BUSINESS

THE ULTIMATE RESOURCE™

BUSINESS
THE ULTIMATE RESOURCE™

BASIC

BOOKS

A Member of the Perseus Books Group

First edition © Bloomsbury Publishing Plc 2002
Second edition © A & C Black Publishers Ltd 2006

Cataloging-in-Publication Data is available from the Library of Congress

ISBN-10: 0–465–00830–5
ISBN-13: 978–0–465–00830–8
Basic Books is a member of the Perseus Books Group
Find us at www.perseusbooksgroup.com

Books published by Basic Books are available at special discounts for bulk purchases in the U.S. by corporations, institutions, and other organizations. For more information, please contact the Special Markets Department at the Perseus Books Group, 11 Cambridge Center, Cambridge, MA 02142, or call (800) 255–1514 or (617) 252–5298, or e-mail special.markets@perseusbooks.com.

Text design by Fiona Pike, Pike Design, Winchester, U.K.
Typeset by RefineCatch Limited, Bungay, Suffolk, U.K.
Printed in China by RR Donnelley

First printing, September 2006
1 2 3 4 5 6 7 8 9 10–

Advisory Board for the First Edition

Publishing, Editorial, and Production Staff

Basic Books

President and C.E.O., The Perseus Books Group
David Steinberger

Vice President and Editorial Director
Jo Ann Miller

Associate Publisher and Marketing Director
John Sherer

Vice President Sales and Marketing, The Perseus Books Group
Matthew Goldberg

Director of Manufacturing, The Perseus Books Group
Melissa Serdinsky

Managing Editor
William Morrison Garland

A &C Black

Chief Executive
Nigel Newton

Managing Director
Jill Coleman

Publishing Director
Jonathan Glasspool

Production Director
Oscar Heini

Commissioning Editor
Lisa Carden

Co-ordinating Editor
Emma Harris

Production Controller
Rachel Murphy

Production Editor
Nicky Thompson

Database Manager
Katy McAdam

Marketing Executive
Suzi Nicolaou

Contributors, Editors, and Proofreaders
Sandra Anderson • Tom Brown •
Stuart Crainer • Steve Curtis •
Des Dearlove • Catherine Gough •
Kate Hardcastle • Rita Herron Brown •
Ruth Hillmore • Jeremy Kourdi •
Ian Linton • Gerry McGovern •
Dena Michelli • Judi Neal •
Antoin O Lachtnain • Julie Plier •
Kate Stenner • Jill Williams

Index
Richard Bird

Contents

MANAGEMENT LIBRARY

BUSINESS THINKERS

MANAGEMENT GIANTS

DICTIONARY

BUSINESS INFORMATION SOURCES

Contributors

Dr. Karl Albrecht is a management consultant, futurist, speaker, and author. He has written more than 25 books on business performance, including the best-selling *Service America! Doing Business in the New Economy* (with Ron Zemke; McGraw-Hill, 2001), which is widely credited with launching the worldwide service revolution. As chairman of Karl Albrecht International, he oversees the practical application of his ideas through a consultancy group, a seminar firm, and publishing company. For more information, please see the Web site: **www.KarlAlbrecht.com**

Keith Alexander is director of the Centre for Facilities Management (CFM) and has a chair in facilities management. He is associate head of Academic Enterprise and a member of the school executive. He is a member of the Research Institute for Business and Informatics, and of Salford University's five-star rated Research Centre for Built and Human Environment. Alexander has been at the forefront of developments in education, research, and practice in facilities management for over 20 years.

A consultant, executive coach, educator, and motivational speaker, **David Allen** has conducted workshops in performance enhancement for more than 500,000 professionals. He is the author of two books, the international best-selling *Getting Things Done: the Art of Stress-Free Productivity* (Viking, 2001), and *Ready for Anything: 52 Productivity Principles for Work and Life* (Viking, 2003), and has published numerous essays and articles on the topic of personal effectiveness.

Christopher Bartlett is Thomas D. Casserly, Jr. professor of business administration at Harvard Business School. Before joining the HBS faculty, he was a marketing manager with Alcoa in Australia, a management consultant in McKinsey and Company's London office, and general manager of Baxter Laboratories' subsidiary company in France. He has published eight books, including (co-authored with Sumantra Ghoshal): *Managing across Borders: The Transnational Solution* (1988)—named by the *Financial Times* as one of the 50 most influential business books of the century; and *The Individualized Corporation* (1997), winner of the Igor Ansoff Award for the best new work in strategic management and named one of the best business books of the millennium by *Strategy + Business* magazine. He has also authored or co-authored over 50 chapters or articles which have appeared in leading journals such as the *Harvard Business Review, Sloan Management Review,* and *The Academy of Management Review*. His academic colleagues have elected him a Fellow of the Academy of Management, the Academy of International Business, and the Strategic Management Society.

Peter Bebb leads the Cedar Business Alignment practice in London, initiating sustainable success through enterprise performance management. He has worked as a director, consultant, and project manager in various industries and companies across the world, including Sema Group Consulting, Proudfoot Europe, Kleinwort Benson Investment Management, and James Martin Associates.

Meredith Belbin is a partner in Belbin Associates, a company known principally as the producer of Interplace—a company-based, team-role advice system, used internationally. He has written several successful business books, including the European bestseller, *Management Teams* (Butterworth-Heinemann, 1996) and, most recently, *Managing without Power* (Butterworth-Heinemann, 2001). He has been a consultant to the European Commission, the U.S. Department of Labor and the OECD, and is senior associate professor at Cambridge University. He is currently External Examiner for the Department of Engineering Management at the University of Bristol, and has been appointed Visiting Professor and Honorary Fellow of Henley Management College, England.

Chip R. Bell is the author or co-author of 16 books, including *Magnetic Service: Secrets for Creating Passionately Devoted Customers* (with Bilijack R. Bell; Berrett-Koehler, 2006), *Customers As Partners* (Berrett-Koehler, 1994), *Managers As Mentors* (Berrett-Koehler, 1998), and *Dance Lessons: Six Steps to Great Partnerships in Business and Life* (with Heather Shea; Berrett-Koehler, 1998).

University Professor and Founding Chairman of The Leadership Institute, USC, **Warren Bennis** is also Chairman of the Advisory Board of the Center for Public Leadership at Harvard's Kennedy School. He has written over 25 books and many articles on leadership, change, and creative collaboration. He is a consultant for Fortune 500 companies and has served on four U.S. Presidential Commissions. His book, *Leaders* (reissue, HarperCollins, 2004), was recently designated by the *Financial Times* as one of the top 50 business books of all time. *An Invented Life* (Addison-Wesley, 1993) was nominated for a Pulitzer. *Forbes Magazine* refers to him as the "Dean of leadership gurus." His recent book, *Geeks & Geezers* (Harvard Business School Press, 2002), is about leaders 70 years and older and 32 years and younger. In 2005, HarperCollins published his series of conversations with the late Bob Townsend, *Reinventing Leadership*. He is now completing a book on leadership judgment. In May 2000, the *Financial Times* referred to Bennis as "the professor who established leadership as a respectable academic field."

Peter L. Bernstein is president of Peter L. Bernstein, Inc., established in 1973 as an economic consultancy to institutional investors. He writes and publishes *Economics and Portfolio Strategy*, a fortnightly analysis of the capital markets and the real economy. His recent books include *The Power of Gold: The History of an Obsession* (Wiley, 2001), *Against the Gods: The Remarkable Story of Risk* (Wiley, 1998), and *Capital Ideas: The Improbable Origins of Modern Wall Street* (reprint; Free Press, 1993; republished by Wiley, 2005). Bernstein's most recent publication is *Wedding of the Waters: The Erie Canal and the Making of a Great Nation* (W. W. Norton, 2005).

General Sir Peter de la Billière began his distinguished career with the Durham Light Infantry during the Korean War and later joined the Special Air Service (SAS) in 1956. He received two Military Crosses and a Mention in Dispatches for his work in Oman and the Far East, and faced important military challenges including the Iranian Embassy siege, and the Falklands War. He was first knighted in 1988. When the Gulf War broke out in 1990, he was appointed Commander the British forces. He was subsequently promoted to General was Knighted again, and became a military adviser on Middle East Affairs to the Government. On leaving the Army he became a Main Board Director of Robert Fleming and Chairman of FARM Africa. He is the author of *Storm Command* and *Looking for Trouble* (HarperCollins, 1992 and 1994). In 2004 he published *Supreme Courage* (Little, Brown).

Drayton Bird is founder of Drayton Bird Associates, an agency specializing in direct marketing. For seven years he was a partner of Trenear-Harvey, Bird & Watson, a firm which was sold to Ogilvy and Mather in 1985. As vice-chairman and creative director, he helped O & M Direct become the world's largest direct marketing agency network, and was elected to the worldwide Ogilvy Group board. Drayton is a celebrated speaker and regularly contributes articles to international journals. His three books include the bestseller, *Commonsense Direct Marketing* (4th ed. Kogan Page, 2000).

Don Blohowiak is executive director of Lead Well, a leadership development firm based in Princeton, New Jersey, which consults with organizations, and coaches executives worldwide. He is the author of six management books, including *Your People Are Your Product* (Chandler House, 1998) and *Lead Your Staff to Think Like Einstein, Create Like Da Vinci and Invent Like Edison: Powerful Real World Techniques That Work!* (McGraw-Hill, 1995). Don is also the award-winning leadership blogger at BNET.com. To find out more about Don, please visit: **www.leadwell.com**

Edward de Bono is the originator of "lateral thinking," and "parallel thinking." He qualified as a doctor, going on to read psychology, and from this basis developed his work in the practical aspect of human thinking. His work in the area of perception provided the basis for the DATT program in business and the CoRT program in schools. His many publications include, *Six Thinking Hats*, (revised edition, Penguin, 2000), and *New Thinking for the New Millennium* (Penguin, 2000). As well as acting as an advisor to various governments, regional governments, cities, and global organizations, he has established the World Centre for New Thinking (**www.worldcentrefornewthinking.org**) in Malta and acted as the Chairman of the Council of Young Enterprise Europe. For more information, please visit: **www.edwarddebono.com**

George Percy Boulden is currently chairman and managing director of Action Learning Associates International Ltd, which he founded in 1980 with Professor Reg Revans and Alan Lawlor to promote the use of Action Learning in solving business problems. He works with clients such as Motorola, ICL, ACE Insurance, Nacco Materials Handing Group, and Roche Pharmaceuticals to help them to design and deliver people development programs. His international work takes him to Japan (where he advises a major Japanese consultancy organization), the United States, and Central and Eastern Europe. He works with many international agencies including the International Labour Organization, EC Phare, UNDP, WHO, and the Know How Fund. George Boulden is a member of the International Foundation for Action Learning and a Fellow of the Institute of Management Consultants. He has written a number of papers and articles on action learning and organizational productivity.

R. Brayton Bowen is author of several books, including *Recognizing and Rewarding Employees* (McGraw-Hill, 2000). As well as being a former senior executive with five major corporations, an author, speaker, and columnist, he leads The Howland Group (**www.howlandgroup.com**), a management consultancy firm based in Louisville, Kentucky, which specializes in organizational strategy, structure, and systematic change initiatives.

Richard Boyatzis is Professor of Organizational Behavior at Case Western Reserve University, Cleveland. He is a bestselling co-author (with Daniel Goleman and Annie McKee) of *Primal Leadership* (Harvard Business School Press, 2002) and *Resonant Leadership* (with Annie McKee; Harvard Business School Press, 2005).

William Bridges is a consultant and lecturer based in Mill Valley, California. Past president of the Association for Humanistic Psychology, he was rated by the Wall Street Journal as one of the ten most popular executive development consultants in the United States. His numerous books include *Managing Transitions: Making the Most of Change* (Perseus, 1991; revised 2003), *Transitions* (Perseus, 1980; revised 2004), and *JobShift: How to Prosper in a Workplace without Jobs* (Perseus, 1994).

Mark Brown is visiting professor of innovation at Henley Management College, England, and managing director of Innovation Centre Europe. His life is divided between consultancy for a range of *Fortune* 500 companies, writing management books and articles, and continuing research at Henley into why some individuals and organizations are more creative and innovative than others. He has contributed to a number of journals, including *Management Today*, *Psychology Today*, and *Creativity Network*.

Peter Brown is the founder and Chairman of Independent Remuneration Solutions, one of the best known specialists in assisting quoted, AIM, and private companies devise the best remuneration structures for their directors. He is Chairman of two quoted companies: Goldshield Group Plc and County Contact Centres Plc; and three private companies Synergy Holdings Ltd, Charity and Fundraising Appointments Ltd, and Gabbitas Educational Consultants Ltd.

Tom L. Brown is the author of the first online book on leadership, *The Anatomy of Fire: Sparking a New Spirit of Enterprise*. He has written more than 400 articles for major journals such as *Across the Board*, Harvard's *Management Update*, and the *Wall Street Journal*. He has been the keynote speaker at major meetings (including the International Association of Management), presented his ideas to many corporations, and lectured at several universities. More about his work can be found at **www.thomaslbrown.com**

Marcus Buckingham is an author, researcher, writer, and expert on leadership and management practices. He was written three bestselling books: *First, Break All the Rules* (Simon & Schuster, 1999), *Now, Discover Your Strengths* (Free Press, 2001), and *The One Thing You Need to Know* (Simon & Schuster, 2005). To find out more, visit his Web site at: **www.marcusbuckingham.com**

Matthew Budman has worked in journalism for nearly two decades, the last nine as managing editor of a Manhattan-based bi-monthly business magazine, The Conference Board's *Across the Board*. The Conference Board is a global, independent membership organization that conducts research, convenes conferences, makes forecasts, assesses trends, publishes information and analysis, and brings executives together to learn from one another.

Dr. Peter Bunce (peterbunce@bbrt.org) is a Chartered Engineer who has worked in industry as a manufacturing engineer and in collaborative research programs on technical and management issues with CAM-I (a U.S.-based research consortium). With Robin Fraser, Jeremy Hope, and Franz Röösli, he is a director of the BBRT, an international research and membership collaborative.

Robert Buttrick is widely known for his refreshing and practical insight into business-led project management. His best-selling book, *The Project Workout* (3rd ed. FT Prentice Hall, 2005), is widely adopted by major corporations and business schools alike, both in the United Kingdom and around the world. It has also been translated into French, Chinese, and Russian. He is also a key speaker at conferences as well as in-company events. Buttrick has lived and worked in countries as diverse as the United States, Yemen, Sudan, Senegal, Mauritius, Bahrain, and Japan.

Sir Adrian Cadbury joined the Cadbury business in 1952, became chairman of Cadbury Limited in 1965 and retired as chairman of Cadbury Schweppes in 1989. He was a director of the Bank of England 1970–1994, chairman of the UK Committee on Corporate Governance 1991–1995, and a member of the OECD Business Advisory Group on Corporate Governance. He received the International Corporate Governance Network Award in 2001 and the Laureate Medal for Corporate Governance in 2005. He is the author of *Corporate Governance and Chairmanship; A Personal View* (Oxford University Press, 2002).

After 20 years in financial and public services, **Terry Carroll** "reinvented" himself as a thought leader and

"Corporate Alchemist," resolving challenges through original thinking and leading edge people technologies. A highly successful motivational speaker, leadership development and business coach, he has also worked with a range of highly successful companies and finance professionals. An established author, his books range from personal growth to finance and risk.

Susan Cartwright is Professor of Organizational Psychology at the Manchester Business School, University of Manchester, England. Her research interests and publications are in the area of occupational stress and organizational culture and change, particularly in the context of mergers, acquisitions, and joint ventures. She has worked extensively with public and private organizations on a range of projects related to stress management and human merger integration. She is the Chair of the British Academy of Management, and an Associate Editor of the *British Journal of Management*. She is the Editor of the *Blackwell Encyclopedia of Human Resource Management* (2nd ed., Blackwell, 2005).

John Case is a veteran observer and analyst of the business world and an internationally-known expert on the subject of open-book management. He is the author of six books, including *The Open Book Experience: Lessons from over 100 Companies Who Successfully Transformed Themselves* (Perseus, 1999), and collaborator on several others. He has also written for a wide variety of periodicals. At present, Case is a consulting writer for Bain & Company and a number of other clients.

James Champy is chairman and head of strategy of Perot Systems consultancy practice, providing strategic direction to the company's team of business and management consultants. He is an authority on management issues surrounding organizational change and corporate renewal. He wrote the bestsellers *Reengineering the Corporation* (with Michael Hammer; HarperBusiness, 2001) and *Reengineering Management* (HarperBusiness, 1996). His newest book is *The Arc of Ambition* (with Nitin Nohria; Perseus, 2001). James moderates programs for the PBS Business Channel and has also been a guest on Wall Street Week. He provides regular columns for magazines such as *Forbes* and *Computer World*.

Cary Cherniss is professor of applied psychology and director of the Organizational Psychology program at Rutgers University. He specializes in emotional intelligence, work stress, management training, organizational change, and career development. His eight books include *Promoting

Emotional Intelligence in Organizations (with Mitchel Adler; American Society for Training and Development, 2000) and *Beyond Burnout* (Routledge, 1995). He has also consulted widely in both public and private sectors.

Subir Chowdhury is executive vice-president at the international consultancy firm ASI (American Supplier Institute). As well as being a renowned consultant in the field of quality management and leadership, Chowdhury has written several books on these subjects, some of them award-winning. His most recent books include *The Power of Six Sigma* (Financial Times Prentice Hall/Dearborn Trade, 2001) and *The Talent Era* (Financial Times/Prentice Hall, 2001). His latest book is *The Ice Cream Maker: An Inspiring Tale about Making Quality the Key Ingredient in Everything You Do* (Currency, 2005).

Clayton Christensen is the Robert and Jane Cizik Professor of Business Administration at the Harvard Business School. He is the author of several bestselling business books, including *The Innovator's Dilemma* (Harvard Business School Press, 1997) and *The Innovator's Solution* (Harvard Business School Press, 2003).

Stewart Clegg received the George R. Terry Book Award of the American Academy of Management (1998) for outstanding contributions to management. He directs ICAN Research (Innovative Collaborations, Alliances and Networks Research) at the University of Technology, Sydney, where Antoine Hermens leads research on strategic alliances and joint ventures. Salvador Porras leads research on business networks and small business at Universidad Autonoma Metropolitana, Iztapalapa, Mexico City.

Jim Collins started his research and teaching career at the Stanford Graduate School of Business, where he received the Distinguished Teaching Award several times. Since 1995 he has operated a management laboratory in Boulder, Colorado, where he conducts multi-year research and works with senior executives. He is the author of several books, including the bestsellers *Built to Last: Successful Habits of Visionary Companies* (with Jerry I. Porras; new edition, Collins, 2004) and *Good to Great: Why Some Companies Make the Leap ... And Others Don't* (Collins, 2001).

Besides his professorship, **Cary L. Cooper** CBE is pro vice-chancellor of Lancaster University, England. He specializes in stress management, regularly contributing to national newspapers, academic journals, TV, and radio. His many publications include *Organizational Stress* (with Philip Dewe and Michael O'Driscoll; Sage, 2001) and he is Editor-in-Chief of *The Blackwell Encyclopedic Dictionary of Management* (1997 and 2004). Cary co-wrote *Managing Workplace Stress* (Sage, 1997) with Professor Susan Cartwright.

Robert G. Cooper is president of the Product Development Institute, professor of marketing at the Michael G. DeGroote School of Business, McMaster University, Ontario, Canada, and on the faculty of the ISBM (Institute for the Study of Business Markets) at Penn State University's Smeal College of Business Administration. Creator of the widely employed Stage-Gate® product development process, he is the author of several books published by Perseus. Robert lives in Oakville, Ontario.

Anne Covey is the owner of Covey & Associates, PC, and adjunct professor at Monmouth University. She is the author of *The Workplace Law Advisor* (Perseus, 2000), and her articles have been published in several magazines. She is also a national commentator, speaker, and trainer on workplace issues. Ms Covey is the first female Member of the Pennsylvania Labor Relations Board since the Board's inception in 1937.

Michael J. Cunningham is president and founder of the Harvard Computing Group, an international strategy and technology consultancy firm geared to creating innovative strategies and developing powerful web-enabled solutions. He speaks and provides consultancy to clients and industry groups internationally and regularly writes articles on web business and e-commerce for publications such as *E-Business Advisor*. He is the author of three books on the topic of e-commerce: *Partners.com: How to Profit from the New DNA of Business* (Perseus, 2001); *B2B: How to Build a Profitable e-Commerce Strategy* (Perseus, 2000); and *Smart Things to Know About e-Business* (Capstone, 2002).

Thomas H. Davenport holds the President's Chair in Information Technology and Management at Babson College, Massachusetts. He is a widely-published author and acclaimed speaker on the topics of information and knowledge management, re-engineering, enterprise systems, and the use of information technology in business. His books include *Mission Critical: Realizing the Promise of Enterprise Systems* (HBS Press, 2000), *The Attention Economy* (with John Beck; Harvard Business School Press, 2001), and *Working Knowledge* (with Laurence Prusak; Harvard Business School Press, 2000), and *Thinking for a Living: How to Get Better Performances and Results from Knowledge Workers* (Harvard Business School Press, 2005).

Stan Davis is the author of several bestselling books, including *Blur: The Speed of Change in the Connected Economy* (with Christopher Meyer; Perseus, 1998).

Charles R. Day, Jr. is the former editor-in-chief of *Industry Week*. A journalist and writer, his career spans more than 32 years including some 25 years covering and commenting on business and management. He has spoken to many audiences, and appeared on radio and television. Day now heads his own firm on Ponte Vedra Beach, Florida, and is researching and writing two books, one on business management and another on the history of the Super Bowl and the professional football merger in the United States. He is also an adjunct professor at the University of North Florida.

Peter Day is BBC News business correspondent; he presents *In Business* on BBC Radio 4 and Global Business on the BBC World Service.

Dinna Louise C. Dayao is a Philippines-based freelance writer and editor. She has authored two books featuring lessons from Asia's best and brightest business leaders and a guidebook to investing in the Autonomous Region in Muslim Mindanao. She has written many articles on business management, health, and the environment.

Alan Downs, Ph.D. is a management psychologist and consultant who specializes in strategic human resources planning and helping business executives reach their maximum potential. He has written numerous books, including *Corporate Executions* (AMACOM, 1995), the much-acclaimed exposé on downsizing, *The Seven Miracles of Management* (Prentice Hall, 1998), *The Fearless Executive* (AMACOM, 2000), and *Secrets of an Executive Coach: Proven Methods for Helping Leaders Excel Under Pressure* (AMACOM, 2005). He has also written on management topics for numerous national newspapers and trade publications, including *Management Review* and *Across the Board*.

Scott J. Edgett is C.E.O. and co-founder of the Product Development Institute and co-founder of Stage-Gate, Inc. As well as a noted speaker and consultant worldwide on new product development and portfolio management, Scott is the co-author, with Robert Cooper, of two books on these topics, including *Product Development for the Service Sector* (Perseus, 1999). Scott lives in Ancaster, Ontario.

Leif Edvinsson is a leading expert on intellectual capital (IC). As former vice-president and the world's first corporate director of intellectual capital at Skandia of Stockholm,

Sweden, he has been a key contributor to the theory of IC and oversaw the world's first corporate Intelligence Capital Annual Report. Formerly, Edvinsson was senior vice-president for training and development of S-E Bank and president and chairman of Consultus AB, a Stockholm-based consultancy company. As a result of his work in these areas, he has been a special adviser to the Swedish Ministry of Foreign Affairs, the Swedish Cabinet, and the United Nations International Trade Center. As well as an international speaker, Edvinsson is co-author of *Intellectual Capital* (with Michael S. Malone; HarperBusiness, 1997), and numerous articles on the service industry and on IC.

John Elkington is the founder of SustainAbility, one of Europe's leading think tank and consultancy firms focusing on business strategies for sustainable development. He has written or co-authored over 30 books and published reports, including bestseller *The Green Consumer Guide* (Gollancz, 1988) and *Cannibals with Forks* (Capstone, 1997), which introduces the triple bottom line. His most recent book, *The Chrysalis Economy* (Capstone, 2001), explores the challenge of integrating societal values and corporate value creation.

Marc J. Epstein is currently distinguished research professor of management at Jones Graduate School of Management at Rice University in Houston, Texas. He has completed extensive academic research and has considerable practical experience in the implementation of corporate strategies, and the development of performance metrics for use in these implementations. Epstein is author of a dozen books and over 100 professional papers. He also provides seminars, executive courses and lectures to senior managerial audiences throughout the world.

Liam Fahey has been adjunct professor of strategic management at Babson College, Massachusetts, and visiting professor of strategic management at the Cranfield School of Management in the United Kingdom. His research, teaching, and consultancy has centered on competitive strategy, macroenvironmental and competitor analysis, with special emphasis on linking strategy, scenarios, and knowledge. He is the author or editor of 8 books and over 40 articles or book chapters, including *The Portable MBA in Strategy* (Wiley, 2001).

Martha I. Finney is the author of *Find Your Calling, Love Your Life* (with Deborah Dasch; Simon & Schuster, 1998) and producer of "Working from the HeartLand," a Web site exploring joy in the American workplace. A veteran human resources reporter, she is internationally recognized as a leading authority in self-actualization through work.

After gaining a languages degree at Oxford University, England, **John G. Fisher** started his business career in direct marketing and the insurance industry, before establishing one of the United Kingdom's leading performance-improvement and incentive agencies. In 1998 he sold the business to the management team to concentrate on consultancy. He went on to specialize in employee incentives, staff communication, and conference/event planning. He is a regular seminar speaker and has written four business books on the subjects of incentives, conferences, benchmarking, and e-commerce, including most recently *E-business for the Small Business* (Kogan Page/Sunday Times, 2001) and *How to Run Successful Incentive Schemes* (2nd ed, Kogan Page, 2005).

Peter Fisk is an experienced strategist and marketer. He jointly leads the London-based strategic innovation firm The Foundation, and was previously C.E.O. of the Chartered Institute of Marketing. His experience includes introducing a value-based marketing framework within Microsoft, the reinvention of food for Marks & Spencer, and a new brand strategy for Shell. He helped Virgin enter the financial services market, Vodafone to enter new international markets, and Philips transform from product-driven technologists to market-shaping innovators. In January 2006, "Business Strategy Review" identified him as one of the leading new business thinkers and his book *Marketing Genius* was published by Capstone in the same year. Visit his Web site at: **www.MarketingGeniusLive.com** or e-mail him at: peterfisk@peterfisk.com

Patrick Forsyth runs Touchstone Training & Consultancy, an independent firm based in the United Kingdom specializing in marketing, sales, and communications skills. He conducts courses for individual clients, public seminars for a number of management institutes, and has worked in a range of industries in many parts of the world. He writes extensively on matters of marketing and management for management journals and is the author of a number of successful books, including *Communicating with Your Staff* (Texere, Orion Toolkit Series, 1999).

Robin Fraser (robinfraser@bbrt.org) is a Management Consultant and co-author with Jeremy Hope of *Beyond Budgeting*, published by Harvard Business School Press in 2003. He was formerly a partner with Coopers & Lybrand (now PwC) in the UK. With Peter Bunce, Jeremy Hope, and Franz Röösli, he is a director of the BBRT, an international research and membership collaborative.

Business strategy and marketing consultant **John Frazer-Robinson** pioneered the movement towards customer relationship management (CRM) and is acknowledged internationally as an authority on marketing, sales, advertising, and customer service. He is the author of several books including *It's All About Customers!* (Kogan Page & Institute of Directors, 2000), and he has worked all over the world as a speaker, trainer, and lecturer. In 1995, he was elected as one of the first honorary Fellows of the British Institute of Direct Marketing.

Mike Freedman is partner and executive vice-president of Kepner Tregoe, Inc., a global consultancy firm. He is responsible for the worldwide strategy practice. Previously he ran practices in Europe, North America, and Japan. He joined Kepner Tregoe in 1982, after ten years as a senior line manager in Xerox. He also spent three years, from 1994–97, as personal adviser to Tom Sawyer (now Lord Sawyer), who was general secretary of the Labour Party at the time. Mike has himself stood for parliament, and has held various community roles.

Robert Fritz is the author of *The Path of Least Resistance* (revised ed. Fawcett, 1989), *Creating* (reprint; Fawcett, 1993), and *The Path of Least Resistance for Managers* (Berrett-Koehler, 1999), *Your Life As Art* (Newfane Press), and co-author of *The Managerial Moment of Truth* (Simon & Schuster). He co-designed (with Peter Senge and Charles Kiefer) the original "Leadership and Mastery" course on which the "Fifth Discipline" is partly based. His firm, RobertFritz, Inc., provides leading-edge consultancy, training, and products which are based on the creative process and structural dynamics. Fritz is also a composer and filmmaker. To find out more, please visit: **www.robertfritz.com**

Michael Gerber is an entrepreneur, small business guru, and the best-selling author of seven books, including *The E-Myth Revisited: Why Most Small Businesses Don't Work and What to Do About It* (revised edition, Collins, 1995), and most recently *E-Myth Mastery: The Seven Essential Disciplines for Building a World Class Company* (Collins, 2005). He is the founder and chairman of E-Myth Worldwide, which since its inception in 1977 has worked with more than 50,000 individual companies around the world.

Giles Gibbons is a founding partner of Good Business, an independent CR consultancy established in 1997. It specializes in CR report writing, developing and embedding corporate responsibility strategies, and creating and managing flagship social marketing programs. It has worked for most major global corporations including Coca-Cola, Nike, and McDonalds.

Ann Gilley is vice-president of Trilogy Consulting Group, a performance consultancy firm, and an associate professor of management at Ferris State University where she teaches courses in management and strategy. Together with Jerry Gilley, she has co-authored five books published by Perseus, including *The Performance Challenge* (2000) and *Beyond the Learning Organization* (1999).

Jerry W. Gilley is a professor of human resource development at Colorado State University, and was a principal at William M. Mercer, Inc. He has written and co-authored 13 books and over 60 articles, book chapters, and monographs. His books include *Philosophy and Practice of Organizational Learning, Performance and Change* (Perseus, 2001), and *Organizational Learning, Performance and Change: An Introduction to Strategic HRD* (Perseus, 2000), which he co-authored with Ann (Maycunich) Gilley, and which won the Academy of Human Resource Development Book of the Year Award for 2000.

Jules Goddard is an independent teacher, writer and consultant in the areas of creativity, strategic innovation and business transformation. He has been a visiting fellow at the London Business School and guest lecturer at INSEAD, as well as Gresham professor of commerce and Mercers School Memorial professor at the City University, and visiting professor of marketing at the École Nationale des Ponts et Chaussées in Paris. He has published various articles on corporate strategy in leading European strategy and consulting magazines.

Seth Godin is a bestselling author, entrepreneur, and agent of change. Godin is author of seven books that have been bestsellers around the world and changed the way people think about marketing, change, and work. Seth is a renowned speaker as well. He was recently chosen as one of 21 Speakers for the Next Century by Successful Meetings and is consistently rated among the very best speakers by the audiences he addresses. Seth was founder and C.E.O. of Yoyodyne, the industry's leading interactive direct marketing company, which Yahoo! acquired in late 1998. He served as VP Direct Marketing for Yahoo! until 2000. He holds an MBA from Stanford, and was called the "Ultimate Entrepreneur for the Information Age" by *BusinessWeek*. Godin is currently founder and president of squidoo.com. Visit his blog at **www.sethgodin.com** (click on his head).

Psychologist **Daniel Goleman**, Ph.D. has written several best-sellers, including *Primal Leadership* (Harvard Business School Press, 2002). He worked for many years for the *New York Times* covering the brain and behavioral sciences; has been a visiting faculty member at Harvard University; helped found the Collaborative for Academic, Social and Emotional Learning at the University of Illinois, and speaks on emotional intelligence and leadership worldwide. Daniel and Cary Cherniss co-chair Rutgers' Consortium for Research on Emotional Intelligence in Organizations. Together they edited *The Emotionally Intelligent Workplace* (Jossey-Bass, 2001).

Edward E. Gordon is a consultant, writer, speaker, academician, and president of Imperial Consulting, a firm specializing in human capital development (**www.imperialcorp.com**). He has taught at three Chicago-based universities and is the author of fifteen books and 200 articles on human capital development issues.

Jim "Gus" Gustafson, Ph.D. is currently responsible for Strategic Leadership Research & Development at U.S. Cellular, and has over twenty years of successful organization development, sales, marketing, operations, engineering, leadership development, channel management, and general leadership experience in public and private companies and has won several awards for his work. He consults, speaks, and writes on a variety of topics, including socially responsible leadership, appreciative inquiry, corporate social responsibility, organizational and team effectiveness, and servant–leadership development. He has recently published a landmark study based upon his doctoral research, entitled *Socially Responsible Leadership: Lifting Humanity to Positively Transform the World*.

Cliff Hakim is the author of *We Are All Self-employed* (Berrett-Koehler, 1994) and the president of Rethinking Work®, a Boston, Massachusetts-based consultancy firm focused in the areas of executive development and career consultancy.

For fifteen years **Katherine Hammer** was the president, C.E.O., and chairman of the board of Evolutionary Technologies International (ETI), a recognized leader in the field of enterprise data integration management software. She joined the Microelectronics and Computer Technology Corporation (MCC) in the mid-1980s, where her research led to the development of technology that automates the exchange of data between incompatible systems. In 1991 Katherine co-founded ETI, and began marketing this new technology, becoming a pioneer in technology

commercialization. Author of *Workplace Warrior* (AMACOM, 2000) and a former columnist for *Fast Company*, Hammer is currently co-authoring a textbook entitled *Fundamentals of Software Integration* (forthcoming, Jones and Bartlett).

Michael Hammer is the originator of both the concept of "re-engineering" and of "the process enterprise." Through his teaching and research, he works with the management teams of leading companies to bring about fundamental change in their organizations.

Richard S. Handscombe is an international business consultant and author, who has worked in some 30 countries and 40 industries. His publications include *The Banker's Management Handbook* (McGraw Hill, 1976), *Productivity Through People*, (ILO 1985), *The Product Management Handbook* (McGraw-Hill, 1988), *Strategic Leadership—Managing the Missing Links* (McGraw-Hill, 1993) and *Your Garden in Spain* (Santana, 2005). He now lives in Spain.

After working as an executive at Shell International, **Charles Handy** became a professor at the then fledgling London Business School. Today he is an independent writer and broadcaster, and describes himself as a social philosopher.

His enduring concern is the implications for society, and for individuals, of the dramatic changes which technology and economics are bringing to the workplace and their wider lives. His most influential books are: *The Age of Unreason* (1989); *Gods of Management* (1992); *The Empty Raincoat* (1994); and *The Hungry Spirit* (1997). Recent works include *Twenty-one Ideas for Managers* (2000), the coffee table tome, *The New Alchemists: How Visionary People Make Something Out of Nothing* (1999), *The Elephant and the Flea* (Hutchinson, 2001), and *Beyond Success: The New Philanthropists* (Heinemann, 2006).

Oren Harari is Professor at the Graduate School of Business in the University of San Francisco where he teaches strategic and global management. Chosen as one of the 40 "best minds" in management in the world by the editors of *Business Minds* (Financial Times, 2001), he consults and speaks widely. His books include *Leapfrogging the Competition* (2nd ed. Prima Publishing, 1999), *Beep! Beep! Competing in the Age of the Roadrunner* (with Chip Bell; Warner, 2000), and *The Leadership Secrets of Colin Powell* (McGraw-Hill, 2002).

Sir John Harvey-Jones joined ICI as a work study officer in 1956, after 19 years in the navy. He rose to be chairman in 1982, and was largely responsible for reshaping the company, doubling the price of ICI shares and turning a loss into a billion-pound profit after only 30 months in the job. Since receiving his knighthood in 1985, Sir John has written several books, including the bestsellers *Making It Happen* (HarperCollins, new edition, 1994) and *Getting It Together* (Ulverscroft, 1992). He also took part in a TV series entitled *Troubleshooter*, where he was invited to visit and advise businesses.

Robert Heller was the founding editor of *Management Today* and editorially responsible for the launch of highly successful business magazines such as *Campaign*, *Computing*, *Accountancy Age*, and *Marketing*. The many books he has written since the best-selling *The Naked Manager* (Sigwick & Jackson, 1971) have confirmed his position as Britain's best-known author on business management. More recent books include *The Seven Summits of Success* (with Rebecca Stephens; Capstone, 2005) and the highly popular Dorling Kindersley series, *Essential Managers* and *Business Masterminds*. Heller speaks frequently to management audiences on many subjects. He has worked all over the world with many of its leading companies.

Tim Hindle is management editor of *The Economist* and the author of several books on business and management. He has also written extensively on Turkey, the birthplace of his wife and the current home of their daughter. Tim and his wife live in rolling English countryside to the west of Heathrow airport.

Chris Hoenig is the author of *The Problem Solving Journey* (Perseus, 2000).

Jeremy Hope (jeremyhope@bbrt.org) is a Chartered Accountant, formerly working with venture capital company 3i and then running his own business. He is the author of four management books, all published by Harvard Business School Press. With Peter Bunce, Robin Fraser, and Franz Röösli, he is a director of the BBRT, an international research and membership collaborative.

Masaaki Imai is one of the most widely acknowledged theorists on incremental change. As well as being a lecturer and consultant, he is founder and chairman of the international Kaizen Institute, an organization that helps Western companies introduce kaizen concepts, systems and tools. As one of the leaders of the quality movement and a champion of the kaizen philosophy, he has written several best-selling books on the subject.

Bill Jensen is today's foremost expert on work complexity and cutting through clutter to what really matters. He's C.E.O. of The Jensen Group (**www.simplerwork.com**), a change consultancy whose mission is: to make it easier to get stuff done. Through his ongoing ground-breaking study, *The Search for a Simpler Way*, he has pioneered such change tools and strategies such as Behavioral Communication and the SimplerWork Index. As well as speaking and conducting workshops all around the world, he's author of such best-selling books as *Simplicity* (Perseus, 2001), *Work 2.0* (Perseus, 2002), *The Simplicity Survival Handbook* (Basic, 2003), and *What Is Your Life's Work?* (HarperCollins, 2005).

Daniel T. Jones is a world expert on supply chain management and co-author of the bestseller *The Machine That Changed the World* (with James P. Womack and Daniel Roos; reprint, HarperCollins, 1991). His main interest has been understanding the differences in industrial performance and the transfer of a set of ideas called lean thinking, from the Japanese motor industry, to a wide range of other industries across the globe. He has led a series of pioneering benchmarking and action research programs, articulating and carrying lean thinking through to pilot implementation. He is Chairman and Founder of the non-profit Lean Enterprise Academy, part of the Lean Global Network, which can be visited online at: **www.leanuk.org**

Sharon Jordan-Evans is founder and president of the Jordan Evans Group, a leadership consulting organization. She is a prominent keynote presenter and executive coach and holds a masters degree in organization development. Beverly and Sharon co-wrote the Wall Street Journal bestsellers, *Love 'Em or Lose 'Em: Getting Good People to Stay* (Berrett-Koehler, 2005) and *Love It, Don't Leave It: 26 Ways to Get What You Want at Work* (Berrett-Koehler 2003). For more information about the authors, log onto: **www.keepem.com**

Robert S. Kaplan is the Marvin Bower Professor of Leadership Development at Harvard Business School. His research, teaching, and consultancy focus on linking cost and performance measurement systems to strategy implementation and operational excellence. With David Norton, Kaplan developed the Balanced Scorecard, an aid to achieving strategy by showing how key measures inter-relate to track progress towards strategy, and both Kaplan and Norton serve as directors with the Balanced Scorecard

Collaborative—a global network to support organizations implementing the method. Their most recent books include *The Strategy-focused Organization* (Harvard Business School Press, 2001) and *The Balanced Scorecard* (Harvard Business School Press, 1996).

Previously director of e-commerce for Great Universal Stores plc (GUS), **Michael de Kare-Silver** is the Managing Director, Europe, for AKQA, a world-leading digital marketing agency. He began his career at Procter and Gamble, then McKinsey and went on to set up his own consultancy operations (Kalchas), specializing in strategy and e-commerce. When the firm was acquired by Computer Sciences Corporation, Michael became vice-president and sat on the CSC European Management Committee, with emphasis on growing e-commerce activities in Europe and North America. Michael has also written widely, most notably *E-Shock* and *Streamlining*. He has been appointed visiting professor in the technology department of Middlesex Business School in London and is non-executive director at Thus Group plc and WIN plc.

Beverly Kaye is C.E.O. and founder of Career Systems International, Inc., a publisher of career development tools. She also works as a consultant, lecturer, and writer, and wrote the classic *Up Is Not the Only Way* (Davies Black, 1997). She earned a doctorate at UCLA and did post-graduate work in organization development at the Sloan School of Management at Massachusetts Institute of Technology.

Lucy Kellaway is the *Financial Times*'s management columnist. For the last ten years her weekly Monday column has poked fun at management fads and jargon and celebrated the ups and downs of office life. She also writes the satirical column, Martin Lukes, which appears in the *FT* on Thursdays. In her 20 years at the *FT* Lucy has been energy correspondent, Brussels correspondent, a Lex writer, and an interviewer of business people and celebrities for the "Lunch with the *FT*" series. She has won various prizes including the Industrial Society WorkWord Award (twice) and the Wincott Young Financial Journalist Award. Her book, *Sense and Nonsense in the Office*, was published by FT Prentice Hall in 1999. *Martin Lukes: Who Moved My BlackBerry™* was published in July 2005 by Penguin.

Allan A. Kennedy is a Boston-based management consultant and writer. He is co-author with Terrence Deal of *Corporate Cultures* (Perseus, reissue 2000) and *The New Corporate Cultures* (Perseus, 1999). He has also written *The*

End of Shareholder Value (Perseus, 2000) and numerous articles.

Debbe Kennedy is an author and president and C.E.O. of Leadership Solutions Companies, an award-winning enterprise since 1990, specializing in leadership and organizational communications solutions. She is also founder of the GLOBAL DIALOGUE CENTER, an online gathering place for people throughout the world with a focus on leadership, professional, and personal development (**www.globaldialoguecenter.com**). Central to her mission is expanding opportunities for inclusion for all people with a special focus on women's leadership. Prior to this, she had a distinguished leadership career with IBM Corporation for over twenty years. She is the author of numerous books and tools with a leadership, humanitarian, goal-directed focus, including *Action Dialogues: Meaningful Conversations to Accelerate Change* and the *Diversity Breakthrough* Series (Berrett-Koehler, 2000).

Peter Killing is professor of strategy at the International Institute for Management Development (IMD). His areas of particular interest are strategy creation and execution, change management, and the design and management of acquisitions and alliances. Much of his work on strategy and change is captured in *Strategic Analysis and Action*, co-written with Professors Mary Crossan and Nick Fry (6th ed, Prentice Hall, 2005). His teaching and consulting has influenced the alliance activities of many companies. At IMD Peter leads the Breakthrough Program for Senior Managers. His most recent book is *Must Win Battles* (FT Prentice Hall, 2005) co-authored with Professor Tom Malnight and Tracey Keys.

Chan Kim, born in Korea, and **Renée Mauborgne**, an American, are based at INSEAD in Fontainebleau, France. Kim is The Boston Consulting Group Bruce D. Henderson Chair Professor of Strategy and International Management, and Mauborgne is the INSEAD Distinguished Fellow and Affiliate Professor of Strategy and Management. Both previously studied and taught at the University of Michigan Business School. They are the authors of the international bestselling book *Blue Ocean Strategy: How to Make the Competition Irrelevant and Create New Market Space* (Harvard Business School Press, 2005).

Karin Klenke is Professor of Leadership Studies in the School of Leadership Studies at Regent University, Virginia, senior principal of the Leadership Development Institute (LDI) International, and Board of Directors of the International Association of Management (**www.aom-**

iaom.org). She has published widely in management and leadership journals, founded and edited several journals including "Journal of Management Systems," and is author of the award-winning book, *Women in Leadership: A Contextual Perspective* (Springer, 1996).

Leslie L. Kossoff was cited by About.com as "one of the most intelligent and perceptive voices on managerial leadership today." A leading international executive advisor with clients ranging from start-ups to Fortune 50s and former associate of Dr. W. Edwards Deming, she is a highly regarded speaker and award-winning author of two books and over 100 articles.

Philip Kotler is S. C. Johnson and Son distinguished professor of international marketing at the J. L. Kellogg Graduate School of Management, Northwestern University. His extensive canon runs to more than 35 books, and includes the classic marketing textbook *Marketing Management: Analysis, Planning, Implementation, and Control* (now in its 12th edition, Prentice Hall, 2005), *Kotler on Marketing* (Free Press, 1999), *Marketing Moves* (Harvard Business School Press, 2002), *Marketing Insights from A to Z* (Wiley, 2003), *Lateral Marketing* (Wiley, 2003), *Ten Deadly Sins* (Wiley, 2004), *According to Kotler* (Wiley, 2005), and *Corporate Social Responsibility* (Wiley, 2005).

He has also published more than 100 articles in leading journals such as the *Harvard Business Review* and the *Journal of Marketing and Management Science*.

Thomas M. Koulopoulos is president and founder of Delphi Group, global business and technology advisers, based in Boston, Massachusetts. He lectures at the Boston College Graduate School of Management, frequently contributes to industry publications and nationally-broadcast technology reports, and is also the author of seven books, his most recent *Smartsourcing: Driving Innovation and Growth through Outsourcing* (Platinum Press, 2006).

Jim Kouzes is the author of numerous books on leadership, and *The Wall Street Journal* has cited Jim as one of the twelve best executive educators in the United States. He is also an executive fellow in the Center for Innovation and Entrepreneurship at the Leavey School of Business, Santa Clara University.

Andrew Lambert is co-founder and director of the Corporate Research Forum. This brings together some 100 major employers to fund research and discussion processes concerning the many employment issues that organizations

currently face. Such challenges include career management, development of talent and leaders, and the psychological contract. He also owns and runs The Lambert Consultancy, a firm specializing in helping companies to manage change, chiefly by integrating their business strategy with the way they manage people and relationships. He writes and lectures on various topics, including organizational change, internal communications, identity and branding, and HR strategy.

Formerly a partner at McKinsey & Company, **Max Landsberg** is now a business author and executive coach. His guide to coaching, *The Tao of Coaching* (HarperCollins, 1996), has become a classic, selling in excess of 100,000 copies and with translations into 12 languages. His other books are *The Tao of Motivation* (HarperCollins, 1999) and *The Tools of Leadership* (HarperCollins, 2000).

Rick Lash is the Hay Group's leader for management development practices in Canada. He has over 20 years' experience in the design of competency-based interventions and technologies to change human behavior and accelerate and maximize the learning process and performance of individuals and organizations. He is a frequent keynote speaker at national and international conferences on topics related to organizational effectiveness has published widely on topics of leadership development and organizational transformation.

Robert Leaf—consultant, international speaker, and writer of numerous articles—established Robert S. Leaf Consultants in 1997. He specializes in advising corporations, their managements, and government bodies on establishing a worldwide public relations strategy and how to make the most effective use of their agencies and internal communications departments. For 40 years, he worked for Burson Marsteller, 25 of which he was head of international operations and opened offices throughout the world including China, Russia and the Middle East. He became one of the industry's most knowledgeable counselors on international public relations, winning the Institute of Public Relations' first Alan Campbell-Johnson award for outstanding contributions in this field, in 2000. He is listed in *Who's Who in the World, Who's Who in America*, and *Debrett's People of Today*. He has a BA in Journalism and an MA in European History, both with honors, from the University of Missouri.

Andrew Leigh's career has spanned marketing, writing business features for the *Observer*, and serving as a senior manager in the public services. He works with a wide range of companies on clarifying and achieving their development needs, and developed the ACE teams computer system for creating team profiles. His books include *The Ultimate Business Presentation Book* (Random House, 1999). Together they started Maynard Leigh Associates in 1989 and they have written several books, including *Leading Your Team* (2nd ed. Nicholas Brealey, 2002).

Bernard Lietaer has had 25 years of professional experience in money systems, from an unusually wide variety of perspectives. For 14 of those years, he was a professional management consultant working with multinational corporations, banks, and governments on four continents. While at the Belgian Central Bank, he was one of the co-designers and implementers of the ECU, the convergence mechanism that has now led to the single European currency. He also served as president of the Belgian electronic payment system. He was professor of international finance at the University of Louvain, and general manager and currency trader for the Gaia Hedge Funds. He is the author of nine books, written in four languages. The most recent of those are *The Future of Money* and *The Mystery of Money* (Munich: Riemann Verlag, 2000). To find out more about Bernard and his work, visit: **www.transaction.net/money**

Christopher Locke is author of *Gonzo Marketing: Winning through Worst Practices* (**www.gonzomarkets.com**), and co-author of *The Cluetrain Manifesto: The End of Business As Usual* (**www.cluetrain.com**), both published by Perseus.

Ian MacMillan is academic director of the Sol C. Snider entrepreneurial research programs at the Wharton School, University of Pennsylvania, and also the Fred Sullivan professor of management. He was previously a chemical engineer and gained wide experience in everything from gold and uranium mines to the South African Atomic Energy Board. His articles have appeared in many prestigious journals such as the *Harvard Business Review*. Rita Gunther McGrath and Ian co-wrote *The Entrepreneurial Mindset* (Harvard Business School Press, 2000).

David H. Maister is a leading authority on the management of professional service firms. For two decades he has advised firms all over the world, covering strategic and managerial issues. He spent six years teaching courses in managing service businesses and production operations at Harvard Business School, during which he published seven books on business topics. He has written and co-

authored several books since then, including *The Trusted Advisor* (Free Press, 2000) and *First Among Equals* (Free Press, 2002). For more information, see: **www.davidmaister.com**

Costas Markides is Professor of Strategic and International Management and holds the Robert P. Bauman Chair of Strategic Leadership at the London Business School. A native of Cyprus, he received his BA (Distinction) and MA in Economics from Boston University, and his MBA and DBA from the Harvard Business School. He has worked as an Associate with the Cyprus Development Bank and as a Research Associate at the Harvard Business School. He is the author of *Diversification, Refocusing and Economic Performance* (MIT Press, 1995), *All the Right Moves: A Guide to Crafting Breakthrough Strategy* (Harvard Business School Press, 1999), *Strategic Thinking for the Next Economy* (Jossey-Bass, 2001), and *Fast Second: How Smart Companies Bypass Radical Innovation to Enter and Dominate New Markets* (with Paul Geroski; Jossey-Bass Wiley, 2005), which was shortlisted for the *Financial Times* Management Book of the Year Award.

Steve Markwell is managing director of Prime Marketing Publications (PMP), a company which specializes in the consultancy and information technology marketplace. The PMP Group provides a range of services for those responsible for purchasing, advising on or marketing IT, and publishes established reports and newsletters.

Michael Maynard has led business and management courses across the United Kingdom and in Europe, specializing in creativity, teams, self-expression, and communication skills. He worked as a professional actor and presenter for nearly 20 years, and is regularly invited to speak at conferences all over the world.

John L. Mariotti is a consultant, writer, and speaker. He is also president and C.E.O. of The Enterprise Group. He is a former corporate president and serves on the boards of six companies. Mariotti writes and publishes a weekly newsletter *THE ENTERPRISE*. His latest books are new editions of *Smart Marketing* and *Marketing Express* (Wiley). For more information, visit: **www.mariotti.net**

Andrew Mayo is a consultant, speaker, writer, and facilitator in international human resources management, having worked for nearly 30 years in major international organizations. He is the author of five books and numerous articles. He currently runs his own consultancy company, MLI (Mayo Learning International Ltd), specializing in organizational strategies for growing human capital and in people-related measures. He is also a fellow and program director for in-company programs for the Centre for Management Development at the London Business School and associate professor of human capital management at Middlesex Business School.

Malcolm McDonald is emeritus professor of marketing and deputy director at Cranfield School of Management, England, with special responsibility for e-business. He is Chairman of six companies and spends much of his time working with the operating boards of the world's biggest multinational companies, such as IBM, Xerox, BP and the like, in most countries in the world, including Japan, the United States, Europe, South America, ASEAN and Australasia. He has written or co-written 40 books, including the best-selling title, *Marketing Plans: How to Prepare Them, How to Use Them* (5th ed., Butterworth-Heinemann, 2002), and many of his papers have been published. His current interests center around the use of information technology in advanced marketing processes and global best practice key account management.

Gerry McGovern is managing partner at Gerry McGovern, a consultancy that focuses on maximizing value from Web content. He has been involved in the Internet since 1994, and has worked on Internet assignments in 35 countries. Gerry has published four books on Web content. His latest is *Killer Web Content* (A & C Black, 2006). To find out more, visit: **www.gerrymcgovern.com**

Rita Gunther McGrath is an associate professor at Columbia Business School. She was formerly a senior technology manager for the City of New York. Her research focuses on economic transformations through entrepreneurship and new technologies. She publishes widely in both scholarly and practitioner publications and has won several awards, including the Academy of Management Review "best paper" award. She teaches and provides consultancy to a variety of organizations.

Ronan McIvor is a Reader within the School of International Business at the University of Ulster. He has carried out extensive research in supply chain management and information systems. He is currently researching in the areas of outsourcing and the application of electronic commerce at the buyer-supplier interface.

Annie McKee is Co-chair and managing director of the Teleos Leadership Institute. She is a bestselling co-author (with Daniel Goleman and Richard Boyatzis) of *Primal*

Leadership (Harvard Business School Press, 2002), and *Resonant Leadership* (with Richard Boyatzis; Harvard Business School Press, 2005).

Regis McKenna (**www.regis.com**) founded his own high tech marketing firm, Regis McKenna, Inc., in Silicon Valley in 1970. Over the next 30 years, his firm evolved from one focused on high tech start-ups to a broad-based marketing strategy firm servicing international clients in many different industries and countries. McKenna retired from consulting in 2000 and is concentrating his efforts on high-tech entrepreneurial seed-ventures. Regis has written and lectured extensively on the social and market effects of technological change. He pioneered many of the theories and practices of technology marketing that have become integrated into the marketing mainstream.

Henry Mintzberg is the John Cleghorn professor of management studies at McGill University in Montreal. He is the author or co-author of thirteen books including *The Nature of Managerial Work* (Prentice Hall, 1973), *Mintzberg on Management* (Free Press, 1989), *The Rise and Fall of Strategic Planning* (Free Press), which won the best book award of the Academy of Management in 1995, *The Strategy Safari* (Simon & Schuster, 1998), and *Managers, Not MBAs* (Pearson, 2004). Dr. Mintzberg has also contributed to many of the major journals in his field, including the *Harvard Business Review* (for which he has won McKinsey Prizes), the *California Management Review*, the *Sloan Management Review* and the *Academy of Management Review*. His most recent book is *The Flying Circus* (Cyan, 2006).

Ian I. Mitroff is the Harold Quinton distinguished professor of business policy and founder of the USC Centre for Crisis Management (which he directed for 10 years) at the Graduate School of Business, University of Southern California. He is also the president of Comprehensive Crisis Management, a private consultancy firm, and he is generally recognized as one of the founders of the field of crisis management. He has published over 300 articles and 24 books, the most recent being *Why Some Companies Recover Faster and Better from Crises: Seven Essential Lessons for Avoiding Disaster* (AMACOM, 2001).

Geoffrey A. Moore is a managing director at TCG Advisors. Geoffrey is a frequent speaker at industry conferences and his books are required reading at leading business schools. These books include *Crossing the Chasm* (revised edition, 1999), *The Gorilla Game* (revised edition, 1999), and *Living on the Fault Line* (2002), published by HarperBusiness, and

Dealing with Darwin: How Great Companies Innovate at Every Stage of Their Evolution (Portfolio, 2006).

Michael Morris, a partner with Covey & Associates, PC, represents organizations in all aspects of the employment relationship from pre-employment through employment separation and defends against employment-related actions. Michael is also the author of several law review articles, litigator, frequent lecturer, and trainer on employment law throughout the United States.

Ken Murrell is professor of management at the University of West Florida and president of Empowerment Leadership Systems. Since 2002 Ken has traveled over 200,000 miles and spent six weeks all over Asia, two months in Europe, and three months in Latin America to experience first-hand the changing world. He also teaches at several other universities and works with doctoral students on three continents. His intellectual passion is focused on what it will take to create better models of self-organizing human systems and the role that empowerment will play in the liberation of spirit in our coming work communities. He can be reached by e-mail at: kmurrell@uwf.edu

Judith A. Neal is the executive director of the Association for Spirit at Work (**www.spiritatwork.com**), which offers networking, publications, research, courses, and consultancy to individuals and organizations seeking a greater integration of spirituality and work. Prior to this, Neal spent some years as manager of organizational development at Honeywell, after which she ran her own consultancy firm, Neal and Associates, and became management professor at the University of New Haven.

Sue Newell is currently the Cammarata Professor of Management at Bentley College in the United States, and a visiting professor of management in the School of Management, Royal Holloway, University of London. She is a chartered psychologist and has previously worked at Warwick, Aston, and Nottingham Business Schools. Her research interests are varied, covering innovation, knowledge management, human resource management and business ethics. Sue has published many journal articles on these topics, as well as a book entitled *Creating the Healthy Organization* (2nd ed.; International Thomson Business, 2001).

John Nirenberg is the author of *The Living Organization* (Irwin, 1993), and was the founding dean of doctoral studies at the University of Phoenix. He has taught at universities in the United States, Malaysia, Singapore, and Australia. His

other books include *Power Tools: A Leader's Guide to the Latest Management Thinking* (Prentice-Hall, 1997) and *Global Leadership* (Wiley/Capstone, 2002).

Kjell Nordström is an Associate Professor at the Institute of International Business, Stockholm School of Economics. He is the co-author of *Funky Business: Talent Makes Capital Dance* (with Jonas Ridderstråle; Financial Times Prentice Hall, 2001).

David P. Norton is President of Palladium, a consulting firm focused on Strategy Execution, and is the former president of Renaissance Solutions, Inc., a management consultancy and systems integration firm. Prior to Renaissance, Norton co-founded and spent 17 years as president of Nolan, Norton & Company, which was acquired by Peat Marwick. Together with Robert Kaplan, Norton developed The Balanced Scorecard, an aid to achieving strategy by showing how key measures interrelate to track progress. Both Norton and Kaplan are directors of the Balanced Scorecard Collaborative, a global network which supports organizations implementing the method. Their most recent books include *The Strategy-focused Organization* (Harvard Business School Press, 2001) and *The Balanced Scorecard* (Harvard Business School Press, 1996).

Joseph O'Connor is an internationally recognized author, trainer and consultant. He is a leading author in the field of Neuro Linguistic Programming (NLP), systemic thinking and coaching, and author of seventeen books published in 25 languages. He is a Master Trainer of NLP, and co-founder of the International Coaching Community (ICC) with coaches in 31 countries. Contact e-mail: joseph@lambentdobrasil.com

Wally Olins is one of the world's most experienced experts on corporate identity and branding. His main interests are the big ideas behind organizations, mergers, and acquisitions, and he has a particular fascination with the branding of regions and nations. His publications include *On Brand* (Thames & Hudson, 2003).

Paul Ormerod built up the Henley Centre for Forecasting with colleagues during the 1980s, and sold it to FTSE 100 company WPP Plc in 1992. His latest book is *Why Most Things Fail* (Faber, 2005).

Hugh Parker is a former managing partner of McKinsey in the United Kingdom, where he worked from 1951 to 1986. For the last 15 of those years he specialized in corporate governance—effective boardroom management, in other words. Parker wrote what was probably the first book on this subject, *Letters to a New Chairman*, published originally in 1970 by the Institute of Directors in London. He is generally credited in the United Kingdom with having pioneered the field of corporate governance.

Sharon Daloz Parks has served in faculty and research positions in leadership and ethics at the Harvard Business School and the Kennedy School of Government. She is the author of several books, including *Leadership Can Be Taught: A Bold Approach for a Complex World* (Harvard Business School Press, 2005).

Perry Pascarella, former vice-president (editorial) of Penton Publishing Inc and editor-in-chief of *Industry Week* magazine, is an award-winning journalist and the author of numerous books on management and leadership. His book titles include *Leveraging People and Profit* (with Bernard Nagle; Butterworth-Heinemann, 1997) and *Christ-centered Leadership* (Prima, 1999). He was the recipient of the 1992 American Business Press J.D. Crain award for a distinguished career in journalism.

Dr. Louis Patler is president of The B.I.T. Group (**www.thebitgroup.com**), an international consultancy firm, and Near Bridge LLC, a strategic research, trend analysis, and corporate training company. He is the author of numerous articles and three books: *If it Ain't Broke. . .BREAK IT! Unconventional Wisdom for a Changing Business World* (co-written with Robert Kriegel, Warner Books, 1991); *TILT! Irreverent Lessons for Leading Innovation in the New Economy* (Capstone, 2000); and *TrendSmart: The 21 Trends That Will Change the Way You Do Business* (Dearborn, 2004).

Jeffrey Pfeffer is the Thomas D. Dee II Professor of Organizational Behavior in the Graduate School of Business at Stanford University, and author of numerous books, including *The Human Equation: Building Profits by Putting People First* (Harvard Business School Press, 1998).

Gifford Pinchot is widely considered the father of the intrapreneuring movement and is the author of *Intrapreneuring: Why You Don't Have to Leave the Corporation to Become an Entrepreneur* (Harper & Row, 1985) and *The Intelligent Organization* (with Elizabeth Pinchot; Berrett-Koehler, 1994). Pinchot & Company, the firm he leads, helps companies to reduce bureaucratic obstacles and to design and implement more effective and sustainable

business practices. He is a worldwide speaker and consultant. For more information, visit: **www.pinchot.com**

B. Joseph Pine II co-founded Strategic Horizons LLP to explore the frontiers of business and to help executives see the world differently. Prior to that he worked at IBM for 13 years, and is now also a visiting professor at the University of Amsterdam. He and his partner are working on a new book on authenticity in business.

Colin Price is a partner of McKinsey & Company, management consultants, and the co-author of several books including the bestseller *Straight from the C.E.O.* (reissue; Nicholas Brealey, 1998) and *Wisdom of the C.E.O.* (Wiley, 2000). Price was formerly global head of the Strategic Change consulting practice at PricewaterhouseCoopers and is a regular speaker at international conferences.

Jeffrey F. Rayport is C.E.O. of Marketspace, a consultancy and information firm that helps executives craft strategies for the networked economy. Before founding Marketspace, a Monitor Group company, Rayport was a professor at Harvard Business School, where he created the first course in e-commerce at a top-tier business school. He has also written and co-written a number of books on e-commerce, including *Best Face Forward: Why Companies Must Improve Their Service Interfaces with Customers* (with Bernard Jaworski, Harvard Business School Press, 2005).

Kathleen Kelley Reardon, professor of management and organization at the University of Southern California Marshall School of Business, has served on the faculty of the MBA, Executive MBA, and International MBA Programs. She is a leading authority on persuasion, politics in the workplace, negotiation, and interpersonal communication. Her five books include *Persuasion in Practice* (2nd ed, Sage, 1991) and *The Skilled Negotiator* (Jossey-Bass, 2004).

John Reh is an Internet management consultant (**www.peoplearecapital.com**) with over 20 years of hands-on management experience in a variety of industries. He has published more than a hundred best practice articles and believes management is as much art as science, but a skill that can be learned. His Web site, **www.management.about.com**, includes a resource library of the best management information on the Internet.

Howard Rheingold is a leading authority on the social implications of technology. A former founding editor of *HotWired*, he has served as editor of *The Whole Earth Review*, editor-in-chief of *The Millennium Whole Earth Catalog*, and online host for *The Well*. He is the author of *Smartmobs: The Next Social Revolution* (Perseus, 2002).

Dick Richards is a consultant, coach, speaker, writer, and ghostwriter who guides people, teams and organizations in pursuit of their aspirations. He has contributed to over fifty organizations of all sizes, in business, social service, health care, government, and education. He has worked in more than a dozen countries to develop leadership, teamwork, and customer service, and to implement strategy. He is the author of *Artful Work: Awakening Joy, Meaning and Commitment in the Workplace* (Berkley, 1997), which won a Benjamin Franklin Award for best business book, and *Setting Your Genius Free: How to Discover Your Spirit and Calling* (Berkley, 1998). He contributes frequently to professional and business magazines and electronic publishing, appears in the media and at conferences, and leads public workshops.

Jonas Ridderstråle is based at the Centre for Advanced Studies in Leadership at the Stockholm School of Economics. He is the author of *Global Innovation: Managing International Innovation Projects at ABB and Electrolux* (IIB, Stockholm, 1996) and *Funky Business: Talent Makes Capital Dance* (Financial Times Prentice Hall, 1999). The latter, co-written with Kjell Nordström, is an international bestseller that has been translated into more than 25 languages and has its own Web site at **www.funkybusiness.com**. The two also wrote *Karaoke Capitalism: Managing for Mankind* (Financial Times Prentice Hall, 2004).

Al Ries and **Laura Ries** are a father and daughter team. Al is chairman and Laura is president of Ries & Ries, a marketing strategy firm located in Roswell, Georgia, which they founded in 1994. They consult with leading companies in the United States and around the world. Their books include *The 22 Immutable Laws of Branding* (HarperCollins, 1998) and *The 11 Immutable Laws of Internet Branding* (HarperCollins, 2000), *The Fall of Advertising and the Rise of PR* (HarperCollins 2002), and *The Origin of Brands* (HarperCollins, 2004).

Gill Ringland graduated as a physicist, researching at the University of California at Berkeley and as a Fellow at Oxford, before joining an expanding software house, where she became chief technical consultant. She worked for a U.S. IT company and a start-up before joining ICL (now Fujitsu), where as Head of Strategy she first used scenarios. As a result she wrote *Scenario Planning* (Wiley), now in

its 2nd edition. She is now Chief Executive and Fellow of SAMI Consulting. She may be contacted on gill.ringland@samiconsulting.co.uk.

Prof. Franz Röösli (franzroosli@bbrt.org) is Head of the Competence Centre for Controlling at the University of Applied Sciences Northwest Switzerland in Basel, Switzerland. He has also held senior positions in finance in several major companies in Switzerland. With Peter Bunce, Robin Fraser, and Jeremy Hope, he is a director of the BBRT, an international research and membership collaborative.

Alan M. Rugman is currently L. Leslie Waters chair of international business at the Kelley School of Business, Indiana University, where he is also professor of international business and professor of business economics and public policy. He is also an Associate Fellow of Templeton College, University of Oxford. He has served as an adviser and consultant to governmental agencies in Canada and international organizations worldwide. Rugman has also published over 200 articles dealing with the economic, managerial, and strategic aspects of multinational enterprises and with trade and investment policy. His numerous books include *The End Of Globalization* (Random House, 2000).

Philip Sadler is vice-president and former chief executive of Ashridge Management College, where for many years he led the team which built the college's reputation as one of the world's leading business schools. He now heads Philip Sadler Associates, a UK-based consultancy firm with core competencies in leadership development, organization design, and strategic human resource management. He has also written several books, including *Designing Organizations* (Kogan Page, 1994) and *The Seamless Organization: Building Tomorrow's Company* (Kogan Page, 2002).

David R. Sadtler is a fellow of the Ashridge Strategic Management Centre, and a teacher and consultant on questions of strategy at both the corporate and business unit levels. He is the author of a number of articles on the issues and challenges of corporate level strategy. He was the co-founder and executive vice president of Medi-Computer Corporation, and served as the first president of Vickers America, Inc. He is a co-author of *Breakup! When Large Companies are Worth More Dead Than Alive* (Capstone, 1997) and *Successful Business Acquisition* (Delta Sierra, 2000). For more information, see: **www.sadtler.demon.co.uk**

James E. Schrager, Ph.D. is a clinical professor of entrepreneurship and strategy at the University of Chicago, founding editor of *The Journal of Private Equity*, and a member of Great Lakes Consulting Group in South Bend, Indiana. He is a board member or adviser to several technology companies and has won numerous teaching awards at Chicago and Notre Dame.

John Seely Brown is a former chief scientist for the Xerox Corporation and a renowned author and speaker. His numerous works include the article *Research that Reinvents the Corporation*, and the books *Seeing Differently: Insights on Innovation* (Harvard Business School Press, 1997), *The Social Life of Information* (Harvard Business School Press, 2000), and *The Only Sustainable Edge* (with John Hagel III: Harvard Business School Press, 2005).

Jane Galloway Seiling MOD is a consultant, writer and speaker, and focuses on the concept of achieving a more open and inclusive workplace community. She is the author of *The Membership Organization: Achieving Top Performance through the New Workplace Community* (Davies-Black, 1997) and *The Meaning and Role of Organizational Advocacy: Responsibility and Accountability in the Workplace* (Quorum, 2001).

Patty Seybold is C.E.O. of the Boston-based consulting firm the Patricia Seybold Group, a worldwide strategic business and technology consulting firm, which she founded in 1978. A regular speaker at senior-level executive summits, international conferences, and industry events, she has 30 years' consulting experience in the computer industry, and is known for her insights into designing customer-facing business processes.

She has written three books. *Customers.com* (Random House Business Books, 1998), written with colleague Ronnie Marshak, examined how leading companies design and implement e-business strategies to make it easy for customers to do business. In her follow-up book, *The Customer Revolution: How to Thrive When Your Customers Are in Control* (Random House, 2001), she argued that successful companies in the future will be those that provide a consistent brand experience across multiple touchpoints, and the ones that use customer metrics and customer lifetime value as strategic management tools, rather than marketing tools. In her new book, *Outside Innovation* (HarperCollins, 2006), Patty Seybold reveals how companies can stay one step ahead by tapping into the innovative power of their customers to help co-design their businesses.

Annette Simmons, M Ed, is president of Group Process Consulting, a firm that helps organizations in the public and private sectors build more collaborative behaviors for bottom-line results. Her books have been translated into nine languages and include: *Territorial Games* (AMACOM, 1998); *A Safe Place for Dangerous Truths* (AMACOM, 1999); and *The Story Factor* (Perseus, 2002; revised ed 2006).

John Simmons is a consultant and author whose books have been internationally influential. A former director of identity company Newell and Sorrell, then of leading brand consultancy Interbrand, he established the discipline of verbal identity as part of a brand. Working with clients such as Diageo, Unilever, 3 Communications, and Air Products, he has helped brands to create a distinctive tone of voice and to tell their stories better. Now an independent consultant and director of brand language at **www.thewriter.co.uk**, he writes regularly for the media and runs writing workshops for individuals and businesses. He is a co-founder of 26 (**www.26.org.uk**), a non-profit collective that champions the cause of better writing in business.

Herbert Simon was Richard King Mellon University Professor of Computer Science and Psychology at Carnegie Mellon. Influential for his work on decision-making, he won the Nobel Prize for Economics in 1978. Simon died in 2001.

Adrian J. Slywotzky and **David Morrison** are senior partners of Mercer Management Consulting, a global strategy consultancy firm that focuses on the development of strategies for growth in changing markets. They are co-authors of several agenda-setting business books, including *How Digital Is Your Business?* (Crown Business, 2000).

David Smith is executive director of the Teleos Leadership Institute, which was founded by Annie McKee in 2001. Prior to that appointment, he worked in leadership positions within healthcare, higher education, and banking before establishing his own consulting practice: David Smith Associates.

Douglas Smith, a consultant, author, executive, innovator, and teacher, has contributed to the success of organizations in more than forty different industries. His books *On Value and Values* (Financial Times Prentice Hall, 2004), *Make Success Measurable* (Wiley, 1999), and *The Wisdom of Teams* (with Jon R. Katzenbach; Collins, reprint, 2003) have been read and used by millions; and his book *Fumbling the Future* (with Robert C. Alexander: William Morrow & Co., 1998) changed forever how large enterprises approach innovation.

John Smythe was founder and chairman of Smythe Dorward Lambert, a leading consultancy firm specializing in employee communication. After leaving in 2003, he worked with his new consultancy firm, Engage for Change, committed to helping everyone within an organization to drive change and raise day to day business performance. He has also worked with McKinsey and Company and lectured internationally, as well as leading many major communication and change programs.

Paul Spenley is founder and managing director of The Leading Change Partnership. He is an engineer and an expert in the practical application of best-practice benchmarking methods to help organizations achieve and sustain competitive advantage. He has an accomplished career in line management, particularly as a system manager for the ICL operation team that won the prestigious EFQM Quality Award, and has many years' experience of implementing change. He has also written three business books, including *Riding the Revolution* (with Robert Heller; HarperCollins, 2001).

David Stauffer heads Stauffer Bury, Inc., a business writing firm that compiles management information and produces business publications for corporate clients. He is the author of several books including *D2D—Dinosaur to Dynamo* (Capstone, 2001) and *Big Shot: Business the Cisco Way* (Capstone, 2001). His numerous articles have been published in journals such as the *Harvard Management Update* and the *Wall Street Journal*. He also teaches business writing as an adjunct professor at Rocky Mountain College in Billings, Montana.

Erik Stern is senior vice-president and managing director of Stern Stewart Europe, a global consultancy firm that specializes in helping client companies to create and measure shareholder wealth through the application of tools based on modern financial theory. He pioneered the development of the EVA® (Economic Value Added) framework and has implemented EVA programs for companies in several industries in the U.S. and Europe. He has written articles for a variety of publications, including the *Financial Times*, and has appeared frequently on TV, including Sky Business News and Bloomberg. With Mike Hutchinson, he co-authored *The Value Mindset: Returning to the First Principles of Capitalist Enterprise* (Wiley, 2004).

Thomas A. Stewart is the editor of the *Harvard Business Review*. Former editorial director of *Business 2.0* magazine and a member of the board of editors of *Fortune* magazine, he is a fellow of the World Economic Forum and has received a number of accolades, including being named one of the world's 50 most influential management thinkers by FT Dynamo, the online community of the Financial Times. He received doctorate of sciences, *honoris causa*, from City University, London. For more information, see: **www.members.aol.com/thosstew**

Paul Stobart, a qualified chartered accountant, spent seven years with a London-based merchant bank before moving to Interbrand, an international branding and marketing services consultancy firm. During eight years at Interbrand he held a number of positions, latterly chairman of European operations. He is now chief operating officer of Sage, overseeing the continuing development of the Sage brand as a powerful marketing tool. Paul is the editor of *Brand Power* (New York University Press, 1994), a book examining the branding strategies of leading international brand owners.

Dr. Paul G. Stoltz has created the most widely adopted method in the world for measuring and strengthening human resilience. He is the originator of, and leading expert on, the Adversity Quotient® (AQ®) theory, measure, and methodology currently in use by industry-leading companies around the globe. Dr. Stoltz founded PEAK Learning, Inc., a global research and consulting firm, in 1987. He coaches, consults, teaches, and collaborates with top leaders, thinkers, and influencers within a broad range of organizations and is the author of *Adversity Quotient: Turning Obstacles into Opportunities* (Wiley, 1999) and *Adversity Quotient @ Work* (William Morrow, 2000).

Florence M. Stone is editor of the American Management Association (**www.amanet.org**), with responsibility for its quarterly journal *MWorld* and its print and electronic newsletters. She is the author of over ten books, including *Coaching, Counseling & Mentoring* (AMACOM, 1998) and *The Mentoring Advantage* (Dearborn Trade, 2004).

Merlin Stone is one of the United Kingdom's most experienced consultants, lecturers and trainers in CRM, database marketing and customer service. He is the author of many articles and thirty books on marketing and customer service, including *Up Close and Personal: CRM @ Work* (with Paul Gamble, Neil Woodcock, and Bryan Foss; Kogan Page, 2006), *Customer Relationship Marketing* (Kogan

Page, 2000), and *Successful Customer Relationship Marketing* (Kogan Page, 2001). He is a Director of WCL, the Database Group Ltd, and NowellStone Ltd. In parallel to his business career, Merlin has also pursued a full academic career, involving senior academic posts at various universities. He is now a Visiting Professor at Bristol Business School – University of the West of England, Brunel University, Luton University, and Portsmouth University.

Donald N. Sull (dsull@london.edu) is an associate professor of management practice at London Business School. His most recent book is *Made in China: What Western Managers Can Learn from Trailblazing Chinese Entrepreneurs* (Harvard Business School Press, 2005).

John Surdyk is Director of INSITE (Initiative for Study in Technology Entrepreneurship) at the University of Wisconsin-Madison School of Business.

Robert I. Sutton is Professor of Management Science and Engineering at Stanford University and author of *Weird Ideas That Work: 11 and ½ Practices for Promoting, Managing and Sustaining Innovation* (Free Press, 2001). Together, they wrote *The Knowing-Doing Gap* (Harvard Business School Press, 2000).

Don Tapscott is an internationally sought authority, consultant, and speaker on business strategy and organizational transformation. His clients include top executives of many of the world's largest corporations and government leaders from many countries. He is President of New Paradigm Learning Corporation, which he founded in 1993, and Adjunct Professor of Management, Joseph L. Rotman School of Management, University of Toronto, Canada. Don has authored or co-authored ten widely-read books on the application of technology in business, including *The Naked Corporation: How the Age of Transparency Will Revolutionize Business* (Free Press, 2003) and *Digital Capital: Harnessing the Power of Business Webs* (with David Ticoll and Alex Lowy; Harvard Business School Press, 2000).

Dan R. Tobin, based in Framingham, Massachusetts, is a consultant specializing in corporate learning strategies. His work focuses on helping companies to make the best use of their most important strategic assets: their people, and the knowledge and skills of those people. Tobin is also an adjunct professor in the graduate management program at Emmanuel College in Boston, teaching courses in leadership, effective teamwork and organizational transformation. He has written several books, including *All*

Learning Is Self-directed (American Society for Training & Development, 2000). For more information, see his Web site: **www.tobincls.com**

Robert M. Tomasko is a former Arthur D. Little consultant on organization and strategy, who now advises major corporations around the world on the challenges of continued growth. A frequent contributor to business and general news magazines, his articles have appeared in publications such as *Newsweek* and the *Wall Street Journal*. Robert has also written several books, including *Bigger Isn't Always Better* (AMACOM, 2006), *Go for Growth* (Wiley, 1996), and *Re-thinking the Corporation* (AMACOM, 1993). He has spoken about the ideas in these books to business audiences on six continents.

Fons Trompenaars' best-selling books include: *Riding the Waves of Culture, Understanding Cultural Diversity in Business*. He is co-author of *Building Cross-cultural Competence* and *21 Leaders for the 21st Century* with Charles Hampden-Turner.

Edward Tse (tse_edward@bah.com), a vice president with Booz Allen Hamilton, is the firm's managing partner for Greater China. He advises multinational and local clients on strategy, organizations, and operations.

Chris Turner partners with a wide variety of organizations to create sustainable learning environments that nurture creative thinking, learning, innovation, energy, fun, and meaning. A native Texan, she spent 16 years at Xerox Business Services, both as a line manager and as the designer and leader of a breakthrough transformation strategy. She recently published *All Hat and No Cattle: Tales of a Corporate Outlaw* (Perseus, 2000). Chris has also been featured in *The Dance of Change* by Peter Senge (Nicholas Brealey, 1999), and *The Circle of Innovation* by Tom Peters (Hodder & Stoughton, 1998).

Bob Tyrrell is chairman of Sociovision UK, the Paris-based consultancy company studying global socio-cultural change. He is also European chairman of the Global Future Forum, a trustee of the Advisory Council of Demos; and a council member of the Conservative Party Policy Forum. He writes and broadcasts regularly, having presented *Analysis* on BBC Radio 4; made his own TV program in Channel 4's "Opinions" series, and written titles including *Things Can Only Get. . .Different?* (Centre for Policy Studies, 2000). He speaks regularly at international conferences and has shared platforms with such luminaries as Tony Blair, William Hague, and Tom Peters.

Dave Ulrich and **Wayne Brockbank** are professors at the Ross School of Business, University of Michigan. They are also partners in The RBL Group (**www.rbl.net**), a consulting firm focused on delivering value through leadership, HR, and organization design. They have conducted research on, and delivered consulting to, hundreds of firms throughout the world. They recently published *The HR Value Proposition* (Harvard Business School Press) and have authored hundreds of articles.

Jim Underwood is professor of management at Dallas Baptist University, and a management consultant with The Dallas Strategy Group, Inc. He has won numerous awards for his work in the field of management and complexity-based strategy, receiving the International Competia Award 2001, for his book *Thriving in E-Chaos* (Prima, 2001). His 2003 book, *More Than A Pink Cadillac*, was a *New York Times* best selling title. He regularly writes articles for business journals, and features on radio and television broadcasts in connection with his work and publications.

Chris Voss is deputy dean of programs and director of the Centre for Operations Management at London Business School. Before moving into academia, he worked in quality and operations management in manufacturing and service companies, and spent five years in consultancy. Voss has taught and researched widely in the areas of operations, service, and technology management. He was co-author of the first UK textbook on service management, and led the UK study which resulted in the "Service in Britain" report. His most recent book, co-written with Per Lindberg and Kate Blackmon, is *International Manufacturing Strategies* (Kluwer, 1997).

John Wells is currently teaching at Harvard Business School. Prior to this, he was a senior partner with Netdecisions, a global strategy and technology company responsible for strategy, knowledge management, innovation, and learning. His career started at Unilever in London, where he trained as a cost and management accountant. During his management career Wells has worked within numerous companies, including the Boston Consulting Group, PepsiCo, and the Thomson Travel Group. He also co-founded The Monitor Company (with Michael Porter and Mark Fuller), a strategy consulting practice, and Datapaq, a leading digital data acquisition company serving the automotive and packaging industries that continues to be a leader in its field.

Margaret J. Wheatley writes, teaches, and speaks about radically new practices and ideas for organizing in chaotic times. She works to create organizations of all types where people are known as the blessing, not the problem. She is president of The Berkana Institute, a charitable global foundation serving life-affirming leaders around the world, and has been an organizational consultant for many years, as well as a professor of management in two graduate programs. She has authored two award-winning books, *Leadership and the New Science* (Berrett-Koehler, 1992, 1999) and *A Simpler Way* (Berrett-Koehler, 1996), and her most recent publication is *Finding Our Way: Leadership For an Uncertain Time* (Berrett-Koehler, 2005). Her articles and work can be accessed at: **www.margaretwheatley.com**

Andy Wibbels is an award-winning blogger, consultant, and author of *Blogwild! A Guide for Small Business Blogging* (Portfolio, 2006; **www.GOblogwild.com**). He has helped hundreds of companies all over the world use blogs, podcasting, RSS, and related technologies to build and market their businesses. His blog is at: **www.andywibbels.com**

Priscilla Wisner is a professor of accounting at Montana State University in Bozeman, Montana, where she teaches classes in managerial accounting, decision analysis, and profit planning and control. Her research interests are focused on the implementation of corporate strategy to improve social, environmental, and economic performance.

Leslie A. Yerkes is author of *Fun Works: Creating Places where People Love to Work* (Berrett-Koehler, 2001) and co-author of *301 Ways to Have Fun at Work* (Berrett-Koehler, 1997). An organizational development/change management consultant with 20 years of experience, she is the president of Catalyst Consulting Group, Inc., based in Cleveland, Ohio (**www.changeisfun.com**). Additional books by Leslie include *Beans: Four Principles for Running a Business in Good Times or Bad* (Wiley, 2003) and *They Just Don't Get It! Changing Resistance into Understanding* (Berrett-Koehler, 2005). Leslie travels internationally as a lecturer and keynote speaker, and has taught at John Carroll University, Baldwin-Wallace College, and Case Western Reserve University in the United States.

George Yip, Professor of Strategic and International Management at London Business School and Lead Senior Fellow of the Advanced Institute of Management Research, is one of the world's leading authorities on global strategy and marketing, internationalization, and multinational strategies for the Asia-Pacific region. His books are widely acclaimed as the definitive works on their subjects.

The late **Ron Zemke** was founder and president of Performance Research Associates, Inc., a consultancy firm specializing in service quality audits and service management programs. He founded PRA in 1972 to conduct organizational effectiveness and improvement studies for business and industry. He was the author or co-author of 28 books, including *E-Service* (AMACOM, 2000) and *Generations at Work* (AMACOM, 1999).

Physicist and philosopher **Danah Zohar** is the author of *The Quantum Self* (William Morrow & Co., 1990), *Rewiring the Corporate Brain* (Berrett-Koehler, 1997), the world bestseller *SQ: Spiritual Intelligence* (Bloomsbury, 2001), which has been translated into more than 20 languages, and *Spiritual Capital: Wealth We Can Live By* (Berrett-Koehler, 2004).

Other Contributors and Advisers

Best Practice
R. Brayton Bowen
Stuart Crainer
Des Dearlove
Robert Heller
Jeremy Kourdi

Management Checklists
Chartered Management Institute,
United Kingdom

Actionlists
Larry Brotzge
Timothy J. Buckley
Charles R. Day Jr
Ian Linton
Gerry McGovern
Dena Michelli
Judith Neal
Bill White

Dictionary
Chartered Management Institute,
United Kingdom

Quotations
James Randall
Sarah Waldram

**Business Thinkers and Management
Giants**
Chartered Management Institute,
United Kingdom
Stuart Crainer
Des Dearlove

Business Information Sources
Chartered Management Institute,
United Kingdom

Business Intelligence
by Daniel Goleman

What special talents allow some people to build a flourishing business from nothing, while others—though given every advantage of background and preparation at the best business schools—run a business into the ground? What abilities allow one person to take a mediocre company and transform it into an industry leader, while others turn great companies into mediocre ones? And what collective qualities let one company flourish year after year while competitors flounder?

The answer must lie not just in luck, breeding or education. Rather there seems to be a certain knack—a preternatural intelligence—at play, one that makes some people naturally talented at the complex demands of business, just as others are naturals at music, math, or soccer. This same ability displays itself at the group level in superlative teams, and at the organizational level in great companies.

This observation leads to the question: could there be a business intelligence—a set of abilities that distinguish those truly outstanding in the world of commerce? Could *business intelligence* be the mark of outstanding individual performers, as well as the building block of the best-performing companies? I raise the possibility in part to inspire debate and research, as business itself has come into its own as a field of inquiry, theory, and practice. Within the last few decades sophisticated theory and sound quantitative methods have been brought to bear on the study of business. In my own work, I've drawn on this new science to understand the role of emotional intelligence in work performance and leadership. But as I ponder the field of business studies, I wonder whether there might be a case for business intelligence as well.

The question of whether there might be a business intelligence is not far-fetched. Serious thinkers like Howard Gardner at Harvard University look at intelligence not in the traditional, early 20th-century mold of a narrow set of intellectual abilities revolving mainly around verbal agility and alacrity at math. Instead, they think of intelligence as specific to various life domains.

Gardner transformed the way we think about intelligence by challenging its definition in terms of the restricted range of abilities that allow some to excel in the academic world or do well in IQ tests. Instead, he argues convincingly, there are *multiple* intelligences that go far beyond that narrow band, including in the world of movement—as in the football star or gifted dancer—and in the universe of music, as embodied in the genius of a Mozart or Yo Yo Ma.

This expands the term "intelligence" to encompass a range of consequential capacities usually thought of as far beyond its scope. Gardner has even proposed an "intelligence" for understanding the world of nature, as in the great naturalists like John Audobon or Linnaeus—and has speculated on the pros and cons of a spiritual intelligence.

Why not, then, a business intelligence? "Intelligence" in its most basic sense refers to the capacity to solve problems, meet challenges, or create valued products. In this regard, business intelligence describes the essential capacity for success in the marketplace: being able to handle the challenges and crises of the day adeptly, to apply the expertise that offers solutions as needed, and to do all that in ways that add value.

Among the criteria for any candidate, intelligence is an evolutionary plausibility for its role in human survival, a role arrived at via a reverse engineering in which selection pressures in evolution are inferred from the current operation of a faculty. Here, for instance, the case can be made that the modern-day talents for business had antecedents in primitive forms of barter and craftsmanship, primal leadership and negotiation, teamwork and cooperation.

Those who excelled in these proto-business abilities in prehistory would very likely be better able to provide for their progeny, the true mark of evolutionary fitness.

Here there is another intriguing bit of data: the evolutionary psychologist David Buss at the University of Michigan has found that in cultures worldwide one of the prime qualities that make a man attractive to women as a potential mate are signs that he can be a good provider. And desirability as a mate makes one that much more likely to pass on one's genes to future generations—the biological meaning of "survival of the fittest."

One mark of any intelligence lies in having a developmental history, a series of landmarks of learning and mastery over the course of life. No intelligence emerges full bloom, but rather is nurtured and developed over the years. When it comes to business, those who emerge as outstanding typically showed signs of a flair for their later talent as far back as their teen years or even childhood. As the biographies of business greats tell us, as they grew they were particularly able learners, refining and honing these natural talents.

The emergence of the human capacity for math speaks to a different criterion for an intelligence: a relevant symbol system. Any intelligence requires a *lingua franca*, a set of symbols that capture the meaningful information needed to operate in that domain—such as musical notation. Historically such symbol systems arose because of a pressing human need. The historical record suggests that the basics of math—counting, adding, subtracting, and the like—emerged to fill the needs of commerce and accounting, keeping track of goods as they were traded and stored. As business has evolved, so too have the symbol systems that serve this intelligence, as they adapt to these dynamic changes.

What might the key elements of business intelligence include? The data trail leads back to the 1970s, when Harvard professor David McClelland first made the argument that what predicted the best performance in business were not traditional academic aptitudes, nor school grades, nor credentials. Instead he focused on the abilities that star performers exhibit, which can differ from job to job, role to role, and company to company—and which have little or nothing to do with academic abilities.

His research showed why academic intelligence matters little as a predictor of success once someone has gotten into a given job—they are largely *threshold* abilities, what anyone needs to enter the field and hold the job. More significant for predicting success are those competencies that *distinguish* the best from the mediocre within a given job, role, or company. If a company wants to cultivate its strengths, it needs to hire, promote, and train people for these distinguishing abilities—just as if we want to succeed in our career, these are the abilities we will need.

Over the last several decades hundreds of studies in organizations of all kinds—from small family-owned retailers to corporate giants, from hospitals to religious orders—have followed McClelland's lead, assessing the capabilities that set the star performers apart from average in jobs within their organization. Those abilities break down into three basic domains: cognitive astuteness, which largely translates into the ability to learn and to think strategically; technical expertise, or the essential crafts we learn to get work done; and emotional intelligence, the ability to manage ourselves and our relationships. Business intelligence, in the sense I propose, subsumes all of these as core sub-abilities—components that, when orchestrated together, create a special business aptitude.

Each of us will inevitably have a profile of strengths and weaknesses across all the varied abilities that make for business intelligence. And each job we hold over the course of a career will have a distinctive set of demands—and so to some extent require a unique recipe of capabilities to excel. As we change jobs and roles, we need to grow our business intelligence through continuous learning—not just to keep up, but also to get and stay ahead.

Of course any intelligence will have its prodigies—those who exhibit the aptitude at its peak. Here the Rothschilds and Rockefellers, the likes of Gates and Branson, make the point. But the simple fact that some have a natural knack for business intelligence, while others have only middling abilities, should not discourage anyone. For one, the abilities that make up business intelligence are all learnable—anyone with motivation can get better. For another, no one need master every element of business intelligence; we can rely on others for much of the expertise we need. And that gets me to my next point: intelligence is distributed.

THE NEED TO KNOW

An ancient proverb holds, "Best is to know—and know you know. Next best is to know that you don't know. Third best is knowing, but not realizing it. Worst is not to know that you don't know." That bit of wisdom certainly pertains to business intelligence, which includes an aptitude for grasping the right expertise at just the right time, for the right business purpose. The best business people know what they need to, and use their expertise with confidence. When they don't have a key piece of expertise, they realize their need to know—and know where to find it. And, frankly, given the complexity of business today, any of us can find ourselves in that position—with an urgent need to know—at any moment.

How well we handle that moment speaks to our business intelligence, which can manifest in knowing the critical piece of expertise a pressing need demands—or knowing how to find it. Such access to expertise sets the best business people apart from those who flounder: star performers have a superlative grasp of just the piece of know-how they need to do their jobs well, while mediocre performers don't even know that they don't know. Indeed, in studies of outstanding performers at work, the very best were able to track down an essential bit of expertise four times faster than it took their less able peers. In short, speed of access to key expertise—a distinguishing quality of business intelligence—typifies business stars.

In today's business reality such access is all the more essential because of a fundamental fact: we each know only a part of the information or expertise we need to get our jobs done. For years Robert Kelley of Carnegie-Mellon University has been asking people who work at a wide variety of companies the same question, "What per cent of the knowledge you need to do your job is stored in your own mind?" Back in the mid-1980s the answer was typically around 75 per cent. But by the turn of the millennium, that percentage had slid to as low as 15 per cent.

This dwindling of what we know most certainly reflects the sheer rate of growth of information. More knowledge has been generated in the last century, it is said, then in all history before—and the rate of increase accelerates. Likewise, when it comes to the information and expertise needed to do business, what we need to know seems ever-escalating.

Given that anyone in business inevitably faces a growing dependence on information and expertise that others hold, access to what others know matters as never before. But luckily, none of us need to keep in our heads the ever-multiplying expertise that business today—and tomorrow—will demand. Cognitive scientists tell us that intelligence—what we know, remember, and can put to practical use—is distributed. Instead of studying for years to learn all that we might one day need to know, we may do as well—or better—simply to know how to get the information or skills we'll need at the time we need it. We can access a particular bit of expertise as called for, rather than spending endless years mastering all of it.

Our business intelligence does not stop at our skin—it resides in the tools such as databases, and our networks of associates, office mates, and colleagues whom we can turn to as needed. But there is an inevitable unevenness to the range and depth of expertise that our information tools and personal networks offer. Each of us needs to find ways to make up for the gaps in our personal network of experts and information—to continue to learn—or learn ways to find out what we need to know, when we need to know it.

The implications of business intelligence go beyond each of us to the companies we work for or the people we work with. Within any human group, knowledge and expertise are distributed. In today's complex business reality, no one person can master all the skills or data the organization as a whole will need to run effectively. The financial officer has one set of expertise, the sales people another, those in R&D still another. And the company will only be as "smart" as the timely and appropriate offering up of those diverse bits of expertise allow.

Today's business reality poses a paradox: the challenge of reconciling information overload with lightning-fast decision making. To survive competitively, each of us individually—as well as any company—must gather expertise as needed, and operate or adapt accordingly. This applies to the smallest corner store and the largest corporation alike. It points to the crucial role of information flow throughout an organization in determining its viability. The sum of what everybody in a company knows, and knows how to do—its aggregate business intelligence—gives a company much of its competitive edge—if it can mobilize that expertise well.

Indeed, battle-worn executives like Andrew Grove of Intel argue that the very survival of a company depends on the ability of its top leadership team to be nimble in their response to the surprises and challenges of the marketplace. And systems theory tells us that in an environment of turbulent change and competition, the person—or company—that can take in information most widely, learn from it most thoroughly, and respond most nimbly, creatively, and flexibly, will be the most adaptive. This business imperative was, no doubt, a force in the emergence of the "knowledge management" movement from within the Information Technology enclave to the further reaches of the organization.

In short, at each step of the way, the ability to access needed expertise makes a critical difference. Where are the gaps in our business intelligence? We can ask ourselves if we are completely current in, say, the best ways to get to know our customers and their needs, or how to make a strategic alliance work, or the ins and outs of relationship marketing. Where would we turn in our own personal network to find the answers?

BUSINESS LITERACY—AND WISDOM

Then there's *business literacy*, a working familiarity with the key thinking and writing that business people need to keep up with. Given the thousands of books and articles published each year for business people, it's virtually impossible to keep current with the explosion of new ideas and concepts—not to mention weeding out the quickly fading fads of the moment. The majority of that unwieldy mass of ideas and insights offered up each year will fall away like leaves in autumn. But year after year there are thinkers whose insights prove

worthwhile, because they make a practical difference—they add to business intelligence, and prove their worth by ways they matter at work.

Business advantage is gained by harnessing smart ideas—not just amorphous data, the latest technology, or a larger-than-life C.E.O. The editors of the *Harvard Business Review* candidly admit that of all the business ideas that have been proposed in their pages, many are mundane refinements of existing concepts. Only a very few qualify as breakthrough: in 1979, Michael Porter conceived his theory of the forces that shape strategy; in 1990 C. K. Prahalad and Gary Hamel wrote about a company's core competencies; in 1995 Clay Christensen proposed the importance of disruptive technologies. All these ideas are now essentials of business literacy.

Failing at business literacy leaves us behind the curve, or defensive when others bring up important business ideas that we, too, should be familiar with. Worse, it can leave us clueless while others act on powerful new concepts. Business literacy feeds and grows business intelligence. In gauging our own business literacy, we need to ask ourselves, how strong is our working familiarity with the key thinking and writing that anyone in business needs to work well?

Finally, consider what might be called *business wisdom*, which can be seen as the sum total of lessons learned over the course of a career. As each of us goes through the ups and downs, crises and triumphs, of a life in business, the brain automatically extracts lessons for confronting similar situations in the future. Over the years we each build up a set of tacitly learned decision rules—life's lessons—which constitute the sum total of our wisdom on the matter.

But each of us has only a specific, limited set of life experiences—and so a restricted set of lessons—informing our business wisdom. We can each benefit from expanding the pool of lessons learned, given the unpredictable nature of challenges we will face tomorrow. Through human history a traditional way of enlarging our wisdom has been by hearing from the "elders"—those who have gone through what we have yet to face. In the business world such wisdom comes from the most highly seasoned among us—both through what they have to tell us, and what their lives in business reveal to us.

Of course business intelligence, literacy, or wisdom are themselves useless unless we can translate them into action—in short, having an answer to the question of what to do come Monday morning. When all is said and done, it is only in the day-to-day demonstration of wise efforts that business intelligence proves its worth.

Here we can ask ourselves how prepared we've been for the major crisis—or opportunity—of the last week, month, or year. What have we done to gird ourselves for the next such moment? Or we can pause to do an audit of our own business intelligence, looking for the gaps that signal where we might want to build more strengths. Or we can reflect on what we know, what we don't know—and where we would go to find out.

ABOUT THE AUTHOR

Daniel Goleman, Ph.D., is the author or coauthor of several bestsellers, including *Emotional Intelligence* (Bantam, 1997) and *Primal Leadership* (Harvard Business School, 2002). A psychologist, he worked for many years for the *New York Times* covering the brain and behavioral sciences. He has also been a visiting faculty member at Harvard University and serves as Co-Chair of the Consortium for Research on Emotional Intelligence in Organizations, Graduate School of Professional and Applied Psychology, Rutgers University. He is a founder of the Collaborative for Social and Emotional Learning at the University of Illinois at Chicago and speaks on emotional intelligence and leadership worldwide.

See also:

☆ Emotional Intelligence (pp. 400–401)

BUSINESS: A User's Guide

Business has been designed to offer a wide range of insights, information, and practical guidance on every aspect of management.

With over 200 contributors, and more than 1.5 million words of text, *Business* is the most comprehensive single volume ever published on the world of work.

Comprised of six distinct sections, *Business* is extensively cross-referenced throughout and organized to help you navigate both across and within topics.

BEST PRACTICE

Putting the Expertise of the World's Leading Business Writers to Work for You

The Best Practice section presents a powerful array of practical business advice and fresh thinking from some of the world's leading business writers and practitioners.

Clockwise from top left: Margaret Wheatley; Jim Collins; Warren Bennis; Patricia Seybold

These essays reflect the full spectrum of issues that define management today, and serve as concise introductions from experts in each respective topic. Each essay features recommendations of related books and Web sites, and is linked to detailed hands-on advice in the Management Checklists and Actionlists section.

The essays have been organized under 12 broad themes: People and Culture, Marketing, Strategy, Finance, IT and Information Management, Systems, Structure, Leadership, Corporate Social Responsibility, Renewal and Growth, Productivity, and Personal Effectiveness.

Each essay leads off with an **Executive Summary** for quick reference, outlining the main points in the article. The **Making It Happen** feature shows how you can apply the principles and concepts in practice. Where relevant, authors have provided illustrative case examples and definitions of technical terms.

This section also includes a number of **Viewpoints**. These pieces are based on a set of exclusive interviews with some of the world's most prominent business authors, as well as forward-looking and agenda-setting articles that explore the future of management in an environment of constant challenge and change.

MANAGEMENT CHECKLISTS AND ACTIONLISTS

Finding Practical Solutions for Everyday Business Problems

The Management Checklists and Actionlists provide you with a comprehensive handbook of practical answers to everyday business challenges. Each list reflects current thinking and best management practice.

The Checklists were developed by experts at the Chartered Management Institute. They provide step-by-step routes to success in a wide variety of practical endeavors, from **Conducting a Performance Appraisal** to **Handling Customer Complaint**s. Each Checklist includes a list of dos and don'ts and "thought starters" to stimulate discussion and critical reflection on the topic at hand.

The Actionlists provide essential instruction for tackling specific tasks and solving problems. They address key management tasks in detail, with an emphasis on e-commerce, marketing, accounting and finance, and personal development. They also include a series of "frequently asked questions" (and direct answers), as well as helpful suggestions on how to avoid common mistakes.

For additional information, each entry offers resource recommendations and cross-references to relevant areas in the Business Information Sources section.

MANAGEMENT LIBRARY

Summarizing the Most Influential Business Books of All Time

There is a vast literature covering business and the world of work, and thousands more new publications emerge every year. However, only a handful of books become landmarks—forever changing the ways in which management is conceived and practiced.

Frederick Taylor and Rosabeth Moss Kanter

This section distills the main lessons from the best and most important business books ever published. It includes both influential new titles such as *The Change Masters* and *Blur*, as well as time-honored classics such as Peter Drucker's *The Practice of Management* and Frederick W. Taylor's *The Principles of Scientific Management*.

Each summary includes a concise overview and analysis of the book's most distinctive contributions to management thinking and practice, along with bibliographic information for the featured title and related works by the author.

BUSINESS THINKERS AND MANAGEMENT GIANTS

Profiling the Top Management Thinkers and Pioneers

This section provides over 100 profiles of the most influential or controversial business writers, entrepreneurs, and managers.

Business Thinkers includes summaries of the careers and insights of the most important and influential writers on management, as well as an assessment of their contributions to business theory and practice.

Peter Drucker

Management Giants is a highly selective gallery of the pioneers who have left their indelible stamp on the business landscape—by inventing new technologies, practices, or even industries. These profiles offer insights on the background, defining moments, and legacies of each of these characters—from John Jacob Astor to F. W. Woolworth. Being nice is not one of the main criteria for selection; being effective is.

John Jacob Astor

a-z DICTIONARY

Defining Business: The Most Up-to-date Global Business English Dictionary

The Dictionary provides jargon-free definitions to more than 7,000 international business terms, abbreviations, and acronyms.

Special features:

- **World Business English to reflect the role of the English language in the globalization of the business world; includes business slang**
- **Abbreviations, acronyms, and their expansions shown in full and cross-referenced**
- **Mini-essays to explain and illustrate complex concepts**
- **Expanded biographical entries to detail the lives and careers of key business thinkers and leaders**
- **Extensive listings of international stock exchanges and trade organizations**

management the use of professional skills for identifying and achieving organizational objectives through the deployment of appropriate resources. Management involves identifying what needs to be done, and organizing and supporting others to perform the necessary tasks. A manager has complex and ever-changing responsibilities, the focus of which shifts to reflect the issues, trends, and preoccupations of the time. At the beginning of the 20th century, the emphasis was both on supporting the organization's administration and managing productivity through increased efficiency. Organizations following Henri Fayol's and Max Weber's models built the functional divisions of personnel management, production management, marketing management, operations management, and financial management. At the beginning of the 21st century, those original drivers are still much in evidence. Although management is a profession in its own right, its skill-set often applies to professionals of other disciplines

BUSINESS INFORMATION SOURCES
Providing the Quickest and Easiest Route to the Best Business Information Available

The final section in the work offers 3,000 sources of the best business information from around the world, organized into over 100 subject areas. These include the best management Web sites, the most informative books, magazines and journals, and the most authoritative organizations.

BUSINESS MONTHLY UPGRADES
Keeping You Up-to-date

As a user of *Business*, you also are entitled to free monthly upgrades. The upgrades are a powerful resource available exclusively to *Business* readers.

These will be sent to you in PDF format, in exactly the same design as this book, so you can either read them on screen, or print and store them. Over time, these upgrades will build up to be a substantial reference work in their own right. In addition, these upgrades will be archived on the Web site, so that you can access them online at any time.

Upgrades will include a selection of the following:
- New actionlists and checklists on the latest management topics
- Best Practice essay on topical business issues
- Interviews and Viewpoints from leading management thinkers
- Summaries of the latest management bestsellers
- The best new Web sites/information sources for managers

These are available from our Web site, *www.ultimatebusinessresource.com*

To receive these valuable updates
All you need to do is go to the registration page on our Web site www.ultimatebusinessresource.com, register, type in your e-mail address, and add in your password: **welch**

FEEDBACK

We welcome any comments you may have about how *Business* might be improved. Let us know, too, if you disagree with any of the points made, or have any correction—we want to hear your views. All e-mails to us will receive a reply; write to us at
newsletters@ultimatebusinessresource.com

BEST
PRACTICE

☆ Best Practice

Putting the expertise of the world's best business thinkers to work for you

The main aim of the Best Practice Section is to provide you with overviews of key problems and business issues you are likely to face at some point in your working life.

With over 100 contributors, this section presents a powerful array of practical business advice and thinking from some of the world's leading business authors and practitioners.

However, don't expect easy answers to every problem. These essays are not designed to be the last word on the subject, but an easy-to-read and practical introduction. There are extensive links to detailed hands-on advice on 'how to do it' in later sections.

We have tried to organise these essays so you can browse them quickly. The section is therefore divided into 12 broad themes: People and Culture; Marketing; Strategy; Finance; IT; Systems; Structure; Leadership; Corporate Social Responsibility and Governance; Renewal and Growth; Productivity; and Personal Effectiveness.

At the beginning of each essay is an **Executive Summary**. This is for quick reference, outlining the main points in the article.

The **Making It Happen** section shows how you can apply what has been discussed in practice. Where relevant, authors have provided examples to show how theories have been implemented.

Each essay provides you with a short directory entitled **For More Information**, as well as quick links to other sections in BUSINESS.

Lastly, we've provided a number of distinguished **Viewpoints**. These are based on a number of exclusive interviews with some of the world's leading business thinkers such as Charles Handy and Fons Trompenaars, as well as more forward-looking articles about the future of business by leading thinkers such as Stan Davis, Jim Collins, Meg Wheatley, Seth Godin, and Chris Locke. Our aim here is to stimulate, to provoke, and to inspire.

Contents

4

BEST PRACTICE

Management in the 21st Century
by Tom Brown

. . . [F]rom the commencement of my management I viewed the population, with the mechanism and every other part of the establishment, as a system composed of many parts, and which it was my duty and interest so to combine, as that every hand, as well as every spring, lever, and wheel, should effectually cooperate to produce the greatest pecuniary gain to the proprietors.
Robert Owen, "Address to the Superintendents of Manufactories"

MANAGEMENT, *THEN*

In the beginning—well, it was complex then, too.

To "manage" resources effectively is a concept, says Daniel Wren in *The Evolution of Management Thought*, which can be traced back to the Babylonian King, Hammurabi. That ancient manager, if you will, issued "a code of 282 laws, which governed business dealings, personal behavior, interpersonal relations, wages, punishments, and a host of other societal matters," says Wren. He points out that "Law 104, for example, was the first historical mention of accounting." Consider it very early B2B thinking, which dealt "with the handling of receipts and established an agency relationship between the merchant and the agent." Another law, amazingly, provided very early consumer protection. Hammurabi prescribed a clear-cut consequence for any builder of a house that collapses on the owner and kills him: "[T]hat builder should be put to death."

As Wren expands the evolution of management to more familiar names (Chris Argyris, Henry Ford, John Kotter, Elton Mayo, William Whyte), it's interesting to note that Wren's analyses, in many ways, reveal the same complex skein of critical factors that challenge anyone today who has tried to convert resources into results. The Chinese general, Sun Tzu, really *was* struggling with the principles of managing a 600 B.C. army; and he wasn't planning to start a consultancy or go on a speaking tour. He wanted to get things done. Simply. Effectively. Correctly. *Now.*

In its familiar definition, management is "getting work done through others." Yet anyone who has tried to manage knows that management is never simple, is only sometimes effective, may or may not be done right the first time, and can never happen fast enough. Management may not be rocket science, but it *is* complex. "Management thought did not develop in a cultural vacuum"; says Wren, "managers have always found their jobs affected by the existing culture." Given the elements of any culture (economic variables, social norms, politics, and so on), managers have always had to think first about current norms—*and only then*—move forward.

The *Oxford English Dictionary* starts its derivative history of *management*, the word as it would be used today, with a 1598 citation; *manager*, it says, was actually in use some 10 years before. It makes more sense to jump to 1813 and to Robert Owen, the first authority cited in *Classics in Management*, a collection of excerpts from the thinkers who most influenced the profession during its formative years. Owen, a Scottish textile manufacturer, was consciously managing in the Industrial Age. His address to his fellow manufacturing magnates shows that he well understood how "inanimate machines" had altered the workscape permanently. "Many of you have long experienced in your manufacturing operations the advantages of substantial, well-contrived, and well-executed machinery," wrote Owen. He talked excitedly about the wonders of a well-oiled manufacturing machine in the way we might boast of the power and beauty of a pulsing new personal computer. He was also well aware of the potential profits from an investment in new technology, "money expended," he says, "for the chance of increased gain."

His 1813 address was far from a paean to technology and profits alone, however; he spent most of his attention on the numerous advantages of managing *people*. "[W]ill you not afford some of your attention," Owen implores, "to consider whether a portion of your time and capital would not be more advantageously applied to improve your living machines?" He argued that a healthy synergy of workplace conditions (including state-of-the-art technology) and workplace humanism ("care and attention to the living instruments") would yield unheard-of profits. Owen promised his fellow manufacturers that, by following his advice, they too would see returns of "not five, ten, or fifteen per cent, for your capital so expended, but often fifty and in many cases a hundred per cent."

Among the many management gurus who followed, Frederick Winslow Taylor (*The Principles of Scientific Management*), Henri Fayol (*General Principles of Management*), Mary Parker Follett (*Freedom and Co-ordination*), and Elton Mayo (*The Social Problems of an Industrial Civilization*) are forebears to the autograph-signing management stars of today. But Owen, even though he knew that management had always operated in the context of economic variables, social norms, and politics, set the essential challenge for all managers thereafter with his elevation of three distinct issues: technology, people, and profits. How do we balance these three elements into the best combination, the most productive combination, the longest sustainable combination: in short, a *winning* combination?

". . . [I]n 1981, . . . I said I wanted GE to become "the most competitive enterprise on earth." . . . In the end, I believe we created the greatest people factory in the world, a learning enterprise, with a boundaryless culture."
Jack Welch, *Jack: Straight from the Gut*

MANAGEMENT, *NOW*

The thousands of management books proffered over the last decade can be easily divided into two stacks. On one side are the numerous bestselling management authors (from thinker Rosabeth Moss Kanter to real-life manager Jack Welch) who often present an overall picture of corporate management doing things exceedingly right. Stellar managers, as presented in some books, have balanced the complexities of technology, people, and profit into distilled and potent commercial certainty. Bookstore racks teem with such tomes; the more cynical readers consider such works "fad books," designed to spawn yet another *program du jour* inside the corporate world. The excellent enterprise may be named General Electric, though it just as well could be called Camelot Inc. Often the same companies and managers are heralded in multiple books by different authors. And those who offer management wisdom gleaned from such paragons seem convinced that managers in any

---

company need follow only a few nicely jotted bullet points to guarantee success.

But amidst the thunderous accolades accorded those few companies and executives that have earned widespread public adulation, many serious observers talk about working and managing with voices pitched harsh, even doleful. In the July 22, 2001, issue of the *New York Times*, Margo Jefferson, focusing on the drama world, posed an interesting question: "How Can the Theater Make Itself Matter Again?" Her answer, in part, was this: "Theater needs new work. It has to catch something of the way we live here and now: take in the facts and the sensations, show us our minds and bodies as they react and realign themselves. And theater needs to take more risks." Change the word *theater* to *management*, and many would argue that Ms. Jefferson's thoughts apply equally to the complex meshing of technology and people to produce profits.

Throughout *The Working Life*, her eminent study of the history of work, Joanne Ciulla also raises some tough issues; she comments that too many people "can't choose when to go to work and what to do at work. They do not deliberate on management policies or decide how to do the task at hand. Worst of all, many still can't plan for the future because they don't know if they will have a job." Richard Donkin spent six years researching the same subject, work, and reached comparable conclusions in *Blood, Sweat & Tears*. "The more I write," he says about the world of work, "the more I ask myself this recurring question: Why on earth do we do it?" Donkin points out, as do others, that management has become such a prized profession that, with salaries and bonuses, some top executives now easily earn "150 times more than their lowest paid employees." But it's not excessive money making that seems to disturb Donkin the most. His introduction relates how he once sat beside "a FTSE 100 company chief, fishing by the riverbank . . . listening to him giving instructions [to his office] on his mobile phone." Says Donkin: "The craziness is that some of these highly paid individuals are working such long hours they rarely have the opportunity to step outside their jobs and enjoy a moment's leisure."

Christina Maslach and Michael Leiter believe that burnout affects far more than tired top execs. When their book on burnout was published (just a few years ago), they offered this challenging thought: "Burnout is reaching epidemic proportions among North American workers today. It's not so much that something has gone wrong with us but rather that there have been fundamental changes in the workplace and the nature of our jobs. The workplace today is a cold, hostile, demanding environment, both economically and psychologically . . . People are becoming cynical, keeping their distance, trying not to let themselves get too involved." There's perhaps good reason not to be too attached to one's job. Citing statistics collected by Challenger, Gray & Christmas, the Associated Press reported at the end of 2001 that job cuts in the United States were the highest in almost a decade. For too many management teams, has strategic planning now been permanently reduced to an exercise in subtraction?

Bill Jensen is actively trying to capture the difference between what the workplace is like and what it *should* be like. He speaks and writes about *Work 2.0*, where people (and managers) need to stop thinking about organizational productivity and start thinking about personal productivity. He says we all need to stop focusing on things like operational excellence and tune into "radical simplicity," an awareness of what people really need to get their work done. In a Work 2.0 world, he stresses

that people are "business units of one." Another vanguard management thinker on how organizations should be is Thomas Stewart, of *Fortune*, who wrote in *The Wealth of Knowledge*: "The modern corporation, like modern art, is over. The postmodern corporation is different." He argues that one of the chief differences lies in how management defines employment. "It's more accurate—and more useful—to think of employees in a new way: not as assets but as investors. Shareholders invest money in our companies; employees invest time, energy, and intelligence."

Arie de Geus, drawing on his long career at Royal Dutch/ Shell, argues in *Business Minds* that management may be suffering a crisis of vocabulary. "[C]ompanies have become trapped in the prison of economic language, which is why so many companies suffer premature deaths . . . [C]ompanies tend to die early because their leaders and executives concentrate on production and profit, and forget that the corporation is an institution . . . a community of human beings." In that same work, Fons Trompenaars argues that, since "culture" today must be defined globally, the basic job of a manager is overdue for a radical redesign. "Just because people speak English does not mean they think alike," he argues. "The international manager needs to go beyond awareness of cultural differences. He or she needs to respect these differences and take advantage of diversity through reconciling cross-cultural dilemmas."

How could modern management, almost 200 years after Robert Owen, be so divided? On the one hand, the biggest bestsellers in management are tied to a daily cartoon strip named "Dilbert" that chronicles the work strife of a high-tech laborer who seemingly debases management for a living. On the other hand, another simple storybook features a cartoon mouse who can't seem to manage a block of cheese. And such contrarian views get even starker. Anita Roddick, founder of The Body Shop chain of stores and a former C.E.O. who has also generated considerable controversy, has written two books about both her trade and her views on management. Her latest work acknowledges that, for many, management has made business "a jungle where only the vicious survive." She laments that, for too many, managing a business is about sitting "in front of computer screens, moving millions of dollars from Japan to New York." She yearns for "a new view of business as a community where only the responsible will lead."

Margaret Wheatley is today more a social philosopher than a management guru. Yet by looking at management practices through the lens of modern physics, her early-1990s book, *Leadership and the New Science*, took "scientific management" to a depth that Frederick Winslow Taylor could never have imagined. Today, she says management is *stuck*. "If we don't change the way we manage business in the next ten years," she says bluntly, "we're dead." A chorus of management thinkers, writers, and managers is there to back her up. W. Chan Kim and Renée Mauborgne, talking about the difficulties of managing strategy in a knowledge economy, believe that a quantum leap in management will come only when "fair process" comes to the modern work world, something that involves "major changes in [behavior] and working practices" which "will not be achieved without people willingly cooperating with the innovation process and making their skills and experience available to a company." It should come as little surprise that Richard Leider these days asks every top exec he meets to answer just one question: *Why would the best people in the world want to work for your company?*

"Success, in my view, is the willingness to strive for something you really want."

Fran Tarkenton

8 BEST PRACTICE

Two Stanford University professors, Jeffrey Pfeffer and Robert Sutton, looking at the corporate world at large, found that, despite all the gleeful chirps by proud executives about their companies being elite learning organizations, there were plenty of organizational examples of the polar opposite. They subsequently wrote *The Knowing-Doing Gap*. Its very first sentence is an indictment of the profession of management today—or, at least, a diagnosis of serious managerial schizophrenia. "We wrote this book because we wanted to understand why so many managers know so much about organizational performance, say so many smart things about how to achieve performance, and work so hard, yet are trapped in firms that do so many things they know will undermine performance." It's as if too few managers (and management thinkers!) had ever read, bothered to think about, act upon, or even recall Douglas McGregor's mournful challenge to the management profession in the closing paragraph of his landmark 1960 work, *The Human Side Of Enterprise*. Forty years before Pfeffer and Sutton's research, McGregor had already concluded: "Fads will come and go. The fundamental fact of man's capacity to collaborate with his fellows in the face-to-face group will survive the fads and one day be recognized. Then, and only then, will management discover how seriously it has underestimated the true potential of its human resources."

As we learn more about life ... Mendel, Darwin, Watson, Crick, Venter ... Will be figures every bit as important as Edison, Einstein, Ford, the Wright brothers ... What they have taught us and produced is changing each of our lives ... How we work, live, and think. You can stand on the sidelines and assume fate will guide things ... (God willing ... Si Dios Quiere ... Insha'Allah ... Shikatta ga nai ...) Or you can help yourself, your family, your company and country navigate ... This wondrous and scary adventure.

Juan Enriquez, *As The Future Catches You*

MANAGEMENT, *TOMORROW*

E-mail and the Internet are two of the technological forces that have altered the job of a manager. Whether the concern be how to manage "virtual employees" who work from home (are they *really* working?) or how to decide who should be able to access the megabytes of intimate corporate data that now course through any modern company, technology is as daunting today as it was for Robert Owen in 1813—with a commensurate impact on people and profits. Yet, for managers, there's an even bigger horizon to glimpse and ponder.

In his role as director of the Life Sciences Project at Harvard Business School, Juan Enriquez has thought deeply about the personal and fiscal import of such society-shaking developments as the recent mapping of the human genome. That may seem like a too-distant subject for someone managing a steel mill, grocery, or factory—or even a software development company. Enriquez thinks otherwise. Referring to the work of Robert Fleishmann and Craig Venter, work that produced "the first genetic map of a living organism," Enriquez reflected that such scientific breakthroughs raise questions that people never even thought they would be able to ask. Robert Owen fretted over how best to control the capital assets and human resources of his manufacturing plant; now people are starting to fret over how, as Enriquez says in his book, "To control ... Directly and deliberately ... The evolution of our species ... and that of every other species on the planet." It's a big jump. Can management, as a profession, make it?

We don't know. What we do know is that every manager today has both new *and* old questions to answer. Andrea Gabor probed the lives of ten individuals (whom she called *The Capitalist Philosophers*) who were management heavyweights of the last century, people like Chester Barnard, Abraham Maslow, and W. Edwards Deming. She concluded that management tomorrow has to find an answer to the question that, at heart, also bothered Owen. Says Gabor: "At the root of the conflict between the humanistic and the scientific are two warring images of the business organization and its purpose in ... society: One sees the corporation as a pivotal institution of democracy with complex responsibilities to a host of constituencies, including its employees, its customer, and the community. The other, much more utilitarian, view recognizes one primary corporate constituent—the shareholder—and a single purpose—profit making."

Technology is now proceeding at a pace that may quickly outstretch management's (and, perhaps, mankind's) ability to decide *what* to do with what we are so rapidly learning *how* to do. The very real prospect arises that many will simply conclude that life and business, both, are irrefutably unmanageable. Owen feared that technology would overpower the human being; Deming feared that human myopia about issues like quality would overpower an organization's technological capability to deliver excellent products. Today, some fear that the push for profit could throttle both technology and humanity. Even a sober thinker like Charles Handy (who calls himself "a reluctant capitalist") talks about "elephants" (large companies) and "fleas" (individuals or small groups with innovative ideas), conceding that "[M]any observers think that the big corporations are now both richer and more powerful than many nation states .... The elephants, people feel, may be out of anyone's control."

AND YET—

And yet one can safely assert that the hundreds of years of management debate have not been without value—that the hundreds of management treatises, the hundreds of management theories, the hundreds of management gurus, the hundreds of management "solutions" (from Theories X and Y to the Managerial Grid to the Eight Principles of Excellence to Business Process Reengineering)—all of this management commotion has not been without a constructive role in society. For the study of management, during the centuries in which it has been active and accepted as a discipline, has always served as the testing ground for how we could and should work, individually and collectively. Management thinking has served as the closest thing to a laboratory where the "genetic code" of human enterprise can be mapped, to see if there are new ways to pool the resources tied to every human endeavor into new vistas of human possibilities. As Robert Heller and Tim Hindle note in their illuminating *Essential Manager's Manual*, "A full understanding of what makes people perform well and of the problems that may affect performance in the workplace is therefore essential for any manager. He or she will need to employ a wide range of skills, both interpersonal and professional, in order to resolve these problems."

The practice of management, through both its scientific standards and its artistic renderings, remains the best way yet to channel the raw energy of human minds, the brute force of vast capital, and the quixotic capability of new technology to transform people by reshaping their perceptions of what's possible

"'Top' management is supposed to be a tree full of owls ... hooting when management heads into the wrong part of the forest. I'm still unpersuaded they even know where the forest is."

Robert Townsend

on this planet, and ultimately, even beyond. The marketplace of ideas about management has always been a free market. Accounting, information, logistics, marketing, manufacturing, organizational culture, research and development, sales, social policy—pick *any* discipline within the profession of management, and you'll find intense debate about the questions that matter most to each particular realm of the corporate world. It is as it always was. It is as it should be.

Thus, whenever a large collection of management thinkers are assembled under one roof, one book, or one Web site, the last thing one should expect is congruence. Management, as it has evolved and is evolving, is a battle of ideas and ideals. Management thinkers and practitioners only align with others when they share common views of how technology can be deployed, how humans can best interact with the machines and systems they have created, and how, when combined, these forces can create new wealth. But wealth follows achievement. Businesses do not prosper because of their strategic planning; they succeed because of their strategic execution and because of the extent to which they can attract both investors and customers to share their strategic purpose. And achievement is very much an exercise in managing for the future.

There are still many questions about management that have not been asked or answered.

The greatest debates about how to manage ourselves and our companies have yet to be staged. The most salient ideas about how to manage both the workplace (and the world!) have yet to be widely disseminated, considered, and tested. Even the largest collection of management information and ideas is simply a mental cake mix until students and practitioners stir themselves into the blend and begin to practice new forms of management—to become, in essence, new kinds of managers.

Management and human enterprise have brought mankind a long way. We travel fast, communicate easily, shop globally, and learn rapidly. Yet, judging mainly by what management has accomplished in the past (and what it hasn't), we can be quite sure that its study will never become passé. The word will never be pulled from the dictionaries because it has become archaic. We need not quake over the prospect that the study of management will no longer be needed because its best practices have accomplished everything that needs to be done. We need not fear terminal success. Whenever enormous problems involving work, people, and organizations crop up, this question will imminently bubble up too: How do we *manage* this problem? The list is endless but undoubtedly starts with . . .

● Some executives do achieve long-term business success. Yet we really don't know how to replace that executive with one just as capable in order to keep the good corporate times going—nor do we know how to transfer an excellent manager's expertise to another company or another industry. We in management own that problem.

● The power of large corporations rivals many nations; their top managers are often more widely known than presidents or prime ministers. Yet corporations don't really know how to wield that power in ways that do not devastate some communities while disproportionately blessing others. We in management own that problem.

● E-commerce is an increasing force in the buying and selling of goods, both between businesses and between companies/customers. Yet we don't know how to e-replicate the relationships and loyalty that used to be the greatest asset of any business: customer goodwill. We in management own that problem.

● Corporations no longer have to be mega in size to leverage global connections; 24/7 workdays and Internet communications make it probable, not just possible, that for many, the worker "in the next cubicle" will be thousands of miles away. Yet few companies have meshed the unique cultural perspectives of a multi-national workforce into a coherent, collaborative team. We in management own that problem.

● Advanced technology has made it possible to fly to outer space and return safely. Yet, all over the globe, people today are struggling with how to fly or drive millions of miles without facing overt terrorism or risking the less obvious terror of enviro-toxic byproducts corrupting the atmosphere permanently. We in management own that problem.

● Even in the most heralded companies boasting a badge of merit that says they are "wonderful" places to work, employees and managers slink to work each day uninspired, even desperate—incapable of connecting the mission of the company with their own mission in life. We in management own that problem.

Management in the 21st century is incomplete, imperfect, and quite often insufficient to meet pressing needs. That makes management tomorrow as exciting as ever, an exhilarating subject to study and a dynamic profession to practice. In almost any corner of your life, your workplace, your community, or your global marketplace, there are problems that simply won't be addressed unless *someone* in management owns them.

Therefore today—right now!—the most important unanswered question in management comes down to four words: *Might that be you?*

FOR MORE INFORMATION

Books:

Adams, Scott. *The Dilbert Principle*. London: Boxtree, 1997.

Ciulla, Joanne. *The Working Life*. New York: Random House, 2000.

Donkin, Richard. *Blood, Sweat & Tears*. London: Texere, 2001.

Enriquez, Juan. *As The Future Catches You*. New York: Crown Business, 2001.

Gabor, Andrea. *The Capitalist Philosophers*. New York: Random House, 2000.

Handy, Charles. *The Elephant and the Flea*. London: Hutchinson, 2001.

Heller, Robert and Tim Hindle. *Essential Manager's Manual*. London: Dorling Kindersley, 1998.

Johnson, Spencer. *Who Moved My Cheese?* London: Vermilion, 1999.

Maslach, Christina, and Michael P. Leiter. *The Truth About Burnout*. San Francisco, CA: Jossey-Bass, 1997.

McGregor, Douglas. *The Human Side Of Enterprise*. Annotated ed. Maidenhead: McGraw-Hill, 2005.

Owen, Robert. "An Address: To The Superintendents Of Manufactories" [1813], *Classics In Management* (ed. Harwood F. Merrill). New York: American Management Association, 1960.

Pfeffer, Jeffrey and Robert I. Sutton. *The Knowing-Doing Gap*. Boston, MA: Harvard Business School Press, 2000.

Roddick, Anita. *Business As Unusual*. London: Thorsons, 2000.

Stewart, Thomas. *The Wealth of Knowledge*. London: Nicholas Brealey, 2002.

Trompenaars, Fons. Interview in *Business Minds*. Prentice Hall, 2002.

Welch, Jack (with John Byrne). *Jack, Straight From The Gut*. New York: Warner Books, 2001.

Wren, Daniel. *The Evolution Of Management Thought*. 4th ed. New York: Wiley, 1994.

"Every hand, as well as every spring, lever, and wheel, should effectually cooperate to produce the greatest pecuniary gain to the proprietors."

Robert Owen

Action Learning by George Boulden

EXECUTIVE SUMMARY

- Action learning is a proven tool for realizing individual and organizational change.
- It combines knowledge that people have been taught with skills that people have learned, often from experience.
- Action learning requires a supportive environment in which to thrive. Once established, it provides a valuable and powerful stimulus for continuous change, enabling organizations to grow and learn dynamically, rather than remaining static or fixed in one set of circumstances or perspectives.

INTRODUCTION

Action learning (AL) is a powerful tool for individual and organizational change. The term "action learning" was originally used by Professor Reg Revans to identify his philosophy of management development. Revans's approach to management training differed from the conventional approach in that it focused on developing managerial skills rather than just increasing knowledge. Revans had recognized from his work in the mining industry that the major factors affecting a manager's job performance were his or her skills (ability to do the job) and attitudes (the will to do what is necessary to optimize effectiveness). Revans's idea was to help managers optimize their performance in a practical way by training managers as they worked to solve real problems. The learning and therefore the development of managerial skills are directly linked to the learner's real needs based on actual experience.

Action learning is based on the concept:

$$L = P + Q$$

Learning [L] comprises **Programmed knowledge** [P] (things that people have been taught or that they have learned through experiences) plus **Questioning skills** [Q] (the ability/willingness to challenge programmed knowledge using the stimulus of real life problems).

In Revans's view, people need the programmed knowledge that they have acquired over the years but, in the conditions of rapid change that we live in today, this is not enough for survival. People, and especially managers, must also constructively question both themselves and those around them so that they can adapt successfully to their constantly changing world.

The basic idea of action learning is simple. Individuals are put in a supportive environment with a problem to solve and a facilitator who will encourage them to question their P and to test themselves and each other. The process of questioning and testing produces experience. Reflection on experience leads to learning. The child learns that the stove is hot, not by touching it (test), but through the pain that comes from the burn afterwards (reflection). Learning is demonstrated if he or she does not touch the hot stove again.

UNDERSTANDING ACTION LEARNING

Key approaches and roles

Action learning creates learning opportunities through which people develop by:

- working on "life" problems;
- being empowered to question what is happening;
- trying out suggested solutions (doing things differently);
- stepping back and reflecting on what is happening and why;
- sharing the experience with others who are also learning by doing.

There are two main models of action learning: the Revans approach, which focuses on individual development, and the "Inplant" or organizational development model developed by Action Learning Associates (ALA), which combines individual development with organizational change. Both methods use the same structure:

- **The problem.** This provides the focus for the activity. It is individual in the Revans model and a team problem (project) in the In-plant model.
- **The client** is the person who owns the problem. In Revans's terms this must be someone who knows, cares, and above all can implement its solution if they wish to.
- **The action learning set.** This is the place where participants meet to share their experience. It is the core of the program;

the questioning, confrontation, challenging, and support which take place in the set provide the encouragement and stimulus for individuals/groups to carry on. It is the meeting place of "comrades in adversity" as Revans calls them.

- **The facilitator** encourages learning through questioning, mirroring, challenging, and supporting. The facilitator is the grit in the oyster which creates the learning pearl.
- **The sponsor** is the senior manager responsible for the program.

Harnessing action learning for individual development

There are several ways in which action learning is used to develop individuals, including:

- **The Own Job model**

  This aims to enable individuals to maximize their personal effectiveness.

  Individuals take a problem into the action learning set and they meet at regular intervals over an agreed period of time with an external facilitator. The learning focus is on helping participants to develop the expertise they need to solve their own problems. An example of this approach is Toyota in Japan. Chu-San-Ren, a Japanese management consulting company based in Nagoya, has been running Own Job action learning programs with Toyota since 1993. A more recent example shows how action learning is being used to supplement a London Business School personal development program in Roche Pharmaceuticals (see Boulden and de Laat below).

- **The P Development (Academic) model**

  This approach aims to maximize the learning opportunities presented while acquiring knowledge (P). The model combines the personal effectiveness development aspects of the Own Job model with the opportunity to acquire new learning. Sets are formed of people who have the same learning goals and have a dual focus: new knowledge coupled with personal learning. This model is now widely used in more advanced management schools and a number of large corporations. An example of this approach is ACE Insurance, which has adopted this model to train its senior managers. The program provides a three-week development activity for senior people from ACE companies around the world. The

"The world can only be grasped by action, not by contemplation. The hand is the cutting edge of man."

Jacob Bronowski

core activity is a major business-related project. The approach reflects a balance of "hard inputs" by specialists, live data gathering, and analysis and self-development.

- **The Inplant Action Learning approach**
While individual action learning programs are very powerful in bringing about individual change, they cannot change organizational culture. One approach to this problem has been to apply the action learning method on an in-plant basis, using problems that exist within the company—real problems which it must solve. The approach uses the typical AL structure, in which directors and senior managers are cast as "clients," middle managers as "set facilitators," and foremen and supervisors as "fellows" in action learning teams. The whole process is coordinated by external "facilitators." Thus all managers and supervisors are involved in a change program at the same time. This structure is classical Revans. The main difference is in the application. The Inplant approach applies action learning to the total management structure of a company in a way which involves everybody.

MAKING IT HAPPEN ▶▶

- First, consider what you want to achieve: do you want to restructure your organization, develop your people, solve specific problems, or something else?
- Read the literature, scan the Web sites, talk to someone who has done it.

- Set yourself some output goals. Note these should be both technical, for example, solving specific problems, and behavioral, for example, participants demonstrating their ability to apply their skills in future projects.
- Design your program. A typical action learning program lasts for about six months and has five main stages:

1 **Introductory workshop**. This is used to launch the program and can vary in length from one day to three weeks. The goal is to get things started and the more effective this process, the quicker the set starts to function effectively.
2 **Investigation and recommendation**. This usually lasts three months and provides the opportunity for participants to analyze the problems, to benchmark against best practice, and to produce recommendations.
3 **Presentation and feedback**. This is usually a two-part stage: the participants present their findings to their clients, and later the clients say what action they would like to sponsor based on the recommendations.
4 **Implementation**. This usually lasts about three months and involves participants in implementing the recommendations agreed upon with the client.
5 **Final review—1 day**. This is an opportunity to review what has or has not been learned or achieved and to agree upon the way ahead.

CONCLUSION

Action learning relies on the team-working and facilitation processes which encourage questioning, empower participants to try something different, and lead to change. The heart of the action learning process is the group, supported by the facilitator. It provides a safe haven from which individuals can emerge to test themselves and return to share their experience, thereby encouraging and supporting change.

Any teamworking or problem-solving activity can be turned into an action learning program, through the simple addition of a facilitation process. Any personal development programs can be greatly strengthened by forming action learning sets and providing facilitation. Why not do it and maximize the value of your investment?

FOR MORE INFORMATION

Book and Journal Articles:
Weinstein, Krystyna. *Action Learning: A Practical Guide*. 2nd ed. Brookfield, VT: Gower, 1998.
Boulden, George P., and Richard De Laat. "Peer Group Learning in Roche Pharmaceutical," *Action Learning: Research and Practice*, Vol. 2, No. 2, September 2005, pp. 1–9.

Web sites:
International Foundation for Action Learning (IFAL): **www.ifal.org.uk**
International Community of Action Learners (ICAL): **www.tlainc.com**

"We do not need, and indeed never will have, all the answers before we act . . . It is often through taking action that we can discover some of them."

Charlotte Bunch

Making Recognition and Rewards a "Whole-Person" Experience

by R. Brayton Bowen

EXECUTIVE SUMMARY

- The 21st century requires a holistic approach to recognizing and rewarding employees.
- It's possible to place too much emphasis on pay and other extrinsic rewards.
- The changing nature of the relationship between employers and employees requires a new kind of "currency."

INTRODUCTION

Managing people is increasingly complex. Markets expand globally. Labor forces grow invisible and offices are virtual. People are less committed to organizations emotionally. And running a successful enterprise has become more difficult and competitive. What are the best ways to engage, activate, and motivate employees?

From hourly wages to piece rates, and profit sharing to gain sharing, the number of incentive programs and pay packages is legion. But why do some employees check out—operationally, emotionally, even physically—while others tune in? Why are some organizations confounded by poor returns while others rocket ahead? The answer lies in a *whole-person* approach.

Effective systems of recognition and reward engage an individual's entire being. They encourage employees to unleash stores of productive energy while exhibiting regenerative qualities that foster creativity, emotional reserves that translate into passion, and even spiritual attributes that result in the inspired performance needed to achieve a larger vision.

Successful managers respect both people and processes. Abandoning command-and-control management, they emphasize relationships. These managers regard employees as part of their customer base, continuously looking for ways to satisfy and retain employee commitment while ultimately inspiring them to peak performance.

THE NEW MILLENNIUM WORKPLACE

Today's labor force is diverse: Boomers, generation Xers, generation Y, former welfare recipients, the Net generation. Add multicultural and multiracial labor pools and the management challenge becomes enormous. Compensation experts and professional managers have realized that a one-size approach to human resources won't fit all. Different people have different values, needs, wants, and expectations, and unless these conditions can be addressed satisfactorily the outcomes can prove disastrous.

Employees are increasingly knowledge workers. No longer can the workplace house all employees under one roof under the watchful eye of a supervisor; workers often telecommute. Furthermore, individual contributors are joining teams, with members scattered around the globe, prompting the need for yet more varied performance management systems and reward programs. Given this diversity, an appropriate blend of recognition and rewards must be available.

THE TRUTH ABOUT CARROTS, STICKS, MOTIVATION, AND REWARDS

Some experts have shown that incentives and alternative pay packages can have a positive influence on employee performance—short-term. Others claim that such packages actually have a negative influence, especially long term. Almost all agree it's essential to pay people fairly and competitively. Some experts are wrong, however, in arguing that pay is the chief motivator. For the welfare-to-work employee and minimum-wage earners, money is a basic need, not a motivator. In reality, motivation is an inside job; money may influence behavior, but it's no substitute for motivation. People require a greater sense of achievement and self-actualization.

Enlightened managers use total reward systems that link direct and indirect payments to performance requirements tied to the organization's success. Such an approach is far more effective than simpler, more restrictive, linear systems that func-

tion on a quid pro quo: produce this and you get x. But even total reward packages won't achieve everything possible if they fail to engage the whole person. Leading systems are holistic.

MINI-CASES
Holistic systems of reward and recognition

Southwest Airlines has a superb record of satisfied customers and upbeat employees. While competitors have succumbed to the downturns and upswings of economic cycles, only Southwest has been consistently profitable. The carrier lavishes attention on its employees (who also hold company stock), displaying plaques honoring those who achieve outstanding performance and promoting a fun-filled culture.

Toyota encourages employees worldwide to generate new ideas at a rate of some 40,000 *per plant* annually, and each is recognized and rewarded according to its operational impact. Moreover, so imbued is Toyota's culture with concepts of quality, teamwork, and empowerment that a single employee can literally stop production for the good of the ultimate customer, without supervisory approval. Indeed, turning the organizational pyramid upside down is nothing new at Toyota, where managers are viewed as resources for team members and an "office" is simply a desk on the production floor readily accessible to the team.

Mary Kay Cosmetics may reward outstanding performers with pink Cadillacs, but it is focused on enhancing the self-esteem and economic independence of women, especially those who represent the company. Moreover, Mary Kay rewards and recognizes women while having fun. The combination of economic opportunity and psychic income resulted in phenomenal growth.

Many other organizations, including Federal Express, The Body Shop, Hewlett-Packard, and Disney, have created environments and traditions that have appealed to the emotional, professional, and economic interests of employees. They use holistic reward and recognition systems via:
- job design
- decision-making processes
- pay equity

"Commitment to objectives is a function of the rewards associated with their achievement."

Douglas McGregor

- performance planning and management systems
- self-direction
- communication
- leadership styles
- professional development

A holistic system is open to incorporating anything that influences employees to unleash their motivation and passion. Holistic systems work especially well with free agents.

THE RISE OF THE FREE AGENT

For some time companies have been downsizing—essentially, firing large numbers of employees wholesale—to ensure profitability, even survival, during harsh economic times. Many middle managers have lost their jobs. People that remain, managers and nonmanagers alike, have had to demonstrate their value to their organization to stay employed. Gone is the old-style psychological contract for lifelong employment. As one manager expressed it, "Loyalty is dead. We can no longer afford it."

The bad news: While companies have been getting meaner and leaner, worker commitment and personal drive to go all out have been lost. The good news: Employees have become more resourceful at finding ways to demonstrate and increase their worth to current and prospective employers. Smart employees see themselves as free agents and are continuously looking for ways to improve their skills, competencies, reputation, and marketability.

IN SEARCH OF NEW CURRENCY

Smart managers recognize the needs of free agents by engaging in practices that say: "I'll meet your needs; I expect you to meet mine. Let's work together!" Free agents want flexibility to move through organizational systems without being locked in to one department. They want to be recognized and valued for the talents they bring and for results achieved. They prefer teams in which they can realize a more self-directed environment than they can in a single job reporting to a supervisor. While rewards are important, so, too, are responsibility, respect, recognition, and relationships. Moreover, because of their concern for independence and marketability, they have a critical need to protect their reputation; they gravitate to assignments that enhance their standing in the eyes of others.

The new currency that managers must use in today's workplace is based on respect. Even when organizations are known to or intend to downsize, smart managers understand the importance of respecting people's

intelligence and telling it like it is. They work collaboratively with employees. They make conscious decisions to join forces instead of subordinating or dominating. As newer systems such as skill-based pay, total-reward programs, pay-for-performance plans, and open-book management become more mainstream, the challenge for management will be to avoid any suggestion that they are manipulative or disrespectful. In fact, placing too much emphasis on pay and pay systems will detract from the intrinsic value of work itself.

WORK AS ITS OWN REWARD

Recognizing the short-term nature of employment and the need to influence peak performance, organizations have generated elaborate programs to motivate employees, including informal awards (spontaneous shows of appreciation, thank-you gifts for special services) and formal awards (bonuses, prizes, trophies, service awards).

These are all extrinsic awards, providing recognition by means of factors external to the work itself; other examples include:
- base-pay packages
- variable pay plans
- incentives
- cash and cash equivalents
- benefits
- gain-sharing plans
- profit-sharing plans
- commissions
- stock options
- alternative pay programs

Intrinsic rewards, by contrast, are inherent to the nature of the work itself and the context or environment in which it is performed. They are innately energizing and satisfying, either because the work is pleasurable or because it fulfills individuals' desire to support the organization's mission or value system or their own relationships with coworkers. Enlightened managers know the importance of responsibility, respect, recognition, and relationships; these are intrinsically rewarding. In the rush to motivate employees, any number of managers have invested heavily in extrinsic rewards, overlooking the enormous value of intrinsic rewards.

Indeed, one intrinsic value of work is that at some level it is a creative expression of self. That's why some people "love" their work. It helps them feel a sense of mission in their life. Consequently, by aligning personal needs, desires, and expectations with the needs of the enterprise, work can be performed, analyzed, and redesigned continuously to create a win–win situation for employer and employee.

The hard reality, however, is that it takes willingness on the part of managers and involvement on the part of employees to construct work assignments and processes that add value for all stakeholders. Indeed, in the new workplace employees will require more respect—and that means more recognition—to feel passionate about their work and motivated to excel. The shared objective for both managers and employees must be to find work that employees can come to love and that they feel valued in doing.

MAKING IT HAPPEN ▸▸
- Begin with a mindset that's passionate about making a difference in people's lives, not just the bottom line.
- Design an environment that encourages people to give their best—because they want to, not because they have to.
- Think big picture! Integrate rewards, benefits, and recognition with the entire work experience.
- Unless you've done it before, get professional help. Do not be thrifty at the expense of the company's future.
- Involve employees in the redesign process. Inclusion is the quintessential form of recognition.

CONCLUSION

True recognition is a whole-person experience. Said one employee, "I appreciate that my manager asks how I *feel* about a situation, then what I *think* about it, and lastly, what I want to *do*." The approach is holistic. It begins with feelings. Smart managers know they may engage the head, but they must also engage the heart of every employee. It's the only way to recognize and reward employees in the workplace of the new millennium.

FOR MORE INFORMATION

Books:
Kohn, Alfie. *Punished by Rewards*. Boston, MA: Houghton Mifflin, 1999.
Pfeffer, Jeffrey. *The Human Equation*. Cambridge, MA: Harvard Business School Press, 1998.
Zingheim, Patricia K., and Jay R. Schuster. *Pay People Right*. San Francisco, CA: Jossey-Bass, 2000.

Web sites:
American Management Association: **www.amanet.org**
WorldatWork: **www.worldatwork.org**

"They [employees] have to feel the rewards that go with winning—in the soul as well as in the wallet."

Jack Welch

Downsizing with Dignity by Alan Downs

EXECUTIVE SUMMARY

- Downsizing is a toxic solution. Used sparingly and with planning it can be an organizational lifesaver, but when used repeatedly without a thoughtful strategy it can destroy an organization's effectiveness.
- One outcome of downsizing must be to preserve the organization's intellectual capital.
- How downsized employees are treated directly affects the morale and retention of valued, high-performing employees who are not downsized.
- Downsizing should never be used as a communication to financial centers or investors of the new management's tough-minded, no-nonsense style of management—the cost of downsizing far outweighs any benefits thus gained.

INTRODUCTION

Make no mistake: downsizing is extremely difficult. It taxes all of a management team's resources, including both business acumen and humanity. No one looks forward to downsizing. Perhaps this is why so many otherwise first-rate executives downsize so poorly. They ignore all the signs pointing to a layoff until it's too late to plan adequately, then act hastily to reduce the financial drain of excess staff. The extremely difficult decisions of who must be laid off, how much notice they will be given, the amount of severance pay, and how far the company will go to help the laid-off employee find another job are given less than adequate attention. These critical decisions have as much to do with the future of the organization as they do with the future of the laid-off employees, so they must be considered carefully.

So what happens? These decisions are handed to the legal department, whose primary objective is to reduce the risk of litigation, not to protect the morale and intellectual capital of the organization. Consequently downsizing is often executed with a brisk, compassionless efficiency that leaves laid-off employees angry and surviving employees feeling helpless, demotivated, and poorly prepared to start rebuilding the business.

Helplessness is the enemy of high achievement. It produces a work environment of withdrawal, risk-averse decisions, severely impaired morale, and excessive blaming. All of these put a stranglehold upon an organization that now desperately needs to excel. Thus downsizing becomes a contributor to an organization's downfall rather than a catalyst for growth and profitability.

AVOIDING THE PITFALLS

Ineffective methods of downsizing abound. Downsizing malpractices such as those that follow are common; they are also inefficient and very dangerous.

Allowing Legal Concerns to Design the Layoff

Most corporate attorneys advise laying off employees on a last-hired, first-fired basis across all departments. The method for downsizing that is most clearly defensible in a court of law, for example, is to lay off 10% of employees across all departments on a seniority-only basis. This way no employee can claim to have been dismissed for discriminatory reasons. Furthermore, attorneys advise against saying anything more than what's absolutely necessary to either departing employees or survivors. This caution protects the company from making any implied or explicit promises that aren't then kept. By strictly scripting what is said, the company protects itself from verbal slips by managers who are themselves stressed at having to release valued employees.

This approach may succeed from a legal perspective, but not necessarily from the more important one of organizational health. First, laying off employees by a flat percentage across different departments is irrational. How can it be that accounting can do with the same proportion fewer employees as human resources? Could one department be externalized and the other left intact? The decision of how many employees to lay off from each department should be based on an analysis of business needs, not an arbitrary statistic.

The concept of laying off employees strictly on the basis of seniority is also irrational. The choice of employees for a layoff should be based on a redistribution of the work, not the date the employee was hired. Sometimes an employee of 18 months has a skill far more valuable than one with 18 years' seniority.

Giving As Little Notice As Possible

Out of fear and guilt many executives choose to give employees as little forewarning as possible about an upcoming layoff. Managers fear that if employees know their fate ahead of time, they may become demoralized and unproductive—they may even sabotage the business. However, there is no documented evidence that advance notice of a layoff increases the incidence of employee sabotage.

The lack of advance notice, however, does dramatically increase mistrust of management among surviving workers. Trust is based on mutual respect. When employees discover what has been brewing without their knowledge or input (and they will when the first person is let go), they see a blatant disrespect for their integrity, destroying trust. By not giving employees information that could be enormously helpful to them in planning their own lives, management initiates a cycle of mistrust and helplessness that can be very destructive and require years to correct.

Acting As If Nothing Happened

Many managers believe that after a layoff, the less said about it the better. With luck, everyone will just forget and move on. The reality is that surviving employees will talk about what's happened whether the management team does or doesn't. The more the company tries to suppress these discussions and act as if nothing has happened, the more subversive the discussion becomes. Remaining employees will react to what has happened regardless of whether the management does.

Recovery from a layoff is greatly hastened if managers and employees are allowed to speak their minds freely about what's happened. In fact, it can be a great opportunity for the survivors to pull together and renew ties. When management refuses to acknowledge what has really taken place, it appears emphatically heartless, feeding the employees' sense of helplessness. If management won't talk about it even after the fact, what else is it hiding?

"To downsize effectively you have to have empathy with the people who are losing their jobs . . . What you say to them has a lot to do with the attitude of the survivors: whether they see the company as a money-machine or keep their respect for it."

Percy Barnevik

DOWNSIZING EFFECTIVELY

An organization that isn't functioning at optimal efficiency and is thinking that a layoff is needed must keep in mind a few key principles.

Is the problem too many people or too little profit?

This is the critical first question to ask before any layoff. Using a layoff as a cost-cutting measure is utterly foolish: throwing away valuable talent and organizational learning only makes a bad situation worse. When your business lacks revenue, annihilating intellectual capital and thus reducing the efficiency of remaining resources as well as the potential for future growth is not the solution.

If the answer is too many employees, then you've begun the process of a well-thought-out strategy for change. To legitimately determine if you have too many employees, look at the organization's business plan, not its head count. What product and services will you be offering? Which of these products and services is likely to be profitable? What talent will you need to run the new organization? These questions will help you plan for the post-layoff future. These issues will enable a quick turnaround from the inevitably negative effects of downsizing to positive growth in value and efficiency.

What will the post-layoff company look like?

Having a clear, well-defined vision of the new company is imperative *before the layoff is executed*. Management should know what it wants to accomplish, where the emphasis will be in the new organization, and what staff will be needed.

If not directed according to a clear vision of the future, the new organization is likely to carry forward some of the same problems that initially created the need for the layoff. Unfortunately, many managers underestimate the momentum of the old organization to recreate the same problems. Without a clearly defined, shared vision of the new company among the entire management team, the past will be likely to sabotage the future and create a cycle of repeated layoffs with little improvement in organizational efficiency.

Always respect people's dignity

The methods employed in many poorly-executed layoffs treat employees like chil-

dren. Information is withheld and doled out. Managers' control over their employees is violated. Human resource representatives scurry from one hush-hush meeting to another. How management treats laid-off employees is how it vicariously treats remaining employees—in a layoff, everything is done in the arena, with everyone observing.

Why does this matter? Because successful planning will keep the new organization going and improve its results. You must keep exceptional talent, who are also the employees most marketable to other organizations. When they see the company treating laid-off employees poorly, they'll start looking for a better place to work.

Respect the law

While it's important not to allow the legal department to design a layoff, it's nevertheless important to respect the employment laws. In different countries such laws include entitlements tied to civil rights, age discrimination, disabilities, worked adjustment, and retraining. These laws should be respected for what they intend as well as what they prescribe—or proscribe. If you plan your layoff according to business needs, and not on head count or seniority, you should have no problem upholding the law. You will almost always find yourself in legal trouble when you base your layoff on factors other than business needs.

MINI-CASES
Good examples

During the merger of *BB&T Financial Corporation* and *Southern National Corporation*, redundant positions were eliminated through the strategic use of a hiring freeze.

Hewlett-Packard implemented a so-called fortnight program in which all employees were asked to take one day off without pay every two weeks until business revenue increased.

Bad examples

Eastman Kodak has laid off thousands of employees in the past 20 years without seeing any significant rise in productivity or profitability as a result. Virtually all the layoffs were administered by company-wide mandated percentage of employees to be laid off.

Perhaps the classic bad-case example remains *Scott Paper*. It conducted a layoff of 10,500 employees in the mid-1990s. In the years that followed Scott was unable to introduce any new products and saw a dra-

matic decrease in profitability, until it was eventually bought out by competitor Kimberly-Clark.

MAKING IT HAPPEN ▸▸
- Plan for the future, including a shared vision of the company post-layoff. Consider how best to motivate and reward employees after downsizing and how to retain the most talented and valuable employees.
- Treat all employees with dignity and respect. Communicate too much rather than withholding information.
- Research applicable laws and follow the spirit of the legislation.
- Afterward, give employees the psychological space to accept and discuss what has happened.
- Understand what the downsizing process must achieve—and what it must avoid.

CONCLUSION

There are two important factors to keep in mind when planning a layoff: respecting employee dignity, and business planning. No one, from the mailroom to the boardroom, enjoys downsizing; but when it is unavoidable, a layoff can be accomplished in such a way that the problem is fixed and the organization excels.

FOR MORE INFORMATION

Book:
Saleni, Ray. *Leading After a Layoff*. Avon, MA: Adams Media, 2005.

Web sites:
American Management Association:
www.amanet.org
Human Resource Planning Society:
www.hrps.org

"Brain cells create ideas. Stress kills brain cells. Stress is not a good idea." Doug Hall

Managing Stress
by Cary L. Cooper and Susan Cartwright

EXECUTIVE SUMMARY

- Recognizing the symptoms of stress is an essential measure in taking immediate action to improve the situation.
- Understanding the causes and common sources of workplace stress is vital in preventing it becoming an issue.
- The changing nature of work makes stress more complex, varied, and quite possibly more common—and dealing with it quickly, early, and effectively is more important now than ever.
- There are a range of techniques and approaches to managing personal stress and these are explored in this section.

INTRODUCTION

The enterprise culture has entailed a substantial personal cost for many individuals. The cost is captured by a single word "stress." Indeed, stress has found as firm a place in our modern lexicon as "fast food," "cell phones," and "CDs." "It's a high-stress job," someone says, awarding an odd sort of prestige to his or her occupation. But to those whose ability to cope with day-to-day matters is at crisis point, the concept of stress is no longer a casual one; for them, stress can be translated into a four-letter word—*pain*.

BEHAVIORAL AND PHYSICAL SYMPTOMS OF STRESS

Pressure is motivating, stimulating and energizing, but when pressure exceeds an individual's ability to cope we are in the stress arena. When a number of the following behavioral and physical symptoms are frequently or nearly always experienced by an individual, it can indicate that he/she has crossed the line between mere pressure and harmful stress.

IDENTIFYING THE SOURCES OF WORKPLACE STRESS

Once an individual acknowledges that they are not coping with the everyday pressures of work, the next step is to identify the source(s) of the stress at work. Once this is done, the individual can draw up a plan of action to minimize or eliminate the excess pressure or damaging source of stress. Table 2 identifies some possible daily hassles at work. There are of course more significant problem areas as well, such as coping with job loss, dealing with a bullying boss, or trying to cope with a dysfunctional corporate culture (for example, excessive working hours, autocratic management style).

PERSONAL STRESS: MANAGING THE DAILY HASSLES
Time Management

Of all the daily hassles experienced by managers, one of the most stressful is poor time management. Time wasters fall into several categories, requiring different solutions.

The Mañanas. Individuals in this category cause themselves problems because they procrastinate, preferring to "think" about work rather than "do" it. Procrastination often stems from boredom, a lack of confidence, or reluctance to seek clarification. For Mañanas, here are some basic tips to effective time management:

- Break up overwhelming tasks into smaller jobs.
- Draw up a "to do" list of all the tasks you need to complete in the short term (that is, within the next week) and in the long term.
- When planning your work schedule, attempt to balance routine tasks with the more enjoyable jobs.
- Accept that risks are inevitable and that no decisions are ever made on the basis of complete information.

The Poor Delegators. Individuals in this

Table 1

Behavioral Symptoms	Physical Symptoms
Constant irritability with people	Lack of appetite
Difficulty in making decisions	Craving for food when under pressure
Loss of sense of humor	Frequent indigestion or heartburn
Suppressed anger	Constipation or diarrhea
Difficulty concentrating	Insomnia
Inability to finish one task before rushing into another	Tendency to sweat for no good reason
Feeling targeted by other people's animosity	Nervous twitches, nail biting, etc.
Feeling unable to cope	Headaches
Wanting to cry at the smallest problem	Cramps and muscle spasms
Lack of interest in doing things after returning home from work	Nausea
Waking up in the morning and feeling tired after an early night	Breathlessness without exertion
Constant tiredness	Fainting spells
	Impotency or frigidity
	Eczema

Table 2

Daily Hassles at Work	
Trouble with client/customer	Traveling associated with the job
Having to work late	Making mistakes
Constant people interruptions	Conflict with organizational goals
Trouble with boss	Job interfering with home/family life
Deadlines and time pressures	Can't cope with inbox
Decision making	Can't say "no" to work
Dealing with the bureaucracy at work	Not enough stimulating things to do
Technological breakdowns, e.g. computer	Too many meetings
Trouble with coworkers	Don't know where career is going
Tasks associated with job not stimulating	Worried about job security
Too much responsibility	Spouse/partner not supportive about work
Too many jobs to do at once	Family life adversely affecting work
Telephone interruptions	Having to tell subordinates unpleasant things,
Traveling to and from work	e.g. layoffs

"One is more likely . . . to perceive a situation of overload when one has many things demanded . . . than when fewer things are demanded."

Rabi S. Bhagat

category waste a considerable amount of their time doing work that could easily and more effectively have been done by somebody else. They should consider some of the following:

- Delegation does not mean abdication.
- Always take time out to explain exactly what is required; poor delegators are often also poor communicators, which is why they are frequently disappointed with the efforts of others.
- Having delegated a job, leave the person to get on with it.
- Avoid taking on unnecessary work that does not fulfill their objectives or that could be done by others, by learning to say "no" politely and assertively.

The Disorganized. Individuals in this category are instantly recognizable by the mounds of paper that form barricades around their desks. Disorganized individuals frequently miss or are late for appointments. They frequently think their problems are due to work overload rather than their own poor organizational skills: They need to:

- plan effectively before taking action;
- make a "to do" list regularly at the start of each day and review it each evening;
- stick to one task and finish it!
- think before they telephone and draw up a list of all the information they require from the caller;
- identify their prime time for working, when their energy levels are high for the complex task, and save the trivial routine tasks for non-prime time;
- when making an appointment in their diaries, enter a finish time as well as a start time.

The Mushrooms. Individuals in this category are usually unclear about the purpose and objectives of what they are required to do. They constantly speculate and inwardly question what they should do rather than do it. They basically lack assertion and communication skills. The two most important things for them to do are:

- learn to say "I don't know," when you don't know something;
- learn to say "I don't understand" when you don't understand a task, a role or objective.

Managing Interruptions

Another source of personal stress at work for many managers are "constant interruptions," from the telephone, e-mail, drop-by coworkers, etc.

Technology

With voice mail, e-mail, cell phones, and the like, it is important to manage the technology rather than let the technology manage you. There are some general rules that apply to each of the technologies most of us work with and which create unnecessary personal pressure.

For telephone calls: batch phone calls; plan what you are going to say and need to know in advance; and deliberately discipline yourself by placing specific time limits on the length of a call.

For voice mail: use this when you need space to perform complex tasks requiring your full attention, and don't be tempted to access your voice mail messages every ten minutes! Also deal with those messages that are most important first; deal with the others later.

For e-mails: prioritize your e-mails in terms of your objectives, then reply to them in this order. All too often, individuals reply to e-mails in order of their arrival and not in terms of their importance.

For cell phones: don't have your cell phone on all the time, as it could interrupt some important meeting or activity. Use it on journeys or during other periods of downtime to deal with work that would otherwise have to be dealt with back at work.

Drop-by Coworkers

Although being interrupted can provide a welcome diversion from a boring or tedious task, too many interruptions are a waste of time, distracting, and frequently irritating. There are a range of strategies for controlling these kinds of interruptions.

- Establish quiet hours during which you can work undisturbed. This may mean closing your door and putting a notice outside.
- Establish visiting hours when you are available for drop-in visitors.
- Arrange meetings away from your desk or office; this enables you to take control and leave when you want to.
- Do not hesitate to curb wafflers, in a polite and friendly manner, by asking them to make their main point(s).
- When unexpectedly interrupted, ask the person how much time he or she needs and, if you haven't got the space, then rearrange the meeting.

Interruptions

Interruptions occur for a number of reasons. The person involved may

- want to exchange information;
- need reassurance or clarification;
- lack confidence about a task;
- want a casual chat because they need a break or are bored, etc.

It is important to attempt to differentiate these; so, if it is important to their doing their job properly, you may need to spend some of your time with them, if not, then use some of the above suggestions.

THE CHANGING NATURE OF WORK

Finally, one of the major overriding sources of stress for managers and others today is the fact that jobs are no longer for life—that job security is a vestige of the past. Under the terms of the "new" psychological contract, organizations expect employees to be more flexible, more accountable, and to be hardworking and committed; at the same time, employers offer increasingly limited (or no) assurances or expectations of employment security and career development opportunities. It is not hard to imagine that for significant numbers of future workers the job is likely to become a freelance activity in the form of a series of temporarily or discretely defined tasks or projects undertaken either successively or concurrently for single or multiple employers. For this, the individual receives financial payment, negotiated in advance, either on a fixed-cost basis or dependent on results achieved.

For individuals currently working in "de-layered" organizational structures, coping with changed career expectations requires considerable personal adjustment: one must accept that the onus for career management and training now rests with oneself rather than with the organization. This requires a greater degree of self-initiative and personal planning and control. Although the prospect of pursuing a self-determined career outside the structure of an established organization might seem daunting, research evidence based on experiences of midlife career changes suggests that increased job and life satisfaction is frequently gained from a move to freelancing and self-employment.

MAKING IT HAPPEN ▸▸
To minimize and handle your own stress you should:

- **Understand yourself**—understand what causes *you* stress, when you are likely to become stressed, and how you can avoid these situations. To help, it can be useful to think about previous times that were stressful for you and remember how you felt, how you reacted and behaved, what the result was, and whether, with the benefit of hindsight, you handled it in the best way possible.
- **Take responsibility**—too often people either deny their problem, in which case it will almost certainly worsen, or blame someone (or something) else. Even if it is the fault of someone else, *you* are being affected and *you* need to resolve it. People are often too afraid, ashamed,

"I think in every country that there is at least one executive who is scared of going crazy."

Joseph Heller

or uncertain to admit that they are suffering from stress, but the longer they delay, the worse the effects of the downward cycle.

- **Consider what is causing stress**—is it resulting from the job, your role, work relationships, change, or something else, perhaps not work-related at all? Knowing the symptoms and acknowledging the existence of stress is really only the start: the next key step is to identify the source of the stress. This is often complicated by the fact that stress is often caused by an accumulation of factors. The solution is to rationally consider how to take down the wall that is encircling you, brick by brick. Stress is rarely removed in one go but often requires action in a range of areas.
- **Anticipate stressful periods (either at work or home) and plan for them**—this may include getting temporary resources or people with specific skills to help during a particular period.
- **Understand and use management techniques to prevent or reduce stress**—time management and assertiveness are two of the most important skills in reducing and handling stress, as many difficulties are caused either by time pressures or relationship issues that could be prevented by more assertive, controlled behavior. Communication, decision-

making and problem-solving also have much to offer once the problem has been acknowledged and the sources of stress identified.

- **Relax**—easier said than done, but the key is to understand that you need to *work* at relaxing! This may mean planning a holiday or finding a hobby or club that suits you, and then *absorbing* yourself in it. Time away from the causes of stress can help to put the situation in perspective and lead to a new approach that provides a solution.

If you are responsible for preventing and reducing stress within organizations, you should:

- **Acknowledge stress in others**—as a leader you should not be afraid to comment to someone if you think they are suffering from stress, and then be prepared to help and support them in breaking the downward cycle. Often, just acknowledging the existence of stress and showing understanding can provide enough energy to see the solution, remove the stress, and ultimately overcome the problem.
- **Build a positive team or work environment**—as a leader it is possible to reduce stress for others by developing good communication systems, a supportive team approach, a blame-free environment, and a clear sense of involvement and responsibility.

Other factors that can also help include mentoring programs that prevent, identify, and treat cases of stress; appraisal systems and simply knowing and understanding the people that work with you. For some senior managers in large organizations this may not be possible, in which case these values need to be passed down the chain of command so that they are supported throughout the organization.

CONCLUSION

In the end, we should begin to truly understand what John Ruskin said in 1851:

"In order that people may be happy in their work, these three things are needed: they must be fit for it; they must not do too much of it; and they must have a sense of success in it."

FOR MORE INFORMATION

Books:
Cooper, Cary L., and S. Palmer. *Conquer Your Stress*. London: Chartered Institute of Personnel and Development, 2000.
Cooper, Cary, and P. Dewe. *Stress: A Brief History*. Oxford: Blackwell, 2004.
Cooper, Cary, and W. Starbuck. *Work: Contexts and Consequences*. Thousand Oaks, CA: Sage Publications, 2005.

"If we cannot be powerful and happy and prey on others, we invent conscience and prey on ourselves."

Elbert Hubbard

Fringe Benefits by John G. Fisher

EXECUTIVE SUMMARY

- Fringe benefits now account for over 30% of average executive remuneration in value terms; they include a wide range of elements.
- Offering non-salary benefits is seen as crucial in recruiting and retaining staff in a virtually full-employment market.
- Flexible benefits packages offer significant advantages in the management of employee benefits, but administration is still the big issue.
- E-benefits applications are now available to handle administration via the Internet.
- The balance between cash and non-cash within the benefits package is changing.
- Personalized remuneration through flexible benefits will become the norm in the 21st century.

INTRODUCTION

Employee welfare policies, or benefits, as they are known today, were initiated in the late 19th century as an attempt by Victorian patriarchs to retain staff and to refute the often-made suggestion that industry exploited the working classes without providing any financial or social security. So strong was the pressure on employers to play a paternal as well as an economic role that successive administrations brought in legislation throughout the 20th century to ensure that some fringe benefits were statutory rather than optional.

But the days when employers could get away with offering only paid vacations, severance, sick days, or even pension plans are long gone. Today's employees have much higher expectations, driven by the double-income way of life. Benefits consultants are often asked to research employee attitudes to fringe benefits before implementing new plans. The main drivers of benefits choice in most employee groups are more time off, loss of health, making ends meet, flexibility should circumstances change, value for money, job security, prospects for advancement, and status (both perceived and actual). These findings are reflected in the wide range of fringe benefits now being offered by employers.

TODAY'S RANGE OF FRINGE BENEFITS

The Reward Group, a remuneration research agency, conducted a survey of 35,000 members of the U.K. Chartered Institute of Personnel Development to establish which fringe benefits were the most popular. Measured by employee takeup, the following ranking of preferences emerged in questions about family-friendly benefits:

1 paternity leave
2 parental/domestic leave
3 stress management
4 telecommuting
5 job-sharing

The following rank order was recorded for benefits relating to career and health advice:

1 health screening
2 mentoring
3 stress management
4 career counseling
5 bereavement counseling

These are all life-event concerns and should rightly form the core of any modern benefits program. But less essential elements are also common, for example, dental insurance, legal advice, daycare, elderly parent support, health-club membership, household insurance, automobile insurance, home computer, automobile, parking, continuing education, relocation assistance, gas, to name a few.

But the offer of such benefits has significant cost implications that are often overlooked by employees. In the late 1980s Chrysler calculated that up to $800 per car produced was spent on hidden employee benefits such as life insurance, pensions, and sickness/disability insurance. Often these benefits were underappreciated and misunderstood by employees. Costs were spiraling out of control. In order to reduce costs the company began to present the benefits to employees with specific costs attached in the form of benefit credits. This led to offering employees a choice of how much of each benefit they wanted up to a prescribed limit depending on their personal circumstances. Similar programs sprang up in other parts of the United States, Canada, and Australia, as trade journal articles extolled the virtues of benefits transparency. Known as *flex plans*, these pro-grams opened up the debate on the efficiency of employee benefits as a retention and loyalty device.

FLEXIBLE BENEFITS

The principle of flexible fringe benefits is that one size does not fit all; the more personalized your benefits package, the more likely employees are to value it as part of their remuneration. A single person under 30 has a very different way of life from a 45-year-old married main-income earner with children. Senior directors have different priorities from junior data-processors. The solution is to offer a portfolio of benefits up to a set value, the elements of which employees can mix and match according to personal circumstances.

A major U.K. telecommunications company with more than 10,000 employees was spending over $70 million a year on benefits that were largely unappreciated by employees. They included the usual collection of insurance, pensions, and automobile allowances that everyone was given regardless of circumstances. With a new company initiative to treat employees as individuals, the company decided to flex its benefits. Within their specific benefits credit level, employees were allowed to choose varying levels of pension, life insurance, health and dental care, paid vacation, company car, and childcare. Subsequent research showed that employees were genuinely appreciative of being able to choose benefits to suit their own circumstances.

ADMINISTRATION AIDED BY THE INTERNET

Until quite recently running flex plans was a complex, expensive job involving external benefits consulting companies and significant internal systems enhancements. But thanks to the recent accessibility of applications over the Internet, the management of such programs can now be outsourced to online benefits agencies that not only administer the detail, but can liaise directly with staff via an intranet or the Internet itself. Companies such as Probusiness.com and Onlinebenefits.com offer a basket of benefits products from which the employer can choose what to offer staff. Such services are of particular interest to companies that operate internationally and wish to manage common cross-border benefits administration.

"We listen to what our employees want and it shows up in everything from the layout of our offices to the benefits and amenities."

Raul Fernandez

THE FUTURE OF FRINGE BENEFITS

Many employees now enjoy fringe benefits never dreamed of by their grandparents. As society becomes more affluent and the economy perhaps more efficient, employers will need to be more open about what fringe benefits they offer within an increasingly competitive job market. We'll see more job ads showing salary-plus-benefits level as the standard format. The ability to deliver benefits glitch-free at the individual level, both domestically and cross-border, will be a basic requirement for every major employer in the 21st century.

MINI-CASE

Proper Communication is Vital

When Saatchi & Saatchi decided to introduce a flex plan into its North American subsidiary, not everything went as expected. Managers gave themselves only three months to introduce it, and by their own admission did little to consult with staff or think through the communications process. The existing benefits were simply repackaged. The new program had a poor take-up, with most employees perceiving the subject as irrelevant and boring.

A new approach was tried, involving 22 focus groups and a thorough features versus advantages analysis from the point of view of the potential recipients. Flex choices could be made onscreen, so participants didn't have to have an appointment with human resources to get things going. Five new benefits were offered, reflecting the lifestyle of different employee groups. Everyone was included in the new program, not just management. Promotions included telephone-booth information points dotted around the office, where participants could put specific questions about their individual situation directly to human resources. Office posters, brief memos, and eye-catching flyers were devised to get the key points across on an ongoing basis. Team briefings were held at crucial times of the financial year.

MAKING IT HAPPEN ▶▶

In introducing a flexible benefits plan, it's important to take a few key steps.

- Consult with staff through focus groups before going live.
- Recognize employee needs for time off, healthcare, making ends meet, flexibility if circumstances change, value for money, security, prospects for advancement, and status (both perceived and actual).
- Offer family benefits from the following list (ranked in order of preference): paternity leave, parental/domestic leave, stress management, telecommuting, job-sharing.
- Again in order of preference, choose from these health and career benefits: health screening, mentoring, stress management, career counseling, bereavement counseling.
- Create both formal and informal advice mechanisms.
- Decide how the features can be promoted as advantages.
- Monitor the cost of benefits with great care; use flexible provision, with employee choice, to optimize cost-effectiveness.
- Consider outsourcing management of a flexible plan to an online benefits agency that will administer the detail and liaise directly with staff via the Web.
- Communicate throughout the year, not just at the launch, and use research to check that your benefits plan is achieving high employee satisfaction.

FOR MORE INFORMATION

Books:
Armstrong, Michael, and Helen Murlis. *Reward Management.* Milford, CT: Kogan Page, 2005.
Fisher, John. *How to Run Successful Incentive Schemes.* Milford, CT: Kogan Page, 2005.
Nelson, Bob. *1001 Ways to Reward Employees.* 2nd ed. New York: Workman, 2005.

See also:

Making Performance Appraisals a Win-win Experience
by Patrick Forsyth

EXECUTIVE SUMMARY

Despite the clear necessity for performance evaluation, many managers dislike conducting appraisals. Worse, many people rate their appraisals as worthless—or something even less flattering. In reality appraisals are a major opportunity for both managers and staff. This article will review the following:
- Why appraisals are necessary and will examine the benefits to managers and staff. Primarily, they ensure and improve future performance.
- How effective appraisals should be planned and undertaken to maximize their positive impact while avoiding negative pitfalls.
- The impact of appraisals on the long-term success of the organization. Appraisals provide considerable opportunity for improving ongoing operations, effective management, and catalyzing change.

INTRODUCTION

There are many reasons why appraisals are necessary. Positive reasons include the opportunity to:
- review individuals' past performance;
- plan their future work and role;
- set and agree on specific individual goals for the future;
- identify development needs and arrange for development activity;
- provide on-the-spot coaching;
- obtain feedback;
- reinforce or extend the reporting relationship;
- act as a catalyst to delegation;
- focus on longer-term career progression;
- underpin or increase motivation.

Often a negative reason is the close relationship between appraisals and employment legislation (for example, lack of appraisal may make it impossible to terminate someone's employment). This is also a factor to keep in mind.

Overall the underlying intention is to improve future performance. The good appraisal presupposes that even the best performance can be improved, and seeks to increase the likelihood of future plans being brought to fruition.

PREPARE CAREFULLY

Unsurprisingly, the key to effective appraisals is preparation by both parties.

The *appraiser* must:

- Spend sufficient time with staff during the year.
- Communicate clearly and thoroughly the purpose and form of the appraisal so people know what to expect. Employees should understand the need for appraisal, its importance, the specific objectives it addresses, and how both parties can get the best from it.
- Prepare throughout the year, keeping clear records. Keeping an appraisal collection file means you don't have to rely on memory. In this, you should note matters that can usefully be raised at appraisals, making notes and filing copies of documents that will assist the process.

The *appraisee* should keep running records and should plan in detail the kind of meeting he or she intends to have.

Successful appraisal is the culmination of a year's worth of thinking. Recalling every detail of a subordinate's working year is difficult, but being seen to be conducting an interview on the basis of incomplete information risks loss of credibility. Managers can only appraise successfully by being informed.

Relevant background information needs checking, for example, the appraisee's job description (which may need amendment after the appraisal), specific past objectives, possible changes to the job, its responsibilities, or circumstances, and the records of any previous appraisals.

Sound preparation gives appraisal meetings structure.

WORK THE SYSTEM

It is not the purpose here to specify exactly how formal measurement in appraisal systems should work. But the measurement—rating scale—must ensure consistency, clarity, and fairness.
- Create a good, manageable system or familiarize yourself with what you must use.
- Make its constructive purposes clear.
- Communicate all procedures, documentation, and action clearly to appraisees.
- Use the process objectively.

Details matter; for example, many favor rating scales with the total number even to eliminate the temptation to rate too many criteria as average.

Ultimately you may need to balance what suits you best and what the system you use necessitates. Attention to detail is vital; the following outlines a systematic approach likely to work well.

BEFORE THE APPRAISAL INTERVIEW

- *Prepare written notification.* As well as confirming mutually convenient timing, this should recap the purpose of the appraisal and highlight background information. Distribute copies of any documents or forms you intend to use or refer to during the meeting.
- *Study the individual's file.* Make sure you have all the information you need about what was supposed to happen during the year and what actually did happen. Make notes of points needing discussion and see to it that you can navigate the documents easily as the meeting progresses.
- *Check performance factors.* Review agreed-on standards and identify any that are no longer relevant or that need to be changed.
- *Draft a provisional assessment.* Brief notes can provide a starting point, prompt the agenda, and link to the system. Don't prejudge the discussion or make decisions prematurely.
- *Critique your initial thoughts.* Check your rationale, asking yourself a why question

---

"It is much more difficult to measure nonperformance than performance." Harold S. Geneen

about anything noted at this stage. If no clear answer comes, more research may be necessary.

- *Consider specific areas of the appraisal.* It may be clear that some training is necessary, for example. Again without prejudging, it may be useful to check out what might be appropriate and formulate a suggestion before the meeting.
- *Think ahead.* Remember that the most important part of the discussion will be about the future. You may need to plan particular projects and tasks, taking both development and operational considerations into account.
- *Consult with others.* Speak to those who work or deal with the appraisee to get a complete picture.
- *Be clear about the link with pay review.* Many managers feel this should be kept for a separate occasion. Otherwise it can be difficult to stop appraisees from thinking all that matters is the potential raise.

SETTING UP THE INTERVIEW

- *Allow enough time.* You need to do the job and also to reflect the importance of the occasion. Few appraisals will be accomplished properly in less than an hour; some may last two or three hours or more—and will still be time usefully spent.
- *Allow no disturbances.* Pausing to take even one telephone call sends out the wrong signals.
- *Create the right environment.* Appraisals should be held somewhere comfortable, perhaps less formal than across a desk, yet suitably businesslike.
- *Put the individual at ease.* Recognize that even with good communication beforehand, appraisals may be viewed as somewhat traumatic. Anything that can be done to counter this is useful.

DURING THE MEETING

- *Spell out the agenda and how things will be handled.* Ask what priorities the appraisee wants recognized.
- *Act to direct the proceedings.* Do not, however, ride roughshod over the appraisee.
- *Ask questions.* Open questions prompt and focus discussion.
- *Listen.* The meeting is primarily an opportunity for the appraisee to

communicate. In a well-conducted appraisal, the appraisee should do most of the talking; the manager's job is to make that happen.

- *Keep primarily to performance factors.* Don't indulge in amateur psychology or attempt to measure personality factors.
- *Use the system.* Use systems and appraisal forms to guide the meeting; working through the form systematically will ensure that most of what needs to happen does.
- *Encourage discussion.* Consider the appraisee's personal strengths and weaknesses, successes and failures, and their implications for the future.
- *Set out action plans.* Describe those that can be decided there and then (who will do what, when); note those needing more deliberation in terms of when and how action will be taken. Deal with each factor separately, for example, by devoting time to development action.
- *Explain the basis of assessment.* Make the basis and reasons for your assessment clear. Be firm about your decisions.
- *Conclude on a positive note.* Always thank the appraisee for the role he or she has played and for the past year's work. Link this to any subsequent documentation.

AFTER THE MEETING

There is one key action here: to complete all documentation and confirmations that are necessary promptly after the meeting. Send copies to the appraisee, flagging any opportunity for further discussion. Copy to central departments such as personnel as well as your own file.

MAKING IT HAPPEN ▶▶

- Make sure that everybody understands the need for appraisal, its importance, its objectives, and its mutual benefits.
- Prepare throughout the year, keeping clear records and notes to assist the appraisal process.
- Keep primarily to performance factors, getting the appraisee to do most of the talking—while you listen hard.
- Concentrate the appraisal process on future performance, and don't confuse it with discussion of remuneration.
- Link appraisal deliberately with training and development, and with

consultation, counseling, mentoring, and motivation.
- Follow up appraisals promptly, sending all necessary written material to the appraisee and flagging any opportunity for further discussion.

CONCLUSION

Appraisals are not one-shot deals. No manager can afford to heave a sigh of relief afterwards and forget about them for another year. Appraisals achieve most when placed in a long-term context and linked to ongoing operations. Consider

- the ongoing management relationship: an effective appraisal should make all management processes through the year easier;
- the link with training and development: consultation, counseling, mentoring, and informal discussions are all just as important extensions of appraisal as formal training;
- motivation: appraisals must themselves be motivational, and what stems from them must assist ongoing motivational activity.

For whatever reasons (and there may be many, such as unease with the process, or inflexibility of systems), the considerable opportunity of appraisals is often missed or diluted.

Appraisals are not only a vehicle for change, one that can be precise and powerful, they're also a catalyst for effective management, and thus effective performance. The benefits are considerable and tangible.

FOR MORE INFORMATION

Books:
McKirchy, Karen. *Powerful Performance Appraisals.* Reprint. Franklin Lakes, NJ: Career Press, 1998.
Neal, James E. *Effective Phrases for Performance Appraisals.* 10th ed. Perrysburg, OH: Neal Publications, 2003.

See also:
☆ Matching Pay to Achievement (pp. 383–384)
☆ New Yardsticks for Performance and Productivity in an E-world (pp. 366–367)

Improving Company Performance with an Older Work Force
by Beverly Goldberg

EXECUTIVE SUMMARY

- The workforce is getting older and this is having a significant impact on the corporate world.
- Those companies that recognize the value of older workers now and create a flexible workplace aimed at attracting and retaining them will have an enormous advantage when the baby boomers begin to reach 65 in 2010.
- Older workers have many clear advantages that prove an invaluable means of using resources effectively and securing competitive advantage. Statistically, older workers have been shown to bring experience, flexibility, loyalty, and reliability, as well as providing a cost-effective means of financing specific projects.
- Despite these advantages, the harsh economic reality facing organizations is that to meet increased and changing future demand, companies will need to address the shortfall in younger employees to meet customer demand. It is essential, therefore, that companies shed their erroneous, stereotypical view of older workers and adopt a strategy of attracting and retaining them. Future success will depend on it.

INTRODUCTION

The months before the collapse of so many dot-coms in 2001 were marked by the influx of senior executives into a once totally youthful culture. These new companies, usually started by twenty-somethings with brilliant, innovative ideas, suddenly brought in older business managers to help them to weather what seemed like bumps on the fast road to success. For all too many it turned out to be too little, too late. The lesson is clear: experience counts. The world's industrial societies remain youth-oriented, even though the so-called baby boomers, the group that brought about this orientation, are now in their mid-fifties.

The aging of the baby boomers, born between the end of World War II and 1964, will bring a dramatic change in the age makeup of both the general population of the industrialized countries and the workplace. For example, in 2025, more Italians will be over than under 50 years old. In 2010, in the United Kingdom there will be 25% more workers aged between 45 and 49 than aged 25 to 29. The median age of the U.S. workforce reached 40 in 2005, and in 2010 50% of all prime-age workers will be over 45.

Moreover, people in the industrialized nations have been retiring well before the usual retirement age. The message: companies that don't retain and recruit older workers won't be able to meet demand, let alone grow.

Older workers, however, are not just bodies to fill vacancies. Companies need older workers for their experience, institutional memories, work ethic, and, perhaps surprisingly, their ability to accommodate change and to focus—moreover, they're likely to remain with an organization longer than younger workers.

A VALUE-ADDED PROPOSITION

Many beliefs about older workers result in companies deciding that younger workers are a better-value proposition when it comes to hiring, training, and retention—these beliefs are patently false.

- **Older workers cost more.** While the actual salaries of new, younger replacements may be lower, there are hidden costs of replacing older workers, for example, severance pay and agency fees for replacements. Corning Glass spends around $40,000 replacing each lost worker. Merck estimates that retraining a successor costs about one-and-a-half times the new person's average salary.
- **Older workers are less creative.** While younger workers may come up with a larger number of ideas in meetings, fewer of those ideas prove to have value. Some have already been tried and failed, others don't work in the company's culture. Measuring the value of new ideas is more important than measuring their number.
- **Older workers don't learn as well as younger workers.** Surveys show that the ratings of older workers increased between 1985 and 1994: the percentage of older workers rated excellent for flexibility rose almost 20%; the percentage of older workers who are comfortable with new technology rose almost 15%. One problem may be that the average age of trainers is 33, also people learn differently depending on their age. For example, older workers unfamiliar with a classroom setting may do better learning one-on-one or on the shop floor.
- **Older workers aren't worth retraining, because they won't be around for long.** Today younger workers move from job to job quickly, because they haven't been raised in an environment in which corporate loyalty is a part of their thinking or tradition. Older workers remain longer, partly because they are more concerned about finding a new job if there is an economic slowdown.
- **Older workers have poorer attendance records.** Human resource managers report that older workers are less likely to be late or absent than younger workers. Also, workers over 55 account for 13.6% of the workforce, but only 9.7% of on-the-job injuries, and workers over 50 file far fewer worker compensation claims than younger workers.
- **Older workers are resistant to change.** False. The fastest-growing group of Internet users is people over 50. When training programs are made available to older workers, such as the programs offered by Microsoft Skills 2000, the Green Thumb, Inc., and the federal government, the number of applicants is far greater than the number of openings. More than 350,000 people between the ages of 50 and 64 were full- or part-time students pursuing degrees in the United States in 1998.
- **Older workers have less to contribute.** Not only do older workers contribute, but when organizations are concerned about maintaining their institutional history and values—and maintaining skills and techniques when those remain constant—they turn to older workers. Older workers

"*Experience*, n. The wisdom that enables us to recognise as an undesirable old acquaintance the folly that we have already embraced."

Ambrose Bierce

can train new workers by working side by side with them and pass on the expertise and experience accumulated over long years, often reducing formal training time. Moreover, it takes an institutional memory to answer such questions as: Why were certain decisions about processes made? Why don't we do business with company X? These are things that don't get captured in memos or expert systems; they're the stuff of history, stored in memory, and they're invaluable.

ATTRACTING OLDER WORKERS

No matter how much companies may want to keep older workers, however, they are likely to discover that many such workers don't want to stay—at least, not under the same conditions they had in the past. Many no longer want to devote their lives to work. Even though life expectancy has increased dramatically so that people are no longer afraid they'll never have time to do the things they've always wanted to if they put off retirement, the urge to enjoy life while they're fit and hearty is strong. People want to take that exotic vacation, spend time with grandchildren, take courses, or pursue hobbies now. And often work has become tedious and dull, partly because companies don't offer older workers training opportunities, leaving them bored and interested in any form of change.

This is where companies need to be imaginative. We've been hearing about the new flexible organization for a decade, and now it's time for companies to apply the concept of flexibility to employment, to wake up to the fact that they can hold on to valuable older workers by being creative. Some companies have adapted, and they're better positioned to take advantage when the baby boomers consider retiring. Flexible arrangements include:

- part-time permanent work, sometimes known as "bridge retirement"—these jobs are scheduled for less than 40 hours a week, whether fewer hours a day or fewer days a week. For those of actual retirement age, it might involve a contract reducing the number of workdays by one day a week for the first three months, two days for the next three, and so on until full retirement is reached.
- full-time and part-time temporary work— an interesting development is the creation of in-house temporary agencies for workers who have retired from the company. Travelers Corporation set up an agency two decades ago and has enjoyed considerable success, encouraging other companies to adopt similar programs.

- contract work or consulting—this covers temporary assignments on specific projects rather than temporary work for different companies on an as-needed basis. Companies looking for workers for specific assignments often entice retired workers to return for the life of the project because they understand the corporate culture.
- telecommuting—working at home at least part of the time. For older employees, at-home work can make life easier, but it doesn't provide the social interaction that can make work attractive.
- on-call work—this arrangement, found most often in organizations such as hospitals that must be fully staffed at all times, involves a guaranteed minimum number of hours. It usually involves varying shifts, so is ideal for older workers who have few specific demands on their time.
- special assignments—these include temporary assignments, for example, serving on a disaster recovery project, representing the company in a community project, or working abroad. Whirlpool finds it less expensive to hire retired workers for short-term assignments abroad than to relocate full-time workers, while Quaker Oats has used retirees for a project in Shanghai. GTE has also tested this approach and plans to expand it.

MAKING IT HAPPEN ▸▸
Train older workers

Kevin Doran, vice president of human resources and government and public affairs at Philips in Somerset, New Jersey, says that the company has not found it necessary to take age into account when it comes to retraining. For example, when Philips adopted new enterprise software companywide, everyone received "equal training regardless of their demographics. We don't see any difference in the ability to learn by age."

Take advantage of experience and institutional memory

Texas Refinery Corporation, based in Fort Worth, Texas, hires older workers as independent contractors (as well as full-time employees). In 1995, 500 members of its 3,000-person sales force were past retirement age. The independent contractors who work for the company receive commissions and benefits on the basis of their sales. The company likes these arrangements because it believes that older salespeople have a distinct advantage when it comes to client relationships and that they are inclined to be self-starters.

Be flexible

Neuville Industries of Hildebrand, North Carolina, set up a job-sharing program for employees over the age of 62. The program, which was initiated in the early 1990s, is aimed at employees with at least five years of experience. It provides for job-sharing with younger employees and allows employees to continue working for as long as they want to.

CONCLUSION

Over the next three decades the workforce in general will become older, and the baby boomers will begin to think strongly about retiring. Experience, people skills, focus, a strong work ethic, and the desire and ability to learn make these older workers extremely valuable. Attracting and then finding ways to hold onto the best and brightest is going to be the key to success. Organizations must begin to address misconceptions about older workers and put in place programs to address their needs and aspirations.

FOR MORE INFORMATION

Books:
Ahlrichs, Nancy S. *Competing for Talent: Key Recruitment and Retention Strategies for Becoming an Employer of Choice.* San Francisco, CA: Davies-Black, 2000.
Hale, Noreen. *The Older Worker: Effective Strategies for Management and Human Resource Development.* San Francisco, CA: Jossey-Bass, 1990.
Bass, Scott A., ed. *Older and Active: How Americans over 55 are Contributing to Society.* New Haven, CT: Yale University Press, 1995.
Zemke, Ron, Claire Raines, and Bob Filipczak. *Generations at Work: Managing the Clash of Veterans, Boomers, Xers, and Nexters in Your Workplace.* New York: AMACOM, 1999.

Web sites:
www.aarp.com: if you want to know what is happening in the world of those over 50.
www.thirdage.com: this site provides a great deal of information for older workers.

"A company needs smart young men with the imagination and the guts to turn everything upside down if they can. It also needs old figures to keep them from turning upside down those things that ought to be rightside up."

Henry Ford

Viewpoint: Fons Trompenaars
Redefining What It Means to Manage Globally

Introduction

In the global business world, how cultures interact in a business setting remains a strangely overlooked area of study. Fons Trompenaars, who works alongside the British academic Charles Hampden-Turner, leads the way in promoting better understanding of the complex dynamics of multiculturalism. Fons has a Ph.D. from Wharton School, University of Pennsylvania, and worked with the Royal Dutch Shell Group in nine countries. He is now director of the Trompenaars Hampden-Turner consulting firm, which has offices in the Netherlands, the United Kingdom, and the United States.

Who is the most important person to have influenced your thinking?

Though he is not well known, my honest answer is that Hasan Ozbekhan, my Ph.D. supervisor, most influenced my thinking. Hasan is Turkish and comes from an oral tradition rather than a written one. Though he has written a lot, it has never been published. Russ Ackoff also influenced me, but Hasan's intellect was particularly impressive and he had a more European outlook. Both Russ and Hasan were heads of the social systems sciences department at Wharton, where I spent two years doing the formal part of my degree.

I then did my research at Shell, a period during which many of the roots of my thinking were laid down. In terms of influential books, *The Phenomenology of the Social World* by phenomenologist Alfred Schutz is one I think almost everyone should read. Schutz argued that the big advantage of a natural scientist over a social scientist is that atoms and molecules don't talk back. We social scientists are observing a reality created by human actions, while natural scientists can't ask a molecule what it thinks about something. In social sciences you need to involve people—though consulting firms tend to forget that even now.

I am more of a talker myself, though I do force myself to write sometimes—I write a column for the Dutch equivalent of the *Financial Times*, for example. But as with most of these things, the combination is important. People have different learning styles. I get my inspiration from talking; writing becomes easier when I have talked about something.

My last big mentor is Charles Hampden-Turner. Charles and I make a wonderful combination. There is no conflict between us, although we are completely

different. I think that Charles' intellect should be known to more people, and I am an intermediary in making that happen. Part of our work is to make things practical as well as conceptual.

I have learned so much from Charles, who I met through Shell. The head of group planning suggested I read an article in a Shell magazine on the effects of culture on marketing. It was called "A tale of two paradigms" by Charles Hampden-Turner—he was a consultant to Shell at the time. It was depressing: I'd worked for five years on my Ph.D., and in one ten-page article it was all summarized and written in much more elegant English!

So I called Charles, and sent him my Ph.D. He came back and said, "Fons, I think we can work together. I reconciled all of your seven dilemmas". That was in 1983; 15 years later I realized the importance of what he'd said.

Completely different again, but highly complementary and synergistic, has been my collaboration with Peter Woolliams, another U.K. university professor. Peter's strengths are his unique analytical skills and insights, which he can translate into software. He has helped with advanced techniques of data mining, neural networks, and now linguistic analysis. Together we have built software tools which have enabled me to get closer to our clients through web-based interviews, and to capture thousands of business dilemmas across the globe.

How will business be different in the 21st century?

My Ph.D. was in the typical Anglo-Saxon, Western tradition of dividing culture into sections labeled separately with names such as "individualism," "communitarianism," and so on. But Charles argued that cultures can combine. If you're an individualist, why

---

"We need a readiness to enter a room in the dark and stumble over unfamiliar furniture until the pain in our shins reminds us of where things are."

Fons Trompenaars

can't you also be a communitarian? Look at the success of the semi-conductor industry: that takes individualists and forms very creative teams out of them. Reconciling such differences is at the heart of our work and of business in the 21st century.

An example Charles uses is that of centralization and decentralization. A company only centralizes when it is decentralized. One value is always connected with its opposite; that's the essence of our work. Typical MBAs and educational systems teach that a person is in one category or another. How many so-called psychological tests or questionnaires place you in one box or another? You might be that one thing, but does that mean you don't also have characteristics from the opposite box?

I'm very hopeful that things will change. Look at the demand for our services. We help managers see the beauty of integration, of reconciliation. Such an outlook means that you do not have to say you are against shareholder value; instead you see that the only way to achieve shareholder value is to integrate it with its opposite. In other words, long-term shareholder value, by definition, is stakeholder value. I've never heard that discussed.

Our consulting firm has some competitors. The worst of them do not take the approach far enough. They say to clients, "Let me tell you what the French are like"; then they leave saying, "Good luck, you now understand them better." In fact it is usually worse, or the client understands the French better and thinks, "Now I know why I hate them"! You see the same thing frequently in the M&A world, where consultants are very good at diagnosing where the problem is . . . but that's where they stop.

The beauty of our work is that, once you have explained about reconciliation, you can offer a methodology for achieving it, codifying it step-by-step. So once you identify a dilemma, you can chart it, you can stretch it, you can analyze it, and then come up with action points to resolve it.

We have been saying for a number of years that it would be a mistake to under-estimate the counter forces of globalization. You can't live with the belief that there is just one best way of doing things. That kind of attitude is part of what causes upsets like the anti-capitalism protests in Seattle, Geneva, and so on. Becoming international needs to be reconciled with local cultures. Globalization needs to become reconciliatory rather than imposing, if it is to be effective.

What new skills will be required?

For a long time, it's been known that an either–or attitude is not enough; and–and was far preferable. However, and–and is now not enough either; the approach should be through–through. So it is not a matter of shareholder value and stakeholder value, it is shareholder value through stakeholder value. It is not marketing and R&D, but marketing through R&D. Business should be asking through–through questions rather than and–and questions.

Why do leaders face such dilemmas and why are they important? All organizations need stability and growth, long term and short term decisions, tradition and innovation, planning and *laissez-faire*, order and freedom. The challenge for leaders is to fuse these opposites, not to select one extreme at the expense of the other. As a leader you have to inspire as well as listen. You have to make decisions yourself but also delegate, and you need to centralize your organization around local responsibilities. You have to be hands-on and yet hands-off. As a professional, you need to master your materials and at the same time you need to be passionately at one with the mission of the whole organization.

What new management questions are there?

I wish we were better educated in asking the right questions. This is a good question. MBA education is answer-driven. I annoy MBA students by giving them a test after five or so lectures. I ask "What is the best question you can ask? Please ignore the answer, it doesn't matter." They get upset and say that I should be asking the questions, not them. But our work is about questions rather than answers.

MBA students are often taught to give the most brilliant answers to what are fundamentally the wrong questions. We need to go beyond that. You can personally become more demanding of yourself.

There are thousands of consultants who are very intelligent, but their intelligence is often restricted to one value. Companies also need to think more broadly instead of concentrating on the single issue of shareholder value. Or at least they need to realize that, in the long term, shareholder value is only created by social responsibility. That pays back—though you still need to meet the bottom line to meet social goals. It is like a circle. You can argue about where you start the circle and where you end it. In that sense I'm optimistic. We are no longer working for pure physical survival.

> We help managers see the beauty of integration, of reconciliation. Such an outlook means that you do not have to say you are against shareholder value; instead you see that the only way to achieve shareholder value is to integrate it with its opposite.

This Anglo-Saxon model of working for two years in one place and two years somewhere else has created other types of loyalties. People are loyal to their profession, rather than to the company. This is a pity, because you don't feel the consequences of many decisions you take . . . you just leave.

How can companies promote enterprises which are profitable and, at the same time, good places for people to work?

Let me give you a simple example. There are conferences with titles entitled things like, "Should we believe in shareholder value?" You shouldn't even ask the question. Obviously the answer is "no," if it is only shareholder value. Everyone who works in business knows that your business is dying if shareholder value is your only value. It leads to short termism.

"It's a gross distortion of nature to conceive of corporations as if they were Newtonian machines."

Charles M. Hampden-Turner

I sometimes say that shareholder value is creating value for people who never share. I am not against shareholder value, but it should be considered alongside the value of other stakeholders. Similarly, if you overdo the emphasis on the other stakeholders, you also run into trouble. That applies to any dilemma that is unreconciled. In addition to the main Trompenaars' cross-cultural database, over the past four year we have collected and indexed some 6,500 dilemmas faced by our client respondents in their respective organizations across the world. Coding and subsequent analysis of these dilemmas reveals a frequently recurring series of "Golden Dilemmas" that provide a basis for a structured approach to diagnosing organizational challenges that owe their origin to cultural differences.

The really exciting part of this third wave, based on our new dilemma database, is that we have been able more recently to converge on a number of key diagnostic measures that reveal how these meta-level dilemmas manifest at the operational level and link to bottom-line business performance. We first help participants make such "Golden Dilemmas" explicit and therefore tangible through our structured "Dilemma Reconciliation Process." We are now in a position to evaluate business benefits against the costs, time scales to realize benefits, and the degree to which the dilemma solution is located in one profit center, or whether it involves cooperation across a number of business units. This type of analysis provides an objective evaluation of where the highest return on investment can be achieved and thus secures the best benefits to the business. Is this the "Holy Grail?" Not yet. We are now researching a fourth phase in which we can quantify the dilemmas between the organization and its societal responsibilities.

FOR MORE INFORMATION

Books:
Trompenaars, Fons, and Peter Woolliams. *Business Across Cultures*. Oxford: Capstone Publishing, 2003.
Trompenaars, Fons, and Charles Hampden-Turner. *Building Cross-cultural Competence*. New Haven, CT: Yale University Press, 2000.
Trompenaars, Fons, and Charles Hampden-Turner. *21 Leaders for the 21st Century*. New York: McGraw-Hill, 2001.
Trompenaars, Fons. *Did the Pedestrian Die? Insights from the Greatest Culture Guru*. Oxford: Capstone Publishing, 2003.
Trompenaars, Fons, and Peter Prud'homme. *Managing Change Across Corporate Cultures*. Oxford: Capstone Publishing, 2005.
Trompenaars, Fons, and Charles Hampden-Turner. *Managing People Across Cultures* . Oxford: Capstone Publishing, 2004.
Trompenaars, Fons, and Peter Woolliams. *Marketing Across Cultures*. Oxford: Capstone Publishing, 2004.
Trompenaars, Fons. *Riding the Waves of Culture: Understanding Cultural Diversity in Business*. 2nd ed. New York: McGraw-Hill, 1997.

Web site:
THT Consulting: **www.thtconsulting.com**

See also:
☆ Boosting Business Success through Diversity (pp. 28–29)
☆ Choosing the Best Training Curriculum for You (pp. 426–427)
☆ SQ: Investing in Spiritual Capital (pp. 43–44)

Boosting Business Success through Diversity

by Debbe Kennedy

EXECUTIVE SUMMARY

- Creating a great place to work and a welcoming place to conduct business for your customers are competitive essentials for today's global organizations.
- Developing a culture of inclusion that embraces the many dimensions of difference is a key success factor. The business reasons are twofold: attracting and keeping the best people is a must to drive creativity and innovation; serving the changing needs of an increasingly diverse set of customers requires an organization that understands, relates to, and responds to people across a wide spectrum of cultures.
- With practice, you can develop three diversity leadership disciplines to boost business success: first, make a culture of inclusion a core business priority; second, lead by example; third, ensure diversity and inclusion are organizational habits in all work.

INTRODUCTION

Regardless of your business, organizational goals, or where you live and work in the world, we share two undeniable areas of common ground as leaders. We all have a mission and we all have an increasingly diverse set of "customers" to serve, both inside and outside our organizations. Whether your goals are bringing product and service innovations to the marketplace, serving communities or nations, creating new wealth, or just getting better and better at your brand of excellence in any endeavor, it is clear that our leadership calling is to forge new paths—to lead the way, embracing new faces, cultures, and a broad array of differences in order to fully participate in the opportunities of the 21st century.

Interestingly, we have been talking about such realities all over the world as if they were some new phenomenon. In fact, this leadership calling is not new. Great leaders have always been able to tap into the best in people. You can see examples in the history and success stories of enduring global corporations like IBM, Hewlett-Packard, and General Electric of the United States, Kyocera Corporation of Japan, and SAP of Germany, just to name a few. Each of them built success upon deeply held beliefs and values about people, striving to create an environment of mutual respect.

Today, leading corporations are expanding their focus on diversity and inclusion worldwide. Their purpose, which touches every organization today, is to attract and retain multicultural, multitalented workforces and to connect and serve a multitude of new *customers* in emerging unexplored *markets,* reaching people, places, and potential that will ensure their continued business success.

The next bold steps into a more richly diverse world rest with leaders like you. So, what is the link between diversity and business success? What can you learn from what others are doing to make diversity and inclusion competitive advantages? What diversity leadership disciplines are essential? These are the important questions we will explore.

THE BUSINESS CASE

Don't make the mistake of seeing diversity and inclusion as "nice to do" moral issues, dismissing them as North American problems. Not today. It is true that across the world we may need to deal with unique issues of difference in our workplaces, marketplaces, and communities. Our way of creating an inclusive environment may also be unique, but in principle a *culture of inclusion* operates in a similar way anywhere. *No one is left out.* More importantly, there is increasing evidence that the business case for diversity and inclusion transcends geographic boundaries.

One of the most compelling presentations of the new business thinking about diversity and inclusion comes from the research of futurist Joel A. Barker in his landmark film, *Wealth, Innovation, & Diversity.* He discovered some startling evidence in history, science, and industry that proves that innovation is driven by diversity and creates new wealth through:

- sustainability
- variety
- innovations
- efficient resource utilization
- new thinking
- lowered risks
- increased predictability
- improved productivity
- economic wealth

Leading companies are recognizing these truths and acting on them to position themselves for success. They are also realizing that more and more companies want to do business with organizations who value people and demonstrate it in the way their businesses are operated.

DIVERSITY BUSINESS LEADERSHIP BEST PRACTICES

Below are four companies that serve as examples for all of us. Each has a history of leadership in valuing people, reflected in their beliefs, policies, and practices. Each is positioning itself for leadership in the 21st century, translating their enduring values into a new level of commitment to diversity and inclusion. Here is a sampling from their efforts.

MINI-CASES
IBM (corporate H.Q. United States)

IBM's diversity commitment extends to all the countries where it does business. To reinforce the link between the marketplace and the workplace, IBM developed a Global Diversity Council that established six global challenges to guide their actions:

- the global marketplace
- multicultural awareness and acceptance
- diversity of the management team
- advancement of women
- work–life balance: dependent care and work flexibility
- integration of people with disabilities

"Today, our definition of diversity includes global cultures. Our boundaries are dissipating. Our ability to do business will be weighted heavily by respect and driven by technology. As we start to connect the people in IBM with people of their culture around the world, we start to see synergies

"Cultural competence refers to the ability to be able to harness and use culturally diverse myths, symbols, rituals, norms, and ideational symbols creatively to add to an organisation's activities."

Stewart Clegg

in relationships and we start to see IBM growing in understanding of the importance of respecting and valuing and understanding the elements of different cultures."

J. T. (Ted) Childs, Jr., Vice President, Global Workforce Diversity

Hewlett-Packard (corporate H.Q. United States)

Hewlett-Packard continues to strengthen its long-held commitment by establishing diversity and inclusion as key business priorities for its organizations throughout the world. Its expanded focus incorporates diversity and inclusion in the marketplace, workplace, and the community, maximizing the opportunity for creativity, invention, profitability, and fulfilling their vision of "being the best place to work and the best place to conduct business."

"Our goal has always been to integrate diversity and inclusion into the fabric of HP—into all our processes, into day-to-day business practices—creating a mindset within every employee and manager so they think about diversity and inclusion in everything they do."

Emily Duncan, Vice President, Culture and Diversity, Hewlett-Packard

Kyocera Corporation (Global H.Q. Japan)

The "Kyocera philosophy," based on a strong belief in people, led to global expansion, serving a diverse set of customers, and a legacy of business success.

Respect the divine and love people. Preserve the spirit to work fairly and honorably, respecting people, our work, our company, and our global community. As a leader, you must clearly indicate your unselfish stand. You should set a meaningful goal for your group and follow it yourself.

Kazuo Inamori, Founder and Chairman Emeritus, Kyocera Corporation

To capture the power of innovation, SAP prides itself on investing in the development of diverse teams with a strong belief in valuing what each employee brings to the company.

"As a global company, SAP believes the world in which we live is growing ever closer together. Technology has connected organizations and individuals all over the world in real time—which makes mutual respect and the protection of diversity a necessity." SAP Diversity and Inclusion Statement

---

MAKING IT HAPPEN ▶▶

"We are what we repeatedly do. Excellence then, is not an act, but a habit." (Aristotle)

To make embracing differences and creating an inclusive environment a *habit* of your personal excellence requires developing a commitment to a few leadership disciplines. The rationale is best illustrated with a story.

Some years back, I visited Sue Swenson, President, International Operations, and C.O.O., Amp'd Mobile, to discuss her approach to diversity and inclusion. "As a practice, I don't do disconnected programs and separate launches of initiatives," she told me. "I have been on the receiving end of such headquarters-driven programs. As a young manager, I was continuously asked to put energy into new programs. If I had responded to every one, I would have done none of them well. As a leader, I've personally taken responsibility for finding ways to engage the organization—integrating fairness, openness, diversity, and inclusion into our business strategies, measures, recruiting practices, new hire orientation, management training, employee development, recognition programs, and our common protocol of behaviors and expectations for everybody. What has convinced me that this approach works are the results."

So, what can you do to take such an integrated approach? Below are three leadership disciplines that when practiced will become *habits of excellence.*

- **Make a culture of inclusion, trust, and mutual respect.** Start by internalizing company values and beliefs that support a culture of inclusion. Learn to express what they mean to you. Set expectations for everyone's behavior by example and through your messages. Guarantee that everyone who does business with you, or who works for you, will experience a culture of inclusion, trust, and mutual respect. Tolerate nothing less.
  How to practice: Let your beliefs and values become part of your day-to-day dialog. Develop your own style of integrating them, perhaps subtly, into your messages, conversations, business planning considerations, and interactions to keep beliefs, values, and expectations in the forefront.

- **Lead by example every day.** See every day as an opportunity to set an example for others. Develop a genuine interest in your employees and customers. Look for the good in others. Appreciate their differences. Model inclusiveness more by your actions than your words. As Gandhi said, "Be the change you want to see in the world."

How to practice: Make a habit of reviewing your behavior and actions at the end of each day. Evaluate your effectiveness as a role model for the culture of inclusion you are working to create.

- **Ensure diversity and inclusion considerations are key organizational** *habits* in all work. Integrating diversity and inclusion into your mainstream business starts with thinking and questioning. Keep it simple. Begin by asking questions that cause you to consider diversity and inclusion implications in such practices as hires, job assignments, promotions, development opportunities, meetings, recognition and awards, pay, who you invite into your inner circle, who you talk with, spend time with, and get to know. Your attention will communicate the importance you place on creating a culture of inclusion. It will also help others in the organization develop their own discipline of thinking about diversity and inclusion in all their work.

How to practice: Help yourself develop your own diversity and inclusion thinking and questioning *habits.* Create a reminder on the back of a business card. Keep it where you can see it as you work through your day. Commit to practicing for two weeks to develop your skill and make it a habit.

CONCLUSION

The great leaders of the 21st century will be those who incorporate considerations of diversity and inclusion into their *habits of excellence* as leaders and into the mainstream of their organizations.

FOR MORE INFORMATION

Book:
Coffman, Curt, and Gabriel Gonzalez-Molina, Ph.D. *Follow This Path: How the World's Greatest Organizations Drive Growth by Unleashing Human Potential.* New York: Warner Business Books, 2002.

Web site:
www.DiversityInc.com: a resource for diversity news in the marketplace, workplace, and community.

See also:
☆ Generation Veneration (pp. 39–40)
☆ Viewpoint: Christopher Bartlett (pp. 45–46)
☆ Viewpoint: Jim Kouzes (pp. 397–399)

"In today's multicultural world, the truly reliable path to co-existence, to peaceful co-existence and creative cooperation must start from what is at the root of all cultures."

Václav Havel

Making the Workplace Flex, Not Break

by Ken Murrell

EXECUTIVE SUMMARY

- Today's workplace community must have enlightened leadership to build and support agile and responsive organizations that stay competitive in the rapidly changing global economy.
- The rapid rate of change in global business has suddenly become very real to nearly every organization. Nowhere is this more obvious than in those companies that are under intense economic pressures in a world that has now linked itself effectively together as one large market, with new global suppliers of about every good and service imaginable.
- Flexibility in the workplace occurs through thoughtful design and an empowered workforce that cares about its work and invests in a spirit of learning, which helps the organization remain competitive.
- Over time success depends on a workplace that has the capacity to change quickly and to create and nurture a workforce that can step up to the challenge of leading change in its own areas of expertise while taking on expanded responsibilities.

INTRODUCTION

Never in history has business played such a central role and been such a globally competitive endeavor. It's also very likely that what we are experiencing today is an easier time for business compared with what is projected to occur in this new century. Dee Hock, founder and C.E.O. of Visa International, is correct when he says, "Fasten your seat belts, the turbulence has barely begun." And as Tom Friedman demonstrates so tellingly in his new book *The World Is Flat*, very soon everyone will be able to compete. The fall of the Berlin Wall made it possible to create one giant global market that is tied directly together over vast networks of fiber-optic cables that connect Beijing, Bangalore, Birmingham, and Baltimore like never before.

Staying competitive isn't just about hiring and developing the very best people you can. It's much more than that it's about building the workplace that allows these talented individuals to create a sustainable organization that has the capacity to learn and to stay a step ahead. And today that requirement to stay competitive has just been moved up several levels. Currently we see it in manufacturing in particular, but we will see it increasingly in service industries also. Very soon a whole new landscape of global competition in the knowledge industries will be upon us.

The roadsides of business growth will be littered with the debris of organizations that once enjoyed success but then couldn't change. Often the failure will have occurred because in the process of building success the organizations broke their people. In the past this breakage was most often a matter of physical breakdown; now more often the breakdown is in the spirit of the workforce. Sadly, this also creates a disintegration of the workplace community often to an irrevocable degree.

How to create flexible and highly competitive workplaces is challenging the best minds in business and the applied behavioral sciences. The Center for Effective Organizations at the University of Southern California, the London School of Economics, the Swedish School of Economics, and countless research universities and consulting companies around the world are grappling with the challenge of creating new forms of organization for the business environment of the 21st century.

WHAT'S NEW? MAYBE OUR WAYS OF RESPONDING

What is the problem? It's the same problem as always! Competitive organizations depend upon people for everything but short-term successes. Market forces and monopolistic positions can generate success for a quarter or even a year, but a healthy workplace is needed for long-term growth. Simple enough to say. Not so easy to do. The challenge is in thinking beyond the current pressures and building the effective workplace as a community in which empowerment occurs naturally. Also needed is a place in which the soul and spirit of the workforce are nourished as they produce the excellence that is required of them.

All of this carries with it an obligation to recreate the meaning of work and to base that recreation on the wisdom developed from the knowledge and experimentation among some of the world's most successful organizations. In today's competitive environment, it is essential to transform the workplace. This will necessarily involve a departure from many previous assumptions. Being creative and taking risks produces the learning needed to help drive the change process.

SETTINGS THAT EMPOWER BRING OUT A FLEXIBLE LABOR FORCE

Being competitive requires the full engagement of the workforce. If an organization has to hire and pay management to continually instruct workers, the game is lost: the cost alone would prohibit successful competition with companies in countries in which the wage scale is a fraction of its own. Efficiencies must be found everywhere; managerial overhead costs that do not add value to the product or service must be reduced.

Jim Collins and Jerry Porras have identified 18 "built-to-last" companies that have done all these things well over the years. One such company is GE, whose "workout" system brings the workforce directly into the organizing process. Workouts are offsite sessions at which facilitators help management and workers to look deeply into issues and jointly arrive at new solutions and workable plans of action. Motorola does much the same thing in getting enhanced employee involvement and building ownership for its Six Sigma quality initiatives. Although costly, the investment has a high return.

Companies that become great often have a culture that promotes flexibility. Fad programs are ineffectual: empowerment comes from employees who are able to pursue organizational goals that they're aligned with. In doing this they develop their own work

---

"Flextime is the essence of respect for and trust in people." David Packard

spirit and create a community of others who believe in what everyone—together—is doing. Flexibility comes from people free to do right, with an agreed value base to help guide them. Real settings where this has been created can be found around the world.

The principles in all successful empowerment cases seem to be the same: there must be sincere respect for the people who work for a company, and management must request that people offer their voices as well as their labor. To create such a flexible workplace is possible; and when it is working well the stressfulness of each job is balanced by a shared desire on everyone's part to provide a performance level that guarantees the success of the company overall.

MINI-CASES

Interface Carpets, headquartered in Atlanta, Georgia, has become a poster child for sustainability. This company, following its President, Ray Anderson, has demonstrated not just that it is good business to be environmentally conscious, but that *learning* how to do its business in the right way can create a blueprint for flexibility. This global company now understands the change process and is meeting its corporate responsibilities to the planet in ways few companies can. Its sustainability drive and its dedication to the triple bottom line of profit, people, and the planet have created an organization that is much more capable of learning and changing. Interface is now a model of a flexible and agile global competitor. This company had seldom been heard of before the world discovered its success at taking out waste and reducing its environmental footprint, but is now rated the third most recognized sustainable company in the world. Its workforce is excited about change and is competing on terms that few companies can even imagine.

The *Toyota* facility in Ontario, Canada (along with its sister sites in many other countries) represents some of the best examples not only of this flexibility but also of the power of *kaizen*, the practice of continuous improvement. Dozens of countries are represented in the plant. The spirit of creating a new way of work and a culture that shows full appreciation for the gifts of each worker has won the facility many awards for learning how to flex and change as each of the company's models requires. The workers understand and adapt without stringent supervision; Toyota has learned to be both flexible and supportive of its workforce.

In Europe, numerous Scandinavian experiments in worker democracy have created the flexible yet empowering work environments that regularly attract study teams from around the world. A work research institute in Norway is also a leading center for such experimentation and change. New research centers are being developed all over the world. In both Singapore and Korea, these centers are being built from the ground up to compete at a global level with special niche markets. They are also being designed with an educated workforce that is trained to keep up to date with state-of-the-art skills and knowledge in their fields.

CREATING MORE EFFECTIVE AND EFFICIENT SELF-ORGANIZING SYSTEMS

Creating a workplace and a workforce that have the capacity to change via flexible self-management requires fundamentally new working principles for a new work environment. The following issues need to be addressed:

- Workforce environments built on command-and-control assumptions must yield to the higher performance potential of workplace communities. Research indicates there is no one best model; what's needed is a commitment to discover the ideal form that fits the unique culture and work performance. Most of these centers are now, by necessity, global, and have workers from every corner of the world.
- Spirit and soul of work are not just interesting phrases but are also necessary conditions for the full investment of the workforce in its work. Work that does not have meaning or cannot give something back to the worker is counter-productive. Work that inspires through meaning and in relationships with others is effective. Inspirational work is a competitive force. Interface, for example, wanted to build better products and as part of that quest also created a much better and more energized workforce. Deadening work leads to a broken workforce and the recent layoffs of thousands at GM demonstrates how disruptive it can be when a company can't manage to stay flexible and adapt to new ways of thinking and doing business.
- Work itself is being redefined. As work increasingly depends on knowledge, the place it plays in people's lives is becoming more complex. The whole person must be considered in order to build effective knowledge work. Balance of work and life is

the goal and the knowledge worker appreciates a place to work as much, or more than, any generation of workers. The difference now is that worker can literally find work anywhere in the world. That kind of mobility makes it imperative to create organizations that the best people in a given field want to work in. To keep these special talents takes a flexible learning organization.

- The wisdom to know how to lead a new workforce requires careful study and a great deal of self-awareness. Knowing others first requires insight into self.
- The changing global economy demands transformational thinking and outside-the-box ways of creating new work environments. These are best created as partnerships in which both workers and managers are expected to change. These partnerships are also often cross-continental and being multinational is a given.

MAKING IT HAPPEN ▸▸
Six Key Principles

- Align work priorities with a clear vision, and a vision that inspires the talented and versatile workforce that organizations need to compete.
- Involve everyone in deciding those priorities. Bring in an inclusive process and design it around where the best talent is, and where the buy-in is needed.
- Define and publicly state how people will work with one another. Create social and psychological contracts that help align the workforce and its leadership.
- Promote the idea of the whole person at work. Be sensitive to the whole family that often supports that person.
- Reward risk-taking to enhance experimentation and discovery. Value conflict for its creative spark and manage it openly.
- Boost performance by boosting learning and by making a serious commitment to workforce development in its many forms.

These are not simple or easy principles, but within them lie the answers to the questions that each organization will have to address in the future. Leadership is key to facilitating and guiding the process, but a commitment to creating an empowering workplace is necessary to start the process. Following these key principles will insure success.

"There's an underutilized work force of well-qualified women who want to work part time. We've created job opportunities that allow parents to balance work and family life."

Gun Denhart

Moreover, as a manager you must:

- share information and educate employees about corporate goals;
- develop a guiding structure, not a controlling one;
- lead with others and invite many to join in creating leadership at all levels;
- support and encourage involvement;
- select the best people with the best skills and the ability to continue lifelong learning;
- be sure the process is adequately resourced in terms of time, money, and team development.

Finally, inform everyone of the global realities of business and the attendant increasing competitive pressures. Help your organization recognize that there are no guarantees and that as business becomes more and more globally competitive—which it must—the only hope for a long-term future is to stay ahead of the economic realities. Cheaper imported products, outsourcing savings, and new technologies keep all businesses on their toes and the need to stay flexible and adaptive has never been higher. To succeed, everyone's help is needed.

Working together is the only way to survive against global pressures, pressures which are nonetheless making business better the world over.

CONCLUSION

Although the task might appear daunting, there is much help available. The emergent global economy is forcing all organizations to move in this direction. The best are already moving quickly, and they represent potential resources for benchmarking or comparing notes. Finally, it is essential that workplaces have the capacity to create and recreate themselves. This work will always be important; in essence, this is true job security. It is also the work that creates in the leader a spirit and a potential for finding personally satisfying work. When the only constant in business is change, building a flexible workplace that can adapt to and thrive in the rapidly changing business environment will be the cornerstone of successful companies in the future. To build long-term competitive advantage, the whole company needs to move in the right direction. Successful organizations are characterized by a flexible culture; brittle ones will break and will be left by the roadside.

FOR MORE INFORMATION

Books:
Collins, James C., and Jerry I. Porras. *Built to Last: Successful Habits of Visionary Companies*. New York: HarperBusiness, 2002.
Friedman, Thomas. *The World is Flat: A Brief History of the 21st Century*. New York: Farrar, Straus and Giroux: 2005.
Hock, Dee. *Birth of the Chaordic Age*. San Francisco, CA: Berrett-Koehler, 1999.
Wheatley, Margaret J. *Leadership and the New Science*. 2nd ed. San Francisco, CA: Berrett-Koehler, 2001.

Web site:
www.Spiritatwork.com: offers resources for people who "walk between the two worlds."

See also:
☆ Converting Anonymity into Participation in a Membership Organization (pp. 239–240)
✔ Moving Sideways: Benefiting from a Lateral Move (pp. 889–890)
☆ Power Struggling and Power Sharing (pp. 126–127)

"Organisations need talented women in their core jobs . . . because many will have the kinds of attitudes and attributes that the new flexible organisation will need. If they screen out the women they will handicap their futures."

Charles Handy

Finding and Keeping Top Talent
by Philip Sadler

EXECUTIVE SUMMARY

Just as organizations have changed dramatically in nature over the last 25 years, so have people's attitudes to their employers—and the attitudes of the most talented people are no exception.

- Talented employees are increasingly aware of their value and are prepared to move to other organizations if they feel they will receive greater respect and reward. Cradle to grave loyalty, if it ever existed at all, is certainly very scarce.
- Knowledge is more important than ever before and a major source of competitive advantage. Attracting, finding, and retaining talented people is therefore vital for success. Not only are people the most decisive and expensive resource, they also determine the success of every activity within the organization.
- Although money remains important, talented people value much more; an increasingly complex range of factors affects their loyalty, motivation, and effectiveness.
- A disappointingly large number of talented people are already within organizations, their potential largely unfulfilled.

INTRODUCTION

In the past, the typical wealth-creating enterprises of the advanced industrial societies were either labor-intensive—such as coal mining or textiles—or capital-intensive—such as chemicals and steel. Today, many of the world's major corporations are best described as knowledge-intensive or talent-intensive. The obvious examples are companies in fields such as software, pharmaceuticals, business and professional services, investment banking, music publishing, entertainment, and professional sports. Many of the dot-com companies such as Amazon, Google, and eBay fall into this group. In such organizations, the principal assets consist of the knowledge and special skills of talented people, rather than the tangible assets of financial reserves, capital equipment, buildings, and stocks of the so-called old economy. The management of knowledge has become a lucrative field for management consultants and academic gurus in recent years and it is obviously important that a company should exploit its knowledge capital to the greatest extent possible. Sooner or later, however, all today's knowledge is obsolete. The competitive edge lies with companies that are focused on creating new knowledge. The value of a research laboratory to a potential investor is the ability of its scientists to make new discoveries and develop new products in the future.

In a world in which there is no shortage of capital for investment, talent is the only remaining scarce resource. However, the kind of talent needed by many of today's businesses is not necessarily of the kind that was in demand in the past. Fashion designers, international footballers, creative writers, successful investment analysts, inventors such as James Dyson, entrepreneurs such as Richard Branson, boy bands, Web site designers, and others possess marketable skills that have little to do with their ability to absorb knowledge. This explains why outstanding performers in many fields did not enjoy academic success in their schooldays.

CHARACTERISTICS OF TALENT-INTENSIVE ORGANIZATIONS

Talent-intensive organizations share several characteristics:
- Their principal assets (that is, their talented people) do not appear on the balance sheet (although they are, or should be, the main determinants of the company's market valuation).
- These key assets are mobile. They can, despite contracts of service, simply walk away.
- Talent-intensive organizations rely particularly on creativity and imagination.
- The success criteria for talent-intensive organizations stretch far beyond the accountants' bottom line. Winning a Nobel Prize, an Oscar, a fashion design award, or the World Series may weigh far more than profit or cash flow does.

The International Dimension

Like so many other activities, recruiting is now affected by globalization. Companies increasingly understand that they must adapt their human resources policies to a highly competitive global market for talent. There is a constant flow of talented people from countries with lower living standards or higher levels of personal taxation to countries where talent can enjoy a higher reward—the so-called "brain drain." Recruiting managers should try to include at least one global candidate in every key search. They should also consult with senior management on the question of where in the world the work (and the workforce) should be positioned in order to maximize its cost effectiveness.

RECRUITING AND FINDING TALENT

The distinction between recruiting talent and finding it is important. Sometimes an organization looks outside for new talent when the potential for outstanding performance already exists unrecognized among existing employees.

Recruitment itself can be separated into two quite distinct processes. The first is that of attracting people whose exceptional talent has already been established and recognized elsewhere. This can be called the transplanting type of recruiting—equivalent to digging up a mature tree in the quest for an instant garden. In such instances, companies often make the mistake of assuming that the cash nexus is the most important factor. While it is obviously true that an outstanding performer in any field is unlikely to move from one organization to another if it involves a drop in remuneration, it remains the case that other factors are seldom given enough weight or consideration. For example, in the case of highly talented people, a key influence on the decision whether or not to move jobs is the reputation of the recruiting organization in its particular field; is it at the leading edge, does it set the pace for its industry, does the individual feel honored to have been approached? Reputation building, therefore, is a key element in recruiting strategy. Top companies like Starbucks, Intel, Cisco, Mar-

> "There are two important factors in building a self-motivated team of people—the opportunity to learn through increased effort and trust in the management to give the utmost support."
>
> Tom Farmer

riott, Dell, Wal-Mart, and Microsoft have been focusing on employment branding for years. Nothing has a greater impact than being talked about in the media as a well-managed company that is also a good place to work. Research shows that the best source of quality applicants comes from an organization's existing employees. If employees are proud of their employer and enjoy a high level of job satisfaction, the result will be one or two quality employee referrals for every vacancy.

The "Nursery" Approach

The second process can be termed the "seedbed" or "nursery" approach: recruiting young people straight from high school or college, nurturing or developing their emerging talent and bringing it to fruition. This is clearly a longer-term approach and one fraught with obvious risks, one of which is the difficulty of predicting ultimate success. The obstacles in the way of successful prediction are many, including:

- different rates of maturing of individuals' abilities—late developers are often missed;
- the relative weakness of psychometric tests when it comes to predicting things like creativity and entrepreneurial ability;
- the tendency to give too much weight to academic qualifications;
- failure to value diversity with regard to the workforce—a great deal of fine talent is overlooked among ethnic minorities, particularly when the selection process involves using psychometric instruments that have been validated within the Anglo-American culture;
- the fact that motivation and drive may well be more powerful determinants of performance than sheer ability.

Talent Spotting

Somewhat less risky is the process of finding talent among existing employees. Assuming they have been in employment for some time, a well-designed appraisal and development procedure can be effective in selecting promising candidates for accelerated development.

Michael Howe, Reader in Human Cognition at Exeter University, England, is one of the world's leading experts on the subject of talent. He points to the danger of seeing talent in any field as a gift which you either have or not, as the case may be. "We are easily convinced that the most striking feats

must depend on circumstances which, except for certain rare individuals, are entirely unattainable. Some of the most widespread beliefs about exceptional people revolve around the view that certain individuals are not only remarkable but inherently so, while the remainder of us are doomed to ordinariness." (Howe, 1990) Howe challenges such beliefs and produces compelling evidence that appropriate training and development can bring about exceptional performance. His views are borne out by the achievements of participants in the TV series *Faking It USA* in which, for example, a go-go dancer with no previous experience of horse riding became a successful show jumper within a few weeks.

KEEPING TALENT

When it comes to retaining talent, it goes without saying that there has to be an adequate compensation package. What makes the real difference in keeping talented employees loyal is the extent to which the company provides them with a working environment favorable to creativity, self-expression, and the exercise of initiative. The paradox facing organizations, particularly very large ones, is that they are hierarchical, bureaucratic, and conformist in order to achieve efficiency and uniformity, yet it is just these characteristics that turn off highly creative people.

The term "skunk works" has entered the language of organizations to describe small, informal, tightly knit teams that are shielded from standard company practices and rules in order to foster their creative energies. Warren Bennis gives a graphic description of the very first skunk works, established by Lockheed to develop the first U.S. jet fighter during World War II. Lockheed's chief designer selected a team of 23 engineers and 30 support staff. They built makeshift quarters from discarded engine boxes roofed with a circus tent. They worked in secrecy, doing their own cleaning and secretarial work. Bennis describes the designer Johnson as "a visionary on at least two fronts: designing airplanes and organizing genius. Johnson seemed to know intuitively what talented people needed to do their best work, how to motivate them, and how to make sure the desired product was created as quickly and cheaply as possible." His unit was characterized by the egalitarian treatment of people, an absence of paperwork,

informality of dress, and open debate. The culture of an organization is an important factor in its ability to retain talent.

The chief characteristics of a culture that nurtures talent are the following:

- highly cohesive work teams
- authority residing in expertise and competence rather than rank or status
- elites recognized without elitism in that talented people respect and recognize the contribution of those less gifted coworkers who support them
- respected leadership: talented people are critical people who do not follow blindly, and know when the emperor has no clothes
- freedom, autonomy, space, and flexibility
- openness and trust
- encouragement of risk-taking

In other words, the right approach for organizations anxious to retain their most talented people is not so much to create a skunk works inside the company, but to make the company as a whole as much like a skunk works as possible.

FOR MORE INFORMATION

Books:
Bennis, Warren, and Patricia Ward Biederman. *Organizing Genius: The Secrets of Creative Collaboration*. Cambridge, MA: Perseus, 1998.
Deems, Richard S. *Hiring: How to Find and Keep the Best People*. Franklin Lakes, NJ: Career Press, 1998.
Howe, Michael J. A. *The Origins of Exceptional Abilities*. Oxford: Blackwell, 1990.

"Surround yourself with the best people you can find, delegate authority and don't interfere."

Ronald Reagan

Managing Today's Angry Workforce
by Florence M. Stone

EXECUTIVE SUMMARY

- Organizations contribute to the anger and violence in the workplace by their demands for more work in less time and a throwaway attitude toward employees.
- The high-stress work environment is causing angry outbursts and violent behavior to grow at epidemic levels.
- Managers need to be sensitive to the levels of stress employees are under, recognize danger signs, and address issues of stress and anxiety before anger evolves into violence.
- Companies need to have recognized protocols and processes for managing all levels of anger in the workplace, including a zero-tolerance policy for threats of violence.

INTRODUCTION

Shareholders and board members expect corporate growth, no matter the state of the economy. To make that growth happen, top managements are putting pressure on their workers, using employee cutbacks to increase profits if there aren't any other ways. The backlash is twofold. Where jobs are plentiful elsewhere, employees leave. If employees are stuck, and are unable to do what is demanded, they react emotionally with endless complaints, angry outbursts, and even fistfights with coworkers.

This may explain why anger in today's workplaces has grown to epidemic levels. The movie *Anger Management*, with Adam Sandler and Jack Nicholson, made hot-headed behavior seem amusing, but in real life it is far from funny. In a recent Gallup poll, two out of every ten employees admitted that within the past six months they were angry enough with a coworker to "hurt" him or her.

According to an article in June 2005 issue of *HRMagazine*, anger is a factor in many of the 1.7 million violent assaults in U.S. workplaces. These include incidents involving customers and other non-employees. Beyond the hurt to those involved, each case costs around $700,000.

TICKED OFF

Conflicts aren't new in the workplace—indeed, disagreements can help select the best among good ideas—but today's offices seem more prone to excessive conflict. This doesn't mean that the anger always erupts into violence. According to Dr. Teri Domagalski, associate professor of management at Florida Institute of Technology, anger and violence aren't synonymous. When conflict is unchecked, however, it can lead to trashed offices and acts of violence against coworkers. Domagalski's research has found that feelings of powerlessness, unjust treatment, and domineering incivility are causes of much expressed anger. Anger is triggered in managers and supervisors when they feel caught between lack of support from the top of the organization and poor performance from the lower ranks.

Some individuals are speechless when angry, while others yell themselves hoarse; still others have to take some physical action. Regardless of the way they respond, the factors that trigger anger seem to be common. Anger is triggered by the threatened loss of something greatly valued. In the workplace, this comes down to five factors:

1 downsizing or the threat of job loss
2 the pressure to do more with less, or the loss of existing resources
3 unrealistic expectations, with deafness to pleas for help
4 disempowerment or the loss of control over the work to be done
5 lack of confidence in those in charge whose demands shift from day to day

The high-stress conditions in today's offices make it difficult to achieve teamwork or creativity, but the bigger problem is that they set the stage for unstable people to act out their anger, pushing them over the edge to violent behavior. Circumstances ranging from an unresolved conflict with a coworker or supervisor, to a bad performance evaluation, to a major change in work procedures can contribute to heightened anxiety and, in turn, to raw anger. If an individual has a predisposition to aggressiveness and perceives the workplace as a hostile environment, experiencing stress can trigger violent behavior, according to Anthony Baron, C.E.O. of Baron Center, a California-based organization of trainers specializing in workplace and school violence protection.

"Boss-icides" continue to grow in number. On average, workers murder three to four supervisors a month, double the number a little more than a decade ago. Unfortunately, according to security experts, most violence-prevention programs are initiated *after* an incident, not beforehand. Many years ago, a troubled and angry employee at U.S. Foodservice in East Allentown, Pennsylvania, shot three managers, killing one, before fatally shooting himself. To avoid a repetition of the incident, U.S. Foodservice undertook a major training effort, teaching managers at its branches about violence in the workplace and how to spot the warning signs of a violent employee. The company also instituted zero-tolerance guidelines on violence in the workplace. A policy on violence existed before the shootings but it was rewritten in plainer language so that there were no misunderstandings.

DEFUSING ANGER

Needless to say, companies should initiate such programs before workplace anger impedes corporate performance or violence erupts.

Reference checks in the case of both new hires and promotions are also important to minimize the likelihood of violence. We can expect a skill war in the near future and, with it, there will be a shortage of talented workers. Companies shouldn't let the rush to fill vacancies cause them to ignore reference checks, opening the way to negligent hiring or promotion.

Among corporate policies should be one that demands an immediate response in the event of a threat to a coworker or manager. Equally important, executives and managers need to be trained to handle on-the-job conflicts and outbursts and consequently avoid the dangers associated with them.

Finally, companies with Employee Assistance Programs (EAPs) need to be sure that their EAP is equipped to identify and address personal and work-related problems that might trigger violent behavior. And managers need to be instructed on how best to use the EAP organization.

"Rash and incessant scolding runs into custom and renders itself despised."

Michel Eyquem de Montaigne

36

BEST PRACTICE

A MANAGEMENT PROBLEM

Besides the physical danger and damage associated with anger, there are management problems that excessive conflict can create. Its existence in the workplace can increase absenteeism and decrease productivity of both assailants and their victims. According to one study (Pearson, Anderson, and Porath, 2000), 53% of targets of anger lost work time from worry about the incident or future interactions, 22% put less effort into work, 10% spent less time at work, and 12% quit to avoid the instigator. Bernie Golden, a clinical psychologist and founder of Anger Management Education in Chicago, described how anger can damage morale and diminish staff attention and even impair judgments, which could mean unnecessary job errors and accidents.

So coping with anger in the workforce is a management issue as well as important to securing the workplace. How should companies start?

Warning Signs

To begin with, managers and executives need to know when someone might be a good candidate for anger management training. Warning signs are relatively straightforward, such as being chronically irritable, impatient, short-tempered, argumentative, or sarcastic. Such people confuse assertiveness with aggression, and think that they are responding assertively to a situation rather than exhibiting passive-aggressive or aggressive communication styles.

But not all angry staff members use verbal abuse to express their feelings. Because they don't want to get fired or disciplined, they will express their anger through backstabbing, rumor-mongering, and engaging in turf wars with peers.

Corporate programs are less likely to identify individuals who have difficulty expressing their anger as assailants in the making, according to Ari Novick, president of the AJ Novick Group in Laguna Beach, California. In an interview in *HRMagazine*, he observed that "for some, rage is less an explosion than a slow burn." Still, this shouldn't discourage corporate effort to address anger in the workplace. Consider workers throughout the organization, from entry-level employees to top-level executives. According to psychologists, the one thing that many of these individuals may have in common is unrealistic expectations. They work hard and they expect to be rewarded for their efforts. When their efforts go unacknowledged, they lose control and become resentful and angry.

As an individual, if you find yourself provoked to anger, you need to learn to take a "time out." Practice deep breathing or visualize a place with positive connotations to regain control over your emotions. Ask yourself, "What can I do to respond to this situation that might help resolve it rather than make it worse?" If you have one of two choices—to lose control or walk away—then choose to walk away from the situation. To identify what situations trigger a heated retort, write down those incidents to identify a pattern. Certainly, don't threaten the other party. If you find you can't control your emotion, then seek out help through your organization's EAP.

Corporate Training Efforts

According to security experts, an organization that conducts training seminars on preventing workplace violence should go beyond spelling out policies. Top management should be quick and stern in dealing with violations. One security expert compared corporate response to the heightened use of the police and military to fend off terrorist attacks. Employees need to be trained to understand that threats aren't appropriate and will be dealt with very seriously. Employees can be placed on unpaid leave or fired if found guilty of making remarks perceived as threatening, since they challenge a company's responsibility to secure the workplace and protect the other employees.

Companies need to take seriously the issue of growing anger and uncivil behavior among coworkers. Left unchecked, in certain individuals it can trigger violent incidents that can be costly beyond the safety of coworkers and customers. Businesses are facing recent judicial trends that find employers liable for acts of violence due to negligence in hiring, supervision, or retention.

Aside from instituting violence prevention/anger management programs, companies need to look more closely at surveys that show pervasive anger within their rank and file. Anger in the workplace is a signal that there's something wrong in the company's culture. It is management's responsibility to investigate the corporate climate, identify the causes, and with its workforce, collaboratively and collectively seek effective solutions.

MAKING IT HAPPEN ►►

Companies need a tandem effort of prevention and protection to defuse and guard against workplace tension.

- Review hiring processes, including background checks, reference

verifications, and applicant screening for propensity toward violence.
- Review and implement policies and procedures that ensure that under the worst of circumstances employees are treated with dignity. Many of those who exhibit violent behavior attribute it to actions they say stripped them of their dignity in some way.
- Institute handgun policies covering the carrying of concealed firearms on the premises.
- Institute training programs to educate managers on early-warning signs and emergency procedures.
- Create a safe environment by establishing workplace violence policies, including a zero-tolerance policy on threats of harm. Provide for an employee assistance or counseling program for workers who threaten or harass fellow employees.
- Create a threat management team to detail a specific plan of action to be taken every time a threat is reported, with participants from human resources, security, the EAP, and legal counsel.

FOR MORE INFORMATION

Books:
Carter, Les. *The Anger Trap: Free Yourself from the Frustrations That Sabotage Your Life.* New York: Wiley, 2003.
Hershorn, Michael. *60 Second Anger Management.* Far Hills, NJ: New Horizon Press, 2002.
Nay, W. Robert. *Taking Charge of Anger.* New York: The Guilford Press, 2003.
Potter-Efron, Ronald T., and Pat S. Potter-Efron. *Letting Go of Anger: The 10 Most Common Anger Styles and What to Do About Them.* Oakland, CA: New Harbinger Publications, 1995.

Web site:
www.angermgmt.com provides information about anger management, and offers a range of services and products including courses, counseling, and a questionnaire measuring your anger level.

See also:

☆ From Crisis Management to Crisis Leadership (pp. 379–380)
☆ Making Cultures Behave (pp. 51–52)

"There is a rage to organize which is the sworn enemy of order." — Georges Duhamel

Creating Fun in the Workplace
by Leslie A. Yerkes

EXECUTIVE SUMMARY

- Many bosses feel there's no place for fun at work. Today's employees demand that work be fun. The challenge is to reconcile these two conflicting expectations.
- Fun and work are not incompatible: they can coexist. Work is most productive when it's fused with fun.
- In creating a sustainable organization fun should be a core essential, not an add-on or a reward for hard work.
- Fun can be an essential element to conducting business, retaining customers, enhancing external perceptions of the business and brand, attracting and retaining talented employees—and helping to build competitive advantage.

INTRODUCTION

The perception is still widespread that work should not be fun, that fun is something you earn only after you've worked hard. That position, once the bedrock of workplace behavior, is changing. Companies such as Southwest Airlines, Skandia, Isle of Capri Casinos, and Pike Place Fish have shown that the integration of fun and work not only improves the day-to-day relationships and atmosphere of the workplace, but also it can positively improve the net worth of the company.

Our attitude toward work is not an absolute. Work and our perception of work have changed and evolved. Each of us adopts the attitude toward work that our parents taught us, or assimilate the attitude held by whoever is exerting the strongest current influence, perhaps our peer group or our employer. For many of us, work has become who we are. It's how we define ourselves.

ATTITUDES TOWARD WORK ARE CHANGEABLE

When we look at the timeline of work attitudes we can see that work has evolved from Aristotle's "work is for slaves" to Calvin's "work is a commandment," through "work is a virtue" to "work is who I am." Since general attitudes toward work merely reflect the times, people can intentionally alter their individual attitudes. Specifically, it's possible to reintegrate fun into our work.

Historically, fun and work have long coexisted. During the agricultural age, for example, work songs helped turn dreary tasks and repetitive actions into activities that, if not fun, at least contained an element of anticipation and comfort. Barn raisings changed a task impossible for one or two people into a picnic-style community event. The element of fun turned an impossible task into an eagerly anticipated one, one at which friends, family, and neighbors worked side by side for the common good, caught up on old times, and shared food with one another. Vestiges of this behavior are seen when people get together on a Saturday to clean up a ball diamond, paint a senior citizen's house, or build a playground.

The concept of work is again in the midst of change. We are rediscovering that fun belongs with work, and that when it's isolated, work isn't fun. Fun and work naturally go together: fun works, and work is more productive when it's fun.

MINI-CASES

Pike Place Fish is one of three fish markets on the Public Market Dock on Puget Sound in downtown Seattle, Washington. When John Yokoyama bought out the previous owner in 1965 for $3,500, Pike Place Fish was simply a fish market, unremarkable in many ways. "Everyone here hated their jobs. I can remember the owner counting out loud the number of steps it took him to get a dozen clams for a customer and then complaining about it. For a long time, no one working here had fun. I was an angry manager; I was an angry owner. All the tools in my managerial toolkit were fear-based."

When the collective group of owners, managers, and employees decided to become world-famous they began to act the way world-famous fishmongers would act. John transformed himself from a yelling whip-cracker into the Fish King. His job evolved: he checks the mood and makes sure energy is present that allows employees to be themselves—and to have fun!

Pike Place Fish is now valued at 1,000 times more than the original purchase price. During the Christmas season it transacts more business per square foot than any competitive grocery chain in the area. The business has expanded successfully into e-commerce, speaking engagements, training, and consulting. It's served as the setting of numerous films, television commercials, and print ads. Leveraging its image and reputation for fun has generated a strong brand and an enviable position in the market.

Employease is an Atlanta-based application service provider offering proprietary human-resources services. Between its September 1998 startup and June 2000, it enrolled more than 1,000 companies without spending anything on advertising. The secret is twofold: an innovative Web-based product and a company attitude that trusts both people and the process to perform.

Employease is a diverse mix of human-resource and IT experts of all races, ages, backgrounds, sexes, and home states. Employees are trusted to be accountable for their actions and responsible for their results, and to take ownership of their jobs. Employease is an egoless company with low political pressures. Its work ethic says, "I'll trust you to do your job, you trust me." In this high-trust environment fun naturally emerges as the social glue that cements the relationships of the diverse staff.

Isle of Capri Casinos has become one of the darlings of Wall Street, going from $2 a share to between $25 and $30 a share in 2006, and from $800 million in earnings in 1999 to just over $1 billion in early 2006.

Guests who visit an Isle resort aren't looking for a company that exhibits corporate financial security. They're looking for excitement, entertainment, and a good time that includes gambling, shows, and good food. What Isle of Capri Casinos does to make guests return is to ensure that the experience is greater than the anticipation—that it's fun.

The Isle of Capri brand is deeply rooted in a philosophy called Isle Style. When guests arrive at an Isle of Capri Casino, the door of

their car is opened by an enthusiastic employee who smiles and welcomes them to Isle Style. After check-in their bags are carried by a bellhop who asks on the way to the room how they like their coffee. Do they like fluffy towels? Do they prefer a special kind of soap or shampoo? Within minutes the bellhop returns with extra towels and the appropriate cream for the coffee. The goal is to make guests feel that their every need has been attended to. This creates a fun experience that encourages repeat business year after year.

Skandia is the world's largest asset gatherer of nonproprietary market-linked insurance policies. Its goals are to attract the best money managers and financial planners to use Skandia's services and to attract and retain the best employees in order to make that happen. Attracting good people is made easy by success in the marketplace combined with a wide variety of day-to-day amenities—from a world-class gym to upscale coffee bars on each of five floors in their U.S. headquarters. But the method it chooses to retain employees is celebration.

Various awards all celebrate achievement through cash, parties, and plaques. To make each day fun, employees order in food, go to baseball games en masse (covering for each other's work to make it possible), and decorate the offices in anticipation of coming holidays.

"It all comes down to believing and trusting in people," says C.E.O. Wade Dokken. "You have to trust them if you want them to succeed. Then you need to reward them. We celebrate success by giving credit to others. To be successful, you need to share and give power freely. And you need to celebrate their successes."

MAKING IT HAPPEN ▶▶

Successful companies like these have learned that integrating of fun and work:

- stimulates creativity and innovation;
- fosters commitment and ownership among all members of the organization;
- creates and secures employee morale;
- increases productivity;
- counters the effects of stress;

- guards against burnout;
- becomes the glue for social relationships;
- mends conflicts;
- stimulates renewal and activity;
- reduces absenteeism;
- creates stronger, deeper, longer-lasting customer relationships.

The successful integration of fun and work comes from the following principles:

- **Give permission to perform**—because of our attitude that fun isn't appropriate in a work environment, fun won't appear unless it's invited. It's essential to give permission to individuals to bring the best of themselves to work each day. This requires a superb leader to create the vision, set the tone for the journey, and believe that only by integrating fun and work can the best results be achieved.
- **Trust the process**—fun takes root in organizations that are high-trust rather than high-fear. The more trust we show, the more fun there is; the more fun there is, the more trust we show. Fun is an energy force that can't be mandated or controlled by rules. If you trust people with your company's most valuable assets, why not trust them to use their judgment in blending fun with work?
- **Be authentic and conscientious**—because we're changing mindsets, this requires initial effort. The integration of work and fun requires a *being* state, not a *doing* state. Attitude isn't a veneer that's applied to a new employee, it's an intrinsic quality that emerges naturally. Search out authentic people who enjoy life and enjoy being around people, and then train them in specific job skills after they've been hired.
- **Celebrate**—what gets recognized gets repeated; what gets celebrated becomes a habit. Individual recognition and group celebration fuel high performance. Make an effort to compliment people doing something right. There's nothing more fun than celebrating a success.

CONCLUSION

The objective observation of the case companies supports the premise that business works best when fun and work are successfully integrated. It disproves the commonly held perception that there's no place in the work environment for fun. No longer do we believe that the only time we can have fun is when the work is over, or that the only way we can have fun is to earn it through hard work.

Companies that integrate fun and work are best able to attract and retain peak performers in an economy that promotes and rewards the rapid and constant changing of jobs.

FOR MORE INFORMATION

Books:
Crother, Cyndi. *Catch! A Fishmonger's Guide to Greatness* San Francisco, CA: Berrett-Koehler, 2004.
Lundin, Stephen C. *Fish! A Remarkable Way to Boost Morale and Improve Results*. New York: Hyperion, 2000.
Schrage, Michael. *Serious Play: How the World's Best Companies Simulate to Innovate*. Cambridge, MA: Harvard Business School Press, 2000.
Weinstein, Matt, and Luke Barber. *Work Like Your Dog: Fifty Ways to Work Less, Play More, and Earn More*. New York: Random House, 1999.
Yokoyama, John. *When Fish Fly*. New York: Hyperion, 2004.

"We are speeding up our lives and working harder in a futile attempt to buy the time to slow down and enjoy it."

Paul Hawken

Generation Veneration
by Ron Zemke

EXECUTIVE SUMMARY

- At no time in history have so many different generations with such different views, values, and approaches been asked to work together.
- The once-linear nature of power at work, from older to younger, has been dislocated by changes in life expectancy, longevity, and health, as well as changes in lifestyle, technology, and knowledge base.
- Understanding generational differences is critical to managing people effectively.

INTRODUCTION

There's a new challenge facing your organization. It doesn't come from downsizing, rightsizing, change, new technology, or competition. It's a problem created by a clash of generational values, ambitions, views, mindsets, and demographics.

The workplace today is awash with the conflicting voices, views, and learning styles of the most diverse workforce the industrialized world has ever known. Look around you. Your customers and your coworkers are a far more age-diverse group than ever before—and more organizationally integrated. Many senior employees are older today than senior employees were in the old days, and these older employees are filling positions once staffed by younger employees—and vice versa. Young employees with mission-critical knowledge and skills are increasingly coming to occupy leadership and management assignments that would have been deemed beyond their years just a few years ago. The new, more horizontal, less segregated-by-function workplace has stirred the generations into a mix of much richer and different proportions than at any time in the past.

According to Walker Smith and Ann Clurman, "New generational differences are causing business upheavals, bringing new categories and ways [of work] into being at warp speed and causing old ones to shrink or disappear." The old way—strict hierarchy, slow promotional tracks, and short life spans—that used to keep one generational cohort together and isolated from others, no longer exists, or exists in a much less rigid, more permeable form. Knowledge, skill, and merit have quickly overcome time as the power factor in today's workplace.

THE PLAYERS

It isn't uncommon today to find four distinct generations working together on the same project. These four generations—known as *veterans*, *boomers*, *Xers*, and *nexters*—are differentiated not solely by their dates of birth, but by events and experiences that at an early age set their values and views on life. In the words of Canadian demographer David Foote, "We look more like our times and our peers than we do our parents and their views." The 80 years that these four generations span cover an amazingly rich and diverse body of history and social change.

Each generation has a unique perspective, particularly on work. Each has its own views about what makes an attractive work environment and what kind of team is worth joining. Perhaps most confounding for a manager, each generation has unique preferences for acquiring, digesting, organizing, and distilling information and skills; each espouses firm ideas about how a career should develop. Understanding these generational differences is critical for leaders who would enroll the participation of all employees in working for the organization and not against it. These differences are also significant for managers who must meld these different viewpoints with the values, philosophy, and know-how upon which the smooth running of any modern organization is premised.

It is worth emphasizing that these classifications are generalizations, but they are surprisingly accurate and valid. They are also *perceived* as being accurate and affecting workplace attitudes and behavior.

The Veterans (Born 1922-43)

The Veterans were born, and some came of age, before and during the Great Depression and World War II. They're the classic keepers of the grail; they form an irreplaceable repository of lore and wisdom, practical wiliness, and more than a few critical extra-organizational contacts. Their preferred style is formal. From the hiring process to performance reviews, they like things done by the book. They aren't interested in bucking authority, but when asked they'll tell you where the weak spots of a plan are. Though past, at, or nearing retirement, they're nonetheless much interested in continuing to work part-time on projects or as mentors for younger employees.

The Baby Boomers (Born 1943-60)

Baby Boomers were the postwar babies. They're now graying, and they'd really rather not be seen as the problem in the workplace—though they frequently are. They invented "Thank God, it's Monday!" and the 60-hour workweek. Boomers are passionately concerned about participation and spirit in the workplace, about bringing heart and humanity to the office, and about creating a fair and level playing field for all. And they hold way too many meetings for the average Gen-Xer's taste. Gen-Xers frequently report that they see Boomers as too wedded to ceremony and ritual and too controlling. Boomers are interested in creating a personal legacy or completing that one last great project before turning their attention toward retirement.

The Xers (Born 1960-80)

The Xers grew up in the post-1960s era of Watergate, latchkey kids, and the energy crisis. Their need for feedback and flexibility, coupled with their hatred of close supervision, is but one of the many conundrums they present employers. At the same time they're personally adept and comfortable with change—after all, they've changed cities, homes, and parents all their lives. They are indeed the new change masters. And they're much more inclined to keep their own counsel than are their Boomer predecessors.

Xers are very clear about the meaning of balance in their lives. Work is work. And they work to live, they don't live to work. "It's just a job" is a mantra often heard from Xers. Their loyalties revolve around them-

selves and their friends and families, not their jobs, not your organization. The biggest Xer challenge is retention. The marketplace wants them, almost fights over them, and they have a natural wanderlust fueled by opportunity and fired by the need to add experience and competence to their personal portfolios. A recent study found that 77% of Xers would like to find a company where they could work for a long time, yet 42% described loyalty to one employer as foolish, if not foolhardy.

The Nexters (Born 1980+)

They may be the smartest, cleverest, most-wanted people to have yet walked the face of the planet. They're an optimistic bunch who express doubt over the wisdom of traditional racial and sexual categorization. They have Internet pen pals in Asia whom they can, and do, contact at any hour of the day or night. Those now in the workforce—think fast food, movie theaters, grocery-store carryout, yard work, babysitting, Web-page building, and internships—seem destined to become what Neil Howe and Bill Strauss call "good scouts." They will be a very welcome relief to any organization currently struggling with the Boomer–Xer conflicts. But be aware that they come with their own agenda. Members of the class of 2001 clearly see themselves as entrepreneurs-in-training. They expect fantastic training, job counseling, and career planning as part of the job.

Nexters have lived a very organized life, with classes and activities carefully planned out by mom, dad, and school. They expect the same at work. They're eager workers, but not the self-sufficient workers that Xers are. They're very comfortable with collaborative work and are uncomfortable with a competitive atmosphere. They see no reason why everyone can't win.

THE CHALLENGE

These four generations have unique work ethics, different perspectives on work, distinct and preferred ways of managing and being managed, and idiosyncratic styles. They also have unique ways of viewing such work—world issues as quality, service, and, well, just showing up for work. *Managing* this mélange of values and views is an increasingly difficult task. For one thing, few of us are able to understand our own generation in context. It's difficult to look at your own life as part of a segment or trend or era—or generation. Each of us feels unique and individual. According to Howe

and Strauss, "People of all ages feel a disconnection with history. Many have difficulty placing their own thought and actions, even their own lives, in any larger story." This is diversity management at its most challenging. However, it is this diversity and character that shapes the modern workplace and, when managed effectively, it can be used to enrich organizational effectiveness.

MAKING IT HAPPEN ▶▶

Companies that successfully nurture cross-generational workplaces exhibit common approaches. They are successful at making their environments generationally comfortable and focusing their people's energies on the business: accommodating differences, exhibiting flexibility, emphasizing respectful relations, and focusing on retaining talented employees. A successful approach to harnessing the power of cross-generational workplaces is encapsulated in the acronym *ACORN*. These potent precepts form the acronym *ACORN*:

Accommodate employee differences.

In order to retain employees, the most generationally friendly companies treat their employees as they would customers—they find out everything they can about them, work to meet their specific needs, and serve them according to their unique preferences. Each generation's icons, language, precepts are acknowledged, and language is used that reflects generations other than those in power.

Create workplace choices.

Generationally friendly companies allow the workplace to shape itself around the work they do, the customers they serve, and the people they employ. Dress policies tend to be casual, bureaucracy is decreased, and the atmosphere is relaxed and informal. This is implemented sensitively, in the least offensive way.

Operate with a sophisticated management style.

Generationally friendly managers have little time for circumlocution. They give those who report to them the big picture, specific goals, and measurements; then they turn their people loose, giving feedback, rewards, and recognition as warranted.

Respect competence and initiative. Generationally friendly companies

assume the best of their people, treating all employees—from the greenest recruit to the most seasoned veteran—as people who have a lot to offer and are motivated to do their best. In the most successful companies this approach becomes a self-fulfilling prophecy.

Nourish retention.

When you consider how difficult it is to find good, conscientious employees in today's job market, you realize why many companies treat employee retention with the same focus as on finding and retaining customers. Generationally friendly companies concern themselves constantly with retention and with making their work environments magnets for excellence. They encourage lateral movement throughout the organization and offer broadened assignments.

CONCLUSION

Generationally savvy organizations value the differences between people and look at differences as strengths. Generationally balanced work groups—balanced not in the arithmetic, but in the human sense—respect and learn from yesterday's experiences; understand today's pressures, dilemmas, and needs; and believe that tomorrow will be different still. The mixed-generation workplace can be thought of as a horror or as a joy of creativity and positive energy. The difference is in how well you embrace and master this important new challenge.

FOR MORE INFORMATION

Books:
Howe, Neil, and William Strauss. *Millennials Rising: The Next Great Generation.* New York: Vintage, 2000.
Martin, Carolyn, and Bruce Tulgan. *Managing Generation Y: Global Citizens Born in the Late Seventies and Early Eighties.* Amherst, MA: HRD Press, 2001.
Tulgan, Bruce. *Winning the Talent Wars: How to Manage and Compete in the High-tech, High-speed, Knowledge-based Economy.* New York: W. W. Norton, 2001.

See also:

"The man who views the world at fifty the same as he did at twenty has wasted thirty years of his life."

Muhammad Ali

Viewpoint: Christopher Locke
The Case for Business Criticism

Introduction

It's easy to see what's unique about Chris Locke. One of the many Web sites dedicated to his work says that he is "Chairman of The Titanic Deck Chair Rearrangement Corporation (NASDAQ: TDCRC)." Somehow, this is exactly what one might expect from this popular author.

What is one to make of someone whose point of view diverges so strongly from standard wisdom? That, Locke would probably suggest, is not the main question. In this Viewpoint, he asks rather: Why hasn't the business world developed its own form of rigorous business criticism? Says Locke about the "logic" of business: it "has become toxic, a dysfunctional complex of neurotic behaviors and primitive defense mechanisms." He urges us to establish a new genre of business writing "that recognizes the profound connections between commerce and culture . . ."

Business and society often seem worlds apart, each operating under a separate set of principles that has little to do with the interests of the other. As business becomes more global, and global networks underscore its world-spanning effects, the results of this radical disintegration are approaching a critical pass. Yet where are the critics to contextualize and make sense of the changing relations between business and the human societies it both depends upon and shapes?

Any mature field of knowledge has developed a critical community that looks at its history, schools of thought, concepts, categories, language, and practices. Substantial bodies of criticism focus on art, literature, music, and media. Why not business criticism? The counter-intuitive answer seems to be: because we don't take business seriously.

A Web search for "business critic[ism]" returns mostly pages denigrating business as a whole. This is not so for other types of criticism. Art critics may deeply dislike particular artists, but few are anti-art. Anthropologists may argue about what "culture" means, but none is anti-culture. Such critics share the basic aims and interests of both practitioners and their audiences. However, most "business critics" are unabashedly anti-business. As a result, they are largely preaching to the choir. Because such criticism is unaligned with the assumptions of business, business tends to ignore it altogether.

The lack of business criticism constitutes a glaring gap in our understanding of today's world. We have data reporting on the financial markets, economic treatises, and business journalism of the who-what-when-where-why variety. However, unlike other forms of criticism, this sort of business writing typically does not take history into account. It tends to focus almost exclusively on current events, ignoring the larger context that shaped the present business

environment. We need to begin thinking critically about business—not to deny its place in the world, but to consider that placement more thoughtfully.

Art, music, and literature date back millennia. While trade and commerce have similarly long histories, the business we know today is barely 150 years old. When it first emerged in the middle of the 19th century, it had no pedigree whatsoever. The period after Reconstruction saw the establishment of the form of legal incorporation currently recognized in the U.S., and the rise of so-called robber barons such as Andrew Carnegie, John D. Rockefeller and Cornelius Vanderbilt. Many of these proto-capitalists were subjected to intense ostracism—not just because they were unschooled, but because they were unlanded. The derogatory label *nouveau riche* implied that they lacked "culture" and "cultivation"—terms rooted in an earthier sense of culture: agriculture.

They were not the powerful titans of industry portrayed in high school civics classes, but embittered, embattled, defensive, and paranoid. Business was not only rejected by society, it made the rejection mutual. Unhappy with the reception it had received, it began to develop a long-term strategy for revenge.

In short, business realized it could buy the status it had been denied. What conferred the most status in the 19th century was science, which, since the European Enlightenment, had overturned ecclesiastical authority and made mankind (women, non-whites, and the "lower classes" excepted) the center of a suddenly knowable universe. The power of science lay in abstraction. Scientific method used hypothesis, observation, and repeatable experiment to establish facts, then employed mathematics and logic to arrive at first principles. Suddenly, the "laws of nature" could be expressed as powerful mathematical abstractions—which also conferred prestige and legitimacy.

"They are not the workers, nor are they the white-collar people in the usual, clerk, sense of the word. These people only work for the organization. The ones I am talking about belong to it as well."

William Whyte

The application of such principles enabled companies to survey rail lines, pump oil, smelt ore, charge interest. Business favored this practical approach over the sort of liberal education fostered by the old agrarian elite. Andrew Carnegie wrote: "While the college student has been learning a little about the barbarous and petty squabbles of a far-distant past, or trying to master languages which are dead, such knowledge as seems adapted for life upon another planet than this as far as business affairs are concerned, the future captain of industry is hotly engaged in the school of experience, obtaining the very knowledge required for his future triumphs . . . College education as it exists is fatal to success in that domain." (Quoted in Laurence R. Veysey, *The Emergence of the American University*, University of Chicago Press, 1965, p. 14.)

Following this sentiment, Carnegie, Cornelius Vanderbilt, Leland Stanford, and others founded their own business schools. Beginning with Wharton in 1898, business schools grew and prospered through the largesse of wealthy industrialists who wanted to pass along their hard-won knowledge to future generations. The current cachet of the MBA degree, once a humble technical certificate, has made their revenge complete.

In 1911, Frederick W. Taylor claimed to have developed scientific principles. His "scientific management"—with its clipboards, stopwatches, graphs, and charts—reduced complex work to just two abstract dimensions: time and motion. This later became known as "industrial engineering." To leverage the power such abstraction provided, it was necessary to ignore "human factors." Any area of study that involved human beings was folded into an overarching category called social science. However, the social sciences were far less prestigious, and increasingly came to be considered "soft." Economics was once a social science, typified by economists like Thorstein Veblen, who wrote about "conspicuous consumption" and railed against the degradation of university education by business administrators, and Max Weber, who warned of the "iron cage" inevitably created by corporate bureaucracy. For these sins of softness, they have since been reclassified as sociologists.

Science introduced a new level of mathematical abstraction, powerful for business because it supported equations, formulae from which it was possible to construct standard procedures. All the intractable, uncountable stuff about workers and customers—the human factors—got factored out. Business became a paint-by-numbers puzzle-solving exercise; operations experts and bean-counters came into the corporate ascendant, and a mountain of stuff got mass produced and mass marketed. This form of applied scientific abstraction worked like a charm.

Ironically, in turning toward such abstraction, business was only following in the footsteps of the society that had previously ostracized it. "High culture"—the cultured and cultivated cadre who delighted in looking down on business—was doing exactly the same thing at the same time. This was called modernism, a reaction against the Enlightenment's goals of rationality and progress filtered through the darker aspects of early industrialism and World War I.

This proscription of social context—often expressed by the slogan "Art for art's sake"—was no less strange than the attitude business adopted toward another kind of abstraction at roughly the same time. "The business of America is business," said president Calvin Coolidge in 1925. In other words: business for business's sake. Through "scientific management," business could ignore those ultimately soft "human factors": people. In the hands of business, abstraction became infinitely more powerful than it did in the world of art. It enabled repeatable procedures, and grounded command and control on powerful principles, equations, formulae, and finally algorithms—the "recipes" underlying computer software.

Like modernist art, business convinced itself it could ignore everything outside the frame—in the case of business: maximize profit. But fixed categories don't work any more. There is no world of art, no world of business—nor of science, politics, religion, music, literature. These "worlds" never existed. They are abstractions. In partial evidence of this, the interdisciplinary field of "economic sociology"—which Max Weber founded many years ago—is enjoying a remarkable resurgence. Trying to understand human beings as strictly economic, non-social entities doesn't work any better than trying to understand them in strictly social, non-economic terms.

While many fixed categories—sociology, economics, anthropology, business—long ago outlived their usefulness as stand-alone disciplines, much of business continues to depend on their rigid segregation. This "logic" of business as usual has become toxic, a dysfunctional complex of neurotic behaviors and primitive defense mechanisms. In a global economy held together by global networks, it is a fatal mistake for business to isolate itself from society.

Understanding the impact and importance of such errors requires a form of business criticism that is largely lacking today. Half a century ago, we had better examples of what such criticism might look like: *The Lonely Crowd* by David Riesman (1950), *White Collar* by C. Wright Mills (1951), *The Organization Man* by William H. Whyte, Jr. (1956). These works appealed to broad audiences, not just to microscopic specialist readerships. They showed how business and society constitute context to each other. Business is embedded within a deeply social and historical context. The societies in which we live are deeply influenced by corporate actions.

Business depends on both workers and markets, both of which are invisible to abstract algorithms and formulaic procedures. Without a business criticism that recognizes the profound connections between commerce and culture, such blindness will continue, and we will never accomplish the increasingly urgent task of re-integrating business and society.

FOR MORE INFORMATION

Book:
Locke, Christopher. *Gonzo Marketing: Winning Through Worst Practices*. New York: Perseus, 2001.

"In every era, society must strike the right balance between the freedom businesses need to compete for a market share and to make profits and the preservation of family and community values."

Hillary Clinton

SQ: Investing in Spiritual Capital
by Danah Zohar

EXECUTIVE SUMMARY

- The central crisis facing capitalism is non-sustainability. Patterns of thought and practice designed for the 18th century will destroy us in the 21st.
- The corporate soul is not about religion. It is about finding and using meaning, deep purpose, and fundamental values in and through our work.
- In the spirited workplace, private corporations will function more as for-profit public service institutions.

INTRODUCTION

We've all heard of the Midas touch. Most of us wish we had it. But the original King Midas's ability to turn everything that he touched into gold was a curse placed on him for his greed. When Midas touched his wife and children, they turned to gold. When Midas touched his food, *it* turned to gold, and the cursed king starved to death.

Today, all of us in business or who are *touched* by the ethic of business, are under a Midas curse, put upon us not by the gods but by the dictates of capitalism and business-as-usual. Present-day assumptions of capitalism are (1) that humans are primarily economic beings who thrive in an environment dominated by money and (2) that humans are selfish beings who will always act rationally to improve their own financial best interests. Greed and a justification of greed are built into our capitalistic system. But if everything we have and are is turned to gold, we too, like Midas, will starve to death—emotionally, spiritually, and ultimately even physically.

To lift the curse of contemporary capitalism, we must envision a broader and deeper view of what it means to be human and what motivates human beings. We are not primarily economic beings; we are fundamentally creatures of *meaning*. Our brains are designed to ask deep, existential questions such as *What is the meaning of life? Why was I born? What am I here for? Why must I die?* We are designed to seek an overarching "story" about ourselves that gives meaning, value, and a sense of purpose to our lives.

A MATTER OF INTELLIGENCE

Intelligence is meant to be the tool with which we cultivate our lives and win control over or cooperation with our environment. But IQ alone won't access meaning, value, and purpose: it measures rational, logical, linear intelligence designed to solve practical or abstract problems. EQ (emotional intelligence) enables us to use feelings to boost and complement our IQ. But SQ (spiritual intelligence) allows us to tap into and use our most fundamental needs. To transcend the crisis created by modern capitalism, business has to use its *whole* brain—IQ, EQ, and especially SQ. Spiritual intelligence is the ultimate intelligence needed to elevate the corporate soul.

Why Today's Capitalism Is Unsustainable

Bolstered by Newtonian science and its accompanying technology and by Darwinian "survival of the fittest," capitalism's own "laws of motion" (competition, profit maximization, capital accumulation) have locked business-as-usual into a ruthless pursuit of competitive advantage in a world whose resources its own practices are constantly diminishing. This is not sustainable. Like a monster eating its own flesh, business is destined to consume first its own resources, then itself.

Why is Business-as-usual Unsustainable?

Six major reasons explain why:

- **Finite resources.** The Western ethic has been that the earth and its resources are there for human use and control. But the earth's resources are finite, while the assumption of business-as-usual is that they are infinite. We arrogantly assume continued and constant growth using our present practices.
- **Environmental damage.** Global warming, floods, holes in the ozone layer, air pollution and its attendant side effects on health, and extreme weather patterns are the result of our reliance on technologies that pollute our own nest.

- **Inequality.** The assumption that human beings are primarily consumers favors the big consumers over the small, those who can pay over those who can't. This deepens inequality between rich and poor nations and between rich and poor groups within nations. Such inequality breeds crime, family breakdown, political instability, and mass, illegal immigration. These things are all bad for business.
- **Leadership crisis.** Making ever more money is not in itself high on the list of what motivates people. The best, most thoughtful, most idealistic people, the best leaders, want to serve something greater than themselves, want their lives to *mean* something—they become doctors, teachers, heads of international aid organizations, go into politics or research. They are seldom found guiding private organizations; there is a critical shortage of great leaders in business today.
- **Short-term thinking.** Concern with maximizing short-term stockholder value deprives business of long-term perspective. It doesn't plan ahead or look at the "big picture." Time comes in quarterly chunks, severely limiting consideration of research needs, long-time viability, and future growth.
- **Human factor.** The mistaken notion that humans are primarily economic creatures increases the stress and exhaustion of the "winners" who serve the existing system. Other values—time with family, time to relax, to nourish inner needs, to enjoy accumulated wealth, to find fulfillment or a sense of fundamental purpose—are all sacrificed to the fast buck. Stressed and exhausted people miss work, suffer disease and premature death. They have reduced creativity and productivity. Stress is bad for business.

Developing Spiritual Capital

If challenged about the prime motive of profit maximization, most business people look dumbfounded, saying, "It has always been that way!" But business as we know it today is only 200 years old. Today's capitalism was conceived by a small handful of 18th century Enlightenment philosophers inspired by Newtonian mechanism. Their idea of capital was solely *material capital*—measured in money.

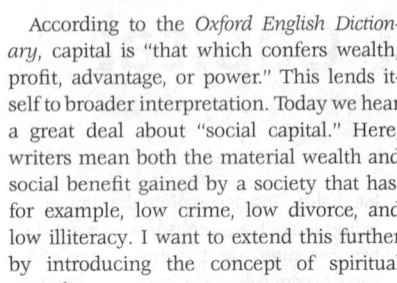
According to the *Oxford English Dictionary*, capital is "that which confers wealth, profit, advantage, or power." This lends itself to broader interpretation. Today we hear a great deal about "social capital." Here, writers mean both the material wealth and social benefit gained by a society that has, for example, low crime, low divorce, and low illiteracy. I want to extend this further by introducing the concept of spiritual capital.

Spiritual capital challenges capitalism's assumption that we are primarily economic creatures and argues instead that human beings are essentially creatures of meaning and purpose. The spiritual qualities of a business or a life are those that show a need for dialogue with meaning, vision, fundamental values, and deep purpose. Spiritual capital takes these as the crucial commodities of exchange.

A company or a person that acts in accordance with meaning, vision, purpose, and fundamental values—*while making a profit*—is invested with spiritual capital. Its primary assumption is that companies can make *more* profit by doing more good. We act on this assumption by using our spiritual intelligence.

Criteria for a High SQ

We are all (if healthy) born with a potential for high SQ. It is a basic, innate capacity of our brain; but like all our innate capacities, it needs nurture and development. To encourage the further development of the spiritual intelligence and build the means for companies to commit more deeply to it, we can identify ten criteria for high SQ. The criteria are:

- self-awareness (awareness that we have a "deep" self);
- spontaneity (emergence, self-organization);
- leading from vision and fundamental values;
- holism (seeing the web, the system, the connections);
- compassion (sense of community, sense of belonging to the flow of life);
- field-independence (standing against the crowd);
- celebration of diversity;
- asking fundamental "Why?" questions;
- reframing (seeing the whole, or big picture);
- using, and thriving on, adversity.

Spiritual Leadership in the Future of Business

Does business today need "spiritual" leaders? Definitely yes! Those who managed old-style capitalist systems, with their sterile assumptions about human nature and narrow reliance on mechanistic philosophies, cannot lead us through the human and global challenges facing business today. We need a new kind of leader for a new kind of "servant capitalism."

Taking for granted that global business has the money and the real power to make a significant difference in today's troubled world, elevating the corporate soul envisages business raising its sights above the "bottom line," becoming more service- and value-oriented (largely eliminating the assumed distinction between private enterprise and public institutions), and having a higher proportion of "servant leaders,"—leaders who serve not just coworkers, employees, products, and customers, but the community, the planet, humanity, the future, and life itself.

The bottom-line criterion for business will always be material solvency and a decent profit. Business *is* society's engine of wealth creation. But wealth is broader than *mere* money. Solvency and profit leave room for maximizing meaning, service, quality of life, health, enjoyment of work, for amassing not merely material but also social and spiritual capital, and thereby contributing hugely to the common well-being and self-organizing creativity of life on earth. That, I believe, is the true purpose of business.

MINI-CASES

Here is a small set of companies whose manufacturing or trading behavior elevates the corporate soul.

- Amul markets the Indian state of Gujarat's 11,000 milk cooperatives. A peasant with only one bucket of milk to sell per day can earn his vital 20 rupees, competing in his own right, and regardless of caste, with larger dairy farmers. An embodiment of Mahatma Gandhi's social and economic principles, Amul sales are $672 million annually.
- Vancity, Vancouver's largest credit union, channels lending funds to customers and causes marginalized by mainstream banks—inner city development, risky small business ventures, environmental

protection projects, disadvantaged women, and investment funds for the developing world—and has a commitment to corporate social responsibility.
- Coca-Cola has put its distribution network in India at the service of the Indian national government to distribute polio vaccine to remote rural areas. It has a similar project in Africa to distribute AIDS medication, providing, at no extra cost, enormous gain in spiritual capital.
- BP/British Petroleum adopted a new motto, "Beyond Petroleum," making it an energy company instead of an oil company. Its heavy investment in developing hydrogen and other alternative energy technologies that both reduce dependence on scarce and damaging hydrocarbon fuels and provide energy for the post-petroleum future, keeps its profits high *by way* of reducing environmental damage.

MAKING IT HAPPEN ▶▶

- Facilitate a corporate conversation that enables habits and a structure for reflection on deep values and fundamental purpose.
- Create corporate infrastructures that respond to a wider environment.
- Learn to negotiate rather than to suppress conflict and difference. Identify and use the "sand in the oyster."
- Cultivate the individual soul—read, reflect, experience.

FOR MORE INFORMATION

Book:
Zohar, Danah, and Ian Marshall. *Spiritual Capital: Wealth We Can Live By*. San Francisco, CA: Berrett-Koehler, 2004.

"I think that business practices would improve immeasurably if they were guided by 'feminine' principles—qualities like love and care and intuition."

Anita Roddick

Viewpoint: Christopher Bartlett
Helping Managers to Assess the Value of Human Capital

Introduction

A long-standing faculty member at Harvard Business School, the Australian Christopher Bartlett is best known for his ground-breaking work with the late Sumantra Ghoshal. Their 20-year writing partnership—a rarity in academe—has produced a steady stream of highly influential articles and books based on in-depth research among practicing managers.

In their most recent work Bartlett and Ghoshal argue that the old corporate model oriented around strategy, structure, and systems is now undergoing a process of rebirth. As human capital usurps financial capital as the key strategic resource, the new model, they say, will be built around purpose, people, and process.

What has had the greatest influence on your thinking on management?

Before I became an academic I used to work for an honest living as a line manager. That evolved into working as a consultant with McKinsey & Company. But the experience as a line manager, with bottom-line responsibility and working with people across the organization, has had the biggest influence on my thinking. That gave me a frame of reference and a great respect for where the learning really occurs in organizations—in the trenches. It has informed my work. My academic career has been based on clinical field-based research: going into companies, talking to practicing managers. I think sometimes there is an arrogance in business books: the authors imply that they know best. I have the opposite view: that we learn most about management from the people who are making it work on a daily basis.

Who has influenced me most? I'd have to say the hundreds of managers I've interviewed. There is so much I've learned from them. People like Jack Welch, Percy Barnevik, and Bill Gates are the Alfred P. Sloans and Pierre Du Ponts of their generation. I use them as examples because they are icons that people know, but there are many others whose names are less well known from whom I have learned.

How will business be different in the 21st century?

In *The Individualized Corporation*, my last book with Sumantra Ghoshal, we wrote about a management revolution that's in its early stages. Behind the turmoil of restructuring and re-engineering, we argued, is the corporate model that is in rebirth. The fundamental shift is that companies are trying to reorganize themselves around what is now the scarce resource—human capital.

Traditionally, there has been an assumption that financial capital is the scarce resource and that companies should be organized around its effective use. That is reflected in the way that companies have been managed in the past. Return on investment, earnings per share—all the measures we've got are about controlling and managing financial capital. Companies used to create sophisticated systems designed to haul the information to the top of the organization so that senior managers could make decisions about the allocation of financial capital.

It's not that financial capital is no longer important; it's that it is no longer *the* constraining resource. The constraining resources, and therefore the strategic resources, are information, knowledge, and expertise. And unlike financial capital, which you can allocate, measure, and control, the knowledge and expertise reside deep down in the organization, in the minds of individuals and in the relationships between people who are closest to the customers, the competitors, the technology, and the regulatory environment. That is what companies are trying to capture, use, embed, and diffuse through the organization—and that's a very different task.

The company of the 21st century will have to learn how to manage human capital rather than financial capital as a strategic resource. This shifts our whole mindset from one that is about appropriating value to one that is about creating value. Creating value is about generating ideas and innovation, and capturing and leveraging the scarce knowledge, expertise, and best practices that reside inside the organization.

The old strategic models were about the external market. Michael Porter's "Five Forces," which dominated strategic thinking for years, were about industry structure and competitive dynamics. That was the model that was embedded in the 1970s and dominated through the 1980s. But by the time we got into

the 1990s, we started to think about a very different model of strategy laid on top of that external strategy, and that was looking at organizational capability—core competencies if you like.

That new strategic framework was about looking internally to examine how to build sustainable competitive advantage through hard-to-imitate organizational capabilities, and not just about the external environment. I think it is now becoming clear that these internal processes depend on the ability to attract, motivate, and retain individuals with the requisite knowledge and expertise.

What new skills will be needed to cope with these changes?

The old model of the hierarchical bureaucracy was all about measuring, allocating, and controlling financial capital. The skills required were very much about having accountability for things that were put under your direct control. As we move toward this very different model of organization—and very different sources of competitive advantage—managers will require different skills from those needed for vertical control processes.

There are three core internal processes that they will have to be able to manage. First, they will need to create a process to elicit entrepreneurial initiative—not just top-down internal directives—although those will remain in terms of the direction and objectives. In the past directives often extinguished the ability for bottom-up initiatives. In the future we will have to create organizations that enable entrepreneurial initiators on the front line, rather than those who follow the traditional "salute and implement" model of management.

The second management skill is being able to link and elicit knowledge and expertise in such a way as to diffuse them, and to develop people and relationships as a source of organizational capability. That's very different from the vertical, financially driven control processes.

The third skill is the ability to self-obsolete. Traditionally, what managers have done is to drive their organizations up the learning curve, to get better and better at what they've always done. In future it will be much more about jumping learning curves and being willing to constantly redefine the business, the product, and processes, and to self-renew.

Those are the three skills that I think will be at the heart of the next generation of management.

Are there new management questions that we should be asking?

There's a fundamental question that faces corporations and management. Today the assumption is that corporations are primarily responsible to their shareholders, and legitimately so, because shareholders have historically been the providers of the financial capital that was the scarce strategic resource. Companies had to compete for it and justify their use of it to the shareholders. But as we shift the primary way of

gaining competitive advantage from appropriating value to creating value through intellectual capital, the constraining resource becomes people rather than financial capital. Then the question becomes what does this mean for the distribution of the value created?

The assumption at the moment is that the value should be distributed to the owners of the scarce capital resource. But, increasingly, that assumption is starting to fray at the edges. Companies are asking: if the people are so important for the creation of value, then don't we need to find ways to distribute more of the value to them? But we're still measuring, evaluating, and rewarding them by the old rules. Increasingly, companies are using stock options and making their people shareholders. And that's legitimate. But I think the real question is: is the balance moving to the point where we need to think about the distribution of the value to them not as a secondary responsibility but as a primary responsibility—a byproduct of maximizing shareholder returns—and an objective of the organization? I think it is.

That's what sole proprietors do; that's what partnerships do; that's what small start-ups do. It's what the large corporations haven't done. They are stumbling toward it with options. But they are a pretty blunt instrument, with lots of risks attached, as the 2000 "tech wreck" demonstrated.

How can companies best promote enterprises that are a) profitable and b) good places to work?

Companies will *only* be profitable if they are good places to work. Talented people will be attracted to places that engage them and give them meaning and development; that, in turn, will allow those companies to be profitable. How they distribute that financial profit is a question we've already talked about.

"Nobody is sure anymore who really runs the company (not even the people who are credited with running it), but the company does run."
Joseph Heller

Tackling Sexual Harassment in the Workplace

by Anne Covey and Michael S. Morris

EXECUTIVE SUMMARY

- Sexual harassment is conduct that results in a "tangible employment action" such as hiring, firing, promotion, or demotion, or is sufficiently frequent or severe to create a hostile work environment.
- A revolution is underway in the United States and other countries where organizations are investing in their employees to provide harassment-free workplaces by providing training. States such as California and Connecticut have enacted legislation requiring sexual harassment training. Other states, such as New Jersey, have mandated sexual harassment training through judicial fiat.
- There are two types of sexual harassment recognized by the United States judicial system: Quid Pro Quo and Hostile Work Environment.
- Quid Pro Quo sexual harassment occurs when submission to sexual conduct is made a term or condition of an individual's employment or when sexual conduct by an individual is factored into any employment decisions affecting the individual.
- Hostile Work Environment harassment occurs when unwelcome sexual conduct has the purpose or effect of unreasonably interfering with an individual's work performance, or creates an offensive working environment.
- A recent study determined that a typical sexual harassment case costs a *Fortune 500* company $6.7 million and costs the United States Federal Government over $327 million.

INTRODUCTION

Sexual harassment knows no cultural, political, religious, gender, or geographical boundary. The United States Supreme Court has observed: "Everyone knows by now that sexual harassment is a common problem in the American workplace."

However, sexual harassment can take on numerous shades of legal interpretation. Historically, a person had to be the target of sexual harassment to bring an action. Today, courts have expanded the zone of harassment to include those persons beyond the target, for example, those who observe or overhear the sexually harassing conduct. If beauty is in the eye of the beholder, then harassment is in the earshot of the listener. Organizations are legally responsible to their employees for making them feel uncomfortable by creating a sexual environment. There is no better incentive for organizations to eradicate sexual harassment.

PRACTICAL AND LEGAL CHANGES IN THE WORKPLACE

Sexual harassment, once thought to be just male against female, now includes any sexual conduct against employees of either gender confronted by an employee of either gender. Similarly, in education, the sexual harassment microscope has switched focus from teacher on student to student on student.

The defined parameters of independent contracting are also under siege. In Danco, Inc. versus Wal-Mart Stores, Inc., 178 F. 3d 8 (1st Cir. 1999), the court held that an independent contractor had the right to bring a racial discrimination claim against an employer based on the employer's non-management employees creating a hostile work environment. In the near future, employers may face legal action not only from their employees, but also from their independent contractors. Thus, an outside accountant performing, say, a year-end audit may sue the client, if he/she is subjected to sexual harassment. Organizations may therefore be responsible to their contractors too, despite not formally employing them.

In a recent legal case, the New Jersey Supreme Court determined that an electronic bulletin board may be so closely related to the work environment that sexual harassment there should be policed as heavily as in the physical workplace. Inventions are perceived as a means of advance. Ironically, the Internet is becoming another potential legal liability for organizations as it provides a site of workplace sexual harassment.

E-mail, another means of improving communication among diverse employment locations, is now fraught with legal implications. For example, an employer may be liable for an e-mail sent to a worker that is opened by another employee who is appalled by the contents of the message or attachments. Lawsuits based on such electronic messages are increasing at an alarming rate. Every employer must now have an electronic mail and Internet policy addressing content which is acceptable, while specifically prohibiting use of its equipment for harassment or other discriminatory purposes.

Technological advances have now become possible legal nightmares for uninformed corporate decision-makers. Each such advancement must now undergo legal scrutiny to determine if liability attaches to the latest development.

ESTABLISHING THE HARASSMENT-FREE WORKPLACE
The Perils of Ignoring Workplace Harassment

Cari M. Dominguez, Commission Chairwoman of the Equal Employment Opportunity Commission, stated: "Sexual harassment in the workplace is not a thing of the past. To the contrary, it continues to be a serious problem for working women. Employers should ensure that all employees are aware of their policies prohibiting discrimination, including sexual harassment. In addition, employers should monitor adherence to those policies to prevent such unlawful conduct from occurring." The seriousness of the problem when left unchecked can be readily seen in the monetary settlements by several *Fortune 500* companies: Coca-Cola—$192.5 million (racial discrimination); Mitsubishi—$34.0 million (the current EEOC record holder for sexual harassment); and Ford Motor Company—$8.0 million (sexual harassment).

A typical sexual harassment case costs a *Fortune 500* company $6.7 million. The overt expenses are the awarding of astro-

"Women's presence in the office work force challenged the Victorian ideal of separate public and private worlds for men and women."

Angel Kwolek-Folland

nomical jury awards and punitive damages. However, the hidden expenses are loss of productive use of employee time and degeneration of employee morale. Some costs can be absorbed while other expenses such as damage to a company's reputation cannot. Management must commit not only to providing a workplace environment free of sexual harassment, but also to taking affirmative steps to ensure its extinction.

Ensuring a Harassment-free Workplace

The goal for employers is to ensure a harassment-free workplace, complete with effective monitoring devices. To do this, corporations must be proactive, not reactive. They must develop appropriate regulatory policies that work to restrict harassment. Policies must be published and clearly state the responsibilities of both the employer and the employee. Just as advertising is used to disseminate information about the product in the marketplace, so too must employers highlight, promote, and distribute their sexual harassment policy. When a problem arises with a defective product redress must be prompt, thorough, and confidential. This same approach is applied to sexual harassment complaints.

The key to addressing any sexual harassment complaint is to provide an effective complaint mechanism. All such redress formats must lead to corrective action based upon fairness to all parties. Corporate ombudsmen are replacing the traditional model of redress. Ombuds are third-party entities who process the complaint from intake through investigation to ultimate resolution. The goal is to provide a mechanism that encourages employee complaints to an entity outside the corporate structure, thereby fostering belief in a system that is beyond corporate manipulation.

The Importance of Education, Corporate Culture, and Monitoring

Companies are implementing proactive management concepts to remedy the lethal virus that is workplace harassment and prejudice. Education lies at the center of reversal and remedial action. Training has become the cornerstone for establishing and maintaining a healthy corporate culture. States such as California and Connecticut have enacted legislation mandating employers to provide two hours of training on sexual harassment. Where legislatures have not enacted training requirements, the Courts have issued opinions requiring sex-

ual harassment training. Some organizations are identifying specific persons within the organization to oversee and monitor the workplace environment while others are hiring outside resources.

Much of humankind's advancement has been through trial and error. However, in times of expensive litigation costs, trials must be avoided and errors pared to a minimum. Organizations seldom realize that the best asset an organization possesses never shows up on any financial statement—the employee. An employee empowered in the workplace, and educated to a sufficient degree, will pay untold dividends in the prevention of potential lawsuits.

MINI-CASES

Coca-Cola is investing approximately $280,000,000 in reforming its corporate culture to provide a harassment-free workplace. Watershed initiatives include: partnership with the United Negro College fund; founding of a "Diversity Leadership Academy"; funding for minority businesses; funding of a "Supplier Mentoring Program"; and financial assistance for minority-oriented nonprofit organizations. Coca-Cola seeks to eradicate racial discrimination and harassment from its corporate image and culture through its monetary commitments.

As a result of a complaint, Mitsubishi implemented a Zero Tolerance Policy and Equality Objectives. Mitsubishi was required to implement a policy to monitor its supervisors' performance based on their handling of harassment issues. This included making it a criterion for qualification as a supervisor that a candidate should make a "commitment to equal employment opportunity." In addition, training was mandated for supervisors on an annual basis, all new employees, and senior management. This resulted in supervisors' advancements within Mitsubishi being based on their sensitivity toward employee multiculturalism as well as their productivity.

Ford Motor Company trains all its employees on job discrimination, estimating an expenditure of $10 million to accomplish this goal. As a result of an incidence of sexual harassment, Ford agreed to increase female supervisory positions by 30% within a three-year period, revise its policies and procedures on harassment, and submit its corrective actions to a three-member panel of independent monitors to oversee and execute the agreement. Through education and independent monitoring Ford anticipates revolutionizing its work environment.

MAKING IT HAPPEN ▶▶

To reform your corporate culture into a dynamic, modern, and prejudice-free environment that can also deal readily and effectively with incidences of harassment:

- develop effective and responsive policies and procedures, and enforce them appropriately;
- educate and train management and nonmanagement employees;
- review the organization and the way in which it is managed to ensure fairness and equality;
- immediately investigate sexual harassment complaints;
- remedy fully and completely any harassing workplace conduct;
- monitor achievement of goals by independent third parties;
- make financial commitments to eradicating traditional stereotyping.

CONCLUSION

What is the future for sexual harassment? Achieve tolerance among employees, regardless of their race, religion, sex, sexual orientation, and national origin, or the high costs of intolerance will continue to be paid. As multiculturalism takes hold on the workplace, the permutations become greater for lawsuits. Ignorance of the law is no excuse, nor is ignorance of common respect and decency. Through the use of proper educational tools and proper monitoring devices organizations can and must provide a working environment with zero tolerance for sexual harassment.

FOR MORE INFORMATION

Books:
Covey, Anne. *The Workplace Law Advisor: from Harassment and Discrimination Policies to Hiring and Firing Guidelines—What Every Manager and Employee Needs to Know.* Cambridge, MA: Perseus, 2000.
Orlov, Darlene, and Michael T. Roumell. *What Every Manager Needs to Know about Sexual Harassment.* New York: AMACOM, 1999.

Web sites:
Equal Employment Opportunity Commission: **www.eeoc.gov**
Overlawyered.com:
http://overlawyered.com

"I was extremely lucky that my first two bosses were people who believed in me as a person and felt that gender was totally irrelevant."
Nicola Horlick

Managing Intellectual Capital
by Leif Edvinsson

EXECUTIVE SUMMARY

- Intellectual capital is already gaining significantly in recognition and acceptance, as a means of valuing and developing the key intangible assets of a business.
- Surveys indicate that two thirds of all U.S. companies have started to look proactively for new ways to collect and report non-financial data, including intellectual capital.
- At least a third of the current investment decisions by U.S. companies are considered partly on the basis of intangibles. Statistics suggest that greater reliance on nonfinancial measures results in more accurate earnings forecasts.

INTRODUCTION

Intellectual capital (IC) is an offspring of the knowledge era. It is still in its formative phase, having first been formally recognized in 1991 when the large Swedish corporation Skandia started implementing a comprehensive set of innovative knowledge practices to account for its intangible assets. The pioneering initiative, championed by Jan Carendi and Bjorn Wolrath, resulted in Leif Edvinsson being appointed as the world's first Director of Intellectual Capital (IC). How will business assets be evaluated over the next decade—will they take account of those assets that are frequently and simultaneously both the most important and the most intangible? It is worth considering:

- why just a handful of the millions of companies started since 1900 achieved solid growth for two decades, and why most of them failed within less than five years
- why managers try to achieve results by imposing financial goals and controls, while knowing next to nothing about their company's products, technologies, and customers
- how managers succeed without having any idea of the return on investments in network relationships, the costs of seeking information, or the state of their IC-index

UNDERSTANDING INTELLECTUAL CAPITAL
How Intellectual Capital Has Developed

The roots of the IC concept run deep. Norris Kronfeld and Arthur Rock wrote about it in an article featured in the November 1958 edition of *The Analyst's Journal*. The econo-mist John Kenneth Galbraith discussed the term "Intellectual Capital" in 1969, and Peter Drucker spoke about "knowledge workers" before that. Though systems for recording IC are now proliferating, the concept is still mysterious to most wage-earners.

The Importance of Non-financial Measures

The importance of non-financial measures is self-evident. W. Edwards Deming, legendary creator of the quality circles concept, has criticized managers in the United States for spending over 97% of their time analyzing figures, and less than 3% on the intangibles that really matter. In other words, they spend 97% of their time trying to figure out 3% of what is going on.

Every third Nordic company now takes these "soft values" into account. The IC network plays its part in this global value evolution. We work with hundreds of consultants and researchers along two mainstream lines: we assist organizations that are installing IC routines and we cultivate and improve our tools by developing IC ratings and using intellectual labs like the growing net of Future Centers.

Powerful institutions, like the U.S. Federation of Accounting Standards Board (FASB) and the Securities and Exchange Commission (SEC) in Washington, are now endorsing supplementary accounts. The influential Brookings Institution explores the issue systematically. In Denmark, a government proposal has made it a matter of legislation. When the international magazine *Business Week* ranks business schools, it features indicators of intellectual capital. Since present financial indicators just refer to the past, they create perilous gaps be-tween the bottom line and long-term goals. They offer a frail groundwork for the strategies of leading-edge companies. Clearly, the key to future productivity is to recognize the interplay of psychological, sociological, and political values in entrepreneurship.

To the extent that customers get involved as co-producers, knowledge that used to be external and distant becomes ever more internal and intimate. Obviously, such changes cannot be handled by traditional accounting practices.

Monetary economies and accounting practices have provided mankind with efficient tools for complex social organization. The present challenge is to make them more multidimensional. Instead of being just black boxes, they could become compasses for charting the course toward tomorrow. The bottom line may be useful when a bank considers lending money to a company. It is not useful for running a company. Cash is only the beginning and the icon of the value-creating process. It is a wonderful enabler, but it can make us forget the reasons for doing something, for creating meaning.

It takes patience, perseverance, and painful re-examinations to make a vision like IC consistently operative. To date, it has been mainly the large and lucrative companies that have taken intangibles into account. Unfortunately, some of them seem to get it all wrong. Instead of using the indicators to advance employee competence or increase surplus and stockholder value, they often exploit them chiefly as seminar exercises for top management.

This is dangerous, since the emerging talent war has triggered a brain drain from large companies to small and medium-sized enterprises. The future business battles will be about ideas and non-traditional thinking, turned into knowledge innovations.

Certainly, figures cannot be faked as easily as words and symbols. Some people fear that before global standards are established, IC audits will open the gates for arbitrary, even fraudulent practices. Probably, yes. But in the absence of IC, vast areas of corporate reality remain in the dark, just visible to insiders. You might as well argue that IC is just what the doctor ordered to restore public confidence in the stock and securities markets.

> "The only irreplaceable capital an organization possesses is the knowledge and ability of its people. The productivity of that capital depends on how effectively people share their competence with those who can use it."
>
> Andrew Carnegie

A corporate rush to cut the brain's lead times is the name of the competitive game now. One way to win is to start learning before new skills are required. To make qualified guesses, and invest in the supposed future. Buying such intellectual options will be a key strategy in the knowledge economy.

The Internet now defies the established control of distribution channels and intellectual property. It undermines anyone whose status depends on privileged access to information. It leverages IC by offering extraordinary opportunities to start new businesses and see prompt returns. It is doing all that, and is likely do it much better and faster tomorrow. Maybe it is time to replace Adam Smith's famous metaphor of the market—the invisible hand—and talk about the invisible brain.

Though stock market booms and busts distract attention from what is really happening, the industrial laws of gravity are being supplanted by rules dictated by knowledge. As the costs of copying and distributing products approach zero, old value chains will break or become obsolete.

There is much to be done before IC standards achieve the sophistication and reliability required to earn general respect. Nevertheless, they are already worth their weight in gold. As financial capital becomes ever more questioned and volatile, sustainable earnings capabilities and new wealth will tip the scales in favor of IC.

MAKING IT HAPPEN ▶▶

There are a variety of approaches to managing intellectual capital, and as a starting point, it may be helpful to consider the following questions:

- **Can you identify your intangible assets and do you understand what they contribute to your organization?** It is worth considering that stockholders and other stakeholders value them, and they affect market perceptions of the business's value. There is therefore a powerful reason for measuring and actively managing your portfolio of intangible assets.
- **How might you measure and monitor the value of your intangible assets, your intellectual capital?** You can't manage what you can't measure, and given the importance of IC it should be continuously valued and developed.
- **How could you manage and develop the value of your intellectual capital?** At a time of commodity production and information overload, intellectual capital is a major source of competitive advantage, a key differentiator, and this can deliver significant benefits in terms of customer retention, acquisition, and innovation.

It is valuable to audit your intellectual capital, understanding its place and significance in the fragmenting value chain, and helping to decide a strategy for managing it. The key to making it happen is to nurture your reputation, people, and other key assets, focusing on how these resources can be fully employed and also developed and grown.

CONCLUSION

How will economic assets be distributed, if the main social distinction is between those who know things and those who do not, rather than between owners of capital and employees? IC may not be a sufficient answer to that question, but it might provide us with instruments to handle it with.

IC is not just any fashionable management fad, like benchmarking, reengineering, or quality circles. It is not something you can choose to apply or not, as conditions and feelings change. It is more generic.

Classic cost management and accounting was not widely practiced in the business world until the fifties. Let's call these approaches the first generation of knowledge management tools. The costs of failing to change them into second generation IC tools may assume massive proportions. To trade knowledge according to the old financial scorecards is like navigating an airplane just using the fuel meter, and ignoring data about altitude, position, etc.; like accounting for the cost of a check while ignoring the loss of the capital it draws from; or as awkward as building with Lego bricks while wearing boxing gloves.

Jack Welch, the former C.E.O. of General Electric, said that we must globalize our intellectual capital, and one way to achieve this is to work toward an international IC system. The key challenge for corporate and political leaders who want to make a difference is not only to develop contexts for future growth. It will take more than communicating intangibles to stakeholders in a repetitive, auditable, and trustworthy way. In the face of coming institutional failures, social entrepreneurship will be a critical concern. The real future space—the IC of nations—will demand significant knowledge innovations.

FOR MORE INFORMATION

Books:
Cusumano, Michael A., and Constantinos C. Markides, eds. *Strategic Thinking for the Next Economy.* San Francisco, CA: Wiley, 2001.
Edvinsson, Leif. *Corporate Longitude.* Englewood Cliffs, NJ: Financial Times Prentice Hall, 2002.
Marr, Bernard. *Perspectives on Intellectual Capital: Multidisciplinary Insights Into Management.* Woburn, MA: Butterworth-Heinemann, 2005.
Stankosky, Michael. *Creating the Discipline of Knowledge Management: The Latest in University Research.* Woburn, MA: Butterworth-Heinemann, 2005.

See also:
Chris Argyris (pp. 1180–1181)
Intellectual Capital (p. 1104)

"Intellectual capital is the sum of everything everybody in a company knows that gives it a competitive edge."

Thomas A. Stewart

Making Cultures Behave
by Robert Heller

EXECUTIVE SUMMARY

- Corporate cultures are the major obstacles to successful change and must themselves change.
- Organizational obstacles can be changed far more easily than human psychology.
- Human resistance can be readily overcome if four preconditions of change are met.
- Cultural change should embody a major shift of emphasis from looking inwards to looking outwards.
- Many cultural change programs are constructed the wrong way around—culture first, behavior second.
- Proactive cultural management bars obstructive behaviors and, instead, supports, reinforces, and rewards constructive ones.
- The leader's personal behavior must be consistent with the demands of cultural change.

OBSTACLES TO CHANGE

Managements wanting to transform their organizations face a fundamental difficulty. Their common problem is that organizational cultures run counter to people's individual inclinations. For example, as customers, everybody wants high standards of quality and service, and knows well what these standards entail. People serving customers are also sensible enough to realize that they cannot expect to receive what they are unwilling to provide themselves. But unless you change the culture, so that it supports rather than obstructs service excellence, the latter will not be achieved.

Conventional wisdom, which portrays culture changes as intrinsically difficult, is therefore mistaken in seeing human resistance and conservatism as the greatest obstacle. Resistance to change is itself cultural, collective as opposed to individual. Above all, it involves the deadening impact of organizational obstacles, such as:

- excessive hierarchy;
- order-and-obey, command-and-control management;
- unresponsiveness to market changes;
- lack of essential skills.

All these can be changed far more easily than human psychology.

BUILDING A NEW CULTURE

Building a new culture is, in this sense, technical. It involves a three-stage process:

1 knowing what to do;
2 knowing how it should be done;
3 actually doing it.

The first two stages are relatively easy: most

managers are fully aware of the need to respond faster and more effectively to the market, for example. Most also know what actions will have this effect. Their subordinates are mostly just as well informed. But time and again the organization gets in the way of informed action.

An overall change philosophy which aims to remove the four cardinal faults listed above is therefore easy enough to state, but very hard to execute. It demands dismantling four pillars of the traditional organization. While people as individuals see the drawbacks of this corporate system, as a collective they will close ranks in its defense and resist its overthrow by acting to:

- flatten the hierarchy;
- empower the workers;
- get close to customers;
- train, train, train.

Each part of this quartet of banners is a precondition of a successful cultural program. If you miss out on any of the four, the program will almost certainly fail. The banner headlines are meaningless unless translated into actions that not only impact the culture in real life, but are seen by all to accomplish transformation. Tests include the following:

1 How close does your new flattened structure come to the ideal minimum?
2 Has all responsibility been delegated to the lowest level at which it can be effectively exercised?
3 Are all activities being designed, monitored, and improved in efficiency in relation to customer needs and satisfaction?

4 Is a high level of continuous training now the clear personal responsibility of everybody in the company and of their leaders?

The four tests sound simple. But their radical nature is extreme. For example, on flattened structures, James Champy (famous for his work on Business Process Reengineering) advises only three levels:

1 "enterprise managers," who are responsible for decisions;
2 and are helped in reaching them by "people/process managers"; the latter plan and implement with the aid of
3 the "self-managers" who execute the decisions.

All three levels are backed by supporting "expertise managers," like accountants and technologists.

Radical the answers to the four questions may be. But in the early 21st century, it is hard to envisage a change program that does not embody this major shift of emphasis from looking inwards to looking outwards. The internal program also requires you to shift totally from what Douglas McGregor described as Theory X (which concentrates on order and discipline to achieve results) to the Theory Y approach, which says work and getting results are as natural as play. Theory Y makes change management much easier further down your organization, because it points people in directions in which they want to go.

This does not remove the need for leadership. The role of the leader under Theory Y is even more important than under Theory X. But you need a different kind of leadership to manage change by getting the best out of a true team. Managing in the new way is much harder than command-and-control management, because self-restraint by the leadership is required to enable "coworkers" to contribute to their full potential.

The object is to change behavior, which in turn changes culture. Many cultural change programs are constructed the other way around—culture first, behavior second. Small wonder that they so often fail. To change the behavior of others, the leader must first change his or her own behavior as a key enabling factor, as illustrated in the table on the next page.

"If a group's survival is threatened because elements of its culture have become maladapted, it is ultimately the function of leadership to recognize and do something about the situation."

Edgar H. Schein

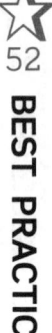

52

BEST PRACTICE

BEFORE	Play an active part in all the unit's work
AFTER	Concentrate on strategy and overall direction
BEFORE	Intervene in day-to-day decisions and operations
AFTER	Leave details of daily operations to those responsible
BEFORE	Make all decisions personally without consultation
AFTER	Endorse and insist on consensus decisions made by the team
BEFORE	Examine and often countermand team proposals
AFTER	Always approve what the team asks for short-term tasks

This formula is the way to achieve the desired and desirable combination of change with order. As it happens, the cultural developments discussed here are being necessitated by the pressures of the early century. Increasingly, companies need people to form and work in changing teams, drawn from all departments and from all the talents, without any consideration of either seniority or status. They want those teams to change from project to project, as do strategies. Companies are even prepared to separate their innovative teams completely from the parent organization (which is probably essential for important and radical innovations).

But reactive change is not enough. Proactive cultural management starts with objectives which embody a vision of the future of the organization. Next, it bars obstructive behaviors and instead supports, reinforces, and rewards constructive ones. These include:

- the creation of a "learning company" whose members stay in the vanguard of knowledge about the business, its environment, and its management.
- abandoning rigid procedures and principles which are defended as a matter of course and habit.
- substituting an emphasis on creating and sharing new ideas and experimentation.
- recognizing the need for successful behavioral change in the formal or informal assessment and reward of managers, and in planning and budgeting.

It should go without saying that the leader's personal behavior must be consistent with these four foundational attitudes. They must also be reflected in the actions which constitute the cultural change program. How decisions are made and implemented, in particular, will determine its success.

MINI-CASE

In a relatively short corporate life, Compaq Computer had developed a very strong "can-do" culture, based on top-end engineering and premium products. When competition from cheaper IBM "clones" undermined this model and losses followed, a new chief executive, Eckhard Pfeiffer, faced the need to change the culture, using an exceptionally high level of communication as a foundation. He acted swiftly to alter behavior; lower costs and prices became the new targets, with "best-of-breed" engineering supplanted by cost-effectiveness, especially for a new low-priced range of PCs. But the major cultural breakthrough came at the meeting called to inform Texas workers that "Project Ruby" would be made in the Far East. The Texans challenged the management decision, requesting and winning the right to bid for the work. Their successful bid was instrumental in establishing and sustaining a new and immensely successful corporate culture.

MAKING IT HAPPEN ▶▶

- Reduce the executive hierarchy to two basic levels, with (1) "enterprise managers" in charge of decisions and helped in reaching them by (2) "people/process managers."
- Make the "people/process managers" responsible for planning and implementation with and by (3) the "self-managers" who execute the decisions.
- Insist that leaders exercise self-restraint so that "coworkers" can contribute to their full potential.
- Counter personal fears and insecurities by a genuinely positive program in a culture built on full and free flows of information.
- Promulgate objectives which embody a clear vision of the future of the organization.
- Bar obstructive behaviors and instead, support, reinforce, and reward constructive ones.

CONCLUSION

The logic of cultural change built on these lines is hard to escape. But powerful, illogical emotions are also active in organizations, including fear. Often, this has no basis in fact. But, whether justified or not, personal fear—say, of job losses or greater insecurity—is both real and serious, and can only be countered by a genuinely positive program. In a culture which is built on full and free flows of information, irrational fear should be far less common, while rational anxieties should be more readily allayed.

There is also the issue of risk. Change always involves risk, ranging from disruption to disastrous error. Staying put sounds and looks much safer. For better or worse, however, organizations no longer have that option. Failure to change involves even greater risk: that of falling fatally behind the competition (and the customer's demands). Fear is the enemy of creativity, innovation, and productive change, without which survival into the second decade of the new century is deeply uncertain. Optimistic realism is the friend of the future, and the foundation of cultural excellence.

FOR MORE INFORMATION

Books:
Kotter, John P., and James L. Heskett. *Corporate Culture and Performance.* New York: Free Press, 1992.
Schein, Edgar H. *The Corporate Culture Survival Guide.* New York: Jossey-Bass, 1999.
Senge, Peter M. *The Fifth Discipline: The Art and Practice of The Learning Organization.* New York: Doubleday, 1992.

See also:
 Boosting Business Success through Diversity (pp. 28–29)
☆ Creating Fun in the Workplace (pp. 37–38)
☆ Managing Today's Angry Workforce (pp. 35–36)
📖 Organizational Culture and Leadership (p. 1141)
💡 Edgar Schein (pp. 1260–1261)

"Changes are not without cost."

Charles Koch

China's Five Surprises
by Edward Tse

EXECUTIVE SUMMARY

In the world's fastest-growing economy, the last 10 years are not the best guide to the next 10 years.

"The test of a first-rate intelligence is the ability to hold two opposed ideas in mind at the same time and still retain the ability to function," F. Scott Fitzgerald once wrote. He might as well have been describing the future of China. There are at least two prevailing views about this country's emerging global identity. Believers assert that by 2030, if not sooner, China will be the world's largest economy. It is already the fastest growing, averaging a 9% GDP increase annually over the past 20 years. Skeptics respond that its growth is bound to falter, soon, amid the environmental, social, and political problems brought on by rapid expansion.

These two perspectives are persuasive and compelling—but simplistic. Like Japan in the 1980s, China has become difficult for outsiders to see clearly in the 2000s. In part, that's because China is not a static business environment. It is rapidly transforming from a planned economy to a market economy. Capable and competitive Chinese companies are emerging, the consumer marketplace is growing, sales and distribution channels are being developed, and the regulatory context is changing, all at accelerating rates. Thus, the lessons of the last 10 years will not necessarily be relevant for the next 10 years. As foreign companies attempt to do business in China, their success depends on their ability to get inside the minds of their Chinese competitors (or partners).

There are at least five "surprises" in China's future: facets of life and global business, stemming from the cultural, economic, and political evolution of this unique country, that will turn out differently from the way most outsiders suspect. These surprises are:

- **"Why not me?"** The intensity of Chinese entrepreneurialism is propelling many companies, even now, beyond a role as producers of low-cost commodities.
- **Fearless experimenters:** China's emphasis on rapid-fire research and development makes it a seedbed for original products and services in the future.
- **China's "brain gain":** The ability to attract and retain executives from around the world has provided a higher level of competence for China's enterprises.
- **Out from *Guanxi*:** Outsiders still view China as a largely patronage-based economy, in which connections and ethnic background determine success, but increasingly (at least in some sectors), high-quality management and transparent governance structures count more.
- **China's overseas ambition:** The country is taking on a role as a catalyst of sustained economic growth in the emerging markets of the developing world.

"WHY NOT ME?"

Many foreign investors base their business plans on the assumption that their Chinese counterparts are simply low-cost competitors. They will be surprised by the ability of some of these companies to compete on product and service differentiation as well.

The most critical factor for Chinese competitiveness is the historical source of the present-day Chinese mindset. Beginning in the mid-1800s (the latter part of the Qing dynasty), there was a period of relative technological and economic stagnation in China, capped after 1949 by more than 40 years of economic standstill under Communism. Only in 1992, when Deng Xiaoping made his now-famous "southern visit" to the city of Shenzhen, was the current wave of economic momentum unleashed.

By now, the momentum has grown so strong, it feels as if holes have been punched into a steam pipe that was building up pressure for a long time. After growing up on a steady diet of two ideas—"Life is good under Communism" and "Acceptable behavior is determined by the authority of the parent, boss, and leader as outlined by Confucius"—Chinese businesspeople are now calling into question the effectiveness of those values.

One question is in the mind of every fledgling entrepreneur in the high-tech start-ups of Beijing's Zhongguancun neighborhood, the fabrication hubs of Wenzhou, the industrial region of Dalian, and dozens of other Chinese business centers: "Why not me?" Success is all around them. The recent Nasdaq I.P.O. of Baidu, a Chinese search engine company led by young entrepreneurs, generated front-page acclaim in the Chinese press. Young Chinese businesspeople are driven by materialistic desires, eager to "catch up" with the rest of the world, and almost giddy with a sense of multiplying opportunity. They have read Internet chronicles of the triumphs of Yahoo, Silicon Graphics, and Google. They see themselves as the creators of the world's future Intels, Apples, and Microsofts, and some of them probably will be.

Because they are in such a hurry to make a place for themselves, and because it is still early in the life cycle of their ambition, Chinese entrepreneurs tend to give the impression that they don't care much about quality. However, that is not universally true. Many of them recognize the trade-offs among cost, quality, and time that exist for any startup, and they have explicitly chosen designs and processes that sacrifice quality for the sake of speed and cost savings.

But this doesn't mean that China will always be a nation of commodity enterprises; indeed, many Chinese businesspeople know the price of a Motorola phone in Chicago or a pair of Nike sneakers in Manhattan. They ask themselves, "If I can make these things, why can't I sell them for higher prices?" Some of them are already laying the groundwork for the evolution of their industries from low-cost producers of shoes, handsets, and components to branded enterprises.

Within China, some industries are already developing a maturity that their Western counterparts took decades to reach. In automobiles, for example, full-service retailers have emerged (formerly, they were state-owned enterprises or joint ventures between the government and foreign manufacturers like Volkswagen). Chinese vehicle manufacturers are establishing global vehicle brands, such as First Auto Works, the world's foremost producers of midsized heavy-duty trucks. The Wanxiang Group (a

---

"Without establishing the appropriate networks in China, it will be virtually impossible to penetrate a market that is significantly different from that in the Western world."

Rosalie L. Tung

privately held manufacturer of auto parts from Hangzhou) is acquiring ownership stakes in American, European, and Japanese companies to build a global supply chain and develop a global brand. Chinese component suppliers are consolidating; some are establishing themselves globally. Most significantly, according to a Booz Allen Hamilton analysis of cost figures, price competition in China (along with price competition from India) has put enough pressure on margins that vehicle manufacturers will probably need to reduce costs by 8% per year within the country to stay profitable, even as annual sales volumes increase by 10% or more per year. Similar consolidation is taking place in appliances, electronics, and textiles. These are the hallmarks of a maturing set of enterprises.

And many Chinese business leaders are eager for that maturation. Yes, they want to get rich quickly, but they don't want an anarchic, free-for-all atmosphere; they want sustained, stable growth. Of course, they won't reach full stability very soon; too many entrepreneurs are trying too many new things. But the best Chinese companies will develop sophisticated supply chains, brands, research labs, and financial infrastructure more quickly than most observers suspect. Even if only a small percentage of the mass of Chinese entrepreneurs cross this threshold, it will have a striking impact on the global business community.

FEARLESS EXPERIMENTERS

Not every Chinese company is good at technological innovation. But those that are can take advantage of several factors unique to China right now. Chinese universities are churning out engineers. Between 1996 and 2001, the country practically doubled the number of engineering and science Ph.D.s it graduated. Many of these individuals are willing to start their careers at relatively low wages, conscious that their fortunes could rise dramatically in the future if they hitch their wagon to the right entrepreneurial star. The anarchic "hungry spirit" of Chinese culture currently provides a supportive intellectual climate for invention, not constrained by the conventional wisdom of existing technological or market paradigms. And the needs of Chinese consumers are often latent and quickly evolving, which makes them open to purchasing the experimental and low-cost products that local innovators produce.

Financial support for research and development is also burgeoning. Cities such as Shanghai, Beijing, and Shenzhen are regular stops on Asian pilgrimages made by foreign venture capitalists. Chinese local governments have built business incubators offering cheap rents and technical infrastructure to small and medium-sized enterprises in Zhongguancun, Shanghai's Zhangjiang High-Tech Park, and similar locations. The national Ministry of Education has promised to quadruple the number of technical universities to which it gives financial support in hopes of raising them to world-class status. And it has introduced incentives to encourage universities, professors, and returning students to commercialize their research. With all this public and private money in play, China recently became the nation with the world's third-largest R&D investment, after Japan and the U.S. And there are many indications that this money is spent more frugally (and thus more productively) in China than it would be in the U.S. or Europe. (See "Money Isn't Everything," by Barry Jaruzelski, Kevin Dehoff, and Rakesh Bordia, for more on the cost-effectiveness of R&D spending.)

Hence, a surprise is coming for those who regard Chinese companies primarily as imitators, prone to borrowing ideas from other businesses or infringing on patents. These habits infuriate Western companies, but many Chinese are less concerned because they view it as a step in their enterprise development.

The most salient quality of the new Chinese innovators is not their imitativeness, but their willingness to take chances and learn from failure, especially compared to their more risk-averse Western counterparts. They require a relatively low burden of proof when deciding to invest in a new product or technology. "Let's try it," they say. Then, if they see it doesn't work, they abandon it immediately and try something else. Speed characterizes every action. They also learn from one another; word travels quickly about practices and results. The ability to replicate successes and rapidly move up the learning curve has already given Chinese companies an advantage against today's Western entrants in China.

Many Chinese entrepreneurs seek to create the kind of technological "killer apps" that can establish them as global competitors. Sooner or later, incremental innovation-and the sheer number and speed of their unfettered experiments-will lead to breakthroughs that appear far more original than anything emerging from China today. Some technological developments will seem to come out of nowhere, not aimed at American or European markets at all. Those surprises, like the Chinese inventions of paper and gunpowder, could have transformative effects everywhere.

CHINA'S "BRAIN GAIN"

A glance at the upper management ranks of China's leading homegrown businesses yields a startling view: not much gray hair. Youthful leadership is the norm because China stopped all formal education from the late 1960s through most of the 1970s (the years of the Cultural Revolution) and thus lost a generation of highly educated managers. To make up for this gap, in a time when managers are needed more than ever before, Chinese enterprises feel an explicit need to recruit and develop responsible business expertise in a hurry.

Often, that expertise is imported. Lured by economic reforms, by the excitement of building a nation, and by the central government's incentives, foreign-trained and expatriate managers are bringing credibility, leadership, and financial and marketing skills to the executive suites of Chinese companies. Microsoft Chairman Bill Gates, during a panel discussion at the Microsoft Research Tech Fair held on April 27, 2005, in Washington, D.C., talked about this phenomenon in the context of his own company's new research centers in India and China. "[Those R&D centers] are giving us an exposure to the quality of [Indian and Chinese] students—most of whom, historically, would have come to the United States. But more are either not coming at all, or coming here and then going back."

This represents the acceleration of a 30-year trend. Today's economic success in China owes a great deal to its diaspora—to the Chinese who live abroad. Even when the economy looked permanently stalled, overseas Chinese sent money home. They were also realists; they saw China as a source of cheap labor, and of relatives, however distant, whom they could trust to handle logistics and money. As opportunities expanded in China, these expatriates began to return in person. Entrepreneurs from Hong Kong, Taiwan, and Macau opened factories back home; students who had won positions in American or European firms returned to China to start their own companies, bringing with them technological and management knowledge, as well as Rolodexes full of contacts—including contacts with one another. In one study of immigrant professionals in Silicon Valley, AnnaLee Saxenian, dean of the School of Information Management and Systems at the University of California, Berkeley, found that 73% of Chinese immigrant profes-

"Five rules for doing business in China: 1. Think small—focus on one region at a time. 2. Skip the manager, talk to the clerk. 3. Study the side streets. 4. Get the goods to market. 5. Above all be flexible."

Anonymous

sionals said they would consider establishing businesses back in their homeland—and a large number had already done so.

Edward Tian is a notable example of the influential role that some globally experienced Chinese executives play, even in government-supported enterprises. After earning a Ph.D. in ecology at Texas Tech University, Mr. Tian started a high-tech venture in Texas. The Chinese national government then recruited him to be the C.E.O. of China Netcom, originally a small startup telecommunications firm based in Beijing. In 2002, China Netcom merged with a major part of the incumbent China Telecom, the then-state-owned primary national telephone utility, to form a new, giant-scale China Netcom, with Mr. Tian as the president. Another example is Fu Chengyu, the president of China National Offshore Oil Corporation (CNOOC), who led that company's 2005 bid to acquire Unocal. Mr. Fu holds a master's degree in petroleum engineering from the University of Southern California. Early in his career at CNOOC, he led the joint management committee, which oversaw joint ventures between CNOOC and global leaders such as BP (then BP Amoco) and Shell.

For its part, the Chinese government realizes that, to turn startups or state-owned enterprises into world beaters, it needs to build strong management capabilities. Executives of state-owned enterprises regularly attend management and leadership training sessions, held either in China or at top academic institutions overseas. They are thus exposed to cutting-edge Western management philosophy and techniques. Meanwhile, the government's "go out" policy encourages corporate executives to acquire foreign assets—not to exploit, but to learn from. The oil industry, in particular, will continue to be on a global watch for companies that will help China build up its strategic reserves in management as well as in oil. China, in short, is no longer an isolated place, and its bridge to the outside world is this growing cadre of people who are comfortable in both places.

OUT FROM "GUANXI"

China's business environment is far more diverse than it seems at first glance. Japanese, Korean, European, Australian, and American multinationals compete against overseas Chinese and local Chinese state-owned and privately owned players. The mix of strategies and tactics has created the world's biggest management laboratory.

However, the most successful participants are not always the Chinese. There are two types of Chinese industries. Wherever the government has a policy of restricted commercial ownership—in industries such as energy, telecommunications, financial services, and banking—the ethnic Chinese still have a home field advantage. For example, although there is a timeline for relaxing restrictions on it, foreign ownership of telecommunications companies is still limited.

In the second category of industries, including consumer products, personal computers, handsets, and pharmaceuticals, there is a much more level playing field. These industries are open to competition from companies all over the world, including Western multinationals, Asian multinationals, overseas Chinese, and local Chinese enterprises. They compete on products, brands, sales and distribution channels, and services, and they often need to bring their best capabilities to China to win. In these open industries, the winners are sometimes the foreign multinationals and sometimes locals. The key to success is effective management and corporate governance practices that can succeed in the marketplace rather than through government favoritism.

Recognizing this, many Chinese companies deliberately use their acquisitions to gain management expertise and good governance structures from abroad. When Lenovo, China's largest computer hardware maker, bought IBM's $1.25 billion personal computer division, one goal was openly acknowledged: gaining IBM's skills, structures, and experience with marketing, research, and probity. The new company has headquarters in New York, research centers under way in North Carolina and Beijing, and a former IBM executive, Steve Ward, as its C.E.O. Some state-owned enterprises are privatizing specifically for the sake of performance improvement. Private owners can bypass the costly shackles that keep enterprises from making money, which include guaranteed employment rules, guaranteed housing, and limited compensation for high-performing individuals. The new managers are also better equipped to make reforms in corporate governance, and to address some of the toughest issues that state-owned enterprises face: human capital, measurement and rewards, and social responsibility.

Together, government liberalization (in some industry sectors) and global integration have changed the rules of the game. Conventional wisdom makes much of the mystique of guanxi—a word that strictly translates as "connections," but usually implies that success is based on relationships, favoritism, and patronage. But in the relatively unfettered sectors today, while knowing the nephew of a Communist Party leader can still open some doors, the trends are toward transparency and merit. What you know is already more important than who you know, and will be more so in the future.

CHINA'S OVERSEAS AMBITION

The CNOOC bid for Unocal focused attention (and resentment) on China's drive for American acquisitions. But the more significant trend is China's increasing investment in other countries, particularly in the developing world: Asia, the Middle East, Latin America, and Africa.

Three obvious objectives underlie Chinese overseas investment: to secure the supply of resources such as oil and raw materials; to enter new markets (often by acquiring local brands and distribution networks); and to gain new skills and technological competence. But the country's overseas investment initiatives also have a surprising impact: China plays a key role, deliberate or not, in accelerating the growth and industrialization of the developing world. This is happening not through grand, World Bank-style investments, but rather through private investments conducted with the same fast pace, experimentation, and pragmatism that have become so common within China. Some of this investment represents a "soft power" of the new China. But much of it is simply the natural consequence of unfettered entrepreneurialism. Instead of mercantile competition with Europe and America, Chinese capitalists are seeking a far bigger prize: becoming the provider of choice for the newly comfortable people of Africa, Asia, and Latin America. Like Henry Ford with his $5-per-day wage, they are gambling that raising the living standard of people in the developing world will pay off enormously.

In Africa, for example, China's economic, commercial, and political relationships with Zimbabwe, Angola, Sudan, South Africa, and Nigeria have grown rapidly in the last few years. The country now imports about a quarter of its oil from Sudan, Nigeria, and Angola. State-owned and privately owned Chinese enterprises have invested in a variety of African businesses in textiles, telecommunications, hotels and tourism, and construction and engineering.

RENAISSANCE NATION

Of course, all five of these trends will be surprises only because they are often un-

---

"The test of a first-rate intelligence is the ability to hold two opposed ideas in mind at the same time and still retain the ability to function."

F. Scott Fitzgerald

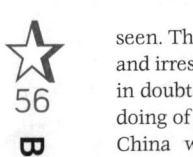

56

BEST PRACTICE

seen. The forces creating them are so strong and irresistible that the outcomes are hardly in doubt. Still, they will probably be the undoing of many businesspeople from outside China who come expecting an isolated, inward-looking country.

The smartest business executives who come to China from different corners of the world have responded with their own willingness to embrace the same qualities that lead to success in China: intense entrepreneurialism, unfettered experimentation, rapid-fire ambition, openness to outside leadership and alliances, and attention to emerging markets. By responding in this way, these outside business executives have also helped to create the new Chinese business culture. In the end, rather than either dominance or weakness, China is facing something altogether different: its first chance of a real renaissance in more than 100 years.

*This article has been adapted with permission from **strategy + business**, the award-winning management quarterly published by Booz Allen Hamilton. **www.strategy-business.com***

FOR MORE INFORMATION

Web site:
Strategy+Business:
www.strategy-business.com

See also:
☆ How to Get Lucky (pp. 101–103)
▱ The Theory of Economic Development (p. 1162)
☆ Toward a Total Global Strategy (pp. 134–136)

Culture Clashes
by Tim Hindle

EXECUTIVE SUMMARY

Companies' different cultures are coming into conflict more and more these days:
- Mergers and acquisitions continue to increase, and they almost inevitably involve one company adopting the culture of another in the process of integration.
- More and more mergers and acquisitions are taking place across national boundaries, as part of the process of globalization. This increases the chances that cultures will clash.
- Companies are involved in a growing number of joint ventures, loose alliances and outsourcing contracts that force them to work in close contact with different cultures.
- Companies themselves are seeking to build a more diverse workforce, recruiting more women and minority groups. This too is increasing the chances of culture clashes within corporations.

To change a company's culture is a very long, slow, and difficult process. But there are some steps that can be taken to reduce clashes if they threaten the well-being of a company.

INTRODUCTION

"When a conqueror acquires states in a province that is different from his own in language, customs, and institutions, great difficulties arise, and excellent fortune and great skill are needed to retain them." Niccòlo Machiavelli, writing in 1527, was not the first to realize that mixing cultures is not easy. Today's cross-border conquerors are more likely to be large corporations than helmeted armies, but they also discover that different cultures, albeit of the companies that they come into contact with, give rise to "great difficulties." It requires careful management to prevent different cultures from clashing, for corporate managers as for Machiavelli's prince.

WHAT IS CULTURE?

Corporate culture has been defined in many ways. Geert Hofstede, a Dutch academic who studied the subject intensively, defines it as "the collective programming of the mind which distinguishes the members of one organization from another." Edgar Schein, a professor at MIT's Sloan School of Management, says it is what a corporation "has learned as a total social unit over the course of its history." Many managers, more prosaically, say it is "the way we do things around here." Others prefer to call it the set of values that the company holds most dear.

Having a strong culture is a mixed blessing. It can drive a company forward with single-minded ambition, but it can also blind a whole company to its own faults. In the 1960s and 1970s, employees at IBM not only looked alike—in their blue suits, dark ties and white shirts—they also thought alike. At first their narrow focus on selling computer mainframes drove IBM to the pinnacle of success. For a while it was by far the most valuable company in the world. But the form of "groupthink" that arises in organizations that become too blinkered by their culture was enough to bring IBM to its knees in the late 1980s. It failed to realize that the personal computer was about to make the mainframe redundant.

Today companies want to develop a strong culture because they believe it is the glue that holds their employees together. As responsibility is more and more devolved down the line, the culture, the way things are done in any one particular organization, is what steers employees in their decision-making. Some 40% of IBM's employees today are "mobile"—that is, they do not report daily to an IBM site. While on the road, these mobile employees have to make decisions all the time, guided mostly by their perception of their company's culture.

Where Cultures Clash:
a) Externally

There are many more opportunities for cultures to clash today than there were a decade or two ago. Not only are there many more mergers and acquisitions, the classic source of culture clashes, but there are also many more ways in which companies interact with each other, and these too give rise to clashes. For example:

- The number of joint ventures in which different companies take stakes in a new enterprise in order to undertake research together, or to develop jointly new products and services, has increased dramatically. This reduces the cost of R&D and the risk of failure for each company in the venture, but it increases the chances of culture clashes slowing down the company's progress
- Many companies have handed over the manufacturing of their products to others. Nike, for example, does not itself make any of its shoes. It relies on other manufacturers to produce them to its specifications. These manufacturers are mostly located in poorer developing countries where national and corporate cultures are very different. Nowadays more and more companies are handing over to others the services that they used to provide—outsourcing them, again often to poorer countries abroad. Call centers in India, for example, provide many of the customer services for Western manufacturers and financial institutions. Conversations between customers and these call-center staff are notorious sources of cultural misunderstanding.

b) Internally

At the same time, as the opportunities for culture clashes between different companies are growing, so too are the chances of clashes occurring within companies. On the one hand companies are seeking to increase diversity in their recruitment policy. More and more women are joining the lower management ranks and, especially in the United States, minority groups are also increasingly represented. This is bringing female and Hispanic influences, for example, to bear on cultures that have traditionally been framed solely by aging white men.

In addition, as companies become more global, they are embracing more cultural diversity within themselves. Multinationals are behaving less and less like imperialists. Gone are the days when they sent expatriates from the country of their headquarters to run anything and everything that they did abroad. That has become too expensive. Young employees are more reluctant to uproot themselves. Those who want to see the world take a Thomas Cook's tour. Hence multinational companies are finding more

---

"When a conqueror acquires states in a province that is different from his own in language, customs, and institutions, great difficulties arise, and excellent fortune and great skill are needed to retain them."

Niccòlo Machiavelli

and more of their managers in the regions in which they operate.

Some of these recruits are rising to the top. A Brazilian, Carlos Ghosn, ran the Japanese car company Honda before he moved to the helm of the French car company Renault. A Welshman, Lindsay Owen-Jones, headed the quintessentially French company L'Oréal, while Jacques Nasser, a former boss of the Ford Motor Company, was raised in Australia. Even Coca-Cola (briefly) had an Australian boss. Many more such instances can be expected to occur in the future.

The opportunities for cultural clashes to occur are increasing, and it is becoming more and more important that companies learn how to defuse such clashes while at the same time reaping the benefits that the interplay of cultures can bring.

c) After mergers and acquisitions

Historically, the time when culture clashes were most likely to occur within corporations was after a merger or an acquisition. The acquiring company would inevitably wish to impose its way on the acquired, which (with almost equal inevitability) would try to resist. In some cases the clashes were so severe as to eradicate any hope that the merger had of creating value.

Cross-border mergers and acquisitions were particularly susceptible to such clashes, especially when the merging companies spoke different languages. At least one Anglo-French merger was completely scuttled by such hostility. When the Walt Disney Company brought its theme-park formula to Europe it took many years of acclimatization before the Disney culture was honed to European tastes.

The likelihood of such clashes occurring depends to some extent on how the company defines its culture. If the definition welcomes diversity then the injection of an alien culture will also to some extent be welcomed. General Electric's legendary leader Jack Welch said that "what sets GE apart is a culture that uses diversity as a limitless source of learning opportunities . . . At the heart of this culture is an understanding that an organization's ability to learn (and translate that learning rapidly into action) is the ultimate business advantage" That perhaps helps explain how Mr. Welch was able to make GE so successful through a long series of mergers and acquisitions. His GE was continually reinventing itself through the purchase and sale of different companies. Only a culture that expressly welcomed such activity could thrive as GE did.

CONCLUSION
Changing Cultures

It is not easy to change a company's culture. And there is no single wonder drug that can be taken for a cure. Any program of change takes time and has to contain a number of different elements:

- Culture is created largely at the top of an organization. If the C.E.O. decides that exclusive parking spaces for senior managers are to be abolished, that sends out a clear signal that the organization intends to be more democratic. If the boss wears an open-neck shirt to meetings, others tend to follow.

- The type of people that a company recruits sends out strong signals about its culture. If it hires masses of over-confident MBAs straight out of business school and puts them on fast-track careers then it is likely to cause offense to other less favored employees. In practice, of course, companies' recruiters tend to recruit people like themselves (because, after all, what's wrong with them?). Hence there is a continual tendency to reinforce the existing culture.

- Some businesses have a distinctive culture that others try to change at their peril. California's Silicon Valley has set the style for the computer industry, for example, where hierarchy is kept to a minimum and the dress code is casual. The movie industry, by contrast, is populated by moguls and stars, with a strict caste system and more formal dress. When AOL, a software company, and Time Warner, a publishing and film-production business, came together in the late 1990s, the contrast between their two distinctive cultures almost brought the merged business to its knees. Some industries' cultures have been changed by new arrivals with a distinctive approach. The traditional national airlines, for example, have become much less stuffy since the appearance of Virgin and the low-cost airlines, and online retailers have thoroughly shaken up industries from newspapers to auction houses.

- Changing the external environment can change a culture. Move a U.S. manufacturing plant south of the border into Mexico and watch the change. But the move need not be so far. Most new U.S. auto-manufacturing plants today are being built in the southern states of the United States where the culture (and particularly the attitude of the labor unions) is very different from that of Detroit in the north, the nation's traditional home of auto-manufacturing.

FOR MORE INFORMATION

Books:
Deal, Terrence, and Allan Kennedy, *Corporate Cultures*. Boston, MA: Perseus Books, 2000.
Kotter, John, *Corporate Culture and Performance*. New York: Free Press, 1992.
Schein, Edgar H., *The Corporate Culture Survival Guide*. San Francisco, CA: Jossey-Bass, 1999.

See also:
☆ China's Five Surprises (pp. 53–56)
🖱 Corporate Culture (pp. 1719–1720)

"The new theory of organisation relates to a corporation as though it has characteristics of its own, such as intelligence, ability to learn, and a culture."
Michael McMaste

Whoever Tells the Best Story Wins: The Subjective Side of Business

by Annette Simmons

INTRODUCTION

Story is a uniquely powerful way to reveal subjective truths and, in the process, improve collaborative decision making and problem solving. Any task or initiative that involves more than one person is, by its very nature, going to involve participants with different perspectives and interpretations of the situation. In an impasse, for example, facts and analysis often spiral deeper into disagreement. A story, however, can collectively raise perspective to a higher level.

A BRIDGE OVER IMPASSE

I adopted my dog Larry from the racetrack. You don't want to know what happens to the ones that don't get adopted. When Larry first came to live with me, he didn't know how to be a pet. He had never seen a bone before. When I gave him one, he chased it nose down across the back yard until he made the intellectual leap that a well-placed paw could keep it still. One thing he has never learned—and shows no sign of learning—is that when he is on a leash and walks on one side of a telephone pole and I walk on the other, we aren't going anywhere. Larry just looks up at me with his puzzled dog face. I could tell him all day to back up. I could explain the benefits of backing up. I could even pull rank, but he's not going to back up until I back up. Once I back up, he follows. Only then can we disentangle ourselves and move on.

C.E.O.'s, senior managers, truck drivers, telemarketers, and nurses alike understand that this story is not really about Larry the dog. With the right delivery and good timing, a story like this can help rescue a group from impasse and prompt introspection, self-awareness, and behavior change. C.E.O.'s back off ultimatums. Truck drivers lean forward. Nurses unfold their arms. A more direct approach—"As long as your egos are attached to being right, you'll never reach agreement"—just doesn't work as well as a story.

Tools for crunching numbers and generating facts have improved business immeasurably. Unfortunately, the tools for generating feelings and shifting perspective are way behind. Business success is a function of both facts and feelings. Feelings are subjective, a function of interpreted experience and individual perspective. Remember the buzzwords "paradigm shift?" We had the right idea . . . but lousy tools. Good ideas—visions, values, and missions—were reduced to laminated cards, hypocritical meetings, and endless word crafting. Objective tools reduce subjective truths into meaninglessness. Some people did it right, but current cynicism in the workplace is often a result of lousy implementation of subjective ideals—promises that never delivered. Many attempts to make things better only made things worse. Why? Perspective and feelings operate according to different principles than objectivity, logic, and facts.

The Larry story tunnels beneath resistance and shifts perspective to a bigger picture. It prompts introspection without risk. Saving face is a very important (and often neglected) aspect of shifting perspective. All of these factors—resistance, perspective, introspection, and saving face—are highly subjective.

RESPECT IS SUBJECTIVE

A company's new IT system had created a roomful of "winners," who didn't need to change a thing, and "losers," who felt like they had to relearn their jobs from scratch. Implementation fell six months behind, because the people who didn't like the system ignored it completely. Tensions rose. At one point, the group got sidetracked about who said hello in the morning. The energy about who said hello was fierce. Suddenly, one very senior manager showed more feeling than intended when she shouted, "No one ever tells ME hello in the morning!" A hush descended and everyone stared, until one of the IT guys gave some lame explanation about her being so busy no one wanted to bother her. No one believed his explanation. Objective truth was not the issue here. The moment called for someone to say something, and his explanation was as good as any. The real impact was the shift in the group's perspective. People began to see that everyone in the room was feeling neglected (even the dragon lady). Saying hello was a metaphor for respect. People did not want to cooperate with anyone who didn't respect them enough to say hello in the morning.

This particular story articulates a subjective truth lost in objective language. Many work groups are dysfunctional simply because individuals do not feel respected. This story validates respect as a legitimate expectation and simultaneously demonstrates that everyone—the dragon lady included—is feeling neglected. No one ever kneels, whispers *mea culpa*, and begs forgiveness from coworkers—but the shift in perspective alters behavior. Subjective shifts often occur without objectively measurable evidence. Genuine respect is subjective: some days it means saying hello, and some days it means discreetly excusing a coworker from this social convention. Forcing people to provide measurable outcomes for subjective shifts will distort, even destroy, your ability to target subjective issues.

OBJECTIVE IS WHAT, SUBJECTIVE IS: HOW AND WHY?

There are few managers who couldn't improve their leadership with better listening skills. Yet objective, skills-based active-listening courses only seem to teach people how to nod, paraphrase, and hold eye contact—in other words, how to fake listening. I was poking fun at these skills-based courses with a group of consultants in Hungary. One of the women in the group raised her hand and said, "Exactly. Listening is just like sex." I had to know. "How so?" She continued in her Zsa Zsa Gabor accent, "When the desire is there, the skills will follow."

That story is a beautiful example of how objective, what-to-do training courses can miss the subjective essence of *how* and *why*. Story has the power to fill in between the lines, to breathe feelings of human *experience* into outcomes, strategic plans, and objective goals so people can see, hear, and feel enough for it to feel real. Once a goal feels real in their imagination, people are much more likely to do what it takes to

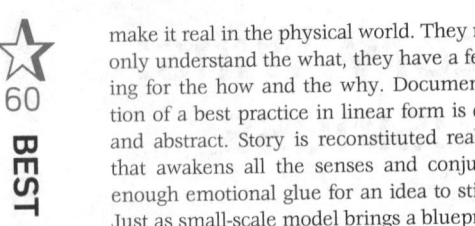
make it real in the physical world. They not only understand the what, they have a feeling for the how and the why. Documentation of a best practice in linear form is dry and abstract. Story is reconstituted reality that awakens all the senses and conjures enough emotional glue for an idea to stick. Just as small-scale model brings a blueprint to life, so does a story bring a list of year-end goals to life.

A story is a narration of events that simulates a visual, sensory, and emotional experience that feels significant for both the listener and the teller. If experience is the best teacher, then story is second-best.

Story takes thinking backward and then forward again through a subjective human experience in a way that prompts new conclusions. Until humans are created with flip-top heads into which you can feed your desired conclusions, the practice of storytelling is the fastest way to prompt people to rethink current practices and reach their own conclusions about how and why they should pursue new initiatives and strategies.

BUSINESS IS OBJECTIVE AND SUBJECTIVE

A so-called merger of equals was not going well; the 30 faces of senior management were a cocktail of anxiety and aggression. They sat around a u-shaped table in a hotel conference room with little faith in this—third—attempt to create a collaborative plan. The C.E.O. had fired the last consulting firm, and when he introduced me as "a young lady from North Carolina," I winced. He clearly saw the dilemma as *us versus them*, and considered me (hired by the chairman of the board) as one of *them*. His sabotage of the process had begun in earnest. Military language like "necessary losses" had placed lines of demarcation and created an impasse. His military training told him that leadership meant clear direction, objective measures, and a firm hand. They hated him. Worse, he didn't care. He was gone in a year.

Many mergers have failed, not because the numbers weren't there, but because the cultures didn't—wouldn't—merge. "Right" answers are useless if people don't accept them. We intuitively know subjective truths have a profound impact on our success. What we *don't* seem to know is what to do about it. One reason is that our business-school training has elevated objective truths over subjective truths for so long that we tend to label time spent making the "right" decision as "real work," and time spent on subjective issues as something less (even ir-

relevant). When faced with the unreliability of subjective truths we tend to default to objective criteria, or exclude the factor completely. By the rules of objective reality, something is either true or it isn't. So a negative result must mean false, right? Wrong! In the subjective world, something can be true one day (I like this merger) and false the next (I hate this merger).

Story has the capacity to access and influence subjective truths. A story can help you stay connected at a human level—even when you are on opposite sides of the facts. If the C.E.O. had been ready to balance clear directions with subjective stories about feeling conflicted when he fired their much-loved sales manager, or how choosing the system architecture was a gut feeling about what ultimately could only be a shot in the dark (perhaps a story about how he, too, had spent years working on something only to discover it was obsolete when a design decision didn't go his way), it might have made a difference. If he had tools to tend to subjective feelings, he might have survived . . . might even have succeeded.

SUBJECTIVE ISSUES NEED SUBJECTIVE TOOLS

Most of us agree that kittens are cute . . . about 50–70%, since that's how true subjective truths tend to run. So imagine this little white kitten, chasing after a ball of string or hiding behind a chair so he can pounce on his brother. This kind of cute can lure the attention of children from 6 to 60. Suppose we want to use our objective analysis to understand the subjective truth *cute*. That would be like cutting the kitten in half to analyze both sides, understand the components, and then try to re-create cute from what we learned. When we try to analyze subjective truths by breaking them down, we destroy that which we seek to understand.

It's a common mistake in business to tackle subjective problems with rational thinking, root-cause analysis, and cost/benefit studies. Objective tools introduce a terrible gold-into-lead alchemy into subjective issues. For a subjective issue like trust, root-cause analysis translates into placing blame and makes the problem worse, not better. Rather than helping, the increased application of objective tools—like better agendas, more objective measures, and clearer outcomes—sabotages our ability to see and tend to subjective problems/opportunities in organizational life. Subjective tools require that you understand how objective and subjective reality are different. Counterintuitively, trust is better achieved with a story

about how you screwed up one day than it is with a résumé of past achievements.

Objective Reality	Subjective Reality
Quality of decision—a decision derived from objective facts, analysis	Quality of acceptance—a decision people like and want to implement
Right/wrong, true/false	It depends—true 50–70% of the time
Root-cause analysis	"Blame game"
Facts	Feelings
Analysis of components = understanding	Kittens
Accuracy (function of rational analysis)	Faith (beyond rational evidence)
Bullet points/charts/statistics	Story and metaphor, laughter, doughnuts
External proof—can prove it is true	Internal experience—you just know

Lightning-fast mental routines that rely too much on objective criteria often cause us to ignore our natural-born wisdom about subjective truths like faith. People don't want more information. They want faith—faith that you know what you're talking about and you mean what you say. Faith is a subjective judgment based on personal experience. Since most people can't experience every aspect of the organization personally, you need to give them a story that inspires faith. Even in a business meeting we are all human beings who have loved and lost, trusted and been betrayed. When you share stories that reveal your humanity, you connect at the level of human experience—the messy, confusing, emotional reality of real people living real lives.

Story is not the only tool to address subjective issues. You probably use many tools you haven't validated as tools. Doughnuts, beer, and pizza, are all very effective subjective tools. Cartoons, jokes, and social time give you access to one of the most powerful tools: laughter, the solvent of negative emotions. As the ambiguity of business and life continues to become more apparent, we will find that our ability to understand subjectivity and to alter subjective feelings will become more important. In other words, whoever tells the best story wins.

FOR MORE INFORMATION

Books:
Simmons, Annette. *The Story Factor: Inspiration, Influence and Persuasion Through the Art of Storytelling.* Cambridge, MA: Perseus, 2002.
Simmons, Annette. *Territorial Games: Understanding and Ending Turf Wars at Work.* New York: AMACOM, 1997.

Viewpoint: Philip Kotler
Making Marketing Manageable

Introduction

A professor at the J. L. Kellogg Graduate School of Management, Northwestern University, Kotler's reputation as one of the world's foremost marketing experts is substantially based on the definitive textbook *Marketing Management: Analysis, Planning, Implementation, and Control.* He has published over 25 other books, covering such topics as the marketing of persons, places, social causes, cultural institutions, professions, higher education, and health care organizations.

Kotler has done more than virtually anyone to cement marketing's reputation as a serious business discipline. "When I am asked to define marketing in the briefest possible way, I say marketing is 'meeting needs profitably.' A lot of us meet needs—but businesses are set up to do it profitably . . . marketing is the homework that you do to hit the mark that satisfies the needs of the target market exactly."

What is the most important thing and who is the most important person to have influenced your thinking on business and management?

Businesses are finally grasping that winning companies choose target segments and customers and make them central to developing their strategy and operations. Customer focus is critical in a world no longer marked by a shortage of goods but by a shortage of customers.

I am deeply influenced by the late Peter Drucker, who observed some decades ago that "marketing . . . is the whole business seen from the point of view of its final result, that is, from the customer's point of view." Drucker insisted that a company has only two functions: innovation and marketing. I have been called the Father of Modern Marketing. But if that's the case, Peter Drucker is The Grandfather of Modern Marketing.

Compared to the last 50 years, how will business be different in the 21st century?

Technology will have the deepest impact on business. We have already witnessed the impact of lean and flexible manufacturing, computers, the Internet, and wireless. Business success in the future will require knowledge workers who are skilled in specific technologies that might confer a competitive advantage to the firm.

What effect has the advent of the new economy and the Internet had on your thinking and on marketing?

I became fascinated with the potentials of e-commerce and e-business for business success. At first I thought that pure click operators such as Amazon and Yahoo would have a tremendous competitive advantage, as they owned few physical assets. My mind changed when I saw how much they had to spend on marketing to build their brand and attract and keep customers.

I believe that the Internet will fundamentally change business and marketing practice. The price transparency of the Internet will put great pressure on prices. The growth of business-to-business Web sites and extranets will reduce the number of salespeople involved in routine sales work. Companies will increasingly differentiate their product and service offerings to different tiers of customers according to estimates of customer lifetime value.

> At first I thought that pure click operators such as Amazon and Yahoo would have a tremendous competitive advantage, as they owned few physical assets. My mind changed when I saw how much they had to spend on marketing to build their brand and attract and keep customers.

In my 12th edition of *Marketing Management,* I show how customers, companies, competitors, and marketplaces are impacted in the information age. The changes will be more profound, with improvements in broadband and m-marketing where cellular phones become our source of e-mail, the Internet, chatting, and even a payment system replacing credit cards.

Are these changes reflected in your current research?

I am doing research on the ability of companies to manage their future through information. I have formulated a concept called "holistic marketing," where companies are able to find, create, and deliver value by linking demand management, resource planning, and partner alliances. Central to holistic marketing is the use of the Internet, the company Intranet, and

"The demands for new knowledge and skills will be constant, no longer a value added element, but the essential factor in determining organizational survival." Meg Wheatley

various Extranets to drive the company to profitable growth.

My research is taking two directions. One is to develop real-time marketing information "dashboards" where managers can continuously monitor sales, prices, and costs in different geographical and segment markets. This will help managers spot growth opportunities as well as problems emerging in the field.

The other research direction is to create "planning dashboards," to be used by brand and product managers to develop stronger marketing plans. They can click to find out how to do any procedure, such as test a marketing concept, develop a sales promotion, test the effectiveness of an ad, or run a test market. The planning dashboard would open a marketing encyclopedia of best marketing practices on the computer screen.

What new skills will be needed to cope with these changes? How can managers best develop these required skills?

Marketers will need skills beyond the four traditional ones of marketing research, sales management, advertising, and sales promotion. Needed are skills in:
- database marketing and data mining;
- customer relationship management (CRM);
- partner relationship management (PRM);
- telemarketing and call center management;
- integrated marketing communications (IMC);
- public relations marketing (including event and sponsorship marketing);
- profitability analysis applied to customers, market segments, channels, geographical area, and order sizes;
- customization of offerings, services, and messages;
- experiential marketing (creating a total experience).

Are there new management questions we should be asking? If so, what are they?

Here are a few questions, not necessarily new ones, that management should think through better:
- How much should companies invest in social responsibility programs? How can the payoff be measured?
- Would companies be more profitable if they spent less on advertising and promotion and more on innovation and improving their products?
- How can companies move more of their customers to using less costly channels?
- How can companies speed up the digitalization of their production, marketing, and distribution and service systems?

What will happen to the concept of the career in the future? What career advice would you offer tomorrow's managers?

Fewer managers will spend their whole career within one company. Managers will be more attached to their knowledge specialty than to their current company. There will be active markets for each knowledge specialty, and managers will be on the lookout for advancement opportunities. The key then is for tomorrow's managers to study the various knowledge specialties and choose the one that will yield the most long-run market value and personal satisfaction. Companies will need to develop better inducement packages and conditions for retaining their most valued knowledge workers.

How can companies best promote enterprises that are a) profitable and b) good places for people to work?

Profitability and a good place to work are more compatible than profitability and a bad place to work. In the old days zero sum thinking prevailed, in that a manufacturer thought that he would make the most money by paying the least to his suppliers, employees, and distributors. But this led to poorer inputs and outputs and lots of resource turnover. Smart companies today practice positive sum thinking and make their suppliers, employees, and distributors into partners who are motivated to deliver superior value. "Win-win-win" thinking will prevail over "I win, you lose" thinking.

> Fewer managers will spend their whole career within one company. Managers will be more attached to their knowledge specialty than to their current company. There will be active markets for each knowledge specialty, and managers will be on the lookout for advancement opportunities.

FOR MORE INFORMATION

Book:
Kotler, Philip. *Marketing Management: Analysis, Planning, Implementation, and Control.* 12th ed. New York: Prentice Hall, 2005.

See also:
☆ Avoiding the Mistakes of the Past: Lessons from the Startup World (pp. 164–165)
☆ Infusing a Company with Cutting-edge Strategy (pp. 110–111)
☆ Marketing: The Importance of Being First (pp. 69–70)
☆ The Business Web (pp. 182–183)
☆ The New Frontiers in Old-economy Industries (pp. 130–131)
☆ Virtual Collaboration (pp. 203–204)

> "A business's flexibility in adapting to change and market dynamics will mark the winners and losers in this fast-changing Internet Age."
>
> Michael Dell

Managing 1:1 Marketing
by Drayton Bird

EXECUTIVE SUMMARY

- Direct marketing is a special marketing discipline, not just a medium.
- The objective is to increase customer value.
- It focuses on individuals, not masses.
- Direct marketing builds brands; it must be integrated with other disciplines.
- Its principles apply to e-commerce.
- Building and enhancing the database is key.
- Testing and accurate measurement reduce risk and increase return on investment.

INTRODUCTION

In late 2000 *Advertising Age* revealed that one in 11 of all new jobs being created in the United States was in direct marketing. Virtually all organizations in advanced economies—and many in less developed ones—use it.

Today's direct marketing is really a fusion of traditional mail-order selling and direct mail. Yet it's more than a sales process or medium: it's a marketing discipline with special characteristics. It uses all media. It's personal, focusing on individuals, not masses. Every message is coded, so you can gauge return on investment exactly. And it looks to long-term customer value rather than the value of individual sales. It is growing in importance because e-commerce, also conducted directly with individuals, is accelerated direct marketing. Brands like Amazon, Dell, and eBay are all direct marketers.

Increasingly, as businesses face greater competition and products and services can be copied fast, direct marketing makes great sense, because it focuses more on the customer than on what is actually being sold. It is not always a cheaper way of marketing. But when properly managed, it directs your efforts more accurately, giving you more for your marketing money. It does this in three stages.

Three Steps to Success

1 First, you identify those customers, including organizations and the individuals within them, that your offering is most likely to appeal to. You store relevant data about them on a database, which you continually enrich with added information. Thus you can offer what they are most likely to want when they are most likely to want it with growing confidence, eliminating junk messages.

2 Second, by communicating with customers in an increasingly relevant way as you learn more, you strengthen and lengthen your relationship with them. This is important, since retaining customers is far more profitable than attracting them. This fact has helped fuel today's greater focus on the customer.

3 Third, you reduce risk by rigorous measurement, testing on small numbers before spending big money, and comparing different approaches. Seemingly trivial changes can make big differences. Adding—or removing—an element in a mailing may increase return on investment by as much as 90%. Running one TV commercial rather than another, or changing the time it runs, may transform loss into profit. Changing just one word in a headline can have the same effect. Altering the timing and heading to an e-mail can increase response as much as 260%.

WHERE AND HOW IT WORKS

Direct marketing is ideal for anything complex calling for detailed explanation to be studied at leisure. It also works where potential customers feel pressured by salespeople. Insurance and investment are good examples—financial services are the biggest direct marketers.

It's a good technique to use when distance is involved. It's also good for products people are shy about buying in person—weight-loss and other health-related products, or exotic lingerie.

Since the database means you can vary messages to suit individuals, direct marketing works well if you sell to businesses where decisionmakers have varying motives—value for the money matters to financial managers, while executives may care more about efficiency.

Direct marketing complements personal selling. You can use various means—direct-response advertising, faxes, banner ads on a Web site, the phone, e-mail, or direct mail—to acquire leads, keep in touch with customers between calls, or deal with lower-value customers who don't merit expensive personal visits.

Direct messages are advertising and can build brands fast—Dell is a good example of this. Direct marketing must be integrated with other disciplines. The creative work need not slavishly follow your advertising, but should have the same tone and positioning.

Long copy generally works best, because you're seeking an immediate response, by using and repeating every relevant argument. That's why effective mailings often incorporate many pieces. The letter, being personal, is normally the critical element in a mailing. Response rates vary greatly depending on the proposition: getting someone to buy something costly is far harder than offering them a free chance to win a lottery.

THE DATABASE IS CENTRAL

At the heart of direct marketing lies the database, holding details of each individual or business. You use it to communicate with people by mail, e-mail, fax, or phone. Recording all relevant information is vital. Success turns on how persuasive, relevant, and timely your messages are, and this is determined largely by how well you capture, store, and use the right details.

You develop your database in the same way you develop your knowledge of other people. It starts as just names and addresses; each added scrap of information makes it more valuable. You overlay it with data already in the public domain or gathered by private enterprise.

Valuable data can derive from the likely characteristics of different addresses. Some areas are more prosperous than others; generally speaking someone living in a house is wealthier than an apartment-dweller; and a

property-owner is more prosperous than a tenant.

You enrich your database with relevant facts, such as who buys what, how often, and when; how long they remain loyal customers; what else they have bought—thus building a complete picture of their nature and value. This information also helps you to predict behavior; similar individuals behave similarly.

CUSTOMER LIFETIME VALUE

Strategically, the most interesting aspect of direct marketing may be its emphasis on customer value. Whereas companies have traditionally measured performance by current sales or profits, direct marketers have always thought in terms of how profitable a customer is over time.

One reason is because the best early direct marketers were book clubs and catalog companies. They lured customers with incentives, which obviously made the first transaction unprofitable—their strategy was to lose money initially in order to make money in the long run. Incentives to buy, or inquire, or simply give information, are important in direct marketing. Thus, an automobile manufacturer may want to know what car a prospect has, what car he or she is thinking of buying next and when, and how much money the next car is likely to cost.

The early direct marketers measured loyalty (how long a customer stayed with them—usually between five and seven years) and what they could afford to pay to acquire a customer. In the same way banks, credit-card companies, and insurance companies look to long-term relationships, and automobile manufacturers look to keep customers buying their make repeatedly.

Customer value varies enormously. A small percentage of customers generally buys most of any product or service, and by identifying those individuals you can concentrate your efforts and reap disproportionate rewards. You can lower or eliminate expenditure on less valuable customers and increase it on more valuable ones.

A MORE PRECISE TOOL

Direct marketing is more precise than mass advertising. Mass advertisers concentrate on the most effective media (those more likely to be read or viewed by customers),

but this is inevitably imprecise since they're always looking at masses or groups.

Direct marketing aims to isolate individuals and place them in groups. The categories will vary according to your purpose. Thus, on a database you could isolate all the individuals over 50 with an annual income above $75,000 within 15 miles of a designated city and offer them the opportunity to buy a car direct from their nearest showroom. Thus you eliminate waste.

Marketers often spend millions on huge campaigns without knowing in advance what will happen. Intelligent speculation or a hunch can be backed by research predicting likely customer behavior. Very often, though, research fails. Customers can tell you what they think or believe, but not what they will do when asked to part with money, especially with a new product.

The direct marketer tests on a small scale first. Test results tell you pretty exactly what will happen—before you spend. You can discover which creative treatments and media work best and when. Nobody knows in advance which message will work best— and there's often great discrepancy between the media that research ranks as best and those that generate most response. Equally, customers recruited in different media or with different messages usually tend to have differing lifetime value.

There's ample room for confusion because different organizations use different names for very similar activities. Some names describe the process, for example, as database marketing, dialog marketing, and one-to-one marketing. Others, such as loyalty marketing and relationship marketing (often labeled customer relationship management), relate to the objective. All rely on direct-marketing methods, but some neglect testing and measurement.

MAKING IT HAPPEN ▶▶

- Identify the customers and organizations (and individuals within) most likely to want your offering, and store the data on a continually enriched database.
- Use direct marketing to strengthen and lengthen your relationship with profitably retained customers.
- Reduce marketing risk by rigorous testing before spending big money.
- Use direct response advertising, phone, fax, e-mail, or direct mail to

complement personal selling by getting leads, keeping in touch, and serving lower-value customers.
- Generally, treat the personal letter as the critical element in a mailing.
- Put your emphasis on customer value— how profitable a customer is over time—not on current sales or profits. Customer value is the cornerstone of long-term success.

CONCLUSION

Direct (or one-to-one) marketing involves market segmentation down to the smallest element: the individual. Individuals with similar characteristics are placed in groups, which are analyzed carefully, leading to a more detailed understanding of their needs and wants. They are then communicated with based on the knowledge gained. This makes messages more relevant, leading to greater profitability and long-term competitive advantage. Good direct marketers test and measure constantly to optimize ROI. Without direct marketing, many organizations will not maximize their potential. Even packaged good marketers wedded to mass advertising like Procter and Gamble, Nestlé, and Mars realize that direct marketing has a role to play. No intelligent marketing strategy should ignore it; some depend completely on it. As markets become increasingly global, diverse, and complex, direct marketing has become increasingly valuable in creating effective marketing strategies.

FOR MORE INFORMATION

Books:
Bird, Drayton. *Commonsense Direct Marketing.* 4th ed. Dover, NH: Kogan Page, 2000.
Stone, Bob, and Ron Jacob. *Successful Direct Marketing Methods.* 7th ed. New York: McGraw-Hill Professional, 2001. (8th edition due 2007)

See also:
☆ Avoiding the Mistakes of the Past: Lessons from the Startup World (pp. 164–165)
☆ Delivering and Delighting—A New Spirit at Work (pp. 91–93)
☆ The Business Web (pp. 182–183)

"The new system takes us a giant step beyond mass production towards increasing customization, beyond mass marketing and distribution towards niches and micromarketing."

Alvin Toffler

Relating to the Public
by Robert S. Leaf

EXECUTIVE SUMMARY

- Discovering the real perceptions of your key audiences, whether they be the government, the financial community, customers, or your own employees, is a valuable guide. If the perception is favorable, the challenge is to enhance it. If it is unfavorable, try to change it. If there is no perception, work to create it.
- Write down a clearly defined program that is realistic and achievable with adequate budgets and has measurable, specific objectives. Assign responsibilities clearly, internally and externally; review the program at least quarterly; change it if and when necessary.
- Prepare for crisis management before crisis strikes—don't wait for it to happen. And if it does, move quickly to defuse it.
- Get a thorough grounding in the different media—don't just leave it to the experts.
- Rehearse before any major media interview, and remember that the rehearsal should be for message training, not media training. What are the key messages you want to get across in the specific interview?
- Relating to the public is a self-fulfilling prophecy: focus on it and things are likely to improve; ignore it and they will almost certainly worsen.

INTRODUCTION

Business has changed radically in recent decades and is becoming much more sophisticated. The public relations of today has become perception management. Communicators have increasingly come to the conclusion that perception is what really counts. You might run a great company, but if analysts don't feel that way the stock does not go up. And your product or service might in reality provide great benefits, but if the customer doesn't perceive it that way, it remains on the shelves.

THE INCREASING VALUE OF PR
PR is Part of the Total Communications Mix

While there are certainly examples where the effective use of public relations by itself was used to solve a problem, public relations, to be most effective, should be part of the total communications mix. Martin Sorrell, C.E.O. of WPP, the world's largest communications organization, says: "Today's sophisticated client demands that every possible form of communications works together to achieve their key objectives." And he is right, because times have changed. Previously ad departments or ad agencies saw PR departments or PR agencies as threats to their egos. Now they appreciate that working together is essential.

The Growing Need for Communications with Key Employees

The one public that has grown the most in terms of the need for effective communications are the key employees. The reason is simple. COMPANY LOYALTY IS DEAD. No company will promise lifetime employment. Anyone can be fired and, since they know that, the good employees are nearly always considering other options. And as demographics have changed with a smaller proportion of people in their 40s and 50s it is vital to keep those people. So why do employees stay with a company, if it is not out of loyalty? They stay because they believe in the vision of the company and how they are involved in making that vision happen. So management, whether through the written or spoken word, must continually communicate that vision to the key people and underline their role in making it happen.

Media Relations

Like them or hate them, the media are here to stay. Once the chairman of a British company, upset by what was a somewhat unfair piece of reportage in the *Financial Times*, said to me, "I am not going to deal with the *FT* anymore." I explained to him, tactfully of course, that he didn't have that option. One of the things he was being paid to do

was deal with the *Financial Times*. In dealing with the media there are some key rules. Know the key media and reporters covering your company and decide who within the company should interface with them. Ordinarily this will be a number of people. It is important to understand that not everyone in the organization is equally skilled at media relations, so pick those best qualified. This can vary according to type of medium.

Often it is not the chief executive you want for a particular interview, but the C.E.O.'s overall image is very important. A Burson-Marsteller C.E.O. Reputation study showed that 94% of analysts asked said they would recommend a company's stock because of the C.E.O.'s reputation. And the C.E.O.'s reputation can count for up to half of the corporate reputation. European managements had always been more reticent than their U.S. counterparts to have programs that include active relations with media but this has changed dramatically.

CHECKLIST: PREPARING A PUBLIC RELATIONS PROGRAM

For your public relations campaign to be successful, you must first understand the real perception of your key audiences. There are only three major categories of perceptions, but these can vary in degrees. If the perception is favorable, you want to enhance it. If it is unfavorable, you want to change it. If there is no perception, such as with a new product, you want to create it. This underlines the need for intelligent research before any significant program is undertaken.

One key to a successful PR program is: don't wait for a crisis! Too often, public relations is relied upon to help solve a problem. A crisis has occurred. The stock price has plummeted. Employees are leaving in droves. New competitors have arisen. But just as you should have checkups when you're healthy, so you should have an active public relations program when times are good. This could make sure times don't become bad. The key is to decide which of your publics need the greatest emphasis and how to reach them effectively. To be successful, your PR activities should take the following issues into consideration.

"Some are born great, some achieve greatness, and some hire public relations officers."

Daniel J. Boorstin

Balancing Internal and External Resources

Years ago the chief internal public relations officers viewed PR consulting firms as a threat to their position. They feared they would have access to top management that they themselves often didn't have. Times have changed. As the understanding of PR has grown dramatically, so has the internal function. Internal PR departments are smaller but more effective. The top PR executives are much more qualified and better paid and work closely with the management. They are usually an integral part of the planning process. What had been the norm was for in-house people to want to move to agencies as a step forward; now the reverse is true. And it is they who now not only want outside help but also have the major say in agency selection. A key rule is: don't hire an agency for what can be done in-house.

When selecting an agency, it is important that you do your homework and use contacts in the PR industry. In the United Kingdom, the Public Relations Consultancy Association and in the United States the Public Relations Society of America maintain lists you can review. You should also provide a carefully prepared brief. The emphasis should not be on what you want to know about them but on what you feel are your needs and how they would plan to fulfill them. If time allows, it is advisable to call them in for a discussion before they make a presentation. The list of prospects should then be narrowed down to three.

You should allow time for questions, because it is usually then that you get a better understanding of who really understands your business and its needs. Make sure to find out exactly who will be on your account and the proportion of their time that will be spent working for you. That is far more important than who is making the presentation because you might never see them again. Also ask the hourly rates of those on the account because, in addition to expertise, a PR company is also selling time.

The Internet

The Internet can be used to reach every public of importance, including your own staff. New uses are appearing all the time such as launching a new product or ad campaign, supporting takeovers or IPOs, reporting to Wall Street or the City, fighting elections, and fashion shows. Increasingly journalists are using it for updates on companies and background for articles they are preparing. An international study by *Fortune Magazine* and Burson-Marsteller showed 91% of C.E.O.s log on, spending an average of six hours a week online. So the question is not whether to use the Internet but how do it most effectively. Here are some guidelines.

- The use of a company Web site calls for a public relations strategy all its own. Who do you really want to reach and how?
- There is a need for continuous updating, which can be costly.
- It is ideal for monitoring competition.
- It is a major vehicle for advocacy groups, some of whom might be hostile to some aspect of your company, so you must be prepared not only to monitor but to react to claims.
- As the number of Web sites grows, giving the user more and more choice, the need for professionalism will continue to increase if your site is to be successful.

Crisis Management

Burson-Marsteller's Crisis Management Division lists the characteristic causes of a crisis as: surprise, insufficient information, escalating flow of events, loss of control, intense scrutiny from outside, siege mentality, panic, and short-term focus. There are key principles in handling any crisis:

- centralize/control information flow coming in or going out;
- isolate a crisis team from daily business concerns;
- define the real problem short term and long term;
- recognize the value of a short-term sacrifice;
- resist the combative instinct;
- be willing to admit error and be 100% sure of any facts you issue;
- assume a "worst case" planning position;
- depend on no one individual fully;
- understand each of the media's role and purpose;
- remember all constituencies, internal and external (for example, unions, employees, family, local community residents and leaders, local authorities, and so on);
- and remember in the Chinese language there are two characters which together make up the word "crisis." The first means "problem" and the other means "opportunity."

CONCLUSION

The future of public relations/perception management remains very exciting. Companies, communities, governments, government bodies, NGOs, and individuals are appreciating a greater need for handling it more professionally and are expanding their efforts. The key now is for those using perception management to make sure they do everything possible to use it as effectively as possible.

FOR MORE INFORMATION

Books:
Cunningham, Michael J. *Partners.com: How to Profit from the new DNA of Business*. Cambridge, MA: Perseus Publishing, 2002.
Stack, Jack, and Bo Burlingham. *A Stake in the Outcome*. New York: Currency/Doubleday, 2002.

Web site:
www.bls.gov/oco/ocos086.htm: created by the Bureau of Labor Statistics within the U.S. Department of Labor, this is a general outline of a public relations professional's job.

"PR cannot overcome things that shouldn't have been done."   Harold Burson

How to Plan Marketing
by Malcolm McDonald

EXECUTIVE SUMMARY

- Organizations operate in a complex and fast-changing environment and managers need some way of interacting with their environments.
- Marketing planning is merely a managerial process for coping with environmental uncertainty.
- Strategic marketing planning needs to precede tactical marketing planning.
- The output of the process (the plan) spells out how an organization expects to achieve its objectives.
- Academic researchers agree that there is a link between marketing planning and long-term organizational success.
- The planning process is universal, although the formality of its implementation may vary between organizations.
- Organizational culture is the biggest barrier to implementing effective marketing planning.

INTRODUCTION

All organizations operate in a complex environment in which hundreds of external and internal factors interact to affect their ability to achieve their objectives. Managers need some understanding or view about how all these variables interact. They must try to be rational in making decisions, no matter how important intuition, feel, and experience are as contributory factors. Most managers accept that some kind of procedure for planning the organization's marketing helps to sharpen this rationality, making the complexity of business operations manageable and adding a dimension of realism to the organization's future plans.

This procedure is known as marketing planning.

THE ESSENCE OF MARKETING PLANNING

The contribution of marketing planning to the success of an organization, whatever its area of activity, lies in its commitment to detailed analysis of future opportunities to meet customer needs. It offers a wholly professional approach to selling to well-defined market segments those products or services that deliver the desired benefits. Such commitment and activities shouldn't be mistaken for budgets and forecasts, which have always been a commercial necessity. Marketing planning is a more sophisticated approach concerned with identifying what sales are going to be made in the longer term and to whom, in order to give revenue budgets and sales forecasts a real chance of being achieved.

MARKETING PLANNING IS A MANAGERIAL PROCESS

In essence marketing planning is a managerial process, the output of which is a marketing plan. As such it is a logical sequence, a series of activities leading to the setting of marketing objectives and the formulation of plans for achieving them. Conceptually, the process is very simple and is achieved by means of a planning system. The system is little more than a structured way of identifying a range of options for the organization, of making them explicit in writing, of formulating marketing objectives consistent with the company's overall objectives, and of scheduling and costing the specific activities most likely to bring about the achievement of the objectives. The systemization of this process lies at the heart of the theory of marketing planning.

TYPES OF MARKETING PLAN

There are two principal kinds of marketing plan:

1 **The strategic marketing plan**
A strategic marketing plan is a plan for three or more years. It is a written document outlining how managers perceive their own position in the market relative to their competitors (with competitive advantage accurately defined), what objectives they want to achieve, how they intend to achieve them (strategies), what resources are required (budget), and what results are expected. Three years is the most common strategic planning period. Five years is the longest, but is becoming less common because of the speed of technological and environmental change. Strategic marketing-driven plans are not to be confused with scenario planning or the kind of very long-range plans formulated by a number of Japanese companies (which often have planning horizons of between 50 and 200 years!).

2 **The tactical marketing plan**
A tactical marketing plan is the detailed scheduling and costing of the actions necessary for achieving the first year of the strategic marketing plan. The tactical plan is thus for one year.

THE CORRECT SEQUENCE OF MARKETING PLANS

Research into the marketing planning practices of organizations shows that successful companies complete the strategic plan before the tactical plan. Unsuccessful organizations often don't bother with a strategic marketing plan at all, relying largely on sales forecasts and the associated budgets. The problem with this approach is that many managers sell the products and services they find easiest to sell, concentrating on those customers who offer the least resistance. By developing short-term tactical marketing plans first and then extrapolating them, managers merely succeed in extrapolating their own shortcomings. This is just about acceptable when markets are growing rapidly or are regulated in such a way that little effort is required to grow sales. Today, however, few such markets exist. Preoccupation with preparing a detailed short-term marketing plan first is typical of companies that confuse sales forecasting and budgeting with strategic marketing planning.

THE CONTENTS OF A STRATEGIC MARKETING PLAN

The contents of a strategic marketing plan are the:
- **mission statement,** setting out the raison d'être of the organization and

---

covering its role, business definition, distinctive competence, and future indications;

- **financial summary,** summarizing the financial implications over the full planning period;
- **market overview,** providing a brief but important picture of the market, including market structure, market trends, key market segments, and (sometimes) gap analysis;
- **SWOT analysis,** analyzing the strengths and weaknesses of the organization compared with competitors against key customer success factors, and considering opportunities and threats, usually for each key product or segment;
- **issues to be addressed,** derived from the SWOT analysis and usually specific to each product or segment;
- **portfolio summary,** offering a pictorial summary of the SWOT analysis that makes it easy to see at a glance the relative importance of each of the four elements; it is often a two-dimensional matrix in which the horizontal axis measures the organization's comparative strengths and the vertical axis measures its relative attractiveness;
- **assumptions,** listing the underlying assumptions critical to the planned marketing objectives and strategies;
- **marketing objectives,** usually consisting of quantitative statements (in terms of profit, volume, value, and market share) of what the organization wishes to achieve; they are usually given by product, by segment, and overall throughout the organization;
- **marketing strategies,** stating how the objectives are to be achieved; they often involve the four Ps of marketing: product, price, place, and promotion;
- **resource requirements and budget,** showing the full planning-period budget, giving in detail the revenues and associated costs for each year.

THE CONTENTS OF A TACTICAL MARKETING PLAN

The contents of a tactical marketing plan are very similar, except that they often omit the mission statement, the market overview, and SWOT analysis, and the plan goes into much more detailed quantification by product and segment of marketing objectives and associated strategies. An additional feature is more detailed scheduling and costing of the tactics necessary to achieve the first year's planned goals.

STRATEGIC MARKETING PLANNING: A REVIEW OF CURRENT THINKING

From an extensive review of the current research into strategic marketing planning, five principal conclusions emerge:

- There is a clear consensus about the desirable outputs of the strategic marketing planning process.
- Strategic marketing planning and the marketing orientation that accompanies it are clearly associated with improved organizational performance across most market situations.
- In unsuccessful companies the prescriptive process of strategic marketing planning is poorly adhered to in practice and is frequently used as a pretext for inadequate budgeting and tactical programs.
- The primary barrier to strategic marketing planning lies in the organizational culture of the company and the values and artifacts that stem from that culture.
- Although the degree of formality of the process can range from a highly creative, entrepreneurial approach to the more structured, rational process described here, there is universal consensus among strategic thinkers and planners that some kind of managerial planning process has to be used to manage the link between an organization and its environment.

Hence, in large, multinational, multiproduct, multicultural organizations it is usual to find a structured process for marketing planning; in smaller organizations the management of the process tends to be much less formalized and structured. The process and the steps, however, are the same in all consistently successful organizations.

MINI-CASE

Everyone has an opinion about why the once-mighty IBM lost billions of dollars in the 1990s. Indeed, the two books about IBM published at the time both predicted the end of the company. The arrival of Lou Gerstner as chairman and C.E.O., however, heralded a reversal in its fortunes. Like all good managers, he stopped the financial bleeding by introducing operational efficiencies. He came from a consumer-goods background, and it wasn't long before he insisted that his business unit managers introduce the kind of classical market-based planning procedures described here, including the major basis for successful marketing planning—market segmentation. IBM is, due to Lou Gerstner, once again a major global player in the communications market.

MAKING IT HAPPEN ▶▶

- Identify what sales will be made in the longer term and to whom, in order to turn revenue budgets and sales forecasts into reality.
- Analyze your strengths and weaknesses compared with competitors' against key customer success factors, and similarly review opportunities and threats.
- Complete the strategic marketing plan before the tactical plan. Write your strategic marketing plan to cover three or more years, defining competitive advantage, objectives, strategies, and budgets.
- Build marketing strategies around the four Ps of marketing: product, price, place, promotion.
- Write a tactical marketing plan, detailing schedules and costing for the specific actions necessary to achieve the first year of the strategic plan.

CONCLUSION

Successful marketing planning is the cornerstone of developing strong, durable, and robust organizations. Overcoming an organizational culture that acts as a barrier to effective marketing planning is essential if performance is to be optimized and long-term goals are to be achieved. Given the complexity of the rapidly changing business environment and the high number of variables that influence business performance, it is necessary for managers to have an effective means of making the situation manageable. Thorough and detailed analysis of how to meet future customer needs provides a sophisticated and reliable method for building long-term success. Marketing planning enables the organization's vision to become a reality.

FOR MORE INFORMATION

Books:
McDonald, Malcolm. *Marketing Plans: How to Prepare Them, How to Use Them.* 5th ed. Woburn, MA: Butterworth-Heinemann, 2002.
Piercy, Nigel F. *Market-led Strategic Change.* 3rd ed. Woburn, MA: Butterworth-Heinemann, 2002.

See also:
King Camp Gillette (pp. 1302–1303)

"Marketing strategy is a series of integrated actions leading to a sustainable competitive advantage."

John Sculley

Marketing: The Importance of Being First by Al Ries and Laura Ries

EXECUTIVE SUMMARY

- Most managers believe the basic issue in marketing is convincing a prospective customer that you have a better product or service. Not true.
- The basic issue in marketing is creating a new category in which you can be first.

INTRODUCTION
Who's Really Best?

Who has the best rent-a-car service? The best cola? The best ketchup? If you are thinking Hertz, Coca-Cola, and Heinz, you agree with most customers who make these three companies the leaders in their fields. In fact, there is a strong axiom, or belief, in the minds of consumers that "the best product or service wins in the marketplace." After all, this is so logical and so obvious, who could disagree?

We could.

There's a paradox in marketing. While everyone believes that the better product will win in the marketplace, the worst possible strategy for any company is to try to produce a "better product." Why? Because the leader in your field already has the perception of producing the better product. If you try to claim that your product is better, the prospect thinks, "No, it can't be better, otherwise *they* would be the leader." Yet what do most companies try to do? They try to: (a) produce a better product, and (b) communicate that difference to customers and prospects. It's easy to do (a) but it's almost impossible to do (b). Is Royal Crown Cola better tasting than Coca-Cola? Royal Crown thinks so, and their research shows that prospects prefer the taste of Royal Crown to Coca-Cola Classic by 57% to 43%. That's a pretty big difference. Yet Royal Crown Cola has only 2% of the market. What they need to do, you might be thinking, is to communicate that difference. Well, they've tried, and it doesn't work; prospects too easily conclude: "If Royal Crown was better tasting, *they* would be the leader, not Coke. There must be something wrong with the research."

WHAT'S IMPORTANT: WHO'S FIRST?

It's our experience that 90+% of all market-ing programs are based on communicating the essence of the better product or service. Unless you are already the leader, these programs are bound to fail because the prospect assumes that the leader must have the better product or service. But how did the leader achieve its leadership? Not by introducing a better product or service; invariably the leader in the category got to be the leader by being the first brand in the category. Companies such as Coca-Cola, CNN, Dell, Hoover, Pizza Hut, Rolex, and Xerox are all globally recognized as leaders in their respective fields. Some consultants have called this leadership phenomenon, "the first mover advantage," but that is not so. It's an advantage, but it's not the reason that most leader brands were first in their categories. It's the "first minder" advantage. That is, the brand that gets into the mind first is the winner, not the brand that is the first in the category. For examples: Duryea was the first automobile on the road, but never got into the mind. Ford was the first automobile in the mind. MITS Altair 8800 was the first personal computer, but never got into the mind. Apple was the first personal computer to get into the mind. Du Mont made the first television set. Hurley, the first washing machine. But these and many other brands failed to get into the minds of their prospects. You don't win in the marketplace. You win in the mind.

EXAMPLES ABOUND

If you weren't first in your category and you can't win by being better, what can you do?

The answer is obvious: start a new category you can be first in. Marketing is more a battle of categories than it is a battle of products. Winning companies think category first and product second. They try to categorize what they do, not in terms of being better, but in terms of being different.

When Procter & Gamble introduced Tide many years ago, they could have called the product a "new, improved soap." Tide was a soap then, and Tide is a soap today, in the sense that soap is a "cleansing agent." But Tide was made from synthetic materials rather than the fats and lye found in traditional cleaning products like Ivory, Oxydol, and Rinso. Tide could have been called a synthetic soap, but that would have nailed the brand to the soap category. So Procter & Gamble called Tide the "first detergent," a totally new category and even today Tide is the leading brand of detergent.

When Charles Schwab established Charles Schwab & Co., he could have focused on providing better service to stock buyers. But he didn't. Instead he decided to launch the first discount stock brokerage company, and today Charles Schwab & Co. is one of the leading stock brokerage companies in the country.

When Michael Dell founded Dell Computer Corporation, he could have sold his "better" products through conventional computer stores, but he didn't. Instead he launched the first brand of personal computer sold direct by phone. Today Dell is the world's largest seller of personal computers and still doesn't sell any computers through conventional computer stores.

HOW TO START?

Before you launch (or relaunch) a new product or service, ask yourself the following questions:

1 What is the name of the category? Not a name that you might like, but a name the industry gives the category.

2 What is the brand name of the leader in the category? Not necessarily the sales leader, but the brand that customers perceive to be the leader.

3 If there is no dominant brand, or at least not a dominant brand in the mind of most prospects, jump right in with your product or service and try to quickly establish your leadership. Cut prices, cut deals, hire sales people, launch massive publicity campaigns, do everything you can to seize the leadership position before someone else does.

4 Promote your brand as the leading brand. "It's so easy to use," says AOL, "no wonder it's number one." Leave no

---

"Implementers aren't considered bozos anymore."   John Sculley

piece of paper or Web site or TV advertisement or radio commercial without mentioning your leadership. Leadership is the most important aspect of any marketing program. Why? Prospects assume the better product or service will win in the marketplace. Therefore, if you are the leader, you must have the better product.

5 If there is a dominant brand, then move on and establish a new category you can be first in. But make sure you have a new name to match the new category. You can get into serious trouble if you try to use an existing name.

6 You can't dictate the category name. Only the industry and the media can do that. Therefore you have to launch your new brand with publicity and get the media to establish the category name for you.

MAKING IT HAPPEN ▶▶

There's almost always a way to establish a new category. Unfortunately, most companies refuse to even consider the possibility of a new category because "there's no market." Of course, there's no market. If there were, it wouldn't be a new category. This presumed "logic" is the most difficult thing to overcome. You have to have faith that you can succeed in getting acceptance for a new category. What was the market for personal computers sold by phone before Michael Dell launched Dell Computer Corporation? Zero. What was the market for sports drinks before Gatorade was launched? Zero. What was the market for discount brokerage companies before Charles Schwab was launched? Zero.

Furthermore, a new category doesn't necessarily represent a big, technological advance. Soapsoft, the first liquid soap, was a big commercial success. How

difficult is it to take a tub of soap and liquefy it? How difficult is it to take regular beer and add water? Miller Lite, the first light beer, was a big success, but ultimately paid a big penalty for its success. Instead of creating a new brand to match the new category, they used a line extension name which just about killed their regular beer brand (Miller High Life) and caused them to lose their light beer leadership to the competition. A new category needs a new name.

The IBM PC was the first 16-bit, serious, office personal computer, but the line extension name caused IBM to ultimately lose their personal computer leadership to first Compaq and then Dell Computer Corporation. VisiCalc was the first spreadsheet for personal computers when all personal computers used 8-bit operating systems. Lotus 1–2–3 was the first spreadsheet for 16-bit, IBM-type personal computers, but lost its leadership to Excel, which was the first spreadsheet to use Microsoft Windows.

Listerine was the first mouthwash, but it was a bad-tasting mouthwash, hence the slogan, "the taste you hate, twice a day." Except for Procter & Gamble, all competitors in the category thought that mouthwash had to taste bad. P&G introduced Scope, the first good-tasting mouthwash, which is neck and neck (or mouth and mouth) with Listerine for leadership in the category.

CONCLUSION

Marketing is not a battle of products. Marketing is a battle of perceptions. And to win the battle of perceptions you have to become the leader in a category. Prospects assume the leader must be better because "everybody knows the better product or service will win in the marketplace." How do you become the leader? You launch a new category you can be first in. It doesn't

have to be a big technological advance. Sometimes the simple ideas are the easiest to get into the mind. And where do you win the battle? You win the battle inside the mind of the prospect.

FOR MORE INFORMATION

You don't learn to become a marketing expert by reading books, ours or anyone else's. You learn to become a marketing expert by studying case histories and asking yourself: "Why did this company win and why did that company lose?" The best place to find these case histories is in the pages of general business publications. Every serious marketing person should subscribe to some, if not all, of the following (and be sure to check their respective Web sites):

- *New York Times*
- *The Economist*
- *Wall Street Journal*
- *USA Today*
- *Investor's Business Daily*
- *Fortune*
- *Forbes*
- *BusinessWeek*

Viewpoint: Seth Godin
The New Marketing

Introduction
Author of seven global bestsellers, Seth Godin has changed the way people think about marketing, change, and work. He is a renowned speaker, and was recently chosen as one of 21 Speakers for the Next Century by *Successful Meetings*. Seth was founder and C.E.O. of Yoyodyne, the industry's leading interactive direct marketing company, which Yahoo! acquired in late 1998. He served as VP Direct Marketing for Yahoo! until 2000. He holds an MBA from Stanford, and was called the "Ultimate Entrepreneur for the Information Age" by *BusinessWeek*. He is founder and president of squidoo.com.

- Advertising used to be the tactic marketers employed in order to spread their ideas.
- Advertising is no longer effective because of clutter, lack of trust, increased parity among competitors, and the fragmentation of the media.
- Now, the best marketing tactic is to create remarkable products that consumers choose to tell stories about.
- Remarkable is in the eye of the beholder, not the marketer.
- The best stories are authentic, and match the worldview of the consumer.
- Faced with diminishing power, the best marketers succeed by delivering anticipated, personal and relevant messages and treating consumers with respect.

For fifty years, advertising (and the pre-packaged, one-way stories that make good advertising) drove our economy. Then media exploded. We went from three channels to 500, from no web pages to a billion. At the same time, the number of choices mushroomed. There are more than 100 brands of nationally-advertised bottled water. There are dozens of car companies, selling thousands of combinations. Starbucks offers 19,000 different ways to order a beverage, and Oreo cookies come in more than nineteen flavors. In the face of all this choice and clutter, consumers realized that they have quite a bit of power. So advertising stopped working.

One insight is that marketing with permission works better than spam. In other words, delivering anticipated, personal and relevant ads to the people who want to get them is always more effective than yelling loudly at strangers. *Permission Marketing* addresses this issue.

Once an idea is in the hands of people who care about its success, it may be lucky enough to benefit from digitally-augmented word of mouth. I call this an "ideavirus." Modern ideas spread online and off, and this is faster and more effective than the old-fashioned centralized way of selling. *Unleashing the Ideavirus* is the most successful eBook of all time and you can buy the paperback for about $10. Feel free to look for the eBook online. It's free.

It's remarkable products that get remarked on. That seems obvious, but it flies in the face of the way most goods and services and business items are created and marketed. Boring is invisible. *Purple Cow* is all about this.

The thing that makes something remarkable isn't usually directly related to the original purpose of the product or service. It's the *Free Prize Inside*; it's the extra stuff, the stylish bonus, the design, the remarkable service, or the pricing that makes people talk about it and spread the word.

The controversial *All Marketers are Liars* isn't about lying at all. It's about telling stories that people want to believe. It's about the fact that people want bottled water, not tap, iPod Nanos, not Rios, and politicians who talk straight, regardless of the consequences ... But most of all, it's about authenticity. The challenge facing marketers who take advantage of the power and leverage of the new marketing is that it's easy to be fake. And fake marketing works for a while ... then crashes and burns. Authentic marketing, however, can stand up to the multi-dimensional scrutiny that the Internet brings. Authentic marketing amplifies your story and makes it more likely to spread once people become familiar with your product or service. When consumers smell a fake—a politician who lifted a speech or a fashion company that uses slave labor, for example—they flee.

Most of all, I believe that it's possible to enjoy your job, to do the right thing, to be transparent, to give more than you get and to be successful, all at the same time. In fact, that's sort of the definition of success, isn't it?

"No one writes a sales formation law."

What is The New Marketing and Why is it Important?

The New Marketing starts from the assumption that the TV-Industrial Complex is dead. This virtuous cycle enabled marketers—those that sell to consumers and to businesses as well—profit by interrupting prospects with advertising and marketing messages that they did not necessarily choose to get. Spending $1 on interruptions could make you $2, which allows you to hire more salespeople, run more ads, and make more stuff. This system has gone from positive to negative—the interruptions cost too much and are not effective enough.

Can Any Company Embrace the New Marketing?

No. Not companies that have ordinary products. Not organizations that need to fake or defraud in order to earn attention. And if your products are perceived as commodities by the producer and the user, forget it. If it's boring, why bother?

In the face of this requirement, many companies that embraced a more commodity-oriented approach are struggling.

What is the Best Way to Embrace the New Marketing?

First, build a permission asset. A group of people that want to hear from you about your new remarkable offerings. These are the "sneezers," the people who will spread the word. As you gain a larger and larger base of sneezers, you can shift from finding customers for your products and start finding products for your customers—a happier, more profitable, better place to be.

Second, invent stories that your customers will want to tell themselves and their friends. These stories must be authentic—they must stand up to scrutiny—and they must engage the worldview of the audience you seek to reach.

What are the Implications for Organizations Large and Small?

I would suggest four main considerations. First, it is crucial to hire right. Imagine that you are no longer running a factory. Instead, you run a fashion atelier. So someone who shows up on time isn't as important as someone who challenges the status quo and creates the remarkable. Second, stop being selfish. You're no longer in charge. Get over it. Third, make it easy for your story to spread. If a satisfied consumer can't easily spread the word, the word won't get spread. And fourth, think small. If you leverage the many tools you can be smaller. Smaller organizations can change faster and can have more employees empowered to act like the boss. Which means treating the outside world with more respect.

To conclude. . .you don't have to like what has happened to the engine of your organization's growth. But you cannot profitably deny that it *is* happening. And the sooner you embrace the new realities, the faster you can profit from them.

FOR MORE INFORMATION

Books:
Godin, Seth. *All Marketers are Liars: The Power of Telling Authentic Stories in a Low-trust World.* New York: Portfolio, 2005.
Godin, Seth. *Free Prize Inside: The Next Big Marketing Idea.* New York: Portfolio, 2004.
Godin, Seth. *Permission Marketing: Turning Strangers Into Friends and Friends Into Customers.* New York: Simon & Schuster, 1999.
Godin, Seth. *Purple Cow: Transform Your Business By Being Remarkable.* New York: Portfolio, 2003.
Godin, Seth. *Unleashing the Ideavirus: How to Turn Your Ideas into Marketing Epidemics.* New York: Hyperion, 2002.

Website:
Visit Seth's blog at: **www.sethgodin.com**

See also:
- Direct Marketing (pp. 1730–1731)
- Marketing Management (pp. 1827–1832)

"Don't sell the steak, sell the sizzle." Elmer Wheeler

The Genius of Business
by Peter Fisk

EXECUTIVE SUMMARY

You need to be a genius to succeed in today's business world. Markets are incredibly complex; customers demand ever more; competition is intense; imitation is instant; margins are under pressure; and the expectations of stockholders are unrelenting. Marketing, in the forms of strategy and innovation, brands and connections, has never been more important.

INTRODUCTION

From the vision of Apple to the insight of Zara, the passion of Nike and irreverence of Jones Soda, the entrepreneurship of Jet Blue, and thrill of Agent Provocateur, today's leading brands think and act differently.

The genius of business today lies in the ability to connect outside and inside, markets and business, customers and shareholders, creativity and analysis, promises and reality, today and tomorrow. Customer insight and creativity are important, but must be combined with the analytical and commercial rigor that drives strategy, innovation and profitable growth. Today's business leaders, like Einstein and Picasso before them, see things differently, and by applying intelligence in more imaginative ways can do extraordinary things.

BLINKERED BUSINESS

Too many businesses are obsessed with their inside—how to do what they do better, reduce their cost base, automate their processes—rather than their outside. This important but limiting preoccupation—plus the blinkers of functional silos and industry conventions—means that businesses often miss what matters most.

Yet in a fast-changing world incrementalism can lead to irrelevance. Ask Kodak, the market leader in photographic film for many decades, who within a handful of years found that its market had disappeared, swallowed up by alien digital worlds led by the likes of Sony and HP. They had not even been on Kodak's radar screen until it was too late.

The best opportunities and biggest challenges are outside, not inside. Market change and its implications are often discontinuous, requiring more significant responses. They should be the starting point of any business strategy rather than a consequence. Market thinking should be at the heart of decision-making, and market thinkers at the heart of business.

Apple watched the market for music fragment and blur into chaos, as new technologies disrupted the industry model, consumers rebelled, new entrants challenged the economics, and old formats quickly became obsolete. Apple brought together an innovative solution in the form of hardware and software—iPod™ and iTunes™—to offer a way through this turmoil, redefining the industry dynamics with a compelling and profitable solution.

CUSTOMER POWER

While borders have blurred and markets merged, within markets there is a shift from economies of surplus demand to those of surplus supply. Customers now call the shots. Most of us, in the Western world, typically have everything that we need, so our wants are more emotional and unarticulated. Customers are more different too, more informed and less tolerant. Gone is the day when we fit into a macro segment, or adhere to average market research statistics. Customer expectations are sky high, and their loyalty is rare.

The noise in markets is deafening, as we are bombarded with at least 1,500 commercial stimuli every day, many causing resentment through the deluge of direct mail and intrusive telemarketing. A young person is likely to have seen around 150,000 different ads by his or her 18th birthday. Indeed kids have learned to cope with more. Research shows that they can typically deal with 5.2 activities at once, whereas adults can only survive with 1.6, and men even less. Therefore we need to address each differently.

We surf through 300 channels of television, dispersing our lifestyle patterns, and destroying the predictability that advertisers used to rely on. And neuroscientists have found that consumers typically choose which brand to buy within 2.6 seconds, not long to turn marketing promises into profits. And the competitive response has been to work harder rather than smarter, with more products, more options, more campaigns. Product lifecycles have typically fallen by 70% in the last decade, while 75% of customers now turn to personal recommendation, rather than anything a brand might tell them.

MARKET LEADERS

So what should business leaders do? How can they throw off their blinkers and address the emerging market landscapes and the new balance of power?

The essence of genius is to apply intelligence in a more imaginative way. Imagination is required to see the uncharted waters, the bigger picture, to drive more sustainable innovation and differentiation. However, business also requires more intelligence than ever in order to make sense of complexity and provide focus amidst unlimited opportunity.

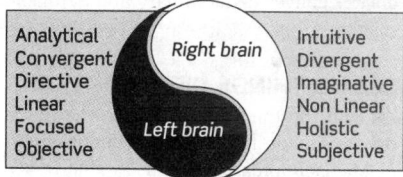

Analysis and creativity are richly complementary, despite our often seeking to label people in one way or another. Human beings have evolved with brains that can do both, and as result perform better. Analysis helps focus creativity on areas of most impact; creativity helps to break through data to find insight and direction. It requires the left and right brain to work harder together, and to embrace the yin-yang opportunities.

Today's geniuses must combine the scientific mind of Albert Einstein, with the creative touch of Pablo Picasso, one a phenomenal mathematician who could only reach new places through hypothesis, the other a radically unconventional artist but with a technical training. So how would such figures approach the challenges of today's markets?

Perhaps king of movies and technology, Steve Jobs, designer-cum-philosopher Philippe Starck, or accountant turned

---

"A mediocre idea that generates enthusiasm will go further than a great idea that inspires no one."

Mary Kay Ash

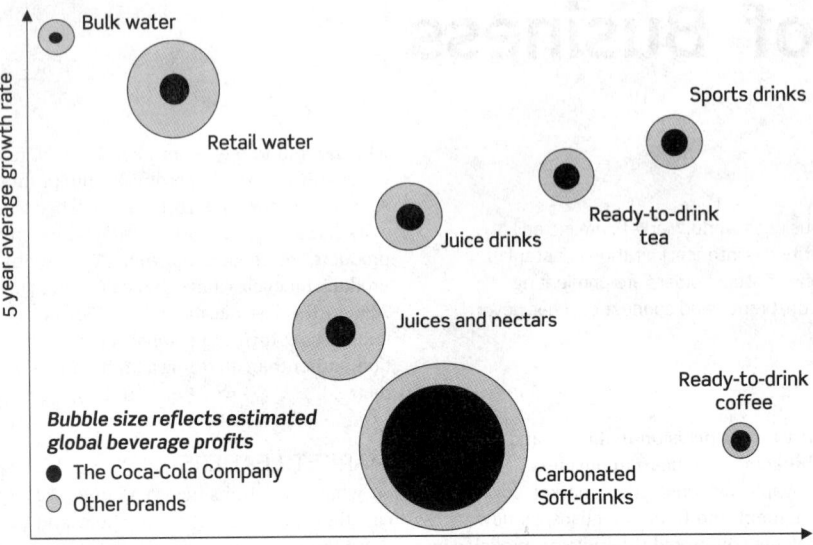

Source: coca-cola.com

marketer Phil Knight of Nike can give us some clues. However, it should not be limited to the special few. Indeed you too can achieve "genius" in your everyday decisions and actions. A genius thinks more intelligently by making sense of chaos, and acts more creatively to cut through the noise and engage the skeptics, and as a result is able to deliver extraordinary and definable results.

SEEING THINGS DIFFERENTLY

As with the theory of relativity, the Alessi orange squeezer, or the brand endorsement of Michael Jordan, a genius is able to see things differently, and thereby has the opportunity to do extraordinary things.

In business, the starting point is to see the world from where customers stand—to see products and services, business and sectors, the way real people see them. The obvious questions then no longer have simple answers—which market are you in, who are your customers, what do they want, how do they use your products, who are your competitors, what is your difference, where to focus, what will happen next? Even the world's leading brand, Coca-Cola, has recognized that it must reframe its market context, and that juices and teas, rather than carbonated drinks, will more likely drive its future success.

The magic however, is not just in the insight but in the actions that can follow. A business leader who sees a new landscape, with appropriate direction and stimulus, develops the belief and conviction to act differently—to disrupt the industry conventions,

to do what everyone else has avoided, to innovate the market rather than just a product.

DOING EXTRAORDINARY THINGS

Strategies become more directional and flexible, but with stronger focus on the best opportunities, existing and emerging. Planning starts to work from the future back, rather than extrapolating from today. Doing the right thing matters more than doing things right. And doing it right and fast, before somebody else grabs the new ground or the best ideas. Knowledge becomes a commodity, the ability to turn insight into innovation creates the advantage.

Look at the leaders of Dell or Tesco, eBay or Zara—they are market-thinking people by background, who intuitively "start with the customer and all else follows" (as Google defines its number one principle). They bring an outside-in approach, starting with

the market rather than what they have done before, obsessed with their customers and competitors, championing the brand and innovation, constantly searching for new ways to stay ahead.

Indeed when the C.E.O. comes from a marketing background, then the impact can be even greater. Recent research shows that such companies generate 5.9% better stockholder returns than those led by people with an inside-out, operational perspective.

THE "OUTSIDE-IN" BUSINESS

An outside-in approach to business starts with the market. A market strategy—defining where and how to compete, and what to do for short- and long-term commercial success—must sit at the core of a business's decision-making framework. This requires fundamental choices, about which markets to focus on, and how to be positioned within them—less about legacy or capability, and more about opportunity and customers.

An outside-in brand defines what it does for customers, rather than what it does itself. Outside-in innovation starts by redefining context before considering products and services. Outside-in communication is less about blanket campaigns, more about customer-initiated dialogues. Outside-in channels are no longer an extended arm of suppliers, but trusted agents of customers. Outside-in relationships are based more on communities than transactions.

Amazon, for example, uses its intelligence and imagination to anticipate and meet the needs of each customer. Not only did Jeff Bezos and his expeditionary marketers seize the new "whitespace" by leveraging virtual technologies and physical delivery, but they harnessed customer power, fundamentally doing business on customer terms, and doing it profitably.

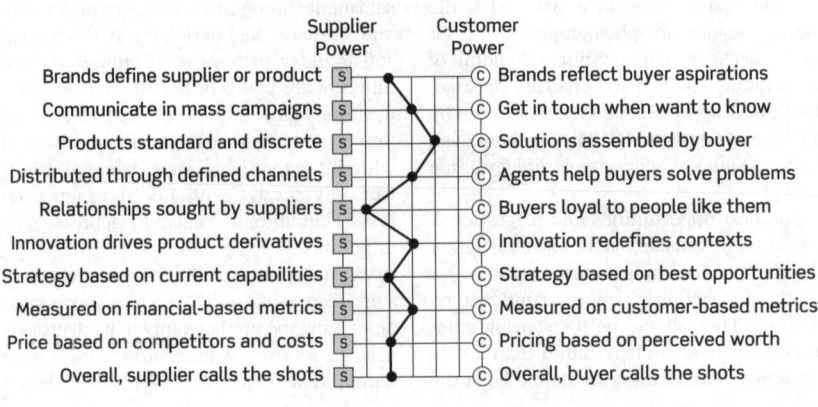

THE "TODAY TOMORROW" PARADOX

While customers must be the orientation of business, performance is ultimately measured financially. This only becomes a tension when the two goals get out of kilter. Over the longer term, creating exceptional value for customers is the only way to create significant value for shareholders. Profitable growth enables this virtuous circle.

Stockholders invest in companies in order to get a return on their money. They look at the future earning potential of a company, the cash the company is likely to generate over future years, the new markets and products which will drive it, and the strong brands and relationships which make it more certain. They take a long-term view.

Yet in business, we spend most of our time focused on the short term. Of course, this matters because cash is needed to pay the bills, and provide some indication of future success. However the long term matters more. Marketers, in particular, end up torn between the short and long term, between sales promotion and brand building, product derivatives and real innovation.

Indeed stockholders look for the things that the forward orientation of marketing provides: profitable growth through market and brand strategy, innovation, and relationships.

When P&G acquired Gillette in early 2005, only $6 billion of the $57 billion purchase price was for its tangible assets, the vast majority of the value being in its brands and relationships. On average 86% of market value is intangible, which is the real measure of the worth of new ideas, the right market choices, and the brands to ensure future success in them.

GENIUSES WANTED

In today's incredibly complicated world, every business faces enormous change, uncertainty, and opportunity. The best ideas will make companies great. Customers, rather than capital, are increasingly the scarcest resources. Market strategy and brands, relationships and innovation are the most significant drivers of economic value.

As organizations, genius is about sensing the best opportunities, then responding in ways that drive short- and long-term results. As individuals, genius is about engaging left and right brains to see and think differently, and responding by turning the best, most radical ideas into practical actions, and to inspire people to deliver them.

The genius of business is about seeing the things everyone has seen, but thinking what nobody has thought, engaging the whole brain to turn great ideas into profitable implementation, creating tomorrow while delivering today. There has never been a more important time for new market thinking, or a more exciting time to lead a business.

10 STEPS TO GENIUS

1 **Leadership.** Bring an outside-in mindset to business, driving focused decision-making and inspiring more enlightened action.
2 **Strategy.** Consider a broader context, focusing on the best few existing and emerging markets, and how to be positioned in them.
3 **Brand.** Define your brand by the benefits it offers customers rather than the functional description of your business or solution.
4 **Customers.** Engage more deeply with customers, observing and collaborating to discover emerging and unarticulated needs and wants.
5 **Innovation.** Reframe opportunities in ways that create new spaces in which to innovate products and their market applications.
6 **Channels.** Invert channels so that they become the trusted partners of customers, creating solutions based on more personal knowledge.
7 **Pricing.** Actively manage perceived value, changing the frame of reference so that a premium price structure still offers "value for the money"
8 **Communications.** Build dialogue with customers on the customers' terms and in their time and place, rather than product-push, mass-market campaigns.
9 **Relationships.** Build loyalty between, rather than with, customers through branded communities of people who want to come together.
10 **Performance.** Invest in markets, brands, and innovation that create a virtuous circle of more value for customers and stockholders, short- and long-term.

Sensing / Responding — Organization / Individual

- **Outside in** Market Competitive Customer
- **Inside out** Business Capabilities Finance
- **Right brain** Concepts Creative Holistic
- **Left brain** Facts Analytical Specific
- **Long term** Market driving Strategic Value
- **Short term** Customer driven Tactical Sales
- **Radical ideas** Conceptual Possibilities Development
- **Practical action** Operational Priorities Delivery

FOR MORE INFORMATION

Books:
Fisk, Peter. *Marketing Genius.* Chichester: Wiley, 2006.
Fisk, Peter. *The Complete C.E.O.* Chichester: Wiley, 2006.

See also:
Marketing Management (pp. 1827–1832)

Creating Powerful Brands
by Paul Stobart

EXECUTIVE SUMMARY

- A brand is defined as the sum of the functional and emotional characteristics that a consumer attributes to a product or service.
- Brands are important both to companies, as a source of competitive advantage, and to consumers, as an aid in making purchase decisions.
- A critical factor in creating powerful brands is a company's ability to differentiate the product and/or service elements of its offerings from those of its competitors.
- Key building blocks in the creation of a brand are brand proposition, brand positioning, and brand identity.
- Brand managers have a number of tools at their disposal, including product design, packaging, and advertising.
- It is important for companies to track their brand equity over time, particularly brand awareness and brand image measures.
- The Internet represents a powerful new medium for creating brands, but it's also encouraging consumers to demand a two-way dialog with brand owners.

WHAT IS A BRAND?

Put simply, a brand is the difference between a bottle of sugared, flavored, carbonated water and a bottle of Coca-Cola. It is the sum of the functional and emotional characteristics, both tangible and intangible, that a consumer attributes to a product or service. These characteristics are embodied in a name, trademark, symbol, or design, or any combination of these.

However, this definition is being increasingly stretched. As the Internet grows ever more pervasive, many online brands have virtually no tangible attributes. It could be argued that brands such as Amazon and Yahoo! exist purely in virtual reality. Moreover, the concept of branding can no longer be restricted to products and services. Movie stars, politicians, and company executives are all realizing that success is dependent on their ability to market themselves as brands.

The Organization as Brand

Many companies, and particularly those that have system brands, are realizing that creating a successful brand franchise involves mobilizing the entire organization. Every aspect of the organization, from the premises through the behavior of the employees (particularly those who work in customer-facing roles) to company letterheads and formal marketing communications, should reflect and reinforce the values of the brand.

A good example of the organization as brand is Sage, a leading supplier of accounting and payroll software. Unusually for the software industry, where marketing tends to focus on product features, Sage's brand identity communicates a feeling of confident control, leading to peace of mind. Most customers who buy Sage software also purchase an annual telephone support contract. When they phone the hotline the support technician's ability to resolve their problem serves to reinforce the brand promise.

WHY ARE BRANDS IMPORTANT?

For most companies brands are their primary source of competitive advantage and their most valuable strategic asset. Without brands we'd live in a world of commodities—undifferentiated products that are traded solely on price, according to the laws of supply and demand. Branding enables companies to actively influence the demand side of the equation by encouraging consumers to base their purchase decisions on factors other than price.

Brands are also important for consumers. They enable consumers to make informed purchase decisions and help them to navigate their way through the bewildering number of alternatives that exist in any product category. It can also be argued that brands enrich our lives. In a world in which our basic needs have been satisfied, brands give us something to which we can aspire and help in defining our own identities. This, however, is a question of ideology, and many would disagree.

SOURCES OF DIFFERENTIATION

Differentiation is the most important concept in the creation of powerful brands. Essentially brands can be differentiated in terms of product and/or service, leading to four generic types.

1 One in which an offering is differentiated neither in terms of product nor service, it is a **commodity**. Precious metals and staple food products are still largely traded as commodities (though the increasing demand for organic produce is changing this).

2 One in which an offering is differentiated in product, but not in service terms, it is a **product brand**. Product brands can be further differentiated in terms of intrinsic (or functional) benefits and extrinsic (or emotional) benefits. In practice most consumer goods are product brands, and most contain elements of both intrinsic and extrinsic differentiation. Hi-fi manufacturers focus primarily on the functionality of their products, while most mainstream soft-drink brands are differentiated largely in terms of image. The marketing of automobiles, one of the most potent symbols of status and way of life, plays on both function and emotion.

3 An offering based on providing an intangible service is a **service brand**. Financial services are classic examples. Creating service brands can prove difficult because, unlike packaged goods, delivering a service to the consumer relies heavily on humans and humans are a lot less standard than products. Service brands are most often measured in terms of their perceived value and/or perceived quality of the experience.

4 An offering differentiated in both product and service terms is a **system brand**. The McDonald's experience is based on a combination of the quality of the food, the speed of the service, and the cleanliness of the restaurant.

THE BUILDING BLOCKS OF BRAND CREATION

The **brand proposition** is the statement of the functional and emotional benefits that a company believes its product or service offers to the consumer. Coca-Cola's brand proposition is a mixture of functional bene-

---

"When you build a brand it is often tempting to force-fit success—you want it to jump and you want it to jump fast."

Ric Simcock

fits (taste, refreshment) and emotional benefits (good wholesome fun).

Brand positioning is a description of those at whom the brand is aimed (the target audience) and where it stands relative to the competition.

Brand identity (or **brand image**) is the aggregation of the words, images, and ideas that the consumer associates with a brand. There is an increasing tendency to personify brands, and companies talk about brand personality and brand attitude. This is particularly important in youth markets, in which consumers regard brands as statements of their beliefs and preferences.

THE BRAND-BUILDER'S TOOLBOX

Successful brand creation starts with product design. But it's not just about how the product performs, it's also about how it looks. When Dyson turned the vacuum cleaner market upside down, it was due not only to the revolutionary technology, but also to the fact that its products looked like nothing else on earth!

In the fast-moving consumer-goods sector, packaging is also a key source of differentiation, both as a powerful tool for creating brand identity and as a means whereby brands can stand out from the crowd on increasingly cluttered supermarket shelves.

Advertising is perhaps the brand manager's most potent tool. Print and broadcast media not only represent a cost-effective mechanism for reaching mass audiences, they also have the power to influence consumer behavior. The press is a particularly effective medium for communicating complex messages, while TV advertising, with its beguiling interplay of sounds and pictures, is ideal for building brand image.

In recent years, however, the brand manager's task has become increasingly complex. Brands have proliferated, media have fragmented, and consumers have become more cynical. Brand owners have had to become more innovative, constantly reinventing their brands to keep one step ahead of their competitors and their consumers.

Technology such as iTV, the arrival of the Internet into more than 50% of our homes and the growing power and penetration of 3G mobile phone technology has facilitated increasingly sophisticated segmentation as well as 24 hour messaging and communica-

tion. With the power of database profiling technologies, many brand owners are being able to jump the chasm from a one-to-many to a one-to-one marketing model.

MEASURING BRAND EQUITY

If brands are a company's most valuable strategic asset, it makes sense to take good care of them. While it is difficult to prove a statistical relationship between advertising and sales because of the sheer number of variables involved, it is possible to prove a relationship between advertising and awareness and between awareness and sales. For this reason most companies track brand awareness levels, together with other measures such as brand loyalty and purchase intention.

It is also important to track brand image, to make sure that the differentiating elements of brand identity a company is attempting to communicate are being received accurately by the consumer. One reason for doing this is to gauge to what extent brand equity can be leveraged into line extensions or new products. Virgin is the classic example of this, with the brand now spanning airlines, trains, soft drinks, and financial services.

In recent years many brand owners have attempted to assign an economic value to their brands on the balance sheet. The brand consulting company Interbrand has been at the forefront of this process, though the accounting profession has yet to fully embrace the concept.

BRANDS IN THE NEW ECONOMY

The Internet was heralded as the brand manager's dream but a new more sophisticated, more pervasive and more personalized channel to consumers has taken the lead by virtue of its attractiveness—the 3G mobile phone. Like the Internet, it is instantaneous, enables direct one-to-one communication, is interactive, and is multimedia, integrating text, sound, and images. Its most unique feature is that it offers 24-hour access from virtually anywhere in the globe while mobile.

MAKING IT HAPPEN ▸▸
- Seek above all to differentiate the product and/or service elements of

your offerings from those of your competitors.
- Build the brand proposition from the functional and emotional benefits you believe your product or service offers to customers.
- Use sophisticated consumer segmentation techniques to move from a one-to-many to a one-to-one marketing model.
- Track brand image to make sure that the differentiating elements of brand identity are being received accurately by the consumer.
- Harness the Internet to extend the customer franchise of your most successful offline brands.
- Work on every aspect of the organization, from employee behavior to premises, so as to reflect and reinforce brand values.

THE FUTURE OF BRANDS

While brands are undoubtedly here to stay, there is growing evidence of a consumer backlash. Ironically it's the Internet that's encouraging consumers, sick of being marketed to by faceless corporations, to demand a dialog with brand owners.

Moreover, disgruntled consumers are using the Internet to undermine the brand equity that has been expensively created by these same faceless corporations. These voices of dissent range from the humorous to the more sinister (**www.aolwatch.org/aolwatch15.htm**).

FOR MORE INFORMATION

Book:
Aaker, David A. *Building Strong Brands.* New York: Simon & Schuster, 2002.

See also:

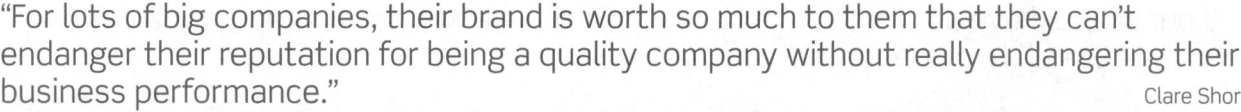

"For lots of big companies, their brand is worth so much to them that they can't endanger their reputation for being a quality company without really endangering their business performance."

Clare Short

On Writing as an Essential Business Skill
by John Simmons

EXECUTIVE SUMMARY

- Brands need to manage both visual and verbal identity (images and words) to achieve recognition and differentiation.
- Creative management of a brand's written language—tone of voice—can build loyalty with audiences.
- Tone of voice needs to develop from the brand's personality and values, and to be consistent across all media, internal and external.
- Inconsistent application through everyday contacts can undermine a brand's credibility.
- All individuals represent a brand through the words they use—it is important to at least recognize when the right tone of voice is not being achieved.
- Champions—individuals able to write in the brand's tone of voice and to tell the brand's story—need to be established through development and training.
- Creativity, particularly the creativity of its own people, is the main means by which a modern business can make itself distinctive.
- Nurturing of creative writing skills at work achieves business objectives and provides opportunities for personal development.

INTRODUCTION
Why Words Matter
Words are the essential tools of communication. But they are so much more. They convey information, they express emotion; they influence, persuade, motivate. They do all the things that a successful business wants to do—if they are used well. Or, if they are used badly, they undermine a business.

After decades of obeisance to the notion that we "live in a visual world," the word has struck back. From "a picture is worth a thousand words," business is returning to a position closer to that articulated by Bill Bernbach in the 1950s: "But not necessarily worth one word. The right word."

VERBAL IDENTITY
Many businesses, particularly those that adhere to principles of branding, now attach equal importance to words and images. Visual identity—the consistent use of logos, colors, typefaces, photography—is an established management discipline. Verbal identity—managing a brand's tone of voice through style, vocabulary, names, the use of stories—is in its relative infancy.

Combining the visual and the verbal provides the means to make brands that really work. A prime objective of any modern brand is to create better relationships with its consumers. Companies use their brands to create and maintain better relationships

through conversations, just as individuals do. Many of those conversations are conducted in written form, whether in print, in e-mails or on the Internet. But, as "conversations" implies, they need to be written as if they were spoken—a more informal approach to language than business practices of the previous century.

The words used in those conversations—through all experiences, including the Internet—are reflections of a brand's personality. When products and services are basically similar, words can be the principal means of differentiating one company from another.

A Case Study
In 1998 three British college friends formed a company that makes fruit smoothies. A very simple business and, at that time, a tiny market for the product. They called the company Innocent Drinks. They had little money to spend on visual identity, but the founders had a playful approach to words. They channeled their creative effort into writing words—humorous little stories—that appeared on the labels of their products.

Innocent's verbal identity begins with its name. They are innocent in the sense of being the little guys up against big corporations—but also in believing in the natural goodness of pure fruit, with no nasty addi-

tives. All their words reinforce this proposition through the disarming use of humor. A very clear sense of the Innocent personality emerges through every word they use, even down to a distinctive, honest but funny way of listing the ingredients of their products.

The news about Innocent spread, appropriately enough, by word of mouth. People talked about them, shared the humor of the labels (which changed constantly) and became loyal fans. Innocent got other things right too, particularly distribution. In a matter of a few years they were ubiquitous, the United Kingdom's fastest-growing food and drink company.

WORDS ARE SLIPPERY
Many businesses have since tried to copy Innocent, but Innocent's success is built on the consistency of its tone of voice and its absolute rightness for what it does. Different brands need different personalities and different words. Those words also need to be consistent across the brand's disciplines and range of activities. Otherwise the wrong words can undermine a brand.

It is relatively easy to manufacture a tone of voice that works in external communication such as advertising. People regard advertising—particularly on TV—almost as a form of entertainment. Naturally good advertising uses words creatively. But there is a danger if a brand's advertising sends a message of, say, off-beat friendliness and if a consumer's subsequent encounter with a brand representative or communication is disappointingly dull or unfriendly.

THE INDIVIDUALITY OF WORDS
A brand's tone of voice needs to work from the inside outwards, if it is to have real credibility. It should start with a brand personality that is distinctive and owned by the individuals responsible for shaping the company. But every individual has a role to play, because everyone represents the brand through the words that they choose to use. If a brand such as Apple promises to "Think different," for example, this places responsibility on the behavior of everyone representing the brand. The consumer has a

right to expect a degree of creativity from all the brand's representatives. And words are the most *available* creative resource for any company to use.

Content matters as well as style. Even if, for example, Apple and Innocent had created an identical brand personality for themselves, their words would be made different by the fact that Apple would describe music or computer technology, whereas Innocent would write about fruit and the making of juice. Content influences vocabulary, the choice of individual words. These words are further ordered by structure and they are connected by style.

For a brand to achieve true differentiation in its tone of voice, all these elements need to be combined with craft. The outcome should be a playful richness of language rather than approaches that masquerade as verbal identity by restricting vocabulary to an approved list of words. Brands, and their representatives, need to see what they do as storytelling.

TELLING THE STORY

Stories are one of the most fundamental forms of communication. Through stories individuals and businesses can understand the world better and engage more effectively with audiences. Stories can be used to achieve a number of important business objectives:

- provide starting points for brands and continuing touchpoints of inspiration as companies grow;
- become a means of encouraging personal creative expression by employees, and therefore increased motivation;

- clarify the purpose of a business and inspire greater internal and external loyalty;
- illuminate the meaning of business strategies and principles so that they are more easily understood.

DEVELOPING SKILLS

It is clear that the need to establish a distinctive verbal identity (including the use of storytelling) makes demands of a company and its individuals. Not everyone can be a fluent, skilful writer. But we all use words as part of our work—it is an inescapable fact of modern working life.

Companies need to look at the way they manage the words that individuals produce on their behalf. Champions—discipline by discipline, department by department—have to be given responsibility for setting and maintaining a high standard of written communication, internal and external. They need to create and adhere to an agreed tone of voice that projects a consistent brand personality. Skills need to be nurtured through guidelines, training, books, and online learning.

CONCLUSION
Creativity Is Fundamental

Fifty years ago, "creativity" was required only in an advertising agency. Today every business needs to be creative and it needs to inspire and harness the creativity of all its people. This is not an optional extra, but an essential requirement for survival, growth and reinvention. Businesses that lack creativity will increasingly struggle to survive.

Creative skills therefore need to be nur-

tured and developed in businesses of all kinds. Writing is the creative skill that is, literally, closest at hand for any business. By developing people to express themselves more creatively through words, businesses can unlock the potential of innovation, increase the impact of communication and become more effective in winning business.

The business benefits are reinforced by the additional advantage of personal development. Businesses are increasingly reliant on the quality of people, and they need to make sure that people feel that they are fulfilling their potential. Writing is an effective way to help people in a business to achieve personal development.

FOR MORE INFORMATION

Books:
Ogilvy, David. *The Unpublished David Ogilvy.* Revised ed. New York: Crown, 1987.
Simmons, John. *Dark Angels.* London: Cyan Books, 2004.
Simmons, John. *The Invisible Grail.* Revised ed. London: Cyan Books, 2006.
Simmons, John. *We, Me, Them & It.* Revised ed. London: Cyan Books, 2006.
Vincent, Laurence. *Legendary Brands: Unleashing the Power of Storytelling.* New York: Dearborn, 2002.
Whyte, David. *Crossing the Unknown Sea: Work and the Shaping of Identity.* New York: Penguin, 2002.

See also:
David Ogilvy (pp. 1340–1341)
Marketing Management (pp. 1827–1832)

On Value and Values: How a Blended Values Strategy Drives Sustainable Performance

by Douglas K. Smith

EXECUTIVE SUMMARY

- Strategies whose sole objective is value creation fail.
- "Value" (profits, shareholder value, wealth) is just one of the overall social, political and economic beliefs and behaviors determining organizational success in markets and networks.
- Strategists who isolate value from other values subordinate a plural ("values") to a singular ("value")—an impossibility that fosters beliefs and behaviors that destroy value.
- In contrast, blended values strategies identify the integrated set of beliefs and behaviors demanded of 21st-century success.

INTRODUCTION

Shareholder value extremism is an ideology demanding the pursuit of value as the sole objective of strategists. It enriches executives and some shareholders over the short term. But it fails to generate sustainable gains for shareholders, customers, and employees because it perverts the social, political, and economic beliefs and behaviors required for 21st-century success. Strategists seeking to avoid the pitfalls must act on the following:

- Strategy is an integrated set of values—of beliefs and behaviors—that drive sustainable performance.
- Sustainable performance must benefit all organizational constituencies as both means and ends to one another's success.
- By exalting one constituency above others, shareholder value extremists subordinate social and political values to economic and financial value causing "the way we do things around here" to become unsustainable.
- *Blended values strategies* help organizations migrate away from shareholder value extremism to sustainable performance.

STRATEGY AS AN INTEGRATED SET OF BELIEFS AND BEHAVIORS, THAT IS, VALUES

"Value-obsessed strategists" have two bad habits. First, they pursue *value as the sole objective* of strategy. Second, such strategists confine their work to *making choices* (for example, about markets, products, services, customers, competitors, alliances, technology, distribution, people, ideas, competencies, and networks). Strategic choices, however, do not implement themselves. People do. In addition to making choices, strategists must also specify the integrated set of people's beliefs and behaviors demanded for sustainable performance. For example, a "low cost" strategy demands beliefs and behaviors directed at building cost advantages, and a "Web-based strategy" requires beliefs and behaviors favoring Web presence and distribution. Moreover, the full set of required beliefs and behaviors must integrate and reinforce one another. For example, 3M's innovation strategy for decades reflected an integrated, reinforcing set of beliefs and behaviors that fostered and commercialized new products and services.

Instead of splitting off concern for financial and economic value and then subordinating all other values, blended values strategies are clear about the mutually reinforcing contribution to be made to the strategy and performance of the enterprise by the following categories of values:

- social
- political
- economic and financial
- family-related
- environmental
- legal
- medical/health
- technological
- creative and self-fulfilling

SUSTAINABLE PERFORMANCE BENEFITS ALL CONSTITUENCIES EQUIVALENTLY

Successful 21st-century organizations pursue strategies in which employees deliver benefits to customers who, in turn, provide returns to shareholders who, in turn, generate opportunities for employees who deliver benefits to customers . . . And on and on and on—each constituency serving and being served by the others. Performance is sustainable because real people make and implement choices grounded in the following Golden Rule of blended values strategies: *As executives/employees, do unto others who are customers and shareholders what you would have them as executives/employees do unto you as customers and investors.*

SHAREHOLDER VALUE EXTREMISTS SUBORDINATE AND DISTORT THE SOCIAL AND POLITICAL VALUES DEMANDED OF SUSTAINABLE SUCCESS

Shareholder value extremists promote the interests of shareholders as the ruling objective of strategy. Their strategies consider employees as a means to promote customer interests that, in turn, are means to promote shareholder interests. Shareholders have no role or purpose other than wealth-gathering.

This linear view is not sustainable because it subordinates and perverts the beliefs and behaviors of the executives and employees on whom it depends for success. For example, strategies grounded in core competencies, movement, initiative, continuous improvement, innovation, and quality must be "owned" by the people of the organization. Such "ownership" demands enthusiastic and constructive responsibility that is impossible when shareholders have no obligation to the people of the enterprise, but only to their own self-enrichment.

"The mind thinks, not with data, but with ideas whose creation and elaboration cannot be reduced to a set of predictable values."

Theodore Roszak

Value-obsessed strategies foster excessive executive compensation; diminished wages, salaries, benefits, and job security; secretive, hierarchical decision-making; destructive organizational politics; illegal and unethical practices; poor customer service and quality; and capital market takeovers, attacks, and disruptions. Executives and some shareholders get rich in the short run-but sustainable performance is never achieved. Consider Enron, WorldCom, Adelphia, Tyco, Martha Stewart, Merrill Lynch, Citigroup, Arthur Andersen, KPMG, Pfizer, Shell, ABC, Firestone, Boeing, AOL Time Warner, Nortel, Health South, Freddie Mac, Dynegy, ImClone, Computer Associates, Knight-Rider, El Paso, Global Crossing, Hollinger, Lucent, JP Morgan Chase, Sunbeam, Xerox, NY Stock Exchange.

BLENDED VALUES STRATEGIES FOSTER SUSTAINABLE PERFORMANCE

Blended values strategies choose and implement an integrated set of beliefs and behaviors that produce sustainable organizational performance. Performance is guided by SMART outcome-based goals that tell *a sustainable story about how and why shareholders provide opportunities for the people of the enterprise (and their strategic partners) to deliver benefits to their chosen sets of customers who generate returns to shareholder who provide opportunities to the people of the enterprise-and so on, iteratively in perpetuity.*

Blended values strategists (1) make choices about where and how to compete in markets and networks; and, (2) specify the blend of economic, financial, social and political values required to implement those choices. Political values include beliefs and behaviors about decision-making, problem-solving, voice, consent, responsibility for implementation, and membership. Social values include beliefs and behaviors about relationships, trust, dignity, respect, integrity, and responsibility. Economic and financial values include beliefs and behaviors critical to product and service quality, price, profit, capital, and market and network competi-

tion and cooperation. And, as indicated earlier, there are comparable specific beliefs and behaviors critical to strategic success that derive from other categories of values such as family, technological, environmental, legal, medical and so forth.

Blended values strategies answer, "What difference does our organization make to the larger world?" How does the common good of our organization (that is, our mission, vision, strategy, and operations) contribute to the greater good of the planet?

MAKING IT HAPPEN ▶▶

The following questions guide strategists to shape and implement blended values strategies:

For a single business:
- Who are our chosen set of customers, what do we provide them, and at what price?
- Where and how will we compete for those customers?
- What do we have to be really good at in order to succeed?
- How can we take the best parts of our past and blend then into the best parts of our future?
- How do our employees, our strategic alliance partners, our customers and our shareholders and supporters benefit from this strategy? How do the benefits of each of these constituencies work to the advantage of the others?
- What are the social, political and economic/financial values that will underpin success?
- How would anyone know we have succeeded at this strategy?
- How do our strategy and our success contribute to the greater good of the planet?
- How can we translate our strategy and values into a specific set of beliefs and behaviors that, once integrated and woven together, will produce sustainable performance?

For a multi-business enterprise:
- What are the shared resources that

matter to the success of each of our single businesses?
- Of these shared resources, which are non-strategic and why? Which are strategic and why?
- How does the aggregation of our various businesses make a demonstrable difference to the constituencies of those businesses as well as the constituencies of our multi-business enterprise?
- How does the success of our multi-business enterprise contribute to the greater good of the planet?

CONCLUSION

In the late 20th century, technology, global capital and political upheaval transformed the geographic boundaries and local/national legal structures on which strategists had depended for advantage. Strategy shifted away from position to movement-and from physical assets to human capabilities. The initial wave of "competency-based" strategies were focused solely on value creation and tapped into the powerful force of self-interest in markets. But value-obsessed organizations—and especially those dominated by the self-interest of executives and shareholders—turn self-destructive. Blended values strategies reflect choices about values that recognize trade-offs between "me" and "we." They explicitly address what each constituency in the 21st-century enterprise (shareholder, employee, customer) seeks from, and can give to, the others as well as how and why the organization's success contributes to the greater good of the planet.

FOR MORE INFORMATION

Web site:
www.douglasksmith.com

See also:
↝ Innovation and Creativity
(pp. 1774–1777)

"The substitution of monetary values for all other values is pushing society towards a dangerous disequilibrium."

George Soros

How HR Adds Value
by Dave Ulrich and Wayne Brockbank

EXECUTIVE SUMMARY

- HR practices, organizations, and professionals must be transformed to succeed.
- The heart of this transformation is that HR must add value.
- Value is defined by the receiver more than the giver and comes as HR responds to a new set of criteria and demands.

INTRODUCTION

As the pressure to do more with less increases and as the human or organization factors become ever more important, human resources (HR) must be transformed. The transformation of HR matters to C.E.O.s and other line managers who want to turn strategy into sustained results. The transformation of HR matters to employees who want to develop the competencies necessary to do their jobs and want to better focus their commitment on activities that enhance personal performance. While these two internal groups (line managers and employees) recognize that HR must be transformed, the realization now goes outside the firm as well. Customers who desire to maintain long-term and increasingly complex relationships with a supplier recognize that a supplier's HR practices help assure a steady flow of desired products and services. And investors who realize that intangibles determine a large source of a company's wealth, increasingly look to HR as a source of a firm's market value. For each of these stakeholders—line managers, employees, customers, and investors—the transformation of HR revolves around a simple idea: value. All HR investments in a firm (practices, departments, and professionals) must deliver value. As the administrative and transaction work of HR is being automated and/or outsourced, the remaining work must create value.

To create value, we propose a 5-stage architecture for the HR Value Proposition (see Figure 1). Using the logic in this figure, we may then specify 14 criteria for HR transformation. In doing HR transformation, the ideal logic is to move through these five elements sequentially, following the solid lines in the figure, but sometimes it is useful to follow the dotted lines instead. For example, you might start your transformation of HR with a competency assessment of your staff (shown in stage 5 of Figure 1), but to ensure that this competency assessment leads to an integrated transformation, it must be connected to the other elements of the overall blueprint. Or, you might start by investing in e-HR (stage 4 of Figure 1), then move to the other four stages to complete the transformation.

Each of the five basic elements defines criteria for what makes an effective HR function. In presentations and team meetings to initiate your HR transformation, these criteria should be discussed as a way to envision the future. (Note that this logic can be applied to other staff groups by changing HR to IT, Marketing, Finance, Legal, and so forth. Each of the five stages could be used to create a template for transformation any staff function.)

EXTERNAL BUSINESS REALITIES

HR actions inside a firm must reflect and influence business realities outside that firm. Over the long run, nothing that matters on the inside of a firm matters unless it ultimately responds to product or service demands on the outside. HR professionals should be able to cogently discuss these external realities—the technological, regulatory and economic factors, and demographics of the global business environment—and connect them to their day-to-day work. Knowing business realities makes it possible to put HR practices in context, tie them to competitive challenges, and relate them to concerns facing line managers. These contextual factors offer the rationale for why a transformation should occur. Everyone in your HR function should be conversant with both the realities of the external world and how HR actions will

Stages in HR Transformation

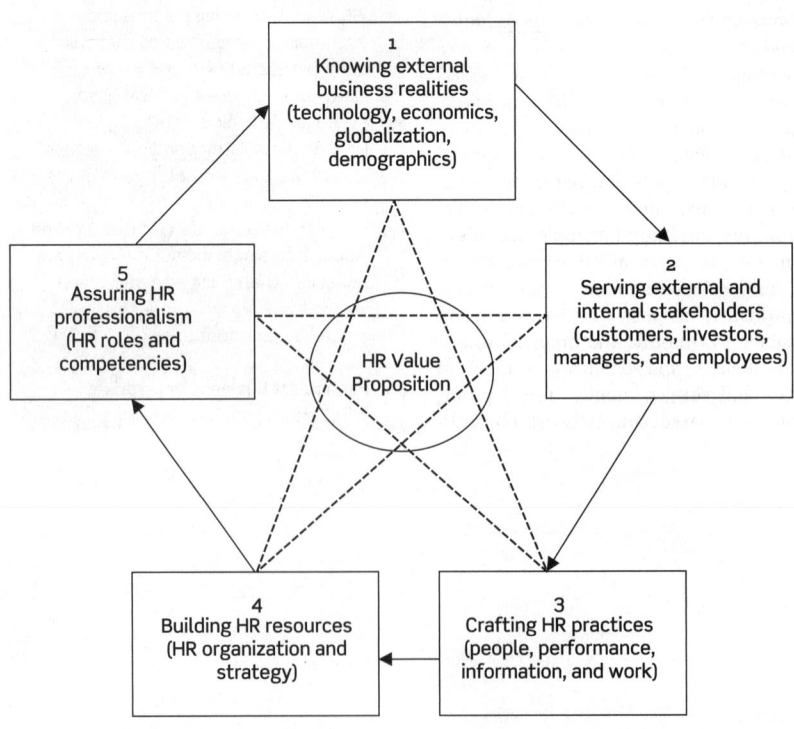

help your firm compete in this changing context.

- Criterion 1: An effective HR function has HR professionals who recognize external business realities and adapt HR practices and allocate HR resources accordingly.

STAKEHOLDERS

Value is defined by the receivers of HR work—the investors, customers, line managers, and employees—more than by the givers. HR is successful if and when it creates value for stakeholders and its stakeholders perceive value from it. Delivering what matters most to stakeholders focuses on the deliverables (outcomes of HR) rather than on the doables (activities of HR). The deliverables of HR involve investor intangibles, customer share, organization capabilities, or individual abilities.

- Criterion 2: An effective HR function creates market value for investors by increasing intangibles.
- Criterion 3: An effective HR function increases customer share by connecting with target customers.
- Criterion 4: An effective HR function helps line managers deliver strategy by building organization capabilities.
- Criterion 5: An effective HR function clarifies and establishes an employee value proposition and enhances individual abilities.

HR PRACTICES

HR practices institutionalize beliefs and values and make them real to all stakeholders. They create and focus organizational energy on key business strategies and initiatives. For example, the way you hire, train, or pay people or the way you organize work sends messages to employees about what matters most. By creating practices around people, performance management, information, and work flows, you shape an organization's identity and personality. These HR practices deliver value to internal and external stakeholders when they are appropriately aligned with your organization goals. They also ensure that the organization outlives any individual leader. They create and sustain the cultural pillars for your organization.

- Criterion 6: An effective HR function manages people processes and practices in ways that add value.
- Criterion 7: An effective HR function manages performance management processes and practices in ways that add value.
- Criterion 8: An effective HR function

manages information processes and practices in ways that add value.
- Criterion 9: An effective HR function manages work flow design and processes in ways that add value.

HR RESOURCES

Your HR function needs a strategy and structure that will deliver value. The strategy will help you focus attention on key factors and respond appropriately to business realities; the structure will organize HR resources in ways that govern how HR work is done. The strategy and structure of your HR department will ensure that HR resources are deployed where they add the most value.

- Criterion 10: An effective HR function aligns its organization to the strategy of the business.
- Criterion 11: An effective HR function has a clear strategic planning process for aligning HR investments with business goals.

HR PROFESSIONALISM

Each HR professional in your organization must learn to play a role and master competencies to deliver value. Roles represent what people do; competencies define how they do it. HR functions are only as good as the people who inhabit them, so having clear roles and distinct competencies ensures that they will deliver they value they intend. With a clear definition of the required HR roles and competencies, HR departments can then invest in developmental efforts that enable HR professionals to deliver the full HR value proposition.

- Criterion 12: An effective HR function has HR professionals who play clear and appropriate roles.
- Criterion 13: An effective HR function builds HR professionals who demonstrate HR competencies.
- Criterion 14: An effective HR function invests in training and development of HR professionals.

With these criteria in place, leaders and HR professionals may now turn the desire for transformation into action. They can do so by assessing their HR departments on the 14 criteria and by then investing in ways to assure that HR professionals add value. When such a process is followed, leaders can rest assured that HR professionals, practices, and departments will be designed and delivered in such as way as to create value, for employees, line managers, customers, and investors.

The picture of HR we present here may

seem unfamiliar to many organizations, but it is, we believe, what is needed to meet the demands of the current and foreseeable business environment. It has implications for general managers, HR executives, and professionals working in HR, and for the profession of HR itself.

MAKING IT HAPPEN ▸▸ Implications for General Managers

General managers set expectations for HR departments, practices, and professionals. When general managers demand value from HR investments, they set high standards. They require that their HR executives be clear, exact, and powerful thinkers about the human and organizational issues. They require high value-adding aspirations from their HR professionals. These expectations shape what HR professionals do and how HR professionals act. General managers should continually follow up on standards to ensure that HR measures up. This follow-up engages general managers in HR issues and holds HR professionals accountable for them. When general managers are aware of the value that HR produces for them and for their organization, they encourage and advocate HR actions.

To have value-driven HR in your organization, your general manager should recognize HR's impact on investor, customer, business, and employee results. This awareness should show up in talks and presentations both inside and outside the company. It means that HR issues should be part of every manager's performance scorecard. It means that general managers need to accept ownership for HR's efforts by personally referring to them as "my" work not "HR" work. It means that organization capabilities and individual abilities are not just rhetoric but action.

For HR to have maximal effectiveness, general managers must base their reputation and identity on their ability to deliver value through people. In private conversations with other business leaders, general managers need to discuss and hold them accountable for their HR actions. The general manager is a cheerleader for people and organizations, and also a coach who helps design the HR processes and a player who helps implement them. As a result, the company's leadership brand will include people and organization issues.

"You're useless in business with just an academic background. You're also useless if you spend too much time in the military."

Ken Olsen

Implications for Senior HR Executives

Senior HR executives have many conversations that lead to action. With the HR value proposition as a foundation, these conversations focus on results relevant to each stakeholder.

- With investors, conversations focus on how intangibles become a determining factor in the creation of sustained market value. Actions focus on intangibles audits and translating the audit results into specific insights on how to improve shareholder value.
- With customers, conversations focus on meeting customer needs and on aligning HR practices with customer expectations, with a view to increasing customer share. Besides adjusting practices, action may involve ways to engage customers in designing and delivering HR practices.
- With line managers, conversations center on delivering business strategies through prioritizing and creating organization capabilities. Actions follow as the concept of capabilities translates into investments of budget, time, and energy.
- With employees, conversations provide insight into an employee value proposition that assures that if and when employees deliver value, they will receive value. Actions may then be specified to ensure that employees have both the ability and the attitude to do what is expected of them.
- With HR professionals, conversations capture both the roles and competencies they require to deliver value. This helps HR professionals realize their roles and demonstrate their competencies.

Each of these conversations is then sustained by creating HR strategies, organizations, and practices that endure. HR strategy that offers a clear line of sight from business realities to HR practices is designed by HR and owned by line managers to complement an existing business strategy, and it is supported by an HR organization that delivers HR transactions with efficiency and HR transformation with effectiveness. Investments in people, performance management, information, and work flow processes deliver sustained value as guided by the strategy. With strategies, organizations, and practices in place, conversations turn into commitments and rhetoric into results.

Senior HR executives also need to develop more powerful HR agendas as laid out in the HR value proposition and then develop HR professionals able to deliver on the agendas. Individual HR professionals should avail themselves of job assignments and career moves as well as high-impact training experiences that cover the full range of the HR value proposition.

Implications for HR Professionals

Most HR professionals want to add value. When roles are clear, HR professionals can describe what they do in ways that set expectations of themselves and others. When competencies are defined and demonstrated, HR professionals can ensure that they know how to deliver value.

To be competent in your role, you need a mental model of the value you create, you should constantly be assessing yourself against that model both formally and informally and you should continually develop greater knowledge and skills that enable you to add greater value. Engage in daily and weekly personal reflections about what worked and what did not. Connect choices and consequences, then take corrective action and make yourself responsible for improvement. With this kind of learning and accountability, you become an HR professional who is respected not only for what you know and do, but also for the value you deliver.

Careers for HR professionals who fully grasp and deliver value may vary widely. They may concentrate in one domain (people, performance management, information, or organization flow practices) or in one organization structure (a center of expertise or a line of business). Or, more likely, they will move across domain and organizational boundaries in differing role assignments. Increasingly, we envision top HR professionals moving into and out of formal HR positions. We would not define the success or "arrival" of HR by the number of HR professionals who move into senior line management jobs (that actually belittles the importance of HR), but nonetheless HR professionals who fully deliver value will be able to work outside HR as well. Some companies—Unilever, Procter & Gamble, Royal Dutch Shell, Baxter Healthcare—already regularly move HR professionals into and out of line management roles.

Implications for the HR Profession

Given the technological, economic and regulatory, and demographic realities of our global world, HR contributions have been pushed to the forefront of business success. Leading thinkers, admired firms, and respected executives converge on issues central to HR. Good to great companies, leaders who execute, firms with reputations as best places to work, and leaders in management's hall of fame all exist because of the people and organization practices that are put in place.

Now more than ever, business success comes from HR. And the DNA for HR success is the HR value proposition. With this value proposition, the HR profession can have a powerful point of view about what can be and should be for all stakeholders, a set of standards about how HR investments in strategy, structure, and practices should be made, and a template for ensuring that each HR professional contributes. The HR value proposition is the blueprint for the future of HR of high value added HR.

FOR MORE INFORMATION

Book:
Ulrich, Dave, and Wayne Brockbank. *The HR Value Proposition.* Cambridge, MA: Harvard Business School Press, 2005.

Web site:
The RBL Group: **www.rbl.net**

See also:
☆ Return on Talent (pp. 144–145)

"We seriously undervalue the passion . . . a person brings to an enterprise. You can rent a brain, but you can't rent a heart."
Mark McCormack

Managing the Customer
by Merlin Stone

EXECUTIVE SUMMARY

- As competition in all its forms intensifies, customer management holds the key to increasing revenues *in a way that also drives profitability.*
- Whether cross-selling or upselling additional products to customers, retaining existing customers, attracting new ones, using customers to help develop new products, or simply providing the same products more efficiently and at less cost—the importance of customer focus and management is without parallel.
- At a time when the number of sales channels is increasing significantly and many other factors are impacting on traditional sales and marketing issues, the need for customer service that is 24/7 and manages the customer is as challenging as ever.

INTRODUCTION

There's no ideal way of managing customers. Marketers have been brought up on consumer-goods branding, retail marketing, and sales-force management. Along comes customer-relationship marketing with the claim to replace or substantially supplement these tried-and-true ways of doing business. However, there are many ways of managing customers. The main ways are listed below. In practice many companies combine several.

MODELS FOR MANAGING THE CUSTOMER
One-on-one

Here most aspects of the marketing mix are actively attuned to the individual, based on information given by the individual before or during contacts, perhaps supplemented by other data (for example, inferred data). Some—but not all—customers are considered receptive to this, that is, customers have different propensities to respond in terms of returning more value. The principles work when applied to large customers whose value justifies the degree of customization implied by this approach.

Transparent Marketing

Many customers would like to manage their relationship with companies rather than the other way around. They try to do this by soliciting information from them and customizing the offer made to them (content, timing, etc.), but they're not usually allowed to do so. Where it is possible (for example, via advanced call centers or the Web) some customers are very responsive. However, most companies do not offer this to their customers, and even waste large amounts of money trying to guess what customers want based on inadequate information.

Customer-relationship Marketing (CRM) Through a Few Segmented Offers

This is still the aspiration of most companies. Although most companies make slower progress than they would like, many get solid gains by prioritizing those areas of the relationship in which the offer for target customers (for example, positive- and/or high-value) is most at variance with the need. This model recognizes that the relationship is only one part of the marketing mix, and that there are often situations in which classic elements of the marketing mix are more critical for marketing success.

Personalized Communication and Targeting

Campaign selection and tailored packaging of standard offers are examples of personalized communication and marketing. The practice grew from good practice in direct mail and telemarketing. It involves good use and management of customer data. It can raise response and conversion rates and save communication costs. In its most advanced form, data given by the customer at the point of contact is used to create or modify the profile and hence the offer made.

Top Vanilla

In this method, leadership is gained by offering excellent customer management (before, during, and after the sale), but to a standard available to everyone in the target market rather than just a few selected customers. In some cases this is combined with one of the other approaches for one or more small segments of highly valuable customers. This approach is characteristic of companies that manage their customers entirely by direct-marketing techniques such as telemarketing, direct mail, and the Internet.

Spot-sell within Managed Roster

For some or all of the products they buy, some customers prefer to get the best deal (value for the money, not necessarily lowest price) at the time of purchase, but only from a selected roster of suppliers. This is characteristic of heavy users of fast-moving consumer goods or shopping goods, but also of many industrial purchases in which a roster of suppliers is used to guarantee optimal variety, product quality, and service. In such situations attempts to develop behavioral loyalty (so that a customer buys more than the usual proportion from one supplier) usually require some promotional incentive.

Branding is usually a critical determinant of inclusion in the roster. For products bought through intermediaries, the supplier's goal is to guarantee availability through intermediaries in the customer's roster. Note that the final customer may have a roster of products/brands and a roster of intermediaries. In this model, marketing focuses on getting on the customer's roster and providing best value compared with other companies on the roster. Top vanilla service can add competitive edge. CRM can be used to reinforce the supplier's or intermediary's position in the roster, though it may not help in gaining profit. However, if the supplier's product or the intermediary's offer is good value for the money, a fair share of the business can be obtained, so the returns to CRM can be good.

Spot-sell Managed by Agent

In some cases drawing up the roster can be a complex task, with which customers feel they need the help of an agent, whether for expert advice, bargaining expertise, or just to delegate some of the transaction management. Some modes of purchase may require the customer to sign on as a registered customer (for example, buying over the

---

"The key to using the Internet to extend and build relationships is to view ownership of information differently—you need to bring customers inside your business to create information partnerships."

Michael Dell

telephone or on the Web), but the customer prefers to register with an independent agent rather than the original product or service supplier. So the customer appoints one intermediary to act as an agent, and the agent then draws up the roster. However, CRM techniques can be used very successfully with the intermediaries. This approach can often be combined with top vanilla service for final customers and agents. In an increasing number of cases, the agent may be Web-based.

Pure Spot-sell

Here the customer rejects all relationships and buys (whether from original supplier or intermediary) purely on the basis of current perceived value. This in turn is strongly influenced by classic marketing-mix variables—brand, perceived product quality, price (including promotional discounts), availability, etc. To avoid being drawn into this situation, suppliers must seek to differentiate their offer such that the customer sees pure spot-buying as being risky.

The Partnership Model

This is a model that seems to have a very good pedigree, but it is quite difficult to implement. It is suggested as a model where both supplier and intermediary have strong visibility of and to the final customer, as in the automotive industry or in financial services.

CLASSIC MARKETING MODELS

There are several classic marketing models in which the nature of customer management is not specified explicitly but there is a very strong implicit model of customer management. These include:
- retailing;
- sales-force management;
- mail order;
- consumer-product and company-brand management;
- business-product management (closely related to technical innovation models).

ADOPTING THE RIGHT APPROACH

Obviously, these approaches to managing customers overlap, and suppliers may find they need to combine them in different ways for managing different customers and for different products. However, each has characteristic and very different patterns of marketing investment and return.

The choice is affected by factors such as the following:
- **state and rate of change of product technology,** which can lead customers to require uncertainty reduction—available through relationship or agents—but it can also create big differences in spot value;
- **underlying production and distribution techniques and costs,** for example, costs of variety, economies of scale;
- **rate of entry of new-to-category customers,** which affects the role of experience;
- **market structure fundamentals,** for example, patterns of competition or regulation;
- **transfer of learning and expectations of customers** between different paradigms of management that customers know;
- **customer behavior and psychographics** or, more simply, what they think and feel, how they buy, their need to give or take control, and associated way-of-life and life-cycle issues;
- **timing issues**—how quickly customers' needs can be identified, and how quickly they can be responded to;
- **customer expertise**—whether customers are good at identifying their own needs (and if so, how long it takes) and associated learning issues;
- **sector**—the strong tendency in some complex business-to-business relationships for customers to prefer a CRM-managed repertoire with spot-buying;
- **state of intermediation**—type of intermediation (for example, by agents, Web-based) and amount and type of value added by intermediaries;
- **relationship between risk and value,** for example, whether customers have high risks (credit, insurance, etc.) attached to them as individuals; what the balance is between good and bad customers and between good and bad customer characteristics;
- **data issues**—quality, legal issues;
- **staffing**—current skill levels, possibilities of recruiting new skill sets, training options, etc.;
- **systems culture of the supplier,** for example, whether managers are able to cope with the latest call-center and Web-based technology.

MAKING IT HAPPEN ▶▶
- Build customer management by combining different approaches in

different ways for managing different customers and products.
- Treat one-on-one marketing as an ideal target rather than a practical means of returning more value.
- Don't guess what customers want, but build an accurate picture from well-researched data.
- Recognize that the customer relationship is only one part of the marketing mix, and that other elements may be more critical.
- If possible, offer excellent customer management (before, during, and after the sale) to everyone in the target market, not just a few.
- Review the success of different approaches in your own and parallel markets as part of general corporate strategy reviews.

CONCLUSION

No one paradigm dominates another. Our research indicates that companies should consider the variety of models of customer management that might work in their market, identifying which might be best for their market as a whole and for particular segments. They should review the extent to which these approaches have really been successful in their own and parallel markets. This review should take place as part of a general corporate strategy review, for each paradigm requires its own operational structure, processes, systems, and policies. There's no point choosing a marketing model that sits badly with other functional strategies. Perhaps most important of all, companies should keep a close watch on the preferred paradigms of their most valued customers—but with a skeptical eye. Often a paradigm only works because customers have been offered nothing better.

FOR MORE INFORMATION

Journal Article:
Stone, M., et al. "The Future of Relationship Marketing: Towards Transparent Marketing?" *Journal of Database Marketing* 6, 1 (1998): 11–23.

See also:
☆ Managing the Challenge of E-service (pp. 223–224)

"We should never be allowed to forget that it is the customer who, in the end, determines how many people are employed and what sort of wages companies can afford to pay."

Alfred Robens

Viewpoint: Patty Seybold
Taking Managers Online for the Customer Revolution

Introduction

Patty Seybold is best known for her 1998 book *Customers.com*. The book's timing was impeccable. At a time when many companies were wrestling with the strategic and operational implications of the Internet, she argued that customers should come first. "What's the formula for success?" she asked. "Make it easy for customers to do business with you!"

In her new book, *Outside Innovation*, Patty Seybold reveals the next huge leap forward in business strategy. Companies are accelerating innovation and staying ahead of the pack by engaging with customers at every level of their business to co-design products and services, business processes, information and knowledge as well as distribution and business models.

What is the most important thing and who is the most important person to have influenced your thinking on business and management? Why?

My father, John W. Seybold, taught me how to spot and understand emerging technologies, to envision how they would transform businesses and industries, and how to build consensus and shared vision among cross-functional teams to achieve business transformation one step at a time. He also taught me the basic information architecture design principle of keeping form, content, and business rules separate and allowing them to dynamically reformat appropriate offerings based on context.

He developed a tagging system for text, which allowed him to reformat the same text in different ways for different purposes. One of the first texts he worked with was the Bible. The tagging system meant that he could reformat it in lots of different ways. His seminal work in this area paved the way for the creation of SGML, HTML, and the World Wide Web.

Robert Fritz taught me how the creative process works and how to harness structural tension to achieve business goals. From him I learned the principles of designing a "path of least resistance" that enables people to achieve their shared goals without struggle.

Nancy Post, the founder of Systems Energetics, taught me that the principles of Chinese acupuncture work as well in human systems as they do in human beings. Information, combined with spirit, flows through organizations. This organizational Ch'i can either heal and keep the organization vital, or become blocked and cause dysfunction. I discovered on my own that customer information and interactions are the most cleansing and healing form of organizational information flow. If you truly bathe your organization with customers' input, feedback, priorities, and out-comes, you can keep it vital and thriving. So, we use customers' most critical scenarios, outcomes, and moments of truth to inform the priority-setting and consensus-building within the companies with which we work. We use customer metrics to keep employees, partners, and suppliers focused on delivering a high-quality customer experience with profitability.

Fernando Flores, the Chilean-born philosopher and cognitive scientist, taught me that people and information systems use the same commitment management protocols across cultures (request/offer, negotiate conditions of satisfaction, agree, perform, report completion, assess, accept). This understanding of how humans manage their work together, despite cultural differences, enables me to help clients design new business processes that combine information, technology, and people.

Doug Engelbart, the father of the ARPAnet (which preceded the Internet) and inventor of most of the tools and concepts we are still perfecting today, taught me how to use networked technology to augment human intelligence, and how to observe and improve knowledge creation and management.

How will business be different in the 21st century?

At the end of the 20th century, the most successful companies were the ones that "made it easy for customers to do business with them." In the 21st century, the most profitable businesses will be the ones that have discovered how to "make it easy for customers to get things done." Instead of designing our business strategies from the inside out, our strategies will be designed from the outside in—by customers seeking to transform and streamline their own lives and business processes. For example, Lego invited its customers to co-design its next generation Mindstorm NXT product line so that it would meet their needs,

ensuring a blockbuster success with built-in customer champions.

Successful companies will be highly adaptive and customer-centric. They will be what I call "sense-and-pro-act" organizations. They will recognize new patterns very quickly—especially in customer behavior. To do so they will require real-time information about that behavior. Being able to identify and act on these new patterns and trends more quickly than their competitors will be vital to their success. At Cisco Systems, for example, all senior managers are now required to spend at least 50% of their time talking to customers.

The way that companies are organized will also change. Federated and networked organizations—extended enterprises—will be the norm. In the past, companies have either been highly centralized, with command and control structures, or highly distributed with autonomous business units, and they have tended to swing from one extreme to the other. They are now beginning to figure out how they can combine the best attributes of these two models to create federal organizations.

Another important change will be a more sophisticated approach to measuring profitability. There will be a move toward customer P&Ls (profit and loss information) rather than product line P&Ls. How we understand a brand will also shift from the notion of brand that is evoked through advertising to one that views the brand as a customer experience. So companies will make operational changes based on enhancing the branded customer experience.

This involves a move to what I call Quality of Customer Experience (QCE) management. Concepts like total quality management and reengineering became movements as companies recognized that they had to adopt them to remain competitive. But TQM didn't really translate into service industries. QCE management will be the variant that takes root in service companies, but it also applies to manufacturing. It is much more dynamic than TQM. QCE management means being prepared to change processes in response to customer demands. Companies will reorient themselves around two-way relationships with customers.

This will lead to customer-managed relationships rather than customer relationship or sales management. This will also pave the way for just-in-time customization of most products and services

What new skills set will be needed to cope with these changes?

I've already talked about the ability to sense and respond quickly to new patterns and to customer demands. This has implications all the way up the supply chain. There are, for example, 200 or so sub-component suppliers for a Nokia handset. If there is a change in the market, the commitments in the supply chain need to be renegotiated very rapidly. The ability to manage dynamically changing commitments across organizational boundaries will be vital.

The ability to identify, codify, package, use, and continuously improve core knowledge, services, and/or capabilities will also be very important. Successful companies will be adept at self-examination to

identify what their core competencies are—again it's dynamic because customer behavior will be changing in real time—and then repackage them to meet new and emerging customer requirements. Say that a company recognizes it has a core competence in project management. The next question is, how can that be repackaged as a service that meets a customer need? In the old economy we were dealing with the allocation of scarce resources. In the customer economy the key resource is knowledge about and relationships with customers. That is infinite. The more you give the more you get. It is an infinite resource.

So the intellectual capital I'm interested in is customer capital. That will be embedded in the minds of employees and in the organization, but it will also be embedded in the company's relationships with its customers. The more customer capital you have, the more successful you are likely to be in meeting customer needs. It's not a case of just milking the knowledge, it's about building relationships which create new value for customers. Leaders will also need the ability to combine vision and strategy and attention to customer-critical detail in day-to-day operations.

How can managers best develop these required skills?

The best way to cultivate these skills is to apprentice with those who already have them. Managers-in-training should be rotated through positions under the people who already embody these skills, rather than being rotated through functional or geographic responsibilities.

Are there new management questions we should be asking? If so, what are they?

What's our customer strategy? Which types of customers do we want to have deeper relationships with? Which types of customers would we like to attract? Do we know what our customers' and prospects' underlying emotional motivations are? Do we know what outcomes our customers need to accomplish? Are we measuring ourselves on our ability to help our customers achieve their outcomes? Do we know which customer scenarios are most important for each group of customers? Are we monitoring the quality of customer experience we're delivering on these customer-critical scenarios? How are we doing on the quality of the branded customer experience we're delivering? How are we doing in increasing our value to customers and the profitability of our customers for our business? These are the questions that managers should be asking.

How can companies best promote enterprises that are a) profitable and b) good places for people to work?

Employees will be drawn to enterprises that care about and deliver value to their customers. They will want and value clear customer-focused goals and metrics. These include metrics for customer value, customer outcomes, and the quality of customer experience. Customer-focused companies give employees a sense of mission, purpose, and value, and they are the most profitable companies in the world.

Viewpoint: B. Joseph Pine II
Transforming Business by Making It an Experience

Introduction

Joe Pine has the distinction of having written not one, but two books that will be seen as seminal in the 21st century. In *Mass Customization*, he showed how companies can efficiently provide individually customized goods and services. And, with co-author James Gilmore, Joe advanced the idea in *The Experience Economy* that goods and services are no longer enough—they're becoming basic commodities; what customers want today are experiences. Here, Joe tells not only what these books mean to management, but how they essentially interconnect and project what they will mean to leaders in the businesses of tomorrow.

As big a shift as is happening in business today, in 50 years the business world will undergo an even more dramatic shift.

It was almost exactly 50 years ago that the economy shifted from an industrial base to a service base. It was the mass production of goods that made America the number one economic power in the world, but beginning around 1950, more people began to earn their incomes from delivering intangible services than from making physical goods or extracting natural commodities. It took, however, almost 30 years for the trend to be fully recognized, at which time many pundits and professors decried the very notion that an economy could be built on anything other than the hard and tangible. Remember all the complaints about manufacturing jobs going away, about production moving offshore, about the very hollowing of America? We don't hear those particular protests any longer, even though the goods and commodities sectors combined have shrunk to less than 15% of employment and GDP. Indeed, it was the very loss of such jobs that opened the door to all the entrepreneurial talent that has made today's business world such a dynamic place through service innovations.

No, what we hear today are the exact same complaints about service jobs! They're now the ones going away, being automated and offshored, once again bringing dismay and raising concern. The cause behind both issues is the same: commoditization. Customers—whether consumers or businesses—want them sold at the lowest possible price, with the greatest convenience, and the least amount of time. Therefore, companies must lower their costs, and that means get rid of as many people as possible.

That also means it's time to shift to another level of economic value, beyond commodities, goods, and services. What customers do value today are experiences—memorable events that engage them in an in-

herently personal way. The prototypical experience is, of course, going to Walt Disney World. Sure, one buys food and parking services, and goods as memorabilia; but the reason one goes is for that shared family experience that lasts for months and even years afterwards. Hard Rock Cafés serve food against the backdrop of staging memorable musical moments. Recreation Equipment Incorporated (REI) places 60-foot climbing mountains in its stores to get consumers to experience the goods before they buy them. And look at Starbucks. It takes the core commodity of its business—coffee beans worth two or three cents per cup—and turns the brewing of them into theater within the ambience of its venues and now can charge two to five dollars per cup! We are now entering an Experience Economy; those businesses—whatever their good or service line—that miss the shift to experiences will be marginalized.

But now let's look 50 years into the future. Then, experiences will also become commoditized, and businesses will need to shift again to sell a fifth and final economic offering: transformations. The Transformation Economy will be one in which companies guide customers to life-transforming experiences—where the customer is the product. It may sound like something out of H. G. Wells, but think more of Michael Douglas's film, *The Game*, in which the main character willingly plays a game that takes him way out of his comfort zone, challenges him as a human being, and transforms him at the end. Many companies are already naturally in the transformation business, in-

> **But now let's look 50 years into the future. Then, experiences will also become commoditized, and businesses will need to shift again to sell a fifth and final economic offering: transformations.**

"The professional service firm—with its obsession on clients and projects—must be the new organizational model."

Tom Peters

cluding fitness centers, hospitals, schools, and consultants. But today each of these charge for the mere service or experience, not for the transformation. In the future, they'll be paid based on the demonstrated outcome their customers achieve—and there is no greater economic value to be gained than helping someone achieve their aspirations.

So what's happening in the business world means that managers need a completely new skill set in order to prosper in the emerging Experience Economy and forthcoming Transformation Economies. They'll need a new skill set even to participate.

First, managers must realize that work is theater. I'm not using a metaphor here. Whenever workers are in front of guests, they are acting, and need to act in a way that turns the interaction into a memorable event. Managers, therefore, must help their workers take on a role, characterize that role, rehearse it, and then perform it on the bare stage of business.

Then, in terms guiding transformations, the key skills required are caring and empathy. We used to talk about understanding a customer's problems and then providing solutions. This is much more. Managers must care for individuals enough truly to understand their aspirations, and to help them achieve those aspirations. It was, I believe, a Woody Allen character who said "Sincerity—if you can fake that, you've got it made." Well, what I'm suggesting is no joke—you won't be able to fake empathy. The new economic landscape demands authenticity. Why? Educated, demanding customers simply will not deal with businesses that are little more than smoke and mirrors.

In this regard, my close friend and business partner, Jim Gilmore coined the term "worldview segmentation" to describe what's starting to happen in the business world. Jim's point is a good one: customers increasingly will not buy from, nor support, a business that does not share their own worldview. In the same way, people will not work for companies that are at odds with their worldviews. They'll do business with or work for only those enterprises that have the same set of values and make the same moral choices as they do. So everything that Jim and I talk about has both external and internal implications. Just as companies must stage experiences and guide transformations to forestall commoditization in their industries, so they must stage authentic, life-transforming internal experiences to enable employees to achieve their work aspirations, and become better workers, in all the senses that word implies. And just as companies must mass-customize their economic offerings to attract and keep customers, so must they mass-customize their compensation systems, development plans, and other internal resources to attract and keep their workers.

Mass-customization is not at all ancillary to this discussion. My work there led to the discovery of experiences and transformations as distinct economic offerings. I recognized that mass-customizing a good automatically turned it into a service, that mass-customizing services turned them into experiences, and mass-customizing experiences turned them into transformations.

Therefore, I owe a great debt to Stan Davis, who first coined the term "mass-customizing" in his compelling and terrific 1987 book, *Future Perfect*. I first read it when I was a strategic planner at IBM in the late 1980s, and it changed my life. During the development of the AS/400 computer system, I managed a cross-functional team that brought customers and business partners into the development process. And through that project I learned that every customer was unique. They wanted different characteristics for their systems, they wanted different software, they wanted to integrate the systems in different ways. We had designed the system for a large, homogenous marketplace that simply did not exist! So when I read Stan Davis's book, it suddenly all made sense. I worked to get his ideas into IBM's plans and strategies, and when the company sent me to the Massachusetts Institute of Technology (MIT) to get my master's degree, I spent that entire time investigating the subject further. I eventually turned my thesis into my first book, *Mass Customization*, for which I was proud that Stan consented to write the introduction.

As I think back to that time, what's amazing is how it all really connects. Building a physical good that's unique for each and every customer—as IBM learned to do with computers—is part and parcel of providing a special experience that connects in a unique way to each and every guest. As we move to the Experience Economy and, eventually, through it to the Transformation Economy, it's crucial to understand that experiences happen *inside* each person individually—and aspirations *belong* to each person in unique ways. Goods and services are becoming commodities today; there's nothing special about them. Leaders who want to make their businesses stand out will have to do more. They'll have to stage memorable experiences for their customers, and they'll have to help their customers become the people (or businesses) they desire to be.

FOR MORE INFORMATION

Books:
Davis, Stan. *Future Perfect*. Boston, MA: Perseus, 1997.
Pine, B. Joseph II. *Mass Customization*. Boston, MA: Harvard Business School Press, 1999.
Pine, B. Joseph II, and James H. Gilmore. *The Experience Economy*. Boston, MA: Harvard Business School Press, 1999.

Web site:
Strategic Horizons: **www.strategichorizons.com**

See also:

"There is far more involved in the relationship with customers than just providing good products and services."

Mark Moody-Stuart

Delivering and Delighting—
A New Spirit at Work
by Richard C. Whiteley

EXECUTIVE SUMMARY

- Although much has been written about customer-centered companies and although many have tried to create them, even today few organizations have broken through to become truly customer centered.
- Often the underlying reason for a corporation's inability to put the customer at its center is what appears to be a standoff between its leaders and employees.
- The key to ending this impasse is to determine what conditions need to exist for employees to embrace the customer-centered way of operating and to teach or encourage corporate leaders to create those conditions.

INTRODUCTION

In speeches and company visits over many years, I have often been asked the same questions. Lower level managers, usually in a service function, ask; "How can I get senior management to believe in delighting customers as much as I believe in it?" With executives, the question flips: "How can I get our people to pay attention to our customers?" These questions mirror the frustration of many organizations trying to reorient themselves around customers. Too often, neither leaders nor employees seem to be committed; worse, each side seems to be blaming the other. Managers must create four conditions to help employees feel a genuine passion for serving the customer; happily, there are three best practices that leaders can employ to create this most desired attitude.

CREATE CONDITIONS FOR CHANGE

The complexity, challenge, and time required for an organization to become truly customer-centric are usually underestimated. It is not just about introducing a new program, training customer contact people to smile over the phone, or conducting a few customer focus groups. Rather, it is about changing the culture of the organization, a challenge that may seem as difficult as, say, rewiring your own DNA. The most successful and dramatic transformation of an organization's culture I have witnessed took place in the 1980s and was led by Sir Colin Marshall at British Airways. When he arrived at the government-owned airline BOAC, it was losing money, abusing cus-

tomers, and not doing well by its employees. Several years after Sir Colin privatized the company, it was commended for having the most improved service in the industry and for being the most profitable airline in the world. By any standard this remains one of the classic cultural turnarounds.

Study the BA success and others like it and patterns emerge of management actions that help create conditions that assist each and every employee to commit to the new direction and engage in the personal change that is required to bring the customer into the equation at all levels of the organization. These actions are to

1 articulate and promote the new direction;
2 make sure that each employee knows what is expected;
3 see that each employee has the skills to do what is expected;
4 motivate each employee to do what is expected.

Looking at these four conditions, it is clear that they are deeply based in common sense. But you would be amazed at how difficult it is to implement them. Common sense, it has been said many times, is unfortunately not common at all.

MAKING IT HAPPEN ▶▶
Articulate and Promote the New Direction

A study by Bain & Company asked C.E.O.s to rate their level of confidence in their ability to perform various aspects of their job. Of those asked, 85% felt they handled strategy development well; strategy

execution, conversely, dropped off dramatically to 40%. When asked about aligning their people with their company's strategy, the response was an anemic 10%. Articulating and promoting the new direction speaks directly to this deficit.

- **Create a clear vision and value statement to direct the organization.** This is not a new idea (and for many managers it may fall into the category of been there, done that); many organizations have vision and value statements that seem to have little influence on day-to-day operations and decisions. It helps to have a vision and values audit to test the extent to which adopted vision and values are truly guiding the company and having a positive impact.

- **Share the strategy of the organization with all employees.** Ironically, a company's strategy is often deemed so confidential that it is not shared with employees, the people who have to make it happen. Sam Walton knew better; his policy was to share each Wal-Mart store's vital performance information with all employees, even part-timers. He reasoned that they were directly responsible for Wal-Mart's success.

- **Actively promote the new direction.** When Sydney Electricity first won Australia's national quality award, I asked C.E.O. John Gillespie what his most difficult challenge was in achieving this honor. He responded that continually selling the vision, repeating it with enthusiasm over and over again at every meeting with one or more of his employees, was the hardest. It simply is not good enough to send an e-mail to all employees stating the new direction.

Make Sure Each Employee Knows What Is Expected

In a multiyear research program that studied 400 organizations, 80,000 managers, and over one million employees, the Gallup Organization found that one of the factors that correlated

---

"Both suppliers and customers must be treated as partners and collaborators."

Michael Dell

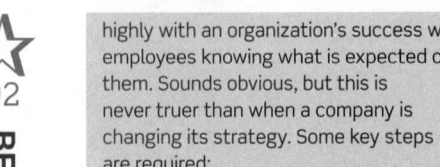

highly with an organization's success was employees knowing what is expected of them. Sounds obvious, but this is never truer than when a company is changing its strategy. Some key steps are required:

- **Use the chain of command to discuss and explain what is expected.** When Michael Abrashoff, the commanding officer of the U.S.S. Benfold, took command of the beleaguered, poorly performing destroyer, he first had to establish new standards of behavior. He met in small groups with his 300 officers and enlisted men and women to make sure that they understood the rationale for the changes he was implementing and what their personal impact would be. Under his command the ship went on to establish training, readiness, and retention records and won the coveted Spokane Trophy for operational readiness.
- **Use your hierarchy to communicate new expectations.** Have all managers meet with their people and explain the rationale for the change and what this means for them. The more a picture can be created of appropriate new behavior, the more it is likely to become part of each employee's daily routine.
- **Have employees create a line-of-sight map between them and your customers.** A simple yet powerful exercise: ask employees to start with their location in the organization and create a visual trail direct to customers. While most are not in direct contact with external customers, they all have internal customers within the organization. Employees soon realize that a glitch in the internal customer relationship inevitably leads to a problem for external customers.
- **Put the spotlight on early adopters.** In any organizational change there are fence sitters and early adopters. Fence sitters do little but sit around, complain about another program du jour, and adopt an attitude of "Change is good . . . you go first." In contrast the early adopters make a sincere (though sometimes awkward) effort at trying on the new behaviors to make the strategy work. Since peer success is a powerful influencer, purposely seek out these early adopters and publicly praise their efforts to change. Don't wait until all results are in; it's the effort to try things differently that

you are actually rewarding. Results will follow.

See That Each Employee Has the Skills to Do What Is Expected

Once people have an idea of what is expected, it is a mistake to assume that they actually have the necessary skills to accomplish the stated goals. Van Kampen Investments, a mutual fund company that consistently wins its industry's top award for customer service, believes that the key to this success is employee training. How to start?

- **Conduct internal best practices research.** Identify best performers in each job category and compare them with their marginally performing counterparts. Identify what superior performers do distinctly. Once critical competences are identified, training exercises can be created to develop these skills in every employee.
- **Conduct a strategic training audit.** This simple process will pay great dividends. Create a matrix that lists the critical competencies required for each job in your company on the left vertical axis and each of your training programs along the top horizontal axis. Then, on a scale of 1 to 5, simply rate each program's contribution to the development of each competency. This will help purge redundant programs and fill gaps in competency development.
- **Make your employees your best trainers.** Rather than assigning all development to your company trainers, make it part of employees' jobs to help. Pret A Manger is a highly successful chain of sandwich shops in the United Kingdom (and now the United States) with legendary service. Many frontline staff (half!) have been promoted to Team Manager Trainer, responsible for training new hires.

Motivate Each Employee to Do What Is Expected

Now comes the hard part: getting people to actually use newly developed skills. Assuming that the compensation and reward system is running smoothly, what are some of the other practices that can create an organization-wide passion for serving the customer?

- **Get everyone in the game.** In recent years much has been written about participative management. Why? Because it works. This means engaging in practices like asking employees to

help create the vision and values, seeking their opinions on strategic issues, inviting them to innovate and create new processes, and authorizing them to solve problems now—without having to go through layers of approval. A survey of 551 large employers by Watson Wyatt found that people are more motivated when they believe they have an important place in the organization.
- **Introduce the face of the customer.** Of course, appropriate metrics based on customer behavior and feedback are also essential. While the *voice of the customer* continues to be a critical driver here, consider introducing *the face of the customer*. This means finding ways to personalize the metrics. For example, videotape focus groups and share the results with every employee. Medical products manufacturer Medtronics keeps employees focused on its real purpose by bringing doctors' patients and their families into the company to share their stories of survival. Such sessions are both inspiring and moving.
- **Make it fun.** With the seriousness and sometimes outright fear caused by downsizings, mergers, stock price collapses, increased working hours, and a near-maniacal focus on quarterly earnings, all too often the fun has been squeezed out of work. Last year the United States lost $1.5 billion in productivity to stress-related absenteeism. This is more than the total profitability of the *Fortune* 500. It is the unquestioned responsibility of leaders to help put the fun back in to work. In a survey of 1,000 peak performers, Louis Harris and Associates asked what kind of workplace they would be reluctant to leave. Their answer? One that promotes fun.

CONCLUSION

Changing an organization's culture is always a complex, even daunting, task. In order to become customer-centered the leaders of a corporation must first be willing to change themselves. It is their responsibility to create the four conditions cited above that will support each and every employee in understanding the new direction, knowing what is expected, and having the skills and motivation to do what is expected.

"One's own employees should be one's best customers."

FOR MORE INFORMATION

Book:

Sobel, Andrew, and Jagdish Sheth. *Clients for Life: How Great Professionals Develop Breakthrough Relationships*. New York: Simon & Schuster, 2000.

Web site:

www.theRITEstuff.com: an excellent resource that summarizes important research on customer, people, investor, and global best practices.

See also:

☆ Avoiding the Mistakes of the Past: Lessons from the Startup World (pp. 164–165)
✔ Extending a Product with Service (pp. 753–754)
✔ Handling Customer Inquiries (pp. 704–705)
✔ Implementing a Customer Relationship Management Strategy (pp. 708–709)
✔ Increasing Customer Lifetime Value (pp. 706–707)
☆ Managing 1:1 Marketing (pp. 63–64)
☆ Marketing: The Importance of Being First (pp. 69–70)
☆ Overcoming the Difficulties of Managing a Virtual Organization (pp. 241–242)
☆ The Second Coming of Service (pp. 104–105)

Marketing in the Internet Age
by Regis McKenna

EXECUTIVE SUMMARY

- Traditional marketing is event- rather than process-oriented. A new form of information logistics is replacing the old marketing. Marketing people haven't as yet caught on.
- The Internet offers a major new vehicle for marketing to reassert its central role in enhancing company value around core assets such as customers, value propositions, partnerships, and brands.
- Successful marketing companies use technology to build, leverage, and promote a powerful, customer oriented business infrastructure.

INTRODUCTION

Most everyone recognizes the Internet as a powerful communications tool, but when it comes to marketing, two questions need to be asked:

1. How does the Internet affect or change the marketing process?
2. How is marketing practiced on the Internet and what room is there for improvement?

Perhaps the most important thing to say at the start is that *true* marketing is not about hype. Hype, of course, dominates the way many people think of marketing and, in particular, Internet marketing. Buzzword solutions, promoted as brands themselves and dispensed by branding consultants, proliferate. Terms such as "viral marketing" and "buzz" are some of the latest marketing buzzword brands used as new tactics for gaining the customer's attention. Too often, they end up cluttering the customer's inbox with junk mail. Don't go there. Marketing via the Internet offers the potential of a real-time connection to the customer and the enterprise value chain; the Internet increases the urgency and criticality of that role. Marketing should embrace activities ranging from managing the product/service analysis and user feedback, real-time interchange with solution partners, and alliances scaling demands, supply logistics, relationships management, and other key business processes that get little mention in the Internet marketing debate. If anything, Internet marketing magnifies the need for focused attention on the core essentials.

THE INTERNET: A UNIQUE VEHICLE

The Internet affects every facet of a company's value-delivery system, providing critical feedback and insight about the company and its partners/channels: the effi- ciency and effectiveness of its product/service design and delivery; who the customers are, what they think, and what they value; and how the competition is performing. Companies become great because they build sustainable business and service infrastructures that are superior to their competitors and leverage those infrastructures to deliver more value to each customer. The infrastructures that matter most are processes such as logistics, distribution, and services. The quality and customer's experience resulting experience of those business process is what customers perceive as a company's "position." Marketing should be critically linked to, if not driving, these processes, because it is visible to the customer and shapes the customer's perspective of the brand.

The Internet is, above all else, a unique vehicle for facilitating and enhancing the customer's role as an integral part of the processes and market infrastructure. I like to think about the network as a "learning channel" whereby the customer learns about the benefits of your products and service and you, the producer, gain knowledge about your customers in order to be responsive. It helps companies with strong and targeted value propositions develop much richer dialogue with their customers and, as a result, improve innovations in products and services to make the consumer experience richer and more relevant. An excellent example of this is Lego, which leveraged the Internet to develop and launch blockbuster products like Mindstorms. It also helps multi-channel companies like Intuit to deliver packaged software (Quicken, Quickbooks, and Turbo Tax) to enable consumers and small businesses to manage their financial activities and operations as well as link account information interactively to their banking and financial services. Companies like Wal-Mart and Dell, with thousands of customer interactions each day, have become places where those in charge of their Internet site must be total access architects stitching the entire corporate infrastructure to the advantage of the online customer. For example, Wal-Mart updates its customer database every 90 minutes and uses that to keep its inventory supple. Old-style marketing could never keep track of a customer that rapidly, and neither could companies that simply market by buzzwords.

CURRENT INTERNET MARKETING: MUCH ROOM FOR IMPROVEMENT

Much of today's marketing activities such as branding and media advertising are, in my view disconnected from reality. As consumers, we are well aware that rarely do products and services meet, much less exceed our expectations. Promotion, however, must have a certain "unreality" about it in order to attract attention. However, attention does not necessarily lead to brand loyalty. Advertising, for example, is often considered "the sizzle" and not the "steak." Too many marketing people are not prepared for the information age. Too many know very little about the real benefits of the product/service they are promoting, or about the competition's strengths and weakness, or about the support infrastructure required to achieve consistent customer satisfaction. As a result, much of promotion we see today is pure, cosmetic fantasy—that's essentially what many marketers call branding.

Because it is a radically new landscape, the networked marketplace or Internet has yet to see a consistent set of marketing principles applied to it. As a result, a series of myths have grown up around the Internet as a marketing medium, myths that have proven expensive and often disastrous to many marketers who have not taken the time to understand this new medium.

Myth 1: The Internet Is a Great Customer Acquisition Vehicle.

True, it is easier and cheaper to use the Internet than, say, television advertising. However, I would content that long-term customer relationship building is an investment and must be continually adapted, constantly renewed and reviewed, as well as addressed in multiple ways and modes. The

Internet is a great communicating vehicle once the customer has established a need or want. But even that does not build long-term loyalty. Loyalty or brand building is not easy. "Brand," by its very nature, implies loyalty over time. That means that the producer and consumer must establish a history of reliable and responsive experiences. On the other hand, the Internet encourages competitive shopping and has an anonymity that screens the customer's decision-making process from direct influence. In effect, the Internet often encourages disloyalty because of the almost limitless choices it presents. The consumer abandons a very high percentage of online "shopping carts." This new media is presently an entirely new experience for both producers and consumers.

Myth 2: The Internet Is a Great Messaging and Advertising Medium.

The Internet is more complex than any broadcast media. First of all, the Internet is real-time interactive. Second, whereas a few hundred channels limit broadcast media at most with fixed content, there are millions of channels (sources of information) available to access on the Internet and those channels are not limited by geographic boundaries. Second, the content on the Internet is a virtual tsunami of information that is—by in large—generated by the consumers themselves. Third, the Internet is not limited by "viewing times." Most studies show today that consumers are multiplexing their time. That is surfing the Internet while listening to music or watching television or talking on their cell phones. This is particularly true of younger consumers. Search engines have become the new "link" to engaging the consumer. As the consumer surfs the Internet, his or her *interests* are responded to by the intelligent listening nature of the search engine that links those interests to specific products or solutions. The consumer—or what I call "market driven," not "marketing driven," drives the process. Thus, access replaces broadcast. We are still learning how to use this new medium effectively and wisely so as to engender trust from the consumer.

Myth 3: The Internet Makes 1:1 Marketing a Reality.

The programmability aspect of computers and software applications makes 1:1 marketing possible. CRM (Customer Relationship Management), after all, is a software approach to managing a large customer base as well as enabling those services repre-

sented in software to adapt to each customer's need. "Web services" is the infrastructure management system that coordinates all the underlying functions for compliance, security, referencing customer history, and so forth. Companies such as BEA Systems, IBM/WebSphere, SalesForce.com, Siebel, and others have pioneered the new information age marketing infrastructure. Listening and responding technologies are now pervasive, from the ATM to the checkout counter to the remote network-management console. Marketing as a promotional game has yet to recognize these systems as the new tools for building brand.

MARKETING IN THE INTERNET AGE

Such myths make most current Internet marketing practices only marginally valuable and successful. We need to think not about Internet marketing but about *marketing in the Internet age*—the totality of the marketing challenge in an age where business processes are increasingly mediated by the Internet and its underlying intelligent infrastructure.

The challenge for marketers in the Internet age is *marketing at the core*. It requires an understanding of customer pain points (an ability to listen rather than talk), a more-than-passing familiarity with the economics of cost-to-serve and, above all, an approach to customers that is based upon a life-cycle relationship management process.

As an example of the importance of marketing as a repository of customer business process expertise, Citibank has one of the more highly developed Internet-based innovation and marketing strategies in the financial services sector. The company has applied superior marketing insight into the way technology can completely change the value proposition to a key target market: corporate C.F.O.s. These customers have traditionally been served by "service-silos" in which one service is not coordinated or even aware of the other within the same business, but customers want one interface access to multiple services. Innovative marketers like Citibank understand that C.F.O.s are really interested in managing their day-to-day activities in a much more integrated fashion. The result has been measurable share gain in corporate financial services. Instead of driving temporary product *differentiation*, they have used Internet platforms to deliver sustainable business value to customers via effective process *integration*.

MAKING IT HAPPEN ▶▶

To separate hype from true Internet marketing, you must answer at least seven questions:

- How does the Web deliver value to customers, business partners, and my own company?
- Who am I serving with my Web presence, and do the economics deliver enough return to the value network to justify the use of the Web?
- What is the whole product that I need to bring to my Web business, including, where necessary, non-Web components and partnership components?
- How do I guarantee extraordinary value delivery on the Web, manage that value delivery over time for my customers, and build brand value from that total customer experience?
- How does the Web fit into that total relationship with the customer and why? What roles should it play at different stages of the relationship?
- Where should the Web fit organizationally so that it leverages and enhances my total marketing strategy and implementation plan?
- How do I measure success in terms of new customers, repeat customers, loyal customers, total revenue and margin growth, new product success rates, partner business and profitability growth?

The Web is indeed a revolutionary technology: millions of people are now online worldwide. The next millions will surely be from emerging economies in India, China, Latin America, and elsewhere. This expansion will present yet another challenge for marketers. All the new technologies such as search engines, CRM, and Web services have emerged from software developers and not from the traditional sources of marketing expertise. Future marketers will have to learn how to apply creative skills within the context of real-time information networks where the consumer controls the dialog.

CONCLUSION

Marketing, like TQM, has become "everybody's job." From the C.E.O. and C.I.O. to the salesperson and retail partner, the strategy and implementation must be well understood and renewed everyday. Competition is going to get more global and more intense, and only those who excel as a total business entity will be successful.

"Marketing takes a day to learn. Unfortunately, it takes a lifetime to master." Philip Kotler

Finally, the new, interactive and digital technologies have enabled the convergence of marketing and IT. With that in mind, I suggest marketers redefine marketing as a continuous process of organizational learning and the subsequent adaptation of the business to technological, market and customer ever-changing dynamics.

Marketing is a business process rather than an event, enabling product and service providers to acquire and apply knowledge efficiently by interacting with customers and the marketplace. They are then able to innovate and respond competitively, reliably, consistently, and profitably.

FOR MORE INFORMATION

Web site:
Regis.com: **www.regis.com**

See also:
☆ The Business Web (pp. 182–183)

Viewpoint: Charles Handy
Elephants and Fleas

Introduction

Charles Handy remains the genteel, civilized voice of management. His first book, *Understanding Organizations* (1976), gave little hint of the social and philosophical enquiries to come. In *The Age of Unreason* (1989) and *The Age of Paradox* (1994), Handy coined some of the most useful management concepts of recent years and explored federalism in an engagingly accessible way.

For all his gentleness, Handy's ideas have a subversive edge. In *The Elephant and the Flea* (2001) he returned to the theme of the changing landscape of working life, focusing on the symbiotic relationship between large companies (elephants) and small businesses (fleas), which include free agents and entrepreneurs inside and outside the organization.

What is the most important thing and who is the most important person to have influenced your thinking?

I read lots of things and listen to lots of people and absorb them. I take bits and pieces. I like a lot of what Gary Hamel says, for example, but probably because it confirms my own prejudices.

The major influences on my thinking have been my life experiences and my wife Elizabeth. She pushed me to step outside organizational life and focus on what I do best—which I think is writing—and to make a business out of that. So I'd say it was the experience of my own life, prodded by my wife, and then influenced by people like Peter Drucker, Gary Hamel, and the American social critic Jeremy Rifkind.

How will business be different in the 21st century?

It will be more shapeless, in the sense that in the past 50 years we had things called companies, and they really were companies—groups of people bound together with roughly the same purpose. Businesses now are much more a collection of globules—partnerships and alliances.

I see business now as much more of a federal creation than it was—a series of autonomous organizations that includes universities, government, and different groupings of people. We are groping toward new ways of thinking about businesses.

What new skills will be needed to cope with these changes?

Key skills will be the ability to win friends and influence people at a personal level, the ability to structure partnerships, and the ability to negotiate and to find compromises. Business will be much more about finding the right people in the right place and negotiating

the right deals. So in a funny way the functions that will be the most important are recruitment and purchasing. It's ironic that neither of these has traditionally been seen as the star.

Conceptual skills are also becoming much more important. There used to be a big distinction between managerial and technical skills. The ability to analyze numbers was considered most important then. In the last 20 years, the softer, human skills have become more important. But it is conceptual skills that are now coming to the fore. They are what the federal organization is all about.

The new workforce wants to contribute to humankind in some way as well as earning a livelihood. Finding a way to describe a cause is important and useful. The why is as important as the what and the who.

> Key skills will be the ability to win friends and influence people at a personal level, the ability to structure partnerships, and the ability to negotiate and to find compromises. Business will be much more about finding the right people in the right place and negotiating the right deals.

Does this change the role of leadership?

A good C.E.O. spends at least half his or her time on people. The shift now is to the C.E.O. as teacher and missionary, persuading people that his or her priorities are important to them.

Conceptualizing is increasingly important. I think strategy now is much more to do with defining—or conceptualizing—what your organization is all about. A lot of the old thinking about strategy is out of date.

Look at Jack Welch. He is a great self-publicist. He had great conceptual skills. His strategy in the early

"We were not destined to be empty raincoats, nameless numbers on a payroll . . . If that is to be its price, economic progress is an empty promise."

Charles Handy

days was that he only wanted businesses that were number one or number two in their markets. But he later reversed that. He realized that GE was becoming complacent, so he reframed his message. He said to his people: "Redefine your market so that you only have 10% market share." He forced them numerically to stretch their horizons and broaden their outlook. That sort of conceptualizing is increasingly import-ant. His human skills were also very important.

How do you develop these sorts of skills?

I once said that education is experience understood in tranquility, and I think that's true. The only way people learn these conceptual skills is by being pushed into roles that are just beyond their grasp, so they are out of their depth and have to stretch them-selves. You need to support them, of course, and for-give them when they get it wrong. I don't like the words mentor and coach. Michael Young has a term "educational companion," which I prefer. Organiza-tional companions could be one way to help man-agers learn these skills.

Are there new management questions we should be asking?

The new management questions aren't really new but they have a new urgency. In my new book I talk about the disappearing middle. The middles of whole indus-tries are disappearing. Take publishing, which is one I am familiar with. At present there is a long chain of processes and organizations between me as an author and the reader. Everything in this chain of distribution is now in doubt, apart from the beginning and the end—the author and the reader. How the first con-nects with the second is now open to a wide range of options.

We could dispense with the physical bookstore, the option focused on by Amazon.com and its imitators. Jeff Bezos says I can connect these two points in dif-ferent ways. The publisher too could choose to bypass wholesalers and bookstores and publish electronic-ally. Or, if I was intrepid enough as the author, I could bypass the lot of them and put my words on a Web site for anyone to download for a fee.

This phenomenon of disappearing middles—disin-termediation—allows newcomers to insert them-selves into the gaps. The question for managers is: how do we redefine ourselves if we're in the middle?

It's quite hard for elephants to do. That's where fleas come in. Elephants are there to connect the tal-ent to the customer, so the fleas need the elephants. But the elephants need the fleas, too, to create new value and to spur innovation.

What will happen to the concept of the career in the future?

It will be a professional career path and not an organ-izational one. People increasingly define themselves by their profession, and the definition of profession is much wider. It includes everything from beauty tech-nician to chef and even sanitary engineer. We're all professionals now.

Very few jobs in future will be defined as jobs. Those that are—like checkout cashier—will disappear. There will be customer relationship managers or something like that. So people will either be profes-sionals or entrepreneurs—fleas in short.

To promote your career you may work in a large or-ganization—an elephant—for a while to gain skills and expertise. You may go back to elephants periodically to upgrade your skills or credentials. But you will have to take responsibility for your own career and life.

It starts as a mental thing. So think customers, not jobs. Think skills, not grades. What can you sell that is useful to other people? One day you will need to do that. One day you will be a flea.

How can companies best promote enterprises which are a) profitable and b) good places for people to work?

Elephants have to become venture capitalists for the people within their own organizations. If people come up with a good idea that fits with the brand, the organ-ization should back it with money and time.

Look at what Ricardo Semler has done with Semco. "We don't have a strategy," he says, "it emerges from the initiatives that come up from the front line." For example, the company makes and erects cooling towers. From talking to cus-tomers, the Semco people heard lots of complaints that the towers kept breaking down because of mainten-ance problems. "We know how to maintain them," they thought. So they said to the customers: "If we take on maintenance we want 60 percent of the saving you'll make from preventing breakdowns". Then they went to the Semco board and said: "We want to keep 20% of the 60% ourselves". The board said OK. So Semco is acting like a venture capitalist for its own people.

Or look at GE. When Jack Welch said "redefine your market so that you have less than 10%," GE was ba-sically acting as a VC to its people, encouraging them to look for new business opportunities. It's more than just money. It's about persuading people that they can build a business, create something new. People have to believe they can leave a footprint in the sand.

> **The new workforce wants to contribute to humankind in some way as well as earning a livelihood. Finding a way to describe a cause is important and useful. The why is as important as the what and the who.**

FOR MORE INFORMATION

Books:

Handy Charles. *The Age of Unreason*. Boston, MA: Harvard Business School Press, 1989.

Handy, Charles. *The Age of Paradox*. Boston, MA: Harvard Business School Press, 1994

Handy, Charles. *The Elephant and the Flea*. Boston, MA: Harvard Business School Press, 2002.

Handy, Charles. *Myself and Other More Important Matters*. London: Heinemann, 2006.

"Managers have been brought up on a diet of power, divide and rule. They have been pre-occupied with authority, rather than making small things happen."
Charles Handy

Strategy in Turbulent Times
by Costas Markides

INTRODUCTION

In our turbulent and uncertain times it is tempting for companies to wonder whether they do actually require a strategy. They do.

By way of proof, imagine that you find yourself in the middle of a dark and hostile jungle. If you want to get out of the jungle, do you need a strategy?

Think about it. In the dense foliage you cannot see farther than a few feet. You want to get out of this jungle, but you don't know how and you don't know which way to turn. There is total uncertainty. How then can you get out alive? Well, the last thing you want to do is to stay still, paralyzed by uncertainty. You need to analyze your position based on the available information and then decide on a direction. That's the first principle of strategy—the need to make difficult choices based on what information you have at the time. You take stock, gather information based on that, and then start walking. The worst thing is to stay still. That's the second principle of strategy—the need to stop analyzing and start doing, even if you are not entirely sure that what you are doing is going to turn out to be the right thing.

After you start walking, new information comes your way. The new information may allow you to revise your original direction. That's the third principle of strategy—the need to learn as you go along and modify your strategy through trial and error. If you meet a wild animal or run into a canyon, your strategy (or direction) has to change. Therefore, strategy is all about making difficult choices in the face of uncertainty and then learning as you go along and adjusting your original choices. When you think of it like this, it's obvious that you need a strategy—even (or especially) in times of uncertainty.

THE SEARCH FOR DIFFERENCE

If strategy is necessary, the next question is how to come up with a *differentiated* strategy.

In many industries competing companies have the same suppliers, are structured in much the same way, receive their information from the same sources, use the same consultants, and so on. They receive much the same information. And yet some pursue genuinely different strategies.

The difference lies in mental processing. How companies process the information around them will determine what they do.

Indeed, this is what differentiates the innovators from other companies. Most companies try to become better than their competitors. But for almost all companies other than the established leader, being better is not the right way. They need to play a different game. Look at EasyJet, e*trade, or Schwab. These are companies intent, not on being better, but on playing a different game. They thought of new ways of playing the game. The managers of these companies face the same information as everyone else in their industries, yet they process this information differently and come up with differentiated strategies. Companies get the same inputs, but it's what they do with the inputs to change the rules of the game that matters.

ESTABLISHED BUT DIFFERENT

Many established companies develop a winning strategy and then spend all their time trying to improve it and make it better. They rarely consider "cannibalizing" their current strategy in favor of a different one. They judge the risks of doing so too high. Yet all around us established companies are being toppled by newcomers that adopt different strategies.

The solution? Companies must continue to improve their existing strategies, but they must also continuously strive to discover new or different strategies. They should try to be better and different at the same time.

PLAYING TWO GAMES

The question is, How can a company play two games simultaneously? Harvard Business School's Michael Porter suggests that doing this is so difficult that most companies that attempt it will fail. His advice is for companies to focus on only one game. His Harvard colleague Clay Christensen suggests that a company can play two games at the same time, but that the new game needs to be separate from the main business.

My own research suggests that although it's difficult, companies can still play two games without necessarily separating them. More importantly, it implies that when es-

tablished companies are attacked by a new way of playing the game, they do not necessarily have to respond by adopting the new game.

What established companies need to appreciate is that the new, disruptive ways of playing the game are not God-sent. The new ways are not preordained to win out. Established companies could respond by killing off the new ways. For example, why is Internet banking the game of the future? Is it more convenient or more efficient than traditional banking? Why don't banks respond to Internet banking, *not* by adopting it, but by making their traditional operations so good that consumers simply wouldn't find banking over the Internet an attractive proposition?

CASES IN POINT

Look at what happened with Gillette back in the 1970s when it came under attack by Bic. The strategy adopted by Bic was certainly different from Gillette's. But Gillette didn't respond by adopting the Bic strategy. Instead, it invested $1 billion in its existing strategy to develop a superior product—the Mach 3—which was then used to destroy Bic and the disposable razor threat. Who buys disposable razors now?

Consider also the case of Swatch. In the 1970s the Swiss watchmakers competed on the basis of their craftsmanship. Then Japanese companies (like Seiko) attacked by offering better prices, the latest technology, more features. Everybody thought that this would be the end of the Swiss watch industry. Instead, Swatch hit back at the Japanese. But rather than trying to compete with them on their terms (that is, price and features), Swatch introduced a new competitive dimension—style and design—as the basis for competition.

Consider Merrill Lynch today. It competes on the basis of research and advice. Schwab and e*trade have now attacked it on the basis of cheaper transaction costs and faster execution of trades. Merrill Lynch will not succeed against them if it, too, chooses to play the price and speed game. What it has to do is innovate and discover new competitive dimensions—different reasons why a customer should buy from Merrill Lynch.

"Leaders with unruly, lowly minds will project and create turbulent and contaminated environments in their spheres of action."

S. K. Chakraborty

CONFUSING CREATIVITY AND INNOVATION

One of the problems is that the difference between innovation and creativity (or invention) is often misunderstood. Coming up with new ideas is not innovation—it's creativity. Innovation is deciding which ideas to select and implement to create value. A lot of research tends to emphasize creativity rather than innovation.

Innovation is about coming up with ideas and then finding ways to scale them up to create mass markets out of them. For example, consider the market for PCs. Who is the innovator in this market? Most people think the answer is Apple, or perhaps Osborne. But who really created the mass market for PCs? Who should be credited with the fact that the personal computer is not some high-tech gimmick that only nerds use, but is instead a fixture in every home? The answer is simple—IBM. IBM scaled it up. IBM created the mass market. Yet nobody considers IBM as an innovator.

Therefore, innovation is not just coming up with ideas but also scaling them up to create big markets. Most of the dot-coms failed because they didn't know how to sell to customers, to bring ideas to a mass market.

The trouble is that while coming up with ideas is celebrated as innovative, the act of scaling them up into big markets is not. Even worse, scaling up—rather than coming up with new ideas—is what big companies are good at, but they often forget this and try instead to become brilliantly creative like the small startups. Instead of taking the ideas of others and converting them into big markets, they focus on coming up with ideas themselves. Unfortunately, this is what small firms excel at.

CONVERTING BIG FIRMS INTO SMALL FIRMS

Over the last ten years we have tried to convert big firms into small firms. There's a lot of talk about injecting big corporations with the entrepreneurial culture of the small firm, or breaking up the big ones to make them as agile and flexible as the small ones. This won't happen. The big firm will never become as creative as the small firm. What the big corporation is good at is scaling up, not creativity. Our attention should shift toward making the big corporation better at what it is good at—not making it like the small ones.

We have a cultural bias in favor of coming up with ideas, and a real lack of appreciation for the challenging task of taking the idea and converting it into a mass market. Similarly, there is a bias in defining innovation as something new. But the real trick is how to convert something new from being a plaything of the few into the mass market.

MAKING IT HAPPEN ▸▸

If you ask a group of C.E.O.'s how to make their organizations more innovative, you'll get a long laundry list of ideas on how to do it—allow experiments, reward new ideas, don't punish mistakes, and so on. The problem is not that they don't know how to do it, but that it doesn't happen.

So why don't they do it? Senior executives know what they can do to promote innovation, but the personal risks are simply too high. Innovation carries a huge personal risk; how many people will actually put themselves on the line? After all, what they get evaluated on at the end of the year isn't generating innovative ideas, it's delivering the numbers.

Over and above this, we tend to forget that innovation is an art. Even if you have all the ingredients, it doesn't guarantee that you'll get innovation. The key is how you put it all together. The baking of the cake is more important than its raw materials.

To make it happen we need to train

people *how* to think, not what to think. We also need to give people a sense that organizations are not there simply to make money for individuals and the company, but that they have a social purpose in the community. The important thing is for young people to get into business not only because it's a good way to make money, but also because through their companies they can help create something that improves the state of the world.

Take the young people who worked as a team to develop the Apple Mac as an example. They weren't just making a computer, they were on a mission to change the way people thought about computers. In the end, galvanizing people isn't about money, but about having a purpose beyond money. Making money is implicit.

The modern corporation is very delicate. It must be able to make an accurate assessment of the external environment so it takes the right strategic position. In addition, the organization must also remain true to its unwritten moral contract with employees. This contract promises to provide employees with an environment that sustains them and allows them to grow as individuals.

This delicate balancing act requires a new kind of corporation, one with different structures, processes, mindsets, and behaviors than has been the norm for the last fifty years. We need to totally rethink how we manage corporations.

If they are to be flexible and fluid, companies need to become amoeba-like—able to move one way while always responding to local stimuli and changing direction in response to new information from the environment.

This can only be achieved by giving people autonomy and the freedom to monitor what's going on around them and respond as they see fit.

"When competencies are not developed at all levels, companies often get into trouble."

Ron Ashkenas

How to Get Lucky
by Donald N. Sull

EXECUTIVE SUMMARY

- Luck is too important to leave to chance.
- The most successful terms use the strategy of active waiting instead.
- Whatever your chosen strategy, remember that timing is everything: too early can be as bad as too late.

INTRODUCTION

In highly volatile markets, a company's success or failure is often attributed to luck. As no one can foresee the twists and turns the future holds; it is all a bit of a crap shoot. Turbulent markets produce opportunities and threats, whose timing, nature, and magnitude managers can neither predict nor control. In such a competitive casino, you place your bets and hope for the best.

The importance of luck in volatile situations is not new. Napoleon explained that he consistently won battles despite the disorder, uncertainty, and friction of war because he picked lucky generals. At first glance, this seems an odd explanation. How was Napoleon able to pick lucky generals any more than directors are able to pick lucky C.E.O.s?

Yet Napoleon was on to something important. Some companies consistently seize major opportunities and skirt crises that undo less fortunate competitors. Over the past six years I have studied more than twenty pairs of comparable companies in unpredictable industries (for example, telecommunications, airlines, enterprise software) and countries (for example, China and Brazil). By pairing similar companies, I could study how they responded differently to unforeseen threats and opportunities that both faced. Indeed, the more successful companies were luckier, in the sense that they consistently responded more effectively to volatile factors that influenced performance, such as unexpected shifts in regulation, technology, competition, and macroeconomics. They did not win through greater insight into the future—the executives at the more successful companies strenuously denied their ability to pierce the fog of an unpredictable future.

Luck is too important to leave to chance. The most successful companies exemplified *active waiting,* a strategy in highly unpredictable markets that consists of anticipating and preparing for opportunities and threats that executives can neither fully predict nor control. Rather than deluding themselves that they could make long-term predictions, executives in the more successful companies proceeded like generals leading armies forward into war: They conducted reconnaissance into the future to anticipate threats and opportunities that might emerge; they built a reserve of capital and managers to deploy when a golden opportunity or life-threatening crisis arose; they kept the troops battle-ready during lulls in the action; and periodically they committed their reserves to seizing a golden opportunity.

TIMING IS EVERYTHING

An executive is sometimes compared to the captain of a ship, standing at the helm in clear weather, peering through a telescope to the distant horizon and setting a clear course for the future. In many markets, however, the future is obscured by dense fog, and managing resembles driving a race car along a treacherous route in an impenetrable mist. The fog descends when multiple variables interact in ways that produce unpredictable opportunities and threats. Consider the telecommunications industry. Shifting regulations, continuous technological change, entry by non-traditional competitors like Google, competitive thrust and parry among established players, and shifts in consumer preferences combine and recombine in countless permutations to produce a steady stream of unforeseen opportunities and threats.

The good news is that unpredictable markets generate opportunities. Demand for automobiles in China, for example, arose from the confluence of increased disposable income, government investment in infrastructure, rising middle class aspirations, easy credit, and the demise of employer-provided housing. Turbulent markets often generate new resources, such as innovative technology like the Internet. Shifting contextual factors open new gaps in the market and new resources enable companies to fill these gaps.

But these opportunities are not created equal. Scientists studying a variety of complex systems have found that the frequency of an event tends to be inversely related to its magnitude—tectonic fault lines, for example, experience many small tremors, regular mid-sized earthquakes, and the rare major one. The same holds for volatile markets. Companies face countless small opportunities, regular mid-sized ones, and the periodic golden opportunity—a chance to create value disproportionate to the resources invested in a short period of time. Typical golden opportunities include acquisition of a major competitor to gain global scale; seizing explosive demand in an emerging market like China; pioneering a new product or service such as the iPod™; or consolidating an industry as Oracle has done in enterprise software.

Golden opportunities are rare; they occur only when external circumstances open several windows at once. Consider the golden opportunity for middleware—software linking an enterprise's disparate applications—an opportunity that IBM and BEA converted into billion dollar businesses. The middleware opportunity arose when, simultaneously, the Internet created demand for software that could link applications; available technology was up to the task; early leaders like NCR and Novell were distracted by other markets; and the paucity of venture capital at that juncture prevented a few startups from chasing the same market. Golden opportunities are the mirror image of major crises—when multiple variables go south simultaneously. The crisis in the global airline industry, for example, resulted from the unfortunate combination of 9/11, SARS, and rapidly rising fuel prices.

Golden opportunities are not only rare, they are also fleeting. Timing is everything when going for the gold. Too early can be as bad as too late. Had IBM or BEA entered the middleware market a year or two earlier, customers' pain would have been less acute

and the technology fix less developed. A few years later, and new entrants flush with venture capital cash might have established a lead, or early leaders might have focused their effort on the segment.

THE STRATEGY OF ACTIVE WAITING

Seizing a golden opportunity can provide a company with a decisive advantage. But there is a catch. Executives can neither predict nor control the precise form, magnitude, or timing of these golden opportunities. Executives can rarely open the contextual windows that give rise to golden opportunities. Even mighty IBM could not have affected the speed of Internet adoption, stopped venture capitalists from funding startups, or deterred NCR or Novell from building on their early lead. Executives should, of course, take whatever steps they can to nudge a golden opportunity along, by, for example, lobbying governments, guiding industry standards, or preempting competitors. But it is rank hubris for an executive to think he or she can conjure up a golden opportunity when the core business is declining or investors are clamoring for a big hit. Attempting to force an opportunity when the contextual stars are not aligned generally ends in tears.

That said, there is much executives *can* do to prepare their companies to capitalize on a golden opportunity (or weather a major crisis) when one arises. The secret to success lies not in heroic efforts in the midst of storms, but rather the quiet actions taken during periods of relative calm between them.

MAKING IT HAPPEN ▶▶

Keep the vision fuzzy. Managers must first acknowledge that they cannot predict or control how the future will unfold by articulating a fuzzy vision—a company's domain, geographic scope, and aspiration—in broad terms: "We aspire to global leadership (or excellence or quality) in our industry." A fuzzy vision provides general direction and sets aspirations without prematurely locking the company into a specific course. In contrast, overly detailed long-term visions cause more problems than they solve. They induce executives to bet too big too early, distract employees from emerging changes inconsistent with the vision, and provide a false sense of security that the world is more certain than it is. A crystal clear long-term vision often ensures that

companies get to the wrong place faster than their competitors.

Keep the priorities clear. In unpredictable markets, managers often try to hedge against every possible contingency by running multiple experiments and unleashing a flurry of new initiatives. Taken in isolation each initiative makes sense, but collectively they lead to priority proliferation. Employees and managers find themselves overwhelmed by multiple, often conflicting priorities. In attempting to pursue too many priorities simultaneously, organizations spread their chips too thin and hinder coordination across units. The point of prioritization is not to choose what to do and what not to do, but what to do *when*. Managers must exercise discipline and choose a small number of objectives to pursue first, and let others wait for now (recognizing that changing circumstances could force a reordering of priorities). Equally important, managers must decide what to stop doing to free up time, attention, and resources so that the critical objectives are met.

Conduct reconnaissance into the future. Reconnaissance, in military parlance, is the activity of sending troops ahead of an advancing army to investigate the terrain, enemy disposition, and other factors that lie ahead. Reconnaissance into the future is the process of probing the fog to discover an emerging situation. Four principles capture the essence of conducting reconnaissance into the future.

1 **Jump into the action:** Rather than spending years conducting market research, companies should make exploratory forays by investing or partnering with startups, or conducting small-scale experiments to test the market.
2 **Send out multiple probes:** A prudent general sends out probes in different directions to broaden the search for opportunities. Executives should likewise avoid betting the company in pursuing a single path.
3 **Interrogate anomalies:** When conducting reconnaissance, managers must above all remain alert to anomalies: new information that surprises them or doesn't jibe with expectations; things that should work but don't or that shouldn't work but do. In turbulent markets, a manager's mental map can quickly become outdated. Anomalies provide clues as

to where a mental map is wrong, and managers who discover and act on these clues can seize the initiative from competitors slower to abandon their assumptions. When managers observe an anomaly, they must investigate it firsthand until they are satisfied they understand the source of the discrepancy.

4 **Pass surfaces but swarm gaps:** Reconnaissance into the future resembles a process of probing a wall of resistance for gaps. Most of the time, a company encounters hard surfaces, for example, competitors who won't get out of the way, customers who don't want to buy, technologies that won't work. Rather than exhaust resources trying to smash through the wall, executives should probe for gaps. When they do find a gap, managers should swarm it, pulling other resource in their wake.

Keep a reserve. During periods of relative calm, executives should build a war chest of cash to deploy quickly when faced with a golden opportunity or sudden-death threat. Building and preserving a war chest requires restraint. To avoid spreading a company's chips across too many probes, thereby leaving little cash in reserve, senior executives should scrutinize the company's resource allocation process, monitor the number of probes, cap the investment allocated to probes, and increase investment only after explicit evaluation. Managers must also build sufficient credibility with investors to allow them to hold onto the cash.

Keep the troops battle ready. During periods of active waiting, executives must relentlessly drive operating improvements—cutting costs, strengthening distribution, improving products. The cumulative effect of incremental operating improvements can prove decisive in the long run. Efficient companies can survive long enough to have a shot at the next golden opportunity. Operating improvements during lulls contribute to the war chest, of course, but also build the credibility required to seize the golden opportunity.

Declare the main effort. One of the greatest challenges in active waiting is deciding when to commit reserves and go for broke. Executives conducting reconnaissance into the future will detect countless opportunities and threats that

never rise above the routine. Periodically, however, they will encounter an opportunity or threat so important that it demands the company's full focus. Executives provide this focus by declaring the opportunity or threat the main effort for a period of time. This creates a sense of urgency, focuses the organization, prioritizes resource allocation, lays the groundwork for coordinated effort, and increases the odds of winning big. Declaring the main effort requires judgment. If managers wait for complete certainty before they commit, nimbler competitors will seize the initiative. Many leaders say that

declaring a golden opportunity the main effort was the most difficult decision they ever made. Playing it safe in the short term, however, can prove hazardous in the long term. Companies that pass on every golden opportunity will eventually find themselves eclipsed by players that can both wait actively and strike decisively.

CONCLUSION

Leading a company into the fog of the future remains risky. By waiting actively during periods of relative calm, however, executives can increase their chances of success.

FOR MORE INFORMATION

Book:
Sull, Donald N. *Made In China: What Western Managers Can Learn from Trailblazing Chinese Entrepreneurs*. Cambridge, MA: Harvard Business School Press, 2005.

See also:
- China's Five Surprises (pp. 53–56)
- Forecasting and Scenario Planning (pp. 1759–1760)
- The Living Company: Habits for Survival in a Turbulent Business Environment (p. 1112)

The Second Coming of Service
by Karl Albrecht

EXECUTIVE SUMMARY

- Executives are discovering that IT is not the magic wand they had been led to believe, and that misapplying it can lead to wasted resources, loss of focus, and even disastrous business results.
- Established, successful companies are making effective use of IT by concentrating on their key strategic priorities and making technology their servant, not their master.
- Strategic customer focus—concentrating on customer value as the primary driving concept—can serve as a powerful organizing principle for reinventing businesses in the age of the Third Wave.

INTRODUCTION

Many companies, particularly in the United States, ran off their rails, strategically speaking, during the Internet craze of the late 1990s. Hypnotized by the e-commerce story, many dot-com businesses made strategic blunders that would be unforgivable on the part of first-year MBA students. Executive teams of many established companies, gripped by the fear of being left behind, threw money at anything that looked as if it might qualify as an Internet strategy.

Apart from the loss of billions of dollars by investors and ill-advised expenditures by established companies, the biggest victim was the customer. Internet operators set back the cause of service quality by a good ten years in some sectors, and the implosion of dot-mania left an ideological vacuum in the minds of many executives.

A more realistic appraisal of the role of IT in business has forced a return to basic principles: focus on the customer and value creation, culture building, skillful execution of quality practices, and inspired leadership. This return to basic truths may unfold as a second coming of customer focus.

WHAT HAPPENED TO SERVICE?

In 1985 the business world embraced the concept of service management with remarkable enthusiasm. There were books, articles, conferences, seminars, training programs, videos, newsletters, consulting companies, and even professional societies and academic research programs aimed at making customer focus a critical and permanent part of Western management thinking. Even the management gurus, established names on other topics, were moved to declare the primacy of customer value.

The wave didn't last. The service revolution was hijacked somewhere along the road to victory. Like most other management movements before it—management by objectives, participative management, productivity, and quality management—customer focus became the object of intense flirtation by many companies, but ultimately the infatuation faded. The same fate befell several other revolutions: TQM, reengineering, and ISO 9000.

The real value and potential impact of the service management model are yet to be realized. We're coming to a stage in business worldwide, in which we will need its principles more than ever. Western management thinking has lost its way in recent years, particularly with the mindless infatuation with all things digital. There is a deep underlying need, only partly articulated, to return to the most basic and timeless precepts of leadership, management, and enterprise thinking.

THE TECTONIC SHIFT AWAY FROM SERVICE

Around 1995, when TQM, ISO 9000, and service quality movements were fading, U.S. business began to feel the pressure of a more primitive shift in emphasis. U.S. enterprises, and to a lesser extent companies in other countries, moved into a reconstruction phase. An unprecedented period of mergers, acquisitions, and the dramatic growth of retail giants got mixed in with business breakups, spinoffs, delayering, outsourcing, and partnering. A growing economy coupled with low unemployment rates and a remarkably flexible workforce enabled U.S. companies to rearrange themselves to maximize their strengths.

Key phrases such as "core competencies," "strategic partnering," and "supply-chain management" replaced the language of service, quality, and customer value. Thus began an ideological drift in U.S. management thinking toward *resource-based* rather than *value-based* competition. A large banking corporation finds it difficult to win more customers by adding value or reinventing its service package, but it's easy to find profit growth by buying up its smaller competitors. Why have competing banks on opposite sides of the street? Let's just buy out the other bank, close its branches, and add its customers to our inventory.

Why should a large airline try to offer better service when all airlines have conditioned their customers to make their choices solely on the basis of price? Why not buy up or force out the smaller airlines and relieve the pricing pressure? Why waste time changing customer service programs that just fizzle out anyway?

This is not to suggest that no companies are interested in service quality as a competitive factor: surely companies like Federal Express are still in a class by themselves. However, the example set by the giant companies, namely buying their competitors and kidnapping their customers, has drawn more attention in recent years.

THE PENDULUM RETURNS?

Has the so-called new economy lived up to its image? Or is it an intellectual chimera?

Actually, there was never any such thing as a new economy (or an old economy) as preached by the Internet hucksters, who managed to separate several billion dollars from investors, venture capitalists, and corporate executives. This warped notion of two economies will eventually be seen as one of the most serious conceptual blunders in business thinking of the last 50 years.

There has only ever been one economy: the ever-new, ever-evolving economy of continuous creative destruction, described by theorist Joseph Schumpeter. Information is, and will continue to be, an important resource for economic development, but it is not in itself a—and certainly not *the*—new economy. Nor is the high-tech industry the primary driver of economic growth, as so many business writers have declared. Even Peter Drucker, the *eminence grise* of man-

"I view today's economy as the Value Economy. Adding value has become more than just a sound business principle; it is both the common denominator and the competitive edge."

Arthur Levitt, Jr.

agement theology, wrongly characterized the U.S. economy as information-based. When the fantasy begins to fade, economists, business leaders, journalists, and management theorists will see the information phenomenon in a more realistic perspective: as an inseparable part of the economic structure, but not the magical engine of it.

Information is one of the five key factors of economic growth and development: land, capital infrastructure, energy, labor, and information. Why arbitrarily declare one factor profoundly more important than the others? It is impossible to do anything with information—create it, manipulate it, store it, duplicate it, transmit it, or present it for consumption—without also consuming energy, usually in the form of electricity. Information is not free, and on a macro scale it isn't even cheap.

As business leaders return to the idea of customer value as the ultimate driving force of business success, they will turn a new page in their understanding of the potential of IT, online technology, and abundant information. Instead of trying to turn their businesses into vending machines and building an impersonal digital moat around their companies by replacing people with software, they will begin to see a wholly different set of strategies for using information as a strategic weapon. This understanding will change the meaning of the customer-value focus and reshape our thought processes as they relate to the use of information in business.

MINI-CASES

USAA is the premier provider of insurance services to U.S. military personnel. Founded in 1922 by a group of army officers, the company has never lost its focus on delivering value to its special population of customers with their special needs. It has stayed at the forefront of applying information technology—with a human face—to the insurance business. Its excellent customer retention rates mean that it has over five million members and $81 billion in owned and managed assets.

REI (Recreational Equipment, Inc.) is the outfitter of choice for over a million outdoor

sports fans and adventure enthusiasts. Successful since 1938, the company has recently achieved a brilliant convergence of bricks and clicks by marrying online technology and its existing experience of interactive retail stores. Customers can interact seamlessly with its 78 retail outlets and its in-depth resources for ordering, advice, and information on its Web site.

MAKING IT HAPPEN ▶▶

- **Refocus on the customer.** Are you conducting customer research on a regular basis? Do people understand what customer value is in your line of business, and do they know how to deliver it? Do you have a workable system for measuring customer perceptions of value? Do you share findings throughout the organization?
- **Reinvent the service strategy.** What is your core benefit premise, that is, the *customer value proposition* on which you base your business model, the design of your service systems, and the operation of the enterprise? Does it make sense? Does everyone in the organization understand it and take it seriously? Is it time to rethink the business model or realign the priorities?
- **Build organizational intelligence.** Conduct a comprehensive review of your operating systems and an audit of their capacity to deliver on the business strategy. Look for evidence of system craziness, or lack of intelligence. Align the systems, the processes, and the people to the critical success factors of the business.
- **Reenlist the people.** Too many crises, priorities, and brushfires can distract the leaders of the enterprise and put them out of touch with the culture. How well do you understand employees today? What do they want? What do they seek in their jobs and careers? What frustrates them, inhibits them, or demotivates them? Are they switched on, switched off, or just glowing at half-wattage? Get the energy up and get the heads all pointing in the same direction.

CONCLUSION

In the present confusing and rapidly changing business environment, enterprise leaders at all levels must learn to see beyond fads and folklore and concentrate ever more tenaciously on the timeless truths of business:

- make sure you are selling what the customer wants to buy;
- concentrate your resources on the strategic advantage;
- align the systems to meet the mission;
- mobilize the culture.;
- make technology your servant, not your master;
- stay on message.

The winning enterprises of the next decade won't be those whose leaders chase fads and fantasies, but those who can integrate new knowledge and new possibilities with their own trusted understanding of the basic truths of business success.

FOR MORE INFORMATION

Book:
Albrecht, Karl. *Social Intelligence: The New Science of Success* New York: Pfeiffer, 2005.

See also:

"To take full advantage of the potential in e-business, leaders must lead differently, and people must work together differently. Let's call this new way of working e-culture."

Rosabeth Moss Kanter

Organic Growth Versus Acquisition
by Peter Bebb

EXECUTIVE SUMMARY

- If they are to survive and succeed, businesses need to find ways to rapidly, radically, and measurably change their strategy, processes, and roles. Individuals need to know precisely what to produce and what reward they'll get for doing so.
- Companies acquiring, merging, and demerging need long-term ways of enhancing stockholder value once the initial and obvious savings have been made.
- Organic growth and growth by acquisition should be complementary strategies. The successful execution of both depends on aligning everyone and everything around a single set of corporate goals, and so achieving these goals faster, better, and cheaper.
- Many organizations suffer from acquisition indigestion, having failed to absorb and make the best of their acquisitions or mergers. All organizations have more scope for organic growth than they realize.

INTRODUCTION

Organizations exist in a rapidly changing environment, necessitating responsive and often radical strategic capabilities. To realize potential, organizations can be beset with common difficulties, such as strategic confusion and preoccupation with day-to-day activities. Despite many attempts to push organizations forward, stockholder value often stagnates or even declines. The solution lies not in focusing on improving the current situation but rather in taking the step changes necessary to realize the future requirements of the organization.

UNDERSTANDING THE PROBLEMS
Dysfunctional Organizations

Most people have difficulty stating their organization's strategy: what the organization wants to become, how it would like its people to behave, and what it will provide to which customers in the future. The reality is that the organization's business and operating units march to priorities different from, if not contradictory to, those implied by its strategy. The majority of the people in an organization focus on day-to-day operational matters and their individual aspirations. Consequently the strategy is never realized.

Frustrated by the lack of forward progress, executives launch new communication, reorganization, process redesign, or technology initiatives. Everyone is doing more, and yet performance stagnates or even declines.

Losing the Value of Mergers and Acquisitions

A recent report by the consultancy KPMG found that, though 82% of respondents believed the deal they had transacted was a success, 83% of the same mergers failed to increase stockholder value. Of these transactions, 30% produced no discernible difference in stockholder value and 53% actually reduced value.

Acquiring, merging, and demerging companies need long-term ways of enhancing stockholder value once the initial and obvious savings have been taken. But they usually focus on tactical integration, (for example, of organizational structure, support services, policies), rather than on strategic integration (customers, products, people, systems). However, to succeed, both are needed.

The Performance Management Gap

There is a gap between business performance *management* and individual performance *management* in all businesses, leading to a gap between business performance and individual performance. Business performance management is usually driven through an annual business planning process, which sets financial targets without specifying how they are to be achieved. Individual performance management is carried out through a performance appraisal process that sets mainly nonfinancial personal targets without explaining how they link to financial targets. Both focus on improving the present situation rather than initiating the step-change today's organizations must make if they want to succeed in the future.

THE SOLUTION: TRANSLATING STRATEGY INTO ACTION
Business Alignment

Business alignment is a unique new approach that:

- defines the issues and resources that are of value, allocating crystal-clear responsibility for them and measuring progress toward their delivery;
- empowers people to set their own objectives in the context of corporate goals;
- creates a results-oriented performance culture, rewarding the delivery of outcomes rather than the management of resources;
- organizes around results rather than skills;
- challenges and justifies partners' and support units' outcomes, replacing adversarial service-level agreements;
- integrates and automates planning, budgeting, resourcing, measuring, reporting, and rewarding, thus releasing managers and support staff to deliver growth outcomes;
- combines business and individual performance management;
- identifies core processes and prioritizes initiatives;
- continuously reveals duplication, streamlines processes, and optimizes the allocation of resources;
- aligns information technology with the business through the IT alignment matrix;
- integrates people and other resources around common goals after a merger or acquisition.

Business alignment gets everyone to specify what their organization needs to do to produce what it needs to deliver to stakeholders in the future. It defines precisely what should be done to extract value from a merger or acquisition once the initial cost savings have been taken, and so enables long-term growth in stockholder value.

By applying business alignment before a merger, the organization goes into the merger negotiation knowing more precisely what it wants out of the merger, and thus is better prepared to extract value from the merger after the event.

APPLYING THE BALANCED SCORECARD

Translating strategy into business results with the balanced scorecard is a four-part process:

1. Leaders build and align around an architecture for change.
2. Required outcomes are linked to the activities that will deliver them, and re-

"Worldwide, IT companies embarking on the non-organic growth mode have understood the wisdom of mergers and acquisitions on the threshold of the Digital Age."

Narayana Murthy

sources are allocated to perform these activities.

3 Change architecture is cascaded and the organization mobilized for action.

4 A feedback and learning system is built to make strategy development and implementation a continuous adaptive process.

Building and Aligning Leadership

Building an architecture for change involves defining strategy as an integrated set of hypotheses that describe an organization's evolution from the present to the future. The hypotheses are captured in a balanced scorecard, which defines the causal relationships between the things of value to the business, thus enabling value-based and activity-based management. It also defines how these things of value should be measured, thus providing key performance indicators.

Linking to Business Planning—Making Strategy Operational

Business process reengineering, activity-based costing, and workflow

The organization's leaders decide on the corporate processes and initiatives required to deliver the outcomes. They use these to assess the relevance of current corporate processes, to prioritize existing initiatives, and to define new initiatives needed for achieving the strategy. Some initiatives and processes are found to be irrelevant to the future of the organization and can be removed. Activity-based costing is used to determine which resources are released by the removal of the activity, and workflow software is applied to the new and remaining processes after their definition or improvement.

Focusing on Organizational development

Processes are associated with the outcomes they deliver, and in so doing they suggest an organization that allocates resources to the delivery of strategic outcomes. This is usually radically different from, and more productive than, the functional organization.

IT alignment matrix

The IT alignment matrix (ITAM) defines the knowledge communities of the future and the structure and content of the data warehouses required to inform them. The ITAM reveals the gap between the current databases and systems and those required to deliver the future outcomes defined in the balanced scorecard.

Enterprise resource planning

The types of resource—people and things—needed to deliver the future outcomes are then identified and valued in monetary terms to define a budget. Note that this turns the business planning process on its head, since the traditional process starts with money (and involves too much guesswork). Starting with outcomes enables a rational debate about what should be produced and in what quantity. Information from enterprise resource-planning systems is used to calculate the budget.

Investing in people

Discretionary pay and bonuses are dependent on the delivery of balanced scorecard outcomes and targets. At the executive level the change is the addition of nonfinancial targets. At lower levels the change is more significant, involving specific rewards for deliverables that individuals can influence.

Business alignment integrates individual with business performance management by empowering individuals to say what they can contribute to corporate outcomes. Instead of being told what to do, people are invited to say what they can produce. Consequently they have a real opportunity to create their own careers.

Cascading and Mobilization—Linking the Boardroom to the Front Line

Now the organization is aligned around the strategic outcomes. There is no formal reorganization in the traditional sense. Instead, individuals are appointed to lead the delivery of the strategic themes, and the rest of the organization is invited to say what it can produce that will assist the delivery of the themes.

Over time, status and rewards are aligned with the delivery of outcomes that help to deliver the themes, and people and other resources gravitate toward the themes. Level by level, organizations achieve strategic focus and alignment.

Feedback and Learning

People at all levels are now aligned to the strategy. What remains is to link them through feedback and learning, using a dynamic enterprise performance-management system. Information about outcomes, activities, and resources is stored electronically, enabling the organization to outpace its peers. Measures, progress assessments, recommendations, and insights flow from the grassroots to the executive team. Meetings only for reporting results become working sessions to solve problems of which everyone is already aware.

FOR MORE INFORMATION

Books:

Bakker, Hans, Martijn Babeliowsky, and Frank Stevenaar. *The Next Leap: Achieving Growth Through Global Networks, Partnerships and Co-operation.* New York: Cyan Books, 2004.

Bruner, Robert F. *Deals from Hell: M & A Lessons That Rise Above the Ashes.* New York: Wiley, 2005.

Hammer, Michael, and James Champy. *Reengineering the Corporation: A Manifesto for Business Revolution.* Revised ed. New York: HarperBusiness, 2001.

Kaplan, Robert S., and David P. Norton. *The Balanced Scorecard: Translating Strategy into Action.* Cambridge, MA: Harvard Business School Press, 1996.

See also:

☆ Building Great Internal Partnerships (pp. 362–363)

✷ C. K. Prahalad (pp. 1256–1257)

▱ Competing for the Future (p. 1082)

☆ Infusing a Company with Cutting-edge Strategy (pp. 110–111)

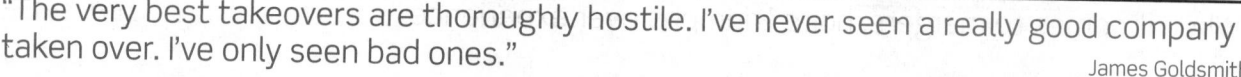

"The very best takeovers are thoroughly hostile. I've never seen a really good company taken over. I've only seen bad ones."

James Goldsmith

Why Mergers Fail and How to Prevent It
by Susan Cartwright

EXECUTIVE SUMMARY

- Mergers and acquisitions (M & A) are increasing in frequency, yet at least half fail to meet financial expectations.
- The United States and the United Kingdom continue to dominate M & A activity. As the number of cross-border deals increases, however, many other national players are entering the field, further highlighting the issue of cultural compatibility.
- Financial and strategic factors alone are insufficient to explain the high rate of failure; more account needs to be taken of human factors.
- The successful management of integrating people and their organizational cultures is the key to achieving desired M & A outcomes.

INTRODUCTION

The incidence of M & A has continued to increase significantly during the last decade, both domestically and internationally. The sectors most affected by M & A activity have been service- and knowledge-based industries such as banking, insurance, pharmaceuticals, and leisure. Although M & A is a popular means of increasing or protecting market share, the strategy does not always deliver what is expected in terms of increased profitability or economies of scale. While the motives for merger can variously be described as practical, psychological, or opportunist, the objective of all related M & A is to achieve synergy, or what is commonly referred to as the 2 + 2 = 5 effect. However, as many organizations learn to their cost, the mere recognition of potential synergy is no guarantee that the combination will actually realize that potential.

MERGER FAILURE RATES

The burning question remains—why do so many mergers fail to live up to stockholder expectations? In the short term, many seemingly successful acquisitions look good, but disappointing productivity levels are often masked by onetime cost savings, asset disposals, or astute tax maneuvers that inflate balance-sheet figures during the first few years.

Merger gains are notoriously difficult to assess. There are problems in selecting appropriate indices to make any assessment, as well as difficulties in deciding on a suitable measurement period. Typically the criteria selected by analysts are:

- profit-to-earning ratios;
- stock-price fluctuations;
- managerial assessments.

Irrespective of the evaluation method selected, the evidence on M & A performance is consistent in suggesting that a high proportion of M & As are financially unsuccessful. U.S. sources place merger failure rates as high as 80%, with evidence indicating that around half of mergers fail to meet financial expectations. A much-cited McKinsey study presents evidence arguing that most organizations would have received a better return on their investment if they had merely banked their money instead of buying another company. Consequently, many commentators have concluded that the true beneficiaries from M & A activity are those who sell their shares when deals are announced and the marriage brokers—the bankers, lawyers, and accountants—who arrange, advise, and execute the deals.

TRADITIONAL REASONS FOR MERGER FAILURE

M & A is still regarded by many decision makers as an exclusively rational, financial, and strategic activity, and not as a human collaboration. Financial and strategic considerations, along with price and availability, therefore dominate target selection, overriding the soft issues such as people and cultural fit. Explanations of merger failure or underperformance tend to focus on reexamining the factors that prompted the initial selection decision, for example:

- payment of an overinflated price for the acquired company;
- poor strategic fit;
- failure to achieve potential economies of scale because of financial mismanagement or incompetence;
- sudden and unpredicted changes in market conditions.

This ground has been well trodden, yet the rate of merger, acquisition, and joint-venture success has improved little. Clearly these factors may contribute to disappointing M & A outcomes, but this conventional wisdom only part explains what goes wrong in M & A management.

THE FORGOTTEN FACTOR IN M & A

The false distinction that has developed between hard and soft merger issues has been extremely unhelpful in extending our understanding of merger failure, as it separates the impact of the merger on the individual from its financial impact on the organization. Successful M & A outcomes are linked closely to the extent to which management is able to integrate organizational members and their cultures and sensitively address and minimize individuals' concerns.

By representing sudden and major change, mergers generate considerable uncertainty and feelings of powerlessness. This can lead to reduced morale, job and career dissatisfaction, employee stress, and uncertainty. Rather than increased profitability, mergers have become associated with a range of negative behavioral outcomes such as:

- acts of sabotage and petty theft;
- increased staff turnover, with rates reported as high as 60%;
- increased sickness and absenteeism.

Ironically, this occurs at the very time when organizations need and expect greater employee loyalty, flexibility, cooperation, and productivity.

PEOPLE FACTORS ASSOCIATED WITH M & A FAILURE

Studies like the one conducted by the British Chartered Management Institute have identified a variety of people factors associated with unsuccessful M & A. These include:

- underestimating the difficulties of merging two cultures;

"When it comes to mergers, hope triumphs over experience."   Irwin Stelzer

- underestimating the problem of skills transfer;
- demotivation of employees;
- departure of key people;
- expenditure of too much energy on doing the deal at the expense of postmerger planning
- lack of clear responsibilities, leading to postmerger conflicts;
- too narrow a focus on internal issues to the neglect of the customers and the external environment;
- insufficient research about the merger partner or acquired organization.

DIFFERENCES BETWEEN MERGERS AND ACQUISITIONS

In terms of employee response, whether the transaction is described as a merger or an acquisition, the event will trigger uncertainty and fears of job losses. However, there are important differences. In an acquisition, power is substantially assumed by the new parent. Change is usually swift and often brutal as the acquirer imposes its own control systems and financial restraints. Parties to a merger are likely to be more evenly matched in terms of size, and the power and cultural dynamics of the combination are more ambiguous. Integration is a more drawn-out process.

This has implications for the individual. During an acquisition there is often more overt conflict and resistance and a sense of powerlessness. In mergers, however, because of the prolonged period between the initial announcement and actual integration, uncertainty and anxiety continue for a much longer time as the organization remains in a state of limbo.

CULTURAL COMPATIBILITY

The process of the merger is often likened to marriage. In the same way that clashes of personality and misunderstanding lead to difficulties in personal relationships, differences in organizational cultures, communication problems, and mistaken assumptions lead to conflicts in organizational partnerships.

Mergers are rarely a marriage of equals, and it's still the case that most acquirers or dominant merger partners pursue a strategy of cultural absorption; the acquired company or smaller merger partner is expected to assimilate and adopt the culture of the

other. Whether the outcome is successful depends upon the willingness of organizational members to surrender their own culture and at the same time perceive that the other culture is attractive and therefore worth adopting.

Cultural similarity may make absorption easier than when the two cultures are very different, yet the process of due diligence rarely extends to evaluating the degree of cultural fit. Furthermore, few organizations bother to try to understand the cultural values and strengths of the acquiring workforce or their merger partners in order to inform and guide the way in which they should go about introducing change.

MAKING IT HAPPEN ▸▸

Making a good organizational marriage currently seems to be a matter of chance and luck. This needs to change so that there is a greater awareness of the people issues involved and consequently a more informed integration strategy. Some basic guidelines for more effective management include:

- extension of the due diligence process to incorporate issues of cultural fit;
- greater involvement of human resource professionals;
- the conducting of culture audits before the introduction of change management initiatives;
- increased communication and involvement of employees at all levels in the integration process;
- the introduction of mechanisms to monitor employee stress levels;
- fair and objective reselection processes and role allocation;
- providing management with the skills and training to sensitively handle M & A issues such as insecurity and job loss;
- creating a superordinate goal which will unify work efforts.

MINI-CASE

Paul Hodder was involved as director of human resource management in the formation of Aon Risk Services, a merger of four rather different retail-insurance-broking and risk-management companies. A major theme of their integration process was the formation of a series of task groups to re-

view and identify best practice. Another part involved an organization-wide training program to provide individuals with life skills to help them initiate and cope with change, to improve teamwork, and to develop support networks. Enthusiasm for the program provided several hundred change champions to lead change projects and assume support and mentoring roles. Good communication of early wins and successes has reassured organizational members that the changes are working and are beneficial.

CONCLUSION

Despite thorough pre-merger procedures, mergers continue to fall far short of financial expectations. The single biggest cause of this failure rate is poor integration following the acquisition. The identification of the target company, the subsequent and often drawn-out negotiations, and attending to the myriad of financial, technical, and legal details are all exhausting activities. Once the target company has been acquired, little energy or motivation is left to plan and implement the integration of the people and cultures following the merger. It seems nonsensical to waste all the resources and energy that has gone into the merger, through inadequate planning of the integration stage of the process, yet all too often organizations do just that. Without a properly planned integration process or its effective implementation, mergers will not be able to achieve the full potential of the acquisition.

FOR MORE INFORMATION

Books:
Cartwright, Susan, and Cary L. Cooper. *Managing Mergers, Acquisitions and Strategic Alliances.* 2nd ed. Woburn, MA: Butterworth-Heinemann, 1996.
Cooper, Cary L., and Alan Gregory, eds. *Advances in Mergers and Acquisitions.* Vol. 1. New York: JAI Press, 2000.
Stahl, Gunter, and Mark E. Mendenhall, eds. *Mergers and Acquisitions.* Stanford, CA: Stanford University Press, 2005.

See also:
☆ Building Great Internal Partnerships (pp. 362–363)
☆ Workers without Borders: Creating Bonds When Workers Have No Loyalty (pp. 237–238)

"The big danger in mega-mergers is that they are seen as a mating of dinosaurs."

Peter Bonfield

Infusing a Company with Cutting-edge Strategy

by Oren Harari

EXECUTIVE SUMMARY

- Strategic planning by itself does not guarantee either competitive advantage or business success. Too often companies' strategies simply mimic each other; they are not exciting or inspiring, their execution is poor, or they're built on obsolete premises.
- Strategy is nonetheless relevant. In today's hypercompetitive global economy, infusing a company with a clear, compelling, cutting-edge strategic direction is critical.
- Whether a company is publicly traded or privately held, effective strategy creates value for stockholders and customers. In the New Millennium Economy, value-creation follows new and different paths. Today, one's strategy should generate *unique* value, *breakthrough* value, *startling* value, *personalized* value, *turbo-speed* value, and *employee-driven* value.

INTRODUCTION

We've made strategy far more complicated than necessary. Smart people with advanced degrees and high salaries generate elaborate documents containing complex analysis, algorithms, heuristics, scenarios, and projections which seldom yield competitive advantage. More than 50% of the 1980 *Fortune* 500 companies—each with elegant, complex strategic plans—no longer exist. And literally 60–80% of megamergers—with strategies of impeccable depth, logic, and financial wizardry—have been empirically shown to diminish stockholder value.

What's Wrong?

First, strategies often wind up looking pretty much the same. It becomes difficult to distinguish oneself in a crowded marketplace. No amount of numbers, graphs, and jargon can stop many strategic plans turning out to be ordinary, with uninspiring results for customers and investors.

Companies often find that, even if their strategic plan makes sense, their execution fails. Bureaucracy, organizational inertia, and resistance to change subvert or delay noble goals, even those representing genuine competitive opportunity.

It gets worse. Companies often find their strategies have become obsolete "overnight." The long-term growth strategies of the major music recording labels, for example, were based on a known product (the compact disc), a known distribution chain, a known set of competitors, and a known

"way of doing things." Then came MP3 formats, P2P file-sharing systems, and other Web-based innovations.

FINDING THE CUTTING EDGE

Strategy is far from irrelevant. Effective strategy creates significant value. But in today's fragmented, hyper-competitive, global economy, value creation follows new and different paths. Singly or combined, these new sources of value creation lead to sustained growth and returns, investor enthusiasm, customer fanaticism, and market "buzz." A cutting-edge strategy:

- **Generates *unique* value.** In crowded markets, where competitors are everywhere and customers are overwhelmed with choices, the most important strategic issue is uniqueness. A cutting-edge strategy demonstrates that the company is doing something special and different. It suggests best-of-breed and greatness.

  In the 1990s, Dell Computer's built-to-order product customization and direct-to-customer sales channel were so unique that they restructured conventional value propositions and value chains, and in the process catapulted the company to a dominant role in the technology sector. Even today, amidst the rough seas of the post-September 11 environment, Dell maintains a powerful "best-of-breed" position. Further, it continues its innovative march by using the Web to conduct 75% of its total business, and by applying the company's core skills to new digital niches.

For example, it recently announced plans to embed Vodafone technology into laptops for its European customers.

Where fragmentation, saturation, and upheaval exist, *unique* equals value.

- **Provides *breakthrough* value.** What do FedEx, CNN, Siebel Systems, and Palm have in common? They created new markets. With so many competitors vying for customers' attention, significant value comes not from incremental improvements, but from marketplace breakthroughs. Once, customers didn't ask for overnight delivery, cable news, or Personal Digital Assistants. Smart companies initiated those and profited handsomely. Cutting-edge strategies demonstrate value by leading markets, which includes leading customers, not just by responding to their current desires.

- **Provides *startling* value.** Increasingly, products and services are becoming "me-too" commodities. Companies with cutting-edge strategies create value by providing things that inspire excitement, intrigue, and joy via exceptional functionality, design, and execution. Sony's PlayStation with its functionality, design, and marketing execution set off a $20 billion computer game industry. Swatch's mission has nothing to do with selling wristwatches; it's about providing joy in life through fashionized timepieces and, more recently, through Web-accessible watches that allow you to "save time," not merely tell it.

- **Provides *personalized* value.** Mass (as in mass-production and mass-marketing) is dead as a value-driver. Nowadays, it's all about "markets of one." Cap One has 29 million holders of its credit cards, and no two have the same terms. The company's digital capacity allows it to canvass thousands of possible combinations instantaneously, so that a person with a bad credit history and a fondness for fusion jazz gets a card with an entirely different set of financial and marketing arrangements from someone with a great credit history and a love of the Chicago Bulls.

  GE Power Systems allows a purchaser of its turbine engines to build-to-order and

---

"Mold-breaking strategies grow initially like weeds, they are not cultivated like tomatoes in a hothouse."

Henry Mintzberg

follow the path of the product's construction, all online and while receiving one-to-one online and face-to-face consulting help from GE throughout the process. Customized products and services are increasingly the primary way that customers conclude that they are receiving true value.

- **Provides *turbo-speed* value.** Whatever winning organizations do, they do *very* fast. They see competitive advantage in how rapidly they can capitalize on changes in technologies, customers, competitors, demographics, and capital markets. Or how dramatically they can shrink decision and cycle times. Or how quickly they can disseminate information and knowledge throughout the organization, put together a team or alliance, implement a change, start an experiment or pilot, and get to market. Winners think about time the way most conventional companies think about costs. They do strategy "on the run."

Pharmaceutical Novartis launched four new drugs in just one year, including a breakthrough leukemia drug after only 32 months of clinical testing. Medtronics' quick capitalization on new opportunities in the medical products arena has resulted in 70% of its revenues coming from products that didn't exist three years ago. Recognizing that operational speed was critical for competing in the U.S. personal computer market, Fujitsu partnered with FedEx and reduced its order-to-delivery cycle from 30 days to four.

- **Provides *employees-driven* value.** The traditional scenario of a few high-ranking executives and high-priced consultants determining strategy, then pushing it down for others to execute, is destructively anachronistic. Real value and its corollary, competitive advantage, accrue to organizations that fully invest in and capitalize on the talents of their people. Top management sets broad strategic priorities and directions, as well as clear values and culture. But within those parameters, cutting-edge strategy and accountability, a.k.a. value, bubbles up from anywhere. This is a quantum departure from conventional "empowerment" and "employee participation."

At Applied Biosystems (formerly PE Biosystems), the long run of 20% annual growth rates is fueled not by a grand plan, but by the personal initiatives of engineers, scientists, and marketers. Their efforts result in a large number of projects going on simultaneously, none of which requires any initial approval from top management. As soon as a promising concept emerges, Applied Biosystems quickly galvanizes the resources to rush it to market. Copenhagen-based Oticon takes the same approach to leading the hearing-aid market; the self-propelled, cross-disciplinary structure is called a "spaghetti organization."

Value can be created by all-hands strategic involvement. At GE Capital and Cap One frequent meetings of entrepreneurially minded employees are held to bat around "crazy" business-enhancement ideas and put together project teams to take those ideas to fruition. Intel and Merck take that idea a step further by funding employee-driven startups. Intel has provided over $100 million in seed capital to different employees who have put together viable plans for high-growth businesses that fit into Intel's mission.

All-hands-driven strategy is not one detailed grand plan, but rather an organizational template. Executives still define the fundamental direction and take on primary fiduciary responsibility. But employees are viewed as genuine partners, which means that they have immediate access to any information (including financials); training and development (talent is viewed as an appreciating asset); opportunity for self-control (taking full responsibility for initiatives and outcomes); and a healthy dose of outcome- and performance-based compensation (including profit-sharing and equity ownership).

MAKING IT HAPPEN ▶▶

- Have regular and frequent policy-making conversations with coworkers that address the following questions: What are we doing—or what do we need to do—that is unique? That generates market breakthroughs and indicates best-of-breed? That sets us apart from the rest of the pack? And, most important, do customers and investors recognize all that? Build strategy around the answers.
- Concentrate your strategic goals and organizational systems on achieving 100% customized products and 100% personalized services.

- Make speed a strategic priority in goal-setting and execution. Regularly canvass how long it takes to make a decision, launch an investigation or pilot, collect and disseminate relevant information, bring something to market, cut a deal, etc.
- Allow strategic initiatives to emerge from anywhere in the organization. Insist that everyone be responsible for improving the company's competitive position. Make certain that all hands receive sufficient tools, technology, training, direction and freedom.

CONCLUSION

A cutting-edge strategy is grounded in constant innovation and customer-centricity. *What* a cutting-edge strategy does is offer unique, breakthrough, startling, and customized value. *How* it does this is by "collaboration on the run": all hands working together as strategic partners, obsessing on speed. When this process is ignited and fueled by top management, something wonderful happens. Strategy becomes an agile, market-centric collaborative process. It also becomes a lot of fun.

FOR MORE INFORMATION

Books:
Birol, Andrew. *The 5 Catalysts of 7-Figure Growth: Propel Your Business to the Next Level.* Franklin Lakes, NJ: Career Press, 2006.
Christensen, Clayton, and Michael E. Raynor. *The Innovator's Solution: Creating and Sustaining Successful Growth.* Cambridge, MA: Harvard Business School Press, 2003.
Roos, Johan. *Thinking from Within: A Hands-on Strategy Practice.* London: Palgrave Macmillan, 2006.

See also:

"Challenging the status quo has to be the starting point for anything that goes under the label of strategy."

Gary Hamel

The Only Sustainable Edge
by John Hagel III and John Seely Brown

EXECUTIVE SUMMARY

We are only now beginning to grapple with the full implications of a globalizing economy. Tom Friedman captured our imagination with the powerful metaphor communicated in the title of his new best-selling book—*The World Is Flat*—but he tells only part of the story. In the process, he may leave many with a misleading impression. The world is not just flattening; it is also creating significant new opportunities to innovate and build strategic advantage. Much has been written about globalization and innovation as distinct topics, but few analysts have focused on exploring the connection between the two. Those who understand this connection—whether they are well-established Western enterprises or entrepreneurial companies in emerging economies like China and India—will be able to create economic value on an unprecedented scale.

INTRODUCTION

Many companies in China and India are pursuing a radical, yet very pragmatic, bootstrapping approach to build capabilities while addressing near-term market opportunities. "Bootstrapping" refers to an array of techniques designed to help companies to get better faster with limited resources, including rapid incremental innovation designed to get revenue and market feedback quickly, and leveraging the resources of other companies wherever possible to move even faster with one's own resources. In a world of intensifying competition and increasing uncertainty, even the very largest companies need to master these bootstrapping techniques to compete successfully.

This leads to **three contrarian messages**:

First, **bootstrapping is not just for small, entrepreneurial companies**. Large enterprises are most in need of bootstrapping techniques if they are to evolve successfully in this flattening world.

Second, **the United States is no longer the global center of innovation in management practices**. The private entrepreneurial sector in China is rapidly emerging as the global center of management innovation, pioneering management techniques that most U.S. companies are struggling to understand, much less master. In part, this innovation stems from necessity—especially the lack of a well-developed financial system to serve the needs of privately held, entrepreneurial companies.

Third, **product innovation is not the most powerful form of innovation**, even though this is what most Western executives focus on when they think about innovation. In a globalizing world, product life cycles are compressing. While product innovation remains critical to survival, any individual act of product innovation has diminishing impact in the marketplace. In this environment, innovation in management practices becomes much more powerful because it provides the key to accelerating and sustaining product innovation. As we will discuss in more detail below, it also provides the key to getting better faster as an institution so that more value can be generated from the products or services offered to the market.

In fact, the deeper we get into our research agenda, the more we find ourselves coming up with contrarian observations that challenge conventional management wisdom. These observations are not contrarian for the sake of being contrarian, rather they reflect more fundamental changes occurring on the global landscape as a result of the convergence of IT innovation with public policy shifts reducing barriers to movement. These changes are forcing us to re-examine some of the most basic assumptions we have about our institutions, whether we are talking about corporations, schools, government bodies, or social institutions. In effect, we are seeing the emergence of a new common sense model, requiring a new, and often quite counter-intuitive, set of assumptions.

In this overview of our research agenda, we have organized our insights into a series of contrarian observations that we hope will shed light on the key assumptions that will be required to shape our view of the world, and therefore the actions that we take in our efforts to achieve impact, more productively. We have focused on the key assumptions themselves rather than the many examples that help to illuminate why and how these assumptions are changing. We discuss a wide range of examples in our recent book—*The Only Sustainable Edge*—and the articles that we have published as part of our research efforts.

MAPPING THE CONTEXT

The edge is becoming the core. Edges—on many levels—are becoming much more important:

- **Edge in the sense of strategic advantage**. Traditional sources of advantage are eroding and we all face the challenge of identifying new sources of advantage that can sustain superior performance.

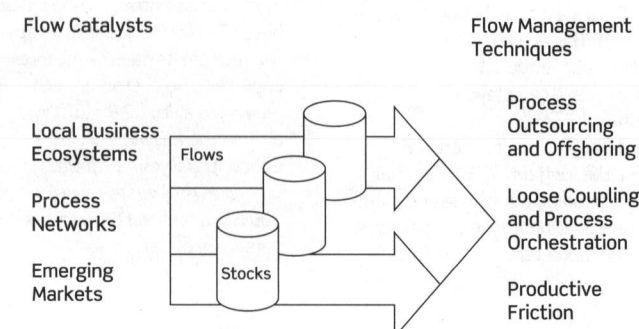

Shifting from Stocks to Flows

Flow Catalysts

Flow Management Techniques

Local Business Ecosystems

Process Networks

Emerging Markets

Flows

Stocks

Process Outsourcing and Offshoring

Loose Coupling and Process Orchestration

Productive Friction

"In the long term, economic success depends on improvements in our financial, environmental, *and* social performance."

Jeroen Van der Veer

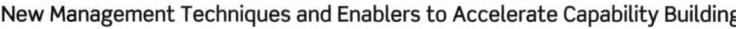

New Management Techniques and Enablers to Accelerate Capability Building

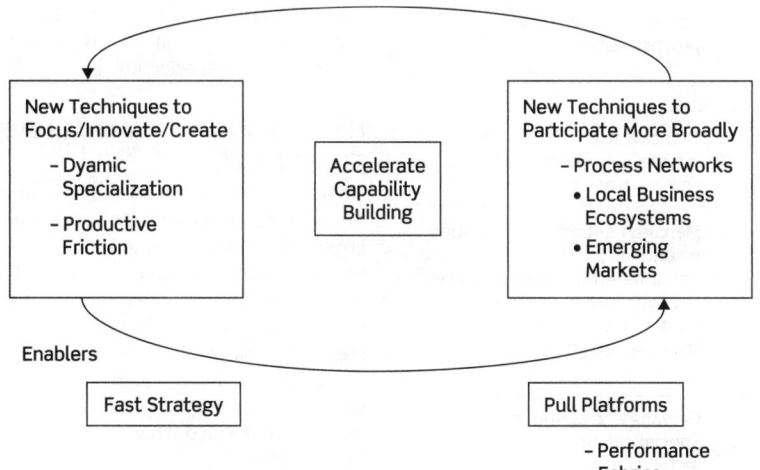

Blowback" in the first quarter 2005 issue of *The McKinsey Quarterly*.

Who we know is more important than what we own. Traditional business strategies are delivering diminishing returns. We are all wrestling with the Red Queen effect and searching for new sources of advantage that can amplify, and not just sustain, our performance. We need to harness the potential for innovation, rather than simply focusing on our existing assets and cost-cutting initiatives.

- As change accelerates, our stocks of physical assets and knowledge depreciate at a more rapid rate. Flows of new knowledge become critical to competitive success and these flows occur only in the context of relationships. Successful strategies will depend on privileged positions in rich networks of relationships. In this world, the primary value of assets is their ability to help us build and sustain relationships.

- Whatever our existing capabilities, we will only succeed in the future by finding ways to get better faster than others. No matter how good we are internally, we will be able to get better even faster by working with others at the edge because people with complementary capabilities can help us to find creative ways to deepen and extend those capabilities.

Unbundling the firm enables even more rapid growth. We are witnessing another wave of specialization that will paradoxically lead to higher levels of concentration in large

- **Edge in the sense of peripheries**. Peripheries, while often relatively marginal in terms of current revenue generation, represent centers of innovation because they provide early insight into new needs and new capabilities. These peripheries can take many different forms, whether as the edges of our existing institutions, geographic edges like emerging economies, or demographic edges represented by younger generations bringing new needs and behaviors to markets around the world.

- **Edge in the sense of boundaries**. Boundaries become fertile areas for innovation because they provide opportunities for people with different experiences, beliefs, and needs to encounter each other.

- **Edge in the sense of performance limits**. Innovation provides the catalyst to push the performance limits of institutions.

As competition intensifies and we seek to build new sources of advantage, peripheries and the boundaries that separate us from others will become more central as sources of innovation. Our institutional cores will remain important, but increasingly their importance will depend on their ability to help us explore and engage with others on the edge. By paying more attention to the edge, we will be better able to refresh and redefine our core.

Western companies generally approach emerging economies much too narrowly. Most Western companies view large emerging economies like China and India as strategic growth engines that compensate for slower growth in more developed economies. Yet they miss the most

important role of these emerging economies. These economies will become catalysts for significant product and business innovation. This innovation will not only be helpful in more effectively serving customers within those economies, but it also has the potential to provide a platform for aggressive attacker strategies to compete with established players in the United States and Western Europe and to take significant share in these more developed economies. Few Western companies appreciate the risk and potential of this phenomenon described in more detail in our article on "Innovation

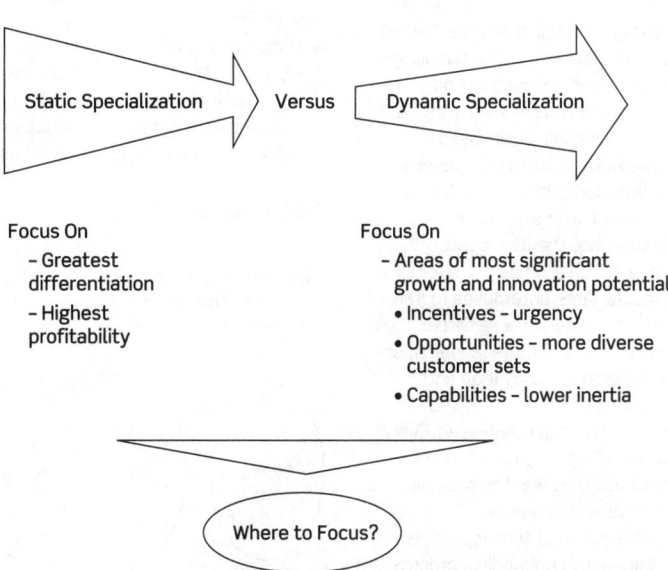

Alternative Views of Specialization

"Challenging the status quo has to be the starting point for anything that goes under the label of strategy."

Gary Hamel

Contrasting Approaches To Business Process Management

	Hard-wired business processes	Loosely coupled global process networks
	From	To
Roles	Controller Limited, all-purpose service providers	Orchestrator increasingly specialized service providers
Rules	Management of micro-activities instructions (push) Full information transparency	Management of macro-entities incentives (pull) Selective information visibility
Renewal	Infrequent benchmarking Infrequent reengineering (every 5–10 years)	Continuous benchmarking Dynamic reconfiguration
Rewards	Experience effects Diminishing returns	Growing and continuous specialization Increasing returns

portions of the global business landscape. The companies that understand this dynamic will be able to create powerful growth platforms.

- *The shedding has already begun.* Large enterprises around the world are actively shedding their infrastructure management businesses to specialized providers. These businesses are high-volume, routine processing activities like managing manufacturing assembly lines, logistics networks, or many forms of customer call centers.
- *The scope of unbundling is expanding.* We are already starting to see some companies shed their product innovation and commercialization businesses to specialized product design firms, as illustrated by the rise of Original Design Manufacturers (ODMs) in Taiwan. This will represent the next wave of unbundling—separating product innovation and commercialization businesses from customer relationship businesses. This unbundling will lead to another level of specialization, extending Adam Smith's original insights on the virtues of specialization into the 21st century.
- *Unbundling will be an imperative for all companies.* All large enterprises represent an unnatural bundle of these three types of business—infrastructure management businesses, product innovation and commercialization businesses, and customer relationship businesses. Every company will ultimately have to choose which business they want to specialize in.
- *Unbundling need not lead to fragmentation.* Rather than leading to fragmentation, this unbundling process will lead to even higher levels of consolidation

and concentration because two of the three types of business—infrastructure management businesses and customer relationship businesses—have significant economies of scale and scope. As an example, look at the concentration emerging in logistics businesses like package delivery (e.g., Federal Express or UPS) or in contract manufacturing businesses (such as Flextronics and Solectron). Online businesses like Travelocity and Expedia illustrate the potential for concentration in customer relationship businesses. Product innovation and commercialization is the one domain where fragmentation is likely to prevail given the desire of creative talent to work in smaller, more intimate, organizational settings.

- *Unbundling creates platforms for more rapid growth.* Unbundling thus creates an opportunity for much more rapid growth by focusing on one type of business, rather than sub-optimizing across multiple,

incompatible businesses. The ability to establish richer relationships with world-class companies in complementary businesses will further amplify the growth potential from specialization.

HARNESSING NEW MANAGEMENT TECHNIQUES

Western companies will need to master new management techniques pioneered largely by Asian companies in order to build a sustainable edge. Our recent book, *The Only Sustainable Edge,* focuses on three key management techniques pioneered largely in Asia. Western companies tend to fall short when they seek to implement these management techniques because they misunderstand where and how to capture the value:

- **Western companies are leaving a lot of value on the table in their process outsourcing and offshoring activities and, in many cases, are actually weakening their business**—more and more companies are moving operations to offshore locations but many are disappointed with the results they have achieved. This is a particular concern since outsourcing and offshoring no longer focus just on peripheral activities but involve the core operating processes of the firm, including manufacturing and product design.
- *Cost reduction is not the primary reason to go offshore.* Western companies still focus too narrowly on cost reduction, rather than viewing these options in terms of providing opportunities to participate in networks of relationships that can accelerate skill building—a key focus of our recent book.

Be wary of captive facilities. Western companies too often tend to build sub-optimal captive facilities, in part based on a false belief that this will reduce risk. They under-estimate the benefits of outsourcing to more specialized providers that can get

The Innovation Agenda

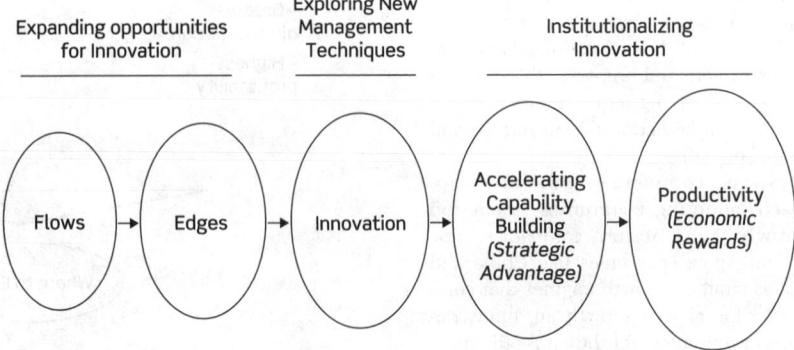

better faster by drawing on the learning that comes from a more diverse customer base.

- *Don't forget your own operations.* Even if they outsource activities, Western companies tend to ignore the need to accelerate capability building in the retained activities. It is often much too easy to complain about the limitations of the other party rather than concentrating on your own limitations.
- *These are strategic, not operational, choices.* Most Western companies still view offshoring and outsourcing choices as near-term operating decisions versus long-term strategic choices—they lack understanding of the strategic implications of unbundling the firm.

Conventional supply chain management techniques of Western companies will undermine their ability to compete with companies pioneering more modular process management techniques—these new techniques provide creative ways to connect highly specialized participants from around the world in global process networks to mobilize resources more flexibly and enhance the potential for innovation in extended business processes.

- *Conventional approaches narrow the number of participants.* Western companies have tended to narrow their external relationships in the quest for efficiency.

This makes sense if the sole objective is to reduce operating costs within conventional process management approaches. The complexity overhead that arises from tight specification and monitoring of activities makes it prohibitive to involve more business partners. Also, reducing the number of business partners enhances bargaining power to obtain lower prices by offering more business to a single supplier.

New approaches are designed to dramatically expand the number of participants. By pioneering more modular and loosely coupled approaches to organizing business processes, orchestrators of these global process networks have found a way to effectively mobilize hundreds and even thousands of participants, creating new opportunities to:

- tap into much deeper specialization;
- create much greater operational flexibility to tailor value;
- unleash significant innovation at multiple levels in the process.

They operate successfully in the most demanding markets. These process networks operate in some of the most demanding and un-

certain global markets, including consumer electronics and apparel. *The Only Sustainable Edge* discusses examples of these global process networks in detail. *They build trust by focusing on future opportunities.* In contrast to the supply chain operations and business partnerships of Western companies, these networks operate with a different incentive structure that accelerates the building of trust.

- Participating companies focus on getting better faster by working together in long-term relationships to come up with innovative approaches to delivering greater value to the marketplace. Unlike their Western counterparts, they view the potential for product and process innovation to be virtually unlimited.
- With the prospect of an expanding pie and through deepening the capability of individual participants, traditional issues of rent distribution and business risk (for example, hold-up and failure to perform) become less severe. Also, since global process networks focus on building long-term relationships they create the expectation of continuing transactions and a disincentive for short-term opportunistic behavior that might threaten the relationship.

This is not just about supply chain operations. These global process networks are not just in supply chain operations but are helping to re-shape both product innovation and customer relationship business processes on a global scale. *Current forms of pull operations are much too limited.* The development of these modular process management techniques represents a broader shift from push to pull models of resource mobilization that go well beyond the existing "pull" approaches pioneered in lean manufacturing—they are pulling resources from thousands of highly specialized business partners. This more aggressive form of pull is discussed in greater detail in our article, "From Push to Pull: The Next Frontier of Innovation" published in the third quarter 2005 issue of *The McKinsey Quarterly*.

Our current approaches to strategy are actually a barrier to building strategic advantage. Traditional approaches to business strategy actually slow down the learning and capability-building process. By challenging traditional approaches to defining corporate strategy, a FAST (Focus, Accelerate, Strengthen and Tie Together) strategy approach provides a way to focus organizational learning based on a limited

set of operational metrics and to balance longer-term direction setting with high-impact near-term initiatives.

- *Shift in time horizons.* Under this new approach, the one-to-five-year time horizon becomes much less relevant. Executives instead need to focus on two other time horizons: a five-to-ten-year horizon and a six-to-twelve-month horizon.
- *From sequential to parallel initiatives.* Rather than proceeding sequentially from strategy development to operational execution, this new approach defines longer-term strategic direction and short-term operational initiatives in parallel.

Fundamental transformation can only be achieved through pragmatic migration paths. Given all the changes outlined above, corporations will end up looking and acting very differently. For many analysts, the conceptual discontinuity described earlier requires radical discontinuities in practice. Radical reconstruction efforts rarely succeed. The best way to manage through discontinuous change is through incremental radicalism. By harnessing the new management techniques and new generations of IT discussed earlier, companies will be able to fashion a pragmatic migration path to compete successfully in a more challenging global economy. While the specific steps will vary depending on the company and industry, companies will broadly pursue three waves of change:

- **Deepening specialization**—Use process outsourcing and offshoring to make strategic choices among the three business types outlined earlier.
- **Harnessing connectivity**—Master the management techniques required to participate more effectively in global creation networks.
- **Accelerating capability building**—Use the techniques of productive friction to get better faster by working with others and to participate in emerging global learning ecologies.

FOR MORE INFORMATION

Book:
Hagel III, John, and John Seely Brown. *The Only Sustainable Edge*. Cambridge, MA: Harvard Business School Press, 2005.

See also:
ꝏ Corporate Strategy (pp. 1606–1723)

116

BEST PRACTICE

Maximizing a New Strategic Alliance
by Peter Killing

EXECUTIVE SUMMARY

- Over 60,000 strategic alliances have been formed in the past decade. About half were joint ventures. Only 40% meet or exceed their partners' expectations.
- To be successful with strategic alliances you must be clear about your objectives, get the alliance design right, and manage the alliance effectively after it is formed.
- There is an important difference between shallow and deep alliances, and you should know which type you need and why.
- Alliance success depends in large part on skilled managers who are good with people, have a high tolerance for ambiguity and conflict, and are patient yet persistent.
- The clearest sign of alliance success is growing trust between the partners.

INTRODUCTION

More than 60,000 strategic alliances were formed in the 1990s. About half of these were joint ventures. The other 50% were nonequity arrangements such as technology licensing agreements, joint marketing arrangements, and joint research or development projects. Most of these alliances were international, so it's no surprise to learn that the world's largest multinationals are heavy alliance users: IBM (254 alliances), General Motors (138), Mitsubishi (233), Toshiba (147), Philips (207), and Siemens (200) are just some examples.

Clearly the ability to create and manage strategic alliances is an important skill for most management teams. If you cannot make effective use of alliances in today's world, you will be at a serious competitive disadvantage.

GETTING IT RIGHT

A 1999 study by Andersen Consulting indicates that only 40% of alliances achieve or exceed the initial expectations of their partners, which suggests there's a lot of room for improvement. One of the reasons for the relatively low success rate is that there are many different aspects of the design and management of alliances that you need to get right, from clearly understanding your objectives to managing the alliance after it is formed. They can be grouped into three sequential steps:

1. **Clarify objectives.** What do we need and for how long? Is an alliance the best way to get what we need?
2. **Design the alliance.** What type of alliance should we create? What should our role be?

3. **Manage after the deal is done.** How do we effectively manage the alliance? Can we build trust?

Clarify Objectives and the Need for the Alliance

The first challenge is to be clear about what your company needs to fulfill its strategy, which may be different from what others in your industry need. The second challenge is to decide whether an alliance is the best way to get what you need. Three common reasons for forming alliances are:

- **To enter new markets.** One of the classic purposes of joint ventures is to enter foreign markets. Typically the foreign company finds the local market attractive, but does not feel confident enough to enter without local knowledge, and so takes a local partner. In some countries the government insists on such a relationship. In China, for example, joint ventures between foreigners and local companies are prevalent. Often, as foreign companies gain confidence in their ability to operate locally, they end the joint venture by buying out their local partner and creating a wholly owned subsidiary. In this case the alliance is a step on the road to something else.
- **To create new technology and set industry standards.** In technology-intensive industries like computing and telecommunications, companies often use alliances to attempt to create a new technology that will become the industry standard. An example is Symbian, a joint venture formed in 1998 by Psion, Ericsson, Nokia, and Motorola. Symbian's objective is to create an operating system for wireless

devices to exchange information efficiently. Microsoft has also shown an interest in this area and has considered building its own alliance around its CE operating system with partners including NTT DoCoMo and British Telecom. The competition has shifted from company versus company to alliance versus alliance.
- **To shape consolidation.** In consolidating industries such as airlines, telecoms, and the automotive industry, alliances are often formed between companies that fear they are too small to continue independently (and that do not want to be taken over) and those that intend to play a dominant role in the consolidation. The alliance between Fiat and GM was formed for precisely this reason. This deal involves cross-ownership holdings between the two companies, two 50–50 joint ventures, and a variety of smaller cooperative arrangements. Fiat also had an option to sell itself to GM (before agreeing a "divorce" worth $2 billion in 2005). The immediate motives behind such alliances are to gain economies of scale and global reach, to eliminate excess capacity, and to keep the smaller company out of the hands of predators.

Why Use an Alliance?

Alliances are often the least-preferred choice of the companies that enter them. Many companies would rather enter a new market themselves, or perhaps make an acquisition. GM, for example, would probably have preferred to buy Fiat, but the company was not for sale. Alliances are often seen as difficult to manage, ambiguous in terms of control and decision making (and as a result slow moving), and requiring an extraordinary amount of management time and attention.

The usual motives, positive and negative, for proceeding with an alliance are:

Positive
- to harness the partner's energy and knowledge;
- to set an industry standard by involving partners;
- to learn something;
- to gain economies of scale or global reach;
- to reduce risk;
- to gain speed.

"You should never underestimate the challenge of operating a multicultural business."

William T. Esrey

Negative

- government insists on alliance;
- acquisitions are too expensive or not available;
- it's the only financially affordable alternative;
- the company fears being acquired;
- an alliance will prevent a competitor's acquisition of, or alliance with, the partner;
- closing the business is too expensive; an alliance provides a more graceful exit.

You should be clear on your own motives as well as your partner's. There are no data on this issue, but alliances formed for positive motives may have a higher success rate.

Design the Alliance

There are many types of alliance. The simplest are straightforward license agreements and shared marketing deals; the most complex are multipart arrangements such as cross-ownership positions, joint ventures, and cooperative projects between partners. Faced with an abundance of choice, managers entering an alliance need to make a key decision: whether they want a shallow alliance or a deep alliance.

Shallow Alliances—Traveling Light

A shallow alliance might be thought of as a flirtation—a low-commitment alliance that doesn't have a lot of resources devoted to it and that can be broken on short notice. As an example, think of current airline alliances such as the Star and One World alliances, which seem to feature new partners every month. Or consider Cisco and its Internet-related businesses. Cisco often cannot judge if a young company's fledgling technology will prove to be important a year later. The shallow alliance solution is to buy 10% of the company's stock in a friendly transaction and get a seat on the board and an option to buy the remainder of the equity. The assigned board member can then assess the company's management, its market prospects, and its technology. If it looks good, they buy the rest of the company. If not, they leave. Shallow alliances thus create options for companies in fast-changing industries in which the way ahead is not clear. The alliances are not usually intended to be permanent.

Deep Alliances—Commitment

At the other end of the spectrum are deep alliances involving high levels of financial and managerial commitment by the partners. Deep alliances feature many links between the partners, usually including one or more seats on the board of directors, cross-ownership positions, at least two or three joint ventures, and many less formal but important cooperative projects. Deep alliances are generally slower-moving than shallow alliances, more difficult to manage, and more difficult to end. The benefits of success can be high, but so can the costs of failure. Deep alliances are not for the timid.

Manage After the Deal Is Done

Once you've formed an alliance, you'll sooner or later discover that you have brought together partners with different ways of doing things and somewhat different objectives, priorities, and performance standards. These differences make the management of alliances a difficult task. The single most important thing you can do to maximize the probability of success is to assign some of your very best people to work on it. "Best" means managers with excellent people skills, cross-cultural sensitivity, and a tolerance for ambiguity and frustration. Alliance managers need to be patient, yet persistent.

Six months into the life of your alliance you should look closely at the relationship between the partners. Is trust starting to develop? If not, why not? Where are the trouble spots? Many texts advise that when choosing a partner you should choose someone you trust. This is difficult to do unless you have worked together before. The real question is whether or not you can develop trust over time. The best predictor of the future performance of any alliance is the current level of trust between the partners.

Finally, don't assume that the alliance is done when the deal is signed. This is just the beginning. Be flexible and open to change and learning. There will be plenty of opportunity for both.

MAKING IT HAPPEN ▶▶

Strategic Alliances are increasingly popular, even necessary, however they are often a high-risk strategy. It is worth viewing the alliance in three distinct phases:

- **Before the deal is struck:** the vital period when goals are considered, resources prepared and partners considered. Internal agreement on the goals, strategy, and resources to be used is important, as is choosing the right partner and evaluating them thoroughly through due diligence.
- **Negotiating the deal:** the terms of the agreement and, significantly, the expectations of each partner and the

spirit of the agreement, will be decisive in determining the effectiveness of the alliance.

- **Post-agreement management:** Successful agreements are those that are consistently and attentively resourced, managed, and valued. If they are not, they are unlikely to survive normal commercial pressures.

Some key questions to consider include:

- Have you formally assessed the aims and benefits of the strategic alliance?
- How does the alliance fit with your overall commercial strategy?
- Who needs to be informed of the alliance—and when?
- Have you sought the advice of professional advisers?
- Have you taken time to understand the target and the commercial implications?
- To what extent should the alliance be integrated into your existing business? Who will lead this?
- Do you have a fully costed and resourced plan for managing the alliance? What are the targets and success criteria for the alliance?

FOR MORE INFORMATION

Books:
Cauley de la Sierra, M. *Managing Global Alliances: Key Steps for Successful Collaboration.* Reading, MA: Addison-Wesley, 1995.
Doz, Yves L., and Gary Hamel. *Alliance Advantage: The Art of Creating Value through Partnering.* Cambridge, MA: Harvard Business School Press, 1998.
Lewis, Jordan D. *Trusted Partners: How Companies Build Mutual Trust and Win Together.* New York: Free Press, 2000.

Web sites:
www.alliancestrategy.com: this site offers resources and readings on alliance strategy and management. It is maintained by Ben Gomes-Casseres, author of *The Alliance Revolution*.
www.smartalliances.com: this site gives a variety of practical advice and useful information on the fast-growing world of Strategic Alliances, linking users to books, conferences, perspectives, and experts.

"We are always willing to be trade partners, but never trade patsies." Ronald Reagan

Viewpoint: Jean-Claude Larréché
Beyond Strategy: Market-based Capabilities

Introduction

Beyond strategy, great business leadership requires building intangible assets for sustainable long-term success. Market-based capabilities are intangible assets that influence the competitive success of a firm in its markets. In this piece, Jean-Claude Larréché, the Alfred H. Heineken Chaired Professor of Marketing at INSEAD in Fontainebleau, France, sets out his views on four selected key issues concerning market-based capabilities: the concept, measurement, the emergence of capability gaps in specific business sectors, and the development of distinctive superior capability profiles.

Ever since the advent of modern management, the business community—corporations, consulting companies, and business schools alike—has been striving to understand what makes some companies more successful than others. From Peter Drucker's first book in the late 1940s through *In Search of Excellence* and several generations of other bestsellers, ample guidance has become available on this most important subject. And, "strategy" has now become more of a buzzword in business than in the military.

Jack Welch, as the new chairman of General Electric, came to his first meeting with financial analysts with a "big" message, organized in two parts: "hard" issues—the strategic requirement of being no.1 or no. 2 in each business unit—and "soft" issues—such as the human element. While the soft issues were essential to General Electric's success for the next decades, the analysts' reaction was cold. In Jack Welch's words: "About halfway through, I had the impression that I would have gotten as much interest if I'd talked about my Ph.D. thesis on drop-wise condensation."

Since that time, the more progressive business leaders and observers have, fortunately, become more enlightened and followed Jack Welch's example. In the search for key success factors, there has been a growing recognition of the importance of intangible assets, or capabilities, such as human resources, customer orientation, corporate culture, or brands. Simultaneously, there has been an increased focus on evaluating these capabilities in terms of their impact on the competitive success of the firm in its markets, not in terms of technically defined criteria. This is emphasized in the expression "market-based capabilities."

Some companies have capabilities that are "technically correct" but ineffective when it comes to winning in the marketplace. For example, they may have an impressive well-written mission statement with all the "right" ingredients, which nonetheless causes confusion or cynicism resulting in reduced effectiveness. They may have sophisticated systems based on the latest technologies with wonderful real-time features, but to no avail if these are seen by front-line staff to be more of a competitive handicap than a competitive advantage. On the other hand, companies like Virgin Atlantic, First Direct, or Amazon .com have great competitive fitness capabilities from relatively small investments. There is no need to be a large firm to have great fundamental capabilities. In fact, sometimes the opposite is true; in large firms the muscles can turn to fat so the firm becomes heavier, ineffective, and handicapped in the market place.

The opportunities for improving market-based capabilities for most companies are huge. Opportunities are uncovered by asking a few fundamental questions, not typically asked in the "normal" process of running a business: How fit, in the absolute and relative to my competitors, are these capabilities that are the life blood of the unit I am leading? What progress has been made in the last five years? What is the current trend? What am I going to do about it? At times, responding to these opportunities requires investment, but in other cases it is more a matter of doing less and focusing more. The executive or manager cannot escape responsibility for the competitive fitness of the unit he or she is in charge of. This responsibility is at the core of leadership.

An important leadership gap is the inability to measure intangible capabilities. In the Competitive Fitness of Global Firms initiative at INSEAD, a

> A competitive advantage in terms of capabilities is the ultimate form of competitive advantage.

"The last remaining source of truly sustainable competitive advantage lies in what we've come to describe as organizational capabilities."

David A. Nadler

framework and an assessment methodology have been developed to evaluate the fundamental capabilities driving the success of the modern firm. This work has been based on available published research, long-term analyses of about 40 corporations, in-depth case studies, and the cooperation of selected firms.

The Competitive Fitness of Global Firms framework includes 12 fundamental capabilities: Mission and Vision, Customer Orientation, Corporate Culture, Organization and Systems, Planning and Intelligence, Human Resources, Technical Resources, Innovation, Market Strategy, Marketing Operations, International, and Performance. The measurement methodology is based on a diagnostic tool containing 182 indicators to estimate scores on the 12 capabilities. The methodology is available for use by executives at any level in a firm.

From 1998 to 2002, a survey was conducted annually to provide international capability benchmarks on which executives can compare their scores with competitors. The Report on the Competitive Fitness of Global Firms, based on this survey, was published annually for 5 years, and covered eight sectors comprising more than 300 of the largest firms from Europe and North America.

A competitive advantage in terms of capabilities is the ultimate form of competitive advantage. Products and technologies are visible and well defined and can be imitated by those ready to make the investment. By contrast, capabilities are often intangible and made up of elemental parts—innovation, human resources, corporate culture. Capabilities also tend to endure and provide a competitive edge for a firm in various markets, not just a specific area or segment. A capability advantage is pervasive and sustainable and can therefore be an important engine of value creation for the short and long term.

In the past, "industry practices" prevailed in separate sectors. There was an acceptable way to run a bank, a chemical group, or a consumer goods company. Industry associations, management transfers, and the leadership of large companies contributed to the establishment of these norms. We can now observe a wider gap being created between the capabilities of different firms in the same sector, and recognize that the trend leaders are not always the largest firms.

The *Report on the Competitive Fitness of Global Firms* provides some illustrations of this phenomenon in many sectors. Many financial services firms still believe in an old industry "truth" that innovation advantages are not possible because products are imitated easily. In reality, some firms find ways to go from strength to strength while others lag behind in innovation and other key capabilities. These latter firms are unaware of their sliding competitiveness as they do not have access to a quantified benchmark. They run the risk of realizing it only when their performance suffers, by which time it will be even more difficult to correct the situation.

Does this mean that all the fittest firms need to be equally strong on all capabilities? Certainly not. The *Report on Corporate Competitive Fitness* shows that the fittest firms very often have a personality, a distinctive competitive fitness profile. There is a unique "capability look" about the fittest companies in a given sector, reminiscent of a specific face, silhouette, or fingerprint.

In addition to a vast array of observations on market-based capabilities, the *Report on the Competitive Fitness of Global Firms* contains the capability profiles of more than 60 firms in 8 sectors. These are the fittest firms among those included in the survey. Companies such as Diageo, Exxon Mobil, and Eli Lilly score highly on overall corporate competitive fitness. They are above their sector's averages on most of the capabilities. In addition, they have a strong atypical profile, the expression of a unique personality that is the result of strong crafting. It may have been achieved over generations or through recent transformations and actions, but such competitive fitness profiles are not developed just through the "normal" way of running a business. It requires strong leadership to invest in what Jack Welch called "soft values." Beyond strategy, the selection of priorities for further capability development is a crucial task of leadership.

Beyond short-term results is strategy; beyond strategy are market-based capabilities. By focusing on short-term results, or on a narrow strategy, some businesses are cutting into both fat and muscle. In the process, they are digging the hole into which they will eventually collapse. The challenge of great leadership is to deliver at all three levels: results, strategy, and market-based capabilities. The latter are the most important for sustainable long-term success. Unfortunately, market-based capabilities are also the most difficult element to comprehend and the easiest to neglect. Effective management of a business's intangible assets requires the three steps described in this article: measuring market-based capabilities, monitoring the emergence of capability gaps in relevant business sectors, and investing in the development of a distinctive superior capability profile.

> **Beyond short-term results is strategy; beyond strategy are market-based capabilities. By focusing on short-term results, or on a narrow strategy, some businesses are cutting into both fat and muscle.**

FOR MORE INFORMATION

Web site:
StratX.com: **www.www.stratx.com**

See also:
☆ Viewpoint: Warren Bennis (pp. 249–250)
💡 Warren Bennis (pp. 1184–1185)

Outsourcing
by Ronan McIvor

EXECUTIVE SUMMARY

- Outsourcing has become critically important to many organizations due to the strategic implications.
- Many organizations have not achieved the desired benefits from outsourcing.
- Typical problems include no formal outsourcing process, limited cost analysis, and core business definition.
- Outsourcing should be carried out from a strategic perspective and integrated into the overall strategy of the organization.
- Definitions of the core and noncore activities of the business must be linked with corporate strategy.
- Relationship management is a crucial element in ensuring effective management of the outsourcing process.

INTRODUCTION

One of the key issues for many organizations has been the growing importance of outsourcing. The drive for greater efficiencies and cost reductions has forced many organizations to increasingly specialize in a limited number of key areas. This has led organizations to outsource activities traditionally carried out in-house. Although the term "outsourcing" has become popular in recent years, organizations have always made decisions about determining their the boundaries. Outsourcing has progressed from involving only peripheral business activities toward encompassing more critical business activities that contribute to competitive advantage.

However, there is evidence to suggest that organizations are not achieving the desired benefits from outsourcing. Recent research has revealed that outsourcing decisions are rarely taken within a thoroughly strategic perspective, with many companies adopting a short-term perspective and being motivated primarily by the search for short-term cost reductions. Also, some commentators have expressed serious concerns over companies that have embarked upon extensive outsourcing without fully understanding the concept (Barthelemy, 2003).

THE DECISION TO OUTSOURCE

The conceptual basis for outsourcing is Williamson's (1975) theory of *transaction cost analysis*. This combines economic theory with management theory to determine the best type of relationship a company should develop in the marketplace. The central theme of transaction costs theory is that the properties of the transaction determine the governance structure. Asset specificity refers to the nontrivial investment in transaction-specific assets. For example, the level of customized equipment or materials involved in the transaction relates to the degree of asset specificity. When asset specificity and uncertainty are low and transactions are relatively frequent, transactions will be governed by markets. High asset specificity and uncertainty lead to transactional difficulties, with transactions held internally within the company—vertical integration. Medium levels of asset specificity lead to bilateral relations in the form of cooperative alliances between the organizations.

A term that is frequently used in connection with outsourcing is "core competence." The ideas of core competence and its relationship to outsourcing have evolved from the work of Prahalad and Hamel (1990). Prahalad and Hamel argue that the real sources of competitive advantage are to be found in management's ability to consolidate corporate-wide technologies and production skills into competencies that empower individual businesses to adapt rapidly to changing business opportunities. Core competence is important to the study of outsourcing, as it has proposed the internal organization of the company as the potential for competitive advantage. Obtaining, creating, and developing certain capabilities is central to the core competence approach and has important implications for what activities should be kept within the company and which should be external to it.

KEY PROBLEMS WITH THE OUTSOURCING PROCESS

Many companies have failed to take a strategic view of outsourcing decisions, deciding to outsource for short-term reasons such as cost reduction and capacity constraints. A number of problems encountered by companies in their efforts to formulate an effective outsourcing decision are listed below:

- **No formal outsourcing process.** Many companies have no firm basis for evaluating the outsourcing decision. In many instances, the choice of which parts of the business to outsource is made by ascertaining what will save most on overhead costs, rather than on what makes the most long-term business sense.
- **A fragmented piecemeal approach.** Many companies have failed to integrate outsourcing decisions into their overall corporate strategy. This has led to a fragmented and piecemeal approach with no coherent strategy on how outsourcing should contribute to strategic objectives.
- **Limited cost analysis.** Cost analysis of the outsourcing decision involves comparing the important costs associated with internal work and outsourcing. However, in many cases these calculations tend to focus primarily on manufacturing costs and do not provide a true reflection of the total costs involved. Also, other more qualitative factors, such as the long-term strategic implications and the workforce reaction to outsourcing, may have a greater impact on the decision.
- **Core business definition.** The embedded skills that give rise to the next generation of competitive products cannot be "rented-in" by outsourcing. Too many companies have unknowingly relinquished their core competencies by cutting internal investment in what they mistakenly thought were "cost centers" in favor of outside suppliers. Outsourcing may provide a shortcut to a more competitive product, but it typically contributes little to build the people-embodied skills that are needed to sustain future product leadership.

KEY REQUIREMENTS FOR EFFECTIVE OUTSOURCING
Core Activity Definition

Companies must identify their core and noncore activities. A core activity is central

"Thinking must be the hardest job in the world. What people want to do is outsource it to a mantra or a methodology like reengineering."

Eileen C. Shapiro

to the company successfully serving the needs of potential customers in each market. The activity is perceived by the customers as adding value, and therefore being a major determinant of competitive advantage. Distinguishing between core and noncore activities is a complex task, and care must be taken to ensure the long-term strategic considerations and true benefits are assessed. This process of identifying the core activities should be carried out by top management with inputs from teams at lower levels in the organization. Each team should encompass a broad section of members—functionally, divisionally, and hierarchically. Noncore activities for which the company has neither a critical strategic need nor special capabilities should be outsourced. Companies adopting this approach, such as Honda and Dell, build their strategies around their core activities and outsource as much of the rest as possible.

Capability Analysis

Each core activity must be benchmarked against the capabilities of all potential external providers (both suppliers and competitors) of that activity. This will enable the identification of the relative performance for each core activity along a number of selected measures. Resources should be focused on the activities where pre-eminence can be achieved and unique customer-perceived value can be delivered. For example, Eastman Kodak has world leadership in two of its core activities—chemical and electronic imaging. Thus, these activities are held within the company in order to maintain and build upon this leadership. A key strategic issue in the outsourcing decision is whether a company can achieve a sustainable competitive advantage by performing a core activity internally on an on-going basis. Many companies assume that because they have always performed the activity internally, then it should remain that way. In many cases, closer analysis may reveal a significant disparity between their capabilities and those of the world's best suppliers.

Cost Analysis

All the actual and potential costs involved in sourcing the activity, either internally or externally, must be measured. This encompasses all the costs associated with the acquisition of the activity throughout the entire supply chain and not just the purchase price. It is important to consider costs right from idea conception, as in collaborating with a supplier in the design phase of the component, through to any costs (for example, warranty claims) associated with the component once the completed product is being used by the final customer. The data requirements for this stage are quite formidable. Management must break down the company's functional cost accounting data into the costs of performing specific activities. The appropriate degree of disaggregation depends upon the economics of the activities and how valuable it is to develop cross-company comparisons for narrowly defined activities as opposed to broadly defined activities.

Relationship Management

As a result of increased outsourcing, companies have become more dependent upon their suppliers, thus making supplier relationship management a key success actor. Many companies have been attempting to develop collaborative relationships with suppliers as they seek to reduce the risks associated with outsourcing.

Companies may establish a collaborative relationship with a supplier in order to exploit their capabilities. For example, a company may wish to maintain the knowledge (design skills, management skills, manufacturing, etc.) that enables the technology of the activity to be exploited, even when another partner is providing it. Also, it is possible for a company to develop a core competency by learning from partners. For example, NEC top management determined that semiconductors would be the company's most important "core product." Hence, it entered into strategic alliances aimed at building competencies quickly and at low cost. In some circumstances it may be more beneficial to pursue a relationship where the company holds the balance of power rather than pursuing a relationship based upon equality and the mutual sharing of benefits. For example, a company may use its influence to obtain reductions in inventory and cost, which in turn have a positive impact on the achievement of its own competitive position. Also, this may ensure greater flexibility in that the company will not get locked into a long-term relationship with a supplier whose technology or processes may become uncompetitive.

MAKING IT HAPPEN ▶▶

- Take a strategic view of outsourcing decisions—don't act on short-term factors such as cost reduction and capacity constraints.
- Outsource what makes the most long-term business sense, not for what will save most on overhead costs.
- Identify core activities by supporting top management with lower-level teams with broad functional, divisional, and hierarchical membership.
- Benchmark each activity against the capabilities of all potential external providers (both suppliers and competitors).
- Keep a core activity internally on a continuing basis only if you can achieve a sustainable competitive advantage by doing so.
- Measure all the actual and potential costs involved in outsourcing the activity—not just the purchase price.

FOR MORE INFORMATION

Books and Journal Articles:
Barthelemy, J. "The Seven Deadly Sins of Outsourcing" *The Academy of Management Perspectives* February 2003: 87–98.
Feeny, D., M. Lacity, and L. Willcocks. "Taking the Measure of Outsourcing Providers." *Sloan Management Review*, 46, 3, 2005: 41–48.
McIvor, Ronan. "A Practical Framework for Understanding the Outsourcing Process," *International Journal of Supply Chain Management*, January 5, 2000: 22–36.
Prahalad, C. K., and Gary Hamel. "The Core Competence of the Corporation," *Harvard Business Review*, July–August, 1990: 79–91.
Quinn, J. B., and F. G. Hilmer. "Strategic Outsourcing," *Sloan Management Review*, Summer, 1994: 43–55.
Williamson, Oliver E. *Markets and Hierarchies*. New York: Free Press, 1975.

See also:
☆ Competing on Costs (pp. 146–147)

"Thinking must be the hardest job in the world. What people want to do is outsource it to a mantra or a methodology like reengineering."

Eileen C. Shapiro

The Power of Identity
by Wally Olins

EXECUTIVE SUMMARY

- Corporate identity is the unique identity of a company that differentiates it from its competitors; it is a valuable asset and influences the organization's strategy, structure, and vision. Today, it is often replaced by the word "brand."
- A corporate identity or branding program enables a corporation's individual identity to be managed and projected.
- In order to develop an effective identity or branding program, organizational builders must have a clear idea about what drives the organization—they must have a vision and a sense of strategic direction.
- Organizational builders can consciously construct a structure that enables the organization to project its identity both internally and externally.

INTRODUCTION

Organizations have a unique identity that can be employed as a valuable asset. Corporations currently face challenges to their identity from all sides. These challenges are increasingly prompting company boards to regard identity or brand as an important topic. These are the most common problems regarding identity management:

- Products and services are increasingly becoming more similar, persuading customers to purchase products on an emotional basis—a projected sense of corporate personality and rapport with customers boosts business. How can Shell, Texaco, and BP differentiate their products from each other so as to provide competitive advantage?
- Corporate mergers are on the rise, disregarding local boundaries and charging leaders with the problem of how to create a new identity from two old ones. Daimler Chrysler is a good example.
- Organizations are forced through changing technologies, deregulation, and globalization to alter the nature of their business and to manage corporate identity through change and uncertainty.

Corporate identity or branding provides a bedrock of valuable resources, such as goodwill, loyalty, and respect among customers, while internally providing a strategic direction.

WHAT IS IDENTITY?

Every organization carries out thousands of transactions every day: it buys, it sells, it hires and fires, it makes, it promotes, it in-

forms through advertising and the Web. In each transaction the organization is in some way presenting itself—or part of itself—to the various groups of people it deals with. The totality of the way the organization presents itself can be called its identity. What different audiences perceive is often called its image.

Because the range of its activities is so vast, and the manifestations of identity are so diverse, the corporation needs to actively and explicitly manage its identity or brand. Identity management, like financial management or information systems management, is a corporate resource embracing every part of the organization.

Identity can project four ideas:

- who you are;
- what you do;
- how you do it;
- where you want to go.

The Four Vectors

Identity or brand manifests itself primarily through:

- products and services—what you make or sell (think of BMW);
- environments—where you make or sell it (Hilton Hotels);
- communications—how you talk about your product (Coca-Cola);
- behavior—how you behave to your employees and the world outside (Southwest Airlines).

The balance among these four is rarely equal, and an early priority in creating any identity program is to determine which predominates.

The Central Idea/Vision

The idea behind an identity program is that in everything the organization does or produces, it should project a clear idea of what it is and what its objectives are.

Name/Logo

At the heart of the visual identity is the hierarchy and identification system and the way it is reflected in symbols, logotypes, and marks. The symbol is highly visible. Its prime purpose is to present the idea of the corporation with impact, brevity, and immediacy.

It is sometimes necessary to change the symbol in order to signify a change in direction, as, for example, BP did. In other cases (for example, Renault or Shell) modification may be more appropriate.

Sometimes it's appropriate to change the name of a corporation for legal reasons or for clarity. Name changes are, however, frequently misunderstood and always excite high levels of emotion, particularly in the media.

Audiences

The audiences of an organization are those people who come into contact with it in any way. It is often assumed that the most important audience for any corporation is its customers. In a service business, however, employees are by far the most significant audience. They transmit the identity of the organization to customers, so they have to live it.

There are both internal and external audiences. The internal audience comprises staff members and their families. External audiences include stockholders, competitors, suppliers, and partners, the financial world, and opinion-formers of all kinds. These audiences are not always separate and independent; to some extent they overlap.

Types of Corporate Identity (or "Brand Architecture")

The identity of most corporations can be assigned to one of three general categories: monolithic, endorsed, or branded.

Monolithic identity. Here the organization uses one name and one visual system throughout all of its interactions. Because everything that the organization does has the same name, style, and character, each

"Our brand awareness went from 81 percent to 65 percent in one year. We weren't advertising so we know exactly what to blame."

Chris Moore

part supports the other. Virgin is the most high profile example of this type of identity. The name and identity of Virgin is not associated so much with what it does, but with what it is, how it behaves, and what it seems to stand for.

Endorsed identity. Most corporations grow at least partly by acquisition. The acquiring corporation is often eager to preserve the goodwill (equity) associated with its acquisitions. Under an endorsed identity strategy, the parent endorses its subsidiaries with the corporate name and sometimes its visual style. Accor is an example of an organization that uses the endorsed system.

Branded identity. Some companies, especially those in the consumer products field, separate their corporate identity from the identities of the brands they own, for example, Unilever, Diageo, and LVMH. The final customer identifies with the brand, other audiences with the corporation. Brands have names, reputations, life cycles, and personalities of their own, and they may even compete with other brands from the same corporation.

STARTING AND MANAGING A PROGRAM

The following points should be considered when implementing a corporate identity program:

- Is it part of a corporate turnaround?
- Does it inspire, invigorate, and create more cohesion internally?
- Is it intended to increase the share price?
- Is it focused on helping to integrate newly acquired companies?
- Is it a response to competitive pressures?

When a corporate identity program is initiated, a senior individual in the organization must be appointed to manage it, and change should be implemented in a clear and goal-focused manner. Most organizations will need outside assistance from branding, identity, or design consultants. As with every corporate activity, the identity program needs a power base, financial controls, and clear lines of authority. A working party should be formed, which should report to a steering group.

THE STAGES OF WORK

Stage One: Investigation, Analysis, and Strategic Recommendations

The organization has to take an objective look at how it is perceived by its various audiences and how these perceptions compare with its aspirations. If the existing identity is seen as unclear, old-fashioned, or ineffective, senior managers need to agree on

the action required to change perceptions. Stage One ends with recommendations for action.

Stage Two: Development

Depending on the results of Stage One, it may be necessary to change the identity of the corporation completely, including name and visual style (Accenture), to keep the same name but change the identity visually (BP Amoco), or simply to make some changes.

Changes of name and visual style are expensive and time-consuming, and they clearly signal to the marketplace that the organization is making a new promise or moving in a new direction. This kind of change makes a promise of changed performance that has to be fulfilled. Never promise more than you can deliver.

On the basis of the recommendations made in Stage One, consultants develop an identity system based on the endorsed or branded model. The identity system usually consists of a name (or names), mark or logo, main and subsidiary typefaces, and colors. These will be applied to materials such as letterheads, Web sites, and products.

Stage Three: Implementation

The new identity has to be codified so that it can be used in the organization and by relevant outside suppliers. Manuals are prepared containing all the identity elements and their precise specifications for a variety of applications. The manual should also demonstrate the spirit that lies behind the organization.

Stage Four: Launch

If the new corporate identity program is to work, it has to be launched with enthusiasm and commitment. The launch is the first major opportunity for the company's leaders to present the identity as a significant corporate resource and to integrate it into the organizational structure.

Never trivialize your corporate identity. Explain that the new identity is the outward sign of change and explain what that change means. Internal audiences want to know what, why, and particularly how it will affect them as individuals. External audiences only want to know why and how much.

MINI-CASE

The Spanish oil company *Repsol* was formed in the 1980s from Instituto Nacional de Hidrocarburos (INH). INH was a state monopoly with low standards of service, old and badly maintained service stations, and a

plethora of names and identities. The central idea/vision emerged naturally from the corporation's new positioning. Spain had just entered the European Union and the corporation had to defend its position. INH had to be revitalized and eventually privatized. Repsol had the opportunity to become and be seen as an industrial and commercial flagship for a revitalized Spain. This was the vision that was presented to and agreed on by the board.

The naming structure and visual identity followed from this brief. The name INH was abandoned in favor of one of the company's brands, Repsol, and a monolithic identity structure was adopted in order to give the organization strength and coherence. A new design was part of the program.

MAKING IT HAPPEN ▸▸

- Develop your corporate identity to project the company's approach, values, distinctiveness, and direction.
- Concentrate primarily on three "tangibles": your products and services, the environments where you make or sell them, and communications.
- Treat the intangibles of behavior—how you behave to your employees and the world outside—as vital.
- As a priority, determine early which of the above four tangible and intangible factors predominates.
- Before starting a corporate identity program, decide what you want it to achieve in the longer term.
- Construct the program in the four stages recommended above.

CONCLUSION

All corporations have an identity, irrespective of whether they control it or effectively manage it. By concentrating on developing a desirable corporate identity, projecting it to customers, and employing it as a tool to provide internal direction and orient strategic development, organizational efficiency can be raised. Remember that a corporate identity program harnesses and manages a valuable corporate asset.

FOR MORE INFORMATION

Books:
Olins, Wally. *On Brand.* London: Thames & Hudson, 2003.
Schultz, Majken et al., eds. *The Expressive Organization.* New York: Oxford University Press, 2000.

"Corporate identities must not be shortlived."

Clive Chajet

Switching Strategies
by Louis Patler

EXECUTIVE SUMMARY

- Today good strategy is more important than ever to sustain success in the marketplace.
- The "strategic givens" and fundamental questions—and their answers—shape good strategy.
- The givens and answers, revisited regularly, also provide early signs whether to stay with or to change strategy.

INTRODUCTION

A five-year-old software company sells for more money than Ford paid to acquire Volvo. American Express announces the creation of a new senior-level vice president of customer listening. In a matter of a few weeks a loan information company moves from not-com to dot-com to hot-com to no-com.

What do all these three cases all have in common? They all have lessons to teach us about the nature of strategy—the pathways or direction to productivity and profitability. As such, strategy is more macro than micro, more compass than map.

We live in a business world taken over by ironies and oxymorons, a world of walking contradictions in which the line between conventional and unconventional wisdom is drawn with disposable pens filled with invisible ink. The rules that once seemed so useful now ebb and flow like a hyperactive harvest moon. With the advent of e-commerce, Internet access, and cell phones, today's economy evolves and changes before our eyes, and we dare not blink for fear we will miss something.

In the face of such exponential change we have witnessed a commensurate rise in the importance of strategy for the growth and profitability of any enterprise. Sony, for example, took an exponential strategic leap when it realized that it was in the miniaturization business as well as the electronics and entertainment business. In fact, the traditional planning process has often been bolstered with a strong commitment to well-conceived strategic planning and research.

This said, the rise of the importance of strategy did not come easily, since conventional wisdom is replete with axioms that lobby for the status quo. If it ain't broke, don't fix it. Never change horses in midstream. The inherent problem with these

supposedly tried-and-true concepts is that they have indeed been tried, but they are often no longer true.

Would you want to fly with an airline with the motto, "If it ain't broke, don't fix it?" Would you want to be on an aging horse in a rising stream of rapids and white water?

The real challenge today is to develop strategies that are both sustainable and flexible, implementable yet nimble. The growing tendency of companies to change their strategic plan, core products, and organizational culture with alacrity typically leaves stockholders bewildered, customers underwhelmed, and employees confused.

Further, the challenge of developing good strategy is exacerbated by the growing tendency of companies worldwide to change direction far too often, thereby confusing flexibility with sloppy thinking and the absence of due diligence.

Against this backdrop let's look then at three practical topics affecting strategy formation and change in more detail. First, what are the assumptions that underlie modern strategic thinking? Second, how do you know when it's time to change strategy? And third, what is "good" strategy?

THE "STRATEGIC GIVENS": ASSUMPTIONS OF MODERN STRATEGY

It's helpful to identify and understand the broad assumptions that underlie your strategy, to know what the basic cornerstones of your paradigm are. Here are five useful indicative assumptions for the modern business world:

1 **Today the rate of change is exponential, not incremental.** This is a crucial starting point. Things are changing at a fast pace. This makes it very difficult to use conventional modes of thought,

measurement, or planning. Often things don't build up or add up, they just explode to a new level.

2 **Things will never "get back to normal"—this is normal!** The so-called glory days of the past have gone. And they won't be back. So, the new Thoughtware says, "Get over it! Get used to it! THIS is normal from now on!"

3 **Plan as we may, the future has plans of its own.** Because exponential change is here to stay, we have to look down the road with 20/20 vision, focusing on the next 20 minutes and the next 20 years simultaneously. The bad news is that the number of senior executives and key managers who possess 20/20 vision is minimal. The good news is that this is a learnable skill that a few training programs can teach you.

4 **Organizations that learn how to learn, ask the right questions** *at the right time*, and find out how to find the answers that will thrive in a global economy. Astute organizational strategists know that an organization's verbs will supplant its nouns; that is, diverse methods and responsive processes will be more powerful than tried-and-true facts and off-the-shelf systems. And asking the right questions at the right time will determine the most sustainable and viable answers.

5 **The productive organizations that will excel will be ones that value flexibility, diversity, integrity, cooperation, and innovation.** It's no longer sufficient to add value to products; we have to add values to both the process and the product. Customers, creditors, consumers, and our conscience now require it.

WHEN TO CHANGE GOOD STRATEGY: TO DISMOUNT OR TO RIDE ON?

The seven questions listed below help place parameters around good strategy (good strategy is strategy that is implementable and drives success, growth, and customer loyalty). But remember that these are not seven easy questions, nor are their answers cast in stone. I advise managers to ask these questions—all of them—at least twice a year.

"Strategy making is an immensely complex process involving the most sophisticated, subtle, and at times subconscious of human cognitive and social processes."

Henry Mintzberg

Even if the answers haven't changed significantly, at a minimum you'll be thinking on the right level with some regularity. Then, once you have the perspective that this combination of answers offers you, you're ready to act and make hard decisions, because you'll know *why* you're doing what you're doing, and your decisions will be based on sound strategic thinking. Remember, too: strategy is not tactics, it's directionality.

Conversely, by regularly revisiting these seven questions you'll have additional, crucial information to detect the early warning signs of good strategy that has taken a turn for the worse. If, for example, two or more of your strategic givens and/or answers to these seven questions change significantly, it's often an early indicator that shifts in strategy are appropriate.

MAKING IT HAPPEN ▶▶

There is strategy and then there is good strategy, and understanding the difference between the two rests on the ability to answer seven fundamental questions:

- **What business are you in?** Many companies are in more than one business and/or offer a variety of products and/or services without knowing it. Others have a single focus or a few well-conceived products or services. It's important to understand the business you are in, the competition, and the most innovative practices in your industry. What is the "big idea" that shapes your business? Sam Walton started Wal-Mart to bring popular brands to smaller communities at low prices.
- **What *other* businesses are you in?** Many companies don't see their business through a wide enough lens. They fail to capitalize on other business opportunities that can accrue from little more than a change in thinking. For example, trucking companies are in the transportation business; banks are in the transaction management business; soccer teams are also in the entertainment business. If Ford and GM make more profit from their automobile financing products than their cars, are they not a financial services company also?
- **What are your core competencies?** Knowing the core competency of your company will give you an incredible

competitive advantage. Competencies are not mere strengths. Every company has its strengths, but only a very few strengths are true competencies that are going to give you an edge over the competition, market differentiators that separate you from others. But core competencies are often very subtle: a billion-dollar computer-connector manufacturing company took much of its skyrocketing growth from an unnoticed core competency—the ability to acquire companies and hold onto their key employees and customers. Acquisition and integration were their core competences.
- **What are your core values?** Isolating and identifying core values is crucial. If your core value is short-term profitability, you need to organize your company accordingly. If you value long-term relationships with customers, this requires a different strategy, compensation package, and organizational chart. What you value should inform your strategy through and through. Southwest Airlines has a people-oriented culture, so they hire for hospitality skills and humor.
- **Which competitor will be your next partner?** Necessity is the mother of odd couplings. It may be to your advantage to form a strategic partnership with a competitor on a specific product, R&D, or other aspects of your business in order to remain a player in your field. The world has changed, and a past competitor can be a future ally. Good strategy is open to new realignments, even with a current competitor. Further, when you research a competitor as a potential partner, you will see that company's strengths and weaknesses in a new and strategically important light. When Sun Microsystems looked at some competitors' strategies, it moved to outsource all facilities management functions, realizing that the company wasn't well suited to be in the real estate business.
- **Are your short-term goals and long-term strategies aligned?** Public companies tend to think from quarter to quarter in order to please financial analysts and stockholders. The pressures of the next quarter too often conflict with the opportunities of the next few years. Companies need to align short-term results with long-term

profitability, short-term profits with long-term customer satisfaction. When Barclaycard realized that it had a long-term strategy of individualizing transactions with customers, it altered its credit-card product array significantly.
- **Do your answers to the foregoing questions complement (or negate) one another?** Too often a company will provide a viable answer to one or two of these questions. The real advantage, however, will go to the company that continuously examines itself in the context of several of these questions. For example, are core competencies, goals, and values working together to meet both long- and short-term goals?

CONCLUSION

Strategy is becoming increasingly important to business success. Good strategy is the result of: knowing the assumptions of your business model; sound investigation; open, curious, and broad thinking; and asking the right questions—often. Though strategy is often changed precipitously, in today's world it is far better to be useful than to be correct. Old ways die hard, so *strategy under constant scrutiny* is best understood as an agent of change.

FOR MORE INFORMATION

Books:
Collins, James C., and Jerry I. Porras. *Built to Last: Successful Habits of Visionary Companies.* New York: HarperBusiness, 1997.
Hamel, Gary, and C. K. Prahalad. *Competing for the Future.* Cambridge, MA: Harvard Business School Press, 1996.
Kaplan, Robert S., and David P. Norton. *The Strategy-focused Organization: How Balanced Scorecard Companies Thrive in the New Business Environment.* Cambridge, MA: Harvard Business School Press, 2000.

See also:

"Whatever you shoot is dead for a while before it starts to stink. The same goes for strategies. How many organizations carry this dead thing around with them, unaware of its irrelevancy until it is too late?"

Gary Hamel

Power Struggling and Power Sharing
by Jonas Ridderstråle

EXECUTIVE SUMMARY

- Power has now transferred from producers to consumers and from capitalists to competents, that is, individuals who possess competencies crucial to success.
- Success requires enhancing the value of human, structural, and customer capital.
- E-business may be the future, but *e* must stand also for *emotion*.

INTRODUCTION

Information technology (IT) opens many opportunities for wealth creation but, from a more general economic point of view, IT in general—and the Net in particular—is best thought of as profit enemy no. 1. The current trends of digitization, deregulation, and globalization are altering the balance of power between those who sell and those who buy, on the one hand, and between capital and competence investors on the other. Combined, these changes make it increasingly difficult for companies to show a profit. Companies must respond by coming up with imaginative strategies to enhance the value of their intellectual capital.

MARKETS MEET MARX

Welcome to the information jungle, where markets flourish because they feed and breed on information. Some 30 years ago only 40% of all individuals lived within a market system. Now around 90% do so. The advent of what we might call global marketification has caused three identifiable trends:

1 *Overcapacity* is often the norm: numbers may vary, but we've seen spikes as high as 40% in automobiles, 100% in bulk chemicals, and 140% in computers.
2 While more products and services are available, they're often incredibly similar: *commoditization* rules.
3 The costs to find the best deal are falling dramatically; thanks to search power, comparison shopping has become a picnic.

In effect we're moving closer to a state of perfect competition. Power is transferred from those who sell to those who buy. The new consumer is a demanding dictator. The concept of the humble and loyal customer, tied to one and only one vendor, is about to die.

Knowledge is our most critical resource:

and we, as individuals, are the owners of our brains. Karl Marx was right: people now control the most critical resources—though individually, not collectively. Modern companies depend heavily on their *core competents*, that is, individuals who make competencies happen. Bill Gates once claimed that if 20 people left Microsoft, the company would risk bankruptcy. Competents are walking monopolies. They stay only as long as the organization can offer something they want. Power is now in the process of being transferred from capital owners to competence owners.

Companies will accordingly do business with demanding dictators, and negotiate salaries and stock-option plans with the business world's equivalents of Madonna and Tiger Woods. Indeed, one plausible hypothesis is that the more Web-based and knowledge-intensive the business, the less chance that any of the eventual profits will end up in the pockets of the purely financial investors of the company.

Any organization relies on a mix of financial and intellectual capital. Now exchange rates are changing. Financial capital is in the process of being devalued. To prosper, organizations must counter the forces of consumer and competent control by boosting their intellectual capital in three primary ways:

1 attracting human capital;
2 transforming it into structural capital, while simultaneously;
3 building customer capital.

HARNESSING HUMAN CAPITAL

Talented individuals have alternatives every minute, every day. Where competition in the labor market is increasingly generic, we're all players in a great global attraction game. Success is contingent on exploiting the fact that human beings simultaneously

want to express their individuality and their need for belonging.

Individual Personalization

Attracting talent calls for a more personalized company. Today smart people hire organizations rather than vice versa. Competents have a choice: the organization is disposable, a temporary home. And human beings are not bulk goods. We differ. Companies either manage this differentiation or watch their most precious resources walk away. The consequence is that each and every little system needs to be personalized.

Organizational Tribalization

Peter Hagström has helped shaped my thinking on this immeasurably. Not only are people individualistic creatures, we also want to belong. Companies with a future will build organizational tribes in which employees share common traits or interests—rewards, ownership, culture, whatever. Today we see successful companies recruiting people with the right attitude, then training them in skills. Look at Hell's Angels or Greenpeace. These organizations hire for attitude, because the half-life of knowledge is coming down fast, and it's easier for most of us to change our skills than our values.

SECURING STRUCTURAL CAPITAL

From the outlook of the company, human capital is best thought of as a liability, while structural capital is definitely an asset on the balance sheet. Companies must therefore transform both the know-how and know-who components of their knowledge bases.

Knowledge Codification

The typical company may suffer not from knowing too little, but rather from not knowing what it knows. A critical task is thus to turn core competents into core competencies that are shared throughout the entire organization. Codification means collecting the knowledge of competents or *competeams* and transferring it to the organizational level. This way the company not only provides others in the organization with an opportunity to learn, but becomes less dependent on a few competents.

Corporate Socialization

By working in teams and spending time together after work, people in groups soon develop tacit knowledge. Tacit knowledge makes it more difficult for competitors to imitate, and for competents to quit with their skill-sets intact. When knowledge is a combination of know-how and know-who, part of it will be nested in a network of relationships with existing coworkers. Anyone threatening to leave can thus only bring the intrapersonal skills along. Socialization = tacit knowledge = knowledge handcuffs.

CREATING CUSTOMER CAPITAL

In a world of customer control, companies will have to come up with new ways to deal with these demanding dictators. Once again the dual nature of humans, comprising elements of both individualism and collectivism, must be exploited.

Customer Tribalization

We all grew up in a world in which physical proximity ruled. Yesterday's tribes were geographically structured: Russians and Americans. The new tribes are biographically structured: they are global tribes of people who actually believe they have something in common, no matter where they were born. In a geographically structured world, companies competed for the local average. Smart companies today go for the global extremes.

A second kind of global tribe is more transactional—*buyographical* rather than biographical. While demanding dictators may constitute powerful forces individually, just imagine what happens when they link up. And in a networked world they will. Tribes of customers will interact and create customer unions. So entrepreneurial companies provide platforms on which customers can indeed aggregate their demand. Just look at LetsBuyIt.com, an Internet auction house/coshopper. The company allows you to link with other consumers (anywhere!) who are interested in buying the same product. Whether LetsBuyIt or someone else will eventually dominate the market is beside the point. Coshopping sites will become to global buyographical tribes what traditional co-ops once were to blue-collar workers in the industrial society.

Total Customization

Within a consumer tribe there must be room for personalization and individual differences. Niches are becoming ever smaller in our fragmenting world. Recent technological developments open up many new opportunities for mass customization. But total customization involves more than the customer offering—it must encompass the entire experience. Innovative organizations help people avoid information overload and aid them in making smart choices. Either companies focus on internally producing this service by employing experts, aggregating information, and comparing prices (the way Pricerunner.com does), or they choose to more actively involve the consumers in the process (as does Amazon.com).

ALL YOU NEED IS LOVE

Given today's almost endless choices for customers and competents, only those companies that realize success rests with capturing the emotional human being will stand a chance. Moving from abundance to affection is a question not of applying more reason, but of fusing functionality with ethics and aesthetics. Logic leads to conclusions. Emotions trigger action. Sensibility rather than sense is the road ahead.

Sounds too touchy-feely? Research in neuroscience shows that the brain's limbic system, which governs our feelings, is more powerful than the neocortex that controls intellect. The traffic instructions in our brains are clear: emotions have precedence.

MAKING IT HAPPEN ▶▶

- Define your organizational tribe by asking: Who are we and where do we want to go?
- Hire people for attitude and then train them for skill.
- Replace job descriptions with motivation descriptions.
- Personalize all aspects of all systems and contracts for all competents.
- Get competents to share their competencies—collect, codify, and communicate.
- Promote socialization at and away from work to develop knowledge handcuffs.
- Invite customers to join your tribe—and then constantly reinforce the bond.
- Customize the entire experience for the consumer, not only the customer offering.
- Remember that people differ. Figure out what makes customers and competents mad, sad, and glad. Then ask yourself that question—over and over again.

CONCLUSION

As digitization, combined with deregulation and globalization, perfects the global market economy, IT is enabling many of the strategies outlined above. Yet for a company to exist just on the Web is a bit like having a restroom back at the office—necessary, but not sufficient for the creation of a sustainable competitive advantage. IT merely provides the means to an end. The road to the future may end up in Silicon Valley, but it must start in Soul and pass through Values on the way to e-(motional) business.

FOR MORE INFORMATION

Books:

Downes, Larry, and Chunka Mui. *Unleashing the Killer App: Digital Strategies for Market Dominance.* Revised ed. Cambridge, MA: Harvard Business School Press, 2000.

Edvinsson, Leif. *Corporate Longitude: Discover Your Position in the Knowledge Economy.* Upper Saddle River, NJ: Financial Times Prentice Hall, 2002.

Lindstrom, Martin, and Patricia B. Seybold. *Brandchild: Remarkable Insights into the Minds of Today's Global Kids and their Relationships with Brands.* Milford, CT: Kogan Page, 2004.

Pooler, Jim. *Why We Shop: Emotional Rewards and Retail Strategies.* Westport, CT: Greenwood, 2003.

Sartain, Libby, and Mark Schumann. *Brand from the Inside: Eight Essentials to Emotionally Connect Your Employees to Your Business.* San Francisco, CA: Pfeiffer Wiley, 2006.

"In the United States, though power corrupts, the expectation of power paralyzes."

J. K. Galbraith

Globalization and Regional Business Strategy

by Alan M. Rugman

EXECUTIVE SUMMARY

- Globalization is misunderstood—it does not, and never has, existed in terms of a single world market with free trade.
- Triad-based business is the past, current, and future reality.
- Multinational enterprises operate within triad markets and access other triad markets; they have regional, not global, strategies.
- National governments strongly regulate most service sectors, thereby limiting free-market forces; the extent of regulation is not decreasing.
- Businesses need to think local and act regional; they should forget global.

INTRODUCTION: THE MYTH OF GLOBAL STRATEGY

Recent research suggests that globalization is a myth. Far from taking place in a single global market, most business activity by large companies takes place in regional blocks. There is no uniform spread of U.S. market capitalism, nor are global markets becoming homogenized. Government regulations and cultural differences divide the world into the triad blocks of North America, the European Union, and Japan. Rival multinational enterprises from the triad compete for regional market share, and so enhance economic efficiency. As a result, top managers now need to design triad-based regional strategies, not global ones. Only in a few sectors such as consumer electronics is a global strategy of economic integration viable. For most other manufacturing sectors (automobiles, for example) and for all services, strategies of national responsiveness are required, often coupled with integration strategies, as explained in the matrix framework below.

The real drivers of globalization are the network managers of large multinational enterprises. But their business strategies are triadic, or regional, in scope and are responsive to local consumers; they are not global and uniform.

Specialty chemicals and the automotive industry are triad-based, not global. There is no global automobile: more than 90% of all automobiles produced in Europe are sold in Europe, and regional production and predominantly local sales are also the norm in North America and Japan. Successful

multinationals now design strategies on a regional basis; unsuccessful ones pursue global strategies.

SOME COMMON GLOBAL MISUNDERSTANDINGS

Globalization has been defined in business schools as the production and distribution of products and services of a homogenous type and quality on a worldwide basis. Simply put, it involves providing the same output to countries everywhere. And in recent years it has become increasingly common to hear business executives, industry analysts, and even university professors talk about the emergence of globalization and the dominance of international business by giant multinational enterprises (MNEs) that are selling uniform products from Cairo, Illinois to Cairo, Egypt, and from Lima, Ohio to Lima, Peru.

To back up their claims these individuals often point to the fact that foreign sales account for more than 50% of the annual revenues of companies such as Dow Chemical, Exxon, Hewlett-Packard, IBM, Johnson & Johnson, Mobil, Motorola, Procter & Gamble, and Texaco. (For more on these companies, see the *World Investment Report*.) These are accurate statements, but they fail to explain that most of the sales of so-called global companies are made on an intra-regional basis. For example, MNEs that are headquartered in North America average 77% of their revenues within NAFTA; the European MNEs average 63% of their sales in the European Union (EU); the Asian

MNEs average 74% of their sales in Asia. Overall, the world's 500 largest companies average 72% of their sales in their home regions. Of these companies, only nine are global, whereas the vast majority are home-region oriented. Recent research gives ample supporting data.

1 More than 85% of all automobiles produced in North America are built in North American factories owned by General Motors, Ford, or Daimler-Chrysler, or by European or Japanese MNEs. More than 90% of the cars produced in the EU are sold in the EU. More than 93% of all cars registered in Japan are manufactured domestically.

2 In the specialty chemicals sector, more than 90% of all paint is made and used regionally by triad-based MNEs. The same is true for steel, heavy electrical equipment, energy, and transportation.

3 In the services sector, which now employs approximately 70% of the workforce in North America, Western Europe, and Japan, business activity is all essentially local or regional.

Another misunderstanding about globalization is the belief that MNEs are globally monolithic and excessively powerful in political terms. Research shows this is not so. MNEs are not monolithic; in fact, the largest 500 multinationals are spread across the triad economies. Of the world's largest 500 companies, 198 are headquartered in NAFTA countries, 156 in the EU, and 125 in Japan/Asia. Further, these triad-based MNEs compete for global market share and profits across a wide variety of industrial sectors and trade services. And this process of regional competition erodes the possibility of sustainable long-term profits and the possibility of building strong, sustainable political advantage.

A third misunderstanding about globalization is the belief that MNEs develop homogenous products for the world market, and through their efficient production techniques are able to dominate local markets everywhere. In truth, multinationals have to adapt their products for local markets. For example, there is no global automobile. Instead there are regionally based North

"Globalization requires that organizations adopt a cross-cultural perspective to be successful in accomplishing their goals in the context of a global economy." Rabi S. Bhagat

American, European, and Japanese factories supported by local regional suppliers that provide steel, plastic, paint, and other necessary inputs for producing the automobiles for their respective geographic triad regions. Even pharmaceutical companies, which manufacture medicines that are often regarded as universal products, have to modify their goods to satisfy national and state regulations, thus making centralized production and worldwide distribution economically difficult.

WORLD TRADE IS HIGHLY REGIONAL

World trade provides a good example of just how regional MNEs are. The amount of trade in terms of exports and imports has grown rapidly over the last decade, but it continues to be dominated by the triad. The latest data show that in 2002 these three broad regions accounted for about 60% of world trade. Most of the world's trade is regional, not global. Within the EU, intra-regional trade accounts for 61% of all exports. Within NAFTA, intra-regional exports are 57%. In Asia, intra-regional exports are 50%. In contrast, only 15% of NAFTA's exports go to the EU, and only 11%

of EU exports go to NAFTA. Due to the large amounts of Chinese manufactured exports to the United States, Asia has 25% of its exports going to NAFTA, with only 17% of NAFTA's exports going to Asia. These trade figures replicate the company-level sales data reported earlier—both data sets deny pure globalization and support the regional dimension of international business.

MAKING IT HAPPEN ▶▶
It is possible to offer some practical strategies for managers who want to increase their company's international revenues and profits. The most useful lessons learned are these:

- Be prepared to design strategies that take into account regional trade and investment agreements such as NAFTA and the single market of the EU.
- Learn to deal with different cultures and become nationally responsive when necessary.
- Develop new thinking and knowledge about regional business networks and triad-based clusters instead of always developing pure global strategies.

- Make alliances and foster cross-cultural awareness in your senior managers.
- Develop analytical methods for assessing regional drivers of success instead of globalization drivers: regional drivers may be more useful in the future in gaining and holding market share.
- Encourage all your managers to think regional, act local—and forget global!

FOR MORE INFORMATION

Books:
Ohmae, Kenichi. *The End of the Nation State: The Rise of Regional Economies.* New York: HarperCollins, 1996.
Rugman, Alan M. *The End of Globalization.* New York: AMACOM, 2001.
Rugman, Alan M., and Joseph R. D'Cruz. *Multinationals as Flagship Firms.* New York: Oxford University Press, 2000.
Rugman, Alan M. *The Regional Multinationals.* Cambridge, U.K.: Cambridge University Press, 2005.
Yip, George S. *Total Global Strategy II: Updated for the Internet and Service Era.* 2nd ed. Englewood Cliffs, NJ: Prentice Hall, 2002.

"The United States is just one part of a global marketplace today. There isn't any offshore anymore; it's all onshore."

Walter Wriston

The New Frontiers in Old-economy Industries by Adrian J. Slywotzky and David J. Morrison

EXECUTIVE SUMMARY

- Many old-economy companies have hesitated to go digital because they believe that digital business is primarily about technology.
- Digital business is about using digital technology to expand a company's strategic options.
- Digital business design offers even old-economy companies a way to use digital technology to achieve improvements long considered unattainable.

INTRODUCTION

Well into a new century, many old-economy companies are still reluctant to go digital. Over the past two decades, the advent of the personal computer, the proliferation of e-mail, the growth of enterprise resource planning systems, and the popularity of the Internet have created a growing awareness of digital technology as both a creative and a disruptive force. Old-economy companies, in the meantime, have tended to be more impressed by the perils than the promise of digital technology. However, there is no reason for them to fear digitization. What digital business can deliver is an expansion of your company's capabilities, its strategic options, greater efficiencies and, above all, improved customer service.

Why are old-economy companies hesitant about going digital? Most people equate digital business with particular technologies or consider it simply the sum total of the high-tech innovations multiplying around us. If they're not themselves involved in high-tech industries, they may not only be intimidated by digital technology, but may fail to see its relevance to them.

What old-economy companies need to realize is that digital business is not about technology per se. It's not about wiring everybody in the company, providing all your salespeople with laptops, converting your R&D and manufacturing facilities to CAD/CAM, selling products through your Web site, or allowing employees to telecommute from their homes. Digital business design is about using digital technologies to expand your company's strategic options. It's about serving customers, creating unique value propositions, leveraging talent, achieving massive improvements in productivity, and increasing and protecting profits. These should be the overriding concerns of any business, old- or new-economy.

THE POWER OF DIGITAL BUSINESS DESIGN

Let's consider two companies that most people would classify as new-economy PC manufacturers, Dell and Compaq. Going into the year 2000, there was a real contrast between the two. At that time, in terms of the way they operated, Dell could be called a digital business—Compaq not.

Compaq relied almost exclusively on retail outlets to sell its products. It guessed what demand would be, produced the number of machines it thought customers might buy, and then tried to sell them through its distributors. By contrast, Dell used its online configurator (a digital system that allows customers to design their own PCs) to enable the company to build computers quickly and accurately to customer specifications without stockpiling. Via this now widely used approach, the customer pays in full before the machine is manufactured. Thus, from the start, Dell was able to use the upfront income to finance production. Compaq, on the other hand, relied on traditional methods of financing to produce machines that it then shipped via its distribution channels, hoping that retailers would eventually pay for them.

Though the PC marketplace has changed, this same guesswork remains prevalent in industries that operate by the seat of their pants as well as those that spend millions on market research. The reliance on guesswork can have unfortunate results. A visit to any auto dealer in the fall offers a vivid illustration: rebates, sales, and financing plans that are unprofitable for the producer all wheeled out in an effort to get rid of unsold inventory to make room for next year's models.

Digital business design uses digital technology to enable companies to know what their customers want and to produce only those products, to do away with the guesswork and the waste of unsold inventory, and to enjoy increases in productivity, profits, and growth. Companies whose feet are planted squarely in the physical world can achieve this just as easily as those that inhabit a purely digital world.

MINI-CASES
Digital Pioneers from the Old Economy

In industries from cement to financial services, innovative companies are using digital business design to achieve breakthrough performance.

Consider the cement business, the last place you would expect to find a digitally driven company. The Mexican company *Cemex* has turned the production and delivery of a basic commodity into one of the world's most sophisticated and innovative businesses. By forging information-intensive links among its customers, production facilities, and truck dispatchers, Cemex has elevated itself to brand-name status, taken significant market share from its competitors in Mexico and elsewhere, and dramatically outpaced the competition in terms of profit margins and revenue growth.

In the office furniture industry *Herman Miller* has similarly made innovative supply-chain thinking the heart of its strategy. Using proprietary software called Z-Axis, Herman Miller created an interactive choice-board selection system for its customers, introduced greater speed and accuracy into its ordering and manufacturing processes, and leveraged these new efficiencies into faster, more reliable delivery. The operating unit that Herman Miller created to develop these innovations was generating annual sales growth of 25% (more than three times the industry average) and producing a remarkable 40 inventory turns (against an industry average of 20) when it was integrated into the company's larger operation in 1998.

"New markets open not only because of novel technologies; shifts in values and culture also are potent sources of innovation."

Stewart Clegg

In financial services, the German company *MLP* used digital technologies to increase revenues and profitability. MLP's growing array of digital tools gives customers opportunities for self-service while adding value to the service its financial consultants provide. By targeting a rapidly growing market of young professionals who are attuned to digital technology, MLP achieved revenue and net income growth at a compounded annual rate of 43% between 1995 and 2000, while its market capitalization increased at a rate of 96%.

ACHIEVING TANGIBLE BENEFITS FROM E-BUSINESS

Companies that exemplify digital business design by integrating a smart business model with business-driven exploitation of digital options produce profit margins that average more than 10 points higher and growth rates almost 20 points higher than their best competition. These are very large differences. And the gap may grow wider as the early advantages gained by digital reinventors are consolidated and used as the basis for taking and holding even greater market share.

The pioneers of digital business have achieved such results by taking advantage of eight specific concrete benefits of digital business design, represented by the following shifts:

- **From guessing to knowing**. With digital business design, the basis of a company's decision making shifts from guessing what customers want to knowing exactly what they want. Using interactive online choiceboards, companies can know what products their customers want before having to manufacture and distribute them, use this knowledge to improve customer satisfaction, and mine real-time customer information to find new opportunities.
- **From mismatch to perfect fit**. A major source of frustration for customers lies in the mismatch between what they actually want and the compromises that they are often forced to accept in choosing from a fixed product line. With digital business design, the value proposition that companies offer their customers shifts to a perfect fit.
- **From lag time to real time**. The need for speed in obtaining information and sharing it within a company is no secret. Digital business design enables the flow of information to shift to real time.
- **From supplier service to customer self-service**. More and more customers actually prefer the convenience of online ordering and customer service to relying on the supplier to perform these tasks. With digital business design, a company's customer service model shifts to customer self-service.
- **From low-value-added work to maximum talent leverage**. Having employees perform routine, repetitive work today is a waste of critical resources. Digital business design shifts employees' time to the most productive, customer-centric tasks.
- **From fixing errors to preventing errors**. Mistakes in order processing, manufacturing, and other processes create frustration for customers and higher costs for suppliers. With digital business design, quality control systems shift to preventing problems and errors.
- **From 10% improvement to 10x productivity**. Incremental improvements in efficiency pale beside order-of-magnitude leaps in productivity. As digitization has taken hold in industry after industry, we've seen productivity growth patterns shift from a norm of 10% improvement to 10x gains.
- **From separate silos to integrated system**. No organization can respond to the challenges and opportunities of a rapidly changing environment without being able to share vital information and act on it with minimal delay. Such rapid organizational response depends in turn on internal integration. With digital business design, organizational structure shifts from a collection of separate silos to an integrated system in which ideas and solutions are shared.

These shifts drive results that go far beyond opening a new sales channel via a Web site or achieving incremental cost reductions by automation. Taken together, they offer a means to achieve differentiation, including the ability to become unique.

- Where I must manage bits, how can I develop bit engines that will manage every one of those bits electronically? (Bit engines can include a wide range of technological tools and systems, from internal databases of product and service information to e-commerce switchboards and electronic marketplaces.)

CONCLUSION

Harnessed to solve your most pressing business issues, digital technologies offer opportunities for any business in any industry. By using digital business design to offer a better deal for customers, create a better system for employees, and generate a better risk-adjusted return for investors, even traditional businesses in unprofitable or slow-growth industries can achieve goals that were long considered unattainable. Digital business design is the wheel with which old-economy companies can spin straw into gold by combining great business design with smart digitization.

FOR MORE INFORMATION

Books:
Annunzio, Susan. *eLeadership: Proven Techniques for Creating an Environment of Speed and Flexibility in the Digital Economy*. New York: Simon & Schuster, 2001.
Olsen, Kai A. *The Internet, the Web, and eBusiness: Formalizing Applications for the Real World*. Lanham, MD: Scarecrow Press, 2005.

Web sites:
Cisco.com: **www.cisco.com**
Dell.com: **www.dell.com**
MercerMC.com: **www.mercermc.com**
Schwab: **www.schwab.com**

MAKING IT HAPPEN ▶▶

To get started in digital business design, ask the following questions:

- What are the most important business issues facing my organization?
- What are the smartest business design choices for responding to those issues?
- Where might digital, particularly online, technology open up new strategic options for my company?
- Which of my current activities involve managing atoms and which involve managing bits? Where can I add bits to atoms or replace atoms with bits?

"In place of 'industry,' I suggest an alternative, more appropriate term: 'business ecosystem.' The term circumscribes the microeconomics of intense coevolution coalescing around innovative ideas."

James F. Moore

Corporate-level Strategy

by David R. Sadtler

EXECUTIVE SUMMARY

- The parent company should add more value than other owners could.
- The skills at the center need to match the improvement opportunities in the businesses.
- Geographic and sectoral diversification are to be avoided; there are other ways to grow.
- Vertical integration is unlikely to succeed.
- When value added no longer seems feasible, demerge or break up completely.
- Good central managers never stop demanding real and substantial value added.

INTRODUCTION

Implementing a successful corporate-level strategy has become an urgent priority for all conglomerates. Parent companies must demonstrate that they are creating stockholder value by their own actions and initiatives, and not just reaping the profits of the businesses in their charge. The sanctions for being seen to fail in this challenge can be severe. At the very least, stock prices will suffer; at the other extreme, predators will force a breakup.

A Framework

The challenge of corporate-level strategy is to ensure that value is being added to every business in the company's portfolio. That value must, of course, be in excess of its cost. Conglomerates with good corporate strategies do even better: they add more value than other companies in the same businesses.

Insuring that this value-added process is productive requires several actions by top management:

First, it must identify ways in which each business can be helped. This help must make possible a major improvement in business performance. Without an understanding of where improvement potential exists, the search for value added cannot be real and substantial. These improvement opportunities should be identified and agreed on through managerial dialogue and business-planning systems.

Second, central management must make sure that it possesses the skills to provide the help needed. Different kinds of improvement opportunities require different forms of help. Management must see that it has those capabilities.

Third, it must construct a portfolio of businesses in which this constructive fit—useful skills attuned to the needs of the businesses—exists. How businesses can be helped is bound to change over time. The strength of the fit must be continually reappraised.

Fourth, management must ensure that it is sufficiently familiar with the requirements for the success of each business and that it will not damage that business, whether by approving the wrong investment proposals, appointing the wrong general managers, or giving poor strategic guidance.

Questions for Management

The pursuit of added value often presents managers with challenging issues to resolve.

How can we grow if our core business is limited in terms of further expansion? This question arises when management has divested businesses that didn't fit and is left with one core business. If it has a commanding market share, competes in a nongrowing market, and has little opportunity for overseas expansion, the dilemma can be a real one. This is especially true in an era in which capital markets reject diversification and demand that companies stick to their knitting.

Capital markets are wary of any form of corporate diversification. They are simply being pragmatic: experience has shown them that diversification doesn't work well. What is the single-business company to do to find growth opportunities? There are four possible answers:

First, seek a way to reinvent the business by looking for new customers, new markets, new ways to present the product, and a better package of customer value to offer. Even commodity products can be differentiated by offering them in a different service con-text. First, make certain that growth limits really have been reached.

Second, consider moves into related businesses that share existing resources and skills. Such initiatives should possess the same requirements for success. If not, the management skills both at the business-unit level and in the parent company may be inadequate to the challenge.

Third, operate a nursery of new ideas. Business unit managers are always on the lookout for new products and markets. The more promising should be regarded as new-product research and development initiatives. Those that offer promise can then receive modest investment until there is a persuasive reason to make a serious commitment.

Finally, although unconventional in today's environment, it may be smart simply to operate the existing low-growth business for cash flow, eschewing major growth aspirations. Mature industries can often be sustained for a long time without heavy investment and achieve above-average returns.

What's wrong with vertical integration as a way of extending the opportunities for a stagnant business? In other words, why shouldn't we acquire our customer to guarantee an outlet for our products?

Vertical integration has increasingly lost favor among thoughtful managers. While it may seem like a sensible proposition to guarantee a supply of raw materials or markets for your products, vertical integration frequently exhibits three major shortcomings:

First, when one division sells products to another division, disagreement often arises about transfer pricing and product and service quality. The selling division realizes it has a captive customer and often works less hard to retain the business. Much time is wasted resolving such intramural issues.

Second, entry into new upstream or downstream businesses often involves competing with your existing customers. Several corporate breakups have been the result of the realization that this problem was insoluble under the existing ownership arrangements.

Third, entry into new businesses often involves dealing with differing requirements for success; it thus requires a new

range of managerial skills and capabilities, both at the business-unit level and in the parent company. Mistakes are made, and the business suffers competitively.

Is it wise to limit the number of eggs in our basket? Management teams often seek positions in different industrial sectors simply to spread risk. They reason that when one sector is unattractive owing to a cyclical market turndown, other sectors can take up the slack. While this can give comfort to management teams, it's an unwise strategy in today's markets. Capital markets will say: "We can spread our own risk; you do what you know how to do." The management team that focuses its effort and investment on areas in which it has demonstrable skills will be rewarded appropriately in capital pricing.

The pressures to build a bigger company are enormous: managers are taught to believe that their enterprise must grow or die; ambitious executives want new challenges; they expect to get paid more when the company gets bigger; and they may believe that economies of scale are always the reward from sheer size. But the pressures of bureaucratic cost, operating manager motivation, decision-making complexity, internal competitive conflicts, suspicion of remote top managers inequitably enriching themselves, and the like all represent potential downsides to great size. To be responsible stewards of stockholder interest, directors and top managers must continually examine and manage this implied trade-off. Failure to do so can be the ultimate destroyer of value added strategy.

Demerger and Breakup

When it becomes clear that a failed corporate strategy is in place—when you recognize that substantial and discernible value is not being added—the question of portfolio changes arises. In some cases this may involve simply a trade, sale, or demerger of the business for which there is no fit. Sometimes, when the value-added formula has substantially dissipated, total breakup is indicated: the company ceases to exist in its entirety and breaks into several pieces.

Successful corporate strategists believe in the primacy of value added. They constantly seek out ways to provide the kind of help the businesses in the corporate portfolio need. They continually search for major improvement opportunities among the businesses. They adjust both their portfolio of businesses and the capabilities of the parent company to provide a continuing match between the needs of the business units and what the parent can provide. And when the businesses need no further help of the sort they can offer—and this often happens—they wish them Godspeed and release them into the outside world.

MINI-CASE

The U.K. conglomerate Hanson Trust offers a superb example of how to do it right. During the 1970s and 1980s it built a portfolio of low-tech, mature businesses by means of acquisition and disposal. It sought out undermanaged companies with major positions in mature businesses who were looking for opportunities to strengthen their competitive position by tight disciplined management. When its acquisitions brought in businesses that didn't fit Hanson's profile, they were disposed of. Hanson was clear about its value-added formula: it found businesses whose fortunes could be dramatically improved through tight financial discipline and strong general management motivation. It worked well and stockholders benefited greatly.

In the 1990s it became apparent that the formula no longer had much to offer stockholders. Major opportunities for the Hanson treatment were waning, especially in the United Kingdom and the United States. All the fat targets had been exploited. At the same time computer-facilitated financial control systems made Hanson's approach an ordinary corporate capability. Finally the businesses in the Hanson stable became so well run that there was little improvement potential left. Realizing that the value-added formula had become obsolete, the company broke itself up into five pieces, each one of which has thrived competitively on its own.

The same caution should be applied to overseas diversification. Some management teams intentionally direct investment to different parts of the world in order to limit exposure in any one area. Unless such geographic expansion is initiated to strengthen one's competitive positioning in a particular global marketplace, the investment community is likely to scorn this form of expansion. There are simply too many downsides to investment abroad to undertake it without a solid competitive business rationale. Currency exposure, entry into alien market environments, and bone-wearying travel all represent significant costs of expanding internationally.

MAKING IT HAPPEN ▸▸

- Make sure that value is being added to every business in the portfolio by identifying ways in which each can be helped to achieve major improvement in performance.
- Restrict the portfolio to activities in which a constructive fit—useful skills attuned to the needs of the businesses—exists at the center.
- If growth prospects appear limited, try reinvention, moves into related businesses, new ideas, or a cash-cow strategy.
- Consider vertical integration as a way of extending strategic opportunities.
- Focus effort and investment on areas in which you have demonstrable skills: don't diversify into unknown areas.
- When substantial and discernible value is not being added, change the portfolio.

FOR MORE INFORMATION

Books:
Galbraith, Jay R. *Designing Organizations: An Executive Guide to Strategy, Structure, and Process.* San Francisco, CA: Jossey-Bass, 2002.
Goold, Michael, et al. *Corporate-Level Strategy.* New York: Wiley, 1994.
Kare-Silver, Michael de. *Strategy in Crisis.* New York: New York University Press, 1998.
Kraines, Gerald A. *Accountability Leadership: How to Strengthen Productivity through Sound Managerial Leadership.* Franklin Lakes, NJ: The Career Press, Inc., 2001.
Mintzberg, Henry. *The Rise and Fall of Strategic Planning.* New York: Prentice Hall, 1994.
Useem, Michael. *Leading Up: How to Lead Your Boss so You Both Win.* New York: Crown Business, 2001.

See also:
☆ Building Great Internal Partnerships (pp. 362–363)
☆ Intrapreneurial Warriors Versus Traditional Managers (pp. 160–161)

"The essence of strategy is not the structure of a company's products and markets, but the dynamics of its behavior."
Tom Peters

Toward a Total Global Strategy
by George Yip

INTRODUCTION

In the 1980s and the 1990s, many companies were still debating whether they should globalize. For most, this debate has now ended. Companies assume that they should globalize unless they can find very good reasons not to.

The spread of the Internet and the Web provides one compelling reason. Any company that creates a Web site has instant global reach, with corresponding demands for delivery and service. In addition, evidence shows that companies that globalize achieve better competitive and financial performance.

But globalizing, in the sense of spreading activities around the world, is not enough. Companies also need to be globally integrated. They need globally coherent strategies, global networks, and the ability to maximize profits on a global basis. However, turning a collection of country businesses into one worldwide business that has an integrated, global strategy is not easy. It presents one of the stiffest challenges for managers today. Developing and implementing an effective global strategy is the acid test of a well-managed company.

THE CASE FOR GLOBALIZATION

Whatever the anti-globalization protestors may say to the contrary, a range of forces is driving companies around the world to globalize. Many managers view this as expanding their participation in foreign markets. But companies also need to globalize in another sense. They need to integrate their worldwide strategy. This contrasts with the traditional multinational approach.

In the past, multinationals have tended to set up country subsidiaries that design, produce, and market products or services that were tailored to local needs. But this model is now in question. Increasingly, the multinational approach is seen as a "multilocal strategy" rather than a truly global strategy.

Today, a growing number of managers are asking, if they are in a global industry, whether their business should have a global strategy. Better questions are: how global is our industry, and how global should our business strategy be? This is because virtually every industry has aspects that are global or potentially global. But some industries have more aspects that are global, and more intensely so.

Similarly, a strategy can be more or less global in its different elements. An industry is global to the extent that there are inter-country connections. A strategy is global to the extent that it is integrated across countries. Global strategy should not be equated with any one element—standardized products, or worldwide market coverage, or a global manufacturing network. Instead, global strategy should be a flexible combination of many elements.

BEYOND THE MULTINATIONAL MODEL

Recent and coming changes make it likely that in many industries a global strategy will be more successful than a multilocal one. Indeed, having a sound global strategy may well be the requirement for survival as the changes accelerate. These changes include: the increasing convergence of consumer tastes across countries; the reduction of tariff and non-tariff barriers; technology investments that are becoming too expensive to amortize in one market only, and competitors who are moving from country-by-country competition to global competition.

In the 1990s, the world saw greater convergence in customer needs and tastes; the drastic reduction of many government barriers to free trade and investment; an acceleration of enablers in communications, and a surge in globally applicable new technological products and services. All this does not mean that every industry has become entirely global. But today, nearly every industry has a significant global segment in which customers prefer products or services that are much more global in nature.

Around the global segments, however, regional, national, or sub-national niches still exist. The size of the global segment varies, from very large in the personal computer industry, to relatively small in many parts of the food industry. But the global segment is increasing in size in nearly all cases.

TUMBLING BARRIERS TO TRADE

Around the world, trade barriers continue to fall. The most important examples include: the North American Free Trade Agreement among the United States, Canada, and Mexico; the continuing integration of the European Union; the formation of the new World Trade Organization in 1995, and China joining that body in 2001. The Asian Crisis of 1997 to 1999 has also helped to open up economies such as Japan and South Korea.

At the same time, the rise of the newly industrializing countries (NICs) such as Hong Kong, Taiwan, South Korea, Singapore, Thailand, Malaysia, Mexico, and Brazil has increased the number of viable sites for sophisticated manufacturing operations with low labor costs. Even China and India are beginning to join the industrialized world and the global market economy.

Almost every product or service market in the major world economies now has foreign competitors. They compete to sell everything from computers, to fast food, or medical diagnostic equipment. Increasing foreign competition is itself a reason for a business to globalize in order to gain the size and skills to compete more effectively. But an even greater spur to globalization is the advent of new global competitors who manage and compete on an integrated global basis.

THE GLOBAL REVOLUTION

In the 1980s these global competitors were primarily Japanese. Their central approach to global competition was one of the factors that allowed Japanese companies to conquer so many Western markets. In the 1990s, American and European companies responded to the Japanese challenge by focusing much more on quality. This was exemplified by the adoption of "six-sigma" quality by General Electric and Motorola. In addition, a growing number of American and, especially, European companies began to develop new models of globalization that were more flexible than the centralized Japanese approach. Companies such as Asea Brown Boveri, for example, developed networked models that combined the benefits of both global integration and national responsiveness.

In recent years, the communications and information revolution has also made it much easier to apply a globally integrated approach to management. Improvements in air travel, computers, satellites and telecommunications make it much easier to communicate with, and control, far-flung operations. Today, in a world where e-mail

"By a progressive, I do not mean a man who is ready to move, but a man who knows where he is going when he moves."

Woodrow Wilson

has become pervasive, it is easy to forget the dramatic impact of the humble facsimile machine. Its immediacy plugged every executive's desk into the global market. The Internet and the Web completed this revolution.

CASES IN POINT

Gillette, the U.S. shaving products company, provides one of the most aggressive examples of globally standardized strategy. While many corporate strategies still regard local adaptations as essential to their success in foreign markets, Gillette minimizes adaptation for cultural differences. The company sells the same products, uses the same production methods, enforces the same corporate policies, and uses the same advertising in every country where it conducts business.

The results are impressive. The company now dominates the shaver market with a 70% market share worldwide. The main advantages of this business model are scale and flexibility, most notable in research and development costs and leveraging intellectual capital across the globe. In addition, the company is more nimble. This was demonstrated during the Asian crisis in the late 1990s. Rather than maintain advertising expenditures in an area with flat to negative growth, Gillette chose to shift its marketing funds to Eastern Europe, where better sales growth was forecast. It is because the company treats the world as one region that it has such flexibility in its operations.

Toyota is another company that has benefited from an integrated global approach. It recognized early that in the automobile industry, where some local customization is essential, a global strategy requires multi-regional production. In the late 1990s, Toyota spent over $10 billion on global expansion in an aggressive effort to become the first truly globally organized car manufacturer. The company developed manufacturing hubs in the three major markets—North America, Europe, and Asia—with the ability to customize vehicles for regional markets.

Such extensive coverage now allows Toyota to react quickly to local tastes, bypass regional trade barriers, and utilize locally based suppliers to increase cost efficiencies. The company set up an assembly plant in the United States as early as 1987 and continued expansion at a number of sites there and in Canada throughout the 1990s.

In Europe, by 2001, Toyota had a regional parts center in Belgium, and manufacturing plants in the United Kingdom, France, and Turkey (two more opened in Poland in 2002 and 2006, and the first Russian plant is scheduled to open in 2007). This local production allows Toyota to bypass tariffs and locally produce Toyota's "Europe Car." In Asia, a local network of suppliers and assembly hubs allows Toyota to build sturdy, simply designed, low priced cars that appeal to the Asian consumer.

MAKING IT HAPPEN ▸▸

So how can companies create truly global strategies? For most, there are three separate stages involved.

1. **Developing the core strategy**: this is the basis of sustainable strategic advantage. It is usually, but not necessarily, developed for the home country first. Without a sound core strategy to build upon, a global strategy cannot be successful.

2. **Internationalizing the core strategy**: this stage involves the international expansion of activities, and adaptation of the core strategy. Companies need to have mastered the basics of international business before they can attempt a global strategy (because the latter often involves breaking the rules of international business).

3. **Globalizing the international strategy**: this involves integrating the strategy across countries to leverage the company's total global potential.

Multinational companies are usually adept at the first two steps. What they are less familiar with is the third stage. For one thing, total globalization runs counter to the accepted wisdom of tailoring for national markets. Yet, it is this third step that is vital to creating a successful total global strategy.

The first step towards a global strategy, then, is the creation of a viable core strategy. This involves several key elements:

- selection of the type of products or services that the business offers;
- the types of customers that the business serves;
- the geographic markets served;
- major sources of sustainable competitive advantage;
- functional strategy for each of the most important value-adding activities;
- competitive posture, including the selection of competitors to target;
- investment strategy.

At the second stage, a business expands outside its home market and needs to internationalize its core business strategy. The key to internationalizing is to select the geographic markets in which to compete. This choice has much more importance for an international business than for a national business.

For most businesses, international market selection presents issues that are much more challenging. These include the role of barriers to trade—such as import tariffs and quotas, and foreign ownership rules—as well as differences from the home country in laws, language, tastes, and behavior. Other aspects of internationalization strategy involve how to adapt products and programs to take account of foreign needs, preferences, culture, language, climate, and so on.

Typically, the end result is that the company ends up with strategies and approaches that involve large differences among countries. These differences can then weaken the company's worldwide cost position, quality, customer preference, and competitive leverage.

This is where a global strategy comes in. It involves strategic integration across all markets to leverage competitive advantage.

A key issue here is: what aspects of strategy should be globalized? Managers can answer this question by analyzing industry conditions or "industry globalization drivers." This provides the basis for evaluating the benefits and costs of globalization, and creates a clearer understanding of the different ways in which a globalization strategy can be used through the use of "global strategy levers."

Industry globalization drivers are externally determined by industry conditions or by the economics of the business. They fall into four groups—market, cost, government, and competitive drivers.

Taken together, these represent the industry conditions that determine the potential and need for competing with a global strategy. Each group of drivers is different for each industry and can also change over time.

Global strategy levers, on the other hand, are the choices available to the business. They operate along five dimensions:

- market participation—involves the choice of country-markets, and the level of activity;

"Strategic market management is a system designed to help management both precipitate and make strategic decisions, as well as create strategic vision." David A. Aaker

- products/services—involves the extent to which business offers the same or different products in different countries;
- location of value-adding activities—involves the choice of where to locate each of the activities that comprise the entire value-added chain, from research to production to after sales service;

- marketing—involves the extent to which a business uses the same brand names, advertising and other marketing elements in different countries;
- competitive moves—involves the extent to which a worldwide business makes competitive moves in individual countries as part of a global competitive strategy;

A global strategy should aim to ensure that all global strategy levers are optimally positioned relative to the industry drivers, and relative to the position and resources of the business and its parent company. In this way, a company ensures that the global whole is greater than the sum of its local parts.

Strategic Agility by John Wells

EXECUTIVE SUMMARY

- Whenever there's an economic slump, management focus shifts to cutting costs.
- This is only of benefit if at the same time the opportunity is taken to build a more agile business platform.
- There are several different levels of approach to cost management, from talking about it to taking the long-term strategic view.
- Most of these approaches have an impact on systems architecture—or they should.

INTRODUCTION

With the crash of technology stocks turning into a general economic slump, top management focus shifted from investing in new technology and business ideas to cutting costs. However, badly directed cost-cutting delivers return on investment no better than the speculation in e-commerce that was so characteristic of the technology boom. When the pressure is on to cut costs, a C.E.O. has a tough choice to make: simply make bold cuts without consideration of future needs, or invest in taking the first steps to building a much more agile business platform that will allow the company to exploit future opportunities and respond more quickly to change.

How quickly times change. How short investors' memories are. One minute the stock market is booming and companies are being driven to invest in e-commerce at almost any cost to protect their stock rating. The next minute the e-bubble has burst and no C.E.O. who wants to stay on the job is talking about new e-commerce initiatives. It's time for consolidation, focus, cutting costs.

This is unfortunate, because e-commerce, wisely deployed, provides a powerful competitive weapon in a downturn as well as in boom times. But this is not what investors want to hear. They insist that now is the time for bold announcements to cut costs and reduce head count, and there are several approaches to choose from.

MAKING IT HAPPEN ▶▶
Level Zero cost management: talking about it

The simplest and least-disruptive approach to cost-cutting is to talk about it but not actually do much. This is common practice in companies that acquire other businesses with the promise of major

cost-reduction synergies that then fail to materialize. For instance, Bank of America, which grew from Nations Bank into the number one U.S. consumer bank in a 30-year binge of more than 100 acquisitions, never realized major cost synergies until a new management came in.

Level One cost management: arbitrary cuts

A more dramatic approach to cost management is to cut all discretionary expenses (consultants, bowls of fresh fruit) and demand head count reductions across the board. But cutting costs without tackling the underlying causes is often a short-lived solution. Costs have a nasty habit of growing back. Savings promised by the majority of cost-reduction programs disappear within two years, never delivering the returns required to justify the high price paid for them.

Level One cost management is fast, decisive, and sometimes very necessary in a crisis, but it's seldom optimal. While it may be a short-term palliative for investors, it is seldom in the best long-term interests of the corporation.

Level Two cost management: redesign business processes to meet today's needs

Rather than simply cutting costs, the challenge is to deal with the underlying causes of cost. This takes reengineering business processes to design costs out. Rather than simply reducing the amount of resource allocated to an old process in the hope that it will work harder, the objective is to redesign the process so that it requires less resource in the first place. This is more thoughtful—and more effective—cost-cutting.

Level Three cost management: redesign business processes to meet tomorrow's needs

There is a danger of changing processes to meet today's immediate needs without paying attention to the future, so that when business improves another expensive process redesign is required. Every C.E.O. knows there are a host of actions that must be taken if the company is to prosper, but some must be deferred until financial conditions improve and stockholders have more of an appetite for investment. The process redesign should take these into account, ensuring that the company is ready to expand its activities when the time is ripe.

Level Four cost management: meeting unforeseen needs

But how can an organization *really* be future-proof? What about those unforeseen events that demand sudden changes? It's not possible to design a set of business processes to meet every eventuality. And yet an organization can't afford to redesign all of its processes every time it encounters change. The challenge is to shape a process architecture that can be more easily adapted to change.

The way to achieve this is to shape processes in a way that decouples them from each other as much as possible, allowing local changes to be made in a single process without major redesign of the total system. This is component-based process architecture.

Level Five cost management: self-adaptive systems

Decoupling processes also allows the team of people responsible for operating each process to look for improvements continuously. If they are incentivized to behave in this way, then when changes occur the process is quickly modified to meet the new needs. The process and the people who operate it form a component of the organization.

To be really adaptive, the component team must have the ability to modify and improve the process themselves. This makes for really rapid response. The component, and the organization as a whole, then become much more agile and adaptive.

"Creative strategies seldom emerge from the annual planning ritual. The starting point for next year's strategy is almost always this year's strategy . . . the company sticks to what it knows, even though the real opportunities may be elsewhere."
Gary Hamel

MINI-CASE

Wells Fargo saw the opportunity to offer loans to small businesses on the Web, collecting credit-check information on each applicant in real time to decide on whether to approve a loan. The company envisaged an automated loan manager and backroom support service that were much more cost-effective than the human variety.

The initial service was very well received. Not only did it cut costs, but it provided much quicker response to the customer, and it began driving up market share.

The next challenge came when Wells Fargo wanted to change its criteria for making loans. This process had traditionally taken up to six months, limiting flexibility and responsiveness to changing market demands. One solution would have been simply to wire in the new loan criteria. However, sufficiently dissatisfied by its past experience, in this phase Wells Fargo sought to componentize the system, isolating the criteria from the rest of the system so that they could be changed more easily. Moreover, rather than simply inserting a new set of criteria into the criteria module, the company built a criteria generator. Instead of requiring expensive IT resource to change the criteria, the department managers could do it themselves, taking days instead of months.

Far from limiting the number of criteria, Wells Fargo made its solution even smarter by making sure that the criteria component allowed the addition of more, as yet unidentified, criteria, providing the system with the agility to react to the unknown. The bank avoided the temptation to implement a Level Two solution and moved directly to a Level Five solution, dealing with known changes and changes as yet unknown, while empowering the management team to look continuously for improvements.

The Implications for Information Systems: Componentized Systems Architecture

Redesigning processes almost always means changing the information systems that support the processes. And the trouble is that old legacy systems get in the way. Hence the frustration with IT departments. Rather than being seen as the driver of change, IT is often seen as the greatest impediment to change in large organizations.

Old legacy platforms are typically hugely complex systems tied together to help run the company. A minor change in one part of the system can have major and unpredictable impact on other parts, rather like the proverbial butterfly that starts a hurricane in the Caribbean by fluttering in South America.

The challenge for legacy IT systems is the same as for organizational processes: to be able to break them down into loosely coupled components, so that each component can be changed without affecting the organization as a whole.

The IT components must map 100% onto organizational process components, so that when a department component sees opportunities for improvement it can change without disrupting the whole organization. The IT system can be adapted in parallel to support the change without changing the whole IT system. The capacity for change when this alignment is achieved is obviously very large.

CONCLUSION
Deal with Today's Challenge with Tomorrow in Mind

When a company is facing major economic challenges, how can it find time to worry about componentizing its IT platform? The reality is that a company must be guided by its component architecture whenever it makes change. Take the current plethora of legacy systems and identify the role each will play in a more flexible componentized architecture. In the context of a clear long-term view, legacy systems can be changed in ways that contribute to the long-term agenda.

FOR MORE INFORMATION

Books:
Laudon, Kenneth C., and Carol Guercio Traver. *E-Commerce: Business, Technology, Society.* 2nd ed. Reading, MA: Wesley Publishing Company, 2003.
Turban, Efraim. *Electronic Commerce 2006: A Managerial Perspective.* 4th ed. New York: Prentice Hall, 2005.

Web site:
http://cor-ex.com/sites/bestchng: with help from Amazon.com, the Best Corporate Change Resources site acts as a gateway to a wide variety of resources—books, journals, and Web sites—all on the topic of information technology and change.

"Failing is a learning experience. It can be a gravestone or a stepping stone." Bud Hadfield

The Human Value of the Enterprise
by Andrew Mayo

EXECUTIVE SUMMARY

- People are often spoken of as assets, but are generally treated as costs, because we have no credible system of valuing them.
- The problem is that in today's knowledge-based organizations value is driven more by people than by any other factor.
- There are five main approaches to building a measurement system for people, or human capital.
- The attempt to value people financially not been successful; however, an index of value factors provides a necessary balance with seeing people as costs.
- Current best practice looks at connecting the value of people in terms of their characteristics (and the value they produce in both financial and nonfinancial terms) via measures of their engagement and motivation.

INTRODUCTION

Our people are our most important asset. This frequent statement from chief executives is often received with justifiable cynicism. The problem is that people within an organization do not always experience decisions and policies in their everyday work life that support such a belief. The accountant who once described people to me (admittedly with a smile) as "costs walking about on legs" is often closer to the reality of organizational experience. The very term "human resources" reinforces this concept of people. Organizations driven by an often understandable drive for increased efficiency and minimized costs see "headcount" as the easy target.

There are many reasons for this. One is the domination of management by current targets for bottom line results—often resulting in a very short-term mindset. Such single-mindedness is illogical because it is out of balance; the desired final outcomes are driven by satisfying other demands that generally get much less attention. A powerful system of financial processes and targets dominates the life of most managers. Measures of intangibles, such as employees' capability or customers' loyalty may exist, but they are frequently excluded from the monitoring and control systems in any serious way.

Another problem is that people do not fit the strict financial definition of an asset. They cannot be transacted at will, their contribution is individually distinctive and variable (and subject to motivation and environment), and they cannot easily be valued according to traditional financial principles. However if we view "assets" as value creating entities, and in an era where knowledge and its application is the key competitive advantage, we will arrive inevitably at the foundational role people play. Organizations do employ some just for "maintenance," but the vast majority are value adding. Some indeed should be seen as investments rather than costs—but management accounting rarely recognizes this.

Perhaps the greatest problem is the lack of credible measures that relate to people and their value. We know in detail what they cost; we have no balancing quantity for their value. We feel it when it has been lost; but often too late.

THE VALUE OF PEOPLE
Is There a Problem to Be Solved?

There is indeed a major problem. The valuation of companies has progressively changed over the last 20 years, putting a much higher proportion on intangible assets like knowledge, competence, brands, and systems. These assets are also known as the *intellectual capital* of the organization. The issue is that we have no comparable system of measurement that enables us to give these the same balanced attention we give to financial matters. The result is that decisions about investment and resources are not necessarily in the long-term interest of the stockholders, even though they may appear to be at the time they are made. A classic case is laying off key people, particularly after mergers and acquisitions, only to hire them back when the value they contributed is suddenly recognized.

David Norton, coauthor of *The Balanced Scorecard* says of his experiences in working on performance management, that: "the worst grades are reserved for the typical executive team for their understanding of strategies for developing human capital. There is little consensus, little creativity, and no real framework for thinking about the subject. Worse yet, we have seen little improvement in this over the past eight years. The asset that is the most important is the least understood, least prone to measurement, and hence the least susceptible to management".

People-related Measures

No standardized approach has become widely accepted as yet, but the various ways in which systematic measurement has been applied to people can be summarized as follows.

- **Attempting to value people financially as assets: human resource (or asset) accounting**. This will be discussed in more detail below.
- **Creating an index of good HR practices and relating them to business results.** Researchers including Mark Huselid of Rutgers University and consulting firms such as Watson Wyatt have shown positive correlation between investment in HR management and stockholder value.
- **Statistically analyzing the composition of the workforce and measures of employees' productivity and output.** The best-known proponent here is Jac Fitz-Enz of the Saratoga Institute, California, who has extensively deployed ratios of all kinds and conducts a worldwide benchmarking practice.
- **Measuring the efficiency of HR functions and processes and the return on investment for people initiatives and programs.** Dave Ulrich of the University of Michigan is the champion of a measurement-orientated HR function, and Jack Philips the leading proponent of RoI for HR initiatives and programs.
- **Integrating people-related measures through a performance management framework.** These are frameworks that look for balance in performance measures between the needs of the different

"Everywhere in the world the industrial regime tends to make the unorganized or unorganizable individual, the pauper, into the victim of a kind of human sacrifice offered to the gods of civilization."

Jacques Maritain

stakeholders, or in relation to the component parts of the total intangible assets. The best known is Kaplan and Norton's *Balanced Scorecard*. An alternative approach comes from Karl-Erik Sveiby of Sweden, whose *Intellectual Capital Monitor* chooses a small number of measures for three kinds of intellectual capital—customer, structural, and human.

The most comprehensive approach to the human dimension is found in Mayo's *Human Capital Monitor*. This links three areas of measurement:

- the human capital that people lend to organizations in exchange for the value added to them;
- the financial and nonfinancial value for stakeholders that this human capital produces;
- the motivation and commitment of the people, which depend primarily on the environment in which they work.

Valuing People As Assets

There are three criteria for defining any asset:

- It must possess future service potential.
- It is measurable in monetary terms.
- It is subject to the ownership and control of the company, or it is rented or leased.

Traditional methods of coming to a valuation include:

- *cost-based*. This method typically looks at acquisition or replacement cost. The costs of recruiting an employee can be assessed and then depreciated over the expected future service of the person hired. Alternatively the person's gross remuneration can be used as a base.
- *market-based*. The price to be paid in an open market must be a reflection of the value of a person. Value is very difficult to assess, however, and does not take account of the value of service continuity in itself.
- *income-based*. The cash inflows expected by the organization related to the contribution of the human asset, calculated as the present value of the expected net cash flows. This is good for individuals whose efforts are directly related to identifiable income.

Human resource accounting, or human asset accounting, has been primarily developed in the United States under the guidance of Professor Eric Flamholz. He sees the value of a person as the product of two interacting variables—his or her conditional value and the probability that the person will stay with the organization for x years. *Conditional value* is the present worth of the potential services that could be rendered if the individual stayed with the organization, and is a combination of productivity (performance), transferability (flexible skills), and promotability. The latter two elements are heavily influenced by the first. This figure is then multiplied by a *probability* factor: the probability that the person will stay for the x years. This gives the *expected realizable value*, which is a measure of the person's worth. There are a number of difficulties with this approach, not least of which is the estimation of potential future services. It also leads to lower values for older and more experienced people who have less time to render future services. This is not necessarily the reality.

The truth is that this is not a well-known discipline, and has not been generally adopted by either the financial or HR communities.

A more useful approach was originally developed by U.K. researchers Giles and Robinson in 1973. They developed a factor called the human asset multiplier, which is applied to gross remuneration. This reflects a number of intrinsically valuable attributes of individuals. Mayo, in his 2001 book, came to similar conclusions, namely that whereas it would be really helpful if we could have a realistic, generally accepted, absolute financial formula, this is unlikely to be achieved. But it would be a major step forward if we could at least enable people's relative values to be compared against their costs. He proposed a formula for what he called the human asset worth (HAW), where

HAW = EC (employment cost) × IAM (individual asset multiplier) ÷ 1,000

(The divisor of 1,000 is used so that the resulting number does not look like a financial one.)

The *individual asset multiplier* is designed to reflect the relevant factors that make individuals valuable in their current context. These factors are not universal and vary for each group of employees sharing a common value output. Examples, however, include:

- specialized knowledge, skills, and experience
- personal skills and behaviors
- contribution to stakeholder value
- potential to grow and contribute at a higher level
- personal productivity in relation to stakeholder value
- alignment with organizational values

Each of these factors can be assessed on a scale, weighted for importance, and then added together to give the multiplier.

Such a formula can lead to tools such as a *human asset register*, which can monitor changes and compare teams and units. The process of analyzing the individual components may lead to strategies for change in the organization. It can be argued strongly that such tools are at least as important as those used for cost management.

A Framework of Measures

The following characteristics are suggested as criteria for a framework of people-related measures:

1. with the exception of workforce statistics, measures should not stand alone but be connected to other outcomes for the organization—particularly the value created for stakeholders;
2. a framework should be *useful* for the users. These might be external (investors, analysts, benchmarking) or internal (managers, other functions). Their needs are different, so more than one framework may be needed. Usefulness means informing actions to be taken;
3. the underlying collection, definitions, and presentation of data need to be valid and reliable, and have credibility with the users;
4. they should not be compiled through the lens of an accountant. Quantification does not equate necessarily with dollars. Value added can be both financial *and* nonfinancial.

None of the approaches described above meet all these criteria. An attempt to do so is found in Mayo's *Human Capital Monitor*. This links three areas of measurement for specific groups of employees:

1. the human capital that people lend to organizations in exchange for the value added to them. This is measured by the Human Asset Worth approach;
2. the motivation and engagement of the people, which depend primarily on the environment in which they work. Outcome measures are used, such as attrition, absenteeism, opinions, and management judgment—and also "input" measures of the factors that make a difference to the group under study;
3. the financial and non-financial value for stakeholders that this human capital produces—often measured as a productivity factor.

This provides a tool for managers which stands alongside their financial statements and informs them about people-related actions.

CONCLUSION

The term *human capital* can be used to describe the asset value of your people. Maximizing human capital through acquisition, retention, growth (and sometimes reten-

tion) should be a major priority of all executives, not an area left to the HR department alone. It is the area in which measurement is least well understood.

This is all about sustainable stockholder (or public sector beneficiary) returns. People are the one factor of value growth that drives all others. The value that a company creates results from the way that people apply their skills, energies, and expertise to the capital and raw materials that customers want. Of all the business levers available to leaders, the greatest potential to build value is offered by people. It is time indeed to recognize this through demanding a rigorous and credible approach to both valuing this most significant asset, and linking that value meaningfully to the benefits for stakeholders. What gets measured gets managed—and we need reality behind the rhetoric about our people.

FOR MORE INFORMATION

Books:
Becker, B. E., Mark Huselid, and David Ulrich. *The HR Scorecard: Linking People, Strategy, and Performance* Cambridge, MA: Harvard Business School Press, 2001.
Davenport, Thomas O. *Human Capital: What It Is and Why People Invest It*. San Francisco, CA: Jossey-Bass, 1999.
Fitz-Enz, Jac *The ROI of Human Capital*. New York: AMACOM, 2000.
Flamholtz, Eric G. *Human Resource Accounting: Advances in Concepts, Methods, and Applications*. 3rd ed. New York: Kluwer, 1999.
Mayo, Andrew. *The Human Value of the Enterprise: Valuing People As Assets— Monitoring, Measuring, Managing*. Naperville, IL: Nicholas Brealey, 2001.
Phillips, J., et al. *The Human Resources Scorecard: Measuring the Return on Investment*. Oxford: Butterworth-Heinemann 2001.

Human Capital by Edward E. Gordon

EXECUTIVE SUMMARY

- Accountants and economists are struggling to find a way for a business to measure the intangible assets of human-capital development. What is their added value to the business?
- But what *is* human capital? It is the sum total of individual intelligence built on the acquisition of skills, training, and educational experience over a lifetime. It's the application of this human knowledge to the workplace that creates real value.
- The merging of three types of capital ("human," "organizational," and "customer") creates the desired outcome—an organization so aligned and balanced as to produce the highest possible financial capital (value).

INTRODUCTION

The high performance workplace over the past two decades has been driven by two titanic forces: globalization and an increasing pace of technological change.

At the beginning of the 21st century these factors have combined to demand a new kind of well-educated knowledge worker, as profound a change as that wrought by the early Industrial Revolution on the role of manual labor in the 1800s.

In this environment, harnessing the human capital—the accumulated skills, experience, wisdom, and capabilities of all of the people employed in the organization is fundamental to success. This may seem obvious—after all, why pay for the most expensive resource in terms of results than any other, without using it to the full? However, at a time when skills are more complex and transferable, traditional loyalty is reducing, and the significance and value of knowledge is rising, there is a premium and renewed focus on managing human capital.

The U.S. departments of labor and education now estimate that 80% of all jobs in the high-tech workplace require at least 13th-grade reading, math comprehension, and applications skill levels. Unfortunately, the National Adult Literacy Survey (NALS) reported that 48% of U.S. adults fail to meet these criteria.

Though this problem can be found in many countries, it is most acute in the United States. The international Organisation for Economic Co-operation and Development (OECD) ranked the United States 15th out of 47 major industrial nations in the education and training levels of its citizens. This study showed about half of the U.S. adults reading below eighth-grade level, with much of the population performing below sixth-grade level.

In another comparative study of 18 nations, the OECD found that of U.S. high-school graduates who do not go on to acquire further education, nearly 60% perform below a literacy level that international experts consider necessary to cope with the complex demands of the modern workplace. That percentage was the highest among the nations studied, with Finland the lowest at 10% and other countries falling in between—20% in Germany, 35% in the United Kingdom, 50% in Poland. Instead of becoming knowledge workers, it would seem that many members of the current U.S. workforce, as well as students about to emerge from school, are in danger of becoming the new techno-peasants. "Investment in human capital is necessary for any nation to reap the benefits from information technology," says John Martin, director of education for the OECD. In this section, we will assess the importance of human capital: what it is, where it is, and how it can be managed to best effect.

WHERE ARE THE KNOWLEDGE WORKERS?

The world is rapidly approaching a 2010 crossroad. In that year, a demographic time bomb will begin its potential meltdown of the world's economy. The U.S. Census Bureau, Department of Labor, and Immigration and Naturalization Service concur that the population younger than 34 is declining. Between 2010 and 2020, 70 million Americans will retire and only 40 million will enter the workforce causing a dramatic knowledge-worker shortfall. The same trends hold true in the United Kingdom, Western Europe, and Japan. In some countries the total population may even decline. After 2015, the working-age population in China and India will begin to shrink.

With skilled workers in such high demand, U.S. companies have repositioned operations overseas, and they now lure up to 65,000 skilled workers to the United States on temporary H-1B visas.

The United States projects a shortfall of 2 million IT workers by 2005, while the European Union (EU) forecasts a 1.5 million worker labor gap. The United States and the EU share the same human-capital strategy—import the workers. But there aren't enough IT workers worldwide to fill the knowledge-worker gap. A so-called skill war is now starting, one that will see nations bidding up salaries just to attract these workers from a diminishing world supply.

To create real value, businesses must better leverage their human capital by helping develop larger numbers of their employees into better-educated workers, who will then be able to create more high-value-added products and services at extremely low cost.

DEVELOPING HUMAN CAPITAL: AVOIDING THE PITFALLS

The learning organization has largely failed in the boardroom for two reasons. First, presidents, C.E.O.s, and small-business owners still see no connection between company profit and investing in their human capital, because they believe you can't measure it. Second, training programs often don't improve employee performance, because they aren't based on the most recent advances in teaching critical-competency and problem-solving skills.

Complex and multilayered workplace performance issues need to be stated in a language and format that will move more business leaders to give them their personal support. Poll after poll shows that people in the United States support the concept of better education in general, but it is in realizing the concept that support falls apart.

Many of the world's leading industrial powers are beating the United States at its own game simply by understanding that knowledge equals profit. Rather than ignoring the relationships, they are acting on the critical interactions among technology, smarter employees, and return on investment (ROI). They invest extensively in student career education and employee-retraining programs—and reap the short- and long-term profits.

The key is high-quality reeducation pro-

"Owning the intellectual property is like owning land: You need to keep investing in it again and again to get a payoff; you can't simply sit back and collect rent." Esther Dyson

grams that motivate employees to use their own learning by applying innovative thinking on the job. This strategy will increase personal performance, better their lifetime careers, and in turn give business a high ROI in human capital.

TAKING RESPONSIBILITY FOR HUMAN CAPITAL DEVELOPMENT

In *Training* magazine's 2004 survey of corporate training and development, 67 percent of the top 100 companies measured training effectiveness through ROI. Accenture Consulting developed their own ROI calculator to analyze all the training for 261,000 employees over the history of the company. Their analysis factored out the effects of inflation, market cycles, experience, and employee levels to isolate the training effect on each person. Accenture determined that for every dollar invested in training, there was a return of $3.53 in net training benefits. They also found that their better-trained employees had a higher number of billable client hours and stayed with the company longer.

But how do you do the ROI calculations? There are many free training ROI worksheet tools available online. The web site **BenefitNews.com/education** offers a variety of these calculators on the "Measuring Training's Return on Investment" page on their website. One of these tools, "A Human Capital ROI Worksheet," was developed by the author and a team of experts. Since its introduction in 2000, thousands of businesses around the globe have used this spreadsheet. Access the latest, upgraded versions of the worksheets free of charge at **www.imperialcorp.com**.

MINI-CASES

Trident Precision Manufacturing of Webster, New York, is one of the smallest companies ever to win a Malcolm Baldrige National Quality Award (in 1996). Over a period of six years, Trident invested 4.7% of the payroll in educating its employees. This custom-product sheet-metal company taught workers blueprint reading, trigonometry, and English as a second language (ESL). Product defect rates improved from 3% to 99.994% defect-free, annual revenue rose from $5 million to $19 million, and revenue per employee shot up by 73%.

Equimeter, based in the United Kingdom, invested its human capital in its Pennsylvania operations by providing a group of engineers with a *kaizen*-team-training program in order to improve the quality and productivity of a gas-meter assembly line. The company achieved a 16% productivity im-

provement and 22% space savings, reduced the work in process by 10%, and solved three safety issues. The estimated ROI of this training program was 31.6%.

Human-capital investment by thousands of other organizations, including Allied Signal, Elco Industries, Hampden Papers, Hardy Industries, Lumonics, MacLean-Fogg, the Northeast Illinois Metropolitan Transit Railroad Authority (METRA), Warner-Lambert, and Will-Burt, more clearly demonstrated the direct correlation of skills, training, and education with increased productivity and profit.

FedEx has established learning and growth as one of its four key business strategies. FedEx Quality University is a global learning system. More than 140,000 employees worldwide have access to its content. When FedEx employees can't find a suitable e-learning course in the Quality University, they can take classroom courses from outside sources that are paid for by the $2,500 annual Personal Learning Fund that FedEx offers every employee. By offering these career development opportunities, FedEx has been better able to retain valuable employees and leverage its available human capital.

innovation by leveraging structural capital and human capital in new combinations. The company benefits from a steeper learning curve at its critical cutting edge: the friction points where people grapple with operational productivity issues. Critical competencies are generated in-house that encourage people to create new procedures, services, products, and intellectual properties—the competitive ideas of business success that generate real profit.

CONCLUSION

Unless businesses invest in people to reverse the dangerous trend of discounting the value of human capital, both technology and management systems will fail as they become more complex and require more people who can think for themselves and adapt information. By investing in their most critical intangible—human capital—businesses will rise to the challenges of technology and globalization and speed up the process of building a knowledge economy in their own communities and across the world.

FOR MORE INFORMATION

Books:
Becker, Brian E., Mark A. Huselid, and Dave Ulrich. *The HR Scorecard: Linking People, Strategy and Performance*. Cambridge, MA: Harvard University Press, 2001.
Conger, Jay A., and Beth Benjamin. *Building Leaders: How Successful Companies Develop the Next Generation*. San Francisco, CA: Jossey-Bass, 1999.
Edvinson, Leif, and Michael S. Malone. *Intellectual Capital: Realizing Your Company's True Value by Finding Its Hidden Brainpower*. New York: HarperBusiness, 1997.
Fitz-Enz, Jac. *The ROI of Human Capital: Measuring the Economic Value of Employee Performance*. New York: AMACOM, 2000.

Web site:
www.astd.org: this American Society for Training and Development site publishes ongoing research regarding the return on investment of human capital.

See also:
☆ Creating Value through People (pp. 153–154)

"Companies . . . have a hard time distinguishing between the cost of paying people and the value of investing in them."

Thomas A. Stewart

Return on Talent
by Subir Chowdhury

EXECUTIVE SUMMARY

- The performance of an organization is determined by the performance of its employees.
- Organizations must therefore measure return on talent as well as return on investment.
- Knowledge is one of the most important factors for business success. If knowledge assets are increased, related factors such as sales will also increase.
- Talent—or intellectual capital—has fast become one of the most significant areas of business activity and competition.

INTRODUCTION

The performance of an organization is entirely determined by the performance of its employees. This bold statement deserves further study. If the determinant of corporate performance is not its employees, what is? Is it strategic intent? Core competencies? Manufacturing? Is it proprietary technologies? The best equipment and laboratories? A visionary C.E.O.? Yes, it's all of these things. And all of these things are created and constantly improved by employees. Talented employees are the change agents. Good employees join in to help implement new initiatives. Others follow at various times, depending on when they can break the bonds of their comfort zone to enter the area of change, uncertainty, and opportunity. They fall by the wayside because they were in the wrong job.

It is broadly recognized that past performance is not a reliable indicator of potential or future success. Yet many organizations continue to use past performance to identify high-potential employees. How much true talent is overlooked by this practice? Overlooked and misplaced high-potential employees stagnate. The problem of identifying, positioning, and compensating high-potential employees spans all disciplines and levels, from the loading dock to the boardroom. Lost and underused employees represent enormous, largely unattended financial loss. A second problem is the difficulty in measuring the financial contribution of employees beyond global measures such as revenues per employee.

To focus a successful organization, managers must use a new tool called return on talent (ROT). Most organizations focus on return on investment (ROI) and fail to understand the key strategy of how to increase ROI by increasing ROT.

HARNESSING TALENT

ROT has the power to revolutionize business. ROT is calculated by dividing the knowledge generated and applied by the investment in talent. You need to address the dilemma of how to measure an intangible asset and how to generate high ROT value. For decades, organizations have used key metrics like ROI and ROA (return on assets) to determine value. But increasingly an effective new-economy organization will use ROT. Current business measurements merely measure the use of capital, but ROT is expressed as follows:

$$\text{ROT} = \text{knowledge generated } \& \text{ applied} \div \text{investment in talent}$$

If you have talented people, knowledge is just one component. The generation of knowledge is the most important thing talent can provide. Now you may realize that knowledge generated by the talent doesn't equal knowledge applied, right? And if knowledge isn't applied, the company loses most of the market value of that knowledge. Whatever knowledge a person generates in a year divided by how much is invested in that particular person is the value.

If an employee generates many innovative ideas but never implements any of them, that person fails to generate any value, because the return to the company is zero. Knowledge generated does not necessarily mean knowledge applied. So value is knowledge generated *and* applied. Knowledge becomes an asset only when it's captured and used effectively; if it isn't effectively applied, it can't generate any yield or ROI. Generating a lot of knowledge within organizations doesn't add any value unless that knowledge is used in effective strategy formulation. Knowledge assets, like money or equipment, are worth cultivating only in the context of strategy. You can't de-

fine and manage intellectual assets unless you know what you are trying to do with them. This is the backbone of the knowledge economy; success in this field depends on mastery of talent, just as success in manufacturing relies on the skillful employment of plant and supply chains.

THE VALUE OF KNOWLEDGE
1. Return on Talent

The value of knowledge generated increases with its effective deployment. Effective knowledge generated means high ROT. It leads to a creative workforce, innovations, smooth processes, continuous product improvements, and improved communications. It helps management to be flexible, to capitalize on opportunities, and to keep pace with the changing business climate. Talented people influence those around them, and their knowledge is shared over time. Top knowledge generators should be rewarded. If managers expect top talent to achieve their maximum performance and produce maximum return, they must not place them in routine jobs.

ROT measures the payback from investment in people; it shows whether managers are hiring the right people and how effectively they use them to achieve business success. It can be a quantitative or qualitative measurement, based on management's viewpoint. Are managers getting the maximum payback on their investment? If managers want to see quantitative results, they need to put a price on knowledge generated, based on the results achieved. Talent generates knowledge, which is one of the greatest assets in the global economy. True knowledge brings creativity and innovation and adds value to the company. Knowledge has become a key production factor, along with traditional resources such as raw materials, buildings, and machinery. Companies that measure the knowledge generated and applied by their talent can make their investments in talent more profitable. Further, companies cannot improve what they do not measure.

Effective managers use ROT measurements to make their investments in talent more profitable. ROT measurements help monitor performance, forecast opportunity, and determine the profitability of their investment in talent. To make their invest-

ment more profitable, management must constantly measure ROT, continuously improve ROT, and nurture, develop, and refresh talent.

2. Return on Knowledge

Return on knowledge generated and applied is more difficult to calculate and track. Knowledge creates real wealth through multiple applications, for example, repeating the same application pervasively through a corporation, or finding new applications to new situations. Knowledge applications have breadth (across organizations) and length (in time). Years may pass between the generation of knowledge and its first application, let alone subsequent applications.

In order to properly account for the value of knowledge generated, initial estimates need to be made and refined yearly as applications appear on the horizon and then are realized. Leading indicators of return are based on projections of the probability of each anticipated application and the monetary value of each application summed over all anticipated applications.

Forward-looking projections and backward-looking allocations are both judgments, and there's no reason to believe that one is any better than the other. Indeed, projections made while focusing on the knowledge generated may be the more reliable of the two. It is certain that the combination of early projections, after-the-fact allocations, and annual updating and tracking between knowledge generated and the first of a series of applications, greatly improves the capability to measure and link return on knowledge generated and applied and investment in talent.

MAKING IT HAPPEN ▶▶

1 **Build a team focused on developing talent.** To reach high ROT scores, you need a talent team. Often you find one or two good people who can generate knowledge and perhaps even apply that knowledge, but you don't have a talent team that can leverage their ideas. Most of the individual talent in a company can be innovative if the team dynamics are right. If you have a low ROT score, you may have a dysfunctional team. ROT scores are not fixed; they change over time.

2 **Measure and monitor ROT.** If you are a manager who hires and invests in talent, you need to monitor ROT closely. In a company the size of General Motors or General Electric, you probably view salaries as a regular fixed cost that is standard. The portion that may vary is how much you invest in certain ideas. If you see that certain employees are not generating enough knowledge and success relative to your investment in them, that should be a big red flag, because your ROT value might become negative, or much lower than your competitor's ROT value.

3 **Decide how to increase ROT throughout the organization.** If you were hired to manage talent with a low ROT score (perhaps even a negative value), you need to do some things to boost the ROT fast. How do you turn around an organization and achieve higher ROT scores? You do it person by person, function by function. You have to assess the talent on your team and find out who and what is bringing the most profit to the company, who and what is winning and keeping the best customers. Your first task is to perform talent diagnostics. You might easily spend six months identifying all your talent and determining which ones you can work with to turn the company around. But usually you don't have six months to do talent diagnostics. So you need to do it faster, even in a large company. There is much to be said for focusing on quick, high-profile actions that build support and momentum behind the need to increase ROT.

Many managers assess employees' talent intuitively—they don't necessarily need a measurement tool. Every manager, however, benefits from having a tool to measure and monitor ROT. Apple soared when Steve Jobs was C.E.O., and faded when he left. It soared again when he returned as Apple's C.E.O. It doesn't mean that Jobs was a good or bad person. He was a very effective person in that environment. Many good C.E.O.'s fail in environments in which there is no structure. They go by intuition. After you identify the key talent, give them the authority and resources to boost the ROT team score. The talent diagnostic may show that in one division you have a lot of talented people, while in a different division you have very few. You have to cross functions, making sure you balance the talent according to the needs of the organization, and then challenge each talent and team to reach a financial goal.

CONCLUSION

Organizations that constantly improve ROT grow at a rapid rate. Management can monitor the performances of individuals as well as teams. Knowledge is one of the most important factors for business success. If knowledge assets are increased, then all other related factors like production and sales will be automatically increased. Consequently, organizations should try to improve ROT continuously to sustain sales growth. ROT is a superb key performance indicator, and one that is set to be measured and managed in much the same way as financial issues.

FOR MORE INFORMATION

Books:
Becker, Brian E., Mark A. Huselid, and Richard W. Beatty. *The Workforce Scorecard: Managing Human Capital to Execute Strategy.* Cambridge, MA: Harvard Business School Press, 2005.
Brockbank, Wayne, and David Ulrich. *The HR Value Proposition.* Cambridge, MA: Harvard Business School Press, 2005.
Kaplan, Robert S., and David P. Norton. *Alignment: Using The Balanced Scorecard to Create Corporate Strategies.* Cambridge, MA: Harvard Business School Press, 2006.

See also:
☆ Retaining Employees (pp. 229–230)
☆ Snapping Managerial Inertia (pp. 322–323)

"All our talents increase in the using, and every faculty, both good and bad, strengthens by exercise."
Anne Brontë

Competing on Costs
by Dinna Louise C. Dayao

EXECUTIVE SUMMARY

- Many companies cut costs out of a sense of crisis. However, companies like Air Asia, Aravind Eye Hospital, Jollibee Foods Corp., and Toyota Motor Corp. don't wait for tough times before they act.
- Instead, these companies choose to be low-cost leaders. They gain their competitive advantage from being able to produce goods and services at the lowest cost.
- Low-cost leaders shave off costs at every element of the value chain. As a result, they can pass on the resulting savings to their customers in the form of low prices.

INTRODUCTION

When Carlos Ghosn became chief operating officer of Nissan Motor Company in 1999, the Japanese automaker looked as if it were headed for the junkyard. Nissan had lost money for six of the preceding seven years. Its market share had fallen for 27 consecutive years. Its debts totaled $20 billion.

Today, Nissan is deemed one of the automobile industry's most striking turnarounds. In 2004, Nissan had a record operating profit of $8 billion, up 4.4% from 2003. Its operating profit margin came to 10%, which is at the top level among global automakers. It had zero debt.

Nissan, like many companies, cut costs out of a sense of crisis. However, companies like Air Asia, Aravind Eye Hospital, Jollibee Foods Corporation, and Toyota Motor Corporation don't wait for tough times before they act. Instead, these companies choose to be low-cost leaders, gaining their competitive advantage from being able to produce goods and services at the lowest cost.

Low-cost leaders understand very clearly the bare bones of their businesses. They rethink the very core of their companies' internal value chain—the distinct activities needed to create their products or services. They determine what controls the cost of each activity. They shave off costs ruthlessly at every element of the value chain.

As a result, low-cost leaders make real and lasting breakthroughs. They benefit from increased productivity, reduced cycle time, and lower input costs. And, crucially, they can produce goods or deliver services more cheaply than their competitors. This translates into better profitability and potentially more cash flow.

SUCCESS SECRETS OF LOW-COST LEADERS
Air Asia: Making It Possible for Everyone to Fly

In late 2001, Tony Fernandes mortgaged his home to buy Malaysia's Air Asia, a failing carrier with two planes and an $11 million debt. Airline analysts thought he would crash and burn. Even before the events of September 11, the world's airlines were in trouble.

Well, Fernandes not only survived, he has thrived. By 2002, Air Asia broke even, with all past debts cleared. Profit has since jumped by about 20 million ringgit a year. An initial public offering in November 2005 was oversubscribed by 130%. Today, Air Asia is the region's biggest low-cost carrier. It has flown about 15 million passengers and expanded its fleet to 28 planes flying to sixty destinations in 8 countries.

Behind the carrier's huge success is Fernandes' simple concept: everyone should be able to fly. So the entrepreneur dreamed up all kinds of ways to save money and to offer Asians cut-rate fares that would encourage them to fly more.

Fernandes slashed fares on heavily traveled routes, turned around planes much faster than before, and stopped serving complimentary food and drinks. His pilots are trained to land lower and slower to conserve fuel and reduce wear and tear on tires. He pays his flight attendants, not special crews, to clean planes. This not only lowers costs but chops the time spent boarding at terminals to 25 minutes—about half that of the major airlines.

Approximately 40% of Air Asia's tickets are sold over the Internet, eliminating travel-agent fees. When a professional aviation construction outfit asked for $20 million to build a hangar at Kuala Lumpur's airport, Fernandes asked the small contractor who built his home to do it instead for $500,000.

Fernandes's penny-pinching ways have pared down Air Asia's cost per available seat kilometer (ASK) to 2.13 U.S. cents. In the airline industry, "cost per ASK" is comparable to "unit cost." Air Asia claims it to be the lowest cost achieved by any airline in the world. These savings have boosted the carrier's profitability for the first half of 2005 to 54 million ringgit (roughly $14 million), a whopping 11% above full year profits for 2004.

Aravind Eye Hospital: Providing High-Quality, Low-Cost Eye Care to the Masses

In a surgery room at Aravind, India, a single large microscope swivels between two operating tables to make the most of the time each doctor can operate. As soon as doctors complete one procedure, they turn to the next table and begin work. Meanwhile, the table used previously is prepared for the next patient.

Such efficiency enables Aravind's network of five hospitals to perform more than 200,000 operations each year. The procedures cost $50 to $100 each. These prices are a mere fraction of the equivalent cost in the United States—more than $2,000. What's more, 70% of Aravind's patients pay little or nothing. Well-to-do patients are charged the higher fee, which partially subsidizes operations for the poorest.

Aravind's success proves that it is possible to provide high-quality, low-cost eye care to the masses. The hospital's key to keeping costs down? The huge volume of surgeries and the efficient system the doctors have developed. After doctors perform the surgery, paramedics stitch and dress the wounds. Also, doctors are spared from administrative or routine tasks. This frees them up to do more surgeries. As a result, each Aravind surgeon carries out about 2,000 cataract operations annually, compared with an Indian average of 250. The "assembly-line" procedure is efficient without sacrificing patient care. Though Aravind puts two or more patients in an operating room at the same time, it hasn't experienced any problems with infections.

"Economics is a 'dismal science,' we don't believe things are perfect, we don't believe there are free lunches. We believe there are trade-offs and costs and sacrifices."

Laura D'Andrea Tyson

Aravind's efficiency was the subject of a case study at Harvard Business School. Several U.S. medical programs send residents to the hospitals for training. Health officials from China, Nepal, and Indonesia—among others—have come knocking at the door of founder Dr. Govindappa Venkataswamy for advice. The World Bank, sponsor of a multimillion-dollar blindness-control project in India, has enlisted Aravind in its training efforts.

Jollibee Foods Corp.: The Logistics Master

Tony Tan, head of Jollibee Foods Corp., is known for trouncing McDonald's in the Philippines. His 508-outlet hamburger chain sells more than half a million burgers everyday and is the market leader. McDonald's has about 250 outlets in the Philippines, by comparison.

Jollibee beat the international burger chain by basically copying the very things that made McDonald's successful. The ever-present Jollibee mascot welcomes customers to bright yellow and orange stores. The crew in colorful uniforms cheerfully greets diners. Jollibee's offerings include French fries, fried chicken, and burgers.

To this recipe, Tan added a new ingredient: fast food aimed at Filipino tastes and offered at a much lower price. Filipinos like stronger-flavored burgers, sweet spaghetti topped with hot dogs, and rice porridge with chicken bits. All this Jollibee provides and at affordable prices, too.

Jollibee controls costs by keeping an eye on logistics. Behind the cheery, relaxed face of the company is an efficient back-office infrastructure. It ensures that a hamburger cooked less than 12 minutes earlier awaits any customer at any Jollibee store. And it lets Jollibee managers know the sales per item per hour, on a daily basis.

In 2002, Jollibee moved to a shared-services model to support its finance, human resources, purchasing, and information. Using this model, instead of each business unit owning its own IT group, they all buy some (or all) of their IT products and services from a central group. In this manner, business units save money by sharing employees and software licenses and eliminating layoffs.

While cost savings have yet to be quantified, they can be significant. International studies have shown that shared-services operations can trim expenses associated with receivables and credit services by 25%, and by 45% for payables and general accounting. Beyond cost savings, shared services can improve the quality of service, writes author and consultant Dean Meyer in *C.I.O.* magazine: "Perhaps most importantly, a consolidated organization can support a higher degree of staff specialization. Greater specialization leads to performance improvements as widespread as greater speed, lower cost, higher quality and more innovation."

These strengths will surely help Jollibee run what has become the Philippines' largest fast-food network with total revenues of 26.2 billion pesos in 2004. Aside from its burger chain, the company has 838 stores in nine countries including Chinese fast-food chain Chowking, pizza parlor Greenwich, sandwich chain Delifrance, Yonghe King chain in China, and the restaurant Red Ribbon.

Toyota Motor Corp.: Eliminating Waste . . . and Competitors

Katsuaki Watanabe, Toyota Motor Corp.'s president, is the company's chief cost-cutter. He is the brain behind an initiative called "Construction of Cost Competitiveness for the 21st Century," or CCC21. This program forced suppliers to slash the prices of 180 key parts by at least 30%. CCC21 helped the automaker save $10 billion over the past five years. Thanks in part to that effort, profits hit a record $10.7 billion in 2004.

Toyota's relentless drive to cut costs stems from a philosophy that views waste as unacceptable. Toyota's engineers, managers, and line workers work together closely to continually tweak the system. They then make little changes to make work go more smoothly. Toyota roots out wasted costs, effort, and time—as well as excess capital investment. As a result, it makes more automobiles with more efficient workers and leaner factories than its competitors.

Harbour Consulting, a Michigan-based company that analyzes factory efficiency, reported that in 2004 the average Toyota automobile in North America needed about 19.5 hours of labor for assembly. Each GM automobile, on the other hand, took about 23 hours. And each Ford needed about 24.5 hours.

Toyota's North American factories built 1.44 million vehicles in 2004. That number is 107% of Toyota's theoretical capacity. In contrast, GM and Ford factories used only 86% of their rated plant capacity in 2004. This suggests they could have invested more efficiently to avoid expensive excess space and machinery.

Toyota's legendary efficiency and innovation have left other automakers in the dust. It is the world's first and largest maker of hybrid automobiles. It can barely keep hot models such as the Prius hybrid in stock. And it's on track to overtake GM as the #1 automaker as soon as 2008.

MAKING IT HAPPEN ▶▶

- Understand the bare bones of your company. Ask the most basic questions about each activity needed to create your product or service.
- Distinguish between low-cost and high-cost activities. Determine what controls the cost of each activity.
- Keep the activities that add value. Compress, eliminate, or outsource those that don't.
- Identify cost-reduction opportunities and implement those ideas.
- Aggressively pursue cost savings throughout the value chain.

CONCLUSION

These success stories demonstrate that low-cost leadership is a proven approach to successful competition in the marketplace. By asking fundamental questions about the processes that create your product or service, by grasping which activities are low-cost and which are high-cost, by eliminating process steps that truly do not add value, and by leveraging all cost-reduction opportunities, any company can compete with a low-cost advantage.

FOR MORE INFORMATION

Books:

Charan, Ram. *Profitable Growth Is Everyone's Business: 10 Tools You Can Use Monday Morning.* New York: Crown Business, 2004.

Liker, Jeffrey. *The Toyota Way: 14 Management Principles From The World's Greatest Manufacturer.* Englewood Cliffs, NJ: McGraw-Hill, 2003.

Womack, James P. and Daniel T. Jones. *Lean Solutions: How Companies and Customers Can Create Value and Wealth Together* New York: Free Press, 2005.

Web sites:

C.F.O. Asia: **www.cfoasia.com**
Lean Enterprise Institute: **www.lean.org**

See also:

☆ Infusing a Company with Cutting-edge Strategy (pp. 110–111)
☆ Outsourcing (pp. 120–121)
☆ Why EVA Is the Best Measurement Tool for Creating Shareholder Value (pp. 166–167)

"Too many companies are expending enormous energy simply to reproduce the cost and quality advantages that global competitors already have."
Gary Hamel

Viewpoint: Stan Davis
Current Lessons in Business Leadership

Introduction
Stan Davis is an independent author, speaker, and consultant best known for linking the fundamentals of science and technology to likely futures in business and management. Davis has written three books with Christopher Meyer: *Blur: The Speed of Change in the Connected Economy* (Perseus, 1998) and *Future Wealth* (Harvard Business School Press, 2000), and *It's Alive: The Coming Convergence of Information, Biology, and Business* (Crown Business, 2003). In this article, he reflects on the challenges facing leadership in the face of global terrorist threats and recession.

Since 2001, we've experienced powerful economic recession, the bubble bursting on the dot-com boom, the terrorism of 9/11, a raft of major corporate scandals, and a pervasive financial panic in the stock markets. If ever there was a time for leadership, it's now.

Ask around the business world, however, and what you get is something different from our usual approach to leading. What's striking is the general lack of answers and direction, much more pervasive than creative new approaches to the problems at hand. No major new theme, strategy, or technique has captured the imagination of the business world. No one is leading us to a great leap forward. Leadership is taking one step back to take two steps forward—but we're still at the one-step-back point.

What we hear is a return to focusing on fundamentals. In our search for answers to allay our discomfort, we go back as far as necessary to find solid beliefs we feel we can trust. Paradoxically, this has "led" us back to the past: the only motif that has currency now is the retro-theme "back to basics."

The focus on basics is meaningful and true. It is a retrenchment, a falling back to someplace where we feel a solid footing, so we can lead ourselves back to a better state.

The "Real" Economy
A healthy example of this is our renewed appreciation for the "real" economy. The real economy is measured by jobs and production, the market economy by financial performance and the stock market. Most commentary says that the real economy is strong but is being dragged down by the financial economy. The good news is that "back to basics" has us focusing on the real more than the purely financial aspects of our businesses. The bad news is that this focus will do little to improve companies' stock prices. remedial back to basics in our financial accounting—for example, expensing executive stock options and C.E.O.-signed responsibility for what the books say—will also have salutary effects. in time the net effect should be a healthier balance between the two economies.

Moving Forward
The temporary mantra, "one step back to basics," should put us back on track, readying us to take those two steps forward. As a necessary corrective it is not misguided. It positions us for moving ahead, but it doesn't tell us what those forward steps need to be. Here are some suggestions.

First, companies are simultaneously both businesses and organizations. A business is what you do, and an organization is how you do it. Businesses are about resources, products and services, customers and markets, and they are about competition. Organizations, on the other hand, are about things like chains of command, departments and committees, structures and processes. Business leadership should focus on business at least as much as on organization, if not more.

> **A business is what you do, and an organization is how you do it.**

Second, while you're taking a business focus: Which is more important to your company, innovation and growth or efficiency and productivity? The current emphasis on fundamentals is more closely tied to efficiencies than to growth. As we go forward, a key element in business leadership will involve knowing which one to emphasize and knowing when to shift focus. Long-term health will require corporate leadership that can innovate and grow companies.

Third, businesses exist out there in the marketplace, while organizations focus their attention internally. The major events of the past year are what economists call "externalities," whereas most steps business leaders have taken are internal organizational ones. A select few business leaders create policies to deal with the externalities and the systemic issues they raise. The majority of us, however, fail to resolve this contradiction. We are constrained to lead from within our organizations, while our companies would fare better if more internal employees would lead with an external focus on the business. Even if we're terrific leaders for the people around us, at best we affect the 30 or 40 percent of corporate problems that reside inside the organization, while not touching the 60 or 70 percent of our problems that lie outside, external and beyond the reach of individual actions.

> **Even if we're terrific leaders for the people around us, at best we affect the 30 or 40 percent of corporate problems that reside inside the organization**

"The blur of business has created a new economic model in which returns increase, rather than diminish."

Stan Davis

Fourth, leadership isn't the exclusive preserve of those at the top. On 9/11 the firefighters embodied leadership as much as New York Mayor Giuliani did. Too much of the stuff on leadership is about C.E.O.s, presidents, and generals. I wonder how an ordinary person is supposed to apply what they learn from them to their own lives and work. Jack Welch, for example, was probably the greatest business leader in the second half of the last century, and he was also very vocal about leadership. But how many of his leadership skills got applied outside of GE by ordinary people like a local sales manager in Kansas City or a plant supervisor in Milwaukee? So another leadership lesson should be to focus more on leadership by ordinary people.

Fifth, new forms of management and organization spawned by the information age are just beginning to take root in corporate America. These include shifts in organization from hierarchy to network, from centralization to decentralization, and from independence to interdependence. September 11 taught us the uncomfortable truth that terrorists have embraced these new forms more completely than has our own private sector.

The negative events of 2001 knocked the hubris and confidence out of us. So there's plenty of room for leadership: leadership by ordinary people, leadership that focuses both externally and internally, leadership that balances business growth and productivity, and leadership that builds new forms of organization.

FOR MORE INFORMATION

Book:
Meyer, Christopher, and Stan Davis. *It's Alive: The Coming Convergence of Information, Biology, and Business.* New York: Texere, 2003.

See also:
Blur (p. 1074)
Jack: Straight from the Gut (p. 1105)

"The difference between buyers and sellers blurs to the point where both are in a web of economic, informational, and emotional exchange."

Stan Davis

Budgeting

by Jeremy Hope, Robin Fraser, Peter Bunce, and Franz Röösli

EXECUTIVE SUMMARY

- **The "Command and Control" model.** This management model emerged in the early 1900s to help companies meet rising demand and maximize profitability. With its main focus on efficiency, it introduced division of labor, incentives linking pay to performance, functional organization, and centralized decision making. It led to dramatic increases in productivity, but it also dehumanized work. The annual planning and budgeting process that ties it all together is its defining characteristic and the source of many of its problems today

- **The changing environment.** In conditions of discontinuous change, unpredictable competition, and fickle customers, few companies can plan ahead with any confidence. Yet most organizations today remain locked into a traditional "plan-make-and-sell" management model that involves a protracted annual planning and budgeting process based on negotiated targets and resources, which act as a constraint on responsiveness.

- **The barriers to change.** Organizations need to find a new model that effectively empowers frontline managers to make quick decisions based on fast, relevant information. But the annual planning and budgeting process and the resulting "fixed performance contract" act as barriers to change, both mental and systemic.

- **The "Devolved Leadership" model.** A number of companies have broken free from the traditional model and created a model that is much better aligned with today's competitive success factors. They have done this by devolving accountability to frontline managers and replacing annual planning and budgeting with alternative steering mechanisms. The BBRT has studied these cases; seen what huge competitive advantage they have gained from this model; and identified the principles on which it operates.

- **Making it happen.** The BBRT has identified some of the best cases worldwide (for example, Svenska Handelsbanken and ALDI, which have been operating for over three decades, and UBS Wealth Management and Business Banking, which has only recently started) and developed a pragmatic, scientifically-based approach to implementing the model and gaining real competitive advantage from it.

THE COMMAND AND CONTROL MODEL

The traditional Command and Control model was designed to execute a *producer-led* approach to business. It was influenced to a large extent by Frederick W. Taylor and the Scientific Management movement. The multidivisional organization (or M-form) coped with increasing complexity by placing the activities of each distinct product line, region, or technology into a separately managed compartment (for example, a business unit or division) and subjecting all these compartments to the financial discipline of a strong corporate staff. The underlying thread was control. The mission statement agreed on by senior executives was translated into the strategic plan by the planners and handed down the hierarchy to operational managers, who then prepared their plans and budgets. Once these were agreed on, all that was demanded was adherence to the plan. Head office did not like surprises. Control reports were constantly fed back up the line, and if they showed that performance was veering off track, new directives would be issued.

The model led to dramatic increases in productivity, but division of labor led to the "dehumanization" of work. Ways have been found to ameliorate this problem to some degree, but the design of the model is fundamentally one that works *against*, not *with* the best in human nature. Douglas McGregor maintained in the 1960s that most managers tend toward Theory X (assuming the worst in human nature) and generally get poor results, while enlightened managers use Theory Y (assuming the best), which produces better performance and results,

and allows people to grow and develop. Much of his message was misinterpreted or ignored, but he hoped that a time would come when significant changes in leadership philosophy would become a requirement for survival, because they would benefit organizations and workers alike. Today, these conditions exist. Workers are no longer the un-automated parts of production processes, as they were in the industrial age. Most are now "knowledge workers" (i.e. professionals). As Peter Drucker forecast decades ago, they must lead in the information age, and this leadership has to be visionary and completely different from the traditional ways of leadership and management applied in the Command and Control model.

THE CHANGING ENVIRONMENT

The traditional model worked well when market conditions were stable, competitors were known and their actions predictable, relatively few people made decisions, prices reflected internal costs, strategy and product life cycles were lengthy, customers had limited choice, and the priority of stockholders was good stewardship. But these conditions no longer apply. Today's competitive climate is far more uncertain, many people are required to make decisions, the pace of innovation is increasing, costs reflect market pressures, customers are fickle, and stockholders are more demanding. To compete more effectively in the information economy, companies must transform their centralized, functional hierarchies into networks of relatively autonomous units accountable for customer outcomes. They must also break free from the incremental planning and budgeting mentality, and involve all their people in building a new platform for sustainable improvement.

THE BARRIERS TO CHANGE

While most senior executives want their organizations to be more adaptive (and thus more devolved), few know how to turn management rhetoric into operating reality. While they talk about fast response, empowerment, innovation, operational excellence, customer focus, and stockholder value, their management processes (for example, targets, plans, measures, and rewards) all too often remain stuck in a time

warp of command and control. Fixed strategies prevent fast responses; rigid organizational structures turn off managers who seek challenge and development; bureaucracies stifle innovation; entrenched functions undermine cross-functional processes; an emphasis on product targets works against customer loyalty programs; and short-term performance contracts fail to support long-term value creation. Nor do the millions spent every year on reengineering, team-building, enterprise-wide systems, customer relationship management, value-based management, and balanced scorecards seem to overcome these problems. In fact, the vast majority of these initiatives fail for exactly the same reason—they support the rhetoric but get slaughtered by reality as they collide with the immovable forces of centralized decision making and "fixed performance contracts."

THE DEVOLVED LEADERSHIP MODEL

The Devolved Leadership (or Beyond Budgeting) model is designed to overcome these barriers and create a flexible and adaptive organization. Unlike the Command and Control model, Devolved Leadership works with, not against the best side of human nature (McGregor's Theory Y); it is suitable for post-industrial knowledge-based organizations; it supports the success factors that must be met in highly competitive business conditions; and it is also consistent with cybernetics and systems theory—the most relevant management science. Twelve principles provide managers with a robust, albeit empirical framework for evaluating where their organizations stand today, and guiding them toward an alternative management model.

Principles of the Devolved Leadership model

Leadership principles

1 **Customers.** Focus everyone on improving customer outcomes, **not** on hierarchical relationships.
2 **Organization.** Organize as a network of lean, accountable teams, **not** around centralized functions.
3 **Responsibility.** Enable everyone to think and act like a leader, **not** merely follow "the plan."
4 **Autonomy.** Give teams the freedom and capability to act; **don't** micromanage them.
5 **Values.** Govern through a few clear values, goals and boundaries, **not** detailed rules and budgets.

6 **Transparency.** Promote open information for self management; **don't** restrict it hierarchically.

Process principles

1 **Goals.** Set relative goals for continuous improvement; **don't** negotiate fixed performance contracts.
2 **Rewards.** Reward shared success based on relative performance, **not** on meeting fixed targets.
3 **Planning.** Make planning a continuous and inclusive process, **not** a top-down annual event.
4 **Controls.** Base controls on relative indicators and trends, **not** variances against plan.
5 **Resources.** Make resources available as needed, **not** through annual budget allocations.
6 **Coordination.** Coordinate interactions dynamically, **not** through annual planning cycles.

MINI-CASES

Since its formation in 1998, the Beyond Budgeting Round Table (BBRT) has made numerous case studies of organizations that have moved or started to move toward a Devolved Leadership model. Here are three examples:

Svenska Handelsbanken, the most successful Nordic bank, introduced its "Devolved Leadership" model in 1970. Although a regional rather than a global player, Handelsbanken's performance is nevertheless quite exceptional. They have achieved their corporate goal of making a higher return on equity than the average of their competitors every year for the last 33 consecutive years. Their cost-to-income ratio is well below 45%: the lowest among European banks. In Sweden, they have had more satisfied customers, both business and private, than the average of their competitors in every single year since 1989. They have had lower loan losses than their competitors since the early 1980s. And they are rated Aa1 by Moody's and are thus among the five highest rated nongovernmental banks in the world. But the key point is that their sustained, high performance, through good times and bad, results directly from their "Devolved Leadership" model. At Handelsbanken their model is their strategy and the main source of their competitive advantage. Theirs is a coherent model, and under consistent leadership for over three decades, they have evolved and deepened it.

ALDI, with Wal-Mart, is the most successful retailer in the world. Its founders, Karl and Theo Albrecht, are the wealthiest men in Europe, and the third-richest in the world, according to Forbes. Their model has been derived from the thrift and entrepreneurship that was necessary at the time the business was founded. It has evolved into what has been described as the retail idea of the century. The fundamental principle is always to keep it as simple as possible. Continual improvements ensure that the "simple" is not only well executed but perfected. The customer is always the prime consideration in all decisions. They reduce the amount of communication and coordination and the risk of bad decisions being taken remotely by establishing small autonomous units. It allows closer contact to the market and customer as well as being faster. It is also one of the best ways to reduce unnecessary complexity, and it enables many more people to feel they are "running their own business." They achieve this through "cell division" from ALDI headquarters, as soon as a certain size is reached in a region (50 or 60 branches, for example). Chiefs of staff and controllers for supporting responsible line managers do not exist. Their leadership is recruited from inside the company. Accordingly, they have an outstanding knowledge of the business, a common doctrine and an unconditional interest in the company. The strong company culture gives ALDI a strategic and competitive advantage which is not easily imitated. They manage by means of their culture and values; there are no budgets and formally agreed plan and there never have been any.

UBS Wealth Management and Business Banking realized, after a period of managing costs successfully, that growth can't be achieved through bureaucracy. They are now in the process of creating an entrepreneurial culture among their 44,000 people worldwide, and re-engineering their management processes to support it, including totally abandoning budgeting. To quote them, they say they are "replacing budgets with leadership." They are in effect reconstructing their entire management model to support significant, sustainable growth in profitability. Roughly a year after the project began, Quarter 3 results in 2005 for UBS Group showed record annual growth of 71%, although other factors contributed to this too.

MAKING IT HAPPEN ▶▶

A well-functioning management model is a delicate and intricate system. Every part of it must steer in the same direction. Only then can the organization minimize its

---

BEST PRACTICE

internal conflicts and maximize its potential. You cannot, therefore, "pick and mix" among the principles. All twelve are necessary to bring about and sustain a complete change from the Command and Control model to Devolved Leadership. Unless the model is coherent, it will not be fully effective and it may regress. So, "making it happen" requires:

- **Initiation.** Build awareness of the gravity of the problems with the organization's management model; raise a real sense of urgency to improve it; and make a compelling case for change.
- **Change process.** Create a coalition of people in the organization that is strong enough to guide the changes needed; work with them to create a clear vision of the new model; communicate it credibly and widely; and importantly "do it together," rather than impose it from the top.
- **Design.** Tackle the design *holistically*; address the leadership issues before the management processes and the management processes before the systems and tools. Each element must cohere to support the new, not the existing model.
- **Implementation.** Don't implement anything until an overall vision and outline design have been agreed by the leadership, including the guiding team. Use "trial and error" rather than "delayed perfection," to find the most workable solutions.
- **Evolution.** Don't let go until the model is implemented and embedded into the organization. Even then the model must be continually improved and deepened if the organization is to sustain competitive advantage from it.

CONCLUSION

Devolving accountability for results and replacing "fixed performance contracts" with more adaptive steering mechanisms will create a management model that will enable an organization to:

- respond more quickly to change and be better able to deal with increasing levels of uncertainty and complexity;
- attract more talented managers and potential strategic partners;
- generate a far better climate for breakthrough strategies aimed at improvement and growth;
- operate at lower cost;
- find and keep the right customers;
- minimize dysfunctional behavior, and encourage ethical behavior
- create sustained growth in stockholder wealth.

It is always a risk to make changes as profound as those required in introducing a Devolved Leadership model, but the greater risk in the long run is to continue to use a management model that is not aligned with today's critical success factors (CSFs), and works against human nature. As increasing numbers of organizations adopt a management model that supports today's competitive success factors, those who do not must fall behind and eventually be forced to change, or fail to survive. Those who adopt it early will gain the greatest relative advantage, because its potential benefits are so great and it is very hard to copy. So it is not really a matter of whether or even when: it's now! Its time has come.

FOR MORE INFORMATION

Web sites:
BBRT: **www.bbrt.org**.
You can also participate free of charge in the BBRT Benchmarking Project at **www.bbrt.org**.

See also:

Creating Value through People

by David H. Maister

EXECUTIVE SUMMARY

- The financial performance of a business is not something you can or should directly control. It is achieved by providing superior value to the marketplace.
- Marketplace value is a consequence of energizing and focusing employees to create and deliver value.
- To make money, managers should not spend their time managing money, but should instead devote their efforts to the things that produce the money: the enthusiasm, commitment, and drive of the labor force. Don't manage money. Manage people.

INTRODUCTION

Which of the following does your company report on, monitor, and react to most frequently? Which consume the most management time?

- Client satisfaction levels
- The strength of key client relationships
- Employee motivation and energy
- Levels of collaboration among staff
- Financial results

If you're like the overwhelming majority of businesses, you will focus primarily on financial results. Consequently, you're making less money than you could!

Why? Because managing a business by looking at financial results is like trying to win a game by keeping your eye firmly fixed on the scoreboard. Financial results are just that: results. They are the *outcome* of excellence (or the lack of it) in the key processes that produce the value that your customers and clients pay for. What you must manage are the things that produce value: energized employees who deliver outstanding quality and service to the marketplace. Does this mean that you don't monitor finances in great detail? Of course not. Financial discipline is the bedrock of business success, but it's not all of it, and maybe not even the greater part of it. The real key is the ability to get your people sufficiently focused so that they eagerly and willingly strive for high standards.

CHALLENGES AND OPPORTUNITIES

Over the years, I've been trusted to see the strategic plans of many direct competitors. Remarkably, they are almost always identical. Everyone figures out correctly which client sectors are growing, which services are in rising demand, and which dimensions of competition, such as client service or innovation, clients are looking for. The strategy documents are the same because everyone's smart! Everyone knows what needs to be done.

If this is so, then what is competition really about? It's about who can best complete the work that need to get done. And this in turn is determined by the following set of closely related concepts:

- energy
- drive
- enthusiasm
- excitement
- commitment
- passion
- ambition

Where these exist the discipline can be found to engage in diligent execution and thereby outperform the competition. The role of the manager is to be a net creator of enthusiasm, excitement, passion, and ambition. Alas, all too often managers are destroyers of excitement. If all they ever talk about is finances ("How are your billings?" "What's happening to receivables?"), it can deaden the spirit. That doesn't mean they don't need to talk about these things—they do. But they shouldn't talk *only* about these things. It's the manager's job to inspire, cajole, exhort, nag, support, critique, praise, encourage, confront, and comfort, as individual people (and groups of people) struggle to live their work lives according to high standards.

All strategies, at some time or the other, involve a tradeoff between short-term cash and executing the strategy. If you're going to get the benefits of a strategy, you need to be willing to make hard choices and act as if you truly believe it. You must be willing to

practice what you preach, both when it's convenient and, most importantly, when it is not.

Many people don't believe that their leaders truly want them to act strategically. Whenever a choice needs to be made between strategy and short-term cash—and it always does—most people feel under significant, if not irresistible, pressure from management to go for the cash. Usually the message from the company's leadership is clear: strategy can wait for tomorrow (if we can get paid for competence, why strive for excellence?). Rather than leaders being a source of encouragement to execute the strategy, they're all too often the biggest obstacles to the implementation of strategy.

If you want to be known as excellent at something, you have to be reliably, consistently excellent at it. Business life is filled with daily temptations, short-term expediencies, and wonderful excuses for why we can't afford to stick to high standards today. We take in work that's off-strategy (after all, it's cash!), we defer training until some more convenient time (often never), we postpone investments until the ever-escalating profit goals are met, and the marketing principle is: we never met a dollar of revenue we didn't like!

There is nothing inherently wrong about making these choices, but you shouldn't fool yourself. If you're willing to sacrifice value to earn short-term cash, you won't create a market reputation for superior quality. It takes courage to believe that a reputation for excellence is worth more in the long run than incremental cash. In their vision, mission, and strategy documents, companies say that they are aiming for excellence, but that's not how they operate.

Managers must have the courage of the convictions they espouse, maintain a long-term focus, and intervene personally whenever there are departures from the values and vision that create excellence. The problem with the implementation of strategies is the absence of certain and recognizable consequences for noncompliance. If the manager doesn't have the courage to tackle individuals who aren't behaving in accordance with the strategy, others will quickly realize that the new strategy is not something they have to do. They'll quickly cease

"The return from your work must be the satisfaction which that work brings you and the world's need of that work."

W. E. B. Du Bois

striving to comply, and the benefits of the strategy will never be attained.

Great managers give their people individually and collectively the confidence that greater success, fulfillment, accomplishment, and profits are indeed attainable. They give their people the courage to try. Change is threatening, however, and many, if not most, people operate well within their comfort zone, reluctant to abandon the old habits that brought them to their current success. If managers are often demanding, they must also be supportive. They must manage with a positive, supportive style.

Just as management involves a delicate balance between being supportive and being demanding, it also requires a style of insistent patience; it's the difference between saying Rome wasn't built in a day and insisting that we *are* building Rome. People must believe that the manager has the courage to believe in something and, more importantly, will stick with it. There's no greater condemnation of managers than to say that they're expedient, and no greater commendation than to say that a manager truly lives and acts in accordance with what he or she preaches.

BEING EFFECTIVE—AND SUCCESSFUL

An effective manager must be:
- articulate and vocal about his or her personal beliefs;
- disciplined about standards;
- even-handed and even-tempered;
- genuine and sincere;
- able to read people's characters and skill levels effectively;
- honorable, with high integrity.

What do the most successful managers believe?
- First you build your people, and the rest will come.
- Fun and discipline combined get the job done.
- It's important how people treat each other: monitor it and manage it.
- People have to trust management and trust each other.
- Success is about character, respect, integrity, trust, honesty, empowerment, confidence, loyalty, and keeping promises.

- You must bet on the long term and not get stampeded by short-term pressures.
- You need to balance your focus on people, clients, and finances.
- You should live up to your values every day.
- Your agenda as a manager is to create a great place to work, not to work at making your own star rise.

Finally, here are the rules on which the most successful managers model their behavior:
- Act as if not trying is the only sin.
- Act as if you want everyone to succeed.
- Actively help people with their personal development.
- Always do what you say you are going to do.
- Do what's right over the long term for clients and for your people.
- Don't regard yourself as separate and distinct from your people.
- Facilitate, don't dictate.
- Let people know you as a human being, not just as their manager.
- Show enthusiasm and drive; they're infectious and addictive.
- Speak regularly about your vision and philosophy so that people know where you stand.
- Take work seriously, but don't take yourself too seriously.
- Understand what drives individuals.
- Know all your people as individuals.

MAKING IT HAPPEN ▶▶

To get started take out the documents that describe your company's mission, vision, values, and strategy. Turn them into a questionnaire and ask your people how well they think you're currently living up to the things you espouse. If you find out that there are some things that you're not doing so well, either fix them or drop them from your declarations: there's no point lying, pretending to advocate things you're not willing to live up to. Practice what you preach! Make it the short-term immediate priority to make the company live up to its overarching vision.

Another vital step is to involve as many people as possible in the process of implementing, if not actually setting, strategy. The task of energizing, mobilizing, and motivating action is easier with people feeling involved, rather than being imposed on from above.

CONCLUSION

A person doesn't build a business. A person builds an organization that builds a business. Many managers are appointed because of their financial skills, their business development skills, or their technical excellence. However there comes a point where the central question is, "Can you manage?" Are you a net creator of energy, drive, and ambition in others? Can you cause others to strive to achieve high standards?

FOR MORE INFORMATION

Books:
Collins, James C., and Jerry I. Porras. *Built to Last: Successful Habits of Visionary Companies.* New York: HarperBusiness, 2002.
Heskett, James L., W. Earl Sasser, Jr., and Leonard A. Schlesinger. *The Service Profit Chain: How Leading Companies Link Profit and Growth to Loyalty, Satisfaction, and Value.* New York: Free Press, 1997.
Kaplan, Robert S., and David P. Norton. *The Balanced Scorecard: Translating Strategy into Action.* Cambridge, MA: Harvard Business School Press, 1996.
Pfeffer, Jeffrey, and Robert I. Sutton. *The Knowing–Doing Gap: How Smart Companies Turn Knowledge into Action.* Cambridge, MA: Harvard Business School Press, 2000.

Viewpoint: Robert Hormats
On Booms, Busts, and the Value of Good Judgment

Introduction

Robert Hormats is vice chair of Goldman Sachs (International). Before joining Goldman Sachs, he was a presidential advisor, an assistant secretary for economic and business affairs in the U.S. State Department, and a staff member of the National Security Council. He has been a member of the Trilateral Commission and is on the board of directors of the U.S.-Russian Enterprise Fund, the Human Genome Sciences Corporation, Englehard Hanovia, and the Council on Foreign Relations. In this piece, he writes about the instability of financial markets and their influence on the future.

In the first part of the 1890s, the United States financed and built 70,000 miles of rail track. In the second part of the 1890s, companies that had built 40,000 miles of that track went bankrupt. Competition to build rail track got way ahead of demand; there wasn't enough stuff to put over those rails, so companies went bankrupt. The similarity between rail track then and fiber optics now (and other components of the telecom and information infrastructure as well) are striking. But there is also a hopeful side to the analogy. Despite the bankruptcies, the rails are still there. Someone bought them and consolidated them—the Harrimans and others. They knew how to manage a continental rail system, so they bought cheap properties from bankrupt companies and put them together to make money. Now we have a well-developed telecommunications and IT infrastructure, plus a lot of very talented engineers, scientists, and programmers who can be mobilized—at prices a lot lower than a few years ago. They will sustain the technology boom—but on a more realistic basis, with less hype, less debt, and less "irrational exuberance" in the stock market. The rail industry did not end with the bankruptcies of the 1890s; it got stronger with consolidations and good management. The telecommunications/Internet industry will not end with the crash of the last couple of years; it will thrive with new configurations, new management, and new business opportunities.

One of the key points of a transformative technology is not that the individual people who develop the technology make the money. Some do, many don't. The key point is that transformative technology enables other people in other sectors to become more productive and to make money. In other words, it is a technology that has broad productive uses for a large portion of the economy. Often it's not the first mover who profits most; it's those who use the technology most effectively to improve their own existing business models or to develop new ones. For instance, AOL was not the first of the online companies. We don't even remember what the first companies were; they're mostly forgotten.

One of the big mistakes people make is to think of financial markets as highly efficient. While they can be efficient over the long term, they can be very inefficient for sustained periods of time. They experience big booms and big busts—and are rarely at equilibrium. Money is often allocated for very inefficient uses or to finance excess. But markets generally are good at enabling people to allocate risk. If you are starting a company, you can then take that company public or to venture capitalists and spread the risk around instead of taking all or most of the risk yourself.

This is part of the entrepreneurial process. Is it an efficient way of allocating capital? No, not always. But it is a critical part of the way capitalism works and technology evolves. If you could not spread the risk, you probably wouldn't have made the initial investment to begin with or developed the company as rapidly. If you are Bill Gates, you couldn't finance the rapid rise of Microsoft all on your own. You have to have others participate in the equity.

In the 1990s the public equity market became, in effect, a venture capital market. In the history of American capital markets, most companies don't come to the public market until they are making money or are about to make money. They get money from banks before that. Generally speaking, very few companies come to the public market without some sort of track record. After Amazon and Netscape, though, many high-tech companies came to the public market with no profits and only the vaguest expectation or hope that they had short-term or medium-term or even long-term prospects for making profits. So the high-tech, overly exuberant investors, in effect, became venture capitalists, buying companies at a much earlier stage than they would have 10 to 15 years ago. A lot of people regarded this as a get-rich-quick approach, and really didn't have sufficient appreciation of the high risks involved. They were becoming venture capitalists without the sophistication—or very deep pockets.

Most people have learned their lesson and won't go back to buying those kinds of stocks very soon. Average investors will steer clear of start ups for a long time to come. In the future investors will be more cautious and they'll have much more diversification

> **One of the big mistakes people make is to think of financial markets as highly efficient.**

"Gentlemen, you have come sixty days too late. The depression is over."   Herbert Hoover

in their portfolios among categories of stocks, and between stocks and bonds. It will slow the whole capital-raising process down. I think it will make equity capital raising for many companies much more difficult in the next 10 years.

The Economy Will Likely Grow Again, but at a Slower Pace

If you go back to the railroad and electricity booms, the economy did build on these technologies quite successfully. We are in, and will continue to experience, a period of very substantial technological progress. But for a while it will be harder to raise equity capital, except for extremely good technology companies with good business plans and good management. There will be a continued dynamism in many sectors of the economy. The "new economy" wasn't just about technology; it was about better management practices, better business models, more efficiency, globalization, more immigration. It was about combining many factors to achieve high productivity. That progress will continue. And the U.S. economy will grow thanks to the remarkable resiliency of its people and an attitude that accepts that risk is part of economics—and that in the long run taking risks may produce some dislocations and failures but over time it also produces dynamic growth.

The knowledge we have gained from financing these new technologies, as well as from the technologies themselves, has been dramatic. Someone said to Thomas Edison: "Mr. Edison, you have done 50 experiments and haven't developed a light bulb. Are you concerned about these failures?" Edison replied: "What failures? We have learned 50 different ways not to make a light bulb." This is a great part of the American entrepreneurial spirit. Try, fail, learn from mistakes, and then do it better.

A New Level of Transparency Is Evolving between Companies and Their Customers

The corporate sector will become much more responsive to the concerns of its stakeholders and will, in its own right and through governmental lobbying pressure, make changes. If you are a corporation, you're operating in an environment today where you have to be more environmentally minded because more and more consumers are environmentally minded. The Internet exposes any indiscretions, any violations, and any polluting that is being done around the world. It also exposes the way you treat your workers, or conduct your human-rights policies. The bright light of exposure on corporate policies and the growing numbers of people—particularly younger people—who are socially minded and obtain information in real time off the Internet will make a difference to the way corporations act. It will place them under continuous pressure to adhere to high standards of social responsibility.

You don't have to wait until the government tells you to do it. Look at BP. They have been a very progressive company on environmental practices. Toyota developed the Prias, a hybrid car that is very gas-efficient and very cool. And it is working on fuel cells for the next generation of cars with high environmental standards. I think you will see a lot of companies doing this.

Companies are also under pressure to improve workplace standards. The notion put about by the antiglobalization forces that foreign investment brings down workplace, environmental, or other standards is a myth. Generally these companies introduce higher standards than are commonly found in local companies. Moreover, if workers are treated badly in, say, a factory run by an American company in Guatemala, kids all over the United States know about it in minutes, because it is on the Internet. They talk about it in school, and they won't buy the company's products.

I think transparency is here to stay. The Internet is just a sliver on the information timeline. The church and the king dominated books until Gutenberg, and then books were developed for large numbers of people. More and more people learned to read because there were more books. And more and more writers came forth to write books that interested large portions of the population. Magazines and pamphlets were instrumental in getting support for the American Revolution. Television and radio exponentially increased the number of people exposed to information—and helped win the Cold War by penetrating the Iron Curtain. King and church controlled information for the first half of the last millennium. Once moveable type was developed, they couldn't do that anymore. I think the Internet is the latest stage in that process of democratizing information—and it has had its effect quickly and globally. It provides individuals with access to others around the world—and no one, no country, no group can control it.

> **The Internet exposes any indiscretions, any violations, and any polluting that is being done around the world.**

Keeping Perspective . . .

I think what happens is that when things start looking good, too many people downplay and disregard risk. It always happens when you get a boom. That is why there are busts—people borrow too much and invest too much in high-risk enterprises with the expectation that the boom will continue indefinitely.

Some argued that more information would prevent this from happening, because it would enable investors to assess the prospects of companies better or shift out of bad investments more quickly thus cutting their losses. But information is not a substitute for good judgment. Tom Friedman has made the point that there should be a warning label attached to information technology that says, "Judgment not included." He is right. There is a lot of information available—and the key now is to exercise good judgment in evaluating it and deciding how to act on the basis of it.

So far we haven't found the substitute for human judgment. Investors and companies made a lot of

mistakes. They got greedy and careless—and a lot of people lost perspective about risk. For many it was a financial tragedy. If you had $1 million and put $100,000 into the dot-coms or other technology companies and lost much of it, that was unfortunate but probably not catastrophic. That was risk money. The real problem is that people who had $100,000 put $90,000 into these kinds of stocks, which is really where the human tragedies occurred. That's where you get the heartrending stories of this period. Things were going so well they thought they could afford to take that kind of risk. And they not only lost their money, but also in many cases—in light of the Enron and WorldCom abuses—concluded that the deck was stacked against them. One casualty of this period has been investor faith that markets are fair; to many, the C.E.O.'s of the companies in which they invested treated them with contempt, and so did many of the so-called gatekeepers. Restoring confidence will not be done by legislation or pronouncements by committees; it must be done one C.E.O. at a time, one company at a time, one audit at a time, one analyst at a time.

The lesson is that the potential for loss is often forgotten when everything is going well. You need to be very diversified. Don't invest more than you can afford to lose, and recognize that there are real risks. And demand that corporations, accountants, bankers, and government regulators adhere to high standards of ethics, transparency, and corporate conduct. The problem is that most companies did adhere to these standards—but the few that did not tarnished the overall image of corporations and corporate governance. For the small investor especially, that image will take some time to recover. And for everybody there is a risk that overregulation could stifle risk taking and entrepreneurialism.

FOR MORE INFORMATION

Books:
England, Robert Stowe, foreword by Robert Hormats. *Global Aging and Financial Markets: Hard Landings Ahead?*. Washington, D.C.: Center for Strategic & International Studies, May 2002.

*This essay was adapted from an interview undertaken with Mr. Hormats by Peter Leyden, knowledge developer at Global Business Network (**www.gbn.com**). The publishers gratefully acknowledge the support of Global Business Network in making these ideas and insights available.*

"A depression is either a 12 percent unemployment rate for nine months or more, or a 15 percent unemployment rate for three to nine months."

Alan Greenspan

Allocating Corporate Capital Fairly
by John L. Mariotti

EXECUTIVE SUMMARY

- The principal job of management is the allocation of scarce resources—people, time, and money—to opportunities that yield the greatest returns.
- There is always a shortage of capital and an excess of worthy projects. There are many methods of capital allocation, but most do not fund the best opportunities.
- The key task is to allocate capital to support the greatest opportunities, those that match strategic objectives.

INTRODUCTION

The appetite of organizations for capital is insatiable. Understanding the nature of capital and its effective allocation is essential to organizational success. Classical economics defines land, labor, and capital as the determinants of wealth, each being exclusive to its owner. Now there is a fourth determinant of wealth—information—and it is nonexclusive. The more information is shared, the more valuable it becomes. Business is a competition in which the score is kept in money, and thus allocation of capital, in all its forms, is a critical success factor.

The challenge is to decide which division, project, or acquisition gets the scarce capital. The challenge varies with the source of capital. Venture capitalists' and hedge funds' tolerance for risk is offset by their high return expectations. The low risk of municipal bonds and banks is matched by low returns. Hedge funds make increasingly larger "bets" while equity investors carefully consider exit strategies in capital allocation decisions. Privately owned companies strive to enhance shareholder value, matching investment choices to their investors' expectations. Public companies are servants of the public stock markets and investment analysts. Each master has different expectations, and thus capital allocation must vary accordingly.

ALLOCATING CAPITAL

If capital is allocated foolishly, or to poorly defined projects, it is wasted. The game is a simple one: invest the least possible amount, borrow the rest, and put it in projects with the greatest potential return (or occasionally the lowest risk). Deciding which ventures to invest in has always occupied management attention. There are many quantitative methods for allocating

capital. Most of these remain valid, but they share one problem: they all depend on a forecast of future events, which is uncertain. The challenge is to allocate capital to the best opportunities, given the risk-reward profile of the investors, and to choose projects that have the best chance of earning good returns.

The Typical Plan: Allocation for Strategic Purposes and Objectives

Capital allocation must be aligned with the strategic purposes and objectives of the investor. The implication is that these are well defined and clearly understood. However, this is frequently not the case. Often the strategies and goals are unclear or poorly understood.

The Typical Practice: An Artifact—The Capital Budget

Organizations develop capital expenditure budget needs for annual review by boards and lenders. A common breakdown of a capital budget is by category or type of expenditure—for example, new products, new facilities, maintenance of existing products or facilities, and infrastructure needs. This is a theoretically sound method, since each category has a different strategic purpose: for example, sustaining current activities or revenue streams, creating new revenue streams, or providing infrastructure to support current or new business needs. These category splits are intended to allow senior management and boards to allocate capital fairly according to the company's strategic needs. The problem is that there is an enormous gap between developing those artifacts of bygone eras—capital budgets—and the actual intent of the investments. This traditional route is a sure path to sustained mediocrity or steady decline.

MAKING IT HAPPEN ▶▶
The Capital Appropriation Process

When management has determined what it believes is an effective use of capital, it must find a means to communicate that need and its worthiness relative to other needs. Larger organizations use a formal capital appropriation process. This process involves documentation of the intended use, description of the assets to be acquired, time frames for the investments, and benefits to be gained. A financial analysis is a required part of the capital appropriation request.

The methods used to compare and evaluate capital investments are based on projections of future revenue streams and a calculation of some combination of:
- internal rate of return (IRR)
- net present value (NPV)
- breakeven
- economic value added (EVA)
- economic profit created (EP)
- risk-adjusted return on capital (RAROC)

This approach rewards the best analysts, politicians, and sycophants, but not the best projects. The most innovative, high-potential projects are seldom easy to analyze and quantify. Yet these are the very ideas that turn out to be outstanding—but only in retrospect—and only if they ever get funded. In traditional allocation, the capital tends to be spent either protecting the past or perfecting the present, with precious little left for funding the future. For reasons of personal or organizational pride, differing goals, or political power, appropriation requests often do not match corporate goals. Competing executives or organizations will scuffle for scarce capital, and even if their intentions are good (which they usually aren't) the resulting conflicts can be ugly. Who is to resolve these conflicts?

Approvals and the Capital Appropriation Committee

In some companies the authority level for heads of business units is high—assuming funds have been budgeted—in the category needed. This means there is a chance that good, innovative ideas might receive financing. In central-control-

"Investing is an act of faith. We entrust our capital to corporate stewards in the faith—at least with the hope—that their efforts will generate high rates of return on our investments."

John Clifton Bogle

oriented companies spending approval levels are kept low, forcing corporate reviews of most investments.

Appropriation requests go up the ladder to be approved by successively higher levels of management, and the higher one goes, the less informed the management tends to be. The originator's chain of command includes gatekeepers from finance and accounting. Other functions affected often have sign-off rights, too. This creates a time-consuming, bureaucratic and often contentious process that wrings the creativity out of any proposal, replacing it with conservatism, caution, and capital "constipation."

After running the divisional bureaucratic gauntlet, the appropriation goes to the corporate capital appropriation committee, where it is subjected to more scrutiny by eve less informed people. This review is supposedly based on alignment with corporate strategies, return versus competing capital needs, and the requesting unit's budget. The larger the organization the more levels there may be, but the process varies surprisingly little from company to company.

When small companies grow rapidly, capital allocation is efficient and effective—and involves only a few well-informed people. As the company gets larger or is acquired by a larger entity, it implements a more formal capital approval process. This process now includes approval at higher authority levels. While this is considered necessary; it is noticeably slower and less efficient. The successive layers of capital appropriation processes and committees can slow down or even kill most creative projects and divert capital to safer, less rewarding uses.

Historically, depreciation was designed to fund the replacement of assets by expensing non-cash charges, thereby reserving the cash (capital) for new expenditures. Thus the norm was for capital allocation to equal depreciation. To spend more is equivalent to putting in new money, and to spend less is in effect using up the business. Many lending agreements also contain restrictive covenants that limit capital spending to formulae—the right spending level is a function of what happened in the past adjusted by management or investors' wishes. The obvious corollary is that, if the company is struggling, it is often starved of the necessary capital to rebuild itself.

Other Challenges

Cash-rich companies also have a problem. A low return on conservatively invested cash reduces overall returns. Companies are expected to earn higher returns than banks. A common alternative is to repurchase stock, a less than exciting capital allocation. In other cases, company treasurers are tempted to use high-risk investments like derivatives to elevate returns on excess cash. Multinational companies encounter another issue: currency exchange rate fluctuations, which can negate the best analyses. Hedging currency by buying futures can protect the downside, but, like all insurance, this too comes at a cost. Then there are fiascos in which capital allocation is based on equity markets and stock prices. The dot-com deals involving stock swaps quickly revealed the flaws here: huge profits disappeared overnight, replaced by unexpected write-offs. Misadventures like Enron illustrate how easily a bogus capital structure can tumble like a house of cards.

Furthermore, what happens to budgeted but unspent money? The government model—use it or lose it—is often used. The rush to spend unused budgeted capital results in waste, misallocation, or both. Alternatively, a passive indecision deprives the enterprise of funding for its growth or rejuvenation.

Nonmoney "Capital"

Finally, there are critical non-capital resources to be allocated—people, knowledge, or time. The people part is often called "human capital," an appropriate name. If this human capital is in short supply, all the monetary capital in the world will not help. Capital must be spent wisely or allocating it well is useless. People spend the capital, and thus the most important question to ask is not what it will be spent on, but who will be spending it and what is their track record? Choosing the right people to bet on is the critical decision.

An Alternative to Allocation?

In the bubble era of 2000–2001, capital flowed freely to those perceived to deserve it; those perceived as undeserving were starved. Many decisions were bad, but consider the concept. Instead of allocating capital, think of "earning it and/or deserving it." Innovative ideas seldom survive bureaucratic battles, particularly if they threaten to cannibalize existing businesses. Harvard's Clayton Christensen has written at length about "disruptive technologies" and their impact on markets. In the real world, an idea should either be able to attract capital or not. No corporate committee says yea or nay. The idea must prove that it deserved the capital by being successful. That is capital allocation's model for the 21st century.

CONCLUSION

Companies usually allocate capital on the basis of one of three mindsets.
- The first is *protecting the past*, in which case they will always be following the competition and reacting to a leader's moves, simply trying to hang on to past glories.
- The second mindset is the attractive trap of *perfecting the present*. Such moves are always easier to analyze, and make short-term goals, except when new, disruptive technology or competitor enters the fray upsetting the applecart.
- The third mindset is the critical one, to allocate capital by investing in *funding the future*. This is harder and riskier, but it is the only true path to success. The capital need must attract the needed capital based on its potential success.

Few traditional appropriation processes accommodate this approach, which is why so few companies succeed over the longer term. Companies trying to fund the future are often led by "escapees" from the other kind of companies—people seeking outlets for creative brilliance and thwarted by bureaucratic, inwardly focused capital appropriations processes, policies, and committees. The best rule for capital allocation is to allocate very little to protecting the past and just enough to perfecting the present, leaving plenty to spend on funding the future. That is where real wealth and excitement lies—if only management and boards will finance it.

FOR MORE INFORMATION

Books:
Hamel, Gary. *Leading the Revolution.* Cambridge, MA: Harvard Business School Press, 2000.
Hamel, Gary, and C. K. Prahalad. *Competing for the Future.* Boston, MA: McGraw-Hill, 1996.
Selden, Larry, and Geoffrey Colvin. *Angel Customers & Demon Customers.* New York: Portfolio, 2003.

"Capital as such is not evil; it is its wrong use that is evil. Capital in some form or other will always be needed."

Mahatma Gandhi

Intrapreneurial Warriors Versus Traditional Managers
by Gifford Pinchot

EXECUTIVE SUMMARY

- New ideas don't generally fit neatly within existing organizational boundaries; thus they require innovators to cross the boundaries in search of help, resources, and permission.
- Many good ideas are lost when progress is blocked by the need to use resources from other parts of the organization.
- Getting people from other parts of the organization to contribute time and resources to an innovation requires either raw power or the skills and mindset of an intrapreneurial warrior.
- The skills of the intrapreneurial warrior can be learned.

INTRODUCTION

As we leave the industrial era, work is increasingly about innovation and doing something different for customers. Dull repetitive jobs are being eliminated by machines and computers, leaving only the more human work of dealing with the shifting desires and needs of people in a world of rapidly emerging technical possibilities.

Almost all the good jobs now require imagination and getting things done in new ways. Traditional bureaucratic expertise is not enough to achieve the rate of innovation needed to compete. What is needed is skill of the intrapreneurial warrior.

TECHNIQUES FOR GETTING RESOURCES: THE QUIZ

Your project has come to a screeching halt, because the people in another department don't understand its importance. You know the ROI for the company would be great. You need their help or their permission, but they are too busy to help. *What can you do?*

Which of these seven options would you select? Pick the top three, then let's score the effectiveness of each choice.

1 Plead with your boss to lobby the resource owners for what you need.
2 Explain all the glorious implications of the idea so that resource owners recognize how important it is.
3 Ask resource owners for advice on your project before asking them for resources.
4 Express gratitude for whatever help you get.
5 Broadcast your idea and see who steps forward to help.

6 Build a network of friends and coworkers.
7 Seek out another project with more powerful sponsors.

Plead with your boss?

Well, you've probably tried asking your boss already. If it worked, fine, but before you ask your boss to spend precious political capital on your behalf, ask yourself if you have made the job as easy as possible.

When your boss requests project resources from someone in another area, it's going to be easier if you have pre-sold the idea to the people who will do the work. Have you converted those people to your cause—are they supportive? Getting someone to lobby others on your behalf may be part of the solution, but it is not the place to begin.

Intrapreneurial Warrior Score: 0 points

Explain the glorious implications?

It's tempting, when visualizing the positive impact of your project, to tell the world about it, but the effect of your excitement may be to scare people. If, in its fully realized form, the implications of your project will change everything—their department, their job, and the comfort of familiar ways of doing things, you cannot blame them for being cautious. If you make your project seem too world-changing, they will respond with delaying tactics and requests for more information, not action or help.

Intrapreneurial Warrior Score: –3 points

Ask resource owners for advice?

The danger of premature glorification is neatly matched by the danger of premature requests for resources. Ask too soon and

there is a good chance that you will get some version of "No!" Once someone has denied you resources, rationalization sets in: if they refused to provide resources, then your idea must be bad. If it was good, then they, a good manager, would have found a way to help.

This vicious cycle of rejection can easily be turned around. Simply ask for some form of help that will not be refused. *The request for help least likely to be refused is a request for advice.* When someone gives you advice, they are contributing to your project. If they contribute to your project one of two things must be true:

1 Your project is worthwhile, so their helping makes them good managers.
2 Your project is worthless or destructive, in which case helping is a poor use of time, and therefore they are a poor manager.

The attraction of seeing oneself as good manager will win out almost every time. Keep asking for things they will agree to and be careful not to ask for too much too soon. The more someone contributes, the more the project becomes their own. So start with advice and build your requests gradually until you can ask for resources. The intrapreneurial warrior gets people involved before asking them for anything of significance.

Intrapreneurial Warrior Score: +5 points

Express gratitude?

Gratitude cements the value of whatever help you have been given, and can even dissolve overt hostility to a project. When someone in a position of power criticizes the project of an intrapreneurial warrior, the intrapreneur takes careful notes. After some time to cool off and a bit of checking, the warrior finds truth in some of the criticisms. In some small way the plan is changed.

The intrapreneur then goes back to the critic and thanks him or her for picking up on a problem that could have sunk the project: "Without your help, we might have . . ." Your critic may have tried to define himself or herself as your enemy, but you have reframed the criticism as a form of support. To balance things out they rationalize that there must be good in your project. Few can

"Competition rarely puts anyone out of business—a man usually puts himself out of business either by not making a good article or by wrong methods in sales or finance."

Harvey Firestone

resist the praise, *if it is delivered with total sincerity.* Thanking critics for their contribution sincerely requires the generosity of spirit to genuinely forgive and appreciate. Don't try it until you have done so.

Intrapreneurial Warrior Score: +4 points

Broadcast your idea?

It seems smart to "run your idea up the flagpole and see who salutes." It makes sense, but it doesn't work. Every innovation involves a bit of creative destruction; the new way replaces the old. Those who will benefit from the new order don't really get the implications of the change; and those whose privileged positions will be challenged by the new order recognize it at once and come forward with spears sharpened. The lesson is this: premature promotion of your idea triggers the immune system. The grander you make your idea sound and the more widely you distribute it, the more people it will frighten.

Intrapreneurial Warrior Score: –4 points

Build a network?

Gone is the era of the lonely innovator. The intrapreneurial warrior knows that when you are not in charge of everything you need, your success hinges on the quality of your relationships with the other players (and the referees). The warrior is alert to the feelings of others and distributes credit widely. (The more you give away, the more comes back in the long run.)

The intrapreneurial warrior keeps everyone in the coalition fully informed, takes time to check up on everyone, and keeps relationships alive even when there is no immediate need for help. Building a network of friends and coworkers is "Innovation 101."

Intrapreneurial Warrior Score: +3 points

Seek out another project?

Every innovation passes through dark and discouraging days. Intrapreneurial warriors don't give up easily. They find ways around obstacles; they don't knuckle under to them.

There are fake intrapreneurs who only want to head large projects with an impressive staff roster. They jump from project to project depending on what is in favor. If the project hits a political snag, they blame others and move on. This may be a good career strategy in some companies, but it will not lead to effective innovation.

Intrapreneurial Warrior Score: –5

Points Scoring

Add the points from your three choices; if the total is

–4 or less: *Bureaucrat*: Stay in safe bureaucratic jobs or break out by starting a

whole new career outside of large organizations.

–3 to 1: *In transition to the 21st century*: Take more time off from work and spend time learning to build relationships.

1 to 7: *Emerging Intrapreneurial Warrior*: Get an intrapreneurial mentor. Build your network. Get smart about handling the immune system.

7 or more: *Intrapreneurial Warrior*: Keep up the good work!

The Intrapreneurial Warrior

To be an intrapreneurial warrior, one must have:

- an inspiring vision
- integrity, trustworthiness
- an inner compass guiding one toward the vision
- the courage to follow this compass
- the emotional intelligence to understand others
- the wisdom to use diplomacy
- the stealth and cunning to avoid organizational backlash
- the generosity of spirit to make and keep allies across bureaucratic lines
- the business judgment to make good use of resources

MINI-CASE

It Can Be Done!

DuPont's Medical Products department sold equipment to test for HIV. One of its customers, the New York Blood Bank, asked for help. If HIV were found, the source of the blood must be located. The Blood Bank needed a massive database to track all blood from collection to transfusion—and they wanted it in 90 days!

The department sought help from information technology and from corporate staff. Neither could meet the deadline. However, the medical products' account executive had heard of a special intrapreneurial team in DuPont's fibers department. Traditionally, a staff group from one division does not do major jobs for another division. But, since this was considered an emergency, IEA got the job. It provided the blood-tracking database within deadline, and Medical Products solved its customer's problem successfully.

Furthermore, as IEA's reputation spread, the group found itself working with many other departments to solve their information problems. Ultimately, IEA became an intraprise (an independent enterprise within the corporation); it went on to provide new and better information technology services for every division of DuPont and spread learning across the organization.

MAKING IT HAPPEN ▶▶

The intrapreneurial warrior makes it happen by building relationships across the boundaries of the organization.

1 Build your network across organizational boundaries. Keep up with old friends when jobs change, and be curious about others' work; interest is a key currency.
2 Give credit widely: express gratitude, and give others credit.
3 Always gauge requests for help so the answer you get is yes. Ask for advice before asking for resources, and build collaborative relationships gradually.
4 Be trustworthy, and make sure your partners come out winners too.

CONCLUSION

Getting help and resources for your project is more about relationships and trust than it is about the quality of your ideas. The intrapreneurial warrior treasures a reputation for integrity, for without trust innovation is impossible. The intrapreneurial warrior is somewhat modest about the idea and its potential, lest others be scared by it. The intrapreneurial warrior asks for advice before resources, because advice is the form of help that people are most willing to give.

FOR MORE INFORMATION

Books:
Bellman, Geoffrey M. *Getting Things Done When You Are Not in Charge.* 2nd ed. San Francisco, CA: Berrett-Koehler, 2001.
Pinchot, Gifford. *Intrapreneuring: Why You Don't Have to Leave the Corporation to Become an Entrepreneur.* New York: Harper & Row, 1985.

Web site:
www.intrapreneur.com: Pinchot & Company's site, which is devoted to intrapreneuring.

"There are no secrets to success: don't waste time looking for them. Success is the result of perfection, hard work, learning from failure, loyalty to those for whom you work, and persistence."

Colin Powell

Managing 21st Century Financials
by Terry Carroll

EXECUTIVE SUMMARY

- C.F.O.s have to balance long-term planning with short-termist behavior in the markets.
- In order to do this, it's essential to have a good business model, a clear understanding of business risk, sustainable revenues, and proper communication.
- Failing to manage the financial information systems well can seriously damage your brand. Getting it right will please both short- and long-term investors.
- Matters have been complicated by the globalization of standards and reinterpretation of company accounts.
- Tangible value creation remains top of the agenda. When investors are frightened or lose faith, they can destroy value much faster than you can create it.
- Relationship management is one of the most important new skills to acquire on the road to success.

INTRODUCTION

Corporate purpose, for most companies, is to create and sustain long-term stockholder value. However, markets can be driven by fear or euphoria. Stuck in the middle are top managers, especially the C.F.O.s. They have to balance long-term planning with "short-termist" behavior in the markets. How can this be achieved? What are the new metrics for survival and sustainable prosperity?

As some companies have destroyed value, some have begun to question whether stockholder value should be a goal, or rather a consequence of excellence. In both quoted and private companies, you need a clear, understandable business model that works; to be able to explain it easily and consistently; to understand strategic business risk and make it work for you; to generate sustainable revenues, income, and cash with rapid and reliable reporting, and no surprises!

MANAGING INVESTORS' EXPECTATIONS

Managing stockholder value is also about managing expectations. The major long-term players (institutions, pension, investment, and insurance funds) are advised by analysts. Short-term investors, traders, and the public are more influenced by news flow and market movements. How can we reconcile these forces? By timely financial information, "no surprises," always having cash, and finally, having a credible, understandable business model.

FINANCIAL REPORTING IN THE COMMUNICATION AGE

Great companies produce rapid, reliable, succinct, simple, usable financial information. Internally, more than three days to report is too long. The Internet or intranets can provide "always-on," real-time connection for the whole company. Management and financial reporting tools and technology allow fast collection, collation, interpretation, and distribution of results. Now, three factors are converging internal with external reporting: urgency, transparency, and consistency.

Global markets and the pace of change mean management needs reliable financial feedback, fast. Meanwhile, external reporting periods are shortening. This is spilling into Europe. Information is a global property, especially when it "leaks." Global brand management demands control of your own destiny. The market wants information as fast as you get it. Too much conversion for external consumption takes time, unsettling management and investor alike. Meanwhile, market regulation requires transparency and "equality" of distribution.

Investors want financial information consistent with expectations. The more frequently it is released, the smaller the mismatch. Regular, progressive business and financial news flow, along with rational enhancements to the business model, can lead to out-performance. When there are surprises, markets wonder whether management is competent.

Uneven information flow; profit warnings

or their lack; information released to analysts before the market; lack of comment on speculation; all these unsettle investors and regulators, sometimes causing sharp movements in stock prices. News and specialist market services supply corporate information 24 hours a day. Analysts interpret it as fast as it is produced. The changes in Accounting Standards, Sarbanes-Oxley, Basel 2, and other complications mean more reliance on expert interpretation. While some have argued about the validity of new Standards, industry leaders and others have got on with it, to create a sustainable advantage.

Some C.F.O.s may need to wake up to the new paradigm. Others will see it as an opportunity for skilled relationship management, making the financial information systems work for the company as another weapon in the public relations armory. The swift can capitalize on the lethargy of the slow. Brand is everything. Failing this new challenge can seriously damage yours. The right approach will please both short- and long-term investors.

CASH IS KING

Investors will demand that companies report quicker. This is a challenge for accounting standards and governance. Historic price/earnings multiples have been replaced by forecast revenues and EBITDA (earnings before interest, tax, depreciation, and amortization) as the currency of decisions. As accounts become almost impenetrable, the metric we all understand is cash. How much cash was generated last period; how much remains in the balance sheet; what is the NPV of sustainable future cash flows?

EVERYBODY NEEDS A BUSINESS MODEL

Apart from cash, the other factor that brings together short- and long-term interests is a credible, explainable business model. If you don't have one, analysts will create their own (or worse still, transport it from another company unlike your own). For example, good TMT (technology, media, telecommunications) stocks have floated up and down with the bad on the waves of market volatility. Some values were absurd, for good or ill.

Nortel (U.S.) and Bookham (U.K.) were both top 100 stocks in their own markets. They were both linked to building communications networks. Nortel's market capitalization peaked at around $282 billion in 2000. It has fallen 95% since the dot-com bubble burst. Bookham Technology was also a darling of the FTSE, floated in July 2000 at roughly $18. Its shares rocketed to $94 in a few months, based on the NPV of forecast revenues for a business model that few people understood. The price was driven by over-optimistic analyst estimates, blind faith, and greed. Its price fell 99% and its market capitalization from $11.4 billion to around $88 million. Like Nortel, it was buffeted by fear and optimism. Unlike Nortel, it has never made any money and has moved to the NASDAQ to try and escape its past.

There are other examples: insurance companies have ebbed and flowed with each other, washed by pension fund and capital adequacy fears. In personal finance, Cattles and Provident Financial's recent fortunes have been very different. Both are described as "doorstep lenders" even though this is now less than 10% of Cattles' business. Unless you regularly communicate a clear differentiation and a plausible business model, you may remain at the whim of the market.

So it's the financial model that really counts, especially generating and sustaining cash. It's lack of cash that busts companies, not lack of capital. When you don't have enough cash to survive a recession and the market isn't receptive to new issues, you have to start slashing costs—"eating yourself"—to stay alive. This can damage the business model, undermine the stock price, and become a vicious spiral toward death, or at best consumption by a sounder business model.

VALUING THE BUSINESS

There has been much theoretical talk in the past about "value added." The theory is that every company should be focused on protecting, creating, and sustaining value. Failure could mean stock price falls, cash calls, unwelcome bids, or business failure.

So the C.E.O., C.F.O., and colleagues need vision and courage. Value creation is top of the agenda. It involves generating the value and protecting it. Brand, fear, technical and fundamental analysis of markets have assumed more significance than the internal business plan, budgets, and the annual report. When investors are frightened or lose faith, they can destroy value much faster than you can create it.

This is why cash generation is critical. Stock prices already eroding due to poor results or loss of confidence in a business model fall dramatically faster when you have to raise cash in an unreceptive market. Investors share your wish to sleep easy at night.

Some C.F.O.s cite short-termism as the real driver of value, therefore. They castigate "teenage scribblers" and analysts for not understanding their business. Some make errors of judgment, not only in their handling of such relationships, but also in silence or, worse still, nasty surprises.

Marconi was the classic case in the United Kingdom. For months investors expected a profit warning. The company continued to make reassuring noises. Investors continued to sell against an expectation of bad news. Eventually trading in the stock was suspended. Dreadful news was released. Returning from suspension the price was savaged. It had fallen from over $20 to under 35 cents in a year. In early 2004, it was recapitalized by its bankers, a shadow of its once great self.

MAKING IT HAPPEN ▸▸
Messages for managers

Creating and protecting stockholder value are even more important in the 21st century. Volatility, expectations, speed of reporting, and a hungry investor demand for "real-time" information have changed the dynamics. The C.F.O. needs new skills. These include strategic thinking; proactive risk management; and communication and interpersonal skills of a high order.

Value creation is about having a clear strategic and business focus, flexible and adaptable as appropriate. The C.F.O. and executive colleagues must recognize the importance of having a sound, understandable business model. The financial model must be based on value creation, ideally measured in sustainable revenues, income, and especially cash. Reporting should be rapid and transparent, using the speed of technology, with no surprises.

You can create long-term value, but investors can take it away in the short term when fear overrides faith, if you don't heed these messages. Relationship management with analysts, investors, and the media is the critical skill that wasn't mentioned when the C.F.O. trained as an accountant. When you understand and manage strategic business risk and the macro-economic factors, you may at least anticipate the challenge of analysts, whether or not they understand your own unique business model. If the unforeseen occurs, report it rapidly and accurately, with a clear understanding of the factors and a plan to manage the consequences.

Finally, much of this message relates to private companies too. Investment of private capital is accelerating. A clear business model is fundamental to accessing the cash for investment and growth, especially if you plan eventually to come to market.

CONCLUSION

All companies can follow this best practice to prosper in the 21st century:
- fast, reliable reporting against a sound business model;
- proactively anticipating and managing investor interest;
- investing in relationships to differentiate your company;
- being clear, informed and consistent;
- creating and sustaining long-term corporate and brand value.

FOR MORE INFORMATION

Books:
Carroll, Terry. *The Role of the Finance Director*. 3rd ed. Englewood Cliffs, NJ: Financial Times Prentice Hall, 2002.
Bierman, Jr., Harold, *Corporate Financial Strategy and Decision Making to Increase Shareholder Value*. New York: Wiley, 1999.
Conger, Jay A., Edward E. Lawler III, and David L. Finegold. *Corporate Boards: New Strategies for Adding Value at the Top*. San Francisco, CA: Jossey-Bass, 2001.
Moore, Geoffrey A. *Living on the Fault Line*. New York: HarperBusiness, 2002.

Web site:
CFO.com: **www.cfo.com**

"Business is all about putting out money today to get a whole lot back later."

Warren Buffett

Avoiding the Mistakes of the Past: Lessons from the Startup World

by James E. Schrager

EXECUTIVE SUMMARY

Congratulations if you didn't personally feel the hardship of the dot-com implosion. Many millions went to their demise but at least left behind a legacy of what not to do. Fear not if you won't be using the Internet in your next venture. Many of these lessons generalize well beyond their former faulty incarnations. For those of you with a new product, technology, or division to launch, most translate into corporate organizations.

INTRODUCTION

Failure is a wonderful teacher. The new-economy revolution had many of the trappings of a genuine economic revolt: vast fortunes forged in a fortnight, dashing young heroes and heroines, rotten institutions brought to their knees. It held such great promise, yet today even the dreams feel thoroughly eviscerated. What to learn from the revolution that never was? What lessons can be applied to new ventures?

There is no better place to look for historical clues than the business plans presented by aspiring business managers. These serve as the revolutionary documents of record, holding within their propositions the seeds of ultimate success or failure. We will reassess these pillars of revolutionary wisdom.

THE LESSONS TO LEARN
We Will Establish First-mover Advantage

The problem with this mantra is that first mover by itself means little; what matters instead is the power of your strategy. The first team to execute a dumb idea has accomplished nothing. In some cases, when you have an exceptional new technology, being first brings power. In other cases—say, when your strategy is nothing more than another way to sell books—being first has little effect. Post revolution, you can safely ignore the first-mover boasts. Instead, worry about the inherent strength or weakness of the business strategy.

Amazon was concerned with being the first big player selling books on the Web. However, Amazon's profit struggle has shown that being first made little difference. If you have an invention, for example, the xerographic copy process, being first is wonderful. But note the difference: Xerox got a patent for its process, thereby making it not only the first, but also the only company to offer a plain-paper copier. Since no one could duplicate its service, it was able to charge a premium. Amazon will never be the only seller of books, so its margins will always be subject to pressure. First mover is fine when defensible, but meaningless without a way to stop competitors entering the market.

Our Strategy Will Be to Grow Quickly

Wrong. Growth isn't a strategy, it's a goal. But the hard part isn't making goals. Rather, it's developing a way to make those dreams come true.

Getting big is the goal of most companies. In some business models, however, it's a requirement: eBay had to get big fast because it needed lots of both buyers and sellers to be the auction site of choice. How to do this?—eBay did it by buzz, by having a willing stock market, by being in the right place at the right time, and by sheer luck. Make your business plan rely on something other than perfect timing.

We Will Be the Technology Leader

Venture capitalists (VCs) are at their best when making carefully calibrated bets on technology companies. They have mostly ignored the rough-and-tumble world of retail business on their way to investments in computer memory chips, software codes, medical devices, pharmaceuticals, genomics, magnetic storage media, telecom satellites, optical bandwidth, and truly new technologies. In each case, tech-company founders had to produce something new and wonderful that worked as promised, would be in great demand, and could be protected via patents, trade secrets, or switching costs. Internet retailers may claim to have some bits of technology in a one-click purchase screen or real-time chat lists, but these are hardly protectable. As such, e-retailing cannot be the basis of a technology strategy.

Claims of new technologies that cannot be protected are not worth much. Instead, strategies may center on building a brand; however, this is expensive to construct and requires constant maintenance to remain viable.

We Will Create a Powerful Image

Instead of worrying about technology that can be protected, retailers concentrate on the precise construction of a tailored image to appeal to a consistently fickle public. Priceline discovered how expensive it is to spend for a national audience and capture just a tiny slice. The overreach inherent in most mass-media advertising makes it a very dull tool for carving a startup's image. So how will the image be created? Post revolution business plans need to find a more efficient way than simply throwing money at the problem! Your marketing plan must also develop a carefully conceived media approach to allow for your image to be built in an economically efficient manner.

We Will Attract the Best VCs—with Their Reputations We Can't Fail

As long as VCs can sell the idea to Wall Street, they'll build the company. When they cannot, they'll do their best to be long gone. Post revolution, VCs who dabbled in e-commerce look just like other Wall Street pawns, appearing to be infallibly brilliant when the market goes up and hapless fools when the market collapses.

The final customer for your product rarely cares who was behind the financing. It's clearly better to have a brilliant idea funded by people no one has ever heard of than a specious idea promoted by a well-known VC shop.

"The mistakes of the great, promulgated along with the discoveries of their genius, are apt to work havoc."

Erwin Schrödinger

We Plan a Full-scale National Rollout to Leverage Our First-mover Advantage and Insure Our Ability to Grow

An accurate market test is your very best insurance against a giant belly flop. But don't think you'll impress anyone by faking it. For example, a pacemaker distributor in Japan gauged demand for a new product by displaying it to its current customers. Even though the doctors involved in the test showed overwhelming approval of the new device, it didn't meet sales projections once launched. In looking at why the test failed, the distributor noticed that the new device sold almost exclusively to existing customers. The distributor failed to realize the extent to which doctors are brand-sensitive. Make it a real test or don't bother.

We Will Form Alliances with Key Players

This is a fine idea, except that in the early days no one knows who will win. In times of rapid change, even an alliance with a leading company may not deliver the promised advantages. The underlying business strategy, not just its alliances, must be more carefully understood. Very few partnerships in which the giving and taking aren't balanced will survive.

The Internet Changes Everything

Well, not really. The information superhighway is certainly here to stay, and we'll use it more and more, but gone are the stories of TheStreet.com buying Dow Jones, e-STEEL buying Bethlehem, and Amazon buying Wal-Mart. Other than Wall Street bonuses, the immediate changes wrought by the Internet were fairly modest and will play out over a much longer period than the matter of weeks we were promised at the outset.

In fact, it's comforting to know that the Internet won't change everything overnight. The pace of change continues, even though not all change is progress. The Internet does enable very rapid access to information and the rather carefree exchange of e-mail messages. If either of these two attributes can drive your business plan further or faster, by all means use the Internet to get there. But what the Internet will not do is take people out of the center of the business process.

MAKING IT HAPPEN ▶▶

- Protect any new technology with patents or trademarks—create barriers to market entry.
- Determine your strategy, then your goals (growth isn't a strategy; it's a goal).
- Aim to reach your target market in an economical way.
- Promote your marketable idea, not your financial backers.
- Stage an accurate market test.
- Use the Internet if it can drive your business plan further or faster.
- Be realistic: by all means, consider different scenarios, but do not lose sight of reality.

CONCLUSION

The basic rules of business strategy remain intact and do indeed apply to the Internet. Like selling things in a store, selling products on a computer screen isn't about technology. A technology business develops something new that cannot be easily imitated. This is the great lesson of the Internet failures. New businesses can be understood by looking at success and failure patterns of the past. A careful review of the strategy you propose can help.

FOR MORE INFORMATION

Books:

Gupta, Udayan, ed. *Done Deals: Venture Capitalists Tell Their Stories*. Cambridge, MA: Harvard Business School Press, 2000.
Slywotzky, Adrian, et al. *Profit Patterns: 30 Ways to Anticipate and Profit from Strategic Forces Reshaping Your Business*. New York: Random House, 1999.

See also:

"The man who makes no mistakes does not usually make anything."

E. J. Phelps

Why EVA Is the Best Measurement Tool for Creating Shareholder Value

by Erik Stern

EXECUTIVE SUMMARY

- Economic value added (EVA) has transformed the corporate finance scene and business practice by transferring modern business theory from classroom to boardroom.
- Traditional metrics, with their roots in accounting, distort economic reality. For example, crucial long-term intangible investments often fall foul of traditional metrics.
- If stockholder value is the goal, then the key to any metric must be the cost of capital, or stockholders' required return.
- At its best, EVA is not just a financial metric, it is a complete management system focused on value creation.
- Incentive-based EVA uniquely aligns the interests of managers, employees, and stockholders. Studies show that EVA companies, after implementation, have increased their market value over peers by some 50% over five years.
- Bold implementation of EVA signals the beginnings of transparency and accountability, though it is too often the subject of lip service. Implementing EVA half-heartedly or without incentives spells disappointment.
- A balanced scorecard demands EVA as the balancing mechanism. EVA covers everything managers can influence, and therefore all drivers of value.

INTRODUCTION

Financial measuring tools are many and varied. The media and equity analysts focus on financial accounting metrics such as sales and sales growth, margin, operating profit and operating profit growth, bottom-line earnings and its partner earnings per share (EPS), market value, return on equity, and return on assets or cash flow.

Each of these metrics is flawed. Neither sales nor operating profit accounts for the financial requirements necessary to achieve them, in terms of either annual expenses or capital invested. Bottom-line profits and EPS take no account of the fact that equity has a cost. Market value ignores the capital employed to create it—invest more, and of course market value rises, without necessarily creating value. And yet each is popular.

Why is so fundamental a series of misapprehensions so widespread? The answer lies in the past. Accounting operating profit is conservative—literally. It focuses on collateral, or at least what would be left of a company after bankruptcy. This is a more than adequate measure for a bank, but it is misleading for an investor. The theory of modern business is founded on the blindingly simple insight that business is primarily about economics, not accounting.

THE PROBLEMS WITH EXISTING CORPORATE FINANCE MEASURES

Debt-inspired measures are misleading because they *expense*—write off as expenses—those aspects of business that are becoming increasingly important. Long-term intangible investments (training, brand building, and so on), in particular, create much of the value of companies today. Yet traditional accounting procedures expense these rather than treating them as investments. Additionally, investments in acquisitions (goodwill) and in restructuring (extraordinary items) are expensed. This is a mistake. A focus on value demands that long-term investments should appear on the balance sheet for the current year, taking the cost of capital into account.

Unless they take into account the cost of capital, return measures can become inflated. Furthermore, concentrating on percentages can lead to a misguided focus—for example, reducing capital investments (especially intangibles) calculated to create profits in the future.

If the hurdle rate for returns is very high, increases may discourage optimal creation of value. If the hurdle for returns is very low, increases may destroy value. If return objectives are above the required returns of

investors—the right benchmark—then managers may forgo investments that create value. If returns are the objective and an increase fails to meet this required return, value destruction results.

Of other measures, cash flow will not provide the right answers in growing businesses. When Wal-Mart was growing rapidly, new stores cost more than the existing cash flow, yet no one demanded that the company stop investing and growing. Furthermore, the net present value of free cash flow emphasizes success in the terminal value of the equation rather than the horizon that managers can visualize and experience. Free cash flow, in other words, is not a flow measure.

MVA

The best measure of corporate performance is market value added (MVA), because this measure differentiates between the total market value, including debt and equity, and the total capital invested: MVA is the difference. (MVA may also be viewed as management value added—the value managers have added to a company.)

The problem is that MVA is strongly affected by stock price, which is notoriously independent of senior executives. This makes MVA less useful for encouraging the creation of value, since it has limited operational use.

THE NEED FOR A MEANINGFUL FINANCIAL MEASURE

An alternative is necessary, one that focuses on what managers can influence rather than what they cannot. The measure should differentiate between financial inputs—what enters a company over time—and outputs—the value created. Clearly our choice should not be a driver of value such as the financial accounting metrics that managers can influence. Consider instead output, on an annual basis, as operating profit after tax, with certain adjustments for intangible and other long-term investments and other accounting anomalies, and input as the annual rental charge on the total capital employed, both debt and equity. The rental charge or required return, known alter-

natively as the hurdle rate for investments or the weighted average cost of capital, is the true benchmark against which all investments and management should be measured. This is economic value added (EVA).

UNDERSTANDING EVA

EVA covers all that managers can influence, all drivers of value. This is seen more easily if we view EVA as the capital investment multiplied by the difference between the actual return and the required return. If we think in addition about the required return as a mix of business risk and financial risk (where financial risk, or debt level, has a potential benefit also), then we have four of the major components of market value as defined by Merton Miller and Franco Modigliani. These are:

- the cost of capital for business risk;
- the amount of debt;
- the current level of operating profit;
- capital expenditure.

The other components look at future EVA (investor expectations for future growth) in the current level of EVA, what we call FGV, or future growth value: they are the expected return on new investment, and the time horizon for excess growth in profitability or EVA. Managers can influence more or less imperfectly the debt, operating profit, capital expenditure, and future returns. They influence the horizon and business risk little, if at all.

The Value and Scope of EVA

EVA covers profit and loss and the balance sheet, differentiating intangibles and growth, and thus covering all factors of production. Growing or improving EVA is the goal, with historic investments viewed as sunk. Hence, managers should focus on growing when the returns are greater than the cost of capital, redeploying capital when the returns are less than the cost, and improving returns on existing capital, as well as having an optimal capital structure (debt versus equity).

If value creation is key, then EVA is the answer, and EVA improvement is the goal. How managers achieve this or choose to accomplish this depends on what they think is victory for their business. Of course the answer may depend on the state of the economy. In reality, investing and containing costs are crucial everywhere in the economic cycle. However, criticism thrives in a falling market and falters in a rising one. A falling market puts failing companies under the microscope, and a rising market forgives all but the worst performers.

In other words, containing costs increases current and near-term EVA, and is always crucial. But investing determines near-term and future EVA and is also always crucial, if the cash is available.

Performance measurement is the bedrock of business. Since people manage what they measure, EVA can form the foundation for a more transparent and accountable management system, especially when combined with powerful incentives to improve EVA at every level, in every activity, across all functions, and independent of geography. With rights to make decisions accurately allocated, a fair system of transfer pricing in place, information flowing freely, and the appropriate tools and training offered, responsibility joins transparency and accountability through robust control and performance evaluation. Pay for the right performance, and value-based management results.

Under EVA, budgeting gives way to long-term planning. Control of the ends and the means is relinquished respectively to externally and objectively determined investor expectations and to management choice and opportunity that allow managers to bet their own success on their meeting or beating stockholder requirements.

MAKING IT HAPPEN ▸▸

- Start using EVA as the key financial measure: subtract input (annual rental charge on the total capital employed) from output (adjusted operating profit after tax).
- Employ EVA as the foundation of a more transparent, responsible, and accountable management system, with robust control and performance evaluation.
- With the right to make decisions accurately allocated, put a fair EVA-based system of transfer pricing in place.
- Couple continuous restructuring of existing businesses to milk value with cautious investing in future businesses.
- Focus managers on growing where returns exceed cost of capital and on redeploying capital where returns are less than its cost.
- Insist on improving returns on existing capital as well as on having an optimal capital structure (debt versus equity).

CONCLUSION

EVA is, in short, the best measurement tool for creating stockholder value. A balanced scorecard of metrics allows for a big-picture view, but what is the balancing mechanism? If value creation over the long term is the goal—and if it isn't, stockholders should run—then EVA must be the balancing mechanism. Sales, margin, operating profit, and bottom-line profit simply fall short. Market value lacks levers. Return measures give the wrong answers. Only EVA can change companies.

Indeed, EVA correlates better with stock price than any other measure: by 50%, compared with up to 30% for other metrics. Since EVA charges for all the factors of production, continuous improvement in EVA always furnishes investors with an increase in value.

Clearly if an organization pays lip service to EVA and blindly measures it without thinking about the behavioral consequences and the need to balance simplicity and accuracy, or else provides poorly considered or misguided incentives to create EVA, the outcome will disappoint. However, a robust system adhered to in times of boom and bust will provide the foundation of sound decision making and business practices.

FOR MORE INFORMATION

Books:
Bloxham, Eleanor. *Economic Value Management: Applications and Techniques.* New York: Wiley, 2003.
Stern, Joel M., and John S. Shiely. *The EVA Challenge: Implementing Value—Added Change in an Organization.* New York: Wiley, 2004.
Young, David, and Stephen F. O'Byrne. *EVA and Value-Based Management: A Practical Guide To Implementation.* New York: McGraw-Hill, 2000.

Web site:
www.eva.com: a site set up by Stern Stewart & Co., the global consulting company which pioneered the development of the EVA framework.

"One of the soundest rules to remember when making forecasts in the field of economics is that whatever is to happen is happening already."

Sylvia Porter

Viewpoint: Peter L. Bernstein
The Case against the Long Run

Introduction

Peter Bernstein is a pre-eminent authority on capital markets and the real economy. His journal, *Economics and Portfolio Strategy*, is read by managers and owners of assets valued at more than five trillion dollars.

In 1974, Bernstein was the founding editor of *The Journal of Portfolio Management*. After graduating from Harvard and doing research for the Federal Reserve Bank of New York, he taught at Williams College and the New School in New York.

In 1997, he received the Award for Professional Excellence from the Association for Investment Management & Research, AIMR's highest honor. In 1998 he was given both the annual Graham and Dodd Award for Excellence in Financial Writing and the Clarence Arthur Kelp/Elizur Wright Memorial Award from The American Risk and Insurance Association (ARIA) for his contribution to the literature of risk and insurance.

"In the long run" is one of the most popular phrases in business and finance. It is also one of the most elusive, and has been used with contradictory meanings. Although many people assume the long run to be an essential part of both business and investment decisions, perhaps it deserves to be tossed into the dustbin.

Sometimes it shows up as a bad-weather friend. When business is rotten or the stock market is depressed, we hear reassuring reminders that things always get better over the long run. Yet when business is great and the market is booming, emphasis on the temporary character of the short run is anathema. Everyone wants good business to last forever. The frequency with which people refer to the long run is a reliable measure of business and investor sentiment.

There is a more important meaning to the long run. Business decisions, where the rubber meets the road, also distinguish between the short run and the long run. Short-run decisions are those we can reverse without much difficulty. When we are locked into something, we are entering the deep waters of the long run. Accumulating inventory, executing a repo, or hiring a temp are clearly short-run decisions. Launching a new product, issuing a 30-year bond, building a new plant, and opening an office in Thailand are clearly long-run commitments.

The two uses of the concept of the long run appear to have nothing in common. The first says "This, too, shall pass." The second says "We are locking ourselves in to this situation." Yet a common thread runs between the long run as a nostrum against bad news and the long run as a policy move reaching out in time: the key word is reversibility. This simple word reveals a great deal about the long run and how to put it to good use in shaping the future. It is important to expose each of these faces of the long run, how they interact, and how to employ them to focus on the doughnut

rather than the hole. A close examination reveals that evoking the long run as a security blanket makes far less sense than its application to strategic business decisions—and even then the concept is mushy.

It is a truism to say that bad times will not last forever. Nothing lasts forever, including good times. Such a statement is little more than incantation, useless for forecasting or planning. John Maynard Keynes well understood this. He was not being facetious when he uttered his famous aphorism: "In the long run we are all dead. Economists set themselves too easy, too useless a task if, in the tempestuous seasons, they can only tell us that when the storm is long past the ocean will be flat." In a naturally volatile system characterized by uncertainty, we are inevitably trapped into the short run. Or, to put it another way, the long run is nothing more than a sequence of short runs.

Much of the appeal of the long run is in its resemblance to an average—the notion of regression to the mean over the long run appears to promise us that the good times will somehow come along after a while and bail us out. But averages are dangerous, useful in decision making only when they summarize a random sequence of events, like dice throws or spins of the roulette wheel. The dice and the roulette wheel have no memory. On the other hand, what happens today is the consequence of yesterday's decision, and what we do today determines what is going to happen tomorrow; hence, passive dependence on averages to hoist us out of trouble can lead to a perilous trap.

This little theoretical digression contains the moral of the whole story. History is notable for the fluctuations from good times to bad, but history is not a random sequence of events. Nothing in the past happened without a cause. The great prosperity of the 1990s developed out of the 1980s—widespread deregulation combined with the flood of restructurings,

takeovers, shutdowns, consolidations, layoffs, and, most of all, the revolution in the boardroom and the new emphasis on shareholder values. The impact of the high-tech revolution of the 1990s has been great, but I would argue that the dynamic of innovation would never have taken a grip on the economy without the intensely competitive environment created by the 1980s. Those profound changes in both government and business were necessitated by the terrible errors of the 1970s, errors of both public policy and heedless over-expansion by business. And so on and so on, all the way back to the beginning of time.

Which of these past heterogeneous states of the world are the ones we will have to confront over the long run that lies ahead? No one knows. Have we learned so little that we will replay the horrors of World War I, the 1930s, or the 1970s? Is the unique experience of the glorious 1990s likely to lead to anything that would closely resemble one of the eras of the past? But if the long-run past consists of nothing but experiences with no significance for today's world, then the long-run average derived from past events is also without significance.

We can learn from the past, but the experience of the 1990s is the launching pad of the future. Do not depend on the ocean being flat one day. Equilibrium is an economist's construct, irrelevant for executive planning. Even though nothing goes up or down forever, there is no predictable point, in space or time, to which matters will regress.

When we enter the sacred precincts of the corporate boardroom, the context of the long run changes. Corporate leaders specialize in the search for empty space and disequilibrium, because that is where opportunity lies: undeveloped markets, products, or production and marketing techniques waiting to be exploited. Great economic changes result in displacement, not more of the same.

Once taken, the commitment to spend money filling empty spaces or capitalizing on disequilibrium does not readily lend itself to second thoughts. It is a scary business to decide to build a new factory, open a new market in a foreign land, launch a new drug, acquire a major company in another line, or redesign an entire production process. If you are wrong, embarrassing write-offs will confront you. People who cannot stand the heat of such largely irrevocable decisions tend to go to work on Wall Street or in the City, where assets are liquid and decisions more easily reversed.

Seen from this vantage point, long-run business decisions look a lot riskier than the reversible ones. Yet, from other vantage points, the long-run moves may be less risky than the short-run moves. It all depends on how we manage the risks of irreversibility. Two elements are involved in that process: information and control. Both are essential in making the long run our servant.

The long run would be riskless if the future were known. And if the future were known, irreversibility would be irrelevant. But that is fantasy—we never have complete information. More information, however, is always better than less. Furthermore, we almost always have the option of postponing action while awaiting further information. Up to the point where we start actually writing checks, the arrival of new information has more value than the same information would have after the die has been cast. Decisiveness is admirable, but so is a sense of when to procrastinate before striding into the long run.

What is procrastination worth? Think of procrastination as an option to wait, or even an option not to act at all. The primary determinant of the value of an option is the volatility in the possible outcomes. Highly volatile outcomes add value to an option because a bad outcome would cost no more than the time spent waiting for information, while a good outcome could have enormous benefit. Consequently, the value of the option to procrastinate is a function of the uncertainty surrounding an irreversible decision. As the option expires at the moment when the corporation sinks its money into the new project, waiting for more information may often be preferable to a "damn-the-torpedoes-full-speed-ahead" approach. Indeed, the option of procrastination is properly part of the cost of capital or hurdle rate, justifying careful estimation of the long-run outlook.

The second element of risk management in long-run decisions is—rather, must be—control. In the typical investment in a reversible asset like a stock or bond, the owners or creditors play a passive role, in reality having no say over the management of the corporation involved. In contrast, the management of the corporation itself has the power after the fact to vary the fundamental parameters of irreversible decisions and illiquid assets for which they carry responsibility. For example, they can change their prices, redesign the product line, or replace executive personnel, among other options.

There are few decisions whose outcomes are so ironclad they are totally immune to revision. That matters. The ability to make revisions in essence means the ability to break the long run into a series of short runs. The greater the control, the shorter the run.

Despite its irrepressible popularity, the concept of "the long run" is in many ways misleading and without substance. The long run of the past tells us almost nothing about the long run facing us in the years ahead. But the long run clearly matters in business decisions. Even here, however, we should not overestimate the apparently risky character of the sunk costs and irreversibility looming over long-range plans to build new facilities, open new markets, or launch new products. Given sophisticated employment of information and control, such moves will almost always open up opportunities to crack that long run into shorter time periods, providing enhanced flexibility and reduced risk to the ultimate outcome.

FOR MORE INFORMATION

Book:
Bernstein, Peter L. *Against the Gods: The Remarkable Story of Risk*. New York: Wiley, 1996.

"Economists are about as useful as astrologers in predicting the future (and, like astrologers, they never let failure on one occasion diminish certitude on the next)."

Arthur Schlesinger, Jr.

Managing by the Open Book
by John Case

EXECUTIVE SUMMARY

- Companies in a knowledge economy need better ways of managing people. Open-book management is a powerful new approach.
- The open-book system focuses everybody's attention on business targets. Employees learn to be businesspeople rather than hired hands.
- Open-book management has caught on among only a few large companies for several identifiable reasons. But many young, entrepreneurial companies have adopted it and are now reaping the rewards.

INTRODUCTION

Companies in the 21st century are groping for new ways of helping people work together effectively. This is hardly surprising: the old hierarchical, command-and-control management systems were devised for industrial enterprises, where most people's jobs consisted purely of doing what they were told. Today's knowledge-intensive companies ask employees not only to do their assigned jobs, but also to take responsibility for world-class quality, impeccable service and continuous improvement and innovation. Thus employees find themselves in cross-functional groups and self-managing teams, charged with running their own projects or work areas as well as with solving their own problems.

But this situation presents a series of difficulties. Most employees don't really understand the business that they're in. They can't read a financial statement or a budget. They have never learned to understand the connections between operational performance and financial results. They don't have a good handle on the costs they incur (and must somehow manage) every day. They lack business acumen, because they have never had the occasion to acquire it.

The approach known as "open-book management," pioneered and developed over the past 20 years primarily by small and midsized companies is designed to solve this problem. Open-book companies teach *and expect* their employees to think and act like businesspeople, and to manage themselves accordingly.

THE ESSENTIALS OF OPEN-BOOK MANAGEMENT

"Open book" is a way of running a business; it means far more than just communicating financial results to employees. The following elements are essential:

- **Determine the critical numbers.** Every businessperson—every manager—has a few key numbers that he or she always keeps a close eye on. In small companies the critical numbers are usually financial: sales, margins, cash flow. In departments or divisions of larger companies, some key numbers are operational—they may include metrics such as units shipped, defect rates, machine uptime, and customer acquisition costs. Savvy managers and business owners know their critical numbers intuitively, and track them from week to week and quarter to quarter. They also understand the relationship between operational metrics and financial performance. Hotel executives know they make money when revenue per available room crosses a certain threshold. Seasoned plant managers estimate profitability simply by watching the number of trucks at the loading dock. Listen to J. Robert Beyster, founder of Science Applications International Corp. (SAIC), the big global research and engineering company based in San Diego, California: "What are SAIC's critical numbers? . . . Time sold, or what is more commonly called labor utilization, drives our business . . . If our time-sold targets are not met, we face staff reductions."

- **Communicate these numbers, and teach people what they mean.** SAIC—one of a handful of large companies that practice open-book management—sends out biweekly reports on each division's time-sold performance. SRC Holdings Corp., a midsized remanufacturing company headquartered in Missouri, puts charts on the wall. For example, at an SRC subsidiary that rebuilds electrical equipment, a green chart shows plant-wide efficiency, and a red one shows how much of the finished product was composed of used parts (a larger percentage means more savings). Teaching the "meaning" of the numbers essentially means explaining the connection between operational indicators and financial performance, and that, in turn, means providing people with a grounding in the basics of business. Employees of SRC, which has practiced open-book management since 1983, actually learn to read an income statement and a balance sheet; wall charts at the company show income and expense breakdowns as well as the operational indicators. A New York City marketing communications company asks its employees to be "C.F.O. for a day," not only to learn the financial numbers but also to explain them to fellow employees. A Massachusetts manufacturer prepares profit-and-loss statements for each team of production employees, so they can learn to track their contribution to company profits, day in and day out.

- **Give employees the power and responsibility to manage the critical numbers.** Many companies these days claim to "empower" people. But empowerment for what? It doesn't do any good to empower people to halt an assembly line or solve a customer's problem unless they understand the business costs and benefits involved. Indeed, empowerment without such understanding can be counterproductive. One manufacturer empowered employees to do "whatever it took" to ensure on-time delivery of product. It wasn't long before managers discovered that the company's margins were being destroyed by expediting costs and overnight-delivery expenses.

For most companies, the best system of empowerment is regular unit meetings to review and discuss key numbers. If the numbers aren't moving in the right direction, what needs to happen? Who has an idea? At least some of the numbers discussed at these meetings must be financial, precisely to avoid the kind of problem created by the all-out effort for on-time delivery. Indeed, veteran open-book companies such as SRC actually build rudimentary income statements at such meetings: unit representatives report their results for the previous time period and

---

"The average employee can deliver far more than his or her current job demands and far more than the terms 'employee empowerment,' 'participative management,' and 'multiple skills' imply."

Tom Peters

discuss how to correct any unfavorable variances from plan.

- **Establish (or communicate) appropriate rewards for outstanding business performance.** Open-book management asks employees to learn new skills and take on new responsibilities. Employees naturally ask "what's in it for me?" and if the answer is "nothing," the system won't work. Small and midsized companies committed to open-book management typically establish substantial bonus programs pegged to targets on key numbers. These targets can vary from year to year, since any business's priorities vary from year to year (for example, sales growth one year, profitability the next, quality improvements in a third). Whatever the target, the bonus must be transparent, equitable, and nondiscretionary. Employees must be able to see how they're doing on the key indicators over time. They must know that they will be paid the bonus if they make the targets.

Units of large companies may have to plead with the human resources department for flexible compensation plans, and unionized companies may need to negotiate bonus terms with the union. (The difficulties of both are one reason why relatively few large companies have been able to capitalize on the open-book approach.) Another useful tool for open-book management is an employee stock ownership plan or broad stock-option program. Insofar as employees *are* owners, they have a built-in incentive to think and act like owners, which is exactly what open-book management requires. The job for managers then is to spell out the connections between financial performance and the stock price.

OBSTACLES AND PAYOFFS

Open-book management makes a good deal of sense on paper, but so far it has been adopted by a minority of small companies and only a few big ones. The reasons stem from both intrinsic difficulties and institutional obstacles. To "go open book" is a big change for a company. Managers, remembering the maxim that information is power, are accus-

tomed to keeping what they know to themselves, and sharing it only when it suits them to do so. Many employees, for their part, still expect to come to work and do only what they're told; they don't want more responsibility or involvement. Open book is a system that must be learned, and changing people's expectations and behavior requires time and patience. In a large company, moreover, it involves change on many fronts—new training, new compensation arrangements, and new procedures for sharing and discussing information. Unit managers often must navigate a thicket of corporate policies and procedures just to reward employees for hitting a business target they all agree on.

And yet open-book management continues to spread, without much help from consultants or professors, primarily among new, growth-oriented companies. For example, *Inc* magazine has found that about half of the businesses on its annual listing of the 500 fastest-growing private companies in the United States practice open-book management. The reason is simply that the payoffs are substantial:

- It focuses employees' attention on the basics of the business
- It builds a collaborative environment—open-book companies report less of an "us versus them" attitude and less office politics
- It taps the wisdom and experience of employees at every level
- It helps create a more fun, more satisfying atmosphere in which everyone is working toward common goals.

Most of all it produces results. "By opening the books," wrote Fay Wu, chief financial officer of Toronto-based Castek Software Factory, "we focused everyone's attention on business performance ... Castek has successfully doubled its size every year by moving the 'numbers' in the right direction."

MAKING IT HAPPEN ▶▶

These are some first action steps you can take toward achieving open book:

- Determine your business's critical

numbers. Chart the relationship between changes in these numbers and financial indicators (margins, costs, and so on)
- Put key numbers up on a chart or on your company's intranet. Hold lunchtime discussions to explain why these numbers are important to financial performance
- Set short-term targets for key numbers, and review progress at weekly meetings. Begin to involve employees in establishing longer-term targets
- Investigate your company's compensation plan to see how much flexibility you have. Meantime, see whether you can pay small bonuses or rewards out of your budget—and if so, set up a short-term, unit-wide "game" to hit a certain business goal. Pay the bonus if the goal is attained.

CONCLUSION

Companies searching for a new way of managing people in the knowledge economy can learn much from the small, entrepreneurial companies that have developed open-book management. Open book can be challenging to implement, particularly in a large corporation, but the payoffs are substantial.

FOR MORE INFORMATION

Books:

Case, John. *The Open-book Experience: Lessons from Over 100 Companies Who Transformed Themselves*. Cambridge, MA: Perseus, 1999.

Schuster, John P., et al. *The Power of Open-book Management*. New York: Wiley, 1996.

Stack, Jack, with Bo Burlingham. *The Great Game of Business*. New York: Doubleday/Currency, 1992.

Web site:

Science Applications International Corporation (SAIC): **www.saic.com/about/obm.html**

"You've got to figure out a way to manage the complexity of large projects yet still allow your core teams to focus on the essentials."

Steve Jobs

Viewpoint: John Seely Brown
Changing the Workplace into a Meaningful Community

Introduction

John Seely Brown is not your typical scientist, but rather a blend of scientist, artist, and strategist. Combining the worlds of digital culture, ubiquitous computing, and organizational learning, he serves as chief scientist for the Xerox Corporation and was director of the Xerox Palo Alto Research Center (PARC) from 1990 to 2000. His acclaimed *Social Life of Information*, a book he coauthored, is transforming the way people think about information. Offering a rare perspective on the human contexts in which technologies operate, he maintains change does not always represent genuine progress.

What is the most important thing and who is the most important person to have influenced your thinking on business and management?

Actually, two people come to mind—each operating in different domains from the other and both radically distinct in their views.

The first is Elizabeth Teisberg, now at the University of Virginia's Darden Graduate School of Business Administration. Taking "real options evaluation" theory from the world of finance and capital management, she demonstrated how options thinking could be applied to the funding and evaluation of research and development initiatives. The concept is very dynamic and, truthfully, there's nothing I do any day that is not influenced by her model.

Real options analysis represents a merging of *investment* decision making with *strategy*. It enables us in effect to value two sources of *learning*: learning by *doing*, which allows us to determine if there are any unexpected problems with an undertaking; and learning by *waiting*—to see how the market develops and learn what customers really want.

By using these techniques companies can take calculated R&D risks, in the form of options on the future, without "betting the farm" or making full-scale strategic commitments initially. Indeed, it encourages the creation and exploration of opportunities, while providing a discipline for continuously assessing whether the options being created are *real*—having potential for significant returns and being worthy, therefore, of further investment. Most importantly, real options thinking strongly implies that viewing risk-taking as "betting" is a mistake!

As we begin to incorporate options thinking, we're continuously *staging* and *gating*—creating opportunities and determining checkpoints for making "go" and "no-go" decisions. This is a very useful concept in

the world of R&D, particularly when you're concerned with cash flow. It establishes a dynamic system for scaling an investment as well as exiting a project altogether. The process effectively shapes conversation around managed risk-taking and the reserving of options for the future. It also favors a bias for innovative thinking, while eliminating much of the politics underlying the innovator's dilemma.

> In a world of accelerating change and dynamic tension, we need disciplines in which we can be playful—frameworks for choreographing the delicate dances of opportunity and commitment.

In a world of accelerating change and dynamic tension, we need disciplines in which we can be playful—frameworks for choreographing the delicate dances of opportunity and commitment. For me, the appeal has been in my being able to take the world of research management to a new plane—allowing for a sort of *creative abrasion* between acts of creation and evaluation.

The second person is Professor Lucy Suchman of Lancaster University's department of sociology. An anthropologist, ethnomethodologist, and author, Professor Suchman completely blew away a corner stone of artificial intelligence with her analyses of situated action. She elaborates on these findings in her book *Plans and Situated Actions: The Problem of Human-machine Communications*.

Drawing on ethnomethodological studies of all types of work, from the seemingly mundane to the most complex and intellectually demanding, she successfully uncovered the specific culturally and materially embodied identities, knowledge, and practices that make up technical systems. Her research helps us to understand how work gets done and to honor the

context and situations in which workers find themselves. For example, at Xerox we were interested in the role and importance of business processes. Dr. Suchman conducted analyses as a participant observer and then returned to ask that community of practice if certain office procedures were helpful. They affirmed they were. But she found the procedures were not being used as originally intended. Workers did not follow the step-by-step instructions; instead, they improvised around the "unexpected," while ensuring the ensemble of improvisations created a result that looked like what they would have gotten had they followed the overall procedure.

I came to the conclusion that many practices in which employees are engaged in the workscape today are driven by improvisation and can't be reduced to written procedures—simply because workers are continuously problem solving, improvising, and interpreting what is going on in the contexts of their environment. That realization moved me to appreciate the inherent creativity of people "at work" and to conclude that *practice makes process* and not the converse.

What will business need to do differently in the 21st century?

We will need to transform the workscape into a place of *meaning*. It will be incumbent upon managers to view the work environment as "communities of practice." They must recognize their existence, and build environments that are genuinely supportive of continuous learning and identity formation. *Their challenge will be to architect the workscape of the future utilizing the triadic elements of social, physical, and informational space.* Those who understand will come to lead organizations that are enormously successful and truly beneficial to all stakeholders.

I believe the pathway to the future will require "looking around"—managers will need to eschew the sort of tunnel vision that "sees" only *one* system or solution for getting there. Let's be frank! Real innovation is not born of logic, but of aesthetics based on a sort of playfulness and constant interpreting of the world in which we operate.

Creating joy, innovation, and meaning in the workscape requires that managers see and think contextually. They will have to unlearn old styles of managing and create, instead, workscapes that foster emergent communities of learning by honoring worker improvisation and knowledge formation.

What new skills will be needed to cope with these changes?

One's ability to unlearn is constrained by *tacit beliefs*. Successful managers must not assume they know someone else's frame of operation. Instead, they will have to appreciate the profound significance of seeing the environment through the eyes of the other person—whether employee, customer, or resource provider. They will have to determine what matters most to others and move to satisfy their needs.

As in sailing, it's a matter of "triangulation." When navigating through unfamiliar waters, managers need to reference various points continuously to get their bearings. Dead reckoning and triangulation are principal methods by which we can learn, but doing this is almost an art form. To be sure, in the corporate world there's a thin line between joy and terror, and it takes a skilled navigator to keep from going over the edge.

Managers must move increasingly to the mode of win-win. Consider Li & Fung Limited in Asia, a highly successful global sourcing company, that orchestrates an entire network of some 6,500 shops in 100 countries to produce goods for their corporate clients. They can take an order from a retail customer and determine the best source according to craft skills, materials used, product quality, and turnaround times. Li & Fung have mastered a deep knowledge of their producer communities. By playing to individual strengths rather than forcing each to a uniform standard or to a least-cost basis, Li & Fung foster an environment where everyone wins and learns. Successful managers will need to become proficient in this regard and emulate the skills of orchestrators like Li & Fung rather than controllers of work practices.

Are there new management questions we should be considering?

Two questions relate to how well an organization is managing its own "periphery"—both *within* and *outside of* its own walls. The first periphery deals with finding the "radicals" who live on the fringes of the organization—customer contact people, for example, who make discoveries every day. Good ideas come from lots of different places. Managers need to honor those on the margins of the enterprise and centralize their knowledge for the sake of the business.

The second periphery has to do with looking and listening to the marketplace—looking at competitors, especially new entrants. It's so easy to discount the smaller players, but often they're only "small" relative to one's interpretation of the market.

A third consideration relates to how effectively managers challenge one another to think about strategic surprises they can launch at their competitors and, in turn, surprises the competition may be planning for them. This line of questioning is an effective way of getting people to think out of the box.

How can companies best promote enterprises that are both profitable and good places to work?

The answer relates again to the idea of creating a learning milieu. By paying serious attention to *people* in an organization—on the fringes, serving customers, in the trenches—roles get reversed, as potentially marginalized ideas and competencies become central. Work becomes meaningful for everyone, and both individual and corporate intelligence grows. By understanding the contextual aspects of work, honoring the creative abilities of employees, and reserving opportunities for the future, managers can produce enterprises that are both successful and satisfying. Of course, the icing on the cake comes with building information systems that facilitate the flow of ideas and nurture the social capital of the enterprise.

"We had the experience but missed the meaning."   T. S. Eliot

Viewpoint: Paul Saffo
The New Service Economy

Introduction

Paul Saffo is a writer, business adviser, and technology forecaster, studying long-term information technology trends and their impact on business and society. Author of *Dreams in Silicon Valley* and *The Road from Trinity*, his essays have appeared in numerous publications, including *The Harvard Business Review*, *Wired Magazine*, *Civilization Magazine*, *The Los Angeles Times*, *The New York Times*, and *Fortune*. He also serves on a variety of boards and advisory panels, including the AT&T Technology Advisory Board, the World Economic Forum Global Issues Group, and the Stanford Law School Advisory Council on Science, Technology, and Society. Here, Paul Saffo assesses the profound social and economic effects resulting from the convergence of communications and technology. He argues that the real impact of computing is the blurring of products and services, with significant implications for producers and consumers alike.

The Next Big Shifts in Communications

So far, the Internet has barely touched our lives. The Internet arrived on the one piece of real estate we've been trying to get away from for the last 20 years: our desktops. It has not gone much further. This is what makes wireless and broadband so important, because both put us in an always-on world, unlike dialup. For example, wireless devices, such as cell phones and personal digital assistants, deliver the Internet to where we actually live, work, and play. That has profound implications for our life and also for the medium. So far, the Internet has barely touched our lives.

The other big shift is in the *nature* of communications. Before deregulation in the 1980s, communications was synonymous with people talking to other people. The symbol was a telephone handset on a desk. Along came the Internet in the 1990s, and the leading edge of communications was no longer simply people talking to people; it was people accessing information, and people accessing other people in information-rich environments. We have saturated those activities. Would you like to receive *more* phone calls? Do you feel like you don't have enough Web pages to surf? These are saturated for the people who have them today. The only growth in delivering the Internet lies in getting it to people who don't already have it.

The *real* growth is not going to come from people talking to other people or people accessing other information—it's going to come from machines talking to other machines on people's behalf. I think what we're going to start seeing in ten years, and really visibly in 20, is an enormous drop in the total communications traffic on the planet attributed to humans. The vast bulk of communication will be machine to machine. In two decades, the amount of communications traffic attributable to human beings will be below the rounding error of your average corporate telecommunications accountant.

Cheap Sensors Will Connect Cyberspace to the Real World

So far, we have two parallel universes: the physical reality that each one of us occupies, and cyberspace, where our machines live. The two worlds barely touch. In fact, the place they touch is so constrained that it is literally a piece of glass called an interface. We peer through the portal of our computer-screen interfaces into cyberspace, but we don't immerse ourselves in it. We look through the window at stuff, and for the most part, the computers don't look out at all. They have no idea that there is anything on the other side of the glass.

Now, do something as simple as putting a video camera on the computer, and make it aware that there are people in the room. Put a GPS chip into a cell phone and make the cell phone aware of where it is in the world, and it can do interesting things for you. When you call emergency, they don't have to ask where you are because your phone will have already told them. A cell phone that knows where it is isn't just a good safety device, it is also a candidate for interesting location-based marketing, certain to delight advertisers but drive the rest of us crazy.

The revolution in geographic information systems (GIS) is happening because of cheap sensors. We're about to connect GIS to ordinary consumer life. Consider this example. It's 4:45pm on Friday, you're walking down Sutter Street in San Francisco and your phone chirps at you. It's an e-mail chirp. You look at the screen and it's not an e-mail—it's an electronic coupon from a Chinese restaurant a block and a half away in your direction of travel. They know you like Tsingtao Beer, and it says, "Get in here in 15 minutes and you get half off Tsingtao, and free appetizers!" Whether or not that is something that we want is another story, but I can assure you that it will be offered to you.

Another example: You're driving up U.S. Highway 101 and discover that your car, unbeknownst to you, has been sending telemetry on its operating condition back and forth to the manufacturer. Just south of Redwood Shores, your screen lights up and a voice comes on and says, "Hey, dude. Your car is 2,000 miles past its oil change. If you get off at the next exit, there is a mechanic standing by at Autobahn Motors. They will have you in and out in 15 minutes. Oh, by the way, we know you like Starbuck's eggnog lattes.

"Long-range planning does not deal with future decisions. It deals with the future of present decisions."

Peter F. Drucker

It's November, and, though it's a little early for it, we've taken the liberty of brewing up an eggnog latte, and it is waiting for you while your oil is being changed."

In the long term, the car ceases to be a product—it's a *vehicle for service*. One can easily imagine, at the extreme, people selling you a car at or below cost because they know they'll make it up in service.

Let's consider what's happening in the area of white goods. For the last couple of years, every white-goods manufacturer on the planet has had a top-secret program to put Internet connectivity into their washers, dryers, and refrigerators. Why? Well, they didn't quite know why, but it was cheap to do and they were desperate for product differentiation. Your washing machine craps out, and you've got to buy a new one. You go down to the store and the high-end model has a big sign on it that says, "Internet ready." You say under your breath, "Do I look like Bill Gates? I don't need my washing machine to talk to the Internet."

But, in fact, you buy that washing machine because it has some other feature you want. So they install it. As the delivery people are carrying out the cardboard box, your washing machine wakes up. Unbeknownst to you, there's a little radio transponder in it that is listening for 802.11 and a couple of other frequencies, and it picks up the radio signal from the 802.11 box on the side of your house that you've already put in for your wireless computer network. It establishes communications and says, "Hi, I'm a washing machine. Would you mind if I borrowed some of your bandwidth from time to time to talk to my manufacturer?"

So your washing machine is now regularly talking to your manufacturer. One morning, you're late to work. You swing open the door and almost knock over the Maytag™ repair person who is about to knock on your door. You say, "What are you doing here?" They reply, "Gosh, your washing machine didn't tell you? It's got a flat bearing. It sent me an e-mail last night screaming for help. Would you mind if I drop in and fix it?"

Companies like Electrolux did tests a couple of years ago. They said, "Gee, young people don't want to go down to the wash-o-mat unless they want to socialize, but they don't want to buy a washing machine and carry it through life either. We're going to use this to transform the nature of the experience, almost like the car. Instead of selling you a washing machine, we will loan you a washing machine. We retain title, and the machine will tell us every time you use it. At the end of the month, we'll put a charge on your credit card based on the number of uses. It will either be the same price or slightly less than the wash-o-mat that you go to." That's an oversimplified scenario, but that is where things are headed.

The Service Economy Finally Arrives

This is where the real transformations come. I'm a technology forecaster, but my interest is in what technology does to society. In general, even the most anticipated of futures tends to arrive late and in completely unexpected ways—if it ever arrives at all. It's what makes us all so humble as forecasters.

For example, in the 1970s, everybody was writing about the leisure society. What were we going to do with all of our time after robots took over our jobs and computers took over our paperwork? I can't wait. I would love for someone to deliver a leisure society. In the 1980s, there was this thing called the service economy. The forecast was basically that everybody would either be flipping hamburgers at McDonald's or they would be consultants—which, of course, didn't happen.

Now, pull a thread through all these themes: wireless, bandwidth, sensors, increasingly autonomous smart effects. Pull that through, and suddenly the service economy just arrived in a completely strange and unexpected way. We're still buying physical products, but those products are actually concealed services. When you buy a cell phone, you think you're buying an artifact. In fact, you're buying the point of service for the thing that's truly valuable, which is communications. The car ceases to become a product; rather, it's a transportation service. So the service economy finally does arrive, hidden in physical products.

Why should we care? Now I shift from being an observer to an advocate—suddenly it puts wheels on the goals of issues like closed-loop recycling, a green economy, and design for disassembly.

For example, the car dealer wants to retain title to the car in the same way Interface Carpet retains title to the carpets it sells. I have a box full of old cell phones in my garage because I get a new one every nine months. I really want to send the old phone back to the manufacturers and have them send me a new one. I don't even want to own the darn thing. You guys keep it; you dispose of it. The same goes for a car or a washing machine. Look what has happened with disposable cameras. You buy the camera, you shoot the roll, you send the camera back with the film. Kodak actually recycles a huge percentage of the pieces of that camera. They basically just peel off the paper and repackage the thing.

It gives us a chance to change the stream of commerce. The thing that persists is the service, and the thing that is transitory is the physical object, which goes back and gets reused in the stream.

FOR MORE INFORMATION

Saffo.com: **www.saffo.com**
*This essay was adapted from an interview undertaken with Mr. Saffo by Peter Leyden, Knowledge Developer at Global Business Network (**www.gbn.com**). The publishers gratefully acknowledge the support of Global Business Network in making these ideas and insights available.*

See also:
Budgeting (pp. 1683–1684)

"You've no future unless you add value and create projects." — Rosabeth Moss Kanter

Enterprise Information Systems
by Thomas H. Davenport

EXECUTIVE SUMMARY

- Enterprise information systems are the backbone systems supporting business transactions all across an organization.
- They support broad business processes and cut across such organizational structures as business functions and business units.
- Increasingly the successful implementation and use of these systems is the key to organizational productivity, to customer and supplier relationships, to the successful execution of competitive strategy, and certainly to electronic commerce.

INTRODUCTION

Information systems have become an integral part of how organizations work and compete. They now support every business objective and process. Those systems that support core business activities for the entire organization are known as enterprise information systems or enterprise resource planning systems. Without them, no organization could easily take orders from customers, procure goods from suppliers, make sure that there is sufficient inventory, or keep track of employee compensation and vacation balances. Enterprise information systems consist of some of the following types of system, many of which are linked in the contemporary organization's technology architecture:

- accounting and financial
- human resource management
- sales and order management
- logistics and supply chain
- manufacturing
- inventory management
- customer relationship management

Enterprise information systems do not include those systems that serve only a small part of an organization—say, a standalone system to manage the legal department. They also would not generally include systems for analyzing data or supporting decisions, or for sharing knowledge within an organization. Enterprise systems are primarily focused on core business transactions. Because of their importance and complexity, enterprise systems have turned the usual formula for business change on its head. It used to be that companies decided what they wanted to do, then built systems to accomplish it. Now they must think first about what they can accomplish with systems, and then they proceed to do it. Of course this raises significant issues for how companies manage and compete.

MAKING IT HAPPEN ▶▶
Getting Them in and Getting Value

Almost all companies that implement enterprise systems do so by buying and installing a package. Companies such as SAP and Oracle supply application packages that are an integrated collection of modules—one for accounting, one for human resources, and so on. companies attempt to configure the packages to fit their particular organizational situations. Because of the complexity of the packages, it is not generally advisable to modify them beyond the limits of the configuration process—hence the constraints that these systems impose on organizational flexibility. Some organizations, however, develop their own proprietary modules and interface them with their packages, although this can be a difficult undertaking as well.

The configuration process has been challenging historically, since both the packages and the organizations they support are complex. Vendors often provide a preconfigured set of choices that a particular organization can select from—for example, what currency to use, or whether revenue will be recognized across geographical units or product groups. The choices are complex, and deciding what options a particular company needs to fit its organization and way of doing business requires both business and technical decision making, and a high level of communication between technical and business managers. Many business executives do not understand these systems or the importance of not modifying them a lot. The idea that they should change their way of doing business to suit the limitations of an information system is often hard for them to understand. But for business people to withdraw from the configuration process almost guarantees that a system will not meet business objectives.

One of the key challenges with such systems is to achieve real business value in the implementation process. These systems are capable of delivering such benefits as radically improved business processes, reductions in inventory, increased sales (through one-stop ordering and prevention of stockouts), and better management of financial and physical assets. Most organizations, however, fail to achieve these benefits—in part because simply installing the system often becomes the overriding objective. This was particularly true for the organizations attempting to install enterprise systems before the Y2K bug took effect. Yet these systems are expensive—usually costing in the tens or hundreds of millions of dollars for a large organization—and managers of the projects must not lose sight of the potential benefits. The key to achieving benefit is to view the project not as a technical initiative, but as a business change project with clear objectives and measures.

Changing Everything at Once

The secret to both the opportunity and the difficulty of enterprise information systems is their tight integration with the business they support. Enterprise systems, to be effective, must be closely aligned to a company's business processes, information, organizational structure, and strategy. While this integration is positive in the sense that businesses can get higher-quality information than ever before, it is also challenging to deal with, both at the time of implementation and thereafter.

During implementation, the integrated nature of these systems means that organizations must "change everything at once." That is, they must make sure that

all aspects of the organization that will be affected by the system are consistent with their objectives for them, and that the system fits each aspect. For example, most companies will have objectives for process improvement and for greater consistency of key processes across the organization. In most cases, some change is desired from the current state. An organization may wish or need in the course of its enterprise system project to develop greater consistency in definitions of key information across different business units, for example. At the same time it may want different units to share the same process for reporting financial matters. Identifying and bringing about these changes in the business may be much more difficult than simply configuring and installing a new system, but it is the system project and its managers that get saddled with the responsibility for making the changes.

Because the project involves business change as well as a new system, many organizations put a senior business executive in charge of the project, such as the chief operations officer or financial officer. If the desired changes primarily involve a single functional area, it may make sense to put a functional executive in charge, such as the head of logistics or manufacturing. Putting an IT executive in charge is a good way to ensure that little business change gets accomplished, even if the system gets installed.

The Implications for Competitive Advantage

It has been estimated that an enterprise systems package can support up to 70% of an organization's information needs. Since these systems come as packages and are similar from one company to another—even after the configuration process—the question arises how companies can obtain competitive advantage from their systems and the processes they support, if they are all essentially alike. The answer is that competitive advantage can still be achieved, but it is difficult.

Some companies tailor their enterprise systems to fit the needs of their business, and rely on being the first to install the systems in their industry. Reebok, for example, added size and color information to the basic SAP system, and was the first company in the athletic shoe industry to implement a package with these capabilities. Its rival Nike also installed SAP, but completed its implementation several years later.

Another alternative is to implement enterprise systems only in those "commodity" business functions that are not associated with competitive advantage. Intel, for example, believes that its primary advantages over competitors come from its product design and manufacturing processes. When implementing an enterprise package, it did not use any package capabilities in these business functions, but rather developed its own systems internally.

What's Next for Enterprise Systems?

Enterprise systems have thus far been implemented primarily to support internal operations. In the future, it is likely that systems will be integrated across organizations. If a supplier's systems can interface with a customer's without human intervention, companies could better coordinate their logistical and production processes, and the costs of supply chains could be reduced. Some companies are already beginning to work on this integration, either on a one-to-one basis or with multiple other companies through an intermediary.

Given the similarities across businesses in areas supported by enterprise systems, it is likely that we will begin to see new business arrangements wherein several companies collaborate on common business transactions and enterprise systems. For example, six oil exploration companies in the North Sea, including BP and Conoco, have combined their accounting and financial processes and enterprise information systems in a joint effort to share services. They have outsourced the operation of these services to an external professional services company.

The other key direction for enterprise systems is for vendors and implementing companies to add increasing amounts of functionality to their systems. Today, for example, many companies are working at adding customer relationship management (CRM) and supply chain management (SCM) capabilities to their base enterprise systems. They have integrated their enterprise systems with the Internet, so that core transaction systems can be employed in electronic commerce. They are also making enterprise systems information more easily available through portals and data warehouses. It is also likely that many companies will eventually add product life-cycle management functions to their core systems. The tight grip that enterprise packages have on business information systems is likely only to increase.

CONCLUSION

For an organization that has yet to implement a system, the following steps will help it get under way most effectively:

- Create the project as a business change initiative, not a systems project—and start by identifying the business objectives that the new system will enable.
- Select a package from a well-established vendor that has all the functionality your organization needs, and limit the changes to the configuration options provided.
- Don't put off the changes in business processes and organizational structure until after the system is installed.
- Tie incentive compensation of the project team, sponsoring executives, and any consultants used to the successful accomplishment of business objectives.

For companies that have already installed enterprise systems but did not receive sufficient value, it's not too late to organize a project to optimize the system and deliver more benefits. The steps include:

- Identify the areas of the business in which value from the system should have been achieved, but was not.
- Create a process improvement or reorganization initiative to bring about the desired business changes.
- Reset the configuration of the system to fit the new process and organization.

FOR MORE INFORMATION

Books:
Davenport, Thomas H. *Mission Critical: Realizing the Promise of Enterprise Systems.* Cambridge, MA: Harvard Business School Press, 2000.
Norris, Grant, et al. *E-business and ERP: Transforming the Enterprise.* New York: Wiley, 2000.

Journal Article:
Davenport, Thomas H. "Putting the Enterprise in the Enterprise System." *Harvard Business Review,* July–August, 1998.

Web site:
www.cio.com/research/erp: the Web site of C.I.O. Magazine's Enterprise Resource Planning Research Center.

"Many individuals and organization units contribute to every large decision, and the very problem of centralization and decentralization is a problem of arranging the complex system into an effective scheme."

Herbert A. Simon

Developing an Internet-era Mindset throughout the Organization
by John Nirenberg

EXECUTIVE SUMMARY

- Because the Internet, telecommunications, and computer technologies enable us to behave so much more knowledgably and almost instantaneously, our organizations must mirror this behavior internally to reach peak effectiveness and competitiveness.
- The Internet is changing the way we think about our environment and how we organize to compete.
- The Internet-era mindset involves the integration of learning, imagination, and the capacity for radical innovation into the internal processes of the organization and the cognitive behavior of its work partners.

THE IMPACT OF THE INTERNET

It is now obvious that computer, electronics, and telecommunications technologies are influencing every aspect of our lives in dramatic and inescapable ways.

While we admire the Internet's presence, the hardware that connects us, and the enormous capabilities of the fiber-optic vines and cell towers rapidly covering the planet, we have yet to integrate our observations of this new external world into the reality of our personal internal world and organizational processes. But our survival depends on coming to grips with how the Internet has fundamentally changed the way we compete, who we compete with, and how we'll need to organize even to stay in the game.

The new Internet environment is turning our traditional models of life and work upside down. While we've been used to linear time, incremental growth, slow face-to-face relationship building, top-down hierarchies of personal power, formal communications, and mostly centralized, unilateral command-and-control decision making, we now must adjust to an instantaneous world with massive, simultaneous, multitasking, parallel-processing capabilities made possible by technological innovation.

Add to that the frequent surprises of new products and services that sometimes appear suddenly and from unexpected quarters, and we find ourselves in an unprecedented competitive environment. With the Internet we face a world of revolutionary change, viral growth, and instant intimacy with people we may never see. The new communications environment is a lateral, multinodal, collegial network acti-vated by Web pages, e-mail, and instant messaging. The challenge to organizations today is therefore twofold:

1 to master the capabilities of an external Internet world;
2 to create an organization with the same internal qualities that reflect the Internet's driving forces, most notably reach and simultaneity.

Indeed, if we don't develop an Internet-era mindset, our organizations will fail.

THE INTERNET MINDSET

The Internet has three levels of impact. First is the now common but still incredible exchange of information globally, conveniently, and instantaneously. The second is building partnerships, creating synergies with suppliers and customers, and developing the ability to anticipate new competitive threats and solutions for emergent market needs and product/service efficiencies. The third level is the very reformulation of the nature of relationships and the creation of new realities that emanate from cyberspace that, among other things, dramatically reduce transaction costs.

In this new context a new nonlinear, non-traditional logic drives the development of meaning. Richard Ogle calls this the "Intercosm: a new kind of space for the creation of meaning and value, a space determined as it is by near-universal interconnection, interdependence, and the interplay of multiple emergent factors." This new arena for sense-making and world creation has profound effects as it overcomes geographic, cultural, and traditional forms of thinking, behaving, and creating meaning. All aspects of life become subject to intentionally constructing our reality, much like customizing a product or service to meet our individual desires. This postmodern idea that almost anything goes is tempered only by the agreements and negotiated outcomes of individuals freely choosing to associate. Harnessing this new force is one of the biggest challenges for organizations today.

HOW TO DEVELOP AN INTERNET-ERA MINDSET

If the impact of the Internet is obvious, unavoidable, and demanding of our adaptation, the implications for managerial behavior are equally revolutionary and transformational. There is simply no way to survive in this protean environment by conducting business as usual. Thus an Internet mindset must begin with the willingness to alter old hardwired patterns of human behavior. Organizations need to consider new ways for their members to communicate, build trust, share knowledge and experience, and work together, and create a shared understanding of their ever changing reality. The Internet era requires that organizations become fully intentional—deliberate in their processes, inclusive of the contributions of each work partner, and responsive to all stakeholders.

Required organizational response to Internet-era mindset	
Driving Force	**Organizational Response**
Global opportunities	Global sourcing
Radical innovation	Flexibility/parallel processing
Competitiveness	Speed
Complexity	Teamwork
Accessible information and personal technologies	Decentralized decision making and personal responsibility
Continuous change	Continuous learning
Thorough professional socialization	Partnership/collegial orientation

"Just having a great Web site is only one step in a company thinking of itself as an Internet company . . . The people at the desk . . . the knowledge workers, need to work in a different way."

Bill Gates

This new environment demands teamwork, collaboration, a distribution of power to those closest to its application: accountability based on performance, expertise, and creativity freely used for the benefit of the group and not just oneself. The measure of success is defined by outcomes, not obedience. The purpose of controls is to ensure that resources are appropriately deployed toward meeting objectives, not conforming to a job description. Indeed, job descriptions become obsolete in an unpredictable world. These internal changes are necessary to successfully match the demands of the external world of constant change, innovation, and hyper-competitiveness.

How will it change? First, efficiency of resource use, speed of innovation, responsiveness to customer and employee needs, and intentional knowledge creation, management, and distribution will be essential. This will dismantle rigid hierarchies and conventional protocols and build networks of self-managing teams with access to whatever information they may need in order to respond as quickly as possible to customers and coworkers.

We can understand how our managerial mindset and behavior need to shift by looking at computer hardware providers as an example of the global reach required to support corporate activities on a global scale by using intranets and the Internet.

In the case of, say, Apple or Dell, design may take place in California or Texas, while data is carried over intranets to component manufacturers in Taiwan for chips, Hong Kong for housings, and Peru for copper wiring, to ship to a power-source manufacturer in Korea, all to be assembled in Malaysia and shipped to Guadalajara, Mexico, New Jersey, and Vancouver for warehousing and distribution.

Meanwhile, logistic data is stored in Madras, human-resource administration is based in Dublin, and the worldwide sales and customer service headquarters is in South Africa, all connected through the company's intranet. The complexity of this arrangement—which is driven by the need to keep costs down, source where worldwide supply is available, and meet the demands of a global marketplace—is made possible by vast improvements in the Internet and other technologic, logistic, communications, and supporting infrastructure, from wireless tools and fiber-optic cables and communications satellites to state-of-the-art industrial parks and the availability of educated professionals worldwide.

But the very complexity of this arrangement requires the power of a network itself driven by decentralized and self-managing teams that also requires a high level of professionalization, well-established working relationships, whether face-to-face or virtual, and the ability to manage the network for the mutual gain of the organization and its internal and external customers. Of course all of this must reflect the instantaneous nature of the Net.

CREATING AN INTERNET-ERA MINDSET IN YOUR ORGANIZATION

Organize
- structures based on deliverables, not function;
- self-managing teams that take responsibility for their output.

Provide
- access to information;
- rewards based on team and individual performance;
- education and development opportunities to assimilate the necessary personal and organizational changes.

Create
- stimulating development experiences for each employee;
- offline time to think;
- exposure to challenging input about changes in other organizations and the environment.

Convey
- a sense of shared meaning;
- authenticity and genuineness;
- respect.

Encourage
- innovation, creativity, and collaboration;
- consultative practices;
- personal and professional growth;
- career opportunities and challenges;
- fun.

Learn
- to communicate and lead in a virtual environment;
- to make sense of the Internet-era possibilities and create a shared reality with coworkers, including an intentional workplace of shared agreements, understandings, and commitments;
- how to "read the world," to know what to pay attention to and where changes emanate from.

MAKING IT HAPPEN ▸▸
- Create an Internet mindset that includes developing divergent thinking skills—the ability to see new and different possibilities—and help each employee to become more curious, connected, inventive, trusting, and communicative.
- Integrate the Internet style of openness, accessibility, and knowledge sharing into your work life and your organization.

CONCLUSION
The Internet changes everything. The most obvious change is the ability to communicate and gather data instantaneously around the clock and around the world. Organizations need to create internal processes, structures, and procedures that mirror the world being created in the Internet era.

FOR MORE INFORMATION

Books:
Hamel, Gary. *Leading the Revolution.* Cambridge, MA: Harvard Business School Press, 2000.
Kelly, Kevin. *New Rules for the New Economy: 10 Ways the Network Economy is Changing Everything.* New York: Penguin, 1999.
Levine, Rick, et al. *The Cluetrain Manifesto: The End of Business As Usual.* Cambridge, MA: Perseus, 2001. (See **www.cluetrain.com.**)
Ridderstråle, Jonas, and Kjell Nordström. *Funky Business: Talent Makes Capital Dance.* Paramus, NJ: Financial Times Prentice Hall, 2000. (See **www.funkybusiness.com.**)

"The electronic highway is not merely open for business; it is relocating, restructuring, and literally redefining business in America."

Mary J. Cronin

Integrating Real and Virtual Strategies
by David Stauffer

EXECUTIVE SUMMARY

- Today's competitive climate increasingly requires corporations to integrate virtual- (clicks) and physical- (bricks) world initiatives.
- Internally, the corporation's virtual units must drive more business to or through physical facilities, while bricks units must similarly boost virtual channels.
- Externally, customers must be able to interact with the corporation through virtual or physical channels, switch between channels, and receive the same products, services, and prices through any channel.

INTRODUCTION

Not long ago experts predicted the demise of long-established companies as relics of the Industrial Age. Then, as high-tech companies faltered, observers concluded that digital outfits weren't such world-beaters after all.

Today corporations young and old are demonstrating that success in the 21st century may most likely spring not from either old virtues or new technologies, but from a potent blend of the two. The ways in which any business effectively intertwines its real and virtual strategies—its bricks and clicks—uniquely reflect its history and its strengths. But an examination of companies that have successfully married clicks to bricks suggests that the key elements of a blissful union are:

- early and unflagging support from the top of the organization;
- meticulous strategic planning based in part on what other organizations have done;
- a clicks-side operation that strives to boost bricks-side business—and vice versa;
- technology employed not to replace workers, but to empower them;
- a structuring of products, services, and functionalities that allows customers to switch from clicks to bricks and back again at will.

How can you make each of these elements part of your powerfully integrated bricks and clicks strategies? Here are the essentials.

Taking it from the Top

Integrating bricks and clicks involves hard work, insight, and more than a few frustrations. Your effort won't necessarily succeed with the strong backing of corporate leaders.

But it will certainly fail without that backing. Someone at the next level can, and probably should, be put in charge of implementing bricks and clicks integration. But the continuous, driving impetus must be exerted from the top.

Benchmarking and Best Practices

You've probably been advised more times than you can count not to reinvent the wheel. That's in part because it's sound advice endorsed by super-successful C.E.O.s. Former Ford C.E.O. Jacques Nasser borrowed best practices from other industries in leading his organization's bricks and clicks integration. Among his initiatives was setting his managers' sights on emulating the build-to-order business model that made Dell successful. The Net-based enterprise FordDirect.com is structured along lines of Dell's build-to-order concept.

Do some exploring in business publications—on the Web and by networking. Which companies are marrying clicks and bricks in a way you might emulate? Who's strongest where you may be weakest? What opportunities can you offer for a fair exchange of best practices? How can you encourage internal units to exchange their best ideas? Someone has already invented the wheel that's right for you. Find it.

A Virtuous Spiral of Mutual Aid

Provide incentives for your virtual-realm people to drive business to traditional outlets and for facility-based folks to generate online traffic. That's what Office Depot has accomplished. This Delray Beach, Florida office products retailer achieved its bricks

and clicks synergy by getting things right when it first went online.

- *Office Depot made its Web unit an integral and equal part of its overall organization.* "That meant we weren't fighting over who got which customer or made which sales," says Monica Luechtefeld, the company's head of business development and IT. By providing online access to information about store locations and inventory, Office Depot's Web sites have increased store traffic. The stores, in turn, promote the Web sites.
- *Office Depot committed additional time and expense to fully integrate Web functionality with its existing information infrastructure.* Luechtefeld asserts that this is a largely unseen and often neglected strategy that can aid Net success. Now an Office Depot customer, even one new to Web purchasing, has online access to the past 18 months of purchasing history, from bricks as well as clicks.

Office Depot's experience suggests these strategies:

- Provide incentives for extending clicks efforts to the bricks side and vice versa. For example, tie part of sales reps' incentive pay to customer use of e-commerce.
- Make Net-based sales channels equivalent in structure and status to traditional channels.
- Tie Web functionality fully into existing systems as it's introduced.

Technology: It's a People Thing

New technology is often viewed as a way to reduce manpower. Some dot-coms even trumpeted the fact that they needed no employees at all (other than a few geniuses at the top). But some corporations that have achieved the most from emerging technologies view new capabilities as ways to further empower their people.

One of these is Inditex SA of La Coruña, Spain, a manufacturer and global retailer of hip clothes for fashion-conscious young people. Best known for its Zara stores, Inditex employs the clicks of digital technologies to link its people and operations worldwide and thereby boost sales from its bricks— over 2,800 stores on five continents.

"Like the anthropologist returning home from a foreign culture, the voyager in virtuality can return home to a real world better equipped to understand its artifices." Sherry Turkle

Inditex starts with computers in every store, into which managers and sales reps enter notes on their sales-floor observations, not just on what's selling, but on the when, how, and why of selling. Fashion consultants similarly report from the favorite haunts of target customers. All of the input is analyzed in La Coruña by designers and production managers. They're empowered to make decisions on what to make, how to make it, and where to send it. Result: an incredibly short four-week lag between field observations and delivery of new fashions based on those observations.

Instant global communication is the enabler of Inditex's speed. But the key to its success is trusting and empowering employees.

Corporate leaders must provide their people with the technological capabilities that transform them from order takers or bean counters into experts with a stake in contributing to the company's success.

Customers See Only Seamlessness

Do you see new technologies as strange and different channels for conducting business, channels used by strange and different people? If so, you're right—at least in the early stages of a digital initiative.

But experience has increasingly shown that companies make distinctions between bricks-customers and clicks-customers at their peril. For one thing, few customers now dwell in only one of these worlds. And even those who do deal with a corporation through only one channel want the same products and prices offered in the other.

Charles Schwab learned that lesson after it set up its first online unit, e.Schwab, as a separate unit. Online customers got a break on stock-trading fees, but paid for that saving by having access to fewer services than those available to branch-office customers. E.Schwab succeeded at first, but soon stalled. Chairman Charles Schwab told *Forbes*, "Customers didn't feel good about the nonintegrated services."

So Schwab took a gamble by terminating e.Schwab and recognizing the online and offline customer as a single individual. That meant offering the lower online trading fee on the bricks side and extending enhanced

services to the clicks world. Revenues plunged initially, but the gamble eventually paid off in new customers, new assets, and rocketing revenues.

The way to view customers, Schwab's experience shows, is holistically. Whether a customer interfaces with you by bricks, clicks, or both, that customer wants to be equally valued and get equal value. Make sure you provide it.

MINI-CASES
Bricks—Clicks Combinations that Soar

Cemex SA, a Monterrey, Mexico, cement maker that uses global positioning system (GPS) satellite technology to overcome the once-intractable obstacles of traffic and weather, delivering cement to construction sites within a 20-minute window.

Rosenbluth International, a Philadelphia corporate travel manager that used technology to pioneer the call-center concept. It has since incessantly applied technological innovations to automate the tedious aspects of workers' jobs and simultaneously serve customers better.

Snap-on Incorporated, a Kenosha, Wisconsin, manufacturer and distributor of mechanics' tools that uses the Internet to make its dealers the main focus of digital initiatives. Its online catalog recruits new customers for dealers and provides dealer commissions on most sales.

Tesco, the United Kingdom's #1 supermarket chain, which is the world's sole example of a profitable purveyor of foods to customers who place orders online. It's simultaneously growing its bricks side by building ultramodern hypermarkets in Asia and Eastern Europe.

MAKING IT HAPPEN ▸▸
- Launch your bricks and clicks integration with an enthusiastic, ongoing commitment from the top of the organization.
- Explore what other companies have done to make clicks work with bricks. Avoid their missteps; adapt their successes.
- Insist that bricks and clicks become mutually supportive, with incentives on

each side to boost business on the other.
- Implement new technologies, not to replace employees but as a means of benefiting from their ground-level expertise and judgment.
- Blur customers' perceived distinctions between your bricks and clicks channels until they see no distinction.

CONCLUSION

We tend to view technological capabilities as something quite apart from the physical environment of factories, warehouses, trucks, and stores. Accordingly, most companies at first managed their clicks and bricks as nonintersecting universes. We know now that this distinction is not only incorrect, but it misses out on synergies. As bricks and clicks are treated as occupying one world, they can boost each other—and your business—to unprecedented success.

FOR MORE INFORMATION

Books:
Bovet, David, and Joseph Martha. *Value Nets: Breaking the Supply Chain to Unlock Hidden Profits.* New York: Wiley, 2000.
Earle, Nick, and Peter Keen. *From.com to.profit: Inventing Business Models That Deliver Value and Profit.* San Francisco, CA: Jossey-Bass, 2001.
Seybold, Patricia B. *The Customer Revolution: How to Thrive When Customers Are in Control.* New York: Crown, 2001.

Web site:
www.bricksplusclicks.com: the Web site of consultants Bricks Plus Clicks, which provides Internet tools enabling small bricks-and-mortar businesses to bridge the digital divide.

See also:
✔ Collecting Consumer Data on the Internet (pp. 653–654)
✔ Implementing an E-commerce Strategy (pp. 610–611)
✔ Involving Customers in Product or Service Development (pp. 741–742)

The Business Web by Don Tapscott

EXECUTIVE SUMMARY

- In the industrial economy, the basic building block of economic activity was the vertically integrated corporation. These companies performed virtually every function in-house because the cost, risk, and hassle of contracting or partnering with outside companies far outweighed the benefits.
- Because the Internet slashes the cost of sharing knowledge, collaborating, and meshing business processes among corporations, companies can now focus on their core competencies and partner or outsource to do the rest.
- Together, in industry after industry, teams of companies—what I call a "business web"—are proving more supple, innovative, cost-efficient, and profitable than their traditional competitors.

INTRODUCTION

The headline-grabbing dot-com fireworks of the 1990s were largely a distraction, representing only a thin sliver of the businesses exploring the power of the Internet. Unfortunately, a get-rich-quick mindset distorted the assertion that "the Internet changes everything" (which is true) into the hope that "all things done on the Internet will prove lucrative" (which is rubbish).

It's now clear that a new vehicle of wealth creation is supplanting the corporation as the starting point for strategic thinking. It is a system of meshed entities—suppliers, distributors, service providers, infrastructure providers, and customers—using the Internet as the basis for business communications and transactions. Usually one company choreographs the activity and enjoys the lion's share of web profits, but all participants are essential, contributing according to their core competencies.

The key to competing in the digital economy is business model innovation that exploits business web power. Smart companies use the Net to achieve goals they have striven toward for 25 years, focusing on core competencies, reducing transaction costs, innovating more effectively, and gaining new ways to achieve deep customer relationships.

It's clear that profound changes are impacting corporate deep structures. The C.E.O. of Boeing says his company is a systems integrator, not an aircraft manufacturer. LEGO, through its Mindstorm robot products, brings customers into its business web, enabling them to co-create products. Schwab moved from being a tightly integrated financial services provider to an Internet-based aggregator of financial ser-

vices (and stole huge market share!). IBM is a computer company that doesn't manufacture computers—its partners do.

Yet most of this underlying restructuring has either been unnoticed or underappreciated by the financial media and business schools. They remain shellshocked at the rise and collapse of Nasdaq; and since Nasdaq and the New Economy are so frequently (but incorrectly) treated as interchangeable terms, the Nasdaq collapse is often cited as proof that the New Economy is a bogus notion. As for eBay, Amazon, Linux, Napster, and others, they are dismissed as Internet aberrations.

Many executives moving their companies incrementally (and often unconsciously) in the business web direction talk of closer links with customers and how they can now outsource more functions to suppliers because the Internet enables close collaboration. But these efforts often fall short of their potential. Only by addressing the fundamental customer value proposition will the most effective business web construction be evident.

THE LESSONS OF COASE

To understand the superiority of business webs, one must first ask: "Why do companies exist?" If, as Economics 101 suggests, the "invisible hand" of market pricing is the epitome of efficiency, why doesn't it regulate *all* economic activity? Why isn't each person at every step of production and delivery an independent profit center?

Nobel laureate Ronald Coase asked these provocative questions in 1937. Coase blames *transaction costs* for the contradiction between the theoretical agility of the market and the stubborn durability of the

company. Companies incur transaction costs when, instead of using their internal resources, they go to the market for products or services. Transaction costs have three parts, which together—even individually—can be prohibitive.

1 **Search costs.** Finding what you need takes time, resources, and money. Determining whether to trust a supplier adds more costs. Intermediaries who catalog products and product information could historically reduce, but not eliminate, such search costs.

2 **Contracting costs.** If every exchange requires a unique, separate price negotiation and contract, the costs can be totally out-of-whack with the value of the deal.

3 **Coordination costs.** This is the cost of coordinating resources and processes. Coase points out that with "changes like the telephone and the telegraph," it becomes easier for geographically dispersed companies to coordinate their activities.

Coase says that companies form to lighten the burden of transaction costs. He then asks another good question: *"If company organization cuts transaction costs, why isn't everything one big company?"* He answers that the law of diminishing returns applies to company size: big companies are complicated and find it hard to manage resources efficiently. Small companies often do things more cheaply than big ones.

All this leads to what I call "Coase's Law": a company will tend to expand until the costs of organizing an extra transaction within the company become equal to the costs of carrying out the same transaction on the open market. As long as it is cheaper to perform a transaction inside your company, keep it there. But if it's cheaper to go to the marketplace, don't try to do it internally.

BEYOND THE CORPORATION

Despite the Net's dramatic growth in functionality, ubiquity, and bandwidth, it is still primitive. Nevertheless, any business that has tasted its benefits is hooked. No company has integrated the Internet into its business model and concluded the predigital way of doing business was better.

In every sector of the economy the competitive ground has shifted, and business webs are clearly established as the new

"The companies that fully capitalize on the promise of the Internet will be those that look at their businesses as more than building and selling products and services. In the virtual economy, collaboration is a new competitive imperative."

Michael Dell

     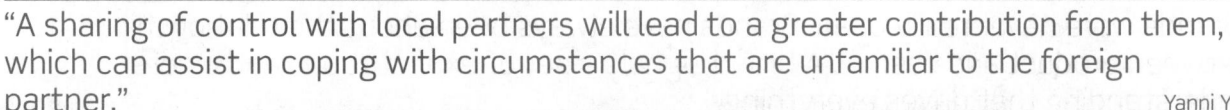

mechanism for winning in the marketplace. To be sure, many companies—of both the Old and New Economies—have set up Web sites and been disappointed by the results. However, a Web site is the digital era equivalent of a business card—nothing more. Businesses that obsess about having "sticky" sites with elaborate multimedia content miss the point.

The power of the business web is that it allows companies to focus on their core competencies. Often the bulk of the employees in a given corporation have nothing to do with the company's core competencies. They attempt to build up and "make do" with design, manufacturing, marketing, and other capabilities that are often not best of breed. Now, with the Net, business functions or large projects can be reduced to smaller components and farmed out (often simultaneously) to more specialized companies around the world, with virtually no transaction costs.

This captures the enormous benefits brought on by the competitive environment. Suppliers strive to reduce costs and increase quality and innovation. They know there are other specialized workers and companies around the world keen to do the work.

By contrast, insisting a project stays in-house often means it is comparatively more difficult to mobilize resources, even with a high-performance intranet. Employees are pressed into jobs unrelated to their skills, as managers try to "make do" with the workers on hand. Alternatively, adding new employees to the payroll is time-consuming and costly. Approvals must be sought, reporting structures developed, workspace arranged, and so on. Every manager knows these internal rigidities increase corporate costs and stifle innovation.

MAKING IT HAPPEN ▶▶

How do you develop a high-performance business web? How do you know which functions to keep or shed? The first step is to disaggregate the value proposition that the end customer receives and experiences. Think about the genuine *customer needs* that your product or service addresses, not just the "thing you do" to get the business. Avoid preoccupation with the production or distribution channels that stand between you and the real customer. Dissect the end customer's experience in terms of your value proposition—as well as the enabling goods, services, resources, business processes, and organizational

structures—into individual components. Honestly face the weaknesses inherent in the Industrial Age mind- and tool-set. Reconfigure the components to radically transform the value proposition for the end customer's benefit.

Ask fundamental questions about the business system in question:

- Why does it exist at all and should it continue to exist?
- Who benefits from it?
- What are its strengths and weaknesses from the customer perspective?
- How could we improve it?
- Who can help us, or who could improve it and kill us?

A business value proposition differs from its products and services. The "value" that a customer needs endures, regardless of the particulars. When a traveler needs to get from A to B, how he gets there matters much less than actually getting there. For your marketspace, what value is offered, delivered, and consumed that justifies a business's right to exist? There are three guidelines:

- Focus on the essence, rather than on a small, fascinating, or rarefied aspect of it. For example, in publishing, describe the underlying value of the publication to readers rather than the printed page or the table of contents.
- Begin with the end in mind, as in how to improve radically the value that the "real" end customer receives from your business. Nothing less will ensure your survival as a winner in the 21st century.
- Prepare and inform all steps of this process with a review and assessment of customer/market/channel trends; supply-side trends; competition; current and expected product/service innovations; industry use of human, relationship, and structural capital; business events (for example, consolidation); environmental issues; and regulation.

Ask the following four questions to drive a "customer-down" approach to the current value proposition:

- Who are your *end customers*, as opposed to intermediary customers? Define the customer categories and who else is serving them, regardless of value proposition.
- What *product* and *service* offerings does the current business system provide its customers?
- From the customer's standpoint, what *value propositions* can you attribute to these product and service offerings?

List only the top ones that come to mind. Once you have listed several dimensions of the value proposition, construct a concise catch-all statement that accommodates all of them. This summary should nail your current business, its *raison d'être*.

- From the end-customer's perspective, what are the main *strengths* and *weaknesses* of the value proposition and the enabling products and services? Who else delivers more value, and in what ways?

CONCLUSION

With business webs, issues such as partnering, distribution channels, industry restructuring, and strategic repositioning are suddenly much more complex. Strategists will no longer look at the integrated corporation as the starting point for value creation. Rather, they will start with a customer value proposition and a blank slate for the production and delivery system. They won't reject value proposals out of hand as being unfeasible, because the art of the possible is dramatically changed through the business web.

FOR MORE INFORMATION

Books and Journal Articles:
Coase, Ronald. *The Firm, the Market, and the Law*. Chicago, IL: University of Chicago Press, 1990.
Downes, Larry, and Chunka Mui. *Unleashing the Killer App: Digital Strategies for Market Dominance*. Cambridge, MA: Harvard Business School Press, 2000.
Malone, Thomas, and Robert J. Laubacher. "The Dawn of the E-lance Economy," *Harvard Business Review*, Volume 76, Issue 5, 1998.

See also:

"A sharing of control with local partners will lead to a greater contribution from them, which can assist in coping with circumstances that are unfamiliar to the foreign partner."

Yanni Yan

Viewpoint: Jeffrey F. Rayport
Making Customer Satisfaction and Loyalty a Managerial Imperative

Introduction

Jeffrey Rayport's academic background in international relations, American civilization, and business history has provided him with an unusual lens through which to explore and analyze the dynamics of an economy increasingly defined by technology. As an associate professor at Harvard Business School in the mid-1990s, his popular courses on e-commerce reflected pioneering research on the relationships between emerging information technologies and service and marketing strategies. Now serving as C.E.O. of Marketspace LLC, a business unit of Cambridge-based Monitor Group, he continues to research, write, consult, and educate on issues of doing business in the networked economy.

When I was just out of high school, I managed to secure what seemed the proverbial nightmare summer job—selling series books over the phone. As it happened, this job turned out to be bizarre and fascinating. The employer was Time-Life Libraries, a unit of what was then Time Inc. (now AOL Time Warner), which sold to consumers across the country.

I was assigned to a small call center in Washington, D.C., where we "outbound telesales reps" would call housewives and retirees across the country to pitch series about gardening and collectibles. We worked in four-hour shifts; mine was 8:00 p.m. to midnight. On that shift, we would change time zones every hour, moving progressively westward from Hartford to Honolulu to ensure that our calls came in just at or past the dinner hour. It was genius.

That telemarketing experience in the 1970s introduced me to business conducted through nonphysical, nontraditional channels. It was, in its own way, a version of electronic or technology-mediated commerce. And the striking thing was how effective it was: intimate, persuasive, and cost-efficient.

At the time, however, this was exactly the battle that was playing out: the war between the telemarketers and the direct mailers. There was little question at the time that this new approach was a powerful alternative to traditional direct-mail marketing. It was easier and more efficient than licking stamps or knocking on doors. What I realized then is the power of technology-based interfaces to substitute for (or even eliminate) face-to-face interactions in business. Technology-mediated interactions enable companies to manage deeper and richer relationships with customers and markets than ever before, whether it's through the phone, the Web, or the ATM. In contrast to my Time-Life days, technology interfaces can do more than enable communication; they're often able to deliver the product or service itself, whether that's music, financial services, textbooks, or any other information products (such as this encyclopedia). That's a radical, mind-bending shift, and we're still only beginning to understand the implications of it.

If the first half of the 20th century involved automation of physical processes (such as manufacturing, assembly, and transport of materials), then the second half involved automation of information processes (such as accounting and control functions, bill paying, and electronic communications). So where are we going from here?

The biggest change we're going to see is technology transforming the "front office" aspects of business enterprise. This may sound like a modest claim, but it is huge.

Most technology revolutions in business have been "back office" affairs until now—involving the automation or reengineering of existing back-office operations, from manufacturing processes on the factory floor to payment processing at corporate headquarters. Indeed, the application of technology to routine tasks is a still-amazing tale of productivity enhancements. The boosts to productivity come in two ways: machines often perform repetitive tasks better than humans; and their deployment in business results in lower operational costs. And now the application of technology to business is entering its most profound phase: its substitution of capital for labor—of machines for people—not just in back offices, but in those aspects of business that touch customers and markets. Where we once marveled at machines' ability to build a car or assemble a PC; now we are entering an age where the machines will come out of the back room. They will manage a company's relationships with us, their customers.

Some may find the idea of a future dominated by

"Brands were never really dead. Brands have always been about the relationship between product and user . . . A brand signals a set of expectations and a core understanding that drives everything."

Shelly Lazarus

machine-mediated interfaces and services cold and impersonal, but smart companies won't let it evolve that way. Even now, it's clear that technology can create highly personal and satisfying service experiences that have a double productivity bonus: they are lower-cost channels than traditional service delivery, and more pleasant and satisfying than people-mediated services. ATMs, for example, have largely replaced the human teller, and few people miss the experience of visiting a bank. Likewise, smart ATM-like gas pumps have improved the gas station experience; Web sites have made booking travel a pleasure; and soon we'll see that a large-format, touch-screen interface will replace the teenage service worker who takes your order at McDonald's or Taco Bell.

This gets even more interesting in the context of faster data interchange. Broadband connections mean richer, smarter, more engaging virtual service providers. In a decade or two, the Taco Bell interface is likely to be more personable for many of us than the real person. The same thing will happen across every sector of services—from fast food to airlines, from medicine to law—in one way or another.

Looking ahead, we will surely mark 2001 as the year when graphics and animation became movie stars. We've long had special effects, but this year two blockbuster movies came to us from the synthetic world of electronic games, and one, "Final Fantasy," involved an entirely lifelike, but thoroughly virtual, cast. It was a big-screen version of what we can expect from many media experiences as they evolve, such as network news (watch Ananova, a virtual newsreader on the Web, who provides frequent updates on demand; if you don't like her hair, change it); operator services (Wildfire, a unit of mobile telephone operator Orange, provides a virtual assistant who lives inside your phone and responds to voice commands; she also makes snide comments and occasionally talks back); directory services (a regional Bell telecommunications company, Verizon, uses voice-recognition-based services from TellMe.com to meet its subscribers' needs without human intervention), and even person-to-person remote communications (a California start-up just announced a holographic form of videoconferencing).

The use of technology to manage and mediate customer relationships can, in many businesses, give managers the tools and data they need to understand evolving customer needs and desires in real time.

Some might argue that delegating customer relationships to technology represents a wholesale abdication by managers of responsibility for customers' experiences. On the contrary, asking a machine to do anything—as any computer programmer knows—requires a deep understanding of the task in hand. To create compelling screen-to-face interfaces requires managers to anticipate much of what the customer will want. Managers need to shift from thinking "How do I sell my product?" to "How do I meet my customer's need?" to "What kind of experiences do I want to enable?"

It makes it essential for managers to be obsessed with the demand side of the business equation (customers and markets), while still maintaining the supply side (delivering products and services).

Of course, the problem is that there is no one final answer regarding customer preferences and needs. They change constantly, just as the market context in which customers experience their preferences also is in a continuous state of dynamic flux. Hence, managerial obsession with customer needs must be continuous, not sporadic. And that is hard work.

There is good news, however.

Consider the TV home-shopping channel QVC, a virtual channel business long before there was a World Wide Web. QVC airs live 24 hours a day, displaying six to ten products an hour and taking incoming calls from viewers to register orders. The channel has little regard for audience ratings because viewership is not the measure of its success; phone calls to its call centers—and converting those calls to orders—is. That means that QVC managers have their finger on the pulse of customers' desires, literally every second. When the phones ring, they know they have a winning product; when the phones don't ring, they know they're marketing something no one wants, and they pull it off the air. Everyone in the company has a real-time awareness of, and ability to react to, the live pulse of the business. The culture and management is driven by demand, not supply.

And it's driven by customer desire in near real time. Real-time tracking of consumer need is the mainspring of the business. Imagine a two-hour delay in QVC's ability to respond to customer trends; this would mean leaving the wrong products on air for too long, promoting them with the wrong hosts, and positioning them at the wrong price points. It is the ability to adjust in real time to the market that makes QVC so successful—and makes it an exciting place not just to shop but to work.

With annual revenues now exceeding $4 billion and margins greatly in excess of any traditional retailer, QVC has a winning model. It's also the model of the future—a demand-driven approach to business. That's why company and manager should aspire to respond in real time to customer demand.

Rational businesspeople have always asked, "What are my resources at hand, and how can I get the most out of my scarcest resource?" Traditionally, that question has been applied to physical and capital resources, and executives have responded with a variety of measurements such as ROI and ROA to keep track of how successful they were. As industry evolved over the last hundred years, firms developed strategies for maximizing returns, such as vertical and horizontal integration, which in turn aimed to maximize a company's access to scarce sources of supply.

These days, supplies of goods and services are abundant. For the half century after World War II, the challenge for companies was making enough products to meet the rising tide of consumer and industrial need. The problem now is reversed; it's sourcing demand. Today, companies face rapid commoditization of products and brands; customers have an endless

"People were sceptical about the new technology. They wanted it to be de-risked."

Jon Florsheim

proliferation from which to choose. Simply put, demand is now the scarce resource.

As a result, it's time to measure success differently. For as long as business requires capital, return on investment and return on assets measures will remain relevant. But in a world where capital is more easily found than customer demand, we should measure success according to return on customer relationship or return on customer desire. In the first case, a company is measuring how much of the full theoretical value of a customer relationship it has successfully realized through a lifetime of interactions. In the second, a company would measure how completely it had harvested, in economic terms, the desires of the customers whose needs it met.

These new "return on" measures would give rise to an entirely new, customer-focused, and demand-centric discussion about how companies plot strategy and establish competitive advantage. Measurements of this kind—and questions of this nature—will change the way we do business. And for our customers to get what they want, this kind of new thinking will be essential.

That means that every manager should ask:

- Who are my customers? How well am I doing at acquiring or retaining them?
- How much is each lifetime relationship worth?
- What share of the lifetime value of each customer is my company realizing?
- How can I raise that proportion?
- In what ways can I increase the duration or enhance the profitability of the relationship?

Companies are valuable because their customer relationships are valuable—and company valuations increasingly will reflect the full value of their portfolio of customer relationships. Paying attention to customer satisfaction and loyalty then becomes an obvious managerial imperative.

So there is no point in asking if you can do well by doing good, or if a company that puts its people first can also make money. Instead, the questions should be "How do we do it?" and "When do we start?"

Some people assume that "doing well by doing good" belongs only in the nonprofit sector. The truth is it's the other way around. When was the last time you flew on an airline where all the staff were rude and then picked up the paper to read that the airline was insanely profitable? Good working environments and good business outcomes go hand in hand.

There are many reasons for this. The obvious is that most people who are happy in their jobs tend to have several attributes in common: they are in the right job; they know the goals; they want to and do learn on the job (training matters, but only for people who care about learning); they have shared values with those around them, and they are in a position to "win" for their customers or accounts.

All of this may seem simple, but it's amazing how few companies realize these basics. Interestingly, it's even more amazing to consider this collection of attributes and identify any one that is not simultaneously good for people and good for business. Would anyone want to work in a job where the fit was no good? Would anyone want to build a career among people without a shared vision, let alone shared values?

Yet the challenge here is more pertinent now than ever before. How people feel on the job matters much more for service businesses than for industrial operations. In the late 19th century, Andrew Carnegie and Henry Frick developed a technique for steel production in their Pittsburgh mills called "hard driving." It meant running furnaces at ruinously high temperatures and working men in the mills long shifts to harvest "abnormally" elevated output. Workers suffered to the point of staging massive strikes, ending in violence. But the steel produced by these workers did not suffer in quality as a function of poor conditions and outraged emotion—only their well-being did. Indeed, for Carnegie's steel business, hard driving made the operation more profitable than ever before, and it shaped industry practices worldwide as a result.

But that was in industrial businesses. In service businesses, there are higher prices to pay for hard driving; service businesses where employees are not happy usually fail. Why? Because success is highly dependent on human factors, the people who interact with the firm's customers. Trite as it may sound, happy employees—in a restaurant, hotel, airline, hospital, bank—make for happy customers. And disgruntled employees do the opposite. Of course, there is a danger of our repeating some of these disastrous lessons in the service sector as we deploy technology to run customer relationships for companies. A kiosk at a fast-food restaurant for order-entry can run "hard" without any adverse consequences, but only to the machine itself. Most services ultimately connect machines to people, just as the kiosk helps consumers place orders that human workers must assemble, package, and deliver to the register.

So there is a lesson here: always in business, there is a human factor. And that means that goodness (how companies treat employees) should always correlate with wellness (how companies perform for stakeholders). Yet technology can sometimes make it easy to forget this.

These ideas are important to keep in mind, especially regarding the service sector, not least because it represents more than four-fifths of gross domestic product output in the United States and a similar proportion in most other industrialized countries. Moreover, among industrial firms the largest numbers of jobs are generally in service positions. Put these together, and we are describing, pure and simple, a service economy. That means that we compete on people. And in service businesses this comes down to how workers feel, what they find motivating, and how well we equip them, with technology and otherwise, for success with their customers.

FOR MORE INFORMATION

Web site:
Marketspace: **www.marketspaceglobal.com**

Making B2B Your New Operational Standard by Michael J. Cunningham

EXECUTIVE SUMMARY

- Why should transaction and collaborative commerce systems co-exist?
- How can they be used to improve productivity across the enterprise and supply chains?
- How are work practices changing as a result of these technologies?

INTRODUCTION

Given the challenges of the marketplace today, executives are looking for solutions that will give them a key advantage over their competitors. Part of this advantage is clearly based on identifying ways to use technology and innovative work practices to improve productivity, reduce costs, and improve service to employees, partners, and consumers. Understanding business-to-business collaboration technologies and how they integrate with transaction systems is one way to gain a competitive edge.

WHY COLLABORATIVE COMMERCE IS IMPORTANT

Collaborative commerce technology is the glue that keeps employees, customers, and partners communicating and informed. In particular, the rise of self-service applications that deliver relevant information to those that need it has created tremendous value over recent years.

Market Conditions

Market conditions are changing faster than they ever have, yet we seem to find it harder than ever to adapt and deal with these changes. Despite the fact that information technology solutions are mature and available, the gap between the organization that wins the first time out and the others continues to widen. How can operations such as COVISINT create tremendous value using technology to support their business needs, yet others spend millions and still fail to get it right?

Many organizations today are concerned about the possibility of failure with their e-business systems. Given the dramatic change in market conditions during 2000 and 2001, confusion has continued to reign supreme in many e-business decision cycles across the globe. Often, it appears that the very large benefits to be gained from e-business technologies are reaped when a combination of technologies are deployed in unison. For example, many companies now understand that implementing customer relationship management (CRM) technologies *without* a supporting knowledge base creates only another touch point for information, and not high-impact benefits. The latter are created only when technology and support systems work in harmony to provide relevant information to the person who needs it.

ACCELERATION

The e-business economy, often cited initially as a separate market, is increasingly being recognized as a hybrid. Existing business operations and practices mutate into new forms, some recognizable from earlier business models, while others change much more dramatically. The successful systems that develop from this strategy focus on accelerating both the business relationship and the cycle.

Leading suppliers in today's economy not only embrace the concept of change; they aggressively try to modify the behavior of a marketplace. The successful ones mix a potent cocktail that includes:

- knowledge of how their market (or supply chain) is currently working, and consequently what needs changing;
- a desire to collapse entire existing business processes and systems, or segments thereof (such as supply chains, work processes, decision cycles);
- technology to effect the change;
- marketing and distribution skills to deliver the new product;
- partnership with others to gain rapid adoption of the new model;
- the ability to change and support new work processes and practices to build solutions.

The business benefits associated with these changes are not only desirable, they are also strategic weapons for e-business systems.

COLLABORATIVE CONTACT

By connecting the power of collaborative commerce tools with tools that build, deliver, and manage the procurement or sales process, significant benefits can be leveraged from buyer and supplier relationships. Many e-business relationships begin by automating the procurement process, so optimizing these relationships using additional tools may seem like a natural extension. However, because the entry points and reasons for collaborative commerce are often separate, many organizations miss out on the benefits of a more integrated strategy. Using collaborative commerce often creates opportunities to improve the efficiency of business relationships, and can radically cut costs and unnecessary steps out of existing processes.

Over time, the effectiveness of any business relationship can be easy to measure. However, seeing what is failing and where improvements need to be made in the short term is much more difficult and is often only visible once serious problems arise.

Using collaborative commerce as a means of communication can help in identifying and resolving these issues rapidly. In addition, the development of the relevant content bases, training materials, and support procedures can often accelerate the speed at which the buying, supply, and sales processes become integrated, reducing the potential for misunderstandings and problems along the way.

TRANSACTION SYSTEMS

Over the last couple of years, the use of the Internet as the basis for transaction tools has expanded. The transaction tools developed include marketplaces, auctions, Web-based EDI, and electronic catalogs. Compared to traditional EDI, transaction systems affect a greater number of phases in procurement or selling life cycles. The good news, however, is that the RFQ, proposal responses, and communication between purchaser and supplier can all be conducted electronically. This cuts the time required to complete the evaluation phases and the supporting tools allow the specialist to manage relationships with more suppliers or customers.

COLLABORATION TOOLS

The tools discussed thus far support import-

"I would advise young companies, particularly the small dot.com companies, to pay close attention to their service levels."

Lillian Vernon

ant phases in the transaction life cycle. They fit within an organization's processes and support certain tasks; in general, they do not require the company to make large process or organizational changes to utilize them. Collaborative tools extend beyond the task level to all the phases in the transaction life cycle.

It is important to view them as modules that fit together to form solutions. These modules are often extensions of existing systems or other collaboration tools. For example, a workflow system will utilize e-mail to notify individuals that they need to take action. These are not a replacement for transaction systems. Rather, they are a way of extending the information and value of a transaction system throughout the enterprise and beyond to its trading partners. By implementing these tools to complement transactions systems, an organization will create a collaborative transaction network.

The collaborative transaction network gives all members of the trading network access to data. Even more importantly, it extends the knowledge of the specialist throughout the life cycle and in other major organization processes.

Until recently, most of the technology being implemented by corporations to aid transaction life cycles has been complementary to existing processes. Organizations have successfully implemented EDI and e-business systems without making significant organizational or process changes. This is no longer enough. In order to stay ahead, companies must not only implement new transaction technology, but must also review and change their work processes and the supporting collaborative technology.

MAKING IT HAPPEN ▸▸
Work processes

Assessing the effect of new technologies on operational processes begins with a clear understanding of the capabilities being introduced. Most corporations understand that potential benefits can be achieved through systems that facilitate staff interaction with critical information and processes. However, enhanced or newly-enabled capabilities to access information, obtain status, self-serve, and collaborate can dramatically affect not only productivity of existing procurement processes, but the manner in which the work is conducted.

Best practices are emerging from the ability to apply one, or a combination, of these newly developed methods to existing transaction requirements. For example, proactive, real-time polling

supports the ability to maintain point-of-use restocking and pay-on-consumption/receipt systems. Access to EDI or Web-linked information provides the ability to share demand forecasts and resource schedules. Self-service capabilities enable supplier-managed inventories and supplier self-qualification systems.

Procurement driven by function

At this stage of development, transaction systems effectively increase a corporation's ability to procure high-quality items at the right time and place and at a fair price. Supply chain activities have evolved as a series of tasks integrated by processes and systems designed to take advantage of advances in connectivity and enterprise-wide databases.

Supply chain integration

More significant improvements often stem from enhanced capabilities in sourcing, procurement, and materials management. Representative strategies include:

- workflow facilitated and self-service processes that provide increased transparency and accessibility between purchasing, suppliers, and materials management
- sole sourcing, supplier pre-qualification, and dynamic bidding processes that tend to lower the acquisition cost of procured items
- coordinated forecasting, planning, and component replenishment processes that tend to lower the retained cost of procured items.

These benefits dramatically improve the efficiency and effectiveness of work processes required to attain business goals. As such, they can be characterized as "collaborative-based" processes that utilize the increased connectivity, accessibility, self-service, and parallel-processing capabilities of new transaction-based solutions.

These types of collaborative strategies tend to de-emphasize the impact and inefficiencies found in serial supply chain operations, through the promotion and use of enhanced data accessibility, concurrent processing, and mutual accountability. Reflecting a more holistic supply chain approach, these systems and strategies increase productivity through the use of new processes that enable tasks to be accomplished simultaneously.

Trading partner benefits

Effective collaboration tends to reduce overall process cycles and costs by improving the level of accountability, and monitoring and controlling duplicate activities. All parties have to realize process efficiencies rather than bottom-line pricing as a primary source for operational savings. Once freed of historic concerns and boundaries, collaborative transaction systems establish the beachhead for a wide variety of strategies leading toward the benefits of comprehensive supply chain integration. Among the most important will be those that link with back office ERP systems and real-time, automated transaction settlement. Ultimately, the benefits should result in lower inventories, faster processes, and higher-quality products and services.

The stakes are particularly high for systems like e-procurement and collaborative commerce that involve increased cooperation with clients and business partners. While traditional EDI has been at the leading edge for some businesses in the past, Internet-based systems open the door for almost any organization to revolutionize the way it does business. For many, changing the way they do things is more than just an opportunity—it will be a necessity for staying in business.

CONCLUSION

- It is essential for executives around the globe to understand the opportunity presented by the combination of collaborative commerce technologies and revised business processes.
- Just "waiting for it to happen around them" may produce very undesirable results.
- The competitive edge will go to those who understand and exploit these technologies and who change their business practices to leverage them in the marketplace.

FOR MORE INFORMATION

Books:
Cunningham, Michael. *B2B: How to Build a Profitable e-Commerce Strategy.* Cambridge, MA: Perseus, 2002.
King, Dave, Jae Kyu Lee, Efraim Turban, and Dennis Veihland. *Electronic Commerce: A Managerial Perspective.* 4th ed. London: Financial Times Prentice Hall, 2005.
McKay, Judy, and Peter Marshall. *Strategic Management of eBusiness.* New York: Wiley, 2004.

"Dotcom will become in our corporate language like Inc. or Co. or Corp.—a generic way of describing a company, in this case a company that does business on the Internet."

Clive Chajet

Marketspaces by Jeffrey F. Rayport

EXECUTIVE SUMMARY

- With the advent of new communications technologies, most notably the Internet, the traditional marketplace has expanded into a new, virtual sphere of management and commerce: the market*space*.
- The marketspace is exerting an increasingly profound impact on business strategy, particularly on the ways companies interact with their customers.
- Though technology enables the marketspace, successful companies will treat technology not as an end in itself, but as one among many components in their overall strategy to build and manage customer relationships.

INTRODUCTION

From the Athenian agora to the mall of America, the places where buyers and sellers negotiate their transactions have for thousands of years been just that: places. But over the past two centuries, and especially since the advent of the Internet and the World Wide Web, technology has given rise to an alternative to the marketplace: the virtual market*space*.

More and more transactions that once took place only in the marketplace now occur in the marketspace, largely free from the bonds of space and time. As a result, there are exponentially greater opportunities—and expectations—for deeper, more frequent interactions between companies and customers. With the growth of a service-based economy in which products are increasingly commoditized and differentiation ever-harder to achieve, successfully managing company-to-customer interactions is not just advisable—it's critical. Indeed, there is a dialectic between the rise of the marketspace and the growth of the service-based economy: each feeds, and feeds off of, the other and they must be considered together.

Thus, the marketspace presents both challenges and opportunities. Companies that either underestimate (the Internet is overhyped; nothing much has changed) or overestimate (technology changes everything; all the old rules of business are obsolete) its significance stand to suffer. On the other hand, companies that understand that the marketspace demands creative new strategies, yet relentlessly test those strategies against fundamental principles of service management, are likely to prosper. Even in the technology-enabled marketspace, using service to manage relationships with customers will only become a greater virtue.

FROM MARKETPLACE TO MARKETSPACE

A marketplace consists of three basic components:
- sellers, offering something of value (goods, services, or information);
- buyers, offering something of value in return (cash or any of the above);
- a physical location (store, exchange) where the two come together.

In the marketspace, buyers, sellers, and the value they exchange remain the same, but the time and space constraints disappear. In the marketspace, their transactions take place virtually any time, anywhere, thanks to a variety of technology-mediated interfaces (not just the Web) such as the telephone, wireless device, and personal computer. If a transaction takes place and you cannot say with confidence *where* it occurred, it happened in the marketspace.

One could say that the marketspace was born more than 150 years ago, the first time that a lone Morse code operator telegraphed an order to a supplier. Succeeding generations of communications technology—telephone, fax, pager, cell phone, even the fast-food drive-through microphone—expanded the universe of transactions that could take place outside of the marketplace.

The marketspace as we know it today is chiefly enabled by the kind of "screen-to-face" interactions offered by the Internet in general and the Web in particular. It should be noted, however, that the first (and still one of the most successful) screen-to-face technology predates the Web by more than a decade in the form of the humble ATM. In spitting out cash at more and more locales around the world, the automated teller machine performed first, on a widespread basis, what many marketspace interfaces are doing today: it represented a substitute of capital for labor, thus threatening to make bank tellers an endangered species.

Banks originally positioned ATMs as a service channel for their least profitable customers, assuming that account holders with substantial means would continue to talk with live tellers. They soon discovered, however, that customers of all stripes enjoyed banking at the machines—and the number of machines, networks linking them, and services they provided mushroomed. The result of retail banking's shift from marketplace to marketspace was nothing less than a transformation of the entire industry's competitive dynamics. As the ATM became the dominant interface between customer and company, consumer loyalty to individual bank brands eroded. The network trumped the brand as the locus of both customer relationships and economic value, which is why we are more interested in spotting Cirrus or NYCE on the side of an ATM than a placard for our particular bank.

By the early 1990s, even before the emergence of the Web, virtual channels were beginning to transform businesses and industries and create significant new sources of value. This is why, in 1992, fellow Harvard Business School professor John Sviokla and I, convinced that the old paradigms for teaching the first-year marketing course were increasingly outmoded, sat down and hatched a new term (and a new course) to describe the brave new business world: marketspace.

Since that afternoon, bubble economies and Wall Street manias have come and gone. But today, I have no doubt that the marketspace is a very real and powerful phenomenon—one that is here to stay.

THE MARKETSPACE *IS* TRANSFORMING BUSINESS

Just as the ATM changed the competitive dynamics of the banking industry, the emergence of the (so far) ultimate screen-to-face interactive medium—the Internet—represented an opportunity for radical reengineering and productivity gains across

the full breadth of the economy. Today, it is the Internet that is the key technology enabling and propelling the explosive growth of the marketspace.

The Impact of the Internet and Technology

The Internet allows millions of customers to interact with a company at any hour, from any place, via millions of distributed digital interfaces, on devices such as the PC. At any given moment, for example, thousands of people from around the world are simultaneously logged on to Amazon.com, buying CDs, selling food processors, browsing books, comparing prices, applying for credit cards, downloading music, registering for wedding gifts, sending electronic greeting cards and so on. Much like the back-office reengineering revolution of the 1980s, the Internet represents a front-office reengineering revolution. It allows—in fact, it *mandates*—a ground-up rethinking of how companies interact with and create experiences for their customers. What drives this rethinking is clear from the success of automated-interface businesses, from banking with ATMs to bidding on auctions at eBay. It's no longer frontline service workers who have a monopoly on management of customer relationships in the service sector—it's machines that are increasingly doing the managing.

The widespread deployment of technology makes deep insight into customer experience possible, and necessary. Literally and figuratively, screen-to-face interactions augment the value of service, making it possible for companies to deliver service at lower cost and at higher quality. In a sector that has long been characterized by diseconomies of scale, machine-mediated interactions make scale economies possible. Given the importance of the service sector in the world's economies—it represents more than 80% of gross domestic product output in the United States, for example—this is a revolution of real magnitude and scope. Moreover, customer relationship management via machine gives businesses around the world a competitive weapon at a time in economic history when service is more crucial than ever.

The Rise of Mass Personalization

With the accelerating commoditization of products and brands, it is not supply, but customer demand, that is the scarcest and most valuable resource. As we continue to move toward a service-centered economy, companies are increasingly dependent on the quality of their customer relationships.

Even for product-based businesses, service, more and more, is the key differentiator. Such iconic brands as IBM and Xerox that once made their money selling boxes (mainframe computers and copying machines) now sell those boxes at a loss; they rely almost exclusively on follow-on service, maintenance plans, financing, and even consulting services for their margins (indeed, the lion's share of IBM revenue is derived from services). Even Microsoft, famous for its ruthless pursuit of profit, has launched its game console, the Xbox, with a business plan for our times. Analysts estimate that every Xbox sold will cost Microsoft nearly $200 in negative margin, but that Microsoft will make up the difference—and ultimately reach profitability on the platform—by selling games, upgrades, and networking services.

That's why personalization has become such a hot concept; it's the ultimate frontier in the delivery of human-mediated or technology-mediated services. And, once again, technology can help marketers defy commoditization by enabling deeper and richer relationships with customers than ever before. For example, technology known as collaborative filtering allows online retailers to predict the products and services their customers may want to buy, based on their previous choices and on the preferences of other like-minded consumers. Or take Ritz-Carlton: the upscale hotelier can elevate its renowned personal service to new heights through its online customer database. A consumer who has stayed only at the Ritz in San Francisco, for example, can walk into its Washington, D.C., property to find that her credit-card and frequent-flier numbers, preference for non-smoking rooms, and desire for an extra chocolate on her pillow have preceded her. Can other high-end hotel chains afford not to follow suit? Clearly, companies that fail to exploit the power of marketspace technology to make them more customer-centric are forfeiting a key competitive advantage.

... But Success in the Marketspace Means Paying Attention to the Fundamentals

The advent of the marketspace has already had a significant impact on business—particularly on the way that companies interact with their customers. However, that does not mean (as was famously proclaimed about the Web not long ago) that the marketspace exists independently of the fundamental laws of economics. In the end, the marketspace is not about new rules for a new economy, nor even about the Internet

or the Web; it is about using the tools of digital technology to achieve a fundamental goal that is as old as the marketplace itself: the creation and nurturing of profitable customer relationships.

In the marketspace, just like the marketplace, the name of the game is providing value to customers; if anything, the marketspace makes the age-old business axiom "serve the customer" even more paramount. Technology must be used to create customer interfaces that deliver higher levels of customer-perceived value (relative to competitive offerings), thus driving rising levels of satisfaction and loyalty. The challenge for managers is to understand the full spectrum of interfaces available to them—both screen-to-face (online) and face-to-face (offline)—as well as how to manipulate those interfaces to optimize the customer's experience.

Technology, in other words, is simply another, albeit immensely powerful, business tool. Successful managers will seek out new and creative ways to integrate it into their company's overall strategy to build and manage strong, loyal customer relationships in a high impact yet cost-effective manner.

MINI-CASES
eBay
By bringing together buyers and sellers who would likely never meet in a physical place, the auction Web site eBay has become one of the best-known and most successful marketspace enterprises. Sellers list their wares in eBay's databases, which are then searched by prospective buyers. Technology facilitates the transactions: would-be buyers can sign up to be notified by e-mail when the object of desire comes up for auction, and they can have their bids automatically set (and reset and reset, as the bidding warrants). It makes little difference whether seller and buyer live across town or across the globe; they are linked by the electronic network of the Internet. In the end, eBay connects physical entities (people and products), but it does so in a highly efficient manner. It outsources to customers all the physical aspects of doing business—merchandising, inventory management, inventory carrying costs, shipping and handling, and logistics—thus keeping its margins extremely high. Moreover, eBay's reach and efficiency would be impractical, or even impossible, to realize in the physical world.

Charles Schwab
With the launch of Schwab.com in January 1998, discount broker Charles Schwab became one of the first companies in the

brokerage sector—or in the general retailing sector—to create integrated online and off-line offerings. When it did so, it kept its eye squarely on the customer, not the technology. Its Web site, for example, was designed not to showcase technological bells and whistles, but to provide easy-to-find, quick-to-download information to its core customer segment: the investor who wants to make fast, informed investment decisions without paying for advice. Ultimately, by embracing the Internet while staying focused on its customers, Schwab was able to use technology to offer superior service at lower prices to its target segment. Moreover, Schwab was the first to demonstrate unequivocally that the marketspace extends and augments the marketplace, but seldom replaces it. A case in point: Schwab's success online was real, but research showed that two-thirds of new accounts, which would be accessed largely online, were nonetheless opened offline. As a result, even at the height of the Internet boom, when retail banks were closing branch offices by the dozen, Schwab was building new offices in key locations. Schwab drew the blueprint for the integration of the physical and the virtual—offline and online—for consumer-facing businesses.

MAKING IT HAPPEN ▸▸

As we have outlined, building and managing customer relationships is at the same time increasingly important, reliant on technology, and complex. Some of the issues to consider may include:

- **How the Internet is shifting the balance of power to your customers.** It is important to realize that customers are now much more able than ever before to choose from a global marketspace, and as a result are often much more demanding in their expectations for service. The Internet offers customers richness and reach at the same time. E-commerce blurs the traditional trade-off between reaching large sections of customers with limited information, and only a few customers with large amounts of information.
- **The Internet is revolutionizing sales techniques and perceptions of established brands**—what are the consequences, either risks or opportunities, for your business in terms of such issues as the ability to sense customer needs and to build brand loyalty?
- **Modern marketspaces are now open 24/7.** The pace of business activity and change is rapidly accelerating, and the need to be flexible, adaptive, customer-focused, and innovative is now at a premium. The Internet compresses time and it is useful to consider how well-prepared and configured your business is. First, the Internet is always available and working; second, there is a culture of urgency and the ability to elicit immediate feedback, if required; and finally, the issue of immediacy means that issues, both trivial and important, need to be actioned swiftly as the trivial can fast become urgent.
- **There is a premium on managing knowledge.** Now more than ever, managing and leveraging knowledge is a key skill, and knowledge is a vital strategic resource that needs to be nurtured and developed.
- **Is it possible to extend the business in order to add value for current and potential customers?** Many organizations are now able to reevaluate factors as fundamental as their objectives, markets, and competencies, all of which may have been altered by the new marketspace opportunities and realities.
- **The Internet is increasing interactivity among people, customers, companies and industries.** It may help to assess the extent to which your business can—and could—forge new, valuable links with key groups.

CONCLUSION

These days, the traditional marketplace has a virtual counterpart: the marketspace. The advent of the marketspace fundamentally alters the ways companies can interact with, and manage, their customers. Companies must refine their corporate strategy accordingly. The proliferation of technology-mediated or "screen-to-face" service interfaces offers myriad opportunities for companies to manage customer relationships both more efficiently and more effectively. In this era of ever-accelerating competition and commoditization, service is the ultimate weapon.

FOR MORE INFORMATION

Books:
Gershenfeld, Neil A. *When Things Start to Think*. New York: Owl Books, 2000.
Heskett, James L., et al. *The Service Profit Chain: How Leading Companies Link Profit and Growth to Loyalty, Satisfaction and Value*. New York: Free Press, 2003.
Kurzweil, Ray. *The Age of Spiritual Machines: When Computers Exceed Human Intelligence*. New York: Penguin, 2000.
McLuhan, Marshall. *Understanding Media: The Extensions of Man*. New York: MIT Press, 1994.
Rayport, Jeffrey F., and Bernard J. Jaworski. *e-Commerce*. New York: McGraw-Hill/Irwin, 2000.

"At its most basic level, a market represents an agreement between two people. For that market to sustain long-term health, those two people must honor that agreement . . . it's useless if basic trust does not exist."

Arthur J. Levitt, Jr.

Creating a Company Web Site That Delivers Real Value
by Gerry McGovern

EXECUTIVE SUMMARY

- Boom or bust, hype or not, the Internet has become a fundamental tool of business.
- Unfortunately, many organizations still treat their Web sites like a glorified brochure or a dumping ground for content.
- One of the best ways to manage your Web site is to focus on the key tasks your customers wish to complete.

INTRODUCTION

Every day customers are leaving Web sites, turned off by out-of-date, poor quality content. People would never leave bowls of rotting fruit in their reception, yet they constantly leave out-of-date content on their Web sites.

The Web is a very functional, task-driven place. A Web site works best when it helps people complete important tasks quickly and simply. The Web is all about self-service, and self-service works best with a clean, no-frills design. To ensure that your Web site delivers real value, focus on what your customer genuinely needs from it. Avoid marketing fluff and get straight to the point. Remember, the word that best describes people when they're on the Web is: IMPATIENT!

E-COMMERCE AND COMMERCE

The key difference between e-commerce and commerce is that commerce is selling with people, while e-commerce is selling with content. In traditional commerce there is a lot of flexibility because people are involved. The customer can ask questions. The sales person can support and guide. Often, the customer isn't sure what they want. It's said that great selling is having a customer walk into a store wanting to spend $100 on one item, and walking out happy having spent $500 on five items.

The problem with commerce is that it can involve a lot of inefficient and costly processes. The classic "old-time" commerce example is the local shop. This was the ultimate in relationship marketing. The friendly shop owner knew everybody and was always ready for a chat. The local shop

was all well and good, but the big supermarket replaced it because it gave the customer more choice at cheaper prices.

E-commerce is like bringing the big supermarket idea to its logical conclusion. A professional e-commerce Web site has the content required to answer your questions. What price is it? Is there a discount if I buy ten? What size does it come in? What are its key features? When is it available? How long does it take to deliver? What do other customers think of it? What kind of reviews has it received in the media?

E-commerce is difficult to do right. An e-commerce Web site has to be as simple as possible to use, while having a robust and reliable back-end, and a depth of content that answers the most important questions customers have. It has become clear that no matter how well designed the Web site is, customers are often wary of purchasing particularly high-ticket items online. They like to talk to or e-mail someone if only to know that there are "real" people running the operation. So, perhaps ironically, one of the most important parts of your Web site will be your contact section. (Just make sure that when people send you an e-mail, you get back to them promptly.)

An e-commerce strategy becomes more effective when:

1 the company is already an established brand;
2 the company can efficiently combine its offline assets with its Web site;
3 the product requires relatively little human support to sell;
4 the customer does not wish to touch and feel the product;
5 the product can be delivered electronically (software, music);

6 the product can be well described by written content and simple images;
7 the cost of delivery for the product is a small percentage of its price;
8 the product is targeted at an affluent, highly educated marketplace;
9 the product is niche, with its customer-base geographically spread.

CLICKS 'N' MORTAR: THE BEST OF BOTH WORLDS

Launching a Web site is like opening a shop on the North Pole. Nobody knows you're there. So, if you're a new brand, don't expect that when you launch your Web site, lots and lots of visitors will come rushing in.

Those businesses that combine their offline business assets with their Web site increase their chances of success. A clicks 'n' mortar strategy combines the distribution and physical presence strengths of the offline business with the convenience of online shopping. The result is better service and reduced cost of sale. Dell, for example, found that people who had visited its Web site and then rang Dell, were converted into purchasers quicker than people who had not visited the Web site.

MINI-CASES

Ryanair.com is, in my view, one hell of an ugly Web site. It is also one of the most profitable and fastest growing airlines in the world. It does most of its bookings through its "ugly" site. Here's a little secret. People are cheap, and they are particularly cheap when they're on the Web. Many of the most successful Web sites heavily discount because that's a key aspect of the self-service model. Amazon discounts, and what is eBay if not the biggest discount store in the world? Pile 'em high, sell 'em cheap works well on the Web.

Google has a very simple homepage. Just a big search box. Google does a lot more than search. Here's a small sample of what else it does: Alerts, Local, Answers, Maps, Blog Search, Mobile, Book Search, News, Catalogs, Scholar, etc. Does Google clutter up its homepage with all these secondary ser-

---

"The rush by marketers to establish World Wide Web sites at times resembled the Gold Rush that sent the 49ers west in search of riches."

Stan Rapp

vices? No. It knows that people are highly impatient and want to quickly find the primary thing they came to a Web site for. What is the primary reason people come to *your* site? Put it on the homepage.

Istockphoto.com is a wonderful example of a Web business. You can buy royalty-free top-class stock photography for a couple of dollars. Istockphoto.com does something many of the successful Web businesses have done: it brings together thousands of buyers and sellers in a well-organized marketplace. Photographers can easily add their images. People looking to buy are given lots of powerful tools to search, organize, and buy. Everything is kept as simple as possible, including the copyright notice! Istockphoto.com is just one more reason why the Web is here to stay.

Intranets: Making Your Staff More Productive

A good quality intranet can deliver cost savings while improving staff productivity. Intranets shift the business away from manual processes to self-service ones, thus reducing costs. If an intranet is well planned and organized, it can help staff complete key business tasks more quickly, thus making them more productive.

Unfortunately, intranets have rarely reached their full potential within organizations. To tap their full potential, make sure you focus on the following:

- **good management.** Managers—particularly senior managers—need to develop clear intranet strategies. For an intranet to succeed, it must have proper senior management buy-in.
- **quality content.** Many intranets are used as dumping grounds for poor quality content. Remember, you want quality, not quantity here. Less is more. Don't let your intranet becomes a mess of links on the

homepage, and the home for substandard material you wouldn't want to be seen elsewhere.

- **your staff.** Don't let your intranet become a haven for vanity publishing. What are the most important tasks your staff come to your intranet to complete? Make sure they can complete them as quickly and efficiently as possible.

MAKING IT HAPPEN ▶▶

The Internet is here to stay. Properly used it can increase efficiency and drive profit. However, it is no magic wand that for little cost and effort will transform your company. Like most other things in business, it rewards long-term planning and hard work.

Here are five principles that will be useful when you are developing your Internet strategy:

1 **Be customer-centric.** Find out what your customer really needs from your Web site. Focus relentlessly on these needs, rather than the internal politics of your organization.
2 **Content is critical.** Maximize its value. In terms of content management, manage the content, not the software. If commerce is selling with people, then e-commerce is selling with content.
3 **Simplicity.** Keep it simple. Again, quality, not quantity, is what you should be aiming for. Make your Web site less cluttered so that things are easier to find. Remember, people are impatient and their favorite button is "Back" . . .
4 **Task completion.** What are the three most important tasks people come to your Web site to complete? Measure how long it takes them to successfully complete these tasks.

5 **Leadership.** Successful Web sites require genuine management and leadership. You must have a vision and then communicate that vision in a clear and compelling manner.

CONCLUSION: THINK PUBLISHING

A Web site is a publication. An Intranet is a publication of vital content for staff, just as an Extranet is for suppliers, and an Internet Web site is for customers. A quality Web site allows staff, customers, and all relevant stakeholders to complete the tasks they came to the Web site to complete. They complete these tasks by reading content.

When all the hype is drained away, the day-to-day job of a Web site is about delivering the right content to the right person at the right time at the right cost. Such content will help staff work smarter. It will make customers more educated about the organization's products, and thus more likely to purchase.

The best Web sites keep it simple. The best Web strategies are fully integrated with the organization's overall strategies.

FOR MORE INFORMATION

Books:
McGovern, Gerry. *Killer Web Content*. London: A & C Black, 2006.
Nielsen, Jakob. *Designing Web Usability: The Practice of Simplicity*. Indianapolis, IN: New Riders, 2000.

Web sites:
Alexa.com: **www.alexa.com**
MarketingProfs.com
www.marketingprofs.com

See also:
☆ Blogs and Business: What You Must Know (pp. 194–195)

"I could see the Internet was going to be massive so clearly having your own identity seemed obvious."

Jason Drummond

194

BEST PRACTICE

Blogs and Business: What You Must Know
by Andy Wibbels

EXECUTIVE SUMMARY

- Blogs are instantly, easily updated Web sites that help businesses save time, money, strengthen customer relationships and improve search engine ranking. More and more companies are using blogs inside and outside the organization for quick publishing and communication.

INTRODUCTION
What Exactly Is A Blog?

In the past several years, blogs have gone from the geek underground to a main attraction for media, marketers and businesses. Talking heads babble on the TV about "what the bloggers are saying" and companies are flummoxed on how they can leverage blogs to promote and grow their business. Blog is short for "web-log." A blog is an easily, frequently and instantly updatable Web site. It looks like an online diary with the most recent entries (called *posts*) on the front page leading to monthly or categorized archives. Each entry has its own Web page and can have a comments form for readers to talk back to the author to agree (or rebut) their ideas. Blog posts are written in a warmer, more informal voice than a traditional, sterile corporate Web site and can give readers a more personal and conversational impression of a company.

HOW BLOGS WORK

Usually blogs are dismissed as diaries or the realm of rabid political punditry, but that misses the big deal: a blog can be updated anytime, anywhere from any Internet connection on any computer in the world. You log in to the system that manages your blog (called a *blog platform*) and fill out a simple online form with your latest post. You then click "publish" and within seconds your post is available online for anyone in the world to read. Further, the blog platform updates the blog's front page and re-shuffles the archives automatically. This leaves you to get back to managing your business-not your Web site. You can always go back and edit or revise your posts as needed and accept, remove, or moderate any comments. You can also easily add links, pictures, audio, and video to your blog to make it a multimedia presence.

THE ADVANTAGE OF BLOGS

The four main reasons that businesses turn to blogs are to save time, save money, strengthen customer relationships, and improve search engine ranking.

Because updating a blog doesn't require the intervention of the IT overlords in your company, you are able to save time, routing around a labored change control process. Since a blog allows you to publish online with inexpensive software, you don't have to wait for your Web designer to get off from Starbucks which will also save you money. Because of the informal voice of blogs, they can provide a warmer face to the client, increasing trust and reputation. Finally, the underlying architecture of a blog's pages make them fantastic for instant search engine optimization, which will enable you to rank higher in relevant online searches.

USING BLOGS INSIDE THE COMPANY

In addition to the main advantages of blogs, they can also be used inside a company in the following ways.

- **Project management.** Blogs can provide an instant snapshot of a project's status, an archive of past reports and an easier way to access deliverables. You won't be annoying your employees by clogging their inbox with an eight gigabyte PDF.
- **Intranet news.** Internal announcements and initiatives from the top brass can be communicated faster and managed more easily across business units or down the organization.
- **Knowledge management.** Blogs can be used for sharing industry research, test-driving ideas, and documenting policies and procedures. Information can be quickly published, categorized and archived in an instantly searchable database.
- **Organizational development and learning.** Blogs can function as touch-points for manager development, performance management and on-the-job training so that employees can share what they are learning and how it is impacting their performance.
- **Distributed workgroups.** With project teams scattered around the world, a blog can provide an instant update on status and needs as the workday moves from time zone to time zone. Collaborative features help collect ideas, provide version control, distribute deliverables, and track dependencies.

USING BLOGS OUTSIDE THE COMPANY

Blogs are great inside the enterprise but become even more useful when unleashed outside the organization chart.

- **Crisis management.** When a public relations challenge comes calling, your PR team needs to get information published quickly and correctly. A blog provides a quick platform for defusing potential PR conflicts before they affect a company's brand or products. Plus, if you are finding backlash from bloggers, using a blog is a great way to meet them on level ground and earn their respect.
- **An additional PR channel.** Journalists and news organizations are increasingly turning to blogs for industry buzz, news, and views. A blog can become a key way for your company's products and services to get noticed and covered by the media. Stories that are littering the evening news were fermenting among blogs a week before.
- **Customer outreach and education.** Blogs can easily manage information that prospects need to know when they are doing product research, and they can also relationships *after* a purchase through customer education, product demos, and customer support.
- **Thought leadership and visioning.** A

company's leaders can utilize blogs to communicate their organization's or business's vision. Being a media-savvy C.E.O. is more important than ever for businesses and a blog provides a more informal conduit than a traditional press release. Customers, shareholders, and the media get to experience a company's top brass in their own voices and on their own terms.

- **Research and development.** Blogs can provide an in-progress view of upcoming products and services. They allow customers to provide instant feedback and suggestions for further features. Rather than spending money on customer surveys and waiting for reports, you can quiz your target audience and start getting feedback within minutes.

UTILIZING BLOGS WITHOUT HAVING A BLOG

Often companies think that the only way for them to start using blogs is for them to start their own blog. Perhaps your company won't start one, but might want to use the collective "hive" of blogs (often called the *blogosphere*) to keep track of what's being said about your brand and products—and find your biggest fans.

Buzz Making

Send influential bloggers product samples, promotional items (often called "swag"), and press kits for new products. Bloggers love to get a scoop, so give them early notice of events or product demos. Allow bloggers to apply for press passes and they'll delight in the extra access.

Customer Surveys

Track what bloggers are saying about your company, your leaders and products with alerts so you always know how you are being perceived online and offline. Read bloggers who are your company's target audience. What are their needs and concerns? What can you glean from reading their blogs?

Corporate Intelligence

Along with tracking your own company's reputation online, you can also use the blogosphere to track the news and views of your competitors. You'll be able to track the reputation of your competitors compared to yours.

Advertise on Blogs

There are several services out there that allow you to advertise on blogs related to your industry or products. This careful alignment of content, audience and advertising can help promote ideas and products.

THE BIG FEAR

Most companies are scared of blogging because it subverts the usual top-down communication style that they are comfortable with. Blogs provide equal platform across an organization and the Internet, inviting two-way conversation with real flesh-and-blood people, instead of carefully programmed PR robots. Blogs and outside criticism or discussion is often seen as a vital threat to a company's integrity and bottom line. Are you willing to talk to your customers like they are real people? Are you willing to hear that maybe some of your products might actually suck? The clincher is: your customers are *already* talking about you. Clincher # 2: they *want* you to talk to them. You might as well join the discussion as a partner and stop hiding behind your brand.

GETTING STARTED QUICKLY

Here's a quick mini-project plan to get you going.

- **Choose a blog platform.** You can start a blog in 15 minutes using low-cost tools and services. Blog platforms like Google's Blogger (**www.blogger.com**), TypePad (**www.typepad.com**) or WordPress.com are free to low-cost and include hosting.
- **Choose your bloggers.** Approach some forward-thinking folks in your company and see whether they'd be interested in being guinea pigs. You probably already have some bloggers in your midst—you might be surprised.

- **Set up expectations.** You can tell them how often to post, what to post about and how to engage with other bloggers. Or you can just set them loose and see what happens. The important thing is that they are able to blog honestly and openly and engage readers in a true discussion.
- **Track metrics.** Most blog platforms have some sort of statistics and traffic system so you can see where hits are coming from, what bloggers are linking to you and what search engine results are finding you.
- **Highlight your bloggers.** Once the bloggers are up and running, start bringing them into the marketing process. Have them write supplements to press releases; have them interview industry experts, satisfied users, or topic gurus. Let your bloggers highlight other bloggers that are writing about your products or industry.

CONCLUSION
Start Starting

There are ton of other options and configurations available but the important thing is to start getting started. Blogging is a powerful medium to get past your brand and let the world see the personality of the people that make up your organization. Your passionate employees and satisfied customers are your best sales force. Let them start talking to the rest of the world about your products and services and see what happens!

FOR MORE INFORMATION

Book:
Wibbels, Andy. *Blogwild! A Guide for Small Business Blogging.* New York: Portfolio, 2006.

Web sites:
Blogwild book site: **www.GOblogwild.com**
Andy Wibbels' main blog: **www.andywibbels.com**

See also:
☆ Creating a Company Web Site That Delivers Real Value (pp. 192–193)

"A quotation is what a speaker wants to say, unlike a soundbite which is all that an interviewer allows you to say."

Tony Benn

Viewpoint: Howard Rheingold

Smart Mobs: Pervasive Computing, Mobile Communications, and Collective Action

Introduction

Howard Rheingold is a leading authority on the social implications of technology. A former founding editor of *HotWired*, he has served as editor of *The Whole Earth Review*, editor-in-chief of *Millennium Whole Earth Catalog*, and online host for *The Well*.

Smart Mobs, the title of my 2002 book, refers to my term for the way groups of people are using cell phones and the Internet to organize collective action, from collaborative research that targets diseases like AIDS and malaria to political demonstrations and electoral campaigns that depose and install heads of state. The two billion telephones in the hands of the world's citizens, the increasing capabilities of co-ordinating services via the Internet, and emerging social practices have enabled a variety of innovations, from emergent collective response to natural disasters to knowledge collectives like Wikipedia. The thesis of my book was that these political, social, and economic phenomena are only the early indicators of a large-scale shift in the way people get things done. Since the book was published, events around the world added to my list of indicators. Consider the range of instances from the past several years:

- Millions of Philippine citizens self-organized demonstrations that contributed to the fall of the President; Korean citizens used e-mail and text messages to get out the vote and tip their presidential election in favor of the eventual winner; Spanish citizens self-organized via SMS (text messaging) an upset in their presidential elections; and elections in Africa have been monitored by citizens with cell phones.
- SETI@home has amassed 20 teraflops (twenty trillion operations per second) of computing power by asking volunteers to link their personal computers via the Internet. Biomedical researchers use folding@home to help tackle computationally intensive problems around protein folding through similar online computation collectives.
- Open source software production by self-elected communities of online volunteers has created the free Linux operating system and Firefox Web browser, challenging Microsoft's dominance through volunteer labor that uses neither market incentives nor the structure of the company.
- Flash mobs of young people, organized online and co-ordinated through cell phones, swept the world in the summer of 2004—frivolous exercises that may nevertheless signal a new trend in self-organized public entertainment. Considering that the computer game industry brings in more money than Hollywood, self-organized entertainment could prove to be an economically significant force.

- eBay created a multi-billion dollar market where none existed before, using its feedback system to enable buyers to rate sellers' performance-a "reputation" system that enabled 150 million people to trust each other, in the words of founder Pierre Omidyar. Omidyar is now transforming philanthropy by using online networks instead of foundations to disburse funds and organize projects.
- InnoCentive, an online "solutions market," enables qualified experts to submit bids for problems in chemical synthesis that are proposed by "seekers." A difficult pharmaceutical synthesis was provided, in exchange for financial compensation, by a petrochemist in Kazakhstan who had been working on it for different reasons. Hewlett-Packard uses an internal "predictions market." with their employers buying and selling stock for predictions, to forecast sales of various products.
- Within hours of the Asian tsunami, a Weblog and Wiki enabled people on the site of the disaster and concerned citizens around the world to self-organize their own humanitarian response, in parallel with official responders. Ad hoc communities of volunteers used the online classified ad community Craig's List to enlist aid to Hurricane Katrina's victims.
- Riots in China, Nigeria, and Australia were inflamed and spontaneously organized by people via text messages.
- OhMyNews deploys 50,000 citizen reporters and a full-time staff of 50 professional editors; the community votes on which reports will rise to the top. This journalistic online community is credited with tipping the Korean presidential election in 2003.
- Thousands of volunteers have created more than two million articles in more than 200 languages for Wikipedia, a free online encyclopedia. The goal of the Wikipedia community is to create a free encyclopedia for all the people on Earth, in their native languages.
- Tens of millions of people have taken to publishing online commentaries and essays in Weblogs, known popularly as blogs. The "blogosphere," as the extremely varied collection of publications is known, was instrumental in toppling Trent Lott and Dan Rather from power. The first photographs of the London bombings of July 2005 were sent directly to the Internet from a camera cell phone. The era of online, instantaneous, ubiquitous citizen journalism is already upon us, although it is only in its infancy.

I've cited a wide variety of early examples in order to illustrate that the use of technology to augment collective action has already begun to catalyze systemic change. The ways in which people gather news, buy and sell products and services, collect knowledge, win elections, respond to disaster, and entertain them-

"If a man carefully examines his thoughts he will be surprised to find out how much he lives in the future."

selves are all already undergoing change. Since the days of 64K RAM personal computers and 1200 baud modems, we've learned that microchip-based technologies can grow tens of thousands of times more powerful as the price of devices drops. Today, there are two billion telephones in the world, with another 600 billion estimated to be sold in 2006. Ten years from now, more than half the world's population are likely to be carrying or wearing global multimedia communications devices that also wield as much power as today's supercomputers. If new forms of widespread collective action such as science and constitutional democracy were catalyzed by the alphabetic literacies unleashed by the printing press—what new forms of widespread collective action will smart-mob technologies catalyze?

Hardware and software furnish platforms, the stages on which to act. The scenarios are enacted by people. How will people do business, grab power, help one another, commit violence, or conduct journalism in a many-to-many world?

There is no technological or political destiny that guarantees the shape of the wireless global infosphere that started to emerge over the past ten years and which will take at least another ten years to settle into a more concrete shape. Eventually, wealth, power, and influence will settle into another temporary basin of attraction. Right now, no player controls nor can even predict the results. When trying to look at what might happen to smart-mob technologies and practices over the next ten years, I've taken a lesson from the Global Business Network—to look for predetermined factors and critical uncertainties. And I've borrowed a lesson from Institute for the Future—aim for insight that provides foresight, not prediction.

The known economics of microchip production and global marketing are predetermined factors: cell phones are going to grow cheaper and more powerful, and the people who don't already own one are going to get them. Chinese citizens alone already own close to half a billion cell phones. Uncertain is whether political or economic incumbencies can find ways to contain or neutralize revolutionaries and entrepreneurs: the Chinese government's censorship of Internet chat rooms and filtering of words sent via SMS is one example of this conflict. Another example is "digital rights management" that attempts to bake a pay-per-view sales strategy into both law and hardware. Politically and economically, the struggle is between established powerful groups who have an interest in maintaining a population of passive consumers whose choices are limited to which brand to buy or channel to subscribe to, and opposed by the same force of human ingenuity that led to the user-created phenomena of the personal computer and the Internet. The old-style telephone monopoly is the model for one side of this conflict. The entrepreneurial inventiveness that motivated Bill Gates and Steve Jobs is the model for the other side.

Another uncertainty grows from our ignorance of human social behavior. Science knows a great deal more about how atoms behave than about how humans behave. An interdisciplinary study of cooperation and collective action, somehow converging findings from biology, economics, sociology, computer science, and psychology, could lead to a much more detailed and comprehensive understanding of how people use media to accomplish collective action. However, even if a large-scale interdisciplinary inquiry into the dynamics of cooperation were to succeed, one of the things that isn't known at present is whether knowing about cooperation, and the obstacles to it, ever enables people to act more effectively.

What insights can we gain by looking at the instances I've cited here? The social temperature of cities is "heating up," NYU's Professor Anthony Townsend has pointed out, as people use the same amount of time to make more appointments, check more voicemail, have more meetings while driving in cabs. Telenor researcher Rich Ling has noted that those who live with mobile communication devices experience a "softening of time" in which appointments and plans are fluidly renegotiated via SMS up to the last minute. Whenever there is an opportunity for individuals to choose or start groups, and to coordinate collective action among the members of the group, economic or political action can follow. For better and worse, cascades of smart-mob events are out of control. Perhaps most important, even when the manufacturers of communication media invest research into understanding how people use new technologies, it is a near certainty that groups of people will appropriate the media for their own, unpredicted purposes. That was true of the telephone, the Internet as a social medium, and of SMS.

Given a new medium to communicate, people will find new ways to do things together, at new scales and paces. Some of the things people do together are hideously destructive. Some of them advance freedom and enhance life. We know a little about the ways the telephone, the personal computer, and the Internet are merging into a new medium, and a little about the kinds of things people are beginning to do. What, if anything, can be done to encourage more humane and democratic use of this nascent medium, and to discourage its more destructive use?

FOR MORE INFORMATION

Book:
Rheingold, Howard. *Smartmobs: The Next Social Revolution.* Cambridge, MA: Perseus, 2002.

Web site:
Rheingold.com: **www.rheingold.com**

See also:
☆ Trend Innovation Management (pp. 353–354)

"My fundamental belief is that if a company wants to see the future, 80 percent of what it is going to have to learn will be from outside its own industry."

Gary Hamel

Intellectual Capital by Thomas A. Stewart

EXECUTIVE SUMMARY

- Intellectual capital is knowledge that transforms raw materials and makes them more valuable.
- To be considered intellectual capital, knowledge must be an asset.
- Intellectual capital's raw materials might be physical or intangible, like information.

INTRODUCTION

Intellectual capital is just that: a capital asset consisting of intellectual material. To be considered intellectual capital, knowledge must be an asset—able to be used to create wealth. Thus intellectual capital includes the talents and skills of individuals and groups; technological and social networks and the software and culture that connect them; and intellectual property such as patents, copyrights, methods, procedures, archives, etc. It excludes knowledge or information not involved in production or wealth creation. Just as raw material such as iron ore should not be confused with an asset such as a steel mill, so knowledge materials such as data or miscellaneous facts ought not to be confused with knowledge assets.

INTELLECTUAL CAPITAL AS AN ASSET

From the standpoint of traditional accounting, intellectual capital frequently does not fit the definition of an asset. Generally, under accounting rules, an asset must be tangible; it must have been acquired in one or more transactions, so that it has a known cost or a market value, and it must be under the control of the party whose asset it is said to be. Thus scientific skill is not an accounting asset, but laboratory equipment is.

Intellectual capital theory argues that this definition is too narrow and hinders businesses from seeing, managing, or building knowledge assets. This in turn inhibits companies' ability to compete and prosper in an economy in which knowledge has become an important source of profits. The intellectual capitalists use a looser definition: an asset is something that transforms raw material into something more valuable. It is a magician's black box. Inputs get put in—a few handkerchiefs, say; the asset does something to transform them; and out come outputs worth more than the inputs—rabbits, maybe. The question of ownership and control matters less than the question of access. A corporation might not own scientific

expertise (in the form of a cadre of employees, for example), but it has the use of it and can exert a quasi-proprietary influence over how it is used.

Intellectual capital, then, is knowledge that transforms raw materials and makes them more valuable. The raw materials might be physical—knowledge of the formula for Coca-Cola is an intellectual asset that transforms a few cents' worth of sugar, water, carbon dioxide, and flavorings into a dollar's worth of refreshment. The raw material might be intangible, like information. Knowledge of the law is an intellectual asset; a lawyer takes the facts of a dispute (raw material), transforms them through his knowledge of the law (an intellectual asset), to produce an opinion or a legal brief (an output of higher value than the facts by themselves).

Though financial accounting does not measure intellectual capital, markets clearly do. Stock in companies in the pharmaceutical industry, for example, generally trade at a high premium over the book value of their assets, and the companies' return on net assets is abnormally high; but if their spending on research and development is added to their capital, both their market-to-book ratios and their returns on assets come to resemble those of less knowledge-intensive companies. (There is a slowly growing movement to find ways to account for intellectual capital and report it to stockholders. Scandinavian countries, particularly Denmark, are leaders in the field.)

Indeed, it was the unusual behavior of the equities of knowledge-intensive companies that first drew the attention of analysts to intellectual capital. The term seems to have been employed first in 1958, when two financial analysts, describing the stock-market valuations of several small, science-based companies, concluded that "The intellectual capital of such companies is perhaps their single most important element," and noted that their high stock valuations might be termed an "intellectual premium."

(Morris Kronfeld and Arthur Rock, "Some Considerations of the Infinite," *The Analyst's Journal*, November 1958, p. 6.) The idea lay dormant for a quarter of a century. In the 1980s, Walter Wriston, the former chairman of Citicorp, noted that his bank and other corporations possessed valuable intellectual capital that accountants (and bank regulators) did not measure.

INTELLECTUAL CAPITAL ANALYZED

Karl-Erik Sveiby, a Swede, intrigued by the anomalous stock-market behavior of knowledge-intensive companies, began an investigation that produced the first analysis of the nature of intellectual capital. Sveiby, his colleagues, and *Affärsvärlden*, Sweden's oldest business magazine, noticed that the magazine's proprietary model for valuing initial public offerings broke down for high-tech companies. Sveiby concluded that these companies possessed assets not described in financial documents or included in the magazine's model. With a like-minded group of associates, he sat down to puzzle out what these might be. In "Den Osynliga Balansräkningen Ledarskap" ("The Invisible Balance Sheet"), 1989, they laid the foundation stone for much of what has come after by coming up with a taxonomy for intellectual capital. Knowledge assets, they proposed, could be found in three places: the competencies of a company's people, its internal structure (patents, models, computer and administrative systems), and its external structure (brands, reputation, relationships with customers and suppliers).

After some tinkering by others—the pieces are now usually called human capital, structural (or organizational) capital, and customer (or relationship) capital—Sveiby's model still stands. It has made managing intellectual capital possible by naming its component parts. Shortly thereafter, Leif Edvinsson, an executive at the Swedish financial services company Skandia, persuaded his management to appoint him "Director, Intellectual Capital"; Skandia became the business world's most conspicuous laboratory for intellectual capital studies.

Ideas whose time has come flower everywhere at once. Ikujiro Nonaka and Hirotaka Takeuchi in Japan began investigations of how knowledge is produced that resulted in "The Knowledge-creating Com-

pany" (*Harvard Business Review*, November-December 1991) and Thomas A. Stewart synthesized U.S. research in intellectual capital in "Brainpower: How Intellectual Capital Is Becoming America's Most Important Asset" (*Fortune*, June 3, 1991).

Every company or organization possesses all three forms of intellectual capital. Human capital consists of the skills, competencies, and abilities of individuals and groups. These range from specific technical skills to "softer" skills, like salesmanship or the ability to work effectively in a team. An individual's human capital cannot, in a legal sense, be owned by a corporation; the term thus refers not only to individual talent but also to the collective skills and aptitudes of a workforce. Indeed, one challenge faced by executives is how to manage the talent of truly outstanding members of their staff: how to use it to the utmost without becoming overdependent on a few star performers, or how to encourage stars to share their skills with others. Skills that are irrelevant to a company's business—the fine tenor voice of an actuary, for example—may be part of the individual's human capital, but not of his employer's.

Structural capital comprises knowledge assets that are indeed company property: intellectual property such as patents, copyrights, and trademarks; processes, methodologies, models; documents and other knowledge artifacts; computer networks and software; administrative systems; and so forth. A data warehouse is structural capital; so is the decision-support software that helps people to use the data. One knowledge-management process is converting human capital—which is usually available to just a few people—into structural capital, so it becomes shareable. This happens, for example, when a team writes up the "lessons learned" from a project so that others can apply them. Some structural capital can be said to be owned in common; open-source software is an example. In general, however, proprietary assets, whether intellectual or otherwise, are of more strategic value than assets equally available to competitors.

Customer capital is the value of relationships with suppliers, allies, and customers. Two common forms are brand equity and customer loyalty. The former is a promise of quality (or some other attribute) for which a customer agrees to pay a premium price; the value of brands is measurable in financial terms. The loyalty of a base of customers is also measurable, using discounted cash-flow analysis. Both are frequently calculated when companies are bought and sold. In a sense, all customer capital should eventually reflect itself either in a premium price or a sticky buyer–seller relationship.

Every organization possesses intellectual capital in all three manifestations, but with varying emphasis, depending on its history and strategy. For example, a chemical company might have as a knowledge asset the ability to concoct custom chemical compounds that precisely match its customer's needs. That asset might be people-based, residing in the tacit knowledge of dozens of skilled chemists; it might be structural, found in an extensive library of patents and manuals, or databases and expert systems; it might be relationship-based, found in the company's intimate ties to customers, suppliers, universities, etc. Most likely, of course, the asset—skill at making custom chemicals—is a combination of the three. A company that takes a strategic approach to intellectual capital will examine its business model and the economics of its industry to manage the combination of human, structural, and customer capital in such a way as to create value that competitors cannot match.

At least three characteristics of intellectual capital give it extraordinary power to add value. First, companies that use knowledge assets deftly can reduce the expense and burden of carrying physical assets, or can maximize their return on them. For example, transportation companies can use information networks and skill in logistics and load management to maximize their utilization of assets like rail cars and containers. Second, it can be possible to get enormous leverage from knowledge assets. The value of an aircraft can be realized over just one route at a time, whereas that of an airline's reservation system is limited only by the number of people in the world. In a study of the chemical industry that examined 83 companies over 25 years, Baruch Lev, professor of accounting at New York University, found that R&D spending (one form of investment in intellectual capital) returned 25.9% pretax, whereas capital spending earned just 15% (about 10% after tax, approximately the cost of capital).

Third, human and customer capital are the primary sources of innovation and customization. The increasing sophistication of machinery and information technology has led to the automation of more and more repetitive tasks. These manufacturing economies of scale are sources of competitive advantage in industrial processes. At a certain point, however, their value diminishes: the more it is possible to do a task the same way twice, the harder it is for one company to differentiate its offerings from its competitors'. When this happens the value of innovation, customization, and service increases; all are highly dependent on intellectual capital.

MAKING IT HAPPEN ▶▶

- Treat knowledge as an asset only if it is capable of yielding an economic return.
- Build human capital by developing skills, competencies, abilities of individuals and groups who deliver value to customers.
- Convert human capital into structural capital, by organizing the exchange and sharing of knowledge.
- Optimize customer capital—the value of relationships with suppliers, allies, and customers—by building brand equity and customer loyalty.
- Use knowledge assets to reduce the expense and burden of carrying physical assets, or to maximize return on those assets
- Look for competitive advantage from innovation, customization, and service rather than from economies of scale.

FOR MORE INFORMATION

Books:

Davenport, Thomas H., and Laurence Prusak. *Working Knowledge: How Organizations Manage What They Know.* Cambridge, MA: Harvard Business School Press, 2000.

Edvinsson, Leif, and Michael S. Malone. *Intellectual Capital.* New York: Harper Business, 1997.

Mayo, Andrew. *The Human Value of the Enterprise: Valuing People As Assets—Monitoring, Measuring, Managing.* Naperville, IL: Nicholas Brealey, 2001.

Stewart, Thomas A. *Intellectual Capital: The New Wealth of Organizations.* New York: Doubleday, 1997.

Stewart, Thomas A. *The Wealth of Knowledge: Intellectual Capital and the Twenty-First Century Organization.* New York: Doubleday, 2003.

Sullivan, Patrick H. *Value Driven Intellectual Capital: How to Convert Intangible Corporate Assets into Market Value.* New York: Wiley, 2000.

Teece, David J. *Managing Intellectual Capital.* New York: Oxford University Press, 2002.

Web site:

www.intellectualcapital.nl: this is a truly global Web site with links to dozens of IC resources.

"Companies . . . have a hard time distinguishing between the cost of paying people and the value of investing in them."

Thomas A. Stewart

Project Management by Robert Buttrick

EXECUTIVE SUMMARY

- Make sure your projects are driven by your strategy.
- Use a staged approach to manage your projects.
- Place high emphasis on the early stages.
- Engage your stakeholders.
- Encourage teamwork and commitment.
- Ensure success by planning for it.
- Monitor against the plan.
- Formally close the project.

INTRODUCTION

Today, managers may spend as much time in interdisciplinary, cross-functional project teams as they do in their usual positions—project management has now become a core competence for all managers. This applies not only to projects undertaken for customers (external projects), but also to those undertaken for the development of the organization itself (internal projects).

Many factors have contributed to this. Among them is speed, coupled with the increased complexity of organizations and the closer relationships within and between companies, their customers, and suppliers. We now need evolutionary change at revolutionary speed, necessitating skillful project management.

As a vehicle of change, project management is well suited to meet these needs. However, it is too often perceived as a necessary technical discipline rather than the powerful business tool it really is. This section looks at the challenges of project management, and potential responses.

THE CHALLENGES TO BE FACED

All organizations have problems with the ways they tackle change within their businesses—these may be related to technology, people, processes, systems, or structure. During the late 20th century, there has been a variety of techniques and offerings available to managers to enable them to do this, most notably CMMi, Six Sigma, total quality management and business process reengineering.

Unfortunately, not all organizations secure the enduring benefits initially promised by techniques. Many remain ineffective at managing and controlling change in order to achieve sustained benefits from such initiatives. Organizations must continually act to solve particular problems or

achieve specific objectives, but many fail. The initiatives often fail because they cost too much, take too long, are inadequately thought out and specified, or simply don't realize the expected benefits.

This amounts to failure on a grand scale, costing billions every year, and results in the demise of some organizations. For two reasons. Organizations don't know *how* to tackle these initiatives: there's no company-wide way of organizing this. Also they don't know *what* projects they should be doing: there's no clear strategy driving decision making.

Project management gives you the environment to solve the first of these root causes, and by its proper implementation will prompt you to think about the second.

PRINCIPLES OF PROJECT MANAGEMENT

Make Sure Your Projects Are Driven by Your Strategy

You should be able to demonstrate explicitly how each project you undertake fits your business strategy. The screening out of unwanted projects as soon as possible is essential. The less clear the strategy, the more likely unsuitable projects are to pass the screening: hence there will be more projects competing for scarce resources, resulting in the company losing focus and risking its overall performance.

Each project should have a project sponsor who is accountable for directing the project and ensuring the expected benefits fit the strategy and are likely to be realized.

Use a Consistent Staged Approach

Rarely is it possible to plan a project in its entirety. You should, however, be able to plan the next stage in detail and to the end of the project in outline. As you progress

through the project you gather more information, reduce uncertainty, and increase confidence. The typical framework comprises the following progressive steps, or stages:

- *proposal*—identifying the idea or need;
- *initial investigation*—a brief overview of the possible requirements and solutions;
- *detailed investigation*—undertaking a feasibility study of the options and defining the chosen solution;
- *development and testing*—building the solution;
- *trial*—piloting the solution with real people;
- *operation and closure*—putting it into practice and closing the project.

You should use the same generic stages for all types of project. This makes the use and understanding of the process familiar and easier, avoiding the need to learn different processes for various types of project. This generic framework should then be tailored to take into account the content of each project, the level of activity, the nature of the activity, the resources required, and the stakeholders and decision makers needed. The *gates* are entry points to each stage, and are the key checkpoints for revalidating a project and committing resources and funding.

Placing high emphasis on the early stages of the project might mean that between 30% and 50% of the project's life cycle is devoted to investigative stages before any final deliverable is physically built. Research clearly demonstrates that placing heavy emphasis up front significantly decreases the time to market/completion. Good investigative work means clearer objectives and plans. Decisions taken at the early stages of a project have a far-reaching effect and set the tone for the remainder. In the early stages, creative solutions can slash delivery times in half or cut costs dramatically. Once development is underway changes can be very costly.

Engage Your Stakeholders

A stakeholder is any person involved in or affected by a project. The involvement of stakeholders such as users and customers adds considerable value at all stages of the project. Engaging them is a powerful mover for change; ignoring them can lead to failure. When viewed from a stakeholder perspective, your project may be just one more problem they have to cope with in addition to fulfilling their usual duties; it may appear

---

"The chief executive . . . like a juggler keeps a number of projects in the air: periodically one comes down, is given a new burst of energy, and is sent back into orbit."

Henry Mintzberg

irrelevant to them, or even regressive. If their consent is required to make things happen, it is unwise to ignore them.

Always Address All Aspects, Not Just Technology
Projects are not just about technology; they should cover every aspect required to achieve the expected benefits. These will include culture, systems, processes, and structures. Stakeholders should be identified to cover every base.

Encourage Teamwork and Commitment
Be sure to encourage teamwork and commitment at all times. The need for many projects to draw on people from a range of functions means an integrated team approach is essential. The more closely people from different disciplines work and the more open the management style, the better they perform. Although this is not always practical, closeness can be achieved by frequent meetings and good communication, often through Web tools or video-conferencing.

Ensure Success by Planning for It
The more functionally structured a company, the more difficult it is to implement effective project management: project management by its nature crosses functional boundaries. To make projects succeed, the balance of power usually needs to be tipped toward the project and away from line management.

Monitor Against the Plan
Good planning and control are prerequisites for effective project management. There must be guidance, training, and support for all staff related to projects, including senior managers who sponsor projects or make project-related decisions. Core control techniques include planning, managing risk, issues, scope change, schedule, cost, and reviews. Planning as a discipline is essential. If you have no definition of the project and no plan, you're unlikely to be successful. It will be virtually impossible to communicate your intentions to the project team and stakeholders. Furthermore, if there is no plan, terms such as "early," "late," and "within budget" have no real meaning.

Risk management is key: using a staged approach is itself a risk management technique, with the gates acting as formal review points at which risk is put in the context of the business benefits and cost of delivery. Projects are risky. It is essential to analyze the project, determine which are

the inherently risky parts, and take action to reduce, avoid, or, in some cases, insure against those risks while looking to exploit any opportunities that arise.

Despite all this foresight and care, things will not always go smoothly. Unforeseen issues do arise that, if not resolved, threaten the success of the project. Monitoring and forecasting against the agreed plan is a discipline that ensures that events do not take those involved in the project by surprise. This is best illustrated by the "project control cycle." The appropriate frequency for the cycle (daily, weekly, biweekly, monthly) depends on the project, its stage of development, and the inherent risk. Such monitoring should focus more on the future than on what has actually been completed. Completion of activities is evidence of progress, but is not sufficient to predict whether milestones will continue to be met. The project manager should continually check that the plan is still fit for the purpose and likely to realize the business benefits on time.

Manage the Project Control Cycle
Monitoring should focus more on the future than on what has actually been completed. Completion of activities is not sufficient to predict whether milestones will continue to be met. The project manager should continually check that the plan is still fit for the purpose and likely to deliver the business benefits on time.

Many projects are late or never even get completed. One of the reasons for this is scope creep: more and more ideas are incorporated into the project, resulting in higher costs and late delivery. Changes, even beneficial ones, must be managed to guarantee that only those enabling the project benefits to be realized are accepted; you must communicate this to the team and stakeholders so they are absolutely clear what the current project comprises.

Formally Close the Project
Finally, every project must be closed, either because it has completed its work or because it has been terminated early. By explicitly closing a project you make sure that all work ceases, lessons are learned, and any remaining assets, funding, or resources can be released for other purposes.

MINI-CASE
One company that has a product leadership strategy terminated a new product before launch, because a competitor had just released a superior product. It was better to abort the launch and work on the next generation product than to continue with a new

product that could be seen by the market as inferior. If they had done so, their strategy of product leadership would have been compromised.

MAKING IT HAPPEN ▶▶
Common mistakes include:
- intrafunctional thinking—not taking the helicopter, or not having a company-wide view;
- having too many rules—the more project rules you make, the more people will break them;
- disappearing and changing sponsors—continual changing of the driver will cause you to lose focus and forget why you are undertaking the project at all;
- ignoring the risks—risks don't go away, so acknowledge and manage them;
- rushing in prematurely to get something going; resist the temptation to confuse activity with progress;
- analysis paralysis—you need to investigate, but only enough to gain the confidence to move on;
- untested assumptions—all assumptions are risks, so treat them as such;
- executive's pet projects—make no exceptions. If an executive's idea is really so good, it should stand up to the scrutiny all the others go through.

Your project will run much more smoothly if you focus on a few basics:
- define strategies clearly so you're better able to eliminate low-leverage, low-value projects;
- plan through progressive stages: proposal, initial investigation, detailed investigation, development and testing, trial, operation, and closure;
- concentrate on the early stages of the project, when the decisions taken have a far-reaching effect on the outcome;
- analyze the project, determine which are the intrinsically risky parts, and act to reduce, avoid, or, in some cases, insure against the risks;
- to make projects succeed, tip the balance of power toward the project and away from line management and the hierarchy;
- focus progress monitoring more on the future than on completion of activities, which doesn't predict whether future milestones will be met.

CONCLUSION
The success of an organization rests on its ability to direct and manage projects effec-

---

202

BEST PRACTICE

tively and efficiently. The interdisciplinary nature of project teams combined with the significance and sensitivity of their impact places considerable demands on management. Acquiring key skills will ensure that the process runs smoothly, minimizing costs and maximizing benefits, while securing stakeholder involvement and commitment. Responsiveness is an increasingly significant source of competitive advantage, and a fast, flexible, and focused project management capability is essential for every organization. Tomorrow's successful corporations will be founded on the efforts those organizations dedicate to the way they

research, plan, and execute new initiatives and projects.

FOR MORE INFORMATION

Books:
Buttrick, Robert. *The Project Workout.* 3rd ed. with CD-ROM. Upper Saddle River, NJ: Financial Times Prentice Hall, 2005.
Obeng, Eddie. *All Change! The Project Leader's Secret Handbook.* Upper Saddle River, NJ: Financial Times Prentice Hall, 1996.

Buttrick, Robert. *The Role of the Executive Project Sponsor.* Upper Saddle River, NJ: Financial Times Prentice Hall, 2002.

Web site:
Project Workout:
www.projectworkout.com

See also:
☆ Avoiding the Mistakes of the Past: Lessons from the Startup World (pp. 164–165)
☆ Intrapreneurial Warriors Versus Traditional Managers (pp. 160–161)
☆ Keeping Control in Nonhierarchical Organizations (pp. 231–232)

Virtual Collaboration
by Stewart Clegg, Antoine Hermens, and Salvador Porras

EXECUTIVE SUMMARY

- The Internet suits collaborative organizations.
- Customers want fast, flexible solutions rather than being hooked into a "single-vendor-provides-all" relationship.
- The value that e-business models create resides in the network of partners.
- Collaborative e-business requires a win–win–win outcome for suppliers, companies, and customers.
- Governance of alliances needs to develop time and culture accounting.

INTRODUCTION

Bureaucracy needn't last much longer. Today the new economy is generating strategic opportunities and organizational forms based on collaborative networks that defy bureaucracy's rationale. E-commerce is more than a way of Web-enabling existing business practices—it creates new opportunities and demands hitherto unknown organizational competencies. The business model for new economy companies is collaborative.

The Internet offers opportunities for smaller players to compete within global networks. Virtual villages are emerging in which small enterprises form and re-form alliances to provide high-tech services to larger companies. London-based Sohonet stretches such electronic adjacency further, sharing high-capacity data links to participate in the Hollywood and West Los Angeles creative milieu. High-speed digital exchange of film, video, and sound enables post-production operations to be carried out in London in direct competition with Californian companies. The open networked nature of the entertainment industry of southern California is a lower-tech version of the IT networks in northern California.

It's not only small businesses that use networked capabilities. Cisco's Global Networked Business Model enabled the company to build interactive knowledge-based relationships with potential clients, customers, partners, suppliers, and employees such that they are now one of the most networked and collaborative of companies globally.

THE PARADOX

- *Technologically*, the shift to e-commerce serves to drive transaction costs down.
- *Commercially*, where this occurs no organization has much advantage beyond

that of being a first mover since every competitor drives down everyone's transaction costs.
- *Organizationally*, to obtain advantage organizations have to add value over and above the costs of transactions stripped out by the use of digital technology.
- *Paradoxically*, e-technology doesn't add value, but erodes it by driving transaction costs down, so the only way of increasing value in the e-economy is by reinstating transaction costs. Organizations must *turn transactions into relationships through collaboration*.

WHY DO COMPANIES COLLABORATE?

Rapid economic and technological change, declining productivity growth and increasing competitive pressures, global interdependence, and the blurring of boundaries between distinct legal organizational entities, all facilitate collaboration. Collaboration is a response to turbulence that individual organizations are unable to manage because of a lack of resources or an inability to control externalities.

Low collaboration and high competition increase the risk that one party will act against others. The best strategy for organizations is high collaboration and high competition, with the major benefit of mutual learning for participants.

Trust plays an important role in collaborative networks. Transactions take place among organizations involved in reciprocal, preferential, mutually supportive actions. Such relationships are different from markets in that transactions involve joint, bilateral coordination of plans and activities. They differ from companies or hierarchies in having no single actor-participant in control; organizations maintain their independence, coordinating through negotiation and broad information interchange.

Successful collaborations combine the strength of two or more companies. They outclass competitors by establishing de facto standards, and avoid the risk of large stand-alone investments. One reason for forming such a network is to *co-market*. Network members market products under a common brand name and portal while otherwise retaining their independence. The benefits of networking can include pool selling of products and services, pool buying of supplies and equipment, joint research and development resources, and improved quality objectives—summed up in the slogan, "Joint solutions for common problems through collaboration."

UNDERSTANDING THE BENEFITS

Collaborative arrangements aid organizational learning and the transfer of intangibles such as knowledge, organizational routines and skills, experiences, reputation, and goodwill. Companies gaining access to new technologies or markets are more likely to collaborate, benefiting from economies of scale in joint research, production, and marketing, and gaining complementary skills by tapping into sources of know-how located outside the boundaries of the company. Other advantages include sharing risks in activities and gaining synergy by combining different strengths.

Strategic partnerships are a critical measure of a company's ability to compete in the new economy. Paradoxically, inter-company differences, such as knowledge, skills, technologies, core competencies, and resources, usually form the underlying strategic motivation for entering into collaboration and remain essential for maintaining it. Differences in partner characteristics may have a negative impact on collaborative longevity and effectiveness. The erosion or convergence of these differences destabilizes the relationship. Confidence and trust in partners are recurring elements in successful collaboration.

MANAGING ELECTRONICALLY ENABLED COLLABORATION

Collaboration has certain disadvantages. Sharing expertise with others can reduce management control. Increased dependence on external organizations can lead to

greater need for more bureaucracy in order to manage what becomes virtual. Greater financial ties can lead to restricted access to other organizations and their capabilities.

Collaboration may increase one partner's competitive edge over the other(s). As businesses increasingly turn to a *fast-alliance* strategy the vast majority of alliances will fail to deliver on their promises. Complementary objectives and learning are vital to the success of an alliance. When partners are equally intent on internalizing each other's skills, distrust and conflict may spoil the alliance.

WHAT ARE THE RISKS?

Participants may take advantage of a collaborative relationship and play side games: the relationship might finish and one partner benefit by copying others. There is the risk that one party will gain all the benefits from the venture.

A lack of understanding of partners can lead to resistance and conflict. If cooperation is lacking, opportunistic behavior will become the norm. Partners may relinquish their competitive position by loss or transfer of core competencies as a result of a sense of security or rationalization pressures. The most desirable alliance arrangements are between partners approximately equivalent in terms of their size, profitability, and status in their own industry and that possess complementary know-how and resources.

Some alliances have been criticized for being too flexible, thus causing a situation in which individual partners may have insufficient details on how to collaborate, little irreversible commitment, unclear property rights, or a weak authority structure. Partners may join competing groups. The advantages of a high level of rigidity, especially through equity investment, include increasing incentives and commitment, aligning the partners' interests, and deterring opportunistic behavior. Such rigidity may seem especially paradoxical when the enabling technologies promise virtual flexibility.

THE FRAMEWORK FOR COLLABORATION

Collaborative business models are crucial for value creation. The more codevelopers, the quicker problems and opportunities can be identified. Over the duration of the relationship partners can share benefits and control, contributing in one or more key strategic areas.

The loss of proprietary information, substantial organizational disruption, and conflict help to explain the structural insta-

bilities of business-to-business relationships. Alliances involving access to knowledge or ability are more likely to dissolve as the party gaining access acquires its own internal skills through the partnership. Collaborations designed to gain benefits of scale or learning in performing an activity have a more enduring purpose.

Collaboration among businesses in the new economy with complementary resources, while creating substantial risks, is necessary for survival and growth. A realistic view of collaboration sees alliances as built on a foundation of dualities. Alliances are

- temporary *but* often produce long-lasting relationships;
- both cooperative *and* competitive weapons;
- strategically determined *and* emergent;
- likely to have emergent benefits that are more important than the intended purposes.

They are dialectical systems whose stability is determined by balancing multiple tensions within systems of accountability that handle tension without stifling innovation.

MAKING IT HAPPEN ▸▸

Organizations need to create value for all participants, including partners, suppliers, and customers. Partnering companies need to focus on the key value drivers, efficiency, complementarities, lock-in, and novelty. Success comes from:

- adopting the customer paradigm;
- optimizing the value chain;
- achieving time to market;
- creating effective governance mechanisms;
- measuring progress and effectiveness;
- processing the inputs of environmental, market, and customer knowledge and expertise;
- delivering barriers that lock out competitors;
- following an open-system model;
- incorporating innovation and entrepreneurship;
- spanning boundaries between industries;
- blurring lines between suppliers, customers, and the company.

There is a paradox, however: blurred lines lead to unclear relations, easily broken. The paradox can be resolved by developing relations into ties that not only bind, but also add value, through the nature of the governmental norms embedded in the alliance culture. Ties that add value require inductive reasoning from

past experiences, where no algorithm exists, and so, in such situations, organization members must work through reflexive capacities, to design something enabling from scratch.

CONCLUSION

Organizations need to design virtual, reflexive strategies of interorganizational ties and self-governance. These must be managed by twin methods: accounting on a time basis (on a professional-practice model that delivers the best value for partners with a client focus) and cultural design of a meaningful context of collaboration that keeps the values of the collaboration uppermost. Managers with reflexive capacities account for their time and act in accordance with cultural values consciously designed to frame the specific collaboration project.

FOR MORE INFORMATION

Books:
Child, John, and David Faulkner. *Strategies of Cooperation: Managing Alliances, Networks, and Joint Ventures.* New York: Oxford University Press, 1998.
Ebers, Mark, ed. *The Formation of Inter-organizational Networks.* New York: Oxford University Press, 1999.
Hamel, Gary. *Leading the Revolution.* Cambridge, MA: Harvard Business School Press, 2000.

Articles:
Clegg, Stewart R., Tyrone Pitsis, Thekla Rura-Polley, and Marton Marosszeky. "Governmentality Matters: Designing an Alliance Culture of Inter-Organizational Collaboration for Managing Projects." *Organization Studies*, 23:3 (2002): 317–337. "Constructing the Olympic Dream: Managing Innovation through the Future Perfect," *Organization Science*, 14:5 (2003): 574–590.

Web site:
Amit, Raphael, and Christoph Zott. "Value Drivers of E-commerce Business Models." Available at **www.wharton.upenn.edu**.

See also:
☆ Developing an Internet-era Mindset throughout the Organization (pp. 178–179)
☆ Overcoming the Difficulties of Managing a Virtual Organization (pp. 241–242)
☆ Viewpoint: Philip Kotler (pp. 61–62)

Managing by Individual Objectives
by Richard S. Handscombe

EXECUTIVE SUMMARY

- Managing by individual objectives (MIO) is imperative for all organizations in a competitive world, whether a multinational or one person organization.
- The generic concepts and processes can be applied to anyone's work and private life.
- MIO has maximum impact when introduced as *the way we manage and implement strategy*.
- The original ideas of Peter Drucker are timeless, as will be increasingly recognized following his death in 2005.
- Best practice is tough for even the best organizations.
- To be successful, MIO needs to be kept simple and constant.
- Unfortunately, it's easy to dodge the basics!

THE NEED

For the last century there has been a general understanding that unless managers know where they are going and why, no one can expect them to perform optimally, either individually or as a team. But this does not always happen. There's a wide gap between best and average practice in both public and private sectors worldwide. Improvement is imperative in the competitive and complex world that managers now work and live in.

This article considers the evolution of MIO, what constitutes best practice, and the success factors for its effective introduction and operation.

A GENERIC DEFINITION

At its simplest, MIO can be defined as *the proactive setting and timely updating of individual objectives by a manager in order to understand, cope with, and benefit from the future.*

The benefits can enhance personal satisfaction in terms of:

- contribution to the organization in which the manager works;
- use and development of personal capability;
- career development, recognition, and rewards;
- improved private life and way of life when in paid employment, voluntary work, or retirement;
- improved time management.

Most managers would not disagree with the concept. Many self-motivated managers have always striven to manage themselves that way, even applying the same discipline

to their education and retirement. In reality the skills required for MIO are generic and apply to all people in all walks of life, whatever their age or status.

Managers, even the self-employed, do not work in isolation. But they may have different visions, priorities, and ambitions influenced by their status and function. Often the end result is not teamwork, but unproductive friction, frustration, and despair. The best-managed organizations have long recognized such problems. For decades they have provided managers with a common sense of purpose and direction and made sure that they had challenging careers based on clear objectives. Average organizations and managers seek to achieve the same outcome but many fail because of the simplicity, creativity, and day-to-day dedication involved.

A MAJOR BREAKTHROUGH

Although Peter Drucker's renowned *The Practice of Management* was first published in 1954, its insights, ideas, and ideals are as relevant today as they were 50 years ago. Drucker laid down basic guidelines for MIO that are still best practice:

- a continuous focus on current and future external and internal customer needs;
- focus through corporate and unit strategy. Achievement of strategy through management by objectives and self-control. A focus on key result areas;
- exceptional teamwork vertically, horizontally, and diagonally within the organization;
- reward in line with results.

EXPANSION OF DRUCKER'S IDEAS

From the early 1960s many organizations sought to introduce MIO formally or informally, some on a worldwide basis. But often they were short of well-qualified managers, not only for line positions, but for the expanding functions of information technology, marketing, and human resources. These companies often sought outside help, and many academics and consultants started to research, write lectures, and consult in the area of MIO.

Drucker's most prominent early disciples were: George Odione in the United States, John Humble (Europe), and William Reddin (Canada). Among them they developed approaches applicable to both small family businesses and major multinationals, charities, churches, governments, etc. In addition to Drucker's research they drew on the work of Grainger (hierarchy of objectives), Rensis Likert (integration of objectives), Douglas McGregor (theory X and Y), Abraham Maslow (hierarchy of needs and ambitions), and others.

Other consultants soon followed, and many brands of MIO were marketed in the 1960s and 1970s, such as achieving business results, managing by objectives, management effectiveness, management by direction (France), action centered leadership, improving management performance, executive target setting and appraisals, and the one-minute manager. Each had its own processes, documentation, and terminology. The best programs worked because they were led by the chairman and chief executive, supported by internal or external change agents with a good grasp and experience of general management as well as MIO theory and practice. MIO has survived the decades in many well-run companies. In successful small companies, the chief executive has acted as the coach, change agent, and mentor.

In others the result was less successful, often because top management support was merely lip service and MIO entered the organization as an objective-led management appraisal system via the human resources department. The links with the objectives of the organization were often slim, and as a result MIO died young. Too often there has been a gap between the theory of the business plan and style of leadership and reality.

"A good goal is like a strenuous exercise—it makes you stretch."   Mary Kay Ash

In many cases the generic MIO processes and skills have been integrated into strategic leadership, total quality, and reengineering programs as the means of securing a genuine, wide-ranging commitment to results.

MIO BEST PRACTICE—WHERE ARE YOU NOW?

The personal audit given in Table 1 includes a summary of best practice.

Use the questionnaire to:
- develop an appreciation of best practice;
- evaluate the effectiveness of your own current practices;
- identify where improvements are required.

Evaluate your position against each of the statements in turn and allocate a score as follows:

0 No evidence of concept.

1 Some evidence, but only lip service is paid.

2 Exists but is not very effective.

3 Exists and company results demonstrate benefits.

4 I believe what we do is best practice.

Your unit may be the overall company, a subsidiary, a business division, a product group, or a department, branch, or project group.

1 Visible management leadership.

2 Continuity of senior management.

3 Stability of the system.

4 Ownership of the system and subprocesses by line management, not finance or human resources. Support from all functional heads.

5 Challenging objectives set for all functions, whether line, service or corporate support.

6 Senior management acting as coaches, not prima donnas.

7 Simplicity of documentation and guidance notes.

8 A balanced set of objectives established for each manager that is specific, quantified, realistic, and measurable, for example:

Enabling

Launch product A in South America by 03/01/2007.

Market survey of Brazil by 06/01/2007.

Support

Reorganize sales department by 03/01/2007.

Complete installation of system B by 05/01/2008.

Development

Gain commercial fluency in Spanish by 09/01/2006.

Table 1: Personal Audit

I and all the members of my team have . . .	Score
1. a clear understanding of the strategy, priorities, and key objectives and structure of the total organization.	
2. a clear understanding of the contribution expected from my unit in terms of its mission, key result areas, and quantified objectives.	
3. agreement to support and receive support from other units in achieving our respective objective.	
4. agreed statements of integrated personal objectives for the next 6, 12, or 18 months to which each is committed and dedicated.	
5. consistently achieved agreed objectives over the last three years.	
6. effective information/intelligence for tracking progress and identifying emergent opportunities and risks.	
7. effective scheduled and ad hoc team and pair meetings* to review progress, reduce risks, and update objectives (* pair relates to you and your superior and you and each of your team members).	
8. a personal development program to provide the knowledge, skills, experience, and authority essential to achieving individual and team objectives.	
9. an annual performance review that is objective and fair.	
10. rewards that reflect achievement of objectives directly and fairly.	

What do you think should be changed over the next 12 or 24 months to improve the performance of yourself, your team, and the overall organization?

SUCCESS FACTORS FOR MIO

Numerous factors determine the success or failure of MIO systems. The following have been highlighted by many surveys (introducing and sustaining the system is not a soft option!).

All team members to attend performance management workshop by 10/01/2006.

9 Effective priority setting. The Pareto rule. Aiming for the things that matter.

10 Tough objectives supported by a rigorous action plan and risk analysis.

11 The objective-setting process for new managers implemented as a learning process with appropriate support.

12 A direct link between objectives and

budget, making sure that funding is available to provide the resources required to achieve agreed objectives.

13 Good baton passing between managers when changes occur due to promotion, special assignments, or departure to other companies.

14 MIO update and reinforcement sessions included in internal conferences, leadership programs, and workshops.

15 Managers empowered to act.

16 Performance reviews happening when planned. They are coaching sessions, not courtrooms.

17 Links between a manager's achievements and rewards are seen as fair.

18 If tough objectives are set, the reward for achievement needs to be significant compared to that achieved with minimum effort by a nonperformer.

19 Continuous reinforcement of the strategic direction and priorities of the organization.

20 Participation used to stimulate and harness continuous challenges, vision, and imagination. Changing mindsets to think beyond the obvious and enrich reality.

21 Regular audits to check that the MIO processes are still productive and add value. If not, revive the system before disbelievers undermine MIO by declaring it the latest fad or merely an appraisal system.

Introducing an alternative approach can take years—if one in fact exists. Attempts to overcomplicate a basically simple concept can be fatal!

MAKING IT HAPPEN ▶▶

- Use MIO to enable managers to understand, cope with, and benefit from the future.
- Have the MIO system and subprocesses owned by line management, not by finance or human resources.
- Insist that senior managers act as coaches, not prima donnas.
- Establish for each manager in every unit or function a balanced set of objectives that is specific, quantified, realistic, and measurable.
- Set tough objectives supported by a rigorous action plan and risk analysis, and with significant rewards for achievement.
- Directly link objectives and budget to insure funding of the resources required to achieve agreed objectives.

THE WAY AHEAD

Whether you aim to improve your own objective-setting process, improve the processes of a total organization, or teach leadership and management, recognize that the core MIO concept and skills are generic, serving as foundation stones for good management. Success requires leadership, insight, dedication, and a determination to keep it simple but rigorous.

FOR MORE INFORMATION

Books:

Blanchard, Kenneth, and Robert Lorber. *Putting the One Minute Manager to Work: How to Turn the Three Secrets Into Skills.* New York: HarperBusiness, 2000.

Drucker, Peter. *The Practice of Management.* New York: HarperBusiness, 1993.

See also:
- ☆ Avoiding Your Worst Career Nightmare (pp. 404–405)
- ☆ Choosing the Best Training Curriculum for You (pp. 426–427)
- ☼ Stephen R. Covey (pp. 1192–1193)
- ☆ Urbane Renewal: Trusting Your Own Wisdom—A Competitive (and Satisfying) Advantage (pp. 406–407)
- ☆ Viewpoint: Tom Brown (pp. 253–254)

"Men do not live only by fighting evils. They live by positive goals, individual and collective, a vast variety of them, seldom predictable, at times incompatible." Isaiah Berlin

The True Total Quality
by Masaaki Imai

EXECUTIVE SUMMARY

- It is important to recognize the importance of the commonsense approach of gemba (shop floor) kaizen to quality improvement, as against the technology-only approach to quality practiced in the west.
- The production system (batch production) employed by over 90% of all the companies in the world is one of the biggest obstacles to quality improvement. A conversion from a batch to a JIT (just-in-time)/lean production system should be the most urgent task for any manufacturing company today in order to survive in the next millennium.

INTRODUCTION

The differences between Knowledge and Wisdom are very important to our thinking about Total Quality Management. Knowledge is something we can buy. We can gain knowledge by reading books and attending seminars and classroom lectures. Knowledge remains just knowledge until we put it into action. On the other hand, wisdom is something we learn by doing. Practice is the best way of learning, and wisdom emerges from practice.

I have observed that Western management has tended to stress teaching knowledge in the classroom over wisdom through doing, whereas the Japanese approach for quality management has been to provide both knowledge and wisdom to employees. This latter approach is particularly effective in solving quality problems in gemba (shop floor).

GEMBA KAIZEN

"Gemba" means the place where real action occurs. In manufacturing "gemba" means the shop floor. In my book *Gemba kaizen: A Common-sense, Low-cost Approach to Management* (McGraw-Hill, 1997), I pointed out the three major activities to support good gemba management, namely: standardization, good housekeeping, and *muda* (waste) elimination. Let me explain the difference between wisdom and knowledge, citing an example from the housekeeping activities.

One of the five steps of housekeeping in gemba is *seiso*, or cleaning, meaning the involvement of operators in cleaning the machines they work with. As they do so, operators often discover oil leaks or loosening of bolts on the machine This gives them the opportunity to take corrective actions and eventually develop maintenance stand-ards. This is learning by doing, and the operators gain valuable wisdom about machine maintenance, which is an important step for quality improvement.

I have observed that many managers often neglect these three foundations of good gemba management and are interested in pursuing sophisticated approaches instead.

There are five Golden Rules of Gemba Management:
- when a problem (abnormality) arises, go to gemba first;
- check with *gembutsu* (relevant objects);
- take temporary counter-measures on the spot;
- find the root cause;
- standardize to prevent recurrence.

Fabricated Data

In managing gemba, the most critical part is for managers to go to gemba and have a good look. Managers who stay away from gemba, and seldom take the trouble of going there, are in contact with the reality of gemba only through indirect means, such as reports and conferences. In such cases, managers are making decisions based on fabricated data.

When you go to gemba where an abnormality occurred, you do not need any data, because what you see there is the reality. A manager on the shop floor is right in the midst of reality, and chances are that the problem may be solved on the spot and in real time by following the five golden rules.

Collect and Analyze Data

Another effective approach for problem solving in gemba has been to collect and analyze data.

Generally speaking, when these down-to-earth activities in gemba are carried out, the reject rates should go down to a tenth of their original levels. And yet, I find most Western managers do not take advantage of these effective gemba practices and pursue more academic and sophisticated approaches for quality improvement.

CONVERSION FROM BATCH TO JIT/LEAN PRODUCTION

The second and perhaps more acute issue facing most manufacturing companies today is the fact that their current production systems are the biggest hindrance to achieving quality management.

Today, most manufacturing companies subscribe to the traditional batch production system. I define batch production as an antiquated paradigm patterned after agriculture. In agriculture, farm products are sown, grown, harvested, and stored in batches. The more grain you have in the warehouse, the better. Agriculture must take into account the shifting seasons, and it is taken for granted that the lead-time of growing and harvesting grain must be long.

When modern manufacturing emerged, it was patterned after this agricultural mentality. Raw materials were bought, processed, and stored in batches. Not much consideration was given to establishing a flow of work, and no effort was made to shorten the lead-time of production. Keeping a large inventory was taken for granted as a way of doing business. Even today, good inventory means high inventory to some managers.

As long as the varieties of products offered to customers were small in number, this type of production did not pose many problems. As customers have come to demand diversified products to be delivered on time and in different volumes, it has become increasingly difficult to develop flexibility to meet such demands in the context of the batch production system. To cope with the new demand, efforts have been made by management in such areas as shortening set-up time, quality improvement, adding more lines, and even building new plants.

Unfortunately, even to this day, more than 90% of all manufacturing companies in the world still subscribe to batch production, a system that is one of the biggest obstacles to establishing good quality management.

"It is not the pace of technology or the brilliance of innovation that guarantees the success of our markets, but rather an unyielding commitment to quality . . . markets exist by the grace of investors."

Arthur Levitt, Jr.

The Drawbacks of Batch Production

The following features of the batch production system stand in the way of quality management:

- **Large inventory**: As the name batch production suggests, the system is based on producing large batches of inventory at every production process. As a result, 100% quality-control inspection is nearly impossible. Even if quality defects are found at a later stage, it is almost impossible to go back to the previous process which produced the defects, seek out the root cause, and take corrective actions, since such rejects were made several days earlier. Also, the quality of products or parts deteriorates over time when stored in inventory, the only exceptions to this, of course, being red wine and whisky.
- **Long lead time**: The long lead time required by the batch production system makes it difficult to take prompt and flexible action to meet the customer requirements for quality and delivery. For instance, the batch production system is far less flexible when design changes are called for.
- **Isolated islands**: Batch production is necessitated because each manufacturing process is separated from the others—each on its own isolated island. This necessitates transport between processes, causing damage. Again, the isolated islands make it difficult to diagnose quality problems in real time. When operators do their jobs surrounded by inventory, housekeeping is difficult to maintain, which in turn leads to lower morale and less self-discipline of employees.

It becomes clear from the reasons given above that no matter how much effort management may make toward improving quality, batch production destroys those efforts.

JUST-IN-TIME PRODUCTION SYSTEM

The JIT production system was developed as an antithesis to batch production by Tai-ichi Ohno at the Toyota Motor Corporation and, along with many other practical tools like *kanban*, *poka-yoke* (fail-safe device) and *jidohka* (automation), is supported by the following three pillars of production:

- *takt* time versus cycle time (theoretical time versus actual time for processing one work piece);
- pull production versus push production (producing only as many items as the next process needs versus producing as many as can be produced);
- establishing production flow (rearranging equipment layout and processes according to the work sequence).

Just-in-time is really a revolutionary production system, and is in every sense just the opposite of the batch production. It employs minimum materials, equipment, manpower, utility, space, time, and money. It produces products within a shortest lead time and meets the diversified demand of customers and delivers the products just-in-time.

Quality is ensured by keeping small inventories and through the use of flow production. Small inventories eventually lead to one-piece flow, namely one work piece moving from process to process. This enables operators to make a 100% inspection of each piece. In flow production, unlike in the isolated islands approach of batch production, processes are arranged in a flow, and any quality reject created in one process can be identified in the next process immediately.

MAKING IT HAPPEN ▶▶

How many quality managers and engineers realize that the production system of their own company is a major cause for many quality problems they have to deal with? A review of the production system currently in use should be the first action taken by those engaged in quality improvement.

- To solve quality problems, help employees to gain wisdom, as well as knowledge.
- Base total quality on good "gemba" (shop floor) management—meaning standardization, excellent housekeeping and effective elimination of "muda" (waste).
- When a problem (or abnormality) arises, always go to "gemba" first, and never rely on secondary information—reports, meetings, etc.
- When at "gemba," check "gembutsu" (relevant objects), take temporary counter measures on the spot, find the root cause, and standardize to stop problems recurring.
- Recognize that batch production itself is one of the biggest obstacles to good quality management.

- Replace the batch system with Just-in-time production, arranging processes in a flow, so that any quality reject created in one process can be immediately identified in the next.

Conclusion

- Quality is everybody's job, even though it is often regarded as the responsibility of the quality manager alone. When serious quality problems arise, the quality manager is the first to be sacked.
- There is an axiom: don't get it, don't make it, and don't send it. Another is: the next process is the customer.
- Inside a company, the flow goes through three processes: the supplier (previous process), one's own process, and the next process (customer).
- When the supplier sends a defective product or information, the next process—which is receiving the product or information—is a customer to the supplier. He or she is entitled to send back what he or she has received and request better quality.
- After adding value on what you have received in your own process, before you send it to the next process (your customer), inspect it and make sure that you are sending only good quality items.
- Only when everybody subscribes to this commitment do you have a good quality assurance system in operation at work. Management need to realize this. The quality manager establishes the framework of quality and the line manager executes it.

Developing such a mindset requires self-discipline. For this reason, good housekeeping is one of the basic activities to be carried out in gemba, as it helps employees to develop that self-discipline.

FOR MORE INFORMATION

Books:
Imai, Masaaki. *Gemba Kaizen: A Common-sense, Low-cost Approach to Management.* New York: McGraw-Hill, 1997.
Imai, Masaaki. *Kaizen: The Key to Japan's Competitive Success.* New York: McGraw-Hill, 1986.

"Quality is not a program that can be simply imposed on an operation; instead it is a way of operating that permeates a business and the thinking of its employees."

Theodore B. Kinni

The Good, the Fad, and the Ugly
by Lucy Kellaway

EXECUTIVE SUMMARY

- All senior managers despise management fads, yet most senior managers are guilty of following them.
- A few fads are valuable, many are not—and all are practical, frequently obvious, common sense approaches to business management.
- The ability to spot a fad and use it is as important as the ability to spot a fad and keep well clear. The ability to spot a peddler of fads is useful as well.
- Big fads often spawn little fads and fads should be treated carefully. There are many ways to treat a situation—and a one-size-fits-all approach may be anti-competitive.

INTRODUCTION

All senior managers despise management fads. Yet most senior managers are guilty of following them.

The attitude of business toward the management fad is a complex mixture of cynicism and optimism. This conflict is evident in the very language used to discuss them. The term "management fad" is derogatory. When managers use this term it is because they are going to say something cynical. They are going to talk about the sheep-like behavior of other companies, and other fads, or fads in general. But when they are describing their own recent adoption of the latest management fad, the f-word is replaced by the word "idea," "concept," "theory," or "solution."

FADS DON'T WORK

Most academics will tell you that management fads, in aggregate, do not work. Not only does the company that has implemented the fad not achieve the expected increase in productivity, profitability, staff retention, or whatever, often the effect is actually negative. There are all sorts of reasons for this:

- The fad is not the right one for the company.
- The fad has been poorly or inconsistently implemented.
- It conflicts with other fads simultaneously being pursued.
- Management is not committed to it.
- Expectations of its likely effect are unrealistic.
- The fad was a bad idea in the first place.

So Why Do Companies Use Them?

Partly they use them out of fear of being left behind. They use them because they are as fashion conscious as the average teenager. If their peers are using them they feel that they must too. They also use them because they crave concrete ideas; they want to have a story to tell. Senior managers are more likely to be highly rated by their stockholders, peers, and employees if they are seen to be doing something. To establish a new system always looks more impressive than simply maintaining the status quo.

They also do it because they are seduced by the amazing success stories that come with every fad: benchmarking—the measurement craze—comes complete with a story of what it did for Xerox; Six Sigma—a variant on Total Quality Management—comes with a glowing case study from Motorola, and so on.

And if this is not enough to hook them, there will be a hard sell from many armies of consultants who have a vested interest in making sure that yesterday's fad is smartly replaced by that of today.

How Many Fads Are There?

There are a lot, however you count them. The *Economist Guide to Management Ideas* covers 100 fads which have attracted mass followings over the last few decades. Yet this list is nowhere near exhaustive. Fads come in all shapes and sizes—hard, soft, big, small, reasonable, and stupid.

Whatever the exact number, there are far too many for any manager—even the most dedicated follower of fashion—to keep up.

WHICH ARE THE GOOD ONES?

There is—unfortunately—no correct answer to this question. Most of the fads are based on a solid idea or a reasonable assumption. The idea may not be new or original—indeed the most successful fads are based on ideas so achingly obvious it is amazing that they need spelling out at all.

Total Quality Management

This has been around since the 1950s. Its passage from pioneering idea to mass adoption to rejection is one that has been followed again by all the major fads.

Developed by W. Edwards Deming, it was practiced initially in Japan. By the 1980s and 1990s almost every Western manufacturer was doing it too. TQM is based on the rational notion that there is no point in just measuring the quality of the finished product. Every single process within a company should be monitored in terms of how it conforms to customer requirements. Managerial processes get measured in the same way as manufacturing ones, with the goal of reducing all errors to almost zero.

For a brief moment at the end of the 1980s TQM had the status of a religion. Everyone believed it was the most important and beneficial management fad ever. The backlash set in at the start of the 1990s, as companies started complaining at the amount of paperwork and bureaucracy. Even companies that had successful TQM programs started having second thoughts. Florida Power & Light, which won an award for its quality program, subsequently abandoned it when it turned out just how much its employees hated it.

Reengineering

As TQM drifted out of fashion reengineering came in. It was the brainchild of two U.S. academics, Michael Hammer and James Champy. They argued that companies should go back to the drawing board, look at all their processes, and redesign them from scratch. This seemed to be a solution to all ills. Here was a way of cutting cost, and improving quality service and speed at the same time. It sounded unbeatable.

Only what actually happened was that reengineering became synonymous with the job losses that almost always accompanied it. Within four or five years this fad had gotten such a bad name that even its creators distanced themselves from it. They noted that senior management tended to make itself exempt from any reengineering, thus rendering the whole exercise useless.

This was one of the fastest trends to come

"A powerful new idea can kick around unused in a company for years, not because its merits are not recognised, but because nobody has assumed the responsibility for converting it from words to action."

Theodore Levitt

and go. The time from the publication of the original article to the mass adoption of reengineering to its being largely discredited was barely five years.

Knowledge Management

This became the big idea of the late 1990s. It is based on the notion that the most valuable asset a company has is its knowledge: its intellectual property, ideas, and experience. This knowledge exists in files, databases, and in the heads of people. Knowledge management is about how to manage all this in a systematic way. Much of it is to do with creating better IT systems, so that one part of the company can know what other parts are doing. Some of knowledge management is cultural—about getting people to generate more ideas, and share their ideas and their knowledge with their coworkers.

The general idea of knowledge management is hard to argue with. Indeed few do argue with it, and it is still, broadly, in favor. However, many of the knowledge management programs put in by different companies have come under attack for being needlessly complex, for saving too much useless information.

Vision, Values, and Mission

Aficionados might take these three categories separately, but all have a common theme. The idea once again is pretty simple. It is that by trying to define what a company is about, that company will learn something about itself. Odd as it might seem, this is often the case. If senior executives sit down and try to work out what their company is—and is not—trying to do, what it exists for, and what are its common values, then so much the better.

However, mission statements in fact have done little to change the corporate world for the better. In practice one company's mission looks uncannily like that of another—a predictable mixture of motherhood and apple pie. Even when the statement is appropriate and distinctive, taken alone it is powerless to bring about change. People do not change by dint of a statement, no matter how carefully drawn up it might be.

Hard Fads

For each of these big fads there are scores and scores of smaller ones. There are many other technical measurement fads like TQM—Six Sigma (a quality variant, hard to understand let alone implement), balanced scorecard, and benchmarking. All of these are about numbers, spotting your target and measuring it. All are sensible. Benchmarking yourself against other comparable companies is so sensible, it is extraordinary that it ever had any status as a fad. All companies should always benchmark—at least they should know roughly how they are doing relative to others. Measurement is important and necessary, but on its own it is not going to guarantee much change in performance.

Soft Fads

This is the biggest growth area among fads. It seems that every week there is a new pat solution that will help managers manage their people better. Management by Objectives got replaced by Management by Walking Around, and then, still more ludicrously, with Management by Hanging Around. Senior managers started frequenting the cappuccino bars in the hope that this would lead to closer-knit teams.

Most soft fads are based loosely around the idea of personal growth. Since hierarchies went out of fashion 20 years ago, all management styles are meant to include coaching and mentoring.

MAKING IT HAPPEN ▶▶
- Treat all fads with caution. Always act suspicious when introduced to a new fad.

- Never take up a fad because a management consultant has persuaded you it is a good idea.
- Never expect miracles from your fad.
- Always consider how well it fits with your company's culture. Any new fad in isolation is never going to change people's behavior.
- Never do it by half.
- Believe in the motto "If it ain't broke . . ." And even if it is broke, you don't need to mend it the same way as everybody else.

CONCLUSION

We know that happy employees are productive ones. According to the fashionable view, people are happiest when they are given responsibility and respect. Thus we have empowerment—the idea that everybody in the organization should be able to wield some power. This was all the rage in the 1990s, and is still fairly popular, especially with wide-eyed human resources people. The difficulty is that very few organizations can pull it off. Empowerment conflicts with some of the less positive aspects of human nature—senior managers do not want to let go, and many underlings do not want more responsibility.

FOR MORE INFORMATION

Books:
Dearlove, Des. *The Ultimate Book of Business Thinking*. San Francisco, CA: Capstone, 2002.
Hindle, Tim. *Guide to Management Ideas*. 2nd ed. New York: Bloomberg Press, 2003.

See also:
☆ Avoiding the Mistakes of the Past: Lessons from the Startup World (pp. 164–165)
☆ Who's Guiding Your Corporate Destiny? (pp. 255–257)

"And I think one of the powers of fad surfing is that it really is a kind of managerial prozac. It allows managers to say, I am doing something therefore I am managing and leading."

Eileen C. Shapiro

Designing Corporate Systems for Success
by Leslie L. Kossoff

EXECUTIVE SUMMARY

- Organizational systems, their policies, procedures, rules, and instructions, can and should be designed to promote the limitless success of the organization.
- Management owns the systems and only they can ensure that the systems are designed to assist everyone in creating success.
- By establishing an ongoing internal and external dialog, management can create an organization that never rests on its laurels and is designed to succeed.

INTRODUCTION

In the best of breed organizations, no matter what industry or sector, the two questions everyone always asks are: "What more?" and "What else?" Then, they go there—no matter where "there" is. Because they can. Because they have designed their management and decision-making systems—from personnel and payroll to IT and R&D—to ensure that the organization and everyone in it is set up to succeed.

ASSESSING THE IMPACT OF ORGANIZATIONAL SYSTEMS

One of the single largest, most consistent management oversights is not understanding that the corporate and organizational systems—those written and unwritten policies, procedures, and instructions to which everyone operates—are a crucial part of the strategic and operational plan of the enterprise. Very simply, if your corporate systems are not designed, implemented, and consistently reviewed and enforced with your organizational strategy in mind, then you're guaranteed to put unnecessary obstacles in your own way.

Corporate systems, in and of themselves, seem harmless. They provide guidance on everything from compensation, vacation entitlement, attendance, and retirement programs to supplier and customer relation systems, product and service policies, and procedures and more.

The intent of the systems is positive. They're there to protect the organization and its employees from harm and to ensure as fair and positive a workplace as possible.

The problem is that they develop in a patchwork over time—usually in response to a particular need or problem of the day which may or may not exist any longer. But the system continues to exist—and it has little or no connection with the strategic direction and needs of the enterprise today.

By stepping back and reviewing your systems from a strategic perspective, you'll be able to quickly identify those systems that are working toward your goals—and which are not. It's easy. Simply ask yourself: How does this policy/procedure/instruction help us to achieve our strategic goals, vision, and mission? If you can identify how—and clearly see that its implementation is consistent with that goal—then keep it. If not, there's your opportunity for positive change. And when you make that change you'll have created a direct line to new worlds of innovation and profit increases.

TECHNIQUES FOR IMPROVING CORPORATE SYSTEMS

Improving corporate systems is no different from improving any other aspect of the enterprise. It begins with an assessment, leading to specific actions that remove obstacles and create new opportunities. Where the difference appears is in the far-reaching outcomes of seemingly simple improvements. Remember, these are systems—not just single actions. Each time you make a change you're creating a ripple effect that positively impacts everyone within and outside the enterprise. That makes systems improvement all the more exciting and satisfying to pursue.

Understand the impact of organizational systems

To understand how your corporate systems are impacting the organizational, you first need to put the systems in context. That means that, before you look at what you want to change, you first have to take an overarching look at the enterprise. Whether you are the most senior executive, small business entrepreneur, or member of a management team, you need to take an objective look at what you are responsible for—in effect the part of the organization you own—then ask yourself: Is the organization operating the way I want it to? Are we, in fact, designed to succeed? Once you take that objective look and give yourself an honest answer, you're ready to take on the corporate systems that are affecting your ability to succeed.

From that point, the next questions are:
- Which policies, procedures, rules, regulations, and instructions within the organizational systems infrastructure support the organization's strategic goals? Which do not?
- Which systems cannot be changed, for example, because of law or government regulation?
- Of those systems that can be changed, what must we do to make sure that the systems that direct and drive the organization are designed to help us succeed?
- Which systems have been unintentionally imposed or supported and can now be let go?

Once you have the answers to those questions, you're ready to move toward active improvement—and you have a good head start on how to achieve it quickly, painlessly, and profitably.

Align your systems with your strategy

Once you've identified the systems to which you're working, assess how each is helping—or hindering—the strategic goals of the organization. Just as you tie your strategic plan to operational and execution plans, slot the systems into place within that larger context. If the systems aren't working to-

> "Running a company is a constant process of breaking out of systems and challenging conditioned reflexes, of rubbing against the grain."
>
> Mark McCormack

ward your goals, they need to be changed. If they are imposed by law or government regulation, find out whether your interpretation is correct and if there's any way to maneuver within those laws and regulations to give you more room to succeed.

Review your metrics

Take a close look at how your organization is measured. Look at the metrics used internally and externally. Each of the corporate systems is tied to a measure—whether you know it, like it or not. As you identify the systems to which the organization operates, you should also be able to identify the specific measures impacted by those systems. Whether the measures are internally designed and driven or the types that analysts use when assessing publicly held companies, each system has a measurable—and financial—impact. So, as you review your metrics, also take a look at the costs attached. That, too, will drive your decisions regarding the priority order of the systems change process.

Create an active systems redesign process

Once you know where to put your attention, create an ongoing system that reviews the systems in place and continually assesses whether they are serving the best interests of your organization—whether by function or for the overall enterprise. With each review of the strategy, incorporate a review of the systems and their progress toward improvement or dissolution. Make sure that your customer and supplier data are incorporated into this process as well. They, too, account for a great deal of your success—financial and otherwise.

MINI-CASES

From first establishing your systems to setting up ongoing mechanisms for review and enforcement, corporate systems development is an ongoing job that must always be tied to the strategic goals of the enterprise. By doing so, your organization is designed to achieve its goals—and even more.

eBay is the poster child for ongoing assessment of systems—and using that process to build out the business even further than anyone could ever have imagined. It began by understanding that the "customers" of eBay constitute a community—with all that that implies. Rules and regulations for a group of people, technically not

belonging to the organization but central to its success, had to be developed so that the company was protected. This protection had to address everything from the revenues to eBay's reputation. Moreover, once the rules and regulations were set, the company ensured that they were enforced on a consistent, ongoing and public basis. When you do business with eBay you know you have the good faith of the company behind you, protecting your interests—because they understand that your interests are theirs, if they want to keep succeeding.

And for all those countries—yes, countries—that find themselves moving out of manufacturing and into service-based economies, they are looking for their Nordstrom moment. Nordstrom is a retail department store located in various states in the United States—but their impact extended even to those who, to this day, have never visited the store. Nordstrom management understood that they offered the same products as their competition. From cosmetics to men's and women's clothing, management understood that their customers had a choice—which led them to become dedicated to making Nordstrom first choice based on a service difference. From return policies to employee follow-up with customers, let alone the legendary stories of late-night home or hotel deliveries in cases of sartorial emergencies, Nordstrom became the bellwether for all forms of service. Whether in retail or your home's gas and electricity provider, customers knew what to expect in excellent customer service—because Nordstrom had taught them the difference through their corporate-designed customer service systems.

MAKING IT HAPPEN ▸▸

Organizational systems are owned by management—which means that only management can do anything about them.

However, it really isn't difficult to ensure that the systems are in alignment with the organization's strategic and operational goals. The process is straightforward, whether applied on a cross-organizational or department-specific basis. The following measures will help you improve the situation:

- Understand the current position: the scope of the system, why they are there, and the impact they have. Is the net effect of each rule positive?
- Consider how to mitigate the effects of

necessary rules or systems which may have some challenging or potentially frustrating consequences.
- Involve people: systems are devised by people for people, so don't ignore them.
- Keep the process of reviewing, replacing, and enforcing rules dynamic. It is not an advantage simply to review the changes once and then leave well alone. Times change; so do systems.

CONCLUSION

To be best of breed, whether a small local business just starting up or a multi-national looking for ever larger pieces of the global market, you have to make sure that all your pieces fit and that the glue that holds them together—your corporate systems—are designed to help every step of the way.

The more stakeholders—within and outside the organization—you involve, the more and better the information you'll get, and the more and faster you'll be able to streamline how you do what you do. From hiring the best of the best to making your customers ecstatic, it all comes from devising, implementing, managing, and enforcing corporate systems that are designed for organizational success.

FOR MORE INFORMATION

Books:
Collins, Jim. *Good to Great: Why Some Companies Make the Leap . . . and Others Don't*. New York: HarperCollins, 2001.
Drucker, Peter. *Management Challenges for the 21st Century*. New York: HarperBusiness, 2001.
Juran, J. M. *Juran on Leadership for Quality: An Executive Handbook*. New York: Free Press, 1989.

Web sites:
About.com:
http://management.about.com
JimCollins.com: **www.jimcollins.com**
Kossoff.com: **www.kossoff.com**

See also:
☆ From Crisis Management to Crisis Leadership (pp. 379–380)
☆ Viewpoint: Christopher Bartlett (pp. 45–46)
☆ Viewpoint: Henry Mintzberg (pp. 292–293)
☆ Viewpoint: Jim Collins (pp. 287–288)

"You can only raise individual performance by elevating that of the entire system."

W. Edwards Deming

Facilities Management
by Keith Alexander

EXECUTIVE SUMMARY

- Facilities management should be considered as a strategic business discipline.
- Organizations need greater flexibility, improved connectivity with customers and better working conditions for employees. Good facilities management can deliver on all these objectives.
- Managers need to consider not "how do facilities benefit occupiers?", but more, "how do occupiers secure maximum benefits from facilities?"
- Research is now beginning to show the relationship between effective facilities management and improved stock value.
- Facilities also play a leading role in fulfilling the social and environmental responsibilities of an organization.
- A business case can be made for facilities management either on grounds of efficiency and the ability to control costs or, alternatively, to improve the return on fixed assets.

INTRODUCTION

In order to respond to today's fast-moving and rapidly changing business environment, organizations need greater flexibility, improved connectivity with their customers, better working conditions, and more choice for employees—all backed by a quality environment and excellent service. The concepts, discipline, and practice of facilities management is evolving to meet these challenges, and is becoming increasingly sophisticated in offering "integrated workplace strategies" and in arranging the provision of "serviced accommodation" to meet these contemporary business needs.

THE IMPORTANCE OF CONTEXT

Facilities—a company's physical settings, support services, and environmental conditions—must be used effectively to add value to business objectives, strategies, and processes. This becomes increasingly important in this rapidly changing economic environment as organizations seek greater flexibility, seek to assimilate new workplace technologies, and reconsider their strategies toward facilities and property. However, the question is less, "how do facilities benefit occupiers?" and more, "how do occupiers secure maximum benefits from facilities?" It is a management issue rather than a design or technical issue.

Many organizations are still completely driven by stockholder return, and research is now beginning to show the relationship between effective facilities management and improved share value. But there are two other very significant factors in the business equation: corporate culture and motivational factors (for example reward, responsibility, job security). An organization's facilities and the services provided to support its operations should reflect that culture and must not disrupt motivational factors.

MAKING A BUSINESS CASE

The business case for facilities management can be made in a number of different ways. However, the emphasis is still generally on the contribution to financial performance and stockholder value. For many years, the emphasis has been on the office as an overhead cost, divorced from its contribution to output. The predominant trend has been to make a case on grounds of efficiency and the ability to control and reduce costs or, alternatively, to improve the return on fixed assets.

Clearly, facilities have an important impact on a company's profitability. As facilities are usually an organization's second largest expense, most facilities managers concentrate on seeking to reduce occupancy costs. Indeed, it is likely that their role and responsibilities in the organization are defined in this way. In many organizations, every facilities management decision must be justified in terms of impact on the profit and loss account. The emphasis is more on cost efficiency than on cost effectiveness.

Alternatively, in some organizations a business case will be built around the return on investment, and facilities are seen as a fixed asset or business resource, with a value on the balance sheet. Traditionally, buildings are seen as a capital asset. In this case the key measure is return on asset, and is an important determinant of stockholder value. However, research has shown that companies with lower property holdings derived superior stock-market value.

Facilities can also be considered as a factor of production. They can make a prime contribution to improving the effectiveness of individuals and teams and to enhancing productivity. Facilities managers have usually concentrated on reducing the office cost per employee and increasing the occupancy per square foot of office space, without sufficient regard to the impact this might have on people's performance and the all-factor productivity of their organization.

However, studies have shown that the total cost of providing office space is less than one-tenth of staff costs, and that operating costs are only one-hundredth of staff output. The importance of buildings in supporting the effectiveness and productivity of office workers has been underplayed, largely because of the lack of available evidence to support the business case. Organizations such as PricewaterhouseCoopers are collaborating in projects that develop tools for measuring the performance of facilities and for evaluating the productivity of office environments.

Facilities are important to public and industrial relations and play a large part in setting the corporate identity and image. Britain's National Health Service has had to reconsider the strategic role of hospital cleaning in recognition of how important cleanliness is to customer confidence in the healthcare received, as well as to cut down on infections. It is increasingly recognized that facilities are a means of improving confidence and morale among employees, customers, and visitors.

Other organizations recognize how essential it is to plan facilities in order to insure business continuity and assess and manage business risk. There are increasing corporate concerns about the power, energy, and transportation infrastructures, and the consequences to business of failure. Contingency and disaster-recovery planning are

---

"Communication is best achieved through simple planning and control . . . Most conversations . . . drift along; in business, this is wasteful; as a manager . . . seek communication rather than chatter."

Gerald M. Blair

essential elements of a coherent business continuity plan.

Facilities management strategies are developed around each of these dimensions of business performance, individually or in combination. Each will have an impact on share value. A more balanced approach is required, and methods and tools are needed to enable the facilities manager to maximize the output from an office and so contribute to the strategic performance of their organization. Many organizations are introducing a balanced scorecard approach in order to ensure they are driven by indicators of business performance other than merely financial ones.

INTELLIGENT CLIENT ROLE

From a practical perspective, facilities management is normally considered as the coordination of functions and integration of multi-disciplinary activities. Many definitions emphasize the practical and operational concerns. But as facility management has become aligned with the core business objectives of public and private organizations, it has had to become increasingly strategic and business oriented.

There are several strategies for dealing with facilities management. Over the past ten years there has been a significant shift toward the outsourcing of facility services in both the public and private sectors. Research suggests that global corporations are considering increasingly radical options for simplifying the facility supply chain. This increases the level of skill needed within an organization to create the conditions for innovation and continuous improvement.

Some organizations, both public and private, treat flexible working initiatives and new workplaces as a strategic issue—one which aims to create an organizational culture suited to the knowledge economy. Management theorists such as Peter Drucker argue that these trends form part of a wider economic restructuring linked to the growth of specialist knowledge-based organizations.

MINI-CASE
The U.K. bank Abbey has 750 branches across the United Kingdom but the portfolio numbers 1,400 sites in total. As well as major office sites, call centers, and IT sites, many of these are offices above branches and are counted separately from the retail sites below. In 2000, Abbey (formerly Abbey National) sold its entire property portfolio to a third party in order to guarantee operational and strategic flexibility, without the future risk of uncertainty over the cost of reconfiguring its property portfolio. The deal involved around 6.5 million square feet of space.

Abbey saw the project as a major step toward being able to alter its property requirements, radically if required, in order to meet its customers' future business needs, thereby significantly enhancing its competitive position. The deal was the first significant transaction of its kind in the private sector in the United Kingdom.

It was about a sustainable approach to property management over the long term—"We are in the banking business, not the property business." The project was also about the management of risk: "It means that we will limit a substantial area of liability from the start of the deal, without losing the flexibility that our business strategy requires." For Abbey, the immediate and long-term benefits of the agreement were substantially reduced exposure to property risk, improved operational flexibility and secured property costs for the foreseeable future.

Abbey has set new standards in property management. The bank has also aligned its property strategy to that of the business, rather than looking at a property portfolio and its liabilities in isolation from its business strategy, as in so many other companies. In short, Abbey engineered a deal that achieved the high level of flexibility its business requires.

MAKING IT HAPPEN ▶▶
- Make a business case by identifying the value added by facilities management.

- Plan facilities strategically to maximize the business benefit.
- Demonstrate the contribution facilities make to achieving organizational objectives.
- Manage change so that FM initiatives and workplace solutions fit the organizational culture.
- Develop the intelligent client role.
- Develop performance management systems consistent with the corporate climate.
- Create service partnerships to promote innovation and continuous improvement.

FOR MORE INFORMATION

Books:
Park, Alan. *Facilities Management: An Explanation*. 2nd ed. New York: Palgrave Macmillan, 1998.
Raymond, Santa, and Roger Cunliffe. *Tomorrow's Office: Creating Effective and Humane Interiors*. London: Spon Press, 2000.
Robertson, Ken. *Work Transformation: Planning and Implementing the New Workplace*. New York: HNB Publishing, 1998.
Rondeau, Edmond P., et al. *Facility Management*. 2nd ed. New York: Wiley, 2006.
Teicholz, Eric, ed. *Facility Design and Management Handbook*. New York: McGraw-Hill, 2001.

Web site:
www.fdm.com: the Facilities Design & Management's Web page is devoted to keeping facility managers informed about current issues and helping them track future developments. Along with the site, you can subscribe to their magazine of the same name.

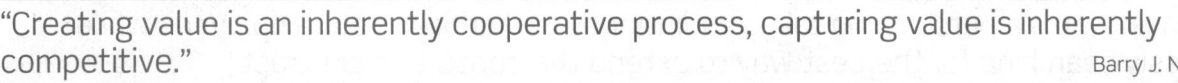

"Creating value is an inherently cooperative process, capturing value is inherently competitive."
Barry J. Nalebuff

216

BEST PRACTICE

Working from the Outside In
by Bill Jensen

EXECUTIVE SUMMARY

- Life is just too short. More to the point, it's just too damn precious.
- There is a great and grave difference between employee satisfaction and satisfying employees' work needs. The new covenant between employers and employees is about that difference.
- In the new war for talent, employees see themselves as investors. Every day, they invest scarce and precious assets—their time, attention, ideas, knowledge, passion, energy, and social networks—to make our companies go. They will work wherever they get the best returns on those assets.

INTRODUCTION

Shortly after the September 11, 2001 attacks on New York's twin towers, I had a gut-wrenching conversation with a fellow airline passenger. She was angry and frustrated at having to be on the plane. Even though she is one of the most senior execs at a *Fortune 50* company, she felt like she didn't have control of her own life. She was traveling 3,000 miles just because the C.E.O. said she had to. "What if something happens on this plane?" she said. "I don't want to leave my two girls believing that life is about sucking up and doing the right thing just for a paycheck or a career. This company just doesn't get that."

That same conversation is rippling across every workplace, in every sector, at every level of the organization. A lot of people are asking with new urgency, "Why am I doing this? Am I really making a difference? Is this what I want out of life? Out of my career?"

The events and aftermath of September 11 have altered forever the public conversation about how companies and individuals serve each other. The very covenant and rules of engagement between employee and employer are being questioned. However, the new rules were emerging long before we got that tragic wake-up call.

During the past decade I have studied how thousands of companies get work done. And a startling shift and major inequity have occurred during that time. The people most companies want to attract and retain are bringing with them never-before-seen levels of sophistication and insights about the design of knowledge work. They know more than most leaders about how to collaborate, how to organize information, what they need to get stuff done, how to

communicate and how decision making really works. Technology, marketplace, and social changes have trained, enticed, and forced them to hone these skills.

Yet, for more and more employees, *the more they invest in their company, the more they lose control of their own destiny*. They have focused on customers. They have drunk the corporate Kool-Aid™, and they have worked hard. But the overwhelming majority of the tools, structures, and support they get are *still* designed to ensure corporate success—not necessarily theirs.

A New Contract Emerges

This inequity is forcing a new covenant. Under the new work contract, employees see themselves as investors. Every day, they invest scarce and precious assets—their time, attention, ideas, knowledge, passion, energy, and social networks—to make our companies go. They watch today's leaders wasting these assets and, like Wall Street, they want better returns.

Decent pay, appropriate benefits, feeling appreciated, being treated and rewarded fairly, and being part of a great team will always be important. But our best employees are moving beyond entitlements and nurturing. They know that they have to be more productive, more efficient, and deliver more better and faster every day. They also know that each day contains only 1,440 minutes with which they can make a difference.

So, in return for those minutes, they're looking at:
- how easy it is to make a big impact;
- how much of their time is spent doing great and important work;
- how much and how fast they can learn;

- how challenging, rewarding, and exciting their work remains;
- how much personal success and balance they achieve—however they choose to define these things;
- how well, or poorly, your company uses their 1,440 minutes;
- how much control they have over their own destiny.

Since there are no guarantees with any employer, employees are beginning to see your company as a middleman between them, their team mates, customers, and the marketplace. Your company is a tool to connect all these constituencies. And the new contract says it's time for you to start acting like an elegant tool.

Whoa, does this add a new dimension to the basic covenant! There is a great and grave difference between employee satisfaction and satisfying employees' work needs. The new contract is about that difference.

Wrenching uncertainty and tough economic times have not disguised the fact that—especially as you slash budgets and reduce headcount—you are using employees' time, attention, and energy as working capital to meet your company's short-term obligations. They know it. And your best talent is seeking more in return than just a job, a paycheck, or benefits—all of which may be yanked from them without notice.

People are seeking more in return for their time . . . because life is just too short. More to the point, it's just too damn precious.

The War for Talent Changes

If we begin to think about our employees as investors, many efforts to attract and retain talent come up short.

Do you waste any of your talent's time, attention, ideas, knowledge, passion, energy, or social networks? What is the daily/weekly/monthly return your talent gets for investing their assets in your company? The new war for talent will be fought over who provides the best returns on life's precious assets. Among the coming changes . . .

- **Employees are seeking to participate in infrastructure specs.** Your technology, processes, information flows, and

everything that connects your employees and organizes their work are being examined from the user's perspective. Sun Microsystems is one company where this is happening. They formed a Workplace Effectiveness group to track how their workspaces and tools are viewed by the people who use them. Every six months, Sun surveys up to 6,000 employees worldwide on issues such as the factors behind personal productivity.

- **Employees are seeking more input into who manages them.** IBM's Extreme Blue student interns have made it clear they won't tolerate "loser managers." And some companies, like PepsiCo, are allowing high-potential talent to select their own managers. Smart companies are beginning to change the rules of how managers and employees are paired and developed.
- **Employees are seeking more input into how they collaborate.** Smart companies also understand that new standards are being set daily for what is valued in work exchanges-for example, what content is most valuable, and what social connections, timing, tips, and tools are needed, and what type of coaching would be most helpful. Companies like Cisco and Dell are designing entire learning structures based upon workforce feedback on what they say they need.

MAKING IT HAPPEN ▶▶

A new war for talent is emerging through tougher examination of work itself. For years, our companies have operated on the premise that there's *work* and there's *life* and it's up to employees to balance the two. Since September 11, it has become clear that this view is no longer acceptable. The very act of using someone's time assigns new accountabilities to each of us.

This creates new rules in how you fight the war for talent. Among them . . .

Great workplaces respect life's precious assets: Smart companies are beginning to attract and retain people with an amazingly simple idea: improve business results and create a great place to work by improving how they use employees' time and energy. This means embracing a bottom-up asset revolution.

Great workplaces get better results by giving people better control over their own destiny: Business must focus on personal, not just organizational, productivity. The future of work is increasingly customized, personalized, and tailored to each individual.

This means the future war for talent will be anchored by My Work My Way—delivering business success by customizing more and more information, work tools, and experiences to individual needs. As long as the future includes heavy knowledge work, where personal choices are integral to success, My-Way approaches will be critical.

Great workplaces get more out of collaboration by putting more into it: Today's centralized, top-down approaches to planning collaboration infrastructure and tools are simply not keeping up with the rate of change in how peers want and need to collaborate with each other. If you are going to add value to peer-to-peer exchanges, you must be willing to design budgets and strategies around what the people doing the work find most valuable. You need to focus a lot more on how you deliver peer-to-peer value.

The leaders of great workplaces accept accountability for life's precious assets: Those whom we will follow in the war for talent are "extreme leaders." What makes leadership "extreme" is greater accountability for performance through greater willingness to be challenged on, and address, work-level details. Partnering with employees who have no fear about pushing upward. Extreme leaders acknowledge that the route to corporate success includes changing the path employees must take for their personal success.

New metrics for great places to work

The SimplerWork Index™ tracks six new dimensions of great places to work. Beyond being nice to your employees, this index tracks what it takes to do great work in a knowledge-based economy. Each measure focuses on how well you enable people to work smarter and faster *while also* giving each employee greater control over his or her own destiny. Unfortunately, the percentages below* illustrate how much today's companies must still improve.

- **Competing on clarity 49%**—evaluates manager's effectiveness in helping individual employees to work smarter and faster;
- **Navigation 29%**—evaluates company's effectiveness in helping individual employees find who or what they need to work smarter and faster;
- **Fulfillment of basics 25%**—evaluates company's effectiveness in work-oriented communication and knowledge management;
- **Usability 19%**—evaluates company's effectiveness in all that it designs to help people get tasks done (tools, technology, training, instructions and so on);
- **Speed 18%**—evaluates company's effectiveness in enabling employees to work in a 24/7, ever-faster world;
- **Time 12%**—evaluates company's respect for employees' time as an asset to be invested.

* 2006 survey of over 50,000 individuals in more than 180 companies

CONCLUSION

No one has a crystal ball. Nobody knows perfectly how to juggle stockholder needs, customer needs, employee needs, and corporate strategies. And certainly, the whole story of the war for talent is far more complex than space here allows.

Yet one signpost on the path ahead is undeniable. Our best employees will no longer tie themselves to any organization that doesn't give them greater control over their own destiny, or respect all of life's precious assets that they put to use each and every day.

The future of business success is tied to every individual's success. We win together, or not at all.

FOR MORE INFORMATION

Books:
Morris, Edmund. *Theodore Rex*. New York: Random House, 2001.
Orwell, George. *1984*. New York: New American Library Classics, 1990.
Toffler, Alvin. *Future Shock*. New York: Bantam Books, 1991.

"It is always easier to talk about change than to make it. It is easier to consult than to manage."
Alvin Toffler

Lean Manufacturing by Daniel T. Jones

EXECUTIVE SUMMARY

- Lean production is the generic version of the Toyota Production System. It has a long history, beginning in the United States before being fully developed by Toyota.
- It is based on managing the product value stream from raw material to end customer, rather than focusing on managing separate assets and companies.
- The objective is to eliminate waste through reconfiguring operations into continuous flow cells linked by leveled pull systems.
- The gains are defect-free products, on-time delivery, big reductions in inventories, and freed-up people, machine time, and space.

INTRODUCTION

Although the terms "lean production" and "lean manufacturing" have only been in circulation since the publication of *The Machine That Changed the World* in 1990, the concepts and practices have a much longer history. Indeed, the core idea of lining production steps in process sequence can be traced back to Colt's armory in Hartford, Connecticut, in 1855. What Henry Ford later called "flow production" reached its peak at his plant in Highland Park in 1915, where every machine making parts and every step toward assembling them were lined up in single-piece flow, so that it took a matter of hours from raw casting to the finished product.

This system could not offer customers enough choice. So when Ford built his next plant at River Rouge in 1931, it was organized quite differently. Large machines able to make large batches of different parts were grouped together in separate departments, maximizing efficiency by ensuring there was always work waiting to be done. Batches of products wandered from department to department and throughput times stretched from several hours to several months. Long lead times entailed making to forecast and selling from several months' stock of finished cars in dealer lots. Thus the world of mass "production" was born and became the dominant model as long as producers could sell everything they made.

DISCOVERING LEAN PRODUCTION

Across the Pacific the founders of Toyota, Sakichi Toyoda and his son Kiichiro, were working on their own version of flow production in the 1930s. They formulated the two key pillars of what later became the Toyota Production System (TPS): automatic machine and line stopping whenever a mistake is made so that no bad parts are passed forward to interrupt the downstream flow (a system they called *Jidoka*), and a pull system in which only parts that are actually needed are made (called *just-in-time*). Later on, the third pillar, involving leveling the workload in a mixed model production flow, was added (called *Heijunka*).

It was not until after World War II that Taiichi Ohno, the production chief at Toyota, implemented these principles. Ohno was determined to overcome all the obstacles to producing a range of products in low volumes, using simple equipment laid out in process sequence. His 20-year experiment started in the engine plant before extending to pressing, body welding, and assembly. Only when Ohno needed to extend the TPS to the supply base in the early 1970s was it written down for the first time, though it was another decade before it was published in books and articles.

Toyota's steady and continuing rise to become the largest automaker in the world led others to try to follow its example. This could only be done by understanding the principles behind TPS and then selecting the right tools in the right sequence. Lean production is the generic version of TPS and lean thinking describes the principles behind not just TPS but the whole Toyota business system, including product development, supplier coordination, and customer management. These principles are based on five key insights.

The Five Principles of Lean Thinking

1. Specify value from the standpoint of the end customer.
2. Identify the value stream for each product family.
3. Link value-creating steps so the product can flow.
4. Enable your customers to pull what they need.
5. Manage toward perfection—where every action and asset creates value.

If you define value from the standpoint of the end customer, you realize that only a tiny fraction of actions and time actually create value. In a typical factory this might be 5% and in a whole value stream (from raw material to end customer) it is usually less than 1%. The rest of the steps are only necessary because of the way companies are currently organized and because of past decisions about assets and technologies. So the greatest opportunity for performance improvement is to reconfigure operations across the value stream to remove these wasted steps.

Taiichi Ohno's Seven Wastes That Consume Value

1. Overproduction
2. Inventories
3. Defects
4. Waiting
5. Excess Transportation
6. Excess Movement
7. Excess Processing

If you identify the whole value stream for a given product (both the flow of orders upstream and the flow of products downstream) you see that optimizing each asset and activity in isolation creates huge amounts of waste elsewhere. It is only by optimizing the product value stream that you can identify ways of eliminating these interface wastes and can begin to rethink the appropriate equipment, technologies, and locations for the future.

The ideal way to organize waste-free production is to line up the value-creating steps so the product flows through them in the shortest possible time. This, in turn, means that every activity must be standardized and repeatable, and that every machine must be fully capable of delivering exactly what is needed and fully available to operate when needed. Where machines cannot be colocated and serve several product flows, then products need to be pulled directly as required from the upstream step. Time compression of every step is the only way to maintain these disciplines and to ensure that waste does not creep back when attention shifts elsewhere.

Multiple decision points and time lags in processing orders lead to amplification of

"Large consumption is at the basis of saving in manufacture, and hence high wages contribute their share to progress."

Thomas Brackett Reed

the variance in orders passed upstream, which in turn requires larger inventories and excess capacity to cover demand spikes. Time compression and direct pull systems are the key to eliminating this amplification and to being able to move away from make-to-forecast and sell-from-stock toward true build-to-order systems able to deliver what customers want within the time available.

The final insight is that reconfiguring the value stream to eliminate waste is a step-by-step process: the more waste you remove, the more you can see to remove next time. It starts by understanding the current state of your operations and defining an achievable future state in a short space of time, which then becomes the current state of the next improvement cycle. However, this cyclical process also needs to be guided by a vision of the perfect state to which you should be headed, in which every action and asset creates value for the end customer.

IMPLEMENTING LEAN PRODUCTION

Lean production is by no means widespread, even in Japan. Indeed, it was only after 1973 that the rest of the Japanese auto industry recognized that Toyota was following a different path. By 1987 the first companies in the United States began to make serious progress with the help of several of Ohno's disciples, who had by then left to become consultants. The early lean conversion stories of Pratt & Whitney, Wiremold, and Lantech are described in *Lean Thinking*. Since then lean production has spread across the automotive, aerospace, and engineering industries and, following Alcoa's example, to raw material processing. It is now also being used in insurance and financial services, utilities, health-care, and government departments.

Many companies began implementing lean production by involving the workforce in team-based problem-solving and *kaizen* or continuous improvement activities. Putting the spotlight on operations should certainly lead to the removal of the most obvious wastes in the organization. However, lean production only really begins when you use value-stream mapping to learn to see the product flow from door to door, and when you give someone the responsibility for reconfiguring operations into continuous flow cells linked by leveled pull systems.

Once progress has been made within the plant, it is time to involve your suppliers, by linking plants using simple pull systems and your customers, by linking them directly to production using build-to-order systems. Beyond this it is possible to envisage rethinking and compressing the value stream using different technologies and right-sized tools colocated close to the point of use. We have in truth only just begun to realize the full potential of lean production.

MAKING IT HAPPEN ▸▸

- Putting the spotlight on all of your operations should eliminate the most obvious wastes and deficiencies in the value chain—from the start of the process to the customer.
- For a more comprehensive assessment of the areas where your organization's processes may improve, use value stream mapping to clearly show product flows.
- Ensure that there is one person with overall responsibility for reconfiguring operations into continuous flow cells, linked by leveled "pull" systems.
- Knit together different parts of your value stream, using build-to-order mechanisms.
- Compress your value stream through the development of new and ongoing strategies—and the application of new technologies—to eliminate wastage and continuously improve efficiency.
- Regularly review your activities—ideally from a customer or end user perspective—to make sure that they are delivered in an effective and profit-centered way.

CONCLUSION

Managing lean value streams is harder than managing individual operations. However, the gains are substantial, particularly when they are replicated across the whole value stream. First, your customers get defect-free products on time. Second, your suppliers get leveled orders and can deliver to you on time. Third, inventories at every point down the value stream can be cut in half. Fourth, you free up a lot of resources—people, machines, and space—that will not appear on the bottom line until they are used. The challenge in sustaining progress toward lean is to grow the throughput and bring operations in house as you free up those assets.

FOR MORE INFORMATION

Books:
Shook, J., and M. Rother. *Learning to See*. Brookline, MA: The Lean Enterprises Institute, 1999.
Womack, James P., and Daniel T. Jones. *Lean Thinking: Banish Waste and Create Wealth in Your Corporation*. 2nd ed. New York: Free Press, 2003.
Womack, James P., et al. *The Machine That Changed the World*. New York: HarperCollins, 1991.
Womack, James P., and Daniel T. Jones. *Lean Solutions: How Companies and Customers can Create Value and Wealth Together*. New York, Free Press, 2005.

Web site:
Other lean manufacturing classics are listed at **www.lean.org**. Here you will also find an online community of those actively implementing lean production and the key workbook to help you get started in mapping your value streams.

See also:
⋅⋇⋅ Genichi Taguchi (pp. 1268–1269)
⋅⋇⋅ Eiji Toyoda (pp. 1360–1361)

"No manufacturing company will ever do well if they are concerned only with calculating profits."

Shoichiro Toyoda

Getting All Your People Committed to Change and Transformation
by John Smythe

EXECUTIVE SUMMARY

- The first age of internal communication: the application of external marketing techniques to internal employee audiences.
- The shift in the role of internal communication from one of replicating management's view of the world to one of creating work place cultures that help organizations achieve their ambitions, not least by creating a compelling place to work.
- The shift from an information-driven concept of communication—conveying messages—to one which releases the energy and creativity of employees; moving in dialog from compliance to commitment.
- Six practical insights to help leaders to create commitment in themselves, in management and all their coworkers.

INTRODUCTION

Internal communication as a management practice is probably no more than 20 years old. It came into vogue when "command-and-control" styles of leadership began to be questioned. Yet most of what is practiced under the banner of internal communication is the internal application of external marketing techniques—internal PR.

In the boardroom, communication is still the final item on the agenda. Directors ask, "What's our line on this?" The function of internal communication is to make sense of decisions after they've been made. Invariably, it's a matter of varying degrees of veracity. The driving metaphor is still largely that of the internal press officer, contriving sense about decisions post hoc and packaging them in a way which offends fewest around the top table. As such, internal communication has been useful in at least putting the communication needs of employees on the leadership team's agenda.

Current best practice enacts the belief that if you are able to communicate and mobilize people quickly and effectively around vision, strategy, change and transformation, then you have a robust internal marketing process. You will be rewarded by feedback which credits the leadership with keeping everyone on the same page as them.

COMMITMENT IS VITAL

The age of compliance at work is over and the essential task of internal communication has to change—in some organizations is changing—from one of replicating the view of the few to the many. Now it's about releasing people's energies in the interests of the organization.

The central challenge of leading people today is creating a work culture that releases people's creativity in a way which benefits both the employee and the organization. The organization that can score a 10/10 for strategy, 10/10 for effective organization and 10/10 for commitment will be not only a great place to work, but commercially very powerful.

You can be sure that the style of internal communication in your organization will reflect leadership style. Thus, the organization which has chaotic communication processes and which is always behind the facts is telling you much about its leadership style. So will the autocratically directed spin machine which whirrs into overdrive when the control freak sneezes. The only difference between the dumb control freak and the smart one is that the smart one has communication sewn up.

Like it or not, the leadership team is the most influential communication team.

THE CHIEF ENTERTAINMENT OFFICER

The C.E.O. could henceforth be called the Chief Entertainment Officer. The C suite—as the leadership team is known by some—has a massive influence on mood. People in the company become aware of the mood of the Chief Executive even if they are thousands of miles away.

Internal communication used to be about managing "news" and information. But with so many sources of information a company has to manage its information in a way that is accessible, timely, honest, and, maybe even entertaining, if it wants to win the war for employees' attention.

I use the idea of the C.E.O. as chief entertainer to bring attention to the fact that many employees are choosing between employment offers by asking themselves, "What culture will bring the best out in me?" It's not that one culture is necessarily "better," but that one will be more suitable.

Consequently, when it comes to winning the battle for the most talented employees and keeping them satisfied and productive, providing a dynamic, entertaining and up-to-date information system can give your company the competitive edge.

WHAT HAVE MOOD, STYLE, CULTURE, AND COMMITMENT GOT TO DO WITH COMMERCIAL SUCCESS?

The answer is—plenty. Having the right strategy and a good organization isn't enough. Without commitment, strategy stays firmly on the ground.

Most C.E.O.s will tell you that turning around a failing business is difficult. It requires the making of hard decisions, made with people who may be part of the problem. These C.E.O.s will also tell you that change when the business is good is much tougher because people ask, "Why jump over that cliff when things are good here?"

Whether reductive or offensive change, the C suite needs to manage the mood around it. To manage it you need to read it, and so it's vital to be a fast listener who recognizes the unstated. The prime job of C.E.O.s is to swing the mood behind them, which means:

- turning the instigators of change (often a bunch of gung-ho types in the program office) from robots into evangelists;
- seducing spectators and victims into being enthusiastic implementors;

- making converts of blockers;
- seeing themselves turning from lonely heroes to "becoming enablers" of the vision and energy of others.

SIX TIPS FOR BUILDING COMMITMENT

1 Agree on the change/transformation story.
2 Map your change or transformation journey.
3 Be clear about who is to be involved.
4 Model the desired change.
5 Engage and entertain.
6 Get your story told.

There are no easy answers to getting commitment, but some of the ideas below may bring value.

1. Agree on the Change/Transformation Story

It is astonishing the number of leadership teams which believe that among themselves they share the vision or the story of change. So often a surface gloss of agreement hides real or imagined tensions and implementation plans are signed off with real agreement around the table merely assumed. The inevitable resulting tensions are felt by the whole organization.

Achieving real commitment in any team requires an investment in outing all the stories or pictures that individual team members have in their heads but may not know until they tell their version of the story to themselves and each other.

I liken this process to concluding a peace treaty. In the heat of apparent agreement around the table, the protagonists rush out to implement, each with his or her own story, which each is sure is the real truth. Alas, all too often the real negotiations end up taking place in the messy arena called implementation, and it seems to everyone that "decisions" keep getting opened up again.

This process of agreeing the story together saves much time. It can act as a team-building exercise and so avoids airing factionalism in a very public way.

2. Map Your Change or Transformation Journey

Too often the energy of the peace treaty is diluted in the environment of implementation. Deadly critical paths put paid to a crusade of change. This is when the idea of a journey of rich experiences is more useful than a monochrome critical path. The instigating team should map the journey together, taking care to plot the mood swings likely to be encountered along the path.

This "journey" or "mood map" then becomes the basis for actively planning the journey to minimize the downs and maximize the ups, because the journey is mapped as it will be experienced by different constituents or stakeholders.

3. Be Clear About Who Is to Be Involved

Involvement is now a very hot topic. The key point for leaders is the development of a coherent approach to involving people in the design and implementation of change.

In my experience, and perhaps yours, most leadership or change teams take one of three approaches to involvement or consultation.

1 They promise much, set false expectations and drive it all from one point.
2 They involve endlessly but never implement.
3 They promise little involvement and live up to it.

Increasingly, the wiser team will deliberate carefully about "the nature of the invitation" which will provide maximum benefit in terms of both the nature of the change and the extra motivation that results in better sustained implementation.

4. Model the Desired Change

The problem with "programs" or "projects" is that often a hit team is assigned which consists, or is influenced by external advisers with entirely different values and with a very clear mission. Within hours of entering into the "chaos" of the client, the advisers are behaving like an alien nation, hell-bent on delivering, whatever the human cost.

On the one hand you're really happy that they are shaking the place up. On the other, a key team member has just walked to your biggest competitor because of the way he was treated by your pet project. It's all about behavior. Attempts at defining behaviors and getting people to live them are largely unsuccessful because they are seen as lip service and tokenism. Descriptions of "new behaviors" are rarely taken seriously by the leadership. An alternative route is to create a set of measurable service standards for the project. These are laid down as success criteria and are used to demonstrate that success is about the style of implementation as well as what is delivered.

Other approaches include that of basing desired behavior on brand or corporate values. One thing is certain: "rolling out" behavior programs in the manner of a marketing campaign is unlikely to have an impact on the subsequent experiences of employees or external groups. Equally, intensive approaches to behavioral change, using group and individual coaching, can become wearisome processes. I believe that the secret here lies in personalizing the nature of the behavioral change required rather than trying to "infect" people with the jargon provided by an internal "brand/values/behavior" team in association with consultants.

Avoiding the behavioral element is not the answer because the behaviors modeled by influential figures will soon become norms. And none more so than those modeled by individuals with any kind of power over others, be that specialist power, power over reward, network power, etc. The key is to think through what kind of program is likely to get take-up in your organization. It is highly unlikely to be an off-the-shelf formulaic approach.

Of all the ways of getting commitment, the behavioral must take account of past efforts, personalities and espoused barriers. A degree of experimentation may well be necessary. A formalized process including tools like coaching, 360-degree appraisals and so forth may be fine in some settings and laughed out of court in others, where, say, a shift in behavior by a significant figure does the trick.

5. Engage and Entertain

Leadership and change teams are competing with many entertaining stimulants, such as surfing the Internet, reading newspapers, watching CNN, and so on. The best thing we can do to make sure that the erudite vision, or strategy, or change process, or new product strategy stays in the files is to BORE everyone with a grimly corporate communication process.

The purpose of getting the change instigators to think through the journey milestones, and to keep change alive, is to create the basis for a lively engagement program which astutely allows for periods of reflection, moments of learning and outbursts of sheer exuberant fun. And I would emphasize the mix of learning, reflection, sometimes mourning, and fun. To engage correctly the activity must be sympathetic with the decisions which the organization is trying to make and implement.

Remember, participants in a change process see the experience as their own personal journey. If the organization can help employees make it a very personal journey on which they can take time to reflect and personalize, those employees are much

---

"Anyone in a large organization who thinks major change is impossible should probably get out."

John P. Kotter

more likely to identify with the process and help to make it happen.

This "participants' shoes" perspective is vital in the design of engagement processes which succeed in de-institutionalizing the change experience, and vital if we are to energize change processes which are so often so Kafkaesque.

6. Get Your Story Told

Much has been written recently about the power of stories in conveying identity, work practices and social links between generations. In premodern times, story was the main social glue and the only method of learning aside from observation and experience.

A characteristic of the story is that people listen and hear their own story. In turn, they internalize it and convey it onward with their own interpretation—which is of course what happens at work regardless of whether there is any effort to manage, influence or spin by management.

The lesson for management is that they have a responsibility to be a credible, fast, and authoritative source of stories which affect people's motivation. But bearing in mind the countless other sources of data, the best you can do is be one source which, by virtue of its integrity, earns a readership and a dialog alongside other sources.

MAKING IT HAPPEN ▶▶

If you are planning to lead a major change initiative in your organization the following steps can be useful to consider:

- **Is it necessary to establish a sense of urgency?** This can often help to start overcoming apathy and inertia. It also highlights the need for attention and commitment. This might mean identifying and discussing crises or potential crises; examining recent market pressures and trends, as well as highlighting potential opportunities, and the benefits of rapid, urgent change.

- **Consider who will guide the change process.** A united, coordinated and respected group within the organization should have the authority to make decisions, lead, and ensure that the right things happen.

- **What is the vision that will guide the change effort?** It needs to be practical, simple, powerful, and consistent with the broader goals of the organization.

- **How will the vision for change be communicated?** This needs to be done in a way that gains people's understanding and commitment; initiates and drives change, unlocking people's energies and guiding their actions.

- **Are people empowered to act?** As we said, leaders alone cannot deliver change. It needs to come from the roots of the organization and people need to feel able—empowered—to make the necessary changes. To empower people it can help for the leader to remove obstacles in the organization, change systems that undermine the vision for change, and encourage risk-taking and innovative thinking.

- **Are there short-term wins that can be achieved?** These often help to build enthusiasm, motivation, and momentum behind the change initiative. Successes and the people behind them need to be valued and recognized.

- **Are successes being consolidated and used as stepping-stones to more change?** The change process needs to move at the right pace, neither too slow nor too fast, and careful thought needs to be given to sustaining it. Hiring, promoting, and developing effective people can help, so too can reinvigorating the change process with new projects and themes.

- **Are the new approaches being anchored in the organization's culture?** A key danger is finishing too soon. This can be avoided by explaining the links between the new behaviors and organizational success. Supporting a climate of continuous improvement is also valuable in achieving success.

CONCLUSION

The new role of communication is no longer about spin. It is about helping to bring about useful change; change which is good for the organization and productive and engaging for the individual. Organizations have managed to make change a dismal experience in which creativity is stifled. Communication should be employed to make the change experience stimulating and even fun.

FOR MORE INFORMATION

Books:
Cross, Rob. *The Hidden Power of Social Networks: Understanding How Work Really Gets Done in Organisations.* Cambridge, MA: Harvard Business School Press, 2004.

Maister, David H. *Practice What You Preach: What Managers Must Do to Create a High-Achievement Culture.* New York: Free Press, 2001.

Wenger, Etienne, Richard A. McDermott, and William Snyder. *Cultivating Communities of Practice.* Cambridge, MA: Harvard Business School Press, 2002.

Yerkes, Leslie. *Fun Works: Creating Places Where People Love to Work.* San Francisco, CA: Berrett-Koehler, 2001.

Web site:
Knowledge@Wharton:
http://knowledge.wharton.upenn.edu

See also:
☆ Now! The Role of Urgency in Creating Positive Change (pp. 330–331)
💡 Philip Crosby (pp. 1194–1195)
💡 Soichiro Honda (pp. 1310–1311)

"Changes are not without cost. It produces reactionaries that fight to block progress. We have found it possible to minimize resistance by establishing a culture based on core values."

Charles Koch

Managing the Challenge of E-service
by Chris Voss

EXECUTIVE SUMMARY

- Customer expectations, in terms of service delivery and other key factors, have increased dramatically in recent years, as a result of the promise and delivery of the Internet. Even after the "dot-com crash" these raised expectations linger.
- The growth in the application and acceptance of Internet-driven technologies means that delivering an enhanced service is more achievable than ever before, however it is also more complex and fraught with potential costs and risk.
- The Internet introduces customers to a new perception of business time as always "on," available 24/7, and demanding an urgent and rapid response. The challenge for managers is to reconcile their business and their own personal perceptions of time with the perceived reality of Internet time.
- The Internet has decisively shifted the balance of power to the customer.
- The Internet is revolutionizing sales techniques and perceptions of leading brands, and the Internet is intensifying competition in all its forms.
- Companies are continuing to use the Internet to add value for their customers: but in order for this to work effectively—maximizing opportunities, reducing risks and overcoming problems—an e-service strategy is required.

INTRODUCTION

The growth of the Web and Internet as new channels, the growth in their use by customers, and the flood of companies entering the market, presents a series of key challenges to companies. It is easy and cheap to put up a Web site. But to create an environment delivering effective service on the Web to a significant proportion of your customer base requires an e-service strategy.

Any strategy must be based on understanding customers and markets. This means having arrangements for collecting data to help understand customers, to track their preferences, and to improve segmentation.

Technology provides the opportunity to track and interact with anyone contacting an organization via the Web and to explore customer needs in new ways.

TECHNIQUES FOR IMPLEMENTING AN E-SERVICE STRATEGY

The challenge is to develop a strategy for the right combination of value-added, personalized and proactive service. Keeping e-service customers will require high levels of service, a positive experience and trust in your organization. How can these be delivered? A strategy for e-service should be part of the overall electronic commerce strategy of the organization. In preparing for e-service, there are nine key steps:

1 Upgrade current service interaction.
2 Understand your customer segments.
3 Understand your customer service processes and interactions.
4 Define the role of live interaction (and hence areas for automation).
5 Make the key technology decisions.
6 Prepare to deal with the tidal wave of increased customer interaction.
7 Train customers and create incentives for them to use the appropriate channel.
8 Address the issue of channel choice and "brick versus click."
9 Exploit the Web to create relationships and a real customer experience.

MEETING THE TECHNOLOGICAL CHALLENGES—CHOOSING THE RIGHT CHANNEL

For many companies, the toughest stage is the fifth: *technology*. As one company said to our researchers: "One of our biggest implementation issues is the integration of Web-enabled technology with our legacy systems, both technology and business processes." Technology is moving rapidly so companies need to make tough decisions:

- Do we pilot now and learn and invest later, risking loss of position, or move quickly and risk major problems to gain market space today?
- Do we go for full integration, and if necessary throw out today's legacy systems?

There are two crucial questions regarding channel choice. The first is whether to offer the customer options, for example, face-to-face, mail, phone, and Web. In any industry there may be a variety of different approaches. For example, many retail banks allow the choice of managing current accounts through the branch, mail, or on the Web. Others have single channel accounts—for example, phone only. Others allow constrained choice, for instance, phone and Web, but enroll new customers only via the Web.

The difficulty in getting high levels of service when adding new channels has led many in the past to start new ventures separate from existing channels and systems. Informing this decision are both the costs of the different channels, and importance of customer relationship management (CRM) databases. In most customer service environments, the quality and scope of the CRM database is central to the successful delivery of service. There is pressure therefore not to operate new channels separately, but to integrate existing channels around a single CRM database.

IMPLEMENTING AN E-SERVICE STRATEGY AND BUILDING CUSTOMER RELATIONSHIPS

No strategy can be effective without attention to implementation. Two of the main lessons from our research are as follows:

- business process and transaction analysis is essential for effective e-service design;
- you must get implementation right first time. If not, people will revert to the phone.

Important areas for implementation include organization and culture. Just as e-commerce changes the organization and power in markets, it can do the same within organizations. Another aspect of organization and culture is the need to realize that in the new environment, alliances and partnerships play a much-increased role.

Companies need to develop key metrics to set standards and measure performance in the following areas:

"If I had a brick for every time I've repeated the phrase 'Quality, Service, Cleanliness and Value,' I'd probably be able to bridge the Atlantic Ocean with them."
Ray Kroc

- *Security/Trust:* measured through surveys and focus groups.
- *Response time:* Internet customers may expect faster response.
- *Response quality:* difficult to measure.
- *Navigability:* one of the most important determinants of service.
- *Download time:* the maximum time that a user will tolerate for any page may be less than 30 seconds!
- *Fulfillment:* is it fast and are the promised goods delivered?
- *Up-to-date:* out-of-date information may quickly turn off users.
- *Availability:* Can the user reach the site 24 hours a day, seven days a week?
- *Site effectiveness and functionality:* Is the Web page intuitive and easy to use? What is the effectiveness of the site from the user's point of view?

BUILDING AN INVESTMENT CASE

Many large companies have found building a case for investment in e-service and e-commerce extremely difficult. This difficulty arises from a number of factors—uncertainty over the data and trends, using the wrong baseline, lack of vision, and lack of knowledge and skills of senior management. One recent survey concluded that while in the United States directors took the competitive threat seriously, those in the United Kingdom and France were in "a state of denial."

In building an investment case against a baseline of today's business, the investment costs are often high, whereas the returns are often not visible in the short term. There are two alternate baselines:

1 **Buying an option on the future.** In an uncertain world, investment in new media and channels could be viewed as buying an option on entry to future markets and in mastering future technologies. In the short term, this allows a company to build expertise and infrastructure without major investment or structural change. However, to profit from this, the option must be exercised before it expires.

2 **What will happen to your business without investment—the costs of not investing.** If your market is being attacked by new players, using new technologies and with different cost structures, and not bound by legacy systems

or policies, then the baseline case for investment may be much lower than extrapolation of today's business.

In every market that we looked at, from utilities to banking, we found organizations wanting to break into the market or change the way the market operates by using new technologies. These organizations are quick to see both the weaknesses of the current marketplace and new ways of doing business, and to challenge underlying assumptions about customer behavior. Too often, the ability to change is constrained by an organization's unwillingness to make tough decisions about its legacy systems and procedures. That is no way to exploit the available dot-com strategies. Instead:

- ignore unattractive, expensive channels;
- cherry-pick segments, differentiate segments;
- pick products/services where the Web adds value;
- offer services worldwide;
- capture or create intermediary roles;
- use strength of portal;
- create affiliate programs, selling products via other people's Web sites;
- Use incentives;

Organizations must view their investment in e-service not just in cost/benefit terms, but also in comparison with doing nothing. By putting yourself in the shoes of a potential entrant, you can gain major insights into what might comprise a service vision.

MAKING IT HAPPEN ▶▶

- Use technology to track and interact with anyone contacting the organization via the Web and to explore customer needs and expectations in new ways.
- Ask "What is our strategy for e-commerce and e-service and how should it be implemented?", not "Should we invest in e-service?"
- Develop a strategy for the right combination of value-added, personalized and proactive service.
- Train customers and provide them with incentives to switch, or disincentives to continue using existing channels.
- Create relationships via tailor-made sites for customers, proactive service offerings, communities of users, and

extension of relationships beyond the company.

CONCLUSION

The Internet makes it easier to achieve three key elements of customer-loyalty: making it easy for customers to do business with you, satisfying your customers, and keeping them coming back to you. Furthermore, these can all be accomplished at a fraction of their normal cost, and, by building greater customer loyalty, sales costs will often be reduced.

Customer care includes routine or mundane features (such as the need to provide a variety of payment methods), through more significant issues (such as responding to queries reactively or up-selling and cross-selling products proactively), to the downright vital—ensuring that customers' security and privacy are respected and maintained. Critical among these factors is the need to *support* customers and to instill *confidence*, and these can be achieved by:

- managing customers in a subtle and flexible way, for example by offering a variety of delivery options;
- ensuring adequate (meaning both capable and ever-present) customer support so that consumers and businesses find online shopping stress-free;
- providing security and privacy for online transactions

FOR MORE INFORMATION

Books:
Evans, Philip, and Thomas Wurster. *Blown to Bits.* Cambridge, MA: Harvard Business School Press, 1999.
Greenberg, Paul. *CRM at the Speed of Light.* 3rd ed. New York: Osborne McGraw Hill, 2004.
Godin, Seth, and Don Peppers. *Permission Marketing.* New York: Simon & Schuster, 1999.
Swift, Ronald S. *Accelerating Customer Relationships.* Upper Saddle River, NJ: Prentice Hall, 2000.

See also:
✓ Delivering Quality Online Customer Service and Support (pp. 612–613)
✓ Implementing a Customer Relationship Management Strategy (pp. 708–709)
☆ Managing the Customer (pp. 85–86)

"E-commerce, E-business, or whatever else you may want to call it is a means to an end. The objectives, as with IT, are to improve or exploit unique business propositions."

William (Walid) Mougayar

The Critical Factors That Build or Break Teams

by Meredith Belbin

EXECUTIVE SUMMARY

- "Team" and "teamwork" too easily become glib terms. Check their meaning.
- Find out what work really requires a team.
- Some people flourish in teams, others don't.
- Teams need to be empowered and enabled to work within boundaries.
- Balanced teams need to be developed into mature teams.
- Effective teams need to understand both team roles and work roles.

INTRODUCTION

The problem with the word "teamwork" is that it has become too popular and has therefore lost its meaning. A person deemed good at teamwork is all too often someone who fits into a group and keeps out of trouble. Ideal behavior is often judged as complying with majority decisions and being willing to do anything that's required. Yet if everyone behaved like that, you'd have good reason to doubt that the team would function effectively. A flock of sheep may hang together well, but their only accomplishment is to eat grass.

For anyone interested in productive teamwork, it's often better to start with the work rather than the team. First of all, does the work call for a team? There are many types of repetitive operation, unskilled work, and specialist activities that are best performed by loners. Rounding up such people and making them members of a team risks producing a double disadvantage: their personal productivity falls and their privacy is invaded. Such social engineering may accord with the prevailing culture, but it's difficult to see any other benefit. Of course, it may be argued that isolated workers need a social dimension to their work. If this is true it implies that individuals engaged on such jobs have been wrongly placed. Introverts need work suitable for introverts, while extroverts need work appropriate to extroverts.

DESIGNING WORK TO FIT THE PERSON

It is important to make sure that people have the right fit in the organization, if not, difficulties may arise. The example below provides an illustration of this.

Introverts and extroverts look for different things in a job. Lighthouse-keeping and leading tour groups are contrasting jobs calling for different personalities. In the case of most jobs, of course, the relationship between work demands and personal characteristics is less pronounced. The reality is that most jobs entail some degree of individual work and responsibility along with a degree of liaison activity and some shared responsibilities. Such a mixture of demands not only makes it difficult to find candidates with the ideal profile, but there are intrinsic problems in setting up jobs encompassing such different constituents. Most employers make few attempts to define the boundaries, and, even if they are laid down in advance, people who work in close association are inclined to move them at will. That's why coworkers are often cited as the biggest aggravation at work. When conflicts result, one party or another will be blamed as a poor team player.

The best starting point for establishing good teamwork is to begin with the principal demands of a broad work area. What are its structural characteristics? Do some responsibilities need to be shared? If so, which responsibilities, and with whom? Which responsibilities can be assigned to individuals and made subject to personal accountability? Which tasks are critical in their timing and mode of treatment and require a prescriptive approach based on best practice? These are all basic questions. They can either be asked and answered with the manager as the sole decision maker, or such decision making can be carried out in consultation with others. Either way, there's a risk that a busy manager will cut corners and make hasty decisions that are out of touch with operational realities. That's why it is often better to assign a group of workers to address these basic questions and seek to find answers. Those at the sharp end will be most familiar with the demands and pressures of the work. They are often better placed to decide how work should be shared.

MINI-CASE

I was engaged on a project to facilitate the introduction of a cargo-handling computer system at a large airport. The perceived problem was that the workers whose jobs were to be converted were both computer-illiterate and highly unionized. Devising a suitable form of training proved a challenge, but once this had been accomplished the introduction went without a hitch. The main problem arose in the way in which the design engineers had devised the work itself. The physical arrangement required these sociable workers to sit in isolation at consoles. They soon tired of it and chose instead to bypass the information system by riding on the mechanical handling equipment in order to conduct personal inspections of the cargo bays. Such bravado may have been exhilarating, but it was also dangerous practice.

Clearly, it is not only vitally important to understand the nature of the work being undertaken, but also the skills, experience and approach of those doing the work. Taking account of people's strengths and motivations can certainly help to build or break teams.

TEAMS NEED TO BE GIVEN SCOPE

The team approach for organizing work depends on empowerment; it relies on trust, the confidence that a manager places in the qualities and caliber of the workforce. It also depends on how well members of a group have developed an understanding of each other's strengths and weaknesses. That's why training in teamwork is so important and why it helps to understand the language of team roles. People make different contri-

> "One man can be a crucial ingredient on a team, but one man cannot make a team."
>
> Kareem Abdul-Jabbar

butions to teams, and it's important that every team plays to the best strengths of its individual players. Diversity in the range of available team roles lays the foundation for a balanced team. But diversity does not automatically produce harmony or balance. It can just as well produce conflict as different individuals strive to do their own thing. This is where the manager becomes so important, in creating the vision and the ethos. The role of the manager is to turn a potentially balanced team into a mature team.

Mature teams have the capacity to make local decisions in distributing the overall workload and its various elements appropriately. This is impossible unless the manager has set the stage, believes in empowerment, and knows how to put it into effect. The key to success lies in managing the interface between team roles and work roles. The manager has to understand this before the team can be expected to respond with appropriate action. Managers sometimes fear that workers will lack the will to take tough decisions, for example, when one person is not up to a particular aspect of the job. The surprise is often that workers prove more intolerant of a slacker or a poor performer than the manager. The group builds up a body of opinion that's a powerful force in its own right. Such a force can operate against the interests of management, but it can equally well reinforce the policies and strategies that management favors. The more autocratic the management, the greater the likelihood that the group will combine to become a counterforce. The greater the level of empowerment, the more likely will be the team's sense of ownership and pride, and the greater its commitment to the responsibilities undertaken. Without empowerment, balanced groups cannot be developed into mature teams.

REWARDING TEAMS APPROPRIATELY

All teams need to be assessed. The question is, how should it be done so that it is positive and constructive?

One way is to set objectives for teams and judge how well these have been met. Such a view prevails in the top-down school of management and is given added impetus by performance-related bonuses. The argument put forward is that teams need fixed incentives to perform well, an assumption linked with the converse view that without such an incentive the team will not perform satisfactorily.

This mechanistic view of human motivation is mistaken and is likely to backfire. Success in meeting given criteria depends partly on circumstances and contingencies. Success may not be commensurate with effort or skill. Objectives may be too easy to reach or too difficult. In the end, people may focus more on the shortcomings of the incentive than on the sense and purpose of their work. Retrospective awards for teams performing well are better received than prospective rewards for teams given set targets.

MAKING IT HAPPEN ▶▶

- Start with the work, not the team. Ask first whether the work calls for a team at all.
- If a team is required, determine which responsibilities need to be shared and by whom.
- Decide which remaining responsibilities can be assigned to individuals, and make them subject to personal accountability.
- Use training in teamwork and team roles to ensure that every team plays to the best strengths of its individual players.
- Understand the team's strengths, weaknesses, and sense of "self-awareness" to improve.
- Maximize empowerment to develop ownership, pride, and maximum commitment to the team's responsibilities.

- Delegate work efficiently, and enable people to succeed.
- Understand what motivates the team, providing them with impetus and momentum.
- Give retrospective rewards for teams performing well rather than incentive rewards linked to set targets.

CONCLUSION

In recent years we have developed an approach to work that hinges on understanding and mastering two languages: the language of contributors to team effort—team roles—and the language of the work demands themselves—work roles. Essentially this approach offers a framework for deciding who does what. Unless people decide for themselves, or at least share in that decision making, there will be no commitment to the work itself.

FOR MORE INFORMATION

Books:
Belbin, R. Meredith. *The Coming Shape of Organization*. Woburn, MA: Butterworth-Heinemann, 1998.
Katzenbach, J. R., and D. K. Smith. *The Wisdom of Teams: Creating the High-performance Organization*. New York: McGraw-Hill Education, 1998.

Film:
To facilitate an understanding of these issues, Belbin Associates have made three films in association with Video Arts: *Building the Perfect Team* (1991), *Selecting the Perfect Team* (1993), and *Does the Team Work?* (1999).

See also:
☆ Keeping Control in Nonhierarchical Organizations (pp. 231–232)

"Dividing enemy forces to weaken them is clever, but dividing one's own team is a grave sin against the business."

Henri Fayol

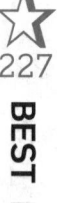

The Composed Organization
by Robert Fritz

EXECUTIVE SUMMARY

- The most influential factor in organizational performance, both for individuals within the organization and the organization as a whole, is the underlying structure.
- Organizations typically exhibit either *oscillating* or *advancing* behaviors. In organizations that oscillate, success is eventually neutralized and reversed. In advancing structures, organizations build on previous successes; both success and failure evoke learning that translates into greater competence and effectiveness.
- We can redesign an organization's underlying structure so that it can move from oscillating to advancing.

INTRODUCTION

In the 1938 movie, *The Dawn Patrol*, Errol Flynn played an easy-going First World War pilot who, with his fun-loving buddy David Niven, flew dangerous missions during the day and caroused in town at night. He had another sport too: driving his serious squadron leader, Basil Rathbone, crazy. Ultimately, Rathbone took revenge, for he so hated the Errol Flynn character that he named him the new squadron leader when Rathbone was transferred. Soon, Flynn began to act as seriously as did Rathbone.

Now here's a movie that understands a common experience—one that all managers have encountered on occasion—*that a position sometimes seems to dictate the behavior of the people who fill it more than the people themselves do.* No matter the background, a new supervisor suddenly acts surprisingly like his or her predecessor. Here is the common pattern: A person is not working well; management does everything to help improve performance, but to no avail. Finally, the person is replaced. Six months later, the replacement is performing exactly like his or her predecessor.

THE IMPLICATION

This pattern contradicts our most cherished ideas about human motivations. How do we explain how such people act? Is it psychology, DNA, cultural background, education, life experiences, values, aspirations, talents, or abilities? Their astrology, numerology, biorhythms, age, gender, generation? We test the potential and predisposition of employees before we hire them and track their performance; yet, when it comes to replacements, though they are different in

generation, gender, genetic code, temperament, experience, maturity, life situation, or work history, the pattern prevails.

The implication is that *no matter a person's individual traits, the architecture of the position is more causal that any of those traits.* This is not always the case. We can see that a change of individual can sometimes make a profound difference in performance. But we can learn something useful by thinking about how often good people and good professionals conform to "positional" behavior.

ELEMENTS OF PERFORMANCE

Performance has two dimensions. One is *execution*, and that's where talent, experience, know-how, and competence come into play. The other dimension is *design*, how organizational parts are put together. Since design and execution are independent, here are all the combinations that exist:

Good Design / Good Execution
Good Design / Bad Execution
Bad Design / Good Execution
Bad Design / Bad Execution

Often our bias is that weak performance is a matter of bad execution. Such bias comes from thinking we *can* control execution, and we are not used to thinking like architects or composers. So often we have seen what is obviously a very stupid policy or directive given to members of an organization which they have no possibility of achieving. "Increase production and reduce capacity" is the war cry of downsizing. "How can they do it?", one is prone to ask. "They will become more efficient and innovative," comes the answer, barely able to be said with a straight face. *Yeah, right.* And if you believe that I've got some land . . .

ORGANIZATIONAL PATTERNS

Just as individuals put into the same position can perform identically, so can entire organizations. Here, there are also two major patterns: *oscillation* and *advancement*. In an oscillating structure, the organization first moves in one direction but later moves in the opposite direction. It builds up capacity, then downsizes, then builds up capacity again. It decentralizes decision making, centralizes it again, but later decentralizes. The pattern is clear, but organizations often have trouble seeing it. When major change efforts are tried, the change (albeit successful elsewhere) is rejected. In oscillating organizations, success seldom succeeds. Come a reversal and success is soon neutralized—heroes and heroines become failures and villains.

An advancing organizational pattern is one in which each success creates a platform for future success. Every failure becomes a building block for learning and developing. As people learn, they become better performers: more capable, more team players, more creative, and more valuable.

CAN ORGANIZATIONS CHANGE?

When I began to work in organizations I asked why some oscillate and why some advance, and whether we could help an oscillating organization shift to an advancing one. The happy answer is, yes, organizations can actually change their fundamental pattern of behavior. But the type of change that is required is not on the same level as dictating new prescriptions for behavior or attempting to impose new systems on faulty structures.

For lasting change, we need to change the underlying structure. An oscillating structure contains critical conflicts of interests. As one interest is served, a competing interest is denied—creating a state of non-equilibrium which produces a shift, just as a rocking chair shifts from forward to backward movement. Typically organizations are fragmented and self-organize into competing interests often competing for the same resource base. If traditional management leads to fragmentation, which leads to self-organizing systems of conflict, then how do we change this condition?

Organizations are much like musical

"Authoritarian organizations tend to develop dependent people and few leaders. Participative organizations tend to develop emotionally and socially mature persons capable of effective interaction, initiative, and leadership."

Rensis Likert

BEST PRACTICE

compositions, whether you think of them as Beethoven symphonies or works by Duke Ellington. Senior management has often not properly "composed" the organization, and people do not know what their parts are or how their parts fit with the other parts and with the whole. In fact, a telltale sign of bad management is that departments within the same organization are competing for the same resource base. Another sign is that there is no formal relationship and coordination between sales goals and capacity limitations in production. Another telltale sign is across-the-board percentage downsizing, an admission that management doesn't know how much its capacity is costing and doesn't know whether the real problem is to try to grow revenues or to blindly cut costs.

The enemy here is not "command and control" as it's often talked about; the enemy is *mindless* in the form of uncoordinated directives that are pushed down an organization's throat. They are often arbitrary rather than strategic, contradictory rather than reinforcing, and unfocused rather than focused. Bad design structure creates oscillation, with failure quickly chasing any short-term successes.

REDESIGNING THE ORGANIZATION

Organizations can be restructured from oscillation to advancement by a combination of clarity, design elegance, and discipline. Just as in writing music, the major theme is the purpose of the organization as expressed through business strategy, which drives the management strategy, which drives the various local-departmental strategies. And the local strategies support the management strategy, which supports the business strategy, which, in turn, supports the purpose.

Some talk about organizations as if they are *so* complex that they defy a compositional approach. But such enterprises only seem complex when you don't know how to design the parts, and then execute the performance. If I had to fix my auto's engine, it would seem complex; fortunately, there are mechanics in the world.

MAKING IT HAPPEN ▸▸

Over 20 years ago I created the model called *structural tension* (or as my friend and colleague Peter Senge liked to call it in his book *The Fifth Discipline*, "creative tension"). I was doing a lot of painting at the time, and I used the artistic process as the archetypal form of the creative process. How does a painter create a

painting—and could managers use the same process? *Yes!* Structural tension is formed by the difference or contrast between the vision that we have—our goals—and the current situation that exists (current reality). A painter has a vision of the finished painting, but he or she must also be aware of the current state of the painting. The relationship between the desired state (the vision) and the actual state (current reality) is a structural dynamic formed by the tension between these two elements.

Tension *seeks* resolution, and the painter is managing structural tension throughout the painting process. He or she has the vision of the end result in mind, while also having a clear and accurate understanding of the current state of the painting. The painter takes action to change the current state so that eventually it conforms to the vision. At this point, the tension is resolved, and the actual state and the desired state for the painting are the same. When a painter signs the painting, he or she is saying, "This painting matches my vision."

Structural tension is not the same as psychological tension or stress. Instead, we can feel the dynamic energy that comes from the contrast between our desired state and the actual state. We translate that energy into actions, which become well motivated and have a sense of direction.

The way we can "compose" the organization is to establish "master structural tension charts" that include:

1 the major goals;
2 current reality relevant to those goals;
3 action steps that need to be taken to accomplish the goals;
4 the due dates of each action step;
5 the person who is accountable for accomplishing that action.

This is a simple "composition" to construct and understand. *But it is not simplistic.* It is elegant. The actions can be developed and managed, and the broad design can then be deployed throughout the organization.

In this system, we can understand the parts within the context of the whole. Details are developed by telescoping the charts. There is a high level of organizational control without having to be controlling or micromanaging. That's the beauty of it. People know what they need to do, how it fits within the broader frame, when it needs to be done, and why.

They also begin to get into the habit of thinking in terms of relationships rather than fragments.

MINI-CASE
Observing Design and Execution

Dell Computer Corporation's success is based on their very clear sense of business strategy, which generates all of their managerial decisions. Dell has a strict focus on minimal finished inventory and direct sales. This has led it to be one of the most successful companies worldwide. It has changed the face of the PC industry.

Gateway, Inc. lost its once solid brand position when it expanded into the business computing market, where it was not competitive. Gateway lost focus on the home and family market, and its brand identity drifted.

Citicorp/Citibank has had a long history of understanding the relationship between a technological vision and current market trends. This understanding has led the company to invest over $1.75 billion, which has enabled it to become the largest integrated financial service company in the world.

CONCLUSION

Structure will lead to oscillation or advancement. Any change effort in an organization structured to oscillate will be neutralized. To accomplish change, the organization must first redesign itself to become an advancing structure. The parts must fit together, rather than work against each other.

FOR MORE INFORMATION

Books:
Mintzberg, Henry. *The Rise and Fall of Strategic Planning.* New York: Prentice Hall, 1994.
Senge, Peter, et al. *The Dance of Change.* New York: Doubleday, 1999.

Web site:
Society for Organizational Learning: **www.solonline.org/connections**

See also:

"The organization exists to restrict and channel the range of individual actions and behaviors into a predictable and knowable routine."
Theodore Levitt

Retaining Employees
by Sharon Jordan-Evans and Beverly Kaye

EXECUTIVE SUMMARY

- Regardless of whether the economy is sagging or booming, employee retention remains a major concern across all industries and countries.
- The keys to retaining talent are well researched. Most of them lie within the manager's control.
- Managers aren't using these keys. They need coaching, some focused accountability, and training.
- The emerging workforce has different attitudes and expectations from the last generation. With the growth of self-reliance individuals are in charge of their own careers. Savvy leaders had better understand their new-millennium workers and shift the way they manage and mentor these golden assets.

INTRODUCTION

A decade ago the leaders of organizations seldom talked about the business issue that now reportedly keeps them awake at night: the challenge of retaining talent.

Research reveals that, while pay and benefits matter, you can't count on money to retain talented people who have employment options. Key motivators include challenging and stimulating work, a chance to learn and grow, a good boss, and great people to work with. Managers can influence these major retention factors. The problem is that many managers don't believe they have the power to hang on to their best and brightest. Yet retention is a hot issue for good reason:

- Talent is the only differentiator. It separates you from your competitors and ensures your company's place in the future. While capital is abundant and technology is easy to access, brainpower becomes the major asset for most businesses.
- The global talent shortage is expected to last for at least the next decade. In the United States there will be an estimated shortage of 40 million workers by 2015, assuming 2% economic growth and current retirement conditions. Fertility is now below replacement level in 61 countries.
- Good employees don't even have to leave their desks to find new jobs. The most popular log-on time for popular job-search sites like Monster.com is between 9 and 5. Headhunters and corporate recruiters practice a multifaceted science complete with firewall-breaking strategies to identify and steal top talent.
- Experts agree that replacing a talented

employee costs at least two times his or her annual salary. The hard costs include search companies and sign-on bonuses. Softer opportunity costs include lost customers, contracts, or business. Replacing platinum employees (those with specialized professional skills) will cost you around four to five times their annual salary.

- You've seen talent loss following major organizational change or downsizing and know that you're at risk. Remember those talented employees who left 6 to 12 months after your last downsizing? They were overworked, demoralized, and pessimistic about the organization's future. If you're facing major change, you'd best double your retention efforts.

TECHNIQUES FOR RETAINING EMPLOYEES
Understand What Motivates People

We've asked over 15,000 people why they stayed in an organization for "a while." Here are the top five responses:

- exciting, challenging work
- career growth, learning, and development
- great people
- fair pay and benefits
- good boss

These answers are no surprise. For more than 50 years researchers have studied the factors that satisfy, motivate, or engage their talented workers, and their findings match ours. Abraham Maslow identified basic survival needs and found that, once those needs are met, people focus on social needs and self-actualizing work. Frederick Herzberg identified "hygiene factors" like decent work environment, pay, and benefits as potential dissatisfiers when they're inadequate, but these are not necessarily motivators.

Keep the Motivational Import of Remuneration in Perspective

If employees aren't challenged or growing, or if they don't get along well with the boss, their paycheck probably won't keep them for long. Even lucrative stock options (golden handcuffs) are being bought out today (golden hellos) by companies wanting to steal talent.

Know Where the Buck Stops

Nine out of ten managers will say that what keeps people is money. Some believe it; others hope it will absolve them of responsibility. They can then point the finger at senior management, human-resources professionals, or the compensation committee. Those players all have a role in retaining talent, but experts agree that the manager is central to attracting and retaining talent. How does a manager begin to do that?

First, you need to find out what individuals on your team really want. Don't guess, and don't assume they all want the same thing (like pay or promotion). Try this. Tell all your key employees, one at a time, how critical they are to you. Maybe you've told them before. If so, tell them again, "You matter so much to me and to this team. I can't imagine losing you. So, what will keep you here, and what might entice you away? What things do you want/hope for/need to stick around for a while?" You may not have opened that conversation for fear they'll ask for something you can't deliver.

So how will you respond if your top guy says he wants a 20% increase and you don't have the power to give it to him right now? Too many managers respond with something that shuts down the dialogue and makes a key employee feel diminished. Be honest, but let him know you care enough to look into it. For example, you might say, "You're worth that and more to me. I am facing some budget constraints right now, but let me investigate the possibilities. Let's meet next Friday to talk more about your request. Meanwhile, what else matters to

230

BEST PRACTICE

you?" Usually there will be at least one thing he wants that you can give. The key is that you've shown this talented employee that he is worth the time and effort to *try* to fulfill his request.

Select the Right People and Support Their Growth

- Get the right people in the door in the first place and don't resort to desperation hiring. Remember that today's hiring mistake is tomorrow's problem.
- Enrich and enliven their work. When the thrill is gone, so are they.
- Allow employees to grow, or they'll find an employer that will. Think about how you can develop your workers' talents. Remember to ask individuals what and how they want to learn. Mentor them, and they're twice as likely to stay. Encourage, nurture, and teach them how to be successful in your organization. Link them to mentors, coaches, leaders, or coworkers.
- Identify options other than promotion or "up." Help your key employees to uncover multiple options, including lateral moves, special projects, or growing while in place.

Develop a Management Style That Inspires Loyalty

- Loyalty is still possible but it is increasingly complex. New-millennium employees can be committed to the team, the project, the boss, the mission, and, yes, even to the company—that provides just what they want and need.
- Show respect in many ways. Treat people fairly "not identically" and trust them; they'll prove to be trustworthy. Create a culture of inclusion, valuing different experiences, and attitudes. Guard against negative behavior that might turn off or turn away your talent.
- Provide feedback. Talented people want to know how they're doing and how you think they could improve and grow. Give feedback clearly, truthfully, and respectfully; in return get feedback from them about your own strengths and opportunities.
- Reward creatively. Use the universal reward: praise. Use it often and authentically with every one of your talented people. Then individualize rewards. Don't guess what people want—ask!

Create a Work Environment That People Love, Enjoy, and Respond To

- Many busy, high-stress organizations admit they've become a fun-free zone. Ironically, fun may be just what they need to ease the pressure and stress. It's definitely what they need if they are to retain their fun-loving employees. Find ways to make the workplace enjoyable.
- Information is power. Give it as freely, openly, and often as you can.
- Give people space. Provide freedom to get the job done in ways that work best for them. Trust them, negotiate with them, open your mind to really hear their requests, and brainstorm creative solutions.
- Encourage people to have a life outside work. You'll get employees who show up refreshed and ready to work.
- Uncover and discover new opportunities inside your organization so employees don't have to seek them outside.

MINI-CASES

Senior leaders at a high-tech company are expected to spend 30% of their time on engaging and retaining talent.

At a large bank 1,000 managers have received retention training. They have significantly reduced their turnover rate.

One credit-card company reduced staff turnover in its call centers with career-development conversations between managers and employees.

IT executives at a telecommunications company agreed to visit more sites, expanded their recognition services, and increased the amount of training employees are encouraged to take in response to feedback from their IT staff.

A large medical center of Nebraska involves managers and employees from all functions in specific retention assignments that apply across its organization.

A major U.S. retailer has focused on involvement, recognition, and celebration. All managers are held accountable for retention.

MAKING IT HAPPEN ▸▸

- Recognize the importance of retention. Understand how people feel now and what action is needed before it is too late.
- Remember: it's more than pay.
- Customize retention strategies to the needs and circumstances of each individual.
- Be accountable: it's no good blaming someone else; if you want the person to stay, then you need to act to retain them.

- Provide training, coaching, and regular feedback for the managers you count on.

CONCLUSION

Your success depends on keeping your best people. The keys to retaining talent are known, but are unfortunately seldom practiced. If you manage others, you have phenomenal influence over their decisions to stay or go. If you have managers reporting to you, they may need help in becoming retention-focused, retention-savvy leaders. Be clear about what keeps people. Customize your retention strategies to individual needs and wants—and pass the message and method on to anyone who manages others in your organization. The success or failure of many organizations is increasingly determined by this single issue.

FOR MORE INFORMATION

Books:

Buckingham, Marcus, and Curt Coffman. *First, Break All the Rules: What the World's Greatest Managers Do Differently.* New York: Simon & Schuster, 1999.

Catlette, Bill, and Richard Hadden. *Contented Cows Give Better Milk: The Plain Truth About Employee Relations and the Bottom Line.* Germantown, TN: Saltillo Press, 2000.

Coffman, Curt, and Gabriel Gonzalez-Molina, Ph.D. *Follow This Path: How the World's Greatest Organizations Drive Growth by Unleashing Human Potential.* New York: Warner Business Books, 2002.

Gubman, Edward L. *The Talent Solution: Aligning Strategy and People to Achieve Extraordinary Results.* New York: McGraw-Hill Professional, 1998.

Harris, Jim, and Joan Brannick. *Finding & Keeping Great Employees.* New York: AMACOM, 1999.

Herman, Roger E. *Keeping Good People: Strategies for Solving the #1 Problem Facing Business Today.* Winchester, VA: Oakhill Press, 1999.

"The common wisdom is that . . . managers have to learn to motivate people. Nonsense. Employees bring their own motivation."

Tom Peters

Keeping Control in Nonhierarchical Organizations
by Karin Klenke

EXECUTIVE SUMMARY

- The archetypal formalistic bureaucracy is increasingly outdated. Flatter organizations are now the norm.
- New organizational structures are constantly emerging that represent the antithesis of the traditional hierarchical form of organization.
- Twenty-first-century organizations must be in tune with the business environment and take on a multitude of shapes, from entrepreneurial companies with no fat to elephants of the old economy with thick layers of excess fat.
- Keeping organizations controlled and focused is essential for an integrated, motivated, and effective organization.

INTRODUCTION

Nonhierarchical organizations have many advantages over their conventional, stratified counterparts. For example, experience and expertise are often shared; creativity and new ideas are fostered, tested and discussed. These organizations are more cohesive and collaborate; empowerment is a key feature; and they can be highly supportive of multiple stakeholders in global environments.

However, flatter organizations also have several potential pitfalls. "Group think," or the herd mentality, can prevail; implementing decisions can be difficult since flatter organizations serve multiple constituencies and stakeholders; and many flatter organizations are team-based, often geographically dispersed and electronically networked.

MANAGING IN HIERARCHICAL ORGANIZATIONS
1. Understand the Value of Flatter Organizations

Traditionally, control is achieved through a number of classical management principles, including division of *labor, formalization* (the extent to which work rules are specified, written, and enforced), and *centralization* (the decision-making authority in the hierarchy of the organization). Centralization for the purpose of tight control provides stability, continuity, and predictable career paths and reward systems. In addition, each manager has a clear, unambiguous span of control (the number of employees they can effectively supervise),

which creates a set of obligations and role differentiation, with the manager as the brain and the worker the hand. Control is reinforced by a dictatorial top-down, command-and-control leadership style.

The sheer size of the hierarchies in large traditional organizations, coupled with top management's distance from the market, makes this type of structure unresponsive. Many of the reasons for the failures of old-economy leaders in the steel, automotive, and consumer-electronics industries can be directly traced to the structure of fat organizations. Similarly, much of the renaissance of companies such as Xerox and Hewlett-Packard can be attributed to throwing off the shackles of vertical integration.

In the new economy speed is of the essence and the time frame for decision making has been dramatically reduced. Hence, bureaucratic hierarchies are being deconstructed. What will tomorrow's organizations look like? What radical surgery may be necessary to transform the vertically integrated structures of the industrial paradigm into designs of the future? How can organizations learn today the skills they need for tomorrow? Answers to some of these questions are found in flat, or nonhierarchical, organizations.

2. Building Nonhierarchical Organizations

21st-century organizations tend to adopt the flatter structures that have become possible as more and more information within an organization comes online. Instead of a man-

agerial hierarchy with seven to ten or more layers of fat, flat organizations have three or four levels. Flat organizations are a cross between a spider's web (interconnected networks) and a leaping frog, able to jump into innovations, reinvention, and renewal.

Flat organizations have been called boundaryless, networked, lattice, ameba, and virtual organizations or global heterarchies (the opposite of hierarchies). They are structured around self-directed or self-managed, multidisciplinary, cross-functional work teams, in which power flows from expertise, not position. In flat organizations, a decentralized approach to management is emphasized, as is high employee involvement in decision making. Flat organizations are structured around customers, teams, problems and opportunities, adaptiveness, horizontal connections, and networking. They decentralize authority, share information, diffuse and distribute competency, and use reward systems that are primarily team-based. Their strategies consistently emphasize growth, innovation, product customization, and technological leverage, rather than cost containment and operating efficiency.

3. Exploit the Benefits of Networked Organizations

Worldwide networking within and across organizations, linking companies, suppliers, customers, designers, and sometimes even competitors, is common in building collaborative advantage and global connectivity. Although by definition competitors are fighting over the same bone, your competitors are probably the only people who know as much about your business as you do. Take Pomarfin, a Finnish shoe manufacturer that markets the Ten Toes brand. The linked company consists of five competitors that share their hidden knowledge in a way that strengthens their ability to compete. Such partnerships and strategic alliances blur traditional hierarchies.

The joint ventures and partnerships established through interorganizational networks are less formal, nonhierarchical, less permanent, and more opportunistic, since the companies within a network band to-

gether to meet a specific market opportunity. AOL Time Warner, Wal-Mart, and Procter & Gamble, and Disney's Celebration City have created conglomerates with fluid boundaries between the participating organizations for the purpose of sharing resources (financial, intellectual, and human) or inventing new businesses.

4. Devolve Responsibility and Set Parameters for Action

Control in flat organizations lies in the mutual agreements that establish the parameters of discretion and performance expectations. Control is dispersed throughout the organization, with emphasis on self-control and problem solving. People own their work—they are self-managing, self-organizing, self-designing. They take personal responsibility for work outcomes, continuously monitor their own performance, seek corrective action when necessary, and take the initiative to help others improve their performance. They also design and control their careers by defining the social contract with the organization, as opposed to having the organization determine individual career paths and progress. In short, in nonhierarchical organizations the main incentive of work is work itself.

Leadership in flat organizations constantly espouses the values of collaboration. It is shared, lateral (as opposed to top-down), and dispersed among organization members. It is a reciprocal investment process between leaders and collaborators. Through the processes of leadership making and team making, individual employees are integrated into cohesive adaptive units at the work level and larger competence networks at organization level. People take responsibility for the development of their leadership and collaborative skills, facilitate the leadership of others, and cultivate leadership processes, functions, and roles that maximize team performance. Leaders as designers, coaches, collaborators, and catalysts influence the workflow through coalition building and value consensus. In flat organizations, the larger-than-life, omnipotent individual leader is often replaced by executive teams, which form a key mechanism for managing the organization of the future.

5. Be Careful, Cautious, and Realistic

Managers must design effective organizations and create superstructures within which the company's work takes place. In

today's flatter companies trust is the glue that holds organizations together. Trust is important, because decentralized discretion implies that managers can no longer maintain the level of control they have been accustomed to in the past. When management does not control, but only monitors, it needs the trust of the workers, especially when they are geographically dispersed without face-to-face contact.

In both fat and flat organizations managers, as designers, must understand their industries' dominant technologies, economic prospects, and degree of organizational uncertainty. They must be capable of navigating in the fog, as former Hewlett-Packard C.E.O. Carly Fiorina put it, in order to make effective choices about organizational design. Effective organizational structures are aimed at enhancing and maximizing the company's capacity for innovation and change. Although the Internet is provoking companies to dynamically restructure their infrastructures, don't expect technology alone to radically change organizations and managerial practice.

Put simply, there's no such thing as a one-size-fits-all organizational design. Organizations must instead be in tune with their environments. A hierarchical organization will not work in a creative, rapidly changing e-commerce environment, although it may work in a standard business-as-usual environment. Similarly, large hierarchical organizations can be managed as if they were small, while mature conglomerates like General Electric can grow like startups. Organizational structures must change to facilitate growth.

MINI-CASES

Before restructuring, *Motorola* had 12 layers of management. Even when the company decided to cut some of the fat by reducing the levels of management, top management was concerned with how such efforts would affect the organization's core values such as protecting employees who had served the company well in the past.

Saturn plants consist of semiautonomous teams of between 6 and 15 people, each of which is responsible for every aspect of its area. Showrooms guarantee no-pressure sales and eliminate haggling.

Edward Jones financial services has an organizational structure that has been called a confederation of highly autonomous entrepreneurial units bound together by a highly centralized core of values and services. The company is a network of thou-

sands of brokers, each of whom works from a wired office.

CONCLUSION

Even the aging dinosaurs have to change and adjust to the rugged landscape of the global economy. Businesses can do so by decentralizing and splitting into smaller and smaller configurations and more adaptable units. Organizations of the future must innovate, therefore they must take risks. One of those risks is reinventing themselves when necessary. Leaders and managers must be able to create organizational environments that encourage out-of-the-box and contrarian thinking, cultural dexterity, knowledge sharing, and diffusion of ideas.

FOR MORE INFORMATION

Books:
Duck, Jeanie Daniel. *The Change Monster: The Human Forces That Fuel or Foil Corporate Transformation and Change*. New York: Three Rivers Press, 2002.
Kanter, Rosabeth Moss *Confidence: How Winning Streaks and Losing Streaks Begin and End*. New York: Crown Business, 2004.
Lipman-Blumen, J. *The Allure of Toxic Leaders*. New York: Oxford University Press, 2005.
Myers, David G. *The American Paradox: Spiritual Hunger in an Age of Plenty*. New Haven, CT: Yale University Press, 2001.

Web sites:
Fast Company: **www.fastcompany.com**
Center for Collaborative Organizations, University of North Texas:
www.workteams.unt.edu

"Finding the right balance of hierarchical looseness versus control is a central task of leadership in the boundaryless organization."

Ron Ashkenas

Managing in a 24/7 Organization
by Thomas M. Koulopoulos

EXECUTIVE SUMMARY

- Ubiquitous and portable computing, global operations, and increased competitive pressure have resulted in an around-the-clock mandate for nearly every industry.
- Companies will need to invest heavily in tools that ease the burden of connectivity by helping employees, customers, and partners to control, manage, and personalize their interactions.
- New approaches such as personalization, workflow, e-learning, and knowledge management will help us to cope with the 24/7 workplace.

INTRODUCTION

For better or worse, our work lives and our personal lives are entwined through electronic connections. Many employers expect —or even mandate—that their employees' work will be boundaryless. It's not unheard of for employment contracts to stipulate that certain employees responsible for critical business processes, projects, or clients be available around the clock through laptop, PDA, cell phone, and pager.

But it's not only a technology problem. The flattening of organizations and the personalization of desktop computing have resulted in a thinning of administrative support infrastructure. We are being forced to become our own administrators and support staff. Like the fighter pilot whose airplane can exceed the G-force limits of physical endurance, we need to understand our limits and build enterprises that acknowledge them.

Yet how can any enterprise competing in a free market escape the gravity of 24/7? There's no substitute for time. If your competitors are open on Sundays, if their support lines are answered in the early hours of the morning, if their R & D works around the clock, you have little option but to follow suit. We may have no choice in the matter, but, as Dylan Thomas wrote, "Do not go gentle into that good night".

THRASHING—TOWARD TERMINAL VELOCITY

The acceleration of business cycles, increased attention to customer service as a competitive differentiator, and instant responsiveness to market volatility are all given as the upside of a 24/7 economy. What's not as often addressed is the very real human toll that 24/7 can exact from workers and consumers. The question now is how to cope with what increasingly appears to be the *terminal velocity* of business.

The most profound effect of 24/7 has been the thrashing that results from our inability to manage and neatly compartmentalize the sheer quantity of information and resources to which we suddenly have instant and unabated access. Each of us is constantly juggling a multiplicity of priorities and tasks across what used to be solid boundaries. The result is a constant bouncing from project to project, application to application, information source to information source—in short, thrashing. The price of thrashing is high. It devours our attention, derails our focus, and compromises our creativity.

Psychologists have long known that as the noise factor around us increases, our filtering mechanisms also increase. It's what scientists refer to as signal-to-noise ratios. As the background noise of our world increases, we need to become better at identifying relatively weaker and weaker signals. Yet filtering without accompanying focus can be a dangerous proposition—the equivalent of blinkers on an angry horse.

Compounding this volume and velocity of information are increasingly shorter windows in which to make decisions. We are weaving the web of our lives ever tighter by dedicating smaller and smaller intervals of attention to each task and responsibility. It's what I call the "uncertainty principle": as the volume of opportunity increases, the time to act on each individual opportunity decreases proportionately.

Most of us walk through life tagged like wildlife with our pagers, PDAs, and cell phones latched to our belts—not just connected, but tethered. And this phenomenon is even more pronounced in Europe and Asia, where wireless technology is far more advanced and accepted than it is in North America, partly because the value of community is far better understood in these older cultures.

From an organizational standpoint the same principle seems to apply. Value chains are becoming far more intertwined, creating a level of complexity that makes discerning critical events and actions nearly impossible. It's as though we just built a super-highway and then put traffic lights at every on/off ramp.

The situation is not dissimilar from the early days of most new technologies. During its early years the automobile imposed a heavy burden on its owners by requiring that they spend as much as half of their time on maintenance. Keeping a car on the road meant a commitment far greater than just learning to drive. Although an automobile could get you to your destination faster than horse and buggy, the aggravation of getting there was rarely worth it. The image of a automobile driver off the road in a ditch kicking his rims while the horse and buggy driver disdainfully passes by is a familiar caricature. Although laughable in retrospect, it's not that far removed from the mixed feelings many workers have when it comes to the use of wireless laptops, PDAs, and other devices intended to make work faster, but in the end just seeming to add more frustration to their lives.

MINI-CASE

Based on data from the U.S. Federal Communications Commission (FCC), over the past two decades telephone use has increased nearly tenfold, while simultaneously the length of a phone call has shrunk by nearly 30%! It could well be claimed that attention management, the exercise of capturing "mind share" against the ever-increasing din of background noise in the marketplace, is among the most pressing issues for the deluge of a 24/7 economy.

MAKING IT HAPPEN ▶▶

Companies will need to invest heavily in tools that ease the burden of connectivity by helping employees, customers, and partners control, manage, and personalize their interactions in the face of ever-increasing access. These tools are available and are increasingly being run by highly competitive organizations.

"The key to running an entrepreneurial business with feet on four continents lies in constant access to information."

Lycourgos Kyprianou

Personalization

The question is not how to break away but, rather, how to better integrate and manage the accessibility and complexity that technology provides. Companies operating 24/7 take care to create environments that provide tools for personalizing every experience of their workers, customers, and partners, cutting through the clutter to the essence of what matters to each person. This paves the way for what has quickly become a new generation of *my*-based experiences. It's hardly a surprise, then, that one of the most popular prefixes for Web sites has become the word "my."

Technologies such as portals offer a single point of personalized access to myriad online resources and are a key factor in coping with a 24/7 world. With a personalized portal you can create anytime, anywhere, online access to all the information, people, processes, and applications you need for doing your job, making decisions, and collaborating with others. Personalization is essential to managing the increasing burden of 24/7 complexity and access.

Workflow

Since 24/7 often implies that we're juggling more individual activities than ever, we need more help with how we keep everything up in the air. Workflow provides the foundation for changes in the way we work by automating much of the routing, follow-up, and scheduling of activities. More importantly, workflow allows this change to occur in ways that improve the general quality and rhythm of our lives by alleviating much of the need for process administration.

Of greatest relevance is the use of roles in helping to define how work should be routed when a particular individual is not available. Most of our systems, from e-mail to organization charts, have used the individual as the designated recipient of work. As a result work often waits until a specific person can respond. Role-based workflow systems route work to the skills of the role, not to the individual. If we shift our focus from the *delivery* of work to the *coordination* of work, technologies such as workflow may actually improve our lives by proving that work is best accomplished when integrated with our lives.

E-learning

In a 24/7 economy we have less and less time to unplug from our tasks and take part in a formal training or education program. Since every task is sliced into smaller pieces of time, our learning has to be sliced into finer intervals. E-learning is a relatively new approach to just-in-time delivery of learning as an integrated part of a value chain. Unlike traditional forms of online learning that have simply delivered classroom materials and instruction on CD-ROM, DVD, or through the Internet, e-learning synchronizes the learning needed for a given task with the performance of that task, resulting in significant time savings.

Knowledge management

Knowledge management was once summarized as "just a bunch of answers all waiting for the right question to be asked." We've all had the experience of hopelessly navigating a large enterprise, bureaucracy, or community trying to get to the right person.

Knowledge management systems provide a mechanism by which organizations and industries can bridge the gap between those who know and those who need to know. In a 24/7 economy, making these connections will be the difference between organizations that succeed and those that fail. However, they will also yield enormous economy of time by connecting those who need to know with those who know.

Globalization

The greatest challenge and accomplishment of the 20th century was building the infrastructure for the massive movement of people to where the work was. The greatest challenge and accomplishment of the 21st century will undoubtedly be building the infrastructure for the movement of work to where the people are. In a 24/7 organization this is clearly the greatest single opportunity since it helps to focus an enterprise on doing the right work with the right resources. Yet it is a daunting challenge to consider all of the implications this involves, from the cultural and social, to the management and technical. What is clear at this stage is that we have entered a new era of globalization, which at least offers the potential for greater global prosperity and economic growth. Realizing that potential will require us to rethink the very nature of work and how we build a new generation of workers and global organizations.

CONCLUSION

By integrating personalization, workflow, e-learning, and knowledge management with a human-centered organization, the quality of life in a 24/7 economy and the opportunities it presents to individuals improve measurably. Rather than spending ever-increasing amounts of time administering, navigating, searching, and accommodating the 24/7 organization, workers are now able to focus on the tasks that can most benefit from their intellectual capital.

Still, it's a difficult future to understand. As Dee Hock, founder and chairman emeritus of Visa International, said, "The old rules no longer apply, but the new rules are not yet known." Indeed, it's like trying to describe color to the inhabitants of a black-and-white world.

Imagine yourself going back in time and trying to explain the concept of jet lag to a citizen of the 19th century. They would have no framework for understanding what it meant to move at a speed that could get you to your destination before you had left.

For all our efforts there's a new generation who are going to regard the way we make decisions today in organizations as anathema. We wonder how we're going to survive at the pace of 24/7. They won't even question it.

FOR MORE INFORMATION

Books:
Davenport, Thomas H., and John C. Beck. *The Attention Economy: Understanding the New Currency of Business*. Cambridge, MA: Harvard Business School Press, 2001.
Rifkin, Jeremy. *The End of Work: The Decline of the Global Labor Force and the Dawn of the Post-Market Era*. Los Angeles, CA: JP Tarcher, 1996.

"The parking is easy, there are no checkout lines, we are open 24 hours a day, and we deliver right to your door."

Anonymous

Self-managed Teams: How They Succeed or Fail

by Andrew Leigh and Michael Maynard

EXECUTIVE SUMMARY

- Many companies have tried self-managed teams, with mixed results.
- When they're successful, self-managed teams can be 15–20% more productive than conventional teams.
- Despite the title, these teams usually have some form of official or unofficial leadership.
- It takes considerable effort and time to refine the concept to make it work well.
- In launching the self-managed concept it's important to understand the natural development cycle of groups.

INTRODUCTION

Procter & Gamble kept self-managed teams a commercial secret for years. Hundreds of companies have tried to make them work, with mixed results. Consultants extract large fees for either recommending them or unraveling the mess from the ones that failed.

Self-managed teams (SMT), often called self-directed work teams (SDWT), have acquired a momentum all their own. More than half of the largest companies in the United States now have them, from the automaker Saturn to Federal Express. The United Kingdom is no slouch, either, with companies such as Land Rover and The Body Shop showing the way.

Such arrangements are not for the fainthearted. They represent a switch from the boss–worker relationship to a collaborative approach. Once the self-managed idea gets underway everything tends to be challenged, from supervision to setting wages, from existing production targets to persistent hierarchies. In principle these apparently leaderless teams are simple to understand. You empower everyone in a team to take responsibility. Instead of a supervisor or some distracted middle manager directing events, the team runs itself. Well, that's the theory. Now for the reality.

ESSENTIAL TECHNIQUES

1. Be Committed and Practical

Creating a self-managed team is a marathon, not a sprint. You stand a better chance of succeeding with an entirely new team than you do with a long-standing one. Managers who have introduced the self-managed principle usually say it's a time-consuming business that needs careful nurturing.

Self-management demands a new mindset, one where you stop thinking in terms of managing per se and focus on empowering or motivating. If you're fond of command and control as a management style, self-managed teams are definitely not for you.

So what exactly is a self-managed team? Broadly, it's a work group of around 5 to 15 people sharing responsibility for a task. It could be building an automobile or processing insurance claims. The assumption is that the members possess the skills and authority to supervise themselves. An important feature is that everyone tends to learn all the tasks required. In this it differs from the traditional team, in which jobs are broken into smaller elements, each assigned to an individual with specialist skills. When self-management works, productivity rises above conventional teams by anything from 10 to 20%. In addition, employee satisfaction increases and employee turnover falls (which explains why the originator, Procter & Gamble, kept quiet about it for so long).

A particular challenge that this work arrangement poses for Western cultures is our passion for independence, self-sufficiency, and competitiveness. These often come at the expense of shared goals and collaboration.

2. Understand the Team Cycle

To make self-managed teams succeed you need to know some basic principles of groups and how they reach peak performance. The chart shows the seven stages that all teams experience, though some stages may dissolve seamlessly into the next.

Whenever someone leaves or joins, in effect you have a new group. A renewed effort needs to go into rebuilding relationships, clarifying working arrangements, establishing trust, and going through some or all of the development cycle. Teams switch between various stages of development as they encounter new issues.

There are different views concerning the evolution of successful teams, but most tend to follow the same pattern. The one that is used most frequently and perhaps most clearly defines the development of teams has four stages:

1 **Forming**—the team is a collection of individuals that are just starting to form into a single unit. The ice is carefully being broken, people are introducing themselves and are generally quiet, polite, and are getting the measure of others in the team.

2 **Storming**—conflict starts to emerge as people display their attitudes and set boundaries. This is an inevitable phase as people get to know others in the team and find their own identity.

3 **Norming**—norms are developed as people understand each other's strengths, weaknesses, and patterns of behavior. The group functions as a team and tasks are accomplished. Often teams settle at this level.

4 **Performing**—the team starts excelling and performing at its very best. This largely results from a steady accumulation of trust, respect, and understanding, combined with a common sense of purpose and some successes.

To these four stages can be added a fifth—reforming—which refers to the process of renewing and reinvigorating the team, perhaps after failures, difficulties, or major changes.

3. Visit a Self-directed Team

If you like the idea of self-directed teams, visit some existing ones to gain a practical feel for the challenges you will inevitably encounter. For example, self-management implies that no one is really in charge, when

---

"A team is not a bunch of people with job titles, but a congregation of individuals, each of whom has a role that is understood by other members."

Meredith Belbin

236

BEST PRACTICE

in reality this is seldom true. Invariably there is someone providing leadership.

4. Understand and Resolve Problem Areas

Mature teams can handle responsibilities that once kept the traditional line manager in business. For example, at Motorola, teams determine members' pay raises based on performance appraisals. At Honeywell, teams start by being responsible for such basic areas as material replenishment, quality at source, and on-the-job training. From there they progress to dealing with conflict resolution and scheduling vacations. Later they may take responsibility for selecting team members, cost control, and performance appraisal. This evolution depends on some early successes, which help motivate the desire to stick with it. There are, however, several issues that have to be resolved en route.

Many teams resist self-management, particularly when it's imposed by senior management. Employees, comfortable with conventional line management and having no desire to take on extra responsibility, can be intransigent. It's essential to offer them clear benefits and structured education.

5. Sustain Momentum

Newly created self-managed teams often produce quick results. Many problems emerge later once the excitement has worn off. Now the team faces the same challenge as any long-term group. It needs to focus on creating and maintaining self-motivation or creating a list of people who are in turn responsible for continually revitalizing the team.

How long it takes before the team is truly self-managing may depend on factors outside the team's own control; such factors influence teams no matter how they are managed. For example, in a U.S. survey of 400 organizations, about half complained of inadequate resources, just under half said they had no or low rewards, and a similar proportion reported lack of decision-making authority.

6. Allow Teams to Make Appropriate Decisions

Long-serving managers must learn to let go and trust people. They may also need to transform their style into a supportive and facilitative approach and learn to allow decisions to emerge naturally. Third, they need to respond to mistakes and crises by turning them into genuine learning opportunities instead of using them as an excuse to punish or even grab back decision-making control.

As companies increasingly rely on talent, brainwork, and virtual teams that hardly even meet, self-management has many attractions. The lessons so far are that self-managed teams can be highly productive and extremely satisfying to work in. Paradoxically, though, it takes particularly good management to allow them to succeed.

FIVE MYTHS ABOUT SELF-MANAGED TEAMS

- **They don't need managers.** They need managing through coaching, facilitation, and other forms of support.
- **They don't need leaders.** Leadership is essential and is often shared ingeniously across the group.
- **They make leaders powerless.** Leaders must exercise power differently and rely more on influence than authority.
- **They're cheap.** They cost more in the short term and have high setup costs such as training and troubleshooting.
- **They're quickly established.** They can take years to get right, needing constant refinement.

MINI-CASE

When mining machinery manufacturer Boart Longyear opted for self-managed teams it had to learn the hard way. Team preparation involved at least 60 hours of training, but no single person emerged as the informal leader. The result was delays in decision making. One of the greatest sources of frustration was that employees felt comfortable only when they were told what to do. When they hit a problem their first reaction was to demand help from a supervisor. The benefits were:

- Individual team members really pulled their weight, because they didn't want to appear to be underperforming.
- Former supervisors shifted roles. They became resource providers rather than rationers and spent their time obtaining information and securing resources.
- Productivity rose by around 10–15%.

MAKING IT HAPPEN ▶▶

- Stop thinking in terms of managing and focus instead on empowering and motivating.
- Visit some existing self-directed teams to gain a practical feel for the realities that you will inevitably encounter.
- To overcome resistance to self-management, offer employees clear benefits and education.
- Be sure to clarify what each person in the self-managed team does and where jurisdiction begins and ends.
- Invest time in developing communication skills and establishing best practice for conducting meetings and making decisions.
- Respond to mistakes and crises by turning these into genuine learning opportunities.

CONCLUSION

Self-managed teams and team-based working have developed into the normal way of structuring organizations and undertaking tasks, yet it is a difficult and complex aspect of leadership and is usually developed through experience. When developing a high performing, self-managed team it is valuable to have an understanding of:

- **the benefits of team building**—what it can achieve and what the leader should be striving for;
- **team roles and dynamics**—how teams work toward and achieve their greatest success;
- **the key stages of team development**—what they are and how to support the team in each stage;
- **the features of a successful team and team leader;**
- **how to avoid potential problems and pitfalls.**

Team building is a continuing process requiring energy, commitment, feedback, and review. Factors affecting the team change constantly, and the team needs to have the leadership and support that breeds flexibility and confidence. It is often useful to consider one's own career and reflect back to when you were in a successful team: what made it work and how could it have been better? Could your current team be improved?

"A good team is a great place to be, exciting, stimulating, supportive, successful. A bad team is horrible, a sort of human prison."
Charles Handy

Workers without Borders: Creating Bonds When Workers Have No Loyalty
by Perry Pascarella

EXECUTIVE SUMMARY

- The death of worker–company loyalty leaves business leadership grasping for ways to align people with the organization.
- Painful but necessary, this "death" gives birth to the possibility of more meaningful bonds for working effectively.
- Converging corporate and personal needs for creativity, collaboration, and commitment set the stage for stronger, though not lifelong, bonds.
- Leaders can take specific steps to create bonds for working together effectively—bonds built on person-to-person relationships.

INTRODUCTION

We see growing evidence from all quarters that many companies are not loyal to their employees and that employees are less and less likely to express loyalty to their companies. People in leadership positions are challenged to find some basis other than company loyalty to hold an organization together and accomplish its objectives.

On the corporate side we see sweeping organizational flux because of the application of new technologies by traditional and new competitors, the impact of globalization and the rapid flow of capital within and across national borders. Product lines are abandoned in the quest for greater profitability; corporate giants downsize, removing tens of thousands of workers from the payroll; companies relocate headquarters or plants; acquisitions and mergers result in job losses.

Quite often such corporate measures have an impact on employment across national boundaries. Workers in Northern Ireland, Mexico, or France may lose their jobs when, for example, a U.S. company reduces its labor force.

MINI-CASES

LTV Steel, crippled by steel imports that exacerbated other difficulties, is seeking government assistance as it files for bankruptcy for the second time in recent years. Tens of thousands of workers, some of them third-generation steelworkers, are threatened with job loss; retirees face adjustments in their pensions.

Boeing, thriving in the world aircraft market, announces it will move its headquarters from Seattle to be better located for managing its other lines of business. About half of the 1,000 corporate employees are not expected to be taken to the new location.

LOYALTY VERSUS GLOBALIZATION

At the same time we see significant changes in behavior and expectations on the worker side of the loyalty equation:

- employees' willingness to relocate and change employers;
- a more entrepreneurial approach to careers, with the growing possibility of pursuing multiple careers over a lifetime;
- a search for the transcendent connection, community, and intimacy that people haven't found in traditional workplaces;
- resistance to the segmentation of work and personal life.

It has become obvious that companies can no longer promise lifelong employment and that fewer and fewer workers truly seek it. Workers and managers alike are increasingly apt to operate without borders, whether on the global map or on the organizational chart or in their mix of work and nonwork interests.

A TRANSITION TO SOMETHING BETTER

While it might be interesting to trace the causes of the death of the old loyalty or implicit contract in the hope of restoring it, there is little value in doing so. It's more valuable to recognize the present situation as a possible transition period between one kind of bond between worker and organization and something far more effective and rewarding to both parties. What we are experiencing is a painful aspect of the transformation in our concepts of work and organization.

Under the old loyalty system, managers controlled and workers complied in organizations built on alliances of reluctant adversaries. Workers submitted to corporate demands in exchange for financial compensation. In such an atmosphere *loyalty* was a cruel misnomer. *Compensation* was truly that—a counterbalance or recompense to make amends for something given up—as employees separated their work from other aspects of their lives and performed tasks that required them to be less than their full selves. These conditions fostered competition and even hostility both between employees and the organization and among employees.

This kind of bond hardly optimized what people could do in an organization. It was tolerable only in situations in which the leader's primary function was maintaining the status quo. As we turn to the future, however, a premium will be placed on creativity and innovation. Leaders will be challenged to find or create a far more meaningful bond than the one forged by control and rigidity.

CONVERGENCE OF CORPORATE AND INDIVIDUAL NEEDS

The apparent parting of the ways between the organization and the individual masks the convergence of corporate and personal needs. The drive for innovation invites three key factors in organizational life:

1 **Creativity** arising out of an interplay of learning and doing in a risk-taking environment.
2 **Collaboration** that opens the way to

"The bond between a man and his profession is similar to that which ties him to his country; it is just as complex, often ambivalent, and it is understood completely only when it is broken."

Primo Levi

innovation, from generating ideas to implementing them. It is widely recognized that innovation emerges through group process—"communities of practice"—more often than individual pursuits. Charles Ehin points out how this differs from the traditional workplace: "The production of intellectual assets depends primarily on voluntary relationships instead of competition."

3 **Commitment** to shared purpose. In an era of worker mobility and corporate flux, leaders have to find ways to get people to commit, for a time, to mutual goals and common values.

These three ingredients match basic needs shared by most individuals; leaders do not need to inject them into people. To be creative, to collaborate with others, and to have something meaningful to commit to are common human desires. Leadership therefore implies discovering ways to capitalize on this convergence of needs and align people in ways that allow them to fulfill their inner needs while serving those of the organization.

BONDS BUILT ON TRUST

What will be the basis for building bonds, with others and with the organization that will allow personal and corporate needs to be met? To a large degree this will come primarily through personal bonds, between leader and follower and among followers. These bonds will depend on more than warm feelings toward others. They must be fashioned through working relationships in which individuals can rely on one another to work together toward some common purpose. People need something they can deeply commit to, even if only on a relatively short-term basis. They need a group purpose—something more substantive than the pins, pizza parties, and propaganda extended by so many quality and productivity improvement programs. Relationships won't be structured by corporate designers, but will have to grow naturally in human dimensions. This means that leaders face the challenge of revealing their humanity and recognizing the humanity of others in order to sow the seeds of trust.

MINI-CASE

Integrity establishes the trust that is so critical to the human relationships that make our values work. With that trust employees can take risks and believe us when we say a *miss* doesn't mean career damage.

In today's *General Electric*, the rewarded behavior has changed from being the exclusive originator of an idea as a vehicle for

standing out among coworkers—to, more importantly, finding a better idea and eagerly sharing it across the entire company.

MAKING IT HAPPEN ▶▶

A leader's ability to earn trust depends not simply on inner character, but on outward expressions—that is, what the individual does and how he or she does it. Here are some suggestions for being proactive about earning trust.

Be open about facts and feelings

- Share information. Work at informing others so that they can be more effective. Don't hoard information to build up personal power.
- Share your feelings. Admit your concerns and fears.
- Share the bad news as well as the good. Beat the grapevine in conveying bad news and put it into a perspective that will enable people to continue functioning effectively.
- Share what you know about where the organization is going. Explain strategy in terms people understand. Organizations need leaders who can give meaning to day-to-day activity. If you are operating without benefit of a clear corporate mission or strategy, you can at least explain what you know.

Explain how you make decisions

- Show consistency in the basic values that guide your decision making. Trying to please everyone increases the risk of straying from your basic values.
- Consider all the alternatives. Your coworkers are more likely to forgive wrong decisions based on careful consideration than those based on shooting from the hip.
- Describe how and why you're shifting management styles to fit a given situation. Depending on the situation, effective leaders shift among a variety of roles: team player, boss, leader, and individual player.

Be a resource

- Build your competence. Learn enough so you can speak the language and be part of the team.
- Prove your commitment. No matter how skilled you are, people will look first at your level of commitment to the endeavor.
- Earn the support of top management. Know what it considers important.

Respect and care for people

- Demonstrate that you're working in others' interests as well as your own. It won't surprise anyone that you want something from the organization, but peers, subordinates, and bosses will look at your track record to see if you generally work for the corporate good.
- Set high standards for all, including yourself. Being the object of high expectations raises people's performance. If you don't set appropriate standards, you will neither achieve maximum results nor keep everybody happy.
- Show that you value other people's ideas. Countless others may have information and viewpoints of value to you and the organization. Be a magnet for ideas.
- Support your subordinates' decisions. When subordinates err, follow up immediately to help them to improve.
- Clear bureaucratic roadblocks. Pay attention to what your followers need to do their work.

CONCLUSION

The strength of an organization will depend increasingly on its level of openness and risk taking. Rather than looking to formal organizational structures to provide energy and direction, leaders will have to nurture bonds among people who have no set borders for where they work, on where they fit into the group or on how their work fits into their lives. Earning trust is the first step in generating the bonds needed for strong, creative working relationships. The resulting loyalties will be more genuine than the old company loyalty despite the fact that in a fluid world they offer no lifetime guarantees. The new loyalty will go much further than the old in promoting risk taking and creativity.

FOR MORE INFORMATION

Books:
Ehin, Charles. *Unleashing Intellectual Capital.* Woburn, MA: Butterworth-Heinemann, 2000.
Stewart, Thomas S. *Intellectual Capital: The New Wealth of Organizations.* New York: Doubleday/Currency, 1999.

See also:

"There has to be some kind of continuity and some sense of belonging . . . unless we develop a more sophisticated model of the organization, the corporation will become just a box of contracts with no commitment on anyone's part." Charles Handy

Converting Anonymity into Participation in a Membership Organization
by Jane Galloway Seiling

EXECUTIVE SUMMARY

- An informed and increasingly demanding workforce is insisting that working together has to get easier.
- Organizational members want to integrate their own beliefs and direction with those of their organization. They want to identify with its overarching design (mission, goals, strategy, culture).
- The principles of membership—contribution, motivation, decisioning, relationship, leadership, accountability, and advocacy—support the members' efforts to connect to other organizational members and the organization they represent.

INTRODUCTION

Organizations are learning that it is essential to value and develop the interests, skills, and abilities of each individual and to provide opportunities for learning to be used. Members who identify with their organization want to contribute to their own welfare and the welfare of those around them and their organization as best they can. They no longer want only to be hands, to do only what they are told to, to work in silence and in anonymity. They want to think and do.

They want to partner with workplace members at all levels, making it possible for all to benefit from a communally designed future. Anonymity and mediocre work no longer satisfy the more demanding new workplace members. They want to *work with* instead of *work for*, in an environment in which their expertise, suggestions, and concerns are valued. They want to be given opportunities to perform at new levels of contribution. They want to work in a membership organization.

LOOKING AT THE MEMBERSHIP ORGANIZATION

Membership suggests voluntariness: working here because I want to, not because I have to, heightens performance and enrollment to a degree impossible in the old disconnected way of working. In membership organizations people seek reliable ways

of working beneficially with others. An overarching design creates an uncommon way of understanding and sustaining messages of why and what performance is in this place. All workplace activities are considered in the light of this overarching design.

The language of membership invites new understandings of beneficially working together. The old language of being an employee or boss signaled designated locations of power, control, and authority. Crossing the line uninvited was frowned upon, even punished, by superiors and coworkers alike. Successfully being together requires an atmosphere of partnering and working with instead of working for.

Membership recognizes the three common desires of workplace members: to be treated with dignity and respect, to be acknowledged and appreciated, and to know that what they do matters to the performance and success of their organization. By striving to address these desires, organizational leaders make it possible for members to connect to their organization and comembers. Failure to address these desires makes anonymity and disconnection inevitable.

PRINCIPLES OF MEMBERSHIP

In order to identify with the purpose and goals of their organization, members look

for guidelines. Without a common understanding, personal responsibility and productivity suffer. In the membership organization the principles defined by the collective membership also define what a successful contribution is. An example of these principles might be:

- contribution—all members, wherever they are in the organizational circle, contribute to the wellbeing of the workplace community;
- motivation—members are personally and collectively empowered to take action and feel that they and their work are significant to the overall achievement of the organization;
- decision making—long-term and short-term decisions are made with consideration for the three bottom lines: human, social, and financial;
- relationships—a relational approach is important to working with others; it's the responsibility of every member to establish connecting relationships that work, adding energy and respectful connection to relationships;
- leadership—leaders may be chosen or assigned, but leadership happens at all organizational levels;
- accountability—members are willingly and individually responsible and accountable for working toward organizational goals;
- advocacy—members' willingness to promote comembers and the workplace community positively influences the performance of individuals, groups, and the organization.

Through defined principles, membership takes participation and involvement to a higher level. New expectations become actualities when they are formed and performed together. Although formal leaders still exist, leading and following are no longer separate functions; all members share in the responsibility of running a successful organization. Organizations can no longer afford to separate, even isolate, the doers from the thinkers.

HEIGHTENED RESPONSIBILITY AND ACCOUNTABILITY

Members make choices to sign on, get out, rebel, or be anonymous. These decisions are consciously and unconsciously shared with others. People recognize that the amount of energy put into a task is often adjusted by the amount of respect held for the person, organization, or process. A minimally responsible person (low-energy, nonparticipative, anonymous) doesn't identify with a group or an organization. This matters because a lack of identification with an organization stifles the drive and dynamism of the business, as well as disenfranchising people and bringing poorer performance.

Responsibility

Within membership, actions of personal responsibility leading to informal leadership are normal occurrences, recognized as vital to the success of the group and the overall workplace community. Members' opportunities to perform are limited only by the extent of the individual's willingness to be personally responsible. Members are encouraged to question the status quo and are challenged to stretch and grow. It's potentially dangerous to be highly responsible and contributive in the hierarchical status-quo organization. In such organizations it may be best to choose anonymity.

Accountability

In the find-and-punish accountability of the old workplace, accountability is reserved for assigning blame which kills the desire to participate at a higher level. Accountability as a process is important to the success of members and the organization alike. Constructive accountability as an ongoing tool for exchanging information is an opportunity for members to learn and serve together. Constructive accountability is the activation of ongoing conversations that indicate project status, questions, exchanges of learning, the checking of statements, and the search for resources. It is the involvement of others in accomplishment—the opposite of anonymity.

Constructive accountability provides vital performance parameters. It gives performers a way of openly seeking information while sustaining dignity and respect. It's the first step to real empowerment. Empowerment requires both hearing and telling the truth in a supportive environment in which decisions are made at the place of need. Constructive accountability that includes recognition of contributions as well as new learning provides opportunities for giving and getting support.

THE ROLE OF LEADERSHIP

Moving from anonymity to membership requires leaders to address safety and security issues. It requires a genuine willingness to step back from rigid control, a belief that giving up control is beneficial. Members must now believe there are leaders-of-the-moment everywhere, even change agents, and that deep participation is consistently supported and encouraged. Leaders (who are also members) are either facilitators or barrier creators in the process of moving toward becoming a membership organization.

MINI-CASE

Southwest Airlines is often cited as an exemplary workplace. Southwest's goal is long-term employment of people who make a difference, while serving loyal customers—who are advocates for Southwest to other potential customers. Through these commitments to their members and their customers, according to Libby Sartain, vice president for people, "We get growth and profits. The result is a sustainable company where it is fun to work." This is a membership organization, where employees share in the corporation's purpose and identify with its success.

MAKING IT HAPPEN ▶▶

Considering membership as a new workplace reality raises important issues of belief, commitment, stamina, investment, and involvement. It derives from purposeful movement toward change. To make it a reality:

- involve, educate, and value member input in the overarching design of the future organization; provide extensive training and education opportunities;
- blur the lines of status and title; make it possible to become collaborative and cooperative—invite membership thinking;
- create new language, principles of performance, and deep involvement that indicate a valuing, respectful environment;
- encourage formal and informal leaders to reflect on and demonstrate these performance principles in all phases of their work performance and relationships;
- support personal and organizational change as a continuous, beneficial movement toward membership instead of a threatening, radical change that makes people fearful;
- move toward a genuine belief that all members understand the new philosophy and want to perform in responsible and accountable ways;
- understand that mistakes and setbacks will happen; acknowledge and understand what's happening. Be positive and consistent in the desire to forgive and move forward toward membership;
- be willing to take action when action is needed. It may be necessary to disconnect those unwilling to make the change.

CONCLUSION

Becoming a membership organization requires leaders to partner with organizational members at all levels to imagine and create an accomplishing, relationship- and performance-based organization. An overarching design anchors the process of steadfastly moving toward membership. The principles of membership, as designed by members, create new understandings of involvement, participation, and behavior. Anonymity, isolation, and mediocre performance are impossible when people choose to participate as members instead of employees. Membership creates and sustains hope in a beneficial future for the individual, the group, and the organization.

FOR MORE INFORMATION

Books:
Goudge, Peter. *Employee Research: How to Increase Employee Involvement Through Consultation.* Milford, CT: Kogan Page, 2006.
Schuster, Frederick E. *Employee-centred Management.* Westport, CT: Greenwood, 2002.

"From leaders, we need clear, consistent and honest attention to the identity of the organization. Identity shows up in our actions, our visions, our relationships inside and out of the organization. Identity gets deepened as we do the work."

Walter Wriston

Overcoming the Difficulties of Managing a Virtual Organization
by Jim Underwood

EXECUTIVE SUMMARY

- In the new economy, accelerating rates of change and increasing levels of complexity pressure companies to move employees closer to the customer while at the same time keeping a close watch on costs.
- The accelerating frequency of major disruptions related to nature (weather), terrorism, and possible pandemics make the case of necessity for creating "virtual capability" in all organizations.
- Emerging technologies will make virtual management easier; at the same time technology will create new management challenges.
- In the future more attention will need to be paid to how people are organized, motivated, and managed.

INTRODUCTION

The decades from 1980 to 2000 presented the business world with a sequence of serious challenges. In the early 1980s it was total quality. In the 1990s it was a new, connected world. By 2000 the problem was chaos: the reality was that managers of organizations had to learn to change with the technology-driven environment or be consumed by it. In response to each cycle of change few, if any, management theorists produced a coherent system for success.

Another reality was the dispersion of the work force. Achieving the speed necessary for success required that either employees would be located closer to the customer, or the customer would be brought closer through the use of technology. In either case many companies found themselves going virtual with no idea of how to maximize organizational performance. However, this brought significant problems. Customers generally seemed to prefer to deal with a human being, not an icon on a Web site. Similarly, dispersed employees seemed to miss the opportunity to interact with coworkers. Many felt their lack of interaction with managers did not bode well for their careers.

The changes brought about by the technological innovations of the 1990s and early 2000s have affected all aspects of business. There was a time when people had a choice as to whether they would be linked electronically. Today it's expected.

In the new wired world, technologies allow people to interact and deal with press-ing issues electronically instead of attempting to find a common time and place for a group meeting. In fact, regardless of location, whether they're in close proximity or not, people tend to do business as if they were dispersed.

MINI-CASE
Competing Globally at the Lauck Group

In 1997 the *Lauck Group*, an interior architecture company, was confronted with a challenge: to design ten offices in the United States and Europe for a major client, quickly. The team had to include professionals of different nationalities knowledgeable about the standards and requirements of their respective countries.

The Lauck team found top professionals in each country and then did something ingenious. They created a virtual workspace for all the constituents. During evening hours in the United States, the European teams would do their work and post it to the virtual workspace. When the U.S. teams came to work they'd log in and provide their input. The project—built on a 16-hour workday—was delivered on time and met every client requirement.

A Lesson from Katrina

2005 brought a lot of challenges to the U.S. Gulf Coast. One of those challenges was a hurricane named Katrina. The city of New Orleans is one of the few cities in the world that are actually located below sea level. In spite of local, state, and national govern-ment recognition of the problem related to a possible direct hit by a hurricane, little had been done to actually prepare the city and its businesses for such an event.

After the hurricane hit New Orleans in August 2005, the planning deficiencies became alarmingly clear. One glaring problem was the University of New Orleans. While other universities had been systematically creating a virtual presence that would allow classes to continue in case of a hurricane, this one had no such presence.

It has been abundantly clear that businesses must be capable of operating virtually if they are to remain competitive. A virtual strategy often enhances the company's talent pool while at the same time enhancing productivity. Now we know that the "virtual capability" of a company may impact its ability to survive catastrophic events as well.

CHALLENGES FOR THE VIRTUAL ORGANIZATION

In spite of the advantages created by virtual organizations, there are also inherent problems. For example, managers at Nortel Networks and Sprint PCS talk about the difficulties of responding to between 100 and 200 daily e-mails. Subordinates become frustrated, feeling "lost" in their managers' inboxes.

If communication consists of four levels— *spoken* or *written words*, *emotional pitch*, *nonverbals*, and *attitude*—the problems associated with communicating electronically with customers or coworkers become obvious. Three of the four are not easily discernible in an electronic message unless the author of the communication pays a great deal of attention to including them.

Les Carter and I have developed a concept we call the "significance principle." Every person has a driving need to be recognized, valued, and appreciated. There is a critical link between organizational performance and a company's practice of this principle. It's no accident that companies like Southwest Airlines continue to perform well. Their people are committed to the company's success because the company is committed to each employee's success. This

---

"The workplace is undergoing rapid change. So are American workers. Technology, globalization and new demographics are constantly redefining what work is."

Alexis M. Herman

also appears to be the case at the "Top 100 Best Companies to Work For."

Today's virtual world does not lend itself easily to such recognition. Managers as well as coworkers must be acutely aware of the needs of others, and this may be achieved in a number of ways:

Managers

- Send a personal note recognizing people's accomplishments (and copy the message to the team or your superior).
- Create special awards and recognition for team members who collaborate on corporate wins. This can be especially important for lower-profile remote contributors.

Colleagues

- Periodically post a comment about the contribution of a coworker.
- Communicate appreciation and value of coworkers.
- Try to avoid communication that might be misunderstood.

EMERGING TECHNOLOGY

Many marvel at the new connected economy. Surprisingly, the change over the next three to five years is likely to be even more dramatic. Massive changes are about to hit the technology arena.

Just five years ago we were talking about the possibilities of DSL (digital subscriber line) and how home communication speeds of up to 1.5 GB were going to change communications. In that short period of time, many (like this author) have "fiber to the premises" capabilities that offer 15 GB download speeds. That same service can offer up to 100 GB speeds. That means that the virtual workspace can now include broadcast quality video.

In the early 1990s Texas Instruments' senior executive team envisioned the world undergoing a massive technology shift. One of the key drivers, they concluded, would be DSP (digital signal processor) technologies. Basically, DSPs convert an analog signal, such as a voice over a telephone, into a digital signal that can be sent or forwarded to almost any device.

A DSP could take a voice message and convert it into a fax and send it. Or it could take a voice message or a fax, convert it into a digital format, and forward the message anywhere via e-mail. The implications of DSPs for the virtual world are overwhelming: geography no longer matters.

Home fax, home voice mail, office fax, office voice mail (plus cell phone messages), and pages can now all be forwarded to one common location. But it gets better—

what about FIDs? FIDs, or fully integrated devices, are also going to play a major role in the virtual organization. Imagine this: a PDA (personal digital assistant), a pager, a computer (with full Internet capability), and a cell phone all rolled into one. Not only can remote or dispersed contributors receive all information anywhere, but they can also use the same devices to respond.

The new 3G networks will allow the FID to send and receive video streaming. These new networks will facilitate at least 30 frames per second (the same as broadcast-quality videoconferencing). The FID will double as a portable videoconferencing device and will be about the same size as existing PDAs.

MAKING IT HAPPEN ▸▸

Management has changed from traditional planning, organizing, leading, and controlling to learning, transformation, and performance. Success is no longer tied to focusing upon historic competencies, but rather to the ability of an organization to rapidly anticipate changes and then transform itself into a completely new entity. As a result, leaders must be able to facilitate organizational learning, focusing on such things as the future of the organization, or competitive and technological challenges. Once the organization has learned, its derived knowledge must be actualized by transforming the organization from what it is into what it needs to be. Actualization of learning will produce maximum performance.

Some top-performing companies have leaders who understand this process: Southwest Airlines, A. G. Edwards, and Cisco Systems are three. The key steps allowing organizations and leaders to compete effectively in the new virtual world include the following.

- Focus on the basics: learning, transformation, and performance.
- Emphasize leadership, not management. Controlling approaches to managing a virtual organization will stifle performance. Organizations that genuinely value and appreciate their people will consistently outperform those that do not.
- Make technology transparent. Never implement a technology just because it's there.
- Recreate the workplace in the virtual world. In order to facilitate organizational learning, one company has a virtual brainstorming area on its

wide-area network. Another has an intelligence board where people can post information on products and competitors.

- Never forget excellence! Great organizations are great because inspirational leaders establish clear standards of excellence and expect their team to win.

CONCLUSION

Technological change accelerates overall environmental change. Rapid technological change, combined with drastically changed market forces, has driven massive shifts through the competitive environment. Each shift changes the rules of the game. The rules of the game for managing change correspondingly: constantly and chaotically.

Since 1980 the business world has had to face a series of challenges. One of the most pressing has been how to manage employees in a virtual organization. Using new technologies and new ways to manage, a virtual organization can not only be successful but can also achieve an extraordinary level of excellence.

FOR MORE INFORMATION

Books:
Goldberg, Beverly. *Overcoming High-tech Anxiety: Thriving in a Wired World.* San Francisco, CA: Jossey-Bass, 1999.
Petzinger, Thomas, Jr. *The New Pioneers: The Men and Women Who Are Transforming the Workplace and Marketplace.* New York: Simon & Schuster, 1999.

Web site:
www.soho.org provides information about technologies for virtual organizations.

"Managing intellectual assets has become the single most important task of business."

Thomas A. Stewart

Viewpoint: Francis Fukuyama
Toward Global Governance: The Paradox of Legitimacy

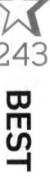
Introduction

Francis Fukuyama of the Johns Hopkins School of Advanced International Studies is renowned for his insightful, provocative, and ground-breaking views on the development of international politics, economics, and commerce. His book *The End of History and the Last Man*—developed from an article of the same name—ignited debate about the future of the world political order in the post-Cold War era. In recent years, Francis Fukuyama has focused on the role of culture and social capital in modern economic life and on the social consequences of the transition into an information economy. In this article, he argues that civil societies, through a variety of channels, are becoming much more involved in setting global norms of behavior for corporations. The result is an informal system of global governance that is emerging alongside official institutions such as the World Trade Organization, and this has significant implications for the way that global corporations do business.

The most obvious development regarding global-level policy in the last few years has been the direct participation of civil society in establishing things like corporate codes of conduct. A good example is the Nike sweatshop issue. Instead of legislating labor policy through the World Trade Organization, change was brought about by grassroots efforts in Honduras, where a nongovernmental organization (NGO) supporting workers' rights staged a protest and Nike accepted a new code of conduct.

The idea that companies can do well by doing good issue is at the heart of Peter Schwartz's book *When Good Companies Do Bad Things* (Wiley, 1999). Companies have an interest in protecting their reputations, and none wants to be vilified in the way that Shell was, for example, for dumping oil into the North Sea. However, the consequences of this need careful thought. Nobody wants overt international regulation because no one has figured out how to do it in a way that is remotely responsive and flexible, avoiding excessive bureaucracy. On the other hand, more informal kinds of self-regulation by the private sector have problems because in many areas it is hard to bring pressure on companies to improve their conduct. In other cases it is not clear that the NGOs that are pressuring the companies to adopt new codes of conduct actually represent the real interests of the people. This is the paradox of legitimacy.

For example, Ethan Kapstein points out in an article in *Foreign Affairs* that it's not clear whether the anti-child-labor code adopted by Nike is actually doing these countries any good. Nike promises not to hire anyone under the age of 17, but mandatory schooling in most of Central America ends at about age 12. In effect, Nike is saying that it will no longer employ these out-of-school kids who were supporting their families by working for a Western multinational. It's a complicated issue. It may be appealing to say that we have alternative ways of effecting global governance, but how to do it equitably and legitimately is something that is still unclear.

We have democratic institutions like Congress, elections, and political parties that have evolved over a long period of time because they were the best way anyone could figure out to represent all of the different societal interests and at the same time make the representatives accountable. You can unelect your representative if you don't like what he or she is saying in your name. The NGO sector doesn't have that kind of accountability. Perhaps you could make them accountable, but then you start regulating them, and they become part of the problem rather than part of the solution.

It is difficult to balance the need for a system that is flexible and participatory against the need for one that is legitimate and representative. Often the two are enemies. The reason we have formal, hierarchical, well-established institutions is to make them transparent and legitimate. But once they become formalized and hierarchical, they also become slow, inflexible, and hard to modify. There's not an easy way to reconcile those kinds of competing demands.

From the standpoint of any multinational corporation, global governance will be a central issue in the next few years. They are going to have to spend a lot of time worrying about how to deal with NGOs, how to deal with the backlash against globalization, and how to make their activities seem legitimate in all sorts of different markets.

Coexisting in a Fragmenting World: The New Difficulty in Finding Consensus

It has always been the case that culture and social norms are difficult and slower to change than technology, so it's not as if dealing with technological change is a new problem. In many ways, the kinds of social changes that took place in the United States between 1850 and 1900 were more momentous than the changes that took place between 1950 and 2000. That is when everybody essentially moved from the family farm to the city to work in factories. I don't think that the Internet even compares to that kind of change in people's lives, or the kinds of norms that accompany this different kind of urbanized, industrialized life.

What's new is that we have more cultural diversity

> "At the level at which entrepreneurs like Henry Ford, Andrew Carnegie, or Ted Turner operate, consumption is not a meaningful motive . . . money is more a symbol of their ability as entrepreneurs rather than a means to acquire goods."
>
> Francis Fukuyama

and a bigger and more complex society. That makes it extremely difficult to generalize about what is going on. You can get pockets of cultural adaptations or cultural stasis that all coexist in the same society. People who don't like change will simply wall themselves off and live in a community where they don't have to deal with it.

Getting society-wide consensus on certain issues is therefore much less likely now than in earlier generations. On the other hand, it may not be necessary in many cases. From a business technology standpoint, for example, you can have a high level of innovation, diversity, and social change in the San Francisco Bay Area while other parts of the country are virtually left out of it, and the latter don't hinder the former. This is also highlighted with the example of India, with a top tier that is world class, absolutely competitive in a globalized world in IT, and then you've got half the country that are failing basic literacy.

One of the reasons that this is significant is, of course, because it does pose a major problem with social justice. I've always thought that "cyberpunk" novelist Neal Stephenson's dystopias were really very apt, because what he describes is a world that is extremely fragmented. The old dystopia used to be an Orwellian vision where everything was regimented. In Stephenson's world everything is fragmented, and you get pockets with high degrees of social order next to very chaotic communities. They all somehow coexist with each other. I think that's a more accurate vision of where the world is actually going.

FOR MORE INFORMATION

Books:
Fukuyama, Francis. *Our Posthuman Future*. New York: Farrar Straus & Giroux, 2002.
Fukuyama, Francis. *The Great Disruption: Human Nature and the Reconstitution of Social Order*. London: Profile Books, 2000.
*This essay was adapted from an interview undertaken with Dr. Fukuyama by Peter Leyden, knowledge developer at Global Business Network (**www.gbn.com**). The publishers gratefully acknowledge the support of Global Business Network in making these ideas and insights available.*

See also:
☆ Trend Innovation Management (pp. 353–354)

"In the future the optimal form of industrial organization will be neither small companies nor large ones but network structures that share the advantages of both."

Francis Fukuyama

Viewpoint: W. Brian Arthur
Placing Bets in a World of Uncertainty

Introduction

W. Brian Arthur is Citibank Professor at the Santa Fe Institute, and currently serves on its board. From 1983 to 1996 he was Dean and Virginia Morrison Professor of Economics and Population Studies at Stanford University. His work on increasing returns won him a Guggenheim Fellowship in 1987 and the Schumpeter Prize in Economics in 1990. Arthur is also one of the pioneers of the new science of complexity. His main interests are the economics of high technology; how business evolves in an era of high technology; cognition in the economy; and financial markets. In this article, he discusses the interplay between complexity and uncertainty in our world today.

For about 300 years we've had a reductionist version of science. We've been looking in finer and finer detail—organisms, then organs, then cells, then organelles, and DNA—each time understanding mechanisms. At the same time, there have always been people curious about how some of these elements come together to make patterns. Rather than taking larger patterns and saying that they are made of elements, it means looking from the bottom up, not the top down, and asking how these elements make a difference.

In the early 1980s we all got desktop workstations, and it turned out for the first time that in physics or mathematics, or for that matter economics, we could start to look at these elements coming together and forming patterns. The elements might be dipoles or atoms or stars and galaxies, but each element is reacting to the aggregate pattern that those elements together create.

Most earlier science, and certainly economics in particular, just looked at static equilibrium patterns—for example, what prices and quantities of goods on the market would be held in equilibrium by the other prices and quantities of goods; what strategies could you or I adopt if we're running companies; where can I change my strategy and improve against the pattern your strategies are creating.

Complexity is about patterns coming into existence. It's not about equilibria. If you just drop water in a tray, you're only going to get one outcome. But if you polish the tray and put a thin film of water on it, you get a known linearity, or positive feedback, because some molecules under surface tension attract others, but gravity will tend to pull them apart again. Conduct that experiment again under identical conditions and the beads may gather in a slightly different pattern. What makes complexity interesting is that these interacting elements may settle into different patterns. In complexity theory, we're interested in the whole idea of how patterns come into being.

The El Farol Problem

In my own area, economics, I began to apply this pattern formation approach to forecasting models. There are a lot of examples in economic systems. The stock market is one where your behavior—whether you buy or sell Intel or Cisco—depends very much on what you think Intel or Cisco stock will be worth in three days', three months', or a year's time. Similarly, you buy a house based partly on what you think it might be worth in 10 years' time.

There's a bar in Santa Fe called El Farol. On Wednesday nights they used to have Irish music, but the bar gets terribly stuffy and crowded if too many people go. Imagine that 100 people are thinking about going to El Farol. The bar only holds 60 comfortably, so each person is trying to forecast how many other people will be there that evening. You have 100 people separately and without communication trying to figure out if they are going to go to El Farol that evening. If each one of them thinks it will be fewer than 60, then they will show up. If each one is expecting more than 60, then they will not go.

Now let's imagine that nearly everybody is forecasting that it will be crowded tonight. Nearly everyone won't go, so that will negate that forecast. Let's say that 85 people are expecting fewer than 40 to show up. Then those 85 will show up, which will negate the fewer than 40. So, if people have similar forecasts—and economics is built on this notion, that we all will do the same thing under the same circumstances—those similar forecasts will negate each other. For me, the theoretical problem was: How does one form forecasts in a situation where, if we all form the same forecast, that forecast would be immediately negated?

Navigating Through the Fog

Now apply this line of thinking to business. Imagine all the C.E.O.s in a certain area are all going into wireless technologies or proteomics or genomics—something trendy. All 20 of these people are on the prow of the ship. There is a kind of fog of technology into which they are heading. No one knows how well the technology is going to work, or who else is going to be in the game or who their competitors are going to be. They don't know how their technology is going to work. They don't know whether the public or other businesses will be interested. They don't quite know what the regulatory atmosphere will be. Each has ideas about all of these factors, but none of these is particularly well known. All of that creates a fog of technology. This is the world of indeterminacy in which all high-tech entrepreneurs live.

If technology C.E.O.s are *not* confused they aren't

being truly smart. The El Farol problem comes into play when the problem gets serious and it's about more than going to a bar at night. When you're talking high-tech the problem can be whether or not to build a fabrication plant at $4 billion a go.

As the ship moves forward through the fog the C.E.O.s can start to see the outlines of a city. But actually the city is created, or the future is created, by the actions the other C.E.O.s are going to take, and those are predicated on their beliefs. Each C.E.O. is trying to form beliefs, forecasts, or, more generally, a guiding vision about a situation that is, in turn, forming from the visions of others.

Place Your Bets

To illustrate the dynamics of decision making in this context of uncertainty I created a metaphor I called "the casino of technology." Imagine that all technology strategizing takes place in a big casino. There are gaming tables everywhere, and the Larry Ellisons and Bill Haseltines of the world are all wandering from table to table wondering which game to join.

Imagine there is a new game forming. Let's say it's "broadband" or "digital banking." Bill Haseltine runs Human Genome Sciences. Suppose he's the first to the table and he says, "I want to play this game." The croupier says, "Fine, Mr. Haseltine. You can play."

Haseltine says, "Well, how much will it be to ante up?" The croupier says, "For you it will be $4 billion." Haseltine replies, "Fine, who else will be playing?" The croupier says, "We do not know until they arrive." So Haseltine says, "OK. What products are we going to be playing with?" The croupier says, "We do not know until we see them." Haseltine asks, "How well will they work?" The croupier says, "No one knows that until the future." Haseltine replies, "What are the rules?" The croupier says, "The rules will be formed when people sit down."

Haseltine has to decide whether to play or not. If he waits until the game is fully in progress, it will be too late. Under a condition like that, whether you take very smart people like Haseltine or Bill Gates or Craig Barrett or anyone else, there is no correct answer. So what a C.E.O. in a high-tech venture has to do is figure out scenarios or figure out backup strategies.

I think the reason I am so interested in the El Farol problem is that it's starting to make sense. El Farol turned out to be the simplest situation that I could cook up that had that kind of diabolical twist to it—everyone thinking the same way and therefore negating each other.

One theme that emerges from this line of thought is that any economy is driven a great deal by what economists call expectations—somewhere in between forecasts and visions, if you like, or notions about the future. Sometimes these visions can be self-fulfilling; at other times they can be self-negating. Self-fulfilling could be positive or negative. If everybody is open, the system stays open and free trade flows. Then we're expecting that to keep going and it becomes self-fulfilling. But if something goes badly wrong, people then are expecting bad times, and then things get closed and shut down and that can become self-fulfilling. You can switch between those two regimes.

This essay was adapted from an interview undertaken with Mr. Arthur by Peter Leyden, Knowledge Developer at Global Business Network (www.gbn.com). The publishers gratefully acknowledge the support of Global Business Network in making these ideas and insights available.

FOR MORE INFORMATION

Book:
Arthur, W. Brian, ed. *The Economy As an Evolving Complex System II*. Boulder, Co: Westview Press, 1997.

"At the point where order and chaos most closely resemble one another, there exists the greatest possibility for broadening the human capacity to adapt to instability and uncertainty."

Daryl R. Conner

Reorganizing the Company Without Destroying It

by Colin Price

EXECUTIVE SUMMARY

- Pressures to change and compete frequently result in organizations needing to transform their structure. This transformation may occur quickly or over an extended period. Whether the organization is expanding, contracting, or simply refreshing its focus, the process needs to be handled very sensitively.
- Recent research has found that one year after a major reorganization, 70% of chief executives are disappointed or significantly concerned by the results of their efforts.
- Important factors influencing motivation among senior executives can be fundamentally affected by restructuring, impacting on issues such as the organization's values and culture, the need for differentiated compensation, and the level of freedom and autonomy enjoyed by managers.
- There are four adversarial mental traps to avoid when restructuring, as well as ten basic principles to observe in transforming performance.

INTRODUCTION
Reorganizations Have a Bad History

We all know that reorganizations have a bad history, not just at McKinsey and not just recently. As long ago as 1990, a study found that more than 50% of companies reported stagnant or reduced productivity after downsizing. In 1995 a study by INSEAD Business School reported that only 46% of 1,005 downsized companies surveyed had actually cut expenses, and fewer had increased profits or productivity. In 1996 *The Economist* reported research by Monitor looking at companies that had outperformed their industry over a ten-year period. Researchers found that nine out of ten had stable structures with no more than one reorganization.

Despite these failures, the imperative to change is still with us. We need to transform the corporation without losing the things that made it work. I'll discuss the mental traps that I believe cause these failures and the elements you need to consider. The goal is to achieve a transformation that fundamentally shifts an organization's strategy, business system, and culture to deliver measurable and sustainable improvements.

The Awful Law of Unintended Consequences

The law of unintended consequences states that any change will be accompanied by a set of consequences that cannot be accurately predicted. The reason this law is awful is that the consequences have a strong tendency to destroy all the value of your planned change.

The problem stems from two sources: the objectives of the change and the process. Major programs of change are often begun for unpopular reasons—downsizing, business process reengineering, and takeovers all seem unattractive and threatening to staff. The process is often unpopular because it disenfranchises people within their own organization. Morale sinks, productivity drops, people lose their trust in management, and the value of the change is lost. If we're going to avoid these problems in our own programs, we need to understand the underlying causes and design our own process so that we can reorganize the company without destroying its soul. This memo outlines four mental traps we need to avoid and ten rules we need to follow to avoid the awful law of unintended consequences.

Four Mental Traps

1 **People versus Performance.** Many change programs are stuck in the old paradigm of improving despite people. Successful companies recognize that you can only improve *through* people. This recognition comes from two main forces. First, the move toward a service economy and the growth in the value of intangible assets mean that these days the people *are* the organization—you can't change without changing them. Jack Welch said of the merger with Honeywell that GE would be bringing its "social architecture" to bear in driving the integration. This is a real acknowledgement that the people and the program are inseparable in creating effective change.

2 **Structure versus System.** Many change programs are overly focused on rearranging the formal organizational structure. The change will only be effective if the structure is part of a broader systemic transformation. In our ten-year survey of companies, structure was only one of several levers (with strategy, execution, culture, talent management, leadership, innovation, and growth through successfully managed mergers and acquisitions) that led to dramatic performance improvements.

3 **Us versus Them.** The role of the leader in crafting a transformational process is to create an environment in which people can take leadership of the changes wherever they are able. Talented people are motivated by freedom, autonomy, and the opportunity to rise to challenges. They can bring your transformation to life, particularly if you have a strong story they can dramatize. This is more engaging and compelling than their simply rolling out your program for you.

4 **Concurrent versus Consecutive.** Because the elements of the transformation program are complementary, you cannot achieve successful change by tackling them one at a time. Improvements to leadership, culture, and management processes will reinforce the changes you make to customer management, operational processes, and organizational design. Effective transformations work simultaneously on more than one element of the change to unfold a sequence of related chapters in the program.

"You can build a lasting competitive edge through the excellence of your organization structure."

Percy Barnevik

WHAT MOTIVATES TALENTED PEOPLE? Percentage of top 200 executives rating factor absolutely essential			
Great company	**%**	**Compensation and lifestyle**	**%**
Values and culture	58	Differentiated compensation	29
Well managed	50	High total compensation	23
Company has exciting challenges	38	Geographical location	19
Strong performance	29	Respect for lifestyle	14
Industry leader	21	Acceptable pace	1
Many talented people	20	**Great jobs**	**%**
Good at development	17	Freedom and autonomy	56
Inspiring mission	16	Job has exciting challenges	51
Fun with coworkers	11	Career advancement and growth	38
Job security	8	Fit with boss I admire	29

MAKING IT HAPPEN ▶▶
Ten Golden Rules

Although every transformation is different, from our experience we have abstracted ten basic principles that you should observe in transforming performance.

1. **Confront the facts continuously.** Make sure you understand the reasons for your current situation, however good or bad. Take time and be open-minded in analyzing the organization's current performance. Remember the world doesn't stop to wait for your transformation.

2. **Build a coherent and compelling transformation story.** Staff, customers, analysts, and investors need to see for themselves why the organization needs to change, where it is going, and how you plan to get there. Successful transformations are built on compelling stories that confront the existing facts, bring alive the point of inflection, threat, or opportunity that the company faces, and chart a clear course toward a new reality.

3. **Use the collective wisdom of the organization.** Transformation is far more effective when people discover a new reality for themselves and adopt new ways of working. No matter how convinced you are of the superiority of your business model, think carefully before imposing your views on the company—ultimately your transformation will take only if it taps into the organization's collective energies and insights. This isn't just a matter of buying in, it's one of genuine discovery.

4. **You can hold a few elements of your transformation sacrosanct, but be flexible about the rest.** As the organization changes, its final form won't be clear. The process of revelation is a necessary part of change, and your design must be flexible enough to accommodate it. But you need to be clear about the few elements that are nonnegotiable, and see that they're not compromised by any element of the transformation.

5. **Work through leaders at all levels.** Leadership is critical, but this is not just about your role as C.E.O. The transformation needs leaders throughout the organization building commitment to the new possibilities that emerge and engaging people in the story of the change.

6. **Get the right balance between action and reflection.** Action and reflection are both vital elements of the transformation process. Without sufficient action the process will lose momentum and fail, but you also need reflection to furnish renewal, check that the change continues to respond to the reality of the situation, and make sure that lessons are learned.

7. **Demonstrate early success.** It's not enough to talk about change—people need to experience it. Inertia can often be overcome by demonstrating early progress in microworlds that deliver visible improvements in operating and financial performance, increase customer satisfaction, and spark enjoyment and motivation in employees participating in them.

8. **Make the change process unique.** Your organization is unique, your people are unique, and your transformation is unique. This means that you must follow a tailored, dynamic change process that meets your needs and responds to events as they unfold. You need to design the change process so that it works for your situation, leveraging the leaders available and the balance of action and reflection to allow you to learn and develop on the journey.

9. **Expect resistance—listen constantly, but be clear about the boundaries.** Transformation is not easy. People, probably including some members of the leadership team, will almost certainly undermine the process, either through active opposition or through passive but visible lack of support. Many transformations fail because top management refuses to listen to these people. Nonetheless, it's up to you to limit the space in which people explore and the degree of resistance that's acceptable. Ultimately people who refuse to join the process must be moved aside.

10. **Measure progress at every stage.** To be effective in your role as leader of the change, you need access to real information about how things are going. Constantly and rigorously measure progress against specific milestones, changes in organizational energy and alignment, operational performance, and financial performance. Make all of these results widely visible in the organization.

CONCLUSION

These principles are based on observation of organizational changes; they encapsulate lessons learned from the successes and failures of others. For the whole of the last century we were collectively stuck in the paradigm that insisted the role of leadership is to drive hard for performance and brush aside resistance. The time has come to abandon this limiting model. Our research on motivation and performance is conclusive: the best people are turned on by a strong performance ethic and an open, trusting, and supportive culture. Performance orientation and people orientation are not opposites. They aren't even choices. Instead they're the two components that will enable us to achieve outstanding, sustainable results.

FOR MORE INFORMATION

Journal Articles:
Day, Jonathan D., and Michael Jung. "Corporate Transformation Without a Crisis." *McKinsey Quarterly*, no. 4 (2000). (See **www.mckinseyquarterly.com**.)
Kets de Vries, Manfred, and Katharina Balazs. "The Downside of Downsizing." *Human Relations* 50:1 (1996): 11–50.

"The inexorable forces of competition and change catch up again with companies that restructure but do not revitalize, that cut people but do not fundamentally alter their ways of working."

Sumantra Ghoshal

Viewpoint: Warren Bennis
Leading Managers to Adapt and Grow

Introduction

Warren Bennis is practically synonymous with leadership. A student and protégé of Douglas McGregor, he was invited by McGregor in 1959 to establish a department of organization studies at MIT's Sloan School of Management. After serving in administrative positions in the 1960s and 1970s, he returned to research and teaching in 1979, joining the University of Southern California, where he continues to pursue his groundbreaking work on leadership, organizational life, and personal development. He is author of dozens of articles and over 30 books on leadership, including *Leaders, On Becoming a Leader, Geeks and Geezers, Managing the Dream*, and *Organizing Genius*. Here he reflects on the factors that have most profoundly influenced this thinking, as well as on the qualities that people and organizations must nurture in order to create meaningful work.

Like everyone else, I'd have to say that there's no one thing that has influenced my thinking. And that's probably true of life. In my own case, I think there were several factors that came out along the way and that, in looking back, seem like a set of eccentric precursors instead of kind of a singular willful, purposeful, I-know-what-I-want-to-do path. I'll start off from how I grew up. There were giants in the air. It was during World War II and these iconic figures dominated the world—some for great evil and some for great good. We happened to be on the side of great good, when you think about Churchill and Roosevelt. I'm reminded of how grateful we should be for their examples of leadership and how wary we should be of dictators and demagogues like the Hitlers and Mussolinis. In those days, very like as recently as September 11, 2001, we turned our eyes to public figures.

This was true when I was a young person. As I was born in 1925, it was very clear that the Depression and World War II were influential in my development. Those of us growing up in those formative years saw horrors with Mussolini, Hitler and, later on, with Stalin. Listening to Hitler giving his speeches during the 1930s before World War II was very, very scary.

So, I grew up at a time when you saw how influential leaders could be and how influential their activities, their political entities, their organizations could be—potentially virulent and toxic; how much pathogen could be spread by one person and how many healthy white cells by the other. That was just part of it, part of the zeitgeist, part of the era. It was very important, though largely unconscious to us.

There were other things—of a more "micro," interpersonal nature. I happened to go to a college where the president was one of the men who laid the foundation for our field of organizational behavior and leadership. That was Douglas McGregor, who was the president of the college that I went to and had come from MIT. Well, it was no accident that I also became a college president and also did my Ph.D. at MIT. He was very interested in group dynamics and leadership—wrote a lot about it—and certainly the "McGregorian chants," as I called them, were very influential. Being at MIT, being in Cambridge, Massachusetts, during the 1950s and 1960s certainly influenced my thinking. I was fascinated by how, under certain conditions, groups can do the most creative, the most spectacular things and reach the most extraordinary heights of achievement—if they can create the right conditions for it. *Organizing Genius*, for example, was really the fruit, the result of those early years of thinking about groups. I became very interested to see how organizations, where we spend at least a third of our life, if not more, can be less toxic, more healthy, and provide more opportunities for people's growth, so that they can reach the frontiers of human possibility.

> I happened to go to a college where the president was one of the men who laid the foundation for our field of organizational behavior and leadership. That was Douglas McGregor, who was the president of the college that I went to and had come from MIT.

Three words leaders have trouble dealing with: "I don't know." I think good leadership will often start with questions whose answer is: "I don't know, but we're going to find out."

Even before September 11, we were living in a world

"You can be very bold as a theoretician. Good theories are like good art. A practitioner has to compromise."

Warren Bennis

characterized by mystery, doubt, complexity, uncertainty, and chaos. Think about the transformation from an analog to a digital society. In 1989, for example, there were only 400 users of the Web; now, as Shakespeare wrote in the 16th century, "we are a girdled globe." Before September 11 there were something like forty ongoing border disputes around the world. Globalization. Disruptive technologies. People are going to have to deal with doubt and uncertainty.

Organizations, organizational leadership, and organizational culture will have to be people factories—generating, nourishing, and nurturing terrific talent. They have to be education factories where that talent will be continually going to school. They will have to be led by leaders with enough emotional intelligence and cognitive capacity to be able to hold two divergent ideas in their heads at one time. I think those are going to be the critical aspects.

I'm going to add from my own work what I consider to be four critical aspects of leadership, which came out of a study about leadership and learning. I think they're important. And I want to argue that these four factors, which I think are critical for leading in this new world, are context- and culture-free. One is the adaptive capacity, which I think is probably the *sine qua non*, absolutely the most essential and central aspect of leadership in this environment of complexity and turbo-change. The adaptive capacity has a lot of things under it. It means a sense of resilience, hardiness, and creativity. It means seizing opportunities. It means learning learning. The second critical ingredient is the capacity to engage followers in shared meaning—to align the stars around a common, meaningful goal. Not just any old goal. Think Henry V at Agincourt: "a mission from God." Third, leaders are really going to have to spend a long time—and it's a continual process—finding out who they themselves are: learning their own voice, learning how they affect other people, learning a great deal about emotional intelligence. And finally, leaders will have to rely on a moral compass, a set of principles, a belief system, a set of convictions. Every good leader is going to have to—one way or another—learn these capacities. Now, I do think there are contextual and cultural factors,

but I'm saying that, regardless of culture and context, these four factors are essential. They are necessary, but not sufficient. For example, if you're interested in leading a ballet company, you must know something about choreography and about the art world. There's a whole ecology around ballet, around science, around being a baseball manager. Nevertheless, these four factors are, across the board, essential, whether talking about George Washington or Margaret Thatcher.

Managers need to ask themselves: Do you really want to lead? Are you aware of the sacrifices, the time demands, the complexity? Do you have a true commitment to abandon your ego to the talents of others? Do you love what you're doing? Do you enjoy trying to understand the social etiquette of bureaucracy? Do you really enjoy engaging others?

Any great place to work can be profitable. In fact, the most profitable *are* great places to work. I remember a former president of MIT once said to me, without a trace of grandiosity, that MIT "has had the habits of success." There's something about being successful that tends to perpetuate itself. I think that what will make a workplace great is when people really feel down deep that the company is on their side, that they will be treated equitably and fairly, that they are being given many opportunities for self-development and organizational development, where people are encouraged to "talk truth to power." If they're going to be putting in a lot of work at a place, not only do people need to have a license to tell the truth, they want to be in a place where they really feel they're going to be learning. People want to feel nurtured, that they're growing, and that there are enormous developmental opportunities available to them. To use my friend, Charles Handy's, book title, I think we're all "hungry spirits." Deep down, we all want to make a difference; if there's no meaning at work, people will check their hearts at the door.

> Organizations, organizational leadership, and organizational culture will have to be people factories—generating, nourishing, and nurturing terrific talent.

"Leaders are the most results-oriented individuals in the world, and results get attention."

Warren Bennis

Emotional Intelligence and Leadership

by Rick Lash

EXECUTIVE SUMMARY

- Effective leaders create organizational climates that foster superior performance.
- Creating climates for performance requires leaders to demonstrate high levels of emotional intelligence (EI)—the capacity to manage one's own emotions and the emotions of others.
- Developing EI is a journey demanding a commitment to personal growth and development.

INTRODUCTION

Most organizations are not the stable, predictable structures of the past. Keeping people motivated and committed in an era of unrelenting and accelerating change are among the most difficult challenges leaders at all levels now face. Companies need to be far more agile and flexible in how they operate both internally and externally. This changing nature presents a whole new challenge for those in positions of leadership. To meet these challenges, leaders must be able to create organizational climates that foster not only performance but also a sense of pride and purpose.

Research indicates that up to 30% of business results come from the climate a leader creates—defined as employees' perceptions of their work environment that impact their ability to do their jobs well. And up to 70% of organizational climate is driven by the competencies of the leader. These competencies can be wrapped up in a skills "package" called emotional intelligence (EI).

Defining Emotional Intelligence

To quote Daniel Goleman, bestselling author of *Working with Emotional Intelligence*, emotional intelligence is defined as "the capacity for recognizing our own feelings and those of others, for motivating ourselves, for managing emotions well in ourselves and in our relationships." Specific competencies that make up EI have been identified, including emotional self-awareness, empathy, self-confidence, self-control, and listening skills.

For many leaders, EI is not an easy concept to accept. Yet studies have shown that EI has real impact on bottom-line results,

sometimes doubling and even tripling productivity. For example, in a study done for the American insurance industry, the most successful companies (judged by growth and financial results) had C.E.O.s with a critical mass of emotional intelligence capabilities. By comparison, the C.E.O.s of companies with just average results lacked these strengths. The difference seems to have been in the climate created among those who worked in the companies, with the high-EI C.E.O.s creating a workplace where people gave their best.

In another study, sales agents with high EI competencies sold twice the amount as average performers. This same study has also shown that EI, unlike IQ, can be increased over time. The key to such improvement is the developmental approach that is used.

Developing Emotional Intelligence

Emotional intelligence is a complex set of skills and requires time to develop. There are seven critical factors in developing EI:

- gauge readiness
- motivate
- make change self-directed
- establish manageable goals
- encourage practice
- arrange support
- provide models

Gauge readiness: Many organizations pay little attention to whether someone they send for training is ready to learn and change. Frequently, only 20% of a group is committed to personal change at any given time. In truth, people will learn what they want to learn when they want to learn it.

Learning requires interest, motivation, and commitment and an emotional investment in the process to make it happen.

Feedback tools that highlight EI competencies, such as 360-degree feedback, are particularly helpful in affirming what the individual does and does not know, and the level of interest in closing the gap between current state versus future state.

Motivate: People invariably want to know, "What's in it for me?" They are motivated when learning is aligned with their values, aspirations, and goals. Personal and professional goals are major factors.

Meaningful and lasting change happens when participants have first identified their personal and professional values, goals, and needs. People develop EI when goals are personally meaningful. Although all seven guidelines are important, this one is particularly important and requires time and attention. This can be done through exercises where people write down their ideal or dream job, or identify times in their lives when they felt engaged and truly alive. Their pictures of success will also include needs around family, community, and leisure activities, as well as their work.

Make change self-directed: Learning EI is very personal, yet most training in organizations is designed as "one-size-fits-all." The commitment to learning—emotional investment—will increase with a greater opportunity for the individual to control the method and pace at which he or she learns. This honors the competencies of EI in respecting people's levels of achievement, self-confidence, and need to "direct themselves." To support this, determining the person's "learning style" and then designing or adapting the program to match is critical.

Nor should EI training be limited to the classroom. Learning EI skills requires social interaction with others. Taking participants outside the classroom to environments that put them in real-life situations that require active listening, empathy and self-control skills is a highly-effective technique for achieving both a commitment to action and the retention of new knowledge, because the control sits with the student and not the trainer.

"People desperately felt the need for connection, for empathy, for open communication. In the new, stripped-down, every-job-counts business climate, these human realities will matter more than ever."

Daniel Goleman

Establish manageable goals: Too often, people set goals that are too large and unwieldy. While their desired goal is not out of line, the sheer scope can be overwhelming and the individual can't see how he or she can get there. Goals should be specific and behavioral. Imagine a goal of achieving higher levels of empathy. At first glance, many would see the task as overwhelming and one may not know where to begin.

In developing empathy, the goal may be to have three conversations with people over the next week simply practicing listening without interrupting or jumping to conclusions. Next, the goal may be to reiterate what you heard and check for understanding or seek feedback from several trusted coworkers on your empathy skills. Small successes also build self-esteem and confidence.

Encourage practice and arrange support: Some believe that behavioral changes in EI will occur after a one, two or three-day program. It seems just a little ambitious to expect adults—usually with 20 or more years of life experience determining their current behaviors—to change to any great degree in a matter of days.

Good musician—practice. Good golfer—practice. Good public speaker—practice. The same applies to any desired result around behavioral change, although this is too frequently ignored in training programs. It requires support and direction from others, which can be delivered by establishing peer coaches, study groups and support networks or, in some cases, a trained personal coach.

To change complex competencies such as those found within EI can take three to six months for maximum effect.

Provide models: It's important to remember that those who teach should embody the behavior they wish to see in others. Nothing is more demotivating than being asked to behave in a certain way by those who do not embrace the same behavioral practices.

People tend to model their behavior on those who are more senior within the organization, negative as well as positive habits. Leaders need a high level of self-awareness and skills in persuasion, and must demonstrate consistency and reliability.

Organizations utilizing EI for leadership:
- At Johnson & Johnson, all 20 EI competencies were significantly stronger in a group of "high potential" mid-career executives than in a comparison executive group.
- At a global division (with 400 branches in 56 countries) of the German electronics

conglomerate Siemens, four EI competencies distinguished the star leaders, whose growth in revenues and return on sales put their performance in the top 15%. They were significantly stronger in the drive to achieve results, initiative, collaboration and teamwork, and leading teams. Not a single technical or purely cognitive competency emerged as the unique strengths of outstanding leaders.

- As part of a program to help the Defense Finance and Accounting Service of the U.S. Government prepare future leaders to handle a new organizational structure, downsizing, and new technology, a program on Developing Competencies for Leadership Success (emotional intelligence competencies) was delivered to 20 high potential middle level managers. This program followed the principles for developing emotional intelligence put forth by the Consortium on Emotional Intelligence, and it included seven contact days over a period of 14 months. The outcome was overwhelming. Participants not only reported that the program was helpful in preparing them to deal with the challenges they were facing, but they increased significantly (from pre and post assessments) in 19 of the 20 EI competencies, as measured by a 360-degree assessment.

A Personal Journey

Emotional intelligence is developed by reflecting on experiences, learning about oneself and practicing new behaviors. This raises a key point—developing EI is a journey that unfolds in stages. It is all about personal transformation. Like all great stories of personal transformation, there is the call to adventure, crossing the threshold into the unknown, embarking on a road of trials and tests, coming face to face with one's greatest weakness, and ultimately transforming oneself.

The benefits that come from developing emotional intelligence are profound. Individuals gain new knowledge and skill, a deeper understanding of themselves, greater wisdom and, perhaps most importantly, a broader perspective.

People who have developed their EI tend to be less self-focused and more community focused; less concerned with their own needs and more concerned about positioning others for success and becoming catalysts for change in their organizations and communities. They are less fearful and more courageous, less blaming and more willing to take accountability.

CONCLUSION

In times of rapid change, leaders must possess the skills and knowledge that create a climate for outstanding performance. Emotional intelligence—the capacity to recognize and manage one's emotions and show empathy toward others—are the foundation upon which organizational leadership is based. Developing EI demands personal commitment to long-term growth. It's a journey worth taking, for becoming more emotionally intelligent enriches both ourselves and the organizations and communities in which we live and work.

FOR MORE INFORMATION

Books:
Cherniss, Cary, and Daniel Goleman, eds. *The Emotionally Intelligent Workplace.* San Francisco, CA: Jossey-Bass, 2001.
Goleman, Daniel. *Working with Emotional Intelligence.* New York: Bantam Books Doubleday Bell, 2000.
Goleman, Daniel, Richard Boyatzis, and Annie McKee. *Primal Leadership: Realizing the Power of Emotional Intelligence.* Cambridge, MA: Harvard Business School Press, 2003.

Web sites:
Hay Group: **www.haygroup.com**
EI Consortium: **www.eiconsortium.org**

"Too seldom does the world pause to consider how much kinder and more humane business has become since women invaded the marketplace." — Edith Johnson

Viewpoint: Tom Brown
Management after Drucker

Introduction

In late 2005, the business world lost probably its most influential guru when Peter Drucker died. In this article, the prolific business journalist and author, Tom Brown, ponders Drucker's contribution to management and describes his own meetings with the *Ur*-guru.

The name, even now, conveys a depth, an astuteness—*an authority*—beyond that of anyone else in the field of management. In a speech to fellow managers, it is always safe to quote Drucker to support your views. Need a book for a new supervisor? Give them *The Daily Drucker*; no one will challenge your judgment. And, if you want to offer indirect criticism to your own supervisor, you can send a Drucker essay with a quick note: "He sure makes a lot of good points here! Maybe we could talk about this sometime soon?"

Author Web sites can easily become overstated PR platforms; but on **www.peter-drucker.com**, this seems almost an understatement: "Experts in the worlds of business and academia regard Peter Drucker as the founding father of the study of management." The author of 35 books and hundreds of shorter pieces, Drucker died at the age of 95 in 2005. His passing leaves both a legend to revere and a puzzle to reflect upon. In terms of the legend, most of the 80,000 Google links revere him and his writings. The greater intellectual exercise for us to consider is this conundrum: Why was Peter Drucker, throughout his life, so handsomely praised but his advice so seldom taken?

In its encomium to Drucker, *The Week* (November 25, 2005) recounted a telling event. Soon after he published *The Future of Industrial Man* in 1942, General Motors asked him to study how it operated as a corporation. He spent more than a year on the endeavor and ultimately wrote *Concept of the Corporation*. Never shy of saying exactly what he thought, Drucker made a number of pointed observations about GM. *The Week* summarizes them nicely: "Drucker recommended that decision-making be decentralized, that managers be hired from 'a wide cross section of per-

sonality types,' and that long-term goals be met via a series of short-term objectives. He also said that a manager's most important quality was 'integrity.'"

Considering that Drucker said all this in the mid-1940s, one might be able to forget "that GM refused to implement his recommendations." All his suggestions (and many others to come) preceded faddish (though commendable) corporate programs like empowerment, diversity, and authenticity. Yet, weighing GM's 1940s reluctance to implement Drucker's counsel from the perspective of 21st-century management, one wonders how GM would have fared had it ever fully acted upon Drucker's advice. (Hmmm. Might much the same be said about your own company?)

As the millennium approached, I conducted an informal poll of as many business leaders and thinkers as I could. Many of them were well-known, widely published scholars; but I also queried line managers whom I considered well read. My single question: what was the best management book of the 20th century? It was not hard to name a winner: Drucker's fifth book, *The Practice of Management* (1954), was just about everyone's pick.

The book remains my own personal favorite. In 2000, Drucker broke into laughter as he recalled for me the initial reaction of his editor when he submitted the book for publication. "Peter," said Ordway Tead, "this is not a business book! There's not a single table in it. It does not focus on how to make money. What's selling now are books about how to train salespeople or how to run a factory". We're blessed that the editor overlooked his own misgivings, although Drucker would undoubtedly have found another publisher for this masterwork.

While meeting one-on-one with Peter Drucker in both 1993 and 2000, I was struck by the simple ele-

---

"Marketing is not a function, it is the whole business seen from the customer's point of view."

Peter Drucker

gance of his house and his person as well as by his ability to recount people, places, and situations that were part of his life far in the past. He was as quotable in person as he was in his writings; my hand repeatedly cramped from trying to capture all his comments using only pen and paper. On videos I've seen, Drucker's bearing is proper, his voice stern. In person, I recall a warm human being, quick to grasp the humor in a story as well as its eternal truth. His intellect was steep; his demeanor was one of extreme confidence. Yet his comments often belied his own feeling that life was always more a question mark than an exclamation point. Peter never substituted rote dogma for perceptive thinking. Perhaps that's why his own writing was always more broad than just business management; half his books deal with society, economics, and politics (he even wrote two novels!).

On my second visit, to discuss his lifetime achievements, Peter offered as much time as I needed. Early on, he commented that what drove him to write it was a void: "I not only saw the gaps in the profession of management, I invented the gaps!" he said. "Nobody had any real experience in defining the practice of management. I had a little." He continued, "I would say that companies during that time were 'fitfully managed.'" He noted that many companies, mid-century, operated as a mirror of one or a few powerful figures who mixed their common sense, business sense, and personal whims into some unpredictable kind of operating policy.

In the book itself, Drucker was even more blunt on how little was known and understood in the 1950s about the practice of managing successfully: "Even the people in a business often do not know what their management does and what it is supposed to be doing, how it acts and why, whether it does a good job or not." Drucker went on to write that most people's view of what happens in the "front office" is often akin to "the medieval geographer's picture of Africa as the stamping ground of the one-eyed ogre, the two-headed pygmy, the immortal phoenix, and the elusive unicorn."

I quickly inferred that Drucker's motivation for writing the book was to answer all the questions he could not answer and that everyone else wasn't yet smart enough to ask. By extension, I'd argue that the thread running through all of Drucker's management books since *Practice of Management* is not a series of prescriptions but an abundance of questions.

Drucker stressed to me that what made his 1954 book so revolutionary was that it considered business as something more than people pulling together just to make money. Yet, many corporations seem to be led by managers dedicated only to profit making and taking. What, asked Drucker repeatedly, is a business? What is the role of business in society? He wondered why so many managers seem to act erratically, often in spite of agreed-to goals, not in pursuit of them. He wondered if chief executives and boards of directors were truly in touch with the hundreds, even thousands, of employees populating their corporation.

Moreover, he questioned whether they had a full sense of the impact their companies made on the communities in which they operated.

He wondered if it was acceptable, even logical, for someone to be hired as a manager and then allowed to, in essence, wither in effectiveness because he or she was never developed to achieve their potential. He wondered why so many people in the business world are lifeless, unenthusiastic, and bored. He asked what, exactly, was the role of work in a person's life. Drucker always elevated human beings over organization charts. He was concerned about peak performance, work/life balance, and motivation before they were chapters in some dry management text. Moreover, while "spirit" is still considered an avant-garde concept in management classes, Drucker was baffled that the subject wasn't an essential component of every Management 101 class.

Given his declining health, it was not possible for me to interview him again as indictments and headlines followed one another, broadcasting the numerous Enrons and WorldComs that have cost investors and workers billions of dollars and soured millions of others on the fundamental nature of corporate management. Yet he surely took the bleak news about corporate corruption with head-shaking disbelief. For Drucker must have been puzzled that so many corporate titans had missed his insistence that the "business enterprise must be so managed as to make the public good become the private good of the enterprise."

Drucker envisioned a profession of managers, distinctive because of their actions and beliefs, not their rank or pay grade. He envisioned managers as engaged and energetic, competent yet considerate, never satisfied until the goals of the corporation were fully achieved because enough managers and workers inside the company fervently believed those goals made worthwhile contributions to society. A happy customer, for Drucker, was simply the first step toward a healthy society.

It would be a disservice to Peter Drucker's life to say that his influence was minimal—*it was enormous*; that his advice and recommendations were all ignored—*many have tried to live his words*; that his legacy has devolved to "what might have been"—*Drucker, indeed, invented management as a science and an art*. Peter Drucker will remain vibrant in the profession of management until all his questions have been answered, more fully and better than they have been answered so far.

FOR MORE INFORMATION

Book:
Drucker, Peter F. *The Daily Drucker: 366 Days of Insight and Motivation for Getting the Right Things Done*. New York: HarperCollins, 2004.

See also:
Peter Drucker (pp. 1198–1201)

Who's Guiding Your Corporate Destiny?

by Don Blohowiak

EXECUTIVE SUMMARY

- A shortage of organizational leadership looms on the horizon as economic and demographic forces converge to keep the pool of talented leaders small—just when they're needed most.
- Executives must act now to stop a leadership vacuum from developing and preventing their organization from competing in a most demanding and unforgiving marketplace.

INTRODUCTION

Organizations worldwide face a troubling demographic challenge. In blunt, politically incorrect plain talk: too many entrenched, old-style views, too few young leaders.

Population trends conspire to leave a huge hole in managerial ranks. Baby boomers, those born between 1946 and 1964, will soon retire from the full-time labor force, leaving a huge talent vacuum, with the greatest impact likely to be felt about 2010.

For many well established organizations, notably government agencies, utilities, and older corporations, the effect will be like a demographic tide washing away, in many cases, 25% or more of the managerial staff. As these armies of managers retire in just a few years, they will leave behind a significant leadership void.

Throughout industrialized nations boomers have failed to replace themselves with a baby boomette. The 1970s pop-culture mantra of zero population growth apparently took root in fertile soil. The birthrate for nearly all developed countries continues to decline below the replacement rate of 2.1. This shrinking labor pool comes just as many nations see their economies cranking along at near-full throttle, straining the means of production to meet demand. Most companies already sense the coming shortage; some are acutely aware. But far too many have adopted a strategy to address their impending leadership crisis that's more "pray and hope" than plan and execute.

DEBOSSED CAN'T MEAN AN END TO LEADERSHIP

But wait, isn't the "flat" organization, delayered of paper-shuffling, non-value-adding middle managers, solving the shortage problem? In short, no. Expectations for high performance results from customers and the financial markets alike mean that leadership is in increasing demand just as the labor pool evaporates.

Team- or process-oriented organizations may need fewer bosses, but they depend on bountiful cadres of *leaderful* people to make their teams and task forces productive. As Tom Peters recently opined, "We're going to see leadership emerge as the most important element of business—the attribute that is highest in demand and shortest in supply."

THE NEED FOR LEADERSHIP

A quick scan of the business landscape reveals a loud cry for leadership. Today's market decrees that an organization can survive only by consistently demonstrating increasing capacity for such hard-earned virtues as speed, innovation, responsiveness, value, productivity, quality, and teamwork.

The means to achieve such virtues lies in the province of leadership. They include:
- clarity of direction and priorities;
- decisiveness;
- adaptability to changes in technology, customer expectations, and society at large;
- proficiency of the workforce;
- consistency of execution.

Leadership sustains life in an organization struggling to endure in a cruel market of demanding customers and ruthless competitors. Weak leadership condemns an organization to death.

LEADERSHIP VOID

This obvious need for leadership comes at a time when C.E.O. tenure is increasingly measured in months as impatient investors look for substantial results instantly and then constantly.

The irony, of course, is that results actually derive from leadership and competent execution by people who toil far from the executive suite. Most of them were sweating in the trenches before the latest C.E.O.'s arrival, and most will still be there when this one is replaced by yet another water-walking hopeful.

An organization that's going to be consistently successful must be led consistently well throughout its ranks. That means cultivating leadership skills deeply and broadly in the workforce at large so that the whole organization can amplify, bring to life, and continuously make real the inspired musings of its visionary top leader. With fewer titular leaders at the very time that organizations need more leadership, the gap must be closed by more people, many without rank, being *leaderful*. And that means going beyond empowerment. It is not enough to empower employees; it may even be dangerous to do so. If empowered employees are not adequately prepared to exercise the rudiments of leadership as requisite underpinnings for their conferred power, they're tantamount to fully authorized but unguided missiles.

DEEP LEADERSHIP IN THE REAL WORLD

Some organizations grasp that leadership can't be the sole province of the executive suite, or even vested in the shrinking ranks of its heavily burdened middle managers. Others are beginning to uncouple the false relationship between position and leadership.

We may never live in a bossless world—and that surely isn't the goal—but, as these organizations demonstrate, we should strive to create a world where more people act leaderfully regardless of the hierarchy's depth.

With a leadership tradition spanning more than two centuries, the *Marine Corps*, operating in relatively small numbers, usually under hostile conditions, understands that its formal leaders can be lost just when they're needed most. So while vesting

---

"What I love about magazines is that an individual can change the destiny of an entire business."

Duncan Edwards

official authority in top ranks, the Marines make leadership development at all levels a priority. Personal leadership by all Marines is an ethic that is constantly on the agenda. It is reflected in continual training, in the culture of daily life, and in formal celebrations to mark what the Corps values most: honor, initiative, and accomplishment by the *team*. The Marines do not aggrandize their formal bosses. (Just try to name a famous Marine Corps general.)

Far removed from the Marines' frontline artillery, the finance organization of *Motorola* has put personal leadership on its agenda. It encourages its accountants, analysts, and other professionals at all levels to be leaderful in their work regardless of whether they have any personnel management responsibility.

Likewise, *CUNA Mutual Group*, the financial services giant that supports credit unions worldwide, has created training and assessments to engage individual contributors in developing leaderful competencies. CUNA Mutual requires all its employees to understand its current challenges and opportunities and to know and apply the company's mission and vision to their own work. In addition, the company makes it clear that contributors can't merely be passive recipients of orders from their managers. "All employees are required to work with their manager and others to set goals and plan their workload—and to apply sound reasoning to make effective decisions and suggest process improvements where appropriate."

BUILDING LEADERSHIP IN YOUR COMPANY

Because every individual works and learns differently, there is no universal leadership development panacea. And no one becomes a better leader instantaneously as the result of a singular event or experience, no matter how intense, memorable, or expensive.

But the author's experience, combined with studies conducted by Linkage, the Center for Creative Leadership, and Development Dimensions International, indicate that the following methods are most likely to build more leaderful associates from well-meaning people regardless of rank:
- opportunities to practice leading. Surgery, driving, and leading are all developed by supplementing instruction and coaching with actual practice.
- evaluations (objective, from validated instruments; and subjective, through feedback from coworkers);
- instruction from credible leadership

teachers, ideally including respected senior executives.

A program for making it happen includes the following steps:
- **Identify the leadership capabilities you need to accomplish your organization's business objectives.** They may vary from those typically considered standard leadership competencies. If your organization doesn't truly value teamwork, preaching its virtues will ring hollow. Don't ask the middle to be better than the top, or you'll get two sure results: demoralized would-be leaders, and departing talent.
- **Secure senior management support of, and participation in, the leadership development process.** If you can't readily point to the leadership qualities you're advocating in your company's own senior ranks, reconsider the development effort until it has registered an impact at the most visible level of management.

Get top managers to put leadership development on their priority agenda and to become involved in the design and delivery of the leadership curriculum—not to talk about leadership theories, but to share their own very personal experiences with leadership challenges in their careers, especially their darkest and lowest moments. If you can't get senior managers to actively participate in the development program, it's not important. Save everyone a lot of time, energy, and money and avoid putting ambitious, hopeful people into a process that is bound to disappointment them.
- **Craft a uniquely tailored leadership development program.** It should:
  - tie in closely with your business needs. Don't try to build an idealized leader based on a pop business guru's overly generalized and unattainable model.
  - integrate multiple coordinated development mechanisms (see below);
  - welcome all interested associates— allow otherwise overlooked potential leaders to declare themselves;
  - teach and cultivate appropriate leadership skills. Someone wrestling with decisions about whether to merge with a competitor isn't drawing on the same leadership competencies as someone consumed with making sure a package gets shipped by 6p.m.;
  - integrate personalized coaching and mentoring. The coaching should come from credible independent coaches, either outside providers or well-trained internal staff. Mentoring should be provided by experienced individuals in your organization who are both exemplary in their leadership

accomplishments and who have been trained in effective mentoring methods;
- hold current leaders accountable for developing themselves and the next wave of leaders by tying financial incentives to active participation in developmental activities. "Talent management" is a top leadership responsibility, not the sole purview of the human resources department.

Develop leadership capacity in your company's people. Use methods to increase the odds of delivering meaningful learning with tangible business results. Provide your associates with opportunities to:
- participate in special assignments or work on special projects outside their normal work duties to give them exposure to new groups or departments (and most especially to talented senior managers);
- rotate into new full-time assignments—a fresh view comes from a new vantage point;
- teach or mentor others; a mentoring or teaching assignment provides great opportunities for people to pay greater attention to and reflect on what they do and why they do it that way;
- receive coaching or mentoring; this personal, interactive learning experience could be in a one-on-one relationship with a more senior manager or could come through participation with a group of peers;
- attend external development courses and learning events;
- go to in-house training courses and leadership development programs;
- volunteer for service to a charity or nonprofit organization to expose them to other perspectives and nonroutine challenges, some of which may well be bigger in scope than currently offered by their day job.

CONCLUSION

Leadership, like luck, is a secret ingredient in every successful enterprise. Unlike luck, leadership can be cultivated and grown. But it doesn't happen quickly. Given the growing need for and the shrinking supply of future leaders, smart business-people will give immediate priority to intentionally and programmatically developing leadership skills at all levels of their organization.

The important elements of encouraging leaders at all levels include voicing and demonstrating your expectation for leaderful behavior and providing people with quality instruction, useful feedback, and rewards for practicing leadership. In the

---

"Control your destiny or die."   Jack Welch

very near future a high-performing organization will be a leaderful organization. Build yours now.

FOR MORE INFORMATION

Books:

Carter, Louis, David Ulrich, and Marshall Goldsmith, eds. *Best Practices in Leadership Development and Organization Change: How the Best Companies Ensure Meaningful Change and Sustainable Leadership.* San Francisco, CA: Pfeiffer, 2004.

Coffman, Curt, and Gabriel Gonzalez-Molina, Ph.D. *Follow This Path: How the World's Greatest Organizations Drive Growth by Unleashing Human Potential.* New York: Warner Business Books, 2002.

Daniels, Aubrey C., and James E. Daniels. *Measure of a Leader: An Actionable Formula for Legendary Leadership.* Atlanta, Georgia: Performance Management Publications, 2005.

Fulmer, Robert M., Jay Alden Conger. *Growing Your Company's Leaders: How Great Organizations Use Succession Management to Sustain Competitive Advantage.* New York: AMACOM, 2003.

Tichy, Noel M., and Eli Cohen. *The Leadership Engine: How Winning Companies Build Leaders at Every Level.* New York: HarperBusiness, 2002.

See also:

☆ Generation Veneration (pp. 39–40)
☆ Setting Objectives for a Business (pp. 391–392)
☆ The Good, the Fad, and the Ugly (pp. 210–211)
☆ Viewpoint: Christopher Bartlett (pp. 45–46)
☆ Viewpoint: John Seely Brown (pp. 172–173)

Deciding Key Operational Questions
by Mark Brown

EXECUTIVE SUMMARY

- Think "white-light," not just "gray" goals.
- Think "future now"; create a "paradise paradigm."
- Nurture frames and not cages of mind.
- Encourage constructive dissent.
- Apply open-thinking tools.

INTRODUCTION

The information and knowledge latent within an organization are valuable resources for resolving key operational questions, making effective decisions, solving problems, and ensuring success. Applying these resources to key operational issues is an important and valuable but challenging leadership task. It is worth considering how best to harness the intellectual capital, knowledge, skills, and experience of people within the organization for effective action. This needs to be done routinely and in a productive way, taking account of the needs of varied tasks, how people behave, time factors, and the need for actions to be specific, achievable, dynamic and, very often, competitive.

This can be achieved by using the process outlined in the Executive Summary, which forms the focus for this section.

The Imperative—Think!

Think about thinking. Here's a simple and useful four-stage model of thinking:

1 goal
2 ideas or options
3 decision or selection
4 action

You go through these stages automatically time and time and time again.

For example:

- goal—to choose a vacation
- ideas—Mexico, Monaco, Morocco
- decision—Monaco
- action—off you go

Or, in a business context:

- goal—to attract and retain customers
- options—new and improved products, packaging, new pricing strategy, etc.
- selection—new product
- action—launch the product

The rate of change is exponential. Tom Peters named the 1990s the Nanosecond 90s. We now live in the mad mayhem of a new and probably crazier millennium.

Who will win in this new world? Those individuals and organizations that have the greatest passion for their work, combined with an unremitting ability to think smartly and outthink their competitors.

To create passion, make work worthwhile and meaningful. To outthink others, start to "metathink," that is, think about thinking, and manage your own and your organization's thinking. What follows are some ideas for thinking about and managing thinking.

Think "White-light," Not Just "Gray" Goals

Think about *where* to think. You often automatically start to think when faced with a problem. Much thinking is problem solving—gray-driven, not opportunity-driven white light. You can solve numerous problems without particularly affecting your organization for the better. Or you can focus on one white-light opportunity—for example, to attract and retain substantially more customers—and have a real impact.

Although some problems do have to be solved, as a rule of mind you need to shift to more *white-light* thinking: what is it that would more radically shift or step-change the organization? *Gray* problem solving prefers to wait for necessity to be the mother of invention. White-light thinking says: Never allow necessity to be the mother of invention. Invent and think now.

Think "Future Now"—Create a Paradise Paradigm

Think about the future now. Two of the more obvious white-light goals in many organizations are the vision and mission statements. Many such statements can be vapid, uninspiring, untransformational rather than step-changing or paradigm-shattering. Even if people do begin to think about the goal, that thinking will be largely *past now* thinking that takes their past experience and familiar patterns and builds or extrapolates from there in an evolutionary manner. As a result you usually get more of the same.

If you want to engage people's hearts and minds to create a radically different and massively more positive future, generate a goal or image of the future that is *tinglingly tangible, head- and heart-grabbing.* It should be so stretching and challenging to the patterns of the past that people have no choice but to think in discontinuous, revolutionary ways.

Thereby you begin to nurture *future now* thinking, in which you work back from the future to the present. The *paradise paradigms*, also called BHAGS (big, hairy, audacious goals), shatter the old patterns. Incrementalism is simply not enough. The paradise paradigm encourages revolutionary breakthrough thinking. The impossible becomes possible—and, given enough revolutionary imagination, probable—and is then achieved. Remember:

"This nation should commit itself to achieving the goal, before this decade is out, of landing a man on the moon and returning him safely to earth."

John F. Kennedy, 1961

NURTURE FRAMES AND NOT CAGES OF MIND

Don't be a victim of your thinking. A paradise paradigm can usefully act to disrupt the patterns of the past. This is not to say the patterns of the past are always foes to be vanquished. Without past patterns, precedents, mindsets, or paradigms, the world would be frighteningly and incomprehensibly chaotic. Past patterns more often than not help us to make sense of today and in turn predict the future. I recall a history teacher who used to explain that we study the past to understand the present and so predict the future.

So mindsets are often useful. But here's the bad news: they're no longer as useful as they once were. The patterns are helpful only if the past is largely the same as the present. The danger arises when we rely on

"I try to create an environment in which others make decisions. Success means not making them myself."

Ricardo Semler

outdated frames of reference or models of the world. Our thinking and decision making can become limiting, and in retrospect even absurd. And as the world is changing, ever-faster models and frames need ever more challenging and rethinking.

"There is no reason for any individual to have a computer in their home." Kenneth Olsen, president and founder of Digital Equipment Corporation, 1977.

"We don't like their sound. Groups of guitars are on the way out." Decca Records, rejecting the Beatles, 1962.

"Computers in the future may . . . perhaps only weigh one-and-a-half tons." Popular Mechanics, forecasting the development of computer technology, 1949.

"Stocks have reached what looks like a permanently high plateau." Irving Fisher, professor of economics, Yale University, October 17, 1929.

"[Television] won't be able to hold onto any market it captures after the first six months. People will soon get tired of staring at a plywood box every night." Darryl F. Zanuck, head of 20th Century Fox, 1946.

"Everything that can be invented has been invented." Charles H. Duell, U.S. commissioner of patents, 1899.

As Gary Hamel neatly summarizes:

"Experience is valuable only to the extent that the future is like the past. In industry after industry the terrain is changing so fast that experience is becoming irrelevant and even dangerous."

Never has it been such a challenging time for more mature managers. Their models and frames may be based on terrains long since perished.

Now you might think that surely once you become aware that the past pattern is no longer useful for making sense of the present or predicting the future, you'll drop the old frame and adopt a new one. This is often not the case. Frames of reference are very sticky and tricky, and once formed they easily become cages of reference within which we become prisoners. This is because the thinking system has a built-in confirmatory bias that works hard to subsume and make sense of now in the light of the patterns of the past. We selectively perceive and uniquely create our own worlds, constantly seeking evidence that confirms those constructs. What a coincidence so

many people agree with themselves and yet often disagree with others!

Old-world, more autocratic organizations that may still encourage conformity of word and thought can exacerbate the problem of outdated mindsets in senior managers. Reporting staff may select and pass upward information that sits comfortably with and confirms their managers' outdated world view. The mind selects the easily fitting. People often communicate up the organization only that information that is acceptable.

Human beings and organizations find it only too easy to operate with closed minds. So how to deal with these self-sealing and unchanging mindsets?

Encourage Constructive Dissent

To think better, dissent more. First of all, encourage constructive dissent and debate. Our own consulting firm, Innovation Centre Europe, has built on the groundbreaking organizational climate research of the Swedish psychologist Goran Ekvall. We've developed his work in the form of the Innovation Climate Questionnaire, which establishes how well you score on 13 critical dimensions that predict how clever and innovative your organizational climate is. One of the key dimensions is constructive debate, encouraging people to challenge and constructively knock around ideas (not people!).

Practically, you can encourage everyone to constructively challenge all the sacred cows, the way you do things around there, the way you think about things. If it ain't broke, break it!

I recall a client in a unit of General Electric who wanted a simple way to help people to "work out" (in other words, get rid of) unhelpful processes and procedures. I came up with the following very simple routine.

ABC

Abolish.

How can we do away with this system, procedure, or process?

If you can't,

Blockbust.

Here's the opportunity for radical, revolutionary creativity. Think outside the square. Think back to the original purpose of the system, procedure, or process and go back to basics. Produce a much smarter/easier/more cost-effective alternative.

If you can't,

Change.

Here's the opportunity for incremental, evolutionary creativity. Think within the square. How can the system, procedure, or process be simplified and/or modified to be smarter/easier/more cost-effective?

Apply Open-thinking Tools

Think openly. As well as encouraging people to challenge other people's mindsets, you can also try to pull yourself up by your own bootstraps and challenge your own mindsets. Some of the following may help:

- if everyone sees it that way—beware;
- if everyone is doing it—think afresh;
- pay attention to and read at the edge of your field and beyond;
- assume a blip may signal a new trend;
- make explicit every assumption you hold— and challenge each assumption.

MAKING IT HAPPEN ▸▸

Issues to consider when resolving key operational questions are:

- **what actions and additional resources may be needed** to increase the likelihood of success—who will do what, when, where and how?
- **how to mobilize and enthuse people** to take effective action;
- **what parts of the operational decision and response may be delegated**—and how;
- **the importance of timing** and the need to develop a sense of timing;
- **where thoughtful analysis is required and where immediate, direct action is needed;**
- **the value of communication and empowerment**—an inclusive approach can often be the preferred method of deciding key operational questions, as it gives ownership of the answer to those people who will deliver the action.

FOR MORE INFORMATION

Book:

Collins, James C., and Jerry I. Porras. *Built to Last: Successful Habits of Visionary Companies.* New York: HarperBusiness, 2002.

"Executive: A man who can make quick decisions and is sometimes right."

Frank McKinney Hubbard

Viewpoint: Richard Boyatzis, Annie McKee, and David Smith

Resonant Leadership

Introduction

Richard Boyatzis and Annie McKee are the bestselling co-authors (with Daniel Goleman) of *Primal Leadership* (Harvard Business School Press, 2002). David Smith is executive director of the Teleos Leadership Institute, which McKee co-founded in 2001. In this article, all three explore some of the key themes of *Resonant Leadership*, Boyatzis and McKee's most recent book.

The world is a very different place than it was ten years ago. Advances in technology and communications have made life and work easier, more exciting, yet much more complicated. Change is occurring simultaneously in multiple arenas. It is also happening at an unprecedented pace, requiring people to be alert to new data and agile enough to respond to it quickly and effectively. These are new challenges for leaders as well as new opportunities for growth, partnerships, and business. These changes also make it difficult for our institutions to keep up, forcing us to rethink, even transform our organizational models.

What does this mean for leaders today? It means, first and foremost, that leading as we did in the past may not be as effective in this era of global change. If "command and control" ever worked, it certainly doesn't in an age that requires us to inspire people to respond to ever-present challenges with speed, optimism, and ingenuity. Today, we need *resonant leaders*—who inspire passion and excitement, leaders who create strong, positive relationships while guiding the energy, emotion, behavior and even the cultures of their organizations.

Resonant leaders are inspirational, moving people to think expansively and to reach for dreams and possibilities that may not have seemed feasible earlier. *Resonant Leadership: Renewing Yourself and Connecting with Others through Mindfulness, Hope and Compassion*, coauthored by Richard Boyatzis and Annie McKee, explores resonance deeply, looking at real leaders, real challenges, and how to sustain excellence in the face of the problems of today. Resonant leaders are highly attuned both to themselves and to the external world. They are committed to learning and have the courage to change their own behaviors when they see they are not producing the desired results. Resonant leaders are able to build strong relationships inside and outside their organizations. They communicate clearly and compellingly, and people around them respond with enthusiasm to the call for action.

Because emotions are contagious, resonance generated by leaders expands within the organization resulting in greater collaboration and a healthier organizational climate. When this occurs, there is a positive impact on organizational culture. People see the opportunities before them and are eager to embrace strategies to seize these opportunities. There is an increase in trust; people believe in their leaders and in the ability of their organizations to be successful.

Colleen Barrett, the president of Southwest Airlines is a resonant leader who recognized that effective, positive organizational cultures do not happen by accident. During the 1970s, when Herb Kelleher asked her to join a team to build Southwest Airlines, Colleen had a positive team experience that influences her leadership today. During the building years, she learned that it takes time, energy, focus, and planning to build and sustain healthy working relationships. Maybe most importantly, she saw that healthy working relationships are essential to building a resonant work culture, and that this culture is linked to results.

Colleen took ownership of key processes within Southwest that guided people's behavior with customers *and* with each other. She deliberately and consciously focused on building the *spirit* of the company and put value on people treating one another with respect and compassion. Today, Colleen continues to model this behavior in her own leadership and minimizes the importance of hierarchy. She builds strong relationships and teams all around, and she makes sure that the fierce competition within the airline industry does not prevent people from finding time for reflection, fun, and celebration. These experiences sustain her—and the culture—and keep the company vibrant and alive.

The results of her leadership speak for themselves. While many airlines have struggled over the past few years, Southwest has had sustained success for over three decades, meeting goals and generating profits. The spirit that Colleen helped create through her resonant style is visible when you interact with Southwest employees. They are excited about being in the Southwest family and are motivated to provide the

> **Today, we need *resonant leaders*—who inspire passion and excitement, leaders who create strong, positive relationships while guiding the energy, emotion, behavior and even the cultures of their organizations.**

highest customer service possible. They are passionate about what they do and deeply committed to their airline. This has generated positive business outcomes at Southwest, showing a strong linkage between resonant cultures and results.

So how does Colleen manage to sustain her own—and her company's—effectiveness over the long term? This is no easy feat. Our work with leaders shows that even when resonant leadership is developed, it is difficult to maintain. This is tied, we think, to the nature of leadership itself. Leaders are constantly called upon to give of themselves and to exert influence, often under ambiguous circumstances. In fact, the constant challenges of the leader's role can result in a special kind of pressure. When unchecked, the unending stress can cause leaders to become trapped in the Sacrifice Syndrome: responsibility, crises, stress, dissonance, and more stress.

Colleen Barrett has managed to avoid the pitfalls of dissonant leadership by consciously and consistently managing the *Cycle of Sacrifice and Renewal*. She has cultivated habits of mind and behavior that actually counter the effects of chronic stress, not just the usual power stress that comes with leadership but also the tremendous stress inherent in the airline business. Specifically, Colleen has developed the capacity to live and work mindfully, while seeking experiences that foster hope and compassion in herself and others. These three factors—*mindfulness*, *hope*, and *compassion*—actually spark physiological and psychological renewal, and enable a leader to sustain resonance even in the face of constant pressure.

Mindfulness means being awake, aware, and attentive to ourselves and the world around us. It means paying close attention to the context in which we are leading, being aware of ourselves and the people around us. For Colleen, mindfulness means recognizing the value of each person and acknowledging individual contributions. She knows that people value personal relationships deeply, in the workplace as well as at home, and she has diligently built an organizational culture that supports connection, collaboration, and celebration.

Resonant cultures, and resonant leadership, are also characterized by a hopeful, optimistic outlook. In fact, *hope* is also a key element that enables people to sustain resonance, even when things are tough. People react differently to change and to the uncertainty that accompanies it. While some individuals are able to manage themselves well, many others find change to be disconcerting and troubling. Colleen, as a resonant leader, offers hope to the people at Southwest, which is highly valued in an industry under fire. She has been able to give hopeful messages continually, even during dark times, which enable people to feel hopeful themselves. They are then able to believe that the future they imagine for themselves and for Southwest is possible.

Having seen Colleen in action with her people at Southwest, we also know that she brings a great deal of *compassion* to her interactions. Like hope, compassion sparks a physiological process that counters the negative effects of stress. Colleen cares deeply about her people and customers and clearly enjoys working on teams This is reflected in how the people at Southwest treat each other. They follow the golden rule, treating each other as they'd like to be treated themselves.

Colleen Barrett is a resonant leader who sustains her effectiveness by consciously renewing herself, while supporting the people around her. Colleen's resonant leadership and attention to mindfulness, hope and compassion have resulted in an upbeat, respectful workplace, one that Southwest employees embrace.

Colleen consciously avoids the pitfalls of the Sacrifice Syndrome. But she, like many leaders, knows that it is easy to slip into dissonance. When dissonance sets in, people cope with their stress by developing defensive routines. When we are defensive, we are not mindful. This results in paying less attention to our own individual behavior as well as important feedback from others. Key information that during resonant times is welcomed and heeded is now ignored. In the same way that resonance produces more resonance, dissonance can have the same impact and a downward spiral can occur. When negativity and stress are sustained, dissonance is reflected within the organization and the work culture suffers.

What can a leader do when he or she slips into dissonant behavior? Leaders who pull themselves out of the Sacrifice Syndrome describe personal renewal journeys where they reinvigorate their spirit, take care of the things that matter most to them, and pay attention to what worked for them in the past. They embrace mindfulness, hope, and compassion as part of their conscious renewal process.

When leaders become more mindful, they recognize that they have been ignoring key data points while sliding into dissonance. They have missed the cues, whether in the office, with their health, or in important personal relationships. Things were not going well, but they did not notice. Sometimes, an important event serves as a wake-up call for leaders that things need to change. When this occurs, people recognize that they need to be more mindful and more attentive to both themselves and others.

Other leaders, like Colleen Barrett, don't wait for the wake-up call; they develop habits of mind and body that keep them resonant and renewed. Colleen found a way to sustain resonance by paying attention to what customers say to her about their experience with Southwest. Travelers often have excellent customer service experiences with Southwest, and they often write letters of appreciation. Colleen *reads* these letters and they help her feel a sense of hope even on days when things are tough.

Reconnecting to her own hope enables her to share this hope with others at Southwest. Since she cares deeply about employees at all levels, she empathizes with their issues and feels compassion for the difficulties they and their customers face. Rather than simply acknowledging this within herself, Colleen takes the time to write notes to her people, thanking them for

their efforts. She cares, and people recognize it. Simple acts like this help keep Southwest a resonant company.

While it is true that the world is changing at a pace not seen before in human history, this does not mean that individuals and organizations have to be overwhelmed. What we need is a new kind of leadership behavior, one that starts with a deep understanding of ourselves and the world in which we live. Leaders like Colleen Barrett, who are mindful, who share their hopes and dreams and who are compassionate with those around them are those who are best suited to lead their organizations through these changes and into bright futures ahead. Building resonant relationships with those around you, through mindfulness, hope, and compassion, not only results in exciting and adaptive organizations, but in leaders and others who can renew themselves along the way. They can live to lead another day!

FOR MORE INFORMATION

Book:
Boyatzis, Richard, and Annie McKee. *Resonant Leadership*. Boston, MA: Harvard Business School Press, 2005.

Web site:
Teleos Leadership Institute: **www.teleosleaders.com**

See also:
Emotional Intelligence (p. 1089)
Leadership (pp. 1798–1803)

"I am a leader by default, only because nature does not allow a vacuum." — Desmond Tutu

The One Thing You Need to Know
by Marcus Buckingham

EXECUTIVE SUMMARY

There is so much clutter in today's business world that focus, insight, and clarity are vital for success. Getting to the heart of the matter, and, in particular, knowing the specific requirements of each role in an organization, are essential to being able to win and keep winning. Several other issues are also significant:
- The role of the leader and the role of the manager are completely different.
- It is counterproductive to demand that everyone be a leader.
- To ensure that their vision of the future succeeds, leaders need to tap into people's common hopes and fears.
- Messages and actions need to be so clear and simple that everyone understands them.

INTRODUCTION

Much has been written about leadership. We are surrounded by books and articles emphasizing how critical leadership is to success. Indeed, some management gurus convince us that we should all be leaders, no matter what our organizational roles are. Yet, is there any real evidence for these claims? Given the unprecedented level of tough, global competition, it is essential to evaluate the factors contributing to success and to decide on the role of leadership in achieving that success. It is time to address the question: has the leadership card been overplayed?

CHALLENGING CURRENT VIEWS

A great deal of misunderstanding and unrealistic expectations surround the issue of leadership. Unfortunately, few business experts dare to challenge the revered status accorded to leaders. Exceptions to this are Jim Collins in *Built to Last and Good to be Great* and Peter Drucker in *Managing for the Future*. They acknowledge that leadership is important but emphasize that other factors are also critical to success. Warren Bennis believes that at least 15% of an organization's success can be directly attributed to the leader. While agreeing over the basic point that great organizations require great leaders, we part company over the need to separate the responsibilities of leaders and managers. Leadership is a specific and difficult task. If managers, at all levels, are preoccupied with being leaders, then this will distract them from their main focus and contribution to organizational success. My research has led to the inevitable conclusion that leadership and management are not interchangeable roles. Indeed, success relies on this distinction being maintained.

THE ROLE OF THE MANAGER

Great managers have one thing in common: they all excel at turning an individual's talents into improved performance. They are catalysts that speed up the reaction between employees' talents and organizational goals. It has been argued that they are in the unenviable position between the company's targets and individual's needs, and that they must always default to supporting the company. However, good managers instinctively know that organizational goals can only be achieved by serving the individual's needs first. Consequently, supporting their staff is of paramount importance.

Too often, the results of management are confused with the essence of management. Delivering excellent quality, customer service, and standards are all outcomes of good management; while they can be used to measure success, they are not the cause of it. The starting point is always transforming each employee's talents into performance. The only way to achieve this is to make each employee believe that his or her success is your main goal. Essentially, people matter to good managers, who are themselves naturally skilled at developing people through understanding, supporting, challenging, and stretching their employees. This coaching instinct is a core skill of good managers that underpins their role of transforming talent into productivity.

THE BASICS OF GREAT MANAGEMENT

Managers need to tap into the power of individualization. Capitalizing on each person's talents promotes time efficiency, accountability, and teamwork. In addition, managers need to:

- select good people who possess the required skills and attributes;
- define clear expectations frequently;
- recognize and praise behavior immediately and regularly, to reinforce successes;
- show they care for their people, as individuals are more productive and loyal when they feel others care for them;
- confront poor performance early.

THE ROLE OF THE LEADER

If the manager's unique contribution is to make other people more productive, what is the leader's contribution? Business experts are adept at listing the many qualities of leaders. While these attributes, ranging from creativity and initiative to courage and integrity are important, they are desirable qualities that each of us may possess in whatever role we undertake. They do not, however, define the essential and unique contribution that leaders bring to their organizations. Fundamentally, great leaders rally people to a better future.

Leaders are preoccupied with the future. While leaders undoubtedly possess many skills (including management skills) it is their image of the future that propels them forward. I would argue that a person is a leader only when he or she is able to rally others to his or her vision of the future.

Underpinning this overarching contribution are optimism and ego. Leaders see the future so vividly and believe in it so passionately that their optimism necessarily spills over. They also believe that they can overcome the challenges of the present to reach a better future. Some experts downplay the value of ego and many egotistical leaders have wreaked havoc, as the Worldcom and Enron fiascos attest. Yet, ego remains a critical attribute. Successful leaders channel their ego into achieving their vision.

THE BASICS OF GREAT LEADERSHIP

Leaders need to address key elements of their organization and decide on their vision of the future to convey this vision clearly and successfully. Great leaders decide:
- who the organization serves;
- what the core strength is. This allows for the most effective management of assets;

"Managing is getting paid for home runs someone else hits." Casey Stengel

BEST PRACTICE

- what the "core score" is—by focusing on one measurable and clearly understood policy, people know what they are working toward and success is more likely;
- what actions need to be taken immediately—the fear of the unknown must be addressed and actions taken that are clear, unambiguous, and comforting. These actions can be symbolic, to provoke thinking and enthuse, or systematic, to redirect people's routines to promote new activities and methods.

At the core of leadership is an ability to cut through individual differences and focus on the common needs and feelings that run through groups. Unlike managers, leaders are not intermediaries: they are instigators of change. Whereas managers focus on individuals, leaders must cut across these differences and exploit common interests, enabling everyone to follow one vision of the future. To achieve this, leaders should consider the five universal aspects of human nature:

1 their fear of death and the need for security
2 their fear of outsiders and the need for community
3 their fear of the future and the need for clarity
4 their fear of chaos and the need for authority
5 their fear of insignificance and the need for respect

CAN LEADERSHIP BE LEARNED?

Given the pivotal role of optimism and ego in leadership, it is difficult to see how great leadership could be learned. Someone is either optimistic by nature or they are not. Great leaders are born. This may be disheartening for some but enables us to identify and nurture potential leaders. Of course, leaders can be coached to improve in certain skills, but they cannot be taught to have a vision of the future or the self-belief that they are the ones to realize that vision. However, there are essential skills that leaders should address and hone to improve their effectiveness.

CLARITY LEADS TO SUCCESS

Why is clarity such an important skill for leaders? Our need for community, authority, and respect means we respond well to clarity. We feel confidence and trust in a clear, compelling vision, which we follow with persistence, resilience, and creativity. Hearts and minds are never won without complete clarity. It is essential for a leader

to convey clearly who the company serves, the organization's core strengths and targets, and any action that is to be taken. There are several steps that will enable leaders to distill their complex work into a clear message for others.

- Take time to reflect on the issues. This is not wasted time. It allows a myriad of factors to be properly processed and understood, ideas to be explored, and conclusions to be reached with confidence.
- To influence the behavior of employees, it is important to select carefully the people you choose to recognize and reward, as others will take their cues from your choices. This sends a clear message of the qualities and achievements you value.
- Practice how you will deliver your vision. Consider and refine your message, so that you choose images and stories that resonate with your audience and have maximum impact.
- It is essential to avoid ambiguity and subtlety. These have no place in rallying others to a vision of the future, as they lead to misinterpretation and confusion.

SUSTAINING PERSONAL SUCCESS

No matter what their roles are in organizations, successful people shape what they do, experimenting with new roles and responsibilities, to ensure they spend their time doing what they love. We must all learn to make course corrections by evaluating our own strengths and dislikes in order to sustain our success and fulfillment and to maximize our contribution. To achieve and sustain this level of personal success and fulfillment, it is important to:
- find and employ the right tactics;
- find your flaws and fix them;
- discover your strengths and cultivate them;
- discover what you don't like doing and stop doing it.

MAKING IT HAPPEN ▶▶

Managers should focus on developing and supporting individuals by:
- identifying individuals' talents and helping them develop these skills to become more successful and productive;
- focusing on their coaching instinct to support and develop others;
- communicating confidence in each person's abilities and then challenging him or her to achieve more;

- considering how things could be changed to ensure each person is able to succeed;
- challenging assumptions.

CONCLUSION

Leaders need to win hearts and minds to ensure that their vision of the future is understood and followed by everyone. A leader should:
- identify the fundamental elements of the organization: who it serves, its core strength, and the core score;
- assess what actions need to be taken today to move everyone toward the future. Using systematic and symbolic action will rally people;
- be optimistic, confident, and decisive;
- tap into the universal aspects of human nature to instigate change;
- above all, be clear.

Clearly, the roles of managers and leaders are distinct. While each is critical to success, the focus of each is necessarily different. To excel as a manager, you should arrange roles, responsibilities, and expectations to capitalize on each person's unique strengths and contributions. Harnessing the individual's talents to raise productivity is undoubtedly the main focus for managers. The opposite is true for leaders. To excel as a leader, you must call upon the needs we all share. The leader focuses on the future and then rallies others to this vision, through clear messages, images, and actions. When moving between roles, it is important to remember this distinction and switch focus accordingly. Focus, discipline, and courage are required companions along this journey.

FOR MORE INFORMATION

Books:
Buckingham, Marcus. *The One Thing You Need to Know.* New York: Free Press, 2005.
Collins, James. *Good to Great.* New York: HarperCollins, 2001.
Drucker, Peter. *Management Challenges in the 21st Century.* New York: HarperCollins, 1999.

"When the rats are running for cover, you must ensure that, as captain, you know what they are doing."

Dennis Stevenson

Leadership
by Peter de la Billière

EXECUTIVE SUMMARY

- Clarity without ambiguity is the essential ingredient in the executive mission statement.
- Communication is both lateral and up and down the chain of command. It is the lifeblood of an efficient company.
- Leadership is an extension of the personality and can be developed through training throughout a person's career.
- Delegation requires courage, but without it you will fail to exploit the potential of your managers.
- Change for change's sake spells disaster. The true leader sees necessary change as a challenge and as the foundation for growth and expansion.
- Moral courage is the backbone of a leader in peace or war.

INTRODUCTION

Leadership is exercised not only in a commercial business environment (although that is probably the biggest single area of activity where leaders are to be found), but in virtually every area of life, from the cradle to the grave. Principles of leadership apply in any sphere of activity, including public service, charitable work, the military, education, science, and other fields.

Nowadays leadership means getting the best from people—managing people so that they work together to move in the direction that the leader sets. Leadership is increasingly recognized as a transferable skill: it can be taught. This belief has gained enormously in popularity over the last thirty years, promoted by distinguished writers such as John Adair and Warren Bennis. By contrast, the so-called Great Man theories of leadership that used to predominate are now seen as largely irrelevant to the fast-moving, complex, and much less hierarchical world that has developed.

THE NATURE OF LEADERSHIP

The most effective leadership is example, and this kind of leadership is within the reach of anybody. I am told that in one of the now-crumbling concrete pillboxes that sprang up over the United Kingdom as that country prepared grimly and alone to hold it against the invader, was to be read this rough inscription:

Hitler has taken Poland,
Hitler has taken Denmark and Norway,
Hitler has taken Holland, Belgium, and France,

He will not take this pillbox.
Signed J. Smith, Corporal, Home Guard

"We still have a lot of Corporal Smiths—and Mrs. Smiths. It doesn't matter what level a person is on from director to office boy, from works manager to factory hand, he can be a leader, a leader by example by the way he tackles the job."

This is a quotation from a radio broadcast given by that redoubtable leader in military, political, and civil affairs, Field Marshal Lord Slim. He spoke in England in 1947 when times were hard, yet after a long uphill pull the British people triumphed over their hardships and overcame their difficulties.

My leadership in the military was directed toward persuading others to implement plans in the face of death. Yours, perhaps less dramatically but not less importantly, is to persuade others to create profits for the success of your enterprise and your country. The ultimate goal of us all, however, is the same—we are today asking others to do for us, as their leader, something unselfish that is not necessarily in the immediate personal interest of those whom we lead. If you accept that, then the business and military objectives are identical and our means of obtaining them have many parallels.

MISSION STATEMENT

Nobody can lead anything effectively without a clear vision of where they are going. In the military every operation is preceded by a goal or objective, clearly stated, unambiguous, and undivided. From my first days in the army I was brought up to understand that a mission statement containing an *and* was a divided goal and therefore unlikely to succeed. A business or military operation, or even a small military patrol, must possess a clear goal, whether it be strategic or tactical. This goal must be clearly understood by everybody participating in the mission. In my first days at Robert Fleming as a merchant banker, John Manser, who had recently been appointed chief executive, collected together all the senior executives in the bank and told them that his goal was to make Fleming's the largest U.K. bank in the City of London with the best-paid employees within five years. This was clear, unambiguous, and easy to remember, and it caught the imagination. He did not achieve it by a short margin, but we all knew where we were going over the next five years and all played a part in making Fleming's one of the most expensive buys in the U.K. banking world when it was sold in 2000.

For myself, I always made everybody write down the goal when I issued it and I made sure that it was consistently repeated as frequently as possible. You would be surprised how short are people's memories.

LEADERSHIP TRAINING

In the services we select and promote people not only for their professional competence, but ultimately for their inherent demonstrative leadership skills and potential. Too often I have noticed in industry that people are promoted because of professional competence, and they are unable to manage the increased leadership responsibilities flowing from that promotion due to shortcomings in personality, training, or leadership experience. A successful business must ask itself questions concerning the value it places on leadership.

- Are you recruiting people of technical quality combined with the personality needed for senior positions?
- Is leadership an obligatory discussion subject in selection interviews? Do you offer training in, and discussion of, leadership during an executive's career? Leadership should be a thread throughout all training sessions.
- Is leadership given a place of importance in the annual review of employees aspiring to management?

"Leadership can be felt throughout an organization. It gives pace and energy to the work and empowers the workforce."

Warren Bennis

COMMUNICATION

No leader is effective without being able to communicate and remember that communication is a two-way process consisting of listening as well as transmitting. Very often managers over-talk and under-listen. During the Gulf War my most valuable moments were those daily occasions when I traveled to ships, air bases, and military units to talk to audiences of all ranks. It was the question-and-answer session after an address or during the tour of a ship or unit when I had the opportunity to listen to individuals: it was then that I truly learned what the concerns, ideas, and views of my servicepeople were. An individual's views might not change the conduct of the war, but a consistent message from those who have to carry out the risky fighting business influences my own planning and thinking. Some of the best ideas come from the bottom up.

Leaders must communicate and listen with a daily consistency and an unambiguous clarity of purpose. This clarity of purpose must stretch to the very humblest in their business, and even to those who have recently joined. It is not an easy task, and is one that frequently goes unrecognized.

DELEGATION

People who cannot delegate deserve no further promotion. Delegation and risk-taking are close allies, for when you delegate you pass on to others the right to make decisions on your behalf. Sometimes mistakes will be made, and then the courage of the true leader is demonstrated when he or she backs a subordinate. If you are unable to do this when they make genuine mistakes, they will make sure they make no mistakes by failing to use the authority you may wish to give them, and you will have failed as a delegating leader. The effectiveness of your business and the power of command when you reach senior positions is not what you are able to do yourself, but what you are able to motivate others to do for you. Achieve this and you will have harnessed the energy, drive, and initiative of your senior management and your employees— and your company will prosper.

MANAGING CHANGE

How often have we seen the new broom arrive in the business, instantly making changes before taking time to fully understand the complexity of the task ahead? Change for change's sake is the sign of a weak leader and a bully. This said, change should never be shirked, and a true leader will never accept things as they are simply because all is on an even keel and going well. It is too easy to leave the status quo unquestioned. A leader will see creative change as an opportunity and a challenge.

Change may be of a strategic nature, for example, our move from a defensive position after Iraq invaded Kuwait to one of offensive warfare designed to defeat Saddam's armies and eject him from Kuwait. On the other hand, change may be of a tactical nature. This was the case on my first patrol against the Chinese in Korea, a well-planned patrol designed to sweep the valley in front of our lines and to ensure that there were no Chinese battalions forming up for a dawn attack. Change was forced upon us when we walked into an ambush, found ourselves under heavy fire, and suffered a tactical defeat. Change, therefore, can be caused by forward planning and thinking, or it may be forced by the enemy or the business competitor. The former requires courage and leadership combined with vision; the latter requires instant response and leadership through decisive directions and initiatives.

COURAGE

There are two aspects of courage: physical and moral. In the services both are required to a high degree. In industry moral courage is the primary requirement. As Winston Churchill wrote, "Courage is a moral quality. It is a cold choice between two alternatives, the fixed resolve not to quit. Courage is willpower."

If your leaders lack the moral courage to stand up for their subordinates when they make genuine mistakes, or fail to confront their employees face-to-face with unpopular decisions, or fail to speak out clearly for what they believe to be the best interests of their company, then your leaders are not people of courage: they should be replaced.

MAKING IT HAPPEN ▶▶

Effective, consistent leadership relies on the following factors:

1 Avoiding the pitfalls of poor leadership. These include the danger that leaders can stifle innovation and reduce confidence by being too overbearing. Leadership can also lead to a cult of personality in which the leader is revered, usually to the detriment of the leader, the people he or she is leading, and the task they are all trying to accomplish. The final danger is that leaders who are too tough, ruthless, or macho will conflict with others, usually their peers, and split teams and the organization.

2 Empowering leadership. Developing an involved, committed, and ultimately successful workforce requires empowering leadership, the key attributes of which are:
- a belief in constant learning and the development of high self-esteem in others;
- a willingness to ask questions, admit weaknesses, and listen to answers;
- strong interpersonal skills, including an appreciation of other people and sensitivity to individuals;
- an ability to engender trust, build relationships, and inspire others;
- the ability and desire to develop leadership in others;
- the capacity to handle criticism by listening and drawing out people's concerns;
- a capacity to develop an effective vision of the future;
- an approach that values and nurtures innovation and initiative;
- the ability to communicate well at every level.

3 Being clear and focused on what you want to achieve. It is important to understand that leadership is a dynamic process and relies on leaders creating a vision and gaining people's commitment to that ideal. There are few certainties with leadership, and leaders therefore need to be clear about their goals.

4 Understanding present realities. It is easy for the leader to focus on a distant utopian vision—a dream—and ignore the immediate obstacles. Quite often these start with the leaders themselves. Initially many leaders may not feel comfortable with their role and may lack the confidence or respect vital for success. In general, therefore, leaders need to understand where they are starting from and what needs to be done immediately in order to start moving in the right direction. It is worth remembering that everyone can develop innate leadership potential, and trust and respect are there to be earned.

5 Understanding your own leadership style, and recognizing the different leadership needs of individuals. It is vitally important for successful leadership to match the leadership style to both the situation and the people involved. There are different times and situations for leading by consensus, control, directing, or

"I'll tell you what leadership is. It's persuasion and conciliation, and education, and patience."

Dwight D. Eisenhower

delegating, and they are best not confused!

6 Leading from the front, by example. It is important to confirm yourself as a leader, building trust and respect, by setting a clear example to your team. This means treating others as you would wish to be treated yourself, and it means developing and exhibiting a range of attributes and abilities such as demonstrating good work habits, understanding and valuing your staff's work, handling pressure, clearly demonstrating the values and goals that you hold dear, encouraging initiative and enthusiasm, providing regular, considered feedback, and listening and learning.

CONCLUSION

Decisiveness, vision, understanding, and confidence are at the core of successful leadership, and the leader needs to be able to use these qualities combined with additional skills relevant to each situation. The best leaders communicate their vision clearly and often: they are open to new approaches and ideas, but they know the direction in which the team and organization should be heading. They create a vision, communicate it, and guide their team to achieving their goal.

FOR MORE INFORMATION

Books:
Buckingham, Marcus, and Curt Coffman.

First, Break All the Rules: What the World's Greatest Managers Do Differently. New York: Simon & Schuster, 1999.
Collins, Jim. *Good to Great: Why Some Companies Make the Leap . . . And Others Don't.* New York: HarperCollins, 2001.
Kotter, John P. *Leading Change.* Cambridge, MA: Harvard Business School Press, 1996.

Web site:
www.hbsp.harvard.edu/products/hbr: this site contains an online version of the current edition of the *Harvard Business Review*, including a synopsis of many articles on leadership and management.

See also:
John Adair (pp. 1176–1177)

"A leader is a man who has the ability to get other people to do what they don't want to and like it."

Harry S. Truman

Viewpoint: Manfred Kets de Vries
Analyzing Organizations

Introduction

Manfred Kets de Vries is one of Europe's leading business thinkers. A Dutch academic and INSEAD professor, he brings a unique perspective to the crowded arena of leadership theory. His expertise spans economics, management, and psychoanalysis.

A Clinical Professor of Leadership Development, he holds the Raoul de Vitry d'Avaucourt Chair of Leadership Development at INSEAD, France, where he is Program Director of the top management seminar "The Challenge of Leadership: Developing Your Emotional Intelligence," and the program "Mastering Change: Developing Your Coaching and Consulting Skills." He has received INSEAD's Distinguished Teacher Award five times. He has also held professorships at McGill University and Harvard Business School.

Professor Kets de Vries is the author, coauthor, or editor of 20 books, including *Power and the Corporate Mind* (1975); *The Neurotic Organization* (1984); *Organizations on the Couch* (1991); and *Life and Death in the Executive Fast Lane* (1995)—a collection of essays on organizations and leadership. His more recent books include *Struggling with the Demon* (2001), *The Leadership Mystique* (2001), and *The Happiness Equation* (2002). He has also published over 180 scientific papers, and his work has been featured in publications including the *New York Times*, the *Wall Street Journal*, *The Economist*, the *Financial Times*, and *Fortune*.

Leadership is a very crowded field. What is distinctive about your approach is the eclectic mix of disciplines you bring to the subject. How did that come about?

Really, it is an evolution of trying to work in two main areas—management and psychoanalysis. I basically started as an economist, so I did a doctorate in economics at Amsterdam, which wasn't all that inspiring. But I went to the Harvard summer school when I was 17 and really enjoyed the experience, so I talked my way into the business school after my studies in Holland. Initially, I was in a program called the "International Teachers' Program," which was one year of studies—aimed at spreading the Harvard case method message around the world. At that time, I took an elective on psychoanalysis and management that was taught by Abraham Zaleznik, who came from production management but had become a psychoanalyst. I found the course very interesting.

At that point I decided to retrain, which was very difficult—particularly, in those days, if you were not a psychiatrist. So I did my MBA and DBA at Harvard Business School. Then I went to INSEAD for two years, followed by a year back in Harvard, and then Professor Henry Mintzberg persuaded me to move to McGill University in Montreal, where he was based. There I did my psychoanalytic training. I basically spent seven years with psychiatrists and some clinical psychologists. That was a very different experience from my previous work.

Trying to teach organizational behavior with traditional training in a doctoral program, you really don't learn that much about human beings. But when you are exposed to people who have a serious pathology, that's a really interesting contrast. It made a big impression on me. So that combination of disciplines resulted in me having a particular slant. In those days I didn't know it would be useful. I knew it was interesting, but I didn't know if it could really be applied.

What was the breakthrough?

The first serious application of the two fields of management and psychoanalysis was in the book I did with Danny Miller, entitled *The Neurotic Organization*. Although it was written in 1984, in many ways it has been a seminal book for management. People know me because of that book.

That was the first time that someone had tried to show in a systematic way the relationship between personality, leadership, corporate culture, and strategy. At that time, too, Henry Mintzberg had produced his book *The Structuring of Organizations*, in which he classifies organizational types—adhocracy, machine bureaucracy, and so on. So it is not surprising, given Henry's influence, that we came up with the darker side of his configurations—how organizations go wrong, in other words. All the organizational forms he described enjoyed a period when they were successful, but eventually they went down the drain for one reason or another. So we were stating some kind of organizational life cycle.

Where did that lead you?

From there, Danny and I wrote one more book together called *Unstable at the Top*, which was a popularization of *The Neurotic Organization*. It was not a great book in some ways, but it was still in the days of *In Search of Excellence* and every publisher thought the next bestseller was just around the corner. So we fell into that trap, by publishing a book that tried to use the ideas in a more populist format.

Danny and I then went our own ways. I left Canada and went to INSEAD, where I extrapolated from some of the ideas and wrote a series of books. I became a sort of corporation pathologist, where people would ask me to look at organizations that they thought were

---

"The American brand of democratic leadership doesn't work so well in Europe, where executives have a psychological need for more autocratic leadership."

David Ogilvy

going wrong, and I edited a book called *Organizations on the Couch*. I'd written some books before—*Prisoners of Leadership* and *Leaders, Fools, and Imposters*—but they were looking at the darker side of organizations, and particularly the darker side of leadership—how do leaders derail, what goes wrong? How can you recognize the signals, and are there things you can do about it?

Around that time, I also wrote a book on family businesses, which was a bit of a sideline. It was a reflection of my work consulting for smaller family businesses, that had real soap operas going on, which made my clinical knowledge very useful. Usually there were major Greek dramas taking place, from Medea to Oedipus, and to have a sense of the psychodynamics of social systems was very helpful. So I started to focus on the clinical orientation to management—what I call the clinical paradigm.

When they think of psychoanalysis, most people probably think of Freud. But who really influenced your thinking?

I use the concepts of psychoanalysis—although not necessarily traditional psychoanalysis. Of course, I cannot deny that Freud's contributions influenced me, but one of the advantages of my training in Montreal was that it was a place where different schools of thought could be applied. I was particularly influenced by Heinz Kohut (1913–1981), who was a pioneer of self-psychology, and, to some extent, Melanie Klein (1882–1960) and her successors. They went away from classical psychoanalysis, which is very drive-centered, to a more interpersonal centered approach. When I was at Harvard I was also very much influenced by Erik Erikson (1902–1994), the great old man of the human life cycle—who coined the phrase "identity crisis." It's due to the influence of those people that I call my approach the clinical orientation. In that respect I am quite a pragmatist, in that I try to do things that work. After all, I am a professor at a business school.

What sorts of practical issues do you use the clinical paradigm to address?

As an analyst, you get a little bit skeptical about the speed of change. I wanted to find new methods of dealing with it. At INSEAD I started a program called "The Challenge of Leadership: Developing Your Emotional Intelligence." Now, of course, emotional intelligence has been popularized by Daniel Goleman. But emotional intelligence has always been there. Any decent clinician has always been involved with emotional intelligence.

I decided that after working with middle managers it would be useful to work with C.E.O.s, because if you want to create change in an organization, you stand a much better chance if you have their collaboration. So for 12 years now, I've been running a seminar in which I work with 20 C.E.O.s. That has been a major source of research for me, because traditionally when you write cases about executives they tell you the party line. But when you have people together three

times a year for a five-day period, with follows-ups years after, you talk about things that really matter. Otherwise, they wouldn't hang around—given the cost of their time.

How has your writing evolved since you've been working closely with C.E.O.s?

Because I had previously specialized in looking at the negative side, I felt that I should try to write about what makes a great organization. So my books *The New Global Leaders* and *Struggling with the Demon* deal with aspects of this question. I even wrote a book called *The Happiness Equation*, which is very different from what I've written before.

You mentioned the importance of emotional intelligence in clinical psychoanalysis. In the past, corporations tried to keep emotions out of the workplace: is that changing now?

It has been changing for a while. I think the emotional intelligence movement has influenced that shift, but there is also a growing recognition that emotional management is required to effect change. Another program I am involved with at INSEAD is called "Coaching and Consulting for Change." My original idea was to aim it at consultants six years into their careers. They are usually brains on a stick, analytical machines, but they have to know something about emotional management if they want to be really effective. The program also attracts people who are involved with implementing change programs. So there are three main groups on the program—consultants, HR directors, and senior executives involved in major change programs.

What they realize is that they have to be very good at emotional management. I've learnt in my two programs that you can only change people if you hit them in the stomach and in the head: cognitively and emotionally. If you don't use a two-pronged attack, nothing is going to happen. The best programs realize this. But many MBA programs still go their own merry way and are totally cognitive.

It is ironic that MBAs love functional courses—the latest technique in financial analysis or marketing. But 10 years afterwards, when they come back to our school for executive programs, the only thing they are really interested in is people management, because that's what it's all about. And they haven't learned that in MBA programs, because to give this type of education is too costly.

Do 21st-century leaders need different qualities and skills from previous generations?

You need to know some different things when you live in a networked world. You probably need a slightly different approach. But I've always said that many of the leadership techniques of Alexander the Great are still highly applicable. In fact, I just wrote a book on Alexander the Great, as I was curious to know whether I would have to eat my words . . . but happily, it's true. Leaders still need to walk the talk—set the example. They still need to speak to the collective

"To grasp and hold a vision, that is the very essence of successful leadership—not only on the movie set where I learned it, but everywhere."

Ronald Reagan

imagination of their people to create a group identity. They need to create an executive role constellation. The use of language—symbol manipulation—also remains very important.

However, when you work in a knowledge society, you have to be careful. If you have a highly skilled workforce, then old-fashioned, autocratic practices are not going to be appropriate—you will lose your people. Also, because most leaders have so many sub-contracting relationships and strategic alliances these days, you need to know how to lead people who don't work for you. So it's a much more subtle style. And it doesn't hurt if you know something about the business, and you love it—if you go beyond being just a financial engineer.

Do you think there is too much emphasis on the financial aspects of the C.E.O. role?

It has been a problem recently. Many of the business leaders who have fallen from grace were financial engineers, rather than people managers. Twenty years ago, most C.E.O.s came through the operations route—and really knew their people. Now, most come through the financial engineering route, and have no sense of the people. That's very different. Derailment at the top is rarely because of lack of marketing or financial skills, it's a lack of interpersonal skills.

Has our understanding of leadership advanced in the past 50 years?

What is different is that, if you look at what effective

leaders do, there is much more awareness of the larger context. That was not explicitly stated in the past. It was quite mechanical. Leadership was characterized as highly task-orientated or highly relationship-orientated. The best leader was the one who could do both. It was probably true but it didn't go much further.

Now, however, more leaders see themselves as the high priests of corporate culture. Probably, intuitively, people were already that in the past. But it is now much more explicit. The turning point came in 1981 with the book the *Art of Japanese Management*, by Pascale and Athos. And then *In Search of Excellence* followed very soon after. Those two books were very influential in making people aware of the role of corporate culture. Nobody had explicitly thought about it until then. Now we know it.

FOR MORE INFORMATION

Book:
Kets de Vries, Manfred. *The Happiness Equation*. London: Vermilion, 2002.
Kets de Vries, Manfred. *The Leader on the Couch: A Clinical Approach to Changing People and Organizations*. New York: Wiley, 2006.

See also:
The Age of Unreason (p. 1068)
Richard Tanner Pascale (pp. 1250–1251)

Meaningful Leadership
by Kjell Nordström

INTRODUCTION

Employees no longer snap to attention when ordered to do so. They don't passively fall into line, and intimidation and threats do not work. The fact that the work force is no longer subservient doesn't mean that leadership is redundant, however. On the contrary, the new world of work requires even more thoughtful and meaningful leadership.

Leaders must challenge people to depart from the patterns of the past and to create new ones. This new form of leadership is about stirring the pot instead of putting on the lid. The new leaders are creators of chaos as much as originators of order. It is the job of great leaders to support the organization in combining order and chaos.

DIRECTION

Direction is not a matter of command and control, but of focusing—allowing and encouraging people to focus on what really matters. It is spiritual management rather than micromanagement. In a chaotic world, people cry out for individuals who can provide meaning to their private and professional lives.

All organizations need a shared idea of why they exist, who they are, and where they're going. In modern businesses this is usually expressed through a vision. The problem is that most companies don't have an operationally potent vision. Most so-called vision statements are generic wish lists whose length is matched only by their emptiness. Visions should be unique. They should differentiate.

To provide direction, a vision should be clear, continuous, and consistent. It should inspire commitment and be continually communicated. Scott McNealy of Sun Microsystems has a favorite formula: 0.6L. Every time information reaches a layer in the organization, only 60% gets through to the next layer. This quickly adds up—especially in hierarchical firms.

With the onus on communication, leaders must distill the company direction into the most potent capsule. At Disney the vision is to "make people happy." 3M focuses on "solving unsolved problems," while AT&T talks about IM&M—"information movement and management." These statements are simple enough to be shared by all employees, and clear in saying what the companies should *not* be doing.

In addition to visionary bullets, companies need short-term goals that inspire change and that themselves change over time. Jim Collins and Jerry Porras, in their book *Built to Last*, call these "big hairy audacious goals (BHAGs)." They come in many shapes and forms, and can be quantitative or qualitative. In the early 1990s, Wal-Mart set its sights on "becoming a $125-billion company by the year 2000." Almost a hundred years ago, Ford decided to "democratize the automobile." BHAGs can be geared toward a common enemy, as was Nike's "Crush Adidas" in the 1960s, or they can use role models as a benchmark. In the 1940s, for example, Stanford University decided to try to "become the Harvard of the West." General Electric adopted a more inwardly oriented focus in its 1980s goal to "become number one or two in every market we serve, and revolutionize this company to have the strengths of a big company combined with the agility of a small company."

Besides being the distilled essence of what a company is and what it stands for, visions and goals should ignite and inspire commitment. People must want to belong.

Communicating a vision not only involves repetition and a carefully distilled message, it demands the ability to tell a story. True leaders realize that metaphors and language are incredibly powerful. Stories and myths contain a built-in tension that draws people in and ensures that the message sticks. Stories are adaptable and open to an array of interpretations; they are universal and eternal. They communicate more than mere facts. Leaders should give rise to and spread stories.

EXPERIMENTATION

Business life has until now been built around spurts of creation and extended periods of exploitation. Companies exploited natural resources, technologies, and people. We are good at exploitation because we have hundreds, perhaps thousands, of years of experience. We know exactly what to do when we find a gold mine. We put structures and systems in place and get to work. When it is exhausted, we look for the next gold mine.

In contrast, we're not very good at creation. Our societies are not built for it, our organizations are not designed for it, and most people are not trained for it.

By its very nature, creation involves a departure from traditional structures and frames. In a world of creativity-sucking board meetings, past structures have ruled the roost. Now we have to be prepared to depart from the agenda. Exploring routes other than the one most traveled can prove worthwhile. After all, Viagra was discovered when scientists were looking to develop a drug to relieve high blood pressure, Columbus was actually trying to reach India rather than America, and Fleming's penicillin was the result of a "failed" experiment.

Innovation requires experimentation, and experiments are risky. So an innovative environment must have an exceptionally high tolerance for mistakes. The trouble is that traditional organizations are not the most forgiving of environments. This not only stops people from failing—it stops them from trying. It leads to the building of systems that act against innovation instead of nurturing it.

The challenge for leaders is to make it less risky to take risks. Work at Decision Research, a company based in Eugene, Oregon, studying risk-management strategies, suggests that people are more likely to accept risks that they perceive as voluntarily undertaken, controllable, understandable, and equally distributed. Conversely, people are less willing to take on risks that they don't understand and that are unfairly distributed.

EDUCATION

Education is a competitive weapon—for individuals as well as firms. If you want to attract and retain the best people, you have to train them.

Already companies are setting up their own universities to train tomorrow's executives. There are now 1,200 corporate universities worldwide, covering virtually every industry. Amid this welcome, and overdue, maelstrom of activity, the nature of education has fundamentally changed, and it will continue to do so.

Since a lot of knowledge is tacit and difficult to communicate, learning can by no means be restricted to the classroom. We

must learn also on the job. Education is as much about improving the processes in which we work and getting to know the people around us, as it is about reading yet another book or listening to yet another lecture. Development is about mentoring, training disciples, and coaching. It is the job of leaders to create new leaders. The distinction between learning, working, and living is gone.

PERSONALIZATION

To attract and retain good men and women, we have to treat them as individuals. The word "individual" originates from Latin and literally means indivisible. We are moving toward one-on-one leadership. The consequence is that every little system needs to be personalized. People can be approached, evaluated, rewarded, and inspired in a number of different ways.

Motivation is increasingly based on values rather than cash. The challenge for organizations is that values are more complex than mere money. By having and communicating a clear set of values, the organization becomes self-selecting—it primarily attracts people who share that attitude.

If people and their motivations differ, rewards must differ. We are used to differentiated contracts in every other market, but not in the labor market. While standard contracts are acceptable in a mass-production context, they are hardly applicable to a building full of highly charged brains with widely different reasons for being there. Working contracts are increasingly individual and individualistic. People express themselves through their contracts. You are your contract, and your contract is you.

Today's employees are more questioning and demanding. They are confident enough to air their concerns, grievances, and aspir-

ations. If they were customers, we would call them sophisticated. It is perhaps significant that we tend not to. Maybe we should. Perhaps we must.

MEANINGFUL LEADERSHIP IN ACTION

Telling Stories

Ikea's founder Ingvar Kamprad uses storytelling. Many people know how Kamprad travels by bus to and from airports to save money. It's a simple story, but its ramifications and message are very powerful. Here is a rich man who is still in touch with reality, who is concerned with value, who is the same as us. Kamprad's bus journeys are a metaphor of the values embodied by Ikea.

Encouraging Innovation

3M is famed for its 15% policy—researchers can spend up to 15% of their time on their own projects. This is called, among other things, "the bootleg policy." It may also be called a competitive advantage, because it's helped foster so many good ideas—most notably the Post-it Note.

"The object is to spur as many ideas as possible, because perhaps one in a thousand will turn out to fit," explains Post-it Note developer, Art Fry. "An idea might be perfectly good for another company, but not for yours. Putting together a new product is like putting together a jigsaw puzzle of pieces such as raw material suppliers, distributors, government regulations, the amount of capital you have to spend. If one part doesn't fit, the whole project can fail."

Caring for Human Capital

The software company SAS Institute in Cary, North Carolina, has no limits on sick days. You can even stay home to take care of sick family members. The firm is responsible for the largest daycare operation

in the state. People work a 35-hour week, and there are baby seats in the lunchroom. Pampering? Sure, but if you can't pamper your own people, you're hardly likely to pamper your customers and go that extra mile to enhance their experience.

MAKING IT HAPPEN ▸▸
Direction

Distill your company's vision down to the smallest communicable capsule.
Communicate continually; tell stories.

Experimentation

Encourage and reward failure.
Enable and encourage people to pursue off-beat ideas and projects.
Seek inspiration from other disciplines.

Education

Encourage and support continual learning.
Emphasize the potential of on-the-job learning.
Use mentoring, training, and coaching to develop a cadre of future leaders.

Personalization

Lead, recruit, and reward people as individuals.
Recruit by attitudes, values, tastes, and aspirations.
Listen—people differ, and the only way you can understand their differences is by listening to them.

FOR MORE INFORMATION

Ridderstråle, Jonas, and Kjell Nordström. *Funky Business*. 2nd ed. Upper Saddle River, NJ: Financial Times Prentice Hall, 2002.

Leading in Interesting Times
by Chris Turner

EXECUTIVE SUMMARY

- Companies continue to talk about teams, thinking out of the box, and empowerment, while modeling management and leadership styles which are controlling, structured, and hierarchical.
- Neither model is right or wrong, but we must think and act in ways that recognize the paradoxical nature of converging approaches.

INTRODUCTION

There is an old Chinese saying that is considered both a blessing and a curse:

"May you live in interesting times."

And that is where we find ourselves—in a world that is messy, unpredictable, often incomprehensible, and incredibly interesting; a world where old ideas of leadership and management no longer serve us; a world that calls for a rethinking of all our assumptions about the nature of organizations and our roles within them.

Most agree that new technologies have affected us in profound ways. Just a few years ago, the Internet was merely a playground for techies. And despite the fact that many dot-coms have folded, the Internet has permanently shifted the way we live and work. Its very existence challenges the fundamental operating assumptions of many organizations.

The Internet originally sprang from people's need to communicate and share information. It is a network of relationships and conversations: dynamic, emergent, adaptive, complex, collaborative, and self-organizing. Nobody is in charge. By nature, the Internet is an organic and feminine phenomenon.

Most business enterprises, by contrast, have roots in the Industrial Age. The mindset leans toward the mechanistic: control, predictability, and internal competition are valued. Even in flattened organizations, reporting lines and hierarchy are carefully defined. These companies are laced with masculine norms and values.

Yet ask any C.E.O. what's required to succeed in the future and he or she will inevitably say that the ability to innovate, to change direction on a dime, and to manage across cultures are imperative. They will talk of tapping the power of the Internet; but many fail to recognize the dissonance created when systems with very different operating assumptions converge: masculine versus feminine; controlled versus messy; engineered versus self-organizing; convergent versus divergent. Michael Lewis's book, *Next*, illustrates how the very existence of the Internet challenges institutions as we have known them.

Neither the Industrial Age model nor the Web model is right or wrong. This is not an either-or proposition. To be successful in the future, we must think and act in ways that recognize the paradoxical nature of converging approaches.

MAKING IT HAPPEN ▸▸

Because I work in many companies, I have the opportunity to observe individuals who navigate this paradoxical world quite well, who are leading effectively in these interesting times. Some lead from powerful positions; others lead informally and have huge influence on their organizations—yet all of them share certain mindsets and practices that are worth noting.

Leaders don't take themselves too seriously

Sometimes I ask people "Did you ever feel like a big sham?" Leaders inevitably have hilarious stories about such moments.

One friend tells about being invited to a very prestigious conference. When he mentioned the meeting to friends and family, their responses were maddeningly similar, "How did *you* get invited?"

He recalled that during the big gathering he kept waiting for everyone to turn to him and say, "You don't belong here. You're nothing but a big sham. Please leave."

Leaders sometimes manage grudgingly

These leaders are imaginative, visionary, and have active intellectual lives. They will often say that managing is both the most rewarding and the toughest part of the job, and they tend, over a career, to move between management and nonmanagement positions.

One of the finest leaders I know recently sold his enterprise for big bucks but has agreed to stay around for four to five years to ensure success. I asked him what he wants to do next. He put his head in his hands and said, "Anything where I don't have a bunch of people reporting to me." It was one of those days.

Leaders are good at relationships

These leaders have mastered the art of hanging out. They make opportunities for casual conversation. They do lunch. They nurture relationships. They aren't all extroverts, nor do they walk around slapping people on the back. On the contrary, many seem quiet when you first meet them. Their approach is often gentle, sometimes even deferential. But because they are great listeners, people gravitate to them.

An organization is really nothing more than a network of conversations and relationships, so it is unsurprising that these "hanger-outers" become the go-to people in enterprises. They know what's up, they know how to make things happen, they can get things done. They move comfortably through chaos.

Leaders don't hang onto their own assumptions and beliefs

Despite the fact that these leaders are powerful, either formally or informally, they don't get overly attached to their own assumptions about "the way things are."

Recently in a meeting with a C.E.O. and his senior staff, the C.E.O. was under incredible pressure. When his colleagues suggested that a planning process would take several weeks, he snapped, "We can finish that in fifteen minutes." A soft-spoken staffer commented, "Well, it's just not that easy." The C.E.O. retreated and within moments was laughing at the absurdity of his statement. He is a person of strong opinions with a powerful job; yet people are not afraid to challenge him because he is down-to-earth, self aware, and really smart. He listens—even when he doesn't like the message.

"Here lies one who knew how to get around him men who were cleverer than himself."

Andrew Carnegie

Leaders are politely tenacious

These new leaders are quietly upbeat. That's not to say they don't get discouraged, even depressed at times. But their funks are brief. If they think an organizational approach is misguided, they either figure out how to work around the craziness or they focus on how to present their viewpoints more convincingly. They ask questions like, "Help me understand why you think this strategy will be successful." They probe the assumptions that have led the organization to a certain place and remain open to seeing things differently. At the same time, they are not afraid to challenge the status quo or to accept responsibility for their own mistakes.

Leaders thrive on ambiguity

Although many of these leaders have grown up in organizations that are obsessed with control and prediction, they themselves tolerate ambiguity quite well. They analyze; they look at data; they study the situation; they pick people's brains; they solicit feedback. If they need approval, they are masterful at selling their ideas—even within risk-averse organizations. They understand that most decisions are about playing the odds— that nothing is a sure thing.

Leaders are curious, always learning

The next time you take a trip, notice the person across the aisle madly tearing articles out of newspapers and quizzing the flight attendants on the airline survey. The odds are that this person is one of these new leaders I'm talking about. These people are hugely curious and ever in search of new information, new points of view. Walk into their offices and you'll see stacks of books and publications; prepare yourself to hear stories about their latest discoveries. They are ever learning.

Many of these leaders seem to have minds that are more divergent than convergent. Engineers are often convergent. They work to connect all the dots. Artists are more commonly divergent. If they even see the dots, they figure that trying to connect them perfectly is a waste of time. In one of Gore Vidal's essays, republished in his most recent book, *Empire*, he contrasts the convergent mind of Jimmy Carter with the divergent minds of Kennedy and Clinton. He suggests that Carter's obsession with connecting all the dots contributed to his ineffectiveness in a dynamic role.

Whatever a leader's style, he or she is careful to surround himself or herself with and listen to colleagues with diverse points of view. He or she understands the value of balance.

Leaders understand that fear is corrosive

Leaders are never punitive. The Chilean biologist, Humberto Maturana, says that "love is the only emotion that expands human intelligence". Leaders understand this at a gut level—although some might hesitate to use the word love.

As managers, these folks are careful about the way compensation policies are designed. They understand that sharing the wealth creates more wealth, not less. If someone is in the wrong job or underperforming, these leaders help the person find another position or figure out a way for them to depart gracefully with a generous package. They recognize that punitive behavior creates fear that, in turn, stifles the creativity they so value.

Leaders talk like real people

Companies are like families; they each have their own language, their own acronyms, their own shorthand. Sometimes people in organizations become so steeped in buzzwords and jargon that, to the uninitiated, they sound like soulless droids from outer space.

These new leaders have a knack for avoiding institutional language. They talk in plain speak. This is part of their appeal, part of the reason that people gravitate to them. They are accessible. They have no need to impress others with insider words. They understand this quote from *The Cluetrain Manifesto* (Perseus, 2001): "In just a few years, the current homogenized 'voice' of business—the sounds of mission statements and brochures—will seem as contrived and artificial as the language of the 18th century French court".

Leaders understand the power of context

Workplaces are embedded with messages. I'm always amazed to hear people say they want their organization to be more innovative while working in offices that are absolutely dismal. To inspire innovation, these companies typically schedule creativity workshops.

If we think of an organization as a fish tank, many efforts to improve enterprises focus on the fish and ignore the water. The true power for change resides in the water, the environment in which the fish live. The water is the context.

I was recently with a group who were ruminating about leadership, wishing for discipline in their organization. When their lunchtime meeting was over, they all departed leaving their lunch mess behind. With this particular group, their leadership efforts need to start with cleaning up after themselves. Their lack of discipline in caring for the physical environment sends signals that affect the organization exponentially.

As Malcolm Gladwell points out in his great book, *The Tipping Point*, "we are all more than just sensitive to changes in context. We're exquisitely sensitive to them". Alan Kay, one of the original innovators in Silicon Valley, says, "Context is worth 50 IQ points". Leaders pay attention to environmental details. They invest in making the workplace more inviting, whether by painting it in bright colors, putting good art on the walls, or taking interior desks so the windows can be shared by everyone. They are attentive to how meetings are conducted, the forms their communications take, the culture's graphic identity. They tell stories and encourage storytelling because stories contribute to context. They tinker with the environment constantly. Recently a C.E.O. showing me around her facility paused to pick up a scrap of paper on the stairs. She didn't see the paper as paper; she understood it to be a message about the organization.

CONCLUSION

I don't have a neat seven-step approach to cultivating the attributes and behaviors detailed here; but what I notice about these leaders is that they are acutely self-aware and very present. They think. They recognize their own strengths and weaknesses. They constantly look for ways to improve themselves—not so they'll be more professionally successful but because they subscribe to the discipline of personal mastery. Their leadership comes from who they are as much as what they know.

FOR MORE INFORMATION

Books:
Ehrenreich, Barbara. *Nickel and Dimed.* New York: Metropolitan Books, 2001.
Gladwell, Malcolm. *The Tipping Point.* New York: Little, Brown, 2002.
Lewis, Michael. *Next.* New York: W.W. Norton, 2001.

"Leadership, unlike naked power wielding is thus inseparable from followers' needs and goals."

James MacGregor Burns

Learning the Art and Practice of Adaptive Leadership Through Case-in-Point

by Sharon Daloz Parks

EXECUTIVE SUMMARY

- "Adaptive leadership" is a new kind of leadership needed in an age of change and moral questioning, and the most effective way of learning how to lead adaptively is through a new theoretical perspective called "case-in-point."
- Case-in-point uses the student's immediate situation and experience as a basis for learning in the midst of practice.
- Adaptive leadership is all about leading and learning at the same time. It involves personal humility and reflection on one's own mistakes, as well as exercising authority, dealing with conflict, and exploring new possibilities.
- In this age leadership is an art, and leaders can learn more from models from the arts, especially the improvisational and collaborative arts, than from traditional command-and-control models.

INTRODUCTION

"Adaptive leadership" signals the reach for a new kind and quality of leadership to meet the challenges embedded in the realities that all managers now face: issues of scale, accelerated change, intensified complexity—all compounded by a deepening hunger for moral courage that is not naive. This call for a practice of leadership that is a match for current conditions leads into a set of critical questions: Can such leadership be learned—and, if so, can it be taught? If the 21st century requires new ways of thinking and acting on the part of management at all levels (and some begin to question whether the MBA is obsolete and conventional "exec ed" fails to yield satisfying results), how do we re-imagine the formation of leadership to meet both immediate and long term needs?

MEETING THE LEADERSHIP CHALLENGE

Among those who have waded into these questions are Ronald Heifetz, Marty Linsky, Dean Williams, and their colleagues at Harvard University. They have developed an approach to recasting the purpose and practice of leadership that is framed by four critical distinctions:

- authority versus leadership
- technical problems (amenable to

knowledge already in hand) versus adaptive challenges (requiring new learning, innovation, creativity, conflict, and loss)
- holding and wielding power versus making progress on tough issues (as the criterion for success)
- personality versus presence (a shift from a focus on personal traits to a focus on effective participation)

This framework, along with multiple competencies delineated within it, makes considerable progress in rethinking the practice of leadership in relationship to the radically systemic, interconnected, and dynamic reality in which every business must operate.

But, unlike many other theoretical perspectives, this approach has engaged head-on the yet more fundamental questions of the implications of this perspective for learning, teaching, and becoming—in the midst of practice. Heifetz and his colleagues have developed a method called "case-in-point" in which the immediate situation (class or workplace) may become a crucible for learning and an immediate experience of a system within which one is challenged to make progress on the toughest (and often hidden) issues at hand. When the work is to learn how to practice leadership more effectively, case-in-point is an invitation to "mobilize the group" to move from a

familiar but no longer functional pattern to a more adequate but yet undiscovered pattern of operation—a difficult move because people don't necessarily resist change, but they do resist loss. Moreover, it is particularly difficult to undergo loss when there is no experience or "vision" of how a new pattern will actually take form. Yet in unprecedented conditions, "vision" becomes a problematic requirement in the practice of leadership, though precisely for this reason, clarity of purpose is crucial.

LEARNING ADAPTIVE LEADERSHIP

In learning how to practice adaptive leadership, one has to give up the assumption that the teacher-authority will by "telling" (and entertaining and reassuring) take responsibility for the task at hand. The student has to begin to take responsibility for his or her own perceptions and participation and their effect in relationship to the work of the group. In this view, and in whatever context, the practice of leadership becomes, in large measure, the management of a learning process (even on the part of the "leader"), typically involving also the management of loss and grief as the group surrenders familiar expectations. This kind of leadership and this kind of learning require a willingness to work on the rim of what is known and what has not yet fully emerged into view—a place where curiosity, commitment, and a necessary courage must be tempered by compassion for oneself and others.

Competencies inherent in this kind and quality of leadership practice include the capacity for reflection in the midst of the action—moving continually between "the balcony and the dance floor"; the ability, at one and the same time, to hold steady, to "find the shapes in the fog," to identify and engage the factions, to control the conflict, to use oneself as a barometer of what is happening in the group, to exercise the functions of authority (formal and informal), to pace the work, to surrender the illusion of ultimate control, to build partnerships and alliances and find appropriate confidants,

"Leaders must invoke an alchemy of great vision. Those leaders who do not are ultimately judged failures, even though they may be popular at the moment."

Henry Kissinger

276

BEST PRACTICE

and to intervene in ways that will enable the system itself to achieve success.

Learning these kinds of capacities happens best, this approach contends, in a relentless reflection on one's own experience of failure and disappointment in the midst of attempting to lead—the case-in-point. Moreover, such reflection becomes most productive when it takes place not only in a personal coming-to-terms but also in public—that is, among professional peers in a "safe enough" setting.

CASE-IN-POINT LEARNING AND THE ART OF LEADERSHIP

The traditional case-study method is a powerful research and teaching tool. Its limitations stem from its tendency to foster an arrogance (and consequent vulnerability) that arises from the repeated experience of being able to crack the case by analyzing after the fact what someone else should have done in real time. Case-in-point learning, in contrast, requires in real time not only smarts, but also an elegant mix of courage and humility—qualities resonant with what Jim Collins has identified as hallmarks of the most effective business leaders he studied. These qualities are required of both the students and the teacher(s). In case-in-point, even the teacher's assumptions and actions are open to scrutiny on behalf of learning, and the teacher cannot fully plan or control what will take place in the process.

Case-in-point teaching and learning does have a structure that must be maintained fairly rigorously. This structure is characterized by a trustworthy "container" within which the work can take place (including responsible practice of authority on the part of the teacher) and clear guidelines, norms, boundaries, and assignments that shape expectations and create multiple opportunities for observation and experimentation. As such, in the case-in-point learning milieu (though it may be located in a setting that appears much like a typical classroom or corporate meeting room) the feel and tempo of the work may resemble something more akin to an art studio.

Indeed, it is my growing conviction that our times call for a laser-beam focus on a well used but under-recognized phrase: "the *art* of leadership." To be sure, more than two decades ago, Donald Schön observed that outstanding practitioners are not credited with more knowledge but with more "wisdom, talent, intuition, or *artistry*." But he also observed that these become junk categories used to elude explanation. Thus he argued, "Artistry is an exercise of intelli-

gence, a kind of knowing though different in crucial respects from our standard model of professional knowledge. It is not inherently mysterious; it is rigorous in its own terms."

Heifetz and Linsky have, on the one hand recognized that leadership is "an improvisational art." What has not been fully recognized and articulated, however, is how much those who would lead in today's world have to learn from artists as conventionally understood. Perhaps most significantly, perceiving the work of leadership through the lens of art, artists, and artistry is a way of responding to the growing necessity for an understanding and practice of leadership with new myths and rituals.

THROUGH THE LENS OF ART

The heroic command and control models that still dominate our imagination of leadership are sustained in the absence of a compelling alternative. This deep command and control myth, anchored in the well-recognized and reassuring roles of shepherds, warriors, and kings and queens is powerfully resonant with the functions of authority. Now, however, as we must create the modes of enterprise and the institutions that will be fitting to the ways in which we have come to live, a new myth that can more adequately take into account the dynamism of the creative process is sorely needed.

What might the practice of artistry teach us that is relevant to management and leadership? Every artist, for example, must have a profoundly interdependent relationship with the medium with which he or she works—be it clay, stone, ice rink, orchestra, or the cast and stage crew of a theater production. You can't make clay, ice, actors, or crew do just anything you want. Your success is dependent upon an intimate knowledge of the medium—you must know its strengths and limits and always be prepared for surprise.

Artists must also constantly work on the edge of what they have done before and cannot quite yet do. Replicable action becomes craft—the technical dimension of art. Art brings through something that has not existed before, which often has to be struggled for and requires experimentation and practice. In many business settings there is a growing brittleness, which does not allow for experimentation and practice. But it is through mistakes and failed attempts that artist-leaders "worry the gap" between current cultural/operational patterns and provide an essential element in what is required to achieve a competitive advantage, a more just society, and a more viable, sustainable global marketplace.

The forms of artistry in leadership that are most relevant to today's business environment convey, first, that art is not something that only "artists" do, but rather that the capacity for creativity is integral to being human—we are creative agents. Many people, however, though intelligent and trained, have lost touch with this dimension of their own experience, often through forms of "learning" and "management" that blunt it, defer it to others, or discount it altogether.

Second, only a distorted perception of artists presumes that artistic endeavor is a mere extension of ego and an isolated, merely personal, asocial activity. Great art emerges within and on behalf of a social context. Theater, music groups, sports teams, and schools of painting, dance, and architecture reveal the power of the collective imagination grounded in individual commitment, courage, and excellence that cannot be understood apart from the systemic, interdependent reality that we are.

CONCLUSION

New ways of perceiving the art of leadership that foster our adaptive capacity and forms of learning, such as case-in-point, that serve to re-awaken our creative capability provide vital steps toward the kind of thinking and acting—the breakthrough consciousness—that the business sector and the wider life of today's global commons now require.

FOR MORE INFORMATION

Books:
Daloz, Laurent A., Cheryl H. Keen, James P. Keen, and Sharon Daloz Parks. *Common Fire: Leading Lives of Commitment in a Complex World.* Boston, MA: Beacon Press, 1996.
Heifetz, Ronald A. *Leadership without Easy Answers.* Cambridge, MA: Harvard University Press, 1994.
Heifetz, Ronald A. and Marty Linsky. *Leadership on the Line.* Cambridge, MA: Harvard Business School Press, 2002.
Parks, Sharon Daloz. *Leadership Can Be Taught: A Bold Approach for a Complex World.* Cambridge, MA: Harvard Business School Press, 2005.
Schön, Donald. *Educating the Reflective Practitioner.* San Francisco, CA: Jossey-Bass, 1987.
Williams, Dean. *Real Leadership: Helping People and Organizations Face Their Toughest Challenges.* San Francisco, CA: Berrett-Koehler, 2005.

See also:
Leadership (pp. 1798–1803)

"The difference between a leader and a boss is the difference between good and bad management."

Henry Kissinger

Walking on the Leading Edge without Falling off the Cliff
by Judith A. Neal

EXECUTIVE SUMMARY

- The complexity of today's world requires people to walk in many different worlds.
- Edgewalkers are leaders who sense the leading edge and have the courage to take action on their vision.
- It's important not to get too far ahead of the pack; walking on the edge only succeeds when others are motivated to follow.
- Walking on the leading edge is frequently the only way to succeed. Innovation, risk, and an ability to push beyond comfort zones can often be decisive.

INTRODUCTION

The complexity of the business world today is astounding. Nothing is predictable. The rules of the game are changing. Just when you think you've figured out how to have a competitive advantage, a competitor develops a new technology. Just when you think you've found the right motivation tool, the values in your workforce seem to shift. Just when you think you've found the right geographical area for the expansion of your internationalization efforts, political turmoil erupts.

Yet some people seem to have an uncanny knack for knowing what's going to happen before it unfolds. They're able to create new rules for the game instead of following the rules everyone else follows. They're able to plan a strategy that seems absurd to most people at first, and is later called brilliant when it's successful. They are a part of an unusual breed of leaders called edgewalkers.

An edgewalker is someone who walks between two worlds. In ancient cultures each tribe or village had a shaman or medicine man. This was the person who walked into the invisible world to get information, guidance, and healing for members of the tribe. This was one of the most important roles in the village. Without a shaman the tribe would be at the mercy of unseen gods and spirits, the vagaries of the cosmos. The skill of walking between the worlds hasn't died out, in fact it's even more relevant today. Organizations that will thrive in the 21st century will embrace and nurture edgewalkers. Because of their unique skills, they are the bridge-builders linking and facilitating different approaches, strategies, and techniques.

Walking on the Leading Edge

Five key skills form the hallmark of an edgewalker:
- visionary consciousness
- multicultural responsiveness
- intuitive sensitivity
- risk-taking confidence
- self-awareness

1. Visionary Consciousness

Edgewalkers begin with *visionary consciousness*. All their other skills are in the service of a sense of mission about something greater than themselves. They feel called to make a difference in the world. The visionary skills arise out of a strong sense of values and integrity. Often these values are developed through some kind of painful experience or loss, and the edgewalker becomes committed to helping other people who may be going through similar kinds of experiences. Typically, the edgewalkers have gone through a major personal or career change that requires them to develop new skills that were never needed previously. Edgewalkers are the consummate integrators of seemingly unrelated ideas, skills, and fields.

2. Multicultural Responsiveness

Edgewalkers must have strong *multicultural responsiveness*. They're bilingual in the sense that they can understand the nuances of different worlds or cultures. They span conventional boundaries and act as translators. Edgewalkers know how to pick up on subtle cues that are different from their own. They pay minute attention to people different from themselves and have an open, warm curiosity about people from other cultures. They look for commonalities more than differences, and they want to know more about the worlds of others.

3. Intuitive Sensitivity

Edgewalkers have strong *intuitive sensitivity*. They're natural futurists. Because they're avid readers they are constantly integrating information from many sources and looking for underlying themes and patterns. Like the shamans of old, they've learned to pay attention to subtle, perhaps invisible, signs of potential change. They have an uncanny knack of making the right decisions, often taking action that seems counterintuitive to others. But, when asked how they knew what to do in a particular situation, they have difficulty explaining. They reply, I just "knew." Intuitive skills are gained through the practice of deep listening. When listening to others, edgewalkers listen as much for the unsaid as the said. They also look for coincidences, patterns, or synchronicities that might provide clues to guide them in their decision making.

4. Risk-taking Confidence

Another strong skill that edgewalkers display is the skill of calculated *risk-taking confidence*. Edgewalkers have a strong sense of adventure and experimentation. They're always attracted to the next new thing. Like entrepreneurs, edgewalkers are easily bored with stability and are attracted to what's over the horizon. They're constantly asking what's next and trying to figure out how to be part of it. Because they're able to walk in two worlds, the world of practicality and the world of creativity, the risks they take to jump into the next new thing are based on information and intuition. Having a clear vision guided by strong values helps the edgewalker take risks that might not make sense to others.

5. Self-awareness

The most important edgewalker skill is that of *self-awareness*. A principle that edgewalkers understand is that each person is a

---

"I am a risk taker but only within rules. I just like the support that an organisation gives, combined with the freedom to express myself."

Guy Hands

microcosm of the whole. Leaders who are edgewalkers know that if they're experiencing a vision or dream or hunger, it's most likely arising in others as well. The challenge for the edgewalker is to find others who have the same passion and to work together to make a difference. Leaders who are edgewalkers have a strong sense of being connected to something greater than themselves.

These five skills can be taught. However, the leaders who tend to learn best strongly value their own personal development and have low control needs.

Avoiding Potential Pitfalls

Edgewalkers can often get too far ahead of the pack. If this happens, they lose their credibility and the opportunity to influence others to do creative work. It's nice to have someone say you're ahead of your time, but there are few rewards for being too far out there. The most successful edgewalkers can remain in the real world and can remember established language and values so they can be a bridge to new ideas. For this reason, you should:

1 Watch for signs that you may be getting too far out on the edge; if this seems to be happening, revisit your own past experience, current priorities and future aspirations.

2 When you have a new idea that you want to implement, talk to people who are likely to disagree with you or try to block you.

3 Create relationships with people who can provide a good reality check.

4 Have patience with people who don't want to move as fast as you do; take time to build relationships with them and specifically ask for their support.

5 Cultivate the skill of honoring people who disagree with you; listen for any pearls of wisdom they have to offer.

6 Be very aware of your highest values and have a strong commitment to integrity. Even if you get too far out on the edge, you will know you are doing it for the right reasons.

If you feel blocked at every turn by people committed to the status quo, consider finding a different organization to work for, or even going out on your own. Being an edgewalker can feel very lonely. Connect with other edgewalkers for support and inspiration.

MINI-CASES

There are many interesting examples of people who successfully walk the leading edge.

Tom Aageson is the executive director of the Museum of New Mexico Foundation. When Tom turned 50 he was a highly successful executive at the Mystic Museum in Connecticut. For his birthday he went on a week's retreat to contemplate the rest of his life. He realized that his mission was to do whatever he could to eradicate poverty in the world. That led him to a position as the executive director at Aid to Artisans, which helps artists and craftspeople in developing countries to design and market products that respect their cultures and improve their economic situation.

Bill Catucci is the leader of Regulatory Data Corp. and former C.E.O. of AT&T Canada. When Bill first came to work for AT&T Canada, the company was losing a significant amount of money. His first act was to send a check for $75 to every employee, saying that it was a token of appreciation for what they had already contributed to the company and that he looked forward to working with them to turn the company around. He turned AT&T Canada from a company losing $1 million a day into a winner—and inspired his people as part of that. Then he turned around Equifax, raising the value of the company by over $3 billion during a time when the stock market was stagnant.

John Lumsden is the C.E.O. of Metserve in New Zealand. John is originally from Scotland and served as an executive in Canada for a number of years; he's truly learned how to walk in different cultural worlds. On the first day of every professional meteorological training course for new employees, there is a Maori welcoming ceremony focusing on Tawhiri-Matea, the God of the Winds. John holds regular "advances" (as opposed to retreats) for his management team, at which people spend time reflecting on deeper questions of life and work. They aim to have a lean and meaningful organization: lean to be competitive; meaningful for the users as well as for the employees.

Jennifer Cash O'Donnell is director of organizational strategy and professional development for AT&T's Asia-Pacific group in China. Walking between the worlds of operations and organizational development, she helps AT&T achieve great results through a focus on human relationships and teambuilding, using Barry Heerman's Team Spirit process. Her success at AT&T Solutions with this team-based program led to her promotion to the directorship in Asia. This provides her with yet another opportunity to be an edgewalker.

CONCLUSION

Edgewalkers are the leaders of the future. They are the corporate shamans who bring wisdom and guidance for their organizations. It's not an easy role to play, but it's one that's essential to the success of your organization—and one that can make you feel fully alive.

FOR MORE INFORMATION

Books:
Moxley, Russ S. *Leadership & Spirit*. San Francisco, CA: Jossey-Bass, 2000.
Ray, Paul H., and Sherry Ruth Anderson. *The Cultural Creatives: How 50 Million People Are Changing the World*. New York: Three Rivers Press, 2001.

Web site:
www.spiritatwork.org: Spirit at Work has numerous resources for people who "walk between the two worlds."

"Corporate risk takers are very much like entrepreneurs. They take personal risks to make new ideas happen."

Gifford Pinchot

Business Ethics by Sue Newell

EXECUTIVE SUMMARY

- Business ethics focuses on identifying the moral principles by which we can evaluate business organizations.
- Corporations often behave unethically, having a harmful effect on people or the environment.
- Unethical behavior is typically not caused by a single "bad apple," but is rather the outcome of complex interactions between individuals, groups and organizations.
- Ethical behavior can be defined either as behavior that maximizes happiness and minimizes harm or as behavior that is motivated by principles of duty.
- While behaving unethically may have some short-term benefit for a company, in the long term it will harm stakeholder support.
- Long-term sustainability comes from concentrating on the *triple bottom line*: being concerned with the social and environmental as well as the economic impact of a business.

INTRODUCTION

Look in the newspaper on virtually any day of the week and you will find at least one business scandal in which a corporation appears to have violated the rules or standards of behavior generally accepted by society. Company finances have been manipulated in order to show a better balance sheet than actually exists, toxic waste has been allowed to flow into a river, bribes have been paid in order to secure a business deal, child labor has been used to assemble a product, discriminatory practices have prevented the employment or promotion of members of a particular group, businesses regularly behave unethically, that is, they behave in ways that have a harmful effect upon others and in ways that are morally unacceptable to the larger community. Moreover, the impact of companies is increasing as they become larger (indeed, global) and as profit-making concerns take over functions that were once publicly controlled such as the railroads, water utilities, and healthcare. Increasingly it is the private sector that determines the quality of the air we breathe, the water we drink, our standard of living, and even where we live and how easily we can move around.

COMMON ETHICAL PROBLEMS WITHIN CORPORATIONS

Given the increasing social impact of business, business ethics has emerged as a discrete subject over the last 20 years. Business ethics is concerned with exploring the moral principles by which we can evaluate business organizations in relation to their impact on people and the environment. Trevino and Nelson categorize four types of ethical problems common in business organizations (*Managing Business Ethics*, 3rd ed. Wiley, 2003).

First are human resourcing ethical problems, which relate to the equitable and just treatment of current and potential employees. Unethical behavior here involves treating people unfairly because of their gender, sexuality, skin color, religion, ethnic background, and so on.

Second are ethical problems arising from conflicts of interest. Here, particular individuals or organizations are given special treatment because of some personal relationship with the person or group making a decision. A company might get a lucrative contract, for example, because a bribe was paid to the management team of the contracting organization, not because of the quality of its proposal.

Third are ethical problems that involve customer confidence, with corporations behaving in ways that show a lack of respect for customers or a lack of concern with public safety. Examples here include advertisements that lie (or at least conceal the truth) about particular goods or services, and the sale of products, such as drugs, that a company knows to be unsafe (or at least not completely safe).

Finally, there are ethical problems surrounding the use of corporate resources by employees who make private phone calls at work, submit false expense claims, take company stationery home, etc.

The financial scandals that have rocked the corporate world in recent years (Enron, WorldCom, Parmelat, for example) involve a number of these different ethical issues. In these cases senior managers have engaged in improper bookkeeping, making companies look more financially profitable than they actually are. This increases the stockholder value of the company so that anyone with stock profits directly. Those profiting will include those making the decisions to manipulate the accounts and so there is a conflict of interest. However, the fall-out from the downfall of these companies affects stockholders, employees and society at large negatively, with innocent people losing their retirement reserves and/or savings, and employees losing their jobs.

ACCOUNTING FOR ETHICAL AND UNETHICAL BEHAVIOR

While it may be very easy to identify and blame an individual or small group of individuals and see these individuals as the perpetrators of an unethical act—the "bad apple"—and hold them responsible for the harm caused, this response is an oversimplification. Most accounts of unethical behavior that are restricted to the level of the individual are inadequate. Despite popular belief, decisions harmful to others or the environment that are made within organizations are not typically the result of an immoral individual seeking to gain personal benefit. While individual influences such as the employee's level of moral maturity or the locus of control may be factors, we also need to explore the decision-making context in order to understand why an unethical decision was made. Group dynamics, for example, very often influence the decision-making process.

A particularly important group-level influence is *groupthink*, a phenomenon identified by Irving Janis in his research on U.S. foreign policy groups (*Groupthink: Psychological Studies of Policy Decisions and Fiascoes*, Houghton Mifflin College, 1982). The research demonstrates the presence of strong pressures toward conformity in these groups; individual members suspend their own critical judgment and right to question, with the result that they make bad and/or immoral decisions. Janis defines groupthink as "the psychological drive for consensus at any cost that suppresses dissent and appraisal of alternatives in cohesive decision-making groups".

The degree to which decisions are ethical

is also influenced by organizational culture. Smith and Johnson differentiate three general approaches that organizations take to corporate responsibility (*Business Ethics and Business Behaviour*, International Thomson Business Press, 1996):

1 **social obligation**: the corporation does only what is legally required;
2 **social responsiveness**: the corporation responds to pressure from different stakeholder groups;
3 **social responsibility**: the corporation has an agenda of proactively trying to improve society.

In a company in which the dominant approach to business ethics is social obligation, it is likely to be difficult to justify a decision based on ethical criteria; morally irresponsible behavior may be condoned as long as it does not break the law. Legal loopholes, for example, may be exploited in such a company if these can benefit the company in the short-term, even if they might negatively influence others in society.

ETHICAL DILEMMAS

In some instances it is clear that a business has behaved unethically, for example, where a drug is sold illegally, the company accounts have been falsely presented, or where client funds have been embezzled. Of more interest, however, and much more common, are situations that pose an ethical dilemma; situations presenting a conflict between right and wrong or between values and obligations, so that a choice is necessary. For example, a corporation may want to build a new factory on a previously undeveloped and popular tourist site in a location where there is large-scale unemployment among the local population. Here we have a conflict between the benefits of wealth and job creation in a location in which these are crucial and the cost of spoiling some naturally beautiful countryside. Philosophers have attempted to develop prescriptive theories providing universal laws that enable us to differentiate between right and wrong, and good and bad in these situations.

PRESCRIPTIVE ETHICAL THEORIES

Essentially there are two schools of thought. The consequentialists argue that behavior is ethical if it maximizes the common good (happiness) and minimizes harm. Opposing nonconsequentialists argue that behavior is ethical if it is motivated by a sense of duty or a set of moral principles about human conduct—regardless of the consequences of the action.

Consequentialist Accounts of Ethical Behavior

Philosophers who adopt the consequentialist approach (sometimes also referred to as utilitarianism) consider that behavior can be judged ethical if it has been enacted in order to maximize human happiness and minimize harm. Jeremy Bentham (1748–1832) and John Stuart Mill (1806–73) are two of the best-known early proponents of this view. Importantly it is the common good, not personal happiness, that is the arbiter of right and wrong. Indeed, we are required to sacrifice our personal happiness if doing so enhances the total sum of happiness. For a person forced with a decision choice, the ethical action is thus to weigh up the impact on others of all the possible options and choose the one that maximizes happiness and minimizes harm. Common criticisms of this approach are that it is impossible to measure happiness adequately and that it essentially condones injustice if this is to the benefit of the majority.

Nonconsequentialist Accounts of Ethical Behavior

Philosophers who adopt a nonconsequentialist approach (also referred to as deontological theory) argue that behavior can be judged as ethical if it is based on a sense of duty and carried out in accordance with defined principles. Immanuel Kant (1724–1804), for example, articulated the principle of *respect for persons*, which states that people should never be treated as a means to an end, but always as an end in themselves. The idea here is that we can establish moral judgments that are true because they can be based on the unique human ability to reason. One common criticism of this approach is that it is impossible to agree on the basic ethical principles of duty or their relative weighting in order to direct choices when multiple ethical principles are called into question at the same time.

MAKING IT HAPPEN ▶▶

While these two approaches to evaluating behavior are clearly different, they can be integrated to create a checklist that will help an individual or group make sound ethical decisions.

- Gather the facts: what is the problem, and what are the potential solutions?
- Define the ethical issues. (This is a step that is often neglected, so that the ethical dilemmas raised by a particular decision are never even considered.)
- Identify the various stakeholders involved.

- Think through the consequences of each solution: what happiness or harm will be caused?
- Identify the obligations and rights of those potentially affected: what is my duty here?
- Check your gut feeling.

The last step is crucial. Those involved need to ask themselves what they would feel like if friends or family found out they had been involved in making a particular corporate decision, whether personally or collectively.

WHY BEHAVING ETHICALLY IS IMPORTANT FOR BUSINESS

Choosing to be ethical can involve short-term disadvantages for a corporation. Yet in the long term it is clear that behaving ethically is the key to sustainable development. When you're faced with an ethical dilemma in which the immoral choice looks appealing, ask yourself three questions:

1 **What will happen when (not if) the action is discovered?** Increasingly the behavior of corporations is coming under scrutiny from their various stakeholders —customers, suppliers, stockholders, employees, competitors, regulators, environmental groups, and the general public. People are less willing to keep quiet when they feel an injustice has been done, and the Internet and other media give them the means to make their concerns very public, reaching a global audience. Corporations that behave unethically are unlikely to get away with it, and the impact when they are discovered can be catastrophic. This leads to the second question.
2 **Is the decision really in the long-term interests of the corporation?** Many financial services companies in the United Kingdom generated short-term profits in the 1990s by mis-selling personal pensions to people who would have been better off staying in their company's pension plan. However, in the long term these companies have suffered by having to repay this money and pay penalties. Most significantly, the practice has eroded public confidence.
3 **Will organizations that behave unethically attract the necessary employees?** Corporations that harm society or the environment are actually harming their own employees, including those who are making the decisions. For example, corporations that pour toxins into the air are polluting the air their employees' families breathe.

Ultimately a business relies on its human resources. If a company cannot attract high-quality people because it has a poor public image based on previous unethical behavior, it will certainly flounder. Behaving ethically is clearly key to the long-term sustainability of any business. Focusing on the triple bottom line—the social and environmental as well as the economic impact of a company—provides the basis for sound stakeholder relationships that can sustain a business into the future.

FOR MORE INFORMATION

Book and Journal Articles:
Elkington, John. *Cannibals with Forks: The Triple Bottom Line of 21st Century Business*. Gabriola Island, BC, Canada: New Society, 1998.
Trevino, Linda K. and Katherine A. Nelson. *Managing Business Ethics: Straight Talk About How to Do It Right*. New York: Wiley, 2004.

See also:
- Business Ethics and Codes of Practice (pp. 1689–1549)
- ✔ Codes of Ethics (pp. 510–511)
- Frank and Lillian Gilbreth (pp. 1210–1211)
- Konosuke Matsushita (pp. 1328–1329)
- ☆ Workers without Borders: Creating Bonds When Workers Have No Loyalty (pp. 237–238)

"He has made a profession out of a business and an art out of a profession."

Clifton Fadiman

Viewpoint: Derrick Bell
Ethical Ambition

Introduction

Derrick Bell is one of the most forthright and best-known commentators on race and ethics in the United States. A prolific author, his autobiography is entitled *Confronting Authority: Reflections of an Ardent Protestor*. Bell, a visiting professor at New York University's School of Law, attracted headlines when he became the first tenured black professor at Harvard Law School in 1971, only to leave in protest about the lack of black women on the faculty. He also resigned as dean of Oregon Law School after the School refused to hire a qualified Asian American woman.

In this interview with Stuart Crainer, Derrick Bell talks about the ethical questions now facing the corporate world in the wake of Enron, Worldcom, and other scandals.

As a lawyer and academic, people might question your credentials to talk about business ethics.

True. It's one thing to preach about living an ethical life in the world of academia—sure there's some power plays there and politics—but it's nothing like business. People might ask what do I know about this slug-it-out, beat-to-the-bottom-line, winner-takes-all world. I have avoided working within it. But it seems to me that the principles are similar. You won't succeed unless your primary concern is keeping hold of your integrity.

So you're right to think that the field of business is different, but I don't think it is possible to live a life without an ethical code. You need to look in the mirror.

So how can ambition be ethical? Aren't ambition and ethics mutually exclusive?

Ethics can be an integral part of your ambition. There is no lasting success that isn't ethically founded.

Ethical ambition means simultaneously honoring our values, our dreams and our needs. It requires critical compassion and honesty toward ourselves and others. It can be achieved only by thoughtfully and candidly assessing who we are, what we believe, what we value, and what we desire. It also involves sacrifice—not only of time and energy, but of inaccurate or outdated perceptions of ourselves and our lives. Many of us are thwarted in achieving our goals because when our values and desires clash, we are paralyzed. Others are disappointed with their lives because they surrender things—like hopes and convictions—that seemed to stand in the way of more material goals.

There are no universal codes of ethics are there? Nepotism, for example, is acceptable in Mexico but not in the United States.

That's a good example because nepotism inevitably leads to its own difficulties, even if no laws are broken and some of it works out okay. I guess the Ford family is a good example, though there are always excep-

tions. Basically, if you bring people in and shoot them up to the top, there are negative reverberations all the way down.

Looking back at your career, have you always looked in the mirror?

Of course, when I look back I see there were times when I thought I was doing right. At one point, for example, I was handling hundreds of school segregation suits and my marriage was probably a little shaky because my family hardly ever saw me. I was saving the world so far as I could see.

As I look back over those years I think, why didn't I recognize that I wasn't the white knight riding into town filing these suits? What I was doing was taking away leadership opportunities from people who were pretty much sidetracked waiting for this litigation to happen.

If some of the executives who are in so much trouble now had been able to look in the mirror, they might have sensed that what they were doing was not only wrong but would lead to disaster.

But isn't greed central to capitalism?

Perhaps we should use a word which is a little subtler! There was a guy, who I talk about in my book, who was determined to avoid the rat race of the big law firms—even though he had spectacular credentials and he joined a firm which had a reputation for treating people well. He did well there but he realized that, although he hadn't intended it, over time his primary goal became making money. That was the measure. He warned people about this.

It is the subtle things. You're doing the same job each time and you can do it in 15 minutes rather than an hour, but still bill an hour. Little things like that build up and build up. It's impressive but discouraging. It happens all the time. The secretaries who help themselves to stamps and paper. A small thing. But you'd really feel better about yourself buying your own goddamned pencils!

The question is good and my answer, though not very satisfying, is my answer. You don't have to sacrifice your integrity. When you do, even if it works and no-one catches you, there is a price to pay.

Is too much emphasis now given to shareholder value?

Placing a high priority on shareholder value, while seemingly a valid basis for corporate policymaking,

all too frequently serves as a shield for actions that, at best, are unethical and, at worst, criminal.

Such dealings include mergers like the hotly-contested combining of Hewlett Packard and Compaq, the principal benefits of which, according to opponents, will be increased profit through the dismissal of thousands of employees, and exorbitant payments to the top executives of the merging companies. With no apparent shame or remorse, businesses are setting up headquarters in Bermuda and other off-shore locales, as the toolmaker Stanley Works is attempting to do, so as to avoid U.S. taxes. To compete effectively, we are told, corporate America must move its manufacturing plants to third-world countries to exploit low labor rates and, coincidentally, take advantage of lax health and environmental laws.

But don't such measures benefit shareholders?

These and far more complicated tactics often serve to benefit company executives while placing shareholders at risk. The various maneuvers of Enron, aided and abetted by a major accounting company, Arthur Andersen, are examples of strategies that are hugely profitable for a time and then, when uncovered, are devastating to both employees and shareholders. The executives, unless indicted and convicted (quite difficult under U.S. laws), walk away, perhaps chastened, but still very rich.

So shareholder value is more a diversionary mantra than a guiding principle for many American corporations. Rather, the guiding principle is profit—however gained—that by the very nature of our free enterprise system, transforms reasonably honest business leaders into unbridled money grubbers ... particularly when government supervision is deregulated or rendered ineffective by political inaction and inadequate funding of regulatory agencies. Business executives of great intelligence, substantial business experience, and great wealth involve themselves in financial schemes that are not only unethical, but downright stupid.

What can be done?

As the scandals grow in number and in their blatant character, it is reasonable to ask whether anything can and should be done to clean up corporate America. The answer, beyond disgrace for those apprehended and small reforms in regulatory laws, is very little. Major corporations control the lives of ordinary citizens far more than the officials they elect, and those officials, with very few exceptions, are beholden to corporations for the funds that keep them in office—a goal evidently far more important to most of them than either personal integrity or making good on promises made when they were running for office. Aware that elections apparently have little to do with the important aspects of their lives, most people don't vote, and those who do are likely to be influenced more by TV ads—sponsored indirectly by major corporations—than by any careful and independent assessment of the candidates' records.

And truth be told, many working class Americans—themselves caught up in the hope that, through the lottery or some other similarly unlikely scheme, they will become rich—tend to admire as much as despise corporate corruption. When even the death of John Gotti, a notorious crime boss, captures the headlines, the interest and—let us say it—the admiration of the masses, public anger at wrongdoing in the executive suites is likely to be both minimal and brief.

And the solution?

There is no easy solution to an economic system that—while encouraging hard work, innovation, and risk-taking in the quest for financial success—develops in some the sense that becoming number one is more important than how you get there.

> **Material success has replaced justice and equality as the overarching social goal.**

There is, though, a challenge for those who view the maintenance of ethical standards for themselves and their companies as not only the prudent course, but the only means of achieving a success unburdened by lies, cover-ups, and the continuing fear that structures built with greed as the glue will come undone. For the rest of us, we can speak out against corporate corruption, encourage those reforms that can be enacted, and support those who find the courage to reveal what they know is wrong.

If, despite the best efforts of expensive lawyers, friendly politicians, and high-powered public relations experts, the corporate scandals manage to generate widespread disgust and a demand for action, perhaps reform advocates can establish a corporate truth and reconciliation commission. In lieu of prosecution, business executives might be offered the chance to explain in detail how they evolved from ambitious

> **[We] often feel that we must constantly choose between our beliefs and our goals, and end up either feeling guilty for succeeding, or morally intact but personally unfulfilled.**

and perhaps ethical young business people to the persons capable of the acts of which they are charged. If the testimony is forthright, society may gain an understanding of how success comes to be measured by wealth, power, and influence, rather than the commitment to integrity based on respect for self and others, that at some point gets jettisoned as the price of getting ahead.

Has the world become overly materialistic?

Material success has replaced justice and equality as the overarching social goal. On one hand, because many obvious barriers to outsider success—overt and legally-sanctioned prejudice—have been lifted or broken, material success *is* possible for those who only a generation or two ago might have had to put most of their energy into merely surviving. On the other hand, we still live in a society where racism,

sexism, homophobia, and other group prejudices remain viable despite public rhetoric to the contrary. In fact, huge disparities in income and opportunity are generally accepted because we believe that those who work hard make it, and those who don't, do not. We even believe this to some degree when we're working hard and not making it! All of this creates profound stress, because those of us who survive those challenges often feel that we must constantly choose between our beliefs and our goals, and end up either feeling guilty for succeeding, or morally intact but personally unfulfilled.

People have been talking about ethics and codes of behavior for decades. There is greater awareness, but it isn't necessarily practiced.

I have no doubt we are going to have some stronger rules. But the ideal set of rules, to keep money out of politics and so on, isn't going to be developed in a few days. Those who feel strongly need to campaign for reform.

The major beneficiaries of instituting higher ethical standards would be businesses, because it would build confidence and what have you, but they do not see that.

So in the short term, the number of abuses and examples of whistle blowing is likely to grow?

Yes. With whistle blowing, people tend to remember the guys who come out looking great and are heralded, but the overall record is not good. Whistle blowers get fired, don't get much recompense, can't prove their case, and then can't find another job very easily.

Are you optimistic that progress will continue to be made, or have things stalled?

Many of these things start off in a dramatic way of black and white but then evolve into other groups. Corporations now embrace diversity in its larger definition. White women have been the real beneficiaries of affirmative action in our country.

There is dramatic change in some areas. Things kind of go in waves, and that's true in the racial diversity issue. The waves are not necessarily motivated by the highest principles, but they're cyclical.

"Now there is one outstandingly important fact regarding Spaceship Earth, and that is that no instruction book came with it."

R. Buckminster Fuller

New Role Models for Enlightened Leadership

by Charles R. Day, Jr.

EXECUTIVE SUMMARY

Role-model executives will be those leaders who are able to:
- reengineer the corporate realm so that working for large companies is fashionable again
- both enunciate core values and hold organizations accountable for living them;
- align their organization's business goals with the needs of their communities to affirm that corporations are forces for good;
- distinguish the full potential of e-commerce to fully harness its opportunities;
- apply teaching skills and the art of persuasion to inspire individual creativity and innovation and build teams that appreciate a measure of structure and policy.

We should make no assumptions about where we will find such role models.

INTRODUCTION

As much as we might like to believe that 21st-century corporate role models will emerge from among executives of high promise at, for example, Sony, Ford, ABB, or Bayer, the odds are that they won't. We might just as well find them among rapidly growing high-tech companies in developing countries. Nor are we apt to inspire the leaders we seek by holding up the most accomplished executives of the late 20th century and declaring, "Do exactly as they do." However, what has been done before may not be what needs doing now.

Political boundaries aren't what they were. Attitudes about globalization continue to shift. So do markets. World currencies now include legal tender that didn't even exist five years ago—the Euro.

Corporate changes are just as striking. DaimlerChrysler confronts vastly different challenges today from those it faced as Daimler-Benz five years ago. The success that India's up-and-coming technology companies enjoy prompts fresh challenges such as leveraging their success to improve the future of fellow citizens along with their businesses. Japan's political and economic difficulties leave its corporations with the formidable task of revising their long-held strategies, attitudes, and practices while preserving their competitive zeal and their renowned work ethic.

Almost any company in any country could offer identical scenarios. Collectively they affirm that the corporate role models of this century will emerge as they did in the last one: by tackling the challenges of circumstances with imaginative strategies that their peers will want to emulate. Role models emerge amid the circumstances that distinguish our times.

UNDERSTANDING HOW CORPORATIONS ARE PERCEIVED

What distinguishes corporate life at the start of this millennium is that so many executives want to avoid it. Striking out as an entrepreneur has never looked so appealing, notwithstanding the risks, long hours, and long odds against success. Mainstream corporations, by comparison, now appear as unsavory as they did in the days of Charles Dickens.

We have laws that enable executives to extend their careers, and advances in healthcare that help them maintain their vitality. Yet executives and professionals rush to retirement or depart the corporate world to launch new ventures. To be sure, new ventures are vital sources of ingenuity. But our corporations also nourish our well-being, and they, too, need leadership.

Two additional factors make this circumstance more alarming: the combination of basic demographics and ruthless dismantling of middle management that have left corporations with fewer executives to groom; and the rise of nongovernmental organizations that pester the corporate world, with the more radical inciting chaos at every opportunity.

Large corporations are derided as the source of the world's ills, not its solutions. This is preposterous. The true means of providing food, shelter, and economic opportunity and of solving energy and environmental problems lie in business tapping its creativity and technology, not in politicians enacting laws. Yet many individuals argue precisely the opposite, and the amount of attention they receive gives their contention legitimacy.

RESTORING APPEAL IS PARAMOUNT

Leaders who restore the appeal of corporate life and make it fashionable again will be our role models. They succeed not just with personal charisma and financial rewards, but by articulating core values worthy of support, by identifying an exciting mission, by painting an inspiring vision, and by arousing passion for their cause. It's noteworthy that this is hardly a new challenge. What business theorists and students yearn for today echoes pleas of 25 years ago.

In this pursuit our new role models will need to reassess the role of the 21st-century business organization—and expand on it. This is a second area that needs attention.

The corporation's role in society has been studied almost as long as there have been corporations. Its importance often rises when economies falter as individuals discover that satisfaction in life isn't measured by income or stock options. Corporations and communities once enjoyed partnerships that nurtured each other. Our role-model leaders need to reconnect these partnerships for their mutual well-being. Certainly stockholders have legitimate interests, which may in fact take precedence over the interests of customers, employees, and communities. But these other stakeholders have valid interests, too. History shows that stockholders who support such initiatives will be rewarded far more handsomely than those who dismiss them as well-meaning but meaningless. Indeed, the opposition to corporations suggests how short-sighted and dangerous this can be.

Role models will also emerge in two other contexts. One is apparent and is the need to *explore the potential of e-commerce*. The other context that will produce role model leaders is *the need for teaching and team building*.

"You just have to be the kind of guy to get people to do things."   Donald Trump

Certainly the notion that the Internet would suddenly challenge traditional retail channels was folly. But it's just as foolish not to discover just what the Net can do. For example, manufacturers envision harnessing e-commerce to deliver diagnostic services to customers and strengthen and extend business relationships far beyond initial purchase. Any number of marketers, meanwhile, are relying on the Internet to build personal relationships with consumers by learning more and more about their needs—after first obtaining their permission. Where this will end we can't imagine. But it starts with someone with the humility to acknowledge that they don't know, and the enthusiastic curiosity to find out.

The very top ranks of young talent may well be better educated and motivated than previous generations, but the masses are probably not. Moreover, a case could be made that many are not as eager to learn, in part because they've grown up more independently and learned to do things their own way. There's also evidence that suggests employees desire more balance in their lives. A study conducted recently by Jobtrak.com asked more than 2,000 college students and recent graduates, Which do you value most in your career decision? The largest number of respondents, 42%, chose balancing work and personal life. Just 26% said compensation, and 23% indicated advancement potential. Such attitudes may well make teaching and team building more challenging, but they also make them more important.

MINI-CASES

Toyota's Web site, Gazoo.com, helps Japan's leading automobile manufacturer to speed up the disposal of used autos as it provides a wealth of customer data that may eventually lead to the development of a new vehicle. Gazoo.com is also helping Toyota

retain young, restless employees who might otherwise strike out for careers in the computer industry.

Cemex, Mexico's leading producer of cement, is demonstrating that e-business has applications in the mature world of commodity products. It's relying on data both to manufacture cement and to deliver it on a just-in-time basis. The company's delivery vehicles are linked to its computers, enabling them to arrive with shipments at precisely the times they're needed. E-business has changed how Cemex conducts all its business and made it the most profitable in its field.

Manco, a Henkel Group company headquartered in Avon, Ohio, musters as much enthusiasm as Duck Tape, its flagship product. Now in its second generation of family leadership, the company generates a plethora of ideas inspired by its duck mascot that inspire employees to say, I want to be part of that. Executives have leaped into icy ponds in March to celebrate milestones, and when the company hit $100 million in sales it treated the entire workforce to a musical performance at a restored downtown theater.

A leading auto producer has put a new twist on a familiar idea. Volkswagen opened its Autostadt complex in Wolfsburg, Germany, in 2000. Adjacent to corporate headquarters, the museum helps VW's customers and community understand the company, its products, and its contributions.

MAKING IT HAPPEN ▶▶

A manager needs to ask:
- What are the organizational core values that guide all your activities?
- What is your organization's mission? What is it in business to do?
- How do you envision your organization acting when it is older?

- Why does your organization matter? Why would it be missed if it disappeared?
- What *won't* your organization do in conducting business? What limits must be set?
- In addition to owners and stockholders, what stakeholders have a stake in the organization's success?
- What operations and procedures might be improved and benefit from e-commerce?

CONCLUSION

Human nature prompts us to believe that role models of 21st-century leadership will mirror those of the past. Most likely they won't, because conditions and circumstances conspire to pose new challenges. Those challenges in turn breed a new generation of leadership.

We should begin our search for corporate role models by studying executives who strive to make corporations not only successful, but appealing. In all likelihood we'll be introduced to some heretofore unknown individuals from unsung organizations.

FOR MORE INFORMATION

Books:
Collins, James C., and Jerry I. Porras. *Built to Last: Successful Habits of Visionary Companies.* New York: HarperBusiness, 1997.
Downs, Alan. *Seven Miracles of Management.* New York: Penguin, 1998.
Levine, Rick, et al. *The Cluetrain Manifesto: The End of Business as Usual.* Cambridge, MA: Perseus, 2001.
Tichy, Noel M., and Eli Cohen. *The Leadership Engine: How Winning Companies Build Leaders at Every Level.* New York: HarperBusiness, 2002.

"The next phase of advanced capitalist expansion will hark back to Robert Owen's enlightened experiments . . . [which proved] that a major investment in employee morale more than paid for itself in productivity."
Theodore Roszak

Viewpoint: Jim Collins
Creating the Vision of Managers Growing from Good to Great

Introduction

Jim Collins's career, since the publication of *Built to Last*, which he coauthored with Jerry Porras, has been meteoric. A bestseller for six years, that book has been through 70 printings and has been translated into 16 languages. More recently, Collins's book, *Good to Great*, has garnered an even wider audience. "Good is the enemy of great," Collins believes. But how a company achieves greatness is a lesson too few managers have taken the time to learn. Collins has dedicated the rest of his career to teaching that lesson to everyone he can. The following text is by Tom Brown; it is based upon one of his many conversations with Jim Collins.

What we have to keep in mind, when we think of what is "state-of-the-art" in management, is that this field is much more science than art. The conditions and the nature of business may change, but the principles of management really do not. So, if you want to think about the world in 2050, it's a sure thing that business will be different, but it's also a sure thing that many of the basic truths of management won't.

Think about the managers—that's what they were, whatever name they used—who built the pyramids. Given the tools and technology they had (and leaving aside labor relations practices we might frown on today!), those Egyptians were using sound management principles to get the work done. You could pick numerous events or personalities throughout history to make this same point. There was a great deal of management required of Christopher Columbus in his daunting expedition involving those three tiny ships, and he managed the challenge admirably. Sure, the scope and complexity of the challenge may be dramatically different, but, essentially, the people managing NASA today are doing the same basic kinds of things that Columbus had to do. So, while the marketplace and organizational conditions under which you manage a group or a process may change, most of the fundamentals that define the superb manager remain the same, at heart, in 1350 and in 2050.

Why this is incredibly important to me is that my own mission in this field of study is to define what's immutable about management and leadership. Perhaps that's why many see my work as different from that of the many other authors who are writing today. Many management thinkers see themselves as engineers; I guess they see management as a form of engineering. Management, to many, is a series of "wheels and pulleys"—and people—that, if configured

just right, will work! I'm much more of a physicist. I'm striving to research and write about the eternal laws, the unyielding principles, that inform sound management thinking.

I am indebted to Jerry Porras in so many ways, not only as a coauthor, but as a mentor. More than anyone else, he set me on a path that I hope to stay on as long as I can continue to make a contribution. But I am indebted to him in one fundamental way, in particular. What Jerry gave me was a lifelong gift—and it wasn't a set of ideas, a list of bullet points, or a point of view. Jerry didn't give me content; he gave me *method*.

Once I discovered the importance of method in the field of management, my career horizons changed. Jerry stressed the importance of taking on a big question and then using the right toolkit to go about answering that question! He stressed—time after time, year after year—that the world will accept the answer to a truly major question only if one has a rock-solid method. So, on *Built to Last*, where Jerry and I spent years trying to outline the immutable laws of visionary leadership, it was the utilization of controlled comparisons that was the breakthrough.

Prior to *Built to Last*, no other piece of management research that I'm aware of tried to look at two sets of companies, one set visionary and the other could-have-beens. Each company under study was matched to a "peer" within its own industry, and we studied what they did and didn't do over their entire life span. What was truly great about the approach was that it developed a new kind of scientific method of inquiry in the field of management, in order to tackle major questions. And, as we all now know, the approach yields insights that can be breathtaking. So, the approach I now have used for years and that I am trying

"In the built to flip world, the notion of investing persistent effort in order to build a great company seems, well, quaint, unnecessary, even stupid."

Jim Collins

to hone each day is quantitative and qualitative—but, most of all, it's scientific. It is a process that leads to true insights, and there is simply no way to cut the cycle time to arrive at compelling, confirmable insights about how to manage and lead.

What, then are the most important management "truths" today that people should be thinking about, reading about, and acting upon?

To answer that, let me go back to 1998. A group of people like me, authors and others who give a lot of thought to the world and leadership in general, came together to talk about our commonly held ideas, if any—or, at least, our commonly held concerns. As so often happens at these events, the discussion turned to what the future would be like 50 years out. When it came my turn to comment, I said that I really didn't know what the world would be like in 2050, but that I had a wish. Wouldn't it be fascinating, I asked the group, if we could know what another group of thinkers—meeting in 50 years—would smile and shake their heads at when they thought about what we, today, hold to be truths about the world? Putting it a different way, I asked this: "What do we, today, take for granted, that in just 50 years our successors will marvel that we actually believed to be true?"

That meeting was held on the top floor of one of the towers of the World Trade Center in New York.

Now, think about that. In just a few years, the assumption has been completely shattered that it would be risk-free to hold a meeting in the United States, because the United States is, after all, a safe cocoon. That's a world view that has been irreversibly changed. The United States now sees the world as those who live in Europe or Israel do or those in Brazil, who have to hire armed guards to surround their houses so they can sleep at night. But all this underscores the need for managers to be ever mindful of the value of adaptability: while you're operating at full tilt, you still have to be ready to confront new and perhaps quite unexpected challenges.

If there is a new key management question for all of us to focus on, it might be this. How does one run any business, government, company, university in an unsafe and terribly chaotic world? I believe the answer to that question inevitably brings leaders to address two priorities that are much closer to home and are, therefore, much more manageable.

In an unsafe and uncertain world, managers must determine what their organization has to contribute to the world that no other institution can. It is terribly important for managers to be emphatically clear about what it is that their enterprise can (1) be deeply passionate about, (2) be the best in the world at doing, and (3) have as a sufficient economic engine to keep the business going forward. I derived this viewpoint after thinking long about Isaiah Berlin's famous essay, *The Hedgehog and the Fox*. Too many businesses are fox-like (fast, sleek, beautiful), but they miss the very essence of greatness because, unlike the hedgehog, they do not understand what it is that makes them unique, powerful, and altogether unassailable.

But there's another point to make. In an uncertain world, managers must find the right people to help them make that special and unique contribution. I commented once, and I meant it, that too many companies spend too much time trying to motivate the right behavior in the wrong people, rather than getting the right people in the first place. For *Good to Great*, a team of researchers and I searched through 1,435 companies to find the small number that made the leap from average results to truly great results and that sustained those results for at least 15 years. The good-to-great companies did not just hire anyone, then try to train them. Instead, they looked, and waited, and looked some more, in order to find the exact caliber of people they needed to make the company operationally strong and financially profitable.

Only then, when they had "the right people on the bus," did they start to fine-tune things like vision, strategy, and structure. It's an important lesson. By concentrating on finding only the right people for your organization and by giving those people liberal access to capitalize on your organization's best opportunities, you create an enterprise which can weather storms of uncertainty because the right people are, in general, focused on what your company does the best—and they are working at their own personal best. It's not an insurance policy against occasional setbacks, but it's the closest thing there is. Study any great company, and you'll find the pattern clear.

You cannot make the world either safe or certain. No one can. But what you can do is to make sure that you, and the people you hire, commit to being the very best at what you do. Don't settle for just being good. There's too much of that already. We have good schools, because people aren't committed to having great ones. There's good government, because people don't want to invest themselves in establishing great government. And too many companies miss the chance to be great simply because they sanction the attitude that "being good is good enough."

I fervently believe that nearly *any* company can become a great one. How greatness is achieved in the organizational world is the scientific breakthrough that I have been privileged to study and write about after investing more than a decade in thinking about what separates great from good. Greatness is not conferred, nor does it come by luck or through an inheritance: it comes when leaders commit themselves and all who work with them to becoming the very best at what they collectively do. Deep, personal commitment precedes greatness. There is no other way.

FOR MORE INFORMATION

Web site:
www.jimcollins.com

See also:
☆ Designing Corporate Systems for Success (pp. 212–213)
☆ Workers without Borders: Creating Bonds When Workers Have No Loyalty (pp. 237–238)

"One of the most important tasks of a manager is to eliminate his people's excuses for failure."

Robert Townsend

Transcending the Glass Ceiling
by Katherine Hammer

EXECUTIVE SUMMARY

- Since the first version of this essay appeared in 2002, women have made little headway in attaining top management positions.
- Although women now hold more than 50% of all management and professional positions, they make up less than 2% of *Fortune* 500 and *Fortune* 1000 C.E.O.s (1.8% of the Fortune 500 and 1.9% of the top 1000).
- Only 16% of women earn six-figure salaries, and only 15% of the dollars loaned to business in the United States are loaned to women-owned businesses, almost none of that coming from venture capitalists.
- While four years is a relatively short period of time, global economic and political factors make it unlikely that men in power will become more open-minded in the not-too-distant future.
- Yet it may be women's superior skills at the "take care" behavior of supporting and rewarding that will allow them to transform the world, but not by withdrawing to home and hearth (as a recent article in the *New York Times* suggested that female undergraduates at Yale are planning to do). Rather the glass ceiling might be considered a boot camp, a rigorous training ground for understanding how things work. Then, if frustrated in their efforts to attain top leadership in business, women have the option of using these skills in addressing social and political challenges.
- While these positions perhaps have fewer perks and glamour than being the C.E.O. of a *Fortune* 500 company, in the long run they have the potential to bring more benefit to a larger group of people.

INTRODUCTION

Catalyst defines itself as "the leading research and advisory organization working with businesses and the professions to build inclusive environments and expand opportunities for women at work." This organization has been consistently ranked No. 1 among U.S. nonprofits focused on women's issues by the American Institute of Philanthropy. In 2002, a Catalyst survey of *Fortune* 1000 company C.E.O.s cited two major factors holding women back:

- a lack of line/management experience (82%)
- the fact that women haven't been in the pipeline long enough (64%)

Almost four years later, women held over 50% of all management positions and made up 57% of the undergraduates on U.S. campuses, where the gap is projected to increase to 60/40 by 2010. Yet despite this progress, in October 2005 Catalyst released a report entitled *Women "Take Care," Men "Take Charge": Stereotyping of U.S. Business Leaders Exposed*, which suggests that the real deterrent to promotion is one of skills rather than experience.

When asked about their perceptions about women's and men's leadership behavior, both women and men considered women to be superior to men in "take care" behavior like supporting and rewarding, and men to be superior in "take charge" behavior like delegating and influencing upward. It is not surprising that women might prefer the type of consensus-based management characterized by supporting and rewarding since they historically come from a weaker base of power. In these situations, solidarity and loyalty are powerful tools that are better nurtured than commanded. However, this difference is less disturbing than the judgments made about the ability to problem solve. While women respondents said that women were better at problem solving than men, men respondents—who are largely responsible for the selection of C.E.O.s—said that "men were most superior to women in problem-solving and effectiveness." And perhaps it is that last word, "effectiveness," that is the most important factor here; as the report suggests, it is the commitment of the subordinates to follow the directions of the leader directing them that determines whether a solution to a problem works.

BREAKING THE GLASS CEILING
Coping with Sexism

There's little doubt that sexism plays some role in all this and sometimes the behavior can be particularly offensive. I was once interviewed for a university teaching position sitting on the edge of a bed in a Chicago hotel while four male interviewers sat on chairs, asking whether I intended to have another child. Four years ago, a woman with her own venture-capital company told me that at board meetings of one of her companies, the other venture capitalists (all male) occasionally call a bathroom break to discuss something without including her. During the entrepreneurial boom of the dot-com frenzy, I belonged to a social group of fifteen or so women in Austin, Texas, all of whom were C.E.O.s or principals of high-tech businesses. Now only one of them remains as C.E.O. of a for-profit business; the rest have gravitated to nonprofits or are seeking their next engagement. I myself recently voluntarily stepped down from the role of C.E.O. of the company I founded fifteen years ago. In working with my hand-picked successor, an extremely bright and talented man of forty, I was regularly irritated by his asking me not to be so emotional (gloss: irrational) when I became impassioned about something, while his expressions of irritation and anger were expected to go unnoticed.

In short, sexism exists. Things aren't fair and that's not news. For some group at every time in history, things have not been fair. The fact that in this case the discriminating factors are connected to gender doesn't change the situation. Fortunately, in most industrialized countries the degree of prejudice has not gone so far as to prevent women from seeking an education or a career. For those of us who have the skill and ambition to get within sight of the glass ceiling, the question becomes this: what can a woman do to increase her chances of breaking through that barrier?

MAXIMIZING OUR CHANCES

In an earlier Catalyst survey, 1,251 women with titles of vice-president and above in *Fortune* 1000 companies (37% response rate) largely attributed their success to several factors:

"Anytime you have a fiercely-competitive, change-oriented growth business where results count and merit matters, women will rise to the top."

Carly Fiorina

- consistently exceeding expectations (77%);
- developing a style their managers were comfortable with (61%);
- seeking out difficult assignments (50%).

Yet the number of women C.E.O.s in venture-backed companies remains exceptionally low. Why? Venture capital is predominantly a man's game, but it's also a game in which success and failure are clearly delineated—and often success requires a public offering. Both in the process of taking a company public and in dealing with the financial analysts after the company is traded, the C.E.O. must consistently exude confidence and authority.

Most women who seek funding don't understand that venture-capital providers are judging how they would stand up to the Street. Any nervousness, lack of conviction—any failing at all—contributes to their concern that a woman doesn't have what it takes. I recall that one of the partners in the company that was to become my company's first venture investor was disturbed that my voice was shaky when I started to present. In short, even as an entrepreneur a woman must mind her manner.

Beyond image and style, a woman must command many business fundamentals to win venture-capital investors. In addition to understanding how private financing works, she must be able to:

- deliver a crisp business plan demonstrating the potential for substantial growth with a good go-to-market strategy;
- attract a strong management team;
- have a vision for a path to liquidity.

A number of organizations and forums exist for helping women attain these skills, including the San Francisco-based Forum for Women Entrepreneurs, and Springboard Enterprises, based in Washington, DC.

One shouldn't underestimate the importance of developing a style that male managers are comfortable with, particularly if the goal is serving as C.E.O. of a public company. In fact, one of the primary concerns that venture capitalists have about the C.E.O.s of the companies in which they invest is not whether the individual in question has the operational management skills (or the ability to attract and work with those that do), but how that individual will be perceived by the financial community.

STAYING THE COURSE

In terms of character, a woman's success tends to be dependent upon her tenacity, her endurance, and her ability to recognize her own failings.

- **Accept that mishaps will occur.** The most important skill the ambitious woman must acquire is the tenacity to persevere. Success grows out of the courage to learn from the misery of failure and come to terms with its major causes—mishap, malice, and miscalculation. There will be *mishaps*—downturns in the economic sector that change customers' spending, technical glitches with the product, unexpected competitors. Such failures will be recognized as coming from external factors and thus will have little long-term effect on a woman's career if she has otherwise performed effectively. The aspiring woman should simply learn from such events and resolve to be more diligent in trying to anticipate such turns on future projects.
- **Recognize the potential for malice.** *Malice* is another matter. There's much historical evidence that jealousy or fear is the cause of many conflicts. Sometimes coworkers may be jealous that the woman in question has been successful, even if she has done nothing to diminish their stature. In this case the harm will probably be slight—gossip in the coffee room—because if the malevolent coworkers had power or were in the game, they'd simply compete. Far more serious is malice that comes from a worthy contender threatened by the woman's success. However, if a woman is committed to beating the statistics, she should expect the path to be difficult.
- **Acknowledge miscalculations—and move on.** *Miscalculation* is one of the hardest sources of failure to acknowledge, because the woman must recognize that her instincts and judgments were flat-out wrong. While the term "mistake" suggests a simple act of omission or oversight, miscalculation suggests that your best efforts at solving a problem were flawed. A woman's success in learning from failures stemming from miscalculation frequently requires her to recognize shortcomings within herself—a tendency to lose her temper or reveal more than she should, a misjudgment about another person's capabilities or passion, or some behavior on her part that instilled malice in someone who could have been, if not a supporter, a bystander.

Successful people transcend the impediments they encounter, whether self-made, external, or a combination of the two. If a woman wants to succeed in obtaining and retaining a top-level position, she should be committed to regularly examining and modifying her own beliefs, skills, and reactions.

Rethinking the Metaphor

While perseverance is key to success, so is the ability to recognize a losing battle and live to fight another day. Sometimes there's no winning, and if the woman is talented and performing, it may well be because the organization has a lead ceiling. In this case if she doesn't recognize the futility of her efforts and leave, she's likely to self-destruct and behave so negatively as to damage her reputation or to give up the fight altogether. The clue to recognizing a losing battle is when a woman continues to encounter resistance and experience frustration even after she has changed her own behavior and won multiple battles. In my own case at Texas Instruments, I had survived the hostility of my first boss and modified my style to deal successfully with my second boss—only to realize that the company's assumptions about how to approach the software marketplace were flawed. Only then did I realize that nothing I did would ultimately make a difference.

However, defeat in one venue doesn't necessarily require withdrawing from the war. The key to a woman's success is the ability to recognize what is really important to her. If it's beating the boys at their own game, a woman's future—for the next few generations anyway—may be limited. But if her goal is to make a difference in the world, a clear-eyed understanding of each defeat can lead to new opportunities because of the skill she gained in the struggle. One should never underestimate the value of resistance. It's resistance that builds muscle in a body, and it's the struggle that builds strength of character. If what's important to a woman is to make a difference in the world, her professional struggles may lead to a different kind of leadership. In fact, in the public arena, the "take care" skills of women may help her win the top post, as suggested by a recent editorial on the election of Ellen Johnson Sirleaf of Liberia and Michelle Bachelet of Chile as their countries' first woman president ("Where Political Clout Demands a Maternal Touch,", the *New York Times*, January 22, 2006.)

> **MAKING IT HAPPEN** ▸▸
> - Develop a plan to master the fundamentals of business. Whether inside a major corporation or with venture capital providers, a woman enhances her chances of success by being able to deliver a good business plan, and thus by knowing how to run a successful enterprise.

"Women are becoming enormously successful . . . They're running their businesses on what we call a familial model, a family, instead of a hierarchical top-down military model. They work with, not over or for."

Faith Popcorn

- Be willing to face mishap, malice, and miscalculation with perseverance. However, this doesn't mean tolerating the status quo. If you're in a losing battle, become an adventurer: look for the new path, new opportunity, new direction that can completely change your opportunities for achievement—success as *you* define it!

CONCLUSION

The statistics for women in business are not heartening. The path is long and hard, and it will be many more generations before things change. But the difficulty can be tempered by attitude. There are two paths to spiritual growth—that of the warrior and that of the adventurer. While both paths require courage and skill, the two result in very different lives. The warrior feels a duty to fight wrong wherever she encounters it, while the adventurer's focus is on the journey and the goal. The adventurer would rather avoid evil or move around or through it, fighting only as a last resort. Given the difficulty of succeeding in business regardless of sex, a woman will be best served if she adopts the path of the adventurer and finds another path to victory rather than spending her creative energy butting her head against a glass ceiling.

FOR MORE INFORMATION

Web sites:
Advancing Women:
www.advancingwomen.com/intlinks.html
Alliance for Business Women International:
www.abwi.org

Catalyst: **www.abwi.org**
National Foundation for Women Business
Owners: **www.nfwbo.org**
United Nations Women Watch:
www.un.org/womenwatch

See also:

Viewpoint: Henry Mintzberg
Taking Management on a Strategy Safari

Introduction

Mintzberg has set the agenda in the sphere of strategic management with a combination of academic rigor and a devotion to seeking out new perspectives, which has generally set him apart from his contemporaries. This reached a climax with the publication of *The Rise and Fall of Strategic Planning*, which sounded the death knell for the strategic planning orthodoxy that had long dominated management thinking and education. One of his more recent books is *Strategy Safari*, coauthored with Bruce Ahlstrand and Joseph Lampel.

Mintzberg has proved a relentless thorn in the side of conventional business school education. The fruit of his dissatisfaction was the International Masters Program in Practicing Management, a thoroughly global program that encourages managers to break free of the limitations of functional, and other, perspectives.

What is the most important thing and who is the most important person to have influenced your thinking on business and management?

I'm not sure I was so much influenced by any one individual. It's not as if I studied under somebody closely or something like that. But probably the most influential thinker for me was Herbert Simon.

He influenced me in two ways. He influenced me positively because his thinking about organizations was so far advanced and sophisticated that it had a very large impact on how I thought about things. And the other way because he eventually took an extreme view of intuition, such a narrow view of intuition, in fact, that his writing drove me in the opposite direction. He had such a strong belief in analysis and analytical processes that it drove me towards a much stronger belief in intuitive and soft processes and really questioning our obsession with analysis. I'm not opposed to analysis at all. I think it's a component. I think management is a practice and craft that uses science wherever it can. But it's not a science, and the emphasis on the analytical is very dangerous. So Simon influenced me both positively and negatively.

As far as the thing that influenced me—that's trickier. My wife was just reading an old article of mine, and she asked to borrow a book by Robert Ornstein, called *The Psychology of Consciousness*, which was the first book that put together key research about the left and right hemispheres of the brain. I think that research—that thing if you like—had a lot of influence on me.

The other thing that stands out is the whole experience around the IMPM—the International Masters Program in Practicing Management that I've been involved with over the ten years. That really grew out of

the fact that I was criticizing MBA programs, and people were saying "What are you doing about it?" The fact that we started doing something about it, and what we've learned from that, has had a big influence on me.

How will business be different in the 21st century?

My feeling about prediction is that anybody who could have predicted the September 11 events should feel free to predict other things. In other words nobody ever predicts anything with any accuracy. So it's simply not worth it. I discovered recently that this is the position that Peter Drucker took, but I've always believed that.

Basically, predictions are based on extrapolations. Optimists extrapolate what they like, and pessimists extrapolate what they don't like. And nobody ever gets it right. But nobody is ever held to account because nobody ever goes back and looks. So I think it's a waste of time to do those kinds of predictions. I can talk about trends that I find positive and trends that I find negative. Which ones are going to dominate? I don't know.

> Basically, predictions are based on extrapolations. Optimists extrapolate what they like, and pessimists extrapolate what they don't like. And nobody ever gets it right.

In the last ten years a trend that I've found extremely negative, for example, is shareholder value and the whole kind of mercenary view of management that has taken over. Economists have taken over the world. That's been a very negative factor because we've got completely out of balance. I would hope another trend, one that is broader, more humanistic, and open to human beings rather than simply inter-

---

"The key managerial processes are enormously complex and mysterious, drawing on the vaguest of information and using the least articulated of mental processes."

ested in maximizing shareholder value, will redress the balance.

What new skills will be needed to cope with these changes?

I don't think they are new skill sets. I think they're probably very old skill sets. I don't think management changes that much. We're in a period of what I would call heroic management: a period where the great hero rides in on a white horse with the dramatic new strategy and the massive merger. These huge dramatic events impress the stock market—at least the financial analysts first and then the market—and then the hero rides off into the sunset with the bonuses while the company collapses a year or two afterwards. Nortel was a classic example.

My hope is that we'll go back to some common sense. I think good managers are very thoughtful people. Some more thoughtfulness wouldn't be a bad idea. Social responsibility as opposed to shareholder value wouldn't be a bad idea. Not social responsibility in terms of sticking to the letter of the law and doing the minimum for everyone except the shareholders, but a responsible stance—nuanced management, where managers appreciate the different sides of arguments and don't just grab at simplistic techniques and simple-minded strategy. What I call "managing quietly." I wrote an article a few years ago about that. ["Managing Quietly," *Leader to Leader*, Spring 1999 (**www.drucker.com**)]

You said in that article that good management is often quite dull, and it is the business press that seeks dramatic leadership. Do you think that's still the case?

I'm not sure that dull is exactly the word; let's rather say quiet and steady and determined to make sure that things get corrected and function well and that organizations get strong. We had a presentation by one of my colleagues, Meg Graham, who wrote a book on Corning with its 50 years of alliances and how it managed alliances, and it's a perfect example of that. Very, very solid. They just kind of worked at it and did it. The press would grab at the techniques, but really it's the culture of those alliances that made that company strong—how they approach things.

Are there new management questions we should be asking?

I'm back to my other comment: there are old management questions we should be asking. I think just looking more deeply at management itself, and organizations themselves, and getting away from all this

hype about technique and heroic leaders and just understanding more in depth. We need to develop managers who are much more thoughtful and believe things and understand things much more deeply than happens now.

How can companies best promote enterprises that are a) profitable and b) good places for people to work?

I have to repeat what I've been saying. What's needed is more thoughtfulness. More of a social bonding process so there's a sense of community in the organization, a belief in what the organization is trying to achieve. Look at the organizations that have sustained high performance—that are just good, remain good, stay good, and keep going. Like Shell, perhaps. There's a sense of depth, there's a sense of a culture, a sense of a deep understanding and belief in the business, a sense of commitment. These are all old-fashioned things, but they are important things.

> I think good managers are very thoughtful people. Some more thoughtfulness wouldn't be a bad idea. Social responsibility as opposed to shareholder value wouldn't be a bad idea.

FOR MORE INFORMATION

Book:
Mintzberg, Henry. *Managers, Not MBAs: A Hard Look at the Soft Practice of Managing and Management Development.* Upper Saddle River, NJ: Pearson, 2004.

See also:

"Professional management is an invention that produced gain in organizational efficiency so great that it eventually destroyed organizational effectiveness."

Henry Mintzberg

Governing the Corporation
by Hugh Parker

EXECUTIVE SUMMARY

- It is often assumed that there is a direct and clear causal link between the actions of the board and the success of the organization, measured in terms of such factors as profitability, reputation, and stock price. In reality, this link to business performance is rarely strong, ranging from satisfactory to weak.
- There is renewed emphasis on corporate governance—not only how well the organization succeeds, but how well it is run and regulated, formally and informally.
- An extensive worldwide survey conducted by McKinsey & Company found compelling evidence that the stock of companies perceived by informed investors to have strong and effective boards of directors command a premium of as much as 20% on their stock price.
- There are six specific ways by which board effectiveness can be enhanced, and one of these—and the most important—is to separate the roles of chair and C.E.O.

INTRODUCTION

"Whenever an institution malfunctions as consistently as boards of directors have in nearly every major fiasco of the last forty or fifty years, it is futile to blame men. It is the institution that malfunctions." (Peter Drucker)

While it is difficult to prove conclusively that there is a direct causal relationship between the effectiveness of a company's board of directors and that company's performance in the marketplace, there is plenty of evidence to show that a weak and ineffectual board—especially one dominated by a powerful C.E.O.—will sooner or later commit strategic or other errors that will seriously damage the company's performance, and in some cases bring it to the brink of ruin.

Partly as a result of such well-publicized shipwrecks, and partly as the result of persistent initiatives by Robert Monks and other so-called stockholder activists, steps have been taken by some companies to obviate some of the more egregious boardroom malpractices. But many of these, like the 1994 "General Motors Board Guidelines of Significant Governance Issues," have been largely cosmetic changes aimed at improving the public perception of a board's effectiveness rather than attacking the problem at its root.

The real problem is that in most U.S. companies today there is a huge imbalance between the effective power of the C.E.O. on the one hand, and the nominal authority on the other hand of the board by which the C.E.O. is appointed and to which he or she is legally accountable. The C.E.O.'s delegated authority becomes absolute power, and the board's authority—vested in it by statute and bylaws—becomes effectively powerless.

WHY BOARDS ARE NOT INCREASING THEIR EFFECTIVENESS

In spite of all the attention focused in recent years on the quality of corporate governance—i.e., on the effectiveness (or not) of public company boards of directors—and in spite of efforts made to improve them, most boards are today only marginally more effective than they were ten years ago. There are several causes for this systematic weakness:

1 **For a long time—and largely by custom—boards have not been in a position to really govern the business.** Boards of directors on both sides of the Atlantic have almost never fully performed the trustee role for which they are legally accountable to the stockholders by whom they are elected. By tradition and long habit, boards of directors have always been more or less honorary bodies of which little action has either been expected or wanted. Board meetings have typically consisted of routine rituals, through which members are led by a chair/C.E.O. who is equipped with information, inside knowledge, and staff support so that they can and generally do control the agenda absolutely. So while boards have the legal authority, it is the C.E.O.s who have the effective power.

2 **Combining the offices of chair and C.E.O. reduces effectiveness.** Combining the offices of board chair and C.E.O. in one person virtually guarantees that the board will be ineffectual. A board can only be as independent and effective as its chair wants it to be and is capable of making it. An independent chair must be able to look his or her C.E.O. in the eye and say "This is my board and I do not agree with you and your management on this issue." But clearly this will never happen if the two offices are combined. Yet this combination is still the norm in over 80% of U.S. companies (but less than 20% of U.K. companies).

3 **Most U.S. boards are simply too big.** In 1998, 70% of the *Fortune* 500 companies had boards with 12 or more members, and 20% had 15 or more. There are several reasons for these high numbers, not least being the realization by some C.E.O.s that the larger the board the less effective it will be in monitoring and controlling his or her performance. Experience has shown that beyond a total of about seven or eight members, a board's effectiveness tends to become inversely proportional to its size.

4 **Too many supposedly "independent" directors are just not qualified to do the job properly.** They often lack the experience, character, and basic financial and other skills required in today's environment. Even worse, although they are elected by the stockholders, in practice they have almost always been selected and nominated by the C.E.O. and rubber-stamped by the board and stockholders. So the wrong people get on corporate boards for the wrong reasons, and their supposed independence is a myth.

5 **Most external directors lack the motivation and/or the time to do the job properly.** Annual fees for directors tend to cluster around $50,000. For an active C.E.O. earning $500,000 or more (plus options) in another company this is too little to justify more than a day or two per month. But for an academic or retired admiral with an income of $100,000

or less, it is too much to put at risk by being too independent, so they tend to support the chair who appointed them.

6 **Lack of relevant information.** Nearly all outsider directors have less information and knowledge about the company and its problems than the C.E.O. whom they are supposed to monitor and judge, and they are entirely dependent on that C.E.O. and his or her management for what information they do have. Thus these outsider directors often only learn about critical strategic and policy issues when things go seriously wrong, by which time it is too late for anything but crisis management and damage limitation. This usually takes the form of replacing the C.E.O., whose successor must then do whatever he or she can to salvage the company.

REEMPOWERING THE LEADERSHIP OF THE BOARD

Corporate governance has evolved differently in each of the major OECD countries. The governance system in each reflects the history, culture, economics, social values, and legal system in that country. One of these variables can be called the degree of "stockholder primacy"—i.e., putting the stockholders' interest first—which today ranges from very high in the United States, moderate in Germany, low in France, and virtually nil in Japan. In the United States

and United Kingdom especially, there are growing pressures from stockholders—which nowadays means the institutional investors—to make the boards of their portfolio companies more responsive and accountable to their stockholders. Hence the current interest in improving corporate governance.

If there is one lesson to be learned by U.S. boards from recent British experience it is the emergence of the independent nonexecutive chair. During the 1970s and 1980s a number of corporate shipwrecks of some highly respected U.K. companies—such as Burmah Oil and Rolls Royce—raised serious questions about the competence of company boards in general, which in turn led to the appointment in 1991 of Sir Adrian Cadbury's "Committee on the Financial Aspects of Corporate Governance." In 1992 this Committee published its "Code of Best Practice" which proposed, among other things, that "There should be a clearly accepted division of responsibilities at the head of a company, which will ensure a balance of power and authority, with no individual having unfettered powers."

The Cadbury "Code of Best Practice" was adopted by the London Stock Exchange. Companies listed on the Exchange are now required to state in their annual reports the extent to which they have complied with each of the code's provisions, and noncompliance must be explained. The growing practice in the United Kingdom of separating the roles of chair and C.E.O. has restored

a better balance between them. It is time for more U.S. companies to adopt this practice.

The most common objection in the United States to this separation of roles is that it is "divisive": that it will lead to indecision and political infighting in the boardroom, that this will undermine the authority of the C.E.O., and that this in turn will weaken the leadership of the company. This view fails to understand that there are two quite different and distinct roles: one managing the board of directors, the other managing the company. The chair is responsible for the former and his or her jurisdiction is confined to the boardroom. The C.E.O. bears full responsibility for managing the company with the authority and powers delegated to the board to which he or she is accountable.

FOR MORE INFORMATION

Books:
Conger, Jay A., Edward E. Lawler, III, and David L. Finegold. *Corporate Boards: New Strategies for Adding Value at the Top.* San Francisco, CA: Jossey-Bass, 2001.
Garten, Jeffrey E. *The Mind of the C.E.O.* New York: Perseus, 2001.

Web site:
www.conference-board.org: the Conference Board created this Web page to list key links to resources on corporate board issues.

Boardroom Roles
by Adrian Cadbury

EXECUTIVE SUMMARY

- The role of the board is to direct, not to manage.
- Balance of board membership and choice of individuals are key.
- The chair is responsible for the effectiveness of the board.
- Nonexecutive directors have a particular contribution to make to the work of a board.
- Board committees are important structurally and for the tasks they undertake.
- Executive directors should be appointed solely for the value they can add to the board.
- Board members have different roles; what matters is how they combine to form the board team.

ROLE OF THE BOARD

The crispest definition of a board's role is that of Sir John Harvey Jones, a well-known British former C.E.O.: "to create tomorrow's company out of today's." A more extensive answer to "What is an effective board?" is provided in *Corporate Boards*, a book I cite more fully later: "The vast majority of U.S. governance practices are concerned with . . . shareholder value," though the authors of that book readily concede that a board only concerned with making profits for owners is a board with "too narrow" a perspective.

Boards are in place to direct and not to manage. They have the task of defining the purpose of their enterprises and of agreeing on the strategy for achieving that purpose. They are responsible for appointing chief executives to turn strategic plans into action, for supporting and counseling them on how to do so and, if necessary, for replacing them. Above all, boards are there to provide leadership, and it is in this context that the roles of board members need to be considered.

BOARD COMPOSITION

A single board at the head of a company is the commonest form of board structure. Unitary boards of this nature are made up of executive and nonexecutive, or outside, directors. (Two-tier boards separate these two kinds of director; their structure is covered briefly in the Mini-case cited below). Given that both executive and outside directors sit on unitary boards, the first issue is the balance between them. Ten years ago the ratio for U.K. boards was around two-thirds executive directors and one-third outside dir-

ectors. This has now moved closer to parity and in future I would expect outside directors to be in the majority. This is already the position in the United States where the chief executive is often the only executive on the board and is usually its chair as well.

In addition to the question of balance, there is the question of size. There is a clear move to smaller boards in both the United States and the United Kingdom. Martin Lipton and Jay W. Lorsch in their "Modest Proposal for Improving Corporate Governance" (*The Business Lawyer*, volume 48, pages 59–77) recommend a maximum board size of ten and favor eight or nine. The argument for smaller boards is that they enable all the directors to get to know each other and to contribute effectively in board discussions, thus arriving at a true consensus. The crucial point is that boards are teams and provide collective leadership. So the balance of membership and choice of individuals are key to forming the team.

MINI-CASE
Two-tier Boards

Two-tier boards constitute a supervisory board whose members are all nonexecutive and a management board made up of executive directors. The management board is responsible for strategy as well as for running the business. The supervisory board appoints and can dismiss the management board and no one can be on both boards. The legal responsibilities of the two boards and of their directors are different, whereas with a unitary board all directors have the same legal duties however the board is structured. Since supervisory boards often have employees as members, this raises the question of their role on boards. In Ger-

many, for example, boards of companies of varying sizes include employees; by contrast, those in the Netherlands tend not to do so. My view is that employees can most effectively participate at levels below the board, where the decisions are taken that affect them most directly and to which they can contribute knowledgeably.

THE CHAIR'S ROLE

The chair is responsible for the effectiveness of the board. This responsibility rests with the chair, whatever the other duties may be. It leads to the point that all companies are different and the issues they face are constantly changing. Individual boards have to follow accepted board principles, but in ways which meet their particular circumstances. It is the chair who has the responsibility of insuring that the make-up of the board is appropriate for the challenges ahead. Similarly, it is the chair who has the task of welding the directors into an effective team. Effective boards are not brought into being simply by seating competent individuals around a board table. Creating effective boards requires effort by board members, but above all coaching and leadership by the chair. This is an argument for the chair not also being chief executive.

The chair is responsible for the running of the board. Responsibilities include the agenda, the provision of adequate and timely information to all directors and the actual conduct of board meetings. The chair is also, provided he or she is not chief executive, responsible for putting in place a means by which the board can evaluate their own performance. Where the chair is also chief executive, his or her duties in relation to their board remain the same, but a deputy or a senior outside director would be responsible for the appraisal of the chief executive and for the review of the board's performance.

ROLE OF NONEXECUTIVE DIRECTORS

All directors are equal in that they all carry the same legal responsibilities. Outside or nonexecutive directors are in that sense no different from their executive colleagues. They do however have particular contribu-

"No other area offers richer opportunities for successful innovation than the unexpected success."

Peter F. Drucker

tions to make to their boards by virtue of standing further back from the business. One of these is reviewing the performance of the chief executive and the executive team; clearly the outside directors are the only board members in a position to do this objectively.

Another contribution is in relation to potential conflicts of interest, such as those between the interests of the executives and those of the shareholders. Examples are directors' pay, dividends versus reinvestment, and whether top appointments should be made from within or outside the company. Decisions on these matters are ultimately the decision of the whole board, but non-executive directors are well placed to offer direction on where the best interests of the company—to which all directors owe their duty—lie.

Nonexecutive directors bring with them their experience in fields which are different from those of the executive directors, and this external experience is of particular value in strategy formulation. The potential advantage which the unitary board has over the two-tier board is that it provides the opportunity to combine, in the same body, the depth of knowledge of the business of the executives with the breadth of knowledge of the nonexecutive directors. Once again, it is up to the chair to make the most of these different viewpoints by the way they structure board debates.

The role of these directors in helping to resolve conflicts of interest does not imply that they have higher standards than their executive colleagues. The difference is simply that they can judge these matters more objectively because their interests are involved less directly.

ROLE OF BOARD COMMITTEES

As the responsibilities of directors have become more demanding, boards have increasingly formed committees to deal with some of their more detailed work. All quoted companies need to establish audit and remuneration committees and, unless they have a small board, nomination committees. These committees strengthen the position of the outside directors, of whom they are made up, and are important for the work they do. The essential point is that they are committees of the board. It is the board which appoints them, sets their terms

of reference and turns their recommendations into decisions.

ROLE OF EXECUTIVE DIRECTORS

The duties of executive directors are the same as those of the outside directors. They are as responsible for the monitoring task of the board as the outside directors, who in turn are as responsible for the strategy and leadership of the company as the executives. This means that executive directors have to take their executive hats off upon entering the boardroom and put on their directorial ones. They should only be appointed for the contribution they can make to the board and they are there to further the company's interests—not those of their function or department. It is not an easy transition to make and executive directors can be helped in the adoption of their new nonmanagerial role through appropriate training or through a nonexecutive directorship elsewhere.

ROLE OF THE COMPANY SECRETARY

The chair and board members should be able to look to the company secretary for impartial and professional guidance on their responsibilities and all directors should have access to the advice and services of a company secretary, who is responsible for ensuring that board procedures are followed.

MAKING IT HAPPEN ▶▶

In their insightful book, *Corporate Boards: New Strategies for Adding Value at the Top* (Wiley, 2001), Jay Conger, Edward Lawler, and David Finegold note that "High performance boards can be created only if the right mix of talent is present on the board". They then lay out the numerous and important considerations that should come into play whenever a board is being constituted—or reconstituted. What is perhaps most important to remember is that the process for arriving at the composition of a board is almost as important as the process of leading and managing the board itself.

Every aspect of board member selection—from how the nominating committee operates to determining what knowledge and expertise are needed to making sure that a true balance of

stakeholder interests—is worth thinking about now. As noted in *Corporate Boards*, the board is a management unit and the strength of the corporation is heavily dependent on making sure that "the board's needs for knowledge, information, power, and opportunity" are addressed. Perhaps the first thing a corporate leader should do is to gain objective, outside assistance to ascertain the strengths and weaknesses of the current board and to develop a plan for developing the corporate board in a reasonable length of time, just as executives routinely do in developing any other corporate business unit.

CONCLUSION

Although board members have different roles, what counts is the way those roles are combined in the board team. This is why board selection is so fundamental. Directors should only be appointed for the value they can add to the board. All directors should have terms of office to enable renewal to take place, although I am against rigid rules tying retirement to age or length of board service. The search for outside directors should be purposeful, with the aim of filling gaps in the experience and backgrounds of the existing directors, and selection should involve the board as a whole. The chair, however, has a particular responsibility for the choice of board members since it is the chair's responsibility to turn them into an effective team.

FOR MORE INFORMATION

Books:
Carver, John. *Reinventing Your Board*. San Francisco, CA: Jossey-Bass, 1997.
Conger, Jay, Edward Lawler, and David Finegold. *Corporate Boards: New Strategies for Adding Value at the Top*. San Francisco, CA: Wiley, 2001.
Demb, Ada, and F. Friedrich Neubauer. *The Corporate Board: Confronting the Paradoxes*. New York: Oxford University Press, 1992.
Shultz, Susan F. *The Board Book*. New York: AMACOM, 2000.
Ward, Ralph D. *21st Century Corporate Board*. New York: Wiley, 1996.

"I get many invitations but I only join the boards of companies where I admire the management and believe in the company."

Jill Ker Conway

Environmental Management
by John Elkington

EXECUTIVE SUMMARY

Some management trends start at the top and cascade down; others evolve from the bottom up. Sustainable development (SD) has come from both directions. In the process it has caught a growing number of well-known companies off balance—among them Shell, Monsanto, and Nike. More positive has been the foundation of the World Business Council for Sustainable Development; and the World Economic Forum in Davos routinely covers sustainable-development issues. But in many respects this business story has only just begun. Consider some of the conclusions from the 2002 Earth summit in Johannesburg; the issues raised then remain squarely on the mind of anyone concerned with the weight of SD issues:

- Demographic pressures will create enormous new risks and opportunities. During the 20th century, the planet's human population rose from 1.6 billion to 6 billion. There is likely to be a further 50% increase by 2030.
- A growing range of environmental problems—including ozone depletion, climate change, the collapse of fisheries, and loss of forests—signals that today's economic and business models are unsustainable.
- The end of communism in many countries means that the one-third of humanity who used to live in the old communist world are now playing a growing role in the global economy. In total, there are some four billion people living in the poorer parts of the world; it will be necessary to meet their needs.
- Business is increasingly in the spotlight—and is expected to play a key role in defining and delivering sustainable development. Paradoxically, the governance vacuum created by accelerating globalization will increase the pressures on brand-name companies and on financial markets to act responsibly and effectively.
- At the same time, however, growing resistance to current forms of economic globalization represents a profound challenge to free market capitalism.
- As a result, growing numbers of companies are adopting *triple-bottom-line* strategies, focusing simultaneously on economic prosperity, social equity, and environmental protection.

THE SUSTAINABILITY AGENDA

Boardrooms have been buzzing with questions since the sustainable-development agenda first began to appear on corporate radar screens. Some business leaders see sustainable development as simply the environmental agenda in new colors, but others speak of a profound shift, with new forms of corporate responsibility and accountability emerging. Here are some key questions and answers.

What Is Sustainability?

The answer, first laid out in the 1987 report of the World Commission on Environment and Development, is that sustainability is the principle of ensuring that our actions today do not limit the range of economic, social, and environmental options open to future generations.

Why Is it Important?

Simply stated, sustainable development is the emerging 21st-century business paradigm. It is increasingly proposed by governments and business leaders as a solution for problems now racing up the international agenda. These range from climate change to human-rights issues.

Surely This Is a Job for Politicians and Lawmakers?

In part, of course, it is, but industry's lobbying over the years for less regulation and in some cases active deregulation may now be coming back to haunt it.

What Has Sustainable Development Got to Do with Capitalism?

Simply put, traditional capitalism dealt with financial and physical forms of capital. In-

creasingly, however, companies are expected to manage, account for, and grow multiple forms of capital, for example, financial, physical, human, intellectual, natural, and social capital.

How Can We Sell this to the Financial Markets?

It's tough, but in the coming decades the world's financial markets will adopt triple-bottom-line models to assess value creation. Insurers and reinsurers have been badly affected by issues like asbestos, contaminated land, and toxic and nuclear wastes. Leading banks are increasingly sensitive both to new forms of risk and to emerging opportunities created by new environmental and social standards. And while some financial analysts have been slow on the uptake, the entry of players like the Dow Jones Sustainability Group is providing a wake-up call.

WHAT THE GURUS SAY

The ways in which the environmental and wider sustainable-development agendas have been engaged by business have reflected the priorities of those held responsible at the time in the corporate world. To help simplify the evolutionary history, let's focus on three main phases.

Phase 1—Denial

From the early 1970s, environmental and social issues were handled on the corporate periphery by lawyers or PR people. Most companies were in denial: pollution problems either were not their fault or, if they were, were seen as the price of wealth creation. Key issues include compliance, a company's license to operate, and risk to reputation.

Phase 2—Cleaning Up

From the late 1970s the spotlight shifted to plant siting, production processes, and products. As a result companies tended look to field planners, engineers, and new product development specialists, who used a growing range of tools such as impact assessments, audits, life-cycle assessments, and so-called clean technology. Ecoefficiency concepts introduced by the World Business Council for Sustainable Development were adopted by a growing number of

"Many leading business people . . . are revelling in the opportunity to put new ranges on the market with "eco-friendly" flashes and a 20 percent mark up."
John Button

companies. Phase 2 activity continues to build, with the European Commission introducing new strategic impact assessment requirements for major industrial projects.

Phase 3—Governance

During the 1990s concepts like that of the triple bottom line began to draw in more senior business people. C.E.O.s and their boards began to pay attention, often because of the difficult tradeoffs involved. A water pollution control investment, for example, might result in higher carbon dioxide emissions, raising climate change issues. Accountants have also been increasingly involved. In the process, the sustainable-development agenda has begun to cross-connect with corporate and global governance agendas.

Most mainstream management writers have overlooked these trends. In their classic text *In Search of Excellence*, first published in 1982, Tom Peters and Robert Waterman made not a single reference to environmental issues. By 1991, however, Peters had published *Lean, Clean, and Green*. Other mainstream management gurus were soon nibbling at corners of the agenda, including Charles Handy (what is a company for?), James Collins and Jerry Porras (guidelines for long-lived companies), James Moore (business ecosystems), Francis Fukuyama (the role of trust and other forms of social capital), Peter Schwartz (the art of the long view, scenarios), Michael Porter (value chains, green competition), and Peter Senge (organizational learning).

However, the greatest impact has come from a number of sustainable-development experts whose books are beginning to be accepted as mainstream management texts. They include Claude Fussler (ecoefficiency, ecoinnovation), Ernst Ulrich von Weizacker (Factor 4–10), and Paul Hawken and Amory and Hunter Lovins (natural capitalism).

Organizations like the World Business Council for Sustainable Development now produce a huge amount of material on the sustainable-development agenda for business (**www.wbcsd.ch**). For those who want to see sustainable development in action, take a look at the work of ecoarchitect Bill McDonough and his colleague Michael Braungart (**www.mbdc.com**). Having designed buildings for companies such as The Gap, Nike, and Ford, McDonough and his associates represent a truly new kind of architectural firm.

MAKING IT HAPPEN ▸▸

- Adopt a triple-bottom-line strategy, focusing simultaneously on economic prosperity, social equity, and environmental protection.
- Make environmental and social issues a central boardroom concern, with compliance, the license to operate, and reputational risk as key issues.
- Take the initiative by adopting policies that will meet the criteria of sustainable development.
- Use tools like impact assessments, audits, life-cycle assessments, and clean technology to obtain ecoefficient plant siting, production processes, and products.
- Consider what sustainable development may mean for your business, the areas to take action, the people to involve, and the benefits that may result.
- Closely monitor the new requirements for major industrial projects stemming from governmental bodies, including the European Commission.
- Accept that difficult tradeoffs may be required, and face up to the consequences sooner rather than later.

CONCLUSION

The floodgates are opening. The first major article in the *Harvard Business Review* on the sustainable-development agenda was by Professor Stuart Hart in 1997; the number has been growing ever since. Some key issues for the coming years include: developing the business case for sustainable development (SustainAbility 2001); exploring the overlap between organizational learning and sustainable-development agendas (**www.solonline.org**); and engaging corporate boards in the governance dimensions of sustainable development. Sustainable development is set to become an increasingly significant strategic priority facing organizations. It offers a more efficient system for growth that is acceptable to stakeholders and is proven to be both viable and commercially advantageous.

FOR MORE INFORMATION

Books:
Brown, Lester R., et al. *State of the World 2001*. New York: W. W. Norton, 2001.
Fussler, Claude, and Peter James. *Driving Eco Innovation: A Breakthrough Discipline for Innovation and Sustainability*. Upper Saddle River, NJ: Financial Times Prentice Hall, 1997.
Hawken, Paul, et al. *Natural Capitalism: Creating the Next Industrial Revolution*. New York: Back Bay Books, 2000.

Web sites:
www.iisd.org: the International Institute for Sustainable Development, an organization that promotes the transition toward a sustainable future through information exchange, policy research, analysis, and advocacy.
www.rmi.org: the Rocky Mountain Institute, an entrepreneurial nonprofit organization set up by resource analysts Hunter and Amory Lovins.
www.worldwatch.org: for other Worldwatch Institute *State of the World* annuals.
www.wri.org: the World Resources Institute, an environmental think tank that seeks practical ways to protect the earth.

See also:
☆ Corporate Social Responsibility: Are You Giving Back or Just Giving Away? (pp. 372–373)
☆ SQ: Investing in Spiritual Capital (pp. 43–44)

"Economic activity should not only be efficient in its use of resources but should also be socially just, and environmentally and ecologically sustainable."

Warren Bennis

X-engineering Success
by James Champy

EXECUTIVE SUMMARY

- Partnerships are more important today than ever. Few companies can afford to invent, manufacture, sell, and service everything that they make without some help.
- So companies come together in relationships, typically called alliances, to complement each other's products and capabilities.
- With attention to harmonizing processes across organizations and with the good fortune of compatible cultures, alliances can work. But truth be told, most alliances now fail.

INTRODUCTION

An example of the joint venture is Concert, formed by AT&T and British Telecom to provide communications services to large multinational companies. The venture made sense on paper. Neither AT&T nor British Telecom had the global coverage that its big customers required. Rather than try to build this capability—at a cost of billions of dollars—and bang heads in competition, it made more sense for these companies to create a jointly owned company out of their combined resources. But in the end, these giants did bang heads, taking the venture apart. It would seem that someone forgot to put terms into the deal about what to do with assets and customers in the event that the alliance failed. About the only thing that the partners seemed to be able to agree on was that it hadn't worked. As Concert wound up its business, it was losing about $200 million each quarter.

What happened? Most observers attribute Concert's failure to a difference in cultures between the two partners. That's certainly plausible. The management styles of both companies are different, and each company has been distracted with its own struggle to maintain share in its local markets. A similar alliance formed by France Telecom and a number of other telecommunications companies also failed after much effort and millions of Euros. In fact, the business landscape is littered with alliance failures.

Research into these failures confirms that differing cultures and management styles are the principal causes for break-ups. But I believe that the problems go beyond different management breeding. Often alliances are the brainchild of sales organizations that are just looking to get access to each other's customers. The word *synergy* is freely used to justify a deal without much appreciation

for what it will take to make the alliance work. Simply agreeing to jointly market products or services isn't enough to sustain an alliance. There is not enough value created for the partners or for their customers.

Even when an alliance is initially successful, it can fall apart when one partner becomes dominant and tries to exercise too much power. This often happens in the information technology industry when large software publishers or hardware manufacturers try to assert control over their smaller channel partners, the systems integrators and consultancies that use their products in delivering services. The big guys just assume that they know more and have superior processes. That behavior causes two problems:

1 Arrogance creeps into the relationship, forcing out the trust and good will needed to make it work.
2 Knowledge is lost.

There is a good chance that a smaller channel partner is closer to customers, knowing what they really want, and having a better process. When one alliance partner starts to assert power over another, the alliance is near its end. Recently I spoke with one large technology company that admitted that only 10 of its 400 alliances produced any significant business.

WHY BOTHER AND WHAT'S CHANGED?

The case for making alliances work goes beyond increasing a company's product offering or virtual size. Alliances can address the enormous inefficiencies that exist in many industries. Companies keep large and depreciating inventories because they don't have visibility into each other's operations. And because companies don't have pro-

cesses that connect well together—such as your selling process not working well with my buying process—lots of unnecessary work and paper is produced. For example, it takes 26 separate electronic and paper documents to make many trans-oceanic shipments. Supply chain reengineering is just scratching the surface of what's possible if companies could work more closely together.

Up to now, it has been difficult to do the kind of collaborative work that a powerful alliance requires. Many economists have argued that the management and transaction costs outweigh the benefits, but that balance may well have shifted with the advent of the Internet. This ubiquitous network is not just about a new channel to market or a place to advertise. Its principal corporate benefit will be as an enabler of a new breed of cross-organizational processes that will dramatically improve business performance. To achieve this benefit will require what I call *X-engineering*. The "X" connotes the organizational boundaries that you will cross.

MAKING IT HAPPEN ▶▶

Making alliances work requires that the partners are culturally compatible. But the partners must do more than be polite to each other and throw resources, processes, people, and customers into a venture. A venture must be thoughtfully designed and implemented and the principles of X-engineering applied. Here's what to do.

- **Do conduct an open assessment of cultures and management styles.** Studies that show cultural and management style differences to be contributors to failure are right. Probe each other's beliefs and values. Ask some simple questions, such as how will your partner handle a breakdown of relations with a customer? How do you both deal with issues of breach of integrity? How will you think about quality, innovation, profitability? Remember, there is no single company culture that is "right." The issue here is compatibility, and hopefully you and your partner will value the same things. In the end, you must choose your partners

> "In large organizations, middle managers serve the purpose of relaying information up and down—orders down, numbers up. But with the new information technologies and more efficient forms of work, their purpose dwindles."
>
> James Champy

carefully. Trust your intuition, and don't fool yourself into thinking that you can influence what your partner fundamentally believes. Company cultures, like country cultures, don't change easily.

- **Make your processes transparent.** Most companies operate under the premise that their processes are unique and should be kept secret. Just the opposite is true. There are very few processes within a company that are unique. Maybe you have a secret formula or a proprietary manufacturing technique, but most of your and your competitor's processes are the same. To operate an alliance, companies must be open so that process relationships can develop. You cannot intimately connect unless you understand how each other operates.

A corollary principle is that you must share good ideas. Forget about who gets the credit. Just put good ideas into the alliance and go on and develop new ones. Just like any business, an alliance cannot be starved—especially by its partners. It may need innovation to maintain its competitiveness.

- **Harmonize your processes.** Being transparent isn't enough. Chances are that your processes and the processes of your partners won't connect easily. For example, if one partner contributes the sales processes to a venture and another partner the service processes, work will have to be done so customers experience these processes in a seamless way. Lots of problems occur in hand-offs. All the processes of an alliance have to be examined to be sure that they are harmonized—that is, that they act in concert with one another. In some cases, totally new processes will have to be developed.
- **Create a powerful business proposition for your customers.** An alliance is only worth doing if it can make one plus one

equal three. The partners have to create a business proposition for their customers that neither could offer on its own. An alliance cannot be sustained because it's convenient for its partners. It requires steady revenues, and that will only happen if it offers a compelling business proposition for customers. An improved business proposition can take many forms. It could be reduced costs and lower prices. That's what Dell and its product partners are doing in Dell's electronic marketplace. Alliances can offer variety and choice. Amazon.com is now a retail channel for Toys-R-Us. An alliance can make service more robust. Many computer hardware manufacturers partner with service providers to handle service problems. Unfortunately, customers don't always experience the benefits of such combinations because the partners haven't harmonized their processes.

THE IDEAL IS POSSIBLE

What does a great alliance look like? It's one that builds on the strengths of its partners, meets a customer need, and avoids the replication of resources or the redundancy of work. Yes, the venture must also make money, but I believe profits will come if the earlier three conditions are met.

MINI-CASE

The *Star Alliance* was formed by a number of major airlines. The Alliance members share few overlapping routes, but they do share information about their customers' travel preferences. This means that they can act as complementors, not competitors. They can offer the intelligent routes that their passengers want. The Alliance also wisely allows passengers to interchange and pool frequent-flier miles from individual member airlines. There is something in the deal for everyone. And because these air-

lines act as complementors, they will avoid spending billions of dollars on redundant jumbo jets to compete for routes. If the members can find ways to share more processes and eliminate redundant work, even more benefits will result.

CONCLUSION

More than ever, businesses need alliances to reduce costs, improve service, and feed innovation. Customers now expect that you can deliver anything, anytime, anywhere; but few companies can do that on their own. The Internet now enables the fundamental cross-organizational change required to reduce costs and create customer value. But relationships must be X-engineered—partners carefully selected, operations made transparent, and processes harmonized. Otherwise, relationships will consume enormous amounts of management time and yield little for companies and their customers. Enter alliances with your eyes and company wide open and expect that they will require an active, continuing negotiation between the partners. Only then will they be worth the effort.

FOR MORE INFORMATION

Book:
Champy, James. *X-Engineering the Corporation: Reinventing Your Business in the Digital Age.* New York: Warner Business Books, 2002.

"I . . . understand the importance of maintaining a balance between information, knowledge, and meaning. Remember what Thoreau said about news: 'If it's important enough, it'll reach you.'"

James Champy

Change Management
by Klaus Doppler

EXECUTIVE SUMMARY

- Change management often meets with resistance and/or is carried out poorly.
- Nevertheless, change remains a necessity. It is the only way for organizations to consistently adapt to new trends, react to competitors, and meet the needs of their customers.

INTRODUCTION

Change management has proved unsatisfactory in many cases. Attempts to implement it have been many and wide-ranging, but the promises made in its name have remained unfulfilled.

There are three main causes for this:
- mistakes continue to be made at shop-floor level;
- bad examples have brought high-level management into discredit. Increasingly nowadays, all top executives start out heavily in the red as far as their credibility is concerned.
- the internal change story, disseminated by company communications in order to awaken the commitment of those affected, is frequently unmasked as pure rhetoric, rhapsodizing about change—with devastating consequences.

The basic challenges, however, not only continue to exist, but have become even more pressing. It is not a question of whether or not to make changes, but of how to implement change most rapidly, most consistently—and with as few undesirable side effects as possible.

In this situation, in order to proceed in a way that promises success, it is necessary to avoid mistakes on the shop floor. Furthermore, a new mental model of change is required that is distinct from the previous, purely engineering-oriented, sequential procedure and has the following main characteristics:
- simultaneous and networked action
- radical decisions as regards line and project responsibility
- thinking about and shaping implementation from the very first step in conceiving the plan
- a carefully-planned communications concept that is worthy of the name and does not simply restrict itself to doling out information

WHY SO MANY PLANS AND PROJECTS COME TO GRIEF

No matter what name they are given—business reengineering, change management, personal leadership, transition management, or organization development—plans for change promise more than they actually deliver. Looking back over the last ten years, the balance sheet is not exactly anything to get excited about: change programs either get stuck or achieve their goal at the expense of severe losses in staff motivation, credibility, and commitment.

Shop-floor Mistakes

If one takes a closer look at the basic concept and concrete implementation of processes of change, one cannot help noticing that the old familiar mistakes are still being made on the shop floor:
- The people affected are drawn into the process far too late and consequently present an obstacle in the most important phase. The process, therefore, becomes unnecessarily drawn out.
- The people affected lack the necessary competence and the requisite abilities to come to terms with the situation successfully, because there are too few opportunities for them to receive information and training.
- The unshakeable motivation and tireless commitment needed to drive things on toward one single significant objective, success, is simply not there. What is lacking in this instance is not training, but a sustained campaign of communication and mobilization.
- The people affected are not sufficiently aware of the problems involved. A sense of urgency is lacking. Pressure is exerted and things are stirred up from above, but the people on the ground do not see what is behind the plan.
- Implementation is not structured

strategically or as a minutely planned roll out, neither is it managed with corresponding precision.
- The so-called hard factors, above all, business-management control indicators, are at the forefront of attention, while the soft factors, such as nonacceptance, discouragement, fear, defiance, open and covert resistance, are neglected.

High-level Change Managers Have Become Discredited

It is always emphasized that change processes only have a chance of being implemented when they are conducted in a consistently top-down fashion. So what happens when the top echelon in a company is suspected of serving only its own interests? Horrendous compensation payments, enormous stock-option plans, and those now familiar cases where data relevant to results are manipulated in such a way as to draw a veil over the actual state of the company and maximize the income of certain individuals—all these do nothing to build trust in staff and stockholders alike. It is not the case that all managements behave in this way, but there have been too many bad examples recently for anyone to overlook this aspect of things.

Rhetoric and Rhapsodizing Befuddle the Brain

It has always been the case that the primary purpose of change rhetoric was to pull the wool over the eyes of the workforce and the public. Words and phrases such as "sense of urgency," "commitment," "synergy," "emotional management," "management of diversity," "passion for excellence," "personal leadership," "vision," "mission," and "values" have in many cases been reduced to slogans. They are used to manipulate ordinary people and make them willing to follow dictates from above more or less uncritically.

THE CHALLENGES REMAIN
General framework conditions

There are three basic reasons why the overall situation regarding the necessity of change will stay as it is.

1 **The consequences of information technology.** Developments in the field

---

"Faced with change, employees have one question: 'What's going to happen to me?' A successful change management communication program will avoid that question."

Scott Adams

of information technology are still proceeding at a terrific pace, and this has a massive effect on the way work processes are organized. In an age where speed and costs are decisive factors for success in all areas of business, any technological development that has a positive influence on one or both of these factors will be seized with both hands. It only needs one trailblazer in any particular industry; the rest are immediately forced to follow. Having information technology as the driver makes constant change inevitable.

2 **Cutthroat competition everywhere.** The market is tight in all industries. There is a surplus of almost every sort of product. Today, if a company drops out, one of its competitors seamlessly fills the gap. Anyone who wants to make a good showing in a crowded market, let alone force a way into it, has to push others aside. Even if someone has a particularly good idea, one thing is clear: nobody occupies the solo spot for long. The competition is always hot on your heels. This is another driver of non-stop movement.

3 **Conflicting customer needs.** Companies spend a lot of money trying to bind customers to them permanently. Clever companies, however, realize that customers are not absolutely dependable and they are by no means consistent in what they need. What applies today will not necessarily apply tomorrow. Moreover, it is a fact that customers are potential two-timers by nature, always looking for an even better offer. A highly reliable communications network with customers is vital to enable you to work out in advance what they want or what you can tempt them with.

The Hot Phase of Change

The consequence to be drawn from the above mentioned factors is: in the future, as now, we shall have to reckon with the fact that changes will take place ever more frequently, rapidly, and radically.

But changes do not (or no longer) take place in distinct, successive waves. Rather, they overlap. Before one project is finished, another is already under way. Objectives alter to some extent in midstream. To launch yourself with full commitment into something that there is no guarantee can be seen through to a clear-cut conclusion, to lay side one project and take up another—ruptures and apparent contradictions such as these are not everyone's cup of tea.

The Basic Human Attitude to Change

Anyone who wants to survive in a business environment should be flexible, adaptable, ready to change and able to live with contradictions. Normal human beings are the exact opposite of this, constantly seeking clarity, repose, and order, opposed in principle to change. They are, so to speak, energy-savers, who only move when they see some real benefit in moving or when they feel the heat on their own backsides—and who immediately shift down a gear when they have the impression that the goal has been more or less reached or the threat has to some extent receded.

Of course, there are exceptions—people who like to perform, are ready to change, and look to the future. But it is fatal if, when we contemplate change, we base our calculations not on normal human beings but on idealized figments of our imaginations. Such undertakings are bound to fail.

CONCLUSION: WHAT IS TO BE DONE—A NEW MENTAL MODEL OF CHANGE PROCESSES

If we assess previous experience with respect to change projects and take seriously the enduring challenges and framework conditions, then we can recognize the outlines of a new model.

The Old Model

The model that has existed up to now is based on the following assumptions:
- processes are separable from each other;
- processes can be put into operation sequentially in accordance with a clearly defined phases model (task delineation, diagnosis, concept development, decision, piloting, roll out, or large-scale implementation);
- exactness and correctness are vital criteria;
- responsibility for the individual sections of the process is divisible;
- objectives are precisely definable;
- action is taken in accordance with defined objectives;
- there is a clear beginning and a clear end to everything;
- as far as possible, processes must be structured from the top down.

These assumptions have the following effects on the manner in which changes are managed:
- process are organized primarily along engineering and *technical* lines;
- planning is given very high status;

- different teams are responsible for planning and implementation;
- project management and line responsibility are clearly separated one from the other.

So called "soft" factors are of very little significance—the people affected are treated as the addressees and objects of change, not as its carriers and co-organizers.

The Current Transitional Model

The following features characterize the current situation in change management:
- the pressure on solutions has risen sharply;
- 100% solutions are not attempted unless absolutely necessary;
- operationally everything is getting more hectic;
- implementation is placed in the foreground;
- change management is regarded as a tool to guarantee and accelerate implementation;
- to underline the significance of change, hierarchical line power is used in the form of power promoters and sponsors.

The New Orientation Model

Many things conflict with one another—values, fundamental orientations, methodological bases, and the roles of the various people affected. Nevertheless, it is perhaps precisely this conflictual element that is one of the crucial new features that we have to learn to deal with professionally instead of regarding them simply as temporary obstacles:
- Projects have neither a clear beginning nor an unambiguous end. Each project must be understood and planned as an intervention into an already existing field of forces. It is a capital error to assume that there is a so-called zero point, from which it might be possible to start afresh.
- It is time to take seriously the principle of moving targets. We live within turbulent and unstable environments—we cannot expect that this fact will have no effect on our planning and projects.
- Instead being able to finish off undertakings in a clear-cut fashion, we shall have to learn more and more often to pass on the baton to some other issue as if in a relay race, but with this vital difference—we shall not know in advance either the time or the place for the baton change.
- Projects should always be structured as micropolitical strategies. Anyone who begins or takes over a project must be fully aware that he or she is entering an existing force field of interests with its own regulatory system. He or she must try to understand this force field before

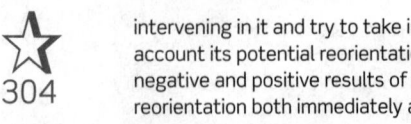
intervening in it and try to take into account its potential reorientation and the negative and positive results of its reorientation both immediately and later on.

- Implementation needs to be thought about from the outset. It is not the final phase in a multistage process, rather its outlines already begin to take shape at the start of the project. This has the following consequences. First, those who will be affected by implementation must be involved in the work of structuring it from day one. Second, the minimum form of involvement is communication—not information. Third, in order to get those affected involved, they need to be identified at the outset with respect to their interests, their knowledge, their attitude toward the project, and their mental state. Fourth, only this way is there any chance of developing a process of mobilization out of a communications program.

- Directly involving the grass roots means that their knowledge can be exploited and the shaping energy required for implementation can be produced. Indirect involvement via the principle known as "cascading" is inadequate. The loss of information at the points of transfer is too great, whether you are working top down or bottom up. The more direct information that the people affected have, the better positioned they are to act autonomously. The maximum possible degree of individual responsibility is called for.

- Project versus line. Clarity with regard to responsibility and ownership are needed. What frequently happens is this: the task is allotted to a project; the power of allocating resources and overall control of implementation remains in the hands of the line. In the struggle for resources and conflicts over the implementation of the outcomes of the project, project management often comes off second best. The alternative? Either the line is from the outset the owner of and task-setter for the project, or project management and line management are put in harness together.

Creating Strategic Excellence
by Mike Freedman

EXECUTIVE SUMMARY

- Organizations need strategy in order to prosper, rather than survive.
- The right environment is essential.
- Strategy, planning, and operational activities must be integrated.
- Develop a strategic culture to guarantee success.

THE NEED FOR STRATEGIC EXCELLENCE
Survival or Prosperity?

Organizations can survive without a strategy, but that's about all they will do. They will never prosper over the long term and will always perform suboptimally—indeed, some may head in the wrong direction fast and finish up nowhere. With a clear strategy, effectively communicated, well planned, and carefully implemented, the chances of superior performance are enhanced immensely. Setting and implementing strategy, however, is not easy, requires considerable time and effort by an organization's leadership, and demands outstanding thinking skills by all involved.

The Right Environment

An appropriate performance environment is required to achieve strategic clarity, coherence, and coordination. The environment needs to encourage and stimulate those involved and balance strategic and operational imperatives, which are often in conflict for time, attention, resources, and thinking efforts. C.E.O.s must lead by example, for there is nothing more important in their role than to make sure that strategy is set and a leadership team is in place to help in that process and subsequently to direct its implementation.

STRATEGY DEFINED

Working on a global basis with many of the world's leading companies and government bodies, we have found that the following definitions have stood the test of time over the past 30 years.

Mission

The mission establishes the overall purpose of an organization in a simple, clear statement of intent. It guides strategy formulation but is not a substitute for it. It must be meaningful. One client had as its mission

"to redefine, build, and own the greetings category globally." This provided direction and motivation and gave a sense of what needed to be covered in its strategic vision.

This compares favorably with the mission of a Japanese car manufacturer: to "kill Porsche." A dramatic statement, but somewhat simplistic.

Strategy

Strategy is defined as "a framework within which the choices about the nature and direction of an organization are made." *Framework* here means boundaries or parameters that help determine what lies inside or outside the scope of the organization's strategy. Clear criteria are developed to apply in this initial decision-making filter. The choices to be made are what products and/or services will and will not be offered, what markets (customers, consumers, and geographies) will and will not be served, and what key capabilities are needed to take products to markets. The *nature* of an organization is its very essence. McDonald's is defined by its fast-food essence, Dunhill by luxury goods, and Goldman Sachs by financial services. *Direction* refers to where an organization is headed and how it might retain or change its nature and/or the scope of its activities.

A MODEL FOR STRATEGY FORMULATION

Having a proven model and the processes to support it eases the burden of a C.E.O. and the top management team and produces a superior result. It also ensures that the necessary links are made and that the organization's mission, strategic vision, planning processes, day-to-day decision making, and human performance system are all aligned. Such an approach also facilitates continuous monitoring, review, and updating of the strategy, vital in today's climate of constant and rapid change.

A Five-phase Model

The model described below has been used effectively by many of the world's great corporations, including the Bank of Ireland, Corning, Hallmark, Hong Kong-based Towngas, the Venezuelan state oil company Lagoven, the Irish Development Agency, Kennametal, and Dunhill.

It has considerable advantages over many other well-known models such as those proposed by Michael Porter, Hamel and Prahalad, the Boston Consulting Group, General Electric, and McKinsey. Each of those focuses on only one or two elements of the Kepner–Tregoe model, typically omitting either planning the execution of the strategy or its actual implementation. They are thus incomplete. Our experience indicates that all five phases must be in place if there is to be a realistic chance of achieving strategic excellence. The model is as follows:

- Phase 1: Strategic intelligence gathering and analysis.
- Phase 2: Strategy formulation.
- Phase 3: Strategic master project planning.
- Phase 4: Strategy implementation.
- Phase 5: Strategy monitoring, review, and updating.

A continuous feedback loop links each phase to the next.

Strategic Intelligence Gathering and Analysis

This phase guarantees that the depth and breadth of information on which strategic decisions are based is up to date, accurate, and relevant; the quality of strategic decisions depends very largely on the quality of this information. The intelligence covered includes competition, technology, markets, macroeconomic, political, and social information and trends, and regulation, among other subjects specific to each organization. Key to this phase is determining the implications of this intelligence for the organization within its strategic time frame.

Strategy Formulation

Using our definition of strategy, this phase results in the creation of a strategic vision or profile that builds on the strategic mission developed as its starting point. Such a vision answers nine key questions:

1 What are our fundamental beliefs and values?

"Beware the manager who proclaims to the world he is a long-termer, beginning today."

T. Boone Pickens

2 What are the assumptions on which we will make our future strategic decisions? (These are drawn from Phase 1.)

3 What products and/or services will we and will we not offer and what are their characteristics?

4 What customers and end-user groups (if they are different) will we serve and not serve and what are their characteristics?

5 What is our geographic scope?

6 What products/services and markets represent the greatest potential for growth and require the most investment and resource allocation?

7 What competitive advantage(s) will enable us to succeed?

8 What key capabilities do we need to make sure that we take our products/services to market and to support our competitive advantage(s)?

9 What financial and nonfinancial goals (for example, market share, technology leadership) do we aim to achieve?

Strategic Master Project Planning

This phase encompasses the development of the plan for strategy implementation.

A significant number of projects emerge (often several hundred), the execution of which leads to successful implementation. Creating a strategic master project plan and developing an optimal project portfolio help to guide the organization in prioritizing, defining in detail, sequencing, scheduling, researching, executing, and monitoring these projects.

A strategic master project plan can contain projects covering a wide variety of activities, including:

- launching new products and markets;
- filling capability gaps;
- aligning organizational structure with strategy;
- reducing complexity;
- managing costs;
- synchronizing planning and budgeting with the strategy process;
- developing functional strategy;
- redefining and realigning IT hardware, software, and information requirements;
- repositioning the company externally;
- branding;
- managing merger, acquisition, and disposal activities;
- creating strategic alliances;
- training and developing middle managers in strategy;
- phasing out products and markets;
- establishing an appropriate performance system.

Strategy Implementation

This phase involves taking planned actions, monitoring implementation, and modifying the strategic master project plan as circumstances change and projects are amended, completed, or abandoned and new ones added. Involving significant numbers of employees in the implementation phase is a vital ingredient in successful execution. The more strongly employees feel ownership of the strategy, the more they will be committed to play their part. Ownership, commitment, and involvement begin with a major communications exercise to see that all employees fully understand the strategy and each can answer the question, "What does this mean for me?" This phase often involves considerable training to empower employees to play their role.

Strategy Monitoring, Review, and Updating

Given the rate and pace of change in the 21st century, this phase is a vital requirement. Continuous monitoring of strategic progress, goals, and indicators of success is a full-time task and a key input to regular, generally quarterly, reviews. Such reviews not only evaluate ongoing implementation, but examine whether the assumptions used to underpin the strategy are still valid and whether the organization's strategic direction is still robust and viable. Strategic updates are an output of the monitoring and review process.

INTEGRATING STRATEGY, PLANNING, AND OPERATIONAL ACTIVITIES

Clearly the strategic dimension of an organization is not an isolated set of activities. Strategic alignment requires the integration of every organizational component. The following model is a guide.

Note: Constant internal and external communication is a key feature of successful strategic leadership and must accompany each phase of the process.

STRATEGY COMMUNICATION

What to communicate, to whom, by whom, when, how, and where are key questions in achieving strategic excellence. Many internal and external constituencies can and must play a role in effective strategy implementation. A precondition is that they all understand the message and know their role and what's in it for them. At Kepner Tregoe we use a communications matrix to

guide this exercise. Each cell in the matrix requires a detailed project plan; this ensures that all key questions are answered. For more information about this, see **www.kepner-tregoe.com**.

Note: The elements of each matrix are different depending on the organization's stakeholders on the one hand and the subjects to be communicated on the other. Check marks indicate a definite need to know, question marks are for debate, and blank spaces represent no need to know.

MAKING IT HAPPEN ▶▶

As the glue to the whole strategic environment, creating a strategic culture helps an organization to achieve its goals. Strategic culture is defined as "the combined effect of behaviors, norms, beliefs, values, heritage, thinking, and relationships and the way they manifest themselves in an organization and its strategic performance." Its facets are:

- basic beliefs and values;
- thinking patterns;
- organizational structure;
- management style;
- management processes and systems;
- education, training, and development;
- goal setting and appraisals;
- reward systems;
- myths, stories, legends, and symbols;
- information and knowledge;
- agendas and meetings;
- behaviors;
- external manifestations to outside constituencies.

When these align with, and support, an organization's strategy efforts, strategic success is assured.

FOR MORE INFORMATION

Books:
Johnson, Spencer. *Who Moved My Cheese?: An Amazing Way to Deal with Change in Your Work and in Your Life.* New York: Putnam, 1998.
Mintzberg, Henry, Bruce Ahlstrand, and Joseph Lampel. *Strategy Safari: A Guided Tour through the Wilds of Strategic Management.* New York: Simon & Schuster, 1998.

Web site:
www.kepner-tregoe.com: has many supplementary articles on strategic approach.

"Vision: Top management's heroic guess about the future, easily printed on mugs, T-shirts, poster, and calendar cards."

Anonymous

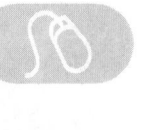

Creating an Entrepreneurial Mindset
by Rita Gunther McGrath and Ian C. MacMillan

EXECUTIVE SUMMARY

- Successful executives will learn to master uncertainty through the skills of entrepreneurial leadership.
- This calls for different disciplines than in conventional management.
- There are five key elements: creating a climate supporting continuous search for opportunity, framing, stocking an opportunity register, focus, and promoting adaptive execution.

INTRODUCTION

Although uncertainty might cause many to freeze, it can be used to your benefit. Uncertain situations are full of new opportunities. Your task is to continuously identify high-potential business opportunities and exploit these opportunities with speed and confidence. Thus, uncertainty can become your ally, not your enemy.

ENTREPRENEURIAL LEADERSHIP: THE MOST IMPORTANT JOB

Entrepreneurial leaders are distinguished from other managers by their personal practices. These fall into three main categories: setting the work climate, orchestrating opportunity-seeking, and moving particular ventures forward personally.

Climate-setting practices create a pervasive sense of urgency for everyone to work on new business initiatives. Dedicate a disproportionate share of your own time, attention, and discretionary resources to finding and supporting new business models. Ron Sim, founder and current C.E.O. of OSIM, one of the fastest growing businesses in Singapore, is a great believer in personally spending time to seek opportunity. As he says, "From a leadership standpoint, it's important to lead by example. I always try to lead by example and walk the talk. Instead of talking too much, put things into action."

Orchestrating opportunity-seeking involves removing uncertainty from your staff by clearly specifying what type of entrepreneurial opportunities are wanted. We call this "ballparking." A Swedish entrepreneur whose small company excelled in CAD/CAM technology defined his company's entrepreneurial playing field as "50 to the power of 4." This meant he was inter-

ested in proposals that had the potential to deliver 50 million Swedish kroner ($5 million) in profits, by capturing 50% market share, with 50% margins in at least 50 countries. The logic was to seek opportunities where he solved a real problem for enough customers that he could capture the lion's share of a defensible global market without having to deal with competition from multinational firms. This gave his people scope, but also kept them focused on those opportunities where he felt that his company could build a strong position.

Specific hands-on management practices recognize that the quest for insight is the single most important source of competitive differentiation a management team can bring to an organization. For example, Robert Brown and Linda Mason, founders of Bright Horizons child care centers, capitalized on an insight that allowed them to create an attractive business model in a traditionally unattractive industry. Instead of focusing on individual families' needs for child care, the couple instead re-

defined their customer as corporations. In 15 years, the venture grew from a concept to a thriving business with over 340 centers.

ESTABLISHING THE ENTREPRENEURIAL FRAME

The entrepreneurial frame defines your goals. The idea is to push you and your team to undertake those initiatives that go beyond mere incremental improvement to really make a difference. Framing has two parts: first, a definition of success; and second, an articulation of strategic direction.

The process for establishing a frame involves working through the following questions:

1. If you were to do something in the next three to five years that you, your boss, and your company's investors would regard as a major win, what would this look like?
2. What is the minimum amount of profit you need from your new ventures (at maturity) to make a difference to your business? What rate of growth must you sustain?
3. What is the increase in profitability you need to achieve in the next three to five years?
4. What return on investment are you seeking?

Next, articulate strategic direction by establishing screening criteria that are consistent with your ballparking definition. Any proposal that has "screen-out" criteria results in "dropping it dead." "Screen-in" criteria represent characteristics that can be described

Establishing a Frame

	Current Performance	Desired Performance	Specification of Success
Last year's profits	200	10% improvement	220
Return on sales	10%	5% improvement	10.5%
Revenues required to produce profits	2,000	220 (above) / 10.5% (above)	2,095
Return on assets	15%	10% improvement	16.5%
Assets required to produce profits	1,333	Profit goal / ROA goal	1,333

"It is more of an entrepreneurial approach where the people close to the market and product create the business."

Kenichi Ohmae

Principles for Redesigning Your Offering

	Basic	Discriminator	Energizers
Positive	Perform at competitive par, watch costs	Pick a few attributes customers will notice and care about to focus on	Execute with vigor and prepare for competitive reaction
Negative	Perform no worse than competition	Perform a little better than competitors	Eliminate yours, capitalize on your competitors'
Neutral	Only keep if cheap, or needed for other segments	Add features that would make the offering complete	No such beast

Source: MacMillan & McGrath, "Discover Your Products' Hidden Potential" HBR, 1997

as "the more the merrier"—the more of these characteristics, the more attractive the opportunity. Think through the following questions:

1 What were the least desirable businesses that you have been involved with? What characteristics made them undesirable? What does this tell you about areas to avoid in the future?

2 What made a particular opportunity very rewarding for you? What does this tell you about areas to pursue in the future?

3 Integrate these statements into a list of (about) ten screen-out statements and ten screen-in statements that capture your experience. A screen out might be: "The opportunity would consume too much time from our key people." A screen-in might be: "This is an attractive market in which we already have a strong position." Try to make your screening statements as specific to your business as possible.

Eventually, your goal is to have about ten screen-in and ten screen-out statements that the organization can agree accurately reflect the types of businesses that are desired and not desired. You can also develop a set of "scorecards" derived from this analysis that can give you a common score across the criteria, as in the example below.

CREATING A WELL-STOCKED OPPORTUNITY REGISTER

An opportunity register is an inventory of potentially attractive new business opportunities. The idea is that at any point in time you'll have a rich set of potential opportunities to choose from, rather than having only the choice of those that managed to survive a corporate winnowing process.

Two techniques are useful here. The first is called consumption chain analysis. The consumption chain is used to map the customer's entire set of experiences with your product or service offering. It begins with the trigger event or circumstance that leads a customer to be aware of a need, and continues through all the steps involved in their being a customer of yours. Any link in the chain has differentiation potential which you can uncover by probing into the customer's experiences at each link.

The second technique is attribute mapping. This captures how well your offering is appealing to customers' needs at the moment. Start simply, by identifying an offering and an important customer segment.

Then analyze the data to see where you could enhance positive attributes and eliminate negative ones.

By using these two techniques, you will typically discover more good ideas than you can execute with the resources you have. The challenge then is to winnow them down to the very best, while bearing in mind that you don't want to over-emphasize either existing businesses or new ones.

CREATING FOCUS USING REAL OPTIONS REASONING

Like investing in a financial option, real options reasoning involves making small investments that give you the right to make a decision later. The idea is to limit your downside exposure until the upside potential of the opportunity is demonstrated. In conjunction with limiting risk, an options approach allows you to create focus and strategic alignment across your portfolio of initiatives. The portfolio addresses whether the market is certain or not, and whether the technological environment is certain or not.

Map the initiatives that your firm is pursuing on the opportunity portfolio chart (overleaf). The mapping should reflect your strategy. If your strategy is to grow the existing business you will want more emphasis on the lower left hand section. If your strategy is exploration, you'll want more options. Firms usually learn from this exercise that they are taking on too many projects and that the projects that are in the pipeline are not consistent with their strategies. One way to fix this is to allocate resources to different sections of the map before projects are approved, then make them compete with similar projects for resources.

PROMOTING ADAPTIVE EXECUTION BY DISCOVERY-DRIVEN PLANNING

Discovery-driven planning is a plan to learn, not to show that you had all the answers

Dimension	Exceptional if . . .	Acceptable if . . .	Unfavorable if . . .	Score Totals
Strategic intent	This opportunity takes us exactly where we want to go in terms of our strategy 9	This opportunity is not inconsistent with our strategy, but offers no engine to drive it 3	This opportunity, even if we succeed, is inconsistent with our strategy 1	
Builds competitive advantage	The idea builds both short-term revenue streams and long-term competitive advantage 9	The idea has either long or short term benefits, but not both 3	The idea provides only short-term benefits and may interfere with a long-term opportunity 1	
Builds knowledge capabilities	The opportunity will help us enhance our capabilities significantly 9	The opportunity will let us build new capabilities, but only in very limited areas 3	The opportunity will not lead us to extend our capabilities in any meaningful way 1	
Use of existing assets	The opportunity requires no investment in new assets 9	The opportunity does require some investment but takes advantage of assets in place 3	The opportunity will require entirely new investment in assets 1	

"Government has an essential role to play in investing in the human resources and infrastructure needed to develop an entrepreneurial culture."

Anthony Giddens

An Opportunity Portfolio

Technical and Execution Uncertainty

	Low (Market)	Medium	High
High	Positioning Options		Stepping Stones
Medium	Platform Launches		Scouting Options
Low	Enhancement Launches		

Market and Organizational Uncertainty

when you wrote the plan. The technique requires the interaction of five processes:

1 determining the frame (objectives) at the level of a project;
2 establishing competitive and market benchmarks;
3 defining operating specifications;
4 documenting assumptions;
5 establishing key milestones.

In uncertain environments, conventional planning makes no sense. Instead, plan with discipline to the next major milestone, then pause and re-plan as new information becomes available.

- Dedicate a disproportionate share of time, attention, and discretionary resources to finding and supporting new business.
- Push yourself and your team to launch initiatives that go beyond mere incremental improvement to really make a difference.
- Seek ten screen-in and ten screen-out statements to accurately reflect types of businesses desired (screened-in) and not desired (screened-out).

- Use the "consumption chain" to map the customer's entire set of experiences with your product or service offering.
- Use "attribute mapping" to capture how well your offering is appealing to customers' needs at the moment.
- Limit your downside exposure to a new initiative until the upside potential of the opportunity is demonstrated.

In all these techniques, the emphasis is on the twin activities of pursuing opportunity while remaining focused.

FOR MORE INFORMATION

Journal Articles:
McGrath, R. G., and I. C. MacMillan. "Discovery Driven Planning." *Harvard Business Review* (July–August, 1995).
McGrath, R. G., and I. C. MacMillan. "Assessing Technology Projects Using Real Options Reasoning." *Research Technology Management* (July–August, 2000).

See also:
- Henry Mintzberg (pp. 1240–1241)
- Viewpoint: Henry Mintzberg (pp. 292–293)

Viewpoint: Michael E. Gerber
So What Are You Obsessed About?

Introduction

Michael E. Gerber is an entrepreneur, small business guru, and the best-selling author of seven books, including *The E-Myth Revisited: Why Most Small Businesses Don't Work and What to Do About It*, and most recently *E-Myth Mastery: The Seven Essential Disciplines for Building a World Class Company* (in each case, "E" stands for "entrepreneurial"). He is the founder and chairman of E-Myth Worldwide, which since its inception in 1977 has worked with more than 50,000 individual companies and is the leading coaching, training, and educational firm in the world focused specifically on Gerber's vision: to transform the lives of small business owners worldwide. In this article, he—pulling no punches—offers a very personal opinion on the parallels between business writing and business creation.

I stopped reading business books a long time ago, and yet I can't stop myself from writing them!

What's wrong with this picture? Well, nothing actually . . . if you understand what motivates me to write business books, and what de-motivates me from reading them.

Let's look at the de-motivated part first. It's fairly easy to understand.

What de-motivates me from reading business books is that I feel they're written by *people* who are interested in being thought of as experts in business. In short, writers of business books have an ulterior motive to *sell* you something under the guise of *teaching* you something.

The idea is that if what they teach you in their book works—and in my view it's rarely been proven that anything they teach you to do in their books will be done by you, the reader—or, if their book is very, very successful, so much so that you will believe it works because so many people are buying it, then you will buy more of what they teach. (That's called the "back end" in the trade; it's what you buy from authors after you read their books.)

So, business books are mainly thought of by the people who write them as sales tools. That's why I don't read them. I know that's why they write them.

On the other hand, if authors were really, really good at selling whatever they're selling in their business books, I *would* probably read them to find out how they did it. That would be interesting to me, given that my business books are also written for the very same reason: I want to sell you something.

Now, don't get me wrong, I don't have any objection to people selling their stuff in a book; that's their business. (And, as I've just admitted, it's also my business!) My problem is I only have so much time, and knowing what I know about business books and the people who write them, my time could be spent better in many other areas of my life. So could yours, I propose.

On the other hand, I know that you probably find yourself reading business books to get some new ideas, since yours are getting a bit rusty. Business books stimulate creative thinking, I'm told. Well, I don't think so. Not at all. Actually, I have rarely read a business book that stimulates creative thinking; 99% of the "new ideas" in business books (not a statistic, just an anecdotal observation) were old long before the book was written. Anything that sounds new will very quickly reveal itself as being very old indeed, simply a dead idea dressed up in new clothes.

There are also those business authors who are academics, they teach business, and they publish new books, or they write in academic journals . . . and, by so doing, their measure goes up in the market of others just like them, and they achieve a sort of graybeard status, a wisdom of sorts, a panache only available to the very determined who wish to be known for seeing all that is to be seen in a splendidly autocratic, visionary way, from far, far, far above.

They, of course, have never grown a business, nor do they ever intend to. They live in a different world than that. They live in a world which *contemplates* the real world, and sends the real-world practitioners (you and me) messages from above.

So, no, I don't read business books any more. Not since—especially not since—they began to be populated by the strangest sorts of beings . . . like mice, and cheese, and little engines that could. They're really not my thing.

Which means, when you come right down to it, that not only do I not like business books, but, I guess, I worry about the people who write them too, because I can't see how they could possibly find joy in writing what they give you to read. There is nothing, absolutely nothing, new to say about business. So, the people who find so much to say about it are, to me, hopelessly uninteresting people.

Which brings me to the question I raised earlier on: why do I continue to write business books if I don't enjoy reading them?

You may well ask! The truth is I love to find myself in the kind of predicament where I've spontaneously

> **Anything that sounds new will very quickly reveal itself as being very old indeed, simply a dead idea dressed up in new clothes.**

begun to write a book, or an article, or a column, without any idea whatsoever of what's going to happen when I'm finally done with it—or, for that matter, where I come face to face with an idea or a thought that just appears on the page without any warning that it's coming up—because, either way, I'm suddenly put into the uncompromising position of having to invent my way out of that predicament.

This is what writers are forced to do all the time. This is what keeps me writing. This is what excites me when I go to my publisher with my next book. This turns me on when they push against me, to tell me that the book I'm thinking about writing has already been written, and when I convince them that *this book*, my book, the book that is sitting somewhere in my body at the moment, about to be born, has never been written, not by anyone, it has just awakened in me, all on its own, and it's beginning to come alive.

I love creating. I love the thought of it, the act of it, the impact of it, the delight of it, the magic of it, the spontaneity of it, the urgency of it, the surprises that come with it, the appearance of it, the strange, remarkable beauty of it—I love the description of something I have never seen, but am just about to.

That's why I keep on writing. I love to create, and it doesn't matter what it is, in fact it could be, of all things, a business. That's the part that's left out of many other books: the all-important fact that a business is nothing more or less than the inspired result of a vivid imagination.

A business is the result of someone's obsession, someone just like you and me who is obsessed with creating anything, anywhere, any time. And, depending upon where we happen to be, what we create could just as easily be a business as a book.

Which means, if you really want to get down to it, that a business is like a book, when that book is created by a writer who loves to write as much as he or she loves to breathe, and regards what he or she creates as something to be cherished both in the making and when it goes forth to play its part in the world.

Book or business, the important thing is that it should spring from an urge to create. So long as it is something you're obsessed about, so long as you start it spontaneously, so long as the words just begin to show up, and you pursue them wherever they're taking you, so long as you're hopelessly dedicated to discovering the end of the story, it will have its own good reason for being in the world. It's not about "the back end"; it's about the front end. It's not about results; it's about what is happening in this very singular moment as I'm writing this piece to you or you're sketching the design for a brand-new product. Forget the books that other people write; just write your own.

> **Book or business, the important thing is that it should spring from an urge to create.**

FOR MORE INFORMATION

Book:
Gerber, Michael. *The E-Myth Revisited: Why Most Small Businesses Don't Work and What to Do About It.* New York: HarperCollins, 1995.

See also:
Entrepreneurs (pp. 1745–1747)
The E-Myth Revisited (p. 1090)

"Many people are inventive, sometimes cleverly so. But real creativity begins with the drive to work on and on and on."
Margueritte Bro

Viewpoint: Michael Hammer
Setting the Agenda for the Next Generation of Leaders

Introduction

Michael Hammer has been, since the early 1990s, one of the most quoted management authors. He co-authored *Reengineering the Corporation*, which has worldwide sales of more than two million. No wonder, then, that *TIME* magazine included him in its first list of America's 25 most influential individuals. In his book *The Agenda*, Hammer delineates nine ways managers can compete more effectively in the 21st century. In his view, "A company can have brilliant leadership and an effective strategy, but these don't guarantee success. What's too often missing—and, therefore, what has always interested me the most—is operations: getting things done. I'm on an eternal quest for more effective ways of executing."

The domain in which I specialize is different from that of most other management thinkers. I often refer to myself as "a plumber." I'm concerned with how companies do and should operate, how best to get work done, and how to organize an enterprise so that work will be done that way. Specifically, I am a believer in process: that it's better for a company to develop a system that will produce an unending stream of results, rather than hope for brilliant ideas and individual heroics.

While many of my colleagues are professors, consultants, or inspirational speakers, I think of myself as mostly a teacher. Trying to discover and communicate the best ways to get work done is what drives me, and is what underlies the educational programs that I present to thousands of managers each year. Instead of selling fish, I teach fishing.

I owe a lot to someone I've never met but respect immensely. David Halberstam and his milestone book *The Reckoning* moved me greatly. I still quote from that book, even though I first read it in the mid 1980s, when I was a technology consultant.

At that time, I had recently left my MIT faculty position, and I was working with companies to help them to use automation and technology more effectively. I ultimately concluded that technology utilization was only a fraction of the real problem, and that the best technology could not help a company that was organized ineffectively and had poorly designed processes. Without rethinking the basics, we would end up paving the cow paths. That's why *The Reckoning* grabbed me so strongly. What Halberstam did in that book was to track the parallel histories of Nissan and Ford. As he looked at the two companies over a long period (roughly 1947 to 1983), his chapters on

Ford were a damning indictment of what was (and is) wrong with many enterprises.

The book was a revelation to me: it confirmed and elaborated my worst fears about large organizations. In the book Ford was depicted as a company more focused on financial issues rather than operational ones. How to design, make, and sell cars was less important than how to manage a balance sheet. Halberstam's insights made me face up to the fact that my technology advice would do little good unless companies rethought their priorities. I still have my copy with my marginal notations; some of the anecdotes in *The Reckoning* are burned into my memory.

> **Trying to discover and communicate the best ways to get work done is what drives me, and is what underlies the educational programs that I present to thousands of managers each year. Instead of selling fish, I teach fishing.**

However, we can't be too critical of companies like Ford (whom I have worked with and, hopefully, helped since reading that book). After all, we still haven't had that much experience with large enterprises, and it is not surprising that we are still trying to figure out how they should be run.

The modern corporation as we know it is a very recent phenomenon, a creation of the 20th century. We're still just beginning to understand how to operate and manage these large enterprises. Furthermore, the world we face today is very different from the world in which the modern corporation was born. Therefore, nothing in conventional business practice should be regarded as set in stone. Indeed, the very

"The revolution that has destroyed the traditional corporation began with efforts to improve it."

Michael Hammer

identity of the corporation is now being called into question. Looking forward, the issue of enterprise boundaries will dominate much of our discourse.

Today most companies still try to be self-contained enterprises. Today's typical corporation believes, as companies have done for the last 100 years, that it needs to do everything required to provide its product or service—and do it all inside the corporation. But that point of view is evaporating, and it will evaporate faster and faster as we move into the new century.

In other words, the question "What is a business?" is now in question.

As products have ever shorter lifetimes, we need to define our companies not in terms of what they produce, but in terms of what they do, focusing on process rather than product. To explain that distinction, let's think about a company that today considers itself in the jet aircraft business. Right now, that company does just about everything required to design, make, and sell jet aircraft. In the future, however, I can envision the managers in that company defining it as being in the business of assembling complex systems (for instance). They would assemble the components of a jet aircraft, but would work closely with other companies who would specialize in selling aircraft, or maintaining aircraft, or financing aircraft purchases by major airlines. In the past this idea was not very practical because of what economists call "transaction costs," the overhead of interfacing and coordinating with other companies. But with the advent of the Internet it is not much harder to work with others than it is to work with yourself—and the advantages of focus make doing so very worthwhile.

As this trend develops, it will change people's perspective of what a business is and what it should be doing. Businesses become parts of systems rather than whole systems in themselves. More than that, it also says that the process by which you do business is the most important part of the business. In other words, your process is your business.

All that this means is that two management skills that today are largely absent will jump to the very top of the leadership agenda. Managers will have to be proficient in designing and instrumenting systems and processes and have an enormous capacity for teamwork and collaboration.

Managers will have to get a whole lot better at looking holistically at operational processes and systems, at designing ones that operate at maximum efficiency, at measuring system performance, and at improving a system once it's up and running. This is a very different emphasis from today's; management takes on much more of an engineering flavor, rather than a financial focus. I see this already starting to take place, as phrases like "business systems engineering" and "process management" enter the par-

lance and organizational charts of more and more companies. I also see an indicator of this shift in the increasing number of executives with engineering backgrounds. I don't think it is an accident that the most influential executive of modern times, Jack Welch, has a background in chemical engineering.

Managers have to shake off once and for all the sense that they are independent actors responsible for a self-contained unit. It used to be that the grade-school child who came home with a report card that had an unsatisfactory grade in "playing well with others" was marked as one with executive potential. No longer. Companies can't afford the infighting and suboptimization that results from giving managers individual fiefdoms and letting them fight it out. Just as people on the front lines need to work collaboratively, so do their leaders. Nor can this collaboration end at company boundaries. As companies integrate their processes with each other, their managers will need to work together closely. To return to our jet aircraft example, the managers of the various companies that design, make, and sell the plane all need to work together.

We need to invoke new questions to guide our thinking. We should all be asking, every day, not only "What should I do?", but also "How can I do it better?" and "What should I not do?"

The way to shake off past traditions that are no longer relevant to tomorrow's business world is to make some hard choices. If your company is to move forward, which customers should you no longer serve? Which products should you discontinue? What things that your enterprise now does should be done instead by some other company?

> **The way to shake off past traditions that are no longer relevant to tomorrow's business world is to make some hard choices.**

This line of questioning will force companies to think of themselves in new ways. And it will also promote an environment in which everyone in the enterprise is thinking hard about how to sustain profitability and make the company the best possible place to work. Ultimately, good management tomorrow will come down to giving everyone in the corporation an understanding of the business, its customers and processes, and where each employee and manager fits. Good management tomorrow will give everyone a sense of connection and a real view of the opportunities that can be seized to generate success.

FOR MORE INFORMATION

Web site:
www.hammerandco.com

Turnaround Strategies
by Sir John Harvey-Jones

EXECUTIVE SUMMARY

- In a crisis situation, the leader of a business tends to be the first casualty and outsiders are brought in to sort out the situation.
- However, remedies are usually best applied by those already within the organization.
- A turnaround situation is one of pointing out a new direction.
- The reason many companies find themselves in trouble is almost always due to problems right at the top.
- Any solution must be one to which all parties (particularly within the company) can offer their support.
- You only get one shot at trying to turn around a business.
- Everything has to be up for grabs, and fear and tradition must not be allowed to inhibit action.

INTRODUCTION

The area of business which, mercifully, few of us have any experience of is turning a business around before it goes under—but when the rocks ahead are clearly visible. In these situations, the first casualty tends to be the current leader. He or she is usually replaced by a hired "hard man" to do the dirty work. The result is all too often far below what could be achieved by someone already within the organization, who would have been aware of the culture which has led to the decline in the first place.

The in-house candidate (a role I have personally filled) is desirable because he or she has the best chance of saving the largest proportion of what may be salvageable. After all, insolvency practitioners, or at least the good ones, could be described as managing turnarounds, but at a cost which most of us would attempt to avoid. The greatest difficulty the in-house employee faces is the problem of analyzing the causes of the downfall with sufficient clarity and over a long enough time. The elapsed time from the first business mistake to eventual collapse varies enormously. Very large organizations can carry on for a surprising time before events overwhelm them, while in the case of the small business retribution tends to strike much more quickly. What is certain is that both the stock market and the banks have less and less tolerance of business mistakes, and the time available to demonstrate an effective recovery plan is becoming ever shorter. Moreover the judgment of the chances of success is made by business analysts and the press, who probably have very little knowledge of the real situation which has led to the visible signs of failure. In reality, these are all too often symptoms rather than causes.

It is the people within the organization itself who know the myriad problems which must be overcome and the actions to be taken. Therefore the turnaround problem becomes one of pointing out the new direction. This is where being able to call on the knowledge, drive, and enthusiasm of existing employees can be so valuable. This is obviously far more difficult when all of your employees are worrying about the future, and the best and most self-confident are voting with their feet for a safer environment. The reason many companies find themselves in trouble is almost always due to problems right at the top. I have yet to meet such a situation which was caused by the employees. Employee dissatisfaction is largely caused by mismanagement or frustration. No employee actually wants to do a bad job, or to be seen to be doing one. Obviously no employee actually wants the company to fail or to find themselves faced with enforced job losses on minimal terms.

Diagnosis and Solution

If you find yourself managing a turnaround, the first two points on which you have to concentrate are your diagnosis of the problem and endeavoring to ensure that you have a reasonable time gap in which to carry out your chosen solution. For the diagnosis, you need every scrap of information, opinion, and statistical analysis you can lay your hands on. The views and openness of those on the shop floor are as important—or in some cases, more important—than those at the top. Individuals in these situations are astonishingly honest with themselves, and it is from this apparently inchoate mass of opinion and fact that a first "rough cut" analysis will appear. The strategy has to be concise and simple, for it is essential that everyone inside or outside the company should understand the goals. The detail is best left to those who will have to deliver it.

Self-evidently you cannot turn around a company by doing more of what has already landed you in trouble, although it is extraordinary how often the existing management blame their own ineffectiveness and not the strategy which has so obviously failed.

Few individuals are so closed-minded that they won't give you a chance if you explain your thinking, and in any case, no recovery plan is a single unique solution. The eventual solution you decide upon can, and must, be one to which all parties (particularly within the company) can offer their support.

Remember that your advent has kindled hope in those who work for you, coupled with probably unrealistic assumptions of a miraculous and speedy change in the situation.

Where Does Everybody Stand?

A positive strategy with clear delegation for action and a lot of trust in your employees can change things surprisingly quickly. The next, and very difficult, action is entirely within your own outfit. It is absolutely vital that everyone knows where they stand. Start with the key 10–20%, who you are sure need to be on board. Make clear that as long as you have a business, you need them and they are as secure as anyone in these times can be. Then address the 10–15% most at risk. It is almost certain you will have to reduce cash, but generally a pay-out of under 20% will do the trick. Remember that starting at the top involves fewer people and releases more money. Those most at risk deserve the earliest warning and the most help. Sharing the task of helping them to find alternatives eases the pain, as does the maximum affordable financial aid.

The remainder should be told that they

are not at immediate risk, and that the risk to them depends almost entirely on the success of the turnaround.

The financial state of the company should be known to everyone, as should the direction and amount of change which will be required. Don't be trapped by the fear of lack of security on data. Bad news travels like lightning and all too often is far exceeded by the rumors and ill-concealed *Schadenfreude* of those in the outside world. You only get one shot at trying to turn around a business, and concealment of the reality is not a help.

Delegation and Trust

Once you have decided the strategy, the goal, and the team, delegate furiously. People have to know they are trusted and that all depends upon them.

Do not allow the inevitable attempts to "delegate upward." You must keep on pushing the problem back to employees, while reiterating your commitment and support for their actions. The world is littered with examples of individuals who have achieved what you and others felt was impossible. Problems are only, and can only be, solved by those who "own" them, and your leadership role is to reinforce that ownership.

Leading by Example

You now enter what is probably the most personally difficult phase of all. Both inside and outside the company, you have to radiate confidence and realism while encouraging people to increase their speed of activity. This is helped by removing the brakes, simplifying the structure, reducing the senior management numbers and levels, and increasing the tempo.

Example is all. You cannot expect every-

one else to throw themselves at the problem if you turn up late and go off early to enjoy a liquid lunch. The drum beat is taken from the top. In my own case, I have reduced my pay level and given back money I had been awarded until the business results had turned. You need a few dramatic examples from the top. Don't expect that stopping tea and biscuits will be greeted with anything other than cynicism. Selling the headquarters or the board cars is more likely to hit a responsive chord.

It is the board that has led the business into the mess, and it is the board who must be seen to take the medicine and be totally committed to the change. In my own case, a 50% reduction in the number of executive board members and a refusal to allow deputies both increased our speed of response and demonstrated that there were no sacred cows.

Everything has to be up for grabs, and fear and tradition must not be allowed to inhibit action.

The whole problem is to achieve ownership of a new plan and a new pace of action—and all must be results oriented. Turnarounds are difficult, and test both the imagination and courage, but once it is evident you have started on the way up again there is no limit to how far and how fast you can go.

MAKING IT HAPPEN ▶▶
- Act in the certainty that people within the organization itself know the myriad problems which must be overcome and the actions to be taken.
- Concentrate first on your diagnosis of the problem and ensure a reasonable

time to execute your chosen solution.
- Ensure that the solution is one which all parties, particularly within the company, can support.
- Start your program by telling the key 10–20% that you need them on board. Then address the 10–15% whose jobs are most at risk.
- Once you have decided the strategy, the goal, and the team, delegate intensively to people who know they are trusted and that all depends upon them.
- Remove the brakes, simplify the structure, reduce senior management numbers and levels, increase the tempo—and implement a few dramatic examples from the top.

FOR MORE INFORMATION

Books:
Deming, W. Edwards. *Out of the Crisis.* Cambridge, MA: MIT Press, 2000.
Garr, Doug. *IBM Redux: Lou Gerstner and the Business Turnaround of the Decade.* Revised ed. New York: Wiley, 2000.
Joiner, Brian L. *Fourth Generation Management: The New Business Consciousness.* New York: McGraw-Hill, 1994.

Web site:
www.turnaround.org: this is the site of the Turnaround Management Association, an international nonprofit association that advocates the use of professional turnaround specialists in a crisis. The site includes a Journal of Corporate Renewal page and links to other sites.

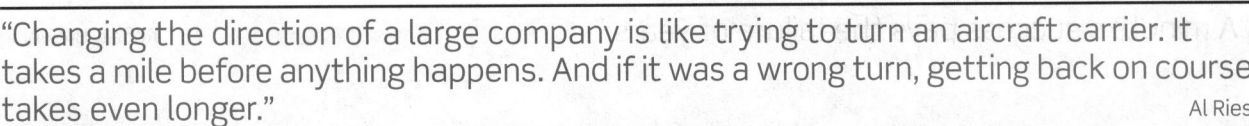
"Changing the direction of a large company is like trying to turn an aircraft carrier. It takes a mile before anything happens. And if it was a wrong turn, getting back on course takes even longer."

Al Ries

Viewpoint: Paul Ormerod
Failure and Success

Introduction
Paul Ormerod was a founding director of the Henley Centre for Forecasting and has been a visiting professor of economics at the universities of London and Manchester, England. He is the author of the bestsellers *The Death of Economics* (St. Martin's Press, 1995) and *Butterfly Economics* (Pantheon, 1999), but in this article focuses on some of the key themes explored in his most recent book, *Why Most Things Fail*.

Failure is all around us. Failure is pervasive. Failure is everywhere, across time, across place, and across different aspects of life. 99.9% of all biological species which have ever existed are now extinct. Failure in this context is measured over hundreds of millions of years. On a dramatically shorter time scale, more than 10% of all the companies in the United States disappear each year. Large and small, from corporate giants to the tiniest one-person businesses, they fail.

Yet, paradoxically, failure at the individual level is the key to the success of the system as a whole. The market-oriented economies of the West are stupendously successful, far more so than any other form of social and economic organization which has ever existed. In the old Soviet Union, everything was planned with great precision. No individual enterprise was allowed to fail. But, eventually, the whole system collapsed. In the West, individual companies fail all the time, but the system as a whole delivers the goods.

Despite this, the existence of failure is one of the great unmentionables. Business gurus eulogize contemporary success, conveniently ignoring that many of these companies often fall on harder times soon after they receive their accolade. Enron, for example, was praised to the skies for its dynamism and innovative thinking right up to the point when it became the epitome of corporate greed and mal-administration.

Books proliferate, and occasionally sell in very large numbers, which claim to have found *the* rule, or small set of rules, which will guarantee business success. But business is far too complicated, far to difficult an activity to distill into a few simple commands, or even some of the more exotic exhortations of the business gurus. It is failure rather than success which is the distinguishing feature of corporate life.

But spectacular and unanticipated success can

happen just as readily. Microsoft's early strategy, announced very publicly, was to link closely with IBM and to develop OS/2 as the standard operating system for PCs. Early versions of Windows were not popular, and attracted bad reviews. Microsoft announced that it would cease development of Windows when version 3.0 was launched, and concentrate on OS/2. Windows 3.0 came out on May 22, 1990. It sold two million copies in the first six months. The rest is history. No one under the age of 35 even remembers the failed OS/2. Everyone knows Windows.

It is this vision, this possibility of success on a stupendous scale, which motivates and drives many people who set up their own companies. Many fail, but some succeed. The person who will eventually destroy Microsoft might be working in her garage at this very moment on the concept.

Such people are the lifeblood of our economy. Small companies, especially new ones, are where all the best new ideas are conceived, the best new products developed. The risks of failure are high, but the rewards can be great.

America has always had a much more positive attitude toward failure. Try a concept and see if it works. If it doesn't, try another. It is this willingness to accept failure which, paradoxically, is the key reason why the United States is so successful.

Peter Mandelson, Britain's current European Commissioner, has called on Europe to be more like the United States in this respect. And he is absolutely right. Fortunately, British attitudes *are* already changing for the better. Bright and energetic young people are now much more open to the idea of starting their own company then they ever were.

A practical example is a bottled beer widely sold in Indian restaurants. Curry has virtually replaced roast

---

"A minute's success pays the failure of years."

Robert Browning

beef as England's national dish. The beer many people prefer with their curry is Cobra. And on Cobra's Web site is the statement: "The scales that weigh every brand were weighted against us." The founder, Karan Bilimoria, still had student debts. Britain was in the grip of the massive economic recession of the early 1990s. The beer market seemed sewn up by the corporate giants. Any business school textbook would tell you the concept was bound to fail. But it worked. Success, like failure, comes in many unexpected ways. All that is needed is a vision of how your product can change the world, a lot of work, and a slice of luck.

It is in the very early years of a company's life when it is most at risk. Elementary mistakes lead to a high death rate amongst small new companies. The single most important cause of failure among small businesses is cash flow. You might have a great idea that will work eventually, but not before you have run out of money. Making sure there is adequate financing at the start is the best way of insuring against initial failure. The sums of money do not have to be large, just enough, in fact, to tide you over the first few fraught months. Another common problem is to ignore any particular quirk of your market. For example, you are reading a magazine at this very moment. You might have a fantastic concept for a new magazine. But unless you realize that as a matter of policy most advertisers will only place material in the second but not the first issue, you are likely to fail.

The upside of all this is that once the first couple of years are successfully negotiated, the chances of a small company going under in any particular year are not much higher than those of the very largest. Size alone offers no guarantee against failure. And neither does age. A company which has survived for, say, 50 years, is almost as likely to go out of business as one which has survived for only 5 years.

Some multi-national giants have escaped extinction by the skin of their teeth. Coca-Cola seems to have been with us for ever. But by the early 1980s, Coke's leading position in the soft drink market was gradually being undermined by Pepsi. After a massive market research effort, Coca-Cola responded by introducing New Coke in 1985. Sales collapsed catastrophically. The company was only saved by the board rapidly abandoning their investment and withdrawing New Coke completely.

It may seem simply bizarre even to consider the idea that British Petroleum, say, could be driven out of business. But such things can and do happen. Almost incredibly, General Motors, once the very symbol of the dynamism and success of the American economy, is in serious difficulties. Each of America's largest 100 companies is very large. Yet every decade, one in every four of these drops out of the top 100, and over the course of a human lifetime half of them disappear.

The fundamental problem facing companies is that the human world is so complex and difficult to understand, much more so in fact than the physical one. So many things can happen that even the most carefully prepared plans come unstuck, as Coca Cola discovered. The popular image of big companies is of

captains of industry steering their giant tankers carefully through the reefs. Reality is much more like white water rafting.

Charles Darwin's theory of evolution explains not why species fail, but why they succeed. In the Darwinian theory of the process of evolution, species gradually become better adapted to their immediate environment, become fitter for survival.

In spite of this, nemesis eventually claims them, and species become extinct. The survival of even the very fittest confronts the Iron Law of Failure. Darwin wrote almost 150 years ago, but it is only very recently that biological theorists have begun to analyze systematically the evidence of failure at the species level. New mathematical models have for the first time made major advances to the Darwinian theory of evolution, explaining subtle and complex features not of evolution but of extinction.

The Iron Law of Failure extends from the world of biology into social and economic organizations. The precise mathematical relationship between the size of companies and the frequency of their extinction, for example, is virtually identical to that which describes the extinction of biological species in the fossil record. Only the time-scales differ.

Successful systems need to encourage change, to promote innovation. Germany is a prime example of a system of social and economic organization which has become ossified. For many years after the war, the German system, with its careful consensus building and reluctance to upset any major stake-holding group, was a great success. But the world in which it operated changed. Britain changed. America became even more dynamic. The Far East finally started on the evolutionary path to prosperity. Yet Germany itself has stood still. No wonder that its unemployment is now over 5 million, higher than at any time since Hitler came to power, and that its growth has stagnated for 15 years.

We need structures which encourage exploration and innovation. We need to accept that in the real world, full of complexity and uncertainty, we cannot plan the future precisely. We cannot know the optimal strategy. Instead, the process of selection and evolution enables us to discover strategies that work. And we need to accept the necessity for failure. It is failure that breeds success.

Karl Marx famously wrote that the motto of capitalists was "Accumulate, accumulate, that is the law of Moses and the Prophets!" As in many other respects, Marx was completely wrong. "Innovate, innovate!" is the guiding principle which companies have used to overcome the inherent uncertainty that surrounds all their decisions. It is the best strategy for successful systems, and it is a strategy from which we all, as consumers and citizens, have benefited immensely.

FOR MORE INFORMATION

Book:
Ormerod, Paul. *Why Most Things Fail: Evolution, Extinction, and Economics.* New York: Pantheon, 2006.

"If you want to succeed, double your failure rate."   Samuel Butler

Value Innovation
by W. Chan Kim and Renée Mauborgne

INTRODUCTION

There are two traditional schools of thought on how to compete and achieve growth. First there is the positioning school, which suggests that companies need to choose an attractive industry and then position themselves within it. This approach takes an industry's conditions as given. It also encourages companies to allow the competition to determine the parameters of their strategic thinking. Competitiveness is based on perceived advantages over the competition.

Then there is the capabilities school, which works from the inside out. This approach takes a resource-based view. Companies identify what they have, and think of what they can do best with it.

These two schools of thought are no longer sufficient. Despite their strengths, neither systematically addresses the strategic challenge of innovation, new demand creation, and—with it—the creation of new market space, or what we call blue oceans. Value innovation is an attempt to start to build this third school of thought.

UNDERSTANDING VALUE AND INNOVATION

Value and innovation are—or should be—inseparable. Value innovation places equal emphasis on value and innovation. Value without innovation can include value creation that simply improves the buyers' existing benefits. On the other hand, innovation without value may lead to bleeding-edge technology or innovation for innovation's sake. But it will not lend itself to mass-market commercial opportunities.

In classical economics, innovation is about random choice; it happens, and so companies tend to rely on people who are very intuitive. However, because innovation is seen as random, strategy has not addressed the challenge of how systematically to build new market spaces and new wealth. Value innovation challenges these assumptions. Value innovation doesn't have to be totally random. Value innovation is the crux of strategy, not the result of one genius.

Another problem is that innovation has been mistakenly equated with advances in technology. There are plenty of examples of

companies that developed technology and then failed to capitalize on it. In video-recording technology, for instance, Ampex Corporation led the way technologically in the 1950s—but value innovators like JVC and Sony brought the technology to the mass market. There are also many examples of true value innovation occurring without new technology. Look at Starbucks coffee shops, the furniture retailer IKEA, the fashion house of Ralph Lauren, or Southwest Airlines. They are in traditional businesses, but each is able to offer new and superior value through innovative ideas and knowledge.

Value innovation can be defined as creating an unprecedented set of utilities at a lower cost. It is not about making tradeoffs, but about simultaneously pursuing both exceptional value and lower costs. It is distinct from either value creation or technological innovation. The power of value innovation is in engaging people to build collective wisdom in a constructive manner.

Value innovation is fundamentally concerned with redefining the established boundaries of a market. If you offer buyers hugely improved value, or create an unprecedented set of utilities in order to give birth to new markets, then the competition becomes unimportant. Instead of playing on the same field, you've created a new one.

Value improvements only get you so far. Value innovation enables companies to shift the productivity frontier to a new terrain. Value innovation is concerned with challenging accepted assumptions about particular markets, changing the way managers frame the strategic possibilities.

CREATING BLUE OCEANS OF MARKET SPACE

The driving force behind value innovation is the willingness of companies to reconstruct industry boundaries to open up blue oceans of new market space.

Yet if you look at strategy literature, industry boundaries are usually taken as given and regarded as central—think of SWOT analysis or Michael Porter's Five Forces Framework.

To explain further, companies have tended to concentrate on differences between

groups of customers. They have divided them into ever smaller and neater segments so they can customize their offerings to meet the needs of those segments.

Value innovators take a different approach. Instead of looking at differences between customers, they focus on the basic commonalities across customers. When companies create unprecedented value on those commonalities, the core of the market is pulled toward them as customers are willing to forgo their individual preferences. Value innovation desegments and collapses established market boundaries by challenging accepted and assumed market order. Unlike the strategy framework built on environmental determinism driven by competition, value innovation takes a reconstructionist view of the market, where its focus is on shaping the market by cognitive reorderings in managers' strategic thinking.

The challenge is to create new demand—what we call *market space*. New market space is about creating a company's future. Companies can continue to mine their wealth from an existing market space—that's maintenance. They can concentrate on market share. But there is something more—the act of creation. Creating new market space will become increasingly vital.

Creating new market space provides growth. There are two paths to growth. One is the mergers and acquisition path, which often leads to growth, but rarely to profitable growth. The other is organic growth, cultivated by creating new businesses. While this path is profitable and necessary, in markets where supply exceeds demand companies are often hesitant because they find it difficult to believe that they can succeed in changing things. Our research on new market space, however, has revealed six patterns or paths that companies can apply to achieve this end. They are:

- looking across alternative industries;
- looking across strategic groups within an industry;
- looking across the chain of buyers;
- looking across complementary products and services;
- shifting the functional-emotional appeal of an industry;
- looking across time.

"Heavy-handed state intervention, the battle between capitalism and socialism . . . is dead and buried. But the idea of values, of collective purpose, and therefore of collective action is not. It is being renewed."

Tony Blair

FAIR PROCESS

Another element is our concept of *fair process*. This has to do with people. Transformation requires that companies earn the intellectual and emotional commitment of their employees. To do this requires a degree of fairness in making and executing decisions. All a company's plans will come to nothing if they are not supported by employees.

If a company violates fair process, it can be devastating. British Airways lost significant ground in employee morale and customer service after it announced a cost-cutting program at a time when its profits were high and its planes were full. There was no engagement, explanation, or clarifying of expectations.

Fair process is based on the simple human need for intellectual and emotional recognition. Without fair process it can be difficult for companies to achieve even goals their people generally support.

To embrace fair process, companies must first ask themselves whether they engage people in decisions that affect them. Do they ask for input and allow people to discuss the merit of one another's ideas? Do they explain why decisions are made, and why some opinions have been overridden? And, after a decision is made, is it clearly stated so that people understand the new standards, targets, responsibilities, and penalties? The big U.S. automakers have a history of violating fair process and have paid the consequences many times over.

CASES IN POINT

The Bert Claeys Group (now renamed Kinepolis) built new market space around Belgium's movie theaters by refusing to accept common perceptions about what was a declining industry. Bert Claeys ignored long-term decline and created the world's first megaplex, with 25 screens and seating for 7,600.

Other value innovators can be largely unknown. Two examples are the Hungarian bus company NABI, which is rapidly dominating the U.S. bus market by changing the value curve of the industry, and Cirque du Soleil, the Canadian circus that has led to a redefinition of the circus industry. Cirque du Soleil collapses the two industries of theater and circus, and in doing so it leapfrogs Ringling Brothers and Barnum and Bailey circuses, opening up the entire adult audience to circus at a price several times more expensive than that of a traditional circus.

There is also the French company JCDecaux, which is the leading provider of outdoor advertising space. JCDecaux created an entirely new industry space by converting bus stops and metro stations into very desirable advertising space. Municipalities win by getting outdoor furniture that is stylish and free, while JCDecaux wins by selling the advertising spaces in these desirable prime-location city stops.

MAKING IT HAPPEN ▶▶

We have created three analytical tools to help managers identify a winning business idea, whatever the market space it occupies or creates.

The *Buyer Utility Map* indicates the likelihood that customers will be attracted to a new idea. This is a matrix based on six stages of buyer experience—from how easy it is to find a product to how easy it is eventually to dispose of it—and six *customer utility levers*—from environmental friendliness to improved customer productivity. The matrix allows companies to assess whether their new ideas address the key blocks to utility and clearly break from the competition.

The *Price Corridor of the Mass* identifies which price will unlock the greatest number of customers. It does this by benchmarking prices not just against similar products, but different products that fulfill the same function. For example, short-haul airlines compete not just against other airlines, but against buses, trains, and cars.

The *Business Model Guide* is a framework for calculating whether, and how, a company can deliver an innovative product or service at the targeted price. It includes options such as cost targeting and opportunities for outsourcing and partnering.

FOR MORE INFORMATION

Journal Articles:

Kim, Chan, and Renée Mauborgne. "Value Innovation: The Strategic Logic of High Growth." *Harvard Business Review* (January–February 1997).

Kim, Chan, and Renée Mauborgne. "Fair Process: Managing in the Knowledge Economy." *Harvard Business Review* (July–August 1997).

Kim, Chan, and Renée Mauborgne. "Creating New Market Space." *Harvard Business Review* (January–February 1999).

Kim, Chan, and Renée Mauborgne. "Knowing a Winning Business Idea When You See One." *Harvard Business Review* (September–October 2000).

Kim, Chan, and Renée Mauborgne. "Charting Your Company's Future." *Harvard Business Review* (June 2002).

Kim, W. Chan, and Renée Mauborgne. "Blue Ocean Strategy." *Harvard Business Review* (October 2004).

Kim, W. Chan, and Renée Mauborgne. *Blue Ocean Strategy.* Cambridge, MA: Harvard Business School Press, 2005.

319

BEST PRACTICE

"Competitive strategy is about being different. It means deliberately choosing a different set of activities to deliver a unique mix of values."

Michael Porter

Core Versus Context: Managing Resources in a Downturn

by Geoffrey A. Moore

EXECUTIVE SUMMARY

- *Core* processes create competitive advantage through differentiation.
- *Context* processes are necessary to meet competitive market standards, but do not differentiate.
- Investors wish the bulk of their capital to go to core processes, as only those can raise stock prices.
- It thus becomes imperative for executives to manage their firm's *core/context ratio*.

INTRODUCTION

Executives well understand the value of focusing on core business issues and activities, although they sometimes fail to distinguish between core as competitive advantage versus core competence. The former is what the market rewards, the latter what the company is good at. One of the toughest challenges in business occurs when core competence is no longer core. Competition has caught up with you to such an extent that what was once core has now become context. The market still demands the process, but it's no longer willing to pay a premium for it.

Companies thus find themselves with an increasing portion of their asset base—sometimes in equipment, always in personnel—that no longer generates attractive returns. What was once differentiated and at a premium has now been commoditized. This in turn causes investors to bid down the value of their stock, since they see an increasingly large portion of their capital going to fund processes that are at best financially inert and are potentially a financial sinkhole.

Every company is subject to erosion of core into context; the very nature of competitive markets works to neutralize differentiation over time as competitors find ways to mimic or substitute for the value created. The knee-jerk response of most management teams is to make or find new core, which is necessary but insufficient. What they must also do is systematically work to shed themselves of context or face a perpetually deteriorating core/context ratio, with loss of attractiveness to investors and, ultimately, an uncompetitive cost of capital. In this section we will outline the impact of core versus context, and the actions that companies must take.

THE IMPACT ON COMPANIES

Companies get trapped by context from various causes, many attributable to organizational inertia. Such processes were once their bread and butter, making it hard to abandon them. Moreover, if the alternative is to outsource the work (the fundamental domain in which context shedding is accomplished), there are inevitable concerns about cost. Rarely do in-house teams *not* assert that they can perform a given function cheaper, faster, and better than outsourcers.

Long term, however, this is not the case. Where one company's context is another company's core, market dynamics ultimately favor the latter's position. That company can invest in productivity-improving systems and processes with full support of its investors, whereas the other company cannot. Moreover, it can attract the best people because it can provide them an upwardly mobile career path, whereas the latter company cannot. Finally, it can amortize investments across a broad base of customers, whereas the other company cannot.

Thus, in the long term, failing to outsource is a losing game. Only in the short term—specifically, in the current quarter—is it often more expensive, in part for reasons of transition costs, in part because prices and offerings are not as competitive as one would want until market forces have a chance to work. The end result: unless the outsourcer makes a short-term sacrifice, it's unlikely the deal goes forward.

Most executives are wise to this game, but few appreciate how pernicious it is to accede to it. They don't see how every context process not outsourced creates a tax on the asset base of the company. Worse, they don't see how failure to manage context aggressively leads necessarily to a loss of agility in their corporate culture and a corresponding rise in stifling administration. Why?

Context processes have no upside, but they do have downside. Context carries liability just as core does. The difference is that core also transfers competitive advantage, which context does not. Thus, if you're managing core, you're always in search of the efficient frontier of risk versus reward. But what is the best strategy for managing context?

Darwinian natural selection will drive context managers to increasingly risk-averse strategies, those being the most suitable for managing processes that have a downside but no upside. As a company's core/context ratio deteriorates, its population of managers will thus become increasingly risk-averse. They are happy for other people to take risks, but not themselves (and not others if that's going to put their area in the line of fire). The result? Large corporations become stultified and unresponsive.

SUCCESSFULLY MANAGING THE CORE/CONTEXT RATIO

The proving ground for outsourcing context today is contract manufacturing in the electronics industry, with companies like Cisco and Dell, and outsourcers like Solectron and Flextronics, leading the way. What these companies are exploiting is the premise that whatever is one company's context can be another company's core. In this relationship, whenever a business process is transferred from one to the other, the investors of both companies applaud, one because it went off their balance sheet, and the other because it went on to theirs.

Drill down into the systems investments that have enabled these early adopters to steal a march on their competitors and we see that they focus on two critical issues: *control* and *visibility*. The following cases provide examples.

"If executives could learn to get things right, and to quit wasting resources doing things over, then there would be work and jobs for all."

Philip B. Crosby

Beyond manufacturing, more companies are looking to outsource IT and financial and human resources services. Payroll has long been a function considered outsource-able. For example, a visible departmental outsourcing deal has been struck by British Petroleum with PricewaterhouseCoopers for human resources. Here, the best strategy is to determine for each function what is still core and what is legitimately context, (particularly critical in the case of IT).

Early outsourcing relationships between EDS and General Motors and between IBM and Kodak provide some important lessons. In both cases, the corporations were fed up with their in-house organization and wanted a better substitute at a fixed price. They made no attempt to segregate core from context. Instead they focused on price, which was negotiated as low as possible. This in turn motivated the outsourcers to cut corners or nickel-and-dime the end users on change requests, leading to bad relationships and bad outcomes. The end result was annoying when it came to context processes, but it was devastating when it ended up holding core projects hostage.

Conversely, outsourcing IT infrastructure looks to be a major growth market, as companies like Exodus attest on the server farm side. Moreover, specialized services like 24/7 performance monitoring and security management both lend themselves to third-party provisioning. These functions, although frequently mission-critical, are almost never core. This is where outsourcing shines.

KEY POINTS WHEN MANAGING THE CORE/CONTEXT RATIO

1 **Be prepared to delegate core activities.** Top management can delegate core to middle management. Of course, it rarely wants to, because this is the fun stuff. The truth is that the middle of the organization has a better view of emerging market trends; if you empower it, it will do a better job than you.

2 **Outsource and manage context.** Top management's most powerful lever is the outsourcing of context. This is not the fun stuff. But middle management is never positioned to act on this directive, as it can't afford to put its political capital at risk. Only top management can drive these initiatives, always with an eye toward repurposing reclaimed resources into the next generation of core work.

3 **Distinguish between mission-critical and supporting activities.** To the distinction between core and context needs, we need to add the distinction be-

tween *mission-critical* and *supporting*. The former applies to processes that can directly damage customer outcomes or corporate capabilities. These must be kept under managerial control. The latter, by contrast, can be readily outsourced with only modest controls.

The big challenge in core/context ratio management comes with the need to outsource mission-critical context. Indeed, executives often confuse mission-critical with core because they're sure they *can't* outsource such processes. But to manage their core/context ratio, they must. This demands new best practices in outsourcing, enabling customers to retain control and visibility while transferring the bulk of work to another organization.

4 **Harness the benefit of technology.** The technology key to the new best practices is for the company and its outsourcer to create information systems that give the company short-term adaptive controls and long-term visibility into its risk positions. The Internet provides a backbone for enabling such systems. The business logic that must ride on that backbone is just now coming to market. Early adopters may well have to write their own systems in order to get ahead of their competition.

Dell has used IT to develop end-to-end visibility into their inventory positions and used their market power to force suppliers to hold that inventory until the last second. This would be intolerable for the supplier were it not for Dell giving them near-real-time visibility into the emerging order mix, which is made possible by configuration software, now Web-enabled, that funnels customer demand from an infinite array of selections into a finite and manageable set of options.

MAKING IT HAPPEN ▶▶

1 First, start with a questioning analysis of core and context activities, at three levels:

Top level: which of our businesses are still core? Which have become context?

Business unit level: which of our line functions are the real basis for our competitive differentiation? Which are not?

Function level: which of our processes are the source of differentiation? Which are driven by more compliance?

Departmental and, if useful, individual levels: how much time is spent on context activities?

2 Next, consider two key ideas to help guide this process, asking the questions:

If we were entirely free of current obligations, what could we do to increase the competitive advantage of our company? This helps people to see the possible sources and types of core activity, and may help start the journey to get there. It also identifies the task work that should be passed on or left alone.

What work would we be willing to surrender if we were assured that someone else would handle it appropriately? This becomes a lightning rod to attract context processes that, once aggregated, can be analyzed for disposal.

3 Finally, implement and monitor the results. It helps to understand from the outset that the process of detailed implementation will invariably result in a course correction later. Also, not only does the process of implementation need to be monitored to ensure that it remains on track, but the core/context ratio needs to be regularly assessed, as competitive markets are far from static. One of the keys to successful implementation is to assemble a sufficient amount of work to motivate an outsourcer to put their best efforts into the work.

CONCLUSION

Executives must learn to manage the core/context ratio. Regardless of how superior their core is, eventually its impact will be dwarfed by an ever-expanding context. It's like cholesterol: if you do not manage context, it will finish you.

FOR MORE INFORMATION

Book:
Christensen, Clayton M. *The Innovator's Dilemma*. New York: HarperBusiness, 2003.

"Companies, like people, cannot be skillful at everything. Therefore, core capabilities both advantage and disadvantage a company."

Dorothy Leonard

Snapping Managerial Inertia
by Jeffrey Pfeffer and Robert I. Sutton

EXECUTIVE SUMMARY

- Despite the billions of dollars that industry spends on executive education, leadership development, and knowledge-management efforts each year, very little change takes place.
- Executives must use plans, analysis, meetings, and presentations to inspire achievement, not to substitute for action.
- To accomplish this, companies must eliminate fear, abolish destructive internal competition, measure what matters, and promote leaders who understand the work employees do.

INTRODUCTION

Why do so many managers understand so much about employee and organizational performance and work so hard, yet do so much to undermine performance? Why do so many companies sponsor training programs and knowledge-management initiatives, yet see no impact from those efforts? Knowing what to do isn't enough. Companies must inspire action to turn all of that individual and collective knowledge into achievements that affect the company's business results.

What happens in many companies is that managers spend so much time fighting internal battles that they have little time left to fight the company's competitors. In too many companies points are scored on the elaborateness of internal presentations (meaning that people spend inordinate amounts of time preparing those presentations to impress their bosses and peers) instead of tangible business results. In many other companies the penalty for failure is so great that managers spend their time preserving the status quo rather than trying to find new and better ways of affecting business results. Further, the "not invented here" (NIH) syndrome prevents people from learning from each other for fear that they'll give credit to some other person in the company who has developed a better method—for fear they'll admit the other person deserves more recognition and, perhaps, a greater share of the available rewards.

It doesn't have to be this way. Many companies are finding ways of overcoming the knowing–doing gap. Knowing how to bridge this gap will make a positive difference to

your company's business results, your employee's morale and performance, and your effectiveness as a manager.

GUIDELINES FOR ACTION
Recognize the Importance of Philosophy

Many companies have undertaken experiments in one division or location to implement high-performance work teams. While many such efforts have shown outstanding results, few of these companies have been successful in transferring these new work methods to other plants, divisions, or locations. A prime example of this is that few of the innovations from Saturn and NUMMI have ever been adopted by other parts of the General Motors organization. What's missing is a company-wide understanding of the basic philosophy of the new methods and a frank and open discussion of why the new methods are important and must be replicated throughout the company.

Companies that don't accept talk as a substitute for action often do one or more of the following:

- promote people who have developed a real-world understanding of the organization's work processes because they have performed them themselves
- build a culture that values simplicity (and doesn't reward complexity), uses simple, clear, and direct language, and values common sense
- use action-oriented language and follow up to ensure that decisions are implemented
- refuse to accept excuses for why things won't work, instead encouraging employees to reframe objections into challenges to be overcome

Act and Teach Others How to Act

Too many companies place great value on conceptual frameworks, fancy graphic presentations, and lots of words, but little value on action. Why are so many change efforts approved in the boardroom and never implemented? Honda puts employees into suppliers' organizations so they can see how the suppliers make parts and what work methods they use. Being closely involved with the supplier is imperative for real understanding and learning.

Plans and Concepts Count Less Than Action

Too many companies are stymied by analysis paralysis, the feeling that plans must be complete and bulletproof before any action is taken. The more successful companies encourage action to foster learning by doing. In many of these companies it is believed that an 80% solution today is better than a 100% solution months or years from now. Former Continental Airlines C.O.O. Greg Brenneman spoke of the airline's turnaround in this way: "If you sit around devising elegant and complex strategies and then try to execute them through a series of flawless decisions, you're doomed. We saved Continental because we acted and we never looked back."

Tolerate Errors as a Sign That Learning Is Taking Place

Does your company treat mistakes so harshly that people continuously analyze and discuss plans instead of taking action? Thomas Edison tried thousands of materials for light-bulb filaments before discovering tungsten. When someone asked him how he overcame so many failures, he said that he never failed—he just learned. Roger Sant, co-founder of AES, fosters a culture of forgiveness, noting, "You would be amazed at how quickly people support and forgive one another here."

Drive Fear out of Your Organization

If employees fear that any new idea that doesn't work perfectly at the first attempt will result in punishment or dismissal, they'll never try anything new. Rapid prototyping is a manufacturing design method in which new ideas can be tried out quickly

"Pusillanimity disposeth men to irresolution, and consequently to lose the occasions and fittest opportunities of action."

Thomas Hobbes

and relatively inexpensively and plans modified based on results. Failure of a new idea is viewed as part of the learning process, not as something to be feared. Successful companies encourage risk-taking and encourage employees to try new ideas without an overwhelming fear of retribution should they fail.

Companies that work to drive fear out of their organization often try some of these approaches:

- rather than shooting the messenger, reward employees who deliver bad news—if the company doesn't know about a problem, it can't solve it;
- punish inaction, not unsuccessful actions—an unsuccessful action should be viewed as a learning experience;
- share failures—when leaders share their failures, they give permission to others to fail and encourage them to try;
- banish anyone, at any level, who humiliates others;
- learn from, and even celebrate, mistakes—especially when trying something new.

Fight the Competition, Not Each Other

Because competitive free enterprise has triumphed as an economic system, many companies have adopted internal competition as a way of life. This is typified by such practices as normal-curve performance rating systems, recognition for relatively few employees, and individual measurements and rewards that set people against each other. These practices take the focus away from the real opposition: external competitors. There are exceptions, however.

Measure Action and What Turns Knowledge into Action

Many companies are awash with data measuring every conceivable action. Amid so many measures employees spend far too much time focused on the numbers and how they'll look instead of on actions that can help to improve the business and meet overall goals. More successful companies focus on a few key measures of company performance, believing that if those key measures are met, everything else will fall into line.

Leadership Is the Key

Successful leaders create a positive learning environment that not only helps employees learn but also helps them apply that learning to their work to make a positive difference in business results. They lead by their own example and teach others how to act.

MINI-CASES

At Men's Wearhouse the emphasis is on team selling; employees succeed only as their coworkers succeed. Customers don't care who gets the commission, they want great service from every employee.

The SAS Institute has a very low turnover rate, based partly on employees' preference not to have to constantly look over their shoulder to see which coworker is getting ready to subvert their work in order to look better themselves.

Southwest Airlines focuses on key measures such as lost bags, customer complaints, and on-time performance.

AES focuses on uptime of their power plants, new business development, and environmental and safety factors.

Measurements that can help to turn knowledge into action include those that are:

- focused on organizational success rather than individual success. This encourages teamwork and interdependence.
- focused more on processes and means to ends, not on end products and final outcomes. This helps to facilitate learning and provides data that can better guide action and decision making.
- focused on the business model, culture, and philosophy of the company. This means that measurements will vary from company to company and will generally depart from traditional accounting-based indicators.
- focused on a mindful, ongoing process of learning from experience and

experimentation. No process is ever viewed as complete or final.

When David Kearns was C.E.O. at Xerox, he applied quality principles to the top management team as he encouraged their implementation throughout the company.

The C.E.O. of General Motors teaches in GM University, demonstrating his personal commitment to knowledge building and sharing.

CONCLUSION

Many readers will finish this article and start nodding: How did they know what's happening in my company? But recognizing that the problems exist isn't enough. Going back over 20 years, Peters and Waterman, in their book *In Search of Excellence*, recognized that the most successful companies have a "bias for action." And that's what you need to snap your company's managerial inertia. Start right now!

FOR MORE INFORMATION

Books:
Kelly, Patrick, and John Case. *Faster Company: Building the World's Nuttiest, Turn-on-a-Dime, Home-grown, Billion-dollar Business.* New York: Wiley, 1998.
Tobin, Daniel R. *The Knowledge-enabled Organization: Moving from "Training" to "Learning" to Meet Business Goals.* New York: AMACOM, 1997.

See also:
☆ Creating Value through People (pp. 153–154)
📖 Management Teams: Why They Succeed or Fail (p. 1115)
☆ Organic Growth Versus Acquisition (pp. 106–107)
☆ Return on Talent (pp. 144–145)
💡 R. Meredith Belbin (pp. 1182–1183)
☆ The Critical Factors That Build or Break Teams (pp. 225–226)
☆ The Good, the Fad, and the Ugly (pp. 210–211)

"Sometimes I am forced to the conclusion that GM is so large and its inertia so great that it is impossible for us to be leaders."

Alfred P. Sloan

The Environment of the Future
by Bob Tyrrell

EXECUTIVE SUMMARY

- Patterns are easily discernible in individual lives, but are less clear on a global scale. However, it's important to try to see the bigger picture.
- Moving into "the second modernity" involves big changes, which in turn cause conflicts in thinking.
- Facing us today or looming over the horizon are an extraordinary range of challenges that will threaten all organizations and even the future of mankind if they are not handled sensitively.
- The best way to steer smoothly into the future is to envisage possible global scenarios. These enable us to predict trends, test theories, and spot possible troubles before they occur.

INTRODUCTION

No one would be surprised to be told that patterns exist in their daily lives, and that these can be easily discerned by observers. Our preferences, the constraints under which we operate, and our habits all help to shape our lives and make them predictable, to a degree.

Things are different when we come to "the global environment." There is much greater complexity; it has fuzzy edges and no one controls it in the way that we control our own lives. The social philosopher Karl Popper went further in his book *The Poverty of Historicism*, seeing great dangers in attempts to discern patterns of global change. He cited as an example Karl Marx's attempts to discern the future course of global capitalism, and how this led to the totalitarianism of communism. He concluded that when people start to play God with the future of the world, we all suffer!

But the skeptics' position is unsatisfactory. In companies and governments, we are all affected by the "bigger picture" and would do better if we were better prepared for what's coming over the horizon. So where and how do we start?

FRAME OF REFERENCE: TWO MODERNITIES

The only way to make sense of a complex phenomenon such as the "global environment" is to simplify it. One way of doing this is to break it into its component parts. The so-called "PESTEL" model is one approach, dividing the world into the political, economic, social, technological, environ-

mental, and legal elements. It has its attractions and supporters but it still leaves you with the need to put it all back together. My favored approach is to abstract from the froth and the surface "noise," to identify the deeper currents at work and attempt to arrive at a gestalt view. A good example of this comes from the German sociologist Norbert Elias, who has characterized the age in which we live as the "Second Modernity."

Sociovision has taken this insight and identified a number of features that differentiate the second from the first modernity. For example in the first, most people "knew their place," belonged to a social class and expected stability. The intergenerational transmission of values was from old to young: sons did as their fathers did; daughters modeled themselves on their mothers. "Institutions" knew what was best and handled matters in the munificent interests of the people. Religious leaders were respected, and traditions structured many aspects of everyday life.

This first modernity dominated the first two-thirds of the 20th century and produced the "industrial society," mass consumption, and the welfare state. Consumers were happy to consume relatively standardized products; employees were prepared to work in regimented conditions; and citizens respected the hierarchy of the family and institutional authority. There was a strong coherence between the family model, the state model, and the managerial model. The first modernity was a "top-down" society where the big ruled the small: big business, big ideology, big institutions, big religion, mass education, mass markets; and where

the rational dominated the emotional—linear careers, structured processes, logical management techniques, and sequenced life stages.

THE NATURE OF THE SECOND MODERNITY

By contrast, the second modernity is more of "bottom-up" phenomenon and less uniform. This era started as early as the mid-1960s. By the early 1970s, the family had begun to adapt itself to the evolution of attitudes among its members, leading to less unquestioned paternal authority, a stronger place for the women, and the possibility for the children to participate in decisions. At the macro level, states progressively gave more freedom to their peoples, freedom of expression, freedom to travel. It is no coincidence that some of the big ideologies, such as communism, started to crumble under the force of new, and increasingly global, social expectations.

Some other characteristics of the second modernity are that people are more concerned about their pleasure than their duty; about participation than belonging; about self-expression rather than fulfilling social expectations. People are less and less attached to formal structures of belonging and find their affiliation needs met in networks, more flexible family arrangements, and in more "organic" associations.

CONFLICT BETWEEN THE TWO MODERNITIES

Because different individuals, societies, and organizations move at different paces, the transition from first to second modernity values produces tensions and can undermine the confidence and clarity of purpose of decision makers. For example, many business and government leaders are still basing decisions on the perceptions of a clearly organized, simple, and hierarchical society. The (largely unnoticed) passage to the second modernity presents these leaders with a huge sense of dissonance. Practical examples of the tensions these differences in mindset create include the clash between:
- Organizational demands for more than full-time commitment to the job, and the

"The earth we abuse and the living things we kill will, in the end, take their revenge; for in exploiting their presence we are diminishing our future."
Marya Mannes

- growing desire on the part of individuals for a work–life balance.
- An approach to leadership that emphasizes command, control, and information holding, and an increasing expectation of empowerment, with the leader as "coach" and facilitator.
- Single-dimensional thinking about the role of business in society (wealth-creation and stockholder value models) and the apparent desire of many employees and consumers to deal with "authentic" and ethical companies.
- The tendency of global organizations to unify their systems and management approaches wherever in the world they operate, and the self-evident reality that different countries and cultures may be going through the modernization process at different rates—or not going through the same process at all.

MAKING IT HAPPEN ▶▶
Dealing with Uncertainty

Having a frame of reference is critical to making sense of a complex phenomenon, but this still leaves us with the problem of future uncertainty: you may now see the pattern, but how will it evolve? This is where scenarios come into play.

Scenarios are less about predicting the future than they are about increasing our sensitivity to the possible twists and turns we may face as we navigate the global environment. Rarely have we faced the need for this sharpening of our senses more than today.

The scenario creation process typically starts with an identification of the predetermined factors. The main purpose of this is not to limit the range of the possible worlds we are going to explore (although it does that); it is more about making explicit the points from which our exploration of the alternatives will start and testing the compatibility of sets of assumptions. For example, one scenario might start from the assumption that "globalization" in terms of increasing economic integration and global communications will continue, but that culturally there will be a return to more locally rooted lifestyles and that national governments will continue to assert their sovereignty. Taken in isolation, each of these assumptions is plausible and evidence can be adduced in their support. The scenario process tests whether all the elements of these worlds can cohabit. This has many benefits:

- The process of developing fully-textured "stories" forces us to think about the way causal processes operate in our world. For example, can we have increasingly global communications and a genuine diversity of culture locally?
- Once we have developed a scenario and tested how far the narrative is "event dependent" (for example, at the time of writing many things hinge on the success of the current war against terror), we are alert to what subsequent "chapters" may hold on the basis of the way the last chapter has ended.
- We are also sensitized to "weak signals" we might otherwise have missed. Without the frame of reference provided by a scenario, many events and trends will either be off our radar screens altogether or we will fail to interpret their significance. For example, lacking a genuinely global view that recognized the growing power of religious belief in the Islamic world, many of the pre-September 11 signals to that awful event were either missed or misunderstood by most people in the West.

CONCLUSION

We live in an extraordinarily complex and uncertain world. In 1989 Francis Fukuyama could write his article "The End of History" to widespread acclaim. He posited that the big questions had been settled and the future would be one of neoliberalism, increasing globalization and, in essence, more of the same—forever. He had seen the future, and it was Reagan's America.

But nothing is forever. There is today a palpable sense that we may be at the end of an era. As recently as five years ago, not many would have questioned Fukuyama's vision of the future. Not now. Facing us today or looming over the horizon is an extraordinary range of challenges that will threaten all organizations and even the future of mankind if they are not handled sensitively. These include:

- The threat of prolonged and synchronized recession in a number of major economies.
- Further terrorist attacks employing chemical, biological, or even nuclear devices.
- Growing ethnic and racial tensions globally and within nation states.
- The threat of global warming.

- The rise of China and its impact on global economic patterns, post its entry to the WTO.
- Dealing with the burden of the aging populations of the West.

We cannot possibly foretell precisely how these challenges will play out either individually or in concert. To react by putting them in the "too difficult" tray would be to abdicate a fundamental responsibility. Thinking about the future is possible, if also hard work. The reward is that we simulate our worst fears rather than experience them, and maximize our opportunities rather than miss them.

FOR MORE INFORMATION

Books:
Bean, Roger, and Russell Radford. *The Business of Innovation: Managing the Corporate Imagination for Maximum Results*. New York: AMACOM, 2002.
Fukuyama, Francis. *The Great Disruption*. New York: Simon & Schuster, 2000.
Gibson, Rowan, ed. *Rethinking the Future*. Naperville, IL: Nicholas Brealey, 1999.
Kelly, Eamonn. *Powerful Times: Rising to the Challenge of Our Uncertain World*. Philadelphia: Wharton School Publishers, 2005.
Malone, Thomas W. *The Future of Work: How the New Order of Business Will Shape Your Organization, Your Management Style and Your Life*. Cambridge, MA: Harvard Business School Press, 2004.
Stewart, Thomas A. *The Wealth of Knowledge: Intellectual Capital and the Twenty-First Century Organization*. New York: Currency/Doubleday, 2001.
Warden, John A., and Leland A. Russell. *Winning in FastTime: Harness the Competitive Advantage of Prometheus in Business and Life*. Montgomery, AL: Venturist Publishing, 2002.

Web sites:
www.gbn.org: the Global Business Network is a worldwide membership organization engaged in a collaborative exploration of the future, discovering the frontiers of knowledge and creating innovative tools for strategic action.
www.wfs.org: the World Future Society Web site is dedicated to providing its users with information about and scenarios of the future so that they will be as prepared as possible when it arrives.

"Perseverance may be just as important as speed in the battle for the future." Gary Hamel

326

BEST PRACTICE

The Future of Money
by Bernard Lietaer

EXECUTIVE SUMMARY

Money is an agreement within a community to use something as a means of payment. A major shift is currently ongoing in the power to create money, from the banking system to private currencies. This could create new possibilities in a wide variety of domains, including in the way business is done and social changes are facilitated.

WHAT IS MONEY?

Economic textbooks define money by what it *does*; that is, they describe its classic functions as a standard of value, means of exchange, and store of value. But what, in fact, *is* money?

Our working definition is as follows: money is an *agreement* within a *community* to use something as a *means of payment*.

From a business perspective, money is also the first objective of a corporation. If a business doesn't manage to have a higher money inflow than outflow, it is doomed to disappear.

Given the amount of effort that goes into trying to capture part of the money flow, it is intriguing that so little time is spent on thinking about where money comes from, or what it is.

TYPES OF MONEY

By our definition, there are already a number of different types of currency in widespread use today. We may distinguish between:

- **Legal tender** "for all debts, public or private." Thus, if someone owes a debt and offers to pay with this currency, the debt can be declared void if the currency is refused. One important debt covered in this respect is tax payments. National currencies are typically the only legal tender in a country.
- **Commercial private currencies.** The most common are loyalty currencies, the best known of which are "frequent-flyer miles." Barter currencies are another type of commercial private currency.
- **Complementary currencies.** Currencies that are accepted in payment, but do not aim at replacing, merely at complementing, conventional national currencies. They are therefore designed to function in parallel with conventional currencies.
- **Social-purpose currencies.** Complementary currencies that aim at

resolving a variety of social problems, such as elderly-care currencies, unemployment currencies, or environmental currencies.

TODAY'S NATIONAL MONEY

The secret of creating modern money is to be able to persuade people to accept one's IOU (a promise to pay in the future) as a medium of exchange. Whoever attains that status can derive an income flow from the process (for example, the interest on the loan that creates the money). Such income is called "seigniorage," a word derived from the right of the lord of the manor (*seigneur* in Old French) to impose the use of his currency on his vassals.

Four key features characterize conventional national money. Today, money is typically (1) geographically attached to a nation-state; it is (2) "fiat" money, i.e. created out of nothing, by (3) bank debt, against payment of (4) interest.

We now have trouble imagining any currencies *other* than those issued by a given country, or in the case of the Euro, a group of countries. However, the vast majority of historical currencies were, in fact, *private* issues made by the sovereign or some other local authority. Sharing a common currency creates an invisible, yet very effective, information boundary between "us" and "them." Thus national currencies are perceived as a distinctive attribute of nationhood.

The simple question "Where does money come from?" propels us into the world of magic. Today's money is "fiat" money. Every unit of every national currency in circulation started as a bank loan, either to the government or to a private entity. Just as the magician needs a handkerchief to wave above the hat before the rabbit can appear, bank money has an additional veil. In the process of creating money, attention will be drawn toward the boring technical aspects, such as mechanisms to foster competition

among banks for deposits, reserve requirements, and the role of the central bank in fine-tuning the valves of the system. While these technical features all have a perfectly valid purpose (so does the handkerchief), they all simply regulate how much fiat money each bank can create (the number of rabbits that can be pulled out of which hat).

The last obvious feature of our money is interest. Here again, we tend to forget that for most of history interest was not a feature of money. In fact, all three "Religions of the Book" (Judaism, Christianity, and Islam) emphatically outlawed usury, defined as *any* interest on money. Applying interest on the loans creating money has a pervasive effect on society. For instance:

1. Interest indirectly encourages systematic competition among the participants in the system, because only the principal is created in a loan, while the interest isn't. When someone pays back interest he or she is using in fact someone else's principal.
2. Interest concentrates wealth by taxing the majority in favor of a minority. It is noteworthy that—when interest became legal—democratic countries felt the need to introduce progressive taxation to counterbalance that wealth-concentration process.
3. Interest continually fuels the need for endless economic growth.
4. Finally, interest programs decision makers to think short term. The "discounted cash flow" technique shows why future income or costs can be discounted into irrelevance when an interest-bearing currency is used.

THE FUTURE OF MONEY

In his massive study entitled *The History of Money from Ancient Times to the Present Day*, Glyn Davies remarks that over the past 5,000 years there have only been two fundamental innovations in the technology of money. The first was paper money, which was invented in China during the 9th century and spread to Western Europe during the late Renaissance. It enabled the transfer of the power of money creation from kings and emperors to the banking system. We are now in the middle of the second fundamental innovation: electronic money. Already today, over 95% of the money existing

in the world resides in the form of bits and bytes in computers at banks and brokers. All the signs are that this new technology shift may also involve a change in the power of creating money.

While conventional bank-debt currencies will in most countries maintain their privileged status as legal tender, other types of currencies could become "common use tender."

Private commercial currencies have indeed already broken the monopoly of conventional money as a medium of payment. Initially, airline frequent-flyer currencies were only a marketing gimmick issued by each airline individually. But today, for example, two-thirds of all British airline miles are cashed in for something other than air travel. Sainsbury's, one of the largest supermarket chains in the United Kingdom, is now accepting them as payment in its shops.

Commercial barter, previously considered a "primitive" form of exchange, is now growing by 15% per year, three times faster than normal currency denominated transactions. *Barter News* estimates that broker-facilitated barter deals now amount to approximately $10 billion per year. More significant still is countertrade (international corporate barter). The U.S. Department of Commerce, the World Trade Organization (WTO), and *The Economist* all estimate countertrade to have reached a staggering volume of between $800 billion and $1.2 trillion per year. This represents between 10% and 15% of all international trade! *Fortune* reports that two out of every three major global corporations now perform such transactions routinely, and have specialized departments focusing on such deals. Social-purpose complementary currencies have similarly experienced explosive growth over the past 15 years.

There is a wide variety of social purposes pursued by such local complementary-currency systems. They vary from care of the elderly to unemployment, from the restoration of a spirit of community in a well-off neighborhood near Washington, D.C. to getting kids off drugs and crime in ghettos in Chicago. They operate in Mexico City and in fishing villages in Canada. They have been designed for small groups of 50 people in Australia, a city of 2.3 million people in Brazil, or prefectures of 10 million in Japan.

While local activists on a shoestring budget started most of these systems, governments now actively support some of them as well.

- The city planning office of Curitiba, the capital city of Paraná in Southern Brazil, has launched and managed for 25 years a local currency that is now providing up to one third of all the income of its citizens, and has been a key to its remarkable development as the "most ecological city in the world" by UN standards.
- In Australia and New Zealand local authorities are funding local currency startups in high-unemployment pockets.
- In the United States, the IRS has declared one such system (Time Dollars) officially tax-free; and 31 states now pay their own employees to start up such systems.
- In Japan, the head of the services department of the Ministry of International Trade and Industry (MITI) has started 40 different experimental "eco-money projects," in order to choose the models that would be most appropriate for general application in the country.
- In the United Kingdom in 2001, the Blair government financed a £500,000 startup for a Time Bank in London.

What matters here is what they have in common:

- Of these systems, 95% are computer-driven.
- They have already proved that they can solve real-life social problems without burdening taxpayers or governmental budgets.
- The vast majority are small-scale affairs that are purposely kept on a local scale. But the only mature system today (the WIR in Switzerland) now has 80,000 members, including one quarter of all small and medium-sized businesses in the country, and enjoys an annual turnover of $2 billion.

Perhaps the most intriguing thing about this phenomenon is that it has proved wrong an implicit hypothesis in economics dating back to Adam Smith: that money is value-neutral. In fact, both empirical fieldwork and theoretical research have proved that *the use of different kinds of currency does significantly affect both the behavior and the relationships of the people who use them.*

These money innovations provide new possibilities for businesses to use their inventories as working capital, or for social issues to be addressed with less taxpayer's money.

We should leave the last word about the future of money to Georg Simmel, a German philosopher and author: "The debate about the future of money is not about inflation or deflation, fixed or flexible exchange rates, gold or paper standards; it is about the kind of society in which money is to operate."

FOR MORE INFORMATION

Books:
Davies, Glyn. *A History of Money from Ancient Times to the Present Day.* Cardiff: University of Wales Press, 2002.
Lietaer, Bernard. *The Future of Money.* New York: Random House, 2001.
Simmel, Georg. *Philosophy of Money.* Revised ed. New York: Routledge, 2004.

"In the past, business was the employer of all those who wanted to work. In the future, there will be lots of customers, but not lots of jobs."

Charles Handy

Competitor Analysis: From Data to Insight
by Liam Fahey

EXECUTIVE SUMMARY

Competitor analysis (CA) has emerged recently as a distinct discipline or area of analysis in leading European, North American, and Asian companies. As it has become more sophisticated, CA has shifted from a pure data focus (gathering data about competitors) to a genuine analysis focus: transforming data relating to competitors into "decision-relevant" insights.

INTRODUCTION

Executives, among others, often misconstrue why competitor analysis is conducted. Its purpose and benefits are not just to learn about one's competitors.

Rivals are analyzed as one means of learning about the broader competitive environment—that is, in order to generate insights into customers, distribution channels, suppliers, technology, and competitive dynamics. In the same vein, CA is also used to reflect on and learn about one's own organization—its vulnerabilities, limitations, and capabilities relative to current and potential rivals.

WHICH COMPETITORS MERIT ATTENTION?

Potential insight is sometimes unnecessarily constrained in many companies because too much attention is devoted to *current* large-market-share competitors and far too little to other types of current and potential rivals. Critical insight into change in customers' buying behavior often emanates from analysis of small(er) rivals or of functional substitute rivals. And, sometimes, it is especially useful to "invent" a competitor that is not yet in the marketplace—for example, one created by the alliance and integration of two smaller rivals, which would then develop and introduce a variety of products new to the market. This "imagined competitor" can be used as a reference point to challenge the company's existing strategy or potential strategy alternatives.

THE PROCESS OF ANALYSIS

The core of the analysis process in CA can be simply stated: identify relevant indicators from competitors' behavior, actions, and words, then draw inferences as to what changes those indicators imply the competitor might make in the future (for example, how it might change its strategy), or what they might suggest about developments in the broader marketplace (such as how fast specific products might come to the market or how quickly other products might penetrate particular customer segments). It is especially important to emphasize that CA is always about detecting change in and around competitors and assessing what that change implies for the competitor itself, for the marketplace in general, or for your own organization.

THE FOCUS OF COMPETITOR ANALYSIS

A central competitor-analysis question confronts every organization: *"What is it about our rivals that we should analyze?"* Or, stated differently, "What do we need to know about our current and potential rivals?" When competitor analysis is driven by a perspective that views it as a source of learning about both the competitive environment and our own organization, however, and not just as a source of learning about our rivals, then a number of other core focal points of analysis quickly surface. We need to learn about:

- The competitor's *marketplace strategy*: how it tries to outmaneuver rivals in the marketplace.
- The competitor's *activity/value chain*: how it organizes itself to develop and execute its marketplace strategy.
- The competitor's *alliances and networks*: what other organizations it aligns with and

how it manages its network of alliances.
- The competitor's *assumptions*: what the competitor assumes about the marketplace and itself.
- The competitor's *assets and capabilities*: what enables the competitor to compete.
- The competitor's *organizational infrastructure and culture*: the nature of the competitor's organization.

CAPTURING RIVALS' MARKETPLACE STRATEGIES

Let us take marketplace strategy to quickly illustrate some key points in how to conduct CA.

Understanding a competitor's marketplace strategy requires you to answer three fundamental, highly interrelated questions related to the rival's marketplace scope, posture, and goals—the three central elements in any company's marketplace strategy:

1 What product-markets does the rival compete in (or want to compete in)?
2 How does it compete in those product-markets to attract, win, and retain customers?
3 What does it seek to achieve in those product-markets?

You can now think about the critical indicators associated with each question. The first question involves indicators associated with products and customers: the variety of products offered; the variety within each product line; the segments of customers reached; differences across the segments, etc.

Indicators that allow posture to be identified depend upon the relevant dimensions associated with its key modes of competing or providing value to customers—product line width, product features, functionality, service, availability, image and reputation, selling and relationships, and price. For example, for a car manufacturer, functionality might involve a number of dimensions, each giving rise to specific indicators: take-off speed (how fast can the car go from zero to 60 mph); braking speed (how fast can you stop the car going at 40 mph); gasoline consumption (how many miles will the car go on a gallon of gasoline); reliability (on average, how often does this type of car have to be repaired).

"Being in front merely gives one the right to try harder. It means that you are setting the pace which every competitor has to follow."

John Harvey-Jones

Indicators that allow marketplace goals to be inferred are also specific to the particular type of goal: product, customer, market share, share of customer, etc.

One great merit of attention to indicators is that they guide you to relevant data sources. The overarching question is always: *What sources might provide data on this particular indicator?* You should always begin by asking which individuals or units within your own organization might possess the required data and what the external sources might be.

For example, a team of competitor analysts in one automobile manufacturer wished to know the terms and conditions associated with purchases of key components from specific suppliers, such as specific types of glass from a well-known international glass manufacturer and specific types of plastic from a local supplier. They discovered that their own internal purchasing department already possessed most of the required data.

The essence of the analysis task then becomes the derivation of inferences from the change detected via relevant indicators. For example, change in a number of indicators of modes of competition (as discussed above) could reveal that a rival is moving to increasingly add value for customers with a broader range of service or through introducing new forms of functionality or by developing more intensive relationships with high-end customers.

ASSESSING RIVALS' MARKETPLACE STRATEGIES

Analysis only generates real insight when it turns to assessing what change in the rival's strategy indicates about current, emerging, and potential change in the broader competitive context, and what such change in turn implies for the company's current and potential strategy, decisions, and actions.

Assessment begins by evaluating the performance of the rival's strategy. Is it resulting in market-share gain? Is it leading to a greater share of individual customers? Is it building greater brand name and reputation (that in turn could be the basis of further market-share gain)?

Assessment then addresses how well the rival's strategy is performing compared to other rivals or to our own company's strategy. For example, with regard to specific customer segments, or even individual customers, is the rival or our own company providing greater value along the modes of competition? Based upon customers' judg-

ments, who is providing superior functionality? Who is providing more useful services? Whose image and reputation is more appealing to customers? It is important to note that these assessments must be based in large measure on the judgments of the customers themselves.

Assessment then aims to determine what change in the rival's marketplace strategy might portend for change in the emerging and potential marketplace. For example, customers' positive responses to a rival's recently introduced product might suggest significant shifts in the value customers will increasingly demand from their suppliers. If the company misses this signal, it could commit extensive investment to products that will be less appealing to the market.

To cite one more illustration, if a rival appears to be committing extensive resources to introducing new product lines, to going after new customer segments, and to seeking a greater share of existing customers, then it may well significantly shift the dynamics of rivalry over time. Its rivals may find that their old ways of competing may no longer be sufficient to retain existing customers, much less attract new ones.

Assessment of change in competitors' marketplace strategy can also lead to strong judgments about what type of marketplace strategy might be required to win in particular product domains or specific geographic regions. For example, in one product area, one computer company concluded from the analysis of a dominant rival's marketplace strategy change, and from the product initiatives of a recent entrant, that the only way any company could succeed in this product/technology was to develop multiple alliances with a range of vendors (so that it could continue to develop state-of-the-art products) and with a range of value-added resellers and other types of retailers (so that it could guarantee rapid access to large customer segments).

Assessment concludes by identifying specific implications for one's own company. For example, do the marketplace implications of change in the rival's strategy suggest that one is missing an emerging marketplace opportunity or that one should be moving faster to penetrate a specific customer segment? Often, assessment reveals key vulnerabilities not just in one's own marketplace strategy but also in one's assets and capabilities.

In summary, competitor analysis can lead to significant new insights into the world around us, as well as into our own organization.

MAKING IT HAPPEN ▶▶
- Focus on analyzing the information gained on rivals in order to reflect on and learn one's own organization's vulnerabilities, capabilities, and future direction.
- Examine six areas of competitor activity: marketplace strategy; activity/value chain; alliances and networks; assumptions; assets and capabilities; and organizational infrastructure and culture.
- Ask what sources can provide the data you need. Look internally for sources of information first.
- Always consider what a change in competitor's activity indicates about the potential change in a broader competitive context.

CONCLUSION

While many managers feel that it's all they can do to collect and analyze information about their own business, one cannot really compete in today's business environment without some understanding of what the competition is up to. Competitor Analysis is a new aspect of a manager's job, and it has rapidly become a respected discipline. However, analyzing the ways of one's competitors is valuable only when a company subsequently makes decisions about how it can perform better, based on a wider view of what's happening in the marketplace.

FOR MORE INFORMATION

Books:
Fahey, Liam. *Competitors: Outwitting, Outmaneuvering and Outperforming.* New York: Wiley, 1998.
Fleisher, Craig S., and Babette E. Bensoussan. *Methods and Techniques for Analysing Business Competition: International Edition.* Upper Saddle River, NJ: Pearson, 2004.
Porter, Michael E. *Competitive Strategy: Techniques for Analyzing Industries and Competitors.* New York: Free Press, 1998.
Yoffie, David B., and Mary Kwak. *Judo Strategy: Turning Your Competitors' Strength to Your Advantage.* Cambridge, MA: Harvard Business School Press, 2001.

Web site:
Competitve Analysis:
www.managementhelp.org/mrktng/cmpetitr/cmpetitr.htm

"What do you do when your competitor's drowning? Get a live hose and stick it in his mouth."
Ray Kroc

330

BEST PRACTICE

Now! The Role of Urgency in Creating Positive Change
by John Reh

EXECUTIVE SUMMARY

- Change happens. It always has happened. You cannot control change; you can only manage your interaction with it.
- Today change happens more quickly than ever before. You must be prepared for change at higher speed and be able to deal with it positively.
- Instilling a sense of urgency in an organization gives it a suite of tools with which to better relate to change and to adapt as necessary to survive.

INTRODUCTION

The speed and extent of changes in the dot-com space, while highly visible, are not unique. The Pony Express was forced out of business in only 18 months because of competition from the telegraph. Japanese automakers almost destroyed several U.S. giants in that industry. And the popularity of the PC pushed Dell and Microsoft past IBM, the company that developed it.

The strengths that got you to the top won't keep you there. Others are always pushing to move past you, to dominate your market, to steal your best customers. You need to stay ahead of them. You need to change with the times—or ahead of them. And that need is urgent.

Business organizations have always had to deal with change. That change now is simply coming faster. Change that occurred in the automobile industry over a period of 20 years starting in the 1960s occurred within less than 20 months in the Internet industry. Change will occur; management must make it as positive as possible.

Businesses are living organisms. Like animals they have certain characteristics that enable them to survive in their environment. When that environment changes the organism must evolve too, or it will die. If the organism is not able or willing to change fast enough, it will be unable to survive in the new environment. Those organisms that can change quickly can survive, however.

CHANGE IS NEVER UNANNOUNCED

Changes always give signs they're coming. Sometimes signs are obvious and we all see them. The more sensitive you are to your environment, the more likely you are to notice the changes. But being aware that change is coming is not enough: you have to be able to react in time.

The environment in which a business operates can change in innumerable ways. Some of the changes are obvious and happen over a long time. For instance, new government regulations that govern your industry are publicly announced, go through a public comment period, and are likely to be revised and republished before they take effect. Few are caught off guard by such changes. We begin to prepare changes to our operations so that we can perform in compliance with the coming regulations.

Other changes can happen more quickly. A competitor may release a new product that captures significant market share almost overnight. A key supplier may suddenly go bankrupt. One of our facilities may be destroyed by a natural disaster. Our latest product may be more popular than expected and our plants unable to keep up with the demand. We develop contingency plans to cover such occurrences.

The better you are at tracking your markets and your competitors, the less likely you are to be surprised by a new product rollout. The more closely integrated you are with your supply chain, the less likely you are to be caught unprepared for a supplier's financial difficulties. The better attuned you are to your customers, the more likely it is that your product demand forecasts will be accurate.

SUCCESS BUILDS COMPLACENCY

Some companies are more sensitive to their environment and better equipped to deal with changes in that environment than their competitors. Sometimes it's an issue of size, sometimes an issue of longevity. Always it's an issue of leadership.

Success can breed complacency, dulling the sense of urgency around the need for change. Procedures that have outlived their usefulness survive because "that's how we've always done it." It's hard to let go of methods of doing things that have contributed to past successes, even though they now waste time and no longer create value.

GET THINGS MOVING

As a manager, you know change will occur. You saw, for example, how quickly the Internet became an essential part of business and how much more quickly businesses that had not properly understood it failed. You also know people have a natural tendency to resist change, a tendency you have to overcome. You have to act to initiate the process of change.

URGENCY: YOUR BEST WEAPON

Nothing is more important in creating positive change than a sense of urgency. It must start at the top, be communicated throughout the organization, and it must be felt by the entire organization.

Urgency is defined as "compelling immediate action; conveying a sense of pressing importance." If you want to blast people and organizations out of their inertia you have to get their attention, give them a compelling reason to act outside their comfort zone, and keep them moving. The sense of pressing importance helps you to move ahead, and that gives you time to recover from mistakes or to change direction early enough, so that only minor corrections are required later.

Once you know a change is needed, urgency keeps you from wasting precious resources on the wrong choices. Failing to communicate a sense of urgency to your organization leaves an avenue open to continue with the status quo. This not only delays the implementation of the needed changes, it consumes resources that will be needed to make them. The most critical of these resources is time.

Those responsible for change must focus

"The tail tracks the head. If the head moves fast the tail will keep up the same pace. If the head is sluggish, the tail will drop."

Konosuke Matsushita

on the roles of the leader, not on the tasks of the manager. Leaders set direction, communicate the vision, and empower people to do what has to be done for the change to succeed. Managers plan how to make the changes happen. They organize, allocate resources, and help people to perform more efficiently. Managers are necessary if a change is going to succeed, but the leader is critical.

MINI-CASES
Urgency at Work
In the summer of 1999, Carlos Ghosn, then new C.O.O. of *Nissan*, set a goal of profitability by 2001. Saying that a sense of urgency was key—"you should come to headquarters and the walls should be on fire"—he set in motion his Nissan Revival Plan (NRP). On May 17, 2001, Nissan announced its best financial results in a decade.

Wal-Mart has a Sundown Rule, founder Sam Walton's twist on the old adage "Don't put off until tomorrow what you can do today." Observing that rule means striving to answer requests the day they're received. It's one reason that Wal-Mart associates are famous for their customer service.

AsiaTrak (Tianjin) is a joint venture of Caterpillar, Itochu, and SNT that provides undercarriage products to the excavator and tractor industries. The company culture recognizes time as a competitive advantage and aims to err on the side of moving too fast rather than too slowly.

Few industries are as time-sensitive as floral retailing. 1–800-FLOWERS.COM uses a Web-based system for transmitting orders and scheduling deliveries. The system, called BloomLink, incorporates real-time chat capability so that florists can ask questions about an order as they receive it.

your actions, but don't hide behind them;
- pushing people out of their comfort zone is high-risk, but can yield high reward;
- help people be brave. Brave people move faster;
- dare to dream. Planning change means visualizing a present that doesn't yet exist;
- reinforce the message by repeating it often and keeping it fresh in people's minds.

People do what they think is in their best interests. You need both positive and negative tactics to create a sense of urgency around your desired change. Show people why the status quo is bad for them. Then show them your vision of the future and why that will be better.

First:
- manufacture a crisis to start the ball rolling;
- allow a very visible (but not deadly) problem to blow up out of control;
- widely publish internal reports that support your position that the status quo is unacceptable;
- make information available that shows how quickly the situation is going from bad to worse.

Then:
- show people the significantly better state that will exist for them after the change;
- reinforce the need for urgency with a good slogan, like the UPS tag line, "Moving at the Speed of Business";
- use time-based metrics to keep up the sense of urgency;
- set targets that are unreachable without the change.

If your goal is to centralize the customer service staff in a single location to reduce costs, build and post graphs so people can track their progress toward the goal. A weekly step chart showing the savings planned from closing smaller facilities, for example, can help people to visualize the goal. Superimposing actual savings on the same chart can vividly illustrate the value of closing one office a couple of weeks early and can help to keep the sense of urgency high.

CONCLUSION
For business strategies to work in practice, organizations need to develop and change: business strategy is not about preserving the status quo, it is concerned with making progress, and this requires change. Combined with this is the fact that, whether it is welcome or not, change is the only constant in business: it is inevitable and needs to be harnessed. If it is not proactively managed, then the effects can be overwhelming.

Leading change is a vital aspect of leadership in general, because it requires dynamic, focused action. Without this proactive leadership, change will fail—or fail even to get started. Leadership is essential to delivering effective change as it provides vision—a clear idea of purpose and direction. Leadership and a sense of urgency are also important to communicate, facilitate, guide, and focus activity; to solve problems; to coordinate and make decisions. In general, to provide a framework that ensures success, the leader must create a sense of urgency and provide the necessary motivation and support.

Change is happening more often and more quickly. The leader's job is to manage that change to create a positive outcome for the organization. Creating a sense of urgency is the best tool for making that happen.

FOR MORE INFORMATION

Books:
Bell, Chip R., and Oren Harari. *BEEP! BEEP!: Competing in the Age of the Road Runner*. New York: Warner, 2001.
Grove, Andrew S. *Only the Paranoid Survive: How to Exploit the Crisis Points that Challenge Every Company*. New York: Bantam, 1999.
Hanna, David P. *Designing Organizations for High Performance*. Boston, MA: Addison-Wesley, 1988.
Kossoff, Leslie. *Executive Thinking: The Dream, the Vision, the Mission Achieved*. Palo Alto, CA: Davies-Black, 1999.
Kotter, John P. *Leading Change*. Cambridge, MA: Harvard Business School Press, 1996.

Web site:
Journal of Organizational Change Management:
www.emeraldinsight.com/jocm.htm

See also:
☆ Getting All Your People Committed to Change and Transformation (pp. 220–222)
☆ Viewpoint: Henry Mintzberg (pp. 292–293)

The Supply Chain by Peter Day

EXECUTIVE SUMMARY

- Once upon a time, the supply chain was invisible simply because it was taken for granted: farm to mill; mill to merchant, merchant to baker, baker to customer or skill to skill, and if the chain broke, people starved or the price went up.
- Modern supply chains are much more complicated. They have their own ideologies and their own gurus. But there is nothing fixed about the supply chain. Its shape and rationale varies from decade to decade no matter how unchanging it may seem when you are in the middle of it.

INTRODUCTION

Let's have a brief history lesson. The family concerns that produced the British industrial revolution in the 18th and 19th century did everything for themselves, because they had to.

It was natural for Henry Ford to control all the elements that fed his production lines. When I interviewed the management guru Tom Peters in a hotel where he was due to address major Ford dealers later in the day, he was much struck by the fact that the convention center was built on the fields where Ford used to raise the sheep to supply the wool for its own automobile upholstery. For a time it was imperative for automakers to own rubber plantations, too. Integration that now seems crazy was seen as the only way to get things done.

The South Korean chaebol are vivid examples of this mentality at work. In a country driven by the urge to climb out of abject poverty at top speed, the founder of one of these huge family conglomerates would start a particular business, usually with the blessing of the president he has helped to gain national power. A builder might start a cement plant. He needed sacks, so one son would start a paper factory to ensure supply. (Importing was hazardous and unpatriotic.) The company needed transportation; another son would start a garage; soon it would be building trucks (and much later, cars). A shipping line would follow; bigger building projects for the company (workers' houses, for example) demanded a construction company; workers' housing developments needed shops, so the chaebol would become a big retailer. Eventually, the youngest son would start a stock brokerage.

In a developing country, it makes perfect sense, say the chaebol. But in a developed world it is perfect nonsense, an organization of frightening inflexibility. And flexibility it what gives the business supply chain its strength . . . and its vulnerability.

THE JOLT FROM JAPAN

Most of what is written about supply chains is technical and detailed, all about how they should be managed. The writers are obsessed with the elimination of corporate or inter-corporate bottlenecks. But there is more to the supply chain than managing it. Just thinking about it sheds much light on organizational development itself.

Supplies have always been a problem. Traditionally companies had a warehouse mentality: security of supply was the pre-eminent requirement. Having many competing suppliers enabled the customer to bargain on prices. Warehousing was uncosted and unanalyzed.

The supply chain as a business idea, something with a life of its own needing specialist management, developed in the 1990s at about the same time that the word "transportation" was being replaced by "logistics." This was logical. The new robotized warehouses were huge investments. Their computerization enabled suppliers to lock their information systems into those of their customers, creating a truly integrated supply chain for the first time.

If warehousing was being reorganized, so were the supplies and suppliers. The speed of technological change meant that there was no longer security in having supplies in-house and on the shelf. As computers followed (Gordon) Moore's Law and halved in price and doubled in power every two years, components on the shelves became not a comforting safety net but a frightening liability. Once, in the 1990s, semiconductor prices plunged from over $70 each to less than $1 in a single year. The supply chain became a threat to a company.

The jolt from Japan also impacted supply chain management. When Western business people went to Japan, they discovered not only Total Quality (imported from the United States, of course) and Continuous Improvement, but also the interlocking relationships between big Japanese companies and their suppliers, often funded or owned by a common umbrella concern, so-called Keiretsu.

These company partnerships were quite natural, and as the geniuses at Toyota carried out decades of warfare on waste in every part and process of their business, what could be more wasteful than supplies on the shelves for eventual use? Out of Japan came just-in-time inventory, nerve-jangling for traditional Western factory managers. It is still enthralling to see less than an hour's supply of car seats stored in a Japanese auto plant, already stacked to match the color of the cars that are on the production line.

Behind that immaculate handshake between need and supply was something more than integrated computer systems. When Japanese automakers started manufacturing in Britain, they trained some local U.K. suppliers to their rigorous needs. But the vital components—the just-in-time car seats, for example—were made in new captive plants built by their customary Japanese suppliers close to the perimeter of the new British plant.

As production migrates from traditional industrial centers to new low-cost tax-efficient countries, suppliers are coming under heavy pressure to send their production abroad as well, whatever it means for their original bases. This is happening now in Spain; local auto parts companies in Barcelona, which were set up to supply the huge foreign-owned car plants 25 years ago, are now being told to migrate with the auto production to central Europe or lose the business.

A "NEW RELATIONSHIP"

Cost pressures forced huge manufacturers such as the auto industry to re-examine their supply chain in the 1980s; they eliminated hundreds of suppliers, promising those that remained a more secure relationship. They devised a theoretically attractive new relationship between big customer and smaller supplier—long-term contracts, close

supervision by the customer of the suppliers' production line, systems integration, joint working to improve the product and the way it was made—a mutual benefit, not just an annual wrangle over prices and quality.

In theory this was a step change in industrial cooperation; many managers say they gained enormous advantage by learning intimately what their key customers wanted. Walk into any surviving medium-sized manufacturing company today, and the preferred supplier certificate will be proudly framed in the reception area, along with the ISO 9000 badge for quality management.

The relationships became close, perhaps dangerously so. Key clients would often gain access to the figures, know the profitability of the components they were buying. Nothing is cozy in industry for long. When automakers hit trouble, they behaved desperately. They made mandatory price cuts on a year's worth of components already supplied to them. The supply chain can be a nasty business when one partner has a one-way advantage.

Recently the supply chain has begun to reverse itself. Dell Computers buys millions of dollars worth of computer semiconductors from Intel every year, but these components are the heart of the machine. It is as though Dell has become a supplier of customers to Intel.

Intel is a clever company and was never more clever than when it woke up to the fact that the rise of the home computer was propelling it into the gadget business. The company replaced its engineer's chips named after their numerical technical capabilities, and gave them brand names such as Pentium™. With aggressive "Intel Inside®" advertising, Intel became one of the most recognized brand names in the world, as the "supplier" became the guarantor of a performance of lesser-known computer assemblers and retail names. This breakdown of traditional flows along the supply chain may happen more and more in the future.

It is a matter of debate whether computers have yet made much impact in the way companies are managed. But when it comes to the supply chain, computers make it real in a way that was not visible before.

Bottlenecks of information become just as important as production bottlenecks.

REVOLUTION?

For a brief moment before the dot-com bubble burst at the end of the 20th century, it seemed as though the supply chain might be about to be revolutionized. For a few years around 2000, Business to Business buying exchanges were touted as the next big thing. Industries claimed to have spent billions setting up information exchanges on the Internet. Companies insisted they would buy everything from transmissions to light bulbs and toilet rolls from the cheapest tendering supplier anywhere in the universe, thanks to the new exchanges. Huge potential savings were claimed.

For a moment it seemed plausible. But as the dot-com bubble burst, the exchanges sank under their own costs and perhaps a reluctance to return to the old days of supplies that could come from anywhere, provided they were cheap. The boardroom asked: Aren't we trying to simplify our supply chain, not recomplicate it?

Meanwhile, surely and silently, the Internet auction service eBay is developing a huge commercial activity. It is a B2B exchange by other means, a supply chain erected for every purchase. Google has similar ambitions, using its current grip on information exchange to exact a tiny slice of every transaction in the world.

The supply chain is under pressure, though I think I would still prefer the people I know and have worked with for years to a supplier whose reputation looks good on the eBay assessment system.

At the same time, the supply chain is beginning to emerge as a point of differentiation for companies which have hitherto relied on their own brands and their own advertising. The Internet is making users or consumers hungry for information that until now has been unfindable.

The wine industry has been disrupted by two information devices: the rise of the single grape varietal wine, and the information-filled back label on the bottle. Both have enabled new wine drinkers in Europe and America to experiment with supermarket

wines with confidence, buying bottles they like from completely new places.

These two separate phenomena have seriously eroded the French grip on the wine industry. Baffled by traditional French appellations, wine drinkers have been able to discover for the first time that the New World wine they liked was made from the merlot grape; the back label told them where and how it was made, and by whom. Suppliers with a clear message to drinkers bypassed the traditions and snobbery of the French influenced trade.

Educated consumers will require increasingly more information about what they buy and where it comes from. Already some leading restaurants are listing their suppliers on their menus.

The sports shoe maker Nike has been troubled in recent years by revelations that its suppliers were paying its workers pittances. In response, it now publishes a list of all 700 of its suppliers' factories on its Web site, with addresses. Inquirers can find out more.

In other words, the supply chain is moving from hidden provider to certified guarantor of good practice. It is a radical break with tradition, and it will happen much more in a big change. Advertisers' claims will be challenged by the consumer activists' cry: "Prove what you say." A transparent and publicized supply chain will be part of the proof.

Meanwhile large companies can themselves use the supply chain as an agent of change. If they demand recyclable packaging, or proof that child labor was not involved in the components they buy, it will happen. The impact is faster than any legislation.

CONCLUSION

The supply chain is changing. It is emerging from commoditized anonymity to become a significant part of what is perceived to lie behind the branded good or service. Educated users will require transparency, information, and integrity from the goods and services they buy. And when customers get even pickier, then the supply chain will have to evolve again.

"An act of God was defined as something which no reasonable man could have expected."

A. P. Herbert

Scenario Planning
by Gill Ringland

EXECUTIVE SUMMARY

- Scenario planning uses possible future outcomes (scenarios) to improve the quality of decision making (planning).
- The emphasis has moved in recent years from building scenarios to successfully using them.
- The techniques for building scenarios are well developed—the challenge is to incorporate an understanding and facility with possible futures into management thinking. This has led to an emphasis on using scenario planning for team development; improving the structural assumptions and data behind planning; and developing techniques for communication of scenarios.
- Scenarios are now widely used in the public and voluntary sectors as well as in business.

SCENARIOS AS MODELS OF FUTURE WORLDS

One of the best definitions of *scenario* is by Michael Porter:

"an internally consistent view of what the future might be, not a forecast but one possible future outcome"

At a time of volatility and change, managers need to be able to step out of their current framework and imagine future worlds—which may arrive sooner than expected. Scenario planning is a set of processes for creating several scenarios or mental models and using them to aid decision making. The scenarios explore a spectrum of different possible answers to core questions facing the organization.

- In 1985, what would the effect of the fall of the Berlin Wall be on the business of an Austrian insurance company?
- What new markets was a manufacturing company supplying copper cable to the telecom industry equipped to tackle?
- In a computer company, what would be the drivers of outsourcing, and what effect would this have?

The scenarios capturing possible answers to these and similar questions are used to improve the robustness of plans (for instance, by exposing implicit structural assumptions in economic or social forecasts) or to create new plans based on newly visible options.

FORECASTING AND SCENARIOS

Scenario thinking traces its history back to just after World War II, when Hermann Kahn pioneered *future now* thinking. This technique, put forward by Kahn to promote debate about nuclear weapons, aimed

through the use of imagination and detailed analysis to produce a report about current events as it might be written retrospectively by people living in the future.

Most current uses of scenarios relate to Kahn's purpose in being used, for example, to:

- stimulate debate about choices;
- develop strategy resilient against several futures;
- test business plans against futures;
- try to anticipate futures as an aid to decision making.

While forecasts or high-growth/low-growth forecasts (sometimes also called scenarios) can be used for any of these purposes, the use of imaginative and qualitatively different worlds is a central theme of most current uses of scenarios. Forecasts aim for accuracy, using techniques such as Delphi; scenarios explore the space of uncertainties in defining possible futures.

Questions often asked include:

- How many scenarios?
- What timescale?

The number of scenarios is bounded on the lower end by the adoption of two qualitatively different worlds, and at the upper by the ability of the team (and its intended audience) to be able to comprehend the differences, maybe up to five. In planning work with numerate groups it is usual to avoid three or five, because planners will often assume that the middle scenario is "right," that is, that it's a forecast. The timescale for the scenarios needs to be longer than the budget or planning cycle of the organization, and certainly longer than the job tenure of the team developing them, in

order to avoid defensiveness. A longer timescale is easier to work with than the medium-term (for example, three years) since many of the defining trends will already be clear and the current complexities still confusing in the medium term.

CREATING SCENARIOS

The creation of scenarios is an excellent management development tool for a team, taking team members beyond defending their current role. It can be useful for management teams to take one or two days to develop scenarios for their business based on existing information within the group as a way of exploring shared perceptions. The classic method for developing scenarios, based on research and analysis by an in-house team or consultants, may take from three people-months to 30 people-years.

A significant advantage for an organization in creating its own scenarios is that wild cards will emerge during the research. These are events that would be calamitous but are judged unlikely to happen. Action to determine the process for dealing with these—for example, which department should have contingency plans—and the subsequent discussions are often beneficial, prompting new insights.

USING EXISTING SCENARIOS

The emphasis in most organizations is moving away from developing new scenarios toward tailoring existing scenarios, working with management teams on the implications of the scenarios for their business or project.

A sample workshop outline to develop strategy-based scenarios is given in Table 1 on the next page.

It is important that these workshops be held offsite to signal their difference from routine work. The two-day format is good to allow time for reflection and absorption.

PLANNING WITH SCENARIOS
Scenarios and Business Plans

Business plans always incorporate the assumptions of the management team, which are often implicit. For instance, will a characteristic that has added competitive advantage in the past continue to do so as markets change? By using scenarios the team can

---

"Scenarios are the most powerful vehicles I know for challenging our mental models about the world and lifting the blinkers that limit our creativity and resourcefulness."

Peter Schwartz

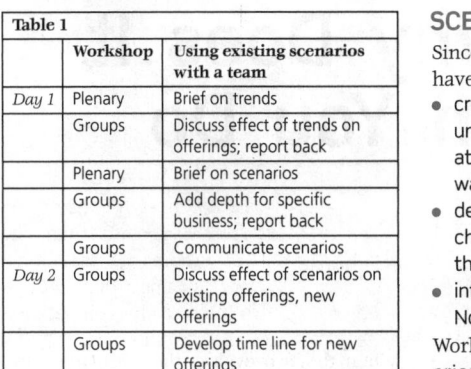

Table 1		
	Workshop	**Using existing scenarios with a team**
Day 1	Plenary	Brief on trends
	Groups	Discuss effect of trends on offerings; report back
	Plenary	Brief on scenarios
	Groups	Add depth for specific business; report back
	Groups	Communicate scenarios
Day 2	Groups	Discuss effect of scenarios on existing offerings, new offerings
	Groups	Develop time line for new offerings
	Groups	Develop time line for new threats
	Plenary	Report back, plan next actions

recognize the future world built into their plan and explore the implications of other possible—or probable—worlds.

Some organizations rework the entire business plan for all (usually two) scenarios. This may be a back-of-the-envelope sketch or a team effort. Back-of-the-envelope calculations can often capture the essential relative viability of a single capital project under different scenarios. Full reworking of the business plan may be needed in organizations in which many divisions and functions will be affected.

Portfolio Management

A market attractiveness/capability matrix is often used to manage a portfolio of businesses within a company:

Table 2			
Market Attractiveness Capability Matrix			
	Weak	*Medium*	*Strong*
High	Double or quit	Try harder	Leader
Medium	Phased withdrawal	Proceed with care	Growth
Low	Withdraw	Phased withdrawal	Cash generation

Examining the portfolio as it would exist in the future under each scenario produces a new position on the matrix for each business. While the discussion of the factors affecting each business is useful, the improvement of the decision process is the main gain.

In assessing the likelihood of a scenario coming true, early indicators are used—events that will occur in the next year or so specifically under one scenario. These might be selected topics already watched by ongoing mechanisms, for example, the patents departments.

SCENARIOS IN PUBLIC POLICY

Since the time of Hermann Kahn, scenarios have been used to:
- create a common language and understanding; for example, in South Africa at the time the African National Congress was poised to take power;
- develop strategy in the face of new challenges, for example, as Canada faced the implications of an information society;
- inform public debate, for example, in Norway on the use of oil revenues.

Workshops associated with building scenarios are widely used to develop public opinion.

COMMUNICATION OF SCENARIOS

When scenarios were used mostly within planning groups, the output was often expressed in tabular form, with a list of factors (for example, growth rate, dominant technology) in the left-hand column and the other columns describing the factors under each scenario. While these were good working tools, they were fatally bad communication tools.

Names are often used to communicate the essence of scenarios. The Chatham House Forum scenarios for the economics of the industrial world in 2020 are called Atlantic Storm and Market Forces; in Atlantic Storm, Europe and the United States are at odds, while in Market Forces a free market dominates.

Newspapers written as if in the future, descriptions of role-model characters, a-day-in-the-life stories, and glossy booklets can all be used to communicate scenarios. Recent work has used film and video clips with interactive choice to explore scenarios with groups of decision-makers.

MAKING IT HAPPEN ▶▶
- Use scenarios for stimulating debate, developing resilient strategies, testing business plans against possible futures, and trying to anticipate futures.
- Allow one or two days for management teams to develop scenarios, based on existing information.
- Hold workshops offsite to signal "different," with two-day residential formats to allow optimum reflection and absorption time.
- For a single capital project, try back-of-the-envelope calculations to capture the essential differences in the viability of alternatives.

- To assess the likelihood of a scenario coming true, use early indicators—events that should be seen in the next year or so.
- Communicate scenarios graphically, for example, by imaginary newspapers written as if in the future, day-in-the-life stories, film, or glossy booklets.

CONCLUSION

Most people who work with scenarios find it to be stimulating and enjoyable. The next stage, making the most of scenario planning, depends on:
- deciding what problem the scenarios are intended to help solve. What are the crucial questions facing the organization, the questions whose answers imply, "I wish I had known this seven years ago?"
- creating or exploiting scenarios that explore the uncertainty space—often in-house scenarios focus on close-to-home and internal problems;
- giving the scenarios effort high enough status by offsite meetings, high-level sponsors, and management feedback;
- using the scenarios to drive decision making by stimulating debate, developing strategy, testing business plans, or anticipating futures;
- using imaginative and frequent communication to embed scenario thinking into discussion and decisions.

FOR MORE INFORMATION

Books:
Ringland, Gill. *Scenario Planning: Managing for the Future.* 2nd ed. New York: Wiley, 2006.
Ringland, Gill. *Scenarios in Business.* Chichester: Wiley, 2002.
Ringland, Gill, *Scenarios in Public Policy.* Chichester: Wiley, 2002
Schwartz, Peter. *The Art of the Long View: Planning for the Future in an Uncertain World.* New York: Wiley, 1997.

See also:
☆ Avoiding the Mistakes of the Past: Lessons from the Startup World (pp. 164–165)
☆ The End of Growth: Why Does It Always End? What Can You Do About It? (pp. 336–338)

"We are self-activating organisms, and can, to some degree, control our own destiny and our own responses to pressures . . . we can select our goals and choose the paths toward them."

Charles Handy

The End of Growth: Why Does It Always End? What Can You Do About It?

by Robert M. Tomasko

EXECUTIVE SUMMARY

- All growth trajectories follow a life cycle.
- Business growth invariably slows.
- If you anticipate the inevitable decline, you can push it further into the future.
- Sustained growth ultimately requires the courage to abandon one growth path for another.

INTRODUCTION

Why do bubbles burst? Because as they grow their surface area becomes so large that increasing amounts of energy are diverted away from keeping the structure intact and into expanding its size. Some bubbles find an equilibrium point and persist, but those that keep trying to grow collapse. This collapse has little to do with outside intervention. It's caused by trying too hard. Many businesses similarly try too hard, fighting the nature of their markets and organization, and find their growth trajectory coming to a crashing halt.

All growth efforts eventually slow. But neither your business nor your career has to decline in tandem with them as long as you stay alert to the dynamics that are in play and cultivate the ability to adapt.

MINI-CASES

Sainsbury, not too long ago the United Kingdom's largest supermarket chain, discovered that an attempt to maintain family control of its top management, while expanding abroad and diversifying at home, was more than its growth path could endure. The result: a fall from the top as the U.K. market-share leader and a change to an outside C.E.O.

Swissair, the longtime standard-setter for classy air travel, attempted to fuel its growth with an ill-thought-out plan to buy parts of a dozen small, struggling airlines. Financial chaos from cascading losses ensued, along with a C.E.O.-firing and resignation of the directors who endorsed such a blind-alley strategy.

THE LAWS OF GRAVITY ALSO APPLY TO BUSINESS

Hitting the growth wall is a problem that eventually plagues every business.

- Wall Street analysts hate hearing from executives with no visibility about their next quarter's prospects.
- Underwater stock options demoralize.
- Unreachable sales quotas squash motivation.
- Just as rapid growth creates its own forward momentum, generating new fast-track career paths, ambitious top performers are often the first to jump ship at the prospect of a business slowdown. Net result: fewer seasoned business growers available to rebound the business.

The cumulative impact of poor publicity, talent loss, and demoralization serves only to reinforce this negative spiral. The dynamics behind the turn-of-the-millennium e-business slowdown aren't all that different from the forces that limited the expansion of the mainframe computer industry in the 1990s, energy companies in the 1980s, consumer-goods makers in the 1970s, and, over a century ago, the steam railways.

Sudden, out-of-the-blue shocks are blamed for many business slowdowns. However, in reality these are few and far between. The Internet, a favorite scapegoat, has caused far more businesses to grow than it has destroyed. Every market runs on a life cycle. So does every business, in a cycle of:

- ramp-up
- rapid growth
- mature stability
- gradual decline

When the two cycles—the company's and its industry's—are out of sync, growth inevitably slows and economic performance suffers. This is the story of Apple Computer before its iPod days, and the Internet-based grocer Webvan. It's a lesson that retailer Target has learned and K-Mart has not. Melding the cycles can keep Amazon.com alive, creating a mature business that matches its mature market. Cataclysmic events and life-cycle misfits are outside-the-company growth retarders. They can sting, but the enemy to be most wary of is lurking within. Most businesses don't need competitors to steal their growth opportunities. They do it to themselves, making errors of both omission and commission.

UNDERSTANDING THE POTENTIAL FOR SELF-INFLICTED WOUNDS

What's most commonly missing among managers and executives of slow-growth companies is the ability to engage in systems thinking.

These people tend to

- treat each happening in the business as an isolated event (or problem to be solved) rather than seeing it as part of a chain extending over a long time period;
- focus on the needs of their own company, department, or job rather than seeing themselves and their business as part of a network of interconnected players.

This mentality puts a brake on growth. It forgets that every driver of growth is accompanied by some kind of limiting process, such as:

- an awakened competitor
- an overtaxed supplier
- an extra-vigilant regulator
- an internal capacity constraint (usually cash or talent)

Plunging ahead in blissful ignorance is a sure way to hit the growth wall. It's what brought Cisco Systems, once the most valuable company in the world, back to earth. As if mesmerized by its we-can-do-no-wrong growth trajectory, the company committed

---

"Growth does not always lead a business to build on success. All too often it converts a highly successful business into a mediocre large business."

Richard Branson

the fundamental sin of doubling inventory in a weakening market, saddling itself with warehouses full of unsaleable merchandise.

It's also important to be wary of growth substitutes. Among the most common are:

- **Accounting trickery**. Managing earnings instead of growth creates the appearance of profit increases through restructuring charges, hidden reserves, and changes in pension-funding policies.
- **Stock buy-backs**. Earnings per share do rise when the number of shares shrinks, but this is not the same as increases due to profitable revenue growth.
- **Merger mania**. Acquisitions and mergers, as Swissair and many other companies have learned, are often more of a long detour than a direct path to real growth.
- **Cost-cutting**. This source of short-term gain destroys more seeds of future growth than any aggressive competitor might.

AVOIDING A TOXIC TREATMENT

Why does cost-cutting bite back? There are times when it's the right remedy, but like some popular medicines it's overprescribed as a cure for stalled growth. Profits can grow in the short-term through cost-cutting, of course, at least until the business runs out of expendables. No amount of downsizing can make up for General Motors' inability to build cars that people really want to buy. Profits resulting from creating hard-to-duplicate benefits that are conveyed to customers are a sustainable, renewable resource. But they are renewable only as long as the business growers who create them are kept in place and motivated. But when the cost-cutting fixer mentality dominates with its often mindless, across-the-board slashes, good growers run for cover. The growth mindset cultivates carefully nurtured, experience-based, invest-now-for-future-return behavior.

Responding to the End of Growth
If you're facing market collapse

- Remember that it's better to yield to some trends, instead of engaging in an unwinnable war. When Intel's bread-and-butter computer memory business was threatened by a wave of cheap Asian imports, Andy Grove accepted the inevitable and just walked away. Instead, he refocused Intel on the much richer business of making microprocessors.
- Even if you're facing total economic collapse, don't throw in the towel until you study the lessons of Brazilian and Lebanese businesses. Both are world-class improvisers—the best strategy when everything seems up in the air.

- If regulatory straitjackets seem insurmountable obstacles, look hard at the ways of northern Italy's virtual keiretsu and France's highly automated manufacturers.

If your market's life cycle is at war with your plans

- Sustain your growth by getting out ahead of the curve.
- Consider the first hints of growth deceleration as nature's way of telling you to shift gears. Nokia did this, growing in the same cell phone manufacturing marketplace that was a quagmire for Ericsson and Motorola.
- When the market seems to have had enough of innovative products, consider reorienting around customer-defined requirements rather than inner vision.
- When growth slows because everyone in the industry seems to be following the same formula, follow the lead of upstarts like Southwest Airlines and Ryanair, and rethink your offerings from the ground up.
- When industry domination becomes too costly to sustain, pick off the most profitable segments, focus exclusively on customers' needs, and reap the high-margin rewards that come to specialist companies like Rolex and Germany's famous Mittelstand.

If your company seems to be its own worst enemy

- Don't throw away that next invitation to a seminar on systems thinking. Go, and you'll never think about your business in the same way again.
- Keep multiple sets of books if you have to (as your country's laws allow, of course), but don't confuse the kinds of growth accountants create with the real thing.
- Resist the urge to merge until it's crystal clear how the acquisition will enable growth. Don't let size become an end in itself.
- Never cut costs as an end in itself, only as a subordinate component of an overall growth plan.
- Never confuse stock-price growth with business growth.
- Don't waste energy whining when the market tanks your stock. High-tech manufacturer Seagate took advantage of a demolished stock price to divorce Wall Street, go private, and restore momentum away from the glare of the financial press.
- "Take no prisoners" is an order that belongs to the movie theater, not the boardroom. Microsoft's growth was much more sustainable when its standard-setting opened up profitable market segments for business allies clustering under its umbrella. Taking a live-and-let-live

perspective on the competition is a great way to expand the size of everyone's market. Coke and Pepsi need each other, and they both know it. Virgin and British Airways do, too, but they may not be quite as aware of the need. Wal-Mart needs vibrant specialty retailers on Main Street, but has ignored that reality, generating opposition to its growth because of it.

MAKING IT HAPPEN ▶▶

The following steps can help to continue or rekindle successful growth:

1. **Review current business activities:** this may involve analyzing strengths, weaknesses, opportunities, and threats, as well as assessing the business's relative market share. It can also mean answering the following questions:

   Where are the most profitable parts of the business?

   What are the prospects in the short-, medium-, and long-term for those products and markets?

   How precarious is the business—for example, does it rely on too few products, customers, or distribution channels?

   How clearly focused is the business—is it over-burdened with too many products, markets, and initiatives, or is it running on empty with too few opportunities?

   What is likely to be the best method of expansion—is it affordable (not just in terms of money)?

   What are the advantages and disadvantages of expanding?

2. **Decide the best method of achieving growth:** discuss the options with senior managers and stockholders, refining potential opportunities and deciding how to approach problems.

3. **Plan for growth:** decide what action is needed to achieve growth. This will certainly involve leadership qualities to communicate and mobilize resources.

4. **Act decisively and consistently:** once the course has been set it needs to be rigorously followed. One of the greatest obstacles to growth is inertia, often in the form of attachment to heritage and past activities. However, Sir John Harvey-Jones, former C.E.O. of ICI and one of the United Kingdom's most successful businessmen, emphasized that any business is only as good as its next three months' order book.

"Growth is like creativity, it doesn't go along very neat, precise plans. You get clogged highways before you figure out a way to open up capacity. You get pollution before you figure out a way to fight it."

Steve Forbes

It is also necessary to pay attention to the details of any strategy for growth. Understand how the changes affect people. Decisive action is vital, but this needs to include an understanding of how to maintain people's commitment and motivation. If people feel threatened, or insecure, then however sensible the strategy for growth and the plan for implementation it simply will not be achieved. It is vital to treat people with respect. It is also worth communicating what is happening to people so that they understand their role and how they can contribute. Also, monitor the situation: time lags need to be understood and planned for, and the strategy needs to be supported in the long term.

CONCLUSION

Growth always ends. For some businesses it comes with a bang, for others, with a whimper. The ideas here will assist in prolonging the endgame. Apply them, but do so with your eyes open. Ramping down is just as much a part of the business landscape as ramping up. Knowing when to let go, and recycling your efforts in a more promising direction, is the secret of long-term happiness in a business career. There are many market, industry, and organizational indicators you can watch for clues that bailout time is near. Look hard at them, but in the end the best litmus test is to ask yourself a simple question: Am I still having fun? If the honest answer is no, then you know what you need to do.

FOR MORE INFORMATION

Books:
Christensen, Clayton M. *The Innovator's Dilemma.* New York: HarperBusiness, 2003.
Greenwald, Bruce, and Judd Kahn. *Competition Demystified.* New York: Portfolio, 2005.
Tomasko, Robert. *Bigger Isn't Always Better.* New York: AMACOM Books, 2006.

Web site:
Robert Tomasko.com:
www.roberttomasko.com

See also:
☆ Scenario Planning (pp. 334–335)

Viewpoint: Mihaly Csikszentmihalyi
On Business As a Privilege

Introduction

Mihaly Csikszentmihalyi is the director of Quality of Life Research Center (QLRC) at the Drucker School of Management, Claremont Graduate University. He is the author of numerous articles and several influential books, including *Flow: The Psychology of Optimal Experience* (HarperCollins, 1991), *The Evolving Self: A Psychology for the Third Millennium* (HarperCollins, 1993, reprint 1994), *Finding Flow: The Psychology of Engagement with Everyday Life* (Basic Books, 1997), *Good Work: When Excellence and Ethics Meet* (with Howard Gardner and William Damon, Basic Books, 2001), and *Good Business: Leadership, Flow, and the Making of Meaning* (Viking, 2003).

Reflecting on the current environment of uncertainty, I suppose the most profound influence for me was World War II, when I realized how the most advanced and scientifically sophisticated societies can go wrong. You can't take anything for granted, you have to strive constantly to advance. In terms of people, in the field of business, Peter Drucker stands out—his common sense and historical rootedness made me realize that there is a way of looking at business and management from a liberal-arts kind of perspective. To be a good manager, you need to have a good idea of what people are like, to appreciate their essential motivations. In that respect, influencers include Hannah Arendt, many of the existential philosophers (Martin Heidegger and so forth), and many psychologists, including Abraham Maslow, who wrote extensively on management.

If it's true that we are moving more and more into a knowledge economy, then it's clear that you have to learn how to manage people who are more demanding and have a greater aspiration for their lives. You have to learn to provide freedom and self-determination. I believe that's true—provided that we are, in fact, moving toward a knowledge economy.

But I think that parallel to this movement, many of the trends show an increase in the number of security personnel—more and more watchers and protectors, especially at the bottom levels of the hierarchy. It's true that the top echelon is moving toward the knowledge economy, but it's not clear that there is saturation to the front lines. There is a discrepancy between top management and the rest. That worries me. There are many trends in that direction; for instance, the notorious book, *The Bell Curve* by Richard J. Herrnstein and Charles Murray (Simon & Schuster, 1996)—I wrote a review of that in the *Washington Post* in which I argued that most people had either misunderstood or not read the book. It's not about racial difference. We have become more and more dependent on intelligence (as measured by IQ) as a way of segregating or stratifying people. In earlier times you could be an honest craftworker or respectable farmer, and these values of honesty and perseverance were considered as important as intellectual abilities. But now, unless you have a degree from a respected university, you cannot feel respected.

There are two stratifying forces: one is the economic, and the other is this intellectual stratification that is getting out of hand. Making decisions on this basis distorts the complexity of human life, especially when you have a single metric—like money—determining who wins and who loses.

In this context, are there new management questions that we should be asking? For instance, who and what am I ultimately responsible to/for? This is partly what we wrote about in *Good Work*. It's so easy to get caught up in your institution's habits of performance or process. You join a company and "this is how things are done," and you end up doing things that way, instead of asking, What is the ultimate outcome of what I'm getting involved in or getting into? Is this really what I want to do or what society needs? Those shouldn't be new questions!

Meanwhile, the more I learn about the self, the less I can say about it. There are all these people talking about the "protean" self—a jumble of half-digested impulses. I can say that there is at least a constructed self that you *believe* represents who you are. At various times that's not the self that is being enacted in your behavior. Without a constructed self, it's hard to operate with integrity; the less variation there is between your constructed self and your behavior, the better off you are. The notion of what you ultimately take responsibility for should be the same at work and at home. Some of the people we talked to in *Good Business* are very clear about it. One of my favorite examples is Aaron Feuerstein of Malden Mills, the Massachusetts-based manufacturer of Polartec, who vowed to keep the company running after a disastrous fire and more recently strengthened it by wisely filing for bankruptcy. He very much disapproves of people who have one set of values and interests at work, and shift to another mode when they get home. He has an almost biblical view: unless you maintain a consistent set of values, your actions are determined by expediency, and you can't continue to sustain either personal or professional integrity.

What about operating on intuition? Intuition really works best when it's based on experience reflected on. It's at the cutting edge of intellect—where intuition moves just beyond what you can rationally justify. It's kind of unpredictable, a loose cannon. You

"Start with your own money and value your intuition. It's all about endurance in the beginning. Your dream and passion to succeed must be stronger than your fear of failure."

Terri Bowersock

have to reflect on experience, and then you can afford to go beyond what you can immediately justify intellectually. Trust in your knowledge and your experience instead of passing the buck to others. To promote this marriage between intellect and intuition, when confronted with a problem or issue, you can train yourself to make an intuitive leap to understand what caused the situation, or what could resolve it. Jot down your intuitive understanding in the moment and then try to deal with the situation intellectually, using all the facts. Then match your intuition to what you discovered intellectually. You can also learn to recognize patterns in your intuition, for example, you may tend to blame others, or to be overly pessimistic or optimistic. Recognizing these patterns can help you harness your intuition.

Currently I am fascinated by the notion of business as a privilege. I'm not a historian or sociologist of power, but it's becoming clear that those who have power end up getting more privileges. Take the clergy, for example. Since medieval times they have enjoyed the bounties of wealth, comfort, and a good life. But when people realize that the bishops and abbots are getting bigger and bigger palaces and we still live in the same hovels our grandparents lived in, the bishops and abbots are out. This scenario plays out over and over again. Eventually people get fed up with those who get away with excesses for their own benefit; then there are restrictions, regulations, or even revolutions. In business we are reaching such a turning point now. Will there be enough business leaders who realize that it will be to their advantage to scale down their excessive behavior of getting away with the privileges and impose some forms of internal restrictions and regulations? If not, the pressure will come from the outside. Consider the threat of a players' strike in major league baseball in the summer of 2002: eventually the fans will say, What am I doing to support this behavior? and find cheaper ways to amuse themselves.

Fundamentally, what's true of business is true of other walks of life. I have discovered four simple and essential aims of successful people:

1 To get to know yourself—good and bad—instead of denying or repressing or deluding yourself, figure out what you really want from life, what you're good at, and what you enjoy doing.

2 To get to do more and more of what you *like* to do, and at the same time learn to love what you *have* to do and get to the point of saying that you look forward to getting up in the morning and facing the day—this is very important to the people I talk to who are successful in life.

3 To respect other people, feel that they are worth helping, feel that the human race is not ready for the slag heap—work for the common good, embrace a sense that life as a whole (the environment) is worth preserving, and recognize that it gives meaning and purpose to your life to give meaning to these things.

4 To be true to yourself—when you have integrity, people will respect you because you try to act in concert with your beliefs.

When I teach MBA students, they're in such a hurry they think that if they don't get their first million by 25, they'll be a failure. They're so impatient and focused that they don't realize they'll be living another 50 years beyond that first million! I started teaching MBA classes in 2000; the difference between that cohort and the one in 2001 was dramatic. In 2000, all of them were sure they would get increasing equity in their firms. That was a hard cohort to teach, because they didn't want to learn anything except how to get into Cisco or Enron. The following year's group, somewhat shell-shocked and not quite sure of anything in the wake of the September 11 attacks, still maintained a remnant of unfounded hope, but were much more interested in traditional business, and even government and nonprofit interests.

One thing that so many of the people I talk to say: If you are looking for a job, look for the best organization in your field and be willing to apprentice yourself to it for a while, even if it means not getting paid. If it's not what you thought it would be, get out of there—cut your losses and move on, and don't settle for less. This is what I mean by being true to yourself.

FOR MORE INFORMATION

Book:
Csikszentmihalyi, Mihalyi. *Good Business: Leadership, Flow and the Making of Meaning.* New York: Viking, 2003.

See also:
Budgeting (pp. 1683–1684)

"[Capitalism] destroys some things and distorts others: it makes new separations, based on privilege and buying power, differences which increase social divisions."

Richard Hoggart

Creating Corporate Creativity
by Edward de Bono

EXECUTIVE SUMMARY

- Creativity is rapidly becoming the most important ingredient in business.
- Creativity is not a mystical talent that only a few people possess, but a skill that can be developed.
- Creativity is not a matter of waiting for inspiration, but a deliberate skill that can be used as needed.
- Feeling free and liberated as in traditional brainstorming is a weak approach.
- Formal creative techniques are based on an understanding of the brain as a self-organizing information system.
- Argument is a crude and primitive way of exploring a subject. Parallel thinking is far more effective.
- In any organization, if creativity is not an expectation it will be seen as a risk.

INTRODUCTION

In my experience with major multinationals and other organizations, the basic behavior is "maintenance and problem-solving." This means running things as they are and solving problems as they arise. A great deal of lip service is paid to creativity but little is done. In surveys I have done at my seminars, 90% of people agree that creativity is important, and 80% claim that little is done in their own organizations.

Three things are becoming commodities in business. Competence is one of those things. If your only hope of survival is that your competitors will continue to be more incompetent than yourselves, you are weak, since there is nothing you can do to stop them from becoming competent. Information has already become a commodity available to anyone willing to pay for it. State-of-the-art technology is a commodity which can be bought or commissioned, with some exceptions such as pharmaceuticals.

When everything is a commodity, what is going to matter is the design and delivery of value created from these commodities. This requires creativity. Six chefs at a cooking competition each have the same ingredients and the same cooking facilities. Who wins? The chef who can create superior value from the basic commodities.

THE USE OF CREATIVITY

Creativity is used to solve problems, design ways forward, resolve conflicts, simplify procedures, cut costs, improve motivation, design new products and services, and fashion strategies. Any situations that require thinking demand creativity. Without it, we are condemned to repeating the standard routines.

In 1971, I suggested at a workshop with Shell Oil in London the concept of horizontal drilling. Today, most oil wells in the world are drilled this way because the yield is three to six times that of a traditional well. (I am not claiming that this change came about as a result of my suggestion, but the chronological fact remains.) After a seminar to Ingwe Coal in South Africa, the senior engineer told me they had developed a new way of cutting coal—the first new way in 80 years. In both cases, there was not a problem, but applying creativity to the usual way of doing things developed powerful new ideas.

A major Scandinavian company used to spend 30 days on their multinational project discussions. Today they do it in two days through using parallel thinking instead of argument. After training in creative thinking, a U.K. television company said they had had more ideas in two days than they had had in six months before. One afternoon, Carole Ferguson (a certified trainer) put together 130 workshops for a steel company. Using just one of the techniques of lateral thinking, they generated 21,000 ideas that afternoon.

A person tied up with a rope cannot play the violin. If we cut the rope, does that make that person a violinist? If you are inhibited, you cannot be creative. If you release yourself from that inhibition, does that make you creative? That is the essential weakness of processes such as brainstorming. Creativity can be a much more structured discipline with specific mental operations that can be used deliberately.

THE BASIS OF CREATIVITY

The purpose of the brain is to be non-creative. Instead, it is supposed to establish routine patterns for dealing with a stable world. If it were otherwise, life would be impossible (there are 39,816,800 ways of getting dressed in the morning with eleven items of clothing). As a self-organizing system the brain allows incoming information to organize itself into routine patterns. We should be grateful for these patterns. But there are side tracks which are suppressed. If, somehow, we manage to move "laterally" to the side track then, in hindsight, the new idea will be logical and obvious. This is why we have never appreciated creativity. Because every valued creative idea is logical in hindsight, we have assumed logic would be sufficient to reach this idea. This is simply not true in the asymmetric nature of self-organizing systems.

DELIBERATE CREATIVE PROCESSES

The techniques of "lateral thinking" are based directly on this understanding of brain behavior. The technique of "random entry" takes us away from the usual starting point to create a new "chance" starting point which allows us to open up tracks we could never have accessed from the usual starting point. That is why the history of science is full of examples of major discoveries that were triggered by an apparently random event.

In any self-organizing system there is a mathematical need for provocation. Otherwise we remain stuck in local equilibria instead of reaching a global equilibrium. The new word "po" signals that something is put forward as a provocation. "Po, you die before you die" sounds illogical but enabled Ron Barbaro of Prudential Insurance, Canada, to develop the concept of "living needs benefits." There are formal ways of setting up provocations. It would be pointless to use "judgment" on provocations. We need to develop the very different mental operation of "movement." There are formal ways of getting "movement" from an idea.

"We want worked out a relationship between leader and led which will give each the opportunity to make creative contributions to the situation."

Mary Parker Follett

"Challenge" is another aspect of lateral thinking. We challenge accepted concepts and perceptions, and then develop alternatives. This was the process that led to the suggestion of horizontal drilling of oil wells. We challenge traditional, accepted and usual concepts, not because they are wrong or inadequate, but because the adequate can hide the better idea.

Alternatives are generated by extracting the concept that lies behind the existing approach. There follows a search for finding a better way of delivering this concept.

"CASE MAKING" VERSUS CREATIVITY

In a court of law, if the prosecuting lawyer thinks of a point which would help the defense case, that point is not going to be made. Conversely the defense lawyer would never mention a point that might help the prosecution case. This is not exploring the subject, but "case making." With parallel thinking, all parties at any one moment are looking and thinking in the same direction. The change in direction is signaled by the symbolic "six hats." Each hat indicates a mode of thinking: for example, white hat for information, red hat for feelings, and green hat for creative possibilities. The result is a much quicker and much fuller exploration of the subject. Every person present is using his or her thinking and experience to the maximum instead of "making a case." This method is now widely used in schools and with senior executives. Why pay someone a large salary if you are not going to use that mind fully?

CREATIVITY IN THE ORGANIZATION

In any organization, creativity is viewed as either a risk or an expectation. If it is not an expectation, it is always a risk. In my experience the culture of creativity needs to be set by senior management. That way, creativity becomes an expectation. Executives and workers are now expected to come up with, explore and develop new ideas. They receive "recognition" for doing that. Failure to explore new ideas means you are not doing your job properly. Training in creative methods then follows as part of the culture.

> **MAKING IT HAPPEN ▶▶**
> - Break out from the trap of "maintenance and problem-solving," or running things as they are and tackling problems as they arise.
> - Recognize that competence, information, and technology have become commodities, and that only creativity adds value.
> - Use creativity to solve problems, design ways forward, resolve conflicts, simplify, cut costs, motivate, design new products and services, and strategize.
> - Challenge traditional, accepted, and usual concepts and perceptions, because the adequate can hide the better idea.
> - Use the "Six Hats" method for parallel thinking, with everybody looking and

thinking in the same direction, and not arguing.
- Lead from the top to create the expectation that executives and other workers will come up with and explore new ideas.

FOR MORE INFORMATION

Books:
de Bono, Edward. *Lateral Thinking: Creativity Step by Step.* New York: HarperCollins, 1990.
de Bono, Edward. *Parallel Thinking.* London: Penguin, 1995.
Clegg, Brian, and Paul Birch. *Instant Creativity.* Milford, CT: Kogan Page, 1999.
Cooper, Robert G., Scott J. Edgett, and Elko J. Kleinschmidt. *Portfolio Management for New Products.* 2nd ed. Cambridge, MA: Perseus, 2001.
Locke, Christopher. *The Bombast Transcripts: Rants and Screeds of Rageboy.* Cambridge, MA: Perseus, 2002.
Mauzy, Jeff, and Richard A. Harriman. *Creativity Inc.: Building an Inventive Organisation.* Cambridge, MA: Harvard Business School Press, 2003.

Web site:
www.thinksmart.com: devoted to innovation, this site will help you, and your company or organization, become more creative and productive with information, articles, and even a creativity test.

"In a restless, creative business with an emphasis on experiment and development, ideas are the lifeblood."

Richard Branson

Viewpoint: Stewart Brand
Globalization and the Really Long View

Introduction

Stewart Brand is a cofounder of Global Business Network and The Long Now Foundation. Best known for founding, editing, and publishing the Whole Earth Catalog, he also has a long-standing involvement in computers, education, and the media arts. He is author of *The Clock of the Long Now*, *How Buildings Learn*, and *The Media Lab*, and cofounder of the All Species Foundation, a non-profit organization dedicated to the complete inventory of all species of life on earth within the next 25 years, and of the Long Bets Foundation, bringing accountability to predictions.

The insight that first made Stewart Brand famous was: take the far view. If you look at something from really, really far away, then not only your view changes, but also your understanding—the shift in your vision will prompt a shift in your mind. Back in 1966, when he was a photographer in San Francisco, Brand started musing one day about what would happen if you pulled your view back from the city so far that you could see the whole Earth from space. That prompted him to ask the question why, ten years after Sputnik, the public had not yet seen a photograph of the entire Earth? And that, in turn, immediately prompted him to launch a campaign (complete with buttons) calling for the image. Thus, some people credit Brand with nudging NASA to release the famous photos taken on Apollo 8.

Today Brand's overarching insight has shifted from "take the far view" to "take the long view"—the really, really long view. When Brand talks about long, he doesn't just mean a five to ten year perspective, which is unusual enough in business circles, he means thinking in centuries, millennia, even in 10,000-year stretches of time . . .

said at a *Fortune* magazine conference in Aspen in 2001, all of the rhetoric of the hyperacceleration of technology absolutely freaks people out. People feel that engineers are messing with their essence, and they're not going to stand for it. They think: "I've got to protect my children. I've got to protect my family. I've got to protect my church. I've got to protect all of these things against the nitwits who think they'll just give us a pill so we can live forever."

They've got a point. The rhetoric is overwrought. Nevertheless, the argument made by Institute for the Future director Paul Saffo and others that we *overestimate* how rapidly change is coming in the short term, and *underestimate* how much change is coming in the long term, continues to be valid. While the United States is focused on stem cells, eight other things are swarming ahead with no attention paid at all. Somebody creates an advanced birth control pill without asking anyone's permission, and it changes the world. Doom is plausible when you take a long-term view, and acceleration matters when you take a long-term view.

They were actually called megatrends once upon a time; they're large trends with sudden manifestations. A major acceleration of everything in ten years' time is a sudden manifestation. There's a mild form of that going on in Japan at the present. They fell out of their bubble economy into a place where they can't pick themselves up. Israel has fallen down and can't get up again.

There's a malaise of progress going on that I think is somewhat part of the long view. It was in a way predicted by cyberpunk science fiction writers. The Bruce Sterlings and the Bill Gibsons saw it coming—that there would be a *noir* version of high-tech that was not going to be glossy, it was going to be ugly; it was not going to be freeing, it was going to be enslaving; it wasn't going to make everybody rich, it was going to make some people rich.

All these are ways of saying that technology acceleration goes on and that contaminant things go with it: the deepening of fundamentalism; liberal re-

The Long View Shows That Accelerating Change Matters, and That Total Collapse Is Plausible

The long view makes the prospect of total collapse seem thinkable. Every now and then, civilizations decline steadily or come to relatively sudden ends. It's normal. In the perspective of centuries, there is nothing special about it. The sense that "that's something those poor fools in history did" goes away, because you realize that, in their way, they were just as smart about what was going on as we are about our times. The fragility of things becomes interesting.

Another thing that emerges by taking the long view is Ray Kurzweil's idea of the self-acceleration of technology and, thereby, of the pace of history. There has been a pretty circular trend of logarithmic increase for many centuries. There is no reason to expect that acceleration to suddenly turn into an S curve that levels off on its own terms. Technology accelerates itself and is accelerating itself more and more, and that singularity offers a way to think about the present that is clear and productive. A whole bunch of technologies accelerate each other to the point where, basically, it's a new world every week.

There are countervailing intelligent, and sometimes not-so-intelligent, forces working against the pace of change. As technology pioneer Jaron Lanier

---

"Like a force of nature, the digital age cannot be denied or stopped. It has four very powerful qualities that will result in its ultimate triumph: decentralizing, globalizing, harmonizing, and empowering."

Nicholas Negroponte

sistance; conservative resistance. Liberal resistance takes the form of building preservation. Conservative resistance is to stop stem cell research or cloning or whatever. It's unlikely that the bioethicists are going to solve all of the problems and that there won't be any new ones. People who say that this is a resistance to Darwinism are absolutely accurate. Darwin knew that he was basically saying, "God is not only dead, he never existed." Humans weren't designed by a great designer; they emerged from 3.5 billion years of mindless mistakes and successes.

We've Got a Global Economy; Now We Need a Global Society

I think we are, in fact, in a long boom. The opportunities of globalization drastically outweigh the downside. It is going ahead and can't be stopped. There will be other avenues that will emerge for managing it. That's what people like former president Bill Clinton and former secretary of state Madeleine Albright are basically bearing down on: How to make a global system that can progress pretty rapidly without breaking.

I'm talking about civilization. We've had a century of a global economy without a global body politic. At least a third of this present century—maybe half, maybe the whole thing—will be spent sorting out the global society in terms of global governance, global civilization, the global frame of reference. We may have one big currency or just a few big currencies. We may all see the same entertainment—or not. What things are increasingly unique? How fine-grained can uniqueness go?

I think one of the interesting things is going to be which states are permitted to fail and which are not. States in central Africa are permitted to fail; Argentina is not. The most hardcore Republicans, holding their noses the whole way and trying to do it almost in secret, will come to the rescue of Argentina when it's in trouble. The system simply will not tolerate it. That's pretty interesting.

It's a centuries-scale project, building a global society. In the past, when civilizations have failed, other civilizations have taken up the slack. When Europe is in a dark age, Islam is having its own renaissance and helps the European renaissance. Once it's an all-encompassing thing, all your eggs are in one basket. If you drop the basket, all of your eggs are broken. You have to build in the comeback capabilities internally. There's a certain rent you have to pay to have a relatively safe global civilization, and we don't know what that is yet.

Science and the Long-term Perspective

Scientific knowledge is increasing and archeology never stops. We know more and more about everything. Science is increasingly able to tell us things like global warming is real, methane at the bottom of the ocean is released or not released and has this effect. These are multicentury, deeply important trends. As soon as you take seriously the idea of the oceans rising x feet in your lifetime, or the Gulf Stream turning off over a period of a couple of years and freezing Europe in your lifetime, it's a different story.

I think that science is giving us this long-term perspective, and it gets out there through the media, through the schools. Kids care about it. That starts to yield a long-term frame of reference in terms of responsibility, in terms of things that are going on for which you can't buy a solution. One nation alone can't unilaterally fix it, or be ignored by the others if it's part of the problem. There's a globalization of concern, and you've reason to think in century terms because science gives you both the need and the tools to do that.

I think part of the increased awareness in long-term thinking is the increasing life span of some people. If an eight-year-old in a couple of years starts to assume that 150 to 200 years is a plausible lifespan for him or her personally, that's going to change thinking and probably behavior. People never used to know their great-grandparents. Now everybody does. That will go on to great-great-grandparents. In turn, they're going to know their own great-great-grandkids. What's life going to be like for them? What will I do now about that? I think that that, in addition to science, creates a personal lengthening of the frame of reference. The "now" of one's life is extending. Things will change around that.

*This essay was adapted from an interview undertaken with Mr. Brand by Peter Leyden, knowledge developer at Global Business Network (***www.gbn.com***). The publishers gratefully acknowledge the support of Global Business Network in making these ideas and insights available.*

FOR MORE INFORMATION

Books:
Brand, Stewart. *The Clock of the Long Now: Time and Responsibility.* London: Weidenfeld and Nicholson, 1999.

Viewpoint: Margaret Wheatley
When Change Is out of Our Control

Introduction
Meg Wheatley has been a business consultant and speaker for over 30 years. She is President Emerita of The Berkana Institute, a global charitable foundation founded in 1991 and dedicated to serving life-affirming leaders, and the author of many articles and books, including *Finding Our Way: Leadership for an Uncertain Time* (Berrett-Koehler, 2005).

Uncertain Times
In June, 2002, the Chief Financial Officer of Oracle Corporation spoke on prospects for the second half of the year. His comments were radically different from the upbeat statements typical of someone in his position: "We are hoping for a revenue recovery in the second half of the year. But I said that same thing six months ago and I have lost confidence in my ability to predict the future." In his humility, this C.F.O. described the new world of the 21st century—this interconnected planet of increased uncertainty and volatility. Organizations are now confronted with two sources of change: the traditional type that is initiated and managed; and external changes over which no-one has control. We are just beginning to experience what it is like to operate in a global environment of increasing chaos, of events beyond our control that have a devastating impact on our internal operations and culture.

The business news is filled with stories of the perils of interconnectedness. One country suffers economic problems, and analysts are quick to say that their problems will not affect other countries. Then we watch as an entire continent and those beyond are pulled into economic recession by the web of interdependence. Or we read how the actions of a few corrupt executives bring down an entire company (and industry), even though tens of thousands of people work there with integrity.

Interconnected systems are always this sensitive. Activities occurring in one part of the system always affect many other parts. The nature of the global business environment guarantees that no matter how hard we work to create a stable and healthy organization, our organization will continue to experience dramatic changes far beyond our control. For example, Contin-

ental Airlines had spent years developing a strong culture. "Our employees believe in this company and will do anything for our president," said one representative I interviewed. But then came September 11, and Continental, like all airlines, suddenly found its entire industry and business model at risk.

There is no company, industry, or nation that is immune to these potentially devastating system effects. One executive in a large corporation commented: "It was always dysfunctional, but it was working. Now it's not. It's a different feeling than years ago. Now we can't influence outcomes. We're 'at the top' but feeling that things are being 'done to' us." Another executive said simply: "What used to work, doesn't. The old strategies don't work."

So, when so much is beyond our control, when senior leaders reveal their own feelings of powerlessness, what skills can we call upon to maneuver successfully and survive the turbulence?

New Organizational Dynamics
In an era of increasing uncertainty, new organizational dynamics appear and old ones intensify at all levels of the organization. It is important to notice how these new dynamics affect employees, leaders, and core operating functions.

Employee Behavior
Uncertainty leads to increased fear. As fear levels rise, it is normal for people to focus on personal security and safety. We tend to withdraw, become more self-serving, and more defensive. We focus on smaller and smaller details, those things we *can* control. It becomes more difficult to work together, and nearly impossible to focus on the bigger picture. And there are

---

"This extraordinary arrogance that change must start at the top is a way of guaranteeing that change will not happen in most companies."

Gary Hamel

physiological impacts as well. Stress deprives the human brain of its ability to see patterns. People become reactive and lose the capacity to understand their work as part of a larger system. We also have difficulty with memory and become forgetful. Then there are the physical manifestations of sleeplessness, restlessness, sudden anger, and unpredictable tears.

Obviously, each of these has negative consequences on work behavior for individuals and teams. As people experience their growing incapacity to get work done well, they often blame themselves for failing to produce. One woman executive expressed that, "So many good people are failing at the changes they're committed to."

Pressure on Leaders

Because of increased fear, many people turn to leaders with unreasonable demands. We want someone to rescue us, to save us, to provide answers, to give us firm ground or strong life rafts. We push for a strong leader to get us out of this mess, even if it means surrendering individual freedom to gain security. But the causes of insecurity are complex and systemic. There is no one simple answer, and not even the strongest of leaders can deliver on the promise of stability and security. We seldom acknowledge that; instead, we fire the leader and continue searching for the perfect one. A troubled male executive described it like this: "We still charge the leader to provide solutions. When he doesn't, we then sacrifice the king/priest to atone for the sins of the system."

It is critical that leaders resist assuming the role of savior, even as people beg for it. This can be extremely difficult as people grow more fearful and fragile. Sophisticated emotional skills are required, especially if people have been directly affected by external events. In these cases, the leader must simultaneously struggle to provide emotional support while also working to maintain decent levels of productivity. If the leader has also been personally affected by recent organizational challenges, it becomes very difficult to inspire confidence. As one woman leader asked: "How do you maintain credibility when you (as the leader) are not sure you want to be there?"

Core Functions

It wasn't long ago that companies engaged in five-year strategic planning. Those sweet, slow days seem very distant now. Many of the primary functions of business, and of human resources—planning, forecasting, budgeting, staffing, individual development plans—only worked because we could bring the future into focus, because the future felt within our control. Shortly after September 11, the C.E.O. of a major technology company reported that it was impossible to do a reliable budget for the coming year, even though they had a very good record at budget forecasting in the past. His proposed solution for dealing with so much uncertainty was to submit five alternative budget scenarios to his board.

It is important to note how many people in organizations have honed their skills at predicting or antici-

pating the future. Businesses have depended upon and rewarded their expertise. But now these skills can be a liability. They may lull the organization into a false sense of security about a predictable future and thereby keep people from staying alert to what's going on around them in the present. Yet even though they may be a liability, often such experts are charged with bringing stability back to the organization which may clamor for new planning tools and processes, and push hard on planning staff to find new modes of prediction. Such staff often suffer severe burn-out as they work zealously on the impossible task of stabilizing an inherently temperamental world. A wise planning executive commented on how he has changed expectations of his function: "I tell people we're not going to get any more clarity. This is as good as it gets."

The Great Paradox

I have painted a fairly grim picture of the new organizational dynamics spawned by tumultuous times. However, there is a *great paradox* that points to the hopeful path ahead. *It is possible to prepare for the future without knowing what it will be.* The primary way to prepare for the unknown is to attend to the quality of our relationships, to how well we know and trust one another. In New York City and Oklahoma City, as well as many other disaster situations, people had engaged in emergency preparedness drills prior to having to deal with the real thing. Working together on these simulations, they developed cohesive, trusting relationships and inter-agency cooperation. They had only prepared for simpler disasters, but, when terror struck, they knew they could rely on each other. Elizabeth Dole, when President of the American Red Cross, said that she didn't wait until the river was flooding at two in the morning to pick up the phone and establish a relationship.

When people know they can rely on each other, when there is a true sense of community, it is amazing how well people perform. This was the experience of the community of Halifax, Nova Scotia on September 11. Forty-two planes were grounded at their small airport, and eight thousand distressed and stranded passengers suddenly appeared on their doorstep. The community's open-hearted response transformed the city, and led to relationships with strangers that will last a lifetime. "It was one of those times when nothing was planned but everything went so smoothly. Everybody just kind of pulled together."

New Organizational Capabilities

In order to counter the negative organizational dynamics stimulated by stress and uncertainty, we must give full attention to the quality of our relationships. Nothing else works, no new tools or technical applications, no redesigned organizational chart. *The solution is each other.* If we can rely on one another, we can cope with almost anything. Without each other, we retreat into fear.

There is one core principle for developing these relationships. *People must be engaged in meaningful work together if they are to transcend individual concerns and*

"Change means avoiding the predictable and known ways of doing things which we learn to adjust to."

John Harvey-Jones

develop new capacities. Here are several ways to put this principle into practices.

Nourish a clear organizational identity. As confusion and fear swirl about the organization, people find stability and security in purpose, not in plans. Organizational identity describes who we are, the enduring values we work from, the shared aspirations of who we want to be in and for the world. When chaos wipes the ground from beneath us, the organization's identity gives us a place to stand. When the situation grows confusing, our values provide the means to make clear and good decisions. A clear sense of organizational (and personal) identity gives people the capacity to respond intelligently in the moment, and to choose actions that are congruent with each other. Times of crisis always display the coherence or incoherence at the heart of our organization. Are we pulling together, or rushing off in many different directions? Are people's actions and choices congruent with the stated values, or are they basing their decisions on different values. If they are using different values, are these the true albeit unspoken values, the real rules of the game?

It is crucial to keep organizational purpose and values in the spotlight. The values come to life not through speeches and plaques, but as we hear the stories of other employees who embody those values. It is important to use all existing communication tools, and invent new ones, to highlight these personal experiences. In the year following September 11, United Airlines communicated this type of story twice weekly as one means to support employees during very difficult times.

Focus people on the bigger picture. People who are stressed lose the ability to recognize patterns, to see the bigger picture. And as people become overloaded and overwhelmed with their tasks, they have no time or interest to look beyond the demands of the moment. Therefore, it is essential that the organization sponsor processes that bring people together so that they can learn about one another's perspectives and challenges. If the organization doesn't make these processes happen, people will continue to spiral inward. This inward spiraling has a devastating impact on performance. People become overwhelmed by the volume of tasks, they lose all sense of meaning for their work, and they feel increasingly isolated and alone. Everybody is busier and more frantic, but the major thing they are producing is more stress. The other serious consequence is that both individual and organizational intelligence declines dramatically as people lose the larger context for their work.

It is important that the processes used for bringing people together should not be formal. People need less formality and more conviviality, time to decompress and to relax enough to be able to listen to one another. Processes such as conversation and story-telling help us connect at a depth not available through charts and PowerPoint presentations. However, people don't recognize how much they need this time, and usually resist such informal gatherings—until they attend one and notice what they've been missing.

Demand honest, forthright communication. In a true disaster or crisis, a continuous flow of information gives people the capacity to respond intelligently as they seek to rescue or save people and property. They are hungry for information so that they can respond well to urgent human needs. They take in the information, make fast judgment calls, try something, quickly reject it if it doesn't work, and then try something else. They call to one another, exchanging information and learning. They contribute what they can to everyone becoming more effective in the rescue effort.

Even though most organizations don't deal with this level of crisis, the lessons are important. People deal far better with uncertainty and stress when they know what's going on, even if the information is incomplete and only temporarily correct. Freely circulating information helps create trust, and it turns us into rapid learners and more effective workers. Often, it is not the actual situation that induces stress; rather, it's the fact that people aren't told what's going on, or feel deceived. The greater the crisis, the more we need to know. The more affected we are by the situation, the more information we need. After every commercial air crash, family who have lost loved ones complain about not being adequately informed by the airlines. They want to know details of how their loved one died, a disclosure that often brings relief to those grieving. Yet the airlines are constrained by potential legal liability from sharing the details that would ease their grief. The families end up suing the airline to get the information, and add emotional damages to their suit. This devastating cycle is fed by feelings of rage and loss that are exacerbated by lack of information.

Prepare for the unknown. The U.S. military has invested large sums of money in the development and use of complex simulations that prepare troops for different battle scenarios. Similar simulations now are used by most civil defense and community agencies. Yet it is surprising how few companies engage in any type of simulation or scenario work. The evidence is dramatically clear that this type of preparation allows people to move into the unknown with greater skillfulness and capacity. While traditional planning processes no longer work, it is dangerous to abandon thinking about the future. We need to explore these newer methods that project us into *alternative* futures. As people engage in processes such as scenario-building or disaster simulations, they feel more capable of dealing with uncertainty. Individual and collective intelligence increases dramatically as people become better-informed big-picture thinkers. And trusting relationships develop that make it possible to call on one another when chaos strikes.

Keep meaning at the forefront. Often in organizations we forget that meaning is the most powerful motivator of human behavior. People gain energy and resolve if they understand how their work contributes to something beyond themselves. When we are frightened, we may first focus on our own survival, but we're capable of more generous and altruistic responses if we discover a greater purpose to our troubles. Why is my

"Only man is not content to leave things as they are but must always be changing them, and when he has done so, is seldom satisfied at the result."

Elspeth Huxley

348

BEST PRACTICE

work worth doing? Who will be helped if I respond well? Am I contributing to some greater good?

Of course, the work truly does have to contribute to something meaningful. People don't step forward in order to support greed or egotists or to benefit faceless entities such as shareholders. We need to know that our work contributes to helping other human beings. My favorite example of this desire to contribute was expressed in the mission statement created by employees at a facility that manufactured dog food. They expressed how their work was serving a greater good when they wrote: "Pets contribute to human health."

Use rituals and symbols. As shrines appear on streets mourning the dead, and other demonstrations of grief flare on TV screens throughout this sorrowing world, we are becoming aware of the deep human need for shared symbolic expression when we experience something tragic. And also the need for celebration when we've experienced something wonderful.

The use of ritual and symbols is common in all cultures, although they almost disappeared in the United States until our lives became so stressful and isolated. Now we are rediscovering this basic human behavior. Because it is so basic to humans, symbols and rituals appear spontaneously, even in organizations. No one department has to create them (a scary thought), but the organization *does* need to notice them when they appear, and to honor them by offering support and resources.

Pay attention to individuals. There is no substitute for direct, personal contact with employees. Even though managers are more stressed and have less time, it is crucial to pick up the phone and connect with those you want to retain. Personal conversations with key people, with experienced workers, with innovators, with those just joining the organization, with younger workers new to the workforce-all of these and more need to know that their leader is thinking about them. When people feel cared for, their stress is reduced and they contribute more to the organization. One of the key findings in the field of knowledge management is that people share their knowledge *only* when they feel cared for and when they care for the organization. It is not new technology that makes for knowledge exchanges, but quality human relationships.

The Difficulty In Investing In Relationships

None of these suggested behaviors is new organizational advice. Most of us have had enough experience in organizations to know the importance of relationships. So why, as the storm clouds thicken, are we not investing in creating healthy, trusting relationships? One answer is that many organizations, as a matter of policy, deliberately distance themselves from their employees. They hold a dangerous assumption, that organizational flexibility is achieved by being able to let employees go when times get hard. The ability to remain efficient is primarily found in the organization's ability to downsize staff. If you need to downsize, so the assumption goes, you don't want to know

your employees or get personally involved with them.

What is most dangerous about this belief is that it is partly true. organizations *do* need to be able to shrink and grow as times demand. But it is absolutely possible to achieve this workforce flexibility without sacrificing loyal, dedicated, and smart workers. Years ago, Harley-Davidson had to let go nearly 40% of their workforce. This was a wrenching but crucial decision for the survival of the company. However, they took the time and paid attention to those individuals who were leaving and those who were staying. Every employee had a personal conversation with the C.E.O., and received complete information about the company's circumstances. People understood why they were being let go, appreciated the personal conversation, and expressed their love and support for the company going forward. Over the years, many of those employees stayed in contact and were rehired as Harley prospered.

There is only one prediction about the future that I feel confident to make. During this period of random and unpredictable change, any organization that distances itself from its employees and refuses to cultivate meaningful relationships with them, is destined to fail. Those organizations who will succeed are those that evoke our greatest human capacities—our need to be in good relationships, and our desire to contribute to something beyond ourselves. These qualities cannot be evoked through procedures and policies. They are only available in organizations where people feel trusted and welcome, and where people know that their work matters. The evidence is all around us, and here's one powerful story.

On September 11th, the Federal Aviation Authority (FAA) cleared the skies of nearly 4,500 planes carrying 350,000 passengers in just a few hours. (75% of them landed within the first hour, more than one landing per second.) It was an unprecedented feat for the agency, one that had not been simulated since the end of the Cold War. And it was the first day on the job for the top FAA official who gave the initial order to clear the skies. Controllers had to land these planes, while also staying vigilant for signs that any other planes had been hijacked. They succeeded through intense co-operation, absolute focus, and dedication, and because they made decisions locally, including some that were outside of policies. In the months following, officials started to try and capture this astonishing feat in new procedures, but then they scrapped the idea. "A lot of things were done intuitively, things that you can't write down in a textbook or you can't train somebody to do." What is the FAA's policy and plan for preparing for another crisis of unknown dimensions? They will rely on the judgment, intuition, and commitment of their controllers and managers.

FOR MORE INFORMATION

Web site:
The Berkana Institute: **www.berkana.org**

Managing New-product Portfolios

by Robert G. Cooper and Scott J. Edgett

EXECUTIVE SUMMARY

- New-product portfolio management is about how you invest your business's product development resources through project prioritization and allocating resources across development projects.
- There are four goals in portfolio management: maximizing the value of the portfolio; seeking the right balance of projects; ensuring that your portfolio is strategically aligned, and making sure you have the appropriate number of projects for your limited resources.
- There are many tools—some quantitative, others graphical, some strategic—designed to help you choose the right portfolio of projects.
- Your new-product process or "stage-gate" system must be working in order to achieve effective portfolio management. It must deliver data integrity and also weed out the bad projects early.

INTRODUCTION

How should you most effectively invest your product development resources? And how should you prioritize your development projects and allocate resources among them? These are crucial issues in new-product portfolio management.

Portfolio management is a critical senior management challenge. Here's why:

- A successful new-product effort is *fundamental to business success*. This logically translates into portfolio management—the ability to select today's projects that will become tomorrow's new-product winners.
- New-product development is the *manifestation of your business's strategy*. If your new-product initiatives are wrong—either the wrong projects or the wrong balance—then you fail at implementing your business strategy.
- Portfolio management is about *resource allocation*. In a business world preoccupied with value to the stockholder and doing more with less, technology and marketing resources are simply too scarce to waste. The consequences of poor portfolio management are evident: you squander scarce resources and, as a result, starve the truly deserving projects.

MAKING IT HAPPEN ▸▸

There are four goals of portfolio management to aim for.

- **Goal 1: maximize the value of your portfolio.** Here the goal is to select new product projects to maximize the sum of the values or *commercial worth* of all active projects in your development pipeline in terms of some business objective. Tools used to assess "project value" include:

Net present value (NPV). Determine the project's NPV and then rank projects by NPV divided by the key or constraining resource (for example, the R&D costs still left to be spent on the project; that is, by NPV/R&D). Projects are rank-ordered according to this index until out of resources, thus maximizing the value of the portfolio (the sum of the NPVs across all projects) for a given or limited resource expenditure.

Expected Commercial Value (ECV). This method uses decision-tree analysis, breaking the project into decision stages—for example, development and commercialization. Define the possible outcomes of the project along with probabilities of each occurring—for example, probabilities of technical and commercial success. The resulting ECV is then divided by the constraining resource (as in the NPV method), and projects are rank-ordered according to this index in order to maximize the *bang for buck*. This method also approximates *real options theory*, and thus is appropriate for handling higher-risk projects.

Scoring Model. Decision-makers rate projects on a number of factors that distinguish superior projects, typically on 1–5 or 0–10 scales. Add the ratings for each factor to yield a quantified "project attractiveness score," which must clear a minimum hurdle. This score is a proxy for the "value of the project" but incorporates factors beyond just financial measures. Projects are then rank-ordered according to this score until resources run out. Typical factors are: strategic alignment; product/competitive advantage; market attractiveness; leverage or synergies; technical feasibility, and risk versus return.

- **Goal 2: seek balance in your portfolio.** Here the goal is to achieve a desired balance of projects in terms of a number of parameters. For example, long-term projects versus short ones, or high-risk versus lower-risk projects. Balance can also be sought across various markets, technologies, product categories and project types. Pictures portray balance much better than numbers and lists, so the techniques used here are largely graphical in nature.

Bubble diagrams: Display your projects on a two-dimensional grid as different-size bubbles (the size of the bubbles denotes the spending on each project). The axes vary but the most popular chart is the risk-reward bubble diagram, where NPV is plotted versus probability of technical success. Then seek an appropriate balance in numbers of projects (and spending) across the four quadrants.

Pie charts: Show your spending breakdowns as slices of pies in a pie chart. Popular pie charts include a breakdown by project types, by market or segment, and by product line or product category. Unlike the maximization tools described under Goal 1, bubble diagrams and pie charts are not decision models, but rather information display. They depict the current portfolio and where the resources are going—the "what is." These charts provide a useful beginning for the discussion of "what should be"—how your resources should be allocated.

- **Goal 3: your portfolio must be strategically aligned.** Being strategically aligned means that all your projects are "on strategy," and that your breakdown of spending across projects, areas, markets, and so on must mirror your strategic priorities. Several portfolio methods are designed to achieve strategic alignment:

"Fashion is something barbarous for it produces innovation without reason and imitation without benefit."

George Santayana

Top-down, strategic buckets: Begin at the top with your business's strategy and from that, your product innovation strategy—that is, its goals, and where and how to focus your new product efforts. Next, make splits in resources: given your strategy, where should you spend your money? These splits can be by project types, product lines, markets or industry sectors, and so on. Thus, you establish strategic buckets of resources. Within each bucket, list all projects—active, on-hold and new—and rank these until you run out of resources in that bucket. The result is multiple portfolios, one portfolio per bucket. Another result is that your spending at year-end will truly reflect the strategic priorities of your business.

Top-down, product roadmap: Once again, begin at the top, with your business and product innovation strategy. But now the question is, given that you have selected several areas of strategic focus (markets, technologies, or product types), what major initiatives must you undertake in order to be successful here? The end result is a mapping of these major initiatives along a timeline of several years—the product roadmap. The selected projects are 100% strategically driven.

Bottom-up: "Make good decisions on individual projects, and the portfolio will take care of itself" is a commonly accepted philosophy. That is, make sure that your project gating system is working well—that gates are accepting good projects and killing the poor ones—and the resulting portfolio will be a solid one. To ensure strategic alignment, use a scoring model at your project reviews and gates (as in Goal 2), and include strategic questions in this model. Strategic alignment is all but assured: your portfolio will indeed consist of all "on strategy" projects (although spending splits may not coincide with strategic priorities). Note that regardless of the strategic approach, all of these methods presuppose that your business has a product innovation strategy, something that many businesses lack.

- **Goal 4: pick the right number of projects.** Most companies have too many projects under way for their limited available resources. The result is pipeline gridlock: projects take too long

to reach the market, and key activities are omitted because of a lack of people and time. Thus an overriding goal is to ensure a balance between resources required for the active projects and resources available. The following are two ways of achieving this goal:

Resource limits: The value maximization methods (Goal 1) build in a resource limitation. Using them means ranking your projects until you are out of resources. The same is true of bubble diagrams (Goal 2). The sum of the areas of the bubbles—the resources devoted to each project—should be a constant, and adding one more project to the diagram requires that another be deleted.

Resource capacity analysis: Determine your resource demand by prioritizing projects and adding up the resources required by each department for all active projects (usually expressed in person-days per month). Portfolio management software enables this roll-up of resource requirements. Then determine the available resources per department—how much time people have to work on these projects. A department-by-department and month-by-month assessment usually reveals that there are too many projects. It suggests a project limit (the point beyond which projects in the prioritized list should be put on hold), and it identifies which departments are the bottlenecks.

YOUR NEW-PRODUCT PROCESS MUST WORK

Before you charge ahead with portfolio management, put first things first: make sure that your new-product process or "gating system" is working well. An effective new-product process is central to portfolio management for the following reasons:

- Regardless of the sophistication of the portfolio models used, your input data must be sound. Look to your new-product process to deliver *data integrity*.
- Your gating process should at minimum kill or cull out the bad projects and, in so doing, yield a better portfolio.

Data integrity means that the up-front homework in projects must be done. Many companies have improved the quality of execution and at the same time provided far better data for project selection by im-

plementing a systematic Stage-Gate® new-product process. Build two stages of homework into your process prior to the beginning of development:

- the scoping stage, which entails a preliminary market, technical, and business assessment;
- building the business case, which involves much more detailed market research (a user-needs-and-wants study, competitive analysis, concept tests) along with technical and manufacturing assessments.

An effective new-product process also means effective gates. In best-practice businesses, this translates into a menu of specified deliverables for each gate; visible "go/kill" and prioritization criteria at the gates (many companies use scorecards to rate projects at gate meetings); defined gatekeepers per gate; clear gate outputs, and even "rules of engagement" for the gate-keeping or leadership team of the business.

CONCLUSION

Portfolio management is fundamental to new-product success. But it's not as easy as it first seems. Not only must you seek to maximize the value of your portfolio, but the development projects in your portfolio must be appropriately balanced; there must be the right number of projects and, finally, the portfolio must be strategically aligned. No one model can deliver on all four goals, and so best-practice businesses tend to use multiple methods to select their projects.

FOR MORE INFORMATION

Books:
Cooper, R.G., S.J. Edgett, and E.J. Kleinschmidt. *Portfolio Management for New Products.* 2nd ed. Cambridge, MA: Perseus, 2002.
Cooper, R.G. *Winning at New Products: Accelerating the Process from Idea to Launch.* 3rd ed. Cambridge, MA: Perseus, 2001.
Cooper, R.G., and S.J. Edgett. *Lean, Rapid and Profitable New Product Development.* Hamilton, Ontario: Product Development Institute, 2005.

Web site:
www.prod-dev.com: this is the official Web site of the widely used *Stage-Gate* Process Model developed by Robert G. Cooper.

"In a small company, one person's hunch can be enough to launch a new product. In a big company, the same concept is likely to be buried in committee for months."
Al Ries

Managing Dynamic Change
by Robert Heller

EXECUTIVE SUMMARY

- Change management has become imperative in the competitive conditions of the early 21st century.
- Change means to pass from one form or phase into another, for which people are perfectly well prepared.
- "Strategic inflection points," demanding radical change, are likely to strike any company or industry.
- Change is synonymous with opportunity.
- The crucial task is to institute change when the company is prosperous, and change does not seem to be required.
- The true test of change management is perpetuating and renewing success.
- The more that change can be measured, the greater the likelihood of achieving successful change management.

INTRODUCTION

Change and its management loom very large in today's business requirements. Corporate success in the 21st century no longer rests simply on the old financial measures: earnings per share, profit growth, and return on capital employed. Shareholder value, service, quality, global market share—these are among the key objectives in world business as it moves forward in conditions of intense and intensifying competition. All the new objectives are inextricably intertwined, creating a dynamic of constant change.

The need to master change is becoming greater by the minute. In a world where Internet usage is doubling every 100 days (to give one phenomenal example of change), organizations and the people in them are most unlikely to succeed, even survive, unless they can manage change. In most cases the necessary changes—what must be done to improve quality, say, or generate added economic value—are obvious. By and large, everybody knows what needs to be done. But it is much easier to say than to do.

It is when an organization finds itself in this situation that change management skills are urgently required. Change management is not about pushing heavy stones uphill. Change means merely to pass from one form or phase into another, for which people are perfectly well prepared. That passage happens all the time, not only in organizational life, but in personal life. Much of today's need for business change springs from the rapid evolution of personal tastes, which alters markets both continuously and abruptly.

STRATEGIC INFLECTION POINTS

Andy Grove, former chairman of microprocessor leader Intel, called monumental change of the Internet type a "strategic inflection point," which occurs when "10 × forces" alter a market with tenfold impact (see Mini-case). Faced with such a phenomenon, you have, in theory, three choices:

1 not to change
2 to change only as and when forced
3 to take charge of your destiny and seek to take advantage of change

In practice the three choices narrow to one—the third. Standing still in changing times is impossible; if you try to tread water in rapids, you'll be moved anyway and you'll probably drown. "Wait and see" or shunning the "first mover" advantage means you lose all control and are condemned to follow, not lead, very possibly forever: the faster the rate of change, the harder it is to catch up. Taking charge of your fate and thus of change, however, means seizing your opportunities.

Change is synonymous with opportunity. In a static market, dominated by established companies, newcomers have virtually no chance of breaking in. When Grove's 10 x forces strike, flux swamps everything. In case after case, industry after industry, newcomers adapt better to radically changed conditions than the existing players.

Strategic inflection points demand the ability to manage change on a dramatic scale. These drastic shifts are becoming less rare—you must constantly look for signs that they are affecting you. But sea-changes do not explain why the spotlight has turned on "how to manage change" in such a big way. Most change is evolutionary rather than revolutionary. All managers have always had to cope with change constantly. Customers, employees, bosses, rivals, products, technologies, regulations, markets, orders; you know that nothing lasts for ever.

MANAGEMENT AND MEASURABILITY

Understandably, however, managers prefer order and discipline to flux, and therefore seek to establish systems that provide predictability and control. That creates a perpetual tension between the real world, which is unpredictable and uncontrollable, and the corporate interior. To put that another way, it builds tension between creativity and organization, which mounts as the latter rapidly degenerates into bureaucracy. What people generally understand by "management of change" is combining chaos and order—changing, yes, but in a planned manner.

The definition of a good change management team is a group of people who know what to change, know how to accomplish that change and, above all, carry it out. It helps to operate technical change under a cultural banner. Total Quality Management (TQM), for example, can be described as a change program that lasts forever, with each year using a new theme (like "Putting the Customer First") to refocus and rejuvenate the program. Banners, themes and exhortations are not the essence of change, but rather part of creating the atmosphere in which real change can take place.

In TQM programs, there is a clear correlation between success and the participation of the topmost management, not just as committed supporters, but as people whose own performance can be changed for the better by quality training and methods. It might seem difficult to find measures for boardroom performance—and TQM hinges on improving measurable and measured statistics—but you can always find such

---

352

BEST PRACTICE

measures. In fact, the more that change can be measured, the greater the likelihood of achieving successful change management.

Closeness to customers, or "customer focus," is a clear example of the importance of measurement. If your company seeks top ratings for RPQ and RPS (relative perceived quality and relative perceived service), it will be forced into continuous, continual change. Studies show that if it succeeds it will also generate increased market share and profitability. Customer satisfaction indices are mere statistics, but achieving the highest proportion of customers who rate your products and services as "excellent," or who call themselves "very satisfied," demands genuine market leadership, perpetually reinvented.

CHANGE FROM THE BOTTOM UP

You cannot manage such changes from the top. The prevailing view of change management has changed dramatically since the early 1980s. It was seen then as an inward-looking process ordained by chief executives who laid down the law from on high. By the end of the 1990s, change management had shifted to a bottom-up process, encouraged by flat organization, relationships of trust, payment for performance, and training. These factors are all inner-directed, but they operate to create an outward-facing organization that is responsive, innovative, and dedicated to high RPQ and RPS performance.

CHANGE BEFORE THE CRISIS

Many managers are sure to find such shifts deeply uncomfortable, even intolerable. Often, as many as half the managers in an organization have to be changed (that is, moved or removed) before change can be achieved. Acceptance is especially hard to obtain at points below the crest of what Charles Handy presents as "the Sigmoid Curve." Similar to Grove's concept of the strategic inflection point, the curve charts the rise of an organization to peak power and profitability, and then the subsequent decline. Unless change management is set going well before the peak (which is difficult, because nobody thinks change is necessary), it will have to be enforced past

the peak, when the organization may be in crisis.

The key to change management is to manage the same way when you are not in crisis as you are forced to manage in crisis, and also to learn the striking lessons of surmounted crisis. Many turnaround cases show that any organization can be changed, for all intents and purposes overnight, even from total aversion to the essential trio—change, risk and action—to the opposite. The results are usually remarkable, but only in the context of recovery. Remember that turning around from incipient disaster is not good management of change. The true test of change management is perpetuating and renewing success.

MINI-CASE
Intel

The strategic inflection point which nearly laid Intel low was the advent of more effective, massive competition in memory chips (its core business) from the Japanese. After a prolonged period of denial and indecision, Andy Grove and his C.E.O., Gordon Moore, asked what a new boss would do. The answer was to exit memory chips altogether. The change took a year to implement as Intel overcame internal resistance and switched all its efforts to the microprocessor. Grove's lessons from this failure turned into brilliant success are invaluable:

1. always have new projects under development as potential replacements;
2. act sooner rather than later;
3. argue out the change plan, but let opponents go rather than compromise the future;
4. treat crisis as opportunity.

MAKING IT HAPPEN ▸▸

- Decide to take charge of your destiny; learn to see change as opportunity—and always take advantage of the latter.
- Watch out for "strategic inflection points"—drastic shifts in the circumstances of your sector or industry—and respond early to their coming impact.
- Form a change management team of people who know what to change, know

how to change it—and who, above all, will carry change through.
- Force your company into continuous, continual change by seeking top ratings for RPQ and RPS (relative perceived quality and relative perceived service).
- Shift from top-down to bottom-up by flattening the organization, establishing relationships of trust, and paying for performance.
- To perpetuate and renew success, manage out of crisis as you are forced to manage in crisis.

CONCLUSION

Study of turnarounds, however, does demonstrate a recurring pattern of eight elements that are also vitally needed for successful change management:

1. Leadership by a single person or united team is the fulcrum, both at the top and at lower levels.
2. Nothing is sacred. Everything is subject to challenge and, if necessary, change.
3. Decisions are made decisively and rapidly.
4. Necessary action is also taken decisively and rapidly: the longer change is delayed, the less likely it is to be effective.
5. What's being done and why is clearly communicated inside and outside the company with maximum commitment.
6. Change is facilitated and symbolized by actions, above all by actions of top management.
7. The basics of the business are subjected to *kaizen* (continuous improvement) and, if needed, *kaikaku* (radical reform).
8. The future of the organization and its businesses is kept firmly in front of everybody's eyes and actions.

FOR MORE INFORMATION

Books:
Hammer, Michael, and James Champy. *Reengineering the Corporation: A Manifesto for Business Revolution.* Revised ed. New York: HarperCollins, 2004.
Pendlebury, John, et al. *The Ten Keys to Successful Management.* New York: Wiley, 1998.

"The toughest thing about success is that you've got to keep on being a success."

Irving Berlin

Trend Innovation Management
by Matthias Horx

EXECUTIVE SUMMARY

- Trend research and futurism, though controversial, are becoming ever more widely used as in aids to strategic decision-making and to innovation generation.
- It is important to decide whether future research should be an activity that is internal or external to the organization, and at what level it should be integrated into the development process.
- While there are various options, the most comprehensive one used by companies with a successful record of innovation is "total trend innovation."
- The two steps to total trend innovation involve establishing, first, a hierarchy of "trend sorts" and, second, a classification of trends.
- There are two ways of operating with this method, through careful analysis or through scatter-gun production followed by a triage of products by customers—a blend of both methods, speeded-up analysis, is likely to produce the best results.

INTRODUCTION

Trend research and futurism research are controversial "sciences" and are seen by many as dark arts with roughly the same reputation as crystal-ball-gazing. Despite this, trend researchers and futurists are getting increasingly popular and receive ever-greater public recognition. Nearly every large organization nowadays works with one or the other forecasting method—maybe even having its own "future department"—or hires some kind of futurist or trend analyst. The reasons why there is now a "trend for looking at trends" are complex, but they are more easily understandable when we consider the fast-moving, ever-changing circumstances of global markets. These demand:

- **better decision-making in strategic management**. Markets and products today are extremely volatile and complicated. To understand their dynamics and react appropriately and—crucially—*at the right time*, you need some help, advice, or a "back-up recognition system."
- **quicker and more precise innovation generation**. While innovation becomes the key element in most markets, driving innovations "to the edge" is a necessity if you want to survive.

FUTURISTS AROUND THE WORLD

Today prognostic and trend services are offered by a wide range of small agencies, think-tanks, and professional groups, some of them with a long history and tradition, such as the Basel-based Prognos. Some are organized in loose networks with gurus in the middle; Peter Schwartz's Global Business Network is a good example. Others work mainly in the political arena, like Demos in London, while some are universalists with a "cross-analyzing" approach, like the German Zukunftsinstitut in Frankfurt and Vienna.

Although there is no real common scientific method among all the futurists and trend consultancies, some cognitive or working similarities can be seen:

- **consumer trend research**. Faith Popcorn, the U.S. marketing guru, is probably the most famous advocate of a "narrative," consumer-centered, sociology-influenced analysis of product and shopping trends. Her findings have indeed led to a lot of innovative products, with some visible success (and some unknown flops).
- **future studies and strategic forecasting**. This has a long tradition going back to the 1960s, when U.S. think-tanks such as the RAND corporation developed war gaming for the future of the Cold War. Shell started to implement scenario techniques into their management strategies. John Naisbitt, who invented the expression "megatrends," founded the "Second Wave" of more managerially orientated futurism in the 1980s. The borderline to "common" consultancies is not precisely clear; every Accenture or McKinsey activity includes some kind of future analysis. Basically, serious futurists in this field know a lot about system theory, complexity theory, and how to connect different branches of modern prognostic science to models of the future (or certain parts of it).

WORKING WITH THE FUTURE

If you want to "work with the future," you first have to decide whether you want the task to be externalized or integrated into your daily business. Second, it is important to define what goal you have. Do you want to empower your core management group with the current trend and future findings? Or do you want to change entire value-creating processes, like the generation of innovative products, in a futuristic way?

Potential options include:

- **external "future tank" method**. This method is especially popular among automobile manufacturers, who in themselves are still production-oriented and like to delegate the future work to "avant-garde pressure groups." For example, ten talented young designers, artists, and trend experts huddle together in a "future lab" in Los Angeles or Shanghai where they exercise their imaginations and create images of wild future cars which will fly and roar. The whole thing is expensive, secret and . . . hermetic. The danger of this method is *disconnection*: the conceptual innovation process *itself* becomes excluded, and the company produces the same old boring cars while the "loonies" in their labs are getting crazier every day.
- **internal "future agents"**. This method is frequently adopted by the "hype-driven" telecommunication companies, but also some big banks and tourist concerns like to work with internal groups who produce a kind of science fiction work about the future of communications/travel/money. These small internal groups (or even "storytelling individuals") paint huge mood boards and evolution charts where you can see that we all will undoubtedly watch a lot of TV and scan our brains into computers in only 20 years' time. All this is put into beautifully designed brochures and presented in "vision days" for journalists and other future-hungry people. Future work in this sense is used first and foremost as a PR and communication tool. There is, however, a problem: future analysis becomes opportunistic and interest-driven for the company. Internal futurists are often just greasing up to the PR departments. There is no reflective element, and it only leads to self-satisfaction and smugness.

- **"strategic management empowerment."** If you "only" want to empower the top management for future challenges, there are plenty of possibilities for future work. These range from the classic huddling in a hut for days with a famous futurist, to well-structured meetings around a special theme. The main technique for this is still—and with still increasing relevance—the scenario technique.
- **collective intelligence trend research.** Some companies like BASF or big pharmaceutical companies, which do not have to deal directly with consumer markets, develop "future sensors" out of the sheer volume of their internal knowledge. This develops in databanks, which are fed constantly by the employees of the company itself. It is a simple and practical "forecast machine" for specific themes, whether they be fluctuating prices for raw materials or lawsuit trends in the United States. The problem? While these instruments are very good at monitoring short-term trends in very isolated and specific fields, they do not give you any clue about circumstances, technology change, interruptions, discontinuities, and so on—the bigger picture, in short.
- **total trend innovation.** Genuinely innovative companies like Virgin, Apple, and Nokia re-created their whole innovation process with trend and future forecasting. There is no difference between the "internal vision" and the "external outlook," nor is the approach of the management of operations different from the management of innovation. Trend innovation encompasses everything from strategic management right down to the last screw on the finished product. Many Nokia mobile phones were created by such a seamless trend innovation process.

TOTAL TREND INNOVATION

There are two steps in the implementation of total trend innovation:

- **Step one.** Analysis and documentation of different "trend sorts" (length, impact, strength, etc.). It is important to know, on which level, in which dimensions, and related to which contexts trends occur. Creating a clean hierarchy allows the innovation process to base its paradigms on the right order.

- **Step two.** The next step is to use the right tools. These are the main categories into which trends should be placed: megatrends, sociotrends, consumer trends, design trends. Out of this background emerges a "world"; a collage which includes the style and functional elements as well as the technological elements of the product to come.

There are basically two different ways to operate with this method in fast-growing and fast-changing markets. One could be called the "careful analytical method." The other could be called "creative trend-speeding." While Siemens, for example, made a lot of effort to find out what the customers might want from mobile phones in the future, a lot of time went by. When Siemens brought their new models onto the market, there were already outdated. Samsung, on the other hand, worked in a different way. The Korean company created a huge amount of output and brought 80 different mobile phones onto the market, of which 80% vanished immediately. The Siemens method is more inside-driven, while the Samsung way, in spite of working with similar, but more creative elements, leaves lots of the end decisions to the customers. Although the Samsung method seems more successful, it is not without risks, because costs are very high, and the method relies on the genuine fashion markets (where the innovation cycle is now 4 weeks, not 6 months, and the products are not so expensive and time-consuming). The best approach would be a clever combination of German carefulness with the more creative approach: or to put it another way, speed up clever analytical work!

MAKING IT HAPPEN ▶▶

If you want to work with trends in the management and innovation processes, remember to:

1 **Define your goals**. You must know which "system" you want to address. Is it collective "management brain" that you want to upgrade with future knowledge? Then more associative, communicative, "mental" ways of working with trends and forecasting are appropriate. To change employees with "future stuff" is not so easy; predictive work has to be "translated"

to work as a motivational instrument.

2 **Beware of trend opportunism**. Never use trends as a guideline for "guaranteed success": you will then become a victim of superficial trend gurus, who can lead you a merry dance. Trends can be used in a very linear way, so that everybody in your business follows the same clichés, and in the end nobody earns money at all! When trend work is properly done, it creates a "mapping of possibilities," which gives you the freedom of decision. Also remember that counter-trends can be more productive than mainstream trends.

3 **Personality matters**. Because high complexity is always an element in prediction, forecasting, and trend research, personality matters a lot. If you work with agencies or trend gurus of your own choice, ask for the scientific and cognitive background of their work. Even if "futuring" cannot be reduced to a mere mathematical tool (you can't calculate the future), trend work and future prediction should be a little more than simply educated guesses. Good forecasting does have intensive theoretical backgrounds, which your guru or future analyst should be able to explain to you properly.

FOR MORE INFORMATION

Books:
Horx, Matthias. *How We Will Live: A Synthesis of Life in the Future*. London: Cyan Books, 2006.
Popcorn, Faith. *Clicking: 16 Trends to Future Fit Your Business and your Life*. New York: HarperBusiness, 1998.
Schwartz, Peter. *The Art of the Long View*. New York: Doubleday, 1991.

Web site:
Zukunftsinstitut:
www.zukunftsinstitut.de

See also:
∽ Innovation and Creativity (pp. 1774–1777)

Viewpoint: Eamonn Kelly
What's Next? The New Challenges for Business

Introduction

Eamonn Kelly is C.E.O. and President of Global Business Network, and he has been central to sustaining the company's thought leadership about the future. He also heads GBN's consulting practice, and has worked at senior levels with dozens of the world's leading corporations in many sectors, as well as with global and national public agencies. He was previously head of strategy for Scottish Enterprise, one of the world's most respected and innovative development agencies. He is the author of *Powerful Times: Rising to the Challenge of Our Uncertain World* (Wharton, 2005) and the *2003 GBN Scenario Book: History in Motion*, and co-author of *What's Next: Exploring the New Terrain for Business* (Perseus/Wiley, 2002) and *The Future of the Knowledge Economy* (OECD, 1999). In this article, Eamonn Kelly highlights the fact that the forces of change—notably including technology and globalization—have presented organizations with a challenging new environment. The solution, he argues, is to learn to anticipate change and to adapt quickly, and this requires organizations to adopt a new set of priorities.

We live in an era of profound transformation. In just a few decades we have witnessed the transition from an industrial, nation-based, resource-oriented economy to a global, networked, knowledge-intensive economy. Corporations have been a powerful catalyst for change: opening markets, promoting privatization, and globalizing goods, services, and production processes. As more parts of the world have adopted market mechanisms to promote wealth creation, millions of people have gained access to new products, as well as technologies, information, and ideas. New economic opportunities have improved the quality of life for many. However, there have also been unintended consequences.

The liberation of markets, driven by the power of corporations, has also created more complex, interconnected economic and social systems that cannot be controlled or predicted. The very forces of globalization, rapid technological advances, increased connectivity, and mounting transparency that businesses have helped to unleash are shaping a new and challenging environment. Global protest movements, demands for greater accountability, increasingly complex geopolitical tensions, wider cultural divides, and rising concerns about environmental and social sustainability, are making the business of business even more complicated. These new realities point to a whole new set of challenges and opportunities for business in the decade ahead.

Foremost among these corporate challenges is a need to move beyond the sole pursuit of competitive advantage to embrace "adaptive advantage" as well. Amidst the economic globalization and deregulation of the past 20 years, companies understandably sought competitive advantage by developing and applying a superior understanding of the marketplace.

Using increasingly sophisticated tools and technologies, they analyzed and modeled the economy, finance, industries, customers, competitors, and options. In the next ten years, businesses will continue to improve such tools, but that alone will no longer be sufficient to ensure success. Instead, businesses must also learn to respond more quickly to an increasingly complex environment in which many political, economic, social, cultural, and technological forces are shifting, interacting, and sometimes colliding. This will entail expanding their peripheral vision to encompass a far broader set of concerns and to focus on the development of *adaptive advantage*, based on a deeper understanding of the world as well as the marketplace. Ultimately, adaptive advantage requires significant improvement in two linked areas: the ability to anticipate and sense change, and the capacity to respond quickly and coherently. For companies this will inform a new set of developmental priorities, organized around *thinking differently, learning differently,* and *acting differently.*

Thinking Differently

When it comes to thinking differently, business leaders will have to increase the complexity of their thought to mirror the complexity of their environment. There are three related ways of evolving one's ability to do just that: *outside-in thinking, connective thinking,* and, finally, *scenario thinking.*

Outside-in Thinking

Strategic or business-development thinking tends to move from the inside out. It typically starts with the organization's purpose and core strengths, then explores its marketplaces and competitive positioning, and finally looks at the broader geopolitical, economic, social, and technological shifts that might matter. Much of the time that trajectory is entirely appropriate, but not when you are seeking to boost your sensitivity to changes in the external business environment. That's because, once you get to the external focus, you have subconsciously introduced so many assumptions about what's important, based on experience, that you see only a small subset of the external world. As a result you can miss the big changes that could be important, such as new security

---

"If global connectivity is the technological breakthrough of our decade, then the outburst of innovation is just beginning."

Mary J. Cronin

risks or seemingly irrelevant scientific and techno-logical developments that could prove advantageous to you—or your competitors. Conversely, by thinking from the outside in you begin with the external changes that might, over time, profoundly impact your markets and organization. Your filters and as-sumptions, though still present, are less restrictive. This encourages more open and imaginative thinking about the full range of potential changes that might matter most to your future.

Connective Thinking

Another thinking skill that is becoming more critical is the ability to make creative connections between apparently disparate ideas and trends—connective thinking. This is closely related to systems thinking, but becomes a different creative challenge when ap-plied to the terrain of future possibilities. It is about connecting dots in new ways to discover new patterns of possibility. For example, the seemingly unrelated trends of rising environmental concerns, continued threats of widespread terrorism, the spreading anti-globalization movement, progress toward a hydrogen economy, and manufacturing at the molecular level together suggest a possible move toward localized ver-sus global production of goods. Chances are the future will not be determined by one big change but by mul-tiple changes that converge. Adaptive advantage, therefore, will partly come from making quicker, smarter connections across varied domains.

Scenario Thinking

Outside-in and connective thinking inevitably lead you to contemplate "What ifs?" about the future. But to do so productively, organizations can neither deny uncertainty and assume that the future will look pretty much like a projection of the past, or be para-lyzed by it—that is, abandon all attempts to take a long view because everything is too complex, too crazy. The well-tested methodology of "scenario thinking" enables us to anticipate the future without the folly of trying to predict it, or the mistake of ignoring it. This "long view" approach involves a process of developing several very different but plausible stories of how the future might unfold, in ways that are relevant to or-ganizations. By providing multiple, plausible perspec-tives on what could happen, scenarios enable you to understand and challenge the organization's domin-ant assumptions. Scenarios, therefore, help to boost our preparedness for different credible futures, while also providing context for discovering new opportun-ities. Above all, scenarios are stories—an ancient and remarkably powerful form of communication that re-veals values and beliefs and sustains communities. In a business setting they help to overcome the inertia and denial that can so easily make the future a dan-gerous place.

Learning Differently

Gaining adaptive advantage requires that business leaders not only think differently, but also learn dif-ferently. This can be accomplished by identifying key *literacies for the future*, establishing *learning networks*, and getting executives out of the office and onto *learn-ing journeys*.

Literacies for the Future

With so much happening in the world, with so many uncertainties and drivers of change, how can over-worked executives identify the limits of their knowledge? Information overload can be channeled productively by creating a specific learning agenda that focuses on a few external developments that may have a low impact on your business today, but could be hugely significant in defining your future. These "literacies for the future" may be very broad, such as emerging geopolitical risks, or bioconvergence—the interactions of bio-, nano-, and info-technologies. Others may focus more narrowly on a specific topic (water resources or China) or technology (quantum computing, fuel cells). Similarly, literacies can be ex-plored in a variety of ways: a series of presentations or debates by internal and external experts, brown-bag lunch discussions, white papers, Web-based conversa-tions, even field trips—all designed to achieve famil-iarity and fluency rather than depth and expertise in a variety of topics and issues.

Learning Networks

Identifying core areas for focused learning is a beginning, not an end. It is equally important to be continually exposed to a broader range of ideas and developments. Learning networks, both internal and external, can serve this function by linking members with a wide variety of expertise and experience. Many networks are organized around a shared interest or expertise to trade information, tools and techniques, and even job opportunities. Learning networks, how-ever, purposely include external experts on a variety of topics—politics and economics, different cultures and religions, science and technology—who provide advance notice of emerging developments in their fields, filter new information, interpret events and issues from different perspectives, and even explore the implications of decisions or actions. Similarly, in-ternal networks can connect people across different business units to leverage expertise, vet options, and facilitate cross-functional teamwork. Some networks are entirely virtual; others periodically come together face-to-face while sustaining their relationships and activities electronically. Also, networks can be a powerful force for action as well as learning. For ex-ample, the World Trade Organization protests in Seat-tle and elsewhere were organized by connecting and communicating with networks of networks using the Internet and cell phones. Although networks are not easy to design—indeed, they tend to take on a life and purpose of their own—it is possible to create networks that will provoke, inform, and accelerate learning and community, fulfilling the old adage, "No one is as smart as everyone."

"If we want a vibrant, inclusive global economy there is no alternative . . . to finding some way between these two extremes. There is no alternative to the pursuit of policies and institutions that will make globalization work . . . for people."

Lawrence H. Summers

Learning Journeys

John Le Carré once wrote: "A desk is a dangerous place from which to view the world." It is crucial for executives to get out of the office and be exposed to forces that might shape the future—or are already shaping the present in ways that are invisible to most of us. "Learning journeys" around a particular theme (such as the biotech economy, clean technologies, converging and diverging cultures, or customers of the future) can stretch thinking far beyond the obvious and everyday. Unlike fact-finding missions or benchmarking expeditions that tend to substantiate preconceptions or prove hypotheses, learning journeys are truly exploratory: they push the envelope on what is known and redefine the boundaries of what is possible by introducing the participants to striking new experiences, places, people, and ideas. Often the most significant insights are subtle; not the presentation given by the head of R&D at a pioneering technology firm, but the fact that she and her colleagues are such a young, diverse, articulate, and energetic group, especially when compared to the bureaucrats at the shabby government lab down the street. Furthermore, because the learning is visceral—derived from an experience rather than a book or lecture—it tends to be more lasting and actionable.

Acting Differently

Thinking and learning differently will have little impact in the absence of changed behavior. In fact, both should inform behavior. So the third pillar of adaptive advantage is behaving in ways that will become increasingly important for business success: *acting experimentally, acting inclusively,* and *acting ethically.*

Acting Experimentally

In the coming decade businesses may have to change even more frequently, rapidly, and dramatically than ever before. This requires a critical new capacity: the ability to act *experimentally.* In evolution, nature experiments through speciation, trying out frequent small-scale changes, or genetic variations that iterate and compound over time. Likewise, science is based on experimentation, as hypotheses are tested and revised through small-scale experiments. Most of these experiments will fail, but they are inexpensive and yield valuable learning. Few businesses, however, have mastered the art and practice of experimentation. Most introduce changes through large-scale initiatives that are typically based on a single approach, consume considerable resources, take a long time to implement, and leave little room for course corrections. Indeed, this approach often works against adaptation—it might even be an adaptive *dis*advantage. Instead, business should follow the lead of nature and science: imagine, design, and execute small-scale experiments in new opportunity spaces; systematically extract the learning from both success and failure; and move swiftly on to the next iteration.

Acting Inclusively

A world of growing interconnection and mutual interdependence demands a more holistic and inclusive approach to thinking and acting. For businesses, taking a more inclusive view of the purpose of your business, beyond making a profit and creating shareholder value, reveals new opportunities for alliances or long-term investments that enhance your adaptive advantage. Similarly, adopting a more inclusive definition of your stakeholders and being open to broader opportunities for dialog and collaboration with them could enhance your business intelligence, standing, and relationships. Perhaps the most promising and challenging long-term opportunity to create adaptive advantage involves engaging the excluded billions of the world's poor—the two-thirds of the world's population that remain disconnected from the economic mainstream despite globalization. On the one hand, the notion of "B24B," or "business to 4 billion" appeals to direct corporate self-interest, since these new markets will allow businesses to sustain high future growth as mature markets evolve toward different patterns of demand. But from a longer-term perspective, businesses need to help create a sustainable business environment by addressing the deep problems found in many parts of the world, laying appropriate foundations for local economic growth, and creating a sense of meaningful opportunity and hope among those currently excluded.

Acting Ethically

In the industrial era, businesses produced widespread economic and quality-of-life improvements through mechanizing, standardizing, automating, and scaling their operations. In most capitalist societies, businesses were considered morally neutral, neither causing deliberate harm nor pursuing a greater social good. Unintended negative consequences of commercial activity, such as environmental degradation, were largely tolerated, even expected. With time, however, there developed a growing disconnect between "economic wisdom"—doing the profitable thing—and "moral wisdom"—doing the right thing. Today, that trend may be reversing as economic and moral wisdom become realigned—enabling and encouraging businesses to "do well by doing good." Many factors are driving this realignment: the sheer scale and reach of market-based business activity, the accumulating evidence of the environmental, social, and cultural consequences of business activity, the unprecedented level of transparency, and a growing sense of public concern regarding the role of corporations and their impact on the world. As we've seen with Enron, Andersen, and WorldCom, it seems inevitable that public scrutiny will grow, leaving fewer places for transgressors to hide or avoid punishment for violating common moral wisdom. Every business could find that its reputation and credibility is constantly in play and at peril. The safest strategy will be to strive for impeccable behavior that over time becomes embedded in your business brand.

This means that business leaders will have to instill a deep ethical consciousness throughout their organization, not merely as an adjunct to business strategy, but as a core organizing principle. Shareholders and

other stakeholders will demand it. However, this will also enhance adaptive advantage because a clear, shared ethical compass will be essential to navigate quickly through the complex terrain of the future business environment. The ability of people at all levels of an organization to develop appropriate options, make rapid decisions, and act swiftly in a changing world will increasingly require a common set of ethical imperatives. Instilling such an ethical consciousness will take more than putting a statement of values on computer mouse pads—the commitment must become embedded in the organization's DNA. Fortunately, promoting ethical behavior does not run counter to the personal instincts of most employees and stakeholders, who want to act ethically in their personal and professional lives. By reinforcing and rewarding ethical standards and behavior, ethical consciousness may prove surprisingly easy to achieve. Moreover, those who move early in this direction can expect to attract and retain great people, which in turn fuels adaptive advantage.

CONCLUSION

Over the last 20 years we have seen businesses large and small, global and local, help to create a vibrant, complex, interconnected, and interdependent world, in which wealth and opportunity have spread globally. Looking ahead to the future it is easy to imagine scenarios of increasing complexity, shaped by the interaction of more elaborate technology, more sophisticated products and services, more diverse global markets, more complicated financial instruments, and more demanding collaborative relationships. It is equally easy to imagine businesses rising to the chal-

lenges created by such complexity and innovating effectively as they continue to thrive. However, it is all too easy to also imagine scenarios in which the increasing complexities and accelerating pace of change that business helped to create, actually compound to undermine the economic, social, and physical environment on which we all depend. So in addition to understanding the world better, businesses will need to address the problems of the world more actively. Collectively, the business sector holds too much power to be morally neutral in its activities. We cannot focus solely on profitability and shareholder value. We cannot ignore the plight of billions of people untouched—or worse, harmed—by the economic progress of the last century. We cannot, in short, simply *adapt* to the changing world—we must use our strengths to influence that change for the better. The next stage in the evolution of business is beginning. Having done so much to create a remarkable new world, we now must play a more active part in nurturing and improving it. This may prove to be the most profound source of sustained success in the twenty-first century.

FOR MORE INFORMATION

Book:
Kelly, Eamonn. *Powerful Times: Rising to the Challenge of Our Uncertain World.* Philadelphia, PA: Wharton, 2005.

See also:
☆ Trend Innovation Management (pp. 353–354)

"Highly-adaptive, informal networks move diagonally and eliptically, skipping entire functions to get things done."

Jacques Barzun

Viewpoint: Clayton M. Christensen
Looking at the Future Through the Lens of Management Theory

Introduction
Clayton Christensen is the Robert and Jane Cizik Professor of Business Administration at the Harvard Business School. He is the author of several bestselling business books, including *The Innovator's Dilemma* (Harvard Business School Press, 1997) and *The Innovator's Solution* (Harvard Business School Press, 2003).

Disruption is a phenomenon, identified in my research, which takes place when innovations that make a product much more affordable and simpler to use take root at the low end, or in the simplest applications, of a market. Generally, this tier of the market is the least attractive to the incumbent leading companies in the industry, because their largest and most profitable customers can't use the lower-performing disruptive products and because these disruptive products yield much lower profit margins than do more expensive, higher-performing ones. As a result, disruptions generally are the least attractive item on the menu of possible investments across which executives allocate corporate resources. For these reasons, the leading companies generally are quite happy to let an upstart company seize the disruptive low ground. Once such upstarts have taken root with processes and an economic model that enable them to earn profit at the industry's lowest price point, they find it very profitable to move up to the next-highest tier in the market. As they launch another attack on the incumbents, the incumbents are once again motivated to hand off to the disruptors the least attractive of the potential investments on their menu, so they can focus on the most profitable investments. Entrants have used disruptions like this to topple the leaders and transform industries as diverse as computers, disk drives, hydraulic excavators, telecommunications, airlines, retailing, automobiles, software, and healthcare.

Several years ago I realized, while examining the list of companies that were coming onto our campus to recruit our graduating students, that the Harvard Business School, where I work, and other schools like ours were themselves being disrupted. Our graduates are extraordinarily capable men and women—as evidenced by the fact that the combined salary and signing bonus approaches $130,000 per year. But when I looked at the companies that were coming onto our campus to recruit our students, I found that fewer and fewer operating companies were coming, because they could not fit the salaries that our graduates commanded into their salary structure. In the language of disruption, we had over-shot the operating-company tier of the market. Increasingly, our gradu-

ates are hired by firms such as McKinsey, Goldman Sachs, venture capitalists, and private equity funds. Operating companies increasingly are hiring undergraduates, and then training them internally, at Intel University, Dana University, and GE Crotonville. When their young managers need an MBA in order to qualify for promotions, they increasingly send them on nights-and-weekends executive MBA programs at local colleges, rather than sending them on a two-year MBA program.

I then wrote a case study about the disruption of the Harvard Business School, to discuss with my students. I began that class ten years ago by asking for a vote of the 100 students in the class: "How many of you think the leading business schools are being disrupted, just like the minicomputer, steel, automobile, and department store companies were disrupted in the past?" Three students raised their hands. I then asked, "How many of you think that Clay is off his rocker, and that we all can be in the 'don't-worry-be-happy' camp?" The other 97 students raised their hands. There were no abstentions.

I then asked one of the three students who had raised his hand why he was worried for our future. He responded, "As you look at this theory, there seems to be a pattern—and I see six elements of the pattern." He had me record these on the board. "These six things happened in these other industries," he continued. "As I read the case, I could see that all six of these things are happening to the business schools. We're still going strong now, but you can see that the disruption already is well underway." He had me check off the elements of the pattern, one by one, on the board.

I then turned to the "don't-worry-be-happy" group and asked, "So why aren't you guys worried?" Everything they cited as reasons related to the facts—the data—that surrounded us at the time. More people were applying than ever before, we were ranked #1, the average graduating student received four job offers, and starting salaries were at record highs. I kept pushing back on them with assertions like, "Isn't that exactly what Den Olsen at Digital Equipment said about the personal computer?" But they always were able to muster data to refute the conclusions of the theory. Finally, I asked a student, "So imagine that you were our dean. What data would you have to see to become convinced that this disruption is real?"

He responded, "I'd look at our market share of the

"In science, the credit goes to the man who convinces the world, not to the man to whom the idea first occurs."

Francis Darwin

C.E.O.s of the global 1000. If it started to drop, then I'd worry."

My question in response was, "When you saw that data, would it be a signal that we should begin to take action, or that the game was over?"

"Oh," he admitted. "I guess the game would be over."

This proved to be an extraordinary exercise for us ten years ago, because it helped us see a flaw in the way we have taught managers to make decisions: we assert that decisions should be data-driven, based upon sound analysis. But the problem with data, we realized, is that it is only available about the past. And when the data is conclusive, the game is over. In teaching managers to be fact-based and analytical in their decision-making, we were condemning them to being able to take action only when it was too late. The scary thing, of course, is this meant that if we were to take timely action it would need to be based upon the predictions of a theory.

The word *theory* gets a bum rap with managers, because it is associated with the word *theoretical*, which connotes *impractical*. But a theory is a very practical thing, because it is a statement of what causes what, and why. Gravity, for example, is a theory and it allows us to predict in advance that if we step off a cliff we will fall and not rise; so we do not need to experiment about that particular question.

Framed in this way, theory is something that managers actually are *voracious* consumers of. Every time they take an action, it is predicated on a theory in their minds that if they do that thing they'll get the result they need. And every time they formulate a plan, it is based upon a set of theories of cause and effect—if they do the things they plan, they'll be successful. Because most managers most of the time aren't conscious of the theories they're using when making plans and taking action, and because they often use inappropriate theories, they often don't succeed as they had hoped. As a result, innovation and attempts to create new growth businesses have acquired something of a stench of riskiness and unpredictability.

The venture capital industry, for example, is actually structured around the belief that innovation is unpredictable. Every time venture investors put money into a company, they think it will succeed. But statistically only two out of ten make it. Hence, they've created portfolios of companies to hedge their bets, having concluded from their experience that venture-investing is unpredictable. In the absence of sound theories that can guide managers to make plans and take actions that will succeed, given the situation they find themselves in, it is indeed random.

In the year AD 1500, aviators had reached a similar conclusion, based upon literally thousands of years of evidence: humans simply could not fly. But after Daniel Bernoulli articulated his theory—that a shape we now call an airfoil creates lift—and after subsequent research established a broader set of theories of cause and effect, humans came to be able to fly quite predictably. The rules are now so clear that today's air-

liners are essentially flown by computer. Aided by the theories encoded in these computers, aviators can collect data from the present, predict what it portends for the future, and make the needed adjustments to keep their aircraft flying safe and true to their destination.

Sound theory has had a similar impact on other industries. For example, 45 years ago there were only 100 or so people in the world who could design a mainframe computer—and IBM employed most of them. Designs were created essentially by trial and error. Using their best experience-based judgment, the engineers would build prototypes and test them. When they didn't work, they'd alter or scrap them, and try again and again until they had iterated towards something that would work. The rewards to the company that employed

> The word *theory* gets a bum rap with managers, because it is associated with the word *theoretical*, which connotes *impractical*. But a theory is a very practical thing

these artisans were enormous. Intel's microprocessor ultimately incorporated within it the solutions to many of the problems that IBM's engineers formerly had wrestled with. During the first three generations of its processor, Intel just sold the single packaged chip—it still took considerable electrical engineering expertise to design a computer around that processor. But starting in the fourth generation, Intel began to sell a chip set and they solved within that set essentially all of the complicated engineering problems associated with designing and building a computer. From that point on, all one needed to start a computer company was a BS in electrical engineering from an average Taiwanese university. The ability to design computers evolved from experimentation and problem solving, into a pattern-recognition mode, and finally into a rules-based regime.

Organic fibers and chemicals have gone through a parallel transformation. If you wanted a new organic fiber or plastic sixty years ago, you basically had to go to the labs at DuPont. Only a hundred or so scientists in the world could design and build one of these molecules, and DuPont employed most of them. One of them would heat up some atoms in a beaker, draw out a fiber, examine it under a microscope, go down the hall and show it to a colleague, and ask, "What do you think this is?" She would respond, "I don't know. But heat it up for ten more minutes and let's see what happens." The miracle molecules we now know as nylon, polyester, and Kevlar emerged from DuPont through a process of experimentation and problem-solving. But as these artists practiced their intuitive craft, patterns of cause and effect began to emerge. This enabled engineers with less intuitive skill to participate in the design of organic molecules. Ultimately, as Quantum Theory came to be understood and applied to the synthesis of organic molecules, the industry moved towards a rules-based regime. Engineers could predict in advance that, if they created a molecule with a particular structure, then the resultant material would have particular properties. This

then allowed them to create software packages that would allow engineers to input the properties of the material they needed, and the software would assist them in designing a molecule that would yield those properties.

This is the model: In almost every industry, the initial methods of development involve experimental, unstructured problem-solving and prototyping. In the second stage, patterns of cause and effect begin to emerge, enabling people whose training is less sophisticated to design and manufacture the products. Ultimately in the third stage scientific progress transforms industries into a rules-based mode, where well-researched and tested guidelines enable people with even less training, experience, and intuition to create even higher-performing products and services than the world's experts could a generation earlier.

How does this apply to innovation? Historically, the ability to conceive and launch successful new growth businesses resided in the intuition, experience, and skill of the best venture capitalists and entrepreneurs in the world. When they succeeded, they *really* succeeded—but 80% of their attempts failed. My colleagues and I have concluded, however, that an emerging body of well-researched theories is shifting the ability to create new growth products and businesses out of the unstructured realm of trial-and-error experimentation into the pattern recognition realm. There *really* are patterns in which plans and actions will lead a company toward success, and which will cause it to fail, in different contexts. There's no cookbook yet—we're not in a rules-based realm. But there are clear patterns. Some elements of this pattern are:

- You beat competitors by disrupting them, not by bringing better products into their markets.
- You can define a product that customers will be sure to buy if you've segmented your market by the jobs that customers are trying to get done, rather than by product categories or customer characteristics.
- For new technologies, the best customers are non-consumers of the traditional product, and the best consuming occasions are those where consumption historically wasn't possible.
- Proprietary architectures are important to success when the functionality and reliability of a product are not yet adequate for what customers need. When these have improved beyond the ability of customers to utilize fur-

ther improvement, then modular, open architectures will dominate.
- What should you outsource, and what should you do in-house? Above-average profitability will always be earned by integrating across the interfaces in the value-added chain where you can better solve a problem that is not yet being solved well enough. The stage in that chain where attractive money can be made today is unlikely to be where the money can be made tomorrow.
- How should you structure your organization to innovate effectively? Functional or lightweight teams work well when you're innovating within an existing architecture. A heavyweight team is the tool needed to create new architectures efficiently. An autonomous unit is required when the business model required to succeed is disruptive relative to the model of the core business.
- New ventures that employ a deliberate strategy process will fail. They need to follow an emergent, discovery-driven process.
- Capital whose owners are willing to incur significant losses in order to grow the business to be very big very fast is bad money—it will cause the venture to fail. Good money is impatient for profit, and patient for growth.

And so on.

The theories that underlie these patterns can help those who understand and follow them to be much more successful, with a higher probability of success, than historically has been the case. In fact, they can constitute a disruptive platform upon which traditional venture capitalists—practitioners of their trial-and-error craft—can be disrupted. They will be disrupted by people with less experience and intuition, who can see into the future with remarkable clarity because their vision will be aided by sound theory.

FOR MORE INFORMATION

Books:
Christensen, Clayton M., and Michael Raynor. *The Innovator's Solution*. Boston, MA: Harvard Business School Press, 2003.
Christensen, Clayton M., Scott Anthony, and Erik Roth. *Seeing What's Next*. Boston, MA: Harvard Business School Press, 2004.

See also:
Innovation and Creativity (pp. 1774–1777)

"The moment a person forms a theory his imagination sees in every object only the traits which favour that theory."

Thomas Jefferson

Building Great Internal Partnerships
by Chip R. Bell

EXECUTIVE SUMMARY

- Organizational success is increasingly dependent on effective internal partnerships as organizations become more complex and as customer demands for improved service make excellence in communication and coordination a necessity.
- The difference between a great team and a great partnership substantially alters the way in which members approach leadership and accomplishment.

INTRODUCTION

When I was a little boy, the TV screen was the impetus for much of our backyard play. My friends and I would watch Batman and Robin and then race to the backyard to reenact what we'd seen on the TV. After what seemed like an hour of arguing over who would be the masked warrior, we'd settle in to battle against evil with our toy guns and pretend Batmobile. Whether it was cowboys and Indians, cops and robbers, or pitchers and batters, TV often shaped the form of our recreation.

A few weeks ago, I was consulting with the C.E.O. of a major high-tech corporation. His company had acquired a smaller software group six weeks earlier to bolster its IT capacity to provide more responsive sales support. The transition had been rocky, and he was now snarling about the infighting between operations and sales. Customer complaints were climbing, field salespeople were frustrated, and the new software enhancements the acquired company was supposed to produce were still stuck in applications development.

"We need better teamwork!" he snapped as he slammed his oversized desk. "Why can't these guys quit arguing in the huddle, just call the play, and get back to basic blocking and tackling?"

It was the Tuesday morning after a popular televised sports event. As I thought of Batman and Robin, I realized the appeal of his reenacting the athletic contest he'd watched on TV had seduced him into reaching for the wrong solution to a common work problem. His problem was not inadequate teamwork but ineffective partnering.

HOW TEAMS DIFFER FROM PARTNERSHIPS

Teamwork and partnership are not the same. Emulating the Dallas Cowboys within

the operations department may heighten synergy and collective productivity. But it is the wrong model for how the operations department works with the sales department. An intact unit uses teamwork. However, synergy between units (whether an external vendor alliance or a relationship with the internal department down the hall) comes from partnership. Using teamwork tactics in a partnership context leads to flawed practices and counterproductive behavior. Here are a few of the key differences.

1. **A team is focused on accomplishing a task and uses an effective relationship as a tool for achieving it.** A partnership is focused on creating a relationship context from which all manner of outcomes can be accomplished. In a team the task is preeminent. In fact, the task a team is engaged on can be so compelling that even a less than excellent team can produce superior performance. In a partnership, excellence cannot be sustained without a superior relationship, no matter how compelling the mission.

2. **A team suspends the individuality of its members in the pursuit of interdependent action.** Collaboration (colaboring) means *two become one*—like two horses harnessed to pull a wagon. In fact, teams work to tone down singleness in their quest to create a new whole; the focus is on mix or blend (as you'd mix yellow with blue to produce green: in green the individual root colors disappear). In a partnership individuality is as meritorious as jointness or union. Singleness is played just as loudly as togetherness, and the focus is on their amalgamation (as you'd create a fruit salad: no matter how hard you toss, apple stays apple and banana remains banana).

3. **Leadership is vital to the effective-**

ness of a team. Generally a great deal of energy is devoted to leadership enlistment—getting associates to accept, value, and respond to followership induction. Even in leaderless teams or self-directed teams, groupings aimed at operating without the formal identification of authority, a sort of pack mentality, encourages the emergence of a leader. In partnerships, followership is less person-centered and more spirit-centered. Partners follow a spirit or energy that may emanate from a partner but is not owned by that partner. It's energy owned by the partnership, providing a force that gives that partnership vitality and drive.

TECHNIQUES FOR BUILDING INTERNAL PARTNERSHIPS

Knowing the difference between a team and a partnership might win you an academic argument, but how does it help with the high-tech C.E.O.'s problem? The implications of these differences are profound. Trying to make a partnership a team is as flawed and problematic as using mules as breeding stock. Below are several key points about the difference between team and partnership that inform practice.

Matching Values, Not Just Talents

Teams depend principally on complementary talents more than congruent values. Partnerships can overcome a mismatch in capacities if the relationship springs from solidly congruent values. "We realized we were two left feet early on," said Frank Esposito, former C.E.O. of the global power sport aftermarket distributor Tucker Rocky Distributing. Speaking of his then company's alliance with a Taiwanese corporation working with Tucker Rocky on a major helmet project, he noted, "Because we shared the same values of honesty, fair play, and commitment, we were able to shore up our mismatch before it derailed our effort." The high-tech C.E.O. we visited earlier asked division heads to write down four work values their unit would refuse to compromise. When both divisions discovered that three of their four values were the same, they found new energy for collaboration and immediately set about

working to accommodate the value that was different. The more they acknowledged values strength, the more their differences seemed minor or petty.

Nurturing Equality, Not Just Synergy

If partnerships are power-free alliances, effort must be devoted to nurturing and bolstering equality. The C.E.O.'s troubles with sales and operations were in part caused by their battles over turf, influence, and recognition. Operations didn't want sales encroaching on their territory; sales didn't want operations getting the right to influence certain decisions that sales considered their purview. *Power over* was the driver, not *power with*. When the C.E.O. later reassured both groups (jointly) that turf, influence, and recognition were not relevant or in jeopardy, they gave up their tug-of-war to decide who was going to be Batman. "If our support staff at global headquarters thinks they have to lose their uniqueness in order to effectively partner with the regional staff in the field, they lose the fruitfulness of their diversity," said Steve Joyce, senior vice president of strategic alliances for Marriott International. "The reverse is equally true."

Negotiating Protocols, Not Just Objectives

Partnerships work because the relationships are anchored to a set of relationship protocols. "Successful partnerships are not built on deals and contracts," said Marriott C.E.O., Bill Marriott, Jr. "They work because of the heart and soul of the relationship." Teams may benefit from some fun-filled ropes course, but partnerships are spawned from hammering out the covenants that guide values and behavior, not just outcomes and results. Honesty, reliability, passion, and support are as vital as goals, roles, rules, and accountability. When the high-tech C.E.O. facilitated a meeting in which sales and operations staff revealed their expectations of each other as well as the no-nos that would sidetrack their relationship, the quality of their communication improved dramatically.

Valuing Early Warnings

Partnerships are purposeful relationships; success hangs on a perpetual focus on their mutual purpose or vision, overriding any zeal for an outcome at the expense of the relationship. Maintenance of the relationship is viewed as being as vital as a clear sense of direction. Great partnerships work

out cues that signal hiccups in the relationship. Such gestures become the preamble to candid confrontation aimed at getting the relationship back on track. Feedback is seen as nurturance (a kind of performance fertilizer) rather than criticism; advice is valued as supportive instruction rather than coercive superiority. A key question our high-tech C.E.O. asked the sales and operations departments was this: "How much time elapses between when your gut tells you there's tension in the relationship and when your partner hears you talk about that tension?" When both divisions agreed to work toward a zero time lapse, assumptions were quickly clarified and innuendoes were traded in for frankness.

Ending Rather Than Stopping

All work partnerships come to an end eventually. Organizations are reshuffled, projects are completed, and new goals dictate new structural designs. The great partnership ends effectively through planning and attention to detail. Far too many internal confederations simply stop, with no consideration given to appropriate closure. This makes the next partnership more difficult and fails to capture the learning important to growth and improvement. Great partnerships acknowledge when the configuration has achieved its purpose or when they have reached a point where continuation would be counterproductive. Debriefings reflect what worked and what didn't, celebrations highlight special people and milestones worthy of public affirmation, and commitments are made regarding ongoing support. The key is to acknowledge completion and bring the relationship to a productive end.

MAKING IT HAPPEN ▶▶

- Choose partners with complementary values, not just synergistic talents.
- Outline relationship agreements regarding communications, trust, and control.
- Assert the truth when behavior or performance wavers from what was agreed.
- Keep your promises or renegotiate them in good faith with ample lead time.
- Honor your partner by sharing credit and seeking ways to affirm contribution.
- Bring continuous passion and attentive energy to the relationship.
- Keep your sights tenaciously on the partnership purpose.

- When the partnership is over, implement a complete and comprehensive closure.
- If the partnership fails, don't burn bridges you may later need.

CONCLUSION

Partnering is the critical success factor of all relationships in today's world of enterprise—in boardrooms, conference rooms, shop floors, half-wall cubicles, and virtual liaisons. These alliances act very differently from teams. Their rise and fall is based far less on the efficacy of their efforts and far more on the success of their synergy. Greatness comes from managing the confederation more with the care of a marriage than with the discipline of a group of athletes.

FOR MORE INFORMATION

Books:
Dent, Stephen M. *Partnering Intelligence: Creating Value for Your Business by Building Strong Alliances.* 2nd ed. Palo Alto, CA: Davies-Black, 2004.

Harbison, John R., Jr., and Peter Pekar. *Smart Alliances: A Practical Guide to Repeatable Success.* San Francisco, CA: Jossey-Bass, 1998.

Lewis, Jordan D. *Partnerships for Profit: Structuring and Managing Strategic Alliances.* New York: Free Press, 1990.

Lewis, Jordan D. *Trusted Partners: How Companies Build Mutual Trust and Win Together.* New York: Free Press, 2000.

Rackham, Neil, Lawrence Friedman, and Richard Ruff. *Getting Partnering Right: How Market Leaders Are Creating Long-term Competitive Advantage.* New York: McGraw-Hill Professional, 1995.

"The desire to stand well with one's fellows, the so-called human instinct of association, easily outweighs the merely individual interest."

Elton Mayo

Raising the Bar: Setting Effective Targets
by Matthew Budman

EXECUTIVE SUMMARY

- Increasing demands on managers results in increasing demands on workers.
- Setting goals often produces higher achievement.
- Work/life shifts and changing technology complicate the issue of productivity.
- Getting more from employees requires more effort and skill on the part of managers.

INTRODUCTION

We want more productivity from workers; indeed, we often need more productivity. As managers we have no choice—we must continue to raise the bar, often under pressure from all sides: enforced cost-cutting, tetchy labor markets, fresh competition from developing nations and, increasingly in-charge customers, etc.

And we have to do it with fewer people and less leverage. While the mass downsizings of the mid-1990s are a memory, their legacy remains. Many workplaces—further shaken by the post-September 11 economic trough—have never regained full staffing, and the specter of layoffs continues to threaten workers at all levels. In a broader sense, the contract that long governed the employer–employee relationship has been torn up forever. In short, downsizing has led to fewer people having to do more work and to permanently heightened expectations of what employees are capable of.

But in asking for more from workers, we frequently make mistakes.

- We fail to understand adequately what workers are already doing, either during or outside the 9-to-5 routine.
- We ask for more while at the same time we undermine trust and commitment through paternalistic electronic supervision and demoralizing layoffs.
- We don't put the necessary thought and effort into managing people and the challenges of the 21st-century workplace.

SCORING WITH GOALS

It's a well-established fact that setting concrete objectives raises workplace productivity; moving the bar upward is practically guaranteed to produce higher returns. People respond to targets by striving to reach them.

But moving goals is a double-edged sword. Workers who fail to meet their objective are likely to suffer disappointment and frustration, particularly if office mates have reached their respective targets. Yet if the goal is met before the specified date, an employee may slacken the pace, since the pressure is off. Either case requires managerial attention.

With many jobs it's not easy to shift annual target numbers higher. Despite a post-reengineering emphasis on accountability and verifiability, knowledge-economy work is not readily measurable. (The Taylorist ideal of timing workers with stopwatches is often irrelevant in the modern office; work is now usually too complex to isolate tasks and measure efficiency in completing them.) Targets must be qualitative, and therefore somewhat subjective, rather than strictly numerical.

Goal setting must be considered regularly. Generally, the subject of new objectives is only raised annually, at performance appraisals—usually dreaded by all participants. Typically there's a space labeled "Goals for Next Year" that must be filled in, an automatic demand for more work.

It's important that new goals don't appear arbitrary or seem to take precedence over quotidian core tasks. They should be produced collaboratively, through manager–employee discussions. Incremental targets, or subgoals, are more effective than distant goals, which may seem daunting.

Setting goals constructively is a tall order. You don't want good people to stagnate; realistically there is no point at which you can tell anyone, "You're doing enough."

LONGER DAYS, LONGER TO-DO LISTS

Don't consider asking more from your people until you understand how much they're already giving you. Many corporations have become "white-collar sweatshops." Your department or company may not fit this pattern, but it might, and you may simply be unaware of it.

There's no question that a general culture of overwork has survived the dot-com bust. We may no longer hear about Silicon Valley entrepreneurs sleeping on cots and working round the clock, but U.K. workers continue to report high levels of stress stemming from increasing demands and hours. Some have estimated that one-third of the working population in Japan suffers from chronic fatigue, and thousands of white-collar workers have died from *karoshi* (death from overwork) in the last two decades.

Why are so many people working so hard? Firstly, under the aegis of empowerment companies have shifted much of the burden of management to workers themselves.(Though Singapore and other countries credit productivity increases partly to worker participation in decision making.)

Secondly, there are fewer people to do the work, and not all of them are top performers. Even after all the downsizings and reengineerings there's plenty of dead wood. Companies announcing layoffs obviously hope to prune only the worst performers, but invariably good people depart as well, partly because they dread the inevitable increase in workload.

Thirdly, employees cite management's tolerance of below-par work as a cause of overwork. Managers' endless patience with mediocrity is easy to explain: it's difficult and unpleasant to fire individuals and expensive to hire and train new people. But unequal distribution of work is a crucial issue for managers to address.

Finally there is the issue of trust. Don't expect people to embrace new demands and goals while the company installs new electronic tools as a result of managerial suspicion. Workers aren't primed to give their all to the company when they know their bosses are reading their e-mail, logging their lunch-hour minutes, counting their keystrokes, watching their Web site use, and recording their voice mail.

"I can charge a man's battery and then recharge it again. But it is only when he has his own generator that we can talk about motivation. He then needs no outside stimulation. He wants to do it."

Frederick Herzberg

TAKING WORK HOME

Technology has allowed both employers and employees to blur the distinctions between work and life; people are working more even as they're enjoying new freedom and flexibility. At the office people surf the Net for sports scores and make personal telephone calls without feeling as though they're exploiting the company.

But in return, they're accountable to the demands of work. They stay at the office later; on the commute home they return phone calls and study spreadsheets on their laptops; they block out time after dinner to read memos and prepare presentations; they check and reply to work-related e-mail and voice mail at all hours.

Managers know whether projects are completed by deadline, and whether people are physically in the office, but it's hard to look over an employee's shoulder and gauge how much work the person is actually getting done. It's especially difficult when that employee is working from home two or three days a week.

Some see this work/home trend as bad for employees, who find themselves not only carrying heavier workloads but, with Black-Berries, cell phones and electronic desk calendars, taking on work responsibilities around the clock. Others insist that workers don't necessarily resent the encroachment of the office on their personal lives, and that many people find more fulfillment and fun in the office than they do outside it.

Either way, these shifts augur more challenges for managers. In conjunction with your input and in line with overall company policies, each worker can arrive at an individual best balance of efficiency and fulfillment. The more options, support, and coaching you can offer, the more productivity you'll get.

PLAYING FAIR

Each worker performs at a particular level and a particular speed. Some thrive under heightened expectations; others grow sullen, believing their supervisor to be impossible to satisfy. The bottom line is that both want to be treated fairly.

What does *fairness* mean? Simply, fair treatment means something different to everyone. Some want special breaks, others no special breaks: for parents, allowing flexible scheduling to deal with children; for singles, ensuring that their workload doesn't rise disproportionately to compensate for the missing parents. Some demand that work be shared equally, others only that they don't have more than they can handle.

For U.S. workers in many industries, heavy workloads used to be an issue handled by union representatives, whose job it was to protect them from unreasonable demands. Today, as machinery takes more and more manual labor out of workers' hands, the strength of unions—both in numbers and by moral weight—continues to decline. This is a trend likely to continue even in countries with traditionally strong organized labor. In France, for instance, union membership has fallen below 10%, lagging behind even the U.S. figure of 12.5%.

And for white-collar workers, technology has rendered union-driven job protections less relevant than ever: productivity is usually measured not by piecework standards but by more intangible and individual methods. Even the issue of working conditions is fuzzy, since work often spills into out-of-office hours, and workspaces sometimes include commuter-train seats and living-room coffee tables.

Without the help of the unions, workers have little official bargaining power when it comes to telling their employers what they will or won't do; often their only defense against increasing demands is to threaten to resign. Obviously, it is best for all parties to avoid reaching that point.

MAKING IT HAPPEN ▸▸

- Familiarize yourself with current workloads and employees' feelings about their responsibilities. It is important to avoid burnout and resentment, especially as your most conscientious people are the ones likely to burn out first.
- Set goals, but be aware of the attendant complications. Collaborate with individual workers on their goals, keeping targets reachable but challenging enough to be interesting.
- In expanding responsibilities for employees, don't overemphasize tasks that aren't directly job-related. If the core fails, the rest doesn't matter.
- Don't assume that slogans or, worse, motivational posters or insincere rah-rah rallies will produce any effect other than cynicism.
- Through coaching and rewards, make it clear that slacking is unacceptable and that you're concerned about all employees feeling that they are treated fairly.
- Work with your staff to arrive at mutually beneficial schedules and workloads that satisfactorily balance work and home lives. A telecommuting

option may be ideal for some; others need the structure of a 9-to-5 office.
- Don't ask for more without making it worth your people's while, either financially or through other means such as a job assignment or, when convenient for all, extra time off work.

CONCLUSION

Is it acceptable and productive to raise the bar through new targets? Empirically, the evidence suggests that where new targets are discussed and set in a realistic, achievable and trusting manner, these targets will be effective. Increasing targets requires greater effort from management; it's your responsibility to put that additional work in context. You can't simply raise the bar and assume everyone will rise to meet the new standards. No size fits all; pushing up standards in a knowledge-economy era of amorphous jobs requires more than cookie-cutter solutions.

The key to setting effective targets is to understand the needs of the team, the individual, and the tasks involved. Managers need to ensure that targets are both realistic and challenging. Nothing de-motivates like failure to meet expectations, while success in meeting targets will generate further confidence and productivity. Reinforcing a positive attitude to abilities will promote future success and a flexibility to engage new and more challenging targets. Setting a clear, unambiguous direction, ensuring that people are ready to meet the new challenges and that they remain on course is not easy. It requires a great deal of attention and keen leadership skills.

This necessitates leadership, not only by example, but also by making a real commitment to keeping staff engaged, productive, and flexible. You'll have to balance what is possible with how much of your people's lives you can legitimately ask for. No small task, but then no one ever said managing was easy.

FOR MORE INFORMATION

Books:
Buckingham, Marcus. *The One Thing You Need to Know*. New York: Free Press, 2005.
Davenport, Thomas. *Thinking for Living: How to Get Better Performances and Results from Knowledge Workers*. Cambridge, MA: Harvard Business School Press, 2005.
Fraser, Jill Andresky. *White-collar Sweatshop*. New York: Norton, 2002.

"To obtain the most from a man's energy it is necessary to increase the effect without increasing the fatigue."

Augustin Colomb

New Yardsticks for Performance and Productivity in an E-world

by Peter S. Cohan

EXECUTIVE SUMMARY

- Setting aside the wide mood swings of the stock market, the Internet remains a tool that lets managers enhance their companies' value to stakeholders.
- In an e-world, change takes place so quickly that managers cannot rely on traditional financial measures alone to chart their organizations' course.
- Several cutting-edge companies have developed more robust performance measurement and incentive systems that enable them to adapt more effectively to this rapid change.

INTRODUCTION

As we move well beyond the dot-com bubble of 2000, it becomes clear that the Internet will not revolutionize all aspects of business. Despite the dot-com crash, the Internet—simply a relatively inexpensive wide-bandwidth global communications network—remains extremely relevant to the way business is conducted. However, the value of the Internet will not emerge from the technology itself. Rather, the value of the Internet will emerge from the ways in which managers use it to enhance the value their companies create for their stakeholders.

Managers need new yardsticks to succeed in a business world thus transformed. Traditional yardsticks such as profitability and productivity have been more important than ever since the market for IPOs shut down in 2000. However, business conditions change so rapidly in an e-world that managing through traditional accounting alone is dangerously akin to driving a car while looking in the rearview mirror. In an e-world, managers need predictive indicators that can pinpoint opportunities and threats to a business before they find their way into the company's financial statements. Managers also need to create the right performance measurement and incentive systems to encourage their people to capture the stakeholder value referred to above.

NEW YARDSTICKS AND MEASURES IN AN E-WORLD

In an e-world, employees need to react thoughtfully—yet rapidly—to customers, suppliers, and stockholders. Consequently employees need new yardsticks to support their decision making. While employee performance measures must support those of managers, they must focus more specifically on helping employees to make decisions that improve the company's competitive position.

Companies have four critical stakeholders:

- **Customers.** Companies can enhance the value they create for customers through initiatives such as lowering product price, increasing product performance to respond to changing customer needs, and/or enhancing customer service.
- **Suppliers.** Companies can enhance the value they create for suppliers through initiatives such as ordering a wider variety of products from a smaller number of suppliers, regular placing of orders, and/or lowering the joint costs of activities such as ordering, invoicing, and billing.
- **Employees.** Companies can enhance the value they create for employees through initiatives such as matching work assignments to an employee's interests and aptitudes, creating an environment that encourages a balance between work and personal activities, and/or offering competitive pay.
- **Shareholders.** Companies can enhance the value they create for stockholders by increasing their stock price and by consistently exceeding analysts' quarterly profit expectations.

Managers should consider three observations about enhancing the company's value to these four stakeholders in an e-world.

Firstly, the Internet serves two roles in an e-world. It's a tool that can enable organizations to enhance their value to each of these four stakeholder groups. In addition the Internet can offer managers a way to measure the company's performance in enhancing stakeholder value.

Secondly, the company's posture toward these stakeholders is likely to change depending on the economic environment. For example, when revenues are growing a company may invest more heavily in retaining employees, whereas when revenues are declining a company may rank employee performance more rigorously and attempt to shed all but the top performers.

Finally, the company's performance affects each of the stakeholder groups in tightly interrelated ways. For example, if a company can enhance the value it creates for customers, revenue growth may accelerate, leading to beating analysts' earnings expectations, thereby raising the stock price. Conversely, if a company creates an environment that frustrates employees, employee frustration may lead to behavior that dissatisfies customers—leading to lower revenues, lower profits, and a decline in stock price.

MINI-CASES
New Yardsticks in Action

Raytheon, the technology and electronics specialist, manages the performance of its e-businesses using eight measurements:

- **Innovation and flexibility.** Average time from concept to start; speed to match a competitor's site; speed at which the competition will match the site; time between new versions of a site.
- **Customer loyalty.** Percentage who return within a year; time between visits; duration of visits; conversion rate; percentage who give personal information.
- **Transactional excellence.** Unique visitors each month; online sales abandoned; percentage of orders correct; time to respond to a customer; percentage of orders filled on time.
- **Customer information.** Percentage of e-mail addresses collected from traffic.
- **Infrastructure reliability.** Time to load a page; network uptime; ease of system expansion.

"There is great potential to improve efficiency using Internet-based e-commerce strategies . . . but no one really knows how big those productivity gains will be, how long they will take to be realized, and who will be the ultimate beneficiaries." Roger W. Ferguson, Jr.

- **Supply-chain excellence.** Inventory levels; inventory turns; order confirmation time; percentage of products built to order.
- **Valuation and financial performance.** Return on invested capital; market capitalization migration (the changing value of the overall business).
- **Digital quotient.** For complementary e-business channels, percentage of total revenue generated online.

Cisco Systems operates in over 70 countries and generated over 80% of its $15 billion in revenue over its Cisco Connection Online (CCO). Cisco measures CCO's performance as follows:

- Register users and measure their CCO visit frequency by counting the days per month a registrant returns.
- Conduct random surveys among customers on their satisfaction with the site. Each page on the Cisco site includes a survey button. Any customer at any time can click on one and fill in comments.
- Survey customers on whether they were able to get their questions answered on the site or had to make a phone call to a company representative.
- Monitor the percentage of total sales that take place on the site.
- Measure the number of orders taken over the site, entered automatically into the ordering system, and forwarded to the factory without human intervention.
- Monitor the time it takes to access the site from 10 different locations around the world.
- Compare the money invested in the site with the revenue it generates.

Schneider National, a trucking and logistics company, began measuring the IT department's overall performance to gauge internal stakeholders' satisfaction, not only to ensure that systems were performing the work business users requested, but also to rate the value and quality of that work. At the conclusion of any IT project, stakeholders fill out a report card that rates deliverables, timelines, requirements, and return on investment. An 18-month invoice-matching project received good marks, for example, in helping to facilitate reimbursement, reducing overhead by 15%, and enabling Schneider National to process 65% of all invoices electronically.

KEY SUCCESS FACTORS

These examples of how systems-based organizations have implemented new yardsticks represent the vanguard of global business. The factors that led these companies to build new yardsticks in an e-world are valuable to general managers.

Successful new yardstick users share the following principles:

- **Involve the right people.** Involve the stakeholders who will produce, consume, and assess the output of the work. Typically, such stakeholders include customers (as Cisco's CCO does), suppliers, stockholders (as in Raytheon's measurement of market capitalization migration), and workers. Involving the stakeholders from the beginning of the process may cause work to proceed a bit more slowly, but the chance of doing the right thing efficiently increases dramatically.
- **Develop a broad set of measures.** Every organization has its own set of measures that are likely to lead to better performance. While all organizations should use traditional measures such as profit and productivity (as Cisco and NCR do), these should be supplemented with nonfinancial criteria that are significant to process stakeholders (such as Cisco's customer-satisfaction measures or Schneider National's measurement of the value and quality of IT work).
- **Understand the links between the measures.** Collect and analyze historical data on the selected measures to gain insights into their interrelationships. Specifically, organizations should identify which variables are leading indicators (customer satisfaction for Cisco and NCR) or financially measurable outcomes (incremental revenue per dollar invested in the system for Cisco, reduced overhead for Schneider National).
- **Tie incentives to performance.** It's a management axiom that what gets measured gets done, but measuring the right variables isn't enough. Managers must deliver more attractive incentives to employees who meet or exceed performance targets than to those whose performance lags. Winning users of new yardsticks put their money where their measurements are (for example, Cisco links employee bonuses to improvements in independently measured customer satisfaction).

MAKING IT HAPPEN ▶▶

Managing the transition from traditional performance measures to new yardsticks is challenging, but essential for companies navigating the e-world's choppy waters. The new yardsticks should include a company's key stakeholders, not just executives; should incorporate nonfinancial measures; and should

explicate the linkages between qualitative measures and financial results.

Here's how to make new yardsticks work for your company:

- Understand how the Internet can improve the way your organization creates stakeholder value.
- Ask stakeholders how they measure your organization's success and how they would like your organization to improve along these lines.
- Assemble a team involving suppliers, customers, employees, and stockholders to identify and implement changes that realize that improvement.
- Track the impact of these changes on the stakeholder measures.
- Understand the relationship between these measures and financial results.
- Link incentives to performance on these measures.

CONCLUSION

The Internet is a useful tool for enhancing the value a company provides for its stakeholders. It's therefore helping managers to realize that they need to develop new ways to measure their corporate performance. The world is changing too quickly to rely solely on financial performance to chart an organization's course. Companies that use new yardsticks focus on enhancing the value they create for stakeholders—a focus that improves financial performance in a turbulent e-world.

"If you sit down and you ask, 'Where is the value center, where is the economic engine for e-commerce?' I guarantee you it is not in cost reduction. Not even close. The economic engine is always in value."

Jay S. Walker

Using Management Consultants Effectively

by Steve Markwell

EXECUTIVE SUMMARY

- Management consulting is a fast-growing industry that can promise more than it can deliver.
- The boundaries are blurring between types of consulting and in the relationships between consultants and suppliers.
- To be effective the consultant's role needs to be carefully defined and managed.
- Successful projects foster a partnership between consultants and their clients.
- Unless organizations feel confident that they can implement and maintain changes after the consultants have left, the project has been a failure.
- The true test of the consultants' worth is whether or not the organization would work with them again—although it may not choose to.

INTRODUCTION

Management consulting is one of the fastest growing, and most controversial, sectors of the service economy. Estimates suggest that the total market for consultancy in the U.K. alone is somewhere in the region of $12 billion.

Management consulting may be lucrative for its practitioners, who unlike lawyers and accountants aren't bound by professional regulations. This can prove a mixed blessing for its clients, some of whom would recognize their own experiences in the description of the management consultant as someone who takes your watch and then uses it to tell you the time.

In order to use management consultants effectively, organizations need to think carefully about what type of consultant they wish to employ and why. They also need to pay close attention to how the relationship with the consulting firm is managed, from its inception through to delivery of the completed project.

THE FIVE TYPES OF MANAGEMENT CONSULTANT

1. Generalist

These are the largest consulting firms, offering a wide range of services from strategy consulting to human resources and IT consulting on a global basis. They cover all the main industry sectors and may also have expertise in highly specialized areas such as Web design or complex project manage-

ment. Examples are well-known names such as Accenture, Pricewaterhouse-Coopers, and PA Consulting. Clients often establish long-term relationships with these consultancies, using different services at different points in their development.

2. Strategy Consulting

This category covers smaller companies such as McKinsey, Bain, and Arthur D. Little. They are more likely to focus on individual industry groups. Their specialty is offering strategic board-level advice to companies as a onetime project.

3. Human Resource Consulting

These companies provide specialist advice on issues ranging from salary and benefit reviews to an analysis of pension planning. They include organizations such as Hay Management Consultants, Watson Wyatt, and William Mercer.

4. IT Consulting

Many former systems development companies and hardware suppliers have enlarged the scope of their operations to include more mainstream consulting advice. Examples are IBM, CSC, and CMG.

5. E-consulting

Traditional bricks-and-mortar companies and startups alike have, in recent years, sought help with e-strategies, design, and implementation. Established consultancies

founded new e-divisions, while the consulting market has also had its own startups.

BLURRED BOUNDARIES

Large accounting companies separated out their audit and consulting practices, partly as the result of regulatory pressure from the Securities and Exchange Commission. Accenture finalized its divorce from Arthur Andersen, while KPMG floated on the NAS-DAQ; and Ernst & Young's consulting arm has been sold to Cap Gemini.

While such moves have created a firewall between companies' traditional accounting activity and consulting, the benefits of other developments are murkier. An increasing number of consulting firms entered into reseller or alliance partnerships with IT vendors, placing a question mark over their ability to provide truly independent advice to clients.

WHEN TO USE A CONSULTANT

Management consulting is by no means a universal cure-all. Some problems respond more positively to consulting advice than others, for example, when a company

- requires skills or knowledge that are in short supply or unusual or are needed for only a short period;
- wants to facilitate and stimulate internal debate, perhaps prior to making significant changes;
- is looking for an objective viewpoint free from company traditions, internal politics, and attachment to previous recommendations;
- is contemplating a move into new areas and is seeking an informed view of current best practice.

Alternatively, some situations are unlikely to be improved by the introduction of management consultants, notably when a company

- is looking simply for confirmation of an existing decision;
- suspects it may need to take unpopular actions and wishes to deflect responsibility for the decision onto a consultant;
- finds its decision making paralyzed because views at senior management level have become polarized.

"Consultants eventually leave, which makes them excellent scapegoats for major management blunders."

Scott Adams

CHOOSING THE RIGHT CONSULTANT

Companies need to select a consulting firm that has the skills necessary to tackle the particular assignment and that has a good cultural fit with the organization's own attitudes. Prospective consulting firms should be asked to

- describe how they would undertake the assignment;
- provide details of the names, qualifications, and industry experience of the staff who will work on the project;
- describe similar projects they have undertaken, plus names of referees;
- provide a draft work program and timetable with an estimate of the fees and other chargeable expenses;
- describe their client liaison and management procedures.

For a successful project outcome the consultants and the client have to be able to work together in partnership, sharing their expertise and resources. The company must be prepared to provide any information or personnel the consultants request, and the consulting firm must provide the staff and resources to which it originally committed.

Client organizations and consulting firms also need to be clear about how they will be managing the levels of risk associated with projects. While consultants will wish to propose solutions that have a reasonable likelihood of success, some companies will be willing to consider more ambitious proposals provided they can contribute the competitive edge they are seeking.

There should be a project committee that meets regularly to review progress and highlight problem areas. The committee should include a senior person from the client, tasked with providing information and assistance and resolving any operational difficulties.

Best practice and signs of success

- Staff members are happy to volunteer information to the consultants because they feel their views are understood and respected.
- Project reviews are held frequently and there is good visibility of progress.
- Action points arising from review meetings are addressed.
- Employees feel they are learning new concepts and adding value to their core skills.

- Project milestones and new concepts are clearly explained.

Warning signs

- Staff members find the consultants' questions time-wasting, irrelevant, or distracting.
- Consultancy project members appear unfamiliar with the industry sector or type of problem.
- It's hard to establish what point the project has reached in its life cycle.
- Consultants seem unwilling to hold review meetings.
- Problems are not remedied quickly.
- Employees feel the consultants are learning more than they are.
- Reports are full of jargon and peppered with acronyms.

Value for the Money

Ultimately the best way to get value for money is to ensure that the consultants' recommendations are implemented. If the client–consultancy partnership has been successful, much of the implementation may be carried out before the consultants leave the company. So long as staff fully subscribe to the new plans and identify with the underlying concepts, they'll be happy to take the necessary actions.

However, once the consultants have left there is still a danger that the benefits of their work may be eroded through neglect, misunderstanding, or a lack of controls. To avoid this it may be helpful to arrange follow-up visits from the consultants to review the implementation process.

MAKING IT HAPPEN ▶▶

- Choose the type of consulting you need before picking a particular company.
- Proceed with consultants to gain missing skills or knowledge, stimulate internal debate, seek an objective viewpoint, or find help in entering new areas.
- Don't proceed in order to get confirmation of an existing decision, avoid responsibility for unpopular actions, or cope with a polarized senior management.
- Make any consultancy you approach prove that it has the necessary skills and will be a good cultural fit.

- Put one of your senior people on a project committee that meets regularly to review progress and highlight problem areas.
- Get value for money by ensuring that the consultants' recommendations are implemented—with much of it done before the consultants leave.

CONCLUSION

Probably the clearest evidence of a successful consulting assignment is the client's willingness to work with the same consultant again—although any new requirement should be evaluated as rigorously as the original project. While some companies do favor a one-stop-shopping approach to purchasing consulting services and look for a single provider who can supply all requirements, others select on "best-in-class" criteria. One-stop-shop fans say their approach reduces management complexity, avoids turf wars between competing consultancies, and opens the way to pricing discounts. Those who favor best-in-class selections say that it leads to better overall performance and a wider choice.

Working successfully with consultants is a matter of planning, not luck. The relationship between consultant and client must be formally defined to ensure a watertight contract; however, it must also be sufficiently flexible during the work itself to enable the job to be done effectively.

FOR MORE INFORMATION

Books:
Kihn, Martin. *House of Lies: How Management Consultants Steal Your Watch and Then Tell You the Time*. New York: Warner Business Books, 2005.
Lerner, Marcy. *Vault Guide to the Top 50 Consulting Firms*. 8th ed. New York: Vault Inc, 2005.
Levinson, J. C. *Guerilla Marketing for Consultants: 100 Breakthrough Tactics for Winning Profitable Clients*. New York: Wiley, 2004.

Web site:
Institute of Management Consultants USA: **www.imcusa.org**

"Some firms hardly dare change the wallpaper without consulting a guru." Anonymous

Making Loyalty Work
by John Frazer-Robinson

EXECUTIVE SUMMARY

- Customer loyalty is critical to business success. Its consequences are profitable, valuable, and of long-term benefit.
- Unlike customer satisfaction, customer loyalty measures customers' actual behavior. The company's goal is to gain—and keep—the maximum amount of each customer's available spend.
- This involves satisfying customers' emotionally based needs, explicitly recognizing their importance to you, and individualizing every contact with them. Managing the total relationship with customers is the business of everyone in the company.

INTRODUCTION

As the business world obsesses itself with customer relationship management, customer loyalty becomes a pivotal focus for those in sales, marketing, and service. It's right that professionals in these disciplines should have loyalty at the forefront of their minds, but it's unfortunate that customer loyalty is left predominantly to them, for just as customer loyalty is a measure of the business as a whole, it should be the concern of the business as a whole.

These fads come and go (take Total Quality Management as an example). And they generally depart from business-practice radar screens with mixed reputations and experiences. But customer loyalty will stand the test of time—and it will demolish the customer satisfactionists.

The fad of customer satisfaction was very annoying, leading as it did to a relentless barrage of mindless questionnaires attached to almost every customer experience. In truth measuring customer satisfaction is about as effective as dipping your toe in a pool.

Measuring customer loyalty is distinct from customer satisfaction in one important regard: it's not the measure of what people say, it's the measure of what they do. Activity—specifically, repurchasing more of the same or purchasing from across the product range—is an important ingredient of customer loyalty.

WHAT IS LOYALTY MADE OF?

Customer satisfaction and loyalty do, however, have five strands in common:
- price
- product
- delivery
- service
- recognition

Each needs thought. Notice that price and product are based in logic, and that service and recognition are based in emotions. Delivery involves both logic and emotions. For the last 30 years, marketing has obsessed itself with the logical elements. Now, in order to concentrate on customer relationships, you have to get your business to become excellent at delivering the emotionally based issues. These should be focused on clearly and individually, as well as how they impact each other.

Price

While price is important, we very often overrate its importance—or worse still, we exacerbate it, simply eroding our own margins into the bargain. This doesn't stop you promoting on value. But get price in perspective. One of the long-term reasons for adopting a customer loyalty strategy is that it shrinks price as a customer priority and replaces it with value.

Product

There's no substitute for delivering a quality product. If the product fails, breaks down, doesn't last as long as it should, or is in any way imperfect, customers won't come back for more, nor will they feel inclined to buy other things from you. One of the stark realities of a customer-driven business is that there are no hiding places. Customer loyalty is built by exceeding customer expectations at every opportunity.

Delivery

If you're a traditional marketer or salesperson, this is what used to be called distribution. Delivery includes distribution, but it encompasses far more. Think of it as the delivery of the whole corporate promise to the customer—every facet of the way the customer feels, touches, and experiences your business.

The significant difference between distribution and delivery is that when you're in business to achieve a series of separate transactions, those transactions take place at the far point of your distribution channel. This is a product-driven process. It distributes your corporate product or service. When you're in business to achieve a managed customer relationship, then what we have is a means of delivering the corporate promise. Transaction marketing effectively switches on to standby between transactions; relationship marketing is permanently fully switched on 24 hours a day, seven days a week, ready for and alert to every customer interaction wherever and whenever it touches the organization.

Service

In a customer-driven business service is paramount, which is why the whole business needs to be obsessive about a customer-loyalty strategy. Size and traditional structures inhibit larger businesses from delivering service. However, small businesses can profit from this. Smaller companies don't have nearly as many protocols as large ones and are much less set in their ways. If a customer wants something different or special, they will do it.

Does this mean a big business cannot become a customer-driven business? No! But it does mean it has more, and more serious, issues to address—management culture, organizational structure, human resources, to name but a few. In short, it has to retain the advantages of size and lose the disadvantages of size. Large corporations have to become as agile as their smaller competitors.

Recognition

Whether you're thinking about customer loyalty and becoming a customer-driven organization for business-to-business or business-to-consumer, the rudiments of developing and managing customer loyalty are the same. We all love to be recognized, not just for who we are, but for other things about us.

"Stop competing on price; compete on value. Deliver total consumer solutions, rather than just your piece of the solution."

Faith Popcorn

Some of the biggest contributions I've seen to the loyalty-building process have come from streaming consistent groups of employees to consistent groups of customers. The result is that the two groups become familiar and their relationships have a far greater chance of success. They know each other!

To boost customer loyalty, it is valuable to work on continuous improvement of the corporate promise, which means all five strands. It means adding to our previous logic-based experiences—product, price, and some delivery issues (essentially those to do with distribution)—and supplementing them with new, *soft-issue* experiences that are emotionally based—service, recognition, and those corporate delivery issues that surround the product at distribution and stay connected with customers throughout their relationship with you. Now we have to examine how we leave customers feeling.

To move from building satisfaction to creating loyalty, you must work on the emotional issues of the relationship. This will gain the most leverage and make the most difference. It is this recognition that exposes the fallacy in the vast majority of so-called loyalty programs.

DECIDE HOW TO MEASURE LOYALTY

Here's a list of the most popular means used to measure loyalty. If your business finds other ways, add or substitute them:

- customer satisfaction—what customers say
- recency—when did they last purchase?
- frequency—how often do they purchase?
- monetary value—how much do they spend?
- customer longevity—how long have they been with you?
- formal and informal (word-of-mouth) referral activity
- share of spend—how much to you and how much to competitors?
- willingness to repurchase

SHARE OF SPEND

Consciously work to build your share of the available and appropriate wallet for that family, household, or business and suddenly the whole picture is transformed. If most businesses had anything like 75% of the available spend of its customers, annual targets would be met in the first month! Most businesses neglect customers, and as a result customers place business elsewhere. When looking at how much they spend remember to look at current and recent transactions, but keep a cumulative figure, too.

Share of spend shares a characteristic with both customer satisfaction and customer loyalty. All three are comparatively fragile until you reach levels of approximately 70–80%. Up to that level, customers are still very vulnerable to competitive offers and propositions; lower than 50% there's no significant value. For businesses available spend is probably the budget for that product or service. For consumers it's their appropriate, affordable, or desired amount. Often this is a notional assessment, but you can easily ask the customer.

CONSIDER HOW FAR CUSTOMERS WILL GO TO HELP YOU

Another valuable piece of information is whether customers will do anything positive or negative to assist you, for example, whether they'll ever pass on positive or negative word of mouth or whether they're prepared to give solicited referrals or testimonials. You often find that customers are more open—more honest, in fact—about whether they would recommend you to someone else than they are about whether they would buy from you again.

MAKING IT HAPPEN ▶▶

- Measure repurchasing more or from across the product range as a key ingredient of customer loyalty.
- Continuously improve the corporate promise and what that means for price, product, delivery, service, and recognition.
- Shape and direct your customer loyalty strategy to shrink price in the customer's priorities and replace it with value.
- Think of delivery as delivering the whole corporate promise in every way that

customers feel, touch, and experience the business.
- Work on the emotional issues of the customer relationship to move from building satisfaction to creating loyalty.
- Seek to raise share of spend, customer satisfaction and customer loyalty to solid levels of 70–80%.
- Consider how to move customers along the value chain, "cross-selling" and "upselling" products.
- Record information about customer intentions, and leverage this to provide a better, more efficient, and tailored service.
- Consider measuring a customer's lifetime value.

CONCLUSION

Understanding the external market and the internal strengths and weaknesses of the business are essential to making loyalty work. First, understanding clearly and monitoring continuously customer needs can enable the business to bond with individuals, retaining them as customers that are loyal and satisfied. Second, the realities of the market are constantly shifting, ranging from technological innovations to competitors' actions, and these need to be closely monitored and understood. It is worth considering the acquisition cost for each new customer, as well as the lifetime value of existing customers. This information may provide a useful target, as well as an indication of the significance of enhancing customer loyalty.

FOR MORE INFORMATION

Book:
Reichheld, Frederick F. *The Loyalty Effect: The Hidden Force behind Growth, Profits, and Lasting Value.* Cambridge, MA: Harvard Business School Press, 2001.

Web site:
InsightExec: **www.insightexec.com**

See also:
☆ Power Struggling and Power Sharing (pp. 126–127)

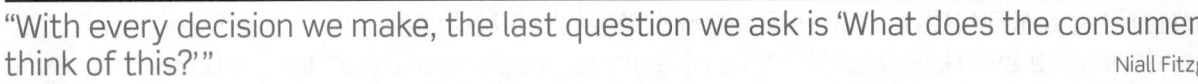

"With every decision we make, the last question we ask is 'What does the consumer think of this?'"

Niall Fitzgerald

Corporate Social Responsibility: Are You Giving Back or Just Giving Away?

by Jim "Gus" Gustafson, Ph.D.

EXECUTIVE SUMMARY

- Many 21st-century global corporations have become bigger and more powerful than the governments of the countries they do business in, and with this shift of resources necessarily comes a shift in responsibility to positively and proactively impact the world around them.
- Corporate social responsibility (CSR) is rapidly becoming an expectation of consumers worldwide that requires a fundamental and holistic change in the way that most businesses currently operate.
- Social and environmental accountability cannot be meaningless words on a dusty mission statement or an afterthought; they must be integrated into all aspects of everyday corporate life.
- Social responsibility and stockholder profitability don't need to be mutually exclusive propositions; if you give back, there's definitely a payback!

INTRODUCTION

Corporate social responsibility (CSR) is one of the most dynamic, complex, and challenging subjects that business leaders face today, and it is arguably one of the most critical. Fueled by the fall of communism and the enormous flow of capital, goods, and services across borders, business is now the most global of institutions. As governments around the world continue to withdraw from operating business enterprises, private-sector companies are increasingly under pressure to take a more active role in making the world a better place to live in, and not only for themselves.

In fact, several global corporations have become so enormous that they have overtaken many nation states as entities with the power and resources necessary to positively impact global change. Yet unlike governments that have been freely elected by and are accountable to a localized group of voters, these massive businesses answer primarily to their stockholders for most of their actions. This combination of enormous wealth and limited accountability makes today's companies extremely powerful.

All of this brings us to a central question, why should these giant corporations—or any company, for that matter—whose primary reason for existence is to maximize profitability for their stockholders, be concerned with becoming good global citizens? The answer is simply, that in addition to being the right thing to do, it is good business.

WHAT EXACTLY IS CSR?

Although there is no single definition of CSR, the term generally refers to an ongoing commitment by business to behave ethically and to contribute to economic development while demonstrating respect for people, communities, society at large, and the environment. In short, CSR marries the concepts of global citizenship with environmental stewardship and sustainable development.

Good *corporate* social responsibility in practical terms means that organizational managers and leaders must:
- be sensitive to the issues that affect the lives of the people they live and work with;
- possess an understanding of the conditions in society that they could have a positive influence on;
- consider the social impact that their financial and business decisions have on a wide range of constituencies, stakeholders, and the environment

- be conscientious about not only what the company produces, but also how it is produced.

Most important, being socially responsible means going beyond awareness of these social impacts by being willing to act on them.

THE CASE FOR CSR

The beginning of the 21st century has witnessed growing societal demand for increased corporate social responsibility and environmental accountability. No longer are companies obligated only to do no harm. Instead they're being called on to actively take responsibility for and positively engage with their communities, the global society, and the environment.

Consequently, today's business leaders are working hard to understand society's changing expectations of corporations in areas that were previously seen as the responsibility of government or nonprofit organizations. Since these leaders are also responsible for delivering profits to stockholders, their CSR efforts must also demonstrate a positive impact on the bottom line.

Many proactive and innovative companies have already discovered that a truly enterprise-wide commitment to CSR yields extremely positive results in both quantitative and qualitative terms. Several recent academic studies and case reports indicate that the value of CSR can be determined in a variety of ways, including:
- significant increase in sales
- increased ability to attract new customers
- improved customer retention rates
- reduced operating expenses
- more motivated and committed labor force
- enhanced brand image
- increased ability to attract talent
- enhanced cross-training of employees
- higher employee retention rates
- increased productivity
- reduced regulatory oversight
- improved quality of products and services

Furthermore, the Social Investment Forum reports that assets under management in

"Few trends could so thoroughly undermine the very foundations of our free society as the acceptance by corporate officials of a social responsibility other than to make as much money for their stockholders as possible."

Milton Friedman

portfolios that use screens linked to ethics, the environment, and corporate social responsibility are growing dramatically—thus allowing these socially responsible companies access to capital that might not otherwise have been available.

GLOBAL CONSUMERS CARE ABOUT CSR

Does the average consumer really care about CSR? The Millennium Poll on Corporate Social Responsibility, a study conducted in 1999 by Globescan (formerly Environics International), indicates an emphatic yes. Interviews with more than 25,000 average citizens of 23 countries across six continents revealed three important points:

1 In forming impressions of companies, people around the world focus on corporate citizenship ahead of either brand reputation or financial factors.

2 Two out of three citizens want companies to go beyond their historical role of making a profit, paying taxes, employing people, and obeying all laws; they want companies to contribute to broader societal goals as well.

3 More than one in five consumers report either rewarding or punishing companies in the past year according to their perceived social performance. Almost as many again considered doing so.

These findings reinforce what a number of companies have already found out the hard way: corporate reputation and sales are both at risk when customers have a negative perception of a company's social behavior.

MINI-CASES

Natura Cosmeticos (Brazil) is recognized as a leader in corporate social responsibility in Latin America for demonstrating commitment to the communities it operates in, creating an empowering workplace, and supporting human rights issues locally. The company focuses on creating partnerships with schools, government organizations, and nonprofits to enhance the quality of children's lives and the public educational systems in the regions it operates in (**www.natura.net**).

BENCHMARKING CSR

Since the concept of social responsibility is as broad as it is complex, it is difficult to find any one standard or system that covers all aspects of CSR. There are, however, several emerging resources for companies to measure themselves against, including:

- **Keidanren Charter for Good Corporate Behavior.** Ten principles from the Japan Federation of Economic Organizations that articulate the kind of corporate behavior that they feel enriches and vitalizes society in the 21st century (**www.keidanren.or.jp**).
- **Principles for Business.** Seven principles from the Caux Round Table that aim to express a world standard of social responsibility against which business behavior can be measured (**www.cauxroundtable.org**).
- **Principles for Global Corporate Responsibility.** Comprehensive benchmarking tool from the Interfaith Center on Corporate Responsibility to hold companies accountable to high standards of international human and labor rights conventions (**www.iccr.org**).
- **Social Accountability 8000.** Standard created by Social Accountability International to enable organizations to develop voluntary standards of social accountability and to become accredited as such (**www.cepaa.org**).
- **Sustainability Reporting Guidelines.** Common framework developed by the Global Reporting Initiative for reporting on the linked aspects of sustainability—economic, environmental, and social (**www.globalreporting.org**).
- **Sustainability Through the Market.** Seven keys from the World Business Council for Sustainable Development that offer companies a guide to implementing and benefiting from sustainable practices (**www.wbcsd.ch**).

MAKING IT HAPPEN ▶▶

To implement CSR, it is useful to consider the following:

- Clearly articulate a relevant CSR philosophy, and incorporate it into your existing guiding principles. Don't hesitate to use any of the benchmarking standards as a guideline or simply decide to adopt one in its entirety as your own.
- Create a social and organizational infrastructure that supports your CSR framework.
- Develop a reward and recognition

system that officially supports socially responsible involvement and behavior throughout the organization.

- Appoint an executive leader as the CSR chief to be the cheerleader, watchdog, and subject expert for your initiatives.
- Make sure the entire senior management team embraces and supports the CSR program.
- Incorporate CSR into your long-range strategic planning to guaranteecontinuity.
- Constantly communicate the results of your efforts to your stakeholders and celebrate your successes.
- Consider partnering with other corporations, community groups, or government organizations to multiply your impact and expand your reach.

And, most important:

- Use the same kind of energy, initiative, and commitment to develop, integrate, and implement your CSR program that you did to build your organization's other core competencies.

CONCLUSION

Today's global corporations have more capital and human resources at their disposal than many governments. As a result, business leaders are beginning to realize that this shift of power and resources also requires a shift in responsibility to becoming better global citizens. CSR is fast becoming a global expectation that is not only the right thing to do, but will also positively add to the bottom line.

FOR MORE INFORMATION

Book:
Tichy, Noel M., Andrew R. McGill, and Lynda St. Clair. *Corporate Global Citizenship: Doing Business in the Public Eye.* Lanham, MD: Lexington, 1998.

Web sites:
Business for Social Responsibility: **www.bsr.org**
GlobeScan: **http://globescan.com**
Social Investment Forum: **www.socialinvest.org**

"So long as commerce specializes in business methods which take no account of human nature and social motives, so long may we expect strikes and sabotage to be the ordinary accompaniment of industry."

Elton Mayo

Corporate Responsibility: A Leadership Approach
by Giles Gibbons

EXECUTIVE SUMMARY

- Corporate responsibility (CR) has moved firmly up the business agenda and the majority of large companies engage in CR activity and publish CR reports.
- In many cases however, the approach adopted is too generic and fails to take account of the particular circumstances of the company. A tailored approach to CR which bolsters and supports core business strategy is much more likely to create real business value.
- Such an approach should include a focus on the opportunities for strategic differentiation created by CR and seize the chance to create social or environmental leadership programs that will deliver significant reputation enhancement.

INTRODUCTION

Corporate responsibility has now been on the business map for a number of years. The debate over the meaning of CR has largely been resolved, and most companies have adopted a definition that runs along the following lines: the extent to which social, environmental, and ethical risks and opportunities are managed to protect and grow shareholder value. Nearly 50% of U.S. companies and 80% of the U.K.'s top 100 companies now publish a CR report and for most international companies having an overall CR strategy has more or less become an expectation.

THE PROBLEM WITH THE STATUS QUO

The problem with so many of the CR "strategies" that companies have adopted is that they are often not really very strategic at all. CR can seem to have claimed ownership of a vast number of issues, from work–life balance to procurement policies to customer service. Many companies find themselves trying to cover all the bases and the result can be little more than a giant box-ticking exercise, with very little business value. There is also a tendency for companies to concentrate on the identification and management of risks, at the expense of any focus on CR-related opportunities for strategic differentiation. This leads to activity that is characterized by a collective approach: compliance with best practice and adherence to common standards. This is important—it helps to ensure that companies comply with society's expectations and protects them from criticism—but it alone is unlikely to lead to significant, sustained competitive and commercial advantage. The upshot of this is that CR is often carried out as an adjunct to core business operations and can sometimes seem to be an exercise primarily designed to generate material for the annual CR report.

ONE SIZE DOES NOT FIT ALL

The best way to ensure that CR is taken seriously, genuinely informs all a company's business decisions, and helps build real business advantage is to devise a strategy that is tailored to the company in question and reflects and compliments its core business goals. The company should seek to address the issues which are most relevant to its business circumstances, rather than adopting a catch-all approach. And, once it has got the basics right by addressing its main issues, it should focus on the strategic opportunities that CR brings into focus. It should consider engaging in activity that exceeds the expectations of its most important stakeholders and could therefore generate real cut-through and significant reputation enhancement, as well as making a real difference to the social and environmental problems of our times.

CONSIDER THE ANALOGY OF A HOUSE

The diagram below provides a useful framework for any company wishing to devise an approach to CR that is both tailored to its particular circumstances and maximizes the opportunities presented by social and environmental issues, while also protecting itself from risks.

The Foundations

Below the line (or ground) and representing the foundations of the house is the ongoing activity that ensures the company runs its core business operations in a responsible way. Conducting this activity will ensure that the company meets societal expectations and protects itself from the risk of negative backlash or imposed regulation.

This activity must be tailored to the particular company in question—reflecting what it does and its individual operating environment. The company will need to cast the net wide at first and identify the whole range of issues for CR. This can be done by conducting research (desk and primary) with key stakeholders, studying the various codes and standards that provide guidance on CR issues (such as the Global Reporting Initiative), and conducting a competitor review. Once all possible issues have been identified they will then need to be filtered for relevance. There is no point in a company actively managing issues which are of no real relevance to its business operations. The issues that remain after the filtering process—those that are material to the company—will then need to be prioritized. First, the issues should be prioritized from a CR perspective (ideally in consultation with key stakeholders). Then the company should put the emergent list of CR issues through the filter of its own business strategy. Issues which relate to its core competitive drivers should be up-weighted. The company should focus on issues which are important from a CR perspective and which also relate to its business drivers.

A few big issues will top the final prioritized list for any given company. These should be things that are central to its business and very much on the radar from a CR perspective. Think obesity for a soft drinks manufacturer or carbon emissions for an energy company. The bulk of CR resources should be directed at actively managing these issues—embedding systems to manage and monitor them into core business operations and performance assessments

---

"No sensible decision can be made without taking into account not only the world as it is, but the world as it will be."

Isaac Asimov

and conducting regular stakeholder engagement sessions around the issue and the company's related activity. Then there will be a number of other, smaller issues which are also material to the company and therefore demand attention. These need to be actively managed and monitored as well. This process is primarily intended to neutralize potentially negative aspects of a company's business.

As part of its annual CR reporting practice, the company should report publicly on all this activity. The sum total of the information should reassure any interested party that the company is aware of its impact upon society and acknowledges its responsibility to manage this impact. Its main audience will be a relatively specialist community including CR experts, NGOs, ethical investors and consumers, industry analysts and opinion leaders.

The House

Above the line (or ground), representing the visible aspects of the house, is activity designed to exceed societal expectations and build competitive advantage. By developing a series of social or environmental leadership programs (the pillars) a company can support its core business strategy and win praise from its key stakeholders. The following three factors will influence a company's choice of program and the size of that program:
- key stakeholders
- key issues
- business strategy

Each of the programs should be designed with one of the company's specific stakeholder groups in mind and may well address the group's key issue(s). The size of the program and the amount of resource it requires will depend upon the relative importance of the stakeholder and the issue and the company's business strategy; programs which support the company's core strategic goals should receive additional focus. If a company's environmental impact is significant, environmental activists are an important stakeholder group, and, environmental leadership chimes with the company's strategic direction, then the "pillar" designed

around the environment will be wider than the others.

An important point to note here is that, while leadership programs can be designed around a company's priority CR issues, they must focus on the positive solution to the problem, not the problem itself. If obesity is the issue, the program might be a groundbreaking way of encouraging young people to lead active lifestyles. All activity above the ground should publicize the positive side of the business. It should be characterized by a competitive approach: innovation, creativity, and the forging of a distinct reputation. The programs should make the most of the company's core strengths and resources, showcasing its capabilities in a new way by demonstrating its power to deliver social and environmental goals.

Nowhere is this more true than for the company's flagship program. This, the roof of the house, is the company's opportunity to design a program directed at its most important stakeholder group (for the bulk of consumer-facing companies and brands this will, by definition, be the consumer) which really sets it apart from the crowd and provides the differentiation that companies are finding increasingly hard to deliver through product and service innovation alone. The flagship program must be designed to inspire large numbers of people and perhaps force them to reappraise a company and see it in a new light. It should have significant, sustained reputational impact. To this end publicity must be one of its core components. The flagship may well not deal with an issue the company faces. It will, however, offer a radical solution to a real problem, showing the world just what the company can do. And it should do this in a way that expresses the values of the organization—bringing to life what it is and what it stands for, and giving it a distinct identity.

A Complete Picture

Any company wishing to develop a coherent approach to CR must start with the foundations of the house. Until it is sure that it is managing its business in a responsible way and meeting the expectations of society, it cannot sensibly forge ahead with

leadership programs. This would be like building a house with no foundations: while it might look impressive, it won't stand the test of time. However to spend time and energy ensuring that the company is run in a responsible way without embarking on any leadership activity is to miss a significant opportunity for public recognition. It's like building solid foundations but then no house: no one will see the benefits.

MINI-CASE

BP is one of the few companies that has grasped the possibilities of CR and gone a considerable way toward building its CR house. BP has been actively managing its CR issues for a number of years with a clear focus on those that are the most important for their business: issues related to climate change. It has built the pillars of the house, for example by developing products and services which tackle climate change issues, such as BP Ultimate—a "cleaner" fuel. And with a high impact campaign around climate change designed to get everyone to do their bit, it has given shape to the roof of its house.

FOR MORE INFORMATION

Book:
Hilton, S., and Gibbons, G. *Good Business: Your World Needs You.* New York: Texere, 2002

Web sites:
Accountability:
www.accountability.org.uk
Business for Social Responsibility:
www.bsr.org
Good Business: **www.goodbusiness.co.uk**
World Business Council for Sustainable Development: **www.wbcsd.org**

See also:
- Business Ethics and Codes of Practice (pp. 1689–1691)
- CSR: More than PR, Pursuing Competitive Advantage in the Long Run (pp. 376–378)

"Education is simply the soul of a society as it passes from one generation to another."

G. K. Chesterton

CSR: More than PR, Pursuing Competitive Advantage in the Long Run

by John Surdyk

EXECUTIVE SUMMARY

- Consumers increasingly expect companies to act in "responsible" ways.
- Because of their scale and reach, companies have unusual opportunities to address social concerns in innovative and productive ways.
- Evidence suggests corporate social responsibility practices produce long-term benefits with financial performance gains.
- Advancing CSR is made easier with modern risk management tools, reporting guidelines, and committed leadership and employees.

THE EMERGENCE OF CORPORATE SOCIAL RESPONSIBILITY

Global greenhouse gas emissions continue to rise. Diseases wreak havoc across entire continents. An entire host of seemingly intractable issues confront governments throughout the world, who are sometimes unable to effect positive changes. With the emergence of companies as some of the most powerful institutions for innovation and social change, more shareholders, regulators, customers and corporate partners are increasingly interested in understanding the impact of these organizations' regular activities upon the community and its natural resources. With the world's largest 800 non-financial companies accounting for as much economic output as the world's poorest 144 countries, the importance of these organizations in addressing trade imbalances, income inequality, resource degradation and other issues is clear. While companies are not tasked with the responsibilities of governments, their scale and their ability to influence these issues necessitate their involvement and create opportunities for forward-looking organizations to exercise great leadership.

In public opinion surveys, consumers admit that they prefer to buy products and services from companies they feel are socially responsible (72%) and that they sell shares of those companies they feel don't pass muster (27%). Challenging Nobel laureate Milton Friedman's notion that companies' only responsibility is to make profit, executives are increasingly seeking ways to combine economic gain with social well-being in ways that will produce more customer loyalty, better relationships with regulators, and a host of other advantages. CSR practices may, in fact, prove pivotal to the success of a company.

Sometimes described simply as "doing well by doing good," corporate social responsibility initiatives gained traction in the 1990s as consumer interest in management practices erupted in the wake of several substantial incidences of executive malfeasance and of escalating environmental challenges. While originally focused on environmental factors, CSR reports increasingly include social measures. Likewise, company leaders today express interest in business models that weave together explicit goals for profit, environmental performance, and social factors, at the same time recognizing that these efforts will likely yield no short-term financial benefits but rather long-term performance improvements.

A CLOUDY CONCEPT BEGINS TO CRYSTALLIZE

The phrase "corporate social responsibility" (CSR) describes both:
- a social movement
- a collection of specific management practices and initiatives

Business leaders, government professionals and others use these principles and tools to assess and report upon organizations' impact on society.

Globally, CSR is an evolving concept without a clear definition, yet it describes a set of corporate obligations and practices somewhere on the spectrum between traditional charitable giving on one hand and merely strict compliance with laws on the other.

While operating definitions remain elusive, the term "CSR" generally refers to a company's efforts to explicitly include social and environmental concerns in its decision-making along with a commitment to increasing the organization's positive impact on society. Beneath these efforts is a realization that improved CSR reporting and better risk-management systems generally promote the transparency and accountability essential to good company governance and improved financial performance. These systems, in effect, enable a company to anticipate and respond to opportunities when it senses that society's expectations aren't being met by the its performance.

BENEFITS FROM CSR

Benefits of corporate social performance reporting can spread over an entire organization.

Areas of greatest gain for a company's market value, operational efficiency, access to capital, and brand value typically come from:
- establishing ethics, values and principles for the organization;
- improving environmental processes or reducing environmental impact;
- improving workplace conditions.

Other efforts, such as better governance measures, also tend to yield positive benefits for companies.

MAKING CSR REAL

Traditional rhetoric about "private versus public" responsibilities is diminishing while companies operate more and more with an understanding of an acknowledged (if tacit) role to play in society. In the United States

"Society never advances. It recedes as fast on one side as it gains on the other. Society acquires new arts, and loses old instincts."

Ralph Waldo Emerson

BENEFITS OF CSR		
Business Area	*Reduce Costs*	*Create Value*
License to Operate	More favorable government relations; reduced shareholder activism; reduced risk of lawsuits	Increased community support for the company's operations ("a bank account of goodwill")
Reputational Capital	Reduced negative consumer activism/ boycotts; positive media coverage/"free advertising"; positive "word-of-mouth" advertising	Increased customer attraction; increased customer retention
Human Resources	Increased employee retention and morale	Enhanced recruitment; increased productivity
Finance		Social screens and investment funds are attracted to companies perceived as good social performers

many people feel companies should be doing more to improve society through changing their business practices.

While implementing CSR initiatives in modern companies is a daunting prospect because of their increasingly complex and global operations, many CSR management frameworks have moved onto the international stage. Approximately 400 companies—including many of the world's largest—use all or some of the Global Reporting Initiative (GRI), and combined environmental and social reports are increasingly common alongside companies' regular sustainability reports. Launched in 1997 by the Coalition of Environmentally Responsible Economies, the GRI report contains 50 core environmental, social, and economic indicators for a broad range of companies. It also offers additional modules with distinct metrics for companies, depending upon their industry sector and operations. The price range for producing a report spans from $100,000 for a basic GRI to more than $3 million for complex organizations like Shell.

Other major initiatives and reporting standards provide helpful guidance and principles, among them are:
- The United National Global Compact
- Global Environmental Management Initiative
- International Standards Organization guidelines (for example, ISO14000)

The continued growth of the socially responsible investment movement, especially in the United States and Europe, is stimulating companies' adoption of GRI and other instruments. In the United States alone, capital available to socially responsible companies reached $2.29 trillion in 2005.

MINI-CASE

Beginning with $1,000 in a garage in 1990, Greg Erickson founded a new energy bar company, Clif Bars, Inc., in Berkeley, California. Committed to exercising environmental stewardship, Greg made expensive investments in organic ingredients and renewable energy while pursuing progressive employment practices such as six-month sabbaticals for employees. Refusing acquisition overtures from other companies, Clif Bars' commitments to corporate responsibility laid a strong, long-term foundation for the growing $100+ million company and its meteoric rise against titans like Kellogg and Quaker Oats.

CHALLENGES TO CSR

The majority of corporations in the world do not produce any reports on their CSR practices. Executives often cite several concerns, including:
- Fear they may undertake a CSR program while competitors do not, meaning they incur expenses and refocus management talent that may place them at a competitive disadvantage.
- No feeling of urgency to act on many societal issues.
- No accepted standard of what type of information should be reported or at what depth.
- Concern that if they only achieve goals they largely establish for themselves, they may appear only half-heartedly committed—or they may even open themselves to lawsuits.
- Trouble identifying stakeholders, meaning the audience for their reports may be ambiguous which may, in turn, undermine the quality of the reporting generally.
- Belief that traditional philanthropy fulfills an organization's commitment to society.
- Reporting upon the entire scope of a company's impact upon society and the environment is increasingly complex.

Recognizing "that one size does not fit all," more companies are exercising greater discretion in reporting initiatives to highlight key information for their sector or the parts of the world in which they operate.

HOW TO GET STARTED

These principles must be grounded in an organization for CSR management frameworks to yield their maximum benefit.
- Ensure long-term organizational commitment by involving the top leadership *and* the employees.
- Don't adopt every reporting system: select one that makes the most sense for your industry and scale.
- Carefully identify stakeholders to help develop feedback loops so you can adjust your course.
- Consider benchmarking against peer companies.
- Communicate your results widely.
- Don't be afraid to revise standards or develop new metrics of your own.

CONCLUSION

Evidence is mounting that CSR provides tangible benefits and lasting competitive advantage to organizations. While difficult to implement, corporate social responsibility practices and frameworks provide companies with a chance to influence the rules of competition positively while playing a crucial—and increasingly expected—role in the world.

MAKING IT HAPPEN ▶▶

There is no consensus among government bodies, companies, or consumers about what precisely constitutes a definition—or even a consistent set of management topics—under the umbrella of corporate social responsibility. Several intergovernmental bodies, company federations, and nonprofits have advanced competing definitions. Among the most influential are:

World Bank. "Corporate Social Responsibility, or CSR, is the commitment of business to contribute to sustainable economic development, working with employees, their families, the local community, and society at large to improve their quality of life, in ways that are both good for business and good for development."

World Economic Forum. "Corporate Citizenship can be defined as the contribution a company makes to society through its core business activities, its social investment and philanthropy programs, and its engagement in public policy. The manner in which a company manages its economic, social, and environmental relationships, as well as those with different stakeholders, in particular shareholders, employees, customers, business partners,

governments, and communities, determines its impact."

Business for Social Responsibility. "CSR is operating a business in a manner that meets or exceeds the ethical, legal, commercial, and public expectations that society has of business. CSR is seen by leadership companies as more than a collection of discrete practices and occasional gestures, or initiatives motivated by marketing, public relations, or other business benefits. Rather, it is viewed as a comprehensive set of policies, practices, and programs that are integrated throughout business operations, and decision-making processes that are supported and rewarded by top management."

Center for Corporate Citizenship at Boston College. "Corporate Citizenship refers to the way a company integrates basic social values with everyday business practices, operations, and policies. A corporate citizenship company understands that its own success is intertwined with societal health and well-being. Therefore, it takes into account its impact on all stakeholders, including employees, customers, communities, suppliers, and the natural environment."

International Business Leaders Forum. "Corporate Social Responsibility means open and transparent business practices that are based on ethical values and respect for employees, communities, and the environment. It is designed to deliver sustainable value to society at large as well as to shareholders."

United Nations. While not advocating a particular definition of corporate social responsibility, the United Nations uses the term "global corporate citizenship" to describe international companies' obligations to respect human rights, improve labor conditions and protect the environment. The UN Research Institute for Sustainable Development, which follows academic work in this area, typically concentrates upon ethical issues and principles guiding how a company's management engages stakeholders

FUN FACTS

The Institute of Business Ethics published a study of FTSE 250 companies, providing evidence that those with an ethical code in place for over five years generated greater economic value and market value than their peers over the period 1997–2000. Source: Simon Webley & Elise More, "Does Business Ethics Pay?" April 2003.

For 79% of fund managers and analysts surveyed in 2003, the management of social and environmental risks has a positive impact on a company's market value in the long term. Source: CSR Europe, Deloitte & Euronext (2003) *Investing in Responsible Business: The 2003 Survey of European Fund Managers, Financial Analysts and Investor Relations Officers,* CSR Europe & Deloitte.

FOR MORE INFORMATION

Book:
United Nations Conference on Trade and Development. *Disclosure of the Impact of Corporations on Society: Current Trends and Issues.* Geneva: New York, 2004

Web sites:
Business for Social Responsibility:
www.bsr.org
CSR Network:
www.csrnetwork.com/default.asp
Ethical Corp: **www.ethicalcorp.com**
Social Investment Forum:
www.socialinvest.com
SustainAbility: **www.sustainability.com**
World Business Council for Sustainable Development: **www.wbcsd.org**

See also:
- Business Ethics and Codes of Practice (pp. 1689–1691)
- Corporate Responsibility: A Leadership Approach (pp. 374–375)

From Crisis Management to Crisis Leadership

by Ian I. Mitroff

EXECUTIVE SUMMARY

- Over 20 years ago, the Tylenol poisonings prompted the field of crisis management. Although much has been learned since, many organizations still have not adopted proactive crisis-leadership programs.
- Until organizations do so, they will be crisis prone, susceptible to an ever-growing number of crises.

INTRODUCTION

Crisis management is no longer sufficient to respond to the crises today's organizations face. The difference between crisis management and crisis leadership is directional: crisis management is largely reactive, responding to crises after they have occurred. In contrast, crisis leadership is proactive, seeking to plan as carefully as possible before crises occur. Crisis management tends to consider individual crises in isolation, while crisis leadership considers the big picture—how individual crises interact.

Unless your organization takes a position of crisis leadership, you cannot respond properly when a crisis hits. Among the more important steps you can take now is anticipating the broadest possible range of potential crises. If your focus becomes too narrow you won't be able to respond appropriately when crises hit—and they will. If you aren't prepared to handle a crisis before it occurs, you won't be able to respond effectively when it arrives.

WHY EVERY ORGANIZATION NEEDS TO HAVE A CRISIS PORTFOLIO

Research demonstrates that crises fall into general categories or families (see table below). Within each general family, the specific crises share strong similarities. On the other hand, there are sharp differences between the general categories, families, or types of major crises.

This table leads us to a number of key lessons that crisis-prepared organizations have learned.

Lesson 1: Prepare for at least one crisis in each of the families

Research has demonstrated unequivocally how the best organizations plan and prepare for major crises. Most organizations consider only one or two crisis families, for example, natural disasters such as fires or earthquakes. This is undoubtedly a major focus because natural disasters not only occur with great regularity, but they're equally likely to strike all organizations. There's no blame associated with them as there is with other types of disaster, for example, workplace violence. Nonetheless, even earthquakes can attract some degree of human blame: humans are still charged with the responsibility of designing appropriate buildings that will withstand their worst effects and with designing appropriate recovery efforts for the survivors.

Lesson 2: It isn't sufficient to prepare only for industry-specific crises

When organizations do broaden their preparations to cover crises other than natural disasters, more often than not it's to cover core or normal disasters specific to their industry. For instance, you rarely have to prod chemical companies to prepare for explosions and fires, which can easily arise from their day-to-day operating experience. No one has to prod fast-food companies to prepare for food contamination and poisoning, since such incidents are an ever-present threat in businesses that handle food. This kind of anticipation, while necessary, is too specific to count as complete preparation.

Lesson 3: Prepare for the simultaneous occurrence of multiple crises

Major crises occur not only because of what an organization knows, anticipates, and plans for, but because of what it does not know and does not anticipate. Even if you've prepared for a particular type or form of crisis, major crises will still occur, because new environmental factors are constantly emerging to give a new wrinkle to old forms. It's not only the crises that you've planned and prepared for that constitute a threat—crises you've never even thought about may be even more serious.

Lesson 4: The purpose of definitions is to guide, not predict

It isn't possible to give a precise definition of a crisis, because it isn't possible to predict with exact certainty how a crisis will occur, when, and why. Nonetheless, as a guiding definition, a crisis is any adverse event that affects or has the potential to affect the *whole* of an organization. If something affects only a small, isolated part of an organization, it may not be a major crisis. In order for a problem to be judged a crisis, it must exact a major toll on human lives, property, financial earnings, the reputation, and the general health and well-being of an organization. Most often, all of these suffer damage simultaneously. A major crisis is something that *cannot be completely contained within the walls of an organization*. A single rogue trader at Barron's Bank had the potential to destroy the entire organization. The Firestone-Ford tire crisis also demonstrates this organizational ripple effect.

Lesson 5: Every type of crisis can happen to every organization

Every organization needs to plan for the occurrence of at least one crisis in each family, because each type could actually happen. Furthermore, you must consider all the types broadly and not literally. Consider, for instance, product tampering, which can impact a company in multiple ways.

"You need to plan the way a fire department plans: it cannot anticipate where the next fire will be, so it has to shape an energetic and efficient team that is capable of responding to the unanticipated as well as to any ordinary event."

Andrew S. Grove

MAJOR CRISIS TYPES/RISKS						
Economic	Informational	Physical (loss of key plant and facilities)	Human resources	Reputation	Psychopathic acts	Natural disasters
Labor strikes	Loss of proprietary and confidential information	Loss of key equipment, plant, and material supplies	Loss of key executives	Slander, gossip	Product tampering	Earthquakes
Labor unrest	False information	Breakdown of key equipment, plant, etc.	Loss of key personnel	Sick jokes	Kidnapping	Fires
Labor shortage	Tampering with computer records	Loss of key facilities	Rise in absenteeism	Rumors	Hostage taking	Floods
Major decline in stock price and price fluctuations	Loss of key computer information relating to customers, suppliers, etc.	Major plant disruptions	Rise in vandalism and accidents	Damage to corporate reputation	Terrorism	Explosions
Market crash	Y2K		Workplace violence	Tampering with corporate logos	Workplace violence	Typhoons
Decline in major earnings						Hurricanes

Source: Pauchant and Mitroff (1992)

Lesson 6: No type of crisis should be taken literally

Product tampering doesn't apply only to food or to pharmaceutical companies. Any organization can be the victim of some form of product tampering. Computers, for example, are integral to every organization, yet the true value of computers is not the cost of the hardware or software: it's the information they contain about customers and other key stakeholders. If someone were to gain access and tamper with these records the company's products and services could be seriously affected. Consider the French publisher Larousse. The French are avid eaters of mushrooms; at times they search the forests with Larousse encyclopedias. One article in the encyclopedia has two facing pages of illustrations, one showing mushrooms that are safe to eat, the other those that are unsafe. Intentionally or not, the labels on the two pages were once reversed. The moral is clear: you ignore any or all of the types of major crisis at your peril.

Lesson 7: Tampering is the most generic form or type of all crises

Tampering—significantly altering the properties of information or of an object, person, product, etc.—is the most important crisis type. Tampering essentially converts properties that are acceptable and safe into properties that are unacceptable or dangerous, thus threatening everything connected with an organization.

Lesson 8: No crisis ever happens in the precise way you plan for it, so it's not crisis planning per se that's important, it's thinking about the unthinkable

Fortunately you don't have to prepare for every specific type of crisis within each of the families. If this were required, then crisis leadership would be overwhelming. It's acceptable to limit your preparations to one or more types of crisis within each of the families. Why? If a crisis seldom happens exactly according to plan, the critical thing is doing your best to think about the unthinkable. This exercise makes you better able to think on your feet when a crisis does hit, and hence to recover faster without being paralyzed. If the specific types of crises within a particular family share strong similarities, giving serious consideration to each of the families is the most helpful kind of preparation. It's still important to prepare for a broader and wider range of crises, although to start on the difficult road of crisis leadership it's not necessary to prepare for everything simultaneously. In fact, trying to prepare at once for every eventuality might well lead you to conclude that the task is overwhelming and hopeless—it's not.

Lesson 9: Every crisis is capable of being both the cause and the effect of any other crisis

The best organizations don't prepare for a single crisis, they attempt to prepare for the simultaneous occurrence of multiple crises. Organizations that are well prepared study past crises, looking for patterns and interconnections. They generate visual maps to understand better how crises unfold over time and how they are interrelated. In today's world, no individual crisis ever happens in isolation and independently of any other crisis. You need to consider the potential impact of every crisis in your organization's crisis portfolio on every other crisis.

Lesson 10: Crisis leadership is systemic

Like total quality management or environmentalism, if crisis leadership is not understood systemically, it is basically not being done, let alone being done well.

MAKING IT HAPPEN ▶▶

- Assemble and train a cross-functional, cross-divisional crisis team.
- Poll individual members of the team about the crises they can envision because of their distinct vantage points.
- Produce at least three or four general maps or big pictures showing how each of the individual crises that the various team members envision might interact so as to set off a chain reaction.
- Referring to the overall maps, determine what pieces of data can be used as early warning signals to announce the beginning stages of each individual crisis and indicate the likelihood that it will set off a chain reaction of other crises.

FOR MORE INFORMATION

Book:
Mitroff, Ian I., et al. *Why Some Companies Recover Faster and Better from Crises: Seven Essential Lessons for Avoiding Disaster.* New York: AMACOM, 2005.

Web sites:
Comprehensive Crisis Management site:
www.compcrisis.com
Center for Global Education:
www.globaled.us

See also:
- ☆ Designing Corporate Systems for Success (pp. 212–213)
- ☆ Managing Today's Angry Workforce (pp. 35–36)
- ☆ Steve Jobs (pp. 1316–1317)

"Financial markets . . . resent any kind of government interference but they hold a belief deep down that if conditions get really rough the authorities will step in." George Soros

Benchmarking   by Paul Spenley

EXECUTIVE SUMMARY

Understanding the scope and power of benchmarking is a strategic imperative in any business, as it allows existing businesses to defend their position, as well as to attack new business opportunities. Benchmarking is used at a number of levels.

- **Strategic benchmarking.** Strategic action teams use benchmarking to drive continuous improvement and refine the overall business strategy.
- **Competitive benchmarking.** For each major business driver, the competitive position is measured against the competition.
- **Customer benchmarking.** Customer perception is all there is—customers never buy just a product. Customer benchmarking enables a business to understand the views of their customers about the organization, relative to the competition.
- **Financial benchmarking.** This comprises key performance measures and the establishment of rankings for each measure. Return on net assets (RONA) identifies which business drivers will deliver the greatest return on the investment needed.
- **Best practice benchmarking.** The minimum process to meet the business driver requirements for time and cost to meet the required outputs.

INTRODUCTION

Benchmarking is a management technique concerned with allowing businesses to establish measures of their performance. This allows companies to analyze their efficiency and compare themselves to competitors and leading companies in the industry.

There are five benchmarking approaches that can be employed independently or together. This section outlines the most effective ways to utilize the principles of benchmarking.

STRATEGIC BENCHMARKING

Benchmarking is the practice of measuring and comparing key aspects of your organization relative to customer expectations. Ideally benchmarking achieves

- knowledge of competitive position
- knowledge of best practice
- a set of targets to achieve competitive advantage
- a customer-focused quality culture

To succeed, the operational and strategic team agrees on a clear mission statement for the business in terms of products and markets. This is done for the immediate one-year period and then for a longer, usually three-year, period. Often, the longer period is considerably more difficult to forecast. However, it is essential to identify the market requirements and product mix for the longer-term future, not just for next year.

Preparing a fishbone diagram is a helpful technique, as it provides a cause-and-effect analysis, breaking down the mission statement by identifying the key business drivers in a clear and concise manner.

COMPETITIVE BENCHMARKING

For each major business driver, the company's actual position is determined in measurable parameters, relative to the competition.

The key is to establish actual and target measures for each business driver. This establishes the degree of difficulty for the operational team in delivering all the customer benchmark elements contained within the business drivers.

The competitive benchmark matrix below provides an outline for this approach. The final, best practice column can include valuable information and ideas from competitors. After all, why reinvent the wheel when the wheel is best?

CUSTOMER BENCHMARKING
Total Product Concept

The total product concept is not new. It's based on the principle that customers never buy simply a product itself, but instead they buy a set of tangible and intangible attributes that they perceive as delivering value.

The total product concept tool is used for each product to identify clearly the things the organization needs to be good at with regard to product, service, added value, and "delight factors" (meaning those factors that really wow customers and help to build a strong customer relationship).

The most consistent business drivers are

- product quality
- delivery performance accuracy
- time to market
- response time to orders
- response time to inquiries, both technical and commercial
- accuracy and timeliness of information

The business drivers need to be reviewed by the strategic and operational teams for each product, then collated into a set of six dimensions such as those identified above.

Most managers realize that the more competitive the market, the more important the level of customer satisfaction. The message is clear: it is absolutely critical for a company to excel in defining its target customers and in delivering a product or service that completely meets their needs.

Customer Surveys As a Part of Benchmarking

The old-fashioned idea that you can measure customer satisfaction by unsolicited customer surveys often does more harm than good, and can actually alienate customers who value a relationship (at whatever level) with the supplier.

The best practice is the 3M top box system, which asks three questions:

1 Are you totally satisfied? If not, why not?
2 Would you buy from us again? If not, why not?
3 Would you recommend us? If not, why not?

The third question is the most important when developing a business—the fact is that word of mouth is the most effective means of persuading new customers to buy from you.

The levels of satisfaction among targeted customers are a good benchmarking indicator of the level of quality of the products and services they're receiving. Nevertheless, the way to raise the level of customer satisfaction from neutral to satisfied, or satisfied to completely satisfied, is not simply a matter of doing a better job of delivering the same value or experience that the company is currently delivering.

Comb Charts

Comb charts reconcile your customers' view of your performance with your own. These benchmark what is important to the customer and your relative performance against those expectations and against the

---

competition. The information which you have gathered needs to be presented in a format that can easily be used to:

- contrast your performance with customers' requirements;
- compare one customer's responses with another;
- compare your strengths with those of the competition.

Comb charts are based on information gathered from surveys requiring your customers to rank areas of requirement in order of importance.

FINANCIAL BENCHMARKING

Using the RONA model it is possible to identify which business drivers will deliver the greatest return on investment. For example, the effect on inventory turns, reductions in WIP (work-in-progress), and finished goods inventory can be calculated to achieve an ongoing financial saving.

Return on Net Assets (RONA)

It is necessary for the strategic and operational teams to establish the RONA plan together. This is crucial in agreeing on realistic performance improvements.

The process of working through the RONA analysis provides a deeper appreciation of the connections between the variables and a better idea of the most appropriate course of action. Reliable financial information is, of course, notoriously difficult to find: what matters here is understanding what seem to be the financial drivers of the industry in general and competitors in particular, and then setting realistic benchmarks and plans to achieve these.

BEST PRACTICE BENCHMARKING

Time and cost are, typically, the most significant drivers of business performance; benchmarking these factors can lead to significant operational improvements in efficiency and performance. The key task is to map out the minimum process required to

deliver the product to the customer, and this can be achieved by assessing performance, setting targets and following through on plans and initiatives focusing on improving the

- cost of waste (errors)
- cost of conformance (prevention)
- minimum process (added value)

MAKING IT HAPPEN ▶▶

The senior management team needs to structure benchmarking activities in such a way that they become a continuous process, driving improvement and helping to build a sustainable business. For benchmarking to succeed:

1. The leadership of the organization should establish teams to lead the process, learning and acting on the results:
   The **strategic action team** is responsible for the strategic direction of the business and needs to review this at monthly meetings.
   The **customer benchmarking team** should be cross-divisional and multilevel and include people at the sharp end of customer contact.
   The **business process teams** are the teams within the company that should have improvement targets.
2. Comprehensive and accurate information on competing businesses needs to be available.
3. the company's internal auditing procedures need to be effective. First, the business needs to understand how they operate in relation to the organizations that are being benchmarked. Second, the organization needs to be able to understand how effective any changes have been.
4. The benchmarks—or performance measures—that are established need to be based on industry best practice. These may differ from the targets set

by the company's business units or departments which may be easily attainable or simply irrelevant. However, the benchmarks should directly relate to the company's overall business plans.

5. Finally, the benchmarks that are established must be flexible and able to change with the external environment.

CONCLUSION

Benchmarking is a fundamental requirement in building a sustainable business, particularly as it allows no room for complacency or "not-invented-here" thinking. The significance and value of benchmarking lies in the fact that building and sustaining a successful business is a battle to keep ahead of the competition. This is only achieved through constant vigilance and a policy from the top of continuous improvement at all levels of the company—and best practice benchmarking provides the framework for this to happen.

FOR MORE INFORMATION

Books:

Calloway, Joe. *Becoming a Category of One: How Extraordinary Companies Transcend Commodity and Defy Comparison.* New York: Wiley, 2003.

Kaplan, Robert S., and David P. Norton. *The Balanced Scorecard: Translating Strategy into Action.* Cambridge, MA: Harvard Business School Press, 1996.

Osborne, Edi, Michael Mard, Robert Dunne, and James Rigby. *Driving Your Company's Value: Strategic Benchmarking for Value.* New York: Wiley, 2004.

See also:

☆ New Yardsticks for Performance and Productivity in an E-world (pp. 366–367)

"The genius of a good leader is to leave behind him a situation which common sense, without the grace of genius, can deal with successfully."

Walter Lippmann

Matching Pay to Achievement
by Peter Brown

EXECUTIVE SUMMARY

- As the war for talent intensifies, the need to match pay to achievement is now greater than ever.
- The history of performance-related pay is variable, and even today, the efforts of many public sector service workers are not involved in performance-related bonuses. This trend is set to change.
- Performance-related pay and bonus programs may vary between senior managers and other levels.
- There are several critical factors that determine the success, failure, or overall effectiveness of performance-related programs, and these are reviewed in this section.

INTRODUCTION

David Ulrich talks about a workplace phenomenon all-too-familiar to anyone who's managed in today's corporate setting. He recalls one occasion when, upon meeting a new corporate group, he led a vigorous discussion about the company vision, its new products, reducing cycle times, and serving customers. To which, he says, one of the participants remarked quietly, "This is all well and good, but what's in it for me?" Matching pay to performance is a well-known issue in today's work world. But when did the trend begin?

The concept of matching reward to achievement took root in the 1960s as society changed due, particularly in the United Kingdom, to a much higher percentage of graduate workers and the outstanding success of young performers in areas such as sports and music, where rewards started to rise dramatically.

As the West moved from a manufacturing to a service-oriented society, the need to differentiate between average and outstanding performers became very apparent to employers in the professional, entertainment, and general service industries. This led to the concept of the "bonus award" linked to the annual salary review.

Some of the old-fashioned systems, like Christmas bonuses that were in no way linked to personal performance and may have been paid in terms of a Christmas hamper or turkey, started to go and companies introduced an annual, often profit-sharing, bonus, which, in a good year, might pay a bonus of between 5% and 10% of employees' annual salary.

It is fair to say that the concept of trying to match pay to achievement arrived with Margaret Thatcher in 1979 in the United Kingdom as her government determined to free the country from the union-dominated collective culture of the past and enthusiastically embraced tax systems to encourage a culture where increased productivity of whatever sort could be awarded with significant, after-tax rewards.

Since 1980, the private sector in the English-speaking democracies, led by the United States, has been moved toward altering pay systems to encourage pay for achievement concepts. In the United States, it is now common for senior executives in publicly quoted companies to have only 20% of their remuneration as salary, with the rest being paid out in performance options, cash bonuses, and preferred or restricted stock which can only be cashed if certain predetermined profit or other targets are reached. The United Kingdom has followed this trend; the belief that this type of pay is likely to enhance the success of the nation as a whole has brought changes in tax policies and encouraged the concepts of performance-related pay of all varieties. Australia and other Commonwealth countries have also followed the trend.

Traditionally, most European countries have been more socialist in their business systems than the United Kingdom and their philosophies of equality and social justice have not encouraged the high bonus culture that has become common in Britain and the United States. However, under pressure from multinational companies and the international employment market, particularly financial and banking expertise, their traditional resistance to this trend has been breaking down fast.

Even in France—with one of the more traditional centralized social models—most managers, including those in the semi-nationalized utilities, are now working in environments that allow them to earn a significant percentage of their pay through performance bonuses.

The use of stock and options is becoming increasingly standard as the payment currency for long-term bonuses across the European Union, including the newer Baltic, Eastern European, and Balkan members.

The area where performance-related pay is still relatively undeveloped is central and local government services in all countries, including the United States and the United Kingdom. While it is obviously difficult to specify the criteria for significant performance bonuses for, say, the armed services or judiciary, repeated attempts are now being made in health, education, and the central bureaucracies to introduce relatively small performance bonuses to staff at all levels. This is a trend which is actively, or passively, opposed by most labor unions who object to any form of assessment and who fight to maintain automatic or incremental salary increases for their members.

One of the problems with performance pay in the public sector is that most attempts in areas such as the police, fire service, and education have centered on the concept of discretionary bonuses amounting to 5–10% of salary, which is insufficient to change the working practices and personal achievement targets of those involved.

It is becoming apparent that the bonus element for government employees is a guaranteed final salary pension, which in 2005 was re-confirmed to start at 60 in the United Kingdom for all current staff when the rest of the nation faces an increase in the normal pension age to 67.

Although this is not a traditional performance pay issue, it is certainly a major "golden hello" and retention payment for older staff across Europe and we expect it to come under attack as governments are forced to recognize that private sector workers will be unwilling to fund over-generous pensions via taxation to public sector coworkers.

RULES FOR MATCHING PAY TO ACHIEVEMENT

"In the just-in-time workplace," says Bruce Tulgan, "you can't expect people to wait around to be rewarded once they've delivered . . . Managers need to reward desired

performance consistently and with speed and creativity." This concept seems to be accepted by more organizations each day, but what are the rules for actually implementing such an ideal?

We now have about 20 years' experience of matching incentive pay to expected outcomes from different groups of staff, and it is fairly clear that certain rules need to be followed if the program is going to be successful. They are as follows.

1 **The relevance of the program to the individual.** The performance of the unit upon which the bonus is based must be one to which the individual can relate and whose output they feel they can influence. Bonuses based on the performance of a holding company make little impact on an individual working in one of the smaller subsidiaries.

If you want to make staff feel they can actually benefit from a performance bonus culture, the targets they need to achieve must be broken down into departmental, divisional, or unit performance triggers, so they can see that their personal input can make a difference.

2 **The scale and value of the performance-related element.** The scale of any performance-related pay needs to be significant in the eyes of the beneficiaries if it is going to affect the way they do their job. Performance-related pay will not necessarily make people work harder, but it will make them work in a more targeted way to deliver the outcomes which the bonus is designed to reward.

It is generally understood that if you want to get individuals to align their personal targets with the organization's preferred objectives, you need to offer at least 15%, and for senior executives 30–50%, of their salary as a potential bonus for achieving, or at least 90% achieving, these objectives.

3 **The reasonableness of the program— and in particular, the time frame.** For senior executives, increasingly you need to structure bonus schemes that pay out over time, as it is very difficult to assess their collective performance over a single 12-month period. For this reason, most consultants have been working on accumulator systems, option plans, or other approaches, whereby measurement of the increasing productivity or profit delivered is made over a rolling three-year period. Bonuses are then paid at intervals over time, with a percentage being banked on behalf of an individual rather than paid out in total; it is only on delivery of the three-year plan that the team involved gets the full bonus award to which it is entitled.

4 **The form of the performance-related bonus.** Because of taxation policy in most sophisticated countries and the need to try to ensure that senior executives feel they are members of the company, most private sector organizations prefer to pay part of their bonuses in stock or options in the company itself. These programs, variously referred to as stock option, restricted stocks, preferred stocks, stock save plans, or employee stock-owning plans, all have the same objective: to pay out a percentage of bonuses in the form of company stock so that the individuals feel part of the organization for which they work.

5 **The need to make schemes inclusive, avoiding divisiveness.** One of the problems with incentive payment programs is that many support staff who work in a cost rather than a profit center are left out of the program architecture. This can often lead to breakdowns in support units and communications behind high-profile sales or dealing teams. It is therefore critically important to make performance-related pay inclusive, despite the difficulty of setting targets for administration and technical staff. If this doesn't happen, breakdowns occur in vital, but relatively mundane, operations that have been overstretched by demands put on them by bonus-driven sales or dealing units.

"Changing how a workforce is rewarded is difficult and not for the faint of heart," say Patricia Zingheim and Jay Schuster, who add that "Pay is a way of gaining understanding, acceptance, and commitment of what people can do to help make a company a success." For this and many other reasons, there seems no stopping the increasing use of performance-related pay in sophisticated democratic societies. To date, it is hard to prove just how effective it has been, but perceived wisdom is that most organizations using this system have in fact achieved higher levels of output than they would otherwise have attained. At the same time, this approach means that if there is a general downturn in demand, an organization is not necessarily saddled with very high fixed salary costs.

> ## MAKING IT HAPPEN ▶▶
> - Ensure that a bonus program is supported by the organization. The first step is for senior managers and directors to recognize that achievement will be rewarded in a way that will be valued by the employees.
> - Relate the program directly to individual and team actions. The bonus needs not only to be meaningful, but achievable, in order to affect people's behavior.
> - The program, or programs, can be imaginative, driving whatever patterns of behavior are identified as priorities, but it must always be reasonable and fair.
> - The type of bonus is important. External factors, such as taxation, can reduce the benefit and perceived value and need to be considered in advance.
> - Programs must be as inclusive as possible: if people are excluded then everyone's performance can ultimately suffer.

CONCLUSION

We expect performance-related pay to increase in importance, though not at the rate it has over the past 20 years, and to spread into public sector areas such as health, education, social services, and the prison system. It is apparent that if the government cannot offer performance-related pay and does not outsource or privatize governmental services to organizations that use this approach, the public sector will have increasing difficulty in recruiting and retaining staff against private sector employers using sophisticated incentive and reward systems. It seems inevitable, therefore, that developed and developing industrial economies will move to systems in which almost everybody, excluding priests, judges, and politicians, is partially remunerated via performance-related pay.

> ## FOR MORE INFORMATION
>
> **Books:**
> Berger, Lance A. *The Compensation Handbook*. New York: McGraw-Hill, 1999.
> Martocchio, Joseph J. *Strategic Compensation*. Upper Saddle River, NJ: Prentice-Hall, 2001.
> Tulgan, Bruce. Interview in *Business Minds*. Upper Saddle River, NJ: FT/Prentice Hall (Pearson Education Limited), 2002.
> Ulrich, Dave, *Human Resource Champions: The Next Agenda for Adding Value and Delivering Results*. Cambridge, MA: Harvard Business School Press, 1997.
> Zingheim, Patricia K., and Jay R. Schuster. *Pay People Right: Breakthrough Reward Strategies to Create Great Companies*. San Francisco, CA: Jossey-Bass, 2000.

"Which of us . . . is to do the hard and dirty work for the rest—and for what pay? Who is to do the pleasant and clean work, and for what pay?"

John Ruskin

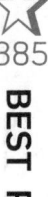
Improving Corporate Profitability Through Accountability

by Marc J. Epstein and Priscilla S. Wisner

EXECUTIVE SUMMARY

- Traditional measures of performance are of limited use to modern businesses, being rooted in evaluating past performance. They are a poor guide to true value, often missing the key factors promoting long-term worth.
- It is essential to include the leading financial and non-financial indicators of performance driving long-term value. This provides broader and more sophisticated information that is better placed to highlight future trends.
- Effectively managing and communicating a broader set of performance measures, reduces uncertainty, ensures better relationships with stockholders and analysts, and enables improved financial performance.
- Full accountability and disclosure combined with improved measures and new systems to drive the process throughout the organization creates greater value for stakeholders, promoting future success.

INTRODUCTION

Improved governance requires the right employees, the right culture and values, and the right systems, information, and decision making. Unfortunately, most organizations are attempting to steer their information-age businesses using industrial-age measurements. Managers have struggled for decades with accounting systems that fail to measure many of the variables that drive long-term value. The historical lagging indicators of performance that are commonly used by accountants are of limited value in determining the value of businesses for external stakeholders, and are of little use in guiding the business internally. Financial data on profitability and return on investment are valuable measures of corporate performance, but they are lagging indicators that measure past performance. A broader set of financial measures is necessary (for example, measurement of intangible assets such as intellectual capital and research-and-development value), in addition to an expanded set relating to customers, internal processes, and organizational measures.

The metrics must include the *leading* financial and nonfinancial indicators of performance that are the drivers and predictors of future financial performance. For example, fines and penalties may be a leading indicator of corporate reputation, employee turnover is a leading measure of future recruitment and training costs, and product

quality is a leading measure of customer satisfaction, which in turn is a leading measure of market share. Each of these factors (reputation, employee-related costs, customer satisfaction, and market share) impacts financial performance.

IMPROVED INTERNAL AND EXTERNAL REPORTING

Just as companies expand their performance measurement parameters, they must also expand their performance reporting models. Employees, stockholders, financial analysts, activists, customers, suppliers, government regulators, and others increasingly demand detailed information about corporate activities, and the Internet has made the dissemination of that information easier and faster. No longer can managers claim they don't have the information. The data are easy to collect, and it's essential to have broader and more forward-looking information to effectively manage the diverse issues that managers now confront daily. Managers should collect this broader array of information on activities and impacts both inside and outside the company and select a set of data to provide adequate disclosure to their various stakeholders. External stakeholders need a broader set of information to effectively evaluate corporate performance, and voluntary disclosure of this information is critical for corporate

accountability. This accountability, both inside and outside the company, through an effective corporate communications strategy, is an essential element of effective and responsible corporate governance.

Proactively managing external disclosures should be a fundamental part of corporate communications strategy. By externally disclosing a more comprehensive set of measures, company executives are seizing the initiative to describe the company's strategy, set expectations, increase transparency, and ensure goal alignment between the company and a broad set of stakeholders. Disclosing performance measures allows investors and other stakeholders to view the company through the eyes of management. A clear, comprehensive communications strategy is highly valued by stockholders and analysts alike.

MINI-CASE

The Campbell Soup Company has continually improved corporate governance.

Changes undertaken in the early 1990s required a majority of directors to come from outside the organization. All directors must stand for election every year and must own at least 6,000 shares of stock within three years of election. Among other provisions, interlocking directorships are not allowed and insiders are banned from certain key committees. In 1995, the board began a rotating yearly performance evaluation of directors, board committees, and the board as a whole. In 2000, the board approved a new director compensation program to closely link director compensation to the creation of stockholder value; only 20% is paid in cash (tied to attendance at meetings). The full set of Campbell Soup's governance standards and current performance review are disclosed in the annual proxy statement to stockholders.

The Cooperative Bank, based in the United Kingdom and with 4,000 employees, has won numerous awards for the high degree of transparency and accountability the company has exhibited. The bank has identified six partners in its quest for corporate value: stockholders, customers, staff and

---

"Good men prefer to be accountable."

386

BEST PRACTICE

their families, suppliers, national and international society, and past and future generations of cooperators. The company surveys all stakeholder groups to determine the critical elements in creating value for each, and performance targets are set on the basis of this information. In 2003, 70 targets were established in three principal areas: delivering value, social responsibility, and ecological sustainability. The Cooperative Bank 2004 Sustainability Report states that 33 targets were fully achieved, acceptable progress was made on 22, and 15 were not achieved. The bank reports progress on each target, providing data and management commentary, and establishes targets for the coming year.

MAKING IT HAPPEN ▸▸

The rewards from building the accountable organization are much like those from building the quality organization—the more committed the managers and workers and the better integrated the concept with company line operations, the greater the benefit. As a first step, managers must build accountable systems and practices within the company. Then they can build bridges to the outside. As they move toward full accountability—well-governed, measured, managed, and publicly responsive—they will position themselves to reap many benefits:

- Executing strategy: the accountable organization articulates each strategy and tactic with specific measures that align direction in ways that broader objectives cannot. The hard measures then give managers objective feedback on what the strategy execution is achieving.
- Improving decision making: the accountable organization generates a wealth of information on performance, which in turn informs decision making with facts, not intuition. People inside and outside the company can make more effective decisions to further company strategy and goals.
- Empowering people: the accountable organization thins the ranks of middle managers that distil and convey information and empowers decision-making authority to the front lines. As management articulates what it wants with concrete quantitative measures, workers have clear guidance of goals and objectives nate to strategy.
- Accelerating learning: the accountable organization installs feedback systems

that yield rapid-fire learning from people both across and outside the company. The company with the most feedback loops—internal and external—is the most successful.

- Communicating the story: the accountable organization delivers its story of value with credible financial and nonfinancial numbers. As senior managers report more numbers externally, exposing performance transparently, stockholders and analysts have less reason to undervalue their stock.
- Inspiring loyalty: the accountable organization markets its value on a basis of reliable performance measures. The no-smoke-and-mirrors approach spurs cooperation and inspires the loyalty of investors, customers, suppliers, employees, business partners, and communities.

CONCLUSION

Once a company has decided to improve corporate governance, measure a broader set of indicators of past and future success, and report internally and externally, managers must develop systems to drive these decisions through the organization. Leading companies are developing integrated, closed-loop planning, budgeting, and feedback systems to help align strategy implementation with corporate performance. While leadership at the top is critical, buy-in at the shop floor is essential for the success of any system implementation. Metrics must be linked to strategy and must be consistent throughout the organization. Companies are increasingly stating desires to become more customer focused or more socially responsible, yet many are still basing employee rewards on meeting revenue and profit goals. If companies expect employees to be more customer focused or more socially or environmentally responsible, part of overall performance evaluations and rewards should be on customer focus or social responsibility.

Accountable managers encourage not only continuous judgment, but continuous improvement. They insist that everyone in the organization participate in decision making. They implement a culture of constant learning and insist on building learning organizations. Accountable managers communicate constantly, setting a tone of forthright feedback and transparency.

Full accountability comes only when a company combines a strong governance structure, improved and broad measure-

ment of relevant performance impacts, timely and full internal and external reporting, and comprehensive management systems to drive the accountability model throughout the organization. By combining these elements companies are creating value for the stakeholders whose support they need in order to prosper—customers, investors, employees, suppliers, communities, the public, regulators, and other government officials.

FOR MORE INFORMATION

Books:
Epstein, Marc J., and Bill Birchard. *Counting What Counts: Turning Corporate Accountability to Competitive Advantage.* Cambridge, MA: Perseus, 2000.
Epstein, Marc J. and K. O. Hanson, eds. *The Accountable Corporation.* Westport, CT: Praeger Publications, 2006.
Monks, Robert A. G. *The Emperor's Nightingale: Restoring the Integrity of the Corporation in the Age of Shareholder Activism.* Cambridge, MA: Perseus, 1999.
Ward, Ralph D. *Improving Corporate Boards.* New York: Wiley, 2000.

Journal Articles:
Sengupta, Partha. "Corporate Disclosure Quality and the Cost of Debt." *Accounting Review* (October 1998).
Epstein, Marc J., and Krishna Palepu. "What Financial Analysts Want." *Strategic Finance* (April 1999).
Hutton, Amy. "Beyond Financial Reporting—An Integrated Approach to Corporate Disclosure." *Journal of Applied Corporate Finance*, Fall 2004.
Engen, Travis, and Samuel DiPiazza. *Beyond Reporting: Creating Business Value and Accountability.* World Business Council on Sustainable Development, June 2005.

Web sites:
Beyond Budgeting Roundtable: **www.brt.org**
Corporate Governance: **www.corpgov.net**
European Corporate Governance Institute: **www.ecgi.org**
Global Corporate Governance Forum: **www.gcgf.org**
Investor Responsibility Research Center: **www.irrc.com**
The Corporate Library: **www.thecorporatelibrary.com**

See also:

Organizational Learning and Performance
by Jerry W. Gilley and Ann Gilley

EXECUTIVE SUMMARY

- As strategic business partners, HR professionals are in a position to influence the direction of the organization as well as enhance the value of HR programs and services.
- Strategic business partnerships are synergistic, mutually beneficial, and long-term oriented. These relationships require HR professionals to develop a responsive, customer-service orientation to better understand and anticipate client needs.

INTRODUCTION

Some human resource (HR) professionals are not perceived as valuable because their programs and services are not linked to the organization's strategic business goals. Other programs falter because HR professionals do not properly communicate the value and benefits of their interventions and initiatives to decision makers within the organization. Although these are contributing factors, most HR programs suffer from a poor image because organizational leaders, managers, and employees do not view the HR department as a vital, contributing part of the organization. When this situation exists, HR is unable to help to improve the organization's performance, quality, efficiency or productivity, or help it to accomplish its strategic goals and objectives.

To address this dilemma, HR professionals need to become proactive. They need to discover ways of enhancing their credibility and thus their effectiveness. One approach is for HR professionals to become strategic business partners. A strategic business partner is a person who "takes part" with others, and partnerships involve the "parts" we each play in our work. Partnerships are essential to the success of any organization.

ELEMENTS OF PARTNERSHIP

There are two primary elements of partnership—purpose and partnering. Purpose defines "why" a partnership is needed, and provides a focus and direction for the partnership. Without a purpose, no partnership exists. Purpose may be quite clear and explicit—as that imposed by an organizational leader or manager, or implicit—as a mutual

exploration of a purpose about to be defined. Purpose, in essence, brings us together.

Partnering occurs when HR professionals and clients pursue a common purpose together. Partnering exemplifies the visible and invisible dynamics between HR professional, client and purpose, the result of clarifying roles and focus. Partnering also embraces underlying assumptions, trust and risk, shared values and expectations. Organizational consultant Geoffrey Bellman suggests that HR professionals and clients who attend to purposes but neglect partnering often fail in their work altogether.

Strategic business partnerships are intra-organizational alliances formed when HR professionals work closely with organizational leaders, managers, supervisors and employees to help the organization achieve its short- and long-term business goals and objectives, as well as to ensure successful completion of the organization's overall strategic plans. These are long-term partnerships that create an interdependence between the HR department and the rest of the organization. They allow HR professionals to better understand and anticipate their clients' needs, to develop a responsive, customer-service oriented attitude toward the client, and to break down the walls between themselves and their clients. As a result, lasting relationships and commitments are forged and investments are made in learning, performance, and change efforts.

Additionally, strategic business partnerships:
- give HR professionals the opportunity to develop personal relationships with clients;
- demonstrate the willingness of HR professionals to learn from clients;

- allow for more effective management of limited financial and human resources;
- produce economic utility, which is measured in terms of increased organizational performance, revenue, profitability, quality, or efficiency.

MAKING IT HAPPEN ▶▶
There are four critical steps in becoming a strategic business partner:

Establish Credibility
The first and most important step in becoming a strategic business partner is to establish credibility within the organization. Improved credibility results from the ability of HR professionals to demonstrate professional expertise, as well as a good understanding of organizational operations and culture. In this way, HR professionals are able to provide real value to the organization.

David Ulrich points out in his book *Human Resource Champions* (1997) that HR professionals need to demonstrate a number of qualities in order to enhance credibility. For example, HR professionals need to be accurate in all HR practices; to be dependable; to meet their commitments in a timely and efficient manner; to establish collaborative client relationships built on trust and honesty; to express their opinions in an understandable and clear manner; to behave in an ethical manner; to demonstrate creativity and innovation; to maintain confidentiality; and to demonstrate mutual respect.

In addition, HR professionals can establish credibility by:
- demonstrating the ability to solve complex problems, resulting in client needs and expectations being satisfied;
- exhibiting professional expertise, along with an understanding of organizational operations and culture, thus establishing respect for their insight and authority;
- securing third-party referrals. These usually come from a network, which is a collection of individuals who can

introduce HR professionals to key organizational decision makers while keeping them informed;

- acquiring an excellent reputation, commonly by delivering results.

Credibility can also be established through an appropriate understanding of the HR professional's and the client's differing roles. Within a partnership, clients are accountable for results, clarity of vision, managing resources (time, energy, money, human talent, materials, equipment, environment), creating structures and systems, and strategic decision making. The HR professional's role combines competence and adaptability. He or she must demonstrate awareness of the organization's needs, assist in developing alternative solutions, reveal new perspectives, model risk-taking, and show knowledge of the consulting process—all while honoring his or her personal purpose and core beliefs. When appropriate roles are defined and maintained, trust and confidence emerge, which deepens relationships and bridges performance uncertainty. Over time, improved efficiency results as collaboration and cooperation replace competition and conflict.

In his book *Competitive Strategy Through People* (1994), Jeffrey Pfeffer cites several examples of HR professionals establishing credibility through partnership. These cases include Advanced Micro Devices, Hewlett-Packard, and Procter & Gamble.

Develop a Customer Service Strategy

The second step in becoming a strategic business partner is for HR professionals to develop a customer-service strategy that satisfies their stakeholders' needs. A stakeholder can be defined as anyone who has something to gain or lose as a result of an interaction with human resources. These gains and losses collectively frame needs and become the target for performance improvement interventions and change initiatives. The typical stakeholders of HR include:

- managers—the primary customer because they endure the cost of programs and services and reap the benefits;
- employees—who participate in programs and services;
- senior managers—who expect programs and services to return value and help the organization to achieve its goals;

- organizations—which need the skills and abilities of all their employees to produce and deliver high-quality products and services at a profit, and rely on employees' capabilities to remain competitive.

A strategy designed in accordance with the stakeholders' expressed interests ensures that the HR department is helping to maximize organizational performance. It also ensures that HR departments will be supported as well as defended by stakeholders during difficult economic periods, and viewed as essential to the organization's long-term success. A customer-service strategy that satisfies stakeholders' needs and expectations consists of six steps:

1. placing the business and professional needs of clients first;
2. listening to clients, responding to their demands, and working with them in a collaborative manner;
3. creating customer-service opportunities through face-to-face interaction;
4. becoming active participants with clients rather than passive observers, using questioning, listening and facilitating skills that lead to viable recommendations and solutions;
5. evaluating feedback from clients regarding their satisfaction with interventions and initiatives;
6. implementing improvements in customer service, based upon the feedback received from clients.

Ultimately, an effective customer-service strategy is an important guiding principle for HR departments, and should direct HR professionals' decisions and actions.

Demonstrate Business Acumen

HR professionals must be able to demonstrate an understanding of business strategies, goals, tactics, and financial performance. Acquiring knowledge of business fundamentals, systems theory, organizational culture, operations, and politics enables HR professionals to think like their clients. In addition, HR professionals possessing business understanding are better able to facilitate change without disrupting the company's operations.

With knowledge of business principles and practices in hand, HR professionals can design and implement programs and services that enhance employee productivity and performance and lead to overall organizational improvement.

Engage in Professional HR Sub-roles

The final step in becoming a strategic business partner is to engage in three sub-roles—influencer, strategist, and problem solver. Awareness of these sub-roles gives the HR professional the ability to respond to unforeseen contingencies, to provide appropriate solutions to complex, sensitive issues, and to conduct a wide range of activities designed to modify or enhance results.

As *influencers* HR professionals are directive in their efforts to influence client thinking, initiate change, or provide specific recommendations that address difficult performance problems. In order to be successful as an influencer, it is important to remain receptive to others' views, ideas, and recommendations. HR professionals should guard against letting their own personal biases and opinions overpower those of others. At the same time, a good influencer encourages organizational members to take risks to achieve their goals and objectives.

As *strategists* HR professionals are responsible for assessing organizational needs, using quantitative and qualitative methodologies, developing and executing business initiatives, and evaluating the effectiveness of performance-improvement interventions and other change initiatives. Additionally, strategists incorporate the ideas of others into directive action plans.

When HR professionals take an active role in the decision-making and change-management process, they are serving as *problem solvers*. In this sub-role, they spend most of their time helping clients make decisions that are beneficial to achieving desired results. Problem solvers strive to make certain that the perceived problem is indeed the one critical to the organization.

These sub-roles are very common ones used by change management and organization development consultants such as Deloitte & Touche, William M. Mercer, Inc., and Towers Perrin.

CONCLUSION

Strategic business partnerships satisfy the needs of internal and external clients alike, while positioning HR professionals in a more positive light within the organization. The principal benefit for organizations is improved performance and efficiency, while HR professionals enjoy increased credibility and influence within the company.

"Because recruiting new leaders is difficult (if not impossible), it is important to use a process to transform the people whom companies already have in place." David L. Dotlich

The Balanced Scorecard
by Robert S. Kaplan and David P. Norton

EXECUTIVE SUMMARY

- The Balanced Scorecard is a powerful framework for aligning strategic objectives, management systems, and corporate performance, resulting in robust long-term growth and value creation.
- Implementing the Balanced Scorecard successfully is a function of five core principles: mobilizing change through executive leadership; translating strategy into operational terms; aligning the organization to the strategy; making strategy everyone's everyday job; and making strategy a continual process.
- The Balanced Scorecard enables organizations to become more adaptive and responsive to the needs of both internal and external constituencies, resulting in greater opportunities for problem solving and innovation.

INTRODUCTION

The Balanced Scorecard is a performance measurement and management system using objectives and measures in four inter-related perspectives—financial, customer, internal process, and learning and growth. We introduced the Balanced Scorecard in the early 1990s because we believed that an exclusive reliance on financial measures in a management system would be insufficient for the 21st century. Strategies for creating value had shifted from managing tangible assets to knowledge-based strategies that created and deployed an organization's intangible assets, including customer relationships, innovative products and services, high-quality operating processes, and the skills, knowledge, and motivation of its workforce.

Organizations such as Mobil North American Marketing and Refining, Cigna Property and Casualty Insurance, Brown and Root Engineering Services, and Chemical (Chase) Bank implemented the Balanced Scorecard, embedded it into their management systems, and achieved breakthrough performance within two years. Our research has revealed a set of five principles, built around the Balanced Scorecard system, that enabled these and other organizations to execute their strategies rapidly.

Principle 1: Mobilize Change Through Executive Leadership
The single most important condition for success is the ownership and active involvement of the executive team. A Balanced Scorecard program starts with the recognition that it is not a "metrics" project; it's a change project. Initially, executive

leaders must *mobilize* the organization, creating momentum to get the process launched. Once mobilized, leadership focus shifts to *governance* to install the new performance model. Gradually a new management system evolves—a *strategic management system* that institutionalizes the new cultural values and processes into a new system for managing. Convergence to the system can take two to three years.

Principle 2: Translate the Strategy into Operational Terms
The objectives and measures on a Balanced Scorecard help executive teams to better understand and articulate their strategies. The scorecard provides a framework for organizing strategic objectives into four perspectives:

1. *Financial*—the strategy for growth, profitability, and risk, viewed from the perspective of the stockholder.
2. *Customer*—the strategy for creating value and differentiation from the perspective of the customer.
3. *Internal Business Processes*—the strategic priorities for various business processes that create customer and stockholder satisfaction.
4. *Learning and Growth*—the priorities to create a climate that supports organizational change, innovation, and growth.

From work done with an initial set of implementers, we developed a strategy map to provide a graphical representation of a well-constructed Balanced Scorecard. A strategy map, a logical and comprehensive architecture for describing strategy, specifies the critical elements and their linkages for an organization's strategy. It creates a common

point of reference for all organization units and their employees.

Organizations build strategy maps from the top down, starting with the destination and then charting the routes that lead there. Corporate executives first review their mission statement (why their company exists) and core values (what their company believes in). From that information, they develop their strategic vision (what their company wants to become). This vision creates a clear picture of the company's overall goal.

Once the strategy map has been defined and agreed to by the executive team, the design of a scorecard with measures and targets is a straightforward process. The strategy map approach illustrates the idea that Balanced Scorecards should not just be collections of financial and non-financial measures organized into four perspectives. Balanced Scorecards should reflect the strategy of the organization. A good test is whether you can understand the strategy by looking only at the scorecard and its strategy map.

Principle 3: Align the Organization to the Strategy
The Balanced Scorecard is a powerful tool to describe a business unit's strategy. But organizations consist of numerous sectors, business units, and specialized departments, each with its own operations and often its own strategy. For synergy to occur across these diverse units, the strategies across these units need to be coordinated. The Balanced Scorecard helps to define the strategic linkages that integrate the performance of multiple organizations. Each unit formulates a strategy appropriate for its target market in light of the specific circumstances it faces—competitors, market opportunities, and critical processes—but that is consistent with the themes and priorities of the corporation or division. The measures at the individual business unit levels do not have to add to a corporate or divisional measure, unlike financial measures that aggregate easily from sub-units to departments to higher organizational levels. The business unit managers choose local measures that *influence*, but are not necessarily identical to, the corporate scorecard measures.

Beyond aligning the business units,

"It is an immutable law in business that words are words, explanations are explanations, promises are promises—but only performance is reality."

Harold S. Geneen

strategy-focused organizations must also align their staff functions and shared-service units, such as human resources, information technology, purchasing, environmental, and finance. Often this alignment is accomplished with a service agreement between each functional department and the business units. The service agreement defines the menu of services to be provided, including their functionality, quality level and cost.

When this process is complete, all the organizational units—line business units and staff functions—have well-defined strategies that are articulated and measured by Balanced Scorecards and strategy maps. This alignment allows corporate-level synergies to emerge, in which the whole exceeds the sum of the individual parts.

Linkages can also be established across corporate boundaries to define relationships with key suppliers, customers, outsourcing vendors and joint ventures. Companies use such scorecards with external parties to be explicit about (1) the objectives of the relationship and (2) how to measure the contribution of each party to the relationship in ways other than just price or cost.

Principle 4: Make Strategy Everyone's Everyday Job

The C.E.O.s and senior leadership teams of organizations that adopted the Balanced Scorecard understood that they could not implement the new strategy by themselves. They wanted contributions from everyone in the organization. This is not top-down *direction*. This is top-down *communication* and bottom-up *implementation*. Three processes are required:

- **Use communication and education to create awareness**. A prerequisite for implementing strategy is that all employees understand the strategy. A consistent and continuing communication program is the foundation for organizational alignment.

- **Align personal objectives with the strategy**. Companies challenge individuals and departments at lower levels to develop their own objectives in light of the broader priorities; in some cases, personal scorecards are used to set *personal objectives*.

- **Link compensation to the scorecard**. To modify behavior as required by the strategy and as defined in the scorecard, change *must* be reinforced through incentive compensation. When the incentive compensation program becomes

linked to the Balanced Scorecard, interest in the details of the strategy increases.

Principle 5: Make Strategy a Continual Process

Companies adopt a new "double-loop process" to manage strategy. The first step *links strategy to the budgeting process*. Managers use the Balanced Scorecard as a screen to evaluate potential investments and initiatives that will develop entirely new capabilities, reach new customers and markets, and make radical improvements in existing processes and capabilities. This distinction is essential. Just as the Balanced Scorecard attempts to protect long-term objectives from short-term sub-optimization, the budgeting process must protect the long-term initiatives from the pressures to deliver short-term financial performance.

The second step introduces a *simple management meeting* to review strategy. As obvious as this step sounds, such meetings didn't exist in the past. Now management meetings are scheduled on a monthly or quarterly basis to discuss the Balanced Scorecard, so that a broad spectrum of managers comes together to monitor organizational performance against the short-term targets for the scorecard's financial and non-financial measures. This process creates a focus on the strategy that did not exist before.

Information feedback systems change to support the new management meetings. Many organizations create an *open reporting* environment, in which performance results are made available to everyone in the organization. Building upon the principle that "strategy is everyone's job," they empower "everyone" by giving them the knowledge needed to do their jobs.

Finally, a *process for learning and adapting the strategy* evolves. As the scorecard is put into action and feedback systems begin their reporting on actual results, the organization tests the hypotheses underlying its strategy, to see whether the strategy is delivering the expected results.

A new kind of energy is created. People use terms like "fun" and "exciting" to describe the management meetings. One senior executive reported that the meetings became so popular, there was standing room only . . . he could have sold tickets to them.

Companies also use the meetings to search for new strategic opportunities that aren't currently on their scorecard. New challenges arise externally, and ideas and learning emerge internally from within

the organization. Rather than waiting for next year's budget cycle, the priorities and the scorecards are updated immediately. Much like a navigator guiding a vessel on a long-term journey, constantly sensing the shifting winds and currents and constantly adapting the course, the executives of successful companies use the ideas and learning generated by their organization to fine-tune their strategies. Instead of being an annual event, strategy formulation, testing, and revision became a continual process.

CONCLUSION

The Balanced Scorecard enables organizations to introduce a new governance and review process—one focused on strategy, not tactics. The new governance process emphasizes learning, team problem solving, and coaching. Review meetings look into the future—exploring how to implement strategy more effectively, and identifying the changes to be made to the strategy—based on what has been learned.

This is a management process attuned to the needs of contemporary businesses. The essential ingredient is a simple framework—the Balanced Scorecard and its representation on a strategy map—that allows strategy to be clearly articulated. The Balanced Scorecard becomes the heart of the management system that strategy-focused organizations will use to build their future.

FOR MORE INFORMATION

Books and Journal Articles:
Kaplan, Robert, and David Norton. "Having Trouble with Your Strategy? Then Map It." *Harvard Business Review* (September–October 2000).
Kaplan, Robert, and David Norton. *The Strategy-focused Organization: How Balanced Scorecard Companies Thrive in the New Business Environment.* Cambridge, MA: Harvard Business School Press, 2000.
Kaplan, Robert, and David Norton. *The Balanced Scorecard: Translating Strategy into Action.* Cambridge, MA: Harvard Business School Press, 1996.

Web site:
www.bscol.com: the Balanced Scorecard Collaborative's Web site.

See also:
✔ Implementing the Balanced Scorecard (pp. 566–567)

"The balanced scorecard is not a way of formalizing strategy. It's a way of understanding and checking what you have to do throughout the organization to make your strategy work."

Robert Kaplan

Setting Objectives for a Business
by Allan A. Kennedy

EXECUTIVE SUMMARY

- Managing inherently involves setting a goal or objective and then executing a series of actions to meet it. Establishing the right objective is critical to successful management of any business.
- Successful long-term businesses almost always started with a set of nonfinancial objectives (sometimes referred to as a vision or mission) and derived financial objectives consistent with pursuit of their broader goals.
- Setting only financial objectives is risky for a business because single-minded pursuit of financial objectives can lead to actions that undermine long-term viability.

INTRODUCTION

Managing is the task of moving an enterprise toward a defined objective. Most of the disciplines of management—budgeting, strategic planning, performance monitoring—take as a given that an appropriate objective has been set. Given the central role that objectives or targets play in most management actions, it is critical that they be set correctly. It may seem trite to point out, but it is none the less valid: if inappropriate objectives are set for a business, inappropriate outcomes will occur.

What constitutes appropriate objectives for a business? As business and management have evolved, thinking about what constitutes an appropriate objective has evolved as well. Throughout this evolution, there has been an ongoing tension between financial goals and objectives and nonfinancial objectives. If business exists primarily or solely to make a profit (a highly quantifiable outcome) then relatively simple financial objectives suffice, argue some. Others say that business exists to serve simultaneously the needs of various constituencies—stockholders, customers, suppliers, employees, communities. The interests of these various legitimate constituencies are not always quantifiable, leading to a school of thought that puts greater emphasis on nonfinancial objectives. The history of business would suggest that both types of objectives are important.

A BRIEF HISTORY OF BUSINESS OBJECTIVES

Most businesses that were launched in the 19th century began their life as some form of family enterprise. As family businesses,

their objectives were quite clear: to provide an ongoing source of income and, where necessary, employment for current and future members of the family.

As the technology of management has evolved, ideas about what constitutes the right objective for a business have changed. In his book *Concept of the Corporation*, first published in 1946, Peter Drucker described the purpose of a corporation as generating the maximum profit achievable from its operations. He went on to comment on the potential conflict between this purpose and society's expectation that the job of business was to maximize the production of cheap goods and services for consumption. To a modern observer, Drucker's thinking seems simplistic.

Drucker based his comments on work he had done with General Motors (GM), then the largest industrial enterprise in the world. The people he worked with in GM were convinced he got it wrong. To set the record straight, the legendary leader of General Motors from 1923 until 1946, Alfred P. Sloan, Jr., wrote his own account of the GM system of management, which he called *My Years with General Motors*. In that book, Sloan described a high-level task force effort he led in 1920 to define the concept of GM's business. He articulated a purpose for GM's business quite different from Drucker's version. "We made the assumption . . . that the first purpose in . . . establishment of a business [is that it] will pay *satisfactory* dividends and *preserve* and *increase* its capital value" [emphasis added].

As a reflection of Sloan's influence in the business world, in the 1950s and 1960s most businesses sought to operate with a conservative balance sheet while showing

steady signs of growth in sales, assets, profits, dividends, and stockholder equity.

During the 1950s and 1960s, new types of companies emerged on the familiar business landscape. These companies were young, entrepreneurial, and managed by hands-on practitioners, each in his own fashion on a mission. This new breed included the likes of Hewlett-Packard, a company set up to make useful technical contributions in a variety of engineering markets. It also included companies like Wal-Mart, whose driving rationale was providing superior value to its customers.

All of these new companies were in business to make a profit, both as a return to their investors and as a measure of the value of what they were doing as a company. These financial objectives were, however, secondary to their broader institutional objectives. Because many of these new companies grew very rapidly and became, relatively speaking, darlings of the stock market, many established companies modified their traditional objectives to focus on achieving specified levels of growth in revenues and profits in an attempt to keep pace.

In the late 1970s, a new theory about appropriate objectives for business was developed by academics specializing in the complex area of accounting. Their theory held that since stockholders owned companies, the real objective of business should be maximizing stockholder value. They went on to point out that conventional accounting measures of profitability, such as earnings per share of public companies, were very poor proxies indeed for the true value of a company. Instead they urged businesspeople to focus on the present value of future cash-flow streams as a truer measure of value. Most managers ignored this advice for all practical purposes, but some specialized investment bankers, who came to be known as "corporate raiders" or "leveraged buyout bankers," took the insights of the academics very seriously.

The immediate result was an unprecedented wave of corporate takeovers during the 1980s. The longer-term result was a fundamental rethinking of what business was all about by most managers, as they adopted stockholder-value thinking as

BEST PRACTICE

a means of defending themselves from the corporate raiders.

Throughout the 1990s and into the 2000s, maximizing stockholder value was the driving purpose of most businesses, and managers did virtually anything they could to ensure that their stock price—the most direct proxy for stockholder value—rose steadily.

LIMITATIONS OF RELYING SOLELY ON FINANCIAL OBJECTIVES

The stock market boom of the 1990s seemed to prove that focusing on stockholder value was the right way to run a business. But the boom of the 1990s gave way to the economic slowdown and stock market corrections of 2000 and 2001. With the change in the business climate, the problems associated with over-reliance on maximizing stockholder value became apparent. With an exclusive focus on rewarding stockholders, many companies simply failed to take care of the legitimate needs of the other constituencies they depended on to provide them with a profitable future. Many of these concerns have persisted with legislation (such as the Sarbanes-Oxley Act in the United States) striving to protect groups such as stockholders. Despite these measures, many other constituencies have rebelled.

Employees, having been treated as commodities by the companies they worked for, stopped being loyal to their employers and sold their services to the highest bidder. Especially for high tech companies in places like Silicon Valley, this change in the labor marketplace forced employers to pay top dollar to get the talent they needed, and left them saddled with the costs inherent in a high-turnover workforce.

Suppliers, who had been forced to accept lower and lower prices for providing ever-increasing amounts of service to their customers, banded together in a last-ditch effort to survive. In some very important sectors like the automobile industry, this led to more concentrated groups of suppliers who had more market power than the customers they served.

Customers, whose choices had been limited by companies intent on pruning product lines and closing outlets to produce higher immediate profits, responded by steadily reducing their loyalty to brands and increasingly shopping for the lowest price available, regardless of the consequences for the companies that supplied them.

Governments, which had once bent over backwards to entice companies to invest, increasingly eliminated investment subsidies and began negotiating tighter and tighter

agreements and strictly enforcing the terms of these agreements.

The net effect of these changes in the business environment is that the path to future growth and profitability is compromised for many of the companies that so excelled in their pursuit of stockholder value.

THE STAYING POWER OF NONFINANCIAL OBJECTIVES

Why do some companies seem to thrive over a very long period of time, while others have a brief moment in the sun and then recede into obscurity? There are a number of factors that account for this long-term pattern of success, including leadership, the quality of management, and the dynamics of the markets they serve. James Collins and Jerry Porras in their landmark book, *Built to Last*, suggest there is one common element. Companies that thrive for a long time all have a nonfinancial vision of what they are in business to accomplish. The 3M company exists to create useful products through innovation. Boeing exists to be at the leading edge of the aeronautics field. Marriott has a mission to make its customers feel like they have a home away from home. Johnson & Johnson exists to help alleviate pain and suffering. All of these companies, and the others cited by Collins and Porras, also work hard to make a profit and return value to their stockholders. However, producing profits and generating value for their stockholders was a byproduct of the broader objectives each of these companies sought to pursue.

Why this should be so is actually quite simple. Most people who work for companies need a broader goal than purely a financial one to motivate them to perform at their best. The companies profiled by Collins and Porras provided their people with just such a broader mission, treated them as full partners in the pursuit of this broader goal, and as a result realized higher levels of commitment and motivation from them. The companies reward this higher level of commitment and loyalty with policies appropriate to maintaining an ongoing partnership. To be viable and successful, every business must set and work hard to achieve a series of financial goals and objectives. But having financial objectives alone will not produce superior performance over the long term.

MAKING IT HAPPEN ▶▶
How can a manager at any level of business decide whether or not the objectives set for the business are sound?

There are no firm rules to rely on, but there are some common-sense tests any manager can apply to determine whether the objectives set are:

- compelling—capable of getting someone's attention;
- motivating—likely to inspire someone to put in extra effort;
- consistent—able to be met without compromise;
- achievable—reachable with reasonable levels of effort and commitment;
- distinguishing—something that when achieved will set the company or business apart from others;
- competitively superior—difficult enough to attain so that the achievement will produce superior rewards from the markets served and the investing public;
- satisfying—of such a nature that the achievement of the objective will produce a personal sense of satisfaction among those who contributed;
- lasting—likely to pass the test of time.

Tests like these are applicable to financial as well as nonfinancial objectives.

CONCLUSION

Making a profit and delivering value to stockholders is motivating indeed for anyone engaged in business. However, it is simply not a sufficient motivator to produce the kind of extra effort over a long period of time that produces superior long-term performance.

FOR MORE INFORMATION

Books:
Collins, James C., and Jerry I. Porras. *Built to Last*. New York: HarperBusiness, 2004.
Davidson, Bill. *Breakthrough: How Great Companies Set Outrageous Objectives—and Achieve Them* New York: Wiley, 2003.
Drucker, Peter F. *Concept of the Corporation*. Reprint. Somerset, NJ: Transaction Publishers, 2001.
Alfred P. Sloan. *My Years with General Motors*. Reissue. New York: Doubleday, 1996.
Roberts, John. *The Modern Firm: Organisational Design for Performance and Growth*. New York: Oxford University Press, 2004.

See also:
☆ Who's Guiding Your Corporate Destiny? (pp. 255–257)

"The goal of a big business person should be to create a new organization that feels and operates like a smaller business, yet retains the resource advantages of big business."

John P. Kotter

Viewpoint: Paul Hawken
Social Entrepreneurship: A Model for Sustainable Growth

Introduction

Paul Hawken is an environmentalist, entrepreneur, and bestselling author, widely respected for his ideas on how corporations can achieve sustainable, ecologically-sound development. His latest book, written with Amory and Hunter Lovins, is *Natural Capitalism: Creating the Next Industrial Revolution.* In it, Paul Hawken highlights the costs and consequences of 200 hundred years of industrial development, introducing four strategies necessary to perpetuate abundance, avert scarcity, and deliver a solid basis for social development. In this article, he argues that a whole range of natural resources and heritage—from the human genome to water and the airwaves—are being dominated by corporations, and he outlines the consequences of this development.

The Antiglobalization Movement Is Really the Fight against the Corporatization of the Commons

The people who are arguing most articulately and vociferously against globalization are protesting the "corporatization of the commons." These commons that are being corporatized include the human genome, seeds, water, food, airwaves, media, and if the draft agendas of the World Trade Organization and other bodies are passed, much more. The commons include stories, music, and culture as well. They include place and self-determination. They include the ability for people to decide what is and what isn't acceptable as a product in a certain locality or region or place. They include tradition. All these areas are being taken over or corrupted by corporations.

Corporatization is caused by the unending and pressing mandate for corporations to grow their capital. If a corporation doesn't grow its capital, there is no change in value—in fact, there would be a loss of value. Furthermore, if financial capital and shareholder value does not grow, then the leaders of a corporation are replaced. Managing a large corporation is like being on a gerbil wheel. As soon as the wheel slows down to a certain level, a new gerbil with fresh legs is brought in.

Not so long ago, if a C.E.O. led a company with a 7 or 8% return on investment, that was considered to be a creditable performance, and they could keep their job. Now, 7 or 8% is seen as unsatisfactory, often leading to a C.E.O. being quickly replaced by someone who promises greater returns. What kind of world is it where, in the words of Hazel Henderson, "capital is divine?" It's a world where capital has the right to grow, and it's a higher right than those of people, cultures, places, and qualities that historically have been our commons. What happens is you have a corporate sector that is way overdeveloped, possessing enormous over capacity.

Corporations are seeking new areas in which they can grow, and they're going into areas that just weren't imagined before. Corporations are continuing to colonize, whether they realize it or not, and this is an extension of Western cultural exploitation that goes back 500 years. This new weight of colonization is having disastrous results. For example, many major multinational utilities want to effectively privatize water supply in many parts of the world. Similarly, three of the world's largest biotechnology corporations want to control 90% of the germplasm of 90% of the caloric food intake of the world. Ted Turner said that in the end there will only be two media companies in the world, and he wants to have a stake in one of them. Rupert Murdoch thinks the same way. McDonald's opens up 2,400 restaurants a year. Right now, one out of every five meals in the United States is fast food, and McDonalds wants that to be the case everywhere in the world. Coke says that it has 10% of the total liquid intake of the world, and its goal is to go to 20%. Or is it 30%? These are absurd and devastating goals for corporations.

These challenges are being answered by people who are suffering, not simply by white middle-class protestors in Quebec, Genoa, and Seattle. In many places in the world where corporations are trying to implement their visions of how to grow capital, they are meeting resistance. They will continue to meet resistance from the world as long as they try to colonize what people have held in common throughout the history of humankind.

The Corporatization of the World Means a Disastrous Loss of Diversity

The way to create healthy, vibrant economies and societies is through diversity. We know that scientifically. Any system that loses its diversity loses its resiliency and is more subject to sudden shocks and changes from which it can't recover. The corporatization of the world is the loss of diversity—it's forcing uniformity upon people. As Arnold Toynbee said, the sign of a civilization in decay is the institution of uniformity and the lack of diversity.

And that's exactly what we're seeing, only it is called "harmonization." The degree to which a company or a corporation honors diversity and then allows it to emerge from a place, a country, locale, culture, tribe, or city is a good thing. The degree to which it tries to enforce a one-size-fits-all formulaic solution to diet or media or agriculture is, in my

"Capitalism, as practised, is a financially profitable, non-sustainable aberration in human development."

Paul Hawken

opinion, going to be seen in hindsight as just as much a criminal act as the deracination of indigenous people by the Spaniards, the genocide of Native Americans, or the enslavement of African Americans. We look back at those things now and feel ashamed. We will look back at what we are doing right now to the world and see it as a violation of humanity.

The economic principle of subsidiarity says that decisions, whether they be economic or political, should always be made at the smallest or closest unit relevant to the issue at hand, because those are the people who not only have the most at stake but who also have the experience and knowledge with which to make an intelligent decision. Of course there are problems with subsidiarity when there's a breakdown like in the Congo or Rwanda. Nevertheless, subsidiarity within a true democratic system is the proper way to make economic decisions.

Rather than talking about globalization, we should be talking about the localization and interdependence of economies. Those corporations that help with localization should do very well. For example, energy companies should introduce technologies to create local sufficiency with respect to energy, to the degree that it is possible. Whether it is a global company or not, it is a company that is helping a region, a locality, a city, or a village. A company that introduces the means to increase self-sufficiency is doing even better. A company that seeks to dominate local economies—to buy out, take over, or make that economy or country dependent on them—is violating humane economic principles.

We'll Remember the Social Entrepreneurs and not the Business People

It is true that this view of the corporation is not a very charitable assessment. Can I imagine corporations as brilliantly adaptive and helpful? I don't have to imagine it: there are 70,000 or 80,000 companies in the United States alone that are doing fantastic work with respect to society, the environment, energy, agriculture, and water. And there are more companies all over the world that are acting similarly. It's just that I can't think of any that are listed on the New York Stock Exchange or appear in the *Fortune* 500. I don't think real solutions scale up in the way that large corporations do.

The truly innovative acts of entrepreneurship that are occurring now and will continue to occur are no longer in business. Social entrepreneurship: that's where the action is. That's where the real innovators are. That's where you'll find the people who will be remembered 50 to 100 years from now. We won't remember a single person who's in business except as a footnote.

Apple says, "Think different." Who are they talking about? People like Gandhi, Einstein, Muhammad Ali. They're talking about people who actually took care of other people, who cared and were compassionate. I've asked myself, when will the Rosa Parks of the business world step up and sit at the front of the bus? It would take an amazing person to do that. Essentially, that person would say that we have marched too long in lockstep with policies and assumptions that are harmful. It's time that we spoke the truth about what we do, about what happens to us as people, about the enormous polarization of wealth, about how we treat people, and about how globalization is a race to the bottom, enforced by rules that nobody agreed to. We'll remember that person, but I don't think they'd have a job for very long.

This essay was adapted from an interview undertaken with Mr. Hawken by Peter Leyden, knowledge developer at Global Business Network (www.gbn.com). The publishers gratefully acknowledge the support of Global Business Network in making these ideas and insights available.

"Sustainable business must be built on recognition of fundamental economic laws. That must include an acknowledgment of competition, of its positive benefits and the severe penalties it can exact."

Mark Moody-Stuart

Profiting From Prices
by Michael de Kare-Silver

EXECUTIVE SUMMARY

- In an attempt to boost profits, many companies have tried to reduce costs through reengineering, outsourcing, downsizing, etc.
- Companies are becoming aware of the opportunity and potential of the top line (as opposed to the bottom line).
- Pricing is an undiscovered weapon in the search for higher revenues.

INTRODUCTION

In recent years many companies have not found it easy to increase revenues. Economic conditions, government policies against inflation, increased competition on pricing (including producers from less-developed countries), and globally more sophisticated customers have all put pressure on volume and price in many industries. Not surprisingly, companies have turned to levers more directly in their control—such as reducing costs and better process management—as sources of profit growth. Hence the fads and focuses on reengineering, downsizing, outsourcing, etc.

But those cost/process levers can only go so far in boosting profits. As their markets strive for growth, companies are increasingly challenging revenue performance and realizing that the top line has not received the same close examination and insight as the bottom line in recent times. There is a growing awakening to the fact that more opportunity and potential may lie on the top line.

What can be realistically achieved? Is the search for higher revenues a futile battle against macro-economic forces and competitive pressures? Analysis shows the contrary. Pricing, especially, is an undiscovered weapon. There is significant profit potential for companies in challenging this area, and in "reengineering" their price position.

OPPORTUNITIES IN PRICING

Research shows two almost contradictory key facts. First, 28% of the top 100 U.K. companies have failed to grow revenues in real terms in the past five years. But, second, the majority (56%) of C.E.O.s in an interview program agreed that:
- insufficient attention is given to challenging revenue opportunities, especially in pricing;
- significant profit upside remains untapped in the pricing area.

Looking at pricing is, in principle, much more attractive than downsizing. There are no severance costs, no people/organization issues, no impact next Monday morning: a quick win flows straight through to the bottom line.

In any event, opportunities to improve profitability principally through cost and process management may have peaked for the time being. Many reengineering projects have disappointed. Research among U.K. and U.S. companies shows that:
- no more than two in ten companies achieve breakthrough improvements in performance;
- less than 30% claim to be satisfied with either the change process itself or the results.

ROUTES TO EFFECTIVE PRICING

The more you know about which products make money and which lose, the more you can adopt a better strategic and selective pricing policy. Three main routes can be identified that lead to more effective pricing:
- exploiting market advantages
- changing the decision-making process on pricing
- testing whether all the different pricing options are being proactively pursued.

Of course, some companies enjoy market or structural circumstances that make pricing management easier. Have they just fallen by luck into those situations, or have their advantages been "engineered" more deliberately? Some companies have used strategic alliances to create market and structural barriers deliberately—by locking up a vital supply of raw materials, say, and making it hard for others to function. Procter & Gamble thus used an alliance to tie up the Japanese supplier of scarce polyacrylate material. As a result, it was able to block competitors and recover market leadership.

Even without market or structural advantage, significant untapped pricing potential exists. How can this be exploited? Many factors are *prima facie* within executive control, and can be changed to enable more effective pricing management. For example, internal structures could be adjusted to facilitate more effective pricing. Several roadblocks operate within the organization—such as:
- responsibility for pricing is left to the sales department. (Who has ever met a salesman who wanted to increase prices?);
- there is little or no finance department involvement to balance decision making;
- senior management's remoteness from the detailed market circumstances makes it difficult to challenge sales views;
- no systems/mechanisms are available to easily assess more aggressive pricing opportunities;
- data on the true net profitability of individual services/products to either company or customer is limited.

Indeed, not only could companies make structural moves that are more easily within their control; research shows that as many as 12 different pricing strategies are available. They often appear to be under-exploited. The challenge is frequently not lack of familiarity with the particular pricing option. It is more about:
- having enough management time to check whether the particular pricing options have been fully considered;
- understanding the pricing relationship to competitors and what drives it;
- examining price opportunities and developing insights on an *individual* product line basis, rather than across a range;
- management's ability to challenge sales-led pricing decisions;
- the effectiveness and rigor with which the pricing strategies are implemented;
- the information base and systems needed to do all this.

PRICING STRATEGIES

Many of the 12 different pricing strategy options are geared to medium/long-term profit-building; few can have immediate effect. They fall into three main groups:

- customer information management
- exploiting structural advantages
- innovation and leadership.

Customer Information Management

There are four approaches to consider:

1 **Category segmentation**: use detailed product-line profitability and pricing to achieve analysis and insight, developed separately for *each* product line.
2 **Customer segmentation**: use detailed customer segmentation to identify pricing opportunities.
3 **Bundling**: in medical products, as core product/service prices have come under pressure, companies have added related products and services where pricing is more robust (and which equally reinforce the core product/service value proposition). Similarly, some leading Internet software suppliers provide free access software but charge for use of related products and services.
4 **Trade terms management**: manage the level of discounts given to customers to get a better return.

Exploiting Structural Advantages

Four options are highlighted here:

1 **Lowest cost/lowest price**: cost advantages enable invaders to price lower and grow share rapidly.
2 **Supply and demand management**: as an illustration, better hotel occupancy/yield management systems have enabled leaders to quote more aggressive room tariffs.
3 **Supplier–customer "balance of power"**: this can be exploited to ensure that suppliers "contribute" to gross margin success. Tough management of the supply price provides greater flexibility in end-consumer pricing.
4 **"Open-book" and partnership-pricing**: the open-book approach was pioneered in the automotive industry. Sharing information about costs has enabled better suppliers to justify and push through selective price increases.

Innovation and Leadership

This area offers two zones of higher comfort:

1 **Branding**: consistent high levels of branding and advertising enable a company to maintain a price premium.
2 **Total value proposition**: where five strategies can be singled out:

Technology-driven: continuous development of niche, technically advanced products can give strong gross margin advantages.

First in: continual focus on being first to market gives initial pricing advantages, as well as other benefits.

Best at: leadership on all features valued by the customer can give price leadership in both "value pricing" of certain products and "premium pricing" for certain others.

Share leadership: restructuring the product portfolio to focus only on market share leaders where you have more control over pricing and other levers.

Innovative consumer value: provide a clear mixing of quality, value, and service to lead in the eyes of the customer.

There are at least a couple of shorter-term options, too:

1 **Price squeeze**: in one turnaround, the new C.E.O. insisted that each product-line price be "squeezed" up 1%. Despite initial internal resistance, this was successfully implemented, immediately impacting the bottom line.
2 **Price elasticity**: is the price/volume equation effectively analyzed and balanced? For example, low-margin products can be priced up relatively aggressively with less impact on contribution from any volume lost.

Research shows that many of these pricing strategies are in fact applicable in most industries and most company situations, but that surprisingly few are being proactively investigated and implemented.

USING PRICING OPPORTUNITIES

How can a company check whether it is fully utilizing its pricing opportunities? This initial checklist looks first internally—for example at the priority that pricing decision making has in the organization:

1 What percentage of senior management time is spent on pricing?
2 How much senior management time is spent with customers?
3 Is there an information base in place which tracks pricing for each product line and its relationship with volume?
4 Is competitor pricing tracked in similar detail?
5 How frequently is pricing specifically and rigorously reviewed?
6 Is the company organized in a way that ensures that a "balanced" pricing decision is made?

The other questions are directed at the external market potential:

1 Are competitors' future pricing strategies and plans understood?
2 Is there a clear understanding and alignment between what the company sees as added value, compared to what the customer sees?

3 Does the company have a clear pricing strategy differentiated for the circumstances and market position of each product group and each customer?

As global competition intensifies, close attention to the detail, the "micro-management," will become increasingly important. "Discovering" pricing and systematizing its proactive exploitation in the business will become a key distinguishing factor among the more successful corporations.

CONCLUSION

Price decisions are too often made by too few people. Only by sharing the responsibility for pricing can managers begin to understand the importance that pricing can have on the success of any business. Ultimately, decisions on pricing must be measured against other critical factors, such as data on customers. In the final analysis, pricing can be an exercise in both innovation and leadership.

FOR MORE INFORMATION

Books:
Dolan, Robert J., and Hermann Simon. *Power Pricing: How Managing Price Transforms the Bottom Line.* New York: Free Press, 1996.
Nagle, Thomas T., and Reed K. Holden. *The Strategy and Tactics of Pricing.* 4th ed. Upper Saddle River, NJ: Pearson, 2005.

"Our policy is to reduce the price, extend the operations and improve the article."

Henry Ford

Viewpoint: Jim Kouzes
Helping Managers Measure Up to the Leadership Challenge

Introduction

Jim Kouzes, along with Barry Posner, has written over a dozen books on leadership, including the bestselling *The Leadership Challenge*, which will appear in its fourth edition in 2007. Based on years of research, involving over 250,000 individual leaders on whom more than one million observers provided feedback, *The Leadership Challenge* is the #1 textbook on leadership, bar none, and the winner of numerous awards and honors. What are the roots of Jim's own view of leadership and does he see the basic shape of leadership changing in the future? Times change, but Jim believes true leadership does not.

If there is one thing I've learned in over three decades of studying and teaching leadership, and in working with numerous outstanding leaders, it's this: *leadership is a relationship.*

So often we treat leadership and teamwork as if they were new phenomena, but we know they're not. Behavioral science research on leadership began during World War II, and while we've learned a great deal since then, most of what we've learned has been built upon the foundations of that early work. It may be oversimplistic to try to summarize over three decades of leadership research in one phrase, but let me be bold enough to give it a try. What we learned in 1940 and what we've learned in 2006 is this: leadership is all about how people mobilize others to struggle for shared aspirations. In order to mobilize others over the long term, especially under conditions of grave hardship, there has to be a relationship between leader and constituent that is grounded in mutual trust and respect.

I'm often asked, "How is leadership different today from what it was when you began your research?" or "How will leadership be different 30 years from now?" Well, there's nothing in the research that would suggest that the practices of leadership were radically different 30 years ago nor that it'll be much different 30 years from now. The *content* of leadership has not changed, but the *context* has changed—and in some cases it's changed dramatically. Each generation, then, has to redefine leadership for its own historical context while accepting that there are fundamentals of human behavior that remain steady and constant. This is not to say that we never learn new methods and techniques or discover new "truths" about our-

selves; we're just saying that we shouldn't be reinventing the leadership wheel every few years.

It's so easy to confuse changing times with unchanging fundamentals. For example, today many seem to think that the Internet will change everything. Well, it makes sense in some ways, but not when it comes to leadership. For example, looking back to the time when the telephone was first invented, someone then might have said that bold leadership is connected to using the telephone. Put a phone on everyone's desk! Put a phone in everyone's home! Hook people up to long distance; enable them to converse across the globe, anytime, anywhere. That'll make them higher performers. That sounds silly now, but it's equivalent to what's been going on with the Internet. Are we better off because we have the telephone? Certainly. Are we better off because we have the Internet. Absolutely. Is the telephone or the Internet the secret to better leadership? Not in the slightest. The principles of leadership are the same; only the context is different.

Our research indicates that to get extraordinary things done in organizations leaders engage in Five Practices. They "walk the talk"—or "model the way" as we call it—setting an example by their own behavior to show others how the organization can best stay true to its vision and values. They "inspire a

> **It's so easy to confuse changing times with unchanging fundamentals. For example, today many seem to think that the Internet will change everything. Well, it makes sense in some ways, but not when it comes to leadership.**

"I am not the one who transforms the company . . . A company requires a leader, but individually no one can pretend to be the driving force."

Michel Bon

shared vision" of the future that followers deeply believe in and embrace with enthusiasm. They "challenge the process" by searching for opportunities to innovate, change, and grow and by experimenting and taking risks, learning from the accompanying mistakes. They "enable others to act," fostering collaboration and strengthening individual capacity, to make a new vision a new reality. And, lastly, they "encourage the heart"—they recognize individuals for their contributions and then celebrate the community of people who care passionately about the destiny of the enterprise.

Leadership is about relationships. It's about working with and guiding people in new directions. It's about achieving the most positive interaction between customers, employees, shareholders, vendors, and other key stakeholders. Several years ago my co-author, Barry Posner, and I invited Irwin Federman to speak to a group of MBA students at Santa Clara University. Irwin, educated in finance, is a former high-technology C.E.O. and now a partner at U.S. Venture Partners. We've interviewed Irwin for a couple of our books, and we felt he had some important insights to share. Irwin said something that day that continues to cause the hairs on the backs of my neck to stand up.

"You don't love someone because of who they are," he said, "you love them because of the way they make you feel. This axiom applies equally in a company setting." Many students looked a little bewildered by these comments. The word "love" coming from the mouth of a C.E.O. and venture capitalist must have come as quite a surprise. It wasn't a phrase they were likely to have heard in their companies or their classrooms. Indeed, Irwin acknowledged how unusual it was. "It may seem inappropriate to use words such as love and affection in relation to business. Conventional wisdom has it that management is not a popularity contest," he said.

Then he hit them with this: "I contend however that all other things being equal we will work harder and more effectively for people we like. And we will like them in direct proportion to how they make us feel." Irwin has it exactly right. We don't need to read mountains of studies on emotional intelligence to understand the truth of his words. We will work harder and more effectively for people we like. And we will like them in direct proportion to how they make us feel.

Where did I learn this? No one single person taught me my current point of view about leadership, but my father comes close to being the one who influenced me the most.

My father, Tom Kouzes, served the United States for over 30 years. In his final career assignment he was deputy assistant secretary of labor. In addition to his regular job, my dad always loved teaching and training, especially in the field of organizational management. Here I was, growing up in the Washington, D.C. area during my formative years, and my dad would bring home books by people like Peter Drucker and talk about them. He was also fascinated by short, experiential exercises that would help people in training

classes to "feel" the leadership lesson and not just think about it. I'll always remember that.

My mother, Thelma, was also a strong influence on me. At home, I would participate in all kinds of discussions about management and political science and world affairs. My mother was a volunteer at the United Nations and, beginning in 1961, we had foreign students live at our home year-round. She also was very active in the civil rights movement, and even took part with Dr. Martin Luther King in the great march on Washington. Now, it's worth noting that all this was happening before the term "diversity" was the hot concept it is now. I'm so thankful that I learned at a young age how important it is to see leadership issues through a global pair of glasses. Because of a combination of influences like the ones my parents provided (and from all the experiences I had becoming an Eagle Scout), I was determined to join the Peace Corps when I was young. There's no question that my service in Turkey helped me to see the critical importance of leaders—how they can improve the world through social action.

There was one other strong influence. Everything that led me to my career followed the path of the applied behavioral sciences. In fact, I think it's safe to say that everything that we read or hear or see today about leadership has its roots in the applied behavioral sciences.

I was especially influenced by David C. McClelland. His work on *The Achieving Society* was seminal. His research and writing definitely tie to the idea that leadership is about relationships. In fact, Daniel Goleman, who popularized the term "emotional intelligence," was a student of McClelland's at Harvard, and Goleman credits Mc-

> **Everything that led me to my career followed the path of the applied behavioral sciences.**

Clelland as the taproot of his own work. Here's just another example of what is old is new again. McClelland's work is a wonderful starting point for anyone who hopes to lead in the difficult and chaotic years ahead. A leader who is capable of managing relationships constructively must realize that there are basic skills that have to be mastered.

I have to add one other point, however. Leadership is not just about skills, any more than any relationship is just about skills. Credibility is the foundation of all relationships. So, you can have all the skills in the world, but, if people don't believe in you as a person, they simply won't want to follow you. We call it the First Law of Leadership: If you don't *believe in* the messenger, you won't believe the message. When we ask people what credibility is behaviorally, the response can always be summed up in the phrase "Do what you say you will do," or DWYSYWD for short. In other words, for people to want to *willingly* follow someone, they have to observe two things: first, the leader has a clear set of values and beliefs, and, second, the leader's behavior is consistent with those beliefs.

Which leads to another practice that too many lead-

"The leader . . . is the translator, facilitator, the articulating point between the group's genius, who is doing great things, producing big and innovative ideas, and the public, the market."

Warren Bennis

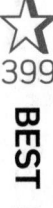
ers discount. Leadership requires self-knowledge. This is a much a more significant point than many first assume. It's amazing how few leaders take the time to answer a very simple but key question: "What do I *really* care about?"

When a leader can answer what it is that he or she really cares about, then it's possible to see the actual leadership face that he or she presents to the rest of the world. Many if not most leaders have some kind of speech about wanting their company to be both profitable and a great place to work. Yet great words in a nice speech are not the same as becoming fully aware of what you really care about. What keeps you awake at night? What ideas or issues grab hold of you and won't let go?

Learn what you really care about and you slowly but surely start to find your leadership voice, to discover your true vision and values.

John Robbins is the son of the co-founder of the Baskin-Robbins ice cream empire. He grew up in a household that sometimes served ice cream for breakfast; he swam in a backyard pool that was shaped like an ice cream cone. But John walked away from all of that. He rejected the lifestyle, and he rejected the production factory approach to how we treat animals. He embraced a whole new lifestyle structured around the profound idea that our diets can help to save our lives and our planet. He is also an eloquent and passionate proponent for a saner approach to how we live, eat, and work in our environment. Now, John didn't wake up one morning with the revelation that this was the way his life should go. He spent 10 years after university on an island, in a one-room log cabin that he and his wife, Deo, built. By being with his thoughts and living a very simple life, he emerged with great clarity about his calling.

Now, I am not advocating that all leaders need to spend a decade alone on an island. But the point to stress is that today's work world is full of so much frenzy, so much noise, that it's nearly impossible for anyone to pause and reflect. But you have to! Winston Churchill, despite all the challenges that confronted him, found time to paint. Guess what he was thinking about when he painted? All great leaders find time to reflect: Lincoln, Gandhi, Martin Luther King. I believe this fervently. Any leader who says I don't have time to reflect is crippling his ability to lead. Why?

People who follow you want a leader who stands for a larger purpose. They want meaningful work, and connecting to a larger purpose ennobles and energizes everyone's efforts. Leadership is about relationships. It's about trust. It's about doing what you say you'll do. So I ask: what do *you* really care about?

> It's amazing how few leaders take the time to answer a very simple but key question: "What do I *really* care about?"

Find the answer to that question and you're on the path to becoming a better leader. Ignore that question, and you're on the road to an empty life. You can't pay people enough to care. People care when they have meaning in their work, when they can connect to a larger purpose. Find a worthy purpose for you and your constituents, and the profits will follow.

FOR MORE INFORMATION

Web site:
Leadership Challenge: **www.leadershipchallenge.com**

See also:
☆ Boosting Business Success through Diversity (pp. 28–29)
☆ Retaining Employees (pp. 229–230)

Emotional Intelligence
by Cary Cherniss and Daniel Goleman

EXECUTIVE SUMMARY

- Emotional intelligence (EI) is the ability to accurately identify and understand one's own emotional reactions and those of others, and to regulate one's emotions and to use them to make good decisions and act effectively.
- The competencies that make the biggest difference in superior individual performance at work are based on EI.
- EI can be improved at any age; in fact, several programs for doing so have been developed and found to be effective.
- However, improving EI takes considerable time and effort.
- To be effective, training and development efforts need to incorporate a number of elements.

INTRODUCTION

Ever since the publication of Daniel Goleman's first book on the topic in 1995, emotional intelligence has become one of the hottest buzz phrases in the corporate world. Many business leaders have found compelling the basic idea that success is strongly influenced by personal qualities such as perseverance, self-control, and skill in getting along with others. They point to sales persons who have an uncanny ability to sense what is most important to the customers and to develop a trusting relationship with them. They also point to customer service employees who excel when it comes to helping angry customers calm down and be more reasonable. Conversely, they point to brilliant executives who do everything well except get along with people, and to managers who are technically brilliant but cannot handle stress, and whose careers are stalled because of these deficiencies.

Many studies have confirmed that the so-called "soft skills" are critical for a vital economy. For instance, the influential report of the United States Secretary of Labor's Commission on Achieving Necessary Skills argued that a high-performance workplace requires workers who have a solid foundation not only in literacy and computation, but also in personal qualities such as responsibility, self-esteem, sociability, self-management, integrity, and honesty (Secretary's Commission on Achieving Necessary Skills, 1991). Emotional intelligence is the basis for these competencies.

But what exactly is "emotional intelligence?" What is the link between emotional intelligence and organizational effectiveness? Is it possible for adults to become more socially and emotionally competent? And finally, what is the best way to help individuals to do so?

WHAT IS EMOTIONAL INTELLIGENCE AND WHY IS IT IMPORTANT?

Emotional intelligence is the ability to accurately identify and understand one's own emotional reactions and those of others. It also includes the ability to regulate one's emotions and to use them to make good decisions and act effectively. EI provides the bedrock for many competencies that are critical for effective performance in the workplace. For instance, one's effectiveness in influencing others depends on one's ability to connect with them on an emotional level, and to understand what they are feeling and why. To effectively influence others we also need to be able to manage our own emotions.

CAN ADULTS BECOME MORE EMOTIONALLY INTELLIGENT?

Many managers and executives who accept the notion that emotional intelligence is vital for success are less certain about whether it can be improved. On the other hand, there are consultants and trainers who claim that they can raise the emotional intelligence of a whole group of employees in a day or less. Who is right? The truth lies somewhere in between. A growing body of research suggests that it is possible to help people of any age to become more emotion-

ally adept at work. However, to be effective, programs need to be well designed, and the change effort requires months, not hours or days.

Several examples of effective change programs can be found in the Model Programs section of the CREIO Web site (**www. eiconsortium.org**). These models, all of which have undergone rigorous evaluation, show that well-designed training and development interventions can produce significant improvements in the so-called "soft skills," and these improvements in turn result in greater productivity and reduced costs. Unfortunately, while it is possible to improve workers' emotional competence, it is not easy to do so. Many programs intended for this purpose fail because they are poorly designed and implemented.

WHAT IS THE BEST WAY TO IMPROVE EMOTIONAL INTELLIGENCE?

To be effective, change efforts need to begin with the realization that emotional learning differs from cognitive and technical learning in some important ways. Emotional capacities like self-confidence and empathy differ from cognitive abilities because they draw on different brain areas. Purely cognitive abilities are based in the neocortex. But with social and emotional competencies, additional brain areas are involved, mainly the circuitry that runs from the emotional centers to the prefrontal lobes. Effective learning for emotional competence has to retune these circuits.

Unfortunately, these particular neural circuits are especially difficult to modify. Emotional incompetence often results from habits learned early in life. These automatic habits are set in place as a normal part of living, as experience shapes the brain. As people acquire their habitual repertoire of thought, feeling, and action, the neural connections that support these are strengthened, becoming dominant pathways for nerve impulses. When these habits have been so heavily learned, the underlying neural circuitry becomes the brain's default option at any moment—what a person does automatically and spontaneously, often with little awareness of choosing to do so.

"The conventional definition of management is getting work done through people, but real management is developing people through work."

Hasan Abedi

Because the neural circuits that need to be modified extend deep into the nonverbal parts of the brain, the learning ultimately must be experiential. Learning to control one's temper, for instance, is like learning to ride a bicycle. Understanding what needs to be done on a cognitive level only helps to a limited degree. It is only by getting on a bike and riding it, falling over, and trying again repeatedly, that one ultimately masters the skill. The same is true for most emotional learning. It usually involves a long and sometimes difficult process requiring much practice and support. One-day seminars just won't do it.

IMPLICATIONS FOR TRAINING AND DEVELOPMENT

Because emotional learning differs from cognitive learning in a number of ways, training and development efforts need to incorporate a number of elements. Below are some of the most important ones:

1 **Practice**: There needs to be much more opportunity for practice than one normally sees in the typical work-based training program. Not only do there need to be many opportunities during the training itself, but also the learners need to practice new ways of thinking and acting in other settings—on the job, at home, with friends, etc. And this regimen needs to occur over a period of months.

2 **Ongoing encouragement and reinforcement from others**: Even with ample practice during the training phase, the old neural pathways can reestablish themselves all too easily unless learners are repeatedly encouraged and reinforced to use the new skills on the

job. The best change programs continue to help participants to apply what they have learned after the formal training phase ends. They also provide periodic reinforcers and reminders to help the participants maintain the fragile new patterns of behavior that they have so recently learned. And effective programs provide social support to help individuals to tinue to work at strengthening the new competencies that they acquired in the training.

3 **Support from the boss**: A learner's bosses play an especially critical role in providing the support necessary for successful change. Reinforcement by one's supervisor can be especially powerful in helping new emotional competencies to take root. Also, supervisors influence transfer and maintenance of new competencies indirectly by serving as powerful models.

4 **Experiential learning**: In addition to sustained practice, feedback, reinforcement, and support, effective social and emotional learning needs to be based primarily on experiential activity rather than more intellectual, didactic approaches. Developing a social or emotional competency requires engagement of the emotional, noncognitive parts of the brain.

5 **Emotionally intelligent trainers and coaches**: Because the competencies involved in social and emotional learning are so central to our personal identities, special care and sensitivity is required in the way that training is presented. The personal nature of what is involved in this kind of learning also makes it critical that there be a trusting and supportive relationship between the learners

and trainers. Trainers need special skills and more than a little emotional intelligence themselves.

6 **Anticipation and preparation for setbacks**: Even when a training program has all of these elements necessary for successful personal change—ample practice and support, emotionally intelligent trainers, etc.—learners will inevitably encounter setbacks. The old emotional memories and social habits will tend to reassert themselves from time to time, especially when people are under stress. Thus, effective training programs also include "relapse prevention," which refers to a set of techniques that help people to reframe slips as opportunities to learn.

CONCLUSION

Emotional intelligence can make a big difference for both individual and organizational effectiveness. However, if the current interest in promoting emotional intelligence at work is to be a serious, sustained effort, rather than just another management fad, it is important that practitioners try to utilize practices based on the best available research. Only when the training is based on sound, empirically based methods will its promise be realized.

FOR MORE INFORMATION

Books:
Cherniss, C., and Goleman, Daniel. *The Emotionally Intelligent Workplace.* San Francisco, CA: Jossey-Bass, 2001.
Goleman, Daniel. *Working with Emotional Intelligence.* New York: Bantam Doubleday Bell, 2000.

"Too many companies believe people are interchangeable. Truly gifted people never are. They have unique talents. Such people cannot be forced into roles they are not suited for, nor should they be."

Warren Bennis

Preventing Your Work Problems from Causing You Stress
by David Allen

EXECUTIVE SUMMARY

- Distracting internal conflict is produced by unexpected, unwanted, and unresolved circumstances, of any size and scope.
- Clarifying the successful outcomes desired and the specific actions next required in these situations eliminates internal conflict.
- Effective personal management of outcomes and actions maintains freedom from stress.

INTRODUCTION

If you're a knowledge worker, manager, or executive, you must constantly think creatively, make decisions, and manage what you and others are doing about it all. Every input triggers these responses, every opportunity invites them, and every crisis demands them. And when you avoid the appropriate thinking and decisions, or don't sufficiently manage the resulting actions, you pay a steep internal price—you lie awake at 3 a.m.

The volume of executive choices in a single day can be astonishing; the typical mid- to senior-level professional makes hundreds. Add the weight of several onerous problems—a 20% staff cut, a customer about to cancel a big deal, and a tax audit next week—and you wonder how anyone gets any sleep at all!

Unproductive worrying doesn't have to happen, however. If you apply a certain thought process and manage the results appropriately with good systems and reviewing habits, you can eliminate the distraction. You can get to sleep in the middle of even the most challenging of situations. But we aren't born knowing how to do this, nor is it taught in school or on the job. There is a learned set of behaviors that can be practiced and mastered. As with tennis, golf, skiing, or sailing, you must learn and apply the basic moves of work to play the game well. And you can continually improve how well you do this.

WHAT KEEPS US AWAKE?

You can't eliminate challenging circumstances in life and work. What you can improve on is how you deal with them—and

how much stress you're willing to allow and endure. There's a difference between stress and intensity. Intensity is concentrated energy focused on dealing with a situation. You can be intensely involved with something and still sleep five minutes later. Stress (the kind that usually keeps people up at night) is infinitely looping inner conflict caused by unfulfilled commitments to yourself.

The broken-agreement syndrome is subtle, though, and not often conscious. Unhealthy stress occurs when some part of you thinks something should be different, but you aren't yet appropriately engaged in making it happen. This kind of stress occurs when:

- you keep something you're paying attention to completely in your head, without acting on it;
- you don't decide and focus on what you want to be true about the situation;
- you don't decide the next physical actions required to move it forward;
- you don't organize reminders of those actions and outcomes to systematically trigger appropriate progressive motion.

GET IT OUT OF YOUR HEAD

If you keep something only in your mind, you file it in psychic RAM, the short-term memory space that has limited capacity for filing and retrieval and operates with no sense of past and future. (You told yourself to clean your garage six years ago, and some part of you thinks you should have been cleaning your garage every day since then!) As soon as your RAM contains more than one current agenda item, it creates inner failure and stress, because you can only do

one thing at a time, and RAM thinks it should all be happening *now*. If that were only two or three things, it might not be very noticeable. But most people have hundreds and sometimes thousands of woulds, coulds, and shoulds piled up internally, forming a kind of free-floating, unproductive tension and overreaction. Capturing something in writing will start to relieve pressure and facilitate intelligent focus.

DEFINE THE GAME AND DECIDE THE NEXT MOVE

Even if you write down something that's bothering you, if you still haven't identified what you really intend to be true about it (the successful outcome), you won't resolve the frustrated feeling. For instance, if you've just found out that a key person on your staff is quitting, just writing down "key person leaving" probably won't make you relax. You must determine what you want to be true, for example, "reorganize staff" or "replace marketing VP." Then you'll have defined the loop that needs to be closed.

This still isn't sufficient, however, to relax your brain. You must also determine the next physical action required to move the situation forward toward closure. What has to happen first to replace your staff person? Send an e-mail? Converse with your partner? Call a recruiting company? Or wait for someone else to do something?

PUT THE RESULTS INTO A TRUSTED SYSTEM

Once it's clear where you're heading with a situation and how to kick-start forward motion, it will feel much better. But there's one final critical element that has to be in place to allow you to let it go in your mind: you need to entrust the management of the outcome and the action to a system outside your own head. You have to know that you'll actually look at "replace marketing VP" written somewhere and think about it as often as you need to. And if your next action is to call recruiting companies, you need to know that whenever you find yourself at a telephone with discretionary time, you'll

see a reminder of that call as an option for what you need to be doing. Or if you've delegated the whole project to someone else, you must trust that the person will do it without fail, or at least that you have a reliable tracking mechanism to remind you in a progress report.

Even if you can't decide what to do about something, action is inherent in finding out what you need to know to make the decision. In the rare case that you really do simply need to sleep on it, you still need to trust that sometime in the future you'll be reminded about it. "Ready to decide about selling the company yet?" could go on your own calendar on a date you think appropriate, and you could then rest. You really just decided not to decide, and your own agreement with yourself is kept.

If you haven't engaged all these steps, your mind simply cannot let go. You can numb it or try to ignore it, but you can't fool it. Your mind knows whether you've made necessary decisions about a problem or situation and whether you have a system in place to manage the results. With anything less, some part of your psyche retains it.

But your head doesn't usually do a very good job of managing these distractions. That part of your mind hanging onto the issue doesn't seem to have innate intelligence. If it did, it would only remind you of a current issue when you could actually do something about it. (Most likely you remember you need batteries when you're trying to use a flashlight with dead ones, not as you're passing the battery display in a store!)

So when you think something needs to be different, you've implicitly made an agreement with yourself. If it remains unrecorded, undecided, and unmanaged objectively, your mind will not stop trying to get resolution, and it does that rather ineffectively. It can occupy your thoughts and still make no progress: you're awake at 3 a.m.

MINI-CASES

Carola Endicott, vice president of clinical operations at the 400-bed New England Medical Center in Boston, said: "A specific tool that has become a way of life for me is the simple question, 'What is the next step?' In all of the hundreds of meetings I attend in the course of a year, I have learned the

power of asking that simple question. Without it, the worry lingers—was I supposed to do something? Capturing and organizing my own next actions is also critical. By knowing these can be easily tracked and reviewed, I can free up my mind for being open to new ideas—and let it take a rest at night!"

Mike Verville, director of retail operations at L.L. Bean, described the dramatic results of learning and implementing these principles: "When I applied these principles [clarifying outcomes and next actions and tracking them appropriately] it saved my life . . . when I faithfully applied them, it changed my life. This is the vaccination against day-to-day firefighting (the so-called urgent) and an antidote for the imbalance many people bring upon themselves."

Robert Stiller, entrepreneur and C.E.O. of the fast-growing Vermont-based Green Mountain Coffee Roasters, has implemented a company-wide training program to instill these principles. He says: "Particularly exciting and successful for me has been training myself to decide the very next action steps on my projects on the front end. In the past I would list things; and when I'd go to do them, I would have to figure out what to do. I'd often get distracted or lose the energy I had for action. Changing my thought process and categorizing the possible actions appropriately really helps in dealing with the work. By collecting, processing, and organizing the things I have attention on, I'm able to look at the day-to-day flow and go on to the higher level context of the work. With my system working and keeping all the issues, projects, and action steps out of my head and before me, it's easy to sleep, and my sleep can actually help me problem-solve."

MAKING IT HAPPEN ▶▶

- Get (and keep) everything out of your head. Whatever you have attention on, write it down. Even the little things.
- Analyze each thing you've collected: does it require action? If not, throw it away or archive it as reference. If it does require action, decide what the next action is and what the successful outcome is that you're committing to. If the action can be done in less than two minutes, do it now. If not, delegate it if you can.

- Organize reminders of the outcomes on a projects list. Organize reminders of work that cannot be delegated, and would take longer than two minutes in lists you can see when you can actually perform the action (for example, be able to see all the calls you have to make when you have a phone and some discretionary time).
- Update your system and review everything that represents outstanding outcomes and actions at least once a week.

CONCLUSION

You don't have to finish something to get it off your mind and sleep well. But stress-free is not free. You do have to stop a distracting thought from rattling in your head by tackling it, clarifying what you're committing to make happen, deciding the next action required to move it forward, and entrusting the results of that thinking to a seamless system.

Getting on top of things that are distracting you requires knowledge work—you must think. You need to discipline your focus to take a minute and answer the key questions—What's the outcome I want here? What's the next action? Then your brain can say, done! There's usually an inverse proportion between the amount of time something is on your mind and the degree to which it's getting done. The more relaxed you are, the more productive you'll be.

FOR MORE INFORMATION

Books:
Drucker, Peter. *Post-Capitalist Society.* New York: HarperBusiness, 1994.
Goldsmith, Marshall, et al., eds. *Coaching for Leadership: How the World's Greatest Coaches Help Leaders Learn.* San Francisco, CA: Jossey-Bass, 2000.

See also:
☆ Raising the Bar: Setting Effective Targets (pp. 364–365)
☆ Urbane Renewal: Trusting Your Own Wisdom—A Competitive (and Satisfying) Advantage (pp. 406–407)
☆ Viewpoint: William Bridges (pp. 410–411)

"To be successful you have to be lucky, or a little mad, or very talented, or to find yourself in a rapid-growth field."

Edward de Bono

Avoiding Your Worst Career Nightmare

by Martha I. Finney

EXECUTIVE SUMMARY

- Employees are more personally and emotionally invested in their work and the outcome of their efforts than at any other time.
- Repeated cycles of vision and failure can wear down resilience and the capacity for renewed hope for a successful outcome in the future.
- Loss of hope can result from the worst career nightmare—and at the same time be an invitation to revolutionary and beneficial change.

INTRODUCTION

What's your worst career nightmare? If you're tempted to say, "Why, losing my job, of course," you wouldn't be alone. Globally, with expanding and contracting economies squeezing once highly in-demand employees out of their careers, millions of productive, talented, and educated workers are dreading the notice that they are about to be fired, laid off, made redundant, or whatever term is in vogue for their particular company.

But losing your job is not your worst career nightmare. The moment you need to worry about is when you lose your hope—hope that you can pay for your basic needs, provide for your family's future, finally find an outlet for your potential, intelligence, and talent—and ultimately achieve success and fulfillment.

HOPE ON THE FRONT LINE OF THE FUTURE

It's not just economic realities that pose a threat to hope. An accident may physically prevent you from being able to do the work you love. Or perhaps your talent might not be equal to the needs of a changing marketplace. War or political strife might force you out of your preferred cultural environment. Corporate politics might make you in conflict with powerful decision makers.

Hope is what drives us forward into our desired future. Hope is usually the last to fall—but when it does, the other side has won. When hope is finally laid down, the personal costs are high, perhaps including:

- loss of mission and vision;
- irrevocably closed doors and destroyed opportunity;

- anger and betrayal at the feeling of a promise broken;
- poor physical and psychological health;
- loss of sense of value and self-worth.

However, hope can be kept alive with a careful and mindful shift in perspective from a feeling of devastation toward one of invitation—invitation to a higher adventure, a more meaningful purpose. The threatened loss of hope frequently provides unexpected benefits—greater self-discovery, new worlds, creative opportunities, a new and more elevated role.

MINI-CASES

Growing up in a small village in northern England, Carol Roberts expected to be a hairstylist. She dedicated her young adult years to training in that field, which she loved, but only weeks into her new job a freak accident cut three tendons in her right hand. Her career was over before it had begun. After searching for unskilled work she became a salesperson. While selling video-game components she identified a need for a special joystick, which she then successfully developed and manufactured. Her new enterprise brought her an enviable and unforeseen life of world travel, creative satisfaction, and income beyond her early expectations.

Jack Zimmerman grew up poor in Chicago. His dream of becoming a trombonist in a symphony orchestra was born of joy-filled summer nights on the lawn of the amphitheater at the Ravinia Festival. Despite studying music for more than 15 years he failed as a professional musician, then briefly edited a music magazine, a job he loathed. Frustrated and depressed, he gave up music altogether and trained as a para-

legal. The weekend of his graduation his phone rang: "Jack, I need a new public relations director who must know the media and love music. Will you come in for an interview?" The call was from the director of his childhood inspiration: the Ravinia Festival.

Franck Malegue graduated from a prestigious French business school and after a short career at L'Oréal realized his passion was to create businesses in Asia. He enjoyed almost a decade of successful startups—he was the first non-Chinese person to joint-venture with the Chinese government importing luxury products—before the Asian economies started to fail. He struggled to stay afloat, but eventually had to close his Asian enterprises. He later described the decision as a "deep release and lightness." Franck has embarked on a journey of self-discovery and rediscovered his passion for work. His new purpose: to help companies and governments to work together for the public good.

MAKING IT HAPPEN ▶▶

The following ideas will help to turn a destructive loss of hope into creative, professional rebirth and success:

- **Keep informed.** Know what's going on in your industry, community, and economic environment.
- **Keep clued in.** Know what's going on in your heart: don't be afraid to understand your own aspirations, motivations, strengths, and weaknesses. What would be your ideal? Use this crisis in hope to understand your inner voice and see in what new directions it might be leading you.
- **Keep connected.** Networking is a powerful and valuable tool: meeting people not only provides tangible help, but also helps to clarify one's thinking, providing perspective and a positive approach. It is also a two-way process; people are often happy to help when they can, treating others as they would wish to be treated. Attend professional chapter meetings, make new

acquaintances, make appointments to meet people for coffee.

- **Keep learning.** Learning new skills, facts, and technologies will do more than help you to stay marketable in an alternately expanding and contracting economy. New learnings will help you connect concepts and relationships in new combinations, spark new ideas, and help you to see your circumstances in new ways.
- **Keep fit.** The psychological effects of exercising and healthy eating are well documented. Rhythmic, whole-body, aerobic exercising—like bicycling, running, or walking—not only releases mood-enhancing endorphins, but it also gives your mind the chance to relax and wander. This is when great ideas are born!
- **Keep creative.** Take up a hands-on hobby that results in a tangible product—needlepoint, model-making, or woodworking. If you're caught up in a hope-challenging situation such as a layoff or a politically charged lose–lose environment, it's easy to start believing that nothing you do makes a difference. A craft that results in a tangible object of beauty uses different parts of your brain and gives you solid evidence that you can make a difference.
- **Keep away from draining negative influences.** Many things—from people to TV advertisements—can act as a distraction or a debilitating influence that saps hope and energy. Avoid them.
- **Keep contributing.** No matter what your skill or expertise there's a need for it in the volunteer community. You can restore hope by engaging your personal purpose in an environment in which it will be received and put to use gratefully!

- **Keep moving.** This doesn't mean you should move away from home, it means you should stay active. Take the time you need to wallow in self-pity, fear, and despair—but then get up. Get out of the house. Fill your calendar with appointments, even if the commitment is as seemingly inconsequential as taking someone to the airport or attending a book-signing. Only by living in the real world will you find opportunities to make progress.
- **Keep the faith.** There are other forces at work to help you to realize your ambitions, but you may not be able to see all of them. Imagine, for instance, a large clock. You can see its face and its hands. If you look carefully at those ever-so-slowly moving hands, you can even see the passage of time. But most clocks don't show you the wheels turning behind the scenes. You don't give much thought to what's not evident, to all the activity that's taking place in secret, but there's activity going on of which you are unaware. Perhaps certain other elements have to shift into place before your gifts and talents can be engaged again in the most productive and beneficial way. Perhaps while you've been forced to wait for your hope to manifest itself, you've been learning a skill—or gathering experience—that will be vital to your new call to action. Every day comes with its own surprises.

CONCLUSION

To manifest your hope and realize your professional objectives, you often need more than sheer, single-minded, determined effort. You need the efforts and influences of others. You also need the accumulation of skills, insights, and experiences that can only be acquired while you're playing the waiting game. And you need the necessary passing of time, while the rest of the world catches up with your vision and the time becomes right. Then the miraculous will happen. Just when you're about to give up all hope, the phone will ring. Or someone will drop by your office door with a proposal. Someone will say "Yes," and hope will flare up again with a bright new light.

FOR MORE INFORMATION

Books:
Frankl, Viktor E. *Man's Search for Meaning: An Introduction to Logotherapy*. New York: Simon and Schuster, 2000.
Jansen, Julie. *I Don't Know What I Want, But I Know it's Not This: A Step-by-Step Guide to Finding Gratifying Work*. New York: Penguin, 2003.

Web site:
MarthaFinney.com:
www.marthafinney.com

See also:
- ☆ Choosing the Best Training Curriculum for You (pp. 426–427)
- ✔ Finding Your Calling and Living Your Passion: The Dream Job (pp. 847–848)
- ☆ Managing by Individual Objectives (pp. 205–207)
- ☆ Urbane Renewal: Trusting Your Own Wisdom—A Competitive (and Satisfying) Advantage (pp. 406–407)
- ☆ Viewpoint: Henry Mintzberg (pp. 292–293)
- ☆ Viewpoint: William Bridges (pp. 410–411)

"If you wanted an easy job, you could be a grave digger or run a graveyard."   Ted Turner

Urbane Renewal: Trusting Your Own Wisdom—A Competitive (and Satisfying) Advantage

by Cliff Hakim

EXECUTIVE SUMMARY

- Whatever position you hold, you're struggling to manage and turn a pressing schedule and hectic pace into a productive focus: products and services. But the swirl of activity can thwart your diehard commitment.
- Urbane renewal can overcome this, providing a satisfying, valuable competitive advantage. *Urbane renewal* is your engagement in ongoing development that ushers forth your own wisdom. Act on your wisdom and you'll get lucky, feel satisfied, and add value to your customers.

INTRODUCTION

The challenge is learning to recognize and trust your own wisdom, not to defer to what your boss thinks, to what an analyst says, or to what the trend or general consensus is. Today you can't wait for the perfect moment for others to act, or for things to align seamlessly before you step forward. You must trust your own wisdom and commit to action—sooner rather than later.

Didn't your company hire you for your individual wisdom? Is your wisdom to lead or manage? To facilitate or advise? To build new systems or to operate them after they're built?

Your wisdom knows the gratifying and productive processes that you engage in to achieve, to produce a product or service. Your own wisdom is rooted in your vulnerability to know what you think, to understand what you believe, and to respond with meaningful actions. Your own wisdom runs deep. On the surface it may appear to be the expression of your skills and talents. Its beat, though, draws from your courage, and to be courageous is to be vulnerable.

There is no such thing as courage without a sense of vulnerability. It is only when you feel unguarded, exposed, challenged, and committed to action that you're really courageous. The people whom I cite below had courage, but first they were vulnerable—they opened themselves up to discovery personally and professionally to increase their satisfaction and significance. All recognized their need to grow and understood the benefits of their growth for their organizations. There are several reasons why organizations need continued wisdom.

WHY DOES YOUR ORGANIZATION NEED YOUR WISDOM?

- The world keeps demanding and changing. Yesterday's accomplishments are no guarantee for tomorrow's success.
- The marketplace is too competitive for dependence or complacency.
- Customers are looking for the highest-quality, lowest-price deal. They'll go elsewhere in this musical-chairs economy if you and your organization don't innovate or can't deliver.

MUTUAL URBANE BENEFITS

The benefits of embracing a program of urbane renewal are:
For the individual
- productive self-confidence;
- an increased ability to trust your own wisdom;
- courage, vulnerability, values, talents, and skills;
- the ability to earn a living by expressing these qualities.
For the organization
- innovative partners;
- a resilient and confident workforce better able to change and compete as the organization reinvents itself and the marketplace shifts.

REAL WISDOM

Popular public figures such as Duke Ellington, Steve Jobs, and Julia Child have all developed themselves and demonstrated their wisdom. Think about how such people have affected you. Each has contributed to your life, not because they followed a pied piper, but because they listened to and capitalized on their own wisdom. I doubt you'd argue with their satisfaction.

Similarly, organizations are filled with wise people. They're leading and managing and developing themselves despite the politics, competition, and chaos. The following mini-cases provide examples of such people and how they work.

MINI-CASES

Natalie Bagdonas, vice president of Technology Systems Engineering at *Fidelity Investments*, taps into her wisdom, using it to lead. Natalie's role, critical to the company's e-business, is concerned with improving the customer's experience when using the Fidelity Web site.

Executive coaching and, specifically, a leadership course called Positive Power and Influence have aided Natalie's development. But mostly she's relied on her experience and intuition to achieve her potential. For example, a challenging staff member was placed in her group. During her first conversation with Natalie, this employee announced that she was reluctant to work for her. Natalie could have covered her vulnerability and allowed the new employee to leave. Instead she knew her challenge would be to respond calmly, giving the staff member a chance. Natalie said, "It may take you months to find another job within the system. In the meanwhile I'd suggest that we talk about some ways to work together, at least temporarily." Natalie's manner and invitation began a planning process. She and her staff member talked about the mission of the group, tasks that the employee was best suited for, and educational programs that might best prepare her. Natalie com-

"Proficient is defined with one word: skilled. In order to become skilled you must have more than knowledge, you need to apply that information."

Jac Fitz-Enz

mented, "I provided empathy and structure that set us both up for success." How could Natalie satisfy her external customers—you and me—if she weren't on a similar journey with her internal ones? Natalie benefited by summoning her intuition. The organizational benefit was a productive new staff member resulting in a congruence between serving internal and external customers.

In the world of consulting, Brad Sweet, former senior partner at *Computer Sciences Corporation* (CSC), recalled a mentoring partnership that influenced his development, leadership style, and ongoing contributions to CSC. Brad advanced to management early in his career. His new role put him in the position of managing several older consultants.

To learn how to manage in this environment more effectively, Brad partnered another staff member who had similar interests in running a productive organization but who had a very different set of skills. His colleague, a senior organizational development specialist, offered Brad his expertise in management, and Brad offered his colleague advice on technical, especially software, issues.

Their initial barter agreement turned into three-hour meetings. The first two hours were evenly split to talk about whatever business issues they brought to the table. During hour three they would eat lunch and socialize.

More than twenty years later Brad managed a larger group. He didn't realize it back then, but he and his colleague developed a mentoring relationship that he now considers to have fortified his management roots. One of Brad's primary management tools was to arrange formal mentoring partnerships in his division.

"I wasn't herding my staff into some artificial training program," Brad said, "but ushering them into a highly relevant, practical relationship and process." Protégés are matched with willing and more experienced partners. They observe their mentors in everyday business interactions and vice versa. In addition they participate in the business at hand. Brad believed, "There's no better teacher than experience guided by a helping hand." Brad benefited by collaborating to learn and excel. The organization benefited from strong leadership and challenged and directed staff.

Steve Ruffing is senior human resource manager for *Medtronic*, the world's leading technology company providing lifelong solutions for chronic disease. He supports 450 salespeople for cardiac rhythm field sales. Steve's satisfaction and significance are derived from his passion—building highly functioning systems or a new organization from the ground up.

"As I evaluate my career history," Steve said, "whether at Honeywell, Northwest Airlines, or in my current role, my success was linked to being thrust into situations in which I had limited knowledge. Staying connected with my network—asking questions and digging and doing research—kept me going. I treated new opportunities like a hobby."

Steve's development wasn't fancy, it was consistent and anchored in his commitment and passion for innovation. He said, "I made a point to talk with others about what they were doing." Steve succeeded by honoring his zeal for building new systems. The organization benefited from his passion, converted to innovation and managing others.

MAKING IT HAPPEN ▸▸

Wisdom is not the end goal, but the means you've engaged to achieve your goals. We both know what it takes—courage, boredom, excitement, uncertainty—to complete an event, produce a product, deliver a service, earn a certificate or diploma, or land a new position or job. You had to dig up your own wisdom to get there.

Right now, consider *when did your own wisdom work for you?* Was it when you satisfied a customer, set a personal-best record, received a standing ovation, supported a friend through a crisis, or wrote a topnotch proposal? Now that you have an example in mind, let go of the accomplishment or event and think about the process. The process—what you believed, thought, and did—contains your wisdom. In the process did you

- trust yourself?
- doubt yourself at first?
- focus?
- relax?
- ramble, staying open and flexible?
- talk with others?
- go one step at a time?
- use your special talents?
- say to yourself, I'll confront my fears?

To further deepen your own wisdom, ask yourself, what skills did I use? Did your skills include the following techniques?

- analysis
- influencing
- managing others
- organizing and prioritizing
- consulting and counseling
- seeing the bigger picture
- interviewing
- incorporating different ideas
- explaining and facilitating.

CONCLUSION

As you become more familiar with your wisdom you can use it again and again, consciously, to create the work life that you want and to make contributions to others. To guarantee the deepening of your wisdom, I encourage you to continue to reflect and dig. As you come to understand your wisdom you'll find it's a well you can draw from to make and sustain your work life.

FOR MORE INFORMATION

Books:
Hudson, Frederic M. *The Adult Years: Mastering the Art of Self-renewal.* 2nd ed. San Francisco, CA: Jossey-Bass, 1999.
Rayman, Paula M. *Beyond the Bottom Line: The Search for Dignity at Work.* New York: St. Martin's Press, 2001.
Reich, Robert B. *The Future of Success.* New York: Knopf, 2001.

"A formal title . . . has less to do with career prospects and success . . . than skills and ideas a person brings to that work."
Rosabeth Moss Kanter

Brainstorming by Jules Goddard

EXECUTIVE SUMMARY

- There is a paradox in modern organizational life: the demands placed on organizations to be creative and entrepreneurial are greater than ever; and yet what we observe today are organizations in the grip of profoundly conservative and risk-averse managerial styles.
- Today's corporations have built up a plethora of routines for administering, aligning, measuring, monitoring, and correcting organizational behavior—but a dearth of techniques for inventing, discovering, exploring, improvising, or inspiring new ways of working or new opportunities for wealth creation.

INTRODUCTION

Since the 1950s, brainstorming has been put forward as a significant antidote to all forms of organizational rigidity and defensiveness—and an important catalyst for liberating organizational creativity. However, in recent years research has cast doubts on the efficacy of brainstorming and this has stimulated some exciting alternatives to it. Electronic brainstorming in particular has the potential to raise the organization's "capacity for strategic innovation."

THE ESSENCE OF BRAINSTORMING

Brainstorming is a particular way of using many brains to storm a singular problem creatively. Its adherents claim that individuals can get to a better solution if they act collectively than if they acted individually.

The virtue that is claimed for brainstorming is that it seeks to distinguish between the two cognitive activities that are intrinsic to all problem solving:
- free conjecture (having ideas)
- rigorous criticism (testing these ideas)

By separating these activities and dwelling exclusively on the conjectural dimension of problem-solving—uninhibited by the threat of destructive criticism—the brainstorming method claims to release the embedded creativity of the group.

Brainstorming is widely practiced—even though recent research has shown unequivocally that "brainstorming groups produce fewer and poorer quality ideas than the same number of individuals working alone" (Furnham, 2001).

THE FOUR BASIC RULES

- **Suspend judgment:** refrain from judging the ideas of others as they are articulated and shared.
- **Record all ideas:** transcribe every candidate solution exactly as it is expressed, however half-baked or far-fetched or ill-formed it may seem at first sight.
- **Encourage "piggy-backing":** let each idea spontaneously spark further ideas and build on the creativity of others.
- **Think "out of the box":** encourage and pursue genuinely "contrarian" lines of thought.

THE STEP-BY-STEP PROCESS OF BRAINSTORMING

In its pure state, brainstorming takes the following form:
- The problem to which a solution is sought is stated in the form of a clear question.
- A group of people come together to address the problem.
- One member of the group takes the role of scribe, recording each idea as it is generated.
- Every member of the group is expected to "storm the problem" by contributing as wide a variety of potential or tentative solutions as possible.
- No one is permitted to criticize or to challenge any of the ideas put forward, however impractical or irrelevant or nonsensical they may at first sight appear to be.
- Only when the flow of ideas dries up, are the candidate solutions reviewed, clarified, amended, and evaluated.

In the event that a host of fruitful ideas emerge, a second stage of brainstorming—sometimes called "reverse brainstorming"—can be applied:
- Each idea deemed worthy of further consideration is posted in its strongest form.
- Group members take each idea in turn and generate all the reasons why the idea may not count as a fully satisfactory solution to the original problem.
- These reservations are then themselves reviewed, clarified, amended, and assessed.
- The reservations that survive are used to filter out the unsatisfactory solutions—leaving only those that have real merit and that are worth taking forward.

THE POPULARITY OF BRAINSTORMING

There are many features of brainstorming that its adherents find attractive:
- *It is inclusive:* it engages the interest and involvement of every member of a work group.
- *It is meritocratic:* it challenges the power structure by assuming that good ideas are not the monopoly of any one level.
- *It is efficient:* it focuses many minds on a single pertinent issue.
- *It is inspirational:* it acknowledges, champions, stimulates, and captures the creativity of each individual.
- *It is synergistic:* it recognizes that creativity is better for being a social activity, where one idea can easily trigger others, and where the total result ends up being greater than the sum of the parts.
- *It is productive:* it maximizes the number of ideas generated by a given group.
- *It is fun:* it promotes the virtues of conviviality and collegiality.

RESEARCH ON BRAINSTORMING

The challenge to brainstorming has come from many experiments that have compared the productivity of "nominal" groups—that is, individuals working alone (whose ideas are only later combined and assessed)—with the productivity of "genuine" groups—that is, individuals generating ideas together in the same room. These experiments, conducted since the 1950s, have shown consistently that nominal groups outperform interacting groups (of whatever size) in terms of both the quantity and quality of their output.

How can this be explained? Which of the many assumptions that underpin classical brainstorming would seem to be at fault?

"Intelligence becomes an asset when some useful order is created out of free-floating brainpower."

Thomas A. Stewart

MISTAKEN ASSUMPTIONS IN BRAINSTORMING SESSIONS

Research has suggested that five particularly "unsafe" assumptions provide, in differing degrees, an explanation for the "failure" of groups to outperform individuals:

- The assumption that personal creativity is enhanced by the presence of others: evidence would suggest however that "social loafing"—the pathology by which the group provides an excuse for individual members to "opt out" and take it easy— often outweighs the opposite effect of "social energizing."
- The assumption that prohibiting criticism is sufficient to encourage individuals to propose provocative and unusual ideas without fear of being judged or made to feel foolish or incompetent ("loss of face"). However strongly the rules of brainstorming are espoused, there is evidence that many individuals are still not comfortable giving free rein to their imagination and remain inhibited.
- The assumption that creativity is contagious and that ideas spark further ideas, especially if group members are encouraged to build upon each other's thinking: but the reality would seem to be that "production blocking" is the stronger effect, as individuals are compelled to wait for others to express their ideas, by which time they will have forgotten their own ideas—or lost confidence in them.
- The assumption that group processes encourage divergent thinking and the confidence to explore uncharted territory: however, group processes can also have the opposite effect, sometimes called "anchoring," by which the creativity of the group is constrained simply to embroidering variations on the first theme to have emerged in the session, rather than inventing radically new themes.
- The assumption that time pressures enhance the creative process: but, if anything, the evidence suggests exactly the opposite—that "hot-housing" the process of discovery produces just the stressed state that generally reduces the capacity of people to think freely and imaginatively.

E-BRAINSTORMING: A REMEDY?

Electronic brainstorming—whereby individuals, each sitting at their own computer terminal, type in their own ideas (before sharing and appraising them) while having easy access to the ideas of others as they are generated—would seem to be an ingenious way of avoiding the problems of social loafing, loss of face, production blocking, anchoring, and hot-housing.

Social loafing becomes a less attractive option if individuals believe that their ideas are likely to be logged and counted; fear of loss of face is alleviated if the principle of anonymity is assured; production blocking ceases to be a problem if individuals can choose for themselves when to create their own ideas and when to pay attention to the ideas of others; anchoring cannot occur where most of the creative work is performed autonomously; and hot-housing is less likely to happen in circumstances where individuals are not permanently fighting for airtime.

MAKING IT HAPPEN ▶▶

The following techniques can help to ensure that brainstorming is fully effective:

- Make clear the goals of the brainstorm well in advance, giving people the chance to prepare their thoughts as well as avoiding too much tension at the start.
- Insure that the people involved are the best ones; check that no one is omitted who could make a valuable contribution to the session.
- Insure that people are relaxed, comfortable and focused—only then will they make their best contributions and generate ideas.
- Make clear the roles and ground rules (for example, avoid criticism of ideas, ensure that everyone contributes and understands the role of the facilitator)—and positively but firmly insure that they are followed.
- As a facilitator, set the tone with a positive, energetic approach.
- Once ideas have emerged, look for patterns and links between ideas that may arise. Morphological analysis, which combines and blends elements from different ideas, often follows on from brainstorming.
- Be prepared to prompt discussion and draw people back to the key issues. Thinking about possible scenarios may help, so too can examples—anything that helps people to think innovatively and "outside the box."
- Agree the actions following the brainstorm: what will be done, who will do it and by when.
- Consider whether other people need to be informed of the results and actions arising from the brainstorm.
- Conclude the session so that everyone emerges from the varied process with a clear sense of value and understanding of what has been achieved.

CONCLUSION

Successful brainstorming encourages people to give vent to all of their ideas on a specific topic, led by a facilitator, in an atmosphere of constructive suggestion rather than criticism, discussion, or even comment. After ideas have been generated, these are then discussed, explored, and prioritized—usually creating new solutions through combining elements from several suggestions.

The key to success is to ensure that the ground rules are clearly understood by everyone and are fairly applied. The facilitator must be expert and able both to draw out contributions and also to recognize where patterns may lie, while the group must possess (or be enthused with) the passion and commitment to participate actively.

FOR MORE INFORMATION

Books:
Correll, Linda. *Brainstorming Reinvented: Corporate Communications Guide to Ideation*. Thousand Oaks, CA: Sage Publications, 2004.
Christensen, Clayton M. *The Innovator's Solution: Creating and Sustaining Successful Growth*. Cambridge, MA: Harvard Business School Press, 2003.
Hamel, Gary. *Leading the Revolution*. Revised ed. Cambridge, MA: Harvard Business School Press, 2002.

"Brains are becoming the core of organisations—other activities can be contracted out."

Charles Handy

Viewpoint: William Bridges
"Work" and "Change"

Introduction

Few grasp how to make sense of life's changes better than William Bridges. His insights and strategies for dealing with difficult, painful, and even scary times are extremely relevant, particularly as we begin a new millennium marred at the outset by enormous adversity and a chilling sense of uncertainty. Indeed, his message is one of hope, compassion, and deep understanding. His book *Transitions*, first published in 1980 and revised in 2004, has sold more than 500,000 copies and continues to be trumpeted as the quintessential resource for understanding the process of surviving and reviving in the face of change. Subsequent books include *Managing Transitions*, *Jobshift*, *Creating You & Co.*, and *The Way of Transition*.

Americans share many of the traits of some of their Old World cousins. Yet, these New World pioneers, in particular, have long been regarded as people on the move. Almost 200 years ago, Alexis de Tocqueville noted, " . . . the American has no time to tie himself to anything, he grows accustomed only to change . . . regarding it as the natural state of man." With my original training in the field of American civilization and my extensive exposure to history, government, and literature, I have been able to draw from a wealth of resources over the years, like de Tocqueville, whose work, *Democracy in America*, is a brilliant study of the American culture.

Similarly, Edward P. Thompson's *Making of the English Working Class* provides extremely valuable information concerning the development of the historical artifact we call a "job." Originally, a "job" was an invention that could go away as easily as it came into existence. The word was first used as a verb, meaning something comparable to "doing." With the advent of the Industrial Revolution, the work people performed could be dissected into discrete tasks, and "job" came to mean something for which people took responsibility, like a possession. This perspective is useful in understanding why the "job" as we know it today— representing more of a function based on a set of activities—is imploding.

While I came to appreciate such *external* analyses of change, I was motivated to examine the thinking of others to formulate my own beliefs with respect to the *internal* experience of it. Those influencing my conclusions included: Arnold J. Toynbee, who helped us understand the process of renewal as it occurs in civilization and in a person; Dutch anthropologist Arnold van Gennep, who first coined the phrase *rites of pas-*

sage; and philosopher Mircea Eliade, whose analysis of religion assumed the existence of "the sacred" as the object of worship of religious humanity—providing a source of power, significance, and value.

Peter Drucker and Charles Handy, two organizational writers, and Ralph Waldo Emerson—all helped to enhance my perspective on what van Gennep referred to as the "neutral zone"—that period between the end of one phase and the beginning of the next in which the greatest opportunity for discovery and renewal is present. What I particularly came to appreciate is the absence of "focusing mechanisms" in our lives today that allow people to "know" where the end points and beginnings are. Our "transitions" are becoming all-consuming. They overwhelm everything rather than providing channeled influences that move us consciously in some new direction. Given the changing nature of work—with increased demands for knowledge, the disintegration of large corporations, and an accelerated pace of change—it is no longer appropriate to think of work as "fixed" jobs. To appreciate this, we have only to consider the dramatic example of *The Wall Street Journal*, whose offices were directly across from the World Trade Center in New York. The very next day following the destruction of the towers by terrorists, the publisher was able to go to press, utilizing an extensive network of cell phones, e-mail systems, fax machines, and remote sites of operation. With that magnitude of integrated technology, we can't think in terms of individual workers arranged in fixed work units producing a product. Instead, what we need to envision is whole communities of people agreeing to assume shifting roles in a highly flexible context.

All to say, these influences, combined with my own

"Yesterday's success formula is often today's obsolete dogma . . . We must continually challenge the past so that we can renew ourselves each day."

Sumantra Ghoshal

research, have shaped the way in which I view "change" and "transition." You see, change is an *event*, whereas transition is a *process* that is always in flux, always disruptive. It forces people to go into a "neutral" role, and it is in this area that business and management have their most important work cut out.

As we begin the new millennium, I predict a dramatic intensification of the trends of the last 10 years. The pace of change has already given business many new advantages. Flexibility and responsiveness are the preeminent qualities of the new workplace. And, while technology enables us to work faster, with fewer jobs and greater productivity, business also has the ability to use more "outsiders." A new construct is well under way as traditional jobs continue to diminish.

Our work habits and lifestyles will change further. We'll need whole new systems of support for employees. To illustrate this: when Washington officials talk about a "safety net" of retirement security, unemployment benefits, and the like, their model is consistently predicated on the old concept of jobs. In the 21st century, *portability*—which allows workers to accrue benefits as they move from one assignment to another—will be terribly important. Business cannot continue to operate in an environment where health insurance, for example, acts as some huge counterweight to the migration of human capital across the workscape.

These are the *external* realities associated with change that I see. The *internal* realities are that people won't be able to keep pace—assimilating the turbulence of a process that gets protracted *ad infinitum*. They may go through the motions, but they won't be into the new work *emotionally*. They'll still be back in the old job. We're seeing this now, and I predict it will continue—slowed only by an occasional crisis—but it will be an unsustainable position leading to all kinds of meltdowns. At the end of the day, there is no end, as "home"—that safe haven from the world outside—is assaulted by beepers, cell phones, and unsolicited sales calls. Families are melting away. I predict other meltdowns, as well—psychological breakdowns, depression, constant fatigue. Even today, large numbers of people are running on empty.

To break this destructive trend, we must work on how the experience of transition can lead to personal renewal. Of course, in the midst of turbulence, usually the last thing we want is transition, especially when we're looking for renewal; but that's how renewal really takes place. We have to learn how to enjoy the ride more, by going *with* the transition—renewing on the fly, so to speak, without necessarily blowing the whistle for a timeout.

New skills will be needed to cope with these conditions. To begin with, *self-management of change* will be essential for everyone. Individuals, as well as businesses, will need to be able to make quick shifts. Leaders in every organization will have to realize how often the rules change, and they will need to assume hugely more responsibility for getting people through these changes successfully—especially for the well-being of the enterprise as a whole. This will involve

every aspect of the change process—communication, timing, training, etc. The old way of "command and control" will be a formula for disaster, particularly if people are allowed to remain stuck in the unfinished mess of transition.

We will also need to reframe the concept of a *career* by incorporating elements that are "change-friendly." We must foster an entrepreneurial spirit that feeds on the change process. Indeed, the *new-style career* will require that everyone know:

- what resources, skills, and abilities they bring to the table;
- where the problems are that are yet to be solved and what the "market" needs;
- what new skills will be needed to bring solutions to these opportunities;
- that we are all "micro-companies," requiring strategic planning, training, financing, etc.;
- that transitions lead to renewal, and we need to be open to traversing many neutral zones.

We will have to find ways to make organizations even more flexible in the future. To do this effectively we will have to facilitate the process by letting go of things that are not servicing us well anymore. We will also have to find ways of getting the most benefit from those who are not in the direct employ of the enterprise. This will involve new forms of recognition and reward sharing. And, finally, management will need to reinvent itself. Rather than assuming responsibility for assigning fixed duties, discrete tasks—like purchasing or human resource management—leaders will do better to shift the focus to cross-functional teams and/or outside workers who, in turn, will assume responsibility for getting work done and adjusting continuously—even more quickly—to change.

In the end, by involving people more in the design of their own work situations and tying rewards to results, people will become more aligned with the goals of the enterprise and more concerned with its welfare. Not only will this approach enable businesses to prosper, it will avert many of the costly meltdowns of human capital. But make no mistake, this will require a major shift from the old-style thinking of one "master" and one "job" to the new reality of *self-managed transitions*.

FOR MORE INFORMATION

Web site:
William Bridges & Associates: **www.wmbridges.com**

"From now on, change will be the constant. The individuals best prepared to succeed are those who can learn, modify, and grow, regardless of age, experience, or ego."

Danny Goodman

Taking Charge of Your Career
by Andrew Lambert

EXECUTIVE SUMMARY

- In an increasingly uncertain world, build on your employability by accumulating skills and experience. Expect to change career direction at least once.
- Don't expect to plan specific job moves far in advance. Be open to new opportunities that may arise, including events you can't control such as mergers and restructuring.
- Be clear about what you want out of life as well as work. Reevaluate this from time to time so that your career genuinely matches your needs as they change.
- Do something you enjoy (you won't succeed for long otherwise) and recognize when it's time to move on.
- Try to stay in control of your destiny—you're the person who's most likely to be concerned about your future. Market your talents with conviction.
- If you're a specialist, beware of dead ends. Alternatively, try not to be too much of a generalist, that is, a jack-of-all-trades but master of none.
- Be realistic about what an employer can offer you (for example, adding value to your résumé) and about whether you want to be your own boss: do you have what that takes?

INTRODUCTION

The quickening pace of market change means that both organizations and individuals need to focus harder than ever on how to adjust, or even reinvent what they do, if they are to continue to prosper. Just as the average life span of employing organizations is decreasing rapidly, with new corporations and public-sector bodies emerging to take the place of those that fail, so individuals face the danger of losing not only their job, but also their knowledge and skills, if they don't attune to the needs of the future.

What is a career in this context? It *is* still valid to envisage a path that follows a broadly consistent direction. However, this is no longer likely to be with one employer, or even in the same industry and specialty. This means being flexible and adaptive, and adjusting any career plan regularly in the light of changing circumstances, both personal and market-related. Additionally, circumstances may require a complete change of direction.

Choosing a Career

With or without economic, peer, and family pressures, some people find it easy to make up their minds early and pursue a path accordingly; others don't, and need time to find a path. Either approach is valid: if you're going to be successful it's important to do something you enjoy, something that will inspire your thoughts and energy.

If you're an early chooser, don't let enthusiasm blind you to some of the hard decisions you may have to make. Research your chosen area thoroughly, identifying the stepping stones and obstacles to making progress, and the life cycle of jobs in the field. Remember also that you may have to shift direction later.

There are advantages in being a late developer in that you can test the waters before committing yourself. Realistically, career planning is often about making opportunistic choices as you progress, not about sticking to a single idea. Many successful people had little idea at the outset that they would end up where they did. They learned from the positive and negative experiences they encountered and made their choices accordingly. However, once they did decide what to head for, they were single-minded.

The importance of academic credentials varies depending on the country you're in and whether or not you are following a specialist path. Some employers see degrees (even MBAs) primarily as a way of choosing among a large number of applicants. As you progress through your career, your track record assumes greater importance.

Specialists and Generalists

If you're expert in something, an employer has a good reason to hire and retain you—at any stage in your career. You will face choices both about how to maintain your specialist edge and how to broaden your managerial skills.

In a corporate context there tend to be two broad types of specialty. Some competences are core to what the organization does (for example, engineering, science, distribution and logistics, trading). Others are the classic support function competences (finance, marketing, IT, personnel, communications, facilities and property management, etc.). All of these have subsets that are more genuinely specialist.

If you continue to specialize, the availability of jobs on offer in companies will steadily reduce until you hit a dead end. You may then need to move into general management or consulting. As you climb the managerial ladder, it's increasingly important to acquire and display general management capabilities such as effectiveness in leading and motivating teams, managing change and projects, and understanding the commercial and systems context.

If you want to lead a support function—such as finance or marketing—first become a generalist within the function by experiencing a number of relevant specialties. If it's your ambition to be a consultant anyway, bear in mind that the real money and status derives from being an owner or partner, and that may not be easy if you enter the arena quite late.

Important Planning Factors

Whether you're moving within or between organizations, you need to provide evidence of your ability to handle varied challenges, demonstrate responsibility as well as initiative, learn from experience, motivate teams, and above all, achieve results. Whatever your level of ambition, be continuously aware of the qualities, knowledge, and skills that will be valuable in the future—don't let yourself become outdated.

Consider:

- what you're working for—job satisfaction, status, material comfort, real wealth, or the buzz of acquiring power;
- whether you intend to have a family at some point (and when);
- whether you feel the need to own a business (large or small), become the leader of an organization, or just be part of one;

"Bureaucratic and risk-averse environments are career killers because of their impact on learning."

John P. Kotter

- whether you want to stay in a certain geographical area or are willing to move;
- personal profiling and psychometric assessment to help you to understand your long-term capabilities and values.

Choosing an Employer

Building your résumé principally means two things: progressing steadily through professional roles, gathering experience and responsibility on the way; and doing so for recognized and well-respected employers. The competition to work for high-profile employers can be fierce.

Money is, of course, a key determinant of people's decisions, particularly early in their careers or when family finances are demanding. Benefits such as pensions and career development are important too, though. However, people choose to leave organizations more often because they're unhappy with the opportunities they face or with the attitude of their boss than on purely financial grounds.

So check out what life is really like inside a company, specifically in the department or division you are joining, before you accept an offer (especially if you're concerned about diversity). Some employers' reality doesn't match their reputation, and getting that name on your résumé can prove punishing, whatever the salary.

Staying in Control

It's ever more likely that an organization you join will undergo takeover, merger, or some other form of restructuring that will affect your career path directly or indirectly. Use any such event as an opportunity to learn—or make sure you move early before the rush. Remember that ultimately you can rely only on yourself to market your talent and achievements—no one else will be as interested as you are!

MAKING IT HAPPEN ▶▶
- Don't expect that your career will be with one employer, or necessarily in the same industry and specialty. Plan accordingly.

- Be rigorous in identifying ways to progress, and form an idea of the stepping stones and the life cycle of jobs in the field.
- Be prepared to make opportunistic choices as you progress instead of sticking to one single idea.
- It's important to become expert at something, and to maintain and expand your expertise, in order to give employers a good reason to hire and retain you.
- Learn how to lead and motivate teams as a manager of change and projects, and to deploy your specialist knowledge in a broad context.
- Fit your career plan to a realistic assessment of your abilities and potential. Be confident of your ability to achieve and succeed. It should also fit the level of your personal and financial ambition.

CONCLUSION

Taking charge of your career is increasingly important at a time when traditional loyalty from employees is much reduced, and when employers are learning (and having to learn) to show greater flexibility about employment patterns. Cradle-to-grave employment and automatic promotions are now, in virtually every area of life, a thing of the *recent* past. So, if your employer is now less likely to map out a career path for you, who will? The answer, of course, is the individual, and to take charge for the future requires a clear focus on oneself. There are several key points to remember when taking charge of your career:

- **Understand, value, and develop your own skills**—know what you do well, what you enjoy, and why. Letting these guide you will help to find a satisfying career path.
- **Recognize all of the factors that are important to you**—for example, geographical mobility, family time, vocational work.
- **Don't be afraid to discuss this with**

others—friends and family can provide a useful sounding board, as they often recognize things about you that you may have missed yourself!
- **Plan your career—but not too much!** See opportunities and cope with change, positive or negative, that may arise and impact on this plan.

Finally, staying in control and making it happen are vitally important. Rarely will anyone else help you out or ensure that your career is looked after exactly as you would wish. The responsibility for acting, or reacting to changing circumstances, is yours.

FOR MORE INFORMATION

Books:
Berman Fortgang, Laura. *Take Yourself to the Top.* Revised ed. New York: Tarcher, 2005.
Brown, Duane. *Career Choice and Development.* 4th ed. San Francisco, CA: Jossey-Bass, 2002.
Farr, Michael, and Lawrence Shatkin. *50 Best Jobs for Your Personality* Indianapolis, IN: JIST Works, 2005.
Handy, Charles. *The Elephant and the Flea: Reflections of a Reluctant Capitalist.* Cambridge, MA: Harvard Business School Press, 2002.
Lore, Nicholas. *The Pathfinder: How to Choose or Change Your Career for a Lifetime of Satisfaction and Success.* New York: Simon & Schuster, 1998.

Web sites:
Monster.com: **www.monster.com**
Career Planning Services: **www.careerplanning.org**

See also:
☆ Choosing the Best Training Curriculum for You (pp. 426–427)
☆ Transcending the Glass Ceiling (pp. 289–291)
☆ Urbane Renewal: Trusting Your Own Wisdom—A Competitive (and Satisfying) Advantage (pp. 406–407)

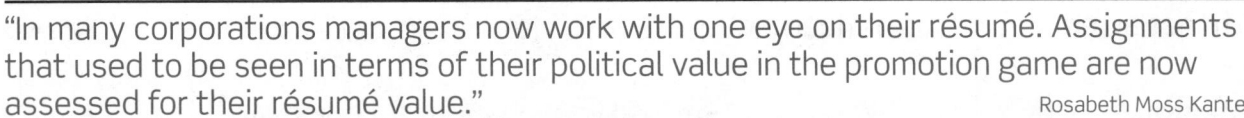

"In many corporations managers now work with one eye on their résumé. Assignments that used to be seen in terms of their political value in the promotion game are now assessed for their résumé value."

Rosabeth Moss Kanter

414

BEST PRACTICE

Mentoring by Max Landsberg

EXECUTIVE SUMMARY

As the traditional career ladder crumbles and is replaced by an increasingly organic and fluid structure, individuals and companies are increasingly institutionalizing the once informal relationship known as mentoring, having a noticeable impact on the way companies implement management and leadership.

- Mentoring is important in developing and retaining employees.
- Corporate mentoring programs match seasoned employees with younger coworkers new either to the organization or to a level of responsibility, designed to have a measurable impact upon the organization.
- Mentors give advice on goal setting and strategizing, sharing their wisdom.
- Mentees gain advice, access to established networks, and broader personal and professional perspective.

INTRODUCTION

Mentoring is defined as the process whereby the leader offers guidance and support to facilitate the understanding of another. Mentoring is vital to delegating and to a range of other management situations—for example, team building, development of people, and managing change.

Most of us probably acquired our mentors more by luck than through planning. But with the erosion of traditional career ladders and the increasingly organic composition of the modern company, individuals and companies alike are seeing ever-greater merits in institutionalizing this once-informal relationship called mentoring.

THE SCOPE OF THE MENTORING RELATIONSHIP

In a corporate setting, a mentoring relationship focuses on skills and career and personal development. At the start of their relationship, neither mentor nor mentee can anticipate all the issues they'll end up discussing. Nevertheless, both parties should be aware of the topics that may emerge.

These topics fall into two broad categories: helping the mentee to achieve learning and career goals, and building the mentee's confidence and self-awareness.

Career issues most typically include:

- whether the mentee's career vision and goals seem relevant and viable;
- how to decode the organization's feedback to the mentee, for example, from an annual appraisal or from a promotion received or missed;
- what experience and expertise to acquire in the short and long terms;
- where to find role models the mentee can identify with;
- whether to accept an internal (or external) job offer;
- how best to promote a corporate initiative that the mentee has conceived;
- how the mentee can best interact with his or her line manager;
- how to react to unacceptable behavior experienced by the mentee, for example, apparent bias, favoritism, or harassment;
- how to deal with the effects of a family problem or disaster, for example, how best to ask for paid or unpaid leave.

Confidence and self-awareness issues may include:

- how the mentee can frankly review personal strengths and weaknesses;
- whether feedback about the mentee's personal style is accurate or not;
- how to overcome apparent career setbacks or feelings of isolation or depression;
- how the to project greater charisma.

Despite this great breadth, mentoring relationships do have their limits. Organizations do not condone nepotistic relationships in which the mentor exerts undue influence in favor of the mentee. The mentor should focus on advice rather than rescue, directing the mentee to a professional counselor if needed.

THE FOUR OPTIONS FOR MENTORING

There are four main types of mentoring an individual may seek or an organization may wish to promote. It's important to recognize that these four models are not mutually ex-

clusive. Furthermore, most people have more than one mentor, and those mentors may play complementary roles.

1 **Informal mentoring** takes place when an experienced person decides to take someone less experienced under his or her wing, often to give career advice.

2 **Positional mentoring** occurs when the mentor is the mentee's line manager.

3 **Formal mentoring** programs emerged during the 1990s in an attempt to gain the advantages of natural mentoring while recognizing the limitations of positional mentoring.

4 **Situational mentoring** provides advice for a specific circumstance, for example, when the mentee has to implement a new computer system or take up an overseas position.

THE BENEFITS TO ALL PARTIES

The benefits of mentoring accrue most obviously to mentees: advice, guidance, access to contacts and networks, reassurance, and a broader perspective.

But corporations also benefit through better recruitment, orientation, and retention of staff, better communication across vertical and horizontal boundaries, faster organizational learning, and a stronger corporate culture.

Finally, mentors often benefit by enhancing their interpersonal skills, gaining insight into the workings of their organization and teams, and enjoying the satisfaction of seeing others grow.

TECHNIQUES FOR ENSURING SUCCESS

The excellent mentor:

- helps the mentee to focus efforts and clarify goals;
- prompts the mentee to develop effective strategies, and acts as devil's advocate to challenge them;
- helps the mentee to identify appropriate resources, contacts, and role models;
- shares knowledge and wisdom based on his or her own experiences;
- acts as a source of inspiration and motivation while maintaining confidentiality.

Mentors do this in the following ways: by asking penetrating questions that help mentees to distinguish real issues from apparent

ones; by accepting the mentees unconditionally, asking *how* or *what* rather than *why*; by listening actively to mentees' feelings as well as their words; and by volunteering observations.

Mentors are unlikely to be effective in the long term if they try to become personal fixers of their mentees' problems.

In obtaining maximum value from the relationship, the three most important attributes of the excellent mentee are openness, initiative, and consideration for the mentor's time.

Mentees clearly need to be open about their objectives and aspirations. But they also need to be open to feedback or other observations by their mentor.

In taking the initiative, the excellent mentee is proactive in meeting with and relating to the mentor, arriving at meetings fully prepared with clear objectives, and taking the lead in suggesting new ways of viewing personal issues. Part of a mentee's task is to follow up on any ideas generated in the meetings and keep the mentor informed about progress.

Finally, the excellent mentee shows consideration for the mentor's investment of time. This involves identifying what the mentor wants to derive from the relationship, accommodating the mentor's schedule when arranging meetings, and providing feedback, praise, and thanks.

ESTABLISHING MENTORING PROGRAMS

Organizations increasingly aim to reap the benefits of mentoring by setting up formal programs. Contrary to natural mentoring, formal mentoring tends to focus on specific objectives and aim at a measurable impact, for example, employee retention. It usually runs for a limited period, involves professional discussions, and is based on pairing, balanced in favor of the mentee.

Such programs typically aim to support employees who are new to the organization or a particular role, or who are part of a group that is in some way specialized or disadvantaged. Formal efforts to provide mentoring for all employees in an organization rarely succeed because of the lack of sufficient mentoring time.

When designing a corporate mentoring program:
- decide whether to adopt a formal program or one that includes an element of natural mentoring;
- develop simple criteria for eligibility to participate and for the maximum number of mentees per mentor;
- agree whether mentees are to choose mentors (recommended) or vice versa, and establish a matching process that is patently fair;
- explain the ground rules clearly, such as commitment to a duration of one year, ability to terminate the relationship at any time without blame, or complete confidentiality;
- provide training for mentors and mentees and specify the expected benefits of the program.

MAKING IT HAPPEN ▶▶
- As a mentor, concentrate on helping the employee to achieve learning and career goals, and to build confidence and self-awareness.
- Some mentoring of team members is desirable, but recognize that the line manager, as a superior, can't provide an impartial view of the relationship.
- Use mentoring to enhance the mentor's own interpersonal skills and insights into the workings of the organization and its teams.
- Consciously move between six roles as needed: coach, motivator, guide, counselor, role model, and (possibly) provider of contacts.
- Ensure that the mentee arranges meetings with the mentor, comes fully prepared, and follows up on any ideas that emerge.

Use formal mentoring programs only for selected employees—there won't be enough mentoring time for everybody. The following factors are critical to the success of corporate mentoring schemes:
- a supportive culture and work environment;
- visible top management commitment, support and leadership;
- participants are volunteers;
- the mentoring program is designed to meet clearly envisioned, critical objectives within an effective time frame;
- agreed terms of reference and ongoing support is provided for mentors;
- the program is regularly monitored and evaluated for successes and drawbacks and inadequacies, and change is implemented on a regular basis.

Key questions to consider when implementing a mentoring program are:
- what are the specific goals of the program?
- have all the people who need to be involved been identified?
- what are the metrics for the program's success and, accordingly, how will the program be evaluated?
- is there commitment from the top management?
- what are the necessary resources, and are they present?
- how will prospective mentors be trained?
- how will mentors and mentees be paired?
- have the guidelines for the program's operation been properly communicated to all parties involved?

Corporate mentoring programs should be goal-focused and, providing the above points are recognized and effectively incorporated into the process, increase productivity and facilitate efficiency.

CONCLUSION

It is important to remember that corporate mentoring programs should be clearly envisioned and constructed to meet the actual requirements of an organization. They are currently being implemented in an increasing number of organizations where they are an invaluable asset—a trend that is sure to continue in the future as old-fashioned management structures are eroded and replaced by organic and dynamic modern constructs. Corporate mentoring programs are a crucial part of such constructs and their benefits are certain to be reaped both in the short term and in the future.

FOR MORE INFORMATION

Books:
Bell, Chip R. *Managers as Mentors*. 2nd ed. San Francisco, CA: Berrett-Koehler, 2002.
Zachary, Lois J. *The Mentor's Guide: Facilitating Effective Learning Relationships*. San Francisco, CA: Jossey-Bass, 2000.

Web sites:
U.S. Coast Guard mentoring program: **http://152.121.2.2/hq/g-w/g-wt/g-wtl/mentoring.htm**
Institute for Management Excellence (search for "mentoring"): **www.itstime.com/oct99.htm**

See also:
☆ Transcending the Glass Ceiling (pp. 289–291)

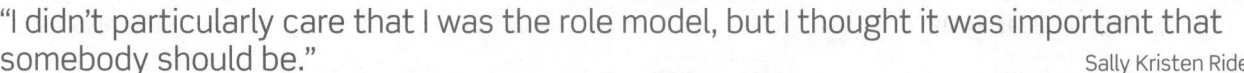

"I didn't particularly care that I was the role model, but I thought it was important that somebody should be."
Sally Kristen Ride

Coaching by Max Landsberg

EXECUTIVE SUMMARY

Coaching is an integrated set of actions, aimed at boosting the performance of an individual or team. Coaching includes:

- a context of trust and understanding
- use of "ask," not only "tell"
- agreement on the goals
- optimizing opportunities to perform
- ongoing, ad hoc, feedback
- periodically, coaching sessions of greater depth
- a recognition by the line manager of the obligation to coach, and the incentives to do so

INTRODUCTION

Coaching is an integrated set of actions aimed at boosting a colleague's performance—so that the person being coached (the "learner") reaches his or her full potential, or even redefines their view of their own potential. In the business world, coaching is a systematic form of on-the-job training, provided by professional outsiders, by peers, or (preferably) by the learner's line manager. Coaching typically aims to build skills in communications (written and oral), problem-solving, teamwork, and selling, or even to enhance personal characteristics such as "impact." In this section we will examine the very elements of successful coaching.

A CONTEXT OF TRUST AND UNDERSTANDING

For coaching to be effective, the coach and learner must first agree explicitly on how the coaching will be delivered. A brief discussion will normally suffice if the coach is the coachee's line manager. However, if the coach is an external professional, a written contract is advisable.

In addition, however, the coach and learner need to trust and understand each other.

First, and most importantly, the learner needs to trust that the coach is not continually trying to evaluate him or her. In corporations or teams in which the culture is highly evaluative, junior people typically do not ask their line managers for coaching support—they avoid showing weakness or ignorance.

Second, the coach needs to understand what motivates the learner to perform strongly in the relevant areas—and whether

any underperformance derives from a lack of skill, or from a lack of will (since the approach to coaching might differ in these two cases).

Finally, the learner needs to understand how the coach most likes to deliver coaching. This topic is often overlooked—but the truly great coach-cum-manager typically helps the learner to understand his preferences.

ASK—DO NOT JUST TELL

In all aspects of coaching, the effective coach will more often ask questions than provide, or "tell," answers. This applies both when providing feedback about the learner's prior underperformance, as well as when generating ideas about how to improve that performance.

AGREE ON SPECIFIC GOALS

Crucial to the coaching process are explicit goals for the learner. This may spring from a recent annual appraisal, from the requirements of a new role, or from some new aspiration by the learner.

It is worth remembering that the best goals are specific, measurable, achievable, results-driven, and time constituted—the memorable "SMART" acronym.

OPTIMIZE OPPORTUNITIES

Practice makes perfect—but feedback alone will not. Central to any increased performance by the learner is the opportunity to confront new challenges in the skill area on which he or she is working. This is why line managers are potentially the best coaches of their team members—they can directly assign tasks which will allow the learner to hone the relevant skills.

PROVIDE AD HOC FEEDBACK

Feedback is one of the coach's most important techniques. Ad hoc feedback means regular constructive and considered comments. Ineffective managers tend to provide feedback using generalities ("Your presentations lack impact."). Such negative forms of feedback leave the learner feeling blamed, defensive, uncertain, and lacking in confidence and self-esteem.

By contrast, constructive feedback focuses on specific skills and improvements needed. It clarifies "where the learner stands" and what to do next, and leaves the person feeling helped rather than merely judged. With this in mind, effective coaches can deliver constructive feedback in three discrete parts.

1 First, the coach is specific in replaying actions that the learner took. ("During your last presentation you avoided answering a direct question and instead presented another chart.")
2 Second, the coach highlights the implications. ("This made the audience feel that you were uncertain about your material and uninterested in their concerns.")
3 Finally, the coach suggests a desired outcome. ("Next time try to allow time for questions and respond to them clearly.")

This three-part approach (*Action, Impact, Desirable outcome*—or *AID* for short), is the key to providing useful feedback. It is particularly effective if the three points can be elicited using "ask" mode, ("Which parts of your presentation worked best? Which parts of it worked least well? What was the impact of this? What could you do differently next time?")

Even when delivering positive feedback (that is, praise), effective coaches use the first two steps of this approach. By specifically highlighting the Action and the Impact, the coachee can more fully understand why he or she has "done a good job."

DELIVER IN-DEPTH SESSIONS

Periodically the coach and coachee will decide to complement ad hoc feedback with a 30–60 minute coaching "session."

To ensure a relevant focus and clear outcomes, effective coaches typically use a four-step agenda that covers **G**oals, **R**eality, **O**ptions, and **W**rap-up.

In the first step (**Goals**), coach and learner agree on the topic for discussion and the objective for the session ("Let's find ways to further develop your presentation skills. Let's find at least three ideas in the next half-hour."). They might also review or amend the longer-term goal ("Let's establish as a goal that you feel able to present the division's results to the board meeting next month.").

In the second step (**Reality**), the coach and learner take stock of the coachee's current strengths and weaknesses. The effective coach invites the learner to do most of the talking, starting with a self-assessment. If the coach does provide feedback, it takes the form of specific examples, either in ask mode ("What did you feel about the question-and-answer session at the end of your last presentation?") or in tell mode ("You could have allowed more time for questions.").

In step three (**Options**), coach and learner both brainstorm ways forward. What can the coachee do to change the situation? What alternatives are there to that approach? Who could help? The coach's role is not primarily to provide answers. It is rather to stimulate creative ideas from the learner—possible actions that the learner will more naturally buy into.

Finally (**Wrap-up**), the coach helps the learner choose an option and commit to action. This involves identifying possible obstacles, making the next steps specific, agreeing timing, and identifying any support needed. In subsequent sessions the coach will naturally vary the length of each step as needed.

UNDERSTAND OBLIGATIONS AND INCENTIVES

The autocratic manager is fast becoming a dinosaur; all managers are now obliged to coach their teams. This stems from two changes in the business climate. Firstly, employees are now even more avid to acquire skills, and even more likely to change employer if they are disappointed. Thus, coaching is crucial to the retention of talented people. Secondly, the rapid pace of business and the greater prevalence of job rotation and cross-functional teamwork mean that traditional off-the-job training can rarely be scheduled in a timely way.

Strong managers recognize their obligation to coach. They also realize the benefits to themselves: more time because of having a stronger team to which to delegate; less time spent on recruiting replacements; a more positive and enjoyable work environment; and stronger interpersonal skills honed through coaching.

MAKING IT HAPPEN ▶▶

There are many questions that coaches can ask to focus the coaching process. The same questions can also be used for self-coaching—all you need to do is consider a major issue or ongoing behavior that you would like to resolve.
- What are you trying to achieve?
- How will you know when you have achieved it?
- Would you define it as an end goal or a performance goal?
- If it is an end goal, what performance goal could be related to it?
- Is the goal specific?
- In what way is it measurable?
- To what extent can you control the result, What sort of things won't you have control over?
- Do you feel that achieving the goal will stretch or break you?
- When do you want to achieve the goal by?
- What are the milestones or key points on the way to achieving your goal?
- Who is involved and what effect could they have on the situation?
- What have you done about this situation so far, and what have been the results?
- What are the major constraints in finding a way forward?
- Are these constraints major or minor? How could their effect be reduced?
- What other issues are occurring at work that might have a bearing on your goal?
- What options do you have?
- If you had unlimited resources what options would you have?
- Could you link your goal to some other organizational issue?
- What would be the perfect solution?

Once the position has been assessed, the time comes to select the best option and take action. The following questions may then be useful:
- What are you going to do?
- When are you going to do it?
- Who needs to know?
- What support and resources do you need, and how will you get them?
- How will the above help you to achieve your goals?
- What obstacles might hinder you and what strategies do you have for countering these?

CONCLUSION

Coaching has much to do with mentoring and it has a great deal to do with counseling. All three are about supporting an individual to overcome problems, achieve success, and realize their full potential. Common skills for coaches, mentors, and counselors are strong interpersonal skills, and include:
- good listening skills
- good questioning—getting the learner to open up by asking open questions and avoiding "yes" or "no" answers
- suspending judgment
- giving constructive feedback
- checking understanding
- providing focus

The value of all these attributes is that they clarify issues, solve problems by creating options, change patterns of behavior, and help the individual to learn.

Coaching relies on the agenda being set by the learners. They should discover their own way forward, and should feel commitment to their course of action because they have been the one responsible for establishing it. Coaching can be seen as having four main phases:

1 Set **goals** both for the overall coaching relationship and for each session.
2 Explore the current position of the learner: the **reality** of their circumstances and their concerns.
3 Generate strategies, action plans, and **options** for achieving the desired goals.
4 Decide **what** is to be done, by whom, how, and when.

FOR MORE INFORMATION

Books:
Landsberg, Max. *The Tao of Coaching*. New York: Economist Books, 2005.
Whitmore, Sir John. *Coaching for Performance*. Naperville, IL: Nicholas Brealey, 2002.

Web site:
www.coachville.com: this site aims to be the definitive coaching portal.

"Lifelong learners take risks. Much more than others, these men and women push themselves out of their comfort zones and try new ideas. "
Bob Guccione

How NLP Can Contribute to Best Management Practice

by Joseph O'Connor

EXECUTIVE SUMMARY

Neuro-linguistic programming (NLP) is the systemic study of human communication. It studies the interrelationship between thinking, language, and achievement and models best practice to make it available to others.

This article will summarize the main contributions of NLP to best management practice.

- NLP helps managers to understand people and how to motivate them.
- It models best practice so that important skills can be passed on to others.
- It models the business system to see how it can be improved.
- NLP helps managers to generate business and personal goals, and to integrate individual and organizational goals and values.
- It gives skills to make meetings shorter and more productive.
- It gives managers the skills to coach their people.

INTRODUCTION

NLP was created in the mid 1970s in California by John Grinder, a professor of linguistics at the University of California and Richard Bandler, a student at that university. They wanted to know: how is it that some people are extremely good at a skill and others are not? The power of this question was in the "how" rather than "why." They modeled some of the best communicators of the time to describe how they were so good, so that the skills could be taught to others.

NLP is now used internationally and NLP practitioners have modeled excellence in many different fields—sports, education, leadership, sales, and, naturally, management. What makes a good manager? What is best management practice? NLP is in a unique position to answer these questions. It does not only study their behavior; it explores the goals, values, and motivations. Nor is NLP satisfied with the rationalizations that people give. Typically the very best in every profession do not know how they do it so well. They show you, they do not tell you.

WHAT IS NLP?

NLP is the systemic study of human communication. There are four main aspects.

1 *An attitude of curiosity.* How do people do what they do? How is it that some days you are very good, and other days you are not? Human thinking is not random; there must be a structure. NLP discovers

this. Then you can have many more of your best days.

2 *A methodology of modeling.* NLP explores the ideas and actions of the person to find out how he or she operates.

3 *A vision.* Everybody has access to the best possible methods. No one has to reinvent the wheel every time he or she assumes a management position. Everybody learns how to learn and be the best he or she can be.

4 *A set of tools.* NLP has a tool set and modeling excellence itself produces more tools.

NLP stands for neuro-linguistic programming.

- "Neuro" is the mind.
- "Linguistic" is language.
- "Programming" is how we put together sequences of actions to achieve goals.

How does this help managers? Management is getting things done through others. Managers stand or fall by the business results they get, but those results are produced by the people they manage, not by themselves. Managers are paid to communicate. The best managers are the best at communicating. This is NLP territory.

MOTIVATION AND COMMUNICATION

"Management practice" is what NLP would call a double nominalization. Both words are abstractions; they cannot be seen, heard, nor touched. Try this small NLP thought ex-

periment. Think of "management." What does it mean to you? Let the pictures, sounds, and feelings that go with this word come into your mind. Now think about "managing." The odds are when you think of the verb, your mental pictures spring to life. Things start moving. Managing is about execution.

The best managers are often not noticed or appreciated. Why? Because there are no dramatics, no last minute saves, no firefighting, no disasters. They seem lucky. Most projects go smoothly. The managers who get noticed are the ones who skirt the edge of disaster, who rescue the project at the eleventh hour. While this may be necessary, the best managers stay away from the edge and are on top of the job well before the eleventh hour.

Good managers motivate and communicate. To succeed, every manager has to balance two elements.

First is task. They need to get the job done, and give clear instructions. Misunderstanding can be very costly. NLP has *the Meta Model*, a series of precision questions to ensure a clear understanding. Most misunderstandings happen because we assume the other person means what we think he or she means, instead of asking questions to clarify.

Second is relationship. All communication is embedded in relationship and NLP has studied how relationships of *trust, rapport,* and respect are developed.

The best managers network well and are respected. They have good relationships. A good relationship makes the task more pleasant and easier. In Western European and U. S. culture, the relationship is supposed to flow from the shared task. In Latin and many other cultures, the best work comes from good relationships that are established beforehand.

MODELING BEST PRACTICE

NLP developed by modeling. The practitioners of NLP search for people who are exceptional in their field and discover how they are able to get the results they do. NLP is pragmatic. An NLP model is evaluated by whether it works or not—you must get the same class of results as the person modeled.

If you want your managers to be the best, don't use a theoretical model, use one that works, one that comes from real managers.

NLP modeling is used in two ways.

1 *Modeling the best people.* For example, model the best managers or salespeople, then using the model to train the average performers to be better. This model can also be used to recruit the people that will be best in the organization.

2 *Systemic audit for the business.* This is an NLP model of the business system that can act as a sophisticated needs analysis. It identifies where the business is working well, and where it is not, by analyzing the communication systems. It analyzes what people do and think, not what they should be doing and thinking. It gives a real-time photograph of the business.

GOAL AND VALUES

Goals are one of the keystones of NLP. Everyone acts to achieve something. They may not be doing it very well and they may not get the results they intend. NLP has a set of principles and tools to ensure that business goals are clear, measured, challenging, and achievable. These goal-setting tools are essential in appraisals, teamwork, and strategic planning.

NLP also gives insight into individual and organizational values. Many businesses have excellent mission and vision statements, but somehow these are never able to connect with the minds and the hearts of the people who are responsible for realizing them. Values are the keys to motivation and creative work. They are the reason companies change hands for millions of dollars when the products and bricks and mortar that comprise the business are worth only a fraction of the price.

Imagine a Monday morning when only 50% of your work force came to work. Disaster. Then imagine on Tuesday, everyone came to work but with only 50% of their energy and creativity. This is still a disaster,

but it is invisible. It never gets noticed. NLP helps to explore and integrate the goals and values of the organization so that everyone is aligned.

MEETINGS

Many business meetings are unnecessary, and many take longer than necessary. NLP has modeled negotiation skills, so people know how to get the most from their meetings. These skills can also be used to deal with difficult people and situations in the workplace, and in negotiations with competitors.

COACHING

Coaching is growing increasingly popular in business and rightly so. It is a cost effective way of getting the best from people. External coaches work with executives and managers to help them to give their best. Managers need coaching skills to get the best from their people.

NLP has contributed a great deal to best practices of coaching, particularly in its study of effective language and the use of powerful questions. NLP helps people to explore how their habitual ideas are holding them back, so that they can become more productive, happier, and effective at work. It also helps them achieve a work–life balance. An unhappy manager will not be so effective, regardless of his or her skill level.

The New Management Paradigm

The old paradigm of management was to get your people to explain the problem to you. You asked questions to help you understand it, and then you told them what to do. The new paradigm, in which the manager is a coach, is to ask open questions to help the person understand the problem so *he* or *she* can find the solution. This not only solves the problem, but also solves the limited thinking that gave rise to the problem in the first place. It makes people more creative, productive, and self sufficient.

CONCLUSION

Here are some of the patterns shared by successful managers:

- *They take multiple perspectives.* They look to the short (next month), medium, (next year) and long term (next five years) when setting goals and assessing plans. They also look at problems from many different viewpoints as well as their own. (for example, customer, shareholder, C.E.O., manufacturer, etc.)
- *They motivate through values.* They do not rely simply on the carrot and the stick. The strongest motivation comes from the inside and people work best when they feel engaged.
- *They are purpose driven rather than problem driven.* They think in terms of achievements and goals rather than what is wrong. They do not blame.
- *They believe in themselves and their business.* They believe in their own skills and they believe in their organization. They are congruent about what they do.
- *They learn on two levels.* They learn how to solve problems and how to stop the kind of thinking that gave rise to the problem in the first place.
- *They balance task and relationship.* They know that both are necessary for the best results.
- *They can tolerate uncertainty and ambiguity.* They know they do not have to know everything. And they do the best they can in the present moment, using all the resources they have.

FOR MORE INFORMATION

Book:
O'Connor, Joseph, and Andrea Lages. *Coaching with NLP.* London: Thorsons, 2004.

Web site:
Lambent.com: **www.lambent.com**

See also:
 Management Styles (pp. 1819–1819)

"Make me a better leader . . . by helping develop larger and greater qualities of understanding, tolerance, sympathy, wisdom, perspective, equanimity, mind-reading, and second sight."

Anonymous

Driving Fear from the Workplace
by Dick Richards

EXECUTIVE SUMMARY

- Disallowing or disowning fear extinguishes the passion needed to achieve organizational goals.
- Engaging human energy, including fear, and connecting it with organizational purpose is a fundamental task of management.
- Engaging human energy is an aspect of the art of management. It requires mastery of skills and techniques as well as intent to value the full spectrum of emotional energy.
- Human energy, particularly fear, can be oriented and employed as an effective tool for success.

INTRODUCTION

In the early 1980s management guru W. Edwards Deming admonished managers to "drive out fear so that everyone may work effectively for the company." He was referring to fear that causes people to distort or ignore unpleasant results. Deming held that such fear stifles learning. Despite Deming's admonishment, fear still stalks workplaces and remains a potent force. The Discovery Group, an opinion survey organization, concluded that "half of all employees do not feel free to voice their opinions openly."

Fear takes many more forms than the one Deming described. It is apparent when we retreat from speaking to someone who does not listen, or when we recoil from saying difficult things to people who are known to shoot messengers. Fear is present whenever we suspect a hidden agenda, or when we are summoned to find a better way of working. It shows up as job insecurity and as dread that our positions might be usurped. It is close by when we feel unwilling to take risks or do what we know is right, and whenever we masquerade as someone other than who we are. Startup companies frequently have an entirely distinct set of fears such as raising capital and making payroll.

Fear originates from different sources: as a consequence of the world we live in; or induced by people who want us to feel fearful; or self-generated in response to a challenge. Whatever its form or source, the effects of fear are insidious and pervasive; it corrupts learning, improvement, innovation, measurement, and relationships. However, fear itself is not the lone culprit. Disallowed or disowned fear, which I refer to as "unacknowledged fear," is another, perhaps more insidious, danger.

FEAR AND PASSION

While it seems that fear ought to have no home in our workplaces, we do want passion. We want excitement about visions. We want enthusiasm for strategic plans. We want the energy that people bring to work when they feel those emotions. It's obvious that emotions are sources of energy that compel action. That's why we welcome passion, excitement, and enthusiasm. When people experience those emotions things get done.

It's less obvious that emotions are inextricably connected to each other. We cannot readily isolate just one emotion. We cannot drive out fear, or any other so-called negative emotion, without the risk of driving out the energy we want—excitement and enthusiasm. Daniel Goleman, author of *Working with Emotional Intelligence*, writes, "When the dictates of a boss determine the emotions a person must express, the result is an estrangement from one's own emotions." For example, when a manager suggests, either directly or subtly, that he or she wants everyone to feel part of one big happy team, but never fearful, angry, or sad, people are likely to shut their genuine emotions down altogether and put on a happy face. Goleman calls this "emotional tyranny." When we fail to acknowledge fear, we also extinguish passion. The result is a robotic workplace.

ENGAGING EMOTIONAL ENERGY

A fundamental task of management is engaging human energy and connecting it with organizational purpose. One popular model posits four kinds of human energy. *Physical* energy is the energy of the body. Engaging physical energy involves deciding

who does how much of what work and when. *Intellectual* energy is of the mind. Engaging it involves such activities as making sense of problems and finding creative solutions. *Spiritual* energy arises from feeling connected to something larger than the self—an idea, a cause, a place, a deity. Engaging spiritual energy is seen in attempts to gain commitment to a vision or mission; these are endeavors to enlist people in a higher calling. Our concern is with the fourth of these—*emotional energy*, and specifically fear. Engaging emotional energy means, first, mobilizing the passion and commitment that spurs people into action and, second, dealing effectively with emotions that create barriers to such action.

George Davis, cofounder of Davis & Dean, a global project-management education company, believes that our prevailing model of management fails when we deal with fear. Davis says, "We reward managers who are warriors. The warrior's orientation is toward short-term goals: win today's battle, take that hill." With such a mentality, Davis believes, induced fear becomes useful because it's a good short-term motivator. "The problem is," says Davis, "if you use it again and again the fear becomes replaced by a sense of helplessness. This is typical of many corporate cultures. It is what employees of large organizations express when they resist change, dismiss change efforts, or become passive and cynical. Induced fear, which seems to work great in the short term, eventually creates apathy, a sense of oppression, and hopelessness."

When induced fear loses its impact, the warrior's impulse is to induce more fear. In the hands of a warrior, Deming's injunction to drive out fear may become a license to make people afraid to be afraid, or at least afraid to admit to being afraid. Rather than engaging emotional energy, warrior managers are likely to kill it.

SELF-GENERATED FEAR

There is little human progress without fear. Psychologist Susan Jeffers said it this way: "The fear will never go away as long as I continue to grow." This is a different kind of fear from the induced fear used to threaten people. This fear is the self-generated consequence of accepting a meaningful challenge. It can be a friend, a harbinger of an

important opportunity. It is stimulating rather than paralyzing and can provide energy to meet the challenge.

Erik Sprotte, former director of human resources for Sears, accepted the challenge of helping to start a Web enterprise called FreeSamples.com. Self-generated fear arises from the challenge of "going where others haven't gone." Sprotte says, "I used to fear making a mistake like not having the facts at a meeting. This new kind of fear is good. It creates discipline and helps me focus on the important things that I really need to do."

THE ART OF ENGAGING FEAR

While fear is an individual experience, people collude with one another in order to allow it to remain unacknowledged. They agree, if only tacitly, that fear should be disallowed or disowned, that "we just don't talk about those things around here." Disallowing and disowning fear thus becomes a cultural norm. Managers can and should take the lead in encouraging people to allow and own their fear. Today's business environment is soaked in challenge. Managers need all the energy they can muster from themselves and from people they manage. They cannot afford to ignore or destroy emotional energy, even when it arrives in an uncomfortable form.

Management, like any other work, is part science and part art. Engaging emotional energy is an aspect of the art of managing. As painters engage the energy of paint and poets engage the energy of words, managers' artistic medium is the energy of the people they manage. So managers must be acquainted with human energy in the same way that a painter is acquainted with how paint behaves, or a poet with the rhythm of words.

MINI-CASES

Many organizations are reluctant to have outsiders know they are fearful, so best practices aren't freely shared. However, Pfeffer and Sutton mention three companies that manage fear successfully:

PSS/World Medical, where managers work to get problems raised faster than they would be in a fearful environment, gives everyone the opportunity to communicate with others and does not punish honest mistakes.

At *SAS Institute*, David Russo, vice president of human resources said, "We punish nothing."

At *Men's Wearhouse*, senior managers believe so strongly in eliminating fear that a transgression such as stealing is often viewed as a signal that development is needed rather than that the transgressor ought to be fired.

MAKING IT HAPPEN ▶▶

Mastery of any art depends on developing certain skills and techniques. Consider the following:

● **Befriend your own fear.** There are three skills involved in befriending fear (or any other emotion): recognizing how it feels physically, putting it into words, and engaging it productively. None is easy in a work context, because most organizations discourage any emotion that seems negative. Find the people around you who are competent at managing their emotions. They are not those who overcontrol, but those who express emotions well and use them to create productive actions. Learn from those people.

● **Facilitate honest dialogue about fears of all kinds.** This requires developing a high level of trust. People won't talk about their fears if there are negative consequences for doing so. Once fear is in the open, treat it as a gift. Treat induced fear as a signal that someone must learn to challenge rather than threaten. Treat self-generated fear as a signal that growth is at hand. It is important to listen and cope with uncomfortable situations.

● **Challenge rather than threaten.** Drive out induced fear and befriend self-generated fear. George Davis argues: "It is far more valuable to challenge people than to induce fear. The person will then create his or her own basket of fears that will spawn creativity."

● **Connect people with purpose.** Erik Sprotte is convinced that people need to believe in what their organization is doing and need to know how their contributions make a difference. He says, "Good managers help others understand their role in keeping the boat afloat. When we know we have a

common goal, and have owned our fear, we can keep each other inspired every day."

CONCLUSION

Mastering the art of management requires developing skills and learning techniques for engaging human energy, including fear. And it requires something more. In *The Art Spirit*, artist and art teacher Robert Henri wrote, "The technique learned without a purpose is a formula which, when used, knocks the life out of any ideas to which it is applied." If we employ skills and techniques to engage the energy of fear, they will work only when coupled with a heartfelt purpose to value the full spectrum of emotional energy. When this is accomplished, your team will have the motivation, discipline, and cooperation required to reach ever more demanding organizational activities.

FOR MORE INFORMATION

Books:
Deming, W. Edwards. *Out of the Crisis.* Cambridge, MA: MIT Press, 2000.
Goleman, Daniel P. *Working with Emotional Intelligence.* New York: Bantam Doubleday Dell, 2000.
Henri, Robert. *The Art Spirit.* New York: HarperCollins, 1984.
Jeffers, Susan. *Feel the Fear and Do It Anyway.* New York: Fawcett Columbine, 1998.
Ryan, Kathleen D., and Daniel K. Oestreich. *Driving Fear Out of the Workplace: Creating the High-trust, High-performance Organization.* 2nd ed. San Francisco, CA: Jossey-Bass, 1998.

Web site:
Articles 911: **www.articles911.com**

See also:

"Increasingly our society does not see social obligation as the primary obligation of the individual. The primary obligation is loyalty to the corporation." John Ralston Saul

Managing Internal Politics
by Kathleen Kelley Reardon

EXECUTIVE SUMMARY

- Advancing business and career goals often necessitates acting politically.
- Those managers who reject—or fail to understand—internal politics do so at their own peril.
- The nature of the political arena affects the productivity, morale, and success or failure of individual employees.
- Career success depends on matching the individual's political style to the company's environment.
- Smart managers familiarize themselves with the warning signs of political pathology before it's too late.

INTRODUCTION

Many of the hurdles managers must face and overcome have little to do with technical competence. Rather, they have to do with politics. Internal politics is a fact of life in organizations, yet many managers and C.E.O.s will tell you their success is largely due to allowing "no politics" in their companies. They'll regale you with stories of how they use and encourage "people skills" to create a desired environment and accomplish organizational goals. What they're really talking about is how they use politics.

In common vernacular, "politics" is used to describe what people do to influence decision makers, accomplish hidden agendas, and surreptitiously advance their careers, often to the detriment of others. But politics is not always so sinister. By its very nature, politics involves going outside usual, formally sanctioned channels to accomplish objectives, but not necessarily in a secretive manner and often to the benefit of all involved. When used to influence people in the service of valid company goals, politics becomes a positive tool indeed. The team leader who makes valuable connections with people who can advance the team's efforts is acting politically.

While a high level of field-based competence is required, given two competent persons, the one who has political savvy, agility in the use of power, and the ability to influence others is more likely to succeed as a senior manager. Indeed, to the successful senior manager in a competitive organization, day-to-day life *is* politics. That's why smart business people think like Caroline Nahas, managing director of Korn/Ferry International, southern California. To be politically astute, you need to "read where the trend lines are" and "be ahead of the game."

Of course, politics is not always positive. Sometimes, people must defend themselves from political maneuvering. When surrounded or targeted by coworkers playing underhanded political games, job survival may require one to respond in politically astute, sometimes unpreferred ways. In organizations where biases or favoritism dictate who gets key assignments and promotions, political-style flexibility is required to get into the loop. The organizational political arena merely requires the use of relational strategies, sometimes uncomfortable ones, to advance oneself. In short, the astute manager must understand how politics functions in organizations and how to advance his or her and the company's own goals.

SIZING UP THE POLITICAL ARENA

The first step in acquiring political acumen is learning to identify the kind of political arena in which you operate. Without this knowledge, managers operate in the dark, wondering why opportunities were lost. All four primary political arenas—minimal, moderate, highly political, and pathologically political—often coexist inside a large organization.

In a **minimally politicized** arena, the atmosphere is amicable. Conflicts rarely occur and don't usually last long. There's an absence of in- and out-groups, and one person's gain isn't seen as another's loss. Rules may be bent and favors granted, but people treat each other with regard and rarely re-

sort to underhanded political means. These are excellent environments for people uncomfortable with aggressive politics. Unfortunately, such organizations are more the exception than the rule.

Moderately politicized organizations operate on commonly understood and formally sanctioned rules. They often include smaller, fast-moving companies and large ones focused on organizational agility. Where customer focus, results, teamwork, and interpersonal trust are priorities, politics are rarely destructive, and often focus on surfacing worthwhile ideas. Achieving objectives via unsanctioned methods isn't unusual, but tends to be subtle and deniable. When conflicts get out of hand, managers will invoke sanctioned rules or shared mores for resolution.

As a manager, however, when such an arena becomes dysfunctional, you will see considerable denial before unspoken political rules surface to where you can identify and address them constructively.

In a **highly politicized** culture, conflict is pervasive. Instead of applying formal rules consistently, political players only invoke them when convenient. In-groups and out-groups are clearly defined. Few people dare to communicate directly with senior managers. "Who" is more important than "what" you know, and work is often highly stressful, especially for those in out-groups. When there's conflict, people rely on aggressive political methods and involve others in the dispute. Highly political organizations usually have difficulty resolving conflicts constructively. They place blame and terminate losers. Such quick fixes rarely alter the dysfunctional pattern.

Pathologically politicized organizations are often on the verge of self-destruction. Productivity is suboptimal and information massaging is prevalent. People distrust each other, interactions are often fractious, and conflict is long-lasting and pervasive. People must circumvent formal procedures and structures to achieve objectives. They spend much time covering their backs. Management uses a carrot-and-stick approach to control people. Subordinates are seen as stubborn, willful—even stupid. In the classic *Harvard Business Review* article, "Asinine Attitudes Toward Motivation," Harry Levinson described this as the "jackass fallacy."

IDENTIFYING POLITICAL PATHOLOGY

To avoid political pathology, managers must recognize its encroachment. Here are five indicators that it's time to alter the political environment in order to save it from self-destruction.

1 **Frequent flattery** of persons in power, coupled with abuse of people in weaker positions.
2 **Information massages**. Anything that might rock the boat is actively discouraged and the common means of communication is hint and innuendo.
3 **Malicious gossip** and backstabbing are common, even where little overt conflict appears.
4 **Cold indifference**, where no one is valued and everyone is dispensable, indicates the area has been systemically polluted by people in charge. Survival is based on obsequiousness, and getting others before they get you.
5 **Fake left, go right**. People, even entire departments, purposely mislead others in order to look good when they fail. Teamwork is absent. Managers sacrifice subordinates' careers to avoid looking bad.

MATCHING POLITICAL STYLE TO POLITICAL CULTURE

The second crucial step in learning to manage politics is identifying individual political styles. The mix of styles and their "fit" with the predominant political arena exert considerable influence on goal achievement.

The Purist

The least political are "purists," who believe in getting ahead through hard work. They shun politics, and rely on following sanctioned rules to get things done. Purists are usually honest and in highly political or pathological organizations are perceived as naively so. They believe in getting ahead by doing their job well. Purists tend to trust other people and prefer to work with those who do the same. Behind the scenes grappling for power and prestige is not of interest, hence purists are best suited to minimally political climates.

The Team Player

"Team players" believe you get ahead by working with others and using politics that advance the goals of the group. They rarely put career needs ahead of group needs. Team players prefer to operate by sanctioned rules, but will trade favors or engage in other relatively benign politics to achieve team goals. Focused on doing the job right and creating conditions for team member advancement, team players are best suited to moderately political environments.

The Street Fighter

An individualist, the "street fighter" believes the best way to get ahead is via rough tactics. The street fighter relies more on subliminal politics than the purist and the team player, but is just as likely to invoke sanctioned rules when they serve personal goals. Street fighters watch their backs, push hard to achieve personal goals, and are slow to trust others. They thrive on the "cut and thrust" of business, enjoy intrigue, and derive gratification from working the system. The street fighter is comfortable in highly political arenas and can survive in pathological ones as well.

The Maneuverer

The "maneuverer" is also an individualist, one who believes in getting ahead by playing political games in a skillful, unobtrusive manner. Subtler than the street fighter, but uninhibited about using politics to advance personal objectives and favored team objectives, maneuverers prefer to do so in deniable ways. They look for ulterior motives in others, have little regard for sanctioned rules, and rely largely on subliminal politics. These smooth operators are less committed to hard work than purists, and only operate as team players when it suits their agendas. People get in the way of a maneuverer at their own peril unless they too are capable of maneuvering. The maneuverer is best suited to highly political and pathological arenas.

The task of all managers with regard to politics is to assess the arena prevalent in their division, and that of the larger organization. Is it becoming highly political or pathological? If so, is this because opinion leaders are of the street fighter or maneuverer styles? There's nothing inherently wrong with street fighters and the occasional maneuverer may be an asset if he or she is not a threat to the group. A predominance of these styles, however, can tip a division or organization closer to pathology, a condition that is difficult if not impossible to reverse. Savvy managers familiarize themselves with political warning signs and they take steps to stem the tide of political self-destruction.

MAKING IT HAPPEN ▶▶

- Assess the degree to which your organization is politicized. Is the atmosphere amicable or distrustful? Is the workforce productive, or does conflict prevent work getting done?
- Recognize the signs of impending political pathology: flattery of superiors, malicious gossip, information massaging, indifference, and purposeful misleading.
- Take steps to detoxify the workplace: communicate more openly and directly, invoke sanctioned rules or shared mores to resolve conflict, emphasize solving problems over placing blame.

CONCLUSION

Politics are a reality in the workplace; and, consequently, one must manage the conflicts that arise from political behavior. Politics, in and of itself, is not bad if it works to serve company goals by making sure that the workplace is productive and that morale remains high. Politics must never be allowed to degenerate into a self-destructive process.

FOR MORE INFORMATION

Books:
Reardon, Kathleen Kelley. *The Secret Handshake: Mastering the Politics of the Business Inner Circle*. New York: Random House, 2001.
Reardon, Kathleen Kelley. *It's All Politics: Winning in a World Where Hard Work and Talent Aren't Enough*. New York: Doubleday, 2005.

"Brutally speaking, our scheme does not ask any initiative in a man. We do not care for his initiative."

F. W. Taylor

Response Ability—How Managers Stay Up When Times Are Down

by Paul Stoltz

EXECUTIVE SUMMARY

- Adversity in business is increasing. A poll of 45,372 managers in dozens of industries worldwide revealed that 98% predict a more difficult, chaotic, uncertain, and demanding future. A separate longitudinal, global survey of 57 different companies shows that the number of adversities a manager faces daily has climbed from seven in 1990, to 13 in 1996, and 23 in 2002.
- Today, managers must have *Response Ability*—the ability to respond optimally to whatever happens the moment it strikes.
- The most important variable in unleashing and growing human capital is how people respond to growing levels of adversity.
- Adversity Quotient (AQ) is a measure of a person's hardwired pattern of response to adversity and a measure of Response Ability.
- AQ can be measured, permanently rewired, and strengthened, impacting individual and collective performance, agility, and resilience.

INTRODUCTION

Adversity, ranging from annoyance to tragedy, has become the rule in corporate life. Adversity is everything that gets in the way of, or blocks, an organization's quest to fulfill its vision, achieve its goals, and accomplish its strategic plan. To keep these imperatives alive requires greater resilience than most managers possess. Given that managing adversity lies at the heart of management's ability to unleash human capital, how can managers learn to harness adversity to launch new levels of opportunity and momentum? As adversity rises, every manager's and organization's resilience and effectiveness hinges on *Response Ability*, the ability to respond optimally to whatever happens the moment it strikes. Response-Able managers thrive amid the same difficulties that paralyze their less Response-Able counterparts.

MANAGING IN ADVERSITY
The Silent Toll

While today's workplace is arguably more dynamic and exciting, it is also exacting a growing toll. A Gallup Poll revealed that 19% of workers are "actively disengaged"—they are delivering a small fraction of their talents at work. Furthermore, 61% (or more) are at least partially disengaged. The estimated cost to corporations in the United States alone is $350 billion; multiply that several times over for a worldwide estimate.

As adversity rises, workers feel increasingly stretched. Their work and their lives become more complex, chaotic, uncertain, and demanding. Their entire world tasks them to do more, faster, and better. The physical toll adversity takes upon the majority of the workforce includes a multitude of dismal symptoms, including diminished immune functions (with increased sick days), sapped energy, insomnia, and stress. Inside most people, today's levels of adversity create a chronic and toxic biochemical reaction that holistically degrades their performance deeply.

The psychological toll of the adversity trend manifests as depression, restlessness, anxiety, and pessimism—all psychosocial phenomena which are occurring at epidemic levels and growing. These conditions are also symbiotic, feeding off and flourishing in each other's presence. Overall the grand-scale toll of adversity in organizations, their capacity, and human capital is inestimable. Fortunately, it is also largely unnecessary.

The Truth about Motivation

Nearly every manager perceives motivating others as an important and essential duty. Yet, intuitively, we know that we cannot motivate others: authentic motivation originates and is sustained from deep within the self. Attempting to motivate others can be like painting your car red to make it go faster. It may *feel* faster, but very little has happened to strengthen performance.

To fully understand the myth and challenge of motivation, we must consider three forms of capacity. A person's *Required Capacity* is what the world demands of them, or what is required of them to perform their job effectively. As adversity mounts, most people's required capacity is growing at an accelerated rate, making it harder to remain fully engaged and motivated.

When we motivate others, we are striving to help them tap and deliver their *Existing Capacity*—their talents, aptitudes, competencies, experience, knowledge, wisdom, and energy—to the challenge at hand. People are hired for their Existing Capacity under two assumptions: that they will tap most, if not all, of it on a regular basis and that they will grow it to meet or exceed the Required Capacity.

The portion of their capacity that a person actually taps and delivers is called their *Accessed Capacity*. Anyone who has hired someone knows that many people fail to access their best abilities at work. This is a chronic source of frustration among managers and the major source of lost or underutilized human capital. The quest of every manager must be to hire and grow Response-Able people who can consistently tap and grow their Existing Capacities. Clearly traditional methods of motivation, screening applicants, and training employees fall critically short of what is required.

ACHIEVING SUCCESS AND RESPONSE ABILITY

Fortunately, there is a way to assess and strengthen how people respond to adversity, or their Response Ability. Beyond your IQ, experience, or skill-set, it is your Adversity Quotient, or AQ, that most directly predicts and determines your ability to weather and harness the current storm for future gains.

AQ is scientifically valid, a reliable measure of your hardwired pattern of response to adversity. More than 100,000 employees in dozens of companies representing a broad

---

"When, in response to deteriorating business, a company blames outside forces or covers up its problems by changing its accounting methods or by using other tricks, it ensures failure."

Charles G. Koch

range of industries have measured their AQs and learned about how their CORE affects their Response Ability, capacity, and resilience.

A Response-Able culture is one in which . . .

1 *People thrive on adversity.* The greater the challenges, the more energized and engaged people become. In fact, people get bored if things are too calm for too long.

2 *Challenges unleash greatness.* People are at their best in trying situations and times. They consistently dig deep and bring out their greatest talents when faced with the impossible.

3 *There's calm in the storm.* There is a norm of cool-headed decision making. People are not easily fazed or thrown off by unexpected turns of events.

4 *There are stories of overcoming.* There is likely to be a history of resilience, with sagas of heroes who overcame adversity to create pivotal advancements.

5 *Managers hire and keep the best.* Self-motivated, fully engaged people are attracted to and are likely to stay with the organization.

A low AQ culture is one in which . . .

1 *People crumble under pressure.* When adversity strikes, people are stunned, angry, resigned, and uninspired.

2 *Situations bring out the worst.* As adversity mounts, people act in selfish, distant, panicked, mean, and disengaged ways. Conflicts arise, panic spreads, helplessness grows, and problems fester.

3 *It seems like a blame game.* Adversity makes people point fingers and sidestep blame. The greater the adversity, the more accountability, trust, and agility suffer.

4 *The bleeding edge moves in.* Despite efforts to reward self-motivated top performers, there is a history of losing these people. Turnover remains a chronic, incalculable loss of human capital and potential.

5 *Excitement reduces to passionless pursuit.* People go through the motions, but the culture lacks passion, excitement, risk-taking, and a compelling sense of purpose. A mere 5–20% of the workforce drives the success of the entire organization.

Adversity Quotient: the CORE of Response Ability

AQ is comprised of four CORE dimensions, which together determine and drive Response Ability. Each dimension plays a

unique role in a person's resilience, performance, innovation, and strength.

C = Control: *To what extent do I perceive I can influence the situation at hand?*

This dimension of AQ assesses perceived control, not actual control. It pinpoints your propensity for self-determination on the one hand and helplessness on the other.

O = Ownership: *To what extent can/ should I play a role in improving this situation?*

This dimension assesses propensity for inner accountability. In contrast to blame, which is about pinpointing the source of the problem, ownership is about playing even the smallest role in improving the situation, regardless of its cause.

R = Reach: *How far does this adversity reach and affect other areas of work or life?*

This dimension pinpoints the perceived size or magnitude of the adversity, which has a dramatic impact on the likelihood of taking meaningful action.

E = Endurance: *How long can you continue to confront adversity in a positive way?*

This dimension provides a reading on how you will deal with the next challenge, obstacle, or difficult personality.

When we measure these four characteristics, individually and collectively, basic patterns emerge. A company can be seen as either having a Response-Able culture, or not.

MINI-CASES
Organizations Building Response Ability

ADC Telecommunications successfully positioned itself to provide vital hardware and services to the prominent warriors (Lucent, WorldCom, Sprint, AT&T, etc.). Yet, when the entire sector lost 70% of its market value in a matter of a few months, ADC's stock plummeted, despite record earnings. ADC decided that creating a Response-Able, resilient sales force would position them for a superior and quicker comeback against competitors. In classes in Singapore, Spain, China, Canada, and the United States, ADC's global sales force from 16 countries learned new ways to get, keep, and grow people who can thrive in a demanding, dynamic industry.

Marriott International recognized that the defining factor in sustaining their aggressive growth curve while maintaining their high standard of service during an economic downturn would be their associates' and leaders' Response Ability.

Many other organizations—including FedEx, Deloitte & Touche, Palm Pilot, and Qualcomm—have focused on how well their

employees and managers handle adversity, resulting in improved performance, retention, agility, innovation, problem solving, resilience, and accelerated change.

MAKING IT HAPPEN ▶▶

Growing a Response-Able workforce that can not only cope with but thrive in adversity-rich times requires a commitment to forego the comforts of mediocrity and the courage to reinvent existing norms regarding Control, Ownership, Reach, and Endurance—the pattern of response to adversity. To start to build Response Ability, managers must:

- assess the Adversity Quotient of their current workforce;
- hire high AQ people;
- grow high AQ, Response-Able leaders;
- pay attention to how people respond to adversity the moment it strikes, assessing Control, Ownership, Reach, and Endurance;
- focus on what facets of a situation can be influenced, no matter how impossible it may seem;
- establish norms for people stepping up to improve and address difficulties the moment they arise;
- contain each adversity in scope immediately;
- be the first to recognize and seize the opportunity embedded in each adversity;
- strategize around worst case scenarios in a matter-of-fact way.

CONCLUSION

Adversity is on the rise, and that's the *good* news! Great companies and managers are—and increasingly will be—those who can harness the force of adversity to create even greater opportunity. They assess and strengthen their Adversity Quotients to become more Response Able. And they use their growing Response Ability to optimize their human capital and to stay up when times are down.

FOR MORE INFORMATION

Books:
Collard, Betsy. *Building a Resilient Workforce as a Competitive Advantage.* Mill Valley, CA: Kantola Productions, 1998. (See www.kantola.com)
Seligman, M. P. *Learned Optimism: How to Change Your Mind & Your Life.* New York: Pocket Books, 1998.

"Prosperity doth best discover vice; but adversity doth best discover virtue." Francis Bacon

BEST PRACTICE

Choosing the Best Training Curriculum for You
by Daniel R. Tobin

EXECUTIVE SUMMARY

- Individuals cannot rely on their employers to provide lifelong employment or a full learning agenda keyed to career opportunities. You must take responsibility for designing your personal learning agenda and finding the learning resources you need to achieve that agenda.
- Within and outside of your company, there is an ever-increasing array of learning opportunities, ranging from traditional training programs and college courses to less formal learning methods.
- To get ahead you must understand your company's and your own personal goals and design a learning agenda that contributes to the company's goals while satisfying your own learning and achievement objectives.

INTRODUCTION

Companies are increasingly questioning their investment in employee education, seeing ever-increasing expenditures with no direct tie-in to the company's bottom line. As a result training is typically high on the list of areas to cut.

Many corporate training groups are rushing to convert their programs to e-learning, which they see as an opportunity to reduce costs in response to (or in advance of) corporate budget reductions. At the same, time e-learning has become a hot commodity on the open market, with dozens of e-learning companies springing up alongside new e-learning ventures from hundreds of universities around the world.

Employees face an ever-increasing array of learning options but receive less and less guidance on how to use these opportunities to advance their own careers. Now more than ever employees must take responsibility for their own learning and understand how that learning can contribute to their own career plans. In this section we will outline key issues relating to personal development planning.

THE FOUR BASIC QUESTIONS

The first step is to consider four fundamental questions:

1. How Does Your Work Contribute to Achieving the Company's Business Goals?

Look at your company's business objectives for the next year and the next five years. What is your role in helping the company to achieve those objectives? To answer this question you need to understand the company's major business processes and your role within those processes—you need to widen your perspective from your narrow functional area to the larger goals of the company. This is an interesting topic of discussion for your manager and your coworkers; you can gain a better understanding of your role in the company and achieve greater job satisfaction as you start making the connections between what you do and the company's business results.

2. What Changes Do You Need to Make to Improve Your Own, Your Group's, and the Company's Results?

Once you understand your role, ask what needs to change to meet individual, group, and corporate goals. Then identify what is necessary to learn. Not every change requires new learning—you may already have the necessary knowledge and skills but never have been given the opportunity to apply them to your work.

In most cases you can't act in isolation; you need to get the approval and support of your manager and/or your fellow workers. Major and even minor business processes rarely change through the efforts of a single individual. Look at both your own and your group's learning needs.

When you see a factory that shows year-to-year increases in productivity over a number of years, you will generally find that workers and managers are constantly assessing the need for change and working together to determine how best to make those changes, experimenting with work processes, inventories, and materials. This is the philosophy behind many Japanese manufacturing plants, and the results extend across the world to factories that have adopted similar team-working and learning environments.

3. How Will You Acquire the Knowledge and Skills You Need?

Once you've identified your learning needs, you need to develop your learning agenda: how and from whom will you learn? Look at what your company offers in the way of formal training programs, and find out what opportunities are available from local colleges and professional associations.

E-learning opportunities are growing exponentially, with many colleges, universities, and e-learning companies providing courses through Internet-related technologies on virtually any technical, professional, managerial, or personal skills topic. However, little formal guidance exists on how to judge the quality of e-learning resources.

There are also many informal learning opportunities available. A learning coach (someone who has the knowledge or skills you want to acquire) in your company or in the community can be a valuable asset whether you're using traditional learning methods or studying on your own. If you can't locate a coach, team up with coworkers who are trying to master the same material so that you can coach each other, or join a discussion group on the Internet. You can find discussion groups on many company Web sites that allow you to team up with other workers at other company locations. There are also discussion groups on professional association Web sites and public discussion forums (for example, **www.groups.yahoo.com**).

With the large number of learning options available inside and outside the workplace, employees must also act as their own consumer advocates. It is unlikely that you will receive any recommendations. Most people

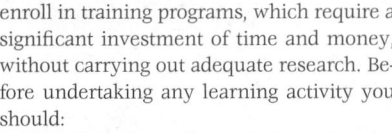

enroll in training programs, which require a significant investment of time and money, without carrying out adequate research. Before undertaking any learning activity you should:

- get reviews from others who have already completed it;
- if possible, talk with the instructor to make sure the program covers what you feel you need to learn;
- ask the instructor to make changes if you find that the learning program isn't meeting your needs;
- find out whether the instructor will be available by telephone or e-mail after the program ends to answer questions that may arise as you try to apply your learning to your work. Also ask other students in the class if they will be available, and offer yourself as a resource to others.

4. How Will You Apply Your Learning to Your Work?

Few employees work in isolation or can apply new learning to their work without affecting the work of others in the company. It's to your advantage to secure allies in your attempts to change the way you, your group, and the company work. Involve your manager, who ideally will be able to coach you and reinforce your learning as you apply it to your job. But even without having mastered the content, your manager can provide encouragement and allow you to experiment without fear of failure. If your manager can't play the coaching role, get one or more coworkers to learn along with you so you can try the new approach together, supporting each other and solving problems together as you apply your new knowledge and skills.

Before trying to apply your new learning to your job, it's important to negotiate an agreement with your manager, recognizing that you need time to try out your new knowledge and skills and that some mistakes may occur initially; you should also set some goals for improved performance based on the new methods. This sets expectations on both sides. From the manager's point of view, this is the payoff for the investment in your learning, while for you it's the promise of support for that learning.

Finally, once you've mastered a new skill or acquired new knowledge, share it with others. Many people interpreted the old saying "knowledge is power" to mean that they should hoard their knowledge—in the belief that it makes them indispensable. But knowledge is a unique economic good. Most economic goods lose their value by being shared: if you give this book to someone you no longer have it. Knowledge is unique in that it increases in value the more it's shared. In today's business climate employees who are known to share their knowledge and bring along other employees are more valued and better rewarded than those who hoard their knowledge.

MAKING IT HAPPEN ▶▶

One of the biggest dangers a leader can make is to assume that there are one or two—or half a dozen—methods for learning; there are in fact many, depending on the situation. Whatever training approach is chosen, there are four useful principles to consider:

1 **Commitment**—a commitment from the senior managers right through the organization to actively train and develop new and existing employees.
2 **Planning**—a plan from the organization detailing how it will routinely include training in its business plan. This includes linking employees' training to the business's objectives and setting targets for training.
3 **Action**—evidence of how the organization has delivered on its plan: how staff training has been completed to meet the organization's objectives, and how development needs are being continuously assessed and met.
4 **Evaluation**—assessing the effectiveness of training activities is the final phase. It involves assessing the original plan against what is actually happening, and also assessing the quality of the training that is being provided and the benefits that result.

The following steps outline some actions that may be valuable:

1 **Appoint a program champion** responsible for managing and overseeing the program.
2 **Undertake a self-assessment** of current training and development activities in the organization; in particular, consider
how well-trained staff are at all levels;
how you decide to train people—the criteria and process that is used;
the methods used to train and develop people;
the overall priority that training is given and the resources that are used.
3 **Produce a plan**, ideally derived from the overall business plan, that details:
the process for assessing and agreeing training needs;
how employees will be trained and developed within their organization;
the resources, including finance, that will be available.
4 **Implement the training program.**

CONCLUSION

Faced with an ever-increasing array of available learning options, you need to become much more adept at choosing the right learning activities, applying them to your work to improve business results, and planning your learning agenda to support your career with your current employer and into your future. By asking yourself the four basic questions given above you can create a personal learning agenda that will help you to succeed in any company in any industry. Companies greatly value people who take the initiative to plan and accomplish their own learning agendas and then apply that learning to make a real difference in business results.

FOR MORE INFORMATION

Web sites:
Thinq: **www.thinq.com**
TrainSeek: **www.trainseek.com**

"It takes less time to put up a factory than to train men of competence to run it."

Indira Gandhi

Developing Exceptional Problem-solving Skills

by Christopher Hoenig

EXECUTIVE SUMMARY

- We live in an era where technology is our primary tool, knowledge is the strategic asset, and problem-solving is the paramount skill.
- The best problem-solvers in any situation or field rely on sophisticated knowledge of how to apply just six essential practices.
- These six practices also represent differing problem-solving preferences, or "personalities." You need all six of them for your problem-solving to be complete and competitive.

INTRODUCTION

Today's business organizations are being challenged by global competition, as well as technological and social change, to solve bigger, tougher problems faster, better, and cheaper than ever. Improved problem-solving capability is the ultimate competitive advantage, and the best organizations are increasing the sophistication with which they systematize their problem-solving processes. Individuals who wish to lead organizations or build successful careers in the digital age will need to build their understanding of problem-solving as a field in itself.

SOPHISTICATED PROBLEM-SOLVING IS BASED ON SIMPLE ESSENTIALS

Knowing how simple elements generate complex results is the ultimate source of power. Three primary colors blend to make up the paintings and films that capture our imagination. Two binary states are the foundation of the digital processing that underpins the information age.

In the same way, there are six essential skills involved in human problem-solving: generating mindset, acquiring knowledge, building relationships, managing problems, creating solutions, and delivering results. The tougher, larger, and more demanding a problem or opportunity is, and the faster and more competitive your environment is, the more important these skills become.

I am not talking about the "old" problem-solving—traditional cookbook approaches that are small-scale, linear, deficiency-oriented, and tactical. Rather, I am talking about a "new," rapidly evolving definition of problem-solving that encompasses large-scale, nonlinear, opportunity-oriented, and strategic work. This is problem-solving in the age of biotech, the Web, smart materials, and the global economy.

We live in an era when information technology is our primary tool, knowledge the strategic asset, and problem-solving the paramount skill. Problem-solving ability is now the most sought-after trait in up-and-coming executives, according to a recent survey of 1,000 executives by Caliper Associates, reported in the *Wall Street Journal* by Hal Lancaster ("Managing Your Career"). To put it bluntly, if you're not a problem-solver, your career potential is limited.

THE PROBLEM-SOLVING JOURNEY

I refer to the problem-solving journey because the mixture of problem-solving and adventure blends two rich sources of knowledge into one. Exactly like an adventure, problem-solving is a journey from a starting point to some distant destination. It is a journey into the unknown—through fear and exhilaration, confidence and disappointment.

Thinking of the solutions to problems (or opportunities) as journeys brings the topic alive. Professional knowledge about problem-solving is, by definition, abstract. But the language, images, ideas, and principles of adventure and exploration make it accessible and invest it with the drama that real problem-solvers experience: the disciplined planning, the long waits, and the moments of crisis and celebration. Moreover, since we have all traveled, this metaphor helps us to tap into our own undiscovered sources of wisdom about the principles and practices of problem-solving journeys.

THE DIFFERENCE BETWEEN THE BEST AND THE WORST PROBLEM-SOLVERS

The difference between the best and the worst problem-solvers is how many of the six essentials they can marshal (by themselves or with others), and how deeply the skills are understood, individually and collectively. Poor problem-solvers understand the skills incompletely and therefore cannot marshal a complete capability. Great ones know the skills well enough to pull together and manage all six, or exhibit one in great depth as part of a team.

The journey from novice to world-class expert in any field begins by understanding the six essentials, practicing them, mastering them at one level, and then moving on toward the limits of your potential.

At some point in this process, the best problem-solvers rise above their profession in a multidisciplinary fashion. Each of the six essentials represents a bundle of habits, skills, and knowledge that come together in problem-solving "personalities." Each personality draws its strength from a variety of specialties and professions.

The six personalities serve as a convenient way to assess yourself and others. They allow you to determine your own personal mix of strengths and weaknesses and how you can put together a complete problem-solving capability. Great problem-solvers know their strengths and weaknesses, and they build teams to compensate for them, creating wholes that are equal to or greater than the sum of their parts.

THE SIX ESSENTIALS
Generate the Mindset (the Innovator)

The **innovator** focuses on moving from self-doubt to innovation by developing potent ideas and attitudes, above all through seeking out alternative points of view. The ability to do this improves your effectiveness in moving creatively through a problem-solving effort. An innovator's mindset sets the stage for discovery, because the combination of commitment and open-mindedness generates the widest possible field of opportunities to consider.

"By blaming others, we fail to find the real solutions to our problems and we do not carry out our own responsibilities."

Jeb Bush

Leading innovators such as Dee Hock, founder of VISA international, Jeff Bezos of Amazon.com, and John Seely Brown of Xerox PARC epitomize the innovator's mindset. Great companies known for a history of innovation, such as 3M, IDEO, and Procter & Gamble, have made it a pervasive part of their culture.

Know the Territory (the Discoverer)

The **discoverer** concentrates on moving from innovation to insight by asking the right questions and getting good, timely information. Better knowledge helps you define problems more effectively, choose the best routes, and identify what's at stake. A discoverer's knowledge of a territory brings understanding and insight, which reveal the most likely problems and opportunities in higher relief. With more investigation, the implications of those problems become more apparent as a foundation for action.

Leading discoverers such as Craig Venter of Celera Genomics, or Nobel Prize winner Dr. Eric Wieschaus, are examples of what outstanding discovery can produce. Great companies and universities that have built a foundation on research and discovery include Bell Labs, MIT, and CalTech.

Build the Relationships (the Communicator)

The **communicator** deals with how to move from insight to community by cultivating quality interaction and so creating an ever-expanding circle of relationships based on service, loyalty, and identity. Communicators develop the support and human context needed to create and implement change effectively. Through their mastery of relationship building, communicators connect potential journeys to their actual implications for real people. They help determine whether a problem-solving effort is worthwhile, for whom, and why. Then they generate a core group that will tackle the journey and a network that will support the effort.

Great communicators like Franklin Roosevelt, or Winston Churchill, demonstrate the power of communication and relationship building in tackling historic problems. Companies that have built worldwide reputations for service because of their attention to communication include Hallmark Cards, L. L. Bean, and Dell.

Manage the Journeys (the Playmaker)

The **playmaker** focuses on moving from building a community to giving that community a sense of direction by choosing destinations and strategies. Fostering an understanding of the stages of any problem-solving journey helps people to set goals, define success, and develop effective plans. Playmakers take the attitude, knowledge, and people brought into play by innovators, discoverers, and communicators, and shape the destinations, direction, and strategies to make the journey a reality.

Playmakers past and present such as Nelson Mandela, Colin Powell, and Jack Welch demonstrate the power of leadership in directing problem-solving efforts. Companies like Kleiner, McKinsey & Company, and American Airlines have institutionalized that leadership in a way that has lasted over decades of business success.

Create the Solutions (the Creator)

The **creator** shows how to move from leadership to power by designing, building, and maintaining optimal solutions. Creators help to bring the best technology, people, and tools together in complete, flexible solutions that will fit the problem you're trying to solve. A creator takes the requirements and goals of a playmaker, which define the journey, and figures out what it will take to get the group where they want to go. When there is more innovation and better knowledge, when there are richer relationships and better-defined problems, then solution design and construction are more focused.

Great creators such as Bill Gates and Paul Allen, Steve Jobs, Steve Wozniak, and Thomas Edison exemplify the passion, talent, and will required to build new solutions. Companies such as Microsoft, Toyota, and General Electric have built corporate systems and cultures that sustain quality creative ability over long periods of time.

Deliver the Results (the Performer)

The **performer** concentrates on moving from power to sustainable advantage through intuitive and disciplined implementation, which allows one continually to exceed expectations. Performers can help to conquer complexity, friction, and scale with simplicity, discipline, and a competitive edge. Performers take the goals and strategies of the playmaker and the solutions of the creator, and work to achieve full resolution of the problem. Innovation, knowledge, and well-developed relationships aid in their efforts. When all the other roles are done well, the performer is able to focus completely on achieving full resolution and not on redesign, unplanned maintenance, or changing requirements.

Great performers such as Lou Gerstner in business, Reinhold Messner in mountain climbing, and Isabelle Autissier in sailing, show the character and savvy it takes to deliver great performances. Companies like Federal Express and McDonald's have built empires on the precision and consistency of performance over time.

MAKING IT HAPPEN ▶▶

- Master the six problem-solving essentials and the stages of any problem-solving journey so that you can locate yourself in problem-solving situations and organize your attack on the problem.
- Diagnose yourself, to understand your strengths and weaknesses and how to compensate for them. Do a free diagnostic self-assessment to find out what type of problem solver you are at www.exolve.com.
- Move in the new direction, and fill the gaps in your problem-solving team.

CONCLUSION

The new professional economy is placing an increasing premium on the mind, body, and soul of the adventurer—the problem-solver—on people who can conceive, organize, and lead expeditions that add value to society, business, and humanity. These problem-solvers have an adventurer's blend of innocence and wisdom, self-reliance and a willingness to collaborate, professional competence and the capacity to scale new peaks, as well as the resilience to persevere through uncharted territory.

And just as in the old economy or the next economy after this one, no amount of buzz, momentum, or technology will cover the lack of problem-solving essentials for long. True problem-solving capability is what drives enduring advantage in any field, at any time, in any place.

FOR MORE INFORMATION

Books:
Bradley, Bill. *Values of the Game*. New York: Broadway Books, 2000.
Dorner, Dietrich. *The Logic of Failure: Why Things Go Wrong and What We Can Do to Make Them Right*. Cambridge, MA: Perseus, 1996.
Senge, Peter. *The Fifth Discipline: The Art and Practice of the Learning Organization*. Revised ed. New York: Doubleday, 2006.

"The problem when solved will be simple."

MANAGEMENT CHECKLISTS

Management Checklists

Finding practical solutions for everyday business problems

The Checklists provide you with a comprehensive handbook of practical answers to everyday business challenges. Each list reflects current thinking and best management practice, and is designed to give you a practical answer to your problem—fast.

The Checklists come from the Chartered Management Institute—one of Europe's largest management organizations—and aim to answer the most pressing everyday problems that you will face at work. They provide step-by-step routes to success, from tasks such as **Planning the Recruitment Process** to **Implementing a Diversity Management Program**. Each Checklist includes a handy list of dos and don'ts, benefits and disadvantages, and thought starters.

Contents

Coaching for Better Performance

This checklist describes the processes involved in coaching as a method of developing skills, potential, and performance.

DEFINITION

Coaching is especially effective used as one of a range of learning activities and training processes when an individual or learner has potential that can best be developed through a focused relationship with a more experienced and senior colleague.

It is both a style and a method of conducting a one-on-one relationship in which a manager empowers and helps a more junior employee develop his or her skills through a series of planned work-based activities. In coaching, a manager works with the learner to identify where the learner could develop new skills to apply in either a current or a future job, and provides support, guidance, and advice to help in achieving the professional aims.

In coaching sessions the manager often works directly with the learner, offering the chance to try things out and supporting the learner in finding areas for further improvement. Coaching effectively may also involve bringing in others with appropriate skills and experience to run specific sessions, with the manager coordinating the overall coaching strategy.

Coaching can be part of mentoring, but they are different training techniques. Coaching is appropriate for passing on specific tasks, skills, or techniques that can be mastered and measured, while mentoring has more to do with longer-term development or progress within an organization.

Coaching also uses assessment skills, but adapts them to a more constructive purpose. Assessment is the neutral and objective observation of success or failure, while coaching is a helping relationship in which the coach provides tips, guidance, and support.

ADVANTAGES

When used selectively and appropriately, coaching:
- is a cost-effective approach to development that is tailored to individual employees;
- develops the skills of existing employees instead of requiring additional staff;
- provides the coach with a sense of achievement and value;
- sends a positive message to other employees about the value the organization places on staff;
- motivates employees, reducing staff turnover and the associated costs of recruitment and orientation;
- helps the learner reinforce and apply theoretical and knowledge-based learning acquired in courses and other training.

Coaches need to:

- be caring, supportive, and patient;
- have good listening skills;
- be aware of their own strengths and weaknesses;
- have good verbal and nonverbal skills;
- be good observers and counselors.

DISADVANTAGES
- Because it is one-on-one, coaching can be a drain on limited resources.
- If there is no real structure to the activity, coaching can become nothing more than the senior person simply lecturing the junior.
- To provide coaching sessions, the coach/manager may need help from other people who may not be committed to coaching as a training technique.

ACTION CHECKLIST

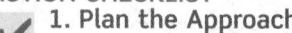 1. Plan the Approach
Hold a preliminary meeting with the learner to establish the ground rules.
- Identify, agree on, and prioritize the learning needs to be addressed by the coaching sessions.
- Agree on and set learning objectives—clearly state what the learner should achieve (for example, "By X date you will be able to explain/demonstrate how to do YZ.")
- Agree on success criteria, or task objectives, specifying the standard against which success will be judged ("By the end you will be able to weld two pieces of pipe to industry standard tolerances.")
- Review the options and make a detailed plan—this is where the coach prepares to demonstrate, explain, and review a task or skill.

2. Identify the Learner's Preferred Learning Style
Everyone learns in different ways. For coaching to be effective, it is essential to understand what these might be for the learner. Explore and test a mixture of methods, including watching, listening, thinking, reading, observing, reflecting, and trying things out, to identify the approach that gives the biggest payback, or the combination that seems most appropriate.

3. Identify Opportunities for Coaching
In coaching, the learner should try out skills in an actual task, so you need to plan the occasion and place to conduct a coaching session. From the identified list of priorities, agree on a time for the first session.

4. Carry Out the Coaching Session
Bearing in mind the learner's preferred learning styles:
- give a clear and easy-to-follow demonstration while explaining to the learner the detail of what is happening and why;
- watch for signs (for example, body language or revealing questions) that the learner has missed something;

"Remember the finish line is at the end of a race. Don't use up all of your energy before reaching it."

Jack Daniels

- summarize and review at appropriate points to help the learner grasp the key points;
- let the learner try out the task, offering support and, if necessary, reminders;
- actively encourage the learner in good performance.

5. Provide Feedback

Feedback is essential for the learner to get the most from the experience. In giving feedback, be honest but sensitive and critical but constructive, and always try to point to improvements.

6. Plan Interim Learning Activities

Plan development activities for the learner to undertake between coaching sessions. Avoid spoon-feeding, but encourage the learner to stay motivated and independently identify opportunities to practice newly learned skills. Agree on improvement targets for the practice sessions.

7. Close the Session

Discuss and review:
- the learner's success against the agreed criteria and standards;
- how well the learner handled the learning process;

- next steps. These may involve more coaching on this task if either the task or the learning objectives haven't been met in full.

THOUGHT STARTERS

- Think about who has coached you in the past and how effective it was—if it worked for you, it can work for others.

- Whom can you think of in your team at work who would benefit from coaching?

- Which tasks and skills would you be best at coaching?

- Who else has skills that others would benefit from developing?

DO
- Carry out a detailed task analysis of the activity you are going to coach, listing all the steps in the process, especially the most obvious (these are easy to overlook when you're experienced in an activity).
- Include all external restrictions and criteria such as health and safety requirements.
- Make sure that the approach, the detailed steps, and the actions within them are discussed and agreed on with the learner—coach and learner have an equal stake in success.
- Accept the learner's mistakes when tackling new tasks. "Learning by doing" means figuring out why something may not have worked, and planning better methods for the next time.
- Remember that coaching is more than instruction: the successful coach relies on a range of other skills, especially the communication skills of questioning, listening, and giving constructive feedback.

DON'T
- Don't confuse coaching with assessment.
- Don't jump in and tell the learner what to do or take over if the learner is experiencing difficulty.
- Don't assume that everyone knows the basics of a task just because you take them for granted.
- Don't forget to include all external restrictions and criteria, such as health and safety rules and requirements.

FOR MORE INFORMATION

Books:
Buckley, Roger, and Jim Caple. *The Theory and Practice of Training and Coaching Skills*. 5th ed. Dover, NH: Kogan Page, 2005.
Hargrove, Robert. *Masterful Coaching: Extraordinary Results by Impacting People and the Way They Think and Work Together*. Rev. ed. San Diego, CA: Pfeiffer, 2002.
Kinlaw, Dennis C. *Coaching for Commitment: Managerial Strategies for Obtaining Superior Performance from Individuals and Teams*. 2nd ed. San Francisco, CA: Jossey-Bass, 1999.
Morgan, Howard, Phil Harkins, and Marshall Goldsmith, eds. *The Art and Practice of Leadership Coaching: 50 Top Executive Coaches Reveal their Secrets*. Hoboken, NJ: Wiley, 2004.
Parsloe, Eric. *Coaching and Mentoring*. New York: Kogan Page, 2005.
Valerio, Anna Marie, and Robert J. Lee. *Executive Coaching: A Guide for the HR Professional*. San Francisco, CA: Pfeiffer, 2005.

Journal Articles:
Kets de Vries, Manfred. "Leadership Group Coaching in Action: The Zen of Creating High-performance Teams." *Academy of Management Executive* 19:1 (February 2005): 61–76.
Sherman, Stratford, and Alyssa Freas. "The Wild West of Executive Coaching." *Harvard Business Review* 82:11 (November 2004): 82–90.
Zweibel, Barry. "A Strategic Coach." *T+D* 59:4 (April 2005): 62–65.

See also:
✔ Empowerment (pp. 444–445)
✔ Mentoring in Practice (pp. 436–437)

"The goals on which hope are based have to be realistic."   Arthur Lydiard

Mentoring in Practice

436

CHECKLIST

This checklist is for managers wishing to explore mentoring as a process for developing people and their potential.

DEFINITION

Mentoring is a relationship in which one person (the mentor)—usually someone more experienced and often more senior in an organization—helps another (the learner) discover more about his or her personal qualities, capabilities, and potential. It can be an informal relationship, with the learner leaning on the mentor for guidance, support, help, and feedback, or a more formal arrangement between two people who respect and trust each other.

Mentoring need not bring together a trainer and a trainee or resemble line management with its attention to seniority and rank. Instead, the mentor's role is to listen, ask questions, and probe for facts and career choices; the mentor is a channel for information, experience, and opportunities from various sources that can benefit the learner.

Mentors are there not to instruct but to provide learners with input to help them form their own views, develop different perspectives, and develop as people and as potential managers.

ADVANTAGES

As a development tool, mentoring has advantages for the mentor, the learner, and the organization.

The organizational benefits of mentoring include:
- support for planning managerial succession and maximizing human potential;
- the likelihood of improving staff retention levels and recruitment prospects;
- improved communication and exposure of employees to the culture of the company;
- cost-effective, personalized staff development.

Mentoring offers the mentor:
- corporate recognition, higher status, and stronger job satisfaction;
- the development of leadership qualities and managerial skills;
- an opportunity to help others develop their careers.

Mentoring offers the learner:
- a sense of being valued by the company;
- an objective, supportive, nonthreatening source of support in developing new skills and exploring new directions;
- access to someone who understands the company's culture, personnel, and ways of working.

DISADVANTAGES

Mentoring has few disadvantages, but some cautions are in order.

- Mentoring does require corporate resources: the process takes time for learner and mentor, and both may need to work on appropriate skills such as planning, reviewing, and communication (particularly listening and constructive feedback).
- Mentoring is a complement to, not a substitute for, more formal training approaches.
- In the hands of an inappropriate mentor, a learner can develop in the wrong direction. You need to be very careful in selecting mentors and matching them to learners.
- A strong personal bond can develop between mentor and learner, to the detriment of both employees as well as the organization.

ACTION CHECKLIST

✔ 1. Make Certain the Mentor Has the Right Skills

It is essential that the mentor has:
- good listening skills;
- sophistication in using different forms of questions—open, closed, probing, etc.;
- the maturity to suspend personal judgment and prejudice so that the learner can choose from a variety of directions;
- experience in giving constructive feedback, covering negative and positive aspects in a way that the learner can act on;
- skill in helping to define objectives and plan ways of achieving them;
- the initiative to use other people's skills and experiences to open up learning opportunities on the learner's behalf.

Consider having the skills of a potential mentor evaluated by an objective party, ideally someone with experience in mentoring. Individuals almost always either over- or underestimate their own competence (especially in communication, where most people believe they shine, even when they are barely adequate).

The mentor must be someone of authority in the organization, an experienced person who can open doors for the learner and offer viewpoints from a valued perspective. If necessary, arrange training and development for the mentor to sharpen and refine appropriate skills.

✔ 2. Clarify the Mentoring Relationship

Make sure that both the learner and the mentor are clear on what the relationship is—and is not—about. Early clarification can help avoid any later confusion and disappointment.

If appropriate, consider drafting a mentoring contract, specifying:
- the participants' respective roles, responsibilities, and commitment;
- the planned number and frequency of meetings, to be reviewed and amended as necessary;
- the participants' obligation of confidentiality within the relationship.

Remember that the aim of the mentor is to help the learner develop, not adopt the mentor's ideas. The

"Cheers hearten a man. But jeers are just as essential. They help maintain his sense of balance and proportion."

Jay E. House

relationship should never become one of dependency—watch out for signs that this might be happening.

3. Open the Relationship

Recognize that in the early stages of the relationship the mentor needs to take a lead; later, as the learner's confidence and understanding grow, the balance shifts. Set objectives for what the mentoring process is to achieve; make the objectives relevant, specific, achievable, and time-limited.

4. Develop the Relationship

At the start of each mentoring session, and each time learners reach a milestone, review not just their current performance or success, but what lessons they learned about themselves and the process. Ask:

- What happened?
- Why?
- What was learned from the experience?

Mentor and learner should jointly identify what needs to be explored in order to achieve each objective. Compare the desired outcome with the current situation, identify the gaps, and outline what needs to happen to get from here to there.

Select and agree on a route to achieving each objective. Possible routes include learning experiences that can be provided or facilitated by the mentor, knowledge that can be passed from mentor to learner, and counseling and feedback to heighten the learner's self-awareness.

It can be hard to identify specific approaches for achieving a knowledge-based or attitudinal objective. In this case explore possible options, discuss experiences, and leave the learner to decide on a plan of action.

If the objective is skill-based, break down the required action into milestones. Hold regular progress reviews, and recognize and celebrate interim successes.

At the end of each mentoring session, articulate achievements so far and specify what needs to happen before the next session, especially if the mentor is to arrange something on the learner's behalf. Over the course of the mentoring, control of the learner's development should pass increasingly from the mentor to the learner: the goal is for the learner to be able to stand alone when the mentoring process ends.

5. End the Relationship

Mentoring relationships between people outside work may flourish for years. Inside the workplace, however, mentoring ends when the objectives are achieved. Having reached this point, celebrate the success of the relationship with a final review of the learner's progress.

437

CHECKLIST

DOS AND DON'TS

DO

- Take the learner's views into account in selecting a well-matched mentor. The mentor needs to be someone the learner respects, trusts, and can open up to.
- Allow the mentor to take a flexible approach in order to focus on the learner's needs and aims.
- Remember that a key part of the mentor's role is to open doors to other people's experience and other learning opportunities.
- Make sure that each session starts with a review and ends with a clear action plan.
- Control the relationship and adjust it as necessary so the learner assumes increasing responsibility.

DON'T

- Don't assume that any line manager can be thrown in as a mentor.
- Don't believe that an individual's direct line manager is an appropriate mentor.
- Don't reveal information you learn during mentoring to people outside the relationship.
- Don't be afraid, as a mentor, to be open about yourself.
- Don't tell the learner what you know or try to supply all the answers—the mentoring journey is one of guided self-exploration.

THOUGHT STARTERS

- Who helped you make sensible decisions about your future, and how did they do it?

- Whom would you like to have as your mentor now? What qualities lead you to choose this person?

- Is your organizational culture one that would welcome an approach that has elements of counseling, personal support, and genuine concern for others? If it clearly isn't, think very carefully before trying to make mentoring work.

- Who in your company has potential and would benefit from working with a mentor?

FOR MORE INFORMATION

Books:

Bell, Chip R. *Managers As Mentors: Building Partnerships for Learning.* 2nd ed. San Francisco, CA: Berrett-Koehler, 2002.

Johnson, Harold E. *Mentoring Greatness.* Torrance, CA: Griffin, 2002.

See also:

 Coaching for Better Performance (pp. 434–435)
 Training Needs Analysis (pp. 476–477)

"They have a right to censure that have a heart to help."

William Penn

Conducting a Performance Appraisal

CHECKLIST

This checklist is for managers responsible for carrying out performance appraisals.

DEFINITION

The focus of performance appraisals has shifted away from evaluation and strict appraisal toward improving performance and developing the employee by means of a well-prepared, honest, and open discussion. This checklist concentrates on the staff development approach.

A performance appraisal usually centers on a face-to-face discussion in which one employee's work is discussed and reviewed by another using an agreed and understood framework. Although peers can appraise each other, usually line managers conduct appraisals of their staff. This is the approach that this checklist takes. An appraisal focuses on behaviors and outcomes, not personality; issues and problems, not subjective gripes; constructive development to improve motivation; and the employee's growth and performance. It generally takes place every six to twelve months.

ADVANTAGES

Employees being appraised will:
- have a clear picture of what is expected of them;
- be able to discuss priorities;
- realize when they are being overloaded;
- receive feedback on their performance;
- be heard and respected;
- be offered constructive guidance on attaining mutually agreed goals;
- receive help in constructing personal development plans;
- take ownership of their performance.

Appraisers will use the appraisal as an opportunity to:
- experience the jobholder's performance firsthand;
- better understand the jobholder's potential and needs;
- motivate the jobholder;
- develop a consistent approach to guidance and encouragement;
- tackle problems more effectively;
- improve the communication process.

Requirements for a successful appraisal include:
- thorough preparation by both appraiser and jobholder;
- the appraiser's skill and tact in not being offensive or drifting into personal attacks;
- reassurance by the appraiser that the jobholder's doubts, fears, or anxieties are unwarranted;
- clarification that the appraisal is not linked to pay (as long as it isn't).

ACTION CHECKLIST

1. Prepare for the Meeting

Much of the hard work of appraising performance should be carried out prior to the meeting itself. If there is an established program, this will provide a framework for action. If not, the following discussion headings provide a starting point.
- Objectives for past 12 months—level of achievement/progress.
- Continuing or unresolved problems during this period.
- Evaluation of professional development during this period.
- Objectives for next 12 months.
- Support required in order to achieve these objectives.
- Personal development objectives that may vary from the above or provide a means to their attainment.
- Any anticipated major concerns in next 12 months.

2. Arrange for the Appraisal Discussion

In a premeeting briefing inform the employee of the purpose of the appraisal and the structure that it will follow.
- Inform the employee of any preparation needed, for example, identifying personal strengths and achievements, weaknesses and failures over the past year.
- Get the employee to prepare a personal assessment of how well the past year's objectives have been achieved and what objectives should be adopted for the next year.
- Ask the employee to reflect on the value and practical application of training or development activities in the past year.
- Explain that this is the opportunity to consider problems and agree on work directions and methods for the next year.
- Most importantly, explain that it is not linked to pay or promotion (unless it is).
- Introduce documentation for notes or record-keeping at this stage.
- Agree the time and place for the discussion.

3. Prepare the Environment

The environment for the discussion should be informal and friendly, private but comfortable, confidential and free from interruption, and nonthreatening.

4. Use a Consultative Approach

Be conversational but positive, discussing specific activities and issues; the focus is on looking forward to improvements. Asking open questions, listening, reflecting back what you hear, and responding appropriately all enable you to exercise a control that is not overt and does not make the employee feel dominated.

5. Start the Discussion

At the start of the discussion, it is important to relax the employee.
- Restate the purpose of the meeting and the structure that it will follow.
- Emphasize that the purpose of the discussion is to help the employee develop and improve.
- Restate the purpose of the documentation—it serves better than memory as a record of the meeting and of

what is agreed, and forms a basis for measuring progress.

6. Develop the Discussion

In theory and with thorough preparation by both parties, the discussion can follow the framework outlined. In practice this does not always happen. Try to:

- encourage self-assessment and help—not lead—the diagnosis of problems;
- maintain and build the employee's self-esteem;
- offer help and suggestions but let the employee arrive at solutions independently;
- concentrate on job performance, not personalities;
- discuss specific examples, not generalities;
- summarize at critical or agreed action points;
- guide and agree on goals and plans.

7. Deal with Difficulties and Focus on Improvements

Rather than raising the question of poor performance, ask the employee to point to any difficulties. Ask not only where and how the employee might make improvements, but also what resources might aid the process. Be prepared to admit that you might be the cause of problems yourself, or could do more to help.

8. Agree on Areas for Improvement

Try to categorize areas that may be in need of urgent remedial attention separately from those that are developmental and progressive. Agree on the preferred outcome of training and development activities, and encourage the employee to identify ways of achieving them.

DOS AND DON'TS

DO
- Remember the appraisal is a discussion.
- Invite the jobholder's comments and views.
- Get the jobholder to analyze his or her own performance.
- Highlight good performance and the reasons why it was good.
- Agree on a need for changed performance before planning action.
- Be aware of your use of language and the potential for misinterpretation.
- Ask for specialist help if necessary.

DON'T
- Don't criticize or try to change personalities.
- Don't skate around difficult moments.
- Don't fall into the trap of holding forth monolog-style.
- Don't use closed, rhetorical questions.

9. Rate the Performance

Some appraisal procedures use performance ratings. They vary in nature and scope and can be useful or destructive, depending on how the rating is done.

If ratings are to be used, they should be:

- fair—reflecting performance against expectations, not other people's work;
- flexible—reflecting the level and extent of the individual's achievements;
- consistent—applying across different sectors of the organization;
- honest—respecting fully what the individual has had to say.

10. Close the Discussion

Ensure that you have reached understanding and commitment on objectives, the means to achieve them, and dates that serve as targets or review points. Ensure, too, that you know who is setting up these activities. Agree on a follow-up date. Ask the employee to write up the objectives and plans so that you can both sign off on it. End on a positive note.

THOUGHT STARTERS

- Are you a good listener, able to extract salient points without making notes all the time?

- Are you satisfied with your own ability to coach and counsel?

- When were you last appraised? What went well? What went badly?

- Are you clear on objectives for your staff and the support they may need in achieving them?

FOR MORE INFORMATION

Books:
McKirchy, Karen. *Powerful Performance Appraisals: How to Set Expectations and Work Together to Improve Performance.* Franklin Lakes, NJ: Career Press, 1998.
Toler Sachs, Randi. *Productive Performance Appraisals.* New York: AMACOM, 1992.

See also:
- Managing Staff Turnover and Retention (pp. 454–455)
- Motivating Your Staff in a Time of Change (pp. 458–459)
- Setting Objectives (pp. 532–533)

"People ask you for criticism but they only want praise."   W. Somerset Maugham

Counseling Your Colleagues

CHECKLIST

This checklist is designed for managers who, in the context of their roles, may be required to help their colleagues by using counseling skills.

Becoming a professional counselor can take several years of training and supervised practical experience. Few managers have this level of qualification, but many of the skills employed by counselors can be put to use by managers of all levels in a work situation. Managers desiring this level of capability should consider some formal counseling training.

DEFINITION

Work often suffers when an employee is personally troubled. Even problems that are not work-related but personal (family issues, debt, illness, and so on) may eventually affect work productivity. Managers dealing with such issues may be able to assist the affected individual or individuals to discover a solution—especially if it is a work-related issue (such as a personality clash or poor communication skills). However, many companies, as part of their employee medical benefits program, allow outside counseling for individuals and circumstances where added professional skills are necessary. Handled successfully, counseling is a process that helps individuals clarify their motivations, worries, and hopes. It also helps them come to terms with their feelings, and enables them to take responsibility for, and begin to resolve, their difficulties.

Counseling is not a process of advice-giving, nor does it involve the counselor providing or managing solutions to the problems experienced by the "client."

ADVANTAGES

Counseling your colleagues:
- may help solve issues that can hamper individual and business productivity;
- helps reduce employee time lost due to low morale, depression, and illness;
- assists in building teams among people having divergent personality styles.

DISADVANTAGES
- It may create the need for more management training.

ACTION CHECKLIST

✔ 1. Make Sure Your Company Supports Peer Counseling

Check your company's personnel policies to make sure that they support peer counseling. Some firms have formal procedures for initiating counseling; it is important to respect these procedures when that is the case.

✔ 2. Find a Suitable Room

It is essential to choose somewhere that is quiet, free from interruption, and appropriate to the nature of the problem. Make sure you will not be disturbed by putting a "Do not disturb" sign on the door, and defer phone calls to avoid interruptions.
- Try to avoid a formal office setting with a desk between you and your colleague.
- If you need to keep an unobtrusive eye on the time, position a clock where you can easily see it.

✔ 3. Allow Sufficient Time for the Meeting

If you know you have to end your meeting at a particular time, inform your colleague of that at the outset. To make sure there is enough time for the session it is sensible to block out the time for such a meeting in advance. Even if there are no time constraints, it is often useful to set a limit of about an hour, to prevent the discussion merely going over the same ground again and again.

✔ 4. Address Your Feelings Toward Your Colleague

Before the meeting, it is essential to assess your personal feelings toward your colleague and put them to one side. Whether or not you like the person is irrelevant.

✔ 5. Open the Meeting by Explaining the Framework

It is important to lay down some ground rules at the beginning of the counseling session. These may include:
- the expectations of the discussion—for example, you may not be able to provide advice or guidance or solve all your colleague's problems;
- time limitations—state again what these are, and whether you will offer a follow-up session if needed;
- note taking—stress that any notes you take are for your own use and will not be revealed to a third party;
- confidentiality—assure your colleague that confidential matters will be treated as such; otherwise the person may hesitate to be candid with you. Explain that the only exception to this will be if you both agree that something needs to be discussed with another party.

✔ 6. Begin to Explore the Issues

The format for a counseling session is not set in stone; each is dependent on the needs of the individual. However, you will find the following skills essential in exploring your colleague's issues.
- Actively listen—what does this person feel? What point of view is being expressed? What seems to be happening to him or her to cause the issue to arise? What does this person do (or not do) in response to that situation? It is essential to understand that, in emotional terms, your colleague's view of the facts or the situation is more important than the facts themselves and that people's behavior may not reflect their true feelings. By rephrasing

"The glad hand is alright in sunshine, but it's the helping hand on a dark day that folks remember to the end of time."

Amadeo Giannini

the concerns your colleague expresses, you demonstrate that you have listened carefully, at the same time you are seeking clarification of the issues involved. Throughout the conversation, occasionally summarizing what has been said will help both of you stay focused.

- Empathize—empathy is not the same as sympathy. Empathy means you recognize and understand the issues confronting your colleague without necessarily becoming an advocate or agreeing totally with the version you are hearing. Your empathy can help encourage your colleague to be more honest and precise in describing the issues.
- Question—there are many reasons for questions, and many types of questions. In a counseling situation, questions enable you to clarify your understanding of the issues, help focus on areas you think may be important, and demonstrate your interest in the other person.

Open, closed, and probing questions are all of value in a counseling session. Open questions can help your colleague begin to talk about an issue and the feelings it provokes. Closed questions help you to establish precise facts, but tend to lead to very short answers. Probing questions enable you to deepen your understanding of an issue and can help to draw out the whole picture.

- Challenge—by occasionally challenging a statement, you force your colleague to reconsider, and possibly rephrase the statement. It is useful to challenge if it appears that the discussion is going around in circles, if your colleague has an unrealistic self-image (either too positive or, more usually, too negative), or if there appear to be contradictions in what you are hearing.

Challenging statements may be based on phrases such as, "You say that you are struggling with your current project, yet I see you as meeting all its objectives and deadlines. Why do you think there is a difference in our views?"

7. Recognize Situations That Are Beyond Your Help

In certain circumstances it may be necessary to refer your colleague to trained counselors or organizations that may be better equipped to help. Be aware of outside resources—names of specific counselors, for example, or a list from the phone directory that you can share with your colleague. Your personnel department or human resources manager may have some information, but be sure not to break a confidence if you ask for a referral.

- Employee Assistance Programs (EAP) have been initiated by many organizations to provide external sources of help, guidance, and advice for their staff. The Employee Assistance Professionals Association Web site is an excellent source of help and a first point of contact if

your organization does not have a program in place already.

8. Help Your Colleague with Problem Solving Skills

Counseling does not mean that the counselor provides solutions to the issues raised by the other person. The counselor can, however, help by bringing problem solving techniques to bear. The discussion should have served to identify the problem area and some possible causes. You can now encourage the individual to set specific objectives to tackle the problem and assign a timetable and means of monitoring progress.

9. Close the Session Constructively

Summarize what has been discussed and what actions have been agreed upon. If appropriate, arrange a follow-up session.

THOUGHT STARTERS
- The greater the perceived level of listening, the more likely the individual will be to accept comments and contributions from you.

- Recurring problems do not solve themselves.

FOR MORE INFORMATION

Web site:
Employee Assistance Professionals Association:
www.eapassn.org

"I always pass on good advice. It is the only thing to do with it. It is never of any use to oneself."

Oscar Wilde

Developing Passive People

This checklist is for line managers handling individuals who are too compliant, too conciliatory, or too self-effacing to make a positive impact. The checklist will help identify the problem and tackle it by making progress toward a more assertive and confident approach.

DEFINITION

Passive people are often superficially very pleasant and eager to please—even too pleasant and too eager, since passive behavior is generally characterized by the desire to avoid conflict and the constant wish to please others. Passive people tend not to want to face up to difficult problems and situations because they are frightened of upsetting others.

They give in to unrealistic and unachievable demands, saying "yes" when they need to say "no" (or at least "but"). They promise deadlines that can't be met, promising to "do their best." They keep problems to themselves and play it safe to avoid any risks. This can lead to a spiraling effect—they gradually lose the confidence of those around them, including their manager. The manager's role is to help such people develop and become more assertive.

ADVANTAGES

There are many reasons for helping passive people change their behavior.

- Passive people become more confident, their self-esteem rises, and, as success breeds success, their newly learned assertive behavior starts to come naturally to them.
- Better communication means the productive airing of problems, fewer missed deadlines, and reduced potential for conflict.
- Passive people learn to make decisions and solve problems that they would previously have referred upward or sideways.
- Creative, decisive, and productive people get better results and cause fewer problems at work.

DISADVANTAGES

The principal disadvantage of helping individuals develop is that it takes time, time, and more time. Passive people require sensitive handling, patience, and a genuine commitment from the manager. Don't avoid the problem and avoid passive people. This may result in:

- the individuals themselves becoming less and less confident;
- a continuous cycle of low self-esteem, underperformance, acceptance of overwork and impossible deadlines, etc., leading to absenteeism and/or illness (often stress-related);
- the loss of their colleagues' confidence and respect, especially if their passivity affects colleagues' work;

- playing it safe or avoiding making difficult decisions, which can have disastrous effects for the organization.

ACTION CHECKLIST

✔ 1. Understand the Problem—Why People Are Passive

Reasons why people behave passively include:

- the mistaken beliefs that they will be disliked if they disagree and that others always like someone who agrees with them;
- the desire to please, sacrificing long-term realism for short-term compliance and agreement;
- the feeling that other people are threatening;
- the failure to understand that they have a right to their own views and ideas;
- a lack of confidence in their own views and ideas;
- a lack of familiarity with assertiveness techniques;
- an inability to see themselves as others see them.

Realize that for most passive people these attitudes and behaviors are deeply ingrained. They cannot be changed overnight, and simply telling a passive person to behave more assertively can make the situation worse. You need to empathize with the person's problems while staying committed to changing his or her behavior.

✔ 2. Understand the Problem—How Passive People React

Passive people often confuse assertive with aggressive behavior and find it very difficult to act assertively themselves. They think if they make a firm statement they are being aggressive, and they equate passive behavior with politeness. It is important to spot these reactions—don't assume a polite smile means everything is fine.

✔ 3. Spot the Problem

Three key indicators of passive behavior are:

spoken language. People who behave passively tend to use expressions like, "I'm sorry to bother you, but . . . " or "I know I'm probably wrong, but . . . "

body language. Telltale signs of passive behavior include:

- an inability to make eye contact;
- stooping and keeping the head down;
- nervous gestures like fingering a collar or playing with a pencil;
- speaking abnormally quietly;
- excessive use of "um" and "er";
- stepping backward when spoken to.

work results. Passive people tend not to want to disappoint or upset people, so they take on too much work, get overloaded, and then can't keep up. They may become unreliable, miss deadlines, or habitually put off difficult decisions or refer them to a superior.

✔ 4. Begin to Address the Problem

All too often managers allow passive behavior to continue unchecked because it poses no immediate problem. However, it is important to start getting to grips

---

"People can place demands upon themselves that create uncertainty."   Rabi S. Bhagat

with it as soon as you recognize it. The first step is to communicate with the person, and in this case communication means more listening than speaking.

Find time to ask questions and listen—quietly and privately—to the person about his or her passive behavior. The idea is to start modifying behavior, which should help gradually to change underlying attitudes.

5. Explain Rights and Responsibilities

Emphasize that everyone has responsibilities and the right to:

- make mistakes;
- say how they feel and what they think;
- refuse certain requests;
- say they don't know, don't agree, don't understand, or need help;
- tell other staff members that their performance needs to be improved, and in what ways.

Help the passive person accept that it isn't helping anyone to relinquish rights and responsibilities; moreover, the team can suffer as a result.

6. Explain the Basics of Assertiveness

On a very basic level, assertiveness means:

- acknowledging the other person's point of view;
- expressing the facts, and your own thoughts and feelings, honestly and openly, without rancor;
- suggesting a constructive way forward when problems arise;
- standing up for yourself if you are being put upon.

7. Be a Role Model

Show how effective assertive behavior can be by demonstrating it yourself. If a passive employee can see that a manager acts assertively, listens to problems, and finds solutions without apportioning blame, the person is more likely to be encouraged to act the same way.

8. Give Your Approval and Encouragement

Make it clear always that the person has nothing to fear. One of the roots of passive behavior is that people are fearful of disapproval and of being wrong. Define your expectations. Make it clear that you will approve of assertive behavior and disapprove of passivity. Given that a passive individual wants to please and conform, establishing acceptable standards of behavior is helpful. Encourage a climate at work that actually allows people to release their fear. A person practicing assertiveness may actually behave aggressively to start with—discourage this carefully without squashing the effort to change.

9. Create the Right Environment

Help people leave passivity behind. Encourage assertiveness by:

- coaching them in techniques and approaches;

- setting up an easy way to increase confidence—for example, a situation in which the passive person can try out new skills and be assured of success;
- giving feedback regularly on the person's performance and progress, and praising assertive behavior;
- clamping down gradually on passive behavior.

10. Implement Training and Development

Training and development are key factors in helping passive staff change the way they behave. Informal coaching is one approach, but if an individual's passivity is particularly deep-seated the person may need to think about getting counseling.

THOUGHT STARTERS
- Do you recognize any signs of passivity in your own behavior?
- Do you want to help individuals enjoy their work more and be more motivated by success?
- Do you ever blame people for their behavior instead of taking an effective management line and aiming to help them develop?

FOR MORE INFORMATION

Books:
Johnson, Larry, and Bob Phillips. *Absolute Honesty: Building a Corporate Culture that Values Straight Talk and Rewards Integrity*. New York: AMACOM, 2003.

Web site:
American Management Association: **www.amanet.org**

See also:

443

CHECKLIST

"Most people live and die with their music still unplayed. They never dare to try."

Mary Kay Ash

Empowerment

CHECKLIST

This checklist has been designed to help line managers move toward a culture of empowerment in their companies.

Empowerment should be seen not as a single initiative, but rather as a climate, atmosphere, and culture in which responsibility and accountability for the job rest with the individual doing it. Empowerment can, however, be construed as a process or style by which people manage, requiring careful preparation, clear guidelines, and understood boundaries.

DEFINITION

Empowerment is more than delegation, it is a genuine opening up of the creative power of your staff. It is based on the belief that employees' abilities are frequently under-used and that given the chance and the responsibility, people want to make a positive contribution.

The goal is to bring staff more into the action at work, in other words, to give them more power and choice to innovate, participate in problem solving and decision-making, and act and work with minimal intervention from their managers.

Empowerment is about:

- letting staff get on with the job;
- allowing staff to take responsibility for customers' experience;
- letting those closest to customers make decisions;
- stripping away unnecessary bureaucracy;
- encouraging and helping staff to put their ideas for improvements at work into practice.

ADVANTAGES

Managed effectively, empowerment can:

- strengthen the commitment of staff as they take ownership of problems and generate their own solutions;
- generate ideas for improving services—staff feel their ideas count;
- help unearth staff talent that has previously lain dormant;
- reduce the amount of time managers spend sorting out other people's problems;
- improve customer service and organizational performance.

DISADVANTAGES

If not handled effectively, the empowerment process may:

- stoke up resentment among managers who feel their role is being downgraded;
- cause anxiety among those you want to empower;
- lead to people innovating well beyond the normal control of their jobs;
- create expectations that cannot be fulfilled, and thus lead to frustration;
- breed resentment because extra responsibility is not accompanied by more pay;
- cause a breakdown in control of staff.

ACTION CHECKLIST

1. Check Your Own Opinions, Assumptions, and Attitudes

Clarify what you mean by empowerment and what you expect to get out of it. Is it an improved consultative process? More active delegation? Is it extended responsibilities for problem solving and decision making? Is your principal concern to develop people and expand their skill base, or is it to improve the bottom line? Let colleagues and senior managers know what you are doing. Do their expectations meet your own?

2. Recognize the Barriers to Empowerment

Barriers may include:

- an unreceptive organizational culture—many organizations are inherently controlling, bureaucratic, and unreceptive to change;
- psychological factors—managers may feel that empowerment means losing control, while staff may fear responsibility;
- rigid routines that discourage people from taking responsibility.

3. Recognize the Need for a Conducive Culture

There is no single formula for a culture conducive to empowerment, but some corporate cultures enable staff to make a positive contribution free from fear or blame better than others. Consider the following archetypes, adapted from the work of Charles Handy (*Understanding Organizations*, 1993) and Edgar H. Schein (*Organizational Culture and Leadership*, 1992).

1. The role culture, with defined functions and specialties and set procedures and job descriptions. This is most appropriate in a stable environment.

2. The task culture, job- or project-oriented, concerned to bring together the right resources and people and let them get on with the job. Reliant on the formation (and dissolution) of teams, the task culture is better equipped than the role culture to generate and respond to change.

3. The fear culture, in which:

- decisions—and truth—come ultimately from senior people;
- relationships are basically vertical and linear;
- each person has a niche that cannot be invaded;
- exchange takes place by agenda and prearranged appointment;
- deference is paid to rank and authority;
- people use the formal communication process to cover their backs.

4. The trust culture, in which:

- ideas come from individuals;
- people are responsible and motivated;

"I'm not wild about accepting responsibility without authority. Why should my people be?"

Bill Creech

- the prevailing atmosphere is informal, with few closed doors;
- mistakes are not met with blame or recrimination;
- opportunities for learning are plentiful.

4. Set Boundaries

Although empowerment allows staff extra autonomy, there should be clear limits to the levels of responsibility and autonomy granted. Wherever the cutoff is defined, retain a mechanism allowing staff to refer problems and suggestions upward. After the boundaries have been set as clearly as possible, it will still be necessary to establish them in practice on a case by case basis so that staff learn when to act without reporting, when to act and report, and when to ask before acting.

5. Raise Awareness

Before the process of empowerment begins, you need to raise employees' awareness of what empowerment entails. Hold meetings and discussion groups to inform everyone what is happening, what is expected of them, and why the process is occurring.

6. Get Staff on Your Side

Reassure employees who are involved and win support from others. Staff who are used to doing what they are told instead of finding solutions for themselves or making independent decisions are likely to feel threatened about such a change in culture. Allow staff to air their anxieties and make sure that they are comfortable with the processes involved. They need to know that channels of communication are open and effective.

7. Audit Staff Skills

Investigate what hidden talents staff have. Draw up a roster of currently under-used talents, including those usually regarded as falling outside the working environment. Ask people about themselves instead of making assumptions.

8. Make Sure Staff Have Resources

Responsibilities for customers, complaints, and operational changes need to be rethought. So do new responsibilities and the levels and types of resourcing needed to allow people to carry out their jobs. You will know whether empowerment is working if your staff:

- seem able to run things without your daily or hourly involvement;
- take ownership of "their" customers;
- come up with ideas for improving the service;
- don't expect you to solve "their" problems.

If your customers are better satisfied and the bottom line benefits, you have further confirmation.

9. Agree on Performance Objectives and Measures

Giving people real responsibility and resources to complete tasks is one thing, setting them adrift another. Empowerment encompasses agreeing objectives with your people and agreeing on the measures of efficiency, effectiveness, and cost effectiveness to deliver excellent customer service.

10. Launch the Initiative

Staff may need a good deal of support in the early stages if they are afraid to take responsibility, but support has to be distinguished from mothering. Managers may need careful handling, too, otherwise they may feel threatened and try to retain control by underhand means. Once the ground has been prepared, empowerment can start to take effect. Encourage the process by acting on ideas suggested by the staff. Boost the success of the process by publicizing what is happening on your intranet or in a company newsletter and by reinforcing examples of good practice.

11. Monitor Developments

Hold meetings to check progress, give and receive feedback, and gather ideas and other support. Establish communication networks to build success and keep the initiative going within the organization. Be prepared to live with the mistakes. They are useful learning experiences for the future—as long as the same errors don't keep recurring.

THOUGHT STARTERS

- How much real authority do you want your people to have?

- Are you sure there is a climate of two-way trust in the organization?

- Are your people being under-used? Are you aware of all their skills and capabilities?

- Does your current reward system encourage empowerment?

FOR MORE INFORMATION

Books:
Blanchard, Ken, John P. Carlos, and Alan Randolph. *The Three Keys to Empowerment: Release the Power Within People for Astonishing Results.* San Francisco, CA: Berrett-Koehler, 1999.
Handy, Charles. *Understanding Organizations.* 4th ed. London: Penguin, 1993.

See also:
✓ Leading from the Middle (pp. 452–453)
✓ Managing Staff Turnover and Retention (pp. 454–455)
✓ Networking and Marketing Yourself (pp. 857–858)

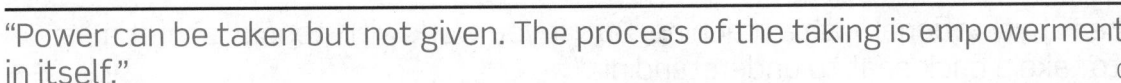
"Power can be taken but not given. The process of the taking is empowerment in itself."

Gloria Steinem

445

CHECKLIST

Emotional Intelligence (EI)

CHECKLIST

This checklist explains the concept of emotional intelligence (EI, sometimes referred to as EQ or emotional intelligence quotient) and why it is becoming more important. It gives an overview of the basic principles and outlines why it is relevant for managers. A brief self-test indicator appears at the end of the checklist.

Emotional intelligence is increasingly regarded as a major key to personal success and as being more important than IQ. Some of the most successful people in life today are those who are regarded as having a high level of emotional intelligence, whatever their IQ. Being able to manage themselves and others successfully is often a crucial factor in their success. With a growing emphasis on soft skills, managers need to be able to handle other people sensitively, both inside and outside the organization.

DEFINITION

"The ability to perceive, to integrate, to understand and reflectively manage one's own and other people's feelings."

(John D. Mayer, quoted in *People Management* (October 28, 1999): 49)

Emotional Intelligence At Work

Most people experience a range of both positive and negative emotions at work, for example:

- satisfaction—you've done an excellent piece of work;
- exhilaration—you've won a major contract;
- pride—you've helped someone out of a difficult situation;
- anger—your work hasn't been appreciated;
- frustration—your recommendations have been shelved indefinitely;
- anxiety—you're having trouble meeting deadlines.

How Does Emotional Intelligence Work?

When an emotion like anger, anxiety, or frustration is experienced, the human brain is programmed to respond to the threat and an emotional response is triggered. However, acting on that first impulse can lead you to say or do things you later regret. Emotional intelligence means that while you acknowledge your instinctive emotional response, you don't act on it, but you step back from the situation and let rational thought influence your actions.

ADVANTAGES

Emotional intelligence can:

- improve your relationships with colleagues;
- help you keep yourself under control;
- help lower stress levels;
- help keep you motivated;
- enable you to communicate well and influence others without conflict;
- enhance your standing in the eyes of your colleagues.

DISADVANTAGES

Emotional intelligence:

- cannot always be learned, though it can be developed;
- is sometimes dismissed as being just another management fad.

ACTION CHECKLIST

 1. Understand the Theories of Emotional Intelligence

Two U.S. psychologists, John D. Mayer and Peter Salovey, first defined the phrase "emotional intelligence" in the 1980s. Daniel Goleman, another U.S. psychologist, later built on their work and published his well-known books on the subject. He also produced a framework for emotional intelligence, which consists of five elements:

- self-awareness—an understanding of yourself, your strengths and weaknesses, and how you appear to others;
- self-regulation—the ability to control yourself and think before you act;
- motivation—the drive to work and succeed;
- empathy—how well you understand other people's viewpoints;
- social skills—the ability to communicate and relate to others.

Other important researchers into emotional intelligence include the British management professors Malcolm Higgs and Victor Dulewicz. They identified seven elements of emotional intelligence, which can be broken down into three main categories:

- drivers—motivation and decisiveness. These two traits energize people and drive them toward achieving their goals, which are usually set very high.
- constrainers—conscientiousness and integrity, and emotional resilience. In contrast, these two traits act as controls and curb the excesses of the drivers, especially if the drivers are very high and are undirected or misdirected.
- enablers—sensitivity, influence, and self-awareness. These three traits facilitate performance and help the individual succeed

(Source: *People Management* (October 28, 1999))

2. Ask What This Means for You

The following competences are considered necessary for managers. They have particular relevance for emotional intelligence. Managers need to:

- be able to manage themselves (self-regulation, constrainers) and not vent their frustration on staff;
- have awareness of their real (not perceived) strengths and weaknesses;
- motivate others as well as themselves;
- counsel or coach others within the organization (social skills, enablers);
- encourage others and offer advice (social skills, enablers);
- develop good working relationships (empathy, enablers).

"You can be totally rational with a machine. But, if you work with people, sometimes logic has to take a back seat to understanding."

Akio Morita

 3. Test and Develop Your Emotional Intelligence

A major problem when testing for emotional intelligence is that there is no one agreed standard definition of the concept. Practitioners and trainers use a widely varying range of characteristics and assessment methods, and many of the tests available for measuring EI (on the Internet, for example) reflect this. These tests are, however, useful in making people aware of the issues involved and can give an indication of where an individual's emotional strengths and weaknesses lie.

Another question is whether EI can be developed. Certainly skills in team building or motivation can be developed—numerous books, seminars, and courses aim to do just that, or at least to give a better understanding of the issues involved. Until more academically rigorous and tested assessment outcomes are developed, it may be safest to say for the time being that only some facets of EI can be learned or taught. Others, like adopting a more understanding attitude or building drive and determination, can only come from within.

Examples of EI tests can be found at **www.eiconsortium.org** and **http://ei.haygroup.com/ resources/topteams**.

The tests usually take the form of questionnaires or psychometric testing, measuring competences or characteristics such as emotional energy, stress, assertiveness, sociability, attitudes, decisiveness, objective judgment, self-esteem, courage, and tolerance of and consideration for others. Some tests are wholly Web-based, others paper-based. A simple test is given at the end of this checklist.

THOUGHT STARTERS
- Do you think your communication with your colleagues could be improved?
- When you're angry, do you say the first thing that comes to mind?
- Do you tend to ignore your emotional responses to events?

DOS AND DON'TS

DO
- Observe your emotional reactions to other people.
- Consider how you might test and develop your emotional intelligence.
- Ask yourself honestly how well you react to the concerns of others.

DON'T
- Don't assume you don't bring your emotions to work with you.
- Don't believe emotional intelligence isn't relevant for your job.
- Don't think your emotional intelligence needs no further development.

FOR MORE INFORMATION

Books:
Caruso, David R., and Peter Salovey. *The Emotionally Intelligent Manager: How to Develop and Use the Four Key Emotional Skills of Leadership*. San Francisco, CA: Jossey-Bass, 2004.
Goleman, Daniel. *Emotional Intelligence: Why It Can Matter More Than IQ*. New York: Bantam, 1997.
Goleman, Daniel. *Working with Emotional Intelligence*. New York: Bantam Doubleday Dell, 2000.
Goleman, Daniel, Richard Boyatzis, and Annie McKee. *Primal Leadership: Realizing the Power of Emotional Intelligence*. Boston, MA: Harvard Business School Press, 2002.

See also:
Daniel Goleman (pp. 1212–1213)

"Use missteps as stepping stones to deeper understanding and greater achievement."
Susan L. Taylor

Handling Conflict Situations

CHECKLIST

This checklist examines the approach to personal conflict and is designed to help line managers handle conflict when it arises.

Conflict can arise from a host of roots and causes, but principally it occurs from differences between people who disagree about ideas or find themselves in difficult situations. "Ideas conflict" can be desirable and creative when handled constructively; "situations conflict" can cause frustration and resentment if not dealt with. Personal conflict can be damaging and destructive unless it is managed with thought and care. Ultimately conflict can cost a great deal of time and money. Most organizations and individuals recognize the need to solve personal conflicts before they become destructive.

DEFINITION

Personal conflict occurs when two or more parties have opposing attitudes or approaches to a particular situation, issue, or person. Sources of conflict range from a difference of opinion, problematic working conditions, or unrealistic work expectations to discriminatory behavior such as racism or sexism, poor communication, or noncompliance with organizational norms or values.

Conflict can occur between a member of staff and a manager, between two or more members of a team, or between departments, sections, or managers. Whether you are involved directly affects whether you negotiate with someone else, apply grievance or disciplinary measures, or mediate between other parties.

Conflict can be covert, taking the form of resentment from a team member passed over for promotion or irritation caused by an individual's personal habits. Such conflict is much harder to detect and easier to ignore. Whichever type it is, all conflict needs to be managed before it becomes a destructive force.

ADVANTAGES

The advantages of managing conflict situations are:
- better motivated staff; staff energies are directed toward work instead of emotions;
- a more positive image of the organization or staff;
- improved teamwork;
- better personal development of individuals.

DISADVANTAGES

The disadvantages of avoiding or failing to manage a conflict situation may include:
- the escalation and spread of the conflict to others;
- the dissipation of staff energy;
- the misdirection of staff energy, contributing to falling productivity;
- the misperception that inaction is the easiest option—the problem will ultimately be harder to solve.

ACTION CHECKLIST

1. Recognize Conflict

To handle conflict you have to spot it. Remember it can be overt, from an obvious or identifiable cause, clearly visible and defined; or covert, from a less obvious or apparently unrelated cause (for example, an employee could seem to be in conflict with colleagues, when the root cause is a perception that the supervisor's treatment of staff is discriminatory).

2. Monitor the Climate

Monitoring the climate at work gives you an early warning system, making it far easier to deal with conflict swiftly and efficiently before it gets out of hand. This does not mean constantly being on your guard; it simply means being prepared and keeping your eyes open. If you see a likely conflict situation, don't ignore it. Early action saves time and stress later.

3. Look Into the Situation

Take time to find out the real cause of the conflict, who is involved, what the key issue is, and what its actual and potential effects are. Empathize—see the situation from other people's point of view.

4. Plan Your Approach

Encourage the parties concerned to examine the interests behind their position and try to create a climate of exchange so that the parties can deal with each other more constructively next time. Devise a strategy based on what this investigation has shown. Managers should decide on the result they want to achieve, bearing in mind that as different evidence emerges their preferred outcome may not always be possible.

5. Handle the Issue

Handling conflict is a difficult process that can create extreme emotions. Use the following techniques.

Stay calm. Take time to respond—don't give a knee-jerk reaction. If necessary declare a time out until people are calm enough to discuss the issues rationally and constructively.

Listen to the points of view of everyone involved and take time to understand all the issues raised by the conflict. Remember that people will usually be more open and honest if they feel they have a receptive and interested audience. Be aware of your body language and spoken language.

Avoid fight or flight. The instinctive human reaction to conflict is either to run away or face it and fight. Neither of these approaches is constructive.
- Fighting back or being aggressive toward one or both parties when you are not personally involved causes greater long-term conflict and intimidates staff.
- Flight avoids solving the conflict and leads to loss of respect.

Stay assertive. This means avoiding being either passive

"It's like breaking up a family row as an outsider."   Gerry Robinson

or aggressive; neither is assertive and each is a short-term approach unlikely to solve the conflict.

- Passive behavior is characterized by apologizing, withdrawn body language, and always accepting the other person's point of view whether it is right or not.
- Aggressive behavior is characterized by being authoritarian and refusing to listen to reasoned argument.

An assertive approach is generally the best way to handle conflict. It means:

- acknowledging the views and rights of all parties;
- encouraging the parties to find the causes of the conflict—and solutions to it;
- trying to make sure that opinions and thoughts are expressed honestly and openly;
- suggesting a constructive way forward.

6. Let Everyone Have a Say

If you have managed to get the parties around a table for discussion in a climate in which exchange is possible, reaching a compromise solution may be feasible. Remember that your desired solution needs to hit a wide range of targets. It should:

- help to build good working relationships;
- be legitimate, nondiscriminatory, and compatible with organizational practice;
- recognize all parties' alternatives;
- help to improve communication;
- help to generate a lasting commitment to the solution.

7. Find the Way Forward

The most important aspect of handling a conflict situation is to find an acceptable way forward. Examine the options and decide what to do next. Can you reach a compromise acceptable to both or all sides? If not, what action needs to be taken to prevent the conflict from continuing? Make sure everyone knows what the conclusion is and what each person is expected to do.

The next steps need to be agreed and spelled out: they could include an individual's need for counseling, the likelihood of disciplinary proceedings, or an agreement to be implemented (even moving a member of staff to another department if there is a deep-rooted personal antagonism). Sometimes problems relate to health or psychology—you have to judge where your limits lie in resolving apparently intractable personal antagonisms.

8. Appraise, Don't Dwell

It is important to learn from conflict situations and move forward. Don't dwell on the past and reopen old wounds.

Appraise the conflict and the way it was handled to see what you can learn. How can similar conflicts be avoided in the future? How could a similar situation be handled

better? Learn from the experience and keep your eye on what has been resolved to stop it flaring up again.

449

CHECKLIST

DOS AND DON'TS

DO
- Tackle conflict early to keep it from escalating.
- Try to avoid instinctive reactions.
- Think the problem through and plan a way to deal with the conflict.
- Refrain from offering your own opinion before understanding the full picture.
- Stay assertive.

DON'T
- Don't avoid the issue and ignore the conflict.
- Don't take it personally (unless it is personal).
- Don't jump in without assessing and understanding the problem.
- Don't fight anger with anger.
- Don't run away.
- Don't handle conflict in public.

THOUGHT STARTERS
- Do you encourage all parties to explore factors common to their respective positions?
- Do you try to enable the parties to deal effectively with their differences?
- Do you try to make it easier for the parties to deal with each other next time?
- Do you encourage the parties to come up with ways of generating mutual gain?
- Do you encourage the parties to come to realistic appraisals of their point of view?

FOR MORE INFORMATION

Book:
Crawley, John, and Katherine Graham. *Mediation for Managers.* Naperville, IL: Nicholas Brealey, 2002.

Journal Article:
Holder, Roy. "How To Turn Conflict to Your Advantage." *Works Management* (March 1997): 28–30.

"When dealing with complexity and uncertainty, trust and openness become critical."

David L. Dotlich

Introducing Flexible Working into Your Organization

> This checklist provides an introduction to the use of flexible working practices within an organization by considering alternatives to traditional working hours.
>
> Employers are continually searching for ways to stay "lean and mean" but effective. Flexibility in working hours is increasingly viewed as a way to manage time and people more effectively within a volatile trading environment, and as a means of recruiting and retaining good people within a more competitive labor market.

DEFINITION

"Flexibility" covers any variation in working hours from the standard nine-to-five working day. The key variants are flextime, which may include a compressed work week, job-sharing, part time employment, comp time, and sabbaticals.

ADVANTAGES

Flexible working can provide:
- recruitment and retention of qualified staff who may not be able to work traditional hours;
- equality of opportunity: standard hours often prevent individuals with family or caring responsibilities and disabled people from working;
- work patterns which can be tailored to accommodate swings in demand or new customer requirements;
- greater success in tackling skills shortages;
- higher return on training investment.

Flextime:
- reduces problems of punctuality and disciplining staff for late arrival;
- reduces one-day absenteeism: staff can use flextime to deal with minor crises or personal appointments;
- creates a greater sense of responsibility and better time management;
- improves efficiency in core times and reduces overtime;
- encourages people with family responsibilities to work;
- increases productivity by making it easier to manage seasonal labor requirements, while allowing control of total hours worked annually.

Compressed work week:
- may improve productivity by increasing the standard hours worked into fewer days;
- may improve employee morale by earning them more days off per month.

Job-sharing:
- brings two sets of skills and experience to one job;
- results in staff who are sometimes more energetic and committed than full-time workers;

- provides greater continuity in cases of sickness or leave.

Voluntary reduced work time:
- opens up jobs to a wider range of people.

Part time employment:
- opens up jobs to a wider range of people;
- encourages single parents, seniors, physically challenged, and students to work;
- benefits the company's bottom line if no benefits are associated with part time work;
- benefits the employee if a health and retirement package accompanies part time work.

Compensation "comp" time:
- avoids paying overtime;
- allows the employee to "bank" a day off with pay at some other time.

Unpaid leave:
- retains the service of staff who would otherwise leave the organization altogether.

Sabbaticals:
- replenish employees' energy and creativity.

DISADVANTAGES
- Arranging cover and scheduling work requires more management time than planning for standard working hours.
- If programs are not handled sensitively and made available to all employees, full time employees may become resentful.

Flextime:
- can encourage people to count the minutes rather than do the job;
- requires more managerial oversight to assure maximum work coordination during core working hours.

Compressed work week:
- requires more coordination of core working hours;
- sometimes creates excess stress on employees working longer days.

Part time work:
- requires more people and more coordination to get the work done.

Job-sharing:
- may lead to communications difficulties;
- can damage continuity if someone starts a task and then leaves it to another person.

ACTION CHECKLIST

1. Secure the Commitment of Top Management

Reach agreement with senior managers on the extent of flexibility and make sure that they are committed to this.

2. Analyze Your Work force

Profiling your existing work force and analyzing its current work patterns may surprise you: you may not

realize the extent of informal flexible working already sanctioned by line managers.

3. Set Up a Working Group

Nominate a working group that represents all types and levels of employee. Use the group to steer through the changes and act as a sounding board.

4. Decide How Flexible the Organization Can Afford to Be

Are you willing to consider all options for flexibility, or do you want to limit employees to a fixed range? Flextime, for example, should apply to everyone at all levels. Keep in mind that once flexible working is adopted, it is difficult to go back to traditional practices. Pilot the program and expand it gradually.

5. Consult All Employees

Seek employees' views on any changes they would like to see, or ask their opinion on specific options. Use questionnaires, workshops, or discussion groups.

6. Have the Working Group Consider Options

- What system will there be for arranging cover?
- What effect will there be on pay?
- Will you allow line managers discretion in interpreting a broad policy, or will there be little scope for variation?
- How will you ensure parity of treatment in training and development, promotion and benefits?
- Will there be a qualifying period?
- Will any additional costs be offset by business benefits?

7. Secure Senior Management's Agreement

Make sure that senior managers are aware of the rationale and the business case for introducing flexibility. Confirm their commitment to the policy outlined by the working group.

8. Communicate the Policies

Publicize the new program to all staff. Use existing examples and role models. Be open and honest about terms and conditions of eligibility for each option and set clear guidelines for their use. Be specific about any particular times or circumstances under which flexible schedules will not be allowed, for example, during the annual parts inventory, harvest season, or at a particularly busy customer demand period.

9. Identify a Coordinator

You will need somebody to retain a general overview of the program and offer guidance on its implementation.

10. Train Line Managers/Team Leaders to Implement the Program

Continuing management control is vital as flexibility is introduced. It is the manager's job to ensure that work gets done; this may mean denying what staff prefer on particular occasions.

11. Monitor and Evaluate the Program

Set up a system to monitor and evaluate the program. Make sure you evaluate its success in terms of the business benefits sought.

12. Consider the Need for Complementary Programs

Think about how the flexible working program fits into the current corporate culture. Do you need to develop a program to change the culture or to support new working practices?

DOS AND DON'TS

DO
- Consult staff first.
- Assume that all jobs can be done flexibly unless a business case can be made otherwise.
- Target the program at all employees.
- Stress the business benefits to line managers at all stages of introduction and implementation.

DON'T
- Don't gear the program exclusively toward women with children.
- Don't make assumptions about employees' needs and wishes.

THOUGHT STARTERS

- Are you tackling flexible working at the three levels on which change needs to operate—culture, policies, and practice?

- Are you making assumptions about what your employees want?

- How will you evaluate the business benefits?

- How would you implement a working group to design the process?

FOR MORE INFORMATION

Books:
Lewis, Suzan, and Cary L. Cooper. *Work-Life Integration: Case Studies of Organisational Change.* Hoboken NJ: Wiley, 2005.

WEB SITE:
HRS Federal Job Search: **www.hrsjobs.com**

See also:
✓ Managing Staff Turnover and Retention (pp. 454–455)

 451

CHECKLIST

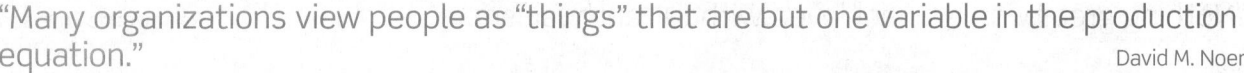
"Many organizations view people as "things" that are but one variable in the production equation."
David M. Noer

Leading from the Middle

This checklist explains the fundamentals of leadership. In today's fast-changing business world, leadership is increasingly seen as a key to improved performance. It is needed at all levels of an organization, not just the top. Think about groups you have observed, and you may be able to identify leaders who were at the bottom of the hierarchy or in positions with no formal authority.

Definable leadership skills exist that, when used purposefully, help managers get the most from their teams. Many companies sponsor programs to improve the leadership skills of staff at all levels, from supervisor to C.E.O. This underlines the point, increasingly understood by organizations in all industries, that leadership is not something we are either born with or not—it can be developed.

DEFINITION

Leadership is notoriously difficult to define, and the link with management is especially difficult. One way of looking at it is to say that "pure" leaders don't have to be good managers, but every manager has to be an effective leader. You may be given a managerial title, but you earn a leadership role. So what makes a good leader?

- Leaders have followers—without followers who trust, rely on, and feel supported by the leader there is no real leadership.
- Leaders have vision—they have a clear, exciting image of the future and set the agenda for their team.
- Leaders show commitment—they generate enthusiasm for the organization and help lead people through times of change.
- Leaders communicate—they are honest, open, and positive, and spend time talking and listening to their people.
- Leaders empower staff—they give staff the room and the confidence to get the job done.

John W. Gardner on leadership:

Although leadership and the exercise of power are distinguishable activities, they overlap and interweave in important ways. Consider a corporate chief executive officer who has the gift for inspiring and motivating people, who has vision, who lifts the spirits of employees with a resulting rise in productivity and quality of product, and a drop in turnover and absenteeism. That is leadership. But evidence emerges that the company is falling behind in the technology race. One day with the stroke of a pen the C.E.O. increases the funds available to the research division. That is the exercise of power. The stroke of a pen could have been made by an executive with none of the qualities one associates with leadership. [John W. Gardner, *On Leadership* (Free Press, 1990).]

ADVANTAGES

Effective leadership:

- is a major factor in successfully bringing staff through turbulent times;
- helps to spread a common understanding of what the organization is about;
- generates enthusiasm and team spirit;
- can be a powerful motivator and get the best out of team members.

DISADVANTAGES

There are no disadvantages to effective leadership, but leaders can abuse their position.

- Domineering leaders tend to trample on other people and stifle innovation.
- Leadership can exert too strong a pull on followers—if the leader is too dominant or charismatic, people may go along blindly with policies or practices that are detrimental to themselves or the organization.
- Charismatic leadership can lead to a personality cult.
- Macho leaders who are in conflict with each other can split teams and the organization.

ACTION CHECKLIST

1. Understand how Leadership Differs from Management

If you are not clear about the distinction, it is difficult to isolate (and therefore improve) the skills unique to leadership.

- Management is really about the day-to-day running of a function, about getting the right people in the right place. It involves many administrative tasks.
- Leadership is more dynamic. It is about creating a vision for that function and gaining people's commitment. There are few certainties in leadership.

2. Be Clear About Where You Are Now

Are you comfortable with the idea of being a leader? If not, where do you think your weaknesses lie? Many people, especially those who have been promoted because they have a technical skill, feel uncomfortable with being leaders. You need to be clear about what you feel about yourself as a leader. Think about whether you feel that leadership is alien to your character, whether you lack the authority and respect to be a leader, or whether you believe that only more senior managers should be leaders.

Remember that everyone can learn how to develop leadership potential—authority and respect are there to be earned. In organizations today, people at all levels are expected to show leadership qualities.

3. Downplay Charisma

Charisma is often spoken of as the key to a leader's success. It is something of a blunt weapon, however, and one that is easily over-used. Charismatic leaders can be destructive. They tend to dominate people and can create slavish followers who are dependent on them for guidance and direction. Organizations need to empower employees to make their own decisions and to develop corporate leaders who have a broad range of leadership skills and styles.

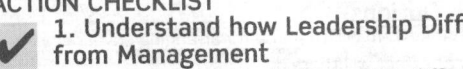

"Nothing great was ever achieved without enthusiasm."   Ralph Waldo Emerson

 ### 4. Recognize That People Have Different Leadership Needs

Work at developing a range of appropriate leadership styles and at matching your leadership style to specific situations and individuals. Different people need different kinds of leadership.

- People who are unwilling or unable to take responsibility need more supervision and direction with specific outcome-oriented work goals and constant monitoring.
- Staff who lack confidence but show potential need coaching. They need you to set goals and priorities, yet be supportive. You need to explain what needs to be done and then reinforce any positive behavior. The aim is to gradually get them to take responsibility.
- Talented but underachieving employees need you to lead by communicating with them. The key is to get them performing better, sharing in decision making, and taking initiative.
- Star performers who are already fully competent need to be left alone to get on with the job.

5. Develop Leadership Qualities

Real leaders demonstrate a range of qualities that encourage others to follow. These include:
- developing and demonstrating good work habits;
- understanding and valuing your staff's work;
- working hard at handling pressure;
- clearly demonstrating the values you hold dear;
- encouraging your staff's enthusiasm;
- providing regular feedback;
- listening and learning.

6. Build Communication Channels

Develop and communicate your intentions and directions clearly, so people understand what you expect, know when they have done well or badly, and feel that they can give you feedback on your own performance. Most research into what makes a good leader stresses that

leaders communicate—and communicate all the time. They create a vision of where the department and organization are going, and they communicate it clearly, and often, by demonstrating it through their actions and by listening to team members.

7. Work Hard at Empowering Your Staff

You need to provide your staff with the support and confidence to achieve things for themselves. Effective leaders work at creating the right circumstances for employees to take real ownership of their work. Ask yourself if you are courageous enough to trust your people to do a good job and to show faith in them. If you are, and can still give them a sense of vision and guidance when they need it, they will begin to see you as their leader.

THOUGHT STARTERS

- Do you know how much your people value your leadership skills?

- Have you tended to rely on one leadership style rather than using a range of styles?

- Do you over-use charisma?

- Are you clear about your values? Are your team members clear about them?

- Are you comfortable encouraging enthusiasm?

- Do you know who in your team needs space and who needs direction?

- Do you know how many of your people are with you?

DOS AND DON'TS

DO
- Match your style to the situation.
- Be clear about your values.
- Keep communication channels open.
- Listen to your people.
- Empower your people.
- Encourage enthusiasm and show it yourself.

DON'T
- Don't be domineering.
- Don't think that leaders have to come up with all the ideas.
- Don't rely solely on your charisma.
- Don't mandate behavior for other people and do the opposite yourself.

FOR MORE INFORMATION

Books:
Bennis, Warren, and Joan Goldsmith. *Learning to Lead: A Workbook on Becoming a Leader.* 3rd ed. New York: Perseus, 2003.
Kellerman, Barbara. *Bad Leadership: What it is, How it Happens, and Why it Matters.* Boston, MA: Harvard Business School Press, 2004.
Northouse, Peter G. *Leadership: Theory and Practice.* 3rd ed. Thousand Oaks, CA: Sage, 2004.
Robbins, Harvey, and Michael Finley. *The Accidental Leader: What to Do When You're Suddenly in Charge.* San Francisco, CA: Jossey-Bass, 2004.

See also:
✔ Empowerment (pp. 444–445)

"Everyone is a potential winner. Some people are disguised as losers, don't let their appearances fool you."

Kenneth Blanchard

Managing Staff Turnover and Retention

This checklist is designed to help managers analyze, understand, and manage staff turnover.

Labor turnover fluctuates with the economic cycle, and often falls during a recession. One advantage of this, a reduction in recruitment costs, can obscure underlying problems such as the retention of dissatisfied staff who would like to move on, or the inability of the company to bring in fresh blood. In a time of low turnover, therefore, it is important to manage these symptoms, even if they do not result in the actual turnover of staff.

Some labor turnover is inevitable and may even be desirable, particularly in today's flatter organizations—for example, because there are few promotion opportunities or because the company prefers to have a regular injection of new talent with fresh minds, enthusiasm, and knowledge and experience of up-to-date developments. Unnecessary turnover, however, is expensive in terms of recruitment costs, production and service inefficiencies, and lower staff morale.

DEFINITION

Turnover can be classified in three ways:
- employer-controlled: dismissal, layoff, and early retirement
- employee-led: dissatisfaction of varying kinds
- employer and employee uncontrolled: long-term sickness, normal retirement, maternity leave, and death in service

ADVANTAGES

Management leads to:
- more effective recruitment;
- reduced costs;
- better staff morale;
- improved knowledge of the labor market as a whole;
- more constructive development of the organization's knowledge base.

ACTION CHECKLIST

1. Determine the Extent of the Problem

Consider using one or more of the measurement techniques commonly used by employers.

- The global turnover rate, otherwise known as the crude wastage index, is the most frequently used measure. It is calculated as follows:

(Leavers in year ÷ Average number employed in year) × 100. The advantage of this measure is that it is widely used, and comparisons can thus be made between companies. It has severe limitations, however, in that it includes all leavers, ignoring factors such as their reasons for leaving and their department, age, and length of service. This technique may leave you with an imbalanced workforce, for example, with all employees over 50 or under 30.

- The stability index is a frequently used additional measure, usually calculated as follows:

(Staff with one year's service or more ÷ Total staff one year ago) × 100

- Cohort analysis takes a homogeneous group of employees who joined at the same time and tracks the way the group behaves over a period. The rate of leaving of this cohort can be plotted as a wastage curve.

- The census analysis method takes a snapshot of the total situation, rather than examining one group over a period. Leavers are studied in groups according to length of service and then plotted as a proportion of total staff in that group.

- Computer models for employment forecasting are used only in large firms and have recently declined in popularity.

2. Benchmark Your Organization Against Others

One way of judging whether your turnover rates are reasonable is to compare them against national, regional, or industry figures. The American Productivity & Quality Center conducts best practice and benchmarking studies. In addition, the *Wall Street Journal*'s Web site maintains a database on industries and hiring trends as well as salary data (www.careerjournal.com/salaries/index.html). Some companies belong to informal employer networks where they exchange information on various personnel topics. If you trade statistics, make sure that you are clear on other firms' definitions, and that like is compared with like.

Monitor general labor market trends to assess how these will affect your organization. These include demographic factors, the number of women, minorities, and graduates in the workforce, and labor mobility.

3. Find Out Why Turnover Occurs

Although external forces such as short supply of some occupational groups may influence turnover, internal factors are usually more significant. Study the work of the motivation theorists. Maslow argued that people have a hierarchy of needs ranging from physical needs to self-fulfillment; Herzberg distinguished between two sets of factors: hygiene and motivation. McGregor stated that bosses tend to treat subordinates according to their own prejudices, specifically their belief either that employees need to be ruled and controlled (Theory X), or that, given the opportunity, all employees can make a significant contribution (Theory Y).

It is important to study physical or hygiene factors such as pay and working conditions, but other issues are just as important (some would argue more important) in determining people's attitude toward their employment. Motivation factors include:

- working for an efficient boss;
- thinking for yourself;
- seeing the end result of work and gaining a sense of achievement;
- getting interesting and challenging work assignments;
- being informed, listened to, and respected.

It is worth bearing in mind, however, that organizations may appear to be following two apparently opposing directions: requiring more commitment and involvement of staff, while also being bent on cost reduction, which may include getting rid of staff. In such conditions it could be argued that motivation factors are being emphasized at the expense of the more fundamental hygiene factors or safety needs of employees.

4. Ask Leavers Why They Are Leaving

Consider conducting exit interviews with leavers or giving them questionnaires to complete. Either tool must be structured carefully and should not be relied on as the only way of collecting data. The trends behind involuntary turnover should not be ignored. For example, a rise in health-related departures may give rise to concerns about health and safety at work.

5. Assess the Effects of Turnover

The most obvious impact of turnover is that of increased costs. These fall into four tangible categories:

- separation costs
- temporary replacement costs
- recruitment and selection costs
- orientation and training costs

Turnover can be self-perpetuating in that it affects the morale of those who stay. Gauge employees' reactions through employee attitude surveys. Turnover also causes inefficiencies, not least because of the disruption caused by resignations.

6. Implement Retention Strategies

Take steps to:

- make sure that pay rates are competitive;
- offer a wider choice of benefits, for example, sabbaticals, career breaks, childcare, and eldercare arrangements;
- review your recruitment literature to make sure it gives an accurate picture of your organization;
- look at the quality of orientation and training you offer;
- improve job design and introduce flexible working practices such as job-sharing, flextime, and telecommuting;
- develop equal opportunity policies.

There are at least eight laws governing hiring policies.

Depending on its size, your organization may be exempt from some discrimination laws. For example, the Age Discrimination in Employment Act only applies to organizations with 20 or more employees.

- Promote career advancement opportunities such as dual career ladders for technical and managerial staff.
- Improve the quality of supervision and management.
- Improve and offer training and education to your employees.

455

CHECKLIST

DOS AND DON'TS

DO
- Distinguish between different types of turnover.
- Understand the difference between hygiene and motivation factors, but make sure that you take account of both.
- Monitor the external labor market.

DON'T
- Don't measure and benchmark without knowing what you want to achieve.
- Don't throw money at the problem without knowing what the problem really is.

THOUGHT STARTERS
- Do you monitor turnover?
- Do you carry out exit interviews?
- Is turnover cyclical, seasonal, or departmentalized?

FOR MORE INFORMATION

Book:
Cohen, David S. *The Talent Edge: A Behavioral Approach to Hiring, Developing, and Keeping Top Performers.* Toronto: Wiley, 2001.

Journal Article:
Rankin, Neil. "Benchmarking Labour Turnover 2005" parts 1 & 2. *IRS Employment Review* nos 817 & 818 (February 11 & 25, 2005).

Web site:
American Productivity and Quality Center: **www.apqc.org**

See also:
- ✔ Attracting and Retaining People Reentering the Workplace (pp. 498–499)
- ✔ Conducting a Performance Appraisal (pp. 438–439)
- ✔ Empowerment (pp. 444–445)
- ✔ Implementing an Effective Change Program (pp. 556–557)
- ✔ Introducing Flexible Working into Your Organization (pp. 450–451)
- ✔ Motivating Your Staff in a Time of Change (pp. 458–459)

"Very few people in the world can be relied upon to work without praise or recognition."
Varindra Tarzie Vittachi

Managing the Plateaued Performer

CHECKLIST

This checklist is concerned with managing employees who have apparently reached a plateau. It is aimed at managers who are immediately responsible for such people.

Plateauing is a familiar corporate phenomenon and is becoming more common with the proliferation of flat organizations, which offer less chance of promotion than traditional hierarchies. The performance of these plateaued employees may decline if it is not addressed, to the disadvantage of the organization and themselves.

DEFINITION

"A performance plateau is a leveling off of growth during which productivity flattens out and results remain stagnant."

(Theodore Kurtz, "Performance plateauing" (1989))

Plateaued performers are employees who have reached a certain level in the company and appear to be stuck there—they have neither the ambition nor the ability to progress further. There may be nothing wrong with their present performance, but they have no new ideas or initiatives and provide no inspiration to their own staff.

The experience of such employees can be very valuable as long as they maintain good performance levels—after all, not everyone can reach the heights. It's tempting to ignore their situation, since it poses no immediate threat. However, there's a serious danger of boredom and staleness setting in, with the result that they simply plod on doing their job in a routine way and cause demotivation in others. It's best to deal with the matter before it becomes a problem.

Staff members should have been plateaued for at least one year, maybe two, before you categorize them as plateaued performers. They are likely to have been in the same job or the same department for some time.

ADVANTAGES

Good handling should ensure:
- at the least, that the employee continues to make a significant contribution to the organization;
- at best, that the person makes new contributions;
- continued job satisfaction for the employee.

DISADVANTAGES

There are many disadvantages of not handling the employee well.

On the part of the individual:
- poor motivation
- decreased job satisfaction
- infrequent generation of new ideas
- possibly declining performance

On the part of the organization:
- reduced productivity

- unoriginal thinking and uninspired ideas
- missing stimulation for other staff

ACTION CHECKLIST

Remember throughout the process that the employee is not yet a problem—don't treat the person like one. Your only aim is to see if and how he or she can rise off the plateau.

✔ 1. Try to Spot the Signs

A plateau is an emerging process; it doesn't happen overnight. No one single incident will present itself as a benchmark or even diagnosis. Be careful not to confuse plateauing with the Peter Principle, the proposition that employees rise to their level of incompetence. Plateaued performers aren't incompetent, they just can't channel their energies or abilities into productive performance.

Ask yourself whether the employee's productivity declined consistently or sporadically. Have you observed a slackening in interest and commitment? Has the person's behavior altered from the norm?

✔ 2. Characterize the Plateau

Use the individual's attitude and level of activity to help you identify the type of plateau involved. Beverley Kaye has described four different types in "Are plateaued performers productive?" (1989).
- Passive: low in energy and activity, being trapped in personal inaction, with the apparent collusion of the employing organization.
- Productive: the opposite of passive, highly active, but busyness does not necessarily equal effectiveness.
- Partial: often concentrating on one small area of interest or responsibility, keeping a personal spark alive in the absence of prospects for promotion or challenge.
- Pleasant: happy with the status quo, doing the job well, in a comfortable groove, but wanting neither challenges nor risks and showing no desire to develop or improve.

✔ 3. Understand the Person

Try to understand what makes the person tick. Ask about outside interests, whether there are personal reasons for the plateau, and whether the person is actually content to stay there or whether, for example, earlier failure to get promotion had a demotivating effect. What are the individual's personal and professional ambitions? Only by knowing the person as a person can you hope to improve matters.

✔ 4. Examine Your Own Relationship with the Person

It may be that there is something in your relationship that is holding the individual back. It can be very difficult to find out if this is the case. It may be possible to ask directly; even if you don't get an answer, the person will appreciate your open and understanding approach.

"The moment you let avoiding failure become your motivator, you're down the path of inactivity."

Roberto Goizueta

It is often necessary, however, to consult other staff at your own level or above.

5. Identify the Problem

Be as precise as you can. There may be various causes for plateauing, for example:

- the company has not offered a stimulating environment;
- the person feels written off by you or other superiors;
- it's a long time since the person has been given a new challenge;
- colleagues largely ignore the person;
- there are problems at home.

There are many other possible causes, but a lack of stimulus is likely to figure among them.

6. Explore How You Can Improve Matters

Start with a positive assumption that improvement is possible, as it nearly always is. If you assume that you are unlikely to be able to do much to help but have to go through the motions, your defeatist attitude is bound to communicate itself. The solution usually includes providing a new stimulus: very few people at any level do not respond to the right stimulus. This might mean nothing more than making the employee's present job more interesting (or pointing out how the person could make more of it), including a new challenge within the person's present responsibilities, or assigning the person to work with a team on a special project. It might mean suggesting a change of job within the company.

7. Continue to Show Interest and Give Support

At the same time you should emphasize that the person must take responsibility for his or her own future and make it clear that you will give your support. A plateaued performer may show a short-term improvement and then sink back again. Show continuing interest without being too obtrusive.

8. Make Supporting Plateaued Performers General Policy

Dealing with one person on your staff is not enough and might even appear to be singling out individuals for special treatment. Bring the matter to the attention of senior management and recommend that supporting plateaued performers be adopted as corporate policy. All managers should be able to identify plateaued staff members at an early stage and learn how they can be helped. This is after all an expression of the organization's concern for its main resource—its people. And success with one or two plateaued performers sends positive signals to other staff.

9. Recognize That You Can't Always Help

Although it is always worthwhile doing what you can to help plateaued performers and although you will achieve some surprising successes, you won't succeed every time. If you can't raise someone's sights after several attempts, you may at least be able to warn the person that his or her behavior is likely to be unsatisfactory to the organization sooner or later and might risk dismissal.

THOUGHT STARTERS

- People are much more likely to get stuck if an organization is stagnant and unstimulating.

- Have you ever been through a plateau phase? If so, how did you get out of it?

- What motivates you to do better?

FOR MORE INFORMATION

Book:
Kaufman, Roger, et al. *Guidebook for Performance Improvement: Working with Individuals and Organizations.* New York: Jossey-Bass, 1996.

Journal Articles:
Clarkson, James G., and Mark E. Haskins. "Beating the Career Blues." *Academy of Management Executive* 14:3 (August 2000): 91–102.
Kaye, Beverley. "Are Plateaued Performers Productive?" *Personnel Journal* (August 1989): 57–65.
Kurtz, Theodore. "Performance Plateauing." *Supervisory Management* (December 1989): 19–22.
Savery, Lawson K. "Managing Plateaued Employees." *Management Decision* 28:3 (1990): 46–50.
Tremblay, Michael, and Alain Roger. "Career Plateauing Reactions: The Moderating Role of Job Scope, Role Ambiguity and Participation among Canadian Managers." *International Journal of Human Resource Management* 15:6 (September 2004): 996–1017.
Zaremba, Denise Karen. "The Managerial Plateau: What Helps in Developing Careers." *International Journal of Career Management* 6:2 (1994): 5–11.

Motivating Your Staff in a Time of Change

This checklist is designed for managers with responsibilities for managing, motivating, and developing staff when organizational structures and processes are undergoing continual change.

In today's turbulent environment, commercial success depends on employees using their full talents. Yet managers often view motivation as something of a mystery. In part this is because individuals are motivated by different things and in different ways. In addition, these are times when delayering and the flattening of hierarchies can create insecurity and lower staff morale. Moreover, more staff than ever before are working part time or on limited-term contracts, and they can be especially hard to motivate.

DEFINITION

Twyla Dell writes, "The heart of motivation is to give people what they really want most from work. The more you are able to provide what they want, the more you should expect what you really want, namely: productivity, quality, and service." (*An Honest Day's Work* (1988))

ADVANTAGES

A positive motivation philosophy and practice should improve productivity, quality, and service. Motivation helps people:
- achieve goals;
- gain a positive perspective;
- create the power to change;
- build self-esteem and capability;
- manage their own development and help others with theirs.

DISADVANTAGES

There are no real disadvantages to successfully motivating employees, but there are many barriers to overcome.

Barriers may include unaware or absent managers, inadequate buildings, outdated equipment, and entrenched attitudes, for example:
- "We don't get paid extra to work harder."
- "We've always done it this way."
- "Our bosses don't have a clue what we do."
- "It doesn't say that in my job description."
- "I'll do as little as possible without getting fired."

Such views will take persuasion, perseverance, and the proof of experience to break down.

ACTION CHECKLIST

✔ 1. Read the Gurus

Familiarize yourself with Herzberg's hygiene theory, McGregor's X and Y theories and Maslow's hierarchy of needs. Read our Management Library digests to gain a basic understanding of their main principles; it will be invaluable for building a climate of honesty and trust.

✔ 2. What Motivates You?

Determine which factors are important to you in your working life and how they interact. What has motivated you in the past?

Understand the differences between longer-term motivators and short-term spurs.

✔ 3. Find out What Your People Want from Work

People may want more status, higher pay, better working conditions, and flexible benefits. But to find out what really motivates your employees, ask them—in performance appraisals, attitude surveys, and informal conversations. You may find that they want, for example:
- more interesting work;
- more efficient bosses;
- more opportunity to see the end result of their work;
- greater participation;
- greater recognition;
- greater challenge;
- more opportunities for development.

✔ 4. Walk the Job

Every day, find someone doing something well and tell the person so. Make sure the interest you show is genuine without going overboard or appearing to watch over people's shoulders. If you have an idea how employees could improve their work, don't shout it out; help them to find their way to it instead. Earn respect by setting an example; it is not necessary to be able do everything better than your staff. Make it clear what levels of support employees can expect.

✔ 5. Remove Demotivators

Identify factors that demotivate staff—they may be physical (buildings, equipment) or psychological (boredom, unfairness, barriers to promotion, lack of recognition). Some can be dealt with easily; others require more time. The fact that you are concerned to find out what is wrong and tackle it is in itself a motivator.

✔ 6. Demonstrate Support

Whether your working culture clamps down on mistakes and penalizes error or espouses mistakes as learning opportunities, your staff need to understand the kind of support they can expect. Motivation practice and relationship building often falter because staff do not feel they are receiving adequate support.

"The task of the leader is to get people from where they are to where they have not been."

Henry Kissinger

7. Be Wary of Cash Incentives

Many people say they are working for money and claim in conversation that fringe benefits are an incentive. But money actually comes low down in the list of motivators, and it doesn't motivate for long after a raise. Fringe benefits can be effective in attracting new employees, but benefits rarely motivate existing employees.

8. Decide on Action

Having listened to staff, take steps to alter your organization's policies and attitudes, consulting fully with staff and unions. Consider policies that affect flexible working, reward, promotion, training and development, and participation.

9. Manage Change

If poor motivation is entrenched, you may need to look at the organization's whole style of management. One of the most natural of human instincts is to resist change even when it is beneficial. The way change is introduced has its own power to motivate or demotivate, and can often be the key to success or failure. If you:

- tell—instruct or deliver a monologue—you are ignoring your staff's hopes, fears, and expectations;
- tell and sell—try to persuade people—even your most compelling reasons will not hold sway over the long term if you don't allow discussion;
- consult—it will be obvious if you have made up your mind beforehand;
- look for real participation—sharing the problem solving and decision making with those who are to implement the change—you can begin to expect commitment and ownership along with the adaptation and compromise that will occur naturally.

10. Understand Learning Preferences

Change involves learning. People rarely learn best by reading a book or taking a course; they learn by practice and experience.

In their *Manual of Learning Styles* (1992), Peter Honey and Alan Mumford distinguish four learning styles:

- activists—like to get involved in new experiences, problems, or opportunities. They're not too happy standing back, observing, and being impartial
- theorists—are comfortable with concepts and theory. They don't like being thrown in at the deep end without apparent purpose or reason
- reflectors—like to take their time and think things through. They don't like being pressured
- pragmatists—need a link between the subject matter and the job in hand. They learn best when they can test things out

Your people will respond best to suggestions that take account of the way they do things best. Developing people against the grain will usually only demotivate them.

11. Provide Feedback

Feedback is one of the most valuable elements in the motivation cycle. Don't keep staff guessing how their development, progress, and accomplishments are shaping up. Offer comments with accuracy and care, keeping in mind next steps or future targets.

459

CHECKLIST

DOS AND DON'TS

DO
- Recognize that you don't have all the answers.
- Take time to find out what makes others tick.
- Encourage and guide staff—don't force them.
- Tell your staff what you think.

DON'T
- Don't make assumptions about what drives others.
- Don't assume others are like you.
- Don't force people into things that are supposedly good for them.
- Don't neglect inspiration and excitement.
- Don't delegate work—delegate responsibility!

THOUGHT STARTERS
- People don't mind being in a rocking boat if they know it's headed somewhere they want to go.
- Staff want a sense of direction, not directiveness.
- Your morale infects others, whether you like it or not.
- Trust your staff to perform 25 percent better than you expect.

FOR MORE INFORMATION

Book:
Katzenbach, Jon R. *Peak Performance: Aligning the Hearts and Minds of your Employees*. Boston, MA: Harvard Business School Press, 2000.

See also:
- Conducting a Performance Appraisal (pp. 438–439)
- Managing Staff Turnover and Retention (pp. 454–455)

"The better people think they are, the better they will be. Positive self-image creates success."

Liisa Joronen

Planning Overseas Assignments

This checklist provides planning guidance to companies sending employees, and to individuals being posted, on overseas assignments.

Selecting, appointing, supporting, and developing managers abroad can be highly complex. Failure rates or noncompletion of assignments have been put as high as 40 percent. In addition, the cost to the employing firm may be considerable, as may the professional and personal price paid by the individual. Creating a positive sense of direction, purpose, and control and reducing uncertainty and ineffectiveness greatly benefits both the company and the individual manager.

DEFINITION

For the purposes of this checklist, working overseas means outside the United States. An assignment means a posting overseas with the current employer for a defined period of more than six months.

ADVANTAGES

- Employee and employer both benefit from minimizing culture shock and attending to detail.
- The potential for failure because of unsuccessful cultural adaptation is minimized.
- The cost of premature repatriation is reduced.

DISADVANTAGES

- The cost of such preparations can be high.
- Unforeseeable changes in political, economic, or environmental circumstances can counteract the preparation.

ACTION CHECKLIST

1. Prepare for the Road Ahead

Be aware of local language requirements and cultural issues, and allow time to prepare for the transition. Preliminary visits for the employee and family (with the organization's full support) are invaluable for gaining an initial perspective, making early introductions, and learning about local facilities, or the lack of them.

Just as the transition is the joint responsibility of both employee and employer, it is vital that both of them:

- understand the task to be accomplished;
- recognize the need for levels of adaptability, maturity, and technical competence;
- understand the need for organizational and family support.

2. Be Aware of Rights Issues

Be aware of the rights of individuals and of the employing organization in the country of destination, especially those covered by existing or pending legislation. It is a good idea to contact the State Department before you plan your trip to find out as much as you can about your destination country. The State Department will be able to give you addresses of your destination country's embassies in the United States as well as contact details for U.S. embassies abroad. Additional resources within each state include the Secretary of State's office, International Trade office, and Small Business Development Centers, many of which are located at community colleges.

3. Define the Personal Characteristics and Requisites for the Job Specification

In *Managing Multinational Corporations* (1974), V. K. Phatak describes the personal characteristics of successful expatriate managers:

"Ideally, it seems, he (or she) should have the stamina of an Olympic swimmer, the mental agility of an Einstein, the conversational skill of a professor of languages, the detachment of a judge, the tact of a diplomat, and the perseverance of an Egyptian pyramid builder. And if he is going to measure up to the demands of living and working in a foreign country, he should also have the feeling for culture; his moral judgments should not be too rigid; he should be able to merge with the local environment with chameleon-like ease; and he should show no signs of prejudice."

Obviously only very rare individuals instantly meet this description. Everyone else selected for foreign assignments must develop the following attributes:

- Knowledge of languages
- International experience. Previous experience can help mental preparation and reduce culture shock. Preliminary visits and existing organizational networks can help the process of familiarization
- Job experience, seniority, and qualifications. In some countries, qualifications—as a recognition and acknowledgment of expertise—are very important
- Flexibility, learning, and lack of prejudice. Employees working overseas need to overcome stereotypical U.S. superiority and insularity and be able to cope with unfamiliar people in unfamiliar surroundings
- Motivation factors:
  – the need to gain foreign experience for career advancement
  – interest in other cultures
  – interest in communication and language learning
- Competence, effectiveness, and capabilities:
  – initiative and capacity for high levels of activity
  – ability to handle stress
  – respect for different opinions and values
  – interest in and liking for people
  – autonomy of action

4. Draw Up the Short List for Candidate Selection

Certain criteria are essential for the selection and elimination process.

- Is the candidate stable, self-reliant, and able to cope with crises?

- Is the candidate willing to adjust to a new way of life?
- Can he or she relate well to people and communicate effectively in the destination culture?
- Does he or she have the required technical knowledge and competence?
- What is the candidate's health record?
- Are problems likely to arise concerning family responsibilities?

The selection process should not focus solely on technical competence, but should also assess personal characteristics such as flexibility, emotional stability, and learning and relational skills.

 ## 5. Devise an Appropriate Training Program

Organizations may prefer job-related opportunities such as international transfers, assignments, or exchanges, but there can be no substitute for a practical, tailor-made, and flexible program that exposes the candidate to a variety of elements, including the following:

- Language training. Teach-yourself tapes and intensive crash courses such as Berlitz have good track records of success if the learner is willing and committed.
- General, national, and business orientation. Awareness of:
  - the global economic order and terms of trade;
  - trends in changing technology and communications, demography, religion, and the environment;
  - the country's historical, religious, ethnic, and political background;
  - the country's attitude toward foreign business;
  - the efficiency of transportation and communications;
  - healthcare, housing, education, and leisure facilities;
  - social and cultural expectations and requirements;
  - international business strategies.
- Family consultation. A stable family life is generally an asset. Where the assignment is for two years or more, the family usually expects to move with the employee. Consider the whole range of domestic arrangements (which on home ground would remain the preserve of the individual). Consider too what the spouse will do in a situation where the employee is cushioned by the very fact of employment, and the spouse exposed to life in the raw without corporate or customary social support.
- Career development preparation. View this experience as a stage of development and not as the end of the road. Both employee and employer should give thought to how this experience will be of benefit and what will follow.
- Pay and benefits. Information should be provided on issues such as the total benefits package during the overseas appointment; tax implications both at home and abroad; medical insurance; hardship and other allowances, for example, for inhospitable climates; accommodations costs; private transportation facilities; leave and travel allowances for home visits; and job security on final return.

6. Support the Manager Overseas

An on-site line manager, subordinate, superior, or peer who acts as a troubleshooter, mentor, and guide in the early stages can be a boon during an otherwise traumatic, worrying, or frustrating experience.

7. Prepare for Repatriation

This is as important for the career path of the employee as for the avoidance of "reentry shock" for the family. Reintegration, or the "coming home" phase, may also require some training, familiarization, and updating in addition to personal effort.

> **THOUGHT STARTERS**
> - Have the political, economic, social, cultural, and market fronts been thoroughly researched?
> - Have facilities and support lines in the foreign country been researched?
> - Is a comprehensive training and familiarization program in place?
> - Has adequate thought been given to what follows the foreign posting for the employee?

FOR MORE INFORMATION

Books:
Guirdham, Maureen. *Communicating across Cultures.* West Lafayette, IN: Ichor Business Books, 2004.
Lomax, Stan. *Best Practice for Managers and Expatriates.* New York: Wiley, 2001.
Mendenhall, Mark E., Torsten M. Kuhlmann, and Gunter Stahl, eds. *Developing Global Business Leaders.* Westport, CO: Quorum Books, 2004.

Journal Articles:
Jun, Sunkyl, and James W. Gentry. "An Exploratory Investigation of the Relative Importance of Cultural Similarity and Personal Fit in the Selection and Performance of Expatriates." *Journal of World Business* 40:1 (February 2005).
Takeuchi, Riki, et al. "An Integrative View of International Experience." *Academy of Management Journal* 48:1 (February 2005).
Mayerhofer, Helene, et al. "Flexpatriate Assignments: A Neglected Issue in Global Staffing." *International Journal of Human Resource Management* 15:8 (December 2005).

Web sites:
Center for International Briefing at Farnham Castle: **www.cibfarnham.co.uk**
Economist.com Country Briefings: **www.economist.com/countries**
Employment Conditions Abroad: **www.eca-international.com**

See also:
✔ Planning Overseas Assignments (pp. 460–461)
✔ Preparing for Business Abroad (pp. 570–571)

461

CHECKLIST

"Planning is as natural to the process of success as its absence is to the process of failure."

Robin Sieger

Steps in Successful Team Building

CHECKLIST

This checklist explores the essential aspects of planning, setting up, and maintaining an effective team for specific projects or assignments.

DEFINITION

Teams are not the same as other groups: they need to be planned, built, and maintained. A number of people who happen to work together in the same place may not operate as a team, and may not need to. A team has a distinct characteristic—it is a group working together to achieve a common purpose, and it may be composed of people drawn from different functions, departments, or disciplines. Increasingly, teams are groups set up for a specific project, are empowered to steer and develop the work they do, and are responsible for their achievements.

ADVANTAGES

Successful team building can:
- coordinate individuals' efforts as they tackle complex tasks;
- make the most of each team member's personal expertise and knowledge, which might otherwise remain untapped;
- raise and sustain motivation and confidence as individual team members feel supported and involved;
- encourage members to spark ideas off each other, to solve problems, and to find appropriate ways forward;
- help break down communication barriers and avoid unhealthy competition, rivalry, and point-scoring;
- raise the level of individual and collective empowerment;
- support approaches such as total quality management, just-in-time management, and customer service programs;
- bring about commitment to and ownership of the task in hand.

DISADVANTAGES

There are circumstances where teams may be inadvisable—for example, they may not fit in some organizational cultures where there are rigid reporting structures or fixed work procedures. A team approach may not be the answer especially:
- where one person has all the knowledge, expertise, and resources to do the job independently;
- when there is no real common purpose, and a group is wrongly called a team.

ACTION CHECKLIST

✔ 1. Decide Whether You Really Need a Team

Just because it is fashionable to talk about team building, it does not mean that every job needs a team to complete it. It may be that a single skilled person working alone and properly supported can achieve the task more effectively than forming a group of people into a team. Consider whether you need a range of expertise and experience, shared workloads, brainstorming, and problem solving. If you do, a team will be your best option.

✔ 2. Determine Your Objectives and the Skills Needed to Achieve Them

Be clear about the broad outcome of the project. Identify the technical and team skills you need and bring together individuals with that range of skills. Whatever the range of personnel available, the key is to pick people with a mix of different skills. These include team skills, personal skills, and technical abilities.

✔ 3. Plan a Team-building Strategy

Invest time at the outset in getting the operating framework right so that the team will develop and grow. There are various areas to consider:
- a climate of trust in which mistakes and failures are viewed as learning experiences, not occasions for blame;
- free flow of information to all those who need to integrate their work with business objectives;
- training in communication, interpersonal, and negotiation skills, and coaching to handle the tasks required and adopt responsibility for them;
- time, not only for regular meetings, but for coordinating activities, developing thoughts, and monitoring progress;
- objectives that are clearly understood by all team members. This is increasingly a case of involving team members in setting the objectives rather than dictating prescribed objectives to them.
- feedback focusing on the positive aspects and suggesting ways of dealing with the negative ones. Team members need to know how well they are doing and if and where improvements can be made.

✔ 4. Get the Team Together

It is important at this early stage that you don't actually try to solve the problem you are confronted with. At the initial meeting you should aim to start to build the group into a team. Discuss and agree on the outcomes the team is to achieve. Clarify the common purposes and make sure that everyone knows what his or her personal contribution to the team's success is, its place in the project schedule, and its importance to the project's success.

✔ 5. Explore and Establish Operating Ground Rules

There will be a need:
- to communicate openly and honestly, with team members feeling free to say what they think and feel without fear, rancor, or anger;
- to listen to others, including those voicing minority or extreme views;
- to agree on which decision-making, reporting, and other processes will be adopted for the life span of the team.

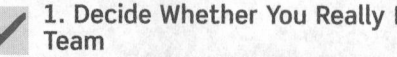 "Team management has been considered as the Chinese approach to enhance collective culture at work."

Zhong-Ming Wang

6. Identify Individuals' Strengths

Audit individuals' strengths so the team as a whole can benefit from all the skills and expertise available. Consider bringing in someone with team-building experience to help with the initial phases, especially if the team's task is important.

7. Include Yourself As a Team Member

Your role is as a member of the team, not just as the boss. Emphasize that everyone in the team has an important role and that yours happens to be the team leader. Act as a role model and maintain effective communication—especially listening—with all members.

It may be helpful for roles to remain fluid, adding to the flexibility of working relationships without team members losing the focus of their individual strengths or objectives. An effective leader may decide to cede project leadership temporarily to another team member when specific skills are required.

8. Check Objectives

Check the team's objectives regularly to make sure that members still have a clear focus on what they are working toward, individually and as a team.

9. Time Meetings With Care

Inessential meetings are a bane, but if there are too few, the project—and the team—can lose focus. Meet regularly but purposefully:
- to provide an opportunity to ask, "How are we doing?"
- to review progress on the task;
- to reflect on how the team is working.

If any gaps or problems arise from the review, plan and implement activity and corrective measures.

10. Dissolve the Team

When the team has accomplished its tasks, acknowledge completion. Carry out a final review to see if the team has achieved the objectives and to evaluate the team's performance; individuals should learn, improve, and benefit next time from this exercise. If all the objectives have been met, the team can be disbanded.

THOUGHT STARTERS

- What excellent (or awful) teams have you worked in? What made them so good (or bad)?

- Does your natural management style fit a team approach, or do you need to adjust—maybe let go and trust individuals more?

- Do you use teams to the best advantage?

- Are you absolutely clear what you want your team to achieve?

- Have you thought through ways to resolve conflict if and when it arises?

DOS AND DON'TS

DO
- Confirm that you actually need a team before you do anything else.
- Take the time and trouble to manage and facilitate the team's development and activity.
- Establish as a team the common aims, objectives, and success criteria for the task, project, or process.
- Clarify regularly who is to do what, and by what date, so that team members understand their contribution to the team's targets.
- Remember that you can't win a team game on your own.
- Communicate freely with all members of the team.
- Manage team meetings so that everyone has a say and feels involved in decision-making and planning.
- Disband the team when objectives have been met.

DON'T
- Don't expect a new team to fire on all cylinders from day one. A team is an entity in its own right, like a new employee who needs orientation and development.
- Don't dominate, however unintentionally or unconsciously.
- Don't exercise such tight management control that you squash creativity.
- Don't let individuals take the credit for the team's achievements.
- Don't let the team feel too exclusive, in case it shuts out other, essential, parts of the organization.

FOR MORE INFORMATION

Books:
Beyerlein, Michael M, and Cheryl L. Harris. *Guiding the Journey to Collaborative Work Systems: A Strategic Design Workbook.* San Francisco, CA: Pfeiffer, 2004.
Lencioni, Patrick. *The Five Dysfunctions of a Team: A Leadership Fable.* San Francisco, CA: Jossey-Bass, 2004.
Miller, Brian Cole. *Quick Teambuilding Activities for Busy Managers: 50 Exercises that Get Results in just 15 Minutes.* New York: AMACOM, 2004.
Romig, Dennis A. *Side by Side Leadership: Achieving Outstanding Results Together.* Marietta, GA: Bard Press, 2001.
Willcocks, Graham, and Steve Morris. *Successful Team Building.* Hauppauge, NY: Barron's Educational, 1997.

Journal Article:
Special Issue on e-leadership (and the management of remote or virtual teams). *Organizational Dynamics* 31:4 (2003).

"To create human capital, a company needs to foster teamwork, communities of practice, and other social forms of learning."

Thomas A. Stewart

Undertaking a Disciplinary Interview

CHECKLIST

This checklist provides guidance for managers who are required to hold a formal interview with an employee to correct a disciplinary problem, such as unacceptable behavior or performance, as part of a disciplinary procedure. It should be read in conjunction with the related checklist Setting Up a Disciplinary Procedure.

DEFINITION

A disciplinary interview is a meeting between at least one manager and an employee (who may be accompanied by a colleague or union representative) to investigate and deal with an employee's misconduct in a fair and consistent manner.

ADVANTAGES

Effective handling of a disciplinary interview:

- tackles the cause of misconduct and provides solutions to remedy it;
- can prevent the need for further and more serious action to be taken against an employee;
- aids general morale (although an ineffective process will have the opposite effect).

DISADVANTAGES

Ineffective handling of a disciplinary interview:

- leaves the employee unclear about the problem or how to improve;
- can lead to claims of unfair dismissal if the employee is dismissed;
- lowers the respect of the manager in the employee's eyes.

ACTION CHECKLIST

✔ 1. Prepare For the Interview

Preparation and planning before the interview are essential in order to be fair and accurate in making a decision on the employee's conduct. The procedure—and the tone—should be as positive as possible in order to improve behavior and help prevent recurrence.

Gather all the facts

Obtain any written evidence (for example, attendance records or production figures) that highlights the employee's misconduct. To obtain a balanced view, look for any special circumstances inside or outside work that may help to explain the problem—low staffing levels, increased demand leading to work overload, or personal difficulties such as caring for a sick child.

Check the employee's record

Find out if the employee has already received one or more warnings under the disciplinary procedure.

Check the organization's disciplinary procedure

Ascertain what options are available if the employee is guilty of misconduct, bearing in mind the person's disciplinary record and the seriousness of the offense.

Look for similar cases and outcomes

Confer with colleagues to see whether they have dealt with similar cases and what the outcomes were. Also try to find out whether the employee is committing an offense that is widespread (for example, persistent abuse of smoking rules or bad timekeeping). Is the employee being singled out unfairly for an offense that should be tackled company-wide?

Structure the interview

Although no two disciplinary interviews will run exactly the same, you should map out a brief structure. Start by trying to define what you need to achieve from the interview. Note important points that you need to cover. Consider the reasons, mitigating circumstances, or excuses that the employee might make and how to record them so you can check them out later. Decide who should be present at the interview, including witnesses.

✔ 2. Inform the Employee

The employee should be informed in writing of:

- the reason why he or she faces a disciplinary interview;
- the time and place of the interview;
- who will be present and who may accompany him or her to the interview.

Determine if everyone present should have access to all documents; in some cases this will not be in the employee's own interests.

Remember to give sufficient notice for the employee to prepare a case. Make sure that an appropriate room is available; it should be large enough to accommodate those attending without congestion. A phone is useful to call witnesses to the interview, but arrange for incoming calls to be diverted to avoid unnecessary interruptions.

Designate and inform a manager to be responsible for taking notes. Call witnesses so they can arrange to be available. If witnesses cannot be present, obtain written statements from them.

✔ 3. Conduct the Interview

Disciplinary interviews are stressful for both the manager and the employee. Their ultimate purpose is to create a satisfactory environment for all employees.

Remember to try to stay calm; do not let the interview develop into a free-for-all. Make certain that the employee is aware that the interview is more than an informal reprimand.

The length of the interview depends on many factors, but it can become clear at any stage either that the problem has been cleared up or that there needs to be further investigation; in either case you should adjourn the proceedings. Similarly, the interview should be called to a halt if the exchanges get heated or unconstructive.

There is no set structure for a disciplinary interview; the following is one approach.

Introduction

- Introduce the people present and the reason for their being there (including the manager acting as a witness and taking notes, and any union representative).
- Communicate the reason for holding a disciplinary inter-

"Stretch and discipline are the yin and yang of business."   Christopher Bartlett

view. Emphasize that it is part of the organization's disciplinary procedure that exists to ensure that all employees are treated equally and fairly.

- Describe how the interview is to be structured—that is, with the case against the employee being presented first, followed by the employee's reply.

Present the case against the employee

- Detail the case against the employee, including specific dates and times that breaches of discipline occurred. If the case has already moved some way along the disciplinary procedure, present an outline of the previous stages, the actions taken, and the results to date.
- Call on any witnesses to state what they have seen or heard, or what they know. If witnesses are unable to attend, read their written statements aloud.

Allow the employee to reply

- Let the employee respond to the case, allowing the person to present evidence, call witnesses, and introduce statements.
- Listen carefully to what the employee has to say. Do not interrupt while the person is speaking.

Discuss the case. Allow both sides to ask questions, particularly about ambiguous issues in the evidence. Ask open-ended questions to gain a general picture and more precise questions for specific information. It is important to ascertain whether there were any sound mitigating circumstances for the employee's behavior that you were unaware of. Allow the employee to suggest ways to overcome the problem.

Summarize the case. After the discussion, reiterate the main points from both sides and summarize the whole case. When both sides have agreed the summary to be accurate, adjourn the interview so you can consider what action to take or whether the case requires further investigation. Try to do this as quickly as possible to keep the employee's anxiety or doubt to a minimum.

✔ 4. Inform the Employee of the Action to Be Taken

Having conferred with colleagues and made a decision, meet with the employee and his or her representative and inform them what action is to be taken, if any. If appropriate, agree on actions for improving the situation (remember that these may involve the employer as well as the employee). Both parties should sign a written copy of the actions to be taken. Set a date for review. If the employee disagrees with the result of the interview or feels unfairly treated inform the person of the company's appeals procedure.

THOUGHT STARTERS

- Do you understand the workings of the organization's disciplinary procedure?

- Have you ever had to discipline an employee before?

- Would you do things differently now?

- Have you ever been disciplined at work?

- Was it handled fairly?

FOR MORE INFORMATION

Book:
Grote, Dick, and Richard C. Grote. *Discipline Without Punishment: The Proven Strategy That Turns Problem Employees into Superior Performers.* 2nd ed. New York: AMACOM, 2006.

Web sites:
HR Guide: **www.hr-guide.com**
HR.BLR.com: **http://hr.blr.com**

465

CHECKLIST

"If people really liked to work, we'd still be plowing the ground with sticks and transporting goods on our backs."

Vic Feather

Using 360-degree Feedback

CHECKLIST

This checklist provides an introduction to the use of 360-degree feedback as an alternative to a traditional performance appraisal system.

Changes in organizational structure in recent years, with flattened hierarchies and greater employee empowerment, have had implications for the appraisal process. Individual managers now often have a greater span of control, so their colleagues may be in a better position to judge their performance than ever before. Hence the increasing interest in the technique of 360-degree feedback, which collects information from all around the employee. It is most often used as a development or training tool, and is not usually tied to pay. It can only work effectively in organizations that have, or are moving toward, an open, supportive, participative culture.

DEFINITION

Strictly speaking, 360-degree appraisal or feedback involves a paper-based appraisal by colleagues above, below, and to the side of an individual employee in addition to self-assessment. In practice it may not include all these elements. Feedback is communicated through a facilitator so opinions cannot be traced to individuals. Some commentators feel, however, that 360-degree appraisal should be an exercise in openness, and that views should not be anonymous.

ADVANTAGES

- Combined opinion gives an accurate, objective, and well-rounded view.
- Some skills (for example, leadership) are better judged by subordinates and peers than by superiors.
- A comment that is hard to accept can't be brushed off or ignored when a number of colleagues have expressed it independently.
- 360-degree appraisal can lead to positive behavior such as more openness and honesty.
- The technique can help motivate people who undervalue themselves.

DISADVANTAGES

- It is time-consuming and costly, so the technique is often restricted to management levels.
- If too many appraisers are used, the results can be hard to interpret.
- It can be destructive unless handled carefully and sensitively.
- It can generate an environment of suspicion unless it is managed openly and honestly.

ACTION CHECKLIST

✔ 1. Decide Which Behaviors to Measure and Whom to Assess

Decide which sets of knowledge, skills, and abilities you want to measure. Should they be competency-based, job-related, or behavior-related? Remember that 360-degree appraisal can be used at any level of the organization, so decide whether you want to assess specific individuals, particular teams, particular levels, or the whole organization. Is it important that everyone who takes part as an appraiser should also be subject to appraisal?

✔ 2. Design a Feedback Questionnaire

In the interest of efficiency, written questionnaires are commonly used for collecting appraisals. Devise the detailed questions or, if you do not have the necessary expertise in-house, consider purchasing a questionnaire or employing a consultant. Make sure that the questions are phrased in a way that elicits descriptive rather than judgmental responses: descriptive comments are less likely to cause offense and more likely to provide useful information to the person being appraised. Avoid asking questions that the majority of the likely appraisers are not qualified to answer, or that contain wording that might be open to misinterpretation.

✔ 3. Communicate the Process and Prepare Participants

Explain the purpose of the process and encourage employees to air their concerns and objections. If necessary, circulate a pilot questionnaire, for example, asking employees for their views on managers in the organization in general. This trial run will demonstrate how the process works and reassure the staff. Appoint a manager to act as a facilitator, and publicize his or her roles and responsibilities. This person should be widely respected and have a reputation for fairness and honesty. If it is not appropriate to nominate an internal manager, consider using a consultant.

✔ 4. Train Your Staff to Give, and Receive, Critical Feedback

Encourage appraisers to be constructive, positive, and specific instead of critical, negative, and general. In describing a colleague's behavior, for example, "I notice that you rarely acknowledge us when you arrive in the morning" is more helpful than "I think you are a bad communicator." "I know you need time and space to yourself, but when you get it you really produce the goods" pinpoints the message in an acceptable way, and is more palatable than "You're too much of a loner." Do not allow the appraisal to become an opportunity for subjective gripes. If the process degenerates, critically appraised people will tend to get their own back when appraising others, especially if they are identified or identifiable.

✔ 5. Let Employees Choose Their Appraisers

Allow employees to select their appraisers from an agreed pool. Since the aim is to achieve a rounded appraisal, make sure that each person being appraised chooses some appraisers they get along with and others

"Positive feedback makes the strong grow stronger and the weak grow weaker."

Carl Shapiro

they do not. Set limits on the number involved in each appraisal, otherwise the exercise can become an administrative nightmare. Instruct appraisers to return their questionnaires to the appointed facilitator. If you have agreed to treat comments anonymously, reassure the appraisers about confidentiality, and honor your commitment. Present the results as soon as possible after collecting the data.

6. Decide How to Present Feedback

Decide how the facilitator should collate and present the appraisers' comments. Is your objective to allow employees to be able to monitor their own performance over time, compare themselves with like employees, or measure themselves against specific competences? Consider whether feedback on a particular activity should be linked to an agreed estimate of how important that activity is to the job. If so, the results need to be weighted accordingly.

7. Provide Counseling and Assistance

Decide whether individuals should identify their own improvement actions or whether they should be offered solutions. If you wish to leave it to individuals, don't show the results to managers without their approval. The facilitator or another trained person such as a psychologist should be available to help employees deal with feedback, particularly to advise them on how to deal with divergent views. Consider holding development sessions in which the people who were appraised can support each other.

8. Set Individual Action Plans

Follow up each appraisal by agreeing on an appropriate program to help the individual improve. These may range from attending a course or shadowing a colleague to temporary internal or external placements. Remember that learners have different needs and preferences.

9. Evaluate the Process

Examine the appraisal process. Take into account the opinion of everyone who participated, including any feedback on completing the appraisal questionnaire or analyzing the data from it. Compare the results of using 360-degree feedback with previous appraisal techniques. Use what you learn from the evaluation to help you improve the next appraisal.

THOUGHT STARTERS

- How effective is your organization's current appraisal system?

- What is upward communication like in your company? How is it received?

- How good is your managers' morale?

DOS AND DON'TS

DO
- Remember that employees may find the prospect of 360-degree feedback threatening and challenging.
- Prepare and support people for their different roles in giving, receiving, and facilitating appraisals.
- Make the exercise nonthreatening by focusing on strengths as much as weaknesses.
- Respect the confidentiality of respondents' replies, if this has been agreed.

DON'T
- Don't allow appraisers to drift into personal attacks.
- Don't treat it as a onetime exercise or leave long gaps between appraisals.

FOR MORE INFORMATION

Books:
Lepsinger, Richard, and Anntoinette D. Lucia. *The Art and Science of 360 Degree Feedback*. San Francisco, CA: Pfeiffer, 1997.
Tornow, Walter W., and Manuel London. *Maximizing the Value of 360-degree Feedback: A Process for Successful Individual and Organizational Development*. San Francisco, CA: Jossey-Bass, 1998.

Journal Articles:
Bracken, David N., Lynn Summers, and John Fleenor. "High Tech 360." *Training and Development USA* 52:8 (August 1998): 42–45.
Fletcher, Clive. "Circular Argument." *People Management* 4:19 (October 1, 1998): 46–49.
Jackman, Jay M., and Myra H. Strober. "Fear of Feedback." *Harvard Business Review* 81:4 (April 2003): 101–7.

"The feedback loop, connecting company and customer, is central to the operating definition of a truly market-driven company."

David Lodge

Using Your Staff to Mutual Advantage

CHECKLIST

This checklist is aimed at managers and looks closely at the building blocks of relationships between those who manage and those whom they manage.

Annual reports frequently pay tribute to "our staff," but practice seldom seems to match the written word. This checklist considers some of the major elements involved in getting the most out of working with others, including the changes in management practice in organizations, the ways in which change affects people, approaches to leadership and communication, and methods of consolidating and improving working relationships.

DEFINITION

"Staff" implies any people or group who are subordinate to a manager at any level.

"To mutual advantage" signifies to the advantage of the manager, to the advantage of the unit (whether company, department, or small firm), and to the advantage of the staff.

ACTION CHECKLIST

1. Recognize Recent Shifts in Management Practice

In the 1980s and 1990s many organizations moved away from models based on differentiating workers from each other. They adopted instead flexible organizational structures that more fully used the experience of their people, often described as the empowered, flatter organization. There are a number of elements involved in this shift away from practices that simply no longer work:

- the autocratic manager to the leader who energizes people
- authority by position to authority by merit
- domination to coordination
- control from the top to participation and collaboration
- self-advancement to self-development
- individual responsibility to the shared responsibility of teamwork
- controlling the work force to giving employees freedom
- power to empowerment

With organizational culture based on trust and initiative rather than on dominance, blame, or fear, the onus is now on the manager to become a team member as well as a team leader.

2. Make Change Work for You

Change means moving from the familiar to the unfamiliar, from the known to the unknown. Be aware of the implications of change and its impact on individuals, particularly when it is imposed.

Psychologists have suggested that any substantial change in our lives involves a sequence of stages.

- Shock—emotional feelings of denial, confusion, and disbelief, a sense that everything is crumbling. Offer understanding and acceptance of the state of shock, convey empathy, create opportunities for grievances to be aired, and encourage the disclosure of feelings.
- Withdrawal or resistance—an attempt to keep the familiar world intact, a search for ways of avoiding change, and a struggle to maintain the status quo. Counsel individuals to disclose frustrations and anxieties. Listen with attentiveness and sensitivity.
- Acknowledgment—a sense of inevitability is accompanied by the recognition of a need to keep in step, of a fear of isolation and rejection by others, of uncertainty and insecurity. Help individuals acknowledge change by reviewing their appropriate skills, competencies, and opportunities for development.
- Adaptation—emotional and psychological adjustment matching the rational acceptance of change. Inner confusion and uncertainty begin to give way as preparations for change get underway, anxieties are reduced, and practical steps forward identified. Help individuals by involving them in the design of new systems and procedures and in gaining familiarity with new resources and equipment, and by getting them to propose new solutions and methods.

Different individuals move through these stages at different rates and in different ways. Understanding the individual nature of reaction to change will help you work with others and encourage them to take advantage of the constantly changing workplace.

Most people will accept change as long as they recognize why it is necessary and are involved in the process—it should be their change.

3. Define the Boundaries of Employees' Responsibility

Someone new to a job is at first dependent on the line manager, but this dependence normally diminishes as the jobholder gains in experience and learns the ropes. Allow newcomers to grow and "feel their way."

As the person gains experience, the relationship becomes interdependent, and interactions arise when the manager needs information on progress or when consultation is required on specific issues. Get your people to report as often as possible, and to suggest potential solutions to problems they encounter.

As time goes on, an increasing proportion of the person's job is characterized by a clear capacity to self-manage without supervision. Encourage the person's independence and the responsibility that goes with it. "Freedom with accountability" is the key phrase.

All three of these elements are present in all jobs. Good practice involves recognizing their shifting balance and

"The more time I spend with our people, the more I find out about our business."

Herb Kelleher

behaving accordingly. Whether your situation is rapidly changing or solid and stable, whether your culture is an empowered culture or not, you must define the limits of the authority enjoyed by the people who work with you. To be wholly effective they need to know which sorts of decision:

- they can make independently, informing you afterwards;
- they can make only after consultation with you;
- they should pass on to you.

4. Identify Your Leadership Strategy

If leadership is about quality and effectiveness, change and development, and focus on the future, effective management is less and less about directing and instructing and more and more about supporting, coaching, and delegating to enable people to own their work and be committed to it. Various techniques or strategies can contribute to your effectiveness as a leader.

- Management by walking around (MBWA)—managers and leaders need to see their main activity as an interactive one, working alongside colleagues where tasks are carried out.
- Work review—this is a nondirected relationship designed to help colleagues develop professional skills through the regular process of reflection on experience.
- Critical friendship—this concept is sometimes used to describe the nature of the relationship between leader and team. It is essentially an active listening role for the leader in which colleagues can explore and clarify aspects of their work experience.

5. Give Feedback

One of the most effective ways of developing others is to help them reflect on their experience in order to learn from it. Feedback is an informal and highly effective way of promoting this process. It is, however, necessary to be aware of some of the psychological implications of giving others information about themselves and their behavior. Among the behaviors and responses managers may encounter are:

- difficulty in accepting responsibility for behavior;
- fear of making mistakes;
- difficulty with uncertainty and change;
- assuming that others know best;
- self-doubt and lack of confidence;
- reluctance to set personal goals for development;
- suspicion of experts and those in positions of authority.

Feedback can be of three basic types:

- Confirmatory—giving information that lets someone know he or she is on course and moving successfully toward his or her goals. It is vital, but often neglected.
- Corrective—giving information that helps someone get back on course when the person is experiencing difficulties or things are going wrong. Corrective feedback should always be positive, not negative.
- Motivating—giving information that tells someone about both successes and difficulties. This combines confirmatory and corrective feedback; the aim is to provide suf-

ficient information to meet the development needs of the receiver and enable the person to make appropriate choices and decisions.

6. Practice Proactive Passiveness!

Getting the most out of relationships for all parties can be an exhausting process: you feel as if you're constantly monitoring employees for feelings of inadequacy, excessive cynicism, inability to express feelings, or a sense of being stuck. While MBWA, work review, and critical friendship may require you to change your behavior substantially, you should be employing other routine interpersonal techniques as a matter of habit:

- active listening, where the listener attempts to gain insights into the perceptual, intellectual, and emotional world of the speaker
- undivided attention, away from telephones and other interruptions
- support, using suggestions and prompts to check meanings, inviting the speaker to continue, and otherwise keeping quietly interested
- conveying understanding, using body language to indicate understanding, acceptance, and agreement

7. Review Your Relationships

Sit down from time to time and ask, "How are we doing?" Talk over work routines and objectives so that you know where you stand in relation to others, and they to you. Focus on moving forward so that the individual, the section, and the organization are all gaining mutual advantage.

THOUGHT STARTERS

- What do my people tell their friends and families about me as their boss?

- What would I hope they would say?

- What do I do that makes it harder for them to do the job I want them to do?

- Am I using all their talents, skills, and capabilities?

FOR MORE INFORMATION

Books:
Murdock, Alexander, and Carol Scutt. *Personal Effectiveness*. 3rd ed. Woburn, MA: Butterworth-Heinemann, 2003.
Whetten, David A., and Kim S. Cameron. *Developing Management Skills*. 6th ed. Upper Saddle River, NJ: Pearson Prentice Hall, 2005.

Web site:
American Management Association: **www.amanet.org**

469

CHECKLIST

"I've got an ego and all that, but I know I need help. So I go and hire the very best people."

H. Ross Perot

The Psychological Contract

CHECKLIST

This checklist introduces the concept of the psychological contract from the employee's point of view. The psychological contract refers to the unwritten expectations that exist between employer and employee.

In the past the psychological contract implied that an employee could expect job security and adequate rewards from their employer in exchange for hard work and loyalty. Today's psychological contract relies more on an unwritten agreement that your employer will assist you in developing your skills in order to maintain your marketability.

The psychological contract is a subtle relationship that shifts over time and is subject to constant change. This checklist focuses on this aspect of negotiation between employer and employee.

DEFINITION

The psychological contract refers to the set of expectations and values that exist between you and your employer. It is most easily defined as "the set of unwritten expectations between an individual employee and the organization." Everyone has some form of psychological contract. The concept addresses those relationships that are very hard to define clearly in a formal employment contract; it can cover:

- knowledge and skills development;
- your work and motivation;
- relationships with your bosses and coworkers;
- the role that you are expected to fulfill;
- the ethical code by which you and the organization will act;
- the support you can expect from the organization and vice versa.

ACTION CHECKLIST

1. Negotiate Your Psychological Contract from the Start

Both sides begin to explore the psychological contract at the job interview. The organization assesses how you might behave in your role and how you're likely to fit in. You in turn have an early opportunity to judge whether you would be comfortable working in the company.

This first psychological contract forms the basis of the others you create with the people you'll work with—colleagues, business partners, and customers.

Think carefully about the organizational culture the company presents and the type of people you'll be working with. If their values and expectations initially appear questionable, it may be because you are seeing these as unfair or unsuitable to you.

2. Inform Yourself About the Organization's Culture and Values

For your first few weeks in the job, the psychological contract develops rapidly as you gather information about others' values and expectations. Watching when, where, why, and how staff talk and act is a good way to assess the realities of the organization's behavior. Don't be afraid to test your understanding by gently pushing against boundaries or asking questions.

3. Compare the Organization's Policies with Your Psychological Contract

The two should be complementary, not mutually exclusive. See whether what is explicit matches what is implicit—for example, does the job description acknowledge your hours of work? Do managers really consult employees about change? Does the company actually fulfill its commitments to quality and customer service? Ask yourself: "Do they do what they say?" "Do they say one thing but expect another?"

If the answers to these questions seem unacceptable, you may have cause to question your future with the organization.

4. Examine the Psychological Contract

Psychological contracts have many parts. Among the most important are the following:

- Knowledge and experience—what are the expectations about what I know and can do, and how I use these? How will I be helped to improve my skills? How am I expected to share skills and knowledge—formally (for example, in reports) or informally (at team meetings)?
- Motivation—what are my real motivations for this job and how do these affect my performance? What motivates the people around me and how can knowledge of this improve my job? What are the rewards and disadvantages of working here?
- Goals (and means)—how do things happen in the organization? Do employees closely follow the rulebook or simply ignore it? Who do I go through to get things done? What happens if I don't follow the expected channels? Would I be happy with this?
- Role—who do I want to be in the organization? What is the real nature and content of the job? How do I avoid being a figurehead and get taken seriously? Do people have emotional expectations of me that weren't communicated at the start?
- Ethics—what are the moral principles that guide the organization? Am I happy with them? Is the company breaking any laws? What morals and principles must I exhibit when dealing with others (including customers and outside agencies)?

5. Review the Psychological Contract

A psychological contract is a description of how well you fit into the organization and how well the organization suits you. If both you and the organization agree

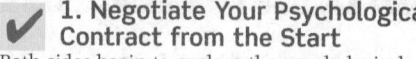

"I trust my employees. They're looking for success as much as I am."   Ricardo Semler

on your role, what is expected of you, and what you expect of the organization, there's a good fit.

But things change. The business environment never stands still, people move on, the type of work changes, or the company implements new policies and practices. You may have negative reactions to any of these changes. If you do, group the factors in your working life and see where problems arise.

- Your boss—are the boss's expectations of you, your role, and your workload now different? Are you unhappy with your supervisor's methods of giving you work or communicating with you? Do you have too many bosses?
- Your coworkers—do you feel left out or sidelined? Are you happy with your colleagues' work? Do employees who have different personalities from yours seem more highly valued than you?
- The physical environment—is it unsafe, overcrowded, or otherwise unsatisfactory?
- Your work—are you bored, overworked, or underused? Have you increased your expertise or knowledge without improving the quality of your output? Are you frustrated

because you can't change something you think needs changing?
- Your private life—is there something at work affecting your private life or vice versa?

6. Resolve Tensions in the Psychological Contract

Be honest with yourself and decide what it is you now want from your work. If you can, tweak or renegotiate the existing contract to reduce tension or conflict.

Use your psychological contract to judge:
- who can help you resolve your concerns and how both the people and the problems should be approached;
- how the organization expects problems to be recognized and dealt with.

THOUGHT STARTERS
- How well do you know your organization's values and expectations?
- What do you expect from your boss and colleagues? What do they expect from you?

471

CHECKLIST

DOS AND DON'TS

DO
- Recognize that a psychological contract exists.
- Review the contract regularly and renegotiate when necessary.
- Realize that the old assumptions about employment relationships have changed.
- Be prepared to share your feelings and opinions with others so you fully understand your role.
- Be willing to adjust your opinions and how you work with others.

DON'T
- Don't expect everyone to share your expectations and values.
- Don't assume people will never change their expectations of you and your role.
- Don't form opinions of others or rely on expectations based on first impressions.

FOR MORE INFORMATION

Books:
Hakim, Cliff. *We Are All Self-employed: How to Take Control of Your Career*. 2nd ed. San Francisco, CA: Berrett-Koehler, 2003.
Makin, Peter J., et al. *Organizations and the Psychological Contract*. Westport, CT: Greenwood Publishing, 1996.

Journal Article:
Altman, Wilf, and Cary Cooper. "New Deal Needed to Secure Commitment." *Professional Manager* 8:5 (September 1999): 38–40.

"If you were to hire household staff to cook, clean, drive, stoke the fire, and answer the door, can you imagine suggesting that they not talk to each other, not see what each other is doing, not coordinate their functions?"
Nicholas Negroponte

Job Cuts—Breaking the News

This checklist provides guidance to line managers who find themselves responsible for informing employees that their job is to be terminated.

The fact that there are to be job cuts rarely comes as a complete surprise to employees, but dismissing individuals is a difficult task that needs to be handled with great care. There are steps to follow, however, that can help make the process as painless as possible.

DEFINITION

This checklist concentrates solely on the termination interview itself, not the process leading up to it. It therefore excludes information about the statutory requirements of an company considering job cuts.

A job is considered to be cut if the employer:

- is ceasing to carry on the business the employment is in;
- is closing down the business at the site where the job is based;
- is transferring the business from the site where the job is based to another location (for example, a company with two offices decides to rationalize at one site);
- requires fewer employees to do a specific type of work (for example, one manager takes over a function formerly divided between two);
- needs fewer employees to carry out the work at the place where it is carried out (for example, the divisional personnel function is closed, but the head office personnel department remains and a personnel manager is appointed for each site).

The basic test for job cuts is whether the employer now needs fewer employees either across the country or at a particular location. In theory, the amount of work need not have changed, but it must be capable of being carried out by fewer people.

Termination interviews are conducted on an individual basis. The purpose of such interviews is to ensure that employees are:

- told the news in a clear and objective manner;
- made aware of the reasons for the termination;
- given information on the time frame of the termination process;
- provided with details of the severance package on offer;
- advised as to employment resources available for all unemployed workers; also about possible public benefits, such as unemployment compensation, that are available to workers terminated through no fault of their own;
- given a letter of recommendation (if it is deserved) so as to better their chances at being hired elsewhere;
- advised—if appropriate to the company's situation—that they could be re-hired by the company in the future, should conditions warrant future workforce expansion.

ADVANTAGES

Careful handling:

- helps to reduce possible animosity and ill will on the part of the terminated employee;
- helps to minimize damage to the company's reputation, by reducing the chances that the terminated employee will "bad mouth" the company in public;
- increases the chances that the terminated employee will have an easier time finding a new job.

DISADVANTAGES

- Takes time and caring on the part of managers, at a time when the company is possibly undergoing other stressful changes.

ACTION CHECKLIST

✓ 1. Prepare Yourself

All managers find it difficult to deliver bad news to their employees. Before breaking such news to an individual it is essential to address your own feelings on the issue, toward downsizing itself and its impact on the employee.

✓ 2. Gather the Information You Need

Before you deliver the news of termination to an employee, make sure you are aware of and understand:

- the reasons for the job cuts;
- the method of selecting employees for termination;
- the details of the severance package;
- the rights, responsibilities and opportunities for terminated employees.

Review the employee's personal details, particularly the person's employment record, before the meeting.

✓ 3. Plan the Interview

Plan the interview carefully in terms of its timing and location and what is to happen immediately afterward.

✓ Timing

Decisions at higher levels may leave line managers with little leeway in choosing the timing of their announcements. Two rules of thumb, however, are:

- avoid holding interviews on Fridays. Few (or no) professional support mechanisms are available to employees over the weekend;
- allow that sufficient time for each interview (while setting a clear time limit) and schedule a gap between interviews.

✓ Location

Make sure that:

- the interviews are held in a quiet place, out of view from and beyond the hearing range of other employees and free from interruptions;
- employees can leave via a different route to avoid embarrassment and to minimize upset between people who

have been told what is happening and those still waiting to see you;

- the interview room is set up in an appropriate way—there are simple ways to avoid giving an overt message that it's "them" against "us!" For example, furnish the room with chairs of equal size and have no desk in between you and the employee. Perhaps have water and tissues available, within easy reach, as an aid for employees who take the news hard and need a moment or two to compose themselves.

Aftermath

You must decide what you want employees to do immediately after they are told they are out. Some organizations require individuals to clear their desks (supervised by their manager or a member of the personnel department) and leave the premises immediately. Others expect employees to work a notice period, but send them home for the remainder of the day on which they are told. Clarify what your organizational policy is or whether special instructions apply to employees in particular positions of responsibility.

Supporting Paperwork

Gather relevant information that employees can take away and read in their own time. This material should reinforce the information given in the interview and go into more detail on such issues as outplacement, support networks, and other services available to dismissed employees.

4. Give the News

It is essential to give news as momentous as dismissal in a clear and unambiguous manner. The individual should come away from the interview knowing that the decision is final.

The amount of information you supply is critical. There is a fine line between overloading an employee with information and leaving someone with unanswered questions. There can be no hard and fast rules about this; each person is different and will react to bad news in a different way.

5. Provide Details of What Is Available

Briefly explain:

- the redundancy package (including the financial settlement, outplacement, and other support);
- the time frame;
- contacts in organizations that may be of help (if no outplacement service is offered).

Give the employee the information you have prepared. If necessary and possible, arrange a follow-up meeting with for the following week to answer further questions or to help with any problems that arise.

6. Check the Employee's Understanding of the Situation and Close the Interview

Make sure that the employee understands the information you have given and ask for any immediate questions. Invite the person to contact you again if (as often happens) further questions arise, but be firm about ending the interview to fit your schedule.

THOUGHT STARTERS

- Have you ever been terminated?

- If so, how was the news delivered?

- Could it have been handled in a better way?

DOS AND DON'TS

DO
- Address your own feelings and be prepared.
- Anticipate and prepare for negative reactions.
- Be firm, clear, and unambiguous.
- Demonstrate sympathy and empathy.
- Provide written details of both the situation and what is on offer.

DON'T
- Don't rush the interview.
- Don't lose control.
- Don't give employees conflicting messages.
- Don't patronize or insult employees ("We just got rid of some dead wood").

FOR MORE INFORMATION

Books:
Steingold, Fred S., and Amy Delpo, ed. *The Employer's Legal Handbook*. 7th ed. Soquel, CA: Nolo Press, 2005.
Stiller, Richard, and Ron Visconti. *Rightful Termination: Avoiding Litigation*. Normal, IL: Crisp Publications, 1994.
Weiss, Donald H. *Fair, Square, and Legal: Safe Hiring, Managing, and Firing to Keep You and Your Company out of Court*. 4th ed. New York: AMACOM, 2004.

Journal Articles:
Dalgarno, David, and Philip Davies. "How to Consult on Collective Redundancies." *People Management* 9:18 (September 2003): 50–51.
Welfare, Sarah. "Communicating Bad News: Managing Redundancy." *IRS Employment Review* no.803 (July 2004): 11–17.
"Managing Redundancy." *IDS HR Studies* no.797 (May 2005).

Web sites:
HR Guide: **www.hr-guide.com**
HR.BLR.com: **http://hr.blr.com**

Arranging for Unemployment and Health Insurance After a Job Loss

CHECKLIST

This checklist is designed as a guide for those wishing to receive unemployment insurance and to continue getting health insurance through their employer, after being laid off from work.

DEFINITION

In broad terms, you can be laid off for one or more of these reasons:

- your employers are ceasing to carry on the business that employs you
- your employers are closing down the business at the site where you work, for example, if a company with four distribution centers decides to close one
- your employers are transferring the business from the site where you work to another location, for example, a company with two offices decides to consolidate at one site
- your employers are selling the business and the new owners decide to "clean house," hiring new employees to replace those laid off
- your employers need fewer employees to do your particular kind of work, for example, they decide to have one manager responsible for sales instead of two
- your employers need fewer employees to do your particular kind of work at the place where you work, for example, the divisional personnel function is closed, but the head office personnel function remains and a personnel manager is appointed for each site

The basic test of a layoff is whether your employers now need fewer employees, either across the company or at a particular location. In theory the amount of work need not have changed, but it must be capable of being done by fewer people.

ADVANTAGES

- Receiving unemployment insurance allows the ex-employee to get by, financially speaking, for at least one-half year.
- It protects the recently unemployed person from experiencing immediate distress, due to their inability to pay for food, shelter and other basis needs.
- Having the ability to continue receiving health insurance benefits under the ex-employer's plan gives the laid off employee the security of being covered temporarily, while seeking other health insurance alternatives.

DISADVANTAGES

- Both unemployment insurance and continued health insurance, under the ex-employer's plan, are temporary benefits.
- Unemployment insurance is substantially less than what a normal pay check would be; it is also considered taxable income.

- While the unemployed person is eligible for health care coverage under their ex-employer's plan, they must pay for the cost of that insurance themselves.

ACTION CHECKLIST

1. Check Eligibility

To be eligible for unemployment insurance, you must meet the following criteria:

- you must be a U.S. citizen, a registered alien, or have permission to work in the United States
- you must have worked for a private employer or for state or federal government; unemployment benefits don't cover those who have been self-employed or who have worked for the railroad
- you must be currently unemployed, and have lost your job due to no fault of your own
- you must have earned sufficient wages during the past year; the exact details of determining your unemployment compensation (both the amount and the duration of benefits) may vary from state to state
- in many states, you must also demonstrate that—if able—you are actively seeking employment
- you must file an unemployment insurance claim with the state in which you reside
- unemployment compensation won't begin until after any employer-paid additional severance wages and bonuses are exhausted

2. Determining the Amount of Payment

Determining the amount of time you may receive unemployment, as well as the amount of compensation, depends on the state in which you live, how long you have worked and how much you earned. In general, benefits last at least 26 weeks (one-half year) but may be extended to a year under certain circumstances. It's best to contact the state department of labor or employment where you live, to be certain of the minimum requirements and benefits available.

Each state also varies in how it determines the amount of compensation someone may receive after being laid off. In general, the applicant for unemployment insurance must have worked at least two of the past four calendar quarters (six months or longer in the past year). The state will determine, based on the wages earned and length of employment, what the weekly benefit amount will be. That decision can be appealed if you think it unfair; you may choose to represent yourself during that appeals process, rather than hire an attorney.

3. Continued Health Coverage Under the Employer's Plan

Losing your job, whether you were laid off, fired, or left for other reasons, doesn't mean you are immediately without medical and health insurance coverage. COBRA (the Consolidated Omnibus Reconciliation Act of 1985) is a federal law that requires your former employer to con-

---

"Business cannot eliminate unemployment, but each business can do its competitive best to expand its own sales and employment."

Henry Ford

tinue to offer you the same plan coverage you had while employed. If a company is small—less than 20 employees—they aren't required by federal law to follow the laws of COBRA. However, many state laws still require small companies to provide something like COBRA for ex-employees, or for those still employed there, but working only part time.

COBRA is not a long term solution; rather, you can opt to receive coverage for between 18 and 36 months, depending on your particular circumstances. For specific details, check with your ex-employer's personnel office as well as the labor or employment department in the state you live. The drawback to COBRA coverage provisions is that you must pay for the insurance coverage yourself. Before you decide to accept that proposition, consider the following options:

- the ex-employer may have alternative, less expensive, plans you could choose instead;
- you may be able to receive coverage under a spouse's plan for less;
- there may be other options available through a non-profit association or from independent insurance companies that would be as effective and perhaps less expensive.

Before deciding whether or not to request COBRA coverage, be sure to also check out the provisions of the HIPAA law (Health Insurance Portability and Accountability Act, of 1996). HIPAA regulates employer group health plans and health insurance companies, most notably in the area of "preexisting conditions."

✔ 4. Tax Consequences

Unemployment compensation is considered income by both federal and state governments, and is therefore taxable. You can elect to have the taxes taken out of each unemployment check, if you wish, but most states do not deduct the tax automatically. You will be sent a form (1099 G) at the end of January, following the year in which you received unemployment payments. You are responsible for reporting unemployment compensation, filing the appropriate forms and paying any taxes due on the income.

There are no negative tax consequences relative to continuing health care benefits under the provisions of COBRA and HIPAA. On the positive side, insurance payments are tax deductible, although they must be sub-

stantial to add up to more than the "standard deduction" allowed individuals and families each year.

✔ 5. Employers' Responsibilities

The only responsibility of the employer when you apply for unemployment insurance is to verify the timeframe and circumstances under which you were employed. They are also required to keep you on their health plan policy temporarily, if you make that request of them with 60 days of leaving the job.

DOS AND DON'TS

DO
- Fully understand your employee benefits package before you leave the job.
- Make sure you file for appropriate unemployment compensation and health insurance (COBRA) coverage in a timely fashion.
- Call the state departments that administer services to the unemployed for assistance and advice.

DON'T
- Don't assume your former employer will be acting on your behalf after you leave the job.
- Don't forget that you have reporting, record keeping and other paperwork responsibilities with these type of programs.

THOUGHT STARTERS
- How can you simplify your life and live with less income during the time between jobs? There are many resources for people in this situation. Start with local and state agencies that specialize in out-of-work issues.

FOR MORE INFORMATION

Book:
Stringham, Jim, and David R. Workman. *The Unemployment Survival Guide.* Layton, UT: Gibbs Smith, 2004.

475

CHECKLIST

Training Needs Analysis

476

CHECKLIST

This checklist lays out the steps for implementing training needs analysis (TNA).

Effective training or development depends on knowing what results are required—for the individual, the department, and the organization as a whole. With limited budgets and the need for cost-effective solutions, all organizations should ensure that resources invested in training are targeted at areas in which training and development are needed and a positive return on the investment is guaranteed. Effective TNA is particularly vital in today's changing workplace as staff exposed to new technologies and flexible working practices need to update their skills regularly.

Analyzing and identifying training needs are prerequisites to any effective training program or event. Simply throwing training at individuals may miss the highest priority needs or cover areas that are not essential. Analysis of training needs is not a task solely for specialists. Managers today are responsible for many facets of people management, including the training and development of their team; they should therefore understand TNA and be able to implement it successfully.

DEFINITION

A training need has two defining features.

- It is any shortcoming, gap, or problem that prevents an individual or organization from achieving their objectives.
- It can be overcome or reduced through training and/or development.

A training need can arise at the organization, the activity, or the individual level. For our purposes an organization means not only the whole company, but any department, section, or team with its own objectives.

At the organizational level a training need is any behavior or lack of skill that hinders the achievement of corporate objectives; for example, a lack of customer service skills that harms the business or a lack of interpersonal skills that negatively affects staff retention.

At the activity level a training need applies to everyone doing the same work. All tire fitters in a company need to learn to use a new piece of machinery, for example, while the members of the sales team do not.

At the individual level a training need occurs when an individual lacks skills, knowledge, or understanding, or when certain behavior prevents someone from being successful. If receptionist A has a professional telephone manner while receptionist B, who does the same job, is abrupt and offhand, then B has a personal training need.

ADVANTAGES

Training needs analysis:

- targets resources at identified priorities;
- enhances organizational ability to plan for and adapt to changes in the workplace;
- helps individuals and teams perform better, improving their job satisfaction, morale, and motivation;
- flows naturally from the appraisal process, in which staff discuss which of their skills need to be improved and how;
- provides a constructive base for improving performance.

DISADVANTAGES

There are no disadvantages, but TNA does require:

- time and energy to plan the analysis systematically and analyze the results;
- the coordination of the results among managers to ensure that an organizational plan reflects corporate priorities, allowing for economies of scale and avoiding duplication across departments;
- the full involvement of, and discussion with, potential trainees instead of faster but one-sided evaluation by their managers.

Ideally, it also means training managers in the process of TNA itself so that they understand what they are trying to achieve and what their approach should be.

ACTION CHECKLIST

Training needs can be sorted broadly into three types:

- those you can anticipate
- those that arise from monitoring
- reactions to unexpected problems

1. Coordinate Training Needs

Training needs that exist in one department are likely to exist in others. It is pointless for individual managers to throw their own limited resources at each problem as it arises, duplicating efforts and dissipating energy. Most organizations have a personnel function that organizes training delivery. You may not be the person who coordinates the system, but you have an important role to play in gathering the best information you can about the training needs of your staff and passing it up the line. At the very least, cooperate with other managers to coordinate your training needs so the company integrates its training and development activities.

2. Anticipate Needs in Your Own Span of Control

Anticipated needs often appear at the organizational or activity level. You know, for example, that a new machine coming into a workshop or office will almost certainly have training implications for everyone using it. Similarly, a company that decides to enhance customer service as part of its corporate strategy knows that a program of training and development is essential for its success.

"I must say that acting was good training for the political life that lay ahead of us."

Nancy Reagan

3. Develop Monitoring Techniques

Some problems that fall into the category of training needs go unnoticed while they creep up on the organization. Active monitoring systems help you spot these.

One approach to monitoring is variance analysis. This sounds technical, but it is a simple tool used by managers to monitor budgets, and it translates neatly to the identification of training needs. When a budget is agreed on, it is broken down into projected monthly expenditure. Any major variance from the forecast—upward or downward—triggers an investigation into why it occurred and what the results will be.

In TNA, the budget numbers are replaced by specific performance standards and indicators. Even in a "soft" issue like customer satisfaction, you can set a standard that 95 percent of customers should feel they received excellent service. Carrying out customer satisfaction surveys allows you to measure any deviation.

Asking questions in appraisal interviews is a form of survey, since the same basic issues are addressed throughout the organization. A fundamental purpose of appraisal is to identify individuals' training needs.

It is also worthwhile to interview staff and customers to help identify specific problems. Regularly ask a random sample of people for their views on the same set of questions relating to general performance, for example, customer satisfaction levels.

4. Keep an Open Mind in Analyzing Problems

Monitoring will indicate where gaps and problems exist, but be careful not to rush into the wrong assumption to explain a particular set of circumstances. As an example, it may seem natural to conclude that unusually rapid staff turnover in a small section is due to shiftwork; however, exit interviews may indicate that cramped working conditions and poor ventilation are to blame. Training cannot resolve this problem, even though the monitoring process has helped you identify it.

5. Identify the Level

A training need might be limited to an individual or an activity, but it is more likely to impact on at least two, and perhaps all three, levels.

If the company generally treats customers as a nuisance, it needs to change its overall approach. Giving one or two people training addresses the training need at the wrong level; organizational development is needed, not individual training sessions.

6. Take Appropriate Action

If the training needs are within your own span of control, probably at individual or maybe at activity level, you can plan action to meet the needs.

If the needs appear to be at a wider level than the one you control, you need to make recommendations and proposals on a wider front.

THOUGHT STARTERS

- How much of the training budget do you think was wasted last year—and why?

- What training do your people need that has not been arranged and is not likely to be? Why is this?

- Have you ever been sent on a course that you felt was irrelevant to your needs?

- Consider the motivational impact on your team of attending an engaging and worthwhile event.

FOR MORE INFORMATION

Books:
Hargrove, Robert. *Masterful Coaching: Extraordinary Results By Impacting People and the Way They Think and Work Together.* Rev. ed. New York: Pfeiffer, 2002.
Peterson, David B., and Mary Dee Hicks. *Leader As Coach: Strategies for Coaching and Developing Others.* Minneapolis, MN: Personnel Decisions International, 1996.

See also:
✓ Evaluating Training (pp. 478–479)
✓ Mentoring in Practice (pp. 436–437)

DOS AND DON'TS

DO
- Take TNA as seriously as you do the delivery of training.
- Coordinate your findings with those of other managers.
- Remember to consider potential needs at the organization, activity, and individual level.
- Include yourself as someone with potential training needs.

DON'T
- Don't arrange any training without first establishing that there is a clear need for it.
- Don't simply send everyone on the same training event that you found useful and enjoyable. Individuals have different backgrounds and experiences—and unique training priorities.
- Don't concentrate on obvious training needs at the expense of those you need to search for (for example, with monitoring systems).

"Education and training are decisive, and the single greatest long-term leverage point available to all levels of government."

Michael Porter

Evaluating Training

CHECKLIST

This checklist provides line managers with ideas and key points to incorporate in their employees' training programs and help assess the effectiveness of training. It should be read in conjunction with the related checklist on Training Needs Analysis. It is not written for trainers themselves.

Virtually all training events end with participants completing an evaluation form. Evaluations may fail to indicate, however, whether the participants actually learned anything useful or how that knowledge can be transferred to the workplace.

Evaluating training is a continuous process of defining training objectives, identifying training needs, delivering programs to meet those needs and objectives, evaluating trainees' reactions to the training, seeking evidence of skills or knowledge learned and their implementation in the workplace, and measuring the effects of training on bottom-line results.

It is not always possible to perform such evaluation in depth, but that is not to say that nothing should be done at all. The key is to have a training objective and put some indicator(s) in place to see whether that objective is met. In this way it should be possible to get some idea of your return on investment.

DEFINITION
Evaluation is an analytical process of estimating the value of something. In the case of training, it focuses on whether the time and money spent on training have achieved the required results.

ADVANTAGES
- Broadly, evaluation can tell you whether what you have done has worked.
- It confirms that financial resources have targeted identified priorities.
- It tells you whether desired improvements in individual performance have been achieved.
- If training has not achieved its objectives, the evaluation provides information that should help you to improve it next time.
- The information gained feeds into the staff appraisal process and helps managers discuss progress with individuals.
- Individuals and teams know what results are expected from training before they start, raising their commitment to, and involvement in, the training itself.
- Evaluation shows clearly where the organization stands in terms of staff development, and provides information about performance to use in planning future training.

DISADVANTAGES
Successful evaluation of training requires:
- a commitment to training as an important and central business function rather than an optional or nonessential activity;
- the adoption of a disciplined and active planning approach rather than a reactive management style distracted by putting out fires;
- the allocation of valuable management time to a careful consideration of what is to be achieved and measured, and how to measure it, before training is planned;
- the commitment of time and resources to detailed analysis afterwards.

ACTION CHECKLIST

✔ 1. Define What You Want Training to Achieve
Remember the evaluation process starts as soon as you begin constructing a training plan. Having identified needs, quantify as specifically as possible what results and outcomes you expect. This can often be relatively easy to define, for example:
- to operate a machine safely;
- to use a graphics package;
- to set up a Web site;
- to construct widgets using new technology.

In many cases these outcomes can be specified and measured by occupational, organizational, or national standards.

It is much harder to set measurable targets when it comes to training designed for teaching skills, transferring knowledge, or changing behavior. Building up knowledge and experience in specific areas is fundamental to development, but it is difficult to quantify. It is essential to work with trainees to specify expected outcomes—for example, more effective selling behavior.

✔ 2. Turn Targets into Objectives
Objectives tell you what is to be achieved, by when. They should be SMART: Specific, Measurable, Achievable, Realistic, Time limited. A training objective specifies what you can realistically expect the trainee to know or be able to do as a result of the training.

If the training is to teach a skill, for example, the measure of success might be that within six weeks of the end of training, the trainee will be able to type a ten-page report containing no more than six mistakes within an hour.

In devising objectives for knowledge-based training, avoid the word "understand"—it is not a measurable concept. Say instead that the trainee should be able to "state," "explain," or "describe" the subject. These are checkable, and the trainee will need to have absorbed the knowledge in order to meet the objective.

✔ 3. Publicize the Objectives
Make sure everyone knows the objectives from the start. "Everyone" includes:

- the trainees, whose should be advised of the objectives in briefings from their managers and any advance materials they receive;
- their managers (if they have not themselves arranged the training), so they know what their staff should bring back from the training program;
- the trainers—this may sound obvious, but they need to design the training based on what it should achieve rather than which areas they have experience in (which may be different). Where the training is to be provided by an outside agency, make sure that the provider can meet the objectives you specify.

 4. Design Methods for Comparing Results with Objectives

The best way to do this is to get people together to come up with one agreed and consistent approach. It may involve a post-training action plan, a debriefing session after trainees return to the workplace, forms, questionnaires, observation checklists, feedback meetings, or statistical data. The key point is that you must design the assessment procedures at an early stage.

Immediate feedback is important, but a realistic time span for evaluating performance improvements is often weeks or even months. You need to allow time for the training to be applied and practiced, leading to the actual outcomes you want to evaluate.

5. Evaluate the Input

Remind trainees to keep their objectives in mind throughout the training and to talk to the trainer if their needs are not being met. If the training is provided by an outside agency, ask the trainees for a summary of their response to the course at a debriefing session when they return. Encourage them to be honest in giving their opinion of the value of the training.

6. Evaluate the Impact of the Training on Performance

The process of evaluation is a matter of comparing results with expectations. Encourage trainees to produce a realistic action plan to implement what they have learned once they are back at work. In the longer term, perhaps three months afterwards, ask the trainees what the training has helped them to achieve.

7. Use the Results

Use the information provided by the evaluation in starting the training cycle again and planning what must be tackled next and how. Evaluation sets out key facts and measures of progress more clearly than any sort of gut reaction or guesswork.

DO
- Specify the outcomes and results required.
- Establish measurements for hard-to-measure activities. Even if the best available measurement is rough-and-ready, it remains the best one available, and it is much better than nothing.
- Design the evaluation procedures at the outset.
- Involve other managers with a stake in the training outcomes.
- Involve the trainees themselves.
- Review with an open mind what the evaluation tells you—mistakes and failures can be more helpful in making continuous improvements than convincing yourself it was really all right when it wasn't.

DON'T
- Don't try to justify poor results with excuses—if there is a lesson to be learned, value it.
- Don't rely on standard written evaluation forms.
- Don't give up—evaluating training is widely regarded as the most difficult aspect of the training function.

THOUGHT STARTERS
- How do you decide now whether training is achieving the right results?

- Wouldn't you like to know which training activities are effective and which can be improved?

- Aren't there some training activities that you already believe either don't work or could be improved, but you haven't got any evidence on which to base a case for improvement?

FOR MORE INFORMATION

Book:
Kirkpatrick, Donald L. *Evaluating Training Programs: The Four Levels*. 3rd ed. San Francisco, CA: Berrett-Koehler, 2005.

See also:
✓ Training Needs Analysis (pp. 476–477)

479

CHECKLIST

"For the bold new world of the 21st century . . . every adult American must be able to keep on learning for a lifetime."
Bill Clinton

Planning a Workshop

This checklist describes how to plan and run a workshop.

DEFINITION

Workshops are not just meetings, lectures, seminars, or discussions, although they may well contain elements of some or all of these things. They are principally gatherings called in order to tackle a problem or achieve an objective in an informal environment conducive to creativity. Workshops are appropriate for the study of broad issues that deserve deeper analysis than can be achieved in ordinary meetings, or of issues that require brainstorming or imaginative thinking.

Workshops do not have a chair or a leader as such, but a facilitator who creates an open, relaxed atmosphere to encourage contributions from those present. A typical workshop has from four to ten or more participants.

A workshop can therefore be a group event, learning occasion, or training session at which participants are the major contributors or learn from each other, or where the experience of those attending is more important than the knowledge of the facilitator.

ADVANTAGES

Workshops are useful when you need to:
- secure group ownership of the objective;
- get maximum contributions from people;
- involve people as fully as possible;
- brainstorm ideas;
- come up with the right questions and constructive alternatives;
- formulate a rough plan of action.

DISADVANTAGES

Workshops are inappropriate if you need to:
- collate or analyze complex or detailed information;
- investigate mistakes or failure;
- make a final decision.

They do not work when some individuals dominate or when people do not want to be there.

ACTION CHECKLIST

1. Select a Facilitator

Determine whether the facilitator should be internal or external. Internal staff can be used if the issue is not too contentious or complex and if you have a staff member who is an experienced facilitator. Otherwise, you should employ an external facilitator.

The facilitator should feel comfortable with running activity-based sessions and should be able to:
- indicate to participants what expected outcomes or targets are;

- formulate clear plans and tactics for moving the group toward them;
- persuade participants to own what they have achieved at the end.

2. Clarify the Necessary Outcomes

Identify the objectives of the workshop, deadlines to be met, and any opposing ideologies to reconcile. Ensure that objectives are measurable.

3. Identify the Participants

Each participant should be able to make a worthwhile contribution. Pay attention to the best mix of people and to any potential conflicts that will need to be managed.

4. Select a Site

The location you choose needs to have appropriate facilities; do not overlook basic features such as equipment, room size, and atmosphere. Look for space that can accommodate a flexible workshop structure, paying attention to appropriate space for group work. When it is important to step aside and think afresh, consider a location outside the workplace—this frees the participants' minds from preoccupation with work waiting for them a few yards away.

5. Gather Equipment

Think of all the small items that may seem trivial but can be enormously helpful when a session is in full swing, for example, glue, scissors, tape, flip charts and pens that work, paperclips, stapler, etc. Make sure the room layout suits your needs. Seating patterns can make a difference to discussion.

6. Establish Ground Rules

This is particularly important with brainstorming sessions and with groups of mixed seniority, but limit the number of rules—too many rules are likely to inhibit free discussion.

7. Prepare the Participants

You may like to set a pre-workshop task, but keep advance information to a minimum, as the focus should be on group activity. Be aware of preconceived ideas and fears, and be prepared to dispel them.

8. Set a Timetable

Workshops can last from half a day to two or three days, depending on the topic(s). Design the time flexibly, allowing for a comfortable proportion of plenary to small-group sessions. Take into account the concentration required of the participants. Try to work a balanced mix between active and passive sessions. Remain in control, but be flexible when events bypass or overrule your scheduling.

Allow adequate time for coffee breaks—participants need time to absorb ideas and chat informally. If the

workshop lasts more than one day, it is often useful to start the first day with lunch so that people can relax and get to know one another.

9. Plan an Opener

An immediate—but appropriate—icebreaker can help establish the atmosphere you wish to create and can also help with introductions. After the icebreaker sets the scene, clarify why you are there and explain the process so that everyone is comfortable with it.

10. Make the Workshop Enjoyable

Everyone will get more from the workshop if it is an enjoyable experience.

MEASURING WORKSHOP OUTPUT

Measuring the success or failure of a workshop goes beyond finding out whether participants experienced an enjoyable and constructive group experience. It is measured in terms of:

- the extent that measurable objectives were progressed, advanced, or achieved;
- the changes in thinking, behavior, or activity that have taken place, will take place, or have been confirmed;
- the action that results from the workshop.

DOS AND DON'TS

DO

- Create an informal atmosphere.
- Focus on getting the group to work collectively.
- Adopt tasks and activities that are meaningful to the participants.
- Allow and encourage participants to solve their own problems.
- Get the group to own their findings and recommendations.
- Finish with a summary of what has been agreed or achieved.
- Allocate responsibilities and arrange for a follow-up.

DON'T

- Don't allow things to become too relaxed.
- Don't worry about an individual's nonparticipation at the expense of overall group success.
- Don't spoon-feed participants.
- Don't seek to dominate or try to impress the group with your knowledge.
- Don't spend too much time lecturing or presenting.
- Don't indulge too many red herrings introduced by participants.

THOUGHT STARTERS

- Do you have more than routine: questions to clarify? alternatives to construct? tactics to determine? proposals to clarify? initial decisions to test and agree? techniques to assimilate? skills to practice?

- Do you have people with appropriate experience who can help to achieve the required outcome?

FOR MORE INFORMATION

Book:

Klatt, Bruce. *The Ultimate Workshop Training Handbook: A Comprehensive Guide to Leading Successful Workshops and Training Programs.* New York: McGraw-Hill, 1999.

See also:

✔ Brainstorming (pp. 584–585)
✔ Performing a SWOT Analysis (pp. 520–521)

"The danger is that people can fall in love with the business they're in and get mesmerised by it. As a result, they don't actually see the business." — Allen Sheppard

Planning Career Assessment and Development Centers

CHECKLIST

This checklist is for managers who are considering the use of career assessment or development centers in their organization. Although assessment centers have traditionally been used for selection and recruitment, companies are increasingly examining their potential role in training and development and even to help support potential candidates for layoffs.

Such centers typically employ such exercises as leaderless group discussions, formal exercises with rotating leaders, business games, role-play, fact-finding exercises, presentations, structured interviews, in-tray exercises, and paper-based and psychometric tests.

DEFINITION

A career assessment center offers a carefully designed program of job-related simulation exercises in which the performance of a group of participants is observed and appraised by specially trained observers who evaluate each participant against predetermined criteria.

Career development centers are similar in design and structure, but have a very different purpose. Because they are designed to help participants learn more about themselves, development centers generally provide much more feedback from observers.

ADVANTAGES

Career assessment and development centers:
- have a proven high level of reliability in predicting future job performance (three times as high as interviews);
- adhere to a clear structure and logic that are acceptable to participants and easily evaluated;
- offer a reliable and objective way of evaluating people against diverse criteria;
- present a proactive image of the company;
- provide insight into the nature of jobs and the culture of the organization;
- make it easier to present negative feedback to participants;
- prevent poorly qualified candidates from slipping through;
- support the company's strategic processes for human resource management.

DISADVANTAGES

They:
- are expensive and demanding to develop and maintain;
- require a high level of expertise;
- necessitate regular training and updating.

ACTION CHECKLIST

✔ 1. Define the Objectives

Clarify reasons for introducing a center and ensure that the necessary resources are available. Do a cost-benefit analysis on the basis of the current cost of poor selection and predicted improvements in selection success. Thus armed, you will need to sell the concept to the rest of the organization. Don't forget to develop some form of policy statement to provide guidance on future plans.

✔ 2. Carry Out Job Analyses

Effective job analysis is the key to successful assessment and development centers. If the behaviors and the criteria used by evaluators are general and unrelated to specific jobs, the probability of success is much reduced.

The special tools that can be used to analyze job roles include:
- direct observation and work study;
- structured interviews;
- critical incident analysis;
- repertory grid analysis;
- job analysis questionnaires.

✔ 3. Design the Activities of the Center

Designing activities for a successful center is an art as well as a science. Designers need to take into account the following factors:
- the relevance of exercises to the job
- the participants' backgrounds
- the relative importance of criteria (weighting)
- an interesting and balanced mix of exercises
- time and resource constraints

Experienced designers like to create a matrix or grid of possible exercises mapped against the criteria. After selecting the most relevant items, they create a script for the center that presents the participants with a coherent experience (for example, the center might focus on a key issue or business simulation). The key stages in designing assessment and development centers are:
- establishing a design team;
- producing the first draft;
- trying out the exercises;
- reviewing and editing the exercises;
- developing guidelines for evaluators.

✔ 4. Train Your Evaluators

No matter how well a center has been designed, its effectiveness ultimately depends on the quality of assessment. Evaluators must be carefully selected and prepared. They should be familiar with the requirements of the job, and are therefore often line managers. Key issues for the organization include:

"There's nothing wrong with people trying, but no one has a right to succeed because they think they are clever."

Alan Sugar

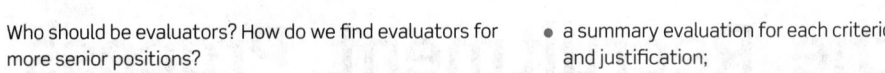

- Who should be evaluators? How do we find evaluators for more senior positions?
- How many evaluators do we need? How many participants will there be? How often will centers be held?
- What qualities are we looking for in evaluators? (Commitment, observational acuity, analytical skills, attention to detail, reputation for fairness, counseling experience, etc.)
- What are our training objectives? (Technical knowledge, standards, ability to record behavior, feedback, objectivity, etc.)
- What should the content of the training sessions be?

5. Plan and Administer the Center

Career assessment and development centers require meticulous planning so that, in theory at least, they will run automatically on the day. Issues that need to be considered by the team include:

- the variety and number of people to be brought together, typically an administrator, evaluators, role-players and resource providers;
- the schedule for exercises, probably starting with a group exercise and incorporating variety, adjustable timing, and flexibility to alter the schedule;
- the master schedule or plan showing the time and location of all exercises and individuals;
- room and equipment allocations;
- procedures for briefing evaluators and participants on instructions and expectations;
- checklists for all concerned.

6. Run the Center

It is important to select an able administrator for the center who can deal with any eventuality smoothly. A typical program might go as follows:

- Start the center—check facilities, label rooms, finalize-/adjust timetables, prepare rooms, provide photos of participants, brief evaluators, and check paperwork.
- Brief participants on the nature of the exercises, the roles of evaluators, expectations, and feedback arrangements.
- Administer exercises, providing periodic opportunities to review progress.
- Hold a closing session for participants. Hand out evaluation forms, explain feedback and follow-up arrangements, and say thank-yous.
- Hold a debriefing session for evaluators. Complete all work, review and reach agreement on overall ratings, document results, resolve disagreements in ratings, and allocate final responsibilities.

7. Write a Summary Report

The center's report should reflect the main purpose of the center. It normally contains:

- a summary of individuals' performance, usually including recommendations;

- a summary evaluation for each criterion, including ratings and justification;
- development needs and action plans.

8. Evaluate and Modify Centers

Career assessment and development centers should continually evolve if they are to serve the organization well. Every center should contain rigorous procedures for quality assurance and there should be regular reviews of the overall design. Jobs change, and new ways of assessing criteria are always emerging.

483

CHECKLIST

DOS AND DON'TS

DO
- Involve key stakeholders in the process.
- Plan meticulously.
- Brief the participants carefully.
- Ensure that participants are provided with clear feedback on their performance.
- Assume that everything will go wrong on the day—plan for all contingencies.
- Question the design at regular intervals.

DON'T
- Don't initiate career assessment centers unless you are prepared to run them properly.
- Don't allow cost to put you off—career assessment and development centers may be cost-effective when compared directly with the hidden costs of traditional methods.
- Don't assume that good managers automatically make good evaluators.

THOUGHT STARTERS
- Have you ever added up the real cost of unsuccessful recruitment?
- Have you ever considered direct assessment as a way of accurately identifying training needs? Or do you leave it to people to suggest training?
- Have you ever considered the possibility of using career assessment or development centers to identify future career paths for those faced with possible dismissal? Can you always afford to lose those who rush to accept voluntary layoffs?

FOR MORE INFORMATION

Book:
Ballantyne, Iain, and Nigel Povah. *Assessment and Development Centres*. 2nd ed. Burlington, VT: Ashgate Publishing Company, 2004.

"I am a big believer in insight and insightful people are hard to find." Ric Simcock

Planning the Recruitment Process

This checklist deals with the recruitment process from the moment the current employee resigns or the hiring of an additional staff member is authorized to the drawing up of a shortlist of candidates to interview.

Recruitment is an expensive process in its own right, but it can also have costly implications in terms of organizational performance and high staff turnover if it fails to identify appropriate people. To minimize these problems, a planned approach to recruitment allows a systematic review of the organization's employment needs and the best way to achieve them.

DEFINITION

The first part of the recruitment process, before conducting interviews, is concerned with verifying that you have a vacancy. Next, identify the sort of person you are looking for and in what capacity. Finally, seek candidates and make a shortlist of those who qualify.

ADVANTAGES

Planned recruitment:
- allows you to verify that you really do have a position to fill;
- offers an opportunity to reevaluate the existing position to see whether the job should be reconfigured;
- lets you decide on what basis you wish to employ somebody;
- ensures that you consider all possible avenues resources for finding the person.

DISADVANTAGES

The process:
- is time-consuming;
- may lead to delays in filling the position.

ACTION CHECKLIST

1. Decide Whether You Have a Vacancy
Determine whether you have a need for the work to be carried out or whether it could be incorporated into another employee's job. If you have a vacancy, decide whether you need a permanent full-time member of staff. Would a temporary or part-time employee be sufficient? Consider using a staffing agency to supply personnel on the basis you want. Another option is to outsource the work altogether.

2. Consult Staff Who May Be Involved
You will probably need to get authorization from senior management to hire or refill the position. Consider other departments in the organization that may have a vested interest in that position—you could decide to make it a joint effort. Talk to the previous holder of the position where possible, as well as to the relevant super-

visor, and especially to the people with whom the new person will work. Consult staff in the personnel department, if you have one, and draw on their expertise. Decide who should interview applicants at various stages in the process.

3. Decide What Sort of Person You Need
List the duties, responsibilities, authority, and relationships the job involves. If you are filling an existing position, decide whether the present job specifications are adequate, or whether this is an opportunity to make changes. Decide what qualifications you are seeking in candidates, what type and length of experience are required, and what personal qualities are important. On this basis you can update the job description and personal attributes desired. Fix a starting date and decide what training you are prepared to give and how soon the new hire is expected to be up to speed.

4. Find Out Whether Your Expectations Are Reasonable
Ask yourself whether you are likely to find the qualities, qualifications, and experience that you are seeking in one person. If so, research the kind of pay and benefits package you will have to offer. This can be done by monitoring local and national advertisements, referring to salary surveys, and networking with other employers in your area and industry sector. This research will also give you a feel for whether you are likely to find qualified candidates locally or whether you will have to look further afield. Start thinking about whether people will want to join your organization and how to attract them.

5. Plan the Search for Applicants
Start within your own organization. Are there any employees ready for this opportunity? Even if your assessment is negative, make sure that you advertise the position internally, both as a courtesy to staff and because they may pass the information on to interested friends or relatives. Word of mouth can be a valuable recruitment method, but guard against the gender and racial imbalances that this practice may perpetuate. Check the files for previous applications, whether unsolicited or not. Draw on any appropriate contacts you have, for example, in relevant community colleges and universities. These can be useful whether you are looking for apprentices or MBAs. Decide at this point whether to use a recruitment agency to find and qualify applicants for you. Your decision will be based on the time and expertise you have available and the fees charged by an agency. Another source for candidates is job fairs. Many hundreds are held annually, all over the world. They can be targeted at particular audiences, such as recent college graduates, for example, or at the public at large. A good Internet search engine will indicate where upcoming fairs are to be held. Employers could then research how to become part of the fair's offering to job seekers.

"The world is full of willing people: some willing to work, the rest willing to let them."

Robert Frost

6. Decide Where to Advertise

If you are going it alone, and you need to advertise, pinpoint the part of the press you need to contact. Do you want to use local or national newspapers? If the position is a specialist one, you may wish to advertise in professional journals or the trade press. Find out how much ads cost for various sizes and decide what you can afford. Use local job or career centers as well as new media such as the Internet, which has an immense number of job listings and employment opportunities.

7. Write the Advertisement

Decide if you and/or other staff are skilled enough to write an ad. If your organization's personnel department takes on this task, stay involved throughout the process. In the case of a senior position or if you are recruiting in large numbers, it may be appropriate to hire an advertising agency to draft the ad and select publications to place it in. It is better to name your organization in the ad instead of using a box number unless you have particular reasons for secrecy, as a box number may deter some applicants. The ad should state clearly:

- the duties and responsibilities of the job;
- the qualifications and experience required;
- the personal qualities sought;
- where the job is based;
- indications of the salary offered;
- what form of reply is required (letter and résumé or request for an application form);
- whether further information is available and in what form.

The ad should present a picture of an interesting and dynamic organization—it should be considered a public relations document with the potential to impact those who read it, candidates and non-candidates alike. More importantly, check that the ad does not contradict any civil rights legislation such as EEO or ADA for example, or discriminate through factors such as race, creed, sex, age, or physical capability. If you intend to ask applicants to use an application form, make sure this form requests all the details you need to assess the candidates. Complete the application form yourself, or get a colleague to do it, from the point of view of an applicant and check its suitability. Prepare an information pack for anyone who asks.

8. Draw Up a Shortlist

Decide on the length of the shortlist, probably five or six people at most. You will probably need help reviewing and prioritizing the applications, either from an outside agency or from other staff, supervisors, or managers in your organization. Apart from the saving time, having feedback on the applicants from others is valuable. When reading an application look out for a close match between the candidate and your requirements, any unexplained employment gaps, the quality of presentation, and whether the applicant has tailored the reply to your particular job and organization.

9. Reply to Candidates

Those whom you have no intention of interviewing should be contacted as quickly as possible and dealt with courteously: they, and their relatives and friends, may be future customers or acquaintances of potential applicants. Those whom you do wish to interview should also be contacted quickly, to affirm that they are still interested in the job and, if so, to arrange a date and time to talk. Make sure they know where to find you and tell them whether you are willing to reimburse them for their expenses. You may wish to keep a small number of candidates in reserve.

THOUGHT STARTERS

- Is there a high turnover of staff in your organization?

- What led to past recruitment mistakes?

- What is your own experience of being a candidate in the recruitment process?

FOR MORE INFORMATION

Books:

Ahlrichs, Nancy. *Competing for Talent: Key Recruitment & Retention Strategies for Becoming an Employer*. Palo Alto, CA: Davies-Black Publishing, 2000.

DeCenzo, David A., and Stephen P. Robbins. *Fundamentals of Human Resource Management*. 8th ed. Hoboken, NJ: Wiley, 2005.

Roberts, Gareth. *Recruitment and Selection: a competency approach*. New York: Beekman, 2000.

Rosenberg, Deanne. *Managers' Guide to Hiring the Best Person for Every Job*. New York: Wiley, 2000.

Shreyer, Ray, et al. *Recruit and Retain the Best*. Waupaca, WI: Impact Publications, 2000.

Sims, Ronald R. *Organizational Success through Effective Human Resources Management*. Westport, CO: Quorum Books, 2002.

See also:
✔ Preparing and Using Job Descriptions (pp. 486–487)

DOS AND DON'TS

DO

- Take the opportunity to review whether there is a job to be filled.
- Have a clear idea of who you are looking for.
- Use assistance from at least one other person.
- Assess the market before advertising.

DON'T

- Don't expose your organization to charges of discrimination.
- Don't forget that the recruitment process has public relations implications.

"One of the qualities I always seek in marketing people is curiosity."   Raoul Pinnell

Preparing and Using Job Descriptions

CHECKLIST

This checklist provides guidance for anyone wishing to write a job description or update an existing one.

A job description gives an overview of the purpose of a job, what it contributes to the organization's aims and objectives, how it fits into the overall corporate structure, and, perhaps most importantly, what its main duties, responsibilities, and reporting lines are.

A well-written job description gives the jobholder and immediate line manager a clear overall view of the position, and the human resources department a recruitment tool to help match applicants with the skills, experience, and competencies required in the job. Job descriptions also form a useful basis upon which to carry out performance appraisals, job evaluation, and job grading, and can help identify the duplication or absence of particular functions or activities across the organization. It is important that the descriptions are structured to allow flexibility and forestall "That's not in my job description!" situations.

With constant change now a fact of life in the work world, job descriptions get out of date rapidly and must be revised regularly to reflect current practice.

DEFINITION

A job description is a structured and factual statement of a job's functions and objectives. It should define the boundaries of the jobholder's authority and include the job title, department, job site, and reporting lines.

ADVANTAGES

Job descriptions:
- clarify duties and responsibilities;
- are useful in recruiting staff;
- help identify gaps or duplication in the company;
- provide an overview of the functions and activities undertaken by the department or organization.

DISADVANTAGES

Job descriptions:
- can create a "That's not in my job description!" environment if they are too restrictive;
- need regular updating.

ACTION CHECKLIST

✔ 1. Inform Staff of the Reasons For Reviewing And Amending Job Descriptions

When you are reviewing existing job descriptions, it is important that you keep staff fully informed. Explain that the exercise will be carried out with the full involvement of jobholders, the objectives being, for example, to:
- identify all interdepartmental working links;
- update existing job descriptions;
- help with job evaluation or job grading;
- give everyone a clear understanding of how the company is organized.

✔ 2. Assign Responsibility

Job descriptions have traditionally been prepared by the personnel department and agreed on with line managers and jobholders. However, many organizations are devolving this responsibility to line managers, with personnel offering guidance and checking for consistency and overlap. The following points should be taken into account:
- Are all key functions and activities listed in order of priority?
- Does each jobholder have a clear reporting line?
- Is there a balance between numbers of staff and any one manager?
- Are there too many reporting levels?
- Is there any overlap within departments or across the organization?
- Are all jobs grouped logically or are some scattered around?
- Are there any gaps or omissions in key functions?

✔ 3. Gather Information

The person responsible for compiling the job description should consider:
- what management wants from the job;
- what the jobholder thinks he or she is doing—and what he or she is actually doing;
- what other employees who interact with the jobholder professionally think he or she is doing—and ought to be doing.

You can most easily get this information from informal interviews. It is possible to use questionnaires, but it often takes longer to analyze written data than it does to interview people, and the results tend to be ambiguous.

✔ 4. Draft the Job Description

The job description should contain the following.

Basic information

Job title and department. The job title should be brief, descriptive, and clear. Remember that employees consider the status of people with similar job titles to be equal.

Reporting relationships. Give the job title of the person to whom the jobholder reports, and job title(s) and numbers of staff reporting to the jobholder.

Location. Specify the location of the job. If travel is involved, give clear and careful details.

Major functional relationships. Where appropriate, use an organizational chart to show how a job relates to other jobs and fits into the company's structure.

"It's good business for our people to have confidence that we will not lay them off just to help our profit short-term."

Ken Olsen

Principal purpose or objective of the job

This should be a short statement describing why the job exists, for example, a sales manager's objective might simply read, "making sure that sales targets are achieved."

Main duties/key tasks/key result areas

Key tasks or responsibilities are those that make a substantial contribution toward achieving the objectives of the job and the organization. They form the main part of the job. Ideally there should be no more than five or six main tasks. Some basic jobs may have only one or two main activities (for example, stocking shelves and working on the registers in a supermarket), though most may have several elements (bringing in new business, managing existing customers, managing staff, liaising with suppliers, etc.). Secondary duties and responsibilities should also be listed.

The description of each task should include three components:

- a "doing" verb highlighting the main activity (for example, to develop, design, implement, advise)
- the object of that activity (stock levels, existing suppliers, a new computer system)
- its purpose (to reduce costs, improve efficiency, generate new income)

An example of a task description incorporating these components might be "to advise on the selection and implementation of a new computer system to forge closer links with key account customers." Include outcomes ("to expand the existing customer base") in the task description, but not quantified targets. Targets are generally negotiated separately and are better incorporated into regular performance systems or reviews.

The key tasks are usually listed in order of importance or by other agreed criteria such as chronology, frequency of activity, or tasks related to a particular activity.

✔ 5. Update and Review

The job description must be kept up to date and should be examined at least:

- once a year when the jobholder is reviewed;
- whenever the job falls vacant, to ensure that the description still meets the department's requirements;
- after a new jobholder has been working for a few months, to take account of any significant changes in the duties assigned to the position.

THOUGHT STARTERS

- Do you know what's in your job description?

- Would you change your job description in any way?

- Is your job description up to date?

DOS AND DON'TS

DO
- Let staff know why job descriptions are being amended or updated.
- Involve the current jobholder.
- Check job descriptions in surrounding areas of work to ensure integration without duplication.
- Update the job description regularly.

DON'T
- Don't restrict the employee's initiative by writing the job description too narrowly.

FOR MORE INFORMATION

Book:
Wood, Robert, and Tim Payne. *Competency-Based Recruitment and Selection.* New York: Wiley, 1998.

Journal Articles:
Fondas, Nanette. "A Behavioral Job Description for Managers." *Organizational Dynamics* 21:1 (Summer 1992): 47–58.
John, Trevor. "Job profiles." *Training Officer* 29:3 (April 1993): 86.

Web sites:
HR Guide: **www.hr-guide.com**
HR.BLR.com: **http://hr.blr.com**

See also:
✔ Planning the Recruitment Process (pp. 484–485)

"Be nice to people on your way up because you'll meet 'em on your way down."

Wilson Mizner

Drawing Up a Contract of Employment

488

CHECKLIST

This checklist details the steps involved in drawing up a contract of employment. It is primarily aimed at new contracts, but many points will also be useful in modifying an existing contract. As with any legal document, it is essential that you seek professional advice before putting a contract into effect.

Legislation does not require that an organization have a formal written contract with its employees, but such a contract can prevent later disputes over terms and conditions, whereas oral agreements are often called into question.

DEFINITION

A contract of employment is a legally enforceable agreement, either oral or written, between an employer and an employee that defines terms and conditions to which both parties must adhere. Areas covered include job title, remuneration, vacation days and holidays, sick pay, location, mobility, and the period of employment. Extra clauses can be added that make a certain qualification or confidentiality a prerequisite of the job, restrain the employee after termination of employment, and so on.

ADVANTAGES

Having well-drafted contracts of employment means that:

- employees can be clear about their rights;
- the employer can avoid the costs associated with disputes over terms and conditions;
- the employer can justifiably terminate employment if an employee does not meet the contract's requirements.

DISADVANTAGES

There are no real disadvantages to contracts of employment. Writing a contract that is watertight while allowing both parties some flexibility is difficult. Contracts require resources to draw up and review, and if they are badly written they can do the organization more harm than good.

ACTION CHECKLIST

1. Analyze the Job to be Contracted

Look at the job description, if there is one, for information on what the job entails. Clauses in the contract must allow the employee to carry out required duties without restrictions. The position may require the person to have a professional qualification—would the person be allowed to continue in the job if the awarding body were to withdraw professional status?

2. Consider Future Plans and Objectives

Do you expect the work force to be cut back in the future? If so, a permanent contract may be inadvisable. An overly specific job title may be inappropriate if the employee might be transferred to a different department—a general title such as "administrative officer" offers more flexibility. If you have plans to open further work sites, you may need to incorporate a mobility clause to cover employees who will be required at times to work away from their usual workplace. Including such clauses helps the company ensure that its work force will adapt to future corporate needs and developments.

3. Look Back at Problems

The organization may have had problems with contracts of employment in the past. Problems often arise from the nature of a company's work: departing employees might take some customers with them, might have created intellectual property of which the ownership is in dispute, or might resist relocation. Such problems are exacerbated when a contractual statement is poorly drafted or lacking.

4. Gather Information and Confer with Colleagues

Try to obtain some sample contracts of employment used in comparable organizations, and research the literature on the current requirements of personnel legislation. Colleagues can offer good advice over what has and has not worked in the past, in both the current organization and others they may have worked in. Union representatives can identify potentially contentious issues. Consult your legal department, if your firm has one; if not, be prepared to go outside—incurring costs at this stage might well save you money in the long term.

5. Incorporate Written Particulars

Neither federal nor state laws require an employer to provide an employment contract to new employees. Nor are employers required to provide an agreement, laying out the particulars of the job. Nevertheless, many employers do provide such things, and employment contracts have become more common. If you're considering an employee contract or agreement, here are some particulars to include:

- the employer's and employee's names;
- the date the employment started and will end (if fixed term), or the period it is expected to last if temporary. Some employers insert an "at will" provision, basically saying that the employer or employee may end the agreement at any time;
- the rate of remuneration, or how it is calculated, and when it is paid;
- terms and conditions relating to hours of work and benefits accrued;

"It is but a truism that labor is most productive where its wages are largest. Poorly paid labor is inefficient labor, the world over."

Henry George

- the notice required to be given by both employee and employer to terminate employment;
- an option to terminate, without discrimination, if a permanent disability keeps the employee from performing the duties for which he or she was hired;
- any collective agreements that affect the terms and conditions of employment—for example, those negotiated by a labor union;
- the job title and job description;
- an item related to employees agreeing to work in the employer's best interest, and that the employee will not simultaneously work for another company in the same industry;
- a nondisclosure clause, which prohibits the employee from divulging company information to anyone outside the business;
- a stipulation about the ownership rights of any inventions, discoveries, or intellectual property developed while the employee is a member of your staff;
- indemnification: the employer needs protection from legal action, should your company hire someone who has violated proprietary rights agreements from a former employer;
- policies and procedures that would include the appropriate steps used by an employee to appeal a disciplinary action taken against them;
- the name of the person or proper outside authorities, namely state or federal agencies, who can be approached, and the procedure to follow regarding any grievance related to employment;
- details of the place(s) of work;
- the length of time and currency in which remuneration will be made if the employee is required to work abroad for a period of more than one month.

The handbook must be accessible—a copy should be given to every employee as part of orientation.

✔ 6. Consider Extra Clauses

Any number of clauses may be included in a contract of employment depending on the nature of the job and the needs of the organization.

- Relocation expenses: it may be appropriate to include a clause requiring employees to repay any relocation expenses if they terminate their employment within a certain period.
- Qualifications: if the jobholder is required to obtain or hold a certain educational or professional qualification by a certain date, define the qualification and the consequences of failing to have it. Employees funded to obtain a qualification may be required to repay the cost if they terminate their employment within a certain period.
- Travel: many jobs require travel to meet customers or clients; you may need to include a clause to cover this.
- Probation: if you have a probationary period for new employees, specify its length and provisions to terminate the contract at the end or an earlier date, or to extend the length of the probation.
- Restraints: in some circumstances you can use clauses known as restrictive covenants to restrain the activities of an employee once employment has terminated. A

common restraint is the prohibition on revealing trade secrets learned while working for a company. Some companies include a "non compete" clause, which restricts the employee from working for any of your company's competitors in the industry for a specified period of time after leaving your company.

✔ 7. Produce a Draft

Have it checked over, preferably by a legal professional. Make certain that all terms are clear and unambiguous and do not contravene any federal or state laws related to employee civil rights, wage and hour restrictions, health and safety regulations, worker's compensation laws, or family leave laws. Finally, make sure the contract or agreement doesn't restrict the employee from carrying out or further developing the role.

✔ 8. Review the Contract

Inform employees that the signed contract is legally binding. Generally, any subsequent changes to the contract or agreement must be confirmed in writing by both parties. Keep an eye on human resource literature for court cases and changes in legislation that may affect current or future contracts.

489

CHECKLIST

DOS AND DON'TS

DO
- Take time to prepare by examining the job and the future of the role.
- Get an idea of the law relating to contracts of employment, both federal and of the state in which you work.
- Use clear and unambiguous wording in the contract.

DON'T
- Don't cut corners—pay for legal advice if it is not available in-house.
- Don't try to restrain the employee too much—allow for some flexibility in the contract.

THOUGHT STARTERS
- Do you know what your contract of employment specifies?

- Have you ever had a problem with your contract of employment? What was it?

FOR MORE INFORMATION

Web sites:
FindLaw Employment Agreements:
www.techdeals.biz.findlaw.com
U.S. Department of Labor: **www.dol.gov**

'Make your bargain before beginning to plow.'   Anonymous

Implementing Job Evaluation

CHECKLIST

This checklist offers guidance on implementing job evaluation or job analysis in an organization. It does not explain the detail of the various approaches to job evaluation.

Job evaluation aims to:
- establish a fair and workable system of differentials between various jobs in the organization;
- eradicate anomalies between similar jobs in different parts of the organization;
- review the jobs that have changed over time;
- calculate the value of a job that is hard to fill.

Job evaluation is a specialized process usually handled by human resource specialists. Department managers and supervisors, however, have a large role to play in helping to define jobs and implementing the results.

DEFINITION

Job evaluation is concerned with the value of a job, especially in relation to other jobs in the organization. It is not about individual employees or their competence or potential, nor is it primarily about pay rates, although it may influence pay structures.

Simple approaches to job evaluation tend to be non-analytical. One such method selects a single job as the benchmark against which all others are compared, and weighs certain factors in every job against the benchmark. Another method is to define a grading structure first, then review job specifications within that framework and make any necessary adjustments.

Analytical approaches involve factor-weighting and point-scoring systems. Each job is examined on a number of key factors such as the size of the budget controlled, the number of supervised employees, the level of direct contact with customers, the technical expertise required, and the potential for affecting the organization's success. Points are awarded for each factor from a predetermined set of specifications (for example, 5 points if 4 or fewer employees report to the position, 12 points for 5–15 employees, etc.) and totaled to indicate the importance of the job. The total is then reviewed to take into account any additional factors that affect the value of the job.

ADVANTAGES

Formal job evaluation:
- results in a relatively objective and unbiased view of the value of jobs;
- gives companies a method to establish a pay scale based on the value of the jobs (rather than on the job title), with more valued jobs getting paid more; simultaneously, it allows the company a means to compare wages paid internally with those elsewhere, for similar work;

- avoids favoritism or patronage as they take no account of individual job-holders;
- irons out current discrepancies and helps to prevent future anomalies between jobs, which can cause bad feeling, resentment, and demands for parity from employees who feel undervalued;
- provides a transparent approach to valuing jobs once established.

DISADVANTAGES

- The process can be lengthy and costly to plan, introduce, and implement, especially if you take an analytical approach or hire an outside consulting firm to do it.
- There can be an emotional backlash if the program is not introduced with adequate consultation and communication.
- Evaluation requires adequate representation from all levels and functions in the organization—individuals should have no grounds for complaining that they feel misunderstood, unrepresented, or neglected.

ACTION CHECKLIST

1. Conduct Some Background Research

Before starting, think through all the implications of job evaluation and make sure that this is the route you wish to follow. If so, decide whether you are going to adopt an analytical or a non-analytical approach.
- Decide what you want job evaluation process to achieve (but keep in mind that it may bring other corporate issues to light).
- Consider whether there is an easier and more direct way of tackling this issue, especially if the inconsistencies between jobs in your company are minor, but make sure that any alternative solution is adequate.
- Try to find one or more colleagues in other organizations with experience of the process.
- If you are planning to use a detailed and analytical approach, research it thoroughly, talk to specialists, and read about it—this is not a route to be followed lightly.
- Once you have all the information, perform a cost-benefit analysis. If the benefits significantly outweigh the costs, move on to the next part of the checklist. If not, go back and think through more appropriate ways of achieving your objectives.

2. Decide on Your Approach

Based on the cost-benefit analysis, decide whether to bring in a consultant with an analytical process or to do what you can in-house, perhaps using a less complex methodology.

Plan the next steps carefully, considering essential details such as:
- whether job descriptions are all up to date or they need revision: they form a major element of job evaluation;
- who will be managing the process in-house, either as the prime mover or as the contact person for a consultant;
- how much time you can give this project;

- how much it will cost (job evaluation takes time and resources even if it is done in-house);
- whether you can afford it now, or whether it is preferable to wait and build it in as a major project in the coming year.

3. Communicate and Consult

Think carefully about what impression any announcement will give to staff. Damage control at the start is preferable to damage limitation later. Consider what employees might read into the introduction of job evaluation and address possible concerns.

Consult wherever it is appropriate. If you need to talk to unions at some stage, start now: sell the benefits and try to work toward an agreement that both sides can live with.

Communicate so all employees are clear about what is happening, why, when, with what aim, and who will be doing it.

4. Draw Up a Project Plan

Remember that there are three basic elements to the process of job evaluation:
- project design
- data collection
- data analysis

List and time all actions so you know the timeline for each, what preparation is needed for each, what depends on it, and what are the key milestones along the way.

Implementing job evaluation is a significant initiative; draw up a separate plan for managing change. Consider the implications:
- What sort of resistance are you likely to encounter?
- Which factors will help you and which are going to block you?
- Whom can you pick as change agents or champions to help spread the word?

5. Implement the Program

An experienced consultant can advise you on what has to be done and how to go about it. If you are paying for expertise, make sure you use it.

If you are handling the project in-house, stay on top of developments in the project and change management plans; if they were well considered at the planning stage, they should ultimately work.

6. Monitor the Program

After the lengthy process of design and implementation, be wary of the program taking on a life of its own and becoming rigid. As jobs evolve or change, their content will impact on your evaluation framework.

Maintain the program as existing jobs change and new ones are created. You may need a panel or team trained in job evaluation techniques to meet regularly to carry out reevaluations.

> **THOUGHT STARTERS**
> - Have there been changes in the nature, structure, and design of the jobs in your organization?
> - Are there people in your company who appear to have the same degree of responsibility but are paid differently?
> - Would you have sufficient time and resources to tackle job evaluation yourself?

FOR MORE INFORMATION

Books:
Armstrong, Michael, and Angela Baron. *Job Evaluation.* Dover, NH: Kogan Page, 2005.
Brannick, Michael T., Levine, Edward L. *Job Analysis: Methods, Research and Applications for Human Resource Managers in the New Millennium.* Thousand Oaks, CA: Corwin Press, 2001.
Brown, Mark Graham. *Keeping Score: Using the Right Metrics to Drive World Class Performance.* Productivity Inc., 1996.

Web sites:
HR Guide: **www.hr-guide.com**
HR.BLR.com: **http://hr.blr.com**

"The one thing I know through experience . . . is that people don't know why they come to work until they don't have to come to work."

H. Ross Perot

Implementing Performance-Related Pay (PRP)

DEFINITION

Performance-related pay (PRP) links additional payments to individual employees to appraisal of their performance. Every employee is set objectives at the beginning of the year. Depending on how well those targets have been met by the end of the year, the employee is awarded a sum of money that is paid on top of the next year's salary.

PRP is appropriate for both individuals and teams. This checklist concentrates on individual PRP.

ADVANTAGES

Relating pay to performance:

- enhances the performance of individual employees;
- creates a strong link between the company's goals and objectives and employees' goals and objectives;
- improves the retention and recruitment of staff—employees are seen to be rewarded for their efforts.

DISADVANTAGES

Performance-related pay:

- may promote competition among employees and undermine team culture;
- may award payments based on inconsistent methods and standards of assessment;
- requires substantial time and resources to administer.

ACTION CHECKLIST

1. Designate a Performance-related Pay Committee

The members of the PRP committee should be drawn from the levels of the organization that will be affected by the new system. Include staff or union representatives and at least one member from the personnel and accounting departments. The committee will manage the design and implementation of PRP. Appoint a coordinator to oversee the process.

2. Define the Scope and Coverage of PRP

Will all staff be eligible for PRP, or only a particular group—for example, middle to senior-level managers?

3. Gather Information

Find out whether members of the committee or other members of your staff have been involved in PRP before; if so, take advantage of their experience. The coordinator should do some background reading on how such systems operate in similar organizations. Remember that a system that works for one organization may not work for another.

4. Draw up a Plan

PRP should:

- be simple and easily understandable by all employees;
- have a clearly defined relationship between the results of the performance rating and the amounts awarded;
- be consistently applied to all staff within departments and throughout the organization;
- include an appeals procedure for employees dissatisfied with their appraisal;
- contain a system of review and evaluation.

Consider the following areas in drawing up the plan:

A method for defining performance measures. Two approaches are available:

- qualitative—based on criteria for individual jobs (such as job specifications) or more general criteria that cover all jobs within an organization (such as customer service, repeat business, or lack of complaints)
- quantifiable—based on targets (usually financial, but can use other measures such as increasing the number of service-users or reducing processing time for invoices)

The method used will depend on the jobs in question—a combination of both methods can be extremely effective. Limit the number of performance measures on which an employee can be evaluated: ten is generally the maximum, otherwise rating becomes complicated and time-consuming.

A scale for rating performance. Whatever method you use to define performance, you must produce a scale to rate it. Most rating systems use a 6-point scale, for example:

Exceptional
Very good
Good
Satisfactory
Poor
Unacceptable

Assign a numerical score to each division of the rating scale (for example, 6 = exceptional and 1 = unacceptable). Score each one of an individual's performance criteria or targets, and add to produce an overall performance rating.

A link between the rating and the pay award. Link the individual's rating directly to the percentage of the employee's salary to be awarded (for example, the award

"He that wants money, means, and content, is without three good friends."

William Shakespeare

for a performance assessment of 2 is 4 percent of salary). Do not make awards for anything less than good performance. Inform employees of their awards in person.

A timetable for appraisal. Line managers should meet with every employee they supervise throughout the year. At the beginning of the year, they should discuss and set criteria and agree on performance objectives. Regular reviews can be used to identify and overcome problems. At the end of the year, line managers can discuss performance and rate employees.

An example of such a timetable might be as follows.

Month 1	Initial meeting and setting of targets/objectives
Months 3 and 6	Performance reviews and identification of problems
Month 10 or 11	Final appraisal and rating
Month 12	Notification to employee of any award due

The first and final interviews should be formally documented, recording objectives and targets; one copy should be given to the employee and another kept on file. Do not discuss awards or ratings during the final meeting; you don't want it to turn into a pay negotiation session. Remember these meetings do not replace an employee's usual development/performance meetings, which are often held informally.

An appeals procedure. It is very important that employees be able seek redress if they feel they have been appraised improperly or unfairly. Let each member of staff know whom to contact if such a situation occurs. This should not be the same person who appraised them; the company's personnel officer is generally the most appropriate person.

✔ 5. Train Managers to Appraise Performance

Training of managers involved in setting targets and conducting appraisal interviews should:
- begin with the principles of PRP;
- cover in detail the ins and outs of the organization's PRP plan;
- coach them in negotiating with employees to arrive at appropriate goals and objectives;
- demonstrate how to conduct an effective appraisal interview and include role-play of performance interviews.

Don't attempt to cover everything in one session. Run refresher courses after PRP is operational, and remember to provide full training for new recruits.

✔ 6. Communicate PRP to All Staff

Use team briefings and individual discussions to spread information about PRP. Write a guide to the company's PRP plan and include it in the employee handbook. Provide the name of a PRP committee member whom an employee can contact for more information.

✔ 7. Pilot PRP

It may be advisable to concentrate initially on one department or level of management. You can use your experience from this pilot to improve the plan before implementing it more widely. Always start PRP at the beginning of your organization's financial year.

✔ 8. Review and Evaluate Your PRP Plan

The PRP committee should meet at the end of each financial year to review how well PRP is working. Obtain the views of employees and line managers to identify any problem areas. Do some managers feel unsure about setting objectives or conducting performance appraisals? Look at the award figures—are some managers being more lenient or more strict than others? Are some managers featuring in the appeals procedure more than others? Take into account any legislative changes that affect PRP. If the plan needs modifying, consult the staff or union representative before making changes and informing all staff.

Most importantly, decide whether PRP is achieving its objective of improving employee performance. If it isn't, decide whether you can improve your particular plan or whether you should replace it with an alternative reward system. If PRP is succeeding, don't rest on your laurels—keep reviewing and modifying it, and consider the possibility of expanding it to cover other departments or levels of staff.

DOS AND DON'TS

DO
- Design the most appropriate plan for your organization.
- Involve staff representatives or union officials.
- Communicate the advantages of PRP.
- Clearly link objectives, effort, and reward.
- Train all staff involved in appraisal.
- Continually look for improvements.

DON'T
- Don't make the plan too complicated.
- Don't allow inconsistencies between managers in appraising performance and applying awards.

THOUGHT STARTERS
- Do monetary incentives motivate employees?

- What are the performance objectives for your organization as a whole?

FOR MORE INFORMATION

Book:
Brown, Duncan, and Michael Armstrong. *Strategic Reward: How Organizations Add Value Through Reward.* Dover, NH: Kogan Page, 2006.

'The one thing I know through experience . . . is that people don't know why they come to work until they don't have to come to work.'
H. Ross Perot

Introducing an Equal Opportunities Policy

CHECKLIST

This checklist provides managers with the basis for introducing an equal opportunities policy. Such a policy is a moral, legal, and business imperative for all line managers.

DEFINITION

An equal opportunities policy is a commitment by an organization to the development of procedures and practices that provide genuine equality of opportunity for all employees, regardless of sex, ethnic origin, age, religion, marital status, or disability. Its reach extends beyond strict compliance with the law and ensures the effective use of all human resources within the organization.

ADVANTAGES

- The ability to attract people with new ways of thinking, leading to a more diverse work force with a richer mix of skills and experience.
- The ability to attract the best talent.
- A more stable work force that retains the best people by seeing that their needs are fully met.
- An improved reputation marking the company as one with high ethical standards.

DISADVANTAGES

- A dissatisfied work force if raised expectations are not met in full.
- Higher recruitment and monitoring costs.
- Resentment or backlash among previously privileged groups in the work force.

ACTION CHECKLIST

1. Secure the Commitment of Top Management

Demonstrate that the organization is serious about equal opportunities by giving overall responsibility to a senior manager, preferably at board level.

2. Designate an Equal Opportunities Officer

Appoint an equal opportunities officer to introduce and implement the policy and coordinate actions on a day-to-day basis. Define the assignment and level of responsibility clearly, even if the position is not full-time.

3. Establish a Working Party to Provide Employee Input

Set up a working party drawn from representative groups within the organization, including union or staff associations, management, human relations, women, ethnic minority groups, and disabled staff members. Make it clear that the group is not a lobbying point for special interest groups.

4. Review Policies of Other Organizations

Obtain copies of the equal opportunities policies of other organizations in your sector. Draw on them to prepare a first draft of your own policy. Include only objectives and commitments that are appropriate to your culture and attainable within a realistic time scale.

6. Conduct an Equality Audit

Conduct a workplace audit to provide information about the composition of the work force in relation to gender, race, age, and disability, and use the information as a baseline for action. If the information is not already held in personnel records, carry out an employment survey, making it clear that any information collected will be used only for equal opportunity purposes. Review how many women and men you employ: in total, by grade and salary, by hours of work, by marital/family status, by age, and by ethnic origin. Use this information to identify existing patterns of employment and under-representation.

7. Draw Up a Plan of Action

Use the information captured by the audit to identify the areas of the organization that need attention. Decide whether you will require positive action. At a minimum, the program needs to cover recruitment, selection, orientation, promotion, flexible working, and assistance for careers and training.

8. Set Targets for Under-Represented Groups

Set targets that are challenging enough to stretch the organization to change but are realistic enough to show existing employees they have a fair chance of promotion.

9. Provide Training

Provide specific equal opportunities training, first to priority groups such as senior executives, personnel specialists, recruiters, reception staff, and other gatekeepers. Where applicable, these groups should then transmit training through line managers to all employees.

10. Offer Flexible Working Arrangements

Assume that all jobs can be done on a flexible basis unless there is a clear occupational requirement for a full-time employee. Make sure that flexibility in hours is available to all employees.

11. Review Job Descriptions

Rewrite job descriptions as positions become vacant. Be objective and base them on the organization's needs, not on the needs or preferences of the person currently doing the job.

"We must earn true respect and equal rights from men by accepting responsibility."

Amelia Earhart

 12. Review Selection and Recruitment Practices

Short-list candidates only on the basis of whether they meet essential skills and knowledge requirements of the job, not on their personal characteristics. Remove personal details from applications before they are reviewed.

 13. Adopt Family-Friendly Policies

Offer plans for parental leave, childcare, and flexible working to all employees.

 14. Monitor Employees' Qualifications and Training Needs

Monitor take-up of training among different categories and grades of employee. Where necessary, make special training available for employees from groups that have traditionally been discriminated against.

 15. Offer Comparable Training Programs at All Levels

Your training programs should provide comparable on- and off-the-job training for all employees at every level. Distinguish between training to improve job performance and training to acquire new skills. Let employees know the link between acquiring new skills and the possibility of being regraded.

 16. Establish a Grievance Procedure

Introduce a grievance procedure that employees can use to pursue allegations of sex discrimination, harassment, or equal pay. The procedure should be written and accessible; publicize it widely among staff. Deal promptly and openly with allegations, and assume all allegations are well founded while they are under investigation.

 17. Monitor and Review Procedures

Your equality audit will give details only of your current work force. Set up monitoring systems to capture details of all job applicants and those recruited; establish performance indicators to review progress against your targets and action plan. Monitor internal and external appointments by gender and ethnic origin: you may also want to include age.

18. Communicate Policies and Practices

Send a copy of the policy to potential and actual applicants, new recruits, and current employees. Use every opportunity to publicize the policy, and include a clear statement of it in the company literature.

GLOSSARY OF TERMS

Affirmative action involves taking action to promote equality of opportunity in gaining access to a job or other opportunity for a previously disadvantaged group (for example, special training to allow ethnic minorities to compete on more equal terms for a particular type or level of work such as management).

Direct racial discrimination occurs if a person is unfavorably treated on racial grounds. These are widely defined to include color, ethnic or national origin, race, or nationality.

Direct sex discrimination occurs if a person is treated unfavorably on the basis of his or her gender.

Indirect racial discrimination occurs when a requirement or condition is applied that only a smaller proportion of people in some racial groups can meet.

Indirect sex discrimination occurs when a requirement or condition is applied that a smaller proportion of one gender can meet than the other can.

Positive discrimination means discriminating in favor of someone from a previously disadvantaged group, for example, a woman or someone of a particular ethnic origin.

Quotas are a fixed percentage of positions reserved for a particular group.

Targets are forecasts of the percentage of ethnic minority, women, or disabled employees that employers realistically aim to have by a specific date.

DOS AND DON'TS

DO
- Consult employees and union representatives regularly.
- Use positive action measures to meet your equality targets.
- Monitor and review progress annually against the targets and consider whether positive action is needed.
- Beware of overt and inadvertent bias in interview techniques.

DON'T
- Don't set unrealistically high targets.
- Don't fall into the trap of positive discrimination when hiring.
- Don't target flexible working hours and childcare programs solely at women.

FOR MORE INFORMATION

Book:
Clements, Phil, and Tony Spinks. *The Equal Opportunities Guide: How to Deal with Everyday Issues of Unfairness.* 3rd ed. Dover, NH: Kogan Page, 2000.

Web site:
U.S. Equal Employment Opportunity Commission: **www.eeoc.gov**

"Inequality is not only about income, where real poverty has grown, it is about self-esteem."

Will Hutton

Implementing a Diversity Management Program

CHECKLIST

This checklist provides a framework for setting up a diversity management program in an organization. It is aimed at managers in all areas and at all levels.

DEFINITION

Diversity encompasses any sort of difference between two or more people in race, age, gender, sexual orientation, disability, geographic origin, family status, education, social background—in fact, any factor that can affect workplace relationships and achievement. Diversity management involves the implementation of strategies that knit a network of varied individuals together into a dynamic work force.

The approach goes beyond that of equal opportunities in that it recognizes an infinite number of differences between people and focuses on the individual rather than various disadvantaged groups.

ADVANTAGES

- A diversity management program enables an organization to keep pace with social and demographic changes such as increasing numbers of female, ethnic minority, and older workers in the labor market.
- Employee recognition can lead to empowerment, motivation, and commitment, and therefore to competitive advantage for the organization.
- Since diversity management leads employees to feel more valued and more content, it reduces staff turnover, thus reducing recruitment and training costs.
- A diverse work force is better equipped to serve a diverse customer base and diverse markets, and facilitates entry into the global marketplace.
- Diversity management can create a flexible work force, increasing productivity.

DISADVANTAGES

- If handled insensitively, a diversity management program may invade employee privacy.
- Implementation of a diversity management program may be expensive in the short term.
- Deep-seated prejudices may be brought into the open, causing short-term tension.
- Conflict and ill-feeling may result from a poorly handled program.

ACTION CHECKLIST

1. Gain Support from Top Management

Approach the directors and managers in your organization and convince them of the advantages of diversity management. Present both the business and social cases for a diversity initiative. If necessary, conduct high-level diversity awareness training to develop the commitment of key decision-makers.

2. Commit Financial and Human Resources

Don't underestimate the time and money needed. Take a long view—the program will spread over years, not months. At an early stage identify as many facilitators as possible who can act as change agents to lead the initiative.

3. Set Appropriate Goals

Decide what you want the program to achieve and set goals accordingly. You may want to use consultation, brainstorming, benchmarking, or literature reviews to help you establish goals. Goals should be specific, measurable, and achievable. For example:

- to increase the proportion of women in the work force to 50 percent;
- to enable parents to take time off to care for sick children;
- to draw from a wider geographical area in recruitment.

4. Establish Current Levels of Diversity Management in Your organization

Plan and conduct a diversity audit to gauge existing levels of diversity management. Assess both qualitative and quantitative evidence, focusing on people, processes, and strategies.

Find out:

- what differences affect the ability of individuals to achieve their working potential in your organization;
- to what extent these differences create disadvantages or advantages for employees;
- how the procedures and strategies of the organization affect different groups of employees.

Data-gathering methods might include:

- questionnaires—design these with your target audience in mind, and guarantee respondents anonymity and privacy;
- individual and group interviews—consider who should conduct these and how to create an informal and frank atmosphere;
- focus group discussions—you could, for example, talk to groups of female, disabled, older employees, or employees of color;
- unobtrusive observation—a discreet walk around the workplace can be very revealing;
- document surveys—examine written procedures, personnel records, customer complaints, publicity material, and any other documentary evidence in the company's files;
- benchmarking—look in organizations similar to your own for examples of best practice to follow and bad practice to avoid.

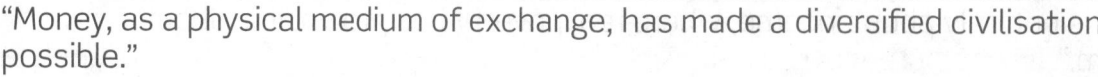

"Money, as a physical medium of exchange, has made a diversified civilisation possible."

Josiah Stamp

5. Conduct a Gap Analysis

Review the audit results to establish how great the difference is between your current position and your goals.

6. Identify Areas That Need Change

Work out the forms of action that are required to achieve your goals. You may need to make changes to:

- processes—for example, revising your recruitment procedure;
- working arrangements—for example, introducing flextime, childcare facilities, or time off for family duties;
- attitudes—for example, combating intercultural prejudice and improving intercultural communication;
- physical environment—for example, creating better access for disabled employees and customers.

7. Write a Diversity Policy

Use these broad change ideas together with your diversity goals to compile a concise written diversity policy. The policy should include:

- a definition of diversity;
- reasons why it is important;
- the goals of the diversity management program;
- the ways in which the goals will be achieved.

Communicate the policy to employees and all stakeholders. Include it in the staff handbook, and, if you have one, on the company intranet.

8. Compile a Diversity Action Plan

Spell out the finer details of the program, specifying how the planned changes will be brought about. Hold brainstorming sessions to produce ideas for action, then write an implementation plan to coordinate and timetable the actions to be taken. Make sure the plan includes regular reviews.

9. Set the Program in Motion

Communicate the plan to employees and put it into action. Appoint program coordinators and publicize their role.

10. Monitor and Review

Monitor the program over 12 months and adjust as necessary. Where problems occur, review the policy and decide whether it should be amended.

11. Establish an Ongoing Program

Schedule an ongoing diversity program for the long term. Allow for the program to be fluid and to change as the organization's internal and external contexts change. Diversity management should become a natural part of everyday life.

497

CHECKLIST

DOS AND DON'TS

DO

- Communicate at all stages of the program. Keep employees, managers, customers, shareholders, and other stakeholders informed: their support is vital to success.
- Involve everyone. This is not an issue for only the personnel department or senior managers: it should concern people throughout the organization.
- Use established change management processes to implement the program.
- Look to the long term. Changes involving attitudes don't happen overnight, and you should expect the program to last for years rather than weeks or months.
- Be prepared to invest money, time, and resources to achieve your goals.

DON'T

- Don't confuse equal opportunities with diversity management. The equal opportunity approach should form a part of any diversity initiative, but the program should go far beyond traditional equal opportunity issues.
- Don't design diversity goals and policies for "them." Think instead in terms of "us."

THOUGHT STARTERS

- List ten differences between yourself and a close colleague. Consider how these differences affect your working life.

- In what ways, if any, does your organization cater to these differences?

- Could your working arrangements, working environment, company policies, and procedures be improved to reduce any negative effects caused by these differences?

- Do you feel respected as an individual in your workplace? Is this respect evident from all levels of the organization?

FOR MORE INFORMATION

Books:
Hubbard, Edward E. *Diversity Scorecard: Evaluating the Impact of Diversity on Organizational Performance.* Burlington, MA: Elsevier Butterworth-Heinemann, 2004.
Loden, Marilyn. *Implementing Diversity: Best Practices for Making Diversity Work in Your Organization.* New York: McGraw-Hill, 1995.

Journal Article:
Thomas, David A. "Diversity as a Strategy." *Harvard Business Review* 82:9 (September 2004): 98–108.

Web sites:
National Association for Diversity Management:
www.nadm.org
U.S. Equal Employment Opportunity Commission:
www.eeoc.gov

Attracting and Retaining People Reentering the Workplace

CHECKLIST

This checklist is an introduction for organizations seeking to attract and retain people returning to the workplace after a prolonged absence.

Women reentering the workplace will continue to make up a large percentage of new entrants into the labor force over the next decade. From that standpoint, organizations will need to develop a range of policies in order to maximize the benefits that all existing and future employees can bring. So, while this actionlist deals more specifically with women, many of the same issues and policy solutions would also be applicable to men, regardless of the reason for their absence from the workforce.

DEFINITION

"People reentering the workplace" refers, in general, to anyone returning to paid employment whether full-time or part-time, after a substantial period away from work.

ADVANTAGES

- You can select from a wider pool of talent at a time of continuing skill shortages.
- Many of these people have maturity and experience, and are likely to be committed and motivated.
- They are likely to be relatively settled and to offer stability: recruitment costs are lower and retention rates higher.
- Women specifically are likely to have good organizational and time-management skills and be well focused.
- Women are especially skilled at multitasking, something many men find difficult.

DISADVANTAGES

- There may be initial costs to update skills or provide confidence-building measures.
- For people with special family or personal circumstances you may wish to offer flexible working practices that could be difficult to extend to all employees.

ACTION CHECKLIST

1. Develop a Broad Human Resources Corporate Policy

Set out clear policies on recruiting and employing a variety of people, in accordance with federal Equal Employment Opportunity (EEO) laws. You may want to develop a subsection especially dealing with those returning to employment after a prolonged absence. With women, it might be because of caring for family, but for women and men alike, there are many other issues involved in having substantial breaks in an employment history. Where possible, try to obtain examples of comparable organizations' policies; learn from their experiences and those of people in your own organization. Emphasize that the policy is a way of meeting human resource needs and retaining specialist skills, and secure support for it at the highest management level. Communicate the policy to managers, then define and set up the mechanisms for implementing it.

2. Establish a Profile of Those Reentering Your Workforce

Establish a profile of the jobs, levels, and occupations of women and men reentering your own workforce after a substantial break in employment. Use this as a benchmark and review these employees annually, as well as those hired subsequently.

3. Win Acceptance for this Type of Employee

Your corporate culture may not fully support this initiative. If there are attitudinal barriers among your staff against employing this type of individual, provide training in equal opportunities (if it is not already available).

4. Imaginatively Review Working Practices

Investigate ways of introducing more flexible hours and flexible working practices to enable anyone with pronounced scheduling issues (for example, family needs, medical appointments, parole and probation meetings) to combine paid employment and other responsibilities: part-time, flextime, job sharing, telecommuting. Make flextime available to all employees, if possible.

5. Improve Employees' Access to Childcare

Only large corporations can offer onsite subsidized childcare, but you can actively help employees to find good-quality care elsewhere. Consider sharing day care facilities with other local employers, reserving a certain number of slots at private nurseries, or offering childcare vouchers. Don't neglect after-school care for older children: could you become a partner in local after-school and Boys & Girls Clubs or church programs, for example?

6. Provide Parental and Caregiver Leave

Modify existing flextime and extended leave programs to take into account the needs of caregivers, whether for children or other family members. Provide a specific period of paid parental leave, with the opportunity for employees to take longer periods of unpaid leave.

7. Provide Appropriate Training

Offer the opportunity for orientation to all those reentering the workforce to include confidence building and skills updating. Once they are working, provide training to enable these employees to develop and qualify

---

"In politics if you want anything said, ask a man. If you want anything done, ask a woman."

Margaret Thatcher

for promotion. Consider family responsibilities when arranging training times. Early morning and evening meetings are often difficult for women, especially single mothers with school-aged children.

8. Examine Your Rules for Promotion

Make sure that the policies and procedures you adopt do not contravene federal and state EEO intentions (prohibiting discrimination based on race, color, religion, sex, national origin, or age).

9. Consider Extending Maternity Leave or Leave without Pay Provisions

Can you provide maternity benefits beyond the minimum to encourage current employees to return after a break? Offer reasonable maternity leave with the option of additional leave without pay for special circumstances without loss of seniority.

10. Set Up a "Stay In Touch" Initiative

Enable women on maternity leave and others with similar excused absences to follow developments at work. Provide a company contact person, and arrange regular phonecalls, mailings with copies of in-house newsletters, magazines, and other corporate communications such as departmental memos and e-mail. If appropriate, the arrangement could involve some

telecommuting work, and you might consider allowing company computer equipment to be used outside the office for this purpose.

THOUGHT STARTERS
- Are you a person who has experienced a long career absence?
- How did your organization help you?
- What more could have been done?

FOR MORE INFORMATION

Web sites:
Equal Employment Opportunity Commission:
www.eeoc.gov
Office of Personnel Management:
www.opm.gov/wrkfam/index.htm

See also:
✔ Managing Staff Turnover and Retention (pp. 454–455)

499

CHECKLIST

"For a woman to attain a high level in a male-dominated profession, she has to work twice as hard and/or be twice as smart."
Elizabeth MacKay

Setting Up a Suggestion Box

500

CHECKLIST

CHECKLIST

This checklist provides guidance for anyone setting up a suggestion box in their company or organization.

Suggestion boxes have been used by companies for a number of years as a way of gathering ideas from their employees to increase productivity, cut costs, and improve working conditions. A successful program has many positive effects: the most important is that employees believe that management cares and listens to them. Implementing a successful suggestion program is not an easy process. It requires careful planning, involving much staff time. A suggestion box should be regarded not as an alternative to regular communication and hands-on management, but as a supplement to them.

DEFINITION

A suggestion program is a planned procedure that enables employees to make known their ideas for improving any aspect of work, from cost savings and operational improvements to new product ideas and better customer service, and that may reward them for their initiative if their suggestions are implemented.

ADVANTAGES

Setting up an employee suggestion box can:
- lead to a reduction in costs and greater efficiency;
- encourage employee involvement, improving morale and motivation;
- help foster an environment in which creativity and innovation can flourish;
- enable employees at ground level (who can often see problems and solutions that management do not) to be heard.

DISADVANTAGES
- Suggestion programs need constant management to be effective.

ACTION CHECKLIST

 1. Designate a Suggestion Box Committee

The suggestion box committee provides input from its conception and helps manage the program. Committee members should represent all levels of the organization. Appoint a coordinator to oversee the project; this need not necessarily be someone from senior management, but should be someone with project management experience who commands respect and can get things done.

 2. Identify Alternative Plans

Ascertain whether any members of the committee have had experience with suggestion programs, and if

so make use of it. The coordinator should, if possible, undertake a literature search to find comparable case studies (remember, however, that a program that worked for one firm may not work for another). A small organization, for example, may not require a formal program at all if employees can communicate ideas directly and easily to the relevant person.

3. Draw Up a Plan

Plan the program, taking into account examples of other suggestion programs and the characteristics of your own organization. Include the following:
- Name of the program—the program should be given a name that will make it instantly recognizable to employees. Design a logo for the program that can be used for posters, leaflets, and suggestion forms.
- Length of program—running a program for set periods of time throughout the year allows you to gear publicity to specific startup dates—it can be difficult to keep a continuous program fresh in the employees' minds. Ideas do not, however, occur only at certain times of the year, so depending on your business cycle and the availability of resources, it is probably advisable to implement a continuous program. Make sure you readvertise it periodically—for example, after Christmas shutdowns.
- Format for suggestions—keep it simple. Encourage contributors to describe their ideas, even complex, technical ideas, in simple language. Details can be filled in later. Position prominently marked suggestion boxes at convenient sites throughout the workplace. Alternatively, invite employees to submit their suggestions to a designated address on the company's intranet. Some programs require that suggestions be signed, and do not accept anonymous contributions.
- Evaluation of suggestions—evaluate the suggestions on a regular basis—for example, monthly. The committee should discuss individual suggestions and develop the most promising ones. It might be helpful to prepare guidelines for the evaluation process. Important factors include the benefits to the organization or department, ease of implementation, originality, and overall cost.

Some suggestions may propose changes in administrative or production procedures, affecting many staff. Consider what retraining or retooling may be required and how and when this might be implemented. In such cases, a cost-benefit analysis may be useful.

Consider any possible effects on external stakeholders such as customers or suppliers.

Send a brief thank-you note to all contributors, successful or not.
- Rewards/awards—monetary rewards or gifts can be given to suggesters. The amount can be linked to cost savings or improvements in efficiency or can be a standard sum for each successfully implemented suggestion.

You can also link the award to the type of suggestion. For example:
- production—methods for reducing costs or increasing efficiency;

- health and safety—ideas for improving health and safety in the workplace;
- environmental—suggestions to make the organization more environmentally friendly.

Consider an award that recognizes the initiative of employees who make a suggestion, whether it is implemented or not. If a number of sites are involved, a "Suggestion of the Year" award could be made that covers the whole organization.

4. Publicity

Publicize the program widely and include details in the staff handbook. Communicate improvements made as a result of successful suggestions. Effective methods include:

- posters and leaflets on bulletin boards and on the company intranet;
- articles in staff newsletters and magazines (include stories about winners);
- inclusion as part of the orientation of new staff.

The initial publicity for the program should communicate the advantages for the employees and dispel any apprehension they may have.

5. Run a Pilot

Conduct a small-scale pilot program. Review it for problems in administration and make any necessary modifications.

6. Implement the Program

Implement the full program. The coordinator should note any problems that occur in running the suggestion box so they can be remedied immediately.

7. Evaluate the Program

At the end of a set period, evaluate the program, looking out for such points as:

- the number and types of suggestions made;
- the number of suggestions taken up and implemented;
- financial savings achieved;
- increases in efficiency achieved;
- costs incurred;
- rewards/awards made;
- problems;
- feedback from employees.

If the program is under-used, investigate why this is the case.

The committee should discuss the evaluation and make any further modifications needed. Submit a report to management detailing the performance of the suggestion program.

The evaluation process should be carried out every year, and improvements and modifications continually made to the program.

DOS AND DON'TS

DO
- Publicize the program regularly.
- Aim to get maximum participation.
- Try to give feedback to contributors as soon as possible.
- Recognize every suggestion, even those that can't be implemented.

DON'T
- Don't undersell the advantages of the suggestion box to employees.
- Don't implement a program without piloting it first.

THOUGHT STARTERS
- How many clever ideas are lying dormant in employees' minds?
- Have you ever wanted to make a suggestion to improve efficiency? What did you do?
- What would encourage you to make a suggestion?
- What would deter you from making a suggestion?

FOR MORE INFORMATION

Book:
Bassford, Robert L., and Charles L. Martin. *Employee Suggestion Systems: Boosting Productivity and Profits (Fifty Minute Series)*. Normal, IL: Crisp Publications, 1997.

Journal Article:
"Suggestion Schemes Study," IDS Study, no. 752 (June 2003): whole issue.

Undertaking an Employee Attitude Survey

This checklist provides guidance for those who wish to undertake an employee attitude survey in their organization.

Employee attitude surveys are used by companies as a way of routinely or occasionally monitoring the views of their employees or of gauging the effect of a new policy. Surveys should not be carried out too often, perhaps no more frequently than every 18 months. Two very important parts of any such survey are to report the results back to employees and to act on those results.

DEFINITION

An employee attitude survey is a planned procedure that enables a company to learn its employees' opinions about a particular issue or the organization itself. The survey is usually carried out in order to be able to take employees' views into account in planning or to make changes that will benefit the firm and individuals alike.

ADVANTAGES

Employee attitude surveys:
- provide data that can be used in problem solving, planning, and decision-making;
- encourage employee involvement, improving morale and motivation;
- allow management to hear employees' opinions, of which they may not otherwise be aware;
- form an effective communication channel;
- act as a sounding board for corporate initiatives.

DISADVANTAGES

Such surveys:
- require a good deal of time to carry out and evaluate;
- incur significant costs in planning, implementation, and evaluation;
- can generate employee suspicion about hidden agendas or the "real" reasons behind the surveys.

ACTION CHECKLIST

1. Define Scope and Coverage

As precisely as you can, identify the subject on which employees' opinions are to be gathered. Be clear on how you will deal with their views once you know them. Bear in mind that a survey entitled, for example, "Introducing telecommuting" may give rise to all sorts of anxieties or expectations and think about how you might deal with these.

Decide who is to be included in the survey—all employees, one department or site, or one type of employee (for example, full-time permanent staff).

2. Identify an Administrator

Appoint an agency to run the survey. This may be your own personnel department if yours is large enough, or a special working party drawn from all levels of the company. If your firm lacks the necessary expertise internally, you can contract the work out to an external consultant; this will probably be more expensive, but it may help persuade staff that the process is impartial and the results will be acted on.

3. Select a Survey Method

Two principal survey methods are available:
- questionnaire—questionnaires that the employees fill in are particularly useful when a large number of people are to be surveyed and when answers to the questions can be framed "yes/no"
- face-to-face interview—these can be on an individual or a group basis. The interactive format allows you to probe attitudes in some depth. But interviews are time-consuming, are impractical for surveying large numbers of people, can suffer from inconsistencies, and can produce results that are difficult to quantify

The choice of method depends on the number of people to be surveyed, the type of information you need, and the resources that are available.

4. Determine Questions and Procedures

Formulate the questionnaire (or guidelines for interviewers, in the case of face-to-face meetings). Ask yourself the following questions:
- Are the questions clear and unambiguous?
- Will this take the employee a long time to complete?
- Do the questions cover the subject thoroughly?
- Will the information obtained be easy to analyze?
- Is confidentiality assured?

Make certain that the questions are not discriminatory in any way; take into account any likely problems with literacy or in understanding terminology.

Devising questionnaires and holding interviews are not tasks for the enthusiastic amateur. Don't be afraid to seek advice.

5. Pilot the Survey

Select a small number of employees to complete the questionnaire (or undertake an interview). Debrief them to see whether they had any problems completing the survey, ask them whether any of the questions were unclear or troublesome, and find out whether they would prefer to think about the issues at work or take the survey home. See whether the information you obtained is what you were looking for. If necessary, modify the questionnaire or provide extra training for the interviewers.

6. Explain the Purpose of the Survey

It is crucial to make sure that all employees who will be involved understand the reasons for the survey

---

"If you can't change your fate change your attitude."

Amy Tan

and the benefits they will gain from it. Sharing information is the best way to alleviate fears and increase participation. Depending on the nature of the exercise, you may want to explain to employees who are not involved why the survey is being carried out.

7. Implement the Survey

Distribute the questionnaires (or arrange for interviews to be held). Maintain impetus by condensing the time frame, allowing sufficient time for employees who are traveling or on vacation. Make help available to deal with questions or problems. Having employees return completed questionnaires to an outside agency will reinforce your commitment to confidentiality and impartiality.

8. Collate and Report Results

Avoid distrust and suspicion by communicating the results of the survey to both senior management and employees. It is usually advisable to summarize the results for employees, who may not want to read a lengthy document. Be sure to include action plans resulting from the survey. Benchmark the results externally, particularly in the case of regular surveys that monitor trends. (Remember, however, that the survey may be so specific that comparison is impossible.) Survey analysis is a specialist task, and you may wish to contract this to an outside agency.

9. Evaluate the Survey

Evaluate the survey questions and your method both quantitatively and qualitatively, looking, for example, at the response rate, the information obtained, and problems in administering the survey. Take the findings into account in planning and designing a follow-up or future surveys.

10. Follow Up

Consider undertaking a second survey once the plans of action have had time to take effect, to see whether the changes have made improvements. This is obviously unnecessary in cases where little or no action was called for in the original survey.

THOUGHT STARTERS

- Have you ever taken part in an employee attitude survey yourself? Did anything productive come from it?

- What would motivate you to complete an attitude questionnaire?

- What would discourage you from taking part in an attitude survey?

FOR MORE INFORMATION

Books:

Connolly, Paul M., and Kathleen Groll Connolly. *Employee Opinion Questionnaires.* San Francisco, CA: Pfeiffer, 2005.

Smith, Frank J. *Organizational Surveys: The Diagnosis and Betterment of Organizations Through Their Members.* Mahwah, NJ: Lawrence Erlbaum Associates, 2003.

Journal Articles:

Morrel-Samuels, Palmer. "Getting the Truth into Workplace Surveys." *Harvard Business Review* 80:2 (February 2002).

Orpen, Christopher. "Our Survey Said." *Chartered Secretary* (January 1998): 29–30.

503

CHECKLIST

DOS AND DON'TS

DO
- Benchmark your employee survey with employee surveys undertaken in other organizations if possible.
- Pilot the survey to test it out before full implementation.
- Report the results of the survey and plans of action to all employees.
- Note any problems in administering the survey so you can do better next time.

DON'T
- Don't use the survey for a hidden agenda.
- Don't implement the survey without careful planning.

"Your attitude determines your altitude."   Stephen Covey

Setting Up Childcare Policies

CHECKLIST

This checklist provides guidance for those responsible for the implementation of a childcare policy within an organization. It focuses on the general principles and considerations involved.

The provision of help with childcare is increasingly viewed as a valuable benefit by employees, as it assists them in balancing work and domestic responsibilities. On the employer's side, childcare is seen as a means of retaining staff and contributing towards equal opportunities objectives.

DEFINITION

A childcare policy is a voluntary program put into practice by an employer to provide, or to help to provide, care for employees' children during working hours. Such a policy allows primary caregivers to work despite childcare responsibilities. Care is available for children of various ages—all day programs for younger children, after-school care for older ones. To comply with equal opportunities legislation, childcare provision has to be made available to both male and female employees.

ADVANTAGES

Providing childcare:

- enables experienced and skilled employees to return to or continue in work, reducing recruitment and training costs;
- attracts a wider range of applicants for vacant positions;
- enhances the firm's reputation as a caring and employee-friendly organization;
- has positive tax implications (tax credits as well as deductions) for both the corporation and the employee.

Buying part of the capacity at local daycare centers:

- eliminates startup costs for employers;
- avoids the responsibility of managing a daycare center.

Childcare allowances:

- cost much less than paying for an onsite daycare center;
- can be used for any qualified daycare center in the parents' local area;
- allow parents to choose the form and location of childcare they prefer.

Employers frequently offer childcare as part of a "cafeteria" benefits plan, whereby employees choose from a list of benefit options, including health care, for which they receive a lump sum allowance each year. The sum does not cover all possible benefits, so the employee must choose from a "menu." This type of plan has a tax advantage over other types of allowances or vouchers, in that the cost for daycare is deducted from employees' wages before taxes are calculated.

Childcare vouchers:

- can be used in much the same way as an allowance or "co-pay" to purchase childcare from qualified providers;
- can be cashed only in exchange for childcare;
- can be used in the parents' local area.

like the other options, use of vouchers also qualifies the employer and employee for tax credits and deductions. Be sure to consult your tax advisor about the best options.

Workplace daycare centers:

- allow parents access to their children at lunchtimes or in emergencies;
- offer a variety of tax benefits (like other daycare options), depending on how the company and the employee work out the details of the cost for the daycare services;
- can provide a beneficial environment for children.

DISADVANTAGES

- If there is no "cafeteria" plan for benefits in place, employees without children may feel resentful of benefits for which they are ineligible.
- Buying part of the capacity at selected local daycare centers can be expensive for the company and may be considered a taxable benefit to the employee; while not as costly as building your own center, providing this benefit to employees will be an added expense, against which you must weigh the advantages.
- It may not be conveniently located for all families.

Childcare allowances:

- may be taxable benefits for employees, unless the allowance is part of a larger "cafeteria" style benefits plan;
- require administration.

Childcare vouchers:

- are of limited usefulness if recipients live in areas with inadequate childcare facilities.

Workplace daycare centers:

- are expensive to set up and run;
- must meet state and local licensing regulations and health codes on an annual basis;
- do not suit parents who don't wish, or find it impossible, to commute with their children to work every day;
- require the allocation of space in the company's own building or nearby, which may prove costly.

ACTION CHECKLIST

1. Examine the Organization's Short- and Long-term Needs

Will a childcare policy benefit the organization in the long term, justifying high initial costs? Is there a demand for a childcare policy?

2. Obtain Management Commitment and Appoint a Project Team

Without strong commitment from the top, childcare policy has little chance of success. Establish who will be responsible for implementing and managing the policy. This is important; the implementation of a childcare policy is a long-term commitment and quality is essential. Consequently the individuals involved must be prepared to be project champions. Assemble a project team to collect and evaluate information and help formulate policy. Include a member of the human resources department.

"My parents . . . gave me the biggest gift a parent can give a child: Confidence."

Elizabeth MacKay

3. Identify the Policy Options

Research the implications of each policy option, including costs, legal implications and local regulations, which options are workable, within a reasonable distance from the workplace, and where your employees live in relation to the workplace.

4. Consult Employees

Present the most practical policy options to employees and get their feedback. Which policy would they prefer, and why?

5. Formulate Policy

Taking the views of employees and the requirements and preferences of the firm into account, choose one or a combination of the options.

6. Draw up a Business Plan Detailing Policy

Set a timeframe for project development, with a budget for setup and ongoing costs. Make sure that the company is adhering to all the laws and regulations that apply, and keep relevant organizations informed of the implementation of the policy. The plan should detail the scope of services provided, as well as the costs to employees, the company contribution, and the hours of coverage available under the plan.

7. Launch the Program

Inform employees of the final policy. Once the program is under way, allow time for parents to adjust to the service and for participation to increase.

8. Review the Program

Evaluate and monitor standards continuously to ensure that childcare policies meet the needs of the organization, the employees, and their children.

GLOSSARY OF TERMS

Childcare allowances are paid directly to individual employees in the form of cash payments or are placed in a childcare fund.

Childcare vouchers are vouchers that are given to employees to pay for any form of childcare they choose. The provider then redeems them from the issuer at face value.

Flexible working means that employees can choose working hours that deviate from the nine-to-five norm. Options include flexible working hours, term-time working, a compressed work week (like four 10-hour days), job sharing, voluntary part-time employment, and "comp" time, where employees who work—but aren't paid for—overtime, take the same number of hours later, when the schedule is less busy.

After-school provision is available for children awaiting a ride home with parents whose work day is longer than the school day. Generally, these services are provided by non-profit community organizations, including churches, YMCA, YWCA, and Boys & Girls Club. The cost to parents for these services is minimal, and is not usually covered by employers.

Purchased places in daycare enables employers to provide their employees with guaranteed places for their children in local daycare facilities. In some cases the costs are reimbursed by the firm, in others they are passed on to the employee.

Workplace daycare is usually onsite or located in nearby premises provided by the employer. It can be run in-house or by a contractor who specializes in childcare. Some organizations work in partnership with other firms to provide these facilities, sharing the costs and management responsibilities.

FOR MORE INFORMATION

Book:
Rosenbloom, Jerry S. *The Handbook of Employee Benefits.* 5th ed. New York: McGraw Hill Professional Publishing, 2005.

Web site:
United States Department of Health and Human Services: **www.hhs.gov**

505

CHECKLIST

Setting Up a Grievance Procedure

CHECKLIST

This checklist provides guidance for those wishing to implement a grievance procedure in their organization.

Many grievances are too complex to be settled by a single meeting. A thorough grievance procedure goes further by providing a process, involving more than one level of management, through which the employer and employee can reach a mutually agreed conclusion to the problem. Settling grievances quickly and fairly means they do not fester and grow.

DEFINITION

A grievance procedure provides an employee with a hierarchical administrative structure for presenting and settling a grievance at work. The procedure defines:

- the type of grievance it covers;
- the individuals responsible at each stage;
- the presentation and documentation of a grievance;
- the time limits by which the grievance must be presented and dealt with at each stage.

ADVANTAGES

By implementing a grievance procedure, an organization:

- complies with, and sometimes surpasses, the requirements of employment legislation;
- can prevent a minor grievance from becoming a major problem;
- conveys a caring attitude toward its employees.

DISADVANTAGES

There are no real disadvantages to implementing a grievance procedure, but remember that such a procedure:

- requires time and resources to be effective;
- can deter an employee from presenting a grievance if it is too formal.

ACTION CHECKLIST

1. Define the Terms of Reference

Decide which types of grievance the procedure will cover. Often, grievance procedures in such areas as sexual harassment, racial discrimination, intimidation or violence, and collective disputes have their own process for settlement. Identify at whom the procedure is aimed and the levels of management that will be involved in settling grievances.

2. Draw Up the Procedure

Consult with other members of the organization, including union representatives, to devise a procedure. Try to obtain copies of the procedures used in other companies. Write the procedure in simple, straightforward language that is easy to understand.

The procedure should contain the following:

Types of grievance.

List the types of grievances the process covers. Refer other types of complaint (such as sexual harassment) to the appropriate administrative or legal entities.

The stages involved.

Initially the complainant should be encouraged to have an informal meeting with the immediate superior to discuss the problem and see if they can work it out without a formal proceeding. If this does not work, the first stage of the procedure should be a formal meeting with the complainant and the immediate superior. Provide an alternative—the personnel manager, for example—in case the supervisor is party to the complaint. If so, the alternative should not be one of the higher levels of referral. Making the immediate supervisor the first point of contact serves to uphold his or her level of authority.

The number of stages in which the employee meets with progressively higher levels of management will depend on many factors, including the size of the organization. There should be at least two stages to provide a minimum of one level of appeal, but too many stages can make the process lengthy and deter some employees. Give the name, or preferably the job title, of the person responsible for grievances at each level.

In the event that the grievance cannot be settled internally, the last stage should be referral to an external body such as an independent arbitrator or conciliator.

Representation at meetings.

A colleague or union representative should be allowed to accompany or represent the aggrieved at each meeting if desired. Specify at what stage the employee is entitled to representation—this can depend on the situation and the relationship between management and unions. The procedure represents the formal acceptance by management of the employee's representative as an equal partner in trying to settle the grievance.

Time limits.

Realistic time limits should be set (in working days) for the presentation of the complaint and the management response at each stage. Time limits should get longer as the grievance moves up the hierarchy to more senior management, since the problem will necessarily be more serious and will require more time to deal with. A proviso might be included permitting the extension of time limits by mutual agreement.

Presentation and documentation of a grievance.

The initial presentation of a grievance need only be made verbally with the immediate supervisor. A written presentation might deter those who feel theirs is a minor grievance. Brief documentation should be kept of this meeting.

For each stage thereafter, a record of information and events, including supporting arguments and evidence, should be kept to pass up through subsequent stages for those not familiar with the grievance. The record should be agreed by the manager concerned and countersigned by the employee and/or the employee's representative.

"Many labor problems have spirit issues at their core, with lack of respect being perhaps the biggest."

Kenneth Blanchard

This helps ensure that there are no misunderstandings when an agreement resolving the problem has been reached.

Guidelines for the interviewer.

Include instructions for the interviewer on the way in which he or she should prepare for and handle the grievance interview.

Status quo clause.

Arrange a status quo clause with the unions so that any industrial action will be deferred until the grievance process is completed.

3. Draw Up an Implementation Timetable

In a large organization it is often better to pilot the grievance procedure on one site or large department before full implementation.

4. Provide Training for Managers and Supervisors

Conducting a grievance interview effectively is not easy. Training should be given to all managers and supervisors who may have to deal with a grievance. Make sure that they are aware of the limits of their and others' authority and that they understand the mechanics of the procedure, for example, the number of working days they have to reply to a grievance and the documentation they should keep.

5. Communicate and Implement the Procedure

Make sure that everyone is aware of the procedure (a letter should be sent to all employees along with a copy of the procedure), the date the procedure will come into effect, and which managers are responsible for grievances at each stage. Explain that the procedure has been introduced to benefit employees by providing them with a systematic way of airing grievances and reaching an amicable agreement in as short a time as possible. The same information should be given to new recruits in the staff handbook or company intranet.

6. Evaluate the Procedure

Regular evaluation of the procedure will help you improve it. Identify the number of grievances and settlements, the subject matter of individual grievances, and any levels of management that seem to have difficulties in handling grievances. Grievance records can help you analyze trends in the causes of grievance. Debrief employees who have used the procedure to settle grievances to see whether they experienced any problems with the process. It is essential to check that the procedure has been applied fairly and consistently.

7. Modify the Procedure As Needed

Alterations should be made to combat any of the problems highlighted in the evaluation. Changes may include offering extra training to certain managers or removing a stage in the procedure. Regularly update the names or job titles of managers responsible for grievances at each stage.

8. Provide Results Feedback

Communicate the success of the evaluation process to all employees and let them know of any changes to be made.

DOS AND DON'TS

DO
- Try to obtain copies of procedures used in other organizations.
- Define the types of grievance the procedure will cover.
- Allow the aggrieved an alternative to the line manager in the initial meeting.

DON'T
- Don't make the initial stage too formal, otherwise some grievances may not be aired.
- Don't set unrealistic time limits.

THOUGHT STARTERS
- Have you ever been party to a grievance at work? What did you do?

- Do you know how to handle a complaint from an employee?

FOR MORE INFORMATION

Books:
Repa, Barbara Kate. *Your Rights In The Workplace.* NOLO: Berkeley, CA, 2005.
Fick, Barbara J. *The American Bar Association Guide to Workplace Law : Everything You Need to Know About Your Rights as an Employee or Employer.* New York: Random House, 1997.

Web sites:
National Labor Relations Board: **www.nlrb.gov**
National Mediation Board: **www.nmb.gov**

507

CHECKLIST

"The microdivision of labour has fostered a basic distrust of human beings." Charles Handy

Setting Up a Disciplinary Procedure

CHECKLIST

This checklist is aimed at managers wishing to implement a disciplinary procedure in their company or organization.

It is essential for an employer to act reasonably in dealing with misconduct or indiscipline. A fair and thorough disciplinary procedure can protect an employer against unfair dismissal claims and their associated costs. Legislation aside, it is good personnel practice to deal with indiscipline quickly and fairly and to offer guidance on improving behavior so problems do not fester and grow.

It is important, however, to remember that good management (for example, spotting problems before they become serious and identifying development needs to improve performance) can prevent many cases from reaching this stage.

DEFINITION

A disciplinary procedure is a structured approach an employer uses to deal with indiscipline at work. It defines the types of behavior it covers, the presentation and documentation of warnings, representation at disciplinary interviews, time limits for investigation, and rights of appeal.

ADVANTAGES

A disciplinary procedure:

- sets standards of conduct at work;
- ensures fair and consistent treatment for employees throughout the organization;
- may prevent minor problems from becoming major ones;
- helps protect the employer against claims of unfair dismissal.

DISADVANTAGES

There are no real disadvantages of implementing a disciplinary procedure, but remember that:

- it requires time and resources to administer effectively;
- the objectives need to be explained thoroughly to staff so they don't worry unduly;
- the procedure should not replace informal warnings and performance monitoring systems.

ACTION CHECKLIST

✔ 1. Designate a Disciplinary Procedure Management Committee

The committee should include at least one person from the personnel department and from each level of management, as well as a person from every union representing employees. The committee will manage the design, implementation, and administration of the disciplinary procedure. Appoint a coordinator to oversee the project, preferably the personnel officer, but certainly someone with project management experience who commands re-

spect, has good communication and negotiation skills, and can get things done.

✔ 2. Define the Terms of Reference

Identify the employees to be covered by the procedure (for example, shop-floor workers only) and the managers who will be responsible for the disciplinary interviews. Define indiscipline (both minor and serious misconduct), clarify legal obligations, and agree on the process to be used to lead up to dismissal.

✔ 3. Draw Up the Procedure

Use the experiences and research of the committee to devise a procedure. Try to obtain samples of procedures used in other organizations. Remember to make the procedure as clear and easy to understand as possible.

The procedure should contain the following:

1. **purpose.** In an initial paragraph, give the reasons for having a procedure, highlighting the benefits to employees of a consistent set of rules and the importance of discipline in the workplace.
2. **types of misconduct.** Spell out the kind of misconduct that would invoke the disciplinary procedure. Distinguish between minor offenses and those that are serious or may constitute gross misconduct, for example,

Minor	Serious
Smoking (where appropriate)	Vandalism
Timekeeping	Fraud
Dress	Alcohol/drugs

3. **warnings.** Depending on the seriousness of the offense, an employee will be faced with a series of warnings:
   - oral (confirmed in writing)
   - written
   - final written

The ultimate penalty after this will be dismissal, although sanctions short of dismissal (such as transfer, demotion, or loss of pay) may be considered.

The warnings will be given to the employee after an interview, usually with the employee's line manager. Many procedures stipulate a length of time after which the warning lapses if the employee does not reoffend, but this leaves the system open to abuse. It is best not to set a time limit and to keep the warning on file. Remember that the disciplinary procedure should not be invoked unless informal warnings from the line manager have had no effect, or the offense is so serious that immediate disciplinary action must be taken. In cases of gross misconduct an employee may be suspended from work on full pay pending an investigation, then dismissed.

representation at meetings. A colleague or union representative should be allowed to accompany or represent the employee at each warning interview. Consider stipulating that the union should be involved unless the employee specifically objects. On occasions when the offense also constitutes a criminal offense, you should also allow a lawyer to be present.

 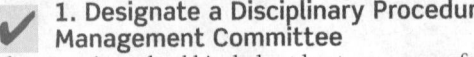

investigations. All abuses of discipline should be investigated before any warning is issued. At the very least this involves hearing the employee's side of the story.

Set a time limit for investigating gross misconduct such as deliberate malpractice. This investigation should be completed within ten working days of the commission of the offense.

documentation. Take detailed minutes at all interviews and keep them together with copies of any investigation into the misconduct and any warnings issued. This documentation is useful for checking whether an employee's behavior improves; it also provides evidence that the company has followed correct procedures.

plans of action. In the case of minor offenses, the company should try hard to help the employee overcome problems, so the disciplinary process need go no further. The procedure should make it clear that at each interview the employee and the line manager will agree plans of action to improve discipline. An evaluation interview will be scheduled at which a more severe warning can be issued if progress has not been made.

appeals. Employees should have the right to appeal against any warning they receive as long as the appeal is made in writing to their line manager within five working days of the issue of the warning.

4. Draw up an Implementation Timetable

In a large organization it is often better to pilot the disciplinary procedure on one site or in a large department before full implementation.

5. Train Managers and Supervisors

Provide training to all managers and supervisors who may have to deal with disciplinary issues. Make sure they understand the mechanics of the procedure, and apply it consistently. Training should cover conducting a disciplinary interview effectively, and also general discipline and control; this will help solve as many problems as possible without going through the full procedure.

6. Communicate the Procedure

If you have disciplinary rules, the law requires that employees be notified. Make certain that staff are aware of the procedure; send a letter to all employees with a copy of the procedure. Explain that it will benefit employees by providing a consistent method of dealing with indiscipline. Tell them when the procedure will come into effect. Include the disciplinary procedure in the staff manual and in the orientation of new recruits.

7. Implement the Procedure

Assign a member of the committee to answer questions, especially during the critical period following the communication of the procedure.

8. Evaluate the Procedure

Regular evaluation of the procedure will contribute to its improvement. Compile figures on the number of times it is used, and identify managers who have difficulty maintaining discipline. Ask for feedback from employees who have been disciplined under the procedure.

9. Make Changes and Give Feedback on the Results

Change the disciplinary procedure in the light of the evaluation. You may want to include extra training for some managers or rewrite some of the steps or phases. Communicate any changes to employees.

509

CHECKLIST

DOS AND DON'TS

DO
- Give examples of both minor and serious misconduct offenses.
- Train managers who will be conducting disciplinary interviews.
- Document every action taken under the procedure.

DON'T
- Don't take disciplinary action until the case has been investigated.
- Don't allow the procedure to replace the need for good management.
- Don't regard the procedure as unalterable—review it at regular periods.

THOUGHT STARTERS
- Have you ever been disciplined at work? What happened?
- Do you know how to handle a disciplinary problem involving one of your staff?
- Are you up to date with the law on unfair dismissal?

FOR MORE INFORMATION

Books:
Delpo, Amy, et al. *Dealing with Problem Employees: A Legal Guide.* 3rd ed. Berkeley, CA: Nolo Press, 2005.
Grote, Dick, and Richard C. Grote. *Discipline without Punishment: The Proven Strategy That Turns Problem Employees Into Superior Performers.* 2nd ed. New York: AMACOM, 2006.
Weiss, Donald H. *Fair, Square, and Legal: Safe Hiring, Managing, and Firing to Keep You and Your Company out of Court.* 4th ed. New York: AMACOM, 2004.

Web sites:
HR Guide: **www.hr-guide.com**
HR.BLR.com: **http://hr.blr.com**

"There could be no worse friend to labour than the benevolent, philanthropic employer . . . sooner or later he will be compelled to close."

Lord Leverhulme

Codes of Ethics

CHECKLIST

This checklist provides initial guidance for managers introducing a new code of ethics or updating an existing one. It applies equally to the public, private, and voluntary sectors.

There is a growing belief that organizations can succeed only if they are seen to observe high ethical standards. As a result, more are choosing to make a public commitment to ethical business by formulating and publishing a code of operating principles. The key difficulty they face in doing so is translating high-sounding principles into practical guidelines and thence into actual practice.

DEFINITION

Codes of ethics are guidelines to the moral principles or values used by organizations to steer conduct. They apply both to the organization itself and its employees, in all their business activities, internal and external.

ADVANTAGES

A code of ethics:

- provides explicit guidance to managers and employees so they know what is expected of them in terms of ethical behavior;
- provides new employees with ethical guidance and a sense of common identity;
- enhances the organization's reputation and inspires public confidence;
- signals to suppliers and customers the organization's expectation of proper conduct;
- promotes a culture of excellence by demonstrating the commitment of the organization to ethical behavior.

DISADVANTAGES

- A corporate code can lead to employee cynicism if it is seen only as a paper exercise.
- Without explicit guidance, different parts of the organization may interpret the code differently, ultimately devaluing it.
- The effective introduction and implementation of a code demands a great deal of time from senior management.
- The code may raise public and employee expectations to a level that the organization is unable to live up to.

ACTION CHECKLIST

✔ 1. Secure the Commitment of Top Management

Without the absolute and public commitment of top management, a code will not be taken seriously by employees. Commitment needs to be seen and felt.

✔ 2. Gain Organizational Agreement on the Primary Purpose of a Code

Is the code mainly for the benefit of employees, or is it to be directed at all stakeholders, including members of the board, shareholders, and even customers? Be clear on your major objectives, and be aware of all the changes that such a code may imply, from a shift in the organization's culture to whistle-blowing.

✔ 3. Identify and Define Existing Sources of Values within the Organization

Consult existing codes, legal guidelines, policy memoranda, and founding statements, and involve both managers and employees in their evaluation. Review the standard codes (for example, those published by the Institute of Management) and those of organizations with operating policies similar to your own. Gain a consensus about the organization's traditions and unwritten rules.

✔ 4. Involve Your Employees

This is best achieved in a small group, but drafting the code should be a dynamic process, so don't exclude comments from employees at any level.

✔ 5. Prepare a Draft Code

The code should include:

- an introduction explaining the code's purpose, the need for such a code, and expectations about its use;
- a clear definition of the organization's mission and objectives;
- guidance on handling relations with each of the organization's constituencies: employees, shareholders, customers, suppliers, the outside community, etc.;
- expectations about acceptable behavior;
- operating principles (use realistic examples);
- a formal mechanism to resolve employees' questions.

✔ 6. Circulate the Draft

Consult widely within the organization, seeking feedback and comments. Be seen to take the feedback seriously. In addition to generating additional ideas, this process reinforces staff awareness of the code. If a significant amount of revision is necessary, circulate a second draft.

✔ 7. Devise an Implementation Strategy

Once the draft is finalized, plan for its implementation. The implementation strategy must be dynamic and continuous. Incorporate the code into orientation, staff training, and management development programs. Bear in mind that implementation, like the preceding processes, may benefit from having a project management champion who can drive implementation forward with purpose, sensitivity, and consideration.

✔ 8. Circulate the Final Code Widely

The code should be sent to all employees, accompanied by a letter from the head of the organization explaining the purpose of the code and expectations about its use.

 "Making money doesn't oblige people to forfeit their honor or their conscience."

Guy de Rothschild

 9. Establish a Procedure for Questions, Concerns, and Complaints

Who is responsible for responding to these—the line manager, human resources, or an ethics hotline? Make sure that an appeal process is built into the procedure.

10. Monitor and Evaluate the Code

Establish a mechanism to monitor and evaluate the code's effectiveness. There is no set formula or time frame dictated by good practice, but nine months to a year after implementation may be an appropriate time to get feedback and reactions and evaluate the impact of the code. Further consultation and one-on-one meetings are useful tools for this process. The code should be monitored regularly thereafter and evaluated for continued relevance: circumstances change, and the code may need periodic amendment.

THOUGHT STARTERS

- Do you really have the commitment of senior management, or are they going to be distracted by other programs and initiatives?

- Does your organization already have a code of ethics?

- Does the code prompt employees to ask themselves the following questions before acting: Would I be willing to tell my family about this? Would I mind if the press found out about it?

DOS AND DON'TS

DO
- Make sure that the code reflects the organization's own values and traditions and that it is in line with staff handbooks and operating manuals.
- Seek employee input at all stages. Encourage a climate that promotes discussion of, and challenges to, the principles of the code without undermining it.
- Use plain language to write the code, avoiding platitudes, jargon, legal and technical phrases, or current buzzwords. Include realistic examples and factual situations to provide guidance.

DON'T
- Don't make the code either too vague or too narrowly prescriptive.
- Don't use the code to impose new or inappropriate values on the organization.
- Don't create an expectations gap between the principles of the code and the behavior of the organization in practice.
- Don't put ethical wallpaper on a decaying wall: an ethical code needs to be real, not cosmetic.

FOR MORE INFORMATION

Books:
Bowie, Norman E., and Patricia H. Werhane. *Management Ethics.* Malden, MA: Blackwell, 2005.
Chryssides, George D., and John H. Kaler. *An Introduction to Business Ethics.* Florence, KY: Thomson, 1993.
Johnson, Larry, and Bob Phillips. *Absolute Honesty: Building a Corporate Culture that Values Straight Talk and Rewards Integrity.* New York: AMACOM, 2003.

Journal Articles:
King, Hans. "A Global Ethic in an Age of Globalization." *Business Ethics Quarterly* 7:3 (1997): 17–32.
Navran, Frank. "12 Steps to Building a Best Practice Ethics Program." *Workforce* 76:9 (September 1997): 120–22.

Web site:
International Business Ethics Institute:
www.business-ethics.org

"Most people sell their souls and live with a good conscience on the proceeds."

Logan Pearsall Smith

Developing a Manufacturing Strategy

512

CHECKLIST

This checklist explains the basic steps in analyzing existing manufacturing operations and reviewing current manufacturing strategy.

Most organizations operate with a business plan and a broad corporate strategy. Not all manufacturing companies have a manufacturing strategy, however, and many that do fail to update it on a regular basis. A superior mix of people, technology, focus, and direction gives manufacturing a competitive edge: a manufacturing strategy addresses all these issues. The extended timescale required for completing a radical manufacturing change demands that you take a long-term view so you can plan investment and implementation.

DEFINITION

A manufacturing strategy is a working document outlining:

- the basis for your competitive advantage;
- key issues affecting your organization;
- your strategic manufacturing aims;
- your broad strategic initiatives.

The last should cover quality, technology, skill requirements, training, and make-or-buy decisions.

ACTION CHECKLIST

1. Appoint a Project Team

Planning strategy requires the full-time attention of a number of knowledgeable people from the management team. Team members need to have a detailed understanding of organizations, products, markets, and manufacturing technology. Skills in competitor analysis are also useful.

2. Understand the Existing Market Position

In order to formulate strategy you need a thorough understanding of your existing products. Ask:

- What strategy does your organization use to compete? The three generic strategies are to compete on cost (cost leadership), on superior features or service (differentiation), or in a subset of the market (niche market focus).
- What product families do you have? Use product life cycles as a framework for thinking about the manufacturing requirements of different products. Plotting product life cycles for existing key products and future projects will begin to fill in a picture of the size and shape your business needs to take on in the future

In addition:

- Measure the performance of each of your products.

Focus on their contribution, market share, and market growth.

- Identify the competitive edge of each product family. Competitive features might include quality, delivery lead time, delivery flexibility, design flexibility, or price. What are the criteria that give you the greatest competitive advantage?

3. Identify the Drivers of Change

Consider:

- business criteria (product performance, market demands, the evolution of manufacturing philosophies, and management structures)
- technological developments
- financial pressures

Analyze external influences on the organization, internal resources and capabilities, and the skills and competencies of staff by undertaking a SWOT analysis.

4. Analyze Your Current Performance

Assessing your performance against competitive edge criteria can be difficult. Some factors are not easy to measure directly, while comparative data may be hard to obtain. Use techniques such as Pareto analysis and activity sampling to facilitate data collection. Focus on product performance features such as quality, delivery, flexibility, material costs, and capital costs. Obtain comparative data through published reports or databases, or by talking to customers and suppliers. Consider destructive analysis of a competitor's product. Participate in benchmarking studies.

5. Identify Critical Components

Identifying the components that are most critical to your long-term success enables you to maximize the use of your investment capital. Range the components along a continuum of high to low business content, placing those of strategic importance at the high end of the scale. Include components with high added value on the list of strategic components; consider buying in those with a low business content.

- Identify the major part families and describe their manufacturing characteristics.
- List the key facilities needed to manufacture the strategic components.

6. Evaluate Your Manufacturing Operation

This can be a complicated task, so give yourself plenty of time.

Examine current practice with regard to a range of criteria. The nine key areas most often covered are:

- facilities
- span of process (the degree of vertical integration)
- capacity

"The idea that commerce and profit may actually be pulling in the same direction is difficult for some people to accept."

Henry Ford

- processes and the way they are organized
- human resources
- quality
- control policies
- suppliers
- new products

Compare the strengths and weaknesses of current practice with your established competitive edge criteria. Where are the gaps?

7. Set New Targets

Without tough targets it is difficult not only to measure achievement, but to maintain the necessary top-down pressure to achieve them. Targets can be wide-ranging; they cover such criteria as tooling costs, the utilization of equipment, defective materials, and inventory.

8. Develop a New Manufacturing Strategy

You are now ready to compile your new manufacturing strategy.

Using your knowledge of your most important product families, your competitive advantage criteria, and the existing performance gaps, identify the weaknesses of your existing policies. Discuss possible actions and strategic choices. Consider running a simulation to test these options.

9. Develop Your Supplier Network

For those components that you have decided to buy in, go through the process of identifying a potential supplier network and evaluating its ability to meet the demands of in-house manufacture. Consider your relationship with each supplier.

10. Review

As with all business plans, review your manufacturing plan annually against the developing business situation and set revised targets.

THOUGHT STARTERS
- Do you have a manufacturing strategy?

- Is it reviewed on a regular basis?

- What are the strengths, weaknesses, opportunities, and threats to your existing product line or range of services?

FOR MORE INFORMATION

Books:
Miltenburg, John. *Manufacturing Strategy: How to Formulate a Winning Plan*. 2nd ed. New York: McGraw-Hill, 1999.
Hill, Terry. *Manufacturing Strategy: Text and Cases*. 3rd ed. Boston, MA: Irwin/McGraw-Hill, 2000.

Web sites:
Advanced Manufacturing: **www.advancedmanufacturing.com**
Manufacturing News: **www.manufacturingnews.com**

513

CHECKLIST

"Those who invest only to get rich will fail. Those who invest to help others will probably succeed."

Art Fry

Developing a Strategy for World-Class Business

514

CHECKLIST

CHECKLIST

This checklist provides an introductory framework for managers whose companies wish to pursue the route to world-class status. The responsibility for a world-class strategy usually rests with the chief executive and senior management.

Becoming a world-class company is not a simple process, and requires effort and commitment from the entire organization. Developing a strategy is essential if world-class status is to be achieved.

DEFINITION

"World-class" is a concept difficult to define. However, an accepted working definition is that a world-class company should be able to compete with any other organization in its chosen markets and aspire to world-beating standards in every department or division. "World-class" also embraces the practice of, and excellence in, techniques such as Total Quality Management, continuous improvement, customer service, international benchmarking, flexible working, and training. World-class organizations also accept the necessity for continuous change.

ACTION CHECKLIST

1. Consider Outside Influences

Identify the factors in the external environment that call for a strategic response from your business. These can be grouped under main headings such as economic factors, demographic trends, environmental factors, technology, suppliers, and competition.

2. Establish the World-class Vision

Determine the core business of your organization—that at which it should excel. Top management should make a vision of excellence clear in a brief statement that is impossible to misinterpret. Besides helping form this vision, the chief executive's role is to clarify the message, push forward change, and champion ideas and capabilities that will beat competitors.

3. Analyze Your Current Position

Benchmark your organization against your competitors as far as you can. This can be very difficult, as much of the necessary information may not be available. However, organizations exist that can help in this process.

Consider the following areas:
- your product
- its price
- its availability
- your customer service
- your policy for continuous improvement

- your costs
- your market share

Do you match your competitors in these areas, or is your organization well below or well above them? Don't limit this measure to competitors in your own country; compare yourself against worldwide competition. Identify which organizations are excellent within these areas and what makes them the best—in order to beat them!

Assess where you stand in customers' eyes. What is their perception of your status compared with the reputation of your competitors?

4. Focus on Core Capabilities

From the analyses of the external environment, the core business of the organization, and the standing of competitors, draw up a list of the core capabilities of your organization that will enable you to compete in world markets. Core capabilities include:
- product knowledge/service skills
- marketing skills
- innovation/research capacity
- financial planning and control
- human resource capabilities (motivation as well as skills)

Determine which of these core capabilities need extra focus and resource their development.

5. Build a Corporate Strategy

Focus on achieving better products or services, better factories or service operations, better organization, better management, and better information and communication.

Ask yourself questions such as:
- Have the key business processes been defined and understood?
- Has a quality or customer focus ethic been established throughout the organization?
- Are quality and reliability of products and services measured?
- Are the key performance measures reviewed? Are they improving?
- Is everyone in the organization informed of results and developments?
- Is customer satisfaction monitored on a regular basis?
- Are employees multiskilled? Are they flexible and willing to adapt?
- Do your employees have continuing personal development plans in place?
- How are creativity and innovation nurtured?
- How well does communication flow?
- Does it flow in all directions?

6. Set High Targets for the Organization

Set imaginative and ambitious targets by identifying where you intend to be in one, three, and five years. If targets are easily achievable there is a danger that you

"In a global economy the challenges and changes are universal."   Robert Heller

will rest on your laurels. Being satisfied with these improvements means never becoming world-class.

- Make certain that organizational targets are translated into divisional and departmental goals that are incorporated into individual objectives.
- Get staff into the habit of setting their own targets—they will usually be higher than those you would set them yourself.

7. Develop Simple Performance Measures

Measurement processes, as simple and as straightforward as possible, allow you to monitor what is happening and report on progress continuously. Performance measures should be relevant to your aims: concentrate on customer service, time reduction, and quality, and remember that within a world-class company, financial measures are not the most important performance measure for achieving your objectives.

8. Adopt Straightforward Reporting Procedures

Complex reports need a lot of preparation and take time to understand: they tend to be produced monthly at best. World-class companies need to be able to act immediately on the results of performance measurement; if a report takes three weeks to generate, then this three-week lead time will impact on continuous improvement. Adopt the one-page management reporting rule.

9. Communicate Your Progress

Nothing inspires and motivates like success. Keep employees fully informed of the organization's progress (get your staff to produce their own progress charts if possible). By adopting simple measurement techniques, results can be given to employees on a daily basis, preferably in a graphic or pictorial form. Progress reports can be an inspirational form of communication; poor communication is responsible for many corporate failures and shortcomings.

10. Revise Your Performance Targets

As your organization raises its performance in the areas you have defined, identify new areas to be improved. As areas improve, their reports should reduce to exception reporting (reports showing only those items that deviate from plan or the established norm), allowing the organization to focus on new needs.

11. Assess Effectiveness

Becoming world-class, though an achievement, is not the end of the process. To be a world-class company you must continue to benchmark yourself against your competitors regularly. If you fail to do this, your organization will slip from the position it has achieved and be replaced by another. Staying world-class is just as hard as becoming world-class, if not harder.

DOS AND DON'TS

DO
- Continue to set challenging targets for your company.
- Remain flexible and adaptable—within limits.
- Have a bias toward action and controlled risk.
- Focus on continuous improvement.
- Keep a constant eye on major competitors.
- Be sensitive to the conditions, context, and methods of local cultures.
- Respect the importance of measures and reports.

DON'T
- Don't become complacent once you achieve world-class status.
- Don't attempt to impose your usual corporate practices across borders.

THOUGHT STARTERS
- Do you know the key performers in your industry?
- What approaches toward guaranteeing and measuring customer satisfaction do you have in place?
- Do you have the means of measuring the quality of your organization's performance?

FOR MORE INFORMATION

Books:
Gronstedt, Anders. *The Customer Century: Lessons from World-class Companies in Integrated Marketing and Communications.* New York: Routledge, 2000.
Harrison, Jeffrey S. *Strategic Management of Resources and Relationships: Concepts and Cases.* New York: Wiley, 2003.
Meister, Jeanne C. *Corporate Universities: Lessons in Building a World-Class Work Force, revised edition.* New York: McGraw Hill, 1998.

Journal Articles:
Calori, Roland, et al. "Innovative International Strategies." *Journal of World Business* 35:4 (Winter 2000).
Markides, Constantinos, and John M. Stopford. "From Ugly Ducklings to Elegant Swans: Transforming Parochial Firms into World Leaders." *Business Strategy Review* 6:2 (1995): 1–24.

Web site:
American Productivity & Quality Center: **www.apqc.org**

"Business now shares in much of the responsibility for our global quality of life."

Roberto Goizueta

Getting Close to the Customer

> CHECKLIST
>
> This checklist is aimed at managers at all levels and explores the steps and principles involved in assessing customers' needs as the basis of any business operation. It focuses on how to identify your customers' needs, but does not extend to suggesting ways of meeting those needs.

DEFINITION

Getting close to (current and potential) customers involves gathering facts and knowledge about them in order to develop an awareness of what they want from you and how they perceive your organization and its products or services. This awareness in turn enables you to continuously strive to meet your customers' demands and secure your organization's long-term survival and profitability.

ADVANTAGES

Being close to your customers allows you to:
- respond to changes in demand and in the market;
- act on facts instead of hunches or intuition;
- develop products or services better tailored to your target market;
- achieve improved sales and increased profits.

DISADVANTAGES

The advantages of being close to your customers far outweigh any disadvantages, but you should take the following factors into account:
- The better you try to get to know customers, the more you risk intruding on their privacy.
- If you ask a customer to reveal personal or valuable information, you'll probably have to offer a reward or benefit in return.
- Customers may resist telling you personal information and may not always tell the truth.
- Surveys and research can be costly and time-consuming.

ACTION CHECKLIST

1. Examine Your Organizational Culture

You are unlikely to get close to your customers unless the culture of your organization encourages such a relationship. Staff should be trained to think "customer first"—those who are not customer-focused can jeopardize the success of the organization by making inappropriate decisions, failing to respond to changing situations appropriately or quickly enough, or neglecting to serve customers in a way that promotes their loyalty.

Remember that every section of your organization has customers. Staff in direct contact with external customers cannot provide effective service without the internal support of colleagues all along the chain. To encourage internal service departments to adopt an outward-looking customer focus, their operators might work for a week or two in the department they service.

2. Identify Your Customers

Your customers are those who use the output of your work. They may be internal to your organization (for example, your personnel function has all employees as its customers) or external (members of the public, other businesses, or government or public bodies). In identifying customers, distinguish between purchasers, those who pay for your product, and end users, those who actually use it.

You will probably wish to compile a database of your customers so you can profile your customer base.

3. Profile Your Customers

A wide range of factors influences customer behavior and choices, for example:
- gender—particularly where the purchaser or end user is not the sole decision maker;
- age—different age ranges being more susceptible to targeting by some products than others;
- marital status—especially combined with other factors such as children and disposable income;
- home ownership—indicating specific needs and responsibilities that relate to buying patterns;
- location—urban consumers differing from rural ones, and regions differing culturally and economically;
- lifestyle—since all customers have individual activities, interests, and opinions.

These factors become more useful when they are analyzed in combination—for example, home ownership, age, and number of dependent children can indicate the likely amount of a customer's disposable income.

Decide how to approach your customers to find out their basic characteristics. It may not be possible to ask every customer individually, but other fruitful approaches exist. For example:
- market research
- questionnaires
- user- or focus-group discussions
- customer audits
- attitude surveys

Take advantage of opportunities to meet business customers at their premises or at yours in a series of open houses or customer care programs or through membership of user groups, industry liaison meetings, or partnerships arising out of new product development.

4. Assess Your Customers' Opinions and Attitudes

Organizations with an inaccurate perception of their customers' needs most likely:
- make untested and unwarranted assumptions about what customers think;
- rely on weak anecdotal evidence;
- accord too much weight to atypical complaints.

If you don't make the effort to find out what your customers think, you can be caught off balance when they go elsewhere. If you don't know why they are going else-

---

"I look in my closet, and if I need it, I design it. If it works for me, it works for the customer."

Donna Karan

where, you can't take corrective actions. Besides basic factual information about them, find out:

- why customers buy your product or use your service;
- how they use it;
- what their opinion is of your product or service;
- why they choose your offering over the competition;
- what their experience is of your product or service in terms of performance and after-sales care.

Attitudes and opinions are hard to quantify. Many factors influence a decision to purchase or remain loyal to a particular brand. Customers may be influenced more by their impressions of service—courtesy, promptness, etc.—than by the quality of a product. Exploring these issues requires detailed research. If you do not have adequate in-house expertise, use an external research agency.

Be sure to listen to your frontline staff, who are on the receiving end of firsthand comments from customers about their satisfaction and dissatisfaction. Consider setting up a procedure for reporting this information.

5. Act on Your Findings

Analyze the results of your research, interpret the data, and publicize your findings. Use your findings to identify where you need to take action to maintain your competitive advantage. Involve all staff in this process; encourage everyone to think "customer first."

Paying attention to your customers' needs is an ongoing process. Consider setting up a regular research project, introducing methods of soliciting customers' suggestions and creating response mechanisms, or initiating procedures that constantly monitor your market.

6. Consider Using the Internet to Improve Customer Focus

The Internet is increasingly used by customers to select items for purchase, specify designs, and submit comments and suggestions on products and services. Used judiciously, the Web permits an organization to get closer to its customers than ever before.

7. Give Feedback to Customers

Let your customers know that you value their needs and their ideas. This may mean publishing a revised mission statement reiterating your commitment to fulfilling their needs, or publicizing survey results and details of new products or product amendments made as a result of the research.

Feedback is not a onetime event. It needs to be a continuous process that informs customers of your organization's response to suggestions, mistakes, and new ideas and that encourages further dialog.

THOUGHT STARTERS
- When was the last time you spoke to, or came into contact with, a customer?
- Do you know who buys your product and why?
- How easy is it for your customers to complain and give feedback?

FOR MORE INFORMATION

Books:
Arussy, Lior. *Passionate and Profitable: Why Customer Strategies Fail and Ten Steps to Put them Right.* Hoboken, NJ: Wiley, 2005.
Barwise, Patrick, and Sean Meehan. *Simply Better: Winning and Keeping Customers by Delivering What Matters Most.* Boston, MA: Harvard Business School Press, 2004.
McQuarrie, Edward F. *The Market Research Toolbox.* Thousand Oaks, CA: Sage, 2005.
Peppers, Don, and Martha Rogers. *Managing Customer Relationships.* Hoboken, NJ: Wiley, 2004.
Smith, Ian. *Meeting Customer Needs.* 3rd ed. Woburn, MA: Butterworth-Heinemann, 2003.

Web sites:
Customer Care Institute: **www.customercare.com**
International Customer Service Association: **www.icsa.com**

"If the shoe doesn't fit, must we change the foot?" Gloria Steinem

Moving the Virtual Organization Forward

CHECKLIST

This checklist is written for managers wishing to gain an understanding of the major philosophies underlying the concept of the virtual organization and the key factors involved in it.

The virtual organization embraces changes to traditional organizational structures and methods of working. Some kinds of organization will find it easier to embrace virtuality, but all managers need to familiarize themselves with what is an increasingly widespread management model; this checklist considers the key factors involved in making a success of the virtual organization.

DEFINITION

There is no single way to define a virtual organization. Most writers agree, however, that a definition should embrace the concept of organizational flexibility unconstrained by traditional barriers of place and time. Essentially the virtual organization relies on exploiting cyberspace, the electronic medium for data exchange brought about by the integration of telecommunications and computer software. It accepts the notion of a hidden reality behind the scenes, one in which results are not achieved in traditional ways. It implies that an organization, team, individual, service, or even product need not exist physically, although it may appear to be material; it is real but not real. "Virtual organization" is actually an umbrella term for various initiatives that organizations are exploring to make themselves more responsive to changes in today's marketplace.

"A virtual company is one where work is performed outside of the definition of *place*. There's no factory floor, no retail store, no conference room, no cubicle farm. Virtual work is primarily the manufacture, retail, and distribution of intellectual property." (Jeanne L. Allert in *Training and Development USA* 55:3 [March 2001], pp. 55–58.)

ADVANTAGES

With a virtual organization:
- distance does not hinder the accomplishment of work, meetings, collaboration, or conferences;
- productivity rises significantly;
- overhead costs are reduced;
- work can be spread across time zones;
- organizations can focus on what they are best at.

DISADVANTAGES

The benefits of the virtual organization cannot be realized unless management:
- empowers and trusts staff members;
- establishes reciprocal loyalty between employees and employer;

- involves all employees, not just knowledge workers;
- questions older, accepted methodologies and explores new ways of working.

ACTION CHECKLIST

 Getting the Platform Right

 1. Don't Mess with Virtual Working

It is either central to your organization's planning and development or it is not. You have to either treat virtual workers as key personnel or not. Virtual workers are not managed by face-time but need to feel part of a collective effort, which comes more from the alignment of shared values than through elaborate forms of co-ordination and control. Virtual workers are judged by results, and the organization's (or team's) recognition and reward system should respond to this.

 2. Get the Training and Support Mechanisms Right

Virtual workers need effective communication, updating, and support mechanisms to enable them to work efficiently. Both technical and team support needs to be fully operational, and each member must have a clear understanding of what they may expect from others, or from the support center (if there is one). Such processes need to be flexible and adaptable, as team members shift with new and evolving projects.

3. Adopt Cultural Diversity

This is no longer a choice but a necessity. Team members will emerge from different cultures as well as different organizations and they will expect to be able to do things their way. They will have varied experiences of working in virtual environments—hence the importance of clarifying goals and processes and getting the support mechanisms right.

Getting the People Right

1. Make Sure the Potential for Chaos is Eliminated

. . . or as much reduced as possible. The steps above would appear to remove much of the older-style control mechanisms that have characterized organizational working for decades. Managing "virtuality" is not so much "laissez-faire" as ensuring that certain shared values—understood rules and expectations—are in place amongst the team members.

 2. Ensure Team Members Have a Core IT Capability

Distance working, which is reliant on communications technologies, cannot be expected from people who sim-

"The revolution people are talking about is one of form rather than substance."

ply do not have the basic core competencies. There are wide ranging levels of technical know-how, but people need to be comfortable with technology as there will be day-to-day problems to resolve, such as with ISPs, software installation, and familiarization with the vagaries of, and patience required with, helpdesks.

3. Get the Start-up Right

When undertaking a virtual project, remember that face-to-face contact is important for building relationships—even if this can only be once at the beginning. Make sure the virtual worker is clear about what is expected, not only in terms of results, but in terms of who is to supply what (e.g. hardware and consumables). A virtual team leader will need to feel comfortable that team members are motivated from within for the task in hand—and there may not be repeat opportunities for reassurance.

4. What Makes the Virtual Teamworker Tick?

Is it just cash? Or is it about being a loner grappling with problems which are a nightmare for others? If the team-

worker has qualities that the organization clearly needs, then it can be a question of finding the key driving factors which will unearth the optimum response or contribution. It could be that the individual's reputation and wish for further contract work is the driver. Early "best practice" suggests that a critical factor could be the challenge of the work to the individual.

5. Make Sure Rules are Understood— But Keep Them Simple

Individuals need plenty of rope if they are to deliver. Leaving them to their own devices on how they deliver does not mean giving them enough rope to hang themselves, or the project. Virtual working is about intellectual property and many individuals are rightly jealous of it. New kinds of agreed control are needed here, defining fair benefit from collective effort—these often take the form of software, access, or reuse licenses.

DOS AND DON'TS

DO
- Ask yourself where the organization will be in five years.
- Consider how IT and telecommunications can change the way you do business.
- Look at what your competitors are doing.
- Weigh up the cost implications of IT/communications technologies.
- Think in terms of genuine trust between colleagues, staff, and partners.
- Remember it's an evolutionary process.
- Look at success stories—the case literature is growing.

DON'T
- Don't ignore how IT and telecommunications can change the way you do business, and change what business you do.
- Don't think in terms of fixed structures or face-time management control.
- Don't underestimate the pitfalls in changing traditional ways of working.
- Don't think that virtual working will go away.

THOUGHT STARTERS

- "How do you manage people whom you do not see?" (Handy, "Trust and the Virtual Organization" [1990])

- "In the future, some organizational functions may exist solely in computer systems." (Barnatt, "Office space, Cyberspace and Virtual Organization" [1995])

FOR MORE INFORMATION

Books:
Hedberg, Bo, et al. *Virtual Organizations and Beyond: Discover Imaginary Systems.* New York: Wiley, 1997.
Heneman, Robert L., and David B. Greenberger, eds. *Human Resource Management in Virtual Organisations.* Greenwich, CO: Information Age, 2002.
Lipnack, Jessica, and Jeffrey Stamps. *Virtual Teams: People Working Across Boundaries With Technology.* 2nd ed. Wiley, 2000.
Neuhauser, Peg C., Ray Bender, and Kirk L. Stromberg. *Culture dot com: Building Corporate Culture in the Connected Workplace.* Toronto, Canada: Wiley, 2000.

Journal Article:
Cohen, Sachs. "On Becoming Virtual." *Training and Development USA* 51:5 (May 1997): 30–37.

"Knowledge building for an organization occurs by combining people's distinct individualities with a particular set of activities."
Dorothy Leonard

Performing a SWOT Analysis

This checklist is for anyone carrying out, or participating in, a SWOT analysis. SWOT is the acronym of Strengths, Weaknesses, Opportunities, and Threats. It is a simple, popular technique that can be used for preparing or amending plans, problem-solving and decision-making, or making staff generally aware of the need for change. The usefulness of SWOT analysis, however, has recently been questioned, and it may be seen as an outdated technique.

DEFINITION

SWOT analysis is a general technique that can find applications across diverse management functions and activities, but it is particularly appropriate to the early stages of strategic and marketing planning.

Performing a SWOT analysis involves identifying and recording the Strengths, Weaknesses, Opportunities, and Threats concerning a task, individual, department, or organization. The analysis typically takes into account internal resources and capabilities (strengths and weaknesses) and factors external to the organization (opportunities and threats).

ADVANTAGES

SWOT analysis can provide:
- a framework for identifying and analyzing strengths, weaknesses, opportunities, and threats;
- an impetus to analyze a situation and develop appropriate strategies and tactics;
- a basis for assessing core capabilities and competences;
- the evidence for, and cultural key to, change;
- a stimulus to participation in a group experience.

DISADVANTAGES

Some commentators argue that SWOT analysis is an overview approach unsuited to today's diverse and unstable markets. They also suggest that it can be ineffective as a means of analysis because it tends to:
- generate long lists;
- rely on description instead of analysis;
- ignore prioritization;
- be overlooked in the later stages of the planning and implementation process.

ACTION CHECKLIST
1. Establish the Objectives
The first key step in any management project is to be clear about what you are doing and why. The purpose of conducting a SWOT analysis may be wide or narrow, general or specific—anything from getting staff to understand, think about, and be more involved in the business to rethinking a strategy, or even rethinking the direction of the business.

2. Select Appropriate Contributors
This is important if the final recommendations are to result from consultation and discussion, not just personal views, however expert.
- Pick a mixed group of specialist and "ideas" people with the ability and enthusiasm to contribute.
- Consider how appropriate it would be to mix staff of different levels.
- Think about numbers: 6 to 10 people may be enough, especially in a SWOT workshop, but up to 25 or 30 can be useful if one of the aims is to get staff to see the need for change.

3. Allocate Research and Information-gathering Tasks
Background preparation is a vital stage for the subsequent analysis to be effective, and should be divided among the SWOT participants. This preparation can be carried out in two stages: exploratory, followed by data collection; and detailed, followed by a focused analysis.
- Gathering information on strengths and weaknesses should focus on the internal factors of skills, resources, and assets, or the lack of them.
- Gathering information on opportunities and threats should focus on external factors such as social, market, or economic trends over which you have little or no control.

4. Create a Workshop Environment
If compiling and recording the SWOT lists takes place in meetings, exploit the benefits of workshop sessions. Encourage an atmosphere conducive to the uninhibited flow of information and to participants openly expressing what they think, free from blame. The leader/facilitator has a key role and should allow time for free flow of thought, but not too much. Half an hour is often enough to spend on strengths, for example, before moving on. It is important to be specific, evaluative, and analytical at the stage of compiling and recording the SWOT lists—mere description is not enough.

5. List Strengths
Strengths can relate to the organization, to the environment, to public relations and perceptions, to market shares, or to people. "People" elements include staff skills, capabilities, and knowledge that can provide a competitive edge or explain past successes. Other people strengths include:
- friendly, cooperative, and supportive staff;
- a staff development and training program;
- appropriate levels of involvement through delegation and trust.

"Organizational" elements include:
- customer loyalty;
- capital investment and a strong balance sheet;
- effective cost control programs;
- efficient procedures, systems, and well developed social responsibility.

"Next to knowing when to seize an opportunity, the most important thing in life is to know when to forgo an advantage."

Benjamin Disraeli

6. List Weaknesses

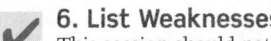 This session should not constitute an opportunity to criticize the organization, but should elicit an honest appraisal of the way things are. Key questions include the following:

- What obstacles prevent progress?
- Which elements need strengthening?
- Where are the complaints coming from?
- Are there any real weak links in the chain?

The list for action could include:

- a lack of new products or services;
- a declining market for your main product;
- poor competitiveness and higher prices;
- noncompliance with or nonawareness of appropriate legislation;
- a lack of awareness of the company's mission, objectives, and policies;
- staff absenteeism;
- the absence of methods for monitoring success or failure.

It is not unusual for "people" problems—poor communication, inadequate leadership, lack of motivation, too little delegation, no trust, the left hand never knowing what the right is doing—to feature among the major weaknesses.

7. List Opportunities

This step is designed to assess socioeconomic, political, environmental, and demographic factors, among others, to evaluate the benefits they may bring to the organization. Examples include:

- the availability of new technology;
- new markets
- a new federal administration;
- new programs for training or monitoring quality;
- changes in interest rates;
- an aging population;
- strengths and weaknesses of competitors.

Bear in mind just how long opportunities might last and how the organization may take best advantage of them.

8. List Threats

The opposite of opportunities—all the above may, with a shift of emphasis or perception, have an adverse impact. Other threats may include:

- the level of unemployment;
- environmental legislation;

- political uncertainty or instability in offshore manufacturing sites or foreign markets;
- exchange rate fluctuations.

It is important to have a worst-case scenario. Weighing threats against opportunities is not an exercise in pessimism; it is rather a question of considering how possible damage may be limited or eliminated. A factor such as Information Technology may emerge as both a threat and an opportunity. Most external factors are in fact challenges, and whether staff perceive them as opportunities or threats is often a valuable indicator of morale.

9. Evaluate Listed Ideas Against Objectives

With the lists compiled, sort and group facts and ideas in relation to objectives. It may be necessary for the SWOT participants to select the five most important items from the list in order to gain a wider view. Clarity of objectives is key to this process, as evaluation and elimination will be necessary to cull the wheat from the chaff. Although some aspects may require further information or research, a clear picture should start to emerge at this stage in response to the objectives.

10. Act On Your Findings

Make sure that the SWOT analysis is used in subsequent planning. Revisit your findings at appropriate intervals to check that they are still valid.

DOS AND DON'TS

DO
- Choose the right people for the exercise.
- Select an appropriate SWOT leader or facilitator.
- Be analytical and specific.
- Record all thoughts and ideas in steps 5–8.
- Take a wide-ranging view of external influences and trends.
- Be selective in the final report.

DON'T
- Don't try to disguise weaknesses.
- Don't merely list errors and mistakes.
- Don't allow the SWOT to become a blame-laying exercise.
- Don't ignore the outcomes at later stages of the planning process.

521

CHECKLIST

"A wise man will make more opportunities than he finds."   Francis Bacon

Planning a Conference

CHECKLIST

This checklist is for anyone who is responsible for planning a conference. Conferences can be productive and memorable if they achieve the objectives of both the organization and the delegates. Alternatively, they can be disorganized, irrelevant, and wasteful of the delegates' time. The difference between the two is careful and detailed planning of the whole process, from the setting of objectives to the studious observation of protocol at the final dinner. If any detail is left to chance and something goes wrong as a result, the conference will be a failure for someone, and this can rebound on the organizers and the host organization.

DEFINITION

Conferences are held for a great variety of reasons—they can be promotional, in-house, educational, or sales-based, to name a few. This checklist concentrates on conferences run for profit.

Basically a conference is a gathering of speakers and delegates meeting to solve particular problems, make specific decisions, discuss or learn about issues of mutual interest, publicize services to potential markets, or discuss cooperation with other bodies.

ACTION CHECKLIST

1. Establish the Need for a Conference
If you have never organized a conference before, be warned: relative to some other methods of achieving your objectives, the planning of a conference can be very expensive and time-consuming. Ask yourself:
- Whom do you want to reach?
- What do you want to say (or ask or discuss), and why?
- How and where do you want to say it?

Your answers will help you determine whether a conference really is the most appropriate and cost-effective way of achieving your objectives, and will establish an initial set of objectives for planning the conference itself.

2. Set Up a Planning Committee
Conferences are best planned by a small committee, which will set detailed objectives and a business or promotional program. Remember, however, that the committee needs to be action-oriented.

3. Appoint a Conference Manager
The committee should appoint a conference manager with full authority to solve problems, make decisions, and negotiate with external parties. This person should have experience in dealing with people at all levels and should like handling conferences, otherwise the work will not be done well. He or she should understand every detail of what is required and should cross-check with the conference committee regularly. The conference manager ultimately has responsibility for the success or failure of the conference.

It is possible to engage the services of a professional conference organizer. Although this can be expensive, it can also prove both desirable and cost-effective for large or complex conferences.

4. Prepare a Schedule
It takes time to organize a successful conference. Appropriate venues are often booked a year or more in advance. The committee and manager should plan a schedule that allows sufficient time to find the right venue, engage appropriate speakers, and send out publicity. The manager also needs to think of the multitude of other considerations that accompany a conference, for example:
- access and parking;
- comfortable space for an unknown (although estimated) number of delegates;
- presentation equipment and visual aids;
- accompanying exhibition;
- information desk;
- access to phones, fax, and e-mail for delegates;
- catering and special dietary requirements;
- varying accommodations requirements.

5. Draw Up a Program
The business program, drawn up by the committee, should meet your objectives completely. Identify a range of speakers who are experienced, sincere, and convincing. Remember that poor presentation of first-class material can destroy a conference session. Plan the schedule so that the presentations hold the delegates' attention (people usually concentrate for a maximum of 25 to 30 minutes before needing a break). Make allowance in the program for:
- breaks between presentations;
- extended refreshment breaks;
- light lunches to prevent delegates from dozing off in the afternoon sessions (if you serve alcohol, do so in moderation);
- a few light relief presentations sandwiched between heavier ones;
- the right balance between interactive, lecturing, and discussion sessions;
- the right balance between work and leisure.

Draw up a social program: it is to the organizer's and delegates' advantage to remain together most, if not all, of the time.

6. Approach and Book Speakers
Approach possible speakers and book them as early as possible. Once a booking is confirmed, agree on the content and format of the speaker's presentation. Approach and book reserve speakers, too, in case of last-minute problems.

Remember to stress (and re-stress) the timing of the presentations, as most speakers overrun. At least one dress rehearsal is advisable—schedule a date and make sure that the speakers can attend.

"In preparing for battle I have always found that plans are useless, but planning is indispensible."

Dwight David Eisenhower

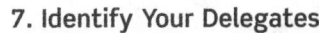

7. Identify Your Delegates

The choice of delegates is closely linked to the conference objectives and is not quite as straightforward as it may seem. A sales conference, for example, will have sales representatives as its delegates, but who else will attend?

8. Select a Venue

Once the format of the conference, the speakers, and the intended delegates have been determined, the conference manager should provide a list of appropriate venues that fall within the financial guidelines set by the committee. Venues can be identified through personal knowledge, word of mouth, or agencies.

The manager should visit the venues to compare them and make sure that they meet all specifications. It is worth remembering that hotels offer special conference rates and are often cheaper off-season and at weekends. More recently, universities have come into their own as conference venues. Many have upgraded dormitories to provide comfortable if not lavish accommodations.

The conference room is of prime importance. The size of the room is the first consideration, but in addition it should have:

- pleasant overall surroundings;
- ceiling height in proportion to the size of room (a low ceiling can depress delegates);
- a first-class PA system (if the system is inadequate, high-quality equipment should be hired);
- efficient but quiet air conditioning;
- efficient room-darkening;
- easy access to convenient exits and entrances;
- comfortable seating.

Inspect the bedrooms, both standard and executive, to check that they are clean and have the facilities your delegates will expect.

Are the catering facilities adequate to cope with the number of delegates who will be attending? Ask for some sample menus. Look at the dining area.

Find out how the hotel will deal with the sudden arrival and departure of your delegates. Ask how they will deal with people who arrive at 2 a.m. A separate conference reception desk can handle this efficiently and can also serve as a conference information desk throughout. Are leisure facilities such as a fitness center and a pool available?

9. Advertise the Conference

Once you are clear about whom you wish to attend and details of the venue and speakers, it is essential to advertise the conference as widely (or as accurately) as possible. The committee should have identified possible advertisers at an early stage.

10. Assemble Information for the Delegates

As soon as arrangements allow, registered delegates should be sent a preconference packet containing:

- the objectives of the conference and an outline of the program;
- arrival instructions;
- hotel details (cost, contact information, map, etc.);
- details of what delegates are expected to pay for;
- the name of the conference manager and assistant and their contact information.

11. Create the Right Atmosphere

Achieving the right atmosphere is vital, although there is no magic formula for it. Panic and last-minute rush are obviously to be avoided; aim instead for calm efficiency, courtesy, and friendliness.

12. Debrief After the Conference

During the conference, the manager should concentrate solely on the administration of the event and the domestic needs of the delegates. Finally, those involved should hold a briefing. Was your conference a success? What lessons did you learn? Add any action points to your checklist for the next conference.

DOS AND DON'TS

DO
- Pay attention to details and recheck them with all concerned.
- Be a perfectionist to the extent of being a nuisance: your conference could easily fail on account of an avoidable error.
- Make contingency plans to deal with unexpected problems such as illness or guest speakers who are unavoidably delayed.
- Plan to collect feedback from delegates for analysis and review.

DON'T
- Don't leave things to chance or assumption: double check all arrangements.
- Don't be afraid to make changes or deviate from the plan when the conference will benefit, or survive, as a result of such action. Take the initiative!

FOR MORE INFORMATION

Books:
Allen, Judy. *Event Planning: The Ultimate Guide to Successful Meetings, Corporate Events, Fundraising Galas, Conferences, Conventions, Incentives, and Other Special Events.* Ontario, Canada: Wiley, 2000.
Appleby, Pauline. *Organizing a Conference: How to Plan and Run an Outstanding and Effective Event.* 2nd ed. Oxford, England: How to Books, 2002.

"There is no better place in the world to find out the shortcomings of each other than a conference."

Will Rogers

Preparing a Marketing Plan

CHECKLIST

This checklist focuses on the standard model of marketing planning endorsed by several writers in the field. The model contains formalized procedures, although the degree to which these are followed will depend on the culture and requirements of your organization.

The discipline of marketing planning has been widely debated. Depending on their standpoint, academics have defended the standard textbook model or proposed alternative versions. Malcolm McDonald, one of the principal writers in the field, acknowledges that "marketing planning is still the most enigmatic of all the problems facing management."

DEFINITION

"Marketing planning is simply a logical sequence and a series of activities leading to the setting of marketing objectives and the formulation of plans for achieving them."

(Malcolm H.B. McDonald, *Ten Barriers to Marketing Planning* (1989))

ADVANTAGES

- Marketing plans encourage a rational approach to making business decisions.
- Everyone follows the same strategy, thus reducing potential conflicts, misunderstandings, and operational difficulties.
- They allow senior management to set out marketing strategy while leaving the day-to-day implementation to junior management.
- They help to highlight areas you might otherwise miss.

DISADVANTAGES

- Marketing plans form a complex process that requires basic knowledge and skills to plan.
- They are time-consuming and therefore costly to construct and follow.
- Firms composed of small business units lose some of their flexibility.
- Procedures can tend to take over and become an end in themselves.

ACTION CHECKLIST

1. Set Strategic Objectives

Traditionally these have been set by top management, although current practice is to employ more democratic processes involving the key stakeholders, if not all the staff. They are not usually within the brief of the marketing planner alone. These objectives need to be kept firmly in mind and the strategies and action plans drawn up need to be broadly in line with them. The marketing process can't go forward without them. The written plan should include a copy of the strategic objectives and the organization's mission statement.

2. Conduct a Marketing Audit

This process enables a company to analyze and understand the environment in which it operates. It is the key to the SWOT analysis, the next stage in the marketing planning process. It is carried out in two parts: the external audit and the internal audit. The external audit should cover the business and economic environment, the market, and the competition; examine the important trends that have affected and will be affecting the market and the industry; and consider searching questions about competitors and customers, now and in the future. The internal audit should concentrate on the planner's own company and cover its operational efficiency and service effectiveness; its key skills, competences, and resources; its products or services; and its core business.

3. Carry out a SWOT Analysis

This is a summary of the audit listed under the headings Strengths, Weaknesses, Opportunities, and Threats, and should be included in the final written plan. Strengths and Weaknesses refer to the company and its internal environment. Opportunities and Threats are external factors over which the company has no control but which it must anticipate, evaluate, and try to exploit. Include only key data.

4. Articulate Your Assumptions

These assumptions are the strategic drivers of the marketing plan. They may relate to economic, technological, or competitive factors. Assumptions should be based on accurate information and sensible estimates of what can be achieved in the light of past performance. Sound information is problematic because the pace of change is making the future discontinuous from the past. Coming up with viable and challenging assumptions involves creative lateral thinking and breaking with the past. Only a few major assumptions should be included in the written plan.

5. Set Marketing Objectives

This is the central step in the marketing planning process. It is important not to confuse objectives (what you want to do) with strategies (how you are going to do it). Marketing objectives are concerned with which products are to be sold in which markets. The setting of achievable and realistic objectives is based on the analysis of the marketing audit; the objectives themselves drive strategy decisions. The objectives should be included in the written plan.

6. Estimate Expected Results

Marketing objectives should be SMART: Specific, Measurable, Achievable, Realistic, and Timetabled, for example, "to gain a 6 percent share of the overall market," or "to achieve 600 customers by the end of the year." Nonspecific terms such as "increase" or "maximize" should not be used unless they can be quantified.

"Running a media brand is about harnessing the value of people . . . journalists, DJs, editors—all of them are the brand."

Vijay Solanki

7. Generate Marketing Strategies

These describe the broad methods by which the marketing objectives will be achieved within a required time. They are generally referred to as the "marketing mix" or the "Four Ps": Product—what its benefits are to the customer; Price—how it is priced to attract the right, or appropriate, customer base; Place—who those customers are; and Promotion—how they can be reached. They should appear in the written plan.

8. Develop Programs

The general strategies must be developed so that they have their own programs or action plans. The combination of these plans and their relative importance will depend on the company. A large company with several different functions or departments may have several plans covering advertising, sales promotion, pricing, etc. Other companies may have a single plan, for example, a product plan embracing the Four Ps. Details of the programs should be included in the written plan.

9. Communicate the Plan

Everyone should understand the plan. It is advisable to communicate it to employees by giving a presentation instead of circulating written copies. If the plan is not effectively communicated, it is likely to be implemented poorly and will probably fail.

10. Measure and Review Progress

Monitor the plan as it progresses. Make sure the measures you collect are meaningful to its success. If circumstances change, revise the plan to include details of how you intend to take advantage of new opportunities or counter new threats; repeat steps 4–9 above in order to do this.

THOUGHT STARTERS

- Is your marketing unsystematic, opportunistic, haphazard, or initiative-led?

- Have you set measurable market targets in the past?

- Are your marketing objectives and tactics known and coordinated throughout the organization?

- Do you really know what your customers think of you?

- Is your market stable and your market position secure?

DOS AND DON'TS

DO
- Be clear on the organization's strategic objectives.
- Analyze information carefully.
- Adjust the plan to suit the size, culture, and circumstances of the organization.
- Consult on and communicate the plan.
- Remember that the plan is a means to achieve objectives, not a rigid control mechanism.
- Be aware that planning is a time-consuming exercise.

DON'T
- Don't confuse objectives (what you want to achieve) with strategies (how you are trying to achieve them).
- Don't spend too long projecting future markets from historical data.
- Don't let the planners alter the shape of the objectives.

FOR MORE INFORMATION

Books:
Hiebing, Roman G., and Scott W. Cooper. *The Successful Marketing Plan: A Disciplined and Comprehensive Approach.* 3rd ed. New York: McGraw Hill, 2003.
McDonald, Malcolm H. B. *Marketing Plans: How to Prepare Them, How to Use Them.* 5th ed. Woburn, MA: Butterworth-Heinemann, 2002.
Westwood, John. *The Marketing Plan Workbook.* London: Kogan Page, 2005.

Journal Articles:
Cousins, Laura. "Marketing Plans or Marketing Planning?" *Business Strategy Review* 2:2 (Summer 1991): 35–54.
Griffin, Tom. "Marketing Planning: Observations on Current Practices and Recent Studies." *European Journal of Marketing* 23:12 (1989): 21–35.
McDonald, Malcolm H. B. "Ten Barriers to Marketing Planning." *Journal of Marketing Management* 5:1 (Summer 1989): 1–18.

Web sites:
American Management Association: **www.amanet.org**
American Marketing Association: **www.marketingpower.com**

See also:
✔ Performing a SWOT Analysis (pp. 520–521)
✔ Strategic Planning (pp. 536–537)
✔ Writing a Business Plan (pp. 538–539)

"Grand business plans are all very well, but nothing beats dipping your toe in the water."

Karan Bilimoria

Producing a Corporate Mission

DEFINITION

There is a great deal of contradiction in the literature over the differences and similarities between vision and mission. It probably doesn't matter what you call it, or whether you treat them separately or as one and the same. It is the process that is important, and this checklist therefore focuses on that process.

In this checklist a corporate mission or vision is taken to mean a description of the road ahead. The mission statement:

- describes the purpose of the organization;
- identifies how an organization defines success;
- outlines the strategy that will be followed to achieve success;
- incorporates the shared values and behavior that the organization expects from employees.

The corporate mission may be known as a corporate philosophy, a credo, or a set of values. Whatever it is called, it should combine the inspiration of where we are going with the realities of where are we now and how are we going to get from here to there. The process of developing a corporate sense of mission incorporates such techniques as strategic planning, developing a corporate culture, internal communication, and empowerment. It involves writing a mission statement, from which appropriate goals and targets can be derived for specific business units and departments. (Strategic planning and setting objectives are dealt with in separate checklists.)

A mission statement does not create a sense of mission. Employees need to feel that they are part of the process, and they will respond to a mission statement only if they can understand it, relate to it, and own it. Developing a sense of mission is usually more successful if it is viewed as a long-term, evolutionary process. However, an organization can develop a mission statement and use it to focus the business. This approach is usually successful only if there has been close consultation with managers as the mission is developed.

ADVANTAGES

It is widely believed that an organization with a sense of mission will outperform those that don't have one.

A well-produced mission:

- outlines clearly the way ahead for the organization;
- informs and inspires employees;
- identifies the business in which the organization will be operating in the future;
- defines success;
- serves as a living statement that can be translated into goals and objectives at each level of the organization.

DISADVANTAGES

Missions fail when:

- the top management team lacks consensus;
- the organization's identity, goals, and strategies are poorly defined;
- communication with employees is ineffective;
- planning and focused implementation are neglected.

ACTION CHECKLIST

The process of establishing a mission is a task for the senior management team. It involves a detailed analysis of the strategy and future of the company. Conducting a SWOT analysis can be helpful in identifying your company's strengths and opportunities.

1. Create a Project Team

The mission team may comprise the complete senior management team in a small organization or a working group of a larger management team. An external facilitator is often useful in assisting the team to reach a consensus.

2. Gather Information

The project team should meet with all the senior managers and research internal and external information on the current strategy and image of the company.

Interview senior management, seeking to identify areas of agreement and conflicts in attitudes, opinions, and strategic thinking.

Obtain an internal view of the organization by talking to a number of influential managers. Research external opinion by consulting press files, analysts' reports, and customers and suppliers.

Compare the views. Use the acquired information to build a broad picture of the company.

The project team should collate this information and prepare a detailed report to present to the senior management team.

3. Build Consensus

The senior management team should work to reach a consensus of a clear vision for the company: an external facilitator can play an important role here. This vision may define direction—a clear declaration of where the management team wants to take the organization. It certainly constitutes a clear message of the firm's intentions to all stakeholders.

Explore barriers that may pose obstacles to the desired direction and agree on appropriate steps and responsibilities for dealing with them. This is the point at which the team begins to own the mission and take responsibility for it. Such obstacles may be perceived at the level of resources: they are probably at the level of core competencies, and appropriate staff development may be needed to overcome them.

4. Draft a Mission Statement

 The mission statement should be written by the senior management team, as it needs to draw on the consensus already reached on the future of the organization. The mission statement is the guide to the company-wide evolution of the corporate sense of mission.

A good mission statement includes:

- a description of the business;
- the mission of the organization;
- the broad strategies to be pursued to fulfill the mission;
- a statement of the guiding values of the organization.

Mission statements often broadly declare the organization's goal of being the best; identify the importance of people, quality, and service; and emphasize the role of innovation, communication, and growth.

Mission statements should be assessed in terms of clarity, succinctness, memorability, credibility, and motivational power, and should be revised accordingly. The mission statement should be worded in such a way that all employees can relate to it.

5. Develop Action Plans and Set Objectives

Action plans should aim to build on the consensus and commitment developed among the senior management team and spread it throughout the organization. Set objectives by asking what needs to be done to realize the mission. Formulate plans to overcome the major barriers to achieving the vision—this is where the mission process meets the strategic planning process. Decide how to communicate the mission.

6. Communicate the Mission

Workshops, internal newsletters, and group meetings are all useful in communicating the corporate mission. It is important to develop a sense of ownership of the mission throughout the organization: it is the employees who bring it to life.

7. Monitor and Review

Developing a sense of mission should be viewed as a long-term process. Introduce mechanisms that allow you to continually monitor the views of all stakeholders so that you know how far the sense of mission has spread, how deep the relevance and understanding of the mission statement are, and to what degree corporate values have spread throughout the organization. Use

regular group meetings to refine your corporate philosophy.

DOS AND DON'TS

DO
- Develop a broad picture of the organization and its goals.
- Gain an understanding of the existing culture of the organization.
- Focus on the core activities of the organization.
- Listen carefully to the views of all stakeholders.

DON'T
- Don't move without a consensus among the senior team.
- Don't see this as a quick process.
- Don't see this as a onetime activity.

THOUGHT STARTERS
- Is there a broad understanding of what the organization's values are and where the organization is headed?
- Is each staff contribution recognized as a key part in the mission?
- Do staff know what the mission of the organization is?

FOR MORE INFORMATION

Books:
O'Hallaron, Richard, and David O'Hallaron. *The Mission Primer: Four Steps to an Effective Mission Statement.* Richmond, VA: Mission Incorporated, 2000. (Includes CD-Rom)

Journal Articles:
Lencioni, Patrick M. "Make Your Values Mean Something." *Harvard Business Review* 80:7 (July 2002): 113–117.
Rangan, V. Kasturi. "Lofty Missions, Down-to-earth Plans." *Harvard Business Review* 82:3 (March 2004): 112–119.

Public Relations Planning

DEFINITION

The Institute of Public Relations defines public relations practice as "the discipline which looks after reputation with the aim of earning understanding and support, and influencing opinion and behavior."

While media relations—building the right profile in the press, on radio, and on TV—is an integral part of public relations, it does not represent the whole picture. Public relations involves sending the right messages about your organization to every audience that could affect your business, whether positively or negatively; media relations is just one way of communicating with some of those audiences. By using public relations, you can "manage" your reputation rather than leaving it to chance.

ADVANTAGES

Effectively managing public relations can:
- influence public opinion of the organization and enhance corporate image;
- create awareness of a product, service, or brand, leading to sales;
- generate support for the organization's work;
- develop long-term business relationships;
- improve staff recruitment and retention.

DISADVANTAGES

There are no real disadvantages to public relations planning, but failure to manage public relations effectively can result in:
- misrepresentation of an organization's activities or products;
- damage to corporate image;
- boycotting of an organization's operations;
- lack of public understanding of the organization, leading to missed opportunities;
- loss of advantage to competitors;
- loss of business and sales.

ACTION CHECKLIST

In order to develop a public relations plan, you need to look at the overall business aims and objectives of your organization. The public relations objectives should support these and link to the overall business plan.

1. Define Target Audiences

These will depend on the nature of your business, but are broadly defined as:
- customers/clients—those who buy or use your products or services;
- the media—press, radio, TV, Internet;
- internal groups—current and future employees, suppliers, distributors;
- community groups and pressure groups;
- government—federal, state, local;
- investors, shareholders, potential sponsors.

2. Conduct Research

It can be valuable at this stage to undertake research among your customers or the groups you wish to influence to establish their current awareness and opinion of your organization, product, or service. The findings will reveal which areas you need to concentrate on, and can then act as a benchmark against which to measure your success in meeting your objectives.

3. Set Public Relations Objectives

Objectives show what you plan to do, while strategies and programs describe how you plan to do it. Objectives should be realistic, measurable, and achievable within a specified time limit.

For example, if your organization has a marketing objective to increase purchases of Product X by consumer group Y by 10 percent over the next 12 months, you could set a public relations objective to improve awareness of the benefits of Product X among consumer group Y within the next 12 months.

4. Decide Key Messages

Decide on the messages that you wish to get across to the different groups your organization needs to communicate with. Outline the concepts you wish to convey—precise wording and presentation can only be determined later when you have chosen your media.

5. Clarify Resources

Establish the financial and human resources available to commit to public relations. Your list should include budget, staff, time, equipment, IT, design, and printing facilities.

Indicate which are in-house resources and which may need to be bought in; then you will be in a position to make choices about where to spend your budget.

6. Select a Program of Activity

The program describes the actions you intend to undertake to achieve your objectives. It should include a timetable detailing planned actions, perhaps classified by phases or activities, on a monthly, quarterly, and yearly basis. The program should clearly prioritize the communication channels you have chosen.

Below are examples of types of activity you might pursue. They are outlined under broad headings for ease of

access, but some of these activities can often be used in communications with multiple audiences, although they might emphasize different messages. For example, a briefing could be used for public affairs and lobbying, but it could also be used to communicate with potential sponsors, staff, and community leaders.

Media relations

- Press releases/statements, articles, radio and TV interviews and discussions, press conferences and briefings, photo opportunities and photographs, press visits, and press interviews (telephone or face to face).

Internal communications

- In-house newsletters, staff briefings and seminars, bulletin boards, memos, briefing papers, training manuals, internal videos, open houses, conferences, intranets, and e-mails.

Public affairs and lobbying

- Briefing documents for senators, members of Congress, and state legislators, submissions to government committees, briefings/presentations to senators, members of Congress, state legislators, and federal and state government officials.

Events management

- Exhibitions, conferences, talks, presentations, road shows, staffing a stand or leading workshops at trade shows, competitions, and awards.

Community relations

- Familiarization visits, community projects, sponsorship of local charities, open houses for community leaders and neighbors, information videos, consultation and discussion groups.

Investor relations

- Reports, accounts, annual general meetings, briefings and presentations, stockholder newspapers/magazines, and corporate videos.

✔ 7. Evaluate Successes and Failures

Making your public relations objectives measurable enables you to evaluate how well various activities have worked. You can measure success in terms of "output objectives"—for example, did you meet your original aim to release a given number of stories to the business media each quarter?

Measuring success by "impact objectives," however, is more valuable in the long term—for example, did you succeed in your original goal of raising awareness within a specific group and affecting its members' behavior? Impact can be harder to measure than output, but the results provide more accurate performance indicators.

You can also put systems in place to measure, for example, the number of leads and sales generated by media coverage or conduct follow-up research to determine changes in awareness and attitudes as a result of a public relations campaign.

THOUGHT STARTERS

- To whom are you talking?

- What message do you want to communicate?

- Why do you want to communicate it—what are the goals and objectives?

- Which activities are you going to use?

- When are you going to carry them out?

- How much will it cost in resources?

- How will you evaluate your success?

FOR MORE INFORMATION

Books:
Cutlip, Scott M. *Effective Public Relations.* 9th ed. Upper Saddle River, NJ: Prentice Hall, 2005.
Caywood, Clarke L. *The Handbook of Strategic Public Relations and Integrated Communications.* New York: McGraw-Hill, 1997.

Web sites:
Institute for Public Relations: **www.instituteforpr.com**
Public Relations Society of America: **www.prsa.org**

"The public may be willing to forgive us for mistakes in judgment but it will not forgive us for mistakes in motive."
Robert W. Haack

Establishing a Customer Service Program

CHECKLIST

This checklist describes the stages in establishing an organizational framework that maximizes the value offered to and derived from customers.

DEFINITION

Successful customer service means making customers want to come back for more, and getting them to recommend products and services to others. It is about not only meeting expectations, but delighting customers by focusing staff energies on offering value, getting it right the first time, and yet improving it in the future.

ADVANTAGES

A comprehensive customer service program impacts on the organization through:
- increased success;
- a developing and satisfied work force.

ACTION CHECKLIST

1. Secure the Commitment of Top Management

Unless top management is fully committed to the concept of customer service, there is very little chance of success. A formal customer service program helps clearly focus roles and responsibilities.

2. Know Your Customers

Excellence in customer service is wholly reliant upon knowing your customers' needs and expectations. Needs are not the same as demands: people don't ask for what they don't expect to get, even when it can be provided. Anticipating real needs can give competitive advantage.

While most companies have internal customers in other departments, divisions, and sectors, establishing external customers' needs can be complex. A range of approaches is available, including:
- feedback directly from customers and staff;
- direct discussion with customers;
- analysis of customer complaints, enquiries, and thank-yous;
- attitude surveys and questionnaires;
- site visits;
- focus-group discussions and customer audits.

3. Assimilate the Major Elements of Customer Service

Customer service is more than just an excellent product or a first-class service; it involves a host of elements that contribute to genuine service and value for the customer. In the sales process these might include:
- clarity of literature on product features, price, payment methods, availability, and after-sales service;
- the way the first contact takes place and is followed up;
- simple ordering procedures designed to be convenient for the customer;
- prompt order processing;
- prompt notification of any changes to specifications or procedures;
- clear invoicing with no hidden charges;
- assistance when the product is delivered;
- easy after-sales contacts.

4. Develop Service Levels

It may be that performance standards do exist but are not formalized, recorded, or audited. It is not good enough to set indicators or levels that put the supplier's convenience before the customer's; such levels should be worked out, discussed, and agreed on with customers. Levels should be challenging but have a realistic chance of attainment. Questions to help set service levels may include:
- How many times does the phone ring before someone answers?
- How many transfers take place before the customer gets an answer?
- How long does it take to process an order?
- How long does it take to respond to a complaint?

Measurements must not gain such a hold on processes that they become a time-consuming nuisance; they should be realistic and helpful in developing a relationship—however short-lived—between supplier and customer. Remember, what gets measured, gets done.

5. Recruit the Right Staff

Your service is only as professional as the people delivering it; attracting new customers and retaining existing ones are tasks for competent people. To focus the recruitment process on customer service, introduce questions at the interview stage, covering, for example:
- candidates' experiences with customers;
- service levels and customer expectations;
- the prioritization of customer needs over in-house activities;
- incentives to motivate frontline staff.

Remember to include customer service in the orientation program.

6. Get Your Communications Right

Top management commitment to a customer service program is no good unless the right message is conveyed to all staff in the right way. If internal communications do not work as well as they should, external communications cannot be expected to be successful. Communications have to be reliable, consistent, and regular. All people then receive the same message and interpret it in the same way and end results will be the same.

7. Convert Complainants Back into Customers

Prompt and sympathetic handling of complaints can turn

"The important product comparisons come from people in the marketplace."

Regis McKenna

a disgruntled customer into a happy—and longer-lasting—one. People whose complaints are fully dealt with are more loyal than those who have no complaints.

Often, those who receive the complaint are not at fault, yet they bear the brunt of the customer's dissatisfaction. It is vital that all employees are familiar and comfortable with the company's procedure, and are fully prepared after receiving a complaint to start converting the customer's dissatisfaction into satisfaction. The complaint must be dealt with promptly, accurately—it may just be a misunderstanding or lack of information—and efficiently, so individuals on the front line must be familiar with seven rules for dealing with verbal complaints.

- Listen patiently—let the customer air the grievance without interruption.
- Acknowledge the customer's viewpoint—even if you don't agree.
- Apologize—say you are sorry if a mistake has been made, but don't overdo it.
- Find a solution—establish what needs to be done to rectify the problem.
- Keep the complainant informed—lack of ongoing information can exacerbate the problem.
- Reach a conclusion to resolve the problem for the customer quickly—a more permanent solution may take longer to find.
- Follow up—check that promised action happens.

8. Reward Service Accomplishments

Build excellent customer service into the culture by recognizing and rewarding staff for superior service performance. Try to recognize smaller accomplishments, not just the major ones.

Customers, too, appreciate rewards for their loyalty, and such rewards will make a significant contribution to their retention.

9. Stay Close to Your Customers

Staying close to customers means:
- carrying out continuous research to learn from them;

- asking questions about the quality and performance of the product at regular intervals after the sale;
- developing procedures to stay up to date with customer needs;
- listening.

10. Train Your People and Work toward Continuous Improvement

Recruiting the right staff is just one step in a customer service program. Training staff to understand customers' needs and tackle their problems, to turn threats into opportunities, is also a prerequisite for effective customer service. Train staff especially in friendly telephone and face-to-face techniques that allow them to be sincere and genuinely helpful instead of parroting empty phrases; it will more than repay the investment.

Publicizing feedback from customers is especially motivating for staff who are not in direct customer contact. Feedback can help you make continuous improvements in how things are done as well as in what is done.

THOUGHT STARTERS
- What irritates you as a customer?

- What delights you?

How can you:

- make ordering/purchasing more convenient for your customers?

- develop more direct relationships with your customers?

- reward loyal customers?

- recognize customer (dis)satisfaction?

FOR MORE INFORMATION

Books:
Arussy, Lior. *Passionate and Profitable: Why Strategies Fail and Ten Steps to Do Them Right!*. Hoboken, NJ: Wiley, 2005.
Barwise, Patrick, and Sean Meeham. *Simply Better: Winning and Keeping Customers by Delivering What Matters Most*. Boston, MA: Harvard Business School Press, 2004.
Bligh, Philip, and Douglas Turk. *CRM Unplugged: Releasing CRM's Strategic Value*. Hoboken, NJ: Wiley, 2004.
Brown, Stanley A. *Strategic Customer Care: an Evolutionary Approach to Increasing Customer Value and Profitability*. New York: Wiley, 1999.

Journal Article:
Rayport, Jeffrey F., and Bernard J. Jaworski. "Best Face Forward." *Harvard Business Review* 82:12 (December 2004): 47–52, 54–58.

531

CHECKLIST

"If you're not happy with yourself, how can you make the customer happy?" — Liisa Joronen

Setting Objectives

CHECKLIST

This checklist is designed for managers who participate in setting corporate objectives and who then have to interpret and apply such objectives to their own functional or departmental operation, including setting objectives with and for the people under their responsibility.

DEFINITION

An objective is an end toward which effort is directed and on which resources are focused. An objective should be specific (so that it is clear to those who are to work toward it), measurable (so that people will know when they have reached it or not), and, usually, tackled within certain time and cost constraints.

Setting corporate objectives means clarifying the strategic and policy requirements of the company and setting and agreeing on complementary operational objectives in relation to them. It is an integrated process that links corporate planning to business operations. As objectives are "rolled down" the organization, they are usually made more specific. Every department, every team, and every individual can and should have objectives.

Much ink has been spilled over the differences between aims, objectives, goals, and targets. There are no real differences except those of scale and time; some may be long-term and high-level, others short-term and low-level. The key is to use the terms that you—and the people you are dealing with—understand. Throughout this checklist we use the term "objective."

In order to have a chance of success, objectives must:
- identify a purpose and an area of responsibility such as improving performance or service;
- be specific and measurable;
- be achievable but challenging within the given time and resources;
- be written down for both clarification and referral;
- be subjected to a process of discussion, compromise, and agreement between those setting the objective and those who are to tackle it;
- be agreed on with the performer—this is not always possible, but is highly desirable because ownership leads to commitment.

ADVANTAGES

These include:
- a better understanding of corporate planning at operational level;
- a clear sense of direction;
- a better understanding of accountability throughout the organization;
- greater understanding in setting priorities;
- improved communication and motivation.

DISADVANTAGES

By failing to manage by objectives you risk:
- not knowing where you are going;
- never knowing what you have achieved;
- not knowing whether what you are doing is in tune with longer-term plans or higher-level objectives;
- confusion and demoralization.

ACTION CHECKLIST

✔ 1. Develop and Communicate the Organization's Mission/Vision Statements

People often confuse a mission with a vision statement. It is quite possible—even desirable—to have objectives relating to both.

The mission statement lays down the purpose for which the organization exists. It provides the umbrella statement for the organization's "standing" objectives.

The vision statement is the expression of an ultimate aim to which the organization aspires. It encapsulates the "change" objectives. For example:
- Our purpose is to make top-quality cars (Mission).
- Our aim is to become the largest-selling car manufacturer in the world by the year 2020 (Vision).

Such statements should be clearly communicated to and reinforced with all personnel, not just senior management.

✔ 2. Identify Corporate Objectives from the Mission/Vision Statement

It is important to link corporate objectives to mission and vision statements. This is usually the purpose of the strategic plan and the function of senior management, although this process is being increasingly decentralized throughout the firm in empowered organizations.

The strategic plan is formulated by an assessment of:
- what the company intends to accomplish and where it intends to be in terms of its market position in relation to the competition;
- how to be in the right markets at the right time with the right product(s) and service(s);
- how to guarantee a sustainable and profitable growth.

Much will depend on the values of the organization: values may be challenged and reassessed when setting high-level objectives, and vice versa—the adoption of new objectives may well lead to a reappraisal of values. The organization's values will influence how it tackles its objectives in terms of the importance it attaches to the environment, the welfare of its staff, and job security and to its public image in general.

In many organizations, however, objective setting still remains a largely top-down exercise. In such cases, objectives should be set out in a plan and communicated to all staff.

✔ 3. Agree on the Objectives for Senior Managers

This is a process of splitting the corporate objectives by function, business unit, or by product or service. It will be necessary to rank the objectives in terms of priority, draw

---

up time frames for achieving them, and identify the resources required to tackle them: this precedes the operational and financial (budgeting) planning of that function or business unit.

4. Make Sure Objectives Reach Departments and Individuals

Again, some organizations make this a two-way process, so that communication on key decisions is bottom-up as well as top-down. Don't wait for ever for top-down objectives; establish your own at department level that reflect the organization's mission and are in harmony with what your customers need and what your resources are geared to deliver.

5. Agree on Objectives with Those Who Are to Tackle Them

Setting objectives should happen not by diktat or decree, but by proposing and seeking ideas, by discussion, negotiation, compromise, and agreement. That is an ideal situation. The minimum that both objective-setter and objective-performer should require from a one-on-one meeting is an answer to each of Kipling's six honest serving men: who, what, where, when, why, and how?

6. Identify Appropriate Performance Measures

Performance measures should allow progress against objectives to be measured. Performance measures (which can be employed on a team or individual basis) should indicate what is expected and how well people are doing in attaining their objectives. Performance measures should be clear, concise, easy to collect and interpret, and relevant in that they should provide information that tells you and your organization how well you are performing.

Measures are usually related to:
- efficiency (how quickly you deliver);
- effectiveness (how good/accurate/relevant the service delivery was for the customer);
- cost-efficiency;
- cost-effectiveness.

They usually cover information relating to:
- finance—costs as well as income;
- customers—new and lost;
- markets—penetration thereof;
- resources—consumed, saved, or required anew;
- processes—how efficiently and effectively tasks and activities are accomplished.

Performance measures should also be agreed on between job-holder and manager and should be reviewed regularly, especially if there are significant changes to the work content. They are of benefit to the organization and the individual in terms of personal development. Managers may need time to help staff understand and interpret objectives for their department or their part of the organization, and even to help them determine what their own contribution to corporate objectives should be.

7. Set up Procedures for Reviewing Performance

With step 6 above, this is the principal content of the performance appraisal. It is in the appraisal discussion that past performance is reviewed, learning opportunities are identified, and new or revised objectives are set for the next period.

DOS AND DON'TS

DO
- Write objective statements that are SMART— Specific, Measurable, Action-oriented, Realistic, Time- (and resource-) constrained.
- Set priorities by ranking what must be done and what you would like to have done.
- Restart the cycle regularly by reviewing and revising objectives.

DON'T
- Don't leave out those who are responsible for achieving the goal from the discussion and agreement process necessary to setting it.

THOUGHT STARTERS
- Are you clear on the "fit" between what you do and where the organization is going?
- Do your people have clear targets that are live issues in the workplace?
- Are targets measured for performance against financial, customer, and personal development indicators?

FOR MORE INFORMATION

Books:
Rouillard, Larrie A. *Goals and Goal Setting: Planning to Succeed.* 3rd ed. Menlo Park, CA: Crisp, 2002.
Smith, Douglas K. *Make Success Measurable! A Mindbook-Workbook for Setting Goals and Taking Action.* New York: Wiley, 1999.

See also:
- Conducting a Performance Appraisal (pp. 438–439)
- Performing a SWOT Analysis (pp. 520–521)
- Strategic Planning (pp. 536–537)
- Writing a Business Plan (pp. 538–539)

"In business as on the battlefield, the object of strategy is to bring about the condition most favorable to one's own side."
Kenichi Ohmae

Strategic Partnering

CHECKLIST

This checklist describes the planning phases of strategic partnering: making the decision to partner, structuring the partnership, and selecting an appropriate partner. The principles apply equally to commercial partnerships and public-private sector partnerships.

DEFINITION

Strategic partnering agreements allow organizations to take advantage of market opportunities and respond to customer needs in collaboration, allowing them to do so more efficiently and effectively than they could separately. Such agreements may be for defined periods of time and may be nonexclusive.

Collaboration is the process by which partners adopt a high level of purposeful cooperation to maintain a trading relationship over time. The relationship is bilateral; both parties have the power to shape its nature and future direction over time. (Spekman)

Partnering means:

- spreading risk and trusting others to act in joint best interests;
- seeking a strategic fit between partners so that objectives match and action plans show synergy;
- finding complementary skills, competences, and resources in partners;
- sharing privileged or confidential information.

ADVANTAGES

Strategic partnering can help an organization:

- find an outlet for excess manufacturing capacity;
- gain quick, low risk access to new markets;
- strengthen its technological base;
- achieve economies of scale through high volume, low cost, and mass distribution;
- overcome geographic, legal, or trade barriers;
- speed up innovation and new product introduction.

DISADVANTAGES

Unsuccessful partnering may result in the following:

- a lack of strategic fit
- an imbalance in the relationship between partners
- implementation problems because of differing leadership styles. Although the fit may appear to be good, traditional control methods may hinder the interdependence strategic partnership requires.
- a lack of trust and confidence
- slow decision making
- key requirements for a market project are concentrated in one of the partners

ACTION CHECKLIST

Phase 1 Making the strategic decision

1. Consider Your Partnering Needs

Few organizations have all the resources or skills to tackle new market opportunities or other initiatives independently and maintain the economies of scale: low cost, high volume, and mass distribution. Going it alone can mean high investment, slower response to changing circumstances, and an infrastructure that may require dismantling, possibly soon afterward.

2. Analyze the Changing Marketplace

Take a good look at your organization in relation to its sector and market position. Understand who is emerging as a market leader and why, which market trends are beginning to dominate, and how the market is likely to develop in the future. The organization's stakeholders—customers, employees, stockholders, and suppliers—provide an invaluable resource to be tapped in this data-gathering exercise.

Carry out a SWOT analysis and look at how you got where you are. Do you need to invest in your technological base, your processing capacity, or new markets? Does market stability—or volatility—make that investment affordable or desirable? Look at what comparable organizations are doing to compete on innovation, service, and value for the customer.

3. Imagine the Future

This may well mean rethinking the business you are in or adjusting your business focus to concentrate on your core strengths. It is important not to be locked into the thinking of the past if you are to express a clear vision for the future. Such a vision should be owned by personnel throughout the organization as the driving force energizing the organization.

4. Look Closely at Your Processes

When considering a strategic partner, remain conscious of what it is really like inside your own four walls. Try to gain a knowledgeable perspective on your company's:

- programs for continuing improvement and development;
- policies and practices of releasing authority to encourage initiative;
- generation, manipulation, and use of key information;
- ability to respond to market changes.

Identify the key processes that you are, or need to be, best at. Identify skills you need to develop and improve. Gaining excellence in a core competence requires years of consistent effort and application and continual renewal. A core competence, however, is probably your greatest bargaining chip in negotiating a strategic partnering agreement.

Phase 2 Structuring the strategic partnership.

1. Decide on the Field of Cooperation

A strategic partnership can take one of three forms: horizontal, vertical, or diagonal.

- Horizontal partnerships are usually formed with former competitors from your industry. Collaboration for the purpose of research and development usually comes under this umbrella.

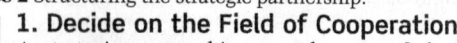

"The Great Principles on which we will build this Business are as everlasting as the Pyramids."

Gordon Selfridge

- Vertical partnerships are usually formed with organizations in the supply-delivery chain such as suppliers, marketers, or distributors.
- Public/private partnerships are formed with organizations from other industries.

2. Decide on the Level of Cooperation
Consider:
- optimal time frames for making the project operational;
- resources available for the project;
- how formal the structure needs to be between partners—the legal form of organization, process and communication procedures, control processes, and organizational structure.

3. Decide on the Level of Involvement
It may or may not be a good idea to restrict the agreement to two partners. Innovation, production, and delivery, for example, may benefit strategically from partnerships with multiple partners, each bringing specific expertise and expanding the richness and the potential of the collaboration. In this case the partnership becomes a dynamic network of contributors. The addition of every extra partner, however, multiplies the possibility of something going wrong.

4. Decide on Measurement and Control
All strategic partnerships need some form of control. Determine:
- which activities which partner will control;
- how much control each partner will exercise;
- how partners will exercise control.

It would be ideal for partners to have similar measurement systems, but this is unlikely. Contribution to, and outcomes from, the partnership may be difficult to apportion precisely when marketing and quality targets and learning objectives are key contributors to financial goals.

Phase 3 Selecting the partner

1. Evaluate Intra- or Extra-industry Players for Basic Fit
This is largely a question of information gathering and analysis. Having decided on a horizontal, vertical, or diagonal approach, search out leading or emerging players that can add their strength to yours in a win-win partnership. Ask yourself questions like these:
- What are the risks of such a collaboration?
- Does this potential partner have a hidden agenda?
- How turbulent is the existing market? What does the future look like?
- Are there other collaborators or associates in the game?

Public-private sector partnerships can involve multibillion-dollar projects. Selection of key partners is critical to concluding such projects successfully, on budget, and on time.

2. Establish a Partnering Champion
The partnering champion should be a senior manager who commands respect at all levels, has outstanding analytical ability, and gets things done. The champion is responsible for establishing the framework for the partnership agreement, promoting ownership

of the partnership, and making it work in the startup phase.

3. Examine Strategic Fit
It is more important that partners share a broad business philosophy than short-term goals. The partnership needs to fit with the overall strategic plans of each organization; joint development of belief systems, business plans, partnership structures, and timescales flow from this agreement.

4. Beware of Hidden Dangers
Cultural incompatibility may lurk beneath the surface of many potentially successful partnerships. Management style, organizational feel, and the way things really get done are hard to quantify and all the more difficult to assimilate, and they are often impossible to impose from the outside.

DOS AND DON'TS

DO
- Do focus on business logic but avoid concentrating on short-term gain.
- Do identify critical issues and potential obstacles.
- Do recognize the importance of cultural fit.
- Do build in flexible processes.

DON'T
- Don't ignore areas of potential conflict.
- Don't underestimate the resources required (money, time) for major projects.

THOUGHT STARTERS
- What changes are affecting your markets?
- How long will these changes last?
- How swiftly can you adapt to such changes?
- Is investment in your own resource levels the best answer?

FOR MORE INFORMATION

Books:
Child, John, and David Faulkner. *Strategies of Cooperation: Managing Alliances, Networks and Joint Ventures.* 2nd ed. New York: Oxford University Press, 2005.
Lendrum, Tony. *The Strategic Partnering Handbook.* 4th ed. Sydney, Australia: McGraw Hill, 2003.
Mockler, Robert J. *Multinational Strategic Alliances.* New York: Wiley, 1999.
Spekman, Robert E., Lynn A. Isabella, and Thomas C. MacAvoy. *Alliance Competence: Maximizing the Value of Your Partnerships.* San Francisco, CA: Wiley, 2000.

"No business enterprise can succeed without sharing the burden of the problems of other enterprises."

Ayn Rand

Strategic Planning

CHECKLIST

This checklist is for managers planning the strategic position and direction of their organization for the first time. It provides a framework of practice to draw on and encourages strategic thinking rather than imposing a sequence of steps to follow.

Such is the pace of change, the growth of uncertainty, and the diversity of customer expectations today that the major risk to survival and success is in not planning. Strategic planning helps you manage the future; if you don't manage the future, the future will manage you.

DEFINITION

Strategic planning goes to the heart of what an organization does, why and how it does it, and where it is going. In *The Strategy-Led Business* (1996), Kerry Napuk describes strategic planning as "a total concept of the whole business involving a framework and process that guides its future." Strategic planning addresses a number of basic questions:

- Where are you now?
- How did you get there?
- What business are you in?
- Where do you want to be in the future?
- How are you going to get there?

ADVANTAGES

Strategic planning provides an organization with a framework for:

- understanding its position in the marketplace;
- moving forward with a sense of direction, purpose, and urgency;
- focusing on key issues such as quality, productivity, and customer satisfaction;
- improving motivation and communication at all levels;
- changing to deliver required results and profitability.

DISADVANTAGES

Failing to plan makes an organization reactive, vulnerable to threats, and closed to opportunities. The strategic plan needs to be:

- flexible—adaptable to change (but too much change can cause havoc);
- responsive—taking account of the market and environmental conditions;
- creative—inspiring commitment and making the organization stand out;
- challenging—but realistic so that people can get to grips with it;
- focused—clear, defined, and understandable to staff and customers.

ACTION CHECKLIST

1. Involve All Managers and Staff

The planning process should not be restricted merely to contributions from senior representatives. All parts of the organization should play a part and all staff will have a contribution to make as stakeholders.

2. Where Are You Now?

Analyze recent performance to identify the current position of the organization in relation to its market and industry sector. Questions should include:

- What is your current market position in relation to your competitors?
- How do customers see you?
- What is your market share?
- What are your strengths (and weaknesses) in relation to your competitors?
- Are you on an upward or downward curve?

3. How Did You Get There?

Assess the reasons and factors that created this situation, for example:

- What did you do right (or wrong) to get there?
- Were you in the right place at the right time?
- What does your success owe to market circumstances?
- What does your success owe to good planning, bad planning, or no planning?

4. Examine Your Corporate Identity

Try to gain a clear sense of identity by asking:

- What kind of people are you?
- What kind of values do you have?
- What people strengths (or weaknesses) do you have?
- What kind of leadership do you have?
- How would you describe morale?

It is important to gain a balanced view of the organization. Do not just see the rosy side—be comprehensive, seek evidence, and base your future planning on realism.

5. Carry Out a SWOT Analysis

Summarize your findings from the external and internal audits conducted in steps 2–4 above under the headings of (internal) Strengths and Weaknesses, and (external) Opportunities and Threats.

6. What Business Are You in?

Question your own marketing literature. Does it make it clear why you are there and what you are there to do? Think of your corporate focus, usually expressed in the organization's mission statement. Is it too limited (a risk in an age of increasing specialization)? Or is it too broad (a risk in an age that requires increasing diversification)? Don't have such a narrow perspective that you lose opportunities, but be wary of too broad a scope, which might lose focus and appeal.

"The essence of a strategy is not the structure of a company's products and markets, but the dynamics of its behavior."

George Stalk

7. Where Do You Want to Go?

Do you want to stay in the same business? Where do you want to be in the future? Do you want to expand into new areas? (Why?) Give priority to your core area? (What is it?) Deciding where you want the organization to be in the future means identifying a target destination that will shape all planning and decisions. Destination is usually expressed in terms of a vision statement.

There is some confusion and a good deal of overlap between missions and visions. Whatever distinctions are drawn, it is up to senior management to make a clear statement of what business the organization is in, where the organization is going, and how it is going to get there.

8. Establish a Time Frame

Visions usually take a rather long-term view. Although an organization needs time to change thinking and shift resources, targets are taking on ever-tighter time frames. As a general guide, visions may take eight to ten years to achieve, but strategic planning should generate objectives achievable within two to four years.

9. Set Objectives

Direction and destination need to be clarified, communicated, and agreed on. Be firm without being so rigid that modification causes failure. Set objectives by asking what needs to be done to contribute to the realization of the vision, covering:

- profitability and return on investment;
- market share and meeting market needs;
- product/service quality and customer service;
- growth and public responsibility;
- participation and commitment.

Your objectives may involve some or all of these elements and should be measurable. They should lead toward attaining the vision.

10. How Do You Get There?

Strategies need to account for the organization's weaknesses and provide the framework to put them right. The focus of the strategy, however, is on the outside world. Think of levels of empowerment and employee development; calculate plant and equipment and the investment needed; review flexible control systems and the information that you have available (or not) to make decisions. The SWOT analysis in step 5 related to the past and the present; now it is time to apply the following questions to the future.

Outside the organization:

- What changes are happening in today's markets?
- What is happening to customers' attitudes and demands?
- What is happening to technology?
- Which market areas give you the best chance of success?
- What will customers want in the future?
- How will you tackle competitors?

And inside:

- What people skills do you need to develop?
- How can you improve your product(s) or service(s)?
- How can performance be improved to meet demand?
- What critical success factors do you have?
- How will you generate the resources to do all this?

11. Communicate and Seek Feedback

Communicate details of the emerging plan throughout the organization. Consultation and feedback are vital to understanding and commitment, and your people on the ground are valuable sources of information about threats and opportunities.

12. Measure, Adapt, and Renew

The end point of strategic action is the combination of product(s), market(s), and technologies that produce results that realize the vision. The one constant is to stay close to the market. That means continuous change for the organization and continuous measurement of progress against the plan. Measurement is a key process. It indicates the levels of change and modification needed as the plan adapts to changing technologies and market forces and evolves to embrace new opportunities. Strategic plans are rolling plans: five-year plans should be rolled over every three years, three-year plans every two years.

THOUGHT STARTERS

- Have you looked at other organizations' strategic plans? If so, do they look credible?

- How well do you know your industry/market sector?

- How close are you to your customers?

FOR MORE INFORMATION

Books:
David, Fred R. *Strategic Management*. 10th ed. Upper Saddle River, NJ: Pearson Prentice Hall, 2005.
Johnson, Gerry, Kevan Scholes, and Richard Whittington. *Exploring Corporate Strategy*. 7th ed. New York: Prentice-Hall, 2005.

See also:

"The task of business strategy is to make the business more valuable by a specific route: that of targeting profitable customers."

Shiv S. Mathur

Writing a Business Plan

CHECKLIST

This checklist is designed as an aid to managers responsible for constructing a business plan, and provides a framework for its compilation. The success of a business plan depends as much on the clarity and realism of the thought behind it as on how it is expressed and put together.

DEFINITION

A business plan is not only a requisite for seeking financing, it is also an essential document for describing aims and objectives and enabling the measurement of progress toward achieving them. The business plan provides the means to:

- appraise the present and future of the business;
- define short- and long-term objectives;
- establish a framework for action to achieve those objectives.

It consists essentially of three elements: a marketing plan, an operations plan, and a financial plan.

- The marketing plan covers how market intelligence will be gathered and makes sure that the organization's strategies will meet market needs.
- The operations plan includes the supply of raw materials, technological requirements, key processes, resource needs, and production and delivery targets.
- The financial plan assesses fixed and variable costs and dictates minimum financial requirements.

ADVANTAGES

Clear business plans:

- form a yardstick by which to measure performance;
- are the starting point for departmental or divisional operational plans;
- provide a framework for offering incentives to managers;
- demonstrate that the organization knows where it is going;
- form the bridge between the organization's strategy and what people should actually do;
- can assist in attracting major customers, financing, and shareholders' support.

DISADVANTAGES

Business plans require:

- detailed thought, research, and application;
- absolutely clear expression that stands up to incomprehension and criticism;
- honest and realistic appraisal of the organization's shortcomings, problems, and obstacles as well as its strengths;
- writing from the reader's point of view, not the writer's;
- regular monitoring and modification if appropriate;
- acceptance by, not just imposition on, all the key players in the organization.

ACTION CHECKLIST

Before you start it may help to carry out a SWOT analysis of your organization or sector; this will help you focus on defining your objectives and drafting the plan. Remember that the SWOT involves not just an analysis of the past and present, but also considers the future, especially in terms of markets, customers, and technology.

As a general rule the plan should be no more than about 25 to 30 pages, focusing most strongly on the management and financial elements. The executive summary should not exceed two pages.

1. Set the Context
Describe the following:

- the background of the business, product, or service and a brief history of the organization
- who the customers are
- the past performance of the organization
- any key or influential elements that might dictate the success of the product or service

2. Define Corporate Objectives
Develop a list of short-term, specific targets that will help to indicate progress towards longer-term ones. Measurability is important.

3. Perform a Market Analysis
Persuade the reader/investor that the product or service will secure a substantial market. Include:

- a brief description of the overall market and the specific market segment targeted;
- detailed information on current and proposed customers;
- names of leading competitors, market share, and alternative products or services;
- market influences—economic trends, seasonal fluctuations, legislation, social factors.

Are you aware of who and where your target market is and of the changes affecting that market?

4. Propose Your Approach to Marketing (the Marketing Plan)
Describe the marketing strategy used to approach customers by detailing:

- the image of the organization you wish to convey;
- the key features that will differentiate the product;
- a description of promotional and publicity material;
- the Four Ps of marketing;
- channels of distribution.

What marketing methods do your competitors use, and how effective are they?

5. Describe Plans for Development and Production (the Operations Plan)
Touch on all aspects of researching, developing, producing, and delivering your product or service. Describe the research, development, and production processes with the expected costs of raw materials, labor, and plant and equipment. Include a brief section on contingency planning for possible disruption scenarios.

"After hard work, the biggest determinant is being in the right place at the right time."

Michael Bloomberg

 6. Clarify the Current Financial Situation (the Financial Plan)

Lay out exactly what is required of investors and lenders. The financial plan is composed principally of data documenting past, present, and projected performance, including startup costs, profit and loss statements, cash flow analyses, and balance sheets. Repayment will be of key interest to investors and lenders, so include accurate break-even projections. It is important to show how sound financial control will be exercised over borrowed and incoming funds. Make sure you can support your sales forecast with reasons for your assumptions, and opt for caution rather than the rosiest scenario.

7. Demonstrate That Management is Committed and Capable

Describe your strengths and skills. An organization chart should note managers' capabilities as well as responsibilities. If there are weaknesses, indicate how you propose to deal with them.

 8. Describe the Ownership of the Organization

An investor or lender will need to know the legal constitution of the organization—partnership, limited liability, corporation. Show how much investment is already being made and by whom.

 9. Discuss Critical Success Factors

Discuss risks and problems, not omitting actual and potential negative factors. Show that you are aware of likely changes in, for example, information technology, markets, or economic circumstances, and will be ready to correct overspending or failure to meet deadlines.

Give a brief account of critical success factors such as:
- the learning environment that generates success;
- specialists and technicians and their knowledge;
- how the team can respond to adversity and turn things around.

10. Conclude on a Positive Note

The conclusion summarizes the key features such as strategic direction, strengths and unique benefits, realistically projected sales, and returns. Include a proposed timetable of events to demonstrate sound planning. Write a strong conclusion that leaves the reader with a positive, dynamic impression.

11. Provide an Executive Summary

Written last, this nonetheless appears first in the final plan. Include the unique features of the product or service; the current, mid- and long-term direction of the organization; the benefits the product or service offers the defined market sector; the qualities and skills of the people who will make it all happen; a financial statement of assets, sales, and profit expectations and how much

capital is required; and, as a conclusion, a statement of return for the investor.

DOS AND DON'TS

DO
- Research the target readership and remember whom you are writing for.
- Consult as widely as is appropriate.
- Solicit help from appropriate sources such as accountants or bankers.
- Point out the "obvious" benefits of the product or service.
- Address fully any possible bones of contention.
- Remember the contingency aspects of the plan.
- Outline the qualities and skills of the management team.
- Keep it short, focused, organized and readable.

DON'T
- Don't make assumptions on the reader's behalf.
- Don't be too optimistic in estimating income potential or expecting an enthusiastic reaction.
- Don't use long words, technical jargon, or overcomplicated sentences.

THOUGHT STARTERS
- What is your main business?
- Who are your main customers?
- What is your main capability?
- How healthy—really—is your current financial situation?

FOR MORE INFORMATION

Book:
O'Donnell, Michael. *Writing Business Plans That Get Results: A Step-by-Step Guide.* New York: McGraw-Hill, 1991.

Journal Article:
Sahlman, William A. "How to write a great business plan." *Harvard Business Review* 75:4 (July-August 1997): 98–108.

See also:
✔ Performing a SWOT Analysis (pp. 520–521)
✔ Preparing a Marketing Plan (pp. 524–525)
✔ Setting Objectives (pp. 532–533)
✔ Strategic Planning (pp. 536–537)

539

CHECKLIST

"Planning, by its very nature, defines and preserves categories. Creativity, by its very nature, creates categories or re-arranges established ones."

Henry Mintzberg

A Program for Benchmarking

CHECKLIST

This checklist is for managers new to benchmarking or for those wishing to review current benchmarking practices.

Benchmarking is a powerful tool for organizations seeking continuous improvement. It is an essential part of many change programs, including total quality management and business process reengineering. A challenging technique to use, it requires careful management and a high level of commitment, but used effectively it can provide companies with a continuous competitive advantage.

Various types of benchmarking exist, including:
- internal benchmarking—the measurement and comparison of practices with similar practices in other parts of the company;
- industry or competitive benchmarking—industry-specific comparisons made either between direct competitors or with target companies with dissimilar products in the same industry;
- functional or noncompetitive benchmarking—the direct comparison of a function in two or more organizations, which may or may not be in the same industry;
- generic or best practice/world class benchmarking—benchmarking of the best practice of recognized world class companies.

Most organizations can use one or a mixture of these.

DEFINITION

Benchmarking is the ongoing structured process of identifying, understanding, and adapting outstanding practices of industry leaders to help a company improve its performance and achieve and sustain competitive advantage.

ADVANTAGES

Benchmarking:
- aids the setting or stretching of performance goals;
- focuses on and accelerates change;
- motivates staff by showing what is possible;
- provides an early warning of competitive disadvantage.

DISADVANTAGES

Benchmarking can fail for a number of reasons, including a lack of commitment, focus, or resources. There are no substantial disadvantages to benchmarking, however.

ACTION CHECKLIST

1. Plan Your Study

Identify the critical performance factors at which you wish to excel; from these select the broad areas in which to benchmark. Focus on those activities that are of real importance to your company, avoiding activities that are irrelevant or are simply easy to measure.

Select a small number of related processes to benchmark. Do not be too ambitious at this stage, particularly if this is the first benchmarking project your company has undertaken. When selecting processes to benchmark, remember the critical success factors: benchmarking must be supported by senior management, be integrated with corporate strategy, and be based on a sound understanding of your own processes.

Consider the legal and ethical issues of competitive benchmarking. Confidentiality and data security are important issues for benchmarking partners and groups.

2. Identify Personnel

Select a benchmarking team and a team leader. Most benchmarking is done by teams to take advantage of the range of skills and knowledge they can offer—use either an intact work group, a cross-functional team, or a functional team. Six members is an average team size. Although much work will be carried out by the benchmarking team, it is advantageous to encourage the participation of all staff, as benchmarking may identify gaps in performance that may require radical change anywhere in the organization. The involvement of process owners ensures they are part of the evaluation process and can become the champions of change.

3. Examine the Process(es) to be Benchmarked

Document the process(es) to be benchmarked to gain an understanding of the activities involved. Simple flow charts can be useful aids to help define the inputs to, and outputs from, the process. Any number of elements can potentially be measured, so it is important for the benchmarking team to determine which ones are true indicators of performance.

4. Plan Data Collection

Data is required in order to make comparisons between organizations or parts of an organization. This information may take the form of statistics, ratios, or detailed case studies and descriptions. As the key to the success of benchmarking projects, the data collection process should be carefully planned. Collect only the data required for decisionmaking: collecting too much information can be as bad as collecting the wrong data.

5. Identify Benchmarking Partners

Consider internal sources (different departments, divisions, or companies within the organization) and external partners (competitors, similar industries, or best practice/world class performers). Sources that can help in identifying partners include trade and industry journals, market research reports, government studies, databases, suppliers, customers, corporate networks, and study tours.

"The most successful innovators are the creative imitators, the number two."

Peter F. Drucker

Consider contacting a benchmarking clearinghouse or a joint interest group.

Solicit the participation of partners. Organizations are often willing to become involved if they can see that they will also benefit from benchmarking—after all, it should be a two-way process. Be willing to share data and findings and to respect requests for confidentiality.

✔ 6. Plan the Comparison Exercise and Gather Data

- Identify the "hard" and the "soft" issues that need to be measured. Hard issues include ratios, time, and costs. Soft issues might include management style, communications, or customer focus.
- Prepare an action plan. Identify who will collect the data, from where and when. The benchmarking team should develop an appropriate survey or interview guide. Questionnaires can be sent by mail or completed over the telephone or on site visits. Decide which is the most appropriate for your requirements.
- Collect the data. It is easy to underestimate the time that data collection requires—err on the side of caution when arranging fact-finding interviews.

✔ 7. Use Data Analysis to Plan Improvements

Draw up a matrix of performance indicators from your benchmarking partners (using spreadsheets and databases can help the analysis).

Compare your current performance against the data. Identify where your company is missing certain elements, fails to match the targets of others, or generally needs to improve. The benchmarking team should try to identify the causes of these failures and, with relevant additional staff, plan to remedy them. It is useful to research case studies of best practice, which can form useful aids to help communicate the objectives of change.

Involve process owners in setting goals to close, meet, and exceed the gaps in performance. The benchmarking team should develop detailed action plans, including measures of success.

✔ 8. Action Improvements

Once the business benefits that would result from change have been identified, communicate the benchmarking findings. If you demonstrate benefits, employees are more likely to support change. Implement the plan, making use of "process champions" throughout the company as catalysts for change. It is at this stage that resources will need to be committed, so it is essential to have senior management support for the project.

✔ 9. Monitor and Review

Monitor the success of the benchmarking in reaching its objectives; the impact of the improvements on the organization; the evidence of a change in the process; the value of the changes to the organization; and the willingness and the barriers to change.

Evaluate the success of the project. Decide if further change is needed. Select the next process to benchmark. Maintaining momentum is one of the most challenging problems in benchmarking.

541

CHECKLIST

DOS AND DON'TS

DO
- Secure senior management support.
- Make sure that benchmarking is a team activity.
- Understand your own processes before starting to look at those of other organizations.

DON'T
- Don't be too ambitious at the start.
- Don't underestimate the need for corporate willingness to change and an openness to new ideas.
- Don't view benchmarking as a tool for providing short-term gains.

THOUGHT STARTERS
- Is the performance of your organization as good as it could be?
- How do you match up to the performance of competitors?
- Are you focusing purely on financial measures or have you considered all your key processes?
- How do your processes compare with those of other organizations?

FOR MORE INFORMATION

Book:
Mard, Michael J., et al. *Driving Your Company's Value: Strategic Benchmarking for Value*. Hoboken, NJ: Wiley, 2004.

Journal Article:
Hanman, Stephen. "Benchmarking Your Firm's Performance with Best Practice." *International Journal of Logistics Management* 8:2 (1997): 1–18.

Web sites:
American Productivity and Quality Center:
www.apqc.org
CFO.com Benchmarking Center: **www.cfo.com**

See also:
- ✔ Deciding Whether to Outsource (pp. 542–543)
- ☆ Outsourcing (pp. 120–121)
- ✍ Outsourcing (p. 1851)

'Whatever a great man does, others imitate. People conform to the standards he has set.'

Bhagavad Gita

Deciding Whether to Outsource

This checklist is for managers addressing the decision of whether to outsource or not, and if so, what and how to outsource. The checklist describes the stages in the process, leading up to drawing up and testing a contract.

Often seen as a threat by employees and an opportunity by companies, outsourcing is becoming more widely accepted. In addition to the inevitable driver of cost savings, many contributory elements lead a company to consider outsourcing, in particular the need for flexibility as demand for products or services rises and falls and as ways of delivering them improve.

DEFINITION

Outsourcing is increasingly understood to mean the retention of responsibility for services by an organization while the day-to-day performance of those services is devolved to an external organization, usually under a contract with agreed standards, costs, and conditions.

In this checklist the organization considering outsourcing some or part of its functions will be called the "Organization"; the external organization designated to take them on will be called the "Agency."

ADVANTAGES

The Organization generally makes the decision to outsource for a number of reasons, including:

- cost and efficiency savings;
- greater financial flexibility through reduced overhead;
- operational flexibility and control through contractual relationships;
- a wish or need to focus on core activities;
- access to better management skills for non-core activities;
- staffing flexibility.

DISADVANTAGES

Outsourcing can:

- reduce corporate robustness by changing support functions;
- require considerable care in coordinating information flow with the Agency;
- reduce the Organization's learning capacity by depleting its skill base;
- impair the Organization's ability to integrate processes;
- compromise the Organization's control over the functions that are outsourced;
- damage morale and motivation as jobs appear to be lost;
- increase employees' insecurity, whether staff remain in the organization or are hired by the Agency.

ACTION CHECKLIST

✔ 1. Create a Project Team

Treat the outsourcing proposal like a project. Select a project leader and team, establish terms of reference, a method of working, and an action plan.

✔ 2. Analyze Your Current Position

Ideally, you should have carried out a radical review of the Organization's processes—you don't want to outsource a function that might be better integrated with one of your core activities. While maintaining a clear vision of where the business is going, evaluate:

- what advantages you can gain by concentrating on core services;
- the minimum corporate involvement necessary to perform functions that don't affect the customer;
- how much control you require over nondiminishing, nonproductive overheads;
- which functions are more viable operated by an external agency.

✔ 3. Pay Attention to People

As the contract stage approaches, your staff will suffer from anxiety and uncertainty. At best their working life will be transferred from one employer to another, at worst their job could be lost. Keep your people's welfare at the forefront of your thinking.

✔ 4. Benchmark

Someone somewhere is probably doing the same thing that you are in a better way, or in the same way at lower cost. Identify appropriate organizations to benchmark against, and establish which activities they are outsourcing.

✔ 5. Come to a Decision

Identify your core areas—Tom Peters says, "Do what you do best and outsource the rest." The principal questions are:

- What is core to the business and to the future of the business?
- What can bring competitive advantage?

Then decide whether outsourcing should become Organization-wide policy for non-core areas or whether it should be used only as the need arises.

✔ 6. Decide What to Outsource

Logically, what to outsource follows from the decision process. If you focus on the core competencies of the Organization, on your uniqueness, then targets for outsourcing become the support, administration, routine, and internal services of the company.

Areas that have traditionally been subject to outsourcing include legal services, transportation, catering, printing, advertising, accounting, and, especially, auditing and security. More recently these have been joined by call centers, data processing, IT services, information

"I don't want to feel responsible to outsiders with financial concerns that may differ from those of the welfare of IKEA."

Ingvar Kamprad

processing, public relations, buildings management, and training.

7. Tender the Package

The tender is an objective document detailing the services, activities, and targets required as well as a selling document designed to attract Agencies that can add to the Organization's capability. Outsourcing is not just a matter of getting rid of problem areas. Once you have defined an attractive package, send an outline specification and request for information to the Agencies that are most likely to be interested. The outline specification should contain the broad intention of the outsourcing proposal and the timescales the Organization has in mind. The request for information is a questionnaire-type eligibility test intended to establish the level of the Agency's competence and interest. The second stage is the invitation to tender, a precise document that spells out exactly what Agencies are required to bid for.

8. Choose a Partner

The tender process should be used to evaluate facts, but choosing an outsourcing partner is much more than choosing a new supplier, because the process involves a customized service, agreement on service levels, and a contract. At this stage the Organization is looking for an Agency with which it can agree on objectives and values, hold regular senior management meetings, and share otherwise confidential information. Harmony of management styles is a key requisite for success.

9. Introduce Your Staff to the Agency

Members of your staff scheduled for transfer to the Agency should meet their new management before any contracts are signed. Allowing employees to air their concerns and ask questions may help to reduce the feeling that they are being cast aside. On the other hand, glaring conflicts in style and personalities may emerge that could affect the contractual stage. Address other issues of terms and conditions of employment, including appropriate compensation if Agency employment is unavailable or not required.

10. Draw up the Contract

If the project team draws up the contract, provide appropriate legal input. The contract should spell out:
- the minimum service levels that the Agency will provide, checks and controls that these are met and clauses including remedies or financial compensation if they are not;
- the demarcation of service responsibilities and boundaries so that both Organization and Agency are clear on who is doing what;
- who owns what in terms of equipment and hardware;
- the fate of the staff to be outsourced and details of their terms and conditions of employment;
- flexibility and allowance for change, for example, if the volume of business changes radically;
- a contract term with a review date and a provision for the outsourced function to revert to the organization;
- a trial period before the contract becomes binding.

11. Test the Contract

Make certain that the contract will stand up to the rigors and complexities of actual operation. A trial period is ideal for making adjustments before the contract becomes final and for judging the likelihood of the partnership breaking down.

DOS AND DON'TS

DO
- Have a clear vision of what outsourcing should achieve.
- Understand the scope of the services to be outsourced.
- Outsource the performance of a function, not the responsibility for it.

DON'T
- Don't outsource strategic, customer, or financial management.
- Don't let the goal of cost savings dominate everything else.
- Don't think that outsourcing is the answer to every problem.

THOUGHT STARTERS
- Have you defined the core areas in which you need to excel?
- Do routine and support functions consume an ever larger slice of overhead?
- Will outsourcing be an extension of your organization's operations or an innovation?

FOR MORE INFORMATION

Book:
Greaver, Maurice F. *Strategic Outsourcing: a Structured Approach to Outsourcing Decisions and Initiatives.* New York: AMACOM, 1999.

Journal Article:
Gottfredson, Mark, Rudy Puryear, and Stephen Phillips. "Strategic Sourcing: From Periphery to Core." *Harvard Business Review* 83:2 (February 2005): 132–139.

Web site:
International Facilities Management Association: **www.ifma.org**

See also:
- A Program for Benchmarking (pp. 540–541)
- Implementing a Service Level Agreement (pp. 554–555)
- Managing Projects (pp. 568–569)
- Outsourcing (pp. 120–121)
- Outsourcing (p. 1851)

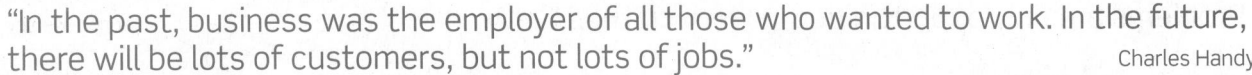

"In the past, business was the employer of all those who wanted to work. In the future, there will be lots of customers, but not lots of jobs."

Charles Handy

Disaster Planning

CHECKLIST

This checklist aims to help managers putting together a disaster plan for their organization. It covers physical disasters such as fires, floods, or terrorist attacks.

Having a disaster plan forces you to make decisions before a disaster strikes, allowing you to spend the first crucial days after a disaster dealing with the situation instead of deciding how to deal with it.

DEFINITION

A disaster plan (DP) aims to prevent or reduce the likelihood of a disaster occurring by identifying threats and taking the necessary preventative action, and to ensure that if a disaster does strike, the organization is prepared to deal with it effectively.

ADVANTAGES

In the event of a disaster, a DP:
- supports the continuity of operations;
- mitigates the financial consequences.

DISADVANTAGES

- Poor planning or an out-of-date plan may be worse than no plan at all.
- The planning process can be time-consuming.

ACTION CHECKLIST

✔ 1. Establish a Disaster Planning Team

This team should include staff responsible for personnel, buildings, public relations, and IT, as well as someone with general management responsibility. You may want to include an external advisor experienced in disaster planning. Appoint a team leader and a deputy. Senior management should clearly commit to the DP.

See that the needs of staff and other stakeholders are taken into account. Identify and prioritize the activities that are necessary to business continuity; consulting staff throughout the organization will help to establish a sense of ownership and commitment.

✔ 2. Carry out a Risk Assessment

Identify particularly vulnerable aspects of your industry, operation, or service and potential internal and external risks to your company. Evaluate and analyze these and act to eliminate or reduce them. Distinguish between areas needing immediate action (the repair of broken windows, for example) and those that can be dealt with over a longer period (the installation of a burglar alarm or sprinkler system). List the extra resources required. Consider appointing a claims adjuster in advance so that the insurance claim process can start immediately in the event of a disaster.

Check and seek professional advice where necessary on your company's:

- insurance coverage (is your existing coverage adequate?);
- maintenance of buildings and equipment;
- security (do your detection and alarm systems work? If you don't have any, should you consider installing them?);
- safety and fire precautions;
- storage systems (are important documents held securely? Is adequate offsite storage available for IT backups?).

✔ 3. Draw up a Disaster Plan

The DP should be simple and easy to understand while containing all the necessary information. It must be developed with the worst case scenario in mind but be flexible enough to be used in less severe cases. Get copies of comparable companies' disaster plans and learn from them. Remember that recovery from a disaster can take a year or longer.

The DP needs to address the following personnel issues:
- key personnel—include out-of-hours contact details (draw up a roster if necessary)
- the responsibilities of the key personnel, and the limits of their authority
- the location of the team's control center, preferably offsite

The DP should contain:
- prioritized functions and activities;
- floor plans;
- evacuation procedures;
- precautionary measures;
- sources and locations of further information;
- procedures for jobs to be done during the recovery period;
- a directory of suppliers of emergency equipment and supplies.

Anticipate the effects on employees, customers, suppliers, and others. Consider every part of your business operation.

Employees
- Make sure managers have employees' telephone numbers and home and e-mail addresses so that they can contact them out of work hours.
- Prepare to offer counseling and other help to deal with the after-effects of a disaster.
- Communicate with staff—overcommunicate if necessary—about progress, moving back into the building, safety, etc. Make sure staff know whom to contact with problems.
- Make alternative arrangements for paying staff if the usual mechanisms are put out of action.

Alternative premises
- Investigate a reciprocal arrangement for sharing space with other organizations.

Continuity of operations and the level of service to be provided
- The company needs to be operational as soon as possible, preferably the next day.

"Problems are only opportunities in work clothes."

Henry J. Kaiser

- Inform customers and suppliers and let them know how to contact you. Customers will desert you if you are unavailable for weeks.
- Brief your public relations spokesperson to deal with the media.

Physical communications

- Talk to your telephone company about forwarding calls.
- Plan for an ad hoc telephone directory and make sure your switchboard operators know what to tell callers.
- Decide where mail should be sent.

Equipment and resources

- Identify critical documents and their location so that vital material can be retrieved from damaged buildings.
- Store backups of important material, including IT information, offsite.
- Identify which resources would be needed during the recovery period and make sure they're available.
- Make sure cash is available at all times. Don't rush out and buy new equipment immediately—rental may be a better option.
- Consider establishing a resource network; identify cooperative partners with whom equipment, storage, and costs might be shared.

Keep copies of the DP in a number of locations for convenience and safety.

4. Pilot the Plan

A test run will reveal anything you've overlooked and indicate whether the plan is practicable. How long does it take to set up the control center? Will the communication systems work, even in the event of a natural disaster? Are the alternative premises suitable? Amend the plan as necessary to take into account any problems revealed by the pilot.

545

CHECKLIST

5. Communicate and Implement the Plan

A member of the disaster planning team should give a presentation to employees to ensure that everyone is aware of and understands the DP and its objectives, and knows what to do in an emergency. The orientation of new staff members should include information about the DP. Rehearse emergency drills and reaction procedures at least once a year to remind existing staff. Deal with any worries staff may have.

6. Monitor, Revise, and Improve the Plan

The DP is not set in stone—it should change with circumstances. At intervals (at least annually) test out individual components and the whole plan and revise as necessary, taking into account the impact of new developments and new technology. Review reported disasters to see what you can learn to benefit your own DP. Communicate any changes to staff.

THOUGHT STARTERS

- Have you ever been involved in a disaster? What can you learn from that experience?

- If a disaster did hit, would your organization survive?

- What risks does your organization face? What can be done to minimize them?

- Can you afford not to have a disaster plan? The costs of a disaster are not just financial—they include interruption to business, wasted time, and lost opportunities.

DOS AND DON'TS

DO

- Be prepared.
- Learn from others' mistakes—and successes.
- Involve staff.
- Make sure that all staff are aware of the plan.
- Communicate—with staff, customers, suppliers.
- Keep copies of the plan in a number of locations—it's no use if the plan itself is destroyed in the disaster!

DON'T

- Don't be complacent—what if it did happen to you?
- Don't assume you've thought of everything; listen to comments and suggestions.
- Don't think of disaster planning as a onetime task. You must keep the plan up to date.

FOR MORE INFORMATION

Books:
Toigo, Jon. *Disaster Recovery Planning: Strategies for Protecting Critical Information Assets.* Upper Saddle River, NJ: Prentice Hall, 2002.
Kaplan, Laura G. *Emergency Disaster Planning Manual.* New York: McGraw Hill, 1996.

Web site:
Federal Emergency Management Agency:
www.fema.gov

"Science writers foresee the inevitable and, although problems and catastrophes may be inevitable, solutions are not."

Isaac Asimov

Effective Purchasing

CHECKLIST

This checklist is designed to help those responsible for purchasing adopt a more effective strategy. This checklist is not intended to itemize the steps in administering a purchase order process; rather it aims to present a proactive approach to purchasing. While directed at those involved in centralized purchasing, the principles apply equally to decentralized buying.

DEFINITION

Most textbooks state that purchasing is about buying the right goods, at the right time, at the right price, in the right quantity, and of the right quality. While these are indeed fundamental requirements, effective purchasing has to deliver more than this. Adopting an effective purchasing strategy turns a reactive buyer into a proactive buyer who adds value to the process.

ADVANTAGES

Effective purchasing:
- is proactive and adds value for your organization;
- improves communication with suppliers;
- gives you a deeper understanding of the marketplace.

DISADVANTAGES

There are no real disadvantages to effective purchasing, but it requires time to:
- gather and sort internal data;
- evaluate suppliers.

ACTION CHECKLIST

Your organization

1. Understand Your Own Organization
Take time to learn how your own company functions and what is important to each department in terms of the supply of goods and services. What are the most crucial factors for each line manager in terms of quality, price, and delivery? Which items do they purchase most often, and what are they used for? How does each department determine its reorder levels?

Gather as much data as you can to provide a sound basis for formulating your strategy. Your internal customers will appreciate your professionalism and increase their sense of involvement in the process.

2. Compile a Purchase History
Use purchase orders and requisitions to compile a history of purchases. Gather data on product types, order quantities, lead times, pricing, order frequency, etc. Use this information to construct a purchasing pattern for key items.

3. Become a Proactive Buyer
Negotiate better deals with suppliers by telling them what volumes they can expect over the year. An-

ticipate reorder dates and do the groundwork in advance. Reduce delivery charges by ordering like products at the same time. Arrange for suppliers to stock frequently used items free of charge, thus reducing your storage requirements, controlling lead times, and giving you the benefit of bulk purchasing. Monitor price fluctuations for seasonal trends.

Your suppliers

1. Evaluate Potential Suppliers
Evaluate suppliers using the following criteria:
- sales and profitability
- how long they have been in business
- who their major customers are (if they are dependent on one customer, what will happen to the business if they lose the account?)
- what percentage of their sales your business will represent
- whether they have any third-party certification
- their quality control policy
- their procedure for handling customer complaints
- their invoicing and administrative procedures
- their level of insurance coverage

2. Visit Potential Suppliers
Find out who would be dealing with your account and how your orders would be processed. Ask to meet the people with whom you will have day-to-day contact. Do they make you feel welcome?

3. Get References
Ask for references. Talk to buyers in organizations that are similar to yours and have similar purchasing patterns.

4. Audit Your Major Suppliers
Perform regular audits on your major current suppliers to evaluate their continued level of performance. Do they still meet the criteria you established at the beginning of the relationship? What improvements have you noticed in the service since then?

5. Maintain Good Communication
You expect your suppliers to keep you advised of delivery dates and problems associated with your orders. Make sure you reciprocate; advise them if you're expecting a sudden decrease in purchases—or indeed an increased requirement. Just as you should tell them exactly what you want from them, get them to tell you precisely what they expect of you.

Show an interest in your suppliers' other accounts. Have they won or lost any major contracts? How are they affected by the economy? Will shipping costs increase as a result of rising fuel prices? Will the price of paper affect the major print job you have scheduled for the end of the year—can you prepurchase the paper to minimize the damage? Good communication and understanding of

your suppliers' business will ultimately filter back into your own.

Get to know your suppliers as human beings. It's much easier to do business and especially to solve problems when you know the person at the other end of the phone (but don't let personal considerations outweigh organizational ones).

6. Use Your Suppliers' Expertise
You can't be an expert in everything. Use your suppliers' knowledge and expertise to help you draw up work specifications.

7. Maintain a Competitive Element
Always review the price and service your suppliers are offering. Let them know they have to remain competitive. Retain documentation proving you sought alternative prices; you'll need it for audits.

8. Compare Quotations
Make sure quotes are based on identical specifications. Check the exclusions such as delivery, installation, training, and insurance. Check the contract period, renewal dates, and how long the price is guaranteed. What provision is made to hold prices at the current level or within the realm of the RPI for long-term contracts? What are the payment terms?

9. Visit Trade Fairs
Visiting trade fairs and reading trade journals are essential for keeping up to date with the market.

10. When Prices Rise, Negotiate
When price rises are inevitable, try to negotiate other advantages such as longer payment terms, prompt payment discounts, quarterly instead of monthly invoicing, management reports, price stability for a fixed period, free delivery, or increased delivery frequency.

DOS AND DON'TS

DO
- Involve your internal customers in the purchasing process.
- Assess and visit your suppliers regularly.
- Build relationships with suppliers based on mutual trust and good communication.
- Establish a clear code of ethics.

DON'T
- Don't allow yourself to be dragged into a Dutch auction by your suppliers.
- Don't stay with the same suppliers because you've always used them—be sure you're using them because they're the best.

Remember, your suppliers want to keep your business and may be able to help in other ways.

General hints/good practice

1. Establish a Code of Ethics
- Respect suppliers' confidentiality—don't disclose their prices and trading practices to their competitors.
- Declare any personal interest.
- Even though it is legally acceptable to receive gifts that would cost $25 or less, it is good practice not to accept gifts from suppliers or potential suppliers. Advise all suppliers of this in writing at the beginning of the relationship and prior to the Christmas period, when most suppliers traditionally send gifts.

2. Protect Yourself
- If you have a rollover contract, make sure you know when you have to give notice if you want to terminate.
- Be aware of the limits on your authority, and don't exceed them.
- Never make assumptions—clarify all details in writing.

3. Keep Your Side of the Bargain
See that your company pays suppliers in accordance with your agreements.

4. Maintain an Audit Trail
Always maintain an audit trail of all purchase documents.

THOUGHT STARTERS
- How much do you know about your organization's annual purchases?
- What is your organization's annual spend with major suppliers?
- How often have you visited your major suppliers?

FOR MORE INFORMATION

Books:
Cavinato, Joseph L. *The Supply Management Handbook*. New York: McGraw-Hill, 2006.
Paquette, Larry. *The Sourcing Solution: A Step-by-step Guide to Creating a Successful Purchasing Program*. New York: AMACOM, 2004.

See also:
✓ Inventory Control (pp. 574–575)

"A business must have a conscience as well as a counting house." — Montague Burton

Establishing a Performance Measurement System

This checklist provides guidance on establishing a performance measurement system for an organization or department.

The purpose of performance measurement is to establish how well an organization or department is accomplishing its mission and objectives. Measuring performance is also a key requisite in any continuous improvement program. Likewise, the information gained may be used to set up a program to benchmark against competitors, other organizations, or previous results.

CHECKLIST

DEFINITION

A performance measurement system provides an organized means of defining, collecting, analyzing, and making decisions regarding all performance measures within a process or activity.

A performance indicator is a level that enables managers to assess how efficiently, effectively, and cost-effectively any operation is performing. Performance measures provide a quantitative gauge of the degree to which you are meeting or exceeding the indicator. They require the collection of raw data and its conversion through a formula into a numerical unit. For example, the target may be to reduce the number of customer complaints from 10 percent of total sales to 5 percent (the indicator). To calculate the percentage of complaints, divide the total number of complaints by the total number of sales and multiply by 100.

ADVANTAGES

Measuring performance enables an organization to:
- understand its current position;
- determine whether improvements have actually taken place;
- identify where improvements need to be made;
- be aware of its processes;
- make sure that decisions are made on the basis of fact;
- know whether or not it is meeting its targets.

DISADVANTAGES

The only drawback to measuring performance may be the resources (staff and time) that it consumes. If you are considering introducing a performance measurement system, you should not underestimate the cost.

ACTION CHECKLIST

1. Designate a Performance Measurement System Committee

The committee will be responsible for the design, implementation, and review of the system. Its members should be drawn from all levels of the organization to map the whole process from beginning to end. Appoint a coordinator to oversee the system.

2. Identify the Process to be Measured

Examples of processes in practice include purchasing raw materials, getting the finished product ready for delivery, invoicing, and handling complaints. Each process usually needs its own performance indicators and measures. Questions for the committee to consider in identifying processes for measurement include:
- What product or service do we produce?
- Who are our customers (internal and external)?
- What exactly are our processes?
- What do we do?
- How do we do it?
- What starts and what ends our process?

3. Identify the Activities to be Measured

From the process flow chart the committee can identify activities that are critical in terms of total process:
- efficiency and cost-efficiency
- effectiveness and cost-effectiveness
- quality, zero defects, or customer satisfaction
- timeliness
- productivity
- safety

Critical activities are those:
- that have to be watched closely and acted on if their performance does not meet specifications;
- that should be continuously improved;
- whose benefits exceed the cost of taking the measurement.

4. Establish Performance Indicators

Establish a performance indicator for each of the critical activities selected for measurement. Remember there may in some cases be legislative standards to meet, for example, in the area of toxic emissions.

Good performance indicators are:
- realistic—meeting them does not require unreasonable effort;
- understandable—they should be expressed in simple and clear terms;
- adaptable—they can be changed if conditions change;
- economical—the cost of setting and administering them should be low in relation to the activity covered;
- legitimate—they should at least meet legislative requirements;
- measurable—they should be communicable with precision.

5. Collect the Data

To determine how the data will be collected, ask yourself:
- What am I trying to measure?

 "Talent is cheaper than table salt. What separates the talented individual from the successful one is a lot of hard work."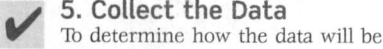

Stephen King

- Where will I make the measurement?
- How accurate and precise must the measurement be?
- How often do I need to take the measurement?

For activities that are undertaken a number of times an hour, it may only be feasible for a sample measure to be taken, for example, every eighth event.

In many cases the data required for the performance measurement already exist, for example, in databases, logbooks, timecards, and checksheets. If additional data are required, the person in charge of that particular area of the activity is usually responsible for collecting them.

In some instances it may be appropriate to install an automated data collection system to provide accurate data without the need for human intervention.

Inform the individuals responsible when they should start collecting data and in what format they should present them, for example, datasheets or spreadsheets. All data should be passed to the committee for analysis.

6. Analyze and Report Actual Performance

Before drawing conclusions from the data, verify that:
- the data appear to answer the questions that were originally asked;
- there is no evidence of bias in the collection process;
- there are enough data to draw meaningful conclusions.

Once the data have been verified, the required performance measurement can be formulated.

Summarize the data and prepare a report. Be sure to:
- categorize the data and use graphs to show trends;
- make the report comparative to goals or standards;
- check that all performance measurements start and end on the same month or year;
- adopt a standard format by using the same size sheets and charts;
- add basic conclusions.

7. Compare Actual Performance to Indicators

Compare the results of the performance measures with the indicator set for each activity.

8. Make Modifications to the Activity

Analysis will reveal whether:
- the activity is underperforming—leave the indicator as it is, but identify the reasons for failure and take remedial action;
- the variance is not significant—set a higher indicator to aim for continuous improvement;
- the indicator is easily achieved—review and raise the indicator. If indicators are not challenging, continuous improvement is unlikely.

9. Continue Measuring Performance and Evaluating the Performance Measures

Continue the process of collecting data and analyzing performance. Increase goals and standards as performance improves; change them as activities change.

549

CHECKLIST

THOUGHT STARTERS
- Did any company you have worked for measure performance? How?

- What are your organization's/department's key activities?

- How can you manage what you can't measure?

DOS AND DON'TS

DO
- Measure only what is important.
- Stress that you are measuring processes or activities, not people.
- Involve staff who are part of the activity to be measured.
- Act on the results of the performance measurement system.
- Review the indicators regularly to support continuous improvement.

DON'T
- Don't set performance measures in stone—modify them as processes and activities change.
- Don't be surprised if indicators are not met immediately—performance measurement should be used to drive continuous improvement.

FOR MORE INFORMATION

Books:
Friedlob, George T., Linda L. F. Schleifer, and Franklin J. Plewa. *Essentials of Corporate Performance Measurement*. New York: Wiley, 2002.
Harbour, Jerry L. *The Basics of Performance Measurement*. Portland, OR: Productivity, Inc., 1997.
Kaydos, W. J. *Operational Performance Measurement: Increasing Total Productivity*. Boca Raton, FL: CRC Press/St. Lucie Press, 1998.

Journal Article:
Barchan, Margareta. "Measuring Success in a Changing Environment." *Strategy and Leadership* 27:3 (May/June 1999): 12–15.

Web site:
Foundation for Performance Measurement:
www.fpm.com

'A best-seller is a book which somehow sold well simply because it was selling well.'

Daniel Boorstin

Occupational Health and Safety: Managing the Process

CHECKLIST

This checklist provides an overview of the key issues to consider in managing the health and safety process in an organization. Effective workplace safety management is not just a corporate legal and moral obligation, but a personal one, as managers are increasingly being held personally accountable in law for the safety of their employees.

The success of a workplace safety initiative depends on the commitment of top management to a coherent strategy that is fully integrated into the general management of the organization.

DEFINITION

Management of the occupational health and safety process involves setting a policy, creating a supportive organizational culture, developing and implementing a occupational health and safety plan, and evaluating the plan's performance.

ADVANTAGES

Managing health and safety in the workplace effectively not only ensures that you meet legislative requirements, but also:

- contributes to the well-being of the organization;
- decreases the risk of injury and ill health;
- reduces lost staff time;
- improves the organization's corporate image and averts negative publicity;
- contributes to a program of continuous improvement.

DISADVANTAGES

The benefits far outweigh the disadvantages, but managing health and safety properly:

- takes up time and resources;
- requires constant review and updating.

ACTION CHECKLIST

✔ 1. Get the policy right

The key to success is developing an effective policy that minimizes occupational health and safety risks to employees and others. Key actions at this stage include:

- undertaking a workplace safety assessment to identify areas that need attention and monitoring;
- familiarizing yourself with relevant legislation;
- allocating responsibilities for creating and revising health and safety policy and procedures;
- giving the health and safety policy the same priority as your other organizational goals;
- resourcing health and safety adequately, using a separate budget if appropriate.

✔ 2. Create a Positive Workplace Safety Culture

Create a corporate culture that involves and motivates all members of the organization in health and safety awareness. All employees need to think "safety first" and consider good health and safety practices a natural part of their working life.

Actions that foster a health and safety culture include:

- appointing health and safety champions to raise the profile of and drive the project;
- setting health and safety objectives and performance standards for all staff (prevention is better than cure);
- involving employees and safety representatives at all stages, from planning through implementation to monitoring and review;
- providing adequate information on health and safety to all staff and keeping them up to date;
- offering refresher training for all staff at regular intervals;
- rewarding employees for good health and safety practice;
- including workplace safety as an agenda item at management meetings and team briefing.

✔ 3. Develop a Plan

You need to:

- produce a written plan for health and safety, coordinating and scheduling all health and safety activities in a single program;
- identify clear objectives and standards;
- set measurable targets;
- identify resources required;
- consider all personnel and all the processes in your organization, from purchasing materials to delivering the product or service, in drawing up the plan;
- review the plan regularly.

The plan may encompass such areas as:

- accident prevention—considering severe hazards such as chemicals and radiation as well as more common hazards such as heavy lifting and trailing electrical leads;
- physical working conditions—including factors such as light, heat, ventilation, seating, hygiene, and computer workstations;
- psychological health—covering areas such as stress reduction, shift working, rest breaks, prevention of bullying, and achieving a balance between work and family;
- health problems of employees—including alcoholism and drug addiction;
- health promotion—for example, exercise and healthy eating;
- emergency procedures—such as fire drills, equipment shutdown, and security procedures;
- specific groups of employees particularly at risk—including young or disabled workers and pregnant women.

Depending on the nature of your business, you may also

"Two basic values, autonomy and solidarity, serve as helpful prompters in any decision-making process."

György Konrád

need to consider extending your workplace safety plan to suppliers and contractors. Any failings on their part will impact on your organization; you might want to introduce a written policy and penalties for noncompliance.

Remember also to consider the health and safety of customers using your products or services and of visitors to your premises.

4. Measure Performance

Once your plan is in place, evaluate its effectiveness. Performance can be measured both proactively and reactively. Proactive measures include:

- auditing your system to ensure that monitoring systems are in place and are effective;
- inspecting your workplace systematically;
- evaluating your training processes;
- talking to staff;
- reviewing relevant portions of minutes of management meetings.

Reactive measures include:

- examining data collected after incidents—accident books, sickness records, and records of near misses;
- checking damage to property, perhaps via insurance reporting.

5. Review Performance

Evaluating the performance of the plan enables you to check that your policy and plans are working efficiently and continuing to meet objectives and respond to changing circumstances. The evaluation process might involve:

- comparing findings with objectives and standards;
- validating findings by talking to staff;
- benchmarking against similar organizations;
- giving feedback to staff and seeking commitment to improvements;
- changing your policy, plan, and procedures to reflect your findings, making sure to give priority to high-risk areas.

Review is a continuous process, but you should set a timetable for formally revising your health and safety plan every year or whenever new legislation or regulations require it.

THOUGHT STARTERS

- How much money are you losing by not managing health and safety effectively?

- Talk to your staff—how aware are they of health and safety risks and issues in your workplace?

- Who is responsible for health and safety in your organization? How accountable is that person?

- Are any incentives in place to encourage good health and safety practice?

DOS AND DON'TS

DO
- Involve all your staff.
- Give health and safety the same priority as your organizational goals.
- Consider health and safety issues when carrying out organizational restructuring—if necessary, arrange training for those taking on new health and safety responsibilities.
- Aim for continuous improvement.
- Include temporary staff and contractors in your planning.

DON'T
- Don't assume health and safety is only for high-risk or hazardous environments.
- Don't believe health and safety is just common sense and therefore everyone understands it.

FOR MORE INFORMATION

Book:
Hartnett, John. *OSHA in the Real World: How to Maintain Workplace Safety While Keeping Your Competitive Edge.* Morton, PA: Silver Lake Publishing, 1996.

Web site:
Occupational Safety & Health Administration: **www.osha.gov**

"Developing a sound and healthy organization requires understanding the environment as much as understanding the organization."

Gary Hamel

Workplace Health: Undertaking a Risk Assessment

CHECKLIST

This checklist provides a plan of action for those carrying out a workplace risk assessment in their company or organization.

By identifying hazards in the workplace and the likelihood (the risk) of an accident or illness occurring, employers can take action to remedy the hazardous conditions quickly. Reducing the incidence of workplace injuries and illnesses benefits both employer and employee by creating a safer working environment. It also leads to savings by minimizing illness and accident claims and loss of time and productivity. This checklist does not aim to cover the complex legal and medical issues of health and safety, for which expert advice should be sought.

DEFINITION

An occupational health and safety risk assessment is a planned procedure in which all hazards in the workplace are identified.

ADVANTAGES

Risk assessments:
- comply with health and safety legislation;
- make accident and work-related illness prevention easier by identifying hazards;
- help improve work force morale by conveying a caring attitude.

DISADVANTAGES

There are no real disadvantages to carrying out a risk assessment, but remember that they:
- can require considerable resources in staff and/or consultants' time to undertake thoroughly;
- need to be updated each time a new piece of equipment or machinery is introduced, and each time an injury or work-related illness is reported.

ACTION CHECKLIST

1. Designate a Workplace Safety Committee

The members of the workplace safety committee should be drawn from all levels of the organization. The committee will manage the implementation and running of the risk assessment. Appoint a coordinator (preferably but not necessarily from senior management—someone with project management experience who commands respect and can get things done) to oversee the project.

2. Define the Scope and Coverage of the Assessment

Use the experience of committee members who have been involved in risk assessment before. All types of risk must be assessed: however, it can be easier (depending on the size of the organization) to identify and concentrate assessments on specific risks (for example, manual handling) at any one time. Decide who is to be included in the assessment at this stage—for example, all departments or one site or one floor. Indicate who will carry out the assessment—a large organization may need a number of individuals, while in a small company one person may be sufficient.

3. Design an Assessment Form

Create a form that the individuals involved in the assessment will use to record risks and/or incidents. Make wording simple and unambiguous. Include a rating scale for the severity of the risk, either in words (for example, "very severe" to "slight" risk) or numbers (for example, 1 = low risk and 5 = high risk). Identify which employees are at risk and, if applicable, any other individuals such as the general public. Leave space for suggestions of ways to minimize the risk. Include a list of common risks to point the assessor in the right direction. In a general risk assessment these may include:
- fire—are there any flammable materials near sources of heat?
- manual handling—are employees carrying items that should be left to machines?
- fork lifts or powered lift trucks—are operators certified? Is the work area well lit and well signed? Are pedestrians trained to work around such equipment? Is the racking system engineered properly to store heavy loads at substantial heights?
- power tools and equipment—are safety precautions, signage requirements and training of operators up to date?
- chemicals—are all hazardous substances stored correctly? Is the ventilation system adequate to take care of any noxious fumes?
- electricity—are any bare wires visible?
- dust—is the HVAC system doing its job?
- temperature (high and low)—do room temperatures reach abnormal levels?
- noise—are there areas of excessive noise? Are employees wearing protective equipment?
- tobacco smoke—are nonsmokers at risk from secondary exposure?
- electronic equipment—are users straining their eyes to see their computer monitors? Do employees have wrist support pads for their keyboards?
- office furniture—are chairs and desks ergonomic? Do they meet health and safety requirements?

The basic U.S. legislation is the Occupational Safety and Health Act of 1970 (Public Law 91–596, 91st Congress, S.2193, December 29, 1970–84 STAT. 1590. There are many federal, state, and local regulations which govern the details. Information on federal legislation can be found at www.osha.gov.

"Anything that promises to pay too much can't help being risky." — Dorothy Fisher

If possible, use the accident book or log of close calls for actual examples.

4. Train Assessors to Identify Risk

Identifying risks in the workplace is not an easy task. If the individual assigned to carry out the risk assessment is not a health and safety officer, it is essential to provide appropriate training from either an internal source or an external agency. Suppliers of equipment, machinery, or chemicals can be a good source of advice.

It is important to train assessors to rate the severity of a risk. Examples of hazards should be discussed with the trainees to achieve some standardization.

5. Communicate the Assessment to Employees

Let all employees know (using newsletters, bulletin boards, e-mail, intranet, and team briefings) that a workplace safety assessment is to be undertaken and who the investigator(s) will be. Invite employees to identify hazards that should be included in the assessment and, if they find any, to inform their supervisor or the person responsible for the assessment in their area.

6. Draw Up a Plan for the Assessments

Plan a timetable scheduling the assessment of various areas and giving a completion date for the assessment. Build into the timetable a schedule noting the availability of risk assessment committee members to guarantee that at least one is always on hand to assist.

7. Carry Out the Assessment and Record the Results

The workplace safety committee should collate all of the completed assessment forms and analyze the results. Look for problem areas such as one department with a large number of high risks, recurring accidents or illness. Create a list of all the risks and incidents in order of severity and report them to senior management. Keep this list as documentation for external occupational health and safety officials and as an internal record to check for changes made.

Look for any difficulties individuals had in completing the assessment; extra training may be needed for future assessments, or the assessment form may require modifications.

8. Report Back to Employees

Let your employees know the results of the assessment. Notify employees of any proposed changes to reduce the risk of accidents.

9. Take Action

Decide what action should be taken to eliminate or minimize the risks identified and draw up a plan for implementing the necessary changes, including budgetary implications.

DO
- Make sure your company reviews all relevant laws and regulations for your industry.
- Involve all employees.
- Check the accident book or log of close calls.
- Seek advice from suppliers of any new equipment, machinery, or chemicals.
- Make sure that workplace assessment investigators are adequately trained.
- Keep written documentation of the assessment.

DON'T
- Don't think of the assessment as a onetime activity—action needs to be taken on the results and reviewed and updated.
- Don't ignore a risk because you assume it is too small.

THOUGHT STARTERS
- Have you ever been involved in an accident at work?
- Can you think of anything in your workplace that is potentially dangerous?
- How could you make your workplace safer?
- Has poor equipment ever caused damage/harm to personnel?

FOR MORE INFORMATION

Books:
Hartnett, John. *OSHA in the Real World: How to Maintain Workplace Safety While Keeping Your Competitive Edge.* Morton, PA: Silver Lake Publishing, 1996.
Tompkins, Neville C. *A Manager's Guide to OSHA.* Menlo Park, CA: Crisp Publications, 1994.

Web site:
Occupational Safety & Health Administration: **www.osha.gov**

553

CHECKLIST

"Confronting reality—no matter how negative and depressing the process—is the first step toward coming to terms with it."
John Ralston Saul

Implementing a Service Level Agreement

CHECKLIST

This checklist is for managers who need to draw up and implement a Service Level Agreement (SLA). Although this checklist draws on examples from Information Technology, it may be used for agreements in any context.

SLAs were originally used mainly for third party provision of information technology services. In recent years, the number and range of services outsourced have grown substantially, as more and more organizations seek to reduce costs by focusing on core activities. Activities outsourced include human resources management, payroll administration, and facilities and fleet management.

An SLA should not be confused with a warranty or guarantee, where the manufacturer or provider determines the level of after-sales service that the customer can expect to receive.

An SLA can be used inter-departmentally within a company, as well as between organizations, providing a valuable baseline for partnership and outsourcing arrangements.

DEFINITION

Andrew Hiles defines an SLA as: "an agreement between the provider of a service and its users which quantifies the minimum quality of service which meets the business need." (*Service Level Agreements*, 1993)

Hiles stresses that this terminology is deceptively simple for several reasons:

- the agreement results from negotiations that recognize the needs and constraints on each side
- the agreement records and measures the level of service to which both parties subscribe as the requirement to meet needs
- the word "minimum" implies "adequate to meet quality needs" (serving the customer's needs and acceptable to the customer)

ADVANTAGES

Implementation of an SLA:

- clarifies understanding as to the basis of meeting expectations;
- requires the provider to be more accountable and responsible for the services delivered;
- commits the provider to plan for the development of services offered;
- commits the user to monitor and measure the efficiency and effectiveness of services from the provider;
- demands that the user be more conscious of the costs of service provision;
- forces the user to plan ahead for services required;
- should help to resolve difficulties in levels of user priority.

DISADVANTAGES

- An SLA can be seen as a threat by the provider.
- The provider may require extra resourcing to meet a minimum level of acceptable service, possibly increasing the cost of provision.
- It is not always easy to predict the level and nature of demand on the provider from all customers.

ACTION CHECKLIST

1. Assess Current Service Provision

Most agreements do not start with a clean slate. They often arise because of past problems. It is as important for the user to define the minimum levels of service required as it is for the provider to assess its current—and planned—resources and the current and planned demand on them. It is at this stage that levels of urgency and priority may be defined.

2. Draw Up an Outline Agreement

SLAs should identify at minimum:

- the purpose of the agreement;
- the parties to the agreement, typically the provider and user of the service;
- the service to be provided;
- the period of the agreement, with notice if appropriate;
- arrangements for monitoring, measuring, and review;
- the mechanism for resolving any conflicts;
- the procedure(s) in case of nonperformance (what happens if either party fails to fulfill the agreement?);
- procedures for change control;
- the degree of contribution and help from the user;
- lines of communication;
- any charges and insurance cover for both parties;
- means of arbitration for unresolved disputes.

The key elements that both provider and user need to clarify are:

- the precise nature of the service to be provided, including timeliness, relevance, accuracy, and format;
- the limits to the extent of the service;
- response times, both expected and deliverable;
- any exceptions to the rule;
- agreed methods for monitoring and measuring.

3. Negotiate the Levels of Performance

The SLA will usually emerge from discussions between both parties in the form of a compromise that recognizes the highest level of service feasible and the minimum that is acceptable. What constitutes unacceptable service should be obvious to both parties, but it is still worth specifying to avoid misunderstandings.

"It is an economic axiom as old as the hills that goods and services can be paid for only with goods and services."

Albert Jay Nock

Equally, a "top-level" service should be discussed—what is desired may be impossible because of excessive costs.

The user must specify the levels of service required and response times for each, for example:
- Priority 1: must take precedence for immediate treatment;
- Priority 2: requires treatment within the hour;
- Priority 3: can wait for a maximum of 24 hours.

 4. Include Change Control Procedures

Information technology will be renewed at an ever faster pace. This will impact on agreement targets and measures, but should also influence the nature of the agreement itself, which should take account of changing hardware and software, and the continuity and improvement of services to the user during the transition phase.

 5. Consider Contingency and Backup Arrangements

Only in an ideal world can problems be solved and errors corrected at the touch of a button. The SLA needs to take this into account. At the same time due attention must be paid to risk management to provide contingency and backup, for example, for temporary operation of user services. Go a stage further and consider the eventuality of a disaster or crisis. Insurance may provide reassurance that things can be put right in due course, but can it answer the immediacy that users normally require?

 6. Measure Performance and Monitor Faults

Agree on a mechanism for measuring the actual performance of the provider against the agreement. This mechanism may oversee speed or effectiveness as well as cost. Precise, mutually agreed performance indicators are useful here in providing a benchmark to indicate whether the existing levels of service are satisfactory or not.

 7. Pilot the SLA

The introduction of the SLA is important: lack of preparation or fine-tuning may well determine its fate. A sensible approach is to run a feasibility study with a pilot user group with a clearly defined level of service need. This trial run should not have the potential to cause widespread damage if things go wrong, but it does need to be large enough for meaningful conclusions to be drawn and modifications to be made before general implementation.

 8. Review the SLA Periodically

Resources, demands, and targets will change over time; the SLA is not cast in stone and should be reviewed on at least an annual basis.

 9. Measuring the Effectiveness of SLAs

Records of speed of response, length of computer downtime, and satisfaction with the solution can be rated against agreed performance indicators. The mean time between the failure and its repair or solution can provide an important indicator for the SLA. Response time can be reviewed against service objectives as agreed in the SLA.

DOS AND DON'TS

DO
- Remember to balance service against cost.
- Explore alternative service levels.
- Pay attention to detail during the initial assessment.
- Review the agreed performance indicators regularly.
- Recognize the resourcing and commitment required from both parties for success.
- Prepare to meet the cost of monitoring minimum quality service provisions.
- Pay attention to definitions with a potential for disagreement.

DON'T
- Don't be satisfied with inadequate measurements.
- Don't accept cumbersome, ill-defined documentation.
- Don't make the SLA too detailed or too difficult to monitor.
- Don't commit yourself to vague or impractical targets.

THOUGHT STARTERS
- Is dissatisfaction with a central support service department widespread but not heard?
- How is your central support service provider monitored and evaluated?
- Is the proposed SLA using a sledgehammer to crack a nut?

FOR MORE INFORMATION

Journal Articles:
Bailey, Diane. "Service Level Agreements." *Training Journal* (August 1999).
Joachim, Aubrey. "Central Office (and SLAs)." *Financial Management Journal* (April 2001).
Pugh, Nigel. "Meaningful Information versus Punitive Damages." *Managing Information* 7:10 (December 2000): 45–46.

See also:
✓ Deciding Whether to Outsource (pp. 542–543)

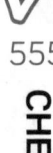
555

CHECKLIST

'Men keep their agreements when it is an advantage to both parties not to break them.'

Solon

Implementing an Effective Change Program

DEFINITION

This checklist covers any type of major change program within an organization. These range from those driven by external forces (changes in the market, customer demands, legislation, or regulation) to those that are internally driven, for example, the decision to introduce a total quality management program.

Change results from the interaction between equipment (technology), processes (working procedures), organizational structure, and people. A change to any one of these elements inevitably causes changes in the others, because the organization is a living, evolving system.

Managing change involves accomplishing a transition from A to B and handling the problems that arise along the way.

ACTION CHECKLIST

1. Agree on the Implementation Strategy

The details of the strategy need to be clear before you embark on change. Is implementation going to be top-down, bottom-up, or both? Will the change be made by division, by department, or in a "big bang?"

2. Agree on the Time Frame

Regardless of whether it is being introduced incrementally or simultaneously across divisions, every change program needs a start date and a finite time span. The timetable must be challenging enough to convey urgency but attainable enough to be motivating.

3. Plan for Implementation

Combine the strategy and timetable to draw up detailed implementation plans with each division or department head. Use the change team as a source of advice and consultation, but empower line managers to determine how they will implement the details of change against the overall goals.

The change program is unlikely to be the only corporate initiative underway. Make sure the strategy and goals behind the other initiatives all point in the same direction. Do employees receive consistent messages about the organization's core values and beliefs from each of the programs?

4. Set Up a Team of Stakeholders

This does not include top management, but will benefit from top management sponsorship. The team should include the key people involved in designing and delivering the service as well as those receiving it. This group is responsible for defining and disseminating the benefits of the change.

5. Establish Good Project Management

Treat change like any project. Set goals and milestones and monitor progress to keep the project on schedule and on budget. Flag potential problems as early as possible and prepare contingency plans. Establish ground rules for the project team, especially on information sharing, decision making, and reporting.

6. Personalize the Case for Change

People will appreciate the case for change only if they can personalize it and relate it to their own job and team. Make sure that your line managers translate the corporate case for change into a real issue for every individual in the company. Consider what change will mean for each employee in terms of status (job title, budget responsibility), habits (changes to working time, new colleagues), beliefs (move to a customer focus), and behavior (new working practices).

7. Promote Staff Participation

Individual employees need to feel they can take ownership of the change program as it evolves. Change can be stressful if it is imposed. Introduce mechanisms that promote staff ownership. Allow criticism and feedback, but provide the means to take corrective action.

8. Tackle Known Blocks to Progress

Create a sense of purpose and urgency to tackle real problems that have prevented progress in the past. Ask what or who is preventing progress and who can really help in removing the blockage.

Think of breaking the code of silence that engenders organizational protectiveness and maintains the status quo.

9. Motivate Your People

Sustained change requires very high levels of motivation. People need to feel valued: their achievements must be recognized, their potential developed, and their skills and ingenuity challenged. Be aware that different rewards motivate different people to change.

10. Be Prepared for Conflict

Change usually brings about conflict of one kind or another, simply because people have different views and reactions. Try to get conflict to surface rather than allowing it to fester; try to tackle it by dissecting and

"Even the best leaders get submerged and stymied in organizations that are highly centralized and highly consolidated."

Bill Creech

analyzing it with those who are experiencing it. Conflict can often be put to positive use through open discussion and clarification.

11. Be Willing to Negotiate

When conflict cannot be resolved through explanation and discussion, you have to negotiate and persuade. This means avoiding taking entrenched positions yourself and deciding how to shift others from theirs. It means getting to an agreed "yes" without either side winning or losing face.

12. Anticipate Stress

It is uncertainty, not change itself, that really worries employees. Provide as much information as possible and quash rumors as soon as they arise.

Any change program is stressful. Fear of the unknown is the major contributory factor. Reduce its impact by being as open as possible about all the consequences of change. See that employees own the changes.

13. Build Skills

View the change program as a learning process and integrate it into the corporate training program. Build both technical and soft skills at all levels within the organization. Set an example by updating the skills of top management.

14. Build in Capability for Learning

Creating goals and plans that everyone subscribes to means that everyone can gain. Turn learning into something that people want to buy into, something that creates a buzz of discovery and involvement in new developments. Don't allow learning to become a chore.

15. Remember Change is Discontinuous

Change is a long process made up of very small and often invisible modifications to behavior and attitudes. Seek innovative ways to remind staff of the overall case for change and to reinforce its value to them.

Accept that change will be a stop/start process. Plan for this and develop strategies to gear the organization up for renewed effort if there are setbacks.

16. Monitor and Evaluate

Monitor and evaluate the results of the change program against the goals and milestones established in the original plan. Are these goals still appropriate or do they need to be revised in the light of experience?

Existing performance measures may transmit the wrong signals and act as a block on change. Design measures that are consistent with the company's vision and goals.

Be honest in your assessment of progress. If the plan's goals and reality begin to diverge, take corrective action quickly. Be open about failure and involve employees in setting new targets or devising new measures.

DOS AND DON'TS

DO
- Appreciate the depth of employees' resistance to change. Plan for resistance and cost it in terms of additional training and communications.
- Select priorities for change instead of attempting to address everything at once.
- Plan to deliver early tangible results and publicize successes to build momentum and support.
- Involve employees at every stage of designing and implementing change.
- Make sure top management sponsors, and is fully committed to, the agreed implementation.

DON'T
- Don't get lost in detail or lose sight of the vision: real change often comes through a simple breakthrough.
- Don't skimp on resources for training or communications.

THOUGHT STARTERS
- Which indicators will tell you if change has really been effected?
- What signals should top management send to employees to show the extent of their commitment to change?
- What messages will indicate successful staff ownership of change?

FOR MORE INFORMATION

Books:
Hussey, David. *How to Be Better At Managing Change.* Dover, NH: Kogan Page, 1998.

Kanter, Rosabeth Moss. *The Change Masters: Innovation and Entrepreneurship in the American Corporation.* New York: Simon & Schuster, 1985.

Kotter, John. *A Force for Change: How Leadership Differs From Management.* New York: Free Press, 1990.

Kotter, John. *Leading Change.* Boston, MA: Harvard Business School Press, 1996.

See also:
✔ Managing Staff Turnover and Retention (pp. 454–455)
✔ Total Quality: Getting TQM to Work (pp. 562–563)

"You can't permit a honeymoon of small changes over a year or two. A long series of small changes just prolongs the pain."

Percy Barnevik

Implementing Business Process Reengineering

CHECKLIST

This checklist provides a synthesis of best practice in the form of an outline guide to the key stages in implementing Business Process Reengineering (BPR).

BPR is multifaceted. At its heart are two fundamental approaches: the understanding that organizations are process-driven, not function-driven, and an appreciation of the far-reaching, quantum-leap approach encouraged by BPR.

Although there have been many BPR-driven successes, there has also been criticism of the relatively high failure rate, where companies have not obtained the expected results. Reasons put forward for failure include: confusing downsizing with changing the way things are done; too much emphasis on reducing staff; poor redesign of processes; continuing with a departmental, rather than a process-driven, customer-focused culture; introducing new technology in isolation; and failing to involve staff at every stage.

DEFINITION

"Reengineering" is a method of initiating and controlling change processes through imaginative analysis and systematic planning.

Any organization, regardless of size, type, or desired objective, operates fundamentally by transforming a collection of inputs (for example, raw materials or raw data) into required outputs (products or services). This transformation involves one or more processes. In order to gain competitive advantage, an organization must transform inputs into outputs more efficiently than its competitors by concentrating on the efficiency of these core processes. This requires regular review and improvement of the relevant processes. In *Reengineering the Corporation*, Hammer and Champy define BPR as: the fundamental rethinking and radical design of business processes to achieve dramatic improvements in critical contemporary measures of performance, such as cost, quality, service, and speed.

The improvements in process quality to be gained from BPR lie in three dimensions: process efficiency (for example, cost, cycle time); product quality (measured, for example, as customer satisfaction, scope, and quality of product); and product development time.

ADVANTAGES

- BPR often creates new markets through the identification of break points.
- BPR encourages creativity and innovation in teams.

DISADVANTAGES

- BPR is effective for products and services that involve logical sequences in production. It may be less useful for highly variable processes.
- BPR initiatives often require a high investment in information technology (IT).
- The high cost of BPR initiatives can speed up the collapse of companies already in trouble.
- The creation of a lean organization through downsizing may actually reduce the organization's capacity to change.

ACTION CHECKLIST

1. Develop the Vision—Think Big
Senior management needs to gain a perception of the problems in the current business. An awareness of customers' expectations, competitors' advantage, and opportunities resulting from IT lead this process. Create a clear, grand vision. Thinking big and bold is the essence of BPR.

2. Establish a Steering Committee
Membership should be cross-functional. Specialists and consultants may be included, but a balance needs to be maintained. Senior managers should lead the project and provide strategic direction. The committee needs to understand the key leverage points in the organization. At an early stage it will need to decide whether it is going to undertake a pilot program or go for an all-embracing project. The committee should outline a preliminary strategy and set goals for the organization. Use appropriate survey techniques to listen to customers, benchmark the competition, and analyze existing processes. Identify points at which there is a gap between performance and customers' expectations.

3. Prepare the Organization for Change
Communication is the key to success in managing change. Present the business case for change, highlighting the objectives and goals of reengineering. Encourage feedback and input from all employees.

4. Analyze Existing Processes
Model current processes in detail. Reaffirm those processes that need to exist and their rationale. This reduces the likelihood that past mistakes will be repeated. Listen to the process owners to identify where problems exist. Document each and every helpful idea and make sure that these are widely circulated. Focus the redesign on the points that can provide the greatest return.

5. Establish Performance Indicators or Baselines
Improvements in performance can be identified only if

"Power is the ability to influence individuals and institutions in ways that change ideas."

Carl McCall

you know where you are starting from. Performance measures include:

- transaction volumes
- cycle times
- defect rates
- customer satisfaction levels

Make sure that the three dimensions—process efficiency, product quality, and product development time—are examined comprehensively.

6. Redesign the Process

Start with the needs of your customers and redesign the process from the outside in. Apply the following guidelines to the redesign process.

- Collect information that is required throughout the life cycle of the process only once, at its point of origin, and make it available immediately to all who need it.
- Reduce the need for coordination by associating individuals with processes, not with departments or functions.
- Improve customer service through genuine empowerment, trust, and delegation of responsibility, allowing partnerships to develop with customers and suppliers.
- Identify the key business outcomes, the business processes required to produce such outcomes, and descriptions of how processes interrelate. It will also be necessary to lay out the infrastructure required to support the change by describing both the management strategy, measurement systems, and reward programs, and the organizational values and individual belief systems that need to be adopted by all concerned.

7. Plan the Implementation

Once a process has been redesigned, an implementation plan can be prepared. Changes need time to be implemented; although BPR aims to achieve dramatic improvement in a short time, the planned schedule of change should not be unrealistically short.

Reemphasize the need for change and communicate the vision to managers and employees to overcome the natural uncertainty that exists. Gain approval and popular support by outlining the expected benefits to be achieved by the proposed redesign.

An implementation plan should take the following into account:

- schedules, budgets, completion criteria, and economic justifications all need to be specified
- training will be vital to smooth the transition
- new control systems need to be established
- immediate feedback on improvements is essential
- contingency allowances are needed to allow for the problems that will inevitably occur
- changes in physical location or layout, work flows and organization structures, plant and IT systems, testing and pilot projects, and a redefinition of roles and responsibilities will result from the process
- the plan should deliver some significant but quick results in the early stages to build commitment

8. Monitor and Evaluate Progress

Monitor the process continually to make certain that the expected benefits are being obtained. Feed back results to employees to let everyone gain by knowing what has and has not worked. Feedback should encourage them and in turn help to identify further areas for improvement.

THOUGHT STARTERS

- Do you know what proportion of resources is spent on the core processes in your organization?

- If you are considering BPR, examine your reasons very carefully—they will indicate your probable success.

FOR MORE INFORMATION

Book:
Hammer, Michael, and James Champy. *Reengineering the Corporation: A Manifesto for Business Revolution.* 2nd ed. New York: Harper Information, 1999.

Journal Articles:
Barnes, David, Matthew Hinton, and Suzanne Mieczkonska. "Managing the Transition from Bricks and Mortar to Clicks and Mortar: A Business Process Perspective." *Knowledge and Process Management* 11:3 (July/September 2004).
Choi, Chung For, and Stephen L. Chan. "Business Process Reengineering: Evocation, Elucidation and Exploration." *Business Process Management* 3:1 (1997): 39–63.

See also:
✔ Total Quality: Getting TQM to Work (pp. 562–563)
✔ Total Quality: Mapping a TQM Strategy (pp. 564–565)

DOS AND DON'TS

DO
- Question all assumptions.
- Choose your consultants carefully.

DON'T
- Don't assume you are on the right BPR track merely by introducing the latest IT.
- Don't settle for automating existing processes.
- Don't focus on individual tasks at the expense of the overall process.
- Don't embark on grand projects without the resources and support to complete them.
- Don't confuse BPR with rationalization.

"Transformational change requires enormous energy."   Robert H. Miles

Implementing Kaizen

CHECKLIST

This checklist is designed to introduce the concept of kaizen and explain its implementation.

In order to be successful, organizations are finding that they must continually improve their quality assurance, cost management, and delivery systems. Increasing competition has made it a priority for every organization to develop and seek an advantage over rivals. Many managers see a culture of continuous evaluation and improvement as an essential tool to achieve and maintain such an advantage. Kaizen is one of the main tools to develop such a culture.

DEFINITION

Kaizen is a Japanese term, which roughly translated means "improvement"—*kai* means "change" and *zen* "good" or "for the better." Kaizen means "continuing improvement in personal life, home life, social life, and working life" (Imai, 1986). Essentially it means continuous improvement, seeking small improvements through the elimination of waste.

Kaizen is a philosophy that inspires the whole company with the instinct for improvement. The culture of seeking continuous improvement should involve everyone from the most senior manager to the most junior employee. Workers participate not for any particular financial reward, although rewards may be a part of the recognition process, but for the satisfaction of using their creative skills to improve the operations they perform and the goods and services they produce. Kaizen incorporates a variety of techniques and principles into the overall culture and philosophy of improvement—improvement as a way of life, not simply the application of isolated techniques. It can help build employees' morale and self-respect. The company benefits from a more motivated workforce and improved financial returns resulting from more efficient operations. Customers benefit from the improved quality of product or service.

ADVANTAGES
- All functions of the organization come under continuous inspection.
- The employees most familiar with a particular operation on a day-to-day basis are the ones evaluating it.
- Employee morale and job satisfaction increase.
- Waste is eliminated throughout the organization, increasing efficiency and reducing costs.
- Product or service quality is improved and is monitored on a continuous basis.

ACTION CHECKLIST
1. Understand the Processes
According to Imai, there are three principal building blocks or keys to satisfying the customer in kaizen:

- a continually improving quality assurance system to meet customer requirements
- a continually improving cost management system to provide the product or service at a favorable price to the customer
- a continually improving delivery system to meet customer requirements on time

These are known collectively as QCD—quality, cost, delivery.

2. Identify Corporate Objectives
The three most important elements in creating the spirit of kaizen are top management commitment, top management commitment, and top management commitment. "Without that, you had better forget the whole thing" (Imai). Kaizen is best introduced as a means of achieving business targets. Senior managers and the board should carry out a SWOT analysis on the company's business program. They should evaluate existing systems and structures with respect to whether they support cross-functional goals and plan necessary changes in organization, planning and control, and personnel practices. They should set targets for the next five years; responsibility for meeting those targets should be agreed on and shared. Senior management should then demonstrate its commitment to kaizen as a corporate strategy by producing a statement of its commitment to achieving functional goals in areas such as quality and cost, the resourcing of the program, and auditing its progress.

Kaizen is often introduced into organizations as a developmental step in total quality management (TQM). In such cases a culture of quality may have been achieved, so that quality is already part of all organizational planning. In order to move toward kaizen, evaluate:
- how successful the quality initiative has been;
- whether everybody understands the key importance of quality;
- whether improvements made have been publicized;
- how employees view quality.

3. Plan the Kaizen Program
A well-planned program is often broken down into three segments representing three different levels—management-oriented, group-oriented, and individual-oriented kaizen.
- Management-oriented kaizen focuses on the most important strategic issues, processes, and systems.
- Group-oriented kaizen is based on small-group activities that use statistical tools to solve problems.
- Individual-oriented kaizen is based on the assumption that each individual can work smarter and can contribute toward the improvement process.

Each segment requires particular consideration as it makes use of different management and personal skills.

"You can't change anything if you don't bring people with you."

Carolyn McCall

4. Allocate Resources

Senior management will need to appoint a director in overall charge of the project and a manager to implement the program, and to introduce training for all employees. It must be prepared to allocate sufficient funding (as well as other resources) to support this.

5. Develop a Training Plan

Explore the training requirements of your employees. A minimum requirement of kaizen is that they understand the continuous improvement process, cross-functional working, and problem-solving techniques. Work with your training department or consultant to draw up a training plan.

6. Communicate with Employees

Bring representatives from all functions and all levels of the organization into the planning process. Kaizen is about cultural change and employee participation, and ownership is an essential part of accepting the change process. Arrange meetings, briefing sessions, and newsletters to promote the objectives of kaizen.

7. Focus Training and Development on the Four Ps of Quality

The four Ps are as follows.

Process control. The management of processes ensures a consistent and reliable level of performance.
- Identify variations and their causes.
- Deal with assignable causes.
- Deal with random variation.
- Undertake process design reviews, making use as necessary of a range of analytical and quality improvement techniques.

Problem identification. Failure to understand the causes of process variation gives rise to incorrect identification of problems. Consider using a range of techniques to identify problems.

Problem elimination. Gain an understanding of problem-solving tools such as Pareto diagrams or cause-and-effect diagrams. Test solutions to see that they work, truly prevent the problem, and do not cause new trouble elsewhere. Implement the solution after gaining an understanding of the dynamics of change.

Permanence. Improvement is a continuous process. You need to ensure that the changes already made stick, and that you go on improving. Processes such as policy deployment, TQM reviews, and quality function deployment are helpful here. Seeing to it that senior managers regularly attend quality improvement group meetings maintains momentum and commitment.

8. Set Up a Suggestion Box

Involving employees is an integral part of individual-oriented kaizen. A suggestion box is a good way of encouraging employee contribution. Be prepared

to listen to all suggestions and give recognition to employees' efforts.

9. Review

Plan to review the development of the kaizen program. Gauge the extent to which a process-oriented culture change has been achieved. Recognize champions and consider further training as required.

561

CHECKLIST

DOS AND DON'TS

DO
- Gain the commitment of senior management.
- Involve everybody in the organization.
- Acknowledge that all organizations have problems.
- View the introduction of kaizen as a cultural change process.
- Remember that the search for improvement is never-ending.

DON'T
- Don't regard implementing kaizen as a onetime exercise; it must become part of the corporate culture.
- Don't underestimate the importance of constant communication to reinforce the cultural change.

THOUGHT STARTERS
- Can you afford not to be interested in improved quality and greater productivity?
- Are you making full use of the creative ability of all your employees?
- Do you use the full range of problem-solving techniques?

FOR MORE INFORMATION

Books:
Imai, Masaaki. *Gemba Kaizen: A Commonsense, Low-cost Approach to Management.* New York: McGraw Hill, 1997.
Laraia, Anthony C. *The Kaizen Blitz: Accelerating Breakthroughs in Productivity and Performance.* New York: Wiley, 1999.

Web site:
Kaizen Institute: **www.kaizen-institute.com**

"There can be no major change in a complex organization unless there are both sufficient resources and substantial readiness."

Robert H. Miles

Total Quality: Getting TQM to Work

CHECKLIST

This checklist provides guidance for those who have mapped a total quality management strategy for their organization and are now seeking to implement it.

DEFINITION

Total quality management (TQM) is a way of managing that gives everyone in the organization responsibility for delivering quality to the final customer—quality being described as "fitness for purpose" or as "delighting the customer." TQM views each task in the organization as fundamentally a process in a customer–supplier relationship. The aim at each stage is to define and meet the customer's requirements, in order to maximize the satisfaction of the final consumer at the lowest possible cost.

ACTION CHECKLIST

1. Decide Whether to Run Pilots

While you need to map a TQM strategy for the whole organization, you will usually introduce it in stages. Select for the pilots significant areas or functions in which you feel TQM will yield results within a year at most: short-term success will be critical in selling TQM to the skeptics.

2. Monitor and Evaluate the Results of the Pilots

Draw up a framework and appoint a management team to assess and evaluate the results of the pilots. What lessons can be learned, and how can these be applied in introducing TQM elsewhere in the organization?

3. Select Tools and Techniques to Use at Each Stage of Implementation

There are four key stages in the implementation of TQM: measurement, process management, problem solving, and corrective action. For each, you need to select the tools and techniques appropriate to the scale and environment of your organization.

4. Select Measurement Techniques

Measurement is critical to the success of TQM in quantifying situations and events and providing a benchmark by which to measure progress. The key is to make certain that measurement is a meaningful process leading to corrective action, not an end in itself. The main techniques are measurement and error logging charts, corrective action systems, work process flow charts, run charts, and process control charts.

5. Select Process Management Tools

Many systems and tools can be used in process management. Some, for example, Gantt charts, flow charts, and histograms may already be used in the organization for other purposes. Select those that are right for your organizational culture.

6. Set Up Mechanisms for Problem Solving

Plan to establish groups throughout the organization to look at improving quality from different angles.
- Improvement groups are regular sessions led by supervisors of natural work groups.
- Key process groups analyze the operation of important processes.
- Innovation groups cross departments and are drawn from different levels within the organization to look at totally new ways of working.

The groups will have a range of techniques available to help them, including brainstorming, fishbone diagrams, and Pareto analysis.

7. Set Up Mechanisms for Corrective Action

The emphasis in TQM must be on identifying the causes of problems and solving them. At the planning stage, build in feedback loops with corrective action.

8. Draw Up a Communications Plan for Announcing the Program

Decide when and how to announce implementation of the program across the organization. Assume that staff may initially be cynical or skeptical, and devise strategies for overcoming employees' doubts. Use "converts" from the pilots to explain the benefits. Spell out the relationship of TQM to other initiatives within the organization.

9. Plan to Create the Right Culture for Quality

Successful TQM depends as much on cultural change as on process improvements. Be aware that TQM will probably need to be accompanied by a general program of information and education targeted at employees, supervisors, and managers.

10. Implement the Education Program

Introduce the education program mapped in your strategy. Target key groups first. Use these as agents of change to disseminate learning through the organization.

11. Empower supervisors

The team leaders will be pivotal to the success of TQM. You need to give them the resources, time, support, and education to become leaders.

12. Consider How to Motivate Employees to Take Ownership

Employees will need to take ownership of quality and act on their own initiative. To achieve this, you will need to create an open culture and drive out fears of failure, of taking risks, and of reprisals. You will also need to be prepared to deal with the possible insecurities of managers who discover that most or all of their work is unnecessary or can be done by staff at lower levels.

 ### 13. Establish a Program of Management Change

Employees will not be able to make the changes needed without profound changes in management style. A new approach based on collaboration, consensus, and participation will be needed under TQM. The largest single change for managers will be from telling to listening, from commanding to empowering.

 ### 14. Set Short- and Long-term Goals for the Implementation Program

Establish a means for monitoring progress. Combine short-term goals to demonstrate progress and more challenging long-term ones to stretch the organization. Include a mix of business and cultural indicators.

15. Maintain the Impetus

Cultural changes will take a long time to show results, but without results staff may be frustrated because they don't perceive much achievement through process improvements. Regularly review and report progress; recognize and publicize successes.

563

CHECKLIST

THOUGHT STARTERS

- Do you need to make changes to the structure of the organization to make clear that quality is the responsibility of everyone?

- To what extent do current reward mechanisms promote employee involvement in quality?

DOS AND DON'TS

DO

- Spell out the relationship between TQM and other initiatives within the organization.
- Find out where the invisible barriers to change are. Be aware of them from the outset and develop a strategy for breaking through them.
- Make sure that systems concentrate on measuring the performance of work processes rather than the individuals engaged in them.
- Pay attention to the soft side of TQM. Changing culture is as important as changing processes.
- Make clear that TQM is not a quick fix, but an ongoing process of continuous improvement: you will never fully achieve total quality because the targets will constantly shift.

DON'T

- Don't view TQM as a precisely defined methodology or a prescribed series of actions to be completed one by one.
- Don't try to bring in TQM alongside other major initiatives if these already make heavy demands on management time.
- Don't lose sight of the ends by excessive concentration on the means.

FOR MORE INFORMATION

Books:

Dale, Barrie G. *Managing Quality*. 4th ed. Malden, MA: Blackwell, 2003.

Campanella, Jack. *Principles of Quality Costs: Principles, Implementation, and Use*. 3rd ed. Milwaukee, WI: ASQ Quality Press, 1999.

Endres, Al. *Implementing Juran's Road Map for Quality Leadership: Benchmarks and Results*. New York: Wiley, 2000.

See also:

- ✔ Brainstorming (pp. 584–585)
- ✔ Implementing an Effective Change Program (pp. 556–557)
- ✔ Implementing Business Process Reengineering (pp. 558–559)
- ✔ Implementing Statistical Process Control (SPC) (pp. 592–593)
- ☆ Outsourcing (pp. 120–121)
- ⌕ Outsourcing (p. 1851)
- ✔ Total Quality: Mapping a TQM Strategy (pp. 564–565)

"All things excellent are as difficult as they are rare."   Baruch Spinoza

Total Quality: Mapping a TQM Strategy

CHECKLIST

This checklist provides guidance on mapping a strategy for total quality management (TQM) for those seeking to introduce TQM to the organization for the first time. A quality strategy combines the "hard" edge of quality—its tools and techniques—with its "soft" side—the cultural changes needed to achieve success. TQM is not just another management gimmick; it is a way of life.

The checklist is intended only as an aid to your initial thinking. Introducing TQM is a major strategic change that requires considerable research and planning. You are likely to need external advice or help to implement it.

DEFINITION

Total quality management, or TQM, is a style of managing that gives everyone in the company responsibility for delivering quality to the final customer, quality being described as "fitness for purpose" or as "delighting the customer." TQM views each task in the organization as fundamentally a process in a customer–supplier relationship. The aim at each stage is to define and meet the customer's requirements in order to maximize the satisfaction of the final consumer at the lowest possible cost.

ADVANTAGES

- TQM vastly improves the quality of the final product or service.
- TQM greatly decreases the waste of resources.
- Productivity rises sharply as employees use time more effectively.
- As products and services are improved, market share should show a long-term increase, leading to sustained competitive advantage.
- The workforce becomes more motivated as employees realize their full potential.

DISADVANTAGES

- TQM is extremely demanding of management and staff time.
- TQM will help only if the organization is heading in the right direction. It is not a tool for turning an organization around.
- TQM is not a quick fix: TQM takes years to implement and is in fact an unending process.
- TQM can lead to too much attention being paid to the needs of final customers and not enough to those of employees.
- TQM can become overly bureaucratic and mechanical, leading to an emphasis on consistency rather than improvement, or a focus on the means rather than the end.

- TQM is likely to cause disruption at various stages, requiring careful handling.

ACTION CHECKLIST

✔ 1. Establish a Planning Team for Total Quality

You will need a quality team to drive through the changes. In a small company this will be the senior management team; in a larger one, it will comprise senior managers representing the major functions. Include in the team known skeptics or mavericks, and make sure that minority views are represented.

✔ 2. Evaluate the Need for Change

Consider the competitive position of the organization. Establish who your key customers are and find out what they expect of you: don't assume that you are currently meeting all of their requirements. Finding out what customers need is a continuous process, not a one-time exercise. Find out, too, how other groups—suppliers, competitors, and employees—view the quality of your product or service.

✔ 3. Define Your Vision

Draw up a vision statement defining where the company wants to be in terms of serving its customers: this vision should be challenging but attainable. Define the principles and values that underpin the vision. Use comparable organizations as a model, but make sure your final draft reflects your own culture and circumstances.

✔ 4. Define the Standard of Service You Aim to Provide

Translate the vision into realistic outcomes. Establish what customers, suppliers, and employees expect the company to deliver in quality of product or service.

✔ 5. Review How Closely You Meet Your Own Standards

There will often be a large gap between customer expectations and reality. Determine the reasons for this across the organization. Key reasons are often external constraints (for example, being let down by suppliers) or internal inefficiencies. It can happen that customers expect too little—you need to assess their needs, not only their expressed wishes.

✔ 6. Audit Current Levels of Waste

Quantify quality failures by securing from heads of department an audit of current levels of waste. All employees should take part in this audit. Collect data as widely as possible, cost the results, and present the findings to the senior management team.

"I could buy companies, tart up their products and put my name on them, but I don't want to do that. That's what our competitors do."

James Dyson

7. Establish the Current Cost of Waste
Calculate how much is currently spent on rectifying internal failure (for example, reworking substandard goods) and external failure (such as handling customer complaints). Include appraisal costs and the time and money spent on inspection and checking.

8. Decide Whether to Seek Third-party Certification
You need to decide whether to include a quality management system in your initiative. If you do, it will lead to third-party certification, which may bring benefits with customers and suppliers or even be demanded by them.

9. Draw Up Your Quality Strategy
Use the results of the waste audit to draw up your quality strategy. This will cover:
- the goals of the strategy, including the revised mission;
- the systems and tools needed to change processes;
- the cultural changes needed to create the right environment for quality;
- details of the resources that can be applied;
- time frames.

Secure senior management approval of the plan.

10. Draw Up a Management Structure for Change
The culture of the organization will be critical to the success or failure of TQM. Plan for the introduction of team-based working: strong, effective teams are essential.

11. Establish an Education and Training Program
Some staff will need training in depth, others less; but everyone should be given a thorough introduction to, and familiarization with, what TQM means. Analyze training needs in relation to TQM and cost the additional training required. The cost can be offset against the expected productivity gains. Plan for:
- general orientation and training of all employees in the principles of TQM;
- coaching of managers, supervisors, and team leaders in the soft skills needed to implement TQM;
- job-specific training in new techniques associated with TQM;
- additional training in customer relations.

An external trainer or facilitator is almost always essential, especially in the early stages.

12. Identify Opportunities and Priorities for Improvement
Set priorities for the introduction of TQM. Select key processes for early analysis and improvement. Start with three processes at the most, choosing at least one that is likely to demonstrate quick returns in business performance.

13. Establish Goals and Criteria for Success
You need both short- and long-term targets. Establish measures of success in both business and cultural terms.

THOUGHT STARTERS
- Is the climate really right for the introduction of TQM? In particular, do managers have the integrity and openness that TQM will demand of them?

- Does your strategy strike the right balance between the needs of your customers and your employees?

FOR MORE INFORMATION

Book:
Dale, Barrie G. *Managing Quality*. 4th ed. Malden, MA: Blackwell, 2003.

See also:
- Implementing Business Process Reengineering (pp. 558–559)
- Total Quality: Getting TQM to Work (pp. 562–563)

DOS AND DON'TS

DO
- Secure commitment from top management from the very beginning.
- Make sure that this commitment is repeatedly conveyed.
- Involve all employees in assessing current failures.

DON'T
- Don't see TQM as a quick fix.
- Don't bring TQM in at the same time as other major new initiatives.
- Don't use TQM (or even appear to use TQM) as a means of downsizing.

'I admire the capacity of American business executives to continually reinvent what they do; it shows they are never satisfied.'

Anonymous

Implementing the Balanced Scorecard

CHECKLIST

Traditionally managers have used a series of indicators to measure how well their companies are performing. These measures relate primarily to financial issues such as business ratios, productivity, unit costs, growth, and profitability. While useful in themselves, they provide only a narrowly focused snapshot of how a company has performed in the past and give little indication of likely future performance.

During the early 1980s the changing business environment prompted managers to take a broader view of performance, and a range of other factors started to be taken into account, exemplified by the McKinsey 7-S model and popularized by Peters and Waterman's business bible *In Search of Excellence*. These provide a broader assessment of corporate health for both the immediate and longer term. This checklist focuses on the balanced scorecard, developed by Robert Kaplan and David Norton in the early 1990s with the aim of providing a balanced view of a company's performance.

DEFINITION

The balanced scorecard is defined as a strategic management and measurement system that measures performance and links strategic objectives to comprehensive indicators. The key to the success of the system is that it must comprise a unified, integrated set of indicators that measure key activities and processes at the core of a company's operating environment.

The balanced scorecard takes into account not only the traditional "hard" financial measures, but also three additional categories of "soft" quantifiable operational measures. These include:

- customer perspective—how an organization is perceived by its customers;
- internal perspective—the areas in which an organization must excel;
- innovation and learning perspective—the areas in which an organization must improve and add value to its products or services or operations.

Measurements taken across these categories are seen to provide a rounded balanced scorecard that reflects organizational performance more accurately than traditional financial indicators, and helps managers focus on their mission instead of short-term financial gain. It also helps motivate staff to achieve the strategic objectives.

ACTION CHECKLIST

Kaplan and Norton have identified a number of stages for the implementation of the scorecard that make use of planning, interviews, workshops, and reviews. The type, size, and structure of an organization determine the detail of the implementation process and the number of stages it entails.

The main steps include the following.

1. Prepare

As the scorecard is inextricably linked to strategy, the first requirement is to clearly define corporate strategy and ensure that senior staff, in particular, are familiar with the key issues. Planning of any other action requires an understanding of:

- the strategy;
- the key objectives or goals to achieve that strategy;
- the three or four critical success factors (CSFs) fundamental to achieving each major objective or goal.

2. Decide What to Measure

Managers should identify the company's major strategic goals. As a guide, no more than 15 to 20 key measures in total should then be linked to these specific goals—significantly fewer measures may not achieve a balanced view; significantly more may become unwieldy and deal with noncritical issues.

Based on the four main perspectives suggested by Kaplan and Norton, a list of goals and measures may include some of the following:

Financial (shareholder) perspective
- Goals—increased profitability, growth, increased returns on assets.
- Measures—cash flows, cost reduction, economic value added, gross margins, profitability, return on capital/equity/investment/sales, revenue growth, working capital, sales.

Customer perspective
- Goals—new customer acquisition, retention, satisfaction.
- Measures—market share, customer service, customer satisfaction, number of new/retained/lost customers, customer profitability, number of complaints, delivery time, quality performance, response time.

Internal perspective
- Goals—improved core competencies, improved critical technologies, streamlined processes, better employee morale.
- Measures—efficiency improvements, development/lead/cycle times, reduced unit costs, reduced waste, amount of recycled waste, improved sourcing-/supplier delivery, employee morale, internal audit standards, number of employee suggestions, sales per employee.

Innovation and learning perspective
- Goals—new product development, continuous improvement, training of employees.
- Measures—number of new products and percentage of sales from these, number of employees receiving train-

"The leader is not just a scorekeeper. He is responsible for creating something new and better."

Bill Creech

ing, training hours per employee, number of strategic skills learned, alignment of personal goals with the scorecard.

Each organization needs to determine its own strategic goals and activities to be measured. A number of organizations have realized that Kaplan and Norton's template does not meet their particular needs and have either modified it or have devised their own scorecards. Public sector organizations, for example, may have different aims and objectives and may need to tailor the scorecard to reflect this.

3. Finalize the Implementation Plan

Further discussions, interviews, or workshops may be required to fine-tune the details and agree on strategy, goals, and activities to be measured, taking care that the measures selected focus on the critical success factors. Other important issues to be resolved before implementation include setting targets, rates, or other criteria for each of the measures and defining how, when, and where they should be recorded.

4. Implement the System

Produce an implementation plan and communicate it to the staff. The scorecard initiative should not come as a surprise at this point: staff should be informed at the beginning of the project and kept up to date on progress. Employees should be made to feel that they have an important part to play in achieving corporate goals. Conversely they should not feel threatened by the measures.

5. Publicize the Results

Collate the results of all measurements on a regular basis—daily, weekly, monthly, quarterly, or as appropriate. The information is likely eventually to comprise a substantial amount of possibly complicated data. Decide whether to make complete data available to senior management, to divisional or departmental heads, or to all staff, or whether to circulate partial information on a need-to-know basis. Determine whether the results can best be publicized through meetings, newsletters, the organization's intranet, or other means.

6. Use the Results

Measurement is not an end in itself; it is a guide to organizational performance that may point to areas that need strengthening. Taking action on the information you obtain is as important as the data in the first place. Management follow-up action is an essential part of the balanced scorecard process.

7. Review and Revise the System

After the first cycle has been completed, review the quality of the information gathered and the success of subsequent actions, and modify the process as required.

THOUGHT STARTERS
- Do you know what measurements are currently taken in your company?

- Do the measurements in place give a holistic view of performance?

- What might be the consequences of not getting a balanced view of your company's performance?

FOR MORE INFORMATION

Books:
Kaplan, Robert S., and David P. Norton. *The Balanced Scorecard: Translating Strategy into Action.* Boston, MA: Harvard Business School Press, 1996.
Kaplan, Robert S., and David P. Norton. *The Strategy-Focused Organization: How Balanced Scorecard Companies Thrive in the New Business Environment.* Boston, MA: Harvard Business School Press, 2000.
Nair, Mohan. *Essentials of Balanced Scorecard.* Hoboken, NJ: Wiley, 2004.
Niven, Paul R. *Balanced Scorecard Step-by-step: Maximising Performance and Maintaining Results.* New York: Wiley, 2002.

Journal Article:
Van de Vliet, Anita. "The New Balancing Act." *Management Today* (July 1997): 78, 80.

Web sites:
Balanced Scorecard Collaborative: **www.bscol.com**
Balanced Scorecard Institute:
www.balancedscorecard.org
Foundation for Performance Measurement:
www.fpm.com

See also:
⚡ Kaplan and Norton (pp. 1226–1227)
☆ The Balanced Scorecard (p. 389)

567

CHECKLIST

"Modern industry seems to be inefficient to a degree that surpasses one's enduring powers of imagination. Its inefficiency therefore remains unnoticed." — E. F. Schumacher

Managing Projects

568

CHECKLIST

> CHECKLIST
>
> This checklist outlines the steps in project management and provides a framework of sequential action for any manager undertaking a project.
>
> Project management is recognized as a special process that differs in approach from general management or change management. The traditional project management focus has been on completing defined work within given time constraints and cost limits. Recently the focus has shifted more to the quality of the final output delivered to the customer.

DEFINITION

"Project management is a specialized management technique to plan and control projects . . . A project is generally deemed successful if it meets predetermined targets set by the client, performs the job it was intended to do, or solves an identified problem within the predetermined time, costs and quality constraints."

(Rory Burke, *Project Management: Planning and Control Techniques* (2000)

ADVANTAGES

Project management techniques provide:
- an appropriate way to bring about sudden, revolutionary, or purposeful change;
- an effective approach for handling single tasks;
- a realistic method for evaluating a proposed plan.

DISADVANTAGES

- Projects often require an extraordinary use of resources—especially money and people—over a finite period of time.
- Projects usually consume more resources than expected.
- Projects can go over schedule by significant margins.

ACTION CHECKLIST

1. Define the Objectives

The management of any successful project demands an understanding of and agreement on the following points by the project sponsor and project manager:
- what needs to be achieved;
- what is to be the outcome and/or what needs to be delivered as a result;
- the dates and budgets for project completion.

Lack of clear objectives will doom the project from the beginning.

2. Appoint the Project Manager

The project manager should be someone who has a proven track record and can command respect and get action from senior management. This person should be able to:

- plan and communicate all aspects of the project;
- motivate with integrity, sensitivity, and imagination;
- gain productivity and trust from shared decision making;
- lead by example, but also take a back seat when appropriate;
- monitor costs, efficiency, and quality without excessive bureaucracy;
- get things done right the first time without being a slave driver;
- get the right people for the right task at the right time;
- use both technical and general management skills to control the project;
- see clear-sightedly through tangled issues.

3. Establish the Terms of Reference

The terms of reference specify the objectives, scope, time frames, and initial scale of resources required. They should also clarify risks, constraints, or assumptions. It is important to make early allowances for cost escalation and plans veering off course, and build in a level of contingency or safety margin.

4. Create the Work Breakdown Structure Document (WBSD)

Having established what the project should achieve, consider how to achieve it.

The WBSD forms the basis of much subsequent work in planning, setting budgets, exercising control, and assigning responsibilities. The key is to break the project down into identifiable phases, then into controllable units for action. Dividing a project into more approachable, discrete units makes it easier to estimate, plan, and control the work. As soon as possible allocate a timescale to each unit of work, being careful to distinguish sequential units (those that need to be accomplished before the next can be tackled) from overlapping units (those that can run in tandem).

5. Plan for Quality

Planning for quality requires both paying attention to detail and ensuring that the project output or outcome does what it is supposed to, or is "fit for its purpose." The work breakdown structure should incorporate micro performance criteria or indicators for discrete units or phases, and macro indicators against which the final outcome can be assessed. Quality measures (systematic inspections against established standards) should be built into the process from the beginning, not later when things (may) have started to go awry. The following formula can run as a continuous sequence throughout the duration of the project.

establish standards > monitor performance > take corrective action.

The key is to guarantee effective quality control that acts as a prevention rather than a cure and enables you to get things right the first time.

"Procrastination is epidemic. The number of people who finish projects three weeks ahead of time you can count on one hand."

Jeffrey P. Kahn

6. Plan Costs

This is a key area, in which the most frequent error is to underestimate costs. Typical cost elements include:

- staff time and wages—usually the largest cost item;
- overhead—general operating costs;
- materials and supplies—the raw materials;
- equipment—the relative advantages of leasing versus purchasing and taking depreciation;
- administration—purchasing, accounting, record-keeping.

One of the enabling functions of a good budget is to monitor costs while a project is in progress.

7. Plan Timescales

In order to calculate the shortest time necessary to complete the project you need to know:

- the earliest time a stage or unit can start;
- the duration of each stage;
- the latest time by which a stage must be completed.

Gantt charts, PERT diagrams, and the critical path method are prominent among a number of project management techniques that can help with effective planning of timescales.

8. Monitor and Report Progress

The monitoring of costs, timescales, and quality is a major consideration throughout the duration of the project. Quality is the hardest to measure and, as such, is prone to neglect.

In addition to progress reports, feedback sessions, and Management By Walking Around, various control tools can help you see that implementation is going according to plan.

- Control point charts ask you what is likely to go wrong in terms of time, cost, and quality.
- Project control charts provide status reports of actual costs against budget with variances.
- Milestone charts show stages of achievement as steps toward the project objectives.

It is important to know what to do when these or other control mechanisms indicate that something is going wrong. Contingency plans are also vital, as conditions change constantly.

9. Deliver the Output

Haynes writes that "the goal of project management is to obtain client acceptance of the project result" (*Project Management*, Crisp Publications, 1997). Steps before delivery of the project outcome may include the compilation of instructional documentation or training packages. The penultimate stage before project completion is ensuring that the outcome of the project is accepted by the customer or sponsor.

10. Evaluate the Project

Building in a final stage of evaluation allows you to gauge the project's success and see what lessons can be learned. Once again the three key areas for review are quality, time, and costs. Others include:

- staff skills gained or identified;
- mistakes not to be repeated;
- tools and techniques of particular value;
- tasks or procedures to be tackled differently next time.

THOUGHT STARTERS

- Does your job or task have a set start and finish date?
- Does it require a budget?
- Does it need other resources: people, equipment, raw materials?
- Does it involve changing something?
- Does it have a clear objective or target?

DOS AND DON'TS

DO

- Take time at the beginning to define objectives, terms of reference, and the work breakdown structure.
- Appoint someone with the right skill mix as project manager.
- Facilitate access to resources needed as far as possible.
- Build in quality checks.

DON'T

- Don't let small changes creep in without assessing the implications.
- Don't lose sight of time targets and budget limits.

FOR MORE INFORMATION

Books:
Burke, Rory. *Project Management: Planning and Control Techniques*. 3rd ed. New York: Wiley, 2000.
Callahan, Kevin R., and Lynne M. Brooks. *Essentials of Strategic Project Management*. Hoboken, NJ: Wiley, 2004.
Graham, Robert J., and Randall L. Englund. *Creating an Environment for Successful Projects*. 2nd ed. San Francisco, CA: Jossey-Bass, 2004.

See also:
✓ Deciding Whether to Outsource (pp. 542–543)

"Beware the manager who proclaims to the world he is a long-termer, beginning today."

Gifford Pinchot

Preparing for Business Abroad

CHECKLIST

CHECKLIST

This checklist aims to stimulate thoughts about some of the implications of doing business abroad—of doing business with people of other nationalities, races, and cultures. Success in doing business abroad often depends on getting the little things right—most importantly, recognizing and anticipating a multitude of cultural differences. The purpose of this checklist is to help you do that by pointing out some general guidelines and some specific examples. It is not a manual on foreign trade.

DEFINITION

For the purposes of this checklist "doing business abroad" involves either transacting business with people from other countries or transacting business in a country outside the United States. In doing business abroad you will be confronted with people of nationalities, races, and cultures other than your own, and probably with customs, practices, and legal systems that differ from yours.

ADVANTAGES

Preparing for business abroad:
- increases your self-confidence in potentially stressful situations;
- enables you to appear informed and international in outlook;
- reduces the chance of your being surprised by suddenly discovering that "they" do things differently;
- lessens the likelihood of you and your colleagues on the one hand, and of your potential business partners on the other, being embarrassed;
- reduces misunderstandings and increases mutual understanding.

ACTION CHECKLIST

1. Identify Sources of Information
Write to, call, or even visit the U.S. embassy or consulate of the country you are visiting. Most have useful background literature about their countries. In the case of smaller countries, particularly those less economically developed, don't count on printed information being completely up to date.

Don't expect all embassies to be like those of the United States or other major powers. Some embassies consist of no more than two or three rooms on an upper floor. If you intend to visit an embassy, phone first and find out what hours it's open to visitors—not all of them are regularly open from 9.00 a.m. to 5.00 p.m. The employees of some embassies speak perfect English; in others they may not—be prepared for this.

Once you've arrived in the country you're visiting, remember the U.S. embassy as a source of information.

Other sources of information include the Internet and newspaper archives, and the *CIA World Factbook*. And don't avoid books intended for the tourist—they may contain useful information that is not available elsewhere. The best source may be someone who has recently been to the country.

2. Learn About the Country
- Identify the principal and minority languages of the country you are visiting—mistaken assumptions can be embarrassing. Spanish is the official language of most South American countries, for example, but Brazilians speak Portuguese.
- Learn something about the country's history, especially the past few decades. In complex regions like the Balkans this may seem daunting, but some knowledge of regional and international relationships will stand you in good stead.
- Discover whether there are significant minorities in the country: their presence can have a major impact on politics and on business and personal relationships. There are, for example, 600,000 ethnic Hungarians in Slovakia out of a population of five million. Don't forget you may be attempting to do business with a member of a minority or mixed group.
- Read up on the country's internal politics, but refrain from expressing your opinions, especially if you do not know the political sympathies of your local contacts. Remember that in some countries expressing dissenting political opinions can put you and/or your hosts in danger.
- Find out about the country's major religions (many countries have more than one). Don't assume that other countries observe the religious holidays that you're accustomed to or that the way a specific holiday is observed is the same in every country. Sundays are not always a day of rest (Israel is one case in point). Many countries have numerous public holidays; find out when they are so that you don't mistime your trip.
- Find out what the temperature and humidity are likely to be during your visit so you can pack appropriate clothing.

3. Ask About Visa Requirements
You may or may not need a visa. Ask your travel agent or approach the country's embassy, which can issue a visa if you require one. Allow plenty of time for this: you are likely to have to submit forms, photographs, and your passport, and possibly pay a fee, and you may have to wait for days or weeks.

4. Decide How to Manage Foreign Currency
Ask your bank or travel agent what form of currency you should take. You may not always need to get local currency before your trip. U.S. dollars are accepted in some countries, and traveler's checks are still a good standby.

If you do take U.S. dollars, take only bills issued during the last five years. In some countries where large numbers of counterfeit dollars have been circulated, older bills won't be accepted. Unless you are a very experi-

---

"A great many American managers are influenced by beliefs, assumptions, and perceptions about management that unduly constrain them."

Richard Pascale

enced traveler, prepare a matrix giving at least approximate exchange rates of:

- the euro
- the pound
- the local currency (know its subdivision)
- the yen

Find out in advance whether, and which, credit cards are likely to be accepted in the country. Ask whether they are accepted in stores and restaurants, whether they can be used to obtain local currency at banks, and whether they can be used in ATMs. In addition:

- be prepared to pay a bank commission if you use your credit card to obtain currency;
- be prepared to produce your passport when you exchange money;
- don't get too much local currency at a time. Some countries do not permit you to take their currency out, and in countries with rapid inflation you can lose money by changing too much at once. Find out in advance what your own bank at home will accept if you bring foreign currency back.

✔ 5. Be Sensitive to Local Culture

To start with, educate yourself about a few basic cultural practices.

- Tips—local custom may or may not require them. The amount and way of giving a tip, especially in restaurants, may not be what you're used to. In some countries tips are given to taxi drivers but not in restaurants, in others it's the opposite. In any case different services usually require different sizes of tip. In some countries expectations differ according to the region or city you are in.
- Find out the locally acceptable practice for giving and receiving gifts.
- Find out what is and what is not regarded as good manners. People are sometimes very critical of their own country—but can be offended if you agree with them. Learn as much as you can before your trip, and be tactful when you are traveling.
- Find out how to negotiate local transportation. It may be local custom (or necessary to protect yourself as a visitor) to agree on taxi fares with your driver in advance, for example.
- Know something about the local police. Do they issue on-the-spot fines? For what?
- Humor doesn't always travel well; be cautious, especially about personal remarks. Some people laugh at themselves, others only at their neighbors. Some people who laugh at themselves don't expect (or like!) others to join in.
- Learn about common physical gestures—a nod in Bulgaria or Greece signifies lack of agreement.
- Don't make jokes about Communists or former nationalized institutions in Eastern Europe: you may be talking to a former Communist about an institution that he or she managed. Your listener's reaction may be reflected only in your order book.
- Accept hospitality carefully—pace yourself, especially when you're socializing over alcohol. Your hosts may be used to whatever you're drinking—you may not.

DOS AND DON'TS

DO
- Remember that people from other countries and cultures are as proud of their histories, culture, and achievements as you are of yours.
- Remember the importance of listening.
- Make sure you know a few words in the language of your potential business partners—especially salutations.
- Try to know what is likely to be making the national news headlines of the country you're in as well as something of the background of those stories.

DON'T
- Don't make assumptions based on your own standards, customs, and practices.
- Don't criticize the country's politicians—your contacts may support them.
- Don't discuss religion.
- Don't patronize your contacts or anyone else.
- Don't disparage sanitary arrangements or standards of hygiene.

THOUGHT STARTERS
- What stereotypes come into your mind when you think of the foreigners you will be meeting? Do they have any basis in reality?

FOR MORE INFORMATION

Books:
Axtell, Roger E., ed. *Do's and Taboos around the World.* 3rd ed. New York: Wiley, 1993.
Earley, P. Christopher, and Miriam Erez. *The Transplanted Executive.* New York: Oxford University Press, 1997.
Walker, Danielle Medina, Thomas Walker, and Joerg Schmitz. *Doing Business Internationally: The Guide to Cross-cultural Business Success.* 2nd ed. New York: McGraw Hill, 2002.

See also:
✔ Planning Overseas Assignments (pp. 460–461)

"Chinese managers and employees perceive that they have as many problems with foreign business representatives as the other way around."   Jan Selmer

Setting Up an Energy Management Program

This checklist provides guidance for managers wishing to control the amount of energy consumed by their company or organization.

Organizations, under pressure to reduce costs and protect the environment, are increasingly turning their attention on both counts to conserving energy. Some companies see energy as a fixed cost that cannot be reduced, but in fact almost all organizations can find ways to use less energy, and a successful energy management program produces benefits for both the organization and the environment.

DEFINITION

An energy management program provides a systematic and continuous method of analyzing, improving, and evaluating an organization's energy usage.

ADVANTAGES

An effective energy management program:
- saves money;
- conveys an environmentally friendly attitude;
- often makes for greater employee workplace comfort.

DISADVANTAGES

There are no real disadvantages to introducing an energy management program, but remember that it takes time to set up and can require a sizeable initial expenditure, and that savings or environmental benefits accrue over the long term.

ACTION CHECKLIST

1. Designate an Energy Management Committee

The members of the energy management committee should be drawn from all levels of the organization. Your finance and purchasing departments should be represented, as should the transportation department, if you have one. The committee will manage the analysis, improvement, and evaluation of energy usage. Appoint a coordinator (someone with project management experience who commands respect and can get things done) to oversee the program. If in-house expertise or resources are limited, consider calling in an energy management consultant.

2. Define the Scope and Coverage of the Program

Depending on the size of the organization, it may be advisable to concentrate initially on one site or building; you can build on this experience to improve energy efficiency throughout the organization. Alternatively, the committee may decide to look initially at only one type of energy consumption, for example, heating or the use of company vehicles.

3. Gather Information

Ask the committee's finance department representative to produce a report of all the company's energy bills over the last couple of years. Check the rates: do they look reasonable, or too high? Look for variations in consumption over the year. Ask an alternative provider for a quote using your own consumption data.

If possible, try to compare your organization's energy usage figures with those of another organization.

4. Undertake an Energy Audit

Examine the way the organization uses energy. Create checklists covering different systems and identify practices that are potentially wasteful.

Cover the following areas:
- Transportation
  Are vehicles regularly serviced, maintained, and tuned?
  Do employees share vehicles when they are traveling to the same place on business?
  Do some drivers appear to use too much gas? Do they need advice on fuel economy?
  In planning trips, is cost-effective transportation a consideration?
  Can diesel fuel or liquefied petroleum gas be used instead of gas?
- Lighting
  Are you using the most efficient light bulbs?
  Could you make more use of daylight by moving workstations nearer windows?
  Are lights switched off when rooms are not in use?
  Are windows cleaned regularly?
- Heating
  Is the heating system serviced regularly?
  Are thermostats functioning correctly, and are they set to the right temperature?
  Is the heating switched off or turned down when the building is empty?
  Are windows energy efficient?
- Air conditioning
  Do you really need it?
  Is the system kept clean and regularly maintained?
  Is it working against the heating system?
- Insulation
  Are wall and roof insulation materials of the correct type and thickness?
- Ventilation
  Do employees open doors or windows to cool the place down instead of turning down thermostats?
  Are badly fitting doors and windows causing excessive drafts?

"Sustainable business has to navigate by more than one parameter. The demands of economics, of the environment and of contributing to a just society are all important for a global commercial enterprise to flourish."

Mark Moody-Stuart

- Equipment and machinery
  Is machinery running efficiently?
  Could you reuse any of the heat/energy produced by processes?
  Are you using the right size of machine for each job?
  Do employees routinely turn off computers and machines when they are not in use?

Every member of the committee should be actively involved in the audit. Members can be assigned to specific departments or sites, or each member can look at one particular aspect of energy use.

 ## 5. Analyze the Results and Make Improvements or Modifications

The results of the audit should highlight areas where action can be taken immediately (turning down thermostats, for example) and areas where investment may be needed to produce long-term gains (for example, buying a more efficient boiler). Instruct the purchasing department to take energy efficiency into account by asking suppliers about the energy consumption of every new piece of machinery or equipment. Ask the department to look for energy-efficient machines that could replace the present ones cost-effectively, and for innovatory products such as systems that switch lights off automatically.

If you don't already have such a system, it is essential to implement a schedule of regularly servicing and maintaining vehicles, machinery, and heating and cooling equipment.

Keep a record of the committee's changes so that improvements in energy usage can be monitored.

 ## 6. Communicate and Train Staff

Communicate the benefits of improved energy management and reduced costs to all employees. Provide

DOS AND DON'TS

DO
- Let all staff know about the importance of reducing energy usage.
- Remember to record the amount the company is spending on energy before the energy management program is launched.
- Make maintenance and servicing a regular program.
- Make sure that purchasing staff look at energy efficiency before making buying decisions.

DON'T
- Don't obscure the results of the program—inform all staff of its success.
- Don't stop after one audit and set of responses—continually look for improvements.

training on ways for employees to reduce energy usage—for example, by turning the heat down instead of opening windows to cool down an office. The checklists devised for the energy audit will help with this. Ask suppliers to provide training on the best ways to maintain and service specialist equipment. Reward staff who suggest successful ways to reduce energy usage.

 ## 7. Evaluate Changes and Look for Further Improvements

Check the energy bills after the program has been implemented and record reductions. Communicate successes to all employees. Hold regular meetings of the energy management committee to look for further ways to save on energy usage.

THOUGHT STARTERS
- Are lights switched off when a room is left empty?
- Are all the radiators and air conditioning units functioning correctly?
- Does your company car use too much gas?
- Remember that turning the heating down by one degree saves fuel.

FOR MORE INFORMATION

Books:
Capehart, B.L., et al. *Guide to Energy Management.* 5th ed. Boca Raton, FL: CRC Press, 2006.
Romm, Joseph J. *Cool Companies: How the Best Businesses Boost Profits and Productivity by Cutting Greenhouse-Gas Emissions.* Washington, DC: Island Press, 1999.

Journal Article:
Por, Otis. "Another Dawn for Solar Power." *International Business Week* (September 6, 2004): 17–21.

Web sites:
Department of Energy: **www.energy.gov**
Future Energy Solutions: **www.future-energy-solutions.com**
Energy Efficiency and Renewable Energy Network: **www.eere.energy.gov**

"There are only four ways to create value in the New Economy, and they're really simple: information, entertainment, convenience, and savings."
Jay S. Walker

Inventory Control

574

CHECKLIST

This checklist deals with some of the major principles of stock control, as it has traditionally been called, or inventory control, as it has become more widely known.

Stock control is important at both ends of the supply spectrum. Too much inventory ties up cash, prejudices cash flow, and in extreme cases jeopardizes the very survival of the company. Too little inventory threatens prosperity and growth if goods cannot be provided to customers. Stock control is therefore very important, although paradoxically it is often neglected.

This checklist is not a manual on stock control. It suggests lines of enquiry for managers seeking to improve their company's management of inventory.

DEFINITION

Stock control is the sum total of the policies, practices, and procedures that a company follows to ensure that its inventory is kept at levels consistent both with meeting predetermined standards of services and with releasing funds for working capital.

Inventory is held by retailers (finished goods), wholesalers (finished goods), manufacturers (finished goods, part finished goods, parts, and raw materials), public bodies (a range of inventory for use); indeed every type of organization.

For the purposes of this checklist, strategic inventory is defined as inventory without which the organization cannot function, that is, essential inventory.

Nonstrategic inventory is defined as basic commodities that are not critical to the overall function of the organization and that can be readily sourced.

ADVANTAGES

The introduction of effective stock control requires the commitment of significant effort and resources. However, stock control:

- releases cash for the major functions of the organization;
- achieves a standard of service consistent with predetermined policy;
- minimizes the costs associated with holding inventory (finance, storage, insurance, handling, obsolescence, pilferage).

ACTION CHECKLIST

1. Understand What Is Involved

Stock control systems vary from the extremely simple, ledger books and card indexes, to sophisticated computerized operating environments.

Establish a system that will provide you with regular reports about current inventory and that records supplies received and sales, deliveries, outputs, and usage. Your system need not be based on precise records for every item held in inventory. Use common sense: the cost of the system and its operation should not exceed the cost of the problem it is intended to solve. However, the following steps must be built into any stock control system:

- the reporting of current inventory levels;
- the recording of receipts/dispatches;
- the identification of reorder levels and quantities (through analysis of lead times, volume discounts, price stability)—this has a cost in itself in the form of higher ordering costs, loss of bulk discounts, and perhaps additional handling charges;
- the establishment of a schedule of regular auditing and inventory checking.

2. Analyze Usage

Analyze usage of all items in terms of:

- volume
- strategic/nonstrategic status

It is important to:

- identify key products that must be available on demand;
- classify products in terms of their importance to sales, not in big product families or in other broad product groupings;
- analyze sales to identify the real money earners: 50 percent probably yields only 10 percent of the total value, so this half requires less attention;
- focus on the items that produce the most profit;
- resist giving equal attention to all inventory items.

Identify the level of inventory you need to hold to avoid the risk of missing core opportunities or failing to supply basic needs. Identify nonstrategic inventory and reduce it through:

- special offers
- nonreplacement
- repackaging
- scrapping for salvage value

In extreme cases, write it off.

Don't spend time monitoring items that yield 5 to 10 percent of annual revenue—reduce stocks of them. The 80/20 rule applies: monitoring the right 20 percent will give you control over 80 percent of the total value of your inventory. Arbitrarily reducing inventory by a fixed percentage across the board is likely to result in reduced service levels without identifying areas of wasted investment.

Identify the level above which excess inventory ties up money and diminishes your return on capital.

3. Plan Your Stocking Area

- Locate frequently used items in an accessible place.
- Train staff in manual handling methods and the operation of mechanical handling equipment.
- Choose appropriate stacking methods—consider pallets, drums, bins, shelving, pipe racks. Do not try to store all items in the same environment.

- Consider storing large or bulky items with your suppliers if you have insufficient space, making sure that availability meets requirements.
- Use an appropriate labeling system for identifying inventory items (this might include bar coding or a simple handwritten label).
- Take shelf life into account and implement a stock rotation system.
- Review environmental conditions such as temperature and humidity.

4. Commit Adequate Personnel

Don't underestimate the staff required for running your stock control system in terms of numbers or quality—too few and you will lose control of your inventory; too many and the cost of running your system will be prohibitive.

575

CHECKLIST

5. Calculate the True Cost of Holding Inventory

Take into account the cost of:

- financing (the cost of funds or opportunity cost);
- storage, including equipment and labor;
- protection from damp, cold, or damage;
- insurance;
- handling;
- obsolescence;
- losses through pilferage;
- forgone rental income from your storage facilities.

6. Use Common Sense

You cannot control every item by quantity—you wouldn't expect someone to count paper clips or screws. Consider classifying such items as consumables and make a policy decision not to count them. Some lines may be controlled by weight.

7. Coordinate with Other Departments

Try to link your stock control system to other departments. A system that works closely with accounting will reduce the workloads of both sections. Good communication with buyers and dispatch departments will lessen the risk of staff and plant being overworked one day and underoccupied the next.

DOS AND DON'TS

DO

- Understand that well-run companies plan inventory levels.
- Think of inventory as cash.
- Relate inventory to known or anticipated sales, deliveries, demand, and usage.
- Consider whether you are carrying excessive inventory.
- Establish and regularly review reorder levels and quantities.
- Designate someone in your company to coordinate the output of inventory, output forecasts, purchasing, and stock control.

DON'T

- Don't assume you aren't suffering from pilferage, excessive waste, or some other form of shrinkage.
- Don't exaggerate the potential consequences of running out.
- Don't assume that every quantity or early delivery discount offered is to your advantage.
- Don't let stock-taking become an annual nightmare—do it regularly on a partial basis.
- Don't think that a stock control system needs to be expensive and complex—a basic system may give you adequate control at a cost below the resulting savings.
- Don't hold inventory only to fill the store or warehouse.
- Don't buy on speculation.

THOUGHT STARTERS

- Who really controls our inventory levels?
- You conscientiously lock the safe because it contains $100. How much thought do you give to the warehouse containing $500,000 worth of inventory?

FOR MORE INFORMATION

Book:
Muller, Max. *Essentials of Inventory Management.* New York: American Management Association, 2002.

Web site:
Modern Materials Handling (including warehousing management): **www.mmh.com**

See also:
✓ Effective Purchasing (pp. 546–547)

"Our key words now are globalization, new products and business, and speed."

Tsutomu Kanai

Taking Action on the Environment

CHECKLIST

This checklist is designed as an aid to the development of an action plan to comply with environmental regulations.

The environment has come to the forefront of industrial and commercial decisionmaking in recent years. The onus and liability are increasingly on senior managers and directors to come to terms with environmental responsibilities by adopting environmental policies and initiating action plans.

This checklist is therefore aimed primarily at senior managers who have, or will have, responsibility for tackling environmental issues.

DEFINITION

An environmental action plan brings together the key elements of environmental management, including:

- the organization's policy statement;
- the environmental audit;
- environmental management systems and standards, including ISO 14001: Environmental Management Systems;
- the setting of targets and the measuring of performance against them;
- the identification and ordering of key responsibilities to set the system in motion.

ADVANTAGES

An environmental action plan will:

- demonstrate commitment to customers, shareholders, and legislators that action to reduce environmental damage is a priority;
- provide a coherent statement of policy and a plan for implementation;
- lead to reduced waste and cost;
- mandate closer examination of processes and raw materials that can contribute to cost savings and improved productivity;
- help to develop improved communications and management systems through better information on sources of environmental impacts;
- lay a foundation for effective management of environmental risk.

DISADVANTAGES

- Staff may not see the need to change established practices.
- Stakeholders may see only the costs as opposed to an investment that will yield benefits.
- Benefits may be slow to accrue while costs are quickly incurred.

ACTION CHECKLIST

1. Gain Top Management Commitment
Make sure that the implications of good—and bad—environmental practice are fully understood by top managers and key stakeholders.

2. Designate a Senior Manager
Allocate responsibility for environmental matters at senior level.

3. Identify Environmental Laws and Regulations
Do your homework on relevant legislation and codes of practice—liability usually means that the polluter pays.

4. Consider Applying for Registration under ISO 14001
Registration provides a recognized framework for environmental management and may give a competitive advantage where there is a need to demonstrate conformance.

5. Review the Environmental Impact of Your Organization's Operations
This will enable you to determine the issues that need to be addressed.

6. Identify the Environment–Business Link
Focus on issues where environmental improvements can be directly related to financial and quality targets, for example, the generation of new or improved product lines by recycling waste, or the justification of price increases for more environmentally friendly products.

7. Establish Your Policy
Draw up a clear statement that covers objectives, improvement programs, audits, supplier and customer liaison, compliance with standards, and responsibility to the community.

8. Build In Measures and Records
These should cover not only outputs (damage to, or impact on, the environment) and inputs (damage created by raw materials), but also process measures (pollution created by outdated or worn-out machinery). Keep detailed records—ISO 14001 or legislation may require evidence of conformance.

9. Develop a Procedures Manual
The manual should be a "who does what and how" of operational control achieved through work instruction, performance criteria, measurements, tests, and verification.

10. Launch an Environmental Training Program
Build the environment into routine operational practice. The organization will benefit from the integration of environmental goals with financial, personal, and operational targets.

"Modern economic thinking . . . is peculiarly unable to consider the long term and to appreciate man's dependence on the natural world."

E. F. Schumacher

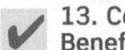 **11. Involve Your Employees**
Work on the commitment of staff by involving them directly rather than issuing remote instructions. Publicize your objectives and targets.

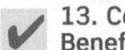 **12. Conduct Regular Audits**
Use audits to see how things are going, to correct what is going wrong, and to publicize what is going right.

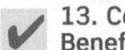 **13. Communicate Environmental Benefits**
Make sure you communicate your successes both internally and externally. Where possible, express environmental benefits in terms of financial savings. The promotion of direct community benefits can also enhance the organization's image and reputation.

MEASURING ENVIRONMENTAL DAMAGE

- Input measures should include indicators, targets, and measures of plant efficiency, materials quality and recyclability, and effectiveness of training in operational procedures.

- Process measures should aim at percentage improvements in reducing waste in manufacturing, finishing, and packaging.
- Output measures record impact on, or damage to, the community, and should measure reductions in waste or pollution discharge. Output measures are those that relate most to the organization's image and reputation and are the ones most likely to be reported outside the organization.

577

CHECKLIST

THOUGHT STARTERS

- "Businesses made a great deal of money fouling the world over the last 200 years. I have no doubt that there are many fortunes to be made cleaning things up over the next three generations." (Sir Crispin Tickell)

- Some 23 billion tons of carbon dioxide are pumped into the Earth's atmosphere every year.

- Tropical rainforests—the world's lungs—are being cut back by 66,000 square miles every year.

DOS AND DON'TS

DO
- Pay attention to ISO 14001.
- Focus attention on all stages of the product life cycle, not just the end.
- Take into account the environmental policies of suppliers, customers, and competitors.
- Try to spread the environmental message far and wide in the organization—action will follow more readily.
- Make sure that staff receive appropriate information and training.
- Communicate what you are doing to the outside world.

DON'T
- Don't assume the environment is irrelevant if you are not in manufacturing.
- Don't wait for legislation or bad press to force you to act.
- Don't impose complicated systems without full consultation and feedback.
- Don't equate measurement and records with bureaucracy. If it gets measured, it gets done.

FOR MORE INFORMATION

Books:
Tibor, Tom, and Ira Feldman. *ISO 14000: A Guide to the New Environmental Management Standards.* New York: McGraw-Hill, 1995.
Thompson, Dixon, ed. *Tools for Environmental Management: A Practical Introduction and Guide.* Gabriola Island, British Columbia: New Society Publishers, 2002.

Journal Article:
Hormozi, Amir M. "ISO 14000: The Next Focus in Standardization." *SAM Advanced Management Journal* 62:3 (Summer 1997): 32–41.

Web sites:
National Council for Science and the Environment: **www.cnie.org**
U.S. Department of Energy Office of Environmental Management (EM): **www.em.doe.gov**
U.S. Environmental Protection Agency: **www.epa.gov**

"While animals survive by adjusting themselves to their background, man survives by adjusting his background to himself."

Ayn Rand

Using Management Consulting Services Effectively

CHECKLIST

This checklist is for prospective users of consultants. It suggests some of the questions you should ask yourself before approaching a consultant to undertake an assignment. There is little doubt that calling on the service of a management consultant can often prove to be a valuable investment, provided that:

- you allow enough time for the whole exercise;
- you have accurately defined the problem area;
- you know what you want the consultant to do and have identified the necessary steps for the task in hand;
- you exercise care in selecting the right consultant;
- you measure progress toward a solution.

DEFINITION

Management consulting is an advisory service contracted for and provided to organizations by specially trained and qualified persons who assist, in an objective and independent manner, the client organization to identify management problems, analyze such problems, recommend solutions to these problems, and help, when requested, in the implementation of solutions.

(Greiner and Metzger, *Consulting to Management*, 1983)

ADVANTAGES

- Expertise. Since consultants are immersed in their specialty, they are well placed to advise on the state of the art. It may be impossible for an organization to tap such expertise in any other way.
- Cost-effectiveness. When help is needed with short-term projects, it may be more cost-effective for a company to buy in skills as and when they are needed.
- Extra resources. A consultant can back up an overstretched management team or pursue a project that would otherwise not be completed.
- Independent viewpoint. An outsider can see things that are unclear to people on the inside or say things that members of staff may fear to articulate. Equally, employees may be more willing to agree to a course of action if they know that impartial advice has been taken.

DISADVANTAGES

- They may be expensive.*Consultants News*, published by Kennedy Information, is a good source of information on industry trends.
- The end result may be unsatisfactory, though steps in the following action checklist will help you guard against this.
- The work may be left to junior consultancy staff once

the assignment starts, or personnel may change during the project.
- There may be resentment among staff over the employment of consultants.

ACTION CHECKLIST

 1. Involve Senior Management from the Beginning
Gain their approval for the decision to use consultants and keep them informed during the selection process. This will help ensure that your choice of consultant will be accepted at the top level.

2. Be Aware of the Number and Scope of Management Consulting Firms
Some offer a wide range of services, while others specialize in particular industries, certain areas of business activity, or smaller or larger organizations.

3. Prepare a Short List of Possible Consultants
Personal recommendation is a common method of finding consultants; you can also consult directories and registers. Make sure you obtain references from previous clients to establish a consultant's track record.

4. Ask Short-listed Consultants for a Preliminary Survey
This should be free, although in certain circumstances a nominal charge may be made. It should enable you to establish the extent to which the consultant can help you, the likely benefits, and the duration of the job. It should also help you study the consultant's approach to the problem and to your organization. Ask for a written report of the survey.

5. Study the Consultancy Proposals Submitted
Each proposal should contain:
- an understanding of your situation or need;
- a program of work;
- an indication of the consultant's management style and approach;
- a timetable for the work;
- details of consultancy staff who will be involved, including relevant qualifications and experience;
- the resources required, for example, time, information, and equipment;
- estimates of fees and costs;
- a summary of the results and benefits to be achieved from the project.

 6. Explain to Staff Why You Are Hiring a Consultant
All staff concerned should be fully briefed on why a con-

"Wall Street is the only place people ride to in a Rolls Royce to get advice from people who take the subway."

Warren Buffett

sultant has been appointed, when the consultant will arrive, and what kind of cooperation is required. Appoint someone as the main contact with the consultant.

7. Ask the Consultant for Regular Progress Reports

Measure actual progress against the agreed objectives of the assignment. Make sure that your requirements are not being overshadowed by the consultant's preferences.

8. Have a Debriefing Session Before the End of the Consultancy

Make sure the consultant summarizes the findings and conclusions of the project either in a report or in a presentation. Make certain that there are no misunderstandings or errors.

DOS AND DON'TS

DO
- Invest time in the whole process.
- Have a clear understanding of what you want to achieve.
- Prepare a checklist of requirements as a basis for reducing your short list to the final selection.
- Establish effective communication and coordination between consultant and staff.

DON'T
- Don't assume that you necessarily need to bring in an outsider.
- Don't accept friendly recommendations without investigating past performance.
- Don't assume that staff will readily accept an outside expert.
- Don't lose sight of your most important objectives.
- Don't become overly reliant on a consultant.

9. Assess the Consultant's Effectiveness

Check that the new development and procedures proposed are being implemented and applied appropriately, and that they are not being undermined by old methods and concepts. Discuss with staff concerned any particular difficulties that arise during implementation. Regularly examine the results being achieved and insist on follow-up visits from the consultant at appropriate intervals after completion of the project.

THOUGHT STARTERS
- Can you define clearly the problem or issue that needs to be tackled?

- Are you sure the expertise needed is not available internally?

- Have you worked with a consultant before? What was the outcome?

FOR MORE INFORMATION

Books:
Kubr, Milan, ed. *Management Consulting: A Guide to the Profession*. 4th ed. Geneva, Switzerland: International Labour Office, 2002.
Schaffer, Robert H. *High Impact Consulting: How Clients and Consultants Can Work Together to Achieve Extraordinary Results*. San Francisco, CA: Jossey-Bass, 2002.

Web site:
Institute of Management Consultants USA:
www.imcusa.org

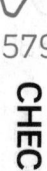

579

CHECKLIST

"I don't think a manager can work with a person day in and day out and not develop some sort of personal relationship."

Mary Kay Ash

Conducting an Information Audit

CHECKLIST

This checklist is concerned with the processes involved in an information audit.

The increasing problems caused by junk mail, information overload, and the need to make decisions ever more rapidly, mean that it is all too easy to take the wrong path in establishing systems for decision support. If accurate information is the key to effective decisionmaking, an information audit will enable you to find out whether your information systems are up to the task.

The audit can take place on an organizational or individual level—approaches to both are presented here.

DEFINITION

An information audit requires an inventory of the way people and technology mix to make sure that the right information gets to the right people in the right form at the right time. It also requires measures to evaluate the costs and benefits of the operational system providing it.

Inventory checks include specialist, and perhaps untapped, human resource skills and processes and information flow charts as well as technological tools, databases, and knowledge stores.

ADVANTAGES

Your organization will discover:
- what information is being circulated but not used to advantage;
- what information is required but not available;
- the differences between what is needed and what is available;
- what needs to be done to match demand with provision;
- how information is best delivered to its potential users.

DISADVANTAGES

- It takes time, skills, expertise, impartiality, and honesty to gain a thorough, flexible, and updatable view of what is happening; where it is good and where bad; and what needs to be done now and continuously.
- Although it is a common practice, it is a mistake to assign value to information on the basis of cost alone. The timeliness, relevance, and accuracy of information, its impact on efficiency and productivity, and its contribution to decision-making are too often taken for granted or ignored altogether.

ACTION CHECKLIST
For Organizations or Departments

1. Carry Out an Initial Investigation
Establish the facts about your situation. Before you can find out where you are going it is essential to know your current position. Gain a picture of the importance information has in the organization and establish an understanding of the organization's objectives and targets, its management culture, and its organizational structure. This establishes a context and perspective for finding out what information resources the organization has and how it uses them, how information flows (or doesn't), and how it is valued.

2. Secure Sufficient Resources to Do the Job
Put together an audit team. You will need people with sufficient knowledge, experience, judgment, and standing in the organization to carry out the investigation. The team will need to establish a method of performing the investigation, securing access to the appropriate people and documentation, winning adequate time to carry out the requisite tasks, and securing support from the top.

3. Establish the Framework of the Audit
In order to guarantee consistency across the organization, set up a general framework of approach. Include the following considerations:
- What information do staff acquire, create, process, or transmit?
- Who and what are involved in these activities?
- What control procedures are in place?
- What is the nature of budget allocation and control?
- Which types of information are used a lot/partially/not at all?
- Which types of information are required but not available?

4. Establish Measures and Values in Order to Assess Effectiveness
Define ways of assessing the importance of the data to be gathered. For example, what significance or value can be attached to the fact that an office keeps files of information? What is done with them? To what use is the information put?

The cost of acquisition, processing, storage, and delivery is an undisputed primary consideration, but it will not necessarily indicate the effectiveness or even performance of the information resource, activity, or result that relates to it. Value or effectiveness may be assessed in more interpretive or qualitative terms such as accuracy, relevance and contribution to decision making, ease of use, and impact on efficiency, as well as return on investment in terms of the bottom line.

5. Get Down to the Detail of the Audit
An information audit should ascertain at least the following:
- What information do staff acquire? From which sources? At what cost? How is it used?
- What information do staff create? What happens to it? Where does it go?

"An individual without information cannot take responsibility; an individual who is given information cannot help but take responsibility."

Wilbert Lee Gore

- What information is stored and why? What purpose will it serve?
- What information is passed on or delivered? To whom? For what purpose? In what form?
- Is there a gap or a match between the information that is available and the information needed?
- What are the skills and responsibilities of the people who carry out these tasks?
- What equipment and tools do they have available?
- Are there any control documents such as policy statements or guidelines?
- Is any of the information superfluous to needs?
- Are any of the information-handling activities nonproductive?
- What budget is available? How was the budget figure reached? How adequate is it? Who controls it? What control measures exist for it?

6. Use the Data Gathered to Map Information Flows

Map out a flow chart to show the areas, processes, functions, and activities through which information passes, clarifying gaps or fault lines that need to be plugged or bottlenecks and overflows that need to be unblocked.

7. Evaluate the Effectiveness of Information Resources and Activities

When the data sets are assembled, ask:
- To what extent does this activity or resource support objectives or help to meet targets?
- How efficient is it in terms of the time and cost required for it?
- Are any positive or negative results directly or indirectly related to it?
- Does it need to be adapted to fit changing needs?
- Is there a good or a bad fit between the resources and the results they produce?
- Are there information gaps between different functions?
- Are there areas where information goes into a black hole?
- Are there gaping holes where results are not forthcoming because no one has identified responsibility for the information process?

8. Report the Findings

Focus on the gravest areas of mismatch—black holes where no useful outcome is visible—and the people, skills, and resources required to correct them. Conclude with recommendations for action.

An Individual Audit
- Are your information needs structured or are they ad hoc, considered only when needs arise?
- Is anyone else aware of your needs or are they a secret?
- Do you review your information sources?

- Do you make do with what you already have?
- Do you add value to the information you process?
- Do you have a say in the hardware or software you use?
- Do you file most of the information you receive? For immediate or eventual reuse?
- When you send information on, do you know what will happen to it?
- Do you get information in the right form for your use?
- Is it reliable and accurate?
- Is it worth keeping for future use?
- Is it worth passing to someone else?
- Could you get hold of it again easily if the need arose?
- Would you know where to go for it?
- If it hadn't arrived, would you (or should you) have gone looking for it?

581

CHECKLIST

DOS AND DON'TS

DO
- Consider the needs of your employees as a key indicator.
- Devise a method of relating resources and activities to objectives and targets.
- Evaluate levels of cooperation.
- Take the culture and structure of the organization into account.
- Think ahead as much as possible—change is coming ever faster.

DON'T
- Don't be influenced by time-honored, fixed ideas, even when they seem persuasive.
- Don't make promises during the data-gathering stage.

THOUGHT STARTERS
- Do you add value to information or just file it, toss it, or pass it on?
- Can you identify specific information that you need but don't get?
- Can you identify specific information that you receive but don't want?

FOR MORE INFORMATION

Books:
Laudon, Kenneth C., and Jane P. Laudon. *Management Information Systems: Managing the Digital Firm.* 9th ed. Upper Saddle River, NJ: Prentice Hall, 2005.

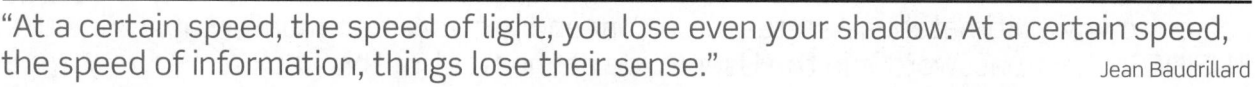
"At a certain speed, the speed of light, you lose even your shadow. At a certain speed, the speed of information, things lose their sense."
Jean Baudrillard

Cash Flow for the Small Business

> **CHECKLIST**
> This checklist is designed to help you understand and control cash flow in your business.

DEFINITION

The flow of cash through a business is roughly comparable to the flow of water through a central heating system. Too little cash/water, or obstruction to a smooth and continuous flow, creates problems. Without an adequate flow of cash, a company may be trading profitably in the shorter term, but it will nevertheless collapse. The figure below illustrates the flow of cash through a business. The flow starts at (1) when the owners or shareholders of the business invest funds, which go into the pool of cash (2).

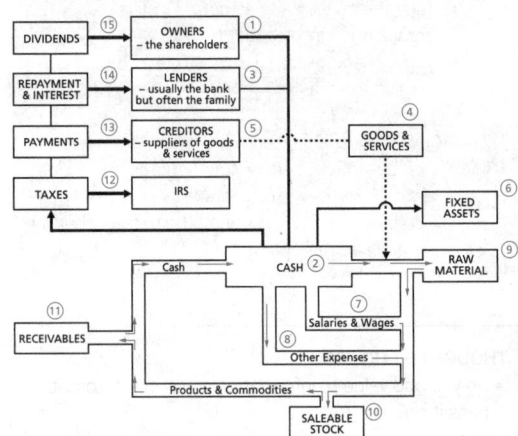

This investment may not be a one-shot occurrence. There may be subsequent injections of cash for a variety of positive (for example, business expansion) or negative (shortage of liquid funds) reasons. Lenders (3) may also put funds into the cash pool at any time. The lenders may be the company's bankers or, in some cases, members of the family or friends of the owners of the business.

Suppose that in order to start trading the company obtains goods and services (4) on credit from suppliers (5), who immediately become creditors. The business may also need to acquire fixed assets (6), perhaps real estate, office equipment, delivery trucks, or cars. If these assets are truly fixed, their purchase immediately immobilizes some liquid capital. Cash also flows out of the pool in the form of salaries and wages (7) and other expenses (8) such as stationery or computer software.

If the new business is in manufacturing, it buys raw materials (9)—another cash outflow, the timing depending on whether materials are paid for immediately or purchased on credit. The expenditure of wages and other expenses (for example, tools), together with some of the raw materials (7), (8), and (9), are used to produce salable

stock (10). If the company does not manufacture products, it may purchase stock for resale. The stocks will rejoin the cash flow when they are sold, probably to customers buying on credit, whose debts immediately become receivables (11). They owe the company the price of the goods or services they purchased until they pay, whereupon cash flows back into the cash pool (2).

Periodically, the cash pool is reduced as cash is withdrawn to pay taxes (12) and creditors (13), repay capital and pay interest to lenders (14), and pay dividends or other rewards to the owners, the original investors (15). The cycle never ends. If it stops, the whole business process stops too. Without an injection of cash, trading ceases and the company goes out of business.

ADVANTAGES

Controlling your cash flow has important advantages:

- you know where your cash flow is tied up
- you can spot potential bottlenecks and act to reduce their impact
- you reduce your dependence on bankers and save interest charges by anticipating and managing your cash needs
- you are in control of your business and can make informed decisions

ACTION CHECKLIST

✔ 1. Identify Potential Cash Bottlenecks

Examination of the figure above suggests some obvious bottlenecks:

- fixed assets (6)
- raw materials (9)
- salable stock (10)
- receivables (11)

Examine these bottlenecks in turn.

✔ 2. Reconsider Your Investment in Fixed Assets

- Is cash unnecessarily tied up in fixed assets?
- Is it tied up in assets that are not used, are underused, or could be disposed of?
- Is it tied up in necessary assets that could be replaced by leasing?
- Is it tied up in expensive assets that could be replaced by something cheaper?
- Has cash been invested in fixed assets for reasons of prestige rather than profit?

✔ 3. Reconsider Your Investment in Raw Materials

Have you tied up cash in raw materials to take advantage of special terms offered by suppliers?

Are you sure that the advantages outweigh the costs of holding raw materials that may not be used immediately? Consider:

- the cost of borrowing money to finance raw materials inventory;
- the loss of alternative uses for the capital;

- the cost of physical storage;
- the risk of shrinkage.

Similarly, reconsider your investment in finished goods.

4. Reconsider Your System of Inventory Control

An adequate system of inventory control does not necessarily require precise records for every line held in stock; common sense dictates the kind of records your company needs. Weigh the cost of the system against the costs and financial risks of the problems it is intended to help solve.

Some form of control is necessary to guard against theft, obsolescence, spoilage, and running out or having too much of a particular good, any of which can damage a business severely. The basic requirements of a inventory control system include:

- a forecast of what you expect to sell and when;
- a knowledge of your present inventory, provided via reports at regular intervals;
- a record of supplies received and shipments dispatched, which should be reconciled periodically with current inventory (this reconciliation need not be of every item, only of selected items in sequence);
- predetermined and regularly reviewed reorder levels and quantities;
- a knowledge of price trends and suppliers' quantity discounts and delivery times.

5. Consider How Credit Works

The amount and length of credit allowed and potential return on capital are directly related. Some business owners assume that in most cases it is more important to turn over capital as quickly as they can instead of producing an additional return on capital made available (actually, lent) to a customer. Make sure your credit policy:

- recovers the cost of extending credit;
- gives customers strong incentives to pay promptly.

6. Consider Your Credit Policy
Policy

- Is there one person in your business who is ultimately responsible for supervising credit and ensuring the prompt collection of monies due, and who is held accountable if your credit position gets out of hand? The exercise of this person's authority should not adversely affect an individual sales rep's relationship with their customers—nor does it reduce their responsibility for seeing that the sales they make are paid for in accordance with the firm's credit terms.
- Do you have a clear-cut maximum credit policy? Is it written down? Is it known to all your sales staff? Are they instructed to make certain that all your customers are familiar with the policy?
- Are you clear in your own mind how you assess credit risks and how you impose your usual limits on each customer's total receivables and overdue accounts?

Bad debts

- Did you know that—assuming you make 1.5 percent of net sales—a loss of $1,500 in bad debts nullifies the net

profit on $100,000 sales and destroys all the effort involved in making those sales?
- Do you realize that an avoidable loss of $1,500 in bad debts almost certainly means that a lot of abortive effort has been expended trying to collect this money before it was written off—and that the cost of this effort is probably hidden and never identified?
- On the other hand, do you recognize that the absence of any doubtful—as opposed to bad—debts probably means that you have been missing out on business by being overcautious?

Granting or extending credit

- Do you methodically check the financial standing of all new customers before executing the first order?
- Do you recheck the financial standing of existing customers whose purchases have recently increased substantially?
- Do you check trade references by telephone? Suppliers will often tell you things over the phone that they would never put in writing.
- Do you understand that salespeople are by nature optimists? Do you therefore rely on other sources of information before establishing (or increasing) customers' credit facilities?

Credit control and collection

- How soon do your invoices go out after the goods are dispatched? Can this be speeded up?
- How soon do monthly statements go out following the last day of the month? Can this be speeded up?
- Are the terms of sale clearly and precisely shown on all quotations, price lists, invoices, and statements?
- What is the actual average length of credit you are giving—or your customers are taking?
- Do you prepare monthly lists of all customers whose settlement is overdue, and do you list the total receivables of slow customers as well as the amount that is currently overdue?
- Do you have a collection procedure timetable?
- Are you politely firm but insistent in your collection routine?
- Do you watch the ratio of total debt on balances on the sales ledger at the end of each month in relation to the sales of the immediately preceding twelve months? Is the position improving, deteriorating, or static? Why?
- Are your sales staff aware that "It's not sold until it's paid for?"

FOR MORE INFORMATION

Books:
Bragg, Steven M., and E. James Burton. *Accounting and Finance for Your Small Business.* 2nd ed. Hoboken, NJ: Wiley, 2006.
Dickie, Terry, and Beverly Manber. *Budgeting for a Small Business.* Normal, IL: Crisp Publications, 1994.
Tracy, John A., and Tage C. Tracey. *How to Manage Profit and Cashflow: Mining the Numbers for Gold.* Hoboken, NJ: Wiley, 2004.

"Start small. If you can succeed with a few thousand pounds, then you can do much better with bigger sums."

Reuben Singh

Brainstorming

CHECKLIST

The purpose of this checklist is to enable a busy manager, without previous experience of the technique and with a minimum of preparation, to introduce brainstorming to a group and then go on to brainstorm a specific problem or opportunity.

DEFINITION

Brainstorming involves a spontaneous, open-ended discussion in a search for new ideas. It is a means of getting a large number of ideas from a group of people in a short time. It can prove valuable for identifying opportunities, for example, for market development, tackling organizational problems, or problemsolving in general. Recent years have seen several variations of brainstorming emerge, such as brainwriting (where ideas are written down by individuals), nominal group technique, electronic brainstorming, and buzz groups.

ADVANTAGES

- Brainstorming rapidly generates a large number of fresh ideas and concepts.
- It actively engages people and allows them to feel they are making a positive contribution.

DISADVANTAGES

- Overbearing individuals can dominate or sidetrack the session.
- Getting people to be noncritical can be a problem.

ACTION CHECKLIST

Preparation

1. Select the Problem/Opportunity to be Brainstormed

Select an issue important enough to justify the participation of others. It should lend itself to an imaginative approach and offer a number of possible solutions.

2. Consider Structure and Objectives

Although a brainstorming session is an open, no-holds-barred discussion, establish where you are going, what you want to achieve, and roughly how to get there.

3. Choose the Facilitator

Choosing the right facilitator is vital. Ideally, it should be an open, outgoing person with the ability to communicate interest and enjoyment. The facilitator need not be the most senior person at the session, but will need to set the scene by relaxing the participants and creating an open, free atmosphere, controlling dominant people, getting and keeping the meeting on track by highlighting the issues, and creating a sense of fun. Perhaps most importantly, the person should be adept at keeping ideas flowing.

The facilitator should feel comfortable running activity-based sessions and should have clear plans and tactics for arriving at expected outcomes. The facilitator must also ensure, as much as possible, that the group works as a team and owns what it has achieved at the end.

4. Select an Appropriate Site

This depends largely on the time set aside for the session. If time is available, somewhere away from the usual place of work is often more appropriate. This often allows a fresh perspective on the business in hand.

5. Invite a Mixed Group

Include people who have little or no knowledge of the problem to be brainstormed as well as those with a specialist contribution to make. Nonspecialists will not be concerned with detail and will offer a fresh approach.

6. Decide on the Size of the Group

There is no right number, although more than ten might be unmanageable when ideas really start to flow, and fewer than five might not be enough for generating creativity. Six to eight is usually about right, although this depends on the style of the facilitator and the nature of the problem to be tackled.

7. Order the Right Equipment

You will need to record the ideas that come up. A tape recorder smacks of Big Brother and may inhibit the free flow of ideas. Use a flip chart—successive sheets can be fastened to the wall to help stimulate further ideas.

8. Design a Relaxed Seating Plan

Do not use a room with fixed rows of seats. Something more relaxed is preferable; a circle or U-shape is fairly usual. A facilitator who is not familiar with the room should check it beforehand and prepare it.

9. Sketch Out a Timetable

Think of your own powers of concentration and remember that brainstorming of ideas can go from dynamic to exhausted and back again. Between 10 and 20 minutes may be needed to get people relaxed. Two hours can be a long time to brainstorm—stop for a break if people show signs of tiredness. Arrange for a 20-minute break after an hour's uninterrupted flow or if and when the flow of ideas slows to a trickle.

10. Select a Productive Time of Day

Unfortunately, advice is difficult here, as we are all different. Some people are better when their minds are less active and more relaxed and when their routine work has been dispensed with. Others may prefer the morning, when collective mental energy is at its highest, or at least is not dulled by the day's toil.

Provide sufficient notice of the session and an outline of the problem to be tackled.

"Intense concentration for hour after hour can bring out resources in people that they didn't know they had."

Edwin Land

The session

 1. State the Problem/Objective

Make sure everyone participating has a clear understanding of the purpose of the session.

2. Restate the Problem

Encourage the group to stand back from the problem, walk around it, and see it from every angle. Suggest rewording it in "How to . . . " statements. Some restatements may be close to the original; others may illuminate new facets.

3. Brainstorm the Problem

Use the following techniques to generate further ideas:

- call for a one-minute break, asking the group to look over ideas already noted before starting the flow again
- offer a target, for example, "We only need six more to make fifty ideas!"
- look back at your restatements to pursue other lines
- freewheel: try to bring the subconscious into play—the wilder the idea, the better
- go for quantity, not quality. Suspend judgment; evaluation comes later. Laugh with wild ideas, not at them
- cross-fertilize: pick up somebody's idea and suggest others leading from it

4. Take Off from a Wild Idea

Ask the group to choose a really wild and apparently senseless idea from the lists you have generated. Using it as a starting point, see how many more ideas you can come up with.

5. Close the Session

About five minutes before the scheduled close, give a warning that the session will soon end. The participants will want to know what happens next. Explain that the lists will be typed up for circulation. Do this within 24 hours to retain freshness and familiarity.

Evaluation

1. Rank Your Ideas and Pick Out the Instant Winners

When you circulate lists of the ideas generated at the brainstorming session, ask the team to rank them: 3 points for ideas that stand out; 2 points for those that have possibilities but need a little adjustment; 0 for those that are obvious nonstarters, clearly require too many resources, or do not meet the original objectives.

2. Sift and Short-list the Feasible Ideas

Reduce the number of 2s to a minimum by applying such criteria as cost, practicability, acceptability, or timescale.

3. Use Reverse Brainstorming

- In how many ways can a particular idea fail?
- What are the negative factors?
- What is the potential downside for the organization?

4. Apply the Key Evaluative Criteria

- What will it cost?
- Will it be acceptable to management, staff, customers?
- Is it legal?
- Is it practicable?
- How long will it take?
- What competition will there be?
- How urgent is it? If it is not done now, will an opportunity be lost?

THOUGHT STARTERS

Does your organization need to:
- become more innovative?
- solve problems requiring creative or imaginative answers?
- get more involvement and participation from staff?

DOS AND DON'TS

DO

In the brainstorming session, the facilitator should:
- encourage an informal atmosphere;
- use a variety of techniques to generate further ideas;
- be sensitive to participants' fluctuating energy levels.

DON'T

The facilitator should not:
- use a tape recorder;
- allow critical or evaluative comments;
- allow interruptions;
- let the session go on too long;
- allow the session to become too "off-the-wall!"

FOR MORE INFORMATION

Books:

Clark, Charles. *Brainstorming: How to Create Successful Ideas*. Hollywood, CA: Wilshire Book Co., 1989.
McCoy, Jr., Charles W. *Why Didn't I Think of That?*. Paramus, NJ: Prentice Hall, 2002.

Journal Articles:

Buzan, Tony. "Constructive Brainstorming Can Jump the Gaps." *Business Marketing Digest* 18:1 (1993): 35–41.
Furnham, Adrian. "Brainstorming Myth." *Business Strategy Review* 11:4 (Winter 2000).
Khan, Mujeeb. "You Got a Problem?" *Quality World* 29:10 (October 2003).

See also:
✔ Performing a SWOT Analysis (pp. 520–521)
✔ Planning a Workshop (pp. 480–481)
✔ Total Quality: Getting TQM to Work (pp. 562–563)

"Our challenge is to stand out from the crowd when the crowd has much more money than you. Ideas are relatively cheap to have."

Dave Hieatt

Designing Questionnaires

586

This checklist is designed for anyone who needs to use a questionnaire to carry out a survey of the opinions or attitudes of a specific group. It is a mistake to take a casual approach to designing a questionnaire; expert advice is not only desirable, but often essential.

DEFINITION

A questionnaire is a means of obtaining specific information about a defined problem so that the data can be analyzed and interpreted. They tend to take one of two approaches: structured (consisting of questions with precoded answers) or unstructured (questions to which respondents can phrase their own answers).

The questionnaire is a vital part of most surveys. Even so, there is no easy way to design a series of questions. It remains largely an art, not a science.

ACTION CHECKLIST

✓ 1. Define Your Research Objectives

The objectives determine the contents of the questionnaire. What topics are relevant to the decision-making task? Which information is essential and which would simply be nice to know?

Questionnaires can be used to gather many kinds of information, including:

- consumption patterns/market trends/reasons for market changes;
- beliefs about specific products or services;
- expectations related to specific products or services;
- general or specific attitudes;
- economic, psychological, or social motivations for behavior;
- influences on people's decision-making;
- competitors' activities;
- media exposure and influence.

✓ 2. Select the Appropriate Method

The most effective method of administering a survey depends on the its subject, the nature of the survey population, and your research budget. The traditional methods are by personal interview, telephone, and mail. Each has advantages and disadvantages (see table below). Other methods include fax, e-mail, and the Web. The Web is most appropriate for lengthy surveys, complex routing, consumer research, and Web site tests. E-mail is appropriate for very short interviews, research on a low budget, employee research, recruiting for Web interviews, and business-to-business research. E-mail surveys benefit from being international, cheaper than mail surveys, faster than the telephone, and automated for data collection, and do not suffer from interviewer influence. There are, however, drawbacks, including technical incompatibilities, the lack of a universal e-mail directory, time delays in completion and return, and low penetration of the population, resulting in self-selecting samples.

✓ 3. Define Your Sample Population

Sources of names, addresses, and telephone numbers include databases, directories, and commercial lists. Consider the spread of your sample with respect to customers/noncustomers, sex, socio-economic groups, and age, if relevant. You can sample a specific population by quota or at random. Random sampling is best, because you can calculate any error in the sample. Pressures of cost, convenience, and time, however, favor quota sampling, in which interviewers must meet numerical targets based on strata within the population.

✓ 4. Decide How to Analyze the Results

Even a low response rate may yield lots of paper to sort or plenty of data to key into a PC analysis package (such as SPSS or SNAP), spreadsheet, or database. Whether the analysis will be done manually or electronically, think in advance of the logistics of data management and the facilities you have to analyze the responses. On the other hand, don't focus so much on ease of analysis that you compromise ease of use for the respondent or the relevance of the exercise. How you will use the responses helps determine the proportion of structured to unstructured questions and the decision whether to put all questions to all respondents—for example, do you need a filter question to establish whether or not respondents use the product or service being surveyed?

✓ 5. Order the Questions

It is good practice to:

- start with one or two easy questions;
- explore present behavior (what is used/done/bought now) before asking about the past or future;

	Face to face	Telephone	Mail
Respondent acceptance	reasonable	doubtful	open choice
Recruitment	controlled	controlled	self-selecting
Response rate	fixed	fixed	variable
Speed	moderate	fast	slow
Variety of sample	poor	very good	very good
Interaction/rapport	very good	good	poor
Complexity of interview	possible	limited	impossible
Interviewer bias	present	present	absent
Interview length	up to 1 hour (prearranged)	10–15 minutes	30 questions (max.)
Demand on staff resources	heavy	substantial	moderate

"The essence of science; ask an impertinent question, and you are on the way to a pertinent answer."

Jacob Bronowski

- follow a logical order so the respondent is not confused;
- position sensitive questions toward the end;
- make sure you don't broach ideas early in the questioning that might influence answers to later questions;
- leave classification answers to the end (for example, "Which age range do you fall into?").

6. Design Precise Questions

Once you have determined which topics to cover and what level of detail to use, consider the following:

- open or closed questions? Questions can be closed or open-ended. The anticipated answers to a closed question are precoded with simple instructions to the interviewee or respondent, for example, "Circle number" or "Please check as applicable." Allow for "Don't know" or "Not stated." It is advisable to precode as many questions as possible—open-ended questions may provide richer data, but the answers still have to be put into coding categories afterward.
- confusion versus understanding. Avoid long, technical words and jargon. Watch out for possible ambiguity. Words such as "frequently," "often," "regularly," or "usually" need to be qualified. Avoid double negatives such as "Would you not drink a nonalcoholic beer?" Stick to one issue per question—avoid questions such as "What do you think of this administration's economic policies, and how do you think they should be modified, if at all?"
- attitude questions. The simplest approach is to put a statement to respondents and ask whether they agree or disagree, for example:

There is a sensible balance between my work and my personal life.

- Agree 1; Disagree 2; Neither agree nor disagree 3; Don't know 4

This scale lacks subtlety, however: you have no idea how strongly those who reply "Agree" do agree, or how strongly others disagree. In order to measure the strength of respondents' attitudes, you need to construct rating scales. Two that are commonly used are the Likert scale and the semantic differential scale.

Likert scale. A statement is put to respondents, who are asked, "Please tell me how much you agree or disagree with this statement," for example:

I have good opportunities for career development.

- Strongly agree 1; Slightly agree 2; Neither agree nor disagree 3; Slightly disagree 4; Strongly disagree 5

The responses are analyzed by allocating weights to scale positions. You might allocate 5 to "Strongly agree," 3 for the midpoint, and 1 point for "Strongly disagree," or vice versa—but be consistent. If the scale battery includes both positive and negative attitude statements, then "Strongly agree" for a negative statement rates 1, not 5.

Semantic differential scale. This is easier to administer and is more meaningful than the Likert scale in rating responses about specific attributes of named products and services. For example, if the product is an automobile, you might construct the following double-ended scale:

Acceleration: Good . . . . Poor.

It is also common to use a point scale:

| Reliability: | Good | 1 | 2 | 3 | 4 | 5 | Poor |

Semantic scales can be either monopolar (bitter–not bitter; modern–not modern) or bipolar (modern–old-fashioned; strong–weak).

7. Consider the Page Layout

Don't cramp yourself—leave room for the answers! A questionnaire administered by an interviewer needs to have clear instructions that cannot be confused with the questions themselves. Instructions should in any case be in a different typeface. An attractive layout is especially important in a questionnaire to be mailed, as it has a significant effect on the response rate.

8. Pilot the Questionnaire

You may have to design a questionnaire without knowing the best questions to ask. A group discussion or a number of in-depth interviews preceding the larger fieldwork program can be helpful. A questionnaire can be tested with as few as 10 to 20 interviews (but the more the better). The pilot identifies ambiguous questions and problems with layout, ordering, etc.

587

CHECKLIST

DOS AND DON'TS

DO
- Keep it to the point, and easy to complete.
- Stress that respondents' answers will be treated confidentially.
- Minimize the nuisance factor for the recipient.
- Thank respondents for their cooperation.

DON'T
- Don't tell respondents the questionnaire will take five minutes if it takes 15.
- Don't ask about more than one issue in each question.
- Don't use jargon or technical language your respondents won't understand.

THOUGHT STARTERS
- What was good about the last questionnaire you were asked to complete? What was bad?

- Don't reinvent the wheel—consult marketing and statistical sources to see whether what you want already exists.

FOR MORE INFORMATION

Books:
Burn, Bonnie, and Maggie Payment. *Assessments A to Z: A Collection of 50 Questionnaires, Instruments, and Inventories.* San Francisco, CA: Jossey-Bass Pfeiffer, 2000.

Hayes, Bob E. *Measuring Customer Satisfaction: Survey Design, Use, and Statistical Analysis.* 2nd ed. Milwaukee, WI: ASQ Quality Press, 1997.

"You know what charm is: a way of getting the answer yes without having asked any clear question."

Albert Camus

Effective Business Writing

CHECKLIST

This checklist is an introduction to the basic principles of business writing. Business writing can take many forms, but what is common to each of them is the importance of conveying the right message to the right audience in the right way—and at the right time. The effectiveness of business writing is measured not by whether the recipient enjoyed reading the communication, but by whether it achieved its purpose.

In an age when business communications are increasingly transmitted in electronic form, it is just as important for ideas and information to be conveyed clearly and concisely. Technology does not remove the need to write well.

DEFINITION

The term "business writing" is used to cover any form of written communication within the context of paid employment, including letters, memos, public relations or marketing materials, and reports. (Report writing is the subject of a separate checklist and is therefore mentioned only in passing here.) Although different organizations may have their own styles, the same principles apply whether the writer is in the public or private sector, a small business, or a large government department.

ACTION CHECKLIST

1. Decide What You Are Trying to Achieve

What is your main aim? How does this relate to the broader context of the organization and the potentially conflicting aims of people within it? Unless you think about this, you will have no reference point by which to judge whether the communication is effective. Relate your objectives to the wider organizational picture.

2. Determine the Outcomes You Want

What do you want to happen as a result of your communication? This will be closely linked to its purpose. If you want to impart facts, how will you know you have been successful? Be explicit about the action, if any, you expect recipients to take.

3. See Whether a Written Communication is the Most Appropriate Medium

Before you begin writing, decide and plan your message, and then choose the right communication strategy. Write only if:

- you need to address a number of people;
- the argument or explanation is complex or needs visual support;
- you need a considered response;
- you need an accurate and permanent record of the communication.

If the message is urgent or one-on-one, or can be expressed simply and without visual aids, consider phoning. If you need to involve several people in an urgent decision, or if action is conditional on presenting an argument to several people, seek a meeting first.

4. Decide Who Should Sign the Communication

The usual assumption is that you are writing the communication. However, its effectiveness may depend on its being seen to come from someone else. Its message may be more powerful if it is signed by someone more senior—or more junior—than you. The important point is that someone with the right credentials for the target readers should sign.

5. Identify the Target Audience

Ensure that your intended audience is the right one to deliver the action you need and that the recipients will be motivated to respond. Do they represent the right constituencies within the organization? Will they have the authority to act? If you are targeting the public, how will you make sure that the right people see the communication?

6. Build a Rapport with Your Audience

Getting readers to deliver what you need, even if it is only their attention, depends on building a rapport with them. You can do this by setting the right tone, and you have three basic choices.

1 Plead for the audience to do something on your behalf.
2 Persuade them to do something by selling its benefits.
3 Appeal to broader organizational interests and invoke the value of teamwork.

The last approach is usually the most effective. Try to establish common ground, and express the issue in terms of its shared effect on both you and the recipient.

7. Build a Convincing Argument

Develop a proposition that is compelling by spelling out the benefits and by anticipating and forestalling objections. See the issue from the recipients' perspective, understand their likely concerns, and show how the proposal addresses these while fitting in with overall organizational strategy. Be realistic about problems and the effort required to overcome them.

8. Prepare an Outline

Note down the key strands of your argument in a few words and build a structure around them. Group key relationships and themes. The structure can be logical (a discussion of the issue followed by evidence and conclusions) or declarative (the conclusion first, backed up by evidence).

9. Guide the Reader Around Your Text

Use the outline to begin writing. Whatever the structure or formality of the document, use clear, eye-

"What do you want from me? Fine writing? Or would you like to see the goddam sales curve stop going down and start going up?"

Rosser Reeves

catching signposts and flags to guide the reader around. Provide an introduction that explains why you are writing and a summary that captures your key points. Separate out your conclusions and recommendations.

10. Make Your Text Easy to Read and Unambiguous

Think about readability. Use short paragraphs and short sentences and avoid long or unfamiliar words. Use simple, clear English. Avoid jargon where possible; where it is unavoidable, explain it. Spell out abbreviations the first time you use them, even if you think your reader will be familiar with them. Use tangible rather than abstract concepts. Use the active instead of the passive voice ("he decided," not "it was decided"), except where it is irrelevant or inappropriate to say who was responsible for the action. Use an occasional image to illustrate a point, but avoid language that is too flowery or informal. Use humor sparingly and tastefully. Be grammatical—grammatical lapses and misspellings irritate readers and hinder their ability to receive messages.

11. Enliven Your Text with Graphics

Use graphics to back up your arguments and convey your key messages—but only if they are clear and easy to read. Incorporate notes in the text telling your readers when to look at them and where to find them. Integrate graphics into the main body of the text, with the exception of detailed statistical tables: place these in an appendix. Don't be tempted to use visual or statistical tricks to bolster a weak argument (for example, by distorting the y-axis of a graph to paint an overly favorable picture of a sales increase). The size of a graphic should relate to the importance of the point you are making.

12. Revise Your Text Once Complete

Your communication will be effective only if it is authoritative. Read over your draft and be self-critical, or, if you have time, ask someone you respect to read the text. Check that your reasoning and arguments form a logical sequence; make certain that all your facts are right; give the source and authority for any opinions you cite; give due weight to contradictory arguments; and cover alternative conclusions or recommendations without being too dismissive of them. Be succinct.

13. Pay Attention to Presentation

As with oral communication, your audience will judge you as much on your presentation as the content of your message. Are you using a clear, easy-to-read typeface (such as Arial or Times) and font size, and good quality paper and ink? Use bold characters to give emphasis to key words and phrases instead of underlining them, and make sure that there is ample white space on every page.

Use indentation, bullets, and one-line paragraphs to break up the text.

14. Follow Up

If the communication is important, follow it up with a telephone call where appropriate. Check that the reader really did receive the message you intended to convey. Make sure that there were no misunderstandings or ambiguities and that the action you needed is under way.

589

CHECKLIST

DOS AND DON'TS

DO
- If possible, find one or two vivid images or phrases that will convey the key element of your message and make it memorable.
- Establish common ground with your readers, and engage their attention and sympathy.
- Be self-critical of your work and be open to other people's comments and suggestions.

DON'T
- Don't undermine the effectiveness of your communication by grammatical, spelling, or typing mistakes. Always print and proofread a communication before sending it. Don't rely on the spellchecker—mistakes show up more clearly in black and white than on the screen.
- Don't suppress arguments that do not wholly support your view, or your readers will distrust you. Confront them and say why you think they are not significant.

THOUGHT STARTERS
- Will a written communication alone be effective in securing what you need to achieve?

- Have you addressed the motivations and concerns of your audience as well as your own?

- Does the communication convey the best possible image of you—and the organization?

FOR MORE INFORMATION

Book:
Simmons, John. *We, Me, Them, and It: How to Write Powerfully for Business.* New ed. New York: Cyan Communications, 2006.

"Later Marx was to recall his mother's words, 'If only Karl had made capital, instead of writing about it.'"

Edna Healey

Effective Communications: Communicating with Groups

This checklist provides an introduction to group communication skills and techniques.

As formal hierarchies break down, managers are no longer able to get things done by passing on instructions to junior staff. The ability to make things happen increasingly depends on being able to adopt different roles, styles, and techniques. It also depends on the manager's effectiveness as a member of different groups both within and outside the organization.

DEFINITION

This checklist covers oral communications with all types of groups.

Within the organization, these range from large formal team briefings to casual encounters between two or three colleagues from different departments.

External groups comprise a very mixed bag of people, from customers and competitors to representatives of suppliers and regulatory authorities. In each context, managers may play a slightly different role, although the principles of effective communication stay the same.

ACTION CHECKLIST

1. Define the Purpose of the Communication

Clarify the purpose of the communication at the outset: is it a meeting to make decisions, a briefing session to impart information, or a brainstorming session to generate new ideas? Some tasks are done better in groups—for example, sifting existing ideas, coming up with new ideas, or involving people in a key decision. Others are best left to individual or written communications, particularly when there is a need to impart large amounts of factual or sensitive information.

2. Limit the Extent of the Communication

Set a time limit, even for an informal encounter, and an agenda, even if it is an unwritten one. Be realistic about what you can expect to achieve within the group, given its representation, and be sensitive to the pressures on other people's time.

3. Make Sure That the Right People Are There

Group communication works best when all the people present have a legitimate reason for being there, have something to contribute to the discussion, and have an interest in the outcome.

Postpone a discussion if the right people can't be present; delay is better than an inconclusive debate. Take the

initiative in doing this yourself if a group leader is reluctant.

4. Get the Right Number of People

For most group discussions, five is recognized as the optimum number for effective debate and decision-making. In a group of this size members can adopt different roles, and a single member can be in the minority without undue pressure to conform.

Getting the right people is, nevertheless, always more important than getting the right number. Think about who can best contribute to the conversation. Is there anyone with relevant experience to share?

5. Facilitate Introductions

If you are leading a group, make clear what people's roles are, why they are there, and what they are expected to contribute. If your expectations turn out to be unrealistic, allow people to leave or suggest alternative members. As a member, define the contribution you expect to make and your authority for making it.

Make clear whether the authority is personal (a function of your own position) or vested (you have been asked to speak on behalf of someone else). Don't claim an authority that is not legitimate or that you can't substantiate.

6. Be Active

If you have agreed to be part of a group, be active in it. Take full responsibility for its success or failure, be energetic, and make positive contributions.

If you have nothing to contribute, admit it and step down: don't waste other contributors' time.

7. Be Rational but Open-minded

Take up a clear position on issues, but be willing to listen to rational argument and be prepared to change your mind—if you do, explain why. Groups work effectively only if participants are open to new information and different points of view.

Give all members the opportunity to speak, even if you have doubts about the likely wisdom of their views. Don't put your own ideas ahead of the group's overriding objective.

Be aware of the dangers of unconscious domination. If the group leader always gives an opinion first, it is possible the others may:

- be unduly influenced from the start;
- be liable to think that this is all sewn up and they aren't required to contribute, only to react;
- get into the habit of not thinking for themselves.

8. Be Brief, Be Simple, and Be Organized

Speak slowly, clearly, and directly in short sentences. Structure your arguments logically. Think what

you are going to say, say it, and summarize what you have said. Link your comments to what has already been said by other contributors. Clarify areas of support for their position or areas of disagreement.

9. Make Good Use of Nonverbal Communication

Use gestures to reinforce your key messages and nonverbal signals to convey attitudes and expressions. Make eye contact with each member of the group. Use nonthreatening but positive body language and convey an impression of calm and confidence. Pay close attention to other people's nonverbal signals: are you irritating them or patronizing them?

10. Stay Calm and Don't Argue

Even if you believe the group is making the wrong decision, stay calm and don't become emotional defending your own ideas. Stress points of agreement and minimize areas of disagreement with a view to finding a way forward.

11. Avoid Personal Attacks

The key to effective group communication is mutual respect. If you believe someone is wrong, criticize the idea, not the person.

- Make your criticism effective by making it palatable: preface it with a word of support or agreement on a related topic.

- Avoid being too negative, even if someone is deliberately putting forward unhelpful ideas.
- Resist the temptation to allocate blame for previous mistakes or failures, otherwise the group dynamics will break down.
- Remember that while group members may be competing to present individual positions, you are cooperating to find an overall solution.

12. Bring the Communication to a Conclusion

Casual encounters in particular often take longer than necessary because the purpose of the communication and its agenda are unclear at the outset.

- Review what you were expecting to get out of the communication and whether you have achieved it.
- If you have to postpone debate, make sure it isn't because the group lacks the people or authority to reach a conclusion.
- Write up a decision and action statement as soon as possible after the meeting and make sure everyone involved has a copy (including interested parties not present).

THOUGHT STARTERS

- How readily can you adapt your communication style to the different roles required of you by different groups?

- Do you rely too much on the authority of your own position to persuade people of the merits of your arguments?

591

CHECKLIST

FOR MORE INFORMATION

Book:
Argenti, Paul A. *Corporate Communication*. 4th ed. Burr Ridge, IL: McGraw-Hill, 2005.

Journal Articles:
De Ridder, Jan A. "Organisational Communication and Supportive Employees." *Human Resource Management Journal* 14:3 (2004).
Stengel, James R., Andrea L. Dixon, and Chris T. Allen. "Listening Begins at Home." *Harvard Business Review* 81:11 (November 2003).

See also:
- Effective Communications: Communicating with Groups (pp. 590–591)
- Getting Your Message Across (pp. 789–790)

"We could have over 520 brains connected in real time across time and space available for any problem."

Robert Buckman

Implementing Statistical Process Control (SPC)

CHECKLIST

This checklist provides an outline of the techniques and benefits of SPC. The actual application of many of these techniques requires more detail than can be covered in a checklist.

SPC is usually understood to operate in a manufacturing context (for example, where production line machinery can be statistically monitored and controlled for deviations from the norm), but it can also apply to some service sector activities.

DEFINITION

Outputs from a manufacturing process may vary from the exact specification, and deliveries from a service differ in quality and substance. These inconsistencies in quality require constant monitoring to see if they are random, regular, haphazard, important, or indicative of a problem. The monitoring and controlling should be applied to the process, not the product, and can be greatly facilitated by statistical process control (SPC). Process control means controlling production by checking its quality while the work is still in process. Implementing SPC means applying statistical techniques and analysis to that control function. Since SPC is about measuring the quality of work in process, its implementation is usually allied to techniques related to quality systems management.

ADVANTAGES

Chaudhry and Higbie, in their paper "Quality improvement through statistical process control," report the following benefits from applying SPC in a chemical plant:
- increased production efficiency
- a more consistent product
- superior reliability
- greater ease in pinpointing problem occurrences
- provision of a usable measure of performance
- clearer communication of objectives
- improved customer relations

DISADVANTAGES

SPC can take time to apply rigorously, but applications show that there are few, if any, disadvantages to SPC. Its application must remain relevant and useful, otherwise it risks becoming a system in place because of inertia.

ACTION CHECKLIST

1. Plan and Communicate the Program

First approach the SPC project by addressing the elements essential to all successful change programs:
- securing proactive and continuous top management commitment

- appointing the right project leader and obtaining the right expertise
- establishing flexible time frames and broad resource requirements
- communicating regularly with the implementation teams and everyone else involved
- preparing an effective and continuous training program

Then adopt a specific operational plan or process:
- locate the process to be tackled
- research the extent of the problem to be controlled
- specify objectives and identify the resources, data, and training required
- select the appropriate technique(s) to control the problem
- plan the equipment, materials, and expertise for the technique(s) chosen
- identify possible causes of the problem
- test possible solutions

2. Identify Appropriate Tools and Techniques

In the toolkit of techniques at your disposal each approach has a particular application. It is important to choose the right technique for the right process: research your options carefully and think about the tools and techniques mentioned below.
- Checklists outline established best practice in a simple sequence so that a process may be checked and controlled for doing the right thing at the right time.
- Flow charts show the sequential steps in a process, how work flows from one area to another, and the when, how, and where (and where not) of activities.
- Cause-and-effect (fishbone) diagrams attempt to relate effects to causes. They examine all related possibilities of a process that is going wrong or a product or service that is not satisfactory.
- Scatter diagrams plot the occurrence(s) of failure, or deviations from the norm, enabling confirmation or dismissal of a suspected relationship between, for example, supply and production or production and delivery.
- Histograms, pie charts, and bar charts show how a process is performing at a moment in time. They are useful for showing the impact of one factor against another, such as faults against a process, or customer calls against sales.
- Run charts show the same data as a histogram but plot the values over time.
- Pareto analysis—according to Pareto, relatively few failure reasons are responsible for the many failures in a system; hence the 80/20 rule. A Pareto chart—a vertical bar chart with the bars representing complaints or defects ranked in descending order—shows the relative importance of a set of measurements, allowing you to focus on the most pressing problems.
- Process performance checks focus on the most recent

"You have more control and less ambiguity today than you are likely to have for the rest of your life."

Daryl R. Conner

observations from the process, offering a glance at a given moment in time.

- Process performance evaluations focus on past performance, using all available historical data to see how a process has been operating and suggest improvements.
- Process capability studies focus on current observations of the process, using control charts to determine the variability and thus capability of a specific process under statistical control.
- Control charts identify continuing and special causes of variation in a process. They can demonstrate that a process is (or is not) currently in control and can warn of causes of variation and signal the need for correction or improvement. Samples of data are needed to calculate limits, expectations, and norms. Different kinds of control chart include:
  - attributes charts: with only two values (right/wrong, pass/fail). Here you need to ask what is being counted, for example, defective items against total items
  - variables charts: average, range (limited or unlimited), and median (the number in the middle of the set). Here you need to ask how many types of measures are to be controlled
- Correlation and regression analysis are methods for determining the type of cause-and-effect relationship between variables.

3. Establish Norms and Indicators
You won't know if something is wrong unless you know what to expect when things are going right. Establish a sample of data from which you can determine acceptable limits, norms, or indicators of performance.

4. Resource Support and Prepare Procedures
Consult the hands-on practitioner and technical and procedural manuals to ensure that you've selected appropriate techniques and that the appropriate technical support is in place, not only for designing and constructing the control charts, but also for analyzing and adjusting the applications.

5. Integrate SPC into Your Quality Management System
Integration is vital if SPC is to succeed. While the tools and techniques used must be perceived to be of practical, operational value and not mere number-crunching exercises, the management of SPC must integrate it into the overall quality management system.

6. Select a Winning Pilot and Don't Rush
Choosing the first process for SPC implementation can be critical for success. Start SPC in a process with the most glaring quality problems and the best anticipated outcome. Poor production records, high costs, high complaints, and high failure levels will tell you where to look. Identify the critical variables to be the subject of the control.

Exercise patience in following through the implementation program. Trying to get results too quickly usually generates the wrong results. Gathering specific data meticulously and paying attention to detail will bring its rewards.

7. Use the Charts for Improvement, Not Just for Control
Assuming that your initial state was problem-free, solving a problem means getting back to where you were—control does not necessarily mean improvement. The evidence SPC produces can indicate what improvements can be made, where, and—with systematic selection of processes—how.

DOS AND DON'TS

DO
- Define clear objectives and pinpoint which process or part of a process you intend to tackle.
- Monitor the process—not the product.

DON'T
- Don't take shortcuts—expertise in whichever statistical method is used is vital.
- Don't seek to place blame on someone once you've solved the problem—fix the process that caused the problem.

FOR MORE INFORMATION

Book:
Levinson, William A., and Frank Tumbelty. *SPC Essentials and Productivity Improvement: A Manufacturing Approach*. Milwaukee, WI: ASQ Quality Press, 1997.

Journal Article:
Chaudhry, Sohail, and J. Richard Higbie. "Quality Improvement through Statistical Process Control." *Quality Engineering* Vol. 2, No. 4 (April 1990): 411–19.

See also:
- W. Edwards Deming (pp. 1196–1197)
- Total Quality: Getting TQM to Work (pp. 562–563)

593

CHECKLIST

"I realised that if you want to change something, nine times out of ten you can change it more effectively from within."
Niall Fitzgerald

Internal Audit

CHECKLIST

This checklist is designed to help managers tackle the process of an internal audit within their organization or department.

Internal audit is an essential (and now much-discussed) part of business life, but not all companies are large enough to have a designated internal audit function. This checklist is aimed primarily at those who are undertaking an internal audit themselves, or those who are responsible for selecting and managing a member of staff who has this responsibility. It applies equally to organizations in the public and private sectors.

DEFINITION

Internal auditing is defined by the Institute of Internal Auditors as an independent appraisal function established within an organization to examine and evaluate its activities, the objective being to assist staff in the effective discharge of their responsibilities. To this end internal auditing furnishes staff with analyses, appraisals, and recommendations concerning those activities. Internal auditing is usually carried out by staff from within the organization.

ADVANTAGES

Internal audit should be a continuous process. It offers several advantages.

- Management's attention will be directed to the key business issues. The audit analyzes weaknesses in the system of control, which become the basis for practical recommendations for improvement.
- It gives management confidence when controls are operating satisfactorily.
- It identifies opportunities for improving efficiency and effectiveness.
- It gives early notice of potential problems. Management can then take action as necessary.

DISADVANTAGES

- Internal audit can be time-consuming and take managers away from their day-to-day work.
- If handled insensitively, internal audit can feel threatening to staff members who may feel that they are being scrutinized with the intention of finding fault.

ACTION CHECKLIST

1. Select Internal Audit Objectives Relevant to the Assignment

Internal audits primarily look at key controls.

- Financial—how is money handled within the organization? Who authorizes payment, for example, and what are the checks and balances to stop unauthorized spending and fraud?
- Administrative—are these conducive to meeting strategic objectives?

- Systems-related—what systems are in place departmentally and across the organization, and how do they fit together?

They look, too, at value for money—is this being achieved through the systems currently in place, or do the systems fail to measure this?

The first step is to make sure your broad audit objectives reflect whichever of these are your priorities.

2. Prepare a Detailed Brief

An internal audit looks at a variety of aspects of the way an organization works. It does not focus solely on financial issues. Write an audit brief or strategy that sets detailed priorities in accordance with the main issues, and give some indication of the proportion of time you expect the auditor to spend on highlighted aspects.

3. Choose Your Auditor

It is usual to appoint an individual from within the organization as the internal auditor. Depending on the issues to be examined, a formal qualification (for example, in accounting) may be appropriate.

4. Brief Your Auditor

Make sure you have all the background information you need before you brief your auditor. Include the following for your organization:

- strategic or business plans
- standing orders
- articles and memoranda of association
- internal procedure manuals
- lists of key personnel
- organization chart

Arrange a meeting with the auditor to confirm that you have provided sufficient information; even if the person is an employee, do not make assumptions about his or her level of knowledge.

The goal of the meeting is to agree on the objectives of the audit. Find out how the auditor plans to meet these objectives. Agree on a timetable and a plan of action and find out if further information is needed.

5. Identify the Key Controls to Meet Audit Objectives

The next stage is to start to look at detail. The auditor needs to look at the organization's existing procedures for controlling the key areas to be examined.

6. Evaluate the Controls

Next, evaluate how effective the controls are. Could they be improved? Are there any omissions? Questions worth thinking about include the following:

- If someone wanted to commit fraud, where and how would they do it?
- If you had bought this product or service personally, would you be happy with the purchase price and the level of service offered?

"When a company's profits slip, its position is tarnished. People are reluctant to buy from companies in financial trouble."

Regis McKenna

7. Test the System

Now test the controls in action. Choose a number of activities or transactions at random, and trace back all the steps that took place. Ask:

- Are there any procedures or rules in place for this transaction?
- Did people follow the procedures?

This will show the degree of compliance with the existing rules and procedures.

8. Select Areas for Further Investigation

From random tests the auditor may find areas of concern that need thorough investigation. The audit should now conduct a detailed examination of these areas: for example, every transaction of a particular type should be examined over a number of months to see whether the random, problematical sample was an exception or a recurring problem.

9. Consider Whether You are Getting Value for the Money

Whatever the overall audit objectives, it is always an internal auditor's job to test whether the organization is receiving value for the money. Look at these kinds of questions:

- Has the market been tested by getting quotes and tenders for goods and services?
- Are the systems working in the most efficient way?

10. Draft a Report

Draft a report of all findings with a set of recommendations. Discuss it with everyone who participated in the audit to make sure that the auditor hasn't misinterpreted any information.

11. Produce the Final Report

The final report should include an action plan to tackle the areas requiring strengthening. Use the knowledge of the auditor as a guide to best practice, and make sure the recommendations are practicable. The report should include a timetable and an agreed time to meet again to monitor progress.

12. Take Action

Act on the findings to improve problem areas, and monitor how effective the remedial actions are. This may well involve changing written instructions, manuals, or procedures, alerting staff to the changes, and seeing that adequate training is given to staff in those areas.

DOS AND DON'TS

DO
- Brief staff on the benefits of internal audit.
- Concentrate on the high-risk elements identified.
- Set an action plan that is realistic.
- Keep staff informed of the findings of the audit and of any positive action that has been taken as a result of it.
- Monitor progress toward accomplishing the action plan.

DON'T
- Don't rely on internal audit as a day-to-day management control mechanism.
- Don't expect internal audit to pick up all the potential weak links in your systems.

THOUGHT STARTERS
- Have you defined the nature and scope of the internal audit?
- Have you established what the system is trying to achieve?
- Have you identified the key controls?
- Are your staff fully informed of what is happening and the actions you are going to take?

FOR MORE INFORMATION

Books:
Moeller, Robert R. *Sarbanes-Oxley and the New Internal Auditing Rules.* New York: Wiley, 2004.
Spencer Pickett, K. H. *The Internal Auditing Handbook.* 2nd ed. New York: Wiley, 2003.

Web sites:
The Institute of Internal Auditors: **www.theiia.org**
U.S. Chamber of Commerce: **www.uschamber.com**

595

CHECKLIST

'Where profit is, loss is hidden nearby.'   Anonymous

Open Systems Thinking

CHECKLIST

This checklist introduces an outline approach to open systems thinking; it does not replace the need for further reading or expert consultation. It is for managers who find that traditional problem-solving techniques are failing to deliver solutions in their organizations or who would simply like to know more about this rather vague term. The approach to open systems thinking presented here is just one way in which it may be used—by definition, open systems thinking should not follow a rigid series of tasks.

Systems thinking has always been valued in some disciplines like biology and information technology, but its scientific connections have tended to make it unattractive to practicing managers. However, systems thinking pervades many of the most radical approaches to modern management, such as total quality management, environmental management, and the learning organization.

Three main reasons may explain why a traditional, mechanistic view of systems fails to work:
- system complexity;
- uncertainty in the environment—not knowing what the future may bring leads to difficulty in accurate forecasting and accounting for risk;
- conflict in human values—many perfect technical solutions have failed because their sponsors have failed to gain public acceptance.

Through open systems thinking, managers can support the strategic management of their organizations by taking advantage of the concepts, tools, and techniques available to systems analysts or management consultants who specialize in this area.

DEFINITION

In *The Fifth Discipline* (1992), Peter Senge describes systems thinking as: "a way of thinking about, and a language for describing and understanding, the forces and interrelationships that shape the behavior of systems."

This checklist distinguishes between the wider approach adopted by Senge and some of the new breed of systems analysts (known as open) and the more traditional techniques used by engineers, information technologists, and systems analysts in the past (where the system in question is finite, or closed, and involves the use of traditional problem-solving techniques).

Traditional approaches are concerned with identifying the "correct" means to an end, defined at the start and taken as fixed. The pace of change, however, has demonstrated that while such an oversimplified view of life might work for engineering or scientific problems, it is totally inadequate for complex systems like organizations. Open systems thinking concentrates on describing the behavior of the system and associated problems before the possibilities for improving the behavior of the system and solving these problems are explored. Open systems thinking is also a learning approach compatible with modern quality philosophies.

ADVANTAGES

Open systems thinking:
- can encourage creative thinking and generate new ways of doing things;
- focuses on reality rather than the idealized mental maps people have of systems and processes;
- is probably the only way to deal with "wicked" problems;
- takes a longer-term, strategic view of organizations, not just a technical one;
- fits well with management practices such as teamwork and continuous improvement.

DISADVANTAGES

Open systems thinking:
- is intellectually challenging and can involve a great deal of time and effort;
- may produce more questions than answers in the early stages and can therefore be disconcerting;
- is not appropriate for situations where the structured problem-solving approach is guaranteed to produce results or where the culture is heavily technocratic;
- usually requires like-minded people to work together as a team.

ACTION CHECKLIST

✔ 1. Find Out about the Problem

Most managers rush into explanations for problems. Open systems thinking leaves explanations until the end. At this stage you should avoid the desire to find cause-and-effect relationships and simply collect the facts. Try to observe all the symptoms in a situation as a dispassionate observer in as wide an arena as possible.

✔ 2. Define the System

- Describe the events that are relevant to the situation. Look at all the symptoms or changes that have occurred in this period, such as accidents or crises, problems with customers or suppliers, or even apparently unrelated events. Pay attention to the climate in the department and organization as a whole.
- Pick out the main trends or patterns. Try to identify the most important variables and attempt to understand what is going on. Are there general trends like increasing levels of customer complaints, loss of customers, a slowing down of market penetration, or increased costs? Mapping changes on time lines will often reveal surprising relationships between key variables and events in time.
- Map the underlying systems or structures. This is a key stage in building effective models of systems. Its aim is to identify the relationships or interdependency between

"The aim of science is not to open the door to infinite wisdom, but to set a limit to infinite error."

Bertolt Brecht

components, and in particular to focus on the feedback loops that control the behavior of the system.

The behavior of all systems, whether living or not, is controlled by feedback loops. Feedback loops tend either to resist change and maintain equilibria (negative feedback loops) or amplify the impact of change (positive or reinforcing loops). Although at this stage you're beginning to look for cause-and-effect relationships, it is important not to make up your mind yet, but to leave ample room for other possibilities. Example: a rise in customer complaints might be linked to a vicious circle in which increased pressure on sales staff may cause them to make unrealistic promises, thereby raising customer expectations that cannot be met.

3. Build Models from Your Definitions

Models are an important part of our everyday lives. We adjust our behavior according to a range of assumptions (models) about the world around us. If our world is not behaving according to plan, we can be sure of one thing—our current models are not appropriate.

Finding the right model to describe complex situations or systems is a real art form. Although technically trained managers often place a lot of emphasis on mathematical or computer-generated models to explain the performance of companies, sooner or later they're usually left scratching their heads when the model fails them in real life. On the other hand, mental models, or even metaphors, can often achieve remarkable results in conveying to others the essence of particular situations.

4. Compare the Models with the Real World

Having generated a model of the system in question, you need to check it out. Go back to the stakeholders and confirm that the model works and takes all the factors into consideration.

5. Identify Possible Actions

It is only at this stage that you should identify possible actions; in systems terms these are not solutions, but ways of improving the behavior of the system.

Example: Customer complaints may be caused by imbalances in the relationship between the production, customer service, and sales departments. The required change may involve shifts in the relationships between departments instead of immediate actions to resolve short-term customer complaint problems.

6. Implement the Action

In the true spirit of learning organizations, managers should spend a lot of time watching the effects of introduced change to see whether they learn any more about the effectiveness of their model.

7. Start the Cycle Again

Treating this approach to problem solving as cyclical is entirely consistent with the philosophy of continuous improvement.

GLOSSARY OF TERMS

Structured systems analysis the use of formal problem-solving techniques to describe systems. Analysts tend to use a top-down approach—breaking a system down into smaller and smaller pieces—to create their solutions. This approach is particularly associated with computer programming.

System a collection of units that interact to form a single operational unit. Systems can be living (organizations or ecosystems) or physical (spacecraft or computers).

Systems analysis the application of special techniques to study systems.

THOUGHT STARTERS

- Organization charts often bear no relation to the real relationships controlling the behavior of an organization. If you were to draw up an organization chart based on the real power relationships within your enterprise, how would it differ from the official one?

- Many organizations consist of systems within systems (recursion). How many levels are there in your organization?

- Delayering attempts to simplify systems, but often fails to reestablish the right sort of feedback loops in the system to promote effective relationships between the units. The majority of business process reengineering projects deliver little or no advantage to the company.

FOR MORE INFORMATION

Books:
Checkland, Peter B. *Soft Systems Methodology in Action.* 2nd ed. New York: Wiley, 1999.
Jackson, Michael C. *Systems Approaches to Management.* New York: Kluwer Academic, 2000.
Senge, Peter M. *The Fifth Discipline: The Art and Practice of the Learning Organization.* New York: Currency/Doubleday, 1994.

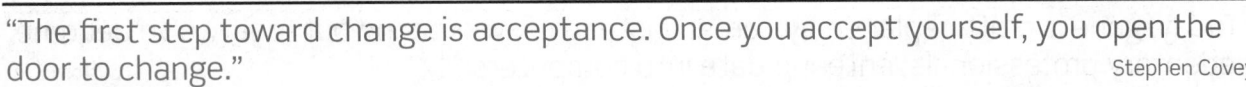

"The first step toward change is acceptance. Once you accept yourself, you open the door to change."
Stephen Covey

597

CHECKLIST

Planning the Replacement of Software Systems

CHECKLIST

This checklist is a starting point for anyone who has to choose a new software package to replace an outdated or inadequate system.

Among numerous reasons for changing software packages are the need for increased flexibility, integration with other systems, greater employee productivity, and improved customer service. Costing should cater for data conversion, customization, installation, training, and the license agreement as well as the package itself. Although you may wish to form a small working party, you should also consult staff throughout the selection process, including those who will have to use the system and senior staff with line and budget responsibilities.

ACTION CHECKLIST

1. Establish Objectives

It is important to have a clear idea of priorities before contacting suppliers. Priorities may change as the project unfolds and learning proceeds, but it is vital to work toward them. A checklist of firm requirements should start to emerge from answering questions such as the following:

- How does your current package hinder customer service improvements and flexibility for future developments?
- How does your current package impede integration?
- Are other systems within the organization going to be upgraded or replaced?
- Who is going to use the package and how?
- What degree of independence from the supplier is required?
- What degree of customization is required compared with a standard off-the-shelf package?
- Must the package fit the existing hardware and operating system you have?
- What improvements would you like to see from your old package?

2. Identify Potential Suppliers

Sources of names may include:

- suggestions from contacts, especially those in similar organizations
- visits to trade shows
- attendance at seminars and courses
- directories and the trade and professional press
- consultants

3. Create a Short-list of Potential Packages

Keep the checklist of requirements at hand and look at a number of systems. Decide which of these would be worth considering in detail. Try to match the size and capability of the package with the size of your organization or department.

4. Send Out Invitations To Tender (ITT)

The ITT is a formal statement of your requirements sent to the suppliers on the short-list, inviting them to reply with a formal proposal. It sets out a timetable for making a final selection, which should include visits to other users of the systems and to the offices of the suppliers.

5. Select the Software

Study each package in detail to assure yourself that the claims of the supplier can be substantiated and to check that it can meet your specific functional needs. Other questions concerning the package in general, the supplier, support, and training also need to be addressed.

The package

- How old is it? Does it offer all that the present system offers?
- Is it modular?
- Are all modules easy to use? Are all modules compatible?
- Is it capable of data exchange? Receiving? Downloading?
- Can it integrate with other packages? With other packages within the organization?
- How often is it upgraded?
- What are the future plans for the package?
- What operating systems does it run on?
- How is it updated? Real time? Batch?
- What is the backup system?
- How many concurrent users can it support?
- How many installations are there? In North America? In Europe? In Asia?
- Can you visit other user sites, particularly migrations?
- What problems have other users encountered? How quickly were they resolved? How do the users react to the supplier and to the package?
- What are the capital and startup costs?

Support

- How long has the supplier been operating?
- Is the supplier financially sound?
- Can the supplier support all modules?
- What is the annual cost of maintenance?
- Do customer support costs appear to be value for the money?
- Does the supplier offer on-site, dial-up, or telephone support?
- How much support is given prior to migration?
- How much work is left to the customer?
- How is the help desk organized?

Training

- Does the supplier offer training as part of the fee?
- Is preconversion training available?

"Today, gone is craft, replaced by career. Instead of workers on our feet, we've become sedentary professionals, entering data into computers."

Clifford Stoll

- Can you rent a machine to train on in advance?

Migration

- What is the size of the migration team?
- What are the skills of the supplier's migration staff?
- Is the conversion process tried and tested?
- How many data migrations has the supplier performed?
- Can you have a trial data conversion?
- Have you planned contingency time, to allow for mistakes?

6. Examine the Contract Terms

Look carefully at the responsibilities and liabilities of the supplier and question any terms that may be open to misinterpretation. Include in the contract details of any modifications you want made to the package and specify any tests you want run before you accept it. Question the level of support and service detailed in the contract and check that the final costs cover all aspects of the purchase, including items like delivery and training.

7. Plan for Implementation

Once you have chosen a package, a further objective will be to minimize the disruption of services upon conversion to a new system. Ways to do this include:

- running trial data conversions;
- planning for a period of parallel running;
- getting training from the supplier for all staff or for the trainer;
- choosing the timing carefully, for example, by avoiding peak vacation periods;
- managing modifications to the package.

8. Manage the "People" Side

From the start to the finish of the project, closely involve staff who will be using the system.

- Who is monitoring the views, reactions, and progress of staff?
- Who is checking that current and developing operational needs are being satisfied?
- Who is coordinating the emerging—as opposed to prescribed—training requirements?

DOS AND DON'TS

DO

- Set up a team of users and consult widely.
- Remember the importance of forward thinking.
- Check out undemonstrated or unsubstantiated claims made by the supplier.
- Be wary of too much customization on your particular application.
- See the products of at least four or five suppliers before short-listing.
- Visit sites where the package is up and running.
- Build in adequate contingency time.

DON'T

- Don't focus too much on your current application.
- Don't let the supplier deter you from your objectives.
- Don't take what the supplier says for granted.
- Don't make assumptions about what is stated or not stated by the supplier.
- Don't skip apparently minor details.

THOUGHT STARTERS

- How old is your current package?

- How often is it upgraded?

- How much customization does your current package include?

- How long is it since you took a good look at alternative packages?

- How good is your current support?

FOR MORE INFORMATION

Book:
McConnell, Steve C. *Software Project Survival Guide.* Redmond, WA: Microsoft Press, 1997.

"A modern computer hovers between the obsolescent and the non-existent."

Sydney Brenner

Six Sigma

CHECKLIST

This checklist introduces the Six Sigma quality technique and presents action points for its implementation.

Companies are increasingly adopting Six Sigma in a bid to improve the quality of their processes and products, and thus achieve competitive advantage. It has been estimated that poor quality, resulting in defects and wastage, can affect 20–40% of production, thus reducing sales revenue. Six Sigma offers a structured and disciplined method for making that percentage significantly lower: in fact, in a perfect Six Sigma state, a company would reduce it to only 10%. While many companies dismiss a zero defects state as unattainable, Six Sigma offers the potential to get very close.

DEFINITION

Six Sigma is both a technique and a philosophy based on the desire to eliminate waste and improve performance as far as is technically possible. At its heart is a statistical method that involves drawing up an optimum specification for each of the processes within the organization, then using statistical analysis to reduce defects in the processes, products, and services to almost zero. This is accompanied by an organization culture that focuses on creating value for the customer and eliminating any processes that do not make a contribution to this final goal. Six Sigma is a registered trademark of Motorola, Inc., which implemented the technique successfully in the 1980s. It is based on the statistical tools and techniques of quality management developed by Joseph Juran.

ADVANTAGES

Implementing Six Sigma can mean that:
- quality, performance, productivity, and competitive advantage are improved;
- costs are greatly reduced;
- wastage and environmental impact is minimized;
- employees become motivated;
- customer satisfaction and retention is increased;
- improvements are sustained over time;
- visible performance goals are created;
- hard data is analyzed and quantifiable evidence of improvements provided.

DISADVANTAGES
- Claims of its potential are so great that it may be met with skepticism as unrealistic.
- It may be hard for employees to understand the technique initially.
- An investment in specialist training will be required.
- It may require a culture change within the organization.
- It is a radical long-term project requiring deep commitment.

- It requires the collection and interpretation of data, which may be a difficult and time-consuming process.

ACTION CHECKLIST

1. Understand Six Sigma

Sigma is the Greek letter used in mathematics to denote standard deviation, or the amount a process varies from the mean. As the level of sigmas rises, the level of variation decreases. A Three Sigma organization achieves 66,807 defects per million, whereas a true Six Sigma organization achieves just 3.4 defects per million. It is important to realize that perfect Six Sigma may not be achieved, but that even a rise from one sigma level to the next will produce significant benefits.

The Six Sigma technique hinges on a continuous reduction of the process and product variation that results in defects. This is achieved by first of all defining and measuring variation in each process, and then discovering its causes. This enables the development of operational means to control and reduce the level of variation. Tools used in this stage include statistical process control, computer simulation, short-cycle manufacturing, supplier qualification, and others.

Six Sigma involves not only reducing existing variation, but also avoiding any future variations that might develop. With this in mind, designers need to "design for producibility," making all new products and processes as little subject to variance as possible. This can be achieved by such methods as "poka-yoke," which aims to design products with minimum opportunity for error. In addition, any potential problems for the organization should be assessed and guarded against. Techniques such as total preventive maintenance and risk assessments are used for this. Before proceeding, the concept of Six Sigma and the goals of the initiative must be defined and communicated, both on a strategic and an operational level.

2. Focus on Organization Culture and Prepare for Change Management

Six Sigma will be a major change initiative, so it is important that employee resistance is overcome and that the culture of the organization is supportive of radical change. As Six Sigma is implemented through project teams, teamworking is a key to its success. A culture of creative thinking and innovation will also aid the process, since many stumbling blocks may have to be removed.

3. Decide on the Extent of Implementation

Although full Six Sigma is organization-wide, there are increasing numbers of companies implementing it in a limited way. Consider whether you might want to focus on manufacturing or engineering processes, or maybe on strategic projects critical to the organization.

4. Select and Train Key Personnel

Teams need to be formed to implement Six Sigma in different areas. Key team members must be trained in

leadership skills. Training traditionally involves three stages.

- Green belt—participants earn green belt status by completing a short course in Six Sigma methodology.
- Black belt—some green belts, usually of managerial status, then complete a project exercise using the knowledge they have gained. Black belts will be responsible for leading and developing teams, advising management, and teaching Six Sigma techniques to team members.
- Master black belt—a select few will need further training to make them the organization's Six Sigma experts, leading the initiative, integrating it into the organization's strategic plans, and teaching the techniques to others.

Some companies use different terminology for these levels of training, and it is important to use names that create the right impression in your organization.

5. Bring the Six Sigma Teams into Action

Once personnel receive training, the teams need to begin to identify processes within the organization. Each process is earmarked as a Six Sigma project. The statistical techniques are applied to each project according to a framework. This usually consists of these key phases: definition of the problem; measurement; analysis; improvements; and control.

In the first phase the team focuses on identifying processes that customers perceive as value-creating. They then need to work out what a "perfect" process would be. For example, a delivery company might aim to deliver all parcels by noon on the day after dispatch.

The next step is to measure how the process is performing in reality. The common measurement used is "defects per unit," which can be applied to virtually any product or process in any area of the company. For example, a unit might be a line of computer code, a sales invoice, a piece of raw material, a finished product, or a delivery. In the last case, a unit is a parcel delivered on schedule; a defect occurs when the parcel is not delivered on time. In a service environment, as opposed to manufacturing, units and defects may be harder to measure.

Tasks should be broken down and ways of quantitatively measuring defects should be created. Use data mining techniques and information technology to make this easier.

This is followed by an analysis that identifies the gap between current performance and the desired goal using statistical techniques. Reasons for this gap must be assessed, perhaps using root cause analysis. Some creativity may be involved. New and better ways to do things must then be devised, and implemented using project management techniques.

6. Integrate Six Sigma into the Organization Infrastructure

If Six Sigma is a company-wide initiative, then it will need to be linked into existing company structures. Consider linking it to pay and rewards, departmental budgets and job descriptions. Modify policies and procedures to reflect the improvements made.

7. Monitor and Evaluate Success

Ensure that projects are monitored and that failures are investigated and successes publicized. Six Sigma is an ongoing, long-term initiative, so constant assessment is vital to make sure that it is heading in the right direction. Ascertain not only what cost savings have been made but also whether employee job satisfaction and customer satisfaction have improved. Remember that customer demands, marketplaces, and business environments are dynamic and changing. You will need to periodically reassess processes that have already been analyzed, to see if defects are creeping in again because of changed circumstances.

THOUGHT STARTERS

- Do you know what proportion of your costs goes on waste that produces no value to your customers?

- Are you aware of consistent errors with a piece of equipment or standard of customer service?

- What are the quality levels of your competitors, and why they are higher or lower than yours?

DOS AND DON'TS

DO
- Secure top management commitment.
- Keep things as simple as possible to make understanding clear and implementation easier.
- Make Six Sigma implementation the responsibility of everyone in the organization, not just black belts.

DON'T
- Don't let the seemingly mathematical nature of Six Sigma deter you, as it can be easily learned, and computer software can perform the calculations.
- Don't forget to teach the soft skills of handling meetings, teamworking, and facilitation that are needed for the statistical analysis to be carried out efficiently.

FOR MORE INFORMATION

Books:
Eckes, George. *The Six Sigma Revolution*. New York: Wiley, 2001.

Breyfogle, Forrest W. III, James M. Cupello, and Becki Meadows. *Managing Six Sigma*. New York: Wiley, 2001.

Larson, Alan. *Demystifying Six Sigma*. New York: AMACOM, 2003.

Pande, Peter S., Robert P. Neuman, and Roland R. Cavanagh. *The Six Sigma Way*. New York: McGraw Hill, 2000.

Thomsett, Michael C. *Getting Started in Six Sigma*. Hoboken, NJ: Wiley, 2005.

"The state of statistical control is . . . the goal of all experimentation."   W. Edwards Deming

Shareholder Value Analysis (SVA)

CHECKLIST

Shareholder value analysis (SVA) is one of a number of methods being used as a substitute for traditional business measurements. SVA calculates the value of a company by looking at the returns it gives to stockholders and is based on the view that the objective of company directors is to maximize the wealth of the company's stockholders. This checklist introduces the financial calculations involved in carrying out SVA and advises on its implementation.

DEFINITION

Shareholder value analysis, or SVA, is a method of financial analysis that measures shareholder value by estimating the total net value of a company based on its present and future cash flows and dividing this figure by the value of its shares. The resulting figure indicates the company's value to stockholders. The fundamental principle underlying concepts of shareholder value is that a company adds value for its stockholders only when equity returns exceed equity costs. Once the amount of value has been calculated, targets for improvement can be set and shareholder value can be used as a measure for managing performance.

ADVANTAGES

Shareholder Value Analysis:
- takes a long-term financial view on which to base strategic decisions;
- offers a universal approach that is not subject to differences in companies' accounting policies. It is therefore applicable internationally and across sectors;
- forces the organization to focus on the future and its customers, particularly the value of future cash flows.

Other, more traditional, measures are cost-based, bearing little relation to the economic income generated during a period.

DISADVANTAGES

- Accurately estimating future cash flows, a key component of SVA, can be extremely difficult. Inaccurate projections can lead to strategic decisions being based on incorrect or misleading figures.
- Developing and implementing SVA can be a long and complex process.
- Communicating the SVA approach to managers can be difficult.
- Management of shareholder value requires more complete information than traditional measures.

ACTION CHECKLIST

1. Understand and Calculate the Company's Shareholder Value

Before adopting shareholder value as a significant financial objective, you need to understand its implications and the best approach for your business. It can be helpful to plan the approach first with professional advisers such as accountants or consultants who specialize in this area.

A company's value to stockholders is calculated by subtracting the market value of any debts owed to the company from the total value of the company.

Total business value has three main components:
- the present value of future cash flows during the planned period;
- the residual value of future cash flows from a period beyond the planned period;
- the weighted average cost of capital.

This is calculated by adding present value of future cash flows to residual value of future cash flows and dividing it by the weighted average cost of capital.

If the result of this equation is greater than one, then the company is worth more than the invested capital and added value is being created.
- Future cash flows

Future cash flows are affected by growth, returns, and risk. According to Alfred Rappaport in *Creating Shareholder Value*, these factors can be explained by seven key value drivers that must be managed in order to maximize shareholder value: sales growth rate, operating profit margin, income tax rate, working capital investment, fixed capital investment, cost of capital, and value growth duration.
- Residual value of future cash flows

The residual value—the price at which a fixed asset is expected to be sold at the end of its useful life—is an important figure that represents cash flows arising after the normal planning period. It has been estimated that as much as two-thirds of the value of a business can be attributed to cash flows arising after the normal planning period (usually 5 to 10 years). Viewed another way, only one-third of the value of a business results from cash flows arising during the normal planning period.
- Weighted average cost of capital (WACC)

The WACC is the cost of equity added to the cost of debt. It represents the return a company needs to earn in order to justify the financial resources it uses; the WACC therefore expresses the opportunity cost of the assets in use. The WACC is entirely market-driven—if the assets cannot earn the required return, investors will withdraw their funds from the business.

2. Gain Top Management Commitment

Underlying SVA is the belief that the creation and maximization of shareholder value is the most important measure by which to assess business performance. Top managers need to commit to this objective for the SVA approach to take root. They should also accept that traditional measures and approaches may fall short of achieving this objective.

3. Identify the Company's Key Value Drivers and Set Targets

Unlocking shareholder value is about maximizing cash flows. In order to achieve this you need to identify the

key value drivers of the business (the seven value drivers are listed in Step 1 above). To take one example, improvements in the operating profit margin are affected by sales and expenses; these in turn are driven by a number of other factors that are themselves subject to other influences.

This analysis of value drivers links financial and operational objectives and provides a framework for:

- setting performance targets;
- assigning responsibility to individual managers;
- reviewing the company's financial performance (and benchmarking against competitors);
- developing strategic plans.

Identifying the key factors influencing each value driver is invariably a process of trial and error. However, this process is fundamental to managing, controlling, and making improvements in the business, leading to improved cash flows.

4. Communicate the Approach and Train Staff

Managers need to understand the broad concept of creating shareholder value, particularly when appraising potential projects, but the technicalities of SVA are unlikely to be of concern to them. Managers should instead understand the importance of identifying, controlling, and improving the performance of the value drivers and the key factors that influence them.

Adopting SVA and setting new targets will probably challenge managers' ingrained habits and approaches and consequently may meet with resistance. Managers will be called on to reevaluate previous approaches and perhaps discard them in favor of new targets.

Unlocking shareholder value is essentially a change process, and it requires line managers (invariably the people making the key operational decisions) to be fully trained.

It is also important when implementing an SVA approach to achieve early, high-profile successes. As with any change process, early successes demonstrate the value of the new approach, highlighting its benefits and winning over skeptics.

5. Change the Company's Information Systems to Monitor and Measure Progress

The company's financial reporting systems and information systems in general usually need to be revised when SVA is implemented. Conventional reporting systems are unlikely to provide all the information required or to provide it in the most effective format. The implementation of SVA requires managers to regularly measure and monitor information about the company's key value drivers and targets.

6. Change Managers' Financial Incentive Packages

Review your incentive packages for managers and revise them to reward performance that adds shareholder value.

Incentives for senior managers should reflect the need to increase shareholder value over realistic time periods instead of focusing simply on short-term profit growth or earnings per share.

7. Monitor and Review Progress

Creating sustained value requires continuous monitoring and redefinition of targets as circumstances change. Appraisals, performance reviews, management meetings, and key decisions should all focus on progress so far achieved and actions required to continue building shareholder value. Without consistent emphasis on value creation, managers may continue to focus on targets that have become irrelevant or are actually harmful to the long-term value of the business.

603

CHECKLIST

DOS AND DON'TS

DO
- Take time to understand what will increase shareholder value in your company—what the value drivers are and what factors influence them.

DON'T
- Don't be impatient—unlocking shareholder value is likely to take time. Some estimates claim two years is the norm.
- Don't cut corners—adopting SVA takes time, energy, and commitment and may require a complete overhaul of the way the business is run.

THOUGHT STARTERS
- Have you set realistic targets for increasing SVA and explained the new approach to the company's stockholders?

- Have you examined your company's strategy, procedures, and processes to make sure that nothing will hinder the adoption of SVA?

FOR MORE INFORMATION

Books:
Manganelli, Raymond L., and Brian W. Hagen. *Saving the Corporate Value Enigma*. New York: American Management Association, 2003.
Rappaport, Alfred. *Creating Shareholder Value: A Guide for Managers and Investors*. 3rd ed. New York: Free Press, 2000.

Web site:
Association of Chartered Accountants in the U.S.: **www.acaus.org**

"Money, *n.* A blessing that is of no advantage to us excepting when we part with it."

Ambrose Bierce

ACTIONLISTS

Actionlists

The Actionlists, written by specialists, provide essential time-saving instructions for tackling tasks and solving problems. They address key management tasks in detail, and include in-depth coverage of e-business, marketing, finance, and personal development topic areas.

The section on personal development will be invaluable if you are looking for practical advice on furthering your career or improving the quality of your working life.

Actionlists include a **FAQs** section, based upon the writers' experience of the most frequent questions asked by managers in the situation, as well as a helpful section on how to avoid **common mistakes**.

If you don't find the precise answer you are looking for, each list provides you with a shortlist of the best sources of management help. Alternatively, you can turn to the **Business Information Sources** section, where we have compiled a carefully selected range of the best management materials from around the world.

Contents

Implementing an E-commerce Strategy

GETTING STARTED

An effective e-commerce strategy combines many separate elements. E-commerce means selling online with content, and this requires a sophisticated content management system. E-commerce purchase, payment, and support systems are required, perhaps with customer relationship management and localization. Proper marketing will be needed for success. Underpinning all this will be a requirement for professional Web site development and management. In implementing e-commerce, keep the following in mind:

- E-commerce is not suitable for every product and service.
- The best e-commerce strategy is a clicks-and-mortar approach, combining offline retail resources with online capabilities.
- E-commerce is complex and expensive to get right: don't underestimate the difficulty involved in designing and managing an efficient e-commerce Web site.

FAQs
What products are best suited to e-commerce?

- digital products such as software and information
- products with a high value relative to their cost of fulfillment
- products requiring a lot of information, such as books, music, travel products, and banking
- products that do not need to be handled or tried on
- products that are difficult to find locally

How difficult is it to establish an e-commerce Web site?

It depends on the scope of what you want to do. You must be able to manage inventory, fulfillment, payment, and security. You must be able to integrate your e-commerce Web site efficiently with your offline business. E-commerce software has improved and become more streamlined, but it is still neither cheap nor simple to get everything running smoothly.

If you set up an e-commerce Web site, will you suddenly be selling to a global marketplace?

No. Selling to a foreign marketplace involves more than setting up an e-commerce Web site.

MAKING IT HAPPEN
Make Sure You Have a Market

Who is going to buy your products online? The best place to start is your current customer base. Will going online make life easier for them? Are you going to save them time and money by allowing them to purchase online? You probably have a basic Web site already; are you getting requests for online buying from potential customers?

It is never truly possible to judge in advance whether a market exists, but there should be at least some indications of a demand for an online presence.

Use a Clicks-and-Mortar Strategy If Possible

The clicks-and-mortar approach is the most effective and economic. This combines offline resources, such as stores, brands, channels, with an online e-commerce presence. The other option—a pure-play dot-com—is now rare. Consumers are looking for brands that they know and trust. They also like the fact that a business has a physical presence, a place where they can go if something goes wrong. Pure-play dot-coms found that they had to spend a lot of money on marketing just to maintain awareness.

Integrate the Shopping Experience

Consumers look to the Web primarily for information; they may use the Web site initially to find out about the product, then buy by phone or in person. However, repeat purchasers more familiar with the Web are more likely to buy online. They will be able to do this more easily if their personal details and purchase history can be stored for use in subsequent purchases.

Plan How You Will Deal with Content, Pricing, Inventory Management, Fulfillment, Payment, Returns, Support, and Security

These are the basics of any business, but there can be added complications online. You need to address the following:

- **Content** is critical to e-commerce and must be updated frequently.
- **Pricing**: if you are selling direct for the first time, you may have problems with your distributors and retailers, who will not want you to underprice them. If you are selling brands by other manufacturers there may be problems involved in selling in foreign marketplaces. Are you going to offer prices in a range of currencies? If so, which?
- **Stock management**: are you going to use the same stock base to sell online and through your physical distribution channels? If so, you need an integrated stock management system.
- **Fulfillment**: when fulfilling, precise information on order status is essential. Each order should have a tracking number so that the customer can get information on the status of the order right up to the point of delivery. If you haven't sold by mail order before, you will have to plan for packaging and fulfillment. This can be a major cost, and needs careful management. If, for cost or other reasons, you decide not to fulfill to certain countries, you must make that very clear on the Web site.
- **Payment**: how will people pay? What credit cards will you accept? How will you manage fraud?

- **Returns**: what is your return policy? Studies indicate that returns can be a major cost for e-commerce.
- **Support**: how will you support the products you sell online? You must plan for a support section on your Web site to answer basic questions from customers. Will you also offer telephone and e-mail support?
- **Security**: security will be a central issue in an e-commerce strategy. Fraud and hacking of computer systems are ever-growing problems.

Develop an Easy-to-Use Purchase Process

An alarming number of consumers abandon their attempts to buy online. One of the reasons given is a badly designed purchase process. Your purchase process must be reliable and very easy to use; a good example is Amazon.com. It is a good idea to tell the consumer upfront how many steps there are in the purchase process, and to keep that information prominently displayed at the top of the Web page. An example of the purchase steps is as follows: "Shopping cart–Account–Shipping–Payment–Verify–Confirm."

Consider Localization Issues

If you want to sell seriously to foreign marketplaces, you will have to localize the Web site. Studies indicate that, without localization, sales will be minimal. More worryingly, returns are very high because of misunderstanding by people who are purchasing in a foreign language.

Consider Customer Relationship Management and Personalization

The Internet offers many opportunities for a better understanding of customers' behavior and for developing a closer relationship with them. Customer relationship management and personalization systems allow for the collection and application of comprehensive information to create a more customized environment for the consumer. While the potential of such systems is substantial, they are complex and difficult to implement, and, if not professionally managed, can lead to the abuse of consumer privacy.

Make Sure You Buy the Right Software

There is no need to do all the work internally, as there is now a wide variety of quality software for e-commerce.

Make Sure You Have a Team in Place

An e-commerce Web site needs day-to-day maintenance. Technical problems must be fixed, new content must be published and old content removed, and the Web site must be constantly marketed.

If You Don't Market, They Won't Come

Opening up an e-commerce Web site is rather like setting up shop at the North Pole: nobody knows you are there. It is not enough just to register with search engines; you will need an aggressive marketing campaign to make your target market aware of what you have to offer. The ideal situation is a seamless integration with the marketing strategy of the offline business.

COMMON MISTAKES

Thinking That It's Cheap to Set Up an E-commerce Web Site

It is not. Back-end infrastructure is expensive to set up and maintain. Without an existing business and brand, marketing costs will be very high.

Thinking That an E-commerce Web Site Has Failed Because It Didn't Deliver Direct Sales

Not necessarily: many businesses have found that their Web sites support the purchase process, but that consumers still like to complete the sale offline.

Thinking That E-commerce Is Just the Same As Ordinary Commerce

It is not, although it has many similarities with mail order. If you have never sold products by mail order before, e-commerce involves a steep learning curve. Packaging and delivery, particularly to many different countries, are difficult to master.

Developing a Poor-Quality Purchase Process

A great many Web sites have poor-quality purchase processes. It is essential to test your purchase process thoroughly to make sure that it is reliable and easy to use.

Thinking That All You Have to Do Is Put Up a Product Catalog

E-commerce is selling with content, and you need a content-rich Web site that is constantly being updated if you want to make sales.

Not Dealing Professionally with Legal and Security Issues

Many consumers are wary of purchasing online because they feel they have better security in a physical store.

611

ACTIONLIST

FOR MORE INFORMATION

Book:
Spector, Robert. *Anytime, Anywhere: How the Best Bricks-and-Clicks Businesses Deliver Seamless Service To Their Customers*. New York: Perseus, 2002.

Web site:
Google: **http://directory.google.com/Top/Business/E-Commerce**

See also:
- ☆ Integrating Real and Virtual Strategies (pp. 180–181)
- ✔ Making Your Web site Secure (pp. 631–632)
- ✔ Managing Payments Online (pp. 616–618)
- ☆ New Yardsticks for Performance and Productivity in an E-world (pp. 366–367)
- ✔ Understanding the Key Principles of Internet Marketing (pp. 651–652)

"Progress, therefore, is not an accident but a necessity . . . a part of nature."

Herbert Spencer

Delivering Quality Online Customer Service and Support

GETTING STARTED

Customer service is increasingly seen as a central concern for e-commerce. For many consumers it is a key differentiator between good and bad e-commerce Web sites. A wide range of online support options is now available to organizations, including e-mail, knowledge base systems, live chat, and phone-back. When designing an online support function, keep in mind

- that the first step in online customer support is a well-structured Web site with comprehensive information;
- that organizations have a poor record in responding to e-mail queries from their Web sites; a lack of response damages your reputation;
- that online support can cause a significant increase in queries, many of which are flippant or of little value. A strategy must be put in place to deal with these and sift out the important queries.

FAQs
Why offer customer support online?

The best-designed Web site in the world will never answer every question a consumer has. Studies in 2000 indicated that over half—and sometimes up to three quarters—of the people who started an online purchase did not complete it. Web sites that have added support facilities have found that the number of people completing transactions increases significantly.

When should you offer support online?

All Web sites should have at least some level of customer support. Cost is a central issue: the lower the margin on the product, the less support can be afforded.

What savings can online support bring?

There are substantial cost savings to be made by dealing with support queries online. For example, customers may be able to find the information they need on a Web site; e-mails from customers can be held over for a few hours until there is someone available to deal with them, while telephone calls always have to be dealt with immediately. It is easier to have a set of generic answers (to frequently asked questions) ready for general or vague queries.

However, all support is expensive. Although there are many benefits from it, publishing high-quality material on a support Web site requires an investment of time and money. It may also be important to ensure that the personal touch remains a part of the relationship between the company and the customer. The key is to target the best-quality, most personalized support at the highest-value customers.

Is online support more appropriate for some consumers than others?

It depends on the type of online support. Online support that is text-based, such as live chat and e-mail, is more appropriate for PC-literate consumers. Chat and e-mail are thus ideal for technology industry customers, who are frequent users of e-mail. New or infrequent computer users can often barely cope with learning to use the browser; asking them to use chat software might just confuse them. For such people, the option to have someone call them and talk them through the Web site can be very comforting.

MAKING IT HAPPEN
Ensure You Have Comprehensive, Well-Organized Web Site Content

A Web site is often described as a library. Libraries have two key components: a selection of well-organized content and a support center where people can ask questions. Person-to-person support is expensive, and the Web site should seek to reduce unnecessary interaction by supplying content that will answer as many questions as possible.

It is widely recognized that quality Web sites can reduce the number of support calls an organization receives. While the entire Web site is there to answer questions, specific support functions include the following:

- Frequently Asked Questions (FAQs): a collection of the most frequently asked questions about a product or service. FAQs should be well written and concise. If there are a lot of them, they should be classified into logical groups, and perhaps provided with a search function.
- Comprehensive Help: a Help link should be prominent on every page. This should lead the person to a section containing information on all the support elements on the Web site. Where people are asked to perform a complex task, such as using an advanced search function, or are performing a purchase process, context-sensitive help should be available: when they click on the Help link, they are brought to the specific page they need.
- Knowledge Based Systems: these approaches seek to take the FAQ model much further. The user can type in a question, rather than using keywords. The response may involve asking the person a series of questions in order to narrow down the area of interest. The Ask Jeeves Web site, **www.ask.com**, is an example of this approach.

E-mail-Based Support

It is often sufficient to use e-mail as the main channel for support on a Web site. A response policy must be established, whereby e-mails are graded where appropriate, and a response time target is specified for each.

However, the ease of sending e-mails can often result in frivolous questions. Organizations receiving a high volume of e-mail and working on tight margins often make extensive use of auto-response. The auto-response e-mail, which is generated automatically, may contain an FAQ and links to support material on the Web site. More sophisticated auto-responders may connect to a

knowledge base that will search for keywords in the e-mail and send back a response based on these keywords. It is advisable for these approaches to include a human-based option so that the inquirer can talk to someone if they need to.

Unfortunately, many organizations don't allocate enough resources to e-mail response, and so messages are responded to late or not at all.

Live Chat

Also known as instant messaging, live chat allows a customer representative to chat with a Web site visitor in real time, using text. The benefits of live chat are:

- many people have only one phone line, so if they call support they will have to disconnect from the Internet: live chat means that they can receive text-based support without having to disconnect;
- support is sometimes complex and may take a long time; live chat can avoid the inquirer having to spend hours on the phone, and can solve the problem in a more logical manner;
- live chat can be an option for international customers who do not have access to a toll-free number;
- an experienced customer representative can handle several chat sessions at the same time.

Live chat can have drawbacks. Response times can be slow, depending on the connection, and novice computer users may not feel comfortable using it. In addition, the quality of the live chat support is dependent on the typing skills and knowledge of the support staff.

Callback Support

With this option the Web site visitor is informed that if they enter their telephone number and details into a form someone will call them back. This option is expensive, and is most appropriate for high-value items. A related and popular option here is to offer the customer a free or low-cost telephone number that they can call.

Co-browsing and Page Pushing

Software is now available that allows the customer service representative to synchronize their browser with the person requesting support. Using live chat or the telephone, the rep can walk the person through a process, changing their Web page as they change their own. This is not appropriate for the sale of low-value items, but can be a valuable feature when complex processes and information have to be delivered.

The Importance of Graduating Customer Service

A fundamental objective of many e-commerce Web sites is to increase sales while reducing the need for person-to-person interaction, thus increasing profit. If there is too much customer interaction, especially with nonserious or low-value customers, the profit will be eaten away. For certain products, margins are so slim that person-to-person interaction must be kept to a minimum.

As a result, it is important that the customer service component of a Web site should be graduated. For example, a person seeking support should be guided to the FAQ section first; if they can't find an answer there, they

should be offered the option of an e-mail, and finally the option of telephone support.

Outsourcing Customer Service

Customer service support functions such as live chat and e-mail support can now be outsourced to countries such as India and the Philippines, where well-educated English-speaking labor is available at low cost. While outsourcing support definitely reduces costs, it can have negative implications. The support staff may not have the in-depth knowledge required to answer complex questions.

Integration of Support Functions

When people are contacting the organization through a number of support channels, the support function can become dissipated. Planning is required to ensure that a single support knowledge base is used, and that all the technologies work in unison.

Training of Staff

Offering a variety of support options requires a well-planned training approach and targeting of staff skills. Training will be required to raise skill levels.

COMMON MISTAKES
Not Responding to E-mails

Surveys indicate that organizations have a poor record in responding to e-mail requests from their Web sites.

Too Many Queries

Online support makes it easier for people to communicate with the organization, and this can substantially increase the number of frivolous queries. Organizations are often not properly prepared to handle the increase in volume, and the important queries can be swamped.

Not Being Able to Answer the Question

A key problem with all customer service support is a lack of trained staff. When customers ask questions, they must be answered quickly and comprehensively; otherwise the whole purpose is defeated.

Lack of Proper Integration

Online support must integrate with the overall support structure. Adding numerous support options increases complexity, and this can lead to integration problems.

613

ACTIONLIST

FOR MORE INFORMATION

Web site:
Business2 E-business Customer Support Guide:
**www.business2.com/b2/webguide/
0,17811,41056,00.html**

See also:
- ✔ Establishing an Enterprise Portal (p. 667)
- ☆ Managing the Challenge of E-service (pp. 223–224)
- ☆ Marketing in the Internet Age (pp. 94–96)
- ☆ Overcoming the Difficulties of Managing a Virtual Organization (pp. 241–242)

"To burn always with this hard, gem-like flame, to maintain this ecstasy, is success in life."

Walter Pater

Developing a Personalization Strategy for a Web Site

GETTING STARTED

Personalization is the process by which some Web sites present customers with selected information on their specific needs. To do this, a personalization system is used to collect personal information on a particular individual. Used properly, personalization is a powerful tool that allows customers to access the right content more quickly, thus saving them valuable time. When considering personalization, keep the following in mind:

- Personalization can only work well if the Web site has quality content that is well structured.
- True personalization is a complex and expensive process, and is financially worthwhile only if the Web site has a large quantity of information and many users.
- Because personalization requires the collection of personal information, it raises key privacy issues.

FAQs

How can I encourage customers to provide the information that I need?

Most customers are willing to give personal information if they know it will benefit them. They need to be confident that the information they give will be properly protected, and that it will be used only for the reasons it was originally collected for. Many studies indicate that privacy is a central issue for people using the Internet. People need to feel confident that they are dealing with a reputable organization that will not abuse their trust.

Can I use the information that customers provide for other sales and marketing activities?

The use of customer information is governed by legislation in each country. Collecting personal information on the Internet, and, in particular, moving that information between countries can be very complicated because different countries have different laws. However, a basic principle is to tell the individual clearly why you are collecting the information and what you will use it for. Only use it for that stated purpose.

Do personalized pages contribute to customer loyalty?

Yes. Studies have indicated that regular customers appreciate personalization options. New visitors are unlikely to use personalization because they are not sure whether they will want to come back to the Web site. However, someone who visits regularly will probably have favorite sections of the Web site; personalization allows these sections to be brought together into a single environment for that user.

MAKING IT HAPPEN
Understanding How Personalization Works

In the basic model for personalization, personal information is collected on an individual, and used to customize the Web site for that person.

Personal information can be collected in two ways:
- A person fills out a personal profile directly, perhaps informing the organization of the type, or types, of products and services he or she is interested in.
- The organization uses software that tracks the way a customer uses the Web site; for example, if you looked at Product X last week, the next time you visit you may be told about a new feature for Product X. A popular method by which such tracking is done is the use of cookies, which reside on an individual's browser and collect information on that person's Web behavior.

Define Clear Objectives and Benefits

Personalization has failed to live up to its original promise of certain profitability. Many organizations spent large sums of money on personalization systems, only to see a very poor return on investment.

There should be a clear set of benefits for the organization and the customer. Personalization makes most sense if a Web site contains a very large quantity of information, which means that visitors are slow to find the information they seek. Personalization also requires a large number of Web site visitors, because systems are complex and expensive to install.

Personalization is a way of improving an already well-structured Web site with high-quality information. It will not solve core problems such as a badly-designed classification and poor-quality content.

Understand Where Personalization Works and Where It Doesn't

Personalization is not always suitable. A study by the Poynter Institute on how people read news-based information on the Internet found that, while many of the respondents had tried personalization, a great number had stopped using it. When asked why, the most common answer was that they felt they might be "missing something."

People are often not sure exactly what they want when they come to a Web site, and their needs can frequently change over time, so past behavior is not always a true indicator of present needs. The following example of a successful personalization strategy by Amazon.com shows where personalization works best.

Amazon.com: Personalization at Its Best

Amazon.com offers millions of books and other products, so it can be hard for customers to find what they are looking for. However, Amazon.com's personalization approach, based on previous browsing or purchasing behavior, shows customers books or other items that reflect those previous choices. Customers may also be sent occasional e-mails informing them of new book or music releases in categories they have previously looked at. The

objective is clear: helping the customer to find quickly the book or item they need and giving them context for their purchase by providing information.

Don't Try to Do Too Much

Personalization can be complex. Start off by personalizing something that is easy to implement and that will deliver an immediate benefit. It is also important to understand that personalization depends on having a well-structured, well-classified Web site that has good-quality, up-to-date information. Without this, personalization is a waste of time and money.

Carefully Plan the Information You Need to Collect

It is essential to plan carefully the type of customer information you need, for two reasons:

- People hate filling out long forms, and are reluctant to provide too much personal information.
- Too much information can be counterproductive if it buries genuinely useful information under a mass of irrelevant detail.

When seeking to develop a profile on a particular customer, the following information may be required:

- name and address
- contact details
- purchase history
- personal interests
- product or service preferences

Develop a Comprehensive Privacy Policy

A clear privacy policy is an essential part of any personalization strategy. It must be made clear why you are collecting the information and how it will be used. If you wish to use the information for purposes other than the personalization of the Web site, such as sending out e-mails on special offers, or sharing the information with partners, you should specifically inform the individual of that intention and give them the opportunity of opting out.

It is good policy to allow individuals to check at any time the information you have on them, and to allow them to delete information on themselves if they wish to do so.

Ensure Proper Security Procedures Are in Place

When collecting personal information on customers, a proper security procedure is essential. Internet security breaches are increasing, and hackers are particularly interested in breaking into systems containing personal information. An organization's reputation can be badly damaged by the theft of personal customer information.

Select a Software Vendor

While it is possible to develop custom-made software for personalization, it is not advisable unless the personalization system is a very simple one. There are a wide variety of vendors selling personalization software. However, it is important not to be too influenced by what may be unnecessary features: keep your objectives clear, and always focus on real needs and benefits.

COMMON MISTAKES

Assuming Personalization Is a Magic Formula

It is a mistake to think that personalization will turn a poorly designed Web site with poor-quality information into a winning success. Personalization is only as good as the foundations upon which it is built. In addition, it is not suitable for every Web site. The benefits must be very clear both from the point of view of the organization and of the Web site visitor.

Not Collecting the Right Information

Collecting the wrong information will ensure that personalization fails. Collecting too much information will frustrate the customer and will make the process of sifting through such information time-consuming and expensive.

Not Articulating a Clear Set of Benefits for the Customer

Many people are willing to give personal information once they can be shown that there are clear benefits in doing so. It is important to explain convincingly to customers why they should give their personal information to a Web site.

Not Having a Comprehensive Privacy Policy

There have been many instances of abuse of privacy on the Internet, and consumers are becoming increasingly wary of Web sites that seek to collect personal information on them. Before personalization can work you must establish credibility and trust. A way of doing this is to have a comprehensive privacy policy and honor it in every detail.

615

ACTIONLIST

FOR MORE INFORMATION

Book:
Kasanoff, Bruce. *Making It Personal: How to Profit from Personalization without Invading Privacy.* Cambridge, MA: Perseus, 2001.

Web site:
Personalization Consortium: **www.consortiuminfo.org**

See also:

"To keep such adaptability while still keeping the initiative, the best way is to operate along a line which offers alternative objectives."

Karl von Clausewitz

Managing Payments Online

GETTING STARTED

If your business sells its products or services online, it's absolutely essential you're your online payment system works well, and works safely. The system must be easy to use, as consumers dislike having to go through long, cumbersome processes to purchase products, but it must also be as secure as possible; it's estimated that, fraud costs an online business three times as much as an off-line one. Remember that:

- consumers may be wary of giving credit card details and other personal information online. Your first step must be to gain their trust;
- fraud and chargebacks are critical issues that can seriously affect an online business;
- there is a wide range of online payment services available, so shop around to make sure you get the best one for you.

FAQs

What is the most common form of payment on the Internet?

For consumer commerce it is the credit card. In the United States it is claimed that over 90% of all online payments are made by credit card. In Europe, the figure is estimated at 70%. For most business-to-business transactions, payment is usually made offline. New forms of payment are emerging, such as prepaid accounts and payments via cell phone.

What are the key issues facing online payments?

- Fraud is a critical concern that must be addressed comprehensively.
- There is no cross-border integration of payment systems.
- People develop payment habits, and are reluctant to change them.
- Can traditional payment methods adapt to the new environment, or is a brand new payment system required?
- There is still no comprehensive hard data on how people pay online.

What is a payment culture?

Within any particular country, and sometimes within states or regions of a country, there are distinct approaches to payment, depending on:

- the range of payment options available locally;
- local payment habits;
- local/national payment regulations.

MAKING IT HAPPEN
Understand Your Marketplace

Depending on the country, or the region/state within a country, people pay for things in different ways. Different countries also have different payment processing approaches and legal obligations. All of these variations are referred to as "payment cultures."

Understand the Types of Payment Options Available

There are a range of payment options that a Web site can use, including:

- credit or debit card payment;
- credit transfer;
- electronic checks;
- direct debit;
- smart cards;
- prepaid plans;
- loyalty plan points-based approaches;
- person-to-person payments;
- cellphone plans.

The approach you choose will depend on your target market. For example, if a Web site targets young people, who often have no credit cards, a prepaid plan can work well. A particular Web site may use a variety of payment approaches, depending on its needs, but the ability to process all the major credit and debit cards is almost always essential.

Check the Characteristics of an Online Payment System

An online payment system should have these key characteristics:

- efficiency and ease of use: a central advantage of doing business online is that it saves time and cuts costs;
- robustness and reliability: because payment is such a critical function, payment systems have to be fully reliable. They can't be "out of action" for any length of time;
- authentication: much online fraud is caused by the absence of proper authentication;
- integration: a payment system must be able to integrate properly with relevant internal information systems, so that, for example, a record of the payment can be added to the account details;
- insurance: facilities such as escrow services must be available to ensure that the seller gets the money and the buyer gets the goods.

Select an Online Payment Service

Finding the most suitable type of online payment service will depend on the volume of business you intend doing and the margins you make on each sale. There is a wide choice of payment services, so it is important to shop around to find the best one. However, whatever service you choose must be able to verify the credit card, process the transaction, and deposit the money in your account.

Key factors to consider include set-up fees, ongoing charges, and software and hardware expenses. Most banks offer some form of online payment service, and can be a good choice. If you don't use a bank, do make absolutely sure that you're dealing with reputable organizations. Those that advertise extremely low charges usually have expensive hidden extras.

"I've always had a place for every dollar that came in. I've never seen the day where I could say that I felt rich. Generally you have to worry about paying the bills."   J. Paul Getty

Offer a Choice of Credit Card Payment Methods

There are two distinct methods by which credit or debit card payments are made for Internet purchases: payment directly online, and payment by phoning or faxing credit card details. The first method is by far the most popular (88%), but it is advisable to offer both options to potential consumers.

When implementing an online credit card system, a comprehensive security system using a secure server with encryption technology is essential. It is equally important to have comprehensive security procedures for the storage of the information. A database containing confidential information on thousands of individuals is far more attractive to a criminal than acquiring a single credit card number.

Keep the Process Simple and Fast

Whatever the payment system you choose, make sure to keep the process as simple and fast as possible. Studies have indicated that many consumers abandon the online purchase process, often because it is too long and difficult to understand. Streamlining the purchasing process is extremely important where repeat business is concerned. Amazon.com, for example, has implemented a patented "1-Click" purchase process for repeat customers, avoiding a lot of form filling.

Consider Business-to-Business (B2B) Payment Options

While there is a wide range of effective business-to-consumer online payment options, payment for B2B transactions is generally made offline. One reason for this is that the amounts of money involved are usually large. However, one of the key reasons businesses embrace online B2B and join e-marketplaces is to reduce costs and to make transactions more efficient. Not being able to complete the payment online adds cost and inconvenience. A range of systems is available for B2B payment online; they focus on ensuring security and authenticity, and some also offer digital signature facilities.

Think About Offering Online Escrow Services

Online escrow services offer to hold payments while the buyer examines the products purchased. If the buyer is satisfied with the products, they then authorize the payment. An online escrow service incurs extra cost because a fee is charged, but it may be worthwhile if it is essential to give the buyer as much confidence as possible.

The system operates by giving the escrow service a tracking number for the delivery. You must agree on the time period allowed to the buyer for examination of the merchandise; you must also establish who pays the shipping fees if the product is returned.

Remember That Fraud and Chargebacks Are Major Issues

Some studies estimate that e-tailers are losing as much as 5% of their margin to fraud—a rate three times higher than for businesses operating offline. For e-tailers on small margins this is a very serious issue. There are many different types of fraud, but a particularly common online form is identity theft, where fraudsters acquire confidential information on an individual and use it to purchase products. Clearly, e-tailers must take great care in this area, otherwise their profits will be eaten away. Fraud detection software is available and should be used.

Chargebacks (disputed payments) are also a major concern. MasterCard claims that, while online purchases represent 4% of total retail transactions, they account for 40% of all chargebacks. Credit card companies have initiated chargeback limits for e-tailers, and penalties are imposed for those who exceed them.

Understand How Payment Systems Work

This is how the process works:

- customers visit your site anytime, during or outside normal business hours;
- they view products and brief descriptions;
- they select products and put them into an electronic shopping cart;
- customers are offered payment options, ideally in their own currency;
- online payment is handled securely, probably by a specialist payment processor;
- payment is approved and confirmed to you and the customer;
- purchases are delivered to the customer.

Choose the Right System

An effective payment system allows your customers to buy online and allows you to manage the process efficiently. A complete payment system includes all the facilities to display products, accept payments, and manage your business. You can also choose systems that can be integrated with existing product display and business management systems. The system should allow you to:

- display products that customers can buy from your Web site;
- calculate any taxes due;
- calculate shipping or delivery charges;
- provide a quick, simple ordering mechanism;
- provide a secure customer payment mechanism;
- accept payment by credit card, debit card, and check;
- handle transactions from customers with approved accounts;
- handle payment for small and large purchases;
- accept payment in local currencies from all the countries where you have customers;
- accept payments in multiple currencies;
- protect your customers and your business against fraud;
- handle customer refunds;
- receive settlement from the payment processor;
- automate stock control;
- simplify administration and accounting;
- expand in line with growth of business;
- minimize the cost of handling transactions.

Select a Payment Processor

You can set up your own payment processing facilities, but if you only handle a small number of transactions or if your transaction requirements are complex this may not be practical. Payment processors can provide you with an established proven system that can grow in line

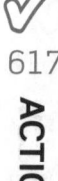

with your business and services of this type are offered by banks and independent specialists.

Using an external provider offers you a number of advantages: there is no need for capital investment from you; there are no hardware, software, and support requirements; high levels of security for your business and your customers are provided; there is a reliable operation, round the clock; and services can expand in line with your business.

Apply for a Payment Account

Many businesses, particularly smaller and medium size operations, can be put off by the complexity of the application process but bear in mind that some suppliers have simpler processes than others. For commercial and security reasons, no company can cut out initial checks but some suppliers have gone out of their way to make the application process as simple as possible. The process varies in a number of areas:

- some independents can make their own internal risk assessment without referring to banks;
- you may or may not have to provide a detailed trading history;
- the proportion of successful applications varies by supplier—independents generally accept a higher proportion of applicants than banks.

Make sure you complete the application forms fully and return all essential documentation, including a customer agreement, direct debit mandate, bank details, and balance sheet.

Offer a clear payment page

Simplifying payment is an important part of the online shopping experience. A clear, easy-to-use order form allows customers to place their orders quickly. The form should include:

- customer details
- delivery requirements
- product details
- quantity
- price
- delivery charges
- total cost
- payment option
- account details, if appropriate
- mechanism to submit the order
- acknowledgment of the order and payment approval

Check the operation of the payment page and insure that any changes to the page layout reflect customer experience and feedback. Also make sure that the page is easy to navigate and simple to complete.

COMMON MISTAKES
Not Understanding Payment Cultures

While credit cards may be very common in the United States, they are not as widely used in Europe. Different countries have different payment habits and payment legislation. Not understanding these is a serious obstacle to online business.

Not Securing Peace of Mind for the Consumer

Consumers are very concerned that their credit card numbers will be stolen on the Internet. They are equally concerned that confidential information that they give to a Web site will not be properly protected. Web sites that fail to show clearly the steps taken to protect customer information are likely to lose potential business.

Underestimating Fraud

Fraud is a pressing issue on the Internet, and can have a serious impact on profit margins.

FOR MORE INFORMATION

Web sites:
Epaynews.com: **www.epaynews.com**
E-payment Systems Observatory: **www.e-pso.info**

Designing a Web Site Effectively

GETTING STARTED

For the majority of Web sites, Web site design is about information, not graphics. The most successful Web sites—Yahoo, AOL Time Warner, Microsoft, Amazon, eBay—have few graphics. Graphics and other high-bandwidth multimedia slow a Web site down, but most people view the Web as a library, not a source of entertainment, and they hate being kept waiting. Web site design should focus on:

- clean, simple, standardized design that helps people find the content they want without delay;
- good page layout that allows people to read the content as easily as possible;
- avoiding fancy graphics and multimedia experiences.

FAQs

What exactly is Web site design?

Web site design is information design. It's about organizing content so that it can be easily found and easily read. Web site design is a form of publishing: presenting content in a way that is attractive to visitors.

Why do so many Web sites seem to be poorly designed?

Because many organizations still don't really understand what their Web sites are intended to achieve. In addition, if the Web site is controlled by graphic design or technical staff, the results may be essentially unusable from a consumer's point of view.

Why should an editor be in charge?

The Web is a publishing medium, and a Web site is a publication. The primary job of an editor is to understand content; the primary purpose of a Web site is to publish content.

What's the main thing people do on the Web?

They search for information, and they read it. Many Web sites still do not fully recognize this fact and make the content harder to read than is really necessary. Overly elaborate color schemes, small fonts, and poor layout are still relatively common. If you think of your Web site visitors as readers, the function of Web site design will become far clearer.

MAKING IT HAPPEN

Design for the Reader/Visitor

Too few Web sites are designed for the needs of their visitors. Remember that the person who visits your site:

- is there to find some information;
- will scan read, moving quickly from one piece of text to another;
- is generally in a hurry, and may not wait for elaborate pages to download;
- may be skeptical because, on the basis of past experience, they expect a Web site to be full of useless material.

Make Sure the Content Is Well Written

When writing for the Web:

- keep it factual, with punchy, descriptive headings and summaries;
- keep it short. Documents should be between 500 and 700 words, paragraphs between 40 and 60 words. Sentences should be short. There should be no more than 9 to 12 words per line of text;
- keep it updated. Out-of-date content is no good.

Make Sure the Content Is Well Organized

Think of your Web site as a directory. If you have lots of products to sell, you must organize them so that people can browse through them easily. Web sites such as Amazon.com and eBay are successful because they organize huge quantities of products properly so that people can find what they want quickly and efficiently.

Metadata, navigation, and search are fundamental to the organization of content on a Web site. Metadata delivers essential information on a document or Web page: publication date, author, keywords, title, and summary. Search depends on metadata to be truly effective, and is one of the most common activities people do on a Web site. Search must be available on every page. Navigation is critical: if people can't easily find their way around a Web site, they will leave.

Make Sure the Web Site Is Interactive

Comprehensive contact details should be prominently available on the Web site, covering the appropriate range of e-mail and telephone contacts. Physical addresses, with location maps, should also be provided. Online community options such as chat, discussion boards, and e-mail discussion lists can enhance a visitor's understanding of the organization and its products. E-mail newsletters can allow the organization to keep in touch regularly and at low cost.

Ensure that Standards Are Developed and Adhered To

Newspaper designers have found that people follow a certain pattern when reading content in a newspaper. This is true of reading content on a Web site too: people navigate and search in a certain way. It is therefore confusing to have different designs in different sections of a Web site, or between Web sites in the same organization.

Some of the emerging standards and conventions for Web site design are included in the following list:

- Essential navigation: every Web page should have a set of essential navigation that is visible when the first screen loads, containing key areas within the Web site. This essential navigation (sometimes known as global navigation) should always begin with a link back to the home page of the Web site. Essential navigation should contain links such as Home, About, Products, Customers, and Contact.
- Slim masthead: the masthead is the top of the page area, and should be slim, like the masthead of a news-

paper. This makes the maximum amount of screen space available for the content—the main reason for a Web site visit. The masthead should contain the logo of the organization, and may also contain the search box and the set of essential links.

- Three-column layout: in the average Web site, a three-column layout is the best means of delivering maximum content in the most readable format.
- Footer on every page: a footer should go at the bottom of every page; it should contain a copy of the essential links, contact information (address, telephone, fax, e-mail), and links to copyright and privacy policy information.
- Maximum accessibility: minimum accessibility standards for Web sites are increasingly becoming a legal requirement. In any case, implementing best practice in accessibility design generally leads to a more effective Web site.
- Effective home page layout and design: a home page has two central functions. First, it provides visitors with the appropriate navigation and search options to allow them to find content quickly; second, it promotes important content. This is done by using short, punchy headings and summaries.
- Consistent document page layout and design: in general, a three-column approach should be used for Web pages that display documents. Every document should have a heading and a summary. Include author and date of publication if appropriate.
- Large sans serif fonts: it is advisable to use sans serif fonts, such as Verdana and Arial, on the Web, because they are easier to read on a screen than serif fonts. Font sizes should not be lower than 8 point for summaries and headings on home pages. The minimum font size recommended for documents is 10 point. The ideal font color is black text on a white background.
- No italic, bold, or underline: avoid using italic, which has a poor appearance on-screen. Avoid using bold in body text, as people may think it's a link. Never use underline, as people will definitely think it's a link.
- Small graphics: graphics should be small, particularly on the home page. If a larger graphic is necessary, consider using a thumbnail approach, with a small graphic and a larger one linked from it, giving visitors the option to view the larger graphic if they want.
- Compatibility with all browsers: although Internet Explorer now has the largest share of the marketplace, it is still important that the Web site can be viewed properly in Netscape Navigator. Test your Web site using both browsers, and different browser versions.
- Light pages: if your Web pages do not download quickly, people will simply leave. Keep pages under 50K in weight; this means small graphics.
- No frames: frames break up a Web page into separate sections. In the words of Web usability expert, Jakob Nielsen: "Frames: just say no."

- No splash pages: a splash page is an introductory or initial page presented to visitors before they can get to the actual home page. It simply forces visitors to go through an extra, redundant stage before they can do what they came to do.
- Lots of hypertext: You should use hypertext liberally, but stick to the standard colors: blue for unclicked, purple for clicked. People are used to these colors.
- No tricks: swirling logos, animated e-mail mailboxes, and page counters are signs of an amateur Web site.

Test, Test, and Test Again

Test out your Web site with potential visitors, and get as much feedback as possible. This is the best way to find out what's working and what isn't.

COMMON MISTAKES
Thinking That a Web Site Is About Getting Attention

Many marketers are used to creating brochures and advertisements that seek to grab attention. However, when someone visits your Web site, you've already got their attention. They don't want to see a swirling logo or splash screen before they get to your home page; they want to find out something about your product or service.

Creating Brochure Ware

Too many people think that Web site design is just like brochure design. Large graphics simply slow down a Web site and turn visitors off. Web site design must allow you to update your Web site with new content easily, so it should be designed more like a newspaper.

Too Many Gimmicks

The majority of people come to Web sites to do things and find out information. Gimmicks may be fun and clever, but too often they get in the way.

FOR MORE INFORMATION

Web sites:
Webmonkey: **www.webmonkey.com**
Builder.com: **www.builder.com**

See also:
✔ Adding Multimedia to a Web Site (pp. 625–626)
✔ Creating a Basic Web Site (pp. 621–622)
☆ Creating a Company Web Site That Delivers Real Value (pp. 192–193)
✔ Developing Appropriate Metadata and Classification for a Web Site (pp. 641–642)
✔ Making a Web Site Easy to Navigate (pp. 643–644)
✔ Writing Well for the Web (pp. 649–650)

Creating a Basic Web Site

GETTING STARTED

A Web site is a way of informing customers and other groups such as suppliers, journalists, or employees about your company. A basic Web site involves delivering essential information that is easy to read and well laid out. In Web site design, simplicity is always best. A Web site must also be actively promoted to make people aware of its existence. When approaching Web site design, ask yourself the following important questions:

- Who are the people that I want to communicate with (your target market)?
- How am I going to structure my information so it is easy to navigate and read?
- How am I going to let people know that my Web site exists?
- How am I going to keep my Web site updated and keep people informed of new content?

FAQs

How much information should I include on a Web site?

Provide the information that your visitors are likely to read. Don't fill your Web site with irrelevant and/or repetitive information as it will clutter your site and make the important information hard to find.

How often should I change content?

You should change your content whenever you have something new and important to say, and whenever content already on the site is out of date. Ideally you should try to publish fresh content every week.

Can I transfer printed copy to the Web site?

Printed copy can be used as a starting point for Web copy, but the structure and length would probably be unsuitable. People like to read short, punchy copy on the Web, so snappy headings and summaries are important. For a Web site to be truly effective, you must also use links (known as "hypertext") so that people can click through for further information if they need it.

MAKING IT HAPPEN
Know Who You Want to Reach

Before you do anything, decide who you want to reach. Prioritize your information for your most important audiences. Ask yourself:

- Do I want to reach new customers? In new markets?
- What can I say on my Web site that will turn a potential customer into an actual one?
- Do I want to offer support for existing customers?
- Do I want to provide information to attract new staff?

Keep It Simple

Web site design is about the design and delivery of information, not about graphic design. Only a small proportion of Internet users have access to broadband, so it is best to avoid fancy graphics and moving images. They slow down a site and frustrate visitors looking for infor-

mation. Good Web site design has simple layout and rich content that is well organized. The best, most successful Web sites in the world (Yahoo, Microsoft, Amazon) don't employ fancy gimmicks; neither should you. Keep it simple. Maximize the content and minimize the presentation.

Structure Your Information Well

When people come to your Web site, they want to find information quickly. They have come for a purpose and they are probably impatient and skeptical. It is therefore essential to make your Web site as accessible and easy to navigate as possible.

A well-structured Web site needs good links that allow the visitor to navigate to other sections of the site. Without these links, a page becomes a dead end.

Include Important Web Site Sections and Links

You should have at least some of the following sections on your Web site. Links to these sections should be provided in a set of essential links placed prominently on every page of the Web site.

Home page

The home page is the first page on your Web site and the most important, as it is usually the first page visitors see. From a linking point of view, the home page is referred to as "Home." It should always be the first link in your set of essential links. The home page itself should be full of punchy, attention-grabbing headings and summaries that quickly inform the visitor of, for example, what you do, what you have to sell, or what special offers you have. The Microsoft home page (**www.microsoft.com**) is a great example of using a home page well.

What's New

This section contains information on important news, events, and press releases. Always keep this section updated, and make sure that you date each entry. You should plan to add an entry for this section at least once a week, but remember to remove old items too.

About

This section should contain essential information about your business or organization. If the section contains a lot of information it should be broken down into manageable subsections. "About" information includes the following:

- mission: a short description of the organization and what it seeks to achieve;
- key strengths: key products, market position, manufacturing, skills, distribution;
- company background;
- management team: pictures and short biographies of key members of the management team;
- financial information: annual results;
- contact and location details: this should link to the Contact section on your Web site.

"The web gives us more choices than before about how we weave society, how we choose, who and what we connect with."

Tim Berners-Lee

Products

This is the core part of your Web site, containing the things you have to sell. It should contain a brief overview of products and services and links to detailed information on specific products or services, containing:

- product/services description;
- product applications;
- business case and ROI (return on investment): how using your product can make and/or save money;
- specifications;
- purchase and delivery details;
- frequently asked questions (FAQs);
- pricing (be sure to specify currency);
- product reviews;
- where you sell to (specify the countries or regions you do or do not sell to).

Purchase

This is an essential link if you have a facility that allows people to buy direct from your Web site. Ideally you should also create a small graphic to be displayed prominently, particularly on the home page, informing customers that they can purchase your products online.

Customers

People want to know who your customers are. Include a list of your key customers and a selection of quotes and case studies.

Partners

If you have a number of partners and joint ventures, you should have a section describing them, explaining how they allow you to deliver a better service.

Contact

This section should contain all your essential contact information including:

- e-mail address;
- physical address and map of location;
- telephone and fax.

Search

If your Web site has more than 50 pages, you need a search facility to enable visitors to find information. Aim to search box on every single page of your Web site, preferably near the top.

Offer an E-mail Newsletter

Every Web site should offer an e-mail newsletter. If visitors give their e-mail address on their first visit, you can send them a regular weekly or monthly e-mail newsletter to tell them what's new.

Use Metadata

Every Web page should have a title. Where appropriate, you should create "metadata" for your content. This is a method of describing your content and it should include: classification (type of information), page title and headings, summary, date of publication, author name, and keywords that appear in the text. Search engines use this metadata to index your Web site properly, so that visitors can find quickly what they are looking for.

Make Sure You Have the Proper Footer Information

The bottom of every page should have footer information containing:

- a list of the essential links for the Web site;
- essential contact details: main address, telephone and fax, e-mail;
- the copyright notice;
- your privacy policy.

Remember to Promote Your Web Site

Promotional strategies include:

- registering with the major search engines (Alta Vista, Google, Yahoo), as well as search engines specific to your industry or sector;
- making sure that your Web site and e-mail address are on all your promotional literature.

Do It Yourself or Get a Design Company

If you are a competent computer user, you may well be able to do most of the work yourself, using packages such as Microsoft FrontPage or Macromedia's Dreamweaver, but you may require a graphic designer to help you with design issues.

COMMON MISTAKES
Being Too Clever

Some sites try too hard to entertain without providing hard information. Animation, multimedia, video clips, and other tricks can obscure important data. Many visitors are deterred immediately by a home page that features animation.

Poor Classification, Navigation, and Search

Good classification, navigation, and search are essential for a successful Web site. Customers expect easy access to the information they want. If they can't find it easily on your site, they will go somewhere else. Structure is critical because it helps people find their way around.

Content That Is Difficult to Read

Many Web sites try to impress by using lots of color, but the easiest text to read is black on a white background. Keep paragraphs, line lengths, and documents short.

FOR MORE INFORMATION

Web sites:
Builder.com, a detailed source of information on design:
www.builder.com
Webmonkey:
http://webmonkey.wired.com/webmonkey

See also:

"The web attacks traditional ways of doing things and elites, and this is very uncomfortable for traditional businesses to deal with."

Martin Sorrell

Building a Web Site Team

GETTING STARTED

All good Web publications are fueled by content, supported by an information architecture and technical infrastructure; the Web site must also be actively marketed and promoted. On a small Web site, all these functions will be performed by a part-time resource, but a large Web site will require dedicated personnel. When building a Web site team, keep the following in mind:

- a Web site should be managed by an editor, who understands content and knows what readers want;
- information architecture skills are vital: the content must be well structured so that it can be quickly found and easily read;
- the need for technical support should not be underestimated, particularly in the area of Web security.

FAQs

Why should a Web site be run by an editor?

E-commerce means selling with content, so if the content isn't right, the customer won't buy. Content is not a technical issue but an editorial one. The primary job of the editor is to ensure that the right content is being created, and that it is being edited and published correctly.

What are the core functions of editing and publishing?

Publishing is about getting the right content to the right person at the right time, and the selection process is vital. Editing is therefore a critical quality control function, rejecting poor content and cutting out unnecessary text. Quality Web sites get the right content up quickly.

What is information architecture?

Information architecture deals with how content is organized and presented. It refers to the metadata, classification, navigation, search, layout, and design of the Web site. Maintaining an information architecture for a small Web site is a relatively simple job but is far more complex for larger Web sites.

What are the key technical resources required to support a Web site?

A Web site that doesn't load quickly and consistently is of little use. Large e-commerce Web sites require complex technical infrastructure that needs constant monitoring. Technical resources include HTML, programming, and systems administration; security is becoming an increasingly important issue.

MAKING IT HAPPEN
Define the Business Requirements

It is essential to establish the business requirements for the Web site and to manage how these requirements are being met. What is the Web site supposed to achieve? If it is modeled on a traditional publication, it will need to generate revenue through advertising and subscription. However, most Web sites exist to support the sale of the organization's products and to promote its brand.

Define the Scope of the Web Site

The people and skills required to run the Web site will depend on its scope.

Editorial Board

It is advisable to establish an editorial board within the organization to establish the content objectives and oversee their implementation. All the main departments and sections should be represented, and senior management should be involved.

The Role of the Managing Editor

A single individual, with an editorial background, should be given overall charge of running the Web site. Specifically the managing editor should:

- manage the content: decide what type of content is to be published, and how often updated;
- manage the staff: hiring, training, motivation, reward, assessment, and discipline;
- champion the visitor: make sure that the Web site focuses on its key visitors. The editor should encourage and make use of feedback from visitors;
- promote the Web site to senior management and within the organization;
- report to management on a regular basis;
- ensure that the Web site is achieving its objectives and evolving to meet changing needs.

Editor

Among other things, the editor should:

- commission and purchase content: make sure that it is delivered on time and to budget;
- edit the content: make sure that content meets editorial standards, clearly communicates its subject matter, and is well written. The editor should check for libel and other legal issues; make sure the metadata is correct; and review, published content;
- publish the content: decide what is to be published and what is not. The editor should decide, in conjunction with the managing editor, what content should be highlighted on the home page and other relevant sections of the Web site;
- manage writers: for many people in the organization, writing is only a small part of their job, so they will require motivation and training. The editor will also deal with hiring, reward, assessment, and discipline;
- champion the visitor/reader: understand what readers want; note and reply to feedback.

Copy editor

Copy editors check for spelling, grammar, and metadata. They ensure that the content is the right length, and rewrite where appropriate.

Writer

Writers must know their subject matter. They should have an ability and enthusiasm for writing, and should be able to suggest content ideas to the editor.

"High-performing companies increasingly believe that teams, rather than business units or individuals, are the basic building blocks of a succesful organization."

Anthony Jay

Contributor

Where the writer is not responsible for adding the meta-data to the content, contributors ensure that the content gets to the editor quickly with all the appropriate metadata.

Moderator

Where online community facilities are available (chat, discussion boards, mailing lists), moderators will be required. Moderators mix editorial and chairperson skills, and also champion a particular mailing list or chat forum.

Information Architect

The information architect is responsible for the information architecture of the Web site, which includes the following:

- Metadata: metadata is crucial to the design of Web sites. How content is classified will directly affect how quickly and effectively it can be found. Defining content templates includes agreeing on vital elements that a particular document should have, such as date of publication, author name, summary, or keywords.
- Navigation: the information architect should decide on the most effective options for navigation. Standards and consistency in navigation design must be maintained. The focus should remain on the main task of navigation—finding an item of content quickly.
- Search: the information architect should design basic and advanced search options where appropriate. Search should be easy to use and deliver accurate results quickly.
- Layout and design: the information architect should ensure that all content is laid out in its most readable format. Simple, elegant design delivers Web pages that are fast to download and easy to read. Consistency of design throughout the Web site is important.
- Usability: the Web site must work for its visitors. Regular feedback and usability testing are essential.

IT Manager/Programmer

This skill will usually be supplied by the IT department or outsourced. Skills are needed most when the Web site design is being implemented, but there is an ongoing need for technical support, so have some sort of programming resource permanently available if possible. A key responsibility of the IT manager is to ensure that the Web site is secure.

Systems Administrator

A site with a lot of traffic requires constant monitoring. Responsibilities include maintaining the network and servers, day-to-day maintenance of all software, backing up the Web site, testing pages for download speed, and checking for broken links or security breaches.

HTML Coder

This skill will vary depending on whether the Web site is being built in pure HTML or content management software is being used.

Graphic Designer

Graphic designers should support the information architect. They should be skilled in creating small, elegant, fast-downloading graphics that support the presentation and readability of navigation, content, and other Web site elements.

Define the Marketing and Promotion Requirements

The marketing department will usually perform marketing and promotion functions. Resources will be required to deal with specific Web-related marketing functions such as ongoing search engine registration, establishing links with third parties, promotion through e-mail newsletters, and development of banner ads.

COMMON MISTAKES

Thinking That a Web Site Is Purely a Technical Issue

A Web site is about communication, and the communications department is where the Web site should reside, supported by the IT and marketing departments.

Not Having an Editor in Charge

The job of the editor is to understand content—the central role in Web design and management. Sites that are run by graphic designers or technologists often push these aspects at the expense of readable content.

Treating Content as a Commodity

Content is the most valuable resource a Web site has, but it must be handled with discretion. Overlong articles, badly written headings, poor metadata—all these reflect a Web site that doesn't care about its content or the person who is supposed to read it.

Not Rewarding and Remunerating Writers

Content is written by people. The creation of content should be part of the job function and remunerated accordingly, otherwise results will be poor.

FOR MORE INFORMATION

Book:
McGovern, Gerry, and Rob Norton. *Content Critical.* Upper Saddle River, NJ: FT Prentice Hall, 2001.

See also:
✓ Maintaining a Web Site (p. 629)
✓ Making Sure Content Is Professionally Created, Edited, and Published (pp. 639–640)
✓ Managing a Web Site (pp. 627–628)
✓ Using the Internet to Create Content Collaboratively (p. 646)

"The role of management is always to identify the weakest links, support them and strengthen them."

Ron Dennis

Adding Multimedia to a Web Site

GETTING STARTED

Multimedia has had problems on the Web, due mainly to limited bandwidth. While the overall environment for Web-based multimedia has improved significantly in recent years, it will still be a long time before rich multimedia can be delivered quickly to the majority of Web site visitors. However, the use of audio, and to a lesser extent video, is increasing steadily, particularly within office environments, where bandwidth tends to be more available. When considering using multimedia, keep the following in mind:

- Never use it as a gimmick. Always make sure it has a clearly defined function that makes it easier for visitors to find and understand information.
- Keep multimedia files as small as possible so that they download quickly.
- Always offer an HTML alternative to multimedia that will deliver the information using text and simple images.

FAQs

Why isn't there more multimedia on the Web?

Many reasons: bandwidth, screen size and resolution, slow computers, the need for special software to view certain multimedia, and the inability of certain browsers to view multimedia. It is only now that people can have the same quality of experience from computer-based multimedia that they currently experience on their TVs. The Web is fundamentally an information-delivery medium. Where multimedia can deliver higher-quality information than text and/or simple images reasonably quickly, it has a real purpose. On a low-bandwidth Web, however, this is difficult.

Isn't broadband now widely available?

People have been saying this since 1995, but it is only now that broadband is beginning to give substantial numbers of Internet users sufficient bandwidth to deal with multimedia over the Web. Although broadband represents a major improvement over dial-up, there is still some way to go before downloading a full-motion video over the Internet will be commonplace. Although there are many more broadband users than there were five years ago, there is still a large group of users using dial-up connections or mobile networks. According to Nielsen's research in March 2005, 43% of U.S.Internet users still connect to the Internet at dial-up speeds.

Why are plug-ins required to experience most multimedia?

Web browsers are not designed to view most multimedia, so extra software, a plug-in, is required. The benefit of the multimedia experience has to be substantial before someone will make the effort to download a plug-in in order to view it.

What is streaming technology?

With streaming technology, you download just enough of the multimedia file to start viewing or listening to it, then the rest of the file is downloaded in the background, reducing, but not eliminating, download time. Streaming can be interrupted if there are bandwidth or server issues.

MAKING IT HAPPEN

Size Really Does Matter

If multimedia on the Web is complex, few people will be able or willing to make use of it. Smaller, but more limited, multimedia is accessible to more people. It depends on your target market: if you know they have the hardware, software, and bandwidth, and that they really want intricate multimedia, then give them exactly that. If, on the other hand, they have an average computer with average bandwidth, and simply need to find information quickly, be careful with multimedia.

Creating Animations with Animated GIFs

GIF (Graphics Interchange Format) is a straightforward method of animating a graphic on a Web site. Its major advantage is that it does not require a plug-in to view, so almost any browser can display it. It is ideal for animating small, simple icons and basic images, and for banner advertisements.

Creating Animations with Dynamic HTML (DHTML)

Dynamic HTML does not require a plug-in to view and, if properly designed, can be viewed by most browsers. However, the significant differences between the Microsoft and Netscape browsers mean that developing Dynamic HTML that will work perfectly across both browser platforms and multiple versions can be a complex task. Like animated GIFs, it is a relatively limited animation tool that often doesn't work well.

Creating Animations with Macromedia Flash

Despite the fact that it requires a plug-in, Macromedia Flash has become the most popular Web animation format. The majority of Web users have the Flash plug-in, but your design depends on the version they have.

Flash is flexible and easy to learn, but requires skill to master. It has a wide variety of built-in animation features that will achieve a basic result quickly. For Web animation, Flash is a powerful tool. It uses streaming technology, so you can view the animation more quickly. It uses vector instead of bitmap graphics: smaller file size and more scalable, although vector graphics do not handle photographs well. It also allows sound to be added to an animation effectively.

Creating Sound for the Web

Full CD-grade sound results in a very large file, so sound must be compressed for delivery over the Web and then decompressed for listening. MP3 is a popular format that has emerged for doing this, achieving high-quality results. There are numerous software packages available

625

ACTIONLIST

for preparing audio for the Web, but the best way to get good quality is to record the audio properly in the first place. The leading audio plug-in is RealAudio. Apple QuickTime and Microsoft Media Player are also popular.

Be careful about sound. Never add it gratuitously to your Web site, but only if it adds real value, for example, an important figure making a speech. (Make sure you provide a text transcript of the speech.) Always give the visitor the ability to stop the audio file.

Creating Video for the Web

Video is very bandwidth-intensive and should be used only when there is a specific need. Basic software-editing packages are available at reasonable costs, but doing the job properly requires very expensive software and equipment. The frame rate that is used for delivering video on the Web is far lower than for television images, sometimes causing a jumpy and distorted picture. To avoid this, reduce movement as much as possible, and avoid zooming or panning.

Create Shortcuts around or Alternatives to the Multimedia Offering

Avoid multimedia intros, but if you must have them, always make sure that there is an obvious link that allows visitors to stop the multimedia and move on to find the information they need.

Many people have little interest in multimedia presentation: they are looking for information, and want to find it as quickly as possible. If a multimedia file contains important information, try to provide it also in an HTML text and simple image format. For example, publish a text transcript of an important interview.

Watch Out for Accessibility Issues

Ensure that your multimedia meets minimum accessibility standards; provide an accessible alternative where appropriate. Multimedia can be a support or a hindrance for people with disabilities: for example, audio files can help people with visual problems. However, when text is created as an image, text readers (which turn text into audio) will not work.

Test with a Variety of Browsers and Computers

The advantage of HTML is its simplicity and open standards. However, even HTML needs to be carefully checked to make sure that it works properly on different browser platforms. Multimedia makes the situation more complex, as many problems can arise between browser platforms and browser versions. Careful checking is essential.

The type of computers also affects the multimedia experience. An old computer with a slow processor can make things happen very slowly. However, newer computers with very fast processors can sometimes have the reverse problem: the animation, for example, plays too quickly.

Inform the Visitor in Advance

When people click on a Web link, they expect to go to an HTML page. If this is not the case, tell them so in advance. If the link is an audio or video file, state this clearly. State the size of the file they need to download and the type of plug-in required, and provide a link to the plug-in, in case they wish to install it.

COMMON MISTAKES

Pushing Boundaries Is Pushing Your Luck

Business is not about pushing boundaries but about making profit. Too many designers focus on creating exciting multimedia that many people are unable or unwilling to view.

Placing Text as an Image

As a rule, text in images should only be used for buttons and certain navigation links. One of the most common mistakes is to place substantial quantities of text as an image. The most readable text is black on a white background, and HTML is more than adequate to achieve this. Text in an image adds unnecessarily to download times, it cannot be searched, and it creates accessibility problems. The only text you should place as an image is, at most, a heading—and even that is not advisable.

Reading While an Animation Plays

Some Web sites seem to be designed to annoy people and distract them from the text they want to read. If there is a quantity of text to be read, avoid animation altogether, or have something animate a couple of times and then stop.

Scrolling Text

Scrolling text looks impressive but is often a gimmick. If you must scroll your text, make sure it moves at a suitable speed for reading.

FOR MORE INFORMATION

Web sites:
Webmonkey: **www.hotwired.lycos.com/webmonkey**
Builder.com: **http://builder.com.com**

See also:

Managing a Web Site

GETTING STARTED

A Web site has to be managed on a day-to-day basis. The work that needs to be done will depend on the size of the Web site and the amount of new content published. However, even small Web sites should be checked briefly each day to ensure that everything is in order. Keep the following in mind:

- Web sites are communication vehicles and should be run primarily by people who understand content.
- Security is a growing concern on the Internet; every site should have a comprehensive security policy.
- Outsourcing can work well for Web site operations, but must be approached with care.
- Visitor feedback should always be encouraged as it will help attune the Web site to visitors' needs.

FAQs

Why should an editor be in charge of the Web site?

Editors understand content, and content drives Web sites. Web site success does not depend on technical issues, important as they are. The ability to find the right content quickly is what makes a Web site work for a visitor. To achieve this, someone is needed who truly understands what the organization does and can consistently publish content on these activities.

Are Web sites a security risk?

Yes. Web sites can open a door into your computer system and require stringent security procedures that are actively policed. Hackers are an increasing threat on the Internet, and if your Web site is not properly secured, the consequences can be very serious.

Why is visitor feedback so important in Web site management?

Web site logs will give some indication of visitor behavior, but it is essential to encourage feedback. In this way, you can find out where visitors are having problems and what improvements they would like to see. A Web site should always be evolving, always seeking to make its processes and structures more customer-friendly.

Isn't outsourcing risky?

Web hosting is a solid and relatively mature business, with many excellent providers of hosting services, but more care is needed when considering outsourcing other Web and Internet functions. Make sure that you are dealing with a stable, well-funded outsource vendor, that you have a comprehensive contract with them, and that they offer quality service and support.

MAKING IT HAPPEN

Hosting Your Web Site

Hosting your Web site means putting it on the Internet so that people can visit it. There are two basic options: internal or external hosting. Internal hosting is often the option when dealing with an intranet, because most of the access to the intranet will be from within the organization. However, you must ensure that there is sufficient bandwidth so that staff working from home, or from hotel rooms, will be able to download pages quickly.

For most public Web sites, it makes sense to use a third-party hosting company. Such companies have mastered the complexities of Web site hosting and can offer excellent, good-value service. When choosing such a hosting company, consider the following:

- Do I need a domain name?
- How many visitors do I expect each month?
- How much space and what access speeds will I need?
- Will I need e-commerce facilities?
- Will I need special programming facilities such as CGI scripts?
- How do I want to deal with e-mail?
- What sort of support is offered?
- What are the price and payment options?

Outsourcing Your Web Site Operations

Hosting externally is a first step in outsourcing your Web site operations. Running a large Web site is a complex technical operation; the key advantage of outsourcing is that it allows you to focus on your core business, while giving you flexibility and removing the need to recruit your own technical staff. Keep the following in mind:

- Web site operation outsourcing is still a new industry with a high failure rate. Choose a company that is solid and well financed.
- It is important to develop a proper outsourcing strategy. This is a serious activity that can have serious consequences if done wrong.
- It takes time to choose the right vendor.
- A comprehensive contract must be in place. Assume that if something is not in the contract, it won't be done.
- Proper metrics as well as a plan for day-to-day management of the outsourcing relationship must be in place.
- Your outsourcer must have appropriate security practices.
- Your outsourcer must have a good track record in providing quality service and support.
- Outsourcing is not a technology strategy, so you will still need experienced technical staff to plan your future technology strategy.

Day-to-day Maintenance of a Web Site

Web sites are constantly evolving and therefore require continual maintenance. The level of maintenance will depend on the size of the Web site and on which, if any, of the Web site's operations have been outsourced. To maintain a Web site professionally:

- the performance of the Web site must be constantly monitored. The home page and other major pages should be checked daily, as should Web site logs, in order to spot any technical problems;
- new content must be published regularly and old content removed. A Web site with out-of-date content makes a very bad impression;

"Procrastination is the art of keeping up with yesterday." — Don Marquis

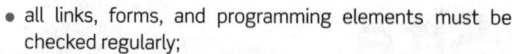

- all links, forms, and programming elements must be checked regularly;
- standards established in the design of the Web site must be monitored, including navigation, search, layout, and graphic design;
- procedures should be in place to ensure regular feedback from visitors. Ideally, usability testing should be carried out regularly;
- Web site accessibility must be monitored;
- Web site security must be policed.

Managing Internet Security

The Internet is a network, and networks are, by definition, open. When approaching Internet security, keep in mind that if you don't have a defined and actively policed Internet security policy, you don't have Internet security. You should also do the following:

- Be ever-vigilant. There is no such thing as the perfect Internet security system. The security threat is constantly changing, so you must monitor the situation constantly.
- Combine software capabilities and human expertise. The best security software in the world still needs human experience and skills, particularly for larger systems.
- Secure internally as well as externally. Many security threats come from inside the organization.
- Keep it simple. Less software and fewer options mean less opportunity for a hacker to find a weakness.

Dealing Effectively with Computer Viruses

Computer viruses are a constant and growing threat on the Internet, costing organizations billions of dollars every year. Every day they become more sophisticated and replicate more quickly. It is now possible to get a computer virus by visiting a Web site or opening an e-mail—previously, you had to open the e-mail attachment. The best approach to computer viruses is that prevention is far, far better than cure. To combat computer viruses:

- install the very latest antivirus software and keep it up to date;
- scan your entire computer system regularly with your antivirus software;
- get the latest software security patches for your computer; if you don't have them, your antivirus software may well not protect you;
- join an e-mail newsletter to get news on new antivirus and software upgrades;
- immediately delete suspicious e-mails;
- don't download anything from the Internet except from highly reputable Web sites;
- back up your data regularly;
- be vigilant.

Managing E-mail Professionally

Not treating e-mail seriously has two main results. First, so much e-mail is generated that its value as an effective communications tool is diminished. Second, many organizations are very lax in responding to e-mail inquiries from their Web sites or elsewhere. Not responding to an e-mail quickly is like leaving a phone unanswered. When managing e-mail, have policies and training in place to ensure that e-mail is used effectively, and implement a policy for responding to e-mails, particularly those received from the Web site.

COMMON MISTAKES
Out-of-date Content

A Web site that has not been updated with fresh content, and/or that contains content that is no longer relevant, makes the organization look unprofessional.

Broken Links and Other Features

Many Web sites do not have procedures in place to check all the parts of the Web site to see if they are functioning properly. Broken links are common on the Web.

Poor Security Procedures

Many organizations do not realize how serious a security threat a Web site can be. Security has, in general, been poor on the Internet; the results of this are seen in the speed with which computer viruses can spread, and the frequency of Web site break-ins.

Not Responding to E-mails

Studies indicate that organizations perform poorly in their responses to people who have contacted them through the Web site. This gives a very poor impression to actual or potential customers.

FOR MORE INFORMATION

Web sites:
Google Web site Management Links:
www.directory.google.com/Top/Computers
Builder.com: **www.builder.com**

See also:
✔ Building a Web Site Team (pp. 623–624)
✔ Coping with Computer Viruses (p. 630)
✔ Creating a Basic Web Site (pp. 621–622)
✔ Hosting or Selecting a Hosting Company (pp. 635–636)
✔ Maintaining a Web Site (p. 629)
✔ Making Your Web Site Secure (pp. 631–632)
☆ New Yardsticks for Performance and Productivity in an E-world (pp. 366–367)

"The only thing experience teaches us is that experience teaches us nothing."

André Maurois

Maintaining a Web Site

GETTING STARTED

The amount of Web site maintenance you will need will depend very much on the size of your Web site and the amount of new content that is being published on it. Web sites are not like brochures or other print material: they change, sometimes because of an action you have taken, and sometimes because of external factors. They must therefore be monitored constantly. Keep the following in mind:

- The performance of the Web site must be monitored.
- New content must be published regularly, and old content removed.
- All links, forms, and programming elements must be checked regularly.
- Standards established in the design of the Web site must be monitored.
- Procedures should be in place to ensure that regular feedback is obtained from visitors.
- Web site security must be policed.

MAKING IT HAPPEN
Test the Web Site from Different Environments

A Web site should be checked at least once a day to ensure that everything is working properly. It should also be regularly tested from different computers, browsers, and bandwidth access points, at different times of the day. Web pages may download quickly in the office environment over a fast connection, but how quickly are they downloading at home or in a hotel room? If pages are slow it may be time to seek more bandwidth.

Managing Your Content

A Web site that doesn't regularly incorporate new content gives a very poor impression to visitors. Content must be created, edited, and published professionally on the Web site. Old content, or content that is found to be libelous or otherwise incorrect, must be removed quickly. The publication schedule for the Web site must be adhered to.

Optimize Graphics

New graphics should be checked for size. The objective is to have the graphic looking as good as possible, at the same time keeping it to the minimum possible file size. You must also make sure that the actual graphic size is being kept within agreed standards.

Check Web Page Download Sizes

It's important to establish a range for the total file size of a page, including all graphics. 35Kbytes to 70Kbytes should do it, with the objective of staying well below 70Kbytes, particularly for the home page. Although broadband connections are now more widely available, many customers will still have dial-up connections. Even broadband users appreciate as fast a download as possible.

Keep a Web Site Accessible

It is important that your Web site is accessible to people with disabilities. Minimum accessibility standards are increasingly required by law. Check it regularly to ensure that it is accessible.

Check Links, Forms, and Programming Elements

Web site links, forms, and programming elements break, so it is important to check them regularly. Links may break because the page that you have linked to has changed or been removed. A wide selection of software that will check broken links is available. The page link may stay the same but the content that you originally linked to changes, so check key links manually.

Forms should be checked on a monthly basis. Put your e-mail address and dummy data into the form, and test that everything works properly. Programming also should be checked.

Manage Web Site Logs

Web site logs are important for tracking visitor behavior on the Web site. However, they can also provide very useful technical information. Check whether:

- any page errors occur that might indicate technical problems or broken links;
- any spikes in visitor behavior may be causing bandwidth shortages.

Web Site Architecture and Management

A set of standards should be established with regard to the navigation, search, layout, and design of the Web site. It is important to monitor these standards to make sure that they are being implemented properly.

Usability and Feedback

Visitor feedback is critical in ensuring that a Web site continues to evolve to meet the needs of customers and other visitors. One of the best feedback methods is to get a small group of customers in a room and observe how they use the Web site.

Make Security a Priority

Computer security is an increasingly critical issue for Web sites. An Internet security policy should be in place, and it should be adhered to strictly.

FOR MORE INFORMATION

Book:
Nielsen, Jakob. *Ensuring Web Usability: Understanding What Users Want.* Indianapolis, IN: New Riders, 2006.

See also:

"I make no secret of the fact that I would rather lie on a sofa than sweep beneath it. But you have to be efficient if you're going to be lazy."

Shirley Conran

Coping with Computer Viruses

630

ACTIONLIST

GETTING STARTED

Computer viruses are a growing threat on the Internet, and if your business operates online they are something you need to bear in mind as they cost companies billions of pounds globally every year. This is genuinely a massive global problem: in January 2005, it was estimated that 15% of all e-mails sent were virus messages. In addition, it is now possible to get a computer virus by visiting a Web site or simply by opening an e-mail. To combat computer viruses:

- ensure that you have the very latest antivirus software and that you scan your entire computer regularly;
- ensure that you have the very latest software security patches for your computer;
- immediately delete e-mails that you are in any way suspicious of;
- don't download anything from the Internet except from reputable Web sites;
- back up your data regularly.

MAKING IT HAPPEN
Understand Computer Viruses, Trojan Horses, and Worms

In its simplest form, a computer virus attaches itself to computer files, and then seeks to replicate itself. Viruses can infect all sorts of files, from program and system files to Word documents and HTML files. The Internet enables viruses to spread with extraordinary speed.

What is known as a "Trojan horse" pretends to serve a useful function, such as a screen saver. However, as soon as it is run, it carries out its true purpose, which can be anything from using the computer as a host to infect other computers, to wiping the entire hard disk of the computer. Never download software over the Internet unless you are sure of its authenticity.

A computer worm does not try to damage the files it infects. Its objective is rather to replicate itself as quickly and as often as possible. Computer worms are a major drain on the Internet because they clog up bandwidth.

Remember That Prevention Is Much Better Than Cure

Viruses can be extremely difficult to get rid of. You may think you have cleaned them out with your antivirus software, but they may well have inserted hidden code in your operating system that is almost impossible to detect. It is, therefore, essential to stop viruses from getting into your computer in the first place. You do this by:

- making sure that you have the very latest antivirus software; popular antivirus software types include McAfee and Norton;
- joining an e-mail list that will inform you of new virus attacks. As soon as you hear of them, check your vendor for the latest updates;
- scanning your entire computer for viruses at least once a week;

- always making sure that you have the very latest security patches for your computer software. Viruses are always at their most potent in the first hours and days after their release, so it is vital to implement software patches as soon as they become available;
- if you use recent releases of Microsoft Windows, regularly checking **www.microsoft.com/security** for news and updates. Microsoft also has a service that will check your computer for security weaknesses. It can be found at: **www.microsoft.com/technet/security/default.mspx**;
- only downloading software from reputable Web sites;
- deleting e-mails you are in any way suspicious of.

Act Immediately If You Become Infected

Deal with the threat immediately. Never wait, as the longer the virus is on your computer the more files it can infect. Some viruses open up your computer system to potential hacking. There is no guaranteed way to know that your system does not contain some malicious code that will be used at a future date, even when the offending virus has been deleted. If a virus of this type has indeed infected your system, and if you want to be absolutely safe, reformat your hard disk and reinstall all your software again.

Cope with Virus Hoaxes

The Internet is full of virus hoaxes that waste time. If you get an e-mail about a new virus, go to the Web site of your antivirus software provider, and check if the warning is real. In order to judge whether it's a hoax, ask yourself the following questions:

- Does the message come from a reputable source?
- Does it ask you to e-mail it on to anyone you know? If it does, it's probably a hoax.
- Does it have a reputable link for more information?

Whatever you do, don't start forwarding on e-mails about viruses before you've found out whether they're real or not. In most cases, e-mails of this type are hoaxes, but you're likely to cause panic among your regular correspondents, especially those who aren't particularly experienced with the online world.

FOR MORE INFORMATION

Web sites:
McAfee Antivirus Software: **www.mcafee.com**
Norton Antivirus Software: **www.norton.com**

See also:

"If you see a bandwagon, it's too late."

James Goldsmith

Making Your Web Site Secure

GETTING STARTED

Internet security is a critically important issue. The Internet is, by definition, a network; networks are open, and are thus vulnerable to attack. A poor Internet security policy can result in a substantial loss of productivity and a drop in consumer confidence. When developing such a security policy, keep the following in mind:

- be continuously vigilant: the perfect Internet security system will be out of date the next day
- combine software and human expertise: security software can only do so much; it must be combined with human expertise and experience
- secure internally as well as externally; many security breaches come from inside the business

FAQs

What are examples of best practice in Internet security?

Consider the following as best practice:

- have an Internet security policy;
- if your system has been compromised, seek immediate independent expert help;
- for complete safety after an attack, the best course of action is to reformat the hard disk;
- strip your computer system down to its bare essentials. The more features, options, and software your system has, the more open it is to attack. This is particularly true for Internet-related software and functions;
- for personal computers, be very careful about always-on connections provided by many broadband suppliers. An always-on connection to the Internet is always open to probing and attack by a hacker;
- do not download software from the Internet unless you are totally confident that it is from a reputable source.

Are cookies a security threat?

Cookies collect information on how you browse the Web, and are a relatively low security risk. However, cookies can encourage lazy security practices, since they remember user-names and passwords.

Can you get a virus by opening an e-mail?

Yes. It used to be impossible to be infected by a computer virus transmitted by e-mail unless you opened the e-mail attachment. However, more recent viruses such as Nimda simply required the opening of the e-mail itself. Be very careful about unexpected e-mails from unfamiliar sources. If in doubt, delete without opening.

MAKING IT HAPPEN
Develop an Internet Security Policy

Keep the following in mind when developing your Internet security policy:

- many security breaches are internal. The fewer people with access to the inner workings of the system, therefore, the better. Those who are allowed access must be recorded and given specific access rights. Immediately delete revoked and inactive users, or users who have left the business;
- put in place a rigorous procedure for granting and revoking rights of access;
- streamline hardware and software: a complex system is more open to attack. In your server software, for example, strip away as many of the optional features as possible;
- have a password policy. Do not allow simple or obvious passwords. Make sure passwords are changed regularly;
- have procedures for data backup and disaster recovery;
- have procedures for responding to security breaches;
- be vigilant. The Internet security threat is constantly changing, and constant vigilance is the best security;
- have your security policy audited by an external professional organization, and have them on call should a major breach occur.

Consider the Benefits of Firewalls

A firewall is software that polices the space between your computer system and the outside world. The design and management of firewalls has become more complex since the advent of the Web because of the vast increase in activity between computers and the Internet. If the firewall is too stringent, it slows everything down and prevents people from carrying out certain legitimate activities; if it is too lax, however, it opens the computer up to attack.

Deal with Viruses

Computer viruses are becoming more sophisticated and widespread. In January 2005, it was estimated that e-mails containing viruses amounted to 15% of all messages sent. Quite clearly, then, it's essential to have antivirus software and to keep it up to date. It is equally vital to upgrade your computer with the latest software security patches. For Microsoft software, more information on such patches is available at **www.microsoft.com/security**.

Deal with Hackers

A hacker's main objective is to gain unauthorized access to another computer. This is done by probing for vulnerabilities on the computer, perhaps the result of flaws in the computer software and/or poor security procedures. The Web is more open than a stand-alone computer, so many hackers now focus on web-based applications. Many of these applications are still relatively new and have not developed robust security measures. Security breaches can range from the hacker changing the pricing in a shopping cart to the theft of credit card numbers. The only way to deal with hackers is to implement rigorous security procedures and to monitor activity on the network constantly.

React Rapidly to a Security Breach

After a security breach there are two basic objectives. First, find out what happened so that you can stop it from happening again. Second, find out who did it so that you

"To be practical, any plan must take account of the enemy's power to frustrate it."

Karl von Clausewitz

can prosecute or otherwise deal with them. It is very difficult to prosecute a security breach without hard evidence, and very easy to contaminate or destroy such evidence. In dealing with security breaches, make sure that:

- you get professional advice, particularly if it is the first time your security has been breached;
- you protect all log information tracking activity on the system;
- the information collected is technically accurate;
- information is collected from various sources to develop an overall picture of what happened;
- no information is tampered with or modified.

In monitoring for security breaches:

- check access and error log files for suspicious activity;
- be alert for unusual system commands;
- be alert for repeated attempts to enter a password.

Guard against Denial of Service Attacks

Denial of service attacks do not seek to break into a computer system, but rather to crash a Web site by deluging it with phony traffic. They are difficult to defend against, and have been directed at some of the best-known Web sites, such as CNN and eBay. Firewalls can be designed to block repeated traffic from a particular source.

Insure you have a Secure Web Server

A Web server is potentially an open door into your network: if someone can break into your server, they are closer to breaking into your entire computer system. Before you set up a Web server you must ensure that you understand and deal effectively with the various security issues. By definition, Web servers interface with the World Wide Web and its potential hazards. They are large, complex software programs that embrace open architecture and that have often been developed at great speed.

From an e-commerce perspective, a secure server is a prerequisite. A secure server uses encryption when transferring or receiving data from the Web. Without a secure server, credit card information, for example, could be easily targeted by a hacker. A secure server will encrypt this information, turning it into special code that will then be decrypted only when it is safely within the server environment.

Equally important is what happens to the confidential information once it has reached the server environment. Once the information has been acted on, it should be stored in encrypted form. In the case of sensitive information, such as credit card details, it should be deleted.

Restrict Access to Your Web Site

You can restrict access to part or all of your Web site in a number of ways. The most common is by implementing a user-name and password system. However, you can also restrict access by IP (Internet) address, so that only people connecting from a certain address or domain can access information. Perhaps the most powerful approach is to use public key cryptography, whereby only the person with the assigned cryptography key can request and read the information.

Consider the Security Implications of Outsourcing

Outsourcing creates an increased security risk. You must establish that the outsource vendor will adhere to your security policy, and that all work done adheres to proper security procedures. Specific questions that you need to ask your outsourcing vendor include:

- What is its security policy?
- What are its data backup and disaster-recovery procedures?
- How is your data safeguarded from that of other customers?
- How is your data safeguarded from the vendor's own employees?
- How is it insured with regard to security breaches?

COMMON MISTAKES
Not Being Eternally Vigilant

There is no such thing as a perfect security system. Without constant vigilance, computer systems become an open invitation for hackers and viruses. An essential part of such vigilance is having the very latest security patches and antivirus software installed.

Thinking That You Won't Get a Virus

Viruses are becoming increasingly common. If you haven't had one so far, either you are tremendously lucky or you have excellent antivirus procedures.

Thinking That You Are Anonymous on the Internet

In general, you are not. When you visit a Web site, you will provide some or all of the following information:

- IP address
- time of access
- user-name (if a user-name and password are used)
- the URL requested
- the URL you were at just before you visited the Web site
- the amount of data you downloaded
- the browser and operating system you are using
- your e-mail address

FOR MORE INFORMATION

Web site:
CERT Internet Security Center: **www.cert.org**

See also:

Outsourcing Your Web Site

GETTING STARTED

As your business grows, you may need to upgrade your Web site to a larger and more sophisticated one. Running a large Web site is a complex operation that requires substantial IT architecture and support. This can take the focus of your business away from its core business of selling, marketing, and supporting your products and services. It will also tie up any technical staff on your team. Outsourcing involves hiring third party professionals to manage and run your Web site's operations for an ongoing fee.

When approaching outsourcing, remember to:
- develop a proper strategy: outsourcing needs a serious approach;
- ensure that a comprehensive contract is in place, and that there are proper metrics and management structures;
- make sure that you choose a robust, well-funded outsourcing vendor with a good track record for service and support.

FAQs
What are the key factors that drive outsourcing?
- The need to focus on core business activities rather than on building up a large IT function.
- Lack of sufficiently skilled staff to run complex Web operations.
- Flexibility: a quality outsource vendor can respond more quickly to rapid changes in customer demand.

MAKING IT HAPPEN
Develop an Outsourcing Strategy
When considering the outsourcing of Web functions, think about exactly why you want to outsource. Is it:

Do you want to outsource:
- to reduce costs?
- to give greater flexibility?
- because you can't find the right IT skills?
- to guarantee a more reliable service?
- to focus better on your core business?
- to keep your IT department as small as possible?
- to reduce staffing levels?

You should have a clear strategy of your vision and objectives long before you start discussions with vendors.

Be Prepared
Deciding on an outsourcer is a complex and time-consuming process, so you must think very carefully about what you want to achieve and why. When developing your strategy, it is best not to be too open with outsourcing vendors. They will naturally want to sell you what they have, and may try to shape your thinking in a way that is not appropriate. It is better initially to go to a quality independent consultant who will help you think through all the issues.

When you finally engage with your shortlist of outsourcing vendors, they will have many detailed questions

on how your operations are currently run. If you cannot answer these questions you will slow the whole process down, and will encourage the vendor to put forward a less fully and clearly defined contract than if it had had all the required information.

Choose a Stable, Well-funded Outsourcer
Choose a company that has a good reputation, is well funded, and has a good track record. When choosing an outsourcing partner, ask the following questions:
- How stable and well funded is it?
- Does it have a satisfied customer base?
- Has it successfully dealt before with the same needs as mine?

Make Certain That You Receive the Right Service and Support
The more you outsource, the more dependent you become on your outsourcer, so it is vital that your chosen vendor delivers comprehensive service and support.

Remember That Choosing an Outsourcing Vendor Takes Time
Outsourcing is a major strategic move involving much research and negotiation, so do not impose tight deadlines on yourself.

Ensure That a Comprehensive Contract Is in Place
An outsourcing contract should be precise, and should describe exactly what is to be delivered. It should state penalties for non-delivery. Legal expertise should be brought in early in the process, ideally when the RFP is being developed, so that everyone understands the legal implications of everything that is being asked for and promised. However, the IT environment is constantly changing, and the contract must recognize this. Quality contracts are designed to facilitate later change and re-negotiation.

Avoid long-term contracts. Vendors will argue that, because they have to bear a high up-front cost, you should sign a five to ten year contract with them. This does not make sense in a rapidly changing IT and e-commerce world; a two-year contract is a more reasonable option.

Determine How This Relationship Will Be Managed and Measured
You must develop a set of metrics to measure how the outsourcer is meeting the objectives set by the contract. By doing this regularly, and addressing issues as they arise, major disputes can be avoided.

Outsourcing is as much about managing the day-to-day relationship between you and the outsource vendor as it is about managing the technology. While a contract is important, prevention, by management that keeps a regular track of what is expected and what has been delivered, is better than cure.

"The way we use the Internet to fight the giants is an afterthought, to be honest."

Stelios Haji-Ioannou

634

ACTIONLIST

Have a Corporate Technology Strategy

You are outsourcing your technology, not your technology strategy, and will always need skilled in-house resources to help you plan your direction from a technological point of view. Your outsourcer cannot do this; if they do, their recommendations will reflect their own strategy rather than yours.

Remember That Outsourcing Is Outsourcing

You can't have the same level of control over the day-to-day running of your IT infrastructure after you outsource it, but some businesses forget that and try to achieve such control. This is counterproductive. You chose your outsourcer because—you hope—they do the job better and more efficiently than you do.

Consider the Security Issues

Outsourcing creates an increased security risk. You must establish that the outsource vendor will adhere to your security policy, and that all work done integrates proper security procedures. Ask yourself:

- What is the outsourcer's security policy?
- What are its data backup and disaster recovery procedures?
- How is your data safeguarded from its other customers?
- How is your data safeguarded from its own employees?
- How is it insured in relation to security breaches?

COMMON MISTAKES
Outsource Vendors Who Promise Too Much

Outsource vendors have been known to over-promise and under-deliver.

Getting Rid Entirely of the Internal IT Web Operation

Some internal IT resource is necessary to take a more strategic view of the Web operation in order to plan its future evolution.

Going for the Lowest Price

Going for the lowest price rarely works out well in the long term. Service and support are critical elements in outsourcing, and the outsourcer that offers the lowest price is also, generally speaking, the one who will offer the least support.

Not Being Able to Deliver the Right Information

To deliver an outsourcing service, the vendor requires very detailed information on your current IT and Web setup. If you can't provide this information, you slow the whole process down, which results in imperfect solutions.

Badly Framed Contracts

Long-term contracts are too often developed on the basis of short-term financial goals, such as cost cutting. What invariably happens is that the contract is unsuitable and renegotiation is required.

FOR MORE INFORMATION

Web sites:
Outsourcing Center: **www.outsourcing-center.com**
Firmbuilder.com: **www.firmbuilder.com/home.asp**

See also:
- Computers, Information Technology, and E-commerce (pp. 1705–1707)
- Facilities Management (pp. 214–215)
- Hosting or Selecting a Hosting Company (pp. 635–636)
- Outsourcing (p. 1851)

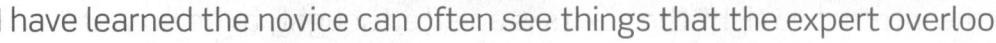

"I have learned the novice can often see things that the expert overlooks."   Tom Peters

Hosting or Selecting a Hosting Company

GETTING STARTED

Hosting your Web site means placing it on the Internet network so that it is available to people who want to visit it. There are two basic choices: internal or external hosting. Hosting a Web site internally is the general option for intranets, where visitors come only from within your organization. External hosting is the usual option for public Web sites.

FAQs

Should I host internally or externally?

External hosting has many advantages. Hosting is a complex activity, and there are many things that can go wrong. There are numerous specialist companies who are experts in the field of hosting, and are able to offer excellent service at a reasonable price because of economies of scale.

What are the key issues to consider when choosing a hosting option?

Ask yourself:

- Do I need a domain name?
- How many visitors do I expect each month?
- How much space, and what access speeds, will I require?
- Will I need e-commerce facilities?
- Will I require special programming facilities, such as CGI scripts?
- How do I want to deal with e-mail?
- What sort of support is offered?
- What are the price and payment options?

What is the most popular and cost-effective hosting approach?

Virtual (shared) hosting. For between $20 and $30 a month there are excellent hosting packages that will work well for many small and medium-sized businesses. If, however, you want to add extra functionality, such as e-commerce, the costs begin to rise.

There are so many hosting companies. How do I choose the right one?

This is not easy. If you have quality technical expertise in-house, you will be able to investigate the various options and choose the one that most closely fits your needs. If not, it is best to go with a big brand.

Key questions to ask are:

- How many customers do they have?
- How long have they been in business?
- How are they funded?
- What is their reputation for support?

MAKING IT HAPPEN
Basic Hosting Options

- Nonvirtual hosting: This is the most basic option, and is provided free by entities such as Geocities. You do not have your own domain name; instead, your address would be: www.hostingcompany.com/yourname. This sort of package is only advisable for very small businesses. A serious drawback is the lack of flexibility: you cannot change your hosting company without changing your Web address, whereas if you have your own domain name, it is yours forever (provided you pay your yearly registration fee), and you can move it wherever you want.
- Virtual hosting (sometimes known as shared hosting): You get space on a network vendor's server that is also used by other organizations. This is a popular and very suitable option for many small to medium-sized businesses. The hosting company agrees to deliver minimum access speeds and data transfer rates, and to perform basic hardware maintenance, but you are responsible for managing the content and software.
- Collocation hosting: This involves placing your own servers with a hosting vendor. You manage everything that happens on your servers: content, software, and the hardware itself. The network provider supplies an agreed access speed to the Internet and an agreed amount of data transfer over a specified period. The network provider will also generally agree to some minimum service, such as ensuring that your server is running, and rebooting should it stop for any reason.
- Managed hosting: This is where the vendor has more responsibility. It can range from the vendor supplying and managing the hardware only, to also supplying and managing the software that runs on it.

Registering a Domain Name

If you are in business you should really have your own domain name. Most of the popular domain names have already been taken, particularly those connected with the .com suffix. Keep the following in mind when choosing a domain name:

- the name should be as short and memorable as possible;
- it's good to have a.com address, but if your primary markets are outside the United States, a domain name specific to these markets should be considered, for example, .co.uk for Britain or .ca for Canada;
- to find out where to register your domain name, you should go to: **http://directory.google.com/Top/ Computers/ Internet/Domain_Names**

If you already have a domain name registered and are setting up with a hosting company, a transfer process will be required. This may take a couple of days, and if you already have a Web site up, or are using e-mail based on your domain, there may be a brief changeover period when your domain is inoperable.

Deciding on Network Speed

How quickly your Web pages download is very important. While the size of your Web pages is a major factor

---

"It is almost genetic in its nature, in that each generation will become more digital than the preceding one."

Nicholas Negroponte

here, the network speed offered by your hosting company is another important element. As a rule, the cheaper the hosting package, the slower the speed. If you know that many of your customers are in, for example, the United States, it may make sense to host there so that pages download more quickly. Another key issue is whether the hosting company has backup and redundancy features, so that if one of its machines or lines to the Internet goes down, it can ensure that service is not interrupted. Network speed depends on more than just the type of the network connection; the overall architecture of the hosting company's systems and how they are connected to the Internet is also critical.

Deciding on Disk Space

Most Web hosting options provide plenty of disk space. If you have a substantial amount of content, estimate how many pages you expect to have. Multiply that by 50K average for each page. If you have 400 pages, the disk space you require will therefore be 20 megabytes.

Deciding on the Number of Web Site Visitors Expected

This is difficult to predict. A hosting company measures this by data transfer—the amount of data downloaded from your Web site. For example, if you expect 1,000 visitors a month, and the average visitor will look at four pages, a total of 4,000 pages will be downloaded. If the average size of a page is 50K, that gives a total data transfer of 200,000K, which would be well within the range of most hosting offers.

Access to E-commerce Facilities

While basic Web hosting can be very good value, it becomes more expensive if you want to add e-commerce functionality. E-commerce requires special software and programming, so you must ensure that your hosting package supports this. If you want to accept credit card information over the Internet, you will need a merchant account and a secure server over which such credit card information can be transferred.

Special Programming Features

If you want to do anything with your Web site that involves special programming, you must make sure that your hosting package supports it. It is essential to check whether your Web site is stored on a machine that supports the UNIX or Microsoft operating systems. Before you select a hosting package discuss with your programmers or consulting company the potential programming that might be involved.

Extra Features That Must Be Considered

There are a number of features, over and above basic hosting, that must be considered when choosing a hosting package. These include the following:

- E-mail management: with your own domain you will want your own e-mail addresses, such as sales@mycompany.com. Depending on your hosting package, you may be allocated a certain number of e-mail addresses. Make sure that this allocation is sufficient.
- E-mail forwarding: Check that the hosting package offers this.
- E-mail auto-responders: if you are away from the office you may want to use an auto-response function, whereby if someone sends you an e-mail they receive an automated response informing them that you are away. Check that the hosting company offers this.
- Microsoft FrontPage: if you are using Microsoft FrontPage as the tool to create your Web site, there are hosting packages available specifically to support this.
- Web statistics: you need to access data easily so that you can use analysis software on it.

How the Hosting Will Be Paid For

Most hosting packages will require a setup fee. The payment structure can vary: some companies require payment monthly, others every 3 or 6 months, while some will ask for 12 months in advance. It is important to check the cancellation policy for any restrictive conditions.

Make Sure of Quality Support

The quality of support is critical. Occasional technical glitches will affect your site. The more you depend on your Web site, the more vital it is to get it back up quickly. If you can, find out what sort of reputation the hosting company has in this area. It is always better to pay a little more to ensure quality support.

COMMON MISTAKES
Going for the Cheapest Option

The cheapest option is rarely the best choice. It is nearly always better to spend a little more to get better infrastructure and support.

Not Planning Ahead

You may not want e-commerce today, but will you want it in six months? If so, you must make sure that the hosting package you choose can provide it or that you can easily migrate to another package with the hosting company. Changing hosting companies is a messy and time-consuming process.

FOR MORE INFORMATION

Web sites:
Business2 Web Site Hosting Guide:
www.business2.com/b2/webguide/0,17811,3713,00.html
HostReview.com: **www.hostreview.com**

Understanding the Key Principles of Content Management

GETTING STARTED

When approaching content management, keep the following in mind:

- in an information economy full of information, workers, and consumers, content management is a critical function for a modern organization;
- content management is about the organization, classification, and storage of digital content, and the publication, navigation, and search of such content;
- management processes that support the creation, editing, and publication of content.

FAQs

Why has content management become so important?

Because there is so much information in the world and so little time. Organizations are producing vast quantities of content every year, and the vast majority of this content is being produced in digital form. By 2001, it was estimated that there were over 550 billion documents on Internet, intranet, and extranet Web sites. Without professional content management it becomes almost impossible to find what you are looking for.

Why has the Web become such an important medium for the publication of content?

HTML, the layout language that is used to present content on the Web, has become the standard by which digital content is now published. The Web browser, through which HTML pages are viewed, is a simple yet powerful tool that is used by millions of people around the world every day.

What are the drawbacks of the Web?

As Steve Case, chairman of AOL Time Warner, has stated, the Web makes every enterprise a publisher. The problem is information overload. Much Web content lacks professional publishing standards. The early Web also depended on HTML for the management of content. HTML is to content management what hand-knitting is to the fabrics industry—beautiful results can be achieved for small amounts of content, but for large amounts of content it is a slow and expensive process. For large quantities of content, content management software is required.

MAKING IT HAPPEN
Develop a Core Business Case

Professional content management is an expensive process. Not all content has the same value. The organization needs to establish the business case for publishing content on its intranet or Internet Web site. A core business case will revolve around statements, such as "Getting the right content to our staff faster will make them more efficient" and "Quality content delivered to our customers will result in more sales and fewer support calls."

Carry Out a Situation Analysis

Before developing a content management strategy, it is important to understand how content is currently being managed within an organization and by the wider industry. If there is already a Web site:

- What content is being published on it?
- Is it up to date and accurate?
- Is it being read?
- What are our competitors doing on their Web sites?
- Are they being successful?
- Are there any standards emerging for content management within the industry?

Focus on Who Is Going to Read the Content

Too often, organizations think of content as a low-level commodity that merely needs to be stored. But content is a critical resource, and its value lies in being read. There is no point in having a great technical document if nobody knows it exists, a Web site full of content that nobody uses. Thus, to make content management work, you really need to understand who the readers are. Who are the people that need to get your content? Ask them what content they need. Always remember that content is consumed by busy people.

Identify the Content You Need

How much content do you need to manage? What's the "must-have" versus the "like-to-have" content?

- How many other languages does it need to be published in?
- What are the media you want to publish it in (Web, e-mail, mobile)?
- What content forms will be required (text, audio, video)?
- Will you need to deal with PowerPoint slides and Word documents? How are these going to be converted?
- What is the sensitivity of the various items of content, and what will the security approach be?

What is the sensitivity of the various items of content, and what will the security approach be? Don't get carried away. You may have 50,000 documents, but maybe only 5,000 of them are relevant to the audience you want to reach.

Develop Professional "Create," "Edit" and "Publishing" Functions

There are a number of options available in relation to creating content, including:

- commissioning content, either from internal staff or from freelance authors;
- acquiring content from third-party sources such as commercial databases;
- online community-created content, whereby content is created from, for example, discussion boards, chat forums, or mailing lists.

Editing content refers to preparing it for publication. This will involve editing for tone and style, checking for

---

638

ACTIONLIST

correct grammar, and checking for such things as libel or copyright infringement. It will involve ensuring that the correct metadata is included. Editing also involves correcting content that is already published, and reviewing published content to ensure that it is up to date.

Define the Content Management Team
Content management software can underpin the publishing processes and make them far more efficient and cost-effective, but if you want quality content you need quality people to create, edit, and publish it. Someone with editorial and communication skills should run a content management project. Another core skill required is information architecture, and other skills will include moderating expertise (if there are online communities) as well as marketing, technical, graphic design, and usability expertise.

Design the Information Architecture
Good design of metadata and classification is crucial to the success of content management. Otherwise, content will end up being piled into a database and it will be almost impossible to find the right content quickly.

When designing metadata it is worth exploring how XML might be used. XML is an emerging metadata standard which facilitates the better organization and publication of content.

Navigation is like a signpost system. It is there to help people to find their way easily and logically around a Web site. Searching is a basic activity on the Web, and its professional design will be crucial to success. Graphic design and layout should ensure that content is presented in a way that is easy to read, view, or listen to. Other information architecture design issues include: multiple language design; content conversion, (e.g. turning Microsoft Word documents into HTML); and integration with internal or external databases, subscription-based publishing design, and online community elements design.

Select the Content Management Software
If the Web site contains more than a couple of hundred pages and needs to be updated regularly, then it will make sense to acquire content management software. On the basis of the previous sections, a set of specifications can be drawn up covering the various content management processes required to achieve a professional result. These specifications will allow the organization to judge which content management software can best meet content management needs.

Define How Everything Is Going to Be Measured
A problem with content is that it is difficult to measure. However, that does not mean that measurables should not be put in place. Measures should be established with regard to how much content needs to be created each week, the quality of that content, and the time it takes to get content published. Information architecture measures include the quality of the metadata, how easy the site is to navigate, how well the search works, and how quickly pages download.

COMMON MISTAKES
Not Having a Proper Business Case
While the Internet boom was in full swing, many content management projects did not have to show a strong business case. That reality has very much changed, and without having a clear business case and return-on-investment model it is unlikely that content management projects will receive the required funding.

Believing That All You Have to Do Is Buy Some Fancy Software and Your Problem Is Solved
Content management software is vital if large quantities of content are involved, but content follows the classic "garbage in, garbage out" rule. No amount of great software will turn poor quality content into good.

Allowing Out-of-date Content to Remain on Web Sites
A key problem on the Web today is out-of-date content. Many Web sites forget to remove old content. This results in a very poor experience for the visitor.

FOR MORE INFORMATION

Book:
McGovern, Gerry, and Rob Norton. *Content Critical.* Upper Saddle River, NJ: Financial Times Prentice Hall, 2001.

Web site:
Business2.com, Web content management, an excellent selection of links to content management vendors, articles, and specialist Web sites: **www.business2.com/webguide**

Making Sure Content Is Professionally Created, Edited, and Published

GETTING STARTED

If your content is not read by the people you want to read it, then your Web site has largely failed. Good content management software can help you create, edit, and publish quality content, but you need the people and processes in place to actually perform the work. After you have identified the type of content and reader:

- establish processes that will ensure that this content is created and/or acquired;
- put editing processes in place that will ensure that the content is of the required standard;
- develop publishing processes that will allow the content to be published on time and presented in such a way that it is easy to find and easy to read.

FAQs

In editing, what is the key tradeoff?

In editing there is always a tradeoff between high-quality content and the time and expense it takes to achieve it. Publishing content to a very high standard is an expensive and time-consuming process. Such an approach becomes economically viable only if you have a large number of readers and/or can derive an appropriate return from a smaller number of readers.

A balance needs to be struck between cost and the need to have content achieve a certain minimum standard of quality.

Can software make creating, editing, and publishing content more efficient?

Absolutely. However, whether you should buy content management software really depends on the quantity of content you are publishing. If there is a lot of content to be published, using an HTML approach with basic software can lead to bottlenecks. Content management software will make this process much faster and more manageable, but there will be significant setup costs.

MAKING IT HAPPEN
Create Content Internally

When creating content internally, keep in mind the following:

- Content written with the Web in mind is far more likely to be read than content written for other sources. It may be more cost-effective to convert such content, but if nobody reads it, what good is it?
- It is necessary to consider what content creation tools are to be used. Is everyone going to standardize around a particular set of software, such as Microsoft Word?
- To ensure consistency, it is necessary to develop a style guide and glossary.

- If people are expected to create content regularly, it must be made part of their job function.
- An appropriate set of policies and procedures must be set in place for copyright and legal issues, and writers must be properly informed of the issues involved.
- A commissioning process must be established whereby editors can request that content be created.

Use Freelance Writers to Create Content

When there are gaps in the organization's ability to create content, freelance writers can be used. Remember that:

- a budget will need to be established, and authority given to the appropriate editors;
- freelance writers can plug gaps, but can become expensive if large quantities of content are involved;
- freelance writers will have the writing skills but not the in-depth knowledge of the organization.

Acquire Content Through Purchase and/or Partnership

In purchasing and/or partnering to acquire content, keep the following in mind:

- For general content, such as industry news or trends, it makes a lot of sense to purchase.
- Too much purchased content can give a generic feel to the Web site; it is important to get the balance right.
- Partnering to acquire content usually works best in a traditional publishing setting. It is not always an option for an intranet or extranet publication, in which case it is usually better to purchase content if it cannot be created internally.

Acquire Content Through Online Community Activities

Discussion boards, chat, and e-mail mailing lists can be effective ways of acquiring content for a Web site. Such online activities can help develop loyalty and a sense of community. The following should be considered:

- Online communities need nurturing and encouragement.
- Moderation is important, to see that the online community does not stray from its objectives, and that sensitive issues are properly monitored.

Establish Professional Editing Processes

Editing is about preparing content for publication. It is an essential though often neglected activity for content published on the Web. There are three editing functions that need to be considered:

- editing content awaiting publication
- reviewing content already published
- correcting published content for legal or other reasons

"The intense, intense passion for excellence and the detail mentality. They're talking my language."

Jeanne Jackson

Edit Content Awaiting Publication

Content that is awaiting publication needs to be edited for the following:

- Metadata: this ensures that the content will be organized properly on the Web site so that it can be easily found. It includes such things as classification, date of publication, keywords, and author name.
- Quality and style: is the content written well and does it properly address its subject? Are the heading and summary snappy? Does it reflect the type of message the organization wishes to communicate? Are there any potential legal issues?
- Accuracy and consistency: are the grammar, spelling, and punctuation correct?

Review Content Already Published

There are a number of ways content already published can be reviewed:

- An expiration date can be set for the content at publication so that it is removed from the Web site after that date. This is suitable for event-type content.
- Related content can be reviewed as new content is published. For example, if a product specification changes then the previously published product specification should be removed from the Web site.
- It is a good policy to have a periodic review of all content on the Web site, perhaps once a year or more often, depending on the nature of the content.

Correct Content for Legal or Factual Errors

No matter how good the editing process, there will always be content that will get through with legal or factual errors. The important thing is to act quickly once these problems are isolated, as this will reduce the likelihood of legal action. Errors may be:

- minor: a date, or the name of a person, may be wrong; these errors should be changed immediately;
- more serious: an important fact may be wrong; a note may need to be attached to the document, explaining the error and the changes made;
- actionable: if charges of libel apply, an apology may need to be published, and the document removed; act quickly and decisively in such situations.

Get Content Published

Publishing content on the Internet can occur in a number of ways:

- Automatically: as a result of the metadata, the content is automatically placed within its classification. The heading and summary may be placed on the home page for a defined period of time.
- By editorial decision: the editor may decide to write special content to promote a particular piece of content on a home page; a number of articles may be grouped together to create a feature focusing on a particular topic or product.
- By subscription-based publishing: a selection of content may be delivered regularly by e-mail or other means to subscribers.

Whatever the means, the objective is to publish content in the most attractive manner possible, so as to ensure that the maximum number of people read it.

The home page is a critical part of any Web site. Studies show that, in the majority of situations, people are not sure exactly what content they want from a Web site. A well-organized home page, with good navigation and search facilities and punchy content, can guide the visitor in the right direction. Keeping that home page updated and lively is a key activity of publishing.

COMMON MISTAKES
Not Having an Editor in Charge

At heart, content is not about technology but about people. Unfortunately, technical people tend to see content as a commodity. They don't really consider that someone somewhere may want to read it. Someone with editorial skills who truly understands the value of content, and how to create, edit, and publish it professionally should be in charge of the content management process.

No Reward for Creating Content

If content creation is not part of someone's job function, quality content will not be created, at least not on a consistent basis. Expecting people to create content and not rewarding them is a recipe for poor-quality results.

Lack of Proper Editing Processes

Too often, Web sites become a dumping ground for content. Many organizations simply do not recognize the negative impact of poorly edited content.

Poor Metadata

The right content is becoming increasingly difficult to find on the Web. This is a result of poor metadata. Content is not being classified properly; keywords are not well thought through; headings and summaries are not descriptive. Add to that the fact that the search functions on many Web sites are poor, and it all adds up to an increasingly frustrating experience for the user.

FOR MORE INFORMATION

Web site:
Clickz content management and design:
www.clickz.com/experts/design/cont_dev

See also:
- ✔ Adding Multimedia to a Web Site (pp. 625–626)
- ✔ Building a Web Site Team (pp. 623–624)
- ✔ Implementing an Effective Search Process for a Web Site (p. 645)
- ✔ Making a Web Site Easy to Navigate (pp. 643–644)
- ✔ Understanding the Key Principles of Content Management (pp. 637–638)
- ✔ Using the Internet to Create Content Collaboratively (p. 646)
- ✔ Writing Well for the Web (pp. 649–650)

"There is mathematics, there are computers, and there are pictures, but the bulk of our communicated thinking is done with language."

Edward de Bono

Developing Appropriate Metadata and Classification for a Web Site

GETTING STARTED

If you have a large Web site—more than 100 pages—metadata is essential to ensure that your content is organized properly, so that it can be found quickly. Without metadata, the Web site becomes increasingly unusable as more content is included. Metadata includes such things as classification (which deals with how content is organized by subject matter), date of publication, keywords, heading, summary, author name, and copyright. The purpose of metadata is to:

- ensure that every document is properly classified so it can be found quickly;
- ensure that all relevant legal and administrative information on a particular document has been collected;
- maximize the chances of a document being indexed appropriately by internal and external search engines.

FAQs

What happens if you don't have good metadata on a Web site?

Without proper metadata it will take longer to find the right content. In fact, if it is a large Web site, then it may be almost impossible to find what you are looking for. Time is the most valuable resource today. As information expands, time seems to be contracting. Waste your customers' time and you will lose their business.

What is XML and why is it so important?

XML (extensible markup language) is an emerging world standard for metadata. It has been described by Bill Gates, founder of Microsoft, as ushering in the third phase of the Internet, because it delivers a common approach to the use of metadata for structuring content. With XML, organizations in a particular industry can agree to structure their documents in the same way. For example, organizations in the financial industry might agree to use the same method of creating documentation such as morning notes. The morning notes (which are short analyses issued daily) would all use the same layout structure, and would all have metadata such as: author name, date, ticker symbols, buy, hold, and sell ratings. Because of this common structure, people receiving these morning notes would be able to search and interrogate them in a far more comprehensive manner.

What are examples of Web sites using quality metadata?

Perhaps the best-known example is Yahoo, which focused on creating a directory classification for the Web, instead of simply depending on search engine software. Yahoo became very popular because it had professional editors selecting and classifying Web sites for its directory. Visitors to the Yahoo Web site did not get an endless listing. Rather, they got a selection of the best Web sites under a particular classification. On the Web, that is what the majority of people want. All the best Web sites focus on quality classification and metadata; other examples are Amazon.com, eBay, and Microsoft.

MAKING IT HAPPEN

General Standards for Metadata Design

When designing metadata, you need to do the following:

- Always keep in mind the type of person that will be looking for the content. How would they like the content classified? When carrying out an advanced search, how would they like to refine their search?
- Only collect metadata that is genuinely useful. Remember, someone has to fill in all the metadata. If you ask for too much metadata, then it will slow the publishing process down and make it more expensive.
- Make sure that all essential information is collected. If copyright information is needed, then make sure that copyright is part of the metadata list.
- Tell people not to abuse metadata. Some will put popular keywords in their metadata just to increase the chances of their documents coming up in a search. However, this is counterproductive, as the document will not be relevant to the search in question.
- Remember that metadata should be strongly linked with advanced search. The metadata becomes the parameters by which advanced search is refined.

Designing Document Templates

To collect metadata, some form of document template will be required which will contain all the relevant metadata fields. Examples of templates would be "Event Template," "Technical Paper Template," and "Personnel Details Template." You will require different templates when you have different metadata to collect. Avoid having too many templates, as it can be confusing. Give templates names that describe their function. Instead of "Template A," for example, call it "Event Template."

Getting Classification Right

Classification is a particularly important form of metadata. A Web site with poor classification is difficult to navigate. Visitors will not be able to find what they are looking for and will leave frustrated.

The top-level classification of your Web site expresses, in the fewest words possible, the nature of your business. Are you selling "products," "services," or "solutions?" Do you offer solutions for "home users," for "small businesses," or for "large businesses?" If you get your classification wrong, your Web site becomes a pointless exercise.

While it is relatively easy to design a classification for 50 documents, designing a classification for 1,000 or more documents is by no means simple. However, throwing your hands up in the air and saying it can't be done is not acceptable. It must be undertaken, and professional advice must be sought where appropriate.

"Many view the Internet merely as a sales channel and treat it as an add-on without fundamentally questioning their current business system."

Alex Birch

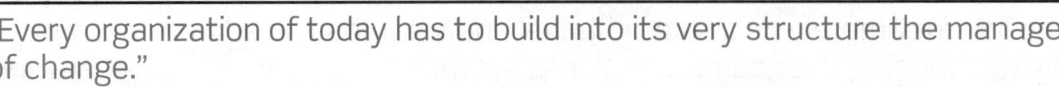
Things to Keep in Mind When Designing Classification

- Make sure that senior management is involved, particularly for the design of the top levels.
- Design from the point of view of the people who will be using the classification. Remember that classification terms that may be understood within the organization may not be nearly as clear to customers and potential customers.
- Focus on simplicity of design. Avoid using as classification terms jargon, ambiguous words, or complex terms.
- If possible, avoid going more than five levels deep for a classification design. Remember that the more levels there are, the more clicks are required to find what you are looking for. In addition, a classification with a lot of levels is prone to error in the classification process.
- As a general rule, aim for no more than 10 classifications at your top level, and certainly no more than 15. You have more flexibility at lower levels, but remember that if you have too many terms at a particular level, you risk confusing the visitor.
- Consider the number of documents you will have under any particular classification. If there are going to be more than 50 in any classification, then maybe that classification should be broken down further.
- Remember that the classification you create will be presented as navigation on the Web site. If possible, make sure that the classification terms at any one level—particularly the top level—are roughly the same length, otherwise the navigation will look awkward.
- Design the classification for the entire content environment, not simply the content you wish to publish at this time. You may have technical papers that you don't intend to publish on the Web site for another six months. However, create the classification term for them in the overall classification design.

Approaching Classification Design

When approaching the design of classification or other metadata:

- do your research. What sort of content do you have right now and in what way, if any, is it classified? How are your competitors classifying content on their Web sites? Are there any industry trends emerging? Make sure you get opinions from your customers on how they would like to navigate and search through your content;
- start at the top and design down. If you don't get the top level of the classification right, all other work is pointless. Make sure you involve senior management in the design of this level;
- mock it up and test it. Classification looks very dry and theoretical until you actually show how it will look on a Web page. It doesn't have to be a fancy design, just enough to illustrate how people might navigate through the classification. Keep changing and mocking up again until you are happy;
- get sign-off for the top level. Don't do any work on the lower levels until you have full agreement on how the top level is to be presented;
- design the lower levels. It may be that individual departments or sections will take on the job of designing the classification for the levels that relate to their areas. However, make sure that everything is coordinated so that the overall design is consistent;
- review and get final sign-off. The classification is the foundation for your Web site. It is essential, therefore, that it is properly reviewed and that the appropriate sign-off is obtained before any content is published that uses the classification. Work done in planning and designing a quality classification pays off handsomely.

COMMON MISTAKES
Regarding Metadata as a Minor Activity

If content can't be found quickly, all the work and expense put into creating it in the first place will have largely gone to waste. Metadata is critical to the success of larger Web sites because it is the foundation upon which those Web sites are built.

Designing Classification for the Organization, Not the Visitor

Many organizations already have internal classification systems. Unfortunately, these may reflect obscure organizational structures rather than something that is useful for the customer or potential customer. When designing metadata, always keep in mind who will be using it.

Designing Too Complex a System

In an ideal world, it would be great to collect as much metadata on a document as possible. However, you have to be practical. If too much metadata is requested, people are unlikely to fill it out completely. Classification design can become very complex, but if it is too complex it will confuse both the visitor who is searching for content and the person who is charged with classifying the content. Remember, if content is continually being misclassified then the whole exercise becomes fruitless.

FOR MORE INFORMATION

Web sites:
Google metadata links:
www.directory.google.com/Top/Reference/Libraries
Business2 Information Architecture Links:
www.business2.com/webguide

See also:
- Developing a Personalization Strategy for a Web Site (pp. 614–615)
- Implementing an Effective Search Process for a Web Site (p. 645)
- Making a Web Site Easy to Navigate (pp. 643–644)
- Understanding the Key Principles of Content Management (pp. 637–638)

"Every organization of today has to build into its very structure the management of change."
Peter F. Drucker

Making a Web Site Easy to Navigate

GETTING STARTED

Web navigation is like a signpost. Without it a Web site becomes just a jumble of content. Keep the following in mind when approaching navigation design:

- Navigation should provide context for content. It should show all the other content that is related to a particular category or item.
- As a rule, navigation should be simple, unadorned, and of a consistent design.
- People like to navigate through content in different ways, so a variety of navigation options should be provided.

FAQs

What is the key principle when designing navigation?

Functionality, not style. Functionality and plainness of design are what people want. What is important is the place they want to get to, not the navigation itself. Navigation should never be flashy and draw attention to itself. It should work in the background, making it easier for people to get to where they want to go.

What is the connection between navigation and classification?

Classification is how content is organized into manageable groups and subject areas. Navigation is how the classification is presented on a Web site. For a particular subject area there may be only one classification term, but it may be presented in a variety of different ways.

What is the connection between navigation and search?

There are two ways for people to find content on a Web site: one is through using search, the other is through using navigation. People often combine navigation and search: they might use search initially to narrow down their options, then use navigation to focus on the content in the subject area they wish to explore.

What would be the print media equivalent of navigation?

A publication's table of contents and index. It is unusual to find a publication without a table of contents. One of the key measures of the professionalism of a larger publication, such as a book or directory, is whether it has a good index. These navigation aids are thus seen as essential to quality publishing.

MAKING IT HAPPEN
Design for the Visitor

Navigation is about helping people to find content. Keep the visitor in mind at all times. Keep it simple, avoid being flashy, and test the navigation to see if people find it easy to use.

Give Visitors a Number of Options

Different people have different needs when navigating through content. Some may want to navigate geographically, some may have a particular subject in mind, some may want to get back to the home page as quickly as possible. A set of essential links (known as global navigation), placed near the top of the page, is always helpful. This allows the visitor to get quickly to key sections on the Web site, regardless of what particular page they are on. There are a variety of other navigation options that need to be employed, depending on the particular focus of the Web site. For example, if the Web site is e-commerce-enabled, then it will require a prominent e-commerce navigation system.

Let Visitors Know Where They Are on the Web Site

Visitors may enter a Web site in a variety of ways. It is important for each page to clearly display what part of the overall classification it represents. If it is the home page, for example, this should be made clear. If it is a page dealing with pricing information for Product Z, then a heading at the top of the page should clearly state that. Such clear and unambiguous headings help put visitors at ease.

Let Visitors Know Where They Have Been

A primary function of hypertext is to indicate to visitors the places that they have already visited on a Web site. This is why hypertext links change color from blue to purple, with purple representing a link that has been clicked on. Avoid changing hypertext colors. People are familiar with blue for unclicked and purple for clicked.

Let Visitors Know Where They Are Going

Navigation should always support visitors in getting around the Web site, pointing them toward places they want to go and away from places they would like to avoid. There are a number of basic rules here:

- When visitors click on a link, they expect to be taken to a standard HTML page. They do not expect to be asked for a password, or to watch as a video or audio file starts downloading. If a link is to a nonstandard page, visitors should be informed in advance. For example, a statement such as "Password required" could be used if that is the case.
- If an image is a link, for example, a company logo linking to a home page, text should appear with a statement such as "Company X home page" when visitors place their cursor over that image.
- When visitors are asked to perform a process, for example the purchase of something, navigation should appear that will indicate to them how many steps there are in the process, and how many steps they have completed.

Provide Context for Visitors

Studies show that only in a minority of cases do visitors know exactly the type of content they want. Visitors may be interested in buying laptop computers, but they may

not know the exact make they require. Navigation assembles all the relevant content for a particular subject area into a well-presented environment. This is where navigation and classification are very much intertwined.

Keep Navigation Consistent
Avoid creating a Web site in which the navigation is constantly changing its structure. If the essential links are placed across the top of the page in one section of the Web site, then keep them across the top of the page in every other section unless you have a very good reason to change them. Lack of navigation consistency is particularly problematic if an organization has a number of Web sites, for example in an intranet environment. Departments and sections may feel a need to be distinctive, so they often make great efforts to create a navigation system that is totally different from those used by other sections. The result of this is confusion, and an environment that becomes increasingly chaotic and difficult and expensive to manage.

Where Possible, Follow Navigation Conventions That Have Emerged on the Web
People who use the Web instinctively see it as a single medium. They like familiarity of navigation design, because what they have learned on one Web site can be carried over to another. Conventions that have emerged on the Web include:
- essential links (global navigation) that are placed on every page: these begin with a "Home" link and usually contain links to "About" and "Contact";
- the organization's logo on every page, usually in the top left, and linked back to the home page;
- a search box on every page, usually near the top;
- a footer on every page containing a copy of the essential links, contact information (address, e-mail, phone), and links to copyright and privacy statements;
- the use of standard hypertext colors: blue for unclicked, purple for clicked.

Never Surprise or Mislead Visitors
Never take visitors down paths that lead to a dead end. For example, if you don't sell to a particular country, inform people of this with a clear statement early on, not after they have ordered a quantity and filled in their address details. Some Web sites ask their visitors from other countries to call an 800 number, which is impossible to do from outside the United States. Also, not every country has ZIP codes. Give visitors an option.

Back Up Navigation with Quality Support
The Web is often compared to a library. If you visit a library, the bookshelves are the navigation system, but librarians are always available to give support if you get lost. If the Web site is a large one, have a comprehensive help section. Make sure that if visitors e-mail the organization in search of a specific piece of content, someone gets back to them quickly. A surprising number of Web sites are extremely poor at responding to visitor queries. Subject-sensitive help is particularly important where you are asking visitors to perform complex tasks. An example would be where a Web site offers advanced search. If visitors are asked to go through a process such as filling out a form, try to isolate any mistakes that are made. For example, if they didn't fill in the address, don't send them back to fill in the entire form, but rather isolate the exact mistake that they made.

COMMON MISTAKES
Constantly Changing the Navigation
It is very frustrating to go back to a Web site and find that the navigation has been changed. Regular visitors get used to the way a Web site is laid out. The more regularly they visit, the more they get used to it (and the more likely they are to be valuable customers!). It is therefore important to plan your navigation well and to stick with it unless there is a compelling reason to change.

Designing Navigation from a Visual Point of View
Too many Web sites treat navigation as some visual branding exercise, rather than as a signpost system for helping visitors to find quickly the content they need. Navigation should be simple and functional. It should be one of the first things to download on a Web page.

Designing an Inconsistent Navigation
Navigation structures that change depending on the section of the Web site you are in, purely for the sake of being different, are of absolutely no help to the visitor. If a large organization with a number of Web sites does not provide consistent navigation, visitors may give up trying to use them. Inconsistency leads to confusion and a sense of disorganization, thereby defeating the purpose of creating the Web sites in the first place.

Making Navigation Overly Complex
New techniques using HTML and Flash make is possible to create sophisticated menus with pull-downs and nested menus. Unless you have a very specific need to use this type of navigation, avoid it if at all possible. Inexperienced users will find it confusing and it is more likely to cause browser compatibility and accessibility headaches later on.

"The conduct of successful business merely consists in doings things in a very simple way, doing them regularly, and never neglecting to do them."

Lord Leverhulme

Implementing an Effective Search Process for a Web Site

GETTING STARTED

Search is one of the most common activities that people perform on a Web site. A quality search process allows people to find quickly the content they need. Getting your search working properly is thus one of the most important tasks you can undertake, particularly when you are dealing with large quantities of content. When designing a search function for your Web site:

- always make sure your search function is prominently displayed on your Web site; ideally, a search box should be available on every page;
- don't build your own; there are many vendors supplying quality search software;
- make sure your search function is effective. Despite search being such an important activity, a surprising number of Web sites do it badly. Don't be one of them.

MAKING IT HAPPEN
Types of Search

There are essentially two approaches to Web site search:

- Basic search: this is sufficient for most smaller Web sites. Any Web site with more than 50 pages of content should consider having a basic search.
- Advanced search: this is an additional option to basic search and is strongly recommended for Web sites with more than 500 pages of content.

General Standards for Search Design

The following general standards apply to search:

- The best font for search is Arial, as it is a narrow font that reads well while allowing the maximum number of characters to be entered into the smallest space.
- After entering their keywords or search term, visitors should be able to initiate a search with the touch of the return key as well as by clicking on a button marked "Search."
- All search functions create an index of the Web site. Make sure that indexing occurs regularly; otherwise recently published content will not be displayed in search returns.

Designing a Basic Search for a Web Site

Search is something people do all the time, so the basic search option should be available on every page of the Web site. Don't hide it behind a link. There are two common places where search boxes are found on Web sites today: at the top right of the Web page or near the top left of the page, directly underneath the organization logo. In a basic search:

- the search box must be sufficiently large to allow a minimum of 20 characters to be entered;
- the font should be Arial, and the font size should be 10 pt, certainly no less than 8 pt;
- there should be a button labeled "Search" at the right of the search box;
- if the Web site has an advanced search option, a text link labeled "Advanced Search" should be placed nearby.

Design an Advanced Search for a Web Site

Advanced search allows visitors to refine their search on the basis of various parameters. The larger the Web site, the more important advanced search becomes. Boolean search, a form of advanced search, allows you to search for a particular word while, for example, excluding another word. If metadata has been collected it may be possible to search by geographic region or subject area, or to search for documents by a particular author during a particular time period, and so on.

Display Search Results

Search is a very functional activity, and the search results page should not contain anything to distract the searcher; it should just give the results. A particular set of search results should include:

- the title or heading of the Web page that the search result refers to, shown in bold type and hyperlinked to that page;
- a two-line summary describing the content on that page;
- the URL for that page;
- the date of publication for that page.

Deciding on Search Software

There is a wide variety of excellent, well-priced basic search software available that is easy and quick to install. Dealing with search for larger Web sites is naturally more complex, with customization demanded where advanced search options are required. A number of companies provide hosted search engine solutions, which do not require the installation of any software on the site to be searched. This may make the implementation easier.

If you have hundreds or thousands of pages or items, then an appropriate search system may be critical to the success of your business. You should be prepared to make a significant investment of time to ensure that you find the right solution, and to tailor it to your specific needs.

FOR MORE INFORMATION

Web sites:
Search Engine Watch: **http://searchenginewatch.com**
WebSideStory:
www.websidestory.com/products/hosted-site-search/search/overview.html

See also:
- ✔ Developing Appropriate Metadata and Classification for a Web Site (pp. 641–642)
- ✔ Establishing an Enterprise Portal (p. 667)
- ✔ Making a Web Site Easy to Navigate (pp. 643–644)
- ✔ Making Sure Content Is Professionally Created, Edited, and Published (pp. 639–640)

"Original research tends to be a novel concept."

Ashok Kumar

Using the Internet to Create Content Collaboratively

GETTING STARTED

Collaborative writing has seen a steady increase since the coming of the Internet. E-mail, in particular, has been a driver of collaboration because it enables writers to communicate cheaply and regularly. When considering the collaborative creation of content, keep the following in mind:

- it is best applied to large, complex-content projects;
- quality results will not be achieved without proper planning and editorial management;
- the people involved must understand the objectives of the project clearly;
- appropriate rewards must be offered to achieve proper motivation.

MAKING IT HAPPEN
Key Benefits of Collaboration in Content Creation

The key benefits are as follows:

- In a complex, ever-changing world, very few people have all the expertise and knowledge required to publish the varied content required for an increasingly demanding readership.
- Alliances, partnerships, and collaboration are seen as key characteristics of the new economy. Publishing collaborative content is an important result of collaboration and partnership.
- Large-content projects can be published more quickly through collaboration.
- Complex issues can be addressed by a variety of experts.
- Various skills and experience can be brought together to achieve superior results. For example, one person may be an expert in the subject area, while another may be a skilled writer who can translate this expertise into a readable format.

Collaboration Works Best for Large, Complex-content Projects

Collaboration is most suitable for large and complex-content projects that require the contribution of many kinds of expertise.

Make Sure Everyone Is on the Same Page

Before starting a collaborative writing project, it is important that everyone involved is clear on what the objectives are. While it is possible for people who have never physically met to collaborate, it is highly recommended that the collaborative group get together at least once so that people know each other better.

Make sure that a common style and tone are agreed. A short document should be prepared that will clearly articulate the intended style and tone. Some sample material should be presented that will illustrate these, such as a style guide and a sample document. A glossary of common words and phrases that will be used should also be prepared. This will establish spelling conventions as well as intended meanings.

Break the Project Up into Definable Segments

Ideally, the project should be broken up into definable segments, each being allocated to a particular individual. One writer may do research for a particular area and write the first draft, while another will take that draft and add to it. Editing functions may be swapped, depending on who has written what. However, be careful about oversegmentation. Simply giving a group of people different sections to write is not collaboration.

Put an Editor in Charge

If collaboration involves only two people, they may well be able to swap editorial functions and agree by consent. Where a larger group is involved, however, there should be an editor in charge who will ensure that the end result reflects the objectives, and that the style and tone are established at the outset.

Establish Clear Reward and Remuneration Structures

In a business setting—and in most other settings—people write for two basic reasons: pay and ego. Pay should be covered because it is part of their job. Ego is about making sure that everyone involved gets the proper credit.

Make Sure Version Control Is Properly Managed

It is frustrating to find that you have been working on the wrong draft of a document. Document management software can be used here, but if this is not available, then the editor should be in charge of keeping the master draft. A useful tool for tracking changes between versions is the Track Changes facility in Microsoft Word, which can be found in the Tools menu.

FOR MORE INFORMATION

Web site:
Guidelines for collaborative writing, a short, informative article on collaborative writing:
www.uncp.edu/home/vanderhoof/syllabus/colab-rt.html

See also:

Setting Up Newsletter and Web Site Subscription Processes

GETTING STARTED

Every organization with a Web site should consider having at least one e-mail subscription service, because that will enable the organization to keep in regular touch with its target market at minimal cost. Some organizations may want to have a number of e-mail services to subscribe to, for different categories of customer.

FAQs

Why have paid-for subscriptions not become common on the Internet?

The difficulty of collecting payments and the complexity of subscription processes is certainly one issue. Another problem is that Web site visitors are likely to be uncomfortable about paying for something they know little or nothing about. Regardless of the price charged however, content must still pay for itself, either directly through subscription or advertising revenues, or indirectly by delivering valuable information that will further the organization's objectives.

When should you consider using a subscription process?

Because intranets and extranets contain confidential information, a subscription process will be required to ensure that the right people are accessing the right information. It is also likely that certain parts of the public Web site will have restricted access. A subscription process defining access rights will be required here. If you are planning a paid-for publication on the Internet, you will need a subscription process.

MAKING IT HAPPEN
Clearly Explain What the Person Is Subscribing To

Outline to potential subscribers what exactly they will get if they subscribe. If they are subscribing for access to a Web site, tell them what sort of content is available on it. If they are subscribing to an e-mail mailing service, tell them what type of content they will receive and how often it will be sent. Depending on the confidentiality of the information, it can be a good idea to offer a sample of the content, and/or a free period of access.

Have a Clear Privacy Policy

Clearly outline a privacy policy in relation to personal information that the potential subscriber is being asked to supply, and be sure to comply with the policy at all times. Privacy is a critical issue for a great many people using the Internet. If they feel a Web site might sell on or otherwise abuse the personal information they give, they will be highly unlikely to subscribe. If a Web site wishes to track a subscriber's use of the site in order to personalize content for them, it must make it clear to the subscriber that this is going to happen.

Keep the Process As Simple As Possible

People hate filling out long subscription forms on the Internet, so if you want to maximize your subscription base you must keep the subscription process as short and simple as possible. It is often enough simply to ask for an e-mail address. However, if you do need to ask a number of questions, consider the following procedures:

- Ask opinion-type questions first. People are more willing to answer opinion-type questions. Place the personal information questions after these.
- Have mandatory and optional questions. Make sure that mandatory questions are clearly flagged. At the top of the form, make a statement such as "All questions marked * must be filled out."
- Don't mandate answers to questions that some people cannot fill out. For example, not every country has a ZIP code. If you do want to mandate ZIP codes, advise those who don't have them to enter "None" in the field.

Support People Who Make Mistakes

People can make mistakes, particularly where they are asked to fill out longer forms. Don't just create a process that says "You have made a mistake." Instead, have the process isolate the error and state, for example, "You have not entered your telephone number. Please fill it in." Have the process check for obvious errors where possible. For example, if someone mistakenly adds characters at the end of their e-mail address, isolate this. Make a statement such as: "The e-mail address you entered—mary@your-company.com—seems to be incorrect. Please recheck."

Use a Double Opt-in Approach

The double opt-in subscription approach is emerging as the industry standard for subscription management. This approach ensures that someone is not maliciously subscribed to a service by a third party. It works as follows:

1. a request for subscription is sent using a Web form or e-mail process;
2. the system replies with a verification message, requesting an affirmative reply to the message;
3. only when an affirmative reply is received is that particular subscription completed.

Always Send a Confirmation Message

When someone has subscribed to a service they should be sent a confirmation message, including:

- a message welcoming them to the service;
- a description of the subscription service;
- how to unsubscribe from the service;
- the e-mail address the person subscribed with, and the username and password, if any, that were used.

Subscribers should be told to store this confirmation message carefully, so that they can access it if, for example, they wish to unsubscribe or forget their password.

648

ACTIONLIST

Make Sure That There Is a Simple and Clear Unsubscription Process

People can get very irate when they find it difficult to end their subscription (or "unsubscribe"). A variety of options should be offered for unsubscribing, including:

- an unsubscription page on the Web site;
- a special e-mail address for unsubscribing;
- a contact for a real person who will carry out the unsubscription if the subscriber is having difficulties.

One of the most common mistakes that people make when trying to unsubscribe is that they forget the exact address they subscribed with. Without this exact address, most unsubscription systems will not allow users to unsubscribe. As part of the unsubscription process, the subscriber should be informed of this mistake before and after the fact so that they can avoid it. To overcome this problem, some e-mail subscription systems offer a feature whereby each mailing has information on the original e-mail address which was used to subscribe. When someone unsubscribes, they should be sent a brief message thanking them for having been a subscriber.

Spend Time Maintaining the Subscriber Base

As the subscriber base grows and matures, various maintenance problems will arise. People will move away from organizations and the e-mail address in the database will be shut down and will return an error. A delivery failure does not necessarily mean that an address has been shut down. It is advisable to wait for a period to see if the delivery problems are temporary or permanent before deleting it from the database. Many list management systems will do this automatically.

Protect the Subscriber Base

A subscriber list is extremely valuable, and careful steps should be taken to protect it. Always make sure that the subscriber list is password-protected. Limit access to it to one or two people at most. Stolen subscriber lists can become a PR disaster, damaging the credibility of the organization. Make sure you create regular backup copies.

Procedures for Managing Passwords

If your site has sophisticated features like restricted content, personalization, or online ordering, it will be necessary for users to have usernames and passwords. Remembering passwords is something that many people find difficult, but they are necessary. Password-protected areas in Web sites should be clearly flagged with wording to such effect. It is very frustrating to click on a link, only to find that it requires a password to get to the content behind it. Cookie software can be used so that subscribers are given an option for the Web site to remember their password, so that the next time they visit they will gain automatic access.

The best process for allocating a password is as follows:

- Ask the subscriber to fill out a username: allow subscribers to use their e-mail addresses as their usernames, as this will be easier for them to remember.
- If it is not possible to use the e-mail address as the username, ask the subscribers to fill out their e-mail addresses, as this will be required in order to communicate vital information to them.

- Have the subscribers create passwords that have a minimum of six characters. Advise the subscribers not to use common words for their passwords. Ideally, they should mix characters and numbers. Show an asterisk for each character entered.
- Present a second password field to fill out to ensure that the password has been filled in correctly.
- People regularly forget passwords. Provide a field which gives subscribers the option of answering one of a selection of common questions: "What is the name of your pet? What is your mother's maiden name?" If people forget their passwords they will be asked the question. A correct reply enables them to create a new password.

RSS Feeds: An Alternative to E-mail Subscriptions

Some site visitors (usually the more technically inclined) may prefer to subscribe to your newsletter using an RSS feed. An RSS feed is a special type of file that can be downloaded to a special program (sometimes called an "aggregator") which is designed to make it easier for the reader to organize his or her subscriptions. Many content management systems now provide inbuilt support for RSS, but the reader still needs to have RSS software to take advantage of it.

Consider implementing RSS feeds now, if there is demand from site visitors. RSS is expected to become more important as major software producers begin to build RSS support into their standard desktop programs.

COMMON MISTAKES
Making the Subscription Process Too Long

People hate filling out long forms. Some subscription processes ask for information that is not really useful. This can have the effect of reducing the number of subscribers.

Not Reacting Quickly Enough to Requests to Unsubscribe

People who get in touch asking to unsubscribe probably tried to unsubscribe themselves, using the automated process, and failed. They are thus already somewhat frustrated. Ignoring their request to unsubscribe can make them very angry. They may claim that you are spamming them, and this will not be good for your reputation.

Not Properly Protecting the Subscriber Lists

Hackers love to steal subscriber lists and publish them. Worse, spammers love to get their hands on subscriber lists and spam to them. Either way, it is a PR disaster.

FOR MORE INFORMATION

Book:
Seybold, Patricia B., and Ronni T. Marshak. *Customers.com.* New York: Random House, 1998.

See also:
- Getting the Best from Loyalty Programs on the Web (p. 656)
- Managing Payments Online (pp. 616–618)
- Using E-mail Marketing Effectively (pp. 661–662)

Writing Well for the Web

GETTING STARTED

People read online material differently than they do standard printed material, and you need to bear this in mind when you're putting together content that will appear online. Surprisingly, very few Web sites take the time to lay out their content in a way that will maximize its readability. Don't forget that it is more difficult to read on a screen than from paper so you must write and lay out your content in a more simple, straightforward manner than you would in print. If you want to make sure that your content has the best chance of being read, focus on:

- shorter sentences, shorter paragraphs and shorter documents;
- plentiful use of short, punchy, and descriptive headings and summaries;
- larger font sizes and sans serif fonts, because they are easier to read;
- straightforward, factual prose.

FAQs

In what way do people read differently on the Web?

Rather than reading every sentence fully, when people read online they scan, moving quickly across text, always looking in a hurry for the content they need. They are very fact-oriented. People don't read on the Web for pleasure—they read to do business, to be educated, to find out something—so they like to read content that gets to the point quickly.

People like reading short documents with links to more detailed information as appropriate. If a document is long, and people really have no choice but to read it, a significant number of them will print it out. In general, however, long documents tend to go unread.

Why do so many people regard Web content as poor quality?

People don't trust the content they read on the Web because they come across so many Web sites with poor publishing standards. The Web gives everyone access to the tools of publishing, but giving someone a word processor does not make them a good writer.

Too many Web sites lack proper editing standards. They also translate documents that were prepared for print directly to the Web; this may save money in the short term, but if people don't read the content, it is pointless. Some Web sites deliberately try to mislead people with their content. All this gives a poor impression to people who use the Web.

Is writing for the Web a difficult skill to learn?

It is not easy to learn how to write well, no matter what the medium is. However, writing for the Web is about concentrating on the facts. You don't need flowery prose; instead, you must be able to communicate the really important information in as few words as possible. This is not an easy thing to do, but with practice most people can master the basics.

MAKING IT HAPPEN

Recognize That If You're Not Read, You're Dead

The connection between writing and reading is one that is not always considered: a surprising number of organizations create vast quantities of content without asking some obvious questions:

- Is anyone interested in reading this content?
- Is it written in a way that is understandable and easy to read?
- How are we going to let people know that we have just published this content?

Realize That Less Really Is More

Writing is rarely about quantity, but it should always be about quality. It is easier to write 5,000 words of waffle than 500 words that are succinct, but 500 words is exactly what is needed on the Web; less is definitely more.

Editing Is Essential

One of the primary functions of editing is to get a long draft into shape. As George Orwell said: "If it is possible to cut a word, always cut it." We all have pet phrases that we love to put into sentences whenever we can. They may sound good to the writer, but very often add nothing to the meaning of what is being communicated. The Web is about functional writing; get to the point as quickly as you can and then stop.

Keep It Short

When writing for the Web:

- documents should rarely be longer than 1,000 words: 500 to 700 is a good length to aim for;
- paragraphs should be between 40 and 50 words;
- try not to let your sentences go over 20 words.

Write for the Reader, Not Your Ego

Always keep your audience in mind when you're writing. Are you writing for a sales rep, a technician, support staff, customers, or investors? Will they understand what you are writing about? Don't write to please yourself—write to please your reader and be clear and precise.

Focus on the Headings

Headings are important on the Web for two central reasons. First, because people scan online, the first thing they often do is to look for headings; if the heading doesn't attract their attention, then they probably won't read any further. Second, people use search engines a lot, and the most prominent things in a page of search results are the headings. The heading really has to sell the web page and convince the person to click for more information.

Writing headings well is an art, but here are a few rules that will help you get the basics right:

- Keep them short. A heading should not be longer than five to eight words.

"What is the short meaning of this long speech?"   Friedrich Schiller

- Make your point clear. For example, "Nasdaq crashes to record low" is more informative than "Apocalypse now for investors!".
- Use strong, direct language. Don't be sensational, but at the same time don't be vague, and don't hedge.
- Don't deceive the reader, for example by using "Microsoft" in a heading just because you think people will then be more likely to read it. Remember, the job of the heading is to tell the reader succinctly what is in the document.

Use Subheadings
In longer documents it is always a good idea to use subheadings, as they break up the text into the more readable chunks that online readers like. Use subheadings every 5 to 7 paragraphs.

Summarize the Who, What, Where and When
Next to the heading, the summary is the most important piece of text. It should be descriptive, not wandering or indirect. Tell the reader what the document is about, and who, where and when the information relates to.

Get Down to Write
"No man but a blockhead ever wrote ... except for money," according to Samuel Johnson. Sound advice. Writing is not easy but someone has to do it. The first rule of writing is reading: if you are asked to write a technical paper, read how other people write them. Read how they are written on your own Web site, on competitors' Web sites, in industry journals. Find a style that works well and copy it; use its techniques and approach to structure. Whatever you do, don't plagiarize and put your own name on someone else's words, but never feel ashamed of finding good quality writing and learning from it.

Learn How to Edit
Even if you have an editor, you still want to send him or her a well written draft. Here are a few steps to follow.
- Get a first draft written and save it.
- Leave it for a while then print it out, or make the font size larger so that the text stands out more.
- Read it as if someone else wrote it. Be severe. Is it written in a way that the reader can easily understand? What is the writer trying to say here? Is this sentence or paragraph necessary? Has the writer covered all the essential facts?
- First drafts are often too long. When preparing the second draft, cut ruthlessly, maybe by as much as half.
- Use your word count carefully. When you are asked to write something, always ask how many words are required. If you are not given a word count then decide on one yourself. Keep it as low as possible.

Explore Collaborative Writing
Computers and the Internet make collaborative writing far easier, and as a result it is becoming an increasingly popular approach to writing content. Collaborative writing works well if:
- the writers spend time working through the objectives of the writing exercise, and reach agreement on such necessary matters as the style, tone, and length of the piece;
- there is a lot of content to be written that can benefit from the input of multiple disciplines;

- people can be given defined segments of content to write, and/or the different skills of different people can be used, for example when one person understands the subject well, while another is a good writer;
- there are professional processes in place to facilitate collaboration;
- the writers know and respect each other.

COMMON MISTAKES
Not Focusing on the Needs of the Reader
A surprising number of Web sites fail to consider who their reader is, simply adding content for its own sake. If you ignore the needs of your reader, then your reader will ignore you.

Putting Non-Web Formats onto the Web
Translating a 40-page Word document into HTML is a simple task; persuading someone to read it is another job entirely. Have you ever tried reading an Adobe PDF file on a screen? It's a painful experience. How many of your customers have read that PowerPoint presentation you translated into HTML?

Putting Every Piece of Content You Can Find on the Web
The Web is not a dumping ground for content. You might have 50,000 documents, with only 5,000 suitable for your Web site. Publishing the other 45,000 simply wastes your readers' time—not something you want to do.

Poor Editing
It is almost impossible to create quality content without sending it through a professional editorial process. No matter how good the writer, his or her content will always benefit by being checked over by an editor.

Long, Rambling Documents
If, after reading the heading and summary, the average Web reader hasn't understood what exactly you are trying to communicate to them, then chances are they will click the Back button. Readers on the Web have become ruthless about their time.

FOR MORE INFORMATION
Book:
McGovern, Gerry, Rob Norton, and Catherine O'Dowd. *The Web Content Style Guide: Style and Usage for Online Writers, Editors and Publishers.* Upper Saddle River, NJ: Financial Times Prentice Hall, 2001.

Web site:
Clickz Writing for the Web: **www.clickz.com**

See also:
- Computers, Information Technology, and E-commerce (pp. 1705–1707)
- Creating a Basic Web Site (pp. 621–622)
- Designing a Web Site Effectively (pp. 619–620)
- Making Sure Content Is Professionally Created, Edited, and Published (pp. 639–640)

Understanding the Key Principles of Internet Marketing

GETTING STARTED

If you work online, you need to think about Internet marketing and what it can do for your business. Internet marketing is about giving, rather than getting, attention. As an adjunct to traditional marketing, it supports and enhances the overall marketing message by providing comprehensive information that answers consumers' questions about a particular product or service. Internet marketing also exploits the networking capabilities of the Web by leveraging online community activities, linking, affiliate marketing, viral marketing, e-mail marketing, and loyalty programs. When approaching Internet marketing, keep the following in mind:

- When visitors come to a Web site they are already aware of the brand. They want information.
- Use Internet technology to understand the needs of your customers, so that you can offer them just the right information and products.
- Remember that the Internet empowers the consumer. A dissatisfied consumer can use the networking capabilities of the Internet to undermine your brand.

FAQs

What sort of products and services is Internet marketing best suited to?

Internet marketing is best suited to:

- products and services that require a lot of information to sell. For example, travel and books are ideal for the Internet. Travel is a very information-intensive product. People want times, prices, and information about the destination. When buying books, they are strongly influenced by reviews, opinions of other readers, tables of contents, and sample chapters;
- products and services that people feel strongly about, such as books, music, and movies. Fans network with other fans in online communities to discuss their favorites. Much of the success of *The Blair Witch Project* was credited to fans getting together on the Internet and promoting it through enthusiastic reviews and dialog;
- products and services that are bought by the Internet demographic. Although the Internet demographic has broadened, it is still generally the domain of the well educated and better off. Those working in technology and academia are very well represented.

What about online advertising?

As a pure branding tool, online advertising does not have the same impact as television or glossy media, because of bandwidth restrictions. Studies indicate that most consumers avoid interactive ads because they simply take too much time to download.

However, the real power of online advertising is not its mass-marketing impact but, rather, its ability to reach niche markets and target the right consumer with the right product. The contextual advertising services like Google AdWords and Yahoo Search Marketing allow even small-scale advertisers to refine their advertising in this way. Advertising success is also claimed by opt-in e-mail-based marketing, where consumers request information on a particular product or service. In online advertising, the scattershot approach is out and laser-point focus is in.

MAKING IT HAPPEN
Recognize That Internet Marketing is Part of the Overall Package

The objective of Internet marketing should be to integrate with the overall marketing strategy, so that it supports and is supported by offline marketing activities. However, that is not to say Internet marketing doesn't have its own unique characteristics. Internet marketing is not about a big idea, some compelling graphics, and a killer catch phrase. Offline marketing brings consumers to the Web site by using such approaches. Consumers' interest has been aroused. They have questions. Internet marketing answers those questions by providing comprehensive information. If people have read the brochure offline, they're not coming to the Web site to read it again.

Understand the Consumer Better

Effective Internet marketing focuses on getting to know the consumer better. The objective here is to understand consumers' exact needs so that exactly the right products and services can be offered to them at exactly the right time and in exactly the right way. The strength of the Internet is also its weakness, though. While people want information, they also suffer from massive information overload. The Internet marketer who can cut through the overload and bring to time-starved consumers the information they need is much more likely to succeed. Find Web sites and e-mail databases that attract the exact type of consumer you wish to target. Analyze statistics generated as a result of consumers visiting your Web site and react appropriately to key trends that these statistics throw up. With more sophisticated Web sites, you can customize consumers' experiences through personalization systems, whereby a unique and finely targeted set of information and products is presented to each visitor.

Back It Up with E-mail Marketing

Since the Web was launched, perceptive marketers have been stressing that every Web site should have an e-mail marketing strategy. Consider that consumers must actively decide to go to a Web site, but with e-mail they join a database in which they can be regularly informed of the products, services, and offers that the organization has available. The key to e-mail marketing success is getting people who want the information to join a database in which they will receive regular e-mail alerts and newsletters. Of course, the information they receive needs to be of a type and quality that they will sign up to get.

"The future of retail is the integration of Internet and digital services with the retail network."

Charles Dunstone

Tap into the Networking Ability of the Internet

The Internet is a community, and it offers a tremendously powerful means for people and organizations to network. Linking is one of the simplest yet most effective Internet marketing devices there is. It underpins affiliate marketing efforts by Web sites such as Amazon.com. Linking is like embedded word of mouth. If another Web site links to you, it is essentially recommending you to its own visitors. Viral marketing is a network effect, whereby groups of consumers create a buzz about a product or service by e-mailing friends and/or creating their own Web sites. Consumers gain a power through Internet networking that they traditionally did not have. There are hundreds if not thousands of Web sites and activist groups established by disgruntled consumers with the objective of attacking particular organizations.

Make Advertising and Promotion Highly Focused

A Web site, because it is not a physical store, faces a constant challenge to achieve and maintain awareness among its target market. Traditional offline marketing, such as press advertising or direct mail, plays a key role here, but so too do specific online marketing strategies. Registration with a commercial search engine is an obvious one. This is an ongoing activity, because the rules by which search engines classify sites are constantly changing. Banner ads can be effective if properly targeted. Banner ad design needs to apply the unique characteristics of the medium and not simply apply traditional advertising principles. A specialist agency can advise on suitable creative approaches. Getting other Web sites to link can be very effective, but this is a slow process, the rewards of which are delivered over time.

Remember that Affiliate Marketing and Loyalty Programs Can Deliver

There is no better example of the success of affiliate marketing than that of Amazon.com. Literally hundreds of thousands of Web sites offer books and other products to their visitors using Amazon's affiliate program. It's a win–win situation. The Web site in question offers an extra service that is easy to establish and delivers a certain amount of revenue. The affiliate sponsor opens up a new channel every time another Web site hooks into it.

However, like all marketing techniques, it's not some magic formula. It needs to be thought through properly and applied professionally.

Loyalty programs can work on the Internet, though they have been over-hyped. Key elements in the management of loyalty programs are the use of customer databases and the tracking of customer purchasing behavior. The Internet facilitates such activities, and can thus be a medium through which loyalty programs can be run. Getting the incentive structure right is critical to the success of loyalty programs.

Use Online Communities to Build Loyalty

Using weblogs ("blogs"), chat, discussion boards, and e-mail mailing lists to bring people together allows you to have a conversation with customers, hear what they want, and to enhance brand loyalty. It can also be a source of unique and cost-effective content. However, it doesn't work in all situations, and online communities that are not properly managed can quickly lose momentum.

Remember that Some Old Marketing Tricks Still Apply

Discounts, competitions, and free offers work as well online as they do offline. While perhaps too much has been offered free on the Internet in order to build business, these traditional marketing techniques, properly used, can be effective on Web sites.

COMMON MISTAKES
Being Flashy

Although the Internet has been around since 1996, it is amazing that there are still a few marketers who think it's TV on a computer screen. On the Web, visitors don't really care about the graphics; they just want the information. Splash screens, audio, video and Macromedia Flash animations should be kept to an absolute minimum.

Not Building and Leveraging a Customer Database

Bringing people to a Web site without strongly encouraging them to join some sort of a database is a serious mistake. Studies indicate that many consumers will visit a Web site once, rarely if ever to return. It's vital to get them into a database to establish ongoing communication.

Focusing on Volume of Visitors Rather than Quality Targeting

In the early years of the Web there was a frantic rush to build visitor traffic to a Web site, without any real focus on issues such as revenue per visitor, numbers who joined databases. Acquisition costs for visitors were high, and as the large number of visitors did not translate into valuable customers, the business model collapsed for many.

Focusing Solely on Purchase Activity

There is a need to understand how a Web site contributes to the overall purchasing process. For example, a great many people visit car Web sites before they make a purchase, but very few will actually make the purchase online. The key is to forget about measuring by crude visitor volume numbers and focus on the quality of the targeting, along with the influence that the Web site and e-mail communications have on purchase behavior.

FOR MORE INFORMATION

Book:
Scoble, Robert, and Shel Israel. *Naked Conversations: How Blogs are Changing the Way Businesses Talk with Customers.* New York: Wiley, 2006

Web sites:
Web marketing information center:
www.wilsonweb.com/webmarket
Adventive e-mail mailing lists: **www.adventive.com**

Collecting Consumer Data on the Internet

GETTING STARTED

If your business has a Web site, you'll find that Internet technologies offer a wealth of ways in which information on consumers can be gathered. Such information can either be collected directly as a result of consumers providing details, or indirectly by analyzing consumers' behavior while on a Web site. If you decide to gather information on consumers this way, keep the following in mind:

- Privacy is a central concern of people who use the Internet, and they are becoming increasingly wary of Web sites that seek personal information.
- The benefit to the consumer needs to be made clear. Consumers are much more willing to offer personal information when a clear benefit to them can be articulated.
- It is one thing to gather information on consumers but another to analyze it properly and use it productively.

FAQs

Why has privacy become such a burning issue on the Internet?

The Internet has lacked a common and comprehensive legal infrastructure and this has led to an unfortunate situation in which basic consumer rights have been exploited. Web sites have gathered information on visitors in a surreptitious manner. Personal data has been sold on to third parties without making the consumer aware. This behavior has resulted in a consumer backlash. Study after study indicates that privacy is a key issue for those who use the Internet.

What are the key benefits of collecting consumer data?

Getting to know consumers better means that you have a better chance of offering them products and services that are more in tune with their needs. This is a key competitive advantage in an information-driven economy. With more and more products becoming increasingly similar in their physical makeup, competitive advantage is achieved through finding out exactly what the consumer wants and meeting those needs precisely. The benefits to consumers are that they receive information and products that more accurately reflect their lifestyles and needs.

Why is it so important to collect information on how a Web site is performing?

A Web site is not like a bricks-and-mortar store in which a manager can walk around and observe what is happening. If there are always long lines at the checkout, and people are leaving the store because of these lines, this will quickly become obvious. People may be dropping out in the middle of a purchase process on a Web site, but unless proper data are coming through and being analyzed, no one will know. The number of people visiting the Web site may be dropping off. How will this be known without proper data? Web sites, like offline stores, need to monitor their performance continuously and adapt where appropriate. Without proper data and thorough data analysis, this cannot be done.

MAKING IT HAPPEN
Use Web site Logs to Analyze Consumer Behavior

Web site logs (server logs) track activity on a Web site. For an average Web site, such log software is simple to install and can be purchased fairly cheaply, though for larger Web sites it is more complex and expensive. It is strongly advisable to use log software, as it delivers vital information on Web site performance.

Unless the Web site is hooked into a personalization system, Web site logs are not able to identify who exactly has visited the Web site. Instead, such logs collect general Web site activity information. Such information includes:

- total number of visits to the Web site during a defined period of time;
- visitor frequency: information on the number of people who visited only once during the period (unique visitors), and those who have visited more than once;
- page impressions/views: information on the total numbers of complete Web pages visited during the period. This is a key measure for advertisers;
- hits: one of the most abused statistics on the Internet, and a totally unreliable measure of Web site visitor activity: every Web page is made up of a number of components—graphics, text, programming elements. Some pages may have anything from 10 to 20 components. Each of these components is counted as a "hit." Therefore, the total number of hits is generally very high and bears little or no relation to the actual visitor activity;
- most frequently visited pages.

Web site logs can deliver a mind-numbing array of data. This will seem very exciting when you first install the software, but can become tedious to wade through every day. It's thus important to isolate what are the key measures required to deliver a better picture of how the Web site is performing.

Use Cookie Software to Track Consumers

Cookies are small files that are sent to reside in consumers' browsers in order to track those consumers the next time they visit the Web site. Cookies are an important component in personalization. A typical example of the use of cookies can be seen when people have subscribed to a service on a Web site. Cookies allow the Web site to remember the username and password information, so that they don't have to keep filling it out every time they revisit. This is clearly a benefit for most people. However, cookies have been abused, collecting

"It is a capital mistake to theorise before one has data. Insensibly one begins to twist facts to suit theories, instead of theories to suit facts."

Arthur Conan Doyle

information on people without their knowledge. When using cookies, clearly explain to people why they are being used and how they benefit them.

Be Cautious about Using Web Bugs that Track Web Site Usage

An alternative technology to cookies is what has become known as Web bugs. Web bugs are not detectable by standard browsers, although there is software that can be downloaded to detect them. Web bugs have been controversial because they are often used in a surreptitious manner. Their very design reflects a desire not to let the person know that they are being tracked. Web bugs are adding fuel to the belief that people's privacy rights are being constantly abused on the Internet.

Collect Information Through the Use of Web Site Forms

Web site forms are used to collect information from a consumer in a structured manner. The following are guidelines to follow when designing a form:

- Keep the forms as short as possible. If you make the form too long, consumers will simply not fill it out, or will skip over large sections of it.
- If forms have to be long, break them up. However, inform the person clearly of how many sections there are in the form.
- Clearly mark mandatory fields. In every form there will be fields, such as e-mail addresses, that must be filled out. The convention is to mark the text associated with these fields in red and/or to place a red asterisk beside the field. At the top of the form, a clear statement needs to be made relating to the mandatory fields.
- Don't mandate information a consumer can't give. Offer an alternative, for example: "If you don't have a ZIP code, please write 'None.'"
- Ask opinion-type questions first. Where the objective of the form is to collect opinion-type information, start off with these questions. People tend to be more open to giving opinion rather than personal information.
- Isolate errors that are made. Everyone makes mistakes, particularly when they are filling out long forms. Never say, "There's an error in your form. Go back and fill it out correctly." Rather say, "It seems you have not filled out your e-mail address. Please fill it out here." Alternatively, you could highlight the field that needs to be completed in another color, which will flag it up quickly for the user.
- Make sure the fields aren't too small. Don't, for example, give people a tiny field when you want their street address, which may be quite long.
- Make sure it's accessible to all. Offer an alternative approach for people with disabilities to complete the information requested; these disabilities can range from issues such as color blindness to physical impairment. Minimum accessibility standards are increasingly required by law.
- Test regularly. You can't just test your forms once before you launch and then keep your fingers crossed. Forms break. Test them regularly as part of your standard Web site maintenance.

Follow Best Practice

People have become rightly uneasy about the abuse of personal information on the Web. To assuage fears and create a win–win situation, put into practice the following:

- Clearly inform people why the information is being collected and what purposes it will be used for.
- Never use this information in a way that was not originally intended.
- Allow the consumer to find out what information has been collected on them.
- Allow them to delete any or all of this information if they desire.
- Publish a comprehensive privacy statement in a prominent position on the Web site.

Protect Consumer Data

Hackers—people who break into computer systems—love to target consumer databases. The reason is that these databases may contain credit card information (it is not advisable to store credit card numbers on a Web site). More usually, hackers know that publicizing the theft of consumer databases will be hugely damaging and embarrassing to the organization. It is therefore vital that any consumer data collected is properly protected and backed up.

Take Care When Collecting Consumer Data on Children

The rules for collecting consumer data on children are quite naturally a lot stricter than for adults. While the law is evolving, numerous companies have been fined for collecting too much information on children who visit their Web sites. It's not enough simply to check your national legislation on this issue. The Web is international and your Web sites should adhere to international standards when it comes to children's privacy rights.

COMMON MISTAKES
Surreptitiously Collecting Data

People have become very wary about their privacy on the Internet. Too many Web sites have collected data on consumers without them knowing. This may produce short-term benefit but has led to an inevitable backlash.

Collecting Too Much Data

Software today can deliver seas of data, and Web sites with large numbers of visitors can easily get flooded. Not focusing on what is the really important data to collect is a common problem. It's important to remember that analyzing data takes time, and that, if tangible benefits are not delivered, then it will be wasted time.

FOR MORE INFORMATION

Web sites:
American Federal Trade Commission Privacy Initiatives: **www.ftc.gov/privacy**
Web Accessibility Initiative: **www.w3.org/WAI**

"Welcome to the new age of datamation—a whole new way to move the prospect to making a purchase, using different strokes for different folks."
Stan Rapp

Delivering the Benefits of Affiliate Marketing on the Web

GETTING STARTED

Affiliate marketing is about paying for performance. In short, it is a type of marketing in which one company induces others to place banners and buttons on their Web sites in return for a commission on purchases made by their customers. Amazon.com is the pioneer of affiliate marketing. It allows other Web sites to publish information of their own choices of books. When people click through to Amazon and buy these books, the Web site in question gets a commission. Affiliate marketing can open up new channels to market for the affiliate sponsor, and be a source of extra revenue for the affiliate Web site. When investigating affiliate marketing, remember that:

- affiliate marketing is more suited to products than services;
- you'll need to work hard with your affiliates if you want it all to work;
- a well-designed compensation package will be critical to success.

MAKING IT HAPPEN

Figure Out If Your Business Is Suited To Affiliate Marketing

Keep the following in mind:

- There needs to be a substantial number of Web sites that are attracting your target market. These Web sites need to show a willingness to join an affiliate program. You might be selling medical supplies but that doesn't mean that hospital Web sites will become affiliates.
- Affiliate marketing is better suited to products than to services. It is much harder to track whether another Web site sent you visitors who, after prolonged negotiation, decide to pay you for your services.
- Is the market already saturated with affiliate programs? It would be difficult to set up one today that offered commission on book sales.

Have a Strong Value Proposition

As with all good ideas, there are a huge number of companies offering affiliate programs. How is your program going to attract new members? The level of compensation/commission you will offer will be important. However, on its own it will rarely be enough. You will need to work hard with your members by organizing regular competitions, special offers, and other incentives that make for an attractive value proposition both for your affiliate members and the end customer.

Keep in Regular Touch with Your Affiliates

Keeping in regular communication with your affiliates is essential in order to build their enthusiasm and trust. You should plan for an e-mail affiliate newsletter. Your affiliate members are your partners, and unless you treat them as such by working closely with them, they will drift away.

Agree a Compensation Approach

Critical to the success of your program will be how the affiliate is compensated. There are various compensation approaches:

- you might pay commission only; for smaller-price items such as books and music, commission is a popular option;
- for more expensive items such as cars, compensation may be based on paying for qualified leads;
- if brand building is also an important objective, then you might also offer compensation every time a visitor clicks through from an affiliate.

When making payments you will need to decide how often you do it. Every month? Every quarter? A problem you may face with partners is that some of them will have achieved very little revenue for a particular period, and it will not be cost-effective to send them a check So you need to inform partners that there is a certain threshold before payment is made, and that commission earned in one period, if below the threshold, will be added to the commission for the next period. You will need an affiliate agreement that will cover these and other relevant issues.

Innovate, Analyze, Test, and Adapt

There is a need to innovate constantly so as to find the best approach. Affiliate software delivers substantial data and this needs to be carefully analyzed. New initiatives need to be properly tested and you need to be willing to keep adapting and refining your offer until you find something that works for both you and your affiliates.

Decide Whether to Outsource or Buy Software

Organizations can have the choice of outsourcing much of the running of the affiliate program or purchasing software and designing it in-house. It is better to outsource, as it allows you to focus on what you do best—selling and marketing your products and services.

THE BEST SOURCES OF HELP

Web sites:
Affiliate Advisor: **www.affiliateadvisor.com**
Associate Programs: **www.associateprograms.com**

See also:

"I think the skills involved in putting together deals are crucial to a start-up. You need wide distribution and many partners."

Rob Herson

Getting the Best from Loyalty Programs on the Web

GETTING STARTED

Loyalty programs reward customers who spend more and/or stay longer with a business. Like much else about the Web, loyalty programs were a gigantic trend that crashed pretty severely. However, much of what went wrong does not reflect an inherent fault in the loyalty model itself, but rather in the vastly overhyped expectations of what loyalty programs can deliver. When considering using loyalty programs on the Web, keep the following in mind:

- you should implement loyalty programs on the Web only after you have your e-commerce fundamentals solidly in place;
- loyalty programs are long-term projects: it can be disastrous to start a loyalty program and then stop it within six months;
- getting the level of incentive right is critical to success—too much and your profits will be hurt; too little and you won't attract members;

MAKING IT HAPPEN
Make Sure Your E-commerce Fundamentals Are in Place First

Top of the list for consumers are service, comprehensive information, appropriate returns policies, and good support. Unless these fundamentals are fully addressed, consumers will see loyalty points only as gimmicks.

Remember That Loyalty Programs Are Long-term Projects

A critical issue with regard to loyalty programs is that, by their very nature, they have to be there for the long term. Loyalty programs ask two key things of consumers: to collect points that will be redeemed at some future date; and to give their loyalty. There is no better way to antagonize a consumer than to start a loyalty program and then six months later—as the member has collected half the points required for that coveted flight—to stop the program. Don't start a loyalty program unless you're in it for the long haul.

Find Out What Makes Your Customer Loyal

If you don't know what makes your customers loyal then you cannot develop a program that will enhance their loyalty. It is also critical to focus on making your most profitable customers more loyal.

Choose the Right Type of Loyalty Program

The following is a selection of loyalty program approaches:

- points systems—a very popular approach that gives points to customers based on what they purchase;
- premium customer programs—customers who spend certain amounts of money and are repeat purchasers of a product or service gain special status. This may involve

them receiving special service offers, discounts, exclusive offers, gifts, and so on. The important thing here is to make the customers feel special—make them feel that they are getting things that those who are not part of the program don't get;

- buyers' clubs—when a certain number of consumers get together to buy a particular product, they will be offered a special volume discount.

Get the Switching Cost Right

If you offer too much in your loyalty program then your margins will be squeezed, and you will be running to stand still from a profitability point of view. If your incentives are too low then the switching cost for your customer will remain low, and the very purpose of the loyalty program will have been negated. It would seem that the problem with a lot of loyalty programs on the Web was that, fueled by venture capital, major incentives were offered in the hope of attracting huge numbers of members.

Create a Loyalty Path for the Customer

Customers can take loyalty programs very seriously. Some customers see it as an important achievement that they have a "Gold Card," or are seen as a "Premium Customer." There needs to be a clear loyalty path to tap into this sort of loyalty psychology. The customers need to see that the more they spend and the longer they stay with you, the more rewards and better treatment they will get.

Keep the Customer Informed

Customers need to be able to check up on their status easily—to see, for example, how many points they have currently accumulated. Keep in touch. Send loyalty club members a regular bulletin that creates a continuing buzz about the loyalty program, announcing competition winners, new competitions, special offers, and so on.

FOR MORE INFORMATION

Web site:
Business 2.0: **www.business2.com/b2/webguide**

See also:

"The Internet has certainly brought us face to face with the consumer. And the consumer has everything to gain here."

Ann Winblad

Applying a Viral Marketing Approach on the Internet

GETTING STARTED

Viral marketing is really another name for word of mouth on the Internet environment. Viral marketing can work in mysterious ways, but what is clear is that the Internet is a medium that offers significant potential for such strategy. Yahoo and Google did little or no advertising in their early years—people told other people they were great resources. News about music-swapping services such as Napster, and the independent movie *The Blair Witch Project*, grew like wildfire within universities. Viral marketing works well when:

- the product is new and genuinely different, and is something opinion leaders want to be associated with;
- the benefits are real—people are telling their friends; they are putting their reputations on the line;
- the product is relevant to a large number of people, and it is relatively easy to communicate the benefits.

MAKING IT HAPPEN
Consider Incentives

Some viral marketing campaigns use an incentive-based approach. This involves rewarding people if they inform their friends and a percentage of these friends purchase the product or fill out a questionnaire, for example. It's very important to have a "cap" on the number of people that the first person is asked to inform, though. For example, ask contributors to tell no more than five people about your product or service. If the process is open-ended then people are more likely to send out thousands of spam e-mails to people they don't know in order to increase their rewards. Spam is the bane of the online world, and one thing you definitely don't want to encourage, even inadvertently.

Create Useful Information That Will Be Quoted and Passed On

People see the Internet as an information resource. A powerful way of building a brand is to publish information that you allow people to quote and redistribute. There is no better way to enhance your reputation than for someone to pass your newsletter on to a friend, recommending that they should read it. The objective is that you be seen as an expert on a particular subject that is directly related to a product or service you offer. To encourage this type of process, create an "e-mail-to-a-friend" function on your Web site, which allows someone easily to e-mail information on something they have just read.

Recognize That Linking Is Viral Marketing

Linking is another form of word-of-mouth. It's one thing for someone to send an e-mail praising your product or information, but the effect is much better and longer-lasting if that person publishes a positive review on their Web site and links back to you.

Remember That Viral Marketing Works Well When There Is Something Free

People love to tell their friends when there is some great new service that is free. The Hotmail free e-mail service and the Geocities free Web site service grew quickly with little or no marketing spend. The appeal of what is free may be losing some of its luster as the Internet matures, but it is still a powerful driver of behavior.

Emulate the Hotmail Approach

Hotmail was a pioneer of viral marketing. Its success was not simply based on the fact that it was a free service. It embedded viral marketing into the product itself. Every time someone using Hotmail sent an e-mail, at the bottom of the e-mail was the compelling message: "Get your private, free e-mail at http://www.hotmail.com." Thus the very use of the product became a vehicle for marketing and promotion.

Think About Integrating Other Approaches

Depending on your type of business, you might want to investigate the option of marketing virally via text messages as well as the Internet. Let's say your business provides information about entertainment options in your local area. You could encourage visitors to your Web site to register their cell phone numbers with you so that you can keep them up-to-date with special offers, new information, and so on via text message. This would be particularly popular in an area with a high student population. However, you must be **scrupulous** about the information you send out via text message—don't, for example, send out "jokey" messages that may be misconstrued in any way by the recipient: in 2004, the games company CE Europe attracted a great deal of negative press when it marketed a "Resident Evil" computer game by a text message that told users that their phones had been infected by a virus. Remember that you must **not** send unsolicited text messages and you must remove numbers immediately from your list if anyone complains (someone else may have registered their number, for example).

Be Wary of Inappropriate Viral Marketing

Done inappropriately, viral marketing can be seen as pyramid selling, chain-letter selling and/or spam. Every e-mail sent needs to make clear that the business is not involved in spamming or other unethical practices or you'll become tarred with the same brush. If you do attract adverse attention from an irate recipient, remain calm and respond to the complainant in a professional manner.

FOR MORE INFORMATION

Web site:
Business2.0: **www.business2.com/webguide**

"Marketing is not a function, it is the whole business seen from the customer's point of view."

Peter F. Drucker

Building Loyalty Through Online Communities

GETTING STARTED

Online communities are seen first and foremost as a social phenomenon, but they are very useful for businesses of all sizes. They allow consumers to engage with one another and with your business through use of interactive tools such as e-mail, discussion boards, and chat software. (Broader and more social online communities are not the topic of this actionlist.) They are a means by which you can take the pulse of consumers to find out what they are thinking, and to generate unique content. As a standalone business, online communities have been found to be weak: they work best when they are supporting the need for the business to get ongoing feedback. Online communities:

- allow the consumer an ongoing voice, thus facilitating greater feedback;
- require moderation and care if they are not to fizzle out, or turn negative;
- offer different options for interaction that reflect the varying ways in which people like to communicate.

MAKING IT HAPPEN
Keep It Moderated

Online communities rarely work if you simply install some discussion board software on a Web site and walk away. The discussion will either quickly dry up, or else drift off to topics that have nothing to do with the company and may well be libelous or otherwise illegal. This is the last thing you need, so the key to success here is to moderate the quality of your online community. Moderators need to combine editorial and chairperson-type skills. They need to be knowledgeable about the subjects being discussed, be enthusiastic, and encourage debate and quality discussion. They require an understanding of legal (particularly libel and copyright) issues, and should have the ability to deal with negative situations where members become overly virulent. Most of all, they need to care and want to make the community work for everybody involved.

Set Up E-mail Mailing Lists

E-mail mailing lists are an excellent way to discuss complex topics over a longer period of time. Members can be drawn from anywhere in the world and come together to share information and experience on a particular theme or subject area. The success of an e-mail mailing list is down to the quality of the contributions and moderation. Done right, it is a powerful way of transferring knowledge. An e-mail mailing list works as follows:

- a moderator establishes a list with mailing list software (this can be bought or rented; renting is usually the best option);
- the theme and focus of the list is published, and people join up, using a Web site form and/or e-mail address;
- the moderator invites contributions and these are duly published by e-mail;

- subscribers react to the initial publication with their opinions and feedback; a selection of these reactions then gets published in the next e-mail sent out;
- if successful, a feedback and opinion loop is created, with new topics of discussion being introduced as older topics have received sufficient discussion.

Set Up Discussion Boards

Discussion boards (also known as newsgroups, discussion groups, or bulletin boards) are areas on a Web site that allow people to contribute opinions, ideas and announcements. They tend to be more general in nature than e-mail mailing lists, and are more suited to casual, one-off interactions. People require less commitment to participate in such boards. They can generally review a discussion topic without subscribing, although they do have to subscribe if they want to contribute something themselves. Moderation is not as essential here, although it is important to watch out for the emergence of "off-topic" subjects—contributions that are unnecessarily negative and perhaps libelous—and copyright infringement.

A prime example of the success of the discussion board approach is how the Amazon sites around the world use it to allow consumers to publish book reviews. Discussion board software is relatively cheap and easy to install.

Set Up Online Chat

Online chat is real-time, text-based communication. Online chat can be effective when:

- there is a specific event occurring that is of interest to people;
- an expert can be made available to talk about a subject or product.

To be productive, online chat needs to be well moderated. It is really only suited to small groups of people (2 to 20) at any one time. Online chat software is relatively cheap and easy to install.

FOR MORE INFORMATION

Book:
Hagel, John, and Arthur G. Armstrong. *Net Gain: Expanding Markets Through Virtual Communities.* Boston, MA: Harvard Business School Press, 1997.

See also:

"Consumers resent it when a company presumes to judge the quality of its products on their behalf."

Andrew S. Grove

Promoting Your Web Site Effectively

GETTING STARTED

Launching a Web site is like opening up a store at the North Pole or in the Sahara Desert. Nobody will know that you are there unless you promote yourself! Web site promotion is not some one-time event that occurs at launch. It is an ongoing activity that demands a keen understanding of promotional techniques that are unique to the Web. It also requires full integration into offline marketing and promotional activities. When approaching Web site promotion, consider the following:

- it requires a range of promotional strategies, both online and offline;
- it's an ongoing activity;
- it should be fully integrated into the overall promotional and marketing strategy.

FAQs
Why is Web site promotion of such importance?

In the property business people talk about "location, location, location." Well, a Web site doesn't really have a location. It's not on a main street where thousands of people walk by every day. Without such physical visibility, a Web site has a major problem attracting consumers. That is one reason why a clicks-and-mortar strategy (combining physical stores with an Internet presence) is deemed so essential for the success of a Web site. In a physical store, and in its related marketing and promotional activity, consumers can be exposed to the benefits of the Web site constantly.

What is banner advertising and does it promote a Web site well?

Banner advertising is the use of rectangular advertisements or logos across the width of page on an Internet site. Businesses often place advertisements of this type on a third party's site to attract users to visit their own.

The jury is still out on the effectiveness of banner advertising. However, prices for banner advertising have dropped significantly in recent years and there is certainly value to be had. It's really down to the target market you are after and whether that accurately matches the profile of visitors coming to a particular Web site. Online advertising systems allow for a level of targeting and measurement that is impossible in much offline media. So, if you can get to the right target market at the right price, then the equation makes sense.

Does online advertising and promotion have to cost a lot of money?

No. Online ads have dropped significantly in price and, with proper investigation, very good value can be had. Online promotion requires dedication, but a few hours spent every week can deliver real results in the longer term.

MAKING IT HAPPEN
Get Linked

Linking is one of the most powerful means of promoting a Web site. A link from another Web site is essentially embedded word of mouth, a recommendation from that site to its visitors also to visit you. The Web is huge, with millions of Web sites, many of them of poor quality. People who use the Internet have become very skeptical and conservative in their behavior. Building credibility is thus of key importance to online success. There is no better way to build such credibility than to have many other Web sites linking to you.

Google, perhaps the Web's most popular search engine, achieved popularity because its search results were seen as more relevant than those of other search engines. The way it achieved better results was by analyzing a Web site and seeing how many external Web sites had linked to it. The more links the Web site had, the higher in the results Google placed it. Thus, if you want your Web site to feature prominently with Google, the more links you can get the better.

But linking is not simply about getting placed higher in search engine results. Think of each link as another "road" to your Web site; another way that the visitor can get to you. Getting links is not easy. It involves finding Web sites that attract your target market and convincing them to include a link to you. Usually, they will not do this unless you have valuable content that could be of interest to their customers. Another approach is to pay for a link, either through monthly fees or through what is called "click through payments"—you pay for every visit that results from a particular link.

Weblogs—or "blogs"—are an increasingly important source of information. They are sites that express a particular person's point of view. Build relationships with blog owners who are relevant to your area to yield links and reviews of your product.

Get Registered with Search Engines

Because so many people use commercial search engines, it's extremely important that your Web site is properly registered. Keep the following in mind:

- There are hundreds of search engines and directories but only a handful that really matter. These include: Yahoo, Google, and Microsoft Network.
- Register with specialist search engines and directories for your particular industry.
- All search engines used to be free to register with, but this is no longer the case for an increasing number. You need to consider if the fee is worth it.
- An increasing number of search engines sell special placements in their search results. You can choose a keyword and when that keyword is input by a searcher, a short promotion for your Web site will appear.
- Search engines need to be monitored regularly, as they can change the rules by which search results are presented. A set of keywords needs to be drawn up and the search engine regularly searched using these keywords.

"The Web site needs to be as sticky as a currant bun."   Carolyn McCall

If you find your Web site is dropping down the results page, you may need to re-register. Also, if you launch a new product or service, you should consider registering that.

- Don't register popular keywords with a Web site just for the sake of increased visitors. It achieves very little, and some search engines will remove Web sites that continuously abuse search registration processes.

Use Banner and Other Online Advertising

As stated above, banner advertising doesn't work for everyone, but it may work for your business. It's particularly useful where a new Web site, product, or service is being launched. Banner ads can be paid for either on a cost-per-thousand (CPM) basis or per click-through, where the seller gets paid wherever a visitors clicks on an ad. Online ads should be a call to action, with the key objective being to get the person to click on the ad. There are a variety of online advertising options:

- banner advertisements. These ads can go across the top or bottom of the page or down the side, like wallpaper.
- interstitials. These are ads that appear before the actual Web page loads. They certainly get the visitors' attention but can be very frustrating.
- pop-under ads. These ads launch in a separate browser window and have been controversial.

Consider E-mail as a Form of Advertising

E-mail can be a very effective form of advertising, particularly when the advertiser is reaching a targeted list that has opted in to receive information on particular products or services. The thing to watch out for in e-mail advertising is spam. Spam is mass distributed e-mail that is unsolicited by the receiver. People are increasingly annoyed at receiving spam, and anti-spam legislation has been enacted or is pending in many states and countries. It's not simply about whether spam is legal or not—but it is certainly unethical, and no reputable organization should use such an approach.

Remember E-mail Signature Files

An e-mail signature is the text at the bottom of an e-mail that contains information about the sender. It is also possible to place a short, two-line ad there (e-mail signatures should not be longer than five lines). E-mail signature promotion was used very effectively when Andersen Consulting changed its name to Accenture. For a period after the name change, every time one of Accenture's 60,000 employees sent an e-mail, there was a short e-mail signature ad notifying the receiver of the change of name.

Integrate with Offline Marketing

Every single piece of offline literature should contain the Web site address and, where appropriate, an e-mail address. This includes: all stationery (letterheads, business cards, compliment slips, receipts, invoices); all product packaging; training and support manuals; all ads that are placed in print, radio, or television. If the organization has physical stores, then promotional material should be placed prominently within these stores informing visitors of the Web site. When planning new offline promotional and marketing activities, you should seek ways to get consumers to go to the Web site. For example, the Web site could be the place where the consumer enters a competition.

Include Competitions and Giveaways

Consumers are as likely to react positively to quality Web-based competitions and special promotions as they do to such tactics in the offline world. Competitions and special offers give the Web site a sense of vibrancy. A key objective of such promotions should be to get consumers to join databases, used in the future to inform people of other special offers and relevant information.

Use Your Home Page

A key objective of a home page is to promote important content, products, and services situated deeper in the Web site. That's the job of sharp, punchy headings and summaries, supported on occasion by small graphics. The Microsoft Web site (www.microsoft.com) is a perfect example of how to use a home page to promote key events, special offers, product launches, upgrades, and so on.

COMMON MISTAKES
Seeking Quantity of Visitors over Quality

In the early days of the Web there was a mad rush—fueled by venture capital—to drive as many visitors as possible to Web sites. A stream of new brands emerged, each one seeking to outdo the next with ad spend. There is still a tendency to consider quantity over quality when it comes to building visitor numbers to a Web site. This is a serious and expensive mistake.

Focusing Purely on Search Engines

Search engines are important, but they should still be only a part of an online promotional strategy. Also, abuse of search engines by bombarding them with popular keywords and other visitor-generating techniques merely serves to bulk up visitor figures. It does little or nothing for the bottom line.

Lack of Integration with Offline Marketing

Organizations miss vital and cost-effective ways of promoting their Web sites by not fully utilizing offline resources.

Lack of Ongoing Commitment

Too many Web sites have been launched enthusiastically, only to be left to wither in the wilderness of cyberspace. To be successful, promotion must be an ongoing activity.

FOR MORE INFORMATION

Web site:
Google: **www.google.com**

See also:
- Applying a Viral Marketing Approach on the Internet (p. 657)
- Delivering the Benefits of Affiliate Marketing on the Web (p. 655)

"We thought the creation and operation of websites was mysterious Nobel Prize stuff, the province of the wild-eyed and purple-haired."

Jack Welch

Using E-mail Marketing Effectively

GETTING STARTED

E-mail should be an essential part of any Internet marketing strategy. If you have someone's e-mail address, you can send them information directly. It's absolutely *crucial*, though, that the recipient has agreed to receive the information you want to send. Remember that:

- e-mail is a relatively cheap, but powerful communications tool—you can send thousands of e-mail newsletters in a simple, cost-effective way;
- e-mail allows you to keep in regular contact with customers and to build up a rapport with them;
- never send unsolicited e-mails (spam). E-mail should only deliver worthwhile information.

FAQs

How often should you contact customers by e-mail?

E-mail is a fast, simple, and cost-effective form of communication, so it is tempting to use it at every opportunity. Unless the information you send is valuable, though, you run the risk of annoying your customers and turning them off—exactly the opposite of what you're aiming for.

Should newsletters be free or chargeable?

It depends on the focus of your business. If you are publishing information, then it is hard to see how a business model can be developed that is advertising only. However, if you are using the information you send to help sell some other product or service, it is highly unlikely that anyone will be willing to pay for it.

What is spam?

Spam is mass distributed, unsolicited e-mail. Spam is a major problem on the Internet today in that it is easy to buy a database of millions of e-mail addresses and send out unsolicited e-mails to them. If you want to be seen as a reputable business, you should avoid sending spam. Legislation is pending in a number of countries to make sending spam illegal.

What do the terms "opt-in" and "double opt-in" mean?

An opt-in approach is where someone actively decides to give you their e-mail address so that you can send them e-mail. However, the emerging convention is double opt-in. What happens here is that when a person receives a request to subscribe to an e-mail address, they reply to that address for verification that the request did in fact come from there. This ensures that the e-mail address was not maliciously set up by a third party.

Is it better to buy software or can it be rented?

Very often it is better to rent. There are a number of organizations that offer professional e-mail management services. To get a list of such companies, go to **http://directory.google.com/Top/Computers/Internet/E-mail/Mailing_Lists/Hosted_Services**.

MAKING IT HAPPEN

Isolate the Information Need

The first step in any e-mail strategy is to isolate the information need of your target market. What sort of information would they find useful? Would they like information on new products and special offers? Would they like information on trends within your industry? What sort of information would make them want to give you their e-mail address?

Define Your Publication Scope and Schedule

Once you have defined an information need, you must make clear what the scope of your e-mail publication is. What exactly will the person get if they subscribe? Unless you are delivering very time-sensitive information, a weekly publication is usually sufficient.

Make the Subscription Process Prominent on Your Web Site

Getting people to subscribe is vital to the success of your e-mail strategy. There should therefore be a prominent subscription box on your Web site encouraging people to subscribe. Also, include subscription details in every mailing that you send out. Don't ask too many questions in the subscription process.

Many successful e-mail newsletter providers only ask for the e-mail address of the subscriber. That makes it a very easy and quick process for the potential subscriber. You can always ask for more information later on, when you have established a stronger relationship with the subscriber. As a rule, the more valuable the information is to the potential subscriber, the more information you can ask of them.

Make the Unsubscription Process as Easy as Possible

It is equally important to ensure that the unsubscription process is easy to use. People can get frustrated and angry if they find it difficult to unsubscribe from a service, and some might think you have started spamming them.

If You're Offering a Paid-for Subscription Service, Offer a Free "Teaser" Subscription

If you plan to offer a commercial service where you charge people to subscribe, then it is a good idea to offer a free e-mail that contains brief summaries of what is included in the commercial offering. It may also be an idea to offer a free trial period, so that the subscriber can get an understanding of what you have to offer.

Decide Whether You Want a Plain Text or HTML Version of Your E-mail

There are two basic options for the format you can use when delivering an e-mail to your subscriber base: plain text and HTML. Plain text is just like a normal e-mail, and is the simplest and easiest to produce. HTML is like send-

---

"It is ironic but true that in this era of electronic communications, personal interaction is becoming more important than ever."

Regis McKenna

ing a web page in an e-mail. It will deliver a lot more impact and color, but it is more expensive to produce, and a number of older e-mail systems find it hard to read HTML. If you do decide to use an HTML e-mail approach, it's a good idea to offer a plain text version as well or a significant number of people may be unable to subscribe to your service.

For plain text e-mail layout keep the line length of text between 65 and 70 characters to avoid breaking lines, which make the layout look very ugly, and keep paragraphs nice and short—five to six lines is optimum. Use capitals for headings. Because plain text e-mails do not allow the use of bold or font sizing, capitalizing is the only way to give emphasis. Use a non-proportional font such as Courier, because it remains constant regardless of the e-mail package being used.

Keep the E-mail Short and Punchy

Think of what you are doing as delivering a publication. You're trying to get people to read something that will make them want to act—to buy your product or use your service, for example. The scarcest commodity today is people's time. Nobody will read an e-mail that goes on and on, so focus on having punchy headings and short summaries. Avoid having articles that are longer than 500–600 words. The entire e-mail should not contain more than 1,500 words, unless you have a dedicated audience that you know is willing to read longer pieces. So keep things short, and always have some sort of call to action.

Have a Strong Subject Line

The subject line is what subscribers see first when they download their e-mail. Because people are so busy they often scan the subject line and, if it's not interesting, delete the e-mail. However, if you are sending out a regular publication you may wish to include the title of the publication and date in the subject line. In the body of the e-mail itself, it's a good idea to have a table of contents near the top that lets the reader know what to expect from the rest of the e-mail.

Use Hypertext and E-mail Addresses

It's a good idea to use a hypertext to link back to your Web site, in order to encourage the subscriber to get more information, purchase your product, and so on. However, when writing out a hyperlink (URL) always use the full URL. For example, don't use "www.mycompany.com"; instead, use "http://www.mycompany.com." The reason is that some older e-mail packages will not automatically turn the URL into a link unless you include the full URL. Also, if you have a URL that is more than 65 characters long, put it in angle brackets (< >). Otherwise, a number of e-mail packages will break the URL onto two lines and make it unusable. If you are including an e-mail address, put in a "mailto": before the e-mail address, as this will turn it into a link to the subscriber's e-mail package. For example: "mailto:tom@mycompany.com."

Include the Essential Things Every E-mail Mailing Should Have

Every e-mail you send out should contain the subject line (title) and date, subscription and unsubscription information, copyright and privacy policies (or links to these on the Web site), e-mail contact details (telephone and address may also be included), links back to the Web site, and brief information on the publication schedule and scope.

COMMON MISTAKES
Using a "Bait and Switch" Approach

Be very clear to the potential subscriber about what exactly they are subscribing to. If you specialize in special offers, e-mail and tell them so. Don't pretend that you're going to send valuable updates on a particular industry, and then just send special offers.

Not Meeting a Real Information Need

Ask yourself the question: why would anyone want to read this? Too many e-mail mailings are full of useless, repetitive, or out-of-date information.

Not Keeping to a Publication Schedule

If you say you will deliver an e-mail every Wednesday, do it. Being late risks losing credibility and subscribers.

Not Managing the Subscription and Unsubscription Process Professionally

Make it difficult for someone to subscribe and they just won't bother. By the same token, if you make it difficult for people to unsubscribe they'll become irate, and with good reason.

Spamming People

Never subscribe people against their will or without them knowing. Sending unsolicited e-mail is a "get rich quick" strategy. It will damage your long-term reputation.

FOR MORE INFORMATION

Book:
MacPherson, Kim. *Permission-Based E-Mail Marketing That Works!* New York: Dearborn Trade Publishing, 2001.

Web site:
Clickz e-mail marketing section:
www.clickz.com/em_mkt/em_mkt

See also:
- Applying a Viral Marketing Approach on the Internet (p. 657)
- Computers, Information Technology, and E-commerce (pp. 1705–1707)
- Managing 1:1 Marketing (pp. 63–64)
- Promoting Your Web Site Effectively (pp. 659–660)
- Setting Up Newsletter and Web Site Subscription Processes (pp. 647–648)

"Electronic communication, as fast and efficient as it has become, does not automatically lead to better communication."

Dan Dimancescu

Getting the Best from E-marketplaces

GETTING STARTED

An e-marketplace is an Internet-based environment that brings together business-to-business buyers and sellers so that they can trade together more efficiently. Used properly, e-marketplaces can make for more efficient purchasing processes, saving time and money for everyone involved. If you're thinking about moving into an e-marketplace, remember that:

- an e-marketplace gives the smaller company access to many more sales opportunities and allows it to compete on equal terms with larger companies;
- the technology is still relatively new, as are many of the companies involved. Caution is necessary before any major decisions are made;
- there are different types of e-marketplaces and you need to decide which is right for you;
- e-marketplaces should not simply focus on getting the lowest price. Collaboration and the supply of quality information are key benefits they can deliver.

FAQs

What are the key benefits of becoming involved in an e-marketplace?

Reduced sales costs, greater flexibility, saved time, better information, and better collaboration.

What are the key drawbacks of e-marketplaces?

The key drawbacks are inertia and resistance to change among key players, costs in changing procurement processes, the cost of applications and setup, the cost of integration with internal systems, and transaction/subscription fees.

What types of e-marketplaces are there?

There are three distinct types of e-marketplace:

Independent: These are public e-marketplace environments that seek to attract buyers and sellers to trade together. Many simply didn't attract a critical mass of buyers and sellers and folded quickly. Such marketplaces have found most success in commodity-based industries, where there are buyers and sellers.

Consortium-based: These are set up on an industry-wide basis, typically when a number of key buyers in a particular industry get together. They often drive an industry-wide move to achieve common standards for the transfer of information.

Private: These are established by a particular organization to manage its purchasing alone. The organization retains full control, though technology costs can be significant.

MAKING IT HAPPEN
Remember That There's More to It Than Buying and Selling

The early e-marketplaces were little more than auction environments. However, as they've evolved, they have sought to help businesses trade more efficiently with partners. This has involved optimizing communication and collaboration; improved time to market as information flows more quickly between parties involved; and better inventory control, through better market feedback.

Consider Joining an Independent E-marketplace

The advantages of joining an independent e-marketplace are:

- you can find new trading partners that you might otherwise not have been aware of;
- it's useful if you need to reduce inventory;
- it can work well when marketing commodity products;
- independents should embrace open infrastructure standards, making them easier to plug into than private e-marketplaces, which may use more proprietary technology.

The disadvantages are:

- a volatile environment, with many independents going out of business;
- they are not really suitable for developing long-term trading relationships;
- confidentiality and security can be an issue;
- many suppliers see such marketplaces as a way to drive down prices and are wary about getting involved. This limits the buying options.

Consider Joining a Consortium-Based E-marketplace

The advantages are:

- less expensive than establishing a private e-marketplace. Charges are usually in the form of subscription fees and/or commission;
- more choice of buyers and sellers;
- cheaper prices, though this isn't always the case;
- enhanced ability to work on industry-wide issues such as achieving common data standards.

The disadvantages are:

- you are setting up a trading environment with your competitors;
- less control than with a private e-marketplace;
- it won't generally integrate as well into backend technology and processes as a private e-marketplace;
- it's more open and thus more generic. If buying/selling relationships are key to your competitive edge, then a consortium-based e-marketplace will not be a huge benefit;
- governments may view such e-marketplaces as cartels or monopolies, depending on the members and their power within the overall marketplace.

Bear in Mind That You Don't Have to Stick with One Type of E-marketplace

Depending on the complexity of your needs, you may

"The greatest risk lies in not knowing what you don't know. In a fast changing marketplace such as the Internet, this trap seems to be so open and so wide."

William (Walid) Mougayar

decide to use a number of e-marketplaces. For example, you might use a consortium-based one for most of your needs, but, when you have unusual demands, use an independent to give yourself greater choice. A trading partner you meet in an independent e-marketplace may end up migrating into your private e-marketplace.

Recognize That Confidentiality Is Key

One of the major worries regarding involvement in either independent or consortium-based e-marketplace is confidentiality. Over time, a picture will be built up of how an organization trades; this is important information, which could be very valuable to competitors. It's essential that proper security procedures are in place.

Consider Content Management

Content management is an important part of an e-marketplace environment. The system will need to deal with requests for proposals (RFPs), quotations, product diagrams and specifications, pricing and delivery information, and so on. It will need to be able to archive everything in an easily accessible way, and to deal with version control so users can receive the most up-to-date information.

Train and Educate Your Staff

E-marketplaces invariably introduce new ways of doing things. There may be resistance within the business and this will require ongoing education and evangelism. Training will be required for the staff who are expected to operate the e-marketplace.

Seller Beware

Sellers have been very cautious about getting involved in e-marketplaces because of their initial tendency to focus primarily on price. Some e-marketplaces have encouraged reverse auctions, whereby sellers bid against each other to sell to a particular customer. However, the right e-marketplace can have benefits for a seller, opening up new markets and customers, and providing a way of reducing excess stock.

Consider General Issues

- What is the procedure if you want to develop a one-to-one relationship with a trading partner you meet within an e-marketplace?
- Will the e-marketplace have any role to play in shipping and logistics?
- What is expected of you as a participant? How, for example, do you deliver content and updates?
- What integration work is involved? And if it doesn't fully integrate, what are the costs involved in new processes?
- How are payments to be made?

- How are the request for proposal (RFP) and quotation processes handled? Does the e-marketplace offer software that makes these processes more efficient?
- Is there a certification process in place to ensure that you are dealing with reputable entities?

COMMON MISTAKES
Forgetting About Corporate Inertia

The expectation by e-marketplace providers that businesses would suddenly change their buying and selling habits upon the arrival of new technology was a serious mistake. Relationships and habits build up over years, and change only slowly in most situations.

Ignoring the Fact That There's More to Buying and Selling Than Price

Product quality, support, and personal relationships are still key in business-to-business situations. E-marketplaces that simply focused on pitting seller against seller found that that approach simply didn't work.

Delays in Getting the E-marketplace Up and Running

E-marketplaces are a lot more complex than was originally predicted. The more partners involved, the more difficult it becomes to synchronize the information and business processes between each entity. Delays in making some of the best-known e-marketplaces fully functional have hurt the image of the industry.

Failing to Provide a Robust Payments Process

Many e-marketplaces lack a process whereby the participants can immediately settle the whole transaction. The fact that some of the trade must then be completed offline means that both offline and online processes need to be maintained, reducing efficiencies and cost savings.

THE BEST SOURCES OF HELP

Web site:
B2business.net: **www.b2business.net/eMarketplaces**

See also:

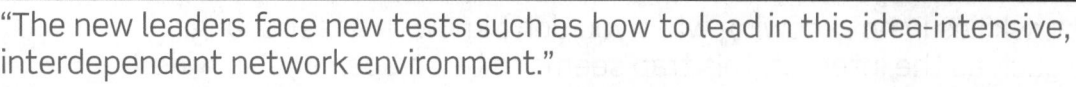

"The new leaders face new tests such as how to lead in this idea-intensive, interdependent network environment."

John Sculley

Making the Most of an Intranet

GETTING STARTED

An intranet is a Web site for your employees. It should contain content and other resources that will make them more informed and productive. Many intranets have evolved in an ad hoc manner, with little approval from senior managers and few clear objectives. Instead of becoming valuable information resources, they have become information dumps. Consequently, staff are not using them and their potential is lost. When developing an intranet strategy, keep the following in mind:

- An intranet can combine internal and external information resources in a one-stop information shop.
- It can become the intellectual capital library of the organization, capturing staff knowledge, facilitating teamwork and collaboration, and providing an excellent induction vehicle for new employees.
- It can allow people to work remotely and still access key information.

FAQs
Should an intranet employ central standards?

Yes. Otherwise an intranet will become almost useless. Some larger organizations now have hundreds of intranets, each with different standards, creating an environment that's impossible to navigate and very expensive and time-consuming to maintain. The approach should be to control key standards centrally, while giving as much responsibility as possible to individual departments for the publication of relevant content.

Should employees be allowed to develop personal content?

Allowing staff space to create their own personal home pages can gain acceptance for the intranet and deepen the sense of organizational culture. However, care must be taken that such home pages are off the beaten track. They should not get in the way of the primary objective: to deliver content that helps employees to do a better job. Nor should they take up too much time.

Should an intranet incorporate security measures?

Yes. Invariably, intranets will be accessed by staff from outside the physical organization—from home, hotels, and so on. So a robust security system is crucial. Passwords need to be changed regularly and access to certain types of information managed properly. However, security should be planned carefully to maintain simple, open communication. If it's too difficult to access the intranet, a lot of people won't bother.

MAKING IT HAPPEN
Achieve Management Buy-in

Unless there is genuine management commitment to an intranet, it will quickly develop into a mess: underfunded, under-resourced and under-used. Experience indicates that employees behave in a "once bitten, twice shy" manner: if they go to an intranet and find it a waste of time, it's much harder to convince them to visit it a second time. It's better to have no intranet at all than one full of badly organized, out-of-date content.

Identify Who Needs Content Most

Organizations create a huge amount of content, not all of which is relevant or productive. The content that should go on the intranet first is that which is most likely to further the organization's objectives. Do salespeople require faster access to more accurate information? Do technical staff spend too long looking for documents that often end up being out of date? Are employee contact details kept in a little green book that nobody can find when they need it? Do support staff find that they're always asking around for answers to customer queries?

Develop Return on Investment Models

A primary reason intranets don't get proper funding is that no one has proved to the finance department that the extra budget should be allocated. Proving that a quality intranet can deliver a quantifiable return on investment (ROI) can loosen those purse strings. Here's a simple example:

Company X has 100 people working for it. On average they spend 12 minutes every day searching for content. The average hourly cost per employee is $50 and they work 250 days per year. Thus, the annual cost in lost productivity due to time spent searching is:

$$100 \times 0.2 \times \$50 \times 250 = \$250,000$$

If a well-organized intranet can reduce searching time by half, that would result in an annual saving of $125,000.

Start with Something Manageable and Likely to Deliver Real Benefit

It's important to start off with something manageable that delivers the most direct and measurable benefit. Find out who within the organization is most concerned about getting the right information. Is it the sales employees, support, research and development? Or is there a facility, such as an online phone directory or appointments diary, that people are screaming out for? Home in on the most burning need; once you prove that a success, it will be much easier to get budget and commitment to expand the intranet. There may also be some easy wins. Perhaps the cafeteria menu would get people checking the intranet every day?

Get Buy-in and Commitment from Staff

Where exactly is all this wonderful content going to come from? Some of it will be created already, certainly. Some may come in the form of subscriptions to magazines or commercial databases. But much of it will have to be created by people within the organization itself. There's no point in assuming that it will magically appear. You need to get approval and commitment from the staff expected to write the stuff.

"The new electronic interdependence recreates the world in the image of a global village."

Marshall McLuhan

Ensure That It Is Part of the Job Function

If the creation of content is not made part of someone's job function, and he or she is not measured on delivery, content quality will inevitably be poor. So reward and remuneration structures need to be put in place. It's not simply about money. If an employee knows his or her good technical paper may get a special feature on the intranet and be seen by peers and managers, that's good motivation. Remember too, writing quality content takes time. If that time is not available, quality content won't get written.

Encourage Collaboration and Interaction

Consider setting up discussion forums, chat facilities and e-mail discussion lists that get people sharing issues and ideas. Encourage collaboratively created content, with several authors working on a document. Remember, collaboration and interaction don't happen on their own. Without quality moderation, discussion areas can quickly become stale and lifeless.

Put an Editor in Charge

An intranet is really a publication: it will live or die by the quality of its content. In the same way that a printer is not in charge of the *New York Times*, a programmer should not be in charge of an intranet. An editor understands content—what staff need or want to read, and how to write it in an accessible, readable way.

Get a Proper Commitment from the IT Department

Even though the central focus is quality content, there will always be technical issues that crop up from day to day. Without sufficient commitment from the IT department, vital content may be delayed or the entire intranet may go down. Not a happy situation.

Focus Design on Metadata, Classification, Navigation, Search and Layout

Forget about fancy gimmicks and bandwidth-hungry applications. Remember that people will be accessing your intranet over those very slow lines from hotel rooms or from home, and just want to get to the facts. Therefore quality classification and navigation, backed up by a robust search engine, are essential. To achieve this, you need the right metadata on every document and page.

Metadata is the content about the content, the who, what, where, and when about each document or page. For example, metadata could include author name, date published, heading, summary, and classification.

Consider Using a Content Management Application

An intranet that has several hundred pages, with more than 20 new pages being published every week, could well do with a content management application. Maintaining an intranet in HTML is fine if the site is small and is updated by only a few people. However if there's a lot of content and lots of contributors, it may become unmanageable. Content management software can streamline the publishing processes, making them much more efficient and cost effective.

Promote It!

If you don't actively promote your intranet, many employees won't even know it exists. Send out a weekly newsletter to all staff informing them of what's new on the intranet. Put up colorful posters in the cafeteria.

COMMON MISTAKES
You Don't Have Management Buy-in

In the early days, intranets grew in the wild, fed by the enthusiasm of a few dedicated staff. However, without proper planning, clear objectives, and management buy-in, an intranet is doomed to failure. Staff will desert it, and management will be left with an information dump.

No Budgets, No Staff Resources

An early Internet assumption was that information is cheap to create. This is far from the truth: quality content is expensive to produce and maintain. You can't expect consistent quality content from people if it's not part of their job function. It's better to have no intranet than one that is poorly funded and staffed.

A Big Launch and No Follow-up

The launch is the beginning, not the end. Too many organizations make a big effort to launch their intranet, only to ignore it. In ignored intranets, out-of-date content grows.

Poor Classification, Poor Standards

Without proper standards and well-planned classification, intranets can become a nightmare to navigate and manage. So when you do find the content you need, it turns out to be red text on a pink background!

No Encouragement of Intranet Use

An intranet is only valuable if employees use it. In many organizations people are not actually aware of the resources available on the intranet, because it has not been properly promoted.

FOR MORE INFORMATION

Web site:
Intranet Journal Magazine: **www.intranetjournal.com**

See also:
✔ Establishing an Enterprise Portal (p. 667)
✔ Setting Up an Extranet (p. 668)

"Experience is a good teacher, but she sends in terrific bills."   Minna Antrim

Establishing an Enterprise Portal

GETTING STARTED

If your business has grown and you employ a number of staff, you may want to investigate enterprise portals. Put very simply, these are Web sites that assemble a wide range of content and services for staff. Some of this content is published by the organization itself, and some will be acquired from third-party publishers. The principle is to bring together all the key information that staff require to do a better job. When considering developing an enterprise portal, keep the following in mind:

- The word "portal" means different things to different people: to some, it's a souped-up intranet, to others it's a nascent e-marketplace; others will see it as part of a customer relationship management strategy.
- Enterprise portals, while great in theory, are complex to develop and expensive to manage.
- An enterprise portal can easily fall into the trap of trying to provide all the information staff could possibly need and providing none of it very well.

MAKING IT HAPPEN
Exploit the Extra Potential

In many ways, an enterprise portal (sometimes referred to as an enterprise information portal) is a fancy name for an intranet. The key difference is that an enterprise portal manages not just internal content, but also external content that may be useful to staff. Such external information could include, for example, specialized news feeds, or access to industry research reports.

Learn from the Public Portals

On the Web everyone is a publisher, but that doesn't mean that everyone is a good publisher or that people will want to read what they publish. Very few public portals have survived, because they have not been able to build a viable business case.

Another portal sector that has seen great change is the much-vaunted "vortal." A vortal, or vertical portal, provides information that is organized around a vertical market sector, such as pharmaceuticals or plastics. Vortals and e-marketplaces have a lot in common, and in many markets may be one and the same thing. Most of these vortals, if they haven't evolved into e-marketplaces, are probably no longer in business.

The lessons that need to be learned from public portals and industry vortals include the following:

- People are very conservative in the way they consume content. The majority of people go to a few trusted brands.
- Running portals is expensive; many have not survived because they did not have a proper business model.

Don't Get Complacent about Having a Captive Audience

The enterprise portal would seem to have a captive audience—employees. But it's not as simple as that. Staff who use an enterprise portal demand high publishing standards. High publishing standards are expensive to maintain, and many enterprise portals are dying because they don't have enough quality content, the content is not being kept up to date, and the whole environment is not properly organized and structured. What many organizations are discovering, to their cost, is that providing all this related information is wonderful in theory, but expensive and difficult to manage in practice.

Know Your Employees' Content Needs

Ask the following questions:

- How are employees' information needs being met at present?
- Are any of these needs not being satisfied properly?
- Can I fill this gap cost-effectively?
- Will my staff trust me to fill this gap?
- Where's the return on investment?

Related information is all well and good, but the key question must be: where is the return on investment? If a member of staff can just as easily get this related information somewhere else, why duplicate the effort? Unfortunately, organizations rarely take the time to examine which content drives the business forward, and which has little effect. But having a Web site is being a publisher, and, if you don't understand the impact of your content, you don't understand publishing.

FOR MORE INFORMATION

Web site:
Business2.0: **www.business2.com**

See also:
- Computers, Information Technology, and E-commerce (pp. 1705–1707)
- Delivering Quality Online Customer Service and Support (pp. 612–613)
- Implementing an Effective Search Process for a Web Site (p. 645)
- Implementing Effective E-learning Within the Organization (pp. 671–672)
- Making a Web Site Easy to Navigate (pp. 643–644)
- Making the Most of an Intranet (pp. 665–666)

Setting Up an Extranet

GETTING STARTED

An extranet is a private Web site between two or more business partners, which aims to enable the partners to share information in an efficient and timely manner. Because this is a work environment and partners will want to get to the information as quickly as possible, the design of an extranet should focus on minimal graphics and maximum content. An extranet will be password-protected in order to maintain confidentiality; security will be a key issue. When exploring the establishment of an extranet, consider the following:

- Extranets are all about the speedy delivery of relevant information.
- Supplying up-to-date, accurate and comprehensive information to a business partner is not a simple process.
- Connecting partners into an extranet can make them more loyal and make it more difficult for them to switch to a competitor.

MAKING IT HAPPEN
When to Establish an Extranet

An extranet makes sense when you have business partners who continually require substantial information from you. By hooking them into an extranet, you are essentially offering them a self-service option. Instead of delivering the requested information by phone, fax, mail, or in person, an extranet allows your partners to get the information they need whenever they want it.

Examples of Extranet Uses

Extranets can range from the relatively simple to the very complex, as shown in these examples:

- A consulting firm may be implementing a job for a client and use an extranet to keep the client fully informed on all aspects of the job.
- A private e-marketplace is essentially a complex extranet whereby products and services can be bought and sold.
- A product design may involve a number of partners. An extranet can be used to share design specifications and to allow effective collaboration to occur.
- An organization may sell a complex product to customers and offer them an extranet that will contain specific information on the product, including support, upgrades, and ways to use the product.

Confidentiality and Security in Extranets

By definition, an extranet will contain confidential information that you wish to share only with identified partners. From a security point of view keep in mind the following:

- An extranet often contains elements of your intranet.

Make sure that it is properly locked off from other parts of your intranet.
- Encryption should be considered: information transferred between parties is specially encoded so that only the relevant parties can read it.
- A joint security policy needs to be agreed with your partners, so that equal standards and procedures are maintained.

The Importance of Content Management

An extranet is only as useful as its information. If the content is not accurate, up to date and comprehensive, then the very purpose of the extranet is undermined. Therefore, quality content management procedures are required. Many extranets fall down because the content is not being updated and managed properly.

Simple, Lean Web Design

Your partners will not be happy if they are left waiting for a page to download because of some fancy animation containing a swirling logo. The design should be even more minimal than for other Web sites, to ensure that content can be navigated and downloaded as quickly as possible. Remember, an extranet is very much a work environment.

Bandwidth May Be an Issue

Extranets are often hooked into intranets, which are generally hosted internally. You will need to make sure that bandwidth is sufficient to allow external partners quick access.

The Need for a Contract

An extranet involves the communication of confidential information. This means a contract is required. Some extranets are designed and maintained jointly by a number of partners. In such a situation, a contract will need to cover who owns what, and who has what obligations from a maintenance point of view.

FOR MORE INFORMATION

Web site:
Intranet Journal: **www.intranetjournal.com**

"Capital, technology, and ideas flow these days like quicksilver across national boundaries."

Robert H. Waterman, Jr.

Adding Value Through E-alliances

GETTING STARTED

E-alliances are partnerships forged between organizations in order to achieve e-business objectives more effectively. There has been a surge in such alliances since the Web took off in the mid-1990s. According to a 2001 study by McKinsey consultants, the most successful e-alliances were those involving traditional offline businesses and online entities—the clicks and mortar strategy. When examining e-alliance opportunities, consider the following:

- It is often faster and cheaper to set up an alliance than to build something from scratch to achieve a particular objective.
- You need to know exactly what you want to achieve from an alliance, how you will measure the objectives, and how to exit.
- About half of alliances end in failure, the key reasons being false expectations, lack of commitment of assets and resources, and unworkable management structures.

FAQs

Why are changes in technology facilitating more alliances and partnerships?

The reasons include the following:

- Internet technologies create a common platform upon which organizations and people can communicate and share information. Such collaboration was more difficult using traditional technologies and organizational structures.
- The huge changes brought by technology mean that modern organizations need to be much more flexible. Alliances can allow an organization to react quickly to an opportunity or threat.
- Trends such as outsourcing are fundamentally dependent on the partnership model.
- Modern technologies have made individuals more independent of the organization. They may work on contract, or go off and start a small company that will offer an alliance with the organization.

Is the trend toward more alliances and partnerships going to abate soon?

All the signs are that alliances and partnerships will continue to be important in the future. Internet use continues to grow, and is by definition a networked environment. Organizations and individuals will use the Internet to become more flexible, not less.

What does this all mean for a manager?

Instead of managing something fixed, like a department or factory floor, you are now managing objectives and relationships. The goal is to achieve the objective as quickly as possible. This should not be limited by organizational resources. Find a partner to fill the gap; form an alliance to get to market quicker than your competitor. You will be judged on achieving your objectives. How you achieve them may well require thinking outside the box.

MAKING IT HAPPEN
Understand Clearly What You Want to Achieve

If you approach alliance building merely because you think it's a "good thing," you may end up having some bad experiences. You really need to be clear about what you want to achieve from any alliance, and what your potential partner wants.

Maybe you both want to achieve the same thing—more sales—but one of you wants much faster sales growth than the other. This will lead to a lot of pain down the line, so be careful that everyone's expectations are managed properly.

Use Alliances to Enter New Markets

Alliances are a key way by which organizations expand globally. Setting up alliances with established players in particular markets can be a much faster way of achieving market share than setting up a large physical presence.

What's in It for the Partner?

Partnership and has to be attractive to both partners, or the relationship will go nowhere. Siebel produces sales and customer relationship management software. From day one it sought partners, such as Accenture and PricewaterhouseCoopers, to implement its solutions. The logic was simple. For every $1 Siebel got paid for software, a consulting firm would receive $5–7 for implementing it. Its partnership program has helped make Siebel one of the fastest-growing companies in the world.

Competitors Can Form Alliances

Competitors may form an alliance to push a particular industry standard. However, in such situations you must be very clear about what the alliance wants to achieve and manage it carefully. A good example is consortium-based e-marketplaces, where competitors come together to achieve greater efficiencies in purchasing.

The Start-up and the Big Organization

Many start-ups seek to form alliances with larger organizations in order to gain more rapid access to markets, funding, and the credibility of being associated with a particular brand. The larger organization gets innovative products and services. The danger for the start-up is that it becomes too dependent on one major customer.

The Clicks and Mortar Alliance

A major study on e-alliances, published by McKinsey in 2001, found that partnerships between traditional offline companies and online business entities were most successful, such as that between Amazon.com and Toys R Us. Toys R Us had the physical infrastructure and brand, while Amazon.com had the online infrastructure and experience in making e-commerce work.

One Alliance Is Rarely Enough

It generally makes sense to have a network of alliances,

"Strategies that succeed are organic. They evolve. They wrap themselves around problems, challenges, and opportunities, make progress and move on."

Robert H. Waterman, Jr.

some involved, some more casual, but all pushing forward your e-business strategy. The key is to be able to judge whether a potential alliance can add value or not, and to manage the network well. Of course, the risk in having too large an alliance network is that you spread yourself too thin.

Alliances Need Ongoing Management and Commitment

Because it is now so easy to establish alliances, many managers focus on the glitzy part—issuing the press release. Some alliances are treated merely as a PR exercise and are pretty much forgotten about after the immediate publicity. But without an ongoing commitment from management, these alliances are dead in the water.

Organizational Structures, Management and Metrics Need to Be in Place

Where do alliances and partnerships fit in the organizational chart? Who is responsible for them? Where is the strategy? What happens in the case of disputes? Some organizations treat alliances as if they are simply ancillary activities, but in this case, the benefits are likely to be negligible. Many partnerships fail because they don't have organizational or management structures in place.

You can't measure success by the number of your alliances. Rather, you need to know exactly what value each partner is delivering, so you will require a set of metrics that regularly measure the success or otherwise of a particular alliance. If negative, you must act on such information quickly, rather than wait for the inevitable big bust-up.

Partnerships Aren't Necessarily About Equality

You don't have to be best buddies to make partnerships work, though a good relationship helps. Partnerships don't have to be with equals. Managing by consensus is all well and good, but if the wrong people are involved, decisions won't get made and momentum will be lost.

Think Long-term, Act Short-term

Because a great many alliances fail to deliver on their promises, it is not advisable to enter into long-term contractual arrangements. It is much better to establish a short-term arrangement with very defined goals. Once these goals have been achieved, a longer-term agreement can be considered.

Be Wary of Exclusive Deals

You need to be confident that a partnership will deliver substantial value before going into an exclusive deal. If your industry is subject to a lot of change, exclusivity is even more risky. If your potential partner wants exclusivity, one option is to create a short-term agreement with very specific objectives: if these are achieved, an exclusive contract can be signed. Another option is to set triggers into the contract. Only if certain objectives—sales

figures, for example—are met within a defined period, does the relationship remain exclusive.

Have an Exit Strategy

Part of knowing what you want to achieve from an alliance is knowing when it has fulfilled its objectives and how to close it down. This needs to be carefully thought through. Both partners should agree on a clear exit strategy, which will include such things as how assets and intellectual capital are to be shared.

COMMON MISTAKES
The E-alliance Press Release

Too often organizations have focused on forming an alliance just so that they can issue a press release and place the partner's logo on their Web site. In the early Internet buzz, such press releases often had an impact. However, since the technology downturn, cynicism is the more common reaction.

You Think an Alliance Is About Signing a Contract

Not making the proper commitment in time and resources is a key reason why partnerships fail. The real work begins after the contract is signed. Making the alliance work takes sustained effort, and it may well develop very differently from what was originally envisaged. Make sure you plan for the longer term, and that your plan is flexible.

You Opt for the Glamour Alliance

Smaller start-ups often believe that an alliance with a large brand will solve all their problems. Big brands are very aware of their status and usually charge a heavy price either directly or indirectly for such associations. Rarely does the smaller player get a bargain.

No Decisions Are Made

Where the decision-making process is overly focused on achieving consensus, the partnership can get bogged down. Thus, it loses a key attribute—speed.

FOR MORE INFORMATION

Book:
Segil, Larraine D. *Fast Alliances: Power Your E-Business*. New York: Wiley, 2000.

Web site:
McKinsey Quarterly: **www.mckinseyquarterly.com**

"Management by trust, empathy, and forgiveness sounds good. It also sounds soft. It is in practice tough. Organizations based on trust have, on occasion, to be ruthless."

Charles Handy

Implementing Effective E-learning Within the Organization

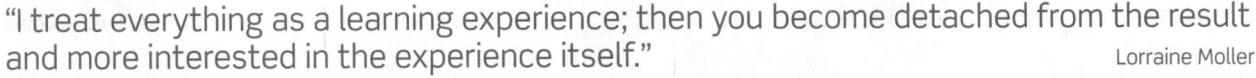
GETTING STARTED

E-learning over the Internet is flexible, cost-effective, and measurable. The global e-learning marketplace continues to grow rapidly, and is now worth more than $25 billion. When investigating e-learning, consider the following:

- E-learning puts learners in the driving seat, allowing them to learn about specific subjects just when they need to.
- To be effective, e-learning needs to involve collaboration with other learners and mentoring from experts. The classroom should not be eliminated, but rather introduced at strategic points in the learning process.
- The e-learning industry has matured very rapidly, and there are many companies offering a wide variety of e-learning content, technology, and services.

FAQs

What are the key factors that drive e-learning?

In an economic upturn, the logic for e-learning is compelling. Change is constant, and there is an ongoing need to keep employees educated and up to date. Quality staff are hard to find, which has two major implications from a learning perspective. First, the best people tend to be focused on constantly improving their skills, so an organization with a comprehensive learning program is more attractive to them. Second, if appropriate staff can't be found for certain positions, an alternative is to retrain current employees. This, again, requires a learning program.

In a downturn, the need to train so many so quickly is not quite as compelling. However, the cost-effectiveness of e-learning becomes attractive here. Traditional classroom-based learning has a high cost in getting people to and from venues, much of which e-learning cuts out. In addition, the effectiveness of classroom-based learning has been difficult to measure. E-learning is seen as more accountable and measurable.

What are the distinguishing characteristics of e-learning?

The following are key characteristics of e-learning:

- e-learning is primarily delivered over the Web;
- it can adapt quickly to meet changing learning needs;
- learners can find what they want to learn, when they want to, at a pace that suits them. (However, some e-learning is instructor-led, when learners log-in at a specific time and are taken through a module by an instructor.)
- many e-learning modules are designed to be 20–30 minutes long, so learners can take them during a break period. By taking a series of modules over a period of time, learners build up a skill;

- learners collaborate with instructors and other learners so as to learn better;
- compared to classroom-based learning, e-learning is a fast and cost-effective way to teach large numbers of people;
- it can deliver learning in multimedia format: text, images, audio, video, interactive and simulation tools;
- material that learners have accessed and completed can be accurately measured, allowing the organization to track who is learning what, and which resources are popular.

MAKING IT HAPPEN

Understand What E-learning Can Do

Organizations invest in learning so that their people can become smarter and thus more productive. The theory is great, but the reality has been described as the "great training robbery." Like the old advertising adage, organizations know that half of their training works, they just don't know which half. E-learning promises to make learning more efficient and accountable by getting the right training to the right people as quickly as possible, measuring the results to ensure it's achieving its goals, and making sure it's done in a cost-effective manner.

Develop a Learning Culture

If there is no learning culture within the organization, e-learning is not going to make much difference. It can only work where staff and management are committed to it. Perhaps many employees feel the only way to learn is in a classroom: they will need to be won over to the benefits of e-learning. Simply installing an e-learning system and waiting for everyone to sign up is not likely to work.

Implement the Components of E-learning

The following are necessary components of an e-learning environment:

- Personalized learning space: learners need their own customized environment in the overall e-learning Web site, so they can check such things as what modules they have completed and have yet to complete; who their mentors are; or what collaborative learning groups they are part of.
- Mentoring: without interaction and mentoring, e-learning can become very dry. Learners need to be able to access experts in order to ask questions and receive guidance.
- Simulation: quality e-learning offers simulated environments in which learners can practice what they have learned.
- Collaboration: interaction with other learners is a fundamental building block of all learning. E-learning needs to facilitate this by actively encouraging collaboration.
- Assessment: important both for the organization and the learner. The organization needs to know if the e-learning

---

"I treat everything as a learning experience; then you become detached from the result and more interested in the experience itself."

Lorraine Moller

is resulting in increased knowledge within its workforce; learners need to have targets and to know where they are doing well and where they need to work harder.

Manage and Administer E-learning

E-learning requires sophisticated administration if it is to be properly managed. The following elements will need to be in place:
- a registration process
- a payment process, or a process by which costs can be matched to budgets
- a monitoring process that allows the manager to track how learners are performing

In addition, a process must be established whereby managers and employees work together to plan and discuss what needs to be learned and how things are progressing. This was traditionally done during annual or biannual staff assessments, but because of rapidly changing learning needs, this now has to happen with greater regularity.

A method of measuring how the new skills learned contribute to a more productive workplace is also required. People may be learning lots of new skills, but, if these are not applicable to their job or their future prospects, they will be wasted.

Mix Classroom-based Learning and E-learning

It is shortsighted to think e-learning will totally replace classroom-based learning. One of the critical functions of classrooms is that people get to know each other and build up contacts. The classic way many people find out about things is to call or e-mail someone. If they don't know who to contact, or don't feel comfortable doing so because they don't know the expert well, that can be a major drawback. A happy medium needs to be achieved: for example, learners could do most of a course through e-learning, but come together in a classroom environment at strategic points.

Create Your Own E-learning or Buy It in

The e-learning marketplace has expanded rapidly and there are many companies who have comprehensive and cost-effective e-learning offerings. E-learning technology is very complex and it will rarely make sense to build your own. A model that has emerged for organizations that have their own training content is to buy or rent e-learning technology.

Select an E-learning Company

The selection process will very much depend on your specific needs. However, in evaluating e-learning companies, the following questions will be useful:
- What are their reputation and brand like? Have they been around for a while, and do they look as if they'll be around in the future?
- What's the quality of their learning content? Is it highly interactive and engaging, with access to experts, or is it like a digitized textbook?

- How comprehensive is the offering? Will this organization meet all your e-learning needs, or will you have to go elsewhere for other courses?
- What is the technology like? Is it robust and scalable? Do the modules download quickly or do they hog bandwidth?
- What sort of global reach do they have? If the e-learning works well in one office, can it be quickly rolled out in other offices around the world?

COMMON MISTAKES
Slow Bandwidth, Poor Machines

A multitude of technical issues often hobble the shining promise of e-learning. E-learning that uses a lot of multimedia elements—sound, video, animation—can cause a lot of delivery problems. Even within the internal network, bandwidth can be scarce.

Doing Training on the Cheap

E-learning does reduce training costs, but few believe that e-learning on its own will meet an organization's entire training requirements. People still need to get together to share ideas and develop friendships. Often, the socializing that occurs after classroom learning is as important as what happened in the classroom itself. Also, e-learning is less suitable for teaching soft skills and those that require a lot of hands-on activity.

Lack of Self-motivation

Not everyone is itching to learn. Some people will always find an excuse for not doing the course. Often the only way that you can get people to focus on learning is to get them into a classroom.

You Forget That Teachers Have Value

Some proponents of e-learning give the impression that teachers are the enemy of education and that getting rid of them is the answer to all training problems. E-learning without active input from mentors and experts can be a very shallow experience.

Lack of Recognition

The e-learning promise of learning when you want often translates into learning after work or at the weekend. Learners work away diligently, but there's no recognition of the effort. A sense of isolation sets in, and, as the day-to-day workload increases, the need to do that e-learning course drifts into the background.

FOR MORE INFORMATION

Web site:
The e-learning jump page contains an analysis of e-learning issues: www.internettime.com/wordpress2

See also:
✔ Establishing an Enterprise Portal (p. 667)

Using Videoconferencing Effectively

GETTING STARTED

Virtual meetings allow a group of people in two or more physical locations to communicate over the Internet or by using video and audio equipment. Videoconferencing has been around since the 1970s but never gained acceptance, mainly because of expensive and unreliable technology and cultural issues. However, with cheaper, improved technology and after an economic downturn, interest in it and other "virtual" options has been renewed. When considering videoconferencing, keep the following in mind:

- Videoconferencing has more benefits than simply saving money on air travel. It can save time and allow for more active collaboration.
- Many people do not understand the many uses of video- or e-conferencing and are nervous about using it for the first time. Training and education is vital if the expensive system is not to be left unused.
- Videoconferencing is still a complex activity, and it will never be of a high enough quality to eliminate the need for people to get together physically.

FAQs

Why has videoconferencing not been more widely used?

- The technology was very expensive and often failed. Many people who tried using it in the early days found it difficult to set up and awkward to use.
- Not enough people were using it. This is what is called the network effect. Videoconferencing is a network technology, and like other network technologies such as fax or e-mail, requires a critical mass of users.
- Face-to-face meetings, which videoconferencing seeks to replace, are where relationships are built and deals are closed.
- Many people feel awkward in front of a camera, or hearing their own voice played back.

What are the new drivers of videoconferencing?

A number of factors have converged to make videoconferencing attractive. These include the following:

- The technology has become cheaper, more robust, and easier to use
- Broadband is becoming more widely available
- PC/Web-based videoconferencing has developed.
- More people are telecommuting.
- The slowing economy has reduced travel budgets; videoconferencing is seen as an affordable alternative.

What are the key benefits of videoconferencing?

The key benefits are:

- it saves time and money;
- less relocation of staff is required, as people can work in virtual teams to a greater extent;
- it is often difficult to get a number of people in the same room at the same time. Videoconferencing makes this easier.

MAKING IT HAPPEN
It's Not All about Saving Money

If videoconferencing is viewed simply as a way to cut costs, then staff may develop a negative attitude toward it. They are likely to see it as something that takes away their perks, a secondhand way of doing business.

Videoconferencing should be promoted in a more positive manner. Staff should see it as a way to:

- get important decisions made more quickly because key people can be brought together more quickly;
- get key people together more often;
- allow people to collaborate and share knowledge more easily and frequently;
- still allow people to meet, even if they can't travel;
- conduct interviews;
- provide or receive training.

Training Is Critical

Videoconferencing is more than having what would have been a physical meeting by video. It can change the way people go about their work, organize their time, and plan their projects. Many people simply don't know how videoconferencing can help them. They are afraid of using it for the first time in case they appear foolish.

What must be emphasized again and again are the benefits for the people involved. Videoconferencing should be promoted as a tool that will make people more productive. Here are some ways of making it more easily understood and more acceptable:

- Make sure that senior management use it. Their presence can be a strong motivator.
- Find a videoconferencing enthusiast and give them scope to promote the technology to other people.
- Have regular demonstrations of videoconferencing to allow people to try it out in a relaxed environment.
- Promote its achievement of practical results by publishing articles and case studies.

Ask People to Examine Their Travel Plans

People should be reminded always to ask themselves: "Can I do this another way rather than get on a plane?" If the trip involves meeting other people within the organization, they should be encouraged to have a premeeting videoconference. After this they can evaluate whether the trip still needs to take place. Even if it does, the meeting is likely to be more productive because of the preceding videoconference.

Get Feedback

Videoconferencing is new to most people, so it is important to track how people are using it and what sort of attitudes are emerging. People should be given evaluation forms to fill out after each meeting. Issues or suggestions should be followed up.

Videoconferencing Options

There are two basic options available for videoconferencing:

"The length of a meeting rises with the number of people present and the productiveness of a meeting falls with the square of the number of people present."

Eileen Shanahan

- Full-blown videoconferencing using ISDN lines, dedicated equipment, and large screens. This is the more expensive option but it guarantees a higher-quality experience. However, this option is complex to set up, and quite expensive.
- PC/Web-based videoconferencing. Sometimes called Internet Protocol (IP) videoconferencing, this is a far cheaper option, since it piggybacks on PC and Internet technology. It is less reliable but improving all the time. It still requires an ISDN line, takes up a small box window on a PC, and is really more like videophone than videoconferencing. Be sure to check minimum processor speeds, video card, and operating system requirements.

Videoconferencing Components

The essential components in a videoconferencing system are:

- a camera
- a monitor
- a microphone
- speakers
- a computer or specialized videoconference terminal, with the appropriate software and user interface
- a codec: a hardware or a software component that compresses and decompresses the audio and video signals (hardware codecs are generally faster)
- a network connection.

The quality of each of these components has an impact on the overall quality of the videoconference. This is why videoconferencing is difficult to get right: everything else may be working well, but the microphone, for example, may be faulty.

Make Sure Security Is in Place

Confidential information will be communicated during many videoconferences. It is therefore important that a proper security process is in place. This is usually achieved by the use of encryption technologies.

Support from the Vendor

Videoconference equipment is liable to break down just at the moment you need it most. Because videoconferencing is so time-critical, having a number to call whenever you have a problem can be very helpful.

Tips for Running a Videoconference

The following are some things to keep in mind when participating in or running a videoconference.

- Get to the room at least 15 minutes before the meeting is supposed to start, to ensure that everything is working well. If this is the first videoconference in a particular location, a trial run is highly recommended.
- Make sure everyone has a proper agenda and all relevant documentation before the meeting.
- Make sure someone in each location is familiar with using the equipment for such techniques as camera zooming and audio control.

- The agenda should be accompanied by a page containing a list of all the relevant contact people and phone numbers in the videoconference locations.
- Make sure everyone gets a proper introduction and that the camera focuses on them as they are being introduced.
- Remember that there is often a slight delay in transmission, so it may be necessary to pause to allow people to digest and respond.
- Make sure people are not being left out.
- If you are showing any text, make sure it is in a large font. Keep graphics simple.

COMMON MISTAKES
A Lot of Things Can Go Wrong

Video- and Web conferencing require many components, cameras, microphones, and speakers, so there are a lot of things to go wrong. You are not depending on your own equipment alone, but on the equipment at the other end also. For example, if another room has a poor camera, then no matter how good your system, the picture will look poor in your room.

Lack of Training and Understanding

Many videoconferencing systems have been underused because of a lack of understanding among staff. Without training the take-up of videoconferencing within the organization is likely to remain low.

Making Your First Sales Call via a Virtual Meeting

Virtual meetings will never replace the need for people to get together physically. If someone is selling a product, the golden rule is to get in front of the potential customer. It is unlikely that sales reps will rely on remote conferencing to make their first vital face-to-face impressions.

Disregarding Teleconferencing

In many situations, people feel that Teleconferencing does the job fine. There needs to be a sufficiently compelling reason why you need to see as well as hear people at the other end. Often there is not, and expensive equipment is underused.

FOR MORE INFORMATION

Web sites:
Microsoft: **www.microsoft.com**
Videoconference cookbook:
www.videnet.gatech.edu/cookbook.en

See also:
☆ Project Management (p. 200–202)
☆ Virtual Collaboration (pp. 203–204)

Exploring Peer-to-Peer (P2P) Commerce

GETTING STARTED

Peer-to-Peer (P2P) embraces the networking capabilities of the Internet. It allows people to share and publish resources directly, and allows the unused processing capability of computers to be shared and used productively. While the concept of peer-to-peer has in fact been around for many years, it has gained a new lease of life with the advent of the Internet. The peer-to-peer model became particularly well known in connection with the original Napster music swapping service and later Skype, which provides high-quality voice calls over the Internet.

FAQs

What exactly is peer-to-peer?

Peer-to-Peer puts every computer on an equal footing, in that every computer can be both a publisher and consumer of information. The traditional model on the Web is the client–server one. The client is a computer and browser that is able only to receive/consume information. The server, on the other hand, serves/publishes information on a Web site. Peer-to-Peer makes a computer both a server and client.

What are examples of peer-to-peer?

Perhaps the best-known example of peer-to-peer is Skype (**www.skype.com**). Skype allows people to make a voice call directly to any other Skype user in the world. There are also a plethora of P2P file-sharing programs. File-sharing programs generally work as follows: Person A could search for and download music from Person B's computer, while Person B could search for and download music from Person A's computer. (The problem with these P2P file-sharing programs is that there is generally no means to control the distribution of copyright material.)

What sort of peer-to-peer options are available?

The following are distinct options for the use of peer-to-peer technologies:

- Information/content: The content on your computer becomes accessible to everyone else in the peer-to-peer environment and vice versa.
- Processing sharing: computers with spare processing capacity network together in order to combine their resources. Using a large number of computers, this can create very significant processing capabilities.
- Communication: a computer user can communicate in various ways with other people in the peer-to-peer network.

Can client-server and peer-to-peer systems work in harmony?

Yes. One does not exclude the other. The best scenario is to exploit the strengths of the client–server model—order, structure, management—and combine them with the flexibility and enabling capacity of peer-to-peer.

MAKING IT HAPPEN
Making Better Use of Processing Power

Studies have indicated that 50% or more of a typical organization's processing power may be unused. Peer-to-Peer is a way of tapping this unused resource for productive purposes. There are indications that commercial organizations see this as one of the most practical uses of peer-to-peer technology. However, bear in mind that such an application of peer-to-peer becomes relevant only when there are major processing needs that an organization is finding difficult to meet. Where such a situation arises, it can be more efficient and cost-effective to spread processing across the computers in the organization than to buy powerful new computers.

The main drawback here is that there will be a setup cost for installing the peer-to-peer technology. Education and training will be needed. When ongoing maintenance is added to this, the costs can begin to mount up, and it may well be that a centralized solution is more cost effective. Whether peer-to-peer is genuinely cost-effective in such situations depends on the amount of processing that is going to be required. A careful analysis is required to establish when a peer-to-peer approach is worth considering.

Collaboration and Communication with Peer-to-Peer

Driven by the rapid growth in partnerships and the need to be more flexible and adaptive, collaboration is now seen as a key attribute of a progressive organization. Peer-to-Peer can prove useful where people are collaborating and sharing resources and content on an active basis. If there is a need to establish a group that might span several organizations, then peer-to-peer technology can be faster and easier to implement and run than traditional approaches.

Content Publication with Peer-to-Peer

It is true that most content today resides on individual computers rather than on servers that publish this content to Web sites. Peer-to-Peer allows you to see all the content within the organization, rather than just what has been published on Web sites. This may be helpful when you are looking for something very specific, but there are some substantial drawbacks.

Much of the content that exists on an individual's computer is either private, in draft form, out of date, or simply not ready for publication or sharing. It is estimated that by 2001 there were already over 550 billion documents published on intranets, extranets, and public Web sites. This in itself is a vast, unimaginable quantity of content. The quantity of content that is on individual computers

"Economics and ethics are not mutually exclusive."   Lionel Tiger

around the world would dwarf this massive amount. Having the capacity to access all this content may sound valuable in theory, but in practice it could make information overload a hundred times worse than it already is.

With regard to content publication, peer-to-peer thinking seems to miss some fundamental rules of publishing. Publishing is not, and never has been, about following an "as much as you can read" approach, but is about selecting the best content and publishing it. A quality publishing house will reject 90% of the content presented to it. It will then polish up the final 10%, and publish it in such a way that it is easy to find and easy to read.

File Sharing with Peer-to-Peer
The classic model of file sharing occurs when someone downloads a file from a central server. This approach can put a lot of strain on bandwidth if there are a large number of people who need to download files. Peer-to-Peer file sharing seeks to use bandwidth more effectively. Let's say Person A and Person B are close together on the network. A downloads an e-learning course. Later, B wants to download the same course. With peer-to-peer, instead of B's request being acted on by the central server, the system looks to see if there is anyone near B on the network who has downloaded the same course. The system finds that A has. So now, instead of B downloading from the central server, B will download from A's machine. This saves time and network resources.

Security and Privacy Are Major Issues
Peer-to-Peer thrives in an open network environment. The problem is that hackers and viruses likewise thrive in that very same environment. Within an organization there may be a whole variety of operating systems and security protocols, and linking them all together in a cohesive and secure manner is not a simple task. Many believe that this is the Achilles' heel of peer-to-peer.

A key aspect of peer-to-peer security is the authentication of users. Trustworthiness is critical. Many peer-to-peer interactions now use encryption, which ensures that the communication is secure as it is being passed from computer to computer.

Privacy is a major issue for people whose computers will be used in the peer-to-peer network. Because most computer users are novices from a technical point of view, they become very dependent on their IT department to make sure nothing is going wrong. This situation is not welcomed by the average IT manager.

Equally, for the individual, the idea that someone else can root around within his or her computer can be unnerving. Making sure that their private files are fully protected is only part of the problem. In essence, it means thinking about the computer differently: looking at one part of it as being public domain and another private.

Peer-to-Peer and Management
Peer-to-Peer technology can allow the organization to investigate its computers and see what resources it has. This could allow an organization to monitor software continually and to distribute upgrades as they become available. It could also allow it to examine the content being created or downloaded by a particular individual, thus giving it more control.

Setting Up a Peer-to-Peer Environment
Certain elements need to be in place for peer-to-peer to function. These include:
- publishing of resources: to make a resource available, it must be published on the computer. This requires that it be identified as a resource that can be shared. Part of this identification involves a proper description that will allow other users to identify it quickly and accurately;
- location of resources: the person who wants a resource must locate it. This can be a major problem in a large peer-to-peer environment where there could be many millions of resources available. Some form of directory classification becomes essential in such an environment;
- utilizing the resource: once the resource has been located, there must be a method by which it can be utilized. If the resource is content, such as music, then it can be simply downloaded. However, if it is processing power, it will require a more complex interaction.

COMMON MISTAKES
The Security Angle Is Overlooked
Peer-to-Peer works best in an open network, but an open network is open to attack. The peer-to-peer structure can allow viruses to spread more easily. If authentication of users is not carried out properly, then hackers or other malicious people can gain access to the network.

You Forget the Napster Example
Part of the original Napster philosophy was that of bringing unsigned artists to the masses, but the reality was that the majority of people just wanted to hear the major acts. When Napster was stopped from illegally swapping commercial music, its usage dropped dramatically. The theory of peer-to-peer is that people are willing to wade through millions of pieces of content to find that precious gem; in fact, most people just want what is popular.

Lack of Standards and Support
Standards tend to vary widely in peer-to-peer technologies, thus making it more difficult to share resources. Without proper standards, a peer-to-peer environment can quickly become chaotic. Because P2P applications are not based on open standards and have a complex architecture, they are difficult to support. Unless you are satisfied that the P2P system is willing to give your organization a support contract, it is unwise to depend on it for business-critical purposes.

FOR MORE INFORMATION
Web sites:
Open P2P.com:
www.openp2p.com/pub/q/p2p_category
Peer Intelligence: **www.peerintelligence.com**

See also:
- Making Your Web Site Secure (pp. 631–632)
- Managing Payments Online (pp. 616–618)

Understanding Legal Issues in E-commerce

GETTING STARTED

In any e-business strategy, it is important to address comprehensively the key legal issues. At a basic level, these are matters such as copyright and libel; at a more advanced level, such things as restrictions pertaining to the sale of your product within particular jurisdictions need to be dealt with. When addressing legal issues on the Web, keep the following in mind:

- Prevention is better than cure. Establishing a sound legal structure early on is much easier than trying to firefight legal problems as they occur.
- Legal systems are getting a grip on the Internet. More and more laws are being passed that deal with doing business online.
- While you can't deal with the unique legal aspects of every jurisdiction, you still need to isolate the key jurisdictions for your online business and make sure you adhere to their relevant laws.

FAQs

Why should you address legal issues from the start?

Because it's important to guard against unpleasant consequences if you get legal things wrong, or just ignore them. Some early e-commerce businesses adopted the latter approach, believing that cyberspace was a kind of laissez-faire utopia beyond the reach of terrestrial governments.

Is it not the case that many laws do not apply online?

Nobody believes that fallacy any more. Which is fortunate, because courts and governments around the world have shown no hesitation about claiming jurisdiction over online activity—in some cases, even when the Web site in question is hosted on another continent. They have applied civil sanctions (such as injunctions and damages) and criminal penalties (fines and even imprisonment) in certain instances.

Is there a pragmatic approach to dealing with legal issues online?

Yes. The practical approach is to get legal advice on three specific types of territory for your Web site:

- the country (or countries) in which your Web operations are principally based, which will often, but not always, be where the site is hosted;
- the countries that are the primary target market of the Web site;
- any other countries which may claim authority over the Web site, and the breach of whose laws might cause unpleasant consequences. The United States is by far the best example of this: its legal regime has a dauntingly long reach.

MAKING IT HAPPEN

Understand the Different Kinds of Web Sites

While there are many different types of Web sites, they can broadly be divided into those with the following attributes:

- shop window Web sites, which provide information about a company and its products, but without encouraging any significant visitor interaction—rather like an online company brochure;
- contributed content Web sites, which allow visitors to contribute content, such as information about their identity, or postings on message boards;
- full e-commerce Web sites, through which visitors can purchase goods or services, either physical products which are delivered offline, or digitized material which is available for download.

Recognize Shop Window Web Site Issues

Even shop window Web sites have legal issues to address. They comprise various types of digitized content, such as graphics, text, images, music and coding, that raise issues which apply to all forms of Web site.

Web site owners must assume that all such content is protected: either by copyright—which, in effect, disallows its inclusion in another Web site without the copyright owner's permission; or, in some cases, by moral rights—which require the author to be attributed, and that the work should not be significantly modified without the owner's permission.

These clearances can take the form of a license or an assignment of copyright from the relevant rights holder, which might be a third-party Web site designer, photographer, journalist, or (in the more difficult case of music) two or more rights-holding organizations.

In addition, you must ensure that content on your Web site satisfies other requirements, including:

- Using the registered trademarks of a third party as part of your Web site's metadata will generally constitute trademark infringement. Even a straightforward reference on a Web site to a third party's trademark can constitute an infringement.
- Hypertext linking, particularly by means of deep linking or framing, to third-party Web sites without the consent of those Web sites should be avoided.
- Misleading price indications, for example where online prices have not been updated, can incur penalties.
- Incorrect product descriptions, where inaccurate statements are made as to the quantity, size, fitness for purpose or performance of goods, can also cause repercussions.
- Unfair comparative advertising, such as comparisons between goods or services that are not intended for the same purpose, must be avoided.

As well as guarding against infringement of third parties' rights, it is important for owners to include wording in

---

"There is no better way of exercising the imagination than the study of law. No poet ever interpreted nature as freely as a lawyer interprets truth."

Jean Giraudoux

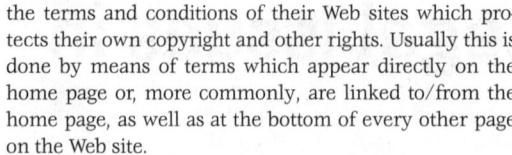

678

ACTIONLIST

the terms and conditions of their Web sites which protects their own copyright and other rights. Usually this is done by means of terms which appear directly on the home page or, more commonly, are linked to/from the home page, as well as at the bottom of every other page on the Web site.

Appreciate Contributed Content Web Site Issues

Web sites that encourage visitors to interact are exposed to several additional forms of legal risk. One of the most basic means of facilitating visitor interaction is a discussion board or chat room. Such environments can pose legal problems, as they are often unchecked and allow visitors to post information without any apparent restriction. You need to recognize that you can find yourself liable, either as a civil matter (where a third party's rights have been infringed) or, more extremely, under the criminal law, unless steps are taken to control material which appears on your Web site.

Some of the most obvious problems here include:
- defamatory statements
- infringement of copyright material
- obscene, blasphemous, threatening, racially discriminatory, and other legally objectionable material

To avoid liability for such material, you need to establish one or more of the following safeguards:
- proactive moderation of material before it appears on the Web site
- a documented "notice and take down" procedure, under which infringing content is removed from the Web site as soon as it has been notified
- regular reviewing of material which has been posted, and removal of any which appears problematic.

These issues all need to be addressed in your Web site's terms and conditions, so that visitors (and potential third-party complainants) are aware of the steps taken to prevent infringement. Many prudent owners also require visitors to register with the Web site before they can post messages. This allows the owner to contact the visitor if a problematic posting is made by the visitor, and, in certain circumstances, to provide that visitor's personal and contact information to a wronged third party, or to a law enforcement authority.

Account for Full E-commerce Web Site Issues

Clearly, there is a wide variety of goods and services which are capable of being traded through a Web site. Further, the seller can be either the Web site owner or a third party trading through the Web site, as in an online auction service.

It is impossible to cover here all the issues which the various kinds of products can raise. Many have specific regulations which have been imposed by governments for social, ethical and fiscal reasons. Examples of these include:
- sale of alcohol
- sale of medicines, particularly prescription-only medicines
- financial services
- betting, gaming and lotteries

- auctions, particularly in various European countries

Depending on the jurisdiction and type of product being sold, a Web site may need to adhere to regulations such as:
- provision of clear information to consumers before the conclusion of a contract, including: the identity of the supplier; the main characteristics of what's being sold; payment and delivery arrangements; and the principal terms and conditions of the contract between seller and purchaser;
- a minimum period during which a consumer may withdraw from the contract for any reason, and reject whatever has been purchased.

Whatever you sell through your e-commerce Web site, it is important that you form a legally binding contract with the purchaser. For example, you might ensure that such a contract is formed by requiring the visitor to scroll through your terms and conditions and click on an "I accept" button.

COMMON MISTAKES
Doing Nothing Because You Think It's Just Too Complicated

It is certainly true that there is a dizzying array of legal issues to ponder when trading over the Web. However, that's not an excuse for doing nothing. There is a basic minimum that can and should be addressed. The key is to understand the legal issues that, if not addressed properly, can have a major impact on your business.

Assuming That the Long Arm of the Law Does Not Reach Online

This is a false assumption. Yes, it is often more difficult successfully to prosecute an organization that is trading over the Web. However, that does not mean that governments and legal systems are ignoring those who they feel are breaking their laws, just because they happen to be on the Web.

Failing to Deal with Copyright and Libel Issues Quickly

If a third party accuses you of libel or copyright infringement, it is imperative that you deal with it urgently. In many courts of law, the longer the libel remains published on the Web site, the greater the penalties.

FOR MORE INFORMATION

Web sites:
Guide to law online, a comprehensive resource from the U.S. Law Library of Congress that has a global focus:
www.lcweb.loc.gov/glin
LLRX.com: **www.llrx.com**

See also:
- Computers, Information Technology, and E-commerce (pp. 1705–1707)
- Implementing an E-commerce Strategy (pp. 610–611)
- Managing Payments Online (pp. 616–618)

"Nothing is illegal if 100 businessmen decide to do it." Andrew Jackson Young, Jr.

Improving Communication with Resellers

GETTING STARTED

To operate effectively, resellers need support. Help your resellers by making it easy for them to access technical support, and give them a helpline and online access to your resources, skills, and experience. Incentive programs can encourage resellers to do more business with you, and certification programs can help to improve reseller performance.

FAQs

Isn't reseller advertising a waste of money?

You have to strike a balance between investing in strong national or regional campaigns, and allocating funds to individual resellers to run their own smaller, local campaigns. If resellers just use funds to run occasional advertisements, the money can be wasted. If the individual local campaigns are well coordinated and planned, they can be extremely effective.

How tightly should you control the use of reseller identity?

Reseller identity is part of overall corporate identity and branding. It should therefore be used consistently throughout the reseller network. Some resellers may argue that their own identity is more important and try to modify your material. In such a situation, you need to stress the benefits of forming part of a nationally recognized brand.

Should you provide funds for specific marketing projects or a general reseller marketing fund?

This question tends to come up when there is a lack of trust between the two parties. Some companies believe that nonspecific marketing funds simply go into reseller profits and have no marketing benefits. They therefore exercise strict control over how the funds are spent. Others trust their resellers' local knowledge to use the marketing funds most appropriately.

Why don't resellers take responsibility for their own training?

Many larger reseller networks do operate their own training programs. However, the aim of training is to improve the performance of reseller staff in selling your product. You have to treat them as an extension of your own sales operation and that makes reseller training an important success factor.

MAKING IT HAPPEN
Support Is Vital

Resellers play a vital link in the supply chain. However, to operate effectively, they need support. Providing the right level of support has a number of important benefits:
- It contributes to high levels of customer satisfaction.
- It makes the company the preferred choice locally.
- It focuses the attention of sales staff on customer requirements.
- It improves the company's competitive position.
- It supports the effective launch of new products.

Resellers have the market awareness and experience to deliver added value, and they play a leading role in providing products and services. Both parties should have access to your full range of products, services, and support.

Scope of Support

A program could contain:
- advertising
- authorized reseller logo
- joint marketing
- financing
- services
- sales training
- technical support
- business education
- sales leads
- helpline
- online presence
- rewards and incentives
- certification
- business and market information

Advertising

You can include resellers in your own advertising programs or allocate marketing funds to reseller advertising campaigns. Such advertising typically generates awareness of resellers among small and medium-sized enterprises and features the reseller emblem.

Authorized Reseller Logo

Resellers can benefit directly from the strength of your own brand name. A reseller logo lets partners use the power of your brand as leverage, and helps them to differentiate themselves from the competition when they communicate with potential customers. The logo can be used in brochures, direct mail, directory listings, exhibitions, trade shows, and Web sites.

Joint Marketing

You can help resellers by driving business in their direction. This can be as simple as generating leads or running reseller advertising campaigns. Alternatively, you can get involved in marketing campaigns aimed at specific market sectors or individual customers.

Financing

Financing can help resellers to market your products and services more easily. You can often help resellers close a deal by providing financing to their customers.

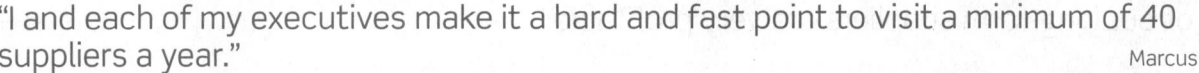

"I and each of my executives make it a hard and fast point to visit a minimum of 40 suppliers a year."

Marcus Sieff

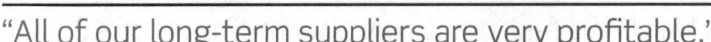

680

ACTIONLIST

Services

Many resellers do not have the skills or resources to provide service and support to their customers. You can help them to deliver services through your own resources in design, installation, and maintenance.

Sales Training

Sales training should be a structured process designed to help your resellers build sales. It should help retailers:
- identify key customer business issues;
- create a solution based on your products and services;
- offer compelling, well-supported sales presentations.

Sales training can be delivered in your own training center, on the reseller's premises, or remotely through the Internet or other media.

Technical Support

Technical support can be crucial, particularly when your products or services are complex, so make it easy for resellers to access your technical support systems. You can provide support tools and information on controlled access areas of your own Web site.

Business Education

A business education program will help your resellers keep up with the latest developments and maintain their product and business skills. Courses could cover:
- executive/management development;
- leadership training;
- product marketing skills;
- sales and marketing tools.

Sales Leads

A formal lead generation program simplifies lead management and delivers qualified leads from a single source in a consistent manner. You could generate leads through your own national advertising or direct mail programs and direct the leads to the local reseller. You should also monitor lead management to make sure that leads are used effectively.

Helpline

A helpline connects resellers with your resources, skills, and experience. It provides a quick response to sales and customer product queries.

Online Presence

Promote your reseller network to prospects and customers on your own Web site. By providing a directory and links to individual resellers, you can direct prospects to a local branch and increase its opportunities for new business.

Rewards and Incentives

Reward programs encourage resellers to do more business with you, while incentive programs can increase revenue for both parties. Some reward programs are designed to provide business development funding equivalent to a percentage of the revenue generated from sales of your products. Resellers can use this funding for a wide variety of approved market development activities.

Certification

Like market development funding, certification programs can help to improve reseller performance. Certification should only be offered to resellers who meet agreed targets in terms of sales, training, skills levels, investment, technical resources, and other factors essential to business success.

Business and Market Information

Resellers should be able to access information on products and availability, prices, order tracking, incentives, marketing campaigns, and sales information quickly and easily. The Internet makes it easy for you to offer resellers support and information electronically. You can offer information on products, pricing, and technical support, as well as various forms of electronic communication, online guides, and publication ordering.

COMMON MISTAKES
Providing Support in an Ad hoc Way

Many companies are faced with last-minute requests to support, for example, a one-time advertisement or a local trade show. While this may seem important to the local reseller, it may have little impact on the overall success of reseller marketing. It is better to provide funds and support for a support program with specific objectives.

Failing to Manage at Local Level

Many companies provide only funds or marketing material to resellers, and leave them to do what they like with the resources. The results are often poor and inconsistent throughout the reseller network. It is far better to provide guidelines, or appoint a manager to work with resellers to develop and control local programs.

Inadequate Funds

Reseller support frequently has a low priority in the overall marketing budget. The result is that small funds are widely distributed and achieve little. If the available fund is small, it may be more effective to concentrate on a smaller number of more focused campaigns.

Poor Campaign Information

Resellers frequently complain that they are not kept informed of national marketing and advertising campaigns. As a result, they miss opportunities to benefit locally from those campaigns. Make sure you keep resellers up to date with all of your company's marketing activities.

FOR MORE INFORMATION

Web site:
The Supply Chain Council: **www.supply-chain.org**

See also:

Getting Better Results from Your Agency

GETTING STARTED

Agencies emphasize a number of factors when trying to win new business. It is important to review agency performance regularly to see that initial promises are being kept and that the original selection criteria are still valid.

FAQs

Should I place all marketing tasks with a single agency or deal with specialists?

Full service agencies claim to integrate all aspects of a client's marketing operations so that clients get a better overall return for their marketing dollar. Specialists, on the other hand, claim to offer a more effective service in critical areas such as creativity, media buying, or below-the-line promotion. If you choose specialists, you have to make sure that they work to consistent standards and do not overlap. If you choose an integrated agency, you may need to compromise on the quality of some of the more specialist areas of activity.

Is agency commission better than a service fee?

Traditionally, agencies were remunerated by the commission received from the media in which they placed advertisements. Any creative, planning, or buying services would be covered by that commission, which meant that these services were effectively free to the advertiser. However, the higher service content of most agency work meant that commission did not adequately cover agency costs. Agencies therefore charged fees to clients and passed some of the media commission to the client. In the absence of fees, agencies might have been forced to reduce service levels.

MAKING IT HAPPEN

Use the Right Criteria to Select an Agency

The most popular reasons for a client's choice of agency include:

- seeing advertising they like;
- recommendation by a colleague;
- information from the marketing/advertising press;
- the agency winning an award;
- using the services of a selection agency;
- using a selection consultant.

Agencies emphasize a number of factors when they are trying to win new business. It is essential to see that they are delivering on their initial claims and promises, which commonly include:

- a good understanding of the business;
- quality thinking;
- involvement of senior staff who will continue to work on the account;
- evidence of sound business and account management skills;
- a powerful creative idea.

Concentrate on the Key Criteria

In reviewing your agency, you should concentrate on key criteria such as those identified in industry surveys:

- creativity
- value for money
- media buying
- quality of account management
- attentiveness and adaptability
- marketing strategy
- coverage of major world markets

According to other research, clients believe the ten most important factors in agency performance are the following:

- Does it take the trouble to understand your business?
- Can it use creativity effectively to sell your products?
- Does it have real creative flair?
- Does it get work done on time?
- Does it have a good understanding of your consumers?
- Does it believe in defining advertising objectives beforehand?
- Does it keep costs within budget?
- Does it use research to aid its creative work?
- Is it strong on media buying?
- Is it thorough and hard-working?

Understand Why Agency/Client Relationships Fail

Reports in the trade press highlight a number of factors that create conditions for a breakdown:

- The agency is not devoting enough time or resources to the account.
- The agency is losing enthusiasm for the account.
- The agency may be faced with working on a conflicting account.
- There may be a personality clash.
- The client believes that advertising does not have the planned effect on the marketplace.
- The agency feels that poor results are caused by problems on the client side.
- The client does not like the advertisements for subjective reasons.
- The agency fails to understand the client's business.
- A failure of communication means the agency cannot respond to the client's real needs.
- Frequent changes in the agency team or client team make continuity difficult.
- Poor agency administration lets down good creative work.
- Relationships can become stale.

Schedule Regular Review Meetings

Review agency performance regularly. Many agencies and clients conduct reviews at three-, six-, or twelve-month intervals, or after each major campaign, to assess both campaign and agency performance.

"Good copy can't be written with tongue in cheek, written just for a living. You've got to believe in the product."

David Ogilvy

Take Action to Improve Performance

If your agency shows poor performance in one or more areas, take remedial action. Suggest a change in remuneration that rewards performance or move part of your account into another type of agency offering specialist services.

Consider Paying Agencies by Results

With the increasing emphasis on accountability, a small but growing number of agencies are including an element of payment by results in their remuneration packages. Variations include:

- part fee and part results-based, for example, based on an increase in sales or awareness;
- part fee and part commission, with the fee based on achievement of agreed measurable objectives.

Although this orientation toward results is attractive to clients, it can be difficult to relate the contribution of the agency to a measurable result, and this trend seems unlikely to replace traditional forms of remuneration.

Switch to Creative Independents

If your agency is weak on creative work, you could consider working directly with an independent creative consulting firm. Creative independents only handle creative work, such as copywriting and design. By specializing, the independents can often achieve more effective advertising than full service agencies. There are three types of creative independent:

- freelance staff, either combined writer/art director teams or individuals
- design consulting firms offering advertising as part of a communications service
- specialist creative independents—small agencies with their own creative teams or who manage freelance teams

Work with a Virtual Agency

As clients demand greater flexibility and an increasingly wide variety of services, they are attracted by the concept of a virtual agency. In some cases, the agency may simply consist of a planning and management team with all creative, media, and specialist services bought in from independent suppliers. Other agencies maintain a central office with specialists based in satellite operations linked by telecommunications and videoconferencing.

Appoint a Brand Consulting Firm

The role of the advertising agency in creating and maintaining brand awareness is being challenged by a new type of marketing services organization known as a brand consultancy. The brand consulting firm brings together skills from a number of different disciplines, including market research, marketing consulting, management consulting, and advertising.

The brand consulting firm claims a number of advantages over the traditional advertising agency approach:

- a longer-term perspective on the development of brands, because they are not limited by an annual advertising budget

- recognition and integration of the different elements that contribute to brand success
- closer working relationships with the whole client brand team

Choose a Media Independent

A media independent, as the name suggests, only handles media planning and buying. By concentrating on media, the independents can often negotiate better deals than full service agencies. In fact, many smaller advertising agencies use media independents to handle their media buying. You would have to handle campaign planning and creative work in other ways.

Appoint an Integrated Agency

Agencies offer integrated services in a number of forms:

- a single integrated agency where all campaigns are handled by the same team
- an agency group where nonadvertising campaigns are handled by specialist companies within the group

COMMON MISTAKES
Failing to Review Agency Performance

Many companies appoint an advertising agency for a fixed period but do not build performance reviews into the agreement. Regular performance reviews provide opportunities to identify and resolve problems before they become too serious.

No Performance Criteria

If you include performance reviews in your agency agreement, make sure you set out the criteria by which the agency will be assessed. The more precise and measurable the criteria, the easier it will be to conduct an objective assessment. It is too easy to say, "I don't like their creative work." If the creative work delivers results and meets targets, it must be judged successful, regardless of personal taste.

Expecting One Agency to Do Everything

Many agencies claim to be good at all types of marketing. They call themselves full service agencies. However, they may not be able to meet your requirements in all areas, so you should consider appointing specialists to handle specific tasks such as media buying, sales promotion, or product development.

FOR MORE INFORMATION

Web site:
American Marketing Association:
www.marketingpower.com

See also:

"I want all our people to believe they are working for the best agency in the world. A sense of pride works wonders."

David Ogilvy

Integrating Advertising with Other Campaigns

683

ACTIONLIST

GETTING STARTED

Advertising is one of a series of interrelated marketing tools that support each other, and in an integrated campaign, advertising becomes a much more flexible medium and can be used wherever it is most effective.

FAQs
Why do some agencies avoid integrated campaigns?

It may be because they do not have the skills to handle the other marketing activities that fall outside the traditional advertising agency role. In some cases, they do not understand how the activities work together.

Is an advertising agency the best choice to handle an integrated campaign?

There are integrated agencies that offer all marketing services from within their own organization. Others may be part of a larger group who can offer the other, nonadvertising services. These types of agency are suitable for handling integrated campaigns. If advertising is not a major part of the integrated campaign, it may be more appropriate to talk to a marketing services company or group that offers all the relevant services.

Why is integration so important? Isn't it better to focus on getting the best results from individual marketing activities?

Results indicate that integration can save money and make better use of a budget. The savings come through multiple use of the same planning and creative work and more efficient use of the available funds. The other major bonus is that integrated activities support each other, improving the efficiency of individual campaign elements against overall objectives.

MAKING IT HAPPEN
Integrate Campaigns

Advertising is not a separate activity but one of a series of interrelated marketing tools that support each other. Although campaigns take many different forms, there are core elements that are crucial to the successful development of an integrated marketing strategy. The most important of these are:
- advertising
- direct marketing
- telemarketing
- press information
- relationship marketing
- sales support
- publications

In the integrated approach, the elements support each other. For example, an advertising campaign with reply coupon is integrated with a direct mail program, which is followed up by telemarketing. Without the support of the other marketing elements, the advertising and direct mail programs would achieve results; but together they reinforce each other to achieve real impact.

Advertising

With an adequate budget and effective media planning, it would be possible to use advertising alone to launch and market a new product. In this situation, advertising would have a number of objectives, which are:
- raising customer awareness of the new product;
- explaining the comparative benefits of the product;
- generating initial requests for information.

The success of the launch would be directly related to the size of the budget and how efficiently it is used. By integrating advertising with other marketing activities, however, the company can use advertising for specific tasks within the overall program and make more effective use of its budget. In an integrated program, advertising is just one of the marketing tools available, and it can be used in whatever capacity is most effective. This could be one of several ways as:
- a national direct response medium, to generate leads for a corporate direct marketing or telemarketing campaign;
- a regional direct response medium, to generate leads for follow-up by local intermediaries;
- part of a selective regional sales promotion campaign that offers prospects incentives for providing database information.

These options make advertising a much more flexible medium.

Direct Marketing

Direct marketing is one of the most flexible tools in an integrated marketing program. It can be used to reinforce the effectiveness of other marketing tools, or used alone in a variety of different ways. Direct mail advertising, for example, can be a viable alternative to press or broadcast media as a way of reaching specific sectors of the market. In an integrated campaign, it can also be used to follow up prospects who request further information. In addition, it can be employed to maintain effective contact and build long-term relationships with customers.

In an integrated campaign, however, direct marketing must be used to strengthen overall effectiveness. As a first stage, it can be integrated with the consumer advertising campaigns:
- as a follow-up to the direct response advertising campaign. The advertisements provide information on warm prospects, which can be used to form a database for future direct marketing programs;
- to make differentiated offers to prospects who respond to the advertising campaign;
- to supplement the advertising campaign's coverage of different target markets;

"Marketing has displaced management as the industry's chief principle, and expenditures on investment advisory services are dwarfed by expenditures on advertising and sales promotion."

John Clifton Bogle

- to reach sectors that cannot be reached efficiently by other media, or to provide increased reach or frequency;
- to reinforce the impact of the advertising campaign by selective follow-up.

Telemarketing

Telemarketing can be used to supplement the advertising and direct marketing campaigns through inbound and outbound programs. It can be used to handle a number of different tasks:

- direct sales to prospects over the telephone;
- maintaining contact with current customers;
- using the relationship to launch new products;
- generating leads from unqualified mailing lists;
- following up direct marketing programs;
- winning back lapsed customers by introducing them to new products that may be of greater interest;
- following up leads generated through advertising or direct marketing, or via intermediaries;
- conducting market research, using surveys to establish consumer response to products or sales incentives;
- maintaining contact with customers as part of a relationship marketing program.

Telemarketing can also provide a point of response for queries generated through advertising or direct marketing campaigns, or to obtain information from respondents as a basis for future database marketing.

Press Information

Press activities can be used in the context of a wider public relations campaign. Sponsorship of sporting or entertainment events, for example, can increase awareness and build a high profile for a company, leaving advertising and direct marketing to focus on direct response and brand-building strategies.

Sales Support

In an integrated campaign, leads can be generated for the sales force by advertising and direct marketing. Sales force productivity can also be improved by using telemarketing to handle routine customer communications. It is essential to back up sales teams with information both on the products and on the marketplace to improve their overall effectiveness. The program includes:

- direct sales force and distributor support;
- standard and customized presentations for different market sectors;
- product/sales guides to improve product knowledge;
- information on the advertising and direct marketing support available in each territory;
- competitor profiles.

Relationship Marketing

Relationship marketing builds on the leads generated by advertising and direct marketing. It also enhances the direct contact of the sales force by increasing customer loyalty. These are its key roles in an integrated program:

- maintaining an existing customer base
- increasing account control

- issuing a regular, planned flow of information
- increasing customer loyalty

Publications

Product publications do not normally form part of an integrated program. However, they form an important part of the communications program. Publications are used to:

- reinforce overall branding;
- provide benefits-led information;
- communicate positioning messages, as well as product information;
- act as sales presentation guides.

COMMON MISTAKES
Running Integrated Campaigns Through Separate Agencies

One of the key benefits of integrated marketing is that the client deals with a single agency for all marketing activities. Dealing with multiple agencies can lead to such problems as different creative solutions or duplicated costs. It is essential that one agency plans and produces the entire integrated campaign.

Defining Integrated Marketing Too Narrowly

Advertising, sales promotion, and direct marketing are viewed as the mainstream elements in an integrated campaign. However, sales support, telemarketing, public relations, exhibitions, and many other activities may have a key part to play.

Failing to Use Data to Plan and Control Campaigns

One of the key elements in an integrated campaign is the database. Information from all campaign activities should be used to identify communications needs, target individual communications, measure campaign effectiveness, and track customer responses. Without this underlying control, campaign funds may well be wasted.

FOR MORE INFORMATION

Book:
Smith, Paul, and Jonathan Taylor. *Marketing Communications: An Integrated Approach*. Milford, CT: Kogan Page, 2004.

Web site:
American Marketing Association:
www.marketingpower.com

See also:
✔ Generating More Leads (pp. 731–732)
✔ Improving the Response to Direct Mail (pp. 718–719)
✔ Planning an Advertising Campaign (pp. 685–686)
✔ Setting Advertising Objectives (pp. 694–695)
✔ Supporting Campaigns with Telemarketing (pp. 771–772)

"In good times, people want to advertise; in bad times, they have to." Bruce Barton

Planning an Advertising Campaign

GETTING STARTED

Any communications campaign needs to have clear, measurable objectives, whether it is designed to communicate product benefits or to support an event. In order to achieve these objectives, it must also be planned carefully. There are eight main stages to consider, from defining the target market to setting a budget.

FAQs

Do I need an advertising campaign?

Often the term advertising campaign is used when the more holistic term "communications campaign" would be more appropriate. Advertising strictly only refers to paid-for space or time in media such as newspapers or radio. On the other hand, direct mail, sales promotions, exhibitions, or any of a variety of communication tools can be used in a campaign to support your marketing. To decide if you need a communications campaign, you should be fairly sure that the problem you want to address can be solved best by communications. For example, finding new customers or prospective customers is often best accomplished by advertising or direct mail, but converting inquirers into customers may be better dealt with by you or your sales team (if you have one) in person.

Who is responsible for campaign planning— the client or the advertising agency?

Both parties contribute. The client sets the overall marketing objectives and the specific communications campaign objectives. The agency develops an advertising strategy based on those, but may seek to modify the campaign objectives. Timings will be determined by the client's product and marketing plans, together with practical considerations such as publication dates and lead times.

Why is it necessary to plan a campaign in so much detail?

To be effective, advertising and communications must meet specific measurable objectives. The objectives affect choice of media, creative strategy, overall budget, and lead times. Overlooking any of those details could weaken the effectiveness of the campaign.

Should planning be applied to the creative process?

There is an assumption that creative work takes place in a vacuum. Like any other marketing activity, it must be directed toward an objective. The more information a creative team has, the more focused its work.

MAKING IT HAPPEN
Set Campaign Objectives

It is important to set clear objectives for an advertising campaign. It is essential to identify a specific task for a specific campaign. This might be:
- raising awareness of a company, product, or service with-

in a clearly identified target market;
- communicating the benefits of a product or service;
- generating leads for the sales force or retail network.

To insure you design a cost-effective campaign that delivers results, advertising objectives should be translated into precise, measurable targets.

Identify Key Planning Activities

There are eight main stages in planning an advertising campaign:

1. Define the Target Market

Who is your campaign aimed at?

An understanding of your audience will influence the media you select and the creative treatment of your advertisement. To define your target market, you should ask questions like these:
- Who buys your type of product?
- Who influences the purchasing decision?
- In business buying, who are the important decision makers?
- Do you need to communicate with the actual buyers or those who influence the purchasing decision?
- How many potential buyers are there?
- How many users are currently buying your product and what is your share of the market?
- Which prospects do you want to reach with the campaign and where are they located?
- What are the characteristics of these people (for example, age, sex, income, job title), and what are their most important considerations in choosing a brand or a supplier?
- What does research tell you about their attitudes toward your company and your products?
- How do they currently receive information about your products?
- What is the role of advertising in reaching the target audience?

2. Select Media

There are four important factors to consider in selecting campaign media:
- how closely the audience profile of the medium matches your target audience
- the comparative costs of reaching the target audience through different media
- whether the frequency of the medium matches the timing of your campaign
- the creative opportunities of the medium for the communication of your message

3. Plan Campaign Timing

When should your campaign run? You have to consider a number of factors first in relation to the purchasing pattern of your products:
- When are your customers making their buying decisions?
- Do you know when your customers hold product/purchasing review meetings?

"Advertising is the very essence of democracy."

Bruce Barton

- If you are launching a new product, when will the product be available?
- Does your advertising campaign have to tie in with the timing of any other marketing activity, for example, an exhibition, direct marketing campaign, or sales force call?
- How quickly will you be able to follow up the campaign?

You also have to take into account production and media lead times:

- What is the next available publication or broadcasting date?
- When does the media owner require your advertisement?
- How long will it take to produce the advertisement?

4. Decide Campaign Frequency

Campaigns raise levels of awareness with each appearance. They also move individual respondents further along the decision making process and maintain contact during an extended process. Campaigns reinforce the impact of the message by repetition and provide an opportunity to communicate multiple or complex messages about the company or the product range.

Frequency is determined by:

- frequency of publication, that is, how often the publication appears;
- frequency of broadcast: radio or television commercials can be broadcast many times during the same day;
- your budget, although a number of appearances in the same medium will earn a discount;
- the behavior of consumers or buyers: if a buying decision is made only annually, then timing may be more crucial than frequency.

5. Plan Creative Treatment

To achieve good results, you must develop a comprehensive creative brief. The main elements are:

- campaign objectives;
- description of the target audience;
- the main concerns of the target audience: why they buy, what they consider, how they view different products and suppliers;
- the main benefits of the product or service: why the product is different from competitive offerings, what is new, why the benefits are important;
- the core message or proposition—what the prospect is being offered: the opportunity to sample or buy, further information, a sales visit, an incentive, or a discount;
- the planned response: should the prospect contact the company, send off an order, wait for a phone call, or simply absorb the information?
- the media—size and mechanical details;
- the supporting activities—telemarketing, advertising, sales follow-up, tie-in promotions.

6. Develop a Response Mechanism

Action is a vital ingredient of any advertising campaign and it is essential that you make it easy for your prospects to respond. First, decide which action they are to take:

- to place an order
- to arrange a sales meeting
- to request further information
- to visit your Web site
- to visit a retail outlet
- to try the product

Review the cost, convenience, and practicality of response options, including telephone, mail, fax, e-mail, and Web site.

7. Set a Budget

A campaign budget will include direct, indirect, and variable costs. Direct costs include the production costs of advertisements, including design, writing and production, and media costs. Indirect costs include the cost of setting up response handling, either by internal resources or an external supplier, and the management costs of planning and controlling the campaign. Variable costs include the cost of handling the campaign response, for example, 800 number costs and telephone resources, or costs of postage paid services; the cost of meeting the response—supplying and distributing the material that is requested; and the cost of servicing the response—sales or telemarketing costs in dealing with the potential volume of new business.

8. Set Schedules

To set a campaign schedule, work back from the launch date and work out how long each individual activity will take.

COMMON MISTAKES
Poor Targeting

Without a clear picture of your target, market advertising can be wasteful. You should always aim for the best match between the audience and your ideal customers—subject, of course, to your budget.

Failing to Integrate Advertising Plans with Other Marketing Activities

Advertising must be integrated with other related marketing tasks. Poor sales force performance, for example, could waste the contribution of a successful advertising campaign that provided a large number of sales leads.

Trying to Achieve Advertising Objectives with Inadequate Resources

If companies try to achieve targets without committing the right budget, it will mean either that advertisements do not appear frequently enough to have impact, or that production quality is sacrificed.

FOR MORE INFORMATION

Book:
Steel, Jon. *Truth, Lies, and Advertising: The Art of Account Planning.* New York: Wiley, 1998.

Web site:
The American Advertising Federation: **www.aaf.org**

See also:
- ✔ Integrating Advertising with Other Campaigns (pp. 683–684)
- ✔ Measuring Advertising Performance (pp. 689–690)

Preparing an Advertising Brief

GETTING STARTED
To get the most from working with an advertising agency, you need to make a start by putting together a comprehensive creative brief. This must cover all aspects of the project: background, objectives, research, competitors, product information, and the target audience. It's worth spending time on making the briefing information as complete as you can, as otherwise you run the risk of wasting time and money on a campaign that has little impact.

FAQs
Why is a detailed brief important?
It will start the campaign on exactly the right foot. An imprecise and insufficiently detailed brief may mean that the work is aimed at the wrong audience. Provide the agency or consulting firm with as much information as possible, so that they can produce a campaign that achieves results.

Who should be involved in preparing a creative brief?
The people who evaluate a creative brief should also be involved in setting or approving the brief. It can be difficult to deal with objections and criticism from someone who does not understand the brief. On the client side, the briefing team is likely to include the marketing executive, sales executive, and any relevant marketing specialists such as promotions or direct mail executives. The person who has the final say must be involved in defining the brief. The team should also include specialists to provide detailed information on the product and prospective customers. The agency team should be involved in preparing the brief, although this does not always happen in practice.

Should an agency brief always have measurable objectives?
The more specific the brief, the easier it is to assess the results of the creative work. It is not always possible to set a measurable objective, but this should be the goal. Agencies may argue that results depend on factors outside their control, but it should be possible to isolate the communications objectives and identify a way of measuring them. A direct response campaign, for example, can be measured by the number of responses, while a corporate campaign could be assessed through attitude surveys conducted before and after the campaign.

MAKING IT HAPPEN
Plan the Campaign Approach
How will you present your message? Most publications and commercial broadcast media carry high volumes of advertising. Your advertisement must achieve immediate impact to succeed. There are three essential checks that can be applied to creative work in any media:
- It must have immediate impact.

- It must meet the needs of the reader or viewer.
- It must stimulate a response.

Provide Background Information
Your briefing of the agency or consulting firm should begin with the background to the project:
- What is the overall objective of the project?
- What threats and opportunities does the business face?
- Why is the project being produced?
- How does the project fit into the overall marketing program?
- Why is it necessary to advertise, and what is the advertising intended to achieve?

The background material should include any research that you have conducted or used. You should ensure that the project works in the context of other marketing activities carried out by you and your competitors.

Produce a Comprehensive Brief
Information of this kind enables writers and designers to approach the creative process in a disciplined, logical way. Great creative ideas may occur in a vacuum, but they are more likely to be a response to a clearly defined problem.

The creative brief is important whether you are using external suppliers or performing the creative work internally.

Set Out Objectives
The brief should set out a number of objectives, including the overall corporate objective and the marketing objective. State the communications objective and how it contributes to the wider marketing objectives. For example you may want to make potential customers in a new region aware of your product in order that sales staff can work more effectively.

The campaign objectives should be detailed and specific. Examples could include:
- generate 3,000 prospects and convert 3% of them;
- make sure that key decision makers understand the product's business benefits;
- raise awareness among 20% of the target audience.

Provide Access to Any Research Information
The creative team should be aware of any relevant research information, including:
- customer surveys, interviews, or analysis;
- industry surveys;
- competitor analysis;
- product reviews;
- press comment on the product or company;
- feedback from focus groups;
- results of previous campaigns.

Include Information on Competitors
The brief should include detailed information on:
- which competitors provide a similar product or service;
- how the competitive offering compares;

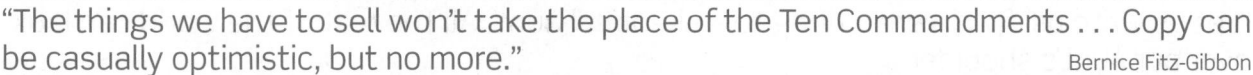

"The things we have to sell won't take the place of the Ten Commandments . . . Copy can be casually optimistic, but no more."

Bernice Fitz-Gibbon

- the product's key benefits against the competition;
- how competitors are perceived by customers.

This information can help creative teams to identify some of the key benefits that will differentiate the product from competitors' offerings. It will also show how other companies have tackled the problem of describing the product.

Provide Comprehensive Product Information

The product or service should be described in detail:

- what it is
- what it is used for
- how it operates
- the main benefits for the customer
- the advantages over competitor products

If the team can use or experience for itself your product or service in the same way as a customer, then this will greatly enhance its understanding.

Describe the Target Audience

Describing the target audience helps the creative team to focus on the key decision makers:

- What types of company buy the product?
- Which business sectors are they in?
- How big are these companies?
- Who are the main decision makers?
- What is their role in the decision making process?
- What are their business concerns?
- What is their perception of your company and its products?

Establish Target Perceptions

The creative team should be aware of any key messages that are important to the target audience. The task of the creative team is not to invent these messages; it is to communicate them as effectively as possible. The brief should therefore set out the perceptions that the target audience have now and those they should hold once the campaign is finished.

Get Approval of the Brief

The brief should be circulated to all members of the group involved in briefing and approving the project. No creative work should begin until the brief has been signed off by everyone involved. Once the brief has been approved, members should not be able to change it without good reason.

Be Clear about Payment Terms

Some agencies will present their ideas without expecting payment, but most would rather not. If you cannot pay for initial ideas, make this clear before expecting anything of value from the team. If, however, you *can* pay, agree the amount and establish who will own the ideas once the initial presentation is finished.

Describe the Review Process

Let the creative team know how their work will be reviewed and evaluated. This can take place at a number of levels:

- review by the agency and client teams
- evaluation in focus groups
- pilot campaigns in test markets

COMMON MISTAKES
Making the Brief Too Specific

It is possible to make a brief too specific, thereby ruling out creative approaches that may achieve outstanding results. For example, setting out the creative approach in the brief before the creative team has had an opportunity to consider it will produce very limited results. The creative team needs information to focus their attention on the problem, not suggestions on how the problem should be solved.

Not integrating Creative Work

Although the brief should allow the agency creative team complete freedom, it is equally important that creative work across different media should be integrated. If advertising is the dominant medium, and a team is working on direct marketing, they should relate their approach to the advertising theme. Repetition of the same creative theme across different media reinforces the key messages and can improve overall awareness.

Concentrating Too Hard on Creativity, and Not Enough on Results

Creative work should be accountable. The agency may have a brilliant, award-winning creative idea, but if it fails to produce the intended results it may be a waste of money. The creative team should therefore be aware of the specific objectives of the campaign; it is not enough just to get attention.

FOR MORE INFORMATION

Book:
Ogilvy, David. *Ogilvy on Advertising.* New York: Vintage Books, 1985.

Web site:
American Marketing Association:
www.MarketingPower.com

See also:
✔ Getting Better Results from Your Agency (pp. 681–682)
✔ Selecting and Working with an Advertising Agency (pp. 691–693)
✔ Setting Advertising Objectives (pp. 694–695)

"Let us write as if we were writing to a skeptical aunt. All the rest of the world can look over our aunt's shoulder."

Fairfax Cone

Measuring Advertising Performance

GETTING STARTED

Advertising is expensive, so it is important to make sure that it provides value for money in terms of effective results. Objectives should be clearly defined; results should then be measured and evaluated in order to establish that these objectives have been achieved.

FAQs

Why is it so important to measure advertising effectiveness?

Advertising budgets represent a major investment for most companies. Measuring advertising allows you to measure the effectiveness of your advertising and your agency. The feedback obtained is invaluable in determining future strategies.

The media publish research on the effectiveness of advertising. Can I use this for my own research purposes?

This type of research is unlikely to be completely objective, since it is designed to promote the medium. However, it can act as a useful guideline for performing a preliminary evaluation of the media. You must measure the results of your own advertising campaign.

Some agencies offer a payment-by-results service. Is this the only way to reward agency and advertising effectiveness?

This type of agency typically runs a high proportion of direct response advertising, where results can be measured accurately. There are other important parameters, but they do not lend themselves to the same simple measurement.

MAKING IT HAPPEN
Set Measurable Objectives

It is important to set clear, measurable objectives for an advertising campaign. There is no single advertising objective, so it is essential to identify a specific task for the campaign:

- to raise awareness of a company, product, or service in a clearly identified target market;
- to communicate the benefits of a product or service;
- to generate leads for the sales force or retail network;
- to encourage prospects to buy directly through a direct response campaign;
- to persuade prospects to switch brands;
- to support a special marketing event such as a sale or an exhibition;
- to make sure customers know where to obtain the product;
- to build confidence in an organization.

Advertising objectives should be measurable for two important reasons: first, to make sure that advertising represents an adequate return on investment and, second, to measure the effectiveness of the campaign itself.

The objectives should be detailed and specific. Examples could include:

- to convert 3% of prospects;
- to make sure that key decision makers understand the product's business benefits;
- to raise awareness among 20% of the target audience.

An effective campaign should have a single focus with a specific measurable result. By mixing objectives, you may achieve only a part of the results you want.

Use Research to Measure Advertising Effectiveness

Research should be used to assess how well your advertising has achieved its objectives. This will enable you to fine-tune your advertising plans. You should conduct research before and after a campaign to evaluate:

- changes in customer awareness of the product;
- advertising recall;
- attitudes to the product;
- the responses to different creative approaches.

Test Creative Treatment

There are three vital checks that can be applied to creative work in any medium: it must have immediate impact; it must meet the reader's or viewer's needs; and it must stimulate a response.

Creative work can be tested in a number of ways, of which the most common are a panel of prospects and customers, test marketing, and measuring the response from pilot campaigns. Important variables to test are:

- size of advertisement
- layout
- creative approach
- position in the publication
- timing
- product offer
- price or discount offer
- response mechanism

Measure Brand Switching

Brand loyalty is a key marketing objective, helping companies to retain customers and increase their lifetime value. Brand switching advertising plays an important role in winning new customers as the first stage in a customer relationship program. It is an important objective that helps you to increase market share or maintain share against competitive actions. It is also important if you are introducing a new product that offers greater benefits than competitors' products. Researching brand switching is therefore an important long-term measure of advertising effectiveness. Published independent surveys that show market share for different suppliers can be a useful starting point.

Monitor Target Perceptions

To find out what your customers consider important about your products and your company, conduct a survey or run a focus group. The survey should ask respondents how they rank the different brand values. It should also ask respondents how they believe your company

"A hard sell advertisement, like a diesel motor, must be judged on whether it performs what it was designed to do."

Rosser Reeves

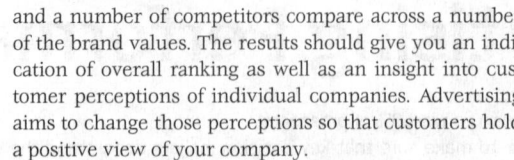
and a number of competitors compare across a number of the brand values. The results should give you an indication of overall ranking as well as an insight into customer perceptions of individual companies. Advertising aims to change those perceptions so that customers hold a positive view of your company.

Customer perceptions change over a period of time, particularly if you are running targeted communications programs, so you should conduct continuous research to monitor changes in customer attitude. This type of research is known as tracking research, and it helps you to measure the effectiveness of your advertising.

Monitor the Right Factors

The corporate reputation is the way a company is perceived by customers, suppliers, and other important groups. You should use your tracking research to monitor customer perceptions of factors such as:

- financial performance;
- the quality of the management team;
- clarity of direction;
- market performance;
- growth record and potential;
- relationships with suppliers and employees;
- manufacturing capability.

Measure Response Levels

Direct response advertising is easier to measure than advertising that is designed to change perceptions over a period of time. Your advertisement will include a call to action, such as:

- send for more information;
- reply within seven days and receive a free gift;
- send for a free report;
- take out an annual subscription now and get the first two issues free;
- call for a free consultation;
- reserve now at a special price;
- order now and get a big discount;
- visit our Web site and find out more.

The most popular mechanisms for press advertisements are:

- Web site address;
- e-mail address;
- toll-free number.

You should monitor the response levels from different sources to see which is the most effective.

Check the Cost of Your Response

You can measure the cost of your direct response campaign by dividing the cost of the advertising or marketing program by the number of responses. You can use the same type of measure to assess factors such as timing, offer, and creative treatment.

Measure Internet Advertising

The advantage of the Internet is that, at little or no cost, you can test your campaign on part of your target audience. You can also experiment with different banner ad sizes. The Internet is ideal for testing messages against your target, gauging the appeal of promotional offers and the type of message that attracts customers who buy. Some advertisers measure effectiveness on click-through rates (CTRs). The average CTR for banner advertising on the Internet is currently 0.2% to 0.4%. Commentators believe that banners that get high click-throughs may not be the best at getting conversions, where the user actually signs up for a subscription or makes a purchase. The real success of your campaign should be based on action, so it is more realistic to use conversions as your measure.

Consider Paying Agencies by Results

With the increasing emphasis on accountability, a small but growing number of agencies are including an element of payment by results in their remuneration packages. Variations include:

- part fee and part results-based, for example, based on an increase in sales or awareness;
- part fee and part commission, with the fee based on the achievement of agreed measurable objectives.

Although this orientation toward results is attractive to clients, it can be difficult to relate the contribution of the agency directly to a measurable result, and this trend seems unlikely to replace traditional forms of remuneration.

COMMON MISTAKES
No Objective Performance Criteria

It is important to set objective criteria for measuring advertising performance. The more precise and measurable the criteria, the easier it will be to conduct an objective assessment.

Failure to Measure Advertising

Companies in consumer and business markets are prepared to spend millions on advertising campaigns but are reluctant to invest in research to measure the effectiveness of them. This has led to a lack of accountability and to problems in reaching a proper evaluation of advertising and agencies.

Using the Wrong Measures

The measures you use are determined by your objectives. If you are running a corporate campaign, measure changes in perception. If you are working on a direct response campaign, measure response rates or direct sales.

FOR MORE INFORMATION

Web site:
American Marketing Association:
www.marketingpower.com

"Never stop testing, and your advertising will never stop improving."   David Ogilvy

Selecting and Working with an Advertising Agency

GETTING STARTED

If your budget will stretch, and you are able to engage an advertising agency to help you spread the word about your product or service, you need to choose an agency that can provide the right selection of services. These can include consulting, strategy, creative work, media, and integration with other communications activities. Important factors in selecting an agency include its approach, reputation, and financial stability. If you choose your agency carefully, you're much more likely to avoid the problems that cause breakdowns in the agency/client relationship.

FAQs

Do I need an advertising agency?

Many small to medium-sized companies don't. However, the skills offered by agencies are just as specialized as those offered by your accountant. Many agencies will be able to offer services other than advertising, including direct marketing, sales promotion, and public relations. Indeed they may not call themselves an "advertising" agency at all. Agencies that offer a wide variety of skills are often called "full-service" agencies. If you know what you want to achieve, but are not sure if advertising is the best course, discuss the issues with a number of different agencies.

I want to work with a specific agency, but they already handle the account of a competitor. Should I work with that agency?

This problem occurs frequently, particularly when agency mergers occur, and the new group finds that its client lists include conflicting accounts. The decision to continue handling conflicting accounts is sometimes taken by the agency, and sometimes by the clients. It can be particularly difficult if the agency is seen as an industry specialist, with considerable expertise in a particular market. Sometimes the problem can be resolved by handling the conflicting accounts through separate agency teams.

How do I know that an agency can maintain its standards in day-to-day business, once they have won the initial pitch?

Sometimes agencies field a special senior team to win new business, and then hand the day-to-day account to a completely different team. Since a good relationship between agency and client is so important, you should insist on meeting the team who will actually work on the business.

Is it essential to appoint an agency to handle advertising campaigns?

A full-service agency may not be essential, particularly if you have the resources to handle part of the task internally. Creative consulting firms, media specialists, or integrated agencies can take on specialist tasks.

MAKING IT HAPPEN
Choose the Right Type of Agency

Depending on the type of agency, you can use a comprehensive service or specific services, including:

- initial consulting;
- development of an advertising strategy;
- creative proposals, copywriting, design, and production of advertisements;
- media planning, negotiation, buying, and administration;
- integration of advertising with other communications activities.

Whatever you decide, ask to see examples of previous campaigns and for an honest appraisal of their effectiveness.

Work with a Full-service Advertising Agency

Full-service agencies handle all aspects of an advertising program. You should select a full-service agency if you do not have any internal skills or resources for handling advertising, or if extensive advertising is important to the achievement of your marketing objectives.

Use a Media Independent

A media independent handles only media planning and buying and so is likely to be interested only if you are spending a considerable amount on buying space in newspapers and magazines or airtime on TV or radio. By concentrating on media, the independents can often negotiate better deals with them than full-service agencies. Many smaller advertising agencies use media independents to handle their media buying. If you can handle campaign planning and creative work in other ways but do not have any internal skills or resources for media planning and buying, then you should use a media independent.

A media independent could prove useful if you spend a large amount of your budget on media, and you want to take advantage of specialist buying skills to get better positions or lower rates. You may find that certain media will not deal with you, because you are an advertiser. In that case, a media agency can provide valuable support.

Choose Creative Independents

Creative independents handle only creative work such as copywriting and design. By specializing in this way, the independents can often achieve more effective advertising than full-service agencies. You would have to handle campaign planning and media in other ways. There are three types of creative independent:

- freelance staff, either combined writer/art director teams, or individuals;

"The more informative your advertising, the more persuasive it will be." David Ogilvy

- design consulting companies offering advertising as part of a communications service;
- specialist creative independents: small agencies that either have their own creative teams, or manage freelance teams.

You should consider using a creative independent if you can handle campaign planning and media in other ways but do not have any internal skills or resources for creative work. If advertising is a small part of your marketing activity, you could develop effective campaigns by taking advantage of specialist creative services.

Work with an Integrated Agency

Integrated agencies handle all aspects of an advertising program and integrate advertising with other media. Agencies offer integrated services in two forms, as:

- a single integrated agency, in which all campaigns are handled by the same team;
- an agency group, in which non-advertising campaigns are handled by specialist companies within the group.

An integrated agency may be suitable if other tools, such as direct marketing, publications, and sales promotion are as important as advertising, and you want all of the activities integrated and handled professionally. Any extra cost incurred will be well worth it.

Use the Media's Own Expertise

One alternative to using an agency is to ask the newspaper, magazine, or radio station to help. Often they will offer basic design or writing services free of charge. However they are rarely as skilled as specialists and you may find it difficult to make your advertising stand out or to maintain consistency over time.

Evaluate Advertising Agencies

There are a number of important factors in selecting an agency.

- Approach: what is the agency's philosophy, and how does it work in practical terms?
- Track record: what campaigns has the agency produced, and how effective have they been?
- Reputation: does the agency have an established reputation in your market? Are you able to approach other clients to give their assessment of the agency?
- Accountability: how does the agency measure the performance of its campaigns?
- Client relationships: what is the current client list, and how many of these clients are enjoying long-term relationships? What is the average length of account tenure?
- Disciplines: does the agency offer all disciplines from within its own resources, and can it offer the full range of services?
- Staff: does the agency have the staff to handle complex, large-scale programs? What is the consulting firm's recruitment and personal development policy?
- Financial stability: what is the agency's recent performance? Does it have the stability and resources to sustain an effective level of service over the long term?

Check Agency Performance

According to research conducted by the U.K.-based Henley Centre, clients believe the ten most important questions regarding agency performance are as follows:

- Does it take the trouble to understand your business?
- Can it use creativity effectively to sell your products?
- Does it have real creative flair?
- Does it get work done on time?
- Does it have a good understanding of your consumers?
- Does it believe in defining advertising objectives beforehand?
- Does it keep costs within budget?
- Does it use research to aid its creative work?
- Is it strong on media buying?
- Is it thorough and hard working?

Obtain Information about Advertising Agencies

There are a number of useful sources of information about agencies:

- The American Association of Advertising Agencies publishes information about agencies.
- Individual agencies provide videos of their agency credentials.
- Specialist magazines publish regular news about agencies and their clients and your own trade publications may mention agencies which specialize in your market.
- Talk to friends and colleagues, even if in different businesses, to find out which agencies are reliable.

Avoid Problems in Client/Agency Relationships

Reports in the trade press highlight a number of factors that create conditions for a breakdown:

- The client believes that the advertising has not delivered results, or not had the planned effect on the marketplace.
- The agency feels that poor results are caused by marketing, product, or management problems on the client side.
- The client does not like the advertisements for subjective reasons.
- The agency fails to understand the client's business.
- A failure of communication means that the agency cannot respond to the client's real needs.
- Frequent changes in the agency team or client team make continuity difficult.
- Poor agency administration can let down good creative work.
- Relationships can become stale.

COMMON MISTAKES
Choosing the Wrong Size of Agency

A large agency may have the resources and scale to support national or international campaigns, but if your account is small, you may get poor service from a junior team. It may be more appropriate to work with a smaller agency, where you will get personal service from the senior people.

Choosing the Wrong Type of Agency

Agencies, like any other business, develop specialties. Their expertise may not coincide with your needs. The most important division is between a consumer and a business-to-business agency but, beyond that, agencies

develop expertise in certain industries or markets. Look carefully at the agency's client list to find the right match.

Relying on a Creative Pitch

Agency selection is frequently made on the basis of a pitch—a presentation that shows how an agency would tackle a specific project. Although the presentation gives an insight into the agency's working methods, it is an artificial guide to potential performance.

Not sharing information with the agency

Clients often expect a lot from a new agency, but can be disappointed when the agency does not know something "obvious" about the client's business. The agency can only know what you know *if you tell them*. If you are concerned about confidentiality, discuss this and get a signed agreement from the agency management.

Not Discussing the Budget in Enough Detail

Agencies work for a fee and, like you, will want to make a profit. You will only get good service when they feel your business is worthwhile for them. From the outset discuss how much you plan to spend and what you want to achieve—competent agencies will tell you from the outset what is possible.

FOR MORE INFORMATION

Books:
Cummins, Julian, and Roddy Mullin. *Sales Promotion: How to Create, Implement and Integrate Campaigns That Really Work.* 3rd ed. Milford, CT: Kogan Page, 2003.
Schultz, Don E. *Sales Promotion Essentials: The 10 Basic Sales Promotion Techniques . . . and How to Use Them.* 3rd ed. New York, McGraw-Hill, 1998.

Web site:
American Association of Advertising Agencies:
www.aaaa.org

See also:
- ✔ Getting Better Results from Your Agency (pp. 681–682)
- ✔ Measuring Advertising Performance (pp. 689–690)
- ✔ Planning an Advertising Campaign (pp. 685–686)
- ✔ Preparing an Advertising Brief (pp. 687–688)
- ✔ Setting Advertising Objectives (pp. 694–695)

"An idea can turn into dust or magic, depending on the talent that rubs against it."

William Bernbach

Setting Advertising Objectives

GETTING STARTED

Clear objectives for a communication campaign are essential, whether it is intended to generate leads or encourage brand switching. These objectives should be in place well before a campaign begins, so that each campaign has a specific task. In addition, the desired results should be measurable so that you can be sure the campaign is worth the investment.

FAQs

Should advertising be judged on sales results?

Advertising should certainly be measured, but there may not be a direct correlation between advertising and sales. Advertising may generate a large number of leads, but the sales force may not be able to convert those leads to sales.

Should advertising agencies be judged solely on the results they deliver?

There has been a trend toward judging agencies on measurable results. This has been driven partly by the increasing importance of direct marketing agencies who claim to be driven by results, and partly by the desire of marketing executives to increase accountability. Some agencies have gone so far as to base their fees on results, rather than traditional agency payment. The problem is that results are dependent on so many other aspects of marketing. An agency could claim that it has no control over the performance of the sales force or the quality of the product. It is essential therefore that you agree on a definition of success.

Is it possible to set a number of different objectives for the same advertising campaign, particularly when budgets are limited?

It *is* possible, but it may not be a good idea. An effective campaign has a single focus with a specific measurable result. By mixing objectives, you may achieve only part of the outcome you want.

MAKING IT HAPPEN
Set the Right Objective

You must have clear objectives for your campaign. There are many different advertising objectives, so identify a specific task for a specific campaign. This might be:
- target market: one million ABC1 prospects
- communicating the benefits of a product or service;
- generating leads for the sales force or retail network;
- encouraging prospects to buy directly through a direct response campaign;
- persuading prospects to switch brands;
- supporting a special marketing event such as a sale or an exhibition;
- making sure that customers know where to obtain the product;

- building confidence in an organization.

Whatever your general objectives, you should be clear how much is dependent on the communications and how much dependent on other aspects of your marketing effort, such as the sales force (if you have one).

Make the Objectives Measurable

To insure you design a cost-effective campaign that delivers results, advertising objectives should be translated into precise, measurable targets, as in the following examples.

Consumer Product
- target market: 500,000 ABC1 prospects
- marketing objective: achieve high level of product understanding
- advertising objective: persuade 15% of targeted prospects to request a free sample

Business Product
- target market: 5,000 specialist machinery designers in (specified) industrial processes
- marketing objective: increase market share to 20% (that is, recruit 1,000 new clients)
- advertising objective: persuade 40% of prospects to request product fact file

Raise Awareness

This objective is usually the starting point for advertisers and is especially important if your company is entering new markets where you do not have an established reputation, or you are trying to influence important decision makers who may not be aware of your company. Awareness advertising can also be used if you are launching new products which appeal to specific sectors of your market, or if research shows that customers and prospects are not aware of the full extent of your products and services.

This type of objective would be important for a company launching a new range of products. For example, to raise awareness of its new range, one company planned to advertise in a group of special interest consumer magazines designed for its target audience. The advertisements included the telephone number of an information line that generated a large number of inquiries. Editorial articles in the same group of publications backed up the advertising by providing more detailed information for consumers. You should, however, be wary of specifying awareness targets. Awareness on its own will not sell products and, if this is your objective, you will have to integrate your campaign carefully with other elements of your marketing to meet your targets. Likewise awareness among the general public is very different from awareness in a very small, specialized market, so you should be clear about who you are trying to reach.

Communicate Benefits

Product advertising should lead with benefits. This type of advertising is important when research shows low

awareness of product benefits. It should also be used if your products have recently been improved, or if you need to counter competitors who have introduced products with similar or better benefits.

For example, if research shows that your company's products are perceived as old-fashioned or poor value for the money, you need to take action to communicate the real benefits of your products.

Generate Sales Leads

Advertising's role is to provide leads that can be followed up by a field sales force or telemarketing team. Lead generation is important if marketing success depends on the performance of the sales force. Sometimes, customers or prospects have a complex decision making structure and you cannot identify some of the decision makers. Advertising that generates inquiries can identify the right people and open the door for the sales team. It can also be used to identify prospects when you are entering new market sectors where you do not have an established customer base. The final use for this type of campaign is to generate leads for agents, distributors, or retailers who handle your local marketing.

Sell Through Direct Response

Direct response advertising is the most measurable form of advertising. The advertising budget provides a direct return in terms of incremental sales. This objective can be important if customers can only buy direct from you. In an increasing number of markets, customers prefer the convenience of buying direct, and you have to decide whether to bypass your existing distribution channels, if appropriate.

In the personal computer market, for example, manufacturers found that businesses and individuals were willing to buy personal computers "off the page" or via the Internet. The products were regarded as commodities and the resulting price competition put pressure on margins. The result was a considerable growth in the level of direct sales with manufacturers using large format advertisements or inserts in computer and business publications. Direct selling meant that the manufacturers could reduce prices by avoiding the cost of selling through retail outlets.

Encourage Brand Switching

Brand switching advertising plays an important role in winning new customers as the first stage in a customer relationship program. It helps you to increase market share or maintain share against competitive actions, and is also important if you are introducing new products that offer greater benefits than competitive products.

Support a Marketing Event

This objective can be important in a number of situations, for example, taking part in an exhibition where an important new product will be launched, or holding a sale, or promoting a seminar or other customer event at which you wish to insure customer participation. Advertising helps to build traffic for your event and insures that the event attracts the right prospects. A company that sponsors senior executive seminars as a way of building its credibility could run advertisements in the business press to promote a seminar.

Help Customers To Obtain the Product

Advertising can help to drive business to retail outlets or distributors, or improve the performance of your distribution network by showing the range of services available from the outlets. It can also counter competitive action, if, for example customers are using other distributors to obtain spare parts and service. To win back this important business, advertising could show locations of retail outlets and explain why the authorized distributor should be the first choice for customers.

Build Customer Confidence

Capability advertising or corporate advertising is sometimes dismissed because it is difficult to measure, but is important when a company has been undergoing significant change, or is entering new markets where it is not established. It also provides support when a company is trying to win key account business, or if competitors are threatening important business.

COMMON MISTAKES
Setting Objectives That Cannot Be Measured

Advertising objectives should be measurable for two important reasons. First, to make sure that advertising represents an adequate return on investment. Second, to measure the effectiveness of the campaign itself, so that future advertising can be improved or modified to deliver better results.

Setting Objectives That Are Too General

A general objective, such as raising awareness, is important, but often is seen as the only objective. Advertising objectives should be closely linked to marketing objectives so that advertising is used to perform specific tasks within an overall marketing framework. You should be sure that what you want to achieve is possible with communications and acknowledge the importance of other elements of your marketing, crucially, the product itself or your pricing strategy.

695

ACTIONLIST

FOR MORE INFORMATION

Books:
Cummins, Julian, and Roddy Mullin. *Sales Promotion: How to Create, Implement and Integrate Campaigns That Really Work.* Milford, CT: Kogan Page, 2003.
Schultz, Don E. *Sales Promotion Essentials: The 10 Basic Sales Promotion Techniques . . . and How to Use Them.* 3rd ed. New York, McGraw-Hill, 1998.

Web site:
American Association of Advertising Agencies:
www.aaaa.org

See also:
✔ Generating More Leads (pp. 731–732)
✔ Preparing an Advertising Brief (pp. 687–688)

"Advertising is the business of telling someone something that should be important to him. It is a substitute for talking to him."

Fairfax Cone

Building One-to-one Relationships

GETTING STARTED

Building one-to-one relationships involves collecting and using information about actual and prospective customers as a basis for a customized selling approach. This provides an efficient and targeted means of maximizing sales.

FAQs

Do I have to tell customers that I am collecting personal information?

You may be bound by guidelines, rules, or legislation to advise customers about data collection and use. In any case, it is good commercial practice to publish a clear privacy policy explaining your procedures. You should also tell customers how you intend to use the data. Experience indicates that customers are happy to part with information if they see some tangible benefit. Concerns about security and privacy issues remain major barriers to the development of e-commerce.

Does one-to-one marketing guarantee customer loyalty?

It cannot guarantee loyalty, but it can make an important contribution. Customers will only remain if they continue to recognize the value of your products and the quality of your customer service. That means continually enhancing the customer experience.

Is one-to-one marketing always the best way to deal with customers?

For one-to-one marketing to work effectively, you need the right level of information on customers. You may not always be able to get that level of information on individual customers. However, if you have sufficient information on groups of customers with common needs, you can use techniques such as direct mail to communicate with a degree of precision. As your information on individual customers grows, you can move toward one-to-one communication.

MAKING IT HAPPEN
Refine Your Target Market

The more information you have about your target audience, the more precise you can make your campaign. In an ideal world, direct marketing techniques would allow you to communicate one-to-one with every prospect, but in practical terms you are more likely to be communicating with groups who share the same characteristics. This enables you to develop a unique relationship that competitors will find very difficult to match. It can also reduce your marketing and customer management costs by reducing wastage to a minimum.

Establish Clear Objectives

One-to-one marketing is designed to:
- improve the quality of customer service;
- strengthen customer relationships;
- maximize the profitability of each customer relationship;

- increase retention rates for customers;
- maximize the return on your investment in marketing and customer service.

Set Up a Database

At the heart of effective one-to-one marketing is a data networking solution that collects, stores, manages, and distributes all relevant customer information via a single, integrated customer database. The database is updated from all customer channels and is accessible by all customer-facing employees.

Keep Capturing Customer Data

The more you know about your customers, the better your chances of increasing lifetime value. Data capture must therefore be an integral part of all your sales, marketing, and customer service campaigns. You can build detailed profiles through campaign responses and customer research, and use the latest database and communications technology to manage, analyze, and distribute information. Take every opportunity to find out more about your customers so that you can build a real competitive edge, based on one-to-one personal relationships.

Invest in Personalization

The rapid development of data storage and data analysis tools means that it is now possible to know far more about your customers—with information well beyond details of income, spending patterns, service preferences, and frequency of use. The information available represents a quantum leap in the ability to profile customers.

Investing in personalization can increase value and loyalty even further.

At the heart of a personalized service is the customer's individual profile. A basic profile covers:
- name and address
- contact details
- purchase history
- personal interests
- product or service preferences

Let Customers Add Their Own Personal Details

If you offer personal pages on your Web site, you can allow customers to add further choices to the profile, using a special checklist. However, it is important to use customer information in appropriate ways. Attempts to increase customer interactions and provide more personalized information have made many consumers concerned about privacy issues. It is essential to let customers control the frequency and scope of interaction. Businesses must understand the difference between using and abusing the information they gather.

Information should be used to meet individual customer needs; customers are aware of the value of their information and are willing to provide it only when they see real benefits. That means giving customers control over their data and the way they interact with your com-

pany. To build trust, you must allow customers to choose how they want to interact and to use the information that they provide.

Develop a One-to-one Relationship

The contact between buyer and seller on the Internet is moving toward the ultimate one-to-one experience. Database technology supports a level of personalization that can deliver highly tailored products and services to specific individuals. Each time a customer logs on to a Web site, for example, the database can pull together purchase history and personal preferences as a basis for a highly personalized response. By giving customers a single point of entry, you can increase customer loyalty and learn more about their purchasing patterns. This provides an excellent basis for adding value and for the development of new products.

Maintain Regular, Targeted Communication

Once you have customer information, it is important to act on it. Maintain regular contact by sending customers information or special offers tailored to their individual needs.

Use E-mail to Maintain Contact

With e-mail you can deliver individual messages cost-effectively. E-mail also commands immediate attention. Most people check their e-mail routinely and generally read or quickly scan most messages. This makes e-mail a powerful marketing tool with a high potential return for a modest investment. Your e-mail goes straight into the customer's in-box, so you don't have to spend money attracting people to your site. When a customer elects to take regular e-mail from you, you have an opportunity to build a strong relationship. This makes online marketing more predictable and gives you the chance to develop a one-to-one relationship.

Allow Customers to Customize Products

Interactive facilities on a Web site allow customers to design their own customized products. Cars and computers are good examples. The customer chooses a basic model, and then selects features and options from a database. The system provides a price for the customized product, then gives the customer the choice of ordering now or storing the specification on a personal Web page for later modification. The high level of interaction gives customers greater choice and provides you with detailed insight into their needs.

Customize Information Services

You can use data on customer preferences as a basis for offering personalized information services. Customers specify the type of information they need, and you alert them by e-mail whenever relevant information is available.

Offer Different Service Levels

One-to-one service allows you to offer different levels of service to each category of customer. These could include:
- privileged rewards for top customers;
- incentives for regular customers to spend more;
- special offers to lapsed customers.

COMMON MISTAKES
Ignoring Privacy Issues

One-to-one marketing is based on the acquisition and use of high levels of personal information. You should publish a privacy policy on your site and you should also make sure that you comply with relevant guidelines, rules, and legislation. When you collect data, tell visitors what you do with the information, and follow best practice on privacy issues.

Failing to Develop Customer Relationships

The primary reason for collecting data is to find out more about customer needs so that you can build long-term relationships and increase customer loyalty. It is essential to act on the information you collect, analyze it, and develop strategies for building a personalized one-to-one service.

Targeting the Wrong People

Marketing programs work most effectively when they are aimed at a specific audience. The more you segment your target audience, the more precisely you can communicate. Different groups within your target market may have different purchasing needs or spending levels. By segmenting your audience and customizing your marketing material, you can address individual needs.

FOR MORE INFORMATION

Book:
Peppers, Don, and Martha Rogers. *Return on Customer: Creating and Maximizing Value from Your Scarcest Resource.* New York: Currency, 2005.

Web site:
The Peppers & Rogers Group's site: **www.1to1.com**

See also:
- ✔ Conducting Market Research (pp. 735–737)
- ✔ Increasing Customer Lifetime Value (pp. 706–707)
- ✔ Making Better Use of Customer Data (pp. 743–744)
- ☆ Managing 1:1 Marketing (pp. 63–64)
- ☆ The Second Coming of Service (pp. 104–105)

"Facts are available to everyone; it is interpretation and implementation that is key."

Ric Simcock

Building Partnership with Business Customers

GETTING STARTED

Partnership can increase your customers' dependence on you and strengthen long-term relationships. It requires long-term commitment by your company, combined with correct structuring and focus. Customer partners are looking for technical expertise, cooperation, and, in some cases, total solutions.

FAQs

How can I use partnership to increase customer dependency?

Put together a dependency checklist to develop a plan that shows how you could strengthen relationships with your customers. List the factors that are most important to your customers, describe how you could contribute to the achievement of their objectives, and prepare a plan for increasing your involvement.

My customers want to achieve market leadership through innovation. How can partnership help them do that?

Your technical skills and resources can help them to develop the right level of innovation without investment in their own skills by using your technical resources to handle product development on a subcontractual basis. This provides them with new technology and allows them to diversify in line with your specialist skills.

Is partnership based only on technical cooperation?

No: the scope of partnership is far wider, and its benefits can include reduced costs, increased capacity, a nationwide distribution network, focus on core business, a stronger supply position, and improved through-life costs.

How does partnership save money?

Through partnership, your customers can become value-for-money suppliers and succeed through competitive pricing. You can help them to reduce overall costs by improving design and manufacturing costs or by handling noncore activities cost-effectively.

MAKING IT HAPPEN

Increase Customer Dependency

Partnership can increase your customers' dependence on you and strengthen long-term relationships. It is important to understand customers' business goals. By showing how your products or services can help them to achieve their objectives, you demonstrate that you can make an important contribution to their business.

Demonstrate Commitment to the Business

The partnership service should be your main business activity, and you have invested in its future growth and development. There must be no internal or external factors that could have an adverse effect on your performance or commitment. You will have a statement of direction showing your long-term plans for development of the business, and you must be able to demonstrate that you have the resources to achieve that development. You will have a record of innovation and excellence and be highly regarded by customers and competitors.

Your customer base will contain a high proportion of long-term customers, and you may demonstrate your readiness to make a major contribution to the future of your industry by means of involvement in industry associations or collaborative projects.

Clarify Your Future Direction

A company's future direction is closely related to its commitment to the business. What plans do you have for growth and for future developments? Information on your future range of products or services will help your partners to develop their own long-term plans.

Focus on Your Market Experience

Your track record is a key factor in any partnership, as it demonstrates that you are capable of understanding your partners' requirements and have already developed successful solutions in that market. You may be the market leader or have a growing market share. Your market knowledge may be specialized—focused on specific niche markets or sectors that are of interest to your partners.

Offer Technical Expertise

Gaining access to a partner's technical expertise is one of the major reasons for forming partnerships. Providing examples of technical innovation or leadership will demonstrate your existing capabilities, but partners are also interested in your potential for future development. Annual expenditure on research and development, a good track record in new product development, and technical and research resources all help to substantiate your claims of technical expertise.

Prove Your Management Capability

Your partners will want to know that you have the resources to manage your business effectively and to insure that they are provided with the highest standards of service. You must have an experienced management team, with a management training and development program in position to insure ongoing development of skills to meet changing requirements. Your managers will have the right level of experience in the partners' business and understand their requirements.

Stress Financial Stability

Partners must have confidence in your long-term ability to provide them with continuing high standards of ser-

vice. Doubts about your financial stability will make them unwilling to commit themselves to a full partnership with you as the sole supplier. Make sure that your partners are fully aware of the financial structure and performance of your organization; if your company is part of a larger group, explain the financial relationship, and use the strength of the group's financial resources to demonstrate your own stability. Provide your partners with regular information on your financial performance.

Highlight Quality Processes

Quality processes insure that your partners enjoy the highest standards of service. You should demonstrate that quality is a key business strategy and that you have implemented recognized quality standards. Your staff should also be committed to quality and should be suitably qualified. Explain your quality principles and demonstrate how these principles are driven by customer needs. Explain how you use customer satisfaction indicators to measure the effectiveness of your quality processes and describe the customer surveys, user groups, or other customer response mechanisms that will form part of the partnership process. Describe how you might apply your quality processes to specific partnership activities and explain how you could integrate your quality processes with those of your customers.

Demonstrate Adequate Resources

Partnership is a long-term commitment, and you must demonstrate that you have the resources to provide the level of service your partners need, both now and in the future. The key facts about your organization—size, number of employees, location, turnover and profitability, national or international network, and infrastructure—will help your partners decide whether you can handle their target level of business. For example, if your customers operate a national or international network of branches, do you have a corresponding network to meet their local needs? Do you have the production resources to handle increasing volumes of business, and can you invest in or automate any processes to increase your capacity? How many staff do you have, and are you using training to develop their skills?

Get Organized for Partnership

It is important to explain to your customers how you will make partnership resources available to them. The structure of your organization must reflect customer needs, not internal requirements. For example, an organizational structure that reflects markets rather than internal divisions shows that you are focused on customer needs. Your organization should help your partners to make the best use of their own resources, and you should make it easy for them to use your services. A single point of contact for all your products and services provides your partners with rapid access. Quality staff who are committed to the highest levels of customer care demonstrate that your company is focused on your partners' interests.

Implement Collaborative Working Tools

Networking solutions such as Internet Protocol (IP) make it easier for you and your customers to collaborate. Project teams in different locations can share files and other material during a videoconference over an IP-based network.

Provide Total Solutions

As well as providing specific products and services, you can support your partners with other added-value services, enabling them to gain maximum business benefits. A total solution might include consulting, project management, implementation, or training and facilities management, and you must demonstrate that you have the skills and resources to provide them.

Demonstrate a Policy of Collaboration

To prove that you can make partnership work, quote other examples of collaboration or partnerships that you have been involved in. Describe the key success factors and show how you have used your capabilities to insure the success of the partnership. By demonstrating involvement in user groups or industry liaison committees, you can also show that you are capable of working closely with other people to achieve joint objectives.

COMMON MISTAKES
Mistaking Selling for Partnership

Selling a product or service does not create a strong relationship with a customer. It is the added-value benefits that increase customer dependency and provide the basis for an effective, long-term relationship.

Failing to Communicate Partnership Capability to a Customer

A partnership is a formal, long-term relationship, with high levels of collaboration and commitment on both sides. Your partners must have a full understanding of your capability and of any developments in your business that affect the partnership.

Focusing on a Narrow Area of Collaboration

Partnership covers a wide area of collaboration: technical cooperation, shared manufacturing resources, joint ventures and development programs, and shared networks. The higher the level of collaboration, the greater the dependency of the relationship.

Neglecting Internal Partnership Processes

Partnerships can fail if internal communications are not used to explain the importance of the partnership and the contributions that different departments make. Quality processes and documented procedures can help to make sure that the company delivers on its partnership commitments.

FOR MORE INFORMATION

Book:
Doz, Yves L., and Gary Hamel. *Alliance Advantage: The Art of Creating Value through Partnering.* Boston, MA: Harvard Business School Press, 1998.

Web site:
U.S. Department of Commerce: **www.doc.gov**

699

ACTIONLIST

"If the U.S. and Japan cannot become partners, then there is a possibility that current trends could eventually make them enemies."
Richard Drobnick

Communicating Customer Service

GETTING STARTED

Your business won't survive without customers, and you need to get across how much you value them. To communicate well externally, you need to have in place a clear, consistent, internal communications strategy too. If you have a team of people working with you, let them know how they each contribute to your business's success, and the way they interact with your customers is a key part of this.

FAQs
Who is responsible for customer service?

Everyone in a business, contributes to overall customer satisfaction, even if their jobs do not involve direct customer contact. Broken delivery promises, inaccurate invoices, or poor telephone handling can cancel out the benefits of a good product or service.

Why are award programs important to the success of customer service?

Customer service staff are in the front line, facing difficult customers and frequent problems. Award programs can help to maintain motivation and demonstrate that their contribution is important.

Isn't customer service the same as marketing?

Certain aspects of customer service—understanding customer needs, delivering a service, tailoring the offer to meet customer requirements—are the same, but the scope of marketing is much broader.

Is customer service just a set of personal skills?

Personal skills are important, but a company can put in place processes and programs that improve the customer's experience and make it easier and more convenient for the customer to do business.

MAKING IT HAPPEN
Communicate Clearly

When a company changes its focus toward customer service, it is essential that everyone is involved. Change creates an atmosphere of uncertainty, so it is vital that everyone understands the important issues and feels that they can contribute to the success of the change. In an atmosphere of uncertainty, customer service levels can be adversely affected.

Build Understanding

Organizational changes can have a significant impact on employees, suppliers, and distributors—so it is vital that they are thoroughly briefed. Change can be a powerful positive factor rather than a cause for concern, and change can demonstrate that a business is committed to improvement and progress.

Encourage Commitment

Implementing a customer service policy requires commitment and involvement from all employees. Before implementing a program, it is sensible to find what the level of commitment is and to include staff in discussion. The most important part of the process is the follow-up. Too many employees believe views will be ignored.

Encourage Improvement

As far as possible, training should be offered to all staff to help them understand the importance of customer care. A customer satisfaction guide could be issued, describing the most important elements of customer service and the standards which apply.

Maintain Motivation

Motivation and award programs can help to maintain high levels of interest in the customer service program and to build a high level of commitment to the program's success. Award programs that reward continued improvement in levels of customer satisfaction maintain momentum and give customer service programs a high profile. They are therefore valuable in building team spirit and a commitment to excellence.

Provide a Vision

Clear visions and strong, motivating language focus attention on the importance of customer service programs. It is also essential that the program is led from the top. A key figure should be involved personally in every aspect of the programs—talking to groups of employees, appearing in company intranet broadcasts, and using every public relations opportunity to raise the profile of the program.

Develop Champions

The leader cannot achieve all the objectives alone, so it is essential that other people with influence can take on the role of supporting the message throughout the business. Management commentators often call these people "champions." Their task is to build commitment and enthusiasm for change. They may be the very people who could undermine change if left out of the process, though.

COMMON MISTAKES
Treating Customer Service As a Departmental Function

Customer service is left to those staff who are directly involved with customers. This is too limited a view, because customer service is relegated to a sales or complaints-handling process.

Managing Customer Service at Departmental Level

If customer service is treated as a line management function, staff will not appreciate its critical importance to the success of the business. Customer service must be led from the top, with the direct involvement of a senior manager.

"Customers do not care about industry boundaries; they want service and convenience."

Peter G. W. Keen

Failure to Develop Customer Service Skills

It's a common misconception that customer service quality depends solely on personal skills. Customer service standards can be improved through training and through the introduction of customer service programs.

Low Recognition

Customer service has long suffered from low recognition. Motivation and reward programs, together with leadership from the top, can help to redress the balance.

FOR MORE INFORMATION

Book:
Reichheld, Frederick F. *The Loyalty Effect: The Hidden Force Behind Growth, Profits, and Lasting Value.* Boston, MA: Harvard Business School Press, 2001.

Web site:
American Marketing Association:
www.marketingpower.com

"Above all, we wish to avoid having a dissatisfied customer. We consider our customers a part of our organization, and we want them to feel free to make any criticism they see fit in regard to our merchandise or service."

L. L. Bean

Handling Customer Problems

GETTING STARTED

Even the most professional service companies will inevitably face a problem with a customer that, if left unresolved, may lead to a loss of business. Customers who know that their problems are taken care of are more likely to be fully satisfied with the services that are available. A key factor in resolving customers' problems is the ability to reassure them that help is on the way. Having in place a process to respond quickly and effectively to a problem enables a company to deliver the highest standards of customer care at a time when the customer most needs it.

This process, sometimes called incident management, is particularly suitable for larger companies or if the customer is likely to suffer a great deal of inconvenience because of the incident. However, the principles can be applied to any business, however small.

- In developing a response and support strategy, you should establish a variety of business objectives.
- The incident management approach is to appoint one person, trained in customer service skills, to deal with a customer throughout an incident.
- The role of the personal incident manager is to take responsibility for the provision of appropriate services.
- An incident management program has two main elements: the infrastructure to deliver the service and the personal skills to provide the right level of customer care.
- Skilled staff members are essential to the effective delivery of the service, and training may be necessary.
- Many equipment manufacturers use incident management techniques to support their customers after a disaster.

FAQs
Should incident management form part of all service offerings?

It depends on the type of service that is offered. If the service is critical to the customer's business process—telecommunications or computing, for example—incident management would be important. Disruption to those services could damage the customer's business.

Why is a personal incident manager necessary?

During an incident, effective coordination of support services and regular communication with the customer are essential. By appointing a single person to take responsibility for coordination and communication, you can guarantee continuity and reassure the customer by giving them a single point of contact.

Is it possible to plan for future incidents?

It isn't just possible; it is essential. Industry research indicates that a high proportion of companies who did not have a documented plan failed to recover lost business. Planning is just as important as quality support services.

MAKING IT HAPPEN
Deal with Customer Incidents

Customers who know that their problems are taken care of are more likely to be fully satisfied with the services that are available and will be happier to deal with the same company in the future. Quality experts found that a key factor in delivering time-guaranteed services was the ability to reassure customers that help was on the way. Customers would then be prepared to wait until help or support arrived, even if there was a long gap between reporting the incident and having it resolved. Other research has shown that customers whose complaints are satisfactorily dealt with are likely to be more loyal than those who had no complaint in the first place.

Identify Opportunities for Incident Management

A number of scenarios can be used to identify situations where support like this could be valuable.

- The customer could suffer a great deal of inconvenience and stress as a result of the incident. Reducing the stress and inconvenience would help to demonstrate high levels of care and increase customer satisfaction.
- The incident could threaten the efficiency of the company business, and measures must be taken to limit the damage.
- The customer does not have the skills and resources to resolve the problems on the spot and is dependent on external forms of support.
- The customer has paid for a support package and has agreed to a certain level of response. The company must respond within the agreed levels.
- The speed of response is seen as a competitive differentiation and is positioned as an integral part of the service package.
- Failure to deal with the incident quickly could have a critical effect on the customer's business or personal activities.
- The incident could have legal implications, and the customer needs high levels of advice and guidance.

Set Objectives for Incident Management

In developing a response and support strategy, you should set a wide range of business objectives:

- to provide the highest levels of quality response and customer support throughout an incident;
- to minimize inconvenience for the customer;
- to make sure that incidents are resolved promptly within agreed time scales;
- to make sure that support resources are deployed effectively to maximize customer satisfaction.

Introduce Incident Management

The incident management approach is to appoint one person, trained in customer service skills, to deal with a customer throughout an incident.

Incident management can be applied to any service-led organization where the customer needs to be kept

"When you stop talking, you've lost your customer. When you turn your back, you've lost her."

Estée Lauder

informed, for example, maintenance and support services for vital equipment or business continuity services where the customer faces difficult and unfamiliar decisions and needs support.

Appoint a Personal Incident Manager

The role of the personal incident manager is to take responsibility for the provision of appropriate services and to reassure the customer that help and support are on the way. In the smaller company, this may be a senior manager, even the managing director, but whoever takes the role must have the authority to take appropriate action. The personal incident manager:

- takes the incoming calls from the customer, establishes the location, and identifies the form of support needed;
- provides individual guidance to the customer on action to be taken with an indication of support provided;
- deals with the customer's immediate queries;
- makes detailed arrangements to put support services into operation;
- monitors the progress of support services and keeps the customer up to date if possible.

Offer Business Continuity Services

Many equipment manufacturers use incident management techniques to support their customers after an incident such as fire, accident, or system breakdown. If the customer loses essential equipment such as computers or telephones for an extended period, this could seriously threaten the future of their business. Industry research shows that only a minority of companies dependent on the computer have a formal disaster recovery strategy and points out that loss of a system for more than a few days could put them out of business.

Plan and Implement Business Continuity Plans

A business continuity program has a number of stages:

- helping the customer to identify critical activities that should be covered in the event of a disaster;
- training staff members and managers to prepare for a disaster by simulating the conditions of an emergency;
- preparing a contingency plan for business continuity;
- providing replacement equipment and services;
- providing support and project management resources;
- providing full support to restore normal service and maintain business continuity.

Throughout a disaster, the customer would have access to an incident manager who would coordinate the rescue and recovery activities and provide advice, guidance, and support. The principle is similar to that of the personal incident manager, where customers are given reassurance that incidents will be resolved and that they can be sure of the highest standards of support throughout the incident.

Create the Infrastructure for Incident Management

The program has two main elements: the infrastructure to deliver the service and the personal skills to provide the right level of customer care. The infrastructure requires a significant investment to make sure that the service can be delivered rapidly and efficiently throughout the country. Depending on the complexity of the project, it might include:

- communications to provide a rapid response to customer questions, and put the service into operation;
- a trained support team to deliver the service;
- quality-controlled suppliers to support the direct response team;
- a control center to manage the operations and coordinate the response;
- a network of contacts and suppliers to provide the specialist services that form part of the response.

Develop the Right Skills

Skilled staff members are essential to the effective delivery of the service. The skills requirements would include:

- incident management skills, to deal with customers who may be in stressful situations;
- project management skills, to coordinate and implement a response;
- technical skills, to deliver the service;
- communications skills, to coordinate the elements of the program.

COMMON MISTAKES
Failing to Communicate with the Customer During an Incident

Research shows that customers who receive regular progress updates feel reassured that they are getting the right level of support. Anxiety levels are high during an incident, but regular communication helps customers to deal with the incident and contributes to overall customer satisfaction.

Not Having an Escalation Procedure

A company should have a formal escalation procedure for dealing with customer incidents. If support staff cannot resolve an incident within an agreed time scale, the incident should be reported to a more senior manager, who would then commit more resources. If there is no escalation procedure, the incident can get out of hand and damage customer relationships.

703

ACTIONLIST

FOR MORE INFORMATION

Books:
Lovelock, Christopher, and Jochen Wirtz. *Services Marketing: People, Technology, Strategy.* 5th ed. Upper Saddle River, NJ: FT Prentice Hall, 2003.
Zeithaml, Valarie A., et al. *Services Marketing.* 4th ed. New York: McGraw-Hill, 2005.

Web site:
American Marketing Association:
www.marketingpower.com

See also:
✔ Communicating Customer Service (pp. 700–701)
✔ Handling Customer Inquiries (pp. 704–705)
✔ Setting Up a Customer Interaction Center (pp. 712–713)

"If a brand screws up, honesty with the customer is the best way to recapture support."

Michael Perry

Handling Customer Inquiries

GETTING STARTED

Businesses need mechanisms to cope with inquiries or requests for help from both existing and potential customers. This actionlist offers some information on the different options open to you.

Helplines are essential for delivering support, service, advice, and information to customers and add value to a business. To provide the best service, use staff with extensive, up-to-date product knowledge and strong interpersonal skills and train them in customer service techniques to ensure they can deal effectively with different types of query or problem. To maximize the benefit to users of the service, deal with queries immediately where possible, or arrange to call the customer back on more complex queries, and ensure that the customer is satisfied with the response at the end of the conversation.

FAQs

Should helpline services be offered free to customers?

Helpline services fall into a number of categories: support, help with problems, advice, and useful information. The support categories should be free because they are essential for customer satisfaction. The information services can also be seen as a customer service, something that adds value to the original purchase. You may feel it strengthens customer relationships to continue offering them free information. Information services offered to the general public are valuable services that can be charged, usually through a premium rate number.

Which staff should work on the helplines?

Trained customer service staff can help customers report a problem effectively and may be able to offer advice or help up to a certain level. When the query goes beyond their level of knowledge, you should have a two-stage process in which the customer service representative takes the initial call and arranges for a specialist to call the customer back within an agreed time.

Can a helpline service be handled by an external organization?

Provided the external organization's team undergoes thorough training, there is no reason why the helpline cannot be outsourced. The practice is common in the computer industry.

MAKING IT HAPPEN
Establish a Helpline

The most important thing about a helpline is that it really needs to *help*, so there are a number of rules to remember when creating one:

- Make it convenient: offer customers an 800 number facility to encourage contact, and set opening times to suit customer calling patterns.
- Get the right staff: use staff with extensive, up-to-date product knowledge, and make sure that they are trained

in customer service techniques so that they can deal effectively with different types of query or problem.

- Provide the right backup: helpline staff need to have access to any existing product, technical, or service databases, as well as guidelines on the actions they can take to deal with different types of complaint. Make sure they also have lists of contacts for authorization of different types of action and information.
- Make the service fast and reliable: deal with queries immediately or arrange to call the customer back on more complex queries, and operate an "escalation procedure" (see below for more information) to deal with complaints that cannot be resolved within agreed time scales.
- Check and double check: follow up to make sure that if a customer was promised a return call within an agreed time scale, it did happen and that he or she is satisfied with the response.

Also investigate what level of support you can offer over the Internet. For example, you could establish a "frequently asked questions" (FAQs) section on your Web site that may be able to tackle most basic questions.

Plan Helpline Staffing Levels

There's nothing worse than getting to a helpline but then being kept on hold for a long time. It really is crucial to get your staffing levels right, so ask your telephone supplier to provide a report on the number of calls to the helpline number, as well as the average waiting time, and then analyze the pattern of calls during the day/week-/month/year, identifying the peaks and troughs. This will help you to determine the current and planned level of calls per day; the ratio of staff to calls, and therefore how many helpline staff you need.

If you have very marked peak and off-peak periods, decide whether you can meet demand using current staff resources, or whether it might be beneficial to use technologies such as voicemail to handle some of the incoming calls. If you can afford it, you could also consider using an external call handling service to manage overload or peak traffic.

Identify Helpline Skills

Make sure that your staff meet a checklist of appropriate helpline skills. These might include product knowledge, telephone technique, and technical, product service, administrative, and customer service skills.

Develop Helpline Skills

Regardless of how good your staff are, there are always ways in which you can help them to improve and develop their skills. Assess the skills required for different types of helpline service, compare these with the current skills of your helpline staff, and identify the areas that need to be improved. Implement training and monitor performance improvements, ensure that staff know how to use any new technology, and obtain customer feedback to evaluate performance.

"I probably spend some time once a month listening in on calls or talking to customers. I encourage my executives to do the same."

Lillian Vernon

Provide Customer Information for Helpline Staff

Your staff will be able to provide a prompt response and personal service if they've been given enough customer information. Make available the information you already have, such as existing customer records, data generated by responses to advertisements or promotional activities, and so on, and make sure it is checked and updated. Take the opportunity to capture customer information each time a customer calls, and add further information that is appropriate to the helpline service, such as service records. Use a simple code to access information quickly, for example, name, account number, and Zip code, and include prompts to contact customers with details of new products and services.

Establish Helpline Escalation Procedures

There are always some calls that cannot be dealt with immediately, so you need to have an escalation procedure in place to make sure they don't slip through the net. Identify critical types of helpline requests, including technical support, complaints, and breakdowns, and set target response times for such queries. Appoint a supervisor to monitor conformance to target response times; escalate any queries that exceed target times to a designated manager; and monitor the responses to escalated queries.

Record Helpline Usage

In order to make sure you are meeting demand properly, you need to record helpline usage. How many calls does your helpline receive per day, per week, per month, per year? What types of call does it receive and what is the volume of each type of call? Which customers are the most regular helpline users? Which media generate most inquiries to the helpline? What is the impact of promotional campaigns on helpline activity? Which products receive most/least complaints, queries, or requests for support? What are the most frequent complaints, queries, and requests for support? Which type of request uses most resources? What is the average call time for different types of request?

Promote the Helpline Service

Above all, make sure customers know what help is available to them. Include the helpline number in advertisements, publications, Web site pages, and other promotional material, as well as on invoices, delivery notes, instructions, user guides, and other product documentation.

COMMON MISTAKES
Putting the Wrong People on the Helpline

The people who run the helpline should have good customer handling skills and a level of product and technical knowledge that enables them to provide the right answer or put the customer in contact with the right specialist.

Inadequate Resources on the Helpline

When customers call a helpline, they are looking for a quick response. Phones that go unanswered for long periods of time show poor customer service. Putting a customer in a queue of other callers is satisfactory only for a short period of time.

Failing to Call the Customer Back

If you cannot deal with queries immediately, let the customer know when someone will get back to him or her, and then check that the return call has been made.

FOR MORE INFORMATION

Books:

Bodin, Madeline, and Keith Dawson. *The Call Center Dictionary: The Complete Guide to Call Center and Customer Support Technology Solutions.* 3rd ed. New York: CMP Books, 2002.

Blackwell, Roger, and Kristina Stephan. *Customers Rule! Why the E-commerce Honeymoon is Over and Where Winning Businesses Go from Here.* New York: Crown Publishing Group, 2001.

Dawson, Keith. *The Call Center Handbook: The Complete Guide to Starting, Running and Improving Your Customer Contact Center.* 4th ed. New York: CMP Books, 2004.

Web site:

CCNG International: **www.ccng.com**

See also:

✔ Communicating Customer Service (pp. 700–701)
✔ Converting Leads into Sales (pp. 733–734)
☆ Delivering and Delighting—A New Spirit at Work (pp. 91–93)
✔ Handling Customer Problems (pp. 702–703)
✔ Setting Up a Customer Interaction Center (pp. 712–713)

"Everything changes when there is a real customer yelling at you from the other end of the phone."

Percy Barnevik

Increasing Customer Lifetime Value

GETTING STARTED

"Customer lifetime value" (CLV or LTV) is a way of measuring how much your customers are worth over the time they buy your products and services. Increases in customer retention can increase sales and profits significantly. It is important to retain customers, but not at the cost of other essential marketing activities.

Putting customers into key categories helps to clarify analysis and acts as the basis for marketing activities designed to improve customer lifetime value.

FAQs

What's the difference between customer lifetime value and customer loyalty programs?

Customer loyalty programs are designed to retain as many customers as possible, regardless of their real value. The customer lifetime value calculation indicates the contribution individual customers make to profitability.

Why are lapsed customers important?

If they can be "revived," they tend to behave like new customers and become regular buyers once again, with good potential lifetime value.

Is customer retention more important than acquisition?

Acquisition should never be neglected, because existing business may decline for reasons outside your control. Industry experience indicates, however, that existing customers make a comparatively greater contribution when marketing costs are taken into consideration.

Do we want to retain all our customers?

Not necessarily. Some customers may not be profitable. Using customer lifetime value, you can calculate the cost and contribution of each customer.

MAKING IT HAPPEN

Apply the Customer Lifetime Value Concept

Customer lifetime value is a way of measuring how much your customers are worth to you, over the length of time that they remain your customers.

The lifetime for customers will vary from industry to industry, and from brand to brand. The lifetime of customers should come to an end when their contribution ceases to be profitable unless steps are taken to revitalize them.

Benefits from Customer Lifetime Value

Industry experience indicates that a number of benefits apply.

- A 5% increase in customer retention can create a 125% increase in profits.
- A 10% increase in retailer retention can translate to a 20% increase in sales.
- Extending customer lifecycles by three years can triple profits per customer.

Identify Categories of Customer

Before calculating customer lifetime value, it is possible to analyze your customers according to four key attributes. This can help to clarify analysis and act as the basis for marketing activities to improve customer lifetime value:

- frequency—how often they purchase (regular customers are more likely to purchase in the future)
- recency—how much time has elapsed since the last purchase (recent customers are more likely to purchase again)
- amount—how much they spend (higher-spending customers are likely to be more committed)
- category—what sort of product they buy (some products will be more profitable than others and some may be one-time purchases)

Calculate Lifetime Value

In a consumer business, customer lifetime value is calculated, in practice, by analyzing the behavior of a group of customers who:

- have the same recruitment date;
- are recruited from the same source;
- bought the same types of product.

In a business-to-business environment, a similar approach can be used.

- Isolate particular customers, and examine them individually.
- Analyze the behavior of different groups, segmenting your customer database by factors such as industry, annual turnover, or staff numbers.

The basic calculation has three stages:

- Identify a discrete group of customers for tracking.
- Record (or estimate) each revenue and cost for this group of customers, by campaign or season.
- Calculate the contribution, by campaign or season.

Refine the Calculation

Other factors can be introduced to make the calculation more relevant. In a business-to-business environment, for example, it may be the sales representatives who generate sales. In this case, the calculation should include the representative's "running costs" and the cost of any centrally produced sales support material.

Evaluate a Campaign

The table overleaf shows the calculations for a group of customers who were recruited through a direct response advertising campaign that ran in the spring of year 1, and tracks their expenditure over a five-year period.

Divide the total contribution by the number of customers in the group. Say there are one thousand customers: the average lifetime value per customer is $7. But this compares favorably with a short term analysis which, in the first year, would show a loss of $3 per customer recruited.

"If you look after the customers and look after the people who look after the customers, you should be successful."

Charles Dunstone

Year	Annual Customer Expenditure	Annual Marketing Costs	Annual Net Contribution
0	$12,000	$15,000	$–3,000
1	$10,000	$6,000	$4,000
Total Year 2	$85,000	$65,000	$20,000
2	$8,000	$6,000	$2,000
3	$7,000	$6,000	$1,000
4	$6,000	$4,000	$2,000
5	$5,000	$4,000	$1,000
Totals	$48,000	$41,000	$7,000

Analyze the Results

A company may offer different products or brands, which are marketed under different cost centers. If a customer is a customer of more than one cost/profit center, there is a choice of approaches:
- Examine customers of each brand and ignore multipurchases.
- Build a more detailed model that combines and allocates the cumulative costs as well as the cumulative profit in the appropriate proportions.

Use Customer Lifetime Values to Improve Marketing Performance

There are four important applications:
- setting target customer acquisition costs
- allocating acquisition funds
- selecting acquisition offers
- supporting customer retention activities

In the example above the decision was taken in Year 4 to reduce marketing costs on this group of customers. Equally valid may be an increase in expenditure aimed at reactivating customers—this is a classic retention activity.

Set Target Customer Acquisition Costs

If a customer is expected to generate more than one sale, the allowable cost can be greater than the cost allowed for the first sale—the classic loss-leader approach to customer acquisition, illustrated in the example table above. However, overspending on customer acquisition can also be ruinous. A reasonable calculation is to recruit only from those sources that yield new customers at less than half the estimated lifetime value. On that basis, the worst sources will have a cost per customer close to a lifetime value, while the average cost per customer should be far lower.

Allocate Acquisition Funds

Different recruitment sources will provide customers with different lifetime values. After identifying those values, spend more on the best sources.

Select Acquisition Offers

The lifetime value of a customer may depend on the type and value of their initial purchase. In turn, this can lead to decisions about which products and offers to use when advertising externally, or when considering how to upgrade existing customers.

Support Customer Retention Activities

Once the typical lifetime value of a group of customers is known, companies can decide how hard to work at retaining them. It is not a foregone conclusion that all customers are worth having. Activities should be tailored to the customers who are most valuable.

Increase Value with New Offers

A financial services company can increase customer lifetime value by cross selling a variety of products and services.

COMMON MISTAKES
Trying to Retain the Wrong Customers

Customer retention costs money in terms of sales and marketing funds, so do bear in mind that not all customers are worth keeping. You should carefully select the customers who are likely to yield the highest returns over a period of time and prioritize the allocation of marketing resources to these.

Offering Customers a Limited Range of Products

When you have identified the most valuable customers, you need to have a wide variety of products or services to offer them. Cross-selling and up-selling are the best ways to increase customer lifetime value, but this can be difficult with a limited product range. Customers are your company's most valuable asset; think about "share of customer wallet" rather than just share of market.

Spending Too Much on Acquiring New Customers

Customer lifetime value analysis reinforces a traditional marketing rule of thumb, that it costs less to retain existing customers than to acquire new ones. Overemphasis on new business development could be a bad move, since existing customers are easier to sell to.

707

ACTIONLIST

FOR MORE INFORMATION

Books:
Reichheld, Frederick F. *Loyalty Rules! How Today's Leaders Build Lasting Relationships*. Boston, MA: Harvard Business School Press, 2003.
Peppers, Don, and Martha Rogers. *Return on Customer: Creating and Maximizing Value from Your Scarcest Resource*. New York: Currency, 2005.

Web site:
Peppers+Rogers: **www.1to1.com**

See also:
- ✔ Building One-to-one Relationships (pp. 696–697)
- ☆ Delivering and Delighting—A New Spirit at Work (pp. 91–93)
- ☆ Making Loyalty Work (pp. 370–371)
- ☆ Managing 1:1 Marketing (pp. 63–64)

"Good customers are an asset which, when well managed and served, will return a handsome lifetime income stream for the company."
Philip Kotler

Implementing a Customer Relationship Management Strategy

GETTING STARTED

Customer relationship management (CRM) is about using people, processes and technology to develop long-term, profitable relationships with customers. The Internet is an important medium through which CRM services are delivered. CRM technology is generally best suited to organizations with a large customer base. CRM requires skilled staff to be able to exploit its features, in order to understand their customers better and deliver just the product or service that such customers require. CRM:

- is growing rapidly;
- has been over-hyped;
- is about a customer-centric view of the world;
- is about people as much as technology;
- is critical to successful e-commerce;
- is for medium and large organizations (smaller organizations should do CRM manually).

FAQs

What makes up a CRM system?

CRM generally includes some or all of the following: customer information systems; personalization systems; content management systems; call center automation; data warehousing; data mining; sales force automation; campaign management systems.

With the emergence of the Web we are seeing what is termed as e-CRM, where there is a strong customer self-service and personalization focus. Ideally, CRM and e-CRM should integrate seamlessly but, because they often use different technologies, this is not always easy to achieve.

Why is CRM so important to e-commerce?

The Internet is a fickle environment. There is no live interaction between the consumer and the Web site. Therefore, a Web site needs to work hard to develop relationships with its customers. It's about anticipating customer information requirements through personalization. It's about answering customer questions in a comprehensive and timely manner. It's about delivering exactly what the customer ordered, on time. It's about suggesting to customers new products that they will be genuinely interested in.

What are the key benefits of CRM?

The benefits of CRM include the following:

- better, faster information on customer needs;
- more cost-effective management of the customer relationship through automating and streamlining of customer processes;
- more empowered customers who can quickly find the information they need
- more profitable and loyal customers.

Is CRM right for every business?

No. A small business should be able to know its customers without having to implement lots of technology. CRM is complex and expensive to install. It is best suited to organizations which have a large customer base, and are already customer-centric. They should have a significant sales force, run a variety of marketing and sales programs, and have strong internal IT resources and quality infrastructures.

MAKING IT HAPPEN

Develop a Long-Term Vision and Strategy

Because of the complexity and expense of CRM, it is not advised to implement an entire CRM system at one time. Rather, your organization needs to develop a vision of where it wants to go with CRM over the long term. Then, the CRM implementation should be broken down into manageable sections prioritizing the technology that will deliver the most immediate benefits in the shortest time.

Develop a Return on Investment (ROI) Model

A significant number of organizations depend on intuition, rather than a clear ROI model, in deciding to implement CRM systems. This is not a good idea. To create an ROI model, establish appropriate metrics and see how they change with the implementation of CRM. CRM metrics include:

- revenue per sales rep
- cost and length of time it takes to close a lead
- revenue/profitability per customer
- length of time customers stay with you
- customer satisfaction ratings

Talk to Your Customers

In developing a vision and strategy, it's critical to talk to your customers. After all, CRM is about focusing on customer needs, and if you don't understand basic customer needs when designing a CRM solution, then chances are you'll get it wrong.

Talk to Employees

It's critical to survey employees internally. CRM covers a broad range of activities, including marketing, sales, support, and IT, so it's vital that key people in all of these areas are engaged. There will always be tradeoffs but a rounded set of requirements should emerge.

CRM can be seen as an IT solution to a sales and marketing problem. Sales and marketing departments can resist such technology-based solutions unless they are brought fully on board and clearly convinced of the benefits of CRM. Getting everyone working together under a single CRM banner may be great in theory, but difficult in practice.

Ensure That Employees are Properly Trained and Educated

Well-trained employees make for successful CRM. The key objective of CRM is not so much to train employees

"There is practically no area of business where the difference between rhetoric and actuality is greater than in the handling of people."

John Harvey-Jones

in how to use the new software, but rather to have a customer-centric view of the world. If employees are not open to embracing a philosophy of making the customer king, then CRM will become an expensive and wasteful exercise. Just as customers are becoming more information hungry, so employees also need to become more information hungry about their customers. Customer data are nothing if they are not analyzed and turned into information and knowledge. Only highly motivated and trained people can do that.

Create a Single View of the Customer

A core objective of CRM should be to create a single view of the customer. Historically, organizations have held isolated pockets of information on individual customers. CRM should be about bringing all that information together into a single, well-organized environment. That means departments sharing and collaborating and ensuring that all relevant staff can make use of this single customer profile.

Carefully Consider Integration Issues

Because CRM can cover such a broad range of technologies and activities, integration becomes a key issue. There is likely to be a range of different software in the CRM solution and this will need to integrate properly. Also, the CRM solution will have to integrate with existing systems—trying to implement what are CRM technologies into an old or poorly managed IT infrastructure will cause serious problems.

Selecting a CRM Vendor

Your organization should have a detailed understanding of what it wants from CRM before approaching vendors. From there a detailed selection methodology should be developed so that all suppliers are appraised on a consistent basis. Here are some key questions:

- Who are the vendor's customers? How happy are they with their implementations? Does the vendor have customers in your industry? (If so, talk to them about their experience.)
- What about support and training, which is just as important as the software itself? What are the means by which it is delivered—in person, by telephone, over the Web)? What support packages are available?
- How long has the vendor been in business? What's their financial situation? Have they been in the news lately? If so why?
- What are the skills and experience of the team that will be involved in implementing the solution?
- What's the pricing? Are payment options available?

The ASP Option for CRM

Technology vending is acronym city. An Application Services Provider (ASP) will offer basically to manage the CRM system for you, and will charge an ongoing fee for that service. Because of the complexity and ever-changing nature of CRM, this can be an attractive option. However, because a CRM system embodies the heart of what an organization does—dealing with customers—the choice of ASP vendor needs to be made very carefully.

COMMON MISTAKES
Forgetting about the C in CRM

Much of the selling of CRM has focused on amazing technology and extraordinary features that do all sorts of fancy things. In all the excitement, the very reason CRM exists—to help organizations develop stronger customer relationships by understanding and meeting customer needs better—is often forgotten.

Not Getting the Staff Approval

The best technology in the world is of little use if the people who are supposed to use it are not properly trained and motivated. CRM implementations have often ignored the core need of changing behavior within the organization. If employees do not have a customer focus and a desire to develop long-term relationships with customers, then CRM is dead on arrival.

Inability to Adapt CRM Solutions Quickly

Surveys indicate that a significant number of organizations have had problems in adapting CRM solutions quickly to changing customer needs. Often, because the systems are so complex, managers are dependent on the IT department to make even simple changes.

Lack of Senior Management's Understanding and Approval

A CRM implementation is crucial to core business functions. CRM projects will run into trouble if senior management is not fully engaged.

Poor Integration

Integration problems with CRM software have proven costly and time-consuming for organizations.

Automation without Common Sense

CRM can automate many sales and marketing processes, but that doesn't mean it shouldn't be carefully monitored. The story is told of a major car manufacturer whose sales department offered deep discounts to get rid of a backlog of lime green cars. The cars began to sell briskly. The CRM system noticed the trend and requested the manufacturing plant to make more lime green cars.

FOR MORE INFORMATION

Web sites:
CRM Forum: **www.crm-forum.com**
ZDNET CRM Update: **www.techupdate.zdnet.com**

See also:
- ✔ Collecting Consumer Data on the Internet (pp. 653–654)
- ☆ Delivering and Delighting—A New Spirit at Work (pp. 91–93)
- ✔ Delivering Quality Online Customer Service and Support (pp. 612–613)
- ☆ Making Loyalty Work (pp. 370–371)
- ☆ Managing 1:1 Marketing (pp. 63–64)
- ☆ Managing the Customer (pp. 85–86)
- ☆ The Second Coming of Service (pp. 104–105)

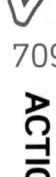

"What makes me *feel* more successful than picking stocks or any of that, is my client relationships."

Grace Fey

Running a Customer Loyalty Program

GETTING STARTED

One of the most important marketing objectives is to retain customers over the long term, because the costs of winning new customers are far higher than those of servicing existing ones. A customer loyalty program is one way of doing this, although it cannot be regarded as a substitute for satisfactory product quality and service levels.

Customer loyalty programs, however, do not simply reward customers for making repeated purchases; they are a powerful tool for gathering information on spending patterns and customer profiles. Because the costs and overhead of such a program are high, it is essential that it is structured and operated effectively.

FAQs
How important are loyalty programs?

It costs considerably more to attract new customers than to service existing ones, so loyalty programs can help to reduce the overall cost of sales. They also offer opportunities to increase the value of individual customers by encouraging them to continue to purchase from your company.

Can you run a loyalty program without investing in database management?

You could run a program simply by offering customers rewards for staying with your company and making occasional purchases. However, the data available from loyalty programs enables you to analyze your customers' purchasing patterns and identify the biggest spending customers. This information can be valuable in developing future marketing and customer service programs.

Isn't it better to invest money in improving quality and service?

Quality and service must be satisfactory before you even think about a loyalty program. If you don't attend to these first, the best you can expect is a temporary rise in sales. However, if these are satisfactory, loyalty programs can add an extra dimension to your marketing programs.

MAKING IT HAPPEN
Reward Loyal Customers

Retaining customers over the long term is a key marketing objective. Customers who are satisfied with the level and quality of service they receive are likely to continue buying from the same company. This can be reinforced by marketing programs that reward customers for their loyalty. The programs can take many different forms, from simple concepts such as discounts on repeat purchases and incentives for multiple purchases to more complex frequent user programs that provide multilevel rewards for customers who continue to use a service.

Establish a Loyalty Program

If you want to make your customers feel welcome, make them members of a loyalty program and offer them benefits that reward their loyalty. Loyalty programs meet a number of different marketing objectives:

- Your customers make regular high-value purchases and you want to retain their business.
- You have customers in a specific age group and you want to retain their loyalty for life.
- There is an opportunity to add value to basic support services.
- Members pay a single annual fee for a service and you want to retain their membership.
- There is an opportunity to make regular offers and sell related products to specific groups of consumers with special interests.
- There is an opportunity to differentiate a product or service by offering customers added-value services that enhance the basic product or service.
- There is an opportunity to offer regular subscribers special benefits.

Offer Customers Real Benefits

You must be certain that the benefits offered by the program are relevant and build the right perceptions. Ideally, they should reflect customer needs identified through research. The benefits should reflect appropriate standards of service, and they should have a degree of exclusivity. They also should add value to the basic product or service offer.

Identify the Costs

Running a loyalty program can represent a significant investment. The major cost areas are:

- recruiting members
- initial offers
- administration
- marketing costs
- full- and/or part-time staff and overhead
- customer offers
- administration
- database management
- cost of interaction, such as a helpline

Consider the Alternatives

Although a loyalty program offers powerful benefits, it may not be the only solution. Consider the following points carefully before committing resources to a program:

- Has customer research highlighted the need for a specific change to the product or service?
- Would such a change help to improve sales and market share?
- Would a loyalty program strongly differentiate your product or service?

"There is no gap in the market unless you have sharp elbows."

Andrew Neil

- Do your competitors offer a similar program?
- Have you got the resources to establish and operate an effective program?
- Would the benefits justify the operating costs?
- Would the customer information available justify the costs?

Manage the Program Effectively

A loyalty program requires careful management to make sure that customers receive the highest standards of service, so training in program administration skills will be important. It is essential that adequate resources are committed to the program—quality customer relationships are essential to its success. The key tasks are:

- identifying the benefits of the program;
- assessing the cost;
- appointing a program coordinator;
- researching customer requirements;
- refining the contents of the program;
- developing a launch strategy;
- introducing the concept of the program internally to build commitment;
- implementing the practical requirements of the program;
- implementing any training required to deliver quality service to customers in the program;
- developing a launch program to guarantee high levels of awareness among prospects and customers;
- implementing a program to make sure that members continue to receive high levels of benefit.

Maintain Interest over the Long Term

A loyalty program is a long-term investment. This means ongoing commitment in terms of people and funding, and a program that will maintain members' interest over time. One way is to offer members increasing levels of benefit—for example, the frequent-flyer clubs run by major airlines.

Use the Program to Improve Understanding of Customers

Loyalty programs can provide you with high levels of information on your customers, and this can prove a valuable basis for future direct marketing.

- Make sure that you capture basic customer data on membership application forms.
- Track members' purchasing patterns and use this to make targeted offers.
- Consider using smart cards to improve data capture.
- Monitor the response to club offers.
- Segment your customer database where possible to improve targeting even further.

Collect Customer Buying Data

Retailers operate programs that issue points to customers based on their expenditure. The points can be accumulated via a smart card, and the customer can use the points to pay for other purchases. The use of technology like this can be used to build a more complete picture of your customers. A smart card can provide detailed information on purchasing patterns that provides a basis for cross-selling other products and services or for tailoring products and services to the customer.

Operate Frequent-buyer Programs

Frequent-buyer programs that also accumulate information on customers are a powerful combination. An example is the frequent-flyer programs run by most of the major airlines. These provide regular travelers with points for every mile they fly which can be exchanged for free leisure travel. Some airlines add a privilege club that offers structured rewards to different groups of customers according to their overall use of airline services. The program includes access to preferential seating, arrangements with hotels and car rental companies, and access to executive airport lounges.

COMMON MISTAKES
Offering Weak Benefits That Competitors Can Match

A loyalty program must offer real, long-term benefits that customers value. If the benefits are not sustainable, the investment will be wasted when customers take their rewards and move on to a competitor's program. Researching customer needs, getting feedback from customers, and monitoring program performance are essential to maintaining a program's success and retaining customers over the long term.

Ignoring the Alternatives

A loyalty program is just one approach to customer retention. The investment may be wasted if the real barrier to customer loyalty is poor product performance or poor customer service. You must research customer attitudes toward your products and your standards of service: if perception is poor, it is essential to put the basics right before setting up reward programs. In the long term, customers prefer quality to rewards.

Failing to Use Program Data

A loyalty program can provide large amounts of data on customer needs and buying patterns. These data should be used to build a better profile of individual customers and to create targeted offers that increase the lifetime value of the customer. The data should also be used to identify and remedy any recurring problems in product performance or customer relationships.

FOR MORE INFORMATION

Book:
Reichheld, Frederick. *The Loyalty Effect: The Hidden Force Behind Growth, Profits and Lasting Value*. Boston, MA: Harvard Business School Press, 2001.

Web site:
Peppers + Rogers: **www.1to1.com**

"Brands are all about trust. You buy the brand because you consider it a friend."

Michael Perry

Setting Up a Customer Interaction Center

GETTING STARTED

The best way to retain customers is through proactive relationship management and outstanding customer service. An integrated approach to customer contact is essential and a customer interaction center integrates people, technology, and customer data. It brings together the staff who deal directly with customers and the support teams into a single, integrated team and gives customers the benefit of a single point of contact. The organization also benefits, as it is able to create "virtual teams" that respond rapidly to requests or queries from customers and is also better placed to share best practice between business units.

FAQs

Why isn't a call center sufficient to handle customer contact?

Call centers were established to handle telephone calls. They are staffed by people trained in telephone techniques and they are designed to deliver a personal service. Customers who communicate with a company via the Web or e-mail may not receive the same level of personal service because of the way electronic communications are routed through the company.

Isn't it best to concentrate resources on a call center because most contact is by telephone?

The trends are changing as more and more people recognize the convenience of ordering electronically, 24 hours a day, 7 days a week, when call centers may be closed. Companies who do not offer the full range of facilities may lose business opportunities.

Who should control the customer interaction center?

The customer interaction center should be more than an extension of the call center. It should be an integral part of the sales or marketing department and should be treated as a strategic resource that contributes to long-term customer retention.

Should the interaction center be limited to telephone and Internet technology?

Customer interaction is getting more and more sophisticated. Multimedia communication is becoming increasingly common in consumer and business markets. The interaction center should be capable of adapting to new technological developments.

MAKING IT HAPPEN
Retain Customer Loyalty

Increasingly, companies recognize that the best way to retain customers is through proactive relationship management and outstanding customer service. A key element in that strategy is an integrated approach to customer contact—a customer interaction center. The interaction center takes the traditional call center a stage further, integrating people, technology, and customer data.

Deal with Multiple Contact

Customers can now contact organizations in many different ways, including the Internet, phone, e-mail, or fax. The integration of the Internet and telephony in multimedia call centers is taking the process even further. On the surface, that level of choice and convenience should lead to better customer service. But, in reality, the opposite is happening. When each channel has its own separate "information silo" on the customer, there is no integration.

Guarantee Consistent Service Standards

If you offer your customers different contact channels and don't integrate your customer information, you could face problems. Here's a situation you might recognize. A customer enters a request via the Web, then calls a customer service representative in a call center to get a status report. If the call center has access only to its own departmental data, it may not even recognize the customer. This could result in an embarrassing phone conversation and possibly a lost customer.

Provide a Single Point of Contact

A customer interaction center brings together staff who deal directly with customers (customer-facing staff) and support teams in a single, integrated location. Staff, backed by sophisticated information and communication systems, provide customers with a single point of contact and access to the combined skills and resources of the whole company.

Bring Together All Customer-facing Staff

Staff from logistics, credit control, accounting, and administration—as well as customer service and technical support—can work together in a customer interaction center. By working more closely, the company can create "virtual teams" that respond rapidly to requests or queries and bring together the right combination of skills for the customer's business. This high level of integration will result in even better alignment between customer service, supply/demand planning and logistics operations. The company can also share best practice more easily between business units.

Speed Up Communication

The center should provide a sophisticated technology infrastructure that will make it easier for customers to do business with the company, by supporting a rapid response and a high quality service. Integrated telephony systems make sure that when a customer telephones, the

call is directed to a named contact with the appropriate skills and knowledge. If the first contact is busy, the customer will be transferred to another team member with the same skills and knowledge. The team member who answers the call will have access to all of the customer's account information on screen, and this information will be updated automatically whenever a customer calls.

Integrate All Customer Information

At the heart of the infrastructure is an interconnected data networking solution that collects, stores, manages, and distributes all relevant customer information via a single, integrated customer database. The database is updated from all customer channels and is accessible by all customer-facing staff. The objective is to make communications simpler and quicker by giving every member of the customer service team access to the most up-to-date information on a customer's business. The solution can also include business rules and workflow functions to make sure that the right level of resources is applied to different types of customer interaction. A solution like this could, for example, assign priorities to key account customers or escalate support requests that have not been resolved within agreed service levels.

Make It Easy to Do Business

Your customers will get consistent service, whichever way they contact your organization. Integrating the center with electronic commerce systems will simplify the purchasing processes even further. Customers who work with a number of different locations or divisions will now have a single point of contact for all their dealings with the company. This is important because customers are looking for ways of simplifying their own purchasing process. Centralized support is becoming more and more important to customers. By providing a single point of contact for sales and technical and service queries, the company can guarantee a rapid, effective response to all customer support requirements.

Develop a More Personal Service

Many traditional personalization initiatives have been built on incomplete customer data. A personal Web page, for example, would probably have been based only on the customer's Internet interactions, completely ignoring any voice contact through a call center. With an integrated strategy, an organization can leverage all its customer interactions, giving it a significant competitive advantage in the drive for personalization.

Plan for Continued Improvement

The center infrastructure can be scaled up to accommodate growth in demand. It also provides a stable platform for developing advanced applications that will allow the company to improve customer service even further.

The interaction center coordinates all forms of customer interaction:
- consistently managing customer interactions through multiple communications channels, including phone, fax, e-mail, Web, and video;
- defining and applying business rules to customer interactions;

- routing customer interactions—according to business rules—to appropriate available resources;
- integrating corporate data into customer interactions.

This approach brings together all the elements needed to strengthen customer relationships and retain loyalty.

COMMON MISTAKES
Limiting the Scope of Communications

An interaction center should cover all forms of communication. It is not a telephone call center with other technology treated as an add-on. From the outset, the center should be capable of communicating via traditional and new media. Plans should also be in place to incorporate emerging media.

Concentrating on the Wrong Standards

If the center is treated as a technology-led function, customer service may suffer. Companies who want to maintain standards should set quality and performance standards that are focused on customer needs, not technical performance.

Failing to Develop a Personalized Service

A customer interaction center provides a great deal of valuable customer information that can be used to develop a personalized service. If the information simply stays on file, the company is losing a great opportunity.

Limiting the Use of Information

The customer interaction center is only a starting point for information management. The information can be used to support decision making and business development throughout a company. Linking the information to what Microsoft calls a "digital nervous system" makes sure that people throughout a company are able to act on the very latest information.

FOR MORE INFORMATION

Books:
Bodin, Madeline, and Keith Dawson. *The Call Center Dictionary: The Complete Guide to Call Center and Customer Support Technology Solutions.* 3rd ed. New York: CMP Books, 2002.
Dawson, Keith. *The Call Center Handbook: The Complete Guide to Starting, Running and Improving Your Customer Contact Center.* 4th ed. New York: CMP Books, 2004.

Web site:
International Contact Center Benchmarking Consortium: www.iccbc.org

See also:

"Make no mistake: customers are in control today." Anne Busquet

Building a Mailing List

GETTING STARTED

The most important element in a direct marketing program is the mailing list, and getting hold of a top-quality one is key. There are several routes you can use. If you have the resources, you can use internal sources to compile a valuable mailing list of both customers and prospects. Alternatively, you can rent or purchase existing lists from sources such as list brokers, Web sites, publishers, or other organizations offering lists of their customers, or you may wish to commission a specially tailored list that matches your requirements exactly. Three of the biggest problems in list management are duplication, incomplete addresses, and out-of-date information.

FAQs

My company has a mailing list of customers and prospects. Can I offer that list to other organizations?

You can market the list to other organizations. However, you should be aware of the implications of applicable legislation and regulations. Customers may have a right to know how their data is being used. Always include a clause asking customers if they are willing to allow their data to be passed to other organizations.

Is it better to buy or rent an external mailing list?

It depends how frequently you plan to mail. Rented lists are for a single use only, charged on a cost-per-thousand basis, and the owners have security techniques to counter unauthorized repeat use. A single campaign may be enough, but experience indicates that multiple mailings generally achieve better results. You would need to compare the cost of buying with renting the list for, say, three mailings.

Is a list compiled internally as effective as a list sourced from a direct mail list specialist?

An internal list is only as good as the sources you have available. However, if your target market is existing customers and good prospects, it may be adequate. An external list supplier may not have the same detailed understanding of that market. However, if you are moving into new markets where you have no existing contacts, it may be more effective to draw on the resources of a company with experience in the market.

MAKING IT HAPPEN
Create an Effective List

The most important element in a direct marketing program is the mailing list. In its simplest form, the list simply includes names, addresses, job titles, and telephone numbers. This can be refined by adding information on buying patterns, lifestyle, and many other factors to provide a comprehensive picture of customers and prospects.

Use Internal Sources of Information

Sometimes your business will already have a mailing list that you could benefit from. Draw on the following sources of information, including:

- customer records
- customer correspondence, including complaints
- Web site requests for information
- warranty records
- service records
- sales prospect files
- requests for information from the Web site
- sales force reports
- records of former customers
- market research surveys
- business information library

Make sure that you are not contravening data protection legislation before you contact these people.

Segment Internal Lists

Customer records can quickly provide you with names and addresses of individuals, but to get more specific information, you will have to conduct further analysis. Simple segmentation might give you categories such as:

- customers who have bought in the last six months;
- former customers;
- customers who spend over X dollars per annum.

Identify External Sources of Information

If you want to compile your own lists, you can use external sources to supplement internal information. These sources include:

- customers' and prospects' Web sites;
- databases and information services available via the Internet;
- general or industry-specific trade directories;
- membership directories for associations and groups;
- local telephone or chamber of commerce directories;
- specialist magazines and yearbooks;
- business reports and industry surveys in newspapers;
- published surveys;
- summaries or reports on consumer surveys;
- government and industry statistics, including census, industry reports, and trade association statistics.

Source External Lists

If you do not have the resources to compile your own lists or if you are moving into new markets, you may be able to make use of existing lists. Lists are available from several sources:

- list brokers who offer different categories of list
- Web sites
- magazine publishers
- directory publishers
- trade associations or professional institutes
- trade show and event organizers
- commercial organizations
- retailers

Assess External Lists

If you plan to use a ready-made list, you should check the following:

- How closely does the list match your customer profile?
- How much wastage will there be—that is, how much of the list falls outside your customer profile?
- Are there any restrictions on the use of the list?

Commission a List

Standard lists may not give you the degree of match you need, and you may wish to commission a specially tailored list. The success of such a list is directly related to the quality of the brief, and you should provide the supplier with a detailed description of your target audience.

Keep Refining Your Lists

Many standard lists and lists you have compiled yourself may not match your requirements exactly. To improve coverage or to make them more precise, you need to refine them continually. These are some of the actions you can take:

- Insure that new customer and prospect data is added to the list.
- Include coupons and other reply mechanisms with every form of communication and add the responses to your lists.
- Encourage the sales force to provide up-to-date customer and prospect information.
- Maintain a search program on the Internet and in publications to identify new prospects for your list.

Segment Your Lists

The strength of direct marketing is that it can provide a high degree of precision—so your lists must be structured carefully. Below is a basic approach to segmenting consumer and business-to-business lists.

Consumer Lists:
- marital status
- income level
- occupation category
- home owner/home value
- car owner/car value
- personal interests
- credit card holder
- shopping patterns
- vacation preferences
- insurance status
- leisure interests
- brand preferences
- recent purchase history
- reading/viewing habits

Business Lists:
- type of business
- size of business
- number of employees
- annual expenditure
- average order size
- purchasing frequency
- head office/local purchasing
- purchasing history
- key contacts
- job title
- budget authority

Check the Accuracy of Lists

To reduce waste in your mailing campaigns, it is important that you regularly check lists for accuracy. Three of the biggest problems are:

- duplication, where the same individual appears several times, possibly in different guises, for example, Ron Smith, R. T. Smith, Mr. Smith. This is not only wasteful, it also irritates the recipient;
- incomplete addresses;
- out-of-date information.

Comply with Legislation and Regulations on Personal Data

The basic premise behind legislation and regulations on the use of personal data is, if you have data, use them properly. Laws and regulations work in two ways:

- They place obligations on data users. They must be open about how they use data and follow sound information handling practice.
- They may give every individual access to information held about them.. They may also allow them to have the information corrected or deleted where appropriate, and may give the right to seek compensation for damage and associated distress through the courts.

COMMON MISTAKES
Using Out-of-date Lists

A mailing list is out of date almost as soon as it is compiled. People change jobs, move, or change interests. List maintenance must be a continuous process.

Failing to Segment Lists

Direct marketing works most effectively when it is aimed at a specific audience. The more you segment your mailing lists, the more precisely you can communicate. Different groups within your target market may have different purchasing needs or spending levels.

Overlooking Internal Sources

Many companies choose to rent or buy external lists without even considering internal sources. Mailing present or past customers can reinforce the benefits of existing communications programs and deliver a high level of response.

715

ACTIONLIST

FOR MORE INFORMATION

Book:
Tapp. Alan. *Principles of Direct and Database Marketing*. 3rd ed. Upper Saddle River, NJ: FT Prentice Hall, 2005.

Web site:
The Direct Marketing Association: **www.the-dma.org**

"GM reportedly has 14 million GM credit card holders being contacted, questioned, tabulated, tracked, and romanced each month when the credit card statement is delivered."

Stan Rapp

Creating Impressive Direct Mail Material

GETTING STARTED

When you are marketing your product or service, you may find you need an effective and precise marketing tool that you can personalize in order to more accurately reflect the needs of customers and prospective customers. If so, direct mail may be what you need. It can be eye-catching and creative, and allows you to include different types of enclosure to provide additional details on the product or service being offered.

Another benefit of direct mail is that it is easy to measure its results precisely, so that you can assess how you've done with a particular campaign or approach. As part of this process, you need to include an easy response mechanism for the customer, such as a business reply envelope, or contact details, such as an e-mail address, so that your customers can give you feedback.

FAQs
Don't customers just throw direct mail in the trash?

No, but attitudes vary enormously. According to research (Direct Mail Information Service, 2004), 60% of people open direct mail, but only 40% open and *read it*. Business managers opened 70% of their direct mail but, on average, filed only 20%. Executives are now also starting to employ growing numbers of direct mail "filterers," who open their mail for them and decide whether it's worth passing on.

Is it possible to create effective direct mail?

Yes, but like any other marketing activity, you'll get the best results from working toward a specific objective. The more information you have, the more focused the work. Direct mail is a very precise medium, so it is possible to create highly customized and attractive mailings that meet the information needs of your chosen prospective customers (prospects).

How far can personalization go in direct mail?

Of course, mailings to a small number of customers can easily be personalized, and should be. Provided you have the budget, larger mailings can be personalized down to individual level (one-to-one marketing). As an example, you could write individual letters to each of your prospects, or include an incentive tailored to their individual preferences. Practical financial constraints usually prevent this degree of personalization, so most companies concentrate on limited customization, addressing specific sector concerns or tailoring special offers to different types of business.

Can the quality of direct mail creative work be measured?

Direct mail is an extremely accountable medium, and the results can be measured precisely, making it possible to

judge whether or not a particular creative approach has worked. However, creative work is only one of the factors that influence campaign success, so many companies test different creative approaches to try to identify how they affect results. Remember, though, that the offer's recipient is more important than the presentation of the offer itself, so targeting should be your priority.

MAKING IT HAPPEN
Create Good Quality Mailing Material

Direct mail is the most precise marketing medium, but campaigns will be effective only if they combine precise targeting with good creative work.

In theory anything can be sent by mail, but most mailings consist primarily of printed material—letters, leaflets, and brochures. Three-dimensional objects can be mailed and can stimulate interest, but they must be relevant and cost-effective. A striking envelope design can also add impact to a mailing.

Use Direct Mail Letters Effectively

Letters are a universal communications medium and an integral element of any direct mail campaign. They can be used on their own as a personalized form of communication, and can also be used to support and personalize other standard mailing items. Letters can be customized easily and cost-effectively to meet different sector marketing requirements.

Personalize Letters

Personalized one-to-one mailings are an ideal form of communication for companies with detailed information on their prospects. The letter should reflect the individual's main interests and concerns, and the offer can be tailored to the individual prospect. Subsequent mailings can build an individual relationship with the prospect.

The key features of this type of letter are:
- it is personalized to the individual reader;
- it offers direct and valuable benefits;
- it builds future relationships with the customer by promising regular offers.

Letters can also be customized by market sector, offering specific benefits to groups of customers.

Use Letters to Support Other Mailing Material

Direct mail letters can also be used to accompany other material—a product brochure, management guide, or even an invoice, for example. The letter can customize the mailing by including information specific to the individual prospect or market sector, or by making a further offer to the prospect.

Include Enclosures

Enclosures can include:
- catalogs;

- sales leaflets or brochures;
- price lists;
- management reports or surveys;
- information on special offers;
- samples, free gifts, or incentives.

There are a number of criteria for selecting enclosures. They should:
- be relevant to the prospect's needs;
- not make the mailing impractical or costly because of size or weight;
- improve response, size of order, or frequency of order—if they do not, they are an unnecessary cost.

Treat Envelopes Creatively

Postal authorities specify a number of preferred envelope sizes which help them to handle mail more efficiently. Companies that wish to use specific mail response services use the preferred layouts. However, using non-standard envelope sizes can add greater impact to a mailing. Envelopes can be designed in a number of ways to achieve greater impact:
- they can include advertising messages;
- addresses can be handwritten to add a personal touch;
- they can incorporate corporate design elements such as logos or company colors.

But be aware of occasions when a clearly, but wrongly identified envelope may depress response, such as if the item looks like a routine statement.

Create Three-dimensional Enclosures

Three-dimensional enclosures can add impact and novelty value to a mailing. They can be used to send product samples by mail, to send promotional items, or to improve response by creating interest. However, it is important that they be relevant to the prospect's needs, that they do not make the mailing too expensive, and that they do not contravene mail regulations.

Include a Response Mechanism

If your mailing is designed to stimulate action, it should include an easy-to-use response mechanism, such as a business reply card, or contact details, such as a toll-free telephone number, e-mail address, or Web site address.

Use Professional Creative and Production Services

Quality and impact are essential to the success of a direct mail campaign. Creating an effective direct mail item requires professional skills, and is best handled by suitably experienced people. Although many of the direct mail processes are straightforward, your company may not have the skills or resources to achieve the best possible results. External specialists provide a variety of direct mail services, including copywriting and design, printing letters, and producing three-dimensional enclosures. Specialists include:
- direct mail agencies
- advertising agencies
- marketing communication consulting firms
- creative consulting firms
- printers

However, there may be occasions when you decide to create simple direct mail items yourself.

Write Persuasive Copy

Use a powerful headline to get the attention of the reader. Words such as "free," "new" and "improved" attract attention, while price benefits such as "sale" and "reduced" are also useful. Keep your writing style simple, with short sentences and paragraphs; in longer mailing items, use headings and subheadings to make sure that the reader picks up key messages without having to read the complete text. Tell your prospects what they need to know in order to make a decision about your product or service. Your message should deal with your customers' most important concerns and requirements. Describe benefits to the prospect, not features of the product: for example, a power drill that features extremely high operating speeds may be technically interesting, but the benefits to a builder are greater productivity and the opportunity to finish a job quickly. Offer the prospect a clear, powerful proposition. Your copy should encourage the prospect to take action—contact the company for more information, or order immediately to qualify for a promotional offer.

Create a Well Designed Layout

Design quality is also important in getting a message to prospects clearly and effectively.
- Keep the layout simple.
- Use photographs, diagrams, or illustrations if they help to clarify a point or create impact.
- Use the most legible type faces and sizes.
- Use bold headings or a larger type size for emphasis.

COMMON MISTAKES
Using Mailing Unnecessarily

When customers already know your company and do business with you, it can be offputting for them to be treated as "prospects." Always check that your mailing is an effective means of communicating.

Failing to Plan

All mailing activity must be planned with sufficient time and resources. Rushing a mailing can lead to embarrassing and costly mistakes. Not anticipating response can lead to disappointed customers.

Failing to Measure

Direct mail campaigns are measured on their results: they should deliver inquiries or sales. If they do not deliver results, even the most creative campaigns should be considered failures. Make sure that you set realistic targets for your campaign. If you do not reach the targets, change the targeting, the offer, the format, or timing until you find one that delivers the results you want.

FOR MORE INFORMATION

Book:
Bird, Drayton. *Commonsense Direct Marketing*. 4th ed. Milford, CT: Kogan Page, 2000.

Web site:
The Direct Marketing Association: **www.the-dma.org**

717

ACTIONLIST

"Time spent in the advertising business seems to create a permanent deformity like the Chinese habit of foot-binding."

Dean Acheson

Improving the Response to Direct Mail

GETTING STARTED

The simplest and most immediate measure of a direct marketing campaign is the response level it achieves. Many different factors can affect response rates; it is important to test the variables before committing all your resources to a particular approach, and you should aim for a realistic figure that is within your budget.

- Do try as far as you can to define your target market precisely. The more precisely you target, the better your response rates will be. Make it easy for your prospects to respond, and test your approach before committing resources to the full campaign.
- Performance can be improved by integrating the campaign with other marketing activities.
- If budget allows, you can develop a series of split campaigns. A series of mailings will make sure that you meet your response targets.
- Getting the mailing list right is vital. Check all internal sources of information and be sure that they are up to date. Customer records invariably generate the highest response rates when they are mailed with relevant information.
- If you are moving into new market sectors, internal lists may not provide the information you need. To achieve a high response rate, check how closely the list matches your customer profile.
- You could decide to commission a special tailored list that matches your requirements exactly.
- Keep refining your lists. To improve response and reduce waste in your mailing campaigns, it is important that your lists are regularly checked for accuracy.
- Personalized one-to-one mailings are an ideal form of communication for companies with detailed information about their prospects.
- Direct mail response levels can increase significantly when telemarketing is used.

FAQs

Why are direct mail responses so low?

The figures quoted are industry averages. They can vary upward or downward, depending on the industry and the type of mailing. Remember that a small percentage of a mass mailing can provide you with a reasonable level of new prospects. To put the response rates into perspective, compare the response and the cost of response with an equivalent amount of spending on advertising.

Should direct mailing always be tested?

If it is practical, test direct mail on a small proportion of the market. Although direct mail is a precise medium, testing can refine the process even further. With so many variables in a mailing campaign, you can test different elements individually and plan your full campaign on the basis of the best response rate.

Should direct mail effectiveness be measured by response or by sales?

The ultimate test of any marketing campaign is an increase in profitable sales. However, direct mail, on its own, cannot deliver sales. Sales depend on pricing, the quality of your products, sales representatives, customer service, competitive activity, and many other factors. Direct mail should be given a specific role and measured by how it fulfills that role.

MAKING IT HAPPEN
Set Target Response Levels

- Response levels as low as 1 or 2% are regarded as the industry norm.
- Response rates in the region of 5% are regarded as high.
- Response rates in the region of 10–20% have been reported by companies who have integrated other forms of marketing communications.

Define Your Target Market Precisely

Do you want to reach all customers and prospects, or specific groups? Direct marketing is a precise medium, so your campaign could be aimed at one key decision maker or thousands of potential users. The more precisely you target, the better your response rates will be.

Integrate the Campaign with Other Marketing Activities

Direct marketing campaigns can run at any time. However, performance can be improved by integrating the campaign with other marketing activities, such as an exhibition, advertising campaigns, or sales force calls. With integrated campaigns, overall awareness levels among customers and prospects will be higher. Your direct marketing offer will have a much higher chance of success.

Choose the Right Campaign Frequency

A mass mailing, telephone call, or direct response advertisement may produce results, but a series of quality contacts will have greater impact and insure you meet your response targets. Multiple direct marketing activities provide a number of benefits:

- They raise levels of awareness with each contact.
- They follow up contacts who have not responded.
- They move individual respondents further along the decision making process.

Make It Easy for Prospects to Respond

If you want to improve response rates, clearly you have to make it easy for your prospects to respond. Web site or e-mail addresses, postage-paid envelopes, and toll-free numbers provide easy-to-use response mechanisms that can boost response. You should monitor the response levels from different sources to see which is the most effective.

"I know half the money I spend on advertising is wasted, but I can never find out which half."

John Wanamaker

Test Your Campaign

To guarantee the success of your campaign, you should test your approach before committing resources to the full campaign. There are a number of variables to test:

- the offer
- the creative approach
- the target audience
- the response mechanism
- frequency and timing
- integration with other communications programs

Improve Your Mailing Lists

Getting the mailing list right is vital. Basic mailing lists simply include names, addresses, job titles, and phone numbers of customers and prospects. The basic list can be refined by adding information about buying patterns, lifestyle, and many other factors, all of which provide a comprehensive picture of customers and prospects.

Check All Internal Sources of Information

Your customer records are probably your most valuable asset, as existing customers invariably show the highest response rate when they are mailed with relevant information. The most important sources are:

- customer records;
- customer correspondence, including complaints;
- warranty records;
- service records;
- sales prospect files;
- Web site registrations;
- sales force reports;
- records of lapsed customers.

Simple segmentation of your internal lists might give you categories such as:

- customers who have bought in the last six months;
- lapsed customers;
- customers who spend over $X a year.

Add External Sources of Information

Your internal lists are likely to yield high response rates, but if you're moving into new market sectors, they may not provide the information you need. External lists are available from a number of sources, including list brokers, magazine publishers, directory publishers, trade associations or professional institutes, commercial organizations, and retailers. To achieve a high response rate, check how closely the list matches your customer profile.

Commission a Special List

Standard lists may not give you the degree of match you need. The successful preparation of a tailored list is directly related to the quality of the brief, so provide the supplier with a detailed description of your target audience.

Keep Refining Your Lists

- Make sure that the list is kept up to date with new customer and prospect data.
- Include coupons and other reply mechanisms with every communication, and add the responses to your lists.
- Encourage the sales force to provide up-to-date customer and prospect information.
- Maintain an active search program in appropriate Web sites, magazines, and newspapers to identify new prospects for your list.

Use Personalized Letters

Personalized one-to-one mailings are an ideal form of communication for companies with detailed information about their prospects. Direct mail letters can be personalized in a number of ways, by:

- including the name in the address and greeting only: "Dear Mr. Jones";
- including the name throughout: " . . . and Mr. Jones, you'll be glad to know that you've won a special prize . . . "

Use Telemarketing

Response levels can increase significantly if direct mail is used in conjunction with telemarketing. It offers a variety of benefits because it is:

- selective: contact can be initiated and maintained with all or selected groups of customers and prospects;
- precise: the calls can be targeted;
- flexible: the offer and the message can be varied;
- fast: calls can be made immediately;
- responsive: because telemarketing is interactive, it encourages response;
- measurable: the effectiveness of a telemarketing campaign can be measured precisely.

COMMON MISTAKES

Setting Unrealistic Response Rates

Direct mail is a precise medium, but it's easy to set unrealistic targets: figures such as 5 or 6% would be seen as extremely high in many industries, for example. If you want a much higher response rate, you may need to use other marketing media or invest more in the campaign.

Failing to Integrate Direct Mail with Other Marketing Activities

Direct mail works most effectively when it is part of an integrated marketing campaign. Advertising can be used to raise the company profile. For example, direct mail would be used to reach specific prospects with a targeted offer, and telemarketing could be used to back up the mailing with follow-up calls. Response rates from integrated campaigns are generally higher because direct mail is given a specific task in that campaign.

Poor Mailing Lists

Good response rates depend on the quality of your mailing lists. If your lists contain duplicate addresses, out-of-date information, or incorrect data, response will be poor. Refine your lists continuously to avoid this.

FOR MORE INFORMATION

Book:
Bird, Drayton. *Commonsense Direct Marketing.* 4th ed. Milford, CT: Kogan Page, 2000.

Web site:
The Direct Marketing Association: **www.the-dma.org**

"It was something you only spoke of in hushed tones. Advertising is a bit of an anathema."

Michael Bungey

Planning a Cost-effective Direct Marketing Campaign

GETTING STARTED

Direct marketing works most effectively when it is aimed at a precise audience that cannot be easily reached by any other medium. A campaign should be carefully planned in accordance with the target market and the product or service concerned. Short-term results can be measured accurately and directly by the level of response, so the effectiveness of a campaign can be assessed quickly. There are, however, many different factors that can affect the outcome, such as product price or the quality of the campaign material. As with any direct approach, it is essential to make it as easy as possible for customers to respond.

FAQs

Is direct marketing the same as direct mail?

No. Direct marketing (DM) is any marketing activity that depends on a direct and measurable response. Conventional advertising can be "direct," as can telephone, fax, e-mail and, of course, the Internet. Direct mail is direct marketing communication sent by mail and therefore often has a poor reputation because of the amount of unsolicited mail that people regularly receive.

Can direct marketing be used to sell products?

There are many situations in which you can use direct marketing to build direct sales. You may not have a sales force or a retail network, so customers can only buy direct from you. If you want to sell to niche markets, or if your customers are widely spread or even global, direct marketing may be the only cost-effective way of reaching them. If you decide to sell direct, you must insure that the products themselves are suitable for selling through direct marketing—that is, that they do not have to be demonstrated, or inspected by the customer.

How does direct marketing build relationships with customers?

The stronger your relationship with your customers, the more opportunities you have to influence the future direction and success of your business. If your company depends on a few key customers for most of its business, you can use direct marketing to improve customer loyalty by building long-term relationships with them. You may also need to use it if your customers want to rationalize the number of suppliers, and you want to remain on the approved list.

Is direct marketing only effective for reaching a small audience?

There are numerous examples of successful large-scale mailings. However, the key to direct marketing success is reaching the right people in a cost-effective way. Large-scale mailings based on poorly researched mailing lists

may yield results, but there will also be a high level of wastage. The more precise your mailing, the more likely you are to succeed.

MAKING IT HAPPEN
Set Campaign Objectives

Direct marketing objectives can be initially expressed in general terms:

- encouraging prospects to buy directly in response to a direct marketing campaign;
- generating leads for the sales force or retail network;
- supporting sales force activity;
- improving the effectiveness of other forms of communication;
- raising awareness of a company, product, or service among clearly identified customers and prospects;
- maintaining effective contact with customers and prospects;
- building relationships with customers and prospects.

However, these general objectives should be translated into precise, measurable objectives, for example:

- raising awareness of your product range among 35% of technical directors in the mechanical engineering sector;
- ensuring that purchasing managers of your ten top corporate customers are contacted at least once every two weeks;
- increasing direct sales of supplies by 15%.

Define the Target Market

Do you want to reach all customers and prospects, or are you targeting specific groups? Direct marketing is a precise medium, so your campaign could be aimed at just a few key decision makers or thousands of potential users. To plan your direct marketing campaign, you should ask questions such as:

- Who buys your type of product?
- Who influences the purchasing decision?
- How many prospective customers (prospects) do you want to reach with the direct marketing campaign?
- How many prospects can you normally convert to customers, and how long does it take?
- How do they currently get information about your products?
- Is direct marketing the best (or only) way of reaching the target audience?

The more information you have about your target audience, the more precise you can make your campaign. In an ideal world, direct marketing would allow you to communicate one to one with every prospect, but, in practical terms, you are more likely to be communicating with groups that share certain characteristics. For example, you could reasonable expect that "all fleet managers in the North East of England managing more than thirty vehicles" would have similar needs in respect to their day-to-day job.

"I think editors are excellent marketers. They know their audience and produce copy to appeal to them—they just don't call it marketing."

David Robinson

Plan Campaign Timing

A direct marketing campaign can run at any time, so you do not have to consider advertisement publication dates. However, timing may be dictated by other factors—lead times for producing mailing material, seasonal purchasing patterns, product availability, or tender dates. These are some of the factors to consider in planning the timing of your campaign:

- When is your customer likely to be making the buying decision?
- How long is the selling or buying process? How many stages are involved? Who is involved?
- Does your direct marketing campaign have to tie in with the timing of any other marketing activity, such as an exhibition, advertising campaign, or sales force visit?
- If you are launching a new product, when will the product be available?
- How long will it take to produce the material that is to be mailed?
- When will you be able to follow up the campaign?
- What will you do if you get fewer responses than you need *or* more than you can handle?

Decide On Your Contact Strategy

A single mailing, telephone call, or direct response advertisement may produce results, but a series of appropriate contacts will have greater impact and insure you meet your objectives. There are several benefits from repeated contracts:

- raising levels of awareness with each contact;
- educating potential clients about your product/service;
- following up those who have not responded;
- moving individual respondents further along the decision-making process;
- maintaining contact during extended decision-making processes.

There is no hard-and-fast rule about the frequency of individual campaigns; a company trying to get a prospect to make a decision may make contact several times a week, while a company aiming to maintain long-term customer loyalty may only need to contact customers monthly or quarterly.

Develop a Response Mechanism

Action is a vital ingredient of any direct marketing campaign, and it is essential that you make it easy for your prospects to respond. First, decide if your prospects are to place an order, request a sales visit, or ask for further information. Then decide which of the five basic types of response mechanism is the most appropriate: mail, telephone, fax, e-mail, or Web site address.

Keep Track of the Campaign

You must be prepared to keep records of every aspect of your campaign. You will have to implement the systems to capture data before your campaign (or test campaign) starts. Aim to know at the very least:

- what was sent (the offer, the pack/letter, and so on) and to whom (the lists used and reason for selection);
- the anticipated response (for example, percentage initial response and percentage purchase);
- the actual response;

- the costs and the return—in other words, did your campaign make a profit?

Test the Campaign

Part of the flexibility of direct marketing is that you can test your approach before committing resources to the full campaign. There are several variables that can be tested:

- the target audience—the most important element;
- the offer—what exactly you are offering for sale (including any incentive);
- the creative approach—the look and feel of the communications;
- the response mechanism—how easy it is to respond, for example, using a toll-free number or business reply mail;
- frequency and timing—including the way you follow up inquiries.

The test campaign can be conducted in a number of ways:

- on a sample of the target market;
- in a defined sales or geographic territory;
- in a particular sector of the target market.

The most effective test campaign is the one that achieves the highest response levels, and committed DM organizations test continuously to drive down their costs and drive up response rates. Indeed, every campaign should be considered a "test" to improve on previous campaigns. Each best-performing campaign then becomes the "control" against which others can be evaluated.

Plan Split Campaigns

Testing your campaign may reveal that different approaches work more effectively in different market sectors. If budget allows, you can develop a series of campaigns that vary the offer, the creative approach, frequency, timing, or other factors, but ensure you keep track of these variables so that you can use the best-performing campaign format next time.

Set Target Response Levels

In the long term, a campaign may increase awareness, improve customer relations, or cut the cost of sales. However, the simplest and most immediate measure of a direct marketing campaign is the response level it generates. In setting your target response levels, you should aim for a realistic figure that is within budget. Note that:

- response levels as low as 1 or 2% are regarded as the industry norm for large companies sending mail to "cold" lists;
- response rates in the region of 5% are therefore regarded as high;
- response rates in the region of 10–20% have been reported by companies who have integrated other forms of marketing communications;
- far higher response rates can be experienced by specialist companies communicating vital information to a very committed list of supporters.

Many different factors can affect the level of response, including price, quality of the mailing list, the promotional offer, and quality of copy and design. A test is very

often the only way to set an initial target response rate for future campaigns.

COMMON MISTAKES
Using DM Unnecessarily

While the principles of direct marketing can help any company in its communications and selling, sometimes direct *mail* is used when the existing channels are preferable. Customers who are used to a personal visit and face-to-face negotiations may feel aggrieved if you try to deal with them at a distance.

Failing to Set Measurable Targets

The results of a direct marketing campaign can be measured precisely by the number of responses. This makes it a particularly accountable medium. It is therefore important to set realistic, measurable objectives. If your target is to generate leads from 2% of the target audience, this will determine how many people you mail, the type of offer you make, and the response mechanism you provide. It will also tell you very quickly if your budget balances—how many of those leads need to convert into customers to cover your costs?

Poor Audience Selection

With direct marketing you can communicate with a single prospect or with 50,000. However, there may be more cost-effective ways of communicating with 50,000 prospects. Direct marketing works most effectively when it is aimed at a precise audience that cannot be easily reached by any other medium, and, crucially, when you want a response. For example, you may find there is a specialist magazine or newsletter that precisely covers your target market.

No Integration with Other Communications

If your marketing budget is split between different communications activities such as advertising, sales promotion, and press and public relations, it is essential that each activity works as effectively as possible. You can use direct marketing in conjunction with other methods of communication. If you place advertisements in publications that only reach a general audience, you can reinforce the advertisements with personalized communications to selected prospects. If your advertisements include a response mechanism, keeping to direct marketing principles will insure effective follow-up. You can also tailor your product and corporate literature to the information needs of different market sectors by including direct marketing material.

FOR MORE INFORMATION

Book:
Bird, Drayton. *Commonsense Direct Marketing*. 4th ed. Milford, CT: Kogan Page, 2000.

Web site:
The Direct Marketing Association: **www.the-dma.org**

See also:
✔ Raising Awareness of Your Brand (pp. 749–750)

Planning a Customer Event

GETTING STARTED

Desk research is no substitute for getting out and meeting customers face to face. Arranging visits or special customer events increases personal contact and improves customer relationships—although events need to be handled professionally to achieve the right results.

FAQs

Who should organize a customer event?

Few companies have the luxury of a special events department, so the task normally falls to the sales, marketing, or public relations department. Events generally form a small part of the overall customer relationship program, so they may not get the attention or the resources they require. Event organization is extremely time-consuming, so it may be better to appoint a special event marketing firm to work with an internal coordinator. Invitations and publicity could be handled internally, while the event firm takes responsibility for venues, staging, and logistics.

Do events provide a good return on investment?

If events reach the right people and help to strengthen customer relationships, they provide a good return. However, many companies organize events simply to get together with customers. Without a specific objective, the event could be a waste of valuable funds.

How do you decide who should be invited to a customer event?

If resources are limited, you may have to select the most important contacts within a customer company. The sales force can provide advice, but you may still overlook influential people and create resentment. Asking customers to nominate their own delegates shifts some of the responsibility, but they may not choose the people you wish to contact. There is always likely to be a compromise, so make sure you check your records carefully and try to keep up to date with the power structure within a company.

MAKING IT HAPPEN
Become Familiar with Customers

How well do you know your customers' businesses, their markets, their plans, their competitors, and their strengths and weaknesses? The more you know, the more easily you can identify their real needs and develop a service that wins and keeps business.

Although you can find out a lot about your customers just by looking in your sales records, desk research is no substitute for getting out and meeting customers face to face. The sales team is doing that all the time, but it is unlikely that they will be responsible for delivering customer service. You need to meet the customers yourself by arranging visits or special customer events. These increase personal contact and improve customer relationships.

Manage Events Professionally

Events such as open evenings, trade shows, and customer receptions are a powerful method of building customer loyalty, but they need to be handled professionally to achieve the right results. By providing the right level of support, you can develop a program of events that is appropriate for the market. This can include:
- the development of suitable promotional and display material;
- choosing the theme for the event;
- the generation of mailing lists and selection of people to be invited;
- support literature;
- personal support by members of the head office team.

Arrange an Informal Customer Visit

Many customers will appreciate the interest you are showing in their business if you visit them informally. Alternatively, invite customers to visit your premises. It provides a good chance for employees who deal with customers to meet their opposite numbers, and meeting people face to face can help to improve working relationships.

Attend Customer Exhibitions, Seminars, and Conferences

You can find out what competitors are up to at the same time. Events like these are a good indicator of what customers believe is important to the success of their business and will give you a good sign of where they see themselves heading.

Make Customer Care Visits

Call on selected customers at intervals to discuss whether they are satisfied with the standard of service they are receiving from you. Ask if they have any specific concerns and insure that you contact them again with an appropriate response.

Conduct Regular Review Meetings

This is a more formal process than the ad hoc customer care visits. Suppliers and customers agree to meet at regular intervals, for example, every year or once a quarter, or monthly, according to the complexity and importance of the business. There is likely to be a set agenda for reviewing performance in specific areas, and there may be agreed standards that are used to measure performance.

Arrange Briefing Meetings for Your Customers

Briefings are not for reviewing progress or performance but for bringing your customers up to date with new developments in your business or industry that might benefit them. For example, you might brief them on a new technical development or on new legislation that is likely to have an impact on them. This type of meeting

"Don't sell customers goods they are attracted to. Sell them goods that will benefit them."

Konosuke Matsushita

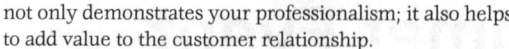

not only demonstrates your professionalism; it also helps to add value to the customer relationship.

Invite Customers to a Webcast
If you run Webcasts on important subjects, you can invite customers to join the event. Provide time, log-in, and other relevant details to your customers well in advance and explain the format and benefits in advance.

Hold a Social Event
Many customers enjoy the chance to meet informally and talk shop. A social event could take place after a more formal meeting or it might be an event in its own right. Although the extravagant side of corporate hospitality has largely disappeared, social events remain an important aspect of business relationships.

Run Regional Events in Retail Outlets
When one manufacturer launches a new range of products, the central feature of the launch is a series of customer events run in conjunction with regional retailers around the country. The outlets are given detailed guidelines on the program and provided with letters inviting customers to the launch event. The outlets put together their own mailing lists using account information, local directories, and database information from head office.

Encourage Employees to Attend
At one event, one of the company's directors attended to make a brief presentation and talk to customers. A group of company sales and technical employees joined with retailer employees to host the evening and meet customers. The company also provided window displays and freestanding display units to insure consistent quality. By providing a professional support service, the company was able to insure a consistent standard and give the retailers the freedom to develop an event that was right for the local market.

Offer Events as Customer Incentives
An incentive program for a bank offered business customers a structured series of special sports prizes. Customers were awarded points for using different types of business banking services and could win a day's free participation and coaching in different sports activities which had high levels of appeal to the target audience, for example, gliding, water sports, auto racing. The local branches could tailor the awards to their own customer base, but they did not have to provide the resources to manage the events themselves. This was handled by a special event organization that could arrange for the events in different parts of the country.

Sponsored Events
Sponsoring an event should be a positive marketing action, not an enforced response to a request for help. Depending on the type of event and its popularity, sponsorship can:

- build the image of an organization or product through association with an event that reflects corporate values;
- raise awareness of an organization or product through the exposure associated with an event.

There are different levels of sponsorship:
- international, national, regional, or local event
- whole event, with unique or joint sponsorship
- program or award sponsorship
- hospitality
- participants, as individuals or teams

Make the Most of Sponsorship
- Issue press releases about the organization's involvement.
- Advertise on the perimeter or program.
- Inform employees and customers.
- Use the event for customer hospitality.
- Consider other promotional activities tied in to the event.

COMMON MISTAKES
Poor Organization
At a customer event, the company is on display. The event must be carefully organized and managed to insure that customers get the right impression of the company. If you are putting on a large or complex event, it may pay to use a professional event organizer. They have the resources and skills to manage all the services and logistics essential to success.

Failing to Set Objectives for the Event
An event must have a specific purpose: for example, to improve relations with key decision-makers or to reward loyal customers. The objectives determine the format of the event and the support services required.

Poor Internal Communication
The success of an event depends on the participation of employees. Make sure that employees who deal with customers are aware of the event, and keep them involved in the planning process. On the day, make sure that everyone is aware of individual responsibilities.

FOR MORE INFORMATION

Books:
Allen, Judi. *Event Planning: The Ultimate Guide to Successful Meetings, Corporate Events, Fundraising Galas, Conferences, Conventions, Incentives and Other Special Events.* New York: Wiley, 2000.
O'Toole, William. *Corporate Event Project Management.* New York: Wiley, 2002.

Web site:
Reed Exhibitions: **www.reedexpo.com**

Running a Networked Conference

GETTING STARTED

Networked conferencing brings people inside and outside an organization together. Although not as effective as live meetings, networked conferencing brings huge benefits in terms of convenience and time savings, and substantial savings on the costs of organizing and travel. Videoconferencing remains the most popular type of networked conference, but Webcasting over the Internet is now a viable alternative.

FAQs

Is networked conferencing a suitable substitute for live meetings?

Live meetings should always be the first choice if you need face-to-face contact or if you aim to motivate people through a dynamic experience. However, time constraints and the cost of staging live events mean that networked conferencing is a far more cost-effective solution for routine meetings or events that need to reach large numbers of people.

Is videoconferencing better than Webcasting?

Each technique has specific benefits. Webcasting over the Internet is a more cost-effective means of reaching a large audience and does not require the use of sophisticated videoconferencing equipment. However, it is not a secure medium, so there is some risk involved for events featuring confidential information.

Videoconferencing is probably more suitable for an internal audience, provided it has access to the necessary equipment. Low-cost, PC-based systems have made videoconferencing more accessible, but it is not such a universal medium as an Internet-based solution like Webcasting. However, Internet Protocol (IP)-based networking, which is rapidly becoming the global standard for networking, can provide a secure environment for reaching people who are linked to the network.

Doesn't networked conferencing just encourage even more meetings?

It certainly makes it easier to arrange meetings, and this can be a good or a bad thing. The reduction in travel time and the problems of getting people together have to be offset against the increased frequency of meetings. Increasing the number of meetings may actually improve the quality of communication.

MAKING IT HAPPEN
Bring People Together

Networked conferencing brings people inside and outside an organization together quickly and easily, wherever they are located. It supports effective teamwork when people operate in different locations or different countries, and it can help people to meet key objectives efficiently and productively. It can also reduce the costs associated with traditional meetings.

Videoconferencing is still the most popular type of networked conference, but Webcasting over the Internet or IP-based networks is now a viable alternative as new technologies develop.

Improve Time Management

Networked conferencing makes it easier to bring groups of people together, even at short notice. With a networked conference, all that is needed is the time for the meeting itself; travel time is eliminated, allowing busy executives and project team members to concentrate on important tasks.

Reduce Costs

The real cost of conventional meetings can be estimated by adding up the salaries of people traveling, the travel costs, and food and accommodations. In an organization that operates internationally, the potential cost savings obtained through networked conferencing are enormous.

Enhance Communications

The freedom and flexibility of networked conferencing means that the organization can arrange meetings whenever such communication is necessary. It is quick and easy to arrange meetings for briefing sales teams, reporting, training or coaching, reviewing progress, or dealing with project issues. Senior executives can communicate easily with people throughout an organization by broadcasting annual reports, for example, or news about significant corporate changes.

Reduce Time to Market

Project teams can speed up the development process by using networked conferencing. Progress meetings, milestone reviews, technical evaluations, or routine meetings can be arranged to suit the team. Networked conferencing is ideal for simultaneous engineering projects where different specialists may work in separate locations. They can exchange information and work on problems at short notice. This eliminates project delays, and can reduce overall lead times, giving an organization a significant competitive advantage.

Enhance Conferences with Webcasting

Businesses can now extend the reach of their meetings by using the Internet and a Webcasting service. The service allows companies to stream traditional audio and video conferences over the Internet or over an IP-based network, incorporating multimedia content and adding interactive capability such as slides, polling, and messaging. Any unexpected increase in participant numbers is not a problem, as a Webcast can reach very large numbers of people in many different locations using sophisticated streaming media. Audio and video streaming is transforming conventional broadcasting and enhancing the distribution of multimedia material to consumer and corporate audiences.

"Even a partial shift towards the electronic office will be enough to trigger an eruption of social, psychological, and economic consequences."
Alvin Toffler

Use the Power of Streaming

Streaming media allows users to view video and other content on the Web without having to wait for it to download completely on to a computer. Before streaming media were developed, the only way to view video or hear audio on the Internet was to download an entire file, which could be a lengthy process over a dial-up connection. Streaming cuts out this delay by continuously downloading content in the background while audience members are viewing or listening; what the audience experiences is a seamless presentation. The technical requirements are simple, as audience members need no complex videoconferencing equipment; anyone with an Internet-connected computer, Web browser, and media player can view a Webcast. New computers increasingly incorporate media players, and this, together with the increasing uptake of broadband, makes Webcasting a very accessible medium.

Include Interactive Multimedia Content

The latest Webcasts combine live and recorded video, with multimedia content such as presentation slides or Web tours. Interactive capabilities, such as question-and-answer sessions and audience polling, create a rich and engaging experience for participants. These new capabilities can help businesses to turn a standard videoconferencing system into an Internet broadcasting tool, ideal for conducting seminars, remote training, employee updates, and large meetings.

Reduce Distribution Costs

Because Webcasting removes the problem of distance, it is a cost-effective way for businesses to extend the reach of their meetings by streaming their messages to hundreds or thousands of participants over the Internet. When its costs are compared with those of staging meetings or taking a roadshow to different locations around the country, Webcasting becomes an attractive proposition. More and more companies are considering how they can use Webcasting to improve their internal and external communications.

Identify Applications

Webcasting is already being used for seminars, focus groups, investor relations, press conferences, financial reporting, training, employee announcements, and product launches. Nor is it confined to the corporate environment; it is being used to broadcast live and archived events such as sports, news, and concerts. One-time events can be broadcast live or prerecorded for later broadcast, while regular programs or items can be recorded and broadcast at specified times. Audio and video clips can be accessed on demand by users around the clock. The programs are broadcast over broadband, giving superb, TV-standard quality.

Check Performance over Different Internet Connections

Although broadband is becoming more widely used, conference participants may have different types of Internet connection, modem speeds, and media players, so it is important to review the transmission in different environments to insure that participants are able to play the audio and video regardless of the technology they have available. Check performance over different types of connections using slower and faster modems, as well as broadband. The companies who provide streaming technology have their own proprietary compression algorithms, and they differ in performance.

Make Sure Participants Can Play the Material

Check what your participants have to do to play the material. In some cases, the preliminary processes may be prohibitive, or their company may place restrictions on viewing.

- Do they have to download special software to play the content?
- If so, how long does it take to download?
- Does the Internet browser have the capability to play rich content? (Not all browsers do.)
- Do company Internet security systems prohibit rich content?

COMMON MISTAKES
Poor Content

When companies stage live events, they aim to create an exciting experience. Networked conferencing rarely gets the same treatment, but the latest Webcasting technologies support a wide variety of multimedia and interactive content. It is important to use the full potential of the medium, because the goal of many events is not just to inform but to motivate people to take action.

Creating Security Risks

Material distributed over the Internet poses security risks because the Web is a public medium. Although Webcasting increases the range of a meeting, and is a cost-effective method of reaching large audiences, the event should not include confidential information. Although videoconferencing is more secure, it may also be broadcast over public networks. Only private links between individual sites or Virtual Private Networks based on IP networking can be regarded as secure.

Failing to Promote the Event

Simply putting an event on the Internet provides no guarantee of reaching the target audience. To attract specific customers or prospects, it is essential that they be aware of the Webcast. E-mail or conventional direct mail and telemarketing techniques can be used to keep people informed.

FOR MORE INFORMATION

Book:
Rayburn, Dan, and Steve Mack. *Hands-on Guide to Webcasting: Internet Event and AV Production.* Burlington, MA: Focal Press, 2005.

Web site:
International Webcasting Association:
www.webcasters.org

"No grand idea was ever born in a conference, but a lot of foolish ideas have died there."

F. Scott Fitzgerald

Running a Sales Force Incentive Campaign

GETTING STARTED

Incentive programs are an integral part of sales management and can either provide general motivation of the sales force or improve performance in specific areas. They can also be used to achieve a new direction or to encourage sales employees to acquire new skills. The type and structuring of the incentive program depend on the desired objectives and the timescale involved.

FAQs

Why does a sales force need incentive programs?

A sales force can improve its general performance through training, encouragement, and higher levels of support. However, incentive programs can be used to improve performance in specific areas. Targeted programs are therefore the most effective form of incentive.

Should incentive programs be used to reward the top performers or the entire sales force?

That depends on the program objectives. If the objective is to encourage the highest levels of achievement, prizes should be restricted to top performers. However, this may act as a disincentive to some members of the sales force. It also may cause problems if some sales representatives appear to have unfair advantages, such as larger territories or customers in growth-market sectors.

Incentive programs designed to raise overall standards should reward all members of the sales force who meet their personal targets, although top-performer prizes should be added to increase motivation.

Don't incentive programs encourage sales employees to increase business at any cost rather than concentrate on improving customer relationships?

A poorly designed incentive program that focuses only on new business can cause problems. The new customers may not be creditworthy or offer long-term growth potential, and they may distract sales employees from existing customers. A good incentive program would take account of this.

MAKING IT HAPPEN
Improve Sales Force Performance

Incentive programs are an integral part of sales management. They can be used to motivate sales employees to improve their overall performance or they can be structured to improve performance in specific areas, such as repeat sales, new accounts, or the acquisition of new skills.

Set the Right Objectives

Ask yourself why you are running the program. Is it because you want to increase overall volume or sales of specific products? Or, do you want to improve performance in other sales-related areas such as customer service, or participation in training programs and other business programs?

Improve Customer Service

You can build both sales and customer loyalty by providing the highest standards of customer care. An incentive program should be carefully structured to improve performance in all the areas critical to achieving that objective. It should cover:

- participation in the relevant training program
- new accounts opened
- percentage of repeat business achieved
- achievement of major contracts
- sales of products identified for special promotion

Encourage Continuous Sales Effort

Sales representatives should be assessed on a series of long- and short-term objectives that help them to build a specific type of business. The same approach can be used to encourage teams to focus on sales of a certain product line. The important point about incentive programs of this type is that they are structured to encourage continuous effort over a period of time rather than achieving short-term objectives. Sales incentives have traditionally been geared to moving inventory quickly for tactical reasons and, as such, they are an essential sales management technique, but they can also be used in a strategic way.

Achieve a Change of Direction

When a European vehicle paint manufacturer wanted to build a broader customer base rather than depend on a few large customers, it developed a year-long incentive program for its sales team. The organization wanted to encourage the sales team to win and retain business from independent garages, as well as the franchised car dealers who represented only a small part of the market. Under the program, points were awarded for opening new accounts with the independents, and a structured bonus system was applied to percentage increases in business with these new accounts. In addition, the sales representatives were given points for increasing business with existing accounts, but these were weighted to count for less in the overall assessment.

The manufacturer also wanted to encourage the sales team to acquire new skills in business development, so that they could form closer working relationships with their customers at senior management level. To achieve this, additional points were awarded for participation in business skills training courses and for reaching different training levels. The incentive program also awarded points for participation in a number of business development programs designed to improve the quality of service to customers. In this way, the incentive program

encouraged overall business development rather than short-term tactical sales.

Select the Right Incentive Program

Incentives have proved to be an effective form of motivation, but they must be managed carefully to provide long-term benefits. The wrong choice of prizes, unclear rules, or poor organization can undo all the good work.

Choose an Appropriate Program Format

- Prizes can be awarded to the biggest earners or the best performers against target.
- Programs that reward only top sales representatives can act as a disincentive to others; programs that reward performance against target give a wider opportunity to win, and can motivate a higher proportion of the sales force.
- A multilevel program that offers many lower-value prizes, with high-value prizes for top performers, can act as a strong motivator.

Make Sure the Prize Motivates People

- Achievable prizes can motivate large numbers.
- The prize structure should offer real variety, and meet many different tastes and interests.
- Quality prizes can be used to reflect the high standards set by a program.
- Popular prizes may have wide appeal but may not have much motivational value.

Define the Rules Clearly

- Set out the scope of the program and the awards.
- Explain what is required to win and how to collect the prizes.
- Include the closing date for the promotion.
- Set the specific targets for each participant.
- Indicate who is eligible for the award.
- State clearly the tax implications of any prize.

Offer Different Prize Levels

To maintain interest in the program, offer different levels of prize. A program like this has depth as well as breadth:

- regular monthly prizes for best sales performance;
- quarterly regional awards for best overall performance;
- regional winners go forward to a national incentive program that rewards high achievers with even more attractive prizes.

Maintain Momentum Throughout the Program

- Send out teaser incentives or gifts during the program to maintain interest.
- Keep participants informed of their progress.
- Use secondary offers to encourage participants who are struggling.
- Publish results and distribute them to all participants.

Reward Effort

A national conference or other event can be used to recognize high achievement. The highlight of this type of program is the individual presentation to the winner by a senior director, an event that represents real status to the winner. The high profile of the program's award ceremony can raise its importance among the whole sales force, and encourage high levels of participation and effort.

Manage the Event

Consider using a professional event management company or incentive specialist to handle the event, and appoint an event team with specific responsibilities for the event itself. If possible, obtain feedback from participants on attitudes to the venue and the event.

COMMON MISTAKES
Putting Too Much Emphasis on the Incentive Program

While an incentive program may result in a short-term increase in sales, it may disguise underlying problems in sales force performance. More training, better regional management, different account allocation, or greater marketing support may lead to even higher levels of performance. An incentive program should not be treated as a short-term fix: it should be integrated with other aspects of sales force management.

Concentrating on Short-term Incentives

Incentive programs can be used to achieve long-term business objectives. If an organization wants to move into new markets, the sales force will have to acquire new product and market knowledge. The incentive program should then be structured to recognize achievement in those areas rather than to reward short-term sales.

Poor Program Management

An incentive program has to be carefully managed. Clear objectives and program rules, attractive prizes, a progressive structure, and sound administration insure high levels of motivation and achievement.

FOR MORE INFORMATION

Book:
Miller, William Skip. *Proactive Sales Management: How to Lead, Motivate, and Stay Ahead of the Game.* New York: AMACOM, 2001.

Web site:
American Marketing Association:
www.MarketingPower.com

Designing a Response Mechanism

GETTING STARTED
Response mechanisms make it easier for prospects to get information, place orders, and respond to offers. Every advertisement, mailing, or other customer communication should incorporate one.

FAQs
Why should every communication include a response mechanism?
Although some advertisements or other customer communications are designed to impart information, it is a courtesy to include a response mechanism. Customers may want more information than you can provide. It is also important to collect customer data. The response mechanism allows you to capture basic details and measure the effectiveness of a campaign.

Why bother with other types of response mechanism when a Web site address is so simple and convenient?
A Web site is convenient. Customers can visit around the clock, download information, and sometimes place orders. However, if they do not register their details when they visit, you have no opportunity to contact them or develop a relationship. If the customer wants to ask questions or discuss a product in more detail, telephone contact may be more appropriate.

Doesn't using a third-party call center take away the opportunity to deliver personal service?
Third-party call center employees are trained to act as personal representatives of your company. They receive full product training and they will become familiar with your company culture and ways of doing business. Customers should notice no difference when they are linked to a call center.

MAKING IT HAPPEN
Include a Response Mechanism
It is important that any advertisement, mailing, or other customer communication incorporates a response mechanism. A response mechanism is a call to action that insures your prospect takes the next step in the buying process. It can also be an effective method of capturing customer data for use in future campaigns.

Encourage Response to Print Advertisements
Include a coupon on print advertisements if you want to capture specific data on prospects, such as name and address, or business details. Also encourage response by including a telephone number, mailing address, Web site, or e-mail address for further information, although this may not give you the same level of data capture. If you do not use coupons, try to capture data through telemarketing techniques. Make it easy for the prospect to respond by offering a toll-free phone number. Capturing e-mail addresses can also be an important first stage in building customer relationships.

Build Response to Television and Radio Advertising
Include a telephone number or Web site address in television or radio commercials if you want prospects to ask for further information, and preferably make the number a toll-free number. If you want to include an address, allow viewers time to take the address down. Repeat the address at least once. If you are encouraging a telephone response, make sure that you have the resources to handle a high volume of calls. Television advertisements have been known to generate high response for a short period immediately after the commercial. If you do not have sufficient internal resources, you can hire a call center to handle the calls during the campaign.

Use the Right Response Mechanisms
There are five basic types of response mechanism:
- mail
- telephone
- fax
- e-mail
- Web site address

Response mechanisms improve the effectiveness of advertising campaigns by making it easier for prospects to get information or place orders, and encouraging prospects to respond to offers.

Consumers feel comfortable with a reply mechanism because it allows more time for consideration and there is no sales pressure. Industry research indicates that customers respond to the range of response mechanisms in different ways. E-mail and the Internet are seen as fast and convenient. They involve little effort and can be used 24 hours a day, seven days a week. Telephone-based services are more immediate and can be more personal. Pay-per-minute information service numbers can be used to provide useful customer information and generate revenue. Business Reply is regarded as suitable for business and financial advertisements.

Encourage Telephone Response
With the toll-free number, prospects and customers call your company from anywhere in the country, free of charge. You can obtain a toll-free number from your telephone service provider and you pay for the calls you receive at the standard rate.

You can also offer customers local numbers. Prospects and customers call from anywhere in the country, and the call is charged to them at local rates. You can obtain a local call number from your telephone service provider and you pay the balance of the charge.

With a pay-per-minute number, prospects and customers call from anywhere in the country and pay a premium rate for prerecorded information. Revenue from each call is divided between your company and the telephone service provider. You can obtain pay-per-

---

minute numbers from your service provider and charges for each call are at an agreed rate. You must publish the charge per minute to the customer, and any offers to children should include a warning that an adult must place the call.

Distribute Information By Fax

Fax back is a convenient way to distribute standard printed information. Prospects and customers call a fax number. When the call is answered, the caller presses the START button and a fax containing information is sent to the caller's machine within seconds. The service can be offered free to customers, using a toll-free number. You can obtain a toll-free number from your telephone service provider; you pay for the incoming calls and the return fax transmission at the standard rate.

Offer E-mail Response

E-mail is a quick, convenient response mechanism. Prospects can either compose their own e-mail and send it to your e-mail address, or complete a form on your Web site. If you want prospects to complete an online form, you must include your Web site address in the original customer communication.

Direct Customers to Your Web Site

Including a Web site address on your customer communications provides an extremely flexible response mechanism. Customers can obtain detailed information direct from the site, reducing your information distribution costs. However, you may prefer to take greater control of the customer relationship. You can also ask customers to register on your Web site. This provides valuable customer data and allows you to choose how to follow up the inquiry.

Keep Data Requirements to a Minimum

Asking for minimal data is a courtesy to customers and increases response. Apart from name and position, the most important information is telephone number or e-mail address. That provides a basis for contact and collection of additional data. Long, complex forms or requests for large amounts of detail could put off potential respondents.

Maintain a Quality Response

Companies that have to handle large volumes of responses and distribute additional material may not have the resources to handle fulfillment internally. Fulfillment agencies specialize in high-volume response programs. The address or telephone number of the fulfillment agency should be included in the response mechanism. If you are selecting a fulfillment house, there are important criteria:

- quality and reliability of service
- capacity to handle the volume of responses

- aftercare service for customers
- management reporting systems

COMMON MISTAKES
Asking Customers for Too Much Information

Customers may be willing to provide basic information, but lengthy questionnaires are time-consuming and can deter people from responding. The most important elements are name, address, telephone number, and e-mail address. If you go beyond that point, you are moving into market research and customers may be less willing to cooperate.

Failing to Integrate Response Mechanisms with Relationship Programs

A response mechanism is simply a starting point for a customer relationship program. A customer may just ask for a leaflet, but that request gives you the opportunity to open a dialog, gather further information, and build a detailed customer profile as a basis for future campaigns.

Poor Follow-up

Your advertising is wasted if you capture customer details and fail to follow up effectively. Customers will feel frustrated if they have to wait a long time for a response. You will also lose the opportunity to develop a relationship while the customer is in buying mood. You should set time limits for responding to requests. If you cannot meet those targets, consider using external resources to handle fulfillment.

Failing to Offer Customers Choice of Response

Before the Internet became a popular medium, the mail and telephone were the only effective response mechanisms. Today, people expect the convenience of an e-mail or Web site address as well as telephone or postal mechanisms. Offering a choice of routes demonstrates good customer service.

FOR MORE INFORMATION

Books:
Kern, Russell M. *S.U.R.E.-fire Direct Response Marketing: Managing Business-to-business Sales Leads for Bottom-line Success.* New York: McGraw-Hill, 2001.
Hughes, Arthur Middleton. *Strategic Database Marketing: The Masterplan for Starting and Managing a Profitable, Customer-based Marketing Program.* 3rd ed. New York: McGraw-Hill, 2005.

Web site:
The Direct Marketing Association: **www.the-dma.org**

"As you seek to change every procedure and job description to aid responsiveness, remember the bygone days when we whipped big competitors by being faster and fleeter of foot."

Ronald Reagan

Generating More Leads

GETTING STARTED

The constant turnover of customers means that generating new leads is essential to keep a business growing. There are many ways of doing this, depending on the product and customer groups involved, but the primary purpose is to provide data on potential customers which can then be followed up.

FAQs

How important is lead generation?

Lead generation is vital to the development of new business. Customers just stop buying, or they move to competitors; this lost business must be replaced, and new customers added, if sales are to grow. Sales teams must have a constant flow of leads in order to maintain or increase business levels.

What is the best source of new leads?

The best source is the one that produces the highest-quality leads; some publications can produce large numbers of leads, but they could all be poor. A publication, a direct mail program, or an event that is precisely targeted is likely to produce the most effective source of leads.

Are incentives necessary to a lead generation program?

They are not essential, but they may help to encourage people to place inquiries. The incentive should not be too generous, since you may attract poor prospects who are more interested in free gifts than in your products.

MAKING IT HAPPEN

Make Direct Response a Priority

To generate leads from your marketing campaigns, include a response mechanism in every communication, and make it easy for prospects to reply. Getting names is a priority, so make sure your communications are designed to deliver.

Generate Leads from Press Advertising

If you want to generate leads, make sure your advertisement includes a call to action, such as:

- send for more information;
- reply within seven days and receive a free gift;
- send for a free report;
- take out an annual subscription now and get the first two issues free;
- call for a free consultation;
- reserve now at a special price;
- order now and get a big discount;
- visit our Web site and find out more.

Make It Easy for Prospects to Respond

To improve response rates, it is essential to make it easy for prospective customers to respond. The most popular mechanisms for print media advertisements are:

- Web site address

- e-mail address
- toll-free number

These facilities provide easy-to-use response mechanisms that can boost customer reaction. You should monitor the response levels from different sources to see which is the most effective.

Use Reader Response Cards

Many publications include a reader response card or helpline number. Readers send back the card to the publication, indicating the products that they are interested in. The usual method is to circle a number which is shown on the advertisement in the publication, for example, "For more information circle # 15." The publication then distributes the inquiries to individual advertisers for follow-up.

Run Advertorials in the Press

An advertorial with a prize is a cost-effective way of generating leads. The advertorial describes a product or service, and customers are offered the opportunity to win a prize in return for supplying basic data or completing a short questionnaire. The questionnaire might take the form of "Give three reasons why product X is the best on the market." The answers could be multiple choice, based on information in the advertorial, or the customer's own opinion. Open-ended questions provide added insight into customer attitudes.

Encourage TV and Radio Response

More and more television and radio commercials now include a response mechanism, such as a phone number or Web site address. Some direct the audience to a source of further information, others to a retailer or other outlet. The response mechanism must be clear, because the audience has only a short time to write down the details.

Use Direct Mail to Target Prospects

Direct mail can be used at a number of stages in a lead generation program. Mailings to lists that have not been qualified should include a response mechanism so that follow-up can begin.

Run Offers on Packaging

Your product packaging can feature special offers. Buyers send in a coupon or other proof of purchase, together with their name and address. Although the person contacting you is, strictly speaking, already a customer, you need to identify that person to build a relationship. Lead generation is just as important here.

Find Out Who Is Visiting Retail Outlets

Visitors to retail outlets are another potential source of leads. Many retail shoppers who buy from you may remain anonymous, so encourage shoppers to provide names and addresses by running competitions or making other special offers.

Encourage Web Site Registration

Web site registration provides high levels of information. When customers visit your Web site, ask them to register their details. The registration form is completed online and submitted by e-mail. In return, you e-mail them regularly with details of products and services that are of interest to them. Incentives such as free reports or free software can encourage higher levels of registration.

Record Exhibition Visitors

Visitor registration should be an integral part of exhibition planning. Establish a process for capturing data on all stand visitors. Establish a database of exhibition contacts, and use it to plan and monitor a contact program after the exhibition.

Monitor the Business Press

Many business publications feature news about recent appointments or interviews with leading executives. This type of information can give you names of potentially valuable contacts. The appointments pages can also alert you to changes in personnel at one of your customer or prospect companies.

Use Telemarketing

Telemarketing can be used to generate new leads and qualify existing leads. The telemarketing team can call target companies and ask for the names of decision makers for follow-up. The team can also call people who have made an initial inquiry, in order to qualify their interest and find out how good the prospects are. However, remember that some people may have placed their names on "do not call" lists and that contacting them by making unsolicited phone calls may lead to significant fines. Make sure you are contacting the right people from the outset.

Integrate Lead Generation with Other Marketing Activities

Lead generation programs can be improved by integrating the campaign with other marketing activities such as an exhibition, advertising campaign, or a call by a member of the sales force. With integrated campaigns, overall awareness levels among customers and prospects will be far higher. Your lead generation program will have an even greater chance of success.

Keep Refining Your Contact Lists

Many of the contact lists you have developed from internal or external sources may not match your requirements exactly. To improve coverage, or to make them more precise, you must make a continuous effort to refine them. These are some of the actions you can take to improve the coverage of your list:

- Make sure that new customer and prospect data are added to the list.
- Include coupons and other reply mechanisms with every

form of communication, and add the responses to your lists.
- Encourage the sales force to provide up-to-date customer and prospect information.
- Maintain an active search program in appropriate Web sites, magazines, and newspapers to identify new prospects for your list.

COMMON MISTAKES
Overlooking Lead Generation

Lead generation could be vital to your company's future. Without it, lost customers will not be replaced, and you may miss major opportunities in new or existing market sectors. Only a small proportion of leads become customers, so lead generation must be an ongoing process.

Paying Too Much for Your Leads

You can measure the cost of your lead generation program by dividing the cost of the advertising or marketing program by the number of leads. Media for lead generation should be assessed in the same way as media to meet other objectives.

No Integration with Other Marketing Programs

Lead generation programs do not work in isolation. Corporate advertising, for example, helps to raise awareness among the target audience, while direct mail and telemarketing can be used to back up lead generation advertising.

FOR MORE INFORMATION

Books:
Carroll, Brian. *Lead Generation for the Complex Sale: Boost the Quality and Quantity of Leads to Increase Your ROI*. New York: McGraw-Hill, 2006.
Jobber, David, and Geoffrey Lancaster. *Selling and Sales Management*. 7th ed. Upper Saddle River, NJ: FT Prentice Hall, 2005.
Zoltners, Andris, Greggor A. Zoltners, and Prabhakant Sinha. *The Complete Guide to Accelerating Sales Force Performance*. New York: AMACOM, 2001.

Web site:
American Marketing Association:
www.MarketingPower.com

"Seize opportunity by the forelock and see where it leads you."

Armand Hammer

Converting Leads into Sales

GETTING STARTED

If you are trying to grow your business, finding leads (that is, potential new customers) is just the beginning. Before they can benefit you in any way, you need to turn those leads into sales. This actionlist offers a systematic approach to doing this and to making sure that the leads are of the right kind in the first place, which will cut down on wasted time and resources.

FAQs

How far can services such as telemarketing take over from the sales force?

These services can be used to handle many of the sales teams' routine functions: conducting initial research, qualifying prospective customers, making appointments, and maintaining regular contact. Despite these benefits, they're no substitute for face-to-face selling if that's important to your customer relationships, so make sure they're appropriate for your business. In addition, remember that some people may have placed their names on "do not call" lists and that contacting them by making unsolicited phone calls may lead to significant fines.

What is the best way to measure lead conversion?

Measuring sales as a percentage of initial leads is too simplistic an approach; it is more effective to measure at each stage of the process. For example, only 50% of initial leads may turn out to be suitable prospective customers. If the leads have been well qualified, the sales team may be able to convert 20% of the final prospect list. Measuring results at each stage helps you focus the right level of resources and plan future lead generation programs.

Should we try to get as many leads as possible?

The quality of the leads is as important as the number. Following up a large number of unsuitable leads is a waste of resources, but getting as many good leads as possible is important to any company that wants to expand its business.

MAKING IT HAPPEN
Qualify Your Leads

Your lead generation program may have given you large numbers of leads, but not all of them will convert to sales. Some may be poor prospects, while others may simply be gathering information rather than planning a purchase. Good prospects have the following characteristics:
- the financial resources to purchase your product;
- the authority to make a purchase decision;
- a genuine need for your product or service;
- the desire to learn more about your product;
- plans to make a purchase in the near future.

Telemarketing can be used to qualify the leads. Call the contact and ask for more details of their inquiry so that you can send information tailored to their needs. Just sending a brochure, with no accompanying letter and no understanding of the prospective customer's needs, is a waste of money. Qualifying questions can include:
- Are you the person who makes the purchasing decision? If not, who does?
- Is your company currently buying this product?
- What quantities do you buy, or how much do you spend on the service?
- When are you likely to make your next purchase?
- What information do you need on our product and company?

Choose a One-step or Two-step Process

In the case of some products and services, the lead generation and sales conversion processes can be combined. These are known as one-step programs, and are equivalent to direct selling operations. They are suitable for:
- inexpensive products
- information services such as newsletters or subscriptions
- office supplies
- software
- low-value financial offers

In a two-step program, the prospective customer (prospect) requests initial information. You send the information and then continue following up until the prospect is ready to buy. Two-step programs are suitable for:
- expensive offers
- complex technical products
- professional services
- high-value financial services

Plan the Conversion Process

Lead conversion can be a long-term continuous process, the duration of which depends on the complexity of the product and of the decision making process. For example, how many people are involved or how important is the product to the customer (or the customer's business)?

For a complex product, the process could be:
- identifying key decision makers;
- sending information to key decision makers;
- arranging meetings with decision makers;
- providing sample products for evaluation;
- bidding for a contract against competition;
- final negotiations;
- purchase;
- after-sales service and support.

You must decide how you will handle each stage of the process, who will be involved in the sales team, and how you will manage communications with the prospect.

Another example could be where the product and the purchasing process are simpler, but the prospect is reluctant to change suppliers. The conversion process could take a long time, so you must plan a program to maintain contact and move the prospect away from the existing supplier. Actions could include:
- personalized direct mail with product information;
- regular updates on new developments in the company;
- targeted special offers to encourage the customer to try the product.

"A salesman has got to dream, boy, it comes with the territory." Arthur Miller

Allocate Responsibility

Normally, the marketing department generates leads and the sales department follows up. It is important for the two departments to work together to integrate their activities and make sure that the company focuses on the kind of high-quality prospects it really needs. Sales departments frequently complain about the quantity and quality of leads. They want as many leads as possible so that the final number of new sales is high; however, they may also complain if too many of the leads are of poor quality and do not meet the right criteria. Collecting a large number of high-quality leads can be a difficult balancing act. Some sales teams prefer to do their own qualifying, while others prefer to leave that to others so that they can concentrate on face-to-face meetings with prospects.

Back the Sales Team with Telemarketing

Telemarketing can be used to enhance the performance and productivity of the sales force. The telemarketing team can be responsible for following up sales leads, qualifying prospects, setting up appointments, and maintaining contact with longer-term prospects. This frees the sales force for increasing the number of face-to-face meetings and for concentrating on the most likely prospects. The integration of telemarketing with the sales force can play an important part in reducing overall sales costs. The cost of keeping a sales team on the road continues to soar, and it may not always represent the most cost-effective way of reaching the right people.

Maintain a Contact Diary

A contact diary can help you plan the conversion process and make sure that the sales team does not miss any important contact opportunities. It also makes sure that the sales backup team integrates its follow-up activities with the field sales force. Computer software is available which allows sales teams to operate a sales diary and record details of meetings and other follow-up activities. The same software can be used by the management team to monitor progress and make sure that no important contacts are overlooked. Contact diaries can include details of the customer, the customer's likes and dislikes, availability for meetings or telephone calls, their buying limits/authorization, and even personal information that helps to maintain a relationship with them.

Track Progress

It is essential to track progress at each stage of the conversion process. If the prospect is important, you may wish to allocate additional resources to win the business. If a prospect is of only minor importance but is taking time and resources, you may want to refocus the efforts of the sales force. The progress from initial lead to customer goes through a number of stages:

- raw lead: an initial inquiry from any source;
- suspect: an inquiry that has been qualified and has the potential to become a paying customer;
- prospect: a lead that has been qualified in more detail;
- inactive lead: a prospect who will not buy now but has future potential;
- dead lead: a prospect who has little potential to become a customer;
- customer.

You might also include lapsed customers in this process as a source of qualified leads.

Choose the Right Contact Frequency

A single mailing, telephone call, or direct response advertisement may produce results, but a series of quality contacts will have greater impact and make sure you meet your response targets. Multiple direct marketing activities raise levels of awareness with each contact. Follow up contacts who do not respond, and move individual respondents further along the decision making process.

Use Personalized Contact

Personalized one-to-one mailings are an ideal form of communication for companies with detailed information on their prospects. The letter reflects the individual prospect's main interests and concerns, and the offer can be tailored to the prospect's needs. Subsequent mailings can build an individual relationship with the prospect.

COMMON MISTAKES
Focusing on the Wrong Prospects

Sales teams have a natural tendency to deal with friendly prospects and avoid the difficult ones. From a business perspective, however, they may be dealing with the wrong people. The qualifying process should be used to identify the most important prospects in order to improve the targeting of the sales force.

Poor Management

Lead conversion can be a long, complicated process, so it is essential to monitor progress and manage the program carefully. Lead conversion can use a lot of sales force and telemarketing resources, and careful planning can make sure that it is performed effectively.

Putting All the Burden on the Sales Force

In some organizations, the sales force has total responsibility for generating leads, qualifying them, and converting them into sales. This may not be the best use of sales force resources. Telemarketing or other tools can be used to supplement the sales force and take over routine tasks.

FOR MORE INFORMATION

Book:
Jobber, David, and Geoffrey Lancaster. *Selling and Sales Management.* 7th ed. Upper Saddle River, NJ: FT Prentice Hall, 2005.

Web site:
American Marketing Association:
www.MarketingPower.com

See also:
✔ Generating More Leads (pp. 731–732)
✔ Handling Customer Inquiries (pp. 704–705)
✔ Supporting Campaigns with Telemarketing (pp. 771–772)

Conducting Market Research

GETTING STARTED

Businesses of all sizes need to keep on top of changes or developments in their chosen markets so that they can make sure that the product or service they offer fits the bill. This actionlist gives you some ideas on how to conduct different types of market research.

FAQs

Can we conduct market research ourselves, or should we use a consulting firm?

Market research is a professional discipline and, depending on your industry and what you need to find out, you may get more meaningful results by using a consulting firm. They are trained to detect possible errors in research results, and their independence is reassuring to people who are being interviewed. The main problem for small businesses is, naturally, the expense. Review your budget and see if you can afford outside help.

You can conduct a limited amount of research yourself, developing and mailing questionnaires or conducting limited telephone interviews. Again, there is a risk that people may feel that your research is a thinly disguised sales pitch.

How do I conduct quick and effective research?

Without incurring great costs, you often have the opportunity to research your own customers. Every time you or a member of your staff meet a customer you can discover important information during the course of a normal conversation. Record this information and create opportunities to share it.

More formal research may include a space on delivery notes or invoices, enclosures with products, or follow-up phone calls to ask customers' opinions. Be cautious about asking for too much (or too personal) information, though, as this puts people on their guard and makes them much less likely to help you.

How reliable are the results from focus groups?

The results are as reliable as the quality of the participants and the people who run the sessions. For example, very bossy or loud participants can dominate a group and influence the course of discussions. Also, if the person running the discussion asks the wrong questions, the resulting discussion may prove worthless. Make sure those in charge are well briefed and know what your goals are.

We have limited resources for research. Should we participate in an omnibus survey so that we can make the best use of our budget?

An omnibus survey is an ideal way to share expensive research resources and reach a large audience. However, you must be sure that the audience is relevant to your company's business. Ask for a profile of the research audience and check the names of other organizations which have used the survey. If there is a reasonable match to your own business, it could be a cost-effective solution.

MAKING IT HAPPEN

Interview Customers by Telephone

Telephone interviews are a quick and cost-effective way to obtain opinions from a sample of customers. They can be used to assess customer reaction to a change in the product or service, or to gauge satisfaction ratings compared to competitors. The make-up of the sample is crucial; it is more important to know the views of valuable customers rather than those who haven't bought from you for a while or who tend not to spend a lot of money on your products and services. Do remember, though, that some people don't like being "cold-called" and may not want to participate. It might be worth sounding out some key customers in advance by e-mail, on your Web site, or via a newsletter if you have one, as you'll get much more useful information from someone who actually wants to take part in your research.

Speed Up Research

The main benefit of telephone research is speed: a large number of interviews can be conducted in a short space of time, and data can be gathered and processed quickly. Telephone interviews also cost considerably less than personal interviews. As long as they are brief and to the point they are non-intrusive and easy to arrange. A customer may be too busy for a personal interview, but willing to spend a short time on the phone. Again, it may be worth sounding people out in advance.

Be careful about a senior decision-maker at another business being contacted by a junior member of your staff or an independent researcher, though—they may prefer to hear from you directly if you have a good relationship with them—and always bear in mind the effect on the customer's relationship with you.

Don't Confuse Telephone Research with Selling

Telephone interviews have limited scope because people may not be prepared to spend a long period of time on the telephone. It can also be difficult to get across complex concepts by telephone.

Follow industry guidelines:

- define the target audience;
- draft a questionnaire and test it with colleagues;
- make the calls at times likely to be convenient for the target audience, but check when you call that it is convenient; if not, offer to call back;
- identify the purpose of the call and give an indication of the likely duration;
- use faxes, if necessary, to send more detailed information for discussion.

Use Mail Surveys or Questionnaires

Questionnaires are very difficult to compile well, and

"Research! A mere excuse for idleness; it has never achieved, and will never achieve any results of the slightest value."

Benjamin Jowett

736

ACTIONLIST

those who do it well have honed their skills over many years. If you feel a questionnaire is that important to your research, it may be worth contacting a questionnaire specialist to help you out. Other types of mail surveys are delivered directly to customers and they can be a quick and relatively inexpensive method of obtaining information. They are ideal for customer satisfaction surveys or detailed surveys that take time to complete, but it can be difficult to obtain a reasonable rate of response and you cannot assume that the responses will be representative of all customers.

Use E-mail
You can reduce the cost of mail surveys even further by using e-mail to distribute surveys and collect responses. You could also upload a research form to your Web site or ask respondents to answer questions by short text messages.

Assess the Value of Mail Surveys
Mail surveys are relatively inexpensive. The costs include outward and return postage and stationery. They are precise and can be targeted at specific customers or prospects. They are also voluntary, because there is no pressure on the customer. The main problem, however, is the low response rate; incentives may be needed to improve it. There is also a risk of questionnaires and survey forms being returned incomplete or being incorrectly completed. You may face a slow response because there is no time pressure on the customer (unless you introduce one, by offering a discount or some such if customers respond within a certain time limit), so you must take this into account in your planning.

Improve the Response from Mail Surveys
Response rates can be influenced by many different factors. For many consumer goods markets less than 5% would be normal and 15% or more would be extremely high. For highly involved customers in some sectors you might anticipate much more. If you need to improve response think about:
- offering an incentive, such as entry into a prize draw, for returned questionnaires;
- simplifying the questionnaire;
- reassuring the customer that information will be kept confidential;
- enclosing a stamped addressed or business reply envelope.

Hold a Group Discussion
In group discussions—sometimes called "focus groups"—existing and prospective customers are invited to discuss a particular topic, usually under the guidance of a researcher. They are ideal for exploring and, possibly, identifying issues or problems which concern customers, and assessing customer reactions to potential changes.

There is no limit placed on what the group can discuss, and this format can highlight important customer issues that the researcher may not be aware of. Many customers welcome the opportunity to discuss products and services with their colleagues and have an opportunity to contribute to change. The disadvantages are that group discussions are not representative, and they can be biased or influenced by a dominant member of the group. It is also difficult to quantify results.

You need to be cautious in planning group discussions. By and large they should not be used to identify only what is wrong with a product or service, and it may cause problems to have several important customers in the same room. Groups composed entirely of customers with grievances will also have limited value: it's unlikely that you'll be able to get past their individual complaints.

To establish a group discussion:
- invite eight to ten customers—this number is controllable, but with fewer people it may be difficult to maintain discussion;
- thank customers for participating and put them at their ease;
- record the discussion if possible, using a tape recorder;
- advise people that their comments are being recorded and that all material will be treated in confidence;
- if conducting a group among consumers (not your customers) you might consider providing participants with a gift for taking part;
- consider using more than one group to gather a variety of views;

You could also consider using an independent researcher to run the discussion.

Conduct Personal Interviews
In a personal interview, a customer and an interviewer work through a series of predetermined questions. The personal interview is ideal for key customers and for obtaining detailed information on attitudes to products and services, or initiating the process of getting feedback. The interview can take place in a customer's home or office, or in a public place. It can be prearranged by telephone, mail, or personal contact.

Personal interviews allow in-depth discussion of complex topics and give you more control over the response. They offer greater accuracy, and results are easy to analyze. Meeting people in a working environment can give an indication of their real purchasing intentions. The main disadvantages are the time and cost of recruiting interviewers and conducting interviews and the risk of interviewer bias.

Before you conduct personal interviews, you should identify the groups or individuals you wish to contact. You should advise the customer about the length of time the interview is likely to take and respect the confidence of the customer.

Use an Omnibus Survey
An omnibus survey is a cost-effective method of researching several topics at the same time. The same survey is used to conduct regular research on different products by telephone or personal interview. They are appropriate for measuring attitudes and behavior toward different types of products and services or monitoring changes in attitude among groups of consumers.

Before participating in the survey, you should check that the other topics in the survey are compatible with your own products and that the overall length of the

"The way to do research is to attack the facts at the point of greatest astonishment."

Celia Green

survey is not excessive. It may reduce costs, but the audience may not give enough attention to all topics.

COMMON MISTAKES

Asking Obvious Questions

Remember that you already know a good deal about your customers and their attitudes and behavior. In a business-to-business market, you may know more than your customer. Before undertaking research, be sure that it is absolutely necessary.

Assuming Formal Market Research Is Necessary

For many smaller companies (and some quite large ones) expensive research does not meet their needs. Companies with just a handful of very important customers would do better to concentrate on their relationship with these key accounts. For example, local retailers will often know their own area well and the best "research" they could do may simply be to talk to their regular customers.

Not Planning Properly

Market research may generate considerable amounts of data, and, to gain any benefit from it, you'll need to have the time and resources to analyze it and turn it into useful information. Alternatively, if you set out without a thorough plan, you may find that you have missed a crucial piece of information and face the embarrassment of having to revisit customers.

Choosing the Wrong Research Technique

Each research technique has different applications, benefits, and disadvantages. You have to decide whether you need depth of information, speedy results, or cost-effective research. A market research consulting firm

may be able to provide advice on an appropriate approach, but you need to have a very clear picture of your needs, and how the information will be used.

Relying on Limited Results

If time or resources are scarce, some research programs may provide limited results. It's important to put the research findings in context and take account of the limited findings when you are making important decisions. Market research consulting firms use proven techniques to evaluate results and should advise you to use their findings with caution.

Using Research to Sell

Too many companies contact customers and prospects claiming to be conducting market research. During the course of the research, the company then attempts to sell a product or service on the basis that the respondent has expressed an interest. This is a betrayal of trust and can prove damaging to valid research and their business's reputation in the long term.

737

ACTIONLIST

FOR MORE INFORMATION

Book:
Brace, Ian. *Questionnaire Design: How to Plan, Structure and Write Survey Material for Effective Market Research*. Milford, CT: Kogan Page, 2004.

Web site:
Marketing Research Association: **www.mra-net.org**

See also:
✔ Building One-to-one Relationships (pp. 696–697)

Profiling Your Competitors

GETTING STARTED

Competitor information helps you to protect and grow your business. To keep one step ahead—or at least at roughly the same place!—as your direct competitors, you need to build a detailed profile of them, their strengths, weaknesses, and relationships with customers, as well as thinking more widely about competition for your customers and their spending. To help you to do this, compare the performance of your business with that of your main competitors by measuring factors that are important to quality of service and use the comparison as the basis for a program of performance improvement.

Whether you sell yourself or you have a sales team, competitor information can be obtained from many different sources. Publications, the press, and the Internet have information readily available that can help you to compile intelligence on competitors, and corporate brochures and annual reports are also excellent sources of published information. Maintain a file of press cuttings on your competitors' activities, using their trade publications or their own Web site news pages as a source.

Published industry surveys can provide a useful insight into purchasing patterns, and competitors' Web sites can provide valuable information on their resources, plans, and capabilities.

FAQs
Why is competitor intelligence so important?

Competitive activity can have a significant impact on your own plans. If you are about to run a marketing campaign or new product launch, competitive activity could limit its effectiveness—so you need to know about it. You may also identify growing threats to important accounts. Unless you monitor activity and take appropriate action, your business faces an unknown risk.

Who are my competitors?

Many small companies already know their main direct competitors. Often they have worked with them or encountered them at trade events or heard of them through customers. It is dangerous, however, to assume you know all the competitors.

It is often useful to think laterally about who might be in competition for your customers. Many products and services could be classed as non-essential and so customers may be choosing to spend their discretionary budget between two very different market sectors. In addition, as a specialist, you could find yourself in competition with a larger company who gives away a competing service as a promotional device.

Should competitor research be conducted internally or by an independent research company?

You can conduct the research internally, provided you have the resources. Much of the source material is in the public domain, so you should be able to obtain it yourself and you must never ignore the wealth of information you already have in your company or can gain through your own contacts. However, if you wish to research customer attitudes (to compare your company to the competition), you may need to use an independent research organization. Customers may not be completely honest with your own representatives.

How reliable is published competitor information?

You have to make assumptions about the accuracy and quality of any published information that is used for research. Much of the material will be published to provide information for customers, so it is unlikely to be misleading. However, realistically, you can only use the latest and best information available.

MAKING IT HAPPEN
Identify the Competitive Threat

Competitor information helps you to identify how you can protect your most important business and, more positively, how you can strengthen your position with customers in situations in which your competitors are currently holding a larger share of the business than you. These are the main questions:

- How many competitors do you have? Are they direct or indirect?
- Who are your major competitors—those that threaten your most important customers?
- How much of your business do they threaten? Quantifying the threat helps you to prioritize.
- Where are your main competitors located? How do they compare in size? Are they growing? Map them and track them.
- How do your products compare with competitive offerings? What about price? Distribution? Image and reputation? Service quality?
- What are customers' attitudes toward your competitors and toward your own company?
- Which customers might switch to competitors, and why?
- How strong are competitors' relationships with key customers or key decision makers? How long have competitors been dealing with them?
- Have you got the skills and resources to overcome the competitive threat?
- Are any competitors making inroads into businesses in which you are currently the dominant supplier?
- Who are your competitors' main customers?
- Have your competitors invested in links with customers that would make it difficult for other suppliers to make inroads?
- Can you (or your customers) identify weaknesses in your competitors?
- Which of your competitors' customers do you want to win?

"I don't meet competition. I crush it."

Charles Revson

Compare Key Competitive Factors

Listed below are a number of factors that are important to meeting customer needs. You can score these factors (0–10, where 10 is the best in the market) to see how your business and your main competitors compare. The results should be used as the basis for a program of performance improvement. As far as possible you should give priority to the things that matter *to your customers* rather than to your own opinions:

- evidence of an excellent service culture, for example, problems quickly resolved by frontline staff rather than reference to higher managers
- high levels of after-sales service and support offered
- product adapted readily to meet customer specifications
- evidence of commitment to quality measurements such as ISO9002, Investors in People, or similar industry programs
- promises made to customers, for example in sales literature offering money-back guarantees or precise delivery schedules
- evidence of feedback encouraged, for example comment forms or toll-free telephone number made widely available
- flexible approach to pricing such as the use of price incentives or financing plans to appeal to different types of customer. Willingness to negotiate prices for important customers
- staff knowledgeable about the product and willing to share this knowledge and give advice to customers
- good reputation with agents, distributors, or other intermediaries
- overall reputation, for example, how do your staff or customers rate the company?

Use the Sales Force

If you have one, the sales force can obtain competitor information from many different sources. By talking to customers, salespeople can find out about competitors' direct sales calls, marketing campaigns, special offers, and new developments. They can also obtain similar information from retailers or distributors. Crucially, they can get a feel for the customers' awareness and attitude toward your competitors.

Analyze Published Information

Information is readily available from publications, the press, and the Internet that can help you to compile intelligence on different aspects of competitors' business, including:

- main markets
- customers
- resources and financial performance
- product range
- new products
- plans for growth

Obtain Competitor Literature

Corporate brochures and annual reports are available for some companies. You can sometimes obtain copies from exhibitions and customers or as downloads from competitors' Web sites. Often by just visiting your competitors' offices you can pick up brochures and leaflets.

Monitor the Press

Maintain a file of press cuttings on your competitors' activities, using their trade publications or their own Web site news pages as a source, or, depending on your budget, you might consider using a press cuttings agency to gather material for you. Smaller companies can give a member of their staff, for example, a sales person, responsibility for gathering and keeping data on a particular competitor.

Analyze Industry Reports

Published industry surveys can provide a useful insight into purchasing patterns in different market sectors. You can sometimes obtain information on competitors, market share, and industry trends.

Check the Internet

Competitor Web sites can provide valuable information on their resources, plans, and capabilities. As well as checking the company information and product pages, you should read any customer case studies on the site and monitor the news section to find out about new developments. Trade publications are increasingly available in electronic editions, making it easier for you to monitor the press.

Visit Exhibitions

Competitors' exhibition stands can be valuable sources of information. Most organizations only participate in exhibitions that are important to their current or future business plans.

Monitor Competitors' Promotional Activities

Analyzing competitors' promotional activities will help you to respond to their plan. By monitoring their advertising, promotions, exhibition presence, press activities, and Internet information, you can assess possible strategies. These are some of the possible scenarios:

- Heavy advertising expenditure could indicate a competitor trying to win greater share or attempting to remedy losses in that market.
- Price promotions may indicate that your competitors want to be perceived as value-for-money suppliers or may be an emergency response to declining sales.
- Press announcements about new production facilities could indicate that your competitors are trying to increase their business significantly. They may become more cost-effective and able to offer lower prices, or may be taking on additional overhead that they must finance.
- Announcements about new branch or dealership openings could mean that competitors are expanding into new territories.
- Recruitment drives may signal a change in direction, a growth strategy, or a sudden loss of staff.

All of these can mean that your competitor is spending more money and you might compare this with published accounts (available through credit reference agencies) to gain an indication of their financial health.

Marketing and trade publications can be useful sources of information on competitor marketing activity.

739

ACTIONLIST

"We need to re-establish the blue water between ourselves and the competition."

Roger Holmes

Appoint a Research Company

If you do not have the internal resources to monitor competitive activity, you can use an independent research company to perform all the tasks outlined above. You can also ask the company to explore customer attitudes to competitors. Customers may be more willing to provide this information to an independent organization.

Consider Benchmarking

Benchmarking compares your performance with that of other, similar companies. Competently done, it will give you a baseline assessment of your company's efficiency and some insight into where competitors may be gaining competitive advantage over you.

COMMON MISTAKES
Overlooking the Obvious Sources

Some competitor intelligence is freely available from the Internet, the press, and other published sources and, most of all, from your staff, your customers, and your competitors themselves. Information from these sources can provide a valuable starting point for developing detailed competitor profiles.

Ignoring Competitor Information

Competitor information is only valuable if you use it to refine your own strategies or take defensive action to protect your business. Simply gathering information without analysis or action is wasteful.

Acting on Incomplete Information

Be cautious about acting on competitor intelligence. Published sources can only provide a partial picture, and more strategic information is likely to be confidential. This means that you may make incorrect assumptions in planning your response to competitor action.

Using Out-of-date Information

Records should be carefully checked and maintained. Using poor quality data can ruin the best campaigns.

FOR MORE INFORMATION

Books:
Hussey, David, and Per Jenster. *Competitor Intelligence: Turning Analysis into Success*. New York: Wiley, 1999.
Smith, D. V. L., and J. H. Fletcher. *Inside Information: Making Sense of Marketing Data*. New York: Wiley, 2001.

Web site:
Marketresearch.com: **www.marketresearch.com**

"Competition is warfare."

Andrew Grove

Involving Customers in Product or Service Development

GETTING STARTED

For some people "new product development" means inventing something new. In reality, though, most new products are modifications of existing ideas. In some cases, "new product development" can also mean adding an element of service onto a product.

The power of new product development is that your business may be able meet a customer's need more closely than the competition. Involving customers creates the possibility of your product or service being tailor-made for them, thereby encouraging loyalty.

FAQs

Is there a risk in letting customers evaluate new products before launch?

There are two risks. First, the customer may be extremely disappointed with the product if quality is poor. Second, there is a risk that competitors could find out about your plans indirectly. The quality issue is one that you should deal with: if a product is not right, it should not be given to customers in any form—it is not enough simply to promise future improvements. The security risk of a leak to competitors can be minimized through disclosure and confidentiality agreements, although these provide no real guarantee. Having said that, the advantages of involving customers outweigh the risks, so evaluation is worthwhile.

How practical is it for customers and suppliers to collaborate on product development?

There are different levels of collaboration. Some may involve regular meetings to provide input and review progress. These meetings can be held on site or remotely, using videoconference links. In some cases, customer staff may work alongside the supplier team for all or part of the project. Collaboration like this can provide other benefits for the customer by improving the technical knowledge of their staff.

Does preannouncement put new product launches at risk?

Some companies, particularly in the IT sector, have put themselves under unnecessary pressure by trying to meet a series of preannounced release dates. The schedule may not allow proper time for development, resulting in failure to meet the date, or the release of a product that is not ready. Both are potentially damaging.

MAKING IT HAPPEN
Ask Customers before You Launch Your Product

If you are planning a new product or redeveloping an existing one, ask your customers for their views on the existing product and what they would like to see in a new

one. By explaining your plans and involving customers in product development, you can strengthen relationships and provide a service that is mutually beneficial. Questions could include:

- How is the product used?
- How can we improve the current product?
- What problems have been encountered?
- What new features would customers welcome?
- Do the plans represent an improvement?
- Would customers make greater use of a product that included the features they have highlighted?

Establish a User Group

You can encourage feedback and build a sense of community by setting up a user group which could operate as a "virtual community" on the Internet or meet at events. The user group can serve as a forum for discussing issues of mutual concern to customers such as quality, performance, standards, and future developments. The group would include representatives from your own company and from a cross-section of your customers. Comments from the user group provide valuable feedback on current performance and help to identify needs that can be met through new product development.

Ask Customers to Evaluate New Products

Customer evaluation, or beta testing, is well established in the software industry. Customers test new products or upgraded versions before they are released to the market. They identify any problems in using the software, thus providing valuable feedback on product performance.

Issue New Product Announcements

Another valuable practice from the IT industry is to preannounce new products. For example, a company will set a number of release dates during the coming year when it will release new versions of products. The company outlines the new products and gives customers the opportunity to provide input to the development process. The major benefit for customers is that they can align their own development plans to the release dates.

Work in Partnership with Customers

Product development can be a joint initiative where you work closely with specific customers to develop products that meet their specific needs. This approach is a valuable one where:

- your customers have developed partnership sourcing to take advantage of your technology;
- your customers have technology and technical skills that complement your own, and a joint project can produce more effective results;
- you want to strengthen relationships with key customers by working in partnership on joint development projects.

"We don't believe in market research for a new product unknown to the public. So we never do any."

Akio Morita

The latest networking systems and collaborative software tools make it possible to create "virtual teams" of key contacts (including suppliers and partners) who can collaborate as appropriate.

Understand Your Customers' Markets

The new products you develop could enable your customers to improve their competitive performance, so it is important to understand their markets. Tell customers about your product plans and ask them for input to your development process. By building a detailed picture of their markets, you can align your own plans with them, and develop products that are tailored to their needs.

- What are their main markets?
- What is their position in the marketplace?
- Who are their main competitors?
- How are their products regarded in the marketplace?
- What are the key success factors in the market?
- What are the long-term product trends?
- What new technical developments will be needed to succeed?
- Could innovation help your customers to succeed?
- Are your customers considering entry into new markets?
- Do you have product development plans that are relevant to the new market?

Understand Customer Strategies

It is equally important to understand your customers' business strategies: their corporate direction and key objectives, and how they aim to succeed. By aligning your product development objectives with theirs, and showing how your products or services can help them to achieve their strategic business objectives, you can improve the chances of your new products being successful.

There are two possible approaches to customer-focused product development. Where your customers want to become market leaders through innovation, your new product programs can help them to develop the right level of innovation without investment in their own skills. Where they want to succeed through competitive pricing, you can help them to reduce overall costs by developing cost-effective products.

Assess Your Products and Services

Products that help your customers to meet their strategic business objectives can increase the chances of new product success. The more your customers depend on your new product, the more demanding they will be. If you can, keep up with their demands, try to anticipate and meet them, and you'll not only help yourself but also create barriers for your competitors.

For example, if your customer must develop new products quickly in order to retain and protect market share, your own new products can be critical to their product development program.

Analyze Your Customers' Technical Requirements

When you're assessing new product development opportunities, think about how your products can help your customers. They can use your skills in a number of ways, such as:

- improving the performance of their own products and services by using your design and development skills. They may gain privileged access to your technical skills to improve their own competitive performance;
- using your technical expertise to enhance the skills of their own technical staff. This enables them to make a more effective contribution to their own product development process;
- using your technical resources to handle product development on a subcontract basis. This provides your partners with access to specialist resources or to additional research and development capacity to improve the performance of their product development programs;
- using your technical expertise to develop new products that they could not achieve themselves. This provides your customers with new technology, and allows them to diversify in line with your specialist skills;
- using your design skills to improve through life costs (the total cost of owning and using a product, including purchase price, maintenance, and any other related costs). By conducting value engineering studies on your customers' products, you may be able to reduce overall costs and improve reliability by designing components that are easier to assemble and maintain.

COMMON MISTAKES
Not Involving Your Customers Sufficiently

Product development should be focused on customer needs. Although most companies conduct research before development, the research may not provide the detailed input that is essential. Product development may also be driven by technology, with no clear market focus. The more your customer depends on your product, the more likely it is to succeed, so involving customers can pay real dividends.

Ignoring User Groups

Many companies established user groups in response to a crisis and then fail to use them. This can be frustrating for customers and wasteful for the companies. User groups provide a valuable perspective on products and services, and their feedback can provide real benefits for the product development process.

FOR MORE INFORMATION

Book:
Ulwick, Anthony W. *What Customers Want: Using Outcome-Driven Innovation to Create Breakthrough Products and Services.* New York: McGraw-Hill, 2005.

Web site:
American Marketing Association:
www.marketingpower.com

See also:
☆ Integrating Real and Virtual Strategies (pp. 180–181)
✓ Introducing a New Product to Market (pp. 755–756)
☆ Managing New-product Portfolios (pp. 349–350)
☆ Power Struggling and Power Sharing (pp. 126–127)

"If you pretest your product with consumers and pretest your advertising, you will do well in the marketplace."

David Ogilvy

Making Better Use of Customer Data

GETTING STARTED

To get full benefit from customer data, analyze it, and make it available to the right people. Review data and focus on questions important to your business. Where possible, create a data analysis team to be responsible for identifying the data required, collecting it, analyzing it, and distributing it.

FAQs

How do I conduct regular data analysis, when I don't have internal resources or the budget to use a research company?

Business intelligence software can speed up and simplify the process of analysis. You could also recruit a research and analysis team from different departments. This would have the added benefit of making sure that data was available and relevant to the company as a whole.

Can I conduct customer data analysis without sophisticated software?

You can use manual techniques to analyze and distribute customer information. Software speeds up and enhances the process. A good information network insures that everyone has access to the same, up-to-date customer information.

Should I make the same information available throughout the company?

Although that seems like a good idea, it can create its own problems. Too much data can overwhelm people. Good software programs include selective reporting processes, allowing you to select the right data for different audiences and to customize reports. In this way, people get the level of information that they need.

Should I put confidential customer data on an intranet or other internal network?

Provided security procedures are in place to protect the data, it is safe to do this. You could, for example, restrict access to a secure area of the network by issuing passwords to authorized users.

MAKING IT HAPPEN

Put Data in the Right Hands

Business and market data can provide a wealth of information about customers and about purchasing patterns. To get full benefit from the data, you need to analyze it and make the results readily available to the people who need it.

Identify Data Requirements

Create a network of other people in the company who can tell you what questions need to be answered and quantified. Make these people responsible for reviewing data and focus on the questions that are important to different groups within the company.

Create a Data Analysis Team

As well as creating a network of reviewers, you need to create a data analysis team, which is responsible for determining what data to collect and analyze. They should understand what metrics are important to the organization and how these are created and applied. They should also feed information to the rest of the organization.

Make Data Accessible

Make sure that the reports can be exported into tools such as spreadsheets, graphics, and slides, and decide how frequently you need to provide analysis. To save time, you may be able to automate the more frequent processes and keep the level of analysis simple. Most people really just want the key points. Your users can drill down through the data to obtain more detailed information.

Provide Self-service Reports

Create a secure area on an intranet for employees to access reports and look up the latest statistics. Store the reports in a format that can be imported easily to standard spreadsheets such as Excel.

Provide Flexible Archiving

Let other members of the company have access to your reports and data and create a discussion group for reviewing the results. Use the feedback to help refine the analysis process and metrics used in analyzing the data. As the volume of data grows, storage and archiving may become more difficult. Networked storage can increase flexibility and access, and this may be a useful route for you to explore.

Keep Analyzing Data

The data becomes more valuable as you continue analyzing it. As your analysis base broadens, you'll be able to track not only how profitable your company has become, but also how profitable it can be in the future through best practice in data management.

Track Customer Satisfaction

Effective business intelligence allows you to identify early indicators of customer dissatisfaction and take action to retain customers for the long term. Customer retention depends on factors that cannot be tracked by mainstream indicators of customer dissatisfaction, such as revenue and growth.

Identify Warning Signs

Business intelligence can identify the early warning signs of customer dissatisfaction, such as late shipments, and the reasons behind complaints, returns, and claims. With this information, customer service teams can increase retention rates for high-profit customers, spot early indicators of customer dissatisfaction, and maximize the profitability of each service relationship.

Measure Delivery

Measuring on-time delivery lets customer service teams

"The importance of collecting data for the purpose of enabling the manufacturer to ascertain how many additional customers he will acquire by a given reduction in the price of the article he makes cannot be too strongly pressed."
Charles Babbage

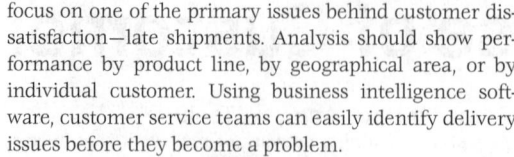

focus on one of the primary issues behind customer dissatisfaction—late shipments. Analysis should show performance by product line, by geographical area, or by individual customer. Using business intelligence software, customer service teams can easily identify delivery issues before they become a problem.

Analyze Complaints, Returns, and Claims

Typically, most individual returns, claims, or complaints can be assigned to a relatively small number of reasons. Establishing categories of problem, rather than analyzing problems case by case, lets customer service teams quickly trace complaints to their source and identify trends. Problems related to a specific product, plant, or production run can be addressed before customer relationships are jeopardized. Analyzing the reasons behind customer complaints makes it easy for customer service teams to be more responsive.

Measure Cost of Service Relationships

Understanding the cost of service relationships lets companies adjust pricing, based on the information that flows through the company. Returns, orders changes, claims, and so on all have an impact on the bottom line. When the true cost of a service relationship is known, pricing can be adjusted to increase profitability.

Measure All Customer-facing Activities

The same measurements can be applied to marketing, customer service, or sales activities. The metrics should also be applicable to all customer channels and distribution mediums. This allows you to monitor the effectiveness of customer marketing or communication programs: for example, comparing the cost per lead on the Web versus direct mail, or cross-selling over the Web compared with the call center.

Develop High-profitability Strategies for Marketing

Business intelligence tools can be the key to developing highly profitable marketing strategies. Special software allows you to understand and analyze issues such as the effectiveness of marketing campaigns, or profit levels by customer. The software enables marketing teams to explore any combination of data—for example, revenues by customer, product, or region—making it easy to spot trends. It helps uncover significant, but often hidden, factors that have an impact on market share, such as price, product design, or packaging. It also provides access to transaction-level data, so that marketing teams can easily explore detailed information to find out what lies behind trends.

Analyze Strategic Marketing Activities

Strategic marketing analysis highlights product attributes and other information that is typically left out of marketing plans. For example, marketing teams can analyze revenue by products, distribution channel, materials, and other factors. This makes it easy to see which products are driving sales and profitability in each market and to focus strategies accordingly. Marketing can identify the factors behind profitability, from the product attribute level up.

Analyze Tactical Marketing Programs

Tactical marketing analysis lets marketing teams evaluate the effectiveness of marketing campaigns. They can explore the impact of marketing messages in different parts of the country by industry type, or by the buyers they are targeting. And, by comparing response profiles against the profile of high-profit customers, they can adjust messaging and media mixes for maximum impact.

Analyze Customer Portfolios

The customer portfolio analysis categorizes customers by profitability and charts their lifetime value to date. Marketing managers can analyze customers by profitability tier, view trends in the profitability mix, and develop strategies to address unprofitable customers.

COMMON MISTAKES
Using Raw Data

Data is only valuable when it is both analyzed and used to address a specific question. Software tools allow you to conduct analysis quickly and easily so as to provide relevant results to answer important questions.

Measuring the Wrong Activities

It may be easy to collect data on a specific activity, but if the activity is unimportant the effort is wasted. By getting agreement from customer-facing groups throughout the company, you can identify important data.

Distributing Data in the Wrong Form

Make sure data is in a form that is useful to the recipient. People don't have time to go through masses of unsifted data to find the information they need.

Limited Analysis

The more you analyze data, the more valuable it becomes. You can uncover different levels of detail, spot trends, or identify recurring problems. You also should make sure that the information is up to date, by continuing to collect data.

FOR MORE INFORMATION

Books:
Berry, Michael J. *Data Mining Techniques for Marketing, Sales, and Customer Relationship Management.* 2nd ed. New York: Wiley, 2004.
Stone, Merlin, et al. *Consumer Insight: How to Use Data and Market Research to Get Closer to Your Customer.* Milford, CT: Kogan Page, 2004.

Web site:
Marketing Research Association: **www.mra-net.org**

See also:
✔ Conducting Market Research (pp. 735–737)
✔ Increasing Customer Lifetime Value (pp. 706–707)
☆ Managing 1:1 Marketing (pp. 63–64)

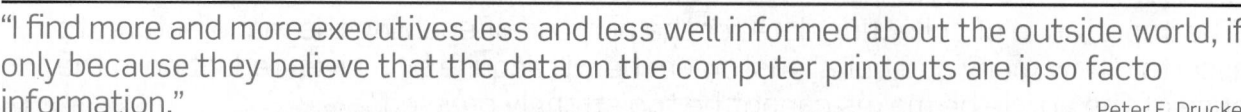

"I find more and more executives less and less well informed about the outside world, if only because they believe that the data on the computer printouts are ipso facto information."

Peter F. Drucker

Profiling Decision Makers

GETTING STARTED

In business purchasing, more than one person influences the choice of supplier. A decision-making team could include a variety of key personnel, and the influence of team members varies at different stages during the purchasing process. It is important to identify the members of the team and communicate with each at the appropriate stage.

FAQs

How can I identify a purchasing team when my sales representatives only meet the purchasing manager?

You need to find out who within your customer's company is interested in your products. Telephone research, direct mail, or advertising with a response mechanism can help to identify other team members. Be careful about direct approaches—purchasing managers may guard their status and resent approaches to other team members that appear to be undermining their position.

My organization sells low-value commodity components. Do I need to identify a complete decision making team?

On the surface, your task should be simple. Just deal with the person who orders the products. However, there may be bigger opportunities. The technical manager may not be happy with the performance of commodity products. The research team or the marketing department may be planning new products, which could change the product specification. You need to monitor changing customer requirements.

My organization needs to talk to senior directors about the strategic importance of our products. How can we do this when our sales team never gets the opportunity to meet directors?

It is unlikely that directors would have time during the normal working day to meet sales representatives or regard a sales meeting as high on their list of priorities. You could arrange a seminar or executive briefing session that would appeal to directors. That would insure you meet the right people and give you the opportunity to find out more about their needs.

MAKING IT HAPPEN
Identify the Decision Makers

In business purchasing, more than one person influences the choice of supplier. Individuals make different contributions to the decision making process and have different information requirements. Many companies have adopted team purchasing structures to deal with high-value purchases and it is important that you communicate effectively with every member of the team.

Depending on the value and complexity of the purchase, a decision making team could include:
- senior executives

- purchasing professionals
- technical employees
- manufacturing managers
- service providers
- marketing employees
- departmental managers

Assess the Importance of the Purchase

As a rough guideline, you are likely to be dealing with a powerful purchasing organization if any of the following conditions apply:
- Your product is a vital component, or strategically important to your customers.
- Your product is technically complex.
- Your product is of high value.

If your product is of relatively low value, purchasing decisions are more likely to revolve around price and delivery, and it is unlikely that a team would be involved.

The influence of team members varies at different stages during the purchasing process:
- Purchasing employees and departmental managers may have considerable early influence when a specification is being drawn up.
- When proposals are being evaluated, technical employees may be more influential.
- Senior executives are unlikely to be interested in detail, but they need an overview of the overall business benefits of the product or service.

Senior Executives

Senior executives need an overview of the business benefits of a product or service and seek reassurance that your organization is capable of supplying their long-term needs—any risk could be detrimental to their own business. Many suppliers try to move discussion of their products and services to board level to demonstrate that they are of strategic importance. This can be a useful exercise in developing business, because it can build a level of dependency that is important to account control.

Purchasing Professionals

Purchasing professionals are usually the key figures in a purchasing team. While they may not take sole responsibility for decision making, they are likely to be the team leaders and will remain your main point of contact.

Many companies operate a preferred supplier program and, to be recognized, you may have to meet a detailed list of criteria. The purchasing department is instrumental in managing the list of approved suppliers. Many of the preferred supplier programs include rating systems to measure suppliers' performance; these are part of a process of developing effective relationships, so that purchasing professionals can provide an even better service to their internal customers.

Finance Executives

Finance executives have ultimate control over purchasing budgets and they're likely to be involved if purchases

---

are complex or entail major capital expenditure. They seek reassurance that they are getting value for their money and that their purchase represents the best return on investment. They may consider alternative methods of financing, and you may be able to improve your competitive position by offering flexible plans such as leasing or deferred payments.

Technical Employees
Technical employees are a vital part of the purchasing team. They are responsible for improving the performance of the company products in order to develop a competitive edge. You therefore need to be closely involved with the technical team at a number of stages. When they are developing new products, you should be involved at the planning stages so you can influence the design. When they are enhancing existing products, you should be developing proposals to improve product performance. If they are moving into new markets, you can support them by handling contract development services or by training their employees. You can provide them with a variety of specialist technical services that enable them to provide a better service to their internal customers.

Manufacturing Managers
If you are introducing an innovative product, or you have identified an opportunity to improve your customers' manufacturing operations or reduce costs, you need to influence manufacturing specialists.

Service Providers
If you provide professional services rather than products, make sure that you are dealing with a service provider. Service providers are responsible for areas such as maintenance, training, administration, logistics, and computers, and other services that enable business processes to operate efficiently. By working with them, you can improve relationships and increase customers' dependency on your organization.

Marketing Employees
Marketing specialists insure that a product or service adds value and helps the company to develop a stronger competitive position. They will play an important part in decision making if your customers are seeking to improve their market position or are entering new markets where you have a specific expertise.

Departmental Managers
Departmental managers are often the users of your products or services. They need to be reassured that they will benefit from dealing with a particular supplier. They play an important role in specifying the product and evaluating the performance of existing suppliers.

Research Decision Makers
Although it is simple to list potential decision makers, it is more complicated to identify who is actually involved in the process. Many decision makers may not have a direct role in a project team or may be involved in only part of the purchasing process, so you need to look carefully at your research processes.

Your sales team in regular contact with the customer should be best placed to identify the key decision makers. There are a number of other techniques for identifying other influencers, such as:
- independent research into how companies buy different types of product or service; the survey may be limited to a specific group of customers, or conducted across a whole industry;
- published industry surveys on buying patterns; these provide broad guidelines to the key decision makers but need to be qualified by specific account research;
- direct response advertising, in which responses are analyzed to identify decision making patterns;
- joint projects, in which members of the customer team work with members of your team; the relationships and approval procedures that emerge provide useful clues about who are the hidden decision makers.

Research like this should be conducted continuously, because purchasing is a dynamic activity. Members of the decision making team may change their jobs and, as the process progresses, individual contributions change.

COMMON MISTAKES
Concentrating on the Wrong People
Don't focus your sales team on the wrong decision makers. Companies rarely make it clear who influences the purchasing decisions. Meetings with the purchasing manager could be wasted if someone else draws up the specification.

Communicating at the Wrong Level
You may think you are just selling your customers a product or a service, but your product may make an important contribution to their business. If it is an innovative component that enables them to develop a new product or enter new markets, your company then becomes a potential strategic partner. Make sure that you communicate this to the right people.

Failing to Keep Up to Date
Purchasing requirements change and so do the people who make the decisions. Customers may launch new products, drop old ones, or acquire other companies. People come and go, and that influences the structure of the decision making team.

FOR MORE INFORMATION

Books:
Parinello, Anthony. *Getting to the VITO (The Very Important Top Officer): Ten Steps to VITO's Office.* New York: Wiley, 2005.
Tuleja, Tad, et al. *The New Successful Large Account Management: Maintaining and Growing Your Most Important Assets—Your Customers.* Revised ed. New York: Warner Books, 2005.

Web site:
Marketing Research Association: **www.mra-net.org**

"Good decisions come from wisdom. Wisdom comes from experience. Experience comes from bad decisions."

Anonymous

Branding a Business Product

ACTIONLIST

GETTING STARTED

Branding is as important in business markets as it is in consumer markets, and buyers feel more confident buying from a reliable company. Indeed, some buyers may be reluctant to buy new products that are not proven.

FAQs

How can I identify brand attributes?

Brand attributes are not always obvious. A good starting point is customer research. What do your customers feel is important when they buy? Compare their requirements against the performance of your own products and your company. Alternatively, look at your competitors and consider your comparative strengths.

What do I do if my brand attributes look poor?

Customers admire a company that is committed to continuous improvement, so start looking for improvements, particularly in the attributes that are most important to customers. Make sure you communicate any improvement.

Is it possible to measure the effect of branding?

In consumer markets, companies use tracking research to monitor changes in customer perceptions of the company. This research can indicate whether customers see your company in a more favorable light. This, in turn, can increase the likelihood of future sales.

My advertising budget is limited. Should I concentrate on product messages or brand-building messages?

Product messages are more likely to generate short-term revenue. That could increase your marketing budget over time. However, it would be wrong to neglect brand-building messages completely. You would be sacrificing long-term business development.

An increasing proportion of sales are coming via the Internet. Does this mean brand values are now less important?

With more and more crowding on the Internet, companies will have to work hard to stand out. Brand values will remain important.

MAKING IT HAPPEN

Why Business Branding Is Important

Branding is as important in business markets as in consumer markets. Business buyers, however, look for a different set of brand values. They ask what a product or service can do for their business.

Using the Brand Values

The following list covers the key attributes. Once you have identified the attributes that are most important to your customers and prospects, you can emphasize them in your communications. If an attribute is important to customers, but is currently weak, you should consider ways of improving performance.

Fitness for Purpose

The product should be fit for its purpose. Does it meet the buyer's specification or conform to industry standards? Approval by recognized authorities is important.

Value for Money and Quality

Value for money may be important to some buyers. That does not mean buyers will always look for the lowest price. Some customers may be happy to pay more for a product with an integral maintenance package. Quality can be an important differentiator. Japanese companies led the way in transforming their brand values with massive improvements in quality. Companies that excel in quality build confidence.

Extendability

If you supply a variety of products or services, brand values should be extendable to the entire range. This can help to build incremental business and strengthen customer loyalty.

Company Reliability

Buyers feel more confident buying from a reliable company. That means solid financial performance, a strong management team, a good industrial relations record, and a track record in effective products.

Proven Products

Some buyers may be reluctant to buy new products that are not proven. They don't like to think that their companies are being treated as proving grounds for product development laboratories.

Investing in Product Development

Customers want to know that products are being continuously improved. They are not necessarily interested in leading-edge products, but they want to know that they are getting the best products currently available.

Distribution and Financing

If distribution is poor, customers can't buy the product. The importance of distribution varies by product, and the recent growth of direct sales via the Internet is reducing its importance. However, certain products, such as components or supplies, continue to depend on effective national distribution. The availability of financing may be important to some customers. Capital goods have long been marketed with a financing package, but financing is also available on many lower-value products. Attractive interest rates or payment terms can differentiate a product.

Service Backup

Service backup is vital to products that a customer de-

"I believe that if you're going to take someone on, you might as well take on the biggest brand in the world."

Richard Branson

pends on. The loss of a critical process can prove damaging, so a customer wants to know that service response will be rapid.

Training
Training helps customers make effective use of a product. Many companies operate their own training departments or develop distance learning packages, to make sure that customer staff become familiar with new products.

Customized Products
Customized products may represent higher value than standard versions. Customers have individual needs and a standard product may not prove an exact fit. By modifying, you can meet needs more effectively.

Partnership
Working in partnership with a customer can increase the value of the relationship. Partnership may mean working on joint development projects or providing a package of services that support a customer throughout the life cycle of the product. Partnership strengthens customer relationships and can weaken the impact of competitive activity. Collaboration on joint projects is now much easier with the growth of videoconferencing and other communications.

Administration and Customer Service
Efficient administration makes it easier to buy from a company. Lost orders, inaccurate invoices, and poor correspondence do not impress customers. Quality of customer service is a key measure of a company's values. Customer service takes many forms, from the way a customer's initial inquiry is handled to the quality of aftercare. In a number of companies, customer service is viewed as a strategic activity, with dedicated staff and documented procedures.

Consulting
Consulting can move a company from commodity supplier to valued partner. Presales advice is critical with complex or high-value products, and the quality of advice can determine where the order goes.

Technical Support
The scope of technical support ranges from advice on the right product for an application, to after-sales user support and problem solving. In complex products, the quality of technical support can be the most important differentiator.

Environmental Issues
Products must conform to environmental legislation, but companies are also measured by the effects of their processes on the environment. Using materials from nonrenewable sources or contributing to pollution can damage a company's image.

Ordering and Product Information
Simple ordering procedures make it easier for customers to do business. Many companies have automated their ordering processes to reduce the time a customer has to spend on administration. Quality brochures, detailed product guides, comprehensive information on the Internet, and clear presentations help buyers make informed decisions.

Delivery
Delivery, like administration, is not seen as a key marketing activity, but it has an impact on brand perceptions.

Customer Base
Buyers assess a product by the customers who already use it. A blue-chip customer list demonstrates product quality and approval.

COMMON MISTAKES
Neglecting the "Soft" Issues
Many companies communicate their strengths in the "hard" attributes, such as quality, performance, and price. Customers may take these for granted, particularly in a commodity market. The "soft" attributes such as customer service or technical support, can prove to be key.

Ignoring Branding
Traditionally, branding has been seen as a consumer marketing discipline. Business marketing was seen as different; buyers were assumed to be rational and decisions were believed to depend primarily on price and performance. Research has shown that business purchase decisions are more complex, and companies base their decisions on a variety of factors. Business-to-business companies ignore branding at their peril.

Concentrating on the Wrong Attributes
It's essential to communicate what customers feel is important. In technology markets, quality of support and commitment to product development may outweigh price and delivery. In commodity markets, support and information can differentiate products with no performance advantage.

Failing to Communicate Brand Strengths
Communications that focus only on the product won't sell important brand strengths. Customer presentations, corporate brochures, public relations activities, and advertising can be used to present a more balanced picture.

FOR MORE INFORMATION

Books:
Hutt, Michael, and Speh, Thomas. *Business Marketing Management: A Strategic View of Industrial and Organizational Markets.* Mason, OH: South Western College Publishing, 2003.
Koehn, Nancy F. *Brand New: How Entrepreneurs Earned Consumers' Trust from Wedgwood to Dell.* Boston, MA: Harvard Business School Press, 2001.

Web site:
American Marketing Association:
www.marketingpower.com

Raising Awareness of Your Brand

GETTING STARTED

Brand awareness is an important factor in customer purchasing decisions. Brand values relate to many areas, from product attributes to less tangible aspects of a company's reputation. By identifying the key values of your brand you can establish how your products, your services, and your company are perceived by different types of customer.

FAQs

Can a small company use branding?

Absolutely. You have to understand your own brand, since you will have a brand or corporate image in your market whether you like it or not! Smaller companies increasingly compete with large, well-known, brands—sometimes globally—so the objective of branding is to differentiate your company or product and to convey its unique attributes.

How important are brand values?

Branding is frequently perceived as a consumer marketing discipline. However, industry experience indicates that business-to-business purchasing is a complex process influenced by intangible perceptions as much as by hard facts on product performance.

MAKING IT HAPPEN

Identify the Most Important Elements of a Brand

The key attributes of a business brand may include the following:

- fitness for purpose—is it the best at what it does?
- value for the money—if not offered at always the lowest price, does it represent a good deal compared to the competition, even if it isn't better?
- quality—is it simply better built or better managed?
- extendability—does the brand work in many related markets?
- company reliability—does the brand come from a good "stable?"
- proven products—is the brand associated with established successes?
- investment in product development—is innovation significant?

Find Out What Is Important to Your Customers

Although these brand values can be applied to business products in general terms, it's vital to understand how individual customers rank the values. This can be determined in several ways, described below.

Talk to Customers

This is the simplest way to find out what they value, but take care not to talk exclusively about the physical benefits of a product. There will almost certainly be aspects of service that are as important. You should also ask "open" questions about the competition for example:

- Who else have you looked at?
- What do you think of them?
- What is their biggest strength or weakness?
- What do other people think of them?

Conduct Customer Surveys

To find out what your customers consider important, conduct a survey; if your budget runs to it, this should be done through a market research company so that respondents feel the survey is independent. It should ask respondents how they rank the different brand values and how they believe your company and a number of competitors compare across these values.

Run a Focus Group

A focus group can be used to cover the same ground as the customer survey, but it enables you to cover the subject in greater depth and to raise issues that you may not anticipate or that would normally be outside the scope of a survey. Focus groups are ideal for identifying branding issues that concern customers, assessing customer reactions to potential changes, or identifying any problems customers are experiencing.

Review Industry Trends

Industry associations and publishers produce regular surveys into buying behavior in their industry sector. These surveys can highlight issues that concern the whole market.

Find Out about Customer Purchasing Requirements

An increasing number of business customers use formal criteria to evaluate potential suppliers and monitor their performance. These purchasing criteria indicate the factors that your customers believe are important and can help to identify the key messages you should include in your own brand communications.

Communicate through All Channels

Advertising and marketing communications are the most important media for raising awareness. However, there are several other direct and indirect channels, including:

- products—the design and brand symbolism can convey significant brand values;
- services—the way you deal with customers can demonstrate your commitment to their needs;
- packaging—can carry messages regarding your brand;
- distribution facilities—can give an impression of your approach and values;
- Web sites—must be consistent with your key brand values;
- customer service facilities—must deliver the promise of the brand.

Assess Your Product Branding

Do your products communicate your key brand values? The most important values are listed above, but brand

"With the strongest brands, the C.E.O. owns the brand. It must be owned by someone, the higher in the company the better."

Shelly Lazarus

values extent to every aspect of your company that your customer may experience.

If customer research shows that you are perceived as poor in any of these areas, or if customers are not aware of your strengths, you must look closely at your product development program. Also review your customer communications to see how customers build their image of your brand.

Brand Your Services
Service capability can also help to differentiate a company from its competitors. Many companies have underestimated the importance of service to their customers and as a result haven't adequately communicated their service capabilities. The right services can help customers improve their own business performance and can supplement their own resources, so raising awareness of service capability is an important aspect of brand communication. You can increase awareness through product advertising, product literature, direct marketing, and product public relations, as well as through service communications.

Communicate Brand Values through Packaging
Packaging raises awareness of brand values by the way in which it reflects the corporate identity. The right packaging can visually support your brand through the use of your logo, slogans, promises and company values.

Don't Forget to Include Your Branding Distribution Facilities
Your distribution facilities can affect awareness of your brand. Again, if your budget allows, vehicles, uniforms, and premises should carry the same logo and key messages as other mediums of communication.

Distribution is an area that is frequently overlooked in branding programs, but it can make an important contribution to customer perceptions of your company. For example, the cleanliness of a delivery van shows a level of professionalism.

Build Brand Values through Your Web Site
An effective e-commerce Web site is one in which the various technical and design components all work together to generate customer interest, build trust, communicate product value, and support convenient profitable transactions. Even if you don't sell directly from your Web site, the key is that your customer must feel they have gained something from the visit that exceeds the "cost" (even if only in time) of visiting.

Brand through Customer Service Facilities
Your customer service facilities have a major impact on the way your customers perceive your company. Customer contact takes place both before and after a sale, and these contacts can prove critical in shaping customer attitudes. When your customer service team handles in-

quiries, orders, or complaints effectively, it creates awareness of positive brand values.

Monitor Levels of Brand Awareness
Customer perceptions change over a period of time. Continuous research should be conducted to monitor customer attitudes. This type of research is known as tracking research, and it helps to measure the effectiveness of brand communications programs.

COMMON MISTAKES
Failing to Monitor Customer Perceptions
Regular research is critical. You must know how you are perceived by your customers so that you can plan the way your brand is represented in the future.

Overlooking Individual Customer Preferences
Industry research may give you a broad view of the brand values that are important to customers. However, it's more important to understand how individual customers—particularly your most important customers—rank individual values. This can be achieved only by continuous detailed research into individual customer needs.

Ignoring Important Communication Channels
Brand values are communicated through many different channels, not just advertising and marketing media. Customers' attitudes and perceptions are shaped by packaging, customer service, distribution, and products as well as by other factors. Make sure every aspect of your business reflects the brand values that are important to your customers.

FOR MORE INFORMATION

Book:
Davis, Scott, and Michael Dunn. *Building the Brand-driven Business: Operationalize Your Brand to Drive Profitable Growth*. San Francisco, CA: Jossey-Bass, 2002.

Web sites:
American Marketing Association: **www.marketingpower.com**
Brand Central Station: **www.brandcentralstation.com**

Creating Product Literature

GETTING STARTED
There are many different types of product publication, each of which has a different role in the sales and marketing process.

FAQs

Who should write product literature?
Product and technical specialists should provide the input and content for product literature. However, it is important that this content is edited or rewritten by a professional writer or communications specialist who understands the information needs of the market.

Isn't it easier to produce a single product catalog rather than a variety of publications?
Not necessarily: for example, if the products change frequently, the cost of updating the catalog could well be prohibitive. Where there are a wide variety of products and customers in different market sectors, a single publication may not provide the depth of information needed.

Does the Internet make product publications redundant?
The Internet has made it easier to produce, update, and distribute product information. However, the comfort factor means that demand for printed publications remains high.

MAKING IT HAPPEN
Choose the Right Type of Publication
There are many different types of product publication, each with a different role in the sales and marketing process.

Leaflets
Leaflets or flyers are simple forms of communication used in the early stages of customer contact. They summarize the key benefits of a product or service and help to create initial interest. They are economical to produce and can be updated easily.

Catalogs
Catalogs give customers an indication of the scope of a product range. A catalog provides an overview and should point to other publications that provide more detailed information. It should be clearly laid out so that customers can find the specific information they want quickly and easily.

Product Brochures
The contents should cover:
- product description
- how the product is used
- main benefits to the customer
- important achievements
- market position
- related products or services
- company information
- commercial information such as price or availability

Data Sheets
Data sheets provide the detailed technical information that customers need in order to evaluate products. They should help customers to understand the benefits of a product and to compare it with competitors' offerings.

Product Guides
A product guide provides a highly detailed description of a product and can be issued to the sales force as well as to customers and prospects. It should include the same information as a product brochure but with a far greater level of detail. It should cover:
- description of the product and its main applications;
- analysis of product features;
- product operation and necessary skills;
- accessories, replacement parts, and support services.

Technical Updates
Technical updates are used to keep customers up to date with information on the products they have bought. They also communicate a policy of continuous improvement. The information that has changed may be important to customers, so it must be shown clearly. Any important safety information should be highlighted.

Help Customers Make Informed Decisions
Your customers may not evaluate a product in the way you want them to. You must explain benefits carefully, particularly those that are less obvious such as reduced maintenance costs.

Educate Customers
If your product is innovative, you may need to reinforce product description with customer education in order to explain the product and its potential benefits.

Provide Practical Guidelines on Usage
Your product literature may need to include instructions or guidelines on use to help customers get the best from the product. You should also include information on sources of technical help or other assistance.

Reassure Your Customers
Customers may be reluctant to change from an existing product or supplier. Case histories, testimonials from satisfied customers, lists of existing users, or approval by official bodies can help to reassure customers.

Stress Price and Quality
Customers don't necessarily want the lowest price: they are looking for value for their money. Stress the quality of your product and show how it can save your customers money.

"We read advertisements . . . to discover and enlarge our desires."   Daniel J. Boorstin

Present the Complete Product Range
Customers may be interested in one specific product, but you should refer to your complete range. It may generate cross-selling opportunities, and it also tells customers that they can obtain all their product needs from a single source.

Present Benefits, Not Features
When customers are making an initial assessment of your product, they want to know how it will benefit them. Features become more important when they are comparing your product with competitive offerings.

Recognize Your Customers' Needs
Your copy should demonstrate that you understand your customers' needs. Describe the business and technical issues facing customers, and show how your product helps customers deal with them.

Brand Your Products
It is important to build customer confidence in your products and your company. Reinforce the brand values that you have established in your advertising and direct marketing. Product literature should sell as well as inform.

Offer Related Services
You can add value to your products by offering customers services such as planning, installation, training, and maintenance. These services will help your customers make more effective use of your products and offer them the benefits of an all-in-one package.

Make Effective Use of Product Publications
A brochure may be the most obvious initial suggestion, but the idea should be carefully examined by laying down stringent requirements for in-house users.
- Ask them to make out a business case for the brochure.
- Levy an internal charge on the brochure which must be covered by an increase in revenue.
- Ask them to define a specific communications task for the brochure.

This process not only eliminates ill-considered requests, it also helps to insure a precise brief that will improve the value and performance of the communication, whatever form it eventually takes.

Consider Alternatives to the Brochure
- Customized presentations, where your company has a small number of key customers. A presentation can be customized for each customer and easily updated. The presentation not only provides relevant, highly targeted information, it also increases personal contact with the customer.
- A customer magazine, where you have a larger customer base and your product range or technology changes rapidly. A regular magazine can easily be distributed to the larger target audience.
- A customer handbook, where you work in partnership with a small number of customers. A customer hand-book, generally in loose-leaf form, includes information on both supplier and customer to increase mutual understanding and awareness.
- A customized information pack, where you have a wide product range and a large customer base in many different sectors and where information requirements are therefore highly diversified. An information pack, consisting of a corporate folder or wallet with inserts specific to the sector or customer, provides a flexible communications tool.
- A targeted literature program, where you have a database that allows you to segment your customer base and track purchasing patterns and campaign response. Use the database to develop a contact strategy that begins with introductory literature and goes on to provide groups or individual customers with product information reflecting their specific needs and purchasing patterns.

COMMON MISTAKES
Producing the Wrong Type of Publication
Different types of publications have specific roles in the sales and marketing process. Giving prospective customers detailed product guides when they are only conducting a preliminary evaluation represents wasted effort.

Overlooking Alternatives to Publications
A publication may not always be the most appropriate communications solution. For example, if a prospect has specific product requirements, it may be more appropriate to develop a customized presentation tailored to that prospect.

Producing Information That Is Too Technical
Product information is read by a wide group of different decision makers, including purchasing managers, general managers, technical specialists, and senior executives. The copy must relate to the information needs of each group. Content should reflect all of these interests.

FOR MORE INFORMATION

Books:
Cyr, Lisa. *Brochure Design That Works: Secrets for Successful Brochure Design*. Gloucester, MA: Rockport Publishers Inc., 2002.
Yadin, Daniel. *Creative Marketing Communications*. 3rd ed. Milford, CT: Kogan Page, 2001.

Web site:
American Marketing Association:
www.marketingpower.com

See also:
✔ Producing a Corporate Brochure (pp. 759–760)
✔ Running a Product Public Relations Campaign (pp. 763–764)

"Dull times are the very times when you need advertising most."   William Wrigley

Extending a Product with Service

GETTING STARTED

"Service" is a business concept that's often overlooked or relegated to somewhere in between maintenance and problem solving. Done properly, though, service can be a key differentiator between your business and the competition. Meeting customer requirements in the most appropriate and efficient way adds enormously to the perceived value of your product and can sometimes increase the profitability of your relationship.

FAQs

My product is a market leader. Why would services be important?

Services can add further value to a product, providing incremental income and increasing customer loyalty. Services provide you with an opportunity to work with a customer long after the initial sale and to develop your relationship with them.

I already offer free installation and maintenance with my products. Does that add value?

Yes. But while some customers may expect this, others may not, or may not value the service. Many companies have recognized the importance of service to certain customers, and have changed their service strategy accordingly. Instead of offering free service to everyone, they have upgraded the services, increased the range of services offered, and therefore, in some cases, started charging customers. Although customers may initially object to being charged for something that seemed to be free, they may see the value of a service that now more closely meets their needs.

I don't have the skills or resources to deliver services. How can I offer my customers a service?

You can either build your own service team through recruitment and training or work in partnership with a specialist organization which will deliver service on your behalf.

My customers have their own internal service people. Why should they want to use my services?

Many companies have internal service departments. They can be expensive to maintain, however, and are sometimes lacking in essential skills. For example, they may not be trained in the latest software. By demonstrating the potential savings and benefits of outsourcing a service, you can persuade them to switch to you.

MAKING IT HAPPEN
Differentiate Your Product with Service

Service is proving to be a key differentiator in many market sectors. In many companies, however, the role of the service department should be more than simply maintenance and problem solving. For example, a company supplying industrial dishwashers to the restaurant trade has to respond quickly to breakdowns—replacing the machine if necessary rather than simply scheduling a repair visit. So, to take full advantage of the service opportunity, it is important to explain the benefits of effective service to customers, and present your service operations as convenient, cost-effective, and strategically important.

Meet Key Service Attributes

These are some of the key features that customers may be looking for in a service offer:
- one contact point, simplifying contact and service administration
- direct contact with a technical specialist, providing an immediate response to problems or queries wherever the customer is located
- quality support to a standard such as ISO 9000, giving independent reassurance that service standards are high
- support around the clock, meaning that it is available when customers need it, minimizes interruption of their business
- service options give a choice of service levels, which can be aligned to customers' needs
- investment in support means long-term commitment to the customer

Provide One Contact Point for Service Resources

Whether your customers have a technical query, a service request, or a product inquiry, or need advice, guidance, or information, they should be able to call one number for direct access to all your support resources. Ideally, you'll have specialists on the spot to deal with their requests. If they can't answer the query immediately, make sure that the right person calls the customer back.

Offer Direct Contact with Technical Specialists

Your customers may have a technical query, and want to talk to an experienced specialist immediately. When they call the technical help desk, they should be talking to a highly skilled person with extensive technical support and field experience. It may mean locating support staff in accessible locations to be able to make visits quickly and efficiently.

Provide Good Quality Support

When your customers have a service request, they should be able to contact a central service point where a service coordinator ensures that the right specialist help is available. Service coordinators should make sure that customers get the fastest and most effective response to their requests. In some cases, service points can deal with requests directly, but if not, they can assign an engineer to visit the customer site within agreed times. All

"A successful product merely gives us a head start in the race."   Sir John Harvey-Jones

754

ACTIONLIST

service processes should be assessed to ISO 9000. If customers have any queries, there should be an "escalation procedure" to move a customer complaint up to a more senior team member if the person dealing with the complaint initially cannot resolve it. This should ensure a prompt resolution of any problems.

Offer Flexible Service Options

You can provide your customers with a choice of flexible service options to suit their operational needs and to increase their loyalty. If your customers have in-house support, you can support their team with an efficient spares delivery service, or manage their spares for them. You can also offer to enhance the skills of your customer's in-house team with training, advice and guidance, technical support, and access to specialists. You may go as far as offering consulting on a fee basis, utilizing your specialist knowledge to help your customer.

Invest in Support

High quality service for your market may require a significant investment in the service infrastructure: the right premises, efficient service communications, and a sophisticated service management system to enable you to enhance your response and performance even further. It may require you to appoint one person with specific responsibility for customer service or, perhaps, develop a dedicated support Web site.

Add Value to a Product

Improving your customer service may add value and help to differentiate your products and services from the competition. By analyzing the products and services in your range (and those of your competitors), you can add relevant value and improve a customer's perception of your business. Some examples are:

- business services that free up customer staff to do more important tasks, or help managers perform their jobs better. Training, for example, can insure that staff make more effective use of the products the company buys;
- complementary services to make a consumer product more attractive. Film processing could, for example, be offered with a camera;
- convenience services added to a basic service to enhance it. Insurance companies, for example, might add a helpline or list of approved repairers to help their customers recover more quickly from an accident.

Develop Product/Service Packages

To add value to products and to increase customer loyalty, put together "bundles" of products and services that reflect customer needs. The list below shows examples of this.

"Adding-in" Services

- special package tours, including flights, hotel, and guides
- cellular service that includes a personal 800 number

"Leaving-out" Services

- quick car care centers, without non-essential services
- real estate brokers that offer fewer services at fixed fees

Added Value Services

- home delivery of fast food or videos
- support and advice through helplines

Changing Distribution Channels

- direct sales, bypassing retailers, such as organic fruit "basket programs"
- electronic delivery, such as delivery of technical drawings and specifications

COMMON MISTAKES
Offering Only Basic Services

Basic services such as installation, maintenance, and upgrades are available from many different service organizations. They do not differentiate you and they do not add value. Higher-value services, requiring skill, knowledge, or experience, are the keys to success.

Failing to Invest in a Service Infrastructure

Customers expect a quality service. That means you have to invest in people and infrastructure. Ideally, your services should conform to recognized industry standards. If you fail to deliver the right standard of service, you could damage customer relationships.

Missing Service Opportunities

Customers require many different services during the time they own a product. Their requirements could include: advice, consulting, and design before the sale; installation and training; then maintenance, upgrading, and other services after the sale. Each of these represents an opportunity to earn incremental income and maintain contact with the customer.

FOR MORE INFORMATION

Books:
Lovelock, Christopher, and Jochen Wirtz. *Services Marketing: People, Technology, Strategy*. 5th ed. Upper Saddle River, NJ: FT Prentice Hall, 2003.
Gronroos, Christian. *Service Management and Marketing: A Customer Relationship Management Approach*. 2nd ed. New York: Wiley, 2000.

Web site:
U.S. Institute of Marketing: **www.usmktg.com**

See also:
- ☆ Delivering and Delighting—A New Spirit at Work (pp. 91–93)
- ✔ Offering Customers Self-Service (pp. 777–778)
- ☆ The Second Coming of Service (pp. 104–105)

"Profit in business comes from repeat customers; customers that boast about your product and service, and that bring friends with them."

W. Edwards Deming

Introducing a New Product to Market

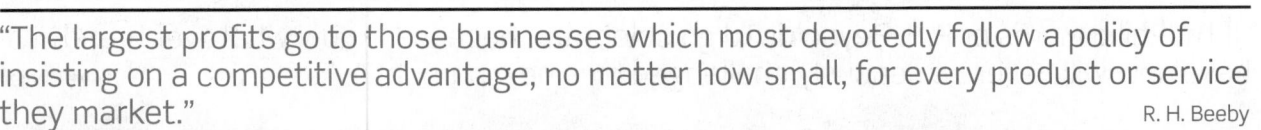
GETTING STARTED

New product launches are crucial to the success of a business and need careful planning. Internal communications are vital to the early success of the program, as is the support of the senior management team.

FAQs

I've heard there is a high rate of new product failure. Is it risky to spend money on a high-profile launch?

Failure to launch properly may be a contributory factor. Provided the product has been carefully researched and developed, an effective launch should contribute to success. It cannot, however, rescue a bad product.

Why spend money on an internal launch, when it is the customers who will determine success?

Unless you have the commitment of the management team and the people who will be responsible for designing, producing, selling, and distributing the product, it is unlikely to get the support or resources it needs to succeed. Internal communication is key.

If a product is good enough, do I need to run sales incentives during the launch period?

Any product has to fight for attention from the sales team and resellers. An incentive may give the new product a vital push during the critical launch period.

MAKING IT HAPPEN
Plan Carefully

New product launches are crucial to the success of a business and reflect a considerable amount of investment. The product launch progresses through a number of important stages:

- internal communications, to guarantee high levels of awareness and commitment to the new product;
- prelaunch activity, to secure distribution and insure that retailers have the skills, resources, and knowledge to market the product;
- launch events at national, regional, or local level;
- postevent activity to help the sales force and retailers make the most of the event;
- launch advertising and other forms of customer communication.

Communicate the Launch Internally

Internal communications are vital to the early success of the program. The new product development team must sell its concepts to the senior management team who will commit resources to the project. They also need to win the support of a number of departments who will form part of the product launch process: manufacturing, design, research and development, distribution, and marketing. Sales and marketing departments involved in the practical launch of the product should be fully briefed on the product so that they can begin the external communications process. Sales staff should be issued with comprehensive sales and marketing guides so that they can identify the most important prospects. The marketing department will use the specification and objectives of the program to formulate other marketing programs and identify the most important sectors for development.

Launch the Product to the Trade

If a product is sold through a distributor or retail network, prelaunch activity is important. The program should include a sales and distributor incentive program to generate high levels of initial interest. Incentives to build high levels of launch inventory are essential. If a product is not available in the retail outlets, consumer launch material is wasted. Launch guides will help to give local outlets an indication of all the key activities that should be performed.

Produce a Launch Guide

A launch guide insures that everyone involved in the launch process understands the product, and the launch itself.

Explain the Background

The first section of the guide should cover the background to the launch and the market opportunities:

- Why is the new product being launched?
- How does it fit into the company's overall strategy?
- What sort of people will buy the product and how do they differ from traditional customers?
- What new opportunities does this give the local outlet?
- How will competitors respond to this product?

Highlight Features and Benefits

The second part of the guide should explain the features and benefits of the product. The guide:

- will act as a sales guide for the local outlet staff;
- will insure that they fully understand the product;
- should include information about the training and product support available;
- will outline the key stages of any training that is to be an integral part of the launch program;
- will identify the people who should be involved in the training program, together with a training schedule.

Describe Launch Support

The third part of the guide should indicate the level of support available for the launch. This will include the launch event itself. Details should be given of national advertising and promotional programs, together with local marketing programs. Advance notice allows local outlets to order support material, and to plan their own

local marketing program, so that it is fully integrated with the national launch.

Outline Launch Activities

The final part of the guide should provide a schedule, and a list of key launch activities, so that the management team can meet all the requirements of the launch program. These launch activities might include:

- inventory and ordering details
- a training schedule
- launch events
- dates for national and local advertising
- suggested dates and formats for customer events
- a schedule for launching marketing activities

Arrange High-profile Launch Events

Hold a national launch event, attended by all sales staff and all retailers, or hold a series of regional events for local retailers. Alternatively, you can introduce the new product to individual outlets through a series of sales calls, or send mailings to individual outlets.

Maintain Momentum through Postlaunch Activity

It is easy to overlook in the emotion of a major launch that the real sales effort has only just begun. Postlaunch sales activities can include promotional support for retailers and ongoing incentives for retailers and sales force, as well as direct marketing programs to help retailers market the new products and local events to reinforce the launch.

Communicate the Product to Customers

The customer launch can be achieved in a number of different ways, including advertising, direct marketing, trial offers, and exhibitions.

Use other forms of marketing to raise initial awareness and get customers to try the new product.

Use Advertising to Build Interest

Advertising can provide a high-profile launch platform. It can be used in a number of ways:

- to announce the new product to raise customer awareness
- to advise customers where to obtain the new product
- to offer customers further information, or a trial of the product, as a way of generating sales leads

Use Sales Promotion to Encourage Product Trial

Sales promotion activities can also be used to encourage sampling and product trial. Curiosity value and novelty are not sufficient to insure the success of a new product launch. The promotional campaign must incorporate strong consumer benefits, together with an incentive to buy that might include money off on trial packs.

Target Key Prospects with Direct Marketing

Direct marketing to key customer groups will allow the marketing group to target their most important prospects. It can be used to make special offers, or to provide detailed information about the new products and feedback on new product performance. The flexibility of direct marketing means that you can evaluate different launch and marketing approaches.

Communicate at the Point of Sale

Consumer information at the point of sale is essential for new products sold through retail outlets. It can be used to reach the prospects and customers who may have been missed in the advertising campaign and to reinforce other media. Point-of-sale material provides additional information to customers and prospects and supports sales development through retail outlets.

Use the Press

A press information program will make sure that the new product receives good coverage in the right publications. It can take a number of forms, including tie-in promotions such as reader offers, competitions, and product information in the form of press releases or feature articles.

Announce on the Web Site

Highlight the new product on your Web site with an announcement on the home page and a link to any product information or launch news stories in the site. You could also add a footer to all e-mail correspondence mentioning the new product and displaying the Web site address.

COMMON MISTAKES
Failing to Motivate the Sales Force

The sales force is critical to the success of a product launch. They need to be committed to the product so that they can communicate enthusiastically with customers and resellers. A new product will form only part of their overall sales target, so motivation is essential.

Overhyping a Poor Product

A new product carries tremendous risk. It is tempting to oversell it to insure a successful launch. However, it is the long-term success of the product that determines a company's market position, so avoid launching for the sake of it.

Losing Momentum after the Launch

A lot of effort and energy goes into a launch, but many companies fail to maintain the sales and distribution momentum. After the initial period, sales may slump to a point where the product fails to recover.

FOR MORE INFORMATION

Book:
Cooper, Robert G. *Winning at New Products: Accelerating the Process from Idea to Launch.* 3rd ed. New York: Perseus, 2001.

Web site:
Journal of Brand Management:
www.henrystewart.com/brand_management

See also:

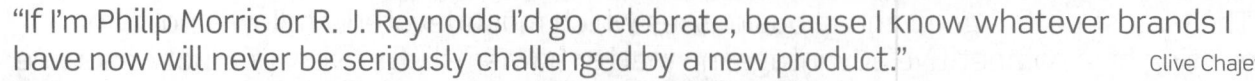
"If I'm Philip Morris or R. J. Reynolds I'd go celebrate, because I know whatever brands I have now will never be seriously challenged by a new product."   Clive Chajet

Planning a Corporate Public Relations Campaign

GETTING STARTED

Corporate public relations raises awareness of a company and builds confidence. It is important when a company has undergone change or is entering new markets. It can also overcome problems of poor reputation.

The corporate reputation is the way a company is perceived by customers, suppliers, and other important groups. Corporate public relations stresses the positive aspects of an organization and seeks to correct any misunderstandings.

The first stage in building a positive corporate reputation is to assess current perceptions. An audit identifies key areas for improving communications performance. A corporate press relations program should communicate:
- professionalism
- technical success
- market success
- corporate stability

It is essential that messages should be communicated consistently in every form of contact with the customer. The program should include information on:
- new appointments and management changes
- investments and other business developments
- business and financial performance

FAQs

If my company has a poor reputation in the market, can corporate public relations overcome that?

Corporate public relations can help to correct wrong perceptions. However, if the perceptions are based on poor corporate performance, the focus should be on improving performance. Trying to mislead the market can be dangerous.

My company's products have an excellent reputation in the market. Why should I worry about corporate public relations?

Success depends on more than a good product range. Your company may have excellent products but a poor delivery record. If demand is growing, customers will ask if you have the capacity to meet new levels of demand. If your company is not making a good profit, customers will ask whether it can invest for the future or even survive in the long term. These are good reasons to keep customers informed about your company.

Who should deal with press inquiries about corporate matters?

Companies deal with this issue in different ways. Some companies appoint a single spokesperson who handles all inquiries. Others refer inquiries to a senior director. It is essential that telephone operators be aware of the correct press contacts. It can be frustrating for journalists to be passed from person to person. An alternative is to route all press inquiries to corporate public relations consultants. If they cannot deal with the inquiry directly, they can refer the question to the appropriate director.

MAKING IT HAPPEN
Plan Corporate Public Relations

Corporate public relations raises awareness of a company and builds the confidence of different groups in the company. It can be important in a number of different business scenarios:
- The company has undergone significant change.
- Research shows that customers are not aware of the company's key strengths.
- The company is entering new markets and there is low awareness among potential customers.
- Research shows that the company has a poor reputation in a number of areas important to its success.
- The company is building key account or partnership relationships and customers need to know that the company can maintain its standard of supply.

Identify the Elements of a Corporate Reputation

The corporate reputation is the way a company is perceived by customers, suppliers, and other important groups. It is based on a number of elements, including:
- financial performance
- the quality of the management team
- clarity of direction
- market performance
- growth record and potential
- relationships with suppliers and employees
- manufacturing capability

Build a Positive Corporate Reputation

Corporate public relations stresses the positive aspects of an organization and seeks to correct any misunderstandings.

Audit the Corporate Reputation

The first stage in building a positive corporate reputation is to assess current perceptions of the organization through research. This is the management summary of a research program into customer perceptions.
- The company is almost as visible as its competitors but is rated only third in all issues associated with image.
- Contact with the customer at all levels is less than professional. According to the customer, the company does not understand its business and its products, and does not communicate its future strategies.
- There is a legacy of poor reputation which has largely been overcome by increased product reliability, but the image persists in the minds of the customer's senior management team.
- The company is perceived as offering lower quality and

"Corporate values are a genuine competitive advantage . . . an enduring factor amid so many changes in products and services."

Rosabeth Moss Kanter

lower performance than competitors, and its users are less satisfied than competitors' users.

- The company is seen as losing ground with important decision makers.
- The company is identified more clearly than competitors with specific product lines, but is not rated most highly as the potential supplier of those products.
- The company's major weakness is perceived as its narrow product line and lack of expertise in certain areas.

An audit like this identifies key areas for improving communications performance. In such circumstances, it is essential that positive messages such as those below should be communicated consistently in every form of contact with the customer.

Communicate Professionalism

The company is a professional organization that understands the customer's business needs and can meet them with a wide variety of high quality products and services. The sample messages below would support this perception:

- The company is investing $X in training over the next year.
- The company is organized into market-focused groups to offer the highest standards of service.
- X number of employees are dedicated to the customer's business.
- The company is committed to total quality.
- The company has developed a broad product range and a full range of support services.
- The new product development program is providing innovative new products.

Communicate Technical Success

The company is technically successful in major projects, developing total solutions and delivering value for the money, on time, every time. The important messages to support this perception include the following:

- The company has an established reputation for innovation.
- The company's products have been selected for the following demanding applications: . . .
- Customers are saving money by using the company's products.
- The company's products conform to national and international standards.
- The company has a research and development budget in excess of $X, and has a team of X highly skilled people dedicated to technical support.

Communicate Market Success

The company is winning share from its competitors. The important messages to support this perception include the following:

- The company has been selected to provide products and services to the following customers: . . .
- The company has recently won a major order worth $X.
- The company has been selected as a strategic supplier to the following customers: . . .
- The company has gained X% market share in the last year, while competitors have lost X% share in the last year.

Communicate Corporate Stability

"The company is successful and financially stable, with a sound management team—a good prospective supplier and business partner." The important messages to support this perception include the following:

- The company's annual results show X% growth in orders, revenue, and profits.
- The company is expanding.
- The company is a member of the following international groups: . . .
- The company is the leading U.S. supplier.

Introduce a Corporate Press Relations Program

A wide variety of press relations techniques can be used to improve corporate relations. They include:

- regular press releases on new appointments and management changes;
- regular press releases on investments and other business developments;
- interviews with senior executives in important magazines;
- encouraging press visits.

COMMON MISTAKES
Ignoring Corporate Public Relations

Many companies fail to recognize the problems caused by a poor corporate reputation. They concentrate on product public relations because corporate matters appear to be intangible. This can make it difficult for a company to rebuild confidence if problems occur.

Waiting until a Crisis before Investing in Corporate Public Relations

If a company hits a crisis, it may try to limit damage by issuing press information. Journalists usually recognize this type of crisis in public relations and this can make the situation worse. By adopting a policy of continuing public relations, it is possible to build effective relations with the press and gain understanding if there are problems.

Ignoring Certain Key Groups

Successful corporate communication depends on building understanding with all the groups that influence the success of your business. This might include investors, employees, pressure groups, distributors, and suppliers—as well as customers. In planning your campaign, make sure that you cover all the key groups.

FOR MORE INFORMATION

Books:
Alsop, Ron. *The 18 Immutable Laws of Corporate Reputation: Creating, Protecting and Repairing Your Most Valuable Asset.* New York: Free Press, 2004.
Treadwell, Donald, and Jill B. Treadwell. *Public Relations Writing: Principles in Practice.* 2nd ed. Thousand Oaks, CA: Sage, 2005.

Web site:
Public Relations Society of America: **www.prsa.org**

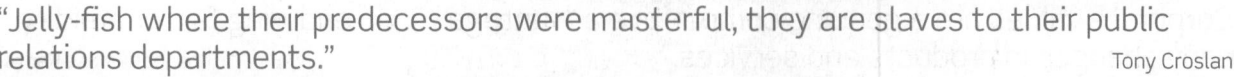

"Jelly-fish where their predecessors were masterful, they are slaves to their public relations departments."

Tony Crosland

Producing a Corporate Brochure

GETTING STARTED

A corporate brochure is a publication that is designed to provide customers with reassurance. Its objective is to present the company as a solid, well-managed business partner offering an excellent product range and possessing the attributes of financial stability, technological innovation, reliability, and customer focus.

FAQs

How important is the corporate brochure?

Many companies produce a corporate brochure before considering any other publication. It is seen as the face of the company and is particularly popular with the sales force. Despite its popularity, however, it is not necessarily the most effective form of communication. A corporate brochure has a role to play in communicating company information, but it should not be used as a substitute for targeted communications.

Corporate brochures can be expensive to produce. Should their use be restricted?

The feeling exists that corporate brochures should be high-quality publications because these will reflect a solid company. These expensive brochures are then often given away freely by members of the sales force. A growing number of companies have introduced internal charging for publications, so that internal customers must now prepare a business case for using publications; the result is that they are used more carefully.

Who should receive corporate brochures?

Corporate brochures can be used as part of an integrated communications program aimed at customers (actual and prospective), suppliers, business partners, distributors, and investors. They can also be used, selectively, as part of an employee communications program.

MAKING IT HAPPEN
Present a Successful Company

A corporate brochure demonstrates corporate success presenting the company as a financially stable, long-term partner. Above all, the corporate brochure should be a statement of confidence: this is a publication that is designed to reassure customers.

A corporate brochure should include the following information about a company:
- a description of its product range
- location, resources, and international activities
- technical and research capability
- manufacturing resources
- success in handling complex projects
- success in terms of innovation or market leadership
- financial performance
- management skills

Present the Product Range

A company must show that its product range meets current requirements and can be developed in response to changing market conditions. The product range should contain a good balance of market leading established products and new products with good growth potential.

Communicate Innovation

Companies who supply technically advanced products must be seen to be at the leading edge of technology: they must convince their customers that their policy of continuous innovation enables them to offer more advanced products than their competitors.

Demonstrate High-performance Products

When customers are trying to improve the performance of their own products, they need to work with companies that can comply with their requirements and meet new technological challenges. High-performance products have to meet stringent quality checks if they are to be accepted. They are often used in safety critical applications where the margin for error is extremely small. In presenting company capability, it is important to show how the company conforms to requirements.

Communicate Investment in Research

Companies should point to their investment in research and development as evidence of their commitment to innovation. A company can enhance its reputation for innovation by becoming involved in industry research and helping to set industry standards. For example, membership of user groups or industry standards associations can help to demonstrate industry leadership and a commitment to progress.

A good research investment record demonstrates that the company is committed to providing increasingly higher standards of service and, in turn, to improving its long-term growth prospects. Investment does not necessarily mean capital expenditure on equipment: investment in people is seen as an increasingly important area for corporate development.

Show That Your Company is Market Focused

Presenting a company as market focused can have a number of important benefits:
- It shows customers that you are concerned about their business.
- It tells investors that your company has the right priorities.
- It helps build staff commitment to customer service.

Market focus is demonstrated by:
- researching customer requirements;
- obtaining customer feedback;
- developing a new product program;
- appointing a senior executive responsible for customer service;
- focusing the organization on the customer;
- communicating customer benefits;
- the right levels of service;
- flexibility of production;

"If figures of speech based on sports and fornication were suddenly banned, American corporate communication would be reduced to pure mathematics." Jay McInerney

- staff training in customer care;
- participation in user groups.

Explain Customer Focus

A market-focused company must first understand the needs of the market through research and consultation with the customer. New product programs are essential to any company, but in a market-focused company they are an integral part of the company culture. The whole organization must reflect the needs of the market, and the principles of market focus must be embodied in a senior executive. A key aspect of market-focused service is that it reflects key customer requirements such as convenience, cost-effectiveness, value for the money, and reliability. A product or service does not need to represent an industry as best in every aspect, but it should reflect the key perceptions identified by research.

Demonstrate Financial Stability

Presenting a company as financially stable can have important benefits:

- It reassures customers that you are a reliable supplier.
- It can help a company win long-term contracts.
- It can provide a company with access to funds.
- It tells employees that the company has good long-term prospects.

Several factors help to demonstrate financial stability:

- membership of a large group
- serving growing markets
- sound financial controls
- good investment record
- share price performance
- stable customer base
- broadly based product portfolio
- record of profitability
- low cost base

Communicate Size and Success

Being a member of a major group can help to reassure customers that your company will remain a reliable supplier. Customers need to know that you have the resources to finance work in progress and that you have access to funds for research and for growth investment. The backing of a major group provides the right credentials.

Market success is another indicator of good long-term prospects. For example, a company operating in sectors in overall decline, such as steelmaking or shipbuilding, is unlikely to have the same long-term prospects as a company in the high-technology sector.

Explain Company Management

A well-managed company should provide a cost-effective service and make reasonable profits to invest in future growth and the development of the service. There are a number of key factors in presenting a well-managed company:

- an experienced team
- commitment to excellence
- clear objectives
- customer-facing organization

- an effective recruitment process
- management development programs

Customers want to know that their suppliers are capable of running their own business effectively and that they understand the business of their customers. A well-managed company should be able to demonstrate a record of sustained growth and profitability and should have a clear sense of direction.

Explain Objectives

Good management begins at the top with effective leadership; if the board is committed, the rest of the management team will have clear guidelines to follow. A company should have a clear mission statement which is focused on service to the customer.

When a company has clear objectives, customers are reassured that future developments are in line with their needs. Many companies publish a statement of direction which tells customers how they intend to develop their business in the future; at the same time, it gives managers and employees a clear sense of direction.

COMMON MISTAKES
Unbalanced Content

A corporate brochure should present a balanced picture of a company: its skills, products, resources, performance, and track record. Customers and prospects use corporate brochures to assess the suitability of a company as a supplier. The brochure should therefore cover all the factors that customers consider important.

Lack of Integration with Other Communications

The messages, treatment, and content of the corporate brochure should be integrated with advertising, product publications, a Web site, and public relations. It is just one part of the communications process.

Presentation before Content

Many companies concentrate on the presentation of a corporate brochure at the expense of its content on the assumption that customers judge a corporate brochure on its appearance. However, high-quality paper, excellent photography, and good print are no compensation for poor content.

FOR MORE INFORMATION

Books:
Cyr, Lisa. *Brochure Design That Works: Secrets for Successful Brochure Design.* Gloucester MA: Rockport Publishers, 2002.
Yadin, Daniel. *Creative Marketing Communications.* 3rd ed. Milford, CT: Kogan Page, 2001.

Web site:
American Marketing Association:
www.marketingpower.com

See also:
✔ Creating Product Literature (pp. 751–752)
☆ The Power of Identity (pp. 122–123)

Producing Press Material

GETTING STARTED

Newspaper, television, trade press, and radio journalists are always looking for stories. Supply information in the form of press releases, feature articles, or advertorials—in the right format and to the right person—and you can gain great publicity for your organization.

FAQs

Will the press be interested in us?

Journalists are always looking for stories and they work under great pressure, so a well-written, informative, and current press release is always welcome. They won't, however, be interested in you unless you have a story to tell. Like customers, editors will want to know what makes your company different from others. Local media will be interested in how you fit in with the community; and the trade press will be more interested in new products and ideas.

It is worth developing a relationship with editors in order to understand how you can help them. By concentrating on the kind of news and story they want, you can save yourself time and increase the chances of your story being published.

Should we produce our own press material or use the services of an external agency?

An external agency can take a more objective view of your press material and may have experience in writing for the publications on your distribution list. That means they can tailor material for individual publications and make sure that it is printed. They may, however, lack product knowledge and require considerable training to achieve the right results. If your company produces complex technical products, you may split the task, keeping technical press releases in-house, and using an external agency to produce company or business material. Do check out their rates and fees carefully before you place work with them, though, as their costs may be well outside your budget.

Can we use the same press release for all the publications on our distribution list?

You can issue a single release, but you will increase the chances of getting into print if you tailor information to the needs of individual publications; for example, your local newspaper will have a different take on your news than a trade publication. By talking to journalist, reading previous issues, and studying publishers' readership data, you can identify the type of material that is likely to be printed or broadcast.

What should we do if an editor does not publish the information in a press release?

There's no cast-iron guarantee that your piece will get published, so don't see it as a "given." There could be a number of reasons for non-publication that are outside your control, such as lack of space, the release missing the copy date, or another story coinciding with your re-lease. Your story may appear in the next issue if space allows. On the other hand, the editor may have decided simply that your information was wrong for the publication or not newsworthy. A quick call to the editor may help you find out the reason. If your material was unsuitable, you may be able to provide something more relevant for future issues.

MAKING IT HAPPEN
Plan Your Press Release

A press release is a piece of information distributed to newspaper, television, or radio journalists, which is published or broadcast as a piece of news. It can cover a variety of topics, including:

- information on new products or services;
- information on developments in a company;
- news of new appointments or promotions.

An effective press release should contain news rather than thinly disguised advertising, and it should reflect readers' interests.

The release may be used without modification if it is newsworthy, timely, and if space permits. The press release may be cut to fit available space without any further reference to you. In some cases, a journalist or editor may contact you for further information and rewrite the item in the style of the publication. It is often a good idea to provide additional background information to help journalists in this task. Information such as product specifications, contact details, or alternative photographs are useful. Some companies offer such information specifically for journalists on a section of their Web site. Sometimes the information may not be used, because it is not newsworthy or not relevant to the readership. Alternatively, although the main press release may not be used, an accompanying photograph may be used with a caption.

Produce Your Press Release

The following guidelines will help you produce an effective press release:

- Press releases should be typed double-spaced.
- The source of the release should be clearly identified.
- A contact name for further information should be provided.
- Any limitations on use or timing of publication should be clearly highlighted, for example, "not for publication before . . . "
- The most important information should be included in the early paragraphs. If an editor is short of space, the press release will be cut as simply and quickly as possible, probably from the bottom upward.
- Quotes are useful and are frequently used by editors.
- Photographs or diagrams add value to the release and may help to insure publication.
- The style of writing, even the length of sentences and paragraphs, should match the targeted publication as far as possible.

"Private enterprise has no press agent. Government does."   Milton Friedman

Distribute Your Press Release

Press releases can be delivered by hand or by mail, depending on quantity. They can also be sent by e-mail or placed on a Web site so that they can be picked up by visiting journalists. Wherever possible, they should be sent to a named individual. Information on editorial contacts, with details of their special interests, is available in publications like *Public Relations Quarterly*, which is updated regularly. If you do not want the information published before a certain date for reasons of commercial security, include an embargo—"not for publication before . . . "

Time Your Press Release

Check the publication dates of magazines or newspapers on your distribution list. This information is available in publications such as *Public Relations Quarterly*. An editorial copy date will be indicated. Make sure that your release reaches the editor by that date at the latest.

Plan Feature Articles

A feature article, which could be 500–2,000 words in length, is published in a magazine and credited to an organization. The article may be on technical or business developments in an industry, or on other subjects that provide practical or topical information for readers. The article may form part of an industry survey. This type of feature provides an opportunity for organizations to demonstrate their expertise and professionalism.

Feature articles can cover a variety of topics, including surveys of new industry or technical developments, practical "how to" articles, or reviews of research projects.

If it is well written, the article may be used without modification; it will be published when space permits, or may be used as part of a special survey. In some cases, a journalist or editor may contact you for more information and rewrite the item in the style of the publication.

Produce Feature Articles

An effective feature article should reflect readers' interests and contain useful information. It should also bring them up to date with recent developments.

The following guidelines should help you prepare a feature article:

- Feature articles should be typed double-spaced.
- Length should be discussed with the editor, but is likely to be between 500 and 2,000 words, with 1,000 words as the average.
- A contact name for further information should be provided.
- Photographs or diagrams, with a caption for every item, add value to the article.

Distribute Feature Articles

Feature articles should only be sent to one publication at a time, although they can be modified for use in other markets. Wherever possible, they should be sent to a named individual. In some cases, the initiative may come from the publication and the editor will provide you with details of requirements.

Time Feature Articles

Check the publication dates of magazines or newspapers on your distribution list. An editorial copy date will be indicated. Make sure that your release reaches the editor by that date at the latest. You should also ask the editor for a list of special editorial features. The article may be suitable for inclusion in a survey.

Produce Advertorials

An advertorial is a special category of feature article, combining advertising and editorial, which is used to promote products and services. These are the key characteristics of an advertorial. It:

- may include a reader offer, such as a chance to participate in a competition;
- should be identified as an "advertisement feature";
- is produced in the form of an editorial rather than in a conventional advertisement format, even though the space is paid for.

The writing guidelines are similar to those for press releases and feature articles but you are paying for the space and you have considerably more control over what is published. Newspapers and journals will often help with the layout.

COMMON MISTAKES
Writing Unsuitable Material

It is important to study the publications that are on your distribution list. Editors know very quickly what is relevant or interesting to their readers. If your material is not suitable, it will not be used. Study the editorial content and check the readership figures, which are usually available from the publication.

Providing Out-of-Date News Stories

"Old news is no news" and that means a story could be wasted. It's easy to get the timing right with a daily or weekly publication, but it can be tricky to decide on the right date to send a news story to a monthly publication. The publication can provide you with the dates when your copy will be required, but you have to make sure that those dates tie in with your own schedules. If you have to release a sensitive news story early to catch a publication date, you can protect your interests by putting an embargo clause on the release, saying "not for publication before . . . ."

Confusing Editorial with Advertorial

A press release or feature article should provide factual, newsworthy information. It should not be a blatant advertisement for the company. Editors dislike items that are thinly disguised advertisements.

FOR MORE INFORMATION

Book:
Treadwell, Donald, and Jill B. Treadwell. *Public Relations Writing: Principles in Practice*. Revised ed. Thousand Oaks, CA: Sage, 2003.

Web site:
Institute for Public Relations: **www.instituteforpr.com**

"Newspapers . . . remain powerful outlets for advertising and information (and political influence) . . . literacy and the printed word are not as out of fashion as many have feared."

Conrad Black

Running a Product Public Relations Campaign

GETTING STARTED

Product public relations is the most frequently used public relations activity, which can be used to support a number of different sales and marketing objectives. There are many different opportunities for improving product public relations across a variety of media.

FAQs

Should I hold a press conference every time I launch a new product?

You should only hold a press conference if the product being launched is critical to your company or will be seen as important in the market. Minor product developments or simple range extensions do not warrant a press conference.

Can I handle my own product public relations?

Many manufacturing companies handle product public relations internally. They have a detailed knowledge of products and services that an external consulting firm would be unable to match.

Should technical specialists write their own product material?

Technical specialists are in the best position to write feature articles that require detailed product knowledge. However, they may write from a technical perspective, rather than a customer perspective, and this may reduce the value of the article. You can take the specialist's material and edit it as necessary.

MAKING IT HAPPEN

Plan Product Public Relations

Product public relations is the most frequently used public relations activity and can be used to support a number of different sales and marketing objectives:
- as part of a new product launch program;
- to raise awareness of a company's product range;
- to correct misunderstandings about a product;
- to build understanding of product applications;
- to encourage wider use of a product;
- as part of a market education program.

Identify Opportunities for Product Public Relations

There are many different opportunities for improving product public relations, such as:
- contributing product information to regular product surveys;
- issuing press releases on new products and new product developments;
- contributing articles on complex product applications;
- contributing how-to articles on different aspects of product usage;
- contributing articles by technical specialists on new developments in the industry.

Support a New Product Launch

A company marketing a new design software tool that will improve engineering design quality and productivity wants to raise awareness and understanding of the product among a group of decision makers, including:
- design engineers who would use the product;
- managers and senior executives responsible for engineering, who would benefit from improved efficiency and productivity;
- marketing directors who would benefit indirectly from better product performance.

The program includes the following elements:
- press releases aimed at publications read by the target audience
- an interview with the company's engineering director, explaining how the product improved internal productivity and performance
- contributions to a number of product surveys on engineering design techniques
- a feature article on developments in engineering design
- a feature article submitted to marketing magazines showing how engineering design influences product and marketing performance

Improve Market Development

A professional services company marketing project services believes that lack of understanding is a barrier to market growth. The company develops a public relations program which includes the following elements:
- case histories of companies using a project management service
- feature articles on using project services to improve deployment of staff
- feature articles on the use of project services in outsourcing programs
- a press release including self-assessment questionnaire, helping prospects to identify the need for project services

Increase Use of a Product

A materials supplier wants to increase the usage of an advanced material which has not been widely used in general markets. The product was originally developed for use in demanding aerospace applications and is believed to be expensive and too good for conventional applications. The campaign is targeted at designers and application engineers in a wide variety of markets. The campaign includes the following elements:
- a press release on an information pack that describes applications of the product
- a feature article, "How to design with the material," submitted to horizontal market design and engineering publications

"We don't know how to sell products based on performance. Everything we sell, we sell based on image."

Roberto Goizueta

- an editorial competition that enables readers to win a special design software package
- a series of application articles written specifically for vertical market publications

Run a Press Conference

A press conference provides an opportunity for an organization to meet journalists and editors in person and give them a detailed briefing on a new product development. However, unless the event is important and the press see a real benefit in attending, press conferences are a waste of time, so planning and preparation are important to guarantee success:

- Invite journalists and editors from publications that reach your most important customers and prospects.
- Give the press plenty of notice, and try to plan the timing so that editorial coverage will appear in the next issue of the most important monthly publications.
- Provide press packs that include background information, specific information on the product, photographs, and other relevant material.
- If necessary, insure that senior executives or other specialists are available for interview or to answer detailed questions.
- If any important press contacts cannot attend, send a press pack and arrange a separate meeting if necessary.

Arrange Interviews with Key Product Specialists

An interview with a senior executive or product specialist provides an opportunity for an organization to meet selected or individual journalists and editors in person and to give them a detailed briefing on a new product development. The advantage to the press is that this process is more selective than a press conference, and it gives them an opportunity for an exclusive interview.

Put Information in Your Online Press Office

Establish a separate page on your Web site where journalists can get the latest news about your products and download press releases, background information, or feature articles. The press office should have a direct link from the home page, and new stories should be featured on the home page. The press page should also feature e-mail addresses and telephone numbers for key contacts.

Alert Journalists by E-mail

Journalists may visit your site regularly if it provides valuable information. You can also alert them to the latest product news by e-mail. Include a link to the press release or feature article on your site, so that it can be easily downloaded.

Issue Reprints of Published Material

If a story about your company's products is covered in the press, television, or radio, include a reprint of the item on your site. Also provide links to the publications that covered the story. Alternatively, e-mail the item to other journalists. This may increase coverage even further. Ask the publisher for permission before you reproduce a complete article.

Run an Online Press Briefing

The problem with conventional press conferences is usually time, but running an online press briefing can overcome that problem. Webcasting allows companies to stream traditional audio and video conferences over the Internet, incorporating multimedia content and adding interactive capability such as slides, polling, and messaging. This enables journalists to attend a virtual press conference without leaving their desks, while the interactive facilities enable them to ask questions—just as they would at a traditional press conference.

Issue Material by Newsletter

If you issue a large number of product press releases, you can include brief summaries of the latest stories in a regular newsletter distributed by mail or e-mail to journalists or customers. The summaries should include a link to the complete release. The frequency of your newsletter depends on the volume of releases you produce each week or month.

COMMON MISTAKES
Concentrating on Product News Rather than Information for the Market

Many companies simply write about their products from an internal point of view, ignoring the implications for the customer. Writing articles about applications or benefits for the market makes the press information more relevant and interesting.

Writing Information That Is Not Suitable for a Publication

It is important to study the publications that are on your distribution list. Editors know very quickly what is relevant or interesting to their readers. If your material is not suitable, it will not be used. Don't assume that all industry publications will be interested in your product.

Failing to Keep Journalists Up to Date

Journalists may not be aware of your company's full product range or of its capabilities. They may receive the latest press releases, but that may give them a limited view of your company. It is important to provide background information as well as the latest product information.

FOR MORE INFORMATION

Books:
Cooper, Robert G. *Winning at New Products: Accelerating the Process from Idea to Launch.* 3rd ed. New York: Perseus, 2001.
Cutlip, Scott M., Allen H. Center, and Glen M. Broom. *Effective Public Relations.* 8th ed. Upper Saddle River, NJ: FT Prentice Hall, 2000.

Web site:
Public Relations Society of America **www.prsa.org**

See also:
✔ Dealing with Press Inquiries (pp. 773–774)
✔ Producing Press Material (pp. 761–762)

"For a successful technology, reality must take precedence over public relations, for nature cannot be fooled."

Richard Feynman

Planning Promotions

GETTING STARTED

Consumer promotions account for around 20% of the value of the average shopping basket. Promotions are popular because they meet the demands of powerful retailers, and they help brand managers to meet volume targets. The strength of the retail trade puts increasing emphasis on trade and consumer promotions.

Consumers prefer instant-win promotions to money-back or collector programs. Instant win has a specific tactical role, but it may not be suitable for more strategic tasks such as brand switching. Cross promotion allows complementary products to be promoted in a cost-effective way.

FAQs

Is sales promotion more effective than advertising for building market share?

Sales promotion can deliver short-term gains in market share, but competitor promotions may wipe those out. Longer-term promotions such as collector programs can encourage customer loyalty for the period of the promotion, but they may also be vulnerable to competitive activity. Advertising, on the other hand, can be used to build longer-term brand awareness and attract new customers. Ideally, the two activities should be integrated, if budgets allow.

I sell my products through retail outlets. Should I run trade promotions rather than consumer promotions?

Trade promotions will help you sell into the retail outlets. If you also give retailers incentives to sell more to consumers, or to improve their standards of service, you may also increase sales to consumers. A consumer promotion may boost sales, but it may not increase sales through your retail outlets.

Who should plan promotions, my advertising agency or a specialist promotions company?

Sales promotion should be integrated with other marketing activities, so it is essential that your advertising agency is aware of the promotion. Your agency may not have the skills or resources to plan and implement the promotion. If you use a specialist company, make sure that the creative theme of the promotion reflects the themes of the advertising and other marketing programs.

MAKING IT HAPPEN
Take Advantage of Promotions

In the consumer sector, items under promotion account for around 20% of the value of the average shopping basket. The strength of the retail trade puts increasing emphasis on trade and consumer promotions. In the United States, the strength of the trade means that some retail-dependent brands allocate as much as 75% of budget on promotions. Promotions are popular because they meet

the demands of powerful retailers and they help brand managers meet volume targets. They are also easy to justify financially because of immediate measurable results.

Identify Promotional Benefits
Promotions:
- attract the attention of retail buyers and sales forces, particularly for smaller brands.
- generate excitement at the point of sale.
- simplify negotiations over margins; promotions may create better volumes than reductions in margins.
- increase the effectiveness of trialing. One survey indicated that 30% of consumers had not tried the brand in the last six months. Another reported that 44% of consumers said they would buy a brand they do not normally buy if it is part of a special offer.

Reflect Customer Views

An industry report indicates that consumers prefer instant-win promotions to money-back or collector programs. The survey, which provides useful data for promotion of branded products, could also provide an insight for companies running business-to-business promotions. The report indicates that instant-win has a specific tactical role, but it may not be suitable for more strategic tasks such as brand switching. Key findings of the report include:
- instant win is most appropriate for products with a high purchase frequency;
- only 5% of consumers felt they would switch brands to participate in an instant-win promotion, compared with 41% of consumers who would switch brands for a price-reduction promotion;
- the main reasons for liking instant-win promotions were: no waiting and immediate knowledge of success;
- the main dislikes were: unlikely to win and likely to be a waste of time.

Avoid Problems Created by a Promotional Culture

The pressure to run promotions can have an impact on overall marketing performance. A review by a major consumer goods company indicated that a great deal of time was required to design, implement, and oversee promotions. It accounted for 25% of sales force time and 33% of brand managers' time. Other problems included:
- supply inefficiencies
- cost of changing packs
- cost of promotional material
- cost of running the promotion
- impact on long-term brand building

Set the Right Promotional Objectives

Promotions must be managed carefully to provide long-term benefits. The wrong choice of offer, confusing rules, or poor organization can undo all the good work. In setting objectives, you should ask:

- Why are we running the program?
- Do we want to increase overall volume, or sales of specific products?
- Do we want to improve performance in other sales-related areas, such as customer service or participation in training programs and other business programs?

Choose an Appropriate Promotional Format
- Promotional offers can be awarded to the biggest spenders or to all consumers.
- Programs that only reward big spenders or large trade customers can act as a disincentive to others.
- Programs that reward performance against target give a wider opportunity to win.
- A multilevel program that offers many lower-value prizes can act as a strong motivator.

Define the Rules Clearly
- Set out the scope of the promotion and the offer.
- Explain what is required to win and how to collect prizes.
- Include the closing date for the promotion.
- Specify the availability of the offer, for example, only available in selected retail outlets.
- Set the specific requirements for each participant.

Use Cross-promotion
Cross-promotion allows complementary products to be promoted cost-effectively. The project can be handled in-house, the samples are cheap, and the cost of the whole promotion is comparatively low. To be successful, this type of promotion should feature products that are complementary and noncompetitive. A database can be used to identify opportunities for cross-promotion—first identify the profile of a product, then look for products with a similar profile.

Maintain Momentum throughout the Promotion
If you are operating a long-term promotion or a promotion that involves a number of stages, you need to maintain momentum.
- Send out teaser incentives or gifts during the promotion to maintain interest.
- Keep participants informed of their progress.
- Encourage struggling participants with secondary offers.
- Publish results and distribute them to all participants.

Guarantee Effective Fulfillment
If you are delivering promotional products to homes or businesses, you need to establish an efficient logistics operation. You can either operate your own fleet, tying up capital and personnel, or subcontract the operation to a specialist logistics company.

Appoint a Fulfillment Agency
If your promotion is likely to generate a large volume of requests, your company may not have the resources to handle fulfillment internally. Fulfillment agencies specialize in high volume response programs.

Assess the Effectiveness of Promotional Programs
- How do you justify spending money on promotions?
- What return on your promotional investment are you looking for?
- What are the related sales objectives?
- How will you quantify them?
- How will you isolate the effect of nonpromotional activities?
- Was the promotional impact evenly spread across your business?
- Were there significant account, sector, or regional differences in impact?
- Did the differences relate to techniques, premiums, value, customer appeal, or communications?
- Is it possible to profile people who used previous promotions as a basis for planning?

COMMON MISTAKES
Setting Too Many Short-term Promotional Objectives
Sales promotion campaigns are judged on the way they change market share. However, any gains in market share can be lost when the promotion stops or competitive activity increases. It is also possible to create an environment in which consumers and the retail trade expect promotion to be a continuous activity.

Failing to Integrate Promotion with Other Activities
Sales promotion works most effectively when it is integrated with other activities. A consumer promotion, backed by a trade or sales force incentive, insures that all parties are aware of the promotion. A direct mail campaign in conjunction with a promotional offer can increase the direct mail response rate.

Choosing the Wrong Type of Promotion
If you run a promotional campaign, make sure that it reflects your brand values. A money-off offer, for example, would do little to enhance a premium product. If you can add value with your promotional offer, the campaign is more likely to be successful. You should also choose the right type of campaign. An instant-win campaign can have an immediate impact on market share, while a collection program encourages longer-term loyalty.

FOR MORE INFORMATION
Books:
Cummins, Julian, and Roddy Mullin. *Sales Promotion: How to Create, Implement and Integrate Campaigns That Really Work*. 3rd ed. Milford, CT: Kogan Page, 2003.
Schultz, Don E. *Sales Promotion Essentials: The 10 Basic Sales Promotion Techniques . . . and How to Use Them.* 3rd ed. New York, McGraw-Hill, 1998.

Web site:
American Marketing Association:
www.marketingpower.com

"Marketing goes wrong when it is perceived by companies as a bolt-on activity."

Michael Perry

Running a Price Campaign

GETTING STARTED

Promotional pricing can be used throughout the marketing process, in order to encourage brand loyalty and increase sales among customers. Pricing programs should be carefully matched to particular marketing tasks.

FAQs

Is pricing more important than brand building?

In the longer term, brand building is likely to be more important. However, price promotions can be used to win market share or quickly establish a new product. They can also be used to rapidly counter competitive activity that could have an impact on market share. Continuing to concentrate on price promotion alone is not a recommended strategy.

Should I always respond to a competitor's price promotion?

If the competitor's promotion is likely to damage your market share, it may be worth responding. However, you should weigh the impact on profitability. It is easy to get drawn into a damaging price war that has no long-term benefit.

Retailers are demanding price cuts. Should I give in to their demands when I'd rather spend the budget on advertising?

It can be difficult to persuade retailers that advertising, direct marketing, and other brand-building strategies are going to benefit them. They frequently prefer a promotion that offers them an immediate return in terms of increased sales. Again, it is a question of balance, meeting both short- and long-term needs.

MAKING IT HAPPEN
Match the Promotion to the Marketing Program

Promotional pricing can be used throughout the marketing process for:
- launching new products
- winning competitive business
- protecting market share
- entering new market sectors
- developing niche markets
- protecting volume and profit in mature markets

Choose the Right Pricing Program

There are five main categories of promotional pricing:
- money off current purchase
- money off next purchase
- cashback
- more product for the same price
- discounts on multiple purchase

Run a Money-off Promotion

This type of price promotion is one of the most commonly used tactics. It is immediate, easily implemented, and is easily understood by consumers. Results are measurable, and pricing levels can be modified for different market sectors. The program is also easy to modify in response to demand. Money-off promotions are acceptable to retailers, and easy to promote at the point of sale.

There are disadvantages. The promotion is easily imitated and competitors can respond quickly. It also has a potential long-term impact on manufacturer and retailer profitability. This type of promotion has no effect on long-term branding, minimal impact on customer loyalty, and does not differentiate the product.

Offer Money Off Next Purchase

This type of price promotion is designed to encourage repeat purchasing and to contribute to brand and customer loyalty. It is easily understood by consumers and can be measured accurately. The campaign is acceptable to retailers and easy to promote at the point of sale. It helps to build a value-for-the-money reputation, and contributes to the development of long-term relationships. However, like promotions giving money off the current purchase, it is easily imitated by competitors and has no effect on long-term branding or on product differentiation.

Make a Cashback Offer

In this type of price promotion, the customer pays the full purchase price, and receives a rebate in the form of cash or a check. The customer can also be offered the rebate in a different form—for example, $400 worth of gas when you buy your next car—although this could be considered a free gift. This type of promotion is designed to encourage purchasers to switch brands, by offering them greater freedom of choice in the way they use the discount.

The promotion has perceived value for both consumers and retailers and encourages brand switching. It is easily understood by consumers and offers them greater flexibility. The offer can be modified for different market sectors and is easy to modify in response to demand. However, the offer is unrelated to brand values and does not encourage repeat purchase. Again, it is easily imitated and offers no product differentiation.

Offer More Product for the Same Price

This type of price promotion is designed to encourage brand switching or increase the volume of purchasing by offering the customer greater value for the money. However, it can be difficult for customers to recognize the value of the offer when packs of different sizes are compared. Apart from this, it is easily understood and offers customers value for their money. Competitors find it difficult to respond quickly to the offer, but it has a number of disadvantages. You may have to modify the product or the packaging, and that can have a potential long-term

"The funny thing is better TV shows don't cost that much more than lousy TV shows."

Warren Buffett

768

ACTIONLIST

impact on both manufacturer and retailer profitability. It can also be confusing to the consumer if competitors offer different pack sizes. Like other price promotions, it has no effect on long-term branding or product differentiation.

Offer Discounts on Multiple Purchase

Although there is overlap between this and extra product promotions, this type of price promotion does not require any physical change to the product or packaging. It is designed to encourage repeat purchase and to increase customer loyalty. The "Buy One, Get One Free" offer takes the promotion to its logical limit. A number of multiple retailers use this offer as the basis for long-term positioning as a supplier of value for the money. The promotion is easily understood, acceptable to retailers, and builds longer-term loyalty. It can, however, have a potential impact on retailer and manufacturer profitability.

Operate Credit Deals and Financing Plans

Credit deals and financing plans can increase sales by making it easier for customers to buy. Although the recession of the mid-1990s made consumers more cautious about unlimited credit, financing plans remain an important method of increasing sales and building customer loyalty. In the business-to-business sector, financing plans such as leasing are often an integral part of a marketing package.

Financing plans can take a number of forms:

- storecards—credit cards that can be used only in named stores;
- loan programs—operated on behalf of stores or manufacturers by finance companies;
- installment plans—operated on behalf of stores or manufacturers by finance companies;
- business financing or leasing programs—operated on behalf of companies by finance companies.

Financing plans make it easier for customers to buy and can increase customer loyalty. They can be used to encourage repeat purchasing, while reducing the impact of price competition. An important bonus is that they provide high levels of customer information as a basis for direct marketing. The disadvantage is that they can be complex to administer and they do not support product branding.

COMMON MISTAKES
Relying on Price As the Only Weapon

Price promotions make little contribution to brand building or customer retention. Most promotions are easily imitated by competitors, and this can create a marketplace in which customers regularly switch brands to take advantage of the latest offer.

Running Price Promotions That Are Difficult to Understand

"Buy One, Get One Free" is a very simple concept. "10% off when you buy more than three in a two-week period" is confusing to customers and retailers. Price promotions must be immediately understandable.

Promotions That Are Difficult to Administer

Retailers prefer promotions that are simple to administer. If they have to return coupons, arrange refunds or rebates, or make complicated adjustments to their own pricing mechanisms, they will be reluctant to run the program. Consumers, too, prefer simple offers. If the program involves redeeming coupons, or posting proof of purchase to claim a rebate, it will be less attractive.

Getting Caught in a Price War

When competitors make similar price offers, this can lead to larger and larger cuts. Although one competitor may gain market share, it may be at the expense of profitability. Since it is difficult to retain loyalty through price promotions, this can be a damaging strategy in the long term.

FOR MORE INFORMATION

Books:
Dolan, Robert J., and Hermann Simon. *Power Pricing: How Managing Price Transforms the Bottom Line*. New York: Free Press, 1997.
Nagle, Thomas, and Reed K. Holden. *The Strategy and Tactics of Pricing: A Guide to Profitable Decision-Making*. 3rd ed. New York: Prentice Hall, 2002.

Web site:
Professional Pricing Society: **www.pricingsociety.com**

"I will build a motor car for the great multitude . . . constructed of the best materials . . . so low in price that no man making a good salary will be unable to own one." Henry Ford

Running Sales Meetings

GETTING STARTED

It is essential to maintain contact with all members of a sales force, wherever they are located, and a sales conference can help sales representatives understand business objectives, products, company policies, and what support is available to them. Conferences also play an important part in motivating sales teams.

National conferences are held for major events, such as the launch of a new product or a presentation of annual results, and, because of their high profile, they can be used to generate high levels of enthusiasm, commitment, and effort. For example, the national conference could be used to reward high achievement by an individual or a team. In addition, they can raise awareness of the organization's overall strengths and help to build consistent standards and performance.

FAQs

Are sales meetings really that important? Isn't it better that sales representatives spend time with their customers?

It's true that sales representatives need to spend most of their time with customers, but if they are not fully aware of company policies, products, and support, that time may be unproductive. Good sales meetings equip representatives with the skills and knowledge to do their job effectively. They also play a key role in motivating sales teams and building team spirit, an important factor for people who spend most of their time working alone.

Should the emphasis in a sales meeting be on excitement or information?

It is easy to present an exciting, theatrical event that motivates but conveys very little hard information. However, such an event may succeed, because it is designed to create impact. Provided it is backed by simpler business presentations that communicate hard facts about new products or corporate development, the "experience" has a place. Sales representatives like to think that their organization cares about them, and a low-key meeting could give the impression that their meeting is not that important.

When networked conferencing makes communication so simple, is the live meeting dead?

Networked conferencing makes it easier to hold regular meetings, saving sales teams' time. For that reason, it will play an important part in the overall sales force communications program. However, personal contact and team building are important benefits of live meetings which means they should also remain an integral part of the program.

MAKING IT HAPPEN
Maintain Effective Contact

To make a sales force work effectively, it is essential to maintain contact with all team members. How many times has the local office accused head office of being remote and out of touch? Can head office employees be certain that local sales representatives are aware of the latest product information or the current operating policy? Is there a feeling that certain members of the team are better informed or supported than others?

Set Meeting Objectives

Formal and informal information channels are used to maintain effective contact with local sales representatives at all levels. The sales conference is a key part of that process, and it should help sales representatives to:
- understand your current business objectives;
- understand corporate operating procedures;
- be aware of the business and marketing support available to them;
- be committed to success;
- acquire up-to-date product knowledge;
- understand how to implement company policies;
- feel that they have a worthwhile career structure within the organization.

Run a National Conference

At national conferences, the entire sales team is invited to attend, and the event may last for a longer period than a normal meeting. The conference is usually held for a major event, such as the launch of a new product or presentation of annual results, and is designed to generate high levels of enthusiasm and commitment. A national conference has the additional benefit of bringing together people from around the country who would not normally meet each other, so it has a considerable team-building value.

Build Team Spirit

A national conference should have purpose and it should be handled effectively. Many product launches have a high theatrical content, because the intention is to create impact. The high point of the event is the launch itself, which needs to be impressive, but the remainder of the time can be spent in building the right level of team spirit within the sales force.

A conference not only brings together employees who are separated by physical barriers but can also raise awareness of the organization's overall strengths and help to build consistent standards and performance.

Reward Effort

The national conference can also be used to reward high achievement. Many organizations run annual incentive and recognition programs for sales employees at different levels—the highlight being an individual presentation to the winner by a senior director, an event that confers real status on the winner. Using the national conference as the occasion for the award ceremony can raise the incentive program's profile and encourage high levels of participation and effort.

"In a good meeting there is a momentum that comes from the spontaneous exchange of fresh ideas and produces extraordinary results. That momentum depends on the freedom permitted the participants."

Harold S. Geneen

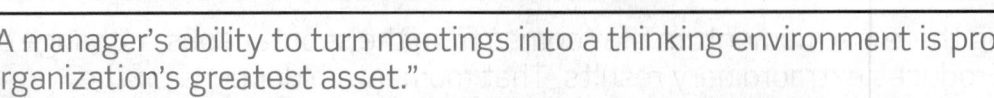

770

ACTIONLIST

Run a Regional Business Meeting

National and international conferences have a role to play, but they can be expensive and time consuming.

Regional business meetings are a valuable format for maintaining personal contact; they allow groupings of local outlets; and they enable an organization to hold a concentrated meeting to bring local sales teams up to date with key events.

Set a Meeting Format

Many organizations adopt a half-day format for their regional business meetings. Delegates arrive at midday for an informal lunch before a series of afternoon briefings covering new products, corporate developments, management changes, promotional activities, pricing, marketing programs, and objectives for the next quarter. The meetings give the head office team an opportunity to update local sales employees on current activities and maintain contact between the teams.

Hold Local Branch Briefings

Although regional business meetings provide a convenient alternative to national conferences for events that do not need a high-profile environment, they still have drawbacks. If an organization wants to brief a local sales team, or if the briefing is applicable only to one particular area, regional meetings may not be practical.

The solution is a presentation tailored to local needs, given at the local office. The location is convenient and the meeting does not take up much of the team's time. Wherever possible, the branch briefing should also be treated as a special event with a dedicated meeting room and professional presentation techniques. It should be formally structured and should resemble the main conference presentation in all but location.

Save Time with Networked Conferencing

A good addition to actual meetings of whatever kind is networked conferencing, which brings sales teams together quickly and easily, wherever they are located. It supports effective teamwork when sales representatives work in different locations or different countries, and it can help teams meet key objectives efficiently and productively. Videoconferencing remains the most popular type of networked conference, but Webcasting over the Internet or a secure IP-based network is now a viable alternative.

With a networked conference unnecessary travel time is eliminated, which allows busy sales representatives to concentrate on customers. Add up the salaries of people traveling to meetings, the outlay on travel, food, and accommodations, and you can estimate the real cost of conventional meetings. If your organization operates internationally, the potential cost savings are enormous.

Enhance Communications

The freedom and flexibility of networked conferencing means you can arrange more meetings, whenever you need to improve communications. It's a quick and easy way of briefing sales teams, reporting, training or coaching, reviewing progress, or dealing with specific customer issues. Senior executives can communicate easily with sales teams throughout an organization by broadcasting annual reports, for example, or news about significant corporate changes.

COMMON MISTAKES
Too Many Meetings

Major events, such as a national conference, are beneficial when there is an important announcement, such as a new product launch or corporate reorganization. However, too many meetings cover routine matters that could be handled through written or networked communications. Networked communications make it possible for sales representatives to participate in meetings without time-wasting travel. You should look carefully at your meeting program to see where you can eliminate unnecessary meetings or arrange alternative virtual events.

Failure to Back Up Presentations

Many conference presentations are designed for visual impact rather than communication. As a result, sales teams may come away impressed but with little hard material to use. You can back up theatrical presentations with business presentations and documentation to guarantee longer term benefits.

One-way Communication

A sales conference should involve more than one-way presentations. It should give the sales force an opportunity to participate and contribute to corporate policy. Discussion groups, question-and-answer sessions, feedback forms, and forums encourage sales force participation and bolster morale.

FOR MORE INFORMATION

Book:
Gitomer, Jeffrey. *The Sales Bible: The Ultimate Sales Resource.* Revised ed. New York: Wiley, 2003.

Web site:
American Marketing Association:
www.marketingpower.com

See also:
✔ Improving Communication with Resellers
(pp. 679–680)

"A manager's ability to turn meetings into a thinking environment is probably an organization's greatest asset."

Nancy Kline

Supporting Campaigns with Telemarketing

GETTING STARTED

Telemarketing can improve the effectiveness of other sales and marketing programs, providing opportunities to increase sales and customer contact; improve service levels; conduct fast, cost-effective research; and reduce overall marketing costs.

FAQs

Can I replace a sales force with a telemarketing operation?

Replacing the sales force would be a drastic move, particularly if face-to-face contact is important. If your company sells low-value products that do not require presales or after-sales support, telemarketing may be appropriate. However, if the sales process is protracted or complex, direct contact is likely to be more effective. Integrating sales force and telemarketing activities can optimize the sales process and reduce overall sales costs.

Can I use an external telemarketing company to contact key accounts?

External telemarketing operations are extremely professional. They would normally receive full training in your products and your company. They would also be briefed on your company's processes and standards. When they make telephone contact, they act as your own company, and the customer should not notice any difference.

Do customers believe telephone research is credible?

There is a risk that customers will feel that research is not independent or objective if it is conducted by an internal telemarketing department. However, this may be outweighed by the speed and simplicity of the research.

MAKING IT HAPPEN

Take a Systematic Approach

Telemarketing involves a systematic approach to campaign support, where the telephone is used as a tool for improving the effectiveness of other sales and marketing programs. According to the Institute of Direct Marketing, telemarketing is twice as effective as direct mail, and the inclusion of a telephone number can increase response by up to 185%. Another survey on telebusiness reported that consumers were becoming more and more aware of the benefits of doing business by phone, and up to 80% saw it as both convenient and easy.

Improve Order Taking

Taking orders by telephone improves speed and accuracy and is more convenient for customers than filling in and mailing forms. The use of fax or interactive voice systems means that orders can be handled around the clock.

Open New Marketing Channels

Telemarketing offers opportunities for "direct" sales to customers. This reduces administration costs and bypasses or supplements traditional distribution routes.

Increase Lead Generation

Offering customers 800 or 888 numbers can increase response. The call information enables campaigns to be monitored and evaluated and provides information for planning future campaigns.

Conduct Market Research

The telephone provides a fast, cost-effective medium for conducting market research interviews. It also provides a valuable channel for capturing database information from helplines, inquiries, and telesales operations.

Speed Up Market Testing

Telephone marketing provides an opportunity to evaluate different marketing and promotional routes and to conduct rapid telephone research.

Improve Sales Support

Telemarketing can be used to enhance sales force performance and productivity. The telemarketing team can take responsibility for following up sales leads, setting up appointments, and warm-calling qualified prospects (potential customers who meet certain criteria: for example, in a particular demographic group; able to afford the products being sold; bought similar products previously). This frees the sales force for increasing the number of face-to-face meetings and for concentrating on top prospects.

Increase Customer Contact

Courtesy calls add a personal touch to the sales process and increase customer contact. They provide an opportunity to offer additional products and services and help to overcome any initial problems.

Support Customers with Customer Service Lines

Customer service lines enable customers to report problems and complaints—a convenient route that demonstrates customer care. Helplines make expertise available to customers, allowing staff to handle minor technical problems and reduce customer downtime.

Integrate Campaign Support

Integration is the key to effective, profitable customer relationship management, with telemarketing services at the heart of integrated campaigns. Your customers receive a consistent, high-quality service on every contact, and the integration can reduce your overall costs. The integrated approach is designed to:
- insure high-impact marketing campaigns;
- increase retention rates for high-profit customers;
- maximize the profitability of each service relationship;

"If the public doesn't believe the message conveyed by your product and its promotion, the marketing game is lost."

Robert Heller

- cultivate customers who generate high profit levels;
- maximize return on marketing investments.

Reduce Marketing Costs

Integration can play an important part in reducing your overall marketing costs, particularly if you have relied on a traditional field sales team. The cost of keeping a sales team on the road continues to soar, and it may not always represent the most cost-effective way of reaching the right people. Research indicates that more and more people accept the telephone as a first choice for doing business. This means you can refocus your sales and marketing activities, using the power and flexibility of telemarketing. You should identify high-cost sales and marketing tasks and look at alternatives based on direct marketing or telemarketing. Wherever possible, set measurable targets so that you can see just how much you are saving.

Focus on Profitable Sectors

You can refocus sales effort by identifying profitable segments, and achieving high penetration levels through direct marketing and telephone follow-up. The average cost of a sale is reduced. Industry research indicates that many consumers prefer the indirect approach to a doorstep sale, adding customer satisfaction to the list of campaign benefits.

Supplement Your Sales and Marketing Resources

You can use external telemarketing resources to supplement your own skills. This gives you the flexibility to tailor individual campaigns and to run fully integrated campaigns, even when you have no in-house resources. You can also pull in extra support when you need to get new products to market in the shortest possible time. By using external call center teams or other resources, you can achieve that vital edge, without investing in recruitment or training. Most reputable call centers employ people who are trained to deliver the highest standards of customer service and are fully immersed in your company's products and culture. They act as professional representatives of your company.

Measure Effectiveness

Start by identifying profitable business opportunities and developing suitable campaigns. You can use emerging technologies to develop new applications and services that can drive your business forward, reducing your costs and improving performance. To help you to plan and evaluate your campaigns, look at the management information available from telemarketing records, including:

- campaign response rates
- regional patterns

- call flow patterns
- call patterns on helplines
- analysis of customer requests

Information like this makes your campaigns fully accountable and measurable, enabling you to integrate them with your marketing and corporate objectives.

COMMON MISTAKES
Duplicating Effort

Telemarketing can be used to supplement other sales and marketing resources. However, it is easy to fall into the trap of duplicating effort, for example, when both the sales force and the telemarketing team contact the customer about the same thing. With careful planning, you can integrate activities to make the most effective use of resources.

Failing to Measure Activities

Telemarketing records can provide a great deal of valuable information, enabling you to measure the effectiveness of campaigns and to identify sales and marketing trends. By measuring performance and comparing alternative communication channels, you can identify the most cost-effective routes to market.

Not Taking Full Advantage of Telemarketing

Telemarketing can be used to support a wide variety of sales and marketing activities. However, departmental rivalries may mean that a company does not take full advantage of telemarketing. Incentive programs and commission programs can also prove to be barriers to effective integration.

FOR MORE INFORMATION

Books:
Bodin, Madeline and Keith Dawson. *The Call Center Dictionary: The Complete Guide to Call Center and Customer Support Technology Solutions.* 3rd ed. New York: CMP Books, 2002.
Linchitz, Joel. *The Complete Guide to Telemarketing Management.* New York: PFS Press, 2000.

Web site:
International Contact Center Benchmarking Consortium: **www.iccbc.org**

See also:
✔ Generating More Leads (pp. 731–732)
✔ Improving the Response to Direct Mail (pp. 718–719)
✔ Setting Up a Customer Interaction Center (pp. 712–713)

"They don't understand that the cold face of the marketing business is about bringing in cash, not just about having big ad campaigns."

Vijay Solanki

Dealing with Press Inquiries

GETTING STARTED

Handling press inquiries promptly, honestly, and efficiently can help your organization to obtain fair coverage in the press. Lack of cooperation can reflect unfavorably on an organization, so respond promptly to press inquiries, because journalists have publishing deadlines.

FAQs

Who should deal with press inquiries?

Some companies appoint a single spokesperson who handles all inquiries. Others refer inquiries to the most appropriate specialist. It is essential that telephone operators are aware of the correct press contacts. It can be frustrating for journalists to be passed from one person to another. Alternatively, route all press inquiries to a public relations consulting firm. If they cannot deal with the inquiry directly, they can refer the question to a specialist.

Does the Internet make management of press relations any easier?

The Internet makes it easier for journalists to obtain information. It also puts the onus on companies to become more transparent in their dealings with the media and also to make sure that their online presence is regularly updated and easy to navigate.

Should we encourage senior executives to hold press interviews?

Interviews with key figures can be valuable for both the company and the press. Although it is important to encourage openness, it can be equally valuable to maintain a degree of exclusivity so that journalists value an interview.

MAKING IT HAPPEN

Deal Positively with Press Inquiries

Handling press inquiries promptly, honestly, and efficiently can help your organization to obtain fair coverage in the press. If there is nobody ready to supply information, the line "No one was available for comment" is used. In certain circumstances, this can reflect unfavorably on an organization.

Provide the Right Contacts for Journalists

Always respond promptly to press inquiries, because journalists have publishing deadlines to meet. Journalists should be able to reach a named contact, and a substitute should be available when necessary. Wherever possible, appoint one spokesperson to handle all inquiries. This will guarantee that the organization speaks with a consistent voice. Include the name of the spokesperson in all press releases and make sure that the switchboard is aware of the press contact or any substitute.

It is important that the spokesperson is fully briefed on current activity. If they cannot provide all the necessary information, let the journalist know that either the spokesperson or someone with more specialist knowl-

edge will call back within an agreed time. Journalists also should be given reasonable access to specialists or senior executives, if necessary.

Make Press Conferences Count

A press conference provides an opportunity for an organization to meet journalists and editors in person and give them a detailed briefing on a new product or corporate development.

Press conferences can be important in a number of situations:

- the launch of a major new product;
- a significant corporate event;
- a news story, such as a takeover, which will have an important impact on the market.

An effective press conference provides mutual benefit to the organization and the press. If journalists have the opportunity to meet contacts or get detailed information that would otherwise be difficult, they see a conference as valuable. From your own point of view, a good press conference provides your organization with direct access to journalists and editors who would normally only be accessible by telephone. It also insures that the event receives effective coverage in the right media. If it is difficult to arrange a press conference at short notice, you can hold a Webcast on the Internet and invite selected journalists to join the event.

Prepare for a Press Conference

Planning and preparation are important to insure the success of your conference. These guidelines will help you prepare for a productive event:

- Invite journalists and editors from publications that reach your most important customers and prospects.
- Give details of time and location and try to confirm who will be attending.
- Try to plan the conference so that editorial coverage will appear in the next issue of the most important monthly publications.
- Make sure journalists understand the importance of the event.
- Provide press packs that include background information, specific information on the subject, photographs, and other relevant material.
- If necessary, make sure that senior executives or other specialists are available to answer detailed questions.
- If necessary, provide facilities for journalists such as telephones, Internet connections, and working areas, so they can produce and transmit material quickly to meet deadlines.
- Provide appropriate refreshments.
- If any important press contacts cannot attend, send them a press pack and—if they're really important—arrange a separate meeting.

Arrange Interviews with Key People

An interview with a senior executive or specialist provides an opportunity for an organization to meet selected

journalists and give them a detailed briefing on a new product or corporate development. The advantage to the press is that this process is more selective than a press conference and gives them an opportunity for an "exclusive." Ideally, there is mutual benefit for the organization and the press, because your company gets its message across to the right people in the right way.

Identify Opportunities for Interviews
An interview can be arranged either at the request of the press, or as part of a planned press relations program. Interviews can be important in a number of situations, including:
- the launch of a major new product;
- a significant corporate event, such as the opening of a new factory;
- a news story, such as a takeover, which will have an important effect on the market;
- the announcement of the financial results of an important organization;
- the appointment of a new senior executive or specialist manager, which might affect the prospects or future direction of your organization.

Prepare for an Interview
You should arrange the interview for selected journalists and editors from publications that reach your most important customers and prospects. If necessary, you can make the interview exclusive by limiting it to one publication only or one publication in each sector. Make sure that the person to be interviewed is fully briefed on the subject of the interview, and provide press packs. As with a press conference, provide facilities for journalists such as telephones, Internet connections, and working areas, so they can produce and transmit material quickly to meet deadlines.

Provide Background with a Press Pack
A press pack should contain background information on an organization and its products. It can be issued to press, television, or radio journalists in conjunction with press releases or feature articles, or distributed on its own.

Press packs can cover a variety of topics, including:
- the company, its products, and its services;
- important recent developments;
- key members of the management team;
- financial and market information.

The information can be used to fill in background if a journalist is writing a news item or editing a press release on the organization. It can also form the basis of a news item or feature article. Whenever you hold a press conference, launch event, interview, or press visit, make sure that journalists and editors have an up-to-date pack. Include any specific information that is relevant to the event. As a matter of routine, send a press pack to any new press contact. Background information included in a conventional press pack can also be placed on the press or media pages of your Web site.

Produce an Up-to-date Pack
Press packs are only useful if they are current and informative. These guidelines will help you produce an effective pack:
- Information should be typed, double-spaced.
- Names and telephone numbers of key personnel should be included.
- A contact name for further information should be provided.
- A selection of product or personnel photographs should be included.

Distributing them properly also is helpful:
- Press packs can be given directly to journalists and editors at events or press visits, or sent separately by mail or e-mail.
- Wherever possible, they should be given to a named individual.
- Maintain a list of contacts who have received press packs and make sure that you send them updated information, whenever it is available.

COMMON MISTAKES
Ignoring Press Inquiries
If a PR problem occurs, it's easy to ignore press inquiries and hope that journalists will go away. They rarely do, and the lack of cooperation from your company could lead to adverse reports in the press. If journalists don't have hard information, they have to rely on their own assumptions, and this could create problems.

Calling a Press Conference for an Unimportant Event
Journalists cannot attend every press conference they are invited to. If your conference is not really newsworthy, you may lose their attention when it comes to later, more important events.

Failing to Keep Press Information Current
Journalists base their stories on the information they have. Press packs and other background material must be amended whenever information changes.

FOR MORE INFORMATION

Book:
Bland, Michael, Alison Theaker, and David Wragg. *Effective Media Relations*. 3rd ed. Milford, CT: Kogan Page, 2005.

Web sites:
Institute for Public Relations: **www.instituteforpr.com**
International Public Relations Association: **www.ipranet.org**

See also:
✔ Producing Press Material (pp. 761–762)
✔ Running a Product Public Relations Campaign (pp. 763–764)

"For a politician to complain about the press is like a ship's captain complaining about the sea."

Enoch Powell

Managing Retailer Marketing Programs

GETTING STARTED

If you are implementing retailer or distributor marketing programs, consistency across the board is important in order to insure the message is not diluted. Central support is therefore vital. There are many steps you can take to help make the program a success, and to make the best use of budgets.

FAQs

Why should local advertising be managed?

It is easy for local outlets to develop and run their own advertisements. This can weaken a brand or corporate identity and give conflicting messages to different customers. A strong management program insures consistent standards and also makes better use of available funds.

Should all local outlets run the same marketing program?

It is not essential to run identical programs in all markets. However, consistent treatment helps local outlets to benefit from repeated communication of the same brand values. Campaigns should be tailored to local market conditions but should incorporate key visual standards and corporate messages.

Who decides how local marketing funds should be allocated?

Individual outlets have the best knowledge of their local markets, but they may not have the skills to plan and operate cost-effective marketing campaigns. By centralizing the management of advertising and marketing programs, local outlets benefit from professional advice and guidance and the cumulative effect of integrated national, regional, and local campaigns.

MAKING IT HAPPEN

Help Distributors Use Marketing Programs

Suppliers can produce a guide to support their programs which enables local outlets to select the ones that allow them to develop their own promotional strategies. The guides should explain the scope and benefits of individual programs; describe the support material available; explain how to order support material; and provide guidelines on running the programs.

Establish a Distributor Marketing Database

The key to the success of local marketing programs is detailed knowledge of the local customer base, so that offers and information can be tailored. Maintain a central database of all local customers and use database management techniques to organize the mailing lists. Local outlets are unlikely to have the sophisticated equipment needed to perform database management operations, so centralizing the exercise is probably more effective.

The database would contain the names and addresses of each outlet's customers, together with variable information such as purchasing patterns, size of expenditure, type of purchase, and number of employees.

Keep Database Information Up to Date

Information for the database can be gathered from a number of sources, including:

- local customer sales records
- replies to advertisements
- responses to special offers or invitations
- applications for membership
- market research

The initial database is unlikely to be complete or to provide information in the most suitable format, so companies who wish to benefit from direct marketing run special campaigns to gather appropriate information. For example, an invitation to an open evening or a prize draw would require customers to provide information that is essential for the database. Local outlets can be given guidelines on the way to build and maintain their own records so that they provide suitable input to the database. A series of mailings can then be done to meet business and marketing objectives. By managing the process centrally and working in close conjunction with retailers, suppliers can make sure that their local outlets enjoy a direct marketing service that is of professional quality, as well as being precisely tailored to their local market.

Operate a Customized Advertising Service

Local or regional advertising campaigns can be customized to suit the needs of the local market. Support can be delivered in a number of forms:

- funds to enable local outlets to produce and run their own advertisements;
- contributions to the cost of joint supplier and local outlet advertisements;
- contributions to the cost of advertisements run by regional groups of outlets;
- production of national support advertisements that incorporate local information and are run on a regional basis;
- support for advertisements run in conjunction with regional radio or television stations.

Offer Funding Options

The level of support depends on the funds available for local support and the outlet's own budget. For example, many independent outlets have substantial advertising budgets of their own and utilize the supplier's budget to supplement these, or to run specific campaigns. Other smaller outlets or franchised outlets without their own budgets rely entirely on the supplier's contribution to run local campaigns. The question of financial support is therefore usually subject to negotiation.

"Acts of marketing insanity such as the U.S. firm that invested heavily in a campaign to sell cake mix to the Japanese—in profound and dismal ignorance of the fact that hardly any homes in Japan have ovens."

Robert Heller

Supply Advertising Material

The more practical forms of support—complete advertisements, logos, artwork, photographs—can be supplied for inclusion in the outlet's own local campaigns. The supplier is likely to be more concerned about the consistency of advertisements than the local outlet and should issue clear guidelines on the use of different elements of corporate identity. Many suppliers provide advertising standards manuals which give examples of layouts for different sizes of advertisements, explain the position and size of the company name and logo, list the typefaces to use, and include sample advertisements for guidance.

Establish a Centralized Advertising Service

Alternatively, the supplier can offer local outlets a central advertising service. This support policy enables suppliers to offer advertising to local outlets at consistent professional standards, incorporating local information (such as name, address, and map), priced offers, product variations, and special offers. Then the local outlet benefits from national advertising and strong branding, but also has advertisements that suit the local market.

Run Regional Advertising Programs

The regional approach can also be used to establish a cooperative advertising program between groups of local outlets. Local outlets pool their budgets and are able to build a higher profile by running larger advertisements or advertising more frequently. Each outlet includes its own name and address, but the advertisement promotes the generic benefits of the group. Some regional advertisements feature priced offers that are available at all the outlets in the group. This requires a high degree of cooperation between local outlets to set the target prices. However, suppliers should be aware that in the United States, the Federal Trade Commission (FTC) may regard this as a form of cartel. Suppliers should therefore seek guidance on the procedure for obtaining FTC approval for joint priced advertisements.

Providing a central form of support for local advertisements not only insures consistency and good branding but can also help to make the most effective use of limited budgets. By purchasing all advertising space or time centrally, the supplier can negotiate more effective rates based on volume purchase and can handle all the administration associated with media planning.

Take Advantage of Direct Marketing

The essence of an effective local support program is that local outlets understand their customers' needs and provide a level of service that is tailored to that market. In terms of customer satisfaction, the most powerful medium available to companies is direct marketing. The information in the marketing database provides a good basis for effective direct marketing programs. By operating them centrally in the same way as advertising, manufacturers can maintain quality and consistency and achieve good results.

Support Local Events

Local events such as open evenings, trade shows, and customer receptions are a powerful method of building customer loyalty, but they need to be handled professionally to achieve the right results. By providing the appropriate level of support, suppliers can help local outlets develop a program of events that suits their local market. The support includes:

- the development of suitable promotional and display material;
- the theme for the event;
- the design and production of invitations;
- generation of mailing lists;
- support literature;
- personal support by members of the head office team.

COMMON MISTAKES

Failure to Control Local Spending

Local outlets frequently run marketing programs to meet ad hoc objectives. This can lead to fragmented communication and poor use of funds. The value of local marketing funds can be increased by integrating different campaigns and reinforcing local initiatives with national campaigns.

No Database

The marketing database is essential to the control of local marketing programs. It supports effective program administration and, more importantly, it allows companies to monitor and measure the effectiveness of programs. Response levels can be measured and compared across different regions and the effects of different spending levels assessed. The database also holds details of local marketing programs as a basis for direct marketing and telemarketing programs.

Poor Administration

Efficient administration is an important part of local marketing support, but it is frequently handled poorly. By setting up a process for ordering marketing support material, booking advertising space, invoicing local outlets, and recording responses, you can gain greater control over the marketing program and make sure that funds are used more effectively.

FOR MORE INFORMATION

Book:
Kotler, Philip, and Kevin Lane Keller. *Marketing Management*. 12th ed. Englewood Cliffs, NJ: Prentice Hall, 2005.

Web sites:
Council of Logistics Management: **www.clm1.org**
The Supply Chain Council: **www.supply-chain.org**

See also:
✔ Improving Communication with Resellers (pp. 679–680)

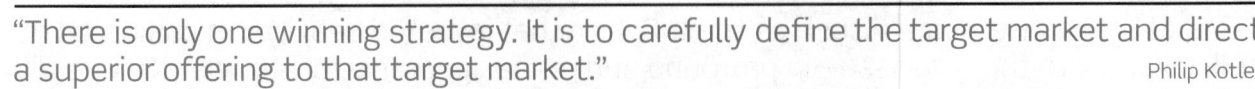
"There is only one winning strategy. It is to carefully define the target market and direct a superior offering to that target market."

Philip Kotler

Offering Customers Self-Service

GETTING STARTED

Offering self-service facilities to customers via the Internet has considerable benefits. For customers, being able to obtain information and place orders whenever they want is extremely convenient. And suppliers can obtain precise data on what customers want, as well as cutting down on administration costs. The only proviso is that the Web site must be constantly available and properly supported.

FAQs

Doesn't self-service weaken customer relationships?

Opinion is divided over the impact of self-service. In the professions, for example, some companies are concerned that their reputation for high-quality personal service is reduced. Other businesses argue that putting simple services online frees staff for more complex customer projects. In industry, the popularity of self-service among customers has convinced some companies that this is the most suitable way to deal with them. The quantity of customer information available from self-service sites is also important, provided it is used to strengthen relationships through tailored service.

If a customer makes a mistake as a result of using self-service facilities, whose fault is it?

Organizations which provide advice and guidance through a self-service facility must assess the risk of mistakes and include warning notices on the site. The warning might take the form of a phrase such as, "You should seek professional advice before taking any action."

Should self-service be the only form of support available to customers?

While self-service support benefits both parties, it may leave customers feeling vulnerable if they cannot get a satisfactory answer from the site. Including a backup telephone facility reassures customers that personal service is available if it is needed. You can discourage unnecessary use by charging a fee for the service.

MAKING IT HAPPEN

Identify Applications for Self-Service

The Internet enables companies to offer customers self-service facilities. Self-service reduces customer support costs and improves convenience for customers. It means companies can deliver service around the clock without tying up key staff. It also enables them to reduce their telephone-based support facilities by transferring support resources to a Web site. Self-service is important in delivery of information, direct sales, sales administration, customer support, and technical support.

Give Customers More Choice

With self-service, customers can obtain information on products, prices, features, and order status from a Web site, then place orders directly. The process is spreading throughout industry as manufacturers recognize the benefits of self-service in terms of cost, control, and customer satisfaction. Self-service gives manufacturers greater control over the sales process and customer relationships, and also reduces sales and distribution costs. Customers themselves recognize the value of these services; many have reported significant savings in productivity through improved support and better asset management. Having such a choice strengthens customer relationships and makes self-service a powerful differentiator.

Gain Better Customer Information

Self-service provides precise information on what customers want, so it is essential to tailor the service to meet those requirements and make self-service a rewarding experience. Support levels, for example, can be customized to individual user profiles, making service delivery more convenient and cost-effective. Customer information can also be used to develop customized, added-value services. For example, business customers can be provided with personalized Web pages that include access to their own product configurations; automated, paperless orders; order tracking; asset management facilities; and individual support tools. Components manufacturers offer services such as online design and specification to their customers, as well as high levels of technical support.

Improve Customer Convenience

Customers now expect service to be available 24 hours a day. They want a choice of services, personalized to their own requirements, and they want these services at competitive prices. Enabling customers to help themselves meets those criteria. Although it appears to reduce the element of personal service that is crucial to customer relationships, the convenience of self-service can add value and give a company even greater control. The challenge is to turn basic self-service into a highly differentiated product. The Internet allows companies to link products, businesses, and services into a database that customers can use to help themselves with routine tasks. By tailoring these products and using the customer information they contain, suppliers can offer a service that is even more personal than traditional face-to-face meetings.

Give Customers Automated Tools

A firm of brokers gives clients a personal minibroking system that they can use any time, day or night. Clients are offered a choice of tasks such as getting a quotation for car insurance. Many of the functions are highly automated, making it quick and easy for clients to get quotes—all they have to do is choose the type of coverage they want. The system provides a selection of quotations and makes it easy to highlight and compare the benefits of different policies. Once the client has accepted a

"There is only one valid definition of business: to create a customer." — Peter F. Drucker

quotation, the system turns it into a live policy. Once credit card payment is completed, customers can print off their own insurance certificate and policy details. This is self-service at its best and provides users with a quick, convenient, around-the-clock service.

Simplify Customer Support

Although support is a critical element in customer relationship management, many organizations see it as an expensive overhead. They want to reduce capital investment and operating costs, and to free skilled resources to focus on other activities. Many of them are therefore turning to self-service support as a cost-effective alternative. Online support tools use the speed and convenience of Web-based contact facilities to simplify support management and improve customer service. So customers can place support requests through various channels, including text, voice over IP, e-mail, fax, and Web forms.

Speed Up Fault Resolution

Self-service support cuts the costs for the supplier and speeds up service for the customer. Customers can solve many problems themselves, by using frequently asked questions or interrogating an online service database. The latest support tools are using the power of data mining and knowledge management to improve fault resolution even further. They insure that all support knowledge and experience is captured and managed on a central database, which is continuously updated. This database insures that users get rapid access to the latest information. It can also distinguish trends as a basis for identifying emerging or recurring problems and providing alternative resources.

Encourage Customers to Help Each Other

A components manufacturer has made significant savings in its customer support costs by enabling customers to serve themselves through an e-commerce site. Customers help themselves to technical support and order status information via personalized Web pages that hold full details of their own products, specifications, component requirements, and technical issues. The manufacturer has added value to this one-to-one service by encouraging community between all of its customers. Customers answer other customers' technical questions and help each other out publicly on the company's Web site. The site also provides shared access to design and technical tools that customers can use in their own projects.

Deliver Consistent Service

It is essential to offer the highest standards of service. In practical terms, that means a Web site that is constantly available, easily accessible information, and high levels of customer support behind the Web site. Although self-service saves everyone time, experience indicates that customers need the reassurance that they can also talk to a specialist if they are having problems. You can provide this backup by including an automatic telephone callback facility on a Web page.

COMMON MISTAKES
Failing to Use Customer Information to Enhance Self-Service

Self-service facilities provide vast amounts of data on customer purchasing habits, support requirements, and information needs. This information should be used continually to enhance the customer experience and develop services and processes that meet customer requirements more closely. Ignoring such data is a wasted opportunity.

Giving Customers Limited Choice

Self-service is just one method of delivering service. You should ask customers how they prefer to deal with you. You can then offer a variety of service and support options with different charges for each level. For example, customer support packages can be offered at gold, silver, and bronze levels, with bronze as the most basic package. Self-service can be part of a portfolio, enabling customers to match your support to their operational needs.

Providing an Unreliable Service to Customers

Customers expect a service that is easy to use, as well as always available and reliable. It must be well supported with appropriate management, infrastructure, and staffing. Any loss of quality could damage your company's reputation.

Putting the Wrong Services Online

Not all services are suitable for online delivery. Simple queries, briefing material, news updates, and frequently asked questions are common, but more complex queries are best handled directly by specialists. Providing only what appear to be standard answers may create the wrong impression of your company.

FOR MORE INFORMATION

Books:
Fleischer, Joe, and Brendan Read. *The Complete Guide to Customer Support: How to Turn Technical Assistance into a Profitable Relationship.* New York: CMP Books, 2002.
Seybold, Patricia. *Customers.com: How to Create a Profitable Business Strategy for the Internet and Beyond.* New York: Crown Business, 1998.

Web site:
Patricia Seybold Group: **www.psgroup.com**

See also:
✓ Extending a Product with Service (pp. 753–754)
☆ The Second Coming of Service (pp. 104–105)

Managing Your Image: Make an Impact

GETTING STARTED

Most of us think image management is for PR consultants and celebrities. The truth is that managing your own image well can enhance your reputation for competence and dependability and multiply the career opportunities available to you.

Image management starts with first impressions: people form remarkably strong and persistent opinions of each other within minutes of their first meeting. It's worth thinking about the kind of impression you want to create and working to project it from the outset, even if you generally shrink from the idea of self-promotion. Starting off on the right foot will make the rest of the process much simpler.

FAQs

I think it's important to be yourself. Aren't you asking for trouble by trying to construct some fake persona for yourself?

Managing your image isn't the same as contriving it. Everything you say and do should feel authentic. Image management is about presenting yourself in the best light, not a false one. We all exercise some control over the way we behave in different situations—this is just another situation in which conscious control can bring advantages.

I want to be judged on the quality of my work, not my appearance. In my professional life, nobody can know me based on a first impression.

In a sense, you're right: it takes time to demonstrate your capabilities and personal qualities. But it's a fact of life that people do judge each other based on physical appearance, not necessarily in terms of their size or shape, but in terms of their self-presentation. The image you present speaks volumes about your motivations and the way you feel about yourself. If you stand in front of a mirror and act out different scenarios, you'll see real differences in how your body responds and how those postures make you feel. Your body language follows your thoughts and reveals a great deal about you.

I'm feeling overwhelmed by an important presentation I have to give. How can I create a good impression in these circumstances?

First, make sure you understand what people's expectations are and aim to meet them. Find out who will be in the audience. Anticipate what sorts of questions they might ask (include worst-case scenarios) and prepare for them. Rehearse your presentation until you're confident of the material. Be sure to wear comfortable clothes that you feel good in. Go into the presentation in a successful frame of mind, and you'll find that you can make it happen.

Although I try to manage the impression I create, people seem to misunderstand me all the time. What's going wrong?

You may be misreading the context or misjudging your own behavior. Stop trying so hard and instead observe people who have a natural aptitude for putting themselves across. You may pick up some clues about where you're going wrong. Alternatively, you could ask for feedback and advice from people you trust on what you could do more successfully.

MAKING IT HAPPEN

Researchers tell us that an impression is created in the first seven seconds of an encounter and that after that it's extremely difficult to change. It's therefore obviously important to learn how to orchestrate those critical few seconds. You may find it helpful to consider the five Cs:

- Context
- Communication
- Credibility
- Clothing
- Composure/confidence

Context

First, understand the context in which you find yourself, the motivations of those present, and the purpose and circumstances surrounding the occasion. Whether you're being interviewed for a job or conducting an important client meeting, it's worth spending time thinking through what your audience's expectations are and how to meet them. Should you take risks to distinguish yourself from the others present, or is it a time when you need to blend in and demonstrate your compatibility with their values?

Communication—Verbal and Nonverbal

Having analyzed the occasion, consider what kind of language is likely to be most effective. Good communicators are able to adjust the tone, tenor, and timing of their speech to maximum effect.

NLP—neurolinguistic programming—has a great deal to say on this subject. It advocates listening to the kinds of words that individuals use; people's words indicate the way they interpret and represent the world. There are five different interpretive modes: visual, kinesthetic, auditory, gustatory, and olfactory, with the first three being the most common. People who "see" things in their mind's eye say things like, "I can see what you're saying," or "I have a clear vision of what this will look like." Those who make "sense" of the world through movement, touch, and feelings use a kinesthetic representational system. They typically use phrases describing touch or motion, for example, "I get a good feeling about this," or

---

"If people don't want to listen to you, what makes you think they want to hear from your sweater."

Fran Lebowitz

"The change in market dynamics will be a blow to the business." People whose world-view is auditory might say, "I hear what you're saying," or "It sounds suspicious to me!"

Your approach can be all the more effective if it matches that of your audience, or at least uses a mixture of the three main representational systems so you reach everyone. Using vocabulary and body language that are compatible with those of the people you are speaking to gives the impression of immediate rapport—which is enormously helpful in creating a positive image.

Remember to make your body language consistent with what you're saying. If you don't believe in your message, your body will show it somehow, and this mismatch is called *leakage*. You often see it when people are nervous or are saying something they know to be untrue. You'll notice their feet shifting, a knee jiggling, or exaggerated gestures to compensate for their discomfort with their own words.

Speak clearly and enunciate your words properly so everyone can hear you without straining. The speed, tone, and pitch of your voice are all signals that will be picked up by your audience.

Credibility

Don't bluff. Stick to what you know and use war stories if appropriate to show the depth of your knowledge. Many of us are trained as children not to toot our own horns or boast about our achievements, but you need to find opportunities to demonstrate the extent of your experience and skills. This means making connections with what's being said and using them as openings to talk about your past experience. Be careful not to overdo it, though; you need to strike a careful balance between demonstrating your capability and being sensitive to how much self-promotion someone can tolerate.

Clothing

Clothes can enhance or destroy a first impression. Too much of a good thing can be a disaster: anything extreme—too bright, too flashy—may stay in the observer's mind as a picture representing you!

Deciding on what to wear largely depends upon the situation. The safest strategy is to reflect the style of those that you'll be meeting with, perhaps erring on the side of conservatism. If the context is creative you have more freedom to be idiosyncratic; but if you aim to engage with an organizational culture, it's best to reflect this in your appearance.

Good grooming is equally vital. Make sure you're well put together. Try to avoid fabrics that show perspiration, an unironed shirt or blouse, and food-stained clothes. Neat and clean is the best bet for most occasions.

Composure/Confidence

Composure comes from confidence. When you know what you want and are well prepared, you feel confident and therefore give an impression of composure. This makes it easier to manage the situation, respond flexibly, and roll with the punches.

Just as bad first impressions are hard to displace, so are good impressions. If you invest in conveying the right image the first time, you won't need to concern yourself with repairing a poor image later. A positive image is relatively easy to maintain.

COMMON MISTAKES
You Try Too Hard at First
Image management is a subtle skill. A common mistake is to try too hard, exaggerating your natural characteristics in order to convey confidence. The best way to avoid this is to practice in front of a friend or trusted coworker and ask for feedback on the impression you're creating. Be open to trying different behaviors. If you have to, practice in front of a mirror. You won't get feedback as such, but mirrors never lie!

You Leave It to Chance
You can unwittingly create a poor image by expecting people to know where your talents or intentions lie without actually telling them. People aren't mind readers, however, and they have no way of knowing you unless you reveal yourself. You have to engage actively in creating an image. If you want others to know about something, find a way of weaving it into the conversation. Provide your audience with a hook that they can remember you by. If you project as bland, you may be remembered as bland. Or you may not be remembered at all!

You Go Too Far
Misreading a situation and drawing attention to yourself in a negative way can be difficult to recover from. If this happens, you may find it best to declare your mistake and start again. Few people can come back from situations like this without any adverse effects.

You Forget that Other People Have Networks
Everyone you meet has a network. If you create a good impression, it circulates well beyond your immediate circle and is likely to benefit you in unexpected ways. A poor impression travels just as far and just as fast. Every time you meet someone for the first time, remember that you're meeting not an individual, but potentially that person's entire network of coworkers, contacts, acquaintances, and friends.

FOR MORE INFORMATION

Books:
Dimitrius, Jo-Ellan. *Put Your Best Foot Forward: Make a Great Impression by Taking Control of How Others See You.* New York: Scribner, 2001.
Mitchell, Mary, and John Corr, eds. *The First Five Minutes: How to Make a Great First Impression in Any Business Situation.* New York: Wiley, 1998.

Web Sites:
About Human Resources:
http://humanresources.about.com/cs/communication/a/profimage.htm
Mental Health Net: **www.mentalhelp.net**

See also:
✔ Developing Presence (pp. 781–782)

"Toughness doesn't have to come in a pinstripe suit."   Dianne Feinstein

Developing Presence

GETTING STARTED

Presence is an elusive human quality that mysteriously enables someone to command respect, or at least attention. Some people believe you're born with presence, others that it develops as a by-product of success. In fact, it's probably a combination of the two—and almost all of us can certainly nurture and develop it in ourselves. It most often seems to result from confidence in what you're doing, when you feel at home with, or passionate about, your role. Presence is most likely to elude us when we're not sure of ourselves and feeling uncomfortable.

FAQs

I'm not very tall. How can I possibly create presence?

Presence doesn't depend on height. When you think of successful political and business leaders, you'll find that many are small people who have compensated for their lack of stature in other ways. Gandhi, Mother Theresa, Nelson Mandela, and Napoleon are just a few examples. Presence can be created by a state of mind: the old adage, "think tall and you will be tall" really does work.

I'm good in some circumstances, but have problems performing well in the workplace. What do I do?

This isn't an unusual phenomenon. Many people who perform well in one context find that they cannot switch their talent on in a different setting. However, there are useful techniques that will enable you to transfer your talent from one situation to another. One that seems to work very well is "anchoring." Briefly, it relies on your ability to capture the feeling when you're doing something really well, and associate it with a gesture, movement, or saying—such as pinching your thumb and forefinger together. This becomes the "anchor," and when you transfer your anchor into a new setting, all the memories of performing well flood back and allow you to do so at will.

I appear to hold real credibility with the people who report to me, but don't have the same effect on my peers and managers. What can I do?

With your subordinates, you have three things that they don't: knowledge, expertise, and authority. When you're with your peers and managers, they probably have the same or more of these things—or create the illusion that they do. This can be sufficiently intimidating to make you lose your confidence. Try the "anchor" technique described above to see if you can transfer your confidence into encounters with your peers and managers.

I have taken many presentation skills courses, but I have problems with creating a consistent presence. How can I address this?

Presence very often comes from being personally aligned with your message. In order to be an effective communicator—both with your body language and speech—you need to be "at one" with what you're saying. You must have the knowledge to explore the area comfortably with your audience, be at ease with your audiovisual aids, and have a real desire to communicate what you have to say. In addition, you need to feel physically comfortable with who you are and how you appear. Practice is essential, especially if you are often nervous as a public speaker. Giving a presentation on a subject that you feel passionate about is a great place to begin.

MAKING IT HAPPEN

Developing presence is a multifaceted challenge that can be categorized in four different areas:

- physical
- mental/emotional
- mastery
- occasion-based

Physical

This refers to how you "manage" your body. People with presence often have good posture, even if they're small. They stand and move well, projecting calm and confidence. Being fit and in good general health are key factors. Exercise, good diet, proper rest, and "centering" practices like meditation and yoga are important allies. Good-quality clothes that fit well emphasize posture and confidence. They don't need to be expensive or conventional, just carefully chosen to suit the occasion.

Nonverbal behavior can reinforce the impression you're trying to create. Steady eye contact, a clear voice, and appropriate gestures are powerful channels of nonverbal communication. People with presence also often create the impression of being larger than they actually are, by the clever use of space. If sitting, they may sit with one arm resting on the back of the chair, their body at an angle, and one leg crossed over the other. This position takes up a large amount of space and is very confident and imposing. Look for opportunities to project a "bigger" persona. Use fuller, sweeping arm movements, rather than just a hand or pointing finger. Exaggerate these gestures in front of a mirror or a friend, so you won't overdo them in public.

The ability to build rapport is invaluable. Good eye contact when engaging with people, even if those in an audience, enables you to make valuable human impressions. Paying proper attention to what people say and demonstrating that you've heard their comments is important. So, too, is remembering people, and the context in which you know them. By deliberately using someone's name when you're speaking to them, you can embed it in your mind.

Mental/Emotional

The mind is one of the most important tools for creating presence. It can create a deep impression—on you as well

"A certain person may have, as you say, a wonderful presence: I do not know. What I do know is that he has a perfectly delightful absence."

Idries Shah

as others—just by "seeing" something. The art of visualization is very effective: our thoughts always precede our actions and behavior so, by making your intention explicit in your mind, you'll already be creating it in reality. Visualize yourself as a person who emanates presence. See your picture in color; examine it in detail. Note the feelings that arise in you, the sound of an audience applauding, the glow of achievement as you make your exit.

Make positive affirmations, "I am confident," "I feel good," "I have presence." These will train your brain to believe what you see in your mind's eye. Repeat your positive affirmations regularly so that they become the dominant messages that you transmit about yourself. Make sure they're in the present tense however. If you say "I will be confident," your brain will believe it to be a *future* scenario, and you may never get there!

Mastery

Know what you know. You've built knowledge and experience over the years and this will enable you to be confident in what you say and do. Ensure that people know your worth in this regard by being open and honest. Share your experiences, tell stories, and engage people at the human level. Be aware, too, of times when others need to have their presence acknowledged. Too often, people on a quest to create presence for themselves stop seeing and listening to others. Try to be inclusive, and "generosity" will also become part of your presence.

Mastering all these elements will open new doors of opportunity for you: people will gravitate to you, offer you new leadership roles, and spread the good word about your qualities and skills.

Occasion

Projecting presence demands an occasion. This may be any type of occasion, from a gathering of a few people to an audience of many. People with presence are able to create a sense of occasion in even the most ordinary of circumstances, such as walking along the production line, chairing a meeting, or giving a presentation. Think through your dramatic strategy, and practice so that you get the timing and pace right.

Presence is about transmitting a quality that others trust and respond to. It makes them feel as if they're gaining something just from being close to you. If it's to be sustained, having presence carries quite a lot of responsibility. For those who look up to you, you'll be providing guidance and inspiring confidence, reflecting their values, and—perhaps—being their conscience. This is

why it's important that you're fully aligned and authentic in your desire for presence.

COMMON MISTAKES
You Mistake Overconfidence for Presence

These two traits are not the same. Overconfidence is about oneself; presence is about others. Overconfident behavior can come across as self-interested and unempathetic, whereas someone with presence is often seen as taking an interest and building relationships. People who demonstrate overconfidence are often lacking in confidence, and are trying to compensate for this.

You Think that Presence Cannot Be Developed

Having a certain amount of natural presence is a gift. Nevertheless, it's a gift that needs attention and development to mature properly. Look for occasions where you can practice the techniques that will help you project the impression you seek. By building up a series of successes, you'll soon be able to join them together and emanate this quality at will. In time, it may become second nature.

You Aren't Fully Prepared

As discussed above, there are physical, mental, emotional, mastery, and "occasion" elements involved in presence. It's important to have all of these aligned in the same direction—if you don't, you could ruin all your good work. Imagine looking good, having a clear intention, having the occasion . . . but nothing to say. Or conversely, having a great story or bit of information, but getting the timing all wrong. Each element assists and supports the others, so pay careful attention to all of them.

FOR MORE INFORMATION

Book:
Demarais, Ann, and Valerie White. *First Impressions: What You Don't Know About How Others See You.* New York: Bantam, 2005.

Web Site:
Mental Health Net: **www.mentalhelp.net**

See also:
✔ Managing Perceptions (pp. 783–784)
✔ Managing Your Image: Make an Impact (pp. 779–780)

Managing Perceptions

GETTING STARTED

We all hold differing views of the world, partly because of our different cultural backgrounds, life experiences, and personal values. Naturally this colors our interactions with others. Our personality, level of social skills, style, and approach further affect our relationships. In the workplace, particularly among managers and supervisors, it is becoming increasingly important to be able to understand and manage the perception others have of us.

This isn't as difficult as you might think. Although it requires a good deal of thought, motivation, and self-awareness, with practice you'll find it easier to communicate with people, to motivate them, and to lead them in a desired direction.

FAQs

Isn't it rather manipulative to manage perceptions?

Most techniques can be either positive or negative, depending on context. We live in a culture in which people and organizations spend enormous sums of money employing others to manage perceptions. You can employ the same skills used by advertising and public relations companies to change perceptions to influence people around you. At the very least, you should be aware of the impressions your behavior creates. At best, you can develop skills that allow you to manage your behavior in a way that furthers your career.

Why is perception management important to my career?

Careers are no longer managed by organizations, but are directed by individuals themselves. You're judged not only on what you do, but on how you do it—so other people's perceptions and evaluations of you play an important role in your career. People who know how to influence others' perceptions of them have a much better chance of controlling their own destiny.

Why do I find it so hard to change others' perceptions of me?

Changing how others view you requires a consistent flow of new messages. People generally hold on to their first impressions, and it's difficult to replace them with something more to your liking. Doing this takes persistent awareness and self-evaluation—both of which take time and energy to develop.

If you wish to change someone's impression of you, you need to understand both that person's existing perception and the one you wish to create. You then need to create a bridge between the two, and find an opportunity to convey a different message. The persona you put forward must, however, be authentic. If you create an impression that is not essentially *you*, the deception will be easy to spot, simply because living a lie is extraordinarily difficult to sustain.

I don't particularly care what other people think about me, I just want to get on with doing a good job.

Fine, but common wisdom suggests that you should take care of your relationships as you move up the career ladder, because you may run into the same people later when you're on the way back down. People can harbor grudges for years, and you don't want to risk encountering an unforgiving individual in a position of influence. If you find it impossible to change your attitude, you'd better have skills that make you indispensable!

MAKING IT HAPPEN
Understand Yourself and How You Are Perceived

To understand how others view you, you need to have an accurate understanding of yourself. Building self-awareness requires courage and commitment.

The first stage is to spend some quiet time with yourself each day, when you can begin to see what is the true you and what is not. The next step is to encourage informal feedback from trusted peers and managers. Remember that people will give subjective views based on their opinion, which may not resonate with you—so you may be surprised at the way you're perceived. Try to remain objective and explore where these views have come from.

You can use more formal tools that enable you to understand yourself, such as psychometrics and personality profiles. The feedback from these is sometimes easier to manage because it's objective and has no third-party relationship standing in the way.

Sometimes 360-degree surveys are used to gather the views of different audiences, both inside and outside the business. These tend to focus on behavior and skill level. Be aware of the differences between the two. While both may be learned and modified, changing the way you behave usually involves altering personality traits and perceptions and may be more difficult than acquiring new skills.

When reviewing test results, try not to concentrate only on personal information that feels hurtful. Look for patterns in your feedback, and reflect on when and why these may have arisen. Stress often allows unintentional behavior to surface. Behaviors you haven't even been aware of may have given rise to the impressions that you'd like to change.

Determine Your Strategy

Before embarking on any perception management strategy, decide what your goals are, how you intend to accomplish them, and how to monitor your progress. Don't be too ambitious at first: focus on one thing that you can change that will create a quick win.

Think of the context in which you're working, and use your feedback to select your initial goals. While there may be indicators and encouragement to change your

"As times change, you want to really revere your heredity, but you don't want to be a shrine—to light candles and kneel."

Kitty d'Alessio

behavior, remember that there may also be reactions to those changes. People are used to the old you and may have difficulty adjusting to the new you. It will help if you concentrate on four tracks:

- **Communicate** your intentions to people who may be affected. If you have a formal annual performance appraisal, make it a learning objective; this is likely to win more support and understanding if things don't work out quite the way you'd planned. You're also likely to receive more praise when you're successful.
- **Gain support** from your manager or key members of your team to help keep you focused. A good support group is essential when you're seeking to change something about yourself—witness organizations such as Alcoholics Anonymous and Weight Watchers.
- **Find a coach** to provide ongoing guidance. A coach can offer impartial observations and encourage you to continue, or change, your strategy as you move forward. Coaching takes time and commitment, so allow for this in your work plan.
- **Evaluate** your progress at each milestone in your plan, either formally or informally. You may wish to keep a daily journal, writing down the kind of details that tend to slip away if they're not recorded. Frequency is important in gathering informal feedback, but make sure you give people enough time to observe your new behavior before asking them for it. You might warn those whom you intend to approach for feedback so they can consciously pay attention to your behavior. A more formal option is to revisit the 360-degree questionnaire and see whether others have noticed the change.

Don't lose heart if the changes you succeed in bringing about aren't immediately recognized by others. It may take months, so consistency and perseverance are key.

A Quick Guide to Perception Management
In a nutshell, perception management is all about creating an impression through conscious activities and awareness of your audience and the impact you have on them. To be successful, define your target audience, overlay your values with theirs, adjust your communication style, encourage feedback, and be aware of how you adapt as changes are implemented.

COMMON MISTAKES
You Become Impatient
It's easy to get impatient for results and give up too quickly. Behavioral change is not as easy as learning a new skill; it requires dedication, commitment, and consistency. Only constant repetition and reinforcement of your new behavior will change people's perceptions of you.

Do	Don't
Increase your own awareness	Act defensive
Be aware of the impact you have on others	React emotionally to the feedback you receive
Learn to interpret other people's verbal and nonverbal signals	Get unmotivated
Know the effect that stress has on you and how this looks to others	Behave aggressively and try too hard too quickly
Be visible at strategic moments	Be ingratiating
Encourage feedback from people you value, without making unreasonable demands	Expect too much
Allow others to make their own choices	Embroil others in your views of yourself
Give yourself adequate time and make perception management part of your personal development	Pester people for feedback
Be consistent, patient, and forgiving	Be political or manipulative in your behavior

You Don't Ask for Feedback
Some people are embarrassed to ask for feedback and advice, particularly when they find themselves in management roles. Remember that much of our behavior is habitual, and to some extent may even have contributed to previous promotions. However, conduct appropriate to some roles may not be right for others. When you move into a management position, for example, relationships suddenly become much more important than technical skills. In this situation, use a new project or a particular aspect of your new role as a test-bed for the new you.

You Go Too Far
In trying to change your way of behaving, it's easy to overdo it and alienate the people you're trying to influence. Pursue your goals for change, but err on the side of subtlety.

FOR MORE INFORMATION
Book:
Demarais, Ann, and Valerie White. *First Impressions: What You Don't Know About How Others See You.* New York: Bantam, 2005.

Web sites:
About Human Resources: **http://humanresources.about.com/cs/workrelationships/a/workallies.htmm**
American Management Association: **www.amanet.org**

See also:
- Managing Perceptions (pp. 783–784)
- Managing Your Image: Make an Impact (pp. 779–780)

Understanding Your Values

GETTING STARTED

During your working life, it's very easy to get so immersed in the day-to-day routine that you forget to think about the larger picture of your life as a whole. You might be very excited to have been offered a new job; you might simply feel grateful that you *have* a job and a regular income; you might be immensely relieved to be one of the survivors after the latest round of layoffs. Any of these situations can take your eye off the really important question: are you in the right job *for you*?

Often this question can be answered simply by whether or not you feel happy and comfortable at work. At other times though, it can be more difficult—you may feel vaguely dissatisfied and restless; looking through your career history, you may have changed jobs a great many times; perhaps you notice that you start a new job with high enthusiasm, only to lose interest or motivation fairly quickly.

All of these scenarios can be the result of a mismatch between your values and your circumstances, so it makes good sense to take a more analytical look at what those values are, and how you can apply them practically to your working life. This actionlist points the way.

FAQs
What are values, exactly?

Values are about worth: they are the principles, standards, and beliefs you are committed to and live your life by; you feel unhappy and dissatisfied when they are compromised.

It's worth remembering that values are not set in stone, however. Some of your values may remain the same throughout your life; other may change through maturity, particular experiences, or as a result of circumstances.

Why is it important to understand my values?

In terms of your job, it's essential to understand your values, because it is they that motivate you to work. If you think of your career as a journey, there are three vital elements involved in that journey—interests, abilities, and values. Your interests tell you what direction to pursue, your abilities indicate how long it will take to reach your ultimate goal, and your values dictate whether or not the journey is worth taking in the first place. If, consciously or unconsciously, your values are telling you that a particular direction is not the right one, you're very unlikely to make a success of that journey!

What is the difference between values and ethics?

In this context, values differ from ethics in that there is not necessarily a moral dimension to values. Values, unlike ethics, do not have to be seen by society as "right" or "just" or "responsible," and so on; they are simply what is right for *you*. So one of your important values might be "a short journey to work," for example—which has no moral

implications whatever. If we take this thought to its logical extreme, then, even if an organization prides itself on its ethical standards or working practices, it *still* may not be the right place for you if your own priorities do not happen to be based on moral issues.

MAKING IT HAPPEN
Assess What Is Important to You

The easiest way to do this is to adopt a structured approach, otherwise your mind tends to jump around all over the place and things get forgotten or confused. A good method is to create a values "scorecard," which helps you identify and prioritize what's important to you.

Think carefully about what each of the words or terms below means to you, and then assess how they relate to what you want from work.

Achievement (accomplishing important things)
Aesthetics (attractive workspace)
Affiliation (membership of organization is a source of pride)
Alignment with boss
Artistic creativity
Autonomy & **independence** (most work self-determined, and limited direction by others)
Change & **variety**
Chaos (loosely defined environment; goals and priorities unclear)
Community activity
Commute
Competition
Creativity
Dual careers (place also offers career opportunities for partner)
Employee benefits
Excitement
Fast pace
Friendships
Glass ceiling (work environment offers all groups potential to work at highest levels)
Global focus (potential to live/work abroad)
Help others
Impact society
Influence people
Intellectual status
Knowledge
Legacy (be remembered for specific achievement by those who follow after)
Lifestyle integration (ability to balance family, career and self-fulfilment)

Location
Loyalty (high level of reciprocal loyalty with organization)
Make decisions
Minimize stress
Mobility (opportunity to relocate when appropriate)
Moral affiliation (work with people of similar morals, values, and ethics)
Moral fulfilment (environment that reflects your own moral standards)
Multicultural affiliation (environment with people from broad range of ages, cultures, etc.)
Physical challenge
Power & **authority**
Precision work
Prestige
Profit & **gain**
Public contact
Pure challenge (work which requires you to overcome impossible obstacles, difficult problems, etc.)
Recognition
Risk
Security
Self-realization (potential for you to realise your best talents)
Stability
Supervision (where you are responsible for planning and managing work done by others)
Time freedom
Travel
Work alone
Work under pressure
Work with others

"Human beings possess the potential to be educated for values." — S. K. Chakraborty

Once you have pondered the meaning of each, list the words or phrases under the following headings—bearing in mind that you may change your opinion several times as you go through them.

Must haves	High wants	Wants	Don't minds	Don't wants

Check Your Values against the Work You Are Doing Currently

Now think about your list of wants and don't wants against your present job. Are your most important requirements being met? If not, is there anything you can do to change the situation? Who might be able to help you—your boss, department head, mentor, HR department? Perhaps you could apply for a different role within the organization to gain more prestige or a higher salary; perhaps you could work flextime to make it easier to fulfill family commitments; perhaps you could move nearer to work to cut down on commuting, or spend more time socializing with colleagues to build up friendships; or maybe a training course would increase your knowledge or give you more intellectual challenge. All of these are just some of the potential options for you, depending on your values.

Many of these values are fairly practical, and even small adjustments in your working conditions could make the difference between them being met or not—with consequent implications for your happiness in your job.

Recognize When You Can't Change Things

Sometimes, however hard you try to alter things, you have to face the fact that the differences between your own values and those of your employer are irreconcilable. In fact, one of the top ten reasons that people cite for leaving their jobs is that their values are at odds with the corporate culture. If this is true in your own case, the most sensible option is to start looking for another job that will suit you better—and preferably sooner rather than later, before the mismatch starts to sap your will to live. No matter what the clash is based on, a lack of congruence with the corporate culture will destroy your attitude at work, and it can be difficult to regain your confidence and enthusiasm once things have gone too far.

COMMON MISTAKES
You Ignore Your Inner Voice

Many of us are brought up to be good, law-abiding, responsible citizens, and even more of us have an innate fear of rocking the boat. We feel guilty if we cause disruption, and we tend to blame ourselves if we're not happy—"I shouldn't make a fuss," "I'm being silly," "I really must learn to apply myself," and so on being common sentiments. However, if you feel restless at work, or are looking for a job and want to make the right decision, it is really important to put yourself and your own priorities first. After all, if you don't make sure that your values are being satisfied, you will never produce anything inspiring in terms of performance—which is hardly in your employer's best interests either!

You Place Too Much Importance on Little Things

Having realized the importance of your own values, you do need to exercise judgment in deciding which are essential to you. Nothing is ever perfect, and you are always going to encounter situations where compromise is required. Say, for example, you think you should have a reserved parking spot at work, but your company operates a first-come first-served policy and everyone parks wherever they can. This is probably not worth going to the wall for (unless perhaps you are physically challenged in some way and have a genuine need to be right outside the office building). This is where prioritizing your values into essentials and nice-to-haves is useful, as it helps you decide just how hard you need to push in different situations.

FOR MORE INFORMATION

Web Site:
About Human Resources:
http://humanresources.about.com

See also:
✓ Developing Presence (pp. 781–782)

"Values serve the process of 'becoming,' in the sense of transformation of the level of consciousness to purer, higher levels."

S. K. Chakraborty

Building Your Self-confidence

GETTING STARTED

For those who have it, there's nothing special about self-confidence. But for people without it, life is often a struggle to develop and maintain a sustaining belief in themselves.

We all have moments of feeling great about ourselves: we know what we want and we're confident of our capacity to get it. When that self-confidence is lacking, however, it's hard to retrieve. The main culprit is fear, which conjures up an endless succession of self-defeating "what if" scenarios. Developing self-confidence is largely a matter of attacking that irrational and debilitating fear.

FAQs

I'm frustrated by a member of my team who doesn't have the confidence to make decisions. Even though this person knows the job well, I'm always having to give directions. What should I do?

This person may have been undermined by having made poor decisions in the past and suffering the consequences. Alternatively, perhaps he or she has been overpromoted. The first thing to do is to stop making other people's decisions. Every time you make a decision for someone, you reinforce this person's dependency. Instead, turn this into a learning exercise to help the person develop, or regain, the confidence to rely on his or her own judgment. Solicit recommendations for solutions, perhaps starting with minor issues and graduating to more important ones as you progressively withdraw your input. Repeatedly validating this person's independent decisions should strengthen your coworker's self-confidence.

I was recently promoted, and although I had lots of confidence in my former job, I'm beginning to doubt my own abilities—this is such new territory for me. What can I do about this?

It's not uncommon for people to lose their confidence when placed in a new work environment, and they're often tempted to go back to their old comfort zone. When a return route isn't open to them, they may try super-imposing familiar activities on to their new role. In this case, the problem is more likely to be a lack of knowledge or skills than not being able to perform well. Asking for constructive feedback, coaching, and rewards for small successes will enable you to make the most of your talent and build the confidence you need to succeed.

MAKING IT HAPPEN
Build a Confident Work Force

You can't fake self-confidence. It has to flow from a well-grounded belief in who you are, otherwise you'll come across as brash and superficial.

Confidence is important in the workplace because it builds trust—trust builds commitment, and commitment builds a quality product or service. Self-confident employees use their initiative and make decisions that support organizational goals. The additional benefits of improved morale and a happier work atmosphere are icing on the cake.

The elements that build a confident work force are:
- people having the knowledge and skills to fulfill their roles;
- clear objectives for individuals and teams;
- authority in decision making and accountability for those decisions;
- recognition for achieving personal goals;
- investment in learning and development;
- opportunities to meet new challenges;
- celebration of meeting organizational objectives.

Boost Knowledge and Skills

Confidence at work comes from knowing what to do, how to do it, and when to do it. Whether this know-how was learned in school or professional training or on the job, it allows people to work within clear boundaries of competence. They become recognized for their abilities, which reinforces their self-image and builds their self-confidence. Putting employees into different jobs or assigning different, less-familiar tasks is likely to shake their self-confidence. Cross-training your people so they have transferable skills is one important way of keeping confidence high.

Set Clear Job Objectives

Success promotes self-confidence, and success can be measured only when an objective has been reached. Clear objectives allow employees to monitor their progress and adjust their focus to help them achieve what's on their work horizon. Without this framework, employees can't enjoy success, because success is never defined. Their enthusiasm and energy diminish, and so does their self-confidence. Poorly articulated objectives cause more personal grief in organizations than almost anything else. It's incredibly demoralizing to pour your energy into a professional void.

Allow Authority and Accountability in Decision Making

Well-managed organizations give employees authority and then hold them accountable for their decisions. This is healthy for the organization, and essential for employees if they're to feel satisfied with their own achievements. Unfortunately, in many organizations, authority and accountability are split, and people are held accountable even when they haven't been given the authority to get the job done. Having accountability without authority is one of employees' chief complaints, and is a source of enormous stress.

Recognize the Achievement of Personal Goals

Although some people are internally driven—they don't need external recognition to make them feel successful—

"By always being optimistic, by having self-confidence . . . you will succeed."

Orison Swett Marden

almost everyone values some form of public appreciation. Even the simplest public gesture proves the worth of their contribution to the business and increases their visibility, reinforcing self-confidence and enhancing their opportunities for promotion and advancement.

Invest in Learning and Development

Many organizations these days are making their employees responsible for job-related learning and professional development. This isn't always as cost-effective as it may seem. Individuals are unlikely to appreciate the complexity of organizational goals or understand how they can best contribute to achieving them. Employees should create individual learning and development plans in collaboration with the organization, which can provide support in the form of advice, time for study, or participation in special projects. Either internal or external training or educational programs may be appropriate, especially when employees need to gain specific skills or knowledge.

Investing in people has a measurable effect on their self-confidence and their ability to add value. Employees need support to develop professionally. Their learning should also challenge them to move beyond their comfort zones so they can master new areas of achievement and continue to meet their own personal goals.

Celebrate Meeting Organizational Objectives

Finally, celebrations are very important. A celebration can be as simple as providing refreshments for a high-performing team during a coffee break or as lavish as the business hosting a big party to celebrate the achievement of objectives or exceptional year-end results. All societies use celebrations to reinforce their shared purpose and reflect on their achievements. Organizational celebrations have the added benefit of ensuring employees that they're an indispensable and valued part of the business.

Work With Individuals

In addition to supporting a self-confident work force, organizations may have a role to play in helping individual employees develop self-confidence, too. This isn't an obvious corporate responsibility, but self-confident individuals promote a broader organizational culture of confidence. Individual coaching or mentoring, buddy systems, and co-coaching are all ways to help individuals develop self-confidence.

Good communication skills are the bedrock of self-confidence. Being able to communicate effectively in any situation—presenting ideas to coworkers, building rapport with clients, getting through to senior management, and engineering win–win solutions—engenders a high degree of self-confidence. Self-assurance leads to both self-respect and respect for others. Developing the communication skills of individual employees pays large organizational dividends.

COMMON MISTAKES
You Can't Let Go

Many managers fear that allowing their people the freedom to make decisions will disrupt the status quo and result in a loss of control. But keeping tight managerial reins on decision making is likely to alienate team members, undermine the confidence they have in their own abilities, and interfere with the team's effectiveness. Learn to let go and create an environment in which future stars can rise and be recognized.

FOR MORE INFORMATION

Book:
Smith, Manuel J. *When I Say No, I Feel Guilty*. Revised ed. New York: Bantam, 2003.

Web Sites:
BusinessTown.com:
www.businesstown.com/people/motivation-team.asp
more-selfesteem.com: **www.more-selfesteem.com**

"I don't really see the hurdles. I sense them like a memory."

Edwin Moses

Getting Your Message Across

GETTING STARTED

Getting any message across to an audience implies some type of transmission process. Transmission alone isn't always an effective form of communication, though, unless what you send is received in the way that you intend. Messages are often conveyed according to our own agendas, and the way we see and experience life impacts on them too. Often we don't take enough account of the context in which the message is spoken or the values, beliefs, and motivations of the recipient. Being aware of and adjusting for these factors can enable you to tailor your communication in the most effective way and enhance your ability to get your message across.

FAQs

I have to prepare the way for a structural change in my department. This will cause some upset but the business reasons for it are sound. How can I get my message across without alienating my team?

Many people are uncomfortable with change and resist any threat of it. You may not be able to get full support immediately, so don't expect too much too soon. Instead, try to make a connection with your team by showing you're aware of how they feel as an entity. For example, you could acknowledge that they've been under too much pressure lately, or that they've been asked to perform tasks that the team was not set up to do. You can then use this mutual touchstone as the basis upon which to explain the pressures and needs of the business and how you propose to accommodate these through structural change, a change that will benefit all parties. Use your political sensitivity and good judgment to decide how much and how far you can go on this occasion; you can always return to the subject and continue the communication at a later date.

I have delivered an important message to my team but they don't act as if they've heard it. What can I do?

Saying something once isn't enough. You need to transmit your message through as many different channels as possible until it's no longer necessary to reinforce your point. If your message is unpopular, you'll have to overcome others' natural lack of response to it, and you can only do this by repeating it. You could do this by sending appropriate e-mails or newsletters, or by arranging meetings with the relevant people. If you take this option, remember that what you say and how you say it will be watched closely and discussed afterwards, so be sure that your behavior mirrors the message you wish to convey. For example, you'll need to maintain eye contact with whoever you're speaking to, as this emphasizes the sincerity of your message. Remember that some gestures are associated with lying and need to be avoided. They include hiding your mouth with your hand, touching your nose, blinking rapidly, and running a finger along the inside of your collar.

MAKING IT HAPPEN

Getting your message across eloquently and elegantly depends on your ability to read a situation accurately and to pick up on the social and political nuances at play in your workplace and among your audience. Some people are able to do this intuitively, while others need some "tools" to help them say the right thing at the right time. Tools may include organizational surveys which feed anonymous opinions back to the relevant people and raise issues that are important to employees without fear of repercussion. On the other hand, you may prefer to talk to a particularly politically astute or well-informed colleague to guide your approach.

There are many different situations—ranging from performance appraisals to negotiations to debates—in which the accurate transmission and receipt of a message is vital to progress. In all of these situations, there's a "space" between the speaker and the listener, and this is filled with personal views, interests, and investments in a particular outcome, all of which can lead to misunderstandings or conflict. Manage this space to your best advantage by considering some of the points listed below.

Set the Scene

If you're engaging in a negotiation or meeting, it's a good idea to make clear to your audience why you're talking to them. This helps to address or sideline any alternative agendas or confusion. If you're working on any particular assumptions, make them clear and check that everyone else shares them. This will save a lot of time and potential crossed wires in the long run, as it makes sure that everyone knows where they stand. Clarifying your objective will also help you to refocus the meeting if things start to go awry.

Check Your Assumptions and Explore the Context Properly

Sometimes you may need to make a strong personal connection with your audience before you deliver your message. To do this, you need to be aware of their concerns or expectations. Ask them what they think of the topic in question and find out about their related hopes and fears. Once you understand your audience's interests and motivations, you'll be able to work out the best way of getting your message across. It's often a surprise to find that others don't share our assumptions, so making this initial check will make sure that you don't inadvertently press the wrong buttons.

Meet the Recipients Where They Are

Very often, messages don't get across well because the recipient can't relate to their content or purpose. If there's no point of identification or common interest between speaker and listener, there's equally no ground in which to root the message and, as a result, its relevance gets lost. To get around this problem, it's a good idea to begin your speech with a phrase that tries to bridge the gap, such as "As we're all aware . . . " or "No doubt you've

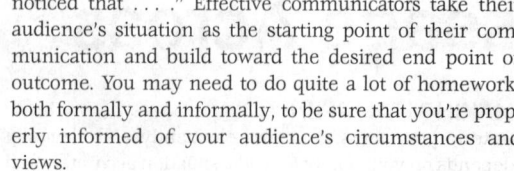
noticed that . . . ." Effective communicators take their audience's situation as the starting point of their communication and build toward the desired end point or outcome. You may need to do quite a lot of homework, both formally and informally, to be sure that you're properly informed of your audience's circumstances and views.

Use Simple and Elegant Language to Reduce Ambiguity

People who are experts in a particular field often baffle their audience with technical language or jargon on the assumption that it will have the same resonance for their audience as it does for them. Find out how familiar your audience is with the topic you're speaking on, and then adjust your vocabulary accordingly. Use plenty of examples, anecdotes, analogies, and metaphors if the audience isn't as "techie" as you. Remember that you can also make your message clearer by using visual aids (such as PowerPoint, overhead slides, or simple handouts). Humor and a touch of drama can sometimes help but it's best to use these sensitively and sparingly. Less is more.

Repeat Key Messages Using Several Different Channels of Communication

Generally, people can take away about three key points from any communication. These three points may be represented in different ways so that all preferred styles of communication can be accommodated. In addition, they may be offered using different channels of communication so that the message is reinforced from many angles. For example, you could follow up a presentation by writing an article for a company newsletter or intranet or by putting up a poster. All of these things will mean that no one can avoid what you're trying to say, even if they don't agree with it!

Listen to Others and Show Respect for Their Point of View

Getting across your message successfully depends to a large extent on your ability to listen well to other people. We very often assume that we know what others are thinking and what they're about to say. However, these assumptions can "deafen" us to what's *really* being said, and we end up as poor communicators as a result. Avoid this, then, by listening properly to other people. Don't jump to conclusions or make snap judgments about their position, but instead respect where they're coming from and nurture a real desire to hear and be heard without the "white noise" of misperception getting in the way.

Address Questions or Concerns Directly

In the same way that we must learn to hear our audience, we also have to help them hear us. Unless they're given an opportunity to have their concerns addressed honestly and constructively, they'll go away feeling negative and may also be ready to damn what you say to others who haven't yet been able to hear you speak. Help your audience by being sure of both your subject and of your objectives in making the communication. Convey the necessary information accurately and remember that you have to seem convinced by it yourself if others are to share your belief. It's a good idea to close the communication "loop" by asking your audience to summarize what they think you've said. This gives you a valuable opportunity to correct any misunderstandings and to run through your key points one more time. Using language that's familiar to your recipients will enable them to act as another mouthpiece for your message.

Summarize and Confirm Any Resultant Actions

There's an old adage about presentations that says "tell them what you're going to tell them, tell them, then tell them what you've just told them." Although this may sound like overkill, it's actually a valuable way of conveying messages in a straightforward and powerful way.

In short, use noncomplex language to convey up to three points at a time repeatedly. Color these points with examples, anecdotes, and analogies and be aware of how your message is going down; if people look confused, adjust your style and explain things in plainer terms. If you see that people are straining to hear, speak louder. It's really important at all times to listen, observe, and respect your audience and their point of view, even if the latter is at odds with your own.

COMMON MISTAKES
You Over Do It

In our urgency to get our message across, we frequently rush in and speak without thinking things through. This will come across as arrogant and high-handed and will immediately set your audience against you. Rushing in like this is often motivated by fear of failure and a compensating thought that, if we assert ourselves strongly enough, there'll be no room for disagreement or dissent. Wrong. In fact, if you do feel this fear, the best thing you can do is tread carefully. Show that you respect your audience, and that you understand their situation and identify with it personally if you can. This will ease any likely resistance, especially if you ask them for their views and listen carefully to them.

You Don't Allow Enough Time

Rushing what you're saying in a message often defeats its objective and leaves people feeling bullied and unmotivated. When you're planning and timing a speech or presentation, make sure you factor in some time for your audience to ask questions or raise concerns at the end. You need to put people at ease so that they feel able to address what you've said. Don't be defensive if people ask you questions (remember that they're perfectly entitled to!), but try to use their point to build upon or illustrate another facet of your message.

FOR MORE INFORMATION

Web Sites:
1000ventures.com:
www.1000ventures.com/business_guide/
crosscuttings/talking_main.html
Mind Tools: **www.mindtools.com**

"If an organization is to work effectively, the communication should be through the most effective channel regardless of the organization chart."

Tom Peters

Communicating Assertively in the Workplace

GETTING STARTED

Do you find that people get the better of you at work, that you're always the one that gets pushed around and ends up doing things that you'd rather not do? Does this make you resentful or unhappy because you feel helpless and unable to represent yourself strongly enough in the way you communicate?

Assertiveness is an attitude that honors your choices as well as those of the person with whom you are communicating. It's not about being aggressive and steamrollering your coworker into submission. Rather, it's about seeking and exchanging opinions, developing a full understanding of the situation, and negotiating a win–win situation. Ask yourself these questions to determine your level of assertiveness:

- Do you feel "put upon" or ignored in your exchanges with coworkers?
- Are you unable to speak your mind and request what you want?
- Do you find it difficult to stand up for yourself in a discussion?
- Are you inordinately grateful when someone seeks your opinion and takes it into account?

If you answer "yes" to most of these questions, you may need to consider becoming more assertive.

FAQs

Won't people think me aggressive if I change my communication style?

There are four types of communication style:

- aggressive—where you win and everyone else loses
- passive—where you lose and everyone else wins
- passive/aggressive—where you lose and do everything you can (without being too obvious) to make others lose too
- assertive—where everyone wins

If you become more assertive, people won't necessarily think that you've become more aggressive because their needs are met too. All that will happen is that your communication style becomes more effective.

I have had a lifetime of being passive. How can I change that now?

If you don't change what you do, you'll never change what you get. All it takes to change is a decision. Once you've made that decision, you'll naturally observe yourself in situations, notice what you do and don't do well, and then you can try out new behaviors to see what works for you.

I just don't have the confidence to confront people. Will becoming assertive help me?

This is a bit like the "chicken and egg." Once you become assertive, your confidence level will be boosted, yet you need to have sufficient levels of confidence to try it in the first place. Just try the technique out in a safe environment first so that you get used to how it feels, then you can use it more widely.

It's all right for people who have presence, but I'm small so I'm often overlooked. How can I become assertive?

Many of the most successful people, in business and in entertainment, are physically quite small. Adopting an assertive communication style and body language has the effect of making you look more imposing. Assume you have impact, visualize it, feel it, breathe it, be it.

I find it hard to say "no" to people. How can I change this?

Until you get used to being assertive, you may find this difficult. However, one useful technique is to say, "I'd like to think about this first. I'll get back to you shortly." Giving yourself time and space to rehearse your response can be really helpful.

MAKING IT HAPPEN
Choose the Right Approach

Becoming assertive is all about making choices that meet your needs and the needs of the situation. Sometimes it's appropriate to be passive. If you were facing a snarling dog, you might not want to provoke an attack by looking for a win–win situation! There may be other occasions when aggression is the answer. However, this is still assertive behavior as *you*, rather than other people or situations, are in control of how you react.

You may find it helpful to investigate some specially tailored training courses so that you can try out some approaches before taking on a coworker or manager in a "live" situation. This sort of thing takes practice.

Practice Projecting a Positive Image

Use "winning" language. Rather than saying "I always seem to get the bum deal!" say "I've learned a great deal from doing lots of different things in my career. I'm now ready to move on." This is the beginning of taking control in your life. Visualize what you wish to become, make the image as real as possible, and feel the sensation of being in control. Perhaps there have been moments in your life when you naturally felt like this, a time when you've excelled. Recapture that moment and "live" it again. Imagine how it would be if you felt like that elsewhere in your life. Determine to make this your goal and recall this powerful image or feeling when you're getting disheartened. It will reenergize you and keep you on track.

"We should do everything both cautiously and confidently at the same time."   Epicetus

Creating a Positive Impression Prompts Others to Take You Seriously

This can be done through nonverbal as well as verbal communication. If someone is talking over you and you're finding it difficult to get a word in edgewise, you can hold up your hand signaling "stop" as you begin to speak. "I hear what you're saying but I would like to put forward an alternative viewpoint . . . " Always take responsibility for your communication. Use the "I" word. "I would like . . . ," "I don't agree . . . ," "I am uncomfortable with this . . . " Being aware of nonverbal communication signals can also help you build rapport. If you mirror what others are doing when they're communicating with you, it will help you get a sense of where they're coming from and how to respond in the most helpful way.

Use Positive Body Language

Stand tall, breathe deeply, and look people in the eye when you speak to them. Instead of anticipating a negative outcome, expect something positive. Listen actively to the other party and try putting yourself in their shoes so that you have a better chance of seeking the solution that works for you both. Inquire about their thoughts and feelings by using "open" questions, that allow them to give you a full response rather than just "yes" or "no." Examples include: "Tell me more about why . . . ," "How do you see this working out?", and so forth.

Assertiveness also helps you learn to deal with people who have different communication styles. If you're dealing with someone behaving in a passive/aggressive manner, you can handle it by exposing what he or she is doing. "I get the feeling you're not happy about this decision" or "It appears you have something to say on this; would you like to share your views now?" In this way, they either have to deny their passive/aggressive stance or they have to disclose their motivations. Either way, you're left in the driver's seat.

If you're dealing with a passive person, rather than let them be silent, encourage them to contribute so that they can't put the blame for their discontent on someone else.

The aggressive communicator may need confronting but do it carefully; you don't want things to escalate out of control. One option is to start by saying "I'd like to think about it first": this gives you time to gather your thoughts and the other person time to calm down. When you're feeling put upon, it's important to remember that you have as much right as anyone to speak up and be heard.

Conflict is notorious for bringing out aggression in people, but it's still possible to be assertive in this context. You may need to show that you're taking them seriously by reflecting their energy. To do this, you could raise your voice to match the volume of theirs, then bring the volume down as you start to explore what would lead to a win–win solution. "I CAN SEE THAT YOU ARE UPSET and I would feel exactly the same if I were you . . . however . . . " Then you can establish the desired outcome for both of you.

COMMON MISTAKES
You Go Too Far at First

Many people, when trying out assertive behavior for the first time, find that they "go too far" and become aggressive. Remember that you're looking for a win–win, not a you win and they lose situation. Take your time. Observe yourself in action. Practice and ask for feedback from trusted friends or colleagues.

Others React Negatively to Your Assertiveness

Your familiar circle of friends will be used to you the way you were, not the way you want to become. They may try to make things difficult for you. With your new assertive behavior, this won't be possible unless you let them get away with it. If you find you're in this situation, try explaining what you're trying to do and ask for their support. If they aren't prepared to help you, you may choose to let them go from your circle of friends.

You Bite Off More Than You Can Chew and Get Yourself into Situations That Are Difficult to Manage

If this happens to you, find a good way of backing down, go away and reflect on what went wrong, rehearse an assertive response, and forgive yourself for not getting it right every time. The more you rehearse, the more assertive responses you'll have in your tool kit when you need them.

FOR MORE INFORMATION

Books:
Alberti, Robert E., and Michael L. Emmons. *Your Perfect Right: Assertiveness and Equality in Your Life and Relationships.* 8th ed. Atascadero, CA: Impact Publishers, 2001.
Burley-Allen, Madelyn. *Managing Assertively: How to Improve Your People Skills: A Self-Teaching Guide.* 2nd ed. New York: John Wiley, 1995.
Michelli, Dena. *Successful Assertiveness.* Hauppauge, NY: Barron's Educational, 1997.
Paterson, Randy J. *The Assertiveness Workbook: How to Express Your Ideas and Stand Up for Yourself at Work and in Relationships.* Oakland, CA: New Harbinger, 2000.

Web sites:
Assertiveness.com:
www.assertiveness.com
Oak Tree Counseling:
www.oaktreecounseling.com
TUFTS University:
www.tufts.edu/hr/tips/assert.html

See also:
✔ Getting Your Message Across (pp. 789–790)

"Whether you believe you can, or whether you believe you can't, you're quite right."

Henry Ford

Preparing Presentations

GETTING STARTED

Presentations are useful in many situations, such as pitching for business, making a case for funding, and addressing staff meetings. Few people like speaking formally to an audience, but there are many real benefits, and, as you gain experience in giving presentations, you'll probably find that it becomes less of a worry, and even enjoyable. This actionlist will give you some suggestions for preparing the content of your presentation, looking at the objectives that you hope to achieve, pitching it right for your particular audience, and getting your points across in the best way.

FAQs
What objectives should I set?

The starting point for any presentation is to set clear objectives. Ask yourself why you're giving the talk, and what you want your audience to get out of it. Also consider whether using speech alone is the best way of communicating your message, and whether your presentation would benefit from using visual aids and slides to further illustrate its main points. When you're planning and giving the presentation, keep your objectives in mind at all times—they'll focus your thoughts. Having clear reasons for giving the presentation will make sure that you're not wasting anyone's time, either your audience's or your own.

What do I need to know about the audience?

Before you plan your presentation try as best as you can to find out who is going to be in your audience, and their expectations. For example, the tone and content of a presentation to the managing director of another company will be very different from one addressed to potential users of a product. It's important that you know the extent of the audience's knowledge about the topic you'll be discussing. Their familiarity with the subject will determine the level at which you pitch the talk. Try to appeal to what will motivate and interest these people.

MAKING IT HAPPEN
Write Your Speech

When it comes to presentations, there is no substitute for detailed preparation and planning. While everyone prepares in different ways, all of which develop with experience, here are a few key points to bear in mind while you're preparing.

Start by breaking up the task of preparing your speech into manageable units. Once you know the length of the presentation—say 15 minutes, for example—break the time up into smaller units and allocate sections of your speech to each unit. Then note down all the points you want to make, and order them logically. This will help you to develop the framework and emphasis of the presentation.

Keep your presentation short and simple, if you can, as it'll be easier for you to manage and remember. If you

need to provide more detail, you can supply a written handout to be given out at the end. A shorter presentation is usually more effective from the audience's point of view, too, as most people dislike long speeches, and will not necessarily remember any more from them.

Avoid packing your talk with facts and figures—your audience may become confused and you could lose the thread as well. If you do need to back up what you're saying, you could use graphs or charts to get across the message in a clear, pictorial form. Aim to identify two or three key points, and concentrate on getting these across in a creative fashion.

Visual Aids and Equipment

With any presentation, you'll need to consider whether to use visual aids, which can range from the simple—such as transparencies for an overhead projector (OHP)—to the more sophisticated—such as a computer package like PowerPoint. Remember that visual aids should only be used as signposts during the presentation, to help the audience focus on the main point. It's important not to cram too much information on to one visual aid, as you'll probably lose the attention of your audience while they try to read everything on it. Make sure the audience can see the information by using big, bold lettering, and bear in mind that images are often far more effective than words.

At its most basic, a personal computer can be used to develop and produce a series of slides which can be printed onto transparencies for use on an overhead projector. A more common usage is to link up the PC with a projector in order to show the information on a large screen.

If you're going to use slides, you should try to standardize them to make them look more professional. Use templates where possible to make sure that they don't blend together, and again, try not to put too much information onto a single slide, or it will become difficult to read. A sensible guideline is to include no more than six points per slide, and to keep the number of words you use for each point to the absolute minimum. Think of what you're writing as the prompts for what you want to say.

The most common presentation packages are Microsoft PowerPoint and Corel Presentations. Both of these will allow you to develop a presentation using slide templates and give you the option of using charts, graphics, or even photographs to bring your information alive. Packages such as PhotoShop or Paint Shop Pro will also allow you to scan in or manipulate photographs, or you could also use some of the available animations for transitions between slides.

You should pay particular attention to the layout and text on the slides and remain consistent throughout. Select a background that contrasts well with the text, and colors that are strong and stand out. It may also be a good idea to include the business's logo on all of the slides. It's important, always, to proofread your slides and transparencies. There is nothing more noticeable, or more

"Speeches measured by the hour die within the hour."   Thomas Jefferson

unprofessional, than a typo or grammatical error projected to ten times its original size on a screen!

Practice as many times as you can to make sure that you're very familiar with your speech; allow plenty of time for rehearsal before the event. Once you're confident that your presentation is right, resist the temptation to change it. Remember, *you* may have heard the speech many times, but the audience will be hearing it for the first time. It's also a good idea to practice your speech using the equipment you intend to use; slide projectors and video machines should be tested in advance to make sure you know how to operate them. Make sure you have a contingency plan to cope with any unforeseen mishaps. For example, you could take acetates of your slides along with you so that if your computer breaks down and there's an OHP to hand, you can show them that way. Finally, during your rehearsals, time your speech so that you can check that it's neither too long nor too short. Remember that you'll probably need to allow time at the end for a question-and-answer session. Resist the temptation to bring your script into the presentation and instead write the main points on numbered cards, known as cue cards, to provide reminders.

Prepare the Venue

Make sure that an appropriately sized room has been organized for your presentation; take into account the number of people you're expecting, and check that there is enough seating, lighting, ventilation, and heating. If you're presenting at your office or on other "home turf," provide some refreshments for participants such as tea, coffee, and water.

You also need to make sure there will be no interruptions, for example by phone calls, fire drills, or people accidentally entering the room. Whether you're presenting at your own office or elsewhere, you must make sure that any equipment or props you need are available and set up properly before the presentation starts. If you're presenting away from your office, at a conference or a client's premises, for example, it's a good idea to visit the site beforehand to make sure it provides the necessary facilities.

COMMON MISTAKES
Not Researching Your Audience

A good knowledge of the audience is absolutely crucial in finding the correct pitch. It's no good blinding your audience with technical jargon if they only have a basic grasp of the subject. Similarly, a very knowledgeable audience will soon switch off if you spend the first few minutes going over the basics.

Long Presentations

If your presentation absolutely has to be longer than 20 minutes, it may be a good idea to insert some breaks so that your audience remains fresh and interested.

Not Checking the Room and Equipment

This can be disastrous! Imagine, for example, arriving and finding that there is no facility for delivering Power-Point presentations, and you have no other method of showing slides. Make sure you're familiar with the environment in which you'll be presenting.

FOR MORE INFORMATION

Book:
Wilder, Claudine, and Jennifer Rotondo. *Point, Click and Wow! A Quick Guide to Brilliant Laptop Presentations.* 2nd ed. San Francisco, CA: Wiley, 2002.

Web Sites:
Mind Tools:
http://www.mindtools.com/CommSkll/ PresentationPlanningChecklist.htm
SpeechTips.com:
www.speechtips.com/preparation.html
Toastmasters International: **www.toastmasters.org**

See also:
✔ Delivering Presentations (pp. 795–796)
🖱 Presentation/Speaking (pp. 1865–1866)

"Speak clearly, if you speak at all; carve every word before you let it fall."

Oliver Wendell Holmes

Delivering Presentations

GETTING STARTED

A presentation is an ideal environment for you to promote your ideas, your products, or your services. You have a captive audience, are able to provide them with relevant information, and can answer any questions they may have on the spot. For a presentation to be a success you need to speak clearly and fluently in order to hold the attention of the audience and to leave them wanting to know more.

Some people are natural presenters, while others find it more difficult, but practice and feedback from previous audiences will help you develop your presentation skills. This actionlist will give you some ideas for structuring, preparing, and delivering your presentation.

FAQs

How should I structure my presentation?

Structure is essential for any presentation: there should be an introduction, a main body, and a conclusion. You can be witty, controversial, or even outrageous if the mood of the presentation allows, but, whatever approach you try, your chief goals are to pique the audience's curiosity and to get your message across.

What's the best way to introduce my presentation?

The introduction to your presentation needs to attract your audience's interest and attention. A good opening is also important for your own confidence, because if you start well, the rest should follow easily. Plan your opening words carefully for maximum impact: they should be short, sharp, and to the point. Let your audience know how long your presentation will take, as this will prepare people to focus for the period of time you expect to speak. Summarize what you'll be discussing, so that they can work out how much information they'll need to absorb. Explaining the key points in the first few sentences will also help your mind to focus on the task at hand, and refresh your memory on the major points of your presentation. It sometimes helps to get started if you can learn your first few sentences by heart. Let your audience know if you're happy to interact with them throughout the presentation. Alternatively, inform them that you'll be holding a question-and-answer session at the end.

What should I do in the main body of the presentation?

The main body of the presentation will be dictated by the points that you want to make. Use short, sharp, and simple language to keep your audience's attention and to ensure that your message is being understood. Include only one idea per sentence and pause after each one so as to make a mental full stop. Use precise language to convey your message, but make sure that your presentation sounds spontaneous—it shouldn't sound like a chapter from a textbook. You need to convey your message clearly, without masking the salient points. Stick to your original plan for your presentation and don't go off on a tangent on a particular point, and miss the thread of your presentation. Why not try using metaphors and images to illustrate points? This will give impact to what you say, and help your audience to remember it.

How should I conclude my presentation?

You should close by summing up the key points of what you've covered. The closing seconds of your presentation are as crucial as the opening sentence, as they give you a chance to really hammer home your point. To make the most of this, think about what action you'd like your audience to take after the presentation is over and then inspire them to do it.

MAKING IT HAPPEN
Make Sure You've Practiced

Nothing will make you more confident about your presentation than practicing. Run through it by yourself a few times or, even better, ask a friend, colleague, or family member to listen to you.

Posture and Delivery

Once you've practiced the core part of your presentation, you can move on to think about some techniques to do with your posture and delivery that can be used to increase its impact. First, keep up good eye contact and address your audience directly throughout your presentation. Try to be aware of your stance, posture, and gestures without being too self-conscious. Don't slouch—you'll look unprofessional—stand up straight: this will make you look more confident and also help you project your voice better. Even if you're nervous, don't fiddle with pens, pencils, your hair, or clothes: all these things are distracting for an audience, and will mean that they're missing important points in your presentation.

Remember that your audience has come to learn something, so be authoritative, sincere, and enthusiastic; if *you* don't sound as if you believe in yourself, your audience won't be interested. Also think about the way in which you're speaking. Most people need to articulate their words more clearly when addressing an audience. There's usually no opportunity for the audience to ask you to repeat a word you've missed, so aim to pronounce the vowels and consonants of words clearly. Also be aware of your vocal expression and try to vary volume, pitch, and speed of delivery to underline your meaning, and so that you maintain your audience's interest. Try not to use too many acronyms that are specific to your business or industry, as you can't be completely sure that everyone in the audience will know what they mean. If you do need to use them, introduce them and explain them early in your presentation so that everyone can keep up.

Close Your Presentation

It's tempting (and, if you're a nervous presenter, comforting) to have the full version of your speech in front of you, but it's best to avoid this and use cue cards instead.

These will have a few headings referring to the main subject areas of your speech, and a few key points. In this way you can remember the key points you want to convey, but you have the freedom to talk naturally about them, rather than speaking from an over-rehearsed script, and this will make you seem more spontaneous. You may, though, want to write out the introduction in full on your first card to get you off to a good start.

Be careful when using visual aids and equipment in the presentation, as these can also be distracting for an audience. Use a pen to point out details on the overhead projector itself, rather than the screen, as this is much clearer. Flipcharts should be written on quickly in long hand, but try not to turn your back on the audience as you write. Commonly available presentation packages often have a facility to enable you to link to specific slides. If a specific topic needs further explanation, you could also have a built-in series of links so that you can move to some extra slides to explain a particular point. If you intend to use sophisticated technology, then have a technician on hand to help out. Make sure you have a contingency plan in case your technology crashes: a back-up disk or extra copies of a handout would be a good plan.

Finish on a High Note

As you draw your presentation to a close, remember to summarize briefly your key points and whatever you want your audience to "take away" from the time you've spent talking to them. You might also want to take a few questions from the audience: in fact, taking all the questions at the end is a good idea for nervous presenters, as it means that they won't have their train of thought interrupted while they're speaking.

We all deal with questions in a different way, but some good general pointers are as follows:

- Give your audience an idea of how much time you have to spend on the questions. This may be an issue if you're just one of several people speaking, as, if you run over, everyone will start running late.
- If someone asks you a question and you don't know the answer, be honest and tell them that you'll find out what they need to know and get back to them separately. This will save time, and also prevent you from giving an incorrect answer. Try to get back to them within two working days.
- If the question is a general discussion point, you could always try opening the question to the floor; you may be able to get an interesting discussion going between the members of your audience.

COMMON MISTAKES
Lack of Enthusiasm

If *you* don't have any interest or excitement in your own speech, then don't expect your audience to be interested or excited. Listening to a single voice for 20 minutes or more can be difficult for an audience, so you must try to inject enthusiasm into what you're saying. You could consider planning some kind of interaction with your audience, too, in the form of activities or discussion.

Speaking Too Quickly

Don't rush your presentation; it's important to take your time. It's hard not to rush, especially if you're nervous and want the whole thing to be over as soon as possible, but the audience will find it hard to understand or keep up with you if you talk too fast. Make sure you summarize your main points every five minutes or so, or as you reach the end of a section. This will help to clarify the most important issues for your audience, and it's then more likely that they'll remember the central issues long after you've finished your presentation.

Not Checking Equipment

There is nothing more irritating for an audience who have all made an effort to turn up on time, than to have to sit around and wait while you struggle to get your laptop to work or sort your slides out. Make sure everything is exactly in place well before your audience begins to arrive. If you're planning to use sophisticated technology, it might be a good idea to have an expert colleague on hand just in case.

Not Interacting with the Audience

Be careful not to look at the floor during your presentation, or to direct your speech at one person. Try to draw your whole audience into the presentation by glancing at everyone's faces, in a relaxed and unhurried way, as you make your points. Keeping in tune with your audience in this way will also help you judge if people are becoming bored. If you do detect this, you could try to change the tempo of your presentation to refocus their attention.

FOR MORE INFORMATION

Book:
Wilder, Claudine, and Jennifer Rotondo. *Point, Click and Wow! A Quick Guide to Brilliant Laptop Presentations.* 2nd ed. San Francisco, CA: Wiley, 2002.

Web Sites:
BusinessTown.com:
www.businesstown.com/presentations/index.asp
SpeechTips.com:
www.speechtips.com/delivering.html

See also:
✔ Preparing Presentations (pp. 793–794)
🖱 Presentation/Speaking (pp. 1865–1866)

Presentations: Surviving Worst-case Scenarios

GETTING STARTED

In an ideal world, everything would always go as planned. Sadly the world is anything but ideal and, as a result, hardly anything ever does! This can be pretty disconcerting, particularly if you're in a situation where you're "on display," as you are when giving a presentation. However, there are very few situations that are completely irredeemable—unless you panic.

It's well worth spending some time thinking through all the things that could possibly go wrong and (if possible) taking preventive action, or (if not) planning what to do in the event. This actionlist lays some ground rules.

FAQs

I'm a bit worried about keeping my audience's attention throughout the whole of my presentation. Some of what I'll be talking about is quite complex. How can I keep them interested?

It's good that you're thinking ahead about this. Audiences have a very short attention span—most adults cannot concentrate for more than seven to ten minutes. To prevent people from wriggling, chatting, or switching off, it's a good idea to break your presentation into easily digestible sections and change the pace or create a diversion at regular intervals. If you feel confident enough, you could throw a question to the audience, for example.

Recently I saw a colleague struggle during a presentation when two members of the audience started a conversation between themselves while she was speaking. What should I do if this happens to me?

This is possibly the most difficult disruption you might encounter. If it does happen to you, in the following order:

- ask if anyone has any questions;
- ask the talkers if you can do anything to clarify;
- if they continue, move closer to them;
- if they still don't stop, lower your voice, or pause in what you're saying and look at them;
- if all else fails, call a halt to the presentation and ask the whole group whether a new session should be arranged.

MAKING IT HAPPEN
Make Sure You Can Handle the Technology and Equipment

Technology is a potential problem for every presenter. Even the best designed presentation will fail if the technology you use to deliver it goes wrong, so it's really important to check everything beforehand.

Technology

Unless you're using your own equipment, make sure that your presentation will work on what's provided.

- Have you checked that you can load your presentation onto the computer (does it have a CD drive, for example)?
- Does this machine run the same software version that you use? You may be able to run newer presentations under older versions of PowerPoint, for example, but extra features (such as animations or links to other applications) may not work. Check that they do.
- If you need to link to the Web, can you get Internet access?
- Is the projector a relatively new one? Older projectors may be dim and/or have fewer colors.
- Are there enough power outlets, of the right kinds, and in the right places? Will you need extension cords or extra plug sockets, or do you need to rearrange the room?
- Do the connections between different pieces of equipment—from the computer to the projector, for example—work properly?
- If at all possible, run your presentation through from beginning to end in situ.

Other equipment

- Make sure you have spares of everything you could need—backup disks, spare bulbs, spare batteries, extra handouts, pens, and so on.
- Check that any lectern or stand is at the right height for you.
- Confirm that people will be able to hear properly from all parts of the room, particularly if you're using sound effects or a microphone.
- Have a spare copy of your notes in your briefcase, stapled together and numbered so they can't get mixed up.
- Familiarize yourself with how to operate all the lights, air conditioning, heating, and so on.
- Make sure you know where all the amenities are—coffee rooms, restrooms, reception areas, phones, for example—not just for your own information, but so that you can answer if asked by an audience member.

Be prepared! If you're presenting on home turf, do a practice run-through the day or a few hours before your presentation, so you can check everything mentioned above. If you're presenting elsewhere, get in touch with your contact at the venue to find out as much as you can about what equipment is available and what you'll be expected to bring. Arrive at the venue in plenty of time so that you can practice there too.

Manage the Audience

Arrange the seating sensibly. There's nothing worse, when presenting, than facing an audience that is scattered all over the room or, even worse, huddled into the back rows of seats leaving a great gulf between you and them. Even the greatest speaker will have difficulty building energy or creating rapport in such circumstances. There are a couple of ways you can prevent such a situation from arising:

- If at all possible, find out how many people are coming

"For every failure, there's an alternative course of action. You just have to find it. When you come to a roadblock, take a detour."

Mary Kay Ash

and put out just enough seats, plus a couple of extras. Arrange them in an arc facing you.

- If you have no idea of, or control over, the numbers attending, tape off the back row of seats and put a "Reserved" sign on them. Once the front rows are full, remove the sign and let the last arrivals sit at the back.

Think about the staging. There are a few other tips for staging the presentation which will also help things run smoothly and enable you to engage with your audience.

- Make sure you're not standing with your back to a window, or you'll appear as a silhouette to your listeners.
- Check that you have somewhere—like a table—to put your papers, notes, handouts, briefcase, and anything else you have with you.
- If you need to darken the room, make sure you know where light switches are and how curtains or blinds close.
- Try sitting in different parts of the room to check that all members of the audience will be able to see properly.
- If possible, make sure there's nothing—like a desk or table—between you and your audience. Psychologically it will act as a barrier, and you will have to work that much harder to create rapport.

Deal with disruptions. Interruptions can put you off your stride, so take preventive action before your presentation begins:

- Make sure the room is booked well in advance—you don't want another group of people arriving at the same time expecting to have a meeting there
- Arrange for any phones in the room to be forwarded for the duration
- Put a sign on the door to stop people from barging in unintentionally
- Check that there's no regular interruption planned, such as a fire drill. If there is, plan a break around it, or at least tell the audience what will be happening before hand.
- Fill the seats from the front, as described in the previous section; this has the added benefit of preventing late arrivals from walking all the way to the front and climbing across other people to find somewhere to sit.
- If the presentation is likely to be a long one, make sure you schedule plenty of breaks—preferably on the hour, every hour. This helps to eliminate surreptitious escapes to the bathroom, and maintains people's concentration.

You can never expect to eliminate all kinds of interruption, so the golden rule, if you *are* interrupted, is to acknowledge it rather than trying to carry on regardless. If you pause and laugh while a jet plane thunders overhead, for example, the audience will probably laugh too, and the whole episode will actually work to your advantage by creating a bond between you.

Survive Unexpected Time Issues

Uncertainty about, or problems with, the time available can throw a presenter completely. Say, for example, the meeting before yours runs long and cuts your time severely; what do you do then? The two scenarios below cover most contingencies.

You find you have 20 minutes instead of the hour you planned on

Talking quickly isn't the answer! Decide swiftly what proportion of the 20 minutes each part of your presentation should take. Is there any section that could be omitted altogether? Then keep your eye on your watch as you speak and limit yourself to the key concept in each portion.

A vital member of the audience has to leave before you've reached your key points

Say the financial director, who has ultimate say over whether his company buys your products, tells you he has to leave early. This could be disastrous. However, there's an old rule regarding presentations: tell people what you're going to tell them, tell them, and then tell them what you told them. If you follow this rule when creating your presentation in the first place, you won't get caught out this way.

- Always mention your main point and major supporting points within the first few minutes of any presentation.
- If you're using slides or overheads, always have one that contains the main point and the key points.
- If, however, you've made the fatal error of trying to save the best for last, ask the decision maker for a moment to summarize (anyone will give you a moment if you ask nicely). Then state, in one sentence, the single point you want the decision maker to remember and, if you have a chance, the two concepts that best support that point.

It's always worth considering contingencies when you're creating a presentation. What would you leave out if your time were halved? What would your key messages be if you had five minutes to tell someone about them?

Answer Difficult Questions

Some presenters dread questions from the audience more than anything else, as it's impossible to know what might come up or whether someone might have a particular agenda attached to the question he or she asks. However, most tricky questions tend to fall into one of only a few categories, and, if you recognize these, it will help you know how to answer.

The concealed objection

For example, "How come the price is so high?"

- Don't get defensive.
- Ask them to clarify the objection. For example, "What makes you feel that the price is too high?"
- Put it in perspective. For example, "It's only a few cents more expensive than its nearest competitor . . . ."
- Give the compensating benefits. " . . . and the quality is much higher, so it's actually a better value for the money."

The test question

These questions are designed to test your knowledge. For example, "What are the research findings on side effects for this new drug?"

- Don't bluff.
- Call on an expert colleague if you have one there.
- If you don't know, say so—but offer to find out later, make a note, and then keep your promise.

The display question

This type of question is often intended to demonstrate the questioner's own expertise.

- Play along and don't be afraid to acknowledge how clever they are publicly. "Of course you're right—I didn't mention it, simply because I thought it might be too technical for this occasion."

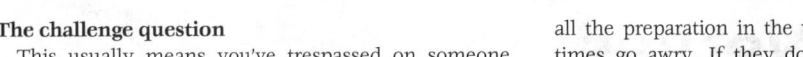

The challenge question

This usually means you've trespassed on someone else's area of knowledge.

- Back down immediately, concede all territorial rights, and perhaps consult that person's opinion. "I'm sorry, I meant the transportation policy in Orange County, not the whole state—which of course you know more about than I do. Would you say it's the same across the board?"

The defensive question

This tends to mean that something you've proposed is a threat to the questioner. For example, "Do you really think it's a good idea to let managers train their own staff?"

- Try to question the questioner. "Could you explain your concerns further, perhaps?"
- Throw the question open to the floor: do other people feel managers aren't qualified to train their staff?
- If it's not within your authority, refer the questioner to someone who can provide answers.

The question you plan to discuss in detail later

- Provide a brief answer, then say that you plan to cover the subject properly later.
- Don't ask the questioner to wait until you reach the point at which you originally intended to discuss the subject, or everyone will focus on the unanswered question instead of listening to you.
- In a meeting setting or small presentation, don't ask people to keep their questions for the end as this suggests that you're not confident enough to deal with interruptions.

If nothing else, making sure that you know your stuff and keeping calm will usually be enough to deal with most questions that you might face.

Don't Let Nerves Get to You

Almost everyone, even a person with lots of experience, suffers from nerves to some degree when they have to present to a group of people. And nerves can make you prone to accidents and stumbling.

However, the key to solving the problem is understanding what causes an attack of nerves: fear, usually fear of what could possibly go wrong. This is why you generally feel better once you get going: your equipment's working OK, the audience hasn't booed you off the stage, you haven't made an idiot of yourself, and so on.

The more you preempt your fear by preparing thoroughly and taking preventive measures against things that could go wrong, the less nervous you will feel, and the less likely you'll be to mess up. However, even with all the preparation in the world, things can still sometimes go awry. If they do, don't panic—you can still succeed overall. Here are some of the most common nerve-induced pitfalls, and what to do about them.

You lose your train of thought mid-sentence

Smile, say "excuse me" or "I'm sorry," and start again. Try not to panic or get flustered: it's not the end of the world, and everyone in the room has lost track of an idea at least once in their lives. People want you to succeed and are generally sympathetic. Keep smiling.

Your throat dries up

Actors have a good trick for dealing with this. Roll a tiny piece of paper into a small ball and place it between your gum and the inside of your cheek at the back of your mouth. It will stimulate the flow of saliva, just like that little roll of cotton wool the dentist uses. Try this in private first, however, so you are sure you are comfortable.

You drop your transparencies on the floor

Make a joke about your clumsiness, pick them up, and take a few moments to put them in order. (Now is the time to be grateful you have numbered them.)

COMMON MISTAKES
You Don't Rehearse

Almost every piece of advice in this actionlist points to one thing: you MUST PRACTICE! With plenty of rehearsal, your confidence will be sufficient to see you through just about any disaster. It's not enough to say your presentation over to yourself in your head, as it's very different when you have to get up and do it in front of an audience. Choose a friend or colleague you trust, and ask him or her if they will watch you and give you honest feedback. As an absolute minimum, stand in front of a mirror and run through the presentation, checking yourself as critically as you can.

799

ACTIONLIST

FOR MORE INFORMATION

Web Sites:
KU Medical Center, online tutorial series:
www.kumc.edu
Strategic Communications:
www.strategiccomm.com/disasters.html
Peterson & Associates, Presentation Tips:
www.passociates.com/visuals_avoiding_a_disaster.shtml

Overcoming Nerves

GETTING STARTED

Being overcome by nerves can be an utterly debilitating experience that sabotages our ability to communicate well and to demonstrate how well we can do our job. The body's nervous reaction to speaking in public, making a presentation to customers or colleagues, or even making an intervention during an internal meeting can, if left unchecked, rob us in just a few seconds of the confidence and experience built up during the course of our career.

If you do suffer from nerves in some work situations, take comfort in knowing that you're not alone and that with the help of a few simple techniques, you can overcome the trembling knees, dry mouth, sweaty palms, and a tendency to ramble. It's always tempting to think that a problem will go just go away, but tackling nerves will offer a range of positive results, including being able to be yourself, contributing to events in the way you know you can deep down. Overcoming nerves is a great first step on the journey to full confidence.

FAQs

I have to make a very important presentation and I'm bound to get it wrong. What can I do to avoid disaster?

If you see yourself failing at something, you're more likely to do so. Try to get your imagination under control and instead of seeing yourself getting it all spectacularly wrong, see yourself succeeding extraordinarily. Your body will follow the cues from your mind, so train your mind to be positive and to "invite" success for yourself. Don't let negative images or words pollute your preparation.

When I get nervous, I speak before I think and say the stupidest things. How can I stop my mouth from running away with me?

Breathe. We're not particularly good at managing our breathing, but it is the key to allowing you the space to observe and hear what's going on. Being sensitive to the needs of others and different situations is an important part of being able to say the right thing at the right time. Give yourself time to take in the information you need and formulate what you're going to say. Don't rush in, breathe calmly, and don't worry about short silences.

I'm an introvert and very shy. What can I do to help myself succeed in public speaking?

Strangely, some of the best performers are introverts and many have severe bouts of nerves before taking the stage and delivering a polished and professional performance. If you're worried, though, one good way of lessening the fear of public speaking is to think of it as having a conversation, rather than giving a talk. It also helps to break the ice by meeting a few people from your audience first; this will help you make a connection with them that you can use and build on while you're on the platform. Be friendly, smile, look people in the eyes, ask questions if appropriate, and take the listening time to breathe, relax, and enjoy the experience if you can.

MAKING IT HAPPEN

Although the effects of a bout of nerves show themselves physically, it's our state of mind that triggers them. Fears that we'll make a fool of ourselves or that we won't achieve our goals commonly drive our nervous reactions, which are often known as the "fight or flight" response. Thousands of years ago, when we were surviving in a physically hostile world that was populated by human predators or enemies, our fight or flight response enabled us to fuel our strength and overpower a beast or build our speed and outrun a being that was threatening us. In the moment of need, adrenalin would be released, our hearts would pump faster, our blood would be super-oxygenated, and our muscles would be fed to achieve higher levels of performance. This is what enabled human beings to survive and build the (relatively) safe, sophisticated, and cerebral world that we enjoy today. However, in spite of our successful emergence from the primitive world, our bodies still react to fear—whether it be real or imagined—in the same way.

When we're giving a presentation, our fear of failure gives rise to the fight or flight response along with its characteristic bodily reactions, but these now have nowhere to go. We don't take flight and neither do we fight, but instead stand still, tell ourselves not to be so silly, and try to combat the panic. By this stage, there's no point in trying to use our mind to control the effects of fear as our body has taken control and is doing its job perfectly well. This lack of control gives rise to further feelings of anxiety and sends a message to the body to try harder because the threat has not disappeared and there is still work to be done. More adrenalin . . . faster heart beat . . . busy muscles . . . and so it goes on. Trying to break this cycle is the challenge of overcoming nerves and it can be tackled in two ways: through the mind and through the body.

Overcome Nerves through the Mind

- Try using visualization as a technique for removing the fear stimulus. Imagine your audience receiving your information enthusiastically, being interested in what you're saying, and applauding when you've finished. Enhance this image with feelings of satisfaction, achievement, and pride. Watch yourself leave the spotlight feeling confident and happy to acknowledge those who come up to you afterwards to congratulate you on your performance.
- Think through your presentation or performance beforehand so that you are both practically and mentally prepared. If you're likely to be asked questions on your presentation, imagine what these might be and prepare some answers. If it helps, write them down, read over them a few times and tick them off your "checklist" of things to prepare.
- Get as much information as possible. This will help you

target your talk appropriately and demonstrate that you understand their needs well and see things from their perspective. Being able to show that you've taken the time to do this will help win them over and put them on your side.

Working through the exercises above will help remove the perceived threat you fear and will fill your mind with positive images. If the threat is removed through visualization, you're unlikely to experience the severe physiological responses.

Overcome Nerves through the Body
Some of these well-known relaxation techniques will help prevent your body from triggering the "fear response."

- Spend a few minutes to calm your breathing and to take attention away from the impending performance. Breathe deeply into your stomach, hold your breath for a few seconds, and breathe out again. Do this several times in a quiet spot away from the action.
- Relax your body. Sit in a chair and concentrate on each muscle group one by one. Working from your feet to your forehead, contract and relax your muscles. Feel the difference. If you find yourself becoming tense again, go back to the problem area and try again, breathing deeply and steadily as you do so.
- Have some water before your performance to prevent you from drying up and keep another glass beside you so that you can refresh your mouth as you go.

Remember that your body language will reflect your state of mind. If you're nervous, you may brace yourself and try to make yourself appear smaller so that your perceived threat won't see you. You may also want to find something to lean against or hang on to so that you get a feeling of support. Resist the temptation to do any of these, though, as they'll actually give off signals of weakness and draw attention to your nerves. Instead, try the following:

- Practice standing solidly, with your knees locked back, and legs slightly apart. Don't be tempted to entwine your legs around each other like barley sugar—you're more likely to fall.
- If you need to take notes on-stage, use cards rather than floppy bits of paper that will rustle and quiver as your hands shake.
- Open body gestures make you look larger and stronger. Point from the shoulder. Find an opportunity to open your arms in an inclusive gesture. Take up more space on the stage by taking one or two steps from time to time. Look your audience in the eyes and try to find a connection that will build your confidence.
- Project your voice well. Your tone and pitch will convey how much you believe in your message. Talk to the back of the room to achieve the right level of projection. If you have the opportunity and the venue is new to you, ask a friend or colleague to stand at the back as you practice and indicate that they can hear you.
- Dress comfortably and appropriately. Don't take risks with your image until you're sure you can carry it off—this isn't the time to experiment with complicated clothes.

Overcoming nerves isn't an easy task but is one well worth aiming for. Success removes obstacles to your personal and professional development and means you're free to express yourself without hindrance.

COMMON MISTAKES
You Put Yourself under Too Much Pressure
Putting ourselves under too much pressure to overcome our nerves can be counter-productive. Set reasonable goals, take things one step at a time, and give yourself an opportunity to celebrate each small success and build upon it incrementally. If you challenge yourself in extreme situations, you run the risk of failing in those extremes and it can be very difficult to recover from that. Be gentle with yourself and try to build your confidence steadily and soundly.

You Pretend You Don't Suffer from Nerves
When people want to appear confident and competent, they often deny that they suffer from nerves and end up playing a part, rather than being themselves. This is a common mistake which at best makes it seem as if you're suppressing the real "you," but at worst, can make you seem arrogant. Putting on masks can be helpful in some situations, for example, if the real you is hidden somewhere in the role that you've decided to act out, but removing who you are by "being someone else" isn't a good way to overcome nerves. Hiding yourself away won't help and in fact sometimes it's just better to acknowledge your perceived short-comings and find yourself a role model, mentor, or coach who can help you find a way through.

You Think the Problem Will Go Away
Many would-be presenters who are overcome by nerves avoid dealing with it, thinking that they just have to get through their ordeal and somehow arrive at the other side. This is perfectly true, but it can be life-enhancing to face your fears and find a dignified way through. Often when we look our fears in the face, they begin to subside, especially if we practice techniques to master them. Rehearsing is extremely helpful, whether it's in front of friends, family, or even the mirror. If you're able to video yourself rehearsing, so much the better; you'll learn a lot.

FOR MORE INFORMATION

Web Sites:
businessknow-how:
www.businessknowhow.com/growth/public-speaking.htm
fearofpublicspeaking.net:
www.fearofpublicspeaking.net/public_speaking_nerves.htm

See also:
✔ Delivering Presentations (pp. 795–796)
🖰 Presentation/Speaking (pp. 1865–1866)

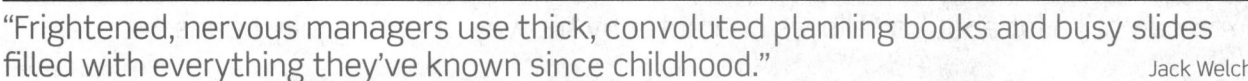

"Frightened, nervous managers use thick, convoluted planning books and busy slides filled with everything they've known since childhood."

Jack Welch

Boosting Your Message with Your Body Language

GETTING STARTED

We all know that real communication is not just a matter of making a noise. But did you realize just how little impact what we actually say has on people we're speaking to? In a face-to-face situation, like a presentation, between 55 percent and 65 percent of your meaning is communicated by your body language—your posture, movements, and facial expressions—and 38 percent comes from your tone of voice. That leaves just seven per cent to be conveyed by the words you use!

In addition, researchers also agree that the verbal part of the communication is used to convey information, while the non-verbal part is used to convey values, feelings, and attitudes—the things that build rapport.

It's obvious, then, that if you can learn to understand and control body language in a conscious way, you can make an enormous difference to the impact you have on your audience. This actionlist will help you to use the different forms of non-verbal communication to help get your message across effectively and to build rapport with your listeners.

FAQs

I prefer to give presentations on "home ground," but realize I have to get used to doing them elsewhere. How can I make things a bit easier for myself?

People, like animals, are territorial and instinctively perceive new spaces—like an unfamiliar presentation room—as hostile territory. As a result, it's natural, if you have not been in the room before, to decrease your speed as you enter it, and this can make you look as if you lack confidence. There are a number of things you can do about this:

- be in the room first, before your audience arrives, so that you already "own" the space;
- familiarize yourself with the room before the presentation, so that when you do enter you are more relaxed and in charge;
- make a point of going into the room at an even speed, or even stopping at the door before entering.

I do get nervous before I present, but try to hide the signs as much as I can. Can others still pick up on my nerves?

They may do, but it's not the end of the world and there is a lot you can do to help yourself. One of the biggest giveaway indications of nerves is your posture. And interestingly enough if you look nervous, rather than getting people's sympathy, you tend to make your audience inclined to feel hostile towards you. Self defense teachers know this: they teach their pupils to carry themselves in a self-confident and upright manner, as people who walk in a timid or frightened way are much more likely to be victims of attack.

To make sure that your posture doesn't betray your nerves:

- **Stand up straight** with your feet slightly apart; keep your head up, and think generally about taking up as much space as you can. It might help to keep in mind the saying, "think tall and you'll be tall"—this will automatically help you to adopt a confident posture.
- **Don't hold your arms in front of your body too much.** People feeling nervous or unsure of themselves will often "protect" themselves: in other words, they adopt a posture that protects a vulnerable area. Men might stand with their hands clasped in front of their genitals, and women tend to fold their arms across their chests. Nothing can make you look more nervous than standing in front of a presentation audience with a folder clasped to your front!

Also, if you can avoid it, don't have any piece of furniture or other object between you and your audience—it can act as a barrier and create a distance between you. However, if you find you have a tendency to shuffle your feet nervously, try positioning a table behind you where you can lean back on the edge of it.

MAKING IT HAPPEN
Be Natural with Gestures

It's easy to worry too much about gestures. With a few exceptions, most gestures are fine—providing they feel natural to you. After all, for most people, gestures are an extension of their personality and it can make you feel uncomfortable and unnatural if you try to repress them.

This issue can affect people in all areas of life. Neil Kinnock, the former leader of the U.K. Labor Party, gave an intriguing example of someone trying to repress his natural gesturing habits during the 1992 general election campaign. His tendency to wave his arms around was interpreted by some as a sign of impetuousness when in fact his objective was to show he could be trusted to run the country and command the respect of other world leaders, so campaign organizers advised him to grip the sides of the rostrum. Camera shots from the rear, however, show clearly how he slid his hands up and down and gripped the edges during his speeches as he tried to keep a grip on his enthusiasm. It clearly wasn't comfortable for him to have his natural exuberance restrained in that way.

Having said this, there are a few useful things to remember about gestures:

- Never make a rude one, obviously!
- Try not to make the same gesture too many times, or it will turn into a mannerism that will distract your audience. They might find it tempting to count how many times you wag your forefinger, rather than listening to what you're saying.
- Be on the look out for distracting habits you acquire only

"You can tell a lot about a fellow's character by his way of eating jelly beans."

Ronald Reagan

when you're under stress, such as foot shuffling or lip licking. If you know what these are, you might be able to eliminate them, or at least minimize them.

- If you find it difficult to know what to do with your hands, you could try using a "prop." Many people use props to reinforce their messages, the most common being extensions of the hand such as a pen or pointer. Using a prop extends the space taken up by your body—and hence your territory—and you are perceived as more confident and powerful.

Finally, no matter how nervous you are, try to avoid hand-to-face gestures such as touching your nose or rubbing your eye. These often mean you're not entirely comfortable with your subject matter, and can signify that you're not being completely honest about something. Even if your listeners don't know this consciously, they will pick up on your discomfort.

Keep Up Eye Contact

It's true of all human interactions to say that the more eye contact we have with someone, the closer we tend to feel to them—and they to us. Often we will avoid eye contact with someone we don't like, and, if we do make it, we will adopt an unemotional stare, rather than a friendly gaze.

When you're giving a presentation, keep your eye contact with people as normal as possible. Look at everyone in the room, not just the person in the middle at the front who you feel is on your side. That way each member of your audience will begin to feel that they have forged some sort of personal bond with you, and will be more receptive to your message.

Watch Your Timing

In normal conversation, another element that conveys information (often unconsciously) is the speed at which you talk. Speaking slowly can sometimes indicate that you're uncertain of what you're saying; speaking quickly may show that you're anxious or excited. These rules still apply to some degree when you're making a presentation, which may make you feel as if you're stuck between a rock and a hard place. As ever, though, going for the middle ground is much the safest option.

Although it's important to speak slowly enough to enable your audience to hear what you're saying, don't overdo it or you'll sound hesitant. Conversely, you also need to guard against gabbling—it's a natural tendency to speak faster than usual if you're nervous and, if you're normally a fast talker anyway, you can completely lose your audience!

Think About Your Tone and Mannerisms

The *manner* in which you speak during your presentation is almost more important than anything else. If you think about it, even a simple word like *hello* can have multiple different meanings—friendly, hostile, surprised, suspicious, offhand, and many others—depending on how you say it, so you need to be careful about what tone of voice you use. There are a number of things to think about here.

- Try to sound friendly, but not so casual that you lose your authority.

- At the same time, don't be too bossy—this is a presentation, not a lecture.
- It's better to be too loud than too soft: nothing is more trying for an audience that a mumbling presenter.
- Ask someone you trust to listen to you and check that you are not swallowing words (easy to do when you're nervous)—in other words, that the ends of your sentences don't die away and become inaudible. To a listener, this makes it seem as if the presentation is repeatedly grinding to a halt.
- Bear in mind that too many "ums," "ers," and hesitations make you sound unprofessional and can be irritating to listen to. Plenty of rehearsal should solve this issue.

As with physical gestures, most catch phrases—"as I say," "basically," "you know," for example—are fine unless they're used too frequently, when they become a distracting mannerism. Again, when you practice, ask someone to keep an ear out for things like this. You'll be so used to saying them, that you won't notice you're doing it!

Remember Your Facial Expressions

As with eye contact, people's emotions towards us are influenced by our facial expressions. In fact, this is so much the case that if someone continually shows the "wrong" facial expressions, or doesn't change their expression at all, we find it hard to warm to them.

While this doesn't mean you should grin manically at your audience throughout your presentation, it does mean that you don't have to be too guarded in your expressions—and it won't ruin your image or make you appear unprofessional if you smile occasionally. In fact, smiling will help put you and your audience at ease. It's not appropriate at all times, of course—if you're delivering bad news of some type, for example—but in the normal run of things, it does no harm.

Match Your Clothes to the Occasion

According to the experts, people form 90 percent of their opinion about someone within the first 90 seconds of meeting them, which means that your audience will be making judgments about you long before you even open your mouth.

What you wear is therefore your first means of communicating something about yourself, and will help your audience to relate to you ... or not. As a rough rule of thumb, people tend to like people who are like them—so it's best to dress in the same sort of way as those you'll be presenting to. If you're presenting informally to a group of colleagues, for example, you can wear normal office attire, while a more formal suit might be better for a meeting of government bureaucrats.

If in doubt, it's probably best to err on the side of restraint. That way, the worst you can do is to present a blank canvas that doesn't distract your audience from what you have to say. After all, you want your *message* to be the point of focus in your presentation, not your personality.

COMMON MISTAKES
You Lack "Congruence"
Because body language is something that occurs naturally, whether or not we are conscious of it, it's impossible

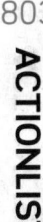

"The ability to control impulse is the basis of will and character." Daniel Goleman

804

ACTIONLIST

to control every last aspect of it. This means that, if you are talking about something you don't really believe in, or if you're not entirely comfortable with what you are saying, your body language will subtly "leak" this somewhere along the line. This lack of "congruence" between your words and your body language will be picked up on by your audience, and they are likely to feel suspicious and distrustful of you and your message. The only answer is to be authentic in what you say and your body language will reinforce that message naturally.

You Overdo Things
When you become conscious of all the ways in which you communicate non-verbally with others, it can suddenly become terribly easy to overdo them . . . your eye contact is a little *too* intense, your posture a little *too* confident, your gestures a little *too* controlled, and so on. And, just as is the case with a lack of congruence, this can make you come across as insincere and inauthentic and may turn your audience against you. To be effective, body language must be subtle and seem completely natural—and the only way to achieve this is to practice

over and over again. Try watching yourself in a mirror as you rehearse your presentation, or ask someone you trust to observe you and give you honest feedback. Eventually, if you practice enough, controlling your body language will become second nature to you.

FOR MORE INFORMATION

Web sites:
Culture at Work: **www.culture-at-work.com/nvcnegotiation.html**
NLP training and resources:
www.altfeld.com/mastery/seminars/desc-sb1.html
The non-verbal dictionary of gestures, signs, and body language:
http://members.aol.com/nonverbal2/diction1.htm
PPI Business NLP: **www.ppimk.com**
Rider University Clinical Psychology Department:
www.rider.edu/users/suler/bodylang.html

Structuring and Writing Good Reports

GETTING STARTED

The art of writing good business reports doesn't come easily to everyone, and, as a result, many people consider the task boring and difficult. Inexperienced writers often feel they have to produce great tomes that include everything they know, rather than elegant documents that meet their objectives. Unsurprisingly, this can result in over-long documents that are a nightmare both to write and read. Writing reports *can* be a satisfying experience, though. Try to bear in mind that their purpose is to present relevant information that allows good decisions to be made, or to outline the effects of decisions that have already been made. Good reports are succinct, helpful, and written with the reader and his or her context firmly in mind. They should be structured so that the logic of their arguments can be followed easily. Don't leave out too much information in your pursuit of elegance, however; paring down too much is just as unhelpful as putting too much in.

FAQs

I have a report to write that covers issues that could become large and unwieldy. How do I control the process and arrive at a neat solution?

Controlling a document's scope can be tricky, but try the following:

- Get a proper brief from the commissioner of the report. This may mean a long conversation, but it sets your parameters.
- Think about your audience, their perspective, their background knowledge of the topic, and their likely investment in it.
- Work out your desired outcome. This will help you to organize your information and arguments.
- Structure the report carefully. Make sure it has a beginning, a middle, and an end. Plan the sections and subsections carefully and logically.
- Find, organize and analyze the information that you want to include. Exclude anything you don't really need.
- Write, check, and double-check your work. If at all possible, ask someone else to proofread it for you.

I work in a technical area and much of my data is numerical. How can I make this come alive for the reader?

Readers can quickly switch off if confronted by reams of numbers and formulas. Make the data come alive by describing the meaning behind the numbers in words if possible, or by turning it into graphs, charts, or other illustrations.

I've been asked to write a report and if I do it well, it could enhance my reputation and offer me further career opportunities. How can I show myself in the best light?

Producing a highly professional document may help you meet this double agenda, but don't fall into the trap of thinking of the report as your résumé—it's a vehicle to show your professional expertise, not an excuse to show off. Keep it simple and use straightforward language. Don't pepper the document with the latest acronyms and jargon—your audience may not be as familiar with them as you. If you *do* need to use this type of language, make sure that you explain the full meaning of an acronym at least once toward the beginning of the report, and you could also include a brief glossary at the back. Language aside, make sure the document follows a logical sequence and leave the reader with some questions or pointers that lead them to recognize your expertise. For example: "The current debate about [relevant subject] goes beyond the scope of this report, but my conclusions take account of the relevant aspects of these issues."

MAKING IT HAPPEN
Know Your Objective

To write a good report, you need to be clear about your audience, what they know already, and what they'll learn from your final document.

You may be writing for a number of different reasons, but each will inform the approach you take. For example, you could be justifying a decision that has already been made and reviewing its effectiveness. Alternatively, you may be developing a persuasive argument in support of a particular decision, or you may be disseminating information in order to provide background knowledge for a debate or a decision in which you have no investment. Each option offers a basic structure that will act as an organizing framework.

Visualize your finished document at the outset and get a sense of how you'd like the reader to feel as they read through it. This will help you decide what to include, what to leave out, and what tone will work best.

Set the Context

Your first task is to draw readers into the material and to remove anything that would detract from them understanding it fully. One way to do this is to create a "frame" through which readers view the topic. Often this frame appears in the form of a summary of the purpose, scope, and structure of the report. It is also helpful to state any assumptions on which the report is based. You may also like to include an outcomes statement to set expectations and guide the reader on how the contents of the report should be considered or applied. For example, you could say: "It is intended that this report will contribute to the

"The leader's unending responsibility must be to remove every detour, every barrier to ensure that vision is first clear, and then real,"

Jack Welch

debate on [relevant subject]" or "This report will set out the rationale for making a decision on [relevant subject] . . . and conclude with a recommendation on what this decision should be."

Present the Key Issues

Reports become difficult to read and understand if the arguments presented are unclear. Rather than crisscross themes, introduce and address each key issue separately and develop your argument logically. Try not to conflate personal opinions with the facts; be accurate and objective in the way you present your data, findings, or discussion points. Identify the themes that will be developed in the main body of the report and signpost the sections in which this will be done.

Understand the Underlying Issues

Now that you've identified and explained the key factors, you need to expand on their underlying causes and on the issues that emerge as a consequence of them. Next, explore possible solutions, being careful to mention fully any implications, including costs. (These are often overlooked.) By taking this tack, your logic will pull the readers along and help them to come to the same conclusions as you. If your report is designed to favor one option out of many, this is clearly the way you want to go!

Appraise the Future

Some people aren't natural decision makers and feel uncomfortable when weighing a number of options. Help them along by having a forward-looking section that allows you to explain why one decision is better than another. Sometimes, you can do this most effectively by painting a picture of the future if the "ideal" decision isn't made. If you do take this approach, however, you must be absolutely sure that your logic is watertight, as any gaps will give others an excellent opportunity to launch counterarguments.

Conclude and Make Your Recommendations

A good report alerts the reader about what to expect, informs and argues the case in line with the purpose of the report, and ends with a conclusion or recommendation that draws all the threads together. Powerful conclusions reiterate the points made and assert what needs to be done next.

Think About the Executive Summary or Synopsis

Although the executive summary usually comes at the beginning of any report, it's actually much easier to write it and then insert it into the proper place when you've finished the rest of the document. By this stage, you'll have thought through all your arguments to their logical conclusions, all of which should still be clear in your mind, so it should be a relatively simple task. Remember that the summary need only be a few paragraphs long and its main objective is to give the reader a brief overview of the report's content and outcome.

Here's a quick checklist covering the main structural points along with some items to consider when reviewing your document.

- **Context:** Have you considered the purpose of the report and clarified its scope and expected outcome? Have you considered the readers and understood their needs, perspective, and motivations for reading the report?
- **Organization:** Have you made sure that your document is ordered logically and that your arguments are robust? Is there an obvious beginning, middle, and end to your report? Is there a logical thread linking your report together?
- **Presentation:** Have you made sure your document is presented well? This includes the layout, the formatting, and the use of tables, figures, and illustrations. It's true that pictures can say a thousand words but make sure they're relevant and add something to the report. Make sure there is enough white space to make the document inviting to the readers
- **Content:** Have you covered all the key issues? Have you differentiated between fact and opinion? Have you outlined your assumptions? Are your facts accurate? Are your arguments clear and free from personal or unreasoned bias?
- **Style:** Is your writing clear and concise and is meaning easily conveyed? Often "less is more" when communicating through the written word. Have you laid out your document effectively and consistently? Have you checked your spellings and grammar?
- **Conclusions and Recommendations:** Are your conclusions a natural outcome of the arguments in your report?
- **Finally . . .** Have you included a succinct executive summary or synopsis? Does the report look good and is the format of the report stable as you flip through a final time?

COMMON MISTAKES
You Include Everything You Know

Many people assume that they must include *everything* they know about a topic or issue in a report. Remember that "less is more" and include only information that is essential to the logic and purpose of the report, or that helps to build important background to the issue at hand.

You're Not Objective

It's easy to weave too much of yourself into a report, especially if you feel strongly about the subject or have a vested interest in it. Try to avoid this if you can, though, as you'll end up creating something that isn't objective or helpful for your audience. Your credibility is on the line if your writing is filled with unsubstantiated facts or emotional assertions, so don't go there. Use good examples to support your points and if you want to refer to other pieces of work (for example, Web sites, books, or articles), include these prominently so that readers can research further if they'd like to.

You Assume Others Think Like You

Report writers often assume that their audience thinks the same way that they do and that it will therefore see an argument along the same lines. Don't fall into this trap; remember that others approach things with their own

"I take the view . . . that if you cannot say what you are going to say in twenty minutes you ought to go away and write a book about it."

Lord Brabazon of Tara

perspective and logic. What you can do, though, is to "head them off at the pass," if you like, and try to address potential counterarguments to your own within the body of the report—this will show you have a grasp of others' views. It's a good idea to ask someone else to read through your draft and test your arguments.

FOR MORE INFORMATION

Book:
Alred, Gerald, et al. *The Business Writer's Handbook*. 8th ed. New York: St Martin's Press, 2006.

Web Sites:
About Writing Business Reports:
http://freelancewrite.about.com/cs/prmarcom/a/busreport.htm
Idaho State University:
http://cob.isu.edu/cis300/reportWriting.htm
TVI Community College:
http://planet.tvi.cc.nm.us/ba122/Reports/Report%20Writing.htm#Effective

See also:
✔ Writing Great E-mails (pp. 808–810)

Writing Great E-mails

GETTING STARTED

Even though e-mail is probably the backbone of business communication these days, many people do not know how to use it well. As it's an "instant" way of getting in touch with others, it's easy to overlook the basics of business correspondence, such as spelling, grammar, and punctuation, in e-mails, but it's important that you maintain high standards however you communicate with others. The style you use for a message will, clearly, depend on the recipient, but take time in judging what you're writing to whom so that your company's image or reputation is always enhanced, never diminished.

FAQs

I'm extremely busy at work, and don't have time to spend ages on writing e-mails. I just tell people what they need to know or ask the questions I need answered. Surely no one will mind?

While nobody could object to a succinct, straightforward e-mail, impolite ones are another thing altogether. However busy you are, it doesn't take much to address and close messages properly, or to say "thank you" if you're asking for help. Obviously you don't need to be formal with people you know very well or work with very closely, but, if you're contacting people for the first time or trying to attract new business, it clearly makes sense to be polite.

I have to ask a colleague with a notoriously short attention span a complicated question via e-mail. What's the best way to do this?

Summarize all the key information you need to share with your colleague and then attach a document with background facts and figures. Make sure you have a powerful subject line in your e-mail and then set out an overview of your question, taking care to highlight exactly what you need to know and when. If your question is based on a string of other events or has supporting evidence, list all of this out separately in an attachment, and tell your correspondent what you've done. If they have lots of e-mails to read, they may not even notice you've attached something, so add a reminder. Once you've sent the e-mail, follow up politely after a few days if you've not heard anything by sending the e-mail again, asking for a response. If your colleague has an assistant and the e-mail is urgent, you could also ask him or her to draw it to their boss's attention.

MAKING IT HAPPEN
Clearly Identify the Subject of the E-mail

As e-mail grows in popularity, people in business receive a high volume of messages each day. To deal with this potential flood, they have to prioritize and decide what's important. Make sure, then, that every e-mail you send has a clearly-identified subject.

Most popular e-mail packages include a subject line, so use that to state as concisely as possible what your e-mail is about. Examples include:
- new date for meeting
- price changes on the ABC range
- sales monthly report
- order for Customer XYZ—delivery status
- new managing director appointed

These are brief and to the point but they indicate clearly what the e-mail is about. Even if you're on reasonably friendly terms with the recipient, if you're writing a *business* e-mail, try to avoid using "Hello" in the subject line. It annoys some people and they'll put off reading the message.

Some e-mails cover a subject that changes over a period of time, such as the content of a new brochure or the status of project. To help everyone keep track of the changes and to make sure they read the latest version of information, add a date or version number to the title. For example:
- new brochure copy—draft 4
- project status—July
- revised personnel guidelines—effective December

Be As Concise As Possible

An e-mail is, first and foremost, a *short* form of communication. It should be brief and to the point and the recipient should be able to understand the main points of your message in the first few lines.

As most e-mails will be read on a small computer screen, it can be difficult and inconvenient to follow long passages of text. If you need to go into more detail, send a document as a separate attachment or tell the recipient to contact you for more information. If you need to go into some detail and sending an attachment *isn't* possible, break your message into small "chunks" with a heading before each new section. This will make long passages of information easier to read and understand on screen and your correspondents will be able to pick out the information most relevant to them.

Let's say you're thinking of creating a new project and would like your correspondent to be a contributor. To save them wading through a dense paragraph, you could give a brief overview of the project and then highlight key points:

Your role

To overhaul our annual product catalog, working with teams in-house on content and delivering a final PDF to the printer.

Budget

$800.00 (40 hours at $20.00 per hour)

Deadline

Final PDF delivered no later than September 30th.

Check Your Spelling and Punctuation

An e-mail is a form of business correspondence that has the same status as letters and other printed material. In the hands of a customer, it reflects on the image of the

"The highest art of professional management requires the literal ability to smell a real fact from all others."

Harold S. Geneen

company, so a message riddled with spelling mistakes and bad grammar isn't going to show you or your company in the best light. With this in mind, take a few minutes to check your message for mistakes and sense before you send it. Many popular e-mail programs include spell-checkers to help you do this, but if your system doesn't have one, you could prepare your message in a word-processing program, check it, and then copy the final version into your e-mail.

The popularity of text messages and text message speak is beginning to creep over into e-mail. While most people will understand what you mean if you send them a message along the lines of "C U at 10" or "mtg off," it's best not to include this type of abbreviation in messages to external clients or contacts. Remember also to use upper and lower case letters in your messages to business contacts. Writing a message completely in lower case gives an impression of something written in haste. Your correspondent might think that you just couldn't be bothered to spend any time on it (and, by extension, them).

Lastly, try not to use acronyms too much. They may be understood by your colleagues, but meaningless to other people. If they're essential or completely unavoidable, explain what they mean at the outset of your message so that your correspondent can work out what's going on.

Use an Appropriate Style

Clearly, there's no single style for e-mail that you can adopt every time you compose one. You could use a friendly, chatty style when you're contacting a colleague or friend, but it's more appropriate to adopt a more formal style when you're contacting someone for the first time or dealing with a customer or an external contact.

For colleagues or regular, familiar contacts, you could open with "Hi," "Hello," or just a name ("John" or "Sarah"). In more formal e-mails, you would use "Dear Mr./Mrs./Miss/Ms . . . ," or "Dear John/Dear Lisa" if you're on first name terms with the recipient.

At the close of the e-mail, tailor your sign-off to your relationship with the recipient.

Different ways of signing off		
Informal	**More formal**	**Very formal**
Cheers	Best	Yours
Thanks	Best wishes	Sincerely
Tnx	All best	Yours sincerely
Ta	All best wishes	Yours faithfully
All the best	Many thanks	
Later	Regards	
See you	Kind regards	
	Best regards	

E-mail styles, like all other forms of communication, will differ from country to country. If you have lots of international correspondents, remember that some cultures are naturally more formal than others, so take a lead from the messages your contacts send to you and copy their tone and style. This will mean that you're less likely to offend anyone inadvertently.

Request the Action or Information You Need

Some of your e-mails give information to the recipient, while others make a request for action or information. If you need to find something out from somewhere, make sure you've phrased your request clearly so that they know exactly what you want. For example, "Could you please send me the latest sales report by November 22nd," or "Please discuss this with Tim, Omar, and Emma and let me have your views by 2:00 on Thursday."

If a number of people are involved in a joint process, you may need to give them individual instructions so that everyone understands their wider role. For example:

For the team to deliver the new product by July, we need to meet the following targets:

Justin—complete the software by March

Helen—get the test results by May

Seema—request additional funding from the Financial Director by April

Explain How Urgent Your Message Is

Make clear whether your e-mail is urgent, important, or routine. With so much e-mail traffic, people need to prioritize their reading and response, so state the level of urgency.

Some e-mail packages allow you to highlight the level of priority, but, if you do use this facility, don't abuse it. It's easy to mark every e-mail as urgent or as highly important in the hope that it'll receive attention, but if you do it too often it'll have a "crying wolf" effect: people will start to disregard messages that you mark as urgent, even if one of them actually is. Use the facility carefully (and honestly) and you'll get the results you need. To overcome possible reader inertia, you could include an indicator in the e-mail subject line such as "product review—decision needed by Thursday." This is informative and gives the recipient a clear instruction.

Don't use too many capital letters to indicate urgency and importance. E-mails like this can prove difficult to read on screen and, again, recipients can become immune to the technique. Also, the use of capital letters in e-mails is regarded by some people as "virtual shouting" and your correspondents may misread your mood and respond in kind.

Use Attachments to Provide Detail

E-mails that include longer documents, photographs, audio, or video take the form of a message plus an "attachment." Attachments allow you to send detailed information to your correspondent, but you should use this facility with caution.

Some attachments can take a great deal of time to transfer and the recipient may have problems downloading them, particularly if they don't have broadband (which allows fast transmission of large amounts of data). Bear this in mind if you have suppliers who have small businesses or who work from home. Attachments that could pose difficulties include:

- video clips
- publications converted to Portable Document Format (PDF)

809

ACTIONLIST

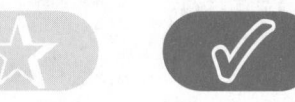    

- presentations spreadsheets
- photographs

Before you send attachments, check with your correspondents that their systems can handle these types of files.

Include Further Contact Details

Some e-mail programs allow you to include a "signature" at the end of your messages. In some cases, this can be a scanned version of your signature, but mostly it's a few lines that allow you to show information that the recipient may not always have easily to hand, such as your job title, mailing address, telephone and fax number, and Web site address. Adding a "signature" is particularly useful if you're writing to someone for the first time, as it provides some extra context about what you do or who you work for. A "signature" can also be used to advertise a new product. You can draw your correspondents' attention to it by mentioning where they can find out more about it on your Web site.

COMMON MISTAKES
You Let Your Standards Drop

E-mail is an instant medium, so it's easy to create a message quickly without considering the impact on the recipient. Abbreviations, acronyms, minimal punctuation, and unchecked spelling save time in the short term, but poor standards can damage a company's reputation.

Your Messages Are Hard to Read

E-mails are normally read on a computer screen, so any information must be concise and clearly laid out. Use upper and lower case letters and a legible typeface for clarity and avoid using capital letters too much. If you have a long message, guide the recipient by using headings for different topics.

FOR MORE INFORMATION

Book:
Danziger, Elizabeth. *Get to the Point! Painless Advice for Writing Memos, Letters and E-mails Your Colleagues and Clients Will Understand.* New York: Three Rivers Press, 2001.

Web Sites:
Albion.com: **www.albion.com/netiquette**
CC Consulting:
www.crazycolour.com/os/emailedge_02.shtml

See also:
✔ Dealing with Difficult E-mail Situations (pp. 814–815)
✔ Integrating E-mail with Other Forms of Communication (pp. 816–817)

Managing Your Inbox

GETTING STARTED

E-mail has completely changed the way we work today. It offers many benefits and, if used well, can be an excellent tool for improving your own efficiency. Managed badly, though, e-mail can be a waste of valuable time. Statistics indicate that office workers need to wade through an average of more than 30 e-mails a day, while managers or people working on collaborative projects could be dealing with a much higher figure.

This actionlist sets out steps to help you to manage the time you spend dealing with e-mail so that you can get on with other tasks. It offers help on prioritizing those incoming messages and deciding how quickly you need to respond. It tells you how to file e-mail according to its value or function and encourages you to clear the inbox regularly. Despite your best efforts, unsolicited e-mail or spam can clutter up the most organized inbox and infect your computer system with viruses, so this section gives guidance on protecting yourself. It also offers alternatives to e-mail that offer the same benefits of speed, convenience, and effectiveness.

FAQs

Does it really matter how many e-mails I have in my inbox?

Actually, it does. Firstly, you're not making life any easier for yourself by having hundreds (or thousands!) of messages sitting there unfiled, unread, or not acted on. If you need to find something quickly, you'll have to comb through the whole lot to find what you need; even if you search electronically, the more messages you have for the software to look through, the longer it will take. Taking control of your inbox is a way of taking control over your work as well. Secondly, if you have hundreds of e-mails you don't really need, imagine how many there are in all your colleagues' inboxes. Hundreds of thousands if not millions, and these will clog up your company's computer systems and cause programs to crash. You know that collective groan that goes around when a system goes down? By not pruning your e-mails, you're contributing to it!

MAKING IT HAPPEN

Prioritize Incoming Messages

If you're regularly faced with a large volume of incoming messages, you need to prioritize your inbox—identify which of the e-mails is really important.

- Check the names of the senders. Were you expecting or hoping to hear from them? How quickly do you need to deal with particular individuals?
- Check the subject. Is it an urgent issue or just information? Is it about an issue that falls within your sphere or responsibility, or is it something that should just be forwarded to someone else?
- Check the priority given by the senders. Do they really mean it's urgent? Remember that some people have a tendency to mark all of their messages "important," even if they're anything but.

- Is it obvious spam? Can it be deleted without reading?
- Check the time of the message. Has it been in your inbox a long time?

An initial scan like that can help you identify the e-mails that need your immediate attention. The others can be kept for reading at a more convenient time.

Reply in Stages

Because e-mail is an "instant" medium, it can be tempting to reply immediately, but that might not always be necessary. You can reply in stages, with a brief acknowledgement and a more detailed follow-up. If you do this, give the recipient an indication of when you'll be able to get back to him or her and try to keep to this deadline wherever possible.

If the e-mail simply requires a brief, one line answer, then by all means reply immediately. For example, if all you need to say is, "Yes, I can make the 10a.m. meeting," or "Thanks, that's just the information I needed," do it. If you're unable to reply there and then or choose not to, let the sender know that you've received the message and will be in touch as soon as possible. This is a useful method of dealing with a query when:

- you need to get further information before replying in full;
- you need time to consider your response, rather than giving a rushed answer;
- you're angry, upset, frustrated, or confused about a message you've received and need a cooling-off period before you make a thoughtful response.

Taking a staged approach is useful, as it allows you to maintain contact while not interrupting other work that may be more important. It also gives you a bit of breathing space if you're feeling under pressure or worried about the issue under discussion.

Set Specific Times for Dealing with Incoming E-mail

Good time management is essential in all areas of our life, and e-mail is no exception. If you're completely overwhelmed by the volume of messages in your inbox, dedicate a certain amount of time each day to dealing with it.

If you don't work in a traditional office setting, you may have "dial-up" e-mail, where you contact a service provider to check your inbox. Set a pattern for checking your inbox that fits in well with the type of work you do and the number of e-mails you expect, and stick to it.

If you have a broadband connection that is "always on," your computer will let you know when you receive a new message. Think about whether to review the new messages immediately or wait till a predetermined time. For example, if you've preferred working patterns or core working hours—times when you need to be available for contact with overseas clients, for example—you may decide to dedicate a certain portion of the day to dealing with your e-mail.

If you spend a lot of time in meetings, you may find

"When you have nothing to say, say nothing."   Charles Caleb Colton

ACTIONLIST

that you have short spells between meetings (say 10 or 15 minutes) that would otherwise be wasted time. Use these breaks to catch up with your e-mail so that you don't have a flood of them waiting for you at the end of the day.

Use a Filing System to Manage Your Messages
What do you do with incoming messages once you've read them? If the information is important, you may want to keep it for future reference. However, hoarding all your messages in no particular order will not only slow you down when you're looking for information, but is also likely to make your computer system unwieldy and likely to crash.

Check whether your company has a policy for retaining and storing e-mails. Archiving may be essential for legal reasons and, if there is a policy in place, you must comply with it. Your company may have a central facility for storing or accessing archived e-mails; so investigate with your technical support department. You'll be making their lives easier as well!

If you have a lot of important information you need to hang on to (deals done over e-mail for example, or sign-offs from partners that need to be kept), create your own filing system. For example, you could sort messages into folders arranged by:
- customer or supplier name
- project name
- date of receipt
- research topic

Using subfolders will help you to keep organized too: for example, for each project it may be useful to subdivide everything into monthly or yearly folders. This will also make it easier to see what should be archived and when.

To save space in your inbox, you might want to copy important e-mails relating to a specific project or program into other applications. For example, you could create a Word document called "project communications," in which all relevant e-mails or messages are held centrally. Everyone will then be able to access the information if you're away for any reason and you'll all be able to find what you need quickly.

Practice Good Housekeeping
If you don't file your incoming messages as described above, make sure you comb through your inbox regularly. If your inbox is full of every message you've received during the course of a working week, a simple search for an important message could take a lot of time.

Unless you need to keep messages for legal reasons, it's generally good practice to delete them regularly. Regular "pruning" will help you keep on top of things. To help you do this, some e-mail applications offer an option that asks you if want to empty your deleted items folder every time you exit the application. This useful option will ease you into good e-mail management practice!

Remember to:
- set time limits for keeping messages in your inbox;
- file or archive any messages that you need to keep;
- make sure that you've replied if a response was necessary;

- keep any valuable information, such as contact names or phone numbers;
- send unwanted messages to the "deleted messages" section of your e-mail system, but check again before you finally clear that section.

Make Arrangements for E-mails When You're Away
Opening your inbox after a vacation or a few days away can be an intimidating experience. "You have 90 new messages"—where do you begin? Prioritizing is a good starting point, but a few minutes spent making arrangements before you leave the office will save you a lot of time on your return.
- Leave an "out of office reply" on your system. This responds automatically to incoming e-mails, telling the sender that you're away and will deal with the message on your return. It won't stop the first message from a particular sender, but it may prevent further material or messages from the same person asking why you haven't replied.
- As part of your "out of office reply," state when you'll be back in the office so that your correspondent has a rough idea of how long you'll be away. If you're expecting a lot of messages or are at a crucial stage in a big project, ask one of your coworkers if you can nominate them to be an alternative point of contact during your absence, and if your coworker agrees, give his or her e-mail and telephone number in your "out of office reply."

Alternatively, ask a coworker to check your inbox regularly for particular types of message and either acknowledge them or deal with the issue, if possible. This will make sure that urgent items receive the right level of attention.

Offer Alternatives to E-mail
Although e-mail is one of the most popular and convenient ways of communicating quickly, there are practical and effective alternatives:
- instant messaging, which allows short messages to be communicated between connected computers on a network—ideal for brief communications, such as "meeting changed to 11a.m." or "send me the latest sales figures"
- voicemail, which again allows the caller to leave messages that you can respond to when you're ready
- teleconferencing, where a number of people can join in a telephone discussion and make decisions without long e-mail chains
- introduction of informal meeting areas which promote real collaboration

A good deal of e-mail communication comes from external sources, but think about how many e-mails you send each day to your coworkers in the office, or receive from them. Are they all absolutely necessary? If not, why not take the initiative and ask whoever is responsible for company-wide e-mail management to instigate some basic rules that will cut down on internal e-mails? The policies could cover:
- mass copies of e-mail to recipients who don't really need it (for example, sending an e-mail about a project to

---

"Today, communication itself is the problem. We have become the world's first overcommunicated society. Each year we send more and receive less."

Al Ries

everyone in the business when only a small group of people need to be kept informed);

- personal e-mail;
- limits on the "thread" of a discussion which covers every point made by every recipient.

Protect Against Spam

Spam or unwanted e-mail, like the unsolicited direct mail that you may receive at home, is a tremendous waste of time and can clog up your e-mail system. It is a real and growing problem for businesses all over the world, and workers can spend up to an hour per day deleting spam from their inboxes. To free up that hour for more useful activities, think about the following ways to limit or prevent spam:

- Use a filter supplied by your Internet service provider. This can block e-mails that contain certain terms or other attributes that identify the message as potential spam.
- If it's practical, set rules for your incoming e-mail. Some rules block all incoming e-mail except messages from addresses you've nominated. This is helpful to a certain degree, but can cause problems for new legitimate contacts or organizations that have changed their addresses.
- Unsubscribe to any services or newsletters that that you do not wish to receive. The incoming e-mail should provide you with details of how to do this.
- Do not give permission for your e-mail address to be passed on to other parties when you subscribe to or register for a new service. At some stage in the registration or subscription process, you should be asked whether or not you give permission for this to happen, normally in the form of a short statement plus a preference box that you need to check. Read any such requests very carefully.
- As a last resort, change your e-mail address. It might take less time to send a new e-mail address to everyone on your contact list than it does to delete your daily spam load.

Not only does spam e-mail clog up your inbox, but it can pass on viruses that may spread throughout your computer system. You should immediately delete any suspicious e-mails and then empty your "deleted items"

folder. Most companies will have invested in the most up-to-date anti-virus software they can afford, but, if you work from home or are self-employed, it's up to you to make sure your machine is virus-free. Scan your computer regularly for viruses and make sure you have the relevant software and security patches. The links at the end of this actionlist will help you find out more about this.

COMMON MISTAKES

You React Immediately to Every E-mail

Like a ringing telephone, it can be hard to ignore a new incoming message. It takes discipline to wait for a convenient moment or scan the message and reply later, but once you've decided on a new approach to dealing with e-mail, stick to it.

You Don't Clear Your Inbox Regularly

The list of incoming messages can very quickly grow to unmanageable proportions. Clear the inbox regularly or develop a filing system that allows you to respond appropriately and retain useful information.

You Have No Protection Against Spam

Spam doesn't just waste your time and fill up your inbox, it can also introduce harmful viruses into your computer or your company network. Make sure you're protected against unwanted e-mail and seek advice from your technical support team or Internet service provider if you have any concerns.

813

ACTIONLIST

FOR MORE INFORMATION

Web Sites:
McAfee Antivirus Software: **www.mcafee.com**
Norton Antivirus Software:
www.symantec.com/index.htm

See also:
- ✔ Coping with Information Overload (pp. 835–836)
- ☆ Preventing Your Work Problems from Causing You Stress (pp. 402–403)

"The fewer the data needed, the better the information."

Peter F. Drucker

Dealing with Difficult E-mail Situations

GETTING STARTED

The immediacy with which e-mail allows us to communicate with others is both one of its great advantages and one of its disadvantages. Sometimes, especially when time is short, people feel under pressure to reply to e-mails as soon as they land in their inbox, and this can cause all sorts of problems.

This actionlist sets out to offer advice on what to do if you find yourself in a difficult situation that has been caused or made worse by e-mail, including sending an e-mail to the wrong person and replying in haste or anger.

FAQs
I get so many messages that I don't have time to read them all properly. What is the best way to tackle this?

This is actually quite a common problem. If you have lots of demands on your time, it's all too easy to misread e-mails, especially if they're badly written or unclear in tone or layout. While replying promptly to messages of any kind is something we all aim for, beware of writing back too quickly if you're not 100% sure of what your correspondent is requesting or asking about. Use a "staged" approach to acknowledge e-mails, request clarification if you need it, and reply fully when you're up to speed with all the relevant information.

MAKING IT HAPPEN
Check You Are Replying to the Right Person

If you are involved in an exchange of e-mails between a group of people, take great care when you reply.

If you're annoyed or exasperated by a group e-mail, resist at all costs the temptation to write while you're still angry. Give yourself some cooling off time first. If you do choose to reply, reply to the group only if it's absolutely necessary and, if you reply to just one person, make doubly sure before you send the e-mail that the addressee is the right person. For example, some of your correspondents may have similar first or surnames, so check before you click "send."

Also take care if you are replying to personal e-mails at work. There are always horror stories in the newspapers about people who think they're writing to friends or partners but who inadvertently send highly personal messages to everyone in their address book or click on "reply to all" rather than just "reply to sender." This not only causes acute (and very public!) embarrassment, but also puts the writer in the firing line back at the office. Always take time to check, but, better still, send personal e-mails from a nonwork e-mail account.

Be Careful When You Forward Information to Other People

In the same way that you need to take care when originating or replying to an e-mail, watch your step when you forward information to another person, especially if he or she is an external client or customer. As mentioned above, double-check you are sending the e-mail to the right person.

In some cases, where the "thread" of e-mail conversation is quite long or you have only been copied in for some part of it, you might not realizes if some of the comments or content interleaved aren't appropriate for passing on. These comments could range from the relatively harmless ("I hope we tie this up soon: the negotiation's gone on for longer than I'd hoped") to the disastrous ("I hope we never have to work with these people again").

Make sure you aren't passing on anything that comments unfavorably on the external party's capabilities or judgment. Also double-check that there are no personal, offensive, or defamatory remarks (such as any that criticizes appearance, or is racist or sexist).

Treat Confidential Information Sensitively

E-mails have been described as electronic postcards—their contents can be easily read by anyone—so be certain you read through external e-mails before you send them to make sure you haven't inadvertently included confidential or sensitive information.

If you do need to send confidential information to a correspondent, you can include it in your e-mail as a password-protected attachment.

Check your company's policy on confidentiality and security. It should set out what can and cannot be sent by e-mail. It will also set out the disclaimers or warnings that should be included in every e-mail.

Deal Immediately with E-mails Sent in Error

Despite your best efforts, sometimes (especially if you have an extensive mailing list) you may write or send something to the wrong person. In many cases, this may be perfectly harmless, but, if the information is confidential or critical of the accidental recipient or their company, you may have a problem.

Many companies put a disclaimer on all outgoing e-mails saying that the information they contain is intended for the recipient only. The disclaimer might also say that the information is confidential. Even with these disclaimers, though, the damage is done as soon as the e-mail has been sent, so you need to act quickly.

If you've sent a potentially damaging e-mail by mistake, contact the recipient as quickly as possible, either by phone or by e-mail.

If the material is confidential, ask the recipient to destroy it securely, if possible.

Apologize if the material contains critical or offensive remarks and offer an explanation.

If you can, try to speak to your manager as soon as you

"Mistakes are a fact of life. It is the response to error that counts."   Nikki Giovanni

can so that they're prepared in case the other party wishes to make a complaint. You may find this embarrassing, but in the long run it will save time and help to put a "lid" on a situation.

If you find yourself in a situation like this, your aim is to resolve the situation as quickly as possible, with minimal damage and inconvenience. Don't be sarcastic, try to make too much of a joke of it (jokes often don't travel well online), or be rude. If you feel that things are escalating beyond your control, talk to your boss, explaining exactly what happened and when.

Don't Involve Other People Unnecessarily in an Argument

"War by memo" has now evolved to "war by e-mail." The practice of sending copies of communications to as many people as possible in order to impress or embarrass is much simpler with e-mail but is a waste of time, energy, and inbox space.

If you have a problem with a colleague or external client, write to them directly. (Calling them may actually be the best way to reach a solution as the voice can convey nuances that e-mail will never be able to.) There's no need to copy in everyone in your team unless there is an essential business reason for you to do so.

COMMON MISTAKES
You Scan Your E-mails, Rather Than Reading Them Properly Before You Reply

If you receive large numbers of e-mails daily and are under time pressure, you might think you're saving time by scanning the messages for key words and then replying. In some cases this will be fine, but in others it will set you off on the wrong foot. Don't reply in a rush, especially if it's an important message: send an acknowledgment and write back properly when you have more time to dedicate to writing a great e-mail.

You Allow a Difficult Situation to Escalate

If you receive an angry or rude e-mail, it can be tempting to reply in the same tone, but this will just make things worse. Keep cool, act professionally, and reply in measured language. If you feel that you've been rude already and have some ground to make up, apologize to your correspondent.

FOR MORE INFORMATION

Web sites:
A Beginner's Guide to Effective E-mail, webfoot.com: **www.webfoot.com/advice/email.top.html**
Emailreplies.com: **www.emailreplies.com**
Tiger Computing Ltd: **www.tiger-computing.co.uk/email.pdf**
"Top 10 e-mail mistakes," ibiztips.com: **www.ibiztips.com/email31AUG00.htm** and **www.ibiztips.com/email04SEP00.htm**

See also:
✔ Coping with Information Overload (pp. 835–836)
✔ Writing Great E-mails (pp. 808–810)

"Experience teaches slowly, and at the cost of mistakes."   James Anthony Froude

Integrating E-mail with Other Forms of Communication

GETTING STARTED

E-mail is a powerful medium in its own right, but it can also be used to enhance other forms of communication. Sometimes, e-mail may not be the most effective approach, so you need to consider whether a telephone call or a conventional letter might be more appropriate.

A telephone call may be more appropriate, for example, if you need to have a two-way discussion with someone. But you can use e-mail to exchange background information and summarize the outcome of your discussion. Write a letter if you wish to include confidential information or if you're covering a formal topic and you want to ensure that the recipient has a printed copy of the information you're sending.

FAQs
What is the role for e-mail on my company's Web site?

An important one. Including e-mail facilities within the site makes it easier for site visitors to contact you or request additional information. Make sure that you always include an e-mail address at the end of your company advertising. When customers contact you, you can capture their details and open up a sales process.

If you send direct mail to customers, you can use e-mail to follow-up the mailing and improve the effectiveness of the campaign. For example, your company may use telemarketing to contact customers or sales prospects initially and then follow up with e-mail.

MAKING IT HAPPEN
Use Telephone and E-mail Together for Detailed Discussions

Although e-mail is a very quick, effective method of communicating information, it may not always be the most appropriate medium if you need to have a detailed discussion with someone. In this situation, using the telephone may be more suitable. You can, however, use e-mail *in conjunction with* the telephone to help you have a more effective discussion.

If you want to hold a detailed discussion with one or more people, e-mail them in advance to outline the key points you wish to discuss and arrange a convenient time for the call. This gives the other parties time to prepare and gather information so that they can make a useful contribution to the discussion. It also gives them the opportunity to make some space in their schedule when they can speak to you without interruption.

During the telephone call, you can e-mail information that might help the discussion along—a set of figures, a diagram, or other material that would be difficult to describe by phone. After the discussion, you can send an e-mail summarizing the main conclusions and action points from the discussion. Alternatively, if you're using a voice-conferencing service, you can ask the service provider to record the call and e-mail participants an electronic copy of the discussion as an attachment. This facility is particularly useful for confirming the points of long, complicated discussions.

Send a Letter As Well As an E-mail for More Formal Communications

For certain types of formal correspondence, such as commercial agreements, appointments and dismissals, confirmation of contracts, and other material which might be legally binding, you may find it more appropriate to send a conventional letter. Although techniques such as digital signatures have given e-mail increased status as legal documents, a printed letter with a handwritten signature continues to carry greater weight in law.

Include E-mail Facilities Within your Web Site

Web sites are a proven, cost-effective method of giving visitors access to large amounts of complex company and product information. However, if a Web site includes no facilities for communication, those resources can be wasted.

E-mail opens up a channel of communication that can turn browsers into buyers. Each site should include a "Contact us" page or section that displays the company address, telephone, and fax details. It should also include an e-mail address such as sales@abc.com, info@abc.com, or feedback@abc.com.

Adding an electronic form to your site that encourages visitors to register their details can prove even more valuable. Don't ask visitors for too many details, as this will irritate them, but ask for some basic ones, including their e-mail address. Once you have that, you can e-mail them with details of products that might be of interest or special offers. This can create valuable sales leads which the sales force can follow up on.

You can also give visitors the option of subscribing to e-mail alerts. Here visitors register their interest in particular products or services and receive a personalized e-mail whenever there is a new development.

Include an E-mail Address on Your Advertisements

If your company uses advertising to promote products and services, you can increase the return on your expenditure by including an e-mail address in the advertisement. The e-mail address encourages readers to respond by requesting further information. This is known as "direct response advertising."

Some advertisements include postal addresses or telephone numbers as a "response mechanism." E-mail has an advantage over these mechanisms because it's quick and easy to use. Remember that advertisers have to overcome a high inertia factor, so employ the simplest technique possible.

"It took me fifteen years to discover that I had no talent for writing, but I couldn't give it up because by that time I was too famous."

Robert Benchley

Including an e-mail address on advertisements also enables you to measure the effectiveness of your campaign in terms of the number of responses. You can measure overall responses or compare the performance of different media by using a different e-mail address on each publication such as info1@abc.com or infotv@abc.com.

Use E-mail in Conjunction with Direct Mail

Some companies send information to customers and prospects via conventional mail. This is known as direct mail and it's used as an alternative to advertising to communicate with smaller or more specialized groups of customers and sales prospects.

Using e-mail can increase the effectiveness of direct mail campaigns. By sending a "teaser" message, you can encourage the audience to watch out for the main mailing. For example: "In just over a week, you'll find out how you could save your company thousands of dollars." After the direct mail has been sent out, follow up with an e-mail reminder: "We hope you received details of our great special offer. Don't forget to reply by November 10th to qualify for a massive discount."

Once a prospective customer has responded, you can then e-mail them on a regular basis with product updates or future special offers.

Improve Telemarketing with E-mail

Telemarketing is the use of the telephone to carry out market research or to sell products and services to customers and prospects. Telemarketing is proving to be more effective when it's used with other media. For example, if you or your staff are responsible for making calls of this kind, you can send, as e-mail attachments, product information such as data, diagrams, or other illustrations that help the prospect to understand what you're offering.

After making a telemarketing call, send an e-mail thanking the prospect for their time and confirming any product, price, or delivery details that have been discussed or agreed.

Establish an E-mail Forum for Customers

An Internet forum is a discussion group for people with similar interests. In business, it's increasingly used to build stronger relationships with customers.

As an example, a technology company could set up a forum where customers were able to exchange technical information with each other and discuss questions of mutual interest. The forum could also be used to resolve problems that a number of different customers experienced.

E-mail is an ideal medium for forum discussions. The company that hosts the forum sets up an e-mail facility on its web site and manages the process. E-mails are posted on a notice board and members can contribute to any relevant discussions.

COMMON MISTAKES
You Use E-mail in the Wrong Circumstances

E-mail is seen as a communications tool suitable for all situations. There are, however, some occasions when a letter or telephone call may be more appropriate. Assess the circumstances and make sure you're using the right method of communication at the right time.

You Don't Recognize the Contribution E-mail Can Make to Other Communications

E-mail is now well-established as a tool for day-to-day business communications. It can also be used to support your sales and marketing processes. By using e-mail as part of advertising, Web sites, direct mail, and telemarketing campaigns, you can make your marketing budget go further and get great results.

"Broadband is like a narcotic. Once you have it, you won't be able to give it up."

Lynn Forrester

Negotiating with Confidence

GETTING STARTED

We all negotiate a lot more than we think we do, in all areas of our lives, and developing negotiation skills is an essential part of moving up the career ladder.

Negotiating is the process of trying to find an agreement between two or more parties with differing views on, and expectations of, a certain issue. Good negotiations find a balance between each party's objectives to create a "win–win" outcome.

Negotiation can be "competitive" or "collaborative." In competitive negotiations, the negotiator wants to "win" even if this results in the other party "losing"; this can ultimately end in confrontation. In collaborative negotiations, the objective is to reach an agreement that satisfies both parties, maximizing mutual advantage.

There is no one right way to negotiate, and you'll develop a style that suits you. Most negotiations will be a mixture of the collaborative and competitive approaches. In situations where you're negotiating the terms of an ongoing relationship (rather than a onetime deal), it's generally more productive to lean toward collaboration rather than competition.

FAQs
What is competitive negotiation?

This type of negotiation may have an unfriendly atmosphere and each party is clearly out to get the very best deal for him- or herself—the other party's objectives tend not to come into the equation. If you find yourself involved in a competitive-style negotiation, bear in mind the following:

- **Opening**. If you can, avoid making the opening bid as it gives a great deal of information to the other party. Try not to tell the other party too much and aim to keep control of the meeting's agenda.
- **Concessions**. Conceding in a competitive situation is seen as a sign of weakness, so do this as little as possible. The size of the first concession gives the opposing parties an idea of the next best alternative, and tells them exactly how far they can push you.
- **Conflict**. If conflict flares up, negotiators need to use assertiveness skills to maintain a prime position, and to defuse the situation.

What is collaborative negotiation?

Many people see negotiation as a battle where the stronger party defeats the weaker party, that is, there is a winner and a loser. In some cases, negotiations can break down altogether, such as in industrial disputes which result in strike action. In this scenario, nobody wins, so there are only losers. It needn't be like this, however. In collaborative negotiation, conflict is minimized and the whole idea is to reach a solution where everyone benefits. This approach tends to produce the best results, mainly because there is much better communication between the parties. In addition, it makes for better long-term relations if it's necessary to work together over a long period.

The opening will involve gathering as much information as possible but also disclosing information so solutions can be developed that are acceptable to both parties. This involves:

- considering a number of alternatives for each issue;
- using open questions (which do not have yes/no answers);
- being flexible;
- helping the other party to expand their ideas about possible solutions.

Both parties will make concessions if necessary, normally aiming to trade things which are cheap for them to give but valuable to the opposing party, in return for things which are valuable to them (but may not be so cheap for the other party).

By listening, summarizing, paraphrasing, and disclosing in collaborative negotiations (for example, "I would like to ask you a question . . . " or "I feel that I need to tell you that . . . "), conflict will be kept to a minimum, enabling a mutual advantage to be reached.

MAKING IT HAPPEN
Prepare Yourself

As with many business situations, good preparation will help to reduce your stress levels. Don't think that preparation time is wasted time; it's anything but. Begin by working out your objectives, and making sure they are specific, achievable, and measurable. It's also important to have a clear idea of what you're expecting from the other party. Be sure that your expectations are realistic and that their results are easy to assess. It's a good idea to write down objectives and to put them into an order of priority. One way to do this is to classify them as "must achieve," "intend to achieve," and "like to achieve." For example, a new photocopier has been bought for the office. It breaks down after a week and you need to contact the supplier to sort out the problem. The objectives can be defined as:

- **Must achieve**: The use of a photocopier that works.
- **Intend to achieve**: Get the photocopier repaired.
- **Like to achieve**: Get a replacement photocopier.

Ahead of any negotiation, gather as much information as possible about the subject under discussion. The person with the most information usually does better in negotiations. For example, two people have each prepared a very important document. Let's see how this situation can progress.

They both need to have them processed by the one desktop publishing operator in the company and couriered to the destination for the following morning. However, there is only time to have one job finished before the daily courier collection at 4p.m., so the two argue over whose document is the more vital. If they argue too long, neither job will be finished on time and both would "lose." The staffer could pull rank, resulting in the junior being the "loser," with the possible loss of his or her future cooperation.

If they obtained more information, they would find out

"Make a suggestion or assumption and let them tell you you're wrong. People also have a need to feel smarter than you are."

Mark McCormack

that the courier company runs an optional 6p.m. collection, which also guarantees delivery before 11a.m. the next day. A "win–win" situation could then be achieved.

Discuss and Explore

At the beginning of a meeting, each party needs to explore the other's needs and make tentative opening offers. Remember that these need to be realistic or it's unlikely that the discussion will progress to a successful conclusion for everyone. If both parties cooperate, progress can be made; however, if one side adopts a competitive approach and the other does not, problems may arise. You need, then, to analyze the other party's reaction to what's said.

An opening statement is a good way of covering the main issues at stake for each party, and allows the discussion to develop naturally. At this stage, the issues are just being discussed and not yet negotiated. What you're trying to do is develop a relationship with the other person. Ask questions to help you identify their needs and keep things moving. As a way of doing this, ask open-ended questions that the person can reply to fully, rather than closed questions to which he or she can only answer "yes" or "no." For example, you could begin by saying "Tell me your thoughts about [the issue under discussion]."

Make a Proposal

Once both parties have had chance to assess the other's position, proposals and suggestions can be made and received. Remember that you need to trade things and not just concede them. The following phrase is valuable:

"If you (give to, or do something for, us), then we'll (give to, or do something for, you)."

Look for an opportunity to trade things that are cheap for you to give but of value to the other party, in return for things which are valuable to your business. For example, if you are a painter and wallpaperer who needs to rent a reasonably priced apartment, you could negotiate with the landlord to paint certain rooms in return for a lower rent. Or say you need to publicize a product and would like to engage someone to do some work for you, but you can't quite afford to pay the job rate they had in mind. If you or your business have a Web site, you could offer to put a click-through link from your Web site to theirs so that anyone who reads their article can find out more about them and perhaps offer them more work.

Start the Bargaining

After discussing each other's requirements and exchanging information, the bargaining can start (as in the first example above). Generally speaking, the more you ask for, the more you get, while you'll concede less if you don't offer as much at the beginning. For example, let's say you've something to sell to another party. You know you have a premium product, but you're not sure quite how blank the other party's check is. If you know you'd be happy to sell for $200, you might want to start off by asking for $300, knowing that:

- you'll be able to look as if you're giving ground to the other party;

- they think they're getting a bargain;
- you may even get a better deal than you'd thought!

If conflict arises when the bargaining starts, explain that the opening position is just that, an opening position and therefore not necessarily the one that will be adopted at the end of the negotiation. Ultimately, an agreement can be reached only when both parties find an acceptable point somewhere between their individual starting positions.

When you make an offer, be very clear about what's on the table. Avoid using words such as "approximately" or "about," as an experienced negotiator will spot an opportunity to raise the stakes quite dramatically. Don't make the whole process harder for yourself. For example, if you can only offer $600 for something, say so, or before you know it you'll be being pressed into agreeing to go up to $700.

Similarly, when the other party makes an offer, make sure you find out exactly what it includes. For example, if you're negotiating with a supplier, check whether or not the cost the supplier is quoting you contains delivery, sales tax, and so on. Ask for clarification if there's anything you're not sure about and check that the offer matches all the criteria that you noted down during the preparation stages as being on your list of requirements.

Communicate Clearly But Openly

When you're negotiating with someone face-to-face, use open body language and maintain eye contact. Try to avoid sitting with your arms folded and your legs crossed, for example. Also, try to think through what you're about to say before you say it. Don't use language that will annoy the other person. For example, try to avoid using words like "quibbling" and "petty." Even if you think someone is doing or being either of these things, using these words to them will only make the situation worse. Don't be sarcastic or demean them, their position, or their offer.

Similarly, if you feel that the main discussion is losing its focus and that people are starting to make asides to colleagues, address this by saying "I sense there's something you're unhappy about. Would you like to discuss it now?"

Listen!

Sometimes when you're nervous about something, you become so focused on what you want to say that you don't pay enough attention to what's being said to you. This can cause all manner of problems, including knee-jerk reactions to problems that aren't really there but which you think you've heard. Active listening is a technique that will improve your general communication skills and will be particularly useful to practice if you have to negotiate a lot. To become an active listener, practice the following:

- Concentrate on what's being said, rather than using the time to think of a retort of your own.
- Acknowledge what's being said by your body language. This can include keeping good eye contact and nodding.
- Emphasize that you're listening by summarizing your understanding of what has been said and checking that this is what the communicator intended to convey.

"Never corner an opponent, and always assist him to save his face . . . Avoid self-righteousness like the devil—there is nothing so self-blinding."

Basil Henry Liddell Hart

- Empathize with the communicator's situation. Empathy is about being able to put yourself in the other person's shoes and imagine what things are like from their perspective.
- Question and probe to bring forth more information and clear up any misunderstandings about what's being said. If you want to explore someone's thoughts more thoroughly, open questions are helpful. "Tell me more about . . . ?", "What were your feelings when . . . ?", "What are your thoughts . . . ?" These questions encourage the speaker to impart more information than closed questions, which merely elicit a "yes" or "no."
- Don't be afraid of silence. We often feel compelled to fill silences, even when we don't really have anything to say—yet silence can be helpful in creating the space to gather thoughts and prepare for our next intervention.

Call a Break If You Need To
Sometimes a short break of 10 or 15 minutes may be a good thing if a negotiation is proving to be more complex or contentious than you'd previously thought. A break will give everyone a chance to cool down or recharge his or her batteries as necessary. It'll also give everyone an opportunity to take a step back from the issue under discussion and return to the discussion with some ideas if there has previously been an impasse.

Reach Agreement
As the discussion continues, listen for verbal indications from the other party such as "maybe" or "perhaps"—these could be signs of an agreement being in sight. Also look out for nonverbal signs, like papers being put away. Now is the time to summarize what has been discussed and agreed and not to start bargaining again.

Summaries are an essential part of the negotiation process. They offer a way of making sure that everyone is clear on the decisions reached and also give all participants a final chance to raise any questions they may have. As soon as possible after the negotiation, send a letter that sets out the final, agreed decision. A handshake on a deal is fine, but no substitute for a written record. Make sure your letter mentions:
- the terms of the agreement;
- the names of those involved;
- relevant specifications or quantities;
- any prices mentioned plus discounts, and so on;
- individual responsibilities;
- time schedules and any deadlines agreed.

COMMON MISTAKES
You Open Negotiations with an Unreasonable Offer
Both parties need to see a reasonable chance of getting

what they want from the negotiation process. By starting off with an unreasonable offer, you risk killing the process before it starts.

You Begin Negotiations without Enough Information About What the Other Party Wants
The early discussion and information gathering phases need to be used properly to ensure that both parties aren't "talking past each other." Before negotiation begins, you need to have a broad view of the points you might need to concede on, and what you want the other party to concede to you. These can then be "traded" in accordance with your bottom line.

You Lose Your Temper
Some people are much easier to negotiate with than others and there's a difference between a serious, probing discussion and a bad-tempered shouting match laced with sarcasm. If someone is rude to you while you're negotiating with him or her, don't take the bait (even though it can be tempting). Instead, address them politely but assertively, and challenge their behavior. You could say something like "I think that comment was inappropriate and unhelpful. Shall we return to the issue?"

You Try to Rush Negotiations in Pursuit of a Quick Agreement
Both parties need to feel comfortable with the pace and direction of negotiations as they develop. This could mean that one or other party might need time to consider certain points or options before moving on to others. You should respect this need, while at the same time making sure that both parties observe a flexible timeframe for resolution. Endless negotiations will only waste time and money.

FOR MORE INFORMATION
Book:
Fisher, Roger, William Ury, and Bruce Patton. *Getting to Yes.* 2nd ed. New York: Penguin, 1991.

Web Site:
The Negotiation Skills Company:
www.negotiationskills.com/articles.php

See also:
Negotiation (pp. 1838–1840)

Coping in Difficult Negotiations

GETTING STARTED

However experienced you are at handling negotiations, you'll occasionally run into difficulties. The number of potential difficulties is legion, but the most common ones fall into two categories: difficult people and difficult situations.

Again, the range of possibilities is wide, but some general principles will emerge in each case.

FAQs

I dread negotiating with one particular supplier as she is so abrasive. What can I do to change this?

People are difficult for several reasons. They may have unresolved issues in their personal life that affect their attitudes and commitment to the negotiation. They may lack empathy and make insensitive or inappropriate remarks, or they may simply be unskilled in negotiating and make mistakes. Whatever the cause, try not to overreact and make the situation worse.

MAKING IT HAPPEN
Decide Whether You Want to Save the Situation

You've had a long day and things aren't going well. Do you want to rescue what's left of the negotiation? If not, suggest postponing the negotiation to another day. If you do want to persevere, try the following approach.

Look at the diagram below. It shows two possible ways of behaving when working with others. When someone asks us for help, or appears to need it, the natural tendency of most people is to try to offer a solution. We generally produce one of the three kinds of behavior in the top half of the diagram:

- we advise people what to do;
- we tell them;
- we offer to do something for them under certain conditions.

This is called "solution-centered behavior" because it focuses principally on finding an answer. Sometimes this works, but it is rather easy to produce a brilliant solution to what later turns out to be the wrong problem. And when this happens, it is, of course, your fault!

An alternative approach is to use "problem-centered behavior," which means going "below the line" shown in the diagram, and questioning the other person about how he or she understands the problem.

You can do this either by consulting ("What exactly is the problem?", "When did it occur?", "What might have caused it?" and so on) or reflecting ("I can see that you're very angry about this, what's causing it?", "What aspect of the problem is troubling you most?"). The key message here is to consult about facts, reflect on feelings. The purpose is to make sure that you both share a clear understanding of what the problem is. In fact, helping the other person to clarify his or her thinking about the problem often allows the answer to emerge as if by magic. The other party then feels as if they "own" the solution,

so they feel committed to it and you may not need to use the solution-centered behavior at all. Even if the answer does not appear automatically, though, you can now direct or advise from a much better understanding of the issues.

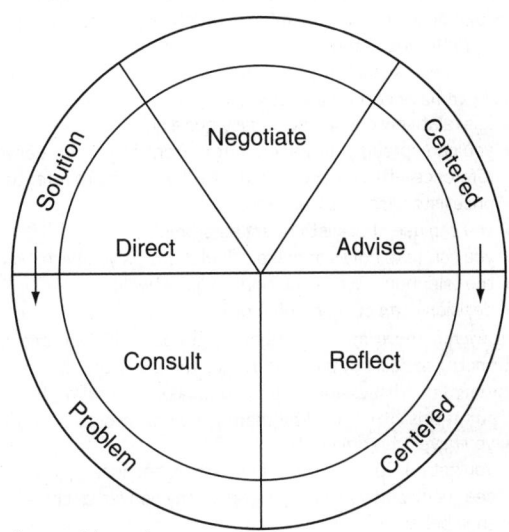

Source: Margerison

Tap Into the Power of Questions

The key to the "below-the-line" approach is that it obliges you to ask questions, which is always a good idea if you have to deal with difficult people, as it enables you to control the conversation—if you ask a question, people will usually answer it. This approach avoids confrontation, and it may get you valuable information about the person or the negotiation.

Remember the Guidelines

- When in doubt go "below the line": consult and reflect.
- Ask good, useful, open questions: plan them carefully.
- Ask for the other party's proposals or ideas—don't give yours first.
- Ask for clarification of the other party's proposals rather than saying what is wrong with them.
- Ask about their goals and objectives rather than telling them about yours.
- Ask how you can help them.

Have a Backup Plan If All Else Fails

If the other person is still being "difficult" and hindering the negotiation, more drastic action is needed. Either he or she doesn't want the negotiation to succeed, or is unable to conduct the discussion properly at this time. In any case, you need to do something to move things along.

Acknowledge that there seems to be a problem and ask three key questions:

- Does he or she want to continue the discussions?

- Would it be better if you spoke with someone else? A more senior member of staff, for example?
- Is there anything you can do that will help him or her feel more comfortable with the negotiation?

Deal With Difficult Situations

Not all negotiations take place face-to-face these days; in fact, most negotiations happen over the phone or by e-mail. Here we'll look at negotiating by phone. People sometimes opt for this to save time, but it's very much a second-best situation: avoid it as much as possible, except for simple negotiations.

For these straightforward discussions, telephone contact can have certain advantages:

- it is relatively cheap and usually quite quick;
- you can spread your papers out in front of you for easy reference—this is especially useful if you need to refer to price lists, discounts, and so on ;
- you can use checklists to act as prompts;
- you can take notes or make calculations as you wish;
- the telephone forces you both to listen well;
- decisions can be made promptly.

However, there are a number of general disadvantages for both parties, but particularly for the party that has not initiated the discussion. You need to take account of these if put in this situation. The main problems are:

- you have little time to think;
- you get no "feel" for the other person, because you can't see them, and you can't pick up on any nonverbal clues in their behavior;
- the telephone is impersonal; it is difficult to use the "personal domain";
- many standard negotiation tactics are less effective over the phone;
- it is difficult to set and keep to an agenda;
- people are more inclined to say "no" on the phone because they don't get that little extra reassurance that comes from face-to-face contact;
- "what if . . . ?" questions and searches for a "better deal" can be more difficult on the phone—there is a tendency to stick to the specified business;
- it can be difficult to coordinate within your own organization;
- there is a danger of distractions: visitors, noise, pending appointments, and so on;
- many people feel pressured by time during a phone call;
- silences are more threatening in a phone call (and in some countries, may lead to the connection being lost) ;
- you feel as if you have to make decisions too quickly;
- the line may be bad, disrupting the flow of the negotiation, and you don't know who else is listening;
- if you forget something, it may be difficult to come back to the point or introduce it later: telephone calls tend to be "linear" (that is, you may have only one opportunity to

say or raise something), whereas face-to-face conversations can go around in loops.

If you *have to* negotiate over the phone, arrange a time that will allow you to do some preparation beforehand. If someone "ambushes" you and you're caught off guard, ask if you can call them back in half an hour or so.

Have all the necessary paperwork close at hand. For example, if you're discussing the renewal of a contract, make sure you have a copy close by that you can refer to. Also have plenty of paper nearby that you can make notes on.

Make sure that you won't be disturbed. If you have an office, close the door. If you work in an open-plan office, see if you can book a meeting room elsewhere in the building so that you won't be distracted by other people's conversations around you.

Even though the other party can't see you, use the body language you would use if they were there in person, for example nod if you agree, move your hands as you speak. All of this will filter back in the tone of your voice.

Take a break and arrange to call the other person back if things are getting heated or you've reached a stalemate. Once agreement has been reached, follow up in writing as you would do if you'd conducted a face-to-face negotiation.

COMMON MISTAKES
You Battle On When It's Just Not Worth It

While everyone aims to tie up negotiations with the least amount of fuss and wasted time possible, some days it just won't work. On those days, it's important to recognize this, cut your losses, and rearrange for another time.

You Don't Get to the Bottom of Why Someone Is Being "Difficult"

Even though your patience may be stretched to its absolute limit, try to put yourself in the other party's shoes to find out why they are acting in the way that they are. Also ask questions that allow the other party to disclose their concerns and motivations—you may actually be able to help them, thus achieving that ideal win–win goal.

FOR MORE INFORMATION

Web sites:
The Negotiation Skills Company:
www.negotiationskills.com/articles.html
Work911.com: www.work911.com/cgi-bin/links/jump.cgi?ID=3323

See also:
Negotiation (pp. 1838–1840)

"Total commercial honesty always costs something, but total or partial dishonesty will cost more."

Robert Heller

Negotiating with People from Other Cultures

GETTING STARTED

With business becoming "global" and increasing numbers of international mergers and acquisitions taking place, it probably won't be long before you find yourself having to negotiate with people from other cultures. Going abroad to seek new customers or business partners is the obvious example, but receiving potential clients or suppliers from overseas or even doing business with other parts of your own company—if it's multinational—will involve you in cross-cultural negotiations.

Remember that it's not up to the other person to adapt to *you*: not attempting to understand and take account of the other party's cultural background may be felt as an insult. On the other hand, most people will notice if you make the effort and give you generous credit for it.

FAQs
What is the best way to prepare for cross-cultural negotiations?

The very best way is to spend some time living in the other culture, or to find a reliable local mentor or partner. Clearly, it's not always possible to do this, but there are other routes you can take to improve the probability of success and minimize the risk of mistakes. Careful planning and attention will pay dividends.

MAKING IT HAPPEN
Investigate Social Conventions

Wherever you are traveling to on your business trip, finding out more about the social conventions of a country or region is invaluable.

Obvious differences in cultural style are easy to spot, but it's the more subtle distinctions that usually cause problems. For example, unintended rudeness or failure to observe little politenesses can quickly make the negotiations competitive. There are a small number of general areas in which these subtleties usually occur, so observe these things carefully when you're in the country, and investigate them as much as you can beforehand.

Meeting and greeting procedures

Watch how these work. For example, you need to think about:

- who introduces whom;
- whether gestures such as bowing are appropriate;
- whether you're expected to shake hands, and if so, how;
- whether women shake hands;
- whether there are set greetings and responses.

As a general rule, hold back if you are not sure about how to proceed. Be guided by your hosts and avoid any physical contact until you're sure it's acceptable. Also, don't be too enthusiastic in adopting local customs—it may make some cultures suspicious and feel that you're mimicking them, rather than trying to match your approach to fit theirs.

Watch your (body) language!

Remember that a lot of the non-verbal clues we give to our colleagues or friends when we communicate with them won't always travel that well to other countries. While a smile can rarely go wrong, bear in mind that some cultures:

- find the "ok" sign (that is, thumb and forefinger closed together to make a circle) offensive.
- also find the "thumbs up" sign offensive.
- use a nod of the head to mean "no" and a shake of the head to mean "yes."
- think that standing with your hands on your hips (as many people do in repose) means that you're angry.
- are less offended by a lack of personal space than others. For example, you may find that people come and stand right up close to your face while they're talking to you. This can be disconcerting if you're not expecting it.
- prefer a kiss on both cheeks to a handshake.
- value silence more than others. In the West, we often feel duty-bound to fill any gaps in a conversation with chit-chat, whereas in Japan, for example, silence is important and designates "thinking time." In the context of a negotiation, saying too much is a bad move. Say only what you really need to.
- are reluctant to make eye contact as they feel it's insulting. This is particularly the case among some Latin American and African countries.
- get to the point more quickly than others. In some countries, there may be a long exposition to the negotiation that, if you're in a rush, may drive you mad. Be patient, however, and adjust to a different pace.
- are offended by people who chew gum or keep their hands in their pockets during conversations.
- are much more tactile than others.
- won't sit with their legs crossed (as many people do to show they are at ease), as this may mean that the sole of their shoe is pointing at someone. This is considered extremely rude and should be avoided.

Ideas about time

Observe local customs about timing of meetings, particularly:

- the rules about appointments. Do you turn up *on* time (Europe); *before* time (China); or a little *after* time (Africa)?
- how time is used—rigidly or flexibly? Does a half-hour appointment mean exactly 30 minutes, or anything up to an hour?
- how your host will indicate that your time is up. How and when can you can politely take your leave?

Role of women

Some cultures have embraced the role of women in business more than others, and may have very clear conventions governing gender relationships. You need to know:

"Never apologize and never explain—it's a sign of weakness."   Frank S. Nugent

- how women's role is defined in the country you're visiting. Don't comment on this, whatever your views may be.
- the roles women play in business.
- any "rules" covering relationships between men and women at work and socially.

Eating and drinking etiquette

In many cultures, eating with others has symbolism and rituals that can be culturally very sensitive. Sometimes these are based on religion, sometimes on historical tradition. If you're invited to a meal, find out beforehand from a reliable source what the etiquette is, particularly

- what form the meal will take, that is, whether it's formal or informal;
- customs such as washing, which hand to use when eating, formal ceremonies, if there are prayers before meals, and so on;
- what people normally drink with their food (that is, whether alcohol is permissible or not) ;
- whether it's polite to eat/drink everything or whether you should leave something on your plate;
- whether business is discussed over meals;
- any dress conventions.

Gifts

This can be a sensitive area: some cultures will tend to perceive a gift as a bribe, others as an embarrassment. Therefore, find out

- what is the attitude to gifts—are they accepted or expected?
- the type of gift that is appropriate. Be particularly careful about gifts to one's host or hostess if invited to someone's home;
- customs for receiving gifts yourself.

This is one of those areas where, sadly, no -one will notice if you get it right, but everyone will be aware if you get something wrong. Do as much groundwork as you can to avoid this.

Humor

Even if you are trying to break the ice, don't make jokes until you're sure you understand the jokes made by the other party. Be aware that irony or sarcasm often isn't picked up easily by people who don't share your first language, so it is best not to take refuge in either of them too much.

If worst comes to worst and you feel you've made a gaffe, don't try to "rescue" the situation by making another joke. It is best to just move on and pick up the threads of your earlier conversation or start a new one.

Understand Business Practices

Although there's increasingly a common core to ways of doing business internationally, there are certain important conventions and habits that distinguish one culture's way of doing business from another. If you're working in new markets you must be able to answer the questions below. Get help or advice if you can't; guesswork is not recommended.

National characteristics

Since the end of the Cold War many new countries have been created, and new markets opened up for business. Some of these countries have no recent history of dealing with foreigners and little experience of international trade, so doing business there can be very tough. But forewarned is forearmed: find out what you can about cultural attitudes and be ready to deal with them patiently. Look particularly at

- their understanding and acceptance of outsiders;
- who controls business and how it works ;
- how decisions are made. Is the culture one where compromise is sought or is it more competitive?
- how their legal, technical, and financial systems differ from your own. Are there any special conditions that will have to be met?
- whether support systems (transport, banking arrangements, and so on) are adequate to deliver the deal, and does the other party have reasonable control of them?

Language

Negotiate in your own language if you can: fluency gives power, but be aware that the other side has already made a concession to you.

Don't underestimate the dangers of missing subtle points when you have to work in another language. Use this to your advantage: slow things down, ask for clarification frequently.

In most cultures you will "gain points" for speaking their language—but many will be less forgiving of "cultural errors" if you do. You might decide not to disclose your knowledge of their language if it isn't fluent.

Confirm all concessions: check for accidental misunderstandings. Finally, if you do work in your own language, check regularly that the other party has understood you properly. Use questions or summaries to do this.

Working with an interpreter

If you feel it's appropriate, hire an interpreter. Make sure that he or she:

- is professionally neutral and properly skilled;
- understands what negotiating is about and what the objectives of this negotiation are;
- can translate not just words but also meanings through gestures, tone, and so on.

Rehearse with your interpreter to create familiarity with likely events. Don't accept the other party's interpreter if the negotiation is an important one: impartiality is very important and it may be worth finding an independent interpreter. Finally, plan plenty of breaks: long negotiations in a foreign setting are very tiring.

Keep the Basics in Mind

- Don't be in too much of a hurry. Give yourself plenty of time to deal with the unexpected, to recover from travel, get used to the climate, and so on.
- Decide under whose law contracts will be applied (preferably your own). If you have to accept the other party's law, check out the implications carefully.
- Be sure that technical, professional, safety, and environmental standards accord with the other party's national standards, and are acceptable to your own company.
- Make sure you've established a good line of communication with your home base.
- Don't try to take on the style of the other culture. Be aware of it, but retain your own (cultural) style and play to your strengths.

"Place a higher priority on discovering what a win looks like for the other person."

Harvey Robbins

COMMON MISTAKES
You Think You Can Wing It
Taking the time to find out more about another culture may seem like a hassle, but any preparation you do will be put to very good use. Imagine how embarrassed you'd be if a negotiation came to nothing because of a gauche remark or gesture you made? Courtesy is essential in business: you would expect it of others, and they will expect it of you.

You Try to Cover Uncertainty with Jokes
Remember that some jokes just won't work when translated into another language, and may make things worse if a situation is getting heated. If you know your opposite party well, that's one thing, but err on the side of caution if you're meeting someone for the first time or if the negotiation is particularly fraught.

825

ACTIONLIST

FOR MORE INFORMATION

Web sites:
BusinessCulture.com: **www.businessculture.com**
Business Know-How:
www.businessknowhow.com/growth/body-language.htm
ExecutivePlanet.com: **www.executiveplanet.com**

See also:
⌕ Negotiation (pp. 1838–1840)

"If you have to boil down your negotiating attitude to two things, you can do a lot worse than question everything and think big."
Mark McCormack

Coping with Stress

GETTING STARTED

Regardless of the general balance of your life, there will be times that are stressful. Learning the practical steps to cope with stress is important to help you get through these episodes. It isn't recommended that you accept and try to cope with an everyday pattern of stress over a long period of time, since this can be very detrimental to your health. Get the balance right first and take steps to deal with stress comfortably.

FAQs

What can I do to beat "after-work" stress?

Agree with your partner or friends when you want to spend time together and then block it out in the diary. An exercise class is another good idea since it occurs at a set time and it's a good social activity if you enjoy time with others. Even if you spend a relaxing hour in the bath with some candles and a book, you'll feel more ready to handle the demands of others. Say goodbye to "false friends"—cigarettes, coffee, alcohol, and chocolate are all likely to add to the negative effects of stress over time. Give them up and get some help if you need it.

I often find it hard to speak up if I don't agree with someone. How should I tackle this?

Believe in the value of your perspective and opinions. Remind yourself: "there are many perspectives on any situation and my point of view is worth hearing; people may need my perspective too."

MAKING IT HAPPEN

Identify the main sources of stress

Pressure can be positive, providing challenges and building confidence as you achieve them. How you see the situation can make the difference between whether you experience pressure or stress. It's important to understand which situations you're finding stressful and to identify the elements within them that cause the stress. General sources of stress at work, home, and in balancing different roles are:

- conflict between people
- handling difficult behavior
- performance worries
- demanding routines
- increased requirements on your attention or time
- financial worries

Identify sources of everyday stress that fit into each of these categories for you and work out how you can eliminate or alleviate it.

Major life changes have also been shown to cause a disproportionate amount of stress, especially where three or more occur within the same two-year period. The most stressful life events are:

- death of your partner
- divorce or separation
- legal proceedings against you
- a prison term
- personal injury
- marriage
- having/adopting a baby
- losing/changing jobs
- retirement
- moving home
- death of family member

Think about the life events that have affected you in the last two years. The process of adapting to these will inevitably take a toll on your welfare, as you understand, respond to, and live with the change. Think about each life event and how you've dealt with it, but without dwelling too much upon it. Give yourself plenty of relaxation time for recovery, using it to do something that you enjoy, unrelated to the change you're facing. Many people will be going through similar life changes. Even those who aren't can understand that this is a difficult time for you and will want to help, so don't isolate yourself.

Sort out stressful relationships

Contact with others is crucial for getting things done at work, but some people are a lot easier to deal with than others. Your support network outside work can help you to deal with pressures and actually reduce your stress, so getting relationships in good working order is well worth doing.

1. Criticism

Do you have to put up with a constant stream of criticism or put-downs from one person? People who are always negative about you or your ideas are probably feeling insecure. Reminding others of their faults is used to deflect attention from their own perceived failings. Perhaps they feel their position is threatened or feel that they need to compete with you. People like this may feel frustrated or have low self-esteem, and they often don't like to see others enjoying success or higher self-esteem than them.

- When someone makes a personal attack, rise above it and remain cheerful, rather than reacting to it negatively.
- Use phrases such as "that's an interesting perspective" to show that you've heard without agreeing.
- Repeat back a negative comment to the person who gave it. Very often they'll notice the destructive effect of their words and will tone down what they've said about you or qualify it. Listen carefully, as this could be useful feedback. Perhaps you've said or done something that they find difficult to cope with.
- When your critic uses sarcasm, interpret what they're saying to check what they're implying and then ask "why do you say that?" to clarify their meaning. This also highlights their negative tactics, which may be enough to stop the behavior.
- Confront persistent critics directly. Describe the criticism you've been receiving, disclose how it makes you feel, suggest what you would like instead. "You have been sarcastic and critical of me on a number of occasions recently, which I find hurtful. If you have a problem with

something I do, come and tell me directly so we can discuss it."

- At work, make a log of events, including your attempts to confront and resolve the problem.

2. Anger

Do you cope well with angry people? Here are a few simple tips that will help you to draw positive outcomes from difficult situations.

- Keep calm yourself, concentrate on breathing slowly, listening carefully, and keeping your body language open.
- Disarm the immediate mood by responding and showing concern: "I can see that this has really upset you; let's discuss it so I can understand fully and see what we can do about it."
- If someone is too upset to listen there's little point wasting your energy. Ask them to come back when they've calmed down so that you can discuss their problem properly.
- Find a good time and place to discuss persistent anger problems. Warn the people concerned first about what you want to discuss, so they can prepare themselves. Work out why the person uses inappropriate behavior, what they hope to gain or what their angry tactics have won for them before. Plan what you'll say to them before you challenge their difficult behavior. Remind yourself that they may have a real grievance or frustration that you can deal with.
- Describe your observations of the problem and why it causes difficulties for you and/or others. Explain what you want them to stop and what you would like to see instead. Ask them if there are any problems with making this change and discuss what you can do to help them. Compromise and negotiation may be required for a solution.

3. Dead battery

Can you identify people in your life who act as a dead battery, draining you of your energy while giving little in return? Sometimes we can simply "unhook" ourselves from a negative or an unresponsive person and have less to do with them. It can be difficult or impossible to do this if they're in our work team or family. The issue has to be dealt with rather than avoided. Find or create a good time to talk to them, preferably with just the two of you and no distractions. Describe your observations of their behavior and disclose how it makes you feel. Explain what you think would make the situation better and ask them if there are any barriers to this happening.

Real life example

Harry finds that Pete's withdrawal from usual family conversations worries him. His attempts to include his son in what he is doing, or to get conversations going are met with negativity or silence. Harry worries. Pete is clearly unhappy and the problem is affecting the family atmosphere. Harry sends the rest of the family out on an errand. He describes what he has noticed and how worried it has made him feel. He describes Pete's former positive outlook and how great it was to be with him. Harry asks if there's anything getting in the way of a return to this. They discuss a particular problem that was affecting Pete at school and how to deal with it. Though Harry feels that Pete held a lot back in their conversation,

the progress was a relief and the atmosphere was immediately better.

Communicate assertively

Prioritization and self-organization can reduce your stress and help you to manage a demanding workload. In a nutshell, promising less can mean that you get more done. But what if you find it hard to say no or to ask for the help you need? As with any skill, practice improves performance, so here are some exercises that will improve your ability to assert yourself.

- Be assertive in your body language. Stand (or sit) tall, taking up plenty of space. Breathe deeply and easily, making eye contact with an open expression. Don't fiddle with your hands or cross your arms or legs. Clasp your hands lightly, relaxing your shoulders.
- Practice projecting your voice strongly. Start by exhaling all the air in your lungs, which will trigger your body to take a deep breath before you talk. Enunciate consonants clearly, keep your voice soft but turn up the volume. Drop the pitch of your voice (without dropping the volume) at the end of the phrase to convey your conviction in your own words.
- Until you get used to communicating assertively, you may want to give yourself time to consider your response with useful phrases like "Possibly, I'll get back to you on that," or "I need to think about that, I'll let you know."
- If people interrupt you while you're talking, raise a hand to signal "stop," increase the volume slightly and finish your sentence with conviction. If this continues to happen, you can say "please let me finish" as you put up your hand, to draw the person's attention to what they're doing. Keep your cool and continue your point, "I was saying that . . . ."
- Recognize the other's point of view while saying what you think. It's important to express yourself honestly but constructively. A useful phrase could be: "I realize that you . . . but I feel that . . . ."
- When asked to do something, state clearly what your answer is, what you're prepared to do and what you are not. Don't feel that you have to justify yourself; it's the request that you're turning down, not the person. Repeat the message until the other person accepts it.

Develop stress-busting habits

Biochemicals are released in response to stress to prepare your body for action. If "fight" or "flight" aren't required to deal with the situation they may continue to affect the whole body even after the stress has gone. Taking exercise as part of the working day is the single most effective stress reliever. Regular exercise boosts your energy and gives you increased stamina. It removes the effects of the biochemicals adrenaline and cortisol. Exercise will relieve stress: following a stressful meeting, take a brisk walk to burn them off before resuming your day.

A routine that includes aerobic, anaerobic, and stretching exercises is ideal but the best exercise of all is the kind that fits in with your lifestyle. A walk to work, a policy of using the stairs rather than the lift, and a lunchtime stroll are ways to fit exercise into the working day. A Saturday cycle ride and a couple of visits to the gym or exercise

---

"What the banker sighs for, the meanest clown may have—leisure and a quiet mind."

Henry David Thoreau

828

ACTIONLIST

class during the week are all it takes to release the nor-adrenaline and endorphins which relieve the tension caused by a frenetic daily routine. You'll improve your circulation and digestion at the same time, making a good night's sleep more likely.

COMMON MISTAKES
You're available 24/7
Deal with phones and e-mails during set periods of the day only. Turn off the "message alert" message on your computer and turn off your cell phone in between times so that you can concentrate on other things. This still means that you're giving people a reasonable response time but in managed chunks of time that will keep you sane.

You don't prioritize your e-mails
With e-mails, a full inbox can be overwhelming, so start with a trawl through to delete spam and other unimport-ant "noise" from your mail. Then "classify" the e-mails that remain: some require an instant response and some require only a couple of lines and can be dispatched straight away. File longer e-mails that require your considered response or ones with reading matter attached, so that you can give them appropriate attention; make a quick note in your "To Do" list to remind you. Prioritize the mails that are left and deal with them as effectively as you can.

FOR MORE INFORMATION

Web Sites:
Assertiveness.com: **www.assertiveness.com**
Mindtools.com: **www.mindtools.com/smpage.html**
National Mental Health Association—Stress:
www.nmha.org/infoctr/factsheets/41.cfm

Managing Your Time

GETTING STARTED

Time is a human concept. Animals don't understand the idea. They live *in* time; they are in the moment; the present is all that counts. Remembering this can be useful in the business world: being able to focus on the present is often an effective way of getting through laborious tasks and not worrying about the past or future.

In business, time is money. Paradoxically, as technology proliferates (with the promise that it will increase productivity), it makes managers' responsibilities more complex—at the same time that there are fewer support staff to perform the work. The only realistic solution is to make better use of time.

FAQs

How can I be a better time manager?

The *desire* to be good at time management is half the battle, but you need to be aware of the choices you have to make. These relate to your overall life balance and the values you hold.

Look at what you're being asked to do and why. If some requests are outside your area of responsibility or expertise, you may need to meet with your boss to clarify boundaries. If additional responsibilities become a permanent part of your workload, something else will have to give way—unless you can improve your time management skills or delegate some of the tasks.

Maybe you'll have to be more realistic about your strengths and capabilities. Instead of submitting to external deadlines, try to have input into setting realistic ones. Build some slack into the schedule to give yourself the best possible chance of meeting deadlines.

One of my team members seems incredibly disorganized. What can I do to help?

A good team leader often needs to work with individual team members to help them understand what's expected. Set realistic goals and give them adequate time and resources to complete the work. Additionally, if possible, ask them to examine their performance objectively and identify patterns of behavior that contribute to being disorganized. Often time management requires a change in habitual behavior. This can only be achieved by building awareness, charting a clear route, and rewarding success.

I've recently invested in a computerized scheduler but find I am still using my old appointment book as well. How can I get away from using redundant systems?

Plan the time it will take to learn the new technology and transfer your information. Ask for a tutorial from someone who has made the leap already. Then, over a period of a month, wean yourself off the dual system by omitting the appointment book. You'll probably be converted to the versatility and convenience of the computerized scheduler long before the month is out.

MAKING IT HAPPEN
Conduct a Time Audit

You may find it useful to conduct a time audit on your life. What's the balance between the demands placed on you at work and those that define your private life? Does this balance satisfy you, or do you find yourself sacrificing one element for another? One key to good time management is being aware of the wider world in which you live and how the constituent parts relate to one another. Another key is prioritizing—if in fact there isn't enough time to satisfy all the competing demands—and then choosing how you apportion your time.

Take a large sheet of paper and write your name in the center. Write all the demands of your life around it. Include work hours, commuting, socializing, eating, sleeping, household responsibilities, and family commitments. Remember that taking time for family and friends, exercise, hobbies, vacations, and just plain fun is important. Mark the number of hours you devote to each of these areas on an average day, month, or year. This chart graphically represents your life in terms of the choices and tradeoffs you actually make in areas that are important to you.

Ask yourself whether this is how you want to live your life. You may decide to sacrifice some important areas in the short term, but be aware of what might happen when a particular phase of your life comes to an end. For example, how will you manage if you get married or divorced; when children are grown and leave home; when you get transferred to another position or take another job in another company or state; when you have an accident or long-term illness; when you retire?

Decide What Action Needs to Be Taken

Take a highlighter and mark those areas on your chart that need attention. If, for instance, you're spending too much time at work, you need to review your professional objectives and decide how to achieve a better balance.

Life is all about choices. You may find that you can recapture more time by telecommuting, if your employer will permit it and your family will respect the necessary home–work boundaries.

You can probably find other ways to prune wasted hours. For instance, if you like sports or fitness activities, consider finding a club near work where you can go early in the morning instead of having to fit exercise into your evenings.

Look for patterns in the way you use your time. You may find that you're constantly in meetings that run late or that you pick up a lot of extra work because you aren't assertive enough in saying no. If you don't have enough time and your own behavior is contributing to the shortage, change your patterns of behavior.

Learn to Use the Right Tools

Time management tools and techniques are only as useful as the time you invest in using them. Common ones include:

"It's not the hours you put in your work that count, it's work you put in the hours."

Sam Ewing

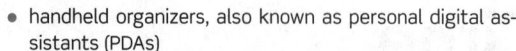

✓

830

ACTIONLIST

- handheld organizers, also known as personal digital assistants (PDAs)
- organizers, both computer-based programs and paper appointment books or schedulers
- "to do" lists
- prioritizing work according to its importance and focusing only on what's essential

If you're a person who tends to concentrate on what's in your in-box or on today's schedule, you may find it useful to stand back and look at the big picture. Your activities don't happen in a succession of unrelated present moments; they mesh into a continuum of past and future. Develop and keep some perspective on how this broader context affects your choices in deciding how you spend your time.

Some Dos and Don'ts of Time Management

If too much work is the issue, look at your workload, prioritize, and refer back to how it fits your job description. Decide, perhaps together with your manager, which things you're doing add value to your job and career potential and which would be better delegated to others.

Do	Don't
Conduct a time-management assessment on yourself	Spend time on unnecessary activities or those that don't serve your purpose
Be honest about how long things take	Take on more than you can handle
Build in time for reflecting and learning	Blame others for your own disorganization
Build in time for yourself	Get hung up on process
Delegate wherever you can	Make commitments you can't meet
Anticipate the pressure of commitments you make	Expect others to make up for what you can't do
Communicate with others when you have time conflicts	Give up
Plan ahead	

The central point is that planning is essential, and being very conscious of time is a necessary first step.

COMMON MISTAKES
You Buy a New Gadget but Still Rely On Old Time Management Tools

If you're going to buy a new device to help you plan your time better, you need to be disciplined in mastering it and using it daily. Don't buy something just for the sake of having it and leave it to gather dust.

You Expect Too Much of Yourself and Become Discouraged

Change is difficult and often requires a new set of skills. The principles of time management sound completely logical and straightforward, but in fact we lead extremely complex lives, and these simple principles are hard to put into practice. Don't overwhelm yourself by trying to change everything at once. Instead, establish a series of small, clear goals, and achieve them one by one.

You Have Trouble Breaking out of Old Patterns

Old habits do die hard, and one of the hardest to break is the way we structure and use our time. Everyone knows people who are always late or always early, who jump right onto tasks or are terrible procrastinators, who are stressed-out workaholics or who always seem miraculously refreshed and relaxed. The choices we make in managing our time are connected to the way we view ourselves and the world: making different choices affects our sense of identity and our relationships. Take it slowly, look to family, friends, and coworkers for support in making these changes, and don't discount the value of taking workshops or seeking out a consultant to help you.

FOR MORE INFORMATION

Books:
Allen, David. *Getting Things Done.* New York: Viking, 2001.
Tracy, Brian. *Eat That Frog! 21 Great Ways to Stop Procrastinating and Get More Done in Less Time.* San Francisco, CA: Berrett-Koehler, 2002.

Web sites:
Mind Tools:
www.mindtools.com/pages/main/newMN_HTE.htm
Steve
Randall:**http://members.aol.com/rslts/tmmap.html**
Time Management Guide: **www.time-management-guide.com**
Total Success:
www.tsuccess.dircon.co.uk/timemanagementtips.htm

See also:
✓ Delegating without Guilt (pp. 833–834)

"The key is not in spending time, but using it."

Arthur Bryan

Maintaining a Healthy Work–Life Balance

GETTING STARTED

"Time flies when you're having fun" goes the adage. Time also flies when you're very busy—but, rather than having fun, you can soon find yourself stressed out in a way that affects not only your mental and emotional well-being, but your physical health. When there isn't enough time in the day, something has to give: but is it to be your work or your personal life? Achieving a balance has become one of the burning issues of the day.

Here are some of the main reasons why more and more people are addressing the topic of work–life balance:

- More women joining the workforce means more demands on parents to juggle job and family.
- More people living longer means more workers with the care demands of elderly relatives.
- More pressure and longer hours at work on account of modern technology (for example, overflowing inboxes, Internet information deluge, and ringing phones) mean people "burning out" younger.

The broad argument for greater balance and flexibility at work is that greater satisfaction among employees will lead to fewer stress-related illnesses, less time taken off for sickness, lower staff turnover, and higher productivity. People with a good balance between their work and other responsibilities and interests tend to be more motivated and productive: in other words, happy people work better.

FAQs
What is work–life balance?

Work–life balance is about modifying the way you work in order to accommodate other responsibilities or aspirations in other areas of your life. Although there has been much attention of late on making things easier for parents of young children or people who care for dependents, quality of life is important for everyone, and achieving a happy work–life balance is an important part of that.

I don't know if my boss cares about my work-life balance. Do the "people in charge" really take it seriously?

Thankfully, growing numbers of businesses are becoming aware of the importance of allowing their employees to strike a balance between their work and personal lives, and hopefully your boss will wake up to this. If you want to talk to him or her about it, explain that flexibility in the workplace is actually driven by a business need—working cultures and attitudes are changing in many parts of the world, and employers are beginning to see that they have to adapt to this if they are to recruit and retain their number one asset: their people.

I'm worried that my boss won't even consider my application for flexible working. How can I get what I want without jeopardizing my current position by being sidelined?

A popular way of approaching negotiations of any type is to draw up a wish list for your successful outcome that contains an ideal solution, a realistic one, and an absolute minimum. If you show that you're prepared to be flexible, your manager may be willing to meet you halfway. Be realistic but also be ready to compromise.

If you're worried that your boss may disapprove, find out if your organization will allow you to bring a union representative with you to a meeting to discuss your application. If you do invite one along, make sure he or she has read a copy of your application and any related documents from your place of work so that he or she is up to speed.

MAKING IT HAPPEN
Assess Your Work–Life Balance

Planning is essential in order to gain a perspective on how your current lifestyle fits in with your ambitions and requirements inside and outside the workplace. Reflect on your work situation—where you are in terms of your career, how fulfilling you find it, how much of yourself you put into it—and then set yourself some career goals, giving yourself a realistic timescale in which to achieve them.

You also need to consider your personal life. What are the most important elements? Who are the most important people to you? How much are you getting out of it? By asking yourself these profound but crucial questions, you can work out what's lacking in your life and what are unwelcome infringements upon it. Decide what you'd like to spend more time on, what you'd like to spend less time on, and then plan how to do it.

It's only once you've established what your goals are and the length of time needed to achieve them, that you can address how changing your work patterns may help you to get there.

Be Aware of the Options

There are several key areas in which you can address your work–life balance needs and preferences. These include the following:

- **Flextime working.** People working on flextime schedules are able to vary their start and finishing times, providing they work a set number of hours during a specific time period. This is not only great for parents trying to manage a household as well as a job, but for anyone who finds working within a strict and continuous routine depressing and demotivating. Everyone's energy levels fluctuate during the day, but not necessarily at the same time, and so flextime is a good solution to making sure

"The life-fate of the modern individual depends . . . increasingly upon the corporation in which he spends the most alert hours of his best years."

L. Wright Mills

people always work at their peak. Another great advantage, particularly for city-workers and commuters, is that flextime gives them the opportunity to avoid the rush hour—probably one of the most time-wasting and stressful parts of the day.

- **Part-time working.** Employees with a part-time arrangement may decide between working fewer days each week or fewer hours a day. This option also works well for people with parental or caring responsibilities. The other people who benefit greatly from part-time working are those returning to work after looking after young children or recovering or suffering from illness, and people who are trying to pursue other interests or careers.

- **Job sharing.** This involves two people dividing between them a full-time workload, with each working part-time. This is beneficial if you want to maintain something of your career while being able to spend more time with your children or pursue other interests outside work.

- **Working from home or telecommuting.** Many jobs now involve computer-based activities that can be done as easily from an Internet-linked PC at home or in a remote (telecommuting) facility. This style of working benefits not only parents and caregivers, but can help many people without those kinds of domestic responsibilities to work more productively, especially in tasks that require a great deal of concentration and uninterrupted peace and quiet. It's unusual for someone to work from home or remotely full-time, but some employers do find it a cost advantage to themselves through the reduced need for fixed office space.

Make an Application for Flexible Working Hours

Do your research. First of all, make sure that you qualify for flexible working arrangements. Not every organization or region will offer them.

If such an option is open to you, check the staff manual or with your human resources department (if you have one) to see what the preferred method of application is.

Once you've checked out your company's policy, speak to friends or colleagues who have applied for flexible working hours or who are already working under a new arrangement. How did the successful applicants approach their request? Are they finding it easier or harder than they'd anticipated to work in a new way? Bear in mind that if your working arrangements are changed, these changes are permanent unless otherwise agreed between you and your employer.

Make a persuasive case. Prepare your case and try to anticipate the questions your manager may ask you when you meet to talk about your application. Requests can be turned down because managers fear that flexible working arrangements may affect the business, so be prepared to give well thought-out, positive responses to questions such as the following:

- Will you still be able be an effective team member?
- How would a change in your working hours affect your colleagues?
- What will be the overall effect on the work you do?
- How could a change in your working hours affect the business positively?

Think about when you would want any new arrangement to start and give your company as much notice as you can. This will convey the fact that you're still committed to the company and are thinking about how the potential changes to your working life will fit in overall.

Stress that the quality of your work and your motivation will not change, even if your working hours do. In fact, you'll be more productive as you'll suffer from less stress and will need to take fewer days off to look after your children or dependants when they are sick. You could also explain that, as part of a reciprocal arrangement whereby all parties benefit, you'd be willing to work extra or longer in times of heavy demand. Finally, but no less importantly, explain how much knowledge and expertise you've built up while you've been working there and how much the company benefits from it.

Follow up. If all goes well and an agreement is reached, your new working arrangement and an agreed start date should be set down in writing and copies given to all relevant parties (you, your manager, and the HR department or representative if you have one).

If your request isn't granted, investigate any appeals process open to you

COMMON MISTAKES
You Don't Prepare Well Enough

As with all types of negotiation, you need to make sure that you've done your groundwork when you make an application for flexible working hours. First, be aware of your rights by researching the issue thoroughly. Second, check your company's stance on the issue, and make sure you follow the procedures properly when submitting a written application. Think through the questions your manager might ask about the effects of flexible working on your workload and that of your colleagues.

You Aren't Flexible

Bear in mind that in some places you only have the right to *request* flextime: it's not guaranteed that you'll automatically get them. If you're flexible when you meet with your manager and open to compromise if your ideal scenario isn't possible, then it's more likely that you'll end up with a result that suits everyone.

You Don't Think Through All the Financial Implications

Don't forget that when you reduce your hours, it's not just your salary that may be affected. Pension contributions and other benefits may change too. Be sure that when you make the decision to apply for flexible working hours, you'll be able to cope financially if your application is granted.

FOR MORE INFORMATION

Book:
Drake, John D. *Downshifting: How to Work Less and Enjoy It More.* San Francisco, CA: Berrett-Koehler, 2001.

Web Site:
Monster.com: **http://wlb.monster.com**

"Total commitment to family and total commitment to career is possible, but fatiguing."

Muriel Fox

Delegating without Guilt

GETTING STARTED

If you have a team working for you, you need to get to grips with delegation. It's a key skill to develop. Delegation isn't about giving tasks to others because you can't be bothered to do them yourself. It *is* about getting a particular job done, clearly, but it's also about encouraging people to learn new skills and reach their potential, all of which helps a business to grow.

Many of us like being in control of everything and find it hard to let go of things we know we can do well ourselves. However, if we want to be successful managers—and preserve our own sanity—that's exactly what we must do.

FAQs

Why do people find it difficult to delegate?

There are many reasons why you may find it difficult to delegate. Often, it seems quicker to perform the task yourself than bother to explain it to somebody else and then correct his or her mistakes. You might worry that the person will make a mess of it, and it'll take a long time to put right the mistakes they make. On the other hand, you may feel threatened by the competence of a person who is quick on the uptake and does well. You may fear that the employee may take over the role of being the person the rest of the staff go to with their problems. They may even find something wrong with the way *you* do things.

If you lack confidence, you may find it hard to give instructions and you'll put off delegating. If you do delegate, and problems arise because the employee fails to do what you've asked him or her to do, you may doubt your own ability to confront the person about his or her actions. If staff have been given increased responsibilities and have done well, you may not be confident of being able to reward them sufficiently. Conversely, you might be reluctant to delegate tasks that you think are too tedious.

Finally, you may realize that delegation is necessary, but you don't know where to start, or how to go about it. You need some kind of method to follow. The following paragraphs will help to put you on the right track.

How can delegation help me?

Delegation offers many benefits. Done well, it will allow you to concentrate on the things you do best and also give you the time and space to tackle more interesting and challenging tasks in the future. You'll be less likely to put off making key decisions and you'll be much more effective. Your staff will benefit too; everyone needs new challenges, and by delegating to them, you'll be able to test their ability in a variety of areas and increase their contribution to the business. Staff can make quick decisions themselves, and they'll develop a better understanding of the details concerned. Done well, delegation should improve the overall productivity of employees.

It's all too tempting to withdraw into "essential" tasks and not develop relations with your team. The bottom line is that it's wasteful for senior staff to be given big salaries for doing low-value work, and passing tasks down the line is essential if other people are to develop. Not knowing how to do this is recognized as one of the biggest obstacles to small business growth. By delegating, you'll have much more time to do your own job properly.

Delegation doesn't make things easier (there will always be other challenges), but it does make things more efficient and effective. Essentially, it represents a more interactive way of working with a team of people, and it involves instruction, training, and development. The results will be well worth the time and effort you invest in doing it properly.

When should I delegate?

Delegation is fundamental to successful management—look for opportunities to do it. If you have too much work to do, or if you don't have enough time to devote to important tasks, delegate. When it's clear that certain staff, particularly new employees, need to develop, or when an employee clearly has the skills needed to perform a specific task, delegate.

What tasks should I delegate?

Begin with any routine administrative tasks that take up too much of your time. There are likely to be many small everyday jobs which you've always done—you may even enjoy doing them (for example, sending faxes)—but they're not a good use of your time. Review these small jobs and delegate as many of them as you can. Being your company's point of contact for a particular person or organization, which is important but can be time consuming, is also an excellent task to delegate.

On a larger scale, delegate projects that it makes sense for one person to handle; these make good tests of people's ability to manage and co-ordinate tasks. Give the person you delegate to something he or she has every chance of completing successfully and, if possible, something for which he or she has a special aptitude. Do not delegate an impossible task at which others have failed and which may well prove a negative experience for the delegatee.

Who should I delegate to?

Make sure you understand the person you're delegating to. He or she must have the skills and ability—or at least the potential—to develop into the role and must be someone you can trust. It's a good idea to test out the employee with small tasks that will help show what he or she can do. Also make sure that the employee is available for the assignment—don't put too much pressure on your most effective workers. Spread out the tasks you delegate among as many people as possible: two or more people could even share a task if it's particularly complicated.

MAKING IT HAPPEN
Be Positive

Think positively: you have the right to delegate and,

"Do not delegate an assignment and then attempt to manage it yourself—you will make an enemy of the overruled subordinate."

Wess Roberts

frankly, you must delegate. You won't get it 100% right the first time, but you'll improve with experience. Be as decisive as you can, and, if you need to improve your assertiveness skills, consider attending a course or reading one of the many books on the subject. A positive approach will also give your employees confidence in themselves, and they need to feel that you believe in them.

If you expect efficiency from the person you delegate to, organize yourself first. If there's no overall plan of what's going on, it'll be hard to identify, schedule, and evaluate the work being delegated. Prepare the ground before seeing the person (but don't use this as a ploy to delay!). Assess the task and decide how much responsibility the person will have. Assess the person's progress regularly and make notes.

Discuss the Task to Be Delegated

When you meet the person or people you're delegating to, discuss the tasks and the problems in depth, and explain fully what's expected of them. It's crucial to give people precise objectives, but encourage them to seek these out themselves by letting them ask you questions and participate in setting the parameters. They need to understand why they're doing the task, and where it fits into the scheme of things. Ask them how they'll go about the task; discuss their plan and the support they might need.

Set Targets and Offer Support If Necessary

Targets should be set and deadlines scheduled into daily planners. Summarize what has been agreed, and take notes about what the person is required to do so everyone is clear. If he or she is given a lot of creative scope and is being tested out, you may decide to be deliberately vague, but if the task is urgent and critical, you must be specific.

How much support you offer and give will very much depend on the person and your relationship with him or her. In the early stages you might want to work with the person and to share certain tasks, but you'll be able to back off more as your understanding of the person's abilities increases. Encourage people to come back to you if they have any problems—while it's important to have time alone, you should be accessible if anyone has a problem or the situation changes. If someone needs to check something with you, try to get back to him or her quickly. Don't interfere or criticize if things are going according to plan.

Monitoring progress is vital—it's very easy to forget all about the task until the completion date, but, in the meantime, all sorts of things could have gone wrong. When planning, time should be built in to review progress. If more problems were expected to arise and nothing has been heard, check with the employee that all is

well. Schedule routine meetings with the person and be flexible enough to changes deadlines and objectives as the situation changes.

How Did It Go?

When a task is complete, give praise and review how things went. If an employee's responsibilities are increased, make sure he or she receives fair rewards for it. On the other hand, there may be limits to what can be offered, so don't offer rewards you can't deliver. Also bear in mind that development can carry its own rewards. Such career development issues can be discussed with the employee in periodic reviews, and the results of delegated tasks noted for this purpose. If the person has failed to deliver, discuss it with him or her, find out what went wrong, and aim to resolve problems in the future.

COMMON MISTAKES
Expecting Employees to Do Things Like You Do

Managers often criticize the way things are done because it isn't the way they would have done it themselves. Remember that people prefer working in different ways; concentrate on the results rather than the methods used to obtain them.

Not Giving People a Chance

If you're giving someone something new to do, you must be patient. It'll take time for employees to develop new skills, but it's time that will pay off in the end. Have faith in the people around you.

Delegating Responsibility without Delegating Authority

It's unfair to expect results from someone with one hand tied behind his or her back. If you're going to delegate responsibilities, make sure that those involved know this, and confer the necessary authority upon the person you're delegating to.

FOR MORE INFORMATION

Web Sites:
businessballs.com:
www.businessballs.com/delegation.htm
jobserve.com:
www.jobserve.com/news/NewsStory.asp?SID=2009
Mind Tools: **www.mindtools.com/tmdelegt.html**

See also:
- Getting Things Done (p. 1095)
- Small and Growing Businesses (pp. 1905–1909)
- The Critical Factors That Build or Break Teams (pp. 225–226)

"Not the least among the qualities in a great king is a capacity to permit his ministers to serve him."
Cardinal Richelieu

Coping with Information Overload

835

ACTIONLIST

GETTING STARTED

The amount of information available to us wherever we go is increasing rapidly, and, as a result, we're all expected to absorb and respond to more information than ever before, for a number of reasons:

- There are many more means of instant communication and data access. Cell phones, the Internet, voice-mail, e-mail, instant messaging, and tele- or videoconferencing have all contributed to the vast and fast flow of information.
- Despite this increased access to information, fewer people are employed to manage it. Secretaries and personal assistants have been replaced by laptops and PDAs.
- Everybody expects information much more quickly. For example, customers are getting used to completing transactions at the click of a button, within just a few minutes. They no longer have to wait for endless copies of paperwork to pass through several pairs of hands before they can place an order.
- Business structures have changed so that many projects are now outsourced, demanding clear and rapid communication between many groups of people at once. If an employee's role dictates that he or she is involved with several projects at once, he or she could be deluged with information from all sides!
- Globalization and deregulation have given rise to new opportunities, but they've also increased competition and the need to understand the changing market.

The problem is that we've all had to deal with this influx without any preparation, training, or time! Often, we find it difficult to process the flood of information—we feel as though we're drowning, struggling to find time for more important tasks. The good news is that there are steps you can take to keep your head above water.

FAQs
What's the scale of the problem?

Although information overload is a fairly recent phenomenon, it's already claimed casualties. Many of us feel that we have to keep up with the information flow in order to perform well, yet increasing amounts of time are required to help us wade through the massive amounts of data available. This time pressure is resulting in stress and, in some cases, burnout. A worldwide survey conducted by Reuters found that two thirds of managers suffer from increased tension and one third from ill health because of information overload.

What's the result?

Information overload contributes significantly to workplace stress. This is turn affects all areas of your life, as it manifests itself in many ways, including increased levels of anxiety, short-term memory problems, poor concentration, and a reduction in your decision making skills.

MAKING IT HAPPEN
Take Control of the Problem

Information management, like time management, is a matter of discipline. To get on top of things, you need to set boundaries around how much time you're prepared to spend processing information.

First of all, decide what your limits are and create a personal information management system that works for you. This may be setting boundaries around the time you spend responding to e-mails, filtering them through your assistant (if you're lucky enough to have one), or responding only to those e-mails that hold high importance for you. Draw up some criteria to work out what you allow through your filter and what you want to screen out. This may mean putting priorities on your e-mails and deleting those that are low priority, returning calls only to those people you need to speak to, and only looking at a piece of data once before deciding what to do with it. If you miss something important, don't worry; if it's really that important, it'll come back to you in one way or another.

It's also a good idea to identify time-wasting information and eliminate it. For example, you could ask to be removed from your company's list of often unnecessary "everyone" e-mails; request a good spam filter from the IT department; or ask for a summary of overly long minutes or reports.

Seek Information Efficiently

Whenever you're looking for information, keep the "Pareto principle" in mind. This holds that 20% of what has been accessed probably holds 80% of the information you need. So much information is now at our disposal that anxiety about missing something prompts us to spend far too much time wading through every piece of data available. Remember that before the Internet, people used to make decisions in ambiguous situations; it was considered to be a management skill. Aim to develop your instincts along with your knowledge—both will stand you in very good stead.

As part of your new, efficient approach to knowledge-seeking, find your own preferred places for accessing information and discipline yourself to go there *only*. You already know the high-quality sites for your particular field of work, so why waste time elsewhere? Failing this, you could make use of the reference librarians in the library of your professional body, if you have one. They're experienced at finding relevant information and can often save you a great deal of time.

Finally, only look at data that is relevant to your job, the project you're working on, or the decision you're making. Bear in mind the principles of time management, as they're just as effective for dealing with information overload. For example, surfing the Web is incredibly seductive, with each link taking you further and further into fascinating but unnecessary detail. Decide how much time you'll spend in each session, print the information that is relevant, and leave the rest in the ether.

"Information is like an oyster. It has its greatest value when it is fresh."   Carl Shapiro

836

ACTIONLIST

You often pick up all the information you need in a few hits, the remainder being less fruitful. Remember that the more specific you make your searches, the more efficient they will be—you'll probably pick up most of the information you need in the first ten minutes or so.

Learn to Say "No"

Try not to be the dumping ground for information that others don't want to wade through. This will involve being polite but assertive and also by being sensible; if you're snowed under as it is, don't even hint at being receptive to this type of task. Take control of what passes over your desk and decide not to be held hostage by a piece of data.

Limit Your Availability

To give yourself some much-needed space, leave your cell phone switched off for periods during the day when you can be quiet and restful or let your voicemail field calls for you. This way you can decide who to speak to and when to schedule the conversations. Anyone who needs to speak to you urgently will find a way of getting through to you.

Learn to Throw Things Away!

Don't be a hoarder. Have the courage to throw data away or delete files when you've exhausted their usefulness. You can always access the same data again and, probably when you do, it will have been updated.

Use Some Tools to Help

It may seem rather self-defeating to resort to technology to solve a problem that technology produced in the first place, but there are useful electronic devices that can help alleviate information overload. Handheld organizers are one example. They have many functions that can be accessed while traveling, making use of otherwise "dead" time: you can read your e-mails, edit documents, plan meetings, write reports, and even read the newspaper. Any changes can be automatically transferred to your PC when you get back to the office.

COMMON MISTAKES
You Get Bogged Down in Detail

Getting drawn into the detail of all the information that's available wastes a lot of time. People often fear they'll miss an essential piece of information if they don't comb through every available source, but in fact this rarely happens. Resist the temptation to scrutinize every piece of information that appears on your screen or arrives on your desk.

You Don't Prioritize

Being able to prioritize information will save you hours, and you may even find that you can delegate some of the processing to a member of your team, outlining what they should focus on and report back to you. Remember to give your colleague clear instructions and a deadline and try not to contribute to their information overload problem!

You Never Switch Off

Not being able to switch off from the need to absorb or generate information can be tiring and stressful. Blood pressure can rise, mental faculties can deteriorate, and any patience you may have had can disappear altogether. Just as the body needs time to relax, so does the mind—and not just when it's in the sleep state. Quietening the mind through techniques such as meditation or yoga has been proven to increase health, improve memory, and stimulate creativity. It has also been linked to increased productivity and a sense of wellbeing. If these techniques don't appeal, try other recuperative pursuits such as listening to music, reading, or taking gentle exercise. Anything that allows the mind to "freewheel" will help a great deal.

FOR MORE INFORMATION

Web Sites:
Microsoft Windows Mobile:
www.microsoft.com/windowsmobile/default.mspx
Palm: **www.palm.com**

See also:
☆ Managing Stress (pp. 16–18)
✔ Managing Your Inbox (pp. 811–813)
✔ Managing Your Time (pp. 828–830)

"The new source of power is not money in the hands of the few, but information in the hands of many."

W. W. Rostow

Managing Meetings Effectively

GETTING STARTED

Meetings are a necessary evil in everyone's working life. Handled well, they can help those gathered examine a difficult situation, agree on action, and act positively. Handled badly, they can be a complete waste of time. In essence, most people want short, effective meetings that allow them to get on with the rest of their day.

This actionlist offers advice for anyone who has to plan and chair a meeting. Special arrangements need to be followed for large meetings such as board meetings or annual meetings, so here we focus only on the type of meeting held most commonly in an everyday work situation.

FAQs

I hate going to meetings, but my boss thinks they're really important. Are there other, more time-efficient ways to get decisions made?

In some cases, meetings are not always a good use of people's time and effort. If someone suggests that a meeting be held to discuss an issue related to your project, team, or department, think hard about whether gathering the attendees in one place is really the most efficient way forward. There may be more efficient alternatives to gathering everyone together for a meeting. For example, you could try:

- conference calls or videoconferencing: if you have access to these facilities, or can afford them, they offer a good way of holding a discussion without having to disrupt the attendees' day too much;
- discussing the issue via e-mail by sending a message to all relevant parties: your e-mail should set out the issue clearly, ask for a response, and give a deadline—and double-check that you've included everyone before sending it!

If all else fails, though, and a face-to-face meeting seems to be the best and least unwieldy way of arranging a plan of action for the issue at hand, prepare as much as you can in advance and delegate where appropriate.

MAKING IT HAPPEN
Think Carefully About Who to Invite

Good planning is the best way to make sure that your meeting goes well, and an important first step is to draw up the list of invitees. Remember that the most productive meetings are usually those with the fewest number of people attending, so try to limit the numbers by only inviting those who *really* need to be there. These will be people directly involved in the decisions that need to be made during the meeting, those significantly affected by those decisions, or those who have some specific knowledge to contribute. If the agenda is lengthy and covers a variety of issues, consider asking people to drop in and out when their relevant section comes up.

Give the Attendees All the Relevant Information in Good Time

Give everyone plenty of notice of the meeting's time and venue and circulate a draft agenda outlining the topics to be discussed and the time limits assigned to each topic. A good agenda will make sure that all the attendees are clear about the purpose of the meeting and why they've been called together, and should state what needs to be accomplished between starting and finishing. Time limits create a healthy sense of urgency. By stipulating the start and finish time of the meeting, as well as setting time limits for each topic on the agenda (particularly important if you're holding a lengthy meeting and asking people to drop in and out), you'll encourage people to stay focused. Sticking to these fixed times is essential, of course, for this to work.

Other information you should provide your attendees with prior to the meeting includes:

- directions to the venue in case they haven't been there before;
- information on who else is attending (this will be particularly helpful if you're going to be joined by people external to your company such as consultants, freelance contributors, or designers) ;
- background information or relevant documents to the meeting. For example, if you're going to discuss a long-overdue overhaul of your product catalog, send everyone a copy of your existing brochure in case they no longer have copies of the original. You could also include other similar publications whose style you admire to see if anyone can think of new ways of presenting your products.
- your contact details and those of one other person in the office (such as your assistant, if you have one) in case of emergency.

Think About Catering Requirements

If you think your meeting will take longer than a few hours, or if it's likely to take place over lunch, remember to ask all attendees whether they have any special dietary requirements. This will save a lot of time and stress on the day. Research shows that the best time to hold a meeting is just before lunch or toward the end of the day—this motivates attendees to focus on the agenda and keeps the meeting from running long.

Delegate Taking the Minutes

Try to find someone other than yourself to take the minutes so that you're free to steer the meeting as appropriate. If the person designated as the minute taker is new to the project or issue you're going to discuss, run through some relevant key words or acronyms so that he or she is not baffled by the jargon—you and the other attendees may be well versed in the relevant vocabulary, but don't expect the same from a "newcomer."

Find and Prepare the Venue

Once you know that a formal meeting is in the cards, find an appropriate space in which the meeting can be held.

"Whoever invented the meeting must have had Hollywood in mind. I think they should consider giving Oscars for meetings: Best Meeting of the Year, Best Supporting Meeting, Best Meeting Based on Material from Another Meeting."   William Goldman

Some companies have a "booking system" for meeting rooms, so give yourself enough time when planning the meeting date to make sure that you can get an appropriately sized room for when you want. Don't assume that it will be free when you're ready!

As the meeting draws near, make sure that:

- the room is tidy;
- you have enough tables and chairs to accommodate everyone;
- the flip chart, if you're using one, has enough paper and pens ready;
- there is enough light, heating, or ventilation for the time of day and year;
- there are enough power outlet, and that they're in the right place if you're going to be using an overhead projector or laptop;
- any equipment in the room is ready to use and is working properly.

Make further catering arrangements once your numbers are confirmed. If your company has a restaurant, book in early for someone to bring refreshments such as coffee and water to the meeting. If your organization is small or doesn't have a restaurant, ask a coworker or assistant to stay close by at the start of the meeting and to go out to a nearby coffee shop or café to fetch what's needed. Again, this will free you up to attend to other tasks.

Start As You Mean to Go On

On the day of the meeting, arrive in plenty of time so that you can double-check that everything is ready. Once the attendees have arrived, set the pace and tone of the meeting by following these steps:

- Begin on time.
- Welcome everyone, and briefly explain basic issues such as where the washrooms are located (particularly helpful for anyone who hasn't been to your offices before) and what the catering arrangements are.
- Ask everyone to check that they've turned off their cell phones so that the flow of discussion isn't interrupted.
- Reiterate the reason the meeting is being held, what you hope to achieve in the meeting, the timescale, and finishing time.
- Frame each item on the agenda by explaining its objectives.

Keep a Tight Rein on Proceedings

While obviously you need to give everyone an opportunity to contribute to points raised on the agenda, there are steps you can take to make sure that you keep roughly on schedule (and on topic). For example:

- Make sure that attendees keep to one agenda point at a time.
- Summarize at appropriate intervals and restate agreed-upon points clearly (the person taking the minutes will be particularly grateful for this).
- Firmly but politely move the discussion forward if a subject has become exhausted.

Don't Let One Person Dominate the Conversation

Meetings can often be hijacked by one or two vociferous attendees, so in your role as chair you need to make sure

that there is only one discussion at a time. Sometimes, people start their own "private" meeting during the main session. This may range from a few whispered asides, to notes being passed around the table, to a full-blown separate discussion taking place. Stop these diversions by addressing directly the people involved and asking them politely but assertively if there's something they'd like to raise. For example, you could say: "I think there may be an issue you're not happy with. Would you like to raise it now before we go any further? We have a lot to get through today."

Strategies for dealing with difficult people	
The talkative	In the case of people who just like the sound of their own voice, you must be assertive enough to interject politely but firmly, reminding everyone of the agenda point you're discussing and steering the discussion back to it. Also mention your target finish time and how the meeting is progressing in relation to it.
The passionate	The same goes for dealing with people who feel very strongly about the issue under discussion and who may feel that others do not share their interest and commitment. Again, make sure that they get the opportunity to voice their point of view, but also that they give others the chance to express theirs too. Interject as appropriate and summarize if you sense they're about to repeat something. Remember that a meeting is a discussion with objectives, not an opportunity for attendees to rehearse an extended monologue.
The angry	If the topic you're discussing is particularly contentious, tempers may flare. If you feel a situation is getting heated and that insults rather than well-considered opinions are being traded, step in to defuse the tension. Suggest a break outside of the meeting room for 15 minutes or so, which will give most people time to calm down and assess what has happened. If voices are being raised, match your voice to the level of other people's, then reduce the volume back down to a normal speaking pitch. This will allow the discussion to get back to a more stable footing.

Wrap It Up

Wrap up the meeting by thanking everyone for their attendance and contribution. If possible, also let attendees know when the next meeting is to be held (should you need one); this will encourage the attendees not to forget about the topics discussed the moment they leave the room.

Make Sure Everyone Is Clear on Any Follow-up Action Required

Ask the person taking the minutes to write them up as soon as possible so that they can be distributed to all the attendees promptly. Bear in mind that most of the attendees will only glance briefly at the meeting minutes, or refer back to them in order to locate a specific piece of

"What is a committee? A group of the unwilling, picked from the unfit, to do the unnecessary."

Richard Harkness

information. This means that they need to be extremely concise and clear. The key things to note are:

- agreed-upon actions;
- the people responsible for them;
- deadline (if appropriate);
- date of next meeting if you agreed to arrange another.

COMMON MISTAKES

You Leave Preparations to the Last Minute

You're not saving time by leaving the arrangements for your meeting to the last minute—you're wasting it. If you plan in advance, you can make sure everything is in place early and spend the time you'd otherwise be wasting by rushing about aimlessly doing something more productive instead.

You Think You Can Squeeze in Taking the Minutes

You're not shirking responsibility if you ask someone else to take the meeting's minutes for you. On the contrary, if you're freed up to make sure that the meeting starts and ends on time, is well organized, and achieves its objectives, you'll have made everyone's life a lot easier and you'll also end up with a set of minutes (and notes) that mean something.

You Lose Track of Time

Don't be afraid to move things on as appropriate if the meeting seems to be getting bogged down in one particular area. Everyone else will be eager to finish on time and get on with the rest of their day, so, in your role as chair, it is your responsibility to shape the discussion and sustain the meeting's impetus.

839

ACTIONLIST

FOR MORE INFORMATION

Book:
Robert, Henry M., et al. *Robert's Rules of Order, Newly Revised in Brief.* New York: Da Capo Press, 2004.

Web Sites:
it-analysis.com: **www.it-analysis.com/article.php?articleid=3728** and **www.it-analysis.com/article.php?articleid=3729**
MeetingWizard.org: **www.meetingwizard.org**

See also:
✔ Managing Meetings Effectively (pp. 837–839)
🖱 Meetings (p. 1833)

'A committee is a thing which takes a week to do what one good man can do in an hour.'
Elbert Hubbard

Solving Problems

GETTING STARTED

Problem solving is a key element in all levels of management, as well as of many other jobs. Without problem-solving capabilities, no organization could exist for very long. Intelligence, common sense, and education help us solve problems in our individual lives, and those same elements can also help us with organizational problems. However, if you're attempting to do something complex, such as reorganize the business or implement a total quality management program, you need a systematic approach to problem solving, a process that allows people at all levels to contribute to finding solutions. This actionlist looks at a variety of issues, techniques, and resources to help you to find your own best approach.

FAQs

Why shouldn't I just allow people to solve problems in their own way?

In most situations, it's good to allow people to understand and then solve problems in their own way. However, using proven techniques of problem solving—ones that are plainly mapped out and used uniformly—makes it easier for others to understand the way in which the problem area is being explored. The process ensures that, whether talking about customer service or production quotas, others can get actively involved in solving the problem at any stage.

Each problem is different; is it really possible to use the same problem-solving technique in each case?

While problems *are* always different, there are some common approaches and processes for solving them. Problems can be diagnosed and the various elements can be mapped—whether you're talking about a manufacturing roadblock or an IT systems failure. Obviously, as an organization grows in size, so too does the need for more sophisticated techniques.

Isn't problem solving just for those people who like to spend lots of time thinking? Surely finding a quick and ready solution is more important?

It's true that we often notice the solution more than the problem. That's because problems cause us headaches and can hold us up; solutions allow us to move forward. However, in order to be sure of having the *right* solution, spending time on using problem-solving techniques means you can be certain that you know the full extent of the problem, the possible chain reaction, and the priorities for managing the situation.

Doesn't a structured approach stifle creativity?

Problem solving isn't just about logical deductions; it's about finding new and alternative ways of resolving a situation. In fact, creativity can flourish through a structured process. Structure can also be limiting, though, so you must be mindful not to preclude a full exploration of the possibilities. If, for example, you're working in a group, don't allow members to become judgmental about ideas and dismiss them too early in the process. Practice letting go of your assumptions, and allow everyone to contribute in a way that suits them best.

MAKING IT HAPPEN

Problem solving is best done in groups, to ensure that a true win–win situation is achieved. Any problem-solving process requires the following steps.

Identify the Problem

Understanding a problem requires an ability to see it in its entirety—in breadth, depth, and context. Here are a number of ways to evaluate the scope of a problem:

- **recognition**—can you see or feel the problem? Is it isolated, or part of a bigger problem?
- **symptoms**—how is it showing itself?
- **causes**—why has it happened?
- **effects**—what else is being affected by it?

The task then is to break the main problem down into smaller problems, in order to determine whether you're the right person or team to handle it. If not, you need to transfer the problem-solving process to those better equipped to deal with it. If the answer is yes, you need to ask additional questions, including: Do you have the right resources? How long might the process take? What are some of the obstacles? What's the anticipated benefit? Once you get answers, move on to the next step.

Find the Best Way of Gathering Data

There are two important questions here: what do you need to know, and how are you going to get it? Most information can be accessed, but there are often time and resource issues involved with collecting and analyzing it. Remember that data collection may involve investigating the symptoms of the problem, its underlying causes, and/or its overall effects. Each of these may have different implications for how the problem is viewed. Data-gathering techniques include:

- workflow analysis;
- surveys and questionnaires;
- flow charts;
- group and/or one-on-one interviews.

Brainstorm the Problem

In any problem-solving exercise, there will be a need for brainstorming. There are five golden rules for the brainstorming process:

- **anything goes**—no evaluation or judgment by others
- **hitchhike**—build on the ideas of others
- **quality**—strive for quality
- **be off the wall**—encourage wild and wacky ideas
- **inclusiveness**—include other people and encourage participation

---

"Problems are the price of progress. Don't bring me anything but trouble. Good news weakens me."

Charles Franklin Kettering

Explore Options and Solutions

Thinking outside the box can play an important role in understanding the perspectives of a problem and their implications. Look at what others have done in the past, and don't ignore what may seem a crazy idea. It's best to cast a wide net when exploring solutions, so that there is a richness of ideas and possible options.

Evaluate Priorities and Decisions

Taking time to identify the most appropriate solution from your range of options is very important. Suggestions need to be winnowed down to a shortlist, containing only the most realistic possibilities.

To do this, take some quantitative measurements. Try to determine the costs and benefits of the suggested solutions. If, for example, you feel that outside investment is needed to solve a particular problem, calculate the payback period. You can then gauge whether your senior management team will accept it.

Always understand that each possible solution has consequences, some of which may cause additional problems themselves..

Select the Best Solutions for the Situation and Context

The chosen solution needs to meet some key criteria. Do you have the necessary people, money, and time to achieve it? Will you get a sufficient return on investment? Is the solution acceptable to others involved in the situation? You should draw up:

- a rationale of why you've reached your particular conclusion
- a set of criteria to judge the solution's success
- a plan of action and contingencies
- a schedule for implementation
- a team to conduct, be responsible for, and approve the solution

Implement the Solution and Make It Happen

Implementation means having action plans with relevant deadlines and contingencies built in, also referred to as a "Plan B." Any implementation needs constant review, and the implementation team needs to be sure it has the support of relevant management. Keep asking the following questions:

- Are deadlines being met?
- Are team members happy, and is communication strong within and from the team?
- Has the team been recognized for its achievements?
- Are the improvements measurable?
- Is the situation reviewed regularly?

Evaluate the Solution

This is where the two most important questions are asked:

- How well did it work?
- What did we learn from the process?

All experience can be valuable in terms of adding to an organization's learning and institutional knowledge.

Canvass people's opinions regarding the effectiveness of the process and its outcome. Ask for areas of improvement that could be incorporated into a second phase. Don't be afraid of involving your clients in any evaluation; this can convey a positive message if handled properly, and builds trust in your ability to troubleshoot problems and implement solutions.

Be Aware of the Pitfalls of Problem Solving

There are, of course, pitfalls that can make for ineffective problem solving. These are:

- failing to involve the right people at the right time, particularly those outside the immediate group;
- tackling problems that lie beyond the control of the team;
- jumping to conclusions before truly understanding the depth or scope of the problem;
- failing to gather sufficient data, either about the problem itself or some of the proposed solutions;
- failing to "right size" the problem; people often work on problems that are too general or too large;
- failing fully to support the conclusions reached or the solution identified.

COMMON MISTAKES
You Use Too Many Techniques

Don't try to use too many techniques. Find one that you feel will work well in the business. Often, when running workshops, the process becomes more important than the ideas and intellectual discussion. Getting the balance right is important.

Your Team Is Too Narrow in Scope

Don't limit your team to the people you like. Try to get representatives from different parts of the business to give a different angle on the problem. Remember that:

- Often the exciting part of problem solving is identifying innovative solutions. But it's important to focus on the full picture, from problem identification through to final implementation and evaluation. Your ideas are only as good as the results you get.
- Creativity can often derail a problem-solving process. Getting the balance right between understanding the problem and finding imaginative solutions requires strong facilitation.
- Your solution will have an impact on other parts of the business, or the client. Make sure you think through the implications of the proposed solution and the implementation plan.

FOR MORE INFORMATION

Book:
de Bono, Edward. *Six Thinking Hats*. Revised ed. New York: Back Bay Books, 1999.

Web Sites:
dmoz open directory project:
http://dmoz.org/Reference/Knowledge_Management/Knowledge_Creation
Edward De Bono: **www.edwdebono.com**
Innovation tools: **www.innovationtools.com**

See also:
✔ Making Sound Decisions (pp. 842–844)

841

ACTIONLIST

"Every obstacle yields to stern resolve." — Leonardo da Vinci

Making Sound Decisions

842

ACTIONLIST

GETTING STARTED

Some people are naturally more decisive than others. For them, it's relatively easy to respond to a situation, weigh the pros and cons of various ways of tackling the issue, make the decision, and move on. For the indecisive, though, the process can be nightmarish, stressful, and eat up an awful lot of valuable time. The trick here is to find a decision-making style that means you spend enough time on a decision to make sure it's a good, well-considered one, but that you cut out the procrastination. Avoid the temptation to make knee-jerk judgments: you may think you're creating a good impression by looking decisive, but it's the quality of the decision that counts in the end.

This actionlist sets out to help you if you find decision-making a challenge. While you may not always be able to predict or control the everyday circumstances that you face, and, clearly, some decisions are a lot easier to make than others, there are skills you can learn that will improve how you respond. As you practice these skills and habits, they'll gradually become second nature. The result will be less stress, more decisiveness, less time wasted, and more focus in your working life.

To make the best decision possible, be clear about your goals, the problem in question, the options open to you, the possible consequences, the timescale, and the outcome of previous decisions on the matter. The process combines your intuition (to initiate your response and come up with innovative options) and your analytical ability (with which you scrutinize and quantify your options).

FAQs

How can I cope with a difficult decision that comes completely out of the blue?

No one can always predict or control the everyday circumstances that you and your business face, but there are skills you can learn that will improve how you respond. As you practice these, they'll gradually become second nature. The result will be less stress, more decisiveness, and more focus toward your long-term business goals.

You can make the best decision possible by being clear about your goals, the problem in question, the options open to you, the possible consequences, and the outcome of previous decisions on the matter. The process combines your intuition (to initiate your response and come up with innovative options) and your analytical ability (with which you scrutinize and quantify your options).

MAKING IT HAPPEN

Understand What You Want Your Decision to Achieve

When you're faced with a difficult issue, try to look past your immediate objective and take in your longer-term goals as well. For example, let's say you work in sales and have dealings with a wide variety of customers. If a cus-

tomer requests that you drop your price to an uneconomical level, you need to think about how important the sale is in the long run. If that customer doesn't feature in your business priorities, then you might only damage your reputation among competitors and other customers by dropping your price too low. On the other hand, if the customer is in a sector that you want to break in to, then a low-margin sale may give you an important foot in the door for future business.

Once you've defined the objectives of your decision, then you're in a position to determine its level of significance. This is important for deciding the amount of time and resources you should spend in making the right decision.

Different decision levels	
1 Strategic	Decisions about strategy are concerned with long-term goals, philosophies, and the overall plan of masterminding the future direction of the business. They therefore tend to be more theoretical than practical, more unpredictable in outcome, and more risky. This makes them of great importance.
2 Tactical	Tactical decisions are concerned with short- to medium-term objectives, and usually involve the implementation of strategic decisions and planning. The long-term risks are fewer and the significance, therefore, more moderate. However, as tactical decisions turn strategic decisions into reality they're more likely to involve the direct and great responsibility of overseeing and handling budgets, people, schedules, and resources.
3 Operational	Operational decisions are concerned with day-to-day systems and procedures and so tend to be more structured—to the extent that they can be routine or pre-programmed. As the third level in the decision chain they're used to support tactical decisions. The outcomes of operational decisions therefore tend to be immediate to short-term, and involve few risks (although a series of decision errors will mount up and cause more damage).

Find the Information You Need

Give yourself as much time as you can to research your decision, and resist the temptation to promise a quick decision to other people. You may think you're creating a good impression by looking decisive, but it's the quality of the decision that counts in the end.

Identify the sources of information you'll need and make sure they're near at hand. Get advice from experts or colleagues, and be honest about those areas where you don't have the answers. Ask coworkers for help if it looks as if you might run out of time or ideas—a brainstorming session is often a good idea. Often people who are new to an issue may see a solution that you've overlooked because you're so close to it. Wherever possible, avoid assumptions: check your facts. This might look like an extra hoop to jump through, but it's a valuable one. If you base a decision around a factor or number of factors that actually turn

---

"A wrong decision isn't forever; it can always be reversed. The losses from a delayed decision *are* forever; they can never be retrieved."

J. K. Galbraith

out to be unreliable, you'll have wasted hours of work anyway.

Six thinking hats: This powerful technique, developed by lateral thinking pioneer, Edward de Bono, will help you to look at decisions from many perspectives. Allocate each individual—alone or in a group—one of a series of imaginary hats, which represent different outlooks, according to color. This forces people to move into different modes of thinking.

- White hats focus on the data, look for gaps, extrapolate from history, and examine future trends.
- Red hats use intuition and emotion to look at problems.
- Black hats look at the negative, and find reasons why something may not work. If an idea can get through this process, it's more likely to succeed.
- Yellow hats think positively. This hat's optimistic view helps you to see the benefits of a decision, providing a boost to the thinking process.
- Green hats develop creative, freewheeling solutions. There is no room for criticism in this mode; it's strictly positive.
- Blue hats orchestrate the meeting—you're in control in this hat. Feel free to propose a new hat to keep ideas flowing.

Outline the Alternatives and Their Consequences

Get a few options down in writing, then explore the positive and negative consequences of each; give special attention to the unintended consequences that might arise, especially if you're considering a course of action that you haven't tried before. You may find it useful to list these in columns alongside the options.

Force field analysis: This is a useful technique for examining pros and cons. By looking at the forces that will support or challenge a decision (such as finances or market conditions), you can strengthen the pros and diminish the cons. Draw three columns, and place the situation or issue in the middle. The pros push on one side, and the cons push on the other. Allocate scores to each force to convey its potency. This allows you to measure the overall advantages and disadvantages of any given action.

SWOT analysis: Here's another handy grid technique, that works by identifying the strengths and weaknesses of a decision, and examining the existing opportunities and threats. You can find more information on these techniques online (see the Web sites listed at the end of this actionlist).

Judge Each Alternative By Your Goals

Remind yourself of what your priorities are in this situation. This will force you to always consider your longer-term goals when making your shorter-term decisions, and ensures that they're "pointing in the same direction."

Measure the merits and problems in each alternative—this may be a case of estimating financial costs and benefits, or it may involve less tangible factors like goodwill or publicity. This involves a forward-thinking process of predicting what will happen as a result of your decision.

Make a note of these expectations, as they'll be important when you review your decision later on and judge with hindsight whether it was a good one.

Compare the alternatives and decide which one comes out best in the light of the information available.

Decision trees: These are a great way to help you examine alternative solutions and their impact, especially when decisions are required in situations where there is a great deal of information to sift through. Start your decision tree on a piece of paper, with a symbol representing the decision to be made. Different lines representing various solutions open out like a fan from this nexus. Additional decisions or uncertainties that need to be resolved are indicated on these lines and, in turn, form the new decision point from which yet more options fan out.

Make the Decision and Implement It

Make sure that everyone involved is informed about the decision you've made as soon as possible; the value of a good decision is often undermined if your staff or colleagues hear about it through inappropriate channels. You'll normally need to inform the more senior people first, but speed is often of the essence when letting people know; plan your timing carefully and control the process firmly.

Explain the reasons why the decision was made, especially if the decision is contentious. Outline what benefits you expect as a result, as well as any other implications that the business needs to anticipate. Be honest but positive if your decision will cause inconvenience of any kind, even if it's only likely to be for a short time. While news like this will never be popular, it's best to announce it openly than let it dribble out over time.

Finally, get the right people onto the job of implementing the decision, so that it gets the best possible chance of success.

Review the Consequences of Your Decision

Estimate how long it will take before the decision will have an effect, and plan an assessment at that time to review how well it went. Make sure that some measurement is being made as you go along, as this will be helpful in any assessment you make.

For example, let's say that you've decided to invest in a promotional mailing, as you're about to launch a new product. You need to make sure that:

- someone is collecting information on the impact of that mailing on daily orders;
- someone is registering respondents' contact details if you asked for them and if they've given you permission to use them;
- someone is fulfilling any orders that come in.

When you come to review the effects of your decisions, remember that you're embarking on a learning exercise for everyone concerned with making the decision and implementing it. Try to get as many of these people as possible involved in the review process. This will help them when a similar decision needs to be taken next time; it will also advance their own decision-making skills and enhance their value to the business.

"A complex decision is like a great river, drawing from its many tributaries the innumerable premises of which it is constituted."

Herbert A. Simon

ACTIONLIST

844

COMMON MISTAKES
You Put Off Making a Difficult Decision

Procrastination will seldom lead to a decision becoming easier to make. Give the decision some thought as early as you can, and give yourself a deadline for making it—based on how long you think you need to gather the necessary information and input, and how important a decision it is.

You Make Snap Decisions Under Pressure

Making any decision without enough thought is risky, but if you're in a high-pressure office situation, there is the added danger of not being able to see the whole picture. If you make a very quick decision, you may not spend enough time considering important consequences of your actions.

You Don't Consult Those Who Will Be Affected

Nothing is quite as demotivating for staff as feeling that their input isn't valued or their feelings aren't respected. Before you begin to address a decision, think carefully about each of the people who are—or could later be—affected by its outcome. Make sure that you include them—not necessarily all of them—at every step, but leave them with no doubt that their input is appreciated.

You Let Your Bad Decisions Overshadow Your Good Ones

Everyone makes mistakes, and there will always be the occasions when your decisions don't work out as you'd intended. Try to see these times as part of the learning process, not as indications of failure. If you learn from a bad decision, that in itself is a good outcome. Don't be too hard on yourself and remember that it's unrealistic to expect a perfect decision every time.

FOR MORE INFORMATION

Book:
Hammond, John, et al. *Smart Choices: Practical Guide to Making Better Decisions*. Boston, MA: Harvard Business School Press, 1998.

Web Sites:
businessballs.com:
www.businessballs.com/problemsolving.htm
Mind Tools:
www.mindtools.com/pages/article/newTED_00.htm
Time Management Guide: **www.time-management-guide.com/decision-making-skills.html**
VirtualSalt: **www.virtualsalt.com/crebook6.htm**

See also:
✔ Solving Problems (pp. 840–841)

Choosing the Right First Job

845

ACTIONLIST

GETTING STARTED

Your first job sets the tone for the rest of your career. It is extremely important to choose the right first job. If you aim low, your career path may be limited as a result. If you choose the wrong company, your choice could haunt you for years.

The following points are questions to consider as you prepare to network and to market yourself:

- What kind of a career have you prepared yourself for?
- Are you financially able to hold out for the best job?
- How prepared are you to launch a professional job campaign?

FAQs

Why is my first job so important?

The average person works for seven or more companies in their lifetime. When you are looking for your second job, employers will evaluate you by your job title and by the prestige of the company where you first worked. It is extremely difficult to go from a low-level position at an unknown organization into a much higher position in a well-known organization. However, it is much easier to go from a good professional position at a well-known company into a better professional position at an even more successful organization.

What if I want to work in a non-profit organization?

Your first job is still important. There is a hierarchy among non-profit organizations in terms of prestige, power, status, and success, just as there is in for-profit organizations. This hierarchy may not influence career choices so heavily, but it still has an effect. Ideally, you are better off establishing your career by working for a well-known and successful non-profit organization than by working for a small, idealistic, but unknown and unconnected organization. If you truly want to have a positive impact on the world (which is most people's motivation for working in a non-profit organization), you are probably better off if you can do that in an organization with resources and clout.

What about the idea of being a big fish in a small pond?

If you are not very ambitious, or are more comfortable in small organizations, then you might want to take a higher level position in a smaller organization as your first job. One of the benefits of doing this is that you learn more about the total organization than if you have an entry-level position in a large organization.

What key question should I be asking myself in order to plan my career strategy when I look for my first job?

The key question you should be asking yourself is "Do I want to be a specialist or a generalist?" If you have chosen a particular field to pursue (such as biology, engineering, finance, music, or nursing) that you are really passionate about, then you probably are a specialist. If, on the other hand, you are interested in eventually becoming an organizational leader or an entrepreneur, you are probably more of a generalist. As a specialist, you would want to choose a first job that allows you in time to progress more deeply in your field. As a generalist, you would want to choose a first job that will offer you opportunities to learn more about other fields, and to expand your leadership abilities.

MAKING IT HAPPEN

Take Time to Think about the Kind of Life and Career Path You Want to Have, Even Before You Begin Your Job Campaign

At this point, you have already done a great deal of career preparation through your education and perhaps through some additional training. Think back and remember why you chose this field. Is it still relevant? Will it give you the kind of lifestyle you want in terms of how you spend your time and how much money you want to make?

Write a "Work Purpose Statement"

The following exercise is adapted from *Zen and the Art of Making a Living* by Laurence Boldt:

Complete each of the following sentences:

- The way I want to contribute is . . .
- The people I want to serve are . . .
- The scale I want to work at is . . . (for example, individual, community, national, global)

Now combine the essence of each of these sentences into one statement about your work purpose that includes who you want to serve, the way you want to serve them, and the scope of the impact you want to make.

Explore Possible Career Roles

Make a list of at least 10 different career roles that would be compatible with your "Work Purpose Statement." Now select the three that are most interesting to you.

Learn about the Lifestyle Associated with Each of these Career Roles

Use the Internet, the library, and personal contacts to get a better understanding of what it would be like to work in each of these potential career roles. Find out what a typical day is like for someone who does this career role.

Assess Your Financial Situation and Your Timescale

Determine how long you have to find your first job. If you do not have the financial support to wait for the "perfect" first job, then decide on your minimum criteria for accepting a position. These criteria could be financial, working conditions, geographic, or any other criteria. At the very least, if you are accepting a job that does not fit your "Work Purpose," then be sure that it gives you the time and opportunity to keep looking for a better position.

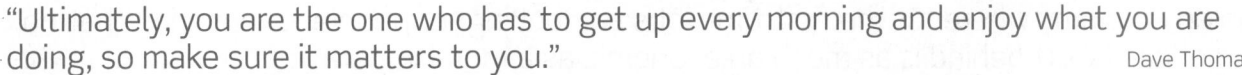

"Ultimately, you are the one who has to get up every morning and enjoy what you are doing, so make sure it matters to you."

Dave Thomas

846

ACTIONLIST

Prepare to Launch Your Job Campaign
See other actionlists in this section to create a professional résumé, make your contact list, prepare for your interview, and create your networking plan.

COMMON MISTAKES
You Choose a Career that Someone Else Thinks You Should Pursue
All too often, people choose a career path that their parents or a favorite teacher thinks they should pursue. Someone may say to you, "Your father and grandfather and uncle are all lawyers (or doctors, or teachers, or businessmen). Of course that is what you will do. It's family tradition." But this does not take into account your unique gifts and talents. It does not take into account what you feel called to do.

You Take a Job Because it Pays Well
If you are lucky enough to be offered several alternatives when you are looking for your first job, it is tempting to take the one with the highest salary. When you are starting your career, this is what seems to make the most sense. But it is short-term thinking. If the job does not fit your personality or your sense of purpose in life, you will either be looking for another job, or you will stay and be miserable. It's much better to take a long-term view when you accept your first job and to ask, "How will this job help me to develop my abilities so that I can best fill my work purpose and my personal and professional goals?"

You Jump at the First Offer
It is a mistake to take the first offer if you have applied for several jobs. But sometimes people lack confidence and think "a bird in the hand is worth two in the bush." They are afraid that if they ask a potential employer to wait, they will lose that opportunity. But employers understand this situation, and are usually willing to give you some extra time while you wait for other offers. Also, even if you get an offer from your number one pick, it is usually a good idea to say to them, "Thank you so much. I'm really interested in your offer, but I would like to take a couple of days to think about it." If you eagerly accept a position without taking a little bit of cooling-off time, you may be jumping into something when you haven't considered some of the possible pitfalls.

You Go to Work for a Family Member or a Friend Because That's the Easiest Thing to Do
Everybody expects you to join the family business. Or your parents encourage a family friend to hire you. It seems so easy to fall into this. But that is putting your career and your life's direction into someone else's hands, and it is not taking responsibility for yourself. It may be that one of these opportunities is the perfect one for you. Take time to analyze and follow the steps above, so that you are making a rational and informed decision.

You Avoid Trying to Find the Kind of Work You Would Really Love, Because People Tell You that the Job Market Is Bad or It's Not Practical
It is amazing what you can do if you are determined to make your dream come true. You can be incredibly creative and resourceful. It may be that you will have to work harder and take a little longer to find the kind of work you would really love to have, but it will be worth it in the long run.

FOR MORE INFORMATION

Books:
Boldt, Laurence. *Zen and the Art of Making a Living: A Practical Guide to Creative Career Design.* Revised ed. New York: Penguin USA, 1999.
Bolles, Richard. *What Color is Your Parachute? A Practical Manual for Job-Hunters and Career-Changers.* Revised ed. Berkeley, CA: Ten Speed Press, 2006.

Web site:
Job Hunters Bible: **www.jobhuntersbible.com**

See also:
✔ Identifying Your Marketable Skills (pp. 865–866)
🐭 Job Hunting (p. 1793)
🐭 Planning Your Career (pp. 1863–1864)
✔ Researching the Job Market (pp. 855–856)

"In an economy where for the first time jobs are looking for people . . . ensuring that no American is left behind is as much an economic as a moral imperative." Lawrence H. Summers

Finding Your Calling and Living Your Passion: The Dream Job

GETTING STARTED

Do you wake up in the morning full of excitement and enthusiasm about your day? Or do you dread going to work? If your job is sapping the life out of you, then it is time to reassess your life and your work. If you feel like an old dream is stirring and just won't go away, then it is time to discover and pursue your calling. The following questions provide thoughts for reflection as you take the first steps in responding to your calling:

- What keeps you in your current job, even though you are unhappy?
- What skills and talents are unused?
- What dreams have you buried because they weren't "practical?"
- What would a "dream job" look like to you?
- What are you willing to sacrifice in order to have a dream job?

FAQs

Isn't work supposed to be painful? Isn't that why they call it work?

No, work is not supposed to be painful. If you believe that, then you will settle for less and never be completely satisfied. Work is as natural to human beings as breathing. We feel bored, dissatisfied, and empty if we cannot contribute to the world in some meaningful way. Freud said that there are two important things in life: work and love.

I'm just getting started in my career. Don't I have to pay my dues first before I can find work I truly love?

Certainly you shouldn't expect to jump into the job of your dreams straight out of school. Unless, of course, you started the company! You do need to spend time in a new job learning the ropes and making connections. But don't ever think of it as "Paying My Dues." This kind of thinking encourages staying in a job that may not really suit you. You should expect to be excited about going to work each day.

I'm getting near retirement. Isn't it a little late to be thinking about finding my calling?

Many people who are nearing retirement grew up in a culture where work was expected to be drudgery. You may have sacrificed your dreams for most of your life, but now is your chance to take the time to do something you really love. You might consider volunteer work, being a mentor to someone getting started, or finding a company that really appreciates the wisdom of older people.

MAKING IT HAPPEN
Assessment

Begin by assessing your skills and talents. Make a list of all the things you have been good at. On this same piece of paper, make three columns. The first one is labeled "Current Job." In this column put a check next to all the skills and talents you are currently using. The second column is labeled "Joy and Meaning." Here put a check next to any skill that brings you joy and a sense of meaning when you are using it. This includes skills that you may not currently be using in your job. The third column is labeled "Dream Job." In this column put a check next to any skills that you would like to use in a "dream job." As you are doing this exercise, you may think of other skills and you can add them to the list. After completing the checklists, make some notes for yourself about any thoughts and ideas that came up about what a dream job might be.

Dream

Think about the dream you may have buried because it wasn't practical. Dreams can come true, but you have to be willing to believe in them. Read stories about people who have made their dreams come true. *Find Your Calling, Love Your Life* by Martha Finney and Deborah Dasch is an excellent source of inspiration. The source of a "calling" often comes from difficult or painful experiences that we have experienced or overcome. It becomes our calling, then, to help other people with similar difficulties.

Be of Service

Focus on the principle of service. All vocational callings have a strong element of service in them. Whom do you serve? How can you use your gifts and talents to serve them? What issues in the community, in business, or in society do you care about? Have you ever wished you could make a difference? These are clues to your calling.

Do What Brings You Joy

In order to be of service to others, we first have to do what brings us joy. So do what pleases you, and you will probably find that you are acquiring knowledge and skills that will help you to be of service to others in the future. And sometimes it is enough just to know that if you do what brings you joy, even if it is not of service to anyone else, the world is a better place. The world could certainly do with a little more joy.

Make It Real

Make your dream real in some concrete way. Write down a description of your dream job. Write in your journal about what "calls" to you. Tell other people about your dream job. You will find that as you get more and more detailed about what you are looking for, opportunities will "coincidentally" appear. Make sure you are paying attention to these opportunities.

"I don't think anybody yet has invented a pastime that's as much fun, or keeps you as young, as a good job."

Frederick Hudson Ecker

Talk To Others

Don't be afraid to tell others about your calling. The more you tell others about your dreams, the more real they become, and the more likely you are to notice opportunities that will help you fulfill your dreams. Also, by telling others about the job you would love to have, you are increasing the chances of finding someone who has the right piece of information, or the right connection for you.

Learn to Fly

Remember the rule of the bumblebee. According to the laws of mathematics and aerodynamics, it is physically impossible for bumblebees to fly. Fortunately, no one ever explained that to a bumblebee. Keep in mind that the most successful business people were frequently told that what they wanted to do was "impossible."

Let Go

In order to follow your calling, there are always necessary sacrifices that must be made. Before you make the move to another job or to starting your own business, spend some time thinking about what are absolute necessities in your life and work. Is it essential that you have high earnings, or are you willing to earn less money to do work that is more meaningful? Is it essential that you have a steady paycheck, or are you excited about the risk and potential in working for a small start-up organization? Is it essential that you work with people, or are you content to work alone? What things are absolutely necessary to you in your work, and what can you do without? Make a list of five things that are necessary and five things that you are willing to do without.

Look In Your Own Backyard

There's an old song that goes, "If you can't be with the one you love, love the one you're with." This can apply to your job too. Many people cannot easily leave their current job. The challenge, then, is how to see your current work as your calling. Once again, the principle of "service" can be very helpful. If you need to stay with your current job, write yourself a brief reminder about how the work you do is of service to others, and keep it somewhere nearby.

COMMON MISTAKES

Many people think that their dream job already exists, and that they just have to look around hard enough until they find it. The truth is that most people who have found their calling have actually created the work that they do. Don't go looking in the classified advertisements for the dream job. You must network, make connections, and tell other people about your dreams.

When you begin to follow your calling, there will always be people who will tell you that you are impractical, unrealistic, idealistic, or selfish. It would be a mistake to listen to them. They are the people who want to tell the bumblebee that it can't fly. Remember that, just because it's never been done before, it doesn't mean that you can't do it.

Beware of a job that is too good to be true, especially if you are being asked to put in your own money or to work for very little money at first. Scam artists understand the hunger that people have for a dream job, and they can play on that. If you are being offered a job that really seems to fit what you are looking for, make sure that you are going to be paid what you are worth.

Sometimes people get too attached to their idea of what a "perfect job" would look like. Beware of being too picky and of passing up opportunities that could turn out to be even better than the job you are looking for. Keep an open mind, but at the same time don't settle for something that doesn't fit your values, or that doesn't really use your most important skills and talents.

FOR MORE INFORMATION

Books:
Finney, Martha, and Deborah Dasch. *Find Your Calling, Love Your Life.* New York: Simon & Schuster, 1998.
Levoy, Gregg. *Callings: Finding and Following an Authentic Life.* New York: Harmony Books, 1997.

Web sites:
Martha Finney's Web site: **www.marthafinney.com**
FastCompany: **www.fastcompany.com**

See also:
☆ Avoiding Your Worst Career Nightmare (pp. 404–405)
☆ Urbane Renewal: Trusting Your Own Wisdom—A Competitive (and Satisfying) Advantage (pp. 406–407)

"Success can be attained in any branch of human labor. There is always room at the top in every pursuit."

Andrew Carnegie

Creating a Career Plan

GETTING STARTED

When jobs were for life, you decided what line of work you wanted, worked hard, and the career path was pretty much mapped out for you. The working world has changed. Now individuals wanting to maximize their potential will take a much more active part in mapping out their career. Career planning today needs to be a frequent, dynamic process of self-awareness, market and trend analysis, planning, development, and self-marketing.

The good news is that career paths are more flexible. Individuals can choose a spiral one, stepping through different fields or functions. Many employers encourage cross-fertilization of ideas through diversity in their workforce. They also value the different perspectives offered by those from outside their industry.

As career breaks are more common today, even transitory career paths are possible. These are popular with people who like variety, novelty, or have other worthwhile priorities. If you require periods of employment, interspersed by breaks, be it for study, travel, raising a family, starting a business, or caring for elderly or unwell family members, this option could be for you.

There are, however, still expert career paths for those who want to specialize in a particular field and linear careers for those who enjoy the challenge, responsibility, and status of climbing the hierarchical ladder. Whatever your set of circumstances, think about this: what does your career need to do for *you*?

FAQs
What's the difference between a career plan and a development plan?

Your career plan maps out long-term objectives, your more immediate objectives, and how you want your life and work to fit together. Your development plan maps out the skills and experience gaps for the different steps along the way and how you will address those. In effect, the development plan enables the career plan to work.

How do I find out what jobs I might be suitable for?

If you are naturally outgoing, start your research by talking to people. Make use of your contacts and ask for names and contact details of people who might be able to help with each of the options you're considering. This approach not only increases your network but it also gets you the targeted information you need. It may also put you in touch with contacts who can often open doors for you.

On the other hand, you may prefer to get started with some Internet or library research and save the networking until you feel a little better informed about your possibilities. Neither approach is right nor wrong, but people who use *both* approaches are likely to be the best prepared, most knowledgeable, and "luckiest" when it comes to opportunities.

Will frequent job moves look bad on my résumé?

It depends on what is "normal" for your market. In IT, for example, regular moves are common. A résumé that shows frequent moves is less likely to be frowned on if the skills offered and achievements shown are relevant to the job you're applying for now. If it is clear that in each job you've occupied you've been promoted or selected for specific strengths or skills, then employers will see you as a sought-after individual rather than a job hopper.

MAKING IT HAPPEN
Be Self-aware

Review your career so far, asking yourself some key questions. For example, what expertise do you have? What achievements are you proud of? What work have you received praise and recognition for? What were the outcomes of these achievements for your clients, team, or organization? What flair or talents have you not yet fully used? Do you have areas of untapped potential?

Also think about the skills you've used throughout your career so far and any differences in the way you've worked from job to job. Go through a typical working week writing down on a separate piece of paper or sticky note each skill, strength, or knowledge area that you have used. Do this for each job you've held. You can then cluster your notes, grouping those that fit together and giving each group a title, such as "Organizing," "Communicating," or "People skills." Doing this will identify and organize your transferable skills and help you to be clearer about what you're offering other employers.

Finally, draw other elements into the mix. What does your career need to do for you (and your family)? What do you value in work? What makes a job satisfying? What would you or do you hate in a job? Thinking about these questions will help you to identify your needs and constraints, such as financial obligations or geographical preferences.

Conduct a Market and Trend Analysis

Next you need to think about the market you're working in and which way that seems to be moving. What do you like about the market you're currently in? What are the trends within the industry? How might these affect your prospects going forward? Think in broad terms about who might have a need for your skills. What goals or problems could you help them with and what else can you offer them?

These are big and wide-ranging questions; so, to help you focus on them, do some research. Use the Internet and your network of friends and colleagues to expand your knowledge of companies and organizations, and of their internal trends and needs. Read all you can in journals and newspapers about the markets you are most interested in and identify relevant professional bodies for information on trends and the market for relevant skills. Libraries can be good sources of local information. The more questions you ask, the more you will know what

"Nothing arouses ambition so much in the hearer as the trumpet clang of another's fame."

Baltasar Gracián

other information you need, and research often gets easier as you go along.

Plan Ahead

Be clear about how you want your research and planning to fit together. Ask yourself what you'd like your life to be like in three years' time and write down what comes to mind in as much detail as you can. Write in the present tense, as if it has already happened. Then repeat this for one year's time, six months' time, and one month's time. This "3161" plan gives clarity and motivation for the long-term future. It breaks down the bigger picture of your life into an actionable plan that you can start on right now.

A "reality check" will help you recognize the right opportunity when it arises. Spend time on this when you are job hunting. Divide a page into four quadrants, headed "Role," "Organization," "Benefits package," and "Boss." Now ask yourself what you want from your next career move. Think about the "ingredients" that make up your ideal role, putting these into the quadrants on your page. Once your criteria are mapped out in this way, you'll have visual aid that will help you to weigh the opportunities that come your way. When you're invited to interview for a new job, you can use the sheet to come up with strong, targeted questions about the job.

Develop Yourself

You have identified your own skills and your immediate and longer-term goals. Is there a direct match already or will employers see gaps? If they might, specify what those gaps are and prioritize them, working out what you need to learn. Divide each missing skill into bite-sized chunks of learning or experience required.

Next, think about how you learn best. Do you prefer to read books, listen to an expert, try things out yourself, or practice with supervision? Knowing your preferred learning style is important to your planning.

Finally, you have to be sure that you're motivated to do this learning. If you are, go back to your "3161" plan and write in what it will be like to have filled these gaps at the relevant stages. If, on the other hand, you have more to do than you think you'll realistically be motivated to do, your plan is unrealistic and needs to be changed. Don't think, though, that all changes need to be drastic—sometimes a realistic timeframe is the only tweak needed to your plan to allow your dream to happen.

Market Yourself

Identify the stage you are at and your objectives. Let's look at three examples.
- During the honeymoon period in a new job, your objective is to establish good communication channels with your new colleagues and contacts and build a practical network. Here, then, marketing yourself will focus on attracting the interest of people who will make your work easier.
- Once you feel established in your new role, your objective is to make sure that interesting work is offered to you, so self-marketing in *this* context will focus more on bringing your successes and achievements to light.
- When looking for new roles, your objective is to attract

offers that meet your criteria. Your self-marketing now will focus on getting noticed by the right employers.

As we can see, self-marketing is continuous, but it will change in nature depending on where you are in your career and what your ideal next step is. Whatever you're doing, though, think about your "audience" and what is important to them. You may be offering to solve problems, deliver a product or service, improve quality or develop something new. To grab and maintain their attention, you need to focus on the relevant outcomes of your activities: increased profits, customer satisfaction and retention, or improvements in efficiency.

COMMON MISTAKES
You Forget to Market Yourself

Don't assume that your work alone will get you noticed. Self-marketing is what makes the difference between a good job well done and a good job resulting in a promotion (if that's what you want). If you are looking for a move up the ladder, keep up the momentum and don't wait to market yourself until you need your next role urgently—try to get into the habit of doing it and of raising your profile gradually but consistently.

You Have Unrealistic Ambitions

If you can't be bothered to identify trends and their impact on your market, you'll end up with a career plan that's completely unrealistic. The wealth of information on the Internet in particular means that there's little excuse for remaining ignorant about issues that may affect your future success. Even if you're not online at home, you can use an Internet café or just visit your local library to find out what you need to know. Make it your business to be informed and don't be afraid to ask "difficult" questions of people in the know.

You Don't Do Anything

A plan works by provoking specific and related actions which together create the desired effect. There's absolutely no point in writing a plan, performing the first action, then leaving it to gather dust.

You're Not Flexible

A plan is there to make your objectives happen, and so is tied in to real life. Just as life shifts and changes all the time, so must you and your objectives. Take time to review your plans regularly so that you can take into account unexpected twists and turns at work or other areas of your life.

FOR MORE INFORMATION

Book:
Jansen, Julie. *I Don't Know What I Want, But I Know It's Not This.* New York: Penguin, 2003.

Web Site:
totaljobs.com: **www.totaljobs.com**

See also:
✓ Finding Your Calling and Living Your Passion: The Dream Job (pp. 847–848)

"The world continues to offer glittering prizes to those who have stout hearts and sharp swords."

Frederick E. Smith

Entering an Entirely New Field

GETTING STARTED

It wasn't so long ago that employment stability was the hallmark of emotional maturity and reliability. Changing jobs frequently, even within the scope of a single career path, was generally frowned upon, unless the transition was on a clearly upward path. Changing careers entirely was almost unthinkable. The prevailing wisdom was "Pick one thing, do it well, and put away your childish notions of further adventures into discovery."

Now, however, most people expect to change jobs several times during their working lives, and some may even change their career. There are many reasons for this shift. We're healthier and more productive longer so we have time to gain experience in several types of work, not just one. The marketplace changes so rapidly that many careers are unrecognizable from their forms even five years ago, and some have disappeared altogether. Some people are being forced into career transitions. But most can't resist the siren call of new discoveries and new opportunities to expand the frontiers of their potential.

The following points are key questions to ask yourself when considering whether you should make a career transition:

- What aspects of your current career do you especially enjoy?
- What attracts you to a different career prospect? Can you isolate those elements and find ways to experience them in your current work?
- Where are you in your career life? Do you expect to have enough working years ahead of you to become fully functional in your new career choice?
- Does the time required for education and training reduce your potential for seeing a return on your investment? If so, is there an alternative choice that can give you the same satisfaction without the necessary investment of years of training before you can start?
- Will the career transition be the change that will give you the happiness you seek? Or are there other issues that you must address as well?

FAQs

Is It Too Late to Change Careers?

This depends on what else you want to do with your life, and what you are willing to sacrifice. It's possible, for instance, to become a lawyer in your late 50s and early 60s, but that would require giving up or postponing the rewards of a leisurely retirement or the benefits of a senior executive position that you have earned in the years you have already invested in your current career.

What Happens If I Make the Change and Discover That I Don't Like It?

It's possible that you can find a way to return to your previous career. Or perhaps you can take your additional self-awareness and launch yourself into yet a third career. Continue thinking of this process as an ongoing journey.

MAKING IT HAPPEN

Focus On What Goes Right in the Career You Have Now

Make a list of the elements of your current work that give you satisfaction. Is it the people you work with? The tasks you perform? The way you feel about yourself when you have achieved a goal? The geographic location of your job? The nature of the industry? How your work benefits your customers?

Isolate Those Things You Dislike About Your Career

Consider the distasteful elements about your current work. Can you simply remove them or reduce them so that the positive elements are more prominent and you can renew your sense of satisfaction in your work?

Remember Your Earlier Dreams

Think back to those careers you dreamed about when you were young. You probably had some big, idealistic ideas for your future as a child, and you might have abandoned them prematurely in favor of more seemingly practical choices. But perhaps the time to realize your dreams has arrived. Refresh your memory of what those early dreams were and how they made you feel about yourself when you imagined doing your dream work. Now that you are equipped with more world knowledge and a more adult intellect, how many different real careers can you list that would realize those dreams?

Research Your Dreams

Use the vast resources available online. The Web continues to expand its content every day, so you should be able to discover the necessary information about any type of career you are interested in. Additionally, you can research the thousands of associations and professional groups that support and promote practitioners in careers that interest you. A good place to start is the American Society of Association Executives: **www.asaenet.org**.

Ask Around

Talk to the people who are already engaged in the work that interests you. Go to association receptions. Arrange interviews with practitioners in the field of your dreams. Don't be shy. Most people who love their work consider it a pleasure and a welcome duty to promote their field to others. Encourage them to discuss their work on two levels: not only the practical how-tos and to-dos, but also the intangible rewards.

Seek Out the Necessary Financial Support to Help You Get the Education You Need

It's possible that you will need to get additional education to prepare for your career transition. That could be an expensive proposition, but there are alternatives to paying for it entirely by yourself. There are sources of financial support available to you, and the Web is a good place to research sources of scholarships, grants, and

"Change is an attitude of mind and the place to start is within ourselves." John Harvey-Jones

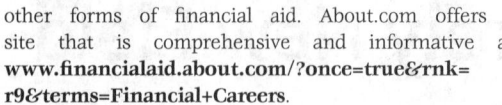
other forms of financial aid. About.com offers a site that is comprehensive and informative at **www.financialaid.about.com/?once=true&rnk= r9&terms=Financial+Careers**.

Keep the Faith

Once you have identified the next career transition that fires your imagination and your passion, continue to cherish that new excitement and vision for yourself and your future. You may go through moments of uncertainty or doubt, but try to consider those feelings as temporary dips in the transition process. Transition is a journey into the unknown, but the rewards will be well worth it.

COMMON MISTAKES
You Are in Such a Hurry to Make a Change That You Neglect to Make an Improvement

Moving from one career to an entirely different one is more than simply changing jobs. It involves changing one of the most fundamental aspects of how you define yourself. You will be changing the environment you work in, many of your social and business contacts, much of your everyday vocabulary, your process of prioritizing conflicting demands. If you're like most people, you entered your first career in a hurry, without full knowledge of all the options available to you. Take this opportunity to make this a positive adventure in discovery, as well as a way of finding a new livelihood.

You Rely on the Wrong Help or Advice

Placement agencies and search firms, for instance, are in the business of filling positions, not helping you discover yourself and your new role. Many career counselors are underqualified and merely process you through questionable pencil-and-paper aptitude tests.

You Rely on No Outside Help or Advice

Do not try to process this adventure by yourself. If you have a high-quality outplacement firm available to you through your employer, be sure to make full use of its services. Additionally, many schools support alumni networking groups where you can investigate the pros and cons of possible new career paths with people already in those fields. Confer with those closest to you—people who have observed those things that have brought you satisfaction and joy throughout your recent years.

You Pursue Careers Mentioned in "Hot Career" Lists, Thinking That They Will Promise Financial Security

Recent history has shown that those "hot career" lists reflect the best of limited thinking for a limited time. As those lists are published, the market experiences a flood of candidates seeking those career options, and suddenly there is not quite the demand for qualified candidates that was originally expected. If you are fortunate enough actually to land one of those hot jobs, you may discover that, financially lucrative as it might be, you are still left with that familiar discomfort that comes with the wrong employment "fit."

You Lose Heart

Try to keep in mind that you are in a far better position to seek out satisfying work the second or third time around than you were the first time you took on a new career. You are more mature, and you are equipped with deeper self-knowledge as well as with additional marketable skills and experience.

Discovering and exploring career options that you might love should never be a one-time exercise. It should be an ongoing part of your life's journey, leading you to even more exciting revelations about your potential to contribute to the world and make a difference, while making a living.

FOR MORE INFORMATION

Book:
Lore, Nicholas. *The Pathfinder: How to Choose or Change Your Career for a Lifetime of Satisfaction and Success.* Columbus, OH: Fireside, 1998.

Web sites:
Monster Career Center:
www.content.monster.com/careerchangers
American Society of Association Executives:
www.asaenet.org
Sources of scholarship, grants and financial aid
www.financialaid.about.com/?once=true&rnk= r9&terms=Financial+Careers.

See also:
✩ Driving Fear from the Workplace (pp. 420–421)

"In every difficult situation is potential value. Believe this, then begin looking for it."

Norman Vincent Peale

Making the Decision to Take a Risky Career Move

GETTING STARTED

Everything in business today is risky. There is no such thing as a safe bet. It is certainly risky to leave a familiar job with routines, expectations, and objectives that you're comfortable with to test the limits of your courage and skills in a strange environment, but, as over thousands of laid-off employees in global companies can attest, it's not exactly safe holding onto a job that is as dependable as a leaky lifeboat.

Whether you should decide to make that risky career move is entirely up to the nature of the risk and your ability to absorb the possible negative consequences. The risk itself may be made up of any number of factors, such as your ability to move into an unfamiliar job or your ability to move into an unfamiliar organization. Are you jumping from an Old Economy position to a New Economy one? Or are you leaping back into the Old Economy world after trying your luck in a high-tech, high-pressure, go-go New Economy environment? Are you considering leaving a stable, secure position that's limited in its prospects in favor of the white-knuckle environment of a bootstrap start-up? Are you about to move from a solid public organization into a family-owned business? Is the family that owns the business your own?

For some people, the notion of going into a shaky entrepreneurial environment after drawing a steady pay check for years would be intolerable. For others, depending on only one income source, as opposed to the multiple sources of revenue available to an entrepreneur, may make them feel vulnerable.

The decision you make is entirely yours. The risk you take is entirely yours.

The following points are key questions to ask yourself while considering whether you should take the risk or not:

- Does the benefit outweigh the potential cost of the risk?
- How many people depend utterly on the regular income your current job provides?
- Is there a backup plan in case your gamble fails?
- Is it possible to return to your original position should you decide that your experiment was not as rewarding as you hoped?

FAQs

How can I be sure that I don't regret my ultimate decision?

Give yourself all the time you need to make your choice wisely and calmly. Think it through methodically, and then make the decision. Whatever the outcome, be sure to learn from it in some way.

I'm not comfortable in risky situations. Is there any way I can avoid this problem?

Not if you intend to grow in your career. Indeed, there are no guarantees in today's marketplace, so taking steps to avoid taking a risk might actually be the worst thing you could do.

MAKING IT HAPPEN

Identify What "Acceptable Risk" Means to You

If you are young and single (with no obligations other than to yourself), you can probably afford to take on a few risky career moves. These high profile actions can give you early boosts that could position you for more momentum-driven rewards later in your career.

If you are older, perhaps with a family, you may not be quite as willing to try your luck with a high-risk/high-reward venture, such as a start-up enterprise.

Your capacity to accept risk is entirely a personal one.

Know Your Goals

Make a list of your short- and long-term objectives. Is your current position more likely or less likely to help you achieve them? If your position is less likely to help you achieve these goals, can you make slight adjustments to your present job in order to position yourself better for achieving your dreams? Or is it necessary to depart from your position entirely, regardless of what you are heading for?

Know What You Value

List your less tangible values. Which opportunity is most likely to help you manifest those values? Your current job or your new possibility? Does one opportunity actually position you to behave in ways that are contrary to those values?

Conduct a Risk/Benefit Analysis

This is the process that will help you determine whether the potential reward outweighs the potential pain. There are several methods for analyzing your potential costs, but the easiest is simply to create two columns. List the potential pain in one column and the potential reward in the other. The column that has the longer list is the one that should receive serious consideration. A variation of this method is to assign points or anticipating dollar values to each item. You can then either compare the grand totals or assess each pain/reward item on its own merit.

Analyze and Compare the Relative Vitality of Prospective Companies

Consider the companies as an investor might. As an employee—even though you may not actually own stock—you are still an investor. You are putting in valuable time and talent in the hope of both short-term return and long-term gain. Is one organization receiving bad press attention which could erode investor confidence? Is one

organization so heavily in debt that it threatens to collapse under the weight of this burden? Which organization is run by the best visionary who inspires confidence from both employees and conventional investors? Which organization creates the product that most directly and indispensably benefits the consumer? Which organization has the business model that you could most easily explain to a five-year-old?

Consider the People You Would Be Working With

Who do you have the most in common with? This is not a question of who you would be most comfortable spending an afternoon watching television or playing tennis with. Rather, whose visions and ideals are most compatible with your own? How does the corporate culture and environment appeal to you?

Consider Which Opportunity Is More Likely to Allow You to Develop Your Latent Talents

Almost all of us feel as though we carry an untapped treasure of talents, energies, and abilities. We are always looking for ways to express our genius. Which opportunity is more likely to give you the chance to develop in ways that you can take with you in the form of a much improved résumé should the worst-case scenario actually take place?

COMMON MISTAKES
You Make a Choice That You Regret Later

As there are no guarantees, there is always a chance that you will make the wrong choice—or at least the choice that feels wrong to you as you begin to experience "buyer's remorse." Have faith in your risk assessment strategy, and carefully watch how that risk plays itself out. There is always something positive to be gained from every adventure.

You Don't Make Any Choice at All

Making no choice is still making a choice. And this is the one that is almost guaranteed to net you no gain at all.

Modern business is full of risky moves. Those who relish the thrill of the risk, shift, and change will be the ones who will ultimately benefit from the growth and added self-awareness that comes from the adventure of being engaged in contemporary commerce.

FOR MORE INFORMATION

Books:
Bolles, Richard N. *What Color is Your Parachute?* Revised ed. Berkeley, CA: Ten Speed Press, 2006.
Borge, Dan. *The Book of Risk.* New York: John Wiley & Sons, 2001.
Dilenschneider, Robert L. *The Critical 2nd Phase of Your Professional Life: Keys to Success from Age 40 and Beyond.* New York: Birch Lane Press, 2000.

Web sites:
"How to Bounce Back From Setbacks," Fast Company: **www.fastcompany.com/online/45/bounceback.html**
Monster.com: **www.monster.com**
Executive Action International: **www.executive-action.co.uk**

See also:
☆ Driving Fear from the Workplace (pp. 420–421)
✔ Moving Sideways: Benefiting from a Lateral Move (pp. 889–890)

Researching the Job Market

GETTING STARTED

In starting your job search, you need to have several different kinds of information. You will need to research industry trends, find out details about the particular companies you are targeting, and perhaps even do some research on the hiring manager. You will want to keep in mind questions such as the following:

- What do I need to know about the industry I want to work in that will help me to ask and answer intelligent questions?
- Where can I find out more information about the companies I have targeted?
- What kind of information do I want to know about each of these companies?
- What would I like to know about the hiring manager that will help me to write a more effective cover letter and to perform most effectively at my interview?

FAQs

Why do I have to research the job market? Isn't it enough to just read the help wanted ads in the newspaper?

Only a small percentage of people find jobs that they love through newspaper ads. If you research the job market thoroughly, you will have a clearer idea of what you are attracted to. You will also be able to design your résumé and cover letter more effectively and intelligently because of the information you have gathered.

Why do I need to research industry trends?

First of all, it will help you to decide whether or not you want to stay in the industry you have chosen, or if you want to move to something entirely new. If the trends show that you are in a declining industry, it may be time for a change. Secondly, when you have an interview, it will help you to ask informed questions (which always impresses hiring managers), and will help you to answer questions from a richer perspective.

How much time should I spend on this research?

It depends, of course, on the level of the job you are looking for. If you are seeking a very high level executive position in the same industry, you may already know most of the required information. If you are seeking a high level position in a new industry, you may need to spend several weeks on your job market research. If you are seeking an individual contributor position, you may not need to know as much about industry trends, but you will want to do several days' research on your targeted organizations.

MAKING IT HAPPEN

Start Broadly and Then Narrow Down Your Research

In the early stages of your research, you will begin by researching industry trends. The main things you will be looking for are:

- the major growth areas;
- the major players;
- the major challenges and problems for this industry.

The first step in doing this research is to visit your nearest city or university library. Ask the reference librarian for help in finding reference guides and publications containing information about industry trends.

If you are not sure which industry you want work in, there are several good references and reports on attractive jobs and desirable companies. For instance, U.S. News & World Report has an annual ranking of the "20 Best Jobs in America." Ronald and Caryl Rae Krannich have written a book called *The Best Jobs for the 21st Century* that provides an overview of trends in different industries.

The major resource guide to information on types of jobs in the United States is the *Occupational Outlook Handbook* published by the U.S. Department of Labor. It describes more than 250 occupations and over 1 million jobs. You might also want to look at the *Encyclopedia of Associations*, which lists more than 100,000 professional and trade associations, organized by industry and the *Encyclopedia of Business Information Sources* which lists trade publications, newsletters, handbooks, associations, and online databases.

The Internet is another excellent resource in learning about industry trends. In the United States, two government Web sites provide very valuable information. The first is the Bureau of Labor Statistics at **www.stats.bls.gov** and the second is the U.S. Census Bureau at **www.census.gov**. In Canada, one of the most valuable Web sites for researching industry trends is **www.canadiancareers.com**. In the U.K., the U.K. Trade & Investment Web site has well-organized information about trends in various business sectors at **www.uktradeinvest.gov.uk**.

Research Your Chosen Companies

The next step is to narrow your research by gathering information about the specific companies that you are targeting in your job search. The key facts you will probably want to know about each of these organizations are:

- size of the organization (sales, profits, market share, numbers of employees);
- strong and weak points;
- key competitors;
- organizational culture;
- how the company is organized;
- key strategic challenges.

Much of this information is now easily available on the Internet, which will save you a lot of time. Once you have found an organization that you are interested in, get hold of a copy of their annual report. You'll probably be able to find this on their Web site, or, if not, simply call the company and ask them to send you a copy.

If you are targeting a local company, find ways to talk to employees about what it is like to work there and what its strengths and weaknesses are. You can also ask them about competitors, and about the key strategic challenges

"I wasn't satisfied just to earn a good living. I was looking to make a statement."

Donald J. Trump

856

ACTIONLIST

that the company is facing. If you don't know anyone who works there, you might consider attending local business meetings, or other professional gatherings.

Large universities also have online databases with company information. For example, Columbia University in New York has an excellent site at **www.columbia.edu/cu/lweb/indiv/business/guides/cpny.html**.

Several "best company" Web sites are listed at the end of this Actionlist will provide information about good companies to target, if you are not sure where to start.

Research Information about a Specific Job

The things you will typically want to know when you are looking for a specific job in a specific company are as follows:

- What would my tasks and responsibilities be?
- What qualifications are needed? What is the typical salary for a job like this?
- What can I find out about the hiring manager?

Most of these questions will be answered when you are at the interview, but if you can gather information about them ahead of time, you are better prepared for your cover letter, your résumé, and your interview. If you saw the job advertisement, then the tasks and responsibilities were probably spelled out. If you know for sure that there is a job opening, you can call and ask the company to send you a copy of the job description.

You will want to find out as much as you can about the hiring manager, and you may be able to do this through some of the business reference books mentioned above, if he or she is at a high enough level. You can also do an Internet search to see if he or she has been mentioned in any publications, or has written any publications in your field. Professional associations may have information on this person if he or she is active in your professional field. And if you know other people in the company, you can use your contacts to find out as much as possible about the hiring manager, before you contact him or her. You are looking for any information that shows that you may have something in common. This is valuable information for the cover letter, and also strengthens relationship-building when you are being interviewed.

COMMON MISTAKES

Your Research Is Not Thorough Enough

If you do not do enough research about the industry, the company, and the job, you may say or do something that shows your ignorance and jeopardizes your chances. If you can demonstrate that you have done your homework, you will really stand out from the pack and will have a better chance of being hired.

You Do So Much Research that You Can't Keep Track of It All

It is helpful to create files for each of the industries and companies that you are researching. Systematize your information so that you can find what you need quickly. This is especially important when you are preparing for an interview. You might want to prepare a set of index cards listing key points that you want to remember. Carry these cards with you wherever you go to help you to learn and remember important information.

FOR MORE INFORMATION

Book:
Bolles, Richard. *What Color is Your Parachute? A Practical Manual for Job-Hunters and Career-Changers.* Revised ed. Berkeley, CA: Ten Speed Press, 2006.

Web sites:
International jobsearch information:
Worktrain: **www.worktrain.gov.uk**
Global Edge: **www.globaledge.msu.edu/ibrd/ibrd.asp**
Canadian Jobs online:
www.justbus.com/canadian_jobs.htm
Fortune.com, best companies to work for:
www.fortune.com/fortune/bestcompanies/index.html

See also:
✔ Choosing the Right First Job (pp. 845–846)
✔ Finding and Working with Search Organizations (pp. 863–864)

"By looking on each engagement as a part of a series . . . the commander is always on the high road to his goal."

Karl von Clausewitz

Networking and Marketing Yourself

GETTING STARTED

Everyone can always benefit from networking and marketing themselves. Business is driven by relationships and marketing yourself requires you to build strong and meaningful relationships—many that will be long term. The following are questions to consider as you prepare to network and to market yourself:

- Why are you networking? What is your personal or professional goal?
- What are your strengths that will help you to market yourself?
- What organizations or events will be valuable places for networking?
- How much time do you want to spend on networking, and when will you do it?
- How will you know when you've been successful?

FAQs

Why should I bother to network and to market myself?

Research has shown that people who have a vast network of contacts, who are involved in professional and community activities outside their business, and who look for opportunities to be visible are more successful in their careers.

Isn't networking the same as politicking, and won't it look bad?

No. Networking is done for the good of your business, rather than for personal gain. If you are a successful networker, people are drawn to you because they know you are well connected and that you have good resources.

When is the best time to network?

Networking should become a way of life, a way of being. You should be networking all the time. As you build professional relationships, be constantly thinking: "What can I offer this person?" "How can I be of help?" The more you try to be of service to others, the more people will want to do things for you, and in the initial stages of a new business this will be a huge help.

MAKING IT HAPPEN

Clarify the Purpose of Your Networking and Why You Are Marketing Yourself

There are many reasons for networking and for marketing oneself. When you are starting up or trying to grow a small business, for example, these reasons may include gaining support for a major project, finding funding, or setting up a partnership with other local businesses. If you are hoping to gain a new job or promotion, you may be looking for someone who can give you expert guidance. Although it is important to continually build relationships, it is much more effective to know from the outset why you are building these relationships and what you hope to accomplish. Everyone has limited time, and this will help you to decide how to prioritize your networking activities.

Make a List of Your Strong Points

It is important to have a sense of who you are and what your strengths are when you are networking and marketing yourself. What are your special skills and abilities? What unique knowledge do you have? What experiences will other people find valuable? What characteristics and beliefs define who you are? Once you have made this list, make copies for your bathroom mirror, for your car dashboard, and for your wallet. Knowing your strengths helps you to remember that other people will value what you have to offer.

Never network from a position of weakness, but from a position of strength. This means having something of value to offer others, so that they don't see you as an annoyance. It's also a good idea to begin networking before you need anything from other people. Join or create a network to build relationships, and do what you can to help others or the organization.

Make a List of Organizations and Events for Networking

Identify professional organizations and events that may be helpful to you in your career or with your project. Look for special interest groups like those for "entrepreneurial women" for example. Get involved. When you are at professional events, make sure that you attend social functions, that you join people for dinner, and that you seek out volunteer opportunities.

Create a Contact List

Keeping in mind your reasons for networking, brainstorm all the people you know who might be of help to you. Prioritize the list according to who is most likely to be helpful. Think about people you have done favors for in the past who might not be of direct help, but who may know someone who can be. After you have spoken to each one, ask him or her, "Who else do you know that can be of help to me?"

Create an Action Plan with a Schedule

Take your list of organizations and events and your contact list, and put together an action plan for making connections. Schedule networking events on your calendar, along with organizational meetings, conferences and so on. Using your contact list, set up a schedule for making a certain number of calls per day or per week.

Meet with People and Attend Events

Before you meet with someone or attend an event, review your list of strengths, and focus on your purpose for networking and marketing yourself. It helps to visualize or picture a successful outcome. Be friendly and professional, but most of all, be yourself. Spend time connecting with people on a personal level before asking for help or sharing your reason for networking. If you are meeting in person with someone on your contact list, always bring a gift—something they can remember you by.

"Forget loyalty. Or at least loyalty to one's corporation. Try loyalty to your Rolodex—your network—instead."

Tom Peters

Network on the Net

The Internet is a valuable place to make connections and to learn fruitful information from colleagues. If you have a special interest or a special field, there is sure to be a newsgroup or threaded bulletin board on your topic. Alternative, you could start your own blog or look out for existing ones of interest.

Market Yourself

The actions you take depend on why you are marketing yourself, but think of yourself as a brand; "Brand You." When marketers are marketing a product, they look for the "Unique Selling Proposition" (USP). A USP is something relevant and original that can be claimed for a particular product or service. The USP should be able to communicate: "Buy our brand and get this unique benefit." When marketing yourself, you need to define who your "customers" are and what your Unique Selling Proposition is. Your list of strengths above should give you some clues, but the USP needs to be stated in a short phrase. People who are closest to you can often give you suggestions. It might be something like: "I help people to realize their dreams," or "My leadership brings out the best in others," or "I solve problems quickly and simply."

Once you know your USP, brainstorm ways that you can market yourself and your uniqueness. The key is to let people know what you have to offer. Write an article for the company newsletter or a professional newsletter related to your USP. Volunteer to give a talk. Design a project that uses your unique talents and propose it to the right people. Be visible.

Assess Your Progress Toward Networking Goals

You may wish to keep a notebook of your action plans and your progress. It also helps to have someone as a sounding board. That person can be a friend, a partner, or a professional coach. When we feel accountable for our actions to someone we trust, we are much more likely to follow through. It also helps to have someone who is willing to celebrate your successes and accomplishments with you.

Always Say "Thank You"

As you network, many people will offer you information, opportunities, and valuable contacts. In your notebook, keep track of the favors that people have done for you and make sure that you write each one a short and simple thank-you letter. People are always more willing to help someone who has been appreciative in the past.

Be Patient

Networking is a long-term activity. Steven Ginsburg of the *Washington Post* describes networking as "building social capital." You may not see results overnight, and at first should expect to give more than you get. But over time, your network will become one of your most valued assets.

COMMON MISTAKES
Not Wanting to Bother Anyone

Remember that people love to help others. Don't take up too much of their time, and come well prepared. When you ask for someone's time, be specific. Say, "I'd like 30 minutes of your time," and then stick to it. Don't outstay your welcome. Whenever you meet with someone, always be thinking, "Is there something I can do to help this person?" Create a win-win situation.

Coming On Too Strong

Networking is not about selling something to someone who doesn't want it. You are looking for opportunities to create a mutual relationship, where there is give and take. In order for networking to be successful, you have to be interested in developing a long-term relationship. Remind yourself that your focus is on relationship building, not on immediate results.

Not Coming On Strongly Enough

You put yourself in networking situations, but never talk about your needs or interests. This may be because you are not clear enough about why you are networking, or you are networking for reasons that are not particularly important to you. Go back to step one and clarify your purpose.

FOR MORE INFORMATION

Books:
Lowstuter, Clyde C., and David P. Robertson, *Network Your Way to Your Next Job.* New York: McGraw-Hill, 1995.
Darling, Diane. *The Networking Survival Guide: Get the Success You Want By Tapping Into the People You Know.* New York: McGraw-Hill, 2003.

Web site:
The Vault Guide to Schmoozing:
**http://www.vault.com/nr/cguides/cguide_
main.jsp?cg_page=1&product_id=535&ch_id=420**

"The people we get along with, trust, feel simpatico with, are the strongest links in our networks."

Daniel Goleman

Building an Awesome Contact List

GETTING STARTED

Throughout your career, you will always need to have an awesome contact list. It is useful for job searching, for marketing and selling products and/or services, and for networking of all kinds. People who have good contacts in their profession are admired and considered powerful. It really is important who you know.

In preparing your contact list and setting up your system, here are some questions to keep in mind:

- What are your major career issues right now?
- What are your major career goals at this point in your life?
- What networks do you have that can be helpful to you?
- What networking activities can you participate in that will build up your contact list?
- What system do you have in place to record and maintain your contact list?
- What do you have to offer to people on your contact list?

FAQs

How can my contact list help me with my job search?

Contacts can help in many ways. They can provide information on industry trends, the rewards and drawbacks of a particular kind of job, the likelihood that a particular organization might be hiring, and on specific job openings. A contact list is integral to a successful job search.

I'm happy with my current job and am not involved in a job search right now. Why do I need a contact list?

First of all, these days you never know when you might suddenly find yourself looking for a job. If you have kept in contact with people while you are gainfully employed, they are more likely to help you when you are job hunting. And contact lists are useful for many reasons besides job hunting.

Your contacts can help you throughout your career. People in your field who are not in your organization can give you a broader perspective on your profession. People who are in your organization can provide important strategic information that will help you make effective career decisions. People who are in professional associations can encourage you to get more involved and can increase your visibility and help you to gain more knowledge.

What is the best way to develop contacts outside my organization?

Generally, the best way to develop contacts is to join a professional association and to get involved by volunteering for committees or running for office.

People tell me that human resources professionals are the best point of contact in an organization. Is that true?

It is true if you are looking for a position in human re-

sources. Otherwise, if you are job hunting, you should be developing contacts with people who make the hiring decisions.

MAKING IT HAPPEN
Identify Your Major Career Issues

It is important to understand your reasons for building an awesome contact list. The two key reasons people use contact lists are (1) job hunting and (2) professional development. If you are job hunting, your contact list will be focused on people who can provide you with information about the job market and who may be able to help you locate specific job openings. If you are not job hunting, you will most likely be using your contact list to help you to learn more about your field, to solve particular professional problems, or to get mentoring from people in your profession.

Develop Relationships before You Need Help

Ideally, you want to begin building your contact list before you need to call on people for help or advice. In today's fast-paced climate, people have limited time to help others and are more likely to respond to someone they know and trust than to a stranger who is asking for help. As you begin to build contacts, keep in touch regularly with people just for the sake of keeping in touch. Then, when you really need their help, they will be glad to give you their time and energy.

Identify Your Different Networks and Create a List of Everyone You Know for Each

We each belong to three basic types of network: a personal network, a professional network, and a work–life network. Create a separate sheet of paper or computer document for each of these networks, and identify everyone you know within each one.

First make a list of people in your personal network, which includes your family, friends, neighbors, and others with whom you interact in your personal life. This might include people who are involved in community organizations in which you volunteer, people from your place of worship, and people connected to your children's school.

Next make a list of people from your professional network. This can include former and current coworkers and supervisors, teachers or professors, and colleagues who are members of professional organizations. You also might add suppliers or customers of your organization, consultants, speakers, and authors in your field.

Finally, make a list of people who are in your work–life network. These are people who are professionals in the career and outplacement field, such as executive recruiters, college placement officers, and career counselors.

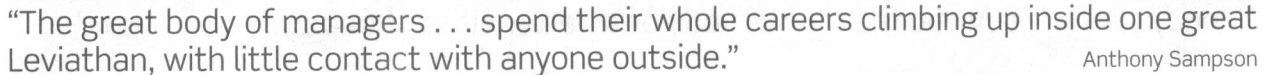

"The great body of managers ... spend their whole careers climbing up inside one great Leviathan, with little contact with anyone outside."

Anthony Sampson

Create a System for Keeping Track of Your Contacts

There are several different types of system that you might consider. The most common systems are:

- index card or rolodex system;
- computer software systems, such as Microsoft Access™ or Microsoft Outlook™;
- personal digital assistant (PDA) or electronic organizer systems.

You must decide whether you will do most of your contact work from your desk in the office or at home, or even when you're out traveling on the road. If you need to be more portable, the PDA is probably the best system to use. Otherwise, it is just personal preference.

Your system should allow you to record the person's name, address, phone numbers, e-mail, Web site address, pager number, and any other contact information that you might need. It also should allow you to include personal information such as birthday, names of family members, hobbies, or other details that will jog your memory about personal connections with this contact. Finally, you need room to include information about when you contacted the person, what transpired, and when you should get back to them.

Consider Creating a "Tickler File"

If you need to connect with people in your contact list on a regular basis, for example, once a month, you might want to create a "tickler" file. Let's say you are using an index card system. Instead of filing names alphabetically, you divide up your contacts into four groups, one for each week of the month. During week one, you call all the people in the first group. During week two, you call all the people in the second group, and so on. This system is particularly good for people who are in sales or public relations, but it also might be useful occasionally for people who are job hunting.

Have Something to Offer the People on Your Contact List

Remember that working with your contact list means working with relationships, and relationships are two-way streets. If you call only because there is something you want, people will eventually think of you as an energy drain and will avoid you. Always think about what you can give. When you ask a contact for help, also ask if there is anything that you can do in return. Each time you call, make sure you take the time truly to listen to the person you have called.

Don't Forget to Say "Thank You"

Every time you interact with someone on your contact list, make sure you find a way to say "thank you." People have so little time these days, and they are much more likely to be responsive to your calls in the future if they feel that their time is respected and appreciated.

COMMON MISTAKES
You Use the "Shoebox" Method of Creating a Contact List

This is the method of writing people's contact information down on a slip of paper and then throwing it in a box or a drawer to look at later. Usually business cards get tossed into this pile as well. The difficulty is finding a particular piece of information when you want it. It's best to set a specific time aside to transfer the information from paper scraps and business cards to your master file on a regular basis.

You Have a Great System, But You Don't Use It

Some people love setting up wonderful systems with color-coding and dividers and cross-referencing and so on, but they find they freeze up when it comes actually to making the call or connection. Commit to a certain time of the day when you will make your calls, and give yourself motivational incentives for doing the work.

You Don't Follow Up

The worst thing in the world is making the initial contact with someone, getting their promise of help, and then not following up. All the hard work is in making the first call. If you don't follow up and keep your commitments to stay in contact, you lose credibility with the people in your networks. This is where the tickler file or a similar system can come in handy. Make sure that follow-up calls are on your calendar or on your daily to-do list.

FOR MORE INFORMATION

Books:
Baber, Anne, and Lynn Waymon. *Make Your Contacts Count: Networking Know How for Cash, Clients, and Career Success.* New York: AMACOM, 2001.

Web sites:
Monster Career Center: **www.monster.com**
The Net Guide:
www.jobhuntersbible.com/contacts/contacts.shtml
The Fourteen Ways to Look for a Job:
www.jobhuntersbible.com/library/hunters/fourteenways.shtml

See also:
✓ Identifying Your Marketable Skills (pp. 865–866)
✓ Networking and Marketing Yourself (pp. 857–858)

Getting the Most from Your Professional Career Consultant

GETTING STARTED

Sometimes the best way to reach a goal is to call in professional help. Professional career consultants can help you figure out what kind of career you should be in, can help you set career goals for yourself, and can help you prepare for a job campaign or for seeking a promotion, if that is what you want. Career consultants come in many shapes and sizes, so you want to make sure that you select someone who is really right for your situation and with whom you feel a sense of compatibility and trust. And they are not inexpensive, so you want to make sure that you get the most for your money. You should consider the following questions as you set out to work with a career consultant:

- What is your goal in working with a professional career consultant?
- What are some of the services typically offered by career consultants?
- How do you find the right person?
- How do you manage the relationship effectively?
- How do you know when your goal has been achieved?

FAQs
When do people typically use a professional career consultant?

Career consultants are most frequently used when someone is considering changing careers or when they are between jobs and looking for a new position. However, career consultants can also be used as a sounding board for your current career. And some people use career consultants once or twice a year for career "tune-ups."

How much does a professional career consultant cost?

Career consultants usually charge by the hour, and their fees generally range from $70 to $200 per hour. Sometimes a consultant might ask you to pay a large fee upfront. Before you agree to do that, you may wish to interview several career consultants and find out what their fees are. The only exception to this is if the career consultant is going to offer you a battery of tests to help you understand your skills and your personality style, and to conduct a self-assessment that can guide you in deciding what kind of career you will be successful in. The battery of tests will cost around $500, but these are not always necessary.

How do I find a professional career consultant?

The very best way to find a career consultant is through personal referral. If you know someone who has successfully used a career consultant, you can ask them to give you the person's name and number. Some people call themselves career coaches or career counselors rather than career consultants, so you can look these terms up in your yellow pages and on the Internet.

MAKING IT HAPPEN
Set a Concrete Goal for Working with Your Professional Career Consultant

Define your goal in results-oriented language. Be as clear and specific as possible so that you will know when you have met your goal. Some examples are:

- to find a new job;
- to obtain a promotion and a raise ;
- to change careers to something more fulfilling.

Become Knowledgeable about the Different Kinds of Services that Professional Career Consultants Offer

First of all, be skeptical of any career consultants who promise a quick fix, easy money, résumés that get speedy results, or other come-ons. Career issues are complex and often take time to work through. And professional career consultants require extensive training and education.

Make a List of Potential Career Consultants and Research Their Qualifications

After identifying sources for finding career consultants as described in the FAQs, narrow your list down by checking on the qualifications of each of the potential consultants. In the United States, Career Consultants are certified by the National Board for Certified Counselors: **www.nbcc. org** and the National Career Development Association: **www.ncda.org**. You also may call potential consultants and inquire about their training and experience.

Select a Professional Career Consultant from Your List

After screening candidates based on their background, conduct a telephone interview with the remaining people on your list and explain your goal to them. Ask them about their methodology, what their costs are, and how their background will help them to help you. Then pay attention to your comfort level with each person and to what your instincts or intuition tell you. You want to select someone that you can trust and who will challenge you to reach your full potential. If you are having difficulty deciding between two or three potential career consultants, then make a face-to-face appointment with each in order to make your final decision. Most professional career consultants will not charge you for an exploratory meeting.

Set Clear Goals and Expectations with Your Professional Career Consultant

Explain your goals to your career consultant. They will describe clear expectations about how they want to work

---

"Don't be afraid to be unique or speak your mind because that's what makes you different from everyone else."

Dave Thomas

with you and what they expect you to do between sessions. If you have any expectations about how you want to work together, make sure that you make them clear from the start. Also get clear on payment amounts and the payment schedule. Will you pay session by session, or will they bill you at the end of each month, for example? Usually, most career consultants expect you to pay something before the sessions as a sign of your commitment, and many will ask you to sign a contract. Only sign the contract if you are comfortable with all elements of it, and feel free to question any items that you don't understand or don't like.

Plan for the Ending of Your Engagement with the Professional Career Consultant

Since you have set a clear goal in the beginning, it will be obvious when your work together is done. However, sometimes new goals arise as a result of your work together, and you may decide to create a new contract. Or you may decide that you want to meet every six months, or on an "as needed" basis. Because the relationship with a professional career consultant can be very personal and rewarding, it's always nice to end with a little celebration or with a gift as a way of showing your appreciation.

COMMON MISTAKES
You Don't Set Clear Goals

Some people go into this relationship because they have been laid off or dismissed from their job and the company pays for them to have a career consultant as part of the severance package. The danger here is that you meet with your consultant regularly just because they are there, and nothing gets accomplished. A really good career consultant will guide you into setting goals right at the beginning, if you haven't done that already. If you find yourself meeting for over a month and not sensing any progress, then it's time to choose a new career consultant.

You Are Not Really Committed to Your Own Career Development

You meet weekly with your consultant and you agree to take certain actions such as working on your résumé or making five phone calls. But the following week when you meet again you have not done anything that you promised you would do. If this becomes a regular pattern, you need to take a serious look at your goal. You may have set a goal that is not really what you want to do. In your next meeting with your career consultant, ask them to help you to evaluate the appropriateness of your goal.

You Don't Know How to Let Go

If the relationship has been really successful, you will have developed a powerful bond with your career consultant, and it will be difficult to terminate the relationship when your goal is met. But it is healthy for you to move on and to begin to apply on your own the things you have learned in this relationship. Having a celebration dinner is a nice way to symbolize the ending of your working together, and you can always schedule career "tune-ups" if you need them.

FOR MORE INFORMATION

Book:
Pickman, Alan, ed. *Special Challenges in Career Management: Counselor Perspectives.* Mahwah, NJ: Lawrence Erlbaum Associates, 1996.

Web sites:
The Five O'Clock Club: **www.FiveoclockClub.com**
National Career Development Association:
www.ncda.org.about/polscc.html#careercounseling

See also:
Planning Your Career (pp. 1863–1864)

"Get the advice of everybody whose advice is worth having—they are very few—and then do what you think best yourself."

Charles Stewart Parnell

Finding and Working with Search Organizations

GETTING STARTED

When you begin the job search process, it is common to feel haunted by the so-called "hidden job market," that exclusive network that links the favored few with the very best job opportunities. There are legitimate reasons for feeling that way. Only a small percentage of open jobs are publicly announced. The very best jobs usually require a special set of skills or background, and companies use refined recruitment techniques to attract candidates for such unique positions.

One of those techniques is the retention of search organizations that specialize in ferreting out the best candidates for the open position. The trouble is that it is not easy to know about, much less apply for, these particular opportunities. And, among the very best search organizations, the general message to the public is: "Don't find us. We'll find you".

Indeed, the mere fact that you reach out to a search organization renders you undesirable in the eyes of many of these companies. Just as banks only like to loan money to people who do not really need it, search organizations like to recruit candidates who are not really looking for jobs.

With that closed-club impression, it is natural to feel as though actively setting out to attract the attention of search organizations is probably counterproductive. However, there are ways to use the connections and power of search organizations to promote your own career.

The following points are questions to consider as you prepare to look for your next job with the help of one or more search organizations:

- Do I need a search organization to help me find my next job?
- How quickly do I need a new job?
- Should I work with a contingency organization or a retained search organization?

FAQs
How much should I expect to have to pay a search organization for helping me?

Nothing. The client is the hiring company. Never pay a search organization. Search organizations receive their fees from the company, valued at roughly 30% of the new employee's first year's salary.

What's the difference between a contingency search organization and a retained search organization?

A contingency search organization only makes its money when it successfully places a candidate. Contingency organizations usually fill junior to middle-level executive positions, with salaries ranging from $50,000 to $150,000.

A retained search organization works with more senior positions, receiving its fee regardless of whether certain positions are successfully filled. Both are legitimate forms of business; however, it is generally agreed that retained search organizations have a higher quality relationship with their client company—a long-term interest in which the mutual goal is the company's prosperity. With a contingency search organization, the emphasis is more likely to be on the individual placement. So both you and the hiring company could find yourselves in a wrong match.

Can I work with more than one search organization at a time?

In most cases, yes. You are the one still in charge of your own future. Seriously reconsider signing with a search organization that insists on an exclusive contract with you. Because you are not the paying client, your own personal interests are not part of the organization's business concerns. Therefore, you should be able to market and represent yourself freely elsewhere.

MAKING IT HAPPEN
Identify the Best Search Organizations for the Type of Position You Are Seeking

Use word-of-mouth and other indirect marketing techniques for identifying the best search organizations and helping them find you. Ask your friends, colleagues, and college career centers to introduce you to the services they found to be satisfactory. Go where search organization consultants go. Attend high-end business receptions, go to human resource seminars in your community or industry. Participate as a speaker (or even a volunteer) at business symposia. Write articles for your industry journal.

Contact the Search Organization

The best way to initiate contact with a search organization is to phone a search organization consultant specifically recommended to you by a friend or colleague. Have an expertly prepared résumé ready to send immediately. If you do not have a personal introduction, send the résumé with a cover letter describing your overall credentials and abilities.

Be Prepared

You may be invited to come in for an interview immediately. Or you may be notified that your résumé has been keyed into the organization's database. Assuming that your résumé contains the important keywords associated with your career path, your information will then come up the next time a suitable position is researched. Working with search companies is likely to be a long-term proposition, where both you and the consultant will find

success if and when a compatible opening is available at a client company.

Know How to Evaluate a Search Organization

When you are contacted by a search organization that you are unfamiliar with, be sure to assess the organization's ability to serve your interests well. An excellent question to ask is who their client companies have been. The organizations you want to work with will freely offer a shortlist of prestigious client companies.

Select Only a Few Search Organizations to Work with

While you should never succumb to the pressure of signing an exclusive deal with only one organization, you also should sign with only a small number of organizations, so that you can stay focused and in control of your schedule of interviews.

Follow Up

After the initial interview with the hiring company, follow up with that company in the standard ways, such as a thank you letter. Search organizations should not try to stand in the way of the relationship you cultivate with the hiring company. The successful hire will benefit all three parties, and it continues to be up to you to do your part to improve the chances of receiving an offer.

Listen to Consultant Feedback and Accept Recommended Advice

The consultant may see you as the best possible candidate for an ideal position; however, there may be a small element in your personal demeanor, grooming, or body language that could spoil your chances. If the consultant's recommendations do not require a fundamental shift in your basic nature or values, seriously consider following the advice.

COMMON MISTAKES
You Waste Your Time with Low-quality Consultants and Search Organizations

Insist on a personal meeting at their offices. If they insist, in return, on a telephone relationship, or if you find that their offices are shabby, these are excellent indicators that their clients will probably not be top-market employment opportunities for you.

You Wait Until You Need to Find a New Job Before Cultivating a Relationship with a Search Organization Consultant

Some of the most successful search organizations receive up to 300 résumés a day, so you have to compete for their attention. Additionally, there may not be any openings for positions that you are best qualified for. The coincidence of availabilities is rare enough that you should be in the search organization's system long before you are desperate for a new job.

You Try to Camouflage a Spotty Past with Finessed Answers

Most consultants and hiring managers have heard the language typically used to camouflage a firing or a dismissal for a company's downsizing. If you are available now because you were dismissed or fired, be as candid as possible.

You Drop Your Search Organization Consultant After You Have Accepted Your New Position

If you have achieved a mutually satisfactory relationship with your search organization consultant, stay in touch with that person. Send them excellent candidates for other positions that may become available. Meet for lunch now and then. You don't have to make that person your best friend. But the days of working for one company for the rest of your life are over. The chances are that you will be searching for a new position within a few years. Use that earlier relationship to keep moving forward along your career path toward your future.

FOR MORE INFORMATION

Book:
Bolles, Richard. *What Color Is Your Parachute? A Practical Manual for Job-Hunters and Career-Changers.* Revised ed. Berkeley, CA: Ten Speed Press, 2006.

Web sites:
Global Executive:
www.economist.com/globalexecutive
Executive Grapevine: **www.askgrapevine.com**

See also:
Job Hunting (p. 1793)
Researching the Job Market (pp. 855–856)

Identifying Your Marketable Skills

GETTING STARTED

Most of us tend to think too narrowly about our marketable skills, and thus undersell ourselves when we are looking for a promotion or a new job. This Career Actionlist will provide you with a step-by-step approach to examining your life and work experiences, so that you can assess which of the many skills you have are the most marketable. As you read this, here are some questions for you to consider:

- What are your personal and professional goals?
- What educational, work and leisure experiences have you had that will help you to reach your goal?
- Do you have a realistic picture of the match between your skills and your career goal?

FAQs

Why is it important to identify my marketable skills?

There are two reasons for doing this. The first, and most pragmatic, is that it will help you to write a more powerful résumé. The second is that it will help you to present yourself more professionally to a potential employer. You will feel confident about what you have to offer and will sell yourself better.

What if I don't want to keep on doing what I am skilled at now?

The steps described below are designed to help you identify the skills that will get you the job you want. If you are planning to change careers, it is important to realize that you may have many transferable skills that will be marketable in a new position. Or you may have skills that you haven't used for some time that could be very useful in a new position.

MAKING IT HAPPEN

It takes a lot of time and energy to identify your marketable skills. It is not an easy task, but it is one of the most important you can undertake because it helps you to plan your job campaign and to target the best potential employers. It also gives you a strong sense of confidence in what you have to offer.

Begin with the End In Mind

In order to identify the marketable skills that you have, you must know what kind of a position you are looking for. This creates the context for thinking about the skills that you want to use in your next job. For guidance, see the Actionlist on finding your dream job.

Write a Brief Life/Work Biography

Take the time to sit down and write a 3–5 page history of your life that includes significant events when you were growing up, important educational experiences, and a summary of your work experiences. As you write about each of these experiences, describe what you liked and what you didn't like and what you accomplished. What

were you most proud of? Also describe what you did during times when you were not working, and how you felt about those activities. Make sure that there are at least seven key events in your biography.

What, if anything, did writing your biography tell you about potentially marketable skills that you might have?

Educational Assessment

Whether or not you included much detail about your educational experiences, here is a useful assessment that may help to highlight some of your skills and interests:

- What teachers did you like best and why?
- What teachers did you like least and why?
- Which subjects did you like best and why?
- Which subjects did you like least and why?
- Which subjects did you get the best grades in and why?
- Which subjects did you get the worst grades in and why?

Based on what you have written, identify five key skills or knowledge areas that you might like to use in your next position.

Work Experience Assessment

Review each of the jobs that you have held and ask yourself the following questions:

- What was my favorite job and why?
- What was my least favorite job and why?
- Which of these jobs would I do even if I didn't get paid? Why?
- Which jobs really challenged me and helped me to develop personally and professionally? Why?

Based on what you have written, identify five key skills or knowledge areas that you might like to use in your next position.

Leisure Activity Assessment

In the times you are not working (whether evenings and weekends, or longer periods of time when you have been between jobs), what do you really enjoy doing with your leisure time? Here are questions to consider:

- What skills have you developed from a hobby that might be marketable?
- What skills have you developed from your travels?
- What skills have you developed from other leisure time activities?
- Is there something you do for fun that you always dreamed of getting paid for?

Again, identify the five most marketable skills you have from your leisure activity assessment.

List Achievements

Now go over what you have written and create a list of at least 10 major achievements in your life. Don't worry about whether or not they are work-related. When you have completed the list, rank your achievements in order, with number one being your most important achievement, number two being your second most important achievement, and so on.

"Focus on operational positions where you have responsibility for profit and loss. That way it's easy to measure whether you're doing a good job."

Fabiola Arredondo

Put It All Together

You can now create your final skills inventory by going over all that you have done so far and putting the information about your skills into the following categories. If you need help identifying other potential skills that you might have, visit one of the Web sites listed below for ideas.

- Make a list of all your skills that are related to management in any way. Although your current job title may not classify you as a "a manager," you may still do some activities that are considered managerial. These can include policy formulation, policy implementation, conducting performance reviews, hiring, firing, project responsibilities, problem solving, budgetary responsibilities, planning, organizing, presenting, and so on.
- Make a list of all of your training skills, including any informal training you may have done. Training can be for individuals or for groups. Also list any certifications you may have received for programs you are certified to teach. Include any other professional training programs, seminars, and symposiums you have attended.
- Make a list of all of your documentation skills where you have prepared reports, manuals, summarized research, conducted studies, and so on.
- Make a list of all your technical skills, which may include operating machines or computers, any specialized knowledge, any manufacturing, sales, engineering, human resources, or other skills that have not been mentioned in any of the categories above.
- Make a list of all your interpersonal skills. Although they are harder to define, these skills can "make or break" an application for a new position. This list could include any of the following skills: communication, facilitation, coaching, conflict resolution, negotiation, team building, and many others.
- Create a category of "other skills" for skills that don't fit into the above categories. Often, these skills are something unique that you have to offer, making you more attractive than other candidates.

Compare the List with Your Career Goals

By this time, you should have quite a long list of potentially marketable skills. Go back through this list and check or highlight the skills that most closely match your career goals. From this list, choose the ten skills that you think are most marketable. Ask yourself "If I were trying to hire someone for this job, are these the skills I would be looking for?" If you are lacking any essential skills for the job you desire, you should develop a plan to acquire these skills.

Take each of the top ten skills you have listed and write a sentence describing how you have actively used this skill. For example: "Used conflict resolution skills to solve a major problem between production and sales"; or "Conducted quality training in the billing department, leading to a 15% decrease in billing errors."

Reality Testing

Through your networking, identify someone who is doing the job that you would like to have. Ask him or her to review your list of skills and see if they agree that your skills are a match for this kind of position. If they do not think there is a match, ask him or her what skills you need to gain. Or you may wish to ask what kind of a job would be a better match for someone with your skills. Another reality check is to ask those closest to you to review your skills and to see if you may have left anything out.

Final Step

Your final step is to turn your list of marketable skills into valuable information in your cover letter and on your résumé.

COMMON MISTAKES
You skip this process and jump into writing your résumé

You may think that you already know all your skills, but this exercise always produces some surprising and creative results that help you to market yourself better. Sometimes it even helps you to see that you may have chosen the wrong job objective, and you are able to alter your career goals to exploit all that you have to offer more fully.

You discount early life experiences

You think to yourself, "It doesn't matter what I did in high school or in my first job. That was so long ago." But often there are clues to your strongest skills and to your life's purpose in these early experiences.

You are unrealistic about the match between your skills and your career goal

You may want to change from a job in information systems to a job in human resources, but if you have not had any specialized training or experience in the new area, you will not be able to make the move. Make sure that you do the reality test before you actually start your job search.

FOR MORE INFORMATION

Book:
Bolles, Richard. *What Color Is Your Parachute? A Practical Manual for Job-Hunters and Career-Changers.* Revised ed. Berkeley, CA: Ten Speed Press, 2006.

Web site:
Skills Identification:
www.mnworkforcecenter.org/cjs/cjs_site/skill.htm

See also:

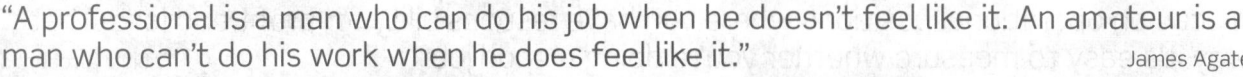

"A professional is a man who can do his job when he doesn't feel like it. An amateur is a man who can't do his work when he does feel like it."
James Agate

Revitalizing Your Résumé

GETTING STARTED

If you're embarking on a job hunt, there are lots of options open to you as you look for the right way to display your fantastic skills and experience. There are many different styles of résumé, but why do you need to know how to prepare them? Because every person's career history is different, and you want a résumé that puts your career history in the most marketable and attractive light. It's important to think carefully about which style to use when you apply for a job. A carefully written and targeted résumé will impress a personnel officer much more effectively than a random story of your life.

Your particular job search and career goals are also unique. The stage you're at in your career is also a factor to bear in mind. As you decide which type of résumé to prepare, think about whether you plan on staying in the same field or whether you're changing careers. Have you had a fairly standard career development, or has your career been less traditional? Is this your first job? Are you aiming for a specific job in a specific company or are you on the look-out for something new and challenging? Is it a while since you've updated your résumé and do you feel a bit behind the times?

All these factors will help you decide which type of résumé is most likely to get you the interview that will lead to your perfect job.

FAQs

How many types of résumé are there?

There are many different types of résumé, but we'll be focusing on the following:

- chronological
- functional
- targeted
- capabilities

A chronological résumé is still the most popular type of résumé by far, but knowing how to put together the other types will stand you in good stead as you progress through your career and come across different job opportunities. These days people may have several different careers (not just jobs) in the course of their working lives, so if you're thinking about changing what you do dramatically, a nontraditional résumé may suit your needs best.

How do the résumé types differ?

You should use a **chronological résumé** when you're staying in the same field rather than making a major career change. This type of résumé also works well when you've progressed steadily up a standard career ladder. For example, if you began your career as a junior designer, you moved on to become senior designer, and you're hoping to become design manager, this is the résumé type for you. You would also use this kind of résumé when you've worked for the same company for most of your career, even though you may have had several different kinds of job within that company. If you're starting off on your career path, looking for your first or second job, this résumé is probably most appropriate to your experience.

A **functional résumé** is the better choice when you're looking for your *first* professional job, as it stresses your skills rather than your experience. It's also a good choice when you're making a fairly major career change, for the same reasons. If you've changed employers frequently, followed a less traditional career path, or are concerned that your career history has been a bit patchy, you may be better off this type of résumé.

You should use a **targeted résumé** when you're very clear about your job direction and when you need to make an impressive case for a specific job. It's hard work writing this kind of customized résumé, especially if you're applying for several jobs, but it can make you and your abilities stand out from all the others in the pile.

If you're aiming for a specific job or assignment within your current organization, the best résumé to use is the **capabilities résumé**. Again, you must be willing to take the time to customize your résumé for the situation.

Do I need to create a résumé for each of these types?

Not normally, no. The only exception to this is when you've created one of the standard formats (either a chronological or a functional résumé), and a unique opportunity comes up for which one of the customized résumés (either a targeted or a capabilities résumé) is better.

What's a job search "objective?"

These were a résumé must-have a few years ago. A job search objective is a short paragraph at the top of your résumé that explains exactly what type of job you're looking for. It's particularly useful if you're writing to someone speculatively, but isn't always appropriate, so think carefully about whether you need to include one or not. If you want to add one to your résumé, make sure it's concise, specific, and above all, honest. For example, the following objective is too general:

Seeking position in broadcasting industry.

That's not going to do you many favors. An improved version could be

An experienced broadcasting professional is seeking a position to make full use of an in-depth background as a television producer, production manager, scriptwriter, and networker. I am looking for a challenging production manager position that will enable me to use and expand my creative skills and international experience in the broadcasting industry.

MAKING IT HAPPEN
Create a Chronological Résumé

- Write your name and contact details at the top. Don't use your work e-mail address as part of these; it will look as if you're taking advantage of your current employer. Use your home e-mail address instead or an Internet-based one such as Hotmail, AOL, or Yahoo.

"A man who lies to himself, and believes his own lies, becomes unable to recognize the truth, either in himself or in anyone else, and he ends up losing respect for himself as well as for others."

Fyodor Dostoevsky

- If you're applying speculatively, you may want to include a job search "objective."
- Write your employment history. Start with your present or most recent position, and work backward.
- For each position listed, describe your major duties and accomplishments, beginning with an action verb. Keep it to the point and stress what you've achieved.
- Keep your career goals in mind as you write and, as you describe your duties and accomplishments, emphasize those which are most related to your desired job.
- Include your education in a separate section at the bottom of the résumé. If you have more than one degree, they should be listed in reverse chronological order. List any professional qualifications or training you've undertaken separately.

If you've been working for some time, you only need to write in detail about your last four or five positions, covering the last ten years or so. It's fine to just summarize the rest of your career history that goes back beyond that.

Create a Functional Résumé
- Write your name and contact details at the top.
- As this type of résumé is well suited to people starting out in their careers, you may want to state your job search "objective" clearly.
- Write between three to five separate paragraphs, each one focusing on a particular skill or accomplishment.
- List these "functional" paragraphs in order of importance, with the one most related to your career goal at the top.
- Provide a heading for each paragraph.
- Within each functional area, emphasize the most relevant accomplishments or results produced.
- Add in a brief breakdown of your actual work experience after the last functional area, giving dates (years), employer, and job titles only.
- Include your education in a separate section at the bottom of the résumé. Again, if you have more than one degree, they should be listed in reverse chronological order.

Using this résumé style means that you can include information about your skills and accomplishments without identifying which employer or situation it was connected to. This is especially helpful if you've signed a nondisclosure agreement with your current or previous employer, in which you undertake not to reveal specific information about a job or project to potential competitors. Nondisclosure agreements are particularly common in high-tech or research companies.

Create a Targeted Résumé
- Begin by brainstorming a list of key points. For example, what have you done that is relevant to your job target? Are you proud of what you've achieved? Have you achieved anything in another field that is relevant to your job target? Think about what you do that demonstrates your ability to work with people.
- Write your name and contact details at the top.
- Think carefully about whether you need to include a job search "objective" here; as this type of résumé is best geared to an application for a specific job, you may not

need to include one and could use the space more usefully.
- From your brainstormed list, select between five and eight skills/accomplishments that are the most relevant to your job target. Make sure that the statements focus on action and results.
- Briefly describe your actual work experience beneath each skills/accomplishment item, giving dates (years), employer, and job titles only.
- Include your education in a separate section at the bottom of the résumé, listed in reverse chronological order.

Create a Capabilities Résumé
- To develop a capabilities résumé, you first need to learn all you can about the internal job that you're applying for.
- List your name and contact details at the top.
- Think carefully about whether you need to include a job search "objective" here; as this type of résumé is best geared to an application for a specific job, you may not need to include one and could use the space more usefully.
- Next, list your five top accomplishments, focusing on actions taken and results achieved that are relevant to the position you're interested in.
- Write a brief paragraph about any relevant work experience you've had in your current position. If you haven't been at the company for long, you should provide a complete synopsis of your work experience as described for the targeted résumé.
- Include your education in a separate section at the bottom of the résumé in reverse chronological order.

Think about the look and feel
Once you've decided on the best résumé type for you and the job you want, spend a little time making sure that you think about the details and present all the information to its best advantage.

- Most résumés are submitted via e-mail these days, but if you're sending your résumé by mail, print the document on high-quality white or cream paper. This will make sure that your résumé can easily be read, photocopied, or scanned by the recruiter.
- Buy your own stationery. Don't use headed notepaper or address labels from your current place of work when you're printing out or mailing your résumé to another company or agency. Just like using your work e-mail as part of your contact details, this will give a strong impression that you're taking advantage of your present employer and his or her facilities.
- Take care with the formatting of your résumé. Use a "clean" looking font that is easy to read (some people prefer a sans serif, such as Arial), and make sure that the type size you use isn't too small. Draw attention to your achievements by using a bold face to highlight positions you've held or qualifications you've gained. Emphasize key points in lists by using bullets.
- Make sure you read over your résumé once you've finished working on it to check for spelling or grammatical errors—these, above all, will mean your résumé ends up in the bin rather than on the right person's desk. It's always a good idea to ask someone else to read over your finished résumé too; he or she may spot something

---

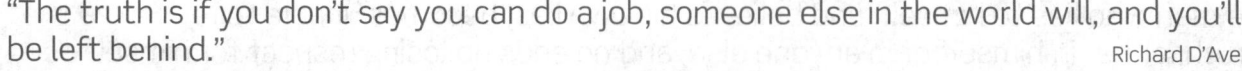

"The truth is if you don't say you can do a job, someone else in the world will, and you'll be left behind."

Richard D'Aveni

you've overlooked as you've become so familiar with what you've written.

- Try not to rely on computer spellcheckers. While they'll pick up on a good many mistakes in spelling and usage, remember that they won't pick up on words that are spelled correctly but used in the wrong way or the wrong place. For example, if you write "there" when you actually mean "their," the spellchecker won't realize that you've made a mistake.
- Unless you're *specifically* asked by a recruiter to submit a hand-written résumé or cover letter, use a computer to give a more professional finish.
- Follow your own instincts. By all means ask friends or family members to read through your résumé but remember that, if you ask 20 people what they think, you'll get 20 (probably different) opinions. In the end *you* are the one who needs to feel comfortable with it.

COMMON MISTAKES
You Try to Include *Everything*

Like many people, you may want to tell a potential employer everything you have ever done to try to impress them. A recruiter or employer will be looking for someone who can get to the point and express him or herself clearly and effectively, though, so remember to keep it simple and focus on those things that are most likely to get you an interview.

You Don't Use Any Particular Format

If you haven't had much experience in writing résumés, you may create one that is a mixture of job listings, skills, and accomplishments. This will only confuse your reader. Rather than leap straight in, work out which type of résumé suits your job search or your target vacancy best.

If you're still concerned about which résumé you think will suit you best, it might be worth visiting a career adviser. If you're still a student, your local further education college may well have a career adviser who can help you for free. Otherwise, the reference library may be able to suggest where to find help. If you're working already, bear in mind that you'll have to pay for this type of service, and rates can vary quite dramatically.

You Don't Follow Up

This is the commonest and most serious mistake. If you said you would phone to arrange an interview in your cover letter, make a note of the date and follow up. Although it can be difficult to make the call because of fear of rejection, you'll never get the job if you don't!

You Become Disheartened

Sales people have learned that you have to take a certain number of rejections before you get a "Yes." Finding a job is the same thing. If you receive a "No" after making a phone call for an appointment, tell yourself, "Well, that's a shame, but it's one less 'No' that I have to hear before I get a 'Yes.'"

FOR MORE INFORMATION

Book:
Bolles, Richard. *What Color is Your Parachute? A Practical Manual for Job-Hunters and Career-Changers.* Revised ed. Berkeley, CA: Ten Speed Press, 2006.

Writing a Great Cover Letter

GETTING STARTED

When you send in your résumé to a recruiter to apply for an advertised vacancy or to let him or her know that you're looking for work, you'll normally send a cover letter or e-mail too.

If you're applying for an existing vacancy, your cover letter should briefly describe the position you're applying for and where you saw it advertised, why you're particularly qualified for the job, and why you want to work for that specific company. If you're approaching an agency to register your résumé as part of your search for a new job, you should describe the type of job you're looking for, the skills you have that would make you an attractive candidate, your current salary, and any preferences you may have in terms of location.

Writing a cover letter is a fairly straightforward process, but there are certain steps you need to follow. If you sound both interesting and interested, you're much more likely to get noticed, interviewed, and employed!

FAQs
Is a cover letter still important these days? Job hunting has changed so much over the last few years.

You're quite right, the way that people look for jobs has changed a lot in a short space of time. In particular, the Internet has had a huge impact for both employers and job seekers; jobs are advertised online, applied for online, and even some pre-interview "weeding out" is done online in some cases. However, remember that the basic premise of the job hunt hasn't changed; however you apply for a job, you have to make yourself attractive to a prospective employer, and a knock-out cover letter works with your résumé to do just that.

A good cover letter can give a sense of who you are that may not come across in a résumé. It's a chance for other people to see how you write, and to gain a sense of how you view yourself and what you understand about them. When you come to write your letter, remember to think about its tone, how you're describing yourself and your skills, and also remember to include the results of any research you've done into the company or field of work you're interested in.

How long does a cover letter need to be?

You don't need to write a long missive. An effective cover letter is usually only two or three paragraphs long; they're best kept short and to the point. Read on to find out exactly what you need to include to make the impact you're after.

MAKING IT HAPPEN
Understand What You're Doing and Why

The cover letter is the very first thing a recruiter or manager reads. It must grab his or her attention and make him or her want to read your résumé and meet you. It's your first chance to stand out from the crowd.

One way of making an immediate good impression is by addressing your letter to the right person. Letters that are addressed to "Dear Sir/Madam" or "To Whom It May Concern" are usually thrown away. If you don't know the name of the precise person you need to write to, call the company to find out, or look it up on the Internet or at a reference library. If you have a copy of the company's catalog or annual report, it may even list key staffers there.

There are a variety of reasons why you might write a cover letter and send a résumé, such as responding to an advertisement, following up on meeting someone, or letting a potential employer know that you're available for work. Sometimes you may need to use your letter for a slightly different purpose, for example:

- when you contact a company to inquire about job openings—in this letter you would ask who you should send your résumé to;
- if you visited an organization in person and filled in a job application and want to follow up;
- when you apply for a job on the Internet—if you apply online via an agency, you may be asked to fill out a form to accompany your résumé attachment. Often you'll just be asked to give your contact details, but some agencies ask for a brief supporting statement to accompany your résumé.

If you're replying to an advertised job vacancy, a cover letter also gives you the opportunity to include details that the advertisement may have asked for but which can't easily be fitted into a résumé format, such as:

- current salary;
- desired future salary;
- notice period;
- preferences for geographical location;
- dates you may be available for interview (you may want to include these if you are about to go on vacation).

Draft the Letter

First of all, you need to say why you're writing. If you're applying for an existing vacancy, begin your letter by describing the position that interests you and explain why you're writing in the first sentence. For example:

- I am very interested in the position of Production Manager as described in your advertisement of September 19 on the *Daily Post* Web site.

Alternatively, if you're writing following a recommendation from someone already working at, or known to, the company:

- I have been given your name by Ms Mary Robertson regarding the position in Human Resources.

Show How You Are Interested in the Job

It's extremely important that you show how interested you are in the job. Take time to show that you've done your homework and that you understand what the company does and what its goals are. Visit the relevant company's Web site (if it has one) and look at any recent news articles, especially its press releases. You should also read business newspapers and trade magazines. These will

---

"You need to have what could be called seduction skills—this is not a world of command and control."

Raoul Pinnell

give you a sense of any industry issues facing the company you're interested in. They may also have particular information about the goals of your target company. Your local library will have lots of newspapers, magazines, and reference books that you can use. They also often have an Internet connection, if you don't have access to the Web at home. Save any articles or printouts on the company somewhere safe so that you can find them easily if you're asked to an interview.

To get across the fact that you've read the job advertisement thoroughly and that you've understood it, match the language you use in your letter to the advertisement itself. For example, if the job description mentions "team leader," use that job title.

Also, make sure you've included all the information requested in the advertisement. If the recruiters want to know your current salary and notice period, make sure you've mentioned them.

Tell Them Why They Need *You*

Describe your qualifications early in the letter to grab the interest of the personnel officer or manager. What will really make a difference is if you explain how you can help the organization achieve its goals. For example:

- I understand that your company is planning on creating a Web presence to support your sales. In my current position as Director of Internet Sales for Speedy Sales Company, I have helped to increase our market share by 13% in the past year.

If you can, show how you and you alone can help this company deal with the challenges it faces.

Request an Interview

Some people feel uncomfortable about asking for an interview with a prospective employer and prefer to wait and see if they're contacted by the company or person in question. A more proactive approach makes a bigger impact, however. If you want to ask for an interview, you could say in your letter that you're going to be in their area on a particular date and that you would be available for an interview. Alternatively, you can simply say something like, "I look forward to discussing how my qualifications can help your organization to be more successful."

Remember the Essentials

Now you've done all the planning, you can put everything together.

- Be yourself. Résumés are factual records of your experiences and skills. A good cover letter is your chance to show your personality and stand out from the crowd of other applicants as the interview shortlist is drawn up. Keep the letter professional, but don't be afraid to show your enthusiasm, your willingness to work hard, and your interest in the position.
- Make sure your cover letter looks professional. Check that there are no grammatical or spelling errors, and read it carefully before you send it off. If possible, ask a friend to check it for you too. Don't just rely on your computer spellchecker!

- As with résumés, most letters are submitted by e-mail these days, but if you're submitting by mail, use the highest quality paper that you can afford.
- Use a standard and easily readable font such as Times New Roman or Arial.
- If you're mailing the cover letter and résumé, send them in a large flat envelope. You may want to send two copies in case the recruiter needs to show your letter and résumé to different people, and photocopies or scans will be clearer if the originals have not been folded.
- If you're e-mailing the cover letter and résumé, remember to check that you've attached the files before you send the e-mail! Also tell the e-mail recipient what type of file you're attaching and be prepared to send it in another format in case they have difficulty opening it.

COMMON MISTAKES
You Use a Cover Letter Template

Reading through examples of cover letters in books can help you to understand what to include, and the layout and tone for different kinds of letters. Do remember to change the letters to fit your particular needs, though. Most managers will have seen hundreds of cover letters and will not want to hear the same old phrases. Make sure you personalize each of your cover letters so that they're targeted at a particular person and company, and so that they represent you and your uniqueness. Some people literally "fill in the gaps," and write a generic cover letter that they "customize" by handwriting the recipient's name and their own signature. No-one will be impressed by this, so don't do it.

You Use the Same Cover Letter for All Your Job Applications

A cover letter is meant to show that you really want to work for one particular company—taking the time to write a personal, company-specific letter will make all the difference to the impression you give! Using the same cover letter for all your applications also increases the likelihood of your making mistakes when you're tired or in a rush—you may inadvertently mention the wrong company in the body of your letter. Tailor your letter to the company you're applying to. It may be more time-consuming than returning to an old document, but this is your big chance to explain why you are the only person worth considering for this job. Why would you want to shoot yourself in the foot?

FOR MORE INFORMATION

Book:
Bolles, Richard. *What Color is Your Parachute? A Practical Manual for Job-Hunters and Career-Changers.* Revised ed. Berkeley, CA: Ten Speed Press, 2006.

Web Site:
Monster.com: **www.monster.com**

"Be bold, be bold, and everywhere, Be bold."   Edmund Spenser

Preparing for Different Types of Interview

GETTING STARTED

Looking for a new job can be a long and tiring process, but when you get to the interview stage, you know that the end is in sight, whatever happens. Quite understandably, some people find interviews nerve-wracking; it's not easy to see your professional life laid out before you on your résumé and then have a series of questions fired at you. Preparation can help, though, and part of that process is being aware of the different types of interviews that you may be asked to attend. Some of them are industry-specific, some are more suitable for experienced employees, some are designed to root out the best first-jobbers. This actionlist gives you an overview of the different types of interview out there and what you need to do to let your natural talent shine.

FAQs

I feel much more comfortable talking to one person than a group of people, but I've been asked to attend a panel interview. I'm really nervous. What can I do to help myself?

First of all, don't panic. You'll just tire yourself out. Keep calm and remember how well you've done to get to this stage—lots of other candidates won't have got this far! Next, find out as much as you can about who you'll be meeting and then plan what you need to say to impress them. This doesn't mean pretending to be someone you're not; rather that you're good at what you do, on top of your game, and you'd like to work with them. If you feel nervous, take plenty of deep breaths before you go in and before you speak. If you don't hear a question clearly or aren't sure if you understand it, don't be afraid to check. Read on for more help!

MAKING IT HAPPEN
Deal with Telephone Interviews

Initial interviews by telephone are becoming more common, but they're quite challenging for both parties. You probably normally use the phone either to talk with friends whom you know, and can visualize, or for business calls with people you don't need to know. Getting to know someone on the phone can be awkward: the absence of visual feedback is disconcerting. As always, preparation and practice will provide some help.

Be well equipped
- Have everything ready before you start: papers, pen, information you'll need to put across accurately, dates, and so on.
- Think carefully about the likely shape of the interview. What information do you need to give? What questions do you need to ask?
- Make sure you find a quiet room to take the call in, where you won't be interrupted or have any distractions. You may need to refer to some notes, but try not to rustle your papers too much. It may be best to arrange to take the call at lunchtime or at home after work. Most HR professionals are used to having to interview clients later in the day, so this may be a good option for you.

Be Aware of Your Own Voice
- It may sound strange, but don't talk too much! Pauses—even very short ones—are awkward on the phone and with no visual cues to guide you it's tempting to fill spaces with words. You may end up saying more than you mean to.
- Take care not to become monotonous—your voice is important because you cannot make an impression visually. As you would in any face-to-face interview, sound positive, friendly, and business-like.

Listen to the Interviewer
- Since you get no visual information on the phone, you should pay careful attention to the non-verbal aspects of speech—tone, pitch, inflection, for example—to pick up clues about what the interviewer is interested in.
- Make notes of important facts and agreements—it's easy to forget things when there is no "picture" to reinforce them

Cope with Competence-Based Interviews

The idea behind competence-based interviews (often called behavioral interviews) is to determine how well suited you are to a job based upon what you've learned from situations in the past. Most interviews incorporate some competence-based questions, because research shows that they seem to be the most effective form of assessment—your knowledge and experience are being judged against the specific criteria of the job. Competence-based questions usually start "Give me an example of when . . . " or "Describe a situation where . . . ."

As a rule of thumb, there are certain competences that almost all employers will be interested in. A shortlist of favorites is planning and organizing; decision-making; communicating; influencing others; teamwork; achieving results; leadership.

Prepare Examples

Given that the interview will focus on past experience, it's useful to think about examples you could use to show how you've developed the core competences outlined in the list above. When you look back at these experiences, ask yourself the following questions:
- What did you do personally?
- How did you overcome barriers or pitfalls?
- What did you achieve?
- Is there anything you would have done differently?
- What did you learn from the experience?

"Business pressures are good for the soul: when it has unburdened itself of them, it plays all the more fully and enjoys life."

Johann Wolfgang von Goethe

While you may not be asked precisely these questions, they'll prepare you for areas of questioning that you're very likely to encounter in the interview.

Know the Job

Before an interview of this type, read the job description very carefully and focus on the specific requirements of the position. Think about the issues and responsibilities related to the job. You can try to anticipate the sorts of questions you may be asked based on those requirements and responsibilities. Also think about your present job and in particular how your role fits within the team.

Cope with Internal Interviews

Some companies like to use an interview process for filling internal vacancies or making career plans. Within an organization there can be all sorts of assumptions that may complicate this process. For example, some people feel that the company should know them well enough from experience and appraisals to make an interview unnecessary. Others worry about the politics of the situation, and the consequences of failure. Some may be inclined to treat it too informally or lightly.

The general rule is to treat these interviews as you would an external application until you have definitive information that things are different. It's much better to err on the side of formality until you're sure what is required.

As ever, remember to do your homework beforehand and find out as much as you can about the job. If you have a human resources department, they'll probably be the best source of information. It's also a good idea to

- talk to your boss about your intended move if your interview is for a job in a different department. It could create a very nasty atmosphere if he or she finds out from someone else.
- find out what's required from you and how the decision-making process works.
- anticipate what the interviewer knows already and what he or she will want to know about your experience and competence. Don't take too much for granted in this area.

Don't Panic in Stress Interviews

Stress interviews involve putting the candidates under pressure to see how they respond to difficult people or unexpected events. Organizations should only use this technique when they can clearly show the need for it, and even then they should be careful how it is handled, taking account of the sensitivities of the interviewee. It can be an unnerving experience, but being aware that this is a recognized interviewing technique for some firms will help you to cope should you come across it. The sorts of industries that may employ this technique include banking and some security firms

Stress questions often come in the form of a role play, when the interviewer, *in his or her role*, may say something like: "I think your answer is totally inadequate: it doesn't deal with my concerns at all, can't you do better than that?" The interviewer is testing your ability to manage surprises and ambiguity. He or she will want to

see you keep the initiative and take responsibility for dealing with the situation appropriately.

The trick is not to take the remarks personally but to recognize that you're required to play a role. Take a deep breath, pause, keep your temper, and respond as naturally and accurately as you can.

Keep your wits about you because the technique is designed to catch you off guard. Create time for yourself to balance logic and emotion calmly in framing your response. If you can, try to anticipate what the next problem will be and keep ahead of the game.

Make Your Mark at Assessment Centers

This method of selection usually involves a group of candidates performing a number of different tasks and exercises over the course of one to three days. Assessment centers were traditionally used at the second stage of recruitment, but nowadays candidates are often asked to one at the first stage.

Assessment centers usually include:

1 Group exercises: role-playing, discussion, leadership exercises

2 Individual exercises. For example:
- written tests (such as report writing based on case studies)
- in-tray exercises (a business simulation where you're expected to sort through an in-tray, making decisions about how to deal with each item)
- presentation of an argument or data analysis
- psychometric tests
- interviews

3 Social events

4 Company presentations

You'll be assessed most of the time—the administrator should clarify this for you—so there's rarely an opportunity to let down your guard.

You can make these events a little less stressful with a few simple rules:

- The organization will probably tell you what they're looking for in their career literature or their invitation. Make sure you've read this, thought about it, and worked out how you show the behavior they're interested in.
- Behave naturally but thoughtfully. Do not attempt to play an exaggerated role—it's never what the assessors want to see!
- Make sure that you take part fully in all activities; assessors can only appraise what you show them.
- Don't be over competitive. The assessors are likely to be working to professional standards, not looking for the "winner." Unnatural behavior quickly becomes inappropriate and boorish.
- Take an overview. Most of the exercises have a purpose wider than the obvious. Try to stand back and look at things in context rather than rush straight in. With the in-tray exercise, for example, you'll probably find that some items are related and need to be tackled together.

Check All the Boxes at Technical Interviews

In this type of an interview you'll be asked specific questions relating to technical knowledge and skills. As you'd imagine, this approach is common and extremely useful

in research and technology companies' selection processes.

The organization will normally tell you in advance that they have a technical interview or if they want you to give a presentation on your thesis or experience. You need to be prepared for "applied" questions that ask for knowledge in a different form from the way you learned it at college. For example, "How would you design a commercially viable wind turbine?" or "How would you implement the requirements of data protection legislation in a small international organization?" Consider the "audience" and how your knowledge fits with their likely interests and priorities. What questions are they likely to ask?

Sometimes these presentations go wrong when interviewers ask very "obvious" questions; or one of them has a favorite or "trick" question. It's easy to be irritated by these, but you should remain calm and courteous. Try to see the interviewers as your "customer" and respond with patience.

As always, preparation and anticipation are the keys to success. Work out what your interviewers will want to know and make sure your knowledge is up to scratch in the correct areas.

Think On Your Feet in Panel Interviews

When you're looking for a job, sooner or later you may be asked to attend a panel interview. These are becoming more popular, as they

- save time and are efficient. Several interviewers meet in one place at one time, so the applicant does not need to be shuffled around from office to office and there is no schedule to follow or overrun.
- provide consistent information. You, as the job applicant, only need to tell your story once instead of repeating it over and over again in private meetings with each interviewer.

Although it can be quite daunting to walk into an interview where several people are present, a panel interview is also an excellent opportunity to show your strengths to a number of interviewers at once. A successful panel interview is one in which you come across as cool and confident and able to handle whatever is thrown your way.

To take the sting out of panel interviews, find out about the organization as well as the position you're applying for. Start with the company's Web site, if it has one, and try to get a copy of its annual report. Talk to people who may be familiar with the organization. Go to the library and see if any recent articles have been written about it.

Next, begin to prepare mentally for the possibility of a panel interview. Ask yourself what your major selling points are. How can you get these across to each member of the panel? This is particularly useful if you know beforehand who you're going to meet and what their responsibilities are. If, for example, you'll be meeting a sales director and a finance director, you might want to explain how you can do things in such a way that you achieve maximum sales of a product or service cost-effectively. If you like, see the panel interview as a type of presentation, and keep your audience in mind at all times.

If the prospect of this type of interview makes you nervous, try to combat your nerves with "visualization." This is a very good way of helping you feel and appear relaxed and confident. Before your interview, imagine what a panel interview might be like. Visualize yourself in a conference room with several people sitting around a large table. Imagine answering each question easily, bonding with each interviewer and having a successful interview.

Some people are uncomfortable using the visualization technique, but it's a really effective method. Remember, Jack Nicklaus claims that much of his golf success comes from mentally rehearsing each shot before he actually picks up a club. What has worked so well for him can work for you, too.

Answer the Questions

Sometimes in a panel interview it can feel as though questions are coming at you from all directions. Try to take the first question, answer it, then build on that answer to respond to the second interviewer. Make sure you answer every question so that none of the interviewers thinks you ignored his or her question.

Clarify questions if necessary. If you find a question confusing, don't be afraid to ask for further explanation; it shows that you're coping under pressure and also it will save time all around. Phrases such as, "Just to clarify . . ." or, "If I understand correctly, you want to know . . ." can help you to understand exactly what information the interviewers are looking for. If you're still unsure, you might want to check that you answers were understood and that you've answered the question fully. Simply ask the appropriate person, "Did I answer your question?"

As you're talking, make eye contact with each member of the panel in turn. This means catching the gaze of a particular member of the panel, holding it for about three seconds, and then moving to the next panel member. In reality, it's actually very difficult to look someone in the eye, count to three, and then move on, all while answering a challenging question, but with some practice it will become second nature. It's a really useful skill to develop for meetings of all types and for public speaking.

Resist the temptation to take the route with less pressure by letting members of the panel do all the talking. Remember, you're there to sell yourself and to do that you need to get your point across. If the people on the panel do all the talking, all they will remember about you is that you may be a good listener. Of course, you should certainly not interrupt members of the panel, but do make sure you discuss your strengths and the reasons they should employ you. Sell yourself as you would in an individual interview.

Keep Calm in "Scenario-Based" Interviews

Most interviewers have been carefully trained to look only for evidence and facts from the candidates past and therefore *never* to ask hypothetical questions. But sometimes—and especially with younger candidates who don't have much past work experience—an organization will be more interested in what the person can become in the future rather than what he or she is now.

There are techniques for doing this. They normally

"Where observation is concerned, chance favors only the prepared mind." Louis Pasteur

     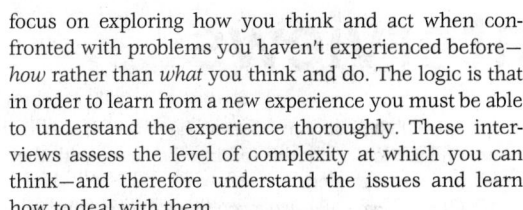

focus on exploring how you think and act when confronted with problems you haven't experienced before—*how* rather than *what* you think and do. The logic is that in order to learn from a new experience you must be able to understand the experience thoroughly. These interviews assess the level of complexity at which you can think—and therefore understand the issues and learn how to deal with them.

Typically you'll be asked in these interviews to take part in a conversation that gets more complex and wide-ranging as it progresses. You build a scenario further and further into the future. There are no right answers of course: the interviewer is looking for an ability to spot the right questions.

Knowing that the interview will take this form is some help, but there is really little that you can do to prepare for it. Being well rested and alert, relaxing and enjoying the challenge are the best tips.

COMMON MISTAKES
You Think You Can Wing It

You can't. You have to prepare for interviews if you want to do well. The amount of preparation you do will depend on the type of interview you're having or the type of job you want, but you have to show that you not only understand what the prospective job is about, but what you can bring to it, what challenges the business faces, what the state of the relevant industry is, and so on. You must be professional and show that you're the complete package.

FOR MORE INFORMATION

Web Site:
The Career Manager:
www.thecareermanager.com/Interview%20Advice.htm

"The cyclone derives its power from a calm center. So does a person."   Brendan Kenelly

Making an Impact in Interviews

GETTING STARTED

Well done! You've cleared the first hurdle in your job search with a great résumé and cover letter, and have been invited for an interview—you've already found some way to stand out from the crowd. Now you need to build on this success. This actionlist will help you prepare mentally and emotionally for your interview. Read on to find out how to make a real impact with prospective employers.

FAQs

Are there any interview questions that I should prepare for whatever type of job I'm going for?

Obviously there are no hard and fast rules about what an interviewer will ask you, but there are a few things that you should get straight in your head as you start your interview preparation. Keep these questions in mind:

- Why do you think you're the best person for the job?
- What is it about this job that attracts you?
- What is it about this organization that has made you apply for the position?
- Who will interview you and what do you know about them?
- What is the appropriate dress and/or image for this organization?

MAKING IT HAPPEN

Refresh Your Memory About Your Résumé or Application Form

As a first step, remind yourself thoroughly of all the information on your résumé or application form (it's a good idea to keep a photocopy of anything you send to a prospective employer for this very reason). It may have been some time since you applied for the job, so it's no bad idea to look back over what you said way back when. Think about what questions you might be asked based on your education or work history. Some questions that might be difficult to answer include, "Why did you choose to study this subject?", "Why did you leave your last job?", or "Why did you have a period of unemployment?". Write notes about what you're going to say and practice your answers with a friend or family member.

Research the Organization

Finding out as much as you can about the company you're visiting will not only help you decide if it's the sort of organization you'd like to work for, but may give you some ideas for questions to ask the interviewer. If you find an opportunity to show that you've done your research, this will signal to the interviewer that you're enthusiastic about the job, as well as knowledgeable about the market.

The best place to start looking is the company Web site. Focus on the annual report, news, press releases, and biographies of key members of staff. This will give you a feel for the organization—its values, its success factor, and its people. If the company doesn't have a Web site, call them and ask to be sent this information along with their most up-to-date catalog.

If you have time, it's also a good idea to cast your net a bit wider and to research current factors that might affect the organization. These can include industry trends, competitive issues, strategic direction, and particular challenges or opportunities.

Set yourself the challenge of finding out about these five essential questions before the interview:

- How large is the organization?
- How is the organization structured?
- What is its main business?
- Who are its major competitors?
- What is the organization's work culture like?

Decide What *You* Want to Get from the Interview

In their nerves before an interview, candidates often forget that there are two sides to the process: clearly, the prospective employer wants to evaluate you, but you too need to work out if you want to work with them. It's a good idea to prepare a list of questions that will help you decide whether or not this job is a good fit for your personality and your career goals. For example, you might want to ask your interviewers what progression prospects they see for the eventual jobholder, what the company's values are, or what the professional development policy is. In general, it's a good idea not to ask about benefits and salary at a first interview, unless the interviewer brings them up. Get the offer first, then talk about money!

You also need to work out the key points you want to make about your strengths and skills. When you prepared your résumé, you listed the principal strengths and skills that you thought an employer would be looking for. Look at that list again, choose a skill, and think of a recent situation you've been in that will demonstrate that strength or skill to an interviewer. If possible, include any concrete results you achieved through using it.

Even though you may feel under pressure at points, always focus on the positive in your answers, even when you've been asked to talk about a difficult situation or your weaknesses. That way, you'll come across as someone who rises to a challenge and looks for opportunities to improve and develop.

Prepare Yourself Mentally

Many people, including athletes and salespeople, prepare themselves for challenging situations by mentally picturing a successful result. This is a great method that can also be used to help you to perform well in an interview.

Before the interview, imagine yourself being professional, interesting, and enthusiastic in your interview. Also imagine yourself leaving the interview with a good feeling about how you did. This will put you in a positive frame of mind and help you to be at your very best in the interview.

Practice!

If possible, ask a friend or family member to role-play the interview with you. If you have a career counselor or coach, they'll also be able to help you out here. Give the other person a list of questions that you think you might be asked (and ask them to throw in a few of their own so that you have to get used to thinking on your feet!), and then role-play the interview, asking your friend afterwards for honest feedback. Videotape the role-play if you can so that you can watch your body language; this is often more telling than you realize.

Start the ball rolling with some standard questions that interviewers often ask:

- Tell me a little bit about yourself.
- Where do you see yourself in your career five years from now?
- What are you most proud of in your career?
- What is your greatest strength?
- What is your biggest weakness?
- Describe a difficult situation and how you handled it.
- Can you tell me about a time when you had to motivate a team?

You don't need to go right back to your junior years if someone asks you to tell them a bit about yourself: use it to give a very brief overview of yourself including a short history of recent employment.

Create a Positive Impression on the Day Itself

When the day of the interview dawns, be punctual. Better still, be early to give yourself some preparation and relaxation time. If you're not sure of the location of the company, you might want to do a practice run of the journey so you can be sure to leave yourself enough time. Have a glass of water, flick through company magazines if they're available, and try to get a feel for the atmosphere, as this will help you to decide if it's the sort of place you can see yourself being happy working in. It will also give you an idea of what to expect in the interview, and the sort of candidate the interviewers will be looking for. If he or she isn't too busy, take some time to talk to the receptionist. They are often asked by recruiters to act as an extra "screen" during the recruitment process; if candidates are rude to the receptionist, they often don't get much further.

Be Enthusiastic

You know why you're interested in this job, and you need to convey that interest to the recruiters—interviewees who are excited about the organization get job offers! Even if it's true, don't say that you're eager to get the job because it pays well. Instead, be ready to talk about what you can offer the company, how the position will expand your skills, and why this kind of work would be satisfying and meaningful to you. Don't overdo it, though, as this may come across as insincere or overconfident.

Be Honest

The overall impression you're trying to create is of an enthusiastic, professional, positive, and sincere person. These things will come across from the word go if you follow the basic rules of giving a firm handshake, a friendly smile, and maintaining good eye contact throughout the interview. Never lie in the interview or attempt to bluff your way through difficult questions—it's just not worth it. Good preparation should ensure that you don't have to resort to this. Speak clearly and respectfully to the interviewers and remember that swearing and flirting are definite no-nos.

Wherever possible, back up your responses to questions with evidence-based replies. For example, if an interviewer asks you how you manage conflict within a team, it's best to give a brief general response and then focus on a specific example of how you've done this in the past. Illustrating your answers with real examples gives you the opportunity to focus on your personal contribution, and will be more impressive than giving a vague, hypothetical reply.

Look and Sound the Part

Even though what you're saying in an interview is the main thing, it's important to look professional as well. You should feel comfortable in what you wear, but it's better to turn up "too smart" than "too casual"—people will take you seriously if you dress respectably. If you're applying for jobs in media or the arts a suit may not be necessary, but dressing smartly will always give the impression that you care about getting this job.

It's always a good idea to take some antiperspirant with you to an interview, as when people are nervous they tend to sweat. You may also find yourself a bit hot and disheveled if you had to rush to get to the interview in good time (although if you've prepared your journey well, this shouldn't happen!). Make sure you have time to freshen up before the interview. This will help your confidence, and spare the interviewers from a sweaty handshake or, worse still, a bad odor when you enter the room. And remember, don't go overboard on the perfume or aftershave—that would count as a bad odor, too.

COMMON MISTAKES
You "Misread" the Interviewer

People tend to underestimate the level of formality and professionalism required in an interview, and some interviewers even create a more social than professional situation to catch you off guard. If you find yourself in an interview with a more casual approach than is appropriate, change your behavior as soon as you notice. The interviewers are more likely to remember your behavior at the end of the interview than at the beginning. On the other hand, if the environment or the interviewer is more casual than you realized, don't worry. You're *expected* to look and act in a highly professional and formal way in an interview. Use your instincts to judge how much you need to change your behavior to show that you'd fit into the company culture.

You Use Humor Inappropriately

To make a situation less tense, people sometimes use humor to lighten the mood. If you've said something you think is funny and received a negative reaction, though, it's best not to call attention to the situation by apologizing. Try to act as if nothing happened and go back to

---

"Things aren't always the way they seem from the outside." Phil Nolan

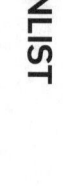

behaving professionally. Whatever you do, don't follow inappropriate humor with more humor.

You Didn't Do Your Homework
You get to the interview and realize that you really know nothing about this organization. Hopefully, you arrived early and have some time in reception. Often, booklets and leaflets found in receptions provide quite a bit of information about the company, its industry, its products and services. Look at them, look around, and learn everything you can. Talk to the receptionist and ask him or her questions that may be helpful to you in the interview. It's possible to learn quite a bit about the organization on the fly, but nothing works better than doing your homework.

You Criticize Your Former Employer
Avoid this at all costs. It gives the interview a very negative feeling, and will leave the interviewer wondering if you would criticize his or her organization when you left. This kind of criticism usually happens when someone is asked why they're leaving (or have left) their last position. The best way to answer this is to talk about the future rather than the past, and to show your eagerness to take on challenging career opportunities.

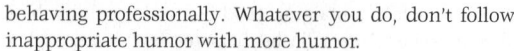

FOR MORE INFORMATION

Book:
Bolles, Richard. *What Color is Your Parachute? A Practical Manual for Job-Hunters and Career-Changers.* Revised ed. Berkeley, CA: Ten Speed Press, 2006.

Web Site:
Monster.com: **www.monster.com**

"The person who knows 'how' will always have a job. The person who knows 'why' will always be his boss."

Diane Ravitch

Answering Tricky Interview Questions

GETTING STARTED

Job interviews are the single most important part of the selection process—for both you and your future employer. Once your résumé (or personal referral by someone whose opinion the hiring manager trusts) has established that you meet the basic skills and background requirements, it is the interview that establishes you as a candidate who will fit well into an organization's culture and future plans.

While most interview questions are generally straightforward, unambiguous inquiries, some interviewers will throw in surprises specifically intended to explore your thinking and expectations at a deeper level. Or they may be meant to throw you off guard to see how you react in high stress or confusing circumstances. Or they may not be intentionally tricky at all. They may merely be invented by the interviewer, or borrowed from lists of questions available on the Internet, with no idea what their value is, or how to assess your response as it relates to the requirements of the job.

How you answer tricky questions could determine whether you will receive an offer from the organization. But it's also important to remember that what those questions are, and how your answers are received, can tell you volumes about whether this is a company you want to work for.

Here are some of the questions you might want to consider as you're preparing yourself for a job interview:

- What aspects of your career do you feel especially good about, and how can you make sure those are discussed in the interview?
- What aspects of your career so far do you feel especially worried about discussing?
- Can you formulate answers to questions about those aspects in advance?
- How can you use the interview to learn about the potential employer?

FAQs
What if I don't understand how the question relates to the job I'm applying for?

Some questions—especially questions in which you are given a scenario and asked to think your way through to a solution—are designed to help the interviewer understand your ability to make tough decisions, or be a leader in high pressure situations.

True, it's reasonable to expect that you won't ever find yourself stranded in a lifeboat, charged with deciding which fellow survivor to throw overboard to conserve rations. But the way you reason out your decision may tell the interviewer much about you—for example, how you would choose which product to take out of inventory to conserve valuable warehouse space. Try to answer these kinds of questions based on business strategy.

Some questions ask me to divulge my greatest weakness. How can I answer these questions without disqualifying myself for the job?

Such questions are usually designed to discover the extent of your self-knowledge. We all have weaknesses, and it's unreasonable to expect you to be perfect in every way. Keep your answer short and dignified. Identify only one area of weakness that you're aware of, but also describe what you are doing to strengthen that area. Don't try to be too clever by turning a negative into a positive, saying things like, "My biggest weakness is that I'm a determined worker and won't give up until the job is done well and completely." You aren't fooling anyone.

Sometimes I get the impression that the interviewer doesn't know why I'm being asked a certain question, and that my answer would be beyond his or her understanding. How do I salvage that situation?

A company that hires unqualified interviewers to select qualified candidates may not be one you would like to work for . . . so you may not want to salvage such a situation. But if you're determined to give yourself the best chance to work at this organization, help the interviewer out by exploring the reasons behind the question and what exactly is being looked for in the way of response.

Even though you may not answer the question itself, you will still benefit from the conversation. You will position yourself in the interviewer's mind as someone who is not rattled by ambiguity, but instead works calmly and cooperatively with team members to arrive at the best possible outcome.

MAKING IT HAPPEN
Understand the Purpose of the Interview

The best job interviews are respectful encounters that allow mutual discovery. It may feel as if the employer has all the power—after all, it's the employer who will decide whether to offer you the job. Ultimately, however, it is you who holds the power, because it will be you who decides whether to accept the job. So interviews are just as important for you in the selection process as they are for the interviewer.

Keep that power balance in mind, and it will help you stay calm when tricky questions are asked.

Assume That the Interviewer Is Probably As Uncomfortable with the Process As You Are

Put yourself in the interviewer's shoes, and assume that he or she is slightly uncomfortable with the process as well. Few people relish meeting someone new and

---

"To ask the hard question is simple."

peppering them with probing questions. You may be the 25th candidate for a job, so the interviewer may feel tired of the same old questions and the same pat, rehearsed answers. Remember also that the interviewer was once sitting in your seat, applying for his or her job in the company and worrying about the same surprise questions that you are. The resulting empathy will help break down barriers

Prepare yourself in advance by identifying the topic areas that might be the trickiest for you. Then think carefully about how you might answer them. Broadly speaking, there are eight areas of questioning that could pose a challenge for you:

- your experience and management skills
- your opinion about industry or professional trends
- the reasons why you are leaving your current job
- financial or other value of your past achievements
- your work habits
- your salary expectations
- your expectations for the future
- your personality and relationship skills or problems.

Imagine which of these areas might be discussed and formulate in advance the general thoughts and responses you want to express. But don't rehearse answers to anticipated questions word for word.

Never Lie
Many interviewers do this work for a living, so they are more experienced at hearing the answers that candidates think they want to hear than you are at delivering them. Be candid and clear, and use lengthy answers only when you see that demonstrating your strategic thought process in detail will add valuable information.

When in Doubt, Try to Understand the Business Reason Behind the Question. Ask Questions of Your Own
"What do you mean?" or "Could you rephrase that question?" are perfectly acceptable queries in any civilized conversation. Job interviews are no different.

Be Prepared to Answer Questions about Salary
During the interview process you want to keep the focus on your worth, not your cost. Early in the process, politely decline to go into details about past salary and future expectations. Many companies have a policy of offering salaries only at a certain percentage above a candidate's previous salary. If your previous salary, for whatever reason, was below market average or below your worth, you shouldn't have to be forced to accept a lower salary in the future.

If a question comes up about your salary expectations, make sure you have done your homework. You should have decided ahead of time on a salary range that is acceptable to you. Make sure the top of the range is well above the figure you would be thrilled to accept, and the bottom of the range slightly above your predetermined "walkaway" figure.

Study Question Lists
Many lists of questions are available online. Interviewers use them, and you can, too. Although you may not be asked those specific questions during the interview, the knowledge that you have done everything you can by preparing in advance will help you feel relaxed, confident, and capable.

COMMON MISTAKES
You Criticize Your Former Employer or Coworkers
If you are asked why you are seeking new employment, focus on your positive ambitions, not any resentments or grudges you may harbor. Talk in terms of what has worked in your career, not what has failed.

You Get Angry or Defensive
A job interview is part gamesmanship, part blind date, part tea party. Use your social skills to smooth over edgy moments or bristly reactions to possibly offensive questions. And don't take anything personally.

You Give Away Your Power
You are at the interview to assess the desirability of the job, just as much as to sell your own desirability to the company. Remembering that will help you to keep your dignity and protect you from feeling compelled to answer inappropriate, irrelevant, or intrusive questions.

You Use Scripted Answers to Anticipated Questions
These are inauthentic, and the interviewer has heard them all before. Original responses, even if they are slightly clumsy, will be more valuable to both you and the interviewer. They are a more accurate guide as to whether there is indeed a match between you and your potential new employer.

FOR MORE INFORMATION

Books:
Deluca, Matthew J. *Best Answers to the 201 Most Frequently Asked Interview Questions.* New York: McGraw-Hill Professional Publishing, 1996.
Fry, Ronald W. *101 Great Answers to the Toughest Interview Questions.* 5th ed. Franklin Lakes, NJ: Career Press, 2006.
Yate, Martin John. *Great Answers to Tough Interview Questions.* 6th ed. Dover, NH: Kogan Page, 2005.

Web site:
Monster Career Center—tough interview questions: **www.content.monster.com**

See also:
✔ Handling Inappropriate Questions in an Interview (pp. 881–882)

"Bromidic though it may sound, some questions don't have answers, which is a terribly difficult lesson to learn."
Katharine Graham

Handling Inappropriate Questions in an Interview

GETTING STARTED

Occasionally, you may get interviewed by someone who is less than politically correct. He or she may ask inappropriate questions, and this always creates a dilemma for the job candidate. Although this happens rarely, it is still useful to have worked through your strategy, just in case it should occur.

Here are issues that you will need to consider when preparing to deal with inappropriate questions:

- What kinds of question would feel inappropriate to me?
- If I get asked this kind of question, what does that say about the culture of the organization I am considering taking a job with?
- What are my options for dealing with inappropriate questions?
- Which of the strategic options fits my particular situation?

FAQs

How frequently do inappropriate questions get asked in an interview?

More than likely, this will never happen to you. Most hiring managers are very professional, and well trained in appropriate interviewing techniques. Nonetheless, it's much better to be prepared.

Is there any group of people who are more likely to get asked inappropriate questions?

Yes. Women are much more likely to get asked inappropriate questions than men, and the questions are generally of a sexual or gender-based nature.

Younger people are more likely to get asked these questions than older people. And people of a non-dominant ethnic group may be more likely to be asked inappropriate questions.

Are inappropriate questions illegal?

It depends on the laws of the country in which you are working. However, many inappropriate questions are discriminatory, and are therefore likely to be illegal. Other questions are considered inappropriate simply because they are of a personal nature and have nothing to do with qualifications for the job.

MAKING IT HAPPEN

In order to prepare yourself for any interview, you need to think through all possible scenarios of what could happen and prepare yourself for those eventualities. Basically, there are two steps in preparing to handle inappropriate questions: deciding what is inappropriate or uncomfortable to you, and deciding how you will respond. The following pointers break this process up into more detailed steps.

Familiarize Yourself with the Law on Questions That It Is Illegal to Ask in an Interview

These are the worst type of inappropriate questions, and it is in order to try to prevent these questions from being asked that legislation has been created. In the United States, these questions fall under the Equal Employment Opportunity (EEO) laws. One of the simplest ways to find a list of these kinds of questions is to look in a human resource textbook. Some examples of illegal questions in the United States are:

- Why would a woman want a job like this?
- Are you planning to start a family?
- How old are you?
- Do you have any physical defects?
- Do you have any religious affiliation?
- Are you married, divorced, single?
- Do you have any children? How old are they?
- Will your husband/wife move if we offer you this job?
- How will you get to work?
- Have you ever been arrested?

There are complex reasons why each of these questions is inappropriate, but the underlying theme is that they might be discriminatory and, as such, illegal.

Make a List of Interview Questions That Would Feel Inappropriate to You

As mentioned earlier, these might be questions that have to do with your personal life. If you are married or cohabiting, they might be questions about your partner or children. If you are single, they might be questions about what you enjoy doing after working hours. But only you can decide if a question feels inappropriate to you. If it is not work-related and if it makes you feel uncomfortable, embarrassed, invaded, or angry, then it is an inappropriate question. By the same token, you also have to decide if the interviewer is just trying to make a human connection with you and is attempting to break the ice.

For example, let's say that your résumé says you worked for Shell Oil in Brazil. The interviewer asks, "What was your favorite thing to do on the weekends in Brazil?" This question has nothing to do with your job experience, but it probably won't make you feel uncomfortable. Perhaps you enjoyed hiking on weekends, and that allows the interviewer to tell you that this organization has a hiking club and that there are many good hiking trails nearby. By contrast, it could be that you worked as a volunteer in hospitals that care for children with AIDS on weekends, and you really don't want to get into a discussion about why you do AIDS volunteer work. In this case, the question might feel inappropriate to you.

Learn to Discern Why the Interviewer Is Asking This Kind Of Question

There are two basic ways to discover the interviewer's

motivation for asking a question that seemingly has nothing to do with the job you are applying for. The more subtle way is to watch for nonverbal cues. Pay attention to his or her body language and the way in which the interviewer uses his or her voice. Watch facial expressions, whether or not the interviewer's body seems tense and closed, and whether he or she makes direct eye contact. Most of us are reasonably good at interpreting these kinds of cues instinctively. You also should pay attention to your own responses. If you have a physical reaction to what is said—if you find yourself holding your breath, or your heart starts to pound, or you find your hands clenching—then your body is telling you there is something you don't trust about this person. The most overt way to discern why an interviewer is asking a question that makes you uncomfortable is simply to ask, "Why do you want to know?"

Be Aware of Your Options for Responding to Inappropriate Questions

Never let an interviewer intimidate you by asking inappropriate questions. You have a right to be treated professionally and with dignity. Your options for responding can include:

- humor: responding to the question as if it were a joke, giving the interviewer an opportunity to save face and to ask more appropriate questions;
- avoidance: ignoring the question and changing the subject;
- compliance: answering the question;
- gentle confrontation: this generally consists of asking the interviewer, "Why do you want to know?"
- strong confrontation: telling the interviewer that the question is inappropriate and that you are not going to answer it.

Decide Which Response Best Fits Your Situation

There are several factors to take into account in deciding how to respond. They include:

- the severity or outrageousness of the question;
- your sense of the interviewer's motivation in asking the question;
- how strongly you desire this job;
- the extent to which you believe that this kind of question is a reflection of the corporate culture.

You will have to weigh these factors and decide whether the question is fairly benign and can be safely ignored on the one hand, or whether the interviewer's behavior crosses ethical lines and must be confronted on the other. If you really want this job, you may overlook the interviewer's question. If the question is so awful that you know you could never work for this company, you may be more likely to be confrontational.

COMMON MISTAKES
You Want the Job So Much, You Will Do Anything to Please the Interviewer

If you are desperate to get a position, you answer a question that you find inappropriate and end up leaving the interview feeling embarrassed, angry, or ashamed. You must avoid feeling this desperate when you are job hunting. Make sure that you have worked hard to create several attractive interview options. Also spend time preparing yourself mentally for the interview, so that you feel a sense of self-worth and self-esteem when you walk in.

You Overreact to the Inappropriate Question

People who have a militant or political agenda tend to do this. A minority may see every comment as a potential insult: for example a woman candidate may perceive interview questions as sexist. With this kind of attitude, an interview is seen as an opportunity to right the wrongs of the world, and the result is that the candidate will not get the job. If you have a tendency to overreact, keep in mind that there are appropriate and inappropriate places to fight your battles, and a job interview is probably not the best place to make a point about your political values, however deeply felt.

FOR MORE INFORMATION

Web sites:
General resources
Careerbuilder.com: **www.careerbuilder.com**
iVillage: **www.ivillage.com/work**
Legal resources
U.S. Equal Employment Opportunity Commission:
www.eeoc.gov

See also:
✓ Answering Tricky Interview Questions
(pp. 879–880)

"Confidence is a mark of respect—and respect is appreciated by anyone of courage and honor."

Anne-Marie-Louise d' Orléans

Understanding Psychometric Tests: A Survivor's Guide

GETTING STARTED

Psychometric tests are often used to help in career guidance and counseling, and to help in selection decisions. There are two basic types of tests: aptitude tests and achievement tests. Aptitude tests measure a person's interests and their abilities to acquire or learn new skills. Achievement tests measure what a person already knows or can do right now. It is helpful to understand the different types of tests that you might run across in your job search and how to approach them. Here are some questions to ask yourself as you consider the implications of being tested:

- How should I prepare for the different types of psychometric test?
- Are there resources that can help me to prepare for a particular kind of test?
- Are there test-taking skills that I can learn?
- What can I do if I don't like the results of the test?

FAQs
Why would an employer use psychometric testing?

Large organizations often use psychometric testing in their hiring and promotion processes as a way of ascertaining whether or not a candidate has the knowledge, skills, and personality characteristics needed to be a good fit for a job. It is frequently an important part of assessment center processes where candidates are identified for future leadership positions.

When can I use psychometric testing in my own career planning?

If you are just beginning your career, or if you are contemplating a major career change, psychometric testing can help you to identify different kinds of career that would fit your interests and personality (see John Holland's self-directed search Web site in "Best Sources of Help" below). University career development offices offer a battery of tests for students and alumni. Probably the most popular career instrument is the Strong–Campbell Index. This is sometimes used by career coaches as well.

How accurate are these tests?

None of these psychometric tests are 100% accurate, but any decent test should have background information on reliability and validity. Libraries have reference books on the various kinds of psychometric tests, what they measure, what research has been done on them, and statistical information on their reliability and validity. If you are taking these tests for career planning purposes, it is best to take several different tests, compare the results, and look for themes and patterns.

MAKING IT HAPPEN
Be Physically Prepared for Taking a Psychometric Test

This might seem like strange advice, since psychometric tests measure psychological and intellectual propensities. However, research has shown that people perform better in all kinds of psychometric tests when they are well rested and in good physical shape. Another interesting fact is that people do better in tests when they are slightly hungry, so eat lightly before taking one.

Prepare for Aptitude Tests

Since aptitude tests measure your interests and your ability to acquire and learn new skills, you can't really prepare for these tests in the way that you would for a math or history exam. Your best preparation is to spend time thinking about your life and career goals, and the things you love to do. Career-related aptitude tests are based on self-awareness, so the more you know yourself, the more likely the test results are to be useful to you. Richard Bolle's book, *What Color is Your Parachute?*, is full of great self-awareness exercises.

Skills-related aptitude tests generally test your problem-solving ability in a particular field. For example, if you are going to be working on equipment, designing with CAD-CAM tools, or doing architectural work, you might be tested on your ability to do spatial reasoning. The best preparation is to be well rested and relaxed so that you can focus clearly on the questions and provide your best answers.

Preparing for Achievement Tests

The two most common achievement tests are those that measure verbal reasoning and mathematical ability. These kinds of test have been used in schools and workplaces for decades and are considered valid and reliable tools. They also have been shown to be pretty good predictors of success in academic work and in certain job situations.

Before you go for the test, find out exactly what skills and knowledge are being examined. There are hundreds of test preparation books on the market, and it is a really good idea to use one for the kind of test you are taking. The books typically explain how the questions are structured, provide test taking strategies, and have sample tests you can take, so that you can evaluate your own level of skills and knowledge. After taking a sample test, you can use the book's study guides to work on strengthening your weaker areas and then retest yourself to see if you have improved. This approach typically increases your score by a significant percentage.

Learn Test-taking Skills

The first lesson of test taking is to read the instructions very carefully. Make sure you understand them

---

"The first steps to becoming a really great manager are simply common sense; but common sense is not very common."

Gerald M. Blair

completely. Don't be afraid to ask for clarification from the person administering the test. You'd be surprised how many people just jump into taking tests, and end up getting a much lower score than they deserve because they missed some important information that could have been helpful.

For example, in some tests, unanswered questions do not count against you. The instructions may tell you that wrong answers will be subtracted from right answers to provide a ratio score for the test. If you understand this, you know that you should skip over questions where you're not sure of the answer, and that you shouldn't guess answers. Some tests are timed and, if so, it's important to know how much time you have left so you can focus on the questions that you are most likely to answer correctly.

One common test-taking strategy is to go through the test the first time answering only the questions you are sure of. When you have gone through the complete test, you can go back over the unanswered questions and tackle the ones that you are pretty sure of. If you still have time after that, you can go through the questions one more time, really taking the time to think them through and to provide your best answer.

Carefully Analyze the Results

If you are taking a test for career guidance, remember to take the results with a grain of salt. No test is completely accurate, and no one knows you better than you do yourself. If the career advice provided by the test seems too far afield, trust your intuition. You may want to take a different kind of career test as a kind of "second opinion."

If you are taking a test as part of a job application process, the organization should at least tell you if you passed or failed the test, even if they don't tell you the specific results. If you failed the test, or if the results lead to placement in a job that seems inappropriate to you, you have the right to question the test. In most organizations, a lot of work has been done to validate tests and make sure they measure what they're supposed to measure. But not all companies do this. As a result some tests have been shown to be discriminatory, and may therefore be illegal.

The human resources department of the organization is responsible for the quality of the tests, so if you have questions about your results that should be your first point of contact. If you are not satisfied with the response, and if you feel that the test might be being used as a way to discriminate against you, you may wish to consult a lawyer.

COMMON MISTAKES
You Decide to Make a Major Career Shift Based on Your Test Results

Test results are only meant to be used as a guideline in decision making about careers, and should be part of a comprehensive career planning strategy. This strategy should include a lot of self-assessment exercises, plenty of personal soul searching, using trusted friends and family as sounding boards, and possibly employing the services of a professional career coach.

You Don't Take the Achievement or Placement Test Seriously

Your résumé looks good, you know some people in the organization, and you have a lot of confidence in your ability to charm the hiring manager—so you don't give much credence to the test you are told you have to take. But you really need to take it seriously. Organizations that use testing typically use the results as the first screen for job candidates. If you don't pass the test, you are not even considered for an interview. If there is a test, be as prepared as possible to do well on it.

You Stay Up All Night the Night Before, Cramming for the Test

This, and a lot of caffeine, was how you got yourself through college, so it has become your standard operating procedure for test taking. The truth is that it wasn't a good strategy then, and it's not a good strategy now. The students who did the best in exams in college were the ones who began preparing for the final exam right after the first night of class. Slow and steady wins the race. So if you are told you will need to take a psychometric test to measure your knowledge and skills, find out as much as you can about the test and study over a period of time on a regular basis. Then don't study the night before you take the test. Relax and make sure that you get a good night's sleep. That way you'll be clear headed and at your best.

FOR MORE INFORMATION

Book:
Bolles, Richard. *What Color is Your Parachute? A Practical Manual for Job-Hunters and Career-Changers.* Revised ed. Berkeley, CA: Ten Speed Press, 2006.

Web sites:
The five rules about taking career tests by Richard Bolles: **www.jobhuntersbible.com**
The Net Guide: **www.jobhuntersbible.com**
SHL Group: **www.shl.com/shl/americas**
Careerzone online assessment center: **www.people-center.com/bydesin.htm**
John Holland's self-directed search: **www.self-directed-search.com**

See also:
Psychological Tests (pp. 1876–1878)

Getting Paid What You're Worth: How to Assess Your Value in the Marketplace

GETTING STARTED

You may be at the beginning of your career, or you may be halfway through it. Wherever you are in your working life, your ability to be paid the salary you want depends entirely on your understanding of how much value you bring to your employer—and how effectively you are able to communicate that value to the person who controls what you are paid.

The subject of money carries with it a great many emotional and psychological issues, and we tend to get overwhelmed and even avoid the mysterious job of assessing what we bring to the marketplace. But just as a store periodically shuts its doors to count its inventory, a regular stocktaking of all those things of value that you bring to your career and organization will help you decide how you need to supplement your skills and how to price them.

You should consider the following questions while you discover your worth to your employer, and decide how to translate that worth into compensation commensurate with your value:

- How can you capture the true value of what you have to offer the marketplace?
- Is there a logical design behind the way your organization pays its employees?
- How important is it to your future prospects to choose your boss when you agree to take a job?
- How much power do you have to position your job as a key contributor within your organization?

FAQs
Aren't salary structures a closely held secret?

Yes and no. Most organizations don't like to broadcast their pay structures. Many employers, in fact, consider their compensation and benefits plans to be a valuable, competitive tool. However, there are ways of finding out what your organization's salary structure is. Sometimes all it takes is simply to ask someone who does a lot of hiring and salary reviewing for the organization about the overall breakdown of the different levels and the reasoning behind them.

If my employer has a formal salary structure, doesn't that limit my ability to negotiate a higher salary?

Not necessarily. You can negotiate above the offered salary by emphasizing more intangible assets that you bring to the table. These might include, for example, the market supply and demand for your abilities, or your institutional knowledge (how long you've been at the organ-

ization and how much valuable information you have in your head), and so on.

Can I count on the organization offering me a salary within the range that is assigned to my job?

Again, not necessarily. As much as organizations want to attract and retain the best possible employees, they also want to save money. So your initial offer may be a figure that your employer thinks you will accept, not necessarily a figure that is "fair" in terms of the salary structure. Therefore, an initial offer to you could be well below the range that is officially assigned to your position.

MAKING IT HAPPEN
Inventory Your Assets

You have assets that carry with them intrinsic worth, regardless of what's going on in the marketplace, your profession, or your organization. They include your education, talents, track record for success (it helps to be able to quantify the financial value of your successes if you can), contacts, public recognition, and passions. This list shows your "fast-moving merchandise"—the goods that your employer already knows you have, and routinely relies on for the value that they bring to the organization.

Indicate on your list which of your assets aren't being used to their fullest potential at present. Then create another list of ideas you have had to benefit the organization's future, as well as interests you have related to the organization but not necessarily to your current job. This list represents your upward mobility, either within your existing range or into an entirely different range.

Inventory Those Behaviors, Skills, and Knowledge Sets That Your Organization Values

Look around you and observe how the "stars" within the organization work and behave. There you will find a clue as to what the informal, unwritten values are in your company. While, on paper, you may have all the necessary skills and knowledge required, you also might have to acquire certain behaviors (such as working late or going to official receptions) that will help you get noticed by the key decision-makers. It's when you are noticed by the people in power that you have the chance to market your worth to the organization. Likewise, if the organization values certain skills or levels of education—and if success within this particular organization is important to you—make plans to acquire them.

"We're overpaying him, but he's worth it." Samuel Goldwyn

Understand How the Organization's Salary Structure Is Designed

The salary structure is not public knowledge, so you must ask around. Someone you know will know how the compensation is arranged within the organization. If you are considering an offer within a new organization or new department, ask frankly where the offer falls within the range assigned to your job title. Expect an answer somewhere around the midpoint of the range. If the answer is vague or dismissive, that could be a sign that you are being offered a salary not within your range at all. Be prepared to negotiate.

Work for a Boss Who Is a "Star" within the Organization

Your prospects are limited by the prospects of your boss. Except in extremely rare circumstances, employees typically do not make more than their bosses. Find a positive, respectful, successful, and supportive supervisor, and your boat will rise with theirs. If, by contrast, you are stuck with a boss who is out of favor or in a department that is routinely underfunded, your own perceived value could diminish by association.

Know What Your Job Typically Pays in Your Marketplace

There are a wide number of variables that affect someone's salary, but, with a little research, general information is available. Trade and professional associations conduct salary surveys that reflect both local and national trends, or salary computation tools are available for free online. Or ask people you know and trust. Don't ask point blank for a specific figure, but talk in terms of ranges. Collect enough range information from enough people, and you will begin to get a picture of what your financial worth is, both to the organization and your bank balance.

Seize the Opportunity to Write Your Job Description

If someone asks you to write your own job description, it is a golden opportunity to position yourself as a valuable strategic player who is helping the organization to meet its objectives. Use verbs that emphasize the things you do to create change within the organization. The more strategic the role that you create for yourself, the higher you will be placed within your range—you might even be bumped up a grade.

Continue to Enhance Your Value in Four Different Ways

As you continue in your work, you can continue to improve your worth to the organization in these ways:
- You are a well-liked and trusted team player, who is both productive and cooperative.
- You are an acknowledged star performer among all the others who hold, or who have held, your job.
- You are irreplaceable—you possess unique skills, talents, contacts, or reputation in your industry.
- Your success track record is superior.

COMMON MISTAKES

You Assume You Have No Power over the Salary You Can Command

You can almost always increase your salary, either by elevating your stature, perceived and real worth, and the respect you are held in within the organization, or by changing employers altogether. If you choose to stay with the same employer, you may have to wait for regularly scheduled increases. But when the time comes, you can take a proactive role in determining what your increase will be.

You Take Your Income and Benefits Personally

Your salary is a reflection of your perceived worth to the organization, not your intrinsic value as a human being, or even as an employee. If you are dissatisfied with your salary, reflect calmly and systematically on the ways better paid employees managed to attract the higher incomes. Then follow their examples.

You Overlook the Worth of Nonfinancial Compensation

Remember that there are other valuable ways of being compensated: the opportunity to work with a prestigious or cutting-edge organization; the chance to do something that is meaningful and important to your personal set of values; tuition reimbursement while you are studying for an advanced degree; paid sabbaticals; the chance to learn important skills that will position you for an accelerated career progression later

FOR MORE INFORMATION

Books:
Chapman, Jack. *Negotiating Your Salary: How to Make $1,000 a Minute.* 5th ed. Berkeley, CA: Ten Speed Press, 2006.
Pinkley, Robin L., and Gregory B. Northcraft. *Get Paid What You're Worth: The Expert Negotiator's Guide to Salary and Compensation.* New York: St. Martin's Press, 2000.

Web sites:
JobStar Central: **www.jobstar.org**
Monster.com Salary Center: **www.salarycenter.monster.com**

See also:

Negotiating Your Salary and Benefits

GETTING STARTED

One of the most nerve-racking parts of the job search process is the moment when it's time to begin discussing salary and benefits. The way you handle this situation will make a major difference in your career. Don't leave these issues to chance. It's important to learn how to ask for what you think you really deserve. Here are some questions that will help you prepare to negotiate the best salary and benefit package possible:

- Do you know your market worth?
- Do you know the potential salary range of the job you are applying for?
- What stage of your career are you at?
- What questions is the interviewer likely to ask when you are discussing salary and benefits?

FAQs

What is the most important thing to remember when I am negotiating for salary and benefits?

Your sense of self-worth is the most important thing to keep in mind. You must do your homework, both mentally and emotionally, so that you feel confident when it comes to discussing what you are worth to the organization.

This will be my first job. Isn't the salary pretty much predetermined?

All jobs have a salary range. The hiring manager will probably try to offer you a starting salary at the low end of that range, but there is always room to negotiate.

Don't I have to take whatever they offer me?

When you go shopping for a box of pencils, you expect to have to pay the price marked on the box. When it comes to salaries and benefits, however, almost everyone acknowledges this as a negotiation situation, and that means that you are not necessarily expected to accept the first offer.

MAKING IT HAPPEN
Know Your Worth on the Market

There are many ways to discover your market worth. If you are just graduating from college, your university career development office will have lots of information on the starting salary ranges for people with various degrees and for different types of career. If you are currently working, it is a good idea to go on at least two job interviews per year, even if you are not looking to change jobs. It is a good way to find out whether your skills and experience are valued outside the organization that you work for, and you can get a sense of your worth from any salary offers you receive. These are external measures of worth.

However, it's also important to have an internal sense of your worth. In preparation for a job interview, you should have made a list of the strengths, skills, and experiences that you can offer this organization. Once the organization is ready to make you a job offer, you will be in a better mental and emotional position to negotiate your salary and benefits if you are confident that you have something of value to give.

Find Out What the Salary Range Is for the Position You Are Considering

There are several ways to do this. Some of the Web sites at the end of this article have salary calculators, but you have to take these with a grain of salt. Several other ways to discover what people doing this kind of job usually get paid are:

- read industry publications—most have an annual report on salaries in the field;
- join an industry or professional association and use that network to get an idea of the salary range for this type of job;
- talk to other people who work in a similar position to the one you are looking at, in person or by joining online discussion boards. Find out what they do and, if possible, how much they get paid or what salary range they are in.

Consider the Stage of Your Career When Preparing to Negotiate Salary and Benefits

The three basic stages of career are early, middle, and late. If you are in the early stages of your career, you may be willing to take a lower salary in exchange for the opportunity to work for an exciting and growing company, or the chance to learn valuable skills—or to work on a project that is deeply meaningful to you.

If you are in the middle of your career, you may be more interested in benefits such as healthcare and retirement than you are in salary. You also may be asking yourself questions about how much further you want to go in your career and how you want to balance work and family issues.

If you are at a late stage in your career, salary may or may not be that important to you, depending on how well you have been able to prepare for retirement. Like the person in midcareer, benefits may be more important than salary. But, often, even more important than either is the opportunity to make your mark and leave a legacy.

So keep your career stage in mind as you figure out what's important to you now and in the future.

Be Prepared to Handle Questions about Your Salary Expectations

You are asked, "What are your salary requirements?" and you don't know what to say. You must expect to face this

---

question. You may have been advised to respond with a question such as, "What are you offering?" or, "I don't know, what does the job pay?" Throwing the question back into the interviewer's lap may seem like a good way to get yourself off the hook, but it can also appear a little too coy and may convey the message that you don't really know what you want. Salary negotiations are an opportunity to demonstrate your professional negotiating skills and, if you handle this well, you will gain the respect of the hiring manager. If you accept the first offer, you may actually convey a lack of self-confidence and an inability to go after what you deserve. If this is your first job, you also should be aware that raises are based on a percentage of current salary, so if you start low you limit your ability to increase your overall salary over time.

If you have done your homework on the job and the organization, you already have a pretty good idea of the range that they are likely to offer. You also should have an idea of your market worth and of the relative importance you put on salary level, benefits, and the work itself. When asked about your salary expectations, be prepared to suggest a range in which the lowest amount is slightly above the minimum you would accept, and the highest is more than you really expect them to offer. This amount shouldn't be too outrageous.

Watch the interviewer's body language closely to assess whether or not your stated expectations are reasonable. If the interviewer balks at the range, be prepared to remind him or her of the unique strengths, skills, and experience that you bring to the organization, and the results you expect to help them achieve. Remember to keep the focus on your worth, not your cost.

Receiving Their Final Offer
You may or may not receive a final offer during the interview. It's almost always a good idea to ask for a day or two to think about an offer, especially if you have concerns about it. You have the right to ask for time, because accepting a job offer is an important life decision. You also want to avoid appearing overly eager or desperate. If you have honest concerns about the offer, then be sure to state them when you call back.

COMMON MISTAKES
You Are Told This Is the Final Offer, and You Accept That
The "final offer" usually refers to the salary offer, but there may be room to negotiate for better benefits. If that also seems like a closed door, then ask if you can come up for review within three to six months with the potential for a raise, based on your performance.

You Have Unrealistically High Expectations of What You Should Be Paid
This mistake is fairly common for young people who are fresh out of college. A visit to a university's career development center can be very helpful for setting realistic expectations, and can usually provide concrete information on typical starting salaries. Even if you have been out of school for a while, your alma mater will still be glad to help you with current salary information. It also helps to check out your salary expectations with other people in the field before you go in to negotiate.

You Accept the Highest Offer, Even Though the Job Is Not That Much to Your Liking
All too often, people think that job decisions should be based only on salary. However, you spend a very high percentage of your waking hours at work, and if you don't love what you do and care about the organization, it can really affect your overall quality of life. No amount of money can compensate for that. When making career and salary decisions, it is important to balance your financial requirements with your need for meaningful and fulfilling work.

FOR MORE INFORMATION

Books:
Chapman, Jack. *Negotiating Your Salary: How to Make $1,000 a Minute.* 5th ed. Berkeley, CA: Ten Speed Press, 2006.
Wendleton, Kate. *Interviewing and Salary Negotiation: For Job Hunters, Career Changers, Consultants, and Freelancers.* Franklin Lakes, NJ: Career Press, 1999.

Web sites:
The Riley Guide:
www.dbm.com/jobguide/salguides.html
Salary.com: **www.salary.com**
Executive Compensation Database:
www.ecomponline.com
Job Hunters' Bible salary page:
www.jobhuntersbible.com/research/salaries.shtml

See also:
- Employee Benefits/Compensation (pp. 1736–1737)
- Finding Out What You Are Worth: Remuneration/Salaries (pp. 1755–1756)
- Getting Paid What You're Worth: How to Assess Your Value in the Marketplace (pp. 885–886)
- Getting the Raise You Deserve (pp. 896–897)

"When a man says he wants to work, what he means is that he wants wages."

Richard Whately

Moving Sideways: Benefiting from a Lateral Move

GETTING STARTED

Today's career environment requires more creativity, flexibility, and originality than ever before. The notion of a "job for life" has vanished. So, fortunately, has the rigid assumption that there is only one way to succeed in a company—that is, by promotion. Previously, if you were not moving up, you were almost certainly fast-tracked in another direction: out the door.

But today both employers and employees are discovering that lateral career moves are a creative way to build exciting companies and rewarding futures. For their part, individuals recognize that the more varied their skill sets and experiences, the more value they can bring to their employers. This translates into increased marketability, as well as additional job security in changing times. Your willingness to move laterally may protect you from being laid off as your company downsizes in one department while expanding operations in other, more profitable divisions.

Employers, by contrast, are coming to recognize lateral moves as a way of retaining valuable employees (as well as protecting themselves from losing valued talent to their competitors). Top talent is difficult and expensive to identify, recruit, and retain. Top talent is also hungriest for new challenges and growth opportunities and will be quick to leave if not fed with them. Employers are beginning to understand that moving eager and interested employees within the organization is an extremely valuable approach to employee development, and one which will serve them well in the future.

The following points are key questions to ask yourself when considering the option to move sideways within the organization—perhaps, in certain circumstances, even down the ladder:

- If your company is downsizing, or if there are other elements in your life requiring more of your attention and energy, will a lateral move help you stay happily employed?
- Will a lateral move give you valuable on-the-job exposure to business functions that will help you to accelerate your upward mobility?
- How receptive is your employer to the principle of hiring from within and providing lateral experience in order to develop employees?
- Is there a monitoring system in place within the management so that your career path will be tracked and your new skills set will be expanded further later on?

FAQs

Wouldn't a lateral move reflect negatively on me?

Not necessarily. As with almost every business decision, you get the best value if you make your choice for strategic reasons and then learn from the experience. A lateral move can be made for any number of reasons, and you may experience some surprising benefits in the process (understanding the ways other parts of the business are run, for example). Capture those benefits as added strategic value and you may actually boost your career prospects in the long run.

How can I be sure that my company won't just assume I belong permanently on the slow track?

Employers that support skills development and communication across the whole business are the most likely to understand the value of placing their high-potential employees in a wide variety of their business operations. After all, the best C.E.O.s are the ones with the broadest exposure to the spectrum of corporate functions. However, if you observe that your company's most senior leaders have achieved their success via single channels of departmental experience, you might consider either staying on your departmental ladder or changing employers if your career plan involves wide variety.

MAKING IT HAPPEN
Identify the Reasons Why You Would Like to Explore the Option of a Lateral Move

Does the next logical upward step in your career path require certain experience that you don't yet have? Have you just finished a protracted period of high-pressure productivity and need a lighter load for a short time? Are you taking demanding classes to increase your market value in the long run and need a less strenuous set of responsibilities during your workday? Are family needs preventing you from keeping up a demanding travel schedule? Are you committed to the company in the long run and want to understand as much of it as you can? Or do you simply want some variety?

Investigate Internal Employment Policies

Find out if there is a policy in place that supports lateral moves. Talk to employees who have made that choice to discover whether their long-term career ambitions are still being protected.

Discover Which Functions and Divisions of Your Company Are Growing

You want to seek out opportunities in areas in which your company is thriving or continuing to expand. Talk to other employees in those divisions to discover what the environment is like and whether senior management is supportive of individual ambition and career development.

Consider the Desirability of the Openings That Are Available

Would you have to take a pay cut? How long do you think you'd remain interested in that particular work? Does the new department show promise for continued growth and

---

"True motivation comes from achievement, personal development, job satisfaction, and recognition."

Frederick Herzberg

opportunity? Is the management team of your chosen department well received and respected among their own superiors?

Identify What You Enjoy about Your Current Work
Think about what you like best about your job as it stands and try to work out if you'll find the same elements in your prospective new assignment. How will you stay in touch with your current team members? Would you be able to return to your present assignment when and if you desire? If not, would that make an important difference to you?

Identify Your Potential for Success and Failure in Your Possible New Assignment
Work out roughly how long it will take to achieve your current level of proficiency in your new assignment. Are the measures of success acceptable to you? Are the requirements for upward mobility on this new ladder attractive to you?

Identify Your Prospects for Development Outside the Company
Does this new ladder present opportunities for expanding your marketability in the external job market? Will it provide you with technical training and experiences to boost your competence, therefore rewarding you sufficiently for the risk you'd be taking now?

Plan for Transitions
Be sure you and your new manager have worked out a plan to integrate you into the new team as smoothly as possible. You may have put a great deal of advance thought and work into making the transition, but your new coworkers may not be so ready for you as a new player.

Don't assume that just because you're a long-standing employee in the company, you're at home in this new division. If you're replacing a beloved former coworker, you may run up against additional resistance to your presence. Do as much as you can to make yourself welcome in the group.

COMMON MISTAKES
You Leave a Secure Position Only to Discover that Your New Job Will Be a Casualty of a Downsizing Exercise
Thoroughly investigate the prospects of this new assignment, just as you would if you were applying for the job from the outside. Understand the roles that this particular position and the department play in the company's long-term plans. If you cannot see how this work serves your employer's mission critical objectives, hold out for another opportunity.

You Become Unintentionally Slow-tracked
If you make a lateral move, especially if it is to reduce your stress load temporarily for a personal reason, you may find yourself accidentally on the list of expendable employees. Be sure to invest time regularly to market yourself to colleagues throughout the business. For example, go to key meetings on a regular basis or have lunch with your former manager to stay in touch with developments in your original department. Stay current with your company's developments and objectives and position yourself to make another jump into a more critical job as soon as you can.

You Make Too Many Lateral Moves with No Apparent Growth or Progression
Remember that, desirable as lateral moves may be, your career path must still show regular upward mobility. When you make lateral moves, try to take a job that pays in some way, even though it's on the same level in the organizational chart. Or take a lateral move to learn more management skills elsewhere, and then return to your original department at a higher rank. Lateral career moves shouldn't be used routinely as a preventative measure against losing your job, or as a way to tread water for longer than during a very short downturn in the economy or your industry. Lateral career moves should be used as a valuable strategic career management tool and, when you're able to discuss your recent career path in those terms, you'll find that a lateral move can be an excellent springboard to an even better future.

FOR MORE INFORMATION
Book:
Bolles, Richard. *What Color is Your Parachute? A Practical Manual for Job-Hunters and Career-Changers.* Revised ed. Berkeley, CA: Ten Speed Press, 2006.

Web sites:
Monster.com:
http://wlb.monster.com/articles/lateralmoves
PersonnelToday.com: www.personneltoday.com

Staying Marketable: Identifying Your Transferable Skills

GETTING STARTED

On a global level, market demands are shifting and changing monthly, weekly, sometimes even from day to day. In recent years, thousands of individuals who trained specifically for sharply defined "hot careers" are discovering that those skills may not be in such strong demand that they warrant such a focused investment of time, money, and education. In such fields as information technology, for instance, disappointing downturns have dissolved what was previously assumed to be a "sure thing"—a "smart" career choice.

Staying marketable in shifting times requires more than a single channel approach to qualifying for certain jobs. It is not enough to have the skill sets required to complete certain tasks any more. To stay marketable, you must be willing both to update those skill sets continually and always to understand the many different roles your growing experience, critical thinking abilities, and interpersonal talents can play in many different market contexts throughout the rest of your career.

As a result, the most important skill that will keep you marketable is your ability to ask yourself fresh questions as circumstances change—and arrive at creative, dynamic answers that will lead you through a prosperous and relevant career. Staying marketable requires you to have enough motivation to invest extra and ongoing effort in keeping your skills not only up to date and transferable but also competitive. As such, your most marketable, most transferable skill is your passion to learn and acquire new skills.

The following points are key questions to ask yourself when considering ways to keep yourself marketable in an era of rapidly changing economic and business conditions:

- Why are you in the field you're in at the moment?
- What aspects of your current work give you the most satisfaction?
- What aspects of your current work give you the least satisfaction?
- Who are you meeting in the natural course of your work whose jobs may be a natural path of transition and growth for you?
- Would you be willing to leave your immediate career path to pursue a more promising or fascinating opportunity on an adjacent path?
- What topic areas fuel your natural, self-motivated curiosity?

FAQs

Why should I bother worrying about transferable skills?

Given the rapidly changing market and economic environments, it's essential to understand how your skill sets fit into your company's immediate objectives and future plans. If those plans don't agree with your own ambitions, you must know how to package and repackage your skills to build your career elsewhere. Transferable skills augment your core function skills to make you desirable across industries and functions.

Will I have to return to school to gain formal education?

Not necessarily. There are many different programs delivering skills training, including training that requires formal certification. Employers offer courses, as do distance-learning institutions. Additionally, old-fashioned "on-the-job" experience and training increase your transferable skill sets. Don't overlook that accomplishment, just because you didn't absorb this extra knowledge sitting in a classroom.

What do I do with an expanded transferable skill, once I have acquired it?

Market that skill. Put it on your résumé. Tell your boss.

MAKING IT HAPPEN

Make a List of All the Skills You Currently Have

Be sure to include skills you're not using at the moment, even those skills you think you'll never want to use again. This is a complete inventory of all your keys to your marketability now and in the future.

Analyze Those Skills

Highlight in one color the skills that help you do the work you love; circle in a separate color all the skills that require regular updating (for example, software, health care, continuing education requirements).

Prioritize Your Skills

Skills that are both highlighted and circled—those skills are your first priority for maintaining and cultivating so they stay current and relevant to the changing job marketplace.

Consider Your "Value Mesh"

Your value mesh is that network of connections and possible next steps for your own career progression (see also "Key Terms" above). Ask the people whose jobs appear in your value mesh what skills are most in demand for the positions you'd most like to consider as next steps.

Volunteer for "Stretch" Assignments That Will Develop Your Key Marketable Skills

Try to find assignments that are slightly beyond your immediate area of operation—in other corporate departments, for instance, where you can also expand your circle of contacts.

"Ninety percent of our jobs are in jeopardy, and corporations are in the middle of unprecedented change. If we simply do the job our bosses want us to do, we may soon find ourselves without any marketable skills."

Tom Peters

     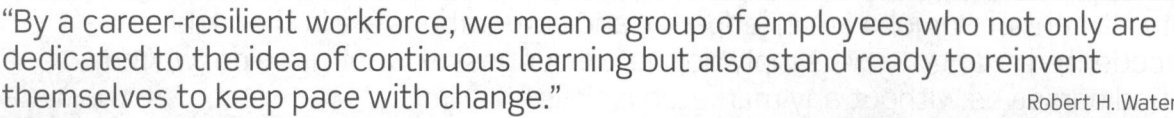

892

ACTIONLIST

Develop References

Remember that in addition to actually having transferable, marketable skills, you must also develop a list of referees who will be happy to confirm that you indeed have those skills. So, as you complete "stretch" assignments, ask your new colleagues for letters of recommendation or introduction, if appropriate.

Document Your Skills

If you intend to continue working with the same employer, ask your "stretch" assignment supervisor to add a report on your performance to your personnel file.

Continue to Educate Yourself

Take advantage of all company-paid or reimbursed training programs to update and/or add to your technical and professional qualifications. Additionally, use whatever tax advantages may be available to support your continuing education.

Stay Involved in Professional Associations

Your skill sets include more than easily measurable technical expertise. It also includes your ability to come up with fresh ideas and innovations based on your overall knowledge and understanding of your industry or profession. For this reason, it is important to attend professional association meetings and development programs.

Make Your Professional Development a Top Priority

When selecting a new employer, choose companies that support ongoing employee development programs. High-quality employers understand that one of the best things they can do for their employees is give them the opportunity to keep their skills at the cutting edge. If potential employers exhibit indifference to this principle, this tells you that your personal potential for growth is likely to meet a dead-end while working for this company.

COMMON MISTAKES
You Are So Busy Doing the Work That You Neglect Your Ongoing Development Needs

With rapidly changing technology and discoveries in almost every profession, it is easy to become obsolete very quickly. As work demands are intense and family needs absorb private time, it is also easy to ignore the need to stay current. It is important to develop and commit to a regular program of professional development (even if the program must be done during your private time) to stay competitive and marketable.

You Are Tempted to Focus Primarily on Acquiring Technical Skills at the Expense of More Conceptual Transferable Skills

Your continued marketability depends not only on your commitment to stay technically up to date but also on your commitment to upgrade continually all of your abilities, including interpersonal abilities such as persuasion or negotiation.

In Your Eagerness to Accept a New Job, You Sign a Noncompete Agreement That Is So Comprehensive It Effectively Takes You Out of the Marketplace

Your skills are transferable only as long as you can offer them in the open marketplace. Unfortunately, employers are currently tending to insist that new employees sign a noncompete agreement, reducing their ability to find new jobs later. Organizations have an obvious need to protect their intellectual property from competitors, and their competitors are a natural pool of future employers for you. So their interest in comprehensive noncompete agreements is understandable.

However, such an agreement could preclude you from working in your profession for an indefinite amount of time. Ask for time to review it with an attorney before signing. If the company makes immediate signing a condition of employment, consider that a negative signal. At the very least, carefully review all the wording in the contract and insist on altering any clauses that would prevent you from using your marketable skills in future jobs.

You Limit Your Own Prospects by Defining Your Potential Based on the Past, Not the Future

To stay marketable and develop your skills, it's important to build on your potential for the future and your passion for growth and learning. Every new experience is an opportunity for additional self-discovery and self-understanding. This is the foundation on which to build your plan for marketing and developing yourself in the future.

FOR MORE INFORMATION

Book:
Bolles, Richard. *What Color is Your Parachute? A Practical Manual for Job-Hunters and Career-Changers*. Revised ed. Berkeley, CA: Ten Speed Press, 2006.

Web site:
The Skills Zone:
www.pch.gc.ca/Cyberstation/html/szone2_e.htm

See also:
☆ Choosing the Best Training Curriculum for You (pp. 426–427)
✔ Identifying Your Marketable Skills (pp. 865–866)

"By a career-resilient workforce, we mean a group of employees who not only are dedicated to the idea of continuous learning but also stand ready to reinvent themselves to keep pace with change."

Robert H. Waterman, Jr.

Making Yourself Promotable

GETTING STARTED

Being good at your job is not enough to guarantee a promotion these days. Being *promotable*, on the other hand, increases your chances of success and assists you in taking the career steps that you desire.

Being promotable draws together your professional skills and competences with your business sense and ability to build good relationships to create the impression of someone who will be valuable to your organization at increasingly senior levels. When you're recognized for your specialist expertise and have a track record of success, you're no doubt likely to be seen as a candidate for the succession line. However, other personal attributes that go well beyond your current role will be taken into consideration. To get ahead, you'll need to demonstrate business acumen, political sensitivity, the ability to manage change, and loyalty to your employing organization. These attributes go hand-in-hand with the need to communicate and network effectively and the ability to cement critical relationships with those who will sponsor and support you as you move along your career path.

FAQs

I am very eager to be promoted and think I have done everything I can to get noticed. Competition is fierce, though, so how can I make sure I'm considered a suitable candidate for a new appointment?

Tooting your own horn too loudly isn't always the most effective way of influencing events. Being clear about what you want and why you deserve to be promoted is, of course, very important, but a subtle approach can also reap rewards. You could, for example:

- find a mentor or sponsor in the organization with whom you can work
- approach your line manager and discuss your development plan in the light of your conviction that you have more to offer the business
- observe those that have been promoted and ask yourself if you're displaying the same personal attributes

Try to become more visible by ensuring that you take the opportunity to mix with decision makers and by sharing stories of your success at appropriate times. Don't make too much of your achievements or you may turn off the very people you need to court.

I am working on becoming promotable but am having difficulty becoming more visible. Do you have any ideas?

While increasing your "visibility" within the boundaries of your organization is important, you don't need to confine yourself to just that. Why not publish articles in your trade or professional magazine, or accept invitations (or volunteer) to speak at conferences? If you want to raise your visibility closer to home to demonstrate your commitment to the community, you could get involved in local politics.

I work in an organization where promotion is a thing of the past for all but a very few. How can I work my way into the senior management tier?

It sounds as if you're working in a flat organization (where there are fewer levels in the hierarchy) or in a matrix organization (where the business is structured according to common activities rather than discrete business units. Project teams are made up from specialists across a business). In these cases, promotability takes on a new meaning as there is often no longer a clear succession route. There may be prestigious and exciting areas to be associated with, however, or some career-enhancing assignments that you could target. Take a step back and examine the patterns and trends of progressive career paths in your organization. Once you've identified the "hot spots," you can figure which suit you best and plan your approach to reach them.

MAKING IT HAPPEN

Making yourself promotable is not an easy task because it implies a very wide development agenda. Aspects of this include familiarizing yourself with the broader business arena and general management issues, developing social and political skills that enable you to build effective relationships, and finding a personal leadership style that you're comfortable with and can develop into a distinctive personal "brand" in the long run.

It's a sad fact that the personal skills and attributes that have carried you to the point in your career where you're looking at a more senior appointment are the very skills and attributes that can sabotage your success at this level. These include having too high a dependence on your specialist expertise, an individualistic approach that differentiates you from your peers, and an inclination to challenge the organizational status quo. Shedding some of these traits, therefore, may be the key to becoming promotable.

In addition to these features, past research has highlighted several derailment factors that can prevent an otherwise capable person from further advancement. These include: "problems with interpersonal relationships, failure to meet business objectives, failure to build and lead a team and an inability to change or adapt during a transition." ("Why Executives Derail: Perspectives Across Time and Cultures," *Academy of Management Executive*. 1995. Volume 9, Number 4, pp 62–72.) Two further derailment factors that were considered to reflect the changing business environment were later identified. These were the failure to *learn* to deal with change and complexity and overdependence upon a single boss or mentor. If you tackle each of these five factors in turn, you can be sure that you'll be building the personal capabilities that will enhance your promotability and distinguish you as a future leader.

Develop Good Interpersonal Skills

As you progress through your career, a shift occurs in the

"An environment which calls for perfection is not likely to be easy. But aiming for it is always good for progress."

Thomas J. Watson, Jr.

balance between the expert contribution you make and your ability to build relationships. More senior positions demand a higher level of political sensitivity because, at this level, relationships go beyond the organizational setting and are more likely have an impact on the long-term viability of the business. Faced with this realization, many potential leaders try to fake it with an overconfident communication style that conveys nothing but arrogance and authoritarianism. Good interpersonal relationships are built by people who have no axe to grind and who aren't trying to create an illusion of confidence and capability. There's no substitute for genuine selfconfidence; people can generally see through bluff and bluster, so it's as well to put the personal development time in to really know yourself well, understand your values, and create a clear picture of what you want. With this knowledge in place, good communication and an easy manner will follow naturally and authoritatively because it will genuinely reflect who you are.

Meet Business Objectives

In order to make yourself promotable, not only do you have to meet the objectives of your role, but you have to contribute to the wider business too. This means showing initiative and taking an interest in areas outside your role boundaries. You could do this by volunteering for an important project, chairing a committee, or facilitating a special interest group. If you're seen to be supportive of, and passionate for, the business, you're much more likely to be noticed as someone who could add value at a more senior level. Although it may be unpalatable to some, you may have to consider (subtle) ways in which you can broadcast your willingness to play a more committed part in the fortunes of your business, such as suggesting or volunteering for a special project. This doesn't mean that you have to be sycophantic, but if you act like someone who occupies the type of role you're aiming for, it'll be easy for others to see you in that role.

Build and Lead teams

One of the essential skills of a senior executive is the ability to build and lead teams. Without this, the cooperative networks that are vital if an organization is to achieve its objectives are damaged. Much of a person's success in this area depends on his or her ability to communicate clear objectives as well as understanding the skills, motivations, and personal values of those in their team. Relationships must be open, with a healthy ebb and flow of feedback to ensure that everyone is aligned with the purpose of the team. Milestones and markers need to be part of the plan so that progress can be monitored and successes celebrated.

Learn to Manage Transition and Change

Business and organizational models change in response to developments in the market and economy. The ripple effects of these changes are felt throughout the organization and have an impact on everyone. Being able to field such changes and use your knowledge and insight to direct people's creative energy toward making them a success are valuable attributes of a leader. Entrenchment and other blocking types of behavior are not perceived to

be helpful, even if you feel that the change is unwise or counter-productive. If you find yourself in a situation like this, you may want to make alternative suggestions and explain the thinking behind them. If your concerns are rejected, though, demonstrate your loyalty by remaining flexible and actively seeking ways of making the changes work. Show that you're prepared to keep people motivated and learn from the new experience rather than demonstrate resentfulness or obstinacy. In short, remaining flexible and actively seeking ways of making (sometimes difficult) things happen, keeping people motivated, and learning from the new experience are all important characteristics of those in the top team. Loyalty and solidarity are values that are prized in cultures that are subject to transition and change.

Build an Effective Network of Champions or Sponsors

We've all seen people who have been promoted on the basis of who they know, not what they know, yet this is no guarantee of future success. Indeed, investing in a nepotistic relationship is all very well when your champion is in favor, but if his or her reputation is damaged for any reason, yours will also be tarnished because of your close association. It's important, therefore, to build a robust network of relationships that will support you purely because of your potential and personal integrity. In this way, you can be sure that you aren't reliant on the perception people have of someone else (over whom you have no control), but that you're judged on your own talent and attributes. Think about your network and identify role models, potential coaches, and mentors for different aspects of your development plan. As you approach them, be open with your request for assistance but beware of projecting self-interest above the interests of the organization. Frame your request in development terms stating that you feel you have more to offer the business and would appreciate their guidance.

In summary, being promotable does not rely on past success but on your ambassadorial qualities as you represent those in the upper echelons of the organization. Neither does it rely on over confidence or bullishness. Being promotable demands that you demonstrate an active interest in the business and an understanding of the strategic issues, an ability to reach stretch targets and build value, a genuinely confident communication style and an ability to build effective personal relationships within your team and among your colleagues.

COMMON MISTAKES
You Irritate the People Who Could Help You

Sometimes, people looking for a move up the career ladder make such a fuss about their ambitions that they make a lot of noise around the people who they think can promote them. This won't help their case, and in fact it's very irritating and counter-productive. There are unwritten "rules" to being promotable, and you need to work these out through observing and adopting some of the tactics of successful people who've gone before you. Find out about the interests of those in authority and reflect these back to them or make yourself known in their phil-

anthropic circles outside the business. For example, if you know that your boss supports a local charity, society, or sports team, why not go along to one of their events?

You're Not Willing to Change

Although a track record of being a maverick may get you noticed, this is usually not a trait that will get you promoted. You need to play down your notoriety and redirect your energies into activities that are seen to support the organization's best interests. If you're hoping to enter a different cultural zone in the organization, you have to make sure you're familiar with the values that operate there and demonstrate that they're part of your value set too.

You Ignore Your Team

It's tempting to focus on yourself as you look toward your career horizon and plan for your own success. You'll be judged on your ability to develop the talent in your team, though, so it's foolish to ignore them. You won't succeed by squashing those with potential, so you must trust in your own abilities and let your team flourish too. Doing

this will create a loyal group who will support you in the long run. Take care to maintain these relationships as you move through the organization, as you never know who you'll be working with (or for!) one day.

FOR MORE INFORMATION

Book:
Rye, David E. *1001 Ways to Get Promoted*. Franklin Lakes, NJ: Career Press, 2005.

Web Sites:
OCJobSite.com:
www.ocjobsite.com/job-articles/promote-yourself.asp
Dauten.com:
www.dauten.com/promotable.htm

See also:
✔ Creating a Career Plan (pp. 849–850)

Getting the Raise You Deserve

GETTING STARTED

You feel certain that you deserve a raise, but you're unsure about how to ask your boss. It's very important to think through a number of issues and to have lots of information available when you make your request. It's also important to know how to respond if you end up receiving a negative answer. Here are some questions that will help you prepare for your negotiations for a higher salary:

- When is the right time to ask for a raise?
- How has your performance been, and what's the evidence of your accomplishments?
- What's the typical salary range for a job such as yours?
- What's the best way to make the request?

FAQs

Why should I even bother to ask for a raise? Won't they give me a raise at my annual performance review if I have performed well?

Organizations have to make a trade off between the need to pay enough money to keep people motivated to stay with the company and the need to keep down labor costs. You have to be your own agent and to promote your own case for why you should receive more money than you're currently making. It's helpful to learn about the salary philosophy of your organization. For example, does it pay the minimum it can to keep costs down, or does it pay higher than market rate in order to attract the best employees? Does it tend to give raises that are close to the cost of living increase for the year (which are really not raises)? Does it require managers to force a ranking among their staff and only give raises to the highest performers? If you have an understanding of the company philosophy, you can come to your performance appraisal well prepared to negotiate for a meaningful increase in salary. If you don't look out for yourself, the chances are pretty good that no one else will.

The company has not given many raises for quite a while. What should I do?

All companies go through boom times and difficult times, and they tend to retrench and cut costs when things are difficult financially. But that doesn't mean that you can't ask for a raise. If you've done a really outstanding job this past year and can point to concrete contributions, it's possible that the company might be able to find some money to reward your hard work.

I'm not good at asking for things for myself. How do I go about boosting my confidence?

If you go into the salary negotiation meeting with well-prepared documentation of your achievements (see "Document your Contributions to the Company" below), you'll have a stronger sense of your worth to the company and will feel more self-assured about asking for a

raise. If you're really nervous about this, you might consider asking someone to role-play the situation with you so that you can practice beforehand. It's also helpful to visualize the meeting ahead of time and to picture what success would look like. Eliminate any negative talk in your head, such as "No one ever appreciates what I do" or "I never get what I want", and replace these ideas with something positive, such as "I have worked hard for this company this past year, and I can present a strong case for why I should receive a raise."

I was offered a promotion without a raise. Should I accept?

There are a lot of factors to take into account in this situation. If the promotion increases your skills, your responsibilities, and your visibility, and if the company is a start-up or is otherwise strapped for cash, you might agree to take the promotion. But you should also get written agreement from your supervisor that you'll have a salary discussion at a predetermined time in the future, for example, in three months.

MAKING IT HAPPEN

Decide on the Best Timing to Ask for a Raise

The most obvious time to ask for a raise is during your performance review discussion with your boss. However, it isn't uncommon for supervisors to put off these discussions for quite a while. It's one of their least favorite things to do. If it has been more than a year since your last performance review and since your last salary increase, you should approach your supervisor about your performance and your salary.

Ask Your Supervisor to Meet with You

Give your boss time to prepare his or her thoughts for this discussion. Don't ask your boss for this meeting in front of other employees, because it puts him or her on the spot. Tell your boss that you'd like to have a meeting to discuss your performance, your career plans, and your salary, and plan for it to last at least 30 minutes. Don't just drop into his or her office and say, "I'd like to talk to you about giving me a raise."

Document Your Contributions to the Company

The best way to do this is to keep a job diary or a file of your achievements regularly throughout the year. It's so easy to forget all that you've done, but if you keep track along the way, you'll have a great record of what you've contributed. When you ask for a raise, you need to build a business case for why the company should pay you more. You need to show what you've done for the business and document why you should be rewarded. Be sure to keep track of measurable results from your actions, such as dollars saved, sales increased, level of quality improved, or percentage of employee retention. Prepare a one-page

"A fair day's wages for a fair day's work: it is as just a demand as governed men ever made of governing."

Thomas Carlyle

executive briefing on your accomplishments to take into your meeting.

Know Your Worth in the Marketplace

When companies calculate how much they typically pay for a job, they conduct wage surveys to compare salaries within the industry and geographic area. They also conduct internal pay analyses to make sure that comparable jobs within the company receive comparable pay. Such wage and salary information is now available on the Internet at sites such as **www.salary.com** and **www.rileyguide.com**. It's a little bit harder to find out information about the internal pay structure, but you can ask the human resources department for information on what jobs like yours typically pay.

Approach Your Meeting with Your Supervisor with a "Win–Win" Attitude

All successful negotiations end in both parties feeling like they received something of value. Your goal is to get a raise. Your supervisor's goal is to have a highly motivated and productive employee. Remember that raises are never given for potential or for what you're "going to do." Raises are given for meeting and exceeding performance goals. When you meet with your boss, you should be thinking about how your actions and accomplishments have helped to fulfill his or her own goals.

Discuss Both Performance and Salary

Begin your discussion with a description of your accomplishments and contributions. Next, discuss how you intend to build on those in the coming year, and what some of your key goals are. Describe your goals in terms of how they'll support your boss and make a difference to the company. Then ask for the amount and percentage of salary increase that you think you deserve and explain why.

Listen

As your boss responds, listen to any objections that are made to your requests. Consider this discussion as a mentoring session and keep an open mind about what you can learn that will help your progress in the company. Before trying to overcome any objections, make sure that you communicate your understanding of those objections through paraphrasing what you've heard. This is the first step in negotiation and objections are a normal response. Be prepared for objections and be prepared to explain why you still deserve a raise.

Know What to Do If You Get a "No?"

If you're told that you won't be getting a raise at this time, then ask what it is you need to do in order to earn one. Write down everything you're told. After the meeting, write a memo thanking your boss for his or her time, and listing the actions you need to take in order to earn a raise.

COMMON MISTAKES

You Threaten to Leave If You Don't Get the Raise You Deserve

Unless you're really unhappy and were thinking of leaving anyway, this strategy can do you much more harm than good. If you threaten to leave, you're sending the message that you aren't that committed to the organization and are basically out for yourself. This approach isn't career enhancing.

You Complain to Coworkers about Your Salary

Most organizations are insistent that all salary discussions take place only with your immediate supervisor. If you complain about your salary to your coworkers, you're very often seen as someone who isn't a team player, and who isn't politically astute. It's very unlikely that you'd get promoted or get a raise under these circumstances.

You Ask Fellow Employees How Much They Make

Unless you're in an "open book" company, most organizations prefer that salary information be kept private. They're concerned that if employees begin to compare salaries with one another, it may lead some to think that they're being treated unfairly and will therefore lead to lower morale. You can get a better idea of your internal worth by benchmarking similar jobs in your organization and then doing a search on the Internet for salary ranges for those jobs.

897

ACTIONLIST

FOR MORE INFORMATION

Books:
Chapman, Jack. *Negotiating Your Salary: How to Make $1,000 a Minute.* 5th ed. Berkeley, CA: Ten Speed Press, 2006.
Pinkley, Robin L., and Gregory B. Northcraft. *Get Paid What You're Worth: The Expert Negotiator's Guide to Salary and Compensation,* New York: St. Martin's Press, 2000.

Web sites:
The Riley Guide to Salaries:
www.rileyguide.com/salguides.html
Salary.com: **www.salary.com**

See also:
- Employee Benefits/Compensation (pp. 1736–1737)
- Finding Out What You Are Worth: Remuneration/Salaries (pp. 1755–1756)
- Getting Paid What You're Worth: How to Assess Your Value in the Marketplace (pp. 885–886)
- Negotiating Your Salary and Benefits (pp. 887–888)
- Remuneration (pp. 1894–1895)

Coping with Job Burnout

GETTING STARTED

Job burnout doesn't occur overnight but when it does happen, it can create an increasing dread of work. In fact, it can become so strong that you can think of little else. The exact combination of symptoms varies from person to person but here are the most common ones:

- You become snappy and irritated over minor things. You may have an increasingly explosive temper with a short fuse and you may lose your sense of humor completely.
- You have overwhelming feelings of helplessness, frustration, and futility.
- You have strong and persistent negative emotions such as frustration, anger, depression, guilt, and fear. You may feel unable to pull yourself out of the cycle of negative emotions.
- You have difficulty in relating to others. You may feel increasingly hostile and react angrily toward others, with emotional outbursts that can damage relationships.
- You withdraw from the company of others. This is a dangerous symptom as strong social supports act as a buffer against the effects of stress.
- You experience effects on your health, including "minor" effects such as colds, headaches, insomnia, cold sores, backaches, and high blood pressure. You may have a general feeling of being tired and run-down. Heart, breathing, and stomach problems are the more serious effects of stress.
- You have problems with chemical "solutions," ranging from coffee, cigarettes, alcohol, and sleeping pills to more addictive and dangerous substances. These can mask the root of the problem.
- The efficiency and quality of your work declines. This can often lead to increased conflict and withdrawal problems, as colleagues and managers attempt to help you reverse the trend.

If you recognize any (or several) of these symptoms, your first step is to be honest with yourself and make a decision to change. Don't be afraid to ask for help.

FAQs
What is job burnout?

Burnout is an extreme reaction to work stress. Exposure to stress produces hormonal reactions in your body. These can be divided into three stages of response, which are not specific to particular stress types and can build over time.

- **Shock and counter-shock phase**: your body reacts to perceived stress with various hormonal changes that increase your respiration and heart rate. "Shock" can be a sudden reaction, but when you are concentrating on the task at hand you may not notice it. If stress continues, your body increases hormone production to cope, and the downward spiral continues.
- **Resistance phase**: your body resists by releasing other hormones that dampen the effects of the shock. This adaptation allows you to cope with prolonged stress.
- **Exhaustion**: if stress is continuous, your reserves of hormones drop, increasing your risk of serious illness

Why does burnout occur?

Burnout can be caused by a lack of balance between important work factors:

- **Demands**: people or tasks requiring your attention and a response
- **Supports**: available resources to help you and your team
- **Constraints**: lack of available resources or barriers to accessing support

The demands and constraints of your work increase stress and the likelihood of burnout, but your supports help you to cope and reduce stress. Each of these factors can be technical, intellectual, social, financial, or psychological. The most stressful jobs are the ones where demands are high, and there is little support and many constraints. The least stressful are not necessarily undemanding, but ones in which the three factors balance each other out.

Why am I suffering from burnout when my colleagues are not?

There are many reasons why stress may affect you more than your colleagues. The way you think or feel about things is important in determining whether stress produces a shock reaction or not. This is known as the person–environment fit. If you believe that you can cope with a particular stressor, you will be less affected by it.

Control offers a protective effect against stress. Feeling trapped will make your job more stressful and, over time, you are more likely to suffer burnout than if you were in a similar job where you have choice and the opportunity to act at your discretion.

Your personality also controls the extent to which you are affected by job burnout. People who are habitually hostile and angry (known as type A personalities) react in a different way to stress from others. They are at greater risk of developing high blood pressure as a reaction to stress and are particularly coronary-prone if action is not taken.

Finally, events from all parts of your life can add to the stress that you are under, and even positive events, such as births and promotions, are major stressors. A poor balance between demands, supports, and constraints mixed together with major life events, can be difficult to cope with.

Can I bounce back?

Yes. Make some immediate changes and create an ongoing stress management plan to make yourself effective in the workplace again and happier in other areas of your life. Work out clearly what stresses you, how it affects you, and what you can do about it.

MAKING IT HAPPEN
Recover Your Health

The first port of call is with your doctor. Once you've discussed your symptoms, he or she will be able to suggest a number of ways forward. For example, you may be referred to a stress counselor, who will help you to talk

"I was actually too exhausted to realize at the moment that my life's purpose had been achieved."

Robert Edwin Peary

about your problems in more depth and find ways to help you cope with your particular set of circumstances.

On the other hand, you may decide you'd benefit from a different tack and that you need a complete break from the demands of your job. If this is the case, you'll need to get a sick note, and, if you feel that you've been treated unfairly (that you've been placed under too much pressure by your manager, for example), the wording of this can prove to be particularly important. Organizations are becoming more aware of stress links to health and are more prepared to help you if you are open about a stress-related diagnosis. When you feel ready to face work again, meet with your manager to discuss your future work regime and prepare well beforehand by coming up with some specific suggestions, such as exploring the option of working from home one day a week.

Identify the Sources of Stress

Stress is any factor to which you have to adapt by changing your hormone levels. To help you tackle the sources of stress in your life, follow this three-stage process:

- Identify the demands that are placed upon you now, not forgetting the positive sources of stress mentioned earlier.
- Identify the supports that you currently use to help you.
- Identify the constraints that hinder you from meeting expectations.

Remove the Sources of Stress and Pressure

In essence, combating job burnout effectively involves decreasing demands, increasing supports, and minimizing constraints in your life, tailoring your approach to suit you best (and not everyone else). For example:

- Consider improving the physical work environment or re-designing your job to allow greater delegation and control. This may involve some structural reorganization or team training, so investigate this with your manager.
- Consider improving role clarity and finally resolving conflicts that crop up time and again. Both of these can make a big difference.
- Time management training, career coaching, and/or stress counseling are good ways to help recovery and long-term comfort and satisfaction.

Minimize the Outcomes of Stress

Energy expenditure at work and exercise in your spare time are both shown to protect against the effects of stress, so look into ways you can incorporate this into your day. For example, you could combine exercise with relaxation techniques via yoga, tai chi, and Pilates. Do check with your doctor before you begin.

Increasing the scope of your discretion through discussion with your boss can also reap plenty of rewards. Explain that having more control over *when* and *how* to achieve your objectives will reduce the impact of work stress on your life.

Increasing your support network can also have a big and positive effect on the way you're feeling: this can range from spending more time with family and friends outside of work to finding a mentor who can bring new insights to the way you live. Maintaining meaningful personal relationships and occupying different roles (such as husband, wife, mom, or dad) are important buffers to stress and will help you focus on your life outside of work.

Through good coaching or stress counseling, you can be taught to cope better with unavoidable stress by changing your perceptions or beliefs, modifying your behavior to gain positive benefits, and negotiating more assertively with others.

COMMON MISTAKES

Those most at risk are the most likely to deny symptoms such as fatigue and distress, and they are unlikely to seek help or change their behavior until a crisis dawns. Avoid this by listening to the messages from your body and allowing yourself time to recover from symptoms caused by stress and pressure.

You Impose Pressure on Yourself

If you have a tendency to be over enthusiastic and ambitious, if you aren't good at asserting yourself or you are a perfectionist, it may take some time to change these habits. Don't expect too much too soon and "rescue" yourself when you realize you have taken on too much. Pace yourself toward deadlines and map out your time, building in sufficient allowance for the other things in life.

You Add to Existing Stress

Psychologists call this "problems about problems": under pressure you become concerned about your work, and, as pressure mounts, symptoms of your concern increase until they become more worrying than the initial trouble. For example, let's say you are finding it hard to sleep because of pressure at work. You then start to worry about the effect of the lack of sleep on your performance, so you take sleeping pills. Now you worry about the effect of these on your health. If you follow this pattern, everything will become worse, so you need to break the cycle. Concentrate on the root of the problem and take action to balance your demands, supports, and constraints.

You Relapse

When you are combating job burnout, give yourself a traffic light system to recognize "green" comfort zone symptoms, "yellow" stretch zone symptoms, and "red" stress symptoms. Notice what triggers you to move between these zones and set aside some time regularly to ask yourself "How do I feel right now? What are the triggers?" Think up some strategies in advance so that you'll know what to do if you feel "amber" or recognize the onset of "red" symptoms. Being prepared will in itself help you to feel more in control of yourself and your situation.

FOR MORE INFORMATION

Book:
Drake, John D. *Downshifting: How to Work Less and Enjoy It More*. San Francisco, CA: Berrett-Koehler, 2001.

"Nobody should be chief executive officer of anything for more than five or six years. By then he's stale, bored, and utterly dependent upon his own clichés."

Robert Townsend

Considering Taking a Career Break

GETTING STARTED

A career break is a period away from the usual working role and its routine, and there are many positive reasons to consider taking one. A new parental role is the most common reason, but study, travel, trying out a business idea, or caring for a sick relative are other positive priorities that trigger people to spend a period away from work.

People may also take a break to get away from negative aspects of their career. Stress and pressure, office politics, and turbulent periods of upheaval can all make employees look for a change of scene. This allows them to recharge their batteries, get back in touch with their core values, and maintain their health.

If you do take a career break, you have some options to think about once you get back; you might return to your old job or look for a new challenge when you're ready. These days companies are more likely to look on career breaks favorably and rather than lose the investment already made in training and development, they agree to career breaks in the hope that their people will eventually return to employment with increased commitment, renewed loyalty, a broader perspective, and additional skills.

FAQs

I've been working for quite a while now. Am I throwing away everything I've achieved if I take a break?

While time off doing nothing will be very hard to sell on your résumé, having and achieving some valuable personal objectives during your time away may well affect your career for the better. You'll often be perceived with respect (and perhaps a little jealousy) for having the initiative, confidence, and determination to realize a dream. You'll need to make sure that you communicate what you've gained from your break clearly and positively, though. Stress the benefits when you describe what you've been doing and quantify your achievements if you can. For example, if you have management skills and you have been working overseas for a charity, you could say: "I helped secure financing for a health center which enabled it to take on three more members of staff and increase its impact in the community."

What are the main obstacles to taking a career break?

Your other priorities are actually the main obstacles. The most common reasons for not taking a long break from work are to do with one's partner, family, house, career, or sports ambitions (if you play regularly for a local team, for example). For most people, giving up work for a period of time means a loss of income on which they have become dependant.

In general, the younger you are and the less routine your life is, the less inhibited you may feel in taking the plunge. At the other end of the spectrum, there are some lucky people for whom a career break of 12 or 24 months can be managed on savings alone, allowing them to return to their previous routine without any material change.

Will my skills be downgraded?

12 months away from a role will not generally leave you with a skills issue. The more technical your role and the longer you spend away from it, though, the more time and effort you will have to put into staying in touch.

Some employers, for example, in healthcare professions, find it so important to retain good workers that they will not only allow them to take lengthy breaks but will fund their skills updates on their return. In other areas, it may be up to you to update yourself. For more specific advice on this area, talk to the relevant managers in your company or organization or contact an industry body for advice. If you belong to a labor union, it may also be able to help.

MAKING IT HAPPEN
Decide on Your Objectives

Step back and take some time to ask yourself why a career break holds such appeal. You need to start off with an idea of what you hope to experience or achieve. What secondary or underlying objectives do you have? Visualize the beginning, middle, and end of your time away and your eventual return to work. Make notes about how you want it to be in an *ideal* situation, but also think about how it might work realistically.

Prepare to Ask Your Employer

When you broach the issue with your boss, be clear in your mind about everything you want. Take along some notes as prompts if you'd find that helpful. Know what you are asking for, including the length of time away, pay and benefits, continuity of employment, possibility of return to the same position, and so on. To make the idea seem as attractive as possible, you need to be able to explain what benefits your break will bring both for you and your employer, and prepare a statement about wanting to return. Make a business case that would encourage your employer to support your request. For example, let's say that you work for a large multinational organization but that you'd like to spend some time abroad learning Spanish. You could say that the language skills you'd gain on your break would be put to good use when you return, as you'd be able to liaise more quickly and effectively with your organization's branches in both Europe and Latin America.

You could also find out whether there's a policy that provides for sponsored sabbaticals. Your employer might be prepared to provide what you request, or suggest a compromise. Be ready to be flexible and to meet your employer halfway. Remember that your request may have come completely out of the blue, so he or she may feel a bit "ambushed."

Be Ready In Case the Answer Is "No"

You have to be prepared for things not going according to plan. If this does happen, first of all find out why you've been turned down. The provision of career breaks is purely at the discretion of your employer, but if they are made available only to women, then they are clearly behaving in a discriminatory manner. If other work colleagues have been granted similar time off for parental or study purposes and you have not been supplied with a satisfactory explanation as to why you have not, you may want to claim a grievance through your personnel department (if your company has one) or your union.

Even though you're bound to feel disappointed at first, look at the positive aspect of your company's decision: freedom. If you're that committed to the idea of the career break, you'll just go anyway, even if your employer won't keep your job open. The obvious downside of your employer agreeing to your break is that you are obligated to return. You may not want to once you've been away for a while, so in a way you've been relieved of that decision.

Consider Other Ways of Achieving Your Goals

Part-time work can free you up to realize your dreams without having to take such a significant drop in earnings. If you stay with the same employer, it can also give you continuity of routine and of your social network, both of which can help to reduce the stress related to big changes in your life.

Working from home, sometimes called "telecommuting," can allow you more time in your chosen environment and it may also give you the flexibility to control when you work. Many people choose this option since it gives them fewer financial headaches than reducing their hours. There is a negative side to it, unfortunately, in that even if you do take this route work will still eat up reasonably large chunks of your time and attention and you may feel isolated outside of your everyday comfort zone. It may also mean that you can't spend as much time focusing on the new challenges you're hoping to explore. It's worth spending some time thinking through an average working week and seeing how that might translate to a home-office setting.

Working abroad can be a great way to satisfy a craving for novelty and variety while furthering your career ambitions at the same time. It is the best way to master a foreign language and to gain an understanding of a nation's culture, as you are totally immersed in it. Don't forget the financial benefits too: you'll still be earning something, so this is a good way to fund your itchy feet. You may choose to work within your usual field through a change of employer, or you may go for a complete change, such as picking grapes or teaching English.

Changing employer can give you the chance to negotiate terms as part of your contract, with a view to a future break. This works for study breaks and for travel abroad but may not be suitable for parental breaks, the timescale for which may already be dictated! If you (or your partner) are already expecting a baby, changing employer could result in a loss of rights to parental leave. This may not affect you right at the moment, but it's worth bearing in mind.

Looking for a new position on your return can give you complete freedom, and it's certainly a good option if you're hoping to take an extended career break. It may also be the most suitable route if you intend to retrain, take a completely new direction in your career, or care for children or other family members in the long term.

Take the Plunge

Look back over the notes you took when you were daydreaming about your career break and prioritize your objectives. Which are most important to you? These are the "core" of what you will achieve. Think about the obstacles that may stand in your way and the contingency plans you'll need to make to deal with them. Obviously you can't see all the potential events that may throw you off course, but attempting to identify the most obvious will bring your plan into the real world.

What is the gap between where you are now and where you want to be? Start breaking it up into manageable chunks and then identify milestones along the way. For example, if you are planning a trip abroad, your first "chunk" is research about your destination(s), and the first milestone is knowing which visas and work permits are required.

Having a plan will help you move efficiently toward your goals, but don't feel you have to stick to it rigidly. You may decide to rethink your objectives as a result of experiences you have early on, so try to remain focused but be flexible too. Once you get used to planning in the way outlined above, you'll find you waste less time worrying or dithering.

Tie Up Loose Ends

If you decide to leave your current job when you go on your career break, make sure that you leave with the best possible reputation so that you'll get a glowing reference. This will also mean that you can apply to your previous employer for work on your return, if you so wish. If you *are* planning to return to the same position after your break, it's even more important to make sure that tasks are properly completed or handed over efficiently, and that you train your successor as well as possible.

Start making a list of important contacts and duties well in advance of your leaving date to act as a helpful resource to others in your absence. If at all possible, arrange for a hand-over period so that your successor can see what you do on an everyday basis.

COMMON MISTAKES
You Don't Keep In Touch

Keeping in touch is vitally important if you want a smooth transition back into your previous job. It's also important if you will be moving on to a new career. Stay attuned to who's who and catch up with relevant communications in your business or industry. This is much easier to do these days, wherever you are, and Web sites, company publications, or trade journals can help with this. If you feel it's right for you, and you are taking some time out to complete a course of study, you could spend your vacation time back at work.

901

ACTIONLIST

"A state without the means of some change is without the means of its conservation."

Edmund Burke

902

ACTIONLIST

Feeling Trapped by Finances

Working out financial matters can be difficult, but it can be done as long as you're clear about your priorities. For example, identify where your money currently goes. What could you achieve with a different plan? Weigh the benefits of continuing as you are, compared to spending on your career break. Are there ways to reduce spending so that you can save for a career break in advance? To release yourself from feeling "trapped," remind yourself of your priorities and choices.

FOR MORE INFORMATION

Book:
Drake, John D. *Downshifting: How to Work Less and Enjoy It More*. San Francisco, CA: Berrett-Koehler, 2001.

Web Sites:
careerbreaker.com: **www.careerbreaker.com**
TEFL.Net: **www.tefl.net**

"If I were a medical man, I should prescribe a holiday to any patient who considered his work important."

Edward O. Wilson

Managing Dual Career Dilemmas

GETTING STARTED

There are many arguments in favor of dual career families. In most cases, two incomes enable partners to provide at least the basic comforts and modest pleasures of modern life. When both partners work, each is able to keep up with his or her career path, stay marketable and competitive, and contribute to postretirement financial security. Additionally, the knowledge that one partner is securely employed gives the other partner the opportunity to quit, if necessary, and seek a better position elsewhere.

However, there are also drawbacks: one member of the couple may have to subordinate their career interests in favor of the other's. Time and energy demands can distract dual career couples from their personal priorities: their marriage, their children, and their interests.

Fortunately, employers are increasingly recognizing the need to implement policies that promote flexibility and tolerance for balancing personal needs with work. As an example, many companies are offering flextime, telecommuting, and day care programs for children, among other initiatives to help working parents balance their jobs with their family life. But, as a member of a dual-career couple, you and your partner must still be the ones to make the choices and decisions that best reflect the values and priorities that you've agreed on as a couple.

Only you and your partner can prioritize the elements of your life together according to your values. But the following points are key questions to ask yourselves as you plan your dual career:

- Is each partner's career a primary career?
- How do family needs and career requirements conflict with each other?
- How do family needs and career requirements enhance each other?
- In the case of conflicting opportunities, how will the decisions be made equitably so that, in the long run, both partners will be able to look back with satisfaction?
- How can you make sure the long-term financial interests of the nonprimary career partner are protected?

FAQs
Is it possible to balance a career that I desire with a healthy relationship?

Yes, but only if you manage each carefully. Have a clear idea in advance about what you want (and agree with your partner) and you'll be able to make your choices consistently with your long-term mission. You'll know later whether you achieved that mission.

How can I have it all at once?

Work–life balance experts say that you probably won't be able to have it all at once. But if you work together with your partner, you stand a better chance of having it all, even if it's only a piece at a time. How much you truly have all at once depends on your willingness to make tradeoffs.

I have heard that dual career divorces are more common than single career divorces. Do I have to sacrifice my marriage for my career?

No. Communication, trust, flexibility, and creativity are important for every partnership and they're especially important for dual career couples.

What should I do if it's not working?

Take a businesslike approach to solving the problem. Living a rough and uninspiring life doesn't necessarily mean you're falling out of love—just as a failed product launch doesn't mean necessarily that your organization is doomed. It could merely mean that you simply need to alter the management of certain parts of your life.

MAKING IT HAPPEN
Approach Your Dual Career As You Would a Complex Business

Understand there are various "departments" in your private life, and manage them effectively. This isn't to suggest that you shouldn't manage them with love and devotion. But budgeting and compartmentalizing certain aspects of your life and time could help you distribute your resources (time, money, and attention) in the most effective way.

Take Advantage of Technology Wherever You Can

Many dual career homes have at least one computer. Install business management software that can also automate certain aspects of the business of your life. There are calendar, organization, and accounting software packages available for average consumers to give them the management advantages enjoyed by big business. You can even keep your grocery list on the family computer.

Consider Your Personal Partner to Be Your Business Partner as well

Just as a company defines long-term objectives and has a mission, work with your partner to determine what your relationship's mission and long-term objectives are. Using long-term missions and objectives as reference points will help the two of you make difficult decisions when an opportunity for one partner involves great sacrifice for the other.

Communicate

You can only expect your partner to fulfill your needs and your priorities if he or she knows what they are.

Get Professional Help When You Need It

Companies outsource services that are necessary but beyond their internal capability. Why not try this at home if you need to? The services available to you can range from chores such as housekeeping and cooking to sup-

---

"I have yet to hear a man ask for advice on how to combine marriage and a career."

Gloria Steinem

port services such as bookkeeping, financial planning, and even marriage counseling.

Use Your Business Skills Training to Help You Manage Your Work–Life Balance

One skill that could serve you well into the future is negotiation. When the two of you take the same course, you'll then negotiate with each other according to the same rules and the same understanding of ultimate shared goals.

Recruit Your Children

There is no reason why dual career couples with children should shoulder the burden of all the little tasks of living. Give your children age appropriate responsibilities. Make them partners in your family's future as well as the beneficiaries of your hard work.

If There Is Going to Be a Primary Career and a Secondary Career, Agree Which One Is Going to Be Which

If you aren't both going to put your careers first, make sure you both recognize this fact. With that understanding, you know who will be responsible for taking care of a sick child, while the other one makes that important meeting. If both careers are primary, it's important to understand that as well. Agreeing how your careers fit on the priority list will reduce the potential for major relationship straining disagreements.

Take Care of Yourself

You're also the C.E.O. of your own life. Remember to fold in your own needs into the larger balance of family, work, and partnership obligations. You're no good to anyone if you aren't good to yourself.

Make Dates and Make Appointments with Your Partner

Dates are for romance. Appointments are for managing the business of your lives together.

COMMON MISTAKES
You Become "Ships Passing in the Night"

It's so easy to get absorbed with the daily details of living and working that you forget to appreciate the life you've built together. Schedule time for each other that is set aside exclusively for enjoying each other's company and remembering the joy of the relationship, regardless of what else is going on in your lives.

You Lose Control of the Small Details of Life

Keeping track of minor details could seem too trivial to prioritize. However, those details could mean the difference between whether or not you'll have an argument over an empty gas tank or milk carton—or a forgotten child still waiting to be picked up at an empty school. Keep "To Do" and "To Buy" lists at a central location where everyone can keep them up to date. Make sure everyone knows whose responsibility it is to complete those "To Do" tasks.

You Feel As Though You Are Carrying the Whole Load, Both at Work and at Home

Be sure you continue to communicate with your partner on both daily needs and long-term career goals. If you find one of you continually is the one to subordinate personal goals and dreams in favor of the other's, check in with your partner to make sure that this trend is acceptable to both of you.

FOR MORE INFORMATION

Web sites:
Anglo Domus, International Relocation Services:
www.anglodomus.com/services/special.html#partner
SelfhelpMagazine:
www.selfhelpmagazine.com/articles/wf/dualcar.html

"In retrospect, for a full-time chief executive to do what is almost a full-time job is extremely difficult."

Clive Thompson

Surviving Job Loss

GETTING STARTED

No matter whether you lose your job with no notice, or you know months in advance that your position is going to be eliminated, the actual event of losing your job can be a shock to your physical system, your emotional health, and, of course, your bank account. The steps you take as soon as you get a hint that your job is coming to an end will help to cushion the impact of one of the most stressful times in your life.

The concept of "strategy" is extremely valuable at this point in your career. It invites you somehow to rise above your sensation of panic and, perhaps, the tendency to feel worthless in the marketplace. It'll also help you take a new, bird's-eye view of your life and career, and see the potential for ultimately better work and greater success. You should consider the following questions as you take important steps to turn this upsetting news into a success story:

- How can you benefit in the long run?
- What can you do to prepare yourself in advance, so you're not taken by surprise?
- What power do you have to decide the terms of your departure?
- Can you be consistent with your own dreams, in the face of a marketplace that is urging you to build a career that doesn't interest you?
- How do your skills, talents, and drive fit into the larger business community?

FAQs

Why is it important to have a strategy in place before I lose my job?

If you're able to design your strategy in a calm environment, you can coolly select the steps and actions to take later when you're most likely to feel panicked and diminished by the event of discovering your employer no longer wants you.

If I'm let go at my company, does that mean my relationship with my employer is over for good?

No. Many employers who are letting their workers go recognize that it's very likely that they'll want to re-hire them when economic conditions improve. Even if that were not to happen, the business world is very small and you will likely run into your employer down the road at a convention, or even at a different organization. In fact, it's not unheard of for the employee who has been let go to be the one to hire their former superior at a different organization months or years later. For this reason, it's important never to burn a bridge!

What should I tell my family?

Hundreds of thousands of excellent employees all over the world face unemployment through no fault of their own. If you aren't completely honest with your family, they won't understand the strain and tension that is suddenly in your home and you'll rob them of the opportunity to support you in your time of crisis. Everyone—down to the smallest child—can contribute to the cause of thriving in temporarily reduced circumstances. This could be a golden opportunity to become closer through the teamwork needed to pull through.

MAKING IT HAPPEN

Try to Be Aware of Lay-off Potential Long Before It Actually Happens

Employers are often reluctant to announce to the workforce that they are letting workers go for fear that everyone will disappear en masse, leaving the organization in chaos. But it's still possible to be aware of trends that might be harbingers of unemployment. Is your local newspaper reporting lower profits out of your company? Is there a merger or acquisition rumored? Is there a sudden spate of "closed-door" meetings? Has your boss, or boss's boss, suddenly lost organizational power, no longer being invited to those closed-door meetings? Is your own job a vital link to the organization's profitability or is it a "cost center?" Is your overall industry—or local economy—suffering a downturn? The answers to these questions might help you assess how secure your position really is.

No Matter How Secure You Think Your Job Is, Always Take Time to Be a Recognized, Respected, and Active Member of At Least One Professional Organization or Association

Have a large and intricate network of contacts that you can always draw from, no matter what your employment circumstances. That network could be your advance warning system, or the conduit for information about other jobs and opportunities in good times and bad. Knowing you have that resource at your disposal will reduce the anxiety and panic, should the worst-case scenario of losing your job actually come true.

Understand You're Part of a "Value Mesh"

"Old economy" market equations would place you in a value chain, where you buy from one and sell to another, almost always in your immediate sphere of commerce or expertise. But in the "new economy" environment, you're actually one connection in an entire mesh—or network—of buyers and sellers from a wide variety of spheres and expertise. With a little imagination, what you do and what you know can be translated into a huge number of marketplaces, not just the one you're doing business in currently.

Don't Sign the Severance Agreement While In a State of Shock

Most employers will tell you the terrible news and then slide a contract under your nose for you to sign before you go away. Remember, they've had plenty of advance warning to devise a separation agreement that benefits the organization. You deserve at least 24 hours to enable

905

ACTIONLIST

"Nothing bad's going to happen to us. If we get fired, it's not failure; it's a midlife vocational assessment."

P. J. O'Rourke

906

ACTIONLIST

you to consider it carefully, perhaps even with an attorney.

Remember That Many Severance Agreements Are Negotiable

Perhaps you can convert your job to a contract position. In most cases, after all, the work still has to be done. By offering to do it on an outsourcing basis, you've found a way to generate cash flow for yourself while staying in touch and on good terms with your former employer. Other negotiable details can include the right to continue to use your office space while searching for new employment (the space exists whether you're there or not, and the illusion of being employed adds to your attractiveness to other possible employers); use of company equipment and services, such as the photocopy machine and voicemail; letters of recommendation or introduction from the organization's senior executives; or a larger severance pay package.

Take Advantage of Company-Sponsored Outplacement Services

The best outplacement services are highly valuable benefits, largely unavailable to the average individual. This is a once-in-a-lifetime opportunity to have free professional help in designing your job search plan of action and to receive state-of-the-art aptitude and skills testing—as well as giving you a place to go to every day, where you'll be in a professional office environment with your peers. Outplacement counselors also know the best and most powerful employers in the area, so you're plugged into a pipeline that's not available to individuals unaffiliated with organizations or outplacement services.

Keep Your Skills Up to Date

If your employer is offering free or subsidized skills training, take advantage of the offer. If you've been out of the job market for even as little as a year, it's likely that your technical and professional skills would benefit from a refresher course. Seize every learning opportunity that's placed before you. It will give you both a technical edge and the confidence to start your job search project.

Keep Your Spirits Up

The "pink slip party" is a new phenomenon of the current round of firings and closings. Throw a party for your fellow sufferers, and invite local recruiters to enjoy the gathering as well. It's good to know you're not alone and, even if recruiters don't have any opportunities at the moment, they'll be glad to collect your résumé and contact information. The economy goes through cycles, and recruiters will always be glad to have a full file of excellent potential candidates.

Forget Those Lists of Promising, "Hot" Careers

They only ever promise a glut on the market of such careers in two to four years' time. Do what you love and build a career around your passions. There will always be a demand for employees who love what they do—they're the most innovative, self-starting, and constantly developing individuals.

COMMON MISTAKES
You Fall into a Disempowered Despair

Don't tie your sense of self-worth to your career or job. You are who you are, regardless of where your salary is coming from. If you fall into a trough of low self-esteem, volunteer your professional expertise to a charity. The time spent with others will get you out of your malaise. Most important, you'll experience the real benefits of your gifts and knowledge, as they'll be received with no other payment than gratitude.

You Don't Take Care of Yourself Physically

Without routine and regular exercise, the sofa and the remote control become increasingly enticing. But if you maintain a regular routine and exercise program, your sense of purpose and minute-by-minute priorities will remain clear. The endorphins resulting from your physical exertion will also keep the blues and fear at bay. Eating sensibly will keep your body strong and resistant to the stress that comes with uncertainty.

You Let Isolation Overwhelm Your Life

Make a point of filling your calendar with business meetings every week. Put on presentable street clothes every day and go to a local coffee shop, if that's all that is available, just to be out among people. Meet at least one new person a week. Find a way to help that individual by introducing him or her to someone inside your own value mesh.

FOR MORE INFORMATION

Book:
Berman, Eileen L. *Dealing Effectively with Job Loss: A Unique Approach to Rebuilding Your Life.* Norcross, GA: Engineering & Management Press, 1999.

Web site:
Laid Off Central: **www.laidoffcentral.com**

See also:
✔ Leaving with Style: Exiting with Dignity (pp. 909–910)

"'You're fired!' No other words can so easily and succinctly reduce a confident, self-assured executive to an insecure, groveling shred of his former self." — Frank P. Louchheim

Returning to Work After a Career Break

GETTING STARTED

People take career breaks for many reasons: to look after family members, for self-development, to satisfy an interest in other cultures, to recover from illness, to complete personal projects, or to recharge their batteries following a layoff. Whatever your reasons for stopping, there comes a moment when your attention turns back to the world of work.

You may have an agreement to return to the same employer after your break or you may be looking for pastures new. Either way, being clear about what you want, as well as what you have to offer, will move you closer to achieving it. Take some time to consider your career plan and your objectives for returning. What is the core purpose of work for you and what else do you hope to get from working? How much of this do you expect to achieve immediately and how much within three years? Think over all of these issues and then review your strengths. What knowledge, skills, achievements, facets of your personality, and potential would you like to use at work?

FAQs
Will my previous experience count, even after several years away?

Many people returning to work after a break worry that their skills and knowledge will be out of date and therefore won't count. If it has been a while since you worked or if you need a license to practice, you may need to refresh your skills. Those with technical aspects to their job will need to put extra effort into updating their knowledge. However, previous experience *does* count. It tells your employer that you are capable of success in the job that you did previously. It's also reassuring to you that you'll be able to perform, since you were successful before.

Will my self-confidence return?

Confidence in your ability to do a good job can drop when you've been away from your work for a while. This is particularly the case after illness, job loss, or a maternity break, and those returning often doubt their ability to cope with their busy and responsible job. Don't worry! Lots of people take up the challenge every year and are successful, enjoying their return to the office. Making sure you are up to date with all the latest policies, technologies, and skills will help you to break back into the working world more easily. The best recipe for building confidence is getting out there and proving to yourself step by step that you can do it.

MAKING IT HAPPEN
Return to the same job

If you're planning to return to the same job, it's a good idea to keep up some regular contact with your team to reassure them of your ongoing commitment and enthusiasm and to keep yourself informed about changes. Step up this contact in the two weeks before you return and make sure that you widen it to include all your regular working contacts.

Be sensitive in the way that you interact with your boss, colleagues, and staff. Some of them may have carried an extra workload in your absence and deserve your appreciation. Some may feel threatened by your return; others may be reluctant to give up tasks and responsibilities they have enjoyed while you've been away. Be tactful and do your best keep open good channels of communication between you.

Return after Job Loss

If your job has been terminated, try not to let it demoralize you. Take some positive action instead that will help you to get back on track. First, think about the market you have been working in. Is it expanding or shrinking? Your answer to this will help you to decide whether to return to the same sector or try your luck elsewhere. Think about your strengths and skills and how you could transfer these to other position. If you're not sure of current trends, ask people you know to give you a steer. Talk to your former boss and colleagues if you have a good relationship with them and ask if they have any recommendations about who you should be talking to as part of your job search. This will help to keep your networks growing.

Prepare a positive statement to use if you are asked during an interview why you lost your job. Ideally, this should be a very short description of the contraction in the market or the restructuring of your department or organization, followed by a forward-looking statement about the skills you hope to build on and where you want to go with your career. Also prepare a description of how you spent your time away from work, how it benefited you, and how the experience will add value to your next employer's business.

Search for a New Position

A gap on a chronological résumé is bound to be picked up and will probably get a knee-jerk adverse reaction, so make sure that you highlight what you've been doing with your time in positive terms. If you find you are still getting negative reactions, try writing a "skills-based" or "functional" résumé. This type of résumé focuses attention on your strengths and achievements; an employer decides whether they're interested in the first few seconds of reading, well before noticing your career break on the second page. Whichever type of résumé you write, you need to get across the benefits your career break has brought whenever the question arises with prospective employers. Perhaps you have demonstrated initiative, patience, people skills, planning and organizing, or

---

"I never think of the future. It comes soon enough."   Albert Einstein

908

ACTIONLIST

confidence and determination. Highlight any new skills, even if you don't feel that they are relevant to the positions you are applying for, as they demonstrate your ability to learn.

Job hunting can be tiring and deflating at times, so it's important to keep yourself feeling upbeat. Do this by making a little progress on your job search every day. Make sure that you make the most of *all* opportunities, replying to advertisements, posting your résumé on Internet job sites, registering with agencies, approaching companies direct, and networking with people you know.

Make the Most of the Honeymoon Period in a New Job

Congratulations, you've got the job! You may have a formal orientation to give you a basic grounding in the information you need but it's still sensible to think about how you can make a good initial impression. In the first week, come to grips with exactly what your objectives are. Clarity is the watchword here. In some jobs you'll be expected to make an impact very early, in other roles the honeymoon period is long. You need to know what's expected of you when, and how your objectives fit into those of the team and the organization. Getting to know specifics about people, like a department head's agenda or a key client's pet hates, will help you to navigate the potential pitfalls and find the easy routes to achieving your goals. Putting all the information together will allow you to understand how and why the organization functions best.

The second week is best spent finding out more about who's who and creating the communication channels you'll need to get your job done. Meet with as many key people as you can, as this will help you to handle any political aspects of your role well. During the third week you can begin to develop a clear picture of how to best play things in your own terms. Ask yourself the following questions:

- What am I going to be doing?
- How am I going to achieve it?
- What do people in this business need to know about me, my skills, and past achievements?
- How am I going to get that message out?

Start a role fresh, in two senses:

- Put behind you the worries that you had in your previous role. For example, if you had a difficult relationship with your boss in your last job, lay that to rest and don't dwell on it. Don't carry old insecurities into your next job—things are different now. Visualize how you want things to be and start on the first day as if they were already so.
- Be well rested, but prepared to go home feeling exhausted. If you're not taking on information like a sponge in the early weeks, then something odd is going on. Plan a very quiet first weekend or two so that you can rest, digest the information, and make sense of what you have learned.

COMMON MISTAKES
You Suffer from Culture Shock

Humans find change stressful, and even changes that we want and actively seek out have an effect on our minds and bodies. Recognize that you may experience culture shock initially when you return to work, and decide in advance how you can help yourself cope. Accentuate the positive when chatting with people at work, both about your time away and about your return. Your colleagues may feel that you are lucky to have had a break and may resent what they see as "whining" about the difficulties of returning. On the other hand, it's important not to bottle up any negative feelings—not everyone can slip back into their old life right away. Find an appropriate and sympathetic friend, coach, or mentor to share your thoughts with and to support you during this period.

You Want to Be the Conquering Hero or Heroine

Some people expect to be greeted with awe and fascination by their team when they return to their old job and are surprised to be facing a very negative atmosphere, one sometimes made up of jealousy, hostility, defensiveness, and, for managers, loss of authority. Try to react with understanding to your colleagues and don't expect too much attention. Throw yourself into your work and have confidence that your performance and your personality will soon bring people around. Be patient and remember that an atmosphere of this sort rarely lasts if you remain positive.

You Don't "Sell" the Benefits of Your Break

Unless you spread the word yourself, people may not recognize what a break has done for you. It may not be clear what additional skills you now have and how these can benefit your team and organization. Whether you're chatting with colleagues or being grilled at an interview by a panel of managers, it pays to have done your homework and to have really thought about what you have gained and how you can persuade others of the benefits. If you raised $X for charity and developed your organizational skills and influencing strategies in the process, say so and be proud of it.

FOR MORE INFORMATION

Web Site:
Monster.com: **www.monster.com**

See also:
✓ Managing Your Time (pp. 828–830)

Leaving with Style: Exiting with Dignity

GETTING STARTED

Probably several times during your career, you will leave one employer for another. Frequently, leaving the organization will be your choice; sometimes it will be the organization's. Either way, it is important for you to exit with style and dignity. Whenever you depart from a job, under whatever circumstances, you want to leave a lasting impression of professionalism. The following are questions you should contemplate as you get ready to leave your current employer:

- How do I want my supervisor and colleagues to remember me after I have moved on to the next job?
- What do I want my supervisor and colleagues to say about me after I leave the organization?
- What specific things can I do to demonstrate my professionalism, even when I know that I am leaving?

FAQs

Why should I worry about "exiting with dignity?" I won't be working there any more anyway

The phrase "never burn your bridges" became a cliché with good reason. You should always leave a job on the best possible terms. People from the organization you are leaving may be called to give you references for future jobs. You want to be able to use past employers for references, and to feel assured that they will speak highly of you.

Remember that, even in large industries, it is still a small world. People (especially at higher levels) know each other, and may casually inquire about a former employee. Staff from your former organization may go to conventions or conferences and meet people from your current organization. If you leave a negative impression at one company, your new employer may very well hear about it.

Also, suppose your new organization were to be bought by or merged with your old one? Mergers and acquisitions are becoming more common. You could end up working for and with some of the same people you left when you resigned from the company. Make sure you can face former employers with your head held high.

My boss has been impossible to work with. Should I discuss his or her management errors in the exit interview?

The simple answer is "no." What will you gain by bad-mouthing your (soon-to-be) former boss? When asked about working conditions or supervision, always begin and end with positive comments. For example, "I think we have a great team in the department, even though we've been under some real pressure lately. If there was a bit less pressure, I think the department could really

capitalize on the creativity that's already there." Say as many positive, accurate things as possible.

Should I help my employer to find my replacement?

If your boss asks you to interview candidates for your job, doing it well can go a long way to leaving a positive lasting impression. When talking to candidates for your job, do not discuss negative aspects of the job, coworkers, supervisors, or the organization. This is the time to be as affirming as possible. Talk about the positive facets of the work and the organization. Remember, the person you are interviewing may get the job, and you want his or her impression of you to be that of the consummate professional.

If the interviewee asks you why you are leaving the organization, never talk about how much more money you will be making, or how much better the working conditions are at your new job. Tell your potential replacement that you were offered an opportunity with some interesting challenges that will build on the skills that you have attained in your current position.

MAKING IT HAPPEN
Prepare Your Letter of Resignation

Always give notice to your employer in writing. Your letter should be brief and professional, and contain the date of your last day of work. End your resignation letter on a positive note by commenting briefly on the valuable learning, or challenging, or growth opportunities the position you are resigning from has afforded you. That's it. Do not go on about how much better the new job is.

Meet with Your Immediate Supervisor

Arrange a time to meet with the person to whom you report directly. Your immediate supervisor always deserves the courtesy of a face-to-face meeting. During this meeting, you should tell your supervisor that you have decided to take another position, and when you will be leaving. This is not the time to tell your boss all the things that are wrong with him or her, how low your salary has been, or how awful the working conditions are in your present organization. When asked why you are leaving, simply state that an exciting new opportunity has presented itself, one that you just could not refuse.

Always be professional in this meeting. If you have had any problems with your supervisor, forget about them now. The best advice ever given about this meeting is "let your supervisor save face." You want your boss to feel as comfortable as possible during this meeting. You also want to assure him or her that you will be finishing certain projects, or continuing to meet with customers, and so on. Perhaps one of the most difficult aspects of exiting with dignity is to keep this meeting positive and upbeat.

"Handled creatively, getting fired allows an executive . . . to actually experience a sense of relief that he never wanted the job he has lost."

Frank P. Louchheim

Continue to Work As If You Were Staying with the Organization

This is the real key to exiting with dignity and leaving an excellent lasting impression. Continue to work as if you were trying for the next promotion. Finish as many projects as possible; attend all meetings; be an active participant in your work. This is not the time to let things slide.

One outstanding example of an impressive and dignified exit was set by a faculty member who did not receive tenure at his university (the academic equivalent of being fired). He attended and actively participated in every meeting, put effort into his teaching, and continued to work enthusiastically with students. In short, he continued to work as if he would be in that job next week, next month, and next year. You should too.

Leave Instructions for the Next Person Who Will Be Doing Your Job

If there are certain projects that are ongoing or you do not complete, leave detailed written instructions. Make the transition for the next person as easy as possible. In doing so, you are leaving the impression that you did not simply "blow off" the work you could not complete; you recognized it, and took the steps necessary to get the job done.

COMMON MISTAKES
Not Giving Enough Notice When You Resign

In a number of professions, the two-week notice is a thing of the past. Many organizations expect a much longer notice. Check to see what the norm is in your industry or organization, and do it discreetly when you start looking for another job. Companies look very unfavorably on employees who give little or no notice before leaving. You should give your employer adequate notice to recruit someone to take over your position.

Talking Excessively about Your Great New Job and Salary to Coworkers

Coworkers will ask you about your new position, and talking about it is natural, but bragging about how much better your new position is than your old one only leaves coworkers feeling resentful and with an overall unfavorable impression of you. Tempting as it is to brag, and excited as you are about your new position, limit your discussions to comments such as "Well, this is a good opportunity for me."

Giving Your Notice or Resignation Via E-mail

Although we use e-mail more and more for office communication, always give your supervisor a formal letter of resignation (see "Prepare your letter of resignation" above). Also be sure to schedule a meeting to give your notice in person to your direct supervisor (see "Meet with your immediate supervisor" above).

FOR MORE INFORMATION

Book:
Levitt, Julie Griffin. *Your Career: How to Make it Happen.* 6th ed. Florence, KY: South-Western Educational Publishing, 2005.

Web site:
Job Hunters' Bible: **www.jobhuntersbible.com**

See also:
☆ Downsizing with Dignity (pp. 14–15)
☆ Driving Fear from the Workplace (pp. 420–421)
✔ Surviving Job Loss (pp. 905–906)

"The final test of a leader is that he leaves behind him in other men the conviction and the will to carry on."
Walter Lippmann

Handling Resignations— The Employer's Perspective

GETTING STARTED

Although it is disappointing to lose key people, resignations give companies a chance to plan ahead and recruit people who can contribute to the organization's growth. Personnel shifts can be a catalyst for taking a fresh look at what's working and what isn't, and deciding what kinds of changes would be most productive.

From the employees' standpoint, resignations allow people to move on in their careers, learn new skills, and take on new responsibilities. An individual leaving a company is not necessarily withdrawing his or her loyalty or influence over its future direction. Indeed, past employees may well be instrumental in instigating joint projects or ventures that will change the fortunes of their former organization.

FAQs

I manage a key individual who has resigned. How can I convey this information to her team without risking a drop in morale?

Convene the team, along with the person who has resigned, to discuss the resignation and its implications. Showing your concern about their feelings and asking for input invites team members' involvement and gives them a sense of control. It will also give you an opportunity to discuss any structural or resource issues arising from the departure.

I run a team of specialists who are hard to replace, and as soon as one left the others started to follow. What can I do to prevent talent from hemorrhaging out of the company?

Take your team's exodus as an opportunity to identify and resolve problems. Are terms of employment better elsewhere? Have conditions in your organization deteriorated without your being fully aware of the slippage? Conducting exit interviews should help you identify your weak points and structure improvements. Invite remaining staff to participate in the planning. This might be a good time to review your company's medium- and long-range strategic plans. Would reorganizing or consolidating departments help reverse the disaffection? Are there others you can promote into these vacancies? Or will your company need to make changes in order to attract new talent?

A member of my team has asked to leave full-time employment and become a contractor to the business on a project basis. Is this a good idea?

Organizations are increasingly turning to contract employees to give them more flexibility and cut direct payroll costs. In many instances, contract employees are responsible for the cost of their own office space off-premises as well as funding their own benefits such as health insurance, vacations, pensions, and so on. However, contract employees will often charge more for their services than they received in salary. The key issues are costs and benefits. Another part of the equation is how you manage the situation with other team members to make sure there's no ambiguity about how work is to be done and who has responsibility.

I was handed a resignation by someone whom I was happy to see leave. However, he's changed his mind and asked to stay on the job. How do I handle this?

If you feel strongly that your organization would be better off without this person, you're within your rights as the supervisor to deny his request. If you think the person might be suited for a job elsewhere in your company, you might advise him to discuss his prospects with the human resources department.

MAKING IT HAPPEN
Be Prepared

Most organizations value a stable work force. Inevitably, however, a certain percentage of your employees will leave every year, taking their skills and experience with them. Handling every one of these departures well is very much in the organization's interest: every former employee is a public witness to the character and culture of your company.

From the employer's perspective, processing an employee out of the organization requires specific steps in order to satisfy policy and legal requirements. Departing employees have needs, too, though, and it's good practice to make the procedure as efficient and straightforward as possible for the person leaving.

Acknowledge the Employee's Intention to Leave

Verbal notice may be acceptable, but it's usual for a resignation to be submitted to the manager in writing. Forward a copy of the letter of resignation to the human resources department so the process of removing the employee from the payroll and preparing a final account of benefits begins promptly.

Confirm the Leaving Date

Notice periods vary according to the position and the seniority level of the departing employee. If the person who is leaving wants to negotiate an early departure, you need to consider your existing resources and the volume of work pending. If work priorities allow, you may be willing to go along with the request.

Transition

Depending upon the nature of the work that the depart-

ing employee was engaged in, you need to plan for a smooth transition of projects and responsibilities. This might range from a simple plan developed jointly by the employee and his or her manager to negotiations involving a broader group of people who will be affected by the resignation.

A transition program may be quite involved. It takes times to brief coworkers, tie up administrative loose ends, and perhaps instigate some training in areas where special skills are required. If the organization is reducing its work force by natural attrition and the employee isn't going to be replaced, the person's responsibilities need to be reallocated.

If the person who is leaving has built a network of relationships important to the organization, you need to plan for continuity. If he or she has developed personal relationships with clients or suppliers, these are likely to continue. Personal loyalties may leave your organization vulnerable to loss of business, especially if the former employee becomes your competitor in the marketplace. Having clients or suppliers meet with the employee's replacement, perhaps with the departing employee present, can help maintain continuity in key relationships.

Conduct an Exit Interview

It's good policy to schedule exit interviews, usually conducted by a member of the human resources team. Invite departing employees to discuss their job, their reasons for leaving, and any other subjects of concern to them.

The exit interview should be a positive experience, even when the employee uses it to air grievances. Listen carefully to what each employee tells you; you may get new information or confirm previous reports of dissatisfaction with company policies or practices. Let exit interviews be learning experiences that clue you in on making the organization a better place to work.

Other Considerations

It is sometimes appropriate to ask an employee who resigns to leave the premises immediately—for example, when the employee has access to confidential information and is leaving to join a competitor, there is risk of disruption or sabotage, or the work has dried up. In these cases it's usual to pay the individual a severance allowance based on two weeks' notice or some other negotiated criterion.

Leaving a job—even under the best of circumstances—is not always comfortable; handling someone's departure

sensitively makes the experience easier. In most instances, it's customary to host a farewell event of some kind and give a gift to show appreciation for the employee's work.

COMMON MISTAKES
You Take it Personally
Taking a resignation personally can lead to distress on both the employee's and employer's side. People leave their jobs for a wide variety of reasons; resigning isn't necessarily an act of betrayal. Try to be open to hearing the reasons behind the decision and exploring the options, if there are any.

You Ignore the Implications of the Resignation
Ignoring the reality of someone's departure can leave you vulnerable. Everyone involved needs to pitch in to make sure that the leaving causes as little disruption as possible, so try bringing those affected by the move together to create a smooth transition.

You're Pleased the Person Is Going, and You Show It
No matter how unlikable, annoying, disruptive, or incompetent the employee has been, try not to show your delight that he or she is leaving: it's disrespectful to the departing employee and demoralizing for those who remain. Behave with professionalism from the moment you receive the resignation throughout the exit process, and leave your ego to one side.

FOR MORE INFORMATION

Book:
Bolles, Richard. *What Color is Your Parachute? A Practical Manual for Job-Hunters and Career-Changers.* Revised ed. Berkeley, CA: Ten Speed Press, 2006.

Web Sites:
FindLaw for Business: **www.findlaw.com**
BusinessTown.com:
www.businesstown.com/people/firing.asp
The U.S. Equal Employment Opportunity Commission:
www.eeoc.gov

Reinventing Yourself

GETTING STARTED

"Reinvention" as a word implies a process of deconstruction, a subsequent reconstruction, and a resultant new thing or (in this case) a new person who exhibits different talents and who pursues different opportunities. The intended "payback" for reinvention is gaining something that you currently feel is missing in your life, which could be anything from a successful career, to a better financial situation, to a happier work–life balance, or a complete change of lifestyle. However, reinventing yourself as a *reaction* to something or a set of circumstances tends to result in a purely cosmetic change as it does not get the root of *why* you want your life to be different. In order to reinvent yourself successfully and for the right reasons, you need to do it consciously and deliberately rather than as a knee-jerk reaction. This doesn't mean for a moment that spontaneity and creativity have no role in a life change—indeed, they're valuable forces in this process—but building in reality-checks as you go along will do you no harm at all.

FAQs

I really dislike my current job and I'm not even sure I want to be on this career path. I do like the company I work for, though. What can I do to reinvent myself in that context?

First of all, think of a career path within your company that you *would* like to pursue and, as part of that process, work out what your transferable skills and attributes are. If you feel there are gaps in your knowledge, think about how you can fill them, either by training or by gaining some experience on-site. For example, perhaps you could arrange to shadow a colleague who does have the experience you're hoping to gain. Once you've done this research and are clear about what you want to do, broach the subject with your line manager or human resources department, if you have one, to discuss how they can support you in making the personal changes you've identified. It's much better to tackle this situation head-on than to languish in an unrewarding job.

I am hoping to change my career direction but my résumé reflects who I *was*, not what I want to become. How can I convince my prospective employers to back me?

There are bound to be elements in your résumé that signpost the direction you'd now like to take, so draw attention to them and explain their relevance to your target job. Also point out factors in your personal life that mean you're suitable for the role. Don't be afraid to share your passions and aspirations with your prospective employers—this will help them see past any omissions in your previous experience. Remember that passion for a role is very attractive to recruiters; just think about how many uninspiring (and uninspired!) applications they have to sift through every day.

I'm feeling increasingly uncomfortable in my job as I've found that my values aren't those of my employer. I have tried to take on the organizational mindset but it isn't working. Is it worth staying on?

Values are strong personal beliefs that aren't up for negotiation. You may be able to *appear* to take on values that aren't your own but, under pressure, your values will reassert themselves. It's essential that your values match those of your colleagues, because otherwise you'll feel continual internal, and possibly external, conflict. Pretending to be someone you're not is too high a price to pay. It's much better to look elsewhere for a new job where your values are shared—it may be tough, but it'll be worth it in the long run.

MAKING IT HAPPEN
Take Stock

Many of us arrive at decision points in our careers unexpectedly. For most people, the planned career path is a myth and it's unusual to find people who decided what they wanted to do with their careers when they were at school and who then followed the recommended route to get there. When people talk about their jobs, it's much more common to hear how amazed they are at what they've ended up doing—listen for how many times you hear the phrase "I just seemed to fall into it!". It's not surprising, then, that many of us eventually realize that we're not doing what rewards us professionally, emotionally, culturally, or spiritually.

The pressures of modern life drive us toward making choices that bring an illusion of security, status, and success. We find a "good job" and are sucked into the promotional slipstream while being paid an increasingly large salary for taking on additional responsibilities. At the same time, we accumulate benefits, such as private health care and company pension plans, which make us reluctant to change our lives radically. Once we realize we're unhappy, we try to rationalize our way out of it, convincing ourselves that we've invested too much in our employing organization and our careers so far to risk starting again at the beginning. So we struggle on, perhaps resentfully, fantasizing about how it could have been. If only . . .

Sometimes, we're "fortunate" enough to be assisted in overcoming our resistance to change. We're laid off, we suffer ill health, our family circumstances change, a significant relationship comes to an end, and so on. This external trigger often results in personal reinvention, and is often perceived to be a blessing in the long run. The challenge for most people is to arrive at the decision to make adjustments in their lives *before* such a dramatic catalyst intervenes. Being able to sense the imbalance in your life, the drawbacks of your current job, and the gulf between who you are and who you've become is key to making meaningful personal changes. In this way, you can be conscious of what you're doing, why you're doing it, and the likely pay-offs or penalties for doing so.

Clothes are our weapons, our challenges, and our visible insult." Angela Carter

Below is a series of steps that may help you through the reinvention process.

Conduct a "Personal Audit"

This is the part of the process where you appraise your life from a personal and professional perspective. You could think of it as a "force-field analysis," where you write your name in the center of a clean sheet of paper and itemize your life's pressures and disappointments on the left and the pleasures and delights on the right. Write down everything you think is relevant, including the interests and aspirations that you had early in your career and all the things that have given you happiness since then. From this activity alone, you may be able to see where unacceptable pressures lie but if you cannot, highlight the "break points" on both sides of the analysis in a highlighter pen so you can easily identify the issues that really need to be addressed. The intention here is to find a way of swinging the balance of your life toward the pleasurable side of the diagram by drawing out the elements of your life that characterize you and your preferred role.

Explore Your Values and Beliefs

If something is preventing you from tapping into your natural talents and living your life in line with them, write it down at the bottom of the sheet of paper. These are the barriers that you have to overcome in order to achieve satisfactory reinvention. They usually manifest as fears, for example: "I will lose my income/pension/benefits," "I have a dependent family and can't risk letting them down," "I have hefty financial commitments and won't be able to meet these if I change my job," or "I can't afford to go back and start something from the beginning at this stage of my career." All these are fears that you hold without question. So question them. Are they *really* true? Do they *really* matter? If you live your life according to these beliefs, how will you feel at the end of your career? Is this acceptable to you?

Think about Your Dream Scenario

Think about what you'd do if you were free from practical or financial limitations and write everything down at the top of your sheet of paper. This is a freeing exercise that may put you in touch with what it is you would prefer to be doing. Don't reject your ideas because you don't have enough money or security to achieve them—don't put more barriers in your way—and remember that, with a little imagination and inventiveness, there are ways around the perceived obstacle of money and security.

Start Making Changes

Now that you've done the thinking, you can start making changes, small or radical. Working through the process above has allowed you to see your life laid out in front of you and should help you pinpoint the areas that need the most immediate attention. If you have a strong feeling about the need to change something that doesn't make any sense to you, don't try to reason your way out it; follow your instincts and see what happens. If you curb your impulses by rationalizing them, you'll end up behaving in the same way time and time again. To others, and indeed to yourself on some levels, your actions may not seem reasonable but see what happens anyway—many people have benefited from taking a risk at points in their life. Taking action first and reflecting later has probably been the pattern of your career to date, so try something new out, see if it works, then adopt or discard your initiative as appropriate.

Live the Changes

It's no good deciding to make changes but then not doing anything about it. Even if the changes seem alien to you to begin with, practice them until they feel normal. Act as if you're the best artist in your field, the greatest writer, the most successful entrepreneur—whatever it is you want to achieve. Once you start behaving like the person you want to be, people will start treating you as if you *are* that person. You cannot change your life without changing your behavior patterns, and this will feel strange to begin with. If you find this too hard, try starting with symbolic changes like your clothing or your car.

Reinvent Yourself

You'll see that reinvention isn't really what's going on here. The *effect* is reinvention; the *fact* is that you're bringing to the surface a latent part of your character that seeks full and happy expression. Make the decision to live the way you want to fully and without apology. What's the worst that can happen?

COMMON MISTAKES
You Rush It

Some people decide to make radical changes in their lives and jump into a reinvention of themselves with brashness and unattractive incompetence. This only leads to disappointment. Although enthusiasm is vital for any attempts at personal change, it needs to be balanced with considered decisions and a deep understanding of yourself. Without these, you'll make changes that don't last and end up feeling disillusioned and de-energized. Work through the process above and ask a trusted friend to help you if you feel you're getting lost along the way.

You Pretend to Be Something You're Not

Reinventing yourself isn't just a marketing exercise, although it may help you to market yourself successfully in your chosen professional area. People are quick to pick up on others who they think are just "putting on" a new personality or way of acting, so be who you really are, for the right reasons.

FOR MORE INFORMATION

Books:
Bolles, Richard. *What Color is Your Parachute? A Practical Manual for Job-Hunters and Career-Changers.* Revised ed. Berkeley, CA: Ten Speed Press, 2006.
Jansen, Julie. *I Don't Know What I Want, But I Know It's Not This.* New York: Penguin, 2003.

Web Site:
FastCompany:
www.fastcompany.com/online/29/reinvent.html

"Keep up appearances; there lies the test. The world will give thee credit for the rest."

Charles Churchill

Freelancing: Setting Up As a Free Agent

GETTING STARTED

Many people are seduced by the idea of commuting in a dressing gown to an office only a few yards away from the breakfast table. On top of this idyllic scene comes the next logical step for many people: leaving their current position to start their own business.

Many people choose to work from home these days, and most new businesses start off in the home of their owner-managers. If you're thinking about basing your company in your house to begin with, you'll need to get used to not only a different way of working, but to being the person with whom the buck stops in all work matters. Could you make it work? To start, ask yourself the following questions:

- How much of my freelance fantasy is based on being unhappy with my current situation?
- What is my "core competency," around which I will begin a freelance business?
- Who employs freelancers in my field of work and do I have enough experience and contacts?
- Who is my competition and what edge do I have over them?
- What are the costs of going into my own business, as well as the benefits?

FAQs
What exactly is a freelancer?

The word "freelance" comes from the old English concept of knights-for-hire, but these days it refers to someone in the service of more than one employer. Nowadays, a freelancer can be a self-employed person in any number of industries, including accounting, writing, film and video, management consulting, software development, and Internet services.

What sort of personality traits and skills must a person have as a freelancer?

You must be—or quickly become—confident, resourceful, enterprising, adventurous, flexible, and organized. As a business owner, you also must be a manager, a bookkeeper, and a promoter. You'll have to be able to "multitask"—juggle a number of diverse projects, each with different deadlines, for your clients.

How do I decide what to charge for my services?

There are books and Web sites that give guidelines about the value of your profession, in terms of an hourly rate. Another way to determine your starting hourly rate is to work out what people in that field earn per hour as employees, then add 25–50% to account for the overhead you'll have (such as taxes, insurance, retirement savings, equipment, and supplies).

Remember, too, that as a business owner, at least a quarter of your workload will involve activities you may not invoice for, such as research, marketing, promotion, and bookkeeping. If possible, find out what established freelancers in your field are charging. You may want to start at a reduced rate for the first year, especially if you're going to be competing against more established freelancers.

MAKING IT HAPPEN
Do Your Research

Making a jump to freelancing requires a kind of "inside-out" approach:

- Be honest with yourself about your motives for the move. If you feel more excitement about the future than dread of where you are now, you're on the right track.
- Look at your personality assets: you'll need people skills, energy, promotional creativity, a love of your chosen profession, and a devotion to detail.
- Your outside research should include canvassing the industry in which you'll offer your services.
- Determine how big a "territory" you'll initially serve, and what sort of companies. If possible, ask the advice of anyone already in that field. In the best of all worlds, knowing someone at those companies who knows you from a prior work relationship (and who can therefore recommend you for future work) is a big asset.

Develop Your Business Plan

Once you decide to commit to a life as a freelancer—but before you leave your day job—develop a business plan. Even if you've lined up a client or two, a business plan will plot the first year's goals and activity.

Some people have found it a good idea to start a freelance business on a part-time basis, so that they can still rely on the income from their other job during the tricky start-up phases. This part-time approach may take on the dimensions of a second full-time job and as a result cut into other areas of your life, but trying it out this way will show you quickly if you have the determination and work ethic to persevere.

Not only will your business plan help you clarify your business's purpose and prepare well for the future, it's also essential if you want to borrow money from the bank or another financial institution. You need to convince other people to be as committed to the business as you are, so remember to

- be as specific as possible about the kind of business you're starting;
- describe your business in terms of a mission statement or "executive summary" that clearly summarizes your business's purpose;
- make sure your purpose can be easily understood by you, your customers, and potential investors. If you can't describe your business in this way, you really need to rethink your business idea and focus on the core activities and direction.

Use as your starting point your vision of where you might want your business to be in five years' time, so that you can show in your plan how you'd start to move toward that point. For example, you might work toward becoming a market leader, an innovator, a specialist, a large concern, or a top-notch supplier.

Market and Promote Your Business

Whether or not your freelance business is in the same industry you're currently employed in, you'll need to develop a target list of companies that you'd like to work for. Once you've done that, learn all you can about each company, its products and services, its financial health, its challenges, and its history with contract employment. Find out who in those companies makes contract decisions. Aim your marketing and proposals at them; invite them to lunch if they happen to live nearby.

Marketing can also include letters, brochures, or e-mails sent to potential customers, as well as personal networking, advertising, and promotional activities, even a Web site. Ideally, you'll have built enough of a network before you start your business to reduce the amount of "cold calling" you must do.

Focus on Customer Service

Making the move to being a profitable freelancer is largely a matter of time: the longer you're in business, the greater the probability that you'll be successful. Remember that it's far better to keep a client happy than to spend the same amount of time finding another one, so being prompt and delivering a professional product or service for the proposed budget are the cornerstones of a successful freelance business.

Keep Up Good Business Practices

As a freelancer, it would be rare to have a consistent client, or set of clients, for a long period of time. Business climates change, and freelancers are vulnerable to shifts in policy and personnel: if your in-house contact moves on, for example, the new person may have his or her preferred freelancers, so you may lose out. Ensure that you always keep on good terms with your contacts, so that they'll want you to "move" with them if the time comes.

Get used to the idea of losing clients and gaining new ones; it's part of the nature of the business, like an animal shedding a winter coat and growing a new one. To protect themselves against this inevitability, freelancers usually have several irons in the fire. As it often takes six months to a year to secure work with a new prospective client, you should discipline yourself to plan at least six months ahead. Learn to anticipate when clients need more service, but also learn to predict when your tenure may be drawing to a close. Have the foresight to build enough diversity in your client base that the loss of one won't spell disaster for your business.

COMMON MISTAKES
You're Cavalier about Your Home Office

Many freelancers begin at home and there's nothing wrong with that. But be very careful (for accounting purposes) to create a separate office that has no other purpose. Keep very good records of things you'll want to list as itemized deductions on your business tax return.

You Rely Too Much on One Client

In the best sense, freelancers bring added value to a company, and companies are willing to pay handsomely for those who can deliver. But don't become complacent—valued as you may feel, freelancers are easier to lay off than employees, so when it comes to budget tightening or changes in administrative personnel be vigilant and be prepared.

You Don't Save for the Lean Times

Inevitably, there will be lean times in your freelance business. Putting aside enough money to get you through, say, two or three months of basic expenses is advisable. Besides that, however, remember that as a freelancer, you're also responsible for paying taxes. Make sure you're aware of what these are likely to be and create a reserve in readiness for this eventuality. However, don't forget to pay yourself, including your subscription to a private health insurer and appropriate provision for your retirement. Try to save for vacations too; we all benefit from a break.

You Let Things Slide

Just as you must be adept and professional about what you bill your client for, you also must become skilled at running your own business affairs. Plan to devote up to 25% of your time on various administrative and marketing-related activities. When business is booming, it's especially easy to get complacent about record keeping, credit card debt, payment of taxes, developing new business leads, and even collecting from your clients on time. If you don't stay on top of your own business details, you could be ruined very quickly when times are harder.

For tax purposes and others, it's well worth the yearly cost of having a respected accountant look at your business. An accountant can tell you how to avoid tax troubles and will often save you more in deductions than you'll pay him or her in fees. Accountants have a lot of experience advising business people about a variety of issues, so feel free to pump yours for information. If they're reluctant to share find another one.

FOR MORE INFORMATION

Web Sites:
Internal Revenue Service:
www.irs.gov/businesses/small
Freelance Work Exchange:
www.freelanceworkexchange.com
Freelancing: Going into Business for Yourself:
www.geocities.com/escapepod.geo/freelance.html
EFA, Editorial Freelancers Association: **www.the-efa.org**

Establishing and Maintaining Your Home Office

GETTING STARTED

Many people choose to work from home these days, and most new businesses start off in the home of their owner-managers. If you're thinking about basing your company in your house to begin with, you may need to get used to a new way of working, especially if you've previously been working in a more formal, structured setting. To start, ask yourself the following questions:

- Can I handle the social isolation of a home office on a full-time basis?
- Am I a self-starter?
- How do I rate as a decision-maker, organizer, bookkeeper, and secretary?
- Could I separate business and personal life if both were under the same roof?
- Am I a workaholic and would an office at home worsen that problem?

FAQs

Is working from home as wonderful as it sounds?

Yes and no. For convenience, cost, and comfort, there's nothing quite like a home office. Low overhead, no commuting hassles, no office politics, and setting your own hours are a few of the plusses. On the minus side, there's only you—and if you're not disciplined, you'll be spending more time with the kids, the pets, or snacking than working where you belong. It can be a simple formula for failure.

How can I make a home-based business seem professional to customers?

It depends on the type of business, but start with a professional attitude and then buy some good-looking business cards and stationery. Think about adding an attractive logo and using a two-color design on business cards, letterheads, and envelopes. Having a well-produced flyer or brochure that describes your business is also a plus: good quality customer service will do the rest.

E-commerce is relatively easy to conduct from a home office, especially with a Web site that attracts customers. Clients don't really need to know whether you work at home or in a sophisticated office building, so long as you get the job done for them. As with your other materials, the Web site should reflect the personality and professionalism of your business.

What sort of investment is necessary to outfit a home office?

This, too, depends on the type of activity you'll be doing—whether it be business or telecommuting, or a personal or family office. But generally, spending between $2,000 and $4,000 should make you well equipped and comfortable. Make a list and plan a sensible budget beforehand. You don't want to blow your entire savings on setting up the office, then have nothing to spend on attracting business.

MAKING IT HAPPEN
Plan the Layout of Your Office

Planning a home office involves deciding where to locate the office, how to decorate it, and how to furnish it. You should give lots of thought to this, as it will be the hub of a small business and you'll be spending a lot of time there. Some people even make a scale drawing of the room they intend to use, then place to-scale furniture in there to work out the best layout.

Take Account of Tax Considerations

As you're planning to use the office for a small business, most government tax agencies allow will allow you to deduct certain expenses connected to the business. For that reason, the office must be completely dedicated to the business and not merely a spare bedroom with a fold-up desk and your cordless phone. Good record-keeping is very important if you plan to deduct expenses and part of the mortgage interest, utilities, and phone bills for business activity.

Make Sure You're Comfortable and Have the Right Equipment

Office décor is important. Besides getting the right atmosphere (lighting, paint/wallpaper, floor covering), think about practical items too: do you have enough phone and electrical outlets in the room to support the office equipment? Beyond that, having comfortable, functional furniture will allow you to work productively.

Your package of office equipment will depend on the type of business you're in, but will probably include computer(s) and peripherals, software, phones and phone service for voice, fax and computer, and perhaps even a separate copier and/or scanner. Add a digital camera if you plan to put photos of yourself or your products on your Web site. Finally, don't forget that you'll need storage space for files, records, and other general office supplies.

Impose Proper Discipline On Yourself

One of the most difficult aspects of the home office is the home itself—it's all too easy to tend to house chores, watch TV, rake the leaves, get involved with family things, snack, and otherwise avoid the work that awaits you in your office. Two factors will help avoid the home trap: being excited about your office space and the work—and discipline. Set regular office hours, have a separate business phone, organize your time, and stick to your deadlines.

Don't Let Yourself Get Isolated

Being isolated in your home office, you may develop a

"There is no reason for any individual to have a computer in their home."   Ken Olsen

tendency to cocoon yourself in there or to avoid reaching out, both of which can be unhealthy.

Having a business gives you plenty of opportunity to break away from the office to meet other people socially and professionally. Even if much of your business is conducted over the phone and by computer, it's still important to network. Invite customers and prospective customers to lunch, if they happen to do business nearby. Join a civic group or professional organization to stay connected and also to generate local interest in your business. Get physical exercise away from the home. Consider taking a class. All these things will help keep you connected, bring in new ideas, and generate lots of personal energy—things you'll value when working alone.

COMMON MISTAKES
Going Halfway with the Office Arrangement

Starting a home office on the dining room table is not a good idea, nor is committing only half-heartedly to making a guestroom into a real office. If you don't treat the office seriously, there's a better than even chance you won't take your work seriously either.

Carve out a separate space and dedicate it as the office. You'll feel better and your work will benefit from that decision.

Succumbing to Workaholic Syndrome

If, while working in an office setting, you've had a tendency to stay there until the work is done, operating from home is a workaholic's dream come true. With the office only a few rooms away, there's a temptation to "get one last thing done" after dinner or on a weekend.

It's important to be professional about your business, but it's also important that you don't let the office become your new home. Set hours, try to manage your workflow into those hours, then shut the door and put up the "closed" sign.

Family Issues

Lots of women see working at home as the answer to two issues—making a living and raising a family. If it were easy to mix kids and work, parents would have been doing it at their business offices long ago.

That said, it isn't entirely impossible either. The trick is balance. You can't afford to be at the beck and call of your children, but you certainly don't want them to feel totally ignored. Racing from the office to untangle toys and do laundry every hour will soon turn your work world upside-down. Closing the door and ignoring the family will have an equally unfortunate effect.

Obviously, day care is an option. Consider it for the days that you might schedule your most critical tasks. On days you set aside for errands, such as paying bills, bookkeeping, research on the Internet, and so forth, you might more easily accommodate the family being around.

Lacking Certain Office Job Skills

When working for other companies, you relied on others with jobs that complemented your own. As your own businessperson, at your own business office, you have a lot more duties besides the specific ones that "bring home the bacon." You'll be responsible for executive and marketing decisions, financial and administrative details and deadlines, as well as clerical and reception work. Until your business becomes profitable enough to employ other people, it's all down to you.

This is where a business plan makes sense. You need to work out the details of how you'll charge for your products or services. Be careful to figure in the "cost of doing business," which includes the clerical and administrative things, too. Add in a "fudge factor" and some profit. Assuming that you'll work a 40-hour week, set your sights on making a living in 30 hours, then use the other 10 hours to take care of the other parts of the business—marketing, promotion, billing, bookkeeping, and business errands.

If you feel you lack the skills to juggle all of these things, or don't have the interest in becoming your own secretary, perhaps you're not cut out for a home business. But if you want to give it a try, you can certainly learn what you need to know about the care and feeding of a small business from books, the Internet, a local chapter of SCORE (Service Corps of Retired Executives), or a nearby community college.

FOR MORE INFORMATION

Books:
Phillips, Barty. *The Home Office Planner*. San Francisco: Chronicle Books, 2000.
Zelinsky, Marilyn. *Practical Home Office Solutions*. New York: McGraw-Hill Professional Publications, 1998.

Web site:
Entrepreneur: **www.entrepreneur.com**

See also:
Computers, Information Technology, and E-commerce (pp. 1705–1707)
Flexible Working/Teleworking/Homeworking (pp. 1757–1758)

"The trouble with corporate America is that too many people with too much power live in a box (their home), travel the same road every day to another box (their office)."

Faith Popcorn

Getting Used to Working from Home

GETTING STARTED

Working from home has become much easier over recent years, especially as technology has become more sophisticated. Some people, especially those who have been used to working in larger companies, can take a while to get used to working in a less structured setting. This actionlist offers some advice on how to get the best from working at home.

FAQs

How can I find out about my tax status?

If your decision to work at home is linked to a decision to work for yourself, you'll find that having an office in the home may qualify you for tax concessions. Tax relief may be available on your mortgage interest, heating, and telephone bills, and the cost of capital equipment and services needed to support your business. Your accountant will guide you on what tax benefits you may be eligible to receive.

MAKING IT HAPPEN
Create Some Boundaries

When you start working from home, it's crucial that you establish a suitable work environment and set boundaries. It's hopeless trying to balance your laptop on your knee in the kitchen while you attempt to avoid intrusions from family or friends; you need to set rules for yourself and others so that everyone can support your efforts rather than sabotage them.

If there are other people at home, be clear about the time you set aside for working. Non-work interruptions can be frustrating when you're trying to get something done to a deadline. Establish boundaries by establishing in advance how you're going to manage your time at home, including things like the beginning and ending of your working day. Having a separate room to work in is key here, as you can close the door and cut down on disturbances. Stick to your guns and people will soon get the message.

If your work requires you to receive visitors, try to find an area where they won't be distracted by your domestic arrangements. Having to ignore the pile of laundry on the kitchen floor can be very off-putting, however friendly you are with your guests. If you're unable to avoid these situations, find a local hotel or restaurant where you can meet for an hour or two. Again, this is about creating boundaries that will enable you to maintain focus and create an impression of professionalism.

If you're an extrovert and enjoy the buzz of having other people around, it's important to recognize and adjust for this. You could try planning a certain number of days in the office and balance these with quieter, more productive days at home. If you're self-employed, you may need to schedule visits and meetings sufficiently regularly for you to feel involved with and energized by others.

Get into a Routine

It's important to differentiate your day between being "at work" and "at home." If your working and resting times become confused, it can feel as if you're always on duty, and when you *do* take a break you can feel guilty that you aren't finishing a project. This differentiation comes naturally when you have to travel to and from work, but when your routine changes you'll need to find a way to make this shift yourself. For example, it could be signaled by a routine; making a cup of coffee, taking it to your desk, closing your door, and switching on the computer. Once you've done this a few times, this routine creates the boundary within which you can work effectively.

Although the idea of wandering into your office pajama-clad may appeal, get up and get dressed as if you were going into the office. Obviously you don't have to wear a suit or very smart clothes, but getting changed is another "signal" that you're starting your working day.

Plan your day so that you don't find yourself wasting time. The advantage of working from home is that you have greater control over interruptions. People will no longer be able to wander past your desk at will and ask you for some information or, worse, to do something for them. A great deal of time is wasted in these "Oh, by the way . . . " moments that happen mostly because you're accessible or visible.

Take Regular Breaks

Make sure you take breaks throughout the day. Most people's concentration starts to diminish after about twenty minutes, and if you continue to work after this time thinking can become a struggle. Taking a break, perhaps a short walk, can re-energize your thinking capability. Of course, breaks need to be balanced by the need to be productive.

Try not to get distracted by picking up something else that needs doing. You'll only end up wasting time and lowering your efficiency by spreading your energies too thinly.

Work at Your Work–Life Balance

Make sure you plan for the end of the day as well. When you work at home, it's all too easy to stay sitting in your workspace well into the evening and to ignore the private side of your life. It can be hard to juggle these two aspects of your life, but everyone needs a break from work. Remember to make time for yourself, friends, family, and other interests; you'll be much happier in the long term.

COMMON MISTAKES
You Lose Your Focus

For those who enjoy dynamic environments and the cut and thrust of being in a busy office, working from home may not be enjoyable. It's tempting for people of this type to create dynamism for themselves by finding activities that distract them from their own company. Flitting around from task to task can create a feeling of being "in the flow," but may not be very productive. If you worry

---

"The brain is a wonderful organ. It starts working the moment you get up in the morning, and does not stop until you get into the office."

Robert Frost

that you may be prone to finding "displacement" activities rather than doing any work, spend a few minutes at the beginning of the day creating a "to do" list. This will focus your energy and make sure that there's a valuable output to the day's activities.

You Can't Switch Off

It's very easy for people to work beyond the call of duty when the office is located in the home. This is especially the case if you've started a new business; the first stages can be really hectic and long hours are often unavoidable. "I'll just go and answer a few e-mails . . . " can become a lengthy session in front of the computer that eats into private time. Try to discipline yourself to keep to the "rules" that you've set, with only occasional exceptions for real emergencies or key deadlines.

You Lose Track of the Time

If you miss the energy you get from working with others, you might turn to the phone as a substitute for their presence around you. It's easy to pass a lot of the day on the phone and to find that, as a result, you have to work late to actually achieve anything that day. Again, this is a question of discipline. Give yourself time to be in touch with others, but keep control of it. A large clock on the wall in front of you is a good reminder of how long you're spending on each activity!

FOR MORE INFORMATION

Book:
Orloff, Erica, and Kathy Levinson. *The 60 Second Commute: A Guide to Your 24/7 Home Office Life*. Upper Saddle River, NJ: Pearson Education, 2003.

Web Sites:
About.com: **http://entrepreneurs.about.com**
Homeworking.com: **www.homeworking.com**
Internal Revenue Service:
www.irs.gov/businesses/small

See also:
๑ Entrepreneurs (pp. 1745–1747)
✔ Managing Your Time (pp. 828–829)

"A man who has no office to go to—I don't care who he is—is a trial of which you can have no conception."
George Bernard Shaw

Working As Part of a Virtual Team

GETTING STARTED

Being a member of a virtual team is becoming more commonplace as organizations extend their global reach and attempt to provide integrated services to their customers. At the same time, co-workers and team members often remain physically isolated from each other because of organizational reluctance to invest time and money in bringing them together.

Although tele- and videoconferencing technology and other forms of electronic communication have improved greatly over the last ten years, these media can't replicate the chemistry of teams by working together to capitalize on each individual's strengths and characteristics. Building successful virtual teams is a relatively new skill that few have so far mastered, but it's one that will need to be developed if this form of cooperative work arrangement is to succeed.

FAQs

I am about to take responsibility for managing a virtual team. What's the best way of getting them to bond and work as a team if they never meet?

In the absence of an opportunity to move through the team-building phases of *forming, storming, norming, performing*, you need to coordinate an activity to replace it. This might take the form of an extensive briefing session run via videoconference or a training program that encourages information sharing and collaboration. This kind of introductory exercise puts team members in a position where they have to build good communication channels and trust among themselves.

I'm a member of a virtual team with colleagues in different time zones. How can I build rapport with people who are asleep when I'm awake?

Obviously it's much easier to build trust and rapport when you can actually see someone and communicate spontaneously. You only need do this once or twice to kick-start your relationship. It's worth having one video-conference with those members of your team who live in compatible time zones and a second with those who couldn't join you at the first conference. Encourage the others to do the same, passing real-time communication around the team like the baton in a relay race. In this way even though you can't meet everyone at the same time, you can still meet each member face to face.

I feel very isolated in my role in a virtual team. What techniques are available to create a sense of comradeship?

Try using some of the virtual group technologies that are available. Each has different attributes, so you may want to try a few before finding one that meets your needs. The technologies create a repository for information, advice, guidance, and war stories that bring a human element to the interaction between you all. They also create

a sense of team identification, because you have to be a member to have access to them. If you go to **www.google.com** and put in the keywords: "virtual teams," "virtual groups," or "e-groups," you'll find lots of information about available technologies.

MAKING IT HAPPEN
Cultivate the Qualities of an Effective Virtual Team

An effective virtual team has the same qualities as a team working in close proximity:

- They are collaborative in their work. They share information, knowledge, ideas, views, and experiences in order for the team to pull together as a unit.
- They are trusting of other members. Each member needs to know that the others will meet their promises promptly without personal agendas getting in the way.
- They are attentive to communication. Each member has to agree on priorities and communicate progress regularly. There should be no withholding of information. Good communication only happens when every member takes responsibility for being part of the team and is committed to the team's purpose.
- They are skilled at building relationships. In the absence of actual face-to-face meetings, the development of strong, trusting relationships depends even more than usual upon excellent communication.
- They are agreed on a modus operandi. All team members should agree on ground rules, written down or not, governing how they operate.

"Meet" All Members of the Team and Get to Know Something About Them

Look for similarities of values, interests, expertise, or experience so you have a bridge into the relationship. Building rapport is the first step to being part of an effective team; without it there's nothing to cement the team together. Share your expectations and agree on the team ethic or terms of your working relationship. Decide how you want to be perceived, what values you want to be known for, and what aspirations you have collectively. This may seem overindulgent when there's work to be done, but it's time well spent. Once you've established a basis on which to build rapport, you can move on to the more concrete work assigned to the team.

Formulate and Assign the Different Roles in the Team

As a group, decide who plays which part in helping the team meet its objectives. Outline the resources and support you need in order to play your part effectively. This exercise demands that all members share their individual talents, capabilities, aspirations, strengths, and competence gaps.

Set Boundaries Around Tasks and Agree On Timeframes

Decide collectively how the team will deal with failures

921

ACTIONLIST

"There is a commodity in human experience. If it has happened to one person, it has happened to thousands of others."

Oprah Winfrey

to meet its objectives. You may need to call emergency meetings to create contingency plans, set new time-frames, or realign the team's objectives.

Agree On a Schedule of Reviews to Make Sure You Stay On Track

Reviews also act as an early-warning system if something is beginning to go wrong. Gain commitment from each team member for these very important sessions.

Discuss the Possibility of Conflict and Decide How You Will Deal With It

Many people are fearful of conflict and tend to ignore the possibility until it actually emerges. Conflict isn't always a negative experience; it can be very creative if handled well.

Celebrate Success

It's all too easy for dispersed teams to forget to celebrate their achievements, but it's important to recognize the attainment of goals. Celebration allows you to release tension, enjoy your success, and move on. You can do this by organizing a videoconference and agreeing to hold a virtual party. Although this may feel a little contrived, it nonetheless allows a form of togetherness and mutual appreciation. It also invites humor as you review what went well and what didn't . . . a great way of letting things go and getting them into perspective.

Learn from the Experience

T. S. Eliot wrote: "We had the experience but missed the meaning." If you don't learn, you don't develop and grow. Take time to reflect on what part you took in the team and what you learned about yourself from doing so.

Draw On Electronic Aids

New electronic communication systems are being developed all the time, many of which can aid the functioning of virtual teams. Most people are familiar with tele- and videoconferencing as means of bringing remote groups together, along with the cell phone, fax, and e-mail. Other useful technologies that can assist in communicating with people who are geographically dispersed include the following:

- **Web conferencing**: this technology enables members of the team to sit at their respective computers and watch the meeting host illustrate his or her message on the screen. This technological aid requires access to two telephone ports, one for the telephone and one for the Web connection, but is otherwise easy to implement and use.
- **Document storage/sharing**: there are a number of online document storage providers that enable team members to store, edit, and access common documents. This way there's no need to create multiple versions of the same document; team members can simply work on the sections they need.
- **Group e-mail**: the ability to send e-mail to one or every member of the team greatly enhances the team's ability to communicate.

- **Message boards**: message or bulletin boards enable group members to go to a central place to communicate with each other and access information.

COMMON MISTAKES
Failing to Build Rapport and Trust

Not spending enough time on building rapport and trust is likely to sabotage any virtual team. It's easy to assume that everyone has the same high level of commitment to the team's formation and purpose as the coordinator or team leader. It's important to give members an opportunity to get to know each other so they can figure out how to mesh their talents and skills to achieve the team's objectives. This means either a physical team-building meeting or a series of virtual gatherings.

Communicating Inadequately

Forgetting to communicate with virtual colleagues is one of the main reasons that virtual teams fail. In the absence of physical proximity and the ability to pass quick messages or information over a cup of coffee in the office, out of sight can quickly become out of mind. Be sure to schedule regular meetings—and hold them without fail.

Not Establishing Clear Understanding of Roles and Expectations

It's important for all members to understand both their role in the team and the expectations that the team leader and the members have of each other. Don't assume that roles and expectations are clear. Making them explicit from the beginning can prevent conflict later on.

FOR MORE INFORMATION

Books:

Duarte, Deborah L., and Nancy Tennant Snyder. *Mastering Virtual Teams.* 3rd ed. San Francisco, CA: Jossey-Bass, 2006.

Fisher, Kimball, and Mareen Fisher. *The Distance Manager: A Hands-on Guide to Managing Off-site Employees and Virtual Teams.* Columbus, OH: McGraw-Hill, 2000.

Lipnack, Jessica, and Jeffrey Stamps. *Virtual Teams: People Working Across Boundaries With Technology.* 2nd ed. New York: Wiley, 2000.

Web Sites:

Wally Bock: www.bockinfo.com/docs/virteam.htm
FastCompany:
www.fastcompany.com/magazine/56/virtual.html
globalchange.com:
www.globalchange.com/vteams.htm

See also:

Handling Office Politics

GETTING STARTED

The old adage "if you want to get ahead, you have to work hard" doesn't necessarily apply in modern organizations, especially those that are predisposed to have a political culture. In these organizations, *who* you know tends to matter more than *what* you know. The *context* in which relationships have been built is also an important factor, because different contexts create different kinds of loyalties (or perceived obligations). Family, school, or social networks that intrude into professional territory can embroil people in all sorts of political maneuverings that eventually lead to a politically charged work environment.

FAQs

I have unwittingly become involved in a political situation which I fear will compromise my reputation in the business. What should I do?

If you are unable to confront the situation directly, it's important to go through the correct channels to avoid compromising yourself further. Communicate with your supervisor or manager and explain what has happened. If the political situation involves your boss, you may want to approach your human resources department to ask their advice. If you have one, a mentor is often a good sounding board for helping you resolve your dilemma.

I am a woman with a management position in a large organization, and I am always battling "male" politics. How can I continue to succeed without getting drawn in to ugly gender battles?

Male networks have controlled the power in businesses for hundreds of years and they sometimes seem impenetrable. You may find it helpful to find a mentor, male or female, inside or outside the business, who will champion you and look out for information and opportunities for you. Build your relationships carefully and find ways in which you can make connections that bring value to your male colleagues. Don't let them get away with abusing your gifts; follow up and ask for feedback. In this way, you will build their respect and hopefully attain parity among them. You might also consider documenting your work output performance carefully, so future reviews will make clear where you are (in terms of pay, promotions, and so on) in relation to male counterparts.

I'm tired of the politics of big corporations, yet I love what I do. How can I find an environment where I can just concentrate my energy on my work?

You may find that a change of scenery meets your needs. This doesn't necessarily mean a move out of the organization entirely, but perhaps you could transfer to a small business unit or specialized department where the likelihood of a different political culture exists. Smaller work units are very often structurally simpler and less political than large ones.

MAKING IT HAPPEN
Watch for Signs of Office Politics

Politics plays a part in all organizations; it's inevitable when you put human beings together in some sort of hierarchical arrangement. Indicators of office politics are often fairly easy to pick up. Employee complaints about discrimination or other unfair treatment may offer clues about how a company actually operates. If you notice that people seem to succeed by flattering their superiors and devoting their energy to self-promotion, you've learned something about the organization's culture and how it rewards behavior.

Find Ways to Discourage Political Behaviors

In any workplace setting, decision making based on politics encourages hypocrisy, double-dealing, cliques, self-interest, and deception. These are the behaviors that need to be reined in if the business is going to thrive in the long term. Here are a few ideas for creating change:

- **Promotions** should be given to the candidates who have a relevant track record of success. Conduct structured, formal interviews and consult with others affected by the decision. Match the successful candidate to the job description. Remember that although a good working relationship is necessary, the talents and values of the individual need not precisely match those of their new manager.
- **Reward and recognition** must be based on performance, not personal relationships or favors. Give promotions and pay raises on the basis of an employee's success in achieving the key performance indicators set during performance reviews. Employees should have access to their own performance data and reviews; there should be no room in the process for hidden agendas or secret evaluations.
- **Communication** should be open and transparent. Only unhealthy organizations hide information and spring unpleasant surprises on their employees. Communicate anything that affects your employees and their performance, including bad news, challenges, and initiatives for change.
- **New initiatives**, projects, and ideas should be initiated on the basis of their value to the business, not on the basis of favoritism or the potential for personal benefit. A formal process for proposing new initiatives and tracing their implementation and evaluation creates confidence in an unbiased outcome.
- **Politicking** can be tempting, especially when you can see an opportunity to benefit either yourself or the organization as a whole. Don't give way to the temptation. If you manage people on this basis you'll destroy your team's trust in you and their collective performance will deteriorate.

"It is the weak and confused who worship the pseudo simplicities of brutal directness."

Marshall McLuhan

924

ACTIONLIST

Guarantee Your Own Survival

If your organization is rife with politics, you can survive by following some simple rules.

- **Observe** the organization's political style without getting involved until you're sure you know what's going on. If you notice coincidences or inconsistencies in the way the organization operates, continue to watch until you can begin to understand what the patterns and motivations are.
- **Be discreet** during this period and stay true to your own values. Don't betray your own sense of what's right in order to blend into the organization—it will eventually lead to stress and conflict. You can't please everyone all the time, so use your own integrity to make decisions.
- **Build a network** of trusted allies. During your observation phase you can identify who these people might be. Build a network outside the organization to create options and opportunities for yourself. Use it to broaden your focus beyond your own company and reconfirm or realign your values.
- **Expose** other people's politically motivated behavior. When coworkers say one thing and do another, or seem to be sabotaging your decisions or work relationships, use your assertiveness skills to challenge their motivation: "You seem to be unhappy with the decisions I've made, would you like to discuss them?" They may deny your assertion or confront it, but at least the issue will be out in the open.
- **Find a mentor** with whom you can discuss your observations and concerns. You may gain a deeper understanding of the political processes at work and some insight into how you can manage these more effectively.

COMMON MISTAKES

You Misread a Situation and Make a False Accusation of Politicking

At best this reveals your naiveté, at worst your own politicking or neuroses. If you think a coworker is politically motivated, observe the person's behavior until you are sure you understand it. You may wish to share your thoughts with someone you trust or if it serves a purpose, confront your coworker. Sometimes, however, it's best to do nothing, and let a political scenario play itself out.

You Build a Network Purely for Your Own Ends

Some people try to short-circuit the path to promotion by building what they believe to be critical relationships. There's a big difference between building professional networks and using your contacts shamelessly in headlong pursuit of your own selfish ends. Remember that if you launch yourself into an early promotion without having developed the skills to be successful, you may be setting yourself up for a very public and career-damaging failure. Build your networks prudently and use them to help develop your skills and open up new opportunities. It may take a little longer, but it will pay off in the end.

You Get Involved in the Politics Too Early

When you first join a new organization, try to remain politically "unattached." Your newness in the business will allow you to ask naive questions that will help you create a picture of the political environment. Keep your relationships open and friendly and build your network with a variety of people. Observe the patterns of relationships closely to understand the power structure. After a few months you will probably have a fairly accurate idea of what is going on and can then decide to what extent you want to get involved in organizational politics.

Communication Channels Are Unclear

Politics in the workplace is sometimes an intentional construct, set up by misguided people. In other cases, the politics is merely a byproduct of other things, largely unintentional. Poor communication is probably the most common unintentional cause of a destructive political culture. In the absence of information or explanation, people fill the gaps with speculation and rumor, which produce bad information, distrust and resentment. The best way to combat this is to maintain clear channels of communication. Internal newsletters, intranet bulletin boards, and companywide meetings are all useful vehicles for getting the word out, along with more local activities such as team meetings and personal briefings.

FOR MORE INFORMATION

Books:
Hawley, Casey. *100+ Tactics for Office Politics.* Hauppauge, NY: Barron's Educational, 2001.
Serven, Lawrence MacGregor. *The End of Office Politics As Usual: A Complete Strategy for Creating a More Productive and Profitable Organization.* New York: AMACOM, 2001.
Wolfe, Rebecca Luhn. *Office Politics.* Normal, IL: Crisp Publications, 1997.

Web site:
"Surfing Office Politics," CareerLink.com: **http://careerlink.devx.com/articles/hc1199/hc1199.asp**

See also:
✔ Building Your Self-confidence (pp. 787–788)
✔ Coping with a Nightmare Boss (pp. 925–926)

Coping with a Nightmare Boss

GETTING STARTED

Many people have a difficult or challenging relationship with their boss. Of all the difficult relationships you may have at work, this will probably be the trickiest and most stressful because of the inherent political dynamic of your relationship. It can be tempting to lay the blame for this unhappy type of situation at the boss's feet because of his or her unreasonable, negative, awkward, or unhelpful behavior. Whether this view is justified or not, the good news is that, as a significant party in the relationship, there is much you can do to end the bad boss nightmare.

FAQs

My boss is always making negative and derisive comments about the way I do my work. What should I do?

See if you can find a private moment when you can explain how this makes you feel and ask your boss to stop doing it. You could suggest that he or she gives you clear guidelines and constructive feedback that will help you to meet his or her expectations and develop your talents. Point out that constant nagging affects the way you work and that you would be much more effective if he or she took a positive interest in what you do. If the negativity continues, you may decide to lodge a complaint of discrimination against your boss. If you take this route, make sure you have a record of the incidents and a note of the witnesses present. You might also decide to seek further advice from your human resources department if you have one.

My boss has favorites and I am definitely not one of them. As a result, I'm not given essential information and I miss out on good opportunities. How can I change things?

Lack of communication often contributes to workplace misunderstandings. Try approaching your boss with information about what you're doing and talk about your methods and goals. If your boss persists in denying you the information you need, you may have a case of bullying against him or her.

I have a boss who is really moody and bad-tempered, making work almost intolerable. Is there anything I can do to change this?

Observe whether there is a pattern in this behavior and try to work out how you could influence the situation for the better. Once you've made your observations, you could try giving constructive feedback, letting your boss know how his or her mood swings affect you. Use assertive language and ask if there is anything you can do to alleviate the cause of the problem. If the behavior persists, you may wish to consult your human resources department to see if there are any formal procedures in place to deal with such a situation.

MAKING IT HAPPEN

Consider the Impact on Your Own Health and Happiness

Rather than deal with the problem directly, many people are tempted to live with the difficulties of having a troublesome boss. Instead of addressing the problem, they brush it under the carpet by looking for ways of minimizing the impact he or she has on their working lives. However, employing avoidance tactics or finding ways to offset the emotional damage can be time-consuming and stressful. Focusing on your own well-being may encourage you to tackle the issue rationally and try to reach an accommodation that will prevent you from jeopardizing your health or feeling that you have to leave your job.

Understand Your Boss

When you come to look more closely at your relationship with your boss, the first thing to do is to realize how much of it is due to the structure of the organization—for example, your boss necessarily has to give you tasks, some of which you may not enjoy—and how much is due to truly unreasonable behavior.

Looking at the wider issues in the organization may provide the key to the problem. "Difficult boss syndrome" is rarely caused simply by a personality clash: more often than not, there are broader organizational factors that can go some way to explaining seemingly unreasonable behavior.

However uncomfortable it may feel, try putting yourself in your boss's shoes. Recognize the objectives that define his or her role and think through the pressures he or she is under. Make a mental list of your boss's strengths, preferred working style, idiosyncrasies, values, and beliefs. Observe his or her behavior and reactions, and watch where he or she chooses to focus attention. This will help you to deepen your understanding. Very often, when we feel disliked or when we dislike someone, we avoid building this understanding and instead look for ways of avoiding the issues.

Compare the Way You Both Perceive Your Role

As part of the process of understanding your boss, compare the perceptions you both have of your role and the criteria used to judge your success. You may feel that you're performing well, but if you're putting your energy into tasks that your boss doesn't feel are relevant, you will be seen as performing poorly.

Take the initiative to explore your boss's expectations and agree on your objectives. This will clarify your role and give you a better idea of how to progress in the organization.

Understand Yourself

Having scrutinized your boss and developed a greater understanding of him or her, try doing the same exercise on yourself. Sometimes a lack of self-knowledge leads to

"One of the most important things about being a good manager is to rule with a heart. You have to know the business, but you also have to know what's at the heart of the business and that's people."

Oprah Winfrey

926

ACTIONLIST

us being surprised by our reactions and the feedback we get. Ask for input from your colleagues while you're doing this. Ask them what they observe when you interact with your boss, how you come across to them, and how you could manage your communication differently. Although their perceptions may not represent the absolute truth about you, it nonetheless reflects the image you create.

Think through some of the past encounters you've had with your boss and reflect upon them objectively, perhaps with a friend or colleague who knows you well. Maybe this situation happens over and over again, which suggests that you harbor a value or belief that is being repeatedly compromised. If you can understand what this is, you can learn to manage these situations more effectively. You may need to consider changing some of your behavior. This often prompts a reciprocal behavioral change in your boss. If you don't change anything about the way you interact with your boss, the relationship will remain unaltered, so this is definitely worth a try.

For example, perhaps you value attention to detail, but your boss is a big-picture person. Every time you ask for more detailed information, you'll be drawing attention to one of your boss's vulnerabilities, and he or she is likely to become uncooperative or irritated by your request. Once you've observed your respective patterns, you can begin to work around them or accommodate them.

Remember That the Relationship Is Mutual
In order to be effective, managers need a cooperative and productive team. But in order to be part of such a team, each member needs their manager to provide the resources and support they need to do their job properly. An unsupportive boss can be just as nightmarish as a vindictive one.

When managers neglect to give their employees the information and feedback they need, employees are forced to second-guess their boss's requirements. This inevitably leads to misunderstandings on both sides. The ultimate effects of this are an atmosphere of distrust and ill-will, and mutual recriminations—not to mention the negative impact on the organization's productivity levels. Ask for the information and resources you require, or find other ways to get these, as this will put you in control of the situation and protect you from the need to improvise.

Nightmare situations can arise when employees' needs aren't met. Some people become angry and resentful of the manager's authority; some find ways of challenging decisions in order to assert their own power; and others develop agendas of their own that are neither helpful nor productive.

One-sided relationships are a recipe for revolution! It is rare in business to find relationships where there is absolutely *no* reciprocal power. Remember that if you're no longer willing to spend time managing your difficult boss, you still have the ultimate power: you can just walk away.

COMMON MISTAKES
You Take Your Boss's Behavior Personally
It is very tempting to take the behavior of a difficult boss personally. However, it is very unlikely that *you* are the problem. It may be something you do, it may be the values you hold, or it may be that you remind your boss of someone he or she doesn't get along with. The only person who loses out if you take it personally is you.

You Don't Remain Detached
Many difficult relationships deteriorate to the point where they are fraught with contempt and confrontation. This is never helpful in a work setting and only makes matters uncomfortable for everyone. If you find yourself being drawn into an angry exchange, try to remain emotionally detached and listen actively to what is being said to (or shouted at) you. It may provide you with clues about why the situation has developed and allow you to get straight to the point of concern. Ask for a private review afterwards to explore the incident. You may find that this brings to the surface issues that are relatively easy to deal with and that will prevent further outbursts from occurring.

You Never Confront the Issue
Because facing up to difficult people is not an easy thing to do, many people avoid biting the bullet. However, this will only prolong a miserable situation. Acquiescence enables bullying to thrive and allows the aggressors to hold power. Break the cycle by taking responsibility for your share of the problem and examining what it is you're doing to provoke conflict between you and your boss. Doing nothing is not a viable option.

FOR MORE INFORMATION
Book:
McIntyre, Marie G. *Secrets to Winning at Office Politics: How to Achieve Your Goals and Increase Your Influence at Work.* New York: St. Martin's Griffin, 2005.

Web Sites:
ImproveNow.com: **www.improvenow.com**
Monster.com:
http://midcareer.monster.com/articles/ careerdevelopment/stresseffects

See also:
✔ Building Your Self-confidence (pp. 787–788)

Dealing with Bullying or Harassment

GETTING STARTED

Anyone who has ever been bullied will know how demoralizing and difficult it can be. When it occurs in the workplace it can be a seemingly inescapable nightmare, the effects of which are sure to take their toll over time on the physical as well as mental well-being of the victim.

Bullying (sometimes also called "mobbing") and physical abuse lie at the extreme end of a continuum, with more subtle forms of harassment at the other end. What is tolerated in the workplace will depend very much upon the culture of the organization and the attitudes of its leaders. Some businesses ignore all forms of harassment; others make a point of creating a culture where intimidation of any sort is cause for reprimand or dismissal. It is worth reflecting on your organization's culture to see what exists, both on and under the surface. This actionlist provides advice both for victims of harassment and the colleagues or managers around them.

FAQs

I've seen a colleague being bullied and no one intervened. What should I have done?

Technically, the decision to deal with the bullying you witnessed rests with the one being harassed, but this is easier said than done. This kind of behavior often affects the whole team, and you therefore have grounds to get involved if you wish. You could start by asking your harassed colleague about the treatment he or she received. The person may indicate that they don't want to make a fuss about it and will leave it at that. Alternatively, you could speak to the bully, explaining the impact of his or her behavior on the team as a whole. When doing this, use good feedback techniques. For example, begin all your statements with "I . . . ," and base them on things that you have personally observed.

How do I know when joking turns to bullying?

The difference between a good joke and bullying can be subtle. However, if the person being bullied is demeaned and disempowered in some way, or if the joke becomes personally critical and destructive, then the line has been crossed.

I feel I'm being bullied, but my boss disguises his actions with jest. How do I deal with this?

Bullies are skilled in undermining confidence, and victims begin to question whether they are doing something wrong, or perhaps imagining things. One way of dealing with this is to write down the incidents in a journal, including the context in which they took place. Ask for feedback from observers and include their comments. Over time, you will be able to see if there is a pattern to the treatment you have been receiving. Also, the record may be useful if you decide to take the matter further.

I've seen victims "asking" to be bullied. How does this happen?

Once someone's confidence has been broken, they become "easy pickings" and can inadvertently help to encourage bullying behavior. If this is the case, you should still approach the victim and express your concern. If the problem persists, you would be wise to bring it up in a staff meeting, or to report it to the person's supervisor—or to another manager of equal or greater rank.

MAKING IT HAPPEN
Understand the Forms Bullying Can Take

The recipient of bullying is often in a weaker position, physically, emotionally, or hierarchically. Victims are usually unable or unwilling to stand up for themselves, due to what they feel will be the unacceptable consequences, such as an escalation of abusive behavior or the threat of job loss. This fear allows the behavior to continue.

Any form of harassment can have a serious impact on the morale of staff in the business, and can affect the performance and health of individuals. Not only is it simply wrong, but it's unlawful, and should be treated seriously.

The various forms of harassment include:
- all manner of physical contact from touching, pushing, and shoving, to serious assault;
- intrusive or obsessive behavior, such as constant pestering, baiting, or dogging a person's movements;
- tricks being played that result in risk or danger to the individual;
- group bullying, where the individual is overpowered by a number of aggressors.

Less direct harassment may include:
- the spreading of rumors, jokes, or offensive personal remarks;
- written statements, letters, or graffiti;
- actions that isolate the individual and prevent them from doing their work effectively;
- non-co-operation, or sabotage of professional objectives;
- pressure for sexual favors;
- obscene gestures and comments;
- the orchestration of situations that compromise the individual;
- manipulative "political" behavior, that may include bribery or blackmail.

Determine When the Line Has Been Crossed

Often, people find it hard to know whether the line of harassment has been crossed. If they confront the perpetrators, they can be accused of "being a poor sport," or worse. Such accusations are often leveled to mask what is going on, and can seriously undermine the victim's confidence.

If you are the one being bullied, seek feedback from those who may have observed any incidents. Their objectivity will help to put perspective on the situation if

---

you're worried that you may be over-reacting. It may be that their account gives you more ammunition to deal with the problem appropriately. Select your witness carefully though—ones you can trust to be allies throughout the ordeal, and who won't "flip" on you under pressure.

If the harassment is infrequent and seems harmless, try not to take it too personally. Bullying says more about the character of the bully than it does about the person being bullied. However, if the bullying is persistent or escalates, you must confront it and report it. Even if you don't wish to face the bully head on, there are likely to be other ways of asserting your rights.

Check in the employees' handbook, if you have one. There are probably procedures in place to assist you in dealing with your situation. You may be advised to report the incident(s) to your manager but, should you feel uncomfortable about this—for example, if your manager is part of the problem—you may wish to go directly to the human resources department. If you decide to lodge a formal complaint, make sure you have a record of the incidents and a note of the witnesses present.

Work to Maintain a Nonbullying Atmosphere

Left unchecked, bullying can destroy the morale of valued employees and put the surrounding people into a state of fear. If you're a manager, you have a responsibility to report bullying elsewhere in the organization, even if it doesn't affect your staff. However, you don't want to create an atmosphere of persecution either. Try to strike a balance between vigilance and freedom of choice.

Bear in mind your legal obligations to your staff. Remember that turning a blind eye to the problem may at some point make you culpable as well. You need to reassure staff that their complaints will be taken seriously and dealt with fairly. Most people are reluctant to report harassment because of the potential impact on their position/job. Explain what steps have to be taken, and estimate the length of time involved in the process.

Remember to give any potential complainant a few days in which to reconsider making a formal complaint. Don't exert pressure to take the issue further if the recipient decides to let the matter go—it's his or her choice and this should be respected. However, make sure that the organization's policy manual spells out how to proceed if the person does decide to pursue the charge. It will probably involve investigating the details to establish what happened, and in what context. This may involve interviews with the victim, alleged abuser, and witnesses. Notes—based on facts, not hearsay and opinions—should be taken and filed with the human resources department or representative.

Cases of serious assault are rare, but when they occur, they may go beyond the scope of the organization to deal with them. It may be necessary to contact a security officer or the police, and you may also need medical intervention and/or counseling for the victim, perhaps the perpetrator, and even some affected colleagues.

The incident could also involve an external third party, such as a customer. It is important to have a plan in place for such events, and then react in as calm and professional a manner as possible. The more serious the problem, the more your employees will depend on you to bring the matter to a close as quickly and judiciously as you can. Minimizing "collateral damage" helps to restore equilibrium more quickly.

COMMON MISTAKES
You Act Before You Know All the Facts

Wading in with accusations when you think you've witnessed an episode of bullying could make matters worse: you may have misjudged the situation. Unless it's a serious incident, it's best to observe and question before intervening. In this way, all parties are given a chance to explain their behavior and resolve the situation calmly.

You Mistake a Genuine Extrovert for A Bully

Extroverts frequently speak their minds before really thinking about what they are saying—which can sound confrontational and be mistaken for harassment. Being extroverts, however, they are often receptive to questioning and eager to point out that they were just testing the boundaries, or joking. By sharing your perception and inviting theirs, it's possible to clarify and dispel the situation without further entanglement.

You Don't Consider That the Bully May Need Help Too

It is easy to assume that bullies are strong characters. Indeed, it's often to create this impression that they become bullies in the first place. In fact, most bullies are insecure and behave as they do to mask a lack of knowledge or skill. Or perhaps they are mirroring behavior further up the organization, thinking that this may help them advance. One way of handling such a person is to offer them coaching, so that they can be helped to understand the underlying cause, and succeed in changing their behavior.

FOR MORE INFORMATION

Book:
Davenport, Noa, et al. *Mobbing: Emotional Abuse in the American Workplace*. Revised ed. Ames, IO: Civil Society Publishing, 2002.

Web Site:
Mobbing USA: **http://mobbing-usa.com**

See also:
✔ Coping with a Nightmare Boss (pp. 925–926)
🖱 Employment Law (pp. 1743–1744)

"Great works are performed not by strength but by perseverance." Samuel Johnson

Turning Around a Poor Hiring Decision

ACTIONLIST

GETTING STARTED

No matter how careful your recruitment process, there are no guarantees that new hires will perform according to your expectations.

A job candidate may perform impressively on tests, interview well, and bring sterling references; none of these can guard you against a poor hiring decision. Once hired, a new employee may reveal values that don't mesh with your organizational culture. The person may not get along with coworkers or have personal problems that spill over into the workplace.

If such problems emerge once a new recruit is on board, you need to act quickly.

FAQs

I believe I've recruited the best person for a particular position, but other members of the team disagree. How can I reassure them?

Your recruit may have a different set of values or way of working from existing team members. If so, you need to work especially hard on integrating the new person. This may mean bringing the team together for some relationship building, and setting expectations around how each will contribute to the team's role in the company. Make this an early priority. Relationships that are allowed to go bad are difficult and time-consuming to repair.

My company recently brought in a senior executive, who relocated at considerable personal and financial cost. It's clear that the hiring decision was a mistake. Where do we go from here?

First, don't allow the circumstances of the hiring decision to affect your response now. Avoiding or fudging the issue is in no one's interest. The executive's employment contract should have a clause specifying what level of compensation he or she is entitled to for termination. Interpret it liberally to minimize the distress and inconvenience the person will undoubtedly face. But once you've decided you made a bad choice, you should bite the bullet and waste no time in issuing notice of termination.

My new employee has some worrisome habits. He frequently smells of alcohol, and often arrives late for work. What's the best approach?

Alcohol abuse is dangerous, and in the workplace it should be dealt with quickly and decisively. If the person is still performing adequately and it's just a matter of the breath and the sloppy timekeeping, perhaps a warning is all that's necessary. But if the problem persists and starts affecting the person's work and relationships, stronger measures will be required. Refer to your employee manual for guidance on the appropriate action to take. The employee's participation in a rehabilitation program and joining Alcoholics Anonymous may suffice. If your organization has no such manual, a professional or trade association might help you, or you might ask a government agency that deals with health and safety issues for advice. If all else fails, you probably have little recourse but to terminate the person's employment.

MAKING IT HAPPEN
Face Up to the Problem

Admitting that you made a bad hire is extremely uncomfortable. You may be embarrassed that in the interview you failed to notice warning signs that seem obvious in retrospect and feel that you've wasted precious time and resources. Furthermore, you may feel frustrated and guilty about what lies ahead—the prolonged process of firing one person while beginning recruitment all over again.

Once you've acknowledged the problem, you need to take several specific steps before you terminate the person's employment.

Set Clear Objectives for the Employee

People starting a new job often find that the job requirements are ambiguous. If you suspect you've made a bad hire, go back to the job description. Make sure it's clear, and satisfy yourself that the new employee understands his or her responsibilities and objectives. Clarify any questions or uncertainties, and keep a close coaching eye on how the person responds.

Review Your Employee Orientation Practices

It's not necessarily easy for a newcomer to feel at home in an unfamiliar organization. Orientation programs can go some way toward easing the transition, but they may not keep new employees from stepping on some sensitive organizational toes and creating a poor first impression. This is unfortunate, because newcomers frequently bring experience and fresh ideas that can usefully shake up stale organizational habits. Managers need to strike a delicate balance between promoting innovative ideas and remaining sensitive to the organization's equilibrium.

Offer Additional Training

It's not at all unusual for there to be a skills or knowledge gap between someone's former experience and new job requirements. The recruitment decision may appear to have been poor when in fact some additional training and development would do the trick. You don't necessarily need to turn to expensive external training programs; it may be a question of having the new employee shadow someone who is successful in the relevant area and arrange for a period of coaching.

"I believe that work is a combination of emotion and reason and you should never exclude how you feel from your decision-making process."

Tamara Ingram

Make Sure You're Providing Adequate Support

People coming into new jobs with lots of background experience are often left to get on with it without a lot of supervision. This doesn't always provide the framework necessary for them to meet their objectives. People need supervision, guidance, and support until they learn how to meet the demands of a new job. After that, they need less support.

Meet the Employee to Review the Situation

A new employee who is performing poorly will undoubtedly be sensitive to a manager's disappointment and anxious about his or her future in the company. An early, one-on-one performance review may be helpful in allowing both parties to raise issues of concern. They should agree on performance targets and time frames for compliance. If the hire eventually turns out to have been a mistake, the record of this meeting will be important evidence in any termination procedure.

Coach the Employee

Coaching is essential if the early signs in someone's employment are disappointing. Although coaching takes time, it's a good investment if it turns the employee's performance around. Good coaching techniques can develop the employee's resourcefulness, and are much more productive than merely telling him or her what to do.

Consider Extending the Employee's Probation

From a practical standpoint, it's much easier to fire someone if the new employee is still in the probationary period; once full employment has been confirmed, the legal requirements are more convoluted. Sometimes it makes the most sense to extend the employee's probation to give other interventions time to work. Make sure the person understands exactly why this extension is being given, and give him or her explicit verbal and written warnings of what the consequences will be if performance doesn't improve.

Create a Contingency Plan to Cover the Job

Most organizations can't afford to leave key positions vacant or in transition for long periods. Formulate contingency plans to cover the job should it be vacated again. These may include bringing in temporary support staff, borrowing someone from another team, or allocating specific tasks to others capable of meeting the performance criteria.

Before you decide to fire the individual, consider whether the person might be better suited to another job in the organization. If not, and the firing comes after the probationary period is over, be sure you follow your company's procedures to the letter to avoid complaints or, worse, a lawsuit.

Prolonging the agony of a bad hire isn't good for anyone. Tackling your mistake promptly and professionally is best for both the employee and the organization.

COMMON MISTAKES
You Don't Explore the Situation Fully

Don't rush to the conclusion that you've made a bad hire without stopping to look at the big picture. Hasty decisions can result in grievances or lawsuits for harassment or unfair dismissal. Take the time to explore the person's poor performance from a variety of angles and to follow your organization's procedures carefully.

It's an Organizational Problem

Underperformance often results from management problems instead of an individual's inability to do the job. If your organization's recruitment process doesn't give new employees every opportunity to perform well, review the process to see how it can be improved.

Performance problems frequently stem from poor communication. Managers must clearly articulate their expectations, thoroughly explain organizational processes and systems, and provide appropriate support to deal with employees' questions or concerns.

The New Recruit Isn't Given Time to Improve

Don't be too hasty in firing new employees. You shouldn't let a bad situation fester, but at the same time you need to give the employee time to understand how seriously you take the situation and help in remedying it. This means giving early feedback, guidance, and advice, and meeting regularly to monitor progress. You should still be aiming for the original outcome of the hire: for the employee to function as a high-performing member of the team.

FOR MORE INFORMATION

Book:
Becker, Brian E., Mark A. Huselid, and Dave Ulrich. *The HR Scorecard: Linking People, Strategy, and Performance.* Boston, MA: Harvard Business School Press, 2001.

Web Sites:
BusinessTown.com:
www.businesstown.com/hiring/hiring-advice.asp
Find Law for business:
www.smallbiz.biz.findlaw.com/hr/hiring

See also:
๖ Coaching, Counseling, and Mentoring (pp. 1698–1700)
☆ How HR Adds Value (pp. 82–84)

"A butterfly is not more caterpillar or a better caterpillar or improved caterpillar: a butterfly is a different creature."

Richard Pascale

Transforming Poor Performance

GETTING STARTED

Poor performance can result from many causes, such as:

- inability to manage perception or pressure;
- failure to prioritize;
- lack of skill, knowledge, or motivation;
- conflict of personalities or styles;
- overpromotion ("the Peter Principle"), where the person is actually out of his or her depth;
- lack of resources, support, or cooperation from others;
- change in performance management systems or processes.

Given the cost of recruiting and training new personnel, helping underachievers move from poor to acceptable performance is almost always worthwhile. This actionlist explores some effective ways to manage poor performance.

FAQs

We've recently restructured our business, and my assistant seems unable to deal with it. What do I do?

People often take time to adjust to new situations, and some cope with change better than others. Talk to your assistant and explore exactly what differences the restructuring has made to his or her job. It's possible that poor communications have left your assistant feeling confused about new responsibilities, unable to prioritize, and lacking support. These are all areas where you should be able to help.

Several members of the sales team I manage consistently fail to meet their targets, which is very demotivating for the rest of the group. What's the best approach?

Some theories about managing salespeople suggest constantly churning the least productive individuals. Managing poor performance is extremely time-consuming, and your time may be better spent supporting your stronger performers. You do need, however, to understand why the bottom group is failing to meet targets, set clear goals, and manage by objectives. If this fails, be prepared to deal with the consequences.

I feel unhappy and unappreciated at work, which is affecting my performance. What's your advice?

The fact that your performance is suffering makes it important to discuss your feelings with your manager. We can often outgrow roles or discover that we need a new challenge to feel rewarded. Enlist your manager to help you understand what's happened. Have your work circumstances changed? If so, your expectations of yourself are likely to have changed, too. Have job pressures intensified, or have you developed different personal goals? What type of recognition or appreciation would be meaningful to you? Remember that it's more cost-effective for organizations to remotivate and align an existing em-ployee than recruit and train a new one, so your boss will have every incentive to help you.

MAKING IT HAPPEN
Understand the Importance of Performance Management Systems

Frequently, by the time poor performance has been identified, the damage has already been done. Prevention is better than cure, so establishing performance management systems—structured methods of identifying and improving poor performance—is the most effective management approach. Simply put, such a system makes sure that each individual has clear objectives, understands how these affect others, knows what's needed to meet the objectives, and is confident of having the necessary skills and experience to deliver.

Putting these systems in place *before* problems arise saves considerable management time and worry.

Define Poor Performance

Poor performance is defined by a variety of factors, some organization-specific, some role-specific. Managers need to decipher which are conduct issues and which are capability/competence issues, since each requires a tailored course of action.

Conduct	Capability/Competence
Lateness, absenteeism	Failure to perform tasks reasonably
Attitude	Failure to perform duties to an adequate standard
Bad language	Failure to provide high standards of customer care
Gender/racial discrimination	Unsatisfactory reviews
Negligence or abuse of company property	Infringement of regulations
Abusive behavior to coworkers, managers, or customers	Failure to observe company policies and procedures

Take Steps As an Organization

The organization must act with consistency and fairness and, where possible, be able to demonstrate that it has provided the employee with guidelines and coaching to achieve the desired actions and behavior. If the problem cannot be resolved, it may be necessary to initiate a disciplinary procedure. Here are some guidelines.

- Conduct a full investigation.
- Hold a formal hearing. Make sure the employee is given written notice of it in advance. The employee is entitled to representation.
- Review all the evidence. Formally outline the disciplinary action to be taken.
- Consider differentiating between conduct and capability in formulating any disciplinary action. In many organizations, an employee with capability issues is given two chances to improve before being terminated, while terms are stricter if the problem involves conduct. Either way,

"Ego-management is a critical tonic for vitalizing organizational transformation."

S. K. Chakraborty

932

ACTIONLIST

be sure to allow time for improvement as part of the disciplinary process.

Take Steps As a Manager
It's always preferable to prevent poor performance instead of treating it. Where prevention fails, the manager needs to:
- be fair and unbiased at all times;
- behave consistently;
- get personally involved in the case;
- understand whether it's a conduct or capability issue;
- work within organizational guidelines and procedures in the event of disciplinary action;
- recognize the importance of training and guidance.

Take Steps As a "Poor Performer"
If you feel that you don't have the skills, experience, or knowledge to achieve the objectives set for you, ask for help before it becomes a performance management issue.

Try to understand why you haven't met your objectives. What support would help you to improve your performance? If your goals are unclear, seek help in redefining them so you can agree on expectations and better focus your efforts.

If your poor performance is attitudinal, try to understand how others react to your behavior. Remember that what works well in one culture doesn't always translate to others. *How* you say something is as important as *what* you say. Try to identify friction points before they become serious performance issues.

Preventative Measures for the Business
The best way to deal with poor performance is actually to take steps to avoid it. For example:
- Maintain clear channels of communication. It's up to the leaders of the organization to articulate overall goals; the managers' job is to unpack these for employees. Individuals need to understand how their own targets support organizational goals, and how their own performance contributes to the organization's success.
- Don't overpromote people. The fact that someone does a great job at one level doesn't necessarily mean that person is capable of succeeding at the next level.
- Encourage managers to spend time with individuals to identify risk areas before they become performance issues.
- Don't overengineer goals. Leave employees room to exceed their objectives.
- Set goals that are aligned with the organizational culture.

COMMON MISTAKES
You Overreact to Poor Performance and Ignore Contributing Factors
No matter how frustrated you feel by poor performance, you need to be completely unbiased, fair, and consistent in dealing with it. Always seek out the underlying factors. Are they part of a pattern, or is this a unique case with a straightforward solution? A rational approach is best: overreacting won't help you, the employee, or the organization.

Objectives Aren't Achievable or Aren't Explicit
Goals should always be achievable and clearly defined. Make sure your expectations are consistent with (and will be supported by) the culture of the organization. Tailor goals to individual employees' capacities. Establish short-term milestones that enable you to monitor progress regularly and intervene before slippage becomes critical. Most important, communicate, communicate, communicate.

You Don't Address Poor Performance Issues Early Enough
Performance needs to be measurable. The easier it is to measure, the easier it is to manage. Check individuals' performance against their targets. Schedule regular reviews and encourage employees to monitor their own performance. Ask them for feedback on their progress. Good performance managers constantly assess risk and identify and address potential failures early.

You Fail to Distinguish Between Poor Performance and Personality Clashes
Personality clashes are difficult to deal with and, if coupled with poor performance, often become highly charged. Where issues are personality-driven, bring in an impartial third party to mediate. Be flexible and open to different approaches to deal with different aspects of the problem, and recognize that resolving one issue is likely to affect others.

In some cases poor performance may be a perceived rather than a real problem. Managers and subordinates or coworkers may operate according to very different systems of internal values or use very different approaches and methods that produce equally effective results.

FOR MORE INFORMATION

Book:
Becker, Brian E., Mark A. Huselid, and Dave Ulrich. *The HR Scorecard: Linking People, Strategy, and Performance.* Boston, MA: Harvard Business School Press, 2001.

Web sites:
business know-how:
www.businessknowhow.com/manage/poorperf1.htm
GovExec.com:
www.govexec.com/dailyfed/0705/070605r2.htm

See also:
- Coaching, Counseling, and Mentoring (pp. 1698–1700)

"People are no longer content to talk merely of 'organizational change' . . . the new aspiration is for 'organizational transformation.'"

S. K. Chakraborty

Addressing Absenteeism

GETTING STARTED

In the United States, the annual cost to employers for time lost due to accidents is almost $100 billion. Absence management is a growing body of knowledge and experience applied to the control and reduction of these costs.

FAQs

Is there anything I can do to manage absence without risking claims of discrimination?

Absolutely. It's not easy, but there are several things you can do to protect your team and organization as a whole, particularly:

- understand the scale of the problem you're facing;
- discover the causes;
- take a positive and methodical approach to solving the problem.

More information about all these points is given later.

Can the effects of absence be measured?

Just as for workplace safety audits, you can measure the number of days lost per department or individual. You can also trace the type of absence, whether injury, illness, or other. These have their uses but are fairly blunt instruments. A different type of measure is the Bradford Factor, which takes account of the fact that persistent short spells of absence are much more costly and disruptive than occasional longer absences. It measures irregularity of attendance using the formula:

Bradford Factor = $S \times S \times D$

where S is the number of spells of absence over the last year and D is the number of days absent in the same period. For example, if an employee is absent for one period of 15 days, the score is $1 \times 1 \times 15 = 15$ points. If he or she was absent for 15 separate days, however, the same person's score would be $15 \times 15 \times 15 = 3,375$ points.

This is perhaps only a crude measure, but one that employers practiced in the art of absence management regard as a realistic comparison of disruption.

MAKING IT HAPPEN

Formulate a Policy

The most effective absence management policies are those based on the following principles:

- balance concern for cost with concern for people
- keep people informed
- collect quality information

Balance Concern for Cost with Concern for People

The value of an absence management policy, if followed and analyzed, is increased productivity and profit for the company. However, the policy must reflect human values of fairness and respect, and management's duty of care for employees. Rather than focusing on policing the policy, and suggesting that people are malingerers, hypo-chondriacs, or cheats, successful approaches emphasize care, positive thinking, and shared responsibility. The policy should be concerned principally with managing the effects of genuine sickness absence, while acknowledging that some may be suspect or exaggerated.

Keep People Informed

Effective programs communicate to employees the objectives of the policy and how it will be applied. Discussions with staff should be about *presence*, rather than absence, and the avenues available to help them get well. Depending on the nature of the absence, benefits and services might include counseling, job retraining, job sharing, extended sick leave, and so on. Remember that federal and state laws are designed to help employees truly in need, and your policies need to be complementary with those laws.

Collect Quality Information

It's essential to know what you're dealing with, both in terms of absolute levels of absence and the patterns shown by individuals and groups. Differentiate between regular days off, frequent short-term absences, and long-term absence—each may need a quite different approach. Supervisors and HR staff should develop skills for discussing absence with employees, not in an adversarial way, but as a means of spotting problems and offering help early. They should also observe patterns of absence and behavior, and particularly changes in these things. Records should be maintained. When managers and others show that they're interested and will follow up, "sickness" rates almost always decline.

The Goal Is Return to Work

The shared purpose must be to get the person back to his or her work as soon as is reasonable. This is especially the case after a prolonged absence, when it will be important to maintain the relationship with the person and help him or her to become productive again. The possibilities for modified or transitional roles to help the employee back into work should be looked at very carefully. If properly constructed, these can be very valuable jobs for all concerned. It's worth creating an inventory of roles that can be modified to meet different physical conditions.

You'll often need to put together a team of people—including the person who's been absent—to handle these cases, as medical and occupational health information will have to be considered alongside working conditions and perhaps legal requirements. The supervisor plays a key role in maintaining contact with the person and identifying suitable transitional work during their recovery and return.

Other Practical Considerations

However you plan your absence management policy, there are certain actions that will always help you to achieve a better result in this area.

"By empowering others, a leader does not decrease his power, instead he may increase it—especially if the whole organization performs better."

Rosabeth Moss Kanter

- **Act early.** If you notice increases or changes in the pattern of absence, investigate and take action before it becomes a major problem. In some companies a certain level of sickness absence has been overlooked for so long that people regard it as an acquired right to extra leave.
- **Seek advice from the outset.** Some complex issues may arise around medical, legal, and contractual situations, so try to think through these with specialists before problems arise. Being able to act with confidence and awareness and avoid ad hoc or impulsive decisions is a significant advantage. Get managers and HR people talking about the issues together—for example about opportunities for transitional roles. And be sure you research the law surrounding these issues. Resource people at state and federal agencies can help, but you may also find people at local business development centers (often at community colleges) or Chambers of Commerce. Consultants, with this particular field of employment law, are another source of advice.
- **Be methodical.** Make an effort to collect data consistently and carefully; to keep good records; to see that everyone receives a "return to work" interview after a lengthy absence; and to communicate fully and regularly with staff about results. This way, fairness and relevance of what you're doing never becomes an issue of contention.

A Case Study
The case concerns a recently privatized business in which staff numbers have been drastically reduced, just as the company refocused its attention on better customer service. The company provides services to residential customers: availability of staff is absolutely critical to the business. It cannot afford to carry previous levels of extra staff to compensate for absence: to meet business goals a 98% attendance (or a 2% absence rate) is required—an undreamed of rate in the industry.

The company decided to construct an absence management policy based on three principles:

- **Culture and values in the company.** The organization has a performance-based work culture, which encourages employees to appreciate the impact their performance (and their absence) has on their colleagues and the business in general. Employees are genuinely involved in an ongoing appraisal of business opportunities, customer service, and team performance. Targets for controlling absence are set and periodically reviewed.
- **A holistic approach.** At the same time, managers express a culture of care. They recognize explicitly that, apart from unavoidable injury and sickness, many other factors contribute to absence—such as family leave, say, for having a child or caring for a spouse, or even job related issues such as stress. The policy emphasizes the value of good employees and invests in an employee assistance program to aid the health and productivity of everyone working for the company. The organization invests in *rehabilitation* to deal with the full spectrum of

employee problems, regardless of whether the problem is caused by the working environment.
- **Reporting and monitoring.** The company's HR information system provides every manager with absence information, including analysis of patterns and trends and their potential impact on results. Because of the firm link established between presence (absence) and business targets, absence management is a fundamental part of all managers' roles. The policy is highly visible to all staff.
- **Results.** In recent years, the company's unscheduled absence rate has been less than half the industry average for the relevant occupational groups. These results have a direct and significant effect on workforce availability and profitability.

COMMON MISTAKES
Ignoring the Issue
There seems to be a tendency for managers to believe that absence is too difficult or dangerous an area to become involved in, when in fact this isn't the case. The benefits of teaching this issue can be very significant, not only in financial terms, but also in building employees' commitment to the business. A good absence management policy may even allow the organization to avoid problems under discrimination or disability legislation by raising awareness of the whole area—and could give a fruitful lead in new areas of concern such as work–life balance issues.

A Lack of Commitment to the Policy
Having a policy in place is a good start, but if sufficient resources aren't allocated at the outset to give the policy time to prove itself, even writing it is just wasted effort. Monitoring such a policy will avoid treating absence arbitrarily, and could avoid legal action brought by employees based on alleged discrimination.

FOR MORE INFORMATION

Books:
Becker, Brian E., Mark A. Huselid, and Dave Ulrich. *The HR Scorecard: Linking People, Strategy, and Performance.* Boston, MA: Harvard Business School Press, 2001.
Fitz-enz, Jac, and Barbara Davison. *How to Measure Human Resource Management.* 3rd ed. New York: McGraw-Hill, 2001.

Web Sites:
employer-employee.com: **www.employer-employee.com/absent.html**
Matrix Absence Management, Inc.: **www.matrixcos.com**

See also:
- Coaching, Counseling, and Mentoring (pp. 1698–1700)
- Leadership (pp. 1798–1803)

Managing Addictive Behavior in the Workplace

GETTING STARTED

Drug and alcohol abuse has been a workplace issue for decades, and employers are increasingly taking action to address its costs in terms of employees' health and productivity.

Statistics published by the Department of Labor estimate that 60% of adults know someone who has reported for work while under the influence of drink or drugs. The impact on those with the problem as well as their colleagues is enormous. In financial terms, alcohol and drug abuse is thought to cost U.S. business over $81 billion annually in lost productivity. In human terms, it is thought that more than a third of all workplace fatalities are related to alcohol consumption.

FAQs

A member of my team is performing poorly. This is uncharacteristic, and I suspect there may be an issue with excessive drinking. What should I do?

Meet with this person to share your observations about his or her performance. Do not mention your suspicions at this stage; give the person an opportunity to allay your fears without becoming defensive. You might explore possible work-related causes to see whether you can elicit an explanation that puts your mind at rest. Failing this you may want to discuss the organization's alcohol policy (see next question) and, if it has one, its employee assistance program, and offer further assistance.

What is the most effective way of dealing with alcohol abuse at work?

If none exists, you might consider drawing up a substance abuse policy and procedures to provide clear guidelines for dealing with alcohol and/or drug abuse at work. Having such a policy can help assure those with alcohol problems that they will be treated considerately and encouraged to seek help. The policy should be drawn up with the input of senior and middle managers and employees or their representatives.

I can recognize alcohol abuse, but I'm less familiar with the signs of drug abuse. What are the signs that suggest someone is taking illegal drugs?

The symptoms are not unlike those related to excessive consumption of alcohol. They include:
- mood swings or uncharacteristic behavior;
- a tendency to become confused and irritable;
- the development of problematical relationships;
- a drop in work performance;
- an inability to arrive at work on time and increased absenteeism.

If you observe these signals you may wish to schedule a performance review, during which you should concentrate on the behavior you have observed and the likely reasons for these changes.

MAKING IT HAPPEN
Realizing the Implications

An adjunct of the World Health Organization states that " . . . all people have the right to a family, community and working life protected from accidents, violence and other negative consequences of alcohol consumption." Alcohol and drug abuse not only affects the individual concerned, but also endangers the circle of people surrounding the abuser, and has the potential to destroy the person's career and relationships.

There is no question that alcohol impairs the brain's proper function. It reduces the ability to make sound judgments or decisions and increases the likelihood of mistakes through the loss of spatial awareness and control of the body. As heavy drinkers or drug users become more unreliable, their absenteeism increases, while their productivity diminishes.

Clarifying the Legal Position

Many organizations now operate a workplace alcohol and drug policy that encourages sobriety and freedom from drugs. In spite of such initiatives the International Labor Organization estimates that 3–5% of the global workforce is alcohol dependent, and that up to 25% of workers drink heavily enough to be at risk of dependence.

There are fairly uniform state laws and some federal regulations prohibiting use of intoxicating substances of any sort while operating motorized vehicles. Likewise, there are federal and state laws about the possession and sale of illicit drugs, but there aren't such laws that cover intoxication in the workplace. Nevertheless, both federal and state laws also require safe workplaces, thus encouraging organizations to implement policies to address the problem of alcohol and drug dependent employees. Most employers see alcoholism and drug abuse as illness and, again, most opt to help the employee seek treatment rather than fire them outright.

Spotting the Problem

Those who have alcohol or drug problems are likely to be identified through a drop in performance, increased absenteeism, or behavior that requires disciplinary procedures. Their behavior may appear erratic or out of character, they may take extended lunch breaks, or they may disappear inexplicably at odd times throughout the day.

What to Do As an Organization

Much can be done from the organizational perspective to raise awareness of the issue of drug and alcohol abuse:
- Post drug and alcohol information and embark on an

"Difficulties, opposition, criticism—these things are meant to be overcome, and there is a special joy in facing them and coming out on top."   Vijaya Lakshmi Pandit

936

ACTIONLIST

education program to ensure that everyone is aware of the issues.

- Outline the potential health and safety dangers to users and their coworkers. You may wish to state that the organization sees drug and alcohol abuse in the same light as any other disease, and that it will be treated in the same way. Encourage early identification of employees at risk.
- Publish the rules about alcohol consumption and drug use at work, and make sure that the message is clearly displayed in places where employees enter the workplace and where people gather.
- Offer advice and assistance to those who feel they have a problem, and outline the help that is available. You may offer a combination of external and internal resources such as medical assistance, counseling services, or your employee assistance program.
- Ensure confidentiality for anyone who seeks advice or assistance.
- Publish guidelines for disciplinary procedures and make it clear what provision will be made for medical leave for treatment.
- Outline the basis on which an individual may return to the same job after treatment, and what the level of tolerance is for repeated offenses.
- Regularly review the organization's stance on drug and alcohol abuse.
- Check the laws and regulations in your state regarding any requirements for treatment of those with abuse problems as well as the relevant regulations about employment termination. If, for example, an employee has lost productivity on the job due to an injury or chronic illness, and the drug prescribed for alleviating pain is the cause of the poor performance, it may be a different set of laws (in this case, the Americans with Disabilities Act) that would define your options, rather than dealing merely with a case of alcohol or illicit drug dependency.

Some organizations perform drugs tests prior to a final recruitment decision; others periodically test employees. This is especially important if the working context is highly confidential, involves complex processes, or must be performed in an environment where physical safety is an issue.

What to Do As a Friend or Coworker

- If you witness a friend or coworker drinking excessively or under the influence of drugs, intervene. This may involve a simple action such as calling a taxi to take the person home. Although this might feel intrusive, you might prevent the person's immediate exposure to personal injury or a serious accident.
- Once your friend is restored to full control, you might want to have a talk with him or her and give the person feedback on their behavior.
- Offer support, but avoid the role of counselor. Helping someone manage an addiction requires professional expertise. The journey to recovery can be rocky, and by taking on too much responsibility you could be jeopardizing a good friendship.

- You may wish to express your concerns to the individual's manager or to the human resources department. Try not to think of it as a betrayal, but as a signal of concern for your friend's welfare.

COMMON MISTAKES
Leaving It Too Long Before Taking Action

Tackling drug or alcohol abuse is difficult, and many people leave it too long before taking action. Avoiding the problem only endangers the individual and his or her colleagues, so it's important not to let things drift. Besides, inaction sends a powerful message to others, who may feel safe in drinking or taking drugs at work because they believe that the organization doesn't take substance abuse seriously. If you are dealing with an individual as their manager or supervisor, schedule an interim performance review and explore the reasons behind the behavior you've observed. Once these are out in the open, the next logical step is to provide the right kind of help.

Not Calling In Professional Help

Being a supportive friend to drug or alcohol abusers may not serve them in the long run and is no substitute for professional help. Dealing with addiction is a delicate business and should be facilitated by a trained counselor. There may be someone in human resources who has experience of this form of counseling, but it may be preferable to enlist the help of a local specialist in substance abuse.

Failing to Provide a Clear Policy

Organizations often don't consider drawing up an alcohol or drug policy until they actually have to deal with someone for whom drugs or alcohol have become a problem. Since these forms of addiction are becoming increasingly commonplace, it's wise to be prepared with a clear policy. Circulating information about alcohol and drug abuse signals the organization's intention to treat drug and alcohol abuse seriously—and may help keep some employees from straying too far in the first place.

FOR MORE INFORMATION

Web Sites:
National Institute on Alcohol Abuse and Alcoholism: **www.nihaa.nih.gov**
U.S. Department of Health and Human Services, National Clearinghouse for Alcohol and Drug Abuse Information: **www.health.org**
U.S. Department of Labor: **www.dol.gov/asp/programs/drugs/workingpartners/stats/wi.asp**

See also:
 Coaching, Counseling, and Mentoring (pp. 1698–1700)
 Leadership (pp. 1798–1803)

Succeeding As a New Manager

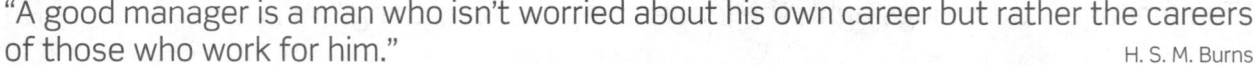
GETTING STARTED

Congratulations, you've been appointed as a manager—either for the first time, or for the first time at this level. You're likely to be responsible for managing a team of up to 15 people, either in a company you already work for, or in a new organization. This is obviously very exciting for you, though you may feel somewhat daunted at the prospect, especially if you were previously a member of the team you will now be managing.

However, provided you follow a few basic rules, there is no reason why such fears shouldn't be easily overcome, and your new role will give you excellent scope to stretch your wings and fulfill your potential. This actionlist is intended to give you these basic rules and help to smooth the path forward into this new phase of your working life.

FAQs

I'm afraid I might not be up to the job. How can I overcome this fear?

It's only natural to have some feelings of this kind; most people do when faced with a new challenge. However it's important to get such worries under control, as a crisis of confidence may affect your chance of success. Try some positive self-talk, reminding yourself of your skills and competence to do the job—after all, the company has recognized them, otherwise you wouldn't have been offered the job! It's also important to look after your health: make sure you get plenty of sleep and exercise, so you feel fighting fit and ready to take on anything.

Is it likely that my new job will affect my home life?

Almost certainly, yes. Moving into any new job can be stressful, and even more so when new or extra levels of responsibility are involved. The trick is to make sure you're prepared for it, and face the fact that your life may be more demanding than ever before. Talk this over with your family and friends at an early stage; it will be a huge help if they are ready to lend their support while you come to grips with your new role, and also to keep "home" distractions to a minimum to let you focus.

Will I need to change my persona at work?

No, not essentially, but you may need to adjust your attitude and the way you think about your job. A lot of management is about standing back from the detail and seeing the "big picture" of what is happening, so that you can make strategic decisions about how to act. Rather than getting involved in the nitty-gritty of individual tasks (as you may have done as a team member), try to cultivate an objective overview. If you can learn to see the forest instead of the trees, this will naturally lead to you behaving in a way that suits the circumstances.

MAKING IT HAPPEN

Research and Plan Your New Job

First things first: if you're moving to a new employer, find out everything possible about the company you'll be working for, the department or section you'll be in, the job itself, and anything else you can think of. Don't pre-judge what you're going to find, and don't be bound by what you've done before, or by how any of your previous employers operated. It's also a good idea to find out a bit about your predecessor: why he or she left, what style they preferred, how people responded to that, what may need to be changed, and so on. (If you're staying in the same company, you may know this already, but it's worth doing some extra research.)

From all this information, try to form at least a tentative plan in advance—it's much harder to do this once you're in the position. What do you want to achieve? How might you need to develop yourself to match the new demands? Reflect as honestly as you can on your strengths and weaknesses: how might you use your qualities and experience to the greatest advantage, and compensate for your limitations?

Engage with Your Team

Once you start your new job, make this your first priority. What is the purpose of your department, team, or unit? What work is being done, how do things stand at present, what customer expectations need to be met? Get all your team members together as soon as possible to introduce yourself, and then arrange meetings with each of them individually. While keeping these meetings as friendly and informal as you can, allow a generous amount of time and plan some kind of framework for the discussion. Listen carefully to what people have to say, and get information about them as individuals. Most importantly, ask each person the question: what should I do or not do to help you to perform your job effectively?

Plan Some "Quick Wins"

Now is the time to plan a few targets that you can hit quickly and easily, which will help you to feel more at home and on top of things. Achieving these also eases the pressure you feel to perform and create a positive first impression, and begins the relationship-building process. Quick wins might include things like familiarizing yourself with systems or ways of working if you're new to the company (for example, the internal e-mail system); setting up an early discussion with your line manager, arranging introductory meetings with suppliers or customers (external and internal), or even taking your team to lunch.

Clarify What Expectations Others Have of You

You may be lucky enough to have been given a detailed job description, but the chances are there are still large gaps in your understanding about the task and priorities, what is or isn't acceptable in the new environment, and on what criteria you will be judged by your boss, peers, customers, and others. Don't be afraid to ask a lot of questions to clarify these issues, and then be very honest with yourself. Can you meet these standards? If not, what

"A good manager is a man who isn't worried about his own career but rather the careers of those who work for him."

H. S. M. Burns

might you need to do? Who could help, and what might the price be?

Beware of "New Broom" Syndrome

While you will evidently be eager to get going and to make your mark, it is important that you tread delicately—at least to start with. Don't assume that your new team will welcome your style or your ideas with open arms, even if your predecessor was unpopular. They need to feel they can trust you and that you respect what they've been doing previously, before you can count on their support and cooperation. Above all, don't depart too dramatically and quickly from established practice.

Show Your Commitment to Individual Development

From your initial meetings with your team, you will know what their individual aspirations and hopes are for their jobs going forward. Follow up by setting a code of management practice that you tell all team members about, and then follow it rigorously. This code might include commitments to assess training needs, to hold regular team meetings and one on one sessions, to set specific goals, and to evaluate performance against these goals.

Support this code by the way you yourself behave toward team members. Make a point of appreciating extra time and effort that people put in, listen closely to what they say, and be generous in your praise of their good qualities or achievements. The point is, by demonstrating to your team that you as their manager are on their side and will do everything in your power to support them, you will gain their trust and acceptance, and the performance of the whole team will be greatly enhanced.

Lead By Example

An effective manager needs to be a role model, so it almost goes without saying that you must be set an example for how you want your team members to behave. Lead by involving people in establishing group objectives, setting standards, and achieving deadlines, and demonstrate your own strong personal commitment to achieving the team's goals. Set an example too by maintaining high standards in your appearance and general behavior, and by establishing warm, friendly relationships.

Take Stock Regularly

At the end of your first week, identify issues that need attention and make a plan for the following week. Get into the habit each week of setting aside time for review and planning. Don't let your mistakes lead to self-doubt: everyone makes them, and good managers learn from them, while bad ones repeat them. The pattern of behavior you set in your first three months will be extremely hard to change later.

COMMON MISTAKES

You Make Promises That May Be Difficult or Impossible to Keep

It is tempting, during the phase of settling in and relationship-building, to make all kinds of promises to your team, boss, or customers in the interests of creating a good impression. However, you will be judged on whether or not those promises are fulfilled, so make sure you exercise caution. Under-promising and over-delivering are infinitely preferable to the other way around.

You Form Alliances Based on First Impressions

Common myth has it that first impressions usually turn out to be accurate, but this is often not true. Your understanding of people and circumstances may change substantially as you learn more about them, and it's important that you don't cement yourself into new relationships that later turn out to be inappropriate or which might alienate other, potentially more useful, allies.

You Maintain Too Close a Friendship with Former Team Mates

Although it's important to create cordial relationships with your team members, it's also important to distance yourself a little from those who report to you, so that you can remain objective and unbiased in your actions. This can be difficult when you have previously been a member of the team yourself, but if you don't, you run the danger of being seen as a manager who has "favorites" and of allowing your personal feelings to affect your judgment. This will not be good for the morale of the team, and you will lose much of your authority. Explain your position to particular friends, be seen to maintain a professional relationship at work, and keep purely social interaction for outside the office.

You Allow Yourself to Be Trapped Into Accepting the Status Quo

No matter what anyone says about "the way things are done around here," the old ways are not always the best. Reserve your right to postpone judgment until you are thoroughly familiar with your team and your job and then, if things need changing, change them, remembering, of course, to be sensitive in the way you do it.

FOR MORE INFORMATION

Web Sites:
HR Guide: **www.hr-guide.com**
HR Next: **www.hrnext.com**
HR Village: **www.hrvillage.com**

See also:
✔ Getting Your Message Across (pp. 789–790)
⌇ Leadership (pp. 1798–1803)

"The manager does things right; the leader does the right thing."   Warren Bennis

Tapping into Passion

939

ACTIONLIST

GETTING STARTED

When people's passion is engaged by their work, they are much more dedicated, much more productive, and much easier to manage because they generate their own momentum. Conversely, when someone's passion is not engaged, he or she is often lethargic, likely to shun responsibility, and unable to meet objectives. It is clearly desirable to have people in roles who are passionate about what they do, and to minimize the number of those who are merely doing a job to fulfill the need for income.

Managing passion is an art that begins with recognizing how people match up with their job, which components of that job resonate with the individual's specific interests, and ensuring that these are in rich supply. In this way, passion can be sustained in the longer term and the benefit to the business optimized.

FAQs

I manage someone who used to be extraordinarily enthusiastic and passionate about her work. Unfortunately, since she was promoted, this attitude has disappeared. What could have gone wrong?

There are a number of reasons why people's attitude could have changed under these circumstances. They may be finding that their new job demands skills that have not yet been developed. Or, they may now be in a setting that conflicts with their values, where there may no longer be a channel for the expression of their passion. This often happens when a natural sales person is promoted to a managerial role. The part of the job that they enjoyed and excelled at is no longer available to them.

I think that "passion" is just an excuse for self-indulgence. I have to manage a team to meet very specific objectives and I don't have time to explore individual passions!

Passion can certainly become self-indulgent if not directed properly, but it can also become a fuel to drive the team's success, if managed well. It is worth considering the consequences of preventing people from contributing in the way that feels most natural to them. What are you losing as a manager, and as a business, if you do not draw employees in to discussions about how to use their individual passions to make the team more effective?

The organization I work for has become very successful on the basis of one individual's passion. However, the business is moving into a consolidation phase where that passion is creating conflict. How can we redirect this energy to create a strong foundation for growth?

Dealing with a founding member's passion and involvement in the business can be very difficult. However, there are places where the expression of his or her passion is extremely useful—in business development, for example. If you can get him or her to be externally focused and channel the passion where it can ignite interest in your products and services, it will take some of the heat out of the business.

I have someone in my team who expects others to take responsibility for all the tasks that don't resonate with their area of interest. How do I manage this?

You need to go back to the job description to ensure that the objectives are clearly stated. If an incumbent is not fulfilling their objectives, ask if they have the necessary skills or resources to meet them. Training or additional support may be required. If the skills and resources are in place, they may need an "attitude adjustment" or help in reorganizing their work with milestones, so that they fulfill your expectations. Any continued lack of cooperation then becomes a performance issue, and further steps may need to be taken.

MAKING IT HAPPEN

The passion "switch" is usually "on" or "off," seldom in between. This makes the successful management of passion a precarious business, especially if "full on" leads to passion fatigue in others and "full off" is disabling for the rest of the team.

There are three main areas to consider when tapping into someone's passion.

Recognition

When confronted with someone who doesn't appear to be fired up by anything, it is easy to jump to the conclusion that nothing in his or her life generates anything other than boredom. However, this is unlikely to be the case. Most people are switched on by *something*; the key is to determine what it is, and then to find a work context in which it can be expressed. You may find clues by observing the person in question. They may have been particularly enthusiastic when running a certain project, organizing a social event, or sitting on a committee. You could explore which aspects of these roles generated the uncharacteristic level of interest and enthusiasm. They may have enjoyed the "expert" status bestowed upon them as a project leader; they may have liked interacting with a wide network of people, or may have preferred structuring a meeting. If these activities are not present in their job then it would be easy to see why they were dispirited.

If you have not seen any evidence of passion in the workplace, you may want to ask them about their interests outside of work, to see if you can find the root of their passion.

Once you have discovered the basis of someone's passion, try to accommodate parts of it in their job. This could be done, for example, by realigning their current job objectives, giving them special projects, or even moving them into a new job where they can engage their enthusiasm constructively.

"If you follow your passion, the money will follow. But if you chase the almighty dollar, you can easily lose that and end up with nothing."

Elizabeth MacKay

Creative Direction

Passion is not always easy to manage. Although you may welcome signs of passion in one of your team, it may be inappropriately directed and therefore disruptive to the other members. Passion needs a framework through which it can be managed. This means creating clear objectives, both for individuals and the team. In this way, a person's inappropriate use of their enthusiasm can be addressed in performance appraisals. The message can be reinforced by managerial guidance (reiterating objectives, for example) and through additional professional training, if necessary.

Rewarding Success

It is not difficult to reward someone for using his or her passion creatively and to the benefit of the organization. Most times, people are satisfied with a "thank you," or, if it is a particularly valuable contribution, a more tangible reward. Bear in mind that absence of any recognition for their contribution and energy is likely to cause offense and hurt.

If someone's passion is different from your own, it is easy to overlook it or even devalue it, so make a conscious effort to learn about the passions of each member of your team. If this is done in a team building session, other members of the team will be able to tap this energy. In this way, new responsibilities can be allocated according to natural aptitude and desire (as well as experience and skill), and everyone can take responsibility for creating a high-performing team.

You may find that you are managing one or two people who don't know what their passions are. This can happen when someone enters a career early and has never really thought about their personal aspirations. Also, in the course of his or her professional life, that person may not have been presented with anything that resonates with their personality. In order to provide these people with an opportunity to explore their nature in more depth, they could be put into a series of situations that trigger different aspects of their talent. Encourage them to network in other parts of the business to see if there are areas that stimulate their interests. A wide exposure to the business may get them thinking more passionately about future career moves and how they could deliver more value through what they do.

If this fails, ask them to think about what they have done in the past that has really given them a buzz. At first, what they come up with may seem wholly unrelated to their professional role, but with careful questioning and a little persistence, it is usually possible to find out what was driving the sense of pleasure or achievement. By getting free of the context, you can see whether this passion is transferable or not.

COMMON MISTAKES
A Lack of Focus

Passion can trigger emotions that range from enthusiasm to anger. These two emotions are deceptively close, and one can turn into another very rapidly. It is easy to get lulled into a false sense of security when channeling someone's passion, but remember the nature of their personal investment and be prepared for an equal but opposite reaction should they be thwarted in its expression. Once tapped, the best way to manage passion is to do so cooperatively. Let the individual know what you're thinking. If any redirection is required, discuss options with them and involve them in the decision making.

Forgetting That Passion Needs Management Too

Expecting someone's passion to overcome any obstacles is unreasonable. Passion does not look after itself, it needs facilitating and managing. Managers often forget that even people with high levels of enthusiasm get frustrated and broken by bureaucracy, politics, and lack of resources. It is a manager's job to orchestrate the work environment so that passion can be creatively and productively directed. This means looking for opportunities to use the workforce's passion and providing the right level of support.

Not Having Empathy for Others' Passion

If someone's passion does not match your own, it can be quite exhausting to maintain enthusiasm and support for that individual. However, if you allow your attitude to show, you risk losing someone who might have been an ally, and risk a drop in his or her performance. If you are approaching this point with someone, be open and discuss your tolerances. They must take responsibility for the personal side of managing this energy, just as you must take responsibility for the professional side.

Developing Your Creativity

GETTING STARTED

Everyone has creative talent, but many people lack confidence in their own creativity. "I'm not very creative" is a common lament, even from people who manage their careers well and are extremely successful in bringing value to the businesses where they work. In fact, developing a more efficient approach to your own workload or introducing a time-saving project management system requires considerable creativity. So the term *creativity* can have a much broader meaning than simply being possessed of artistic talent.

FAQs

I think creativity is born, not made. I'm not naturally a creative person, that's all.

Creativity is certainly born—in all of us. Developing this talent depends on finding a channel for its expression. Think of something you enjoy doing, an interest that you've held for some time but never really explored. Even if it's been in the back of your mind as a vague idea, if you focus on it and keep at it, your creative talent will begin to blossom. Many people start to draw or paint in this way. It starts as a whim, continues with lots of practice, and ends with some wonderfully inspiring works. Most important, regardless of the outcome, newly discovered creativity can bring you personal joy and a belief in your own creative powers.

Some of my coworkers are incredibly creative, but they just don't seem to be able to make anything of it. How can you actualize creative expression in the real world?

Some people love to explore ideas but don't have the interest or patience to turn ideas into action. But ideas in themselves are valuable—in fact, most research and development begins with ideas. Instead of dismissing these people as dreamers, see if there's a niche in your organization where their skill can be encouraged and nurtured. Such people can be very valuable members of a product or service innovation group.

Organizations can't afford to waste time on fluffy, self-indulgent thinking. What's the business case for letting creativity loose?

Even the most logically derived thinking is born of the creative impulse, and in today's business environment, where good ideas are the only way of differentiating yourself from the competition, this creative impulse is incredibly valuable. Some physicists believe that the smallest particle of matter is a thought, that we literally create our own reality. Surely organizations can use this force to generate the kind of innovation that enables them to excel in their industry or market.

I see my children being naturally creative. How can I make sure that this quality isn't squashed in them?

Preschool children don't yet comprehend the rules that tell them they can't do certain things. Try to keep their imagination alive by allowing them to express themselves in their own way. Let them challenge the acceptable, and give them a framework for making their own independent choices. Give them some questions to ask of their rule-breaking activities: could doing this hurt myself or anyone else? What else could I do with this idea? What might happen if I really do this? Giving your children tools for analyzing their actions will help keep them safe and may actually help broaden their patterns of thinking.

MAKING IT HAPPEN
Look at the World Around You

Developing creativity requires the same amount of thought and attention as developing any other skill. Although some people do seem to be more innately creative than others, it's wrong to think that some individuals have it and others don't. Creativity is a natural form of human expression.

Take a look at the world you've created around yourself. Your home and workspace are a creative expression of who you are and so are the social networks you've created for yourself. What about the gifts you give to the special people in your life, or the hobbies and activities you like? Think about your role at work; what have you done differently from others who have held your job? What kind of relationships have you developed with your coworkers? What positive impacts have these had? All these things are evidence of your creativity. All any of us needs to do is to recognize that creativity takes many forms, become aware of the process, and work on making it a conscious activity.

Useful Techniques

A number of conscious techniques have been shown to promote the flow of creativity.

- **Brainstorming.** Brainstorming generates a free flow of ideas, associations, and concepts, however foolish they may seem at the outset. Energy generated by a brainstorming group is contagious, fostering creative leaps and jumps. The speed of the process bypasses the logical circuitry of the left side of the brain, allowing imaginative ideas from the right side—the creative side—to emerge uncensored—perhaps offering possibilities for innovative products or services.
- **Finding the Zone.** Artists, athletes, and craftspeople often experience the phenomenon of being in the creative zone, a state in which it's almost as if they are running on automatic pilot. This usually happens when people are so totally absorbed in what they're doing that their creative energy takes over and generates its own momentum. Total concentration seems to switch something in the brain that enables pure, unrestrained

---

"Minds are like parachutes. They only function when they are open."   James Dewar

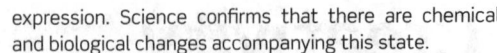

expression. Science confirms that there are chemical and biological changes accompanying this state.

- **Stimulating the Creative Side of the Brain.** The right side of the brain is where intuitive and creative abilities reside; the left side is where logical thinking takes place. A number of techniques exist that allow you to switch consciously from left side to right, thereby enabling you to tap into your reserves of inspiration and innovation. One activity that can trigger this is to write or draw with your nondominant hand, simply allowing your instinct to direct your muscles. The result is a product of the creative side of the brain. Visualization can also be helpful. Close your eyes and draw what's in your mind's eye. Your imagination is also part of your right-brain activity.

Writing down a few pages of your thoughts on a daily basis—whatever comes into your mind—can also open up channels of creativity. It's important not to get in your own way as you write—just let ideas flow without judging or filtering them. You may feel self-conscious or awkward at first, but if you keep at it you'll find that your mind is much freer and your expression more fluid. Your ability to formulate ideas, think abstractly, and make decisions improve, while counterproductive tendencies like having tunnel vision or being judgmental will diminish.

- **Relaxation/Meditation.** Logical thinking generates beta waves in the brain. Meditation and relaxation techniques produce alpha waves, whose myriad positive effects include creative thought. With practice, you can meditate even in the midst of chaos—in an airport or on a city street. Certain breathing techniques can also help clear your mind and change your brain activity from beta to alpha waves. The alpha state has been found to be an exceptionally good way to enhance learning, as it clears the path for new thoughts and inspiration.

Listening to soothing, uncomplicated music is another way of tuning your brain into a different wavelength.

- **Doing Something Out of Context.** Being creative is about breaking habits and being open to new thoughts and experiences. Try doing something that you've never done before—something undemanding like going to an event that you wouldn't normally be interested in, or taking a different route to work. You may be amazed at how such a simple change can open the creative floodgates.

If you're struggling to solve a particularly difficult problem, try asking a child or elderly relative. Without the clutter of knowledge (or, in the elderly relative's case, with the wisdom of experience), someone coming fresh to the problem can often trigger insights that can prove useful.

COMMON MISTAKES
You Don't Keep an Open Mind

People who don't have time for, or don't value, creative talent often miss out on a flow of ideas that just might contain the germ of the next big thing. Allowing creative energy the freedom to express itself without restraint or censure is the best way to reap its benefits.

You Don't Do a Reality Check

Just because an idea is exciting it doesn't mean it will be useful! Organizations looking for a unique product may be tempted to pick up on ideas that really have very little mileage in them. Build a reality check into your development process to ensure that only those ideas that are viable actually end up on the market. If you get the timing or context wrong, you're likely to make big, often expensive, mistakes.

You're Not Receptive Enough to New Ideas

Sometimes ideas are dismissed simply because they threaten the status quo or challenge long-held, never-questioned values. Bottled water is a good example. It was launched at a time when drinking water was considered to be a commodity freely available to all. What originally seemed like a commercial nonstarter has turned into a major sector of the beverage market. Always ask yourself "On what basis am I rejecting this idea?" If your dismissal is coming from habit or old assumptions, step back and think again.

You Give Up Too Easily

Don't expect too much of yourself too soon. Our pragmatic, do-it-now, bottom-line society doesn't always value the creative process. Taking steps to develop your own creativity may feel awkward to you and seem odd to others. Be patient and give yourself exploring time—free from censorship—before abandoning the effort. Rewards are often immediate, but if they aren't, or you feel you need support, seek a teacher or mentor who can help you to unleash the latent power of your right brain.

FOR MORE INFORMATION

Books:
de Bono, Edward. *Six Thinking Hats.* Revised ed. New York: Little, Brown, 1999.
Csikszentmihalyi, Mihaly. *Flow: The Psychology of Optimal Experience.* New York: HarperCollins, 1991.
Von Oech, Roger. *A Whack on the Side of the Head: How You Can Be More Creative.* New York: Warner Books, 1998.
White, Shira, with G. Patton Wright. *New Ideas About New Ideas.* Cambridge, MA: Perseus, 2002.

Web sites:
Creativity at Work: **www.creativityatwork.com**
creativityportal:
http://creativityportal.searchking.com
Creativity Web:
http://members.optusnet.com.au/~charles57/Creative/index2.html
Mind Tools:
www.mindtools.com/pages/main/newMN_CT.htm

See also:
★ Creating Corporate Creativity (pp. 341–342)
✔ Managing Others' Creativity (pp. 943–944)

"Since business is a 'get things done' institution, creativity without action-oriented follow-through is a barren form of behavior."

Theodore Levitt

Managing Others' Creativity

GETTING STARTED

Everyone has a creative spark, but our beliefs often inhibit its ignition. Part of what managers do is to see the spark in their people, encourage its ignition, and then champion its success. In many cases, however, a manager's own dampened spirit makes it impossible to recognize creativity in coworkers. Paradoxically, looking inward is a good place to start for those seeking creativity in others.

Fresh ideas are increasingly the primary means by which an organization can differentiate itself in the market and attain competitive advantage. Rehashing old formulas doesn't cut it. When success depends on expanding knowledge boundaries, knowledge management becomes more and more important.

FAQs

A member of my team is a fountain of new ideas, but instead of helping, he often derails meetings and wastes time. How can I manage his or her creativity?

Some people are naturally creative and just can't help exploring new territory and concepts. Your team member is showing signs of needing an outlet to channel his or her creativity into innovative and practicable solutions. Try to create contexts in which her ideas can be recognized, sifted, and used, so she learns which situations are best suited to the exercise of his or her creative talents.

I would like employees to have an outlet for their creativity, but our products don't lend themselves to innovation. How can I encourage a more creative environment?

Creativity doesn't need to produce transformational or earth-shattering results to be valuable. It can be useful in various ways, for example, thinking of a new process that improves quality or efficiency, restructuring a business area to enhance the work environment, or finding a better way to access stored information.

Raise the subject of creativity at a management team meeting. The team might be willing to arrange an organizational review with the idea of developing creative thinking in every department or business unit. In addition to helping the company think more creatively, such an activity would send a message to employees that management values (and maybe even rewards) creativity.

My job includes finding and facilitating creativity in my team. I find that this quality ebbs and flows naturally, and it's hard to "switch it on" when required. How can I sustain creativity at a high level?

You need to create a creativity-friendly environment by finding ways to break routines so that creativity can percolate, as well as providing opportunities and tools to allow creative thinking to surface. Consciously focus and direct creative activities toward desired outcomes. Intro-ducing visitors to brainstorming or product development meetings can help provoke creative thinking. When people know each other well, they settle into comfortable routines that can become stale. Introducing third parties can stir things up!

MAKING IT HAPPEN
Identify the Blockages

Creative thinking is divergent thinking—a nonlinear process in which our brains make associations and build linkages where none existed before. It allows us to speculate on future trends by expanding the realms of possibility. Managing creativity means sifting through these unrealized ideas and directing them toward new solutions.

As organizations grow, the pace of innovation and creativity tends to slow. In general that's a good thing, because managers need to focus on the business's core products and services. Nevertheless, organizations can go too far the other way and unwittingly construct institutionalized blocks to creativity.

Here are some of the blocks that you may see in your organization:

- **a belief that creativity is only for some people, not everyone.** To a certain degree, what you think is what you get. Depending on how we think about creativity, we can either block its expression or give it wings. New ideas are not necessarily based on a rare kind of brilliance. They often emerge simply from thinking about the same old things from different perspectives and placing them in fresh contexts. This is a talent that anyone can develop.

- **entrenched belief systems.** We seldom question our belief systems. They just exist in our subconscious, and we use them to make sense of the world, to filter and file sensory information according to fairly rigid parameters. We tend not to examine their usefulness unless forced to do so by extraordinary events. Learning to be open to possibilities that lie outside our personal belief system can open us up to creative thought.

- **fear of failure.** People fear making mistakes and being judged foolish—or worse. This fear can have paralyzing effects, inhibiting innovative thought and nurturing mediocrity. In a fear-driven environment, "right" is rewarded and "wrong" is punished. Yet these so-called rights and wrongs aren't absolute, but merely an accepted matter of opinion. Promoting a work culture that applauds creative exploration will help people overcome their fear of failure.

- **ideas with no practical application.** All creative ideas have a life, not just the practical ones. It may take a hundred crazy ideas before one is grounded in a product or service that adds value to the business. That one good idea validates the entire process, even the ninety-nine ideas that needed to be discarded.

- **"knowing" what will work and what will not.** People make judgments based on what they know and what they believe. Judgments can give rise to prejudice, caution, spite, and many other undesirable reactions. Sus-

"Creativity is never enough."

Adrienne Landau

944

ACTIONLIST

pending judgment—on yourself and others—is a means of allowing new thoughts the opportunity to be born.

- **"Yes, but . . ." cynicism.** Sometimes people automatically cite reasons why something won't work. They're so attached to current reality—and perhaps so afraid of expanding their belief system—that they resist anything new. If this cynicism is given free rein (or if your management is infused with nay-sayers), don't be surprised if your organization generates few really good ideas.

Overcoming Blockages to Stimulate Creativity

You can remove these blockages by raising awareness, expanding communication channels, and encouraging people to reserve judgment until new ideas have been fully and fairly considered. This is the skill of listening *for* instead of listening *against*.

Learn to listen

Encourage active listening skills throughout the organization. This means truly paying attention to what's being said and being conscious of your own perceptions. If you don't like someone's suggestion, ask yourself why. Which belief are you so attached to that you protect it from being challenged?

Encourage "Creative Tension"

Creative tension is a concept discussed in Peter Senge's book, *The Fifth Discipline*, and in Robert Fritz's *Creating*. It demands that holders of opposing views challenge their entrenched beliefs and open themselves up to the unthinkable or undoable. Allowing "crazy" ideas room to develop makes it possible for extraordinary solutions to emerge.

Reward Innovative Thinking

To change the organizational culture to one where creativity has free rein, you need to reward innovative thinking—whether it leads anywhere or not. If rewards are contingent on an idea being successful, people will be discouraged from contributing. Ideas can be gathered in a number of different ways—casual comments around the coffee machine, suggestion box programs, or structured brainstorming. However you do it, acknowledge contributors for their efforts. Be sure to follow up, too, and let them see how the ideas are being implemented.

Track Ideas

Creating organizational structures and systems to capture, channel, and track creativity will ensure that fewer good ideas get lost. Having a system to develop and incorporate good ideas keeps an organization from depending on a few individuals to do the creative thinking for everyone.

Value Diversity

It's a commonplace that creators aren't implementers.

The beauty of a healthy organization is that something rare and wonderful comes from variety. What emerges from such a mix of talents and thought patterns isn't always the shortest line between two points. But it's often new and invigorating—and sometimes extremely profitable!

COMMON MISTAKES
Creativity Isn't Harnessed

You can waste a lot of time, energy, and money chasing ideas that have no practical value. In the broadest sense all ideas have merit, but in a commercial setting ideas are there to serve the aims of the business. This implies a need for criteria to decide which ideas will be further explored and which will not. A scattershot approach to ideas generation is rarely helpful.

You Judge Ideas Too Early

Rushing to judgment too early can extinguish good ideas. Institutional memory is a repository of ideas that didn't work, often backed up by war stories that quash new ideas. Authoritative pronouncements on the viability of an idea based on historical experience need to be treated with caution. Contexts change, and what may not have worked in the past may well work now. Create an accepting, open culture so ideas can get off the ground. Only after an idea has been thoroughly discussed should judgment be brought to bear, in the form of prioritization, synthesis, and analysis.

You Overanalyze

Overreliance on analysis can paralyze creative thinking. Your usual approach to problem solving—gathering information, organizing, analyzing, prioritizing, forecasting—actually quashes creative thinking; you may need to suppress your well-trained professional instincts at the early, creative stages of a particular process.

FOR MORE INFORMATION

Book:
Senge, Peter M. *The Fifth Discipline: The Art and Practice of the Learning Organization.* New York: Currency Doubleday, 1994.

Web Sites:
Creativity at Work: **www.creativityatwork.com**
creativityportal: **www.creativity-portal.com**
Creativity Web:
http://members.optusnet.com.au/~charles57/ Creative/index2.html
CREAX: **www.creax.com**
omega23.com: **www.omega23.com/creativity.html**

See also:
☆ Creating Corporate Creativity (pp. 341–342)

"True creativity often starts where language ends." Arthur Koestler

Developing Your People

GETTING STARTED

The case for developing your people is well established; it makes sense for the organization, it makes sense for the team, and it makes sense for the individuals concerned.

From the *organization* perspective, it's clearly beneficial to make the best of the talent held in your community of employees. This is because there are few competitive options other than the creativity and imagination of those contributing to the fortunes of the business. The possibilities of gaining competitive advantage through pricing, distribution, and service levels have been largely exhausted, so differentiation rests with innovations that change the "experience" someone has of a product rather than the "fact" of a product.

From the *team* perspective, harnessing its collective talent increases its effectiveness and motivates everyone involved to learn, develop, and contribute more to their roles.

From the *individual* perspective, development brings new possibilities for career progression as well as personal rewards and recognition for the value that is plowed back into the business as a result. What can be more rewarding that seeing the fruits of your talent flourish within the business, or developing the skills that will enable you to progress inside or outside the business in the long run?

Instigating a culture that welcomes development will also reflect well on the manager who organizes the processes that help people meet tough targets. There are no "losers" if the art of developing people is performed properly, but there are pitfalls that must be negotiated along the route to the business's success.

FAQs

I've been trying to get a particular member of my team to develop some skills that are needed for our collective success but whatever I do, I cannot make her take this seriously. What should I do?

People won't put their energy into something they don't believe in, and you may have stumbled across a clash of values that stops this person from being committed to what you're aiming for. On the other hand, it may be that her interests and aspirations aren't what you'd like them to be, or that her talents aren't what you expect. As a team leader, it's important that you listen openly to this person to learn about her motivations and to find creative ways of tapping into these—or trading with her—to meet your own agenda.

I have been asked by members of my team to pay for some training which I don't believe has any immediate benefit for the business. I don't want to dampen their enthusiasm but I equally don't want to incur unnecessary costs that I can't justify to my line manager. What should I do?

It's good that your team is eager to be developed, but you need to direct their enthusiasm towards serving the business's needs, not just their own. Ask them to explain why they've chosen these training options and encourage them to tell you what benefits these will bring to the business. If they can't justify their choice, try negotiating a way forward that takes in elements of their needs as well as yours.

I'm trying to encourage my high-potential team members to follow a distance learning program that results in them earning a valuable degree, but one of them tends to miss tutorials and never submits work on time. How can I encourage more commitment?

Even though *you* think the degree is valuable, your team member may not. The course may not match up with what he or she wants to do, or he or she may not be suited to a distance learning program. People learn in different ways and you may find that a more hands-on approach works better for this person. Suggest a "stretch" project in a different part of the business. The gains may be achieved in a different way from the one you'd envisioned, but they'll be just as valuable.

I have been running a training program for my team which I feel has been completely ineffective. The evaluation sheets would suggest that the program is a great success, though. What's going on?

Some training programs are enjoyable and get good ratings from participants, but they might not result in anybody learning anything. Other courses are more challenging and get poor ratings but ironically *do* result in behavioral changes. It's all a matter of perception. Are you sure you're measuring the right things? Evaluation sheets are sometimes called "happy sheets," and, as this nickname would suggest, they merely give you a measure of enjoyment. Try focusing on what are known as "learning outcomes" instead; for example, you could ask people to list the learning points they've taken away from the experience rather than whether or not they enjoyed the session leader's style. You may find the results illuminating.

MAKING IT HAPPEN

Development should not be an indiscriminate activity that generates random skills, but rather a focused program that connects the business's objectives with each employee's talents and skills. This focus is necessary if the planned development will help people achieve their goals. It's important, then, to start off the process with a "diagnosis" that highlights the knowledge or skills gaps that are making the organization ineffective or, worse, making it vulnerable to failure or collapse. This diagnosis

945

ACTIONLIST

"Profound sincerity is the only basis of talent as of character."   Ralph W. Emerson

946

ACTIONLIST

is based on the assumption that the organization's mission is clear and that all employees buy in to it.

Diagnosing the need—an organizational perspective

The most obvious indications of a company's need to develop its employees are financial. Forecasts aren't met, the stock price is falling, costs are spiraling, cash isn't flowing, and so on. In addition, competitors may be challenging your once prized position, your market share may be diminishing, or a new innovation may have totally eclipsed your product range. This, along with high absenteeism, loss of key staff, and poor motivation must surely wake up an organization to the need to act decisively and fast. Once the problem has been recognized, an honest and precise appraisal must be undertaken to work out where the development effort needs to be focused for early results and then what longer-term initiatives need to be established to guarantee that a constant stream of talent will be entering the business. These initiatives could include a particular recruitment process, succession plan, or people policy that will allow continual development and the attainment of organizational objectives.

Training needs analysis—a team perspective

A training needs analysis can only be conducted meaningfully if the organizational objectives have been broken down and translated into functional, departmental, and team targets—all players must know their part in order to work out whether or not they're able to play it properly. The gaps in knowledge and skill that are identified create the development agenda and build a picture of what the team lacks as a whole. In matrix or flatter organizational structures (where, as you might guess, there isn't a hierarchy as such), teams tend to be mobile, with members joining and leaving according to the particular project that is being undertaken. One person can also be a member of several teams.

Despite these structural constraints, each team member must be responsible for contributing to the collective success of the team; everyone also needs to be part of the analysis and development solution. It's important to agree team roles that use the individual members' strengths. A full complement of team roles must be allocated or resourced to ensure that all the bases are covered. Those who are particularly strong in one activity may also be useful coaches to new members or those who want to diversify their skills. Once a project has come to an end or a target has been achieved (or not), bring together the team members to analyze the team's performance, distil learning from the experience, and create a development agenda that prepares the team for future challenges.

Performance appraisals—and individual perspective

On a more personal basis, 360 degree surveys (in which all those with a vested interest in a person's performance give him or her feedback) and performance appraisals highlight those areas that need to be addressed by the individual. These should be put alongside their career aspirations, so that they feel passionate about their development plan and are committed to following it to its conclusion. If people aren't motivated to learn new skills or broaden their experience, they'll only create obstacles to the progress happening around them. All parties need to agree on the way forward and provide resources to support people in their development activities. Remember that feedback on development targets should not be reserved for the (probably annual) performance review—giving positive feedback frequently is a good way of helping someone learn and adapt as they go along. Praising good work will help "ground" new behavior in a person's repertoire.

Identify Development Opportunities

The days when the only solution to a lack of knowledge, skill, or experience was a training program have gone. The mindset that "one size fits all" is outmoded, and there's a greater appreciation of the individual's unique talent profile and their personal development needs. Creating a development plan requires more imagination and a higher degree of tailoring if the breadth of talent needed is to be tapped. Not only are there the options of a company-specific or an open program, but there are also opportunities for work shadowing, job sharing, "stretch" assignments, special project allocation, sabbaticals, coaching, and mentoring. Distance learning and attendance of part-time release programs are also options, as are e-learning initiatives that allow people to pick and choose the programs that they feel will build their skills most effectively.

Evaluate Effectiveness

Once an organization has recognized the importance of development and invested in it, it needs to check that it's receiving something in return. This isn't always an easy task, as much of the benefit is "soft." For example, what value do you place on a motivated workforce, good relationships with colleagues and suppliers, and customer satisfaction? Some experts believe that it's possible to estimate the financial value of these results by looking at the cost of *not* having achieved them, while others advocate such a tight tailoring of training objectives to outcomes that it's merely a question of simple mathematics to estimate the return on investment after having accounted for all relevant costs. The bottom line (in all senses) is that development initiatives need to be effective at building a more successful organization.

Review and Follow Up

Once the initial trigger of the need for development has passed, it's easy to lose momentum and the initiatives can lose focus. To maintain this, review all development activities against performance targets and set new objectives to ensure ongoing benefits to the business. It's no good launching an initiative with a fanfare of trumpets only to see it peter out quietly until the next organizational panic forces new action. People get cynical about these patterns and soon they won't put in the effort necessary for successful development. Establishing a performance culture creates expectations and develops a

"It is not the individual but the team that is the instrument of sustained and enduring success in management."

Anthony Jay

language that can be used to maintain momentum. Development plans, taken seriously and discussed frequently, keep them active and alive.

We all collect experiences and learn new things throughout life. Development is a natural human trait that follows us wherever we go, so we may as well make the most of this characteristic and manage it according to our personal aims and objectives. Developing people is easy when you tap into their values and natural enthusiasm or passions. It's also extremely rewarding to see people thrive and grow under your care. Challenge yourself, therefore, to talk to your team to see if you can find a way to work with them in identifying their development needs and sparking off their interest in personal and professional growth.

COMMON MISTAKES
You Impose Your Views on Someone Else
Thinking you know what someone else "needs" and imposing this on them is a sure way of wasting time, money, and energy unless they agree with you. It's important for the person experiencing development to take part in the objective-setting and decision-making process if the rewards are to be felt at the team level.

You Assume Everyone Will Be Motivated
Once a development culture is established somewhere, it's easy to assume that everyone is motivated to learn and is willing to put time and energy into their development plan. This isn't always the case, though, and there will be some who genuinely do not want to take on more responsibility or further their careers. If you find that you're managing someone who feels like this, spend some time trying to understand what rewards they *do* seek from their work and direct them towards those activities that require competent and consistent performance.

You Expect Too Much of Others
Development takes a great deal of time, and, inevitably, choices have to be made that may have an impact on an individual's personal life. The time needed for study may impact an individual's family life, for instance, or impose a level of commitment that results in others, perhaps the individual's colleagues or team members, making choices or sacrifices of their own. Take care not to overload anyone's development plan and don't expect him or her to work all hours in order to meet job and development objectives. Try making some of a person's development targets part of his or her role specification so that one activity serves the other. For example, it's a good idea to teach someone how to create budgets or plan a project in an existent and relevant setting (that is, by giving them a real budget to work out or a live project to plan) than to leave it all in the realms of abstract theory. In this way, you can reduce the burden and also get some immediate value for the business.

947

ACTIONLIST

FOR MORE INFORMATION

Web Sites:
businessballs.com:
www.businessballs.com/traindev.htm
personal-development.com: **http://personal-development.com**

See also:
↪ Training and Development (pp. 1922–1924)

"The man who loses his opportunity loses himself."
George Moore

Managing a Volunteer Workforce

GETTING STARTED

Volunteers are an important part of the national workforce. Organizations use volunteers in many ways to help them meet institutional goals. Beyond economic considerations, however, voluntarism also provides opportunities for volunteers to meet their own personal objectives, acquire new skills, or contribute to their communities.

Volunteers can be found in organizations providing services in a wide variety of fields, including education, the arts, children's welfare, community and church services, healthcare, counseling, economic development, politics and many more.

Knowing how to manage and motivate a volunteer workforce is an essential management skill, particularly in the nonprofit sector, and it differs in significant respects from managing paid employees.

FAQs

I've just begun a campaign to recruit volunteers. What are the main things I should do?

If the number of volunteers is few, it may be possible to incorporate them into the organization without a separate manager. But if you anticipate the numbers to be significant, or that the size of the volunteer workforce will be gradually increasing, you need to make sure that a volunteer manager is hired. Among other things, the volunteer manager develops a program for volunteers—determining with other managers how the volunteer program will intersect with the rest of the business. The manager then recruits, screens, develops an orientation program for volunteers, trains them (or, oversees their training), and supports their integration into the organization. While not mandatory, volunteers are sometimes offered the same health care insurance and other benefits of a full-time employee.

I have a very difficult volunteer who just won't do the work the way we need to have it done. What is the process for dismissal?

Before considering dismissal you may wish to consider whether the volunteer has been assigned to the wrong job or whether other factors might be contributing to poor performance. If so, a move to another part of the organization may resolve the problem. Otherwise you may need to initiate a formal termination process. While not legally obliged to do so, the organization would be wise to have a process that largely reflects the same care and considerations given paid employees. Such steps might include:

- a review meeting to discuss areas that need improvement. Offer support or training if necessary and agree targets and key performance indicators;
- a meeting to give a verbal warning (supplying supportive documentary evidence, if appropriate);
- an official written warning referring to the reasons for the action;
- a follow-up meeting to appraise the situation and give any further support necessary;
- a formal letter of dismissal.

Are volunteers covered by OSHA regulations?

Yes, volunteers are covered by federal OSHA regulations, as well as state laws. Be sure to inquire about the specific health and safety laws governing your organization, as there are some differences from state to state.

MAKING IT HAPPEN
Understand What Motivates Someone to Volunteer

People volunteer their time, skills, and services for a number of different reasons. They may be exploring new career horizons, or they may be committed to a particular purpose or cause. They may have political ambitions, seek personal or professional development, or simply be filling in time between jobs to keep their skills fresh. Whatever is driving your volunteers, your job as their manager is to harness their motivation and put it to the most effective use.

Remember that Fitting Volunteers into an Organization Can Be Challenging

Because volunteers are giving their time and effort freely, they often feel entitled to a say in the way things should be run. This can make managing them a challenge. Unless they're prepared to adopt the shared corporate vision and adhere to the systems and processes embedded in the organization, they can actually be more trouble than they're worth. In order to achieve a productive level of alignment, volunteers need to be trained, coached, and supported.

Volunteers are very often made responsible for their actions, but they are not necessarily held accountable—that responsibility rests with their manager. Because of this it may be necessary to draw boundaries around the level of work they can do.

Manage the Relationship Between Volunteers and Full-time Staff

The relationship between volunteers and full-time staff can be tricky. Ostensibly they both have the organization's goals and objectives at heart, yet the contractual arrangement that holds them there is very different. Sometimes the enthusiasm of a volunteer can outweigh that of a full-time employee, leading to conflicts where the volunteer questions the employee's motivation. Employees may feel irritated by volunteers' naïve and apparently superficial view of the organization. In such instances it sometimes helps to have a meeting that encourages each side to see the other's point of view and to work cooperatively.

"Professionals require little direction and supervision. What they do require is protection and support."

Henry Mintzberg

Match Roles to Talents

Whatever their age, volunteers come to organizations with a variety of experiences and talents and (perhaps) with clearly defined areas of interest. It makes sense to do some screening of volunteer candidates before placing them. An interview that explores the volunteers' skills and experience and matches them with the needs of the organization will help make the relationship rewarding and productive. Assigning a coach who has had a long volunteering relationship with the organization can also help orient and settle a new volunteer.

Acquire the Right Management Skills

Managing volunteers calls for skills that range from human resource management and finance to training and administration. Managers can get training in recruiting and building a successful volunteer workforce, but one of the most effective ways to prepare is to speak to someone experienced in this area. Hearing about details and responsibilities of the job first-hand can be very helpful. You may also be able to develop a mentoring relationship with this person.

As manager of a volunteer workforce, you may also find yourself working outside normal working hours to dovetail with your volunteers' schedule. If this is the case you need to discipline yourself and manage your time carefully.

Instigate Best Practice Guidelines

As a volunteer manager you may want to consider the following best practice steps:

- Write a volunteer policy that outlines the organization's commitment to volunteers. Include your rationale for using volunteers, your recruitment policy, what training and support are available, and an equal opportunity statement.
- Make sure your volunteers understand and adhere to the organization's health and safety policies.
- Let volunteers know what they're getting into. This may mean bringing them in for a trial period to work alongside other volunteers or paid employees, depending on where they'll eventually be assigned. If that's not possible, arrange for them to have a telephone conversation with an experienced volunteer or employee before they start work.
- Outline roles and expectations, just as you would if you were recruiting employees into the business full time.
- See that volunteers understand their boundary of autonomy.
- Develop a program for paid staff who will be working with volunteers, so that they know the parameters of the volunteer program as well as their role in it.
- Establish a volunteer coaching or mentoring program to help volunteers to learn about organizational policies, procedures, and customs.
- You may wish to articulate in writing your organization's attitude toward the personal and professional development of volunteers. Many volunteers hope to leverage their volunteer experience into other, perhaps paid, situations and your organization's commitment to their development is a bonus.
- Make clear your policy on expenses. Although they're not paid, volunteers shouldn't find themselves paying to do the job.
- Get to know the volunteers, and find ways of building the team and making them feel appreciated. You may want to consider team meetings that help them to get to know one another, and include a vote of thanks or a celebration of their efforts.

Keep Volunteers In the Loop

Just as employees do, your volunteers want to know how your organization is performing. Any good (or bad) news will be of interest to them. You may have a special channel of communication for your volunteers (a newsletter, for example), but if this is not so, find a way of keeping them up to date. Remember that their enthusiasm for your organization can make volunteers your most effective mouthpiece—so the more informed and positive they are, the better.

Some organizations allow for a volunteer on a management committee. In this way volunteers can get their views and ideas heard at senior management level and may be able to effect change. Stay close to this network so you don't get any surprises.

COMMON MISTAKES
Not Having a Formal Volunteer Policy In Place

Although often regarded as unnecessary, a volunteer policy can forestall problems that may arise if expectations and procedures aren't explicit.

Forgetting to Manage the Relationship Between Volunteers and Full-time Staff

Many organizations forget that the line between volunteers and staff can be problematic. Full-time employees may be resentful of their "territory" being invaded or having desirable parts of their job reassigned to a volunteer. You would be wise to spend time with your paid staff to outline your approach and volunteer policy.

Sometimes full-time staff maintain that they're too busy to deal with volunteers. Although this can be true, it often masks a different concern, such as fearing their job will be given to a volunteer. If this is the case, try organizing a forum in which these issues can be discussed and addressed directly.

Failing to Understand What Motivates a Volunteer

Remember that volunteers are motivated by their values and beliefs. These are powerful motivators, and you can use them to direct volunteers' energy constructively. Make sure you take time to understand what these values are, and use this knowledge to build your relationship and assign volunteers appropriate jobs.

FOR MORE INFORMATION

Web Sites:
Association for Volunteer Administration:
www.avaintl.org/network/cybervpm.html
Energize, Inc.: **www.energizeinc.com/art.html**

"Motivation, really moving people to do something, needs emotion." — Paul Corrigan

Giving and Receiving Feedback Well

GETTING STARTED

When the thought of having to give or receive feedback arises, most people assume that the experience will be a negative and uncomfortable one. This isn't necessarily the case, though, and in fact it's good practice to highlight positive achievements or traits in any type of feedback situation.

Feedback is, in fact, a gift. If you're giving feedback, your main motivation is usually to see someone change their behavior for the better. Feedback is rarely given with ill intent, and so it can help people understand how they're perceived and how they may make positive changes to influence those perceptions. It is important to bear in mind that perceptions are not always reality, but they're very real in their consequences, so being aware of these will help you to choose whether or not to perpetuate them.

FAQs

I recently experienced some feedback in my performance appraisal that I felt was unreasonable and misrepresented my motivations. What's the best way of dealing with such a situation?

If you're receiving feedback from someone who doesn't understand the process well or who has not had a lot of practice, you may need to coach or guide them by asking them specific questions that will encourage them to express themselves more clearly and suggest ways forward for you. For instance, if they told you that your recent presentation wasn't good, ask them what it was that you did to create that impression and what they think you could do differently another time.

You could also share any political dilemmas that you had in deciding your approach and ask what further ideas they had that you could have considered. For example, you may have had to contend with different interests or agendas among those in your audience, such as those between sales and marketing, or the opposing forces of cost-cutting and achieving quality standards.

Finally, if you feel it's appropriate, tell the person who appraised you how their feedback has made you feel so that he or she has an opportunity to change his or her style.

I find it difficult to speak to my manager and it's hard to make her see me in a better light. What can I do?

If you have a difficult relationship with the person who is giving you feedback, there may be occasions when you feel unable to respond, unfairly judged, or put on the spot. If this is the case, thank your manager for his or her comments and say that you'd like to consider them for a short while (during which you can seek advice from friends or colleagues) and ask for the meeting to be reconvened at a (not too distant) later date.

I'm the manager in a team where one of the team members isn't pulling his weight. This is beginning to cause bad feeling among everyone else. What's the most effective way of dealing with this?

Talk to the person involved as soon as you can, giving feedback from your own perspective, not on behalf of the rest of the team. (For example, use "I" statements not "We") Start with a question like "How do you think the team is working?" This will help you to uncover the person's feelings and give you a useful inroad to the situation. If that approach doesn't help, though, continue with something like: "You really are an important member of the team and you bring a great deal of expertise to it but lately you've seemed rather unhappy. Is there anything you need or would like to discuss?" This acknowledges a positive achievement first, and should protect the recipient from feeling criticized. You can then have a discussion about what's going on, what you'd like to see happen to resolve it, and how you might help to make that happen.

I've just received some 360 degree feedback which concerns me. How can I learn more about why I'm getting certain feedback if I can't confront the respondents?

360 degree feedback is a one-way process and is usually based on a promise of confidentiality. It's a process whereby key colleagues or "stakeholders" in a company comment on someone's performance so that he or she can get a picture of how others perceive them.

Confrontation is not a desired outcome of 360 degree feedback, or indeed of any other form of feedback. As the process is confidential, it allows people to speak freely, but the downside for feedback recipients is that, obviously, they don't know who said what, and this may make them feel frustrated. The positive side of the process is that it may tune you in to common perceptions people have about you and raise your awareness of potential behavioral issues that you may wish to deal with. There is nothing to stop you asking for further feedback from a different audience if you need more input on the perceptions that have been highlighted to you. Try not to preface any requests for additional help with a moan or complaint, though, even if your ego is feeling a bit bruised.

I've recently been given a managerial position which involves conducting performance reviews, and I know that one in particular will be challenging. How do I give feedback in this setting?

Unfortunately, annual performance appraisals tend to be the only time that people receive feedback on how they're doing. It's much better to give and receive feedback more regularly than this so that problems can be ironed out as they arise. If a review is looming, however,

make sure that you're familiar with the reviewee's objectives and that you can back up your feedback (whether positive or negative) with evidence. Do not use hearsay or rumor to inform your feedback and don't get locked into giving your opinion or advice unless your offer of it is accepted or it's asked for by the reviewee. This is a trap that can give rise to defensive behavior and may lead to the review being ended early.

MAKING IT HAPPEN

Giving and receiving feedback is one of many forms of communication that goes on every day at work. However, rather than being abstract, theoretical, or debatable, feedback is essentially extremely personal and thus highly relevant to the recipient. Unfortunately, many people feel that the most common type of feedback they receive is critical. Sadly we rarely receive as much praise as we do criticism, even though we know that someone receiving lots of positive encouragement performs much more effectively than those who are constantly put down.

Feedback is a mechanism for conveying to people how they're experienced and perceived by others. It provides the recipient with an opportunity to make decisions about whether or not they wish to change their behavior and the consequences of doing that. There are two parties associated with feedback: the giver and the receiver. Both may benefit from understanding and learning how to manage the dynamics of feedback.

Giving Feedback

Giving feedback is not easy. The very thought of it may conjure up bad memories if you've been on the receiving end of badly thought out or tactless feedback yourself, and, if it's an area with which you're unfamiliar or uncomfortable, a feedback session can easily spiral into a critical and defensive exchange rather than be a positive and illuminating experience.

Here are some important steps in making sure that the delivery of your feedback is constructive and well received:

- **Find an appropriate venue.** Make sure that the feedback session is held in a private place and that you can speak to the recipient without being distracted or interrupted. If you have an office, turn your phone on to voicemail or ask someone to field your calls, and remember to turn off your cell phone.
- **Make sure the reviewee is prepared.** If you're conducting a performance review, brief the reviewee so he or she has clear expectations on what will be taking place. This is usually built into the process through timed activities and deadlines but it's as well to make a mental check that each party is clear about the purpose and boundaries of the meeting beforehand. You may ask the reviewee to prepare in a particular way for the meeting by describing the objectives they've met and how they've met them, reflecting on how they think they've been perceived and what development or additional resources they need to help them to perform in their roles more effectively.
- **Set the scene and create a conducive context for the feedback.** This would include preparing or copying any relevant documents, setting aside sufficient time, a pri-

vate room, and some water or refreshments. Frame your intervention carefully, so that the recipient understands where you're coming from and what you're commenting upon. Be sure that he or she is willing to receive your feedback before you attempt to give it. If you think you feel defensiveness at the outset, address it directly. "I sense that you're uncomfortable with this process. Is there anything I can do to make it easier for you?" You might want to add some reassurances also such as "Any comments we make today will stay within the confines of this room."

- **Be positive.** Lead with a positive piece of feedback to demonstrate that you've noticed and valued particular behavior. Deliver the feedback, taking care to be sensitive to the recipient's likely reactions and responding with your full attention and consideration. The feedback should be descriptive rather than evaluative and focus on behavior that can be changed rather than on personality. For example: "I've noticed that you've been finding your workload stressful recently," rather than "You were aggressive!" Remember to speak for yourself only, this means using "I" statements rather than hiding behind the views of a colleague or group.
- **Ask for feedback on the way you handled the feedback session.** Even if the session was difficult, it's an opportunity to build bridges and show your willingness to learn.
- **Honor any agreements made during the meeting.** If you've promised some additional resources, greater involvement in a project, or some training, confirm this afterwards in writing and follow it through.
- **Demonstrate the behavior you wish to see.** It's no good asking for something from others that you're not prepared to do yourself. You may want to introduce a culture of ongoing feedback so that issues aren't left for the performance review.

Receiving Feedback

The way we act reflects who we are to the world and when this is criticized or questioned, it can feel like an assault on our personalities. If you receive feedback that you find challenging or hard to deal with, try to see it as information that allows you to make informed choices about how you're perceived by others. In some circumstances, of course, the feedback (or the manner of it) may say more about the person communicating it to you than it does about you, but whether this is the case or not the best thing to do is to thank the person for their feedback and assure them that you'll think about it further. You're not compelled to accept feedback and you may choose to maintain the behavior that feels right for you.

Remember the following when you're receiving feedback:

- **Listen carefully.** Even if you feel under attack, try not to leap to your own defense until you've had a chance to think about and understand the feedback thoroughly. Be genuinely open to hearing what the other person is saying and try not to interrupt or jump to conclusions. Active listening techniques may be helpful for you here.
- **Ask questions to clarify what's being said and why.** You are completely entitled to ask for specific examples and instances of the types of behavior that are at the root of

951

ACTIONLIST

"No organizational action has more power for motivating employee behavior change than feedback from credible work associates."

Mark R. Edwards

the feedback. If the atmosphere is becoming tense, introduce a more positive approach by asking for examples of the behavior your reviewer would like to see more of.

- **Keep calm**. Even if you feel upset, try not to enter into an argument there and then; just accept what's being said and deal with your emotions another time and in another place. Stay calm and focus on the rest of the feedback.

Remember that giving feedback can be an uncomfortable experience too, and people generally don't do it unless they feel that you can benefit from their observations. Try to remain engaged throughout and don't start a "tit-for-tat" exchange.

Receiving feedback doesn't mean that you can't talk to the other person about your behavior. For example, you may want to ask if the giver has any suggestions about what you could do differently. You don't have to accept them, but at least it demonstrates a willingness on your part to take the feedback seriously.

Thank the person giving you feedback for taking the time and trouble to share their perceptions with you.

Honest and well-presented feedback allows people to enjoy good, open relationships. If feedback is a common feature of the way people communicate, issues aren't left to fester and grow out of all proportion. Some organizations have been known to benefit from instigating a culture of "instant constructive feedback." which encourages employees to address issues as they arise rather than leave them to fester or develop into crises. This approach not only diffuses the more destructive or passive-aggressive styles of relating to others, but it can have a genuine impact on profitability as ideas may be freely exchanged and innovative approaches discussed.

COMMON MISTAKES
The Feedback Session Falters Because of a Personality Clash

Giving feedback can very quickly turn into a personality clash when the means of achieving an objective is debated hotly and defensively. This happens when either or both parties believe they are right and are heavily invested in their own approach. In such a situation, people can become entrenched and dogmatic when a suggestion to do things differently is made. Try to maintain good rapport throughout, which includes the free expression of views, a genuine desire to understand each other's per-

spectives, and the absence of premature judgment or closure. If a feedback session veers off track, it can be brought back by calling a "time out" and then clarifying once more what the session is supposed to achieve. Re-assessing what you're doing gives you an opportunity to talk through your values and assumptions and also provides a clear framework for the remainder of the session.

You Make Assumptions

Making assumptions about others' values, motivations, or intentions can quickly lead to the deterioration of rapport. Avoid this by making sure that each person has an opportunity to make these explicit. Don't assume you know the motivation behind someone's behavior but instead give them the chance to explain this early in the feedback session, perhaps as you set the context for your discussion. For example, ask open questions such as, "What were you hoping to convey when you gave your presentation?" From their answers, you can get very useful insights into that person's way of thinking and acting.

You Don't Admit There's a Problem

If things start getting out of hand, acknowledge that things are going wrong. By showing your vulnerability and humility, you'll be able to create a mood of trust and rebuild rapport.

FOR MORE INFORMATION

Web Sites:
Active Reviewing guide:
http://reviewing.co.uk/archives/art/3_9.htm
Giving and Receiving Feedback:
www.mapnp.org/library/commskls/feedback/feedback.htm
SelfhelpMagazine.com:
www.selfhelpmagazine.com/articles/growth/feedback.html
The University of British Columbia: **http://co-op.arts.ubc.ca**

See also:

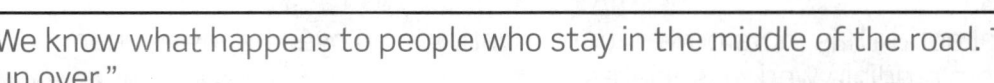

"We know what happens to people who stay in the middle of the road. They get run over."

Aneurin Bevan

Downshifting: Working Less and Enjoying It More

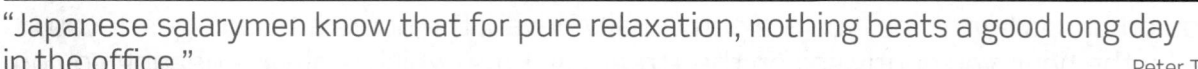
GETTING STARTED

The traditional definition of success is to work hard, get promoted, make more money, and give more and more of your life and your identity to your organization. Some call it "climbing the corporate ladder," or "making good." But in the last few years, there has been a growing number of people who are questioning common wisdom. Instead, they are looking for ways to get out of the rat race and to have a more balanced and fulfilling life.

There are many reasons why you might consider downshifting in your career. Quite often, the reason is family demands. Your children require more attention, or your marriage may be shaky because of the time you spend away from the family. Or perhaps an elderly parent requires more care. Conflicts of values can be another major reason for a desire to downshift. You may have been asked to do something by your organization that goes strongly against deeply held values, and it leads you to question why you are working so hard for this organization. And, finally, you may be near retirement and it feels as if it is time to begin disengaging from your career and building a new life outside of work.

Regardless of the reason for downshifting, it takes a lot of foresight, planning, and courage to make a move toward a simpler life. Consider the following questions as you think through the possibility of downshifting:

- Why do you want to downshift?
- Do you feel called toward something new, or are you wanting to get away from something that no longer works for you?
- What is your current, and long-term, financial situation?
- What are the core values that you want to live by in your new life?
- Do you have a support network of like-minded people?
- What do you want to keep, what do you want to let go of, and what do you want more of?

FAQs

If I downshift, won't I be ruining my career?

If you have to ask this question, then you shouldn't even be considering downshifting. People who downshift generally are no longer interested in climbing the career ladder. It's just not relevant to them. They have emotionally detached themselves from the "corporate game" and are moving toward a slower, less demanding way of life. They are not motivated by the traditional definitions and trappings of success.

I am ready to get off the fast track, but won't everyone say I'm crazy?

Chances are very good that a number of people will say you are crazy. It's as if they are playing Monopoly and you have moved over to another table to play chess. You are each playing by a different set of rules, and, if they think you are still playing Monopoly, then your behavior looks very strange to them. You must constantly check with your own inner voice and your own values to see if this is right for you. Don't worry about what other people think. It is your life to live. Paul Ray and Sherry Anderson have done research on people's values in the United States and Europe. They found that about 26% of the adult population in these areas have a strong interest in living a slower, simpler life that is more in harmony with nature, family, and community life. So you are not alone.

If I decide that downshifting is not for me, will I be able to get back into my old career path?

You take a risk when you downshift. You are stepping into unknown territory and creating a new lifestyle for yourself. You may not be able to go back the way you came. However, chances are pretty good that this new adventure may lead you to other career paths you never even considered. If you decide that a simpler way of life just doesn't suit you, you can use the same risk-taking and imaginative skills you used in downshifting to create the next inventive step on your path.

MAKING IT HAPPEN
Be Clear about Why You Are Thinking about Downshifting and Involve Your Family

The decision to downshift is a major lifestyle decision. Take the time to do soul-searching about why you want to slow down and simplify your life. Then discuss it with your family and anyone else who would be directly affected by such a choice. Explain what you find attractive about this new way of life, and then be willing to listen to their concerns and fears.

Downshifting often occurs as a backlash to a corporate lifestyle that doesn't work for you any more. But be sure that you are not just running away from a difficult situation that perhaps you should face. Successful downshifting occurs when there is also a clear vision of a better and more meaningful life. It is important to be as concrete about the new vision as you can.

Make a Thorough Assessment of Your Short-term and Long-term Financial Situation

Downshifting requires some risk, but you should not be putting your health and your old age in jeopardy. Give careful consideration to what you might need in an emergency or in case of a long-term illness. But also don't turn so conservative that you become afraid to build a life that you've always dreamed of. Make sure that you have something in savings. And wherever possible, think of ways to develop passive income.

When you first make the move toward downshifting, it may mean leaving your organization and being on your

---

"Japanese salarymen know that for pure relaxation, nothing beats a good long day in the office."

Peter Tasker

own for a while. You should have sufficient savings in place to pay your monthly expenses for six months to a year. As a part of downshifting, you will be dramatically reducing your expenses, so your savings should go quite a bit further

Conduct a Work–Life Values Assessment

Downshifting requires some major decision making about your life and your work. If you are going to be happy with your decision, you will need to be very clear about your core values and how your new life will be in alignment with those values.

Evaluate Your Living Situation and Consider a Move

A major way to reduce monthly expenses is to move to a smaller house or apartment. In the process, you will need to go through your possessions and decide what to keep and what to give away or sell. Also think about how a smaller home can simplify your life. Choose a place that requires minimal maintenance, is easy to clean, and has little or no yard work.

Make a Decision about Whether or Not You Want to Leave Your Organization

Downshifting often means leaving your job and becoming a free agent and working out of your home. But it can also mean moving to a lower-pressure less demanding job in the organization. Or you might consider moving to an organization that has a slower paced culture.

Decide What to Keep and What to Let Go of

You can simplify your life by getting rid of possessions you no longer need. There is less to keep track of and care for, and often you can do good by giving these things away. Clean out your closets. Give clothes to charity. Cancel magazine subscriptions. At the same time, be sure to keep things that have significant meaning and value for you. Even if it is not practical, you will want to keep those coffee cups that were passed down from your grandmother.

Create an Action Plan with a Schedule

Once you decide what living and working changes you are going to make, you can prepare a timetable of key actions. These might include putting your house on the market, selling furniture, giving notice at your company, and starting up your own business. As you begin to implement your plan, your life will actually get more hectic before it gets simpler. You will be still living your old life while planning for your new life. Be gentle with yourself

and do not try to rush things too much. That would be defeating the overall purpose of having a slower, less stressful life.

Take an Annual Retreat and Continue Your Life–Work Assessment

At least once a year, take time off with your family to talk about how this new lifestyle is going. Analyze what is working and what you would like to change. Celebrate your courage for taking the risk to move toward a more balanced life.

COMMON MISTAKES

You Get Excited about the Idea of Downshifting and Immediately Quit Your Job

Downshifting is a major life change, and requires a lot of thought and planning. Take your time to really think through the kind of life you want to build before doing anything drastic.

You Try to Do Too Much at Once

Changing jobs and moving are two of life's most stressful activities. If your downshifting plan calls for both of these actions, try not to do them both at once. Plan for gentle transitions where possible.

You Make Only Cosmetic Changes and Then Find Yourself Right Back in the Rat Race

Old habits are hard to break and many of us are addicted to hard work and stress. You might try to simplify your life by eliminating some of the things you normally do, only to find that you have filled up the spare time with new things to do. Revisit your core values assessment and spend time envisioning the simpler lifestyle you pictured. You may need to make a more dramatic change in order to have a truly slower lifestyle.

FOR MORE INFORMATION

Books:
Bolles, Richard. *What Color is Your Parachute? A Practical Manual for Job-Hunters and Career-Changers.* Revised ed. Berkeley, CA: Ten Speed Press, 2006.
Drake, John. *Downshifting: How to Work Less and Enjoy Life More.* San Francisco, CA: Berrett-Koehler, 2001.

See also:
✓ Managing Dual Career Dilemmas (pp. 903–904)

Assessing Your Entrepreneurial Profile: Do You Have What It Takes?

GETTING STARTED

Once you've started thinking about starting a business, you need to start thinking about your own role in it. Are you the right type of person to make a success of a new venture? There's a great deal of romance surrounding the notion of being an entrepreneur, but not everyone has the aptitude. And it's important to understand that there's nothing wrong with *not* being an entrepreneur. The world wouldn't function half as well if it were peopled solely with them.

There are, though, some general personality traits that are essential for entrepreneurs. If the following list seems to fit your personality, you may have what it takes:

- I am persistent, with a great deal of drive and stamina. I see problems as opportunities. I have a good intuitive sense and thrive on new ideas.
- I tend to rebel against authority. I want to be my own boss.
- I am positive, communicate well, and enjoy working with people.
- I have a strong need to succeed, financially and otherwise.
- I'm not afraid to make mistakes, and I learn from them.

FAQs

How can I be sure I've got what it takes?

Before quitting your job and using your savings to start a business, you owe it to yourself to approach your entrepreneurial venture with some practicality. Take a more in-depth personality test and talk to small business advisers—often available at no cost through business associations, community colleges, and organizations such as SCORE (Service Corps of Retired Executives). Also try to speak to people in business already as they'll be able to give you a no-holds-barred account of what day-to-day life is like as an entrepreneur.

How much money will I need?

Whether you want to buy an existing business, purchase a franchise, start your own company, or merely offer services to others from a home office, starting a business depends on first knowing the numbers. People in the same or similar business are a good source of information—use your ingenuity to find out what it cost them to get started, and where they got the funds to do so. Be tactful and don't pester someone with questions if it's clear that he or she doesn't want to disclose this information to you, though. Other sources include trade associations, franchise organizations, business articles in magazines and newspapers, Internet research, or business consultants.

Besides being an ideas person, what else do I need to be good at?

Success in a new enterprise depends on dedication and the consistent application of good business principles. Some of these principles include being good with money; being good with people (investors, suppliers, employees, and so on); being a good promoter (marketing, sales, PR); and being good to yourself. Many entrepreneurs burn out before their businesses take hold. In this game, pacing yourself and your business is important.

MAKING IT HAPPEN
Check That You Have the Right Idea

If you've got a great new idea and no competition in sight, you must be sure that the product or service will be of value to customers—at a price at which you can afford to sell it. There may be no competition for a very good reason . . . If your objective is to enter a field with established competitors, you have to know your own strengths and weaknesses, as well as those of your competition. Be sure that you can provide a better product or service for a competitive price. Finding out all these things is called "market research," and you'll have to do a thorough job of it to succeed.

Develop a Detailed, Professional Business Plan

This is the key to building a successful business. Having a well-considered and systematic plan allows you to recognize problems as they arise in time to be able to take corrective action. The plan should be a living document, flexible over time to adapt to changes in the marketplace and your industry. It should include sections on every facet of your business—whether you're a sole proprietor or the executive director of a new manufacturing venture.

Bankroll Your Idea

Take your ideas and business plan to a variety of people, starting with friends and close supporters. Be prepared for critical feedback, and be flexible. Take the inevitable first few comments of "no thanks" as opportunities to fine tune the next presentation. One of the hallmarks of an entrepreneur is the ability to regroup, rethink, and reach a goal in another way.

Seeking publicity for your business is a way not only to notify potential customers but also to get the attention of possible investors. The more people who know about your idea, the better the chances that you'll attract the right investor.

Be willing to share a portion of the company with the right partners, but be wary of finance companies and investors who want full control, or the lion's share of the proceeds. You could also think about entering into a joint venture with another company, or position your company to attract start-up funds from federal or state sources.

"Entrepreneurs have no frontier other than their own ambition."

Robert Heller

Practice Your Networking

Being entrepreneurial doesn't mean being a lone ranger. Being successful often depends on your ability to network with potential customers, suppliers, new investors, and even those in government who control certain aspects of the business environment.

Plan Your Marketing and PR

An integral part of your business plan involves a marketing plan—how you intend to create the demand for your product or service. While market research tells you the "what" and "where" of your opportunities, the marketing plan outlines the steps by which you will find potential customers and convince them to buy from you. Networking, advertising, and PR (public relations) are all forms of marketing and promotion.

Make Sure You Have the Right Financial and Management Support

Most entrepreneurs are better at ideas than at managing budgets, business operations, and employees. Anticipate that you'll need more capital than you figured at the start, and don't be lavish with spending beyond the company's means. If you find yourself in a questionable position, make sure you have a network of trusted and experienced advisers to help you see the proper perspective and cover the things you are not naturally good at.

COMMON MISTAKES
Setting up Equal Partnerships

Entrepreneurs often share the start-up responsibilities with a partner or partners. However, sharing 50–50 or by thirds or quarters is a big mistake, because conflicts will inevitably arise and need someone in a controlling position to make a final decision. Choose (or hire) a C.E.O.—someone with the experience and skills needed for success—and give that person a greater decision-making authority and a bigger salary, even if it is only bigger by a small margin.

Having Inadequate People and Planning

Entrepreneurs must become strong managers when the company gets going. Many businesses fail because the people in charge don't have the managerial qualities or strength to cope with the challenges. In addition, stress can put a strain on personal relationships and this can make the challenges harder to deal with. Personality assessments can determine if you're cut out for a managerial position, and managerial training can prepare you for your new role as an executive.

Without proper market research and a solid business plan, a business is more likely to fail. The more preparation you do, the better your chances of success.

Relying Too Heavily on One or Two Customers

Having too few customers makes your business vulnerable, because it ties your future to the decisions of other organizations. If their business falters, it puts your hard work and dedication at risk— through no fault of your own. The advice of personal financial consultants is appropriate here. Having lots of customers, even though none of them is gigantic, is healthier in the long run.

Causing Cash Flow Troubles through Insufficient Financing

While some people are successful at jump-starting their own enterprise with little or no outside investment, they do so by being fortunate, being modest in their spending, and by plowing profits back into the business.

The majority of businesses, however, don't deliver the projected first-year sales volume. It's better to overestimate your need for capital resources at the beginning and to underestimate your projected sales figures. It's better to be pleasantly surprised at your success than to lose the business and your house because the money isn't there when it's needed.

When contemplating an expansion of your business, be wary of spiraling costs. If you're in a cyclical business, or one vulnerable to recession, be sure to be very calculating about your expenses—and develop "Plan B" well before you need to implement it.

Failing to Admit Mistakes

Entrepreneurs are sometimes the last to admit that their idea hasn't the sparkle it once had. Having advisers that you trust is important. Cut your losses and move on if your advisers all agree that you should. Doing so may save the company—if you can move quickly enough to capitalize on your mistakes or shift the product or service to take advantage of other opportunities.

Underestimating the Competition

Your competition won't stand still for long, once you've demonstrated their weakness in the marketplace with your product or service. Expect them to plug the hole quickly and even try to outflank you in the process. Your business and marketing plans should anticipate how to deal with new initiatives from your competition. If you conduct ongoing research, product and service evaluations, and marketing campaigns, you should always be one step ahead of the competition.

FOR MORE INFORMATION

Books:
Kushell, Jennifer. *A Young Entrepreneur's Edge: Using Your Ambition, Independence and Youth to Launch a Successful Business.* New York: Princeton Review Series, 1999.
Stolze, William J. *Start Up: An Entrepreneur's Guide to Launching and Managing New Business.* Franklin Lakes, NJ: 5th ed. Career Press, Inc., 1999.

Web sites:
Ewing Marion Kauffman Foundation: **www.emkf.org**
Kaufmann e-venturing: **www.eventuring.org**
Venture Capital Institute: **www.vcinstitute.org**
SCORE (Service Corps of Retired Executives): **www.score.org**
Entrepreneur: **www.entrepreneur.com**

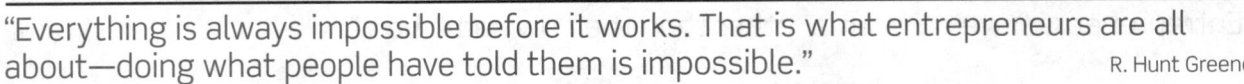

"Everything is always impossible before it works. That is what entrepreneurs are all about—doing what people have told them is impossible."

R. Hunt Greene

Deciding Whether to Start a Business

GETTING STARTED

Setting up your own business can be very rewarding, but there are pressures involved. It's not enough just to have a good, viable idea: you also need to have the right skills and temperament to make the opportunity succeed. Starting your own business is also a risky thing to do, so you need to be aware of what problems to look out for as early as possible. This will help you to decide if you are willing and able to take those risks, and will also help you to apply strategies that will reduce them.

Before you go any further, it's important to find out as much as you can about what sort of person you are. Be honest and objective, and discuss the project with friends, colleagues and relatives. Think about how you have dealt with past challenges, as an indication of your response to difficult new situations. This actionlist will help you to decide whether starting a business is the right thing for you to do.

FAQs

Do I have the right personality to start a business?

While the technical aspects of your business will require specific qualifications, skills, or experience, there are broader demands that are as important. These could include the ability to negotiate with suppliers, mediate between staff, be sociable with customers, be convincing with prospects, think clearly under pressure, take criticism, portray confidence, and use your time effectively.

There is no single type of self-employed person, but experience has shown that there are some characteristics which successful self-employed people often have in common. They tend to be logical, perceptive, organized, and responsible. They are usually extroverted and confident, and able to communicate and get their point across. They are also often sociable, with the ability to lead. Self-employed people are generally single-minded, but able to take advice. They are flexible and adaptable, quick to take opportunities, and ready to take risks. They tend to be tough-skinned, and able to handle failure. They are usually creative and imaginative, always coming up with new ideas for the business, and also hard working, committed, and determined. Finally, they are often individualists, who are not afraid to stand out from the crowd.

Are older people more successful at running a business?

There is no doubt that it helps to have some experience in the workplace, and it's even more useful to have it in the sector in which you want to start a business. Surveys reveal that many successful businesses have been started by people in their 30s who have some management experience. People over the age of 50 (sometimes called "third-age entrepreneurs") are also responsible for many business start-ups and many think about a change of direction after taking early retirement. Having said that, a wide variety of people have established their own businesses successfully and have much to offer. For example, young people have fewer domestic commitments, plenty of energy, new ideas, and the potential to develop and adapt to the challenges of self-employment.

What kinds of skills will I need?

You will almost certainly need technical skills. If you have qualifications relevant to your business activity this will obviously be helpful. Customers, and anyone lending your business money, will be more comfortable if you have the right qualifications. Additionally, certain businesses require exceptional ability, for example design skills, artistic skills, or technical skills.

Business skills are a huge advantage. It is important to understand the principles of business and management, including marketing, strategic planning, accounting, personnel management, and so on. Ideally, you should aim to get some basic training in business administration before you start. If this is not possible (and many people do not have the time or money initially), then read as much as you can to fill the gaps in your knowledge. Leadership skills are important, too. If you expect the business to grow, you will inevitably have to employ people, and the ability to show leadership and to manage people will be critical.

All businesses require an element of selling, and you'll need to develop skills in this area if you do not already possess them. Initially, it is important to persuade people to support you, and crucial to be able to win over potential customers. It is possible to learn basic selling techniques, but being outgoing and articulate are equally important. Your organizational skills will also be essential to the success of your business. To generate sufficient income, small businesses must be well organized and efficient. It is important that you can organize yourself and others, plan ahead, and manage your time. You also need to have the discipline to set and meet deadlines. Try to think laterally about how many of these skills you have, and don't be put off too easily. Starting a business is challenging, yes, but think about the skills you use in everyday life and how you could apply them to a different context. For example, if you are a woman with a family, or one who has juggled full- or part-time work with family life, think about how you have developed your time management skills, probably without even noticing it.

MAKING IT HAPPEN
Assess Your Abilities and Resources

Starting your own business is a risky thing to do, so you should come to grips with the various risks as early as possible. This will help you to decide if you are willing and able to take those risks. It will also help you to apply strategies that will reduce the risk.

"I'm not an entrepreneur. I like rules too much and entrepreneurs break rules." Guy Hands

You need to ask yourself several questions. Do you have the financial resources, and can you afford to risk them? For example, you might take a secured loan based on the value of your home; what are your plans if the business fails and you are forced to sell your house? Do you have sufficient experience and technical skills to perform the core functions of your new business? Are you familiar enough with the market to be able to assess its needs and adapt to its changes? Do you have the tenacity and discipline to see through hard times when cash will be short and demands will be heavy (from customers, bankers, staff, and, crucially, your family)?

Look at Your Motives

Why *do* you want to start your own business? There are many good reasons, but there is often the danger of having unrealistic expectations. Here are some reasons that people often give, and some notes of caution:

- **Independence.** Yes, it can be a pain working for someone else, but you still need to be disciplined and able to get on with others when you work for yourself.
- **Greater job satisfaction.** Self-employment allows you to do the job in your own way, and it is very satisfying when your way is shown to work. You do, of course, also have to take responsibility your way when it *doesn't* work, as is bound to happen at some point.
- **Achievement and success.** There can be some cachet attached to the idea of running your own business, but make sure that you are not trying to prove that you're something you're not. If the venture failed, would you be able to deal with it?
- **More money.** While the thought of being better off financially is naturally attractive, doing it for the money is not usually a good enough motive in itself, and greater wealth is by no means guaranteed. In particular, beware of starting a business when you have no other choice—you'll be putting yourself under even more pressure. If you do go down this route, though, try to be pragmatic about what you can achieve as well as positive.

Be Prepared for the Pressures

The pressures of being self-employed are inescapable. You may have to work long hours, and there will be times when things get on top of you. You may well get into debt in order to finance the enterprise. You will need to maintain your faith in your business, often in the face of other people's doubts.

There will be times when you feel lonely and isolated. If you employ people, you will need to be positive and show leadership all the time. There will be times when you need to be tough and prepared to discipline difficult employees, or make difficult demands of your suppliers. You need to be polite and helpful, even when an awkward customer is giving you a hard time.

Many of those who successfully start their own business have the backing of their family. You will be under pressure, working long hours. Your family must be prepared for the impact this can have on family life. Also, you must be sure that your family can accommodate the risks that self-employment can bring, especially in terms of lower income in the initial stages, and maybe even the implications of the business failing. Take time to talk to all members of your family who might be affected by your choice to be your own boss.

COMMON MISTAKES
Assuming That Being your Own Boss is Easy

Everyone at some point has come across a boss who makes his or her life difficult, but don't assume that working for yourself will be all plain sailing. There are many benefits, to be sure, but you have to get used to the idea that the buck stops with you. Make sure you're ready take on that responsibility.

Doing it for the Wrong Reasons

Don't do it for the money alone. Weigh the pros and cons of your idea and the impact that starting a business will have on all areas of your life. It will take a lot of effort, but you *can* do it—read on to find out how.

FOR MORE INFORMATION

Web Site:
United States Small Business Administration:
www.sba.gov/starting_business

See also:
- ✔ Assessing Your Entrepreneurial Profile: Do You Have What It Takes? (pp. 955–956)
- ℘ Entrepreneurs (pp. 1745–1747)
- ℘ Small and Growing Businesses (pp. 1905–1909)
- ✔ Understanding Business Models (pp. 961–962)

"Entrepreneurs are simply those who understand that there is little difference between obstacle and opportunity and are able to turn both to their advantage."

Victor Kiam

Profiling Your Target Market

GETTING STARTED

Before your business can realistically or effectively begin a marketing campaign, you'll need to be able to answer two vital questions: what is your target market, and what does your target market want or need that your business can provide?

Without detailed and precise answers to these questions you won't be able to define your marketing strategy, or put in place an effective sales and marketing plan. It's worth recalling the classic tale of two shoe sales representatives out exploring opportunities in a country in which their company had yet to establish a market. The first sales representative sent back an initial report saying "Everyone goes barefoot in this country, no market here at all." The second sales representative's report, however, was somewhat different: "Everyone goes barefoot, massive opportunity for us." Who was right?

This illustrates the necessity for any business to understand accurately the needs of its target customers, in terms of knowing enough about them and gathering sufficient information about what they really want. Without this precise understanding your efforts to market your goods and services won't be effective.

FAQs
How do I identify my target customers?

Your first job when profiling a target market is to be able to identify precisely who your audience is. Can you accurately describe the characteristics of your ideal customers? Which clients currently spend the most with you? Why do they do this? If you don't know the answers, you need to find out.

You'll probably already have a good idea about the groups of people or types of businesses that you think you can sell your service to. For individual customers this might be people of a certain age, gender, socio-economic status, occupation, or a group with common or special interests such as sports or hobbies. For business customers these might be located in a specific area, or in a particular sector, or could have similarities in terms of the customer groups they sell to.

Your objective should be to concentrate your marketing on these groups of people, businesses, or existing customers who are most likely to buy your product or service. Doing this in the most profitable way takes experience, but once you have identified this target group of people or businesses, you'll have completed the first step in profiling your market and now have your list of target prospects—your ideal customers.

Is it about quality or quantity of prospects?

A precision-driven marketing approach—where you have a high-quality list of prospective clients or leads—will, dollar-for-dollar of marketing spend, prove far more productive and profitable than an untargeted blanket approach to generate sales.

Quality of leads, based on your understanding, know- ledge, and careful profiling of your customers and their needs, will massively increase your ability to convert them into sales.

MAKING IT HAPPEN
Pinpoint what Your Customers and Prospects Need or Want

Having selected your ideal customer groups you'll now need to be absolutely clear about what they want and need, and exactly what it is that you are going to offer them. This understanding will enable you to develop the specific marketing message and proposition that will most effectively sell the benefits of your product or service to them.

If you get these messages wrong, then it's almost certain that your marketing efforts will fail, as your customers will buy from your competitors instead. Your product, service, or business proposition will have missed the target completely.

Speak to Target Customers Before Developing Your Marketing Strategy

Before you start to develop or choose your marketing strategy it's always worthwhile to speak first to a sample from your target audience. By doing this you'll be able to check that your profile of your intended market has been the right one, and test your assumptions about what you think they want and why they could buy from you.

You could do this by speaking directly to a group of people or you could undertake a survey in the form of a questionnaire, which can be mailed to a sample of target customers. Alternatively, you could talk to passers-by in a location that is frequented by your ideal customers.

Don't forget that you could also speak to your existing clients or, even better, clients of your competitors if that is possible.

Double Check that Your Marketing Message Is Right for Your Target Market

Once you have spoken to a sample of your target market and you are satisfied that you have confirmed your assumptions about their needs, you'll be in a position to create or adapt a marketing proposition to sell the benefits of your product or service to that audience. After you have established the basic proposition, consider carefully whether there is anything further that will make your marketing message even more appealing. Will these communications convince them that your service can provide the benefits that meet their exact needs?

Check that Your List of Prospects Is as Precise as Possible

Your prospects list will only be of real use in your marketing campaign if it accurately reflects the profile of the audiences you are targeting. Have the consumers of your product or service been identified in terms of their geographic and demographic profile, their employment status, profession, special interests, membership of clubs,

---

"To succeed, you have to have confidence in yourself and your product. You have to love what you're doing, and you have to care about your customers."

Mary Kelekis

and so on? Have you compiled a list of your business targets in terms of where they are located, their size, names of the main buyer, repeat purchase rate? Have you identified the best sales channels to enable you to reach these target customers?

Your sales efforts can only be as good as the list of prospects you have selected in your target markets, and that list must reflect the profile of the audience you are developing your marketing proposition to reach.

Insure that You Are Giving Them What They Want

With a thorough understanding of the needs of your ideal customers, you should then strive to create an offering and proposition based on four criteria that will give them a product or service that is

- exactly what they want from you
- precisely when they need it
- in a way that is convenient for them
- at a price they can afford and are prepared to pay

If you are not convinced that your sales proposition meets all of these criteria, then you'll need to study the profile of your customers again and revise your offering.

COMMON MISTAKES
Failing to Test

The most common mistakes made when targeting products and services toward specific users or customer groups are caused by not testing the assumptions you have made about your audience. You'll waste valuable time and marketing budget if you launch a campaign to-

ward an audience when you have not accurately identified who those customers are, and cannot precisely define what they want and why they could buy from you instead of your competitors.

Lack of Focus

Do not buy into a list of unknown prospects, no matter how attractive it seems to get names of thousands of people you can blanket-sell to in the short term.

Find out who they are, where they are located, and test your assumptions about what you believe they want. By testing, you can either confirm that your profiling was right, or you can adjust your offering until you get it right. Being precise will lead to more sales more quickly, and more profit over the longer term. One book you might find helpful when learning to sharpen your focus is *The Discipline of Market Leaders: Choose Your Customers, Narrow your Focus, Dominate Your Market* by Michael Treacy and Fred Wiersema, published by Perseus.

FOR MORE INFORMATION

Web Site:
American Marketing Association:
www.marketingpower.com

See also:
- Market Research and Competitor Intelligence (pp. 1824–1826)

"The key is to get into the stores and listen."   Sam M. Walton

Understanding Business Models

GETTING STARTED

There are four main types of legal status available to you when starting a business. These are sole proprietorship, partnership, limited liability company, and corporation. You will need to take into account several considerations when deciding which of these will be best for your new business. For example, you will need to think about taxation and administration implications, the image of the business, legal requirements, financial issues, and so on. This actionlist shows you how to decide which status is most suitable for your business, and raises some of the issues you may need to consider.

FAQs

When is sole proprietorship status suitable?

There are various advantages to operating as a sole proprietor.

The status of sole proprietor is convenient in situations where just one person will own the business and will have final responsibility for its management and development. It is possible to employ other people if you are a sole proprietor, but ultimately the business is the individual, and there is no separate legal status.

There are various advantages to operating as a sole proprietor. You generally do not have to file any special forms or pay any fees to start your business. However, regulations differ by locale, so check with your Secretary of State and city or county clerk's office regarding business licenses, local tax requirements, home/storefront parking, and other local or state regulations. There is less paperwork to deal with regarding legislation and taxation than for a limited liability company or corporation. As the owner, you are entitled to all the profits made by the business.

When is partnership status suitable?

A partnership is a good vehicle to use when your business will involve two or more people owning a business together. Like a sole proprietorship, a partnership has no separate legal identity and does not generally need to be formally registered with a government office. Experts recommend, however, that any partnership be formalized by a written general partnership agreement (although no law requires one).

There are several advantages to operating as a partnership. The structure of a partnership can be flexible, according to the partnership agreement. There is less paperwork to deal with regarding legislation and taxation than for a limited liability company or corporation. Management responsibilities, risks, and losses are shared. Partners can bring a variety of different skills and experience to the business. More people involved also means that more capital can be raised among them. Partnerships cannot be taken over by other businesses.

There are two other kinds of partnership, a limited partnership and a limited liability partnership (LLP). A limited partnership is a partnership which has at least one partner who is a general partner (that is to say, he or she has management rights and unlimited liability), and at least one limited partner. A limited partner, who may be an individual or a company, contributes a fixed amount (as capital or property) to the partnership, but is only liable for partnership debts or liabilities up to the amount they have contributed. Also, a limited partner may not be personally involved in the management of a company.

A limited liability company (LLC) has the flexibility and tax status of a partnership, but the benefits of limited liability. Business profits or losses are reported on the owners' personal tax returns; the LLC itself does not pay taxes. The liability of all of the partners is limited to their capital contribution to the LLC, so personal assets cannot be seized to settle debts. LLCs are required to register with their state.

When is limited liability company status suitable?

A limited liability company (LLC) consists of stockholder/members whose percent of ownership is based on their capital contribution. LLCs are formed when the business requires outside funding for its operations. Managing member(s) hold management responsibility and unlimited liability. Member liability is limited to their percent ownership.

The main advantage of the LLC structure is that its members have limited liability for the debts of the business up to the value of their shareholding. They are not personally liable for company debts. Filing procedures to create an LLC can be complicated and vary by state. Attorney assistance is recommended.

What is a franchise?

A franchise is a license that has been granted by one business (the franchiser) to another (the franchisee), allowing the franchisee to use the trademark and name of the franchiser, as well as its methods for marketing, managing, administration, and so on, within the business.

There are several advantages to franchising. The franchisee, by investing in a proven business format, can become the owner of a business with a well-known brand name, while at the same time overcoming some of the difficulties associated with a new business. The franchisee also receives help in finding and refurbishing premises. Help will be given in obtaining any planning permission and purchasing inventory and equipment, as well as with staff training, marketing, and advertising. The franchisee is therefore able to concentrate on the day-to-day running of the business. The franchiser will be able to provide specialist managerial advice and guidance to help overcome any problems that a small business is likely to encounter, and the franchisee will benefit from the economies of scale of operating as part of a large organization.

"Traditional business defaults to the familiar; it's easy, comfortable, and bonus-building to rely on old business models, outdated templates, yesterday's strategies." Faith Popcorn

MAKING IT HAPPEN
Establish a Sole Proprietorship

As a sole proprietor, you can simply start operating your business. Contact your state, county and city clerk offices to ensure that you have any licenses required. If you have a storefront, make sure you have all of your necessary property and liability insurance coverage in place. If you operate from your home and will have clients visiting your office, find out about parking restrictions and so on.

Establishing a Partnership

Like a sole proprietorship, when starting a partnership you can simply start operating your business. Partnership agreements with all terms and conditions should be written by an attorney. If you are establishing a limited partnership or limited liability partnership (LLP), contact your state office of corporations, Secretary of State or LLC/LLP office to ensure that you have completed the appropriate paperwork.

Establish a Limited Liability Company

A limited company must be registered with your state before trading commences. This requires certain documents, available from the state office of corporations, Secretary of State's office or LLC/LLP office, to be completed and submitted with a registration fee. An attorney can help you to draw up and submit these documents. A limited liability company must have at least one managing member and corporate officers.

Establish a Franchise

Before you make a decision, talk to existing franchisees to find out more information about the franchise you are considering purchasing. If you decide to go ahead, and your application is accepted, you will probably find that a first interview with the franchiser is required. This is valuable, as it gives both parties the opportunity to appraise one another. Provided both parties wish to continue, there will be a second interview to begin formalizing the agreement. It is a good idea to take advice from a specialist professional adviser before signing any documents.

COMMON MISTAKES
Underestimating your Liability

A sole proprietorship has unlimited liability for the debts of the business, such as bank loans and amounts owing to creditors. This means that if your business fails your personal savings and assets could be at risk. In a general partnership there is unlimited liability, and each partner is personally responsible for the debts of the partnership. As a partner, therefore, your personal assets may be seized to pay off debts. Limited liability companies and corporations must comply with a wide range of complex and detailed legislation that is not applicable to sole proprietorships and partnerships; this can add to the administrative and financial burden.

Mistaking the Protection of a Corporation

Sole proprietors will often decide to establish themselves as a corporation in order to give themselves protection behind the "corporate veil" and protect their personal assets. In fact, the corporate veil provides little or no protection to sole proprietors even if they have established their company as a legal corporation. Thus, before moving from sole proprietorship to corporate standing, speak with your attorney to determine whether you and your business will be given the protection you seek, or if you are just adding unnecessary expenses and paperwork to your operation.

Underestimating the Role of Franchisers

Franchisers exert a fairly high degree of control over the franchise operation, so although the franchisee is legally independent, he or she will never be completely independent of the franchiser.

Thinking That a Franchise Will Be Less Expensive Than is Actually the Case

Franchises can be expensive investments. After the initial fee, there will be ongoing fees for the continuing support provided by the franchiser. Under the franchise agreement the franchisee may be obliged to buy supplies and equipment from the franchiser, which they may have been able to purchase cheaper elsewhere.

FOR MORE INFORMATION

Web Sites:
The Knowledge Exchange:
www.myworktools.com/dept/legal
U.S. Small Business Administration: **www.sba.gov**

See also:

"But markets today are moving targets. The only way to hit them is to launch your business like a cruise missile."

Harry V. Quadracci

Evaluating an Existing Business

GETTING STARTED

It's often thought that buying a business is simpler than starting your own, but remember that many businesses are sold because they have inherent problems that prevent them from generating sufficient income. If you're buying a business, it's vital that you conduct comprehensive research and analysis in the same way as if you were setting the business up from scratch.

FAQs
What's my first step toward buying a business?

Your first step is to decide on the type of business you're looking for. Think about what size of business you want. Are you, for example, looking for a small local business, or are you aiming for a large national one? Also think about what business sector you're most drawn to—is it manufacturing, retailing, or perhaps services? Consider location too. Are you prepared to change your location and travel, or would you prefer to stay where you are and travel relatively short distances?

What should I be looking for in a business?

Look first and foremost for skills and experience. The most common reason for business failure is people taking on businesses outside their area of expertise, so think long and hard about the skills and knowledge that already exist in the potential business, and whether you can add to those skills. You also need to consider the products and/or services that the business provides. Again, ideally, you should be looking for a business which deals in a product or service that you have some experience with, especially if the operation is particularly complex or technical.

Remember to investigate the level of competition facing the business, especially locally. Make sure you know your competitors' strengths and weaknesses relative to the business you're considering buying, and what their share is of the market. Look at the size of the business, and find out how fast it has grown in the past, and whether this rate is likely to continue, increase, or decline.

Another important factor to consider is location. Check that the business is located appropriately, for example, close to its target market (if location is relevant), and within reach of employees with the right skills. You'll also need to judge whether the business needs any major changes requiring a large investment of management time—you may be able to acquire a business at a lower price if this is the case. If the business is already successful, it can probably continue to operate in the same manner, regardless of a change of ownership.

Money is another key issue and you need to calculate how much needs to be invested in the venture. This is a crucial factor in determining whether to buy a particular business. Consider whether you'll be able to secure financing for future investment if it's required. Evaluate too the level of profitability of the business. Does it make

the amount of profit you're looking for; does it have the potential to expand and grow?

How do I value the business?

Many people find it useful to employ a business appraiser or financial adviser when they are having a business valued. The three methods often used are asset value, earnings multiple, and return on capital.

Asset value—To obtain the business's net asset value (that is, what it is worth, in basic terms), the value of the liabilities (that is, a business's financial obligations, such as outstanding debts, loan repayments, outstanding invoices, etc), is subtracted from the value of the assets. The value for the entire business will be the net asset value, plus a value for goodwill representing the business's reputation and existing customer base.

Earnings multiple—The earnings multiple method requires you to apply a multiple to the earnings from the business. Earnings should take into account interest charges to be paid after purchasing the business, and any loans needed to make improvements. To come up with an earnings multiple, divide the company's market price by its after-tax earnings over a one year period.

Return on capital—To find the return on capital, you'll need to define a desired rate of return. (Rate of return can be defined as a ratio of the profit made in a financial year as a percentage of the capital employed.) Then the income of the business before interest and tax should be calculated, and this figure should also be given as a percentage of the capital invested. If the figure is less than the desired rate of return, then any purchase should not go ahead.

MAKING IT HAPPEN
Evaluate the Business

You'll need to conduct some research to evaluate properly any business you're considering for potential purchase. You should be able to obtain much of the information you require from the present owner; ask for details, including the business plan, financial statements, details of established customers, and so on.

It's a good idea to conduct a SWOT analysis (Strengths, Weaknesses, Opportunities, and Threats) on any potential business purchase. Consider the present position of the business in the market, its past performance, and its potential for growth. Look at its available resources, for example money, assets, manpower, and so on. Investigate the training, experience, and skills available within the business. Check its sources of supply, costs, reliability of material, inventory supply, and relations with suppliers.

Find out who the competition is, where it is, and what its strengths and weaknesses are. Research your customers, making sure you know who and where they are, and how loyal they are. You'll need to examine external factors like industry trends, regulations, and political and economic developments. Consider how much money you'll need for advertising and marketing. The way the

---

"Three components make an entrepreneur: the person, the idea and the resources to make it happen."

Anita Roddick

business is promoted may have to change. Look at the business's distribution channels, asking yourself how reliable they are, and whether they can be maintained once the business changes hands. Calculate the profitability of the business after any initial capital outflow for improvements.

Determine a Price

Obviously, if you become interested in purchasing a business, you'll need to value it and determine a reasonable price in conjunction with the seller. The price of a business may be derived from some of the factors mentioned in the previous section. It will also depend upon an appraisal of the land and buildings. The fair market value of the property is affected by a number of factors. These include the business's location in relation to its customers and suppliers, employees, and competition. The condition of the premises, for example whether improvements are necessary to bring them up to legally acceptable standards, is also an important consideration.

Financial considerations, such as the costs of property maintenance, transfer of title, licenses, leases, property taxes, and so on, need to be taken in to account. There may also be problems over the transfer of a lease on premises. Some leases prohibit assignment.

External factors, such as current interest rates and the state of the property market, influence a property's value. So too will the future outlook, for example whether the property will continue to meet the needs of the business as it grows. There will also need to be a valuation of fixtures and fittings. There may be equipment leases that need to be transferred (for example, the photocopier). Check for any contingent liabilities.

Consider Other Factors

You'll need to negotiate the transfer value of the inventory. This should be cost or "net realizable value" (NRV), whichever is lower. For redundant inventory the NRV is zero. A recorded valuation and inventory count should be done by a third party. You'll also need to engage an accountant to evaluate the business's books, bank statements, and tax records to get an accurate picture of the current financial situation and future profitability.

Valuing the goodwill of the business is especially important. Goodwill reflects the cumulative effect of the reputation of the business; its relationship with customers, suppliers, and competition; its market position; and the skills of the staff. You'll need to consider whether the existing staff are suitable for the business, and how they are likely to react to a new owner/manager. Decide

what benefits will be offered, for example, maternity benefits, vacation time, and so on. Income tax withholding (both federal and state), FICA tax, pension plans, and insurance should also be considered.

Make sure that you evaluate the outstanding loans to the business, its relationship with its creditors, and its repayment history. Be realistic about whether you'll be able to obtain financing for the venture, and to repay the loan. Look at pro-forma income statements, balance sheets, and cash budgets. When you estimate how much income the business is likely to generate, it's important to be conservative, especially in the early stages.

COMMON MISTAKES
Rushing Through the Research Stage

If you don't conduct thorough research, you may find you have made the wrong decision. Without enough information, facts and figures, and forecasts, a view of any business's prospects can be easily distorted and misleading.

Not Exercising Due Diligence

You should always exercise due diligence when purchasing a business. You must make sure that what the vendor is saying is correct. Examine all financial statements carefully. Ask yourself whether customers are likely to remain loyal once you have taken over the business, and whether suppliers will maintain the same relationship with you. If you don't exercise due diligence, you'll only have yourself to blame for any problems you could have discovered before the purchase.

Not Setting a Price before Bidding

You should have a price band in mind before bidding, otherwise you'll be at a disadvantage. The seller may state an asking price outright, at which time the buyer must be prepared to negotiate. This way you shouldn't spend more than you can afford.

FOR MORE INFORMATION

Web Sites:
The Appraisal Foundation:
www.appraisalfoundation.org
American Society of Appraisers: **www.appraisers.org**

See also:
↪ Small and Growing Businesses (pp. 1905–1909)

"I wanted to set the world on fire and that would not come about through working for someone else in a nine-to-five job."

Ian Schrager

Financing a New Business

GETTING STARTED

New businesses need financing to cover the cost of equipment and expenses before sales generate enough cash to make the operation self-supporting. This action-list describes the main ways of financing your business. It explains how to work out the amount of financing you need, and what proportion of debt to equity is advisable.

FAQs
What is an angel investor?

An angel investor is someone who is willing to invest money in a business. The amount available from angels is usually much less than from venture capitalists, but they are often willing to take bigger risks.

What is equity financing?

Equity, or stockholder capital, is the money introduced into a business by the owners. If it is a company, then the equity is introduced in exchange for shares. Investors expect a share of the business's profit. In the case of limited companies, this takes the form of dividends. The person starting a business will normally introduce equity capital, but it can also be raised from external investors, including business angels and venture capitalists. Investors will be looking for an annual dividend, which often can be quite small, and a good return when they sell their shares. Equity is best suited, therefore, to businesses that expect to grow quickly.

What is loan financing?

Loan financing is money that is borrowed from a finance company, such as a bank. Loans are repaid over a period of time, at either fixed or variable rates of interest. The lender will usually require security against a business or personal asset. Terms can vary in length from one year to 25 years, and will usually be determined by the asset that is being financed. The interest rate will reflect the lender's perception of the risk in providing the loan. Loan financing can be provided in different ways.

An overdraft is money that a business can borrow from a bank up to an agreed limit. It provides a business with short-term financing, effectively by running a negative balance on the bank account. This is a particularly good way of funding short-term requirements, such as providing working capital during the course of each month.

Term loans are funds borrowed for a fixed term. Usually, such loans are repayable in equal installments over the term of the loan, although sometimes they can be repaid in a lump sum at the end of the term. Term loans are more attractive than overdrafts for long-term borrowing because repayments are fixed and the cost is usually less. However, lenders are increasingly writing into the small print that term loans are repayable on demand. If the loan has been used to finance capital assets, this could cause problems.

Creditor financing is an excellent way of "borrowing" money, effectively at no cost. Typically, suppliers may give 30 to 60 days' credit for their goods or services before payment is due. If you can sell your product or service and get paid before paying your creditors, then it will generate cash into the business. Your business may have to establish a good credit rating before credit is given, and it can be withdrawn at any time.

Debtor financing is particularly useful if your business is growing rapidly and is providing credit accounts to its customers. Instead of waiting for your own customers to pay your invoices within a 30- or 60-day period, you can use the services of a third party invoice discounting or factoring firm. Factoring can be an expensive way of speeding up cash flow, but it may reduce administration costs since the factor normally takes on the role of invoice clerk.

Capital asset financing can often be done through "off-balance-sheet" financing. There are different ways of doing this. Financial leasing allows you to finance the use of an asset rather than owning it. The equipment remains the property of the leasing company; the business has the legal right to use the equipment for the period of the lease, provided that the lease payments are up to date. In a lease purchase arrangement, you have an option to purchase the equipment at the end of the lease period. Through hire purchase, you pay regular installments to a third party, normally a finance company, to purchase ownership of plant and machinery from a supplier. The finance company will own the equipment throughout the period of the agreement, until the last installment has been paid.

MAKING IT HAPPEN
Work Out How Much Capital You Need

The working capital of a business is its current assets (typically stock, cash at the bank, and accounts receivable) minus its current liabilities (typically accounts payable, outstanding loans, and lines of credit drawn upon). This information is summarized on the balance sheet, although this only gives a snapshot of the working capital requirements at a specific moment in time. Generally, this is the financing required for the short-term running of the business.

The amount of working capital needed will vary during the course of the year and even during the course of a month. You need to allow for the maximum likely working capital requirement. Consideration needs to be given to the variation that can occur within each month. As a rule of thumb, it makes sense to aim for minimum working capital of a month's average sales multiplied by the number of months it takes to collect payment. If you want to be more accurate, then use the following procedure:

1 Determine the average number of weeks that the raw material is in inventory.

2 Deduct from this figure the credit period from suppliers, in weeks.

3 Then add the average number of weeks to produce goods or service, the average number of weeks finished

goods are in inventory, and the average time customers take to pay.

4 Take the total, and divide it by 52 (the number of weeks in the year). Multiply the result by your estimated sales for the year. The answer will give you a figure for the maximum working capital required.

It would be more accurate to use the cost of sales (direct and fixed), rather than the full selling price, but the above calculation is close enough. If your business is growing, then you need to use the budgeted sales figures, and it is advisable to calculate your working capital needs on a regular basis.

Understand Leverage and Interest Coverage

Leverage is the proportion of debt to total capital in the business. The more debt there is relative to equity, the higher the leverage. Introducing more equity or retaining more of the profits can reduce the leverage ratio. Most banks look for a leverage of no more than 50%; in other words, your debt should be no more than half of the total capital.

Once you have built up a track record with your bank, you should be able to attract medium-term loans (three- to seven-year loans) to cover the cost of plant and equipment. Established companies may be able to raise long-term debt as a debenture or convertible loan stock, which normally receives a fixed rate of interest and is repayable in full at the end of the term. Long-term debt is usually included with the capital on the balance sheet. The banks will also be more comfortable with a higher leverage, though they still do not like to see it too high. Lease and hire purchase companies will not have as great a concern about leverage as the banks. They will, however, be interested in your cash flow and whether you can afford the repayments.

If you expect to grow quickly and do not have enough of your own money to provide the necessary financing, then you may need to look for equity early on. Banks will be reluctant to keep on providing additional working cap-ital as that simply increases the leverage and increases their risk. Growing too quickly is often known as "over-trading" and is a major cause of business failure. The banks will also want to reassure themselves that you can afford the interest on the loan. So they will look for profits that are at least three or four times the expected interest charge.

COMMON MISTAKES
Not Thinking Ahead

Regularly calculate the total level of funding required for the next year, and split the funding into fixed asset re-quirements and working capital requirements. Think carefully about the term, the cost, the suitability, the timescale, and any security required. Remember that cost should not be the sole criterion. Keep your lenders informed of your financial position, giving ample warn-ing if you are likely to need to increase your loan amount, for example.

Not Changing with the Times

In times of recession, keep as much of your debt as pos-sible as fixed medium-term loans, and keep your line of credit drawn upon to the minimum. In times of expan-sion, when financing is more readily available, it may be more cost-effective to use a line of credit.

FOR MORE INFORMATION

Web Sites:
U.S. Small Business Administration: **www.sba.gov**
U.S. Department of Commerce: **www.commerce.gov**

See also:
- Budgeting (pp. 1683–1684)
- ✔ Preparing a Successful Business Plan (pp. 967–968)
- Venture Capital (pp. 1927–1929)

"Failures are like skinned knees—painful, but superficial."   H. Ross Perot

Preparing a Successful Business Plan

GETTING STARTED

Many new owner-managers write business plans with the sole purpose of convincing a financier to lend them money for starting up. However, a good business plan does much more than that and also helps you to build a stronger foundation for your business. It can help you to clarify your business purpose to yourself and communicate it to your partners and staff; predict future scenarios and address them before they threaten the success of the business; and set targets and objectives so that you can monitor your business performance.

Your plan must be a coherent description of how your business will move from where it is now to where you want it to be in the future. Obviously each business will be different, but the headings below are useful stepping stones to include in your business plan and will make sure that you cover the most important aspects.

FAQs

What should I say about my business?

Be as specific as possible about the kind of business that you are starting. Describe your business in terms of a mission statement or "executive summary" that clearly summarizes its purpose and is easily understood by you, your staff, customers, and potential investors. If you cannot describe your business in these terms, rethink your business idea; focus on the core activities and direction.

What should I use as my starting point?

Try to envision where you might want your business to be in five years' time, so that you can start to move toward that point. For instance, you might work toward becoming a market leader, an innovator, a specialist, a good employer, a large concern, or a supplier of superior quality.

MAKING IT HAPPEN

Make Sure You Cover All the Important Issues in Your Business Plan

As well as being very specific about the type of business you are starting and thinking ahead to where you want to be in five years, there are a number of important elements that you will need to include in your business plan.

Current Market Situation

To earn enough revenue, your business must be able to achieve a share of the available market. To do this, you'll need to have a thorough understanding of your market environment, including its size and the share that you can realistically achieve. The size of your share will depend on:

- market trends—find out what influences your target market now, and how your product can take advantage of this;
- target customers—describe who your target customers

are and how many there are; also justify your estimate of the market share you aim to get;
- competition—list your competitors and describe their products; also describe in detail how your product will be different.

Current Target Customers

Define the characteristics of the target groups of customers that could buy from your business. Make a list of the features that your products have, and the associated benefits that these features can provide to your customers, then build up a picture of your target customers. For individuals, describe them in terms of characteristics like age, income, location, lifestyle, and marital status. For businesses, consider location, numbers of employees, public or private sector, industry type, and turnover. Conduct some research into how many customers there are in your target group and how much they spend, and also try to identify trends that tell you whether this group is growing or shrinking.

Competitor Analysis

Competitors may be in the same (direct competition) or similar (indirect competition) business to you. The level and strength of competition in a market indicates how difficult it will be to gain a share of the market. However, it is not simply the number of competitors that you should be concerned about; analyze the following aspects of each competitor's business:

- Their products: are their products and services the same as yours? Do your competitors provide something that you don't?
- Their customers: are your competitors targeting the same customer segments as your business?
- Their share of the market: how large is it, and could you take some of it?
- Their strategies: how they grow, market themselves, and price their products. Can you learn from how they conduct business, or do it better?
- Their operations and facilities: what levels of service are customers demanding?

Marketing Strategy

With a clear understanding of your market, you can define your overall strategy. Break this down into objectives and targets relating to the volume and share of the market (or market segments) you hope to achieve, and when you intend to achieve them by. Ask yourself, for example:

- Who are your initial marketing targets?
- What products, services or particular deals will you be offering?
- Is there a specific volume, value, or share of these markets that you hope to achieve?
- When do you hope to achieve these targets by?
- Why are you choosing these markets first?
- Who will you target next, in the next 6 or 12 months?

967

ACTIONLIST

"The wisest prophets make sure of the event first."   Horace Walpole

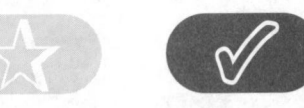    

Marketing Plan

Now that you have a coherent marketing strategy, you need to be clear about how you are going to make it happen. A detailed marketing plan must explain how you go about achieving each of your marketing targets and objectives. Such a plan will include some, or all of the following:

- the methods you will use for each target segment
- the specific action you are going to undertake
- a timescale or timetable for each marketing activity
- who is going to carry it out
- the estimated costs of particular marketing activities
- how you will monitor and review progress
- how you will handle the response to your marketing

It will also be important to identify how you will manage the overall marketing plan, in other words, ensuring that the entire budget is not spent in the first couple of months, monitoring results, adjusting the plan, and introducing new tactics as you go along.

Sales Targets and Objectives

Your marketing plan, when implemented, needs to be converted into perhaps the most important business goal of all: sales revenues. Set out your forecasts in terms of sales of different product types by volume and value; sales from different customer groups; and sales from different distribution channels.

Operational Requirements

Information about your operational requirements will be required for your financial forecasts, while other information will be needed for your basic operational planning. Outline your plans for premises, equipment, staff, suppliers, and compliance and licensing, and estimate the respective costs involved.

Current Financial Requirements and Financial Forecasts

Your business plan should include a breakdown of your financial requirements, the sources of financing you have available to you, and any additional amount that you may need. This breakdown should include: the cost of starting your business; your personal budget; details of your own personal finances that you intend to invest, as well as of additional financing; a detailed cash-flow forecast that will help to estimate how much available cash you will have in any particular month; a profit and loss forecast to help to estimate when your business will start to make a profit (which will be essential to your medium-term success); and a balance sheet forecast to provide you with a snapshot of the trading position of your business, identifying what your business will owe, what it will own, and how financially strong it will be at a particular point in the future.

Management Processes

Even if you are the only person involved in your business, it is still important to consider your key skills, responsibilities, and management processes. Think about:

- Management team—outline skills and experience
- Key staff and responsibilities—summarize roles and contribution to the business. Be sure to cover the following tasks: marketing and sales, financing, recruitment, product development, general management, and administration
- Monitoring and coordination—set out how you plan to monitor performance (against objectives and targets), and to co-ordinate the key roles in the business.

Business Risks

Your plan should include an honest awareness of the risks involved, as well as how you plan to minimize them. Consider which of the following risks are relevant to your businesses: lack of management experience; no trading history; economic uncertainties; reliance on key staff; reliance on a few suppliers; reliance on a small customer base; bad customer debts; partnership difficulties; increased competition; security and insurance against burglary and loss; and failure to meet your sales targets. Show that you have thought about all of these issues and that you have contingency plans in place.

Present Your Plan in a Professional Manner

Once you have researched and drafted all the necessary information, you can compile the plan. Produce a simple but stylish cover for it, not forgetting to include the business name, your address, your phone numbers, e-mail address, and the date. Put an edited, proofed, and double-checked final draft together. Use a transparent plastic cover with a binder, and letter-quality printer and paper. The order should be: cover, title page, executive summary, contents page, contents, and appendices.

COMMON MISTAKES
Producing Unrealistic Sales Forecasts

It is a good idea to produce more than one sales forecast, including one for the worst-case scenario so that you can show how you would deal with that. If you are over-optimistic you may not be able to make the necessary repayments. Also make sure that any market research is comprehensive enough to give you realistic sales targets.

Not Proofreading the Plan

To give your plan the best chance of impressing all the right people, it's essential that it's accurate and mistake-free. Ask two other people to read it through thoroughly to check that nothing has gone awry: if you can, ask a friend or family member who isn't directly involved in your business to check it, as he or she will be able to give you a more objective view.

FOR MORE INFORMATION

Web Sites:
Business Plan Software: **www.brs-inc.com**
Business Plan Software and Sample Business Plans: **www.bplans.com**
U.S. Small Business Association: **www.sba.gov**

See also:
- Budgeting (pp. 1683–1684)
- Financing a New Business (pp. 965–966)

Franchising Your Business

GETTING STARTED

If your business has suitable branded products or services and you're looking to grow it with relatively low risk, then franchising could provide a worthwhile route. the process can involve considerably less capital investment by you than other approaches to growth, because the franchisees you appoint will invest their money—and their time—in creating new outlets under your organizational umbrella. You will, however, need to undertake a considerable amount of planning and research to make sure that your business is suitable for franchising and to enable you to create a successful franchise network.

FAQs

What is a franchise?

In basic terms, a franchise is a legally binding agreement between you (the franchisor) and another business (the franchisee) that enables it to use your trade name and trademark, and supply your branded services or products under license. The franchisee will pay a fee in return for your granting them a franchise license, and they'll have to comply with any terms and conditions set by you in the agreement. The European Franchise Federation describes it as "a system of marketing goods, products, or services, based on a close and ongoing collaboration between legally and financially separate and independent undertakings."

How will I make money from franchising?

There are two sources of income from franchising: fees and the profit you could make from supplying materials to your franchisees. The fees come in the form of a one-time initial payment—the franchise fee—for granting a license, and an annual management charge for the support services you provide, which should include training and development. The latter fee is usually calculated as a percentage of your franchisees' turnover. In order to attract suitable franchisees it's accepted practice to keep the franchise fee low and to provide good value for your management charge. Where the supply of materials is concerned, you can make money by buying in bulk and then reselling to your franchisees, but you must make sure that in doing so, you keep within the law regarding commercial practices. If you have any doubts or queries, take appropriate legal advice and contact the organizations listed below.

What are my obligations to franchisees?

Franchisees will expect you to provide them with a variety of support services in addition to a protective framework that will involve monitoring the quality and standards of your network. Attracting good and reliable franchisees may rely a lot on how seriously you take and fulfill these obligations. The support services should include:

- product and service development;
- marketing, advertising, and public relations;
- protection of intellectual property (such as copyrights, brand names, patents, and trademarks);
- purchasing, financial, and administration services;
- communications between franchised outlets;
- quality control;
- training.

Most franchisees will expect you to help them raise capital for their outlets. One of the best ways to do this is by putting together some sort of support package with a bank. You should also consider putting together a franchise handbook that will set down specific rules and approaches to things like local marketing, use of brand names, and so on. That way, all concerned parties are clear about who is doing what, how, and when.

MAKING IT HAPPEN

Make Sure Your Business Is Suitable for Franchising

Not every type of business is suitable for franchising, but it usually works well where a wide variety of products or services are involved, for example, where there is a strong demand being created for new or innovative goods targeted toward niche or specialist markets. If your business offers products or services with a broad appeal, or which satisfy a common need, franchising may be a good way for you to grow. This would apply, for example, if you have an existing and profitable outlet supplying branded items that have a high profile and a strong reputation with customers. Many household names have managed their growth via franchising, including The Body Shop and Blockbuster Video.

Franchising is not so good a choice if your business supplies products or services with a short market life (if it is catering to the latest fad, for example), or with low profit margins. Similarly, if you offer services that involve high skill levels and prolonged training, such as accounting, or which rely on repeat business from customers with a strong sense of loyalty, franchising is unlikely to be the right option. This might also be the case if the business is dependent on a geographically-defined market, as would be the case with a tourist attraction. Enterprises with high levels of audit and control requirements—a financial institution like a bank, for example—are unsuitable too, as these outlets can't operate as separate legal entities, which is essential with franchises.

Prepare Your Business for Franchising

As part of the careful research and planning you need to do to prepare your business for franchising, you should identify the elements of your operations that can be adopted in each franchised outlet. You can't franchise a concept or an idea, so you should have a business format that has been tried, tested, and shown to have a good track record in a particular marketplace. Your brand name has to be strong enough to attract suitable franchisees. Where appropriate, you should

"It's one of life's ironies that the more you can prove that you don't need a loan, the better your chances usually are of getting one. This is especially true for start-up businesses."

Lillian Vernon

have proven manufacturing processes or distribution systems.

Among the things you'll need to develop are a new accounting system and a business plan for your franchising activities. You'll find it a great help to do SWOT (strengths, weaknesses, opportunities, and threats) analyses for each geographical area in which you'd like to establish an outlet. You'll need to devise and establish support services for your franchisees, as well as initial and ongoing training programs that will enable even relative novices to learn about the various facets of your business and how to then run their own franchises successfully. There will be technical issues in all of these aspects of franchising your business, so you should be prepared to call in professional advice at each stage.

It's advisable to run a pilot operation for at least 12 months, preferably at more than one location, to test the business concept in different geographical areas. When this has been successfully conducted and fine tuning has been done, you can then prepare a prospectus to attract suitable franchisees.

Recruit Franchisees

It will be important for you to be able to attract franchisees of the right caliber to be certain your network is successful, so do be wary of badly run franchise recruiting agencies. Put in place a thorough vetting process for candidates that will allow you to attract highly motivated applicants. You could consider:

- attending franchise exhibitions;
- advertising in newspapers and trade magazines;
- setting up or adapting your business Web site to promote the franchising opportunities;
- registering with reputable franchise centers and brokers.

Draw Up Franchise Agreements

A franchise agreement is a contract between you and the franchisee. You'll be able to negotiate various aspects of the agreement and there are no hard and fast rules about what it should contain. However, it must comply with Federal Trade Commission and individual state regulations. It must also be clear and unambiguous in stating the rights, duties, and responsibilities of you and the franchisee, and reflect the interests of all members of your network.

When evaluating the agreement you should consider the following key issues:

- the rights granted to you and the franchisee
- your obligations and those of the franchisee
- the goods and services provided by you to the franchisee
- the terms, and amounts, of the payments for licenses, management fees, and other costs you impose
- the duration of your agreement
- the basis for any renewal of your agreement
- the terms by which the franchisee may sell or otherwise transfer their interest in a franchise
- the terms by which the franchisee may use your trade names, brand names, logos, store signs, and so on
- your right to adapt the franchise system to meet new or changed methods and market conditions
- the franchisee's right to terminate the agreement before it expires

- the ownership of property, both tangible and intangible, provided by you to the franchisee and provisions for its surrender if an agreement is terminated

Think about whether or not you'll be granting exclusive geographical licenses to franchisees, and how big the respective areas will be. Also think about whether you'll allow them to pursue other business interests, possibly competing ones, at the same time.

Bear in Mind the Advantages . . .

One of the chief advantages of franchising is that it provides you with an opportunity to expand your business for minimal investment. Other major advantages include: a predictable income stream from franchisees; a centralized system that spreads the costs over a wider network thus reducing the individual costs for each franchisee; and the fact that you'll be able to concentrate on developing and growing your business because there is no need for you to be involved in the management of individual outlets.

. . . But Remember The Disadvantages Too

Because you'll have no direct control over the running of individual outlets, one bad franchisee could damage the reputation of your entire network. You should train or recruit specialist staff to conduct the training of franchisees and the central management of your network. The process of starting your franchising operation will be complicated and you'll have to rely on expensive professional or specialist help and advice.

WHAT TO AVOID
Having Unrealistic Expectations

Don't overestimate the early growth rates of your franchise network and don't assume the franchise fee will generate profits, as it's usually the annual management fees that produce real returns. You'll need to have a realistic idea of what your initial costs will be, and these will need to include professional advice.

Seeing Franchising as a Panacea

If your business is experiencing financial or other potentially fatal problems, franchising is highly unlikely to provide a solution. Franchising is a way of growing viable businesses, and a variety of conditions need to be met to enable this to succeed (as explained above).

Appointing Unsuitable Franchisees

Reject applicants who fail your vetting process. A ratio of ten inquiries to one successful applicant is normal, and ratios as high as 100:1 are not uncommon.

FOR MORE INFORMATION

Web Sites:
Federal Trade Commission: **www.ftc.gov/bcp/menu-fran.htm#bized**

See also:
Entrepreneurs (pp. 1745–1747)

"The challenge in a startup is that you always have to spread your wings pretty far to see what will work."

Michael Dell

Buying into a Franchise

GETTING STARTED

One of the most readily available ways of starting your own business is to buy a franchise. Compared to other forms of start-up, this is often a relatively risk-free method of getting established in business, because the development of the product or service has already been done for you by the source company (franchisor). One of the most important things for many people is that franchising gives them an opportunity to become their own boss within the protective framework of a larger organization with a successful formula. When you buy a franchise, however, you should understand that your success or failure in the enterprise will be largely down to your own hard work and the business skills you learn. It shouldn't be seen as an easy option, because to become successful the operation of a franchise requires as much dedication and effort as any other kind of business.

Franchising offers both advantages and disadvantages over other types of business, and there are some basic steps that should be followed in setting up in this way.

FAQs
What is a franchise?

A franchise is basically an agreement between one business (the franchisor) and yourself (the franchisee) that enables you to use the trade name and trademark, and supply the branded services or products, of the franchisor. You pay a fee in return for the granting of a franchise license and you have to comply with any terms and conditions set by the franchisor in an agreement. Typical franchise sectors are fast food chains, fitness centers, grocery and convenience stores.

What should I look for in a good franchise?

Perhaps the most important thing a good franchise opportunity should offer you is a product or service with a proven track record. You should, ideally, gain access to a recognized brand name. All the research and development effort on the service or product should have been conducted by the franchisor, who will also be responsible for maintaining standards and guaranteeing quality control. Other benefits should include access to help, advice, and training, as well as participation in marketing and advertising activities that would be beyond your reach as a small business.

What is a franchise network?

This is an association of independently owned businesses selling a variety of products or services developed by an umbrella organization. They are linked together by the common brand identities and the support activities they share, such as marketing, advertising, and training.

What are the disadvantages of franchising?

There are certain things over which you may have no control as a franchisee. For example, you're unlikely to have any decisive say over the development and introduction of new products or services. The franchise agreement will normally require you to contribute to expenditure (up to an agreed amount) on marketing and advertising campaigns on behalf of the franchise network, and you may have little or no opportunity to influence the way that this is done. Furthermore, the appointment of other franchisees to the network, who you may feel are unsuitable or less competent than you, will be beyond your control (though the franchise agreement should give you exclusive rights over a defined geographic area). Any damage done to the reputation of the network could impact adversely on your business.

What costs should I expect?

Before you begin trading you'll have to pay a fee to the franchisor for granting the initial license. This will normally be followed by an annual premium, called the management services fee, which is likely to be based on a percentage of your annual turnover. You'll be responsible for the professional fees of lawyers, accountants, and business consultants you appoint for negotiating the franchise agreement and setting up your enterprise. The normal overhead of your business will include such things as buying supplies and materials; staff wages; taxes and VAT; rent, rates, and maintenance of machinery and property; vehicle running costs; and any advertising and promotional material you produce under your own steam.

MAKING IT HAPPEN
Look For a Suitable Franchise

You should look for a franchise package that will include all the things necessary to enable you successfully to operate an outlet of an established business. This includes, first and foremost, a commercially viable product or service. Your franchisor should offer you discounts on bulk supplies of products and be able to help you find startup capital (most established franchisors have special arrangements with the banks to help new franchisees) and suitable premises. To enable you to become fully operational—even if you're a novice at the business—you should be offered adequate initial training, after which you should have a program of courses and seminars to continue your development and keep you abreast of changes affecting your sector. As well as giving you help and advice, your franchisor should encourage you to meet other franchisees in the network who'll be able to pass on useful insights and tips about the best way to manage your business.

Choose a Franchise That Best Suits Your Needs

While you may have the dedication and commitment required to run a franchise, you should nevertheless choose one that most closely matches your aspirations and capabilities. There are events and services available that will help you to make the right decision. You could start by

"My own success was attended by quite a few failures along the way. But I refused to make the biggest mistake of all: worrying too much about making mistakes."

Kemmons Wilson

attending a franchise exhibition, where you'll be able to compare and contrast different types of opportunities. Consultants attached to reputable franchise organizations can also help you to make the right choice.

Conduct Some Basic Checks

Before you make your final decision about the franchise to go with, you should check out certain information. This will include examining:

- financial projections for your proposed outlet;
- proof that the franchised product or service is viable and can be traded profitably;
- a list of existing franchisees in the network and their trading performance;
- what training will be available to help you to establish your outlet;
- evidence that the proposed franchise agreement will protect your rights.

Particular care should be taken about joining a network that has no proven track record. However, organizations that are members of the BFA must follow certain rules, which include disclosing the information listed above.

Think About the Franchise Agreement

This is a legally binding contract between you and the franchisor. While you may be able to negotiate various aspects of the agreement, there are no hard and fast rules about what it should contain. However, it must comply with Federal Trade Commission and individual state regulations.

When evaluating the agreement, you should consider the following key issues:

- the rights granted to you and the franchisor
- your obligations and those of the franchisor
- the goods and services provided to you by the franchisor
- the terms and amounts of your payment for licenses, management fees, and other costs imposed by the franchisor
- the duration of your agreement
- the basis for any renewal of your agreement
- the terms by which you may sell or otherwise transfer your interest in your franchise
- the terms by which you may use the franchisor's trade names, brand names, logos, store signs, and service marks
- the franchisor's right to adapt their franchise system to meet new or changed methods and market conditions
- your rights to terminate a franchise agreement before it expires
- the ownership of property, both tangible and intangible, provided to you by the franchisor and provisions for its surrender when an agreement is terminated

WHAT TO AVOID
Being Unrealistic

Running a franchise involves a huge amount of time, effort, and money. Make sure before you take the plunge that you're prepared to commit what it will take to make the business a success. Talk to other franchisees to get a realistic idea of just how great the commitment must be.

Falling for the "Hard Sell"

Don't be taken in by promises and the sales pitch from some organizations that may attend franchise exhibitions. If you find what appears to be a promising opportunity at an exhibition, before you sign anything take your time to think through carefully the proposals put to you. A reputable franchisor will encourage you to reflect before you commit yourself.

Signing Up to a Bad Agreement

Be wary of generalizations in any franchise agreement. Make sure the terms apply specifically to you and your franchise, and that the details cover your particular requirements. Another thing to avoid is signing up to an agreement that does not last long enough to enable you to make a decent return on your investment. You should get a lawyer experienced in this area of commercial law to check the agreement before you sign; this is an added expense but it could save you a great deal in the longer term.

Setting Up Too Close to an Existing Franchise

While your franchisor should make sure that you don't locate your business too close to other franchises in the same network, check that there are no similar outlets operated by other organizations. This can happen in some areas of retailing and food catering, for example, and if you're not careful you could end up with unnecessary competition.

FOR MORE INFORMATION

Web Sites:
American Association of Franchisees and Dealers:
http://aafd.org

Entrepreneur.com:
**www.entrepreneur.com/article/
0,4621,303298,00.html**

See also:
Entrepreneurs (pp. 1745–1747)

"To run this business . . . you need . . . optimism, humanism, enthusiasm, intuition, curiosity, love, humour, magic and fun, and that secret ingredient—euphoria."

Anita Roddick

Understanding the Basics of Project Management

GETTING STARTED

"Project management" is a term that's often bandied about today. It first became popular in the early 1960s, driven by businesses which realized that there were benefits to be gained from organizing work into separate, definable units and from coordinating different kinds of skills across departments and professions. One of the first major uses of project management was to handle the U.S. space program, and governments, military organizations, and the corporate world have all since adopted the discipline.

Although the term is now universally familiar, not many people fully understand exactly what project management involves. We tend to think of it as common sense, and that anyone can manage anything by being calm and well-organized. These are qualities that a project manager definitely needs, but other things are essential too. Project management is, in fact, a structured way of working and recording events that can bring order and coherence to any set of tasks with a predetermined goal. This actionlist sketches the outlines of that structure.

FAQs

Can a "project" be defined in any way?

It can, yes, although it's one of those words that is defined in various different ways by different bodies. However, all sources seem to agree that a project is:

a task or set of tasks undertaken within specific timeframes and cost constraints in order to achieve a particular benefit.

Are there any stages common to all kinds of projects?

Yes; there are three of them, in fact. Think about the following:

- arranging a vacation
- decorating a room
- assembling a garden shed
- moving to a new house
- organizing a party

These are all examples of a project, because they all have three things in common. In each case, you:

- identify a need or benefit first of all;
- start to produce whatever will satisfy the need;
- use, operate, or simply enjoy the fruit of your labors once all the work has been done.

This basic three-stage cycle is common to all projects, large and small, whether you're producing a physical product (such as a bridge or computer system), an event (like a product launch or sporting event), or a change in circumstances (an office move or reorganization, for instance).

What other factors have to be taken into account?

As well as the three stages mentioned above, all projects have three key parameters (or factors) which have to be taken into account:

1 time
2 cost
3 quality (also referred to as "performance" or "specification")

The relationship between these three elements is often shown as a triangle, with each different element joined to both of the others. This is because, throughout the life of a project, the three factors are likely to conflict with one another. You will nearly always find that everyone wants **high performance** within a very **short time**, at **minimum cost**! However, if any one of these factors is absolutely essential, the other two will have to give way to a certain extent—it's impossible to be in all three corners at once, so you have to set priorities for the project, whatever it is.

Say, for example, your project had been to make all your IT systems 2000-compliant in time for the new millennium. Your priorities would probably have been in the following order:

1 **Time**: you'd have needed to get everything ready for midnight on 31 December 1999.
2 **Quality**: it would have been essential that everything worked properly when the clocks changed.
3 **Cost**: you might have had to spend whatever was necessary to make sure the other two parameters were met.

When you're beginning a new project, it's a useful exercise to place it in this triangle to indicate how flexible—or not—you could be with any of the three parameters.

So, from a combination of the three stages and the three parameters, we can see that a project:

- has a finite and defined life span
- aims to produce a measurable benefit or product
- contains a corresponding set of activities designed to achieve that benefit or product
- has a defined amount of resources allocated

The final, vital requirement is that the project also has a proper organization structure with defined responsibilities, so that everyone involved knows what they are doing and why; how it must be done, and by when.

One important thing to bear in mind is that projects are finite—they have a definite beginning and end. If these are unclear and if you and others are working away without a proper goal in sight, it's not a project.

MAKING IT HAPPEN
Understand What Project Management Is

All projects, large or small, are established to create something new to an organization, and, as a result, they create an environment which is unstable and risky.

Without change, though, we'd stagnate. Projects help us to develop, but it's important to keep them under tight control so that they stay focused and achieve what

"Soon the emphasis will be on getting a life instead of a career, and work will be viewed as a series of gigs or projects."

Jonas Ridderstråle

they're supposed to. This is where the project manager comes in!

The whole project management process revolves around three main areas:

1 **Business.** Projects must support your organization's business strategy. If they don't, they shouldn't be started in the first place. To work out whether a project is a good idea or not, there has to be agreement from everyone involved or affected about
- what the project is
- what its targets are
- the benefits to the business

It's the project manager's job to make sure the project has been properly defined and planned from the outset.

2 **People.** Projects revolve around people, and, if the project manager isn't managing the team doing the work and all the other stakeholders, he or she isn't managing the project. Identifying or appointing certain people is also key, such as the project sponsor (the person who's requested the project—usually the one who is paying for it) and "champions" who can support and promote the different areas of the work.

3 **Control.** As soon as authorization is received to start work, the project manager must plan the route of the project, assess what risks are involved, identify what skills and resources are required, then constantly check progress and adjust its course to make sure the targets are reached successfully.

Know What Skills Are Required

The project manager is often seen as a juggler, the person who has to keep all the balls in the air at once—plans, budgets, people, communications, and so on, as well as keeping the balance between the three parameters of time, cost, and quality mentioned above. Project managers therefore need to have a good level of know-how in whatever field their project is in (such as IT or manufacturing expertise, for example), as well as sufficient "clout" to have influence with senior decision makers.

All these requirements can be split into two different areas of skills: business and interpersonal.

Business

The project manager should be able to:
- plan all aspects of the project;
- monitor costs, efficiency, and quality without generating unnecessary extra work for others;
- use both technical and general management skills to control the project;
- make sure that the whole team takes part in decision making, which boosts trust and productivity;
- get things done right first time without being a slave driver;
- get the right people for the right task at the right time;
- see clear-sightedly through tangled issues;
- keep focused on results;
- demonstrate excellent problem-solving skills.

Interpersonal

He or she also needs to:
- lead both by example and by taking a back seat when appropriate;
- negotiate any project requirements (such as suitable timeframes and budgets) with senior decision-makers;
- motivate with integrity, sensitivity, and imagination;
- build excellent team relationships;
- communicate clearly and unambiguously with everyone.

Understand the Project Lifecycle

Any project has a natural progression, following a series of different stages from when it is first established to when it is finished and the benefits are seen. This is known as the *project lifecycle*.

Depending on their complexity, some projects will need more stages than others. Having said that, the same steps can generally be applied to any sort of objective:

- **Evaluate ideas.** This stage establishes the business need for the project; documents the initial idea(s); assesses the benefits; identifies risks which might threaten the success of the project; and outlines how it is going to be done, how long it will take, what it will cost, and whose authority will be needed to proceed.

- **Define and design.** Now you're into the detail. How will you run the project? Who will be needed to do it? How will you divide up the responsibilities? What key measures and milestones will you use to monitor progress? To make sure things don't get missed out, think in terms of what your business/team needs, what customers need, and what your competitors are up to. Do they have any new initiatives that you need to improve on, for example?

- **Build and test.** With all your plans and designs in place and agreed upon, you find and build all the new processes, places, and people involved in the project. At every stage, you test to make sure that everything works as it's meant to.

- **Implement, pilot, and launch.** Here you pilot the project, evaluate how it's gone so far, and refine as necessary. Then you finalize the full-scale launch, prepare the processes and systems that will be required, and provide any necessary training. This is the last point at which your project sponsor(s) can make a final decision on whether or not to go ahead.

- **Evaluate and monitor.** Following the launch, you make sure that the project has delivered the expected benefits. You also record any learning points so that you can manage things more effectively next time—things are bound to go wrong along the way but, if you learn from them, you'll start your next project much better equipped.

Bear in mind that this process doesn't necessarily flow through in one smooth sequence, as you will need to keep evaluating and monitoring plans, budgets, schedules, and so on throughout the life of the project. However it does act as a good "road map," and none of the stages should be left out, even if your project is a small one.

COMMON MISTAKES
You Don't Do Enough Planning

Once the go-ahead has been given for a new project, it's tempting to get overexcited and rush into a frenzy of activity. All projects stand or fall on how well they've been planned and researched from the outset, though, so the early stages of any project (the "evaluate ideas" and "define and design" steps described above) are by far the most important, and it's essential that you place high

---

"The desire for order is the only order in the world."   Georges Duhamel

     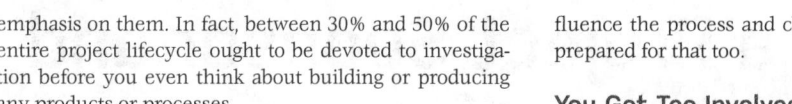

emphasis on them. In fact, between 30% and 50% of the entire project lifecycle ought to be devoted to investigation before you even think about building or producing any products or processes.

Research has shown clearly that time spent on these stages is valuable in several important ways:

- It significantly decreases the time to completion, and can cut costs dramatically.
- It results in clearer objectives and plans, which are more likely to be achieved.
- Since decisions taken at the early stages of a project have a far-reaching effect, it sets the tone for the remainder of the process.
- It minimizes changes being made once development is under way, which can be very costly.

Doing your groundwork properly will lessen the chances of you ending up with a disaster on your hands!

You Underestimate the Impact of a New Project

Because projects, by their very nature, are designed to bring about change, you may meet a lot of resistance from the people potentially affected by it. If you are the project manager, you need to be really sure of what the benefits will be and you also have to be good at getting these across to others. You're also likely to encounter considerable internal politics, with people wanting to influence the process and clashing with each other, so be prepared for that too.

You Get Too Involved in the Nitty-gritty

With so much going on around you, it's all too easy to get distracted by details of each individual activity in a project. It's vital that someone stays in the driver's seat and keeps all the activities together and on course, though, and as the project manager, that's your job. Don't be tempted to get in there and get your hands dirty—you have enough to do already.

975

ACTIONLIST

FOR MORE INFORMATION

Book:
Portny, Stanley. *Project Management for Dummies.* New York: Hungry Minds, 2001.

Web Sites:
4pm: **www.4pm.com/articles**
Mind Tools: **www.mindtools.com**

See also:
☆ Project Management (pp. 200–202)
 Project Management (pp. 1873–1875)

"Project management is the furnace in which successful careers are made."

Thomas A. Stewart

Working with a Project Sponsor and Stakeholders

GETTING STARTED

It's all too easy, when you're managing a project, to become so involved with your team and the work at hand that you overlook a very important group of people. These are your sponsor and stakeholders—in other words, all those who may have an investment or interest in the project's outcome without being directly involved in making it happen.

Neglect them at your peril! This group is likely to have opinions and influences that can make all the difference between success and failure of the whole project. The wise project manager will make sure that he or she knows from the outset who all these people are, what form their interest in the project takes, and their needs and desires, and will then work out how to start and maintain a great working relationship with them. This actionlist shows you how.

FAQs
What is the difference between "project sponsors" and "stakeholders?"

The project **sponsor** is the individual or organization for whom the project is undertaken—the primary risk taker, in other words. This usually means the person or body responsible for financing the project. The project sponsor is far and away your most important stakeholder.

Stakeholders are people who are not directly involved in the project but are affected by it in some way, and so have a vested interest in its successful or unsuccessful conclusion. As a result, they (and their views) have to be taken into account by the project manager and the sponsor. The most common type of stakeholder is the user—that is, the group of people who will be using the end product—but can also include people like your boss, suppliers, customers, and even your family.

Why do I need to have sponsors and stakeholders "on my side?"

There are a number of important benefits to having a good relationship with your sponsor and stakeholders. For example:

- If you consult the most powerful among them early on, you can use their opinions to shape your project from the outset. Not only does this make it more likely that they will support you, but their input can also improve the quality of your work (and stop you from having to do things twice).
- Gaining support from powerful stakeholders can help you to win additional resources—which also means that your project will be more likely to succeed.
- If you keep in touch regularly with stakeholders, you'll know that they fully understand what you're doing and what the benefits are. As a result, they'll probably be willing to support you actively when necessary.

- Through stakeholders, you can anticipate what people's reactions to your project may be and build in plans that will win widespread support.

Good stakeholder management also helps you to deal with the politics that can often come with major projects, and eliminates a big source of major stress.

Does the project manager or project sponsor have the final say in running a project?

This is tricky, and it can be a fine balancing act. If you are managing a project, remember that your sponsor, having the biggest interest in it, does have the right to make decisions—don't think of him or her as being just a "silent partner." If you think these decisions are wrong, be honest about what you think (but don't be confrontational). If, after all that, the sponsor *still* wants it done his or her way, follow instructions and do your best to make sure the outcome is successful.

MAKING IT HAPPEN
Work Out Exactly Who Your Stakeholders Are

It will be perfectly obvious who most of your stakeholders are, but there may well be a few who don't come to mind immediately. It's a good idea to have a brainstorming session with your project team to make sure no-one gets left out of the loop. Think about all the people who are affected by your work, who have power or influence over it, or who have an interest in whether it succeeds or fails.

The table below shows some of the people who might be stakeholders in projects:

Your boss	Your project sponsor	Government
Senior executives	Business partners	Trade associations
Your colleagues	Suppliers	The press
Your team	Lenders	Interest groups
Customers	Analysts	The public
Prospective customers	Future recruits	The community
Your family	Labor unions	Stockholders

Remember that, although stakeholders may be both organizations *and* people, you communicate with people, not buildings. Make sure, then, that you have a contact at any stakeholder organization with whom you can build a relationship.

Analyze Who Takes Priority

If you write down all the people who might fit into the categories above as well as anyone else you can think of who will be affected by your project, you may well end up with quite a long list. You don't have enough time to

deal with them all equally, so how do you decide who takes precedence?

The best thing to do is to categorize them by their power over and interest in your work. Draw a graph, with the y-axis representing "power" and the x-axis representing "interest." Go through the list of people you've identified as your stakeholders, and write their names in wherever seems appropriate. For example, your boss is likely to have *high* power over your project and *high* interest, and will therefore go at the top right hand corner of the grid. Your family may have high interest, but are unlikely to have power over it (so they'll be at the bottom right-hand corner).

Someone's position on the grid shows you how you ought to deal with them:

- **High power, high interest:** these are the people you must make the greatest efforts to satisfy, so make sure you communicate with them very regularly and get them on your side.
- **High power, less interest:** put in enough work to keep them satisfied, but not so much that they get bored with your message.
- **Lower power, high interest:** keep this group adequately informed, and talk to them to ensure no major issues are arising. These people are often very helpful with the detail of your project.
- **Low power, low interest:** check in every now and then with this group to confirm there aren't any problems developing. An overview is usually fine here, so there's no need to go into too much detail!

Understand Your Key Stakeholders

So now you know who they are and what sort of priority they should have for your attention, you need to know more about your stakeholders: how they are likely to feel about and react to your project, and how best to engage them and communicate with them.

Key questions that can help you to understand your stakeholders are:

- What financial or emotional interest do they have in the outcome of your work? Is it positive or negative?
- What motivates them most of all?
- What information do they want from you?
- How do they want to receive information from you? What is the best way of communicating your message to them?
- What is their current opinion of your work? Is it based on good information?
- Who influences their opinions generally? Do some of these influencers therefore become important stakeholders in their own right?
- If they're not likely to be positive, what will win them over to support your project?
- If you *don't* think you will be able to win them over, how will you manage their opposition?
- Who else might be influenced by their opinions?

The best way to answer these questions is to talk to your stakeholders directly. People are usually quite open about their views, and asking their opinions is often the first step in building a successful relationship with them—they'll be pleased that their views are being taken into account.

Plan How You'll Communicate with Your Stakeholders

The next step is to draw up a communications plan, so you can make sure the right messages get to the right people in the right format.

This is vital: there's always a danger that while a project is in progress, the project team slogs away and takes the attitude that "everyone should leave us alone until we've finished, and then we'll deliver a wonderful product." Stakeholders, who are eager to see a successful result, get nervous if they have no indication of how things are progressing.

There are eight different aspects that you need to consider while drawing up your plan. These are:

1 **Stakeholders.** Who are you trying to reach (you'll know this from your initial brainstorming session)?
2 **Objectives.** What are the objectives of the communication? Is it to prompt action, gain approval, or merely to inform?
3 **Message.** What are the key messages you want to get across? These should be targeted at the individual stakeholders according to their influence and interest. Typical messages will show the benefits to the person or organization of what you are doing, and will focus on key issues like increasing profitability or delivering real improvements.
4 **Information.** What information will you communicate? There may be issues of confidentiality which must be addressed.
5 **Channel.** What channels will you use? The choice of channel for a particular stakeholder will depend upon the message, feedback, level and timing aspects, not to mention geography (where they are located relative to you). You probably have a multitude of choices available to you—meetings, videos, e-mail, newsletters, telephone, workshops, and press conferences, for example.
6 **Feedback.** How will you encourage feedback, and what mechanisms should you have in place to respond to it? For example, you could have a dedicated e-mail address for queries that a member of your project team is responsible for.
7 **Level.** How much detail should be provided?
8 **Timing.** When should you communicate? It's no good leaving it until the end and then telling everyone that the project is finished!

The easiest way to organize all this information into an easy-to-follow communications plan is to plot it all into a table of some kind.

Say, for example, your project is to construct a meeting place for a local neighborhood group, and you've decided your main forms of communication will be consultation meetings during design, monthly site meetings, monthly progress presentations, a page in the neighborhood magazine, and an open day. You could set them out as shown below.

You can use simple tables of this type to illustrate various aspects of the communications plan. Keep the stakeholders down the left-hand side and change the column headings as you need to—they could relate to timings, information, message, channel, and so on. There are no set rules: just use whichever layout is most appropriate for your project.

"The more you can do, the greater should be your patience to endure."

Seneca

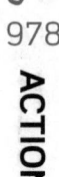

978

ACTIONLIST

Stakeholder	Consulta-tion meetings	Site meetings	Progress presenta-tion	Local maga-zine	Open day
Group leaders	X		X		X
Project sponsor	X	X	X		X
Architect	X	X			X
Builder		X			X
Residents				X	X
Facilities manager	X	X	X		X
County officials	X		X		X

Flag up potential problems as early as you can. This gives everyone time to think through how move forward, and also preserves your reputation for reliability. No one will be happy to be told at the last minute that a project is not going to be delivered on time or to budget.

COMMON MISTAKES
You Go Over the Top

It's just as damaging to relations with stakeholders to go over the top as to provide too little information. The company chairman is not going to be amused to receive every detail of every quote you get in for materials and supplies! Be sensible about judging the level of detail you give to whom, and how much time you spend on managing your stakeholders. It all depends on the size and complexity of your projects and goals, and the time you have available.

You Don't Consider What You Want from Each Individual or Group

Stakeholders are likely to be a disparate lot, and you'll probably need very different kinds of support from each of them. Your family, you hope, will be understanding about you working at weekends (if necessary); your boss, you hope, will be understanding about you *not* giving priority to his or her immediate work. You'll need to communicate with each stakeholder or group of stakeholders in very different ways: there's no point bombarding them all with the same progress presentations if they're just not suitable for everyone.

FOR MORE INFORMATION

Web Sites:
4pm: **www.4pm.com/articles**
Mind Tools: **www.mindtools.com**

See also:
☆ Project Management (pp. 200–202)
🐭 Project Management (pp. 1873–1875)

Building a Cross-functional Team

GETTING STARTED

Most projects require a wide variety of skills to complete the work involved, so if you're managing a project of any type, it's likely that you'll have to work with a group of people from different backgrounds. They may be drawn from different parts of your organization; they may come from a number of separate organizations—wherever they're from, when they come together, they're known as a "cross-functional team."

It's the project manager's job to bring cross-functional team members together and form them into an effective group which operates as one to achieve the overall goals of the project. Unsurprisingly, this can sometimes be tricky. However, there are a number of rules which, if followed, can make team building much easier and more likely to succeed. This actionlist lays out the basics.

FAQs

I'm new to project management and I have to build and lead a cross-functional team. Where do I start to find the right people?

Begin by identifying and engaging a team of people with the right skills and enthusiasm for the project. This list, obviously, will vary enormously, depending on the size of your project and what it entails. Say, for example, you are organizing an office move: you're likely to need floor planners, packers, removal men, electricians to do the wiring, IT people to sort out the computers, and so on.

Your team will probably need to come from all parts of your company, so that you get people with the right skills and also that you get input and involvement from all parts of the business. You may well find that your senior stakeholder (the senior manager who has agreed to the project idea, for example) can help you to find and recruit the right people.

Is it important to get the right mix of personalities, as well as skills, in a project team?

Absolutely. The mix of personalities among a team's members can have a huge effect on whether the team functions properly or not.

Meredith Belbin, the business writer and academic, identified around a dozen common team roles as part of his research in the 1970s.

Ideally, you need a good mix of these types of people in your team (bearing in mind that people can fulfill more than one role at a time), as you're likely to have problems if you have too many of one type. Imagine a team full of judges, or challengers, for instance!

However, don't worry too much if your team does contain quite a few of the same type of people—there are ways around it. For example, you could split your team into smaller "working parties," each of which is responsible for particular tasks that together contribute to the overall goals.

Role and characteristic	Function
Leader—aims to get the best out of everyone	Forms the team; sets objectives; monitors performance; provides structure.
Challenger—rocks the boat	Adopts unconventional approaches; challenges the accepted order; comes up with ideas.
Expert—provides specialist advice	Provides a professional viewpoint, often from an external source (for example IT, accounting).
Ambassador—makes friends easily	Develops external relationships; understands external environment; sells the team.
Judge—down to earth, logical, careful	Listens; evaluates; ponders before deciding; avoids arguments; seeks truth and the best way.
Innovator—provides source of vision, ingenuity, and creativity	Uses imagination; motivates others; evaluates and builds on ideas; deals with complex issues.
Diplomat—steers team to successful outcome	Influential; builds alliances in and out of the team; good negotiator; aids agreement; often becomes leader in difficult times.
Conformer—helpful, reliable, co-operative	Fills gaps; jack of all trades; seldom challenges authority.
Outputter—chases progress	Self-motivated; focuses on tasks and results; imposes timescales; checks progress; intolerant of other people.
Supporter/mediator—focuses on team relationships	Builds morale; resolves conflict; gives advice; supports and encourages.
Quality controller—ensures tasks done well	Checks output; preoccupied with high standards; focuses on quality.
Reviewer—monitors performance	Observes; reviews performance; promotes feedback; looks for pitfalls.

MAKING IT HAPPEN

Learn About the Stages of Team Formation

Teams go through a number of stages after they are first brought together, and these stages can be responsible for different kinds of problems or issues that arise.

Say, for example, your team is going through a sticky patch and you're having to deal with conflict and arguments. If, rather than wondering what on earth is going wrong, you recognize that this may simply be a result of the stage your team has reached, it will help you judge objectively what—if anything—needs to be done about it.

The four stages are:

- **Forming.** Excitement is high; everything is new and fun; no-one knows what they're doing yet.
- **Storming.** Roles are assigned; personalities begin to show; uncertainty of others and their abilities can lead to conflict, which can smolder unless tackled promptly; people don't yet feel safe to be open and honest.

"Teams are now the primary force of organizations. They are worth cultivating at their core. Their core is the *mind* of each team member."

Nancy Kline

- **Norming.** Confidence starts to improve; relationships strengthen; differences of opinion are respected; solutions begin to develop; goals become manageable, and everyone starts to work together to achieve them.
- **Performing.** The team becomes fluid, with people taking it in turns to lead; delegation occurs so team members grow and flourish; goals and targets are reached regularly and effectively.

Help the "Norming" Process Along

In any team, it is important to get the "vectors" aligned. A vector is a force that pulls in a certain direction and every project team member will have their own, created by their individual beliefs, thoughts, and desires. Within a team, it can be disastrous if everyone's vectors are all straining in different directions—and even one "anti-vector" or team member forcing the current a separate way will have an adverse effect.

In your role as a project manager, it's your responsibility to get every team member pulling in the same direction to achieve the project goals—a process known as "vectorship." Although this sounds obvious, it's extraordinary how many projects fail because individuals who are being negative are allowed to go unchallenged!

The best way to get these vectors aligned is to create a working climate in which mistakes and failures are viewed as learning experiences, not occasions for blame, and where every member feels included "in the loop." There are a number of elements which contribute to this type of an atmosphere:

- **A free flow of information.** Make sure that every member receives/has easy access to any information they need to do their job.
- **Open communication.** Don't keep secrets, or allow team members to feel that some people are privy to information that others aren't.
- **Frequent feedback.** People need to know how well they're doing—and where improvements can be made.
- **Regular one-to-one interaction.** Talk to your team members as people, and use the time to make sure they're happy and on side.
- **A listening culture.** Make sure that people feel free to say what they think without fear or anger, and that they will be heard, even when they're voicing minority or unpopular views.

Learn What Motivates People

Motivation is essential for people and teams to work effectively and harmoniously. Studies into what motivates people at work have revealed that motivators and demotivators are not necessarily the same thing. In other words, the things that make people feel motivated and enthusiastic are not always the same things that, if unsatisfactory, make them feel discontented and apathetic.

The table below identifies the top ten motivators for project team members, and the top ten demotivators.

These lists prove the point: some things, if they're good, are hardly noticed—but they cause high levels of dissatisfaction if they're bad.

Go through your list of team members and consider what you think motivates each of them, or small groups of them, if this is more appropriate. Then consider

Motivators	Score	Demotivators	Score
Recognition	1	Relations with project manager	1
Achievement	2	Team peer relations	2
Responsibility	3	Salary	3
Team peer relations	4	Project manager's leadership	4
Salary	5	Security	5
Relations with project manager	6	Work conditions	6
Project manager's leadership	7	Organization's policy	7
Work itself	8	Team subordinate relations	8
Advancement	9	Personal time	9
Personal growth	10	Title/status	10

(R. J. Yourzak, "Motivation in the Project Environment" (1985))

whether any of the demotivators listed are present in your project or organization. What can you do to boost the positives and minimize the effect of the negatives?

Delegate

Delegation is another vital tool for managing your team. It's not something that everyone finds easy to start with, but it does get easier with practice and will help your project to run smoothly. Here are the basic rules:

- Select the most appropriate person for the task. Depending on what the job is, you might not have to always delegate downward, toward your team; you can also delegate upward (to your manager) or sideways (to a peer).
- Communicate clearly to whoever will be helping you, so that he or she is clear about what they should be coming back to you with, and when.
- Break down tasks into manageable chunks, probably with deadlines at each stage where the other person can report back and let you know that things are moving in the right direction.
- Keep proper records so you know what tasks you are delegating and to whom.

And here's a quick summary of how much supervision is needed, depending on a person's experience and motivation:

Level of experience	Degree of supervision required
1 New or inexperienced person, low confidence	Tell the person what to do; show them how to do it; put a plan together, showing each checkpoint when they have to report back to you; review the task and give feedback.
2 Slightly more experience/confidence	Tell the person what your desired outcome is, and plan the steps together. Less frequent checkpoints than (1).
3 More experienced, though needs some guidance and help	Tell the person what your desired outcome is and allow them to plan it, and establish when checkpoints are necessary.
4 Experienced, committed person	Explain the required outcome, timescales, and checkpoints (if any), and leave them to get on with it. But **don't** abdicate all responsibility for a task; you are the project leader, and are ultimately responsible for everything!

"Team player: An employee who substitutes the thinking of the herd for his/her own judgment."

Anonymous

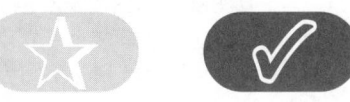

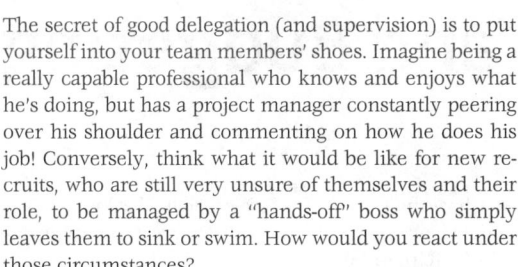

The secret of good delegation (and supervision) is to put yourself into your team members' shoes. Imagine being a really capable professional who knows and enjoys what he's doing, but has a project manager constantly peering over his shoulder and commenting on how he does his job! Conversely, think what it would be like for new recruits, who are still very unsure of themselves and their role, to be managed by a "hands-off" boss who simply leaves them to sink or swim. How would you react under those circumstances?

Resolve Conflict

Projects can be breeding grounds for conflict because they are temporary situations and circumstances within them tend to change continually. Unresolved conflict can be very destructive, so it needs to be tackled immediately. Here's how:

1. Recognize conflict

Conflict can be either overt (clearly visible and stemming from an easily identifiable cause), or covert (bubbling under the surface, from a less obvious or apparently unrelated cause).

2. Monitor the climate

Look out for early warning signals so that you can deal with the conflict quickly, before it gets out of hand. Early action saves time and stress later.

3. Research the situation

Spend time finding out the true root cause of the conflict, who is involved, and what the potential effects are. Putting yourself in other people's shoes will enable you to understand and empathize better.

4. Plan your approach

Encourage everyone involved to be open and understanding in the way they interact with others. It might be a good idea to ask people to write down their thoughts and feelings, so that they can express themselves logically and constructively.

5. Tackle the issue

- Give everyone a chance to express their point of view.
- Avoid fight or flight: fighting back will only make the situation worse, while running away from the situation will show that you don't feel up to resolving the situation, and it may lead to a loss of respect.

- Remember to be assertive. Becoming aggressive will get you nowhere, but neither will passivity.
- Acknowledge the views and rights of all parties.
- Encourage those involved to come up with their own solution—if they've created the solution, they are more likely to buy into it.
- Suggest a constructive way forward.

COMMON MISTAKES
You Don't Involve Your Team Early Enough in Decision Making

Making too many rules and trying to impose your own plans and methods on your team without getting their input is just asking for trouble. You've brought these people together for their skills—so involve them from the start. Not only will they provide information and ideas, but also they will feel as if they "own" the plans, all of which boosts their level of commitment to them.

This doesn't mean that your projects should be planned by committee; rather that you, as manager, plan the project based on all the available experience and creative ideas. Perhaps you could attempt the first level(s) of planning to help you to explain the project to the team and then ask for comments. Then, using these, the final breakdown of tasks could be looked at again by the people who'll actually be carrying them out.

You Micromanage

Don't go there! You'll explode with the effort of trying to oversee every detail yourself, and your team will quickly lose motivation. Delegate the work and supervise it appropriately, but keep your eye mainly on the overall direction of the project—the "big picture."

981

ACTIONLIST

FOR MORE INFORMATION

Web sites:
Belbin Associates: **www.belbin.com**
Experience Based Learning, Team Building Workshops:
www.ebl.org/index.html
Gallup Management Journal: **gmj.gallup.com**
Office of Personnel Management:
www.opm.gov/perform/
teams.asp#Staff%20Recommendations

Planning, Scheduling, and Budgeting During a Project

GETTING STARTED

Estimation—whether in connection with plans, budgets, or schedules—is one of the darker arts of project management. This is because there are always so many unknowns: details that might change, issues that might arise, or events that might happen. However, it is also among the most important skills for the project manager and plays a key role in a project's success.

There are many tools and techniques you can use to overcome the problems of uncertainty, and in this actionlist we'll be looking at the main ones.

FAQs
Is it ever possible to "over-plan" a project?

Not really, no. Taking a lot of time during the early stages of a project to be sure of what you're doing, why you're doing it, and when you need to finish it by is really important. Detailed planning will help you save time and money, and it's a good idea to involve all your team in it so that you benefit from everyone's experience.

What you do need to be wary of, however, is making things more complicated than they need to be. For example, if your project is a relatively simple one, there's no need to use a full battery of complicated planning tools that you don't need. Read on to find out which tool might best suit your needs.

MAKING IT HAPPEN
Think About the Planning Tools Available to You

Drawing up a detailed project plan is your most vital ingredient for a successful, pain-free project. The tools you use to do this will obviously depend greatly on what you're doing—the size of your project, its complexity, and deadline, for example—but here are some of the most useful ones:

Work breakdown structure

This is useful for identifying the individual tasks in your project.
● Get the team together and brainstorm all the tasks that need doing, in no particular order.
● Write them down on sticky notes and put them up on a board or wall.
● Once everyone has thought of as many tasks as they can, arrange the sticky notes into groups under the major areas of activity.

Project logic diagram

Next put start and end notes at opposite ends of the board or wall.
● From left to right between them, arrange the sticky notes in the logical sequence of activities.
● Join the notes with arrows in and out, depending on whether things can be done one after another or at the same time (some tasks may have more than one arrow).
● Under each task, write how long you estimate it will take.

You have now created a "project logic diagram," which should help you identify which tasks are **dependent**, and which are **parallel**:
● **Dependent tasks:** Some activities are dependent on other activities being completed first. For example, it is not a good idea to start building a bridge before you have designed it! These dependent activities need to be completed in a sequence, with each stage being more or less done before the next can begin.
● **Parallel tasks:** These are the tasks which are not dependent on the completion of anything else, and may be done at any time before or after a particular stage is reached.

You can then put these tasks into a simple timetable, or use either of the next two planning tools to create a more formal structure for how the work should proceed.

Gantt charts

Gantt charts are a very popular tool and are most useful for analyzing and planning small or medium sized projects. They:
● help in planning the tasks involved;
● give a basis for scheduling when tasks will be performed;
● allow you to allocate the necessary resources;
● help in plotting the critical path for a project where it must be completed by a particular date.

To produce a Gantt chart, take all the activities for the project that you listed in your project logic diagram and for each task show the earliest start date, estimated time it will take, whether it is parallel or dependent, and if dependent, which other tasks it depends on.

Let's say your project is to manage an office move. Your task list might look like this:

Task	Earliest start date	Length	Type
1 Produce new floor plan	Day 1	2 days	
2 Pack up current office	Day 3	1 day	Dependent on 1
3 Organize facilities	Day 3	1 day	Parallel
4 Transport furniture	Day 4	2 days	Dependent on 2
5 Transport equipment	Day 5	2 days	Parallel, dependent on 4. Any time after
6 Unpack in new office	Day 6	3 days	Parallel, dependent on 4. Any time after
7 Set up IT systems	Day 7	4 days	Parallel, dependent on 5. Any time after
8 Staff move in	Day 10	2 days	Parallel, dependent on 7. Any time after

You can plot the list into a chart, like the one on the next page.

Once you've plotted your chart, you can see if any adjustments are required.

When the project is under way, the chart will be very useful for monitoring progress, as you can see immedi-

---

"If we had had more time for discussion we should probably have made a great many more mistakes."

Leon Trotsky

Task	Day 1	Day 2	Day 3	Day 4	Day 5	Day 6	Day 7	Day 8	Day 9	Day 10	Day 11
1 Produce new floor plan	X	X									
2 Pack up current office			X								
3 Organize new facilities (light, phone etc)			X								
4 Transport furniture				X	X						
5 Transport equipment					X	X					
6 Unpack in new office						X	X	X			
7 Set up IT systems							X	X	X	X	
8 Staff move in										X	X

ately what should have been achieved at a point in time—and take remedial action if things are slipping.

Critical path analysis

Critical path analysis (CPA) is a powerful tool for scheduling and managing complex projects. Its main benefit is that you can use it to identify the tasks that have to be done on time and in sequence in order for the whole project to be completed (the critical path itself). Then you can fit the other non-dependent tasks around them.

Say your project is to launch a new product, and you've listed the tasks as follows:

Task	Type
A. Prepare initial designs	
B. Make prototypes	Dependent on A
C. Test prototypes	Dependent on B
D. Finalize design	Dependent on C
E. Set up production line	Parallel, dependent on A. Any time after.
F. Train operators	Parallel, dependent on E. Any time after.
G. Produce first batch	Dependent on D and F

In order to work out the critical path, you need to work out which tasks are critical.

A task is said to be critical *if its duration cannot be extended without delaying the completion of the project.*

Allow Enough Time!

As a rule, people vastly underestimate the amount of time needed to make a project happen, particularly if they're not familiar with the individual tasks to be performed. They forget to take into account unexpected events or unscheduled high-priority work, and also often simply fail to allow for the full complexity involved with a job. Many people are naturally over-optimistic, so it's all too easy to fall into this trap.

However, it's important to get time estimation as accurate as possible for two main reasons:

1 You'll save yourself and your team a huge amount of stress.

2 You could save yourself a lot of money; if you get your timings wrong and you have to have work done at very short notice, it's highly likely that you'll have to pay a lot more for it.

Also, you'll enhance your reputation as a great project manager if you can deliver by deadline. If you're in a competitive work environment, or if you want to move up the career ladder, making your project successful will really help.

In an earlier guidance point, we looked at assigning lengths of time to the different tasks in your project,

using the expertise and experience of your team to do so. In addition, there are other factors you need to take into account when estimating the overall time for the project as a whole. Again, these will vary dramatically, depending on the type of project you're working on, but they could include some or all of the following:

- detailed project planning
- liaison with other parties
- external and internal meetings
- quality assurance and any supporting documentation necessary
- accidents and emergencies
- vacations and sickness among essential staff
- contact with customers
- breakdowns in equipment
- missed deliveries by suppliers
- interruptions
- quality-control rejections

Any combination of these factors may double (or more than double) the length of time needed to complete a project.

Count the Costs

Costs, like time, are often underestimated. If you get your time more or less right, though, it's easier to be accurate with your costs.

The types of costs you should include in your estimates and in your project plan are outlined in the lists below:

One-time development costs

- Staff costs for the project—usually the biggest expense
- Cost of research undertaken
- Systems development costs, including software/hardware purchase or licenses
- Office re-fitting/re-wiring
- Pilot costs (staff and materials)
- Implementation costs—training, recruitment, communication, etc
- Third party expertise (for example software consultants, marketing agency)
- Government taxes on any third-party services

Ongoing operating costs

Direct costs:

- Overhead—the general operating costs
- New supplies of materials resulting from the project
- New administration—purchasing, accounting, record-keeping, etc.
- Costs incurred before the benefits of the project can be realized

Indirect costs:

- A proportion of the costs of running your business day to

day (for example, office rental, vehicles and expenses, existing staff additional duties)

Identify the Benefits

Wherever possible, try to identify the benefits of your project in financial terms so they can be weighed against the costs.

For example, if your project is to develop a new product or service for your clients, you might estimate that this will bring in extra income of X thousand dollars per annum for your organization. Or if the project is to move offices, you might calculate that the new premises will save the company money in terms of rent, cheaper utilities, better facilities (your own cafeteria, so you don't have to use outside caterers, for example), and so on.

However, not all benefits can be measured financially; so, instead, try to find ways of quantifying them in tangible, measurable terms so that the success of the project can be assessed. Any benefits that form critical success factors (see below) should be highlighted, as these may be just as influential in getting decision-makers to approve the project as the purely financial benefits.

Know the Critical Success Factors

These are the factors that define how the achievement of project goals will be judged. They need to be measurable and unambiguous, so there cannot be arguments over what they mean.

For example:

"Relocation of offices must be completed by August 15, 2007" is a good critical success factor, as it is very clear.

"Work must be completed to a high level of quality," on the other hand, is not, as there's no definition of what "high quality" means and this could be interpreted in all sorts of different ways.

Refine Your Estimates As You Go Along

Regardless of how often you emphasize the fact that forecasts of time and costs are approximate estimates to begin with, there is a continual danger that the words "approximate" and "estimates" get forgotten as the figures get communicated through the business, and everyone thinks you have given them the final "completion date" and "total cost!"

To avoid this particular headache, keep refining your costs and timescales as you work through the project, and then make sure you keep people up to date. Tell any relevant people—your team, customers, or stakeholders, for example—and very clearly too.

It is wise to check your estimates at various stages of the project (for example, initial ball park figure; design stage; implementation stage; launch). It is likely that you will find that the accuracy can improve through the project process. For example, your final time and cost estimates could end up being as much as 50% more or 30% less than you've quoted as your initial ball park figure.

COMMON MISTAKES

You Don't Fight to Protect Your Estimates

It doesn't help your accuracy—and therefore your reputation for reliability—if you allow your estimates to be disrupted unnecessarily by external people or circumstances. Once you have arrived at what you consider to be a realistic schedule or budget, fight for it. Never let the outside world deflect you from what you know to be practical. If someone tries to impose a deadline upon you which is impossible, clearly state this and give your reasons.

However, you may need to compromise instead, since a flat "No" will be seen as obstructive. Look for alternatives, if you can. For example:

- offer a prototype service or product at an earlier date, on the understanding that your finished project would later replace the prototype;
- reduce the complexity of the product, or the total number of units; future enhancements or more units would then be the subject of a subsequent negotiation;
- demonstrate what other (specified) resources would be required if it's vital that the project is delivered to an earlier deadline.

You Overcomplicate Things

It's important to remember that complex planning tools aren't always appropriate. If your project is a relatively simple one, a straightforward timetable or action plan might be sufficient. Over-complicated planning can "blind people with science," and lead to poor communication and muddled projects.

You Don't Allow for a Contingency in your Budget

The earlier on in the project you do your cost estimates, the more likely it is that these will only be "best guesses." For this reason, it's essential to allow a significant contingency, so as an absolute minimum, add a further 20% to what you think the costs will be. Unfortunately, in most cases actual costs tend to be higher than estimated!

FOR MORE INFORMATION

Web Sites:
4pm: **www.4pm.com/articles**
Mind Tools: **www.mindtools.com**
Tools and Examples for Planning a Project:
www.washington.edu/computing/pm/tools

See also:
☆ Project Management (pp. 200–202)
🖱 Project Management (pp. 1873–1875)

"Dreams have their place in management activity, but they need to be kept severely under control."

Arnold Weinstock

Calculating Annual Percentage Rate

WHAT IT MEASURES

The annual percentage rate (APR) measures either the rate of interest that invested money earns in one year, or the cost of credit expressed as a yearly rate.

WHY IT IS IMPORTANT

It enables an investor or borrower to compare like with like. When evaluating investment alternatives, naturally it's important to know which one will pay the greatest return. By the same token, borrowers want to know which loan alternative offers the best terms. Determining the annual percentage rate (APR) provides a direct comparison.

HOW IT WORKS IN PRACTICE

To calculate the annual percentage rate (APR), apply this formula:

$$APR = [1 + i/m]m - 1.0$$

In the formula, **i** is the interest rate quoted, expressed as a decimal, and **m** is the number of compounding periods per year. For example, if a bank offers a 6% interest rate, paid quarterly, the APR would be calculated this way:

$$APR = [1 + i/m]m - 1.0$$
$$= [1 + 0.06/4] 4 - 1.0$$
$$= [1 + 0.015] 4 - 1.0$$
$$= (1.015) 4 - 1.0$$
$$= 1.0614 - 1.0$$
$$= 0.0614$$
$$= 6.14\% \text{ APR}$$

985

ACTIONLIST

TRICKS OF THE TRADE

- As a rule of thumb, the annual percentage rate is slightly higher than the quoted rate.
- When using the formula, be sure to express the rate as a decimal, that is, 6% becomes 0.06.
- When expressed as the cost of credit, remember to include other costs of obtaining the credit in addition to interest, such as loan closing costs and financial fees.
- APR provides an excellent basis for comparing mortgage or other loan rates; lenders are required to disclose it.
- When used in the context of investment APR can also be called the "annual percentage yield," or APY.

FOR MORE INFORMATION

Web site:
Investorguide.com: **www.investorguide.com**

See also:
⌕ Accounting (pp. 1667–1669)

"I finally know what distinguishes man from the other beasts: financial worries."

Jules Renard

Calculating Asset Turnover

WHAT IT MEASURES

The amount of sales generated for every dollar's worth of assets over a given period.

WHY IT IS IMPORTANT

Asset turnover measures how well a company is leveraging its assets to produce revenue. A well-managed manufacturer, for example, will make its plant and equipment work hard for the business by minimizing idle time for machines.

The higher the number the better—within reason. As a rule of thumb, companies with low profit margins tend to have high asset turnover; those with high profit margins have low asset turnover.

This ratio can also show how capital intensive a business is. Some businesses, software developers, for example, can generate tremendous sales per dollar of assets because their assets are modest. At the other end of the scale, electric utilities, heavy industry manufacturers, and even cable TV companies need a huge asset base to generate sales.

Finally, asset turnover serves as a tool to keep managers mindful of the company's balance sheet along with its profit and loss account.

HOW IT WORKS IN PRACTICE

Asset turnover's basic formula is simply sales divided by assets:

sales revenue / total assets

Most experts recommend using average total assets in the formula. To determine this figure, add total assets at the beginning of the year to total assets at the end of the year and divide by two.

If, for instance, annual sales totaled $4.5 million, and total assets were $1.84 million at the beginning of the year and $1.78 million at the year end, the average total assets would be $1.81 million, and the asset turnover ratio would be:

4,500,000 / 1,810,000 = 2.49

A variation of the formula is:

sales revenue / fixed assets

If average fixed assets were $900,000, then asset turnover would be:

4,500,000 / 900,000 = 5

TRICKS OF THE TRADE

- This ratio is especially useful for growth companies to gauge whether or not they are growing revenue, for example, turnover, in healthy proportion to assets.
- Asset turnover numbers are useful for comparing competitors within industries. Like most ratios, they vary from industry to industry. As with most numbers, the most meaningful comparisons are made over extended periods of time.
- Too high a ratio may suggest overtrading: too much sales revenue with too little investment. Conversely, too low a ratio may suggest undertrading and an inefficient management of resources.
- A declining ratio may be indicative of a company that overinvested in plant, equipment, or other fixed assets, or is not using existing assets effectively.

FOR MORE INFORMATION

Web site:
Biz/ed: **www.bized.ac.uk**

See also:
- Accounting (pp. 1667–1669)
- Calculating Asset Utilization (p. 1020)

Calculating Bond Yield

WHAT IT MEASURES

The annual return on this certificate (the rate of interest) expressed as a percentage of the current market price of the bond.

WHY IT IS IMPORTANT

Bonds can tie up investors' money for periods of up to 30 years, so knowing their yield is a critical investment consideration. Similarly, bond issuers need to know the price they will pay to incur their debt, so that they can compare it with the cost of other means of raising capital.

HOW IT WORKS IN PRACTICE

Bonds are issued in increments of $1,000. To calculate the yield amount, multiply the face value of the bond by the stated rate, expressed as a decimal. For example, buying a new ten-year $1,000 bond that pays 6% interest will produce an annual yield amount of $60:

$$1,000 \times 0.060 = 60$$

The $60 will be paid as $30 every six months. At the end of ten years, the purchaser will have earned $600, and will also be repaid the original $1,000. Because the bond was purchased when it was first issued, the 6% is also called the "yield to maturity."

This basic formula is complicated by other factors. First is the "time-value of money" theory: money paid in the future is worth less than money paid today. A more detailed computation of total bond yield requires the calculation of the present value of the interest earned each year. Second, changing interest rates have a marked impact on bond trading and, ultimately, on yield. Changes in interest rates cannot affect the interest paid by bonds already issued, but they do affect the prices of new bonds.

TRICKS OF THE TRADE

- Yield to call. Bond issuers reserve the right to "call," or redeem, the bond before the maturity date, at certain times and at a certain price. Issuers often do this if interest rates fall and they can issue new bonds at a lower rate. Bond buyers should obtain the yield-to-call rate, which may, in fact, be a more realistic indicator of the return expected.
- Different types of bond. Some bonds are backed by assets, while others are issued on the strength of the issue's good standing. Investors should know the difference.
- Zero coupon bonds. These pay no interest at all, but are sold at a deep discount, increasing in value until maturity. A buyer might pay $3,000 for a 25-year zero bond with a face value of $10,000. This bond will simply accrue value each year, and at maturity will be worth $10,000, thus earning $7,000. These are high-risk investments, however, especially if they must be sold on the open market amid rising interest rates.
- Interest rates. Bond values fall when interest rates rise, and rise when interest rates fall, because when interest rates rise existing bonds become less valuable and less attractive.

FOR MORE INFORMATION

Web site:
www.azcentral.webpoint.com/finance offers exceptional explanations of bond yields.

See also:
✔ Calculating Amortization (pp. 1047–1048)

"Economics limps along with one foot in untested hypotheses and the other in untestable slogans."

Joan Robinson

Calculating Book Value

WHAT IT MEASURES
A company's common stock equity, as it appears on a balance sheet.

WHY IT IS IMPORTANT
Book value represents a company's net worth to its stockholders, based on the difference between assets and liabilities. Typically, book value is substantially different from market value, especially in high-tech and knowledge-based industries whose primary assets are intangible and therefore do not appear on the balance sheet.

When compared with its market value, book value helps to reveal how a company is regarded by the investment community. A market value that is notably higher than book value indicates that investors have a high regard for the company. A market value that is, for example, a multiple of book value suggests that investors' regard may be unreasonably high—as was shown in the painful plunge of dot-com companies in 2000 and 2001.

The reverse is also true, of course; indeed, it may suggest that a company's stock is a bargain.

A companion measure is book value per share. It shows the value of the company's assets that each stockholder theoretically would receive if a company were liquidated.

HOW IT WORKS IN PRACTICE
To calculate book value, subtract a company's liabilities and the value of its debt and preferred stock from its total assets. All of these figures appear on a company's balance sheet. For example:

	$
Total assets	1,300
Current liabilities	−400
Long-term liabilities, preferred stock	−250
Book value	**650**

Book value per share is calculated by dividing the book value by the number of shares issued. If our example is expressed in millions of dollars and the company has 35 million shares outstanding, the book value per share would be $650 million divided by 35 million:

650 / 35 = $18.57 book value per share

TRICKS OF THE TRADE
- Related terms include: **adjusted book value** or **modified book value**, which is book value after assets and liabilities are adjusted to market value; **tangible book value**, which also subtracts intangible assets, patents, trademarks, and the value of research and development. The rationale is that these items cannot be sold outright.
- Book value can also mean the value of an individual asset as it appears on a balance sheet, in which case it is equal to the cost of the asset minus any accumulated depreciation.
- Though often considered a realistic appraisal, book value can still contain unrealistic figures. For example, a building might be fully depreciated and have no official asset value but could still be sold for millions, or four-year-old computer equipment that is not fully depreciated might have asset value but no market value, given its age and advances in technology.

FOR MORE INFORMATION

Web site:
investopedia.com: **www.investopedia.com/dictionary**

See also:
 Accounting (pp. 1667–1669)

Calculating Contribution Margin

WHAT IT MEASURES
The amounts that individual products or services ultimately contribute to net profit.

WHY IT IS IMPORTANT
Contribution margin helps a business to decide how it should direct or redirect its resources.

When managers know the contribution margin—or margins, as is more often the case—they can make better decisions about adding or subtracting product lines, investing in existing products, pricing products or services (particularly in response to competitors' actions), structuring sales commissions and bonuses, where to direct marketing and advertising expenditures, and where to apply individual talents and expertise.

In short, contribution margin is a valuable decision-support tool.

HOW IT WORKS IN PRACTICE
Its calculation is straightforward:

sales price – variable cost = contribution margin

Or, for providers of services:

total revenue – total variable cost = contribution margin

For example, if the sales price of a good is $500 and variable cost is $350, the contribution margin is $150, or 30% of sales.

This means that 30 cents of every sales dollar remain to contribute to fixed costs and to profit, after the costs directly related to the sales are subtracted.

Contribution margin is especially useful to a company comparing different products or services (see the example below).

Obviously, Product C has the highest contribution percentage, even though Product A generates more total

	Product A $	Product B $	Product C $
Sales	260	220	140
Variable costs	178	148	65
Contribution margin	82	72	75
Contribution margin (%)	31.5	32.7	53.6

profit. The analysis suggests that the company might do well to aim to achieve a sales mix with a higher proportion of Product C. It further suggests that prices for Products A and B may be too low, or that their cost structures need attention. Notably, none of this information appears on a standard income statement.

Contribution margin can also be tracked over a long period of time, using data from several years of income statements. It can also be invaluable in calculating volume discounts for preferred customers, and break-even sales or volume levels.

TRICKS OF THE TRADE
- Contribution margin depends on accurately accounting for all variable costs, including shipping and delivery, or the indirect costs of services. Activity-based cost accounting systems aid this kind of analysis.
- Variable costs include all direct costs (e.g. labor and materials).
- Contribution margin analysis is only one tool to use. It will not show so-called loss leaders, for example. And it doesn't consider marketing factors like existing penetration levels, opportunities, or mature markets being eroded by emerging markets.

FOR MORE INFORMATION

Web site:
Business Owner's Toolkit: **www.toolkit.cch.com**

989

ACTIONLIST

Calculating Conversion Price

990

ACTIONLIST

WHAT IT MEASURES

The price per share at which the holder of convertible bonds, or debentures, or preferred stock, can convert them into shares of common stock.

Depending on specific terms, the conversion price may be set when the convertible asset is issued.

WHY IT IS IMPORTANT

The conversion price is a key factor in an investment strategy. Knowing it helps investors to determine whether or not it is to their advantage to convert their holdings into shares of stock, sell them on the open market, or retain them until they mature or are called by the issuing company.

At the same time, existing stockholders of the issuing company need to know the point at which the value of their shares could be diluted by the creation of additional shares without the concurrent creation of additional capital.

For companies themselves, a conversion price represents an additional financing option: an opportunity to convert debt into equity, an action that itself has advantages and drawbacks.

HOW IT WORKS IN PRACTICE

If the conversion price is set, it will appear in the indenture, a legal agreement between the issuer of a convertible asset and the holder, that states specific terms. If the conversion price does not appear in the agreement, a conversion ratio is used to calculate the conversion price.

A conversion ratio of 25:1, for example, means that 25 shares of stock can be obtained in exchange for each $1,000 convertible asset held. In turn, the conversion price can be determined simply by dividing $1,000 by 25:

$1,000 / 25 = $40 per share

Comparison of a stock's conversion price to its prevailing market price can help to decide the best course of action. If the stock of the company in question is trading at $52 per share, converting makes sense, because it increases the value of $1,000 convertible to $1,300 ($52 × 25 shares). But if the stock is trading at $32 per share, then conversion value is only $800 ($32 × 25) and it is clearly better to defer conversion.

TRICKS OF THE TRADE

- Conversion ratios may change over time, according to the terms of the agreement. This is to ensure that a convertible asset holder is not unduly advantaged and that the value of existing stock is not diluted—which, of course, would anger existing stockholders.
- Stockholders, in turn, need to monitor closely a company that decides to issue a large number of convertible assets, since the value of their shares could ultimately be undermined.
- Convertible bonds closely follow the price of the issuing company's underlying stock. Often, in fact, the respective prices of the bond and the shares to be exchanged are almost equal.

FOR MORE INFORMATION

Web site:
investopedia.com: **www.investopedia.com**

See also:
✔ Calculating Conversion Ratio (p. 991)

"We haven't got the money, so we've got to think."

Ernest Rutherford

Calculating Conversion Ratio

WHAT IT MEASURES

The number of shares of common stock an investor will receive upon converting a convertible security—a bond, debenture, or preferred stock.

The conversion price may be set when the convertible security is issued, depending on its terms.

WHY IT IS IMPORTANT

Like conversion price, the conversion ratio is an investment strategy tool, which is used to determine what the value of a convertible security would be if it were converted immediately. By knowing a convertible's value, an investor can compare it with the prevailing price of the issuing company's common stock and decide whether it is best to convert or to continue holding the convertible.

By the same token, holders of common stock in the company issuing the convertible can use the conversion ratio to help to monitor the value of their stock. For example, a relatively high ratio could mean that the value of their shares would be diluted if large numbers of convertible holders were to exercise their options.

HOW IT WORKS IN PRACTICE

In the same way as conversion price, the conversion ratio may be established when the convertible is issued. If that is the case, the ratio will appear in the indenture, the binding agreement that details the convertible's terms.

If the conversion ratio is not set, it can be calculated quickly: divide the par value of the convertible security (typically $1,000) by its conversion price.

$1,000 / $40 per share = 25

In this example, the conversion ratio is 25:1, which means that every bond held with a $1,000 par value can be exchanged for 25 shares of common stock.

Knowing the conversion ratio enables an investor to decide quickly whether his convertibles (or group of them) are more valuable than the shares of common stock they represent. If the stock is currently trading at 30, the conversion value is $750, or $250 less than the par value of the convertible. It would therefore be unwise to convert.

TRICKS OF THE TRADE

- Although it is rare, a convertible's indenture can sometimes contain a provision stating that the conversion ratio will change over the years.
- A conversion ratio that is set when a convertible is issued usually protects against any dilution from stock splits. However, it does not protect against a company issuing secondary offerings of common stock.
- "Forced conversion" means that the company can make holders convert into stock at virtually any time. Convertible holders should also pay close attention to the price at which the bonds are callable.
- Conversion ratio also describes the number of shares of one common stock to be issued for each outstanding share of another common stock when a merger takes place.

FOR MORE INFORMATION

Web site:
investopedia.com: **www.investopedia.com**

See also:
✔ Calculating Conversion Price (p. 990)

"Capitalism is using its money; we socialists throw it away."   Fidel Castro

Calculating Days Sales Outstanding

WHAT IT MEASURES

A company's average collection period, or the average number of days it takes a company to convert its accounts receivable into cash. Commonly referred to as DSO, it is also called the collection ratio.

WHY IT IS IMPORTANT

Knowing how long it takes a company to turn accounts receivable into cash is an important financial indicator. It indicates the efficiency of the company's internal collection, suggests how well a company's customers are accepting its credit terms (net 30 days, for example), and is a figure that is routinely compared with industry averages.

Ideally, DSOs should be decreasing or constant. A low figure means the company collects its outstanding receivables quickly. Typically, DSO is reviewed quarterly or yearly (91 or 365 days).

DSO also helps to expose companies that try to disguise weak sales. Large increases in DSO suggest that a company is trying to force sales either by accepting poor receivable terms or selling products at discount to book more sales for a particular period. An improving DSO suggests that a company is striving to make its operations more efficient.

Any company with a significant change in its DSO merits examination in greater detail.

HOW IT WORKS IN PRACTICE

Regular DSO requires three figures: total accounts receivable, total credit sales for the period analyzed, and the number of days in the period (annual, 365; six months, 182; quarter, 91). The formula is:

accounts receivable / total credit sales for the period × number of days in the period = days sales outstanding

For example: if total receivables are $4,500,000, total credit sales in a quarter are $9,000,000, and number of days is 91, then:

4,500,000 / 9,000,000 × 91 = 45.5

Thus, it takes an average of 45.5 days to collect receivables.

TRICKS OF THE TRADE

- Companies use DSO information with an accounts receivable aging report. This lists four categories of receivables: 0–30 days, 30–60 days, 60–90 days, and over 90 days. The report also shows the percentage of total accounts receivable that each group represents, allowing for an analysis of delinquencies and potential bad debts—a figure that appears on a profit and loss account.
- A rarely used related calculation, best possible DSO, shows how long it takes a company to collect current receivables. Its formula is:

  current receivables / total credit sales for the period × the number of days in the period = best possible DSO

  So, current receivables of $3,000,000 and total credit sales of $9,000,000 in a 91-day period would result in a best possible DSO of 30.3 days (3,000,000 / 9,000,000 × 91).
- Only credit sales of merchandise should be used in calculating DSO; cash sales are excluded, as are sales of such items as fixtures, equipment, or real estate.
- Properly evaluating an acceptable DSO requires a standard for comparison. A traditional rule of thumb is that DSO should not exceed one-third to one-half of selling terms. For instance, if terms are 30 days, acceptable DSO would be 40 to 45 days.
- A single DSO is only a snapshot. A fuller picture would require at least quarterly calculations, and some companies review DSO monthly.
- DSO can vary widely by industry as well as company. For example, clothing wholesalers have to have the goods on retailers' shelves for months before they will be sold and the retailer is able to cover invoices. However, a computer wholesaler with a lengthy DSO suggests trouble, since computers become obsolete quickly.

FOR MORE INFORMATION

Web site:
Dun & Bradstreet: **www.dnbcollections.com/kdso.htm**

See also:
Accounting (pp. 1667–1669)

Calculating Debt-to-Capital Ratio

WHAT IT MEASURES
The percentage of total funding represented by debt.

WHY IT IS IMPORTANT
By comparing a company's long-term liabilities to its total capital, the debt-to-capital ratio provides a review of the extent to which a company relies on external debt financing for its funding and is a measure of the risk to its stockholders.

The debt-to-capital ratio is also a measure of a company's borrowing capacity, and of its ability to pay scheduled financial payments on term debts and capital leases. Bond-rating agencies and analysts use it routinely to assess creditworthiness. The greater the debt, the higher the risk.

However, it can be misleading to assume that the lowest ratio is automatically the best ratio. A company may assume large amounts of debt in order to expand the business. Utilities, for instance, have high capital requirements, so their debt-to-capital ratios will be high as a matter of course. So are those of manufacturing companies, especially those developing a new technology or new product.

At the same time, the higher the level of debt, the more important it is for a company to have positive earnings and steady cash flow.

HOW IT WORKS IN PRACTICE
Although there are variations on exactly what goes into this ratio, the most common method is to divide total long-term debt by total assets (total long-term debt plus stockholders' funds), or

$$\frac{\text{total liabilities}}{\text{total assets}} = \text{debt-to-capital ratio}$$

For example, if the balance sheet of a corporate annual report lists total liabilities of $9,800,000 and total stock-holders' equity of $12,800,000, the debt-to-capital ratio is (calculating in thousands):

> **9,800 / (9,800 + 12,800)**
> **= 9,800 / 22,600**
> **= 0.434, or 43.4% debt-to-capital ratio**

Some formulas distinguish different portions of long-term debt. However, that complicates calculations and many experts regard it as unnecessary. It is also common to express the formula as total debt divided by total funds, which produces the same outcome.

TRICKS OF THE TRADE
- If a company has minority interests in subsidiaries that are consolidated in the balance sheet, they must be added to stockholders' equity.
- Debt calculations should include capital leases.
- One rule of thumb holds that a debt-to-capital ratio of 60% or less is acceptable, but another holds that 40% is the most desirable.
- A high debt-to-capital ratio means less security for stockholders, because debt holders are paid first in bankruptcies. It still can be tolerable, however, if a company's return on assets exceeds the rate of interest paid to creditors.
- Do not confuse the debt-to-capital ratio with debt-to-capitalization, which compares debt with total market capitalization and fluctuates as the company's stock price changes.

FOR MORE INFORMATION

Web site:
www.multimedia.calpoly.edu explains debt-to-capital ratio concisely.

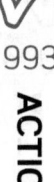
"The debt is like a crazy aunt we keep down in the basement. All the neighbors know she's there, but nobody wants to talk about her."
H. Ross Perot

Calculating Creditor and Debtor Days

994

ACTIONLIST

WHAT THEY MEASURE

Creditor days is a measure of the number of days on average that a company requires to pay its creditors, while debtor days is a measure of the number of days on average that it takes a company to receive payment for what it sells. It is also called accounts receivable days.

WHY THEY ARE IMPORTANT

Creditor days is an indication of a company's creditworthiness in the eyes of its suppliers and creditors, since it shows how long they are willing to wait for payment. Within reason, the higher the number the better, because all companies want to conserve cash. At the same time, a company that is especially slow to pay its bills (100 or more days, for example) may be a company having trouble generating cash, or one trying to finance its operations with its suppliers' funds. Ultimately, companies whose creditor days soar have trouble obtaining supplies.

Debtor days is an indication of a company's efficiency in collecting monies owed. In this case, obviously, the lower the number the better. An especially high number is a telltale sign of inefficiency or worse. It may indicate bad debts, dubious sales figures, or a company being bullied by large customers out to improve their own cash position at another company's expense. Customers whose credit terms are abused also risk higher borrowing costs and related charges.

Changes in both measures are easy to spot, and easy to understand.

HOW THEY WORK IN PRACTICE

To determine creditor days, divide the cumulative amount of unpaid suppliers' bills (also called trade creditors) by sales, then multiply by 365. So the formula is:

(trade creditors / sales) × 365 = creditor days

For example, if suppliers' bills total $800,000 and sales are $9,000,000, the calculation is:

(800,000 / 9,000,000) × 365 = 32.44 days

The company takes 32.44 days on average to pay its bills.

To determine debtor days, divide the cumulative amount of accounts receivable by sales, then multiply by 365. For example, if accounts receivable total $600,000 and sales are $9,000,000, the calculation is:

(600,000 / 9,000,000) × 365 = 24.33 days

The company takes 24.33 days on average to collect its debts.

TRICKS OF THE TRADE

- Cash businesses, including most retailers, should have a much lower debtor days figure than noncash businesses, since they receive payment when they sell the goods. A typical target for noncash businesses is 40–50 days.
- An abnormally high creditor days figure may not only suggest a cash crisis, but also the management's difficulty in maintaining revolving credit agreements.
- An increasing number of debtor days also suggests overly generous credit terms (to bolster sales) or problems with product quality.

FOR MORE INFORMATION

Web site:
Global Investor: **www.finance-glossary.com**

See also:
⅏ Accounting (pp. 1667–1669)

"The Rich aren't like us—they pay less taxes."   Peter De Vries

Calculating Debt-to-Equity Ratio

WHAT IT MEASURES

How much money a company owes compared with how much money it has invested in it by principal owners and stockholders.

WHY IT IS IMPORTANT

The debt-to-equity ratio reveals the proportion of debt and equity a company is using to finance its business. It also measures a company's borrowing capacity. The higher the ratio, the greater the proportion of debt—but also the greater the risk.

Some even describe the debt-to-equity ratio as "a great financial test" of long-term corporate health, because debt establishes a commitment to repay money throughout a period of time, even though there is no assurance that sufficient cash will be generated to meet that commitment.

Creditors and lenders, understandably, rely heavily on the ratio to evaluate borrowers.

HOW IT WORKS IN PRACTICE

The debt-to-equity ratio is calculated by dividing debt by owners' equity, where equity is, typically, the figure stated for the preceding calendar or fiscal year. Debt, however, can be defined either as long-term debt only, or as total liabilities, which includes both long- and short-term debt. The most common formula for the ratio is:

$$\frac{\text{total liabilities}}{\text{owners' equity}} = \text{debt-to-equity ratio}$$

In our example, a company's long-term debt is $8,000,000, its short-term debt is $4,000,000, and owners' equity totals $9,000,000. The debt-to-equity ratio would therefore be (calculating in thousands):

(8,000 + 4,000) / 9,000

= 12,000 / 9,000

= 1.33 debt-to-equity ratio

An alternative debt-to-equity formula considers only long-term liabilities in the equation. Accordingly:

8,000 / 9,000 = 0.889 debt-to-equity ratio

There is also a third method, which is the reciprocal of the debt-to-capital ratio; its formula is:

$$\frac{\text{owners' equity}}{\text{total funds}} = \text{debt-to-equity ratio}$$

However, this would be more accurately defined as "equity-to-debt ratio."

TRICKS OF THE TRADE

- It is important to understand exactly how debt is defined in the ratio presented.
- Like all ratios, debt-to-equity must be evaluated against those of other companies in a given industry and over a period of time.
- When calculating the ratio, some prefer to use the market value of debt and equity rather than the book value, since book value often understates current value.
- For this ratio, a low number indicates better financial stability than a high one does; if the ratio is high, a company could be at risk, especially if interest rates are rising.
- A ratio greater than one means assets are mainly financed with debt; less than one means equity provides most of the financing. Since a higher ratio generally means that a company has been aggressive in financing its growth with debt, volatile earnings can result owing to the additional cost of interest.
- Debt-to-equity ratio is somewhat industry-specific, and often depends on the amount of capital investment required.

FOR MORE INFORMATION

Web site:
www.connex.bdc.ca.eng.ratio_dette.htm defines the ratio, and features a worksheet that guides its computation.

Calculating Efficiency and Operating Ratios

WHAT IT MEASURES

The portion of operating revenues or fee income spent on overhead expenses.

WHY IT IS IMPORTANT

Often identified with banking and financial sectors, the efficiency ratio indicates a management's ability to keep overhead costs low. This measurement is also used by mature industries, such as steel manufacture, chemicals, or auto production, that must focus on tight cost controls to boost profitability because growth prospects are generally modest.

In some industries, the efficiency ratio is called the overhead burden: overhead as a percentage of sales.

A different method measures efficiency simply by tracking three other measures: accounts payable to sales, days sales outstanding, and inventory turnover, which indicates how fast a company is able to move its merchandise. A general guide is that if the first two of these measures are low and third is high, efficiency is probably high; the reverse is likewise true.

HOW IT WORKS IN PRACTICE

The efficiency ratio is defined as operating overhead expenses divided by fee income plus tax equivalent net interest income. If operating expenses are $100,000, and revenues (as defined) are $230,000, then:

$$100,000 / 230,000 = 0.43 \text{ efficiency ratio}$$

However, not everyone calculates the ratio in the same way. Some institutions include all non-interest expenses, while others exclude certain charges and intangible asset amortization.

To find the inventory turnover ratio, divide total sales by total inventory. If net sales are $300,000 and inventory is $100,000, then:

$$\frac{300,000}{140,000} = 2.14 \text{ inventory turnover ratio}$$

To find the accounts payable to sales ratio, divide a company's accounts payable by its annual net sales. A high ratio suggests that a company is using its suppliers' funds as a source of cheap financing because it is not operating efficiently enough to generate its own funds. If accounts payable are $50,000 and total sales are $300,000, then:

$$42,000 / 300,000$$
$$= 0.14 \times 100$$
$$= 14\% \text{ accounts payable to sales ratio}$$

TRICKS OF THE TRADE

- Identifying "overhead" to calculate the efficiency ratio can itself contribute to overall inefficiency. Some financial experts contend that efficiency can be measured equally well by reviewing earnings per share growth and return on equity.
- Some banks identify amortization of goodwill expense, and pull it out of their non-interest expense in order to calculate what is called the cash efficiency ratio: non-interest expense minus goodwill amortization expense divided into revenue.
- In banking, an acceptable efficiency ratio was once in the low 60s. Now the goal is 50, while better-performing banks boast ratios in the mid 40s. Low ratings usually indicate a higher return on equity and earnings.

FOR MORE INFORMATION

Web site:
bizval.com:
www.bizval.com/publications/articlelibrary/
Default.htm

Calculating Payback Period

WHAT IT MEASURES

How long it will take to earn back the money invested in a project.

WHY IT IS IMPORTANT

The straight payback period method is the simplest way of determining the investment potential of a major project. Expressed in time, it tells a management how many months or years it will take to recover the original cash cost of the project—always a vital consideration, and especially so for managements evaluating several projects at once.

This evaluation becomes even more important if it includes an examination of what the present value of future revenues will be.

HOW IT WORKS IN PRACTICE

The straight payback period formula is:

$$\frac{\text{cost of project}}{\text{annual cash revenues}} = \text{payback period}$$

Thus, if a project cost $100,000 and was expected to generate $28,000 annually, the payback period would be:

100,000 / 28,000 = 3.57 years

If the revenues generated by the project are expected to vary from year to year, add the revenues expected for each succeeding year until you arrive at the total cost of the project.

For example, say the revenues expected to be generated by the $100,000 project are:

	Revenue	Total
Year 1	$19,000	$19,000
Year 2	$25,000	$44,000
Year 3	$30,000	$74,000
Year 4	$30,000	$104,000
Year 5	$30,000	$134,000

Thus, the project would be fully paid for in Year 4, since it is in that year the total revenue reaches the initial cost of $100,000.

The picture becomes complex when the time value of money principle is introduced into the calculations. Some experts insist this is essential to determine the most accurate payback period. Accordingly, present value tables or computers (now the norm) must be used, and the annual revenues have to be discounted by the applicable interest rate, 10% in this example. Doing so produces significantly different results:

	Revenue	Present value	Total
Year 1	$19,000	$17,271	$17,271
Year 2	$25,000	$20,650	$37,921
Year 3	$30,000	$22,530	$60,451
Year 4	$30,000	$20,490	$80,941
Year 5	$30,000	$18,630	$99,571

This method shows that payback would not occur even after five years.

TRICKS OF THE TRADE

- Clearly, a main defect of the straight payback period method is that it ignores the time value of money principle, which, in turn, can produce unrealistic expectations.
- A second drawback is that it ignores any benefits generated after the payback period, and thus a project that would return $1 million after, say, six years, might be ranked lower than a project with a three-year payback that returns only $100,000 thereafter.
- Another alternative to calculating by payback period is to develop an internal rate of return.
- Under most analyses, projects with shorter payback periods rank higher than those with longer paybacks, even if the latter project higher returns. Longer paybacks can be affected by such factors as market changes, changes in interest rates, and economic shifts. Shorter cash paybacks also enable companies to recoup an investment sooner and put it to work elsewhere.
- Generally, a payback period of three years or less is desirable; if a project's payback period is less than a year, some contend it should be judged essential.

FOR MORE INFORMATION

Web site:
Business Owner's Toolkit: **www.toolkit.cch.com**

See also:

"Greed is even more contagious than fear."   Bud Hadfield

Calculating Elasticity

WHAT IT MEASURES

The percentage change of one variable caused by a percentage change in another variable.

WHY IT IS IMPORTANT

Elasticity is defined as "the measure of the sensitivity of one variable to another." In practical terms, elasticity indicates the degree to which consumers respond to changes in price. It is obviously important for companies to consider such relationships when contemplating changes in price, demand, and supply.

Demand elasticity measures how much the quantity demanded changes when the price of a product or service is increased or lowered. Will demand remain constant? If not, how much will demand change?

Supply elasticity measures the impact on supply when a price is changed. It is assumed that lowering prices will reduce supply, because demand will increase—but by how much?

HOW IT WORKS IN PRACTICE

The general formula for elasticity is:

$$\text{elasticity} = \% \text{ change in } \times\ /\ \% \text{ change in y}$$

In theory, $\times$ and y can be any variable. However, the most common application measures price and demand. If the price of a product is increased from \$20 to \$25, or 25%, and demand in turn falls from 6,000 to 3,000, elasticity would be calculated as:

$$-50\%\ /\ 25\% = -2$$

A value greater than ± 1 means that demand is strongly sensitive to price, while a value of less than 1 means that demand is not price-sensitive.

TRICKS OF THE TRADE

There are five cases of elasticity:

- E = 1, or *unit elasticity*. The proportional change in one variable is equal to the proportional change in another variable: if price rises by 5%, demand falls by 5%.
- E is greater than 1, or just *elastic*. The proportional change in x is greater than the proportional change in y: if price rises by 5%, demand falls by 3%.
- E = infinity, or *perfectly elastic*. This is a special case of elasticity: any change in y will effect no change in x. An example would be prices charged by a hospital's emergency room, where increases in price are unlikely to curb demand.
- E is less than 1, or just *inelastic*. The proportional change in x is less than the proportional change in y: if prices are increased by 3%, demand will fall by 30%.
- E = 0, or *perfectly inelastic*. This is another special case of elasticity: any change in y will have an infinite effect on x.

There are more complex formulae for determining a range of variables, or "arc elasticity."

Elasticity can be used to affirm two rules of thumb:

- demand becomes elastic if consumers have an alternative or adequate substitute for the product or service;
- demand is more elastic if consumers have an incentive to save money.

FOR MORE INFORMATION

Web site:
Investopedia.com: **www.investopedia.com**

See also:
🖱 Accounting (pp. 1667–1669)

Calculating Expected Rate of Return

WHAT IT MEASURES

The projected percentage return on an investment, based on the weighted probability of all possible rates of return.

WHY IT IS IMPORTANT

No self-respecting businessperson or organization should make an investment without first having some understanding of how successful that investment is likely to be. Expected rate of return provides such an understanding, within certain limits.

HOW IT WORKS IN PRACTICE

The formula for expected rate of return is:

$E[r] = \Sigma_s P(s) r_s$

where $E[r]$ is the expected return, $P(s)$ is the probability that the rate r_s occurs, and r_s is the return at s level.

A simple example, as given below, is far easier to grasp, and adequately illustrates the principle which the formula expresses. It will also probably be of more practical use to most of those who need to calculate ERR.

The current price of ABC, Inc. stock is $10. At the end of the year, ABC shares of stock are projected to be traded:

- 25% higher if economic growth exceeds expectations—a probability of 30%;
- 12% higher if economic growth equals expectations—a probability of 50%;
- 5% lower if economic growth falls short of expectations—a probability of 20%.

To find the expected rate of return, simply multiply the percentages by their respective probabilities and add the results:

$$(30\% \times 25\%) + (50\% \times 12\%) + (25\% \times -5\%) =$$
$$7.5 + 6 + -1.25 = 12.25\% \text{ ERR}$$

A second example:

- if economic growth remains robust (a 20% probability), investments will return 25%;
- if economic growth ebbs, but still performs adequately (a 40% probability), investments will return 15%;
- if economic growth slows significantly (a 30% probability), investments will return 5%;
- if the economy declines outright (a 10% probability), investments will return 0%.

Therefore:

$$(20\% \times 25\%) + (40\% \times 15\%) + (30\% \times 5\%) +$$
$$(10\% \times 0\%) =$$
$$5\% + 6\% + 1.5\% + 0\% = 12.5\% \text{ ERR}$$

Another method that can be used to project expected return is the Capital Asset Pricing Model (CAPM), which is explained separately.

TRICKS OF THE TRADE

- The probability totals must always equal 100% for the calculation to be valid.
- Be sure not to overlook any negative numbers in the calculations, or the results produced will be incorrect.
- An ERR calculation is only as good as the scenarios considered. Wildly unrealistic scenarios will produce an equally unreliable expected rate of return.

FOR MORE INFORMATION

Web site:
investopedia.com **www.investopedia.com**

"Buy stocks like you buy your groceries, not like you buy your perfume." — Warren Buffett

Calculating Future Value

WHAT IT MEASURES
Any amount of any currency.

WHY IT IS IMPORTANT
Future value is a fundamental of investment. Understanding it helps any organization or individual to determine how a sum will be affected by changes in inflation, interest rates, or currency values. Inflation, for instance, will always reduce a sum's value. Interest rates will always increase it. Exchanging the sum for an identical amount in another currency will increase or decrease it, depending on how the respective currencies perform on the world market.

Armed with this knowledge, an organization can make more informed decisions about how to generate the maximum value from its funds in a given period of time: Would it be best to deposit them in simple interest-bearing accounts, exchange them for funds in another currency, use them to expand operations, or use them to acquire another company?

HOW IT WORKS IN PRACTICE
Start with three figures: the sum in question, the percentage by which it will increase or decrease, and the period of time. In this case: $1,000, 11%, and two years.

At an interest rate of 11%, our $1,000 will grow to $1,232 in two years:

$$\textbf{\$1,000} \times \textbf{1.11} = \textbf{\$1,110} \text{ (first year)} \times \textbf{1.11} = $$
$$\textbf{\$1,232} \text{ (second year, rounded to whole dollars)}$$

Note that the interest earned in the first year generates additional interest in the second year, a practice known as compounding. When large sums are in question, the effect of compounding can be significant.

At an inflation rate of 11%, by comparison, our $1,000 will shrink to $812 in two years:

$$\textbf{\$1,000} / \textbf{1.11} = \textbf{\$901} \text{ (first year)} / \textbf{1.11} = $$
$$\textbf{\$812} \text{ (second year, rounded to whole dollars)}$$

TRICKS OF THE TRADE
- Express the percentage as 1.11 and multiply and divide by that figure, instead of using 11%. Otherwise, errors will occur.
- Calculate each year, quarter, or month separately, as our example illustrates.
- It is important always to use the **annual** rates of interest and inflation.
- A more useful tool is "present value," which estimates what future value cash flows would be worth if they occurred today.

Calculating Internal Rate of Return

WHAT IT MEASURES
Technically, the interest rate that makes the present value of an investment's projected cash flows equal to the cost of the project; practically speaking, the rate that indicates whether or not an investment is worth pursuing.

WHY IT IS IMPORTANT
The calculation of internal rate of return (IRR) is used to appraise the prospective viability of investments and capital projects. It is also called dollar-weighted rate of return.

Essentially, IRR allows an investor to find the interest rate that is equivalent to the monetary returns expected from the project. Once that rate is determined, it can be compared to the rates that could be earned by investing the money elsewhere, or to the weighted cost of capital. IRR also accounts for the time value of money.

HOW IT WORKS IN PRACTICE
How is IRR applied? Assume, for example, that a project under consideration costs $7,500 and is expected to return $2,000 per year for five years, or $10,000. The IRR calculated for the project would be about 10%. If the cost of borrowing money for the project, or the return on investing the funds elsewhere, is less than 10%, the project is probably worthwhile. If the alternate use of the money will return 10% or more, the project should be rejected, since from a financial perspective it will break even at best.

Typically, management requires an IRR equal to or higher than the cost of capital, depending on relative risk and other factors.

The best way to compute an IRR is by using a spreadsheet (such as Excel) or financial calculator, which do it automatically, although it is crucial to understand how the calculation should be structured. Calculating IRR by hand is tedious and time-consuming, and requires the process to be repeated to run sensitivities.

If using Excel, for example, select the IRR function.

This requires the annual cash flows to be set out in columns and the first part of the IRR formula requires the cell reference range of these cash flows to be entered. Then a guess of the IRR is required. The default is 10%, written 0.1.

If a project has the following expected cash flows, then guessing IRR at 30% returns an accurate IRR of 27%, indicating that if the next best way of investing the money gives a return of –20%, the project should go ahead.

Now	-2,500
Year 1	1,200
Year 2	1,300
Year 3	1,500

TRICKS OF THE TRADE
- IRR analysis is generally used to evaluate a project's cash flows rather than income, because, unlike income, cash flows do not reflect depreciation and therefore are usually more instructive to appraise.
- Most basic spreadsheet functions apply to cash flows only.
- As well as advocates, IRR has critics who dismiss it as misleading, especially as significant costs will occur late in the project. The rule of thumb "the higher the IRR the better" does not always apply.
- For the most thorough analysis of a project's investment potential, some experts urge using both IRR and net present value calculations, and comparing their results.

FOR MORE INFORMATION

Web site:
http://hadm.sph.sc.edu/COURSES/ECON/irr/irr.html
is a thorough and well-written tutorial on IRR.

1001

ACTIONLIST

"It is not wisdom to lose the capital for the sake of the interest."   Tiruvalluvar

Calculating Marginal Cost

WHAT IT MEASURES

The additional cost of producing one more unit of product, or providing service to one more customer.

WHY IT IS IMPORTANT

Sometimes called incremental cost, marginal cost shows how much costs increase from making or serving one more, an essential factor when contemplating a production increase, or seeking to serve more customers.

If the price charged is greater than the marginal cost, then the revenue gain will be greater than the added cost. That, in turn, will increase profit, so the expansion in production or service makes economic sense and should proceed. Of course, the reverse is also true: If the price charged is less than the marginal cost, expansion should not go ahead.

HOW IT WORKS IN PRACTICE

The formula for marginal cost is:

change in cost / change in quantity

If it costs a company $260,000 to produce 3,000 items, and $325,000 to produce 3,800 items, the change in cost would be:

$325,000 – $260,000 = $65,000

The change in quantity would be:

3,800 – 3,000 = 800

When the formula to calculate marginal cost is applied, the result is:

$65,000 / 800 = $81.25

If the price of the item in question were $99.95, expansion should proceed.

TRICKS OF THE TRADE

- A marginal cost that is lower than the price shows that it is not always necessary to cut prices to sell more goods and boost profits.
- Using idle capacity to produce lower-margin items can still be beneficial, because these generate revenues that help cover fixed costs.
- Marginal cost studies can become quite complicated, because the basic formula does not always take into account variables that can affect cost and quantity. There are software programs available, many of which are industry-specific.
- At some point, marginal cost invariably begins to rise; typically, labor becomes less productive as a production run increases, while the time required also increases.
- Marginal cost alone may not justify expansion. It is best to determine also average costs, then chart the respective series of figures to find where marginal cost meets average cost, and thus determine optimum cost.
- Relying on marginal cost is not fail-safe; putting more product on a market can drive down prices and thus cut margins. Moreover, committing idle capacity to long-term production may tie up resources that could be directed to a new and more profitable opportunity.
- An important related principle is contribution: the cash gained (or lost) from selling an additional unit.

FOR MORE INFORMATION

Web site:
The Motley Fool: **www.fool.com**

See also:
🔖 Accounting (pp. 1667–1669)

Calculating Net Present Value

WHAT IT MEASURES

The projected profitability of an investment, based on anticipated cash flows and discounted at a stated rate of interest.

WHY IT IS IMPORTANT

Net present value (NPV) helps management or potential investors weigh the wisdom of an investment—in new equipment, a new facility, or other type of asset—by enabling them to quantify the expected benefits. Those evaluating more than one potential investment can compare the respective projected returns to find the most attractive project.

A positive NPV indicates that the project should be profitable, assuming that the estimated cash flows are reasonably accurate. A negative NPV, of course, indicates that the project will probably be unprofitable and therefore should be adjusted, if not abandoned altogether.

Equally significantly, NPV enables a management to consider the time value of money it will invest. This concept holds that the value of money increases with time because it can always earn interest in a savings account. Therefore, any other investment of that money must be weighed against how the funds would perform if simply deposited and saved.

When the time value of money concept is incorporated in the calculation of NPV, the value of a project's future net cash receipts in "today's money" can be determined. This enables proper comparisons between different projects.

HOW IT WORKS IN PRACTICE

Let's say that Global Manufacturing, Inc. is considering the acquisition of a new machine. First, its management would consider all the factors: initial purchase and installation costs; additional revenues generated by sales of the new machine's products, plus the taxes on these new revenues. Having accounted for these factors in its calculations, the cash flows that Global Manufacturing projects will generate from the new machine are:

Year 1:	-100,000 (initial cost of investment)
Year 2:	30,000
Year 3:	40,000
Year 4:	40,000
Year 5:	35,000
Net Total:	145,000

At first glance, it appears that cash flows total a whopping 45% more than the $100,000 initial cost, a strikingly sound investment indeed.

Alas, it's not that simple. Time value of money shrinks return on the project considerably, since future dollars are worth less than present dollars in hand. NPV accounts for these differences with the help of present value tables. These user-friendly tables, readily available on the Internet and in references, list the ratios that express the present value of expected cash flow dollars, based on the applicable interest rate and the number of years in question.

In our example, Global Manufacturing's cost of capital is 9%. Using this figure to find the corresponding ratios on the present value table, the $100,000 investment cost, expected annual revenues during the five years in question, the NPV calculation looks like this:

Year	Cash flow	Table factor (at 9%)	Present value
1	($100,000) ×	1.000000 =	($100,000)
2	$ 30,000 ×	0.917431 =	$27,522.93
3	$ 40,000 ×	0.841680 =	$33,667.20
4	$ 40,000 ×	0.772183 =	$30,887.32
5	$ 35,000 ×	0.708425 =	$24,794.88
	NPV =		$16,873.33

NPV is still positive. So, on this basis at least, the investment should proceed.

TRICKS OF THE TRADE

- Beware of assumptions. Interest rates change, of course, which can affect NPV dramatically. Moreover, fresh revenues (as well as new markets) may not grow as projected. If the cash flows in years 2–5 of our example fall by $5,000 a year, for instance, NPV shrinks to $5,260.89, which is still positive but less attractive.
- NPV calculations are performed only with cash receipts payments and discounting factors. In turn, NPV is a tool, not the tool. It ignores other accounting data, intangibles, sheer faith in a new idea, and other factors that may make an investment worth pursuing despite a negative NPV.
- It is important to determine a company's cost of capital accurately.

FOR MORE INFORMATION

Web site:
www.toolkit.cch.com has both tables and additional information about net present value.

"The natural counterpart of a free market economy is a politics of insecurity." John Gray

Calculating Rate of Return

WHAT IT MEASURES

The annual return on an investment, expressed as a percentage of the total amount invested. It also measures the yield of a fixed-income security.

WHY IT IS IMPORTANT

Rate of return is a simple and straightforward way to determine how much investors are being paid for the use of their money, so that they can then compare various investments and select the best—based, of course, on individual goals and acceptable levels of risk.

Rate of return has a second and equally vital purpose: as a common denominator that measures a company's financial performance, for example in terms of rate of return on assets, equity, or sales.

HOW IT WORKS IN PRACTICE

There is a basic formula that will serve most needs, at least initially:

[(current value of amount invested – original value of amount invested) / original value of amount invested] × 100% = rate of return

If $1,000 in capital is invested in stock, and one year later the investment yields $1,100, the rate of return of the investment is calculated like this:

[(1100 – 1000) / 1000)] × 100% = 100 / 1000 × 100% = 10% rate of return

Now, assume $1,000 is invested again. One year later, the investment grows to $2,000 in value, but after another year the value of the investment falls to $1,200. The rate of return after the first year is:

[(2000 – 1000) / 1000] × 100% = 100%

The rate of return after the second year is:

[(1200 – 2000) / 2000] × 100% = –40%

The average annual return for the two years (also known as average annual arithmetic return) can be calculated using this formula:

(rate of return for Year 1 + rate of return for Year 2) / 2 = average annual return

Accordingly:

(100% + –40%) / 2 = 30%

Be careful, however! The average annual rate of return is a percentage, but one that is accurate over only a short period, so this method should be used accordingly.

The geometric or compound rate of return is a better yardstick for measuring investments over the long run, and takes into account the effects of compounding. As one might expect, this formula is more complex and technical, and beyond the scope of this article.

TRICKS OF THE TRADE

- The real rate of return is the annual return realized on an investment, adjusted for changes in the price due to inflation. If 10% is earned on an investment but inflation is 2%, then the real rate of return is actually 8%.
- Do not confuse rate of return with internal rate of return, which is a more complex calculation.
- Some mutual fund managers have been known to report the average annual rate of return on the investments they manage. In the second example, that figure is 30%, yet the value of the investment is only $200 higher than it was two years ago, or 20%. So, read such reports carefully.

FOR MORE INFORMATION

Web site:
www.ricefinancial.com/calcs calculates rates of return required for an investment to reach a desired amount, based on amount invested and time.

Calculating Return on Sales

WHAT IT MEASURES

A company's operating profit or loss as a percentage of total sales for a given period, typically a year.

WHY IT IS IMPORTANT

Return on sales (ROS) shows how efficiently management uses the sales dollar, thus reflecting its ability to manage costs and overhead and operate efficiently. It also indicates a company's ability to withstand adverse conditions such as falling prices, rising costs, or declining sales. The higher the figure, the better a company is able to endure price wars and falling prices.

Return on sales can be useful in assessing the annual performances of cyclical companies that may have no earnings during particular months, and of companies whose business requires a huge capital investment and thus incurs substantial amounts of depreciation.

HOW IT WORKS IN PRACTICE

The calculation is very basic:

operating profit / total sales × 100 =
percentage return on sales

So, if a company earns $30 on sales of $400, its return on sales is:

30 / 400 = 0.075 × 100 = 7.5%

TRICKS OF THE TRADE

- While easy to grasp, return on sales has its limits, since it sheds no light on the overall cost of sales or the four factors that contribute to it: materials, labor, production overhead, and administrative and selling overhead.
- Some calculations use operating profit before subtracting interest and taxes; others use after-tax income. Either figure is acceptable as long as ROS comparisons are consistent. Obviously, using income before interest and taxes will produce a higher ratio.
- The ratio's operating profit figure may also include special allowances and extraordinary non-recurring items, which, in turn, can inflate the percentage and be misleading.
- The ratio varies widely by industry. The supermarket business, for example, is heavily dependent on volume and usually has a low return on sales.
- Return on sales remains of special importance to retail sales organizations, which can compare their respective ratios with those of competitors and industry norms.

FOR MORE INFORMATION

Web site:
Investopedia.com: **www.investopedia.com**

See also:
⌐ Accounting (pp. 1667–1669)

1005

ACTIONLIST

"The Lord gave us farmers two hands so we could grab as much as we could with both of them. "

Joseph Heller

Calculating Return on Assets

WHAT IT MEASURES

A company's profitability, expressed as a percentage of its total assets.

WHY IT IS IMPORTANT

Return on assets (ROA) measures how effectively a company has used the total assets at its disposal to generate earnings. Because the ROA formula reflects total revenue, total cost, and assets deployed, the ratio itself reflects a management's ability to generate income during the course of a given period, usually a year.

Naturally, the higher the return the better the profit performance. ROA is a convenient way of comparing a company's performance with that of its competitors, although the items on which the comparison is based may not always be identical.

HOW IT WORKS IN PRACTICE

To calculate ROA, divide a company's net income by its total assets, then multiply by 100 to express the figure as a percentage:

$$\textbf{net income / total assets} \times \textbf{100} = \textbf{ROA}$$

If net income is $30, and total assets are $420, the ROA is:

$$\textbf{30 / 420} = \textbf{0.0714} \times \textbf{100} = \textbf{7.14\%}$$

A variation of this formula can be used to calculate return on net assets (RONA):

$$\textbf{net income / fixed assets} + \textbf{working capital} = \textbf{RONA}$$

And, on occasion, the formula will separate after-tax interest expense from net income:

$$\textbf{net income} + \textbf{interest expense / total assets} = \textbf{ROA}$$

It is therefore important to understand what each component of the formula actually represents.

TRICKS OF THE TRADE

- Some experts recommend using the net income value at the end of the given period, and the assets value from beginning of the period or an average value taken over the complete period, rather than an end-of-the-period value; otherwise, the calculation will include assets that have accumulated during the year, which can be misleading.
- While a high ratio indicates a greater return, it must still be balanced against such factors as risk, sustainability, and reinvestment in the business through development costs. Some managements will sacrifice the long-term interests of investors in order to achieve an impressive ROA in the short term.
- A climbing return on assets usually indicates a climbing stock price, because it tells investors that a management is skilled at generating profits from the resources that a business owns.
- Acceptable ROAs vary by sector. In banking, for example, a ROA of 1% or better is a considered to be the standard benchmark of superior performance.
- ROA is an effective way of measuring the efficiency of manufacturers, but can be suspect when measuring service companies, or companies whose primary assets are people.
- Other variations of the ROA formula do exist.

FOR MORE INFORMATION

Web site:
MSN Money: **www.moneycentral.msn.com/investor**

See also:
- Accounting (pp. 1667–1669)
- Calculating Return on Shareholders' Equity (p. 1008)

"A stockbroker is someone who takes all your money and invests it until it's gone."

Woody Allen

Calculating Return on Investment

WHAT IT MEASURES

In the financial realm, the overall profit or loss on an investment expressed as a percentage of the total amount invested or total funds appearing on a company's balance sheet.

WHY IT IS IMPORTANT

Like return on assets or return on equity, return on investment (ROI) measures a company's profitability and its management's ability to generate profits from the funds investors have placed at its disposal.

One opinion holds that if a company's operations cannot generate net earnings at a rate that exceeds the cost of borrowing funds from financial markets, the future of that company is grim.

HOW IT WORKS IN PRACTICE

The most basic expression of ROI can be found by dividing a company's net profit (also called net earnings) by the total investment (total debt plus total equity), then multiplying by 100 to arrive at a percentage:

$$\text{net profit / total investment} \times 100 = \text{ROI}$$

If, say, net profit is $30 and total investment is $250, the ROI is:

$$30 / 250 = 0.12 \times 100 = 12\%$$

A more complex variation of ROI is an equation known as the Du Pont formula:

$$\text{(net profit after taxes / total assets)} = \text{(net profit after taxes / sales)} \times \text{sales / total assets}$$

If, for example, net profit after taxes is $30, total assets are $250, and sales are $500, then:

$$30 / 250 = 30 / 500 \times 500 / 250 =$$
$$12\% = 6\% \times 2 = 12\%$$

Champions of this formula, which was developed by the Du Pont Company in the 1920s, say that it helps to reveal how a company has both deployed its assets and controlled its costs, and how it can achieve the same percentage return in different ways.

For stockholders, the variation of the basic ROI formula used by investors is:

$$\text{net income + (current value – original value) /}$$
$$\text{original value} \times 100 = \text{ROI}$$

If, for example, somebody invests $5,000 in a company and a year later has earned $100 in dividends, while the value of the stock is $5,200, the return on investment would be:

$$100 + (5,200 – 5,000) / 5,000 \times 100$$
$$= (100 + 200) / 5,000 \times 100$$
$$= 300 / 5,000 = 0.06 \times 100 = 6\% \text{ ROI}$$

TRICKS OF THE TRADE

- Securities investors can use yet another ROI formula: net income divided by common stock and preferred stock equity plus long-term debt.
- It is vital to understand exactly what a return on investment measures, for example assets, equity, or sales. Without this understanding, comparisons may be misleading or suspect. A search for "return on investment" on the Web, for example, harvests everything from staff training to e-commerce to advertising and promotions!
- Be sure to establish whether the net profit figure used is before or after provision for taxes. This is important for making ROI comparisons accurate.

FOR MORE INFORMATION

Web site:
Investopedia.com: **www.investopedia.com**

See also:
Accounting (pp. 1667–1669)

"If you do anything just for the money you don't succeed." — Barry Hearn

Calculating Return on Shareholders' Equity

WHAT IT MEASURES

Profitability, specifically the percentage return that was delivered to a company's owners.

WHY IT IS IMPORTANT

ROE is a fundamental indication of a company's ability to increase its earnings per share and thus the quality of its stock, because it reveals how well a company is using its money to generate additional earnings.

It is a relatively straightforward benchmark, easy to calculate, and is applicable to a majority of industries. ROE allows investors to compare a company's use of their equity with other investments, and to compare the performance of companies in the same industry. ROE can also help to evaluate trends in a business.

Businesses that generate high returns on equity are businesses that pay off their stockholders handsomely and create substantial assets for each dollar invested.

HOW IT WORKS IN PRACTICE

To calculate ROE, divide the net income shown on the income statement (usually of the past year) by stockholders' equity, which appears on the balance sheet:

$$\text{net income / owners' equity} \times 100\% = \text{return on equity}$$

For example, if net income is $450 and equity is $2,500, then:

$$450 / 2,500 = 0.18 \times 100\% = 18\% \text{ return on equity}$$

TRICKS OF THE TRADE

- Because new variations of the ROE ratio do appear, it is important to know how the figure is calculated.
- Return on equity for most companies certainly should be in the double digits; investors often look for 15% or higher, while a return of 20% or more is considered excellent.
- Seasoned investors also review five-year average ROE, to gauge consistency.
- A word of caution: financial statements usually report assets at book value, which is the purchase price minus depreciation; they do not show replacement costs. A business with older assets should show higher rates of ROE than a business with newer assets.
- Examining ROE with return on assets can indicate if a company is debt-heavy. If a company owes very little debt, then it is reasonable to assume that its management is earning high profits and/or using assets effectively.
- A high ROE also could be due to leverage (a method of corporate funding in which a higher proportion of funds is raised through borrowing than stock issue). If liabilities are high the balance sheet will reveal it, hence the need to review it.

FOR MORE INFORMATION

Web site:
www.fool.com has an interesting discussion of ROE, analysis of ROE, and variations of its basic formula.

See also:
✔ Calculating Return on Assets (p. 1006)

Calculating the Alpha and Beta Values of a Security

WHAT THEY MEASURE
A security's performance, adjusted to risk, compared to overall market behavior.

WHY THEY ARE IMPORTANT
Just as coaches would expect their most accomplished athletes to perform at a higher level than others, investors expect more from higher-risk investments. Alpha and beta give investors a quick indication of just how risky a stock or fund is.

Alpha is defined as "the return a security or a portfolio would be expected to earn if the market's rate of return were zero."

Beta is a means of measuring the volatility (or risk) of a stock or fund in comparison with the market as a whole. The beta of a stock or fund can be of any value, positive or negative, but usually is between +0.25 and +1.75.

Alpha expresses the difference between the return expected from a stock or mutual fund, given its beta rating, and the return actually produced. A stock or fund that returns more than its beta would predict has a positive alpha, while one that returns less than the amount predicted by beta has a negative alpha. A large positive alpha indicates a strong performance, while a large negative alpha indicates a dismal performance.

HOW THEY WORK IN PRACTICE
To begin with, the market itself is assigned a beta of 1.0. If a stock or fund has a beta of 1.2, this means its price is likely to rise or fall by 12% when the overall market rises or falls by 10%; a beta of 0.7 means the stock or fund price is likely to move up or down at 70% of the level of the market change.

In practice, an alpha of 0.4 means the stock or fund in question outperformed the market-based return estimate by 0.4%. An alpha of –0.6 means the return was 0.6% less than would have been predicted from the change in the market alone.

Both alpha and beta should be readily available on request from investment firms, because the figures appear in standard performance reports. It is always best to ask for them, because calculating a stock's alpha rating requires first knowing a stock's beta rating, and calculating beta is a challenge! It is based on linear regression analy-

sis, the week-to-week percentage changes in the given stock's price and the corresponding week-to-week percentage price change in a market index, over a given period of time, often 24 to 36 months. In short, beta calculations can involve mathematical complexities.

If it's any consolation, calculating alpha is far less taxing, provided requisite data is available. The formula is:

> **(actual return – risk-free return) – [beta × (index return – risk-free return)] = alpha**

If a mutual fund with a beta rating of 1.1 returned 35%, while its benchmark index returned 30%, and a U.S. Treasury bill returned 4% (T-bill returns are usually used as the "risk-free investment"), then the fund's alpha would equal 2.4, based on the formula:

> **(35% – 4%) – 1.1 × (30% – 4%) = 31% – 1.1 × 26% = 31% – 28.6% = 2.4 alpha**

TRICKS OF THE TRADE
- The underlying rationale for both alpha and beta is that the return of a stock or mutual fund should at least exceed that of a "risk-free" investment such as a U.S. Treasury bill.
- Stocks of many utilities have a beta of less than 1. Conversely, most high-tech NASDAQ-based stocks have a beta greater than 1; they offer a higher rate of return but are also risky.
- Alpha is often used to assess the performance of a portfolio manager. However, a low alpha score doesn't necessarily reflect poor performance by a fund manager, any more than a high alpha score means that a manager's performance is outstanding. At times, factors beyond a manager's control affect alpha values.

FOR MORE INFORMATION
Web site:
www.zurich.com discusses alpha and beta in greater detail and offers links to additional sites.

See also:
✓ Calculating a Capital Asset Pricing Model (p. 1021)

"Observation of realities has never, to put it mildly, been one of the strengths of economic development."
Jane Jacobs

Calculating the Future Value of an Annuity

WHAT IT MEASURES

The value to which a series of fixed-amount payments made at regular intervals will grow over the specified period of time.

WHY IT IS IMPORTANT

The calculation enables companies to determine the future value of a fund receiving regular payments, such as contributions to a pension fund. Individuals in companies may find the calculation equally useful if they want to establish a fund to pay the cost of future college education: they will know what their annual payments will grow to in a given number of years.

HOW IT WORKS IN PRACTICE

There are several types of annuity. They vary both in the ways they accumulate funds and in the ways they disperse earnings. The following are some examples:

A **fixed annuity** guarantees fixed payments to the individual receiving it for the term of the contract, usually until death.

A **variable annuity** offers no guarantee but has potential for a greater return, usually based on the performance of a stock or mutual fund.

A **deferred annuity** delays payments until the individual chooses to receive them.

A **hybrid annuity**, also called a combination annuity, combines features of both the fixed and variable annuity.

Financial calculators and spreadsheet programs will compute annuity calculations automatically. Manual calculations require a future value of annuity table that contains figures based on the interest rate and period in question. The basic formula is:

amount invested × table value [interest, period] = future value

If, for example, a pension manager puts $1,000,000 at the end of every year into his company's pension fund, the fund earns 8% interest, and there are no withdrawals, at the end of five years it will be worth:

$1,000,000 × 5.867 [table value] = $5,867,000

TRICKS OF THE TRADE

- The formula assumes that payments are made at the end of a given period.
- If a stated interest rate is not an annual rate, it must be adjusted to reflect an annual rate.
- Although their yields are low, annuities are relatively safe investments that provide level streams of cash flow for fixed periods of time.
- In the United States, annuities are tax-deferred, but also often carry an early withdrawal penalty.
- If you are calculating manually, be sure to use the designated future value of an annuity table, and not the future value table; there is a significant difference.
- The mathematical expression for the numbers appearing on a future value of an annuity table is $[(1 + i)^n - 1] / i$; i is the interest rate, and n is the number of years in question.

FOR MORE INFORMATION

Web site:
www.getobjects.com/Components/Finance/TVM/ fva.html offers useful examples and further explanation.

Calculating Working Capital Productivity

WHAT IT MEASURES

How effectively a company's management is using its working capital.

WHY IT IS IMPORTANT

It is obvious that capital not being put to work properly is being wasted, which is certainly not in investors' best interests.

As an expression of how effectively a company spends its available funds compared with sales or turnover, the working capital productivity figure helps to establish a clear relationship between its financial performance and process improvement. The relationship is said to have been first observed by the U.S. management consultant George Stalk while working in Japan.

A seldom used reciprocal calculation, the working capital turnover or working capital to sales ratio, expresses the same relationship in a different way.

HOW IT WORKS IN PRACTICE

To calculate working capital productivity, first subtract current liabilities from current assets, which is the formula for working capital, then divide this figure into sales for the period.

$$\text{sales} / (\text{current assets} - \text{current liabilities}) =$$
$$\text{working capital productivity}$$

If sales are $3,250, current assets are $900, and current liabilities are $650, then:

$$3250 / (900 - 650) = 3250 / 250 = 13$$

In this case, the higher the number the better. Sales growing faster than the resources that are required to generate them is a clear sign of efficiency and, by definition, productivity.

The working capital to sales ratio uses the same figures, but in reverse:

$$\text{working capital} / \text{sales} \times 100\% =$$
$$\text{working capital to sales ratio}$$

Using the same figures in the example above, this ratio would be calculated:

$$250 / 3250 = 0.077 \times 100\% = 7.7\%$$

For this ratio, obviously, the lower the number the better.

TRICKS OF THE TRADE

- By itself, a single ratio means little; a series of them, several quarters' worth, for example, indicates a trend, and means a great deal.
- Some experts recommend doing quarterly calculations and averaging them for a given year to arrive at the most reliable number.
- Either ratio also helps a management compare its performance with that of competitors.
- These ratios should also help to motivate companies to improve processes, such as eliminating steps in the handling of materials and bill collection, and shortening product design times. Such improvements reduce costs and make working capital available for other tasks.

FOR MORE INFORMATION

Web site:
The Motley Fool: **www.fool.com**

See also:
∽ Accounting (pp. 1667–1669)

"Superfluous wealth can buy superfluities only."　　　　　Henry David Thoreau

Calculating Economic Value Added

WHAT IT MEASURES

A company's financial performance, specifically whether it is earning more or less than the total cost of the capital supporting it.

WHY IT IS IMPORTANT

Economic Value Added (EVA) measures true economic profit, or the amount by which the earnings of a project, an operation, or a corporation exceed (or fall short of) the total amount of capital that was originally invested by the company's owners.

If a company is earning more, it is adding value, and that is good. If it is earning less the company is in fact devouring value, and that is bad, because the company's owners (stockholders, for example) would be better off investing their capital elsewhere.

The concept's champions declare that EVA forces managers to focus on true wealth creation and maximizing stockholder investment. By definition, then, increasing EVA will increase a company's market value.

HOW IT WORKS IN PRACTICE

EVA is conceptually simple and easy to explain: from net operating profit, subtract an appropriate charge for the opportunity cost of all capital invested in an enterprise—the amount that could have been invested elsewhere. It is calculated using this formula:

> **net operating profit less applicable taxes – cost of capital = EVA**

If a company is considering building a new plant, and its total weighted cost over ten years is $80 million, while the expected annual incremental return on the new operation is $10 million, or $100 million over ten years, then the plant's EVA would be positive, in this case $20 million:

> **$100 million – $80 million = $20 million**

An alternative but more complex formula for EVA is:

> **(% return on invested capital – % cost of capital) × original capital invested = EVA**

TRICKS OF THE TRADE

- EVA is a measure of dollar surplus value, not the percentage difference in returns.
- Purists define EVA as "profit the way stockholders define it." They further contend that if stockholders expect a 10% return on their investment, they "make money" only when their share of after-tax operating profits exceeds 10% of equity capital.
- An objective of EVA is to determine which business units best utilize their assets to generate returns and maximize stockholder value; it can be used to assess a company, a business unit, a single plant, office, or even an assembly line. This same technique is equally helpful in evaluating new business opportunities.

FOR MORE INFORMATION

Web site:
Stern Stewart & Co.: **www.sternstewart.com**

See also:
- Accounting (pp. 1667–1669)
- Why EVA Is the Best Measurement Tool for Creating Shareholder Value (pp. 166–167)

"But in this world nothing can be said to be certain, except death and taxes."

Benjamin Franklin

Calculating Risk-adjusted Rate of Return

WHAT IT MEASURES

How much an investment returned in relation to the risk that was assumed to attain it.

WHY IT IS IMPORTANT

Being able to compare a high-risk, potentially high-return investment with a low-risk, lower-return investment helps to answer a key question that confronts every investor: is it worth the risk?

By itself, the historical average return of an investment, asset, or portfolio can be quite misleading and a faulty indicator of future performance. Risk-adjusted return is a much better barometer.

The calculation also helps to reveal whether the returns of the portfolio reflect smart investment decisions, or the assumptions of excess risk that may or may not have been worth what was gained. This is particularly helpful in appraising the performance of money managers.

HOW IT WORKS IN PRACTICE

There are several ways to calculate risk-adjusted return. Each has its strengths and shortcomings. All require particular data, such as an investment's rate of return, the risk-free return rate for a given period (usually the performance of a 90-day U.S. Treasury bill over 36 months), and a market's performance and its standard deviation.

Which one to use? It often depends on an investor's focus, principally whether the focus is on upside gains or downside losses.

Perhaps the most widely used is the **Sharpe ratio**. This measures the potential impact of return volatility on expected return and the amount of return earned per unit of risk. The higher a fund's Sharpe ratio, the better its historical risk-adjusted performance, and the higher the number the greater the return per unit of risk. The formula is:

> **(portfolio return – risk-free return) / std. deviation of portfolio return = Sharpe ratio**

Take, for example, two investments, one returning 54%, the other 26%. At first glance, the higher figure clearly looks like the better choice, but because of its high volatility it has a Sharpe ratio of 0.279, while the investment with a lower return has a ratio of 0.910. On a risk-adjusted basis the latter would be the wiser choice.

Meanwhile, the **Treynor ratio** also measures the excess of return per unit of risk. Its formula is:

> **(portfolio return – risk-free return) / portfolio's beta = Treynor ratio**

In this formula (and others that follow), beta is a separately calculated figure that describes the tendency of an investment to respond to marketplace swings. The higher beta, the greater the volatility, and vice versa.

A third formula, **Jensen's measure**, is often used to rate a money manager's performance against a market index, and whether or not a investment's risk was worth its reward. The formula is:

> **(portfolio return – risk-free return) – portfolio beta × (benchmark return – risk-free return) = Jensen's measure**

TRICKS OF THE TRADE

- A fourth formula, the **Sortino ratio**, also exists. Its focus is more on downside risk than potential opportunity, and its calculation is more complex.
- There are no benchmarks for these values. In order to be useful the numbers should be compared with the ratios of other investments.
- No single measure is perfect, so experts recommend using them broadly. For instance, if a particular investment class is on a roll and does not experience a great deal of volatility, a return per unit of risk does not necessarily reflect management genius. When the overall momentum of technology stocks drove returns straight up in 1999, Sharpe ratios climbed with them, and did not reflect any of the sector's volatility that was to erupt in late 2000.
- Most of these measures can be used to rank the risk-adjusted performance of individual stocks, various portfolios over the same time, and mutual funds with similar objectives.

FOR MORE INFORMATION

Web sites:

www.captive.com presents a detailed discussion of risk-adjusted return and lists the formulas used to calculate it.

www.cpadvantage.com discusses the Sharpe ratio and related concepts.

www.finportfolio.com has definitions and detailed information.

www.sortino.com presents a lengthy and technical discussion of the Sortino ratio.

"A bank is a place that will lend you money if you can prove that you don't need it."

Bob Hope

Calculating Exchange Rate Risk

WHAT IT MEASURES

The risk of a gain or loss in the value of a business activity or investment that results from changes in the exchange rates of world currencies.

WHY IT IS IMPORTANT

Each business day seems to bring more international business transactions, generated by an ever-growing number of enterprises from an ever-increasing number of countries. Enterprises in developing nations, especially, are vying for their share of world commerce.

However, the economies of these developing nations can be especially fragile, while economies of mature nations periodically sputter and suffer recessions. Asia, Latin America, and Eastern Europe have all endured economic turmoil in the past decade, while such regions as the Middle East have been volatile for several decades, principally because of the wide swings in oil prices.

Currency exchange rates can be just as volatile and this clearly poses risks to any enterprise conducting business in foreign markets, and any investor holding either stock in a foreign-based company, or an interest in a mutual fund that invests in foreign companies. The effects on a company's earnings, cash flow, and balance sheet can be significant.

The main exchange rate risk to an operation or investment is that any profits realized will be partially reduced—or wiped out altogether—when they are exchanged for the domestic currency, be it U.S. dollars, pounds sterling, the Euro, or Japanese yen.

More often, exchange rate risk will affect a company's price competitiveness in a product or service also offered by a competitor whose costs are incurred in a foreign currency. If the competitor's currency weakens, its relative competitive position improves because its costs decline, enabling the competitor to reduce its price and attract a larger share of a market.

HOW IT WORKS IN PRACTICE

There is a simple way to avoid the risk posed by exchange rates: don't do business abroad! For large companies, as well as an increasing number of small- and medium-sized companies, that would be like sticking one's head in the sand.

A second defense against exchange rate risks is almost as unrealistic: conduct all business in your home currency. Requiring foreign customers to pay up only in, say, dollars, puts the burden of currency fluctuations squarely on the customer's shoulders and completely insulates the selling company from any shrinkage of profits from exchange rate differences. The price for such insulation, however, is likely to be a steady loss of customers.

The practical course of action, then, is to gain a basic understanding of exchange rate risks, if only enough to sort out the reams of opinions on the subject, and to select knowledgeable advisers and use their counsel wisely. This is a sophisticated, complex realm that has been examined for over a century. It is certainly no place for amateurs.

At the same time, however, exchange rates, interest rates, and inflation rates have been linked to one another via a classic set of relationships that can serve as leading indicators of changes in risk. These relationships are:

- The **Purchasing Power Parity** theory (PPP). While it can be expressed differently, the most common expression links the changes in exchange rates to those in relative price indices in two countries:

  rate of change of exchange rate = difference in inflation rates

- The **International Fisher Effect (IFE).** This holds that an interest-rate differential will exist only if the exchange rate is expected to change in such a way that the advantage of the higher interest rate is offset by the loss on the foreign exchange transactions. Practically speaking, the IFE implies that while an investor in a low-interest country can convert funds into the currency of a high-interest country and earn a higher rate, the gain (the interest rate differential) will be offset by the expected loss due to foreign exchange rate changes. The relationship is stated as:

  the expected rate of change of the exchange rate = the interest-rate differential

- The **Unbiased Forward Rate Theory**. This holds that the forward exchange rate is the best and unbiased estimate of the expected future spot exchange rate.

  the expected exchange rate = the forward exchange rate

Other than these yardsticks, defending against exchange rate risk is largely a matter of observation. In the floating exchange rate environment that has existed for nearly the past 30 years, currency exchange rates respond to a host of factors: political climates, the flow of imports and exports, the flow of capital, inflation rates in various countries, consumer expectations, and confidence levels, to name a few. Frequently, limits are placed on exchange rate fluctuations by government policies—actions that themselves can arouse controversy or debate.

Even so, the exchange rate risks these factors create can be arranged into three primary categories:

- **Economic exposure**. Due to changes in rates, operating costs will rise and make a product uncompetitive in the world market, thus eroding profitability. There's little that can be done about economic risk; it's simply a routine business risk that every enterprise must endure.

- **Translation exposure**. The impact of currency exchange rates will reduce a company's earnings and weaken its balance sheet. In turn, the denominations of assets and liabilities are important, although many experts contend that currency fluctuations have no significant impact on real assets.

- **Transaction exposure**. There will be an unfavorable move

in a specific currency between the time when a contract is agreed and the time it is completed, or between the time when a lending or borrowing is initiated and the time the funds are repaid. This is the most common problem that confronts most companies. Requiring payment in advance is rarely practical, and impossible, of course, for borrowing and lending.

To reduce translation exposure, experienced corporate fund managers use a variety of techniques known as currency hedging, which amounts to diversifying currency holdings, monitoring exchange rates, and acting accordingly, depending upon specific conditions. Its advocates contend that taking appropriate action can greatly reduce translation risks, if not avoid them altogether. Currency hedging, however, is also technical and sophisticated.

Transaction exposure can be eased by a process known as factoring. Major exporters, in particular, transfer title to their foreign accounts receivable to a third-party factoring house that assumes responsibility for collections, administrative services, and any other services requested. The fee for this service is a percentage of the value of the receivables, anywhere from 5% to 10% or higher, depending on the currencies involved. Companies often include this percentage in selling prices to recoup the cost.

Commercial and country risks can affect exchange rates, too. Commercial risks include the default or bankruptcy of major foreign customers. While this risk mirrors what can also occur at home, foreign-based companies operate under different laws and relationships with their governments. More worrisome are country risks: political or military interventions and currency restrictions that less stable nations might impose. Insurance is available to address such risks, but it can be costly.

TRICKS OF THE TRADE

- Any number of models have been created to explain and forecast exchange rates. None has proved definitive, largely because the world's economies and financial markets are evolving so rapidly.

- A forward transaction is an agreement to buy one currency and sell another on a date some time beyond two business days. It allows an exchange rate on a given day to be locked in for a future payment or receipt, thereby eliminating exchange rate risk.
- Foreign exchange options are contracts which, for a fee, guarantee a worst-case exchange rate for the future purchase of one currency for another. Unlike a forward transaction, the option does not obligate the buyer to deliver a currency on the settlement date unless the buyer chooses to. These options protect against unfavorable currency movements while allowing retention of the ability to participate in favorable movements.
- A producer facing pricing competition caused by fluctuations in exchange rates can also use currency contracts to try to match competitors' cost structures and reduce costs.
- Companies doing larger volumes of business in a foreign country often establish a local office there to pay expenses and collect revenues in local currencies to reduce the impact of sudden and pronounced exchange rate fluctuations.
- Private-sector subscription services monitor currencies and publish alerts. One U.S.-based service has established numerical ranges that indicate risk, from 100 (no risk) to 200 (extreme risk or an outright currency crisis).
- Exchange rate risks cannot be insured against per se.
- The U.S. Export-Import Bank (Eximbank) may be a source of advice for companies, especially smaller and medium-sized companies, seeking assistance.

FOR MORE INFORMATION

Web site:
www.stern.nyu.edu/~igiddy/fxrisk.htm is a lengthy but well-written analysis that urges companies to engage in currency management.

Calculating Total Return

1016

ACTIONLIST

WHAT IT MEASURES

The total percentage change in the value of an investment over a specified time period, including capital gains, dividends, and the investment's appreciation or depreciation.

WHY IT IS IMPORTANT

Total return furnishes fundamental information that every investor seeks sooner or later: all things considered, just how much did my investment return?

That in itself makes total return rather important. In addition, there are several sound reasons for paying close attention to each of its components. For those who invest to maximize income, dividends will be very important. For those who invest for long-term growth, capital appreciation will be equally important.

Knowing how much of an investment's total return is attributable to each of the components can help in assessing how volatile the fund is likely to be, how tax-efficient it is, and how much steady income it can be expected to produce.

HOW IT WORKS IN PRACTICE

The total return formula reflects all the ways in which an investment may earn or lose money: dividends as income, capital gains distributions, and capital appreciation—the increase or decrease in the investment's net asset value (NAV):

> **(dividends + capital gains distributions +/- change in NAV) / beginning NAV = total return × 100%**

If, for instance, you buy a stock with an initial NAV of $40, and after one year it pays an income dividend of $2 per share and a capital gains distribution of $1, and its NAV has increased to $42, then the stock's total return would be:

$$(2 + 1 + 2) / 40 =$$
$$5 / 40 = 0.125 \times 100\% = 12.5\%$$

TRICKS OF THE TRADE

- The total return time-frame is usually one year, and it assumes that dividends have been reinvested.
- If a fund's capital gains exceed its capital losses for the year, most of the net gain must be distributed to stockholders as a capital gains distribution.
- Total return measures past performance only; it cannot predict future results.
- Total return generally does not take into account any sales charges that an investor paid to invest in a fund, or taxes he or she might owe on the income dividends and capital gains distributions received.
- Rules of the U.S. Securities & Exchange Commission require a company to show a comparison of the total return on its common stock for the last five fiscal years with the total returns of a broad market index and a more narrowly focused industry or group index.
- Total return can be a key yardstick in selecting funds once an investor has set objectives and a time horizon, and made decisions about risk and reward.

FOR MORE INFORMATION

Web site:
The Motley Fool: **www.fool.com**

"Investment is not only volatile, it is the key motor of the economy's prosperity because it has a snowball effect."

Will Hutton

Calculating Price/Earnings Ratio

WHAT IT MEASURES

The price/earnings ratio (P/E) is simply the stock price divided by earnings per share (EPS). While EPS is an actual amount of money, usually expressed in cents per share, the P/E ratio has no units it is just a number. Thus if a quoted company has a stock price of $100 and EPS of $12 for the last published year, then it has a historical P/E of 8.3. If analysts are forecasting for the next year EPS of, say, $14 then the forecast P/E is 7.1.

WHY IT IS IMPORTANT

Since EPS is the annual earnings per share of a company, it follows that dividing the stock price by EPS tells us how many years of current EPS are represented by the stock price. In the above example then, the P/E of 8.3 tells us that investors at the current price are prepared to pay 8.3 years of historical EPS for the stock, or 7.1 years of the forecast next year's EPS. Theoretically the faster a company is expected to grow, the higher the P/E ratio that investors would award it. It is one measure of how cheap or expensive a stock appears.

HOW IT WORKS IN PRACTICE

The P/E ratio is predominantly useful in comparisons with other stocks rather than in isolation. For example, if the average P/E in the market is 20, there will be many stocks with P/Es well above and well below this, for a variety of reasons. Similarly, in a particular sector, the P/Es will frequently vary quite widely from the sector average, even though the constituent companies may all be engaged in broadly similar businesses. The reason is

that even two businesses doing the same thing will not always be doing it as profitably as each other. One may be far more efficient, as demonstrated by a history of rising EPS compared with the flat EPS picture of the other over a series of years, and the market might recognize this by awarding the more profitable stock a higher P/E.

TRICKS OF THE TRADE

- Take care. The market frequently gets it wrong and many high P/E stocks have in the past been the most awful long-term investments, losing investors huge amounts of money when the promise of future rapid growth proved to be a chimera. In contrast many low P/E companies, often in what are perceived as dull industries, have proved over time to be outstanding investments.
- The P/E is an investment tool that is both invaluable, and yet requires extreme caution in its application when comparing and selecting investments. It remains though by far the most commonly utilized ratio in investment analysis.

FOR MORE INFORMATION

Web site:
The Motley Fool: **www.fool.com**

See also:
- ✔ Calculating Yield (p. 1041)
- ✔ Reading the Financial Pages (pp. 1055–1056)

1017

ACTIONLIST

"The higher our income, the more resources we control and the more havoc we wreak."

Paul Carter Harrison

Calculating the Current Price of a Bond

WHAT IT MEASURES
The narrow range within which a given bond price falls, based on that bond's current asking price and bid price.

WHY IT IS IMPORTANT
Current prices of comparable bonds are strong indicators of a bond's buying or selling price. Changes in bond prices are also indicators of economic strength and direction.

HOW IT WORKS IN PRACTICE
The price of a bond depends on several factors.
- Interest rates: as rates rise, a bond's price falls, because it pays less interest than current offerings and is thus less attractive. Conversely, a bond becomes more attractive as interest rates fall.
- The risk perceived for the issuing entity, reflected in its credit rating from one of the major rating agencies. The price of a bond of a company in bankruptcy, for instance, will be low because the company may never be able to redeem it. The price of a bond from a strong company may include a premium over its face or "par value" because it is considered a reliable investment: a bond with a face value of $1,000 might sell for $1,050, indicating a $50 premium.
- The issuing of new bonds by corporations or other bodies (and the ratings they receive) affects the prices of existing bonds.

Daily bond tables vary in format, but list the basic information necessary for comparing prices. Only a small fraction of the outstanding bonds trade on any given day, but these representative prices provide sufficient information to estimate what a fair price would be for the bonds being considered.

When considering bonds, several pieces of information are essential:
- the bond's coupon rate: what it will pay in interest;
- how long before the principal amount of the bond matures, or if there is a call date;
- its recent price and current yield.

Essentially, all the tables provide this basic information. The U.S. Treasury table, for example, would be listed as follows:

Rate	Maturity	Bid	Ask	Yield
7 ¾	Feb. 07	105:12	105:14	5.50
5 ¾	Feb. 07	99:26	99:27	5.44

In the first row, the security is paying its bondholders 7 ¾% interest and is due to mature in February 2007. Prices in the bid and ask columns are percentages of the bond's face value of $1,000. A bid of 105:12 means that a buyer was willing to pay $1053.75, compared to the seller's lowest asking price, 105:14, or $1054.38, a difference of 63 cents per thousand.

Bond quotes follow certain conventions. Prices are given as percentages of face value, but the digits appearing after the colons are not decimals, being expressed in terms of 1/32. So 12/32nds, for example, would equal $3.75, which is appended to the 105 before the colon.

The bid and ask prices indicate that an investor who bought the bond at par when it was first issued can make a profit of more than 5% if it were sold now. The last column gives the yield to maturity, an interest rate summarizing the bond's overall investment value.

COMMON MISTAKES
- A bond's yield and its price are not the same. Price is what is paid for a bond; yield expresses the percentage return on the investment. Yield is most useful for comparing fixed income investments for planning purposes, rather than as an exact measure of the return expected from an investment.
- The number of bond issues outstanding at any given time is far greater than stocks, and most bondholders buy with the intent of holding them until maturity, so the amount of trading is limited.
- There are several bond-rating agencies. A bond's rating indicates its level of risk.
- Listing tables also show the volume traded along with the current yield.
- The Internet offers many calculators for quickly determining bond prices and yields.

FOR MORE INFORMATION
Web site:
www.investinginbonds.com offers an explanation, with examples, of several different kinds of bonds.

See also:
✔ Calculating Amortization (pp. 1047–1048)

"Banking establishments are more dangerous than standing armies."   Thomas Jefferson

Calculating Accounts Receivable Turnover

WHAT IT MEASURES

The number of times in each accounting period, typically a year, that a company converts credit sales into cash.

WHY IT IS IMPORTANT

A high turnover figure is desirable, because it indicates that a company collects revenues effectively, and that its customers pay bills promptly. A high figure also suggests that a company's credit and collection policies are sound.

In addition, the measurement is a reasonably good indicator of cash flow, and of overall operating efficiency.

HOW IT WORKS IN PRACTICE

The formula for accounts receivable turnover is straightforward. Simply divide the average amount of receivables into annual credit sales:

sales / receivables = receivables turnover

If, for example, a company's sales are $4.5 million and its average receivables are $375,000, its receivables turnover is:

4,500,000 / 375,000 = 12

TRICKS OF THE TRADE

- It is important to use the average amount of receivables over the period considered. Otherwise, receivables could be misleading for a company whose products are seasonal or are sold at irregular intervals.
- The measurement is also helpful to a company that is designing or revising credit terms.
- Accounts receivable turnover is among the measures that comprise asset utilization ratios, also called activity ratios.

FOR MORE INFORMATION

Web site:
The Motley Fool: **www.fool.com**

See also:
- Accounting (pp. 1667–1669)
- Calculating Asset Utilization (p. 1020)

"International finance is always looking for new opportunities. The challenge for Africa is not just to be attractive to traders and investors, but to offer opportunities which are more attractive than anywhere else in the world."
Peter Hain

Calculating Asset Utilization

WHAT IT MEASURES

How efficiently an organization uses its resources and, in turn, the effectiveness of the organization's managers.

WHY IT IS IMPORTANT

The success of any enterprise is tied to its ability to manage and leverage its assets. Hefty sales and profits can hide any number of inefficiencies. By examining several relationships between sales and assets, asset utilization delivers a reasonably detailed picture of how well a company is being managed and led—certainly enough to call attention both to sources of trouble and to role-model operations.

Moreover, since all the figures used in this analysis are taken from a company's balance sheet or profit and loss statement, the ratios that result can be used to compare a company's performance with individual competitors and with industries as a whole.

Many companies use this measure not only to evaluate their aggregate success but also to determine compensation for managers.

HOW IT WORKS IN PRACTICE

Asset utilization relies on a family of asset utilization ratios, also called activity ratios. The individual ratios in the family can vary, depending on the practitioner. They include measures that also stand alone, such as accounts receivable turnover and asset turnover. The most commonly used sets of asset utilization ratios include these and the following measures.

Average collection period is also known as days sales outstanding. It links accounts receivable with daily sales and is expressed in number of days; the lower the number, the better the performance. Its formula is:

accounts receivable / average daily sales = average collection period

For example, if accounts receivable are $280,000 and average daily sales are 7,000, then:

280,000 / 7,000 = 40

Inventory turnover compares the cost of goods sold (COGS) with inventory; for this measure, expressed in "turns," the higher the number the better. Its formula is:

cost of goods sold / inventory

For example, if COGS is $2 million and inventory at the end of the period is $500,000, then:

2,000,000 / 500,000 = 4

Some asset utilization repertoires include ratios like debtor days, while others study the relationships listed below.

Depreciation / Assets measures the percentage of assets being depreciated to gauge how quickly product plants are aging and assets are being consumed.

Depreciation / Sales measures the percentage of sales that is tied up covering the wear and tear of the plant.

In either instance, a high percentage could be cause for concern.

Income / Assets measures how well management uses its assets to generate net income. It is the same formula as return on assets.

Income / Plant measures how effectively a company uses its investment in fixed assets to generate net income.

In these two instances, high numbers are desirable.

Plant / Assets expresses the percentage of total assets that is tied up in land, buildings, and equipment.

By themselves, of course, the individual numbers are meaningless. Their value lies in how they compare with the corresponding numbers of competitors and industry averages. A company with an inventory turnover of 4 in an industry whose average is 7, for example, surely has room for improvement, because the comparison indicates it is generating fewer sales per unit of inventory and is therefore less efficient than its competitors.

TRICKS OF THE TRADE

- Asset utilization is particularly useful to companies considering expansion or capital investment: if production can be increased by improving the efficiency of existing resources, there is no need to spend the sums expansion would cost.
- Like all families of ratios, no single number or comparison is necessarily cause for alarm or rejoicing. Asset utilization proves most beneficial over an extended period of time.
- Studying all measures at once can devour a lot of time, although computers have trimmed hours into seconds. Managements in smaller organizations may conduct asset utilization on a continuing basis, tracking particular measures monthly to stay abreast of operating trends.

FOR MORE INFORMATION

Web site:
Powerinvestor.com: **www.powerinvestor.com**

See also:

"Most economists . . . are reluctant to make predictions, and those who make them are seldom accurate. The economy, like the human body, is a highly complex system whose workings are not thoroughly understood."

Alice M. Rivlin

Calculating a Capital Asset Pricing Model

WHAT IT MEASURES

The relationship between the risk and expected return of a security or stock portfolio.

WHY IT IS IMPORTANT

The capital asset pricing model's (CAPM) importance is twofold.

First, it serves as a model for pricing the risk in all securities, and thus helps investors evaluate and measure portfolio risk and the returns they can anticipate for taking such risks.

Secondly, the theory behind the formula also has fueled—some might say provoked—spirited debate among economists about the nature of investment risk itself. The CAPM model attempts to describe how the market values investments with expected returns.

The CAPM theory classifies risk as being either diversifiable, which can be avoided by sound investing, or systematic, that is, not diversified and unavoidable due to the nature of the market itself. The theory contends that investors are rewarded only for assuming systematic risk, because they can mitigate diversifiable risk by building a portfolio of both risky stocks and sound ones.

One analysis has characterized the CAPM as "a theory of equilibrium" that links higher expected returns in strong markets with the greater risk of suffering heavy losses in weak markets. Otherwise, no one would invest in high-risk stocks.

HOW IT WORKS IN PRACTICE

CAPM holds that the expected return of a security or a portfolio equals the rate on a risk-free security plus a risk premium. If this expected return does not meet or beat a theoretical required return, the investment should not be undertaken. The formula used to create CAPM is:

$$\text{risk-free rate} + (\text{market return} - \text{risk-free rate}) \times \text{beta value} = \text{expected return}$$

The risk-free rate is the quoted rate on an asset that has virtually no risk. In practice, it is the rate quoted for 90-day U.S. Treasury bills. The market return is the percentage return expected of the overall market, typically a published index such as Standard & Poor's. The beta value is a figure that measures the volatility of a security or portfolio of securities, compared with the market as a whole. A beta of 1, for example, indicates that a security's price will move with the market. A beta greater than 1 indicates higher volatility, while a beta less than 1 indicates less volatility.

Say, for instance, that the current risk-free rate is 4%, and the S&P 500 index is expected to return 11% next year. An investment club is interested in determining next year's return for XYZ Software, Inc., a prospective investment. The club has determined that the company's beta value is 1.8. The overall stock market always has a beta of 1, so XYZ Software's beta of 1.8 signals that it is a more risky investment than the overall market represents. This added risk means that the club should expect a higher rate of return than the 11% for the S&P 500. The CAPM calculation, then, would be:

$$4\% + (11\% - 4\%) \times 1.8 = 16.6\% \text{ expected return}$$

What the results tell the club is that given the risk, XYZ Software, Inc. has a required rate of return of 16.6%, or the minimum return that an investment in XYZ should generate. If the investment club doesn't think that XYZ will produce that kind of return, it should probably consider investing in a different company.

TRICKS OF THE TRADE

- As experts warn, CAPM is only a simple calculation built on historical data of market and stock prices. It does not express anything about the company whose stock is being analyzed. For example, renowned investor Warren Buffett has pointed out that if a company making Barbie™ Dolls has the same beta as one making pet rocks, CAPM holds that one investment is as good as the other. Clearly, this is a risky tenet.
- While high returns might be received from stocks with high beta shares, there is no guarantee that their respective CAPM return will be realized (a reason why beta is defined as a "measure of risk" rather than an "indication of high return").
- The beta parameter itself is historical data and may not reflect future results. The data for beta values is typically gathered over several years and experts recommend that only long-term investors should rely on the CAPM formula.
- Over longer periods of time, high beta shares tend to be the worst performers during market declines.

FOR MORE INFORMATION

Web site:
www.xrefer.com and **www.contingencyanalysis.com** have analysis, definitions, and links to additional references.

See also:
✔ Calculating the Alpha and Beta Values of a Security (p. 1009)

Calculating Current Ratio

WHAT IT MEASURES

A company's liquidity and its ability to meet its short-term debt obligations.

WHY IT IS IMPORTANT

By comparing a company's current assets with its current liabilities, the current ratio reflects its ability to pay its upcoming bills in the unlikely event of all creditors demanding payment at once. It has long been the measurement of choice among financial institutions and lenders.

HOW IT WORKS IN PRACTICE

The current ratio formula is simply:

$$\text{current assets / current liabilities = current ratio}$$

Current assets are the ones that a company can turn into cash within 12 months during the ordinary course of business. Current liabilities are bills due to be paid within the coming 12 months.

For example, if a company's current assets are $300,000 and its current liabilities are $200,000, its current ratio would be:

$$300,000 / 200,000 = 1.5$$

As a rule of thumb, the 1.5 figure means that a company should be able to get hold of $1.50 for every $1.00 it owes.

TRICKS OF THE TRADE

- The higher the ratio, the more liquid the company. Prospective lenders expect a positive current ratio, often of at least 1.5. However, too high a ratio is also cause for alarm, because it indicates declining receivables and/or inventory—signs that portend declining liquidity.

- A current ratio of less than 1 suggests pressing liquidity problems, specifically an inability to generate sufficient cash to meet upcoming demands.

- Managements use current ratio as well as lenders; a low ratio, for example, may indicate the need to refinance a portion of short-term debt with long-term debt to improve a company's liquidity.

- Ratios vary by industry, however, and should be used accordingly. Some sectors, such as supermarket chains and restaurants, perform nicely with low ratios that would keep others awake at night.

- One shortcoming of the current ratio is that it does not differentiate assets, some of which may not be easily converted to cash. As a result, lenders also refer to the quick ratio.

- Another shortcoming of the current ratio is that it reflects conditions at a single point in time, such as when the balance sheet is prepared. It is possible to make this figure look good just for this occasion: lenders should not, therefore, appraise these conditions by the ratio alone.

- A constant current ratio and falling quick ratio signal trouble ahead, because this suggests that a company is amassing assets at the expense of receivables and cash.

FOR MORE INFORMATION

Web site:
Business Owner's Toolkit: **www.toolkit.cch.com**

See also:
ⅆ Accounting (pp. 1667–1669)

Calculating the Reserve Ratio

WHAT IT MEASURES

In the United Kingdom and in certain European countries, there is no compulsory ratio, although banks will have their own internal measures and targets to be able to repay customer deposits as they forecast they will be required. In the United States, the policy is more prescriptive, and specified percentages of deposits—established by the Federal Reserve Board—must be kept by banks in a non-interest-bearing account at one of the twelve Federal Reserve Banks located throughout the country.

WHY IT IS IMPORTANT

To provide stability. In view of the volume and unpredictability of transactions that clear through their accounts every day, banks and financial depositories must maintain a cushion of funds to protect themselves against debits that could leave their accounts overdrawn at the end of the day, and thus subject to penalty.

As a result of the creation of reserve ratios, periods of financial stress are no longer characterized by runs on banks by depositors.

HOW IT WORKS IN PRACTICE

In Europe, the reserve requirement of an institution is calculated by multiplying the reserve ratio for each category of items in the reserve base, set by the European Central Bank, with the amount of those items in the institution's balance sheets. These figures vary according to the institution.

The required reserve ratio in the United States is set by federal law, and depends on the amount of checkable deposits a bank holds. The first $44.3 million of deposits are subject to a 3% reserve requirement. Deposits in excess of $44.3 million are subject to 10% reserve requirement. These breakpoints are reviewed annually in accordance with money supply growth. No reserves are required against certificates of deposit or savings accounts.

The reserve ratio requirement limits a bank's lending to a certain fraction of its demand deposits. The current rule allows a bank to issue loans in an amount equal to 90% of such deposits, holding 10% in reserve. The reserves can be held in any combination of vault cash and deposit at a Federal Reserve Bank.

A bank facing a reserve deficiency has several options. It can try to borrow reserves for one or more days from another bank, sell marketable assets such as government securities, or bid for funds in the money market, such as large CDs or Eurodollars. As a last resort, it can pledge collateral and borrow at the Federal Reserve's discount window.

In order to meet deposit withdrawal contingencies, many banks maintain a margin of excess reserves above the required reserve ratio, since the required reserves are really not available to meet withdrawal liquidity needs. Excess reserves are higher than those needed to meet reserve and clearing requirements, and provide extra protection against overdrafts and deficiencies in required reserves.

TRICKS OF THE TRADE

- Because reserves earn no interest, they have an adverse effect on bank earnings.
- In practice, the required reserve ratio has been adjusted only infrequently by the U.S. Federal Reserve Board.
- U.S. depository institutions hold required reserves in one of two forms: vault cash on hand at the bank or—more significant for monetary policy—required reserve balances in accounts with the Reserve Bank for their respective Federal Reserve District.

FOR MORE INFORMATION

Web site:
www.xrefer.com offers a variety of definitions and examples of the reserve ratio.

Calculating Capitalization Ratios

WHAT THEY MEASURE

By comparing debt to total capitalization, these ratios reflect the extent to which a corporation is trading on its equity, and the degree to which it finances operations with debt.

While not the focus here, capitalization ratio also refers to the percentage of a company's total capitalization contributed by debt, preferred stock, common stock, and other equity.

WHY THEY ARE IMPORTANT

By itself, any financial ratio is a rather useless piece of information. Collectively, and in context, though, financial leverage ratios present analysts and investors with an excellent picture of a company's situation, how much financial risk it has taken on, its dependence on debt, and developing trends. Knowing who controls a company's capital tells one who truly controls the enterprise!

HOW THEY WORK IN PRACTICE

A business finances its assets with either equity or debt. Financing with debt involves risk, since debt legally obligates a company to pay off the debt, plus the interest the debt incurs. Equity financing, on the other hand, does not obligate the company to pay anything. It is apt to pay investors dividends—but at the discretion of the board of directors. To be sure, business risk accompanies the operation of any enterprise. But how that enterprise opts to finance its operations—how it blends debt with equity—may heighten this risk.

Various experts include numerous formulas among capitalization financial leverage ratios. Three are discussed separately: debt-to-capital ratio, debt-to-equity ratio, and interest coverage ratios. What's known as the capitalization ratio per se can be expressed in two ways:

> = **long-term debt / long-term debt + owners' equity**

and

> = **total debt / total debt + preferred + common equity**

For example, a company whose long-term debt totals 5,000 and whose owners hold equity worth $3,000 would have a capitalization ratio of:

> = **5,000 / 5,000 + 3,000**
>
> = **5,000 / 8,000 = 0.625 capitalization ratio**

Both expressions of the capitalization ratio are also referred to "component percentages," since they compare a company's debt with either its total capital (debt plus equity) or its equity capital. They readily indicate how reliant a company is on debt financing.

TRICKS OF THE TRADE

- Capitalization ratios need to be evaluated over time, and compared with other data and standards. A gross profit margin of 20%, for instance, is meaningless—until one knows that the average profit margin for an industry is 10%; at that point, 20% looks quite attractive. Moreover, if that the historical trend of that margin has been climbing for the last three years, it strongly suggests that a company's management has sound and effective policies and strategies in place.
- Also, all capitalization ratios should be interpreted in the context of a company's earnings and cash flow, and those of its competitors.
- Take care in comparing companies in different industries or sectors. The same figures that appear to be low in one industry can be very high in another.
- Some less frequently used capitalization ratios are based on formulas that use the book value of equity (the stock). When compared with other ratios, they can be misleading, because there usually is little relation between a company's book value and its market value—which is apt to be many times higher, since market value reflects what the investment community thinks the company is worth.

FOR MORE INFORMATION

See also:
Accounting (pp. 1667–1669)

"Never invest your money in anything that eats or needs repainting."

Billy Rose

Calculating Acid-test Ratio

WHAT IT MEASURES

How quickly a company's assets can be turned into cash, which is why assessment of a company's liquidity also is known as the quick ratio, or simply the acid ratio.

WHY IT IS IMPORTANT

Regardless of how this ratio is labeled, it is considered a highly reliable indicator of a company's financial strength and its ability to meet its short-term obligations. Because inventory can sometimes be difficult to liquidate, the acid-test ratio deducts inventory from current assets before they are compared with current liabilities—which is what distinguishes it from the current ratio.

Potential creditors like to use the acid-test ratio because it reveals how a company would fare if it had to pay off its bills under the worst possible conditions. Indeed, the assumption behind the acid-test ratio is that creditors are howling at the door demanding immediate payment, and that an enterprise has no time to sell off its inventory, or any of its stock.

HOW IT WORKS IN PRACTICE

The acid-test ratio's formula can be expressed in two ways, but both essentially reach the same conclusion. The more common expression is:

(current assets – inventory) / current liabilities = acid-test ratio

If, for example, current assets total $7,700, inventory amounts to $1,200, and current liabilities total $4,500, then:

(7,700 – 1,200) / 4,500 = 1.44

A variation of this formula ignores inventory altogether, distinguishes assets as cash, receivables, and short-term investments, then divides the sum of the three by the total current liabilities, or:

cash + accounts receivable + short-term investments / current liabilities = acid-test ratio

If, for example, cash totals $2,000, receivables total $3,000, short-term investments total $1,000, and liabilities total $4,800, then:

(2,000 + 3,000 + 1,000) / 4,800 = 1.25

There are two other ways to appraise liquidity, although neither is as commonly used: the cash ratio is the sum of cash and marketable securities divided by current liabilities; net quick assets is determined by adding cash, accounts receivable, and marketable securities, then subtracting current liabilities from that sum.

TRICKS OF THE TRADE

- In general, the quick ratio should be 1:1 or better. It means a company has a unit's worth of easily convertible assets for each unit of its current liabilities. A high quick ratio usually reflects a sound, well-managed organization in no danger of imminent collapse, even in the extreme and unlikely event that its sales ceased immediately. On the other hand, companies with ratios of less than 1 could not pay their current liabilities, and should be looked at with extreme care.
- While a ratio of 1:1 is generally acceptable to most creditors, acceptable quick ratios vary by industry, as do almost all financial ratios. No ratio, in fact, is especially meaningful without knowledge of the business from which it originates. For example, a declining quick ratio with a stable current ratio may indicate that a company has built up too much inventory; but it could also suggest that the company has greatly improved its collection system.
- Some experts regard the acid-test ratio as an extreme version of the working capital ratio because it uses only cash and equivalents, and excludes inventory. An acid-test ratio that is notably lower than the working capital ratio often means that inventory makes up a large proportion of current assets. An example would be retail stores.
- Comparing quick ratios over an extended period of time can signal developing trends in a company. While modest declines in the quick ratio do not automatically spell trouble, uncovering the reasons for changes can help to find ways to nip potential problems in the bud.
- Like the current ratio, the quick ratio is a snapshot, and a company can manipulate its figures to make it look robust at a given point in time.
- Investors who suddenly become keenly interested in a company's quick ratio may signal their anticipation of a downturn in the company's business or in the general economy.

FOR MORE INFORMATION

Web site:
Business Owner's Toolkit: **www.toolkit.cch.com**

See also:
Accounting (pp. 1667–1669)

1025

ACTIONLIST

"Armaments, universal debt, and planned obsolescence—these are the three pillars of Western prosperity."

Aldous Huxley

Calculating Convertible Preferred Stock

GETTING STARTED

- Evaluating convertible preferred stock is principally an analysis of risk rather than of a company.
- Preferred stocks are listed as equity on a balance sheet, but perform more like bonds than common stock, since most of these issues pay a fixed dividend set at the time of issue.
- While holders of preferred stock are entitled to a fixed dividend, they do not usually have voting rights.
- Preferred stocks are usually repayable at par value, and rank above the claims of ordinary stockholders but behind bank and trade creditors.
- An expensive form of capitalization, preferred stock is typically used to finance growth opportunities and capital expenditures, and to repay bank debt and non-bank short-term debt.
- Preferred stocks are often preferred by venture capitalists because they protect their investments better, and offer them greater leverage and growth opportunities.
- U.S. income tax considerations severely limit the appeal of preferred stock among individual investors, but enhance it among corporations.

FAQs

Officially, what is convertible preferred stock?

It is a share of corporation ownership that give holders a claim prior to the claim of common stockholders on earnings and, generally, on assets in the event of liquidation. It may also be exchanged for a fixed number of shares of common stock. Because no maturity date is stipulated, preferred stock is priced based on a stated dividend yield—in, for example, dollars, pounds, or Euros—or as a percentage of par value.

How does preferred stock compare to common stock?

The dividend on common stock is uncertain and variable: high when a company performs well, low or nonexistent when it fares poorly. Holders of preferred stock, however, get a fixed dividend—and one which, if not paid, accrues until it can be. On the other hand, preferred stockholders are not usually able to vote on pertinent resolutions unless dividends fall into arrears, while holders of common stock have voting rights based on the number of shares owned.

Are there different kinds of preferred stock?

Yes. For example, callable preferred stock may be repurchased by the issuing company, typically at par value or slightly higher, while an indirect convertible may be exchanged for another convertible security, such as a bond that can be exchanged for convertible preferred stock. There are also participating preferred stocks, which entitle holders both to receive specified dividends and to participate along with holders of common stock in receiving additional dividends.

Any other important distinguishing features of preferred stock?

First, there may be an option to receive cash for those who decline to exercise their conversion rights. Most preferred stock also carry lower interest rates than similar fixed-interest securities, since the investor has the opportunity to convert his holdings to common stock and, in turn, to realize a capital gain if its price rises above its conversion price. Some preferred stocks also permit the investor to require the issuing company to redeem the stock after a predetermined time for an amount that gives the investor a modest profit.

Venture capitalists are known to prefer preferred stock. Why?

It gives them preference in the event of a company's liquidation or sale. A typical convertible preferred stock also enables venture capitalist investors to convert their shares into common stock at a predetermined formula and to vote on major stockholder issues such as the election of directors and a change of the company's core business activity.

How are repeated conversions of preferred stock prevented from diluting the value of common stock?

The formula used to convert the convertible preferred stock into shares of common stock typically includes an adjustment mechanism—an "anti-dilution provision"—that protects the investor against any dilution in his percentage ownership caused by sale of cheaper stock to later investors. The nature and extent of the protection afforded can be very important also to the holders of the company's common stock: the greater the protection against dilution given to the holder of convertible preferred stock, the more dilution common stockholders are likely to suffer.

MAKING IT HAPPEN

Like virtually any stock consideration, evaluating convertible preferred stock opportunities and transactions is based on research, market knowledge, and past experience.

It is essential first to understand what a company does and how it generates cash. The next question is determining the likelihood of the company being able to pay its preferred dividends. The tools of choice are, first, a common "coverage ratio" like EBIT or EBITDA and, second, preferred stock ratings.

EBITDA is the acronym for "earnings before interest, taxes, depreciation, and amortization." It usually

measures a company's ability to handle debt service (interest payments), but can easily be adapted to include preferred stock dividends. The ratio is:

$$\frac{\text{EBITDA}}{\text{interest expense}} + \text{preferred dividends}$$

The higher the coverage ratio, the better.

Like corporate bonds, most preferred stocks are rated by such services as Standard & Poor's and Moody's. Each rating service uses a slightly different rating system, but they have a similar basis: "A" is good, "AAA" is better, and so on. A "B" or above is considered investment grade, but anything below that is regarded as very high risk.

Another warning point is that, if a preferred stock is rated only by one of the second-tier rating agencies, the likelihood is that the company's management was unable to get a favorable rating from Standard & Poor's or Moody's. The investor relations offices and Web sites of most corporations will provide the ratings. If they do not, beware—although the Web sites of the rating services themselves will probably list them.

There are also some guidelines to follow. For instance, preferred stocks should have a higher yield than the issuing company's comparable debt (yield is the annual dividend divided by the price). This must be gauged on a case-by-case basis.

There is another long-held contention that higher-quality companies issue standard convertible preferred stock, while lower-quality companies issue convertible exchangeable preferred stock. Similarly, it is maintained that only the "best" companies are consistently able to issue straight debt cost-effectively, while medium-quality companies issue convertible securities, and lower-quality companies or high-risk companies tend to issue additional common stock.

Conversion ratios and prices are other key facts to know about preferred stock. This information is found on the indenture statement that accompanies all issues. Occasionally the indenture will state that the conversion ratio will change over time. For example, the conversion price might be $50 for the first five years, $55 for the next

five years, and so forth. Stock splits can affect conversion considerations.

In theory, convertible preferred stocks (and convertible exchangeable preferred stocks) are usually perpetual in time. However, issuers tend to force conversion or induce voluntary conversion for convertible preferred stock within ten years. Steadily increasing common stock dividends is one inducement tactic used. As a result, the conversion feature for preferred stocks often resembles that of debt securities. Call protection for the investor is usually about three years, and a 30– to 60-day call notice is typical.

About 50% of convertible equity issues also have a "soft call provision." If the common stock price reaches a specified ratio, the issuer is permitted to force conversion before the end of the normal protection period.

Converting preferred stock risks diluting common stock, of course, and among mature companies that is a valid concern. Where a company has a good track record and aggressive growth plans, however, it may benefit both investors and the company, especially if the management can maintain (or increase) profit margin.

TRICKS OF THE TRADE

- Preferred stocks and other convertible securities offer investors a hedge: fixed-interest income without sacrificing the chance to participate in a company's capital appreciation.
- When a company does well, investors can convert their holdings into common stock that is more valuable. When a company is less successful, they can still receive interest and principal payments, and also recover their investment and preserve their capital if a more favorable investment appears.

FOR MORE INFORMATION

Web site:
Equity Analytics Limited: **www.e-analytics.com**

Creating a Balance Sheet

WHAT IT MEASURES

The financial standing, or even the net worth or owners' equity, of a company at a given point in time, typically at the end of a calendar or fiscal year.

WHY IT IS IMPORTANT

The balance sheet shows what is owned (assets), what is owed (liabilities), and what is left (owners' equity). It provides a concise snapshot of a company's financial position.

HOW IT WORKS IN PRACTICE

However they are presented, assets must be in balance with liabilities and stockholders' equity. In other words, assets must equal liabilities and owners' equity.

Assets include cash in hand and cash anticipated (receivables), inventory of supplies and materials, properties, facilities, equipment, and whatever else the company uses to conduct business. Assets also need to reflect depreciation in the value of equipment such as machinery that has a limited expected useful life.

Liabilities include pending payments to suppliers and creditors, outstanding current and long-term debts, taxes, interest payments, and other unpaid expenses that the company has incurred.

Subtracting the value of aggregate liabilities from the value of aggregate assets reveals the value of owners' equity. Ideally, it should be positive. Owners' equity consists of capital invested by owners over the years and profits (net income) or internally generated capital, which is referred to as "retained earnings"; these are funds to be used in future operations (see opposite and below for an example).

LIABILITIES	$
Payables	7,000
Taxes	4,000
Misc.	3,000
Bonds & notes	25,000
TOTAL LIABILITIES	39,000
STOCKHOLDERS' EQUITY (stock, par value × shares outstanding)	80,000
RETAINED EARNINGS	10,000
TOTAL LIABILITIES AND STOCKHOLDERS' EQUITY	129,000

TRICKS OF THE TRADE

- The balance sheet does not show a company's market worth, nor important intangibles such as the knowledge and talents of individual people, nor other vital business factors such as customers or market share.
- The balance sheet does not express the true value of some fixed assets. A six-year-old manufacturing plant, for example, is listed at its original cost, even though the price of replacing it could be much higher or substantially lower (because of new technology that might be less expensive or vastly more efficient).
- The balance sheet is not an indicator of past or future performance or trends that affect performance. It needs to be studied along with two other key reports: the income statement and the cash flow statement. A published balance sheet needs to include prior period comparatives.

FOR MORE INFORMATION

Web site:
Conetic.com: **www.conetic.com**

See also:
 Accounting (pp. 1667–1669)

ASSETS	$
Current:	
Cash	8,200
Securities	5,000
Receivables	4,500
Inventory & supplies	6,300
Fixed:	
Land	10,000
Structures	90,000
Equipment (less depreciation)	5,000
Intangibles/other	
TOTAL ASSETS	129,000

"But what those critics don't know is that these same assets that excite me in the chase often, once they are acquired, leave me bored."

Donald J. Trump

Creating a Profit and Loss Account

WHAT IT MEASURES

A profit and loss account (P&L) represents a company's sales revenues and expenses over a period, providing a calculation of profits or losses during that time.

WHY IT IS IMPORTANT

Reading a P&L is the easiest way to tell if a business has made a profit or a loss during a given month or year. The most important figure it contains is net profit: what is left over after revenues are used to pay expenses and taxes.

Companies typically issue P&L reports monthly. It is customary for the reports to include year-to-date figures, as well as corresponding year-earlier figures to allow for comparisons and analysis.

HOW IT WORKS IN PRACTICE

A P&L adheres to a simple rule of thumb: "revenue minus cost equals profit."

There are two P&L formats, multiple-step and single-step. Both follow a standard set of rules known as Generally Accepted Accounting Principles (GAAP). These rules generally adhere to requirements established by governments to track receipts, expenses, and profits for tax purposes. They also allow the financial reports of two different companies to be compared. Note that in the United Kingdom and several other nations, sales, revenues, and receipts may all be designated as turnover.

The multiple-step format is much more common, because it includes a larger number of details and is thus more useful. It deducts costs from revenues in a series of steps, allowing for closer analysis. Revenues appear first, then expenses, each in as much detail as management desires. Sales may be broken down by product line or location, while expenses such as salaries may be broken down into base salaries and commissions.

Expenses are then subtracted from revenues to show profit (or loss). A basic multiple-step P&L is shown below.

P&Ls of public companies may also report income on the basis of earnings per share. For example, if the company issuing this statement had 12,000 shares outstanding, earnings per share would be $5.12, that is, $61,440 divided by 12,000 shares.

TRICKS OF THE TRADE

- A P&L does not show how a business earned or spent its money.
- One month's P&L can be misleading, especially if a business generates a majority of its receipts in particular months. A retail establishment, for example, usually

MULTIPLE-STEP PROFIT & LOSS ACCOUNT ($)			
NET SALES			750,000
Less: cost of goods sold			450,000
Gross profit			300,000
LESS: OPERATING EXPENSES			
Selling expenses			
Salaries & commissions	54,000		
Advertising	37,500		
Delivery/transportation	12,000		
Depreciation/store equipment	7,500		
Other selling expenses	5,000		
Total selling expenses		116,000	
General & administrative expenses			
Administrative/office salaries	74,000		
Utilities	2,500		
Depreciation/structure	2,400		
Misc. other expenses	3,100		
Total general & admin expenses		82,000	
Total operating expenses			198,000
OPERATING INCOME			102,000
LESS (ADD): NONOPERATING ITEMS			
Interest expenses	11,000		
Interest income earned	(2,800)		8,200
Income before taxes			93,800
Income taxes			32,360
Net income			**61,440**

generates a large percentage of its sales in the final three months of the year, while a consulting service might generate the lion's share of its revenues in as few as two months, and no revenues at all in some other months.

- Invariably, figures for both revenues and expenses reflect the judgments of the companies reporting them. Accounting methods can be quite arbitrary when it comes to such factors as depreciation expenses.

FOR MORE INFORMATION

Web site:
Biz/ed: **www.bized.ac.uk**

See also:
Accounting (pp. 1667–1669)

"Take care to sell your horse before he dies. The art of life is passing losses on."

Robert Frost

Creating a Cash Flow Statement

WHAT IT MEASURES

Cash inflows and cash outflows over a specific period of time, typically a year.

WHY IT IS IMPORTANT

Cash flow is a key indicator of financial health, and it demonstrates to investors, creditors, and other core constituencies a company's ability to meet obligations, finance opportunities, and generally "come up with the cash" as needs arise. Cash flow that is wildly inconsistent with, say, net income, often indicates operating or managerial problems.

HOW IT WORKS IN PRACTICE

In its basic form, a cash flow statement will probably be familiar to anyone who has been a member of a club that collected and spent money. It reports funds on hand at the beginning of a given period, funds received, funds spent, and funds remaining at the end of the period.

That formula still applies to a business today, even if creating a cash flow document is significantly more complex. Cash flows are divided into three categories: cash from operations; cash-investment activities; and cash-financing activities. Companies with holdings in foreign currencies use a fourth classification: effects of changes in currency rates on cash.

A standard direct cash flow statement is shown in the opposite column.

TRICKS OF THE TRADE

- A cash flow statement does *not* measure net income, nor does it measure working capital.
- A cash flow statement does not include outstanding accounts receivable, but it does include the preceding year's accounts receivable (assuming these were collected during the year for which the statement is prepared).
- Add to a cash inflow any amounts charged off for depreciation, depletion, and amortization, since cash was actually spent.
- Cash equivalents are short-term, highly liquid investments, although precise definitions may vary slightly by country. These should be included when recalculating the movement of cash in the period.
- There are alternative ways to present cash flow from operations. Some texts, for example, omit earnings and adjustments, and list instead cash and interest received, cash and interest paid, and taxes received.

CRD, Inc.
Statement of Cash Flows
For year ended December 31, 20__

FLOWS FROM OPERATIONS	
	$
Operating Profit	82,000
Adjustments to net earnings	
Depreciation	17,000
Accounts receivable	(20,000)
Accounts payable	12,000
Inventory	(8,000)
Other adjustments to earnings	4,000
Net cash flow from operations	**87,000**

CASH FLOWS FROM INVESTMENT ACTIVITIES	
Purchases of marketable securities	(58,000)
Receipts from sales of marketable securities	45,000
Loans made to borrowers	(16,000)
Collections on loans	11,000
Purchases of plant and real estate assets	(150,000)
Receipts from sales of plant and real estate assets	47,000
Net cash flow from investment activities	**(-121,000)**

CASH FLOWS FROM FINANCING ACTIVITIES	
Proceeds from short-term borrowings	51,000
Payments to settle short-term debts	(61,000)
Proceeds from issuing bonds payable	100,000
Proceeds from issuing capital stock	80,000
Dividends paid	(64,000)
Net cash flow from financing activities	**106,000**
Net change in cash during period	72,000
Cash and cash equivalents, beginning of year	27,000
Cash and cash equivalents, end of year	**99,000**

FOR MORE INFORMATION

Web site:
International Accounting Standards Consultancy:
www.iasc.co.uk

See also:
∽ Accounting (pp. 1667–1669)

"The eighties was an era when many companies were asset rich and cash poor."

Nicola Horlick

Reading a Balance Sheet

GETTING STARTED

A balance sheet will tell us something about the financial strength of a business on the day that the balance sheet is drawn up. That situation changes constantly, so you could say it is more like a snapshot than a movie. Although the method of producing a balance sheet is standardized, there can be a certain element of subjectivity in interpreting it. Different elements of the balance sheet can tell you different things about the how the business is doing.

This actionlist gives an overview of a balance sheet and looks at a brief selection of the more interesting figures that help with interpretation. It's important to remember that a lot of these figures do not tell you that much in isolation; it is in trend analysis or comparisons between businesses that they speak more lucidly.

FAQs

What is a balance sheet?

A balance sheet is an accountant's view, the book value of the assets and liabilities of a business at a specific date and on that date alone. The term "balance" means exactly what it says—that those assets and liabilities will be equal. In showing how the balance lies, the balance sheet gives us an idea of the financial health of the business.

What does a balance sheet not do?

A balance sheet is not designed to represent market value of the business. For example, property in the balance sheet may be worth a lot more than its book value. Plant and machinery is shown at cost less depreciation, but that may well be different from market value. Stock may turn out to be worth less than its balance-sheet value, and so on.

Also there may be hidden assets, such as goodwill or valuable brands, that do not appear on the balance sheet at all. These would all enhance the value of the business in a sale situation, yet are invisible on a normal balance sheet.

MAKING IT HAPPEN

Here is a very simple company balance sheet:

Fixed Assets		1,000
Current Assets	700	
Less Current Liabilities	400	
Net Current Assets		300
		1,300
Less Long-term Loans		200
Net Assets		1,100
Profit and Loss Account		500
Share Capital		600
Stockholders' Funds		1,100

Define the Individual Elements

- *Fixed Assets*—items that are not traded as part of a company's normal activities but enable it to function, such as property, machinery or vehicles. These are tangible assets (meaning you can kick them). This heading can also include intangible assets (you cannot kick them). A common example is "goodwill," which can arise upon the acquisition of one business by another.
- *Current Assets*—items that form the trading cycle of the business. The most common examples are stock, debtors, and positive bank balances.
- *Current Liabilities*—also items that form the trading cycle of the business but represent short-term amounts owed to others. Examples are trade creditors, taxes, and bank overdrafts—broadly, any amount due for payment within the next 12 months from the date of the balance sheet.
- *Net Current Assets*—not a new figure, but simply the difference between current assets and current liabilities, often shown because it may be a useful piece of information.
- *Long-term Loans*—debt that is repayable more than one year from the date of the balance sheet.
- *Net Assets*—also not a new figure, but the sum of fixed assets plus net current assets less long-term loans. In other words, all of the company assets shown in its books, minus all of its liabilities.
- *Profit and Loss Account*—the total of all the accumulated profits and losses from all the accounting periods since the business started. It increases or decreases each year by the net profit or loss in that period, calculated after providing for all costs including tax and dividends to stockholders.
- *Share Capital*—the number of shares issued, multiplied by their nominal value. The latter is the theoretical figure at which the shares were originally issued and has nothing to do with their market value.
- *Stockholders' Funds*—not a new figure, but the sum of the profit and loss account plus the share capital. It represents the total interest of the stockholders in the company.

Learn to Interpret Them

Note that balance sheets differ between one industry and another as regards the range and type of assets and liabilities that exist. For example, a retailer will have little in the way of trade debtors because it sells for cash, while a manufacturer is likely to have a far larger investment in plant than a service business like an advertising agency. So the interpretation must be seen in the light of the actual trade of the business.

Reading a balance sheet can be quite subjective—accounting is an art, not a science and, although the method of producing a balance sheet is standardized, there may be some items in it that are subjective rather than factual. The way people interpret some of the figures will also vary, depending on what they wish to achieve and how they see certain things as being good or bad.

"Every man's occupation should be beneficial to his fellow-man as well as profitable to himself. All else is vanity and folly."

P. T. Barnum

Look First at the Net Assets/Stockholders' Funds

Positive or negative? Our example, being a healthy business, has net assets of a positive $1,100. Positive is good. If there were 600 shares in issue, it would mean that the net assets per share were $1.83.

If it had negative assets (same thing as net liabilities), this might mean that the business is heading for difficulty unless it is being supported by some party such as a parent company, bank, or other investor. When reading a balance sheet with negative assets, consider where the support will be coming from.

Then Examine Net Current Assets

Positive or negative? Again, our example has positive net current assets (NCA) of $300. This means that, theoretically, it should not have any trouble settling short-term liabilities because it has more than enough current assets to do so. Negative net current assets suggest that there could be a problem in settling short-term liabilities.

You can also look at NCA as a ratio of current assets/current liabilities. Here, a figure over one is equivalent to the NCA having a positive absolute figure. The ratio version is more useful in analyzing trends of balance sheets over successive periods or comparing two businesses.

A cut-down version of NCA considers only (debtors + cash)/(creditors) thus excluding stock. The reasoning here is that this looks at the most liquid of the net current asset constituents. Again a figure over one is the most desirable. This is also a ratio that is more meaningful in trends or comparisons.

Understand the Significance of Trade Debtor Payments . . .

Within current assets, we have trade debtors. It can be useful to consider how many days' worth of sales are tied up in debtors—given by (debtors × 365)/annual sales. This provides an idea of how long the company is waiting to get paid. Too long, and it might be something requiring investigation. However, this figure can be misleading where sales do not take place evenly throughout the year. A construction company might be an example of such a business: one big debtor incurred near the year end would skew the ratio.

. . . And Trade Creditor Payments

Similar to the above, this looks at (trade creditors × 365)/annual purchases, indicating how long the company is taking in general to pay its suppliers. This is not so easy to calculate, because the purchases for this purpose include not only goods for resale but all the overhead as well.

Recognize What Debt Means

Important to most businesses, this figure is the total of long and short-term loans. Too much debt might indicate that the company would have trouble, in a downturn, in paying the interest. It's difficult to give an optimum level of debt because there are so many different situations, depending on a huge variety of circumstances.

Often, instead of an absolute figure, debt is expressed as a percentage of shareholders' funds and known as "gearing" or "leverage." In a public company, gearing of 100% might be considered pretty high, whereas debt of under 30% may be seen as on the low side.

COMMON MISTAKES

Believing That Balance Sheet Figures Represent Market Value

Don't assume that a balance sheet is a valuation of the business. Its primary purpose is that it forms part of the range of accounting reports used for measuring business performance—along with the other common financial reports like profit and loss accounts and cash flow statements. Management, shareholders, and others such as banks will use the entire range to assess the health of the business.

Forgetting That the Balance Sheet Is Valid Only for the Date at Which It Is Produced

A short while after a balance sheet is produced, things could be quite different. In practice there frequently may not be any radical changes between the date of the balance sheet and the date when it is being read, but it is entirely possible that something could have happened to the business that would not show. For example, a major debtor could have defaulted unexpectedly. So remember that balance sheet figures are valid only as at the date shown, and are not a permanent picture of the business.

Confusion over Whether in Fact All Assets and Liabilities Are Shown in the Balance Sheet

Some businesses may have hidden assets, as suggested above. This could be the value of certain brands or trademarks, for example, for which money may not have ever been paid. Yet these could be worth a great deal. Conversely, there may be some substantial legal action pending which could cost the company a lot, yet is not shown fully in the balance sheet.

"I don't know what we have. It becomes so complex that you need to have ten accountants working for two years to find out what you have."

Yoko Ono

Reading a Profit and Loss Account

GETTING STARTED

A profit and loss account (P&L) is a statement of the income and expenditure of a business over the period stated, drawn up in order to ascertain how much profit the business made. Put simply, the difference between the income from sales and the associated expenditure is the profit or loss for the period. "Income" and "expenditure" here mean only those amounts directly attributable to earning the profit and thus would exclude capital expenditure, for example.

Importantly, the figures are adjusted to match the income and expenses to the time period in which they were incurred—not necessarily the same as that in which the cash changed hands.

FAQs
What is a profit and loss account?

A profit and loss account is an accountant's view of the figures that show how much profit or loss a business has made over a period. To arrive at this, it is necessary to allocate the various elements of income and expenditure to the time period concerned, not on the basis of when cash was received or spent, but on when the income was earned or the liability to pay a supplier and employees was incurred. While capital expenditures are excluded, depreciation of property and equipment is included as a noncash expense.

Thus if you sell goods on credit, you will be paid later but the sale takes place upon the contract to sell them. Equally if you buy goods and services on credit, the purchase takes place when you contract to buy them, not when you when you actually settle the invoice.

What does a profit and loss account not show?

Most importantly, a P&L account is not an explanation of the cash coming into and going out of a business.

MAKING IT HAPPEN

Below is a simple example of a profit and loss account for a particular year.

Note that the presence of inventory and purchases indicates that the business is trading or manufacturing goods of some kind, rather than selling services.

Defining the Individual Elements

- *Sales*—the invoiced value of the sales in the period.
- *Inventory*—the value of the actual physical inventory held by the business at the opening and closing of the period. It is always valued at cost, or realizable value if that is lower, never at selling price.
- *Purchases and Other Direct Costs*—the goods or raw materials purchased by the business for resale—not capital items used in the business, only items used as part of the direct cost of its sales. In other words, those costs which vary directly with sales, as distinct from overhead (like rent) which do not.

When a business holds inventory, the purchases figure

Sales		1,000
Opening inventory	100	
Purchases	520	
	620	
Closing inventory	80	
Cost of Sales		540
Gross Profit		460
Wages	120	
Other Overhead	230	
		350
Net Profit before Tax		110
Tax		22
Net after Tax		88
Dividends		40
Retained Profit		48
Retained Profit Brought Forward		150
Retained Profit Carried Forward		198

has to be adjusted for the opening and closing values in order to reach the right income and expenditure amounts for that period only. Goods for resale bought in the period may not have been used purely for that period but may be lying in inventory at the end of it, ready for sale in the next. Similarly, goods used for resale in this period will consist partly of items already held in inventory at the beginning of it. So take the amounts purchased, add the opening inventory, and deduct the closing inventory. The resulting adjusted purchase figure is known as "cost of sales."

In some businesses there may be other direct costs apart from purchases included in cost of sales. For example, a manufacturer may include some wages if they are of a direct nature (wages of employees directly involved in the manufacturing process, as distinct from office staff, say). Or a building contractor would include plant hire in direct costs, as well as purchases of materials.

- *Gross Profit*—the difference between sales and cost of sales. This is an important figure, as it measures how much was actually made directly from whatever the business is selling, before it started to pay for overhead.

The figure is often expressed as a percentage ratio, when it is known as the "gross profit margin." In our example the GPM is 460:1,000—or 46%. Ratios are really only useful as comparison tools, either with different periods of the same business or with other businesses.

- *Overhead*—the expenses of the business which do not vary directly with sales. They include a wide variety of items such as rent, most wages, advertising, phones, interest paid on loans, audit fees, and so on.
- *Net Profit before Tax*—the result of deducting total overhead from gross profit. This is what the business has made before tax is paid on that profit.
- *Tax*—This will not actually have been paid in the year concerned, but is shown because it is due on the profit

for that period. Even then the figure shown may not be the actual amount due, for various reasons such as possible overpayments from previous years. Tax can be a very complex matter, being based upon a set of changeable rules.

- *Net Profit after Tax*—the result after deducting the tax liability—the so-called bottom line. This is the amount that the company can do with as it wishes, possibly paying a dividend out of part of it and retaining the rest. It is the company's reward for actually being in business in the first place.
- *Dividends*—a payment to the stockholders as a reward for their investment in the company. Most publicly listed companies of any size pay dividends to stockholders. Private companies may also do so, but this may be more for tax reasons. The dividend in the example shown is paid out of the net profit after tax, but legally it is not permitted to exceed the total available profit. That total available profit is comprised of both the current year's net profit after tax and the retained profit brought forward from previous years.
- *Retained Profit*—the amount kept by the company after paying dividends to stockholders. If there is no dividend, then it is equal to the net profit after tax.
- *Retained Profit Brought Forward*—the total accumulated retained profits for all earlier years of the company's existence.
- *Retained Profit Carried Forward*—the above figure brought forward, plus the current year's retained profit. This new total will form the profit brought forward in the next accounting period.

How to Interpret the Figures

A lot of accounting analysis is valid only when comparing the figures, usually with similar figures for earlier periods, projected future figures, or other companies in the same business.

On its own, a P&L account tells you only a limited story, though there are some standalone facts that can be derived from it. What our example does show, even in isolation, is that this business was successful in the period concerned. It made a profit, not a loss, and was able to pay dividends to stockholders out of that profit. Clearly a pretty crucial piece of information.

However, it is in comparisons that such figures start to have real meaning.

The example figures reveal that the gross profit margin was 46%, an important statistic in measuring business performance. The net profit margin before tax was 110:1,000, or 11%. You could take the margin idea further and calculate the net profit after tax ratio to sales as 88:1,000, being 8.8%. Or you could calculate the ratio of any expense to sales. In our example, the wages to sales ratio is 120:1,000 or 12%.

If you then looked at similar margin figures for the preceding accounting period, you would learn something about this business. Say the gross margin was 45% last year compared with 46% this year—there has been some improvement in the profit made before deducting overhead. But then suppose that the net profit margin of 8.8% this year was 9.8% last year. This would tell you that, despite improvement in profit at the gross level, the overhead has increased disproportionately. You could then check on the ratio of each of the overhead to sales to see where this arose and find out why. Advertising spending could have shot up, for example, or perhaps the company moved to new premises, incurring a higher rent. Maybe something could be tightened up.

Another Commonly Used Ratio

Another ratio often used in business analysis is return on capital employed. Here we combine the profit and loss account with the balance sheet by dividing the net profit (either before or after tax as required) by stockholders' funds. This tells you how much the company is making proportionate to money invested in it by the stockholders—a similar idea to how much you might get in interest on a bank deposit account. It's a useful way of comparing different companies in a particular industry, where the more efficient ones are likely to derive a higher return on capital employed.

COMMON MISTAKES
Assuming That the Bottom Line Represents Cash Profit from Trading

It does not! There are a few examples where this is the case: a simple cash trader might buy something for one price, then sell it for more; his profit then equals the increase in cash. But a business that buys and sells on credit, spends money on items that are held for the longer term, such as property or machinery, has tax to pay at a later date, and so on, will make a profit that is not represented by a mere increase in cash balances held. Indeed, the cash balance could quite easily decrease during a period when a profit was made.

FOR MORE INFORMATION

Web site:
The Motley Fool: **www.fool.com**

See also:
- Accounting (pp. 1667–1669)
- Reading a Cash Flow Statement (pp. 1035–1036)

Reading a Cash Flow Statement

GETTING STARTED

In their annual report, most public companies must publish a cash flow statement—together with the profit and loss account and a balance sheet. As the name suggests, the purpose of a cash flow statement is to explain the movement in cash balances or bank overdrafts held by the business from one accounting period to the next.

The balance sheet shows the assets and liabilities at the end of the period, with comparative figures for the start of it. The profit and loss account shows how much profit was generated by the business in the period. The cash flow statement is the third part of the financial picture of the business over the period.

FAQs

What is a cash flow statement?

Over an accounting period, the money held by a business at the bank (or its overdrafts) will have changed. The purpose of the cash flow statement is to show the reasons for this change. If you look at the actionlist on profit and loss (**Reading a Profit and Loss Account (pp. 1033–1034)**), one of the common mistakes illustrated was the erroneous belief that the profit was equal to the cash generated by a business. It is not, but the cash flow statement is the link between profit and cash balance movements. It takes you down the path from profit to cash. The figures are derived from those published in the annual financial statements, and notes will explain how this derivation is arrived at.

What does a cash flow statement not show?

In the same way that a profit and loss account does not show the cash made by the business, a cash flow statement does not show the profit. It is entirely possible for a business with a loss to show an increase in cash, and the other way around too.

MAKING IT HAPPEN

Below is a simple example of a cash flow statement for a particular year.

Define the Individual Elements

- *Net Cash Inflow from Operating Activities*—broadly this is the profit of the business, before depreciation plus the change in debtor and creditor balances. There may also be other items included here. In the statutory annual financial statements of companies, there will be an explanation to show how this net cash inflow figure is derived from the profit and loss account and balance sheet. Depreciation is excluded because it does not represent a cash cost.

Debtor and creditor balance changes are included here because they represent an inflow or outflow of cash to the business. Thus, if customers owe you less or more at the end of a period than at the beginning of it, it follows that there must have been cash flowing in or out of the business as a result. A reduction in debtors means that cash has come in to the business, and the reverse for an

Net Cash Inflow from Operating Activities		7,020
Returns on Investments and Financing Costs		
Interest Paid	820	
Less Interest Received	90	
Net Cash Outflow from Financing Costs		(730)
Taxation		(1,060)
Capital Expenditure		
Sale of Fixed Assets	760	
Less Purchase of Fixed Assets	4,420	
Net Cash Outflow from Capital Expenditure		(3,660)
Dividends Paid		(1,530)
Net Cash Inflow before Financing		40
Financing		
New Loans	1,000	
Loan Repayments	(300)	
Finance Lease Repayments	(100)	
Net Cash Inflow from Financing		600
Increase in Cash		640

increase in debtors. The same applies to the creditor balances of suppliers. An increase here means a cash inflow, with a decrease denoting an outflow.

- *Returns on Investments and Financing Costs*—these figures comprise interest received on cash balances, less interest paid on debt. There could be other forms of investment income here, such as dividends on shares owned.

- *Net Cash Outflow from Financing Costs*—this is not a new figure but the net result of the above items, identified as returns on investments. In our example the result is an outflow of cash. That is, the interest paid on debt exceeded the interest received on cash. It could in some circumstances be the other way around, where, for example, a business has substantial cash balances earning interest.

- *Taxation*: self explanatory, this is the outflow of cash arising from corporation tax paid by the business. It can on occasion be an inflow, where the company has obtained a repayment of corporation tax for some reason.

- *Capital Expenditure*—this is cash expended on fixed assets bought for the business, less cash received from the sale of assets no longer required by the business.

- *Net Cash Outflow from Capital Expenditure*—this is not a new figure but the net result of the above items, identified as expenditure on new fixed assets less receipts from the sale of disposals of such items. In our example there is a large outflow, which generally would be the norm. It can happen sometimes, though, that a business realizes more from the sale of fixed assets in a particular period than it expends on items acquired.

- *Dividends Paid*—self explanatory; this is the outflow of cash arising from paying dividends to stockholders.

- *Net Cash Inflow before Financing*—this is not a new figure but a subtotal of the items above. In our example, the figure of $40 shown happens to be an inflow but it could just as easily have been an outflow. There is no typical

---

"I just never got involved with the cash flow thing. My attitude was creativity will see me through."

Adrienne Landau

figure here; it is just as common to see net inflows as outflows.

It is important to understand what this figure represents. It is the net cash result of running the business in the period concerned, after paying tax to the government and dividends to the stockholders. However, as its label indicates, it doesn't include any financing.

- *Financing*—this term includes the raising of new loans, the repayment of old ones and other methods of financing such as issuing new shares. In the example the company borrowed $1,000 in new loans, which creates a cash inflow of that sum, and repaid $300 on old debt plus a further $100 on equipment leases (which are another form of financing), making a net inflow on financing of $600.
- *Increase in Cash* (the bottom line)—adding the net inflow of $600 from financing to the $40 generated by business operations gives us an overall net cash inflow of $640. This is the bottom line. It means that we have $640 more in the bank at the end of the accounting period than at the beginning of it.

Learn to Interpret the Figures

As suggested above, the cash flow statement is the third section of the primary set of accounting documents used to explain and analyze businesses. It is a "derived schedule," meaning that the figures are pulled from the profit and loss account and balance sheet statements, linking the two.

Its purpose is to analyze the reasons why the company's cash position changed over an accounting period. For example, a sharp increase in borrowings could have several explanations—such as a high level of capital expenditure, poor trading, an increase in the time taken by debtors to pay, and so on. The cash flow statement will alert management to the reasons for this, in a way that may not be obvious merely from the profit and loss account and balance sheet.

The generally desirable situation is for the net position before financing to be positive. Even the best-run businesses will sometimes have an outflow in a period (for example in a year of high capital expenditure), but positive is usually good. This becomes more apparent when comparing the figures over a period of time. A repeated outflow of funds over several years is usually an indication of trouble. To cover this, the company must raise new financing and/or sell off assets, which will tend to compound the problem, in the worst cases leading to failure.

Cash is critical to every business, so the management must understand where its cash is coming from and going to. The cash flow statement gives us this information in an abbreviated form. You could argue that the whole purpose of a business is to start with one sum of money and, by applying some sort of process to it, arrive at another and higher sum, continually repeating this cycle.

COMMON MISTAKES
Confusing "Cash" and "Profit"

As mentioned previously, the most common mistake with cash flow statements is the potential confusion between profit and cash. They are not the same!

Not Understanding the Terminology

It is clearly fundamental to an understanding of cash flow statements that the reader is familiar with terms like "debtors," "creditors," "dividends," and so on. But more than appreciating the meaning of the word "debtors," it is quite easy to misunderstand the concept that, for example, an increase in debtors is a cash outflow, and equally that an increase in creditors represents an inflow of cash to the business.

FOR MORE INFORMATION

Web site:
The Motley Fool: **www.fool.com**

See also:
- Accounting (pp. 1667–1669)
- Reading a Balance Sheet (pp. 1031–1032)
- Reading a Profit and Loss Account (pp. 1033–1034)

Defining Assets

WHAT THEY MEASURE

Collectively, the value of all the resources a company uses to conduct business and generate profits.

Examples of assets are cash, marketable securities, accounts and notes receivable, inventory of merchandise, real estate, machinery and office equipment, natural resources, and intangibles such as patents, legal claims and agreements, and negotiated rights.

WHY THEY ARE IMPORTANT

No business can continue for very long without knowing what assets it has at its disposal, and using them efficiently. Assets are a reflection of organizational strength, and are invariably evaluated by potential investors, banks and creditors, and other stakeholders.

Moreover, the value of assets is also a key figure used to calculate several financial ratios.

HOW THEY WORK IN PRACTICE

Assets are typically broken down into five different categories:

- Current assets. These include cash, cash equivalents, marketable securities, inventory, and prepaid expenses that are expected to be used within one year or a normal operating cycle. All cash items and inventory are reported at historical value. Securities are reported at market value.
- Noncurrent assets, or long-term investments. These are resources that are expected to be held for more than one year. They are reported at the lower of cost and current market value, which means that their values will vary.
- Fixed assets. These include property, plant and facilities, and equipment used to conduct business. These items are reported at their original value, even though current values might well be much higher.
- Intangible assets. These include legal claims, patents, franchise rights, and accounts receivable. These values can be more difficult to determine. Accounts receivable,

for example, reflect the amount a business expects to collect, such as $9,000 of the $10,000 owed by customers.

- Deferred charges. These include prepaid costs and other expenditures that will produce future revenue or benefits.

TRICKS OF THE TRADE

- Assets do not necessarily include everything of value, such as the talents of individuals, an organization's collective expertise, or the value of a customer base.
- Classic definitions of assets also often exclude or undervalue trademarks, even though there is universal agreement that these, for example, the three-point star of Mercedes-Benz or Coca-Cola's red logo, can have enormous value.
- Fixed assets are valued at their original cost, because of the prevailing opinion that they are used for business and are not for sale. Moreover, current market value is essentially a matter of opinion.
- Determining the value of patents can be challenging, because a patent has a finite life span, its value declines each year, and its useful life may be even shorter.
- Some experts contend that the principal assets of "knowledge-based" businesses such as consulting firms or real estate development companies are, in fact, its people. In turn, their aggregate value should be calculated by subtracting the net value of assets from market value.

FOR MORE INFORMATION

Web site:
Investorwords.com: **www.investorwords.com**

See also:
Accounting (pp. 1667–1669)

1037

ACTIONLIST

"Human resources are the greatest assets of any company. You can raise tariffs or prevent MNCs from entering, but one can't stop the employees from leaving if they are dissatisfied."

Narayana Murthy

Calculating Cost of Goods Sold

ACTIONLIST

WHAT IT MEASURES

For a retailer, cost of goods sold (COGS) is the cost of buying and acquiring the goods that it sells to its customers. For a service company, COGS is the cost of the employee services it supplies. For a manufacturer, COGS is the cost of buying the raw materials and manufacturing its finished products.

WHY IT IS IMPORTANT

Cost of goods sold may help a company to determine the prices to charge for its products and services, and the volume of business that it needs to maintain in order to operate profitably.

For retailers especially, the cost of the merchandise sold is typically the largest expense, and thus an absolutely critical business factor. However, understanding COGS is an important success factor for any business, because it can reveal opportunities to reduce costs and improve operations.

COGS is also a key figure on an income statement, and an important consideration in computing income taxes because of its close relationship to inventory, which tax authorities treat as future income.

HOW IT WORKS IN PRACTICE

Essentially, COGS is equal to a company's opening inventory of goods and services, plus the cost of goods bought and direct costs incurred during a particular period, minus the closing inventory of goods and services.

A critical consideration is the accounting policy that a company adopts to calculate inventory values, especially if raw materials prices change during the year. This may happen often, particularly when inflation is high. Inventory values under a First In First Out (FIFO) policy reflect original or older prices of materials, while a Last In First Out (LIFO) policy reflects current (and often more expensive) prices. Somebody computing COGS first needs to know which policy is being used, because this will affect inventory values.

COGS for a manufacturer will include a variety of items, such as raw materials and energy used in production, labor, benefits for production workers, the cost of raw materials in inventory, shipping fees, the cost of storing finished products, depreciation on production machinery used, and factory overhead expenses.

For a retail company such as Wal-Mart, COGS is generally less complex: the total amount paid to suppliers for the products being sold on its shelves.

COGS is calculated as follows:

Inventory at beginning of period	$20,000
Purchases during period	+ $60,000
Cost of good available for sale	= $80,000
Less inventory at period end	– $15,000
Cost of goods sold (COGS)	= $65,000

Because the counting of inventory is an exhaustive undertaking for retailers, doing it quarterly or monthly would be open to error. Accordingly, tax authorities allow them to estimate cost of goods sold during the year.

Determining these estimates requires details of the gross profit margin (retailers typically use the preceding year's figure). This figure is then used to calculate the cost ratio.

Begin by assuming that net sales are 100%, then subtract the gross profit margin, say 40%, to produce a cost ratio of 60%: 100% – 40% = 60%. A monthly COGS calculation then is shown below.

Inventory at beginning of month	$10,000
Purchases during month	+ $25,000
Cost of goods available for sale	= $35,000
Less net sales during month	– $28,000
Cost ratio 100% – 40%	= 60%
Estimated cost of goods sold	= $16,800 ($28,000 × 60%)

There is one sample to review, because calculating COGS for manufacturers requires additional factors:

Inventory at beginning of year	$20,000
Purchases during year	+ $50,000
Cost of direct labor	+ $15,000
Materials and supplies	+ $12,000
Misc. costs	+ $3,000
Total product expenses	= $100,000
Less inventory at year end	– $15,000
Cost of goods sold (COGS)	= $85,000

TRICKS OF THE TRADE

- Anyone who wants to determine COGS must maintain inventory and know its value!
- Because goods returned affect inventory values and, in turn, cost of goods sold, returns of goods must be reflected in COGS calculations.
- Merchandising companies may use different inventory accounting systems, but the choice has no bearing on the actual costs incurred; it only affects allocation of costs.
- COGS should not include indirect costs like administration and marketing costs, or other activities that cannot be directly attributed to producing or acquiring the product.

FOR MORE INFORMATION

Web site:
Biz/ed: www.bized.ac.uk

See also:
⌕ Accounting (pp. 1667–1669)

"Business neglected is business lost."   Daniel Defoe

Calculating Working Capital

WHAT IT MEASURES

The funds that are readily available to operate a business. Working capital comprises the total net current assets of a business, which are its inventory, debtors, and cash—minus its creditors.

WHY IT IS IMPORTANT

Obviously, it is vital for a company to have sufficient working capital to meet all of its requirements. The faster a business expands, the greater will be its working capital needs.

If current assets do not exceed current liabilities, a company may well run into trouble paying creditors who want their money quickly. Indeed, the leading cause of business failure is not lack of profitability, but rather lack of working capital, which helps to explain why some experts advise: "Use someone else's money every chance you get and don't let anyone else use yours."

HOW IT WORKS IN PRACTICE

Working capital is also called net current assets or current capital, and is expressed as:

current assets – current liabilities

Current assets are cash and assets that can be converted to cash within one year or a normal operating cycle; current liabilities are monies owed that are due within one year.

If a company's current assets total $300,000 and its current liabilities total $160,000, its working capital is:

$300,000 – $160,000 = $140,000

The working capital cycle describes capital (usually cash) as it moves through a company: It first flows from a company to pay for supplies, materials, finished goods inventory, and wages to workers who produce goods and services. It then flows into a company as goods and services are sold and as new investment equity and loans are received. Each stage of this cycle consumes time. The

more time the stages consume, the greater the demands on working capital.

TRICKS OF THE TRADE

- Good management of working capital includes actions like collecting receivables faster and moving inventory more quickly; generating more cash increases working capital.
- While it can be tempting to use cash to pay for fixed assets like computers or vehicles, doing so reduces the amount of cash available for working capital.
- If working capital is tight, consider other ways of financing capital investment, such as loans, fresh equity, or leasing.
- Early warning signs of insufficient working capital include pressure on existing cash; exceptional cash-generating activities such as offering high discounts for early payment; increasing lines of credit; partial payments to suppliers and creditors; a preoccupation with surviving rather than managing; frequent short-term emergency requests to the bank, for example, to help pay wages, pending receipt of a check.
- Several ratios measure how effectively and efficiently working capital is being used. These ratios are explained separately.

FOR MORE INFORMATION

Web sites:
www.planware.org/workcap.htm is dedicated to working capital issues, and includes calculations, spreadsheets, definitions, and software packages.
www.studyfinance.com was created for students of finance at the University of Arizona, but its wealth of financial information benefits and serves managers also.

"The market economy as such does not respect political frontiers. Its field is the world."

Ludwig von Mises

Calculating Goodwill and Patents

1040

ACTIONLIST

WHAT IT MEASURES
The value of two intangible assets.

WHY IT IS IMPORTANT
Since both goodwill and patents are intangible assets, their values will be whatever negotiators conclude. Still, their values need to be reflected in financial statements.

Goodwill is created in the aftermath of an acquisition, and must appear on a balance sheet. The acquisition of a patent has a cost of its own, be it the price of internal development costs, or the purchase price paid to an inventor.

HOW IT WORKS IN PRACTICE
Ultimately, the assigned values of both assets are matters of opinion, however learned the opinions may be. Each must be considered separately.

Ordinarily, goodwill is completely ignored by accountants. Only when a company has been acquired by another does goodwill become an intangible asset. It then appears on a balance sheet in the amount by which the price paid by the acquiring company exceeds the net tangible assets of the acquired company. In other words:

purchase price − net assets = goodwill

If, for example, an airline is bought for $12 billion and its net assets are valued at $9 billion, $3 billion of the purchase would be allocated to goodwill on the balance sheet.

The buyer will attribute the difference to any number of reasons that give a competitive advantage, such as a loyal and long-standing customer base, a strong brand, strategic location, or productive employees.

A patent's value, meanwhile, will probably be the sum of its development costs, or its purchase price if acquired from someone else. It is usually to a company's advantage to spread the patent's value over several years. If so, the critical time period to consider is not the full life of the patent (17 years in the United States), but its estimated useful life.

For example, let's say that in January 2000 a company acquired a patent issued in January 1995 at a cost of $100,000. It concludes that the patent's useful commercial life is 10 years, not the 12 remaining before the patent expires. In turn, patent value would be $100,000, and it would be spread (or amortized in accounting terms) over 10 years, or $10,000 each year.

TRICKS OF THE TRADE
- Accounting for goodwill can vary by country, an issue to be considered when evaluating or negotiating acquisitions of foreign-based companies. Moreover, the rules may change from time to time. In the United States, for example, goodwill no longer has to be amortized over 40 years.
- The total value of a patent's development costs may stretch over several years.
- The cost of a patent ultimately may have little bearing on the future revenues and profits it brings.

FOR MORE INFORMATION

Web site:
www.patentcafe.com offers a wealth of patent valuation services and information, including links to the U.S. Patent & Trademark Office and to fee-based evaluation services.

See also:
✓ Calculating Amortization (pp. 1047–1048)

"One lady friend of mine asked me . . . 'What do you love most?' That's how I started painting money."

Andy Warhol

Calculating Yield

WHAT IT MEASURES

Shares that pay dividends (note that not all do) will produce an annual cash return to the investor. Simply dividing this cash return by the current share price and expressing that as a percentage is known as the "yield"—that is, the annual percentage income at the current price. As far as newspapers are concerned, the yield figure published there is usually the historical one.

Analysts will often provide forecasts for dividends in terms of earnings per share (EPS) and thus the forecast yield can then be calculated. Forecasts can, of course, go wrong, and consequently there is some risk in relying upon them.

WHY IT IS IMPORTANT

Yield, after the price/earnings ratio (P/E), is one of the most common methods of comparing the relative value of stocks and that is why it is so widely quoted in the press. The majority of investors like to see a cash income from their stocks, although to some extent this is a cultural thing. There are more companies in the United States, for example, that pay no dividends than in the United Kingdom.

HOW IT WORKS IN PRACTICE

You can compare yields against the market average or against a sector average, which in turn gives you some idea of the relative value of the stock against its peers, much like other ratios. Other things being equal, a higher yield stock is preferable to that of an identical company with a lower yield. The higher yield stock is cheaper. In practice of course, there may well be good reasons why the market has decided that the higher yielder should be so—possibly it has worse prospects, is less profitable, and so on. This is not always the case; the market is far from being a perfectly rational place.

An additional feature of the yield (unlike many of the other stock analysis ratios), is that it enables comparison with cash. When you put cash into an interest-bearing source like a bank account or a government stock, you get a yield—the annual interest payable. This is usually a pretty safe investment. You can compare the yield from this cash investment with the yield on stocks, which are far riskier. This produces a valuable basis for stock evaluation. If, for example, you can get 4% in a bank without capital risk, you can then look at stocks and ask yourself how this yield compares—given that, as well as the opportunity for long-term growth of both the stock price and the dividends, there is plenty of capital risk.

TRICKS OF THE TRADE

Care is necessary, however, because unlike banks paying interest, companies are under no obligation to pay dividends at all. Frequently, if they go through a bad patch, even the largest, most well-known household name companies will cut dividends or even abandon paying them altogether. So, stock yield is greatly less reliable than bank interest or government stock interest yield.

Despite this, yield is an immensely useful feature of stock appraisal. It is the only ratio that tells you about the cash return to the investor, and you cannot argue with cash. Earnings per share (EPS), for example, is subject to accountants' opinions but a dividend once paid is an unarguable fact.

1041

ACTIONLIST

FOR MORE INFORMATION

Web sites:
Securities and Exchange Commission: **www.sec.gov**
The Accounting Standards Board U.K.: **www.asb.org.uk**

See also:
- ✔ Calculating Earnings per Share (p. 1060)
- ✔ Calculating Price/Earnings Ratio (p. 1017)
- ✔ Reading the Financial Pages (pp. 1055–1056)

Reading an Annual Report

1042

ACTIONLIST

GETTING STARTED

Every company must publish an annual report to its stockholders as a matter of corporate law. The primary purpose of this report is to inform stockholders of the company's performance. As a legal requirement, the report usually contains a profit and loss account, a balance sheet, a cash flow statement, a directors' report, and an auditors' report. The different elements tell you about different aspects of the company's performance and can be read in particular order to build up a true picture of how it is doing.

Many companies also provide a lot of other nonstatutory information on their affairs, in the interests of general communication. In some cases, this may be little more than gloss, contrived to illustrate the company's wonderful achievements while remaining strangely silent on negative features.

FAQs

Is there any difference between annual reports from private and public companies?

The main difference is usually length. The reports of privately held companies will be far shorter because their mandatory reporting requirements are much reduced. Additionally, they will be less concerned with image and consequently will tend to omit the noncompulsory public relations features that are present in public company reports.

What guarantee is there that an annual report is a true picture of a company's performance and not just propaganda put out by directors?

All annual reports have to include a report from the auditors, independent accountants charged with investigating a company's financial affairs to ensure that the published figures give a true and fair view of performance. Their investigation cannot extend to examining every single transaction (impossible in a company of any size), so they use statistical sampling and other risk-based testing procedures to assess the quality of the company's systems as a basis for producing the annual report. They are not infallible, but they stand between the stockholders and the directors as a way of trying to insure probity in the running of the company.

MAKING IT HAPPEN
Understanding the Main Contents of an Annual Report

The best way to look at this is to take an example. Standard sections in annual reports can vary from country to country, but the following is the contents list of a medium-sized U.S. public company—let's call it X, Inc.
- X World
- Chairman's Statement
- Chief Executive's Review
- Financial Review
- Board of Directors
- Board Report on Remuneration
- Directors' Responsibilities
- Report of the Auditors
- Financial Statements
- Five-year Record
- Stockholder Information

X World—belongs in the PR area. It tells you about the company, its products and markets.

Chairman's Statement—comments on the group results for the year and upon future developments. It also provides detail on earnings per share and dividends.

Chief Executive's Review—goes into more detail about individual divisions, breaking down the operating results from areas around the world. It tells us a bit about discontinued businesses and new ones acquired.

Financial Review—expands on the two previous sections in a more quantitative way, looking at things like cash flow and how it affected group debt; interest charges; the effect of exchange rate fluctuations on profits, assets and liabilities; exceptional items that affect the profits (such as the disposal of a subsidiary company), and so on.

Board of Directors—lists the directors, with a brief description and photo of each.

Board Report on Remuneration—describes the work of a committee of nonexecutive directors, who decide the directors' income and that of other senior employees. Their remit includes looking at service contracts, bonus and stock option plans, plus pension plans. It includes an analysis of the pay of each director, with comparable figures for the previous year plus details of stock options, and so on.

Directors' Responsibilities—is a mandatory statement showing exactly what the directors are obliged to discharge with regard to the annual report, maintaining accurate accounting records, and so on.

Report of the Auditors—is simply what it says. Their findings are published using standard language in this report.

Financial Statements—are the main purpose of the annual report. In the example of X, Inc., these consist of:
- Consolidated Profit and Loss Account. The profit and loss account of all the group as one.
- Consolidated and Company Balance Sheets. The former is the group balance sheet and the latter shows the parent company alone.
- Consolidated Cash Flow Statement. A guide to how the money flowing in and out of the company was utilized.
- Management's Responsibility for Financial Reporting.
- Management's Discussion and Analysis.
- Notes to the Financial Statements. These amplify numerous points contained in the figures and are usually critical for anyone wishing to study the financial statements in detail.

Five-year Record—shows a very abbreviated set of profit and loss and balance sheet figures for the current and previous four years. Some companies provide a ten-year record.

"We can't run the business. We learned over twenty-five years ago to let the business run itself. Commitment, not authority, promotes results."

Wilbert Lee Gore

Stockholder Information—deals with matters such as the registered office, stockholder registrars, brokers, lawyers, dates for meetings and dividend payments, and other points.

Choosing the Right Order in Which to Read the Report

One way is simply to read the report from cover to cover, like a book. However, if you are not experienced with these things, that may lead you to giving equal weight to all the contents and, perhaps, overvaluing the glossy PR bits at the expense of the hard facts shown by the figures.

Start with the Auditors' Report

Remember that this thin gray line of accountants is all that stands between the outside stockholder and the directors. To speed up matters, look at the final paragraph, their opinion. Does that statement give a true and fair view? If so, fine. If not, then it is said to be "qualified." Qualifications vary in depth from the disastrous, meaning that the company has gotten something seriously wrong, to perhaps a difference of opinion between the auditors and the board over some accounting matter. Most auditors' reports are unqualified, but, if there is a qualification present, you will have to judge how much the financial statements can be relied upon as a measure of the company's performance.

Next, Turn to the Five/Ten-Year Review

This is where you build up a mental picture of the company's financial history. Look at earnings per share (EPS)—is it increasing, decreasing, fluctuating wildly? This gives you an idea of how it has been doing over the period. Look at dividends, if any, and consider their pattern. Do they follow EPS or, as is likely, are they showing a smoother picture? Look at company debt, if the information is there, and compare it with stockholders' funds. How is it changing over the years?

Generally, try to build up a view as to whether the company is doing better, worse, or perhaps has no particular pattern over the period. Depending on your reasons for reading the report, a set of prejudices will have begun to develop from this historical picture. If it shows a declining financial situation, this could be a good thing from some points of view—if you wish to acquire the company, for example. If you are an employee though, it would not be very encouraging. So reading reports depends to some extent upon which angle you are coming from.

Now Read the Chairman's and Director's Comments

These will give a deeper feel for the company's business, over and above the raw numerical data. Try to exercise a

degree of skepticism in some areas, because it is natural for directors to attempt to play up the good points and play down the less good ones.

Get to the Heart of the Matter

The kernel of the report comprises the financial statements and the huge number of notes that accompany them. A lot of it is in highly technical accounting terminology, but it gives you the intimate financial detail on the year. Never ignore the notes—they are critical. In fact some investment analysts read the report from the back, because the notes are so important.

Notes have increased dramatically over the years as new legal and accounting standards have been introduced, primarily to enforce standardization so that financial reports are more comparable, but also to avoid "creative accounting," whereby some companies have tried to conceal (legitimately) financial undesirables.

Relax with the Glossy Stuff

Having absorbed all that really matters, settle back and read the glossy parts that tell you how wonderful the company is. Just remember to exercise a mild degree of cynicism here—this is the least important, though no doubt the most visually attractive, part of the annual report. The real picture of the company is the numbers, not the photo of the guy in the hard hat standing on an oil rig!

COMMON MISTAKES
Paying Too Much Attention to Pretty Pictures and Directors' Comments and Too Little to the Accounting Data

This can give a false view of how well, or badly, the company is doing. Understandably, a large number of people have difficulty in comprehending the figures. But if you want to appreciate annual reports properly, then learning to read financial reports is essential.

Some cynics among investment analysts have even expressed the view that there is an adverse relationship between the number of glossy pages in an annual report and the company's actual performance. Maybe that's a little harsh but . . . there might be something in it.

FOR MORE INFORMATION

Web sites:
International Accounting Standards Board: **www.iasb.org**
Securities and Exchange Commission: **www.sec.gov**

See also:
✓ Calculating Earnings per Share (p. 1060)

1043

ACTIONLIST

"It's an unbelievable responsibility to influence decisions, shareholder value and, most important to me, people's careers and livelihoods."

Andrea Jung

Calculating Depreciation

GETTING STARTED

Depreciation is a basic expense of doing business, reducing a company's earnings while increasing its cash flow. It affects three key financial statements: balance sheet; cash flow; and income (or profit and loss). It is based on two key facts: the purchase price of the items or property in question, and their "useful life."

Depreciation values and practices are governed by the tax laws of both national governments, and state or provincial governments, which must be monitored continuously for any changes that are made. Accounting bodies, too, have developed standard practices and procedures for conducting depreciation.

Depreciating a single asset is not difficult: the challenge lies in depreciating the many assets possessed by even small companies, and is intensified by the impact that depreciation has on income and cash flow statements, and on income tax returns. It is essential to depreciate with care and to rely on experts, ensuring that they fully understand the current government rules and regulations.

FAQs
What is depreciation?

It is an allocation of the cost of an asset over a period of time for accounting and tax purposes. Depreciation is charged against earnings, on the basis that the use of capital assets is a legitimate cost of doing business. Depreciation is also a noncash expense that is added into net income to determine cash flow in a given accounting period.

What is straight-line depreciation?

One of the two principal depreciation methods, it is based on the assumption that an asset loses an equal amount of its value each year of its useful life. Straight-line depreciation deducts an equal amount from a company's earnings throughout the life of the asset.

What is accelerated depreciation?

The other principal method of depreciation is based on the assumption that an asset loses a larger amount of its value in the early years of its useful life. Also known as the "declining-balance" method, it is used by accountants to reduce a company's tax bills as soon as possible, and is calculated on the basis of the same percentage rate each year of an asset's useful life. Accelerated depreciation also better reflects the economic value of the asset being depreciated, which tends to become increasingly less efficient and more costly to maintain as it grows older.

What can be depreciated?

To qualify for depreciation, assets must:
- be used in the business;
- be items that wear out, become obsolete, or lose value over time from natural causes or circumstances;
- have a useful life beyond a single tax year.

Examples include vehicles, machines and equipment, computers and office furnishings, and buildings, plus major additions or improvements to such assets. Some intangible assets can also be included under certain conditions.

What cannot be depreciated?

Land, personal assets, inventory, leased or rented property, and a company's employees.

MAKING IT HAPPEN

In order to determine the annual depreciation cost of assets, it is necessary first to know the initial cost of those assets, how many years they will retain some value for the business, and what value, if any, they will have at the end of their useful life.

For example, a company buys a truck to carry materials and finished goods. The vehicle loses value as soon as it is purchased, and then loses more with each year it is in service, until the cost of repairs exceeds its overall value. Measuring the loss in the value of the truck is depreciation.

Straight-line depreciation is the most straightforward method, and is still quite common. It assumes that the net cost of an asset should be written off in equal amounts over its life. The formula used is:

(original cost – scrap value) / useful life (years)

For example, if the truck cost $30,000 and can be expected to serve the business for seven years, its original cost would be divided by its useful life:

(30,000 – 2,000) / 7 = 4,000 per year

The $4,000 becomes a depreciation expense that is reported on the company's year-end tax return.

In theory, an asset should be depreciated over the actual number of years that it will be used, according to its actual drop in value each year. At the end of each year, all the depreciation claimed to date is subtracted from its cost in order to arrive at its "book value," which would equal its market value. At the end of its useful business life, any undepreciated portion would represent the salvage value for which it could be sold or scrapped.

For tax purposes, some accountants prefer to use accelerated depreciation to record larger amounts of depreciation in the asset's early years in order to reduce tax bills as soon as possible. In contrast to the straight-line method, the accelerated or declining balance method assumes that the asset depreciates more in its earlier years of use. The table below compares the depreciation amounts that would be available, under these two methods, for a $1,000 asset that is expected to be used for five years and then sold for $100 in scrap.

While the straight-line method results in the same deduction each year, the declining-balance method produces larger deductions in the first years and far smaller deductions in the later years. One result of this system is that, if the equipment is expected to be sold for a higher

| | Straight-line Method | | Declining-balance Method | |
Year	Annual Depreciation	Year-end Book Value	Annual Depreciation	Year-end Book Value
1	$900 × 20% = $180	$1,000 – $180 = $820	$1,000 × 40% = $400	$1,000 – $400 = $600
2	$900 × 20% = $180	$820 – $180 = $640	$600 × 40% = $240	$600 – $240 = $360
3	$900 × 20% = $180	$640 – $180 = $460	$360 × 40% = $144	$360 – $144 = $216
4	$900 × 20% = $180	$460 – $180 = $280	$216 × 40% = $86.40	$216 – $86.40 = $129.60
5	$900 × 20% = $180	$280 – $180 = $100	$129.60 × 40% = $51.84	$129.60 – $51.84 = $77.76

value at some point in the middle of its life, the declining-balance method can produce a greater taxable gain in that year because the book value of the asset will be relatively lower.

The depreciation method to be used for a particular asset is fixed at the time that the asset is first placed in service. Whatever rules or tables are in effect for that year must be followed as long as the asset is owned.

Depreciation laws and regulations change frequently over the years as a result of government policy changes, so a company owning property over a long period may have to use several different depreciation methods.

TRICKS OF THE TRADE

- With very specific exceptions, it is not possible to deduct in one year the entire cost of an asset if that asset has a useful life substantially beyond the tax year.
- To qualify for depreciation, an asset must be put into service. Simply purchasing it is not enough. There are rules that govern how much depreciation can be claimed on items put into service after a year has begun.
- It is common knowledge that if a company claims more depreciation than it is entitled to, it is liable for stiff penalties in a tax audit, just as failure to allow for depreciation causes an overestimation of income. What is not commonly known is that if a company does not claim all the depreciation deductions it is entitled to, it will be considered as having claimed them when taxable gains

or losses are eventually calculated on the sale or disposal of the asset in question.

- While leased property cannot be depreciated, the cost of making permanent improvements to leased property can be (remodeling a leased office, for example). There are many rules governing leased assets; they should be depreciated with care.
- Another common mistake is to continue depreciating property beyond the end of its recovery period. Cars are common examples of this.
- Conservative companies depreciate many assets as quickly as possible, despite the fact that this practice reduces reported net income. Knowledgeable investors watch carefully for such practices.

FOR MORE INFORMATION

Web sites:
Business Owner's Toolkit: **www.toolkit.cch.com**
Encyclopedia.com: **www.encyclopedia.com**
Bankrate.com:
www.bankrate.com/brm/itax/Edit/tips/Stories/sec179_deduction.asp

See also:
- Accounting (pp. 1667–1669)
- Calculating Amortization (pp. 1047–1048)

Calculating Enterprise Value

WHAT IT MEASURES

It measures what financial markets believe that a company's ongoing operations are worth.

Some people also define enterprise value as what it would actually cost to purchase an entire company at a given moment.

WHY IT IS IMPORTANT

Enterprise value is not a theoretical valuation but a firm and finite value, logically determined. It tells an individual investor the underlying value of his stake in an enterprise. For potential acquirers considering a takeover of a company, enterprise value helps them to determine a reasonable price for their desired acquisition.

HOW IT WORKS IN PRACTICE

Although it is a finite figure, enterprise value can be calculated in two ways. One method is quicker, but the other is more thorough and thus more reliable.

The quick way is simply to multiply the number of a company's shares outstanding by the current price per share. Using this approach, the enterprise value of a company with 2 million shares outstanding, and a share price of $25, would be:

$$2{,}000{,}000 \times 25 = 50{,}000{,}000 \text{ enterprise value}$$

However, this value is based on the market's perception of the value of its shares of stock; it also ignores some important factors about a company's fiscal health. The second, more complete, method is therefore preferred by many experts. This method calculates enterprise value as the sum of market capitalization, plus debt and preferred stock, minus cash and cash equivalents:

market capitalization + long-term debt + preferred stock – cash & equivalents = enterprise value

In turn, if market capitalization is $6.5 million, debt totals $1 million, the value of preferred stock is $1.5

million, and cash and equivalents total $2.5 million, enterprise value would be:

$$(6.5 + 1 + 1.5) - 2 =$$
$$7 \text{ (million) enterprise value}$$

This more thorough calculation recognizes the existence of both a company's debt and of the amount of cash and liquid assets on hand. No matter how a stock may fluctuate, these sums are relatively constant, and the amount of debt can be very significant. Debt—and cash, too—can be just as important during a company's sale, since new owners both assume existing debt and receive any cash on hand. Indeed, more than a few acquisitions are financed in part with funds of the acquired company.

TRICKS OF THE TRADE

- Financial markets often use the market capitalization figure for enterprise value, but they really are not the same thing.
- Experts will occasionally refer to "total enterprise value," but its definition and formula are virtually identical to this second-formula enterprise value. Total enterprise value is only meaningful to those who use the quick method to compute enterprise value.
- A company's value is sometimes expressed as "the total funds being used to finance it." This is increasingly used in place of the price/earnings ratio, and indicates the economic rather than the accounting return that the company is generating on the total value of the capital supporting it. Companies that have borrowed heavily to finance growth, or that have paid large premiums for acquisitions or assets, are more frequently evaluated by this method.

FOR MORE INFORMATION

Web site:
The Motley Fool: **www.fool.com**

Calculating Amortization

WHAT IT MEASURES

Amortization is a method of recovering (deducting or writing off) the capital costs of intangible assets over a fixed period of time. Its calculation is virtually identical to the straight-line method of depreciation.

Amortization also refers to the establishment of a schedule for repaying the principal and interest on a loan in equal amounts over a period of time. Because computers have made this a simple calculation, business references to amortization tend to focus more on the term's first definition.

WHY IT IS IMPORTANT

Amortization enables a company to identify its true costs, and thus its net income, more precisely. In the course of their business, most enterprises acquire intangible assets such as a patent for an invention, or a well-known brand or trademark. Since these assets can contribute to the revenue growth of the business, they can be—and are allowed to be—deducted against those future revenues over a period of years, provided the procedure conforms to accepted accounting practices.

For tax purposes, the distinction is not always made between amortization and depreciation, yet amortization remains a viable financial accounting concept in its own right.

HOW IT WORKS IN PRACTICE

Amortization is computed using the straight-line method of depreciation: divide the initial cost of the intangible asset by the estimated useful life of that asset. For example, if it costs $10,000 to acquire a patent and it has an estimated useful life of 10 years, the amortized amount per year is $1,000.

$10,000 / 10 = $1,000 per year

The amount of amortization accumulated since the asset was acquired appears on the organization's balance sheet as a deduction under the amortized asset.

While that formula is straightforward, amortization can also incorporate a variety of noncash charges to net earnings and/or asset values, such as depletion, write-offs, prepaid expenses, and deferred charges. Accordingly, there are many rules to regulate how these charges appear on financial statements. The rules are different in each country, and are occasionally changed, so it is necessary to stay abreast of them and rely on expert advice.

For financial reporting purposes, an intangible asset is amortized over a period of years. The amortizable life—"useful life"—of an intangible asset is the period over which it gives economic benefit. Several factors are considered when determining this useful life; for example, demand and competition, effects of obsolescence, legal or contractual limitations, renewal provisions, and service life expectations.

Intangibles that can be amortized can include:
- **Copyrights**, based on the amount paid either to purchase them or to develop them internally, plus the costs incurred in producing the work (wages or materials, for example). At present, a copyright is granted for the life of the author plus 70 years. However, the estimated useful life of a copyright is usually far shorter than its legal life, and it is generally amortized over a fairly short period.
- **Cost of a franchise**, including any fees paid to the franchiser, as well legal costs or expenses incurred in the acquisition. A franchise granted for a limited period should be amortized over its life. If the franchise has an indefinite life, it should be amortized over a reasonable period, not to exceed 40 years.
- **Covenants not to compete**. An agreement by the seller of a business not to engage in a competing business in a certain area for a specific period of time. The cost of the not-to-compete covenant should be amortized over the period covered by the covenant unless its estimated economic life is expected to be shorter.
- **Easement costs** that grant a right of way may be amortized if there is a limited and specified life.
- **Organization costs** incurred when forming a corporation or a partnership, including legal fees, accounting services, incorporation fees, and other related services. Organization costs are usually amortized over 60 months.
- **Patents**, both those developed internally and those purchased. If developed internally, a patent's "amortizable basis" includes legal fees incurred during the application process. Normally, a patent is amortized over its legal life, or over its remaining life if purchased. However, it should be amortized over its legal life or its economic life, whichever is the shorter.
- **Trademarks, brands, and trade names**, which should be written off over a period not to exceed 40 years. However, since the value of these assets depends on the changing tastes of consumers, they are frequently amortized over a shorter period.
- Other types of property that may be amortized include certain intangible drilling costs, circulation costs, mine development costs, pollution control facilities, and reforestation expenditures. They can even include intangibles such as the value of a market share or a market's composition: an example is the portion of an acquired business that is attributable to the existence of a given customer base.

TRICKS OF THE TRADE
- Certain intangibles cannot be amortized, but may be depreciated using a straight-line approach if they have a "determinable" useful life. Because the rules are different in each country and are subject to change, it is essential to rely on specialist advice.
- Computer software may be amortized under certain conditions, depending on its purpose. Software that is amortized is generally given a 60-month life, but it may be amortized over a shorter period if it can clearly be established that it will be obsolete or no longer used within a shorter time.

"One way to make sure crime doesn't pay would be to let the government run it."

Ronald Reagan

1048

ACTIONLIST

- Under certain conditions, customer lists that were purchased may be amortized if it can be demonstrated that the list has a finite useful life, in that customers on the list are likely to be lost over a period of time.
- While leasehold improvements are depreciated for income tax purposes, they are amortized when it comes to financial reporting—either over the remaining term of the lease or their expected useful life, whichever is the shorter.
- Annual payments incurred under a franchise agreement should be expensed when incurred.
- The Internet has many amortization loan calculators that can automatically determine monthly payment figures and the total cost of a loan.

FOR MORE INFORMATION

Web sites:
Financial Accounting Standards Board: **www.fasb.org**
U.S. Copyright Office: **www.copyright.gov**
U.S. Patent and Trademark Office: **www.uspto.gov**

See also:

"Human resources are the greatest assets of any company."   Narayana Murthy

Calculating Activity Based Costing

GETTING STARTED

Activity based costing (ABC) attempts to create the big picture—crystal-clear, full, and accurate—by painting assorted little pictures.

- ABC identifies the relationship between a business activity and all the resources needed to conduct it by assigning costs to each of those resources, thus presenting the true total expense of the entire activity.
- ABC can account for so-called "soft" or indirect operating costs, and thus produce a more revealing, and perhaps startlingly different, financial picture than other accounting methodologies such as standard costing might offer.
- Used properly, ABC helps management better to distinguish operations that add value from those that do not, permitting more informed decisions about such matters as pricing, product mix, capital investments, and organizational change.
- In turn, ABC's advocates praise it as a more effective tool to identify and control costs, improve productivity, and increase profits.

FAQs
When did ABC start?

ABC came of age in the 1980s amid manufacturers' furious efforts to raise the quality of their products while simultaneously eliminating every unnecessary cost from their operations. The dramatic improvements realized by manufacturers have led to ABC becoming a widely used tool, especially in the manufacturing industry.

What are the basic steps of ABC?

There are five:

- identify the product or service to be studied;
- determine all the resources and processes that are required to create the product or deliver the service, and their respective costs;
- determine the "cost drivers" for each resource: the cost of labor as well as raw materials;
- collect cost and other data, such as time taken, for each process and resource;
- use the data to calculate the overall cost of the product.

What are ABC's principal advantages?

First, ABC can gauge virtually any activity, be it a manufacturing process, a business process, the performance of a service, or an administrative operation. Second, it considers a much wider variety of resources and materials than more traditional accounting methodologies, and can thus present a more complete picture.

What are ABC's primary weaknesses?

It can be a very time-consuming exercise because of the volume of data it demands. Also, if not managed properly, ABC can transform every manager into an accountant whose energies become fixed on tracking the costs of the activity, rather than on tracking and perfecting the activity itself.

What kind of business sectors use ABC?

The list ranges from accountants to zoologists. It may be especially helpful to knowledge-based businesses that rely primarily on human services and related resources, whose total costs may be difficult to measure with more traditional accounting yardsticks.

What is critical to ABC's success?

Without gaining and maintaining the enduring commitment of all individuals, even a modestly detailed initiative will probably fail. It's also best to start with pilot projects to demonstrate success.

What preliminary steps are needed?

First, an organization must understand its activities and the resources that these require. Second, it must understand thoroughly the amount of information required, and the expense of generating that information. It must also determine what level of accuracy will be acceptable.

MAKING IT HAPPEN

Creating an ABC cost accounting system requires three preliminary steps:

- converting to an accrual basis of accounting;
- defining cost centers and cost allocation;
- determining process and procedure costs.

Businesses have traditionally relied on the cash basis of accounting, which recognizes income when received and expenses when paid. ABC's foundation is the accrual-basis. The numbers this statement presents are assigned to the various procedures performed during a given period. Cost centers are a company's identifiable products and services, but also include specific and detailed tasks within these broader activities. Defining cost centers will of course vary by business and method of operation. What is critical to ABC is the inclusion of all activities and all resources. Once these steps have been taken, the results are often more than satisfying.

Banks and financial services firms, for example, have long used ABC-like methods to confirm that investments in automated teller machines would be both cheaper than continuing to rely on tellers and clerks and in their customers' best interests.

Railroad companies have used the methodology to determine the cost of processing bills of lading by hand, fax, and the Internet. Studying such costs confirmed the wisdom of using e-commerce, generating annual savings of up to $1 million.

Law firms are better positioned to confirm that the hourly fees they charge—no matter how princely they may at first appear—do, in fact, enable them to provide their services profitably.

Finally, healthcare providers use ABC to measure profitability, eliminate unnecessary costs, and plan for change. A medical practice that knows the actual cost of providing a specific service, for example, can make far better decisions about the price of managed health care.

For instance, let's say the Apple-a-Day Medical Clinic

includes three physicians, Drs. Peel, Core, and Stem. Their clinic has an in-house laboratory and a radiology department. All direct revenues and expenses are allocated to the physician who performs the service and incurs the expense. Indirect variable overhead costs are allocated to each physician based on the proportion of total revenues that each generates in a given period. Fixed overhead costs are divided equally among physicians. Because of their respective incomes and expense allocations, each physician would represent a separate cost center.

Additional cost centers for this medical practice could be laboratory, radiology, and administration. As cost centers are defined, they could further be classified as, say, "patient service centers" or "support centers." In this example, laboratory, radiology, and each individual physician's activity would be patient service centers, while administration would be a support center.

Once cost centers are identified, management teams can begin studying the activities each one engages in and allocating the expenses each one incurs, including the cost of employee services. In this healthcare scenario, activities would range from actual treatment by physicians and nurses, X-rays, medical tests and assessments of their results, plus such administrative support services as personnel, bookkeeping, rent, utilities, property insurance, office supplies, advertising, telecommunications expenses, and equipment costs related to the administrative function. Rent, utilities, and property insurance are usually allocated on the basis of the square footage that the particular activity covers.

Tracking and allocating the detailed costs of individual activities and procedures can be accomplished by different methods, with various degrees of accuracy. The more detailed the cost analysis, of course, the greater the accuracy of the data. Then again, as the detail increases, so does the time and expense.

The most appropriate method is developed from time studies and direct expense allocation. Management teams that choose this method will need to devote several months to data collection in order to generate sufficient information to establish the personnel components of each activity's total cost. The cost of this exercise itself can be significant, but also worthwhile. Proponents say ABC has resulted in cost savings worth as much as 14 times the cost of the exercise. More importantly, the exercise has provided solid documentation for decisions that "seemed correct," as a Chrysler Corporation team once reported, "but could not be supported with hard evidence."

Time studies establish the average amount of time required to complete each task, plus best- and worst-case performances. Only those resources actually used are factored into the cost computation; unused resources are reported separately. These studies can also advise management how best to monitor and allocate expenses which might otherwise be expressed as part of general overhead, or go undetected altogether.

Notably, determining how much of an operation's personnel is underused or unused can significantly help management planning, specifically by exposing activities that are overstaffed or understaffed. This can be especially helpful to any knowledge-based business, since payroll is almost always its highest cost. Moreover, in any business, the more efficiently an enterprise deploys its personnel, the more profitable it will be.

COMMON MISTAKES
Getting Caught Up in the Details

Notwithstanding its successes, ABC remains a tool, not an end in itself. Organizations can lose sight of that fact, if they are not careful, and end up allowing it to dominate their working lives.

The enormity and complexity of such a project should never be underestimated. The data requirements alone are daunting. It is all too easy to get caught up in ABC's details and mechanics. In turn, estimating some costs is often recommended, to minimize the level of detail.

At the same time, however, some details are important prerequisites of objectivity and success. For example, if time studies are not used, some other measure must be used to allocate personnel and related costs, as well as indirect costs such as percentage of revenues or income, or the number of customer calls. These methods require far less time for compiling data and are less costly, but drawbacks abound. For one thing, accuracy suffers, and they are almost always subjective, potentially to the point of compromising the entire initiative. Being far less precise, these alternative methods also do not differentiate between used and unused personnel resources, and will not provide information on unused capacity or trends in procedure costs.

Without the aid of computer software that has been developed to automate the process, ABC can be hopelessly time-consuming. Indeed, unaided by technology, ABC might well be hoist with its own petard and exposed as an outrageous waste of time.

Like any cost accounting system, activity based costing is not static. Once established, it needs to be maintained and updated as business conditions and organizations change.

Finally, in delivering its crystal-clear pictures, activity based costing also has the potential to make individual champions of particular products or services squirm, because it may reveal them to be far more expensive than they might otherwise appear. All the more reason for advocating caution: "Watch out what you wish for!"

If a management team is to reduce and eliminate costs, it must first identify them and grasp their impact on specific processes or products. Because activity based costing can paint a single picture that reveals all the individual direct and indirect costs a business incurs in a given operation, it can be a powerful tool for both assessing current operations and guiding prompt and intelligent reactions as circumstances change. In fact, it's also known as activity based management (ABM).

FOR MORE INFORMATION

Web site:
Activity Based Costing Benchmarking Association (ABCBA™): **www.abcbenchmarking.com**

Calculating Price/Sales Ratio

WHAT IT MEASURES

The price/sales ratio (P/S) is another measure, like the price/earnings (P/E) ratio, of the relative value of a stock when compared with others.

WHY IT IS IMPORTANT

Like many such price-based ratios, it does not mean too much in isolation but acquires worth when making comparisons. So a figure of 0.33 does not say a lot on its own, until you start to look at how this matches up to the market average or the sector average, for example.

HOW IT WORKS IN PRACTICE

The P/S ratio is obtained by dividing the market capitalization by the latest published annual sales figure. So a company with a capitalization of $1 billion and sales of $3 billion would have a P/S ratio of 0.33.

P/S will vary with the type of industry. You would expect, for example, that many retailers and other large-scale distributors of goods would have very high sales in relation to their market capitalizations—in other words, a very low P/S. Equally, manufacturers of high-value items would generally have much lower sales figures and thus higher P/S ratios. Like anything to do with share analysis (this being more of an art than a science), it is not always that clear cut . . . but that would be the general trend.

If you rank companies by ascending P/S, you will find usually that supermarket chains figure among the lowest.

A company with a lower P/S is cheaper than one with a higher ratio, particularly if they are in the same sector so that a direct comparison is more appropriate. It means that each share of the lower P/S company is buying you more of its sales than those of the higher P/S company.

Note though, that it is cheaper only on P/S grounds; that does not mean it is necessarily the more attractive share. There will frequently be reasons why it has a lower ratio than another, ostensibly similar company, most commonly because it is less profitable. As far as corporate efficiency goes, this ratio considers only sales, the top line of the profit and loss account. It is a long way from there to the bottom line, the bit that really counts (that is, how much profit the company has made).

TRICKS OF THE TRADE

- A company with a loss would thus still have a P/S ratio, even though it would have no P/E ratio. In consequence, like all investment analysis tools, P/S has to be used with care—but it can be of use for investors. P/S was cited in an extensive study of the New York Stock Exchange as one leading indicator for selecting very long-term shares that perform well.

"Money is certainly too dangerous an instrument to leave to the fortuitous expediency of politicians."

Friedrich August von Hayek

Distinguishing between a Capital and an Operating Lease

1052

ACTIONLIST

GETTING STARTED

Determining whether a lease obligation is an operating or capital lease, for financial reporting purposes, requires that it be evaluated based on four criteria established by the FASB (Financial Accounting Standards Board). The criteria are objective rules for making a judgment about who, the lessor or lessee, bears the risks and benefits of ownership of the leased property. If a lease is determined to be a capital, an asset and corresponding liability is recorded at the present value of the minimum lease payments. The capital asset is depreciated over time, while the liability is amortized as lease payments are made. Rental payments under operating leases are simply expensed as incurred. Due to the complexity of lease agreements, management judgment still plays a large role in distinguishing between operating and capitals.

FAQs
What are minimum lease payments?

The minimum lease payments are the rental payments to be made during the lease term, plus the amount of the bargain price, guaranteed residual value, or penalty for failure to renew the lease at the end of its original term.

In determining whether a lease should be classified as an operating or capital lease, what interest rate should be used?

The interest rate used to discount the minimum lease payments to their present value is the incremental borrowing rate of the lessee, this being the interest rate that the lessee would have been charged if the assets had been acquired by borrowing the purchase price. If the lessor's implied interest rate for the lease is known and is lower than the lessee's estimated incremental borrowing rate, then the lessee uses the implied rate to discount.

MAKING IT HAPPEN
The Four FASB Criteria

Until the 1970s, many companies used leasing as a means to purchase tangible assets without recognizing their ownership or the lease obligation on the balance sheet. In substance, leases were off-balance-sheet financing. Although all leases were required to be disclosed in the footnotes to the financial statements, even long-term finance leases did not appear as a liability. Because the basic measures of leverage do not consider off-balance-sheet obligations, the accounting profession and the investment community believed that there needed to be more stringent guidelines for classifying leases as operating or financing, and in 1976 the FASB issued statement No. 13, "Accounting for Leases." It contains four criteria to distinguish between an operating and finance lease:

- The lease agreement transfers ownership of the assets to the lessee during the term of lease.
- The lessee can purchase the assets leased at a bargain price such as $1, at the end of the lease term.

- The lease term is at least 75% of the economic life of the leased asset.
- The present value of the minimum lease payments is 90% or greater of the asset's value.

If a lease agreement does not meet any of these criteria, the lessee treats it as an operating lease for accounting purposes. If, however, the agreement meets one of the above criteria, it is treated as a capital lease.

Accounting for a Capital Lease

Capital leases are reported by the lessee as if the assets being leased were acquired and the monthly rental payments as if they were payments of principal and interest on a debt obligation. Specifically, the lessee capitalizes the lease by recognizing an asset and a liability at the lower of the present value of the minimum lease payments or the value of the assets under lease. As the monthly rental payments are made, the corresponding liability decreases. At the same time, the leased asset is depreciated in a manner that is consistent with other owned assets having the same use and economic life.

Accounting for an Operating Lease

If the lease is classified as an operating lease, the monthly lease payments are simply treated as rental expenses and recognized on the income statement as they are incurred. There is no recognition of a leased asset or liability.

Clearing Up Remaining Confusion

The FASB's attempt to establish objective criteria for distinguishing between operating and capital leases was a good first step. This has enabled companies to make prudent financial decisions in lease versus buy situations, based on the accounting treatment afforded a specific lease structure. Furthermore, financial professionals now have a framework within which to determine what lease terms create a capital lease. However, the use of financial engineering still occurs. Consequently, many leases that are truly financing leases are recorded as operating leases, because their provisions have been altered to avoid qualification as capital leases.

When in doubt, a manager should always ask whether the risks and benefits of ownership have truly been passed from the lessor to the lessee. Facts that indicate the transfer has occurred are when maintenance, insurance, and property tax expenses are born by the lessee or when the lessee guarantees a specific residual value on the leased property.

FOR MORE INFORMATION

Web site:
Securities and Exchange Commission: **www.sec.gov**

"Forecast: to observe that which has passed, and guess it will happen again."

Frank McKinney Hubbard

Calculating Borrowing Costs and Capitalization

GETTING STARTED

The costs of borrowing are primarily made up of interest and issuance expenses. The interest rate assigned to a particular debt instrument is based on the level of default risk assumed by the investor. Several rating agencies assess the default risk of public debt issuances and provide a rating that is indicative of credit quality. The credit quality is greater for secured/collateralized senior debt than for unsecured subordinated debt issued by the same company, and hence the former typically carries a lower rate of interest. Companies that have higher levels of debt must typically pay higher interest rates to investors to compensate them for the increased risk of default. Capital-intensive businesses can usually maintain greater debt-to-capital ratios for the same level of borrowing costs as businesses that are less capital intensive.

FAQs

What are debt issuance costs and are they always incurred when borrowing money?

Debt issuance costs are the underwriting, legal, and administrative fees required to issue the debt. These fees are significant when issuing debt in the public markets, such as bonds. However, other types of debt, such as private placements or bank loans, are cheaper to issue because they require less underwriting, legal, and administrative support. Consequently, the public issuers of debt are typically *Fortune* 500 companies, while middle-market companies tend to issue debt through private placements.

Do borrowing costs increase or decrease for callable bonds or bonds with detachable stock warrants?

When debt securities are issued with a call feature, the debt can be retired at the discretion of the company until some specified future date. The call feature represents value to the issuing company, much like a call option on equity. The issuer must compensate investors for providing this option. Therefore, the interest rate on callable bonds is typically higher than those on non-callable bonds of the same credit quality. That is, the borrowing costs increase on bonds with a call feature.

The opposite is true of bonds with detachable stock warrants. A stock warrant provides the bondholder with the right to purchase shares of common stock in the issuing company at a specified price during a defined period of time. The warrant's strike price is typically at, or higher than, the current market price of the company's stock. Nonetheless, the warrant provides value to the bondholder in the form of a call option on the company's equity. Because these warrants add to the potential total return on the debt, the stated interest rate is usually lower than that on debt issued without warrants of similar credit quality. Borrowing costs are typically lower on bonds with detachable stock warrants.

MAKING IT HAPPEN

When companies borrow money, they enter a formal obligation to make periodic payments of interest and to repay the principal balance outstanding, according to an agreed schedule. The interest payments are typically based on a stated, annual percentage of the original amount borrowed. The interest paid on such obligations represents the cost of borrowing, along with the costs to issue the debt.

The Difference between Funded and Unfunded Debt

The debt can be classified as funded or unfunded. Funded debt is long-term debt or debt that has a maturity date in excess of one year. Unfunded debt is short-term debt requiring repayment within a year from issuance. Funded debt is usually issued in the public markets or in the form of a private placement to qualified institutional investors. Most unfunded debt is commercial paper or bank lines of credit.

Senior and Subordinated Debt

Debt can also be classified as senior or subordinated, based on its preference to assets in the event of default by the lender. Subordinated lenders have a junior claim to assets in the event of bankruptcy and are paid only after senior creditors' claims have been satisfied.

Senior credit can be secured or unsecured. Much of the corporate debt outstanding is referred to as a bond. However, a true bond is secured by claims against the company's property, plant, and equipment. For example, many airlines secure their public debt by mortgaging their airplanes. In this example, an airline could be forced to sell its airplanes to pay its public debt if it defaults on the bonds. Most public debt is secured by the good faith and credit of the issuing company, and is more accurately called a debenture. A company can also pledge certain assets, like accounts receivable, inventory, or property, as collateral for a loan or debt.

Differing Levels of Risk

Even when debt is secured or collateralized, it still does not guarantee repayment by the issuer. A company's underlying asset value and its earnings may be very volatile, increasing the risk of default in a down business cycle. Because this risk can be different from one business to another, there are several national rating agencies that rate public debt based on the credit-worthiness of the borrower. Investment-grade debt securities are securities that are rated in the top four categories of credit-worthiness by Standard & Poor's or Moody's rating

"Capitalism is an art form, an Apollonian fabrication to rival nature . . . Everyone born into capitalism has incurred a debt to it. Give Caesar his due."

Camille Paglia

agencies. All debt securities rated below investment-grade are considered to be junk bonds.

Different Types of Interest Rate

Debt can have a fixed or floating rate of interest. Fixed-rate debt pays the same interest rate over its term. Most long-term debt is issued with a fixed rate. Many short-term loans are floating-rate instruments based on the prime lending rate, LIBOR (London Interbank Offered Rate), or some other U.S. Treasury security. When the rates on these securities change, the loan rate changes. For example, a line of credit whose current interest rate is 6%, based on one percentage point above the three-year LIBOR rate, will change to 6.25% if the LIBOR rate increases by a quarter of a point. Floating-rate debt is typically used to support a business's working capital requirements.

The Determinants of Credit Quality

The interest rate and, consequently, the borrowing cost is determined by credit quality. Credit quality depends on the type of debt security, the amount of debt relative to total capital, and the capital-intensiveness of a company's business. All other things being equal, a secured or collateralized debt security is less risky than an unsecured obligation. Therefore, investors require a greater return for the additional risk assumed by investing in unsecured debt. Likewise, an investor will require a greater return for subordinated debt than for senior credit.

Credit quality also deteriorates as the level of debt grows on the balance sheet of a company. Intuitively, the greater the debt-to-capital ratio, the greater the risk of default. By continuing to add financial leverage to its business operations, a company increases the risks that in a bad year it may not be able to cover its debt service. In studies on cost of capital, it was determined that companies experiencing debt-to-capital ratios between 25%

and 45% saw their cost of capital increase exponentially, indicating greater risk of financial distress.

Debt-to-capital Ratios

Finally, companies that are more capital-intensive tend to have greater debt-to-capital ratios. For example, automobile and airline manufacturers typically maintain greater leverage than professional services and software companies. The academic explanation given for this circumstance is the degree of industry maturity, lower earnings volatility, and the ability to secure more debt with tangible assets. Consequently, companies within more capital-intensive industries tend to have lower borrowing costs at a given debt-to-capital ratio than those in less capital-intensive industries.

TRICKS OF THE TRADE

- The costs of borrowing are composed of interest payments and issuance costs. Interest paid on outstanding debt is a function of the credit-worthiness of the borrower. The greater the interest rate on a debt security relative to other, similar securities, the lower the credit quality of the issuer. As credit quality falls below investment-grade, the risk of default becomes ominously greater and the costs of borrowing become more exorbitant.

- The company's capital structure is another major determinant of credit quality. There is a direct relationship between debt level and default risk. At a given debt to capital ratio, incremental borrowing costs increase dramatically as the company's risk of financial distress reaches its peak.

FOR MORE INFORMATION

Web site:
The Motley Fool: **www.fool.com**

Reading the Financial Pages

GETTING STARTED

There are two broad areas to the financial pages of newspapers. One consists of a simple listing, primarily of stocks quoted on the stock exchange, shown alphabetically with certain details on each stock.

The other area will contain reports by journalists on individual stocks and other general economic and financial information. Often the article will end with an opinion upon whether or not the stock should be purchased as an investment. How much credence is attached to such opinion is a matter of individual judgment.

To be able to appreciate the data shown in stock market share listings, you do need to have a little understanding of some basic financial analysis—particularly yield and price/earnings ratio (P/E), the two most common measures of the value of a share. We suggest you read the two actionlists on these subjects first.

FAQs
What information is included in the financial pages?

The financial pages of the papers publish tabular price and statistical information about stocks listed on the stock exchange, together with a series of articles on individual stocks and the economy in general. The latter could include an enormous variety of subjects, such as unemployment and interest rates, the effects of technologies on particular types of share, and so on. Individual company stocks will also be discussed, usually around the time when important information about the company is published—such as results or other corporate activity, perhaps a takeover, a profits warning or a new product development.

The statistical listings of financial data may cover more than just stocks quoted on one local stock exchange. They could, for example, include overseas stock exchanges and commodity exchange prices, though the latter are of far less general interest than stock prices.

Are there any rules about how to read these pages?

No. The financial pages are there to provide people with information on the general economy, particular industries, and individual companies. All of these are changing constantly so that there is a perpetual stream of news being published. How much of it is relevant to an individual reader is something that each person will decide for him- or herself.

MAKING IT HAPPEN
General Information about Stock Listings

Here is an actual extract from the stock listing pages of a paper, for a Monday. The actual entries will contain a lot more information than this, but we have selected the key elements.

52 Week High	52 Week Low	Stock	Div.	Yield %	P/E	Close
53.9	22.15	Honeywell	0.75	2.3	dd	32.90
119.75	63.27	Goldman Sachs	0.48	0.6	20	86

The abbreviations at the heads of each column stand for:

- 52 Week High/Low: indicators of the highest and lowest price of the stock over the past year
- Stock: the name of the company
- Div: the annual dividend per share of stock, based upon the company's last declaration
- Yield: the dividend per share, expressed as a percentage of the closing share price
- P/E: price/earnings ratio

Note that different papers may have a slightly different choice of data for each stock but all will have the price—that being the most important fact.

Also the same paper may change its data for different days. The example here appeared on a Monday, and one of the columns shows the weekly change that occurred since the previous Monday. However in editions published on other days, this column would be altered to show the daily price movement that took place on the day prior to publication.

The stock's name should be fairly obvious, even if abbreviated for reasons of space. However the sector in which the share is located may not always be so clear.

How to Interpret the Figures

What is this information telling us about these stocks? We could separate the data into two broad groups, one of which tells us something absolute about the particular stock and the other which enables us to compare the stock with others, although some data falls into both groups.

52 Week High/Low

This gives you an indication of the range within which the share price has been fluctuating. A big range might indicate that the company concerned is operating in a volatile market. It should only be used as an indicator of a stock's value in conjunction with a number of other facts about the company.

Dividend

This is paid by the company to its stockholders. The amount of dividend paid to stockholders is dependent upon a number of factors, but is one important indicator of the long term profitability of a company. Companies with a long history of consistently rising dividend payments and earnings per share are generally considered to be safer bets than companies offering no dividends at all. In the case of Honeywell, "dd" indicates that the company made a loss over the most recent four quarters.

"Freedom of the press is guaranteed only to those who own one."

A. J. Liebling

Yield and Price/Earnings Ratio (P/E)

Briefly, yield represents the historical annual dividend income paid by the share as a percentage of its current price. P/E shows how many years of current earnings are represented in the current price. Both of these ratios will therefore fluctuate with the price of the stock—P/E in direct proportion and yield in inverse proportion.

These are two of the most common ratios used by investors and market commentators in evaluating a stock as a potential investment, both on its own merits and as a comparison with other stocks. For this reason they are widely quoted in the press and almost every serious newspaper will show these figures alongside the price of each stock in the listings.

Close

This is simply the closing market price of the share, in dollars, from the last day of trading. For a Monday edition, this would be the previous Friday.

COMMON MISTAKES
Believing That Share Price Alone Is an Indication of the Value of the Stock

It seems logical to believe that stock for company A, with a share price of $200, is twice as expensive as that of company B, with a share price of $100. This is completely incorrect. The share price alone tells you almost nothing about the stock, which is why P/E is so critically important.

Suppose in the above example, A has a P/E of 12 and B a P/E of 24. Now you can see that in fact B is twice as costly as A, even though it has half the share price. It means that collectively, investors have decided that it is worth paying 24 years' earnings for B but only 12 years' earnings for A. This does not mean that the collective market view is right or wrong, in that a higher P/E is better or worse than a lower one. That is a matter for the individual to decide for him- or herself.

What we are doing when using P/E is relating the price to some other fact about the company, in this case its earnings. Similarly, yield relates the price to the annual dividends paid. There are several other measures that relate the price to something about the stock, examples being assets and sales. It is really only by reference to these that one stock can be compared with another to ascertain which is cheaper or costlier.

Thinking That the Yield Will Apply in the Future

In most cases, the yield figures shown in papers are historical. The exact method varies between papers, but generally it is based on taking the last year's dividends paid, dividing by the share price, and expressing the result as a percentage. But it must be borne in mind that no company is obliged to pay dividends at all.

Assuming That Yield Figures Will Always Be Sustainable

If you look through the tables, you can occasionally discover stocks that appear to give enormous yields like 20%—which, on the face of it, seems to be a fantastic investment. But if you look behind the figures at announcements from the company, you will very likely find that it is going through a bad time and will probably cut, or eliminate, its dividend in the future. The huge historical yield appears only because the share price has collapsed following the bad news, and a falling share price drives up the yield in inverse proportion. So do not make the mistake of assuming that the yield figures are always sustainable in the future, particularly those that appear astronomically high in relation to the rest of the market.

FOR MORE INFORMATION

Web sites:
The Motley Fool: **www.fool.com**
Wall Street Journal: **www.wsj.com**

See also:
✔ Calculating Earnings per Share (p. 1060)
✔ Calculating Price/Earnings Ratio (p. 1017)
✔ Calculating Yield (p. 1041)

"If the creator had a purpose in equipping us with a neck, he surely meant us to stick it out."

Arthur Koestler

Calculating EBITDA

WHAT IT MEASURES

EBITDA measures a company's earnings from ongoing operations, before net income is calculated. EBITDA is an acronym for "earnings before interest, tax, depreciation, and amortization".

WHY IT IS IMPORTANT

EBITDA's champions contend it gives investors a sense of how much money a young or fast-growing company is generating before it pays interest on debt, taxes, and accounts for noncash changes. If EBITDA grows over time, champions argue, investors gain at least a sense of long-term profitability and, in turn, the wisdom of their investment.

Business appraisers and investors also may study EBITDA to help to gauge a company's fair market value, often as a prelude to its acquisition by another company. It also is frequently applied to companies that have been subject to leveraged buyouts—the strategy being that EBITDA will help to cover loan payments needed to finance the transaction.

EBITDA, and EBIT, too, are claimed to be good indicators of cash flow from business operations, since they report earnings before debt payments, taxes, depreciation, and amortization charges are considered. However, that claim is challenged by many—often rather vigorously.

HOW IT WORKS IN PRACTICE

EBITDA first appeared as leveraged buyouts soared in popularity during the 1980s. It has since become well established as a financial-analysis measure of telecommunications, cable, and major media companies.

Its formula is quite simple. Revenues less the cost of goods sold, general and administrative expenses, and the deductions of items expressed by the acronym EBITDA:

revenue – expenses (excluding interest, taxes, depreciation, and amortization) = EBITDA

or:

revenue – expenses (excluding interest and taxes) = EBIT

This formula does not measure true cash flow. A communications company, for example, once reported $698 million in EBIT but just $324 million in cash from operations.

TRICKS OF THE TRADE

- A definition of EBITDA isn't as yet enforced by standards-making bodies, so companies can all but create their own. As a result, EBITDA can easily be manipulated by aggressive accounting policies, which may erode its reliability.
- Ignoring capital expenditures could be unrealistic and horribly misleading, because companies in capital-intensive sectors such as manufacturing and transportation must continually make major capital investments to remain competitive. High-technology is another sector that may be capital-intensive, at least initially.
- Critics warn that using EBITDA as a cash flow indicator is a huge mistake, because EBITDA ignores too many factors that have an impact on true cash flow, such as working capital, debt payments, and other fixed expenses. Interest and taxes can and do cost a company cash, they point out, while debt holders have higher claims on a company's liquid assets than investors do.
- Critics further assail EBITDA as the barometer of choice of unprofitable firms because it can present a more optimistic view of a company's future than it has a right to claim. *Forbes* magazine, for instance, once referred to EBIDTA as "the device of choice to pep up earnings announcements."
- Even so, EBITDA may be useful in terms of evaluating firms in the same industry with widely different capital structures, tax rates and depreciation policies.

FOR MORE INFORMATION

Web site:
The Motley Fool: **www.fool.com**

See also:
⌕ Accounting (pp. 1667–1669)

"Pack lightly and carry a compass."   Raul Fernandez

Calculating Payout Ratio

WHAT IT MEASURES

Dividend cover expresses the number of times a company's dividends to common stockholders could be paid out of its net after-tax profits.

Payout ratio expresses the total dividends paid to stockholders as a percentage of a company's net profit in a given period of time.

WHY IT IS IMPORTANT

Whether defined as dividend cover or payout ratio, it measures the likelihood of dividend payments being sustained, and thus is a useful indication of sustained profitability. However, each ratio must be interpreted independently.

A low dividend cover suggests it might be difficult to pay the same level of dividends in a downturn, and that a company is not reinvesting enough in its future. Negative dividend cover is unusual, and a clear sign of trouble.

The payout ratio, expressed as a percentage or fraction, is an inverse measure: a high ratio indicates a lack of reinvestment in the business, and that current earnings cannot sustain the current dividend payments.

HOW IT WORKS IN PRACTICE

Dividend cover is so named because it shows how many times over the profits could have paid the dividend. To calculate dividend cover, divide earnings per share by the dividend per share:

**earnings per share / dividend per share
= dividend cover**

If a company has earnings per share of $8, and it pays out a dividend of 2.1, dividend cover is:

8 / 2.1 = 3.80

An alternative formula divides a company's net profit by the total amount allocated for dividends. So a company that earns $10 million in net profit and allocates $1 million for dividends has a dividend cover of 10, while a company that earns $25 million and pays out $10 million in dividends has a dividend cover of 2.5:

**10,000,000 / 1,000,000 = 10
and 25,000,000 / 10,000,000 = 2.5**

The payout ratio is calculated by dividing annual dividends paid on common stock by earnings per share:

**annual dividend / earnings per share
= payout ratio**

Take the company whose earnings per share is $8 and its dividend payout is 2.1. Its payout ratio would be:

2.1 / 8 = .263 or 26.3%

TRICKS OF THE TRADE

- A dividend cover ratio of 2 or higher is usually adequate, and indicates that the dividend is affordable. By the same token, the payout ratio should not exceed two-thirds of earnings. Like most ratios, however, both vary by industry.
- A dividend cover ratio below 1.5 is risky, and a ratio below 1 indicates a company is paying the current year's dividend with retained earnings from a previous year—a practice that cannot continue indefinitely.
- The higher the dividend cover figure, the less likely the dividend will be reduced or eliminated in the future, should profits fall. Companies that suffer sharp declines or outright losses will often continue paying dividends to indicate that their substandard performance is an anomaly.
- On the other hand, a high dividend cover figure may disappoint an investor looking for income, since the figure suggests directors could have declared a larger dividend.
- A high payout ratio clearly appeals to conservative investors seeking income. However, when coupled with weak or falling earnings it could suggest an imminent dividend cut, or that the company is short-changing reinvestment to maintain its payout.
- A payout ratio above 75% is a warning. It suggests the company is failing to reinvest sufficient profits in its business, that the company's earnings are faltering, or that it is trying to attract investors who otherwise would not be interested.
- Newer and faster-growing companies often pay no dividends at all in order to reinvest earnings in the company's development.

FOR MORE INFORMATION

Web site:
finance-glossary.com: **www.finance-glossary.com**

"Money is like a sixth sense without which you cannot make a complete use of the other five."

W. Somerset Maugham

Calculating Interest Coverage

WHAT IT MEASURES

The amount of earnings available to make interest payments after all operating and non-operating income and expenses—except interest and income taxes—have been accounted for.

WHY IT IS IMPORTANT

Interest coverage is regarded as a measure of a company's creditworthiness because it shows how much income there is to cover interest payments on outstanding debt. Banks and financial analysts also rely on this ratio as a rule of thumb to gauge the fundamental strength of a business.

HOW IT WORKS IN PRACTICE

Interest coverage is expressed as a ratio, and reflects a company's ability to pay the interest obligations on its debt. It compares the funds available to pay interest—earnings before interest and taxes, or EBIT—with the interest expense. The basic formula is:

EBIT / interest expense = interest coverage ratio

If interest expense for a year is $9 million, and the company's EBIT is $45 million, the interest coverage would be:

45 million / 9 million = 5:1

The higher the number, the stronger a company is likely to be. Conversely, a low number suggests that a company's fortunes are looking ominous. Variations of this basic formula also exist. For example, there is:

operating cash flow + interest + taxes / interest = cash flow interest coverage ratio

This ratio indicates the company's ability to use its cash flow to satisfy its fixed financing obligations. Finally, there is the fixed-charge coverage ratio, which compares EBIT with fixed charges:

EBIT + lease expenses / interest + lease expense = fixed charge coverage ratio

"Fixed charges" can be interpreted in many ways, however. It could mean, for example, the funds that a company is obliged to set aside to retire debt, or dividends on preferred stock.

TRICKS OF THE TRADE

- A ratio of less than 1 indicates that a company is having problems generating enough cash flow to pay its interest expenses, and that either a modest decline in operating profits or a sudden rise in borrowing costs could eliminate profitability entirely.
- Ideally, interest coverage should at least exceed 1.5; in some sectors, 2.0 or higher is desirable.
- Interest coverage is widely considered to be more meaningful than looking at total debt, because what really matters is what an enterprise must pay in a given period, not how much debt it has.
- As is often the case, it may be more meaningful to watch interest coverage over several periods in order to detect long-term trends.
- Cash flow will sometimes be substituted for EBIT in the ratio, because EBIT includes not only cash but also accrued sales and other unrealized income.
- Interest coverage also is called "times interest earned."

1059

ACTIONLIST

FOR MORE INFORMATION

Web site:
The Motley Fool: **www.fool.com**

See also:
Accounting (pp. 1667–1669)

"Markets reduce everything, including human beings and nature, to commodities."

George Soros

Calculating Earnings per Share

WHAT IT MEASURES

The portion of a company's profit allocated to each outstanding share of a company's common stock.

WHY IT IS IMPORTANT

Earnings per share (EPS) is simply a fundamental measure of profitability that shows how much profit was generated on a per-share-of-stock basis. Were the term worded as profit per share, the meaning certainly would be much clearer, if not self-evident.

By itself, EPS doesn't reveal a great deal. Its true value lies in comparing EPS figures across several quarters, or years, to judge the growth of a company's earnings on a per-share basis.

HOW IT WORKS IN PRACTICE

Essentially, the figure is calculated after paying taxes and dividends to preferred stockholders and bondholders. Barring extraordinary circumstances, EPS data is reported quarterly, semiannually, and annually.

To calculate EPS, start with net income (earnings) for the period in question, subtract the total value of any preferred stock dividends, then divide the resulting figure by the number of shares outstanding during that period. Or:

$$\text{net income} - \frac{\text{dividends on preferred stock}}{\text{average number of shares outstanding}}$$

By itself, this formula is simple enough. Alas, defining the factors used in the formula invariably introduces complexities and—as some allege on occasion—possible subterfuge.

For instance, while companies usually use a weighted average number of shares outstanding over the reporting period, shares outstanding still can be either "primary" or "fully diluted." Primary EPS is calculated using the number of shares that are currently held by investors in the market and able to be traded. Diluted EPS is the result of a complex calculation that determines how many shares would be outstanding if all exercisable warrants and options were converted into common shares at the end of a quarter. Suppose, for example, that a company has granted a large number of share options to employees. If these options are capable of being exercised in the near future, that could alter significantly the number of shares in issue and thus the EPS—even though the E part (the earnings) is the same. Often in such cases, the company might quote the EPS on the existing shares and the fully diluted version. Which one a person considers depends on their view of the company and how they wish to use the EPS figure. In addition, companies can report extraordinary EPS, a figure which excludes the financial impact of unusual occurrences, such as discontinued operations or the sale of a business unit.

Net income or earnings, meanwhile, can be defined in a number of ways, based upon respective nations' generally accepted accounting principles.

For example, "pro forma earnings," tend to exclude more expenses and income used to calculate "reported earnings." Pro forma advocates insist these earnings eliminate all distortions and present "true" earnings that allow pure apples-to-apples comparisons with preceding periods. However, "non-recurring expenses" seem to occur with such increasing regularity that one may wonder if a company is deliberately trying to manipulate its earnings figures and present them in the best possible light, rather than in the most accurate light.

"Cash" earnings are earnings from operating cash flow—notably, not EBITDA. In turn, cash EPS is usually these earnings divided by diluted shares outstanding. This figure is very reliable because operating cash flow is not subject to as much judgment at net earnings or pro forma earnings.

TRICKS OF THE TRADE

- Given the varieties of earnings and shares reported today, investors need to first determine what the respective figures represent before making investment decisions. There are cases of a company announcing a pro forma EPS that differs significantly from what is reported in its financial statements. Such discrepancies, in turn, can affect how the market values a given stock.
- Investors should check to see if a company has issued more shares during a given period, since that action, too, can affect EPS. A similar problem occurs where there have been a number of shares issued during the accounting period being considered. Which number of issued shares do you use: the opening figure, the closing figure, the mean? In practice the usual method is to use the weighted mean number of shares in issue during the year (weighted, that is, for the amount of time in the year that were in issue).
- "Trailing" earnings per share is the sum of EPS from the last four quarters, and is the figure used to compute most price-to-earnings ratios.
- Diluted and primary shares outstanding can be the same if a company has no warrants or convertible bonds outstanding, but investors should not assume anything, and need to be sure how "shares outstanding" is being defined.

FOR MORE INFORMATION

Web site:
investopedia.com:
www.investopedia.com/articles/analyst/091901.asp

See also:

"First get in, then get rich, then get respectable."

Bernie Ecclestone

MANAGEMENT LIBRARY

 # Management Library

Summarizing the most influential business books of all time

There is a vast literature covering business and the world of work, and thousands more new publications emerge every year. Managers have little time to read, even if they have the inclination.

The Management Library aims to distil the main lessons from the best and most influential works ever published. They include both well regarded new titles such as *The Tipping Point*, as well as time-honored classics such as Peter Drucker's *Practice of Management* and Frederick W. Taylor's *Principles of Scientific Management*.

Each summary includes a quick analysis of the book's contribution to management thinking and practice, as well as a list of the key points emerging from the work.

Contents

MANAGEMENT LIBRARY

Action Learning

Reg Revans

WHY READ IT?

What is the difference between a puzzle and a problem? According to Revans, there is an existing solution to a puzzle and it simply needs to be found. There is no existing solution to a problem. The solution has to be worked out by a process of inquiry that begins at the point where one does not know what to do next and expertise is no help. *Action Learning* explains that process and offers an alternative method of learning to the traditional one, which is based on programmed knowledge instead of encouraging students to ask questions and roam widely around a subject.

GETTING STARTED

As a young man, Reg Revans competed in the 1928 Olympics and worked in the famous Cavendish laboratories at Cambridge, in the United Kindom, alongside such fathers of nuclear physics as Ernest Rutherford and J. J. Thompson. Action learning is his systematization of the methods used by the Cambridge team to deal with problems. He developed them further when working for the National Coal Board after World War II. He also later went on to become Britain's first professor of industrial administration at the University of Manchester.

Action Learning is all about an alternative to traditional education and training. The method it sets out is a form of "learning by doing," but its proponents are careful to distinguish it from simply "learning on the job" or "learning by experience." It involves a collaborative effort, humility, a "trading of one's confusion with that of others," and deep reflection on one's experience and on the nature of the problem. Its outcome is personal growth as much as a way out of a current difficulty.

CONTRIBUTION
1. Action Learning

The concept of "action learning" is based on a simple equation: $L = P + Q$. Learning (L) occurs through a combination of programmed knowledge (P) and the ability to ask insightful questions (Q).

It does not deny all usefulness to existing knowledge, but its focus is on asking questions. Learning must be opened up. Programmed knowledge is one-dimensional and rigid; the ability to ask questions opens up other dimensions and is free-flowing.

The first step towards asking constructive questions is to acknowledge one's own ignorance. Too many people conceal it under a veneer of knowledge. Instead of hiding our ignorance, according to Revans, we should be bartering it.

The essence of action learning is to become better acquainted with the self through observing what one actually tries to do, endeavoring to ascertain the reasons for attempting it, and tracing the consequences that result from it. Revans said he sought "to focus [his] own doubt by keeping away from experts with prefabricated answers."

2. The Importance of Small Team Learning

The structure linking the two elements in the equation is the small team or set. The central idea of this approach is collaboration within the set; its members strive to learn with and from each other as they confess failures and expand on victories.

3. A Better Way to Develop Managers

Action learning is also the antithesis of the traditional approach to developing managers. We keep solving the same problems because we do not learn from them. We bring in consultants to provide solutions or send managers on courses where they are taught a lot but learn little. Action learning is about teaching little and learning a lot.

4. Collaboration Counts

In industry, managers and workers need to acknowledge the problems they face and then attempt to solve them. When doctors listen to nurses, patients recover more quickly. If mining engineers pay more attention to their workers than to their machinery, the pits are more efficient. It is neither books nor seminars from which managers learn much, but from here-and-now exchanges about the operational job in hand.

According to Revans, "The ultimate power of a successful general staff lies not in the brilliance of its individual members, but in the cross-fertilization of its collective abilities."

CONTEXT

For a long time Revans's ideas were comparatively little known and comparatively undervalued—at least in the English-speaking world. His ideas were received much better in mainland Europe (and in Belgium in particular), however, and he himself spent the final period of his working life abroad. Many management ideas that are currently fashionable, however, such as teamworking, reengineering, and the learning organization, contain elements of "action learning."

One of the critical points about action learning is its relation to action. In a way it appears misnamed. The name at first sight suggests learning in practical situations or performing tasks rather than studying theory. It tends to conceal the centrality of reflection; questioning, especially questioning one's own actions in a deliberate and precise way; ignorance-bartering; and collaborative effort to the process. The solutions that are eventually arrived at must be tested in action, but that is very much the final stage.

Interest in Revans's ideas nevertheless continues to grow in many organizations. The Pentagon is said to be enthusiastic; and General Electric uses action teams to tackle particular problems. There is also the Revans Foundation at the University of Manchester in the United Kingdom, where the theory and practice of action learning are particularly studied.

FOR MORE INFORMATION

Revans, Reg. *Action Learning*. London: Blond & Briggs, 1974.

Administrative Behavior

Herbert Simon

WHY READ IT?

Decision making, according to Simon, is synonymous with management. But what is decision making, and how are decisions made? Simon realized that most people's assumptions were hopelessly unrealistic. He set out to inject some realism into the subject, but not in a merely reductive way; he also elaborated a very modern concept of the organization as an interrelated and intercommunicating body. He said that the ability to make decisions effectively made the difference between effectiveness and ineffectiveness in organizations. On that basis alone, his book must be worth reading.

GETTING STARTED

Herbert Simon, the son of German immigrants to Milwaukee and a graduate of the University of Chicago, won the Nobel prize for economics in 1978 for his work on administrative behavior, the subject of his doctoral thesis and this book. He is said to have been inspired to write it by observations made while working part-time for Milwaukee's recreation department as a student. He is also said to have told the Nobel committee, when collecting his award, that his real interest was in artificial intelligence—the field into which his interest in how decisions and choices are made ultimately led him.

In *Administrative Behavior: A Study of Decision-making Processes in Administrative Organization* (to give the book its full title), he developed a theory of human choice or decision making that aimed to be sufficiently broad and realistic to accommodate both the rational views of economists and the human concerns of psychologists and practical decision makers.

CONTRIBUTION
1. The Problems of Organizational Theory

According to *Administrative Behavior*, the way administration is usually described suffers from superficiality, over-simplification, and a lack of realism. Theorists have refused to undertake the tiresome task of studying the actual allocation of decision-making functions. Instead, they have been satisfied with talking loosely about authority, central-ization, span of control, function, and the like, without seeking operational definitions of these terms.

Classic economic theory also suggests that decisions are made by obtaining all the available information, assessing it, and coming to an objective and rational conclusion as to how the best result can be achieved. In reality, nobody has the time and the mental resources to do this. Instead of aiming for "the best," management is content with what is "good enough," a solution that is "satisficing" (that satisfies and suffices).

2. Organization is Important

Organization is important, first, because in our society, people spend most of their waking adult lives in organizations, and this environment provides much of the force that molds and develops personal qualities and habits.

Second, because it provides those in responsible positions with the means for exercising authority and influence over others.

3. The Complexity of Organizational Interaction

It is not sufficient to regard organizational behavior as a matter of understanding people or measuring the performance of people more effectively. Each act in an organization exists in a complex interaction with the organizational system as a whole.

4. Understanding Decision Making

A complex decision is like a great river, drawing from its many tributaries the innumerable component premises of which it is constituted.

Many individuals and organization units contribute to every large decision, and the problem of centralization and decentralization is a problem of arranging the complex system into an effective plan.

5. The Importance of Relationships

An organization is not an organizational chart, but a complex pattern of communications and other relationships in a group of human beings.

This pattern provides the members of the group with much of the information, as-sumptions, goals, and attitudes that enter into the decisions made by each and every one of them. It also provides them with a set of stable and comprehensible expectations as to what the other members of the group are doing and how they will react to what any individual says and does.

CONTEXT

Simon later observed that he must have had a prophetic gift when he included the words "behavior," "decision-making," and "organization" in the book's full title as they quickly became the fashionable phrases of social science.

Organizational theory had remained deeply embedded in vagueness before the publication of *Administrative Behavior*. Its clearest proponent up to that time had been Chester Barnard who contributed the foreword to Simon's book.

In response, Simon developed a theory of human choice or decision making that aimed to accommodate:

- the rational aspects of choice that have always been the principal concern of the economist;
- the properties and limitations of the human decision-making mechanisms that have attracted the attention of psychologists and practical decision makers.

He thus formed a bridge between the humanists and engineers in management thinking.

His views were ahead of their time. For the next 40 years, organization, in the West at least, continued to be seen as an act of ordering, simplifying, and categorizing rather than as a powerful, dynamic, and ever-changing force.

Only in the early 1990s, partly through the success of Senge's *The Fifth Discipline*, did systems thinking make the leap from academic obscurity to the executive agenda.

FOR MORE INFORMATION

Simon, Herbert. *Administrative Behavior: A Study of Decision-making Processes in Administrative Organization*. 4th ed. New York: Free Press, 1997.

"Organization is not an organizational chart, but a complex pattern of communications and other relationships in a group of human beings."

Administrative Behavior

The Age of Discontinuity
Peter Drucker

WHY READ IT?

Drucker predicted the rise of the knowledge worker long before the term came into common usage. His definition is broader than the IT-led version that is currently used. The book gives a valuable insight into the changing nature of management roles and responsibilities in the knowledge economy.

GETTING STARTED

According to Drucker, the manager as knowledge worker was a new breed of thoughtful, intelligent executive. The manager was reincarnated as a responsible individual, paid for applying knowledge, exercising judgment, and taking responsible leadership within the organization.

The knowledge worker sees him or herself as another professional. While dependent on the organization for access to income and opportunity, the organization equally depends on him or her.

In this book we read that knowledge, rather than labor, is the new measure of economic society—and the knowledge worker is the true capitalist in the knowledge society. Knowledge is not only power, but also ownership of the means of production.

CONTRIBUTION
1. The Manager as Knowledge Worker

Drucker coined the term "knowledge worker." This was a new breed of executive—a highly trained, intelligent managerial professional who realized his or her own worth and contribution to the organization. Drucker bade farewell to the concept of the manager as mere supervisor or paper shuffler. The manager was reincarnated as a responsible individual.

Though the knowledge worker is not a laborer, and certainly not proletarian, he or she is not a subordinate (in the sense that he or she can be told what to do). The knowledge worker is paid, on the contrary, for applying his or her knowledge, exercising

judgment, and taking responsible leadership.

2. The Nature of the Knowledge Worker

According to Drucker, the knowledge worker sees him or herself just as another professional, no different from the lawyer, the teacher, the preacher, the doctor, or the government servant of yesterday. He or she has the same education, but more income—and probably greater opportunities as well.

The knowledge worker may well realize that he or she depends on the organization for access to income and opportunity, and that without the organization, there would be no job. But there is also the realization that the organization depends equally on him or her.

Drucker effectively wrote the obituary for the obedient, gray-suited, loyal, corporate man and woman. The only trouble was, it took this corporate creature another 20 years to die.

3. The Impact of Knowledge Workers

The social ramifications of this new breed of corporate executive were significant. If knowledge, rather than labor, was the new measure of economic society then the fabric of capitalist society had to change. The knowledge worker is both the true capitalist in the knowledge society and dependent on his or her job.

Collectively the knowledge workers—the employed, educated middle class of today's society—own the means of production through pension funds, investment trusts, and so on.

Knowledge was not only power, but it was also ownership.

CONTEXT

The book effectively mapped out the demise of the age of mass, labor-based production and the advent of the knowledge-based, information age. Drucker's realization that

the role of the manager had fundamentally changed was not a sudden one. The foundations of the idea of the knowledge worker can be seen in his description of management by objectives in *The Practice of Management* (1954). Knowledge management, intellectual capital and the like are now the height of corporate fashion. The modern idea of the knowledge worker is a creature of the technological age, the mobile executive, the hot-desker. Drucker provided a characteristically broader perspective. He placed the rise of the knowledge worker in the evolution of management into a respectable and influential discipline.

Drucker continued to develop his thinking on the role of knowledge, most notably in his 1992 book, *Managing for the Future*, in which he observed, "From now on the key is knowledge. The world is becoming not labor intensive, not materials intensive, not energy intensive, but knowledge intensive."

The Age of Discontinuity was startlingly correct in its predictions. Much of it would fit easily into business books of today.

Prior to Drucker's death, management guru Gary Hamel said, "Peter Drucker's reputation is as a management theorist. He has also been a management prophet. Writing in 1969, he clearly anticipated the emergence of the knowledge economy. I'd like to set a challenge for would-be management gurus: try to find something to say that Peter Drucker has not said first, and has not said well. This high hurdle should substantially reduce the number of business books clogging the bookshelves of booksellers, and offer managers the hope of gaining some truly fresh insights."

FOR MORE INFORMATION

Drucker, Peter F. *The Age of Discontinuity*. Revised ed. Woburn, MA: Butterworth-Heinemann, 1992.

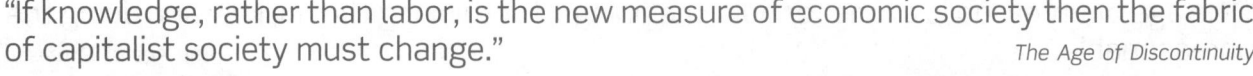
"If knowledge, rather than labor, is the new measure of economic society then the fabric of capitalist society must change."

The Age of Discontinuity

The Age of Unreason

Charles Handy

WHY READ IT?

Written in 1989, this book includes a number of incisive predictions about the way work would develop. The author provides valuable, still relevant, insights into the changes in organizational structures and developments such as knowledge working, outsourcing, and strategic alliances—the hallmarks of the new economy.

GETTING STARTED

In the author's view, the age of unreason is a time when the future is shaped by us and for us. At such a time, a number of organizational forms will emerge; so too will new working patterns, such as outsourcing, telecommuting, the intellectual capital movement, and the rise of knowledge workers.

The portfolio worker will become more important, contributing to a greater work–life balance. A work portfolio is a way of describing how the different bits of work in our lives fit together to form a balanced whole. Portfolio work includes wage work and fee work, homework, gift work, and study work.

Handy goes on to state that the social changes resulting from these developments will be reflected in changing patterns of business, with a mix of small enterprises and large conglomerates. There will also be temporary alliances of large and small organizations to deliver a particular project.

CONTRIBUTION

1. The Concept of an Age of Unreason

The age of unreason is a time when the future, in so many areas, is to be shaped by us and for us. The only prediction that will hold true is that no predictions will hold true. It will be a time for thinking the unlikely and doing the unreasonable.

2. New Organizational Forms

The author suggests that a number of organizational forms will emerge in an age of unreason:
- the shamrock organization
- the federal organization
- the Triple I organization

The shamrock organization is a form of organization based around a core of essential executives and workers supported by outside contractors and part-time help.

The federal organization is a form of decentralized set-up, in which the center's powers are given to it by the outlying groups; the center therefore coordinates, advises, influences, and suggests rather than directs or controls. Federalism is the way to combine the autonomy of individual parts with the economics of coordination.

The Triple I organization is based on Information, Intelligence, and Ideas. This type of organization will resemble a university and will seek to make added value out of knowledge. To achieve this, the Triple I organization increasingly uses smart machines, with smart people to work with them.

3. New Working Patterns

Handy anticipated the growth of outsourcing, telecommuting, the intellectual capital movement, and the rise of knowledge workers. He also foresaw how these developments might impact the individual. His concept of the portfolio worker helped redefine the nature of work, as well as questions of work–life balance.

4. Portfolio Working

A work portfolio is a way of describing how the different bits of work in our lives fit together to form a balanced whole. The five main categories of portfolio work are:
- wage work and fee work, which are both forms of paid work;
- homework, gift work, and study work, which are all free work.

Wage (or salary) work represents money paid for time given.

Fee work is money paid for results delivered. Employees do wage work; professionals, craftspeople, and freelancers do fee work. Fee work is increasing as jobs move outside the organization. Some employees now get fees (bonuses) as well as wages.

Homework includes that whole catalog of tasks that go on in the home, from cooking and cleaning, to children and carpentry. Done willingly or grudgingly, it is all work.

Gift work is work done for free outside the home, for charities and local groups, for neighbors or for the community.

Study work done seriously is a form of work, not recreation.

5. A Broader Portfolio

In the past, for most people, the work portfolio has had only one item in it—their career. This was a risky strategy. Few people would put all their money into one asset, yet that is what most people were doing with their lives. The career had to provide many things at once—interest or satisfaction in the work, interesting people and good company, security, money, and the opportunity for development.

6. Funding the Portfolio

Portfolio people think in terms of portfolio money, not salary money. Money comes in fits and starts from different sources, for example a bit of a pension, some part-time work, some fees to charge or things to sell. They lead cash-flow lives not salary lives, planning always to have enough inflows to cover outflows.

Portfolio people think in terms of barter and know that most skills are saleable if you want to sell them.

7. Changing Patterns of Business

It will be a world of "fleas and elephants"—large conglomerates and small individual entities, or large political and economic blocs and small countries.

A small enterprise can be global as easily as a large conglomerate, but can more easily be swept away. Conglomerates are a guarantee of continuity, but small enterprises provide the innovation.

There will also be ad hoc organizations, temporary alliances of large and small organizations to deliver a particular project.

CONTEXT

The book predicts many of the important changes in working patterns which are now commonplace, including outsourcing, telecommuting, and virtual project teams from different organizations.

It also recognizes the growing importance of knowledge workers and intellectual capital.

FOR MORE INFORMATION

Handy, Charles. *The Age of Unreason*. Boston, MA: Harvard Business School Press, 1998.

"The age of unreason is a time for bold imaginings, for thinking the unlikely and doing the unreasonable."

The Age of Unreason

All the Right Moves
Constantinos C. Markides

WHY READ IT?

Bill Gates once remarked that though his company did good work, the problem was that products aged so quickly. It is plain from this that innovative strategies are vital for survival in business; organizations must differentiate themselves clearly from their competitors. They must also develop strategies that enable them to find and occupy a unique position within their own industry, while at the same being constantly on the watch for new strategic positions. In this book, Constantinos Markides guides readers toward discovering the breakthrough strategy that will work best for them.

GETTING STARTED

Markides describes what makes a strategic position distinctive and how a business can make sure it occupies a unique strategic position within its industry. He demonstrates how established companies can discover and work on new strategic positions in parallel to their old position. On the basis of examples drawn from actual practice, he presents a guide to how a company can allow an old strategy that obviously no longer has a future to "run out" and, simultaneously, prepare the ground for a new one.

CONTRIBUTION
1. No Strategy without Innovation

According to the author, a successful business needs a strategy that enables it to find and occupy a unique position within its own branch of industry. But no position is made to last forever. Ambitious competitors not only copy attractive positions, they create new ones and these, over time, can become so successful that they endanger established positions. A company that is not permanently striving to discover new positions in its field encourages the competition to do precisely that.

2. Building a Unique Strategic Position

Markides suggests that in order to create a unique strategic position and make the best use of it, a company must first define what business it is in. It must then decide what customers it wishes to appeal to and what products or services it intends to offer. The task then is to build up an organizational

environment in which these decisions can be implemented. In his view, all this involves looking at the following areas:

- Core business: Defining one's own business is the starting point for any strategy. As soon as a definition is arrived at, actions follow from it automatically. But after it has been accepted, it has nevertheless to be questioned again and again, and one must always be on the lookout for better alternatives.
- Customers: In deciding who its customers are and what it is selling, the company at the same time marks out the terrain that it does not intend to enter: the customers it is not setting out to attract, the investments it is not going to action. In this way the company protects itself against squandering its limited resources through not having a clear focus or not following a clearly defined path.
- Activities and achieving objectives: The company must try to reach a dynamic understanding with its workforce. It can, for example, encourage internal diversity to develop competences that it then has "in stock" and promote a type of culture in which changes are welcomed.
- Values and capabilities: The values and capabilities that can give a company a lasting advantage are those that it is difficult for a competitor to achieve. They are rare, they cannot be copied, and there is no substitute for them.
- Organization: A company's organizational environment is made up of four elements: culture, structure, incentive systems, and workforce. If all these are to function as desired, then the company must ensure that it shapes the environment in such a way as to support their proper functioning.
- Strategy development: The development of a new strategy involves planning and trial and error. The planning is necessary to identify the parameters within which the experiments can take place. The process of strategy formation is made up of two parts: first, the production of ideas; second, assessment, experimentation, learning, and modification.

3. Preparing Strategic Innovations

The book then goes on to say that, as soon as a company occupies a unique position with-

in an industry, it must try to improve it. While improving its current position, it must be vigilant for new and potentially dangerous positions that its competitors may be adopting.

Since it cannot be taken for granted that new positions will harmonize with previously existing ones, it is often a good idea for established companies to establish their own units for that purpose. When a company takes over a new position and intends to concentrate on it entirely at some time in the future, it should separate itself from its old position through a gradual process of transition.

In developing its strategy, a company must be able to envision itself going through the following cycle:

- First, it identifies a distinctive strategic position within its industry and occupies it.
- Then it does so well in that position that the position becomes more attractive than any other in the industry.
- While carrying the fight to its competitors from its present position, it constantly looks around for new strategic positions in the industry.
- Once it has identified another more promising position, it attempts to maintain the old position and the new one simultaneously.
- As it gradually removes itself from the old position, it completes the transition to the new one and begins the cycle over again.

CONTEXT

The book is based on numerous case studies of companies from different countries over a period of three years. The author has supplemented the results of these with material from other companies as well as generally available information. It is written from a management perspective and describes the thought processes that a manager has to go through to find and develop a new and innovative strategy.

FOR MORE INFORMATION

Markides, Constantinos C. *All the Right Moves: A Guide to Crafting Breakthrough Strategy.* Boston, MA: Harvard Business School Press, 1999.

The Art of Japanese Management

Richard Pascale
Anthony Athos

WHY READ IT?

This book was one of the first business bestsellers. It had a crucial role in the discovery of Japanese management techniques. In its comparisons of Japanese and U.S. companies, it provides rare insights into the truth behind the mythology of Japanese management and the inadequacy of much Western practice.

GETTING STARTED

By the late 1990s, growing Japanese superiority threatened the United States' dominant position in world markets. In the authors' view, a major reason for the superiority of the Japanese is their managerial skill. Japanese managers have vision, something notably lacking in the West. In Japan, visions are dynamic, rather than generic statements of corporate intent. U.S. managers are constrained by their beliefs and assumptions. The seven S framework (strategy, structure, skills, staff, shared values, systems, and style) represents the key categories requiring managers' attention. The Japanese succeeded through attention to the "soft" Ss—style, shared values, skills, and staff, while the West remained preoccupied with the "hard" Ss of strategy, structure, and systems.

CONTRIBUTION

1. Growing Japanese Superiority

In 1980, Japan's GNP was third highest in the world. Extrapolating trends at the time, it looked likely to be the highest by the year 2000.

For the U.S. readership, *The Art of Japanese Management* contains some hard-hitting truths.

If anything, the extent of Japanese superiority over the United States in industrial competitiveness is underestimated.

2. Managerial Skills

A major reason for the superiority of the Japanese is their managerial skills. Among the key components of Japanese management is vision, something the authors found to be notably lacking in the West, where the tools are there but vision is limited.

Beliefs, assumptions, and perceptions about management frequently constrain U.S. managers. The Western vision of management circumscribes our effectiveness.

In Japan, managers enhance their modus operandi via dynamic visions rather than pallid or generic statements of corporate intent.

3. The Seven S Framework

The book is best known for its central concept: the seven S framework.

As a generic statement of the issues facing organizations the seven S framework is unremarkable, though it did gain a great deal of attention. It simply lists the seven important categories that managers should take into account—strategy, structure, skills, staff, shared values, systems, and style.

According to Pascale and Athos, the value of a framework such as the seven Ss is that it imposes an interesting discipline on the researcher.

4. Comparing Management Styles

The seven Ss presents a framework for comparing Japanese and U.S. management approaches.

The Japanese succeeded largely because of the attention they gave to the "soft" Ss—style, shared values, skills, and staff.

The West remained preoccupied with the "hard" Ss of strategy, structure, and systems.

Since the book's publication, the general trend of Western managerial thinking has been directed towards the soft Ss.

CONTEXT

The book played a crucial role in the discovery of Japanese management techniques. Its roots lie in Pascale's work with the U.S. National Commission on Productivity. Having initially thought that lessons from Japan were limited for cultural reasons, Pascale and Athos decided it would be more productive to look at Japanese companies in the United States. The research for the book eventually covered 34 companies over six years.

The authors' championing of vision proved highly influential. It was Athos who really started the entire "visioning" industry in the United States. Soon after *The Art of Japanese Management*, a flurry of books appeared highlighting so-called visionaries. Today, corporate visions are a fact of life.

Leading author Gary Hamel commented, "Japan-phobia has subsided a bit, helped by a strong yen, inept Japanese macroeconomic policy, and the substantial efforts of many Western companies to rebuild their competitiveness. While Pascale and Athos undoubtedly overstated the unique capabilities of Japanese management (is Matsushita really that much better managed than Hewlett-Packard?), they successfully challenged the unstated assumption that the United States was the font of all managerial wisdom. Since *The Art of Japanese Management* hit the bookstores, U.S. companies have learned much from Japan. Pascale and Athos deserve credit for setting the learning agenda."

FOR MORE INFORMATION

Pascale, Richard Tanner, and Anthony Athos. *The Art of Japanese Management.* New York: Simon & Schuster, 1981.

"The Western vision of management circumscribes our effectiveness."

The Art of Japanese Management

The Art of War

Sun Tzu

WHY READ IT?

When the postwar achievements of Japanese industry began to make a significant impression in the West, and Western businesspeople began to examine the thinking that underlay the success of their Eastern counterparts, Sun Tzu's *The Art of War* was a book that was often mentioned. This may seem surprising as it was probably written over 2,000 years ago. But military language and imagery have played an important role in the development of management thinking, and if you wish to gain an insight into strategy, leadership, and survival in a hostile, competitive environment, who better to turn to than a general whose name is a byword for sagacity?

GETTING STARTED

Sun Tzu is thought to have lived over 2,400 years ago, at roughly the same time as Confucius. Historians are generally agreed that he was a general who led a number of successful military campaigns in present-day Anhui Province; the state of Wu, under whose sovereign he served, became a dominant power at that time. Since then, it has become standard practice for Chinese military chiefs to familiarize themselves with his writings.

The Art of War (the book's actual title is *Sun Tzu Ping Fa*, literally "The Military Method of Mr. Sun") is a compilation of the legendary general's thinking on the strategies that underlie military success. His anecdotes and thoughts, which fill no more than about 25 pages of text in all, are divided into 13 sections. Not all of them are relevant to modern-day concerns, but some strike a significant chord. Rather like a proponent of judo, Sun Tzu particularly recommends using the momentum of your enemy's own moves to defeat him.

CONTRIBUTION

1. Get the Strategy Right

Sun Tzu, like most good and seasoned generals, is anything but an adventurer and anything but gung-ho. "Why destroy," he asks, "when you can win by stealth and cunning? To subdue the enemy's forces without fighting is the summit of skill."

His advice shows subtlety and restraint: "A sovereign should not start a war out of anger, nor should a general give battle out of rage. While anger can revert to happiness and rage to delight, a nation that has been destroyed cannot be restored, nor can the dead be brought back to life."

He continues: "The best approach is to attack the other side's strategy; next best is to attack his alliances; next best is to attack his soldiers; the worst is to attack cities."

2. Get Information From the Right Sources

Sun Tzu also gives sound advice on knowing your markets, saying: "Advance knowledge cannot be gained from ghosts and spirits, but must be obtained from people who know the enemy situation."

3. Stay Focused

His view on strategy leaves no room for sentiment or distraction.

"Deploy forces to defend the strategic points; exercise vigilance in preparation, do not be indolent. Deeply investigate the true situation, secretly await their laxity. Wait until they leave their strongholds, then seize what they love."

CONTEXT

So what does *The Art of War* have to offer the manager of a small components factory in, say, Peoria or Nottingham? Sun Tzu's admirers argue that his pithy sayings encapsu-

late basic and eternal truths. According to Gary Hamel, "Strategy didn't start with Igor Ansoff; neither did it start with Machiavelli. It probably didn't even start with Sun Tzu. Strategy is as old as human conflict . . . " Anyone, therefore, who has to devise a plan, anyone who has to give a lead, can do with all the help they can get.

Hamel goes on to add " . . . and, if the stakes are high in business, they're rather higher in the military sphere." One of the attractions of the military analogy and the military role model in business is that they elevate proceedings to a loftier plane. Not only are the issues larger, and the scale more heroic, but it is clear who your enemy is, and when your enemy is clear, the world appears clearer whether you are a military general or a managing director.

Embattled managers in particular may benefit from the stimulus that military authors like Sun Tzu, Clausewitz, or Liddell-Hart, and the writings of modern military leaders like Colin Powell or Norman Schwarzkopf, can give to their civilian imaginations.

Finally, as has often been pointed out, Sun Tzu has long been revered in the East. He is said to be required reading not only for Eastern military tacticians but also for Eastern businesspeople. To know your enemies—or indeed to know your friends, partners, and colleagues—it is useful to have read what they read.

1071

MANAGEMENT LIBRARY

FOR MORE INFORMATION

Tzu, Sun. *The Art of War* (trans. Griffith). Revised ed. New York: Dover Publications, 2002.

"Water flows in accordance with the ground; an army achieves victory in accordance with the enemy."

The Art of War

Barbarians at the Gate

Bryan Burrough
John Helyar

WHY READ IT?

Barbarians at the Gate explores the takeover battle for RJR Nabisco in 1988, one of the largest ever leveraged buyouts (LBOs). It is both a biography of C.E.O. Ross Johnson and an analysis of why the planned LBO went awry. Unknown to Johnson and his supporters, other bidders emerged, including Kohlberg Kravis Roberts (KKR), who were highly experienced at LBOs. For several weeks, these two main groups, among others, fought to control the company. Eventually, KKR's $25 billion was decisive. Johnson initiated the LBO as a cheap way to consolidate his standing—and lost everything. *Barbarians at the Gate* addresses both the financial and human aspects of investment banking. Financial issues are explored alongside "softer" aspects of business, such as negotiating. Like *Liar's Poker*, *Barbarians* teaches the lessons of an entire age. It shows how financial matters are dominated by human characters and captures the culture of competition in the 1980s: a valuable lesson for current and future generations.

GETTING STARTED

Leveraged buyouts are debt-financed transactions (using bank loans and bond sales) to take a public corporation private. It enables a single party to gain control of a publicly traded company, using vast sums of capital to buy out shareholders. Such deals became possible for two reasons. In the early 1980s, the Internal Revenue Code made interest, but not dividends, deductible from taxable income, making it possible to obtain large bank loans. Secondly, the demand for junk bonds exploded in the 1980s, enabling the sale of bonds to raise finance for such transactions. Consequently, the LBO of RJR Nabisco was part of a wider economic trend. What Johnson and his supporters ignored was that if they could use this mechanism to take over a public company, then others would be able to as well. They overlooked economic trends at their peril.

Barbarians at the Gate highlights a milestone in financial history: the LBO of the Gibson Greeting Card Company, when the company was first taken private in 1982. Only 18 months later, it was made public again with a significantly higher share price, despite few managerial changes. LBOs were one of the most lucrative investments throughout the 1980s. Consequently, cor-porations faced numerous takeover battles: the competition surrounding this could be disastrous for their performance.

CONTRIBUTION

The authors draw the following conclusions from this rollercoaster business ride:

1. Never Pay in Cash

Johnson's team underestimated the importance of the initial offer. Theirs was excessively low, proposing to the Board of Directors an LBO at $75/share, after concerns that the price was undervalued at $55. Consequently, rival bidders emerged, who could otherwise have been deterred. By showing his financial position before gaining control over RJR, the authors maintain that Johnson allowed his weaknesses to be exploited. His concern that falling tobacco sales were dragging down the share price was insignificant compared to the threat of losing his stake in RJR Nabisco. The authors speculate about whether Johnson was unwilling to incur the large debt a higher bid would require because of the cost cutting it would necessitate. No valuation put RJR's value beneath $80 a share, and the authors suggest that Johnson's low bid invited better financed parties to tender bids.

2. Never Tell the Truth

The book details how, ignoring Johnson's offer of directorship seats and soaring share holdings, the independent board evaluating the offer issued a press release, rather than keep the deal quiet. The board knew their strengths: any potential buyer would reward them handsomely for their support. Johnson had, in the authors' views, shown his cards too early. This allowed other bidders to enter the fray with a good understanding of how to undermine Johnson and win control of RJR Nabisco. The plan was that nobody would know of the deal until the last moment, by when Johnson would already have gained control. By revealing his plan too early, Johnson undermined his strategy. Nowadays, investors are far more adept at handling the media.

3. Never Play by the Rules

Johnson's key mistake, the authors suggest, was to rely on Shearson Lehman Hutton and Salomon Bros. to support the bid. Both firms were hurt by the 1987 stock market crash and had little LBO experi-ence. Johnson's competitors were KKR and Drexel, the biggest players in LBOs and junk bonds respectively. Now, firms are more diligent about choosing partners. According to Burrough and Halyar, Johnson's decisions were based more on loyalty and personality than due diligence. It would have been better to gain more finance, in case it was needed, while acting more unpredictably. Since KKR could anticipate Johnson's actions, they were able to attack his character in the media, undermining his popularity base. *Barbarians at the Gate* maintains that in a game of mavericks, one cannot win through playing by the rules.

CONTEXT

In many ways, the dot-com bubble of the late 1990s was a repeat of the stock market crash of the late 1980s. *Barbarians* shows how irrational personalities precipitate such economic recessions. While Johnson's failure was on a relatively small scale, it demonstrates the kind of irrationality that leads to fluctuating asset prices. Eagerness to lend unjustifiable amounts of venture capital to high-tech start-ups in the late 1990s was mirrored in the LBO boom, which consumed similarly large sums of capital.

Much of investment banking has changed since the 1980s. Nowadays, shareholders are unlikely to accept such turbulent management, because of the disruption to organizational culture it produces. The LBO wave of the 1980s was defined by an eagerness to make quick gains. Today, the focus is on building sustainable increases in value. Most LBO firms in the 1980s leveraged capital with bank loans or junk bond borrowings. Now, most capital comes in larger quantities from global pension or hedge funds. Now, the philosophy is "buy and build," with bidders often keeping their holdings for three to ten years. They sell for the highest price possible through adding as much value to the organization as possible—and takeovers are usually management-led. However, the lessons from Johnson's failed takeover still apply.

FOR MORE INFORMATION

Burrough, Bryan, and John Helyar. *Barbarians at the Gate*. Revised ed. New York: Harper Perennial, 2003.

"We've got our fee, let's go on with the next deal."

A Behavioral Theory of the Firm

Richard Cyert
James March

WHY READ IT?

The book is a powerful introduction to the complex world of decision making. One of its authors, James G. March, is one of the foremost decision-making theorists of the 20th century. The book evaluates traditional approaches to decision making and puts forward real-world alternatives.

GETTING STARTED

An entire academic discipline, decision science, is devoted to explaining management decision making. Early thinkers believed that the decision process could be rationalized and systematized, and that decision making can therefore be distilled into a formula. However, reality is often more confused and messy, and managers make decisions based on a combination of intuition, experience, and analysis.

CONTRIBUTION

1. The Evolution of Decision-making Theory

Early theories were based on the premise that, under a given set of circumstances, human behavior is logical and therefore predictable.

A profusion of models and analytical tools followed, seeking to distill decision making into a formula. The danger is in concluding that the solution provided by a software package is the right one.

2. The Rational Theory of Decision Making

The authors suggest that the rational, or synoptic, model of decision making involves a series of steps:
- identifying and clarifying the problem
- prioritizing goals
- generating and evaluating options
- comparing predicted outcomes of each option with the goals
- choosing the option that matches best

These models rely on a number of assumptions about the way in which people will behave when confronted with a set of circumstances. The assumptions allow mathematicians to derive formulae based on probability theory. The decision-making tools include such things as cost/benefit analysis, which aims to help managers evaluate different options.

3. Problems in the Rational Theory

Reality is often more confused and messy than a neat model can allow for. Underpinning the mathematical approach are a number of flawed assumptions. The model assumes that decision making is:
- consistent;
- based on accurate information;
- free from emotion or prejudice;
- rational.

4. Real-world Decision Making

According to the authors, the reality is that managers make decisions based on a combination of intuition, experience, and analysis. As intuition and experience are impossible to quantify, the temptation is to focus on the analytical side of decision making.

5. The Relevance of Decision-making Models

This does not mean that decision theory is redundant or that decision-making models should be cast aside.

A number of factors mean that decision making is becoming ever more demanding. The growth in complexity means that companies no longer encounter simple problems. Managers are having to deal with a flood of information: a 1996 Reuters survey of 1,200 managers worldwide found that 43% thought their ability to make decisions was affected as a result of having too much information.

Decision theory and the use of models is reassuring, as they lend legitimacy to decisions that may be based on hunches. However, no models are foolproof; none is universally applicable, or can yet cope with the idiosyncrasies of human behavior.

6. The Challenge for Organizational Decision Making

Business decision-making theory faces a crucial and immediate problem: individuals have goals; collective groups do not. There is a need, therefore, to create useful organizational goals, while not believing there is such a thing as an organizational mind.

Organizations should be regarded as coalitions that negotiate goals.

Creating goals requires three processes:
- bargaining, which establishes the composition and general terms of the coalition;
- internal organizational control, which clarifies and develops the objectives;
- adjustment to experience, which alters agreements in accord with changing circumstances.

Goals are inconsistent for three reasons:
- decision making being decentralized;
- short-term goals taking most attention;
- the resources available to the organization being insufficient to maintain the coalition.

7. A New Decision-making Model

The authors assert that the five principle goals of the modern organization are production, inventory, sales, market share, and profit. There are nine steps in the decision process: forecast competitors' behavior; forecast demand; estimate costs; specify objectives; evaluate plans; reexamine costs; reexamine demand; reexamine objectives; select alternatives. To work successfully, this decision-making model demands that there are standard operating procedures. The procedures can be divided into general ones based on avoiding uncertainty, maintaining the rules, and using simple rules. There are also specifics, such as task performance rules, continuing records and reports, information-handling rules, and plans.

CONTEXT

Much of decision science rests on foundations set by early business thinkers, such as computer pioneer, Charles Babbage, and scientific management founder, Frederick W. Taylor, who believed that, under given circumstances, human behavior was logical and therefore predictable. Based on this premise, models emerged to explain the workings of commerce which, it was thought, could be extended to the way in which decisions were made.

FOR MORE INFORMATION

Cyert, Richard M., and James G. March. *A Behavioral Theory of the Firm*. 2nd ed. Malden, MA: Blackwell Publishing, 1992.

"Managers make decisions based on a combination of intuition, experience, and analysis."

A Behavioral Theory of the Firm

Blur

Stan Davis
Christopher Meyer

WHY READ IT?

Blur is a book about the future, but the authors do not offer prescriptions. Instead they offer a starting point: provocative ideas, observations, and predictions to get you to think creatively about your business and your future.

GETTING STARTED

At the heart of *Blur* are three forces—connectivity, speed, and intangibles—that are redefining businesses and destroying solutions that worked for the industrial world. The forces are known as the blur of desires, the blur of fulfilment, and the blur of resources.

A product offer and exchange were once clear cut, but buyers and sellers are now in a constantly evolving relationship. The entire theory and practice of competitive strategy is changing, and intellectual capital has emerged as the key resource.

Change no longer carries the huge weight it did only a few years ago, and connectivity is speeding the economy up and changing the way it works.

CONTRIBUTION

1. The nature of Blur

At the heart of the authors' Blur theory are three forces: connectivity, speed, and intangibles. These forces are blurring the rules and redefining our businesses and our lives.

Davis and Meyer suggest that they are destroying solutions, such as mass production, segmented pricing, and standardised jobs, that worked for the relatively slow, unconnected industrial world.

The three forces are shaping the behaviour of the new economy.

They are affecting what the authors label the blur of desires, the blur of fulfilment, and the blur of resources.

2. The blur of desires

In the authors' view, the blur of desires has two central elements—the offer and the exchange that were once clear cut.

In the product-dominated age, a company offered a product for sale. Money was exchanged and the customer disappeared into the distance.

Now, products and services are often indistinguishable from each other. Davis and Meyers argue that buyers and sellers are in a constantly evolving relationship—a mutual exchange—which is driven by information and emotion as well as by money.

3. The blur of fulfilment

As organisations change to meet changing demands, so too must the entire theory and practice of competitive strategy.

Connectivity produces different forms of organisation operating to different first principles, in the authors' view.

The blur of businesses has created a new economic model in which returns increase rather than diminish; supermarkets mimic stock markets, and you want the market, not your strategy, to price, market, and manage your offer.

4. The blur of resources

Davis and Meyer feel that intellectual capital has emerged as the key resource.

Hard assets have become intangibles; intangibles have become your only assets.

5. Change is less critical

Built to last now means built to change. However change, and the ambiguity it brings, no longer carries the huge weight it did only a few years ago.

6. The impact of connectivity

The authors suggest that in the information economy, small things are connected in myriad ways to create a complex adaptive system.

Instantaneous, myriad connections are speeding the economy up and changing the way it works. The problem is that the connections are so many and so complex, that they can bring things to a grinding, inexplicable halt.

CONTEXT

From Dale Carnegie to Stephen Covey, Frederick Taylor to Michael Porter, business book readers have been weaned on a diet of prescriptions for success. Books are distilled down to a handful of key points or simple models. The trouble is that lists of the essential ingredients for success are becoming increasingly more questionable.

Uncertainty is uncharted territory and *Blur* is a book of the new breed. *Blur* would not even have been considered as a possible title just a few years ago when blind faith and certainty ruled. It would have been too weak, too suggestive of managerial confusion and impotence, too realistic.

FOR MORE INFORMATION

Davis, Stan, and Christopher Meyer. *Blur: The Speed of Change in the Connected Economy*. Oxford: Capstone, 1999.

The Book of the Five Rings Miyamoto Musashi

WHY READ IT?

Emerging victorious from combat is not a matter of fighting skill, but rather of attitude. Miyamoto Musashi, a 17th-century master samurai swordfighter, says that the fighter's attitude should be characterized by open-mindedness, uprightness, equanimity, and relaxation. The principles he enunciates also apply to managers in modern businesses. From them the perceptive manager can derive useful strategy concepts and rules of conduct for modern business life.

GETTING STARTED

Musashi's work offers the Western reader access to, and an understanding of, the thought, attitudes, and traditions of Japan; and it attempts to show how to achieve and preserve individuality in today's mass society. It is divided into five "books," each assigned to one of the five elements in Japanese tradition and each showing, on the basis of simple principles, how a samurai can defeat an opponent.

CONTRIBUTION
1. The Book of the Earth

Those who wish to learn the art of swordfighting, says Musashi, must follow these rules.

- Never have malicious thoughts.
- Practice constantly to follow the Way.
- Make yourself familiar with all the arts and techniques required.
- Study the ways of all occupations and professions.
- Learn to distinguish between profit and loss in all things.
- Develop your ability to see through things at first glance.
- Endeavor also to perceive the nature of things that remain invisible.
- Never let your attention slip, even when dealing with the smallest things.
- Do not waste time on useless activities.

Only those, Musashi says, who strictly follow these rules, consider each situation in its totality. Constant practice will enable them to control their bodies so that they defeat their opponent physically, and if they have steeled their minds, they will be able to overcome their opponent psychologically as well. If there is a way that leads to invincible self-confidence, that helps the individual to overcome all manner of difficulties, and

brings fame and honor, that way is the Way of the Warrior.

2. The Book of Water

Musashi stresses that in combat your inner attitude should be the same as it usually is. Take good care, he advises, that you are always the same in fight as you are in everyday life. If your body is at rest, do not let your mind remain inactive, but if your body is in violent motion, let your mind remain calm.

In order to defeat an opponent in the correct way, you must first learn the five fighting positions and the corresponding tactics for attack. In this way, he argues, you will develop your judgment and your understanding of rhythm.

3. The Book of Fire

Musashi lists three methods of seizing the initiative.

- Attacking before your opponent does. This is called *Ken-no-sen* (leading by making the first move).
- Seizing the initiative at precisely the moment when the opponent launches an attack. This is *Tai-no-sen* (leading by waiting).
- Still seizing the initiative though both attack at the same time. This is *Tai-tai-no-sen* (leading in a tie).

If you have seized the initiative, says Musashi, victory is as good as assured.

Turning to the broader military picture, Musashi teaches that it is important to recognize the situation and judge whether your opponent is in full command of his forces or already beginning to falter. That involves assessing the fighting spirit of his troops and the positions they have taken up and thus establishing a clear picture of the state he is in, so that you can deploy your own troops accordingly. If you use this strategy, victory is in your hands, because you fight with foresight.

4. The Book of the Wind

He who relies solely on the power of his sword to beat down an opponent, according to Musashi, will strike with unreasonable force and not be in a position to finish the opponent off.

No matter what opponent you are in life-and-death combat with, do not consider whether your blows are strong or weak;

your mind must be set solely on killing him. The Book of the Wind says you should think about nothing else but his death.

All other tricks to bring down an opponent, for example by winding the body, leaping away, or twisting the hand, do not belong in the true art of swordsmanship, according to Musashi.

5. The Book of the Void

The void is that in which nothing exists; it is that which it is impossible for humans to know. If, says Musashi, you know that which exists, you will also be capable of knowing that which does not exist. If, as a samurai, you understand precisely the way of swordsmanship, if daily and hourly you are diligent in training yourself, if you sharpen your wisdom and the power of your mind and learn judgment and vigilance, this will bring you to a state of true emptiness, understood by Musashi in the Buddhist sense as the state of ultimate fulfillment.

CONTEXT

Miyamoto Musashi (1584–1645) was a famous samurai. His *Gorin-no-sho*, or *The Book of the Five Rings* is a manual of swordsmanship, and, in contrast to other samurai texts like the *Hagakure*, it contains little information on the ethical and philosophical principles of the "Way of the Warrior." Musashi was a "masterless," or independent, samurai. For him, there was no superior authority apart from the Way. He remained undefeated throughout his life and shortly before his death withdrew to a cave as a hermit in order to write down his experiences.

Reviews describe Musashi as a cult figure, as a guru, whose disciples now fight in world markets on the same principles that once guided the samurai. Musashi's guide to strategy is treated with great respect in internal seminars held by large Western companies. Japanese business people use it as a handbook for planning sales campaigns.

FOR MORE INFORMATION

Musashi, Miyamoto. *The Book of the Five Rings* (trans. Cleary). Boston, MA: Shambhala Publications, 2005.

"One should pay attention to even the most seemingly insignificant matters."

The Book of the Five Rings

The Borderless World

Kenichi Ohmae

WHY READ IT?

Like *The Mind of the Strategist*, the book gives valuable insights into the strategic thinking behind Japanese corporate success. The author adds new elements to the structure of business strategy, showing how it operates on a global scale.

GETTING STARTED

According to Ohmae, in the global marketplace, the concepts of country and currency are important to business strategy. Fluctuations in trade policy or exchange rates can affect an otherwise brilliant strategy. Strategy is about more than being better than the competition. Big companies must relearn the art of invention in global industries. Customers are not driven to purchase things through nationalistic sentiments, therefore strategy should be formulated around a determination to create value for customers. Global business balances world-scale economies with products tailored to key markets. The role of central governments must be changed to allow individuals access to the best and cheapest goods and services from anywhere in the world.

CONTRIBUTION

1. The Key Elements of Business Strategy

To the three Cs of his previous works (commitment, creativity, and competitiveness), Ohmae adds:

- country—the government-created environments in which global organizations must operate;
- currency—the exposure of such organizations to fluctuations in foreign exchange rates.

These two additional elements are now key to the formulation of any strategy.

An otherwise brilliant strategy can be ruined by a sudden fluctuation in trade policy or exchange rates, leading to a seemingly irreparable hemorrhage of cash.

Making arrangements to deal with fluctuations must lie at the very heart of strategy.

Strategy is creating sustained values for the customer more effectively than the competitors.

2. Invention is Critical

In the author's view, invention and the commercialization of invention are essential. Most people in big companies have forgotten how to invent, but they must relearn the art of invention. This time they must learn to manage invention in industries or businesses that are global, where it is necessary to achieve world-scale economies and yet tailor products to key markets.

3. Going Beyond the Competition

Strategy is about more than simply being better than the competition, which only encourages companies to become fixated on the competition. This fixation drives them to formulate their strategy according to the strategy of their competitors.

Possible strategies should be tested against competitive realities.

Tactical responses to what competitors are doing may be appropriate, but they should come second to your real strategy.

Before you test yourself against the competition, your strategy should encompass the determination to create value for customers.

4. The Interlinked Economy

In the author's view, countries are merely government creations.

In the interlinked economy (made up of the triad of the United States, Europe, and Japan), consumers are not driven to purchase things through nationalistic sentiments, no matter what politicians may say.

At the cash register, people don't care about country of origin or country of residence. They don't think about employment figures or trade deficits.

This also applies to industrial consumers.

5. Declaration of Interdependence

The role of central governments must change to:

- allow individuals access to the best and cheapest goods and services from anywhere in the world;
- help corporations provide stable and rewarding jobs anywhere in the world, regardless of the corporation's national identity;
- coordinate activities with other governments to minimize conflicts arising from narrow interests;
- avoid abrupt changes in economic and social fundamentals.

In addition, governments must deal collectively with traditionally parochial affairs, including taxation.

CONTEXT

The Borderless World explores the new logic of the global marketplace as well as what Ohmae calls power and strategy in the interlinked economy.

This manifesto for the future is as broad ranging as it is, in political reality, unlikely.

The Borderless World has, however, fueled debates about the role of governments, as well as the relationship between governments and the business world, which have yet to be resolved.

Ohmae has since gone on to explore the role of nations still further and now suggests that we have reached a time when the end of the nation state is imminent (see *The End of the Nation State*, Free Press, 1996, and *The Invisible Continent*, HarperBusiness, 2001).

Leading business author Gary Hamel commented, "So the world is becoming interdependent. Hardly news to companies like Dow Chemical, IBM, Ford, or Nestlé. But in 1990 this was still news to Japanese companies (and politicians) who typically defined globalization as big open export markets, and maybe a factory in Tennessee. Kenichi challenged Japanese companies, and myopic executives elsewhere, to develop a more sophisticated view of what it means to be global. Just what balance will ultimately be struck between the forces of globalization and the forces of nationalism and tribalism remains to be seen."

FOR MORE INFORMATION

Ohmae, Kenichi. *The Borderless World: Power and Strategy in the Interlinked Economy*. Revised ed. New York: Collins, 1999.

Built to Last

James Collins
Jerry Porras

WHY READ IT?

According to the authors, companies that enjoy enduring success have core values and a core purpose that remain fixed, while their business strategies and practices endlessly adapt to a changing world. The book shows the importance of developing and sticking to a set of guiding principles, and identifies the qualities essential to building a great and enduring organization.

GETTING STARTED

Values are important in the context of business and corporations, and many companies have long recognized the importance of possessing a set of guiding principles.

In the authors' view, enduring organizations with strong guiding principles have outperformed the general stock market by a factor of 12 since 1925.

Core values are the organization's essential and enduring tenets, and drive the way the company operates at a level that transcends strategic objectives. Such values don't change, although strategies and practices adapt endlessly to change.

Core ideology defines what the company stands for and its very reason for existing. It complements the envisioned future—what the company aspires to become. Any effective vision must embody the core ideology of the organization.

CONTRIBUTION
1. The Importance of Corporate Values

Honesty, integrity, wealth, fairness are all values that we may be able to relate to on an individual personal basis. But what about values in the context of business and corporations?

While the term "corporate values" is a relative newcomer to the business lexicon, the concept of values as an important aspect of corporate life is not. Many companies have long recognized the importance of possessing a set of guiding principles, and the evolution of the concept can be traced

through some of the most influential business books over the last 50 years.

Thomas Watson, Jr., C.E.O. of IBM, observed that any great organization that has lasted over the years owes its resiliency to the power of its beliefs and the appeal these beliefs have for its people.

2. The Qualities of an Enduring Organization

The book sets out to identify the qualities essential to building a great and enduring organization—the successful habits of truly visionary companies.

The 18 companies chosen as subjects had outperformed the general stock market by a factor of 12 since 1925.

Core values are the organization's essential and enduring tenets. These are a small set of guiding principles (not to be confused with specific cultural or operating practices), which are never to be compromised for financial gain or short-term expediency.

Values are timeless guiding principles that drive the way the company operates at a level that transcends strategic objectives. For Hewlett-Packard, for example, values include a strong sense of responsibility to the community. For Disney, they include creativity, dreams, and imagination and the promulgation of wholesome American values.

3. Core Values Don't Change

Companies that enjoy enduring success have core values and a core purpose that remain fixed while their business strategies and practices endlessly adapt to a changing world. This constancy is a key factor in the success of companies such as Hewlett-Packard, Johnson & Johnson, Procter & Gamble, and Sony.

4. A Model for Core Values

The authors recommend a conceptual framework to cut through some of the confusion swirling around the issues.

In their model, vision has two com-

ponents—core ideology and envisioned future. Core ideology, the Yin in their plan, defines what the company stands for and why it exists. Yin is unchanging and complements Yang, the envisioned future.

The envisioned future is what the company aspires to become, to achieve, to create—something that requires considerable change and progress to attain. Core ideology provides the glue that holds an organization together through time.

5. An Effective Vision

Any effective vision must embody the core ideology of the organization. This has two components—core values (a system of guiding principles and tenets) and core purpose (the organization's most fundamental reason for existence).

CONTEXT

Built to Last sets out to identify the qualities, or corporate values, essential to building a great and enduring organization.

The evolution of the concept of corporate values can be traced through some of the most influential business books over the last 50 years.

In *A Business and Its Beliefs*, published in 1963, Thomas Watson, Jr. observed, "Consider any great organization—one that has lasted over the years—I think you will find it owes its resiliency not to its form of organization or administrative skills, but to the power of what we call beliefs and the appeal these beliefs have for its people."

In the early 1980s, Tom Peters and Robert Waterman thought corporate values important enough to warrant an entire chapter in *In Search of Excellence*.

1077

MANAGEMENT LIBRARY

FOR MORE INFORMATION

Collins, James, and Jerry Porras. *Built to Last*. Revised ed. New York: Collins, 2004.

"Companies that enjoy enduring success have core values and a core purpose that remain fixed while their business strategies and practices endlessly adapt to a changing world."

Built to Last

A Business and Its Beliefs Thomas Watson, Jr.

1078

MANAGEMENT LIBRARY

WHY READ IT?
A Business and Its Beliefs: The Ideas that Helped Build IBM was written by the son of the founder of IBM's commercial greatness, who himself led the company into the computer age. It describes the origins of one of the world's most successful corporations and shows how its achievements were built on a strong corporate culture and a passionate commitment to customer service.

GETTING STARTED
Thomas Watson, Jr. went to work for IBM in 1946 as a salesman. He was appointed chief executive in 1956 and retired in 1970, after presiding over IBM's rise to preeminence at the beginning of the computer age.

IBM's origins lay in the Computing-Tabulating-Recording Company, which Thomas Watson, Sr. joined in 1914. The company initially made everything from butcher's scales to meat slicers, but gradually concentrated on tabulating machines that processed information mechanically on punched cards. It changed its name to International Business Machines in 1924.

IBM's development was helped by the 1937 Wages-Hours Act, which required U.S. companies to record hours worked and wages paid. The existing machines couldn't cope; Watson, Sr. developed a solution, the Mark 1, followed by the Selective Sequence Electronic Calculator in 1947. By then IBM's revenues were $119 million and it was set to make the great leap forward to become the world's largest computer company.

As far as management thinking is concerned, what IBM stood for is more important than what it did. Thomas Watson, Jr. took on a hugely successful company with a strong corporate culture built around salesmanship and service. Thomas Watson, Sr. had emphasized people and service obsessively. IBM was a service star in an era of machines that performed badly. This is where the heart of the message of *A Business and Its Beliefs* lies.

CONTRIBUTION
1. Core Values Are Critical
A company's central beliefs (what would now be called its core values) are central to its success. Watson believed that these beliefs help people find common cause with each other, and sustain this common cause and sense of direction through the many changes that take place from one generation to another.

Success, in his view, comes through a sound set of beliefs, on which the corporation premises all its policies and actions. Beliefs must always come before policies, practices, and goals. The latter must always be altered if they are seen to violate fundamental beliefs.

Not only should the beliefs be sound, they should be stuck to through thick and thin. The most important single factor in corporate success is faithful adherence to those beliefs. Beliefs never change. Change everything else, but never the basic truths on which the company is based.

However, Watson argued for flexibility in all other areas. If an organization, he asserted, is to meet the challenges of a changing world, it must be prepared to change everything about itself except beliefs as it moves through corporate life. The only sacred cow in an organization should be its basic philosophy of doing business.

2. Develop a Corporate Culture
The beliefs that mold great organizations frequently grow out of the character, the experience, and the convictions of a single person. In IBM's case that person was Thomas Watson, Sr.

The Watsons created a corporate culture that lasted. IBM, Big Blue, became the archetypal modern corporation and its managers the ultimate stereotype, with their regulation somber suits, plain ties, zeal for selling, and company song.

3. A Passion for Competing
Behind the corporate culture lay a belief in competing vigorously and providing quality service. Later, competitors complained that IBM's sheer size won it orders. This was only partly true. Its size masked a deeper commitment to managing customer accounts, providing service, building relationships, and to the original values laid out by the Watsons.

4. People Matter
The real difference between success and failure in a corporation can very often be traced to the question of how well the organization brings out the great energies and talents of its people. Giving full consideration to the individual employee was one of the enduring beliefs on which IBM's success was built.

CONTEXT
In this book, the author codified and clarified what IBM stands for. The book is a statement of business philosophy, an extended mission statement for IBM.

Though it was published in the same year as Alfred P. Sloan, Jr.'s *My Years with General Motors* it could not be more different. While Sloan sidelines people, Watson celebrates their potential; while Sloan espouses systems and structures, Watson talks of values.

Business guru Gary Hamel commented, "Never change your basic beliefs, Watson argued. He may be right. But the dividing line between beliefs and dogmas is a fine one. A deep set of beliefs can be the essential pivot around which the company changes and adapts; or, if endlessly-elaborated, overly-codified, and solemnly worshipped, the manacles that shackle a company to the past."

FOR MORE INFORMATION
Watson, Thomas Jr. *A Business and Its Beliefs: The Ideas that Helped Build IBM.* Revised ed. New York: McGraw-Hill, 2003.

Capital

Karl Marx

WHY READ IT?

In the capitalist world human labor itself becomes a commodity. *Capital*, the major work by the social philosopher Karl Marx (1818–83), is a thoroughgoing critique of capitalism. Marx recognized the dynamics of the economic process, foresaw economic cycles, and developed a closed theory of economic activity. He was also the first economist to bring economics and history into relation with each other and *Capital* was the book in which he did it.

GETTING STARTED

Marx describes the capitalist method of production in its overall context. He follows Ricardo in positing that only labor can produce value, then develops a theory of added value as the difference between the use value and the exchange value of labor as a commodity. Workers do only a portion of their work for themselves; a large portion goes to create added value, which falls entirely to the capitalist. Capitalists, Marx suggests, attempt to increase added value either by making their workers work longer or by reducing the amount of work time necessary for their workers' subsistence. Workers, therefore, have to earn their livelihoods in a shorter time, so that they can produce more added value. This leads to the exploitation of the working class.

CONTRIBUTION

1. Volume One: The Production Process of Capital

Volume one deals with the development of the laws of added value production. This is the part of *Capital* that has always played the largest role in often heated public discussion of the book.

Capitalist production, for Marx, is the production of goods, that is, production for the market. It is not conducted by small independent producers such as craftspeople, but by non-working entrepreneurs, who control the means of production and who therefore have the ability to make others work for them and to exploit them.

Every commodity, Marx argues, has two characteristics: usefulness (equivalent to its use value) and the property of being produced by human labor. Since use value varies, depending on persons, time, and circumstances, it cannot be the basis of price. Labor must therefore be the criterion of value.

With the development of the exchange of goods, Marx continues, trade emerges as an independent function. In trade, consumption is not the purpose of the act of exchange, as it is in a simple exchange of goods, but profit.

The following paradox, according to Marx, then emerges. The law of value regulating the exchange of goods knows only the exchange of equal values. But in exchange transactions in trade, on the other hand, an inequality must come into play. This can only stem from production. For this to be possible, the capitalist must discover a commodity whose use value is that it creates more value than it actually possesses. That commodity is labor.

2. Volume Two: The Circulation Process of Capital

In the second volume, Marx deals with the circulation of capital as it passes through various stages. Capital must, he says, continually take on and then divest itself of three separate forms in order to be able to function and be of use: money capital, productive capital, and commodity capital. Money capital constantly transforms itself into the elements of the production process—labor and the means of production—and the result of its functioning appears in the form of commodities, endowed with added value, which are once again transformed into money. Acts involving the circulation of commodities take place continually; sales and purchases are always being transacted; goods and money are constantly brought into conjunction. But it is, says Marx, the fact that these acts are transition stages in the circulatory process of capital that makes them functions of capital; it is precisely that which transforms a sum of money into money capital, that makes commodities either productive capital or commodity capital. It is not their material nature that gives them this character, but the economic and historical conditions under which the process takes place. Commodities are not by nature capital, any more than workers are.

3. Volume Three: The Overall Process of Capitalist Production

In this volume, Marx brings volumes one and two into unity. The theoretical category of value, he asserts, is of interest to the capitalist. What the capitalist looks at is the capital advance that must be made to bring about production of a particular commodity. The advance is made up of constant and variable capital and represents, for the capitalist, the cost of the commodity. Capitalists do not calculate added value achieved in relation to the capital used, they simply calculate the surplus achieved against aggregate costs when the goods are sold, the profit.

Added value, says Marx, interests capitalists as little as does value per se. They expect a gain not on the variable capital they advance, but on aggregate capital. The added value on aggregate capital is profit; the numerical relationship of the one to the other is the profit rate.

CONTEXT

Marx came to economics after his political party failed to achieve power in the revolution of 1848–49. *Capital*, published in 1867, became the cornerstone of Marxism, the political doctrine and system named after him. It is, of course, more than pure economic theory. It is a mighty intellectual construct made up of historical, sociological, and economic ideas and propaganda. It was to provide the groundwork for socialism and give a theoretical basis to Marx's other major work, the *Communist Manifesto*. Marx's guiding light was the classless society, communism. As a result, while some honor him as the prophet and advocate of the working class, others refuse to take him seriously as an economist. He has also been blamed for the fact that while concerned in theory with the working class he avoided actual contact with the object of his investigations and never once saw a factory from the inside.

FOR MORE INFORMATION

Marx, Karl. *Capital: A Critique of Political Economy* (trans. Fernbach). New York: Penguin USA, 1992.

1079

MANAGEMENT LIBRARY

"Capital is dead labor."

The Change Masters

Rosabeth Moss Kanter

WHY READ IT?

This book is regarded as an authoritative work on the factors behind successful corporate change. Kanter's work takes a human relations perspective, and was one of the earliest books to focus on the importance of empowerment.

GETTING STARTED

According to the author, "change masters" are adept at anticipating the need for, and leading, productive change. Companies with a commitment to human resources were significantly ahead in long-term profitability and financial growth.

Kanter goes on to suggest that growth problems in U.S. companies are due to suffocation of the entrepreneurial spirit—innovation is the key to growth. New skills are required to manage effectively in innovation-stimulating environments: power skills, the ability to manage employee participation, and an understanding of how change is managed. Empowerment is critical to corporate success.

CONTRIBUTION

1. The Nature of Change Masters

Change masters are those people and organizations adept at the art of anticipating the need for, and leading, productive change. Change resisters are those who remain intent on reining in innovation.

2. The Importance of Managing People

A research program asked 65 human resource directors in large organizations to name companies that were progressive and forward-thinking in their systems and practices, in relation to people. Forty-seven companies emerged as leaders in the field. They were then compared to similar companies. The companies with a commitment to human resources were significantly ahead in long-term profitability and financial growth.

The message is that if you manage your people well, you are probably managing your business well.

3. Innovation as the Key to Growth

Kanter places responsibility for company growth problems on the quiet suffocation of the entrepreneurial spirit in segmentalist companies. She identifies innovation as the key to future growth. The way to develop and sustain innovation is to adopt an integrative approach rather than a segmentalist one.

Three new sets of skills are required to manage effectively in such integrative, innovation-stimulating environments:

- the ability to persuade others to invest information, support, and resources in new initiatives driven by an entrepreneur
- the ability to manage problems associated with increased use of teams and employee participation
- an understanding of how change is designed and constructed in an organization: how the microchanges introduced by individual innovators relate to macrochanges or strategic reorientation

4. The Importance of Empowerment

The extent to which individuals are given the opportunity to use power effectively influences whether a company stagnates or innovates. In an innovative company, people are at center stage.

CONTEXT

Rosabeth Moss Kanter began her career as a sociologist before her transformation into international business guru. *The Economist* (15 October 1994) commented, "Kanter-the-guru still studies her subject with a sociologist's eye, treating the corporation not so much as a micro-economy, concerned with turning inputs into outputs, but as a mini-society, bent on shaping individuals to collective ends."

Kanter's work is a development of the Human Relations School of the late 1950s and 1960s. Through *The Change Masters* (1983) and *When Giants Learn to Dance* (1989), she was partly responsible for the increased interest in empowerment, if not its practice.

The Change Masters has been called "the thinking man's *In Search of Excellence*."

U.S. author Gary Hamel said: "In a turbulent and inhospitable world, corporate vitality is a fragile thing. Yesterday's industry challengers are today's laggards. Entropy is endemic. Certainly *The Change Masters* is the most carefully researched, and best argued, book on change and transformation to date. While Rosabeth may not have discovered the eternal fountain of corporate vitality, she certainly points us in its general direction."

FOR MORE INFORMATION

Kanter, Rosabeth Moss. *The Change Masters.* New York: Simon & Schuster, 1983.

"The companies with a commitment to human resources were significantly higher in long-term profitability and financial growth."

The Change Masters

The Changing Culture of a Factory

Elliot Jaques

WHY READ IT?

This book is based on an extensive study of industrial democracy in practice at the United Kingdom's Glacier Metal Company between 1948 and 1965. The company introduced a number of highly progressive changes in working practice that were ahead of their time and set a pattern for future practice.

GETTING STARTED

The Glacier Metal Company introduced a number of highly progressive changes in working practice, resulting in a form of industrial democracy that was ahead of its time. According to the study, the emphasis was on granting people responsibility and giving them a say in every problem they encountered. The project highlighted the shortcomings of conventional industrial relations practice, and showed that managers should be measured by the long-term impact of their decisions.

CONTRIBUTION

1. Introducing Industrial Democracy

The Glacier Metal Company introduced a number of highly progressive changes in working practice:

- A works council was introduced. This was far removed from the usually toothless attempts at worker representation.
- No change of company policy was allowed unless all members of the works council

agreed. Any single person on the council had a veto.
- "Punching in," the traditional means of recording whether someone had turned up for work, was abolished.

Contrary to what experts and observers anticipated, the company did not grind to an immediate halt.

2. Increasing Personal Responsibility

The emphasis was on granting people responsibility and on understanding the dynamics of group working. Everybody should be encouraged to accept the maximum amount of personal responsibility, and should be allowed to have a say in every problem in which they could help.

3. Anticipating Organizational Developments

The project was a decade ahead of any form of organizational development. It highlighted a number of issues:

- the redundancy of conventional organization charts;
- the potential power of corporate culture (a concept then barely understood);
- the potential benefits of running organizations in a fair and mutually beneficial way.

4. Theory of the Value of Work

"The manifest picture of bureaucratic organization is a confusing one," according to Jaques. "There appears to be no rhyme or

reason for the structures that are developed, in number of levels, in titling, or even in the meaning to be attached to the manager–subordinate linkage."

A solution, labeled "the time span of discretion," contended that levels of management should be based on how long it was before their decisions could be checked. Managers should be paid in accordance with that time, and measured by the long-term impact of their decisions.

CONTEXT

The practices introduced at the Glacier Metal Company were almost a decade ahead of their time. However, they did not ensure the company's survival.

The study's progressive views on the importance of motivation at work have undoubtedly influenced other management writers and practitioners, such as Mary Parker Follett and Frederick Herzberg. Jaques' work was based on long-term scientific observation, in contrast to what he terms the "fantasy fads," the "waffle and fiddling around" of management consultants.

FOR MORE INFORMATION

Jaques, Elliot. *The Changing Culture of a Factory.* Revised ed. Oxford: Routledge, 2003.

"I'm completely convinced of the necessity of encouraging everybody to accept the maximum amount of personal responsibility."

The Changing Culture of a Factory

Competing for the Future

Gary Hamel
C. K. Prahalad

WHY READ IT?

Competing for the Future, named by *BusinessWeek* as the best management book of 1994, is regarded as the definitive book on strategy for contemporary business. It criticizes the narrow mechanistic view of strategy and calls for a broader approach that recognizes a company's core competencies.

GETTING STARTED

This book argues that traditional strategy is too narrow in its perspective. Far from being a simple annual exercise, strategy is multifaceted, emotional as well as analytical, and concerned with meaning, purpose, and passion. Few managers spend enough time looking to the future. They should adopt "strategizing"—a new approach for developing complex, robust strategies, focusing on core competencies.

Today the onus is on transforming not just individual organizations, but entire industries. The true challenge is to create revolutions when you are large and dominant. Small entrepreneurial offshoots are not the route to organizational regeneration. Downsizing is an easy option—growth comes from creating a difference, and vitality comes from within the organization, if only executives would listen.

CONTRIBUTION
1. The Narrow Focus of Traditional Strategy

The authors assert that strategy has tied itself into a straitjacket of narrow, and narrowing, perspectives:

- A huge proportion of strategists, perhaps 95%, are economists and engineers who share a mechanistic view of strategy.
- Strategy is multi-faceted, emotional as well as analytical, concerned with meaning, purpose, and passion.
- Strategy should be looked on as a learning process.

2. Strategy is not Simple

In the authors' view, executives perceive that the problem with strategy is not creating it, but implementing it. Strategy is not a ritual or a once-a-year exercise. As a result, managers are bogged down in the nitty-gritty of the present—spending less than three percent of their time looking to the future.

3. Adopt Strategizing

Instead of talking about strategy or planning, companies should talk about strategizing and ask, "What are the fundamental preconditions for developing complex, variegated, robust strategies?"

Strategizing is part of the new managerial argot of strategic intent, strategic architecture, foresight (rather than vision), and the idea of core competencies.

4. Focus on Core Competencies

Core competencies represent the collective learning in the organization, especially how to coordinate diverse production skills and integrate multiple streams of technologies.

Organizations should see themselves as a portfolio of core competencies as opposed to business units. Core competencies are geared to growing opportunity share whereas business units are narrowly focused on market share.

5. Different Approaches to Strategy

There is a thin dividing line between order and chaos. Neither Stalinist bureaucracy nor Silicon Valley provides an optimal economic system. Silicon Valley is extraordinarily good at creating new ideas, but in other ways is extraordinarily inefficient.

6. Small or Large Organizations?

Small entrepreneurial offshoots are not the route to organizational regeneration. They are too random, inefficient, and prone to becoming becalmed by corporate indifference. Smaller companies have had a revolutionary impact (IKEA, Body Shop, Swatch, and Virgin), but the true challenge is to create revolutions when you are large and dominant. U.S. companies such as Motorola and Hewlett-Packard are more successful at this than their European counterparts. We are moving to more democratic models of organization, to which U.S. corporations appear more attuned. In Europe and Japan there is a more elitist sense of knowledge residing at the top—a hierarchy of experience, not of imagination.

7. Rules for Success

- A company surrenders today's businesses when it gets smaller faster than it gets better.
- A company surrenders tomorrow's businesses when it gets better without getting different.

- Downsizing is an easy option.
- Growth (the authors prefer to speak of vitality) comes from difference, though there are as many stupid ways to grow as there are to downsize.
- The pressure for growth is usually ignited by a crisis.
- Vitality comes from within, if only executives would listen.
- Companies pay millions of dollars for the opinions of McKinsey's bright 29-year-olds, but ignore their own bright 29-year-olds.

CONTEXT

The debate on the meaning and application of strategy is long-running. The 1960s gave us the analytical Igor Ansoff; the 1970s, Henry Mintzberg with his cerebral crafting strategy; the 1980s, Michael Porter's rational route to competitiveness.

Nominations for the leading strategic thinkers of the 1990s would certainly include Gary Hamel and C. K. Prahalad. *Competing for the Future* has been called the blueprint for a new generation of strategic thinking. *BusinessWeek* (19 September 1994) stated: "At a time when many companies continue to lay off thousands in massive re-engineering exercises, this is a book that deserves widespread attention. It's a valuable and worthwhile tonic for devotees of today's slash-and-burn school of management."

The surge of interest in core competencies has tended to enthusiastic oversimplification. Commentators believe companies need to be cautious about where core competencies will lead. They are a very powerful weapon, but can encourage companies to get into businesses simply because they see a link between core competencies rather than ones where they have an in-depth knowledge.

The authors' strategic prognosis falls between two extremes. At one extreme are the arch-rationalists, insisting on a constant stream of data to support any strategy. At the other is the thriving-on-chaos school, with its belief in freewheeling organizations where strategy is a moveable feast.

FOR MORE INFORMATION

Hamel, Gary, and C. K. Prahalad. *Competing for the Future*. Boston, MA: Harvard Business School Press, 1996.

"A company surrenders tomorrow's businesses when it gets better without getting different."

The Competitive Advantage of Nations

Michael Porter

1083

MANAGEMENT LIBRARY

WHY READ IT?

Many consider *The Competitive Advantage of Nations* to be one of the most ambitious books of our times. Said to do "for international capitalism what Marx did for the class struggle," it re-examines the nation state, suggesting that its basic role today is an economic one, and that, even in a global economy, it has a key role to play by ensuring the success of the companies operating within its borders who are the actual wealth producers for the population.

GETTING STARTED

Michael Porter, author of the modern business classic *Competitive Strategy*, has a good deal of experience as a consultant to national governments. *The Competitive Advantage of Nations* emerged from his work on Ronald Reagan's Commission on Industrial Competitiveness. The research for the book encompassed ten countries: the United Kingdom, Denmark, Italy, Japan, Korea, Singapore, Sweden, Switzerland, the United States, and Germany (then West Germany).

The book can be read on three levels as:

- as a general inquiry into what makes national economies successful;
- as a detailed study of eight of the world's main modern economies;
- as a series of prescriptions about what governments should do to improve their country's competitiveness.

It asks crucial questions. What makes a nation's businesses and industries competitive in global markets and what propels a whole nation's economy to advance? Why is one nation often the home for so many of an industry's world leaders? Why, for example, is Switzerland the home base for international leaders in pharmaceuticals, chocolate, and trading?

At its heart is a radical new perspective of the role of nations. From being military powerhouses they are now economic units whose competitiveness is the key to power.

CONTRIBUTION
1. Nations, Competition, and Productivity

According to the author, "Nations don't compete. Companies compete. Nations can make it hard or easy for them to do so." When governments deliberately set out to help companies compete, however, their efforts are often counterproductive. The principal economic goal of a nation is to produce a high and rising standard of living for its citizens. The ability to do so depends not on the amorphous notion of competitiveness but on the productivity with which a nation's labor and capital resources are employed.

2. The Paradox of Globalization

Companies and industries have become globalized and more international in their scope and aspirations than ever before. This would appear to suggest that the nation has lost its role in the international success of its firms. Companies, at first glance, seem to have transcended countries.

While the globalization of competition might appear to make the nation less important, instead it seems to make it more so. With fewer impediments to trade to shelter uncompetitive domestic businesses and industries, the home nation takes on growing significance because it is the source of the skills and technology that underpin competitive advantage.

In addition, it is the intensity of domestic competition that often fuels success on a global stage.

3. The National Diamond

To make sense of the dynamics behind national or regional strength in a particular industry, Porter developed the concept of the national diamond made up of four forces.

- Factor conditions—these would once have been largely restricted to natural resources and plentiful labor; now they also embrace data communications, university research, and the availability of scientists, engineers, or experts in a particular field.
- Demand conditions—if there is strong national demand for a product or service, this can give the industry a head start in global competition. The United States, for example, is ahead in health services due to heavy national demand.
- Related and supporting industries—indus-

tries which are strong in a particular country are often surrounded by successful related industries.
- Company strategy, structure, and rivalry—domestic competition fuels growth and competitive strength.

Together, these four determine whether a nation has competitive advantage or not.

4. Clusters

"Nations succeed not in isolated industries, but in *clusters* of industries connected through vertical and horizontal relationships." Groups of interconnected companies, suppliers, and related industries arising in particular locations contribute substantially to national success. Porter shows how such clusters come into being.

CONTEXT

According to *The Economist* (October 8, 1994), "The book that projected Mr. Porter into the stratosphere, read by aspiring intellectuals and despairing politicians everywhere, was *The Competitive Advantage of Nations*."

Not everyone, however, agrees with Porter on the relationship between the nation and the globalized economy. Kenichi Ohmae believes that the nation state is on its way out, and Gary Hamel commented: "While *The Competitive Advantage of Nations* provides a good account of why particular industry clusters emerged in some countries and not others, it is essentially backward-looking. In a world of open markets, and mobile capital, technology, and knowledge, no firm need be the product of its geography."

Yet on balance, readers around the world have embraced the challenges outlined in Porter's book, and its status and impact as a classic business text cannot be underestimated.

FOR MORE INFORMATION

Porter, Michael. *The Competitive Advantage of Nations*. Revised ed. New York: Free Press, 1998.

"Productivity is the prime determinant in the long run of a nation's standard of living."

The Competitive Advantage of Nations

Competitive Strategy

Michael Porter

WHY READ IT?

Competitive Strategy is a modern classic. It claims to provide a solution to a long-running strategic dilemma, and has put strategy at the forefront of management thinking.

GETTING STARTED

In 1973 Michael Porter became one of the youngest professors ever at the Harvard Business School. He has since acted as a strategy counselor to many leading U.S. and international companies, besides playing an active role in economic policy with the U.S. Congress, business groups, and as an adviser to foreign governments.

Competitive Strategy is one of those books that bases its message around significant numbers—in this case three and five, the three generic strategies (every company must adopt one or lose out to its competitors) and the five competitive forces (that determine what a company must do to remain competitive). Over 20 years after its first publication, the current critical consensus seems to be that the competitive forces are truer to reality than the generic strategies. But strategy, having gone out of fashion in the 1980s and 1990s, may be making a comeback.

CONTRIBUTION

1. Resolving the Strategy Dilemma

Competitive Strategy presents a rationalist's solution to a long-running strategic dilemma. At one end of the spectrum are the pragmatists, who contend that companies have to respond to their own specific situations. Competitive advantage emerges from immediate, fast-thinking responsiveness. There is no pat formula for achieving sustainable competitive advantage.

At the other end are those who, like the Boston Consulting Group, think that market knowledge is all-important. Any company that masters the intricacies of a particular market can reduce prices and increase market share. Porter proposes a compromise, arguing that there are three strategies for dealing with competitive forces: differentiation, overall cost leadership, and focus.

2. Differentiation

Differentiation entails competing on the basis of value added to customers (quality, service, differentiation) so that customers will pay a premium to cover higher costs. It requires creative flair, research capability, and strong marketing.

3. Overall Cost Leadership

Cost-based leadership involves offering products or services at the lowest cost. Quality and service are not unimportant, but cost reduction provides focus to organization.

4. Focus

Focus involves combining elements of the previous two strategies and targeting a specific market intensively.

5. Combining the Strategies

Companies with a clear strategy outperform those whose strategy is unclear or those that attempt to achieve both differentiation and cost leadership.

Sometimes the company can successfully pursue more than one approach, though this is rarely possible. Effectively implementing any of these generic strategies usually requires total commitment, and organizational arrangements are diluted if there is more than one primary target.

6. The Risks of Ignoring Generic Strategies

If a company fails to focus on any of the three generic strategies it is liable to encounter problems. The company stuck in the middle is almost guaranteed low profitability. It either loses the high-volume customers who demand low prices or must bid away its profits to get this business away from low-cost companies. It also loses high-margin businesses, the cream, to the companies who are focused on high-margin targets. In addition, it will also probably suffer from a blurred corporate culture and a conflicting set of organizational arrangements and motivation systems.

7. The Five Competitive Forces

In any industry, whether domestic or international or product- or service-oriented, the rules of competition are embodied in five competitive forces.

- The entry of new competitors. New competitors necessitate some competitive response, which will inevitably use resources and reduce profits.
- The threat of substitutes. If there are viable alternatives to your product or service in the marketplace, the prices you can charge will be limited.
- The bargaining power of buyers. If customers have bargaining power they will use it. This will reduce profit margins.

- The bargaining power of suppliers. Given power over you, suppliers will increase their prices and adversely affect your profitability.
- The rivalry among the existing competitors. Competition leads to the need to invest in marketing or R&D, or to price reductions. These will reduce profits.

The collective strength of these five competitive forces determines the ability of companies in an industry to earn, on average, rates of return on investment in excess of the cost of capital.

CONTEXT

When *Competitive Strategy* was published, it offered a rational and straightforward method for companies to extricate themselves from strategic confusion. The reassurance proved short-lived. Less than a decade later, companies were having to compete on all fronts. They had to be differentiated through improved service or speedier development, and be cost leaders, cheaper than their competitors.

Porter's other contribution proved more robust. The five forces are a means whereby a company can understand its particular industry. Initially passively interpreted as statements of the facts of competitive life, they are now usually seen as the rules of the game, which may have to be challenged if an organization is to achieve any impact.

Influential author Gary Hamel commented, "In *Competitive Strategy*, Michael Porter did a masterful job of synthesizing all that economists know about what determines industry and company profitability. While *Competitive Strategy* isn't much help in discovering profitable strategies, it is an unfailing guide as to whether some particular strategy, once articulated, can be counted on to produce worthwhile profits. What distinguishes *Competitive Strategy* from many other contemporary business books is its strong conceptual foundation. Every MBA graduate in the world can remember Porter's five forces. How many can recall the eight rules of excellence?"

FOR MORE INFORMATION

Porter, Michael. *Competitive Strategy: Techniques for Analyzing Industries and Competitors.* Revised ed. New York: Free Press, 1998.

"Strategy is a choice on how to compete."

Co-opetition

Barry J. Nalebuff
Adam M. Brandenburger

WHY READ IT?

The authors claim that this is the first book to adapt game theory to business strategy. Combining cooperation with competition to produce "co-opetition" is, they claim, an innovative business strategy that will give companies a winning advantage. It is a technique for making the right strategic business decisions in complicated business situations.

GETTING STARTED

The authors explain why game theory provides a valid basis for thinking about business. The theory states that nothing is static; markets are dynamic and evolutionary. Companies can create new models or take on different roles to succeed. Nothing is taken as given. According to the authors, players in the game of business can change the rules to succeed. *Co-opetition* uses game theory to show how companies who cooperate can influence each other's success. Software, for example, becomes more valuable when a complementary company produces more powerful computers. Co-opetition strengthens the interdependence between companies.

CONTRIBUTION
1. The Game of Business

Nalebuff and Brandenburger believe that co-opetition depends on complementary activities. When products stimulate demand for complementary products, companies should cooperate.

They show how the game of business includes customers, suppliers, competitors, and complementors. These organizations form part of a value net with integral dependencies. The value net expands the concept of a company's customers. By taking a multiple perspective, they argue, companies can redefine the role of a customer in a value net.

The authors explain how film companies initially saw video as a threat to their business. Now, they recognize video as complementary to film distribution. Similarly, computers did not create a paperless office, they made it easier to create paper.

2. The Importance of Added Value

To succeed in a game, companies must be able to offer added value. However, say the authors, this must represent what a customer or competitor regards as valuable. If the value is not sufficient, the company can change the game by playing a different role or changing the rules. Perception therefore plays an important part in co-opetition; recognizing what other people believe is important.

Companies must recognize the boundaries of their business and be realistic about their ambitions. According to the authors, companies operating in a lower segment can easily harm their core business by attempting to move into a higher segment.

3. Changing the Rules

The authors suggest a number of ways to change the rules.

A company entering a monopoly market may create competition, but if the incumbent has strong brand values, the new entrant may not gain sales. In those circumstances they recommend "getting paid to play." The new entrant should gain some benefit from entering a market, rather than just acting as a makeweight competitor.

The authors suggest that a company needing sales of complementary products to boost its own sales can influence a market by negotiating favorable prices for its own customers.

As the authors point out, a dominant supplier can exercise a monopoly position: limiting development and supplies to keep customers and suppliers hungry strengthens its own position.

4. Changing the Game

Nalebuff and Brandenburger recommend an action plan for bringing about change:

- look at your own value net;
- identify opportunities for cooperation and competition;
- change the players;
- identify the implications if the players change;
- identify added value;
- see how you can add further value;
- identify the other players' added value;
- see which roles are hindering or helping you;
- identify roles you would like to adopt;
- work out whether you can change the rules;
- work out how other players perceive the game.

CONTEXT

Game theory began in the 1950s with the publication of the book *Theory of Games and Economic Behavior* by Neumann and Morgenstern. Their theories were applied to economics, military strategy, computer science, and evolutionary biology. Game theory has been used more widely in business since the 1990s.

Co-opetition is the first book to use game theory to demonstrate business strategy. Its publication is timely as industry commentators from leading companies believe that the idea of complementary business is still not widely understood.

1085

MANAGEMENT LIBRARY

FOR MORE INFORMATION

Nalebuff, Barry J., and Adam M. Brandenburger. *Co-opetition*. New York: Doubleday, 1996.

"Business is cooperation when it comes to creating a pie and competition when it comes to dividing it up."

Co-opetition

Corporate Strategy

Igor Ansoff

WHY READ IT?

In *Corporate Strategy*, Ansoff codified and generalized his experiences as a strategist at Lockheed. The book develops a series of concepts and procedures that managers can use to develop a practical method for strategic decision making within an organization.

GETTING STARTED

Corporate Strategy integrated strategic planning concepts invented independently in leading U.S. companies. The book provided a powerful, rational model by which strategic and planning decisions could be made. Ansoff saw strategic planning as a complex sequence, or cascade, of decisions and defined two main concepts essential to understanding its nature, and, therefore, to implementing it successfully. The first of these was "gap analysis"—the "gap" being the difference between the current position of an organization and its strategic objectives. The second was "synergy"—the concept that $2 + 2 = 5$.

CONTRIBUTION

1. Integrating Strategic Planning Concepts

Corporate Strategy integrated strategic planning concepts which were invented independently in a number of leading U.S. companies, including Lockheed.

Ansoff saw strategic management as a powerful applied theory, offering a degree of coherence and universality lacking in the more traditional, functionally-dominated management theorizing.

2. New Theoretical Concepts

The book presented several new theoretical concepts such as partial ignorance, business strategy, capability and competence profiles, and synergy. One particular concept, the product-mission matrix, became very popular, because it was simple and—for the first time—codified the differences between strategic expansion and diversification.

3. A Rational Model for Planning Decisions

Corporate Strategy provided a rational model by which strategic and planning decisions could be made. The model concentrated on corporate expansion and diversification, rather than on strategic planning as a whole.

The Ansoff Model of Strategic Planning was a complex sequence, or cascade, of decisions. The decisions started with highly aggregated ones and proceeded toward the more specific.

4. The Introduction of Gap Analysis

Central to the cascade of decisions is the concept of gap analysis, which can be summarized as: see where you are, identify where you wish to be, and identify the tasks that will take you there.

The procedure within each step of the cascade is similar.

- A set of objectives is established.
- The difference (the gap) between the current position of the organization and the objectives is estimated.
- One or more courses of action (strategy) is proposed.
- These are tested for their gap-reducing properties.

A course is accepted if it substantially closes the gap; if it does not, new alternatives are put forward and tested.

5. The Concept of Synergy

Corporate Strategy introduced the word "synergy" to the management vocabulary. Although the term has become overused, Ansoff's explanation $(2 + 2 = 5)$ remains memorably simple.

CONTEXT

Corporate Strategy was published at a time of widespread enthusiasm for strategic planning, and an increasing number of organizations were joining the ranks of its users. Until its publication, strategic planning was a barely-understood, ad hoc concept. It was practiced, while the theory lay largely unexplored. Ansoff also examined corporate advantage long before Michael Porter's dissection of the subject in the 1980s.

While *Corporate Strategy* was a remarkable book for its time, its flaws have been widely acknowledged, most honestly by Ansoff himself. It is highly prescriptive and advocates heavy reliance on analysis.

Some companies have encountered what Ansoff called "paralysis by analysis"—the more information they possess, the more they think they need. This vicious circle dogs many organizations that embrace strategic planning with enthusiasm.

Ansoff regarded strategic planning as an incomplete invention, though he was convinced that strategic planning was an inherently useful management tool. He spent 40 years attempting to prove that this is the case and that, rather than being prescriptive and unwieldy, strategic management can be a dynamic tool able to cope with the unexpected twists of turbulent markets.

Business guru Gary Hamel described Ansoff as "Truly the godfather of corporate strategy," and went on to say, "Though Ansoff's approach may now appear overly-structured and deterministic, he created the language and processes that, for the first time, allowed modern industrial companies to explicitly address the deep questions of corporate strategy: how to grow, where to coordinate, which strengths to leverage, and so on."

FOR MORE INFORMATION

Ansoff, Igor. *Corporate Strategy*. McGraw-Hill, New York: 1965.

Corporate-level Strategy

Michael Goold
Marcus Alexander
Andrew Campbell

WHY READ IT?

Although large conglomerates claim to add value through synergy and economies of scale, the authors suggest this is not the case. They recommend that multibusiness organizations should aim for a tighter fit between individual company strategies and the overall corporate strategy. The book introduces the concept of heartland businesses and shows how it can help corporations improve their overall performance.

GETTING STARTED

The authors argue that most large companies are now multibusiness organizations. Research indicates that the benefits of economies of scale and synergy do not, in reality, exist.

While individual businesses within the organization often have strategies, the corporation as a whole may not. Only a tight fit between the parent organization and its businesses will add value.

There must be a clear insight about the role of the parent organization. "Parents" must concentrate on heartland businesses that they understand. The parent must only intervene on limited issues, and corporate strategy should be driven by parenting advantage.

CONTRIBUTION
1. The Value of Multibusiness Organizations

Multibusiness companies, by virtue of their very size, should offer economies of scale and synergy between the various businesses, which can be exploited to the overall good. The authors' research suggests that in reality this is not the case.

They calculate that in over half of multibusiness companies, the whole is worth less than the sum of its parts. Instead of adding value, the corporation actually detracts from its value. Its influence, though pervasive, is often counter-productive.

This condemnation is not restricted to conglomerates. The influence of the corporate parent is also felt in companies with portfolios in a single industry, or in a series of apparently related areas.

2. Lack of Overall Strategy

A primary cause of this phenomenon is that while individual businesses within the organization often have strategies, the corporation as a whole may not. The proclaimed strategy is often an amalgam of the individual business strategies given credence by general aspirations.

3. Need for a Tight Fit

According to the authors, if corporate-level strategy is to add value, there needs to be a tight fit between the parent organization and its businesses.

Successful corporate parents focus on a narrow range of tasks and create value in those areas, and align the structures, processes, and central functions of the parent accordingly. Rather than being all-encompassing and constantly interfering, the center is akin to a specialist medical practitioner—intervening in its areas of expertise when it knows it can suggest a cure.

4. Success Factors for Multibusiness Organizations

From their analysis of 15 successful multibusiness corporations, the authors identify three essentials for successful corporate strategies:

- There must be clear insight about the role of the parent. If the parent does not know how or where it can add value, it is unlikely to do so.
- The parent must have distinctive characteristics. It, too, has a corporate culture and personality.
- It must be recognized that each parent will only be effective with certain sorts of business—described as their "heartland."

5. The Importance of Heartland Businesses

"Heartland businesses are well understood by the parent; they do not suffer from inappropriate influence and meddling that can damage less familiar businesses," say the authors. "The parent has an innate feel for its heartland that enables it to make difficult judgments and decisions with a high degree of success."

Heartland businesses are broad ranging and can cover different industries, markets, and technologies. Given this complexity, the ability of the parent to intervene on a limited number of issues is crucial.

6. Core Businesses

The concept of heartland businesses is distinct from core businesses." A core business is often merely a business that the company has decided to commit itself to," they say. Though core businesses may be important and substantial, the parent may not be adding a great deal to them.

7. Building Parenting Advantage

The authors continue: "In contrast, the heartland definition focuses on the *fit* between a parent organization and a business: do the parent's insights and behavior fit the opportunities and nature of this business? Does the parent have specialist skills in assisting this type of business to perform better?"

Corporate strategy should be driven by "parenting advantage" to create more value in the portfolio of businesses than would be achieved by any rival. To do so requires a fundamental change in basic perspectives on the role of the parent and of the nature of the multibusiness organization.

CONTEXT

Most large companies are now multibusiness organizations. The logic behind this fact of business life is generally assumed rather than examined in depth.

The authors' research runs counter to the findings of authors such as Alfred Chandler in *Strategy and Structure* and Peter Drucker in *The Practice of Management*.

Gary Hamel said: "Chandler and Drucker celebrated large multidivisional organizations, but as these companies grew, decentralized, and diversified, the corporate center often became little more than a layer of accounting consolidation. In the worst cases, a conglomerate was worth less than its break-up value. In writing the definitive book on corporate strategy, Goold, Alexander, and Campbell gave hope to corporate bureaucrats everywhere. Maybe it really was possible for the corporate level to add value."

FOR MORE INFORMATION

Goold, Michael, Marcus Alexander, and Andrew Campbell. *Corporate-level Strategy*. New York: Wiley, 1994.

"The parent has an innate feel for its heartland that enables it to make difficult judgments and decisions with a high degree of success."

Corporate-level Strategy

Dynamic Administration
Mary Parker Follett

1088

MANAGEMENT LIBRARY

WHY READ IT?

The book provides one of the earliest perspectives on business from the point of view of human relationships. It was written at a time when workers were seen simply as part of the mass-production process. The book provides useful background on the development of concepts such as empowerment and visionary leadership.

GETTING STARTED

In the author's view, management is a social process and should have a special human dimension. The process is based in human emotions and in the interrelations created by working. The working environment has human problems, with psychological, ethical, and economic dimensions.

She goes on to say that workers should be given greater responsibility, which is the great developer of people—and successful leaders must offer a vision of the future and train followers to become leaders.

Relationships, not just transactions, are important in organizations. Knowing this involves recognizing that conflict is a fact of life that we should use to work for us—but integration is the only positive way forward.

CONTRIBUTION
1. Management as a Social Process

"We can never wholly separate the human from the mechanical sides," says Follett. The study of human relations in business and the study of the technology of operating are bound up together. The everyday incidents and problems of management reflect the presence or absence of sound principle.

Management has a special human character. Its nature as a social process is deeply embedded in the emotions of human beings and in the interrelations to which the everyday working of industry necessarily gives rise—both at manager and worker levels and, of course, between the two.

2. Toward Empowerment

Mary Parker Follett believed that, "we should undepartmentalize our thinking in regard to every problem that comes to us."

She continued, "I do not think that we have psychological and ethical and economic problems. We have human problems, with psychological, ethical, and economical aspects, and as many others as you like."

Follett advocated giving greater responsibility to people at a time when the mechanical might of mass production was at its height. "Responsibility is the great developer of men," she said.

3. Leadership Through Vision

The most successful leader of all is one who sees another picture not yet actualized—who sees the whole rather than the particular, organizes the experiences of the group, offers a vision of the future, and trains followers to become leaders.

Leading should be a two-way, mutually beneficial process. "We want worked out a relation between leaders and led which will give to each the opportunity to make creative contributions to the situation," Follett wrote.

4. Relationships Matter

Relationships, not just transactions, are important in organizations. The reciprocal nature of relationships means that a mutual influence is developed when people work together, however formal authority is defined.

Conflict is a fact of life that we should use to work for us. There are three ways of dealing with confrontation: domination, compromise, or integration. Integration is the only positive way forward. This can be achieved by first uncovering the real conflict and then taking the demands of both sides and breaking them up into their constituent parts.

Outlook is narrowed, activity is restricted, and chances of business success largely diminished when thinking is constrained within the limits of what has been called an either-or situation. "We should never allow ourselves to be bullied by an either-or," said Follett. There is often the possibility of something better than either of two given alternatives.

CONTEXT

Published eight years after her death, *Dynamic Administration* is a collection of Mary Parker Follett's papers on management gathered from 12 lectures given between 1925 and 1933. Her work is a humane counterpoint to that of Frederick Taylor and the proponents of scientific management. Follett was a female, liberal humanist in an era dominated by reactionary males intent on mechanizing the world of business.

Bearing in mind she was speaking of the United States in the early 1920s, her thinking can be described as little less than revolutionary, and certainly a generation ahead of its time. During her life, Mary Parker Follett's thinking on management was generally ignored—though in Japan there was a great deal of interest in her perspectives.

Leading commentator Gary Hamel said, "The work of Mary Parker Follett is refreshingly different from that of her peers. She was the first modern thinker to get us close to the human soul of management. She had the heart of a humanist, not an engineer."

To some, Follett remains a utopian idealist, out of touch with reality; to others, she is a torchbearer of good sense whose ideas have sadly not had significant impact on organizations.

Henry Mintzberg commented, "Integration requires understanding, in-depth understanding. It requires serious commitment and dedication. It takes effort, and it depends on creativity. There is precious little of all of these qualities in too many of our organizations today."

FOR MORE INFORMATION

Follett, Mary Parker. *Dynamic Administration*. Revised ed. New York: Buccaneer Books, 1982.

"We should remember that we can never wholly separate the human from the mechanical sides."

Dynamic Administration

Emotional Intelligence

Daniel Goleman

WHY READ IT?

Daniel Goleman challenges traditional thinking, which claims that a high IQ is essential for success. He provides examples of people with high IQs and considerable academic achievement who have failed in business and in life, and, conversely, of those who, though apparently less gifted intellectually, were able to manage and harness their emotional intelligence in order to succeed. Although the book does not specifically relate to behavior in business, its conclusions highlight patterns that can be used to improve personal performance at work. Emotional intelligence is also referred to as the "soft skills," and these are increasingly regarded as important in business, particularly for people in sales, supervisory, or customer service roles.

GETTING STARTED

Goleman describes the evolution of the brain and explains how the two main brain functions that influence behavior—emotion and intelligence—are situated in different parts of the brain. The part of the brain that controls emotions receives external signals before the intelligence functions, and that means that initial reactions to events may be emotional rather than rational. Goleman explains that the brain still retains a primitive "survival mode" that may trigger reactions and responses that are inappropriate. To succeed, he advises, we need to understand those reactions and learn how to control them.

CONTRIBUTION
1. Overcoming Impulses

According to Goleman, emotions have a wisdom of their own that can be harnessed. Although our natural reaction is to respond emotionally, it is important to make use of emotional intelligence to develop more positive responses.

2. A Framework of Emotional Intelligence

Goleman has developed a framework that explains emotional intelligence in terms of five elements:
- self-awareness
- self-regulation
- motivation
- empathy
- social skills

3. Self-awareness

According to Goleman, this element enables you to develop a better understanding of the way emotions affect your performance. You can also use your values to guide your decision making. By looking at your strengths and weaknesses and learning from your experiences, you can gain self-confidence and certainty about your capabilities, values, and goals.

4. Self-regulation

Goleman describes how this element can help you control your temper and reduce stress by acting in a more positive and action-oriented way. This enables you to retain your composure and improves your ability to think clearly under pressure. Through self-regulation, he claims, you can handle your impulses effectively and exercise self-restraint.

5. Motivation

According to the author, by harnessing this aspect of emotional intelligence, you can enjoy challenge and stimulation, and strive for achievement. You will be committed to the cause and seize the initiative. You will also be guided by your personal preferences in following one set of goals, rather than another.

6. Empathy

Empathy is the characteristic that enables you to understand other points of view, and behave openly and honestly.

7. Social Skills

Goleman describes how social skills such as persuasion, communication, listening, negotiating, and leading can be honed.

8. Emotional Intelligence and Management

Goleman claims that people with a higher degree of emotional intelligence are more likely to succeed in senior management. He also believes that emotional intelligence can be developed over a period of time, although this is disputed by a number of commentators.

CONTEXT

Daniel Goleman has built on the work in this book to research leadership styles based on different characteristics of emotional intelligence. These range from coercive leaders who are self-motivated and driven to succeed, to democratic leaders who are good at communication and listening, and coaching leaders who listen well and motivate others. The research is reported in the March–April 2000 edition of the *Harvard Business Review*.

Commentators point out a possible contradiction in Goleman's work. He claims that emotional intelligence is inherent, yet suggests that it can be developed.

Other studies of leaders have pointed out the relationship between high achievement and characteristics such as self-awareness and empathy. In *Emotional Intelligence*, Goleman does not specifically deal with the direct relationship between leadership and emotional intelligence. His subsequent research does, however, analyze the relationship further.

MANAGEMENT LIBRARY

FOR MORE INFORMATION

Goleman, Daniel. *Emotional Intelligence: Why It Can Matter More Than IQ.* New York: Bantam, 1997.

FURTHER READING
Goleman, Daniel. *Working with Emotional Intelligence.* New York: Bantam Doubleday Dell, 2000.
Goleman, Daniel. "Leadership That Gets Results." *Harvard Business Review* (March–April 2000).

"The ability to control impulse is the basis of will and character." *Emotional Intelligence*

The E-Myth Revisited

Michael E. Gerber

WHY READ IT?

Since its publication in 1995, *The E-Myth Revisited* has been an international bestseller, providing insight into how to turn an entrepreneurial dream into a successful reality. By means of its lively, readable, and occasionally anecdotal style, Michael E. Gerber guides the reader through the journey of becoming an entrepreneur: from the skills that are needed initially, to what is needed to ensure that a successful business emerges in its final "mature" stage. Gerber's insight gained as a consultant for small businesses has made this an entertaining, enlightening, and effective guide to creating the modern small business.

GETTING STARTED

The "E-Myth" refers to the entrepreneur myth: the belief that simply having an indepth knowledge of the product or service is all that is needed for a successful business. The author argues convincingly that this just isn't enough, and he outlines the other skills necessary to create a successful business.

In his view, the key principles any entrepreneur should be aware of include working *on* the business, rather than *inside* it, as well as lessons that can be learned from highly successful business franchises, such as providing consistent quality and exceeding customers' expectations. In addition, Gerber offers advice on how to establish effective marketing, work well with others, and reach your "life-goals."

CONTRIBUTION
1. The Entrepreneur Myth

The "E-Myth" refers to the assumption that because a person is a good "technician" within a particular area of expertise, he or she will be successful in owning a business in that field. While being a good technician with a large knowledge base of the product *is* important, Gerber argues that it is only a starting point to becoming a successful entrepreneur.

2. The Characters

A successful business starter must assume the roles of three necessary but diverse characters: the *technician*, the *manager*, and the *entrepreneur*.

The *technician* provides the labor and delivery of the product. While these are vital skills, many technicians start their business without knowledge of how to be a manager or entrepreneur. The important fact for technicians to note is that, to produce a successful business, managerial and entrepreneurial knowledge is vital.

The *manager* provides the design of the business and organizes it into an efficient company operating at maximum performance and productivity.

The *entrepreneur* provides the vision, the audacity, and the drive to support and build the business. The entrepreneur lives in the future and is happiest when allowed to construct images of "what if . . . ?" to explore possible strategies.

3. The Transition between the Four Stages of Business

Gerber argues that a business typically undergoes four phases: *infancy*, *adolescence*, *comfort zone*, and *maturity*. To move successfully between these stages, the strengths of all three characters described above must be utilised. Moreover, the author feels that individuals must be in place to complete any tasks that the business owner cannot attend to. It is important to relinquish some responsibility for difficult tasks to appropriately skilled individuals.

This, in Gerber's view, will allow the business to progress from *infancy* to *adolescence*. Qualified, external help will support the integration of the skills of the technician, manager, and entrepreneur to create a *comfort zone*. This zone inevitably ends when boundaries are pushed and the company becomes more disordered. If it is able to survive this period of turbulence, the author argues, the company can reach the last phase: *maturity*. Maturity, however, does not represent an end to the effort needed. Constant innovation and growth is required for a business to prosper.

4. Working *On* Your Business

Gerber feels that it is important to spend more time working *on* your business than *inside* it. A common mistake is to assume the role of the technician, at the expense of the roles of entrepreneur and manager. Time and external help are necessary to create systems and innovation that will allow the business to grow.

5. Standards for Franchise Prototypes

The author argues that a standardized business will deliver consistent success. The principles of standardization (sometimes also called systemization) are:

- delivering a product or service that will continually match or exceed clients' expectations;
- allowing the work to be user-friendly and accessible to people with low skills and/or experience;
- making sure the business model is free from any potential problems;
- providing a clear, standardized operations manual;
- ensuring a predictable product or service;
- ensuring that marketing, dress code, and facilities remain consistent with each other.

6. The Business Development Program

This is arguably the most important aspect of being an entrepreneur: developing a business that can survive and grow by itself, allowing the owner to step back from the business and focus on other projects or simply to enjoy the rewards of the business.

A successful business development programme consists of several factors:
- the Primary Aim
- the Strategic Objectives
- the Organizational Strategy
- the Management Strategy
- the People Strategy
- the Marketing Strategy
- the Systems Strategy

CONTEXT

The E-Myth Revisited was published before the dot-com bubble burst in the late 1990s. While the title alludes to the cyber connection, it is most telling that this book challenges the flawed foundation of the dot-com dream: that only indepth product knowledge is needed for a successful business.

As a business consultant, Michael Gerber has seen the mistakes he warns against. In *The E-Myth Revisited*, these potential triumphs and pitfalls are shared with the reader, providing an eminently practical guide to becoming a successful entrepreneur.

FOR MORE INFORMATION

Gerber, Michael E. *The E-Myth Revisited: Why Most Small Businesses Don't Work and What to Do About It*. New York: Collins, 1995.

"Success depends on having a product or a service that catches the consumer's imagination."

The E-Myth Revisited

The Fifth Discipline

Peter Senge

WHY READ IT?

This is the book that popularized the concept of the learning organization. More philosophical in tone than most business-oriented books, it adopts a holistic approach. Learning is an individual and a group experience, Senge would claim, much deeper than just taking information in. "It is about changing individuals so that they produce results they care about, accomplish things that are important to them," he wrote.

GETTING STARTED

Peter Senge is director of the Center for Organizational Learning at MIT. *The Fifth Discipline* emerged from extensive research by Senge and his team, but Senge said the "vision that became *The Fifth Discipline*" came to him one morning during his meditation, when he realized that "the 'learning organization' would likely become a new management fad."

The "fifth discipline" of the title is systems thinking. Of the five building blocks of a learning organization, systems thinking connects the other four and enables them to work together for the benefit of business.

CONTRIBUTION
1. Learning is Vital

In Senge's view, as the world becomes more interconnected and business more complex and dynamic, work must become more "learningful." It is no longer sufficient to have one person learning for the whole organization, a Ford, say, or a Sloan or a Watson. It is no longer possible to figure it out from the top, and have everybody else follow the orders of the grand strategist.

The organizations that will excel in the future will be those that can tap the commitment and capacity to learn of people at all levels within them.

Managers should therefore encourage employees to:
- be open to new ideas;
- communicate frankly with each other;
- understand thoroughly how their companies operate;
- form a collective vision;
- work together to achieve their goals.

2. The Five Disciplines

There are five components to a learning organization:
- systems thinking
- personal mastery
- mental models
- shared vision
- team learning

3. Systems Thinking

Systems thinking is a conceptual framework to make patterns clearer, claims Senge. It requires a shift of mind to see interrelationships rather than linear cause and effect. It can help managers spot repetitive patterns, such as the way certain kinds of problems persist, or the way systems have their own in-built limits to growth.

4. Personal Mastery

This idea is based on the familiar competencies and skills associated with management. But it also includes spiritual growth—opening oneself up to a progressively deeper reality and living life from a creative rather than a reactive viewpoint.

As part of this discipline, one must continually learn to see current reality more clearly; the ensuing gap between vision and reality produces the creative tension from which learning arises.

5. Mental Models

These are the organization's driving and fundamental values and principles. Senge alerts managers to the power of patterns of thinking at the organizational level and the importance of nondefensive inquiry into the nature of these patterns.

6. Shared Vision

Senge stresses the importance of cocreation and argues that shared vision can only be built on personal vision. He claims that shared vision is present when the task that follows from the vision is no longer seen by the team members as separate from the self.

7. Team Learning

The discipline of team learning involves two practices: dialog and discussion. Dialog is characterized by its exploratory nature, discussion by the opposite process of narrowing down the field to the best alternative for the decisions that need to be made. The two are mutually complementary, but the benefits of combining them only come from having previously separated them.

8. Creating Learning Organizations

The author argues that transforming companies into learning organizations has proved problematical, principally because it involves managers surrendering their spheres of power and control to the people who are learning. If people are to learn, they must be allowed to experiment and fail. In a blame-oriented culture, this requires a major change in organizational attitude.

The learning organization demands trust and involvement, usually notable by their absence. Real commitment is rare in today's organizations. Experience indicates that 90% of the time what passes for commitment is compliance. One man reported to Senge that by adopting the learning organization model, he made what he called "job-limiting choices." What he meant was that he could have climbed the corporate ladder faster by rejecting Senge's theories and toeing the company line.

CONTEXT

Although the learning organization sounds like a product, it is actually a process. Phil Hodgson of Ashridge Management College commented: "Processes are not suddenly unveiled for all to see. Academic definitions, no matter how precise, cannot be instantly applied in the real world. Managers need to promote learning so that it gradually emerges as a key part of an organization's culture."

The Fifth Discipline has proved highly influential. Though the learning organization has rarely been converted into reality, the idea has fueled the debate on self-managed development and employability, and has affected the rewards and remuneration strategies of many organizations.

Gary Hamel observed that: "While Professor [Chris] Argyris put organizational learning on the management agenda, Peter Senge married it with system thinking and created a language and approach that makes the whole set of ideas accessible to managers. Peter is no mere theorist, his organizational Learning Center at MIT has helped launch thousands of in-company learning experiments. *The Fifth Discipline* would certainly be on my shortlist of the half dozen best business books of the last 25 years."

FOR MORE INFORMATION

Senge, Peter. *The Fifth Discipline*. Revised ed. New York: Doubleday, 2006.

The Functions of the Executive

Chester Barnard

WHY READ IT?

Barnard is regarded as an important management thinker, who, according to Tom Peters and Robert Waterman in *In Search of Excellence*, created "a complete management theory." Though his language is dated, much of his thinking—particularly on the importance of communication—is relevant to modern management.

GETTING STARTED

The author asserts that an organization allows people to achieve what they could not achieve as individuals, as they and their actions are interconnected. One essential ingredient for a successful organization is good, short lines of communication because communication enables everyone to be tied into the organization's objectives. It is also vital that chief executives nurture goals and values and translate them into action; executives should not just ensure conformance to a code of morals, they should create moral codes for others.

CONTRIBUTION

1. People Are Interconnected

Barnard rejected the concept of an organization as comprising a rather definite group of people whose behavior is coordinated only because they are linked together by some explicit goal or goals. "In a community," he argued "all acts of individuals and of organizations are directly or indirectly interconnected and interdependent."

2. Communication

Barnard highlights the need for communica-tion. He argues that everyone needs to know what and where the communications channels are so that every single person can be tied into the organization's objectives.

Lines of communication should be short and direct. He writes: "the essential functions are, first, to provide the system of communications; second, to promote the securing of essential efforts; and third, to formulate and define purpose."

3. The Need to Nurture Goals and Values

The chief executive is not a dictatorial figure geared to simple, short-term achievements. Part of his or her responsibility is to nurture the values and goals of the organization. Values and goals need to be translated into action, rather than meaningless motivational phraseology—"strictly speaking, purpose is defined more nearly by the aggregate of action taken than by words," he writes.

4. A Holistic Approach

An organization is simply a means of allowing people to achieve what they could not achieve as individuals. An organization is a system of consciously coordinated activities of forces of two or more persons.

5. A Code of Management Morality

In Barnard's view, the distinguishing mark of the executive responsibility is that it requires not merely conformance to a complex code of morals, but also the creation of moral codes for others.

CONTEXT

Chester Barnard was a rarity: a management theorist who was also a successful practitioner. He won an economics scholarship to Harvard but, before finishing his degree, he joined American Telephone and Telegraph and after a successful career with that company eventually became President of New Jersey Bell in 1927.

The Functions of the Executive collected together his lectures on management. "It is doubtful if any other book since Taylor's *Scientific Management* has had a deeper influence on the thinking of serious business leaders about the nature of their work," observed Barnard's contemporary, Lyndall Urwick.

Although the language in which the book is written is dated, much of what Barnard argued strikes a chord with contemporary management thinking. His ideas on communication, especially on the importance of short lines of communication, has retained its relevance down to the present day. In arguing that there was a morality to management, Barnard played an important part in broadening the managerial role from one simply of measurement, control, and supervision, to one that is also concerned with more abstract notions, such as values.

FOR MORE INFORMATION

Barnard, Chester. *The Functions of the Executive*. Revised ed. Boston, MA: Harvard University Press, 2005.

"In a community, all acts of individuals and of organizations are directly or indirectly interconnected and interdependent."

The Functions of the Executive

General and Industrial Management

Henri Fayol

WHY READ IT?

Fayol created one of the first systems of management that put management at the center of the organization. His system divides a company's activities into six groups, in which managerial activities are distinct from the other five. The book provides a systematic analysis of the process of management, in which he anticipated most of the more recent analyses of modern business practice. His brief résumé of what constitutes management largely held sway throughout the 20th century.

GETTING STARTED

Fayol created a system of management in which management was the foundation stone of the organization. His system focused on acceptance of, and adherence to, six different functions: technical, commercial, financial, security, accounting, and managerial activities.

He believed that to manage is to forecast and plan, to organize, to command, to coordinate, and to control. His view of forward planning was one of the first examples of business planning in practice.

CONTRIBUTION

1. A System of Management

Fayol created a system of management encapsulated in *General and Industrial Management*.

"Management plays a very important part in the government of undertakings; of all undertakings, large or small, industrial, commercial, political, religious, or any other," he writes.

2. Division by Function

Fayol's system was based on acceptance of, and adherence to, different functions. He said that all activities to which industrial undertakings give rise can be divided into six groups. These are:
- technical activities
- commercial activities
- financial activities
- security activities
- accounting activities
- managerial activities

3. The Nature of Management

The management function is quite distinct from the other five essential functions. To manage is to forecast and plan, to organize, to command, to coordinate, and to control.

Fayol's view of what constitutes management has been highly influential throughout the 20th century and has only recently been challenged.

4. Principles of Management

From his observations, Fayol also produced general principles of management:
- division of work
- authority and responsibility
- discipline
- unity of command
- unity of direction
- subordination of individual interest to general interest
- remuneration of personnel
- centralization
- scalar chain (line of authority)
- order
- equity
- stability of tenure of personnel
- initiative
- esprit de corps

5. Forward Planning

Fayol talks of ten-yearly forecasts, revised every five years—one of the first instances of business planning in practice.

The maxim "managing means looking ahead," gives some idea of the importance attached to planning for the future in the business world. It is true that if foresight is not the whole of management, it is at least an essential part of it.

CONTEXT

Fayol created a system that put management at the center of the organization in a way never envisaged by contemporaries such as Frederick W. Taylor, author of *Scientific Management*.

Fayol's championing of management was highly important. While Taylor regarded managers as little more than overseers with limited responsibility, Fayol regarded their role as critical to organizational success.

In his faith in carefully defined functions, Fayol was systematizing business organization in ways that worked at the time, but proved too limiting and restraining in the long term.

In *The Principles and Practice of Management*, a 1953 study of early management thinking, E. F. L. Brech notes, "The importance of Fayol's contribution lay in two features: the first was his systematic analysis of the process of management; the second, his firm advocacy of the principle that management can, and should, be taught. Both were revolutionary lines of thought in 1908, and still little accepted in 1925."

Igor Ansoff has noted that Fayol anticipated imaginatively and soundly most of the more recent analyses of modern business practice. His brief résumé of what constitutes management largely held sway throughout the 20th century. Only now is it being seriously questioned and challenged.

An extrapolation of Fayol's methods was later exposed by Peter Drucker who observed, "If used beyond the limits of Fayol's model, functional structure becomes costly in terms of time and effort."

FOR MORE INFORMATION

Fayol, Henri, revised by Irwin Gray. *General and Industrial Management*. New York: IEEE Press, 1984.

"To manage is to forecast and plan, to organize, to command, to coordinate and to control."

General and Industrial Management

The General Theory of Employment

John Maynard Keynes

WHY READ IT?

Should the state intervene to combat unemployment? Governments today may ask themselves this question; governments were already asking themselves this question during the 1930s and had even more compelling reasons for doing so, perhaps. Keynes was the first to show convincingly why state intervention to boost employment is sensible and necessary. This book, first published in 1936, lays the foundations of Keynesianism, a demand-oriented doctrine that is still hotly debated and highly influential in both politics and economics today.

GETTING STARTED

Keynes' *General Theory* shows how economic policy can overcome periods of stagnation. He argues in favor of investment being state-directed to ensure full employment. In contrast to the exponents of classical economic theory, he does not believe in the self-healing power of the market. Demand is, for him, the lever of the economy, and in times of crisis it is the state that must operate the lever.

CONTRIBUTION

1. The Error in Classical Economics

According to Keynes, Adam Smith and David Ricardo start out from the assumption that the law of supply and demand regulates the price of goods and of labor. Workers, therefore, are only dismissed when their wages are too high. If they accept lower wages, they are re-employed. The classical economic model always returns to a state of balance: anyone who is unemployed, is so voluntarily.

The world economic crisis of the 1930s could not, however, be explained in this way, Keynes thought. Millions of workers were on the streets, although wages were sinking lower and lower. The "paradox of poverty in the midst of affluence" needed another explanation. Supply was not decisive in achieving economic success; demand was.

2. Aggregate Demand— Consumption and Investment

Demand across the entire economy—the sum of expenditure on consumer and investment goods—has one essential charac-teristic, Keynes argues: it is unstable. Expenditure on consumption depends on income: the higher the income the more money is spent. But, above a particular level of income, the tendency to increase consumption declines. Part of the additional income is saved.

Investments are the second element in aggregate demand, because they increase the potential of businesses to produce. Investments, according to Keynes, depend on the "marginal efficiency of capital." If this is higher than the standard rate of interest in the market, the investor has an incentive to use credit to implement investment plans. In the opposite case, the costs of credit would be higher than the profit, and the investment would not be made.

3. Imbalance between the Markets for Goods and Capital

The market interest rate for investments, says Keynes, results from the population's inclination toward liquidity, that is, their demand for cash. People save for a variety for reasons, to purchase goods, to protect themselves against hard times, or in order to speculate. Speculators keep their savings in cash until prices become low and a favorable opportunity arises to enter the stock market.

Harmonization between the goods and capital markets is the exception; equality of savings and investments a rare and lucky chance. It is not the case, says Keynes, that savings decisions are solely dependent on the rate of interest and that the interest mechanism ensures that all savings are available to be loaned to businesses for the purchase of investment goods. Rather, he argues, businesses expand their production so long as they expect larger sales in the future. More and more investors try to attract the capital of the savers. Interest rates and production costs rise and reduce returns. The suppliers of capital get nervous. Panic grips the markets. The unrealistic expectations of the boom are followed by the hysteria of crisis. Investments fall, employment drops, purchasing power disappears, future prospects become more and more dismal. Businesses do not even invest when interest rates sink to zero. The national economy is caught in the "liquidity trap."

4. The State as Starter Motor of the Economy

To free the economy from this disastrous situation and turn it back in the direction of full employment, aggregate demand must rise, says Keynes, until increasing production by businesses offers all workers employment. If the demand for investment goods rises, this leads to more production, more work, and more income. Higher consumption boosts demand for goods and investment, which means that production and income rise further. A chain reaction begins, an "income multiplier"—an exogenous impulse, perhaps an extra boost to investment, gives rise to a multiple increase in income.

From this, Keynes draws the following conclusion. If entrepreneurs do not invest in sufficient quantities, the state must step forward as an investor to set the economy back in motion. To produce additional investment, the public purse accepts credit and uses it to finance, for example, roads, sewage systems, schools, or hospitals.

CONTEXT

The stock market crash of 1929, the crisis in the world economy, and the Great Depression of the 1930s threw up a number of crucial economic and political questions, which Keynes attempted to answer in this book. It made him the most famous national economist of the 20th century and initiated one of the most influential strands in modern economic thought, Keynesianism. Keynesian ideas provided the framework for the postwar recovery and held sway in many countries during the middle of the last century. Even President Richard Nixon remarked "We are all Keynesians now." It was only in the 1970s that the "monetarist counterrevolution" began, eventually re-enthroning supply-side economics and the market forces whose fallibility it had been part of Keynes' purpose to demonstrate.

FOR MORE INFORMATION

Keynes, John Maynard. *The General Theory of Employment, Interest, and Money.* Cambridge, MA: Prometheus Books, 1997.

"Capitalism is the astounding belief that the wickedest of men will do the wickedest of things for the greatest good of everyone."

The General Theory of Employment

Getting Things Done

David Allen

WHY READ IT?

When faced with a seemingly insurmountable workload, it is easy to feel intimidated. In *Getting Things Done* David Allen presents a number of techniques designed to reduce stress and increase efficiency. With more than twenty years' experience as a management consultant, executive coach, and educator, David Allen has gained almost a cult following with this widely commended guide to "getting things off your mind and getting them done."

GETTING STARTED

The key principles in *Getting Things Done* center around moving "to-do lists" from the mind to actual, physical filing systems, and then making sure that prompt action is taken to deal with problems as soon as they become evident. Allen also emphasises the importance of clear thinking and "horizontal control"—that is, coordinating beteen different projects, tasks, and priorities.

Allen explains that "open loops" are the tasks that we do not tackle and which are often mismanaged and inappropriately prioritized. These act as a constant, often unconscious, source of distraction and stress. He provides three starting points to accomplishing tasks more effectively, to promoting better control of situations and, consequently, to reducing stress:

- rather than trying to keep all the information in your head, write it down so that you have a physical record of it;
- decide actions and outcomes when things *first* emerge on your radar, instead of later;
- regularly review and update the complete inventory of the "open loops" that exist in your life and work.

CONTRIBUTION
1. Coordinate Outcomes and Actions

When in a challenging situation, form a clear and concise picture of the ideal outcome of the situation. This will enable you to decide what action should be taken to achieve this result.

2. Exercise Horizontal Control

Make sure all projects are cohesive and consistent with each other. It is essential to maintain clarity about, and knowledge of, all necessary projects and tasks and how they will interact with each other.

3. Exercise *Vertical* Control

Ensure there is clear understanding of each *individual* task.

4. Understand the Five Phases of Workflow

To maintain horizontal control across all activities that require attention, the author believes that it can be helpful to implement the following five stages:

- *Collect*. Gather and assess everything that requires action, either in an in-tray, computer, notepad, or other filing/collection system. Keep this filing system organized and make sure that you deal with it and empty it frequently.
- *Process*. Decide on the nature of the tasks. Is it possible to take action to complete the task? If it is, then either *do it*, *delegate it*, or *defer it*. If it is not actionable, then Allen suggests that you either *trash it*, *incubate it*, or *reference it* (that is, keep it in a filing system for easy reference in the future).
- *Organize*. Make sure that the results of the previous stages are kept organized.
- *Review*. Decide what options are available to deal with the tasks.
- *Do*. Complete the tasks.

5. Weekly Review

Over the course of a week, create lists to help you simplify thinking and organize workload. Allen believes that in addition, it is necessary to introduce processes to cope with new tasks as they arise. It is important to review and deal with this new data on a weekly basis.

This review should consist of:

- collecting loose papers;
- reviewing notes;
- reviewing existing calendar data;
- creating new calendar data;
- keeping things out of your mind and in a more physical form—make lists of any new projects or activities;
- reviewing any lists that have been made.

6. Create a Filing System

Allen believes that an efficient filing system is crucial to remaining organized and accomplishing goals. The ideal filing system is clear and easy to navigate. Label files alphabetically, unless a more specific method is required. They should not be grouped according to person, project, topic, or company. Remember to clear your files at least once a year.

CONTEXT

With stress now recognized as a major cause of illness and lost productivity, David Allen argues that it is vital to discover how it is possible for a person "to have an overwhelming number of things to do and still function productively with a clear head and a positive sense of relaxed control."

Allen's ideas build on his extensive experience as a management consultant and executive coach. They are perfectly tailored to anyone aiming to boost their productivity by simultaneously sharpening their competitive edge and slashing stress levels. The book's concepts are also effective for anyone struggling to deal with a large and stressful workload.

Although at times reminiscent of Eastern philosophies of clarity, inner peace, and allowing your mind to flow "like water," *Getting Things Done* is based firmly in finding an effective and practical way to deal with today's fast-paced business culture.

FOR MORE INFORMATION

Allen, David. *Getting Things Done: The Art of Stress-Free Productivity*. New York: Penguin Putnam, 2001.

Getting to Yes

Roger Fisher
William Ury

1096

MANAGEMENT LIBRARY

WHY READ IT?

Negotiation is an important skill in many aspects of business and personal life. The authors claim that people can become more effective negotiators by moving from adversarial haggling to constructive joint problem solving, a solution they call "principled negotiation." Both Fisher and Ury have conducted negotiations at extremely high levels in business, politics, diplomacy, law, and international relations. They write with authority and have the experience to offer practical advice and insight into each stage of the negotiating process.

GETTING STARTED

The negotiating principles that the authors claim will lead to successful outcomes are:
- don't bargain over positions;
- separate the people from the problem;
- focus on interests, not positions;
- invent options for mutual gain;
- insist on objective criteria.

CONTRIBUTION
1. The Importance of Effective Negotiation

Negotiation involves everyone, the authors claim. People use negotiation to handle their differences at work and in personal life. However, they believe that standard negotiating strategies tend to leave one or both parties dissatisfied. They describe two types of negotiators:
- soft negotiators who may make easy compromises to avoid conflict
- hard negotiators who want to win at all costs

The authors propose a third way, using what they call "principled negotiation." Its objective is to decide issues on their merits, rather than on the will of the parties involved.

2. Avoid Bargaining over Positions

Fisher and Ury point out that, traditionally, people take positions and defend them. The matter is only resolved through concessions. This approach can harm relationships, and that can be damaging to future negotiations. In this approach, emotions become entangled with logic, so it is important to separate people from problems.

3. Separate People from Problems

The authors prompt us to remember that negotiators are people with emotions. Negotiators are therefore just as interested in ongoing relationships as in dealing with the immediate problem. Understanding the emotions of the other side is important, because they can act as a barrier to rational discussion. It is important to understand the other person's perspective and find out what is important to them. Listening actively and acknowledging the other party's perspective is critical.

The authors explain how successful negotiators try to make the other party own the problem so that they fully participate in reaching a satisfactory conclusion. Communication is an important part of this process, helping to build constructive working relationships that can reduce the element of confrontation.

4. Focus on Interests, not Positions

Fisher and Ury recommend looking for the underlying interest in negotiations. Interests may not conflict, although positions do. They suggest finding out or asking why the other side takes a particular position, and acknowledging those interests as part of the problem.

5. Invent Options for Mutual Gain

The objective of negotiation is a single conclusion, say the authors. Introducing other options may appear to slow down the process, but, they claim, it can make the outcome easier to achieve. Enlarging the pie can help to provide what appears to be mutual gain. They believe that brainstorming can help to determine the options because during brainstorming, no decisions have to be made and creativity is encouraged.

6. Insist on Objective Criteria

Finally, according to Fisher and Ury, it may be possible to decide on the outcome of negotiations by reference to an independent or objective authority. The standards adopted should be fair and acceptable to both sides. Comparable criteria from other negotiations may also be acceptable.

CONTEXT

Negotiation is a critical element of business. The book takes a detailed look at the process of negotiation independently of business processes such as sales, customer service, or union negotiations.

The authors build on their own experience of negotiations in politics, diplomacy, and the law. Although not all of the examples they give relate directly to business, it is possible to apply the same principles to business situations of many types.

FOR MORE INFORMATION

Fisher, Roger, and William Ury. *Getting to Yes*. 2nd ed. New York: Penguin USA, 1991.

How to Win Friends and Influence People

Dale Carnegie

WHY READ IT?

Dale Carnegie was a highly successful public speaker and author of books on public speaking and confidence development. *How to Win Friends and Influence People* provides practical advice on the universal challenge of face-to-face communication. As the familiarity of the title proves, the book has had a great impact. The first edition had a print run of a mere 5,000, but the book has since sold over 15 million copies.

GETTING STARTED

Carnegie holds that it is essential to handle people effectively, and to make them like you to ensure your own success. His book is littered with illustrative anecdotes from the lives of the famous—Clark Gable, Marconi, Franklin D. Roosevelt, Mary Pickford—and the not so famous.

CONTRIBUTION
1. Handle People Effectively

Carnegie presented the fundamental techniques in handling people:
- don't criticize, condemn, or complain;
- give honest and sincere appreciation;
- arouse in the other person an eager want.

2. Make People Like You

He added advice on other ways to make people like you:
- become genuinely interested in other people;
- smile;
- remember that a person's name is to that person the sweetest and most important sound in any language;
- be a good listener;
- encourage others to talk about themselves;
- talk in terms of the other person's interests;
- make the other person feel important, and do it sincerely.

CONTEXT

How to Win Friends and Influence People is the original self-improvement book, and Carnegie was the first superstar of the self-help genre.

Cashing in on his success, he wrote a plethora of other titles on similar themes, including *Public Speaking and Influencing Men in Business* ; *How to Stop Worrying and Start Living* ; *How to Enjoy Your Life and Your Job* ; and *How to Develop Self-confidence and Influence People by Public Speaking*. His successors included Anthony Robbins and Stephen Covey, who studied U.S. success literature (of which Carnegie's body of work is a prime example) before coming up with *The Seven Habits of Highly Effective People*.

Carnegie had done much the same 50 years before, and his principles have a similar homely ring to Covey's. Carnegie's books and his company's training programs continue to strike a chord with managers and aspiring managers, because they deal with the universal challenge of face-to-face communication.

Carnegie was notable in being the first to create a credible long-term business out of his ideas. In creating a flourishing business, Carnegie ensured that his name and ideas should continue to live on and make money after his death.

FOR MORE INFORMATION

Carnegie, Dale. *How to Win Friends and Influence People*. Reissue. New York: Pocket Books, 1990.

1097

MANAGEMENT LIBRARY

"The application of these principles literally revolutionizes the lives of many people."

How to Win Friends and Influence People

The HP Way

David Packard

WHY READ IT?

David Packard was half of the partnership that created one of the business and management benchmarks of the 20th century—Hewlett-Packard. In 1937, with a mere $538 and a rented garage in Palo Alto, Bill Hewlett and David Packard created one of the most successful corporations in the world. This book tells the story behind the company.

GETTING STARTED

According to Packard, the HP secret lay in a simple approach to business. The HP way reflected the culture of the company and the management style they used to run it. It was based on openness and respect for the individual, which was key to the company's success. Management was always available and involved, and conflict had to be tackled through communication and consensus rather than confrontation. Their commitment to people fostered commitment to the company, and HP people at all levels show boundless energy and enthusiasm. The recipe for growth was to make products leaders in their markets. They kept divisions small and didn't do anything too risky. These values worked to save the company when times were hard.

CONTRIBUTION

1. A Simple Approach to Business

HP's secret lay in the simplicity of their methods.

"Professors of management are devastated when I say we were successful because we had no plans. We just took on odd jobs," said Bill Hewlett.

Their legacy lies in the culture of the company they created and the management style they used to run it—the HP way.

From the very start, Hewlett-Packard was guided by a few fundamental principles:

- it did not believe in long-term borrowing to secure the expansion of the business
- its recipe for growth was simply that its products needed to be leaders in their markets
- it got on with the job

"Our main task is to design, develop, and manufacture the finest [electronic equipment] for the advancement of science and the welfare of humanity. We intend to devote ourselves to that task," said Packard in a 1961 memo to employees.

The duo eschewed fashionable management theory: "If I hear anybody talking about how big their share of the market is or what they're trying to do to increase their share of the market, I'm going to personally see that a black mark gets put in their personnel folder."

2. Respect for the Individual

The company believed that people could be trusted and should always be treated with respect and dignity.

"We both felt fundamentally that people want to do a good job. They just need guidelines on how to do it."

HP believed that management should be available and involved—"Management by wandering about" was the motto.

Rather than the administrative suggestions of management, Packard preferred to talk of leadership.

If there was conflict, the company decided that it would be tackled through communication and consensus rather than confrontation.

Their legacy, and Packard's proudest achievement, is a management style based on openness and respect for the individual.

3. Keeping it Small

Hewlett-Packard was a company built on very simple ideas. While competitors were turning into conglomerates, Hewlett and Packard kept their heads down and continued with their methods.

When their divisions grew too big (around 1,500 people) they split them up to ensure that they didn't spiral out of control.

They didn't do anything too risky or too outlandish. For example, Packard was skeptical about pocket calculators though, in the end, the company was an early entrant into the market.

They didn't risk the company on a big deal or get into debt.

4. Strong Commitment to Values

Their values worked to save the company when times were hard. During the 1970s recession, Hewlett-Packard staff took a 10% pay cut and worked 10% fewer hours.

As the book documents, if the company hadn't had a long-term commitment to employee stock ownership, perhaps employees wouldn't have been so willing to make sacrifices. Packard claims that commitment to people clearly fostered commitment to the company.

CONTEXT

Hewlett-Packard has pulled off an unusual double—it is admired and successful. When they were assembling their list of excellent companies in the late 1970s, Tom Peters and Robert Waterman included Hewlett-Packard. When Jerry Porras and James Collins wrote *Built to Last*, their celebration of long-lived companies, there was no doubt that Hewlett-Packard was worthy of inclusion. In the same vein, in 1985, *Fortune* ranked Hewlett-Packard as one of the two most highly-admired companies in the United States. The company is ranked similarly in virtually every other poll on well-managed companies or ones that would be good to work for.

"Wherever you go in the HP empire, you find people talking product quality, feeling proud of their division's achievements in that area. HP people at all levels show boundless energy and enthusiasm," observed Tom Peters and Robert Waterman in *In Search of Excellence*.

According to Louise Kehoe in the *Financial Times*, "Their legacy, and the achievement that Packard was most proud of, is a management style based on openness and respect for the individual."

FOR MORE INFORMATION

Packard, David. *The HP Way*. New York: Collins, 1996.

1 The two alleles of genotyp‹
Rr are located on
homologous chromosome‹

2 ...which replicate in
the S phase of meiosis.

Figure 3.6 part 1
Genetics: A Conceptual Approach, Fifth Edition
© 2014 W. H. Freeman and Company

The Human Problems of an Industrial Civilization

Elton Mayo

1099

MANAGEMENT LIBRARY

WHY READ IT?

The author was part of the team conducting the Hawthorne Studies at Western Electric's Chicago plant between 1927 and 1932, early studies into motivation in the workplace. The book shows the important link between workforce morale and organizational performance, and paved the way for policies and management theories based on teamwork and effective communication.

GETTING STARTED

The Hawthorne Studies offered important insights into the motivation of workers:

- People and their motivation were critical to the success of any business.
- There was a link between morale and output—changes in working conditions led to increased output.
- It is important to restore humanity to the workplace.

Workers selected for a test felt that more attention was being paid to them. They felt chosen, and so responded positively. The feeling of belonging to a cohesive group led to an increase in productivity. Informal organizations between groups are a potentially powerful force.

CONTRIBUTION

1. The Hawthorne Studies

According to Mayo, the studies offered important insights into the motivation of workers. It was found that changes in working conditions led to increased output, even if the changes didn't obviously improve working conditions.

Whatever the dictates of mass production and scientific management, people and their motivation were critical to the success of any business.

2. The Link Between Morale and Output

The researchers were interested in exploring the links between morale and output. The author documents how five women workers were removed to a test room and observed as they worked. The research was initially restricted to physical and technical variables. Sociological factors were not expected to be of any significance. The results proved otherwise.

Removed from their colleagues, the morale of the "guinea pigs" improved. By virtue of their selection, the women felt that more attention was being paid to them.

3. The Importance of Group Cohesion

Mayo reports that the feeling of belonging to a cohesive group led to an increase in productivity. He comments: "The desire to stand well with one's fellows, the so-called human instinct of association, easily outweighs the merely individual interest and the logic of reasoning upon which so many spurious principles of management are based."

Mayo champions the case for teamworking and for improved communications between management and the workforce.

The Hawthorne research revealed informal organizations between groups as a potentially powerful force, which companies could make use of or ignore at their peril.

4. Restoring Humanity to the Workplace

Mayo's belief that the humanity needed to be restored to the workplace struck a chord at a time when the dehumanizing side of mass production was beginning to be more fully appreciated.

"So long as commerce specializes in business methods which take no account of human nature and social motives, so long may we expect strikes and sabotage to be the ordinary accompaniment of industry," Mayo notes.

The research assumed that the behavior of workers was dictated by the "logic of sentiment" while that of the bosses was by the "logic of cost and efficiency."

CONTEXT

The author is known for his contribution to the famous Hawthorne experiments into the motivation of workers.

The experiments were carried out in 1927–32 at the Chicago division of Western Electric. Although they were celebrated as a major event, their significance lay not so much in their results and discoveries but in the statement they made—that people and their motivation were critical to the success of any business.

The findings influenced the human relations school of thinkers, including Herzberg, McGregor, and Maslow, which emerged in the 1940s and 1950s.

The work of the Hawthorne researchers redressed the balance in management theorizing, and the scientific bias of earlier researchers was put into a new perspective.

FOR MORE INFORMATION

Mayo, Elton. *The Human Problems of an Industrial Civilization*. Revised ed. Boston, MA: Harvard University Press, 1946.

"The desire to stand well with one's fellows, the so-called human instinct of association, easily outweighs the merely individual interest." *The Human Problems of an Industrial Civilization*

The Human Side of Enterprise

Douglas McGregor

WHY READ IT?

McGregor was a key member of the Human Relations School of Management whose work significantly influenced management styles from the 1960s on. His most famous concept is "Theories X and Y" which describe two extreme approaches to managing people. The book highlights the potential for a more enlightened approach to human relations management and paved the way for approaches such as empowerment.

GETTING STARTED

Management assumptions about controlling human resources determine an organization's character. Theory X assumes that workers are inherently lazy, needing to be supervised and motivated. Authority is the central, indispensable means of managerial control. Theory Y assumes that people want and need to work and organizations should develop employees' commitment. McGregor argues that the average human being learns, under the right conditions, not only to accept but to seek responsibility.

CONTRIBUTION

1. The Importance of Human Resources

According to the book, the assumptions management holds about controlling its human resources determine the whole character of the enterprise.

2. Theory X—A Traditional Management Approach

Theory X is built on the assumption that workers are inherently lazy, need to be supervised and motivated, and regard work as a necessary evil.

3. The Assumptions behind Theory X

- People inherently dislike work and will avoid it if they can.
- People need to be coerced, controlled, and threatened into making adequate effort toward the organization's ends.
- People lack ambition, preferring to be directed and to avoid responsibility. Above all they want security.

4. The Influence of Theory X

The assumption that authority is the central, indispensable means of managerial control pervades U.S. industry. In the author's view, this is a consequence not of human nature, but of management philosophy, policy, and practice. It is not people who have made organizations, but organizations that have transformed the perspectives, aspirations, and behavior of people.

5. Theory Y—A Humanist Approach

Theory Y is based on the principle that people want and need to work. An organization needs to develop the individual's commitment to its objectives, and then to liberate his or her abilities on behalf of those objectives.

6. The Assumptions behind Theory Y

- Work is as natural as play or rest—the typical human being doesn't inherently dislike work.
- External control and threat of punishment are not the only means for bringing about effort.
- Commitment to objectives is a function of the rewards associated with their achievement.
- The most important reward is the satisfaction of ego, which can be the direct product of effort.
- The average human being learns not only to accept but to seek responsibility.
- The capacity to use imagination, ingenuity, and creativity in the solution of organizational problems is widely distributed in the population.

7. Toward the Learning Manager

McGregor suggests that four kinds of learning are relevant for managers:

- intellectual knowledge
- manual skills
- problem-solving skills
- social interaction

8. Assessing Behavior

The skills of social interaction are outside the confines of normal teaching and learning methods. "We normally get little feedback of real value concerning the impact of our behavior on others. If they don't behave as we desire, it is easy to blame their stupidity, their adjustment, or their peculiarities. Above all it isn't considered good taste to give this kind of feedback in most social settings. Instead, it is discussed by our colleagues when we are not present to learn about it," says McGregor.

CONTEXT

Despite publishing little in his short life, McGregor's work remains significant. His classic study of work and motivation reflected the concerns of the middle and late 1960s, when the monolithic corporation was at its most dominant and the world at its most questioning. The common complaint against Theories X and Y is that they are mutually exclusive. To counter this McGregor was developing "Theory Z" when he died in 1964: a theory that synthesized the organizational and personal imperatives. William Ouchi later seized on the concept of Theory Z. In his book of the same name, he analyzed Japanese working methods. Here he found fertile ground for many of the ideas McGregor was proposing:

- lifetime employment
- concern for employees including their social life
- informal control
- decisions made by consensus
- slow promotion
- excellent transmittal of information from top to bottom and bottom to top with the help of middle management
- commitment to the company
- high concern for quality

Leading author Gary Hamel commented: "Over the last forty years, we have been slowly abandoning a view of human beings as nothing more than warm-blooded cogs in the industrial machine. People can be trusted; people want to do the right thing; people are capable of imagination and ingenuity—these were McGregor's fundamental premises, and they underlie the work of modern management thinkers from Drucker to Deming to Peters, and the employment practices of the world's most progressive and successful companies."

FOR MORE INFORMATION

McGregor, Douglas. *The Human Side of Enterprise*. Revised ed. New York: McGraw-Hill, 2005.

"It is not people who have made organizations, but organizations that have transformed the perspectives, aspirations, and behavior of people."
The Human Side of Enterprise

The Innovator's Dilemma

Clayton M. Christensen

WHY READ IT?

Christensen's book faces up to a fundamental problem facing innovative companies—how to deal with breakthrough technologies when customers may not be ready for them. It argues that normal practice—focusing investment and development on the most profitable products, those that are in demand among top customers—may ultimately be damaging. The risk is that companies may reject innovative products that do not meet this criterion. Christensen explains how to overcome this problem and manage breakthrough products successfully.

GETTING STARTED

Christensen examines a variety of leading, well-managed companies that have failed to capitalize on innovative technologies. The dilemma is that it is often sound decisions by good managers that lead to failure. The author distinguishes between sustaining technologies, which foster improved performance, and disruptive technologies, which represent a breakthrough, but may initially lead to poorer performance. Examples of disruptive technologies include cellular telephones, digital photography, and online retailing.

Part of the problem, according to Christensen, is that the market may not be ready for the new technology. In other cases, leading customers may not be willing to risk a new product. Companies therefore focus on the safe bets, but may subsequently be overtaken by innovation.

CONTRIBUTION
1. Control by Customers

The disk drive industry shows the dilemma in action. The author explains how the major players in the industry used sustaining technologies to offer their customers improved performance.

New entrants introduced disruptive technologies, such as smaller floppy disks that required new computer architecture. These innovations were, however, initially rejected by customers until they became a proven technology. The author concludes that, to a

degree, the larger companies were controlled by their customers.

2. Value Networks

Christensen offers a possible explanation for failure in these cases—the concept of the "value network." This is a technique companies can use to assess the value of a new technology in relation to their current business and customer base. It asks what rewards the company would obtain if it were to reallocate resources away from mainstream products.

The author believes that the problem is compounded by the scope of the company's suppliers and subcontractors. Each may have its own value network based on the needs of its own customers. Innovative ideas that come up from subcontractors may be stifled in the same way as internal ideas.

The author explains how the cost and profit structures in a value network can limit the attractiveness of an innovation. If profit margins are low, the emphasis will be on cost cutting across proven technologies. Innovation would be too risky. The other response from established companies is to move upmarket where they can earn more from existing products.

3. Avoiding Risk

Christensen points out that new entrants have frequently forced the pace of innovation with disruptive technologies. Established companies only moved in when there was a definite market. Disruptive technologies do not initially represent large, high-margin opportunities for established companies and the decision-making structure can rule out innovative ideas.

The author cites five reasons why successful companies fail to capitalize on disruptive technologies:
- Customers control the pattern of resource allocation.
- Small markets do not solve the growth needs of large companies.
- It can be difficult to identify successful applications in advance.

- Larger organizations rely on their core competencies and values.
- Technology supply may not equal market demand.

4. The Importance of Spinoffs

Christensen explains how companies who did harness disruptive technologies used a number of management techniques:
- Projects were handled within another "spinoff organization" that had customers who needed the new technology.
- Those same project organizations could get excited about small markets and small wins.
- Failure was an acceptable part of the process as companies proceeded by trial and error to the right solution.
- Companies looked for new markets and developed the market where the disruptive technology offered value.

The author gives examples of large corporations that establish spinoff companies to exploit new technology. Frequently, the corporation pulls the spinoff back into the core business when it proves successful.

CONTEXT

The book claims that overdependence on customer needs can affect a company's success. This argument runs counter to the marketing and customer service books that put customer focus at the top of the corporate agenda.

Books such as *When Giants Learn to Dance* by Rosabeth Moss Kanter (Touchstone, 1990) have pointed out the problems faced by larger corporations who compete in fast-moving technology markets. Christensen's book is unusual in highlighting the problems inherent in what appears to be sound decision making.

FOR MORE INFORMATION

Christensen, Clayton M. *The Innovator's Dilemma: When New Technologies Cause Great Firms to Fail.* Revised ed. New York: HarperBusiness, 2003.

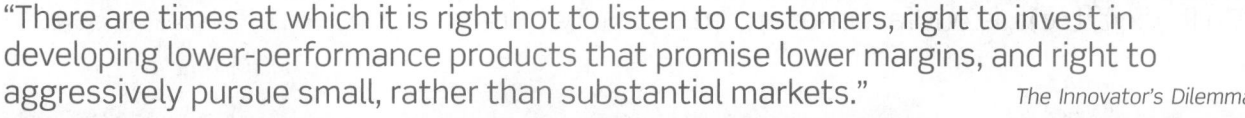

"There are times at which it is right not to listen to customers, right to invest in developing lower-performance products that promise lower margins, and right to aggressively pursue small, rather than substantial markets."

The Innovator's Dilemma

In Search of Excellence

Tom Peters
Robert Waterman

WHY READ IT?

In Search of Excellence is the most popular management book of recent times. Appearing when Japanese competition had brought Western business low, it gave managers new heart and a new direction, reminding them, in Gary Hamel's words, "that success often comes from doing common things uncommonly well."

GETTING STARTED

The book emerged from research conducted by Peters and Waterman with the consulting firm, McKinsey. They identified excellent companies, then sought to distill lessons from their behavior and performance.

The sample was eventually whittled down to 62 (which were not intended to be perfectly representative). The choices were largely unsurprising, including the likes of IBM, Hewlett-Packard, Wal-Mart, and General Electric. The emphasis was exclusively on big companies.

There is a certain irony here, however. Although it celebrated big manufacturing businesses, the book condemned the excesses of dispassionate modern management practice and advocated a return to simpler virtues. The authors later came to feel that their ideas were better embodied in smaller companies.

CONTRIBUTION
1. Success Builds on First Principles

The book attacks the excesses of the rational model and the business strategy paradigm that had come to dominate Western management thinking.

It counsels return to first principles:
- attention to customers;
- an abiding concern for people (productivity through people);
- the celebration of trial and error (a bias for action).

"The excellent companies really are close to their customers. That's it. Other companies talk about it; the excellent companies do it."

2. Achieve Productivity through People

The authors quote a General Motors worker laid off after 16 years making Pontiacs: "I guess I was laid off because I make poor quality cars. But in 16 years, not once was I ever asked for a suggestion as to how to do my job better. Not once."

Excellent companies encourage and nurture an entrepreneurial spirit among all employees.

3. The Management Role

The real role of the chief executive is to manage the values of the organization. Executives nurture and sustain corporate values. Rather than being distant figureheads, they should be there making things happen.

The word "manager" in lip-service institutions often has come to mean not someone who rolls up his or her sleeves to get the job done right alongside the worker, but someone who hires assistants to do it.

4. Keep Things Simple

Excellent companies "stick to the knitting." They remain fixed on what they know they are good at and are not easily distracted.

One of their key attributes is that they have realized the importance of keeping things simple, despite overwhelming pressures to complicate things.

The authors explain what they call the "smart–dumb rule" as follows:

"Many of today's managers . . . may be a little bit too smart for their own good. The smart ones . . . shift direction all the time, based upon the latest output from the expected value equation [and] have 200-page strategic plans and 500-page market requirement documents that are but one step in product development exercises. Our dumber friends are different. They just don't understand why every customer can't get personalized service, even in the potato chip business."

5. Become Simultaneously Loose and Tight

The debate about how to become loose and tight (controlled and empowered; big yet small) has dominated much subsequent business writing. The authors recommend new management vocabulary. Each one turns the tables on conventional wisdom, implying both the absence of clear directions and the simultaneous need for action. They include:
- temporary structures
- ad hoc groups
- fluid organizations
- internal competition
- product champions
- skunk works

CONTEXT

Peter Drucker suggested that the book's simplicity explained its appeal: "The strength of the Peters book is that it forces you to look at the fundamentals. The book's great weakness—which is a strength from the point of view of its success—is that it makes managing sound so incredibly easy."

Gary Hamel said, "The dividing line between simple truths, and simplistic prescription is always a thin one. For the most part, Peters and Waterman avoided the facile and the tautological. Indeed, the focus on operations research, elaborate planning systems, and (supposedly) rigorous financial analysis had, in many companies, robbed management of its soul—and certainly had taken the focus off the customer."

For such a trailblazing book, it is surprisingly uncontroversial. Peters and Waterman admit that what they have to say is not particularly original. They commented that the ideas they were espousing had been generally left behind, ignored, or overlooked by management theorists.

The criteria for selecting excellence were debatable, as all criteria are, and set the authors up for criticism when their excellent companies fell from grace. In 1984 *BusinessWeek* revealed that some had speedily declined into mediocrity and, in some cases, abject failure. But Peters and Waterman had already provided a warning: "We are asked how we know that the companies we have defined as culturally innovative will stay that way. The answer is we don't."

In Search of Excellence created the impetus for the deluge of business books and, in the business world, established customer service as a key form of differentiation and advantage.

FOR MORE INFORMATION

Peters, Thomas, and Robert Waterman. *In Search of Excellence*. Revised ed. New York: Collins, 2004.

Innovation in Marketing

Theodore Levitt

WHY READ IT?

Levitt's views on the importance of marketing are highly regarded. His article "Marketing Myopia" (reprinted in the book) was one of the most popular *Harvard Business Review* articles ever published. It highlights how narrow perspectives result from companies focusing on production rather than customers.

GETTING STARTED

Historical success encouraged the belief that low-cost production was the key to success, but this inevitably leads to narrow perspectives. In the author's view, companies must broaden their view of the nature of their business, and should be marketing-led rather than production-led. The emphasis is on providing customer-creating value satisfactions.

There is no such thing as a growth industry: success comes from being perceptive enough to spot where future growth may lie. Companies fail because they assume continued growth, believe that a product cannot be improved, and concentrate on improved production techniques to deliver lower costs. Mass-production industries aim to produce all they can and marketing gets neglected.

CONTRIBUTION
1. A Focus on Customers

Mintzberg argues that the central preoccupation of corporations should be with satisfying customers rather than simply producing goods. Companies should be marketing-led rather than production-led. Management must think of itself not as producing products but as providing customer-creating value satisfactions. The lead must come from the chief executive and senior management.

2. Problems of Production-led Companies

Henry Ford's success in mass production fueled the belief that low-cost production was the key to business success. Ford continued to believe that he knew what customers wanted, long after they had decided otherwise.

Production-led thinking inevitably leads to narrow perspectives.

3. Narrow Perspectives

Companies must broaden their view of the nature of their business; otherwise their customers will soon be forgotten. The railroads are in trouble today not because the need was filled by others, but because it was not filled by the railroads themselves. They let others take customers away from them because they assumed they were in the railroad business rather than in the transportation business—they were product-oriented instead of customer-oriented.

The railroad business was constrained by a lack of willingness to expand its horizons. Similarly, the movie industry failed to respond to the growth of television because it regarded itself as being in the business of making movies rather than providing entertainment.

4. Taking Growth for Granted

Growth can never be taken for granted, asserts the author. There is no such thing as a growth industry—growth is a matter of being perceptive enough to spot where future growth may lie.

History is filled with companies that fall undetected into decay because:

- they assume that the growth in their particular market will continue for as long as the population grows in size and wealth;
- they believe that a product cannot be surpassed;
- they tend to put faith in the ability of improved production techniques to deliver lower costs and, therefore, higher profits.

5. Problems of Mass-production Industries

Mass-production industries are impelled by a great drive to produce all they can. The prospect of steeply declining unit costs as output rises is more than most companies can usually resist. The profit possibilities look spectacular, so all effort focuses on production.

Concentration on the product, in Levitt's view, also lends itself to measurement and analysis. The result is that marketing gets neglected.

6. Distinguishing Selling and Marketing

There is a distinction between the tasks of selling and marketing. Selling concerns itself with the tricks and techniques of getting people to exchange their cash for your product; it is not concerned with the values that the exchange is all about. It does not, as marketing invariably does, view the entire business process as consisting of a tightly integrated effort to discover, create, arouse, and satisfy customer needs.

CONTEXT

Ted Levitt's fame was secured early in his career with "Marketing Myopia"—a *Harvard Business Review* article which enjoyed unprecedented success and attention, selling over 500,000 reprints.

It has since been reproduced in virtually every collection of key marketing texts. "Marketing Myopia" is a manifesto rather than a deeply academic article. It embraces ideas that had already been explored by others (Levitt acknowledges his debt to Peter Drucker's book *The Practice of Management*).

In the 1980s when marketing underwent resurgence, companies began to heed Levitt's view that they were too heavily oriented toward production. Levitt's article and his subsequent work pushed marketing to center stage. In some cases it led to what Levitt called marketing mania, with companies obsessively responsive to every fleeting whim of the customer.

Many of today's leading thinkers, such as Pascale and Peters, continually re-emphasize Levitt's message that there is no such thing as a growth industry.

Influential writer Gary Hamel said: "If Ted Levitt had done nothing else in his career—and he did plenty—he would have earned his keep on this planet with the article 'Marketing Myopia.' Managers get wrapped up inside their products (railroads) and lose sight of the fundamental benefits customers are seeking (transportation). Equally provocative was Ted's 1983 *Harvard Business Review* article, 'The Globalization of Markets.' While some argue that markets will never become truly global, there are few companies that are betting against the general trend."

FOR MORE INFORMATION

Levitt, Theodore. *Innovation in Marketing*. New York: McGraw-Hill, 1962.

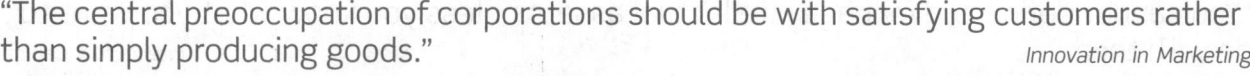

"The central preoccupation of corporations should be with satisfying customers rather than simply producing goods."

Innovation in Marketing

Intellectual Capital

Thomas Stewart

WHY READ IT?

The author is widely regarded as the world's leading authority on knowledge management, and his views are valuable to any organization that wants to improve the return on its "intellectual capital." The book is a useful guide to the strategic and practical issues of identifying, capturing, and using knowledge to improve a company's competitive advantage.

GETTING STARTED

Traditional capital had financial or physical characteristics. In the author's view, however, the emphasis now is on an intangible asset, intellectual capital, that consists of human capital, customer capital, and structural capital.

Human capital resides in the heads of employees; customer capital represents the value of a company's ongoing relationships with customers; and structural capital is the knowledge retained within the organization.

The real value comes in being able to capture and deploy intellectual capital, Stewart argues. However, you cannot define and manage intellectual assets unless you know what you want to do with them.

Knowledge working will change the pattern of careers in the 21st century.

CONTRIBUTION

1. The New Concept of Capital

Traditionally, capital could be viewed in purely financial or physical terms. It showed up in the buildings and equipment owned, and could be found in the corporate balance sheets.

The author suggests that in recent times, the emphasis has switched to an intangible form of asset, intellectual capital. Intellectual capital can be broken down into three areas: human capital, customer capital, and structural capital.

2. Human Capital

Human capital is the knowledge residing in the heads of employees that is relevant to the purpose of the organization.

Human capital is formed and deployed, when more of the time and talent of employees is devoted to activities that result in innovation. It can grow in two ways: when the organization uses more of what people know; or when people know more that is useful to the organization. Unleashing it requires an organization to minimize mind-less tasks, meaningless paperwork, and unproductive infighting.

3. Customer Capital

This represents the value of a company's ongoing relationships with the people or organizations to which it sells. Indicators of customer capital include market share, customer retention and defection rates, and profit per customer.

Customer capital is probably the worst managed of all intangible assets. Many businesses don't even know who their customers are.

4. Structural Capital

Structural capital is the knowledge retained within the organization. It belongs to the company as a whole and can be reproduced and shared.

Structural capital includes technologies, inventions, publications, and business processes.

5. Managing Intellectual Capital

The real value comes in being able to capture and deploy intellectual capital. Knowledge assets exist and are worth cultivating only in the context of strategy. You cannot define and manage intellectual assets unless you know what you want to do with them.

There are ten principles for managing intellectual capital:

- Companies don't own human and customer capital. Only by recognizing the shared nature of these assets can a company manage and profit from them.
- To create usable human capital, a company needs to foster teamwork, communities of practice, and other social forms of learning.
- Organizational wealth is created around skills and talents that are proprietary and scarce. Companies must see people with these talents as assets.
- Structural assets are the easiest to manage but those that customers care least about.
- Move from amassing knowledge "just in case" to having readily available information that customers need.
- Information and knowledge can and should substitute for expensive physical and financial assets.
- Knowledge work is custom work.
- Every company should reanalyze its own industry to see what information is most crucial.
- Focus on the flow of information not the flow of materials.
- Human, structural, and customer capital work together. It is not enough to invest in people, systems, and customers separately.

6. Knowledge Working and Individual Careers

Stewart argues that careers in the 21st century will have a number of characteristics:

- A career is a series of "gigs," not a series of steps.
- Project management is the furnace in which successful careers are made.
- Power flows from expertise, not position.
- Most roles in an organization can be performed by either insiders or outsiders.
- Careers are made in markets not hierarchies.
- The fundamental career choice is not between one company and another, but between specializing and generalizing.

CONTEXT

Thomas Stewart pioneered the field of intellectual capital in a series of articles that earned him an international reputation, with the Planning Forum calling him in 1994 "the leading proponent of knowledge management in the business press."

Intellectual Capital has proved itself as the definitive guide to understanding and managing intangible assets. It explains not only why intellectual capital will be the foundation of corporate success in the new century, but also offers practical guidance to companies about how to make best use of their intangible assets. Since it first appeared, there has been a flood of books on knowledge management.

The term "knowledge worker" is not a new one. In 1994, Peter Drucker wrote that "the true investment in the knowledge society is not in machines and tools but in the knowledge of the knowledge worker. In the knowledge society the most probable assumption for organizations . . . is that they need knowledge workers far more than knowledge workers need them."

FOR MORE INFORMATION

Stewart, Thomas. *Intellectual Capital: The New Wealth of Organizations*. New York: Doubleday, 1998.

"You cannot define and manage intellectual assets unless you know what you want to do with them."

Intellectual Capital

Jack: Straight from the Gut — Jack Welch

WHY READ IT?

Jack: Straight from the Gut outlines what made former General Electric C.E.O. Jack Welch successful. It explores the lessons he learned from leading. Without technical performance models, Welch knew "from his gut" what individuals needed to reach their potential. *Jack: Straight from the Gut* is both a textbook on leadership and on competing and an entertaining and personal account of what made GE one of the most successful companies of the last century. Welch has been a role model for many leaders since becoming GE's youngest ever C.E.O. in 1980, and his vision was critical to the business's success—indeed from when he first addressed city analysts in his new role at GE, he maintained that vision was his main responsibility.

GETTING STARTED

The value of *Jack: Straight from the Gut* lies in learning what made Jack Welch one of the most respected C.E.O.s of the 20th century. Welch argues that the success of GE owed as much to the outstanding people he led as to his own skill as a leader. However, his intolerance of failure and mediocrity—which he calls "superficial congeniality"—and his ability to motivate and communicate an appealing vision was decisive. His evaluation of managerial talent brought about an unprecedented improvement in performance. He classified people into three categories: the best 10%; the critical 70%; and the worst 20%. His vision was to nurture and develop the top 10%, help the 70% meet their goals, and minimize the resources wasted on the bottom 20%. He did not differentiate between the most able 10% of managers, as this would waste perfectly capable talent—exemplifying Welch's policy of recognizing both the benefits and limitations of competition. This enabled Welch to develop people and reshape a massive company into achieving more.

In his efforts to destroy corporate bureaucracy, Welch created a culture of accountability and teamwork. Welch insisted on GE being either first or second in any market. If not, he would remove GE from, or downsize in, that market. Consequently, GE became more efficient and profitable. Unlike other successful entrepreneurs who believe in visionary thinking, Welch's management style is rooted in the real world. By using stock options as an incentive, he forced managers to relate their decisions to the reality of the marketplace. But competing was not Welch's sole contribution: he was also an effective teacher. Many of the executives he developed subsequently became successful C.E.O.s at other Fortune 100 firms.

CONTRIBUTION

1. Competing

In this book, Welch explains how a competitive spirit is fundamental to his own character as well as the GE's organizational culture. It was a component of their success, motivating people to do better and to value excellence. Welch feels that his mother, Grace, was the most influential figure in his life because she taught him to take pleasure in winning and to deal well with defeat. He argues that competing effectively is about learning from one's mistakes, working as a team, and having confidence.

Ambition is important when competing. When he assumed the role of C.E.O., Welch boasted that his team would break all sales and profit records, and that GE's plastics business would grow in profitability more in his first year than in the previous ten years. Such a vision was a key feature of Welch's successful style.

2. Motivating

Welch describes how, in 1963, after three years at GE, he blew up a factory. As the manager, he was responsible and took responsibility. Welch was not punished, however; instead he was encouraged to learn from his mistakes and be honest about them. Bearing this example in mind, Welch explains his view that when people make mistakes, the last thing they need is to be disciplined. Instead, their self-confidence needs to be restored, so they may improve. Motivation is a key theme in this book, and Welch is keen to emphasize that he was always felt he was in the "people business." He feels that any company's greatest resource is its people, and at GE, motivating others enabled him to use his resources more effectively.

3. Focusing

According to Welch, a clear focus is essential if you are to succeed in business. Winning requires a focus on what needs to be done and an elimination of waste. Welch explains how his policy of "fix, close, or sell" involved only operating in areas where GE was first or second in the market. If GE could improve its performance in a particular area to lead the market, they could "fix" themselves; otherwise, they would either be closed or sold. This applied to staff: the best were rewarded, the majority developed so that they could reach their full potential, while the employees who performed worst were made redundant.

Welch tackles this issue in more detail in *Jack*. The number of employees at GE fell by 118,000 between 1980 and 1985. Welch was nicknamed "Neutron Jack" because he eliminated people but left the buildings standing—like a neutron bomb. Welch explains how he hated that name, because it implies he wasn't doing what was best for everybody. He feels his contribution was to make GE a "lean" organization, which meant improving performance. This led to the Six Sigma initiatives, whereby quality was improved to less than 3.4 defects per million operations (99.99966% accuracy). Consequently, GE became known for an unrivalled level of product quality. Often, conglomerate multi-nationals are known for when they make mistakes. GE, in Welch's view, were known for when they didn't.

CONTEXT

In 1980, GE was a massive bureaucracy: the C.E.O.'s office was at remove of 12 levels from the factory floor. Having worked on the frontline, Welch had a strong prejudice against that type of bureaucratic culture. He significantly changed GE by integrating innovative practices into many different areas of the business. Other companies were also developing some of these practices, such as e-commerce or cost-cutting, but GE under Welch's leadership, was unique in focusing on the power of competition to develop people. Welch's search for the best talent to manage GE made a large company both efficient and good at creating new ideas. He created a meritocracy that was the foundation of GE's success. *Jack: Straight from the Gut* ends with Welch's search for an heir, culminating in his retirement in 2001.

FOR MORE INFORMATION

Welch, Jack, and John A. Byrne. *Jack: Straight from the Gut*. Revised ed. New York: Warner, 2003.

1105

MANAGEMENT LIBRARY

The Knowledge-creating Company

Ikujiro Nonaka
Hirotaka Takeuchi

WHY READ IT?

The book focuses on the development of organizational knowledge in Japanese companies. It explains how this knowledge forms the basis of innovations that have enabled Japanese companies to become world leaders in many different market sectors. It shows that the ability to acquire and apply knowledge is becoming a key factor for success in the transition from an industrial economy to an information economy.

GETTING STARTED

Nonaka and Takeuchi believe that historical adversity has forced Japanese companies to pursue a policy of continuous innovation. Organizational knowledge, according to them, is the ability of a company to create new knowledge, disseminate it throughout the organization, and embody it in innovative products, services, and systems. They distinguish between explicit knowledge, such as rules or formulas, and tacit knowledge, which is gained from experience and can rarely be learned. The Japanese, they claim, are very effective at turning tacit knowledge into explicit knowledge that can be shared throughout an organization.

CONTRIBUTION
1. Characteristics of Knowledge Creation

According to the authors, there are three key characteristics of knowledge creation:
- metaphor and analogy;
- the transition from personal to organizational knowledge;
- ambiguity and redundancy.

The use of metaphor and analogy helps companies to visualize difficult concepts and explain them to other people within an organization. The transition from personal to organizational knowledge depends on the successful implementation of teamwork so that individuals can interact with each other. The concept of ambiguity and redundancy means that Japanese companies are happy to take a number of different approaches to innovation, some of which are bound to fail. They use redundancy to encourage creativity and identify what does not work in practical terms.

2. Knowledge Management

The authors review theories of knowledge from ancient times onward. They analyze recent management writing to identify attitudes toward the question of knowledge. They cite Peter Drucker's "knowledge worker" and Peter Senge's "learning organization" as important concepts in knowledge creation. They discuss the concept of core competencies and argue that this can distract companies. Core competencies, they argue, suggest that knowledge is an existing, finite resource within a company. Knowledge creation, on the other hand, emphasizes the importance of acquiring and developing knowledge from as many internal and external sources as possible.

3. How Knowledge Creation Works

The authors claim that there are four key processes in knowledge conversion:
- socialization
- externalization
- combination
- internalization

An example of socialization is the brainstorming camps established by Honda to solve difficult production problems. Externalization is the process of using metaphors or analogies to communicate difficult concepts in product development. Combination is the process of sorting, adding, combining, and synthesizing different types of knowledge to create new knowledge. Internalization is like relearning other people's experiences or learning by doing.

4. The Environment for Knowledge Creation

To create a suitable environment for knowledge creation, the authors stress the importance of vision to guide overall direction and autonomy to allow everyone in the organization to get involved in the process.

They describe a structure called "middle-up-down management" that underpins knowledge creation. This structure contrasts with the bottom-up or top-down management styles of Western companies. The Japanese model puts middle managers at the heart of the process, acting between front-line workers and a visionary senior management team. The authors believe that this structure creates dialog and builds positive relationships between the individual specialists who contribute to a development project.

5. Hypertext Organizations

Nonaka and Takeuchi refer to the concept of a "knowledge crew," consisting of knowledge engineers and knowledge practitioners. Underpinning this is what they call a "hypertext organization." This is an organization with multiple layers:
- a business system layer;
- a project team layer;
- a knowledge base layer.

The business system layer and project team layer generate different types of knowledge, which are brought together in the knowledge base which can be shared throughout the organization.

CONTEXT

A number of books have looked at the process of innovation, trying to identify the factors that distinguish a successful innovator. The authors offer both theoretical and practical insight into the way that Japanese companies use knowledge as the basis for innovation. Their findings are in contrast with the widespread Western view that Japanese success is based on access to cheap capital, lifetime employment, culture, or quality.

The authors draw on a wide variety of Western management sources to highlight the differences between Japanese and Western practice. Among others, they quote Peter Drucker and Alvin Toffler on the importance of knowledge, and Peter Senge on the concept of the "learning organization."

FOR MORE INFORMATION

Nonaka, Ikujiro, and Hirotaka Takeuchi. *The Knowledge-creating Company: How Japanese Companies Create the Dynamics of Innovation.* New York: Oxford University Press, 1995.

"To these companies, change is an everyday event and a positive force."

Leaders: Strategies For Taking Charge

Warren Bennis
Burt Nanus

WHY READ IT?

Warren Bennis is an academic and regular presidential adviser who brought leadership to a new mass audience. He is regarded as one of the most important contemporary thinkers.

Burt Nanus is the founder and director of the Center of Futures Research at the University of Southern California.

In this book, the authors use an eclectic selection of U.S. leaders to offer the readers key lessons on how to become successful. Their message is that leadership is open to all.

GETTING STARTED

Leaders commit people to action and convert followers into leaders. They are usually ordinary people rather than particularly charismatic, as leadership is all-encompassing and open to all.

Successful leaders also have a vision that other people believe in, and communicate it effectively. Instead of being individual problem solvers, they achieve greatness through working with groups. Devising and maintaining an atmosphere in which others can succeed is the leader's creative act.

CONTRIBUTION
1. The Ordinary Leader

In the authors' view, the new leader is one who commits people to action, who converts followers into leaders, and who may convert leaders into agents of change. Leadership is not a rare skill—leaders are made rather than born. They are usually ordinary people, or apparently ordinary, rather than obviously charismatic. Leadership is not solely the preserve of those at the top of an organization—it is relevant at all levels. Leadership is not about control, direction, and manipulation.

2. Common Abilities of Leaders

From a survey of 90 U.S. leaders (including Neil Armstrong, the coach of the LA Rams, orchestral conductors, and businesspeople such as Ray Kroc of McDonald's), Bennis and Nanus identified four common abilities:
- management of attention
- management of meaning
- management of trust
- management of self

3. Management of Attention

This is a question of vision. Leadership is the capacity to create a compelling vision, translate it into action, and sustain it. Successful leaders have a vision that other people believe in and treat as their own.

4. Management of Meaning

A vision is of limited practical use if it is encased in 400 pages of wordy text or mumbled from behind a paper-packed desk. Effective communication relies on use of analogy, metaphor, and vivid illustration as well as emotion, trust, optimism, and hope.

5. Management of Trust

Trust is the emotional glue that binds followers and leaders together. Leaders have to be seen to be consistent.

6. Management of Self

Leaders do not glibly present charisma or time management as the essence of their success. Instead, the emphasis is on persistence and self-knowledge, commitment and challenge, taking risks and, above all, learning. The learning person looks forward to failure or mistakes, which means that the worst problem in leadership is basically early success. There's no opportunity to learn from adversity and problems.

7. A Positive Self-regard

Leaders have a positive self-regard, known as emotional wisdom. This is characterized by an ability to accept people as they are. They also have a capacity to approach things in terms of only the present, and an ability to treat everyone, even close contacts, with courteous attention. They need an ability to trust others, and to do without constant approval and recognition.

8. Leaders and Group Working

Greatness starts with superb people. Great groups don't exist without great leaders, but they give the lie to the persistent notion that successful institutions are the lengthened shadow of a great woman or man. It's not clear that life was ever so simple that individuals, acting alone, solved most significant problems. Instead of the individual problem solver, we have a new model for creative achievement.

9. Changing Leadership Qualities

The leader is a pragmatic dreamer, a person with an original but attainable vision. He or she knows that this dream can only be realized if others are free to do exceptional work. Typically, the leader is the one who recruits the others, by making the vision so seductive that they see it too, and eagerly sign up.

Inevitably, the leader has to invent a leadership style that suits the group. The standard models, especially command and control, simply don't work. The heads of groups have to act decisively, not arbitrarily. They have to make decisions without limiting the autonomy of other participants.

10. The Idealistic Leader

Most organizations are dull and working life is mundane, so groups can be an inspiration. Individual leaders can create a human community that will, in the long run, lead to the best organizations. "A Great Group is more than a collection of first-rate minds. It's a miracle," say the authors. Every person has to make a genuine contribution in their lives and the institution of work is one of the main vehicles to achieving this.

CONTEXT

With the torrent of publications and executive programs on the subject, it is easy to forget that leadership had been largely overlooked as a topic worthy of serious academic interest until it was revived by Bennis and others in the 1980s. Since then, leadership has become a heavy industry. Concern and interest about leadership development is no longer a U.S. phenomenon: it is truly global. The book stands as a humane counter to much of the military-based hero worship which dogs the subject.

FOR MORE INFORMATION

Bennis, Warren, and Burt Nanus. *Leaders: Strategies for Taking Charge*. 2nd ed. New York: Collins, 2003.

Leadership

James MacGregor Burns

WHY READ IT?

In his book *Leadership*, Burns makes an important contribution to management literature by refocusing interest on the nature of leadership. He brings practical insights from both business and politics and has used them to identify two key strands—transactional and transformational leadership.

GETTING STARTED

Burns believes we know too much about our leaders, but too little about leadership. It is a structure for action. It is not the preserve of the few or the tyranny of the masses.

Burns identifies two vital strands of leadership—transformational and transactional leadership. Transactional leadership is built on reciprocity—the relationship between the leader and his or her followers develops from the exchange of some reward. The secret of effective leadership appears to lie in combining the two elements so that targets, results, and procedures are developed and shared.

CONTRIBUTION

1. Problems in Defining Leadership

If we know all too much about our leaders, we know far too little about leadership. There are literally hundreds of definitions of leadership and, as a result, the concept "has dissolved into small and discrete meanings," Burns claims.

2. Leadership As a Structure For Action

Leadership is exercised when people with certain motives and purposes mobilize—in competition or conflict with others—institutional, political, psychological, and other resources so as to arouse, engage, and satisfy the motives of followers. Leadership is not the preserve of the few or the tyranny of the masses. The leadership approach tends often unconsciously to be elitist; it projects heroic figures against the shadowy background of drab, powerless masses. The followership approach tends to be populist or anti-elitist in ideology, perceiving the masses, even in democratic societies, as linked with small, overlapping circles of conservative politicians, military officers, hierocrats, and businesspeople.

Leadership is a structure for action that engages people, to varying degrees, throughout the levels and among the interstices of society. Only the inert, the alienated, and the powerless are unengaged. It is also intrinsically linked to morality—moral leadership emerges from, and always returns to, the fundamental wants and needs, aspirations, and values of the followers.

3. Transformational Leadership

Burns identifies two vital strands of leadership—transformational and transactional leadership.

Transformational leadership occurs when one or more persons engage with others in such a way that leaders and followers raise one another to higher levels of motivation and morality. Their purposes, which might have started out separate but related, become fused. Power bases are linked, not as counterweights, but as mutual support for common purpose. Various names are used for such leadership: elevating, mobilizing, inspiring, exalting, uplifting, exhorting, evangelizing.

Transformational leadership becomes moral in that it raises the level of human conduct and ethical aspiration of both the leader and the led, thus having a transforming effect on both. It is also dynamic, in the sense that the leaders throw themselves into a relationship with followers who will feel elevated by it and often become more active themselves, thereby creating new cadres of leaders.

Transformational leadership is concerned with engaging the hearts and minds of others. It works to help all parties achieve greater motivation, satisfaction, and sense of achievement. It is driven by trust, concern, and facilitation rather than direct control. The skills required are concerned with establishing a long-term vision, empowering people to control themselves, coaching and developing others, and challenging the culture to change. In transformational leadership, the power of the leader comes from creating understanding and trust.

4. Transactional Leadership

Transactional leadership is built on reciprocity. The relationship between the leader and his or her followers develops from the exchange of some reward, such as performance ratings, pay, recognition, and praise. It involves leaders in clarifying goals and objectives, communicating well in order to plan tasks and activities with the cooperation of their employees, so that wider organizational goals are met.

The relationship depends on hierarchy and the ability to work through the mode of exchange. It requires leadership skills such as the ability to obtain results, to control through structures and processes, to solve problems, to plan and organize and work within the structures and boundaries of the organization.

5. Combining Transformational and Transactional Leadership

Their apparent mutual exclusiveness makes transformational and transactional leadership akin to Douglas McGregor's Theories X and Y. The secret of effective leadership appears to lie in combining the two elements so that targets, results, and procedures are developed and shared.

CONTEXT

Burns's book provides an important link between leadership in the political and business worlds. For all the books on leadership, the two have usually been regarded as mutually exclusive. His examination of transformational and transactional leadership also stimulated further debate on leadership at a time when it was somewhat neglected. In the 1980s, it returned to prominence in management literature as a subject worthy of study.

Business guru Gary Hamel commented, "There is no theme in management literature . . . more enduring than leadership. Among the many contributions which Burns makes to our understanding of leadership, two seem central: leadership must have a moral foundation; and the responsibility for leadership must be widely distributed. Self-interested autocrats, whether political or corporate, ignore these truths at their peril."

FOR MORE INFORMATION

Burns, James MacGregor. *Leadership.* New York: Harper Perennial, 1982.

"If we know all too much about our leaders, we know far too little about leadership."

Leadership

Rudolph Giuliani

WHY READ IT?

Leadership covers the lessons former New York City Mayor Giuliani learned from his own experiences both during the September 11 terrorist atrocities in New York and during lifetime of taking the helm effectively. The author describes how the leadership rules he practiced enabled him to gain control on September 11th as well as throughout his term as Mayor. He compares the art of writing and researching to the art of politics—both are about persuading others to interpret things as you do. In *Leadership*, Giuliani explores the events and ideas that influenced him as a leader.

GETTING STARTED

Any leader, whatever the size of his or her business, may use Giuliani's rules for leadership to succeed. Giuliani demonstrated an important characteristic of good leaders during the events of September 11th—emotional strength. With little experience in responding to a national emergency, Giuliani improvised. In his view, being able to learn and to be affected by circumstances is critical to good leadership. While we learn from personal experience, we can also learn entirely new ideas and incorporate them into our approach.

CONTRIBUTION
1. Be Accountable

When he was Mayor of New York City, Giuliani had a sign on his desk saying "I'M RESPONSIBLE." He feels that leaders need to accept the blame if things go wrong—and expect similar standards from others. The accountability systems Giuliani established enabled the police to focus and tackle crime more effectively. Giuliani instituted an accountability system for police command areas that won the 1996 Harvard Innovation in Government Award. Every week, the leaders of the eight command areas would defend their performance to all the other leaders, which gave them a strong incentive to boost their performance and maintain standards. Giuliani recommends that reliable systems must be put in place to provide data on performance, which can prevent disputes over blame.

2. Believe and Deliver

These two tools are about communicating a sense of authority and competence. Successful leaders manage expectations, as well as results. This requires, as Giuliani puts it, "avoiding mentioning what you've done until you've actually accomplished something." Announce initiatives once you know they work. "Underpromising" focuses the internal team. The author cites as an example New York's budgeting process during his time in office: he often projected revenues to fall by up to 2%, to produce a frugal, lean culture. If revenues were higher than expected, the city gained a budget surplus, boosting the economy and the Mayor's popularity at the same time.

Belief is also a powerful leadership tool in Giuliani's view. Many people never develop strong beliefs at work, partly because they fear the consequences of rocking the boat. Consequently, things are done the way they were in the past, which is not, necessarily, the best way. This eliminates creativity. Inspirational leaders communicate positive beliefs to others and maintain firm beliefs themselves, while staying flexible only when uncertain. You can't lead someone if you don't know *where* to lead them.

3. Think and Organize

Most organizational structures do not correspond to the organization's real purpose. Giuliani demonstrates the importance of "aligning the system with the purpose," using the example of the Budget Director's lack of visibility within the New York structure before he took office. The Budget Director controlled annual expenditures of $40 billion yet reported only to the Deputy Mayor. The Budget Director was rarely present at critical meetings, so financial constraints were rarely priorities. Giuliani made the Budget Director report to him directly and encouraged his participation in senior management meetings, which improved efficiency and team performance. Organisational structures must reflect the purpose, rather than generating alternative priorities that distract.

Giuliani argues that when you are making important decisions, it is advisable first to envision alternative scenarios. The longer you have to make a decision, the better chance you have of coming up with a mature and well-reasoned solution. When you are faced with a complex problem, the wisest approach is to reflect in more depth. Disasters occur when decisions are taken without enough thinking or when alternative scenarios are ignored. Giuliani explores how better organization and greater reflection—both part of a much more rational decision-making process—produce spectacular success.

4. Funerals Are Mandatory

Difficult events in the lives of a team require leadership, strengthening the ties that bind people together. Giuliani argues that the real measure of a leader is taken during such tough times as funerals, where our fundamental responses are heightened. Emotional support is critical to effective leadership and wellbeing is key to people's success. During difficult times, weak links break while strong ones are cemented and as Giuliani explains, leaders who contribute during such times gain respect.

CONTEXT

Leadership, like parenthood, is something that many people aspire to. Yet isolating the characteristics of all great leaders is impossible. Different leaders exhibit different traits—the successful are, by definition, unusual. Giuliani's insight into the importance of leading during tough times derives from his experience on September 11th, but his other achievements are well documented: crime rates fell, while living standards and prosperity improved during his tenure as Mayor of New York City. *Time* magazine's "Person of the Year 2001" did not become a great leader on September 11th 2001, when he had almost left office: he had long understood the need to make hard decisions. Giuliani was often satisfied with being unpopular, writing "I thought I was doing a good job if anger was coming from a variety of sources—white collar criminals, mobsters, corrupt politicians, narcotic traffickers. It's not a popularity contest." Instead of chasing shallow popularity by avoiding confrontation, he faced problems head on with "zero tolerance" for failure; important lessons for any leader to learn.

FOR MORE INFORMATION

Giuliani, Rudolph W. *Leadership*. New York: Miramax Books, 2002.

MANAGEMENT LIBRARY

1109

Leading Change

John P. Kotter

1110

MANAGEMENT LIBRARY

WHY READ IT?

Kotter is regarded as one of the world's leading figures in change management. His article, "Leading Change," published in the March–April 1995 *Harvard Business Review*, quickly became the *Review's* best-selling reprint. Readers commented that its analysis defined the real problem of change management. They also found the 8-stage change framework "compelling." The book builds on the success of the article and includes dozens of examples of effective change management in action.

GETTING STARTED

Kotter believes that successful change is based on an 8-stage process:

1 establishing a sense of urgency;
2 creating the guiding coalition;
3 developing a vision and strategy;
4 communicating the change vision;
5 empowering employees;
6 generating short-term wins;
7 consolidating gains and producing more change;
8 anchoring new approaches in the culture.

CONTRIBUTION
1. Why Change Fails

Kotter opines that most business transformations fail if they do not meet the criteria set out in his 8-point plan. These omissions would not be important in a slower-moving world, but the volatile forces of competition mean companies must change to survive and prosper. He believes that the pace of change is driven by forces such as technological development, international economic integration, and the globalization of markets and competition.

The result, according to Kotter, is that there are either more opportunities or more hazards, depending on whether an organization can adapt or not. He then explains how successful change, the sort that enables companies to grasp opportunities, goes through the 8-stage process. He adds, however, that it is essential to go through all the stages in sequence. He also believes that change must be led, not managed.

2. A Sense of Urgency

Establishing a sense of urgency helps to get the cooperation needed for change. A committed group, Kotter argues, can drive change through. He suggests a number of approaches for increasing the urgency level:

● creating a vision;
● setting targets so high they cannot be achieved through business as usual;
● getting staff to talk to customers;
● showing people that great opportunities cannot be achieved by the present organization.

3. Building the Guiding Coalition

Kotter's second stage is the "guiding coalition." He believes that an isolated chief executive or a weak committee cannot cope with the pace of change. The coalition must comprise people with power, expertise, credibility, and leadership. Leadership is key, because change must be led not managed. He explains why the coalition must be built on trust and a common goal, noting that team-building exercises can be an important part of that process.

4. Developing a Vision

According to Kotter, a vision clarifies the direction of change. Other decisions must be in line with the vision. Vision also helps to align individuals and motivate them in an efficient way. He believes that a vision should be imaginable, desirable, feasible, focused, flexible, and communicable.

5. Communicating Change

Kotter argues that a vision has real power only when it is communicated effectively. Effective communication is vital because employees receive vast amounts of information, and communications about change can easily get lost. Kotter's advice is to keep it simple, use metaphors, keep repeating the message, listen, and lead by example.

6. Empowering Employees

Turning the vision into action means removing structural barriers to change so that employees are empowered, says Kotter. That may require training, reorganization, aligning information and systems to the vision, and confronting people who try to restrict change.

7. Short-term Wins

According to Kotter, short-term wins are essential. They are visible and show that change is producing results. They also help to fine-tune the change process, build momentum, and reward the people who are de-livering change. Pressure and challenging targets can help to deliver the gains.

8. Consolidating Gains

Kotter believes that all gains need to be consolidated to keep the process moving. This is particularly important in companies where there is a high level of interdependence. Maintaining momentum also requires strong leadership, effective project management, and support for the people who are effecting change.

9. Anchoring Change

The final stage in Kotter's process is anchoring the new approaches in the corporate culture. He argues that the new behavior should become the norm. Ideally, everyone in the organization should have shared values. Kotter believes that achieving this level of acceptance depends on results. It may even require changing key people.

CONTEXT

The study of change has gained importance as competition has intensified and other structural factors impact the business environment.

Kotter's work demonstrates the positive aspects of effective change. It also shows that strong leadership is essential if change is to succeed. Rosabeth Moss Kanter's book *The Change Masters* (Free Press, 1985) puts a similar emphasis on the importance of strategic leadership.

William Bridges, on the other hand, in *Managing Transitions* (Perseus, 1991), puts more emphasis on management of the personal consequences of change, highlighting the need to reduce anxiety and manage the process he calls "transition."

Hammer and Champy's book *Reengineering the Corporation* (Collins, 2004) took change to a logical conclusion and showed how companies would have to transform themselves to compete effectively. Unfortunately, reengineering has been widely associated with downsizing, and this has given change management negative connotations.

FOR MORE INFORMATION

Kotter, John P. *Leading Change*. Boston, MA: Harvard Business School Press, 1996.

"If environmental volatility continues to increase as most people now predict, the standard organization of the twentieth century will likely become a dinosaur."

Liar's Poker

Michael Lewis

1111

MANAGEMENT LIBRARY

WHY READ IT?

Beyond economic history, *Liar's Poker* explores the characters and forces behind Salomon Brothers' bond-trading empire in the 1980s. This autobiographical account of the author's sojourn working for that company analyzes the costs and benefits of competition between individuals and between firms. He emphasizes how a culture of excessive competition contributed to Salomon's financial collapse, along with the recession following the crash of 1987–88. An entertaining insight into human nature, *Liar's Poker* explores the drivers of success and failure in a complex, dynamic financial environment.

GETTING STARTED

The 1980s saw a boom in the U.S. mortgage market. *Liar's Poker* explains the drivers of that bubble but also explores the personal factors contributing to Salomon's (and the author's) changing fortunes. From his own experience at Salomon's rapidly developing mortgage bond desk, Lewis explains bond trading: buying and selling shares in debt. Salomon made mortgage debt tradable, in a market with few buyers and only them trading, which proved to be a profitable monopoly. The sector reached maturity between 1983 and 1986, with the number of buyers rising; other firms entered the market, increasing competition. Together with worsening economic circumstances, this caused the bubble to collapse.

The book's title is particularly apt. Lewis feels that "In any market, as in any poker game, there is a fool." The person that doesn't know who the fool is, probably is the fool! Salomon failed to use information to understand its competitors. The game of liar's poker is played on Wall Street. People form a circle, each holding a dollar bill to their chest and trying to fool others about its serial number. A player makes a "bid" suggesting, for example, "three sixes"—meaning all serial numbers contain three sixes. Players continue to bid as follows. The next player either makes a bid with higher numbers or challenges, where all players show their numbers. Bidding escalates until a challenge is made. Good players calculate probabilities of number combinations; great players read others' faces to gain critical information.

CONTRIBUTION
1. Culture and Loyalty

In *Liar's Poker*, the reader is shown how an organization's culture is critical to its success. In the 1980s, the culture of bond trading became increasingly competitive and ambitious. Weak traders were exposed by their failures and the strong—"big swinging dicks"—commanded unprecedented salaries and bonuses. Salomon faced juxtaposing its hierarchical structure, culture, and outlook with a competitive, meritocratic environment. Rewarding successful traders became an issue. Lewis explains how most, including chairman John Gutfreund, were unwilling to pay substantial bonuses to successful young traders, despite their sizeable contribution to profits. Denied these benefits, the traders joined competitors, which ultimately caused profits to fall. The author highlights how success relies on managing culture and cultural change and how he himself left Salomon, alienated by their undervaluing his efforts.

2. Communication and Information

Information is critical. In a poker game, reading others' expressions improves the likelihood of success. In a dynamic market, communicating with customers, competitors, and your team is essential. At Salomon, communication was restricted, leaving bond salesmen on the floor below the main trading floor feeling distanced from the "big swinging dicks" above. This reinforced traders' unwillingness to share information and strengthened the culture of internal competition. Furthermore, it created clear winners and losers; underperforming traders were marginalized, being unable to take credit for others' profits. Managing employees' access to information is important. In Lewis's view, the collapse of Salomon Brothers mortgage department was the result of poor communication between business units, a lack of market awareness, and dwindling employee loyalty.

3. Competition and Customers

Actively competing with others is often key to success in a business environment, but competition at the expense of teamworking can be disastrous. Lewis attributes Salomon's difficulties after 1987 to its management's lack of focus and their behaving more like traders than managers—seeking to "manage by the numbers." He quotes a colleague: "Wall Street makes its best producers into managers. The best producers are cut-throat, competitive, and often neurotic and paranoid. You turn those people into managers, and they go after each other." Customers need to come first, and Salomon failed to maintain customer loyalty. Since their traders focused exclusively on commission-based bonuses, they appeared neither to value customers nor to show loyalty to their firm.

CONTEXT

In the 1980s, Paul Volcker's expansionist Federal Reserve drove the boom in the bond market. This policy of floating interest rates made the market volatile, providing traders with profitable opportunities. Another driver was rising debts for federal, municipal, corporate, and consumer borrowers. Trading exploded as traders moved $300 million in bonds each day, compared to $5 million per week in the 1970s. It was the age of greed and ambition. Salomon Brothers profited from structural economic change: Lewis transferred capital, in bonds, from savers outside the U.S. to consumers needing mortgages inside the country. This leveraging brought spectacular wealth.

Salomon's chairman, John Gutfreund, challenged chief trader, Meriwether, to liar's poker: "one hand, one million dollars, no tears." Beating his boss would be a "career-limiting move" for Meriwether: it was a lose-lose situation. Meriwether returned: "if we're going to play for those kind of numbers, I'd rather play for real money. Ten million dollars. No tears." He gambled Gutfreund couldn't stomach the risk. Gutfreund declined. Here, Lewis highlights character traits of a successful trader: a fast, ambitious, and addicted gambler. Trading is about risk; the sole determinant of power is managing and defeating risk. After the dot-com collapse of 2001, *Liar's Poker* has resonance: all good things must come to an end.

FOR MORE INFORMATION

Lewis, Michael. *Liar's Poker: Rising Through the Wreckage of Wall Street*. New York: Norton, 1989.

"In any market, as in any poker game, there is a fool."

Liar's Poker

The Living Company: Habits for Survival in a Turbulent Business Environment

Arie de Geus

MANAGEMENT LIBRARY

WHY READ IT?

The book looks at the problem of corporate failure, presenting alarming statistics on the relatively short life of European and Japanese enterprise.

The author argues that short-term focus on profits, rather than nurturing people, is a key factor in failure. *The Living Company* is the testimony of someone who practiced the human side of enterprise and who believes that companies must be fundamentally humane to prosper.

GETTING STARTED

The author argues that corporations should last as long as two or three centuries, but the reality is that companies usually die young. And focus on profits rather than on human issues lies behind the high failure rate. However, like all organisms, the living company exists primarily for its own survival and improvement.

A successful company is one that can learn effectively, and senior executives must dedicate a great deal of time to nurturing their people.

CONTRIBUTION

1. The Problem of Corporate Mortality

Companies may be legal entities, but they are disturbingly mortal. The natural average lifespan of a corporation should be as long as two or three centuries—for example, the Sumitomo Group and the Scandinavian company, Stora.

The reality is that companies usually die young. A Dutch survey indicated 12.5 years as the average life expectancy of all Japanese and European firms. The average life expectancy of a multinational corporation—Fortune 500 or its equivalent—is between 40 and 50 years.

2. Reasons for Longevity

The high company failure rate is attributed to the focus of managers on profits, rather than on the human community that makes up their organization.

In an attempt to get to the bottom of this mystery, de Geus and a number of his Shell colleagues carried out some research to identify the characteristics of corporate longevity. As you would expect, the onus is on keeping excitement to a minimum. The average human centenarian advocates a life of abstinence, caution, and moderation; and so it is with companies.

The research team identified four key characteristics. The long-lived companies were:

- sensitive to their environment;
- cohesive, with a strong sense of identity;
- tolerant;
- conservative in financing.

3. The Importance of People

There is more to a company and to its longevity than mere money making. The skills, capabilities, and knowledge of people are paramount; capital is no longer king.

4. The Learning Company

A successful company is one that can learn effectively. Learning means being prepared to accept continuous change, and a company can only change if its community of people changes.

Individuals change through learning—requiring senior executives to dedicate a great deal of time to nurturing their people. The author recalls spending around a quarter of his time on the development and placement of people; while the C.E.O. of GE, Jack Welch claimed to spend half of his time on such issues.

According to de Geus, all corporate activities are grounded in two hypotheses:

- The company is a living being.
- The decisions for action made by this living being result from a learning process.

Like all organisms, the living company exists primarily for its own survival and improvement. It aims to fulfill its potential and to become as great as it can be.

CONTEXT

With its faith in learning, *The Living Company* represents a careful and powerful riposte to corporate nihilism.

The book proposes that the wisdom of the past be appreciated and used, rather than cast out in the manner of a cultural revolution.

Contrast this with reengineering, which sought to dismiss the past so that the future could begin with a blank piece of paper. De Geus suggests that the piece of paper already exists, and notes are constantly being scrawled in the margins as new insights are added.

De Geus's arguments are probably at their weakest when he contemplates why companies deserve to live long lives. The average entrepreneur would probably accept a life expectancy of 12.5 years.

The Living Company is the testimony of someone who practiced the human side of enterprise, and who believes that companies must be fundamentally humane to prosper—whatever the century.

FOR MORE INFORMATION

de Geus, Arie. *The Living Company: Habits for Survival in a Turbulent Business Environment.* Revised ed. Boston, MA: Harvard Business School Press, 2002.

The Machine That Changed the World

James P. Womack
Daniel T. Jones
Daniel Roos

1113

MANAGEMENT LIBRARY

WHY READ IT?

Lean production was Japan's secret weapon in the trade war, and it went on to conquer the world. In 1984 a team of researchers at the Massachusetts Institute of Technology (MIT) undertook a study of it. Within the framework of an analysis of the situation and problems of auto manufacturers worldwide, Womack, Jones, and Roos examined the differences between mass and lean production. This widely read and wisely praised book presents their findings.

GETTING STARTED

A new form of manufacturing—lean production—is about to supersede the mass production of goods, the authors announce. Lean production can simultaneously double productivity, improve quality, and keep costs low. The book recounts the history of the rise of lean production, describes its essential elements, and presents the prospects for the spread of this revolutionary management initiative.

CONTRIBUTION
1. The Beginnings of Lean Production

In 1950 Eiji Toyoda, a Japanese engineer whose family had founded the Toyota Motor Company, and Toyota's production manager, Taiichi Ohno, visited the Ford motor works in Detroit, then the biggest and most efficient production plant in the world. The basis of the Ford system was a complete division of labor among a wide variety of specialist operatives. The conveyor belt could never be halted; flaws were dealt with in postproduction.

Toyoda and Ohno felt that there was waste throughout this system: wasted labor, wasted materials, wasted time. Apart from the assemblers, none of the specialists created any value for the car.

On his return, Ohno grouped his workers in teams, to whom he delegated more tasks and who were to work together on improvements. Each worker had a duty to halt the production line if a problem arose that he or she could not deal with. The whole team would then trace the fault back to its ultimate cause and then think up a solution that would ensure it never happened again.

The remedial work required before dispatch was thus reduced to zero, and lean production, the authors say, was born.

2. The Elements of Lean Production

The first element is the organization of the assembly works. A lean factory, the authors report, has two main organizational characteristics. First, it allots a maximum number of tasks and responsibilities to those workers who create actual value in the product on the line. Secondly, it has a fault detection system installed that quickly traces each fault back to its source.

The second element is product development. Lean production, the authors say, is quicker than mass production. The reason lies in basic differences in construction methods.

- Project leadership works on the *susha* system. The *susha* is the team leader, a position of great power in Japanese businesses. In mass-production companies the system is very different. The position of the development manager is too weak to push projects through. Top management often overrides his or her decisions.
- The *susha* creates a small, close-knit team, whose members are drawn from various specialist departments and who remain in contact with them. For the duration of the development project, however, they remain wholly under the control of the *susha*. In mass-production business, development teams consist of individuals on short-term loan from specialist departments.
- Communication too is different, say the authors. In Western mass production, it is only at a late stage in the project that there is any coordination of different interests. In Japan, team members sign formal undertakings to do exactly what the team as a whole has decided. Any conflicts therefore show up at the very beginning of the crisis.

The third element in lean production highlighted by Womack and his coauthors is coordination of the supply chain. In the lean, *susha*-led product development process, all the necessary suppliers are carefully selected, not on the basis of their bids, but on the basis of earlier relationships and proven performance.

Customer relations form the fourth element. Japanese auto manufacturers, the authors point out, have comparatively few sales channels. These are differentiated in terms of their appealing to different types of purchaser. The objective is to establish a direct link between the production system and the customer. Employees in the sales channels are loaned to the development teams, and the dealers have a close relationship with the manufacturer.

The fifth major element in lean production, according to the authors, is the way the lean company is managed. Various framework conditions have to exist:

- There must be money to finance development projects that last several years.
- Career ladders must be available for qualified and motivated employees.
- Decentralised activities must be coordinated worldwide.

CONTEXT

The MIT investigation was at the time the most comprehensive study of a single industry ever conducted.

While it showed the undoubted successes of lean production, it also claimed to have uncovered certain deficiencies in the concept. Lean production, it suggests, overemphasizes the aspects of savings and mechanization and neglects categories such as know-how and innovation. Lean management brings a short-term improvement in efficiency, but not a long-term increase in productivity. In addition, the authors argue, it is unsuited to dismantling complexity. Anyone, for example, who wishes to reduce the complexity of serialized production steps through individualized manufacture must understand ever more expansive processes in their entirety. In theory, the highly innovative and flexible business organization with no hierarchy may count as the company of the future, but in everyday practice the weaknesses of lean production are clearly apparent.

FOR MORE INFORMATION

Womack, James P., Daniel T. Jones, and Daniel Roos. *The Machine That Changed the World: The Story of Lean Production.* New York: HarperCollins, 1991.

"The whole world should adopt lean production, and as quickly as possible."

The Machine That Changed the World

Made in Japan

Akio Morita

WHY READ IT?

Made in Japan is the story of Sony and reflects the changes that took place in postwar business history. Morita and Sony's story parallels the rebirth of Japan as an industrial power. When Sony was first attempting to make inroads into Western markets, Japanese products were sneered at as being of the lowest quality. Surmounting that obstacle was a substantial business achievement.

GETTING STARTED

This book charts the reemergence of Japan as an industrial heavyweight. It helped change the image of "Made in Japan" from shoddy goods to high quality. Sony invented new markets with a pioneering spirit by bringing out product after product, innovation after innovation. Its most famous success was the Walkman, the development of which was based on instinct, not research. Analysis and education do not necessarily help you to reach the best business decisions; sometimes understanding must come before logic. "Japanese people tend to be much better adjusted to the notion of work, any kind of work, as honorable," says Morita. Recruitment is "management's risk and management's responsibility."

CONTRIBUTION
1. The Japanese Renaissance

Morita and Sony's story parallels the rebirth of Japan as a major industrial power.

They helped change the image of "Made in Japan" from something shoddy to something reputable and desirable.

At the time when Sony first tried to break into the Western electronics market, Japanese products were considered fifth-rate. Morita helped Sony not only to overcome this prejudice but to reverse it.

2. Inventing New Markets

Morita and Sony's gift was to invent new markets with a pioneering spirit. "Sony is a pioneer and never intends to follow others," says Morita.

"Through progress, Sony wants to serve the whole world. It will always seek the unknown. Sony has a principle of respecting and encouraging one's ability . . . and always tries to bring out the best in a person. This is the vital force of Sony."

3. The Power of Innovation

While companies such as Matsushita were inspired followers, Sony set the pace with product after product, innovation after innovation.

Sony brought the world the handheld video camera, the first home video recorder, and the floppy disk.

The blemishes on its record were the Betamax video format, which it failed to license, and color television systems.

4. Instinct and Research

Sony's most famous success was the Walkman, the brainchild of Morita. Morita noticed that young people liked listening to music wherever they went. He put two and two together and made—a Walkman.

He did not believe that any amount of market research could have told the company that this would be successful.

"The public does not know what is possible. We do.", he has famously said.

5. Analysis Doesn't Always Pay

Brilliant marketing by instinct was no mere accident.

Morita believes that, if you go through life convinced that your way is always best, all the new ideas in the world will pass you by.

Analysis and education do not necessarily help you to reach the best business decisions. You can be totally rational with a machine but if you work with people, sometimes understanding has to come before logic.

6. Japanese Culture Encourages the Work Ethic

Morita has emphasized the cultural differences in Japanese attitudes toward work. The Japanese tend to have a much stronger work ethic, and see work as an honorable occupation.

In *Made in Japan*, Morita states his belief that management has ultimate responsibility for its staff. If a recession is looming, profit should be sacrificed rather than employees be laid off.

CONTEXT

The book tells the story of the rise of Sony and it reflects the rise of Japan as a postwar industrial power. It looks at the role of quality and innovation as key factors in the success of Japanese companies. Many Western authors have focused on the role of quality in Japan, particularly the influence of people like Deming and Juran.

Richard Pascale and Anthony Athos look at the phenomenon in *The Art of Japanese Management*.

Morita and Sony took the attitude that global markets were important from the outset. Ken Ohmae writes on that subject from the Japanese perspective in *The Borderless World*.

FOR MORE INFORMATION

Morita, Akio. *Made in Japan.* New York: Dutton, 1986.

Management Teams: Why They Succeed or Fail

R. Meredith Belbin

WHY READ IT?

Effective teamworking is now seen as key to the success of all types of organization. Meredith Belbin identified the characteristics of people needed to make a successful team. His recommendations are still used, and the book can therefore help anyone who needs to develop a team.

GETTING STARTED

Corporations have been preoccupied with the qualifications, experience, and achievement of individuals—but it is not the individual but the team that is the instrument of sustained and enduring success in management.

Team performance is influenced by the kinds of people making up a group, and testing indicates that certain combinations of personality-types perform more successfully than others. Nine archetypal functions make up an ideal team—plant, coordinator, shaper, teamworker, completer, implementer, resource investigator, specialist, and monitor evaluator.

Unsuccessful teams can be improved by analyzing their composition and making appropriate changes.

CONTRIBUTION
1. The Preoccupation with Individuals

Corporations have been preoccupied with the qualifications, experience, and achievement of individuals, and have applied themselves to their selection, development, training, motivation, and promotion. However commentators believe that the ideal individual for a given job cannot be found, because he or she cannot exist. It is not the individual but the team that is the instrument of sustained and enduring success in management.

2. The Contribution of Individuals in Teams

Belbin was interested in group performance and how it might be influenced by the kinds of people making up a group. He asked members engaged in a business school exercise to undertake a personality and critical-thinking test and, based on the test results, discovered that certain combinations of personality-types performed more successfully than others.

Belbin realized that given adequate knowledge of the personal characteristics and abilities of team members through psychometric testing, he could forecast the likely success or failure of particular teams. Unsuccessful teams can be improved by analyzing their team design shortcomings and making appropriate changes.

3. Identifying Team Characteristics

A questionnaire completed by team members was analyzed to show the functional roles the managers thought they performed in a team. From this research, Belbin identified nine archetypal functions which go to make up an ideal team.

4. Successful Team Composition

- Plant—creative, imaginative, unorthodox; solves difficult problems. Allowable weakness: bad at dealing with ordinary people.
- Coordinator—mature, confident, trusting; a good chairman; clarifies goals, promotes decision making. Not necessarily the cleverest member.
- Shaper—dynamic, outgoing, highly strung; challenges, pressurizes, finds ways around obstacles. Prone to bursts of temper.
- Teamworker—social, mild, perceptive, accommodating; listens, builds, averts friction. Indecisive in crunch situations.
- Completer—painstaking, conscientious, anxious; searches out errors; delivers on

time. May worry unduly; reluctant to delegate.
- Implementer—disciplined, reliable, conservative, efficient; turns ideas into actions. Somewhat inflexible.
- Resource investigator—extrovert, eager, communicative; explores opportunities. Loses interest after initial enthusiasm.
- Specialist—single-minded, self-starting, dedicated; brings knowledge or skills in rare supply. Contributes only on narrow front.
- Monitor evaluator—sober, strategic, discerning. Sees all options, makes well-considered judgments. Lacking in drive and ability to inspire others.

CONTEXT

The explosion of interest in teamworking during the last decade has prompted greater interest in Belbin's work. The teamworking categories he identified have proved robust and are still used in a variety of organizations. Gary Hamel commented, "High-performing companies increasingly believe that teams, rather than business units or individuals, are the basic building blocks of a successful organization. Belbin deserves much credit for helping us understand the basic building blocks of successful teams."

Antony Jay commented, "Corporations have been preoccupied with the qualifications, experience, and achievement of individuals . . . it is not the individual but the team that is the instrument of sustained and enduring success in management."

FOR MORE INFORMATION

Belbin, R. Meredith. *Management Teams: Why They Succeed or Fail*. 2nd ed. Burlington, MA: Butterworth-Heinemann, 2004.

"It is not the individual but the team that is the instrument of sustained and enduring success in management."

Management Teams: Why They Succeed or Fail

The Managerial Grid

Robert Blake
Jane Mouton

WHY READ IT?

The book made an important contribution to the measurement of management performance. It challenged existing theories and provided organizations with a grid for assessing the types of manager they needed for different positions.

GETTING STARTED

In the early 1960s there was a sizeable gap in management theorizing, especially in terms of leadership and motivation. Douglas McGregor's Theory X and Y had a number of shortcomings in reality, and Blake and Mouton found that a management performance model with three axes provided a more accurate representation of reality. The important axes were concern for productivity, concern for people, and motivation. Accurate measurement is important because of managers' capacity for self-deception and exaggeration.

CONTRIBUTION

1. Challenging Management Performance Theories

While acting as consultants for Exxon, Blake and Mouton concluded that there was a sizeable gap in management theorizing, especially in terms of leadership and motivation. Popular among theories of the time was that of Douglas McGregor and his motivational extremes of X and Y. However, Blake and Mouton believed that many behaviors and motivations fell in the middle of these extremes. Theories X and Y were only a part of the overall picture of organizational behavior.

2. A New Model of Management Performance

Blake and Mouton's conclusion was that a model with three axes, rather than two, was a more accurate representation of reality. The three crucial axes they determined were: concern for productivity, concern for people, and motivation.

Concern for production and people were both measured on a scale of one to nine, with nine being high. The reason a people axis was necessary is that managers achieve things indirectly. They don't produce nuts and bolts themselves, rather they organize others so that the production line can be productive.

Motivation was measured on a scale from negative (driven by fear) to positive (driven by desire).

3. Flaws in Performance Measurement

Blake and Mouton found that, when left to rank themselves, some 80% of people give themselves a 9,9 rating. Once this is discussed and considered, this figure is routinely reduced to 20%. Given the capacity for self-deception, it is little wonder that change programs fail.

4. Key Management Styles

From the grid emerge five key manager styles:

- 1 (production); 1 (people): Do nothing manager. The leader exerts a minimum of effort to get the work done, with very little concern for people or production;
- 1 (production); 9 (people): Labeled the Country Club Manager. This manager pays a lot of attention to people, but little to production. Can be seen in small companies that have cornered the market and some public sector organizations;
- 9 (production); 1 (people): This manager emphasizes production and minimizes the influence of human factors;
- 5 (production); 5 (people): Organization man or woman who diligently fosters mundanity;
- 9 (production); 9 (people): Managerial nirvana. The ultimate, with an emphasis on team working and team building. Personal and organizational goals are in alignment; motivation high.

CONTEXT

When Blake and Mouton examined the behavior of people at Exxon, they concluded that there was a sizeable gap in management theorizing, especially in terms of leadership and motivation. They found that many behaviors and motivations fell in the middle of Douglas McGregor's X and Y extremes. They observed that Theories X and Y were only a part of the overall picture of organizational behavior.

Blake and Mouton's conclusion was that a model with three axes—concern for productivity, concern for people, and motivation—was a more accurate representation of reality.

FOR MORE INFORMATION

Blake, Robert, and Jane Mouton. *The Managerial Grid*. Houston, Texas: Gulf Publishing, 1964.

"Managers . . . don't produce nuts and bolts themselves, they organize others."

Managing

Harold Geneen

WHY READ IT?

Geneen joined the board of ITT in 1959 and set about turning the company into the world's greatest conglomerate. Along the way he became, according to *BusinessWeek*, the legendary conglomerateur. The book relates the management style and culture that helped ITT to achieve that success. In particular, it highlights the importance of knowing the numbers in minute detail.

GETTING STARTED

Geneen's success was based on knowing every single figure possible. He did not invent the conglomerate, but he had an obsessive belief that it could be made to work. ITT bought 350 companies and appeared to be a managerial nightmare—yet Geneen made the nightmare work by fanatical attention to detail.

He only micro-managed the numbers; the people were generally overlooked. However, his success meant that people followed his methods without question. Over 200 days a year were devoted to management meetings held throughout the world.

Success was based on amassing all the facts so that decisions became self-evident— Geneen wanted no surprises.

CONTRIBUTION

1. A Rigorous Management Style

Geneen was the archetypal workaholic. His style was unforgiving, built on a degree of intellectual rigor that bordered on ruthlessness. He pinned his managerial faith on hard work and knowing every single figure possible. For Geneen, detail was everything. Once an accountant always an accountant.

2. Making Conglomerates Work

The conglomerate was not Geneen's invention. But he brought an obsessive belief that it could be made to work. He believed that ITT could manage any business in any industry if it knew the figures.

His career with ITT, described in *Managing*, is a pageant of acquisition and diversification. Under Geneen, ITT bought companies as casually as a billionaire buys trinkets. One acquisition funded another. ITT bought 350 companies, including Avis Rent-A-Car, Sheraton Hotels, Continental Baking, and Levitt & Sons, among many others. By 1970, ITT was composed of 400 separate companies operating in 70 countries. With such huge numbers of companies in such vastly different fields, ITT was hopelessly diversified. To contemporary eyes, the company was a managerial nightmare. Yet, Geneen made the nightmare work by fanatical attention to detail.

3. Managing the Numbers

Geneen only micro-managed the numbers; the people were generally overlooked.

"The very fact that you go over the progression of those numbers week after week, month after month, means that you have strengthened your memory and your familiarity with them so that you retain in your mind a vivid composite picture of what is going on in your company," he wrote.

4. Management Culture

Geneen inculcated a remarkable culture within ITT. His success meant that people followed his methods with the unquestioning faith of true believers.

Between 1959 and 1977, ITT's sales went from $765 million to nearly $28 billion. Earnings for the same period went from $29 million to $562 million, and earnings per share rose from $1 to $4.20.

As part of Geneen's formula, over 50 executives flew every month to Brussels to spend four days poring over the figures. It was calculated that over 200 days a year were devoted to management meetings held throughout the world.

5. Success Based on Facts

The point was to amass all the facts available so that the decisions became self-evident. If you knew everything, you would then know exactly what to do. Facts were the lifeblood of the expanding ITT.

"The highest art of professional manage-ment requires the literal ability to smell a real fact from all others," Geneen believed."Managers should have the temerity, intellectual curiosity, guts and/or plain impoliteness, if necessary, to be sure that what they do have is indeed what we will call an unshakeable fact."

Geneen wanted no surprises. He also hoped to make people as predictable and controllable as the capital resources they must manage.

CONTEXT

Much of Geneen's managerial philosophy and very rigorous practice would appear to be anathema to the contemporary executive.

However, his fundamentalist style of management remains. Management consultants, for example, continue to trade their rational models—pour in all the figures you can find and the right decision will emerge. There is still a temptation to manage by numbers rather than through and with people.

On the positive side, Geneen can be said to have elevated management to a new level. His system required a team of highly numerate, professional managers who had to take responsibility.

The Geneen legacy is most notably evident in the conglomerates that continue to survive. General Electric, under Jack Welch and now Jeff Immelt, may be the most lauded corporation of our age, but it is also a conglomerate with interests in everything from financial services to nuclear reactors and washing machines. Harold Geneen would have regarded the survival of such companies as vindication of his methods.

Others, however, point to the decline of ITT on his departure as a true measure of the long-term validity of Geneen's approach to management.

FOR MORE INFORMATION

Geneen, Harold. *Managing*. New York: Doubleday, 1985.

Managing Across Borders

Christopher Bartlett
Sumantra Ghoshal

WHY READ IT?

Bartlett and Ghoshal map out the new business reality of globalization and the kinds of organizations a "borderless" business world requires. The book is regarded as a classic, and has helped many companies to focus on the type of organization they need for success in the global economy.

GETTING STARTED

According to the authors, changing patterns of international management have led to a new global model, in which enabling innovation and disseminating knowledge in globally dispersed organizations is an important challenge.

A number of organizational forms are now prevalent among global companies: multinational companies offer high local responsiveness; global companies offer scale efficiencies and cost advantages; international companies have the ability to transfer knowledge and expertise to overseas environments that are less advanced; and the transnational company combines local responsiveness with global efficiency and the ability to transfer know-how better, cheaper, and faster.

Integration and the creation of coherent systems for value delivery are the new drivers of organizational structure.

CONTRIBUTION
1. Changing Patterns of International Management

The traditional international management model was simply to export your own way of doing things elsewhere, and companies believed that global operations were simply a means of achieving economies of scale. Local nuances were overlooked in the quest for global standardization: global and local were mutually exclusive. In general, organizations either gave their local operations autonomy or controlled them rigidly from a distance.

2. A New Global Model

Global presence with local responsiveness is now key. Companies face the challenge of enabling innovation and disseminating knowledge in globally dispersed organiza-

tions. Bartlett and Ghoshal identify a number of organizational forms prevalent among global companies.

3. Multinational Companies

The multinational or multidomestic organization offers a very high degree of local responsiveness. A decentralized federation of local businesses, it is linked together through personal control by expatriates who occupy key positions abroad.

4. Global Companies

Global organizations offer scale efficiencies and cost advantages. With global scale facilities, they seek to produce standardized products. They are often centralized in their home countries, with overseas operations considered as delivery pipelines to tap into global market opportunities. There is tight control of strategic decisions, resources, and information by the global hub.

5. International Companies

International companies have the ability to transfer knowledge and expertise to overseas environments that are less advanced. They are coordinated federations of local businesses, controlled by sophisticated management systems and corporate employees. The attitude of the parent company tends to be somewhat parochial, fostered by the superior know-how at the center of the organization.

6. The Transnational Companies

Global competition is forcing many businesses to shift to a fourth model, which they call the transnational. This organization combines local responsiveness with global efficiency and the ability to transfer know-how better, cheaper, and faster. The transnational company is made up of a network of specialized or differentiated units, which focus on managing integrative linkages between local businesses as well as with the center. The subsidiary becomes a distinctive asset, rather than simply an arm of the parent company. Manufacturing and technology development are located wherever it makes sense, and there is an explicit focus

on leveraging local know-how in order to exploit worldwide opportunities.

7. The Importance of Integration

Integration and the creation of a coherent system for value delivery are the new drivers of organizational structure. Companies cannot be left to their own devices, but have to be brought within the fold—while also keeping in touch with their local business environment.

What binds the companies together is a set of explicit or implicit shared values and beliefs that can be developed and managed effectively. There are three techniques crucial to the formation of an organization's psychology:

1 clear, shared understanding of the company's mission and objectives;
2 the actions and behavior of senior managers are vital as examples and statements of commitment;
3 corporate personnel policies must be geared up to develop a multi-dimensional and flexible organization process.

CONTEXT

Managing Across Borders is one of the few business books of recent years that deserves recognition as a classic. When it was published in 1989, understanding of globalization was in its infancy. With its emphasis on networking across the global organization and transferring learning and knowledge, the book effectively set the organizational agenda for a decade and created a new organizational model.

The authors effectively signalled the demise of the divisional organization—which gives divisions independence—first developed by Alfred P. Sloan of General Motors.

FOR MORE INFORMATION

Bartlett, Christopher A., and Sumantra Ghoshal. *Managing Across Borders: The Transnational Solution.* 2nd ed. Boston, MA: Harvard Business School Press, 2002.

"Integration and the creation of a coherent system for value delivery are the new drivers of organizational structure."

Managing Across Borders

Managing on the Edge

Richard Pascale

WHY READ IT?

This book challenges traditional management thinking, which Pascale feels is too complacent for an environment driven by change. He sets out a new perspective for "contention management," which seeks to harness the conflicting energies in an organization to achieve positive change. The book set the management agenda for a decade after its publication.

GETTING STARTED

U.S. managerial history is largely inward-focused and self-congratulatory. Change is a fact of business life, but complacency can cause problems. It is essential to change the management perspective. The incremental approach to change is no longer effective. The new emphasis should be on asking questions. Successful organizations undergo continual renewal by constantly asking questions.

Four factors drive stagnation and renewal:
- fit
- split
- contend
- transcend

"Contention management" is essential to orchestrate tensions that arise between these four factors. Forces locked in opposition can be used to generate inquiry and adaptation and the manager's job is to maintain a constructive level of debate.

CONTRIBUTION

1. The Dangers of Complacency

Nothing fails like success. Great strengths are inevitably the root of weakness. Of the companies listed in *Fortune 500* of 1985, 143 had been dropped by 1990. In the author's view, U.S. managerial history is largely inward-focused and self-congratulatory.

2. The Need for Change

According to Pascale, change is a fact of business life. We are ill-equipped to deal with it and the traditional approach to managing change is no longer applicable. The incremental approach to change is effective when the goal is to obtain more of the same thing. Historically, that has been sufficient. The United States' advantages of plentiful resources, geographical isolation, and absence of serious global competition defined a league in which U.S. companies competed with each other and everyone played by the same rules.

3. Growth of Management Fads

There have been more than two dozen management fads since the 1950s; a dozen emerged in the five years prior to 1990.

4. Driving Stagnation and Renewal

Four factors drive stagnation and renewal in organizations:
- fit—pertains to an organization's internal consistency (unity);
- split—describes a variety of techniques for breaking a bigger organization into smaller units and providing them with a stronger sense of ownership and identity (plurality);
- contend—refers to a management process that harnesses (rather than suppresses) the contradictions that are inevitable by-products of organizations (duality);
- transcend—alerts people to the higher order of complexity that successfully managing the renewal process entails (vitality).

5. Changing Management Perspective

Pascale calls for a fundamental shift in perspective.

Managerial behavior is based on the assumption that people should rationally order the behavior of those they manage. That mindset needs to be challenged. Orderly answers are no longer appropriate.

The new emphasis should be on asking questions. Strategic planning, at best, is about posing questions, more than attempting to answer them. Successful organizations undergo a continual process of renewal.

Central to achieving this is a willingness to ask questions constantly and to harness conflict for the corporate good, through systems that encourage questioning. Companies must become engines of inquiry.

6. Contention Management

Managers are ill-equipped to deal with the contention that arises when fundamental questions are posed.

Contention management is essential to orchestrate tensions that arise. Around 50% of the time when contention arises, it is smoothed over and avoided.

The forces that we have historically regarded as locked in opposition can be viewed as apparent opposites that generate inquiry and adaptive responses.

Each point of view represents a facet of reality, and these realities tend to challenge one another and raise questions.

If we redefine the manager's job as maintaining a constructive level of debate, we are, in effect, holding the organization in the question. This leads to identifying blind spots and working around obstacles.

Truth—personally and organizationally—lies in the openness of vigorous debate.

Organizations are, in the last analysis, interactions among people.

CONTEXT

Managing on the Edge presents a formidably researched and argued challenge to complacency and timidity.

Pascale criticizes Peters and Waterman's *In Search of Excellence* saying, "Simply identifying attributes of success is like identifying attributes of people in excellent health during the age of the bubonic plague."

Passions and obsessions often degenerate into simplistic formulae—for example, acronyms such as KISS (Keep it simple, stupid).

Managing on the Edge set the tone for much of the management thinking of the decade. Its emphasis on the need for constant change has since been developed by Pascale. He now argues that the issue of managing the way we change is a competence rather than an episodic necessity.

The capability to change is a core competence in its own right.

Influential critic Gary Hamel commented, "In *Managing on the Edge*, Richard Pascale provides a number of useful observations on the sources of corporate vitality. One of the things I've always admired about Richard Pascale is that he focuses not on tools and techniques, but on principles and paradigms. While management bookshelves groan with the weight of simplistic how-to books, Pascale challenges managers to think, and to think deeply. Pascale forces managers to deconstruct the normative models on which they base their beliefs and actions."

FOR MORE INFORMATION

Pascale, Richard T. *Managing on the Edge: How Successful Companies Use Conflict to Stay Ahead.* New York: Simon & Schuster, 1990.

1119

MANAGEMENT LIBRARY

"Nothing fails like success."

Managing Transitions

William Bridges

WHY READ IT?

This book focuses on the human aspects of change management. Change is a situation. What the author calls "transition" is the psychological process people go through to come to terms with change. The book stresses that change involves people and that managers and leaders must help people deal with the transition. The author shows, through practical examples, how managers should make people feel comfortable and unthreatened during a period of change and offers advice, as well as case studies, on the best way to achieve this.

GETTING STARTED

The author believes that many companies try to impose change, but fail to manage the transition. Transition means recognizing that things cannot be the same after an organizational change. People must get used to the new ways of doing things. They do this by going through a "neutral zone" before emerging into a new beginning.

CONTRIBUTION

1. Letting Go

The author explains that transition begins with a process of "letting go." However, this is a process that many people in an organization find difficult. They are comfortable with familiar, proven ways of doing things and they fear the unknown.

The first stage, he suggests, is to identify who is losing what, by analyzing what is going to change and identifying the impact on different groups of people. Managers should be aware that people will react in different ways. They should acknowledge the effect of the change on people and, if necessary, make some compensation for their loss. Managers should also acknowledge what was good about the existing processes and emphasize the element of continuity in the most important aspects of the new proposals.

2. The Neutral Zone

Bridges believes that the "neutral zone" is the most difficult part of the transition process, because this is where people's uncertainties and anxieties about change are most acute. He advises managers to give people a clear sense of direction, as well as support to help them through this difficult stage. Moving from an existing routine to a new one can prove difficult without the right help.

Bridges argues that managers can reduce the damaging impact of the neutral zone by setting short-term targets that are achievable. He also believes that they should not expect or demand exceptional performance during a period of transition.

Communication is vital, claims Bridges, at this and every stage of transition. It is also important to encourage creativity during the neutral zone, particularly when there is less pressure on people to perform. Creativity can help to overcome the sense of loss people feel about leaving old routines behind.

3. New Beginnings

When people move to the new system, uncertainties can remain, according to Bridges. There is always a risk in new ways of doing things. It is therefore essential to set out a clear plan with timings and targets. Managers should ensure that everyone has a clear part to play in the new system.

He recommends clear, regular communications to explain the object and rationale for the new system. A vision of the future can help to paint a clear picture for people in the organization. To reinforce the new beginning, Bridges recommends that companies should create a new identity and celebrate success.

The book also includes advice for readers on how to take care of themselves during a period of transition.

CONTEXT

This book is one of a number that deal with the subject of managing the process of change. John Kotter's *Leading Change* (Harvard Business School Press, 1996), for example, reflects on the themes of leadership, vision, and communication.

Bridges' book looks at the human perspective of change and includes a great deal of practical advice on ways of dealing with the personal issues that people face. It also contains a number of useful studies, case histories, and exercises that could be used in workshops.

As such, the book may be more suitable for people in human resources or line management roles. Senior executives who are concerned with the strategic implications of change might find more value in an author such as Kotter.

FOR MORE INFORMATION

Bridges, William. *Transitions: Making Sense of Life's Changes*. 2nd ed. Cambridge, MA: Perseus, 2003.
Bridges, William. *Managing Transitions: Making the Most of Change*. Cambridge, MA: Perseus, 1991.
Bridges, William. *Creating You and CO: Learn to Think like the C.E.O. of Your Own Career*. Cambridge, MA: Perseus, 1998.

Marketing Management

Philip Kotler

WHY READ IT?

Kotler is one of the leading authorities on marketing. *Marketing Management* is the definitive marketing textbook, covering the full scope of contemporary marketing. It is the most widely used marketing book in business schools.

GETTING STARTED

Marketing continues to evolve and expand its scope exponentially. The emphasis is shifting from transaction-oriented marketing to relationship marketing—retaining customer loyalty through continually satisfying their needs. Marketing management is the process of planning and executing functions that satisfy customer and organizational objectives.

Customer-delivered value is the difference between total customer value and total customer cost.

Organizations encounter three common hurdles to marketing orientation:
- organized resistance
- slow learning
- fast forgetting

CONTRIBUTION
1. Marketing Continues to Evolve
The marketing discipline is redeveloping its assumptions, concepts, skills, tools, and systems for making sound decisions.

Marketers must know when to:
- cultivate large markets or niche markets;
- launch new brands or extend existing brand names;
- push or pull products through distribution;
- protect the domestic market or penetrate aggressively into foreign markets;
- add more benefits to the offer or reduce the price;
- expand or contract budgets for sales force, advertising, and other marketing tools.

The scope of marketing is expanding exponentially as is demonstrated by the size and scope of *Marketing Management*. Its contents range over:
- industry and competitor analysis;
- designing strategies for the global marketplace;
- managing product life cycle strategies;
- retailing, wholesaling, and physical-distribution systems.

2. The Change to Relationship Marketing
The emphasis is shifting from transaction-oriented marketing to relationship marketing. Good customers are an asset which, when well managed and served, will return a handsome lifetime income stream.

In the intensely competitive marketplace, the company must retain customer loyalty through continually satisfying their needs in a superior way.

3. Defining the Role of Marketing
Marketing is the social and managerial process by which individuals and groups obtain what they need and want through creating, offering, and exchanging products of value with others. A market consists of all the potential customers sharing a particular need or want, who might be willing to exchange in order to satisfy that need or want.

Marketing management is the process of planning and executing the conception, pricing, promotion, and distribution of goods, services, and ideas, to create exchanges with target groups that satisfy customer and organizational objectives.

4. Analyzing Products
A product is anything that can be offered to a market for attention, acquisition, use, or consumption that might satisfy a want or need. A product has five levels:
- the core benefit (marketers must see themselves as benefit providers);
- the generic product;
- the expected product (the normal expectations the customer has of the product);
- the augmented product (the additional services or benefits added to the product);
- the potential product (all the augmentations and transformations that this product might undergo in the future).

5. Customer Value
Customer-delivered value is the difference between total customer value and total customer cost. Total customer value is the bundle of benefits customers expect from a given product or service. It consists of product value, service value, personnel value, and image value. Total customer cost consists of monetary price, time cost, energy cost, and psychic cost. Combined, the two produce customer-delivered value.

6. Barriers to Marketing Orientation
In order to become marketing oriented, organizations encounter three hurdles:

- Organized resistance—entrenched functional behavior tends to oppose increased emphasis on marketing, as it is seen as undermining functional power bases.
- Slow learning—most companies only slowly embrace the marketing concept.
- Fast forgetting—companies that embrace marketing concepts tend, over time, to lose touch with the principles. Various U.S. companies have sought to establish their products in Europe with scant knowledge of different marketplaces.

7. Achieving Market Leadership
Good companies will meet needs; great companies will create markets. Market leadership is gained by envisioning new products, services, lifestyles, and ways to raise living standards. There is a vast difference between companies offering "me-too" products and those creating previously unimagined product and service values.

Marketing at its best is about value creation and raising the world's living standards.

CONTEXT
Marketing Management is the definitive marketing textbook. Tightly argued and all-encompassing, its content has been expanded and brought up to date through various editions. The eighth edition, published in 1994, maps out the emerging challenges to all those involved in marketing.

The very size and scope of *Marketing Management* demonstrates the exponential expansion of marketing. Gary Hamel commented: "There are few MBA graduates alive who have not plowed through Kotler's encyclopedic textbook on marketing, and have not benefited enormously from doing so. I know of no other business author who covers his (or her) territory with such comprehensiveness, clarity, and authority as Phil Kotler. I can think of few other books, even within the vaunted company of this volume, whose insights would be of more practical benefit to the average company than those found in *Marketing Management*."

FOR MORE INFORMATION

Kotler, Philip. *Marketing Management: Analysis, Planning, Implementation, and Control.* 12th ed. Des Moines, IA: Prentice Hall, 2005.

1121

MANAGEMENT LIBRARY

"Good companies will meet needs; great companies will create markets."

Megatrends

John Naisbitt

WHY READ IT?

Megatrends was written in 1982 before the technology revolution took hold. It attempts to predict the key changes in business and society. Naisbitt correctly anticipated a number of factors such as globalization and the rise of an information economy.

GETTING STARTED

According to the author, we have changed to an economy based on the creation and distribution of information. Speed is a competitive weapon.

We must now acknowledge that we are part of a global economy. The bigger the world economy, the more powerful its smallest player—and in small organizations, we have rediscovered the ability to act innovatively and to achieve results from the bottom up. Big bureaucratic organizations can be beaten. Economies of scale are giving way to economies of scope. The acceleration of technological progress has created an urgent need for a return to human scale.

Empowerment, with responsibility, has become more important for everyone in an organization. We are more self-reliant and less hierarchical. Society is moving towards much longer-term time frames.

CONTRIBUTION

1. Toward the Information Economy

Although we continue to think we live in an industrial society, we have in fact changed to an economy based on the creation and distribution of information.

In the early 1980s however, traditional issues, such as production methods, still held sway. The technological possibilities in information exchange and transfer were contemplated by a small group in West-Coast laboratories.

2. Technology with a Human Scale

We are moving in the dual directions of high tech/high touch; each new technology is matched with a compensatory human response. Heart transplants led to new interest in family doctors and neighborhood clinics; jet aircraft resulted in more face-to-face meetings.

High touch is about getting back to a human scale. All change is local and bottom-up. If you keep track of local events, you can see the shifting patterns.

You can't stop technological progress, but by the same token, you can hardly go wrong with a high-touch response. FedEx has all the reliability and efficiency of modern electronics, but its success is built on a form of high-touch hand delivery.

3. The Emergence of a Global Economy

We no longer have the luxury of operating within an isolated, self-sufficient, national economic system. We must now acknowledge that we are part of a global economy.

We have begun to let go of the idea that the United States is the world's industrial leader as we move on to other tasks.

The global paradox is that the bigger the world economy, the more powerful its smallest player.

4. A Longer Time Frame

We are moving away from a society governed by short-term considerations and rewards to one which deals with things in much longer-term time frames.

5. The Growth of Empowerment

In cities and states, in small organizations and subdivisions, we have rediscovered the ability to act innovatively and to achieve results from the bottom up.

Naisbitt anticipated the fashion in the late 1980s and early 1990s for empowerment with responsibility being spread more evenly throughout organizations, rather than centered on a small group of managers.

6. Greater Self-reliance

We are shifting from institutional help to more self-reliance in all aspects of our lives.

Trends in working patterns suggest that this is becoming the case for a select few professionals with marketable skills.

7. Changing Framework of Democracy

We are discovering that the framework of representative democracy has become obsolete in an era of instantaneously shared information.

Alvin Toffler was suggesting this in his 1970 book *Future Shock*, though there are few signs of reform.

8. Informal Networks Replacing Hierarchy

We are giving up our dependence on hierarchical structures in favor of informal networks. This will be especially important to the business community.

This has become one of the great trends of the last decade as networks are developed in a bewildering variety of ways—with suppliers, between competitors, internally, and globally.

Technology has enabled networks never previously anticipated, with important repercussions. When everyone hears about everything at the same time, we all know that everyone is equally well-informed.

9. Speed as a Competitive Weapon

Linked to this is the entire question of speed, which Naisbitt identified early on as a competitive weapon.

Economies of scale are giving way to economies of scope, finding the right size for synergy, market flexibility, and above all, speed.

10. More Choice for Society

From a narrow "either/or" society with a limited range of personal choices, we are exploding into a free-wheeling, multiple-option society.

11. The Power of Small Businesses

Naisbitt championed the role of small business in generating the wealth of the future. Small companies, right down to the individual, can beat big bureaucratic companies every time.

Unless big companies reconstitute themselves as a collection of small companies, they will just continue to go out of business.

It's the small companies who are creating the global company.

CONTEXT

Megatrends identified ten critical restructurings. Some have proved accurate predictions of what has happened in intervening years, others have proved less accurate.

Naisbitt predicted the rise of the information economy when the technology was still a laboratory product and he identified the emergence of factors such as globalization and empowerment.

FOR MORE INFORMATION

Naisbitt, John. *Megatrends*. New York: Warner Books, 1984.

The Mind of the Strategist
Kenichi Ohmae

WHY READ IT?

The book illuminates the strategic thinking behind Japanese corporate success. The author shows how and why it differs from the Western approach to strategic thinking and explains that Western companies can adapt to this successful model.

GETTING STARTED

The author argues that to a large extent, Japanese success can be attributed to the nature of Japanese strategic thinking. Japanese businesses tend not to have large strategic planning staffs. The customer is at the heart of the Japanese approach to strategy. There are three main players in any business strategy—the corporation itself, the customer, and the competition—collectively called the strategic triangle. Just as events in the real world do not always fit a linear model, the Japanese approach to strategy is irrational and nonlinear.

CONTRIBUTION

1. Strategy Determines Japanese Success

Japanese success can be attributed to the nature of Japanese strategic thinking. This is basically creative and intuitive rather than rational, but the necessary creativity can be learned.

Unlike large U.S. corporations, Japanese businesses tend not to have large strategic planning staffs. Instead they often have a single, idiosyncratic, naturally-talented strategist.

From the dynamic interaction of the company, customers, and competition, a comprehensive set of objectives and plans eventually emerges.

2. The Customer at the Center

In contrast to the West, the customer is at the heart of the Japanese approach to strategy and the key to corporate values.

3. Strategic Triangle

In the construction of any business strategy, three main players must be taken into account: the corporation itself, the customer, and the competition. Collectively they are called the strategic triangle.

The job of the strategist is to achieve superior performance. At the same time, the strategist must be sure that his strategy matches the strengths of the corporation with the needs of a clearly defined market. Otherwise, the corporation's long-term viability may be at stake.

4. Strategy is Irrational

The central thrust of the book is that strategy as epitomized by the Japanese approach is irrational and nonlinear.

In strategic thinking, one first seeks a clear understanding of each element of a situation, and then makes the fullest use of human brain power to restructure the elements in the most advantageous way.

Events in the real world do not always fit a linear model. Hence the most reliable means of dissecting a situation into its constituent parts, and reassembling them in the desired pattern, is not a step-by-step methodology, but the ultimate nonlinear thinking tool, the human brain.

True strategic thinking thus not only contrasts sharply with the conventional mechanical systems approach, but also with the purely intuitive approach, which reaches conclusions without any kind of breakdown or analysis.

5. Gaining Ground through Effective Strategy

An effective business strategy is one by which a company can gain significant ground on its competitors at an acceptable cost to itself. There are four main ways of achieving this:
- focusing on the key factors for success (KFS);
- building on relative superiority;
- pursuing aggressive initiatives;
- utilizing strategic degrees of freedom.

The principal concern is to avoid doing the same thing, on the same battleground, as the competition.

6. Focusing on Key Factors for Success

Certain functional or operating areas within every business are more critical for success in that particular business environment than others.

If you concentrate effort into these areas and your competitors do not, this is a source of competitive advantage. The problem lies in identifying these key factors for success.

Today's industry leaders, without exception, began by bold deployment of strategies based on KFS.

7. Building on Relative Superiority

When all competitors are seeking to compete on the KFS, a company can exploit any differences in competitive conditions.

For example, it can make use of technology or sales networks not in direct competition with its rivals.

8. Pursuing Aggressive Initiatives

Frequently, the only way to win against a much larger, entrenched competitor is to upset the competitive environment, by undermining the value of its KFS.

That means changing the rules of the game by introducing new KFS.

9. Utilizing Strategic Degrees of Freedom

This means that the company should focus upon innovation in areas that are untouched by competitors.

CONTEXT

The author is Japan's only successful management guru. The book was published in the West at the height of interest in Japanese management methods.

Ohmae challenged the simplistic belief that Japanese management was a matter of company songs and lifetime employment. Instead, Japanese success could be attributed to the nature of Japanese strategic thinking.

Bestselling author Gary Hamel commented, "I loved this book! At a time when most strategy savants were focused either on the process of planning (Ansoff and his followers) or on the determinants of successful, that is, profitable, strategies (Michael Porter), Kenichi Ohmae challenged managers to think in new ways. Strategy doesn't come from a calendar-driven process; it isn't the product of a systematic search for ways of earning above-average profits; strategy comes from viewing the world in new ways. Strategy starts with an ability to think in new and unconventional ways."

FOR MORE INFORMATION

Ohmae, Kenichi. *The Mind of the Strategist: The Art of Japanese Business.* Revised ed. New York: McGraw-Hill, 1991.

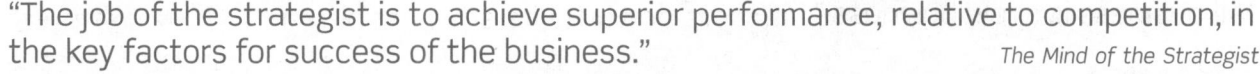

"The job of the strategist is to achieve superior performance, relative to competition, in the key factors for success of the business."
The Mind of the Strategist

Moments of Truth

Jan Carlzon

WHY READ IT?

Jan Carlzon is a Swedish businessman who shot to international prominence by leading a turnaround at the Scandinavian airline, SAS. The turnaround was based on excellence in customer service, and the book contains many practical examples of the way this can be applied. The SAS story is one of the most frequently-used case studies in customer service training and literature.

GETTING STARTED

Carlzon used customer service as a vehicle for turning the SAS airline around. He held that quality service is built around moments of truth—the critical transactions at each stage of the ownership or use cycle. These critical transactions occur at initial contact; first use; problem solving; ongoing support; further purchases; and recommendations to others. Customer satisfaction and value are affected at different points in the cycle. They also vary by customer type.

This approach owes much to the Scandinavian management style—humane and people centered. Scandinavian companies embraced team working and employee participation before they became fashionable: their leaders are anti-authoritarian; they make very effective use of coaching and mentoring, and they also communicate consistently and continually.

CONTRIBUTION

1. Making Customer Service Work

Carlzon actually made customer service work and used it as a vehicle for turning the SAS airline—formerly an indifferent performer—into a world class organization.

Carlzon came up with the phrase, "moments of truth"—the sequence of critical transactions across each stage of the ownership or use cycle. Any time a customer comes into contact with any aspect of a business, however remote, is an opportunity to form an impression.

2. Identifying Moments of Truth

The critical transactions are broken down into:

- initial contact;
- first use;
- problem solving;
- on-going support;
- further purchases;
- recommendations to others.

The key to understanding customer behavior is to: 1) evaluate the degree to which satisfaction and value are affected at these different points in the cycle; 2) understand how they vary by customer type.

Carlzon decided dramatically to prove the company's dedication to these moments of truth by sending tens of thousands of SAS managers on specially-tailored training programs.

3. The Success of the Scandinavian Approach

Like most stereotypes, the image of highly motivated, well-rewarded, hard-working, and contented Scandinavians is only partly true. However, Scandinavian companies have a track record of managing their human resources in innovative ways. Their management style tends to be humane and people centered, and they were champions of team working and employee participation long before they became the height of managerial fashion.

Scandinavians have very stable political systems and fairly homogeneous societies, and problems typically are solved through negotiation. Historically there has been little unrest—but the counter to this is that often, without a crisis, advancement is not achieved.

Scandinavian business culture shares some characteristics with that of the Japanese. Saving face is important and, rather than direct frontal attack, Scandinavians prefer a more indirect and subtle approach.

4. A Scandinavian Leadership Style

Old-fashioned virtues are in. Typically, in one survey cited by Carlzon, U.S. executives rated honesty as the prime business virtue. Swedish executives did not include honesty at all—it was assumed.

The Scandinavian leader tends to be decidedly anti-authoritarian. Highly personal and practical theories, such as coaching and mentoring, find fertile ground; being upfront and communicating openly is expected. With Carlzon and others there is a certain amount of showmanship—they play their roles to perfection. They stand in the middle of their strategy. They don't preach the strategy; they are the strategy. They communicate consistently and continually. They repeat the same messages again and again. But they never grow tired of saying them—there is no sign of boredom, no cynicism, no sarcasm. They give words real meaning. This appetite for communication is clearly linked to a more humane style of management.

CONTEXT

Carlzon set in train SAS's revival, which became a benchmark for international best practice in customer service. The achievement was celebrated, among many others, by Tom Peters in *A Passion for Excellence*.

After Carlzon left SAS, the company's halo slipped a little and Scandinavian role models were thin on the ground for a number of years. During the 1990s, however, there was a steady stream of corporate benchmarks. The new Scandinavian role models—IKEA, Skandia, Oticon, and ABB—remain indebted to Carlzon's example.

FOR MORE INFORMATION

Carlzon, Jan. *Moments of Truth*. New York: Collins, 1989.

Motivation and Personality Abraham Maslow

WHY READ IT?

Maslow introduced the concept of a hierarchy of needs which has formed an integral part of marketing, human resource, motivational, and management literature ever since. The book makes an important contribution to the emergence of human relations as a professional discipline.

GETTING STARTED

There is an ascending scale of needs that provides the basis for motivation. Basic physiological needs come first; once these are met, other needs dominate. At the top of the scale is self-actualization, where individuals achieve their personal potential. Also high up are social or love needs, and ego or self-esteem needs.

The hierarchy of needs provides a rational framework for motivation, and human nature determines that motivation is intrinsically linked to rewards.

CONTRIBUTION
1. The Hierarchy of Needs

There is an ascending scale of needs, which must be understood if people are to be motivated. First are the fundamental physiological needs of warmth, shelter, and food. It is quite true that man lives by bread alone—when there is no bread.

But what happens when there is plenty of bread?

2. Emerging Needs

Once basic physiological needs are met, others emerge to dominate. These can be categorized roughly as the safety needs. If a person's state is sufficiently extreme and chronic, he or she may be characterized as living almost for safety alone.

Next on the hierarchy are social or love needs, and ego or self-esteem needs.

3. Self-actualization

As each need is satisfied, eventually comes self-actualization—the individual achieves his or her own potential.

4. From Motivation to Reward

While the hierarchy of needs provides a rational framework for motivation, its flaw lies in the nature of humanity. People always want more. When asked what salary they would be comfortable with, people routinely—no matter what their income—name a figure around twice their current income.

Instead of being driven by punishment and deprivation, motivation became intrinsically linked to reward.

CONTEXT

Abraham Maslow was a member of the Human Relations School of the late 1950s, which also included Douglas McGregor and Frederick Herzberg.

Motivation and Personality is best known for its hierarchy of needs—a concept that was first published by Maslow in 1943. He argues that there is an ascending scale of needs, which must be understood if people are to be motivated. While the hierarchy of needs provides a rational framework for motivation, its flaw lies in the nature of humanity.

Maslow's hierarchy of needs contributed to the emergence of human relations as a discipline, and to a sea-change in the perception of motivation.

Gary Hamel commented: "However subtle and variegated the original theory, time tends to reduce it to its most communicable essence: hence Maslow's hierarchy of needs, Pascale's seven Ss, Michael Porter's five forces, and the Boston Consulting Group's growth/share matrix. Yet there is no framework that has so broadly infiltrated organizational life as Maslow's hierarchy of needs. Perhaps this is because it speaks so directly to the aspirations each of us holds for ourself."

FOR MORE INFORMATION

Maslow, Abraham. *Motivation and Personality*. 3rd ed. New York: Harper & Row, 1987.

"It is quite true that man lives by bread alone—when there is no bread."

Motivation and Personality

The Motivation to Work

**Frederick Herzberg
Bernard Mausner
Barbara Bloch Snyderman**

WHY READ IT?

Herzberg's work has had a lasting influence on human resource management. Concepts such as job enrichment, self-development, and job satisfaction have evolved from his insight that motivation comes from within the individual, rather than from a policy imposed by the company.

GETTING STARTED

Employee motivation can be improved through greater emphasis on human relations.

Research indicates that motivation at work takes two forms—hygiene factors and motivation factors. Hygiene factors, which cover basic needs at work, include working conditions, benefits, and job security. Motivation factors, which meet uniquely human needs, include achievement, personal development, job satisfaction, and recognition. Improvements in hygiene factors remove the barriers to positive attitudes in the workplace, although hygiene factors alone are not sufficient to provide true motivation to work.

Employers should aim to motivate people through job satisfaction, rather than reward or pressure.

CONTRIBUTION
1. The Importance of Employee Attitudes

"People are our greatest assets" has become one of the most over-used clichés in business. However, before Herzberg, "people issues" took a low priority in management literature. Management thinkers rarely sought the opinions of employees, or considered them worthy of study. Herzberg and his colleagues, Mausner and Snyderman, highlighted the importance of employee attitudes through a study of 203 Pittsburgh engineers and accountants. By asking what pleased and displeased people about their jobs, he raised the wider question: "How do you motivate employees?"

2. Identifying Factors That Motivate Employees

Herzberg made a critical distinction between factors that cause unhappiness at work and factors that contribute to job satisfaction. This distinction was based on his earlier work in public health, where he had concluded that mental health was not the opposite of mental illness. Transferring that concept to the workplace, he suggested that the reverse of the factors that make people happy did not make them unhappy. His research indicated that motivation at work takes two forms—hygiene factors and motivation factors.

3. Hygiene Factors

Hygiene factors cover basic needs at work. They include working conditions, supervision levels, company policies, benefits, and job security. If these are poor or deteriorate, they lead to dissatisfaction with work. Conversely, improvements in hygiene factors remove the barriers to positive attitudes in the workplace. However, improvement in hygiene factors alone is not sufficient to provide true job satisfaction.

4. Motivation Factors

Herzberg discovered that the factors that lead to dissatisfaction are completely different from those that provide satisfaction. He called the positive factors "motivation factors." These meet uniquely human needs and include achievement, personal development, job satisfaction, and recognition. Improving these factors can make people satisfied with work.

3. Challenging the Reward Process

Herzberg concluded that organizations should aim to motivate people through job satisfaction, rather than reward or pressure.

This led to the concept of job enrichment, which would enable organizations to liberate people from the tyranny of numbers and expand the creative role of an individual within the organization.

CONTEXT

Herzberg was one of the humanist school of management thinking, emphasizing the human aspects of organizations, in contrast to the mechanistic views of scientific thinkers. The humanist tradition includes Mary Parker Follett, Elton Mayo, Douglas McGregor, Abraham Maslow, Charles Handy, and Tom Peters.

Maslow's hierarchy of needs, formulated in 1943, influenced industrial psychologists like Herzberg by showing that work can be made more satisfying by giving greater emphasis to affection, ego, and self-actualization needs.

Herzberg's breakthrough was to identify hygiene and motivation factors. His work has had a lasting influence on human resource management: concepts such as job enrichment, self-development, and job satisfaction have evolved from his insight that motivation comes from within the individual, rather than from a policy imposed by the company. It has also influenced organizations' rewards and remuneration packages.

The trend toward "cafeteria benefits" reflects Herzberg's belief that people choose the form of motivation that is most important to them. Many organizations believe that money is the sole motivation for workers; Herzberg offers a more subtle approach. There has been much subsequent academic debate on the extent to which pay or other factors are the most important motivators.

Guru Gary Hamel commented: "Too many organizations believe that the only motivation to work is an economic one. Treating knowledge assets like Skinnerian rats is hardly the way to get the best out of people. Herzberg offers a substantially more subtle approach—one that still has much to recommend it."

Critics of Herzberg argue that pay plays an important part in the motivational equation, and can be used to reinforce other motivational levers. Others point out that people frequently describe good work experiences in terms that reflect credit on themselves—success, greater responsibility, or recognition. Conversely, they will blame bad work experiences on factors that are outside their control, such as poor working conditions or a difficult boss.

Recent commentators believe that the main application of Herzberg's theories has been to nonmanual workers, where the hygiene factors are normally well satisfied. They believe that employees who were well rewarded would tend to emphasize motivational factors as more important.

FOR MORE INFORMATION

Herzberg, Frederick, et al. *The Motivation to Work*. Revised ed. Somerset, NJ: Transaction, 2003.

"If you have someone on a job, use him. If you can't use him, get rid of him."

My Life and Work
Henry Ford

WHY READ IT?

My Life and Work is an account of Henry Ford's life and business philosophy. It provides unique insights into the man who took mass production to new levels and opened up mass markets through consistently low pricing and standardization. It also highlights the risk of a single-product strategy and the problems of autocratic control.

GETTING STARTED

Ford's policy was to reduce the price, extend the operations, and improve the article. He did not bother about the costs. Price forces the costs down. Ford reduced prices by 58% at a time when demand was such that he could easily have raised them instead. Mass production was the consequence, not the cause, of his low prices.

Management and managers were dismissed by Ford as largely unnecessary—but his lack of faith in management, along with its total reliance on the Model T, later proved the undoing of the company.

CONTRIBUTION
1. Pricing and Costs

Ford stated his policy as being, "to reduce the price, extend the operations, and improve the article. The reduction of price comes first. We have never considered any costs as fixed. Therefore we first reduce the price to the point where we believe more sales will result. Then we go ahead and try to make the prices. We do not bother about the costs. The new price forces the costs down. The more usual way is to take the costs and then determine the price, and although that method may be scientific in the narrow sense, it is not scientific in the broad sense. What use is it to know the cost, if it tells you that you cannot manufacture at a price at which the article can be sold?"

Ford's commitment to lowering prices cannot be doubted. Between 1908 and 1916 he reduced prices by 58% at a time when demand was such that he could easily have raised them.

2. Marketing

In a sense Ford was both the most brilliant and the most senseless marketer in U.S. history. He was senseless because he refused to give the customer anything but a black car. He was brilliant because he fashioned a production system designed to fit market needs.

We habitually celebrate him for the wrong reason, his production genius. His real genius was marketing.

3. Standardization

Ford realized that the mass car market existed—it just remained for him to provide the products the market wanted.

Model Ts were black, straightforward, and affordable. At the center of Ford's thinking was the goal of standardization—something continually emphasized by the automakers of today.

4. Problems of a Single Product

The problem was that when other manufacturers added extras, Ford kept it simple and dramatically lost ground.

Henry Ford is reputed to have kicked a slightly-modified Model T to pieces, such was his commitment to the unadulterated version. But the company's reliance on the Model T nearly drove it to self-destruction. The man with a genius for marketing lost touch with the aspirations of customers.

5. Mass Production

Ford is celebrated for his transformation of the production line into a means of previously unimagined mass production.

He calculated that the production of a Model T required 7,882 different operations. Production was based around strict functional divides or demarcations. Ford believed in people getting on with their jobs and not raising their heads above functional parapets. He didn't want engineers talking to salespeople, or people making decisions without his say so.

6. Authoritarian Control

Management and managers were dismissed by Ford as largely unnecessary, and he made a systematic, deliberate and conscious attempt to run the billion-dollar business without managers.

Ford's lack of faith in management proved the undoing of the huge corporate empire he assembled. Without his autocratic belligerence to drive the company forward, it quickly ground to a halt.

7. Innovation in Business

In some respects Ford remains a good role model. He was an improviser and innovator who borrowed ideas and then adapted and synthesized them. He developed flow lines that involved people; now, we have flow lines without people, but no-one questions their relevance or importance.

Though he is seen as having dehumanized work, Ford provided a level of wealth for workers and products for consumers which weren't previously available. He introduced the $5 wage for his workers which, at that time, was around twice the average for the industry.

He had an international perspective that was ahead of his time. His plant at Highland Park, Detroit, produced. But the world, not just the United States, bought.

Ford was acutely aware that time was an important competitive weapon. "Time waste differs from material waste in that there can be no salvage," he wrote.

CONTEXT

My Life and Work is a robust account of Ford's life and business philosophy, although it is notable for the dominance of the former and the lack of the latter. Ford's business achievements and contribution to the development of industrialization are likely to be remembered long after his theories on politics, history, motivation, or humanity.

Leading author Gary Hamel said, "Henry Ford may have been autocratic and paranoid, but he brought to men and women everywhere a stunningly precious gift—mobility. Whatever his faults, Henry Ford was driven by the dream of every great entrepreneur—to make a real difference in people's lives, and to do it globally."

FOR MORE INFORMATION

Ford, Henry. *My Life and Work*. Revised ed. North Stratford, NH: Ayer Company Publishers, 2000.

"I have no use for a motor car which has more spark plugs than a cow has teats."

My Life and Work

My Years with General Motors

Alfred P. Sloan, Jr.

WHY READ IT?

Alfred P. Sloan, Jr. is one of the very few figures who undoubtedly changed the world of management. He was also one of the first managers to write an important theoretical book. *My Years with General Motors* is an account of his remarkable career and the creation of a new organizational form that spawned a host of imitators.

GETTING STARTED

Alfred P. Sloan, Jr., a leading figure at General Motors from 1917, became its chief executive in 1946 and honorary chairman from 1956 until his death in 1966.

When he joined, the automobile market was dominated by Ford, and GM's market share was a mere 12%. GM was then an unwieldy combination of companies with eight models that competed against each other as well as against Ford. Sloan cut the eight models down to five and targeted each at a particular segment of the market. The five ranges were updated regularly and came in more than one color—unlike Ford's Model T. He also reshaped the organization so that it was better suited to deliver his aspirations.

He created eight divisions—five auto and three component divisions. In the jargon of 50 years later, these were strategic business units. Each had responsibility for its own commercial operations and its own engineering, production, and sales department. The divisions were supervised by a central staff responsible for overall policy and finance.

The main interest of *My Years with General Motors* for modern management thinkers lies in how Sloan managed to coordinate the semi-autonomous divisions with the center and balance flexibility with control.

CONTRIBUTION
1. Balancing Flexibility with Control

The policy that Sloan labeled "federal decentralization" marked the invention of the decentralized, divisionalized organization.

The multi-divisional form enabled Sloan to utilize the company's size without making it cumbersome. Executives had more time to concentrate on strategic issues and operational decisions were made by people in the front line rather than at a distant headquarters.

By 1925, with its new organization and commitment to annual changes in its models, GM had overtaken Ford. Sloan's segmentation of the company changed the structure of the auto industry and also provided a model for how companies could do the same in other industries.

2. Commitment to Employees

The book reveals that Sloan was committed to what at the time would have been regarded as progressive human resource management. In 1947 he established GM's employee-research section to look at employee attitudes, and he invested a large amount of his own time in selecting the right people for the job.

3. Problems in Decentralization

The decentralized structure built up by Sloan revolved around a reporting and committee infrastructure that eventually became unwieldy.

As time went by, more and more committees were established. Stringent targets and narrow measures of success stultified initiative. The organization proved quite unable to create and develop new businesses internally. This inability to manage organic expansion into new areas was caused by many factors:

- Operating responsibilities and measurement systems focused on profit and market share in existing markets.
- Business unit managers were not expected to look for new opportunities
- The boxes in the organization chart defined their product or geographic scope.
- Small new ventures could not absorb the large central overheads and return the profits needed to justify the financial and human investments.

As Sloan himself put it: "In practically all our activities we seem to suffer from the inertia resulting from our great size. There are so many people involved and it requires such a tremendous effort to put something new into effect that a new idea is likely to be considered insignificant in comparison with the effort that it takes to put it across."

CONTEXT

Sloan established GM as a benchmark of corporate might, a symbol of U.S. strength and success. "What's good for GM is good for America," ran the popular mythology. Peter Drucker and Alfred Chandler celebrated his approach, but the deficiencies of the model were clear to Sloan himself, and were most obviously manifested in the decline of GM.

By the end of the 1960s the delicate balance, which he had brilliantly maintained between centralization and decentralization, was lost. Finance emerged as the dominant function, and GM became paralyzed by what had once made it great.

Gary Hamel commented: "Can you be big and nimble? The question is as timely today as it was when Sloan took over General Motors. Despite divisionalization and decentralization, Sloan's organizational inventions, GM still fell victim to its size . . . [T]he corporate superstructure that emerged to manage GM's independent divisions was more successful in creating bureaucracy than in exploiting cross-divisional synergies. The challenge of achieving divisional autonomy and flexibility on one hand, while reaping the benefits of scale and coordination on the other, is one that has eluded not only GM, but many other large companies as well."

One thing that should not be forgotten is that Sloan believed in managers and management in a way that his great rival Henry Ford did not. Nevertheless, as *The Economist* said: "Alfred Sloan did for the upper layers of management what Henry Ford did for the shopfloor: he turned it into a reliable, efficient, machine-like process."

Of the book as a whole, Peter Drucker remarked: "It is perhaps the most impersonal book of memoirs ever written. And this was clearly intentional. Sloan's book knows only one dimension: that of managing a business so that it can produce effectively, provide jobs, create markets and sales, and generate profits."

FOR MORE INFORMATION

Sloan, Alfred P. *My Years with General Motors.* Revised ed. New York: Doubleday, 1990.

"I had learned that increased productivity would support higher wages."

Natural Capitalism

Paul Hawken
Amory B. Lovins
L. Hunter Lovins

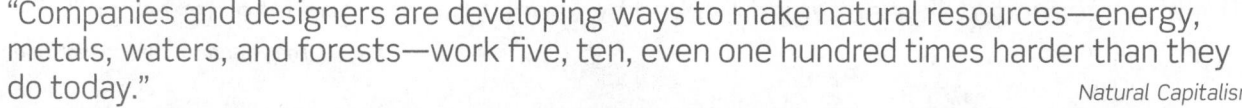

WHY READ IT?

The book offers an environmental perspective on economic activities. It includes practical advice on ways to transform business so that the Earth's resources are protected.

GETTING STARTED

Natural Capitalism recognizes the critical relationship between the traditional creation of financial capital and the maintenance of natural resources. The book suggests an approach for reconciling ecological and economic priorities, one that not only protects the Earth's environment, but also improves profits and competitiveness. Environmental and economic priorities are normally considered contradictory, so that any state of balance requires tradeoffs. However, they believe that the best solutions may be based on design integration at all levels of economic activity, an approach they call "natural capitalism."

CONTRIBUTION
1. The Concept of Natural Capital

"Natural capital," according to the authors, comprises the world's resources, living systems, and ecosystem services. These, they feel, are being depleted at a dangerous rate. They explain how increased resource productivity would enable business and consumers to obtain the same amount of utility from a product or process while using less material or energy. These natural efficiencies go way beyond industry's current marginal performance gains. They believe that, if natural capitalism became widely accepted, resource productivity could grow at least fourfold, allowing people to live twice as well, yet use half as much.

2. The Stages of Natural Capitalism

The authors divide natural capitalism into four key strategies:
- radical resource productivity
- biologically inspired production models
- a solutions-based business model
- reinvesting in natural capital

These strategies, they say, offer benefits and opportunities in markets, finance, materials, distribution, and employment.

3. Radical Resource Productivity

According to the authors, radical resource productivity is the cornerstone of natural capitalism. It means obtaining the same amount of utility or work from a product, while using fewer materials and less energy. In simple terms, this means doing more with less. The authors believe that fundamental changes in production design and technology offer the opportunity to develop ways to make natural resources such as energy, minerals, water, and forests stretch 5, 10, even 100 times further than they do today.

In manufacturing, transportation, forestry, construction, energy, and other industrial sectors, their evidence suggests that radical improvements in resource productivity are both practical and cost-effective. Designers, they believe, are already developing ways to make natural resources work much harder. These efficiencies transcend the marginal gains in performance that industry is constantly seeking as part of its evolution. According to the authors, these revolutionary leaps in design and technology will alter industry itself.

4. Biologically Inspired Production Models

Taking examples from the natural world, the authors show how living organisms can produce complex "products" from recycled materials using minimal amounts of sustainable resources. Some of these products, such as the spider's silk or the cellulose produced by trees, have qualities that outperform their human-made equivalents. They argue that industry should learn from these natural techniques, a process they call "bio-mimicry." This approach seeks not only to reduce waste, but to eliminate the very concept of waste.

They demonstrate how every output, in closed-loop production systems modeled on nature's designs, is returned harmlessly to the ecosystem as a nutrient, like compost, or becomes an input for manufacturing another product. They point out how this compares with the inefficiency of many production processes where as little as 6% of the materials consumed actually end up in the product.

5. A Solutions-based Business Model

The business model of traditional manufacturing rests on the sale of goods: a consumer uses the product for a limited period and disposes of it at the end of its useful life. This process, the authors argue, is extremely wasteful. They offer an alternative model, where a physical product owned by a consumer is replaced by a flow of services.

A simple example might be a washing machine that is owned, maintained, and upgraded by the manufacturer. When its useful life is finished, the manufacturer is responsible for recycling the product. Another example would be providing access to the entire catalogs of music companies by subscription rather than purchasing individual CDs. This shift of responsibility, they claim, would reduce consumption, but improve consumer choice.

6. Reinvesting in Natural Capital

According to the authors, sustaining, restoring, and expanding natural stocks of capital would work toward reversing worldwide planetary destruction, and governments are already recognizing the importance of using resource productivity to achieve this. They use terms such as "Factor Four," which means that resource productivity can and should grow fourfold: in other words, the amount of wealth extracted from one unit of natural resources can quadruple.

CONTEXT

Natural Capitalism is one of the increasing number of books that argue for a more ecologically sound approach to business. Unlike many more confrontational books that attack industry and offer no solution, *Natural Capitalism* shows how industry can adapt by learning from the natural world. While most commentators believe that environmental and economic priorities are contradictory, this book attempts to reconcile them. Above all, it indicates opportunities that could lead to nothing less than a transformation of commerce and all societal institutions.

FOR MORE INFORMATION

Hawken, Paul, Amory B. Lovins, and L. Hunter Lovins. *Natural Capitalism: The Next Industrial Revolution*. Boston, MA: Back Bay Books, 2000.

"Companies and designers are developing ways to make natural resources—energy, metals, waters, and forests—work five, ten, even one hundred times harder than they do today."

Natural Capitalism

The Nature of Managerial Work

Henry Mintzberg

WHY READ IT?

Mintzberg is regarded by many as a leading contemporary management thinker, and this book was the first to explore what managers actually do at work. It goes behind the myths and the self-perceptions to describe the day-to-day work of a manager.

GETTING STARTED

What managers actually do, how they do it, and why, are fundamental questions. Managers believe they deal with big strategic issues—in reality they move from task to task dogged by diversions. Managerial work in general is marked by variety, brevity, and fragmentation.

Managers have three key roles and the prominence of each role varies in different managerial jobs.

CONTRIBUTION

1. What Managers Do—The Myth

What managers actually do, how they do it, and why they do it, are fundamental questions. There are a number of generally accepted answers.

Managers believe:

- that they sit in solitude contemplating the great strategic issues of the day;
- that they make time to reach the best possible decisions;
- that their meetings are high-powered, concentrating on the meta-narrative rather than the nitty-gritty.

The reality largely went unexplored until Henry Mintzberg's book.

2. What Managers Do—The Reality

Mintzberg went in search of the reality. He simply observed what a number of managers actually did. The resulting book blew away the managerial mystique.

Managers did not spend time contemplat-ing the long term. They were slaves to the moment, moving from task to task with every move dogged by another diversion, another call. The median time spent by a manager on any one issue was a mere nine minutes.

3. The Characteristics of the Manager at Work

Mintzberg observed that the typical man-ager:

- performs a great quantity of work at an un-relenting pace;
- undertakes activities marked by variety, brevity, and fragmentation;
- has a preference for issues that are cur-rent, specific, and nonroutine;
- prefers verbal rather than written means of communication;
- acts within a web of internal and external contacts;
- is subject to heavy constraints but can exert some control over the work.

4. Managers' Key Roles

From these observations, Mintzberg identi-fied the manager's work roles as:

- interpersonal
- informational
- decisional

5. Interpersonal Roles

- figurehead: representing the organiza-tion/unit to outsiders
- leader: motivating subordinates, unifying effort
- liaiser: maintaining lateral contacts

6. Informational Roles

- monitor: overseeing information flows
- disseminator: providing information to sub-ordinates
- spokesman: transmitting information to outsiders

7. Decisional Roles

- entrepreneur: initiating and designing change
- disturbance handler: handling nonroutine events
- resource allocator: deciding who gets what and who will do what
- negotiator: negotiating

All managerial work encompasses these roles, but the prominence of each role varies in different managerial jobs.

CONTEXT

Henry Mintzberg is perhaps the world's premier management thinker, according to Tom Peters. His reputation has been made not by popularizing new techniques, but by rethinking the business fundamentals of strategy and structure, management, and planning.

His work on strategy—in particular his ideas of emergent strategy and grass-roots strategy making—has been highly influen-tial.

Influential author Gary Hamel com-mented: "Five reasons I like Henry Mintz-berg: he is a world class iconoclast. He loves the messy world of real companies. He is a master storyteller. He is conceptual and pragmatic. He doesn't believe in easy an-swers."

The Nature of Managerial Work has pro-duced few worthwhile imitators, but Mintz-berg's rigor and originality have given his ideas staying power.

FOR MORE INFORMATION

Mintzberg, Henry. *The Nature of Managerial Work*. New York: Harper & Row, 1973.

"The manager undertakes activities marked by variety, brevity, and fragmentation."

The New Corporate Cultures
Terrence Deal
Allan Kennedy

WHY READ IT?

Deal and Kennedy wrote the first significant book on corporate culture, *Corporate Cultures: Rites and Rituals of Corporate Life*, in 1982. Their later book, *The New Corporate Cultures*, reexamines its role in the light of accelerating changes in the business environment. They set out to demonstrate how organizations with a strong culture have survived and succeeded, despite the impact of globalization, information technology, mergers, and downsizing, and how an understanding of corporate cultures, coupled with strong leadership, can prove an effective model for business.

GETTING STARTED

The authors argue that corporate culture is a unifying factor that enables people to cooperate to achieve a common goal. However, a number of factors have militated against the development and maintenance of an effective culture—the demand for short-term results, the impact of downsizing and mergers, the introduction of outsourcing, and the effect of computers on business relationships. Organizations wishing to regain lost ground must now rebuild their cultures from the bottom up through strong leadership and high performance.

CONTRIBUTION
1. Culture Breeds Financial Success

The authors demonstrate the value of corporate culture by analyzing financial performance. The companies they identified as top performers in 1982 outperformed average stock market growth by nearly 50%.

2. The Impact of Short-term Needs

They also explain, however, how the rise of stockholder value played a key role in reducing the importance of corporate culture. The emphasis on short-term results, coupled with a growth in institutional ownership, meant that long-term actions proved unattractive to many organizations.

Short-termism, they believe, had a significant impact on employee loyalty and productivity, initiating a vicious circle that produced more and more short-term responses. Cutting costs to achieve short-term results led to a wave of downsizing and reengineering. This, in turn, ended the concept of lifetime employment and destroyed trust within organizations.

3. Outsourcing, Downsizing, Mergers, and IT

Downsizing, say the authors, damages a corporate culture by destroying trust and breaking the link between leaders and employees.

Outsourcing, they claim, has a similarly damaging effect, since when organizations focus on their core activities and outsource everything else, employees may be transferred to other organizations, losing benefits and severing their links with the original employer.

The increase in mergers has likewise tested corporate cultures. Mergers create a climate of uncertainty for employees, because there are always winners and losers.

Information technology too has, in their view, had a significant adverse effect. Although personal computers empower the people who use them, they can also isolate people from each other and break the informal links that are an important part of corporate culture.

4. The Effect of Globalization

Globalization, according to Deal and Kennedy, has accelerated the outsourcing and downsizing trends by enabling companies to source from around the world. Management is also affected by globalization, as multinational managers struggle to operate in different cultures.

5. The Need for Cultural Leadership

The authors believe that cultural leadership is key to overcoming the problems that have emerged. Managers must find out what employees really believe about the company and translate that into a statement that represents the company's position. Finding the common ground and turning it into set of shared beliefs helps to shape the overall corporate vision.

6. Challenge People

It is important, the authors suggest, to measure the progress of cultural revitalization in financial terms. Celebrating victories can bring people together. However, performance standards should not necessarily be based on financial targets. Setting people other challenges can help to create a strong culture.

Companies must rebuild trust by emphasizing the importance of employees to

the business. Transparency is an important part of that process. To ensure a high standard of performance, the authors recommend hiring and rewarding the right people. However, they point out that the organizational structure must be right to get the most from people. A rigid divisional structure tends to isolate people, so transferring them can help to redress the balance.

7. Building Teamwork

The authors recommend the introduction of cultural revitalization teams with access to senior management. The team should try to identify subcultures, small informal groups who work together and can form the basis of strong teams. Encouraging formal and informal meetings also helps to rebuild the connections inside a company.

Rebuilding the social context of work helps give people a sense of belonging. The authors explain how job security, job satisfaction, and a socially rewarding environment create a more attractive culture.

CONTEXT

When Deal and Kennedy introduced the term "corporate cultures" in 1982, it received a mixed reaction. Supporters believed it gave a valuable insight into the inner workings of an organization. Critics felt it was a superficial application of the discipline of anthropology to management.

The term is now an accepted part of business language and forms a key element of corporate strategy. Edgar Schein, writing in *Organization, Culture, and Leadership*, believes the only important thing leaders do is create and manage corporate culture.

In 1995, *Fortune* magazine published a survey on corporate reputation and introduced the feature with a comment that robust culture appeared to be the factor that set the top-ranking companies apart.

FOR MORE INFORMATION

Deal, Terrence, and Allan Kennedy. *The New Corporate Cultures*. Reading, MA: Perseus Books, 2000.

FURTHER READING
Deal, Terrence, and Allan Kennedy. *Corporate Cultures: Rites and Rituals of Corporate Life*. Reading, MA: Perseus Books, 2000.

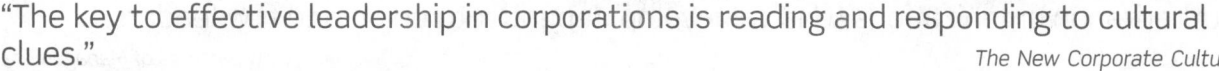

"The key to effective leadership in corporations is reading and responding to cultural clues."

The New Corporate Cultures

1131

MANAGEMENT LIBRARY

New Patterns of Management

Rensis Likert

WHY READ IT?

The author was a pioneer of attitude surveys and introduced an attitude scale that is now widely used in business research. The book explains how he used his research tools to identify patterns of participative management and organization that would bring success in an increasingly competitive environment.

GETTING STARTED

Rensis Likert was a pioneer of attitude surveys and poll design, as well as social research as a whole. According to Likert, there are four types of management style:

- exploitative and authoritarian
- benevolent autocracy
- consultative
- participative

Participative management is the best option, as increased participation and individualism is essential to meet increased competition. Participative groups can improve management and performance. The greater the loyalty of a group, the greater the motivation to achieve its goals.

An organization's style can be linked directly to its performance. The route to understanding managerial performance is improved measurement.

CONTRIBUTION
1. Measuring Attitudes

In his doctoral thesis, written in 1932 while Likert was at Columbia University, and entitled *A Technique for the Measurement of Attitudes*, he introduced a straightforward five-point scale by which attitudes could be measured. The now well-known scale ranges from "strongly agree" to "strongly disagree" and is known as the Likert Scale.

2. The Contribution of Participative Groups

Likert's business research focused on the ways in which participative groups could improve management and performance. It also examined the human systems that exist in organizations.

The greater the loyalty of a group, the greater is the motivation among members to achieve the goals of the group, and the greater the probability that the group will achieve its goals.

3. Management Styles

Likert identified four types of management style each of which tends to mold people in its own image. Authoritarian organizations tend to develop dependent people and few leaders. Participative management was seen by Likert as the best option, both in a business and a personal sense. Participative organizations tend to develop emotionally and socially mature people capable of effective interaction, initiative, and leadership.

4. Organization Style and Performance

"Managers with the best records of performance in American business and government are in the process of pointing the way to an appreciably more effective system of management than now exists," Likert wrote in the book's opening. With the assistance of social science research, it is now possible to state a generalized theory of organization based on the management practices of these highest producers.

5. The Importance of Participation

Increased participation in the workplace and individualism are necessary consequences of increased competition and fast-accelerating technological improvement. Likert asserts that there is much greater need for cooperation and participation in managing the enterprise than when technologies were simple and the chief possessed all the technical knowledge needed.

6. The Importance of Measurement

Management can make a difference, and the route to understanding managerial performance is improved measurement. In the author's opinion, an organization should be outstanding in its performance:

- if it has competent personnel;
- if it has leadership which develops highly effective groups and uses the overlapping group form of structure;
- if it achieves effective communication and influence, decentralized and coordinated decision making, and high performance goals coupled with high motivation.

CONTEXT

Likert's research highlights the importance of participative styles of management. This book bids farewell to the world of blind obedience and corporate man or woman. Likert picks up the mood of individualism, which was to sweep the world later in the 1960s. The book provides a blueprint for the ideal organization, which has largely stood the test of time.

FOR MORE INFORMATION

Likert, Rensis. *New Patterns of Management*. New York: McGraw-Hill, 1961.

"Authoritarian organizations tend to develop dependent people and few leaders."

New Patterns of Management

No Logo

Naomi Klein

WHY READ IT?

No Logo is not a business handbook: it is an analysis of the impact of unchecked globalization. The book posits that nation states have been rendered powerless, while corporations have gained *de facto* power. Klein's controversial political opinions earned her the soubriquet of "Marx for the new millennium." Drawing on four years' research, *No Logo* details the origins of a global economic system and explores anticorporate "resistance." After the collapse of the WTO trade talks in Seattle in 1999 following massive street protests and the now seemingly routine demonstrations that dog any international trade meeting, Klein's message is one to make many a chief executive sit up and take notice.

GETTING STARTED

No Logo sets out to show how three forces have given rise to waves of anticorporate activism to the fore. These forces are: the subverting of indigenous cultures through global branding; the loss of choice as brands overrule demand through predatory franchising, mergers, aggressive advertising, and corporate censorship; and the changes in global labour markets towards cheap labor, temporary working, and "portfolio" careers. Corporate social responsibility is rejected because it "favours only those being responsible." Klein's focus is on the reaction to this and does not blame the suggestion that the world is "getting smaller." Instead, she questions how "small" the world actually is by dispelling the romantic myth of the tribal nomad in a jungle playing video games via a broadband satellite connection, and by drawing attention to the "digital divide." Klein argues that public activism is the only democratic alternative to unchecked globalization.

CONTRIBUTION
1. The Birth of the Brand

According to Klein, the development of economies of scale has required production to shift to locations that can offer suppliers the cheapest prices. Fashion and familiarity are essential to generating sales, as symbolized by Philip Morris's acquisition of Kraft for $12.6 billion—six times the company's real equity. The high price derived from Kraft's brand: its name brought tangible sales. Distinguishing between advertising—merely informing customers of something—

and branding, Klein argues that communicating a powerful, emotionally resonant "image" distorts markets through changing tastes. The number of channels communicating "brands" are increasing: even schools grant exclusive advertising rights in canteens, corridors, and toilets. Klein suggests that brands put image before products: IBM do not sell computers, for example, they sell "solutions." Richard Branson argues that brands revolve solely around reputation: a fragile strategy. If Branson's Virgin Trains are late, though, Klein argues, people will lose trust in his airline, record shops, and financial products.

2. Space, Choice, and Jobs

In Klein's view, big brands force out small businesses by using mergers, predatory pricing, and economies of scale to ensure that they cannot survive. Branding ensures there is only a market for specific "images," which creates monopolies. Only multinationals can employ such anti-competitive measures: gaining ever-greater levels of marketshare, they take over a disproportionate amount of physical space. Starbucks coffee shops operate by "clustering": saturating areas with branches to force local cafes out of the market. Klein suggests that this removes consumer choice and destroys the local culture. A few corporations—a plutocracy—have unprecedented control.

According to the author, this has altered the labour market. After a century of improvements in working standards, corporations in both the developed and developing world are abusing their position. Klein suggests that scenes common during the industrial revolution recur in the developing world today. Child labor, excessive working hours, low pay, and hazardous conditions put a downward pressure on wages globally. "Outsourcing" produces lower wages and higher unemployment in rich countries. Globalization makes this inevitable in Klein's view: maximising profit means producing where labor is cheaper. The author uses the example of Cavite, the Filipino free-trade zone, where workers face rules against talking and smiling and must endure forced overtime. Klein argues that branding prevents consumers from questioning multinational corporations and their unethical actions and removes the incentive to behave responsibly. Now, concern about unethical practices is pressuring corporations into

being socially responsible. One urban teenager said, "Nike, we made you. We can break you." This, Klein suggests, is the new democracy.

3. No Logo

No Logo shows how resistance to brands has developed as consumers feel rising resentment at brands' colonization of their lives, some even suggesting that the backlash is comparable to the civil rights campaigns of earlier generations. There are boycotts against "unethical" companies and activists are "as global and capable of co-ordinated action as the multinational corporations they seek to subvert." Some successful corporations pride themselves on working "responsibly"; Shell, for example, has commited resources to developing "clean" fuels. Klein argues that consumers are becoming cynical, though. Nike has advertised that "high heels are a conspiracy against women," which is often interpreted as a self-serving attempt to be both anti-sexist and justify exorbitant prices. The "brand backlash" has begun.

CONTEXT

Critics view the anticorporate movement as having no common ideology except angry anarchism. When "indigenous" cultures choose development, they are denounced as being "exploited" by "imperialists." In fact, many East-Asian Tiger economies, such as Taiwan and Japan, have become as rich as the societies they trade with. However, if consumers are antagonized by those aiming to serve their needs, something is wrong. If corporations put "image" before delivering value, consumers will lose trust in them. Reflecting the fact that the anticorporate movement is in its infancy, *No Logo* ignores the benefits of the system it condemns—including the greater accountability brands have over local businesses, or technology transfer to low-cost locations—while providing few practical solutions. What it does do, however, is draw its readers' attention to the need for greater—and genuine—corporate social responsibility.

FOR MORE INFORMATION

Klein, Naomi. *No Logo*. New York: Picador USA, 2002.

1133

MANAGEMENT LIBRARY

Now, Discover Your Strengths

Marcus Buckingham
Donald Clifton

MANAGEMENT LIBRARY

WHY READ IT?

Most firms, according to authors, go about things the wrong way when training their staff. They try to make up for their employees' weaknesses. They concentrate on filling in gaps. The right thing to do, the authors advise, is to identify the special talents that employees possess and work on them to build up their strengths.

GETTING STARTED

On the basis of a wide-ranging survey, Buckingham and Clifton claim to have identified over 30 main "themes" of human talent. The particular gifts of each and every human individual can be described in terms of these themes, they say. Their book presents these themes in their various manifestations, explains how a strength profile works, and shows how the results can be translated into the everyday business of management.

CONTRIBUTION

1. The Anatomy of a Strength

Three tools are required, the authors say, to enable you to make use of your own and other people's strengths:

- an ability to distinguish innate talents from things that can be learned;
- a system to enable you to recognize the predominant talents in yourself and others;
- a common language to describe talents.

If you want to build up strengths, say the authors, you need know-how as well as knowledge. Know-how gives structure to knowledge derived from experience, inasmuch as it enables accumulated knowledge to be formalized as a series of steps, which, if followed, will produce results. Know-how enables you to avoid proceeding by trial and error and to incorporate the best insights in your own performance.

Buckingham and Clifton define talent as any persistent pattern of thought, feeling, or behavior that can be made use of productively. Talents, they say, are unique, dependable, and long-lasting.

2. Recognizing the Origins of Strengths

The authors claim that anybody can determine where his or her greatest strength potential lies by using their "StrengthFinder

Profile." It measures over 30 major talent themes. The authors' labels for these include: achiever, activator, adaptability, analytical, belief, command, communication, competition, connectedness, context, deliberative, discipline, empathy, fairness, focus, futuristic, harmony, ideation, input, learner, relator, restorative, self-assurance, significance, and strategic.

3. Making Use of Strengths

The main purpose of the StrengthFinder is to achieve the best possible performance over time. The authors claim, for example, that it is possible to use this system to uncover your own strongest talent themes, get to grips with them, and combine them into strengths. By concentrating on your strengths, you also find ways to manage your own weaknesses.

There are five separate strategies for weakness management, discussed by the authors. These are:

- getting better in the area of weakness;
- developing a support system;
- deploying a strong talent to overcome the weakness;
- finding a complementary partner:
- accepting the weakness.

With the help of the talent themes listed in the book, employees can be successfully managed and their needs satisfied in ways such as these:

- employees with analytical gifts should be presented with precise and well-founded figures and facts, and the logic of any decisions affecting them should be explained;
- adaptable employees should be deployed for short-term tasks that demand immediate action;
- "arrangers" should be given as much responsibility as possible taking into account knowledge and abilities;
- employees with authority should be given as much scope as possible to make their own decisions, but prevented from building up their own little empires;
- cautious employees should be kept away from any tasks that demand quick decisions and instead be made members of teams;
- disciplined employees should be given the opportunity to bring order to a planless or chaotic situation;

- enthusiastic employees should be given scope to bring drive and energy to their job or their team.

4. Building the Strength-based Business

The book describes four steps to constructing an organization built on strengths.

1. Management should spend a lot of time and money finding and appointing the right employees. It is a matter of discovering the "right" talent for every job.
2. The talents of each individual are unique. Consequently the company should concentrate on foregrounding results, instead of trying to press everybody into the same stylistic mold.
3. The main potential for growth in every person lies in the area of his or her greatest strengths. Training, therefore, should be focused on people's strong points and on ways of building these further.
4. Since people are best able to move on in the areas in which they are naturally gifted, management should do its best to find ways of furthering employees' careers without necessarily forcing them up the company ladder or promoting them out of areas where their strengths are most effective.

These four steps, say Buckingham and Clifton, represent a systematic process whereby the values bound up in a company's "human capital" can be maximized.

CONTEXT

The book is based on two long-term studies by the Gallup Institute, in which more than a million employees were surveyed and interviews were conducted with more than 80,000 managers. The authors defined their talent themes on the basis of this material. Their talents make individuals act in particular ways that management can make use of. Ultimately, then, the book is a plea for a very individual style of management.

FOR MORE INFORMATION

Buckingham, Marcus, and Donald Clifton. *Now, Discover Your Strengths*. New York: Free Press, 2000.

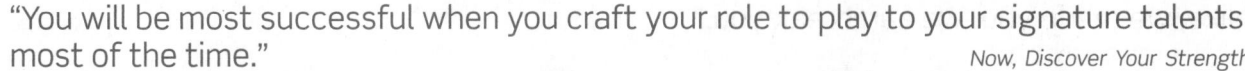

"You will be most successful when you craft your role to play to your signature talents most of the time."

Now, Discover Your Strengths

On Becoming a Leader

Warren Bennis

WHY READ IT?

Warren Bennis is widely respected as one of the foremost thinkers on leadership, and this book is regarded as a classic. It explains how people become leaders, how they lead, and how organizations respond to leadership. It is not based on academic theory, but offers practical advice based on interviews with a mix of leaders from many different fields.

GETTING STARTED

Bennis believes that there is no exact science of leadership. Leaders vary in their background, education, and experience. However, he identifies certain characteristics as essential for success. According to Bennis, leaders should know what they want and should be able to communicate what they want to others in order to gain their support. Leaders should also understand their own strengths and weaknesses and use them to achieve their goals. Bennis explains the phenomenon of leadership by defining its distinctive qualities—especially those that set a leader apart from a boss or manager, by highlighting the experiences that were vital to the development of leaders, by identifying the turning points, and by examining the role of failure.

CONTRIBUTION

1. The Importance of Leadership

Bennis explains that leaders are important for three reasons:
- they are responsible for the effectiveness of organizations;
- they provide a focal point;
- they provide a recognizable constant in the midst of rapid change.

2. Leading and Managing

According to Bennis, the ingredients of leadership are wide-ranging and they include guiding vision, passion, integrity, self-knowledge, trust, and daring. Leaders, he argues, can be highly competent, but fail to win the hearts and minds of the people they are leading.

Bennis believes that there is a significant difference between a leader and a boss, especially a boss who comes up from a results-driven management role. The drive for short-term results can run counter to the effectiveness of a visionary leader.

There are also many important differences between managers and leaders, he argues. The former have short-term rather than long-term perspectives, focus on systems rather than people, accept the status quo rather than challenging it, and exercise control instead of inspiring trust.

3. Leaders and Learning

Leaders, according to Bennis, are their own best teachers. They accept responsibility and gain from their own experience and that of others.

He distinguishes between maintenance learning and shock learning, both of which are familiar to managers, and what he calls innovative learning, which involves listening to others. This type of learning, he explains, means that people are free to express themselves, rather than just explain themselves. True intellect, he believes, is being able to see how things can be different.

4. The Value of Failure

Bennis suggests that leaders also learn from adversity. Making mistakes should not be punished. Leaders must operate on instinct, a process based on the use of the left- and right-hand sides of the brain. Managers, in contrast, rely on tried and tested processes.

According to Bennis, leaders should try everything, even in the face of failure. Few people venture into uncharted waters because of the risk of failure.

5. Achieving Goals

Leaders should be able to shift perspective so that they can see what is most important.

Bennis argues that leadership, unlike any other skill, cannot be broken down into a series of repeatable maneuvers. The creative process involved in reaching a goal is infinitely complex. As he explains, leaders

have to be able to move through chaos and synthesize all the elements needed for success.

6. Gaining Support

Bennis argues that leaders must get people on their side to effect change. Empathy is therefore an important characteristic of leadership. This, he explains, is in contrast to theories of leadership by force.

Leadership, he believes, requires persuasion, not giving orders. This requires an understanding of the needs of other people and the ability to communicate a vision.

CONTEXT

Leadership is now one of the most popular topics in management literature and training, and Warren Bennis has made a very important contribution. Leadership did not attract serious academic interest until the 1985 publication of *Leaders: Strategies for Taking Change* written in conjunction with Burt Nanus.

Bennis's work is based on extensive research with leaders in every field. One of his projects involved interviews with 90 of America's leaders, including astronaut Neil Armstrong, the coach of the LA Rams, orchestral conductors, and businesspeople such as Ray Kroc of McDonald's.

Bennis argues that leadership is not a rare skill. Leaders are made rather than born; leaders are usually ordinary, or apparently ordinary, people rather than obviously charismatic figures. Leadership, moreover, is not solely the preserve of those at the top of the organization—it is relevant at all levels.

1135

MANAGEMENT LIBRARY

FOR MORE INFORMATION

Bennis, Warren. *On Becoming a Leader.* 2nd ed. Cambridge, MA: Perseus, 2003.

FURTHER READING

Bennis, Warren, and Burt Nanus. *Leaders: Strategies for Taking Charge.* 2nd ed. New York: Collins, 2003.

"Leaders today sometimes appear to be an endangered species, caught in the whirl of events and circumstances beyond rational control."

On Becoming a Leader

On the Economy of Machinery and Manufactures

Charles Babbage

WHY READ IT?

Charles Babbage was one of the great minds of the first industrial revolution. He is credited with pioneering the computer, and wrote extensively about the importance of data and manufacturing. The book offers fascinating insights into the early development of manufacturing techniques.

GETTING STARTED

In an age of economic theory, Babbage argued for a highly scientific approach. His emphasis on fact-finding influences not only the practical elements of factory management in the early industrial era, but the formation of interpretive theory. Mechanical principles govern manufacturing, and merchants and manufacturers are the best people to supply the data on which all the reasoning of political economists is founded. People should not fear bad deductions from good facts.

Good factory organization is important, and factories require an entire system of operation.

The most important principle of manufacture is the division of labor.

It is vital to calculate the life expectancy of capital equipment. In five years capital equipment ought to have paid for itself, and in ten it should be superseded by a better version.

CONTRIBUTION

1. Mechanical Principles Govern Manufacturing

Babbage's fundamental approach was highly scientific. He held that mechanical principles regulate the application of machinery to arts and manufacture.

First, he said, it's essential to gather the evidence. Babbage did so through touring factories exhaustively in the United Kingdom and Europe. The book provides helpful hints and a checklist of questions on how to find the best information when touring a factory.

2. Make Use of Facts

Political economists have been reproached with too small a use of facts, and too large an employment of theory. "If facts are wanting, the closet-philosopher is unfortunately too little acquainted with the admirable arrangements of the factory," Babbage wrote. "The merchant and manufacturer are the best people to supply readily, and with so little sacrifice of time, the data on which all the reasoning of political economists are founded."

3. Collecting Data Is Essential

People should not fear that erroneous deductions may be made from recorded facts. The errors which arise from the absence of facts are far more numerous and more durable than those which result from unsound reasoning based on true data.

Babbage encourages managers to follow his example and gather their own data. Collecting data is essential for the manufacturers who want to know how many additional customers they will acquire by a given reduction in the price of the article he makes.

4. Good Factory Organization Is Important

The arrangements that should regulate the interior economy of a factory are founded on deeply-rooted principles. Babbage recognized that the factory requires an entire system of operation. It needs to be organized in a vastly different way to the conventional means of production.

Babbage provides insights in two central areas. First, economies of scale and second, the division of labor.

5. Calculating the Right Division of Labor

Perhaps the most important principle on which the economy of manufacture depends is the division of labor among the people who perform the work.

"The number of operations performed in a given time may frequently be counted when the workman is quite unconscious that any person is observing him," Babbage said. "For example, the sound made by the motion of a loom may enable the observer to count the number of strokes per minute, even though he is outside the building in which it is contained."

6. Life Expectancy of Capital Equipment

Machinery for producing any commodity in great demand seldom actually wears out. New improvements, by which the same operations can be executed either more quickly or better, generally supersede it long before that time arrives. To make such an improved machine profitable, it is usually reckoned that in five years it ought to have paid for itself, and in ten to be superseded by a better one.

CONTEXT

The book was a bestseller of its times. It is one of the first to recognize the importance of factories, economically and socially. In that sense, it is like the first book on the potential of the Internet.

Babbage was a pioneer of modern management. His approach bears more than a passing resemblance to that later adopted by the U.S. champion of scientific management, Frederick Taylor. He beckoned in the industrial era and, in doing so, laid the intellectual groundwork for Marx, Engels, and John Stuart Mill. Contrasts can be made with Adam Smith, whose economic viewpoint remained stuck in the agricultural era.

Joseph Schumpeter called the book "a remarkable performance of a remarkable man."

FOR MORE INFORMATION

Babbage, Charles. *On the Economy of Machinery and Manufactures*. New York: Dodo Press, 2006.

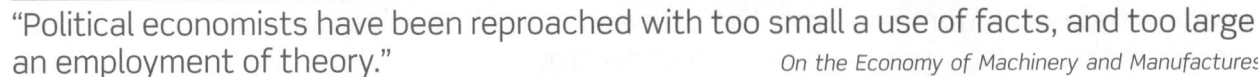

"Political economists have been reproached with too small a use of facts, and too large an employment of theory."

On the Economy of Machinery and Manufactures

The One Minute Manager

Kenneth Blanchard
Spencer Johnson

WHY READ IT?

Blanchard and Johnson start from the idea that the profession of management is not as complicated as it is sometimes made out to be. Following a few simple rules can guarantee increased productivity, profits, and job satisfaction for the employees. First published in 1982, this book has become a popular management classic. It is short, to the point, and the ideas that it advocates can be put into practice straight away.

GETTING STARTED

The "carrot-and-stick" method of motivating employees does not work, say Blanchard and Spencer. It causes confusion and frustration, for two reasons: firstly it is inconsistent, and, secondly, it is unpredictable. And consistency and predictability are what count in human management. This "allegory," as the authors describe it, recounts the story of a young beginner who sets out to find a really effective manager to model himself on. He finds what he is looking for in the One Minute Manager, who has three simple secrets: one minute goal-setting, one minute praising, and one minute reprimanding.

CONTRIBUTION

1. The Search for the One Minute Manager

Really efficient managers deploy themselves and their employees so that both the business and its staff profit from what they do. Effective management, the authors say, is team-oriented. Managers should by and large keep out of decision making by employees. They should be equally interested in results and people, because results are only achieved by people. A good manager, they suggest, acts on the principle that only people who feel good about themselves work well.

2. One Minute Goal-setting

In setting goals the One Minute Manager asks the following questions:
- What goals do I want to achieve?
- What kind of behavior will best help me achieve these goals?

and goes through the following steps:
- writing each individual goal down on a separate sheet of paper in not more than 30 lines;
- reading through the piece of paper setting out the goal again periodically;
- scrutinizing his or her own working methods several times a day;
- deciding, on the basis of self-observation, whether his or her own behavior is helping to achieve the goal or not.

3. One Minute Praising

Praising is effective, say the authors, if it is done like this.
- Always tell your employees what you think of their work.
- If you can praise someone, do it straight away.
- Tell your people what they have done well. Be concrete and go into detail.
- Let them know how pleased you feel about their good performance.
- Stop for a moment so that the person you are praising can share that feeling.
- Tell your employees to "keep up the good work," as a way of letting them know that you actively support the professional success.

4. One Minute Reprimanding

A one minute reprimand works well, Blanchard and Spencer suggest, if this procedure is followed.
- Before the reprimand: tell staff from the outset that you will make absolutely clear to them what you think of their work.
- First part of reprimand: if you have to reprimand someone, do it straight away. Tell the person involved in detail what he or she has done wrong. Stop talking and wait long enough for the silence to become painful, that way the person you are criticizing will share some of the feeling behind the reprimand.
- Second part of reprimand: offer your hand or show by some other gesture that, despite the fault, you are still on the person's side. It is important to make it clear to people that you value them as employees and think highly of them—apart from what they have done in this particular instance.
- After the reprimand: do not hark back. Once the reprimand is over, it is over.

5. Why One Minute Goal-setting Works

Many managers, say the authors, act like this. They know what they want from staff, but do not take the trouble to tell them. They assume the employees will know. This is wrong. A manager should never take anything for granted, where goal-setting is concerned. Goals must be fixed in writing, so that employees can always look at them again to check their own performance.

6. Why One Minute Praising Works

Most managers hold back praise until the employees have done something "exactly right." Consequently, the authors assert, many people never reach their full potential, because their superiors concentrate on catching them out making mistakes. That is wrong. When employees are introduced to a new task, the vital thing is to "catch" them doing something "nearly right," so that they go on to learn how to do it exactly right.

7. Why One Minute Reprimands Work

In many businesses a "blacklist" system operates. Managers collect up instances of unsatisfactory work they have spotted, and then one day—when giving a performance review or if they happen to be in a bad mood—they let the employee have it all at once. That, say Blanchard and Spencer, is wrong. Proper criticism is basically nothing but prompt feedback. Confront the person involved as soon as you have spotted a fault. Reprimands are fairer and clearer if they apply to someone's current behavior. Criticism should also be directed only at the employee's behavior, never at him or her as a person.

CONTEXT

The behavioral perspective in *The One Minute Manager* comes from Blanchard, a behavioral scientist and one of the creators of the situation-determined method of management. The psychological aspects of leadership are handled by Johnson, a specialist in social medicine and communications. Reviews praise the book's compact treatment of insights that are often presented at great length.

1137

MANAGEMENT LIBRARY

FOR MORE INFORMATION

Blanchard, Kenneth, and Spencer Johnson. *The One Minute Manager*. New York: Berkley Publishing Group, 1983.

FURTHER READING

Johnson, Spencer. *One Minute For Yourself*. New York: William Morrow, 1998.

On War

Karl von Clausewitz

WHY READ IT?

Von Clausewitz believed that comparisons between military action and commerce are valid and useful. His book explains this comparison in detail and gives examples based around key concepts such as strategy, use of resources and response to competitors. Other management thinkers agree that military thinkers like von Clausewitz can provide valuable insight for business.

GETTING STARTED

Military and commercial comparisons are valid for a number of reasons. Commerce, like war, is a conflict of interests and activities. Plans must be flexible and take account of competitors—and the best way to achieve flexibility is to operate along a line which offers alternative objectives. Theory is only an aid to decision making, and it is important to achieve results through minimal effort. In both areas, it is important to remember that strategy and tactics are different and that objectives should be concentrated on one at a time.

CONTRIBUTION

1. Military and Commercial Comparisons are Valid

Karl von Clausewitz was firmly of the mind that comparisons between the military and commercial worlds were both valid and useful.

"Rather than comparing it [war] to art we could more accurately compare it to commerce, which is also a conflict of interests and activities," he wrote. "It is still closer to politics, which in turn may be considered as a kind of commerce on a larger scale."

2. Plans Must be Flexible

To be practical, any plan must take account of the enemy's power to frustrate it.

The best chance of overcoming obstruction is to have a plan that can easily be varied to fit the circumstances met.

In order to maintain such adaptability, while still keeping the initiative, the best way is to operate along a line which offers alternative objectives.

3. Theory is Only an Aid to Decision making

Knowing is different from doing and therefore theory must never be used as the norm for a standard, but merely as an aid to judgment.

Pragmatism is combined with a desire to achieve results through minimal effort.

A prince or general can best demonstrate his genius by managing a campaign exactly to suit his objectives and his resources, doing neither too much nor too little.

4. Strategy and Tactics are Different

Von Clausewitz differentiates between strategy—the overall plan, and mere tactics—the planning of a discrete part of the overall plan (the battle, for example).

Grand strategy represents the overall political objectives.

Arguments over the difference between strategy and tactics have raged inconclusively ever since.

5. Concentrate on One Objective at a Time

Success comes through concentrating on one battle at a time.

This is the distant precursor of the managerial theory of management by objectives.

By looking on each engagement as part of a series, at least insofar as events are predictable, the commander is always on the high road to his goal.

CONTEXT

Soldiers have a surprisingly lengthy heritage as managerial exemplars, both in terms of practice and theory. Hadrian, for example, was a champion of "people power" long before the advent of human resource departments: his military reputation was forged on his willingness to share the same conditions as his troops. He was also a globe trotter—he didn't seek to control his empire from Rome but traveled throughout it. In modern parlance, he accepted the diversity of his empire. Hadrian was also reputed to have had an eye for financial management. He built up reserves to fund building projects and social welfare programs. At the same time, he didn't raise taxes.

The Duke of Wellington can lay claim to "managing by wandering around" during the Napoleonic Wars. Historian John Keegan said, "Wellington's methods required a particularly intense managerial style—taking trouble with the battle."

Wellington said, "The general must make himself the eyes of his own army and must constantly change position to deal with crises as they occur along the front of his sheltered line; must remain at the point of crisis until it is resolved and must still keep alert to anticipate the development of crises elsewhere."

More recently, management thinkers have sought inspiration from leading military thinker Basil Liddell Hart, in particular from his 1967 book, *Strategy*.

Management gurus including Richard Pascale have examined military approaches to such issues as leadership, training, motivation and strategy.

FOR MORE INFORMATION

von Clausewitz, Karl. *On War*. Princeton, NJ: Princeton University Press, 1989.

"Rather than comparing [war] to art we could more accurately compare it to commerce, which is also a conflict of interests and activities."

On War
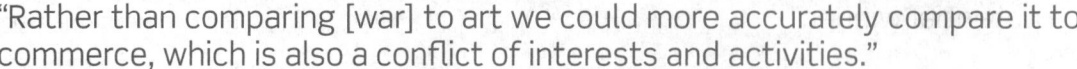

Onward Industry

James Mooney
Alan Reiley

WHY READ IT?

The book provides insights into early thinking about the nature of organizations and their impact on the performance of industry. The authors argue that organization is a universal phenomenon and has a benefit on the overall standard of living.

GETTING STARTED

Organization is a universal phenomenon that has occurred throughout history. The organization of businesses is crucial to prosperity and living standards.

Production without distribution is worthless; the emphasis must be on finding and exploiting markets. Industry should encourage participation in business so that purchasing capacity can be created and extended. Organizational size is less important than knowing what to do with the organization.

CONTRIBUTION

1. Organization Is a Universal Phenomenon

People love to organize, and organization is as old as human society itself. Consider the scalar organization of the Catholic Church, governmental organization, and the evolution of different forms of organization from Roman times to Medieval times, through to the company of the early twentieth century.

2. Organization Is Crucial to Standards of Living

The organization of businesses is crucial to overall standards of living. There is a direct link between industrial prosperity, built on modern management techniques, and the affluence of society as a whole.

"The highest development of the techniques both of production and distribution will be futile to supply the material wants of those who, because of poverty, are unable to acquire through purchase," the authors write. The final task of industry, therefore, is to organize participation in these activities, even in the poorest communities and countries, through which purchasing capacity can be created and extended.

3. Production Without Distribution Is Worthless

Before the 1930s, production was the overarching driving force. Later the emphasis shifted to finding new markets and enhancing and expanding distribution to make inroads into these markets.

4. The Value of Size

Size isn't everything. Modern business leadership has been generally characterized by the capacity to create large organizations, but by failure in knowing exactly how to make effective use of them.

5. Key Organizational Principles

Mooney and Reiley's theory of organizations identified three important organizational principles:

- the co-ordinative principle, leading to effective co-ordination;
- the scalar process, resulting in functional definition;
- the functional effect, leading to interpretative functionalism.

CONTEXT

The book provides an organization model that is firmly of its time. It applies the reasoned science of Frederick W. Taylor to the broader organizational canvas.

The argument that production without distribution is worthless marks something of a watershed. Before the 1930s, production was the overarching driving force. From World War II, the emphasis shifted to finding new markets and enhancing and expanding distribution to make inroads into these markets.

1139

MANAGEMENT LIBRARY

FOR MORE INFORMATION

Mooney, James, and Alan Reiley. *Onward Industry*. Revised ed. Bristol, U.K.: Thoemmes Continuum, 2004.

The Organization Man

William Whyte

WHY READ IT?

From the point of view of the age of uncertainty, the age of downsizing, reengineering, and "discontinuous change," the 1950s and 1960s can easily seem like a golden age. The careers enjoyed by corporate executives were built on solid foundations, workers had jobs for life, suburbia was heaven, and everything seemed set to go on and on and on. William Whyte showed the downside to this corporate utopia. Read his brilliant, witty, and often poignant analysis to get both the postwar past and the present in perspective.

GETTING STARTED

William Whyte joined the staff of *Fortune* magazine in 1946 after graduating from Princeton and serving in the U.S. Marines during World War II. *The Organization Man* is based on articles he wrote for the magazine. He subsequently left *Fortune* and, in his later years, wrote mainly on the subject of urban sprawl, urban planning, and human behavior in urban spaces.

In the 1950s, the United States still publicly and privately subscribed to the idea that rugged individualism was the hallmark of the American character and the foundation stone of American success. According to Whyte, this was a delusion. Average citizens in fact subscribed to a collectivist social ethic that was turning them into organization people—and they needed to realize the fact and do something about it.

CONTRIBUTION

1. The Social Ethic

Whyte believed that the condition he was analyzing did not affect the United States alone: he referred to "a bureaucratization that has affected every country."

The bureaucratic or collectivist ethic rested on three major principles:

- a belief in the group as the source of creativity;
- a belief in "belongingness" as the ultimate need of every individual;
- a belief in the application of science to achieve belongingness.

And above all he believed that, "the fundamental principle of the new model executive is . . . that the goals of the individual and the goals of the organization will work out to be one and the same."

2. The Importance of Loyalty

Gray-suited and obedient, corporate man was unstintingly loyal to his employer. He spent his life with a single company and rose slowly, but quietly, up the hierarchy.

Loyalty and solid performance brought job security. This was mutually beneficial.

The executive gained a respectable income and a high degree of security. The company gained loyal, dependable, hardworking executives.

But while loyalty is a positive quality, it can easily become blind. What if the corporate strategy is wrong or the company is engaged in unlawful or immoral acts? The corporation becomes a self-contained and self-perpetuating world supported by a complex array of checks, systems, and hierarchies. The company is right.

In a remark reminiscent of George Orwell's *1984*, Whyte suggested that the organization man "must not only accept control, he must accept it as if he liked it."

3. Low-risk Environment

Customers, who exist outside the organization, are often regarded as peripheral.

In the 1950s, 1960s, and 1970s, it sometimes seems, no executive ever lost his or her job by delivering poor quality or indifferent service. In some organizations, executives only lost their jobs by defrauding their employer or insulting their boss. Jobs for life was the refrain and, to a large extent for executives, the reality.

Clearly, such an environment was hardly conducive to the fostering of dynamic risk-takers. It rewarded the steady foot soldier, the safe pair of hands, the organization man living with his organization wife.

CONTEXT

Reviewing the book in the *New York Times*, C. Wright Mills wrote: "Whyte understands that the work-and-thrift ethic of success has grievously declined, except in the rhetoric of top executives; that the entrepreneurial scramble to success has been largely replaced by the organizational crawl."

Chester Barnard noted in *The Functions of the Executive* : "The most important single contribution required of an executive, certainly the most universal qualification, is loyalty [allowing] domination by the organization personality."

Twenty years after the publication of Whyte's book, things had not changed very much. When she came to examine corporate life for the first time in her 1977 book, *Men and Women of the Corporation*, Rosabeth Moss Kanter found that the central characteristic expected of a manager was dependability.

Fortune founder Henry Luce commented: "It was *Fortune's* William H. Whyte, Jr. who made the 'organization man' a household word, and the organization wife too. His was a fine achievement in sociological reporting. In it he related the phenomenon of the business organization to questions of human personality and values. The kind of people who are eager to hear the worst about U.S. society assumed that Mr. Whyte was predicting the destruction of individualism by the organization."

Whyte was uneasy about corporate life, which seemed to stifle creativity and individualism. He was uneasy about the subtle pressures in the office and at home that called for smooth performance rather than daring creativity. However, he did not urge the organization men to leave their secure environment. Rather he urged them to fight against the organization when necessary, and he was optimistic that the battle could be successful.

FOR MORE INFORMATION

Whyte, William. *The Organization Man*. Revised ed. Philadelphia, PA: University of Pennsylvania Press, 2002.

"The fault is not in organization, in short, it is in our worship of it."

The Organization Man

Organizational Culture and Leadership

Edgar Schein

WHY READ IT?
Organizational Culture and Leadership clarified the entire area of corporate culture in a way no previous book had. It brought culture into the management debate and paved the way for a plethora of further studies. Even today, its perspectives on culture as a constantly changing force in corporate life remain as disconcerting as they are valuable.

GETTING STARTED
Schein is sometimes seen as the inventor of the term "corporate culture"; he is, at the very least, one of its originators. After a long and distinguished academic career, he is currently the Sloan Fellows' Professor of Management Emeritus at the MIT Sloan School of Management.

In this book, he not only provides a sophisticated definition of culture, but he turns the abstract concept into a tool to assist managers in understanding the dynamics of organizations. In addition, he tackles the vital question of how an existing culture can be changed—one of the toughest challenges for leadership.

CONTRIBUTION
1. The Basis of Corporate Culture
Culture is a pattern of basic assumptions invented, discovered, or developed by a given group as it learns to cope with its problems of external adaptation and internal integration. These assumptions have worked well enough to be considered valid and, therefore, to be taught to new members as the correct way to perceive, think, and feel in relation to those problems.

They can be categorized into five dimensions.
- Humanity's relationship to nature—while some companies regard themselves as masters of their own destiny, others are submissive, willing to accept the domination of their external environment.
- The nature of reality and truth—organizations and managers adopt a wide variety of methods to reach what becomes accepted as the organizational truth.
- The nature of human nature—organizations differ in their views of human nature.

Some follow McGregor's Theory X and work on the principle that people will not do the job if they can avoid it. Others regard people in a more positive light and attempt to enable them to fulfill their potential for the benefit of both sides.
- The nature of human activity—the West has traditionally emphasized tasks and their completion rather than the more philosophical side of work. Achievement is all. Schein suggests an alternative approach—"being-in-becoming"—emphasizing self-fulfillment and development.
- The nature of human relationships—organizations make a variety of assumptions about how people interact with each other. Some facilitate social interaction, while others regard it as an unnecessary distraction.

These five categories are not mutually exclusive, but are in a constant state of development and flux. Culture does not ever stand still for long.

2. Shaping Organizational Values
Key to the creation and development of corporate culture are the values embraced by the organization. A single person can shape these values and, as a result, an entire corporate culture. The heroic creators of corporate cultures include such people as Henry Ford and IBM's Thomas Watson, Sr.

3. Development of Corporate Culture
There are three stages in the development of a corporate culture:
- Birth and early growth—the culture may be dominated by the business founder. It is regarded as a source of the company's identity, a bonding agent protecting it against outside forces.
- Organizational mid-life—the original culture is likely to be diluted and undermined as new cultures emerge and there is a loss of the original sense of identity. At this stage, there is an opportunity for the fundamental culture to be realigned and changed.
- Organizational maturity—culture, at this stage, is regarded sentimentally. People are hopelessly addicted to how things used to be done and unwilling to contemplate

change. Here the organization is at its weakest, as the culture has been transformed from a source of competitive advantage and distinctiveness to a hindrance in the marketplace. Only through aggressive measures will it survive.

4. Changing Corporate Culture
Each stage of the culture's growth requires a different method of change.

If culture is to work in support of a company's strategy, there has to be a level of consensus covering five areas:
- the core mission or primary task
- goals
- the means to accomplish the goals
- the means to measure progress
- remedial or repair strategies

Achieving cultural change is a formidable challenge, one that well-established executives in strong cultures often find beyond them. The exceptional executives who achieve cultural change from within a culture they are closely identified with (such as GE's Jack Welch) are rarities, and are known as cultural hybrids.

CONTEXT
Schein's findings gave rise to a host of other studies of the subject. His basic assumptions are rephrased and reinterpreted elsewhere in a variety of ways. Perhaps Chris Argyris comes closest to him when discussing "theories-in-use."

Gary Hamel says: "It is impossible to change a large organization without first understanding that organization's culture. Ed Schein gave us an ability to look deeply into what makes an organization what it is, thus providing the foundation of any successful effort at transformation or change. *Organizational Culture and Leadership* remains essential reading for all aspiring change agents."

FOR MORE INFORMATION
Schein, Edgar H. *Organizational Culture and Leadership*. 3rd ed. San Francisco, CA: Jossey-Bass, 2004.

"Through debate, dictatorship, or through simple acceptance, if something achieves the objective, it is right."

Organizational Culture and Leadership

Organizational Learning

Chris Argyris
Donald Schön

1142

MANAGEMENT LIBRARY

WHY READ IT?

This book shows why organizational learning is the ultimate competitive advantage. It also explains two of the central paradoxes of business life—how individual initiative and creativity can work in an organizational environment, where rules will always exist, and how teamworking and individual working can coexist fruitfully.

GETTING STARTED

Learning is a key business activity. Many organizational models only achieve single-loop learning, which—while this permits a company to carry on its present policies and achieve its current objectives—is limited to detection and correction of organizational error.

Double-loop learning, however, enables organizations to detect and correct errors in ways that involve the modification of underlying norms, policies, and objectives. With double-loop learning, managers can act on information and learn from others. Most organizations do quite well in single-loop learning, but have great difficulties with double-loop learning.

Deutero-learning is the process of inquiring into the learning system by which an organization detects and corrects its errors. It underpins the concept of the learning organization.

Increasingly, the art of management is managing knowledge—and effective leadership means creating the conditions that enable people to produce valid knowledge. Success in the marketplace increasingly depends on learning, yet most people don't know how to learn.

CONTRIBUTION

1. The Weakness of Single-loop Learning

The authors investigate two basic organizational models.

Model 1 is based on the premise that we seek to manipulate and form the world in accordance with our individual aspirations and wishes. In Model 1, managers concentrate on establishing individual goals. They keep to themselves and don't voice concerns or disagreements. The onus is on creating a conspiracy of silence in which everyone dutifully keeps their head down. Defense is the prime activity in a Model 1 organization, though occasionally the best means of defense is attack. Model 1 managers are prepared to inflict change on others, but resist any attempt to change their own thinking and working practices.

Model 1 organizations are characterized by single-loop learning—the detection and correction of organizational error that permits the organization to carry on its present policies and achieve its current objectives.

2. The Importance of Double-loop Learning

Model 2 organizations emphasize double-loop learning—where organizational error is detected and corrected in ways that involve the modification of underlying norms, policies, and objectives.

In Model 2 organizations, managers act on information. They debate issues and respond to change—as well as being prepared to change themselves. They learn from others. A virtuous circle emerges of learning and understanding.

Most organizations do quite well in single-loop learning, but have great difficulties with double-loop learning.

3. The Challenge of Deutero-learning

Deutero-learning offers even greater challenges. This is the process of inquiring into the learning system by which an organization detects and corrects its errors. The examination of learning systems is central to the contemporary concept of the learning organization.

4. The Importance of Managing Knowledge

Learning is powerfully practical and increasingly, the art of management is managing knowledge. Organizations should not manage people per se, but rather the knowledge that they carry.

Leadership means creating the conditions that enable people to produce valid knowledge, and to do so in ways that encourage personal responsibility. Knowledge must relate to action, rather than knowledge for the purpose of understanding and exploring.

5. The Learning Imperative

There is a natural temptation for organizations and individuals to limit themselves to single-loop learning rather than its more demanding alternatives. However, the need better to understand learning in all its dimensions is now imperative. Any company that aspires to success in the tougher business environment of the 1990s and beyond must embrace learning—yet most people don't know how to learn. Those members of an organization who are assumed by many to be the best at learning are, in fact, not very good at it.

CONTEXT

If you wished to trace the roots of the learning organization, you would invariably find yourself reading *Organizational Learning*.

Organizational Learning grew out of the authors' 1974 book, *Theory in Practice*.

Chris Argyris was part of the human relations school of the late 1950s and involved in the work of the National Training Laboratories. He was drawn to the riddles of human nature—in particular, why do people fail to live up to their own professed ideals? Why is so much human behavior so self-frustrating, particularly within the context organizations?

In the last decade, Argyris's ideas have become fashionable. This is most apparent in the upsurge of interest in the concept of the learning organization.

Organizational Learning appeared in 1978, but it took the 1990 bestseller from Peter Senge of MIT (Massachusetts Institute of Technology), *The Fifth Discipline*, to propel the learning organization from an academic concept to mainstream acceptance.

Charles Hampden-Turner of the University of Cambridge's Judge Institute of Management says, "There is an urgent need for alternative visions of science and Schön's work, along with that of Argyris, provides some of the best ideas and answers. Few have gone so far in reconciling the vigor of relevance and in building a bridge between the isolated academic fortresses of the sciences and the humanities."

Gary Hamel concurs, "If your organization has not yet mastered double-loop learning, it is already a dinosaur. No one can doubt that organizational learning is the ultimate competitive advantage. We owe much to Argyris and Schön for helping us learn about learning."

FOR MORE INFORMATION

Argyris, Chris, and Donald Schön. *Organizational Learning*. 2nd ed. New York: Addison-Wesley, 1995.

Out of the Crisis

W. Edwards Deming

WHY READ IT?

This book is regarded as a classic of literature on quality management. It reflects Deming's experience in introducing quality to Japan, and its goal was to transform the style of U.S. management. Deming is regarded as the leading figure on quality and this book sets out the methods that taught industry the power of quality.

GETTING STARTED

Deming argues that profit comes from repeat customers—and they respond to good quality.

Statistical quality control produces spectacular results, so senior managers must take charge of quality, and quality training should begin at the top of the organization.

Quality is a way of living, Deming says: it is not the preserve of the few but the responsibility of all. He argued that factory workers already understood the importance of quality but were stymied by managers focused on increasing productivity regardless of quality.

Japanese culture is uniquely receptive to the quality message.

CONTRIBUTION

1. The Importance of Quality

Profit comes from repeat customers, who boast about your product and service, and who bring friends with them.

Quality is more than statistical control, though this is important. Statistical quality control produces spectacular results by using tools to improve processes in ways that minimize defects and eliminate rejects, rework, and recalls.

Deming's work bridges the gap between science-based application and humanistic philosophy.

2. The Quality Gospel

The book's quality gospel revolves around a number of basic precepts:
- If consistent quality is to be achieved senior managers must take charge of it.
- Implementation requires a cascade, with training beginning at the top before moving down through the hierarchy.
- The use of statistical methods of quality control is necessary so that, finally, business plans can be expanded to include clear quality goals.
- Quality is a way of living, the meaning of industrial life and, in particular, the meaning of management.

3. Deming's Fourteen Points
- Create constancy of purpose for improvement of product and service.
- Adopt the new philosophy.
- Cease dependence on inspection to achieve quality.
- End the practice of awarding business on the basis of price tag alone. Instead, minimize total cost by working with a single supplier.
- Improve constantly and forever every process for planning, production, and service.
- Institute training on the job.
- Adopt and institute leadership.
- Drive out fear.
- Break down barriers between staff areas.
- Eliminate slogans, exhortations, and targets for the workforce.
- Eliminate numerical quotas for the workforce and numerical goals for management.
- Remove barriers that rob people of pride of workmanship. Eliminate the annual rating or merit system.
- Institute a vigorous program of education and self-improvement for everyone.
- Put everybody in the company to work to accomplish the transformation.

4. The Importance of Empowerment

The simplicity of the Fourteen Points disguises the immensity of the challenge, particularly that facing management: quality is not the preserve of the few but the responsibility of all. Deming was anticipating the fashion for empowerment.

People all over the world think that it is the factory worker that causes problems. He or she is not your problem. "Ever since there has been anything such as industry, the factory worker has known that quality is what will protect his job. He knows that poor quality in the hands of the customer will lose the market and cost him his job. He knows it and lives with that fear every day. Yet he cannot do a good job. He is not allowed to do it because the management wants figures, more products, and never mind the quality."

5. The Problem of Management

Management is 90% of the problem, a problem caused in part by the Western enthusiasm for annual performance appraisals. Japanese managers receive feedback every day of their working lives.

The basic cause of sickness in American industry and resulting unemployment is failure of top management to manage. He that sells not can buy not.

The Japanese culture was uniquely receptive to Deming's message for a number of reasons. Its emphasis on group rather than individual achievement enables the Japanese to share ideas and responsibility. It also promotes collective ownership in a way that the West often finds difficult to contemplate, let alone understand.

CONTEXT

W. Edwards Deming has a unique place among management theorists. He had an impact on industrial history that others only dream of.

Deming visited Japan after World War II on the invitation of General MacArthur, and played a key role in the rebuilding of Japanese industry. During the 1950s, Deming and the other U.S. standard bearer of quality, Joseph Juran, conducted seminars and courses throughout Japan. Deming and Japanese management were eventually discovered by the West in the 1980s.

British author Robert Heller says, "Deming didn't invent quality but his sermons had a uniquely powerful effect because of this first pulpit and congregation: Japan and Japanese managers. Had his fellow Americans responded with the same intense application, post-war industrial history would have differed enormously."

Management guru Gary Hamel adds, "Of all the management gurus . . . there is only one who should be regarded as a hero by every consumer in the world—Dr. Deming. He may have taken the gospel of quality to the Japanese first, but thank God his message finally penetrated the smug complacency of American and European companies. No senior executive ever sat through one of Dr. Deming's harangues without coming away just a little bit more humble and contrite—a good beginning on the road to total quality."

FOR MORE INFORMATION

Deming, W. Edwards. *Out of the Crisis*. Revised ed. Bambridge, MA: MIT Center for Advanced Engineering Study, 2000.

Parkinson's Law

C. Northcote Parkinson

WHY READ IT?

Parkinson's Law, like *The Dilbert Principle*, takes a cynical look at business. The book treats the growth of bureaucracy and red tape in a humorous way, but the findings reflect real life situations, particularly in government organizations.

GETTING STARTED

Companies grow without thinking of how much they are producing and without making any more money. The time taken to complete a task depends on the person doing the job and his or her unique situation. Work also expands to fill the time available for its completion and officials make work for each other.

CONTRIBUTION

1. How Organizations Grow

Parkinson's Law is simply that work expands to fill the time available for its completion. As a result, companies grow, but without thinking of how much they are actually producing.

Even if growth in numbers doesn't make them more money, companies grow and people become busier and busier.

The author contends that an official wants to multiply subordinates, not rivals, and that officials make work for each other.

2. Work Expands to Fill the Time

The notion of a particular task having an optimum time for completion is wrong.

There are no rules—it depends entirely on the person doing the job and his or her unique situation.

An elderly lady of leisure can spend an entire day in writing and dispatching a postcard to her niece.

The total effort which would occupy a busy person for three minutes may, in this fashion, leave another person prostrate after a day of doubt, anxiety, and toil.

3. Administration Expands

Faced with the decreasing energy of age and a feeling of being overworked, administrators face three options:

- resign
- halve the work with a colleague
- ask for two more subordinates

There is probably no instance in civil service history of choosing any but the third alternative.

The number of admiralty officials in the British Navy increased by 78% between 1914 and 1928 while the number of ships fell by 67% and the number of officers and men by 31%.

The expansion of administrators tends to take on a life of its own.

The conclusion drawn is that officials would have multiplied at the same rate had there been no actual seamen at all.

CONTEXT

Parkinson's Law is an amusing interlude in management literature.

It is a kind of *Catch-22* of the business world, by turns irreverent and humorous, but with a darker underside of acute, critical observation.

The book was written in the late 1950s when the Human Relations School in the United States was beginning to flower and thinkers were actively questioning the bureaucracy that had grown up alongside mass production.

Max Weber's model of a paper-producing bureaucratic machine appeared to have been brought to fruition as the arteries of major organizations became increasingly clogged with layer upon layer of managerial administrators.

Gary Hamel had this to say, "Yes, I know that bureaucracy is dead. We're not managers any more, we're leaders. We're not slaves to our work, we've been liberated. And all those layers of paper-shuffling administrators between the C.E.O. and the order-takers—they're all gone, right? Well then, why does a re-reading of *Parkinson's Law*, written in 1958, at the apex of corporate bureaucracy, still ring true? *Parkinson's Law* was to the fifties what *The Dilbert Principle* is to the 1990s."

FOR MORE INFORMATION

Parkinson, C. Northcote. *Parkinson's Law*. Revised ed. Cutchogue, NY: Buccaneer Books, 1993.

"Work expands to fill the time available for its completion."

Parkinson's Law

The Peter Principle

Laurence Peter

WHY READ IT?

This book is one of the most enduring books to take a cynical view of management. It is a humorous book that sets the tone for later works like *The Dilbert Principle*.

GETTING STARTED

According to the author, in a hierarchy, every employee tends to rise to his or her level of incompetence. There are no exceptions to the Peter Principle. In time, every post tends to be occupied by an employee who is incompetent to perform his duties. If at first you don't succeed, you may be at your level of incompetence. There are two kinds of failures: those who thought and never did, and those who did and never thought. There are two sorts of losers—the good loser, and the other one who can't act.

CONTRIBUTION

1. Finding a Level of Incompetence

In a hierarchy every employee tends to rise to his level of incompetence.

A position of incompetence is the apotheosis of a corporate career—or, indeed, of any career in any profession in which there is a hierarchy.

No one in the business world is exempt from the Peter Principle.

The author contends that for each individual, the final promotion is from a level of competence to a level of incompetence. So, given enough time—and assuming the existence of enough ranks in the hierarchy—each employee rises to, and remains at, his level of incompetence.

In time, every post tends to be occupied by an employee who is incompetent to perform his duties.

2. Dealing with Failure

If at first you don't succeed, you may be at your level of incompetence.

If you don't know where you are going, you will probably end up somewhere else.

An economist is an expert who will know tomorrow why the things he predicted yesterday didn't happen.

Human inadequacy is universal, as is the human capacity to build vacuous power structures. In our supposedly leaner and fitter times, there are still hierarchies aplenty. The difference is, perhaps, that we have simply become more adept at disguising them.

There are two kinds of failures: those who thought and never did, and those who did and never thought.

There are two sorts of losers—the good loser, and the other one who can't act.

Fortune knocks once, but misfortune has much more patience.

3. Computerized Incompetence

Computerized incompetence can be either the incompetent application of computer techniques or the inherent incompetence of a computer.

CONTEXT

Cynicism about the way businesses and managers operate is nothing new. For example, *The Dilbert Principle* is simply an accurate and amusing portrayal of corporate cynicism, 1990s-style.

From *Murphy's Law* to *Parkinson's Law*, from Pudd'nhead Wilson to Stanley Bing, a steady infusion of comic skepticism has been injected into the corporate canon.

The Peter Principle is perhaps the most enduring, cynical classic.

The book carries many echoes of that other humorous classic of the 1960s, Joseph Heller's *Catch-22*.

The Peter Principle remains a poignant antidote to the blind optimism and sugary outlook of most business books. It is a reminder that corporate reality is not usually about grand designs and great decisions. It is more mundane and frustrating; too mundane and too frustrating ever to be taken too seriously.

Dilbert creator Scott Adams commented, "Now, apparently, the incompetent workers are promoted directly to management without ever passing through the temporary competence stage. When I entered the workforce in 1979, *The Peter Principle* described management pretty well. Now I think we'd all like to return to those Golden Years when you had a boss who was once good at something."

The book remains relevant today. When Peter refers to codophilia (defined as speaking in letters and numbers instead of words), he could be talking of today's business consultants.

Microsoft's Bill Gates echoes Peter saying, "The art of management is to promote people without making them managers."

1145

MANAGEMENT LIBRARY

FOR MORE INFORMATION

Peter, Laurence. *The Peter Principle*. Revised ed. Cutchogue, NY: Buccaneer Books, 1993.

"If at first you don't succeed, you may be at your level of incompetence." *The Peter Principle*

Planning for Quality

Joseph Juran

WHY READ IT?

Juran, like W. Edwards Deming, was one of the key figures in the quality revolution. In this book he stresses that the human aspect of quality management is as important as statistical control. The book underscores the contribution that quality teams and empowerment give to the quality process.

GETTING STARTED

Unlike the West, the Japanese have always made quality a priority at the top of the organization.

The key elements in a quality philosophy are:
- quality planning;
- quality management;
- quality implementation.

Juran contends that quality is nothing new, but it has become ignored in the West where it is treated as an operational issue. There is more to quality than specification and rigorous testing: it cannot be delegated and has to be the goal of each employee, individually and in teams. Quality can be seen as an invariable sequence of steps. Planning consists of developing processes that will meet customers' needs; the human side is just as important.

CONTRIBUTION
1. National Attitudes to Quality Matter

Talking to Japanese audiences in the 1950s, Joseph Juran's message was enthusiastically absorbed by groups of senior managers—the Japanese have made quality a priority at the top of the organization. In the West, Juran's audiences were made up of engineers and quality inspectors. Quality was delegated downward—an operational rather than a managerial issue.

In the post-war years, U.S. businesses were caught unawares for two reasons:
- They assumed their Asian adversaries were copycats rather than innovators.

- Chief executives were too obsessed with financial indicators to notice or heed any danger signs.

2. The Quality Trilogy

Juran's quality philosophy is built around a "quality trilogy" based on "Company-Wide Quality Management" (CWQM), which aims to create a means of disseminating quality to all. Juran insisted that quality cannot be delegated, and he was an early exponent of what has become known as empowerment.

Quality has to be the goal of each employee, individually and in teams, through self-supervision.

3. The Historical Context of Quality

Manufacturing products to design specifications and then inspecting them for defects to protect the buyer was something the Egyptians mastered 5,000 years before when building the pyramids. The ancient Chinese established a separate department of the central government to establish quality standards and maintain them.

Juran's message is therefore that quality is nothing new. But if it is so elemental and elementary, why had it become ignored in the West?

4. The Human Side of Quality

There is more to quality than specification and rigorous testing for defects; Juran regarded the human side of quality as critical. He developed all-embracing theories of what quality should entail.

5. The Quality Planning Process

Quality planning consists of developing the products and processes required to meet customers' needs. Quality planning includes the following activities:
- identifying the customers and their needs;

- developing a product that specifically responds to those needs;
- developing a process able to produce that product.

Quality planning can be produced through an invariable sequence of steps:
- Identify the customers.
- Determine their needs.
- Translate those needs into our language.
- Develop a product that can respond to those needs.
- Optimize the product features to meet our needs as well as customers' needs.
- Develop a process which is able to produce the product.
- Optimize the process.
- Prove that the process can produce the product under operating conditions.
- Transfer the process to those who will be operating it.

CONTEXT

Juran is critical of Deming (*Out of the Crisis*) as being over-reliant on statistics. Juran's approach is less mechanistic than Deming's and places greater emphasis on human relations. It is based on Company-Wide Quality Management (CWQM), a means of disseminating quality to all. Juran was an early exponent of what has become known as empowerment and believed that quality should be the goal of each employee.

Gary Hamel commented: "The impact of Juran, and of Deming as well, went far beyond quality. By drawing the attention of Western managers to the successes of Japan, they forced Western managers to challenge some of their most basic beliefs about the capabilities of their employees and the expectations of their customers."

FOR MORE INFORMATION

Juran, Joseph M. *Planning for Quality*. New York: Free Press, 1988.

"Quality planning consists of developing the products and processes required to meet the customers' needs."

Planning for Quality

The Practice of Management Peter Drucker

WHY READ IT?

Peter Drucker is regarded as the major management and business thinker of the 20th century. *The Practice of Management* is a book of huge range, encyclopedic in its scope and historical perspectives. It laid the groundwork for many of today's accepted management practices and is an excellent primer in management thinking.

GETTING STARTED

Drucker asserts that management will remain a basic and dominant institution, with managers being at the epicenter of economic activity.

A business's purpose is to create a customer; and the two essential functions of business are marketing and innovation. Organization is a means to achieving business performance and results.

There are five basics of the managerial role—to set objectives; organize; motivate and communicate; measure; and develop people. Management has a moral responsibility, and must be driven by objectives.

CONTRIBUTION
1. The Importance of Management

Management will remain a basic and dominant institution perhaps as long as Western civilization itself survives. Drucker places management and managers at the epicenter of economic activity.

Rarely has a new basic institution emerged as fast as has management since 1900, and never before has a new institution proved indispensable so quickly.

2. A Marketing Attitude Is Critical

There is only one valid definition of business purpose: to create a customer.

Markets are created by businesspeople. The want they satisfy may have been felt previously by the customer, but it was theoretical. Only when the action of businesspeople provides a means to satisfy that want is there a customer, a market.

Since the role of business is to create customers, its only two essential functions are marketing and innovation. Marketing is not an isolated function, it is the whole business seen from the customer's point of view.

3. The Nature of Organizations

Though indispensable, organization is not an end in itself, but a means to achieving performance and results. The wrong structure will seriously impair performance and may even destroy the business.

The first question in discussing structure must be: what is our business and what should it be? Organization structure must be designed in such a way that it's possible to achieve business objectives for 5, 10, 15 years hence.

4. The Managerial Role

There are five basics of the managerial role. These are to:

- set objectives;
- organize;
- motivate and communicate;
- measure;
- develop people.

The function that distinguishes the manager above all others is educational. The unique contribution he or she must make is to give others vision and ability to perform.

5. The Importance of Moral Responsibility

It is vision and moral responsibility that, in the last analysis, define the manager. This morality is reflected in five areas.

- There must be high performance requirements; no condoning of poor or mediocre performance, and rewards must be based on performance.
- Each management job must be rewarding in itself, rather than just a step on the ladder.
- There must be a rational and just promotion system.
- Management needs clear rules on who has the power to make life-and-death decisions affecting a manager; and there should be some way to appeal to a higher court.
- In its appointments, management must realize that integrity is the one quality that a manager has to bring to the job and cannot be expected to acquire later on.

6. Management by Objectives

A manager's job should be based on tasks, the performance of which will help attain the company's objectives. The manager should be directed and controlled by the objectives of performance, rather than by his or her boss.

The manager must know and understand what the business goals demand of him or her in terms of performance, and his or her superior must judge the manager accordingly.

7. Tasks for the Manager of the Future

Drucker identified seven new tasks for the manager of the future. Given that these were laid down over 40 years ago, their prescience is astounding. Tomorrow's managers must:

- manage by objectives;
- take more risks for longer;
- be able to make strategic decisions;
- be able to build an integrated team, each member of which is capable of managing his or her own performance in relation to the common objectives;
- be able to communicate information;
- be able to see the business, and the industry, as a whole and to integrate his or her function with it.

CONTEXT

The Practice of Management laid the groundwork for many of the developments in management thinking during the 1960s, and is notable for its ideas concerning the tools and techniques of management. The book is also important for the central role it argues management has in modern society.

Drucker coined phrases such as "privatization" and "knowledge worker," and championed concepts such as management by objectives. *The Economist* commented, "In a field packed with egomaniacs and snake-oil merchants, he remains a genuinely original thinker."

Before Drucker's death in 2005, influential author Gary Hamel said, "No other writer has contributed as much to the professionalization of management as Peter Drucker. Drucker's commitment to the discipline of management grew out of his belief that industrial organizations would become . . . the world's most important social organizations—more influential, more encompassing, and often more intrusive than either church or state. Professor Drucker bridges the theoretical and the practical, the analytical and the emotive, the private and the social more perfectly than any other management writer."

FOR MORE INFORMATION

Drucker, Peter F. *The Practice of Management*. Revised ed. New York: Collins, 1993.

1147

MANAGEMENT LIBRARY

"Management will remain a basic and dominant institution perhaps as long as Western civilization itself survives."

The Practice of Management

The Prince

Niccolò Machiavelli

WHY READ IT?

Although written over 400 years ago, Machiavelli's advice to leaders remains relevant to managers today, and covers many popular topics such as motivation, dealing with change, and leadership qualities.

GETTING STARTED

Change management, leadership style, motivation, and international management were just as relevant in the 16th century as they are today. Executives continue to see themselves as natural rulers of an organization, and to the leader, presentation is as important as ability.

Introducing change is extremely difficult. It's essential to keep motivation high—success is not the result of luck or genius, but happy shrewdness. Leaders who rise rapidly often fall just as quickly, and people ruling foreign countries should be on the spot to prevent trouble. When necessary, leaders have to practise evil.

CONTRIBUTION

1. Executives Have Not Changed

Machiavelli covers topics as apparently contemporary as change management, leadership style, motivation, and international management. Like the leaders Machiavelli sought to defend, some executives tend to see themselves as the natural rulers in whose hands organizations can be safely entrusted.

Theories abound on their motivation: is it a defensive reaction against failure, or a need for predictability through complete control? The effect of the power-driven Machiavellian manager is usually plain to see.

2. Presenting the Right Image

According to Machiavelli, "It is unnecessary for a prince to have all the good qualities [I have] enumerated, but it is very necessary to appear to have them. It is useful to be a great pretender and dissembler."

3. Managing Change and Motivation

"There is nothing more difficult to take in hand, more perilous to conduct, or more uncertain in its success, than to take the lead in the introduction of a new order of things. A leader ought above all things to keep his men well organized and drilled, to follow incessantly the chase."

4. Managing Internationally

"When states are acquired in a country with a different language, customs, or laws, there are difficulties; good fortune and great energy are needed to hold them. It would be a great help if he who acquired them should go and live there. If one is on the spot, disorders are seen as they spring up, and one can quickly remedy them; but if one is not at hand, they are heard of only when they are great, and then one can no longer remedy them."

5. The Qualities of Leadership

In the author's opinion, success is not the result of luck or genius, but happy shrewdness. He felt that a Prince "ought to have no other aim or thought, nor select anything else for his study, than war and its rules and discipline; for this is the sole art that belongs to him who rules."

"In addition, those who solely by good fortune become princes from being private citizens have little trouble in rising, but much in keeping atop," says the author. "They have no difficulties on the way up, because they fly, but they have many when they reach the summit."

It is all very well being good, the author states, but the leader "should know how to enter into evil when necessity commands."

CONTEXT

The Prince is the 16th-century equivalent of Dale Carnegie's *How to Win Friends and Influence People.* Many of its insights are as appropriate to today's managers and organizations as they were half a millennium ago. Antony Jay's 1970 book, *Management and Machiavelli* developed the comparisons.

The book offers something for everyone. It covers topics as apparently contemporary as change management, leadership style, motivation, and international management.

Gary Hamel has said: "We occasionally need reminding that leadership and strategy are not modern inventions. It's just that in previous centuries they are more often the concerns of princes than industrialists. Yet power is a constant in human affairs, and a central theme of Machiavelli's *The Prince.* It is currently out of fashion to talk about power. We are constantly reminded that in the knowledge economy, capital wears shoes and goes home every night. No place here for the blunt instrument of power politics? But would Sumner Redstone, Bill Gates, or Rupert Murdoch agree? What is interesting is that after 400 years, Machiavelli is still in print. What modern volume on leadership will be gracing bookstores in the year 2500? Does Machiavelli's longevity tell us anything about what are the deep, enduring truths of management?"

FOR MORE INFORMATION

Machiavelli, Niccolò. *The Prince.* New York: Penguin, 2003.

"It is unnecessary for a prince to have all the good qualities I have enumerated, but it is very necessary to appear to have them."

The Prince

Principles of Political Economy

John Stuart Mill

WHY READ IT?

Can liberalization and ethics be combined? Is there a just way of distributing wealth? These are still very relevant issues in the age of globalization and neoliberalism. They also exercised the mind of John Stuart Mill (1806–73) in the middle of the 19th century. He gives lucid and humane expression to the view that the objective of economic policy must be to ensure an appropriate material livelihood for everyone. Rejecting the premises of "homo economicus," the rational maximizer of profit and consumption, and the unrestricted belief in the progress of his age, he evolved a concept of the "good" society that is ultimately a vision of unilaterally cooperative socialism.

GETTING STARTED

Mill deals with the principles of production and distribution, embedding economic issues in a broader sociopolitical context. Free competition is necessary, Mill believed, in order to liberate useful social energies. However, the state is not thereby relieved of all its responsibilities, though the scope of its interventions should be strictly limited. Mill draws together the balance of a whole period of scientific research and connects economic principles with their practical applications.

CONTRIBUTION
1. Production and Distribution

The national economy, Mill argues, has to be redefined. Production and distribution must be separated. Whereas the laws of production may be natural laws, the only laws to be investigated in the case of distribution are human-made.

2. Progress

Belief in progress should not, he believes, be unqualified. A "stationary" state in which economic production stagnates is not a crisis signal or catastrophe for industrialized countries, but an opportunity to develop a more just, leisured, and cultivated society. It is not an unhappy and discouraging prospect but a chance to create a harmonious social order. He confessed that he was "not charmed with the ideal of life held out by

those who think that the normal state of human beings is that of struggling to get on; that the trampling, crushing, elbowing, and treading on each other's heels, which form the existing type of social life are the most desirable lot of human kind or anything but the disagreeable symptoms of one of the phases of industrial progress."

Progressive economic development, Mill thought, is characterized by the continuing and unlimited growth of human control over nature and the constant increase in the security of persons and property.

3. Production and Prosperity

Increase in production remained of significance only for underdeveloped countries, in Mill's view. Distribution was much more important for developed countries. The objective there is not mere increase in the result of aggregate production, but prosperity for all.

Where producers join together to form cooperatives, Mill suggests, the overall productivity of industry increases. A strong impetus is given to productive energy inasmuch as the workers are placed in relation to their work as a single body. But the material benefit is nothing in comparison to the moral transformation of society that would accompany this. Cooperatives reduce the profits of capitalists.

4. Private Property

The principle of private property is, according to Mill, important for three reasons. First, individuals have a right vis-à-vis society, a claim to the rewards of the labor or their frugality. Second, the criterion of economic efficiency is operative in that people are motivated to perform to the best of their abilities when they can appropriate the results of their efforts to their own use. Third, private property develops as a function of individuality itself.

5. State Interference

In Mill's opinion, state interventions in the economy are to be rejected. For one thing, individuals know what benefits them and what harms them; for this reason state interventions are always inferior to private

initiatives. For another, state interventions increase the power of the state and tend to lead to despotic and centralized rule.

6. The Good Society

A happy society is characterized by the following elements. In Mill's words:

- "a well-paid and affluent body of laborers"
- "no enormous fortunes, except what were earned and accumulated during a single lifetime"
- "a larger body of people than at present not only exempt from coarser toils, but with sufficient leisure . . . to cultivate freely the graces of life, and afford examples of them to the classes less favourably circumstanced for their growth"

Modern states, he says, will need to learn the lesson that the welfare of a nation must rest on the justice and the judicious self-determination of its individual citizens. Progress in the future depends on the degree to which they are educated to be able to think for themselves.

CONTEXT

The English economist, philosopher, and logician, John Stuart Mill, is one of the chief exponents of empirically oriented thought and of utilitarianism. He made his name as an advocate of radical reform in political and social life and of equality for women. He wished to unite the political economy of capital with the demands of the working class. His thoroughgoing investigation of the methodological questions relating to national economies made him the epistemologist of the liberal school. His inquiries at the interface of pure economics, social philosophy, and ethics gave liberalism a new social cast and are still relevant today. Mill's reflections have once again attracted attention in the course of the debate on "the limits of growth."

FOR MORE INFORMATION

Mill, John Stuart. *Principles of Political Economy with Some of Their Applications to Social Philosophy*. New York: Oxford University Press, 1999.

1149

MANAGEMENT LIBRARY

"Human improvement has no tendency to correct the intensely selfish feelings engendered by power."

Principles of Political Economy

Principles of Political Economy and Taxation

David Ricardo

WHY READ IT?

David Ricardo (1772–1823) is one of the most important theorists in the history of political economy. *The Principles of Political Economy and Taxation* is one of the cornerstones of the classical approach to the subject. His ideas, especially the theory of comparative cost advantage, formed the basis for the discussion of free trade and protective tariffs throughout the 19th century. His work forms a bridge between that of Adam Smith, who was Ricardo's immediate inspiration, and that of Karl Marx. He is also often said to be the inspirer of the Chicago "monetarist" school that had such a profound influence on the economics and the politics of the late 20th century. The book is still acknowledged as a masterpiece today for its isolation and abstraction of basic principles, its synthesis, and its logic.

GETTING STARTED

In this book, first published in 1817, Ricardo gets to grips with the concept of exchange value and expounds the theory of comparative cost advantage.

His central argument runs as follows: the exchange of goods between two countries is worthwhile for both, even if one country can produce all the goods more cheaply than the other. He uses two trading nations, Britain and Portugal, and two types of good, cloth and wine, as examples. In addition, he sets out criteria for the objective valuation of goods. According to his doctrine, the value of any good is determined solely by how much labor is necessary for its production. He also deals with prosperity and poverty in the social classes, and the connections between the factors of production, labor, land, and capital, and develops general principles of taxation.

CONTRIBUTION
1. On Value

Ricardo states that the value of a good depends on the relative quantity of labor required for its production. By this he means not merely the labor expended in actually creating it, but also that expended on the machines, tools, and buildings that support the immediate work of production.

2. On Foreign Trade

Expansion of foreign trade will not, according to Ricardo, immediately increase the sum of value in a country. As the value of all foreign goods is measured by the quantity of the products of the country's soil and labor expended in exchange for them, it will not possess greater value if, through the discovery of new markets, it receives double the quantity of foreign goods for a specific quantity of its own.

3. On Taxes

Taxes, says Ricardo, are a part of the product of the land and labor of a country that is put at the disposal of the government. They are always paid out of the country's capital or revenue.

Taxes on luxury goods only affect those who use luxuries. Taxes on necessities, however, are a burden on consumers not only in proportion to the quantity they consume, but often in far greater measure. This is because, argues Ricardo, anything that increases wages reduces the profit from capital; taxes on goods consumed by workers tend to bring down rates of profit.

Income taxes likewise increase wages and reduce the rate of profit on capital. Consequently, in Ricardo's view, only those who employ workers contribute to income tax, not money capitalists, nor landowners, nor any other social class.

He also argues, however, that a tax on essential consumer goods does not entail any particular disadvantage insofar as it raises wages and lowers profits. Profits are indeed reduced, but only to the extent of the worker's contribution to the tax, which in any event must be borne either by the worker's employer or the consumers of the products of his or her labor.

4. On Currencies and Banks

The exchangeability of paper money for metal is not essential to ensure its value, Ricardo says. It is only necessary that its quantity should be regulated in accordance with the value of the metal that has been declared as the standard. If gold of a specific weight and fineness is the standard, then the amount of paper money in circulation can be increased whenever gold declines in value or, which is the same thing in its effect, whenever the price of goods rises.

5. On the Influence of Supply and Demand on Prices

Production costs, Ricardo argues, determine the prices of goods, not the relationship between supply and demand. This relationship may influence the market price of a good for a time, until it is delivered in greater or lesser quantities depending on whether demand has risen or fallen. But this will only be a temporary effect.

CONTEXT

In his thoughts on foreign trade, Ricardo went against the spirit of his age. Whereas his homeland, Great Britain, protected its own economy with customs barriers, his theorem of comparative cost advantages argued in favor of free trade. Ricardo's views on foreign trade are a guiding light in the liberalization of world trade even today: his portrait adorns the Web site of the World Trade Organization (WTO).

Ricardo's arguments on the value of goods and his ideas on the division of income between workers, capitalists, and landowners influenced many later economists. In particular, his theory of added value was taken up by Karl Marx and became a weapon in the arsenal of socialism.

Before he began writing, Ricardo was one of the best-known speculators of his time. As a young man, he was a dealer in government securities and made a fortune through the stock exchange. In Ricardo's system of distribution, however, landowners come off best in the long run. He himself acted in accordance with his own principles: he sold his securities and bought an estate.

FOR MORE INFORMATION

Ricardo, David. *The Principles of Political Economy and Taxation.* Amherst, NY: Prometheus Books, 1996.

The Principles of Scientific Management

Frederick Winslow Taylor

WHY READ IT?

At the time *The Principles of Scientific Management* was published, "business management as a discrete and identifiable activity had attracted little attention" as Lyndall Urwick, the British champion of scientific management, said. The book put management on the map, and its influence on working methods and managerial attitudes for most of the 20th century, especially in mass-production industries, was enormous. Taylor's principles have been alternately reviled, rejected, and rediscovered. They remain undeniably significant even today.

GETTING STARTED

Frederick Winslow Taylor was a U.S. engineer and inventor, whose fame rests chiefly on this book. He shares with Henry Ford the dubious distinction of founding an "-ism." Taylorism is the practice of the principles of scientific management, which emerged from Taylor's work at the Midvale Steel Works. It involves rigorous measurement of work processes, total objectivity in the assessment of which methods work best, and the consequent mechanization of work and elimination of the human element. The objective standards arrived at, however, are as binding on managers, who have to enforce them, as on the workers who have to meet them. Like the assembly line, scientific management imposes its discipline on everyone. To most members of the humanistic school of management it is the enemy *par excellence*.

CONTRIBUTION

1. Measuring Work

Taylor's science consisted in the minute examination of individual tasks. Having identified every single movement and action involved in doing something, he could determine the optimum time required to complete a task.

Armed with this information, the manager could determine whether a person was doing the job well.

2. Putting Science Before Opinion

The most obvious consequence of scientific management is a dehumanizing reliance on measurement.

The experts, who first analyze and then accurately time the various ways of doing each piece of work, will finally know from exact knowledge, and not from anyone's opinion, which method will accomplish the results with the least effort and in the quickest time.

The exact facts will have in this way been developed and they will constitute a series of laws, which are destined to control the vast multitude of our daily personal acts which, at present, are the subjects of individual opinion.

3. A System with No Initiative

The Taylorist system envisages no room for individual initiative or imagination. People are labor, mechanically accomplishing a particular task and doing what they are told.

According to Robert McNamara: "those who were so important in the early stages of American manufacturing, the foremen and plant managers, were disenfranchised. Instead of being creators and innovators, as in an earlier era, now they depended on meeting production quotas. They could not stop the line and fix problems as they occurred; they lost any stake in innovation or change." (quoted in *Promise and Power* by Debora Shapley). Taylor's program for objectively determining best practices for every imaginable job could, on the other hand, be said to have freed front-line workers from the capricious discipline of unscientific, turn-of-the-century foremen.

CONTEXT

While Taylor's concepts are now usually regarded in a negative light, the originality of his insights and their importance are in little doubt. He himself announced that he was ushering in a revolution, "a complete mental revolution on the part of the working man engaged in any particular establishment or industry, a complete mental revolution on the part of these men as to their duties toward their work, toward their fellow men, and toward their employees."

Peter Drucker observed in *The Practice of Management* : "Few people had ever looked at human work systematically until Frederick W. Taylor started to do so around 1885. Work was taken for granted and it is an axiom that one never sees what one takes for granted. *Scientific Management* was thus one of the great liberating, pioneering insights."

Lyndall Urwick added: "At the time Taylor began his work, business management . . . was usually regarded as incidental to, and flowing from knowledge of . . . a particular branch of manufacturing, the technical know-how of making sausages or steel or shirts. The idea that a man needed any training or formal instruction to become a competent manager had not occurred to anyone."

The legacy of Taylor's work is most obvious in companies that tend to emphasize quantity over quality. His ideas were enthusiastically taken up by Henry Ford in the development of mass-production techniques.

Drucker goes on to identify two fundamental flaws in scientific management.

"The first of these blind spots is the belief that, because we must analyze work into its simplest constituent motions, we must also organize it as a series of individual motions, each if possible performed by an individual worker; the second that it divorces planning from doing."

Gary Hamel sums up the position thus: "The development of modern management theory is the story of two quests: to make management more scientific, and to make it more humane. It is wrong to look at the latter quest as somehow much more enlightened than the former. Indeed, they are the yin and yang of business. The unprecedented capacity of twentieth century industry to create wealth rests squarely on the work of Frederick Winslow Taylor. While some may disavow Taylor, his rational, deterministic impulses live on. Indeed, reengineering is simply late twentieth century Taylorism. Though the focus of reengineering is on the process, rather than the individual task, the motivation is the same: to simplify, to remove unnecessary effort, and to do more with less."

FOR MORE INFORMATION

Taylor, Frederick Winslow. *The Principles of Scientific Management*. Revised ed. New York: 1st World Library, 2006.

"The determination of the best method of performing all of our daily acts will, in the future, be the work of experts."

The Principles of Scientific Management
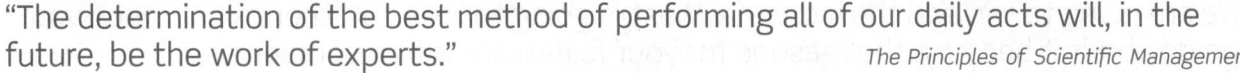

Quest for Prosperity

Konosuke Matsushita

WHY READ IT?

This book describes how Konosuke Matsushita built a global business—Panasonic—from nothing. It contains lessons on customer service, business ethics, and marketing that would benefit any business.

GETTING STARTED

According to the author, customer service is critical to success—customers want goods that will benefit them. Furthermore, after-sales service is more important than assistance before sales.

Business with a conscience cements loyalty. We are using precious resources that could be better used elsewhere unless we make a good profit. Production efficiency and quality products are key. The mission of a manufacturer should be to overcome poverty, to relieve society as a whole from misery, and to bring it wealth.

CONTRIBUTION
1. Building a Winning Business

The Matsushita story is one of the most impressive industrial achievements of the 20th century.

The company's first break was an order to make insulator plates. The order was delivered on time and was of very high quality. Matsushita began to make money. He then developed an innovative bicycle light. At first, retailers were unimpressed. Then Matsushita had his salesmen leave a switched on light in each shop. This simple product demonstration impressed the retailers, and the business took off.

2. The Importance of Customer Service

The company understood customer service before anyone in the West had even thought about it:

- Don't sell customers goods that they are attracted to. Sell them goods that will benefit them.

- After-sales service is more important than assistance before sales. It is through such service that one acquires permanent customers.

3. Efficiency and Quality

Matsushita emphasized efficient production and quality products.

To be out of stock is due to carelessness. If this happens, apologize to the customers, ask for their address, and tell them that you will deliver the goods immediately.

4. Risk-taking Pays

Matsushita took risks and backed his beliefs at every stage.

The classic example of this is found in the development of the videocassette. Matsushita developed VHS video and licensed the technology. Sony developed Betamax, which was immeasurably better, but failed to license the technology. Consequently, the world standard is VHS and Betamax is consigned to history.

5. Business with a Conscience

Matsushita advocated business with a conscience, reflected in his paternalistic employment practices. During a recession early in its life the company did not lay anyone off. This cemented loyalty.

It is not enough to work conscientiously. No matter what kind of job you are doing, you should think of yourself as being completely in charge of and responsible for your own work.

6. The Role of the Leader

Big things and little things are the leader's job. Middle-level arrangements can be delegated.

Matsushita also explained the role of the leader in more cryptic style: "The tail trails the head. If the head moves fast, the tail will keep up the same pace. If the head is sluggish, the tail will droop."

7. The Broader Obejctives of Business

Matsushita mapped out the broader spiritual goals he believed a business should have. Profit was not enough. The mission of a manufacturer should be to overcome poverty, to relieve society as a whole from misery, and to bring it wealth.

He outlined his basic management objective in the following way: "Recognizing our responsibilities as industrialists, we will devote ourselves to the progress and development of society and the well-being of people through our business activities, thereby enhancing the quality of life throughout the world."

Failure to make a profit was regarded as a sort of crime against society: "We take society's capital, we take their people, we take their materials, yet without a good profit, we are using precious resources that could be better used elsewhere."

Business is demanding, serious, and crucial: "Business, we know, is now so complex and difficult, the survival of companies so hazardous in an environment increasingly unpredictable, competitive, and fraught with danger, that their continued existence depends on the day-to-day mobilization of every ounce of intelligence."

CONTEXT

Matsushita created a $42-billion revenue business from nothing. He also created Panasonic, one of the world's most successful brands, and amassed a personal fortune of $3 billion.

The book explains the principles that made his business a success.

FOR MORE INFORMATION

Matsushita, Konosuke. *Quest for Prosperity*. Kyoto: PHP Institute, 1988.

"We are going to win and the industrial West is going to lose out; there's not much you can do about it because the reasons for your failure are within yourselves."

Reengineering the Corporation

James Champy
Michael Hammer

WHY READ IT?
Reengineering the Corporation is seen as the key book in the reengineering revolution. It encourages organizations to take a fresh look at inefficient and outdated processes, and to focus on dramatic improvements in cost, quality, service, and speed. Although the message has been misinterpreted, reengineering remains a powerful tool for change.

GETTING STARTED
In the authors' view, reengineering must focus on the fundamental rethinking and radical redesign of key business processes. Dramatic improvements in cost, quality, service, and speed are the objectives, and organizations must make key processes as lean and profitable as possible, discarding peripheral processes and people if necessary.

Reengineering should go far beyond altering and refining processes: the goal is "to reverse the Industrial Revolution." Organizations should start with a blank piece of paper and map out processes to identify how their business should operate. They should then attempt to translate the paper into concrete reality.

Reengineering puts a premium on the skills and potential of the people at the center of the organization, and should also tackle three key areas of management—managerial roles, styles and systems.

CONTRIBUTION
1. Focus on Improving Core Processes
In the context of a fiercely competitive environment and the ability of IT to transform business processes, the book encourages organizations to take a fresh look at inefficient and outdated processes. Reengineering, according to the authors, is the fundamental rethinking and radical redesign of business processes.

2. Create a Lean Organization
The authors argue that organizations need to identify their key processes and make them as lean and profitable as possible. In some cases, peripheral processes and people need to be discarded.

Unfortunately, many organizations have taken this advice literally and downsized without reengineering. CSC, the consulting firm founded by Champy and Hammer, surveyed more than 600 companies involved in reengineering projects in 1994. In the United States, an average 336 jobs were lost on each project. In Europe, the figure was 760 jobs per project.

3. Achieve a Complete Corporate Revolution
Simple business process reengineering is not enough, say the authors. True reengineering is a recipe for a corporate revolution, and should go far beyond altering and refining processes: the past is history; the future is there to be coerced into the optimum shape.

The authors believe that reengineering is concerned with rejecting conventional wisdom and received assumptions about the past. However, this can mean ignoring the experiences and lessons of the past. Companies are discouraged from trying to understand why they have been successful and building on that.

4. Transform the Future
The authors suggest that organizations should start with a blank piece of paper. They should map out their processes to identify how their business should operate, and then attempt to translate the paper into concrete reality.

In practice, this has proved difficult to achieve. The authors now believe that companies tend not to cast the reengineering net widely; they find processes that can be reengineered quickly and stop at that point. They lack a vision for the future and the revolutionary approach to take reengineering forward.

5. Reengineer Management As Well
Part of the problem, they now believe, is that managers fail to impose change on themselves—they concentrate on tearing down processes, but they leave their own jobs and management styles intact. However, the old ways of management could eventually undermine the very structure of their rebuilt enterprise. The reengineering process should therefore tackle three key areas of management—managerial roles, styles, and systems.

6. Reengineering Should Be Built on Trust, Respect, and People
The authors believe that reengineering actually puts a premium on the people at the center of the organization. Once peripheral activities have been cut away, the new environment puts a premium on skills of the people who are left. Experience suggests that this has not happened so far: downsizing creates a difficult environment in which trust is frequently absent.

CONTEXT
Reengineering is seen by some as an old concept with a new label. Frederick W. Taylor's *Scientific Management* advocated similar change, but at an individual rather than an organizational level. Gary Hamel pointed out that reengineering followed a line from scientific management, industrial engineering, and business process improvement.

The mechanistic theme has been a key focal point for critics, who have made the point that reengineering owes more to visions of the corporation as a machine, rather than a human system. Peter Cohan, a former colleague, said the authors ignored the importance of people, describing them as objects who handle processes.

Christopher Lorenz of the *Financial Times* believed that the authors failed to state whether organizations should undertake behavioral and cultural changes in parallel with reengineering.

It has also been easy to take the book's messages too literally. Reengineering has been seen as a synonym for redundancy, and the book has been blamed for a wave of downsizing.

FOR MORE INFORMATION

Champy, James, and Michael Hammer. *Reengineering the Corporation*. Revised ed. New York: Collins, 2004.

"I tell them what I really do is I'm reversing the Industrial Revolution."

Relationship Marketing

Regis McKenna

WHY READ IT?

Relationship marketing has become one of the most important determinants of corporate success. Retaining customers and maximizing lifetime customer value are critical to long term revenue and profitability. Regis McKenna's book sets out the principles of building successful relationships, using technology to understand and communicate with customers.

GETTING STARTED

Marketing, the author says, is everything. It has moved away from mass marketing to customization and personalization. Technology, he explains, is the enabler in this change, allowing companies to deal with the growing power of the customer and the accelerating pace of change in the marketplace. Products are no longer sufficient. Customers demand solutions. Communication has also moved from monolog to dialog based on a deeper understanding of customers.

CONTRIBUTION

1. Integrating the Customer

McKenna believes that technology and the choices it offers are transforming the marketplace. All companies, he claims, are technology companies, using technology to customize and offer unlimited choice. The knowledge and understanding available through technology are changing the nature of marketing. The objective now is to integrate the customer into the company.

2. Dominating Markets

A strong brand is the reflection of a successful relationship. Owning the market, not just competing in it, is therefore a key goal. Market dominance is vital to attracting customers, business partners and the best employees. The starting point is to define a narrow market and dominate it, before expanding the relationships.

3. Dialog with Customers

McKenna claims that one-way advertising is no longer valid. Companies need to have dialog with customers using trials, user groups, and other feedback mechanisms. He calls this "experience-based marketing" based on a deep understanding of the customer.

4. Merger of Products and Services

The author points out that, in industries like computing, around 75% of the business consists of services such as consulting, systems integration, and customer support. These are essential to customers and form part of a solution that builds relationships.

5. Faster Time to Market

Companies must reduce time to market as much as possible—delay leads to lost opportunities. The marketplace is changing rapidly so it is important to stay close to customers.

6. Market Creation Replaces Market Sharing

Companies must differentiate their products to dominate a market, says the author, which may mean starting with small sectors and acting like entrepreneurs. Market creation also means educating customers and listening to them. However, quantitative information can distract companies from entering small sectors. Qualitative judgment may be more important.

4. Relationships

Relationships are more important with complex high-risk products. Customers need reassurance, education, support, and services to build and maintain their confidence in a company.

8. Dynamic Positioning

The author explains how dynamic positioning differs from traditional positioning:
- Product positioning determines how a product fits into a competitive market.
- Market positioning requires a company to understand the infrastructure, influences, and distribution channels in its market.
- Corporate positioning determines whether a company is perceived as a credible and trusted supplier.

9. Product Positioning

Product positioning must be based on an understanding of the market environment, according to McKenna. It must also focus on the intangible factors that are important to customers. Trust, he argues, is the logical outcome where customers have a strong relationship and continue to buy.

10. Product Success

McKenna cites ten characteristics of a successful product:
- appeals to a new market

- takes advantage of the best technologies
- depends on the market infrastructure for newly-developed technologies
- timing is right
- adapted to market requirements
- developed by small entrepreneurial teams
- customers involved in development
- adopted by early users
- generates a new language
- used in demonstrations, workshops, and user groups

11. Developing Relationships

According to McKenna, successful companies develop relationships with the whole market, not just customers. This is the market infrastructure and it includes analysts, developers, retailers, journalists, suppliers, and other organizations who are mutually dependent. The leaders set the standard for their market and everyone else works with them. McKenna describes these as structural relationships. Strategic relationships with partners are important. For larger companies, the relationships reduce development costs and speed up time to market. For smaller companies, the relationships provide credibility and access.

12. Selling to the Right Customers

McKenna places buyers in four categories:
- innovators
- early adopters
- majority
- laggards

CONTEXT

This book was one of the first to highlight the importance of relationships with customers, suppliers, distributors, and other players in the marketplace. The discipline of relationship marketing has now entered mainstream marketing practice and is an essential tool for companies in very field.

Since the book's publication, the practice of relationship marketing has been further refined by the development of personalization techniques and one-to-one marketing via the Internet. The principles, however, remain the same.

FOR MORE INFORMATION

McKenna, Regis. *Relationship Marketing: Successful Strategies for the Age of the Customer.* Cambridge, MA: Perseus Books, 1993.

Riding the Waves of Culture

Fons Trompenaars
Charles Hampden-Turner

1155

MANAGEMENT LIBRARY

WHY READ IT?

Riding the Waves of Culture is an examination of the cultural imponderables faced by managers in the global village. Based on exhaustive research, it systematically "dimensionalizes" cultural differences, identifying seven areas, such as attitude to rules and awareness of time, in which different nations have fundamentally different conceptions. Anyone whose work involves dealing with people from other cultures would benefit from reading it.

GETTING STARTED

Fons Trompenaars studied at a top U.S. business school where he started thinking about cultural differences. "I started wondering if any of the American management techniques I was brainwashed with in eight years of the best business education money could buy would apply in the Netherlands, where I came from, or indeed in the rest of the world."

Charles Hampden-Turner is an international authority on cross-cultural communication who taught for many years in the United States and, like his coauthor, worked for Shell.

The book is based on meticulous quantitative research (over 15 years 15,000 people from 50 countries were surveyed) and more than 900 seminars presented in 18 countries. Its main contentions are that basic to understanding other cultures is the awareness of cultural difference; that cultural difference can be systematically analyzed; that flexibility, a certain amount of humility, and a sense of humor are needed in dealing with cultures other than our own; and that the reconciliation of difference is the supreme managerial art.

CONTRIBUTION
1. Culture

Culture is a series of rules and methods that a society has evolved to deal with the recurring problems it faces. They have become so basic that we no longer think about how we approach or resolve them.

People should be aware, first, that they belong to a culture and have a specific way of doing things, and they should be prepared, second, for a different response from the one they are accustomed to receiving

when they do business with someone whose culture differs from theirs.

2. Seven Dimensions of Culture

In analyzing cultural differences, the authors identify seven dimensions in which different or contrasting attitudes are particularly crucial. There are:

- universalism vs particularism
- individualism vs collectivism
- neutral vs emotional
- specific vs diffuse
- achievement vs ascription
- attitude toward time
- attitude toward the environment

3. Universalism and Particularism

There are two fundamentally distinct ways of dealing with situations that the book labels "universalism" and "particularism." Universalists (including Americans, Canadians, Australians, and the Swiss) advocate one best way, "what is good and right can be defined and always applies." They focus on rules and procedure. Particularists (South Koreans, Chinese, and Malaysians) feel that circumstances dictate how ideas and practices should be applied. They focus on the peculiar nature of any given situation and on particular relationships.

Universalists doing business with particularists should be prepared for meandering or irrelevancies that do not seem to be going anywhere.

Particularists doing business with universalists should be prepared for rational and professional arguments and presentations and little else.

4. Collectivist and Individualist

The book also contrasts the collectivist mindset with the individualist one.

The United States again comes at one extreme of the spectrum emphasizing the individual before the group. Countries such as Egypt and France are at the other end.

Individualists working with collectivists must tolerate time taken to consult and negotiators who only agree tentatively and may withdraw after consulting with superiors.

5. The Role of the International Manager

Given the wide range of basic differences in

how different cultures perceive the world, it is evident that the international manager is moving in a world riddled with potential pitfalls. There are also profound differences between those who show their feelings (such as Italians) and those who hide them (such as the Japanese), and those who accord status on the basis of achievement and those ascribe it on the basis of family and age.

The international manager needs to go beyond awareness of cultural differences. He or she needs to respect these differences and take advantage of diversity through reconciling cross-cultural dilemmas. The international manager reconciles cultural dilemmas. In the end, the only positive route forward is through reconciliation. Those societies that can reconcile better are better at creating wealth.

CONTEXT

Tom Peters called *Riding the Waves of Culture* a masterpiece. "What's not okay is cultural arrogance. If you come to another's turf with sensitivity and open ears . . . you're halfway home."

Gary Hamel takes the authors to task for their criticisms of U.S. cultural inflexibility: "So Americans will never understand foreign cultures? Funny how American companies are out-competing their European competitors in Asia and Latin America . . . Where I agree with Trompenaars is that the future belongs to the cosmopolitans."

The cultural aspects of managing internationally are likely to gain in importance as the full force of globalization affects industries and individuals. In this respect the value of the book's contribution is undeniable. It has been argued, however, that its stress on cultural relativism and adaptability might become outmoded if capital markets were to enforce "global rules of the game" independent of different cultures.

FOR MORE INFORMATION

Trompenaars, Fons, and Charles Hampden-Turner. *Riding the Waves of Culture*. 2nd ed. New York: McGraw-Hill, 1997.

"Culture is the way in which people resolve dilemmas emerging from universal problems."

The Rise and Fall of Strategic Planning

Henry Mintzberg

WHY READ IT?

Mintzberg shows how an over-emphasis on analysis and hard facts limits strategic planning. Planning should be something visionary and creative. The book has become an influential classic.

GETTING STARTED

Planning is concerned with analysis; strategy making is concerned with synthesis. Strategic planners tend to make false assumptions that discontinuities can be predicted; the future will resemble the past; and strategy making can be formalized. They tend to be detached from action and the reality of the organization.

Planners typically gather hard data on their industry, markets, and competitors. Soft data—such as networks of contacts, talking with customers, suppliers, and employees—have been ignored. Strategy formulation has been dominated by logic and analysis. This narrows options. Intuition and creativity need to become part of the process.

CONTRIBUTION

1. Strategy and Planning

Planning codifies, elaborates, and operationalizes existing company strategy. In contrast, strategy is either an emergent pattern or a deliberate perspective, and cannot be planned. While planning is concerned with analysis, strategy making is concerned with synthesis.

2. The Nature of Planners

Planners do have value, but only as strategy finders, analysts, and catalysts. At their most effective, they unearth strategies in unexpected pockets of the organization, whose potential can then be explored.

3. Problems with Planning Practices

The three main pitfalls are:
- the assumption that discontinuities can be predicted;
- planners are detached from the reality of the organization;
- the assumption that strategy making can be formalized.

4. The Assumption That Discontinuities Can Be Predicted

Forecasting techniques often assume that the future will resemble the past. This gives artificial reassurance, and creates strategies that disintegrate rapidly as they are overtaken by events.

5. Detachment from the Reality of the Organization

If the system does the thinking, strategy must be detached from operations, and thinkers from doers. This disassociation of thinking from acting lies at the root of strategic planning's problem.

6. Hard Data and Soft Data

Planners typically gather hard data on their industry, markets, and competitors. Soft data—networks of contacts, talking with customers, suppliers, and employees, using intuition, and using the grapevine—have all but been ignored.

Hard data are often anything but. There is the fallacy of measuring what's measurable. There is a tendency to favor cost-leadership strategies (emphasizing operating efficiencies, which are generally measurable) over product-leadership strategies (emphasizing innovative design or high quality, which tends to be less measurable).

To gain useful understanding of an organization's competitive situation, soft data need to be dynamically integrated into the planning process. They may be difficult to analyze, but they are indispensable for synthesis—the key to strategy making.

7. The Assumption That Strategy Making Can Be Formalized

The emphasis on logic and analysis creates a narrow range of options. Alternatives that do not fit into the predetermined structure are ignored.

The right side of the brain needs to become part of the process, with its emphasis on intuition and creativity. Planning defines and preserves categories. Creativity creates categories or rearranges established ones.

Thus strategic planning can neither provide creativity, nor deal with it when it emerges. Mold-breaking strategies grow initially like weeds—they are not cultivated and can take root anywhere.

8. The Nature of Strategy Making

Mintzberg defines strategy making thus:
- It is derived from synthesis.

- It is informal and visionary, rather than programmed and formalized.
- It relies on divergent thinking, intuition, and using the subconscious. This leads to outbursts of right-brain creativity as new discoveries are made.
- It is irregular, unexpected, ad hoc, and instinctive. It upsets stable patterns.
- Managers are adaptive information manipulators—opportunists, rather than aloof conductors.
- It is done in times of instability characterized by discontinuous change.
- It results from an approach that takes in broad perspectives and is, therefore, visionary, and involves a variety of actors capable of experimenting and then integrating the results.

CONTEXT

The book reflects a general dissatisfaction with strategic planning. Research by the U.S. Planning Forum found that only 25% of companies considered that their planning was effective.

The book attracted much attention and debate. It also brought a spirited response from the defenders of strategy. Andrew Campbell, coauthor of *Corporate-Level Strategy*, wrote: "Strategic planning is not futile. Research has shown that some companies—both conglomerates and more focused groups—have strategic planning processes that add real value." Campbell further argues that the corporate center must develop a value-creating, corporate-level strategy and build the management processes needed to implement it.

Management guru Gary Hamel commented: "Henry views strategic planning as a ritual, devoid of creativity and meaning. He is undoubtedly right when he argues that planning doesn't produce strategy. But rather than use the last chapter of the book to create a new charter for planners, Henry might have put his mind to the question of where strategies actually do come from!"

FOR MORE INFORMATION

Mintzberg, Henry. *The Rise and Fall of Strategic Planning*. New York: Free Press, 1994.

 "Strategy cannot be planned."

Small Is Beautiful

E. F. Schumacher

WHY READ IT?

Schumacher's book has become one of the most influential works ever on environmental issues and business. It looks at traditional Western economics in a radical way, arguing that big is not always best. His work has struck a chord with politicians, environmentalists, and a growing number of business leaders.

GETTING STARTED

Schumacher argues that the relentless pursuit of profit and progress has resulted in economic inefficiency, environmental pollution, and inhumane working conditions. Instead, he proposes greater use of "intermediate technology," based on smaller work units, communal ownership, and the use of local labor and resources.

CONTRIBUTION

1. The Problem of Production

Schumacher believes that business has not solved the problem of production. Businesses are using up the store of natural capital and he cites the spiraling demands on fossil fuels and other finite natural resources. The proposal to replace fossil fuels with human-made energy sources such as nuclear fuels creates its own problems.

The author's view is that the concept of peace through universal prosperity is also unachievable. He argues that, if prosperity grew in line with population growth, the impact on fuel consumption and subsequent atmospheric pollution would be extremely damaging.

2. Changing the Emphasis of Economics

The solution, he claims, lies in a reorientation of science and technology. The emphasis should not be on concentrating production in larger and larger units, it should be on making technology accessible and suitable for small-scale application. He also believes that technology should leave room for

human creativity, rather than replacing it.

Traditional economic theories are driven by market forces. Schumacher believes that they ignore humanity's dependence on the natural world. Economics, he says, is also overdependent on quantitative measures such as gross domestic product and consequently overlooks qualitative measures such as the impact of the economy on the environment.

According to Schumacher, economics looks upon human labor as a necessary "input" to wealth. Business takes every opportunity to reduce the cost, making work meaningless. An alternative point of view says that work should enable people to utilize their faculties and join in a common cause. This is in contrast to the theory that consumption is the only real end.

3. Toward a Smaller Scale

Schumacher points out that scale is another important element of economic thinking. The traditional theory is that economic organizations, such as businesses, should be as large as possible. He counters that they only need to be big enough to meet real needs.

Schumacher also argues for the more effective use of land. It is not simply a factor of production. He cites the flight from the land as evidence of this misunderstanding.

4. The Efficiency Gap

The author is critical of modern industrial efficiency. The United States, for example, has around 5% of the world's population, yet requires almost 40% of the world's primary resources to sustain its economy.

Apart from the demand on resources, Schumacher argues that this situation also creates problems between producer and consumer countries. An economy that is so dependent on other resources must in the long term suffer.

5. A Human Face for Technology

Schumacher believes that technology needs

a human face. Technology should free people from the burdens of work. He describes how the Intermediate Technology Development Group aims to broaden the use of technology, supporting production by the masses, instead of mass production. This approach, he feels, would be an effective way to support regional economic development around the world.

Despite his emphasis on small-scale regional development, Schumacher accepts that large organizations will remain an important part of the economy. He believes that setting up smaller units within a larger organization could help to overcome any inherent problems of size.

CONTEXT

Schumacher, like Hawken and Lovins in *Natural Capitalism*, highlights the conflict between business growth and the destruction of natural resources. He proposes a system of environmentally friendly business that takes account of limited resources and offers everyone a stake in success.

He draws on a wide variety of influences and sources to develop his themes, including Buddhist economics, Adam Smith, Gandhi, and economists such as Galbraith.

Although Schumacher's work could be regarded as utopian, he proposes practical working solutions, some of which have already been put into successful practice.

1157

MANAGEMENT LIBRARY

FOR MORE INFORMATION

Schumacher, E. F. *Small is Beautiful: A Study of Economics As If People Mattered.* New York: HarperCollins, 1999.

FURTHER READING

Hawken, Paul, Amory B. Lovins, and L. Hunter Lovins. *Natural Capitalism: The Next Industrial Revolution.* Boston, MA: Back Bay Books 2000.

"One of the most fateful errors of our age is the belief that the problem of production has been solved."

Small Is Beautiful

Strategy Safari

Henry Mintzberg
Bruce Ahlstrand
Joseph Lampel

WHY READ IT?

The landscape of strategic management, according to the authors, is a wilderness—confusion reigns, the most heterogeneous forms of thinking coexist, and there is no recognizable order or structure. This book offers itself as a jargon-free guide to those who wish to explore the wilderness. Its objective is to clarify and critique a variety of approaches, which the authors have shaped into distinct schools of thought. It ends with a plea for synthesis.

GETTING STARTED

The authors present eight "schools of strategy" and compare them to one another. They explain their premises, criticize their weak points, and show under what conditions each particular doctrine can bring success. But these theories do not stand alone; they are parts of a larger whole, and the important thing is to integrate them.

CONTRIBUTION

1. The Design School

- Premises: Strategy development should be a conscious process. Control remains in the hands of the chief executive: he or she is the strategist. The model of strategy development must be kept simple and informal. The best strategies are the result of an individualized formation process.
- Criticism: The Design School puts too great an emphasis on thinking divorced from action, because it does not view the strategy-developing process as a learning one.
- Contribution and context: In principle, an individual person is capable of dealing with all the information needed to develop a strategy.

2. The Planning School

- Premises: Strategies result from planning; they are divided into separate steps, which are presented in the form of checklists and conducted by means of concrete techniques. The strategies that emerge from this process are ready formulated.
- Criticism: Plans provide a clear direction and give an organization stability, but they undermine flexibility.
- Contribution and context: Planning strategists make good analysts; they feed the black box with data and scrutinize strategies to see if they are feasible.

3. The Positioning School

- Premises: Strategies deal with generic, general, and recognizable market positions. Strategy development, therefore, is a matter of choosing these generic positions on the basis of analytical calculations.
- Criticism: The perspective is narrow. It concentrates on the purely economic and quantifiable and omits other factors.
- Contribution and context: The role of positioning must be to support the process; it should not be the actual process.

4. The Entrepreneurial School

- Premises: Strategy exists in the mind of the chief executive as a feeling for the organization's long-term direction. Strategy development takes place at best only half consciously.
- Criticism: Strategy development is presented as a process that is "wrapped up in" the behavior of a single individual.
- Contribution and context: Businesses profit from the firm sense of direction and the high degree of integration and definition provided by this approach.

5. The Cognitive School

- Premises: Strategies form in the head of the strategist as ways of seeing—concepts, maps, schemata, and frameworks—that shape the way in which people act on information from their environment.
- Criticism: Strategic management hobbles a long way behind cognitive psychology.
- Contribution and context: Good strategists are creative; they create a world in their heads and then bring it into being.

6. The Learning School

- Premises: The complex nature of the organizational environment excludes conscious control. It is the collective system that learns. There are many potential strategists.
- Criticism: Learning is costly. It takes time, it produces endless meetings and floods of mail, and it runs off in all directions.
- Contribution and context: The research of the Learning School rests on simple methods that are well suited to explaining complex systems.

7. The Environmental School

- Premises: The decisive factor in the strategy development process is the environment, which presents itself to the organization as an array of forces to which it must react.
- Criticism: In reality no environment is simply generous or complex or hostile or dynamic. The attempt to orient strategies in accordance with such general conditions seems foolhardy.
- Contribution and context: Both practitioners and theoreticians have to come to grips with a multifarious world that prompts imaginative action.

8. The Configurational School

- Premises: In a business, phases of stability are interrupted by processes of transformation—there is a quantum leap to another configuration. Over time these become ordered into structured sequences.
- Criticism: It is doubtful whether businesses either are static or change by means of great leaps forward.
- Contribution and context: The Configurational School brings order into the chaotic world of strategy development.

9. Integration

Every strategy-making process demands, say the authors, a combination of various elements from the individual schools. Shaping strategy has mental and social aspects, must take the demands of the environment into account, and is unthinkable without leadership and powers of organization, or without balancing step-by-step and revolutionary development.

CONTEXT

Henry Mintzberg is reckoned to be the *enfant terrible* of the strategy scene and enjoys the reputation of being the scourge of orthodox thinking. In his opinion, businesses are only able to function because people break the rules—not because they act in accordance with them.

FOR MORE INFORMATION

Mintzberg, Henry, Bruce Ahlstrand, and Joseph Lampel. *Strategy Safari*. Revised ed. New York: Free Press, 2005.

"Strategy is a pattern, that is, consistency in behavior over time."

Strategy Safari

Strategy and Structure

Alfred Chandler

WHY READ IT?

Chandler's book is regarded by many commentators as a masterpiece. It demonstrates the critical link between a company's strategy and its structure, and played an influential role in the profitable decentralization of many leading corporations. The book's findings remain relevant to new forms of organization such as the federated organization, the multi-company coalition, and the virtual company.

GETTING STARTED

According to the author, structure should be driven by strategy—and if it isn't, inefficiency results. The structure of many corporations is driven by market forces: so a recognition that production had to be market-driven led large organizations to change to a looser divisional structure.

Increases in scale also led to business owners having to recruit a new breed of professional manager, as professional management coordinates the flow of product to customers more efficiently than market forces can ever do.

A planned economy is important to long-term organizational success.

CONTRIBUTION

1. Structure Should Be Driven by Strategy

Strategy is the determination of the long-term goals and objectives of an enterprise, and the adoption of courses of action and the allocation of resources necessary for reaching these goals.

A company's structure is dictated by its chosen strategy—and unless structure follows strategy, inefficiency results.

A company should establish a strategy and then seek to create the structure appropriate to achieving it.

2. Structure Driven by Market Forces

Organizational structures in companies such as Du Pont, Sears Roebuck, General Motors, and Standard Oil were driven by the changing demands and pressures of the marketplace.

The market-driven proliferation of prod-

uct lines in Du Pont and General Motors led to a shift from a functional, monolithic organizational form to a more loosely-coupled divisional structure.

3. The Rise of the Multidivisional Organization

The multidivisional organization removed the executives responsible for the destiny of the entire enterprise from the more routine operational responsibilities.

It gave them the time, information, and even psychological commitment for long-term planning and appraisal.

4. The Professionalization of Management

The managerial revolution was fueled by a variety of factors: the rapid rise of oil-based energy, the development of the steel, chemical, and engineering industries, and a dramatic rise in the scale of production and the size of companies.

Increases in scale led to business owners having to recruit a new breed of professional manager. The roles of the salaried manager and technician are vital, as the visible hand of management coordinates the flow of product to customers more efficiently than Adam Smith's "invisible hand" of the market.

5. The Importance of a Planned Economy

Organizations and management require a planned economy rather than a capitalist free-for-all dominated by the unpredictable whims of market forces.

CONTEXT

The book is based on Chandler's research into major U.S. corporations between 1850 and 1920. Its subtitle is "Chapters in the history of the American industrial enterprise," but its impact went far beyond that of a brilliantly-researched historical text. Alfred Chandler's *Strategy and Structure* is a theoretical masterpiece which has had profound influence on both practitioners and thinkers.

Chandler was highly influential in the trend among large organizations for de-

centralization in the 1960s and 1970s. While in 1950 around 20% of Fortune 500 corporations were decentralized, this had increased to 80% by 1970. In the 1980s, Chandler's thinking was influential in the transformation of AT&T from what was in effect a production-based bureaucracy to a marketing organization.

Until recent times, Chandler's conclusion that structure follows strategy has largely been accepted as a fact of corporate life. Now, the debate has been rekindled.

Tom Peters said, "I think he got it exactly wrong. For it is the structure of the organization that determines, over time, the choices that it makes about the markets it attacks."

In *Managing on the Edge*, Richard Pascale said, "The underlying assumption is that organizations act in a rational, sequential manner. Yet most executives will readily agree that it is often the other way around. The way a company is organized, whether functional focused or driven by independent divisions, often plays a major role in shaping its strategy. Indeed, this accounts for the tendency of organizations to do what they best know how to do—regardless of deteriorating success against the competitive realities."

Gary Hamel, author of *Leading the Revolution*, said, "Those who dispute Chandler's thesis that structure follows strategy miss the point. Of course strategy and structure are inextricably intertwined. Chandler's point was that new challenges give rise to new structures. The challenges of size and complexity, coupled with advances in communications and techniques of management control, produced divisionalization and decentralization. These same forces, several generations on, are now driving us toward new structural solutions—the federated organization, the multi-company coalition, and the virtual company. Few historians are prescient. Chandler was."

FOR MORE INFORMATION

Chandler, Alfred. *Strategy and Structure*. New York: Beard Books, 1996.

1159

MANAGEMENT LIBRARY

Du système industriel
Henri de Saint-Simon

1160

MANAGEMENT LIBRARY

WHY READ IT?
Henri de Saint-Simon (1760–1825) was a social reformer and a seminal figure in the history both of socialism as a political movement and sociology as an academic discipline. In this work, a collection of essays and open letters which first appeared in 1821, Saint-Simon describes and justifies the claims of "les industriels" to play the decisive role in any society, an *industriel* being, in Saint-Simon's terms, anyone who is in the broadest sense productively active: a farmer or laborer, a craftsperson or manufacturer, a merchant or banker, a scholar or an artist.

GETTING STARTED
The king should reign, but the government should be in the hands of the producers, *les industriels*. They, according to Saint-Simon, are the embodiment of "all manner of useful work, both intellectual and manual, its theory as well as its practical application." In the future state as Saint-Simon envisages it, this class of people is entrusted with two tasks: to take over the leadership role and to emancipate the working class. The nobility, clergy, and the bourgeoisie must be removed from their ruling positions within the monarchy. Knowledge is to be the guiding spirit of society, directing it so that it operates for the good of all and the removal of oppression.

CONTRIBUTION
Workers and Idlers
As Saint-Simon saw it, the basic division in society was between those who were productively active and those who were idle. The active (*industriels*) were those whose income was dependent on their work. (Industrialists in the modern sense are termed *manufacturiers* or *fabricants* by Saint-Simon; his term for modern industry is *fabrication*.)

He contrasted the position of the *industriels* with that of the *rentiers*, those who lived on unearned income, the landowners, the royal dignitaries, and the military. He classified all these as "idlers" (*oisifs*) because they did not contribute to production in any way.

Saint-Simon's aim was to convince the *industriels* that they should rely on the king to be their support, represent their interests, and take care of state business. His parallel aim was to convince the king that the *industriels* were his natural allies and that he could rely on them to guarantee the stability of the monarchy.

Lawyers, he said, occupied all the important offices of state, and provided both the ideas and the leadership for political parties. But in everything relating to the economy, lawyers lacked the necessary technical knowledge. It was therefore incumbent on the *industriels* to form the grassroots of a party of those who work for a living and to organize themselves as an interest group in order to make their views count.

Financial Planning
The best kind of budget, Saint-Simon argued, was one that did justice to the interests of the earning classes. They were the best administrators, because, in contrast to officials, they had to administer, that is, to make productive use of, not only income but also capital assets. The drawing up of financial plans for the state ought therefore, in his view, to be left to the *industriels*. They, in turn, should internalize the power that they represented so that they would no longer hesitate to demand the prominent position to which they were entitled in the administration of public affairs.

Constitutional Reform
Saint-Simon created a plan for constitutional reform that envisioned that the position of minister of finance could be held only by an ordinary citizen. The minister would preside over a council of *industriels*, which was to be called the *chambre de l'industrie* (chamber of industry) and would be made up of experienced members of the productive classes of society. This chamber would meet once a year to debate and decide upon the state budget. The budget would be the basic legislative measure that would determine the policy of the kingdom.

The Working Class
In all the states on earth, said Saint-Simon, the working class was the most numerous class, but its interests were those in which governments had least interest or involvement. The common people needed the basic essentials of life. They must be provided with as great a livelihood as possible, that is, they should be given as much work as possible. Saint-Simon wished to entrust entrepreneurs with the task of deciding on large-scale state projects that would be financed from the public purse.

Bankers
The plans of the entrepreneurs could only be implemented if they were approved by the bankers. Business enterprises, therefore, found themselves in a kind of hierarchy, with the banks at the top. According to Saint-Simon, the class of *industriels* dominated by the banks ought in consequence to draft the budget.

The State
The nobility being politically dead, the state would relinquish its traditional powers in favor of the members of the productive classes who led business enterprises. In the *système industriel*, the attributes of the state would be reduced to the minimum necessary. Long before Karl Marx, therefore, Saint-Simon announced the "withering away of the state."

CONTEXT
Saint-Simon was one of the most influential thinkers of the 19th century. He was an advocate of "utopian socialism," striving for a just society in which rights would be grade in accordance with productivity. He was the founder of the first socialist school, his work prepared the way for the socialist movement and became one of its seminal texts. In contrast to Marx—whose forerunner he is often said to be—Saint-Simon focused on the intellectual superstructure of society rather than its economic substructure.

FOR MORE INFORMATION
de Saint-Simon, Henri. *Selected Writings* (trans. F. M. H. Markham). Westport, CT: Hyperion Press, 1991.

"He liked nobody to be in any way superior to him."

Henri de Saint-Simon

Tableau économique

François Quesnay

WHY READ IT?

Even before the French Revolution, François Quesnay (1694–1774) was setting up what reads like a modern catalog of economic demands: a state guarantee of private property, the removal of high taxes and customs tariffs, the dismantling of state subsidies, free competition, and liberalized access to the market. Quesnay, though originally a barber surgeon by trade, is perhaps the first economist proper. His work influenced Adam Smith. The famous zigzag diagram in the *Tableau économique* is the first macroeconomic model depicting economic activity as a balanced circular flow and demonstrating the interdependence of all economic sectors. Quesnay's "physiocratic" terminology also formed the basis of the technical language of economics as an academic discipline.

GETTING STARTED

Quesnay describes the national economy as a circulatory system. His overall view of a system in which goods, services, and money continually circulate is a groundbreaking one. The model shows the flows of money and goods between various sectors: agriculture (the productive sector), landowners (the distributive sector), and the "sterile" sector (merchants, craftspeople, officials, and factory workers). The productive sector produces added value—"net product"—which also allows net investment. The distributive sector receives a portion of the net product. The sterile sector produces only reproduction costs and therefore no added value. That is the peculiarity of Quesnay's system. Land is, for him, the only production factor that produces added value. It is through agriculture, therefore, that wealth creation processes become transparent and the significance of net investment and capital accumulation are recognized.

CONTRIBUTION
1. The Tableau

Quesnay looks at three types of expenditure, their source, the "advances" that they necessitate, their effect, their distribution, their "reproduction," their relationship with each other, and their relationships with the population, with agriculture, with industry, with trade, and with the mass of wealth of a nation as a whole.

The tableau or table has three columns.

Column one shows productive expenditure on agriculture (annual advances 600 in order to produce 600 units (U) of "revenue").

Column two shows how the revenues are spent (minus tax, they are distributed between productive and sterile tasks).

Column three shows sterile expenditure on industry etc. (annual advances for items manufactured with sterile expenditures).

Quesnay summarizes the results of his calculations using the circulatory system as follows. Reproduced in total: 600 U of revenue; in addition the annual costs of the 600 U plus the interest on the original advance by the landowner, which the land pays back in the sum of 300 U. Thus reproduction runs to 1500 U, inclusive of the revenues of 600 U, which, not taking into account tax and the advances required for reproduction, represents the basis of calculation.

2. Explanatory Notes

Expenditures, explains Quesnay, may preponderate on one side or the other. If they are balanced, then large revenues are renewed year by year through reproductive spending. But it is easy to see how the annual reproduction of revenues would change, depending on whether sterile or productive expenditures preponderated to a greater or lesser extent.

The 300 U in revenue, which in accordance with the regular operation of the table flow to productive expenditure, are a repayment of cash advances, which again produce 300 U net and thus a portion of the revenues of the landowner. This process of circulation and mutual redistribution continues in the same manner down to the last penny of the sums that flow alternately from one class of expenditure to another.

3. Extract from the Rules for the Royal Budget

For such a distribution, according to Quesnay, it is assumed:

- that from the mass of revenues nothing is exported abroad without an equivalent return in money or goods;
- that taxation is not destructive in its effects and does not stand in a false relation to the mass of national revenue; that it is increased only after revenues increase;
- that foreign trade is not impeded by products from the domestic harvest, for as sales are, so is reproduction;

- that the price of foodstuffs and other goods in the kingdom is not artificially depressed, because trade with foreign countries would then become disadvantageous. As the exchange value, so the revenues. From superfluity and devaluation comes no wealth. From scarcity and price rises comes want. From superfluity and high prices comes prosperity;
- that the means to provide for extraordinary needs of the state are to be expected from the wealth of the nation, not from the credit of financiers. Riches in the form of money are hidden riches, recognized neither by the king nor the country.

CONTEXT

The work was conceived under the absolutist monarchy in France. The king's extravagant lifestyle and expenditure on wars led to large state deficits, and the peasants were impoverished by high taxes.

Quesnay was one of the most important exponents of an Enlightenment school of thought known as "physiocracy." The physiocrats extended the idea of a "natural order" to society and concluded that there must be positive laws governing social activities and that scientific knowledge of those laws could be made to serve useful human purposes. They claimed to show how these laws operated in the economy and to reveal economic theory as an exact science.

Physiocracy was also a countermovement to mercantilism, criticizing mercantilist economic policies as being against nature. Its weakness, however, lay in its insistence that agriculture was the only productive sector and its dismissal of trade and industry as sterile. Despite his status as the founding father of economic theory, it is sometimes argued that the practical financial reforms that Quesnay persuaded Louis XV to introduce were more significant than his theoretical writings.

FOR MORE INFORMATION

Quesnay, François. *Quesnay's Tableau économique* (trans. Marguerite Steinfeld Kuczynski and Ronald L. Meek). New York: Macmillan, 1972.

"Great expenditures may cease to be excessive if they lead to an increase in wealth."

François Quesnay

The Theory of Economic Development

Joseph A. Schumpeter

WHY READ IT?

One of Schumpeter's claims to fame—many have rated him one of the greatest economists of the 20th century—is that he was among the first to set out a clear concept of entrepreneurship and its function within an economy. The key factor is innovation. Entrepreneurs innovate. Innovations create dynamism. Schumpeter's work was for a long time overshadowed by that of Keynes, but increased interest in innovation since the 1980s has led to a renaissance of Schumpeterian economics and a renewal of interest in this book in particular.

GETTING STARTED

This book sets out to uncover the forces within an economy that produce endogenous change. Schumpeter explains the processes of economic development by means of microtheory; he bases his study on innovative entrepreneurs and uses them to make large-scale factors, such as capital accumulation, interest, and company profits, understandable as dynamic processes.

CONTRIBUTION

1. Static and Dynamic Phenomena

According to Schumpeter, static general concepts of the workings of national economies are inadequate to explain the periodic changes in their stationary equilibrium, that is, the fluctuations of the economic cycle, and economic progress. This is because such concepts ascribe change solely to external influences. The central element in any overall concept ought, in his view, to be economic development, which alters the existing balance from within.

It is necessary to distinguish between static phenomena, in which no changes take place, and dynamic ones, which lead to changes until counteracting forces bring the economy into a new state of balance. This development is apparent in phases of boom and recession, which, consequently, represent necessary manifestations accompanying economic development.

2. The Stationary Economy

Schumpeter's starting point is a stationary economy, that is, a system in a state of balance that periodically repeats itself. These are some of its features.

- All economic plans are aimed at achieving an optimum and need only be updated from period to period.
- In all households and businesses income corresponds exactly to outgoings.
- In each period only those goods are consumed that were produced in the foregoing period and then exchanged.
- The possibilities of production are fixed in advance, this means that the production function is invariable, with the result that there are no possibilities for improvement or further investment.
- Perfect competition reduces aggregate profit to zero and consequently removes any incentive to entrepreneurial action.

But the function of capitalism is not, says Schumpeter, to administer existing structures, but to change them:

- In the static concept, there is no endogenous mechanism that could lead out of the status quo. Consequently, changes can only be brought about exogenously, that is, by external factors, social, political, and cultural influences, such as population growth, capital growth, or altered preferences and technical or organizational improvements (organic growth).
- In the dynamic concept, economic development originates in innovations. Here too, progress in production methods and organizational improvements play a part, but as a result of entrepreneurial action.

3. Innovations

Innovations, according to Schumpeter, consist of the practical implementation of knowledge, ideas, or discoveries, and rely, therefore, not on inventiveness but entrepreneurial abilities. Technically speaking, technological and organizational improvements could be described as new possibilities for factor combination. The innovation could, therefore, lie in the introduction of new products or production methods, in the opening up of new markets or supplies of resources, or in organizational changes.

These innovations are put into practice by dynamic entrepreneurs; they represent the microfoundation of the macrophenomenon of social development. Schumpeter posits two conditions as necessary for innovative entrepreneurs to appear as economic actors:

- Development takes place by means of individual actions and of incentives and thus appears as the aggregate of the consequences of individual actions. Only when profits can be realized through innovations, will the latter happen.
- Companies must have the opportunity to react to these incentives by changing the way they act. In balanced conditions, all production capacity is fully exploited. Banks must make capital available so that potentially profitable investment opportunities can be realized through a change in the input of resources.

4. The Outcomes of Innovation

Profits from innovation make it possible to meet interest payments. As a result the rate of interest will be determined by the demand for capital and this demand, in turn, by the extent of profitable investment opportunities. Interest rates are consequently an indicator of economic progress. Profit and interest can therefore be explained as outcomes of economic dynamism.

CONTEXT

Joseph Schumpeter (1883–1950) was an Austrian professor of political economy who belonged to the Vienna School of national economics. He later emigrated to the United States and held a professorship at Harvard.

The roots of his theories lay in Marxism, but since Marx's doctrine of the value of labor was in disrepute, he chose the neoclassical theory of value as the foundation for his work. This makes it difficult to assign Schumpeter a place in economic history. He proclaimed the significance of the business organization, but at the same time believed in the victory of socialism, famously answering no when asked if capitalism would survive. He realized himself that his work was likely to be overshadowed by Keynes's, and for most of the latter part of the 20th century this proved indeed to be the case.

FOR MORE INFORMATION

Schumpeter, Joseph A. *The Theory of Economic Development* (trans. Opies). New Brunswick, NJ: Transaction Publishers, 1983.

"Can capitalism survive? No, I do not think it can."   *The Theory of Economic Development*

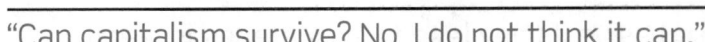

The Theory of Social and Economic Organization

Max Weber

WHY READ IT?

It is quite easy to make Weber's book sound as if it was intended to be a source text for Franz Kafka's novels and Charlie Chaplin's film *Modern Times,* not to mention George Orwell's *1984.* Weber is often incorrectly assumed to have been an advocate of bureaucracy and a mechanistic society, rather than someone who described bureaucracy—with at least some degree of correctness—as the most efficient and rational means of organization. In fact, as R. J. Kilcullen puts it, "bureaucracy was for Weber what capitalism was for Marx, the admired enemy." No understanding of the way modern organizations work would be complete without a study of this book.

GETTING STARTED

Max Weber was a versatile thinker who was a professor of political economy at the universities of Freiburg and Heidelberg in Germany. He is best known today as one of the founding fathers of modern sociology.

The Theory of Social and Economic Organization grew out of his philosophical inquiries into the nature of authority and how it is transmitted. Weber identified three types of authority: the "charismatic," based on the individual qualities of a leader and reverence for them among his or her followers; the "traditional," based on custom and usage; and the "rational-legal" based on the rule of objective law. Bureaucracy is the most efficient way of implementing the rule of law.

CONTRIBUTION

1. How Bureaucracy Works

There are four main principles identified by Weber as characteristic of a rational-legal bureaucracy:

- The organization is structured around official functions which are bound by rules, each area having its own specified competence.
- Functions are structured into offices organized into a hierarchy that follows technical rules and norms for which training is provided.
- The administration is separated from the ownership of the means of production.

- The rules, decisions, and actions of the administration are recorded in writing.

2. The Impersonality of Bureaucracy

The most important feature of bureaucracy—its main strength as well as its main weakness—is its impersonality.

Impersonality is a strength in that it minimizes the potential abuse of power by leaders because:

- offices are ranked in hierarchical order;
- operations are conducted in accordance with impersonal rules;
- officials are allocated specific duties and areas of responsibility;
- appointments are made on the basis of qualifications and suitability for the post.

It is a weakness in that:

- their characteristic information processing and filtering to the top makes bureaucracies cumbersome and slow to react;
- their machinery makes it difficult to handle individual cases, because rules and procedures require all individuals to be treated as if they were the same;
- bureaucratization leads to depersonalization, because the roles of officials are circumscribed by written definitions of their authority, and there is a set of rules and procedures to cater to every contingency.

3. Toward Ultimate Efficiency

The purely bureaucratic type of administrative organization is, from a purely technical point of view, capable of attaining the highest degree of efficiency. It is, in this sense, the most rational known means of carrying out imperative control over human beings. It is superior to any other form of organization in precision, in stability, in the stringency of its discipline, and in its reliability.

CONTEXT

Bureaucratic organization as expounded by Max Weber became the model for the 20th-century organization, and was encapsulated in Alfred Sloan's General Motors and Harold Geneen's ITT. Strictly implemented, and in combination with regimented mass-production as practiced by Henry Ford, who echoed some of Weber's thoughts in his faith

in strict demarcations and his fervently mechanistic approach to business, it could produce a nightmare scenario for the world of work in the 20th century.

Weber himself could see no realistic substitute for bureaucracy. He regarded its triumph with distaste, but as inevitable. Only in the latter part of the 20th century did new and more humane concepts of the organization emerge and start to win adherents. The roots of some of the latest theories are in biology and the new sciences of chaos and complexity, areas unknown to Weber. Today's organizations are talked of in terms of fractals and amoebae—they are imagined as elusive and ever-changing rather than efficient and static.

The regularity of the machine age has given way to the tumult, ambiguity, and complexity of the information age.

Even so, Max Weber remains important. In his book *Gods of Management,* Charles Handy chose as one of the gods Apollo, who is characterized by a Weber-like faith in rules and systems. Aspects of the bureaucratic model remain alive and well in a great many organizations where hierarchies, demarcations, and exhaustive rules dominate.

The influential author Gary Hamel notes: "Every organization wrestles with two conflicting needs: the need to optimize in the name of economic efficiency, and the need to experiment in the name of growth and renewal. Authoritarian bureaucracies, of the sort that rebuilt the Japanese economy after the war, serve well the goal of optimization. While there is experimentation here, it is tightly constrained. Anarchical networks, of the sort that predominate in Italy's fashion industry, allow for unfettered experimentation, but are always vulnerable to more disciplined competitors. Weber staked out one side of the argument; Tom Peters the other. As always, what is required is a synthesis."

FOR MORE INFORMATION

Weber, Max. *The Theory of Social and Economic Organization* (originally published 1924). New York: Free Press, 1997.

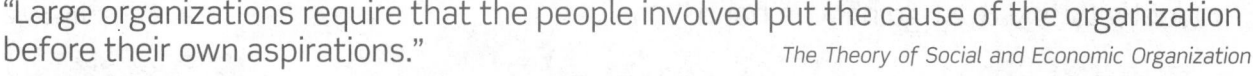

"Large organizations require that the people involved put the cause of the organization before their own aspirations."

The Theory of Social and Economic Organization

Theory Z

William Ouchi

WHY READ IT?

The book is subtitled *How American Business Can Meet the Japanese Challenge*, and the issue is still as important as it was when *Theory Z* was published in 1981. Ouchi believes that one of the major differences between Japanese and Western companies is their respective approach to managing people. He claims that Western companies who adopt the Japanese approach and adapt it to the Western business environment will be able to transform their business.

GETTING STARTED

Ouchi believes that Japanese success is due to a very strong company philosophy, a distinct corporate culture, long-range staff development, and decision making based on consensus. The result, he claims, is lower staff turnover, increased job commitment, and higher productivity—all important factors in determining competitiveness. He argues that Western companies should not simply adopt Japanese practices, but adapt them. These are the companies that he calls Type Z organizations and he gives detailed insights into U.S. companies that have transformed themselves in this way.

CONTRIBUTION

1. The Real Forces behind Productivity

Ouchi believes that productivity is not just working harder. Trust is an essential factor, enabling people to make a contribution that will be respected. Subtlety is also important, allowing teams to balance their skills in line with their roles, rather than seniority. According to the author, intimacy is a feature of all aspects of Japanese life, and this enables people to cooperate effectively at work.

2. Lifetime Employment

The author reports that major companies hire people just once a year. Staff are guaranteed employment until their retirement at 55, and any promotion takes place from within. The employment system is mirrored in the satellite system of suppliers and sub-contractors that surround a major com-

pany and its bank. The trading relationships are permanent and stable.

3. Job Rotation

Ouchi points out that the Japanese employment system features non-specialist career paths so that staff gain a broader experience of the ways of the whole company. This is a form of life-long job rotation. The Western system, he claims, rewards specialists and there is less chance of interaction between staff.

4. Working to Common Objectives

According to the author, the basic mechanism of control in Japan is the corporate philosophy and objectives. All other company policy is derived from that. The company values and beliefs are also derived from the overall philosophy.

5. Decision making by Consensus

Ouchi explains that, in this method of decision making, everyone gets involved. This may not result in the best decision, but it means that everybody understands the reasons for the decision and shares a commitment and responsibility for its success.

6. Japanese and Western Companies Compared

According to Ouchi, the key differences are:
- lifetime employment versus short-term employment;
- slow promotion versus rapid promotion;
- non-specialist career path versus specialist career path;
- implicit control mechanisms versus explicit;
- collective decision making versus individual decision making;
- collective responsibility versus individual responsibility.

7. Type Z Companies

Ouchi uses the term to describe Western companies that have adapted Japanese practices. They encourage employees to stay longer, but have a faster promotion ladder. They substitute "management by walking about" for the job rotation of Japanese companies. Type Z companies encourage collaboration, but still maintain individual responsibility for decision making.

8. Creating a Type Z Company

The author outlines the key stages for leaders who want to transform their company:
- Understand a Type Z company and your own role in it.
- Audit your company's philosophy to detect inconsistencies.
- Define a suitable company philosophy.
- Create structures and incentives to support the new philosophy.
- Develop staff interpersonal skills.
- Involve employees and unions in the transformation.
- Stabilize employment.
- Broaden career path development.
- Encourage participation.

CONTEXT

Comparing Japanese and Western business practice has a long tradition.

W. Edwards Deming, paradoxically, took Western ideas on quality to Japan after World War II. He made an important contribution to Japanese economic recovery and the country's subsequent reputation for quality. It was only when Western observers realized the potential impact of Japan on Western economies that they took notice of Deming's writings.

William Ouchi offers a valuable insight into the human factors that make Japanese business so successful. However, Nonaka and Takeuchi in their 1994 book *The Knowledge-creating Company* caution readers about over-reliance on contributory factors such as lifetime employment. They focus on the management of innovation within Japanese companies as a key competitive weapon.

Richard Pascale's *The Art of Japanese Management*, published in 1981, argues that Japanese success is largely attributable to what he called "soft factors"—style, shared values, skills, and staff. Western companies concentrated on "hard factors" such as strategy, structure, and systems.

FOR MORE INFORMATION

Ouchi, William. *Theory Z*. Reading, MA: Addison-Wesley, 1981.

The Third Wave

Alvin Toffler

WHY READ IT?

The obvious reason for reading a work of futurology more than 20 years after its publication is to see if the futurologist got it right. In many respects Toffler did. But there is a danger there also. Toffler predicted the electronic office and its effects. Now that most people work in electronic offices and live with their effects, perhaps it seems redundant to read a book simply in order to be able to congratulate the author on his foresight. What is startling about *The Third Wave* is that it was written so recently, and yet the technological leaps made since its publication have been so immense. The intriguing thing now is whether the author's broader analysis encompassed the developments that flowed from the developments he immediately foresaw. For many people Toffler's ideas are still intriguing.

GETTING STARTED

Alvin Toffler began his career as a journalist but shot to international fame as a futurologist with the publication of his first book *Future Shock* in 1970. *The Third Wave* appeared ten years later, and *Power Shift* ten years after that.

The "Third Wave" referred to in the title is the super-industrial society that emerged toward the end of the 20th century and is still taking shape. It succeeded the "Second Wave," the industrialized society produced by the Industrial Revolution, which itself succeeded the agricultural phase of human development, the "First Wave." Each new wave was ushered in by the development of revolutionary new technology. Electronics brought in the third.

Though the various waves followed one another in time, they did not affect the whole of the human race simultaneously—many people are still living under First Wave conditions. Toffler's main concern is with the transition from the Second to the Third Wave in advanced societies, but he also deals with possible areas of friction between people coexisting at different stages of development.

CONTRIBUTION
1. Toward Mass Customization
The Third Wave, according to Toffler, is characterized by mass customization rather than mass production.

The essence of Second Wave manufacture was the long run of millions of identical standardized products. By contrast, the essence of Third Wave manufacture is the short run of partially or completely customized products.

The Second Wave strictly separated consumer and producer. The Third Wave will see the two become almost indistinguishable, as the consumer becomes involved in the actual process of production, expressing choices and preferences.

2. The Growth of Flexible Working
Toffler predicted the demise of the nine to five working day.

Machine synchronization shackled the human to the machine's capabilities and imprisoned all of social life in a common frame. It did so in capitalist and socialist countries alike. Now, as machine synchronization grows more precise, humans, instead of being imprisoned, are progressively freed. They are freed into more flexible ways of working, whether it is flextime or working at home.

3. Changes in Working Relationships
A partial shift towards the electronic office will be enough to trigger an eruption of social, psychological, and economic consequences. The coming word-quake means more than just new machines. It promises to restructure all the human relationships and roles in the office.

The Third Wave will produce anxiety and conflict as well as reorganization, restructuring, and, for some, rebirth into new careers and opportunities. The new systems will challenge all the old executive turfs, the hierarchies, the sexual role divisions, the departmental barriers of the past.

4. The Impact on the Corporation
Instead of clinging to a sharply specialized economic function, the corporation, prodded by criticism, legislation, and its own concerned executives, is becoming a multipurpose institution.

The organization is being driven to redefinition through five forces:
- Changes in the physical environment. Companies must take greater responsibility for the effect of their operations on the global environment.
- Changes in the line-up of social forces. The actions of companies now have greater impact on those of other organizations such as schools, universities, civil groups, and political lobbies.
- Changes in the role of information. As information becomes central to production, as information managers proliferate in industry, the corporation, by necessity, impacts on the informational environment exactly as it impacts on the physical and social environment.
- Changes in government organization. The profusion of government bodies means that the business and political worlds interact to a far greater degree than ever before.
- Changes in morality. The ethics and values of organizations are becoming more closely linked to those of society. Behavior once accepted as normal is suddenly reinterpreted as corrupt, immoral, or scandalous. The corporation is increasingly seen as a producer of moral effects.

The organization of the future will be concerned with ecological, moral, political, racial, sexual, and social problems, as well as traditional commercial ones.

CONTEXT

Other studies of the future of working life tend to plunge head-first into celebrations of the miracles of technology with little attempt to understand the human implications. Toffler is aware of them.

Many of his ideas have since been developed further by others. Charles Handy, for instance, has done a lot of work on the rise of homeworking.

Gary Hamel, influential author of *Leading the Revolution*, commented: "The post-industrial society is here! And Alvin Toffler saw it coming in 1980 . . . One of the challenges for anyone reading Toffler, or any other seer, is that there is no proprietary data about the future. Your competitors read Toffler, Naisbitt, and Negroponte too! The real challenge is to build proprietary foresight out of public data."

FOR MORE INFORMATION

Toffler, Alvin. *The Third Wave*. New York: Bantam, 1980.

"Old ways of thinking, old formulas, dogmas, and ideologies, no matter how cherished or how useful in the past, no longer fit the facts."

The Third Wave

The Tipping Point

Malcolm Gladwell

GETTING STARTED

The spread of some products or ideas while others decline is rarely understood. Gladwell's insight into social dynamics provides concrete laws governing the trends of human behavior. He likens rapid growth, decline, and coincidence to epidemics. Ideas are "infectious," fashions represent "outbreaks," and new ideas and products are "viruses." For example, advertising is a way of infecting others. Developing his analogy, Gladwell shows how a factor "tips," that is, when a critical mass catches the infection and passes it on. This is when a shoe becomes a "fashion craze," social smoking becomes "addiction," and crime becomes a "wave." *The Tipping Point* is a manual for understanding and directing change: a revolutionary's handbook, in fact.

WHY READ IT?

The Tipping Point explains Gladwell's "laws of epidemics." Beyond his entertaining anecdotes and illustrations lies an exploration of the forces driving the spread of products, ideas, and other phenomena. The "tipping point" is the dramatic moment when everything changes simultaneously because a threshold has been crossed, although the situation might have been building for some time. Epidemics can be either "good" or "bad." The spread of HIV is catastrophic but it thrives on the same mechanism that spreads positive things—like fashions or health warnings. Underpinning this mechanism lie three fundamental forces driving all epidemics.

CONTRIBUTION
1. The Law of The Few

Epidemics need only a small number of people to transmit their infection to many others. Transmission is not achieved by the majority, or even a large minority; it only takes a very few. This is apparent with the spread of disease: the few people who socialize and travel the most make the difference between a local outbreak and a global pandemic. Word of mouth is a critical form of communication when spreading ideas. Those that speak the most (and speak the best) create epidemics of ideas. Gladwell categorizes these decisive people into connectors, mavens, and salespeople.

Connectors bring people together, using their social skills to make connections. This affords them power over the spread of epidemics, as they communicate throughout different "networks" of people. They are masters of the "weak tie" (a friendly, superficial connection), and can spread ideas far. Since ordinary people form time-consuming relationships, they make fewer of them and affect fewer people.

Mavens (information specialists) are subtly different. They focus on the needs of others rather than their own, and they have the most to say. Examples of mavens include teachers.

Salespeople concentrate on the relationship, not the message, and are more persuasive because they have better sales skills, mastering nonverbal communication and "motor mimicry" (the imitation of another's emotions and behavior to gain trust). The product is not necessarily theirs. An individual might make smoking look "cool" to an impressionable teenager without owning the cigarette company. Without connectors, mavens, and salespeople, epidemics would not reach a "tipping point." Epidemics need surprisingly few such people.

2. The Stickiness Factor

Whereas the law of the few relates to communication, stickiness is about intrinsic qualities or appeal. With a product or idea, the extent to which it spreads and becomes well known depends as much on its attractiveness as it does on how it is promoted. Its "stickiness" determines whether it passes by or catches on. The author explains that to reach a tipping point, ideas have to be compelling. If the idea or product is unattractive, it will be rejected irrespective of how it is transmitted. The information age has created a stickiness problem: the "clutter" of messages we face leads to products and ideas being ignored. For those wishing to create epidemics (such as marketers), it has become increasingly important to pay attention to the way they present their message. If contagiousness is a function of the messenger, stickiness is a property of the message.

3. The Power of Context

We rarely appreciate how our personal lives are affected by circumstances. Changes in the context of a message can tip an epidemic. An example is the "broken windows theory." If people see a single broken window, they may believe there is an absence of control and authority. Consequently, they are more likely to commit other crimes. A broken window or wall covered in graffiti invites crime that is more serious, spawning a crime wave. Yet the origin of the epidemic might not be with the connectors, mavens, or salespeople, nor with the stickiness of the factor (assuming crime is not a necessary human act). It could result from an accident in the environment. Gladwell argues that our circumstances matter as much as character. This means that manipulating the environment can control tipping points.

CONTEXT

Gladwell's experience at the *Washington Post* and the *New Yorker* in business, science, and medicine has left him with some excellent explanations for a diverse range of questions. *The Tipping Point* charts a common course between a range of different phenomena. Successful strategies require improvements in our thinking and a shift from an exclusive focus on cause and effect. Gladwell supports a "systems-thinking" approach. Behind all successful epidemics rests a belief that change is possible. Tipping points underline the power of intelligent action—always an empowering vision.

FOR MORE INFORMATION

Gladwell, Malcolm. *The Tipping Point.* Revised ed. Boston, MA: Back Bay Books, 2002.

FURTHER READING
Shapiro, Andrea. *Creating Contagious Commitment: Applying the Tipping Point to Organizational Change.* Hillsborough, NC: Strategy Perspective, 2003.

"In a given process or system some people matter more than others."   *The Tipping Point*

Toyota Production System   Taiichi Ohno

WHY READ IT?

During the last 40 years, Western automakers have lurched from one crisis to another. They have always been one step behind. The company they have been following is the Japanese giant Toyota, and the reasons for this are explained by Taiichi Ohno in his brief book *Toyota Production System: Beyond Large-scale Production*.

GETTING STARTED

The Toyota Production System was developed to help the company catch up with the United States. U.S. auto workers were producing nine times as much as their Japanese counterparts. The Toyota system differed from the Western approach, emphasizing a reduction in costs rather than an increase in selling price.

According to the author, the company should be seen as a continuous and uniform whole, including suppliers as well as customers. Asking the question "why?" five times at each stage helps identify and solve problems before moving on.

CONTRIBUTION

1. Catching Up with the West

The roots of the Toyota Production System lie in the immediate post-war years.

Toyoda Kiichiro, president of Toyoda Motor Company, demanded that the company should catch up with the United States. He gave his company three years to do so. Otherwise, he anticipated, the Japanese auto industry would cease to exist.

At that time in the auto industry, an average U.S. worker produced around nine times as much as a Japanese worker.

2. A Different Approach to Production

The Toyota Production System evolved by Ohno was strikingly different from approaches used in the West.

In the West, selling price was regarded as the combination of actual costs plus profit.

Toyota, believing that the consumer actually sets the price, concluded that profit resulted when costs were subtracted from the selling price. Their emphasis therefore was on reducing costs rather than increasing the selling price.

3. The Principles of the Toyota System

The system has three simple principles:

- just-in-time production;
- wider responsibility for quality;
- concept of value stream.

4. Just-in-time Production

There is no point in producing cars, or anything else, in blind anticipation of someone buying them; production has to be closely tied to the market's requirements.

5. Wider Responsibility for Quality

Responsibility for quality rests with every individual in an organization. Any quality defects need to be rectified as soon as they are identified.

6. Concept of Value Stream

The company should not be seen as a series of unrelated products and processes.

It should be seen as a continuous and uniform whole, a stream including suppliers as well as customers.

7. The Five Whys

Another central element in Ohno's system was the process of the five whys.

This suggested that by asking "why?" five times and discovering the answer at each stage, the root of any problem can be discovered and solved.

CONTEXT

These concepts were brought to mass Western audiences thanks to work conducted at the Massachusetts Institute of Technology as part of its International Motor Vehicle Program. The MIT research took five years, covered 14 countries, and looked exclusively at the worldwide auto industry.

The researchers concluded that most U.S. automakers remained fixed in the mass-production techniques of the past. In contrast, Japanese management, workers, and suppliers worked to the same goals as each other—resulting in increased production, high quality, happy customers, and lower costs.

This research was the basis for the 1990 bestseller by James Womack, Daniel Jones, and Daniel Roos, *The Machine that Changed the World*. From lean production, Womack and Jones went on to propose the lean enterprise (based on research covering 25 U.S., Japanese, and German companies) and lean management. As with most management fads, it was willfully misinterpreted. It became linked to reengineering and, more worryingly, with downsizing.

The reality is that lean production as introduced by Ohno and Toyota is a highly effective concept. It can provide the economies of scale of mass production, the sensitivity to market and customer needs usually associated with smaller companies, and job enrichment for employees.

The West continues to see lean production as a means of squeezing more from fewer people. This is a fundamental misunderstanding. Reducing the number of employees is the end rather than the means. Western companies have tended to reduce numbers and then declare themselves as lean organizations.

Womack argues that while lean production requires fewer people, the organization should then accelerate product development to tap new markets to keep the people in work.

Inevitably, lean production has its downside. The most obvious one is that its natural home is the mass-manufacturing world of auto making. It can be more difficult to apply in other industries.

The second obvious problem with lean production is that it fails to embrace innovation and product development. It is one thing being able to make a product efficiently, but how do you originate exciting and marketable products in the first place?

Womack and Jones would suggest that the critical starting point for lean thinking is value, but this is effectively one stage beyond the initial one of generating ideas. Even so, lean production has raised awareness, provided a new benchmark, and brought operational efficiency to a wider audience.

Harvard Business School's Michael Porter argues, "Organizations did well to employ the most up-to-date equipment, information technology, and management techniques to eliminate waste, defects, and delays. They did well to operate as close as they could to the productivity frontier. But while improving operational effectiveness is necessary to achieving superior profitability, it is not sufficient."

FOR MORE INFORMATION

Ohno, Taiichi. *Toyota Production System*. Cambridge, MA: Productivity Press, 1988.

"Toyota's emphasis therefore was on reducing costs rather than increasing the selling price."

Toyota Production System

Up the Organization

Robert Townsend

MANAGEMENT LIBRARY

WHY READ IT?

Like any good satire, *Up the Organization* is not only irreverent and wickedly humorous, it is based on shrewd insight and sound common sense. Its questioning of the ghastly stifling orthodoxies of corporate thinking, corporate behavior, and corporate society is, many commentators note regretfully, as relevant now as it was when the book was first published over 30 years ago.

GETTING STARTED

Townsend's first concern is for the people who are trapped in rigid organizational structures and unable to realize anything like their full potential. He has no time for the adornments of executive office or indeed anything that separates a management elite off from the experiences of ordinary workers. Then, turning his attention to more general issues, he suggests that all major organizations are operating on the wrong assumptions.

CONTRIBUTION

1. The Organizational Trap

According to Townsend, in the average company, the boys in the mailroom, the president, the vice presidents, and the girls in the steno pool have three things in common: they are docile, they are bored, and they are dull.

He claims that they are trapped in the pigeonholes of organization charts and that they have been made slaves to the rules of private and public hierarchies that run mindlessly on and on because nobody can change them.

2. The Problems of Business Schools

Townsend's advice to companies is not to hire Harvard Business School graduates.

He believes that this so-called elite is lacking in some pretty fundamental requirements for success: humility; respect for people on the firing line; deep understanding of the nature of the business and the kind of people who can enjoy themselves making it prosper; respect from way down the line; a demonstrated record of guts, industry, loyalty, judgment, fairness, and honesty under pressure.

3. The End of Executive Office Perks

All the special perquisites of executive office are anathema to Townsend.

His list of no-nos includes:

- reserved parking spaces;
- special-quality stationery for the boss and his elite ;
- muzak;
- bells and buzzers;
- company shrinks;
- outside directorships and trusteeships for the chief executive;
- the company plane.

4. The Wrong Kind of Leaders

According to Townsend, those with power, or who think they have power, are dangerous beings.

He claims that there is nothing fundamentally wrong with the country except that the leaders of all our major organizations are operating on the wrong assumptions.

Townsend believes that the country is in this mess because for the last two hundred years it has been using the Catholic Church and Caesar's legions as the patterns for creating organizations.

He argues that until forty or fifty years ago it made sense. The average churchgoer, soldier, and factory worker was uneducated

and dependent on orders from above. And authority carried considerable weight because disobedience brought the death penalty or its equivalent.

CONTEXT

Townsend's genius lies in debunking the modern organization for its excess, stupidity and absurdity. He collected his material in the course of his successful career as a director of American Express and president of Avis Rent-a-Car, then transformed himself into a witty commentator on the excesses of corporate life.

His bestseller *Up the Organization* is subtitled *How to Stop the Corporation from Stifling People and Strangling Profits*. Robert Heller called the book the first pop bestseller on business management. It is in the tradition of humorous bestsellers debunking managerial mythology and the high-minded seriousness of the theorists. In the 1950s there was *Parkinson's Law* ; at the end of the 1960s came Lawrence Peter and Townsend; more recently the Dilbert series has followed in their footsteps.

Townsend also belongs in the tradition of people-oriented business writing. His humor should not blind one to the underlying seriousness of his purpose.

Given that over 30 years have passed since its publication, the book still retains its freshness and originality, and its insights into the blind deficiencies of too many organizations remain sadly apt.

FOR MORE INFORMATION

Townsend, Robert. *Up the Organization*. New York: Fawcett Books, 1984.

"We're in this mess because for the last two hundred years we've been using the Catholic Church and Caesar's legions as our patterns for creating organizations."

The Wealth of Nations

Adam Smith

WHY READ IT?

Many books are claimed to be classics or seminal works: *The Wealth of Nations* is indisputably both. It is a broad-ranging exploration of commercial and economic first principles. In it Adam Smith laid the philosophical foundations for modern capitalism and the modern market economy. There are few economists over the last 200 years—and fewer politicians of a free-market persuasion—who have not been influenced by it. Smith has helped shape the economic policies of British prime ministers and chancellors of the exchequer from the days of Lord North (1770–82) to those of Margaret Thatcher—and even Tony Blair.

GETTING STARTED

Adam Smith was a Scottish philosopher. He was professor of logic and professor of moral philosophy at Glasgow University, but left his university posts in order to travel on the continent as tutor to a young nobleman. In France he was greatly influenced by a school of philosophical economists known as the "physiocrats." Returning to his native town of Kirkcaldy in Fife, he spent the next ten years preparing *An Inquiry into the Nature and Causes of the Wealth of Nations*, which was published—a significant coincidence perhaps—in the same year as the signing of the Declaration of Independence, 1776.

His central thesis is that capital can best be used for the creation of both individual and national wealth in conditions of minimal interference by government. The "invisible hand" of free-market competition ensures, in his view, both the vitality of commercial activity and the ultimate good of all a nation's citizens.

CONTRIBUTION
1. The Invisible Hand

According to Smith, conscious and well-meaning attempts to better the lot of a nation and its population are generally doomed to failure. The unintended cumulative effects of self-interested striving are far more effective. As he puts it: "Every individual is continually exerting to find out the most advantageous employment for whatever he can command . . . [and] necessarily labors to render the annual revenue of the society as great as he can. He generally neither intends to promote the public interest nor knows how much he is promoting it. He intends only his own gain, and he is in this, as in many other cases, led by an invisible hand to promote an end which was no part of his intention."

2. Value and Labor

The value of a particular good or service is determined by the costs of production. If something is expensive to produce, then its value is similarly high.

"The real price of everything, what everything really costs to the man who wants to acquire it, is the toil and trouble of acquiring it. What everything is really worth to the man who has acquired it, and who wants to dispose of it or exchange it for something else, is the toil and trouble of which it can save himself, and which it can impose on other people."

"What is bought with money or with goods is purchased by labor, as much as what we acquire by the toil of our own body. They contain the value of a certain quantity of labor which we exchange for what is supposed at the time to contain the value of an equal quantity."

3. The Division of Labor

Smith's legacy to scientific management was the concept of the division of labor.

"The division of labor occasions in every art a proportionable increase of the productive powers of labor. The separation of different trades and employments from one another seems to have taken place in consequence of this advantage."

"Men are much more likely to discover easier and readier methods of attaining any object when the whole attention of their minds is directed towards that single object than when it is dissipated among a great variety of things."

CONTEXT

For a book that is over 200 years old, there is a surprisingly modern-sounding ring to a great deal of what *The Wealth of Nations* has to say. This is mainly owing to the acuteness and lasting value of Smith's analysis—the book was the first comprehensive exploration of the foundations, workings, and machinations of a free market economy—but also to the familiarity of many of its basic concepts. *The Wealth of Nations* continues to have a role as a right-wing manifesto, a gloriously logical exposition of the beauty of market forces. And the appeal is not only to the right wing in politics.

Smith's system of demarcation and functional separation provided the basis for the management theorists of the early twentieth century, such as Frederick Winslow Taylor, and practitioners such as Henry Ford. They translated the economic rigor of his thinking to practices in the workplace, though in ways and to a scale that Smith could never have imagined.

History has, however, put its own limitations on Smith's theorizing.

- Physical labor is no longer so important.
- The 20th century saw the emergence of management as a profession. It is barely acknowledged by Smith.
- Smith wrote without knowledge of the power and scope of modern corporations, let alone the power of brand names and customer loyalty.
- He also wrote in harder times where self-interest was not a choice but a necessity.

Nevertheless, as Gary Hamel commented: "Revisionists be damned. Citizens from Prague to Santiago to Guangzhou to Jakarta owe much of their new-found prosperity to the triumph of Adam Smith's economic ideals. [He] laid the philosophical foundations for the modern industrial economy. Enough said."

FOR MORE INFORMATION

Smith, Adam. *The Wealth of Nations*. New York: Bantam, 2003.

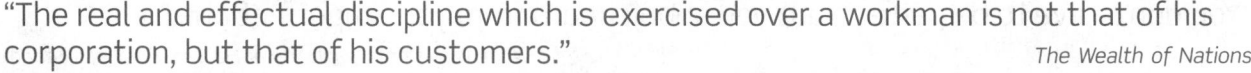
"The real and effectual discipline which is exercised over a workman is not that of his corporation, but that of his customers."
The Wealth of Nations

What They Don't Teach You at Harvard Business School

Mark H. McCormack

1170

MANAGEMENT LIBRARY

WHY READ IT?

What They Don't Teach You at Harvard Business School is neither an indictment of Harvard's business education program nor of the merits of a business education elsewhere, but a testament to the importance of practical experience. Although an alumnus of Yale Law School, in this book McCormack argues that education is useful only when one understands its limitations: in his opinion, ignoring them leads to dangerous arrogance and a lack of understanding about the way the world works. MBAs and high IQs alone often indicate little about future success in business. The value of this book is to learn the lessons McCormack teaches, drawing on his experiences gained throughout a long and successful career. The "street smarts" that McCormack highlights were the critical factor in his business career and in understanding others' behavior.

GETTING STARTED

To get the most out of this book, you have to understand that what you know matters less than how you react to what you do not know. The book comprises many lessons ranging from McCormack's opinion of the best way to dress in a business situation (conservatively) to how to impress and judge others.

McCormack founded the International Management Group (IMG) in the early 1960s with less than $500, few contacts, and a novel idea. This gave birth to a new industry, incorporating the lifestyle sector and, by the early 1980s, generated revenues of several hundred million dollars. IMG's business, in addition to television programming, is to market "sports personalities" as diverse and famous as Gary Player, Tiger Woods, Serena Williams, and Michael Schumacher. While IMG's fortunes are largely tied to their clients' success, it was their ability to construct a successful enterprise with an excellent brand, a deep reserve of talent and a series of winning deals that bred their success.

McCormack shares his practical experience with entertaining anecdotes from his personal career. McCormack presents these as rules, showing how they contributed to the building of IMG, and organizes them into those concerning people, selling and running a business.

CONTRIBUTION

1. People

The author offers advice on different aspects of dealing with people, but the general message is to be observant and diligent to create the right impression, build trust, and obtain winning advantages over your rivals, competitors, and peers. These different skills are categorized into "reading people," "creating impressions," "taking the edge," and "getting ahead." Observing others effectively and influencing them—the "gamesmanship of business"—brings success. Perhaps the most interesting individual lesson McCormack teaches is the value of "working in the mailroom" or similar situations. This will not teach humility or how the company really works, but helps one to understand oneself—those that succeed are those who compete with themselves. However, you do not need to be genuinely the best to get ahead. As McCormack observes, "Carpenters that become contractors have a need to drive a nail straighter and truer than anyone else." However, "some executives, had they started in the mailroom, would still be sorting mail—and misrouting most of it." Knowing others is essential, but it is just as important to understand yourself use this understanding as a practical advantage.

2. Sales and Negotiation

McCormack's advice on selling and negotiating includes tactics such as the importance of silence, to force the other person to talk or to make sure the right pitch is made at the right time. Moreover, it highlights that we are all "natural" salespeople. In school, we persuade peers to accept us and teachers to give us good grades. After this, we excel at selling ourselves to employers. However, when we actually go out to sell we often under-perform for fear of rejection, or underestimate the importance of salesmanship, neglecting "street wisdom" for that of the business school. The rules of selling are described, but the most important lesson is that failure in sales and negotiation usually comes from one's own psychological barriers, such as fear of failure: overcoming these is the secret to success.

3. Running a Business

Much of the literature about building a business is academic, concerning different models for growth, acquisition, entrepreneurship, and countless other factors. However, McCormack uses his own experience in creating and building IMG to distil the realities of successful business management. His lesson is to avoid "reinventing the wheel": it is far better to use your own common sense and apply proven rules to unique situations. Often, general rules—grow prudently, diversify risks and opportunities, manage talent, distinguish between short and long term opportunities, employ systems-based thinking while staying flexible, be efficient, and pay attention to detail—are ignored as managers apply more complicated strategies to gain competitive advantage. Most situations benefit from common sense, rather than complex solutions. For example, when IMG faced a lawsuit regarding their client Bjorn Borg, McCormack refused to seek legal advice, held a meeting with the plaintiffs to discuss their complaints, and eventually settled the matter to everyone's satisfaction.

CONTEXT

This book is not a substitute for real-world experience—it merely distils McCormack's personal experiences and values—but it *is* an autobiography that provokes and inspires. It should do: Mark McCormack was at the top of his game until his death in 2003.

His most valuable lesson is that no-one has to be perfect to be successful, as long as they play to their strengths. This is a key theme: that book-learned knowledge and scientific preparation is less important than being able to get things done in the real world. It may not be necessary to be perfect at something if there is an alternative or if you are at least good enough at that thing. However, worrying about being perfect is an excellent way to destroy confidence and to establish even greater barriers to success. In McCormack's words: "You don't have to be perfect, but you should learn from your imperfections."

FOR MORE INFORMATION

McCormack, Mark H. *What They Don't Teach You at Harvard Business School*. Reissue. New York: Bantam, 1986.

"You don't have to be perfect, but you should learn from your imperfections."

What They Don't Teach You at Harvard Business School

The Will to Manage

Marvin Bower

WHY READ IT?

Marvin Bower is the man who did more than anyone else to create the modern management consulting industry. The book gives a valuable insight into the management practices that made McKinsey and Company such a long-lasting success.

GETTING STARTED

Marvin Bower's success grew on his principle that building trust with clients is critical to the consulting firm's success. The interests of the client should precede increasing the company's revenues: if you look after the client, the profits look after themselves.

He also believed that using values to help shape and guide an organization is extremely important. One of those values is that regard for the individual is based not on title, but on competence, stature, and leadership. Instead of experienced consultants, McKinsey recruited graduate students who could learn how to be good problem solvers and consultants. The company also developed "virtual" project teams, bringing in the best people in the organization wherever they were based in the world. Clear, simple employment policies and change through empowerment helped to maintain high professional standards.

CONTRIBUTION

1. A New Way of Looking at Consultancies

Bower did not change the name of his company, McKinsey, as he shrewdly decided that clients would demand his involvement in projects if his name was up in lights. His vision was to provide advice on managing to top executives and to do it with the professional standards of a leading law firm. Due to a belief that in all successful professional groups, regard for the individual is based not on title but on competence, stature, and leadership, McKinsey consultants were as-sociates who had engagements, rather than mere jobs, and the firm was a practice rather than a business.

2. Building Trust with Clients

The entire ethos of McKinsey was to be very respectable, the kind of people C.E.O.s naturally relate to. Bower's gospel was that the interests of the client should precede increasing the company's revenues: unless the client could trust McKinsey, the company could not work with them. If McKinsey looked after the client, the profits would look after themselves. High charges were not a means to greater profits, but a simple and effective means of ensuring that clients took McKinsey seriously.

Other central principles were that consultants should keep quiet about the affairs of clients, should tell the truth, and be prepared to challenge the client's opinion. They should only agree to do work which is both necessary and which they could do well. Using values to help shape and guide an organization was extremely important.

3. New Patterns of Recruitment

Instead of hiring experienced executives with in-depth knowledge of a particular industry, Bower recruited graduate students who could learn how to be good problem solvers and consultants. This changed the emphasis of consulting from passing on a narrow range of experience to using a wide range of analytical and problem-solving techniques.

4. Developing Virtual Project Teams

Another element of Bower's approach was the use of teams. He thought of McKinsey as a network of leaders. Teams were assembled for specific projects, and the best people in the organization were brought to bear on a particular problem, no matter where they were based in the world. McKinsey's culture fostered rigorous debate over the right answer, without that debate resulting in personal criticism.

5. Clear, Simple Employment Policies

The company's policy remains one of the most simple: seniority in McKinsey correlates directly with achievement. If a consultant ceases to progress with the organization, or is ultimately unable to demonstrate the skills and qualities required of a principal, he or she is asked to leave McKinsey.

6. Change through Empowerment

"There have been thousands of changes in methods, but not in command and control. Many companies say they want to change, but they need to empower people below. More cohesion is needed rather than hierarchy," Bower said in 1995.

CONTEXT

Under Bower's astute direction, McKinsey became the world's premier consulting firm. Recent years have also seen the structure and managerial style of the company receiving plaudits. McKinsey is special because it has developed a self-perpetuating aura that it is unquestionably the best. Marvin Bower was the creator of this organizational magic.

American Express chief, Harvey Golub, says that Bower led McKinsey according to a set of values, and it was the principle of using values to help shape and guide an organization that was probably the most important thing he took away.

FOR MORE INFORMATION

Bower, Marvin. *The Will to Manage*. New York: McGraw-Hill, 1966.

BUSINESS THINKERS AND MANAGEMENT GIANTS

Business Thinkers and Management Giants

Profiling the top management thinkers and pioneers

This section provides over one hundred concise summaries of the most influential or controversial business writers, entrepreneurs, and managers. The Business Thinkers and Management Giants range from pioneer and professor through to performer and pundit. One factor links them all—they have all had an impact on current business practice.

Business Thinkers includes summaries of the career and thinking of the most important and influential writers on management, as well as an assessment of their contribution to business practice. We also provide a list of key works and sources if you need to read further.

Management Giants is a highly selective and controversial gallery of some of the most successful business leaders. As with any list, it is as much distinguished by whom it omits as who is included.

Our aim has been to identify the key figures in a range of industries that by their efforts have transformed the way a business is conducted. Being nice is not one of the main criteria for selection; being effective is.

Contents

John Adair
Action-Centered Leadership

John Adair, best known for his three-circle model of "action-centered leadership," is widely regarded as one of Europe's foremost authorities on leadership in organizations.

Adair believes that leadership can be taught, and his works have been instrumental in overturning the "great man" theories of leadership. He draws a distinction between leadership and management.

Adair's ideas are practical and relevant to all managers.

1176

BUSINESS THINKERS

1934	Born.
1963–1969	Senior lecturer in military history and leadership training advisor, Royal Military Academy, Sandhurst.
1969–1973	Assistant director at Industrial Society; pioneered "action-centered leadership."
1979	Becomes the world's first professor in leadership studies, at the University of Surrey, England.
2005	Becomes first recipient of lifetime achievement in leadership award from Centre of Leadership Studies, University of Exeter, England.

LIFE AND CAREER

John Adair's early career was varied and colorful, and undoubtedly formed the basis for his views on leadership. After joining the Scots Guards he became the only national serviceman to serve in the Arab Legion, where he was adjutant in a Bedouin regiment. Before going to college he qualified as a deckhand and worked on an Icelandic trawler. He also worked as an orderly in a hospital operating room. After studying at Cambridge University, he became a senior lecturer in military history and leadership training advisor at the Royal Military Academy, Sandhurst. He went on to become the director of studies at St. George's House in Windsor Castle, and two years later was appointed assistant director of the Industrial Society, where he pioneered action-centered leadership.

In 1979, Adair became the world's first professor in leadership studies at the University of Surrey. He has been visiting professor in leadership studies at the University of Exeter, and acts as a consultant to many organizations around the world in business, government, education, health, and the voluntary sector.

For over three decades his overlapping, three-circle model of action-centered leadership has been integrated into company cultures and individual leadership styles, and is an established hallmark of management training for many organizations.

KEY THINKING
Action-Centered Leadership

This simple and practical model is based on three overlapping circles, representing the task, the team, and the individual. The model has endured well, probably because it is a fundamental description of the actions leaders must take in order to be effective, which are to:

- achieve the task;
- build and maintain the team;
- develop the individual.

Adair's concept asserts that the three needs of task, team, and individual are the building blocks of leadership, as people expect their leaders to help them achieve the common task, build the synergy of teamwork, and respond to individuals' needs.

- The task needs work groups or organizations to come into being because one person alone cannot accomplish it.
- The team needs constant promotion and retention of group cohesiveness to ensure that it succeeds. The team functions on the "united we stand, divided we fall" principle.
- The individual's needs are the physical ones (such as salary) and the psychological ones of recognition, sense of purpose and achievement, status, and the need to give and receive from others in a work environment.

For Adair, the needs of the task, team, and individual overlap.

- Achieving the task builds the team and satisfies the individuals.
- If the team needs are not met (if the team lacks cohesiveness) performance of the task is impaired and individual satisfaction is reduced.
- If individual needs are not met, the team will lack cohesiveness and performance of the task will be impaired.

He holds that leadership exists at three different levels:

- team leadership, of teams of between 5 and 20 people;
- operational leadership, where a number of team leaders report to one main leader;
- strategic leadership, of a whole business or organization, with overall accountability for all levels of leadership.

Regardless of the level at which leadership is being exercised, Adair's model remains the same: task, team, and individual needs must constantly be considered.

The strengths of the concept are that it is both timeless and independent of situation or organizational culture. It can also help a leader to identify where he or she may be losing touch with the real needs of the group or situation.

The Functions of Leadership

In order to fulfill the three aspects of leadership and achieve success, Adair believes that there are eight functions that must be performed by the leader. They are:

- defining the task: Individuals and teams need to have the task distilled into a clear objective that is SMART (Specific, Measurable, Achievable, Realistic, and Time Constrained);
- planning: Planning requires a search for alternatives, best done with others in an open-minded, positive, and creative way. Contingencies should be planned for and plans should be tested;
- briefing: Team briefing is viewed as essential for creating the right atmosphere, promoting teamwork, and motivating each individual;
- controlling: Excellent leaders get maximum results with the minimum of resources. To achieve this, they need self-control, good control systems in place, and effective delegation and monitoring skills;

"Leadership is about a sense of direction . . . It's knowing what the next step is." John Adair

- evaluating: Leaders need to be good at assessing consequences, evaluating team performance, appraising and training individuals, and judging people;
- motivating: Adair distinguishes eight principles for motivating others: Be motivated yourself; select people who are highly motivated; treat each person as an individual; set realistic and challenging targets; remember that progress motivates; create a motivating environment; provide fair rewards; and give recognition;
- organizing: Good leaders have to be able to organize themselves, their team, and the organization (including structures and processes). Leading change requires a clear purpose and effective order to achieve results;
- setting an example: Leaders need to set an example both to individuals and to the team as a whole. Since a bad example is noticed more than a good one, providing a positive pattern to follow must be worked at constantly.

These leadership functions need to be developed and honed constantly to improve the leader's ability.

Motivating People

In many ways, Adair's ideas in the area of motivating people are in line with those of the classic motivational theorists, such as Maslow, McGregor, and Herzberg.

The 50:50 Rule

Just as the Pareto principle (or 80:20 rule) is the ratio of the vital few and the trivial many, the Adair 50:50 rule (from *Effective Motivation*) states that: "50% of motivation comes from within a person and 50% from his or her environment, especially from the leadership encountered therein."

Adair's view is that people are motivated by a number of complex factors. So, for example, he does not dismiss the "carrot and stick" approach, but sees it rather as one stimulus-response factor among many that might influence a person's actions.

The strength of an individual's motivation is affected by what outcome the person expects from certain actions—and also what he or she would prefer that outcome to be (as demonstrated by Victor Vroom in the 1960s). Conditions in the working environment and the individual's own perceptions and fears are also factors that have an impact on strength of motivation.

Adair's Eight Rules in Motivating People

Adair proposes that understanding what motivates individuals is fundamental to engaging their interest and focusing their efforts. The will that leads to action is governed by motives, and motives are inner needs or desires that can be conscious, semiconscious, or unconscious. In *The John Adair Handbook of Management and Leadership*, the point is made that "motives can also be mixed, with several clustered around a primary motive."

Adair emphasizes the importance of a motivating environment and a motivated individual. Another crucial factor is the role of the leader, who must, he believes, be completely self-motivated. In *Effective Motivation*, eight basic rules are outlined to guide leaders in motivating people to act:

- be motivated yourself;
- select people who are highly motivated;
- treat each person as an individual;
- set realistic and challenging targets;
- remember that progress motivates;
- create a motivating environment;
- provide fair rewards;
- give recognition.

Developing a Personal Sense of Time

Adair's view of time management accords closely with Peter Drucker's, in that he argues that it is essential to manage time in order to manage anything else. He was one of the first management thinkers to emphasize the critical importance of time management and its central role in focusing action and helping leaders to achieve goals. Time management is not simply about being organized or efficient, or completing certain tasks, Adair states. It is about focusing on achievement: time management should be goal-driven and results-oriented.

Success in time management should be measured by the quantity of productive work achieved, and the quality of both the work and the person's private life. Ten principles of time management given in *How to Manage Your Time* are:

- develop a personal sense of time;
- identify long-term goals;
- make medium-term plans;
- plan the day;
- make the best use of your best time;
- organize office work;
- manage meetings;
- delegate effectively;
- make use of committed time;
- manage your health.

Of these 10 principles, developing a personal sense of time and increasing personal effectiveness are central to Adair, again highlighting his emphasis on individual characteristics.

JOHN ADAIR IN PERSPECTIVE

Adair's ideas were very "different" when they first appeared, and for many people their main value lay in the successful challenge they offered to the "great man" theories that dominated then. These theories, because they insisted that leaders were born and not made, eliminated the possibility of training or developing people in leadership skills. So Adair's new ideas were welcomed and quickly became established.

Given the pace and scale of changes in the work environment during the last 20 years, however, it is perhaps not surprising that there has been something of a backlash against Adair, with critics claiming that his approach (developed in the 1960s) has itself now become outdated.

One criticism of action-centered leadership is that it takes little account of the flat structures that are advocated as the best organizational form. It is also judged to be too "authoritarian"—applicable in a formal, military-type environment but less relevant to the modern workplace, where the leadership emphasis is on leading change, empowering, enabling, managing knowledge, and fostering innovation.

Another criticism of Adair's approach in recent years is that his ideas are too simplistic, merely stating the obvious, common sense view. For many people, however, it is exactly this simplicity and clarity about what a leader should do that is so valuable.

1177

BUSINESS THINKERS

FOR MORE INFORMATION

Books:

Adair, John. *Action-Centered Leadership*. New York: McGraw-Hill, 1984.

Adair, John. *The Skills of Leadership*. New York: Nichols Publishing Company, 1984.

Adair, John. *Effective Motivation*. Guildford: Talbot Adair Press, 1987.

Adair, John. *The Action-Centered Leader*. London: Industrial Society, 1988.

Adair, John. *Effective Leadership*. Burlington, VT: Ashgate Publishing,1983.

Adair, John. *Great Leaders*. Philadelphia, PA: Trans-Atlantic Publications, 1997.

Adair, John. *Inspiring Leadership*. London: Thorogood, 2003.

Adair, John. *Understanding Motivation*. Guildford: Talbot Adair Press, 1990.

Adair, John. *How to Manage Your Time*. Guildford: Talbot Adair Press, 1990.

Adair, John. *How to Grow Leaders*. London: Kogan Page, 2005.

See also:

Frederick Herzberg (pp. 1218–1219)

Warren Bennis (pp. 1184–1185)

"The capacity to create a compelling vision and translate it into action and sustain it."

Warren Bennis

Igor Ansoff
Father of Corporate Strategy

The John Carter Brown Library at Brown University, Ansoff's alma mater.

Igor Ansoff was the originator of the strategic management concept, and was responsible for establishing strategic planning as a management activity in its own right. His landmark book, *Corporate Strategy* (1965), was the first text to concentrate entirely on strategy, and although the ideas outlined are complex, it remains one of the classics of management literature.

1918	Born.
1936	Family emigrates to the United States.
1950	Joins the Rand Corporation.
1957	Publishes article "Strategies for Diversification" that presents the Ansoff Matrix.
1963	Appointed professor of industrial administration at the Carnegie Institute of Technology, Pittsburgh.
1965	*Corporate Strategy* published.
1983	Joins U.S. International University as professor of strategic management.
2000	Retires from academic life.
2002	Dies.

LIFE AND CAREER

H. Igor Ansoff was born in Russia in 1918 and his family emigrated to the United States in 1936. His early academic focus was on mathematics, and he obtained a Ph.D. in applied math from Brown University, in Rhode Island. He joined the Rand Corporation in 1950, and moved on to the Lockheed Aircraft Corporation, where he eventually became vice president of plans and programs, and then vice president and general manager of the industrial technology division.

In 1963 Ansoff was appointed professor of industrial administration at the Carnegie Institute of Technology in Pittsburgh. He went on to hold a number of positions in universities in both the United States and Europe. He retired from academia in 2000 and was named Distinguished Professor Emeritus at the United States International University.

KEY THINKING

Until the publication of *Corporate Strategy*, companies had little guidance on how to plan for, or make decisions about, the future. Traditional methods of planning were based on an extended budgeting system that used the annual budget, projecting it a few years into the future. By its very nature this system paid little or no attention to strategic issues. However, with the advent of greater competition, higher interest in acquisitions, mergers, and diversification, and greater turbulence in the business environment, strategic issues could no longer be ignored. Ansoff felt that, in developing strategy, it was essential to systematically anticipate future environmental challenges to an organization, and draw up appropriate strategic plans for responding to these challenges.

He explored these issues in *Corporate Strategy*, and built up a systematic approach to strategy formulation and strategic decision-making through a framework of theories, techniques, and models.

Strategy Decisions

Ansoff identified four standard types of organizational decisions, those related to strategy, to policy, to programs, and to standard operating procedures. The last three of these, he argued, are designed to resolve recurring problems or issues and, once formulated, do not require an original decision each time. This means that the decision process can easily be delegated. Strategy decisions are different, however, because they always apply to new situations and so need to be made anew every time.

Ansoff developed a new classification of decision-making, partly based on Alfred Chandler's work, *Strategy and Structure* (Cambridge, MA: MIT Press, 1962). This dis-

tinguished decisions as: *strategic* (focused on the areas of products and markets); *administrative* (organizational and resource allocating), or *operating* (budgeting and directly managing). Ansoff's decision classification became known as Strategy-Structure-Systems, or the 3S model. (Sumantra Ghoshal proposed a 3Ps model—purpose, process, and people—to replace it.)

Components of Strategy

Ansoff argued that within a company's activities there should be an element of core capability, an idea later adopted and expanded by Hamel and Prahalad. To establish a link between past and future corporate activities (the first time such an approach was undertaken) Ansoff identified four key strategy components as:

● product-market scope—a clear idea of what business or products a company was responsible for (predating the exhortations of Peters and Waterman to "stick to the knitting");

● growth vector—as explained in the section below on the Ansoff matrix, this offers a way of exploring how growth may be attempted;

● competitive advantage—those advantages an organization possesses that will enable it to compete effectively—a concept later championed by Michael Porter;

● synergy—explained by Ansoff as "2+2=5," or how the whole is greater than the mere sum of the parts; it requires an examination of how opportunities fit the core capabilities of the organization.

Ansoff Matrix

Variously known as the "product-mission matrix" or the "2 × 2 growth vector component matrix," the Ansoff Matrix remains a popular tool for organizations wishing to understand the risk component of various growth strategies—including product versus market development and diversification. The matrix was first published in a 1957 article called "Strategies for Diversification" and the example below illustrates what such a matrix may look like:

	Present	New
Present	1. Market penetration	2. Market expansion
New	3. Product expansion	4. Diversification

"Structure will become a dynamic enabler of both change and unchange, the ultimate model of organizational chaos."

Igor Ansoff

Of the four strategies given in the matrix, *market penetration* requires increasing existing product market share in existing markets; *market expansion* requires the identification of new customers for existing products; *product expansion* requires developing new products for existing customers; and *diversification* requires new products to be produced for new markets.

Ansoff's article focused particularly on diversification as a potentially high-growth but also high-risk strategy that necessitates careful planning and analysis before any decision is made. In Ansoff's view it requires organizations to "break with past patterns and traditions" as they enter on "uncharted paths" where, generally, new skills, techniques, and resources will be required. His matrix offered a method of carefully analyzing and evaluating the profit potential of diversification strategies.

Paralysis by Analysis

It has sometimes been suggested that the application of the ideas in *Corporate Strategy* can lead to an over-emphasis on analysis. Ansoff himself recognized this possibility, however, and coined the now famous phrase "paralysis by analysis" to describe the type of procrastination caused by excessive planning.

Turbulence

The issue of turbulence underlies all of Ansoff's work on strategy. One of his key objectives in establishing a better framework for strategy formulation was to improve the existing planning processes of the stable, postwar economy of the United States, since he realized these would not be sufficient to cope with the pressures that rapid and discontinuous change would place on them.

By the 1980s change, and the pace of change, had become a key issue for management in most organizations. Ansoff recognized, however, that if some organizations were faced with conditions of great turbulence, others still operated in relatively stable conditions. Consequently, although strategy formulation had to take environmental turbulence into account, one strategy could certainly not be made to fit every

industry. These ideas are discussed in *Implanting Strategic Management*, where five levels of environmental turbulence are outlined as:

- repetitive—change is at a slow pace, and is predictable;
- expanding—a stable marketplace, growing gradually;
- changing—incremental growth, with customer requirements altering fairly quickly;
- discontinuous—characterized by some predictable change and some more complex change;
- surprising—change that cannot be predicted and that both develops, and develops from, new products or services.

IGOR ANSOFF IN PERSPECTIVE

Although Ansoff's work is frequently referred to by strategists, it has not become as generally recognized as that of other theorists. The complexity of his work and its reliance on the disciplines of analysis and planning are perhaps among the reasons why Ansoff is not popularly viewed as belonging to the top echelons of management thinkers.

Other theorists were working on themes similar to those of Ansoff at similar times. In the 1960s Ansoff's notion of competence (which was later developed by Hamel and Prahalad) was not unique and, although Ansoff seems to have been the originator of his 2 × 2 growth vector component matrix, a similar matrix had been published earlier. It is likely that much work done during the 1980s and 1990s by other theorists on strategy formation under conditions of uncertainty or chaos owed something to Ansoff's theory of turbulence, though it is difficult to evaluate the extent of the debt.

A debate between Ansoff and Henry Mintzberg over their differing views of strategy has been reflected in print over many years, particularly in the *Harvard Business Review*. Ansoff has often been criticized by Mintzberg, who dislikes the idea of strategy being built from planning that is supported by analytical techniques. This criticism is based on the belief that Ansoff's reliance on planning suffers from three fallacies: that events can be predicted; that

strategic thinking can be separated from operational management; and that hard data, analysis, and techniques can produce novel strategies.

Ansoff was one of the earliest writers on strategy as a management discipline and laid strong foundations for several later writers to build upon, including Michael Porter, Gary Hamel, and C. K. Prahalad. He invented the modern approach to strategy, and his work pulled together various ideas and disparate strands of thought, giving a new coherence and discipline to the concept he described as strategic planning. During the 1970s and 1980s, this concept shaped more ideas about management as other writers took up Ansoff's ideas, such as core competence or "sticking to the knitting."

1179

BUSINESS THINKERS

FOR MORE INFORMATION

Books:
Ansoff, Igor. *Corporate Strategy*. New York: McGraw-Hill, 1965.
Ansoff, Igor, Roger P. DeClerck and Robert L. Hayes. *From Strategic Planning to Strategic Management*. New York: Wiley/Interscience, 1975.
Ansoff, Igor. *Strategic Management*. London: Macmillan, 1979.
Ansoff, Igor. *Implanting Strategic Management*. Englewood Cliffs, NJ: Prentice Hall, 1984.
Ansoff, Igor. *The New Corporate Strategy*. New York: Wiley, 1988. (Revised edition of *Corporate Strategy*)

Journal Articles:
Ansoff, Igor. "Strategies for Diversification." *Harvard Business Review*, September/October, vol. 35 no. 5, 1957, pp. 113–124.
Ansoff, Igor. "The Firm of the Future." *Harvard Business Review*, September/October, vol. 43 no. 5, 1965, pp. 162–174.
Hussey, David. "Igor Ansoff's Continuing Contribution to Strategic Management." *Strategic Change*, vol. 8, no. 7, 1999, pp. 375–392.

"History consists of the tracks made by strategy and includes the risks players take, whether they win or lose."

George Konrád

Chris Argyris
The Manager's Academic

Chris Argyris's career may look more like that of a classical academic than that of a management guru, but a stuffy academic he is not. His passionate interest in management and organizational problems makes him one of the most respected management thinkers of our time. He is also as much at home in the factory and boardroom as in the lecture hall.

Argyris is first and foremost a behavioral scientist, and his career has been devoted to understanding how organizations behave and how managers learn.

1923	Born.
1960	Publication of *Understanding Organizational Behavior*.
1968	Moves from Yale to Harvard Business School.
1971	Appointed James Bryant Conant Professor of Education and Organization Behavior, Harvard Business School.
1978	Publication of *Organizational Learning*.

LIFE AND CAREER

Chris Argyris was born in 1923 and at an early age developed an interest in how people learn. "It sounds corny, but I love learning for its own sake," is how he explains it. After service in World War II he returned home and, like so many young men at that time, felt a strong determination to help create a better world. He chose to direct his interest in education toward the needs of organizations and the individuals working in them. His great energy and formidable academic qualifications—a baccalaureate in psychology, a Masters in economics, and a Doctorate in organization behavior—equipped him perfectly for the task, and by the early 1950s he was teaching and carrying out research at Yale University.

By the mid 1960s he was Professor of Industrial Administration at Yale and in 1968 he moved to the Harvard Business School. There, in 1971, he became the James Bryant Conant Professor of Education and Organization Behavior.

His consulting work has been wide-ranging and highly influential. Clients have included IBM, DuPont and Shell, along with the U.S. State Department, other U.S. government bodies and several overseas governments.

KEY THINKING

A staunch supporter of job enrichment, Argyris has always challenged the extremes of Taylorism, especially the suggestion that one "hires a hand," rather than a whole person. Underlying virtually all his thinking is a fundamental belief in people, and he tirelessly reminds us of the mutual benefit that comes when organizations assist and encourage individuals to develop their full potential. He believes that each person already has the "psychological energy" that provides motivation. The challenge, he suggests, is not to find ways of artificially motivating people; it is to recognize and channel this innate energy.

T-Groups

Chris Argyris was the main force behind the groundbreaking T-group experiments in the 1960s. "T-group training" is a phrase used to describe a number of similar training methods, the purpose of which is to increase the trainee's skills in working with other people—and a considerable proportion of time on such a training course is spent in discussing the trainees' relationships with one another. Argyris was not alone in being elated by the success of T-groups, by their power to unfreeze the rigid, authoritarian behavior of so many managers and to generate a feeling of liberation and excitement. However, as we now know, for most people these positive effects are short-lived. Once back in the turmoil of life in their organization, mixing again with those who have not been trained, the resolutions and ideas are quickly forgotten, and people revert to their old ways of doing things.

This rapid return to their original behavior patterns by people who had been extremely enthusiastic about the "new approach" generated by T-group training led Argyris to formulate an idea that has affected people's views about organizational behavior for many years. The way people behave in organizations, he suggests, shows that there is a sharp difference between the beliefs they profess and the beliefs on which they appear to act.

"Espoused Theories" and "Theories-in-use"

Argyris coined the term "Espoused Theories" for things that people profess to believe, and the term "Theories-in-use" for those that they appear to believe when faced with problems in the real world. He concluded, after much research, that, no matter how genuinely we believe in some approach to a situation, at the first sign of threat, embarrassment, or loss of face, most of us fall back on a deep-rooted "master program" of behavior. This behavior, which is characterized by a powerful defensive attitude and a tendency to blame others while struggling to maintain control and save face, is surprisingly consistent across different cultures and classes.

Not only do people slip easily into defensive routines, but they also remain totally unaware that they are doing so. It is a reflex action, an automatic response to any threat or challenge. Argyris argues that the organization can inhibit learning because it imposes—perhaps unconsciously—rules over the ways in which people relate to one another. He maintains that problem solving and decision making can be dominated by an almost unconscious drive to "save face," "protect others," or maintain the status quo. What concerns him most about this behavior is that it blocks any opportunity people have to learn from experience and provides an all too effective strategy for avoiding change.

Single-loop and Double-loop Learning

Concern at people's failure to learn from experience has led Argyris to the theory for which he is best known: the concept of single- and double-loop learning. Developed in collaboration with Donald Schön and described in their book *Organizational Learning* published in 1978, the theory

---

"Individual learning is a necessary but insufficient condition for organizational learning."

Chris Argyris

stresses the importance of human reasoning as a basis for decisions and action.

Their work also produced the idea of a "learning organization." An organization, Argyris and Schön suggest, differs from a mob by having procedures for making collective decisions, by delegating authority to individuals to act for the "collectivity," and by setting out boundaries and rules. Norms and strategies are developed for all this activity, but in a healthy organization these are constantly being tested and challenged as people interact and learn new ideas. When the constant learning of people within an organization is reflected in the way the organization itself changes and develops, then the organization itself can reasonably be described as learning—hence the term "learning organization."

The two types of learning—single-loop and double-loop—refer to the way people respond to changes in their environment. Single-loop learning occurs when a manager responds to a problem with a simple "application of the rules." For example, problem: budgets are being exceeded; solution: cut costs. Argyris uses a thermostat as an analogy for single-loop learning; the thermostat switches the heating on and off in response to temperature changes.

Double-loop learning goes beyond this simple feedback response and questions the assumptions on which the response is based. In the thermostat model, the double-loop approach would be to question the validity of the selected temperature. In the example involving exceeded budgets, the double-loop approach would be to check the appropriateness of the budget figure and the basis on which it was calculated. Speaking to a conference in 1982, Argyris described the theory thus:

"Learning can be defined as occurring under two conditions. First, learning occurs when an organization achieves what it intended; that is, there is a match between its design for action and the actual outcome. Second, learning occurs when a mismatch between intention and outcome is identified and corrected; that is, a mismatch is turned into a match . . . Single-loop learning occurs when matches are created, or when mismatches are corrected by changing actions. Double-loop learning occurs when mismatches are corrected by examining and altering first the governing variables and then the actions."

CHRIS ARGYRIS IN PERSPECTIVE

Argyris's work is rarely a comfort to managers. He raises profound questions about how we run organizations and frequently throws into doubt much of what is widely accepted to be "good practice." And when he does outline solutions they are never simple or easy. What he offers, and what makes his contribution to management thinking so important, is a profound and detailed exploration of the fundamental principles of organization behavior and human interaction in the workplace. He pulls no punches when showing us how hard we will have to work, and how much we will have to change if we are to achieve our full potential; but he is equally convincing when describing the rewards we will receive for our efforts.

Future

In recent years Argyris has been looking at leadership and, after considerable research, he claims the massive literature on this overworked subject has failed to produce anything practical. Such strong views have made his recent book on leadership, *Flawed Advice and the Management Trap*, compelling reading.

He is also taking a lively interest in IT, something he feels will play a key role in learning within organizations. He says, "In the past the one-way, top-down approach gained strength from the fact that a lot of behavior is not transparent. IT makes transactions transparent so that behavior is no longer hidden. It creates fundamental truths where none previously existed."

FOR MORE INFORMATION

Books:

Argyris, Chris. *Personality and Organization: The Conflict between the System and the Individual.* New York: Harper & Row, 1957.

Argyris, Chris. *Understanding Organizational Behavior.* Homewood, IL: Dorsey Press, 1960.

Argyris, Chris. *Reasoning, Learning, and Action: Individual and Organization.* San Francisco, CA: Jossey-Bass, 1982.

Argyris, Chris. *Overcoming Organizational Defenses: Facilitating Organizational Learning.* Boston, MA: Allyn and Bacon, 1990

Argyris, Chris. *Knowledge for Action.* San Francisco, CA: Jossey-Bass, 1993.

Argyris, Chris. *On Organizational Learning.* Cambridge, MA: Blackwell Business, 1994.

Argyris, Chris, and Donald Schön. *Organizational Learning II: Theory, Method, and Practice.* 2nd ed. Reading, MA: Addison-Wesley, 1996.

Argyris, Chris. *Flawed Advice and the Management Trap.* New York: Oxford University Press, 1999.

Journal Articles:

Argyris, Chris. "Teaching Smart People How to Learn." *Harvard Business Review*, May/June 1991, pp. 99–109.

Argyris, Chris. "Education for Leading Learning." *Organizational Dynamics*, Winter 1993, pp. 5–17.

Argyris, Chris. "Good Communication That Blocks Learning." *Harvard Business Review*, July/August 1994, pp. 77–85.

"Managers who are skilled communicators may also be good at covering up real problems."

Chris Argyris

R. Meredith Belbin
Team Builder

R. Meredith Belbin is acknowledged as the father of team-role theory. As a result of research conducted in the 1970s, he identified eight (later extended to nine) useful roles that are necessary for a successful team. His contribution has gained in significance because of the widespread adoption of teamworking in the late 1980s and 1990s.

1926	Born.
1981	Publication of *Management Teams: Why They Succeed or Fail*.
1987	Founds Belbin Associates.
1990	Publication of *The Job Promoters: A Journey to a New Profession*
1993	Publication of *The Coming Shape of Organization* and *Team Roles at Work*.
1997	Publication of *Changing the Way We Work*.
2000	Publication of *Beyond the Team*.
2001	Publication of *Managing without Power*. Visiting Professor of Leadership at the University of Exeter, United Kingdom.

LIFE AND CAREER

Belbin, who was born in 1926, is an academic who has also spent periods working in industry and who now has his own consulting company. It was while working at the Industrial Training Research Unit in Cambridge that he was asked by Henley Management College to conduct some research into the operation of management teams. The college's approach to management education was based on group work, and researchers there had noticed that some teams of individually able executives performed poorly and others well. This impression was reinforced when a business game was introduced to one of the courses. Belbin discovered that it was the contribution of particular personality types, rather than the merits of the individuals themselves, that was important to the success and failure of such teams.

KEY THINKING

There has been a continuing interest in Belbin's work because teamworking is an increasingly important strategy for organizations. There are many reasons for this. Teamworking is variously seen as a means of:

- providing greater worker flexibility and co-operation;
- helping to achieve cultural shifts within an organization;
- improving problem-solving and project management;
- tapping the talents of everyone in the organization.

There are also different types of teams involved in working together, for example, temporary teams, cross-functional teams, top management teams, and self-directed teams. As a result of this interest in teams, the issue of team building, including team selection, group dynamics, and team performance, has become particularly vital. Although there are many models of team relationships, such as the Team Management Systems (TMS) developed by Margerison and McCann, Belbin's model is probably the best known.

Team Role Theory

It is important to remember that Belbin's findings relate to teams of managers rather than other types of teams. Belbin's findings were first published in *Management Teams: Why They Succeed or Fail* and later refined in *Team Roles at Work*. In Belbin's own words, a team role "describes a pattern of behavior characteristic of the way in which one team member interacts with another where his performance serves to facilitate the progress of the team as a whole."

The essence of his theory is that, given

knowledge of the abilities and characteristics of individual team members, success or failure can be predicted within certain limits. As a result, unsuccessful teams can be improved by analyzing their shortcomings and making changes. But it is also important for individuals within the team to understand the roles that others play, when and how to let another team member take over, and how to compensate for shortcomings. Although each of the eight roles has to be filled for a team to work effectively, the eight roles are not needed in equal measure, nor are they needed at the same time. There can be fewer than eight people in a team, since people are capable of taking on back-up roles where there is less need for them to fulfill a primary team role.

The roles themselves are determined largely by the psychological makeup of the individuals who instinctively adopt them. Four principal factors are involved: intelligence, dominance, extroversion/introversion, and stability/anxiety. Each role demands a particular combination of these four, and they can be used to rate any individual. In the list of team role contributions, the ratings for each particular trait are shown.

The Self-Perception Inventory and the *Interplace* System

Belbin devised a self-perception inventory, which has been through several revisions, as a quick and easy way for individual managers to work out what their own team roles should be. It was taken up by organizations and used to determine employees' team types, but it has been questioned whether it is psychometrically acceptable for this purpose. Academics were concerned that it was too subjective and recommended that feedback should come instead from a variety of sources. Belbin answered this criticism by reiterating that the inventory was never designed for this purpose and by developing a computerized system called *Interplace* to cater to the wider needs of organizations.

Interplace is a more sophisticated approach to role analysis than the self-perception inventory because it incorporates feedback from other people, not just the individual concerned. The main inputs to the *Interplace* system use data from self-perception exercises, observer assignments, and job requirement evaluations. *Interplace* filters, scores, stores, converts, and inter-

---

"Teamwork is a constant balancing act between self-interest and group interest."

Susan Campbell

prets the data gathered. It offers advice based on the three inputs with respect to counseling, team role chemistry, career development, and the behaviors needed in certain jobs and team positions. The system works as a diagnostic and development tool for organizations.

Later Theories

In the 1990s Belbin extended his work on teams to explore the link between teams and the organizational environment in which they operate. He suggested that an effective model for the new flatter organization might be a spiral or helix in which individuals and teams move forward on the basis of excellence rather than of function.

He has also very recently devised a system for defining jobs which he calls "Workset." Its objective is to define the boundaries and content of a job through an interactive communication process between the manager and the jobholder. The system uses color to denote different aspects of the job. There should be five key outcomes:

- the facilitation of empowerment;
- the encouragement of greater job flexibility;
- the promotion of teamworking;
- the support of cultural change;
- a continuous improvement process for jobs and job holders.

It is too early to say what impact the Progression Helix theory or Workset system will have. They are undoubtedly a contribution, however, to management in today's delayered organizations and flexible working environments, with their associated need to communicate with and involve staff.

R. MEREDITH BELBIN IN PERSPECTIVE

Although independent recent research has thrown doubt on the existence of eight separate team roles, Belbin's broad findings have not been questioned, nor has the popularity of his theories been disputed. There has been an enduring interest in team role categories on the part of practicing managers in a wide variety of organizations. This is because:

- there is an increasing interest in teamworking;
- Belbin made his ideas accessible to the lay person;
- Belbin is recognized as the first to develop our understanding of the dynamics of teams.

FOR MORE INFORMATION

Books:
Key works by Belbin
Belbin, R. Meredith. *Management Teams: Why They Succeed or Fail.* 2nd ed. Burlington, MA: Butterworth-Heinemann, 2004.
Belbin, R. Meredith. *Team Roles at Work.*
Woburn, MA: Butterworth-Heinemann, 1993.
Belbin, R. Meredith. *The Coming Shape of Organization.* Woburn, MA: Butterworth-Heinemann, 1996.
Belbin, R. Meredith. *Changing the Way We Work.* Woburn, MA: Butterworth-Heinemann, 1997.

Journal Articles:
Belbin, Meredith, Barrie Watson, and Cindy West. "True Colours." *People Management*, 6 March 1997, pp. 36–38, 41.
Furnham, Adrian, Howard Steele, and David Pendleton. "A Psychometric Assessment of the Belbin Team Role Self-perception Inventory." *Journal of Occupational and Organizational Psychology*, vol. 66 no 3, 1993, pp. 245–261 (This article includes Belbin's criticism of the research and the response of the authors).
Senior, Barbara. "An Empirically-based Assessment of Belbin's Team Roles." *Human Resource Management Journal*, vol. 8 no 3, 1998, pp. 54–60.

Web site:
www.belbin.com contains a useful list of answers to frequently asked questions about team role theory, as well as an online team analysis and reports service. It also contains helpful information on Belbin's latest work on Work Roles.

1183

BUSINESS THINKERS

"Corporations have been pre-occupied with the qualifications, experience and achievements of individuals."

Anthony Jay

Warren Bennis
Leadership Guru

Warren Bennis has worked as an educator, writer, administrator, and consultant, besides authoring or coauthoring many books on different topics. He has performed highly respected work in the areas of small group dynamics, change in social systems, T-groups, and sensitivity training, and during the 1960s became a recognized futurologist. Bennis wrote his first article on leadership in 1959, and he has become a widely accepted authority on the subject since 1985, when *Leaders* was published.

BUSINESS THINKERS

1925	Born.
1959	Sets up department for organizational studies at MIT.
1967	Appointed Provost of State University of New York (SUNY).
1971	President of the University of Cincinnati.
1979	Professor of Management at the University of Southern California.
1985	Publication of *Leaders: The Strategies for Taking Charge*.
1989	Publication of *On Becoming a Leader*.
1997	Publication of *Organizing Genius*.

LIFE AND CAREER

Bennis was born in New York in 1925 and educated at Antioch College, Ohio, and the Massachusetts Institute of Technology (MIT). Later, he studied group dynamics, and during the 1950s was involved in the U.S. National Training Laboratories teamworking experiments. His early field of work was organizational development. Bennis was a great admirer of Douglas McGregor and his "Theory Y" approach to motivation. In fact, Bennis became very close to McGregor and was strongly influenced by him. His career path even followed McGregor's to some extent. First, he was an undergraduate student at Antioch College while McGregor was President there, and later, in 1959, he was recruited by McGregor to establish a new department for organization studies at MIT. From the late 1960s, Bennis's career moved for a time from academic research and teaching to administration. He became Provost at the State University of New York (SUNY), Buffalo, in 1967, staying

there until 1971, when he moved to take on the post of President of the University of Cincinnati.

As an administrative leader from 1967 to 1978, Bennis attempted to put McGregor's motivation theories into practice, and found them unworkable without some adaptation in the form of strengthened structure and direction.

During the 1960s, Bennis became known as a student of the future, and predicted (with coauthor Philip Slater in a March 1964 article for the *Harvard Business Review* called "Democracy Is Inevitable") the downfall of communism in the face of inevitable democracy. By the mid-1960s, he was predicting the demise of bureaucratic organization. His 1968 book, *The Temporary Society*, explored new forms of organization, advocating an "adhocracy" of free-moving project teams as a necessity for the future. This idea has since been taken up by other writers, such as Alvin Toffler and Henry Mintzberg.

In an adhocracy, responsibility and leadership are distributed to groups or task forces on the basis of the relevance of members' qualifications or abilities for the specific task or purpose of the group. For Bennis, adhocracy was an important concept as a counter to hierarchy, centralized control, and bureaucratic organization.

KEY THINKING

In his early book on leadership, *The Unconscious Conspiracy* (1976), Bennis highlights how leaders can positively influence others to bring about change. His most distinctive ideas on the subject, however, partly grew out of the broad, general response to a landmark *Harvard Business Review* article of 1977 by Abraham Zaleznik (then Profes-

sor of Social Psychology of Management at Harvard).

The Zaleznik article was entitled "Managers and Leaders—Are They Different?" Bennis's research and writing were extreme in emphasizing a complete, qualitative difference between management and leadership, and he drew up a list of sharp distinctions that ended with the now familiar aphorism: "Managers do things right, leaders do the right thing." While Bennis considers that managers can become leaders through learning and development, he is firm about the functional differences between the roles and the approaches involved, and the distinctions he draws echo throughout most of his writings on leadership.

The Leaders Study

In 1979, on his return to research and teaching as Professor of Management at the University of Southern California, Bennis sought to unravel the lessons of his practical experience of leadership. He explored the subject through a 1985 serial study that was published as a book coauthored with Burt Nanus, called *Leaders: The Strategies for Taking Charge* (1985). While Bennis has written or co-written many other books relating to leadership, these largely expand on the ideas developed in *Leaders*.

Leaders aimed to identify common characteristics among 90 successful U.S. leaders who had all, the authors considered, demonstrated "mastery over present confusion" in their careers. The leaders ranged from an orchestra conductor to Ray Kroc, the founder of McDonald's, and included a baseball player and a tightrope walker, as well as the astronaut Neil Armstrong. It was Bennis's second book on leadership, selling over 300,000 copies, and is still considered an important text on the subject.

In *Leaders*, Bennis and Nanus identify four common factors amongst the subjects, and these form the core of their ideas about leadership.

- Attention through vision—all had an agenda, an intense vision and commitment that drew others in. The leaders also gave much attention to other people.
- Meaning through communication—all had an ability to communicate their vision and bring it to life for others, sometimes using drawings or models as well as metaphor and analogy.

"Empowerment is the collective effort of leadership."   Warren Bennis

  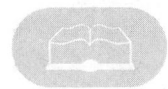   

- Trust through positioning—through establishing a position with a set of actions to implement their vision, and staying the course, the leaders established trust.
- The deployment of self through positive self-regard—the creative deployment of self is essential to leadership, involving an honest appreciation of oneself and one's own worth, and instilling confidence in others.

Positive self-regard is related to "emotional wisdom," and five key skills in emotional wisdom are given as the abilities to:

- accept others as they are;
- approach things only in terms of the present;
- treat others, even familiar contacts, with courteous attention;
- trust others, even where the risk seems high;
- do without constant approval and recognition.

One common quality that Bennis and Nanus particularly identified in these leaders was their way of responding to failure as a learning experience. Karl Wallenda, the great tightrope aerialist, was taken as a main example. The authors illustrate his manner of putting his energies completely into his task, thinking of failure as a mistake from which he could learn, and viewing this experience (of learning based on failure) as a new beginning, rather than the end, for a project or idea.

"Transformative" Leadership

The style of leadership discussed by Bennis and Nanus is termed "transformative," in that it is said to have an empowering effect on others, enabling them to translate intentions into reality. A transformative leadership style is described as one that motivates through identification with the leader's vision, pulling rather than pushing others on.

Four elements of empowerment are distinguished as:

- significance—a feeling of making a difference;
- competence—development and learning "on the job";
- community—a sense of interreliance and involvement in a common cause;
- enjoyment—capacity to have fun at work because it is enjoyable and involving.

The four major characteristics of transformative leaders identified earlier are linked to strategic approaches through which a leader leads.

- The creation of a compelling vision: a leader must develop and communicate an image, or vision, of a credible and attractive future for the organization.

- The translation of meaning into social architecture: social architecture is the intangible variable that translates the buzz and confusion of organizational life into meaning. While similar to culture, social architecture is more precise in meaning, in that it can be defined, assessed, and, to some extent, managed. Three styles of social architecture are distinguished as formalistic, collegial, and personalistic.
- The position of the organization in the outside world: positioning of an organization is described as the process by which it establishes a viable niche in its environment. It encompasses all that must be done to align the internal and external environments of the organization.
- The development of organizational learning: good leaders are experts at learning within an organizational context, and their behavior can help to direct and energize innovative learning within the organization as a whole.

The end result of transformative leadership is, Bennis and Nanus consider, an empowering environment and accompanying culture, enabling employees to generate a sense of meaning in their work. Higher profits and wages, the authors suggest, inevitably accompany this sort of culture, if it is genuinely established.

At the end of the book, five myths about leadership are identified and contradicted.

- Leadership is a rare skill—it is not.
- Leaders are born—they are not.
- Leaders are charismatic—most are ordinary.
- Leadership can exist only at the "top"—it is relevant at all levels.
- Leaders control, direct, and manipulate—they do not. Transformative leaders align the energies of others behind an attractive goal.

Later Work

A later, prominent book by Bennis, *On Becoming a Leader* (1989), looks at learning to lead, developing leadership qualities, and how leadership can be taught. It uses 29 well-known people as case studies to illustrate leadership qualities. Its main message suggests that becoming a leader involves continual learning, development, and the reinvention of the self.

Bennis has since written or cowritten many books and articles that expand on and develop his ideas on leadership. His more recent works focus on the important roles of followers and groups, as well as on leadership. In *Organizing Genius* (1997), a collaborative work with Patricia Ward Biederman, Bennis almost returns to his roots in group work. The book looks at the

history of seven well-known groups in action, including Walt Disney's animation studios, President Clinton's 1992 election campaign, and Lockheed's "skunk works." Common features of these successful groups are highlighted, and the mutually interdependent relationship between great leaders and great groups is stressed.

WARREN BENNIS IN PERSPECTIVE

The importance of Bennis's work in the field of leadership is indisputable, and his informal and easy-mannered style of writing and use of practical illustrations have made his books very approachable. The management writer Stuart Crainer emphasizes Bennis's humane approach to leadership. Bennis views leadership as a skill that can be developed by ordinary people and that centers on enabling and empowering others rather than on control and direction. He is sometimes criticized as a romantic in his approach and has himself affirmed (in *The Director* of October 1988), that he is indeed a romantic, if that term accurately describes someone who believes in possibilities, and is optimistic.

FOR MORE INFORMATION

Books:

Bennis, Warren. *The Unconscious Conspiracy: Why Leaders Can't Lead*. New York: AMACOM Press, 1976.
Bennis, Warren, and Burt Nanus. *Leaders: The Strategies for Taking Charge*. New York: Harper & Row, 1985.
Bennis, Warren. *On Becoming a Leader*. Cambridge, MA: Perseus, 1989.
Bennis, Warren. *Why Leaders Can't Lead: The Unconscious Conspiracy Continues*. San Francisco, CA: Jossey-Bass, 1989.
Bennis, Warren, and Patricia Ward Biederman. *Organizing Genius: The Secrets of Creative Collaboration*. Cambridge, MA: Perseus, 1997.
Bennis, Warren. *Managing People Is Like Herding Cats*. Provo, VT: Executive Excellence Publishing, 1998.
Bennis, Warren. *Managing the Dream: Reflections on Leadership and Change*. Cambridge, MA: Perseus, 2000.
Bennis, Warren, and Robert Thomas. *Geeks and Geezers*. Boston, MA: Harvard Business School Press, 2002.

See also:
- Abraham Maslow (pp. 1234–1235)
- Charles Handy (pp. 1216–1217)
- Douglas McGregor (pp. 1238–1239)
- Henry Mintzberg (pp. 1240–1241)

1185

BUSINESS THINKERS

"Successful executives are great askers."   Warren Bennis

Kenneth Blanchard
The One Minute Manager

The One Minute Manager was first published in 1982. Lambasted as trite and shallow by academics, it has since sold over 17 million copies worldwide, been translated into over 25 languages, and is frequently found on managers' bookshelves. It launched a new genre of management publishing, providing the model for a host of imitations.

1186

1939	Born.
1982	Publication of *The One Minute Manager*.
1984	Publication of *Putting the One Minute Manager to Work*.

LIFE AND CAREER

Kenneth Blanchard graduated from Cornell University in Government and Philosophy and went on to complete his Ph.D. in Administration and Management. In the early 1980s he was Professor of Leadership and Organizational Behavior at the University of Massachusetts, Amherst. He wrote and researched extensively in the fields of leadership, motivation, and the management of change, and his *Management of Organizational Behavior: Utilizing Human Resources* (coauthored with Paul Hersey) is now in its 8th edition and has become a classic text. In the Introduction to *The One Minute Manager* (OMM), Blanchard and his coauthor Spencer Johnson, MD, describe the book as an allegory, a simple compilation of what "many wise people have taught us and what we have learned ourselves."

KEY THINKING
One-minute Management

The framework story of *The One Minute Manager* imagines a young manager going off in search of that holy grail of the aspiring newcomer—an effective manager on whom to model his own thinking and actions. The novice—a cross between *Le Petit Prince* and *Candide*—is caught between the two extremes of the Scientific and Human Relations schools: some managers get good results (but at a price that few colleagues and subordinates seem willing to support),

while others (whose people really like them) have results which leave much to be desired. Our hero, however, soon comes across a manager who gets excellent results as a result of—apparently—very little effort on his part—the One Minute Manager. The OMM has three simple secrets that bring about increases in productivity, profits, and satisfaction—one-minute goal-setting, one-minute praising, and one-minute reprimanding.

One-minute Goal-setting

Although staff cannot know how well they are doing without clear goals, claims the OMM, many are not clear on priorities, and many are spoken to only when they make a mistake. The OMM requires managers to make it clear what tasks people are to do and what sort of behavior or performance is expected of them, and to get staff to write down their most important goals on a single sheet of paper for continued clarification.

One-minute Praising

The second secret—one-minute praising—is the key to improved performance and increased productivity. Instead of criticizing people for doing something wrong, the opposite is recommended: "the key to developing people is to catch them doing something right." There are three steps in one-minute praising.

- Praise someone as close in time to the good behavior as possible. If you can't find someone to praise every day, then you should wonder why.
- Be specific. Make it clear what it was that was performed well.
- Share feelings—tell them how you feel about what they did, not what you think about what they did.

One-minute Reprimanding

The third secret of the One Minute Manager is the key to changing the attitude of the poor performer and there are four aspects to it.

- Immediacy—when a reprimand is necessary, it is best to deliver it as soon as possible after the instance of poor performance that led to it.
- Be specific—don't tell people about your reactions or give vent to your feelings, tell them what they did wrong; admonish the action, not the person.
- Share feelings—once you have established what was wrong, share your feelings.
- Tell them how good they are—the last step in the reprimand. If you finish on negative feedback, they will reflect on your style of behavior, not on their own performance.

The Development of One-minute Management

Putting the One Minute Manager to Work was a follow-up in 1984 by Blanchard and co-author Richard Lorber (an expert in performance improvement) to flesh out some of the basic ideas which had met initial success in *The One Minute Manager*. Subtitled *How to Turn the Three Secrets Into Skills*, the 1984 follow-up focuses on the "ABCs" of management, "effective reprimanding," and the "PRICE" system.

The ABCs

- Activators—those things that a manager has to do before anyone else can be expected to achieve anything, such as goal-setting, laying down key areas of accountability, issuing instructions, and setting performance standards.
- Behavior—or performance—what a person says or does, such as filing, writing, selling, ordering, buying, etc.
- Consequence—what a manager does after performance, such as sharing feelings, praising, reprimanding, supporting, etc.

Effective Reprimanding

A manager has to distinguish between a situation where an employee can't do something—which implies a need for training and signals a return to the activator of goal-setting—and one where an employee won't do something—which implies an attitude problem and a case for a reprimand. Reprimands do not teach skills, they can only change attitudes. Positive consequences on

the other hand can influence future performance to the good. Therefore it is important, as *The One Minute Manager* had already suggested, to end a reprimand with praise, making the employee think about his or her own behavior, not that of the reprimander.

The PRICE System

PRICE takes the three basic secrets of one-minute management and turns them into five steps.

- **Pinpointing**—defining key performance areas in measurable terms—part of one-minute goal-setting;
- **Recording**—gathering data to measure actual performance and keep track of progress;
- **Involving**—sharing the information recorded with whoever is responsible;
- **Coaching**—providing constructive feedback on improving performance;
- **Evaluating**—part of coaching, also part of reprimanding or praising.

Later Works

Leadership and the One Minute Manager stresses that there is no single, best method of leadership, but that there are in fact four styles: directing, delegating, coaching, and support. Whichever style is employed depends on the situation to be managed. "Situational leadership is not something you do to people, but something you do with people." Blanchard turns conventional leadership thinking on its head, using the analogy of turning the organizational pyramid upside down; instead of staff working for their boss, the boss should work for the staff.

The One Minute Manager Builds High-Performing Teams can be seen as a companion to *Leadership* and concentrates on integrating the simplicity of the one-minute techniques into understanding group dynamics and adjusting leadership style to meet developing circumstances.

The One Minute Manager Meets the Monkey deals with the problems of time management and overload. Paying tribute to Bill Oncken, Blanchard's coauthor who created the monkey analogy, Blanchard points the finger at the concept of the manager as the "hero with all the answers," stressing that bosses are not there to try to tackle every problem themselves, but to get others to come up with solutions. The monkey is the problem being passed from subordinate to superior, making the superior rapidly ineffective; the one-minute manager is not a collector of monkeys; rather a facilitator and coach helping others to solve their own problems.

KENNETH BLANCHARD IN PERSPECTIVE

So where does Blanchard sit in the Hall of Fame of management thinkers?

In the early years of the 21st century, much of what Blanchard et al. have to say in the *One Minute Manager* series no longer seems earth-shattering. Countless publications and endless seminars on leadership, change, delegation, and time management have, unsurprisingly, rendered a glance back to Blanchard, an entertaining experience, yes, and a comforting one in its confirmation of what one has learned elsewhere, but—like the key message of a contemporaneous publication *In Search of Excellence* (Peters and Waterman, 1982)—one-minute management is no longer the inspiration it was.

When asked why *In Search of Excellence* did so well, critics and commentators argued that its timing was impeccable: It was published at a time when Western business concepts were being trashed in favor of analyses of the Japanese business boom. If Peters and Waterman were largely about reinvigorating pride in successful U.S. organizations, Blanchard's book was excellently timed for its impact on individual skills and techniques.

It is important to remember that before Blanchard, Peters, and everyone who followed in their wake, management—as far as the hard-nosed manager was concerned—was a stuffy, dry subject reserved for lengthy academic treatises and exposés. Most books—not that there were many of them—focused on building the arguments of the human relations school and tackling the monstrous scientific/bureaucratic establishment so convincingly constructed by Taylor, Ford, and Weber. Books on management were not popular, not widely read, and certainly not best-sellers. It is often claimed that Peters and Waterman changed all that. But Ken Blanchard's contribution was also hugely influential. *The One Minute Manager* may have been panned by the academics, but it did more to make management digestible, readable, and accessible to a wide audience than any of its predecessors. By means of allegory, anecdotes, and allusions, it brought management to a level where many believed they could do it and do it well. Others have followed the storytelling format of OMM, such as *One Page Management* (Khadem) and *Zapp! The Lightning of Empowerment* (Byham) to name but two.

So what is the appeal of *The One Minute Manager*, rejected (like Maslow) by academia, but wholeheartedly adopted (as was Maslow) by practicing managers around the world? Blanchard's book was, first and foremost, short and to the point. Moreover, it was written in readable, everyday language, offering practical, everyday solutions to practical, everyday problems. This was no dry, stuffy theory, but a collection of honest sensible techniques to try out straight away. This is where Blanchard scored a first.

Any author who sells over 7 million copies deserves a place in the Management Hall of Fame. For Blanchard, that place has to be broadly in the human relations school alongside the great popularizers of empowerment on the one hand and the self-help school, stretching from Samuel Smiles and Dale Carnegie to present-day figures like Stephen Covey and, recently, Tom Peters, on the other. Blanchard's message may not be original but few have spread the simple messages more effectively, or to such a wide audience.

FOR MORE INFORMATION

Books:

Blanchard, Kenneth, and Spencer Johnson. *The One Minute Manager*. New York: Berkley Publishing Group, 1983.
Blanchard, Kenneth, and Robert Lorber. *Putting the One Minute Manager to Work*. New York: William Morrow & Co., 1984.
Blanchard, Kenneth, Patricia Zigarmi, and Drea Zigarmi. *Leadership and the One Minute Manager*. New York: William Morrow & Co., 1985.
Blanchard, Kenneth, William Oncken, and Hal Burrows. *The One Minute Manager Meets the Monkey*. New York: William Morrow & Co. 1990.
Blanchard, Kenneth, Donald Carew, and Eunice Parisi-Carew. *The One Minute Manager Builds High-Performing Teams*. New York: William Morrow & Co., 1980.
Blanchard, Kenneth, and Terry Waghorn. *Mission Possible*. New York: McGraw-Hill, 1997.
Blanchard, Kenneth, and Sheldon Bowles. *Gung Ho*. New York: William Morrow & Co., 1998.

Dale Carnegie
How to Win Friends and Influence People

Dale Carnegie's main focus is on dealing with people successfully. His best-known work, *How to Win Friends and Influence People* (1936), puts forward the essential principles for doing this; for example, you should never criticize, complain about, or condemn another person; you should give sincere appreciation to others; in order to motivate people, you need to stimulate a specific desire in them.

1888	Born.
1908	Graduates from State Teachers College, Warrensburg, Missouri.
1912	Teaches first public speaking class at YMCA in upper Manhattan.
1912–1920	Formalizes course in public speaking.
1926	Publication of textbook *Public Speaking: A Practical Course for Businessmen*.
1936	Publication of *How to Win Friends and Influence People*.
1939	Introduces sales course.
1955	Dies.

LIFE AND CAREER

Dale Carnegie (1888–1955) came from a poor, farming background and had to struggle through college. Looking for a way to distinguish himself, he began to enter speaking contests and, despite a shaky start, was soon winning every contest he entered. On leaving college he worked for some time as a salesman, making his territory the most successful one in the company, before deciding to train and work as an actor. This was another false start, however. He gave up the stage to run his own business, and then eventually decided to write novels and support himself by teaching at night.

Carnegie's first courses on public speaking for businesspeople at the YMCA schools in New York were run purely on a commission basis, as he was initially refused any pay. The courses did well, however, and their popularity made him a great success. They were so successful, in fact, that he was able to turn them into a series of popular books that extended beyond his initial sphere of public speaking into the realm of human relations in general. The books, which provided simple rules on how to achieve success with people, using examples from his own and others' experiences and stories about historical figures such as Roosevelt and Lincoln, became runaway successes in their turn. Carnegie went on to found the Dale Carnegie Institute of Effective Speaking and Human Relations to spread his ideas yet further. In 1997, over 40 years after his death, *How to Win Friends and Influence People*, the book that made him internationally famous, was still on the bestseller list in Germany.

KEY THINKING

Carnegie believed that criticism was counterproductive and should never be used to try to change or motivate people. In his view, people who are criticized tend to respond by justifying themselves and condemning the critical person in return. Great leaders such as Abraham Lincoln achieved their success partly because they never criticized others. Carnegie recommended instead the practice of self-control, understanding, and forgiveness. Most importantly, he advised that you should always try to see the other person's point of view.

In order to influence people and achieve your objectives, Carnegie suggests, it is necessary to understand individual motivation. You need to ask yourself what will motivate a person to want to do a task for you, before you attempt to persuade them to do it. He considers most people to be interested only in their own desires, but suggests that, if they are given what they want, they can help the giver to achieve great success in business.

People may simply want to drive a better car or buy a bigger house. For most people, however, the desire to be important is a main, if not the main motivator. It can inspire them to do great things, such as become important leaders or make their fortune in business. It can also take morbid forms. Sometimes individuals become invalids to gain attention or become insane so that they can live in a dream world where their importance is exaggerated by imagination. In any event the urge to be important should not be ignored. Using very human, anecdotal evidence, Carnegie illustrates how nourishing a person's self-esteem can achieve far better results than criticism ever could.

The Rules

How to Win Friends and Influence People has "in a nutshell" conclusions at the end of each section. In them Carnegie summarizes the main messages each section offers in terms of behavior. Some of these are paraphrased below.

Six ways to make people like you:
1 Show a genuine interest in other people.
2 Be happy and positive.
3 Remember that people love hearing the sound of their own name.
4 Listen to other people and develop good listening skills.
5 Talk about others' interests rather than your own.
6 Give others a sincere sense of their importance.

Twelve ways to win people to your way of thinking:
1 To get the best of a situation, avoid arguments.
2 Always listen to others' opinions and never tell anyone they are wrong.
3 Admit it if you are wrong.
4 Show friendliness.
5 Make statements that the other person can agree with.
6 Let the other person talk more than you.
7 Make the other person feel that an idea is their own.
8 See the other person's point of view.
9 Show empathy with others' ideas and desires.
10 Infuse some drama into your ideas.
11 Appeal to the better nature of others.
12 Finish with a challenge.

Nine ways to change people without arousing resentment:
1 Start with genuine praise and appreciation.

"Don't criticize, condemn, or complain; give honest and sincere appreciation; and arouse in the other person an eager want."
Dale Carnegie

2 Draw attention to people's mistakes gradually.

3 Admit that you have made mistakes and then talk to other people about theirs.

4 Don't give direct orders but ask questions.

5 Never humiliate anyone, and let people keep their pride intact.

6 Use plenty of genuine praise and encouragement when there is the slightest improvement.

7 Give people a reputation to maintain.

8 Encourage people. Show them that their task is easy to accomplish.

9 Suggest what you want them to do and make them happy about it.

Becoming a Good Public Speaker

Some of the advice given by Dale Carnegie at the start of his career, in his writing and training on public speaking, is summarized below.

Preparation

From the beginning, Carnegie suggested, you should generate an enthusiasm within yourself for public speaking, whether you have a financial or a social goal in view. Prepare as much as possible for the speech and have it ready well in advance. Begin planning as soon as you can and look for a topic that you know a lot about. Always try to use your own ideas, but bring the topic of your speech into conversation, so that you can explore any interesting stories on the subject that others may be able to tell you. Think about your talk at every possible opportunity and research it thoroughly, using libraries and other sources and collecting more material than you will need.

Do not memorize the talk word for word, as you will then be more likely to forget it. It may also lose much of its effectiveness if it seems too studied. While you should have plenty of material prepared, you should not try to say too much in the talk itself. Your material needs to be structured simply, so that you can talk as if you were in ordinary conversation.

Most people are nervous about talking in public. If you try to act bravely and pretend that you feel more confident than you really do, you will often actually gain in con-

fidence. Practice will help you to feel more certain of yourself, and it is a good idea to rehearse your speech as much as possible, maybe in front of the mirror, or with family and friends as an audience.

Delivery

Dress the part for your speech. Smile, and make sure you are clearly visible to your audience. Show respect and affection for the audience, and let the first sentence capture their attention. Examples of techniques to help you to achieve this are:

- start with a striking incident or example;
- state an arresting fact;
- ask for a show of hands;
- use an exhibit;
- do or say something to generate suspense;
- promise to tell the audience how they can get something they want.

You should not, however, open a talk with either an apology or a funny story. Humorous stories often fail to work, and this is particularly likely to be the case when you are nervous.

Use statistics or the testimony of experts to support your main ideas, but know your audience and do not use technical terms if you are addressing a lay audience. Be eager to share your talk with your listeners, putting passion into your way of speaking and using your emotions without fear. Represent things visually when possible, turning a fact into a picture to help your audience to understand what you are talking about and using specific instances and concrete examples.

Stress important words and avoid hackneyed expressions or clichés. Once your talk is launched, you may feel freer to be humorous when appropriate, but take care to target any fun at yourself rather than others.

Your talk should have some marked form of closure. Summarize what you have said, then use a finalizing climax or close of some sort that is appropriate within the context, for example:

- make an appeal for action;
- pay the audience a sincere compliment;
- raise a final laugh;
- use a fitting verse of poetry or a quotation.

Carnegie's Concluding Advice

- Remember that many famous speakers were originally terrified of speaking in public and that a certain amount of stage fright is useful.
- Predetermine your mind to success and seize every opportunity to practice.
- Remember that as you increase your experience your fear will diminish, so seek opportunities to speak in public, and believe in yourself.

DALE CARNEGIE IN PERSPECTIVE

Carnegie claimed that his theories do really work and that he had seen them transform the lives of many people. Some management writers have, however, dismissed Carnegie's ideas as being simple wisdom dressed up in a commercial coating.

Certainly, Carnegie's ideas are based on common sense and are hardly revolutionary. All his self-help books are based on down-to-earth and simply illustrated basic principles. Despite this simplicity, Carnegie has expressed many general truths which people acknowledge and, whatever his critics may say, the books he wrote are still popular.

In fact, Carnegie created a highly successful business out of his ideas, and his books have sold millions. Even today, much money is still being made from his work, which suggests that people still find him very relevant. Certainly, it is possible to see Carnegie's influence in some of today's ideas about management, particularly in discussions on the treatment of customers, and in approaches to interpersonal skills development.

1189

BUSINESS THINKERS

FOR MORE INFORMATION

Books:
Carnegie, Dale. *How to Win Friends and Influence People*. New York: Pocket Books, 1984 (reissue).
Carnegie, Dale. *How to Enjoy Your Life and Your Job*. New York: Pocket Books, 1986.
Carnegie, Dale. *How to Stop Worrying and Start Living*. New York: Pocket Books, 1985.

"Take a chance! All life is a chance. The man who goes the furthest is generally the one who is willing to do and dare."

Dale Carnegie

Alfred D. Chandler, Jr.
Business History As a Management Tool

The U.S. academic Alfred D. Chandler Jr. is the first historian in the modern era to both forge his own subject area and dominate it for almost half a century. When he stumbled on the genre after World War II, business history was just a virgin cousin of the emerging and wider-based topic called economic history, a largely theoretical discipline that deals with macrofiscal issues as they affect national and international economies.

Harvard University, where Chandler completed his Ph.D.

1918	Born.
1952	Completes Ph.D. at Harvard.
1962	Publication of *Strategy and Structure*.
1970	Appointed Isidor Strauss Professor of Business History, Harvard Business School.
1977	Publication of *The Visible Hand: The Managerial Revolution in American Business*.

LIFE AND CAREER

Chandler was born in 1918 and acquired his first interest in history from Wilbur Fiske Gordy's *Elementary History of the United States*, which his father gave him at the age of seven. He was educated at Phillips Exeter Academy, Harvard College, the University of North Carolina, where he received his MA, and Harvard University, where he completed his Ph.D. in history in 1952. His wartime experience was with a unit responsible for analyzing photographs of gunnery exercises by the Atlantic Fleet and bombing raids in the Pacific.

He acquired an interest in sociology and saw the value of explicit concepts, generalizations, and theories in analyzing human behavior, but it was when he came to choose his dissertation topic that his interest in business history was initially sparked. His great-aunt died suddenly, and Chandler and his family moved into her house, in which were stored the personal papers of his grandfather, Henry Varnum Poor. Poor, whose name survives as one half of the business information company Standard and Poor's Corporation, had been one of the people most knowledgeable about U.S. railroads, having edited the *American Railway Journal* for nearly 20 years. Using Poor's per-

sonal papers, together with the extensive back files of his newspapers and related publications in the Baker Library at Harvard, he produced a classic series of articles, his dissertation, and a book entitled *Henry Varnum Poor: Business Editor, Analyst, and Reformer*. This treatise, a seminal work on U.S. railroad companies during their formative years, enabled him to develop—through his genius at widespread comparative analysis—what became his characteristic way of extracting clear historical patterns that tended toward inductively derived theory.

Chandler's career as a working business historian began at the Massachusetts Institute of Technology, where he had the opportunity of working on the individual histories of Du Pont, General Motors, Standard Oil (now Exxon), and Sears, Roebuck & Co.—a course of study that culminated in *Strategy and Structure*. At Johns Hopkins University he wrote the biography of Pierre du Pont; and in 1970 he was appointed Isidor Strauss Professor of Business History at Harvard Business School, the world's only endowed chair in the field at the time. Since then he has led a growing field of teachers and studies; about 200 U.S. academics now work on the subject.

KEY THINKING

Until Chandler turned to business history as his principal interest, mainstream economic history predominated as the subject matter of business education. There was, admittedly, a detour, the result of imported Western European attitudes, when both popular journalism and academia started to take an interest in the corrupt practices of businesspeople. The perception emerged that they were "robber barons," a viewpoint that only started to change when Joseph

Schumpeter's *The Theory of Economic Development*, which depicted the businessman as a force for positive advancement, was translated from German into English in 1934. Several notable academics started to reevaluate the same robber barons as constructive, daring, and far-seeing "industrial statesmen," who deserved credit for making the United States a predominant economic power able to defend itself and its allies from the totalitarian assaults on freedom of the 20th century. Nevertheless, it was Chandler who made business history a linchpin of the curriculum.

His work has been pioneering in several other respects. It has been conducted in front of a largely unreceptive audience: The majority of management educators long resisted the concept of using the real example of corporate and business history as a teaching tool. With an attachment to the more empirical methodologies dominated by macroeconomics and quantitative analysis, they believed that business historians painted with too broad a brush on too wide a canvas and lacked a solid or explicitly stated methodology. They also accused the genre of being largely irrelevant given the perceived pace of change. Chandler's work has done much to change these attitudes, although it is instructive to note that business and management teachers—unlike educators in disciplines such as the military, politics, music, architecture, sociology, and so on—still widely resist both the concept and the development of history-based experiential learning in their own discipline. Chandler has also spent his life challenging economic thinking, in particular the static equilibrium theory. Although he used the results of quantitative research, he did not employ mathematical notation, remaining skeptical of highly theorized arithmetical manipulations that, he says, while elegantly logical, distort intelligible generalizations about the past.

In shifting the focus of business history, Chandler's work, which in fact specifically addresses the process of evolution and change, uses a systematic and analytical approach that has evolved from an intellectual outlook, which he labeled "managerial enterprise." As he explains it, this concept moves in two directions—forward from the past to the present and backward from the present to the past. Using the former perspective, for example, he examined why

"Regrettably, history is strewn with the visions of such 'new eras' that, in the end, have proven to be a mirage. In short, history counsels caution."

Alan Greenspan

early 19th-century industry did not employ any managers, a phenomenon which changed decisively and for ever in the second half of the 19th century. Using the latter perspective, he questioned the 1950s moves by industry toward decentralization of their functionally-specialized and multidepartmentalized organizations. His answers—in a landmark book entitled *Strategy and Structure*, published in 1962—took business history into a new dimension by establishing a fresh framework and rationale for the subject. He introduced the feature of making comparisons within and between industries and over time, and enabled business history to acquire relevance in a wide variety of related fields.

In *The Visible Hand*, another milestone book, Chandler used the concept of managerial enterprise to illustrate how Germany became the most powerful industrial nation in Europe before World War II, the United States became the most productive country in the world for 40 years until the 1960s, and Japan became its most successful competitor thereafter. For this book he won the Pulitzer Prize. These and other works—including, with Richard Tedlow, *The Coming of Managerial Capitalism*—are routinely used in at least 30 higher educational institutions in the United States and many more abroad.

Business history's role at the operational level, Chandler explains, is not about teaching specific management techniques. It has a more strategic function. Any meaningful analysis of an organization today, he says, must be based on an accurate understanding of its past. "Such data has to come from business history based on company records or from historically based case studies. Certainly a restructuring of enterprises to meet changing conditions requires an understanding of both why and how the existing organization evolved and how and why competitive conditions changed. Managers facing such problems can get insights by observing the working out of such processes in other enterprises." Companies such as McKinsey & Co and AT&T have applied *Strategy and Structure* to this end. The former, for example, has used it to teach its clients about the timing of strategic change and how to adjust their organizational structures, while

the latter put it to use in one of its reorganizations.

At the wider education level, Chandler believes that business history can provide insights into the processes of businesses such as the development of competitive strategy, the restructuring of organizational forms, and the effectiveness of investment and monitoring techniques. His view is that the value of teaching business histories in universities is to make MBA students and those in more advanced management courses aware of recent as well as long-term changes in functional activities such as production, marketing, research and development, finance, labor relations, and the like; also in monitoring and coordinating the activities of the current operations of an enterprise as well as in locating resources for future production and distribution. "Not only can the students learn something about the nature of the functions but also the complexities of carrying out change," he says.

ALFRED D. CHANDLER, JR. IN PERSPECTIVE

For students and practitioners alike, Chandler's name may be remembered principally as the pioneer who placed strategy before structure in his seminal work published in 1962. Not only has he championed the systematic study of modern bureaucratic administration in an original way, he has also turned what is often dismissed as an artless medium into a valid and powerful educational tool. Using the conglomerate history of individual companies to arrive at a historical theory of big business instead of the mainstream—economic—discipline of the day, he revolutionized the fledgling discipline by refocusing attention away from individual entrepreneurs and seeking patterns in the rise of large-scale modern business. Almost uniquely, his work—which has given rise to the term "Chandlerianism"—has had a profound effect on historians and business thinking all over the world, particularly in Japan and Germany. Some of his books have been translated into Chinese and Russian.

Following his lead, U.S. business historians have moved to more thematic areas: for example, how companies formulate and

implement policy; how industries evolve; the impact of administrative hierarchies on the modern economy; industrial evolution across national boundaries; the interaction of business with governmental institutions and regulatory bodies; and organized labor and the consumer.

History will no doubt endow him with the distinction of giving modern management educators a less theoretical way of teaching the business of business. In essence, he has skillfully recycled the tried and tested past to provide both practicing and aspiring managers with an inheritance that has practical corporate application in today's highly competitive world. In truth, history is the only way individuals and companies can learn from experience. And learning from experience is the only way to increase productivity and competitiveness.

1191

BUSINESS THINKERS

FOR MORE INFORMATION

Books:
Chandler, Alfred. *Strategy and Structure*. Cambridge, MA: MIT Press, 1962.
Chandler, Alfred. *The Visible Hand: The Managerial Revolution in American Business*. Cambridge, MA: Harvard University Press, 1977.
Chandler, Alfred. *Managerial Hierarchies*. Cambridge, MA: Harvard University Press, 1980.
Chandler, Alfred, and Richard Tedlow. *The Coming of Managerial Capitalism*. Homewood, IL: Richard D. Irwin, 1985.
Chandler, Alfred. *Scale and Scope; The Dynamics of Industrialized Capitalism*. Cambridge, MA: Harvard University Press, 1994.
Chandler, Alfred. *Big Business and The Wealth of Nations*. New York: Cambridge University Press, 1997.
Chandler, Alfred. *The Dynamic Firm*. New York: Oxford University Press, 1998.
REFERENCES: Both quotations are extracts from private correspondence with Chandler.

See also:
Henry Mintzberg (pp. 1240–1241)
Kenichi Ohmae (pp. 1244–1245)
Michael Porter (pp. 1254–1255)

"Change means movement. Movement means friction."   Saul Alinsky

Stephen R. Covey
The Seven Habits of Highly Effective People

In *The Seven Habits of Highly Effective People*, Stephen Covey offers a holistic approach to life and work that has struck a significant chord with the perplexed manager working in turbulent times. The recurring themes in his various works are the transforming power of principles rooted in unchanging natural laws that govern human and organizational effectiveness; the necessity of adapting every aspect of one's life to accord with these principles; effective leadership; and empowerment.

1192

BUSINESS THINKERS

1932	Born.
1985	Founds Covey Leadership Center.
1989	Publication of *The Seven Habits of Highly Effective People*.
1997	Covey Leadership Center merges with Franklin Quest.

LIFE AND CAREER

Stephen Covey is founder and chairman of the Covey Leadership Center—now part of Franklin Covey—and the Institute for Principle-Centered Leadership in Utah. Born in 1932, he received an MBA from Harvard Business School and a doctorate from Brigham Young University, where he was subsequently Professor of Organizational Behavior and Business Management.

At the Covey Leadership Center, through his writing—chiefly *The Seven Habits of Highly Effective People* (which has sold over five million copies)—and through consulting (he was invited to Camp David by President Clinton), his message has reached millions of individuals in business, government, and education.

KEY THINKING
The Seven Habits of Highly Effective People

The Seven Habits is addressed to readers not only in their capacity as managers but also as members of a family, and as social, spiritual, sporting, and thinking individuals. It offers a "life-transforming prescription," which calls for a reappraisal of many fundamental assumptions and attitudes (paradigms), and builds on the fundamental concept of interdependence. Covey traces a personal development outline from:

- dependence in childhood (many people never grow out of a dependency culture), through . . . ;
- independence in adolescence—self-assurance, a developing personality, and a positive mental attitude, to . . . ;
- interdependence—recognition that the optimum outcome results from each individual giving of his or her best, aiming for a common goal, and sharing the same mission and vision, but having the freedom to use his or her best judgment as to how to go about achieving that common goal.

Habit 1
Be proactive.

Covey distinguishes between proactive people—those who focus their efforts on things which they can do something about—and reactive people, who blame, accuse, behave like victims, pick on other people's weaknesses, and complain about external factors over which they have no control (for example, the weather).

Proactive people are responsible for their own lives. Covey breaks down the word *responsibility* into "response" and "ability." Proactive people recognize their responsibility to make things happen. Those who allow their feelings to control their actions have abdicated responsibility and empowered their feelings. When proactive people make a mistake, they not only recognize it as such and acknowledge it, they also correct it if possible and, most importantly, learn from it.

Habit 2
Begin with the end in mind.

Leadership is about effectiveness—the vision of what is to be accomplished. It calls for direction (in every sense of the word), purpose, and sensitivity. Management, on the other hand, is about efficiency—how best to accomplish the vision. It depends on control, guidance, and rules.

To identify the end, and to formulate one's route or strategy to achieving that end, Covey maintains the need for a "principle-centered" basis to all aspects of life. Most people adopt something as the basis (or pivotal point) of their life—spouse, family, money, church, pleasure, friends (and, in a perverse way, enemies), sports, etc. Of course all of these have some influence over the life of every individual. However, only by clearly establishing one's own principles, in the form of a personal mission, does one have a solid foundation.

Habit 3
Put first things first.

Covey's first major work, *First Things First*, sets out his views on time management. It argues that the important thing is not managing time, but managing oneself, focusing on results rather than on methods when prioritizing within each compartment of work and life.

He breaks down life's activities into four quadrants:

Quadrant 1: Urgent and important—for example, crises, deadlines, unexpected opportunities.

Quadrant 2: Not urgent, but important—for example, planning, recreation, relationship-building, doing, learning.

Quadrant 3: Urgent, but not important—for example, interruptions, meetings.

Quadrant 4: Not urgent and not important—for example, trivia, time-wasters, gossip.

Essentially all activity of effective people should focus on the second quadrant, apart from the genuinely unpredictable quadrant 1 events. However, effective planning and doing in Quadrant 2 should minimize the number of occasions on which crises occur.

The outcomes of a Quadrant 2 focus include: vision, perspective, balance, discipline, and control. On the other hand, the results of placing one's main focus on the other quadrants are:

Quadrant 1: stress, burnout, inability to manage time (and thus loss of control of one's own life).

Quadrant 3: short-termism, loss of control, shallowness, feelings of being a victim of circumstances.

Quadrant 4: irresponsibility, dependency, unsuitability for employment.

Habit 3 is therefore about managing oneself effectively, by prioritizing according to the principles adopted in Habit 2. This approach transcends the office diary or day-planner, embracing all roles in life—as manager, mentor, administrator, strategist, and also as parent, spouse, member of social groups, and as an individual with needs and aspirations.

Habits 1–3 are grouped under the banner "Private Victory." They are about the development of the personal attributes that provide the foundations for independence. Habits 4–6 are described by Covey as the "Public Victory," as they are the basic paradigms of interdependence.

Habit 4

Think win/win.

Interdependence occurs when there is cooperation, not competition, in the workplace (or the home). Covey holds that competition belongs in the marketplace.

Covey points out that, from childhood, many people are conditioned to a win/lose mentality by school examinations, by parental approval being related to "success," by external comparisons and league standings. This results in a "scarcity mentality," a belief that there is only a finite cake to be shared: evident in people who have difficulty in sharing recognition or credit, power or profit. It restricts their ability to celebrate other people's success, and even brings about a perverse satisfaction at others' misfortune.

By contrast Covey advocates an "abundance mentality" that:

- recognizes unlimited possibilities for positive growth and development;
- celebrates success, recognizing that one person's success is not achieved at the expense, or to the exclusion, of others;
- understands and seeks a win/win solution.

Covey argues that, to be true to your ideals, it is sometimes necessary to walk away if the other party is interested only in a win/lose outcome. Covey describes this as "win/win or no deal."

Habit 5

Seek first to understand, then to be understood.

"I just can't understand my son . . . he won't listen to me." The absurdity of this statement is highlighted by Covey in emphasizing the importance of listening in order to understand. Clearly, the parent needs to stop and listen to the son if he or she truly wants to understand him.

However, most people want to make their point first, or are so busy looking for their opportunity to butt into the conversation that they fail to hear and understand the other party. Covey defines the different levels of listening as:

- hearing but ignoring;
- pretending to listen ("Yes," "Oh," "I see . . . ");
- selective listening (choosing to hear only what we want to hear);
- attentive listening, without evaluation (e.g. taking notes at a lecture);
- empathetic listening (with intent to understand the other party).

True empathetic listening requires a great deal of personal security, as one is vulnerable to being influenced, to having one's opinions changed. "The more deeply you understand other people," Covey says, "the more you appreciate them, the more reverent you feel about them."

Likewise, when you feel that someone is genuinely seeking to understand your point of view, you recognize and share their openness and willingness to negotiate and to reach a win/win situation.

Habit 6

Synergize.

The essence of synergy is where two parties, each with a different agenda, value each other's differences. Everything in nature is synergistic, with every creature and plant being interdependent with others.

We also have personal effectiveness where there is synergy at an individual level—where both sides of the brain are working in tandem on a problem or situation, the intuitive, creative, visual right side and the analytical, logical, verbal left side combining to achieve the optimum outcome.

Synergy is lacking in insecure people: they either clone others, or else try to stereotype them. Of such insecurity is born prejudice—racism, bigotry, nationalism, and any other form of prejudging others.

Habit 7

Sharpen the saw.

The seventh and final habit relates to renewal. Just as a car or any other sophisticated tool needs regular care and maintenance, so too do the human body and mind.

Covey uses the metaphor of a woodcutter who is laboring painfully to saw down a tree. The saw is obviously in need of sharpening, but when asked why he doesn't stop and sharpen the saw, the woodcutter replies, "I can't stop—I'm too busy sawing down this tree."

The warning is quite clear. Everyone can become so engrossed in the task in hand that the basic tools are neglected:

- "the physical self"—which requires exercise, a sensible and balanced diet, and management of stress;
- "the social/emotional self"—which connects with others through service, empathy, and synergy, and which is the source of intrinsic security;
- "the spiritual self"—which through meditation, reflection, prayer, and study helps to clarify and refine our own values and strengths, and our commitment to them;
- "the mental self"—building on to our formal education through reading, visualizing, planning, writing, and maintaining a coherent program of continuing personal development.

STEPHEN R. COVEY IN PERSPECTIVE

Commentators have both attacked and applauded Covey's approach for mixing the self-help message, which can be traced back to Samuel Smiles, with the positive self-drive of winning friends and influencing people (Dale Carnegie), current management theories, and religious fervor.

In times of change and confusion, however, when failure, job loss, and unemployment dominate individual thinking and lead to stress, Covey's message offers the individual something to hang on to. *First Things First*, coauthored with Roger and Rebecca Merrill, has achieved twice the sales of *The Seven Habits* over the same period.

He is undoubtedly a philosopher for our times, highlighting the significance of changing industrial and human relations in this postconfrontational era, and recognizing the potential of the untapped resources within each individual.

1193

BUSINESS THINKERS

FOR MORE INFORMATION

Books:
Covey, Stephen. *The Seven Habits of Highly Effective People*. New York: Simon & Schuster, 1989.
Covey, Stephen. *Principle-centered Leadership*. New York: Summit Books, 1991.
Covey, Stephen, A. Roger Merrill and Rebecca R. Merrill. *First Things First*. New York: Simon & Schuster, 1996.
Covey, Stephen. *The Seven Habits of Highly Effective Families*. New York: Golden Books, 1997.
Covey, Stephen. *The Eighth Habit: From Effectiveness to Greatness*. New York: Free Press, 2004.

See also:
Tom Peters (pp. 1252–1253)

"Avoid fight or flight, talk through differences."   Stephen Covey

Philip Crosby
Zero Defects

Philip Crosby wrote the best-seller *Quality Is Free* at a time when the quality movement was a rising, innovative force in business and manufacturing. In the 1980s, his consulting company was advising 40% of the Fortune 500 companies on quality management.

His popularity as a consultant can be partly attributed to his ability to talk about quality management ideas in terms that were easy to understand.

1926	Born.
1952	After war service, begins his career working on an assembly line.
1961	Establishes "zero concepts" while working for Martin-Marietta.
1965	Joins ITT.
1979	*Quality is Free* published. Leaves ITT to found Philip Crosby Associates II, Inc.
1984	*Quality without Tears* published.
1988	*The Eternally Successful Organization* published.
1991	Launches Career IV Inc.
2001	Dies.

LIFE AND CAREER

Crosby was born in West Virginia in 1926. A graduate of Western Reserve University, he saw service in the Korean War, and started his working life on the assembly line in 1952, becoming quality manager for Martin-Marietta where he developed the "zero defects" concept. After working his way up, Crosby was corporate vice president and director of quality at ITT for 14 years.

As a result of the interest shown in *Quality is Free* (1979), he left ITT to establish Philip Crosby Associates II, Inc. and started to teach organizations quality principles and practice as laid down in his book. In 1985, his company went public for $30 million. In 1991 he retired from Philip Crosby Associates to launch Career IV Inc., a consulting company advising on the development of senior executives. He died in August 2001.

KEY THINKING

Quality, Crosby emphasized, is neither intangible nor immeasurable. It is a strategic imperative, something that can be quanti-

fied and put to work to improve the bottom line. "Acceptable" quality or defect levels produced by means of traditional quality control measures, for Crosby, represent evidence of failure rather than an assurance of success. The goal is to meet requirements on time, first time, and every time. The emphasis, therefore, should be on prevention, not inspection and cure.

Crosby's approach to quality was unambiguous. In his view, good, bad, high, and low quality are meaningless concepts in the abstract; the meaning of quality is "conformance to requirements." What that means is that a product should conform to the requirements that the company has itself established based on its customers' needs. He also believed that the prime responsibility for poor quality lies with management, not with the workers. Management sets the tone for the quality initiative from the top.

Nonconforming products are ones that management has failed to specify or control. The cost of nonconformance equals the cost of not doing it right first time, and not rooting out any defects in processes.

"Zero defects" does not mean that people never make mistakes, but that companies should not begin with "allowances" or substandard targets with mistakes as an in-built expectation. Instead, work should be seen as a series of activities or processes, defined by clear requirements and conducted to produce identified outcomes. Systems that allow things to go wrong—and that result in those things having to be done again—can cost organizations between 20% and 35% of their revenues, in Crosby's estimation.

His seminal approach to quality was set out in *Quality Is Free*, and is often summarized as the "Fourteen Steps."

The Fourteen Steps

1. Management commitment: the need for quality improvement must be recognized and accepted by management, who then draw up a quality improvement program with an emphasis on the need for defect prevention. Quality improvement equates to profit improvement. A quality policy is needed which states that " . . . each individual is expected to perform exactly like the requirement or cause the requirement to be officially changed to what we and the customer really need."

2. The quality improvement team: representatives from each department or function should be brought together to form a quality improvement team. Its members should be people who have sufficient authority to commit the area they represent to action.

3. Quality measurement: the status of quality should be determined throughout the company. This means establishing and recording quality measures for each area of activity in order to show where improvement is possible and where corrective action is necessary. Crosby advocated delegation of this task to the people who actually do the job, thus setting the stage for defect prevention on the job, where it really counts.

4. The cost of quality evaluation: the cost of quality is not an absolute performance measurement, but an indication of where the action necessary to correct a defect will result in greater profitability.

5. Quality awareness: this involves making employees aware of the cost to the company of defects, through training and information, and the provision of visible evidence of the results of a concern for quality improvement. Crosby stressed that this sharing process is a key, or even *the* key, step in the progress of an organization toward quality.

6. Corrective action: discussion of problems will result in the finding of solutions and will also bring to light other elements that are in need of improvement. People need to see that problems are regularly being resolved. Corrective action should then become a habit.

7. Establishing an ad hoc committee for the zero defects program: zero defects is not a motivation program: its purpose is to communicate and instill the notion that everyone should do things right first time.

8. Supervisor training: all managers should undergo formal training on the Fourteen Steps before they are implemented. Managers should understand each of the Fourteen Steps well enough to be able to explain them to their people.

9. Zero defects day: it is important that the commitment to zero defects as the performance standard of the company makes an impact, and that everyone gets the same message in the same way. Zero defects day, when supervisors explain the program to their people, should make a lasting impression as a "new attitude" day.

10. Goal setting: all supervisors ask their people to establish specific, measurable goals that they can strive for. Usually, these comprise 30-, 60-, and 90-day goals.

11. Error cause removal: employees are asked to describe, on a simple, one-page form, any problems that prevent them from carrying out error-free work. Problems should be acknowledged and begin to be addressed within 24 hours by the function or unit to which the memorandum is directed. This constitutes a key step in building trust, as it will make people begin to grow more confident that their problems will be attended to and dealt with.

12. Recognition: it is important to recognize those who meet their goals or perform outstanding acts with a prize or award, although this should not be in financial form. The act of recognition itself is what is important.

13. Quality councils: the quality professionals and team leaders should meet regularly to discuss improvements and upgrades to the quality program.

14. Doing it over again: during the course of a typical program lasting from 12 to 18 months, turnover and change will dissipate much of the educational process. It is important to establish a new team of representatives and begin the program again from the beginning, starting with zero defects day. This "starting over again" helps quality to become ingrained in the organization.

Putting Quality to the Test

Crosby often used stories to convey his message and also used audit techniques and questionnaires to clarify organizational and individual understanding.

Below we reproduce a quick "true or false" questionnaire that features in *Quality Is Free* (the answers are given at the end of this piece).

1. Quality is a measure of goodness of the product that can be defined as fair, good, excellent.

2. The economics of quality require that management establish acceptable quality levels as performance standards.

3. The cost of quality is the expense of doing things wrong.

4. Inspection and test should report to manufacturing so manufacturing can have the proper tools to do the job.

5. Quality is the responsibility of the quality department.

6. Worker attitudes are the primary cause of defects.

7. I have trend charts that show me the rejection level at every key operation.

8. I have a list of the ten biggest quality problems.

9. Zero defects is a worker motivation program.

10. The biggest problem today is that customers don't understand.

Later Work

In his 1984 book, *Quality Without Tears*, Crosby developed the idea of a "quality vaccination serum," which would be made up of the following ingredients:

- integrity for the chief executive officer, all managers, and all employees
- systems for measuring conformance, and educating all employees and suppliers so that quality, corrective action, and defect prevention become routine
- communications that enable problems to be identified, progress to be conveyed, and achievement to be recognized
- operations organized in such a way that procedures, products, and systems are proven before they are implemented and are then continually examined
- policies that are clear, unambiguous, and establish the primacy of quality throughout the organization

The Eternally Successful Organization (1988) presented a broader approach to improvements. In it Crosby identified five characteristics essential for an organization to be successful.

- People routinely do things right the first time.
- Change is anticipated and used to advantage.

- Growth is consistent and profitable.
- New products and services appear when needed.
- Everyone is happy to work there.

PHILIP CROSBY IN PERSPECTIVE

Throughout his work, Crosby's thinking was consistently characterized by four absolutes:

- the definition of quality is conformance to requirements;
- the system of quality is prevention;
- the performance standard is zero defects;
- the measurement of quality is the price of nonconformance.

The major contribution made by Crosby to management thinking is indicated by the fact that his phrases "zero defects," "getting it right first time," and "conformance to requirements" have now entered not only the vocabulary of quality itself, but also the general vocabulary of management.

When Crosby's name is not mentioned in the very same sentence as the best-known quality thinker of them all, Deming, then it is almost certain to be mentioned in the next. Crosby's practical and easy-to-read books on quality became—and remain— bibles for many, demystifying a great deal of the jargon formerly associated with quality management. His timing was perfect for the quality movement, and his writing has marketed quality to a wide audience.

ANSWERS TO QUESTIONNAIRE

1. F; 2. F; 3. T; 4. F; 5. F; 6. F; 7. T; 8. F; 9. F; 10. F

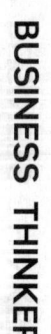

1195

BUSINESS THINKERS

FOR MORE INFORMATION

Books:
Crosby, Philip. *Quality Is Free: The Art of Making Quality Certain*. New York: McGraw-Hill, 1979.
Crosby, Philip. *Quality Without Tears: The Art of Hassle-Free Management*. New York: McGraw-Hill, 1984.
Crosby, Philip. *The Eternally Successful Organization: The Art of Corporate Wellness*. New York: McGraw-Hill, 1988.

See also:
W. Edwards Deming (pp. 1196–1197)

"The great discoveries are usually obvious."

Philip B. Crosby

W. Edwards Deming

Total Quality Management

W. Edwards Deming is widely acknowledged as the leading management thinker in the field of quality. He is credited with being the most influential catalyst of Japan's postwar economic transformation, although it wasn't until much later that the value of his ideas and practices began to be recognized by the U.S. manufacturing and service industries.

1900	Born.
1928	Completes Ph.D. at Yale.
1950	Begins teaching quality management in Japan.
1986	Publication of *Out of the Crisis*.
1987	Receives National Medal of Technology.
1993	Founds W. Edwards Deming Institute.
1993	Dies.

LIFE AND CAREER

Deming obtained a Ph.D. in mathematical physics from Yale University in 1928 and concentrated on lecturing and writing on mathematics, physics, and statistics for the next ten years. It was only in the late 1930s that he became familiar with the work of Walter Shewhart, who was experimenting with the application of statistical techniques to manufacturing processes. Deming became interested in applying Shewhart's techniques to nonmanufacturing processes, particularly clerical, administrative, and management activities. After joining the U.S. Census Bureau in 1939, he applied statistical process control to their techniques, which contributed to a sixfold improvement in productivity. Around this time he also started to run courses for engineers and designers on his—and Shewhart's—evolving methods of statistical process control.

Deming's expertise as a statistician was instrumental in his posting to Japan after World War II as an adviser to the Japanese Census. At this time, the United States was the leading economic power, with products much envied by the rest of the world; it saw no need for Deming's new ideas. The Japanese, on the other hand, recognized that their own goods were shoddy by inter-

national standards. Moreover, after the war, they could not afford the wastage of raw materials that postproduction inspection processes brought about and were consequently looking for techniques to help them address these problems. While in Japan, Deming became involved with the Union of Japanese Scientists and Engineers (JUSE) and his career of lecturing to the Japanese on statistical methods and company-wide quality, a combination of techniques now known as Total Quality Management (TQM), had begun.

It was only in the late 1970s that the United States became aware of his achievements in Japan. The 1980s saw a spate of publications explaining his work and influence. In his U.S. seminars during 1980, Deming talked of the need for the total transformation of Western-style management. In 1986 he published *Out of the Crisis*, which documented the thinking and practice that had led to the transformation of Japanese manufacturing industry. His ideas gained acceptance in the United Kingdom following the foundation of the British Deming Association in 1987. Deming died in 1993.

KEY THINKING

Deming's work and writing constitute not so much a technique as a philosophy of management, one that focuses on quality and continuous improvement, but that has also—justifiably—had a much wider influence.

Below we consider Deming's interest in variation and his approach to systematic problem-solving, which led on to his development of the 14 points that have gained widespread recognition and are central to the quality movement.

Variation and Problem Solving

The key to Deming's ideas on quality lies in his recognition of the importance of variation. In *Out of the Crisis* he states that "the central problem in management and in leadership ... is failure to understand the information in variation."

Deming was preoccupied with why things do not behave as predicted. All systems (be they the equipment, the process, or the people) have variation, but, he argued, it is essential for managers to be able to distinguish between special and common causes of variation. He developed a theory of variation: that special causes of variation are usually attributable to easily recognizable factors such as a change of procedure, change of shift or operator, and so on, but that common causes will remain when special causes have been eliminated and are normally inherent in the design, process, or system. These common causes often are recognized by workers, but only managers have the authority to change them to avoid repeated occurrence of the problem. Deming estimated that management was responsible for more than 85% of the causes of variation. This formed his central message to the Japanese.

Deming's 14 Points for Management

Deming created 14 points that provided a framework for developing knowledge in the workplace and guiding long-term business plans and objectives. The points constitute not so much an action plan as a philosophical code for management. They have been extensively interpreted, both by commentators on quality control and by experts on other management disciplines.

- Create constancy of purpose toward the improvement of products and services, with the aim of becoming competitive, staying in business, and providing jobs.
- Adopt the new philosophy. Western management must awaken to the challenge, learn its responsibilities, and take on leadership for change.
- Cease dependence on mass inspection. Build quality into the product from the start.
- End the practice of awarding business on the basis of price tag alone. Instead, minimize total cost. Move toward a single supplier for any item, based on a long-term relationship of loyalty and trust.

"Only management can change the system."

- Improve constantly and forever the system of production and service to improve quality and reduce waste.
- Institute training and retraining.
- Institute leadership. The aim of supervision should be to lead and help people to do a better job.
- Drive out fear so that everyone may work effectively for the company.
- Break down barriers between departments. People in research, design, sales, and production must work as a team, to foresee and solve problems of production.
- Eliminate slogans, exhortations, and targets, for the workforce, as they do not necessarily achieve their objectives.
- Eliminate numerical quotas in order to take account of quality and methods, rather than just numbers.
- Remove barriers to pride in workmanship.
- Institute a vigorous program of education and retraining for both the management and the workforce.
- Take appropriate action to accomplish the transformation. Management and workforce must work together.

These principles are relevant to management in general, not simply to quality and process control. They contributed to Deming's status as a founder of the Quality Management movement, and attracted an audience much wider than the quality lobby.

W. EDWARDS DEMING IN PERSPECTIVE

Naturally enough, no one as universally acclaimed as Deming escapes without criticism. Some have criticized his approach as being good for improvement but uninspiring for creativity and innovation. Others say his approach is not effective in generating new products or penetrating new markets.

Others—particularly Juran, another quality guru—accuse him of overreliance on statistical methods. Deming's U.S. lectures in the 1980s, however, point time and time again to a mistaken preoccupation with the wrong type of statistics. He argued against figures that focused purely on productivity and control and argued for more evidence of quality, a message that Tom Peters adopted in the 1980s and 1990s.

Deming also stirred up wide interest with his rejection of management by objectives and performance appraisals. Similarly, his attitude toward integrating the workforce led TQM to be perceived as a caring philosophy. Paradoxically, however, his focus on cost-reduction has been pointed to as a cause of downsizing.

Although in the 1980s the United States paid tribute to Deming—not only for what he did in Japan, but also for his thinking and approach to quality management—few U.S. companies use his methods today. One reason for this is perhaps that, by the 1980s, Deming was selling a system that worked, thereby implying that he had discovered the only way to achieve quality; thus he was no longer alert to changes in the problems. In Japan, in the beginning, he had listened to Japanese needs and requirements, showed them respect, and developed his thinking with them. In the United States of the 1980s, he appeared to try to dispense his philosophy rather than readapt it to a different culture.

In 1951, in early recognition of their debt to Deming, the JUSE awarded the Deming prize to Japanese organizations that excelled in company-wide quality. It was not until the 1980s that the United States recognized Deming's achievements in Japan and elevated him to guru status. In 1987 the British Deming Association was founded to disseminate his ideas in the United Kingdom. From the 1990s it seemed as if Deming's legacy was likely to have both a lasting and significant impact on management theory. Why is this?

The first reason must lie in the nature of his achievement. Deming has been universally acclaimed as one of the founding fathers of Total Quality Management, if not the founding father. The revolution in Japanese manufacturing management that led to the economic miracle of the 1970s and 1980s has been attributed largely to him.

Second, if the 14 points make less of an impact today than they did just after World War II in Japan, it is probably because many aspects of those points were adopted, assimilated, and integrated into management practice in the 1990s and have been continuously debated and taught in business schools around the world.

The third reason is more complex and lies in the scope of his legacy. Deming's 14 points add up to a code of management philosophy that spans the two major schools of managerial thought that have predominated since the early 20th century: scientific (hard) management, on the one hand, and human relations (soft) management, on the other. Deming succeeds—despite criticisms of his overuse of statistical techniques—in marrying them together. Over half of his 14 points focus on people as opposed to systems. Many management thinkers veer towards one school or the other. Deming, like Drucker, melds them together.

The originality and freshness of Deming is that he took his philosophy not from the world of management, but from the world of mathematics, and wedded it with a human relations approach that did not come from management theory but from observation and from seeing what people needed from their working environment in order to contribute their best.

FOR MORE INFORMATION

Book:
Deming, W. Edwards. *Out of the Crisis: Quality, Productivity, and Competitive Position.* Cambridge, MA: MIT Press, 2000.

See also:
Philip Crosby (pp. 1194–1195)

1197

BUSINESS THINKERS

Peter Drucker
The Father of Postwar Management

Peter Drucker was known throughout the world as *the* management guru. He did not claim to have invented management—but conceded that he discovered it as a way of life central to the well-being of society and the economy.

He had interests as diverse as journalism, art appreciation, mountaineering, and reading. With more than 33 books published over seven decades Drucker was, by common consent, the founding father of modern management studies.

Year	Event
1909	Born.
1927	Commences study at University of Hamburg.
1931	Doctorate in Public and International Law, University of Frankfurt, Germany.
1933	Moves to London to work as an investment banker.
1937	Leaves for United States to become investment adviser and correspondent for *Financial News*.
1939	Publication of *The End of Economic Man*.
1940	Private consultant to business and on government policy; teacher at Sarah Lawrence College; Professor at Bennington College, Vermont.
1943	Spends 18 months interviewing senior management at General Motors, which results in the bestselling *The Concept of the Corporation* (1946).
1950	Professor of Management at New York University Graduate School of Business.
1969	Publication of *The Age of Discontinuity*.
1971	Marie Rankin Clarke Professor of Management, Graduate School, Claremont.
1974	Publication of *Management: Tasks, Responsibilities, Practices*.
1975	Columnist for *Wall Street Journal*.
1990	Founding of The Peter F. Drucker Foundation for Non-Profit Management.
1999	Publication of *Management Challenges for the 21st Century*.
2005	Dies.

LIFE AND CAREER

Peter Ferdinand Drucker was born in Vienna in 1909 into a high-achieving, intellectual family and was surrounded in his early years by members of the prewar Viennese cultural elite. He began his studies at the University of Hamburg, but transferred to the University of Frankfurt, where he obtained a Doctorate in Public and International Law in 1931.

While still a student in Frankfurt, he worked on the city's *General Anzeiger* newspaper and rose to the posts of foreign and financial editor. Recognized as a talented writer, he was offered a job in the Ministry of Information. Observing the Nazis' rise to power with abhorrence, he wrote a philosophical essay condemning Nazism; this was probably instrumental in hastening his departure to England in 1933. It was in 1937 that he left for the United States to become an investment adviser to British industry and correspondent for several British newspapers, including the *Financial Times*, then called the *Financial News*.

His first book, *The End of Economic Man*, appeared in 1939. In 1940 he began work as a private consultant to business and government policy-makers, specializing in the German economy and external politics. From 1940 to 1942 he was a teacher at Sarah Lawrence College, and this was followed by the post of Professor of Philosophy, Politics, History, and Religion at Bennington College, Vermont.

It was in the early stages of this appointment that he was invited by the vice president of General Motors (GM) to investigate what constitutes a modern organization, and to examine what the managers running it actually do. Although Drucker was relatively inexperienced in business at the time, his analysis led to the publication, in 1946, of *The Concept of the Corporation*, which had a mixed reception but nonetheless confirmed Drucker's future as a management writer.

The period 1950–1972 was a time of prolific writing, teaching, and consulting while he was Professor of Management at New York University Graduate School of Business. In 1971 he was appointed the Marie Rankin Clarke Professor of Social Science and Management at the Graduate School in Claremont, a school that was subsequently named after him. In 1994 he was appointed Godkin Lecturer at Harvard University.

Drucker held decorations from the governments of Austria and Japan as well as 22 honorary doctorates from universities in Belgium, Japan, Spain, Switzerland, the United Kingdom, and the United States. He was also a Fellow of the American Association of Science; an Honorary Member of the National Academy of Public Administration; a Fellow of the American Academy of Arts and Sciences; and a Fellow of the American, British, Irish, and International Academies of Management.

KEY THINKING

Drucker's management writings are phenomenal in their coverage and impressive in their clarity. With over 33 books to his credit, we can provide only a snapshot of his thinking here. His earlier works made a significant contribution to establishing what constitutes management practice; his later works tackle the complexities—and the management implications—of the postindustrial 1980s and beyond. It is that range and development that we have tried to represent in our comments on the books covered here.

The End of Economic Man—1939

The End of Economic Man concentrates on the politics and economics of the 1930s in general and the rise of Nazism in particular; Drucker signaled a warning about the Holocaust and predicted that Hitler would forge an alliance with Stalin. This was his first book in English as sole author; J.B. Priestley said of it: "At once the most penetrating and the most stimulating book I have read on the world crisis. At last there is a ray of light in the dark chaos."

This was followed by *The Future of Industrial Man* (1942), which assumed Hitler's defeat and started to look ahead to peacetime,

> "Leadership is all hype. We've had three great leaders in this century—Hitler, Stalin, and Mao."
>
> Peter F. Drucker

warning of the dangers of an approach to planning founded on the denial of freedom. It attracted the interest of critics, who argued that it mixed economics with social sciences; it was, in fact, the first book to argue that any organization is both an economic and social organ. As such, it laid the foundations for Drucker's interest in management in general and, as it turned out, General Motors in particular.

The Concept of the Corporation—1946

When General Motors invited Drucker to write about the company, it was expected that the invitation would result in a glowing description of GM's success. What in fact emerged was something different, something that recognized success but also looked to the future.

General Motors provided Drucker with the opportunity to test in practice the theory he had propounded in *The Future of Industrial Man*, that is, that an organization was essentially a social system as well as an economic one. *The Concept of the Corporation* questioned whether what had worked in the past—a foolproof system of objective policies and procedures throughout every layer of the organization—would continue to work in a future of global competition, changing social values, and automation, and with the drive for quality and the growth of the knowledge worker.

The assembly line, he argued, actually created inefficiency because activity took place at the pace of the slowest. Demotivation was rife because no one saw the end result, and initiative was stifled by the minutiae of checks, rules, and controls. The layers of bureaucracy slowed down decision making, created adversarial labor relations, and did nothing to create a "self-governing plant community" (the phrase Drucker used for an empowered workforce). Drucker reported the benefits of decentralized operations—an issue that critics were quick to praise and organizations quick to mimic—but suggested that the GM hierarchy of commands and controls would be slow to respond in a rapidly changing future.

The fundamental difference between Drucker and GM was that GM saw the workforce as a cost in the quest for profits, whereas Drucker saw people as a resource who would be better able to satisfy customers if they had more involvement in their jobs and gained some satisfaction from doing them. *The Concept of the Corporation*, consequently, was decades ahead of its time in terms of its espousal of empowerment and self-management. Although Alfred

Sloan—the chief executive and powerhouse behind General Motors' success—had no time for Drucker's book, Drucker was, in the early 1950s, to advise Sloan on establishing a School of Administration at MIT. His criticism of Sloan was implicit rather than explicit, saying he had vision rather than perspective, and implying that leadership had been sacrificed to the rulebook. Sloan was measured in his reply—after all, at the time, General Motors was the largest and arguably one of the most successful companies in the world. His response came in 1963 with the publication of *My Years with General Motors*, which sets out the scientific credo of GM's philosophy, yet talks little of people, transparently because they had little importance relative to the systems they were following.

Another effect of *The Concept of the Corporation* was the establishment of management as a discipline, bringing to the fore the notions of:

- the social and environmental responsibility of the organization;
- the relationship between the individual and the organization;
- the role of top management and the decision-making process;
- the need for continual training and retraining of managers with the focus on their own responsibility for self-development;
- the nature of labor relations;
- the imperatives of community and customer relations.

It is interesting that Japanese industry listened to these messages and U.S. industry did not.

The Practice of Management—1954

The Practice of Management was Drucker's second book on management, and it established him as a leader in his field. It set trends in management for decades, and reputations were built by adopting and expanding on the ideas that he set out. It is still regarded by many as the definitive management text.

Drucker states that there is only one valid purpose for the existence of a business, that is, to create a customer. It is not, he argues, the internal structure, controls, organization, and procedures that keep a business afloat; rather, it is the customer—who pays, and decides what is important—who fills this role. He sets out eight areas in which objectives should be set and performance should be measured:

- market standing
- innovation
- productivity

- physical and financial resources
- profitability
- managers' performance and development
- workers' performance and attitude
- public responsibility

The Practice of Management is probably best remembered for setting out the principles of Management by Objectives and Self Control (Drucker's term, although he didn't coin it)—a management process that has become the accepted basis for management theory and practice.

The book also identified the seven tasks of the manager of tomorrow. He or she must:

- manage by objectives;
- take risks and allow risk-taking decisions to take place at lower levels in the organization;
- be able to make strategic decisions;
- be able to build an integrated team whose members are capable of managing and measuring their own performance and results in relation to overall objectives;
- be able to communicate information quickly and clearly, and motivate employees so as to gain commitment and participation;
- be able to see the business as a whole and to integrate his or her function within it;
- be able to relate the product and industry to the total environment, to find out what is important and what needs to be taken into account. This perspective must embrace developments outside the company's particular market or country, and the manager must begin to see economic, political, and social developments on a worldwide scale.

Management: Tasks, Responsibilities, Practices—1974

Much of the work in *The Practice of Management* is updated, expanded, and revised in *Management: Tasks, Responsibilities, Practices*, which establishes where management has come from, where it is now, and where it needs to go. It draws upon a wide variety of international examples and sets out principles for managers and management. Effectively, it is a complete management handbook.

Moving on from his earlier work, Drucker defines the manager's work in terms of five basic operations. He or she:

- sets objectives;
- organizes;
- motivates and communicates;
- measures;
- develops people, including him/herself.

Top management's tasks are to:

- define the business mission;
- set standards;

"Whenever anything is being accomplished, it is being done, I have learned, by a monomaniac with a mission."

Peter F. Drucker

- build and maintain the human organization;
- develop and maintain external relationships;
- perform social and civic functions;
- know how to get on with the task in hand if and when necessary.

Management: Tasks, Responsibilities, Practices is regarded by many as Drucker's finest book.

The Age of Discontinuity—1969 (reissued 1992)

It is in *The Age of Discontinuity* that Drucker describes the very changes that he had signaled to General Motors 23 years earlier. He writes in the preface: "This book does not project trends; it examines discontinuities. It does not forecast tomorrow; it looks at today. It does not ask: 'What will tomorrow look like?' It asks instead: 'What do we have to tackle today to make tomorrow?'"

The book deals with the forces that change society as new technology impacts old industries, changing social values impact consumer behavior, and markets become international. Drucker advocates privatization, pointing out the ineffectiveness of government in leading and stimulating change; he examines the role of organizations in society in an age of discontinuity and looks at different ways of managing the knowledge worker.

Managing in Turbulent Times—1980

The issues raised in *The Age of Discontinuity* were revisited a decade later in *Managing in Turbulent Times*. Change, uncertainty, and turbulence are the underpinning themes as Drucker highlights the new realities of changing population demographics, global markets, and a "bisexual" workforce.

Drucker issues challenges to junior, middle, and senior management.
- In the knowledge organization, the "supervisor" has to become an "assistant," a "resource," and a "teacher."
- The very term "middle management" is becoming meaningless as some will have to learn how to work with people over whom they have no direct control, to work transnationally, and to create, maintain, and run systems—none of which are traditionally middle management tasks.
- It is top management that faces the challenge of setting directions for the enterprise, of managing the fundamentals. It is top management that will have to restructure itself to meet the challenges of the "sea-change," the changes in population structure and population dynamics.
- It is top management that will have to con-

cern itself with the turbulences of the environment, the emergence of the world economy, the emergence of the employee society, and the need for the enterprises in its care to take the lead in respect to political process, political concepts, and social policies.

Drucker Said It First

Part of Drucker's success and longevity as a management expert was that he had a remarkable knack of spotting trends that were later picked up and made fashionable by others. Invariably, research will trace the origin back to something Drucker wrote ten years—sometimes 20 years—ago. It is interesting that Drucker noted that one of the key aspects of leadership is timing; he, in fact, upbraided himself for being ten years ahead with his forecasts.

The following section is adapted from work by Clutterbuck and Crainer, who summarized the work of James O'Toole, Professor of Management at the University of Southern California. O'Toole said that Drucker was the first to:
- define the role of top managers as the keepers of corporate culture;
- advocate mentoring, career planning, and executive development as top management tasks;
- say that success hinges on the vision expressed by the C.E.O.;
- show that structure follows strategy;
- suggest a reduction of management layers between the top and the bottom;
- argue that success comes from sticking to the basics;
- state that the primary purpose of the organization is to create a customer;
- say that success boils down to sensitivity to the consumer and the marketing of innovative products;
- suggest that quality is a measure of productivity;
- describe the coming knowledge worker;
- state that new approaches to management would be needed in the postindustrial age.

It must be said, however, that Drucker also prophesied the continuing growth of the middle manager as he or she evolved into the knowledge worker of postindustrial society. It has not happened quite like that and the massive delayerings of the early 1990s suggest that Drucker may well have got it wrong . . . so far.

"Druckerisms"

On business:

A business is not defined by the company's name, statutes, or articles of incorporation. It is defined by the want the

customer satisfies when he buys a product or service. (*Management: Tasks, Responsibilities, Practices*)

On leadership:

There is no substitute for leadership. But management cannot create leaders. It can only create the conditions under which potential leadership qualities become effective; or it can stifle potential leadership. (*The Practice of Management*)

On management:

The function which distinguishes the manager above all others is his educational one. The one contribution he is uniquely expected to make is to give others vision and ability to perform. It is vision and moral responsibility that, in the last analysis, define the manager. (*The Practice of Management*)

On decision making:

[In] these specifically managerial decisions, the important and difficult job is never to find the right answer, it is hard to find the right question. For there are few things as useless—if not as dangerous—as the right answer to the wrong question. (*The Practice of Management*)

On the knowledge worker:

Increasingly, the knowledge workers of tomorrow will have to know and accept the values, the goals, and the policies of the organization—to use current buzzwords, they must be willing—nay, eager—to buy into the company's mission. ("Drucker Speaks His Mind," *Management Review*)

[The knowledge worker] . . . may realize that he depends on the organization for access to income and opportunity, and that without the investment the organization has made—and a high investment at that—there would be no opportunity for him. But he also realizes, and rightly so, that the organization equally depends on him. (*The Age of Discontinuity*)

PETER DRUCKER IN PERSPECTIVE

Critical of the business school system in general, Drucker always set himself apart from mainstream management education. He said of himself: "I have always been a loner. I work best outside. That's where I'm most effective. I would be a very poor manager. Hopeless. And a company job would bore me to death. I enjoy being an outsider."

An outsider maybe, but commentators pointed consistently to his gentlemanly old-world charm, his humility, and the fact that he never criticized negatively, always politely and constructively.

Drucker's earlier works no longer strike the reader with the same force that they did in the 1950s, 1960s, and 1970s. But this is entirely to his credit. His thinking was ab-

---

"Intellectual integrity . . . the ability to see the world as it is, not as you want it to be."

Peter F. Drucker

sorbed and adopted as the prevailing wisdom behind the philosophy and practice of modern management.

What does strike the modern reader, however, is the sheer force of his writing, his clear mastery of the subject matter, and the clarity of his expression. It is as well to remember that readable books on management were very few and far between when Drucker wrote *The Concept of the Corporation* and *The Practice of Management*. Texts for managers concentrated usually on technical and industrial engineering, and were too complex to have either a wide readership or the impact or influence that Drucker had.

"For many business leaders across the world . . . he remains the doyen of modern management theory, not so much because he can lay claim to being the founder of any particular concept such as business re-engineering, or total quality management, rather because he has demonstrated a rare ability to apply common sense understanding to the analysis of management challenges and their solutions." ("Interview with Peter Drucker," the *Financial Times*)

One of Drucker's achievements lay in the fact that he, a devotee of the human relations school, recognized the value of Taylor's scientific, work-study approach, and succeeded in striking a balance between the two approaches. Management by Objectives, when performed properly, is an effective marriage of both schools, which attaches significance to culture and to the fact that organizations are held together not just by a dictated vision but by a shared vision of the future.

So, although Drucker awarded the accolade of "guru's guru" to F. W. Taylor, the world of management will always attribute it to Drucker himself. His ability to see management with a long historical perspective and in a broad social and political context is very rare in management writers. With his capacity for demystifying the apparent complexities of management for millions worldwide, he stood, as he said of himself, quite alone.

FOR MORE INFORMATION

Books:
Drucker, Peter F. *The Future of Industrial Man: A Conservative Approach*. London: Heinemann, 1943.
Drucker, Peter F. *The Practice of Management*. London: Heinemann, 1955.
Drucker, Peter F. *Managing for Results: Economic Tasks and Risk-taking Decisions*. London: Heinemann, 1964.
Drucker, Peter F. *The Concept of the Corporation*. New York: New American Library, 1964.
Drucker, Peter F. *The Effective Executive*. London: Heinemann, 1967.
Drucker, Peter F. *The End of Economic Man*. New York: Harper & Row, 1969.
Drucker, Peter F. *Technology, Management, and Society*. New York: Harper & Row, 1970.
Drucker, Peter F. *Management: Tasks, Responsibilities, Practices*. New York: Harper & Row, 1973.

Drucker, Peter F. *Managing in Turbulent Times*. New York: Harper & Row, 1980.
Drucker, Peter F. *The Changing World of the Executive*. New York: Times Books, 1982.
Drucker, Peter F. *Innovation and Entrepreneurship: Practice and Principles*. New York: Harper & Row, 1985.
Drucker, Peter F. *The Frontiers of Management: Where Tomorrow's Decisions Are Being Made Today*. New York: Truman Talley Books/Dutten, 1986.
Drucker, Peter F. *Managing the Non-Profit Organization: Practices and Principles*. New York: HarperCollins Publishers, 1990.
Drucker, Peter F. *Managing for the Future: The 1990s and Beyond*. New York: Truman Talley Books/Dutten, 1992.
Drucker, Peter F. *Managing in a Time of Great Change*. New York: Truman Talley Books/Dutten, 1995.
Drucker, Peter F. *Management Challenges for the 21st Century*. New York: HarperCollins Publishers, 2001.

Journal Articles:
Donkin, Richard. "Interview with Peter Drucker." *Financial Times*, 14 June 1996, p.13.
Johnson, Mike. "Drucker Speaks His Mind." *Management Review*, October 1995, pp. 10–14.

See also:
Alfred P. Sloan, Jr. (pp. 1356–1357)
Charles Handy (pp. 1216–1217)
Henry Mintzberg (pp. 1240–1241)

"No other area offers richer opportunities for successful innovation than the unexpected success."

Peter F. Drucker

Henri Fayol

Planning, Organization, Command, Coordination, Control

1202

BUSINESS THINKERS

Henri Fayol remained comparatively unknown outside his native France for almost a quarter of a century after his death. However, in the 1950s, *General and Industrial Management* was published, and he posthumously gained widespread recognition for his work on administrative management. Today Fayol is often described as the founding father of the administration school.

1841	Born.
1872	Appointed director of a group of mines.
1918	Retires.
1925	Dies.
1950s	*General and Industrial Management* published; Fayol's reputation as "the founding father of the administration school" established.

LIFE AND CAREER

Fayol spent his entire career working for one company, the French mining and metallurgical combine Comentry-Fourchamboult-Decazeville. He began as a mining engineer, was appointed director of a group of mines in 1872, and became managing director in 1888—a post which he held until his retirement in 1918. He retained the honorary title until his death.

When Fayol began his career, the financial health of the mining combine was poor. By the time he retired, however, there had been a complete turnaround and the company was prospering. Fayol's success is often attributed to his development and championing of the "functional principle." This involved:

- preparing yearly and 10-yearly plans, and acting on them;
- preparing organization charts to demonstrate and encourage order;
- recruiting and training carefully to ensure each employee was in the right place;
- adhering to the principle of the chain of command;
- arranging regular meetings with heads of departments and divisions to ensure coordination.

KEY THINKING

Administration Industrielle et Générale—Prévoyance, Organisation, Commandement, Contrôle (*General and Industrial Management—Planning, Organization, Command and Control*)

In his writing, Fayol attempted to construct a theory of management that could be used as a basis for formal management education and training. First, he divided all organizational activities into six functions:

- technical: engineering, production, manufacture, adaptation;
- commercial: buying, selling, exchange;
- financial: the search for optimum use of capital;
- security: protecting assets and personnel;
- accounting: stocktaking, balance sheets, costs, statistics;
- managerial: planning, organizing, commanding, coordinating, controlling.

Although well understood in their own right, none of the first five functions takes account of drawing up a broad plan of where the business is going and how it will operate; organizing people; coordinating all of the business efforts and activities, and monitoring to check that what is planned is actually performed. Fayol's sixth function, therefore, acts as an umbrella to the previous five.

Fayol argued that to manage is to:

1. Plan. A good plan of action should be flexible, continuous, relevant, and accurate. Its function is to unify the organization by focusing on the nature, priorities, and condition of the business; the longer-term predictions for the industry and economy; the intuitions of key thinkers; and strategic sector analyses from specialist staff.

For effective planning, managers should be skilled in the art of handling people, and possess considerable energy and a measure of moral courage. It is also important that they have some continuity of tenure; be competent in the specialized requirements of the business; have general business experience; and be able to generate creative ideas.

2. Organize. Organizing is as much about lines of responsibility and authority as it is about communication flow and the use of resources. Fayol lays down the following organizational duties for managers.

- Ensure the plan is judiciously prepared and strictly conducted.
- See that human and material structures are consistent with objectives, resources, and general operating policies.
- Establish a single guiding authority and lines of communication throughout the organization.
- Harmonize activities and coordinate efforts.
- Formulate clear, distinct and precise decisions.
- Arrange for efficient personnel selection.
- Define duties clearly.
- Encourage a liking for initiative and responsibility.
- Offer fair compensation for services rendered.
- Make use of sanctions in cases of fault and error.
- Maintain discipline.
- Ensure that individual interests are subordinated to the general interest.
- Pay special attention to the authority of command.
- Supervise both material and human order.
- Have everything under control.
- Fight against excess regulation, red tape, and paperwork.

3. Coordinate. Coordination involves determining the timing and sequencing of activities so that they mesh properly; allocating the appropriate resources, time, and priority; and adapting means to ends.

4. Command. Managers who are in charge should:

- gain a thorough knowledge of their personnel;
- eliminate the incompetent (this is not as final as it sounds! Fayol takes pains to point out that any decision to part with employees should be the result of careful thought; that the employees should have

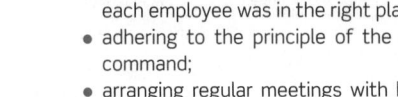

had fairly assigned work for which they were trained; that they should have been appraised fairly and objectively and provided with honest feedback; that they should have been given every opportunity for additional training, offered guidance and—where possible—reassigned to alternative work. Fayol also mentions procedures involving written warnings and protection against bias and "inequities");

- be well versed in the agreements between the business and its employees;
- set a good example;
- conduct periodic audits of the organization;
- bring together senior assistants to ensure unity of direction and focus of efforts;
- not become engrossed in detail;
- aim at making energy, initiative, loyalty, and unity prevail among employees.

5. Control. Controlling means checking that:

- everything occurs according to the plan adopted, the principles established, and the instructions issued;
- appropriate corrective action is taken;
- weaknesses, errors, and deviations from the plan have not slipped in;
- the plan is kept up to date (it is not cast in stone but adapts to changing developments).

Fayol's Principles of Management

Fayol's five-point approach advises managers on their tasks, duties and activities. From his own experience, he established a number of general principles of management, which lend definition to this approach.

- division of work: specialization allows the individual to build up expertise and therefore be more productive
- authority: the right to issue commands, along with the appropriate responsibility
- discipline: two-sided—employees obey orders only if managers play their part by providing good leadership
- unity of command: one man, one boss—with no other conflicting lines of command
- unity of direction: staff involved in the same activities should have the same objectives
- subordination of individual interest to the general interest: the good of the organization must come first over any group, just as the interests of any agreed team should come first over the individual

- remuneration: should be fair and equitable, encouraging productivity by rewarding well-directed effort; it should not be subject to abuse
- centralization: there is no formula to advocate centralization or decentralization; much depends on the optimum operating conditions of the business
- scalar chain: Fayol recognized that although hierarchies are essential, they do not always make for the swiftest communication; lateral communication therefore is also fundamental
- order: avoidance of duplication and waste through good organization
- equity: a "combination of kindliness and justice" in dealing with employees
- stability of tenure: the more successful the business, the more stable the management
- initiative: encouraging people to use their initiative is a source of strength for the organization
- esprit de corps: management must foster and develop the morale of employees and encourage each person to use his or her abilities

HENRI FAYOL IN PERSPECTIVE

It is hard to overestimate the influence Fayol has brought to bear on management thinking and management thinkers. Labeled "the founding father of the administration school," he was the first author to look at the organization from the "top down"; to identify management as a process; to break that process down into logical subdivisions; and to lay out a series of principles to make best use of people—thereby establishing a syllabus for management education.

The fact that Fayol's influence has endured is expressed no better than in the influential classic management formula, POSDCORB, a notion directly derived from his writings. It directs that managers should Plan, Organize, Staff, Direct, Coordinate, Report, and Budget.

Looking more closely at the detail of Fayol's five management activities, it is obvious that the conflicts and concerns, responsibilities and duties, styles, and problems that he identified a century ago are still just as relevant today. How do we "ensure that individual interests are subordinated to (har-

monized with) the general interest?" How do we "encourage a liking for initiative and responsibility?" And if the "fight against an excess of regulation, red tape, and paperwork" was problematic enough for Fayol to regard as a management duty in his day, he would surely be disappointed at how little progress has been made.

Fayol's last two management activities, command and control, have been taken to describe the hierarchical structure and management style that large organizations adopted from the 1950s through to the 1980s. But again, if we look closely at what Fayol actually says—especially about command—it is not too distant from a description of an empowering, rather than a "commanding," manager today.

Fayol's views have been criticized for weakness of analysis and assessment; for the overlap in his principles, elements, and duties; for confusing structure with process; and for an overreliance on top-down bureaucracy. However, his principles of management do not differ greatly from the characteristics of formal organizations as set out by Max Weber. Fayol's influence as the first to describe management as a top-down process based on planning and the organization of people will ensure his prominence among students and practicing managers alike.

1203

FOR MORE INFORMATION

Books:

Brech, Edward. *The Principles and Practice of Management*. 3rd ed. London: Longman, 1975.

Crainer, Stuart. *Financial Times Handbook of Management*. 2nd ed. Upper Saddle River, NJ: Financial Times Prentice Hall, 2001

Fayol, Henri, revised by Irwin Gray. *General and Industrial Management*. New York: IEEE Press, 1984.

Pugh, Derek S., and David J Hickson. *Great Writers on Organizations*. 4th ed. Thousand Oaks, CA: Sage, 1989.

See also:

Frederick Winslow Taylor
(pp. 1270–1271)

"To manage is to forecast and plan, to organize, to command, to coordinate, and to control."

Henri Fayol

Mary Parker Follett
Prophet of Management

Mary Parker Follett was one of the first people to apply psychological insight and social science findings to the study of industrial organization. She viewed business as a pioneering field within which solutions to human relations problems were being tested.

After World War II her ideas were largely neglected, except in Japan. Yet her work foreshadowed current Western approaches emphasizing involvement and cross-functional communications.

1868	Born.
1888	Attends Society for Collegiate Instruction of Women, Harvard.
1896	Publication of *The House of Representatives*.
1890	Spends a year at Newnham College, Cambridge University.
1918	Begins writing *The New State*.
1933	Gives inaugural series of lectures for Department of Business Administration (now Department of Industrial Relations) at the London School of Economics.
1933	Dies.

LIFE AND CAREER

Born in Massachusetts to a well-off Boston family, Follett was a brilliant scholar who graduated from high school at the age of 12. She was educated at the Thayer Academy, Boston, and Radcliffe College, Massachusetts. At 20 she attended an annexe of Harvard University called the Society for Collegiate Instruction of Women. In 1890, as a student of 22, she spent a year at Newnham College in Cambridge, England, and went on to Paris as a postgraduate student. Pauline Graham describes Follett as a polymath, and records that she studied law, economics, government, and philosophy at Harvard, and history and political science at Newnham. While at Cambridge, Follett gave a paper that she later developed into her first book, *The House of Representatives*. This was taken seriously enough to be reviewed by Theodore Roosevelt in the *American Historical Review* of October 1896.

Follett's family life was difficult. Her father, to whom she was close, died when she was in her early teens. Her mother was an invalid with whom Follett did not get along very well. From an early age Follett ran the household and later she also ran the family housing business.

Eventually, Follett broke all family ties and went to share a home with her friend, Isobella Briggs. Over the next 30 years, Isobella provided a stable domestic background, while her social connections were helpful to Follett's work. When Isobella died in 1926, Follett lost her home life as well as her closest friend. Later that year she met Dame Katherine Furse, an Englishwoman who was strongly involved with the Girl Guide scouting movement. Follett later moved to England to share a house in Chelsea with Furse.

Follett the Social Worker

Follett was expected to become an academic, but instead she went into voluntary social work in Boston, where her energy and practicality (as well as her financial support on occasions) achieved much in terms of community-building initiatives. For over 30 years, she was immersed in this work, and proved to be an innovative, hands-on manager whose practical achievements included the original use of schools as centers for community education and recreation after the normal school day. This was Follett's own idea, and the resulting community centers became models for other cities throughout the United States.

Follett established vocational placement centers in Boston schools, and represented the public on the Massachusetts Minimum Wage Board. From 1924 she began to give regular papers relating to industrial organization, especially at conferences of the Bureau of Personnel Administration in New York. She became, in effect, an early management consultant, as businesspeople began to seek her advice about their organizational and human relations problems.

In 1926 and 1928, Follett gave papers for the Rowntree Lecture Conference and to the National Institute of Industrial Psychology. In 1933, she gave an inaugural series of lectures for the newly founded Department of Business Administration (now the Department of Industrial Relations) at the London School of Economics (LSE). Later in 1933, Follett returned to the United States, where she died on December 18 of that year at the age of 65.

KEY THINKING

The New State was written during 1918, and argues for group-based democracy as a process of government. Through this book, Follett became widely recognized as a political philosopher. It was based on her social work experience rather than on business organizations, but the ideas it contains were later applied in the business context.

The New State presented an often visionary interpretation of what Follett viewed as the progress of social evolution, and the tone is occasionally infused with poetical religious feeling. The text argues that democracy "by numbers" should give way to a more valid process of group-based democracy. This form of democracy is described as a dynamic process through which individual conflicts and differences become integrated in the search for overall group agreement. Through it, people will grow and learn as they adapt to one another's views, while seeking a common, long-term good.

The group process works through the relating of individuals' different ideas to each other and to the common interests of the group as a whole. Appropriate action would, Follett held, become self-evident during the consultation process. This would eventually reveal a "law of the situation," representing an objective that all could see would be the best course for the group as a whole to pursue. Conflict and disagreement were viewed as positive forces, and Follett saw social evolution as progressing through the ever-continuous integration of diverse viewpoints and opinions in pursuit of the common good.

The New State envisions the basic group democratic process following right through

to the international level, feeding up from neighborhoods via municipal and state government into the League of Nations. Sometimes, Follett refers to an almost autonomous group spirit, which develops from the community between people.

The Creative Experience was also written during 1918, and again focused on democratic governance, using examples from business to illustrate ideas. *Dynamic Management—The Collected Papers of Mary Parker Follett* and *Freedom and Coordination* were both published posthumously and edited by L. Urwick. *Freedom and Coordination* collects together six papers given by Follett at the LSE in 1933, and these represent the most developed and concise distillation of her thoughts on business organization.

Follett's business writings extended her social ideas into the industrial sphere. Industrial managers, she saw, confronted the same difficulties as public administrators as regards control, power, participation, and conflict. Her later writings focused on management from a human perspective, using the new approach of psychology to deal with problems between individuals and within groups. She encouraged businesspeople to look at how groups formed and how employee commitment and motivation could be encouraged. The participation of everyone involved in decisions affecting their activities is seen as fundamental, in that Follett viewed group power and management through cooperation as the obvious route to achievements that would benefit all.

Views on Power, Leadership, Authority, and Control

Follett envisioned management responsibility as being diffused throughout a business rather than wholly concentrated at the hierarchical apex. Degrees of authority and responsibility are seen as spread all along the line. For example, a truck driver can act with more authority than the business owner in terms of knowing more about the best order in which to make his or her deliveries. Leadership skills are required of many people rather than just one person, and final authority, while it does exist, should not be overemphasized. The chief executive's role lies in coordinating the scattered authorities and varied responsibilities that make up the organization into group action and ideas, and also in foreseeing and meeting the next situation.

Follett's concept of leadership as the ability to develop and integrate group ideas, using "power with" rather than "power over" people, is very modern. She understood that the crude exercise of authority based on subordination is hurtful to people, and cannot be the basis of effective, motivational management control. Partnership and cooperation, she sought to persuade people, were of far more ultimate benefit to everyone than hierarchical control and competition.

Follett viewed the group process as a form of collective control, with the experience of all who perform a functional part in an activity feeding into decision making. Control is thus realized through the coordination of all functions rather than imposed from the outside.

Follett's Four Fundamental Principles of Organization

Follett identified four principles of coordination that she considered basic to effective management.

- Coordination consists in the "reciprocal relating" of all the factors in a situation.
- Coordination should be by direct contact, operating by means of direct communication between all responsible people involved, whatever their hierarchical or departmental positions.
- Coordination should begin in the early stages. It should involve all the people directly concerned, right from the initial stages of designing a project or forming a policy.
- Coordination should be a continuing process, based on the recognition that there is no such thing as unity, but only the continuous process of unifying.

MARY PARKER FOLLETT IN PERSPECTIVE
The Context of Evolutionary Progress

Follett's thinking was ahead of her time, yet was founded on a conviction of social, evolutionary progress, which the course of subsequent history has shown to be flawed. She lived through momentous times, when social and technological change seemed to make a new order inevitable. The destruction caused by World War I also seemed to dictate the clear need for a determined effort to create a social order that would not break down so disastrously. Simultaneously, the war created pressures in both England and the United States for labor participation in management, and led to a growth in internationalist ideas and to the birth of the League of Nations. Like other writers of the time, Follett made leaps of the imagination that grew out of the factual changes that were actually taking place. Her view was rational and progressive, and she could not know the degree to which some things would remain constant, undermining the apparently inevitable dynamic of social "progress."

Looking back on the whole of the 20th-century, of which Follett saw only the beginning, we have all too full a knowledge of World War II and countless other conflicts, of the discrediting of Russian Communism, and of worsening ethnic divisions and continuing human barbarities. The progressive, internationalist vision seems to be, from our contemporary perspective, a fast-receding dream.

Yet, while Follett's optimistic expectations of radical social change were largely mistaken, she drew from it the imaginative vision to transform at least some of her convictions into ideas about ways of living and working that have contributed much to both social and management practice. In fact, it is almost disheartening to read Follett and realize that she clearly and strongly stated, so many years ago, ideas that are being proffered as "new" today and that are still rarely practiced in any sustained way.

FOR MORE INFORMATION

Books:
Graham, Pauline, ed. *Mary Parker Follett: Prophet of Management—A Celebration of Writings from the 1920s.* Boston, MA: Harvard Business School Press, 1995
Parker Follett, Mary. *The Speaker of the House of Representatives.* New York: Longmans, Green & Co., 1896.
Parker Follett, Mary. *The New State: Group Organization—the Solution for Popular Government.* New York: Longmans, Green & Co., 1920.
Parker Follett, Mary. *Creative Experience.* New York: Longmans, Green & Co., 1924.

See also:
Anita Roddick (pp. 1350–1351)

1205

BUSINESS THINKERS

"The most successful leader of all is one who sees another picture not yet actualized."

Mary Parker Follett

Henry Laurence Gantt
The Gantt Chart

Henry Laurence Gantt's legacy to management is the Gantt chart. Accepted as a commonplace project management tool today, it was an innovation of worldwide importance in the 1920s. But the chart was not Gantt's only legacy; he was also a forerunner of the human relations school of management and an early spokesperson for the social responsibility of business.

1861	Born.
1884	Qualifies as mechanical engineer.
1887–1893	Employment at Midvale Steel Company, Philadelphia.
1901	Introduction of task and bonus system.
1917	Contributes to war effort for Frankford Arsenal and for the Emergency Fleet Corporation. Creates Gantt chart.
1919	Dies.

LIFE AND CAREER

Henry Gantt was born into a family of prosperous farmers in Maryland in 1861. His early years, however, were marked by some deprivation as the Civil War brought about changes to the family fortunes. He graduated from Johns Hopkins University and was a teacher before becoming a draftsman in 1884 and earning a degree as a mechanical engineer. From 1887 to 1893 he worked at the Midvale Steel Company in Philadelphia, where he became Assistant to the Chief Engineer (F. W. Taylor) and then Superintendent of the Casting Department.

Gantt and Taylor worked well in their early years together and Gantt followed Taylor to Simonds Rolling Company and on to Bethlehem Steel. From 1900 Gantt became well known in his own right as a successful consultant as he developed interests in broader, even conflicting, aspects of management.

In 1917 Gantt accepted a government commission to contribute to the war effort in the Frankford Arsenal and for the Emergency Fleet Corporation. He died in 1919.

KEY THINKING

Gantt is often seen as a disciple of Taylor and a promoter of the scientific school of management. In his early career, the influence of Taylor—and Gantt's aptitude for problem-solving—resulted in attempts to address the technical problems of scientific management. Like Taylor, Gantt believed that only the application of scientific analysis to every aspect of work could produce industrial efficiency, and that improvements in management came from eliminating chance and accidents.

Gantt made four individual and notable contributions.

The Task and Bonus System

Gantt's task and bonus wage system was introduced in 1901 as a variation on Taylor's differential piece-rate system. Under Gantt's system, employees received a bonus in addition to their regular daily pay if they accomplished the task for the day; they still received the daily pay even if the task was not completed. Taylor's piece-rate system, by contrast, penalized employees for substandard performance. As a result of introducing Gantt's system, which enabled workers to earn a living while learning to increase their efficiency, production often more than doubled. This convinced Gantt that concern for the worker and employee morale was one of the most important factors in management and led him eventually to part company with Taylor on the fundamentals of scientific management.

The Perspective of the Worker

Gantt realized that his system offered little incentive to do more than just meet the standard. He subsequently modified it to pay according to time allowed, plus a percentage of that time if the task were completed within the specified time or less. Hence a worker could receive three hours' pay for doing a two-hour job in two hours or under. But here Gantt brought in an innovation, by paying the foreman a bonus if all the workers met the required standard. This constituted one of the earliest recorded attempts to reward the foreman for teaching workers to improve the way they worked. In *Work, Wages, and Profits* Gantt wrote:

"Whatever we do must be in accord with human nature. We cannot drive people; we must direct their development . . . the general policy of the past has been to drive; but the era of force must give way to that of knowledge, and the policy of the future will be to teach and lead, to the advantage of all concerned."

Gantt was interested in an aspect of industrial education which he called the "habits of industry"—habits of industriousness and cooperation that entailed carrying out work to the best of one's ability, and taking pride in the quality as well as the quantity of work performed.

From his experience as a teacher, Gantt hoped that his bonus system would help to convert the foreman from an overseer and driver of workers to a helper and teacher of subordinates.

The Chart

Gantt's bar chart started as a humble but effective mechanism for recording the progress of workers toward the task standard. A daily record was kept for each worker—in black, if he met the standard, in red, if he didn't. This expanded into further charts on quantity of work per machine, quantity of work per worker, cost control, and other subjects.

It was while grappling with the problem of tracking all the various tasks and activities of government departments on the war effort in 1917, that Gantt realized he should be scheduling on the basis of time and not of quantities. His solution was a bar chart that showed how work was scheduled over time through to its completion. This enabled management to see, in graphic form, how well work was progressing and indicated when and where action would be necessary to keep on time.

Gantt charts have been applied to all kinds of projects to illustrate how schedul-

ing may be best achieved. To illustrate the principle we might take the miniproject of redecorating an office. The operation would be broken down into the following steps:

- establishing the terms of reference and standards of quality, the cost, and the time;
- informing all appropriate personnel and customers;
- arranging alternative accommodations;
- preparing the office;
- redecorating.

Each step would be allocated a specific amount of time that would be represented on the chart. The Gantt chart provided a graphic means of planning and controlling work and led to its modern variation—PERT (Program Evaluation and Review Technique).

The Social Responsibility of Business

After the death of Taylor in 1917, Gantt seemed to distance himself further from the core principles of scientific management and extended his management interests to the function of leadership and the role of the company itself. As his thinking developed, he believed increasingly that management had obligations to the community at large, and that the profitable organization had a duty toward the welfare of society.

In *Organizing for Work*, he argued that there was a conflict between profits and service, and that the businessman who says that profits are more important than the service he renders "has forgotten that his business system had a foundation in service, and as far as the community is concerned has no reason for existence except the service it can render." These concerns led him to assert that "the business system

must accept its social responsibility and devote itself primarily to service, or the community will ultimately make the attempt to take it over in order to operate it in its own interest."

Gantt was hugely influenced by the events in Russia in 1917 and, in fear that big business was sacrificing service to profit, he began to attack the profit system itself, calling for public service corporations to ensure service to the community.

HENRY LAURENCE GANTT IN PERSPECTIVE

Gantt was a prolific writer and speaker. He addressed the American Society of Mechanical Engineers on a number of occasions. One of his papers—"Training Workmen in Habits of Industry and Cooperation" (1908)—has been noted by several commentators as giving a unique insight into the human relations dimension of management at a time when scientific management was at its peak.

His approach to the foreman as teacher marks him as an early contributor to human behavioral thought in a line that stretches back to Owen and forward with Mayo to the present day. His approach to the duty of the company towards society also singles him out as one of the earliest spokesmen on the social responsibility of business. But it is as the inventor of the Gantt chart that he will be remembered.

It has been suggested that his thinking became somewhat vague shortly before his death, as he began to situate the work of the company in a broader national and political context. It seems that there was a struggle in his later years between service and appropriate rewards, on the one hand and socialist control policies, on the other.

Gantt never profited from his enduring innovation, and his books are illustrated with examples of charts showing "work in progress" rather than the lateral project bar chart with which we are more familiar today. He did receive the Distinguished Service Medal from the government, but it was a member of Gantt's consulting firm, Wallace Clark, who popularized the idea of the Gantt chart in a book that was translated into eight languages.

FOR MORE INFORMATION

Books:
Duncan, W. Jack. *Great Ideas in Management.* San Francisco, CA: Jossey-Bass, 1989.
Gantt, Henry. *Work, Wages, and Profits.* New York: Engineering Magazine Co, 1910.
Gantt, Henry. *Industrial Leadership.* New Haven, CT: Yale University Press, 1916.
Gantt, Henry. *Organizing for Work.* New York: Harcourt, Brace and Howe, 1919.
George, Claude S. *The History of Management Thought.* 2nd ed. Englewood Cliffs, NJ: Prentice Hall, 1972.
Urwick, Lyndall. *The Golden Book of Management.* London: Newman Neame, 1956.
Wren, Daniel A. *The Evolution of Management Thought.* New York: Wiley,1987.

See also:
Frederick Winslow Taylor (pp. 1270–1271)

1207

BUSINESS THINKERS

"I've often thought that after you get organized, you ought to throw away the organization chart."
David Packard

Ghoshal and Bartlett
Managing Across Borders

Pioneering research with collaborator Christopher Bartlett into what makes large global organizations tick, and an inquiring mind committed to management as the wealth creator, contributed to the emergence of Sumantra Ghoshal (left) as one of the most respected management thinkers of his generation.

A sought-after consultant, teacher, speaker, and prolific writer, his research played an important role in guiding companies toward the era of globalization.

LIFE AND CAREER

Born in India, Sumantra Ghoshal (1946–2004) studied physics at university before spending 12 years (1969–81) at the Indian Oil Corporation. He demonstrated his appetite for understanding what makes organizations work by obtaining two doctorates, one from MIT, champion of the rigorous scientific method, the other from more pragmatic Harvard, whose approach is based on case studies, observation, and practice.

After lecturing at MIT and INSEAD, Ghoshal became professor of business policy at INSEAD in 1992, and professor of strategic leadership at the London Business School in 1994. He first came to international prominence with the publication in 1989 of *Managing Across Borders*, coauthored with Christopher Bartlett.

LIFE AND CAREER

Christopher Bartlett is the Thomas D. Casserly, Jr. Professor Emeritus of Business Administration at Harvard Business School. Before joining the faculty of Harvard, he was a marketing manager with Alcoa in Australia, a management consultant in McKinsey and Company's London office, and general manager at Baxter Laboratories' subsidiary company in France.

His research interests have focused on the strategic and organizational challenges which managers face in running multinational corporations, and these interests have been reflected in his most successful books.

Managing Across Borders was cited by the *Financial Times* as one of the 50 most influential business books of the century. It remains a classic of the genre.

KEY THINKING
Managing Across Borders

Ghoshal and Bartlett's thinking begins with two fundamental questions:

- What does strategy mean?
- Why do the time-honored business models—exemplified by Alfred Sloan's General Motors—no longer work?

Their initial research involved asking over 250 managers in nine multinational companies how their companies were facing up to the complexities of international competition and the growing global marketplace. They identified a pervasive organizational inability to cope, survive, and succeed in the face of growing diversity and accelerating change.

They found three types of organizational model in operation:

- the multinational model, exemplified by Philips or Unilever—a decentralized federation of local companies held together by posting key people from the center;
- the global model, exemplified by Ford and Matsushita—benefiting from large-scale economies and new market opportunities;
- a more widespread international model—focusing on technology and the transfer of knowledge to less advanced environments.

They concluded that a fourth model was necessary—the transnational—which would combine all the elements of the other three and, in addition, exploit local know-how as the key weapon in identifying opportunities, rather than operating overseas sites as outposts of the center.

Efficiency versus Economic Progress

To understand why the old models no longer worked, Ghoshal examined Alfred Sloan's General Motors, the pioneer of the three Ss

(Strategy—Structure—Systems), emulated by other companies for decades.

The three Ss were designed to make the management of complex organizations systematic and predictable. The top people in the organization crafted the strategy, then designed the structure that enabled it to unfold and the systems that made it operational. The information systems they relied on dealt with facts and reduced the human element to a minimum. Employees on Ford's assembly lines, for example, were viewed as replaceable parts; ITT, under Harold Geneen, abolished the possibility of surprise by constantly establishing "unshakeable facts."

For years, this systematic approach worked. It started to break down only in the 1980s, when converging technologies, fluctuating markets, overnight competition, and technological innovation combined to make its control systems cumbersome, unresponsive, and ultimately a risk to the survival of the organization itself. An article by Ghoshal, Christopher A. Bartlett, and Peter Moran in the *Sloan Management Review*, Spring 1999 ("A New Manifesto for Management," pp. 9–20) pointed out that criticisms of these systems for stifling initiative, creativity, and diversity were valid: "They were designed for an organization man who has turned out to be an evolutionary dead end." (p. 11)

In the same article, the authors implicitly attacked Michael Porter's work. Porter had influenced strategic thinking for over a decade by arguing that organizations must beat the competition by gaining a stranglehold on value, that is, by either reducing competitors' value (perhaps through competitive incremental cost or quality improvements) or buying them out. Ghoshal wrote: "Porter's theory is static in that it focuses strategic thinking on getting the largest possible share of a fixed economic pie." (p. 12) For Ghoshal, companies exist not to appropriate value, but to create it—and they get themselves into a position to be able to create value by "changing the smell of the place."

Fontainebleau and Calcutta: The "Springtime Theory"

Ghoshal developed his "springtime theory" while teaching business policy at INSEAD in the forest of Fontainebleau, south of Paris. During a summer visit to his home city of

---

"Satisfactory under-performance is a far greater problem than a crisis." Christopher Bartlett

Calcutta, he found the humidity oppressive and draining, and likened this to the stultifying atmosphere in control- and system-oriented corporate climates. Later, walking in the woods at Fontainebleau, he realized that the fresh, energizing forest reminded him of the cultural atmosphere of more open and dynamic organizations. From this, he went on to propound his "springtime theory," arguing that managers and approaches to management strongly affect cultures and can create or change the organizational context, "the smell of the place." But how?

The Three Ps

Ghoshal considered that modern leading companies are built around the "three Ps": Purpose, Process, and People. In an interview in *Management Skills and Development*, he claimed that, as shapers of purpose, senior managers need "to create a shared ambition among their staff, instill organizational values, and provide personal meaning for the work their staff do." Creating that shared ambition is an active management process that challenges poor performance, establishes a common goal, demonstrates managers' commitment and self-discipline, and provides "meaning for everyone's efforts." (p. 40)

In the same interview, Ghoshal also stressed the need for organizations to:

- start thinking outside the "strategic planning" box and examining how they actually learn;
- complement vertical information flows with horizontal personal relationships;
- build a trust-based culture by spreading a message of genuine openness;
- share all the information that has traditionally been a source of power.

He said: "You cannot have faith in people unless you take action to improve and develop them. The success of businesses depends now more than ever on the talent of people working for them." (p. 39) In short, organizations need to forge a "new moral contract" with their people.

The New Moral Contract

In the past, the contract between organizations and employees promised relative security in return for conformity. In the 1980s and 1990s, however, this changed: job security was undermined by downsizing and reengineering, while managerial approaches such as Total Quality Management and Customer Focus demanded more involvement and initiative from employees. The new contract Ghoshal proposed is based on developing employability, and providing challenging jobs rather than func-

tional boxes. It should be viewed neither as altruism on the company's part nor as something imposed on employees. It is, rather, a new management philosophy that recognizes that personal development both improves employees' performance and makes them more employable in their future working lives, and that market performance stems from the initiative, creativity, and skills of all employees, and not just the wisdom of senior management.

Such a contract involves a great leap for both organizations and employees. Employers must create a working environment with opportunities for personal and professional growth, within a management environment in which it is understood that talented, growing people mean talented, growing organizations. Employees must make greater commitment to continuous learning and development, and accept that, in a climate of constant change and uncertainty, the will to develop is the only hedge against a changing job market.

Companies As Value Creators

Ghoshal felt strongly that organizations must stop focusing on squeezing out every last cost saving, waste reduction, or improvement in quality or efficiency. That may seem like the ultimate goal of TQM and continuous improvement, but organizations with that sole objective are only good at improving existing activities. Their emphasis is wholly on conservation, which, as Ghoshal pointed out, Jack Welch described as a "ticket to the boneyard" when he was running GE.

The main message of Ghoshal and Bartlett's more recent book, *The Individualized Corporation* (1998), was that the key to competitive advantage in a turbulent economy is a company's ability to innovate its way out of relentless market pressures. As companies shift emphasis from acquiring value to creating it, managers should shift their focus away from obedience, control, and conformity to initiative, relationship building, and continuous challenge of the status quo. Instead of being cogs in a system, they should become facilitators and people developers, drawing creativity from others.

In an interview published in the *Professional Manager*, Ghoshal pointed out that the modern world has brought about an enormous improvement in the quality of our lives and that this improvement—this value—has been created by business. Politicians create the context; they did not, in Ghoshal's view, create value: this came from companies and managers. From this perspective, management is the most important social profession today; the wealth of the

nation depends on it: "The quality of BT's management matters, perhaps matters more than a quarter per cent change in interest rates, because it creates value. If BT, ICI, or Marks and Spencer are poorly managed . . . the U.K. loses, because these institutions are the engines of the country's progress. The most important source of a nation's progress is the quality of its management." ("Professor of the Spring Strategy," *Professional Manager*, May 2000, pp. 20–23)

GHOSHAL AND BARTLETT IN PERSPECTIVE

During the time that Ghoshal came to prominence, his focus shifted from international strategy to the importance of putting people, creativity, and innovation at the top of the agenda and an emphasis on high-quality management as an important social and moral value-creating force. His death in 2004 meant that the management world lost an inspirational teacher, thinker, and collaborator. Christopher Bartlett has the last word: "Borders never meant much to Sumantra."

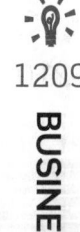

1209

BUSINESS THINKERS

FOR MORE INFORMATION

Books:

Bartlett, Christopher A., and Sumantra Ghoshal. *Managing Across Borders: The Transnational Solution.* 2nd ed. Boston, MA: Harvard Business School Press, 2002.

Bartlett, Christopher A., and Sumantra Ghoshal. *The Individualized Corporation: A Fundamentally New Approach to Management.* Collingdale, PA: DIANE Publishing Co., 1997.

Journal Articles:

Bartlett, Christopher A., and Sumantra Ghoshal. "Changing the Role of Top Management: Beyond Strategy to Purpose." *Harvard Business Review*, November/December, 1994, pp. 79–88.

Bartlett, Christopher A., and Sumantra Ghoshal. "Changing the Role of Top Management: Beyond Structure to Processes." *Harvard Business Review*, January/February, 1995, pp. 86–96.

Bartlett, Christopher A., and Sumantra Ghoshal. "Changing the Role of Top Management: Beyond Systems to People." *Harvard Business Review*, May/June, 1995, pp. 132–142.

See also:

Kenichi Ohmae (pp. 1244–1245)

"It is possible for a business venture to be an island of efficiency in a sea of sloth."

Indira Gandhi

Frank and Lillian Gilbreth

Motion Study Pioneers

Management practitioners today largely ignore the Gilbreths, possibly because the principles pioneered by them are now unfashionable. However, through Frank's concerns that the efficiency of employees should be balanced by economy of effort and minimization of stress, and Lillian's interest in the psychology of management, they laid the foundations for the modern concepts of job simplification, meaningful work standards, and incentive wage plans.

1868	Frank born.
1878	Lillian born.
1885	Frank develops theory of work simplification.
1895	Frank founds engineering consulting company, Gilbreth Inc.
1890s	Frank founds Society to Promote the Science of Management, in conjunction with F. W. Taylor.
1904	Frank and Lillian marry; go on to produce 12 children.
1912–1913	Lillian's book, *Psychology in the Workplace*, published in installments by the Society of Industrial Engineers.
1915	Lillian awarded a Ph.D. in applied management by Brown University.
1921	Lillian becomes first woman member of the Society of Industrial Engineers; later becomes first woman member of the American Society of Mechanical Engineers.
1924	Frank dies. Lillian presents a paper of his at the International Management Conference in Prague.
1925	Lillian continues the work of Gilbreth Inc., conducting seminars on motion study and accepting consulting jobs.
1972	Lillian dies, having been the first and, to date, only female recipient of the Gilbreth Medal, the Gantt Gold Medal, and the CIOS Gold Medal.
1995	Lillian included in the National Women's Hall of Fame in the United States.

LIFE AND CAREER

Frank B. Gilbreth (1868–1924) began his career as a bricklayer and, by the age of 27, had worked his way up through the profession to found his own engineering consulting company, Gilbreth Inc. He had a particular interest in the development of people to their fullest potential through training, work methods, and improving the working environment and tools, as well as through the creation of healthier working conditions. An adherent to the principles of scientific management, Frank was one of the first to find practical applications for it. Although he had disagreements with F. W. Taylor (mostly through Taylor's claiming Frank's work as his own, and then implying that it was nothing new), Frank was an advocate of Taylor's methods and founded the Society to Promote the Science of Management (renamed the Taylor Society after Taylor's death).

Frank and Lillian married in 1904, and were the parents of 12 children (one daughter died of diphtheria at the age of five). Frank apparently informed Lillian that he wanted six sons and six daughters. In an interview with the *New York Post* in 1941, Lillian was quoted as having once asked him, "How on earth could anybody have 12 children and continue a career?" To which Frank had replied, "We teach management, so we'll have to practice it."

Lillian Moller Gilbreth (1878–1972) was an inspirational woman. In what was very much a man's world at the time—particularly in the area of engineering consulting work, which she entered with Frank—Lillian achieved an astounding amount. When she completed a thesis on the psychology of management, the University of California

refused to award her a doctorate unless she returned to campus for a year's residency. This was impractical, so the family moved to the East Coast, where Lillian undertook a Ph.D. in applied management at Brown University, writing a new thesis, entitled "Some aspects of eliminating waste in teaching." Her Ph.D. was finally awarded in 1915.

Lillian worked closely with Frank at Gilbreth Inc., as well as running their household and bringing up their children. Within a few days of Frank's death in 1924, she traveled to Europe to present a paper that he had intended to give at the International Management Conference in Prague. As Frank's widow, Lillian continued the work of Gilbreth Inc. by conducting seminars on motion study and accepting any consulting jobs that she was not barred from taking simply because she was female.

Often called "the first lady of management," Lillian became the first woman member of both the Society of Industrial Engineers (1921) and the American Society of Mechanical Engineers. She was also the first and, to date, the only female recipient of the Gilbreth Medal, the Gantt Gold Medal, and the CIOS Gold Medal. In 1995, Lillian Gilbreth was included in the National Women's Hall of Fame in the United States.

KEY THINKING
Work Simplification

Work simplification was based on respect for the dignity of people and work, and was developed by Frank Gilbreth from the age of 17, when he began work as a bricklayer. He documented the different ways that individuals laid bricks and from these observations determined the most efficient way to perform this task. For Frank, efficiency was of benefit both to the employer through an increase in the number of bricks laid, and to the employee, through minimizing the levels of exertion required, and so reducing tiredness and the risk of injury. Through his extensive analysis, Frank pioneered a new system of laying bricks that increased output per worker from 1,000 to 2,700 bricks per day.

Another application of Frank's efficiency studies can be seen in operating rooms in hospitals around the world today. Prior to the efficiency study he conducted, surgeons would find all the instruments they needed for operations themselves, wasting precious

minutes as the patient lay on the table. Frank introduced the procedure of having a nurse assist the surgeon by passing instruments into an open hand, as they were required.

Frank took his efficiency systems very seriously, even at home. In *Cheaper by the Dozen*, it is stated that he used two shaving brushes to lather his face in order to save 17 seconds on his shaving time. He abandoned attempts to shave with two razors however: While it saved 44 seconds in shaving time, he also had to spend an extra two minutes bandaging his cuts.

Neither were the Gilbreths' children exempt from their parents' efficiency methods. They were all given their own tasks and became individually responsible for duties such as buying the family's birthday presents, or being chairperson of the house budget committee.

Therbligs

In their study of hand movements, the Gilbreths found that terms such as "move hand" were too general to allow detailed analysis. They split hand movements into 17 basic units of motion that could then, through various combinations, form the hand movements being monitored. These units were known collectively as "therbligs"—Gilbreth spelled backwards, with the "th" transposed.

Microchronometer

In the course of their motion study work, the Gilbreths used photographs to record and then analyze workers' movements. To aid in the clear analysis of their films, they developed the microchronometer—a clock that could record time to 1/2000 of a second—which was placed in the area being photographed. This device is still sometimes used today.

Process and Flow Charts

Around the time that the Gilbreths began working, Henry Gantt developed the ideas that grew into what came to be known as the "Gantt chart"—a system of recording the planning and controlling of work in progress. Frank and Lillian used a Gantt chart in their work and, in their turn, added process charts and flow diagrams. These new tools graphically demonstrated the constituent parts that need to be performed to complete a task.

Psychology of Management and Personnel Issues

The importance of employee welfare was reflected throughout the work of both the Gilbreths, ranging from Frank's concern over the minimization of employee fatigue and stress to their mutual interest in incentives, promotion, and employee welfare. Although not the originator of the discipline of industrial psychology, Lillian's research for her doctoral thesis raised awareness of the importance of the human element in industry. Many publishers refused to publish a book by a woman on such a technical subject, but *Psychology in the Workplace* was eventually published in installments by the Society of Industrial Engineers in 1912 and 1913. The Gilbreths' interest in industrial psychology continued throughout their lives and was demonstrated by Lillian's participation in various U.S. government committees, on subjects ranging from unemployment and war production to problems related to aging and disability.

FRANK AND LILLIAN GILBRETH IN PERSPECTIVE

The Gilbreths are largely unknown and uncelebrated in today's modern corporate world, which tends to minimize the importance of measurement minutiae and favors the space and thinking time needed for creativity and innovation. Earlier in the 20th-century, however, management writers from the 1940s on, such as Lyndall Urwick and Edward Brech, had lionized the Gilbreths, along with Taylor and Fayol, as scientific management became the popular gospel.

As we move into the 21st century, any glory for original time and motion work is largely assigned to Taylor, and the work of the Gilbreths is often forgotten or ignored. As the human relations school of management gained in momentum, with the Hawthorne studies and the work of motivational theorists such as McGregor, Maslow, Likert, and Herzberg, people rather than processes slowly became the central pivot for many management thinkers.

The overwhelming influence of scientific management faded from the 1960s onward. The work of the Gilbreths, however, combining the disciplines of both motion study and industrial psychology, deserves to be recognized for its lasting contribution to management thought, and to the ways in which we work today.

1211

FOR MORE INFORMATION

Books:
Gilbreth, Jr., Frank B., and Ernestine Gilbreth Carey. New ed. *Cheaper by the Dozen*. New York: HarperCollins, 2002.
Spriegel, William R., and Clark E. Myers, eds. *Writings of the Gilbreths* (A compendium of various books and papers by the Gilbreths including: *Field System, Concrete System, Bricklaying System, Primer of Scientific Management, Motion Study, Applied Motion Study, Motion Study for the Handicapped, Fatigue Study, Psychology of Management*). Homewood, IL: Richard D. Irwin, 1953.
Wren, Daniel. *Evolution of Management Thought*. 4th ed. New York: Wiley, 1993.
Yost, Edna. *Frank and Lillian Gilbreth: Partners for Life*. New York: American Society of Mechanical Engineers, 1949.

See also:
Frederick Winslow Taylor (pp. 1270–1271)

BUSINESS THINKERS

Daniel Goleman
Emotional Intelligence

1212

BUSINESS THINKERS

Daniel Goleman is usually credited with challenging the traditional view of the IQ (intelligence quotient) by drawing together research on how the brain works and developing this to promote and popularize the concept of emotional intelligence. In *Working with Emotional Intelligence* (1998), Goleman defined emotional intelligence as a capacity for recognizing our own and others' feelings, for motivating ourselves, and for managing our emotions, both within ourselves and in our relationships.

1946	Born.
1984	Joins editorial staff of *New York Times*.
1995	Publication of *Emotional Intelligence*.
1997	Founds Consortium for Research on Emotional Intelligence at Rutgers University.
1998	Publication of *Working with Emotional Intelligence*.

LIFE AND CAREER

Goleman, born in 1946, gained his Ph.D. in psychology from Harvard, where he also taught. His best-selling book, *Emotional Intelligence: Why It Matters More Than IQ*, was published in 1995, and in 1998 this was followed by *Working with Emotional Intelligence*. Goleman has frequently written for the *New York Times* on behavioral science, and currently acts as the chief executive of Emotional Intelligence Services in Sudbury, Massachusetts, which is affiliated with the Hay Group and offers courses in training and assessment for emotional intelligence. Goleman is also co-chairman of the Consortium for Research on Emotional Intelligence, based at Rutgers University.

Goleman's interest in EI arose from a realization that a high IQ is not necessarily a prerequisite for having a successful life. In *Emotional Intelligence* he identifies many people who, while brilliant academically, were nevertheless failures socially or in corporate life. Conversely, he identifies others who were not well qualified or distinguished in academic terms, but were still highly successful in terms of their lives and business achievements. Goleman went on to relate business acumen to emotional intelligence. In *Working with Emotional Intelli-*

gence he later identified 25 EI competencies, or surface behaviors, and discussed how high emotional intelligence can make all the difference between success and failure.

KEY THINKING
Emotional Intelligence and the Brain

In *Emotional Intelligence*, Goleman describes how the evolution of the brain has implications for our emotions and behavioral responses. He outlines how, during its evolution over millions of years, the brain has now come to comprise three main areas.

- The brain stem is situated at the base of the brain and at the top of the spinal cord. It controls bodily functions and instinctive survival responses, and is the most primitive part of the brain.
- The hippocampus evolved after the brainstem and is situated just above it. It includes the amygdala region, the importance of which was identified by Joseph LeDoux during the 1980s. Here, the brain stores emotional, survival-linked responses to visual and other inputs. The amygdala seems able to "hijack" the brain in some circumstances, taking over people's reactions literally before they have had time to think, and provoking an immediate response to a situation. Mammals or human beings who have had their amygdala removed show no signs of emotional feeling at all. The amygdala can catalyze the sort of impulsive actions that may sometimes overpower rational thought and the capacity for considered reactions.
- The neo-cortex is the large, well-developed, top region of the brain which comprises the center for our thinking, memory, and reasoning functions.

Because of this course of evolution, our emotions and thinking intelligence—the

two main functions of the brain regulating our behavior—are situated in separate areas. Furthermore, our emotional centers receive "input" before our thinking centers, and can react very quickly and very strongly in some situations. The results of this for human behavior can be catastrophic in that, unless we are aware of the situation and practiced in controlling our initial feelings, we may allow inappropriate emotional responses to pre-empt behavior based on consideration of more appropriate options. Our emotions have a "wisdom" of their own that we should learn to use more, particularly in terms of the intuitive sense they offer. Yet, when people confront stimuli that prompt, for example, extreme fear, anger, or frustration, their first impulse to active response comes from the amygdala. Unless intelligent control is exerted, the brain moves into survival mode, stimulating instinctive actions that, while possibly right for the situation, are not rationally considered, and may be very wrong.

Today, we usually have no need to fight or run away from dangers of the sort faced by prehistoric people. While some instinctive reactions may be wise in given circumstances, we need to be aware of how the primitive response in the brain's emotional center precedes all rational evaluation and response. Emotional intelligence is largely about understanding this and making use of our EI, while also controlling our responses to take account of it.

Goleman's Framework of Emotional Intelligence

Goleman developed a framework to explain emotional intelligence in terms of five elements he described as self-awareness, self-regulation, motivation, empathy, and social skills. Each of these elements has distinctive characteristics, as outlined below.

- *Self-awareness*: examining how your emotions affect your performance; using your values to guide decision-making; looking at your strengths and weaknesses and learning from your experiences (self-assessment); and being self-confident and certain about your capabilities, values, and goals.
- *Self-regulation*: controlling your temper; controlling your stress by being more positive and action-centered; retaining composure and the ability to think clearly under

pressure; handling impulses well; and nurturing trustworthiness and self-restraint.

- *Motivation*: enjoying challenge and stimulation; seeking out achievement; commitment; ability to take the initiative; optimism; and being guided by personal preferences in choosing goals.
- *Empathy*: the ability to see other people's points of view; behaving openly and honestly; avoiding the tendency to stereotype others; and being culturally aware.
- *Social skills*: the use of influencing skills such as persuasion; good communication with others, including employees; listening skills; negotiation; cooperation; dispute resolution; ability to inspire and lead others; capacity to initiate and manage change; and ability to deal with others' emotions—particularly group emotions.

Goleman claims that people who demonstrate these characteristics are more likely to be successful in senior management, citing research from various sources that suggests senior managers with a higher emotional intelligence rating perform better than those without. He gives several anecdotal case studies to illustrate ways in which emotional intelligence can make a real impact in the workplace.

The Emotional Competence Inventory

Goleman believes that emotional intelligence can be developed over a period of time and he developed an Emotional Competence Inventory (ECI), in association with the Hay Group, to use in assessing and developing EQ competencies at work. The ECI reduces the original five components of emotional intelligence to four:

1. Self-awareness
- being aware of your emotions and their significance
- having a realistic knowledge of your strengths and weaknesses
- having confidence in yourself and your capacities

2. Self-management
- controlling your emotions
- being honest and trustworthy
- being flexible and dedicated

3. Social competence
- being empathetic, being able to perceive another's thoughts and points of view
- being aware of and sensing a group's dynamics and interrelationships
- focusing on others' needs, particularly when they are customers

4. Social skills
- helping others to develop themselves
- effective leadership
- skill in influencing others
- excellent interpersonal communication
- change-management skills
- ability to resolve arguments and discord
- ability to nourish and build good relationships
- team-player skills

Leadership Styles
Goleman, in association with Hay/McBer, has more recently been involved in researching leadership styles, as he reported in a 2000 *Harvard Business Review* article. On the basis of findings with 3,781 executive participants, the research suggests that leaders gain the best results by using a combination of six leadership styles, each of which has a central characteristic feature and uses different components of emotional intelligence.

- *Coercive leaders*—demand instant obedience. Coercive leaders are self-motivated, initiate change, and are driven to succeed.
- *Authoritative leaders*—energize people towards a goal. Authoritative leaders initiate change and are empathetic.
- *Affiliative leaders*—build relationships. Affiliative leaders are empathetic and have good communication skills.
- *Democratic leaders*—actively encourage team involvement in decision-making. Democratic leaders are good at communication, listening, and negotiation.
- *Pacesetting leaders*—set high standards of performance. Pacesetting leaders use their initiative, and are self-motivated and driven to succeed.
- *Coaching leaders*—expand and develop people's skills. Coaching leaders have the ability to listen well, communicate effectively, and motivate others.

The research evidence suggests that the six leadership styles identified are each appropriate for different types of situation, and also that leadership styles have a direct influence on the working atmosphere of an organization, which, in turn, influences financial results.

DANIEL GOLEMAN IN PERSPECTIVE
The conviction that success depends to a high degree on interpersonal skills is not new, and Goleman has often been criticized for taking others' ideas, to some extent, and repackaging them as a new concept. Goleman himself, however, freely discusses the origins of his ideas, and acknowledges fellow academics when he uses their work.

A critical article by Charles Woodruffe in 2001 reviewed Goleman's version of EI, and suggested that:
- Goleman contradicts himself in claiming that emotional intelligence is inherent and biologically based, yet is a skill that can be learned and developed;
- the self-report measures of emotional intelligence used by Goleman have considerable limitations, particularly in terms of accuracy;
- the EI behaviors or competencies put forward by Goleman, such as self-confidence and leadership, are not at all new, and are factors that have often been recognized as commonly associated with high achievement levels.

Whatever truth there might be in these criticisms, Goleman has certainly promoted management thinking on the subject of EI. He has taken some quite complex ideas relating to human behavior and biological evolution, and put these into a more simple and comprehensible format that, under the label of "emotional intelligence," is easy to understand. As a result, many people have found his core proposition, that we can use intelligence to better manage our emotions and draw on our emotional intuition to guide our thinking, to be a helpful approach in both their lives and their work.

1213

BUSINESS THINKERS

FOR MORE INFORMATION

Books:
Goleman, Daniel. *Emotional Intelligence: Why It Can Matter More Than IQ.* New York: Bantam, 1995.
Goleman, Daniel. *Working with Emotional Intelligence.* New York: Bantam, 1998.
Goleman, Daniel, Richard Boyatzis, and Annie McKee. *Primal Leadership: Realizing the Power of Emotional Intelligence.* Boston, MA: Harvard Business School Press, 2002.
Goleman, Daniel. *Destructive Emotions: A Dialogue with the Dalai Lama.* New York: Bantam, 2004.

Journal Articles:
Goleman, Daniel. "Leadership That Gets Results." *Harvard Business Review*, vol. 78 no. 2, March/April 2000, pp. 78–90.
Woodruffe, Charles. "Promotional Intelligence." *People Management*, vol. 7, no. 1, 2000, pp. 26–29.

See also:
✔ Emotional Intelligence (EI) (pp. 446–447)

"A common core of personal and social abilities has proven to be the key ingredient in people's success: emotional intelligence."
Daniel Goleman

Gary Hamel
The Search for a New Strategic Platform

BUSINESS THINKERS

Professor Gary Hamel (1954–) is one of the most respected contributors to the modern debate on strategy. His fresh and often hard-hitting approach to organizational innovation has brought wide acknowledgment from academics and practitioners alike. His reputation developed from the early 1990s, when, with C. K. Prahalad, he began to communicate his revolutionary views on strategy, in the process creating the concepts of organizational core competencies, strategic intent, and strategic architecture.

1954	Born.
1980	Gains a Ph.D. in international business from the University of Michigan, where he meets C. K. Prahalad.
1983	Starts teaching at the London Business School.
1990s	Comes to prominence through journal articles containing revolutionary views on strategy.
1994	Cowrites *Competing for the Future* with C. K. Prahalad.
1995	Establishes Strategos Inc. with C. K. Prahalad; currently acts as chairman.
Present	Visiting professor in strategic management at London Business School.

LIFE AND CAREER

Hamel worked as a hospital administrator until 1978, when he began to study for a Ph.D. in international business at the University of Michigan. While there, he met C. K. Prahalad, who later became his mentor, collaborator, and colleague in research, writing, and business. Hamel first came to prominence through journal articles in the early 1990s, and as the coauthor of the 1994 book *Competing for the Future*, written (like most of the articles) with Prahalad.

Now at the forefront of thinking on strategy, Hamel is visiting professor in strategic and international management at the London Business School, distinguished research fellow at Harvard Business School, and chairman of Strategos Inc., the strategy services company he established with Prahalad in 1995.

KEY THINKING

Why a new approach to strategy?

At the beginning of the 1980s, Hamel argues, organizational development was no longer driven by strategic forces but by incrementalism. Companies were concerned with getting bigger and better through downsizing, delayering, reengineering, and continuous quality improvement, and their goal became to mimic best practice. The result of all these incremental improvements was to squeeze cost efficiencies to the point where there was nothing left to gain.

At the same time, there were various new forces at work that were changing the nature of competition and the base of traditional industries that had enjoyed primacy in the past. These forces included:

- deregulation and privatization, particularly in the airline, telecommunications, and financial services sectors;
- blurring, fragmentation, and increase in newcomers to the computer and telecommunications industries;
- changing customer expectations, in terms of price, quality, and service;
- continuous technological growth, particularly with the Internet;
- shifting boundaries of control and authority, as workforces became more widely distributed, more empowered, and less layered;
- changes in traditional loyalties as people became simultaneously the most valuable, but also the most expendable, asset;
- the lowered value of experience, as change undermined its relevance for the future.

Strategic Questions to Address

Hamel argues that a compelling view of the future is necessary if one is not to be tied to the orthodoxies of the past, and he highlights the number of companies that lost money because they stuck too long to the same game instead of trying to get ahead. Although no view of the future can be accurate or perfect, a view of some sort is essential. This can be developed through addressing questions about the possibility of unleashing the corporate imagination, turning technicians into dreamers, turning planners into strategists, and creating an organization that really lives and makes its decisions in the future.

In a 1996 article Hamel states that, while we can all recognize a great strategy once it is proved to be successful in action, we find it difficult to generate a great strategy in the first place. He argues that strategy generation is not a purely analytical process, but that it is multifaceted and involves risk, gut feelings, intuition, and emotion, as well as analysis. ("Competing in the new economy: managing out of bounds," with C. K. Prahalad, *Strategic Management Journal*, vol. 17, pp. 237–242.)

Strategy As Core Competence

The concept of corporate competencies was highlighted by Hamel and Prahalad in journal articles and in the book *Competing for the Future*. In the latter they argued that, for too long, organizational focus had been on returns from individual business units, as opposed to the conditions, processes, and competencies that enabled those returns. They define "core competencies" as the collective learning in the organization and, especially, the coordination of diverse production skills and integration of multiple streams of technologies.

Hamel and Prahalad ask organizations to look on themselves as portfolios of core competencies by analyzing what it is that they do better than others. Viewing the organization as systems of activities and building blocks means asking:

- How does activity X significantly improve the end product for the customer?
- Does activity X offer access to a variety of applications and markets?
- What would happen to our competitiveness if we lost our strength in activity X?
- How difficult is it for others to imitate activity X and compete with us?

In order to realize the potential that core competencies create, the organization's people must have the imagination to visualize new markets and the ability to move into

---

"Neither Stalinist bureaucracy nor Silicon Valley provide an optimal ecosystem."

Gary Hamel

them, ahead of the competition. One of the keys to core competencies and effective competition is, therefore, the process through which an organization releases corporate imagination. And one of the words that recurs increasingly through Hamel's writing is "revolution."

Strategy As Revolution

In a seminal article, "Strategy As Revolution" (*Harvard Business Review*, July/August 1996, pp. 69–82), Hamel sets out 10 principles that strategy generators should bear in mind.

- Strategic planning is not strategic: Rather, it is a calendar-driven ritual involving plans and subplans, instead of something challenging and innovative that might lead to discovery.
- Strategy making should be subversive: Great strategies come from challenging the status quo and doing something different. Anita Roddick, founder of the highly innovative Body Shop, is quoted as saying, "I watch where the cosmetics industry is going and then walk in the opposite direction."
- The bottleneck is at the top of the bottle: The most powerful defenders of strategic orthodoxy are senior management, and strategy making needs to be freed from the tyranny of their experience.
- Revolutionaries exist in every company: Let everyone have a voice, so that new and young as well as tried and tested contributors are part of strategy making.
- Change is not the problem—engagement is: People will support change and welcome the responsibility for engendering it, if this gives them some control over their own future.
- Strategy making must be democratic: The capability for strategic thinking is not limited to senior people, and it is impossible to predict where a good, revolutionary idea may be lurking.
- Anyone can be a strategy activist: People who care about their organization do not wait for permission to act.
- Perspective is worth 50 IQ points: Subversive strategy means gaining a new perspective on the world, and looking at potential markets through new eyes.
- Top-down and bottom-up are not alternatives: If top-down can achieve unity of purpose among the few involved, bottom-up will bring diversity of perspective. Bring the two together.
- You can't see the end from the beginning: Surprises do not appeal to everyone, but delving into discontinuities and identifying potential competencies will bring about unpredictable outcomes. These will probably not fit the orthodox strategic mold—but strategy making is about letting go.

So how do we begin to put these principles into a framework for creating strategy as a systemic capability?

Creating Strategy

"Strategy innovation is the only way for newcomers to succeed in the face of enormous resource disadvantages, and the only way for incumbents to renew their lease on success." ("Strategy, Innovation and the Quest for Value," *Sloan Management Review*, Winter 1998, pp. 7–14)

While some strategies result from analysis and others from inspiration and vision, many strategies also evolve and emerge. To achieve strategies that are neither too random nor too ordered or ritualistic, Hamel suggests we look to the roots of strategy creation, which he regards as a relatively simple phenomenon amid the complexity of organizational life. In "Strategy, Innovation and the Quest for Value" (cited above), Hamel turns his revolutionary principles into action points, and urges organizations to adopt a new stance through:

- new voices—top management relinquishing its hold on strategy and introducing newcomers; young people and people from different groups bring richness and diversity to strategy formulation;
- new conversations—the same people discussing the same issues over and over again leads to sterility; new opportunities arise from juxtaposing formerly isolated people;
- new passions—people will go for change when they can steer it and benefit from it;
- new perspectives—search for new ways of looking at markets, customers, and organizational capabilities; think different, see different;
- new experiments—small, low-risk experiments can accelerate the organization's

learning and will indicate what may work and what may not.

GARY HAMEL IN PERSPECTIVE

While it is not possible to pigeonhole Hamel, we can place him roughly in the progressive (if sometimes ragged) line of strategic thinking stretching back to Chandler and Ansoff and including Porter and Mintzberg, as well as Hamel's collaborator and colleague, Prahalad. Hamel's curiosity and tendency to challenge the status quo make it difficult to predict where his future research interests may take him next. However, it is likely that he will continue to move in tune with, if not ahead of, the rapidly changing business environment. His recent book, for example, *Leading the Revolution*, is about throwing away the old rule book, imagining a future that others have not seen, and then taking the initiative to act on it.

1215

BUSINESS THINKERS

FOR MORE INFORMATION

Books:
Hamel, Gary, and C. K. Prahalad. *Competing for the Future*. Boston, MA: Harvard Business School Press, 1994.
Hamel, Gary, and Yves Doz. *Alliance Advantage: The Art of Creating Value Through Partnering*. Boston, MA: Harvard Business School Press, 1998.
Hamel, Gary. *Strategic Flexibility: Managing in a Turbulent Environment*. New York: Wiley, 1998.
Hamel, Gary. *Leading the Revolution: How to Thrive in Turbulent Times*. Boston, MA: Harvard Business School Press, 2000.

Journal Articles:
Hamel, Gary, and C. K. Prahalad. "Strategy As Stretch and Leverage." *Harvard Business Review*, March/April 1993, pp. 75–84.
Hamel, Gary, and C. K. Prahalad. "The Core Competence of the Corporation." *Harvard Business Review*, May/June 1990, pp. 79–91.

See also:
C. K. Prahalad (pp. 1256–1257)

Charles Handy
Understanding the Changing Organization

Charles Handy is well known for his work on organizations. Culminating in the formation of a vision of the future of work and of the implications of change, his observation of work in modern society has identified discontinuous change as the (paradoxically) continuing characteristic of working lives and organizations. He has forecast a future—so far, with a good deal of accuracy—where half of the United Kingdom's workforce will no longer be in permanent full-time jobs.

1216

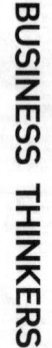

1932	Born.
1967	Founder of Sloan Program, London Business School.
1972	Professor, London Business School.
1974	Governor, London Business School.
1976	Publication of *Understanding Organizations*.
1977	Warden, St. George's House, Windsor Castle.
1985	Publication of *Gods of Management*.
1989	Publication of *The Age of Unreason*.
1994	Publication of *The Age of Paradox*.
1997	Publication of *The Hungry Spirit*.

LIFE AND CAREER

Born in Ireland, Charles Handy is a self-employed writer, teacher, and broadcaster. He is a visiting professor at the London Business School and consultant to a wide variety of organizations in government, business, and the voluntary and educational sectors.

After he graduated from Oxford, his working life began in the marketing and personnel divisions of Shell International and as an economist with Anglo-American Corporation. He then returned to academia at the Sloan School of Management of the Massachusetts Institute of Technology. In 1967 he was the founder and director of the Sloan Program at the London Business School, where he also taught managerial psychology and development. Appointments as professor and governor of the School followed in 1972 and 1974 respectively. In 1977 he was appointed Warden of St. George's House in Windsor Castle, a private conference and study center with a strong focus on the discussion of business ethics. As a

teacher he later concentrated on the application of behavioral science to management, the management of change, the structure of organizations, and on the theory and practice of individual learning in life.

He is a past chairman of the Royal Society of Arts; in 1994 he was U.K. Business Columnist of the Year. He has also been a regular contributor to "Thought for the Day" (a daily brief religious talk) on the *Today* news program on BBC Radio 4.

KEY THINKING

Four of Handy's books in particular consider the structure of organizations in detail, and offer a perspective on the ways in which they work. These are: *Understanding Organizations* (1976), *Gods of Management* (1985), *The Age of Unreason* (1989), and *The Age of Paradox* (1994).

Understanding Organizations

Handy's *Understanding Organizations*—described by publishers and commentators alike as "a landmark study"—is equally valuable for the student of management and for the practicing manager. Among the subjects with which it deals are motivation, roles and interactions, leadership, power and influence, the workings of groups, and the culture of organizations. They are dealt with both as "concepts" and "concepts in application." A "Guide to Further Study" points the way for further examination of each concept.

Gods of Management

Handy identifies some established structures in organizations and suggests new forms that are emerging. He perceives that, currently, organizations embrace four basic "cultures."

- *Club Culture*. This is represented metaphorically by Zeus, the strong leader who has, likes, and uses power, and graphically by a spider's web. All lines of communication lead, formally or informally, to the leader. Such organizations display strength in the speed of their decision making; their potential weakness lies in the caliber of the "one man bands" running them.

- *Role Culture*. This is personified as Apollo, the god of order and rules, represented by a Greek temple. Such organizations are based on the assumptions that people are rational, and that roles can be defined and discharged with clearly defined procedures. They display stability and certainty, and have great strength in situations marked by continuity; they often display weakness in adapting to, or generating, change.

- *Task Culture*. This is likened to Athena, the goddess of wisdom, and is found in organizations where management is concerned with solving a series of problems. The structure is represented by a net, where resources are drawn from all parts of the organization to meet the needs of current problems. Working parties, subcommittees, task forces, and study groups are formed on an ad hoc basis to deal with problems. This type of culture is seen to advantage when flexibility is required.

- *Existential Culture*. This is represented by Dionysus, the god of wine and song. Organizations characterized by a culture of this type are those that exist to serve the individual and in which individuals are not servants of the organization. They consist of groups of professionals, for example, doctors or lawyers, with no "boss." Coordination may be provided by a committee of peers. Such structures are becoming more common as more conventional organizations increasingly contract out work to professionals and specialists whose services are used only as and when required.

The Changing Organization

The link between this analysis of organizational structures and Handy's later work is, in part, provided by the development of "contracting out". This is one of a number of changes that he observes in the world of employment. Another major change is the basing of the quest for profit on intelligence and professional skills rather than on manual work and machines. Yet another is that

---

"Brains are becoming the core of organisations—other activities can be contracted out."

the days of working for one employer and/or in one occupation may be over.

The Shamrock Organization

An example of Handy's changing perception of organizations is provided by his use (in *The Age of Unreason*) of the shamrock. He uses this symbol to demonstrate three bases on which people are often employed by organizations today. The people linked to an organization are beginning to fall into three groups, each with different expectations, each managed and rewarded differently.

The first group is a core of qualified professional technicians and managers. They are essential to the continuity of the organization, and have detailed knowledge of it and of its objectives and practices. They are rewarded with high salaries and associated benefits, in return for which they must be prepared to give commitment, to work hard, and, if necessary, to work long hours. They must be mobile. They work within a task culture, one within which there is a constant effort to reduce their numbers.

The second group consists of contracted specialists who may be used, for example, for advertising, R&D, computing, catering, or mailing services. They operate in an existential culture; and are rewarded with fees rather than with salaries or wages. Their contribution to the organization is measured in output rather than in hours, in results rather than in time.

The third group—the third leaf of Handy's shamrock—consists of a flexible labor force, discharging part-time, temporary, and seasonal roles. They operate within a role culture; but, Handy observes, while they may be employed on a casual basis, they must not be managed casually but in a way that recognizes their worth to the organization.

The Federal Organization and the Inverted Doughnut

The concept of the federal organization was first explored in *The Age of Unreason* and expanded in *The Empty Raincoat*. In it, subsidiaries federate to gain benefits of scale. Federal organizations should not be confused with decentralized organizations, in which power lies in the center and is exerted downwards and outwards. In the federal organization, the role of top management is redefined as that of providing vision and motivating, inspiring, and coordinating; initiative comes from the components of the organization. Handy observes and describes the principle of "subsidiarity"—not handing

out or delegating power, but ruling and unifying only with the consent and agreement of equal partners.

In *The Empty Raincoat* Handy uses the metaphor of the inverted doughnut to demonstrate how those in the subsidiaries must constantly seek to extend their roles and associated activities. The hole in the conventional doughnut is filled by the core activities of the subsidiary; the substance of the doughnut represents a diminishing vacuum into which the subsidiary can expand its activities given the necessary drive, will, and ability.

Portfolio Working and Downshifting

Following on from his work on organizational change, Handy studied the effects of such change on the individual. He coined the concept "portfolio working," based on the assumption that full-time working for one employer will soon be a thing of the past. Embedded in this is the notion of downshifting—the idea that it is possible to exchange some part of income for a better quality of life.

Although Handy has gone on record as saying that more and more individuals will opt out of formal organizations and sell their services at a pace and at a price to suit themselves, he has also admitted that comparatively few may find themselves in a position to take real advantage of this. He argues, however, that there is much that the organization can do to help the individual to get to grips with the new uncertainty. It was in discussion with the Japanese that Handy coined the "theory of horizontal fast track." In Japan, the most talented people are moved around from experience to experience as quickly as possible, so that their talents can be tested in different situations, with different managers and in different cultures. This ensures that they discover what they are really good at and provides a lot of experience.

CHARLES HANDY IN PERSPECTIVE

With his imaginative use of analogy and metaphor, the Handy of the 1990s moved us from the past into the future. He argues that federalist and shamrock organizations can really be successful only if businesses are prepared to invest in their workforces and build relationships of trust.

While he is as much concerned with individuals as organizations, his messages are sometimes disquieting. In *The Hungry Spirit*, he assesses the effects of the com-

petitiveness of capitalism on the individual, suggesting that people can become not only stressed but also selfish and insensitive. But his message is not confined to pessimism about the future. On the contrary, the new capitalism consists of intellectual property—know-how, not merely physical and financial resources; the new knowledge markets enable low-cost entry to those with "a bit of wit and a bit of imagination" and the new products of the knowledge world are not nearly so destructive to the environment as the industrial products of the past.

Handy stands apart from many other management writers by his breadth of vision, his setting of management in a wide social and economic context, and the sheer readability of his writing. He is also ready to modify his views in the light of experience and further thought (he has admitted that some of his expectations have been proved wrong). He is not merely an observer of change but increasingly a catalyst who forces people to stand back from their daily routine, take stock, and view the future through different glasses, acknowledge change, and address its implications.

FOR MORE INFORMATION

Books:

Handy, Charles. *Understanding Organizations*. New York: Oxford University Press, 1985.

Handy, Charles. *The Gods of Management*. New York: Oxford University Press, 1995.

Handy, Charles. *The Age of Unreason*. Boston, MA: Harvard Business School Press, 1989.

Handy, Charles. *The Age of Paradox*. Boston, MA: Harvard Business School Press, 1994.

Handy, Charles. *Beyond Certainty*. Boston, MA: Harvard Business School Press, 1998.

Handy, Charles. *The Hungry Spirit: Beyond Capitalism—A Quest for Purpose in the Modern World*. New York: Broadway Books, 1998.

Handy, Charles. *The Elephant and the Flea*. Boston, MA: Harvard Business School Press, 2002.

See also:

Peter Drucker (pp. 1198–1201)
Stephen R. Covey (pp. 1192–1193)
Tom Peters (pp. 1252–1253)

"Profit has to be a means to other ends rather than an end in itself." Charles Handy

Frederick Herzberg
The Hygiene-Motivation Theory

Herzberg is best known for his "hygiene-motivation" or "two factor" theory of what motivates workers. He invented the acronym KITA (Kick In The Ass) to explain why personnel practices such as wage increases, fringe benefits, and job participation often fail to instill motivation and prove to be only short-term solutions. He also coined the term "job enrichment" to describe a process in which positively motivating factors are built into the design of jobs.

1218

BUSINESS THINKERS

1923	Born.
1945	Enters Dachau concentration camp with U.S. liberating forces.
1946	Graduates from City College of New York.
1951–1957	Research director of psychological services in Pittsburgh, Pennsylvania.
1957	Appointed professor of management at Case Western Reserve University, Cleveland, Ohio.
1959	*The Motivation to Work* published.
1966	*Work and the Nature of Man* published.
1968	"One More Time: How Do You Motivate Employees?" published in the *Harvard Business Review*.
1972	Joins University of Utah's College of Business.
2000	Dies.

LIFE AND CAREER

Frederick Herzberg (1923–2000) was a U.S. clinical psychologist who became an influential management thinker through his work on the nature of motivation and the most effective ways of motivating people. The "overriding interest in mental health" that led him into a career in psychology stemmed from a belief that "mental health is the core issue of our times," a conviction prompted by his posting, while serving in the U.S. forces during World War II, to Dachau concentration camp very soon after its liberation. On his return to the United States, he worked for the U.S. Public Health Service before beginning an academic career. His "hygiene-motivation" theory was first set out in *The Motivation to Work*, pub-

lished in 1959. From 1972 until his retirement he worked at the University of Utah College of Business.

KEY THINKING
The Hygiene-Motivation Theory

The "hygiene-motivation" or "two factor" theory that made Herzberg's name grew out of research he undertook with two hundred Pittsburgh engineers and accountants in the late 1950s.

He asked his subjects to recall times when they had felt exceptionally good about their jobs, why they had had these positive feelings, and what effect they had had both on their performance at work and on their lives outside work. In a second question, he asked them to recall times when their experiences at work had resulted in negative feelings.

Herzberg was struck by the fact that the positive things the respondents had to say about their work experiences were not the opposite of the negative ones. From this, he concluded that there were two factors at work.

He postulated first of all that human beings have two sets of needs:
- lower-level needs as an animal to avoid pain and deprivation;
- higher-level needs as a human being to grow psychologically.

These needs have to be satisfied at work as much as in any other sphere of life. He concluded from the results of his survey that some factors in the workplace meet the first set of needs but not the second, and vice versa. The former group of factors he called "hygiene factors" and the latter, "motivators."

"Hygiene factors" have to do with the

context or environment in which a person works. They include:
- company policy and administration;
- supervision;
- working relationships;
- working conditions;
- status;
- security;
- pay.

The most important thing about these factors is that they do not in themselves promote job satisfaction; they serve primarily to prevent job dissatisfaction, in the same way that good hygiene does not in itself produce good health, but a lack of it will usually cause disease. Herzberg also spoke of them as "dissatisfiers" or "maintenance factors," because their absence or inadequacy causes dissatisfaction at work, while their presence simply keeps workers reasonably happy without motivating them to better themselves or their performance. Some factors are also not to be regarded as true motivators because they need constant reinforcement. Once introduced, they increasingly come to be regarded as rights to be expected, rather than incentives to greater satisfaction and achievement.

"Motivators" (also referred to as "growth factors") relate to what a person does at work, rather than to the context in which it is done. They include:
- achievement;
- recognition;
- the work itself;
- responsibility;
- advancement;
- growth.

Herzberg explains that the two sets of factors are separate and distinct because they are concerned with two different sets of needs. They are not opposites.

Herzberg's hygiene-motivation theory is derived from the outcomes of several investigations into job satisfaction and job dissatisfaction, studies that replicated his original research in Pittsburgh. The theory proposes that most of the factors that contribute to job satisfaction are motivators, while most of the factors that contribute to job dissatisfaction are hygiene factors.

Most of the evidence on which Herzberg based his theory is relatively clear-cut. This is particularly the case with regard to achievement and promotion prospects as potential job satisfiers as well as with regard to supervision and job insecurity as factors

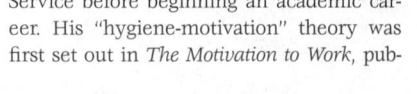

that contribute most to dissatisfaction.

The element that continues to cause some debate is salary/pay, which seems as if it might belong in either group. Herzberg himself placed salary with the dissatisfiers, although the evidence was not so clear in this instance. This would seem to be the more appropriate classification. Although pay may have some short-term motivational value, it is difficult to conceive of it as a long-term motivator of the same order as responsibility and achievement. Most experience (and the history of industrial relations) would point to pay as a dissatisfier and therefore a hygiene factor along with supervision, status, and security.

KITA

In his extremely influential 1968 article for the *Harvard Business Review*, "One More Time: How Do You Motivate Employees?" Herzberg basically lumped all the hygiene factors together with the less pleasant aspects of the working experience under the heading KITA (Kick In The Ass). To explain why managers are unable to motivate employees, he demonstrated again that employees are not motivated by being kicked (figuratively speaking), or by being given more money or benefits, or by a comfortable environment, or by reducing the time they spend at work. These things merely produce movement, the avoidance of pain. What genuinely motivates are things that are intangible, or intrinsic to the work.

Adam and Abraham

Herzberg used biblical allusions to illustrate his theory, especially in his book *Work and the Nature of Man*, first published in 1966 and intended as a psychological underpinning to his workplace-oriented studies. He depicted humanity's basic needs as two parallel arrows pointing in opposite directions. One arrow represents the "Animal-Adam" nature of human beings, concerned with the basic need to avoid physical deprivation (the hygiene factors); the other represents their "Human-Abraham" nature, which is driven by a need to realize their potential for perfection (the motivation factors).

Job Enrichment

Job enrichment was a logical extension of Herzberg's hygiene-motivation theory. Still working on the basic premise that a satisfied workforce is a productive workforce, he proposed that motivators of the type he had always advocated should be built into job design. They included:

- self-scheduling;
- control of resources;
- accountability;
- undertaking specialized tasks in order to become expert in them.

He saw it as a continuous function of management to ensure that people were given the opportunity to become more and more responsibly and creatively involved in their jobs.

FREDERICK HERZBERG IN PERSPECTIVE

Herzberg's work—in common with that of Elton Mayo (known for the Hawthorne Experiments), Abraham Maslow (developer of the hierarchy of needs), and Douglas McGregor (creator of Theory X and Theory Y)—can be seen as a reaction to F. W. Taylor's scientific management theories. These last focused on techniques which could be used to maximize the productivity of manual workers and on the division of mental and physical work between management and workers. In contrast, Herzberg and his contemporaries believed that workers wanted the opportunity to feel part of a team and to grow and develop.

Although Herzberg's theory is not highly regarded by psychologists today, managers have found in it useful guidelines for action. Its basic tenets are easy to understand and can be applied to all types of organization. Furthermore, it appears to support the position and influence of management.

More specifically, it has had a considerable impact on reward systems, first, in a move away from payment-by-results systems, and today in the growing proportion of cafeteria benefits plans, which allow individual employees to choose the fringe benefits which best suit them.

Job enrichment was more theorized about than put into practice. Many plans that were tried resulted only in cosmetic changes or led to demands for increased worker control and were therefore terminated. Nowadays the concept is more one of people enrichment, although this still owes a great deal to Herzberg's original work. His greatest contribution has been the knowledge that motivation comes mainly from within the individual; it cannot be imposed from the outside by an organization in accordance with some formula. Many of today's trends—career management, self-managed learning, and empowerment—have their basis in Herzberg's insights.

1219

BUSINESS THINKERS

FOR MORE INFORMATION

Books:
Herzberg, Frederick. *Work and the Nature of Man*. New York: Ty Crowell Co., 1966.
Herzberg, Frederick. *The Managerial Choice: To Be Efficient and To Be Human*. Homewood, IL: Dow Jones-Irwin, 1976.
Herzberg, Frederick, Bernard Mausner, and Barbara Bloch Snyderman. *The Motivation to Work*. 2nd ed. New York: Wiley, 1959.

Journal Articles:
Cameron, Donald. "Herzberg–Still a Key to Understanding Motivation." *Training Officer*, July/August 1996, pp. 184–186.
Herzberg, Frederick. "One More Time: How Do You Motivate Employees?" *Harvard Business Review*, January/February 1968, pp. 53–62. (This article was republished, in *Harvard Business Review*, September/October 1987, pp. 109–120, with a retrospective commentary by the author. By the time of this republication, the article had sold over one million reprints, making it the most requested article in the *Review's* history)

See also:
Abraham Maslow (pp. 1234–1235)

Geert Hofstede
Cultural Diversity

Hofstede identified four "dimensions" (commonly known as "Hofstede's dimensions") for defining work-related values associated with national culture: power distance; individualism/collectivism; masculinity/femininity; and uncertainty avoidance. He also devised the "values survey module" for use in researching cultural differences, which has been adopted by many other researchers in their work.

1220

BUSINESS THINKERS

1928	Born.
1953	Graduates from Delft Institute of Technology.
1967	Receives Ph.D. from University of Groningen.
1967– 1973	Undertakes massive research project into IBM.
1980	*Culture's Consequences* published.
1991	*Culture and Organizations* published.

LIFE AND CAREER

Geert Hofstede (b. 1928) is a Dutch academic who has also spent long periods in industry, most notably at IBM. He is emeritus professor of organizational anthropology and international management at the University of Limburg in Maastricht in the Netherlands, and he founded the Institute for Research on International Cooperation. He has become known for pioneering research on national and organizational cultures. Much of his subsequent thinking was based on a monumental six-year research project in the late 1960s and early 1970s into the workings of a giant international corporation, originally known by the pseudonym HERMES and later revealed as IBM.

The management of cultural diversity is becoming a significant issue for companies of all sizes, not just multinationals. The rise of global business—leading to an increase in the number of joint ventures and cross-border partnerships, greater cooperation within the European Union, and business's need to embrace people from a variety of ethnic backgrounds and cultures, have all contributed to the need to develop cultural sensitivity. Ignorance or insensitivity in cultural matters can cause serious problems to

international operations. The transfer of Western values to the East, for example, may be inappropriate, and corporate culture and management practices may need modifying to suit local conditions. Hofstede's work has provided a framework for understanding cultural differences.

KEY THINKING
Theory of Culture

Hofstede defines culture as being collective, but often intangible. Nonetheless, it is what distinguishes one group, organization, or nation from another. In his view, it is made up of two main elements: internal values, which are invisible, and external elements, which are more visible and are known as practices. The latter include rituals (such as greetings), heroes (a broad concept that includes not only people but also such things as television shows), and symbols (such as words and gestures). The cultures of different organizations can be distinguished from one other by their practices, while national cultures can be differentiated by their values.

Values are among the first things that are programmed into children. These are reinforced by the local environment at school and at work. It is, therefore, difficult for an individual to change them in later life, and this is the reason why expatriate workers often experience difficulties when faced with another national culture.

The Dimensions of National Culture

Hofstede conducted his research using a questionnaire called the values survey module. From the results, he drew up indices that reflected the national cultural characteristics or dimensions of a country.

(All the quotations in this section are taken from Hofstede's *Cultures and Organizations*, 1991.)

Power Distance: How a Society Handles Inequalities

Power distance is defined by Hofstede as "the extent to which the less powerful members of institutions and organizations within a country expect and accept that power is distributed unequally."

In nations with a low power distance, such as the United Kingdom, inequalities among people will tend to be minimized; decentralization of activities is more likely; subordinates will expect to be consulted by superiors; and privileges and status symbols are less evident. In high-power distance nations, conversely, inequalities among people are considered desirable; there is greater reliance by the less powerful on those who hold power; centralization is more normal; and subordinates are likely to be separated from their bosses by wide differentials in salary, privileges, and status symbols.

Individualism/Collectivism: Behavior toward the Group

"Individualism pertains to societies in which the ties between individuals are loose: Everyone is expected to look after himself or herself and his or her immediate family. Collectivism as its opposite pertains to societies in which people from birth onward are integrated into strong, cohesive in-groups, which throughout people's lifetime continue to protect them in exchange for unquestioning loyalty."

In some societies, people need to belong to a group and have a loyalty to the group. Children learn to say "we." This is true of countries such as Japan, India, and China. In other societies, such as in the United Kingdom, individualism is more important, and there is a lower emphasis on loyalty and protection. Children learn to say "I." In strong collectivist countries, there tend to be greater expectations of the employer's obligations toward the employee and his or her family.

Masculinity/Femininity: Behavior According to Gender

"Masculinity pertains to societies in which social gender roles are clearly distinct;

"Management in a global environment is increasingly affected by cultural differences."

Fons Trompenaars

femininity pertains to societies in which social gender roles overlap."

In a masculine society (Hofstede gives the United Kingdom as an example), there is a division of labor in which the more assertive tasks are given to men. There is a stress on academic success, competition, and achievement in careers. In a feminine society such as France (according to Hofstede), there is a stress on relationships, compromise, life skills, and social performance.

The last 10 to 15 years have seen enormous changes—a "feminization" process—in the behavior of Western democracies. It has also been said that the emergence of developing countries is as much about feminization, as it is about dealing with harder business and economic realities.

Uncertainty Avoidance: the Need for Structure

Uncertainty is "the extent to which the members of a culture feel threatened by uncertain or unknown situations."

In some societies there is a pronounced need for structure. This is because those societies tend to fear the unknown and to possess a high degree of uncertainty. Countries characterized by a low level of uncertainty (such as the United Kingdom) do not perceive something different to be dangerous, whereas, in strong uncertainty-avoidance societies, people will seek to reduce their exposure to the unknown and limit risk by imposing rules and systems to bring about order and coherence. The same thing can be seen in organizations: for example, where there is a need for rules and dependence there will tend to be a pyramidal organizational structure.

Dimensions in Practice

Hofstede is eager to emphasize that his "dimensions" are not a prescription or formula but merely a concept or framework. They equip us with an analytical tool to help us understand intercultural differences, and a very useful one now that, with the rise of global business, many people are working with, or managing, individuals and groups from cultures other than their own. Multinational companies building international teams, for instance, can make use of Hofstede's framework to make sense of the cultural differences they encounter in their practical experience. Knowing about such differences can help to avoid conflict in international management. Using the framework shows that it is always not safe to assume that apparently similar countries in

the same region, for example, Holland and Belgium or Austria and Hungary, have similar cultures.

The dimensions also provide us with a convenient shorthand method of defining the cultural characteristics of a particular organization or country. For example, if someone refers to a country as having a "high feminine index," it suggests that its inhabitants characteristically value having a good working relationship with their supervisor and with their coworkers, living somewhere they and their family want to live, and having job security.

GEERT HOFSTEDE IN PERSPECTIVE

Hofstede's theory has been extensively validated, although the point needs to be made that cultures change and the specific country examples that Hofstede used in the past may no longer be valid today. His framework has been used by other researchers to determine the suitability of certain management techniques for various countries or to make comparisons between countries to understand cultural differences in various areas of management. Mo Yuet-Ha used Hofstede's framework to assess the cultural differences and similarities between East Asian countries. The findings were then used to underpin the understanding of competency-based behaviors in these countries.

Hofstede's original research focused on middle-class workers. Other writers have extended his work by looking at different groups of workers and different countries. Michael Bond took Hofstede's work into Hong Kong and Taiwan, using a Chinese values module devised by Chinese social scientists to test whether Hofstede's work was conditioned by his Western outlook and methods. The cultural dimensions were confirmed, except that of uncertainty avoidance, which may be a theory applicable only to the West. (Other researchers have also cast doubt on this dimension, suggesting that it may have been merely a product of the time at which Hofstede did his original research and may not be as relevant today.) Bond's work led to the discovery of a fifth dimension, long-term/short-term orientation. This dimension measures the extent to which a country takes a long- or short-term view of life. The long-term orientation of Confucian dynamism and thrift correlated strongly with economic growth.

Fons Trompenaars, another noted writer on cultural diversity, has conducted work that shows how national culture influences

corporate culture. For Trompenaars, the major types of culture—the Family (a power-oriented culture), the Eiffel Tower (a role-oriented culture), the Guided Missile (a project-oriented culture), and the Incubator (a fulfillment-oriented culture)—are comparable with Hofstede's model. Hofstede himself has also extended his work into this area by collaborating with Henry Mintzberg, linking Mintzberg's five organizational structures with his own cultural dimensions. This link is intended to show that some organizational structures fit better in some national cultures that in others.

FOR MORE INFORMATION

Books:
Hofstede, Geert. *Culture's Consequences: International Differences in Work-Related Values.* Beverly Hills, CA: Sage, 1980.
Hofstede, Geert. *Cultures and Organizations: Software of the Mind.* New York: McGraw-Hill, 1991.
Hofstede has pointed out that *Culture's Consequences* was a scholarly book, whereas *Culture and Organizations* was written for practicing managers and students. The latter book revisited the basic material of the former and also included some new information.

Journal Articles:
Brown, Andrew D., and Michael Humphreys. "International Cultural Differences in Public Sector Management: Lessons from a Survey of British and Egyptian Technical Managers." *International Journal of Public Sector Management*, vol. 8 no. 3, 1995, pp. 5–23.
Hodgetts, Richard. "A Conversation with Geert Hofstede." *Organizational Dynamics*, Vol 21 no. 4, 1993, pp. 53–61.
Hofstede, Geert, and M. H. Bond. "Confucius and Economic Growth: New Trends in Culture's Consequences."*Organisational Dynamics*, vol. 16 no. 4, pp. 4–21.
Morden, Tony. "National Culture and the Culture of the Organisation." *Cross-Cultural Management: An International Journal*, vol. 2 no. 2, 1995, pp. 3–12.
Mo Yuet-Ha. "Orienting Values with Eastern Ways." *People Management*, 25 July 1996, pp. 28–30.

See also:
Henry Mintzberg (pp. 1240–1241)

"One of the greatest challenges to international business today is how to manage business operations across cultural boundaries."

Jan Selmer

Joseph M. Juran
Quality Management

Dr. Joseph M. Juran is a charismatic figure and a legend in his own time, recognized worldwide for his extensive contribution to quality management. While he is often referred to as one of the leading figures of total quality management, much of his work actually preceded the total quality concept. Regarded as one of the architects of the quality movement in Japan, his influence on manufacturing throughout the world has been substantial.

BUSINESS THINKERS

1904	Born.
1912	Family joins father in United States.
1920	Enrolls at University of Minnesota.
1924	Goes to work for Western Electric at Hawthorne Works in Chicago.
1926	Chosen for inspection training program by visiting Bell Laboratories team.
1928	Produces first work on quality, the training pamphlet, *Statistical Methods Applied to Manufacturing Problems*.
1937	Head of industrial engineering at Western Electric's corporate headquarters in New York.
1941	Assistant administrator for Lend-Lease program.
1945	Leaves Western Electric for New York University.
1951	Publication of *Quality Control Handbook*.
1954	Invited to lecture in Japan.
1964	*Managerial Breakthrough* first published.
1979	Founds the Juran Institute.

LIFE AND CAREER

Juran was born in 1904 in a small village in part of the Austro-Hungarian Empire that is now Romania. He was the third of four children and lived in poverty for much of his childhood. His father left the family in 1909 to find work in the United States and some three years later there was enough money for the rest of the family to join him in Minnesota.

Juran excelled at school in the United States and his affinity for mathematics and science meant that he was soon advanced the equivalent of three year-grades. He enrolled at the University of Minnesota in 1920 and became the first member of his family to enter higher education. By 1924 he had earned himself a B. S. in Electrical Engineering and in 1936 a J. D. in Law at Loyola University. During his career Juran has produced many leading international handbooks, training courses, and training books that have all been widely read and have collectively been translated into 16 languages. He has been awarded more than 40 honorary doctorates, honorary memberships, medals, and plaques around the world. For his work on quality in Japan he was awarded the Second Order of the Sacred Treasure for "the development of quality control in Japan and the facilitation of U.S. and Japanese friendship," and in the United States he has been awarded the National Medal of Technology.

Starting out as a professional engineer in 1924, Juran worked in the inspection department of the famous Hawthorne works of Western Electric, and this first job stimulated his interest in quality. The plant was vast, with some 40,000 workers, 5,000 of whom were in inspection. Juran's unfailing memory soon allowed him to develop an encyclopedic knowledge of the place. His intellectual and analytical abilities were recognized early and he quickly progressed through a series of line management and staff jobs.

In 1926 a team of statistical quality-control pioneers from Bell Laboratories came to the Hawthorne plant to apply some of their methods and techniques. Juran was selected as one of twenty trainees to participate in the training program and was later appointed as one of the two engineers in the newly formed inspection statistical depart-

ment. It was while in this role that he wrote his first work, *Statistical Methods Applied to Manufacturing Problems*.

By 1937, Juran was head of industrial engineering at Western Electric's head office in New York. He became the equivalent of an in-house consultant, visiting other companies and discussing ideas about quality and industrial engineering. Indeed, it was on one such visit to General Motors in Detroit that he realized how relevant Pareto's idea of "the vital few and the trivial many" was to quality management. He eventually described this idea as the "Pareto Principle" (see below).

In 1941 Juran was seconded as an assistant administrator to the Lend-Lease Administration in Washington. This assignment was to last for four years, during which he streamlined the shipment process to reduce the number of documents required and to cut costs significantly. Today such an approach might be called business process re-engineering; Juran has long claimed that there is nothing new about BPR!

Juran left Washington and Western Electric in 1945 with the objective of writing, lecturing and consulting. In 1951 he published his *Quality Control Handbook*. This established his reputation as an authority on quality and increased the demand for his lecturing and consulting services. In 1954 he delivered a series of lectures in Japan at the invitation of the Union of Japanese Scientists and Engineers. Though Juran himself plays down their significance, in Japan it is widely held that these lectures formed the basis of the country's shift towards an economy based on quality principles. The ideas from these lectures were published in his book, *Managerial Breakthrough*, in 1964.

In 1979 Juran founded the Juran Institute with the objective of increasing awareness of his ideas. It was through this Institute that the widely acclaimed video series *Juran on Quality Improvement* was produced, and he continued to write and publish into the 1990s. He played a part in establishing the Malcolm Baldrige National Quality Award and only retired from leading the Institute in 1987.

KEY THINKING
Pareto Principle
In his early days as a young engineer Juran noted that when defects were listed in the order of the frequency with which they oc-

---

"In the language of the industrial leader, quality is primarily a business problem, not a technical problem."

Joseph M. Juran

curred, relatively few types of defect accounted for the bulk of those found. As his career in management progressed he noted the occurrence of this phenomenon in other areas. The idea of "the vital few and the trivial many" was forming. In the 1930s Juran was introduced to the work of Vilfredo Pareto, an Italian economist, who had produced a mathematical model to explain the unequal distribution of wealth. Pareto had not promoted his model as a universal one and did not talk of an 80:20 split, but in preparing the first edition of the *Quality Control Handbook* Juran needed a form of shorthand to describe his idea. Remembering Pareto's work he captioned his description "Pareto's principle of unequal distribution." Since then the "Pareto Principle" has become a standard term to describe any situation where a relatively small percentage of factors are responsible for the substantial percentage of effect. Juran later published an explanation of his error in attributing more to Pareto than the latter had originally claimed, at the same time recognizing the contribution of another economist, M. O. Lorenz. Juran was, in reality, the first to identify and popularize the 80:20 rule (as it has colloquially become known) as a universal principle.

Breakthrough

In his classic work *Managerial Breakthrough* Juran presents his general theory of quality control. Central to this is the idea of an improvement breakthrough.

Juran defines a breakthrough as "change, a dynamic, decisive movement to new, higher levels of performance" (Juran 1994, p. 3). This he contrasts with control, which means "staying on course, adherence to standard, prevention of change" (Juran 1994, p. 1). Not all control is viewed as negative, and not all breakthroughs are expected to be for the good. Breakthrough and control are seen as part of a continuing cycle of events. Juran highlights the importance of managers' understanding of the attitudes, the organization, and the methodology used to achieve breakthrough, and of how they differ from those used to achieve control.

The Juran Trilogy and Quality Planning Road Map

Juran's message on quality covers a number of different aspects. He focused on the wider issues of planning and organization, managerial responsibility for quality, and the importance of setting targets for improvement. Intrinsic to these, however, was his belief that quality does not happen by accident and needs to be planned. The process of quality improvement is best summarized in his "trilogy" concept, based on the three financial management processes of financial planning, financial control, and financial improvement. Various interpretations of the trilogy have been published, and the following represents one version.

Quality planning
- Identify who the customers are.
- Determine the needs of those customers.
- Translate those needs into our language.

Quality control
- Optimize the product features so as to meet our needs and customer needs.
- Develop a process which is able to produce the product.

Quality improvement
- Optimize the process.
- Prove that the process can produce the product under operating conditions.
- Transfer the process to operations.

Juran's "road map" provides a more detailed approach to the steps within the quality planning element of the trilogy. It is made up of a series of actions with corresponding outputs, and emphasizes the need for measurement throughout. In his book *Juran on Quality by Design* Juran describes six activities in the road map: establish quality goals; identify the customer; determine customer needs; develop product features; develop process features; establish process controls; and transfer to operations.

Quality Campaigns

Juran has never been a fan of quality campaigns based on slogans and praise. He viewed the Western quality crisis of the early 1980s as being a result of too many quality initiatives based on campaigns with too little planning and substance. In his view, planning and action should make up 90% of an initiative, with the remaining 10% being exhortation.

Juran's formula for success is as follows.
- establish specific goals to be reached;
- establish plans for reaching those goals;
- assign clear responsibility for meeting the goals;
- base the rewards on the results achieved.

JOSEPH M. JURAN IN PERSPECTIVE

Juran's contribution to the revolution in Japanese quality philosophy helped to transform that country into a market leader. Add to this his influence on Western manufacturing and management in general, and you emerge with a guru who has been influential for more than half a century.

Juran has had a varied career in management and, while his fame centers upon his ideas and thinking on quality issues, his influence in the field of management is far wider. He has played a number of roles—writer, teacher, trainer, and consultant—and has contributed a great deal, over many years, to the field of management. Many of the thousands of managers who have learned from him hold him in near reverence, and management today is infused with his techniques and ideas, even though the name of their creator is not always recognized.

FOR MORE INFORMATION

Books:
Butman, John. *Juran: A Lifetime of Influence*. New York: Wiley, 1997
Juran, Joseph M. *Juran's Quality Control Handbook*. New York: McGraw-Hill, 1988.
Juran, Joseph M. *Juran on Planning for Quality*. New York: Free Press, 1988.
Juran, Joseph M. *Juran on Leadership for Quality*. New York: Free Press, 1989.
Juran, Joseph M. *Juran on Quality by Design*. New York: Free Press, 1992.
Juran, Joseph M, and Frank M. Gryna. *Quality Planning and Analysis*. New York: McGraw-Hill, 1993.
Juran, Joseph M. *Managerial Breakthrough*. Revised ed. New York: McGraw-Hill, 1994.

"In broad terms, quality planning consists of developing the products and processes required to meet the customer's needs." — Joseph M. Juran

Rosabeth Moss Kanter
Pioneer of Empowerment and Change Management

Rosabeth Moss Kanter's writings encompass a wide variety of topics. She views herself, however, as a thought leader and developer of ideas, and is best known for her work on change management and innovation although her current area of research is turnaround management.

Much of Kanter's success is due to a combination of rigorous research, practical experience, and her ability to write in a clear and concrete way, using many illustrative examples.

1224

BUSINESS THINKERS

1943	Born.
1977	Publication of *Men and Women of the Corporation*.
1983	Publication of *The Change Masters: Corporate Entrepreneurs at Work*.
1986–present	Moves from Yale to Harvard Business School. Currently Ernest L. Arbuckle professor of business administration.
1989	Publication of *When Giants Learn to Dance: Master the Challenge of Strategy, Management, and Careers in the 1990s*.
1989–1992	Editor, *Harvard Business Review*.
2001	Receives Academy of Management's Distinguished Career Award.

LIFE AND CAREER

Kanter was born in 1943, in Cleveland, Ohio, and attended the top women's academy, Bryn Mawr. She earned her Ph.D. at the University of Michigan and was associate professor of sociology at Brandeis University from 1966 to 1977. Between 1973 and 1974 she was on the Organization Behavior Program at Harvard, and she was a fellow and visiting scholar of Harvard Law School between 1975 and 1976.

From 1977 to 1986 Kanter was professor of sociology and professor of organizational management at Yale, and from 1979 to 1986, she was a visiting professor at the Sloan School of Management, Massachusetts Institute of Technology (MIT). In 1986, she returned to Harvard as the "class of 1960" professor of entrepreneurship and innovation, and she still holds the post of professor of business administration at Harvard Business School.

Between 1989 and 1992 Kanter was editor of the *Harvard Business Review*, and she acted as a key economic adviser to Michael Dukakis during his 1988 presidential campaign. She has traveled widely as a public speaker, lecturer, and international consultant. In 1977, she and her future husband, Barry Stein, established a management consulting company called Goodmeasure, which has some large and well-known multinational companies as clients.

KEY THINKING

Kanter has authored or coauthored several books and well over 150 major articles. Her doctoral thesis was on communes, and her first books, written during the early 1970s, were sociological. The three books for which she is best known are *Men and Women of the Corporation*, *The Change Masters* and *When Giants Learn to Dance*. There is a logical progression within them, in that the first studies the stifling effects of bureaucratic organization on individuals, while the subsequent titles go on to explore ways in which "post-entrepreneurial" organizations release, and make use of, individuals' talents and abilities. Later books include *The Challenge of Organizational Change* (with Barry A. Stein and Todd D. Jick), *World Class: Thriving Locally in the Global Economy*, *The Frontiers of Management*, and *Evolve*.

Men and Women of the Corporation

Men and Women of the Corporation won the C. Wright Mills Award in 1977 as the year's best book on social issues. It is a detailed analysis of the nature and effects of the distribution of power and powerlessness within the headquarters of one large, bur-

eaucratic, multinational corporation (called Industrial Supply Corporation, or Indsco, in the book). The effects of powerlessness on behavior are explored and the detrimental effects of disempowerment, both for the organization and individual employees, are made clear. Women were the most obvious group affected by lack of power, though Kanter emphasizes that other groups outside the white, male norm, such as ethnic minority members, were also affected.

Three main structural variables explained the behaviors observed within Indsco:
- the structure of opportunity;
- the structure of power;
- the proportional distribution of people of different kinds.

Before this book was published, it was generally assumed that behavioral differences underlay women's general lack of career progress. Kanter's findings made structural issues central, however, and the implications for change management were significant. If all employees were to become more empowered, organizations rather than people would need to change. Accordingly, the book ends with practical policy suggestions to create appropriate structural changes.

While working on this book, Kanter identified the need for organizational change to improve working life, create more equal opportunities, and make more use of employees' talents within organizations.

The Change Masters

The Change Masters puts forward various approaches to achieving these ends. Kanter compares four traditional corporations like Indsco with six competitive and successful organizations, described as "change masters." All findings were weighed against the experiences of many other companies and much other material. From the six innovative organizations, Kanter derives a model for encouraging innovation.

Innovative companies were found to have an "integrative" approach to management, while companies unlikely to innovate were described as "segmentalist" in that they were compartmentalized by units or departments. The difference begins with a company's approach to problem-solving, and extends through its structure and culture. Entrepreneurial organizations:
- operate at the edge of their competence, focusing on exploring the unknown rather than on controlling the known;

- measure themselves by future-focused visions (how far they have to go) rather than by past standards (how far they have come).

Three clusters of structures and processes are identified as factors that encourage power circulation and access to power: open communication systems, network-forming arrangements, and decentralization of resources. Their practical implementation is discussed.

Individuals can also be change masters. "New entrepreneurs" are people who improve existing businesses rather than start new ones. They can be found in any functional area and are described as, literally, the right people, in the right place, at the right time:

- the right people—those with vision and ideas extending beyond the organization's normal practice;
- the right place—an integrative environment fostering proactive vision, coalitions, and teams;
- the right time—a moment in the historical flow when change becomes most possible.

The ultimate change masters are corporate leaders, who translate their vision into a new organizational reality.

The Change Masters advocates "participation management" as the means to greater empowerment. Some major "building blocks" for productive change are identified, and practical measures to remove "road blocks" to innovation are discussed.

When Giants Learn to Dance

When Giants Learn to Dance completes Kanter's trilogy on the need for change which, she considered, U.S. corporations had to confront in order to compete more effectively. The book is based on observation from within various organizations, through consulting projects. The global economy is likened to a "corporate Olympics" of competing businesses, with results determining which nations, as well as organizations, are winners.

The games differ, but successful teams share some characteristics such as strength, skill, discipline, good organization, and focus on individual excellence. To win, U.S. companies would have to become progressively more entrepreneurial and less bureaucratic. Kanter suggested a model for the 1990s the "post-entrepreneurial" corporation, in which three shaping forces would play the key roles:

- the context set at the top
- top management values
- project ideas and approaches coming up through the organization

An "athletic" organization of this kind would be lean and flexible, and would seek to create synergies through the use of team and partnership approaches. The organization would be built on empowerment, and employees would be highly valued within team-based or partnership relationships.

Kanter picks out seven skills, or sensibilities, that characterize individual "business athletes." These are:

- the ability to operate and get results without depending on hierarchical authority, position, or status;
- the ability to compete in a way that enhances cooperation, and aims to achieve high standards rather than destroy competitors;
- the high ethical standards needed to support the trust that is crucial for cooperative approaches when competing in the corporate Olympics;
- a dose of humility, basic self-confidence being tempered by the understanding that new things will always need to be learned;
- process focus, that is, respect for the process of implementation as well as for the substance of what is implemented;
- a multifaceted and ambidextrous approach that makes possible cross-functional or cross-departmental work, the forming of alliances where appropriate, and the cutting of ties where necessary;
- a temperament that derives satisfaction from results, and a willingness to be rewarded according to achievements.

World Class: Thriving Locally in the Global Economy

World Class: Thriving Locally in the Global Economy focuses on world class companies with employees described as "cosmopolitan" in type. These people are rich in the "three Cs"—concepts, competence, and connections—and carry a more universal culture to all the places in which their company operates.

This knowledge-rich breed is compared with "locals," who are set in their ways, and the two groups are viewed as the main classes in modern society. The book is optimistic, in that Kanter believes stakeholders can influence world-class companies to spread best practice around the world.

Globalization, it is argued, offers an opportunity to develop businesses and give new life to the regions. From her studies of regenerative areas, Kanter suggests that business and local government leaders can work together to draw in the right sort of companies to create prosperity.

Later works

The Challenge of Organizational Change: How Companies Experience It and Leaders Guide It, coauthored with Barry A. Stein and Todd D. Jick, draws a distinction between evolutionary and revolutionary change, here described as the "long march" and "bold stroke" approaches.

Rosabeth Moss Kanter on The Frontiers of Management collects Kanter's essays and research articles for the *Harvard Business Review* together into one volume.

ROSABETH MOSS KANTER IN PERSPECTIVE

Overall, Kanter's books present some fairly complex ideas in a way that many people seem to find approachable. They are well-argued and supported with a wealth of practical research evidence. Some of her central ideas, once viewed by some as unrealistic, have now become absorbed into general management wisdom. These include empowerment, participative management, and employee involvement. In *The Frontiers of Management*, she is presented as a groundbreaking explorer who has initiated a revolution in terms of new ways of working. Some managers have yet to cross those frontiers, or do so in aspiration rather than actuality.

FOR MORE INFORMATION

Books:

Moss Kanter, Rosabeth. *Men and Women of the Corporation*. New York: Basic Books Inc, 1977.

Moss Kanter, Rosabeth. *The Change Masters: Corporate Entrepreneurs at Work*. New York: Simon & Schuster, 1983.

Moss Kanter, Rosabeth. *When Giants Learn to Dance: Master the Challenge of Strategy, Management, and Careers in the 1990s*. New York: Simon & Schuster, 1989.

Moss Kanter, Rosabeth, Barry A. Stein, and Todd D. Jick. *The Challenge of Organizational Change: How Companies Experience It and Leaders Guide It*. New York: Free Press, 1992.

Moss Kanter, Rosabeth. *World Class: Thriving Locally in the Global Economy*. New York: Simon & Schuster, 1995.

Moss Kanter, Rosabeth. *Rosabeth Moss Kanter on the Frontiers of Change*. Boston, MA: Harvard Business School Press, 1997.

Moss Kanter, Rosabeth. *Evolve*. Boston, MA: Harvard Business School Press, 2001.

Moss Kanter, Rosabeth. *Confidence*. New York: Crown Business, 2004.

1225

BUSINESS THINKERS

"Power is the ability to get things done."   Rosabeth Moss Kanter

Kaplan and Norton
The Balanced Scorecard

The name of Robert S. Kaplan (left) is almost invariably linked with that of his coauthor, David P. Norton, and with the assessment tool they introduced to the business world in the early 1990s—the "balanced scorecard." Kaplan and Norton argued that adherence to quarterly financial returns and the bottom line alone could not provide the organization with an overall strategic view. The balanced scorecard enables the organization to describe its strategy adequately.

1226

BUSINESS THINKERS

LIFE AND CAREER

Robert Kaplan is Marvin Bower Professor of Leadership Development at Harvard Business School in Boston. He was previously based at Carnegie Mellon University in Pittsburgh, where he was Dean of the Graduate School of Industrial Administration. Kaplan's research work has focused on performance measurement systems, in particular activity-based costing and the balanced scorecard.

David P. Norton is a founder, chairman, and chief executive of the Balanced Scorecard Collaborative, based in Lincoln, Massachusetts. He also founded and was President of Renaissance Solutions, a balanced scorecard consulting firm.

They are jointly recognized as the popularizers of the balanced scorecard concept. Their approach to it was first introduced in a 1992 *Harvard Business Review* article ("The Balanced Scorecard: Measures That Drive Performance"), which began with a variation of the saying "What gets measured gets done"; Kaplan and Norton took as their starting point "What you measure is what you get."

As the story goes, David Norton coined the term "Balanced Scorecard" after a conversation with John Thompson, who was then president of IBM Canada. John Thompson, returning from a round of golf, announced he needed a scorecard just like the one he used during his game to measure the performance of his company. The balanced scorecard grew out of that conversation.

KEY THINKING

In creating the balanced scorecard, Kaplan and Norton argued that strategies often fail because they are not converted successfully

into actions that employees can understand and apply in their everyday work. The problem comes with the search for realistic measures that are meaningful to those doing the work, relate visibly to strategic direction, and provide a balanced picture of what is happening throughout the organization, not just of one facet of it. It is this aspect that the balanced scorecard addresses.

It concentrates on measures in four key strategic areas—finance, customers, internal business processes, and learning and innovation—and requires the implementing organization to identify goals and measures for each of them. Research and experimentation have come up with the following, which seem to be regularly applied in many organizations.

Financial Perspective
● Goals: survival, success/growth, prosperity
● Measures: return on capital, cash flow, revenue growth, liquidity, cost reduction, project profitability, performance reliability

Customer Perspective
● Goals: customer acquisition, retention, profitability, and satisfaction
● Measures: market share, transaction cost ratios, customer loyalty satisfaction surveys/index, supplier relationships, key accounts

Internal Business Process Perspective
● Goals: core competencies, critical technologies, business processes, key skills
● Measures: efficiency measures of working practices and production processes, cycle times, unit costs, defect rates, time to market

Learning and Innovation Perspective
● Goals: continuous improvement, new product development
● Measures: productivity of intrapreneurship, new ideas and suggestions from employees, employee satisfaction, skill levels, staff attitude, retention, profitability, and rate of improvement

The scorecard provides a description of the organization's strategy. It will indicate where problems lie because it shows the interrelationships between goals and the activities that are linked to their achievement. It creates an understanding of what is going on elsewhere in the organization and shows all employees how they are contributing. As Kaplan has said: "The business scorecard seeks to empower all levels of the workforce by educating them about their company's strategy and the small steps they can take to achieve their goals." Providing that accurate and timely information is fed into the system, the scorecard also helps to focus attention where change and learning are needed through the cause and effect relationships it can reveal. Examples of the types of insight achieved were detailed in "Linking the Balanced Scorecard to Strategy."
● If we increase employee training about products, then they will become more knowledgeable about the full variety of products they can sell.
● If employees are more knowledgeable about products, then their sales effectiveness will improve.
● If their sales effectiveness improves, then the average margins of products they sell will increase.

Implementing the Balanced Scorecard

In "Putting the balanced scorecard to work" Kaplan and Norton identify eight steps toward building a scorecard:

1. Preparation. Select/define the strategy/business unit to which to apply the scorecard. Think in terms of the appropriateness of the four main perspectives defined above.

2. First interviews. Distribute information about the scorecard to senior managers along with the organization's vision, mission, and strategy. A facilitator will interview each manager on the organization's strategic objectives and ask for initial thoughts on scorecard measures.

"Over the long run, superior performance depends on superior learning."   Peter Senge

3. First executive workshop. Match measures to strategy. The management team is brought together to develop the scorecard. After agreeing the vision statement, the team debates each of the four key strategic areas, addressing the following questions:
- If my vision succeeds, how will I differ?
- What are the critical success factors?
- What are the critical measurements?

These questions help to focus attention on the impact of turning the vision into reality and what has to be done to make it happen. It is important to represent the views of customers and stockholders, and to gain a number of measures for each critical success factor.

4. Second interviews. The facilitator reviews and consolidates the findings of the workshop and interviews each of the managers individually about the emerging scorecard.

5. Second workshop. Hold a team debate on the proposed scorecard; the participants should discuss the proposed measures, link ongoing change programs to the measures, and set targets or rates of improvement for each of the measures. Start outlining the communication and implementation processes.

6. Third workshop. Final consensus on vision, goals, measures, and targets. The team devises an implementation program to communicate the scorecard to employees, integrate it into management philosophy, and develop an information system to support it.

7. Implementation. The implementation team links the measures to information support systems and databases and communicates the what, why, where, and who of the scorecard throughout the organization. The end product should be a management information system that links strategy to shop-floor activity.

8. Periodic review. Balanced scorecard measures can be prepared for review by senior management at appropriate intervals.

KAPLAN AND NORTON IN PERSPECTIVE

Kaplan and Norton published their first ar-ticle on the balanced scorecard in early 1992. Since then, elaborating, explaining, and applying the basic concept seems to have become a small industry. The jury is, nevertheless, still out on whether it will be an innovation of lasting importance or merely a passing fad. But an increasing number of organizations are trying it out. David Norton has claimed that 60% of large U.S. companies are now using some sort of scorecard that combines financial with nonfinancial measures.

The balanced scorecard should not be regarded as a panacea. In "The design and implementation of the balanced business scorecard: an analysis of three companies in practice," Stephen Letza states that the balanced scorecard should highlight performance as a dynamic, continuous, and integrated process; act as an integrating tool; function as the pivotal tool determining the organization's current and future direction; and deliver information that forms the backbone of its strategy. He also highlights some of the major drawbacks that may be encountered when using the balanced scorecard and points out the need to:
- avoid being swamped by the minutiae of too many detailed measures and make sure that measures do genuinely relate to the strategic goals of the organization;
- make sure all the organization's activities are included in the assessment—this ensures that everyone is contributing to the organization's strategic goals;
- watch out for conflict as information becomes accessible to those who were not formerly in a position to see it or act on it, and try to harness conflict constructively.

The balanced scorecard can be seen as the latest in a long line of attempts at management control, descending from Taylor through to work measurement systems, quality assurance systems, and performance indicators. Commentators claim that the balanced scorecard could become the management tool of the early 21st century, given that it is flexible and adaptable to each organization's use, and that it is practical, straightforward, and devoid of obscure theory. Most importantly, it responds to many organizations' requirements to expand stra-tegically on traditional financial measures, and points to areas for change.

FOR MORE INFORMATION

Books:
Kaplan, Robert S., and David P. Norton. *The Balanced Scorecard: Translating Strategy into Action*. Boston, MA: Harvard Business School Press, 1996.
Kaplan, Robert S., and David P. Norton. *The Strategy-Focused Organization*. Boston, MA: Harvard Business School Press, 2000.

Journal Articles:
Kaplan, Robert S., and David P. Norton. "The Balanced Scorecard: Measures That Drive Performance." *Harvard Business Review*, January/February 1992, pp. 71–79.
Kaplan, Robert S., and David P. Norton. "Putting the Balanced Scorecard to Work." *Harvard Business Review*, September/October 1993, pp. 134–147.
Kaplan, Robert S., and David P. Norton. "Using the Balanced Scorecard As a Strategic Management System." *Harvard Business Review*, January/February 1996, pp. 75–85.
Kaplan, Robert S., and David P. Norton. "Linking the Balanced Scorecard to Strategy." *California Management Review*, Fall 1996, pp. 53–79.
Kaplan, Robert S., and David P. Norton. "Strategic Learning and the Balanced Scorecard." *Strategy and Leadership*, September/October 1996, pp. 18–24.
Letza, Stephen. "The Design and Implementation of the Balanced Business Scorecard: An Analysis of Three Companies in Practice." *Business Process Reengineering and Management Journal*, vol. 2 no. 3, 1996, pp. 54–76.

See also:
- Frederick Winslow Taylor (pp. 1270–1271)
- ✔ Implementing the Balanced Scorecard (pp. 566–567)

1227

BUSINESS THINKERS

"You can only raise individual performance by elevating that of the entire system."

W. Edwards Deming

Theodore Levitt

Marketing

Theodore Levitt has made a key contribution to management theory in the marketing field, stimulating debate on the importance of a pervasive marketing mindset within an organization. Having encouraged an awareness of the marketing concept, Levitt further analyzed the benefits and shortfalls of marketing in a series of articles and books over four decades. His talent for expounding his views clearly and for illustrating his arguments with company examples and metaphors makes his work highly accessible.

1925	Born.
1935	Leaves Germany for the United States.
1959	Lecturer in business administration at Harvard Business School.
1960	"Marketing myopia" appears in *Harvard Business Review*.
1965	Edward W. Carter Professor of Business Administration, Harvard Business School.
1990	Resigns post as editor of *Harvard Business Review*.

LIFE AND CAREER

Born in Volmerz in Germany, Levitt moved with his parents to the United States in 1935, where he later studied economics. In the late 1950s he worked as a consultant in Chicago before being approached by the Harvard Business School. In his very first year there he began to teach marketing, although at the time he had reportedly never read a book on the subject.

Levitt's first article was published in 1956. His tenure at Harvard as an academic lasted for more than 30 years. This period included a stint as a somewhat controversial editor of the *Harvard Business Review*, a post from which he resigned in 1990 following an argument over an article on women in management.

KEY THINKING

Levitt emphasizes the need for a company to achieve a balanced orientation by including marketing in its strategy. He focuses on the need for a marketing outlook to pervade an organization and provide a necessary counterbalance to a preoccupation with

production. His landmark article expounding this theory, "Marketing Myopia," appeared in the *Harvard Business Review* in 1960 and is one of the most requested reprints from that journal, having sold over 500,000 copies. Subsequently, Levitt reiterated and expanded his theory in several articles and books. These partly focus on the methodology of implementing the marketing mode, including the proposition of a "marketing matrix" for assessing the degree of marketing orientation existing in a company. They also explore the theory behind the marketing concept and delineate some of its limitations and problems. Other works concentrate on such topics as "the industrialization of service" (examining the potential benefits of applying the production line and quality control methods of industry to service provision), the nature of the product, advertising, and globalization.

"Marketing Myopia" Explored

Levitt himself described his article "Marketing Myopia" as a manifesto. It challenged the conventional thinking of the time by putting forward a persuasive case for the importance of the marketing approach and the shortsightedness of failing to incorporate it into business strategy.

In an era in which postwar shortages contributed to a concentration on production, most companies had developed a product orientation, which, Levitt believed, was too narrow a philosophy to allow continued business success. A drive to increase the efficiency and volume of production took place at the expense of monitoring whether the company was actually producing what the customer wanted. The article stressed that "customer wants and desires should be a central consideration of any business. The

organization must learn to think of itself not as producing goods or services but as buying customers, as doing the things that will make people want to do business with it."

In order to achieve this, "the entire corporation must be viewed as a customer-creating and customer-satisfying organism. Management must think of itself not as providing products but as providing customer-creating value satisfactions. It must push this idea (and everything it means and requires) into every nook and cranny of the organization."

Levitt highlighted the need for companies to define what business they are in, as this concentrates attention on customer needs. He used the now famous example of the railroads, which, rather than thinking of themselves as being in the business of running trains, should instead have defined themselves as providing transportation. Self-definition along those lines would have helped the railroad companies to be aware of changing customer demand; if they had had that awareness, they might not have suffered so greatly from the rise of road and air transportation. Focusing on the satisfaction of customer needs, Levitt argues, is a better path to continued business success than concentration on the actual product on offer.

Also presented in "Marketing Myopia," as a warning against complacency, is Levitt's belief that "in truth there is no such thing as a growth industry." There are growth opportunities, which can be created or capitalized on, but those companies which believe they are "riding some automatic growth escalator invariably descend into stagnation." The belief that a company is in a growth industry and is therefore secure must never be allowed to overshadow or replace awareness of the need to practice marketing and assert a customer orientation. This is the only route through which a company can hope to achieve sustained expansion.

Of a more practical nature is the "marketing matrix," a device presented by Levitt in *Marketing for Business Growth* to aid the measurement of a company's marketing orientation. A horizontal scale of 1–9 records the degree of customer orientation, and a vertical scale of 1–9 records the degree of company orientation. A score of 9 on both scales is the ideal. Using this method, organizations can assess their incorporation of marketing thinking and determine where

steps are needed to improve their strategy and to become more marketing-oriented.

Ways of doing this include the "industrialization of service," which involves the measuring and standardizing of customer service to a predetermined quality level—in other words, applying industrial-style quality controls to the service process. For example, a production line can be established for service delivery, and service encounters can be standardized and monitored to ensure that they are of a similar quality. This has been accomplished with great success by the McDonald's fast food chain ("The industrialization of service"). To recognize this concept is, writes Levitt, " . . . to introduce a potentially emancipating new cognitive mode and operating style into modern enterprise" (*The Marketing Imagination*). Another factor that is important in enhancing a marketing orientation is relationship marketing (see "After the sale is over"). This revolves around the need not only to acquire customers, but also to keep them and form mutually beneficial long-term relationships with them.

In a 1983 article, "The globalization of markets," Levitt once more produced a forward-looking "manifesto" with a view of the changing nature of the marketplace and the trend, fueled by technological advances, towards globalization. His thesis is that, in order to survive and prosper, companies must offer standardized products around the world, products that incorporate the best in design, reliability, and price. The efficiency of such an approach will outweigh, in his opinion, the benefits of taking into account varying cultural preferences and tailoring products to different national markets. The reason for this is the overlying trend toward world homogenization. "Two vectors shape the world—technology and globalization. The first helps determine human preferences; the second, economic realities. Regardless of how much preferences evolve and diverge, they also gradually converge and form markets where economies of scale lead to reduction of costs and prices."

Thinking about Management, Levitt's 1991 book, contains a distillation of his thinking on effective management, presented in nuggets in the three categories of thinking, changing, and operating. Many of his theories are reiterated here, and the work forms a useful guide to his collected thought.

THEODORE LEVITT IN PERSPECTIVE

A major influence on Levitt's work was the writing of Peter Drucker, who was among the first to see marketing as all-pervasive: "Marketing is not a function, it is the whole business seen from the customer's point of view" (*The Practice of Management*).

However, although influenced by academic thought, Levitt seems to have drawn his greatest inspiration from the real world, examining the companies around him and distilling the examples of good and bad practice that illustrate much of his writing.

Levitt's influence contributed to the rise of the marketing concept in the 1960s and its increasing incorporation into management thinking, initially in the United States but later also in Europe. His subsequent works may not have achieved the fame of "Marketing myopia," but they are nevertheless an important part of the evolving pattern of marketing writing that has gathered impetus through recent decades. By pointing out the myopic vision of many managers, Levitt set in motion a vigorous new way of thinking that was taken up by other management writers and practitioners and culminated in the rebirth of marketing in the 1980s. Other marketing gurus such as Philip Kotler acknowledge the influence of Levitt's work, and he is regularly quoted.

In retrospect, Levitt has been proven to have had remarkable foresight in his anticipation of the importance of marketing to organizations, his initial work predating the marketing boom by two decades. He also successfully predicted the value of relationship marketing, a topic which only became an identifiable discipline in the early 1990s, and the concept of the global village, which is now commonplace.

Levitt's assertion that there is no such thing as a growth industry is another tenet that proved influential, and was taken up by writers such as Tom Peters and Richard Pascale in the 1990s.

 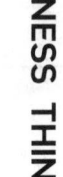

1229

BUSINESS THINKERS

FOR MORE INFORMATION

Books:
Drucker, Peter. *The Practice of Management*. New York: HarperBusiness, 1986.
Levitt, Theodore. *Innovation in Marketing: New Perspectives for Profit and Growth*. New York: McGraw-Hill, 1962.
Levitt, Theodore. *Marketing for Business Growth*. New York: McGraw-Hill, 1974. (first published in 1969 as *The Marketing Mode: Pathways to Corporate Growth*)
Levitt, Theodore. *The Marketing Imagination*. New York: Free Press, 1983.
Levitt, Theodore. *Thinking about Management*. New York: Free Press, 1991.

Journal Articles:
Levitt, Theodore. "Marketing Myopia." *Harvard Business Review*, July/August 1960, pp. 45–56.
Levitt, Theodore. "The Industrialization of Service." *Harvard Business Review*, September/October 1976, pp. 63–74.
Levitt, Theodore. "After the Sale Is Over." *Harvard Business Review*, September/October 1983, pp. 87–93.
"The Globalization of Markets." *Harvard Business Review*, May/June 1983, pp. 92–102.

"Without organizations, there would be chaos and decay."   Theodore Levitt

Kurt Lewin
Change Management and Group Dynamics

Kurt Lewin's output included studies of leadership styles and their effects and work on group decision-making, and he was responsible for the development of force field theory, the "unfreeze—change—refreeze" model of change management, the "action research" approach to research, and the group dynamics approach to training (especially in the form of T Groups).

The Dome at MIT, where Lewin co-founded the Research Center for Group Dynamics.

1890	Born.
1910	Begins formal training in psychology.
1914	Graduates as Ph.D. from the University of Berlin.
1914–1916	Active service with the German army; is wounded and awarded the Iron Cross.
1916–1932	Teaches at the University of Berlin.
1932	Leaves Germany to escape persecution by the Nazis.
1935	Appointed professor of child psychology at University of Iowa.
1939	Researches leadership styles in Iowa.
1944	Cofounds the Research Center for Group Dynamics at MIT. Mother killed in Nazi extermination camp.
1946	Pioneers T-Group approach.
1947	Dies.

LIFE AND CAREER

German-born, Lewin was professor of philosophy and psychology at Berlin University until he fled to the United States in 1932 to escape from the Nazis. There, he taught at Cornell University, and then at Iowa, becoming professor of child psychology at the latter's Child Research Station. In 1944 he went on to found, with Douglas McGregor and others, a research center for group dynamics at the Massachusetts Institute of Technology.

KEY THINKING
Leadership Styles & Their Effects

With his colleagues L. Lippitt and R. White, Lewin studied the effects of three different leadership styles on the outcomes of boys' activity groups in Iowa (1939). Those three styles were classified as "democratic," "autocratic," and "laissez-faire." It was found that in the group with an autocratic leader, there was more dissatisfaction and behaviors became either more aggressive or apathetic. In the group with a democratic leader, there was more cooperation and enjoyment, while those in the laissez-faire group showed no particular dissatisfaction, although they were not particularly productive, either.

Significantly, when the respective leaders were asked to change their styles, the effects produced by each leadership style remained similar. Lewin was aiming to show that the democratic style achieved better results. The possibility of social and cultural factors influencing the results undermined his findings to some extent; nevertheless, the studies suggested the benefits of a democratic style in a U.S. context. They also showed that it is possible for leaders and managers to change their approach, to improve their leadership through training, and to adopt management styles appropriate to their situation and context.

Group Decision-making

After World War II, Lewin conducted research for the U.S. government, exploring ways of influencing people to change their dietary habits and eat less popular cuts of meat. He found that, if group members were encouraged to become involved, discuss the issues themselves, and make their own decisions as a group, they were far more likely to change their habits than if they simply attended lectures where they were given information, recipes, and advice.

Force Field Analysis

Lewin put forward the theory that people's activity is affected by forces in their surrounding environment, or "field." Its three main principles are that:

- behavior is a function of the existing field;
- analysis starts from the complete situation and distinguishes its component parts;
- a concrete person in a concrete situation can be mathematically represented.

A particular feature of Lewin's method of analyzing behavior within a given field (for example, within a situation or an organization) is its identification of the forces at work there as either "driving forces," which will tend to promote change, or "restraining forces," which will tend to hinder it. Such things as ambitions, goals, needs, or fears, that drive a person toward or away from something, constitute driving forces. Restraining forces are different in nature, Lewin asserts, in that they act to oppose driving forces rather than constituting independent forces in themselves.

Force field analysis is used extensively for purposes of organizational and human resources development, because it can help to indicate when the driving and restraining forces affecting people are not in balance, thus creating a situation in which change can occur.

The interplay of the two types of force can produce either stability or instability. Where activities and situations go on from day to day in a regular, stable routine—that is, in what Lewin calls "quasi-stationary processes"—the forces are more or less balanced out and equalized; they fluctuate around a state of equilibrium. Achieving change, therefore, involves altering the forces that maintain this equilibrium. To bring about an increase in productivity, for example, the forces currently keeping production at its existing quasi-stationary levels would have to be changed. This can be done by taking one of two alternative routes:

- strengthening the driving forces, for example, paying more money for more productivity;
- restraining inhibiting factors, for example, simplifying production processes.

Strengthening the drives would seem the obvious route to take, but analysis would show that this could lead to the development of countervailing forces, concern

among employees about tiredness, or worry about new targets becoming a standard expectation. Reducing restraining forces, for example, through investment in machinery or training to make the process easier, might be a less obvious, but more rewarding approach, bringing about change with less resistance or demoralization.

Lewin identified two questions to ask when seeking to make changes within the framework of force field analysis:

- Why does a process continue at its current level under the present circumstances?
- What conditions would change these circumstances?

For Lewin, "circumstances" is a concept with a very broad meaning; it covers anything from the social context and wider environment to subgroups and communication barriers between groups. The position of each of these factors determines a group's structure and "ecological setting" while the structure and setting together determine a variety of possible changes that are dependent on, and can to some degree be controlled by, the pacing and interaction of forces across the entire field.

Model of Change: Unfreeze— Change—Refreeze

Lewin believed that, to achieve change effectively, it was necessary to look at all the options for moving from the existing state to a desired future one, then to evaluate the possibilities of each option and decide on the best one, rather than simply identifying a desired goal and taking the straightest and easiest route to it. His change management model is linked to force field analysis and encourages managers to beware of two kinds of force of resistance, the first deriving from "social habit" or "custom," and the second from the creation of an "inner resistance." These two different kinds of force are rooted in the interplay between a group as a whole and the individuals within it, and only driving forces that are strong enough to break the habits, challenge the interests, or "unfreeze" the customs of the group will overcome them. As most members will want to stay within the behavioral norms of the group, individual resistance to change will increase as a person is induced to move further away from current group values. In Lewin's view, this type of resistance can be lowered either by reducing the value the group attaches to something, or by fundamentally changing what the group values.

He considered that a complex, stepped process of unfreezing, changing, and refreezing beliefs, attitudes, and values was required to achieve change, with the initial phase of unfreezing normally involving group discussions in which individuals experience others' views and begin to adapt their own.

Since Lewin's death, "unfreeze— change—refreeze" has sometimes been applied more rigidly than he intended, for example, by discarding an old structure, establishing a new one, and then "fixing" the latter into place. Such an inflexible course of action fits badly with more modern attitudes to change as a continuous and flowing process of evolution. Lewin's change model is now often criticized for its linearity, especially from the perspective of more recent research on nonlinear, "chaotic" systems and complexity theory. The model was, however, process-oriented originally. Lewin himself viewed change as a continuing process, recognizing that extremely complex forces are at work in group and organizational dynamics.

T-Groups

What is now known as the "T-Group" (or Training Group) approach was pioneered by Lewin when, in 1946, he was called in to try to develop better relations between Jewish and black communities in Connecticut. Bringing such groups of people together was, Lewin found, a powerful way of exposing areas of conflict, so that established behavior patterns could "unfreeze" before potentially changing and "refreezing." He called these learning groups T-Groups. This training approach became particularly popular during the 1970s. Some interpreters of the method, however, have used it in a more confrontational way than Lewin may have intended.

Action Research

Lewin's "action research" approach is linked to T-groups. Introduced during the 1940s, it was seen as an important innovation in research methods and was especially used in industry and education. Action research involves experimenting by making changes and simultaneously studying the results, in a cyclic process of planning, action, and fact-gathering. Lewin's approach emphasized the power relationship between the researcher and those researched, and he sought to involve the latter, encouraging their participation in studying the effects of

their own actions, identifying their own biases, and working to transform relationships within their communities.

"Action research" centered on the involvement of participants from the community under research and on the pursuit of separate but simultaneous processes of action and evaluation. Different variations of this approach have evolved since Lewin's day, and its validity as a scientific research method for psychology is often questioned. Its strengths, however, in offering groups or communities an involving, self-evaluative, collaborative, and decision-making role are widely accepted.

KURT LEWIN IN PERSPECTIVE

Lewin is widely recognized as a seminal figure in social psychology, although his early death obscured his central role in the development of the managerial human relations movement. In the United States and the United Kingdom (especially through the work of the Tavistock Institute), much subsequent management thinking and research has been influenced by Lewin's approaches and ideas. These, following in the tradition of Mayo's 1920s and 1930s Hawthorne studies, underlie the whole current field of organizational development and change management.

1231

BUSINESS THINKERS

FOR MORE INFORMATION

Book:
Lewin, Kurt. *Resolving Social Conflicts and Field Theory in Social Science.* Washington, D.C.: American Psychological Association, 1997.

Journal Articles:
Lewin, Kurt, R. Lippitt and R. White. "Patterns of Aggressive Behaviour in Experimentally Created 'Social Climates.'" *Journal of Social Psychology,* vol. 10, 1939, pp. 271–99.
Lewin, Kurt. "Action Research and Minority Problems." *Journal of Social Issues,* vol. 2, 1946, p. 65.
Lewin, Kurt. "Frontiers in Group Dynamics." *Human Relations,* vol. 1, 1947, pp. 5–41.

See also:
Douglas McGregor (pp. 1238–1239).

Niccolò Machiavelli
The Patron Saint of Power

Throughout most of the five centuries since his death Niccolò Machiavelli has not been a popular figure. There have always been a few people who appreciated his genius, but most have also closely associated him with intrigue and dark deeds. Fortunately, in the last 100 years or so, a more reasoned view of his work has developed, and the enormous value of Machiavelli's philosophy and its remarkable relevance to modern society has emerged.

1469	Born.
1489	Secretary of Second Chancery, Florence.
1512	Falls from grace as Medici family returns to power.
1513	Publication of *The Prince*.
1527	Dies.

LIFE AND CAREER

Niccolò Machiavelli was born in 1469, the son of a Florentine lawyer. He first came to public notice when in 1498, at the age of 29, he was appointed Secretary of the Second Chancery—part of the complex bureaucracy that ran Florence as a city state. His appointment came after the execution of Savonarola, the friar-politician who, after leading a revolt that expelled the Medicis and established a democratic republic, dominated Florentine life until he ran afoul of the papacy and was burned for heresy.

Machiavelli held the post of Secretary for 14 years, during which time his influence was significant. He took part in 30 foreign missions, meeting most of Europe's key politicians and rulers. This opportunity to learn about government, politics, and economics must have been unique. Unfortunately, it was not to last. In 1512 the Medicis returned to power, and Machiavelli lost his post immediately. He was then suspected, quite wrongly, of plotting against the Medicis, for which he was arrested, imprisoned, and tortured. Although eventually found innocent, he was expelled from Florence and forced to spend the rest of his life in exile on an isolated farm. His many attempts to reenter political life failed and he died in 1527, still struggling to regain his lost influence. It was more than 300 years later

that Italy became unified, as Machiavelli had wanted it to be.

While Machiavelli may not have enjoyed his time in exile, the world has gained immeasurably from it. The enforced idleness allowed him to write prodigiously about his experiences and ideas.

His written works include a history of Florence, several plays, and two books that established him as a great authority on power politics: *The Prince* and *The Discourses*. Professor Max Lerner, in his introduction to the 1950 Random House edition of *The Prince* describes the book as "a grammar of power." There can be no more fitting description of this seminal work.

KEY THINKING

Machiavelli presents no instant management theories or clever techniques for solving day-to-day problems. He deals mainly with broad strategies, and to get value from his writing one needs to interpret it and make comparisons. Perhaps the best approach is first to read Jay's introduction on the art of making such comparisons and then to read Machiavelli with a personal checklist of interests and questions.

Some pertinent insights

The following examples show how certain passages in Machiavelli's writing bridge the seemingly huge gap between sixteenth-century politics and twentieth-century business.

Leadership

Machiavelli provides several examples of good leaders and leaves his readers in no doubt about the importance of skillful leadership to the success of any enterprise. He dismisses luck and genius as the key to suc-

cessful leadership and goes for "shrewdness." The dangers and risks a leader faces are dramatically illustrated (happily for us these are less terrifying today than in Renaissance Italy), and comparisons made between the relative ease of getting to a position of leadership and the difficult task of staying there.

Centralization versus decentralization

Anyone who thinks that the problem of choosing between centralized or decentralized control is a modern dilemma will be quickly persuaded otherwise by reading *The Prince*. Machiavelli's examples are drawn entirely from government and from military history, but the comparisons with today's business world are easy to make. Perhaps his best advice comes when he is talking about the government of colonies and outposts.

Poor communications in Renaissance times usually made decentralization the only option in such cases, and Machiavelli's recommendations center on what today we would call "selection and training." A colonial governor must be carefully selected for his experience and loyalty, trained thoroughly in the state's way of doing things and made so familiar with "best practice" that however isolated from "head office" guidance he may be, the job will still get done in a highly predictable way. Shades of William Whyte's *Organization Man*?

Takeovers

The equivalent of a takeover in Machiavelli's world was the conquest of another country or the establishment of a colony. In such matters his advice is very clear. One either totally subjugates the original inhabitants, so that rebellion is unlikely and the cost of garrisoning the place reduced to a minimum, or, and Machiavelli makes clear this is his preference, the conqueror puts in a small team of "key managers."

This team will displace only a small number of the original inhabitants, who being scattered cannot rebel, and the remainder will quickly toe the new management line since they have everything to gain from cooperation and a clear indication of what happens to those who do not cooperate. Parallels with business takeovers are frighteningly stark.

"All empire is no more than power in trust."   John Dryden

Change

Machiavelli has little to offer in the way of ideas for coping with change, but shows very clearly that the problems of introducing change were just as awesome and hazardous in the sixteenth century as they are today. In *The Prince* he says: "It must be considered that there is nothing more difficult to perform, nor more doubtful of success, nor more dangerous to handle, than to initiate a new order of things."

Federations and Bureaucracies

Machiavelli compared the "management" of sixteenth-century France and Turkey. He saw France as a "federal organization"; a collection of independent baronies in which the retainers regarded their baron, and not the king, as the "key manager." Such organizations are difficult to control, impossible to change, and the ruler is easily overthrown. Turkey, on the other hand, was in Machiavelli's time a classic bureaucracy with a highly trained civil service. Civil servants were frequently moved around, hence they developed no local loyalties, and had a strict, hierarchical relationship with "top management." The ruler in such a state, being appointed by the "system," was secure, respected, and powerful. The points of comparison with today's large organizations need little emphasizing.

NICCOLÒ MACHIAVELLI IN PERSPECTIVE

The impact of Machiavelli's writing on politics has been accepted for some time, but the relevance of his ideas to business had to wait until the second half of the nineteenth century, when companies began to operate as large, complex organizations—the equivalent in Machiavelli's terms of a move from a tribal society to a corporate state. An English parson, writing in 1820, compares Machiavelli unfavorably with the devil, yet by the 1860s Victor Hugo was able to say, "Machiavelli is not an evil genius, nor a cowardly writer, he is nothing but the fact . . . not merely the Italian fact, he is the European fact."

Machiavelli's image is not helped by what many see as an amoral attitude toward power. It is easy to take offense when he unashamedly says, "A prudent ruler ought not to keep faith when by so doing it would be against his interest, and when the reasons which made him bind himself no longer exist."

Such statements are easier to accept if we remember they were made in times very different from our own. They were also the words of a man who was a true observer; he reported what he saw and measured results dispassionately in terms of practical success or failure. He had moral views, as can be seen in his other writing, but on political issues he is a cold realist. He had, as Professor Lerner so aptly observed, "the clear-eyed capacity to distinguish between man as he ought to be and man as he actually is—between the ideal form of institutions and the pragmatic conditions under which they operate."

By being so linked with intrigue, cruelty, and opportunism, Machiavelli remains rooted in his own age. However, if we set him aside from the harsh realities of sixteenth-century Europe and look at how he observes human nature and organizations, we see a man who was centuries ahead of his time.

1233

FOR MORE INFORMATION

Books:
Jay, Antony. *Management and Machiavelli*. London: Hodder & Stoughton, 1967.
Machiavelli, Niccolò. *The Prince and The Discourses* (introduced by Max Lerner). New York: Random House, 1950. A number of editions of *The Prince and The Discourses* are currently in print.
Whyte, William H.. *The Organization Man*. Philadelphia, PA: University of Pennsylvania Press, 2002.

BUSINESS THINKERS

"It is a common fault of men not to reckon on storms in fair weather." Niccolò Machiavelli

Abraham Maslow
The Hierarchy of Needs

Maslow, known principally for his theory of the "hierarchy of needs," was one of the first people to be associated with the humanistic—as opposed to task-based—approach to management. As people have increasingly come to be appreciated as a key resource in successful companies, Maslow's model has remained a valuable management concept.

1908	Born.
1934	Receives Ph.D. from the University of Wisconsin.
1935	Returns to New York to work at Columbia University.
1937– 1951	On the faculty of Brooklyn College.
1943	"Hierarchy of needs" first presented in an article in the *U.S. Psychological Review*.
1951	Becomes head of the psychology department at Brandeis University.
1954	*Motivation and Personality* published.
1970	Dies.

LIFE AND CAREER

Abraham Maslow (1908–1970) was a U.S. psychologist and behavioral scientist. He spent part of his career in industry as well as working as an academic. He liked to say that, whereas most early psychologists studied people with psychological problems, he devoted his attention to successful people. The "hierarchy of needs" theory, on which his fame chiefly rests, was first presented in 1943 in the *U.S. Psychological Review*, and later developed in his book *Motivation and Personality*, first published in 1954. His concepts were originally offered as general explanations of human behavior, but quickly came to be regarded as a significant contribution to workplace motivation theory. They are still used by managers today to understand, predict, and influence employee motivation.

KEY THINKING

Maslow grouped human needs into classes and arranged these classes in the form of a hierarchy, ascending from the lowest to the highest. When one set of needs is satisfied, it ceases to be a motivator; motivation is then generated by the unsatisfied needs further up the hierarchy. The classes of needs identified by Maslow are: survival or physiological needs, safety or security needs, social needs, ego-status needs, and self-actualization needs, and they appear in that order in the hierarchy. Today the hierarchy is usually represented as a pyramid, although Maslow himself did not present it in that way.

The five levels within the hierarchy can be broken down as follows.

- Survival or physiological needs. These are the most primitive of all needs, comprising all the basic animal requirements such as food, water, shelter, warmth, and sleep.
- Security or safety needs. In earlier times, these needs expressed themselves in the form of a desire to be free of physical danger. In the modern context, they have been refined and are now felt in mainly social and financial terms; purely physical requirements have been replaced by the need for things such as job security or a living wage.
- Social needs. Most humans need to belong and to be accepted by others. They are essentially social beings and therefore seek membership of social groups, such as work groups.
- Ego-status needs. Most humans also need to be held in esteem by both themselves and others. This kind of need is satisfied by power, prestige, and self-confidence.
- Self-actualization needs. The most sophisticated type of need is the desire to maximize one's skills and talents. This embraces self-realization, self-expression, and self-fulfillment.

There are certain conditions, Maslow wrote, that are immediate prerequisites for satisfying needs, such as the freedom to speak, the freedom to express oneself in other ways, the freedom to defend oneself, justice, fairness, and honesty. Any danger threatening these is perceived almost as if it were a danger to the satisfaction of the needs themselves.

The hierarchy is usually referred to as if it were a fixed order, but Maslow explained that it is not necessarily rigid or universally applicable in its usual form. While most people do experience their basic needs in the order indicated, there are a number of exceptions. Creative people, for example, are often driven by a desire for self-actualization and give it precedence over the satisfaction of "lower" needs in a way that the average person perhaps would not. The hierarchy is often presented in simplified terms, giving the false impression that one need must be fully satisfied before the next need emerges. In fact, as Maslow pointed out, man is a continually wanting animal, whose basic needs are for the most part partially satisfied and partially unsatisfied at the same time. Needs continually overlap; for example, social needs are felt by almost everyone, including those people whose basic physiological needs are not being met. As soon as a need is satisfied, however, it will drop out of the equation and cease to be a motivator.

Maslow's intention all along was to define an aspect of the human condition, but his insights are obviously applicable within a business context. If, for example, a manager is able to recognize which level of the hierarchy a worker has reached, then he or she can motivate the employee in the most appropriate way. Peter Drucker, in his book *Management: Tasks, Responsibilities, Practices* (London: Heinemann, 1973), pointed out that although it becomes less satisfying to obtain economic rewards as one moves up the hierarchy, the need for such rewards does not necessarily become less important. This is because, as their impact as a positive incentive decreases, their ability to create dissatisfaction and act as a disincentive increases. Economic rewards come to be seen as entitlements and, if they are not looked after, can act as deterrents.

ABRAHAM MASLOW IN PERSPECTIVE

Maslow is often mentioned in connection

"In order for an ideal to become a reality, there must be a person, a personality to translate it."

Jesse Jackson

with his contemporaries, Douglas McGregor and Frederick Herzberg, who were also developing motivation theories at about the same time. Maslow admired McGregor, the author of Theory X and Theory Y, although he had strong reservations about the validity of Theory Y. Herzberg suggested that hygiene factors—those that may be causes of job dissatisfaction (for example, working conditions, salary, job security, or company policy) but are not in themselves incentives to improve performance—should be separated from motivators—those that lead to positive job satisfaction (such as achievement, recognition, responsibility, or advancement). Herzberg's hygiene factors can be compared with Maslow's levels one, two, and three, and the motivators to levels four and five.

Maslow's influence continues through the work of later psychologists and writers, such as Chris Argyris and Blake and Mouton. Argyris looked at how individual initiatives and creativity can coexist with organizational rules. Blake and Mouton were the authors of the *Managerial Grid*, which created the concept of the manager who balanced a concern for people with a concern for the task.

Practicing managers have also, on the whole, found Maslow's concept a valuable and sensible one, which helps to clarify their thoughts. It is often used as a basis for questionnaires and checklists to discover an individual's level of motivation, or cited in support of the idea of empowerment. Twyla Dell, in *How to Motivate People* (London: Kogan Page, 1988), listed the ten qualities that people most want from their jobs and included two questionnaires to help readers judge how many of the ten qualities they were receiving and giving in their work. She then matched the ten qualities to Maslow's hierarchy.

Maslow's theory only makes complete sense when applied, as he originally intended, to life in general rather than to the workplace in particular. This is because some of the needs of the individual, particularly the higher needs, may be satisfied outside the workplace. This holistic view is nonetheless important within the workplace, as employers increasingly come to realize that individuals have a life outside their job that impinges on their perform-ance at work. Although Maslow's theory is now over 50 years old, it is still referred to by managers and it offers them useful insights. Along with Herzberg and McGregor, he is recognized as one of the founding fathers of motivation theory.

FOR MORE INFORMATION

Books:
Frick, Willard B. *Humanistic Psychology: Interviews with Maslow, Murphy, and Rogers*. Columbus, OH: Charles E. Merrill, 1971.
Lowry, Richard J. *A. H. Maslow: An Intellectual Portrait*. Monterey, CA: Brookes Cole, 1973.
Maslow, Abraham. *Motivation and Personality*. 2nd ed. New York: Harper and Row, 1970.
Maslow, Abraham. *The Farther Reaches of Human Nature*. New York: Viking Press, 1971.

See also:
Frederick Herzberg (pp. 1218–1219)

1235

BUSINESS THINKERS

"True motivation comes from achievement, personal development, job satisfaction, and recognition."

Frederick Herzberg

Elton Mayo
The Hawthorne Experiments

George Elton Mayo (1880–1949) has secured fame as the leader in a series of experiments that became one of the great turning points in management thinking. At the Hawthorne plant of Western Electric, he discovered that job satisfaction increased through employee participation in decisions, rather than through short-term incentives.

1236

BUSINESS THINKERS

1880	Born.
1911	Appointed lecturer in logic, ethics, and psychology (later Professor of Philosophy) at University of Queensland.
1923	Moves to United States and takes a post at Pennsylvania University; conducts experiments on productivity in a spinning mill, related to working conditions.
1924–1932	Experiments are conducted at the Hawthorne plant.
1928	Moves to Harvard as associate professor of industrial research; becomes involved with Hawthorne experiments.
1929–1930	Deduces that a more listening, caring style of supervision raises morale and boosts productivity.
1930–1945	Develops TWI program.
1947	Retires from Harvard.
1947–1949	Advisor to British government on problems within industry.
1949	Dies.

LIFE AND CAREER

An Australian by birth, Mayo studied psychology at Adelaide University and, in 1911, was appointed lecturer in logic, ethics, and psychology (and later Professor of Philosophy) at the University of Queensland.

Anxious to move to the United States for professional reasons, he took a post at Pennsylvania University in 1923. Here, he became involved in one of the investigations that acted as a dry run for Hawthorne. In one department at a spinning mill in Philadelphia, labor turnover was 250%—compared with an average of 6% in other parts of the company. A series of experimental changes in working conditions was introduced in the department, most notably rest pauses. These changes led to successive increases in productivity and the raising of morale. After one year, labor turnover was down to the average level for the company. It was assumed that this improvement was due to the introduction of rest pauses—a conclusion that was to undergo substantial modification as a result of Hawthorne.

The Hawthorne experiments began in 1924 and Mayo's involvement in them in 1928, after he had moved to the Harvard University School of Business Administration as associate professor of industrial research. Later he became a professor and remained at Harvard until his retirement in 1947. During World War II, Mayo contributed to the development of supervisor training with his Training Within Industry (TWI) program, which was widely adopted in the United States. The last two years of his life were spent in the United Kingdom, as an advisor to the British government on problems within industry.

KEY THINKING

Mayo wrote about democracy and freedom, and the social problems of industrialized civilization. It is as the author of *Human Problems of an Industrial Civilization*, which reports on the Hawthorne experiments, that he is known for his contribution to management thinking, even though he disclaimed responsibility for the design and direction of the project.

Hawthorne

The Hawthorne plant of Western Electric was located in Chicago. It had some 29,000 employees and manufactured telephones and telephone equipment, principally for AT&T. The company had a reputation for advanced personnel policies and had welcomed a study by the National Research Council into the relationship between workplace lighting and the efficiency of individual workers.

The Experiments

The study began in 1924 by isolating two groups of workers in order to test the impact of various incentives on their productivity. Improvements to levels of lighting produced increases in productivity, but so, too, did reversion to standard lighting and even below-standard lighting in both groups. The initial assumption therefore was that increased output stemmed from variation alone.

Other incentives—including payment incentives and rest pauses—were manipulated at regular intervals and, although output levels varied, the trend was inexorably upwards. Whatever experimentation was applied, output went up. Although it had been fairly conclusively determined that lighting had little to do with output levels, the assistant works manager (George Pennock) agreed that something peculiar was going on, and that experimentation should continue.

Early Deductions—Supervision and Employee Attitudes

In the winter of 1927, Pennock invited Clair Turner, professor of biology and public health at Massachusetts Institute of Technology (MIT), to contribute. Turner quickly resolved that rest pauses in themselves were not the cause for increased output, although longer rest pauses gave rise to more social interaction, which in turn affected mental attitudes. Turner attributed the rise in output to the small group; the type of supervision; earnings; the novelty of the experiment; and the increased attention to the workers generated by the experiment itself.

Pennock had been among the first to note that supervisory style was important. The supervisor involved in the illumination experiment had been relaxed and friendly; he got to know the operators well and was not too worried about company policies and procedures. Discipline was secured through enlightened leadership, and an esprit de corps grew up within the group. This was in

"You can't treat your people like an expense item."

Andrew S. Grove

stark contrast to standard practice before the experiment.

When Pennock invited Turner to participate, he also invited Mayo—although it is not known whether this was a result of Mayo's achievements at the Philadelphia spinning mill, or because of a desire to involve Harvard. Visits in 1929 and 1930 indicated to Mayo "a remarkable change of attitude in the group." Mayo's view was that the test room workers had turned into a social unit, enjoyed all the attention they were getting, and had developed a sense of participation in the project.

In order to understand this further, Mayo instituted a series of interviews. These provided the workers with an opportunity to express their views. It emerged that they would feel better for discussing a situation, even if it did not change. Further exploration revealed that some complaints had little or no basis in fact, but were actually indicators of personal situations causing distress.

By focusing on a more open, listening and caring interview approach, Mayo had struck a chord which linked the style of supervision and the level of morale to levels of productivity.

Further Research—Social Groups

A third stage in the research took place in the bank wiring room, with a similar application of incentives to productivity. Here it emerged that output was restricted:

- The group had a standard for output that was respected by individuals in the group.
- The group was indifferent to the employer's financial incentive plan.
- The group developed a code of behavior of its own, based on solidarity in opposition to the management.
- Output was determined by informal social groups rather than by management.

Mayo had read the work of F. W. Taylor, who had already established that social groups were capable of exercising very strong control over the work behavior of individual members (Taylor had called it "systematic soldiering"). The interesting development that Mayo noted, however, was that whereas in the first set of experiments productivity went up as the project progressed, in the other—the bank wiring room—productivity was reduced.

In *The Human Problems of an Industrial Civilization*, Mayo wrote: "Human collaboration in work ... has always depended for its perpetuation upon the evolution of a nonlogical social code which regulates the relations between persons and their attitudes to one another. Insistence upon a merely economic logic of production ... interferes with the development of such a code and consequently gives rise in the group to a sense of human defeat. This ... results in the formation of a social code at a lower level and in opposition to the economic logic. One of its symptoms is 'restriction.'"

The question which needed to be asked, therefore, was, "What was different between the two groups?" The answer was found to lie with the attitude of the observer—where the observer encouraged participation and took the workers into his confidence, productivity went up; where the observer merely watched and adopted the trappings of traditional supervisory practice, output was reduced.

Interpreting Hawthorne

For industry to benefit from the experiments at Hawthorne, Mayo first concluded that supervisors needed training in understanding the personal problems of workers, and also in listening and interviewing techniques. He held that the new supervisor should be less aloof, more people-oriented, more concerned, and skilled in handling personal and social situations.

It was only later, after a period of reflection, that Mayo was able to conclude that:

- job satisfaction increased as workers were given more freedom to determine the conditions of their working environment and to set their own standards of output;
- intensified interaction and cooperation created a high level of group cohesion;
- job satisfaction and output depended more on cooperation and a feeling of worth than on physical working conditions.

In Mayo's view, workers had been unable to find satisfactory outlets for expressing personal problems and dissatisfactions in their work life. The problem was that managers thought the answers to industrial problems resided in technical efficiency, when actually the answer was a human and social one.

Mayo's contribution lies in recognizing that the formality of strict rules and procedures spawns informal approaches and groups with their base in human emotions, problems, and interactions. The manager, therefore, should strive for an equilibrium between the technical organization and the human one, and hence should develop skills in handling human relations and situations. These include diagnostic skills in understanding human behavior and interpersonal skills in counseling, motivating, leading, and communicating.

ELTON MAYO IN PERSPECTIVE

Mayo has been acclaimed by his followers as the founder of the human relations school of management, and criticized by sociologists for not going far enough in his interpretations.

Reading Mayo's conclusions causes no surprise—let alone discovery—at the end of the 20th century; his attitudes are increasingly commonplace among social scientists, labor unionists, and managers alike. But that is perhaps a measure of his achievement, because most commentators agree that he was the first to demonstrate, infer, and provide evidence for the benefits of a shift in management thinking away from the widespread dominance of Taylor's scientific management.

F.J. Roethlisberger said of Mayo that the data were not his; the results were not his; but the interpretations of both were indeed his. Without those interpretations, the results of Hawthorne might still be collecting dust in the archives.

The experiment also gave rise to the term "Hawthorne effect"—a situation that arises because people are "singled out" for special treatment, or a "special situation" is created, in which workers can feel free to air their problems.

Mayo's ideas on the emergence of "informal" organizations were read by Argyris and others as they developed theories about how organizations learned and developed. The discrediting of the "rabble hypothesis" theory led directly to the work of McGregor.

The conclusions drawn by Mayo from the Hawthorne studies established the beginnings of recognition that management style is a major contributor to industrial productivity; that interpersonal skills are as important as monetary incentives or target-setting, and that a more humanistic approach is an important means of satisfying the organization's economic and social needs.

1237

BUSINESS THINKERS

FOR MORE INFORMATION

Books:

Mayo, Elton. *The Human Problems of an Industrial Civilization*. Revised ed. New York: Routledge, 2003.

Mayo, Elton. *The Social Problems of an Industrial Civilization*. Boston, MA: Harvard University Press, 1945

See also:

- Douglas McGregor (pp. 1238–1239)

"The art of leadership is to mobilize people to care about the tasks ahead."

Doris Helen Kearns Goodwin

Douglas McGregor
Theory X and Theory Y

Developer of Theory X and Theory Y, which describe two views of people at work and two opposing management styles, Douglas McGregor's relatively short career has been a key influence for many of today's management commentators. *The Human Side of Enterprise* marked a watershed in management thinking, and laid the foundations for the modern, people-centered view of management.

1906	Born.
1932	Graduates from Wayne University.
1935	Receives Ph.D. in Experimental Psychology from Harvard University.
1948–1954	President, Antioch College.
1954	Professor of Management, Massachusetts Institute of Technology.
1960	Publication of *The Human Side of Enterprise*.
1964	Dies.
1993	Listed as one of the most popular management writers alongside Henri Fayol.

LIFE AND CAREER

Douglas McGregor (1906–1964) followed a mostly academic career, lecturing at Harvard University, Massachusetts Institute of Technology (MIT) and Antioch College, where he became the first Sloan Fellows professor at MIT. Although he wrote only a few publications before his early death, they have had a great impact.

In 1993 McGregor was listed as one of the most popular management writers alongside Henri Fayol (in *Management Gurus—What Makes Them and How to Become One*). Major U.S. writers such as Rosabeth Moss Kanter, Warren Bennis, and Tom Peters, whose writings have much influence on current learning and practice, agree that much of modern management thinking goes back to McGregor, especially the implications of his writing for theories on leadership.

KEY THINKING

McGregor believed that managers' basic beliefs have a dominant influence on the way that organizations are run, and central to this are managers' assumptions about the behavior of people. McGregor argues that these assumptions fall into two broad categories—Theory X and Theory Y. His findings were detailed in *The Human Side of Enterprise*, first published in 1960.

Theory X and Theory Y describe two views of people at work and may be used to describe two opposing management styles.

Theory X: The Traditional View of Direction and Control

Theory X is based on the assumptions that:
- the average human being has an inherent dislike of work and will avoid it if at all possible;
- because of this human dislike of work, most people must be coerced, controlled, directed, and threatened with punishment to get them to make an adequate effort toward the achievement of organizational objectives;
- the average human being prefers to be directed; wishes to avoid responsibility; has relatively little ambition; wants security above all else.

A Theory X management style therefore requires close, firm supervision with clearly specified tasks and the threat of punishment or the promise of greater pay as motivating factors. Managers working under these assumptions will employ autocratic controls that can lead to mistrust and resentment from those they manage. McGregor acknowledges that this approach constitutes a damning statement about the "mediocrity of the masses." He acknowledges, too, that the "carrot and stick" approach can have a place but will not work when the needs of people are predominantly social and egoistic.

Theory Y: The Integration of Individual and Organizational Goals

Theory Y is based on the assumptions that:
- the expenditure of physical and mental effort in work is as natural as play or rest. The average human being does not inherently dislike work. Depending on controllable conditions, work may be a source of satisfaction, or a source of punishment;
- external control and the threat of punishment are not the only means for bringing about effort toward achieving organizational objectives. People will exercise self-direction and self-control in the service of objectives to which they are committed;
- commitment to objectives is a result of the rewards associated with their achievement. The most significant of such rewards, such as the satisfaction of ego and self-actualization needs, can be direct products of effort directed toward organizational objectives;
- under proper conditions, the average human being learns not only to accept but to seek responsibility. Avoidance of responsibility, lack of ambition, and emphasis on security are generally consequences of experience, not inherent human characteristics;
- the capacity to exercise a relatively high degree of imagination, ingenuity, and creativity in the solution of organizational problems is widely, not narrowly, distributed in the population;
- under the conditions of modern industrial life, the intellectual potential of the average human being is used only partially.

Theory Y assumptions can lead to more cooperative relationships between managers and workers. A Theory Y management style seeks to establish a working environment in which the personal needs and objectives of individuals can relate to, and harmonize with, the objectives of the organization.

In *The Human Side of Enterprise*, McGregor recognizes that Theory Y is not a panacea for all ills. But by highlighting such ideas, he hopes instead to achieve an abandonment by management of the limiting assumptions of Theory X and a consideration of the techniques involved in Theory Y.

Theory into Practice

Abraham Maslow viewed McGregor as a mentor, and was a strong supporter of theories X and Y. So he decided to put

---

"Commitment to objectives is a function of the rewards associated with their achievement."

Douglas McGregor

Theory Y (that people want to work, achieve, and take responsibility) into practice in a Californian electronics factory. However, he found that an organization driven solely by Theory Y could not succeed, as some sense of direction and structure was required. Instead, he advocated an improved version of Theory Y that involved an element of structured security and direction taken from Theory X.

Maslow's negative experience with implementing Theory Y must be balanced against that of McGregor himself at a Procter & Gamble plant in Georgia, where he introduced Theory Y through the concept of self-directed teams. This plant was found to be a third more profitable than any other Procter & Gamble plant; it was kept a trade secret until the mid-1990s.

Before he died, McGregor began to develop a further theory that addressed the criticisms made of theories X and Y—that they were mutually incompatible. Ideas he proposed as part of this theory included lifetime employment; concern for employees (both inside and outside the working environment); decision by consensus; and commitment to quality. He tentatively called it Theory Z. Before it could be widely published, McGregor died and the ideas faded.

Theory Z
The work on Theory Z that McGregor began was not completely forgotten. During the 1970s, William Ouchi began to expound its principles by comparing and contrasting Japanese (Type J) and U.S. (Type A) organizations.

Type A organizations, he proposed, tend to offer short-term employment, specialized careers (with rapid promotion), and individual decision making and responsibility. Type J companies, on the other hand, mirror the ethos of Japanese society—collectivism and stability rather than individuality. Those U.S. companies that share Type J characteristics, and indeed have more in common with Type J organizations, were described as Type Z (examples included Hewlett-Packard and Procter & Gamble).

Leadership
Before McGregor, the thrust of writing about leadership focused on the qualities and characteristics of "great people," in the hope that, if those qualities were identified, they could be emulated.

McGregor argued that there were other variables involved in leadership, including the attitudes and needs of the followers, the nature and structure of the organization itself, and the social, economic, and political environment. For McGregor, leadership was not a property of the individual but a complex relationship among these variables. He was one of the first to argue that leadership was more about the relationship between the leader and the situation he or she faced, than merely the characteristics of the leader alone.

DOUGLAS MCGREGOR IN PERSPECTIVE
The Human Side of Enterprise marked a watershed in management thinking that had previously been dominated by the scientific approach of Taylor, and formed the foundations for the current, people-centered view of management.

Theory Y has been criticized for being too idealistic, but if we examine each of the six tenets of Theory Y in turn, we can trace much modern thinking back to McGregor:

1. Work, as a source of satisfaction, means accepting that people need to know not just what or how, but why; the adoption of meaningful objectives is one of the keys to self-motivation.

2–4. Ownership, commitment, and responsibility are three of the cornerstones of empowerment.

5–6. The encouragement for people to be fully exercised in the solution of organizational problems is central to action learning, total quality management, strategic thinking, and knowledge exploitation.

As mentioned above, Moss Kanter (writing on empowerment), Bennis (on leadership), and Peters (on excellence as well as chaos) all acknowledge their debt to McGregor.

Contemporary and subsequent commentaries on McGregor's theories have tended to see them as black and white. Harold Geneen, former president and C.E.O. of ITT, commented that although Theories X and Y propose a neat summary of business management, no company is run in strict accordance with either one or the other. Peter Drucker said that Theory X sees people as immature, whereas Theory Y sees them striving towards adulthood.

The two contrasting theories are best seen perhaps as two polarizing forces with which managers have to grapple. Blake and Mouton expressed this in terms of the managerial grid, where managers constantly have to balance the drives and forces between task (getting things done) and people (how best to get them done for the benefit of the organization and the individuals doing them).

Although Theory Y has been held up as an unachievable goal—with the individual and the organization having convergent aspirations—the successful cases in which this goal is being attempted are growing. It is precisely such a goal that organizations are hoping to achieve through continuous improvement, continuous professional development, and participation plans, operating in climates of empowerment.

It is not going too far to say that *The Human Side of Enterprise* recognizes that although we cannot actually motivate people, we do have a responsibility to acknowledge the elements involved in motivation. What we can do is to attempt to create the right climate, environment, or working conditions for motivation to be enabled.

1239

BUSINESS THINKERS

FOR MORE INFORMATION

Books:
Huczynski, Andreas. *Management Gurus—What Makes Them and How to Become One.* London: Routledge, 1992.
McGregor, Douglas. *The Human Side of Enterprise.* Revised ed. New York: McGraw-Hill, 2006.
McGregor, Douglas. *Leadership and Motivation.* Boston, MA: MIT Press, 1966.
McGregor, Douglas. *The Professional Manager.* New York: McGraw-Hill, 1967.
Ouchi, William G. *Theory Z: How American Business Can Meet the Japanese Challenge.* Reading, MA: Addison Wesley, 1981.

See also:
Elton Mayo (pp. 1236–1237)
Kurt Lewin (pp. 1230–1231)

"The process of developing heterogeneous resources must be continuous; it is never completed."
Douglas McGregor

Henry Mintzberg
A Great Generalist

Often regarded as an iconoclast and a rebel, Henry Mintzberg (1939–) has certainly challenged many traditional ideas. But he does not attack people with whom he disagrees; he simply sets about proving them wrong, with devastating clarity. In his writing—the product of a career devoted to understanding how people actually manage—he resists every temptation to pontificate about how anyone ought to manage.

1939	Born.
1961	Receives a B.Eng. from McGill University.
1961–1963	Operational Research with Canadian National Railways.
1968	Receives a Ph.D. and becomes professor at McGill University; also subsequently becomes director of the Center for Strategic Studies.
1973	Publication of *The Nature of Managerial Work*.
1975	Wins the McKinsey Prize for best article.
1988–1991	President of the Strategic Management Society.
1991–	Holds other positions in management institutions, including that of visiting professor at INSEAD in France.
1995	*Academy of Management* receives the George R. Terry best book of the year award.
1995–2000	Director of International Masters Program in Practicing Management.
1996	Appointed Cleghorn Professor of Management Studies at McGill University.

LIFE AND CAREER

Henry Mintzberg was born in Canada and has spent virtually all his working life there. He studied at McGill University and, after further study at MIT, returned to Canada to take up an appointment with Canadian National Railways in 1961. In 1963 he moved into the academic world and by 1968 was back at McGill University as a professor, a post he holds to the present day. He is also director of the Center for Strategic Studies in

Organization at McGill and has held several important positions in other management institutions, including that of visiting professor at INSEAD, the international business school at Fontainebleau in France. He has been a consultant to many organizations throughout the world and from 1988 to 1991 he was president of the Strategic Management Society.

Mintzberg's major impact on the management world began with his book *The Nature of Managerial Work*, published in 1973, and a seminal article in the *Harvard Business Review*, "The Manager's Job: Folklore and Fact," written two years later. Based on detailed research and thoughtful observation, these two works established Mintzberg's reputation by showing that what managers did, when successfully carrying out their responsibilities, was substantially different from much business theory.

KEY THINKING

Unlike many gurus, Mintzberg's contribution to management thinking is not based on one or two clever theories within some narrow discipline. His approach is broad, involving the study of virtually everything managers do and how they do it. His general appeal is further enhanced by a fundamental belief that management is about applying human skills to systems, not applying systems to people, a belief that is demonstrated throughout his writing.

How Managers Work

In "The Manager's Job: Folklore and Fact," Mintzberg sets out the stark reality of what managers do. "If there is a simple theme that runs through this article, it is that the pressures of his job drive the manager to be superficial in his actions—to overload himself with work, encourage interruption, re-

spond quickly to every stimulus, seek the tangible and avoid the abstract, make decisions in small increments, and do everything abruptly," he writes.

Mintzberg uses the article to stress the importance of the manager's role and the need to understand it thoroughly before attempting to train and develop those engaged in carrying it out.

"No job is more vital to our society than that of the manager. It is the manager who determines whether our social institutions serve us well or whether they squander our talents and resources. It is time to strip away the folklore about managerial work, and time to study it realistically so that we can begin the difficult task of making significant improvements in its performance." In *The Nature of Managerial Work*, Mintzberg proposes six characteristics of management work and ten basic management roles. These characteristics and roles, he suggests, apply to all management jobs, from supervisor to chief executive.

The six characteristics are:
- the manager's job is a mixture of regular, programmed jobs and unprogrammed tasks;
- a manager is both a generalist and a specialist;
- managers rely on information from all sources but show a preference for that which is transmitted orally;
- managerial work is made up of activities that are characterized by brevity, variety and fragmentation;
- management work is more an art than a science and is reliant on intuitive processes and a "feel" for what is right;
- management work is becoming more complex.

Mintzberg places the ten roles that he believes make up the content of the manager's job into three categories.

Interpersonal
- Figurehead—performing symbolic duties as a representative of the organization
- Leader—establishing the atmosphere and motivating the subordinates
- Liaiser—developing and maintaining webs of contacts outside the organization

Information
- Monitor—collecting all types of information that are relevant and useful to the organization

---

"Strategy is not the consequence of planning but the opposite, its starting point."

Henry Mintzberg

- Disseminator—transmitting information from outside the organization to those inside
- Spokesperson—transmitting information from inside the organization to outsiders

Decision Making
- Entrepreneur—initiating change and adapting to the environment
- Disturbance Handler—dealing with unexpected events
- Resource Allocator—deciding on the use of the organization's resources
- Negotiator—negotiating with individuals and dealing with other organizations

The Structuring of Organizations

In his 1979 book, *The Structuring of Organizations*, Mintzberg identified five types of "ideal" organization structures. These were: simple structure; machine bureaucracy; professional bureaucracy; divisional; and adhocracy. The classification was reexamined ten years later in *Mintzberg on Management* and the following, more detailed, view of organization types drawn up:

- the Entrepreneurial Organization—small staff, loose division of labor, little management hierarchy, informal, with power focused on the chief executive;
- the Machine Organization—highly specialized, routine operating tasks, formal communication, large operating units, tasks grouped under functions, elaborate administrative systems, central decision making, and a sharp distinction between line and staff;
- the Diversified Organization—a set of semiautonomous units under a central administrative structure. The units are usually called divisions and the central administration referred to as the headquarters;
- the Professional Organization—commonly found in hospitals, universities, public agencies, and firms doing routine work, this structure relies on the skills and knowledge of professional staff in order to function. All such organizations produce standardized products or services;
- the Innovative Organization—this is what Mintzberg sees as the modern organization: one that is flexible, rejecting any form of bureaucracy and avoiding emphasis on planning and control systems. Innovation is achieved by hiring experts; giving them power; training and developing them; and employing them in multidisciplinary teams that work in an atmosphere unbounded by conventional specialties and differentiation;
- the Missionary Organization—it is the mission that counts above all else in such or-

ganizations, and the mission is clear, focused, distinctive, and inspiring. Employees readily identify with the mission, share common values and are motivated by their own zeal and enthusiasm.

Strategy and Planning

In his 1994 book, *The Rise and Fall of Strategic Planning*, Mintzberg produces a masterly criticism of conventional theory. His main concern is with what he sees as basic failings in our approach to planning.

- processes—the elaborate processes used create bureaucracy and suppress innovation and originality
- data—"hard" data (the raw material of all strategists) provides information, but "soft" data provides wisdom. "Hard information can be no better and is often at times far worse than soft information."
- detachment—it is no use producing strategies in "ivory towers." Effective strategists are not people who distance themselves from the detail of a business " . . . but quite the opposite: they are the ones who immerse themselves in it, while being able to abstract the strategic messages from it."
- strategy—it is not "the consequence of planning but the opposite: its starting point." Mintzberg has coined the phrase "crafting strategies" to illustrate his concept of the delicate, painstaking process of developing strategy—a process of emergence that is far removed from the classical picture of strategists grouped around a table predicting the future. He argues that while an organization needs a strategy, strategic plans are generally useless as one cannot predict two to three years ahead.

HENRY MINTZBERG IN PERSPECTIVE

Henry Mintzberg remains one of the few truly generalist management writers of today. His work covers such a wide perspective that different readers see him as an expert in different areas. For some people, he is an authority on time management, and he has written some of the most practical advice on this subject; for others he is the champion of hard-pressed managers, surrounded by management theorists telling them how to do their jobs; and for yet another group, he is a leading authority on strategic planning.

For most people, however, Mintzberg is the man who dared to challenge orthodox beliefs and who, by the scholarly presentation of research findings and some truly original thinking, has changed our ideas about many key business activities.

FOR MORE INFORMATION

Books:
Mintzberg, Henry. *The Nature of Managerial Work*. New York: Harper & Row, 1973.
Mintzberg, Henry. *The Structuring of Organizations*. Englewood Cliffs, NJ: Prentice Hall, 1979.
Mintzberg, Henry. *Structure in Fives: Designing Effective Organizations*. Englewood Cliffs, NJ: Prentice Hall, 1983.
Mintzberg, Henry. *Power In and Around Organizations*. Englewood Cliffs, NJ: Prentice Hall, 1983.
Mintzberg, Henry. *Mintzberg on Management*. New York: Free Press, 1989.
Mintzberg, Henry. *The Rise and Fall of Strategic Planning*. Englewood Cliffs, NJ: Prentice Hall International, 1994.
Mintzberg, Henry, and J. B. Quinn. *The Strategy Process: Concepts, Contexts, Cases*. 3rd ed. Englewood Cliffs, NJ: Prentice Hall International, 1996.
Mintzberg, Henry, Bruce Ahlstrand, and Joseph Lempel. *Strategy Safari*. New York: Free Press, 1998.
Mintzberg, Henry. *Managers, Not MBAs*. San Francisco, CA: Berrett-Koehler, 2004.
Mintzberg, Henry, Bruce Ahlstrand, and Joseph Lempel. *Strategy Bites Back*. Englewood Cliffs, NJ: Prentice Hall, 2004.

Journal Articles:
Mintzberg, Henry. "The Manager's Job: Folklore and Fact." *Harvard Business Review*, March/April, pp. 163–176. (Originally published in 1975, the article includes a retrospective commentary by the author.)
Mintzberg, Henry. "Crafting Strategy." *Harvard Business Review*, July/August 1987, pp. 66–75.
Mintzberg, Henry. "The Fall and Rise of Strategic Planning." *Harvard Business Review*, January/February 1994, pp. 107–114.
Mintzberg, Henry. "Rounding Out the Manager's Job." *Sloan Management Review*, Fall 1994, pp. 11–26.
Mintzberg, Henry. "Musings on Management." *Harvard Business Review*, July/August 1996, pp. 61–67.

See also:
 Alfred D. Chandler, Jr. (pp. 1190–1191)
Kenichi Ohmae (pp. 1244–1245)
Michael Porter (pp. 1254–1255)
Peter Drucker (pp. 1198–1201)

"Society has become unmanageable as a result of management." — Henry Mintzberg

Ikujiro Nonaka
Knowledge Creation

The work of Ikujiro Nonaka is best known for its focus on the creation of knowledge within organizations. Nonaka believes that this is the most meaningful core capability for a company, particularly because it leads to innovation. He argues that the knowledge generated becomes the key source of competitive advantage for the company.

Nonaka's work has been influential to many industries.

1935	Born.
1958	Graduates from Waseda University.
1995	Publication of *The Knowledge-Creating Company*.
1995	Joins Japan Advanced Institute of Science and Technology (JAIST).
1997	Becomes dean of the school of knowledge science at JAIST.
1997	Named Xerox Distinguished Fellow in Knowledge at Haas School of Business, Berkeley.
2000	Appointed professor in the Graduate School of International Corporate Strategy, Hitotsubashi University.

LIFE AND CAREER

Ikujiro Nonaka (born 1935) is the first professor of knowledge at the Haas School of Business, University of California, where he previously received his MBA and Ph.D. degrees. From 1997 to 2000 he was dean of the graduate school of knowledge science at the Japan Advanced Institute of Science and Technology (JAIST) in Japan. He is a professor at the Graduate School of International Corporate Strategy at Hitotsubashi University, Tokyo.

Professor Nonaka has described his work as comparative research on knowledge-creating processes in companies around the world, and also research on the characteristics of innovative activities in Japanese companies. He seeks to answer questions about what knowledge is, how organizations create knowledge, and how we can promote knowledge creation.

KEY THINKING

In their book *The Knowledge-Creating Company: How Japanese Companies Create the Dynamics of Innovation*, Ikujiro Nonaka and Hirotaka Takeuchi argue that the success of Japanese companies is due to their skill and expertise in organizational knowledge creation, especially with respect to bringing about continuous business innovation. They use the metaphor of a journey, warning that there are new and foreign road signs to follow on the way. The book, which combines theoretical and philosophical analysis with practical case studies, attempts to convey the complex forces at work within creative organizational systems. It is not straightforward to read, but the authors justify this with the declaration that " . . . managers can no longer afford to be satisfied with simplistic ideas about knowledge and its creation."

Explicit and Implicit Knowledge

Nonaka and Takeuchi's starting point is a contrast between Western and Eastern philosophies. In the West knowledge is unambiguous, systematic, falsifiable, and scientific, and a quest for knowledge normally involves the analysis and interpretation of data and information. New knowledge is documented and then transferred by means of formal training. The authors describe this form of knowledge as "explicit." It is primarily managed through databases and manuals. Human expertise, experience, and insights are, they claim, generally ignored as sources of knowledge.

In the East, however, knowledge is intuitive, interpretive, ambiguous, non-linear, and difficult to reduce to scientific equations. Instead of being created through data analysis and interpretation, it grows from the expertise and experience of many people, whose minds are probed for insights. New knowledge is distributed and re-tained through experience. The resulting Eastern form of knowledge is described as "implicit."

In the authors' view, implicit and explicit knowledge are not totally separate but mutually complementary entities. Successful Japanese companies are able to convert implicit knowledge to explicit knowledge, so that knowledge acquired by individuals becomes organizational knowledge shared among colleagues, and explicit knowledge is converted into implicit knowledge by individuals. Nonaka and Takeuchi refer to this interaction between implicit and explicit knowledge as knowledge conversion. They suggest four methods of knowledge conversion, otherwise known as the SECI process:

- socialization
- externalization
- combination
- internalization

These are described as the mechanisms by which implicit knowledge is "amplified" throughout the organization, creating a spiral model of knowledge creation.

Middle-up-down Management Style

Nonaka and Takeuchi argue that the two traditional Western management styles, "top-down" and "bottom-up," fail to foster the dynamic interaction necessary to create organizational knowledge.

Successful Japanese companies acknowledge the vital role played by middle managers in taking the top management vision of "what should be" and the frontline employees' realistic sense of "what is," and developing midrange concepts. Middle managers are, in effect, the real "knowledge engineers" of the knowledge-creating company, serving as facilitators between top and bottom as well as between theory and reality, and playing a key role in innovation.

A "hypertext" organization consisting of interconnected layers is put forward as the ideal structure for knowledge creation. It combines two traditional structures—the hierarchy and the task force. Surprisingly, the model for this organizational form is the U.S. military, which is bureaucratic in peacetime but highly task-oriented in war. Nonaka and Takeuchi provide two case studies of Japanese companies that have attempted to implement a hypertext structure—Kao and Sharp.

"The biggest opportunity is harnessing our knowledge within the organisation to provide better solutions."

Martin Sorrell

Transferring Knowledge

The Knowledge-Creating Company is rich in case studies, which are mostly based on large, well-established Japanese companies, including Matsushita, NEC, Canon, Honda, and Nissan. Many of the case studies describe a "transferring process," in which the organizational knowledge created during new product development in one division becomes transferred to other parts of the company. For example, the knowledge created within Canon while developing the mini-copier in the early 1980s was subsequently used in other areas. The product knowledge generated was applied to other equipment such as printers; the knowledge gained from the manufacturing process led to the automation of copier production; and the organizational knowledge gleaned, especially with respect to the role of middle managers and cross-functional working, influenced the way the company was managed.

The transfer of knowledge can also take place at a global level. The case of Shin Caterpillar Mitsubishi, a U.S.–Japanese alliance, shows how knowledge creation can cut across company as well as national boundaries. It refers to the experience of Mitsubishi of Japan and Caterpillar of the United States when they pooled their resources to develop and market hydraulic shovels. Nonaka and Takeuchi demonstrate that using the four stages of knowledge conversion within the alliance averted potentially damaging clashes of culture, overcame the weaknesses of both sides in knowledge creation, and led to effective knowledge creation and innovation.

Practical Implications

The authors finish with some recommendations as to what Western companies can do to become knowledge-creating companies. They should:

- create a knowledge vision (top management should define the boundaries of organizational knowledge and outline what kind of knowledge ought to be created);
- develop a knowledge crew (of employees with diverse talents);
- build a high-density field of interaction (an environment in which frequent and intensive interactions take place) at the frontline;
- piggyback on the new product development process;
- adopt middle-up-down management;
- switch to a hypertext organization;
- construct a knowledge network with the outside world (meaning external stakeholders such as customers).

The Concept of "Ba" or Shared Spaces

Since the publication of *The Knowledge-Creating Company*, Nonaka has developed the theory of "Ba," which provides a platform for creating knowledge. Ba means "place" or "shared spaces" and can be physical (for example, an office), virtual (for example, e-mail) or mental (for example, shared experiences, ideas, and, by extension, organization culture). Nonaka argues that knowledge cannot be separated from its context and is embedded in these shared spaces.

Nonaka describes four kinds of platform corresponding to the four stages of knowledge conversion mentioned above. Each space supports a particular conversion process and thereby speeds up overall knowledge creation.

- Originating (supports the socialization stage)—physical face-to-face experiences which provide the environment in which individuals share feelings and experiences. These are the key to the transfer of tacit knowledge.
- Interacting (supports the externalization stage)—a team-based environment, where individuals' mental models and skills are converted into common terms and concepts. This assists the process in which tacit knowledge is made explicit.
- Cyber (supports the combination stage)—interaction in the virtual world of cyberspace. This facilitates the exchanging and combining of different forms of explicit knowledge.
- Exercising (supports the internalization stage)—focused training with senior mentors and colleagues which assists the conversion of explicit knowledge into tacit knowledge.

"Knowledge Activists"

Knowledge activists support platforms and cultures by enabling knowledge creation. A knowledge activist can be an individual, group, or department that takes on a particular responsibility for energizing and coordinating knowledge creation throughout the organization. The activist has three roles: to act as a catalyst for knowledge creation, to coordinate knowledge creation initiatives, and to provide overall direction to these efforts.

IKUJIRO NONAKA IN PERSPECTIVE

Peter Drucker first used the terms "knowledge worker" and "knowledge society" in the 1960s and more recently stated that knowledge has become the only meaningful resource. Nonaka acknowledges Drucker's

contribution and takes it a stage further by looking at how knowledge is created and examining the processes and mechanisms involved.

The second half of the 1990s saw a huge surge of business interest in knowledge, led primarily by practitioners rather than academics. Nonaka provided ideas that gave purpose and direction to practitioner initiatives. No other writer in this field has made such a forceful business case for knowledge creation. Also, in contrast with much of the organizational thinking on knowledge management prevalent today, Nonaka reminds us that information technology is not enough and that human experience and implicit knowledge are important in creating new knowledge. Lastly, Nonaka emphasized the importance of middle management in organization information creation as early as 1988, and this was a significant departure from the Western view of middle management as a deadweight, potentially expendable part of the corporate structure.

In these respects Nonaka's ideas have been absorbed into the mainstream of management thinking and are almost taken for granted. Few organizations, however, have embraced his vision in its entirety, or attempted the kind of cultural and organizational restructuring to improve knowledge creation which he advocates.

FOR MORE INFORMATION

Books:
Nonaka, Ikujiro, and Hirotaka Takeuchi. *The Knowledge-creating Company: How Japanese Companies Create the Dynamics of Innovation.* New York: Oxford University Press, 1995.
Nonaka, Ikujiro, Georg Von Krogh, and Kazuo Ichijo. *Enabling Knowledge Creation.* New York: Oxford University Press, 2000.

Journal Articles:
Nonaka, Ikujiro. "The Knowledge-Creating Company." *Harvard Business Review,* vol. 69 no. 6, November/December 1991, pp. 96–104.
Nonaka, Ikujiro, Georg Von Krogh, and Kazuo Ichijo. "Develop Knowledge Activists!" *European Management Journal,* vol. 15 no. 5, October 1997, pp. 475–483.
Nonaka, Ikujiro, Ryoko Toyama, and Noboru Konno. "SEC BA and Leadership: A Unified Model of Dynamic Knowledge Creation." *Long Range Planning,* vol. 33 no. 1, February 2000, pp. 5–34.

1243

BUSINESS THINKERS

"Bureaucratic administration means fundamentally the exercise of control on the basis of knowledge."

Max Weber

Kenichi Ohmae
The Art of Japanese Business

Ohmae's fresh approach to business strategy challenged business leaders to think in innovative, simple, and unconventional terms. His work in the late 1970s and 1980s heralded the arrival of Japanese management techniques in the West. Ohmae was the messenger for the Japanese way of doing business, urging managers to think "out of the box," and challenge accepted norms with clear, simple ideas in order to gain, and sustain, competitive advantage.

1943	Born.
1972	Joins McKinsey & Co.
1975	Publication of *The Mind of the Strategist*.
1987	Publication of *Beyond National Boundaries*.
1990	Publication of *The Borderless World*.
1995	Stands as candidate for governorship of Tokyo.
1995	Publication of *The End of the Nation State*.
1997	Joins UCLA's School of Public and Social Research.

LIFE AND CAREER

Kenichi Ohmae was born in 1943 on the island of Kyushu, and graduated from Waseda University and the Tokyo Institute of Technology before obtaining a Ph.D. in nuclear engineering from the Massachusetts Institute of Technology. In 1972 he joined the consulting firm McKinsey & Co, becoming managing director of their Tokyo office. As well as being a nuclear physicist, he is an accomplished clarinettist and a politician. In 1995, he ran for election as governor of Tokyo and also acted as an adviser to Japan's then prime minister, Nakasone.

Ohmae lives in Yokohama and advises some of Japan's most successful international companies in a wide spectrum of industries. His special interest and area of expertise is in formulating creative strategies and developing organizational concepts to implement them.

Ohmae's seminal book, *The Mind of the Strategist*, was published in Japan in 1975. It was, however, only when interest in Japanese management methods increased dur-

ing the early 1980s that the book was published in the United States. This 1982 U.S. edition was given the subtitle *The Art of Japanese Business*. In *The Mind of the Strategist* Ohmae argues that the success of Japanese companies can be attributed to the nature of Japanese strategic thinking. This, contrary to the Western stereotype of Japanese management, was largely creative, intuitive, and vision-driven. Ohmae went on to explain what this creativity involved and how it could be learned.

The view presented by Ohmae overturned traditional Western perceptions of Japanese managers, and the idea that their success was founded on brilliantly rational, farsighted thinking. Ohmae heralded a revolution based on creativity and innovation, and showed how, in the hands of a single, talented strategist, creativity could transform a major corporation.

In 1990, Ohmae's book *The Borderless World* challenged Japanese companies and corporations around the world to take account of globalization in their strategic planning. He urged businesses to focus less on the competitive aspects of strategy (promoted so effectively by Porter and others), and instead to give greater focus to "country" and "currency," two key elements that in an interdependent world economy can make or break a business strategy. This approach reflected Ohmae's increasing focus on global business and the relationship between business and the nation state. The latter was also the subject of two other books, *Beyond National Boundaries* (1987) and *The End of the Nation State* (1995).

Just as *The Mind of the Strategist* had encouraged innovation in strategy in the 1980s, so *The Borderless World* highlighted

the importance of the global interdependence that dominated trade in the 1990s.

KEY THINKING
The Role of the Strategist

Ohmae has explored a number of features of successful business strategies (usually Japanese), and compared them with their typical counterparts in the West. He identified several key differences.

- Vision and dynamic leadership. Japanese businesses tend to have a single, driving force in the form of an effective strategist, a leader, or a visionary who possesses what Ohmae has described as an idiosyncratic mode of thinking. Through this, company, customers, and competition (described as the strategic triangle) merge into a dynamic interaction from which a comprehensive set of objectives and plans for action eventually emerges. This approach was in marked contrast to the large, strategic planning bureaucracies that were typical of many large Western corporations of the time (the early 1980s).
- Customer focus. The customer is at the heart of Japanese strategy and is virtually enshrined as central to corporate values. The focus of the business needs to be on delivering what the customer wants, or there will be no business.
- Methodology. Ohmae perceived that to develop effective strategies, managers must first gain a detailed understanding of the characteristics of each element in a situation, and then develop a holistic plan tying each part of the business, each separate resource, into a competitive and efficient operation. This is not a systems approach based on linear thinking, but instead relies on detailed analysis ("the starting point") and knowledge, combined with innovation, intuition, and creativity.

The Strategic Triangle

Ohmae claimed that, in constructing any business strategy, the three main players to be taken into account are the corporation itself, the customer, and the competition. Each of these three Cs is a living entity with its own interests and objectives, while collectively they form the strategic triangle. The three Cs influence strategy and planning in a number of important ways.

1. *Strategic business units (SBUs)*. The need for strategic business units that understand

all three elements and to which strategic decisions can be delegated is held to be essential, in order to take adequate account of the strategic triangle. This is particularly the case for a large company made up of a number of different businesses selling to different customer groups (probably with different competitors). The definition of a business unit is always likely to be in dispute, so Ohmae suggests asking three key questions as a test:

- Are customer wants well defined and understood by the industry, and is the market segmented so that differences in those wants are treated differently?
- Is the business unit (an aspect of the corporation) equipped to respond easily to customer wants and needs?
- Do competitors have different sets of conditions that give them a relative advantage over the business unit?

If the business unit seems unable to compete effectively, then it should be redefined to better meet customer needs and competitive threats.

2. *Freedom of operation*. The SBU must have full freedom of operation across the strategic triangle in order to develop and implement an effective strategy. In devising a strategy the SBU must be able to:

- address the total market for its customers;
- encompass all the critical functions of the corporation (i.e. procurement, design, manufacturing, sales, marketing, distribution, and service) in order to respond with maximum freedom to the total needs of the customer;
- understand all key aspects of the competitor so that the corporation can seize an advantage when opportunities arise, and exploit any unexpected sources of strength.

3. *Matching the corporation with the market*. In the context of the strategic triangle, Ohmae sees the role of the strategist as matching the strengths of the corporation to the needs of a clearly defined market. Such matching, however, is relative to the capabilities of the competition. For this reason, Ohmae defines a successful strategy as one that ensures a better or stronger matching of corporate strengths to customer needs than that provided by competitors.

Four Routes to Strategic Advantage

In *The Mind of the Strategist*, Ohmae identi- fies four ways in which a corporation can gain advantage over its competitors.

- A business strategy based on Key Factors for Success (KFS). The business is required to identify what it does to give it an advantage over its competitors, or where the potential for advantage is greatest, and then concentrate resources there.
- Relative superiority. If a business is still unable to gain an advantage over its competitors and the KFS struggle is being waged equally, then any difference between the two competing businesses can be exploited. This might, for example, mean linking products together through the sales network to provide customers with better offers.
- Aggressive initiatives. When a competitor is established in a stagnant, low-growth industry, then Ohmae advocates an unconventional strategy aimed at upsetting the competitor's KFS. This can be achieved by challenging the accepted ways of doing business in the industry—upsetting the status quo.
- Strategic degrees of freedom. Success in the competitive struggle can be achieved by a business strategy based on the use of innovations. This may involve the vigorous opening up of new markets or the development of new products in areas untouched by the competition.

In each case, Ohmae believes that the main concern is to avoid taking the same approach in the same market as the competition.

KENICHI OHMAE IN PERSPECTIVE

Gary Hamel, among others, has recognized Ohmae's immense influence, emphasizing the impact of his challenge to managers to think in new and unconventional ways. It is a testament to the strength and appeal of Ohmae's work that, although the growth of the Japanese economy faltered during the 1990s, his ideas are still regarded as fundamental contributions to strategic management.

It might be argued that Ohmae's emphasis on strategic creativity helped to lay the foundations for the radical, transforming management approaches of the 1980s and 1990s. Certainly, if one accepts the need for an intuitive, innovative strategist, then it seems likely that there will be widespread changes in the ways that organizations are managed. So it was with the arrival of lean production, business process reengineering, and strategies for innovation and empowerment. Ohmae's view of the strategist, in fact, is now the widely accepted norm, and the need for a questioning approach that is not constrained by tradition, fear, or habitual patterns of behavior has filtered down from the strategists themselves to all layers of organizations.

Later works by Ohmae have focused on the rise of the global business and the relationships between business and governments. In a sense, Ohmae has grown away from his starting point and now prefers to write about a time when the end of the nation state is imminent. For many this emphasis on the distant future—rather than on business approaches for the medium-term—is of more relevance to politicians and academics than companies competing today. Even so, his legacy of startlingly simple, unconventional, and effective approaches is still required reading for many executives.

FOR MORE INFORMATION

Books:

Ohmae, Kenichi. *The Mind of the Strategist*. New York: McGraw-Hill, 1982.

Ohmae, Kenichi. *Japan Business: Obstacles and Opportunities*. New York: Wiley, 1983.

Ohmae, Kenichi. *Triad Power: The Coming Shape of Global Competition*. New York: Free Press, 1985.

Ohmae, Kenichi. *The Borderless World: Power and Strategy in the Interlinked Economy*. New York: Harper Business, 1990.

Ohmae, Kenichi. *The End of the Nation State: The Rise of Regional Economics*. New York: Free Press, 1995.

Ohmae, Kenichi. *The Next Global Stage: The Challenges and Opportunities in Our Borderless World*. Indianapolis, IN: Prentice Hall PTR, 2005.

See also:

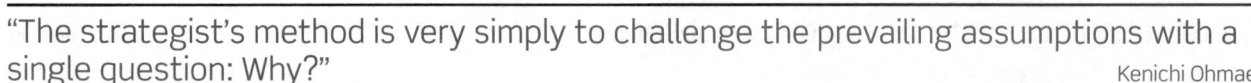

"The strategist's method is very simply to challenge the prevailing assumptions with a single question: Why?"

Kenichi Ohmae

Taiichi Ohno
Toyota Production System

A Toyota production line, much influenced by Ohno.

Japanese manufacturing has gained a reputation for innovative thinking and developments, and the current Western focus on quality, just-in-time delivery, waste and defect reduction, and kanban systems all have their origins in Japanese manufacturing companies. Taiichi Ohno was responsible for much of the background work and thinking that created the now widely recognized and much copied Toyota Production System.

1902	Sakichi Toyoda invents power loom.
1912	Taiichi Ohno born.
1932	Ohno joins Toyoda Automatic Loom Works.
1936–1937	Toyoda starts manufacturing automobiles.
1945–1973	Development of Toyota Production System.
1947	Toyota producing 100,000 vehicles per year.
1956	Ohno visits United States to study production methods.
1990	Dies.
2000	Toyota produces 5.8 million vehicles internationally.

LIFE AND CAREER

The history of the Toyota Production System goes back to the Toyoda Spinning and Weaving Company, established by Sakichi Toyoda in 1918. This company later became the Toyota Automatic Loom Works. From the outset Sakichi recognized that his main competitors were based in the United Kingdom—an early observation of global competition. By 1929 the company had gained a reputation for innovative looms that stopped when there was a quality problem, such as a break in the thread. A British company, Platt Brothers, bought the production and sales rights for this loom for £100,000, a deal that was to have far-reaching consequences. This money was given to Sakichi's son Kiichiro to expand the company and to develop automotive technology. The Model AA was launched in 1936. A year later the Toyota Motor Company was formed.

Kiichiro traveled widely in his search for the best infrastructure for his company and Detroit was a place where he learned a great deal. Ford's assembly line system provided the framework upon which Kiichiro based his early car production, but he recognized the need to adapt it to the particular market conditions in Japan. Toyota was producing cars solely for the internal market, which meant supplying small numbers with high variety. This contrasted with the Ford approach of large numbers "in any color you like as long as it is black." Operating with only limited funds, Toyota was forced to work with supplier partners to generate the necessary capital investment.

It was under these conditions that Taiichi Ohno was brought into the company and one of his initial assignments was to increase its productivity, which was behind that of Ford by a factor of ten. At the end of World War II Kiichiro had decreed that the company must "catch up with America in three years." Ohno realized that Japanese workers could not realistically be working ten times less effectively than their U.S. counterparts. Waste and inefficiency must be prevalent, and if they could be eliminated from the system, productivity could increase by a factor of ten—or even more! The elimination of waste marked the start of the Toyota Production System and is still at its core today.

KEY THINKING

Ohno's early experiments in waste elimination were based within the manufacturing machine shops of which he was in charge. The "one man one machine" approach was seen as the only cost-effective system that a heavily unionized U.S. industry could adopt. The production of large quantities of parts on high-speed, expensive machines creates the potential for an abundance of waste.

Ohno experimented with different machine layouts, encouraging workers to become multiskilled and stopping machines when a job was finished. He encountered many problems during these early stages and learned the need for patience to allow workers to adapt to change.

Later he traveled widely in the United States looking at automobile plants. The knowledge he gained about Ford's assembly line was later to be applied in his ideas on continuously flowing processes. However, according to company lore, his "most important discovery in the U.S. was the supermarket." This has been explained by the fact that he came from a country that, at the time, was unused to self-service. Ohno was impressed by the way customers chose exactly what they wanted, and by the way stores supplied goods in a simple, efficient, and timely manner.

In his later years Ohno often described his production system in terms of a supermarket. Like a supermarket, each production line sets out its produce for the next line to choose from. Each line becomes the customer for the preceding one and a "supermarket" for the following one. Such an approach represents a radical rethink of the production systems of the time. These were primarily "push" systems where the rate of output of the preceding line governed the running rate of the factory. Ohno's ideas amount to a "pull" system whereby demand pulls through resources from the previous line.

The Toyota Production System was developed between 1945 and 1973 and is still evolving. Its basic elements are *muda* (waste control), just-in-time, *ninben no tsuita jidoka* (automation with a human touch), *jidoka* (the quality principle), *heijunka* (production leveling), and *kanban* (the "signboard"—an inventory-control system).

Muda

The philosophy of the Toyota Production System is based on obtaining cost reductions through the elimination of wasteful operations. Ohno divides waste into the following seven categories:

- overproduction
- transporting
- unnecessary inventory on hand
- producing defective goods
- waiting (idle/non productive time)

"Automation does not make optimism obsolete."   Keith Funston

- processing itself
- unnecessary motion

The key to eliminating waste is first to find it and then to ensure that it is recognized as waste by all.

Just-in-Time

The concept of just-in-time (often shortened to JIT) was invented by Kiichiro Toyoda, but it was Ohno who developed its full potential and made it into the system we know today. JIT means supplying to each process what it needs when it needs it and in the quantity that it needs.

Ohno's ideas about just-in-time implementation flowed once again from his experience of the supermarket. Customers visit the supermarket to buy as much of what they want as they happen to need it. When he arrived at Toyota he found that, as in most assembly production at the time, lines producing an item usually pushed their output on to the next stage, whether the next stage needed it or not. Ohno proposed turning this around so that the "process that needs the parts [goes] to get what is needed, when it is needed and in the quantity needed." Thus, the output of a process is replaced as it is transported and consumed by the next process. Storage (inventory) becomes the responsibility of the producer, not the user. Thus workers and their supervisors can clearly see whether they are working too fast or too slow and can act to reduce the waste.

Ninben no tsuita jidoka

"Autonomation" is the second pillar of the Toyota Production System and results from Sakichi Toyoda's earlier invention of the auto-activated weaving machine. The machine would automatically stop if a problem occurred, thus preventing the production of defective products. At Toyota the same principle was carried forward so that all machines were equipped with various safety devices, fixed-position stopping, and poka-yoke foolproofing systems to eliminate defective products.

The concept, however, is applied not only to machinery, but also to the production line and workers. It basically allows workers to stop the production line if a problem occurs. This enables each problem to be fully explored using Ohno's "five whys" (asking the question "Why?" five times to get to the heart of a problem), and makes sure that everyone understands the reason why it has arisen. In the long term this creates an efficient production line.

Jidoka

Jidoka means building quality into the process itself and is a natural extension of autonomation. Inspection teams were the traditional answer to quality control in most manufacturing systems. Ohno believed that quality must flow from production and not inspection. He achieved this by developing the most efficient and safest method of doing every task and training each team member to carry it out in this manner.

Heijunka

Work leveling or load smoothing is the major basis for the elimination of waste. Peaks and troughs in demand create waste capacity; it should be possible to rearrange the production plan and schedule to level out its effects. In this way a process with less work can help out another process that has excess work. In the complex production systems of the car industry the only viable solution, which most manufacturers adopted, was to maintain inventory—itself a waste.

A production line may have cars with different engine sizes, of different colors and with a mix of left- and right-hand drives. Toyota's solution was to equalize not only the quantities but also the types of parts used. This creates an even demand for the different types of components throughout the production cycle. Peaks and troughs are avoided, even in the most minute parts of the process.

Kanban

The kanban system evolved at the same time that Toyota was experimenting with just-in-time and is the method by which the system runs smoothly. Ohno recognized the need for a method of exchanging information between processes in a pull manufacturing environment. By taking the finished product as the starting point, Ohno developed a system of tags or signboards for controlling the transportation of a finished assembly and the production of replacement parts.

A kanban is used for managing and assuring just-in-time production. It is a simple and direct form of communication that is always located at the point where it is needed. Kanbans can be of various shapes as designed by the particular plant. Normally they are a small piece of paper on which is recorded how many of what part to pick up or which parts to manufacture. Ohno built the Toyota kanban system around six rules.

- Do not send defective products to the next process.
- Subsequent processes come to withdraw only what is needed.
- Produce only the exact quantity withdrawn by the subsequent process.
- Equalize production (load smoothing).
- Use *kanban* as a means of fine tuning.
- Stabilize and rationalize the process.

TAIICHI OHNO IN PERSPECTIVE

Taiichi Ohno was an excellent originator of new ideas with his own unique management style. His ability to identify the best of a competitor's systems and to adapt them to the Japanese business environment gave Toyota an unrivalled advantage. The Toyota Production System is remarkable because it was developed in completely the opposite direction to the traditional ways of thinking about production at the time. Ohno was able to build in the quality and the flexibility required in a small but demanding home marketplace by developing a "pull" manufacturing system. The combination of the early example set by his senior managers, his own conscientious research and study of the best of America's assembly line production systems, and his Japanese patience and logic enabled the fledgling Toyota motor company to survive, against its large U.S. competitors.

FOR MORE INFORMATION

Books:

Ohno, Taiichi. *Workplace Management.*. Trans. Andrew P. Dillon. Cambridge, MA: Productivity Press, 1982.

Ohno, Taiichi. *Toyota Production System: Beyond Large-Scale Production*. MA: Productivity Press, 1988.

Ohno, Taiichi, and Setsuo Mito. *Just-in-Time for Today and Tomorrow*. MA: Productivity Press, 1988.

1247

BUSINESS THINKERS

Robert Owen

Pioneer of Personnel Management

Robert Owen is perhaps best known for his model textile factory and village at New Lanark in Scotland. Conditions in early factories were harsh. Long working hours were the norm, with children as young as five working under the same conditions as adults. Factory owners placed more importance on the care of their expensive machines than on the well-being of their expendable employees. Owen's strength was that he saw his employees as every bit as important to the success of his enterprise as his machines.

1771	Born.
1781–1790	Works in various drapery businesses in Stamford, London, and Manchester.
1790	Becomes joint owner of textile factory in Manchester.
1799	Purchases mill in New Lanark from his father-in-law, David Dale, and sets about creating a "model" mill and village.
1808	Keeps the mill open, in spite of the U.S. trade embargo on British goods; mass unemployment elsewhere.
1813	Tries to persuade other manufacturers to follow his example in employment practices.
1815	Attempts to introduce a bill to legislate on working conditions in factories.
1819	Legislation finally introduced, although limited to banning employment of children under nine.
1825	Leaves for the United States; founds New Harmony in Indiana.
1828	Returns to England after project fails due to internal disagreements and bad planning, leaving the settlement in his sons' hands.
1834	Founds the Grand National Consolidated Trades Union.
1858	Dies.

LIFE AND CAREER

Owen the Factory Owner

By the age of 19, Owen was joint owner of a textile factory in Manchester, England. Being new to the responsibilities of management, he learned about the workings of the factory by observing his employees as they performed their work. He wrote: "I looked very wisely at the men in their different departments, although I really knew nothing. By intensely observing everything, I maintained order and regularity throughout the establishment, which proceeded under such circumstances much better than I had anticipated."

In 1799, Owen (with a group of partners) purchased the New Lanark mill from his father-in-law, David Dale. Even though Dale was recognized as a progressive employer, conditions in and around the factory were still very poor. Children from five or six years old were employed through contracts with the local poor house, and working for 15 hours per day was common. Owen immediately withdrew from accepting any further children from the poor house, and raised the minimum age of employment to ten. He also banned the beating of children.

KEY THINKING

Although a paternalistic employer, Owen was a businessperson above all else. He made no changes to employment conditions that could not be justified on economic grounds—all social improvements at New Lanark were funded through the profits of the factory. To achieve this, he required improved productivity from his workforce through changes to the working practices and methods of the factory.

For a workforce that was already working very hard, this was not popular. Owen (uniquely for the time) realized he had to gain the trust of his employees in order to get them to cooperate with the changes to the working environment he wished to achieve. He did this (in the language of today) by persuading "champions." He wrote: "I . . . sought out the individuals who had most influence among [the workforce] from their natural powers or position, and to these I took pains to explain what were my intentions for the changes I wished to effect."

Owen further won the trust of his employees when, in 1808, the United States passed a trade embargo on British goods. Most mills closed and mass unemployment occurred. Unlike other mill owners of the time, Owen kept his employees on full pay just to maintain the factory machinery in a clean, working condition.

This approach of fair management proved to be successful and, as returns from the business grew, Owen began to alter the working environment. Employment of children gradually ceased (as no further children were indentured from the poor house) and those still in employment were sent to a school built for the purpose in New Lanark. The housing available to his workers was gradually improved, the environment was rid of gin shops, and crime decreased. The first adult night school anywhere in the world also operated in New Lanark. Finally, Owen established a store at New Lanark, and the principles behind this laid the basis for the later retail cooperative movement.

Owen the Innovator

Owen's innovations, however, did not merely extend to improving working conditions for his employees. The Industrial Revolution (which began in the mid-to-late 1700s) led to a belief in the supremacy of machines. Owen opposed this growing view by seeking to humanize work.

"Many of you have long experiences in your manufacturing operations of the advantage of substantial, well-contrived and well-executed machinery. If, then, due care as to the state of your inanimate machines can produce such beneficial results, what may not be expected if you devote equal attention to your vital machines, which are far more wonderfully constructed," he wrote.

As already indicated, Owen was one of the first to "manage" rather than order his workforce, and the first to attempt to gain agreement for his ideas rather than impose them on others (a worker could not be fired for disagreeing with Owen). Additionally, he required his managers to behave with some autonomy (possibly the first example of

"Success is a science; if you have the conditions, you get the result."   Oscar Wilde

empowerment at work); managers (or superintendents) were selected carefully and trained to be able to act in Owen's absence.

Owen developed an aid to motivation and discipline—the silent monitor system—which could be described as a distant ancestor of the appraisal plans in practice today. Each machine within the factory had a block of wood mounted on it with a different color—black, blue, yellow, or white—painted on each face. Each day, the superintendents rated the work of their subordinates and awarded each a color that was then turned to face the aisle so that everyone was able to see all ratings. The intention of this plan was that high achievers were rewarded and slackers were motivated to improve.

Owen the Reformer

The factory at New Lanark was spectacularly profitable, with returns of over 50% on investment, and Owen held this to be proof of the validity and importance of his theories. Strengthened by his profitability, he tried to persuade other manufacturers to follow his example in employment practices. This was first attempted through those of influence who visited New Lanark (estimates put the number of visitors at 20,000 between 1815 and 1825) and then, in 1815, via his attempt to introduce a bill to legislate on basic working conditions in factories.

The objectives of the bill were to ban the employment of those aged under ten; to ban night shifts for all children; to provide 30 minutes' education a day for those under 18; and to limit the working day to ten and a half hours. This would have been enforced by a system of government factory inspectors. The bill failed to be introduced in its intended form, as its opponents argued that it would be bad for business and that in any case most employers were voluntarily doing what the bill would require. By the time it was finally introduced in 1819, the legislation was limited to banning the employment of those under nine.

In 1825, disillusioned with his failure to introduce far-reaching employment legisla-

tion but still enthusiastic about his ideals, Owen left for the United States, where he founded New Harmony in Indiana. This, along with other projects, failed because of internal disagreements and bad planning. He returned to England, where in 1834 he founded (and briefly chaired) the Grand National Consolidated Trades Union and continued to push for social reform and the growth of the cooperative movement. Robert Owen died at age 87 in 1858.

ROBERT OWEN IN PERSPECTIVE

Owen occupies a curious position in the history of management thinking. Dismissed by his contemporaries and now little recognized apart from the linking of his name with that of New Lanark, his vision and foresight place him as the pioneer of management practices that are taken for granted today.

Although many influential people visited the sites of New Lanark and New Harmony, the ideas Owen propounded failed to win him immediate followers. There is much debate about the reasons behind this. The New Lanark factory was obviously very profitable (although, as Frank Podmore argued, almost any personnel policy could have been profitable then because profits in the cotton spinning industry at the time were so large), but still none of his factory-owning contemporaries adopted his ideas. Possibly the radical nature of his views contributed to this—if he had instead advocated a step-by-step approach toward improving working conditions and relations with employees instead of an "all-or-nothing" approach, he might have been more successful.

Although it is not too surprising that resistance to his ideas came from factory owners (who may indeed have felt they had much to lose from following them), antipathy was also expressed from across the political spectrum. Some of the most long lasting criticism was expressed by Marx and Engels in their Communist manifesto. The label of "Utopian" that they applied to Owen is one by which he is still well known. The

manifesto expressed the view that his ideas could not work in practice; his success at New Lanark was, they argued, due to luck rather than judgment.

Against these negative views must be set the experiences of those followers Owen did inspire. Although Owen's own partnership with Quakers and Nonconformists at the end of his time at New Lanark failed (because of their wish to impose religious instruction on all), it was this sector of society that produced the people who were most influenced by his ideas. They included Titus Salt, George Palmer, and Joseph Rowntree.

The foresight Owen demonstrated in areas such as motivation of employees, industrial relations, and management by observation was not appreciated until a century later, in the work of F. W. Taylor and Mary Parker Follett, among others. In 1949, Urwick and Brech wrote of Owen: "Generations ahead of his time, he preached and practiced a conception of industrial relations which is, even now, accepted in only a few of the most progressive undertakings."

Owen's lasting contribution may be best seen in the fact that it would be unthinkable for modern employers not to follow the practices he advocated.

1249

BUSINESS THINKERS

FOR MORE INFORMATION

Books:
O'Toole, James. *Leading Change: Overcoming the Ideology of Comfort and the Tyranny of Custom.* San Francisco, CA: Jossey-Bass, 1995.
Owen, Robert. *A New View of Society.* Revised ed. London: Penguin, 1991
Podmore, Frank. *Robert Owen: A Biography.* Revised ed. Hawaii: University Press of the Pacific, 2004.
Urwick, Lionel, and Edward Brech. *Making of Scientific Management.* Revised ed. London: Thoemmes Continuum, 2002.
Wren, Daniel. *Evolution of Management Thought.* 4th ed. New York: Wiley, 1993.

Richard Tanner Pascale
Change, Agility, and Complexity

Richard Tanner Pascale came to prominence in the early 1980s at the time when Peters and Waterman's *In Search of Excellence*, published in 1982, was aiming to redefine the route to corporate success. His *The Art of Japanese Management* (coauthored with Anthony Athos), expounding the virtues of the McKinsey 7-S model, has become a classic, and he has remained at the forefront of management thinking ever since.

1250

BUSINESS THINKERS

1938	Born.
1982	Publication of *The Art of Japanese Management*.
1984	Publication of "Perspectives on Strategy: The Real Story Behind Honda's Success," *California Management Review*.
1999	Publication of "Surfing the Edge of Chaos," *Sloan Management Review*.

LIFE AND CAREER

Born in 1938, Pascale was educated at the Harvard Business School. In the late 1970s he was heavily involved in the evolution of the Seven-S model developed by Peters and Waterman at McKinsey. As a member of faculty at Stanford's Graduate School of Business, Pascale acted as an advisor to the White House and as a consultant to many Fortune 500 companies. More recently he became an associate fellow at Templeton College, Oxford University.

A critic of fads, Pascale, like many of his contemporaries, does not want to be known as a "guru" or "expert." Such labels, he believes, evoke the image of a "hero with all the answers," and he would rather be recognized as someone who keeps addressing questions as they occur and recur. To that end, Pascale spends a number of days every year focusing on questioning, and learning from discussions with, business leaders.

KEY THINKING
Japanese Management and the 7 Ss

A spirit of inquiry brought Pascale and Athos into contact with Peters and Waterman in the late 1970s, when Waterman was driving a McKinsey initiative to seek out new models of corporate success. Peters and Waterman went on to cite U.S. examples of success in their 1981 bestseller, while Pascale and Athos looked at lessons from Japan and how they were being applied in corporate America. What brought the four of them together was the accelerating pace of business change and the increasing inadequacy of corporate information systems that had been sufficient in the past. Both *In Search of Excellence* and *The Art of Japanese Management* expounded the 7-S theory, but it was Pascale and Athos who explored it in greater depth, tracing many of its origins to working practice in Japanese organizations, and particularly in the Matsushita Electric Company.

Comparing Matsushita to ITT, Pascale and Athos found that the two organizations were differentiated more by "softer" elements of management style, staffing policies, skills, and shared values than by their systems, structure, or strategy.

In the early 1980s, the 7 Ss—usually presented in the shape of a circle or diamond—were as original for their juxtaposition of concepts not previously trumpeted as important, as for their communicability through alliteration.

- Strategy—how the organization gets from where it is to where it wants to be.
- Structure—how the company is organized.
- Systems—how information moves around.
- Style—the patterns of behavior of senior management.
- Staff—not just numbers, but the characteristics of those who live and work at the organic center of the organization.
- Skills—the distinctive capabilities of individuals or of the organization as a whole.
- Superordinate goals (shared values)—not so much bottom-line targets as the

meanings and values that are pervasive throughout the organization and "genuinely knit together individual and organizational purposes."

Ambiguity and Uncertainty

In *The Art of Japanese Management*, Pascale and Athos describe how managers are increasingly faced with situations which are neither clear-cut nor susceptible to resolution by the application of rational analysis. These situations arise from the conflicts, ambiguities, and uncertainties that stem from the four Ss of style, staff, skills, and shared values. In such circumstances, the East has something to teach us. Rather than forcing a final solution, the authors suggest, it may be better to accept the lack of clarity in the situation, and simply "decide" to proceed. "Proceeding" should yield further information, and the best course may be to move toward the goal by a sequence of tentative steps rather than by bold, striking actions.

The Honda Effect

Pascale published "Perspectives on Strategy: The Real Story behind Honda's Success" in the Spring 1984 issue of *California Management Review*. This article juxtaposed two contrasting views on the rise of Honda in the United States: the Boston Consulting Group's (BCG's) account and the Honda executives' own explanation. The article stimulated much debate, which was later summarized in "The Honda Effect Revisited," another *California Management Review* article (vol. 38, no. 4, Summer 1996) by Henry Mintzberg and others.

BCG attributed Honda's success to its long-term investment in technology and economies of scale rather than in short-term profitability. Pascale did not aggressively dispute this, but found it did not explain why the then still young Honda had embarked on an apparently reckless U.S. strategy in the first place. Interviewing a number of Honda executives, Pascale became aware that the story was characterized more by miscalculation, chance, and learning-on-the-spot than by a logical, analytical progression of the sort that emerges from BCG's rationalized account.

Pascale explained BCG's interpretation of the "Honda effect" as the result of a Western preference for the oversimplification of reality and linear explanations of events, an

approach that overlooked the process through which organizations experiment, adapt, and learn. This preference leads to a failure to appreciate that the ways in which an organization deals with miscalculation, mistakes, and chance events outside its defined plan are often crucial to its success over time.

The key to Honda's success, concluded Pascale, was organizational agility. He continually returns to this theme, believing agility to be a core organizational competence.

Agility

Pascale's five conclusions summarizing the Honda debate propose the following.

- Organizational agility is increasingly important as a source of renewable competitive advantage.
- Agility resides in what an organization is rather than what it does. In *The Art of Japanese Management*, Pascale cites Harold Geneen's attempt, while chief executive at ITT, to reduce uncertainty through quantification and controls. Matsushita, on the other hand, he pictures as a Pied Piper, more in tune with the uncertainty and imperfection that exist in all organizations, and operating on a basis of shared values and beliefs created by a philosophy linking work to social as well as productive ends.
- The interaction of four key dimensions makes an organization what it is:
  (i) power—can employees really influence the course of events?
  (ii) identity—do individuals identify with the organization as a whole?
  (iii) contention—how is conflict brought out into the open and used creatively?
  (iv) learning—how does the organization handle and develop new ideas?

Within Honda, for example, employees are empowered to take pioneering action and they share an enterprise-wide identity in cross-functional teams, while debate, experimentation, and inquiring attitudes are actively encouraged.

- Strategic intent and agility depend on the norms, values, and behaviors inculcated within the social system of the organization. Pascale refers to Honda's efforts to institutionalize responsiveness, adaptability, and external focus.
- Agility depends on certain organizational disciplines, such as continuing dissatisfaction with the status quo, managing back from the future, uncompromising straight talk and the bringing of differences out into the open, and harnessing adversity by learning from setbacks and adapting to move forward.

Complexity, Chaos, and Letting Go

In an article called "Surfing the Edge of Chaos" in *Sloan Management Review* (Spring, vol. 40, no. 3, 1999), Pascale addresses what he considers to be the biggest challenge facing organizations today—how to increase the number of workable and winning strategic initiatives. He builds on the principles of the science of complexity.

- A complex adaptive system is at risk when it is interfered with and controlled. Equilibrium precedes extinction.
- Complex adaptive systems are capable of self-organization and of generating new methods of operating.
- Some complex adaptive systems can move toward the brink of chaos before new patterns emerge and new forms of organization take shape.
- Complex adaptive systems cannot be directed or strictly controlled.

In drawing parallels between the world of complex scientific systems and the world of organizations, Pascale tests out these four principles against a period of change at Shell, through interviews with Steve Miller, the director driving Shell's renewal initiative. He concludes the article by quoting Miller's words—that is, not by summarizing and generalizing, but by going into the depth and individuality of the organizational context itself. It is interesting to look at some of Miller's comments (quoted below) and relate them to the above four principles:

- "You have to recognize that the top can't possibly have all the answers."
- "The actual solutions about how to best meet the challenges of the moment, those thousands of strategic challenges . . . have to be made by the people closest to the action."
- "The leader becomes a context setter."
- "Once the grassroots realize they own the problem, they also discover that they can help create and own the answers."
- "There's another kind of risk to the leaders . . . the risk of exposure. Before, you were remote from them, now, you're very accessible."
- "Finally, the scariest part is letting go . . . you get more feedback than before . . . you know more through your own people about what's going on in the marketplace . . . but you still have to let go of the old sense of control."

RICHARD TANNER PASCALE IN PERSPECTIVE

Pascale's research, consulting, and exploration continue to lead him to redefine what makes organizations tick, at a time when uncertainties grow at an accelerating pace. He does not fit easily into any predefined category of management theorist and remains both at the front and at the edge in seeking new ways of understanding organizations. Pascale has sought to explore the processes of change by trying to understand their complexities and interdependencies, and not by trying to reduce his findings to mechanistic formulas. In line with his own advice to organizations, he himself exhibits a lack of complacency in his efforts to understand the right pieces, before fitting them into the organizational jigsaw.

He describes his recent work on complexity as a "big idea" and, although it builds on established principles of complexity theory, it will no doubt seem a little strange at first—particularly to those who want to eradicate uncertainty.

1251

BUSINESS THINKERS

FOR MORE INFORMATION

Books:
Pascale, Richard Tanner, and Anthony Athos. *The Art of Japanese Management*. New York: Simon & Schuster, 1981.
Pascale, Richard Tanner. *Managing on the Edge: How Successful Companies Use Conflict to Stay Ahead*. New York: Simon & Schuster, 1990.
Pascale, Richard Tanner, Mark Millemann, and Linda Gioja. *Surfing the Edge of Chaos*. New York: Crown Business, 2000.

Journal Articles:
Pascale, Richard Tanner, Mark Millemann, and Linda Gioja. "Changing the Way We Change." *Harvard Business Review*, November/December 1997, pp. 127–139.
Pascale, Richard Tanner, Tracy Goss, and Anthony Athos. "The Reinvention Roller Coaster: Risking the Present for a Powerful Future." *Harvard Business Review*, November/December 1993, pp. 97–108.

See also:
- Kenichi Ohmae (pp. 1244–1245)
- Konosuke Matsushita (pp. 1328–1329)
- Tom Peters (pp. 1252–1253)

Tom Peters
The Guru As Performer

Tom Peters has probably done more than anyone else to shift the debate on management from the confines of boardrooms, academia, and consulting organizations to a broader, worldwide audience, where it has become the staple diet of the media and managers alike. Peter Drucker wrote more and his ideas have withstood a longer test of time, but it is Peters whose energy, style, influence, and ideas have shaped new management thinking.

1942	Born.
1966–1970	Naval service, including a term of duty in Vietnam and being assigned to the Pentagon.
1973	Leaves Stanford with Ph.D. in organizational behavior; works for White House as senior drug abuse adviser.
1974–1981	Joins consulting firm, McKinsey, becoming a partner in 1977.
Late 1970s	Various collaborative research projects; development of the McKinsey 7-S Model.
1982	Publication of *In Search of Excellence*.
1982–present	Writing, lecturing, touring, and changing his mind; formulates ideas for a management agenda for the future

LIFE AND CAREER

Born in Baltimore in 1942, Peters repaid a navy scholarship to Cornell with a degree in civil engineering and four years' service in the navy, spending a term of duty in Vietnam in 1966 before being assigned to the Pentagon in 1968. He left Stanford in 1973 with a Ph.D. in organizational behavior and worked for the White House for a short while as senior drug abuse adviser. In 1974 he joined the top consulting firm, McKinsey.

Exposed to consulting assignments in America's blue-chip companies, Peters's curiosity and imagination led him in the late 1970s into various aspects of collaborative research, which brought about the development of the McKinsey 7-S Model. This model focuses on shared values, staff, systems, strategy, structure, skills, and style. It was in fact the first expression of the shift—characterizing all of Peters's work—away from the traditional numbers-centered, rational, analytical, and bureaucratic notion of management of McKinsey and many others toward a more innovative, intuitive, and people-centered approach.

In 1982, Peters copublished with Bob Waterman *In Search of Excellence*, which brought him worldwide fame, and set him off on a new career expounding his theories of excellence. Since then, his life has been a whirlwind of writing, lecturing, touring, and changing his mind.

Peters describes himself as gadfly, curmudgeon, champion of bold failures, prince of disorder, maestro of zest, corporate cheerleader, and irritator. *Fortune Magazine* calls him the Ur-guru (the original guru) and *The Economist* the über-guru. He is the founder of the Tom Peters Group and lives on his farm in Vermont, or on American Airlines, or on an island off the Massachusetts coast.

KEY THINKING

In Search of Excellence resulted from the application of the 7-S model in an attempt to discover models of excellence in corporate America. Peters and Waterman identified eight lessons from their research.

- A bias for action—excellent companies get on with doing the job, unconstrained by the bureaucratic trappings.
- Be close to the customer—this has since become a key business "must."
- Autonomy and entrepreneurship—the entrepreneur has freedom to think, act and invest effort in the organization.
- Productivity through people—it was previously believed that large organizations held the key to productivity because only they could handle the economies of scale required for profitability.
- Be driven by hands-on values—the shared values of the 7-S model that matter to employees, as well as making the business tick with managers who are not afraid to get their hands dirty.
- Stick to the knitting—companies should stay with their core competencies, not diversifying for the sake of it.
- Simple form, lean staff—successful companies are not preoccupied with their size or procedures but with keeping things simple.
- Simultaneous loose-tight properties—examples of excellence derived from the faster-moving, more flexible features of smaller organizations, not the more cumbersome aspects of large ones.

When Peters declared in 1987, at the beginning of *Thriving on Chaos*, that there are no excellent companies, it was not only in recognition of the fact that many of the companies he had cited earlier had foundered. It was also because the rules had changed again; there was no single consistent route to excellence. Times change, so companies need to change their approach in order to continue to be successful. Peters has argued consistently that the eight lessons from *In Search of Excellence* remain valid—the companies he cited that later foundered merely failed to follow the lessons through.

A Passion for Excellence was published in 1985, intended as a sequel to *In Search of Excellence*, but this time with the focus on leadership. According to Peters (and his coauthor Nancy Austin) the successful leader becomes passionate about getting the most out of people, takes to heart the full people-centered implications of the 7 S's, and lays the basis for the culture of empowerment. It is also in this book that Peters starts to return time and again to the centrality of the customer.

In *Thriving on Chaos*, Peters was one of the first to describe the emerging world of uncertainty and accelerating change. He was lucky with his timing: it was published in the same month (October 1987) that the stock market crashes in Wall Street, London, and Tokyo brought chaos to the world's money markets. The book was in fact a rejection of the secure world of the past, and a description of the uncertain world of the future. Some of the book's themes were already there in *In Search of Excellence*, cus-

---

"The world's best poker players don't hanker for jobs in casino management." Tom Peters

tomer responsiveness and flexibility through empowerment, for example. But already in 1987, the world was a fast-changing place where increased competition meant speed to market, and that meant fast-paced innovation. Most of all, Peters understood that organizations would need flexible systems to deal with a topsy-turvy world.

Thriving on Chaos encouraged managers to cast off their old thinking and be prepared for a world of change and uncertainty. But Peters had not yet drawn a map of how to get there. *Liberation Management* was his attempt to draw such a map. He advocated flexible, flowing structures that are antihierarchical and based on building up relationships with customers. As he had done in *Thriving on Chaos*, Peters quoted examples of companies that represent the lean, flatter, and responsive organization required now that the old rule-book had been torn up. Again, he focused on the need to innovate, on closeness to customers, and on empowerment. In *Liberation Management* who asserted that knowledge is becoming the key asset, the working capital of the organization.

Peters the Writer

Drucker may have written more, but Peters is beginning to catch up with him. *Thriving on Chaos* is over 500 pages long; *Liberation Management* is over 800. In addition, Peters wrote a column for 10 years as a channel for his thoughts, ideas, observations, and continuing flow of examples of companies.

His style of writing, as well as the content of his work, has changed over the years. One of the attractive features of *In Search of Excellence* was its accessible style. Peters's later works take this style to an extreme and reduce the language of management to monosyllabic expressions designed to shock, excite, provoke, and stir the reader out of conventional thinking. Hence his 1994 title—*The Pursuit of Wow!*

The Guru as Performer

This is an area that Tom Peters has made his own. Many gurus are academics or writers, but few would claim to have the impact of Peters on stage. He has been universally described as a brilliant performer, with great stage presence and unbeatable delivery technique. Sometimes delivering two seminars a day in different cities, Peters is acknowledged for his genuine interest,

concern, even passion for getting people to reflect on the way they manage.

The Tom Peters Seminar: *The Circle of Innovation*

The message that comes over in *The Circle of Innovation* is one that has taken between 15 and 20 years to develop. The book attempts to push the management of organizations to anticipate the topsy-turvy markets that are emerging with global markets, the Internet, and the ever greater closeness of customer and producer.

- Beyond change—be prepared to try things out, but do not expect to get things right first time. Peters acknowledges the role of stability and regularity but attaches far greater importance to agility.
- Beyond downsizing—aim to be big and small at the same time, so that you get the benefits of a large organization (economies of scale, networking, and knowledge-sharing) along with those of the small (speed, independence, and responding to opportunities).
- Beyond empowerment—make every job entrepreneurial.
- Beyond loyalty—everybody learns to think about the future, the customer, and the bottom-line.
- Beyond reengineering—the conversion of units or departments into full professional service firms with responsibility and accountability.
- Beyond disorganization—as the organization spots and responds to opportunities, it becomes a network of partners, distributors, suppliers, and customers with boundaries that are transparent to outsiders.
- Beyond the learning organization—stimulating curiosity and creativity everywhere in the organization.
- Beyond TQM—toward sustainable product/service differentiation to escape the sameness of today's markets through design.
- Beyond management—from management to revolutionary leadership.

TOM PETERS IN PERSPECTIVE

Peters did not actually discover the concept of customers with *In Search of Excellence*, but he and Waterman bucked the dominance of strategy to remind management that customers come first. If he seems all for discontinuity and disorganization, it is principally to remind people not to get stuck in the rut of procedures and routine.

Peters has been criticized for not being thorough or academic enough in support of his assertions, for relying too much on his charisma as a performer, and for "dumbing down" management to a level of mundaneness and banality. However, his antennae have sensed where the world of business is heading before it arrives. It is also widely acknowledged that his approach, style, and energy have popularized management ideas to a wider audience than ever before.

Managers from all levels and from all types of organization say that Peters's influence has been positive rather than negative, and he is spoken of in the same league as Porter, Ohmae, Hamel, Handy, and even Drucker. If he has changed his mind, it is because the world of the 1990s and 2000s has altered radically from that of the 1970s. If he has been inconsistent, he has nonetheless stayed ahead of the management times and foreseen—or helped to set—the management agenda for the fast-changing world of the future.

FOR MORE INFORMATION

Books:

Crainer, Stuart. *Corporate Man to Corporate Skunk: The Tom Peters Phenomenon, A Biography*. San Francisco, CA: Jossey-Bass, 1997.

Peters, Tom, and Bob Waterman. *In Search of Excellence: Lessons from America's Best-run Companies*. New York: Harper & Row, 1982.

Peters, Tom, and Nancy Austin. *A Passion for Excellence: The Leadership Difference*. New York: Harper Collins, 1985.

Peters, Tom. *Thriving on Chaos: Handbook for a Management Revolution*. New York: A. Knopf, 1987.

Peters, Tom. *Liberation Management*. New York: A. Knopf, 1992.

Peters, Tom. *The Tom Peters Seminar: Crazy Times for Crazy Organizations*. New York: Vintage Books, 1994.

Peters, Tom. *The Pursuit of Wow! Every Person's Guide to Topsy-Turvy Times*. New York: Vintage Books, 1994.

Peters, Tom. *Re-imagine!* London: Dorling Kindersley, 2003.

See also:

- Charles Handy (pp. 1216–1217)
- Stephen R. Covey (pp. 1192–1193)

1253

BUSINESS THINKERS

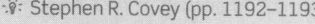

"Progress is mostly the product of rogues."

Tom Peters

Michael Porter
What Is Strategy?

In an age when management gurus are both lauded by the faithful and hounded by the critics, Michael Porter seems to be one of the few who is well regarded both academically and in the business world. Porter has been at the leading edge of strategic thinking since his first major publication, *Competitive Strategy* in 1980.

1254

BUSINESS THINKERS

1947	Born.
1969	Completes a degree in aeronautical engineering at Princeton University.
1971	Receives an MBA from Harvard Business School.
1973	Receives a Ph.D. from Harvard University. Joins the Harvard Business School faculty.
1980	Publishes *Competitive Strategy*, which sets him at leading edge of strategic thinking.
1994	Founds The Initiative for a Competitive Inner City, and becomes Chairman and C.E.O.

LIFE AND CAREER

Born in 1947, Porter completed a degree in aeronautical engineering at Princeton in 1969 and joined the Harvard Business School faculty at the age of 26 after completing a doctorate in economics. He has acted as a consultant to businesses and governments and, like many academics, he has established a consulting company, Monitor.

KEY THINKING

His thinking on strategy has been supported by precision research into industries and companies. Over a period of almost 20 years, his thinking remains consistent as well as developmental—it has not stood still since *Competitive Strategy* became a corporate bible for many in the early 1980s. Before that time, most strategic thinking focused on either the organization of a company's internal resources and their adaptation to meet particular circumstances in the marketplace, or improving an organization's competitiveness by lowering prices to increase market share. These approaches, de-

rived from the work of Igor Ansoff, were bundled into systems or processes that provided strategy with an integral place in the organization.

In *Competitive Strategy*, however, Porter managed to reconcile these approaches and provide management with a fresh way of looking at strategy—not just from the point of view of markets or of organizational capabilities, but from the point of view of industry itself.

Internal Capability for Competitiveness—the Value Chain

Porter describes two different types of business activity—primary and secondary. Primary activities are concerned with transforming inputs (raw materials) into outputs (products), and with delivery and after-sales support. These are usually the main "line management" activities and include:

- inbound logistics—materials handling, warehousing;
- operations—turning raw materials into finished products;
- outbound logistics—order processing and distribution;
- marketing and sales—communication and pricing;
- service—installation and after-sales service.

Secondary activities support the primary and include:

- procurement—purchasing and supply;
- technology development—know-how, procedures and skills;
- human resource management—recruitment, promotion, appraisal, reward and development;
- company infrastructure—general and quality management, finance, planning.

To survive competition and supply what customers want to buy, the company has to ensure that all these value-chain activities link together, even if some of the activities take place outside the organization. A weakness in any one of the activities will impact on the chain as a whole and affect competitiveness.

The Five Forces

Porter argued that in order to examine its competitive capability in the marketplace, an organization must choose between three generic strategies:

- cost leadership—becoming the lowest-cost producer in the market;
- differentiation—offering something different, extra, or special;
- focus—achieving dominance in a niche market.

The skill is to choose the right one at the right time. These generic strategies are driven by five competitive forces that the organization has to take into account:

- the power of customers to affect pricing and reduce margins;
- the power of suppliers to influence the organization's pricing;
- the threat of similar products to limit market freedom and reduce prices and thus profits;
- the level of existing competition that impacts on investment in marketing and research and thus erodes profits;
- the threat of new market entrants to intensify competition and further impact on pricing and profitability.

In recent years, Porter has revisited his earlier work. Such is the acceleration of market change that companies now have to compete not on a choice of strategic fronts, but on all fronts at once. Porter has also said that it is a misconception of his approach for a company to try to position itself in relation to the five competitive forces. Positioning is not enough. What companies have to do is ask how the five forces can help to rewrite industry rules in the organization's favor.

Diversification

Instead of going it alone, an organization can spread risk and attain growth by diversification and acquisition. While the blue-chip consulting companies such as Boston Consulting Group (market growth/market share matrix) and McKinsey (7-S framework) have developed analytical

models for discovering which companies will rise and fall, Porter prefers three critical tests for success.

- the attractiveness test. Industries chosen for diversification must be structurally attractive. An attractive industry will yield a high return on investment, but entry barriers will be high; customers and suppliers will have only moderate bargaining power, and there will be only a few substitute products. An unattractive industry will be swamped by a variety of alternative products, high rivalry, and high fixed costs.
- the cost-of-entry test. If the cost of entry is so high that it prejudices the potential return on investment, profitability is eroded before the game has started.
- the better-off test. How will the acquisition provide advantage to either the acquirer or the acquired? One must offer significant advantage to the other.

Porter devised seven steps to tackle these questions.

- As competition takes place at the business unit level, identify the interrelationships among the existing business units.
- Identify the core business that is to be the foundation of the strategy. Core businesses are those in attractive industries and in which competitive advantage can be sustained.
- Create horizontal organizational mechanisms to facilitate interrelationships among core businesses.
- Pursue diversification opportunities that allow shared activities and pass all three critical tests.
- Pursue diversification through a transfer of skills, if opportunities for sharing activities are limited or exhausted.
- Pursue a strategy of restructuring if this fits the skills of management, or if no good opportunities exist for forging corporate partnerships.
- Pay dividends so that shareholders can become portfolio managers.

National Competitiveness

Why do some companies achieve consistent improvement in innovation, seeking an ever more sophisticated source of competitive advantage? For Porter, the answer lies in four attributes that affect industries. These attributes are:

- **factor conditions**—the nation's skills and infrastructure capable of enabling a competitive position;
- **demand conditions**—the nature of home-market demand;
- **related and supporting industries**—pres-

ence or absence of supplier/feeder industries;

- **company strategy, structure and rivalry**—the national conditions under which companies are created, grow, organize, and manage.

These are the chief determinants that create the environment in which businesses flourish and compete. The points on the diamond constitute a self-reinforcing system, in which the effect of one point often depends on the state of the others, and any weakness at one point will impact adversely on an industry's capability to compete.

The New Strategic Wave

Sometime between 1980 and 1990 a new wave of more subversive strategic thinking—like Gary Hamel's *Strategy as Revolution*, and Mintzberg's "The fall and rise of strategic planning" (*Harvard Business Review*)—emerged to replace the old rulebook. Porter's main contribution to date, *Competitive Strategy*, argues that strategic planning lost its way because managers failed to distinguish between strategic and operational effectiveness and confused the two.

The old strategic model was based on productivity, increasing market share, and lowering costs. Hence, total quality management, benchmarking, outsourcing, and reengineering were all at the forefront of change in the 1980s as the key drivers of operational improvements. But continuing incremental improvements to the way things are done tend to bring different players up to the same level, rather than differentiating them. To achieve differentiation therefore means that:

- strategy rests on unique activities, based on customers' needs, customers' accessibility, or the variety of a company's products or services;
- the company's activities must fit and link together. In terms of the value chain, one link is prone to imitation but with a chain, imitation is very difficult;
- it is important to make trade-offs. Excelling at some things means making a conscious choice not to do others—it's a question of being a "master of one trade" to stand out from the crowd, as opposed to being a "jack of all trades" and lost in the mass. Trade-offs deliberately limit what a company offers. The essence of strategy lies in what *not* to do.

MICHAEL PORTER IN PERSPECTIVE

It is a mark of Porter's achievement that much of his work on *Competitive Strategy*,

researched in the 1970s, still has high value and relevance and still shapes mainstream thinking on competition and strategy.

While his work is academically rigorous, his ability to abstract his thinking into digestible chunks for the business world has given him wide appeal to both the academic and business communities. It is now standard practice for organizations to think and talk about "value chains," and the five forces have entered the curriculum of every management program.

1255

BUSINESS THINKERS

FOR MORE INFORMATION

Books:

Crainer, Stuart. *Key Management Ideas: Thinking That Changed the Management World.* 3rd ed. Upper Saddle River, NJ: Prentice Hall, 1998.

Porter, Michael. *Competitive Strategy: Techniques for Analyzing Industries and Competitors.* New York: Free Press, 1980.

Porter, Michael. *Cases in Competitive Strategy.* New York: Free Press, 1983.

Porter, Michael. *Competitive Advantage: Creating and Sustaining Superior Performance.* Revised ed. New York: Free Press, 1985.

Porter, Michael, ed. *Competition in Global Industries.* Boston, MA: Harvard Business School Press, 1986.

Porter, Michael. *The Competitive Advantage of Nations.* Rev ed. New York: Free Press, 1998.

Journal Articles:

Jackson, Tony. "Dare to Be Different." *Financial Times,* June 19, 1997, p. 23.

Porter, Michael. "Corporate Strategy: The State of Strategic Thinking." *The Economist,* May 23,1998, pp. 21–22, 27–28.

Porter, Michael. "The Competitive Advantage of Nations." *Harvard Business Review,* March/April 1990, pp. 73–93.

Porter, Michael. "From Competitive Advantage to Corporate Strategy." *Harvard Business Review,* May/June 1987, pp. 43–59.

Porter, Michael. "What Is Strategy?" *Harvard Business Review,* November/December 1996, pp. 61–78.

See also:
- Alfred D. Chandler, Jr. (pp. 1190–1191)
- Henry Mintzberg (pp. 1240–1241)
- Kenichi Ohmae (pp. 1244–1245)

C. K. Prahalad
A New View of Strategy

C. K. Prahalad is regarded as one of the most influential thinkers on strategy in the United States. His work stems from a deep concern with the ability of large organizations to maintain competitive vitality when faced with international competition and changing business environments. Many of his ideas on competitive analysis argue against the supremacy of traditional strategic thinking and focus upon the concepts of "strategic intent," "core competence," and "strategy as stretch and leverage."

1256

BUSINESS THINKERS

Year	Event
1941	Born.
1960–1964	Works as an industrial engineer.
1966	Completes an MBA at the Indian Institute of Management.
1975	Completes a DBA at Harvard Business School.
1975	Visiting Research Fellow, Harvard Business School.
1975–1977	Professor and Chairman, Management Education Program, Indian Institute of Management.
1981	Visiting Professor, INSEAD, Fontainebleau, France.
1986–	Professor, University of Michigan Business School.
1994	Cowrites *Competing for the Future* with Gary Hamel.
1994	Receives award from Indo-American Society for promoting goodwill, understanding, and friendship between India and the United States.
1995	American Society for Competitiveness recognizes his contribution to competitiveness in business.

LIFE AND CAREER
Prahalad came to management thinking from the field of physics. He worked as an industrial engineer before completing an MBA at the Indian Institute of Management in 1966 and a DBA at Harvard Business School in 1975. Since then he has been a visiting research fellow at Harvard, a professor at the Indian Institute of Management, and a visiting professor at the European Institute of Business Administration (IN-

SEAD). He is Harvey C. Fruehauf Professor of Corporate Strategy and International Business at the Graduate School of Business Administration, University of Michigan. Over the years he has consulted for many large, multinational companies, including Eastman Kodak, AT&T, Honeywell, Philips, Motorola, and Ahlstrom.

Prahalad's contributions to strategic thinking have been widely acknowledged. *Business Week* wrote " . . . a brilliant teacher at the University of Michigan, Prahalad may well be the most influential thinker on corporate strategy today." In September 1993 the *Wall Street Journal*'s Special Report on Management Education named him as one of the top ten teachers in the world. In 1994 he received the annual award presented by the Indo-American Society for his outstanding contribution toward the promotion of Indo-American goodwill, understanding, and friendship, and in 1995 the American Society for Competitiveness recognized his outstanding academic contribution to competitiveness in business.

KEY THINKING
Competing for the Future
Prahalad sees his book *Competing for the Future* as presenting a new view of competitiveness, strategy, and organizations. It takes the ideas of strategic intent, core competence and strategy as stretch and leverage, and builds on them to create a new strategy model.

Strategic Intent
Strategic intent is described as a way of creating an obsession with winning at all levels and across all functions of the organization. It is a shared competitive agenda for global leadership. Strategic intent uses stretch

targets to create competitive advantage. For example, landing a man on the moon by the end of the 1960s provided the stretch target that gave the United States global leadership in space. It is the role of senior management to develop the organization in a way that closes the gap between ambition and ability. This involves active management processes, which include focusing the organization's attention on the urgency of winning; motivating people with challenges that require personal effort and commitment; using these challenges to create midterm competitive advantage, and applying intent consistently to guide resource allocation. Strategic intent provides the focus for "barrier-breaking" initiatives.

Core Competencies
Core competencies are often confused with core capabilities and core technologies. A core competency is an ability that transcends products and markets, and it results when an organization learns to harmonize multiple technologies, learning, and relationships across levels and functions. Core competencies feed into core products, which themselves can become business units. A core competency provides access to a wide variety of markets, makes a significant contribution to the customer's perceived benefit, and is difficult for competitors to imitate. Examples include Sony's competence in miniaturization, Philips's optical-media expertise, and Black & Decker's knowledge of small electrical engines. Viewing the organization as a portfolio of competencies is seen to lead to strategic advantage.

Strategic Architecture
A strategic architecture is a framework for leveraging corporate resources towards the strategic intent. It draws upon a variety of information to present a view of the evolution of an industry. A strategic architecture identifies the core competencies to build, and their constituent technologies. It provides a framework within which innovation can be planned and managed.

Corporate Imagination
In order to realize the potential that core competencies create, organizations must have the imagination to visualize new markets and the ability to move into them ahead of the competition. The key to competitive

"You might merge with another organization, but two drunks don't make a sensible person."

Gary Hamel

advantage is the process through which organizations release corporate imagination, identify and explore new competitive space, and consolidate control over emerging markets. Prahalad suggests that four elements combine to quicken an organization's imagination:

- escaping the focus on served markets;
- searching for innovative product concepts;
- overturning assumptions about price and performance relationships;
- leading, rather than following, customers.

Escaping Served Markets

Traditionally, organizational concern for existing markets blurs the view of new markets. Such a defensive policy is fine up to a point, but it should not be at the expense of new and potentially lucrative markets.

Innovative Product Concepts

Dramatic innovations in product concepts reshape markets and industry boundaries, creating new competitive space. Such innovations take one of three forms:

- the addition of a new function to a successful product;
- the development of a new form for delivering a proven functionality;
- the delivery of a proven functionality through an entirely new product concept.

Product innovations flow from organizations that view a market in terms of needs and functionalities. This logical process of dissecting a product or service into its functional components is rare in most organizations.

Price/Performance Tradeoff

Most organizations view products and services as price/performance tradeoffs. Radical innovation can be achieved where an organization pursues those products labeled "unattainable dreams." New competitive space can be created by understanding how emerging technologies might allow customers' unmet needs to be satisfied, or their existing needs to be better satisfied.

Leading Customers

Leading customers requires a deep insight into the lifestyles, needs, and aspirations of today's and tomorrow's customers. Traditional modes of market research fail to provide such insights; it is through creative human science studies that such an understanding can be gained. Leading customers to where they want to go, before they know it themselves, provides a huge competitive advantage. This approach involves all functions of the organization. It creates marketeers with technological imagination and technologists with marketing imagination, overcoming the debate about whether an organization should be market- or technology-led.

Expeditionary Marketing

On the premise that being first to market provides a competitive advantage, expeditionary marketing is identified as a tool used by organizations that create competitive space. Expeditionary marketing helps organizations gain an understanding of the particular features, price, and performance of new products that will successfully penetrate the market. Such learning can be gained only when a product—imperfect as it might be—is launched. Expeditionary marketing increases the number of successful products an organization achieves by increasing the number of market opportunities, niches, and product variations explored.

C. K. PRAHALAD IN PERSPECTIVE

The strength of Prahalad's writing lies in the fact that much of it has resulted from debate and development with his joint authors. His belief that there was more to strategy than the existing theories portrayed caught the attention of academics and practicing managers alike. Couple this with a strong belief in the need for business school research to have a strong managerial significance, and you begin to realize why Prahalad is held in such high regard.

Consulting work in corporate America and beyond continually raised the question of how smaller rivals, new to a market, could prevail against much larger, richer organizations. "Existing theories of strategy and organization, while providing a solid base for discovery, do not fully answer these questions," Prahalad argues. These theories help us to understand the structure of an industry, identify the attributes of a transformational leader, and provide a scorecard for monitoring relative competitive advantage. But they do not provide insight into what it takes to redesign an industry, help us understand the role of the leadership team in visualizing the future, or explain the process of competence-building. *Competing for the Future* is a work which aims to fill the gap between theory and reality.

Prahalad's ideas developed at a time when corporate strategy was in crisis and in need of a new face. Organizations were more concerned with improving operational efficiency than focusing on the future, and downsizing for short-term gain meant that many businesses were failing to focus on the potential of tomorrow. It was the recognition that such an approach could not continue that has made large organizations receptive to Prahalad's thinking.

FOR MORE INFORMATION

Books:
Prahalad, C. K., and Gary Hamel. *Competing for the Future.* Boston, MA: Harvard Business School Press, 1994.
Prahalad, C. K. *The Fortune at the Bottom of the Pyramid: Eradicating Poverty Through Profits.* Philadelphia, PA: Wharton School Publishing, 2004.
Prahalad, C. K., with Venkat Ramaswamy. *The Future of Competition: Co-creating Unique Value with Customers.* Boston, MA: Harvard Business School Press, 2004.

Journal Articles:
Prahalad, C. K., and Yves L. Doz. "An Approach to Strategic Control in MNCs." *Sloan Management Review,* vol. 22 no. 4, 1981, pp. 5–13.
Prahalad, C. K., and Gary Hamel. "Do You Really Have a Global Strategy?" *McKinsey Quarterly,* Summer 1986, pp. 34–59.
Prahalad, C. K., Gary Hamel, and Yves L. Doz. "Collaborate with Your Competitors and Win." *Harvard Business Review,* January/February 1989, pp. 133–139.
Prahalad, C. K., and Gary Hamel. "Strategic Intent." *McKinsey Quarterly,* Spring 1990, pp. 36–61.
Prahalad, C. K., and Gary Hamel. "Core Competence of the Corporation." *Harvard Business Review,* May/June 1990, pp. 79–91.
Prahalad, C. K., and Gary Hamel. "Corporate Imagination and Expeditionary Marketing." *Harvard Business Review,* July/August 1991, pp. 81–92.
Prahalad, C. K., and Gary Hamel. "A Strategy for Growth: The Role of Core Competencies in the Corporation." *EFMD Forum,* no. 3–4 1993, pp. 3–9.
Prahalad, C. K., and Gary Hamel. "Competing for the Future." *Harvard Business Review,* vol. 72 no. 4, July/August 1994, pp. 122–128.
Prahalad, C. K., and Gary Hamel. "Competing in the New Economy: Managing out of Bounds." *Strategic Management Journal,* Mar 1996, pp. 237–242.

See also:
Gary Hamel (pp. 1214–1215)

"There is nothing more short term than a 60-year-old C.E.O. holding a fistful of share options."

Gary Hamel

Reg Revans
Action Learning

Reginald Revans was involved in education throughout his long and varied career. Scathing about the value of traditional "chalk and talk" management education that prevailed during the 1960s and 1970s, he argued that people learned most effectively not from books, lecturers, or teachers, but from sharing real problems with others.

Revans was director of education for the U.K. mining industry.

1907	Born.
1926–1929	Studies at Cambridge.
1928	Represents Great Britain in the long jump at the Olympics.
1929	Sets undergraduate long jump record; held until 1962.
1935	Appointed chief education officer for Essex.
1938	Becomes director of education for the mining industry (later the National Coal Board).
1950	Returns to academia to research management of coal mines; develops theories of action learning.
1950–2003	Holds variety of professorial positions in the fields of industrial administration and management; campaigns around the world to spread his ideas; has had influence in countries as diverse as Belgium, India, and Egypt.
1970s–1980s	National output in Belgium surpasses that of many major competitors; credit laid at Revans's feet.
2003	Dies.

LIFE AND CAREER

Revans studied at Cambridge (where he held the undergraduate long jump record between 1929 and 1962) and, during his time there, represented Great Britain in the long jump at the 1928 Olympics. After he obtained his degree, Revans became a research fellow at Emmanuel College and in 1935 he was appointed chief education of-

ficer for Essex. At the end of World War II, he became director of education for the mining industry (later the National Coal Board), but by 1950 he had returned to academia to research the management of coal mines. From the mid-1950s, Revans held a variety of professorial positions in the fields of industrial administration and management. In 1995 he gave his backing to the establishment of the Centre for Action Learning and Research at Salford University.

KEY THINKING
Action Learning Processes

While director of education for the National Coal Board, Revans spent two years living and working with miners trying to identify what their problems really were (rather than what people thought they were). His experiences led him to understand that people learn most effectively through "doing" in groups, and this realization helped him develop the theories to support "action learning."

The learning process may be expressed as:

Learning = Programmed knowledge + the ability to ask "insightful" Questions (or L = P + Q).

Programmed knowledge (P) is conveyed through books, lectures, and other structured learning mechanisms. It is an accessible format for knowledge, but it may take time to find exactly what we need, and in isolation is not sufficient to fulfill all learning needs. Revans argued that it is overvalued in management learning.

Insightful questions (Q) are those questions that are asked at the right time and are based on experiences or an attitude about ongoing work projects, as well as on creativ-

ity that goes beyond acceptance of ready-made solutions. Revans maintained that P is the domain of experts, while Q is the domain of leaders who wish to drive projects forward by getting answers. Revans also noted that P was the initial letter of poppy-cock, platitude, and professor, while Q initiates query and quiz.

Insightful questions are the key to Revans's process. P will not take you very far unless you focus on the reflective side of what you do. Revans argued that it is not just "doing" but learning to learn by doing—Q—that is much more important.

Revans suggested that each participant should have the following (deceptively simple) questions at the forefront of his or her thinking.

- What are we really trying to do?
- What is stopping us from doing it?
- What can we do about it?
- Who knows about (understands) the problem being tackled?
- Who cares (genuinely wants something done) about the problem?
- Who can (has enough power to) get something done about it?

Action learning requires solutions to be implemented, not just recommended. Because it demands probing and sensitive questions, it can also require levels of tact and diplomacy.

Principles of Action Learning

Action learning is a process that, if it is to work, must be owned by its participants. This is because, Revans argued, the participants need to make their own decisions about tasks, in order to learn how to help each other. Besides the important issues of ownership, action learning has other principles that must be adhered to.

- The learning context must be a real working situation, or a defined project meaningful to the participants—not a simulation. Learning to take action involves taking it, not merely making a recommendation on someone else's problem.
- Members of the learning set (the group or team involved) should all be able to make a contribution from their experience.
- The team members need to be ready to continue to learn from one another as they discuss problems and test out ideas through regular meetings. The learning process is not one of isolation: managers learn best from each other.

"Seek to understand each others' problems and develop a sense of responsibility for each other through working in small groups."

Reg Revans

- Scheduled input of knowledge (P) should be kept to a minimum.
- An adviser needs to be present for the life of the team to facilitate, help, steer, or guide when needed, but not to teach or lecture.
- Top management support must be available to respond to the team's findings.

To be successful, action learning also requires:

- commitment from the top—no hidden agendas in which time spent will produce an outcome that has been rejected before it is announced;
- the full commitment of everyone involved—action learning must be voluntarily embraced; it cannot be imposed;
- time for meetings and questions, which necessitates flexibility in terms of scheduling;
- good communication to facilitate enthusiasm and commitment from all participants;
- an atmosphere of trust and openness— team members should be able to feel relaxed about confronting sensitive internal issues.

These are onerous requirements for a learning program, but the benefits offered through action learning make the undertaking worthwhile. Action learning:

- encourages self-reliance and develops people, especially in times of uncertainty and discontinuity;
- is an aid to management development because it helps individuals to prepare for the future by helping themselves;
- develops the organization by changing the way it behaves;
- produces results because it requires team members to take decisions;
- can be a powerful problem-solving tool.

REG REVANS IN PERSPECTIVE

Accepting Revans's distinction between knowledge or didactic learning (P) and insightful questioning (Q), research has revealed those situations in which action learning may be most appropriate. These are situations in which:

- knowledge is changing rapidly;
- a body of knowledge is applied to specific problems;
- the individual is acquiring self-knowledge;
- processes and concepts for thinking and learning are applied.

By contrast, action learning may prove less appropriate where knowledge is relatively stable; when you are building up a body of knowledge, or where the body of uncontested knowledge is well established.

Revans's position of influence on modern-day management remains undefined; he ranges from being underestimated and ignored to being described as a management genius. He campaigned around the world to spread his ideas and had influence in countries as diverse as Belgium, India, and Egypt. In Belgium, his ideas were applied with particular success, National output during the 1970s and 1980s surpassed that of many major competitors, and credit for this was laid at Revans's feet. He had his detractors as well as his devotees, and this is probably as much for his uncompromising style as for his apparently simplistic thinking. But it is on his thinking that posterity should judge him, and there are a number of discernible developments in the domain of business learning that have been influenced by Revans.

Learning Cycle

Developed by David Kolb, this ensures that a learner cannot assume a passive role. Instead, learning is active, following a continuous, cyclical process of experience, evaluation, conceptualization, and experimentation.

Learning Preferences

All learners have different levels of comfort or difficulty in relation to the phases of Kolb's learning cycle. Some may need to practice more than others; some may prefer reading; some observation. Peter Honey and Alan Mumford have identified four basic styles of learning—the activist, the theorist, the reflector, and the pragmatist— which take account of Revans's great emphasis on learning to learn by doing.

Competence Movement

The competence movement in management education is principally about being able to do things better in the workplace, by using work-based problems and situations for projects and assignments. Along with the growth of National Vocational Qualifications and the rise of mentoring plans, the movement must surely acknowledge Revans as one of its main forerunners.

1259

BUSINESS THINKERS

FOR MORE INFORMATION

Books:
Honey, Peter, and Alan Mumford. *Manual of Learning Styles*. 3rd ed. Maidenhead: Peter Honey Publications, 1992.
Kolb, David A. *Experiential Learning: Experience as the Source of Learning and Development*. Englewood Cliffs, NJ: Prentice Hall, 1984.
Revans, Reg. *Action Learning: New Techniques for Management*. London: Blond & Briggs, 1974.
Revans, Reg. *The ABC of Action Learning: a Review of 30 Years of Experience*. Bromley: Chartwell-Bratt, 1983.

Journal Article:
Bourner, Tom. "What Can Be Learned Using Action Learning." *Organizations and People*, vol. 3 no. 4, 1996, pp. 18–21.

See also:
- Chris Argyris (pp. 1180–1181)
- Peter Senge (pp. 1262–1263)

"Unless your ideas are ridiculed by experts, they are worth nothing."   Reg Revans

Edgar Schein
Careers, Culture, and Organizational Learning

Edgar Schein pioneered the concept of corporate culture with his landmark book *Organizational Culture and Leadership* (1985), which sparked off much research into the subject. He also coined the now much-used phrases "psychological contract" and "career anchor."

1928	Born.
1949	Masters Degree in Psychology, Stanford.
1972– 1982	Chairman of the Organization Studies Group of Sloan School of Management, Massachusetts Institute of Technology.
1978– 1990	Sloan Fellows Professor of Management, Massachusetts Institute of Technology.
1985	Publication of *Organizational Culture and Leadership*.

LIFE AND CAREER

Currently the Sloan Fellows Professor of Management Emeritus and part-time senior lecturer at the MIT Sloan School of Management, Edgar Schein has had a long and distinguished academic career. He received his Ph.D. in social psychology from Harvard University, collaborated with Douglas McGregor at MIT, and worked for many years with the National Training Laboratory. In addition, he has made a strong contribution to the "helping" professions, mainly in the areas of organization development, career development, and organizational culture.

Schein has researched and written extensively about the factors that influence individual and organizational performance. The main themes underlying his work are the identification of culture(s) in the organization, the relationship between organizational culture and individual behavior, and the importance of organizational culture for organizational learning. Douglas McGregor invited him to MIT on the basis of his work on the repatriation of POWs following the end of the Korean War. This work strongly influenced Schein's whole career, and re-

emerged forcefully in 1999 in an article for the *Learning Organization* on brainwashing and organizational persuasion techniques ("Empowerment, Coercive Persuasion, and Organizational learning: Do They Connect?" vol. 6, no. 4, pp. 163–172).

KEY THINKING
Corporate Culture

Early in his career Schein found traditional approaches to understanding work behavior and motivation first too simplistic to explain the variety of experiences of individuals in organizations, and, second, too restrictive, since human and organizational needs vary widely from person to person, place to place, and time to time. In *Organizational Culture and Leadership*, he became the first management theorist to define corporate culture and suggest ways in which culture is the dominant force within an organization.

In his view, culture is a mix of many different factors, such as:

- observed behavioral regularities when people interact;
- norms that evolve in working groups;
- dominant values pushed by the organization;
- the philosophy guiding the attitudes of senior management to staff and customers;
- organizational rules, procedures, and processes;
- the feeling or climate that is conveyed without a word being spoken.

In *Organizational Culture and Leadership*, Schein defines culture as a pattern of basic assumptions, and discusses how these fall into five, often oppositional, categories, which are:

- humanity's relationship to nature—some organizations seem to want to dominate

the external environment, while others accept its domination;
- the nature of reality and truth—the ways and means by which organizations arrive at the "truth";
- the nature of human nature—some people seem to avoid work if they possibly can, while others embrace it as a way of fulfilling their potential, to both their own and the organization's benefit;
- the nature of human activity—a focus on the completion of tasks on the one hand, and on self-fulfillment and personal development on the other;
- the nature of human relationships—some organizations seem to facilitate social interaction, others to regard it as an unnecessary distraction.

Organizational Socialization

Schein's thoughts on organizational socialization were triggered when, after arriving at MIT, he asked McGregor for guidance in the form of previous outlines and notes for a course he was preparing. McGregor suggested that Schein should make up his own mind. This lesson in acclimatizing to MIT led Schein to argue that companies should be conversant with their socialization practices and recognize the conflicts they can create for new recruits.

In "Organizational Socialization and the Profession of Management" (*Sloan Management Review*, Fall 1988, pp. 53–65), Schein discusses how, when a new recruit enters the organization, a process of socialization—adaptation or "fit"—takes place. He argues that this process has more to do with recruits' past experience and values than their qualifications or formal training.

Usually, Schein suggested, organizations create a series of events that work to undo the new recruit's old values to some extent, so that he or she is more open to learning new values. This process of "undoing" or "unfreezing" can be unpleasant, and its success may therefore depend on either a recruit's strong motivation to endure it, or the organization's perseverance in making recruits endure it. There are three basic responses to this socialization process:

- rebellion—outright rejection of the organization's norms and values;
- creative individualism—selective adoption of key values and norms;
- conformity—acceptance of the organization's norms and values.

"Market competition is the only form of organization which can afford a large measure of freedom to the individual."

Frank H. Knight

Noting similarities between brainwashing experienced by servicemen captured during the Korean War and the socialization of executives in programs at MIT, Schein argues that many forms of organizational development involve restructuring and change, and have serious implications for the way people work and their relationship with management.

Schein likens such processes to a form of coercive persuasion, or brainwashing, giving people little choice but to abandon, for example, older norms and values that fit badly with the new learning. If we are in tune with the goals and values of the change this will not be a problem, but if we dislike the values, we are likely to disapprove of the brainwashing. Schein concludes that, because the very concept of organization involves some restriction of individual freedom to achieve a joint purpose, the concept of a continually learning, innovative organization is something of a paradox, since creativity and learning are related to individual freedom and growth.

Organizational Learning

Organizational learning, Schein considers, needs to be fast in order to cope with growing market pressures, yet seems to be obstructed by a fear of, or anxiety about, facing change, particularly on the part of senior executives. This feeling is associated with reluctance to learn what is new, because it appears too difficult or disruptive. Schein argues that only a new anxiety greater than the existing one can overcome this, and his "anxiety 2" is the fear, shame, or guilt associated with not learning anything new.

Schein emphasizes the need for people to feel psychologically safe, if change is to happen. Achieving organizational learning and transformation therefore depends upon creating a feeling of safety and overcoming the negative effects of past incentives and past punishments—especially the latter. To learn, people need to feel motivated and free to try out new things.

Psychological Contract and Career Anchors

In *Organizational Psychology* Schein highlights a "psychological contract" (attributing the original concept to Chris Argyris) which he defines as an unwritten set of expectations operating between employees and employing managers and others in an organization. He stresses how essential it is that both parties' expectations of a contract should match, if a long-term relationship that will benefit both parties is to develop.

Closely linked to the notion of the psychological contract is the concept of the "career anchor," a guiding force that influences individuals' career choices and is based on their self-perceptions. Schein proposes that, from their varying aspirations and motivations, individuals—perhaps unconsciously—develop one underlying career anchor, which they are unwilling to surrender. On the basis of 44 cases, he distinguishes career anchor groups such as technical/functional competence, managerial competence, creativity, security or stability, and autonomy.

The Three Cultures of Management

Rather than a single culture, Schein identifies three cultures (or communities of interest) within an organization: the operator culture, which evolves locally within organizations and within operational units; the engineering culture of technicians in search of "people-free" solutions; and the executive culture, which is focused on financial survival.

The three often conflict rather than work in harmony. For example, while the executive culture requires systems and reporting relationships for evidence that operations are on track, the engineering culture attempts to design systems that cut across lines of control and the people manning these.

In his article "Three Cultures of Management: The Key to Organizational Learning" (*Sloan Management Review*, Fall 1996, pp. 9–20), Schein suggests that, in many cases, either operators assume executives and engineers do not understand their work needs and covertly do things in their own way; or executives or engineers assume a need for tighter control over operators and force them to follow policies and procedure manuals. In either case, there is no commonly understood plan, and efficiency and effectiveness suffer.

Schein stresses the need to take the concept of culture more seriously and accept how deeply embedded are the assumptions of executives, engineers, and employees. He proposes that helping executives and engineers learn how to learn about, analyze, and evolve their cultures may be central to organizational learning.

EDGAR SCHEIN IN PERSPECTIVE

Schein's work now spans more than four decades and his great contribution has been in linking culture with individual development and growth, putting the accent on organizations as complex systems and on individuals as whole beings.

Schein was aware that the concept of corporate culture was no cure-all for ailing organizations. The fact, however, that culture is now generally recognized as a central factor in organizational change and development is largely attributable to his work.

1261

BUSINESS THINKERS

FOR MORE INFORMATION

Books:
Schein, Edgar H. *Career Dynamics: Matching Individual and Organizational Needs.* Reading, MA: Addison-Wesley, 1978.
Schein, Edgar H. *Organizational Psychology.* 3rd ed. Englewood Cliffs, NJ: Prentice Hall, 1980.
Schein, Edgar H. *Organizational Culture and Leadership.* 2nd ed. San Francisco, CA: Jossey-Bass, 1997.
Schein, Edgar H. *The Corporate Culture Survival Guide.* San Francisco, CA: Jossey-Bass, 1999.

Journal Article:
Schein, Edgar H. "How Can Organizations Learn Faster? The Challenge of Entering the Green Room." *Sloan Management Review*, Winter 1993, pp. 85–92.

See also:
Warren Bennis (pp. 1184–1185)

"Success goes to those with a corporate culture that assures the ability to anticipate and meet customer demand."

Tadashi Okamura

Peter Senge
The Learning Organization

Popularizer of the theory of the learning organization, first suggested by Chris Argyris and Donald Schön, Peter Senge studied how organizations develop adaptive capabilities in a world of increasing complexity and change. His work culminated in the publication of *The Fifth Discipline: The Art and Practice of the Learning Organization*.

BUSINESS THINKERS

1262

1947	Born.
1975–1990	Research at the Sloan School of Management into ways of learning.
1990	Publication of *The Fifth Discipline*.
1999	Named by the *Journal of Business Strategy* as one of the 24 people with the greatest influence on business strategy over the previous century.
Present	Founding chair of the Center for Organizational Learning at the Sloan School of Management, MIT.

LIFE AND CAREER

Peter Senge is chairman of the Center for Organizational Learning, a nonprofit, member governed organization, based at the Sloan School of Management, Massachusetts Institute of Technology (MIT). He graduated in engineering from Stanford before earning a Ph.D. in social systems modeling at MIT. For many years, Senge studied how businesses and organizations develop adaptive capabilities in a world of increasing complexity and change, but the success of his book *The Fifth Discipline* popularized the concept of the "learning organization."

Published in 1990, *The Fifth Discipline* brought the attention of the world to bear on this rather unassuming man, who suddenly found himself the modern equivalent of a medieval crusader seeking dramatically to change corporate America, and indeed the rest of the world, against all the odds. Senge's message was simple—the learning organization believes that competitive advantage derives from continued learning, both individual and collective. Furthermore, the new challenges of the information age

demand that not only businesses, but also educational institutions and governments, transform themselves radically. Senge describes himself as an "idealistic pragmatist" and spends much time building learning organizations with the top leaders of companies, education, and government.

Although Senge's ideas are utopian, his Center for Organizational Learning has attracted an impressive list of corporate sponsors who have dug deep into their pockets to fund pilot programs.

KEY THINKING
The Fifth Discipline

In *The Fifth Discipline*, Senge suggests that there are five basic ingredients for a learning organization.

Systems thinking: Senge's whole approach to organizations is a "systems" approach that views the organization as a living entity, with its own behavior and learning patterns. He introduces the idea of "systems archetypes" to help managers spot repetitive patterns that lead to recurrent problems or limits to growth.

Personal mastery: Every modern manager recognizes the importance of developing skills and competencies in individuals, but Senge takes this notion further by stressing the importance of spiritual growth in the learning organization. True spiritual growth exposes us to a deeper reality; it teaches us to see the current reality more clearly and, by highlighting the difference between vision and the current reality, generates a creative tension, out of which successful learning arises. In Senge's own words, a learning organization is "a group of people who are continually enhancing their capability to create their future" by "changing individuals so that they produce results they

care about, accomplish things that are important to them."

Mental models: The systems approach is continued with Senge's emphasis on mental models. This discipline requires managers to construct mental models for the driving forces behind the organization's values and principles. Senge alerts his readers to the impact of acquired patterns of thinking at the organizational level and the need to develop nondefensive mechanisms for examining the nature of these patterns.

Shared vision: According to Senge, true creativity and innovation are based on group creativity, and the shared vision the group depends on can only be built on the personal vision of its members. Shared vision occurs when the vision is no longer seen by the team members as separate from the self.

Team learning: Effective team learning involves alternating processes for dialogue and discussion. Dialogue is exploratory and widens possibilities, whereas discussion narrows down the options to find the best alternatives for future decisions. Although these two processes are complementary, they need to be separated. Unfortunately, most teams lack the ability to distinguish between these two modes and to move consciously between them.

Senge's basic premise can be stated very simply: people should put aside their old ways of thinking (mental models); learn to be open with others (personal mastery); understand how the company really works (systems thinking); form a plan everyone can agree on (shared vision); and then work together to achieve that vision (team learning).

Practical tools—The Fifth Discipline Fieldbook

Recognizing that the ideas contained in *The Fifth Discipline* needed to be made more accessible to practicing managers, Senge and his colleagues produced a more practical guide—*The Fifth Discipline Fieldbook*. Throughout the book, the authors stress that anyone who wants to be part of a learning organization must be willing to go through a personal change. To help this process, Senge and his coauthors provide a set of elaborate personal awareness exercises. The *Fieldbook* was designed as a resource for dipping into and it contains many good ideas and case studies. Even if you find Senge's thinking

too general, the *Fieldbook* is well worth scrutinizing for references and new ideas. Here are just a few:

System archetypes and causal loops: The *Fieldbook* devotes a lot of time to mapping processes in organizations, analyzing feedback loops and identifying typical organizational problems (the system archetypes). This process-mapping tool can help employees to work out how complex systems interact, and to develop their "mental models" of the organization. The "beer game" described in *The Fifth Discipline* is a simulation based on these models.

Left- and right-hand columns: By writing down in meetings what you really think (left-hand column) and what you actually said (right-hand column), you can analyze and identify those personal prejudices that get in the way of really productive work.

The ladder of inference: This exercise provides a step model for analyzing our values, beliefs, and actions. Climbing down the ladder helps us to discover why we behave the way we do, and helps us to avoid jumping to dangerous conclusions. The steps on the ladder are:

- I take ACTIONS based on my beliefs;
- I adopt BELIEFS about the world;
- I draw CONCLUSIONS;
- I make ASSUMPTIONS based on the meanings added to my mental models;
- I add MEANINGS (cultural and personal);
- I select DATA from what I observe;
- I OBSERVE data and experiences.

The container: This is a dialogue tool that has proved very effective (if not explosive!) in some organizations. People at a meeting are encouraged to imagine a container that holds everyone's hostile thoughts and feelings. As everyone speaks out, putting their fears, prejudices, and anger on the table, the hostility between different factions is neutralized, because it is exposed in a safe place for all to discuss. In the early days of such experiments, a good facilitator is probably essential.

Learning labs and flight simulators: The *Fieldbook* provides useful references for all those who wish to design effective simulations for training sessions.

PETER SENGE IN PERSPECTIVE

Although Senge's *The Fifth Discipline* was a bestseller, its basic concepts had emerged from extensive research conducted at the influential Sloan School of Management at MIT over 15 years. The success of the "learning organization" concept is a reflection of the times. None of the book's concepts is new, but Senge was able to put them all together and to create a simple but very powerful idea.

Senge is a product of his age, probably greatly influenced by the culture of the 1960s in the United States. His systems approach toward organizations shows the same maturity displayed in the systems analysis tools developed by thinkers such as Peter Checkland at Lancaster University. Here the organization is viewed as a "super-organism" with its own behavior patterns, but also profoundly influenced by the nature of its constituent members. The sad fact is that Senge was one of the first management gurus to make the accepted beliefs of a whole generation of social scientists, biologists, and environmentalists credible to the corporate world.

In his own words, Senge says: "We live under a massive illusion of separation from one another, from nature, from the universe, from everything. We're depleting the earth and we're fragmenting our spirit. The symptoms are pollution, anger, and fear. Everything in our culture is about the management of impressions and appearances, from physical fitness to the way we dress. And yet on another level we know it's all bullshit." Even having just passed the millennium, there is little evidence that the change in attitude needed to achieve Senge's ideals—of long-term corporate sustainability and freedom for all to achieve personal mastery—is in sight: there are very few organizations that have been able to implement his ideas successfully.

The main criticism that can be leveled at Senge's work is the inherent difficulty of applying his models. Senge was trained as an engineer and then became involved in social research. Both require a systems approach, but this cannot be developed easily. In fact systems thinking is about as easy as learning brain surgery in a three-day course. Nor can most companies afford the luxury of their top executives learning to "crash land" for too long.

Breaking old corporate habits is very hard, and therefore transforming an enterprise into a learning organization is highly problematic and not for the faint-hearted. The reason for this is simple—in order to move forward to a new, cooperative learning model, managers have to give up their traditional areas of power and control. They have to hand over power to the learners and allow them to make mistakes. In a blame-oriented culture, this change in attitude remains a major obstacle.

Despite the elusiveness of its ideals, *The Fifth Discipline* has proved highly influential. Its concepts have stimulated the debate and acceptance of issues such as self-managed development, empowerment, and creativity. Its practical impact can be seen in modern human resource management strategies, teamwork principles, and in quality models.

It is more important perhaps to recognize that in life all the most profound truths are deceptively simple, yet almost impossible to apply in practice. The difficulty experienced in applying Senge's ideas does not invalidate them—if anything, it confirms their importance for companies in 21st century.

1263

FOR MORE INFORMATION

Books:
Checkland, Peter. *Systems Thinking, Systems Practice!*. New ed. New York: Wiley, 1999.
Gibson, Rowan, ed. *Rethinking the Future*. Naperville, IL: Nicholas Brealey, 1997.
Kleiner, Art. *The Age of Heretics: Heroes, Outlaws, and the Forerunners of Corporate Change*. Naperville, IL: Nicholas Brealey, 1996.
Senge, Peter. *The Fifth Discipline: The Art and Practice of the Learning Organization*. New York: Doubleday, 1990.
Senge, Peter, et al. *The Fifth Discipline Fieldbook: Strategies and Tools for Building a Learning Organization*. New York: Currency Doubleday, 1994.

Journal Articles:
Senge, Peter. "The Future of Workplace Learning and Performance." *Training and Development USA* vol. 48 no. 5, 1994, pp. S36-S47.
Senge, Peter. "Mr Learning Organization." *Fortune International* 17 Oct 1994, pp. 75–81.
Senge, Peter. "Looking Ahead: Implications of the Present." *Harvard Business Review* September/October 1997, pp. 18–32.

See also:
Chris Argyris (pp. 1180–1181)

BUSINESS THINKERS

"A mistake is an event, the full benefit of which has not yet been turned to your advantage."

Edwin Land

Adam Smith
Founder of Political Economics

Adam Smith published his best-known book, fully entitled *An Inquiry into the Nature and Causes of the Wealth of Nations* but commonly known as *The Wealth of Nations*, in 1776. This is often described as one of the most important texts of our time, and its two main philosophical points stressed the supreme value of individual liberty, and the pursuit of self-interest as ultimately beneficial for society as a whole.

1264

BUSINESS THINKERS

1723	Born.
1748	Appointed lecturer in literature at Edinburgh University, Scotland.
1751	Appointed professor of literature at Glasgow University.
1763	Publication of *The Theory of Moral Sentiments*.
1776	Publication of *The Wealth of Nations*.
1778	Accepts post of commissioner of customs in Scotland.
1787	Elected lord rector at Glasgow University.
1790	Dies.

LIFE AND CAREER

Smith was brought up in Kirkcaldy, Scotland by his widowed mother. At 14, he won a scholarship to study mathematics and moral philosophy at Glasgow University; and then, at 17, to Balliol College, Oxford. In 1748, he was appointed to a lectureship in literature at Edinburgh, and in 1751, became professor of literature at Glasgow University. One year later, he was appointed professor of moral philosophy and, despite a nervous disorder, faltering speech, and a tendency to forgetfulness, became a teacher of high repute. His lectures focused on theology, ethics, and jurisprudence.

In 1763, following the publication of his first book, *The Theory of Moral Sentiments*, Smith was asked to act as tutor and companion to the young Duke of Buccleuch during his "grand tour" of Europe. Through this he met several great philosophers and thinkers, including Voltaire and Rousseau, and his own ideas took firmer shape. On his return from Europe he retired to Kirkcaldy

to concentrate on writing *The Wealth of Nations*.

In 1778, Smith accepted the post of commissioner of customs in Scotland, and was elected lord rector at Glasgow University in 1787. Although Smith had plans to add a third volume (on jurisprudence) to follow the other two, his writings remained limited to reissuing editions of *The Wealth of Nations*.

Smith never married and, despite his impressive mind, became known as somewhat eccentric, largely due to his tendency to forget everyday things, such as changing from his nightclothes into day wear. After the death of Smith's mother, he was looked after by a maiden aunt until his death in 1790.

HISTORICAL BACKGROUND

To understand Smith's thinking fully, it is helpful to know a little about his background. He knew many of the most influential contemporary thinkers, and spent much time debating in the gentlemen's clubs of London. He was a friend of both John Locke and David Hume and was, for a time, a disciple of Quesnay, the leading French physiocrat. *The Wealth of Nations* undoubtedly drew ideas from many such sources.

In the later 17th and 18th centuries, there was increasing interest in the theory of "natural" law. The natural sciences had become established since the publication of Newton's *Philosophiae Naturalis Principia Mathematica* (1687) and there was a strong drive to uncover the natural laws that were thought to guide people's actions.

At the same time, burdensome government regulations were increasingly criticized, and the theory of natural order was being drawn into ideas about society and government. For example, John Locke's *Treatise on Civil Government* (1691) proposed

that men are born free and equal, and are governed by "natural laws," arguing that, while executive power is necessary, this should be only by consent.

Such revolutionary ideas were taken up by many great thinkers, including Hume, Hutchison, the French physiocrats, and Smith himself. It was, however, impossible to prove the existence of a benevolent "natural order," ordained by God for men's happiness. While proponents of the concept considered it to be self-evident, it was always, in fact, an intangible hypothesis wide open to challenge.

The idea that human society should be based on a natural order encouraged ideas about individualism to develop further. The concept of an economic system founded on individual self-interest rather than government control is central to *The Wealth of Nations* and to later social, political, and economic change.

THE WEALTH OF NATIONS
Natural Law and "laissez faire"

The Wealth of Nations followed the French physiocrats in arguing that all human powers are subject to immutable, natural moral and physical laws. These laws, divine in origin, were thought to offer a basis for government that could leave things to work naturally, with results that would satisfy both individual and state interests.

Smith never actually used the term "Laissez Faire," but his book popularized associated arguments for government non-intervention in social, economic, and commercial matters. "Laissez faire" was first used by the French, and essentially meant that the government should let things alone, specifically in terms of trade, production of goods, and quantities or quality of products. This philosophy dominated much 18th and 19th century government, and assumed that:

- natural laws, if left to work freely, would create the best possible society;
- enlightened individual selfishness was ultimately in the public interest;
- men are born equal.

The Wealth of Nations took ten years to write, and the ideas within it challenged Smith's contemporary, mercantilist government and its protectionist laws. The author realized that his book would outrage those with vested interests in business or government, because of its arguments for government-

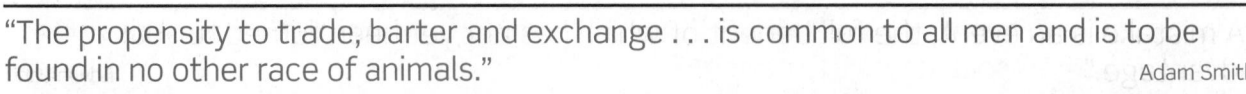

"The propensity to trade, barter and exchange . . . is common to all men and is to be found in no other race of animals."

Adam Smith

enforced competition and against price-fixing.

Although often castigated as such, Smith was neither inhumane nor a proponent of "the law of the jungle" as an approach to social organization. He recognized the worst tendencies of some businessmen who "love to reap where they never sowed," and was extremely aware of how greed could lead to excesses of monopoly and corruption. Smith did, in fact, support some forms of intervention, especially in public areas such as defense. He did not, however, have our benefit of hindsight, or know how the Industrial Revolution would change society, creating some extremely wealthy businessmen, and a mass of extremely poor industrial workers, who would suffer greatly because of their lack of protection from regulatory laws.

The Law of Labor

Natural law was considered by Smith to encompass a "law of labor." According to this, the external environment could provide people with the products necessary for subsistence, in return for their labor, and all people should therefore have the right to perform activities to preserve their existence. Government's only role should be to promote the existence of natural law and to enable its free working.

The natural laws were assumed to work in the same exacting way as mathematical laws. Left to themselves, they should establish an order that would benefit both individuals and society. Individualism, for Smith and the other economists and philosophers of his time, meant relief from the constraints of mercantilism, the right to economic freedom, and the right of a people to legislate for themselves and be taxed by the government they chose.

The Division of Labor

Smith gives many examples of the advantages of the division of labor, with each worker focusing upon a single stage of manufacture rather than, as in traditional crafts, being involved in every stage. His ideas were based on life before 1760, and he did not foresee how the introduction of machinery would make the division of labor even more logical and sometimes a harsh necessity.

The Free Market

Smith's main thesis throughout *The Wealth of Nations* was the inefficiency of government interference, which he demonstrates with reference to the markets for both national and international trade. He envisions a free market as a customer-driven, democratic mechanism through which, by exercising their free choices about purchase or sale prices, people would act to regulate resources fairly. Although it was Dudley North who first related supply to demand and extolled the benefits of free trade, Smith recognized that buyers as well as sellers profit from trade, and saw international commerce as a source of wealth for both importers and exporters.

Smith had a very positive vision of how a free market would eventually realize a state of "universal opulence" for everyone. He argued that each nation should concentrate on those industrial areas where it enjoyed a "comparative advantage." These ideas were taken up by subsequent economists such as Ricardo and Malthus, and can be traced within the thinking of some contemporary strategists, particularly in Michael Porter's work on competitive advantage.

Morality

Smith is often criticized for a lack of moral focus in *The Wealth of Nations* but he did assume that its readers would already know of the moral base given in *The Theory of Moral Sentiments*. The earlier book sought to explore moral judgments within the context of Smith's assumption that people are essentially driven by self-interest, and proposed that we all have "social propensities" for sympathy, justice, and benevolence.

ADAM SMITH IN PERSPECTIVE

The Wealth of Nations had a profound influence on English history, leading to the end of the mercantilist era and catalyzing a social and economic order based on individualism and the "natural laws" supposedly underlying competition and free market forces.

Smith's ideas have often been castigated for the support they gave to later businesspeople who grew very rich while rejecting any regulations to protect industrial workers. He wrote his masterpiece, however, before the Industrial Revolution began to take effect, and it was intended as a polemic against restrictive government policies and monopolistic abuses, rather than as a panegyric for unregulated business. Also, just as Smith's first book, *The Theory of Moral Sentiments*, supplies a moral aspect to complement *The Wealth of Nations*, it is probable that his intended, but unwritten, third volume on jurisprudence could have contributed ideas for legal safeguards to protect the public from abuses resulting from greed and collusion, since he considered these typically to arise out of people's business activities and contacts.

For his time, Smith was actually a social radical, promoting liberty and equality and denouncing various pillars of the existing establishment. From our modern perspective, it is clear there was no factual base for his ideas about natural law and harmony, and that perfect competition could not erase social problems, particularly when factors from a future that Smith could not have imagined (including giant corporations, economic cycles and depressions, mass unemployment, and mechanical warfare) became more pertinent. Despite this, however, *The Wealth of Nations* remains a "milestone" book offering a composite analysis that shaped our social and economic world.

1265

BUSINESS THINKERS

FOR MORE INFORMATION

Books:

Haakonssen, Knud, ed. *The Theory of Moral Sentiments*. New York: Cambridge University Press, 2002.

Smith, Adam. *Inquiry into the Nature and Causes of the Wealth of Nations* (abridged). Indianapolis, IN: Hackett Publishing Company, 1993.

"There is no art which one government sooner learns of another than that of draining money from the pockets of the people."

Adam Smith

Sun Tzu
Strategy and *The Art of War*

Eastern business methods had shaken Western management thinking long before *The Art of Japanese Management* or *In Search of Excellence*. The quality management techniques used by Japanese companies enabled them to put cheaper and better products into American and British stores than their domestic rivals. This led to an understanding that Japanese businesspeople have a different perspective on the marketplace from their Western counterparts.

c. 400 BC	Sun Tzu lived and wrote.
1780	First European translation of *The Art of War* published.
1910	English translation published.

LIFE AND CAREER

Although the precise dates of his birth and death are not known, Sun Tzu is thought to have lived over 2,400 years ago, at roughly the same time as Confucius. Raised in a family of army officers, he became familiar with, and eventually expert in, military affairs. Historians are generally agreed that he was a general who led a number of successful military campaigns in the region currently known as the Anhui Province. It is recorded that the state of Wu, under whose sovereign he served, became a dominant power at that time. Since then, it has become standard practice for Chinese military chiefs to familiarize themselves with Sun Tzu's writings.

KEY THINKING
The Art of War

Sun Tzu's *The Art of War* (the book's actual title is *Sun Tzu Ping Fa*, literally "The Military Method of Mr. Sun") is a compilation of his thinking on the strategies that underlie success in war. It has been translated into many languages, and there are several English versions. This account is based on the translation by Thomas Cleary, published by Shambhala Pocket Classics and available on the Internet. Two further editions, published by Tuttle and Wordsworth Editions respectively, were also consulted.

Sun Tzu's anecdotes and thoughts, which fill no more than about 25 pages of text in all, are divided into 13 sections:

1 strategic assessments
2 doing battle
3 offensive strategy
4 formation
5 force
6 emptiness and fullness
7 armed struggle
8 adaptations
9 maneuvering armies
10 terrain
11 nine grounds
12 attack by fire
13 use of spies

Some of these have less current relevance than others, but they are all worth at least a glance. Hidden among advice such as not to dally in salt marshes when retreating or attacking (11), there is the odd gem that is striking in its modernity. For example: "when a leader enters deeply into enemy territory with the troops, he brings out their potential." (11) The advice given in section 10 on how to proceed in narrow or steep terrain (occupy the high and sunny side to await your opponent) can be quickly passed over, but a little further on in the same section Sun Tzu's castigation of poor leadership is much more pertinent: "When generals are weak and lack authority, instructions are not clear, officers and soldiers lack consistency, and they form battle lines every which way; this is riot."

On Strategy

Many commentaries focus on the first section, strategic assessments, at the expense of the others. It is certainly there that, helped by a little lateral thinking, Sun Tzu seems best to relate to the spirit of modern business. He refers initially to five key factors that determine the result of war:

- politics—that which causes people to be in harmony with their ruler;
- weather—the seasons;
- terrain—distances, difficulty or ease of travel, opportunities or safety;
- leadership—a matter of intelligence, trustworthiness, humaneness, courage, and strictness;
- discipline—organization, chain of command, logistics.

There are also seven issues to be appraised (the postscript following each question has been added to indicate the line most interpretations take).

- Whose moral influence is the stronger? (Whose followers are more willing to subscribe to common goals?)
- Which leader is the more able? (Who has the ability to combine benevolence and compassion with boldness and strict discipline?)
- Which army has greater advantage of nature and terrain? (Whom do politics, economic cycles, investment, and social and cultural factors favor? Who understands the bigger picture?)
- Whose laws and rules are more effective? (Do people understand what is expected as a result of clear instructions and procedures?)
- Whose troops are stronger? (How can things be arranged so that small can compete effectively with large?)
- Whose soldiers are better trained? (Who uses delegation and training for organizational effectiveness?)
- Whose system of rewards and punishments is clearer? (Who is therefore able to generate higher performance and a better competitive position?)

The theme of strategy is picked up again and again, apparently at random. One interpretation stretches section 6 to make it relate to market presence and strategies of deception employed to fool competitor intelligence. Sun Tzu argues that "there is no constant good or bad, right or wrong: therefore victory in war is not repetitious, but adapts its form endlessly . . . so a military force has no constant formation, water has no constant shape: the ability to gain victory by changing and adapting according to the opponent is called genius." (6)

On Information and Intelligence

" . . . to fail to know the conditions of opponents because of reluctance to give re-

---

"Be polite. Write diplomatically. Even in a declaration of war one observes the rules of politeness."

Otto Edward Leopold von Bismarck

wards for intelligence is extremely inhuman, uncharacteristic of a true military leader ... so what enables an intelligent government and a wise military leadership to overcome others and achieve extraordinary accomplishments is foreknowledge ... [which] must be obtained from people who know the conditions of the enemy." (13)

On Tactics

"Making the armies able to take on opponents without being defeated is a matter of unorthodox and orthodox methods." (5)

"The difficulty of armed struggle is to make long distances near and make problems into advantages." (7)

On Competition and Competitor Intelligence

"So if you do not know the plans of your competitors, you cannot make informed alliances." (7)

"So the rule of military operations is not to count on opponents not coming, but to rely on having ways of dealing with them; not to count on opponents not attacking, but to rely on having what cannot be attacked." (8)

On Leadership and People Management

"If they rule armies without knowing the arts of complete adaptivity, even if they know what there is to gain, they cannot get people to work for them." (8)

"If soldiers are punished before a personal attachment to the leadership is formed, they will not submit, and if they do not submit, they are hard to employ." (9)

"Look upon your soldiers as you do infants, and they willingly go into deep valleys with you; look upon your soldiers as beloved children, and they willingly die with you." (10)

"If you are so nice to them that you cannot employ them, so kind to them that you cannot command them, so casual with them that you cannot establish order, they are like spoiled children, useless." (10)

On Communication

"When directives are consistently issued to edify the populace, the populace accepts ... when directives are consistently issued, there is mutual satisfaction between the leadership and the group." (9)

SUN TZU IN PERSPECTIVE

Historians tell us that the *Sun Tzu Ping Fa* is the oldest existing military treatise in the world, predating Clausewitz by 2,200 years. But so what? Does it have any relevance for people in business today? How can the thoughts of a Chinese general who lived two and a half millennia ago possibly inform, enlighten, or inspire a modern manager, or have any bearing on his or her day-to-day concerns? And even if there are interesting links, do they do any more than show us that ancient Chinese strategists did not differ fundamentally from modern businesspeople?

Sun Tzu's supporters, however, insist that his concepts are ageless. Although it is easy to stretch interpretation too far and find meaning anywhere if you look hard enough, such things as strategic intelligence, planning, attention to detail, cunning, deception, and theories of leadership in which the leader earns authority with the led, have universal value and are appropriate to any human arena and any period.

If part of Sun Tzu's modern appeal derives from the constant search for any nuggets of intelligence that may give an organization an edge over the competition, another part lies in the fact that the *Ping Fa* offers an opportunity to gain insights into the Oriental mindset that do not come from someone with a modern ax to grind or reputation to make. In addition, the insights are couched in direct, no-nonsense, hard-hitting language that makes them seem more, not less, pregnant with meaning.

As globalization brings East closer to West, business relationships will hinge on understanding cultures and attitudes that may appear strange at first. And wherever managers set strategic goals, sell their goods abroad, or interrelate with their workforce, *The Art of War* may still have something to say to them. It is finding its way into many MBA programs.

1267

BUSINESS THINKERS

FOR MORE INFORMATION

Books:

Kaufman, Stephen F. *The Art of War: The Definitive Interpretation of Sun Tzu's Classic Book of Strategy for the Martial Artist.* Rutland, VT: Charles E Tuttle, 1996.

Sun Tzu. *The Art of War.* Trans. Thomas Cleary. Boston, MA: Shambhala Pocket Classics, 1991.

Journal Articles:

Crainer, Stuart. "Braingain." *Management Today,* April 1998, pp. 68–70.

Min Chen. "Sun Tzu's Strategic Thinking and Contemporary Business." *Business Horizons,* March/April 1994, pp. 42–48.

"Do not expect everyone to agree with you ... Do not consider all opponents to be enemies."

Wess Roberts

Genichi Taguchi
Veteran Design and Development Engineer

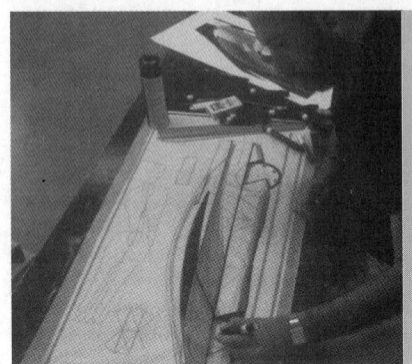

Taguchi is famous for his pioneering methods of modern quality control and low-cost quality engineering. He is the founder of what has come to be known as the Taguchi method, which seeks to improve product quality at the design stage by integrating quality control into product design, using experiment and statistical analysis.

Taguchi's methods have influenced design and engineering around the world.

1924	Born.
1942–1945	Serves in Japanese navy during World War II.
1945	Works in Ministry of Public Health and Welfare and Ministry of Education.
1950	Joins Electrical Communication Laboratory (ECL) of Nippon Telephone and Telegraph Company.
1960	Wins Deming prize for contribution to field of quality engineering (later wins it three more times).
1962	Awarded doctorate by Kyushsu University.
1964	Takes up professorship at Aoyamagokuin University in Japan.
1970s	Develops concept of the quality loss function.
1980s	Visits AT&T Bell Laboratories in the United States; U.S. interest in his methodology established.
1983	Becomes executive director of the Ford Supplier Institute.
1986	Receives Indigo Ribbon from the emperor of Japan; medal from International Technology Institute.
1986	Institute of Statisticians organizes conference in London; Taguchi's ideas become known in Europe.
1987	U.K. Taguchi Club formed (now the Quality Methods Association); ideas adopted widely in the West, particularly in the auto industry.
1995	Honorary member of Japanese Society of Quality Control.
1998	Honorary member of the American Society for Quality (ASQ).

LIFE AND CAREER

Genichi Taguchi, born in Japan in 1924, served in the Navigation Institute of the Japanese navy during World War II. He then worked in the Ministry of Public Health and Welfare and in the Institute of Statistical Mathematics of the Ministry of Education, meeting the renowned statistician, Matosaburo Masuyame, who nurtured his statistical skills.

In 1950, Taguchi joined the Electrical Communication Laboratory (ECL) of Nippon Telephone and Telegraph Company, gaining six years' experience in experimentation and data analysis while developing telephone switching systems. The commercial benefits resulting from his ECL work helped Taguchi to earn the Deming prize in 1960, for his contribution to the field of quality engineering. He went on to win this award, one of Japan's most prestigious commendations, three more times.

In 1962, Taguchi was awarded a doctorate by Kyushu University, after working with industrial statisticians (and beginning his work on the signal-to-noise ratio) at Bell Laboratories in the United States. He continued working for ECL in a consulting role and became part of the associate research staff of the Japanese Standards Association, where he founded the Quality Research Group. In 1964, he took up a professorship at Aoyamagokuin University in Japan, where he spent the next 17 years developing his methods.

Throughout this time, Taguchi was largely unknown outside Japan. He developed his concept of the quality loss function in the early 1970s, but it was during the 1980s that Taguchi's methods became established, when he revisited AT&T Bell Laboratories in the United States, as director of the Japanese Academy of Quality.

After that, interest from U.S. companies such as Xerox, Ford, and ITT in Taguchi's methodology increased. In 1982, Taguchi was involved in seminars for Ford executives, and the following year he became executive director of the Ford Supplier Institute (later known as the American Supplier Institute). He was also further honored in 1986, receiving the Indigo Ribbon from the emperor of Japan for his contribution to Japanese economics and industry, and the International Technology Institute's medal for his work on statistical methods to achieve cost and quality improvements.

Throughout much of this time, Taguchi was also operating as a full-time consultant to various major companies in the United States, Japan, China, and India. Apart from occasional work with, for example, Lucas Industries, Taguchi's ideas only became known in Europe from 1986, when the Institute of Statisticians organized a conference in London. The U.K. Taguchi Club (now the Quality Methods Association) was formed the following year and, since then, Taguchi methods have been in regular and widespread use in the West, particularly in the auto industry. Taguchi himself is now in semiretirement.

KEY THINKING
Taguchi Methods

Taguchi developed methods for both online (process) and offline (design) quality control, which formed the basis of his approach to total quality control and assurance within a product's development life cycle. His approach emphasized improving the quality of product and process prior to manufacture (that is, at the design stage) rather than the more traditional approach of achieving quality through inspection.

Quality Loss Function

Taguchi's approach differed from the traditional one of manufacturing a product within a specification based on tolerances, equally spaced around a target value. He developed a concept of "quality loss" occurring as soon as there is a deviation away from the target value, and worked in terms of quality loss rather than just quality. He defined quality loss as "the loss imparted to

---

"In broad terms, quality planning consists of developing the products and processes required to meet the customer's needs."

Joseph M. Juran

society from the time the product is shipped," and this related the loss to society as a whole. Thus, it included both company costs, such as reworking, scrapping, and maintenance, and any loss to the customer through poor product performance and reduced reliability.

A loss function curve can be calibrated by using information from the customer. A target value is identified as being the best possible value of a quality characteristic. Taguchi associates a simple, quadratic loss function with deviations from the target. Thus:

- the smaller the performance variation, the better the quality of the product;
- the larger the deviation from the target value, the larger the loss to society.

A loss will occur even when the product is within the specification allowed, although it is minimal when the product is on target.

After the design engineer has determined the cost of parts being manufactured out of specification, this information can be used to justify expenditure on quality improvement, enabling decisions to be made on firm cost and quality grounds. Thus, it is possible to estimate whether the "quality gain" from changing a design is worthwhile—although ensuring that a product is produced at a quality level acceptable to the customer remains an important consideration.

Signal-to-Noise Ratio

One of Taguchi's most innovative ideas was to use a quality measure called the "signal-to-noise ratio," which communications engineers could employ to find the strength of an electrical signal. Taguchi applied this measure to everyday products, and used it as a measure to choose control levels that could best cope with changes in operating and environmental conditions, or noise.

Robust Quality of Design

On the basis of the signal-to-noise measure, Taguchi was able to develop the concept of robustness, which enables a product to be designed to be less affected by noise. Given normal variations in process operations, the product in question would be less likely to fail acceptable quality criteria.

Product Design Improvement

During the product design and production engineering phases, Taguchi set out three steps that must be followed.

1 System design. This may involve the development of a prototype design, and will determine the materials, parts, and assembly system to be used. The manufacturing process has also to be considered.

2 Parameter design. Taguchi's parameter design aimed to find the most cost-effective way of controlling noise. Taguchi's process and design improvements are gained by identifying easily controllable factors and settings that minimize performance variation. Controllable factors are design factors that a designer can set or easily adjust. The specified value becomes the signal. Uncontrollable factors are noise, or external variations, and a higher signal-to-noise ratio means better quality. Taguchi found that if controllable factors were set at optimal levels, the product would be robust to external changes. This was achieved through parameter design applied at the design (offline) stage to reduce or remove the effect of noise factors.

Experiments were designed using orthogonal arrays that (rather simply described) were a series of rows and columns allowing the effects of different factors to be extracted and separated out. Taguchi was not the inventor of the orthogonal array, but this type of experimentation moved away from the traditional approach of testing one factor at a time. His new approach dramatically reduced the number of experiments and prototypes required and, in consequence, costs were much lower. He developed various experimental designs that allowed the variability of the noise factors on each controllable factor setting to be simulated. The settings that minimized variability could then be determined.

3 Tolerance design. If parameter design failed, Taguchi suggested using tolerance design to identify the most crucial noise factors. Tolerances could be reassigned so that the overall variability was reduced to acceptable levels.

Invest Last not First

Taguchi placed much emphasis on optimizing the product and process at the beginning, in order to engineer product quality (parameter design) into the system. Using low-cost materials and components was a vital feature of this, and money was spent on higher cost items only when necessary (tolerance design).

GENICHI TAGUCHI IN PERSPECTIVE

It was W. E. Deming who first recognized the importance of moving quality control backward from inspection to proper process control, notably via statistical process control (SPC). Taguchi moved quality control even further back, to the design stage, thus completing the total quality loop. Taguchi's techniques and statistical experimental designs for offline quality improvement complemented SPC, to achieve online quality improvement. Deming's philosophy regarding management quality improvement encompassed both.

It has been said that Deming's work inspired a revolution in the old management culture, while Taguchi inspired evolution. Certainly Deming provided a theory mainly for management, while Taguchi provided important techniques for improving a process at every stage, from design to production, and for keeping the improved processes under control.

FOR MORE INFORMATION

Taguchi, Genichi, Subir Chowdhury, Shin Taguchi, and Rajesh Jugulum. *Taguchi's Robust Engineering: Learn How to Boost Quality While Reducing Costs and Time to Market.* New York: McGraw-Hill, 1999.

Taguchi, Genichi, Subir Chowdhury, and Yuin Wu. *The Mahalanobis-Taguchi System.* New York: McGraw-Hill, 2000.

Ohno, Taiichi, Elsayed A. Elsayed, and Thomas C. Hsiang. *Quality Engineering in Production Systems.* New York: McGraw-Hill, 1989.

Taguchi, Genichi. *Introduction to Quality Engineering: Designing Quality into Product and Processes.* Tokyo: Asian Productivity Organization, 1986.

Taguchi, Genichi. *The System of Experimental Design, vols. 1 & 2.* New York: Kraus International Publications, 1987.

FURTHER READING

Books: *Taguchi Methods: Applications in World Industry*

Logothetis, Nickolas. *Managing for Total Quality: from Deming to Taguchi and SPC.* New York: Prentice Hall, 1992.

See also:
 W. Edwards Deming (pp. 1196–1197)

1269

BUSINESS THINKERS

"The excellent companies treat the rank and file as the root source of quality and productivity gain."

Tom Peters

Frederick Winslow Taylor

Father of Scientific Management

BUSINESS THINKERS

Peter Drucker was often called "the guru's guru." Drucker himself would have suggested that the accolade should be given to Frederick Winslow Taylor (1856–1917). "On Taylor's 'scientific management' rests, above all, the tremendous surge of affluence in the last 75 years which has lifted the working masses in the developed countries well above any level recorded, even for the well-to-do," Drucker wrote in *Management: Tasks, Responsibilities, Practices*.

1856	Born.
1874	Becomes an apprentice pattern-maker and machinist at Enterprise Hydraulic Works.
1878	Takes unskilled job at the Midvale Steel Works.
1881	Gains master's degree in mechanical engineering.
1890	Becomes general manager of Manufacturing Investment Company (MIC).
1898	Becomes joint discoverer of the Taylor-White process, a method of tempering steel.
1911	Publication of *The Principles of Scientific Management*.
1915	Dies.

LIFE AND CAREER

Although Taylor passed the entrance examination for Harvard College, failing eyesight meant that he could not become a student there. Instead he took the unusual step for someone of his background of becoming an apprentice pattern-maker and machinist at the Enterprise Hydraulic Works in Philadelphia.

Following his apprenticeship, Taylor took up an unskilled job at the Midvale Steel Works. After several different jobs and a master's degree in mechanical engineering, he was appointed chief engineer there. In 1890 he became general manager of Manufacturing Investment Company (MIC), eventually becoming an independent consulting engineer to management.

In 1881, Taylor won the doubles championships of the United States Lawn Tennis Association and a year later, the doubles in

the Young American C. C. Lawn Tennis Tournament. Later in his career he developed a passion for golf and, in keeping with his love of experiment, attempted to make a putting green that was reliant on water below the surface rather than on natural rainfall. By the time of his death, Taylor's experiments had led to him filing at least 50 patents and had made him an extremely wealthy man.

KEY THINKING
Scientific Management

Taylor's seminal work—*The Principles of Scientific Management*—was published six years before his death. In it, he put forward his ideas of "scientific management" (sometimes referred to today as "Taylorism"), which differed from traditional "initiative and incentive" methods of management. These ideas were an accumulation from his life's work, and included several examples from his places of employment. The four overriding principles of scientific management are as follows.

- Each part of a job is analyzed "scientifically," and the most efficient method for undertaking it is devised—the "one best way" of working. This consists of examining the implements needed to perform the work, and measuring the maximum amount a "first-class" worker can do in a day. Workers are then expected to do this much work every day.
- The most suitable person to undertake the job is chosen, again "scientifically." The individual is taught to do the job in the exact way devised. Everyone, according to Taylor, has the ability to be "first class" at some job. It is management's role to find out which job suits each employee and train them until they are first class.

- Managers must cooperate with workers to ensure the job is done in the scientific way.
- There is a clear "division" of work and responsibility between management and workers. Managers concern themselves with the planning and supervision of the work, and workers carry it out.

Taylor summed up the differences between his principles of management and the traditional method as: "Under the management of 'initiative and incentive,' practically the whole problem is 'up to the workman'; while under the scientific management, fully one-half of the problem is 'up to the management' ... The principal object of management should be to secure the maximum prosperity for the employer, coupled with the maximum prosperity for each employee." Taylor could justify his methods because he felt that his long-term goal would lead to "diminution of poverty, and the alleviation of suffering."

His main reason for developing scientific management was that he wished to do away with "soldiering" or "natural laziness," as he believed that all workers spent little time putting in full effort. To do this, Taylor aimed to analyze every job in a scientific way so that no one could be in any doubt about how much work could and should be done in a day. He felt that "every single act of every workman can be reduced to a science." Much inconclusive argument has ensued as to whether he was the pioneer of time and motion study. Certainly, time study played as important a part in Taylor's scientific job and task analysis as the examination of a worker's movements and the implements he used.

Inherent in Taylor's management style was the establishment of planning departments, staffed by clerks who ensured that "every laborer's work was planned out well in advance, and the workmen were moved from place to place ... very much as chessmen are moved on a chessboard, a telephone and messenger system having been installed for this purpose." He concluded that, in this way, "a large amount of the time lost through having too many men in one place and too few in another, and through waiting between jobs, was entirely eliminated." Such a policy did, however, require the establishment of a more "elaborate organization and system," which sowed the seeds for Max Weber's bureaucratic organization structure. Taylor's approach consti-

"The more a person can do, the more can motivate them."   Frederick Herzberg

tuted one of the first formal divisions between those who do the work (workers) and those who supervise and plan it (managers).

Management and Workers

For workers on the shop floor, scientific management brought a dramatic loss in skill level and autonomy. As well as being subject to increased supervision, workers were no longer able to use their own tools, which they might have spent many years modifying to suit their own style. In many cases, however, Taylor's ideas were extremely effective. In the case of shovelers at the Bethlehem Steel Works, workers earned higher wages and the company saved between $75,000 and $80,000 per year through greater efficiency.

Although Taylor believed that disputes between managers and workers would be eliminated because what "constitutes a fair day's work will be a question for scientific investigation, instead of a subject to be bargained and haggled over," there were several occasions when his ideas came into conflict with labor organizations. His opinion of such unions was invariably derogatory, as he was convinced that their objective was to limit the output of their members. Because of this, Taylor focused on the individual, believing that where a group of workers was formed, peer pressure would be used to ensure each man did not work to his full capacity. In the Bethlehem Steel Works, he decreed that no more than four men could work together in a gang without a special permit.

Even the way he wrote about unskilled workers was condescending. "Now one of the very first requirements for a man who is fit to handle pig iron as a regular occupation is that he shall be so stupid and phlegmatic that he more nearly resembles in his mental make-up the ox than any other type" is a typical example.

Although Taylor's manner often appeared inhumane, he also wrote: "If the workman fails to do his task, some competent teacher should be sent to show him exactly how his work can best be done, to guide, help, and to encourage him and, at the same time, to study his possibilities as a workman. So that, under the plan which individualizes each workman, instead of brutally discharging the man or lowering his wages to make good at once, he is given the time and the help required to make him proficient at his present job, or he is shifted to another class of work for which he is either mentally or physically better suited."

Contemporary Reaction to Scientific Management

It is easy to see why Taylor's work was regarded as inhumane. However good his motives of bringing about the greater good for the worker on the shop floor, the alleviation of poverty, and the elimination of waste, his methods were extremely hard and sometimes had the opposite effect.

It took him three years to implement some of his methods in the Midvale Steel Works. The workers resorted to breaking their machines in an attempt to prove to management that Taylor was overworking them. In response, he fined anyone whose machine broke, until eventually "they got sick of being fined, their opposition broke down, and they promised to do a fair day's work."

FREDERICK WINSLOW TAYLOR IN PERSPECTIVE

Many of Taylor's ideas are relevant to the modern day. Three in particular, taken from *The Principles of Scientific Management*, stand out:

- Rewards: "A reward, if it is to be most effective in stimulating men to do their best work, must come soon after the work has been done ... The average workman must be able to measure what he has accomplished and clearly see his reward at the end of each day if he is to do his best." In Taylor's view, it was pointless to involve the shop floor workers in end-of-year profit sharing plans.
- Quality standards: The use of written documentation for each part of a worker's job, inherent in scientific management, is strikingly prescient of the procedural documentation used in the ISO 9000 series of quality standards. "In the case of a machine-shop which is managed under the modern system, detailed written instructions as to the best way of doing each piece of work are prepared in advance, by men in the planning department. These instructions represent the combined work of several men in the planning room, each of whom has his own specialty, or function ... The directions of all of these men, however, are written on a single instruction card, or sheet." The main difference is that today's best practice means involving staff in drawing up their own procedures.
- Suggestion plans: Taylor proposed a form of incentive for employees to make suggestions if they felt an improvement could be made, either to the method or the implement used to undertake a task. If, after analysis, the suggestion was introduced into the workplace, the person suggesting it "should be given the full credit for the improvement, and should be paid a cash premium as a reward for his ingenuity. In this way the true initiative of the workmen is better attained under scientific management than under the old individual plan."

At the time of his death in 1917, Taylor's work was the subject of much debate, both for and against. His approach is now frowned on as "Victorian," but it should not be forgotten that he was a man of his times and sought solutions to the problems of his times. The main criticism of Taylor is that his approach was too mechanistic—treating people like machines or as unthinking creatures to be trained like dogs, rather than as human beings.

However, he was one of the first true pioneers of management through his scientific examination of the way work is done, and his thinking led directly to the achievements of other management gurus such as Max Weber and Henry Ford.

FOR MORE INFORMATION

Books:
Kakar, Sudhir. *Frederick Taylor: A Study in Personality and Innovation.* Cambridge, MA: MIT Press, 1970.
Nelson, Daniel. *Frederick W. Taylor and the Rise of Scientific Management.* Madison, WI: University of Wisconsin Press, 1980.
Taylor, Frederick Winslow. *Shop Management* in *Scientific Management* (comprising *Shop Management, The Principles of Scientific Management, Testimony before the Special House Committee*). New York: Harper, 1947.
Taylor, Frederick Winslow. *The Principles of Scientific Management.* New York: W. W. Norton, 1967.

See also:
:ᵥ: Frank and Lillian Gilbreth (pp. 1210–1211)
:ᵥ: Henry Laurence Gantt (pp. 1206–1207)
:ᵥ: Max Weber (pp. 1276–1277)

"You know as well as I do that a high-priced man has to do exactly as he is told from morning to night."

F. W. Taylor

Alvin Toffler
The Futurologist's Futurologist

A leading authority on change, Alvin Toffler is anything but a soothsayer. He carefully avoids words like "trend" and "prediction" in his writing and insists that nobody can tell for certain what will happen in the future. His special gift is an understanding of the effects of change. It comes from a broad and deep knowledge of science, technology, and the arts, and a capacity to deduce what might result when complex technological and social changes impact on entrenched attitudes and vested interests.

1928	Born.
1965	Coins the term "future shock" in an article in *Horizon*.
1969–1970	Works as consultant for AT&T.
1970	Publication of *Future Shock*.
1977	Cofounds Institute for Alternative Futures with Clement Bezold and James Dator.
1980	Publication of *The Third Wave*.
1986	Helps establish Issyk-Kul Forum, the first non-Communist, nongovernmental organization in the former USSR.
1990	Publication of *Powershift*.
1993	Publication of *War and Anti-War*.
1996	Founds Toffler Associates, an executive advisory firm.

LIFE AND CAREER

Alvin Toffler was born in 1928. Though he has traveled widely, he gained all his education and working experience in the United States. He has been a visiting fellow at the Russell Sage Foundation, a visiting professor at Cornell University, a faculty member of the New School for Social Research, and a highly successful business consultant. He has several honorary degrees, and his books have won many awards.

Much of Toffler's work has been created in collaboration with his wife Heidi—as he is always the first to point out. Theirs is a long-standing partnership: both studied English at New York University and then entered the heady Bohemian world of postwar Greenwich Village, where their interests were mainly in writing poetry and planning novels.

Not a scientist by first choice, Toffler understood from a very young age the importance of science and technology in the modern world and took a course in the history of technology.

The Tofflers spent several years in journalism, writing for publications ranging from *Fortune* and *Playboy* to the leading political, scientific, and economic journals of the day. In 1960 an invitation from IBM to write a paper on the long-term social and organizational implications of the computer gave them a lengthy exposure to high technology. From this seminal experience grew the all-consuming interest in change, for which they are now world-famous. *Future Shock*, the first book in Toffler's great trilogy on change, was begun shortly after completing the IBM paper.

KEY THINKING

Though he has published many books and countless articles and papers, Toffler's philosophy, and most of his key ideas, are encapsulated in three books: *Future Shock* (1970), *The Third Wave* (1980), and *Powershift* (1990). Each is a self-standing work in its own right, but they combine to form a trilogy that develops Toffler's ideas about change in a seamless dialogue.

Toffler gives his own brief summation of what the trilogy is all about in the preface to *Powershift*: " . . . the central subject is change—what happens to people when their entire society abruptly transforms itself into something new and unexpected. *Future Shock* looks at the process of change—how change affects people and organizations. *The Third Wave* focuses on the directions of change—where today's changes are taking us. *Powershift* deals with the control of changes still to come—who will shape them and how."

Besides giving a painstaking analysis of change and the many challenges and problems it brings, the trilogy is full of hope. The books argue, convincingly, that the rapid change all around us is not so chaotic or random as it first appears; there are patterns and recognizable forces behind it. Understanding these patterns and forces will allow us to cope "strategically" with change, and to avoid haphazard responses to individual events as they are encountered.

The Trilogy: *Future Shock*

Toffler has described the effect of too much change occurring too quickly so well, that the expression "future shock" has entered the world's vocabulary and is now widely used to define the disorientation, confusion, and breakdown of decision-making capacity that afflicts individuals, groups, and whole societies when they are overwhelmed by change.

In his preface to *Powershift*, Toffler contends that "the acceleration of history carries consequences of its own, independent of the actual direction of change. The simple speed-up of events and reaction times produces its own effects, whether the changes are perceived as good or bad."

Future Shock was written over 30 years ago, and of Toffler's foresight. What we find is quite remarkable; he anticipated the break-up of the nuclear family, the genetic revolution, the "throwaway" society, the resurgence of emphasis on education, and the increased importance of knowledge in society.

The Third Wave

This book explores perhaps Toffler's most elegant theory, adding a "third wave" to the other two great and generally recognized surges in human development.

The first came with the introduction of agriculture, and humankind's revolutionary shift from hunter-gatherer to settled farmer. This released it from the constant struggle for subsistence, providing the stability and security needed to develop the arts and technology that are the basis of civilization as we know it today.

The second was the industrial revolution, the remarkable leap forward in manufacturing methods and the organization of labor that created the industrialized world. The exploitation of raw materials, mass production, and an ever more ingenious applica-

"It is always easier to talk about change than to make it. It is easier to consult than to manage."

Alvin Toffler

tion of technology brought prosperity and comfort to those countries that could embrace the necessary changes.

Toffler's third wave is the post-industrial, information-based revolution that began, he suggests, in the 1950s, with a number of major technological and social changes.

In *The Third Wave*, Toffler predicted with an uncanny foresight both the profound effects of information technology and biotechnology on the economy, and the changes we can now see taking place in manufacturing methods, marketing, and working patterns. He showed particular prescience in foreseeing the development of niche marketing and the increased power of the consumer. He even invented a new word—"prosumer"—to designate the fusion of producer and consumer.

In his introduction to the book, Toffler talks of the seemingly chaotic changes of the 1960s that produced "a culture of warring specialisms, drowned in fragmented data and fine-toothed analysis," and a climate in which synthesis "is not merely useful—it is crucial." It was to address this need for synthesis that Toffler conceived *The Third Wave*. It is, he claims, "a book of large-scale synthesis [that] describes the old civilization in which many of us grew up, and presents a careful, comprehensive picture of the new civilization bursting into being in our midst."

He goes on to say: " . . . the world that is fast emerging from the clash of new values and technologies, new geophysical relationships, new life-styles and modes of communication, demands wholly new ideas and analogies, classifications and concepts. We cannot cram the embryonic world of tomorrow into yesterday's conventional cubby holes."

Powershift

In this, the final book of the trilogy, Toffler carries forward his earlier analysis with an exploration of how individuals, organizations, and nations will be affected by inevitable changes in the way power is perceived and applied. He talks of a "new power system replacing that of the industrial past."

The word "powershift" in the title means something very different from the usual two-word term "power shift." Toffler says that, while a power shift is a transfer of power, a "powershift" is "a deep-level change in the very nature of power." A pow-

ershift does not merely transfer power, but also transforms it.

In *Powershift* we are reminded of the three basic sources of power: violence, wealth, and knowledge. All businesses work in what Toffler describes as a "power-field," where these three "tools of power" constantly operate. The rising importance of knowledge, so eloquently argued throughout the trilogy, has brought about a profound change in the balance between them.

Powershift gives no hint of an early solution to the problems associated with change. Toffler talks about the struggles to come as individuals, businesses, and national economies move away from their traditional sources of power toward a new dependence on knowledge. In his view, the problems will not be over when these power conflicts are resolved. He sees even greater challenges ahead as divisions develop between "fast" and "slow" economies.

Another idea, explored throughout the trilogy but most strongly in *Powershift*, is what Toffler calls "de-massification." By this he means a reversal of the trend toward "mass" solutions prevalent in the late 20th-century. He sees mass marketing giving way to niche and micro-marketing; mass production being replaced by increasingly customized production; and large corporations being broken down into small, autonomous units. Even politics and the concept of nationhood, Toffler believes, will be affected by the pressure to "de-massify," created by the increasing awareness of better-informed individuals and made effective by the unstoppable development of information technology.

ALVIN TOFFLER IN PERSPECTIVE

Influential as Toffler's trilogy continues to be, it must be remembered that the last of the three books was published in 1990; it would be misleading to imply that Toffler's work started or finished at that point. *The Adaptive Corporation*, for example, published in 1985, was built around the report resulting from Toffler's 1969–70 consulting work for AT&T. Ignored by senior management at the time, this report became influential later, at the time of the Bell divestiture. The book deals with questions of organizational change and adaptation through focusing on the case of AT&T.

Other books and articles have appeared

since the trilogy and, from the time of the publication of *Powershift*, Heidi Toffler has allowed her role to be more formally acknowledged; the Tofflers' more recent publications have been under explicit joint authorship.

Their contribution to world politics is something many management commentators neglect. Respected by many world leaders, they have played a significant part in improving East-West relations. Mikhail Gorbachev is an admirer whom they have met several times and greatly influenced.

The Tofflers also visited China and were having a positive effect on Chinese politics until the disastrous reversals following the Tiananmen Square episode. Their books are now banned in China though, of course, banning books often merely serves to increase their influence.

Of the Tofflers' major publications in the last ten years, *War and Anti-War* is usually regarded as the most important. It focuses on warfare, suggesting that changes in the way we do business are matched by a parallel revolution in how we make war—and that, like so many in commerce and manufacturing, these military changes derive directly from advances in information technology. Their ideas have already been proved correct in the Gulf War and elsewhere, but Alvin Toffler's most chillingly accurate prediction came in an interview he gave for the *New Scientist* magazine of March 1994, where he spoke of the inadequacy of conventional military force in controlling terrorist action. To illustrate his point, he quoted a former U.S. intelligence officer as saying that, if he had 20 people and a million dollars, he could shut down America. Seven years later the events of September 11, 2001 provided appalling evidence of this statement's credibility.

1273

BUSINESS THINKERS

FOR MORE INFORMATION

Books:

Toffler, Alvin. *Future Shock*. New York: Random House, 1970.

Toffler, Alvin. *The Third Wave*. New York: Bantam, 1980.

Toffler, Alvin. *Powershift*. New York: Bantam Books, 1990.

Toffler, Alvin, and Heidi Toffler. *War and Anti-War*. New York: Little, Brown, 1993.

Victor H. Vroom
Motivation and Leadership Decision Making

Victor H. Vroom is acknowledged as a leading authority on the psychological analysis of behavior in organizations. His major contributions include work on motivation in the workplace, illustrated by his expectancy model, and research into leadership styles and decision making. From the latter, he and Philip Yetton developed a model for selecting appropriate methods of problem solving for different situations.

1274

BUSINESS THINKERS

1932	Born.
1955	Receives M.A. from McGill University.
1958	Receives Ph.D. from the University of Michigan.
1964	Publication of *Work and Motivation*.
1972	Appointed chairman of the department of administrative science at Yale.
1973	Publication of *Leadership and Decision-Making*, coauthored by Philip Yetton and containing the Vroom/Yetton model.
1973–present	John G. Searle Professor of Organization and Management and Professor of Psychology, Yale.

LIFE AND CAREER

Born in Canada in 1932, Victor Vroom received his bachelor's and master's degrees at McGill University and a Ph.D. at the University of Michigan. He taught at the universities of Michigan and Pennsylvania and the Carnegie Institute of Technology before being appointed John G. Searle Professor of Organization and Management and Professor of Psychology at Yale University's School of Management. He has also acted as a consultant to many large organizations.

Vroom's work spans the two disciplines of management and psychology. He first applied psychology to organizations in a prize-winning doctoral dissertation in 1960. This examined the effects of personality on participation in decision making. His theories were further developed in a 1964 book, *Work and Motivation*, which applied expectancy theory to work for the first time. Expectancy theory maintains that people will be motivated to behave in certain ways if they believe that doing so will bring them rewards they seek and value.

Vroom's study of the causes of people's decisions to act in certain ways at work continued with his collaboration with Philip Yetton to develop what became known as the Vroom/Yetton model of leadership decision making (*Leadership and Decision-Making*, 1973). This is a contingency model that identifies styles of leadership appropriate to different situations. Specifically, it can be used by managers to assess the degree to which they should encourage people to participate in the decision-making process. With Arthur Jago, Vroom further developed this model in *The New Leadership: Managing Participation in Organizations*.

KEY THINKING
Expectancy Theory

In *Work and Motivation* Vroom defines the central problem of motivation as "the explanation of choices made by organisms among different voluntary responses"(p.9). To understand how these choices are made, he defines the three concepts—valence, expectancy, and force—and describes how these work in conjunction to determine how people will decide to act, given possible routes of behavior leading to possible outcomes.

Valence is a term referring to a preference for one outcome over another. An outcome is said to have positive valence when a person prefers attaining it to not attaining it; when he or she prefers not to attain an outcome, then it has a negative valence; and when he or she is indifferent to whether an outcome is attained or not, it has a valence of zero. If a manager particularly wants a promotion, for example, and thinks that successful completion of a certain project will earn that promotion, then he or she will attach a positive valence to completing the project, and be motivated to do so by the perceived value of the reward.

A person's behavior, however, is affected not only by preference for one outcome over another, but also by how likely he or she believes these outcomes to be. Vroom defines expectancy as "a momentary belief concerning the likelihood that a particular act will be followed by a particular outcome" (p. 17). Expectancy can be assigned a value from zero (the belief that the outcome will not follow on from the action) to one (the belief that the outcome certainly will follow on from the action). If someone wants a cup of coffee, for example, and knows that there is a drinks machine in the staff room, that person will walk straight there. The act of walking there has a high expectancy value in terms of obtaining coffee, whereas the act of walking to, say, the post room has a low expectancy value, as the person does not expect to find coffee there.

The third concept that Vroom outlines is force. He argues that a person's behavior is the result of a field of forces, each of which has direction and magnitude. Mathematical values assigned to the valences and expectancies for acts are combined to produce their hypothetical force, and the act that produces the highest level of force is assumed to be the one that the person will choose. The highest levels of force will be produced by actions with high levels of both valence and expectation.

Vroom's model is summed up in an equation:

$$M = (E \times V)$$

where M is the motivational force resulting from the sum of expectancy and valence, E is the expectancy measure and V represents the valence for the individual of a particular outcome. (Source: Martin, J. *Organizational Behavior*. Boston: International Thompson Business Press, 1998.)

Vroom's theory can be put into practice by interviewing individuals or giving them questionnaires to assess their expectancies and valences. These are then scored, and the expectancy score is multiplied by the valence score. The results for all outcomes that could be produced by a particular behavioral alternative are added together to give the expected value (EV) of that alternative. Each possible course of behavior can be assigned an EV in this way, and the model

---

"One more time, how do you motivate?"

Frederick Herzberg

predicts that the one with the highest EV will be a subject's most likely choice.

The primary implication for managers is that, since motivation is closely tied to reward, they should aim to encourage high work performance by tailoring rewards to those things which employees value most—and some research will be needed here to find out just what these might be for each individual. Incentives and benefits should be explicitly linked to actions which are in line with the organization's strategy and which will contribute to its success.

This is a normative model: it can only predict how people should make decisions to act, rather than how they actually do make such decisions. In reality, few people are well enough informed about all the possible choices and all the possible outcomes to make balanced judgments as to which behavior it would be best for them to adopt. As a theory explaining a general approximation of an individual's behavior, however, it has gained much support.

In 1968 Vroom's expectancy theory was extended by L. W. Porter and E. E. Lawler in their book *Managerial Attitudes and Performance* (Homewood: Richard D. Irwin, 1968). Their model emphasized that performance is also affected by factors other than motivation.

Subsequent research has focused on showing that expectancy models can be used quite accurately to predict choice of occupation, levels of job satisfaction, and levels of work effort. An extensive review of recent research on expectancy theory can be found in "Old Friends, New Faces: Motivation Research in the 1990s," by Maureen L. Ambrose and Carol T. Kulik (*Journal of Management*, May/June 1999).

Vroom/Yetton Model of Leadership Decision Making

Vroom's second major model, developed with Philip Yetton, shows how different leadership styles can be harnessed in solving different types of problems.

In *Leadership and Decision-Making* (1973), they developed a set of rules that can be used to determine the level and form of participation in the decision-making process that will support the best solution in different problem-solving situations. New managers may think they must make decisions alone, but Vroom clearly believes that this is not the case. He outlines types of decision-making involved in both group problems that affect a manager's workgroup, and in

individual problems that affect only the manager. The following list from *Leadership and Decision-Making* (p. 13) shows the types of management decision methods for group problems:

- authority decisions—made by the manager alone without involving others. A1—the manager makes the decision on his own using information available at the time. A2—the manager makes the decision alone but obtains his information from subordinates or other group members first.
- consultative decisions—made by the manager after consultation with a group. C1—the manager approaches several other people individually to obtain their suggestions, then makes his own decision. C2—the manager brings several other people together at the same time as a group and collectively obtains their suggestions, then makes his own decision.
- group decisions—made by a whole group in consensus. G2—the manager brings together several other people at the same time and they discuss the problem to arrive at a consensus decision between them.

Five similar methods are defined for individual problems. The Vroom/Yetton model then proposes a decision tree based on seven rules, which managers can use to pinpoint the most appropriate method for a given situation.

By means of a sequence of questions, each requiring a yes/no answer that advances the manager along a decision tree path, the problem is ultimately defined as one of 14 types. Vroom and Yetton then recommend suitable methods of decision-making (from methods A1–G2 above) for each problem type.

Since some types of problem can be solved by more than one method, further means of choosing between them are needed. When Vroom and Arthur Jago revised the model in 1988, they suggested that time is one important factor to consider: person-hours carry a financial cost, and a swiftly made decision may be best; also, a decision might be required urgently, and participative processes may slow down the decision-making process.

The Vroom/Yetton model has been progressively developed by its original authors, and by Vroom and Jago, since its inception. Further factors examined include:

- the extent to which participation benefits the organization by offering development opportunities for participants;

- the influence of a manager's position in the organizational hierarchy on his or her problem-handling style;
- the styles adopted by women managers.

VICTOR H. VROOM IN PERSPECTIVE

Vroom has made valuable contributions in the fields of both management and psychology. His models have been tested and extended, and remain important landmarks in the discipline of industrial psychology. Vroom has explored other, neighboring aspects of industrial psychology, but the two theories outlined above remain his most famous and enduring work. The models proposed by Vroom, and by Vroom and Yetton, have contributed much to managers' understanding of behavior, and to their ability to mold behavior to produce the most favorable outcomes, and so to manage more effectively.

The Vroom/Yetton model of leadership decision making, however, was at the height of its fame a quarter of a century ago and management thinking has changed since then. There is now more emphasis on delegation, empowerment, flatter structures, and matrix management, all of which have implications for managers' choices of leadership style. Vroom himself is not oblivious to change and development, and has actually used it to justify the relevance of his work on the Yale Web site: "Managers seldom live in a static world. They change jobs, change organizations, move from one country to another, from sector to sector. [Such changes] . . . spur new challenges, new opportunities, and place new situational demands on leadership . . . Old habits must be discarded if one is to respond to today's challenges and opportunities."

1275

BUSINESS THINKERS

FOR MORE INFORMATION

Books:
Vroom, Victor. *Work and Motivation*. New York: Wiley, 1994.
Vroom, Victor, and Philip Yetton. *Leadership and Decision-Making*. Pittsburgh, PA: University of Pittsburgh Press, 1973.
Vroom, Victor, and Arthur Jago. *The New Leadership: Managing Participation in Organizations*. Englewood Cliffs, NJ: Prentice Hall, 1988.

Max Weber
The Conceptualization of Bureaucracy

As he was the first to develop the concept of bureaucratic organization, any understanding of the way modern organizations work would be incomplete without at least a cursory study of Weber, who is commonly described as a founding father of sociology and whose work is also of historic importance from a managerial viewpoint. Weber's thoughts on the concepts of leadership, power, and authority are closely linked to his description of bureaucracy.

1864	Born.
1894	Professor of Political Economy, University of Freiburg, Germany.
1897	Professor of Political Economy, University of Heidelberg, Germany.
1904	First publication of *The Protestant Ethic and the Spirit of Capitalism*.
1919	Professor of Political Economy, University of Munich, Germany.
1920	Dies.

LIFE AND CAREER

Max Weber was born on April 21, 1864, the first of seven children, and grew up in a cultured bourgeois household, ruled by a strong authoritarian father. While at university in Heidelberg, Weber studied economics, medieval history, and philosophy as well as law. A period of military service brought him under the care of his uncle, Hermann Baumgarten, a historian, and his wife. Both uncle and aunt acted as mentors to Weber, the former as a liberal who treated him as an intellectual peer, the latter as a person who impressed him with her deep sense of social responsibility toward her charitable work. Both offered a stark contrast to Weber's father, who treated his son with patronizing authoritarianism.

It was probably during this formative period that Weber developed an aversion to the way people then most often gained positions of power and authority—through nepotism and accident of birth—factors he considered were lacking in legitimacy. He started to think of ways to free the individual as much as possible from personal judgments or from judgments clouded by emotion or self-interest.

After periods as a legal scholar at Heidel-berg and then at the University of Berlin, Weber became professor of political economy, first at the University of Freiburg, and later at Heidelberg.

His principal contribution to the study of organizations stemmed from his interest in understanding why people obeyed commands. This interest led him to distinguish between power as the ability to force obedience irrespective of resistance, and authority as the ability to get orders obeyed as a matter of course, apparently voluntarily.

KEY THINKING

Weber describes power as the probability of carrying out one's own will despite resistance or, at its extreme, as the ability to force people to obey. It is not necessarily the same as leadership or authority, but is invariably linked to them. He links organizational power to structure and authority, and considers it inherent in any hierarchy or bureaucracy. Invariably the effects of power depend on who has it, how that person is perceived, and the particular situation in which power is invoked. Weber identified three types of legitimate authority.

Charismatic Authority

The leader is obeyed because of followers' faith in his or her special, "supernatural" qualities. Weber proposed in his *Theory of Social and Economic Organization* that the term "charisma" was associated with someone who possesses exceptional, supernatural qualities and who is thus set apart from ordinary people. These qualities constitute the basis on which that individual is considered to be, and is treated as, a leader.

Commentators at the beginning of the 21st century might conclude that very few business leaders could be said to have supernatural qualities. We must remember, however, that Weber was arguing from a philosophical standpoint, not a current, pragmatic management one; we may therefore understand "supernatural" as being "supernormal" and at the opposite end of a scale balanced by "rational." Although not considered supernatural, many business leaders have been deemed special in some way, and have had attributed to them qualities that set them apart from "ordinary people." Indeed, research in the 1970s and 1980s by Warren Bennis suggested that leaders do have qualities which set them apart, although he did not use the word "supernatural" and went on to suggest that leadership qualities can be developed.

Of his three models of legitimate authority, Weber thought charisma the least stable because its inspirational and motivational qualities disappear when the leader relinquishes the post. For Weber, charisma was not a sustainable option as the basis for authority. He advocated locating legitimacy in something more lasting and systematic.

Traditional Authority

Leaders have authority by virtue of the status they have inherited—the extent of their authority is determined by birth, custom, precedent, and usage. Although Weber derives his theory from a study of history, we can still sometimes witness today how many positions of authority are handed from one generation to another, as companies establish dynasties, and appointments have more to do with family ties than competence. Another characteristic of organizations based on traditional authority is that things tend to be done in a particular way just because "they have always been done like that."

In the competitive world of today, the dangers of this approach are only too apparent: larger organizations get caught up in their own systems and either fail to spot when competitors are catching them up or markets are slipping away, or else simply become trapped by their own inertia. Precedent, rather than rational analysis, becomes the reason in itself for doing things.

Weber's search for a sustainable form of organizational authority based on rational analysis led him to distinguish a third authority system.

"Man is dominated by the making of money, by acquisition as the ultimate purpose of his life."

Max Weber

Rational-legal Authority

Authority within a bureaucracy is both legal and rational when it is exercised through a system of rules and procedures attached to the "office"—the job role—which an individual occupies.

Weber described how bureaucracy-based, rational-legal authority works:

- The organization is structured around official functions that are bound by rules, each area having its own specified competence.
- Functions are structured into offices organized into a hierarchy that follows technical rules and norms for which training is provided.
- The administration is separated from the ownership of the means of production.
- The rules, decisions, and actions of the administration are recorded in writing.

Weber stated that the bureaucracy was technically the most efficient form of organization because, within it, work is conducted with precision, knowledge of files, continuity, discretion, unity, strict subordination, and reduction of friction.

Bureaucracies

Within bureaucracies organized along rational lines, the abuse of power by leaders is minimized because:

- offices are ranked in hierarchical order;
- operations are conducted in accordance with impersonal rules;
- officials are allocated specific duties and areas of responsibility;
- appointments are made on the basis of qualifications and suitability for the position.

Weber was, however, also aware of the shortcomings of bureaucracy, inasmuch as:

- their characteristic information processing and filtering to the top makes them cumbersome and slow to react;
- their machinery makes it difficult to handle individual cases, because rules and procedures require all individuals to be treated as if they were the same;
- bureaucratization leads to depersonalization, because the roles of officials are circumscribed by written definitions of their authority, and there is a set of rules and procedures to cater for every contingency.

Weber recognized that the more efficient a bureaucracy becomes, the more it succeeds in excluding the personal, the irrational, and the incalculable in favor of emotional detachment and "professionalism." Perhaps this goes a long way toward explaining why Weber is held in low esteem in today's business climate of change and uncertainty.

MAX WEBER IN PERSPECTIVE

Weber recognized the dangers of bureaucratization and spoke of how measurement processes could turn people into cogs in a machine. In this respect his reflections are not too distant from Marx's theories of alienation. Although organizational bureaucratization increases efficiency and productive capability, its mechanical efficiency also threatens to dehumanize its participants. Weber also believed, however, that the only way people could make a significant contribution was to subjugate their personalities and desires to the impersonal goals and procedures of large scale organizations. Paradoxically, he believed that the only way to escape such a mechanical future was for a charismatic leader to transform the organization into something new.

Bureaucracy became the model for the 20th-century organization, and was encapsulated in Alfred Sloan's General Motors and Harold Geneen's ITT. Perhaps the mundaneness and regularity of bureaucratic, corporate life was best described in William Whyte's *The Organization Man* (1956), in which the individual is taken over by the bureaucratic machine, in the name of efficiency. A more recent and humorous interpretation of life in a bureaucracy has been depicted by Scott Adams in *The Dilbert Principle*.

The bureaucracy may have outlived its age of supremacy, but it is still hard to foresee a future without any need for the order, procedures, levels of authority, and controls that constitute a bureaucracy. The problem is how to develop systems that combine necessary bureaucratic features with a people-centered, flexible, and imaginative style.

As the foremost social scientist of his day—with little interest in management—Weber would have found it hard to believe that he was to exercise such a dominant influence on the way organizations have been managed. He would have also found it hard to credit the notion that he would be quoted as one of a trinity of management pioneers, along with Henri Fayol and F. W. Taylor, contemporaries whom he would not have known or read.

FOR MORE INFORMATION

Books:

Pugh, Derek S., and David J. Hickson. *Great Writers on Organizations.* 2nd ed. Burlington, VT: Ashgate Publishing, 1999.

Weber, Max. *The Protestant Ethic and the Spirit of Capitalism.* New York: Routledge, 2001.

Weber, Max. *Theory of Social and Economic Organization.* Trans. A.M. Henderson and T. Parsons. New York: Free Press, 1947.

Web Site:

The Dead Sociologists' Society: **www2.pfeiffer.edu/~lridener/DSS/DEADSOC.HTML**

"Bureaucratic administration means fundamentally the exercise of control on the basis of knowledge."

Max Weber

John Jacob Astor

Born in Germany, John Jacob Astor emigrated to the United States in 1780. Arriving with a few dollars and seven flutes, he amassed a fur and property empire that made him one of the richest men of his day. Astor's story is a lesson for all entrepreneurs: provide excellent customer service; be close to markets; buy cheap, and sell wherever the price is best. In a battle with Astor, the government-subsidized fur trade looked as if it would surely be the winner, but Astor won by a knockout.

Then, in his smartest career move, Astor dumped his fur trading interests just before fur became old hat. Moving onto something more fashionable, he bought up property—lots of it—in the way that most people buy groceries. In doing so, he helped shape the development of one of the greatest cities on the planet—New York. When he died in 1848, he was worth over $20 million.

Astor fashioned a fortune from his exploits in the fur trade.

1763	Born.
1783	Sets sail for America. Takes $24 and seven flutes.
1784	Arrives in New York.
1785	Marries.
1786	Opens shop selling pianos and buying furs.
1808	Consolidates holdings and incorporates American Fur Company.
1810	Founds Pacific Fur Company.
1811	Establishes Astoria at the mouth of the Columbia River.
1820s	Fur trade begins to slow down.
1834	Sells entire holdings in fur trade and retires. Develops property.
1848	Dies.

BACKGROUND AND RISE

Born in Walldorf, Germany in 1763, John Jacob Astor was the third son of a butcher. His brother George, the eldest son, left Germany for England to establish a business making and selling musical instruments. His brother Henry departed for New York City. In 1780, John Jacob too left the family farm, made his way down the Rhine Valley and set sail for England, where he joined his brother in business.

> By 1800, Astor was the leading U.S. fur trader. It was a considerable achievement.

In London, Astor learned to speak English, assisted his brother, and saved enough money to take a ship across the Atlantic. In November 1783, at the end of the American Revolution, he set sail for the United States. With him he took $24 and seven flutes. The journey took the standard eight weeks, arriving in Chesapeake Bay in January. Astor's berth was in the crew's quarters, and on the crossing—so the story goes—he befriended another German emigrant who told him about the fur trade and the opportunities it offered.

DEFINING MOMENTS

Arriving in New York in March 1784, aged 21, Astor soon married and established a shop selling pianos and buying furs. His wife would mind the store while Astor ventured into the northern territories, building a network of contacts among the fur traders.

The lucrative fur trade was important not only commercially, but also politically. Canada's patronage from France was dependent on its revenues. U.S., French-Canadian, and British companies—like the Hudson Bay Company and the Northwest Company—dominated the trade. In 1796 a treaty between the United States and Great Britain demarcated trading boundaries along national borders, excluding the Canadians from U.S. territories. Astor moved into the vacuum left by the Canadians.

By 1800, Astor was the leading U.S. fur trader. It was a considerable achievement. As well as dealing with competition from other private traders, Astor was competing with the U.S. government. Eager to make a show of strength to the Native Americans and to keep out the French and English, President George Washington had approved funds to establish the Office of Indian Affairs and a series of government-sponsored fur factories. The problem was that when it came to the actual trading, private traders won hands down. Government representatives like Thomas McKenney insisted on foisting plows—and other implements that were deemed to be intrinsically good or useful—on the Native Americans who, uninterested in sanctimony or agricultural equipment, wanted kettles and muskets. Like all good entrepreneurs, Astor gave them what they wanted and got what he wanted in return—furs. He refused to sell the Native Americans liquor, figuring that they were unlikely to make good trappers if inebriated. Astor also outcompeted on service. The government maintained trading posts some distance from the Native Americans, so Astor's men went upriver to deal with them directly. It was customer service at its best.

At the other end of the supply chain, Astor got better prices for his furs than the government did. While the government sold the furs immediately on the local market, regardless of demand or oversupply, Astor shipped his furs around the world to whatever market paid the best price. The folly of the government's attempts to control the fur trade was revealed when it passed legislation to close down the fur factories and sell their assets.

Already wealthy, Astor expanded his commercial horizons. He obtained permission to trade through ports owned by the East India Company; sent a ship to China in a joint venture, and pocketed $50,000 in profit. The profit was plowed into New York property.

In 1808 Astor consolidated his holdings and incorporated the American Fur Company. This was a precursor to an attempt to control the developing fur trade in the West. Most companies planned to extend their territories to the West. The key would be finding and controlling a route through to the Pacific. A Canadian expedition had set out cross-country and was rumored to be making good progress. Astor thought it would be more sensible to make his way around the Cape of Good Hope by ship and head for the mouth of the Columbia River. To finance his enterprise, he joined forces with some of the members of the Northwest Company and founded the Pacific Fur Company in 1810.

Astor's party arrived at the Columbia River in 1811. Six weeks after they raised the U.S. flag over a hastily erected stockade, christened Astoria, the Canadian expedition arrived. Astoria was to be an essential cog in Astor's international trading plans. No one could accuse him of lacking ambition. His intention was to send goods from New York to Astoria; trade them for furs with the Native Americans; ship the furs to the Orient to be traded for goods; ship the Oriental goods to Europe; trade them for European goods; and ship the European goods to the United States, taking a profit at every stage. It was a brilliant plan that fell at the first hurdle when one of his ships sank, and the 1812 war between the United States and England broke out. The British forced Astor to hand over his fort in Astoria for $58,000.

Other than this setback, Astor did well during the war. Even in his worst year, his revenues were $50,000. By the end of the conflict he had substantially increased his property holdings. After the war, with the help of some friendly government officials and some useful legislation that forbade Canadian involvement in the U.S. fur trade, Astor gained control of all the Northwest Company's holdings that lay within U.S. borders. He continued to take over the interests of other companies, inching his way west. But by the late 1820s, fashions had changed, silk was all the rage, and profits were falling. Never failing

to spot a trend, Astor got out while he could. In June 1834, he sold all his fur trading holdings and retired.

For the rest of his years, Astor dabbled in property speculation. He had always bought parcels of land in New York City when they became available. Now he bought up vast tracts of land on the urban fringes of New York, figuring—correctly—that at the current rate of population growth, the city would soon swallow up his plots. As usual he figured right. He became one of the largest property owners in New York City and, as a by-product, one of the main landlords. He died in 1848, the richest man in the United States. His fortune was some $20 million.

> **For the rest of his years, Astor dabbled in property speculation.**

CONTEXT AND CONCLUSIONS

What Astor considered legitimate trade, modern sentiment labels immoral and unethical. The fur trade, an industry of considerable commercial and political importance at the time, is now considered an anathema in many parts of the world. Astor's dealings with the Native American population and the tenants of his property empire also left much to be desired by today's standards. Nevertheless, Astor is an important figure in business history for a number of reasons. As a champion of private enterprise, his endeavors clearly illustrated the shortcomings of government monopolies. Ultimately he demonstrated that the disincentivized, bureaucracy-ridden, heavily subsidized, government-run fur factories were no match for an agile private enterprise that paid close attention to its customers' needs and promoted innovation as a means to increasing profitability. Astor's actions also helped open the western frontiers of the United States for development. Finally, regardless of his motivation, he was responsible for shaping the development of Manhattan and New York City.

FOR MORE INFORMATION

Books:
Houghton, Walter R. *Kings of Fortune or the Triumphs and Achievements of Noble, Self-made Men.* Chicago, IL: The Loomis National Library Association, 1888.
Irving, Washington. *Astoria; or, Enterprise Beyond the Rocky Mountains.* London: Richard Bentley, 1839.
Smith, Arthur D. Howden. *John Jacob Astor: Landlord of New York.* Philadelphia, PA: Lippincott, 1929.
Terrell, John Upton. *Furs by Astor (John Jacob Astor).* New York: William Morrow & Co., 1963.

"Work alone qualifies us for life."

Zoë Akins

Jeffrey Bezos

Jeff Bezos, the founder and C.E.O. of Amazon.com, is the most famous son of the e-commerce revolution. The company he created became the best known online brand in the world.

After graduating, Bezos worked for a variety of investment firms. By 1992 he had made it to vice president, yet he gave up his Wall Street career to chase a dream. Amazon.com opened for business in July 1995, and soon became the flagship for the New Economy.When the tide turned against dot-com stocks in 2000, Amazon.com looked as if it might be washed up. Yet Bezos battened down the hatches and by the following year seemed once more to be steaming ahead towards profitability. Never afraid to branch out from its core business of books, in 2006 Amazon.com offered shoppers over 30 different product categories.

Amazon has gone from strength to strength under Bezos.

1964	Born.
1986	Graduates from Princeton.
1990	Youngest vice president at Bankers Trust.
1992	Senior vice president at D. E. Shaw & Co.
1995	Amazon.com opens for business.
1998	Net sales of $252.9 million, an increase of 283% over the same period in 1997.
1999	Amazon.com, Inc. has a market capitalization of $6 billion. Voted *Time* person of the year.
2000	Adds toys and electronics to product range.
2001	Amazon.com, Inc. posts first quarterly profit and achieves highest ever score for service business in American Customer Satisfaction Index.
2001	Industry protest as Amazon.com seeks patents to protect systems for online payments and advertisement allocation.
2005	Bezos' net worth estimated to be $5.7 billion.

BACKGROUND AND RISE

Born on January 12, 1964 in Albuquerque, New Mexico, Jeffrey Preston Bezos was a clever child. At a very early age he took a screwdriver to his crib and dismantled it. This set a pattern. When his grandfather bought him a Radio Shack electronics kit, he concocted a "burglar alarm" to keep his siblings out of his bedroom. Moving on to the garage, the venue of choice for so many budding entrepreneurs, he built a microwave oven driven by solar power. There is no record of how well it cooked.

> **Amazon.com opened for business in July 1995, and soon became the flagship for the New Economy.**

Mike Bezos, Jeff's father, was an engineer with Exxon, and the family moved several times because of his work. Jeff attended high school in Miami and spent most summers on his grandfather's Texas ranch, living the life of a cattle rancher and driving the tractors.

DEFINING MOMENTS

In 1986, after graduating in electrical engineering and computer science from Princeton, Bezos headed for Fitel, a high-tech start-up company in New York, where he built a computer network for financial trading. After Fitel he joined Bankers Trust, becoming their youngest vice president in 1990. From there he moved to D. E. Shaw & Co. The Wall Street firm interviewed him on the strength of a recommendation from one of its partners, who suggested, "he is going to make someone a lot of money someday." At Shaw, Bezos described his role as a "sort of an entrepreneurial odd-jobs kind of a person," looking for business opportunities in the insurance, software, and Internet sectors. He excelled in the role, and becoming senior vice president in 1992.

Then came his epiphany. While surfing the Internet one day, Bezos came across an astounding fact. According to usage statistics, the Internet was growing at a rate of 2,300% a year. Online commerce, he realized, was a natural next step. Being a combination of Wall Street insider and computer nerd, he was perfectly positioned to cash in.

Bezos compiled a list of 20 products suitable for selling online, which included CDs, magazines, PC software and hardware—and books. The shortlist was quickly whittled down to two—books and music. In the end, he decided upon books. His logic was twofold. With more than 1.3 million books in print as against 300,000 music titles, there were simply more to sell. Perhaps more important, the major book publishers appeared less intimidating than their record company counterparts. The six major record companies had a stranglehold on the popular music distribution business, but the biggest book chain, Barnes & Noble, had only 12% of the industry's total sales.

"We are pioneers and the history of pioneers is not that good."

Jeff Bezos

Quitting his job, Bezos headed out to Seattle. "I will change the economics of the book industry," he is reputed to have told one venture capitalist. Ironically, some of the fundraising took place in the coffee shop of a Barnes & Noble bookstore.

With no state tax, a wealth of high-tech talent, and a major book distributor on the doorstep—Ingram's warehouse in Oregon—Seattle seemed a perfect place to start his new business. In the garage of his rented home, Bezos and his first three employees booted up their computers and began writing software for the new business. He originally planned to call the company Cadabra. Fortunately, his friends convinced him that, while the name might have magical connotations, it sounded very similar to "cadaver." Instead, Bezos opted for Amazon, after the world's largest river.

The company, according to its Web site, "opened its virtual doors in July 1995 with a mission to use the Internet to transform book buying into the fastest, easiest, and most enjoyable shopping experience possible." By the beginning of 1999, Amazon.com, Inc. had a market capitalization of $6 billion—more than the combined value of Barnes & Noble and Borders, its two largest bookstore competitors. The fourth quarter of 1998 brought net sales of $252.9 million, an increase of 283% over the same period in 1997. With Amazon awash with revenue, analysts seemed unperturbed by the absence of profits.

Bezos, meanwhile, was a model of reassurance. Amazon would reach $1 billion in sales by 2000, he confidently asserted, and sure enough it did. Yet details about when Amazon would make a profit were hazier. Amazon was, said Bezos, still in "an investment phase." For a while, investors were more than happy to go along for the ride.

Then, in June 2000, cracks began to appear in the almost unanimous support enjoyed by the star child of the Internet revolution. Holly Becker, e-commerce analyst at Lehman Brothers and a longtime Amazon believer, switched her recommendation on the company from a buy to a neutral. She was, she said, "throwing in the towel on Amazon." Many saw Becker's change of heart as a turning point in the company's fortunes.

Yet Bezos may well have the last laugh. With some 21 million satisfied customers in the first two quarters of 2001, revenue over the same period up by 16%, and a strategic alliance with Internet Service Provider AOL in the bag, Warren Jenson, Amazon.com's chief financial officer, correctly predicted operating profitability in the fourth quarter of 2001. Customer satisfaction was officially recognized when Amazon achieved the highest-ever scores for a service industry in 2001 and 2002. The Amazon range is growing too, with the introduction of toys and electronics in 2000, jewelry in 2004, and, more recently, gourmet foods. Bezos, however, came under fire for holding back the broader development of e-commerce when he applied for patents to protect Amazon's "Honor" online payment system and the system for allocating advertising space from multiple bidders. After several roller-coaster years, the group announced its first full-year profit in January 2004. Whether Bezos will go down in the business history books as the creator of a viable and long-lived Internet business, or simply as an e-business pioneer, remains to be seen.

CONTEXT AND CONCLUSIONS

Amazon is the totem stock of the Internet evangelists. Critics say that through smoke and mirrors, PR, and puff, one man has succeeded in making a fortune through hyping his online business to unthought-of heights. What he created, after all, was nothing more or less than a virtual bookstore, and one that in its first five years didn't turn a profit. But Amazon.com isn't a bellwether stock without reason. Bezos is the quintessential dot-com icon. He proved to the business world that the Internet was about more than knowledge. He proved that it is possible to overcome fears about purchasing online, to drive down transaction costs, and to build an international e-commerce business. Bezos is one of the great business pioneers. He had the courage to attempt something that people doubted could be done. Amazon has firmly entrenched itself as a dominant force in e-commerce and, as a result of product additions and strategic alliances, is now a virtual marketplace. The question is whether it can profitably exploit its position consistently.

> **Holly Becker, e-commerce analyst at Lehman Brothers and a longtime Amazon believer, switched her recommendation on the company from a buy to a neutral. She was, she said, "throwing in the towel on Amazon."**

1281

MANAGEMENT GIANTS

Scott Blum

A colorful character, Blum survived a brush with the SEC while at his company Pinnacle Micro and went on to found buy.com. buy.com epitomized the gung ho, blindly optimistic philosophy of dot-com mania with its "make money by losing money" strategy. The idea was to sell goods on the Internet at a loss and make money through advertising. Critics sniggered. The "losing money" part went well; unfortunately the "make money" element was lacking. Critics laughed openly. Meanwhile Blum stepped down as C.E.O. in March 1999, and as chairman in October of the same year. He put his less than 50% of the stock into a blind trust, raised $100 million in financing, and moved on to Enfrastructure.com, providing "scalable, full-service technology and infrastructure for high-growth companies."

FOR MORE INFORMATION

Books:
Marcus, James. *Amazonia*. New York: The New Press, 2004.
Spector, Robert. *Amazon.com*. Revised ed. New York: HarperBusiness, 2002.

Web site:
Amazon.com: **www.amazon.com**

Warren Buffett

1282

Warren Buffett (1930–) had an eye for a deal from an early age. He progressed from childhood race tipster and paper-route king to property owner and stock picker extraordinaire. By the age of 14 the young Buffett had already accumulated enough money to buy 40 acres of farmland. Now in his seventies, he is a multibillionaire—though not one to flaunt his wealth. The Coca-Cola-swilling, ukulele-playing Buffett lives a modest life, occupying an average house and preferring to drive an older car rather than the latest model, even though his personal fortune makes him one of the richest men in the world. He is justly one of the most influential people in the finance world.

Buffett's advice on the stockmarkets has been invaluable to millions.

1930	Born.
1934	Publication of *Security Analysis* by Ben Graham and David Dodd.
1950	Attends Columbia Business School.
1951	Graduates; starts to invest for a living.
1965	Acquires Berkshire Hathaway (invests $10,000; it is worth $51 million by 1999).
1967	Berkshire Hathaway buys National Indemnity Company and National Fire & Marine Insurance Company.
1969	Winds up investment partnership to concentrate on Berkshire.
1995	Buys major stake in McDonald's.
1996	Acquires GEICO, the sixth-largest U.S. automobile insurer.
1998	Buys Executive Jet Corporation.
2001	Becomes the United States' second richest man behind Bill Gates.
2001	Announces 21st-century investment strategy focusing on bricks, paints, and housewares.
2002	Berkshire Hathaway announces first ever negative coupon security.
2003	Continues investment strategy by acquiring furnishing goods giant, Burlington Industries.
2003	*Forbes* names him world's second richest man with net worth of $30.5 billion.
2004	Agrees to act as economic adviser to John Kerry during presidential elections.

BACKGROUND AND RISE

In 1952, an aspiring 21-year-old money manager placed a small advertisement in an Omaha newspaper, inviting people to attend a class on investing. He figured it would be a good way to accustom himself to appearing before audiences. He even invested $100 for a Dale Carnegie course on public speaking. Twenty others showed up that day. If he were speaking today, the building would be besieged. He was Warren Buffett, one of the greatest investors of all time.

Born on August 30, 1930, in Omaha, Nebraska, Buffett exhibited the talents that were to make him wealthy at an early age. Aged six, he would buy six packs of Coca-Cola for a quarter, break them up, and sell the individual bottles for a nickel each. Stricken with a mysterious illness, he lay in bed figuring out how to get rich. On his recovery he roped his friends into a number of money-making enterprises he had thought up.

He looked for lost golf balls, packaged them up, and sold them. He also became one of the youngest racing tipsters in the United States when he published *Stable Boy Selections*. His record for picking winners is not known, but if it was anything like his later talent for picking stocks, he must have made a few gamblers very rich.

When Warren was 12 his father, Howard Buffett, won a seat in Congress and the family moved to Washington, D.C. The move was initially unpopular with Buffett. However, he changed his mind when he realized the commercial potential of the U.S. capital. He took on five paper routes at once, delivering a staggering 500 papers each morning and earning the equivalent of a man's full-time salary of $175. When he was still only 14 he had earned $1,200—enough to enable him to buy 40 acres of farmland in Nebraska and rent it out for farming.

DEFINING MOMENTS

After another business foray in high school, installing overhauled arcade games in barbershops, Buffett decided to enhance his natural flair for commerce with a formal business education. He was admitted to the Wharton School at the University of Pennsylvania.

But Buffett found the theoretical aspects of business dull and discovered nothing in the curriculum to slake his thirst for practical knowledge. He left Wharton and fin-

---

"Never is there just one cockroach in the kitchen."

    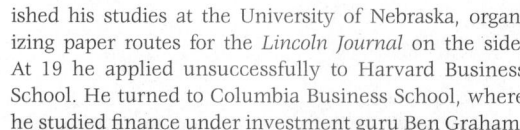

ished his studies at the University of Nebraska, organizing paper routes for the *Lincoln Journal* on the side. At 19 he applied unsuccessfully to Harvard Business School. He turned to Columbia Business School, where he studied finance under investment guru Ben Graham.

It was in reading the stock market that Buffett found his true vocation. His first foray into stocks had been as a boy of 11 (it helped that his father was a stockbroker). Young Buffett bought three shares in Cities Service preferred at $38 a share; the stock promptly fell to $27. When it recovered to $40 he sold, making a small profit. The stock then rose to $200, leaving the boy kicking himself and teaching him the value of long-term investment.

Determined to make a living by investing, Buffett plowed his energy and all the savings amassed from his various enterprises into the stock market. From 1951 to 1956 he turned $9,800 into $140,000. News spread about the new whiz-kid investor, and more and more people asked him to invest their money for them. What started with friends spread to the general public, and soon Buffett was forming limited partnerships and taking a 25% cut of any return above 4%.

Once Buffett started investing as a career, he developed his own personal investment strategy. He began by looking for stocks that offered outstanding value—those that were relatively cheap given their asset value—and then holding the stock for the long term. "Lethargy, bordering on sloth, should remain the cornerstone of an investment style," he has said. He was heavily influenced by the theories of Ben Graham, his former teacher at Columbia and the coauthor of the investment classic *Security Analysis* (1934). Buffett eventually took Graham's strategies a step further by seeking out companies whose stock was inexpensive compared to their growth prospects. This approach required assessing a company's intangible assets, such as brand value. In this Buffett was ahead of his time. The area of intangible assets is now the subject of growing interest from business academics, but in the 1950s it was largely neglected. Buffett, however, was not unduly interested in theoretical niceties.

Theory was all very well, as Buffett had noted at Wharton, but how would his strategy work in practice? The answer proved to be: phenomenally well. Between 1957 and 1966 the investment partnership that Buffett managed posted an amazing 1,156% return—against 122.9% over the same period for the Dow Jones Industrial Average. A partner's investment of $10,000 would, after deducting Buffett's share, have returned $80,420. Buffett continued to outperform the market, making a 36% return in 1967 and 59% in 1968 in a speculative market, not particularly suited to his particular investment strategy.

In 1969, to the surprise of his managers, Buffett called it a day. Concerned about maintaining his performance in an uncongenial investment climate, he decided to wind up the partnership.

Since 1969 his attentions have been focused entirely on his investment vehicle Berkshire Hathaway, the publicly listed company he acquired in 1965. The markets may go up or down, but over time Buffett has delivered consistently for his stockholders. His legendary, almost uncanny, knack of picking stocks has earned him the epithet "the Sage of Omaha." On the strength of his

company's performance, it's a tag he undoubtedly deserves. A $10,000 investment in Berkshire Hathaway in 1965 would have been worth over $50 million by the end of 2000. Investors who backed the S&P 500 Index would have accumulated some $500,000, a paltry amount by comparison. Along the way, Buffett has picked stocks such as Coca-Cola and American Express when they were at a low ebb. The only downside, so far, has been investments in insurance companies, which have hit problems since 2002. On the other hand, he has resisted the temptation to be drawn into media-fueled stock bubbles such as the Internet boom of the 1990s. "As a group, lemmings have a rotten image," notes Buffett, "but no individual lemming has ever received bad press."

He remains determined to avoid the technology sector: "We have embraced the 21st century by entering such cutting edge industries as bricks, carpets, insulation, and paint—try to control your excitement." Since 2001, he has invested in companies like Fruit of the Loom, Pampered Chef and, in 2003, Burlington Industries, part of that "household" portfolio.

Buffett himself has remained relatively unaffected by the plaudits heaped upon him. A modest man, he has few indulgences other than a corporate jet. Even then he bought a small, used plane for Berkshire; when he traded up to a more expensive model, he named it "the Indefensible." Modesty apart, he moved into the position of the United States' second richest person in 2001, behind Bill Gates. He lives in an average home in Omaha, famously drives an old car, and maintains a fairly small office with few staff. His main hobby, it seems, is reading company reports, in which he reportedly maintains an avid interest despite the many thousands he's undoubtedly plowed through. In 2004 he acted as economic adviser to John Kerry, Democratic candidate in the presidential elections.

> His legendary, almost uncanny, knack of picking stocks has earned him the epithet "the Sage of Omaha."

CONTEXT AND CONCLUSIONS

Warren Buffett is one of the greatest investors of all time. What lifts him above his peers is a determination to stick to his investment principles. Companies have risen and fallen. Unlike so many other investors who are nursing their burns, Buffett let the dot-com train roll on by. Famously, he refuses to invest in businesses that he doesn't understand—which includes most high-tech companies. Instead Buffett has made a fortune for himself and his stockholders by investing in undervalued companies for the long term. It's Buffett's willingness to buck the trend that makes him worthy of his "Sage of Omaha" tag.

FOR MORE INFORMATION

Book:
Lowenstein, Roger. *Buffett.* New York: Doubleday, 1996.

Web site:
Berkshire Hathaway: **www.berkshirehathaway.com**

"The market will pay better to entertain than educate."   Warren Buffett

Andrew Carnegie

Andrew Carnegie (1835–1919) was one of the finest of his generation. A significant proportion of his achievements fell within the 19th century, yet his impact on the commercial revolution that took place in the United States as the 19th century gave way to the 20th is huge. Carnegie was arguably the first of a generation of businessmen who pioneered industrial growth in the United States, and throughout the world, on the back of steel manufacturing and the building of railroads. At the end of his long career he had built the largest steel company in the United States and amassed a vast personal fortune.

Carnegie forged a business empire from steel.

1284

MANAGEMENT GIANTS

1835	Born.
1848	Family moves to Allegheny near Pittsburgh, Pennsylvania. Carnegie, aged 12, takes job in cotton mill.
1870	Builds first blast furnace. Experiments with the Bessemer process.
1874	Opens steel furnace at Braddock.
1880	Plant operating for 24 hours a day with profits of $2 million.
1881	Company reorganizes as Carnegie Bros & Co.
1882	Carnegie acquires coke-producing interests of Henry C. Frick.
1886	Writes *Triumphant Democracy*.
1889	Moves to New York to conduct R&D into the steel manufacturing process. "Gospel of wealth" article published. Steel production 332,111 tons.
1899	Steel production 2,663,412 tons. Carnegie buys out Frick.
1901	Frick and J. Pierpont Morgan purchase the Carnegie Company for $500 million.
1919	Dies.

BACKGROUND AND RISE

Andrew Carnegie was born in Dunfermline on November 25, 1835. In 1848 economic depression persuaded Carnegie's father to emigrate with his family to the United States. The family settled in a colony of Scots gathered at Slabtown, Allegheny, near Pittsburgh, and the 12-year-old Andrew took work in a local cotton mill.

Leaving the cotton mill, he got a job at the Pittsburgh Telegraph Office as a messenger boy. Thomas A. Scott, superintendent of the western division of the Pennsylvania Railroad at the time, spotted Carnegie's potential and appointed him as his secretary at $50 a month—in those days a handsome salary for one so young. It was Scott who set Carnegie on the path to riches by showing him the likely gains of investing in startup companies. Acting on a tip from Scott, Carnegie bought stock in the Adams Express Company using money from his mother, who remortgaged her house. Shortly afterward he borrowed money to invest in a successful railroad sleeping car venture.

During the Civil War, Carnegie served with Scott in Washington. Then, with the Union victory secured, he took Scott's old position as superintendent of the western division of the Pennsylvania Railroad. But his entrepreneurial instincts were not satisfied, and he soon left the railroads to establish an iron bridge building firm, the Keystone Bridge Company. He was also involved in several other speculative ventures that proved successful.

DEFINING MOMENTS

While Carnegie was busy in the United States, Henry Bessemer, an inventor and businessman, was working on a manufacturing process in England that would change industry the world over. The Bessemer process allowed the industrialized production of steel from iron. Carnegie often visited the United Kingdom, and on one visit he came across the Bessemer converter. It was a revelation.

Hurrying back to the United States, Carnegie formed Carnegie, McCandless, & Co., built his first blast furnace in 1870, and began experimenting with the Bessemer process. He opened a steel furnace at Braddock and, by 1880, the plant was operating 24 hours a day and producing annual profits of $2 million. In 1881 the company reorganized, becoming Carnegie Bros. & Co. Carnegie held the controlling interest. In 1882 he acquired the coke-producing interests of Henry C. Frick, who became his most trusted associate.

In 1889 Carnegie moved to New York to continue his research into the steel manufacturing process. He also spent six months of the year with his family in Scotland. In his absence Carnegie left Frick, as chair of Carnegie

Bros., in charge of the day-to-day running of the company. When Frick took over, the company was a collection of disparate threads—the threads being individual mills and furnaces dotted about Pittsburgh. Frick wove these threads together into a fabric: an organization that would become the biggest steelmaking enterprise in the world. He centralized the management structure and integrated production. The firm was transformed into the Carnegie Steel Company, valued at $25 million.

Unfortunately for Carnegie, Frick also presided over one of the most notorious incidents in U.S. corporate history. In an attempt to drive down costs and boost profits, Frick reduced piecework rates. Incensed, the Amalgamated Iron and Steel Workers Union called its members at the Carnegie Homestead plant out on strike. Instead of settling through negotiation, Frick inflamed the situation by arranging to bring in 300 strikebreakers.

When the day came and the strikebreakers arrived on barges down the Monongahela River, complete with armed guard, all hell broke loose. At the end of a day of pitched battle, ten men lay dead and a further sixty were wounded. Homestead was placed under martial law.

Carnegie, in Scotland at the time, was irate. It was not just the disruption to the company that he rued; Frick had gone against his explicit instructions not to use strikebreakers. For Carnegie it was a matter of personal ethics. Nevertheless, being the controlling owner and, as such, ultimately responsible, he had to bear the dark stain of the workers' blood on his reputation for many years after the debacle.

Although Carnegie refrained from criticizing Frick in public, their relationship never recovered. The company continued to thrive, improving annual production of steel from 332,111 tons in 1889 to 2,663,412 in 1899, and profits from $2 million to $40 million. But, because of the deteriorating relationship between them, Carnegie took the opportunity to buy Frick out for a handsome $15 million in 1889. Even this act of severance failed to quell the personal animosity between the two men. In 1901 Frick returned with the backing of the notorious J. Pierpont Morgan and purchased the Carnegie Company for $500 million, establishing the U.S. Steel Corporation which, valued at $1.4 billion, was the biggest steel company in the world.

CONTEXT AND CONCLUSIONS

Carnegie played a leading role in the industrialization of the United States. As a poor Scottish boy who became one of the wealthiest men in the world, his rise from rags to riches was extraordinary. In his time he was criticized and praised in equal measure. Some saw him as a smug, tyrannical, autocratic, arrogant slave driver; others as a wise, benevolent, enlightened entrepreneur. Of the many qualities Carnegie possessed, one in particular stands out: he was an opportunist who acted on his instincts. He took any opportunity to promote his business interests. When he invited the Prince of Wales to ride a Pennsylvania Railroad engine, for example, he did it to secure business favors rather than to increase his social standing.

Carnegie will be remembered as much for his philanthropy as for his business adventures. In later life, guided by his ethical beliefs, he gave away the greater part of his fortune. He established a trust fund "for the improvement of mankind." The Carnegie Institute of Pittsburgh, the Carnegie Institute of Technology, the Carnegie Institution of Washington, and three thousand public libraries were built with this trust money.

When the "King of Steel" died in August 1919, he had already given away $350 million of his fortune.

> Carnegie was arguably the first of a generation of businessmen who pioneered industrial growth in the United States, and throughout the world, on the back of steel manufacturing and the building of railroads.

> Some saw him as a smug, tyrannical, autocratic, arrogant slave driver; others as a wise, benevolent, enlightened entrepreneur.

1285

MANAGEMENT GIANTS

FOR MORE INFORMATION

Books:
Carnegie, Andrew. *The Empire of Business*. New York: Doubleday, Doran, & Co., 1902.
Mackay, James. *Andrew Carnegie: His Life and Times*. New York: Wiley, 1998.

Web site:
Carnegie Corporation of New York: **www.carnegie.org**

"There is no business in America . . . which will not yield a fair profit if it receives the unremitting, exclusive attention, and all the capital of capable and industrious men."

Andrew Carnegie

Stephen Case

MANAGEMENT GIANTS

Steve Case, born in 1958, is cofounder and former C.E.O. of America Online (AOL). A political science graduate, he worked in marketing and sales before starting Quantum Computers, which offered online services to users of Commodore computers.

Renamed America Online (AOL) in 1989, the company went public in 1992 with 150,000 subscribers. By 1996 that figure was 4.6 million. In 1998 Case wiped out a chunk of the competition by buying CompuServe and its 2.5 million subscribers, as well as Netscape. By 2001 AOL had 30 million subscribers worldwide.

The pinnacle of Case's deal making came in early 2000 with the shock announcement of a $166 billion merger with media giant Time Warner. However, the merger was slow to succeed and continuing poor results led to his resignation in 2003.

Case at the height of his success.

1958	Born.
1979	Graduates from Williams College, joins Procter & Gamble.
1983	Gets job at Control Video.
1989	Quantum Computers renamed America Online (AOL).
1991	Case becomes C.E.O. of AOL.
1992	America Online I.P.O.
1996	4.6 million subscribers.
1998	Acquires CompuServe.
1999	Acquires Netscape.
2000	Announces merger with Time Warner.
2001	AOL has 30 million subscribers. Launches new improved AOL 7.0.
2002	AOL launches broadband services.
	Restates pre-merger profits prompting U.S. Justice Department inquiry into accounting practices.
	AOL TimeWarner announces largest ever corporate loss of $100 billion.
2003	Case resigns as C.E.O.

BACKGROUND AND RISE

Steve Case, born August 21, 1958 in Honolulu, is a world apart from the Marc Andreessens (Netscape) and David Filos (Yahoo!) of the New Economy. Instead of taking the usual geekster's path to billionaire status by studying computer sciences or engineering in a West Coast tech hotspot like Stanford—he majored in political science at Williams College, Massachusetts.

> **The pinnacle of Case's deal making came in early 2000 with the shock announcement of a $166 billion merger with media giant Time Warner.**

He followed this by working in marketing and sales, first at Procter & Gamble (haircare products) and then at PepsiCo (the Pizza Hut division). It was only then that Case paid any attention to the Internet.

Recalling the first time he logged on, Case said: "I thought it was magical then, I still think it's magical today. The center of my world is consumers. Every day I wake up and say, 'How can we make America Online more interesting, more useful, more fun, more affordable, so that it will attract a broader audience?' Because I still remember that excitement 13 years ago when I first connected to an online service."

After his taste of the corporate world, Case joined a small video games service company, Control Video, in 1983. He had always had a touch of the entrepreneur. As a kid he sold lime juice from his backyard, took charge of the obligatory paper route, and started a mail-order company with his brother Dan.

While the video company wasn't a storming success, it did introduce Case to Jim Kinsey and Mark Seriff. It was the perfect combination: Seriff had technology in his blood (he had worked on Arpanet, the forerunner of the Internet), Kinsey was a finance man, and Case provided the sales and marketing know-how. Together the trio founded Quantum Computers. The company provided online services to users of the soon-to-be defunct Commodore computer. Commodore imploded, but America Online (AOL), as the Quantum business was renamed in 1989, went from strength to strength.

DEFINING MOMENTS

Case instinctively knew what the customer wanted. Not burdened with a technological background, he could pitch the product at the average consumer, and make the consumer experience as user-friendly as possible. "Our strategy has always been crystal clear," he said in 1998. "Consumers want one place where they can find good

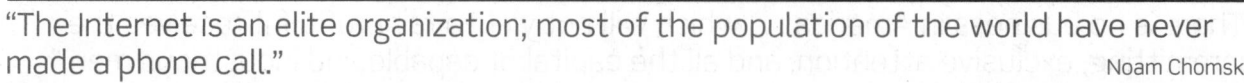

"The Internet is an elite organization; most of the population of the world have never made a phone call."

Noam Chomsky

Internet content and meet interesting people. And they want someone to make it easy for them."

America Online entered the market in 1992. At the time it had a membership of some 150,000. By 1996, with the help of an innovative marketing strategy involving the shipping of AOL CDs offering a free trial, 4.6 million had signed up.

AOL dominated its main rivals, CompuServe and Prodigy, although Microsoft's MSN was still a distant threat. Yet success brought its problems. AOL replaced usage charges with a flat-fee structure and usage figures shot up. People spent more time online, the systems couldn't cope, and the service caved in under the pressure.

Case hired Bob Pittman, cofounder of MTV, to take over the day-to-day running of the company. Pittman was a media man who understood content delivery. He also knew how to deal with a corporation the size of AOL. Making money out of the subscriptions, however, proved a tough nut to crack. The more users AOL signed up, the more AOL spent on infrastructure and maintaining quality of service. Case and Pittman formulated a business model in which content sucked in subscribers who then spent money. Surely if they had a captive audience, advertisers would be falling over themselves to get onto AOL. That's what they figured, and they were right.

Pittman attacked costs, driving down customer acquisition costs from $400 per new subscriber to below $100. Concessions were sold: 1–800-Flowers bought the flower concession for $25 million; Amazon paid $19 million to be the exclusive bookseller on the external aol.com Web site; Barnes & Noble went one better, paying $40 million to be the exclusive bookseller inside.

Active on the acquisitions trail, Case engineered a takeover of rival CompuServe in 1998 (adding 2.5 million subscribers), and in the same year acquired Netscape for $4.2 billion. Then, in early 2000, AOL made the shock announcement of a planned $166 billion merger with Time Warner. However, the merger failed to produce instant success and in 2002, posted record charges of $54 billion. Further financial troubles hit the company in 2002 when it re-stated pre-merger profits, prompting a U.S. Justice Department enquiry into accounting practices.

AOL, meanwhile, continued to expand its operations, adding broadband services in 2002. Roughly 80% of the world's online users log on to AOL in some way. And while they are traipsing around the online shopping malls, they part with over $10 billion dollars a year. By 2002, more than 35 million subscribers worldwide were spending an average of 70 minutes a day on AOL, adding up to more than 1 billion subscriber hours each month. Despite that success, Case's position had become untenable and he resigned from AOL Time-Warner (now Time Warner Inc.) in January 2003. A high-profile figurehead, Case felt that he had become a "distraction", explaining that "Some stockholders continue to focus their disappointment with the company's post-merger performance on me personally." The downturn in his fortunes continued when he and Richard Parsons, his successor at Time Warner, were subpoenaed by the U.S. Securities and Exchange Commission regarding the company's accounting practices.

CONTEXT AND CONCLUSIONS

Steve Case did not pore over circuit boards in the garage to build his tech empire—he took an alternative route to IT stardom. When he saw the Internet, he figured there would be plenty of people who would struggle to get to grips with the technology. Until the advent of the Internet, most home entertainment involved turning on a switch and choosing a channel. The Internet changed the rules. For a start, access was via a computer, which had to be correctly configured, and then there were the browser and the URLs, the server addresses, the e-mail protocols, and much, much more. For the uninitiated, logging on to and navigating the Internet was the equivalent of string theory and quantum mechanics. Case changed all that with the AOL CD. He made the Internet experience easy for millions worldwide, and in so doing built a company that was effectively able to take over one of the world's largest media companies, Time Warner.

1287

MANAGEMENT GIANTS

Jeffrey Wilkins

Trading a job in the burglar alarm business for one in the IT industry, Wilkins founded CompuServe in 1969 to provide excess computer capacity to other corporations. It shifted in 1978 to providing services to the owners of personal computers, and again in Internet age to become a provider of online services. The first to offer e-mail and real-time chat, they were bought out by AOL in 1998. Wilkins meanwhile had left to found Metatec International, "a full-service information distribution company offering businesses optical disk manufacturing, supply chain solutions, and Internet-based information and software distribution services."

William Von Meister

Von Meister founded a phone-in data service for PC owners—the first purely consumer online service—called The Source. The Readers Digest Association bought it in 1980 for $6 million and in 1988 sold it to CompuServe, who closed it down. Von Meister also founded Control Video Corporation in 1981. The company was funded, among others, by Dan Case II, Steve Case's brother, a banker at Hambrecht & Quist. Von Meister was ousted from the company in 1983. He died in 1995.

FOR MORE INFORMATION

Web site:
AOL: www.aol.com

"America has caught Internet fever."

John A. Roth

Michael Dell

Michael Dell (1965–) was always going to be a winner. After all, how many high school students earn more than their teachers? Dell progressed from selling newspaper subscriptions to selling computers.

Yet it wasn't the product that made him wealthy, it was the way he sold it. The Dell corporation pioneered direct selling of computers. It is also an excellent example of a company succeeding by sticking to its founding principles: build to order, keep a low inventory, sell direct, understand your customer. And the Internet was a godsend for Dell. What better way of reaching the global consumer? Dell's success with the direct selling business model made him the youngest C.E.O. ever of a *Fortune* 500 company.

Dell's direct approach was a hit with his customers.

1288

MANAGEMENT GIANTS

1965	Born.
1977	Aged 12, sells stamps by catalog.
1983	Enters the University of Texas at Austin.
1984	Drops out of college to found Dell Computer Corporation.
1988	Dell Computer's first year revenue is $257.8 million.
1994	www.dell.com launched.
1997	Dell's online sales, begun in 1996, exceed $3 million a day.
2000	Online sales reach $50 million.
2000	Problems with supply of Intel chips, Dell stock price falls.
2000	Accelerates investment strategy of acquiring companies in networking and storage.
2000	Introduces computers with open-source Linux operating system.
2003	Launches managed networking services.
2004	*Forbes* rates him as world's eighteenth richest person with a net worth of $13 billion.
2004	Steps down as Dell's C.E.O., but remains as company chairman.

BACKGROUND AND RISE

Michael Dell started his business career as a boy. Born in Houston, Texas, on February 23, 1965, he came across his first commercial opportunity when he was just 12 years old. Like many children his age, Dell was an enthusiastic collector of stamps. Where he differed from his peers was in his approach. Dell didn't trade stamps with his friends at school; he contacted the auction houses and sent them his catalog. When anyone placed an order he went out to find the required stamps. His direct sales method and entrepreneurial acumen were an early sign of what was to come.

Dell brought new focus and intensity to his early commercial forays. As a summer job he sold newspaper subscriptions for the *Houston Post*. He quickly realized that calling people at random using the list of telephone numbers supplied by the company was not the best way to win new business. Instead he targeted two distinct groups, newlyweds and new homeowners. He obtained lists of applicants for wedding licenses from the local courthouse. From another source he compiled a list of people who had recently applied for mortgages. He then wrote a personalized message and conducted his own direct mail campaign. Subscriptions poured in. When the new school term began Dell was asked as part of an economics assignment to complete a tax return. After calculating his profits, Dell estimated his income at $18,000. His teacher, assuming a mistake, corrected his return by moving the decimal point. She was dismayed to discover that the mistake was hers. Dell earned more than she did.

DEFINING MOMENTS

Dell's career really started while studying at the University of Texas in Austin. By then the boy who had dismantled and reassembled the motherboard of his Apple II computer at 13 had grown into a fledgling entrepreneur, making money from his computing hobby. Dell would rebuild computers and sell them. Still at college, he started a company called PCs Limited, headquartered in his dorm room. Ignoring his parents' advice to concentrate on his studies, he decided the lure of business was too great and concentrated his efforts on his PC company.

In 1984 the Dell Computer Corporation was founded with just $1,000 in capital. With such a small investment, Dell was forced to develop a business model that required little capital outlay. He decided to build to order. This eliminated the need to tie up working capital in inventory. The company carried only around 11 days' worth of inventory—and still does. Compare this to the 45 days' worth of inventory in an average, nondirect distribution

channel, and the cost savings are obvious. Building to order also allowed Dell to cut out the middleman, retaining more profit and reducing selling costs from a typical 12% of sales to a mere 4–6% of sales.

Low costs and high profit margins are a recipe for an exceptional business. In its first eight years Dell Computer grew at an astonishing annual rate of 80%. Even when it slowed down, it was still growing at over 50% a year. By the middle of 2000 its yearly sales were up to $27 billion.

Such a successful business model has attracted its imitators. Companies such as Compaq and Gateway have adopted a similar model. None, however, seem to be able to capture the Dell magic. "There is a popular idea now that if you reduce your inventory and build to order, you'll be just like Dell. Well, that's one part of the puzzle, but there are other parts too," Dell has said. He explains the company's success as "a disciplined approach to understanding how we create value in the PC industry, selecting the right markets, staying focused on a clear business model, and just executing."

Dell has built more than a simple direct sales company. His company's success is closely linked to its relationship with the customer. He knows that the company must not only sell but deliver. Dell Computer has made good use of its direct communication with the consumer. The result? A strong brand, low customer acquisition costs, and high customer loyalty. Dell asks his customers to complain so he can keep the company at the cutting edge of consumer needs. The company once ran an ad that said, "to all our nit-picky, over-demanding, ask-awkward-questions customers. Thank you, and keep up the good work." Few computer companies—or any other company, come to that—would have the confidence to run an ad like this.

With his innate enthusiasm for technology Dell was quick to realize the potential of the Internet. Harnessing its power to reach a wide audience at little cost, the company swiftly moved its selling operations online. "The Internet for us is a dream come true," Dell has said. "It's like zero-variable-cost transaction. The only thing better would be mental telepathy." The figures support the point. Dell began e-commerce in 1996. By 1997 the company's online sales exceeded $3 million a day. The comparable figure for 2000 was $50 million. Half the company's sales are Web-enabled.

When it comes to strategy Dell is no slouch. As the year 2000 approached all the talk in the industry (apart from Y2K worries) was about the imminent demise of the PC. Analysts predicted that PC sales would slump as consumers sought mobile computing solutions. Donald Selkin, chief investment strategist at Joseph Gunnar, the New York securities and banking firm, said of Dell Computer, "I believe its glory days are over; I hate to say it, but it's old technology."

Others believe that Dell's success is founded on a business model rather than a particular product. As if to prove the point, Dell has expanded into areas such as servers and storage network devices. In the quarter ending April 30, 2000, for example, sales of these products accounted for 48% of the systems sales total. There was a 100% increase in sales of storage products, and Dell's machines accounted for 40% of the worldwide industry growth in the server market. Michael Dell says, "I believe we have the right business model for the Internet age. We have a significant lead in dealing direct with customers and suppliers."

In 2000, he reaffirmed the company's commitment to its core strategy of beating components on price and performance, but also indicated that he was accelerating investment into networking and storage companies. He also started to offer Linux open-source operating systems on PCs, broadening the appeal of the range. In 2003, he launched Dell-managed network services to strengthen the company's position in corporate computing. Despite those changes, the company was damaged by a shortage of Intel chips in 2000 and suffered its first stock price fall.

The Dell Computer Corporation had been consistently ranked number two in the world in terms of liquidity, profitability, and growth among all computer systems companies, and number one in the United States. With that sort of performance, many a C.E.O. would be pleased to take a bow and enjoy the applause. Michael Dell has made his first step toward that, and in March 2004 announced that he was stepping down as C.E.O. He will, however, remain as chairman—and one "deeply involved" in the business at that.

> Low costs and high profit margins are a recipe for an exceptional business. In its first eight years Dell Computer grew at an astonishing annual rate of 80%.

1289

MANAGEMENT GIANTS

CONTEXT AND CONCLUSIONS

As the youngest C.E.O. ever to run a *Fortune* 500 company, Michael Dell joined the ranks of the most revered entrepreneurs in the United States. He is credited as the man who took the direct sales model and elevated it to an art form. Dell Computer may not be the biggest company in the world—yet. Nor are its products the most innovative. Yet Dell has built a benchmark company, demonstrating how best to structure a business in order to reap the most reward from new technologies.

> As the youngest C.E.O. ever to run a *Fortune* 500 company, Michael Dell joined the ranks of the most revered entrepreneurs in the United States.

FOR MORE INFORMATION

Book:
Dell, Michael, with Catherine Fredman. *Direct from Dell: Strategies That Revolutionized an Industry*. Revised ed. New York: Collins, 2006.

Web site:
Dell: **www.dell.com**

"When a business goes wrong, look only to the people who are running it."   Michael Dell

Walter Elias Disney

Walt Disney (1901–1966) started with an idea for a cartoon and finished with a film studio. Over a 43-year career in Hollywood, he and his studio won 48 Academy Awards and 7 Emmys as well as a host of other awards. He pioneered the cartoon as an entertainment medium with full-length cartoon features like *Snow White and the Seven Dwarfs*, *Dumbo*, and *Fantasia*. Under his guidance the Disney entertainment machine also produced family film favorites such as *Mary Poppins* and wildlife features such as *The Vanishing Prairie* among its 100-plus films. Today the company that Disney created spans a huge entertainment industry that even his, the most fertile of imaginations, could never have conceived.

Disney and one of his most popular creations.

1901	Born.
1918	Tries to enlist for World War I, at age 16, but is rejected.
1920	Creates his first original animated characters.
1925	Marries employee Lillian Bounds.
1928	Creates Mickey Mouse.
1937	First feature-length musical animation, *Snow White and the Seven Dwarfs*, premieres.
1940	Disney and over 1,000 staff occupy the Burbank Studios.
1955	Disneyland opens.
1964	Conceives Experimental Prototype Community of Tomorrow (Epcot).
1966	Dies.
1971	Disney World opens in Orlando, Florida, with Epcot to follow in 1982.

BACKGROUND AND RISE

Born in Chicago, Illinois, on December 5, 1901, Walt Disney was raised by his parents on a farm near Marceline, Missouri. As a child he showed above average ability. At the tender age of seven he sold sketches to neighbors. His interest in the arts continued at McKinley High School in Chicago where he concentrated on drawing and photography. In the evenings he studied at the Art Institute of Chicago.

When World War I arrived, Disney tried to enlist in the U.S. Army. Unable to produce his birth certificate, he was rejected as being too young. Instead he traveled to France with the Red Cross and spent his time driving an ambulance decorated with his own cartoons.

Settling in Kansas City after the war, Disney embarked on a career as a cartoonist. In 1920, while working for Kansas City Film Ads, he created his first original animated characters. In May 1922 he started his own company, Laugh-O-Grams. The laughs were short-lived as the company quickly ran into financial difficulties, and Disney decided to skip town. Emboldened by the spirit of youth, he left for Hollywood armed only with his drawing equipment, an idea for a cartoon, and the suit on his back.

> When World War I arrived, Disney tried to enlist in the U.S. Army. Unable to produce his birth certificate, he was rejected as being too young.

DEFINING MOMENTS

Disney's new venture began where so many great U.S. corporate dreams have started—in a garage. Together with his brother Roy, Disney launched Disney Brothers Studio. He started out with $500 borrowed from his uncle, $200 from Roy, and $2,500 from his parents, who mortgaged their house to raise the money. Before long Disney was out of the garage and into the back of a Hollywood real estate office. The first work that he sold was a series of featurettes based on Lewis Carroll's Alice character.

Mickey Mouse was born in 1928. There are several versions of how Disney came up with the idea of the little mouse. The most frequently recounted story is that a flash of inspiration came to him on the way home from a disastrous business meeting in which he was forced to relinquish control of his most successful character at the time—Oswald the Rabbit. Daydreaming on the train to Hollywood, he recalled the mice that had been frequent visitors to his old office. Disney wanted to call his new character Mortimer. His wife—displaying a more acute instinct for marketing—persuaded him to christen his creation Mickey Mouse. Mickey made his debut in the first-ever sound cartoon *Steamboat Willie*. It was November 1928 and Disney was just 26.

Disney continued to innovate within the cartoon medium. *Silly Symphonies* introduced Technicolor to cartoons, and in 1937 he premiered the first feature-length musical animation, *Snow White and the Seven Dwarfs*.

     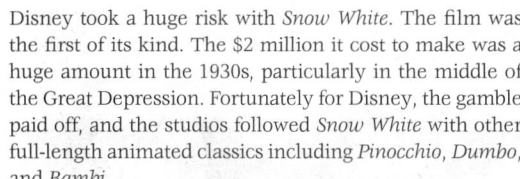

Disney took a huge risk with *Snow White*. The film was the first of its kind. The $2 million it cost to make was a huge amount in the 1930s, particularly in the middle of the Great Depression. Fortunately for Disney, the gamble paid off, and the studios followed *Snow White* with other full-length animated classics including *Pinocchio*, *Dumbo*, and *Bambi*.

By 1940 Disney and over 1,000 staff had occupied the Burbank Studios. For some time Disney's role had been that of a catalyst; he no longer drew any of the studio's output, nor had he done so since the early 1920s. In his own words he was "a little bee. I go from one area to another, and gather pollen and sort of stimulate everyone." The worker bees in Disney's hive weren't always impressed with him. Many resented his reluctance to acknowledge the contribution of the studio artists. Indeed, he wasn't an easy man to work for. Frequently neurotic and obsessive, he imposed strict rules at his studio. Anyone caught cursing in mixed company was fired on the spot, and despite Disney's own preference for a pencil mustache, facial hair was forbidden for all male employees.

During the 1940s the Disney studio became embroiled in a series of labor disputes. Disney was a member of the Motion Picture Alliance for the Preservation of American Ideals—an organization which sought out "communists, radicals, and crackpots" in the movie business. In 1947 he testified before the House Un-American Activities Committee (HUAC), denouncing a number of employees at his studios as communist sympathizers. The fallout from these events took years to dissipate.

World War II had temporarily sidelined the Walt Disney studio's output. During the war most of the Disney facilities were given over to the making of propaganda and health films commissioned by the U.S. government. The studio's small nongovernmental output consisted of comedy shorts to pep up morale. After the war, Disney continued to hone his craft and vary the studio's productions. Cartoons were joined by films combining live action and animation, and "true-life adventures" portraying animals in their natural habitat.

In 1955 Disney took his brand in a new direction. The Disneyland theme park in Anaheim, California, was to be a living embodiment of the Disney movies: a magical land where children and adults could mingle with their favorite cartoon stars from the big screen. Disney's investment was $17 million. It was another big risk for him, but Disneyland was a great hit, with Mickey and his friends greeting a million people in its first seven weeks and many millions more since.

At the same time, Disney continued to push his products on television. He supplied television with the *Wonderful World of Color*, exploiting the lack of programming in what was still a comparatively new medium—color television.

From the mid-1960s onwards, one project consumed the final years of Disney's life. The plan was to build a Disney World with a social dimension. Disney was interested in solving the problems afflicting urban living in the United States. His answer was the Experimental Prototype Community of Tomorrow (Epcot)—the equivalent of a gigantic Ideal Home Exhibition for urban life.

Disney World opened in October 1971. Located in Florida, it was built over 43 square miles and included an amusement theme park, hotel complex, airport, and, 11 years later, the futuristic Epcot Center. Like its Californian relation, Disney World was a success. Disney, however, was not present to witness the fruition of his plans. He died on December 15, 1966.

CONTEXT AND CONCLUSIONS

Walt Disney is an icon of the 20th century and a U.S. folk hero. To many, his name conjures up an image of wholesome homespun entertainment laced with good old-fashioned family values. While this may have been true of his studio's output, Disney himself was a tough, tenacious, and driven businessman with a sizeable ego.

His innovative work ranged from celebrated animated feature films to futuristic amusement parks. The magic of Disney is, however, nowhere more evident than in the fact that such a complicated and often difficult man could attract such talented individuals to his studios and somehow persuade them to produce their very best work. Critics may carp about his management style, but the vision and drive that spawned a billion dollar international entertainment company came down to one man—Walt Disney.

> The Disneyland theme park in Anaheim, California, was to be a living embodiment of the Disney movies: a magical land where children and adults could mingle with their favorite cartoon stars from the big screen.

1291

MANAGEMENT GIANTS

FOR MORE INFORMATION

Books:
Byrne, Eleanor, and Martin McQuillan. *Deconstructing Disney*. London: Pluto Press, 1999.
Giroux, Henry A. *The Mouse that Roared: Disney and the End of Innocence*. Lanham, MD: Rowman & Littlefield, 1999.
Nardo, Don. *Walt Disney*. San Diego, CA: Lucent Books, 2000.
Schickel, Richard. *The Disney Version: The Life, Times, Art, and Commerce of Walt Disney*. Chicago, IL: Ivan R. Dee, 1997.
Sherman, Robert B., and Richard M. Sherman. *Walt's Time: From Before to Beyond*. Santa Clarita, CA: Camphor Tree Publishers, 1998.

Web site:
Disney.com: **www.disney.com**

"Of all the things I've done, the most vital is coordinating the talents of those who work for us and pointing them towards a certain goal."
Walt Disney

George Eastman

"You push the button, we do the rest." The well-known advertising phrase was coined by George Eastman, the U.S. industrialist who brought photography to the masses. Before Eastman's intervention, photography was the province of a small number of specialists who could both understand and physically maneuver the cumbersome technical machinery necessary to take a small picture. Eastman reduced photography to a simple process, making it accessible to all. In addition to his role as an innovator, he brought enlightened management practices to his company, the Eastman Kodak Company—practices that were far ahead of their time.

Eastman developed a camera. The world did the rest.

1854	Born.
1874	Starts work at the Rochester Savings Bank on $15 per week.
1878	Takes up photography.
1880	Patents a dry plate and a machine for mass-producing it.
1881	Takes Henry A. Strong as partner.
1884	The Eastman Dry Plate and Film Company incorporated.
1885	Advertises his revolutionary new photographic film.
1888	The word KODAK registered as a trademark.
1899	"Wage dividend" strategy implemented.
1919	Hands one-third of his company holdings—$10 million—to his employees.
1932	Dies.

BACKGROUND AND RISE

The youngest of three children, Eastman was born in the village of Waterville, 20 miles southwest of Utica, in upstate New York. At age five, Eastman moved with his family to Rochester. Sadly, his father died unexpectedly, leaving the Eastman family in financial straits.

Finishing school at 14, Eastman was forced to get a job to contribute to the family finances. After a period with an insurance firm, he decided to study accounting at home in the evenings to increase his chances of earning more than $5 a week. In 1874, five years after starting in insurance, his studies paid off when he was offered a position as a junior clerk at the Rochester Savings Bank on a weekly salary of over $15.

DEFINING MOMENTS

Eastman's life-changing moment came at age 24. He was planning a vacation in Santo Domingo when a colleague suggested making a photographic record of the trip. Eastman bought the equipment needed to take a photograph using state-of-the-art wet-plate technology. This comprised a camera the size of a 21-inch computer monitor and tripod, together with the glass plates on which the images were captured, and the chemicals, glass tanks, plate holder, and other paraphernalia required for developing them. There was also a tent in which the developing had to take place before the wet plates with the photographic emulsion on could dry out. To learn how to use all the equipment cost $5—a week's wages for Eastman only a few years earlier.

Eastman never made it to Santo Domingo. Instead he became obsessed with photography. Before long he was busy perfecting a dry-plate process in which a photographic plate was covered with a veneer of a special gelatin emulsion. This emulsion remained sensitive even when it was dry, enabling the plate to be exposed whenever the photographer wished, unlike the wet-plate process in which the print had to be developed immediately. It was an idea that Eastman had read about in a British magazine. He took the idea, perfected it, and in 1880, after three years of experimentation, patented a dry plate and a machine for mass-producing it. He gave up his job at the bank and at the beginning of 1881 took on a partner, Henry A. Strong.

Quick to recognize the commercial possibilities of his innovation, Eastman leased a building on State Street in Rochester and began to turn out dry plates for other photographers. Early on the company was faced with a crisis when the dry plates provided to dealers proved defective. Eastman recalled all the faulty plates and replaced them with good ones. "Making good on those plates took our last dollar," he later said. "But what we had left was more important—reputation." In 1884 the Eastman Dry Plate and Film Company was incorporated.

It dawned on Eastman that he could do more than make life easier for professional photographers. He

"Innovation is the specific instrument of entrepreneurship . . . the act that endows resources with a new capacity to create wealth."

Peter F. Drucker

could, in his own words, "make the camera as convenient as the pencil."

When Eastman perfected the transparent roll film and roll holder, the days of cumbersome plate photography were numbered. Photography was at last within reach of the amateur. Eastman had a hand in all aspects of promoting his new photographic film. He wrote the ads and came up with the famous slogan: "You push the button, we do the rest." He even dreamed up the word Kodak, registering the trademark in 1888, and devised the yellow color scheme associated with it. Its origins have been a subject of speculation ever since, but Eastman appears to have invented the name out of thin air. "I devised the name myself," he told his biographer. "The letter 'K' had been a favorite with me—it seems a strong incisive sort of letter. It became a question of trying out a great number of combinations of letters that made words starting and ending with K. The word Kodak is the result."

The KODAK camera was released in 1888 and before long KODAK advertising was inescapable. One of the first electric advertising signs in Piccadilly, London, bore the legend KODAK. In 1892 the company was renamed the Eastman Kodak company of New York.

Eastman built his business using an enlightened humanitarian management style far removed from that of some of his contemporaries. In 1899 he distributed to his entire work force a substantial sum from his own pocket. It was the first act of Eastman's "wage dividend" strategy, a plan to reward employees in proportion to the dividend paid on the company stock. Continuing in the same vein, in 1919 he handed a third of his company holdings—worth some $10 million—to his employees. At the same time he instituted retirement annuities, life insurance, and disability benefits.

George Eastman's philanthropy extended beyond the confines of his corporation. The Massachusetts Institute of Technology (MIT) was particularly favored as two of its graduates, Frank Lovejoy and Darragh de Lancey, had become valued assistants to Eastman. He gave the institute $20 million under the name of "Mr. Smith"—and for years after there was intense speculation over the identity of the mysterious benefactor. Eastman was confident enough of his anonymity to join in a toast to Mr. Smith at an annual MIT alumni dinner.

On one day alone in 1924 Eastman signed away $30 million to the University of Rochester, MIT, Hampton University, and Tuskegee Institute. As he laid down the pen he said, "Now I feel better."

In his final years Eastman was plagued by disability resulting from damage to the lower spinal cord. His inability to lead an active life frustrated him so much that he shot himself on March 14, 1932. He was 77.

CONTEXT AND CONCLUSIONS

Eastman took a cumbersome scientific process and turned it into a commercial mass-market product.

Through his pioneering and innovative work on photographic technology he brought the means of capturing the moment on film to the general public at a price it could afford. Eastman was also the father of a particular type of "trust what's in the box" branding. That first Kodak promise, with its suggestion that consumers simply need to provide their imagination to complement its technology, is echoed by both Microsoft's "Where do you want to go today?" and "Intel Inside." Both draw on Eastman's early inspiration that consumers could be persuaded to trust the brand to take care of the technological side, leaving them free to personalize the product to suit their own lives.

Eastman's slogan captured a turning point in the history of consumerism unlike any other. Previously consumers had understood—even if only at a rudimentary level—how the products they bought worked. But in the late 19th and early 20th century, an explosion of new and technically complex inventions—which included the telephone, the electric light bulb, and film processing—changed the situation forever.

An enlightened manager, Eastman introduced business practices well ahead of his time. He recognized the importance of crisis management when faced with complaints from customers. He also understood that acknowledging the contributions of the work force with remuneration above and beyond their basic salary would in turn benefit the company. Few companies the size of Eastman Kodak were forward-thinking enough to implement employee stock ownership programs and the variety of employment benefits he instituted.

> **Eastman never made it to Santo Domingo. Instead he became obsessed with photography.**

> **An enlightened manager, Eastman introduced business practices well ahead of his time.**

1293

MANAGEMENT GIANTS

FOR MORE INFORMATION

Books:
Ackerman, Carl W., and Edwin R. Seligman. *George Eastman: Founder of Kodak and the Photography Business.* Boston, MA: Houghton Mifflin Co., 1930.
Brayer, Elizabeth. *George Eastman: A Biography.* Baltimore, MD: Johns Hopkins University Press, 1996.
Collins, Douglas. *The Story of Kodak.* New York: H. N. Abrams, 1990.

Web site:
Kodak.com: **www.kodak.com**

Thomas Alva Edison

"Genius is 1% inspiration and 99% perspiration," declared Thomas Alva Edison (1847–1931), the inventor and entrepreneur. It was a maxim he clearly lived by. Unlike many inventors, Edison was a great businessman. By the end of his extraordinary career he had accumulated 1,093 U.S. and 1,300 foreign patents. The inventor of the phonograph and the incandescent light bulb also found time to start up or control 13 major companies. Directly or indirectly, his endeavors led to the creation of well-known corporations like General Electric and RCA. Consolidated Edison is still listed on the New York Stock Exchange.

Edison's genius lit up the world.

1847	Born.
1854	Family moves to Port Huron, Michigan.
1859–62	Sells newspapers on the Grand Trunk Railway.
1863	Works as a telegraph operator; travels across the United States.
1868	Patents his first invention, an electric vote recorder.
1869	Takes up inventing full time; moves to New York City; and starts his first business, making telegraph equipment.
1871	Opens a factory and laboratory in Newark, New Jersey.
1874	Develops a quadruplex system for the telegraph.
1876	Moves to Menlo Park, New Jersey.
1877	Invents the phonograph.
1879	Develops the first commercially viable electric light bulb.
1882	Opens Pearl Street Central Power Station in New York City.
1889	Forms Edison General Electric, and invents the kinetograph (an early motion picture camera).
1892	Edison General Electric merges with Thomson-Houston to create General Electric. Edison sells his interest.
1910	Invents a nickel–iron–alkaline storage battery.
1931	Dies.

BACKGROUND AND RISE

Thomas Edison was born in the town of Milan, Erie County, Ohio, of Dutch and Scottish ancestry. The youngest of seven children, he was effectively an only child since his siblings were much older. His schoolteacher mother was loath to let the young Edison out of her sight and educated him mainly at home.

He was a voracious reader. Newton's *Principia Mathematica*, Parker's *Natural and Experimental Philosophy*, and Gibbon's *Decline and Fall of the Roman Empire* had all been devoured before he reached the age of 12. It was a pattern that continued as Edison embarked on a lifetime of discovery and self-education.

From an early age he displayed an entrepreneurial spirit. When, due to economic hardship, the family was forced to move to Port Huron, near Detroit, he sold vegetables from his home garden; operated a newspaper concession on the Grand Trunk Railroad; and eventually printed his own paper, the *Grand Trunk Herald*. In his spare time he conducted chemical experiments. In one particular episode, he set fire to a train's boxcar. The guard, who had to put out the fire and burned his hands in the process, became so angry that he struck Edison on the ear, bursting his eardrum and leaving him partially deaf.

DEFINING MOMENTS

Telegraphy turned out to be the catalyst for Edison's greatness. He was a natural with the Morse key, becoming one of the fastest transcribers of his day. As a night-duty telegrapher, he was required to key the number six every hour to confirm he was still manning the wire. Instead he invented a machine that automatically keyed the number, and he spent the nights indulging himself at local bars. After being fired from a succession of jobs, he crossed the United States working as a freelance telegrapher, finally coming to rest in New York. He had by this time filed his first patent—an automatic vote recorder for the Massachusetts Legislature.

It was in New York that Edison formed his first partnership, with Frank L. Pope, a noted telegraphic engineer, to exploit the potential of their inventions. The partnership was subsequently absorbed by Gold & Stock (a company controlled by Marshall Lefferts, former president of the

"The real measure of success is the number of experiments that can be crowded into 24 hours."

Thomas Edison

American Telegraph Company) who paid $20,000 to the two partners for this privilege. Recognizing Edison's ingenuity, Lefferts conducted a side deal with him, securing Edison's independent patents for the then princely sum of $30,000.

In 1870, with the benefit of some financial security, Edison hired the talents of Charles Batchelor, an English mathematician, and John Kruesi, a Swiss machinist. He signed patent agreements with Gold & Stock and Western Union; took on a business partner, William Unger; moved into a four-story building at Ward Street, Newark, New Jersey; and started inventing on a grand scale. The fertile mix of minds at Ward Street quickly produced a stock printer, quadruplex telegraphy, and a machine to enable the rapid decoding of Morse.

By 1876 the 29-year-old Edison had 45 inventions to his name and was worth some $400,000. Domestic life did little to change his work habits. Indeed he appeared to work even longer hours. Edison was notorious for his devotion to seeking a solution to the problem in hand. Not only would he work, sleep, and eat at the company premises, but he would lock the lab doors and tell his staff they were staying until they arrived at an answer.

The 1870s were the most creative years of Edison's life. Needing to expand his premises, he moved into buildings at Menlo Park, New Jersey. It was there that he and his team perfected the phonograph. The patents were filed in December 1877, but developing a commercially viable product proved difficult. Finally the phonograph came to market in a selection of models from large to miniature, motor-driven or hand-cranked. The product was a huge success—so much so that Edison's creditors began creeping out of the woodwork.

Barely pausing to draw breath, Edison continued to invent. In early 1877 he began experimenting with incandescent filaments and glass bulbs. Some time before developing the light bulb, he managed to persuade a consortium that he could design a marketable lighting system based on such a product. As a result he signed a rights and remuneration agreement that laid the foundation for the Edison Electric Light Company.

In reality he was far from developing this product. Time passed with Edison making favorable noises about progress while actually making little headway in the lab. Feeling the pressure, at one point he retired to an under-stairs closet, took a dose of morphine, and slept for 36 hours.

It was on Wednesday, November 12, 1879 that Edison finally lit a bulb that lasted long enough to be considered of commercial value. It lasted for 40 hours 20 minutes and within two months Edison had extended its lifetime to 600 hours. Countless visitors trekked to Menlo Park to gaze in wonder at the lights that lit the roadway. Sadly, what followed for Edison was not the triumph of invention but a period of protracted patent litigation that lasted over ten years.

The invention of the light bulb and the formation of the Edison Electric Light Company mark the pinnacle of Edison's achievements. He did continue to invent. In the years that followed, a succession of innovations emerged:

DC generators, the first electric lighting system, electrical metering systems, alkaline storage batteries, cement manufacturing equipment, synchronized sound and moving pictures, and submarine detection by sound. His labs also hosted a great number of prodigious minds, most notably Nikola Tesla, famed for his work on the Tesla coil and AC induction motors. The wizard of Menlo Park, however, never quite recaptured the brilliance of his earlier years. Edison died, working to the last, on Sunday, October 18, 1931.

> He was a voracious reader. Newton's *Principia Mathematica*, Parker's *Natural and Experimental Philosophy*, and Gibbon's *Decline and Fall of the Roman Empire* had all been devoured before he reached the age of 12.

CONTEXT AND CONCLUSIONS

Part of Edison's genius lay in the realization that innovation alone was insufficient for commercial success. Edison focused on creating a commercially viable product. To do so, he assembled a team of brilliant minds at Menlo Park. In effect he created the first product research lab—a forerunner of facilities such as the celebrated Xerox PARC at Palo Alto, California. It was a practical and commercial approach to invention that proved immensely successful.

> Domestic life did little to change his work habits. Indeed he appeared to work even longer hours.

Edison's pragmatism also extended to patenting his ideas. He understood the value of intellectual property and the importance of being able to assert ownership of ideas.

A legend in his own lifetime, his achievements were acknowledged shortly before his death in a nationwide celebration attended by luminaries such as President Hoover, Henry Ford, John Rockefeller, and George Eastman. He remains an inspiration for inventors and entrepreneurs to this day.

FOR MORE INFORMATION

Books:
Baldwin, Neil. *Edison, Inventing the Century*. Revised ed. Chicago: University of Chicago Press, 2001.
Israel, Paul. *Edison: A Life of Invention*. New York: Wiley, 1998.
Jenkins, Reese V., et al., eds. *The Papers of Thomas A. Edison*. Baltimore, : Johns Hopkins University Press, 1989.
Josephson, Matthew. *Edison: A Biography*. New York: Wiley, 1992.
Millard, Andre. *Edison and the Business of Innovation*. Baltimore, MD: Johns Hopkins University Press, 1990.

Web site:
Con Edison, Inc.: **www.conedison.com**

"Genius is one percent inspiration and ninety-nine percent perspiration."   Thomas Edison

Henry Ford

Henry Ford (1863–1947) was part engineer, part inventor, and part entrepreneur. Curiosity and a talent for engineering drove Ford to develop a prototype automobile in his garden. His flair helped him found the Ford Motor Company to develop his prototype. By 1924 Ford had sold ten million Model T Fords—the car famously available in a choice of colors so long as it was black. On his way to ten million sales, Ford broke the land speed record and the mold of manufacturing. During his lifetime his introduction of mass-production assembly line methods irrevocably changed the nature of manufacturing, something for which, for once, the use of the phrase "paradigm shift" is wholly justified.

Ford on the road to another great achievement.

1863	Born.
1884	Attends business school for three months.
1896	Chief engineer at Edison electric factory in Detroit. Drives first vehicle out of garden shed.
1901	Drives to victory in Grosse Point car races.
1903	Founds Ford Motor Co.
1905	Model A Fordsmobile produced.
1908	The first Model T rolls off the production line.
1914	Introduces wages for unskilled workers at a minimum of $5 a day.
1918	The River Rouge plant built.
1919	Ford's son, Edsel, becomes president of the company.
1924	Ten millionth Model T produced.
1928	Brings out second Model A.
1945	Hands over power to his grandson Henry Ford II.
1947	Dies.

BACKGROUND AND RISE

Ford was born in 1863 on his father's farm at Greenfield, near Detroit, Michigan. As a boy he showed great interest in mechanics and engineering. He delighted in dismantling his friends' watches and then reassembling them, and while still a schoolboy built an engine from junk. He was always looking for ways to improve things. "Even when I was very young I suspected that much might somehow be done in a better way," he later observed. "That is what took me into mechanics."

Leaving school at 16, Ford went to work as an engineer for James Flower & Co. in Detroit. To supplement his meager $2.50 a week, he worked at a jeweler's in the evenings. Nine months of grueling hours later, Ford moved to the Dry Dock Engine Works to try his hand at a different type of engineering. By 1896, he was chief engineer at the Edison electrical factory in Detroit. Finding himself unable to confine his engineering to work,

Ford continued to tinker with engineering projects at home.

Ford's strategic planning skills appear to have been underdeveloped at this early stage in his career. His first prototype automobile was the Quadricycle, built in his garden shed. But the innovative horseless carriage was too big, forcing him to dismantle part of the shed to remove it.

For eight years Ford continued to work 12-hour days and then come home to improve his invention. Yet despite the potential of his automobile, no one could be persuaded to invest in it. The turning point came when Ford built a car for the Grosse Point automobile races. Although inexperienced, Ford entered the races, drove the car himself, and won emphatically. He repeated the feat the following year, in 1902. The victory attracted financiers and, after a couple of corporate false starts, the Ford Motor Company was up and running. On the way Ford broke the world land speed record for a four-cylinder automobile, driving a mile over the frozen Lake Sinclair in 39.2 seconds, seven seconds faster than the existing record.

> His first prototype automobile was the Quadricycle, built in garden shed.

DEFINING MOMENTS

Ford's idea was to produce a car for "everyday wear and tear," suitable for the masses. "Anything founded on the idea of the greatest good for the greatest number will win in the end," he said. Rival models like Cadillac cost many thousands of dollars—well beyond the reach of the majority of ordinary people. Ford's first commercial automobile was the Model A Fordmobile, introduced in 1905. Priced at $850, it undercut its rivals and its basic but solid design appealed to the mass market. It was followed in 1908 by the Model T.

The overwhelming demand for the Model T forced Ford to modify the production process and make it more

---

efficient. Initially the cars moved along the production line on cradles. At each stop, men climbed over the cars attending to different tasks. Ford simplified the process and made it more predictable. First, he delineated tasks so that one man performed one task repeatedly, instead of several. Second, he roped the cars together so that they traveled at a steady speed through the plant. These simple but effective measures resulted in an increase in production from 100,000 to 200,000—with, at the same time, a reduction in the workforce of nearly 1,500 men.

Production line work was arduous and monotonous; staff turnover was high. In 1914 Ford reluctantly increased wages for unskilled workers to a minimum of $5 a day, a move that brought in workers from far and wide. Tens of thousands joined the Ford automobile company. So many prospective employees queued up at the factory gates that the fire department had to use its hoses to disperse the crowd.

Ford's management style was not, however, benevolent. The company had its own Sociological Department to watch over the workers—making sure, among other things, that they were mindful of good personal hygiene. Ford's coercive managerial style grated among the workforce. To sweeten this he introduced profit sharing and an extensive welfare program.

He stopped short of allowing the workers to form a labor union, however. When Roosevelt introduced the Wagner Act of 1935, allowing the unionization of the motor companies, Ford resisted the legislation bitterly, refusing to let labor unions operate at Ford auto plants. It was only after adverse publicity as a result of the infamous Battle of the Overpass in May 1937, in which several United Auto Workers' officials were badly beaten—allegedly by Ford employees—outside the River Rouge plant, that Ford was forced to back down and permit union organization at the company.

By 1924 Ford had manufactured 10 million Model Ts and built a new plant at River Rouge, with wages raised to $6 a day. Increasingly he spent less time managing—his son, Edsel, had become president in 1919—and more time pursuing his socially idealistic interests. He built an experimental rural idyll, a model village named Greenfield Village. He also launched the Peace Ship in an attempt to end World War I, and hobnobbed with other magnates and entrepreneurs such as his good friend Henry Firestone. Although a pacifist, Ford was drawn into war manufacturing after Pearl Harbor, when the Willow Plant was built to produce B-24 bombers. This gigan-

tic production plant, with its mile-long assembly line, produced one plane every hour, with a total of 86,865 aircraft between May 1942 and the end of the war. In 1943 Ford returned as C.E.O. after Edsel died.

More at home on the factory floor addressing engineering problems, Ford lacked the managerial skills and flexibility necessary to keep the company ahead of the competition. He was unable to keep pace with the beast he had created. Fixated on the Model T, he waited too long to develop the company's next model, the revamped Model A (launched in 1927), and so lost the initiative to General Motors. Like many entrepreneurs Ford was reluctant to give up his company. A poorly-managed succession further damaged the company, with Ford finally handing power to his grandson Henry Ford II in 1945. Ford died at the age of 84 on April 7, 1947.

> So many prospective employees queued up at the factory gates that the fire department had to use its hoses to disperse the crowd.

CONTEXT AND CONCLUSIONS

Henry Ford is frequently cited as one of the most important and influential businessmen of the 20th century. Although he didn't invent that icon of modern society, the automobile, he was responsible for turning it into a mass-market commodity. Once the sole province of the wealthy, the car was, in its pre-Ford incarnations, a toy—unreliable, poorly engineered, impractical, and above all expensive. Ford changed all that. The champion of mass production, he started an entire industrial revolution of his own, founded on his Model T. It was a revolution that made Ford $1 billion richer and made travel a reality for millions.

MANAGEMENT GIANTS

FOR MORE INFORMATION

Books:
Graves, Ralph H. *The Triumph of an Idea: The Story of Henry Ford*. New York: Doubleday, Doran & Company, Inc., 1934.
Ford, Henry, and Samuel Crowther. *My Life and Work*. New York: Doubleday, Page & Co., 1923.

Web site:
Ford Motor Company: **www.ford.com**

"Sometimes it is the men 'higher up' who most need revamping—and they themselves are the last to recognize it."

Henry Ford

Bill Gates

Bill Gates's contribution to the development of computer technology is beyond dispute. At the age of 13 he was already plotting his business future, forming the Lakeside Programmers Group with some school friends. Its goal was to seek commercial opportunities for their computer skills. His early programming brilliance, his alliance with Microsoft cofounder Paul Allen, and his departure from Harvard to start Microsoft are well known.

Microsoft is one of the most successful companies the world has ever seen. As the Internet market exploded, he beat off Netscape in the browser wars. But perhaps his biggest challenge to date has come from the Department of Justice and its antitrust lawyers. Despite protracted litigation, Gates has so far managed to keep Microsoft intact, and enabled it to hold on to its dominant position.

Bill Gates—cyber visionary.

1298

MANAGEMENT GIANTS

1955	Born.
1977	Drops out of Harvard to focus on computer software company with Paul Allen.
1980	Agrees to license operating system to IBM.
1995	Windows 9X series introduced.
1997	Microsoft ordered to supply Windows 95 without a browser.
2000	Microsoft found guilty of anticompetitive behavior. Judge orders break-up of Microsoft.
2001	Break-up ruling set aside by appeals court. Launch of XP generation of OS and X-Box game console.
2002	Gates Foundation donates $300 million to world health research.
2003	Major focus on security of Windows operating system. Commitment to mobile computing.
2003	Microsoft passes $200 billion market capitalization.
2004	European Union instructs Microsoft to undergo series of anti-monopoly measures.
2005	Microsoft celebrates its 30th birthday.

BACKGROUND AND RISE

William Henry Gates III was born in Seattle on October 28, 1955. He was a precociously brilliant boy. Before his tenth birthday he had read the family's encyclopedia from beginning to end.

At Lakeside, the exclusive private school he attended in Seattle, he developed an obsession with computers. Gates, then still only 13, and some of his computer friends formed the Lakeside Programmers Group, dedicated to using their programming skills to make money.

> **He was a precociously brilliant boy. Before his tenth birthday he had read the family's encyclopedia from beginning to end.**

At Lakeside he developed a friendship with another boy two years his senior. The boy, whose obsession with computers matched Gates's, was Paul Allen.

Gates left Lakeside in 1973 to study law at Harvard. Law was a lot less appealing, however, than computing. He contacted Allen and the two teamed up to develop a version of an early computer language—BASIC. Gates dropped out of Harvard in 1977 to focus on a small computer software company with Allen. They called it Microsoft.

DEFINING MOMENTS

A brilliant strategic decision in 1980 set Microsoft on the road to global dominance. At that time IBM dominated the IT industry through its mainframe business. By the late 1970s Microsoft was licensing its software to a number of customers. But the prevailing wisdom was that hardware was the business to be in and software merely an adjunct. Apple at the time was developing a proprietary in-house operating system (OS) that would provide a competitive advantage. Its strategy was to maintain control over what it regarded as its superior hardware by running it with its own software. Gates thought differently. As far as he was concerned the more people that used Microsoft software on their machines the better. So when IBM approached Microsoft to develop the operating system for its first PC, Gates recognized what an enormous opportunity this presented. IBM's dominance of the IT market meant that its PCs were destined to set the standard—both for hardware and for the OS. IBM failed to realize that, when the end user switched on the machine, the part of the computer he or she interacted with would be the OS, supplied by Microsoft. Gates capitalized on the situation, cannily retaining the right to license its OS to other PC manufacturers.

The decision by IBM to use Microsoft's MS-DOS was a turning point for both companies. From that point onward, the fortunes of IBM, which singularly failed to

> "If the 1980s were about quality and the 1990s were about reengineering, then the 2000s will be about velocity."
>
> Bill Gates

grasp the significance of the OS, would inexorably decline, until Lou Gerstner came to its rescue as C.E.O. in 1993. For Microsoft the only way was up. Endorsed by IBM, MS-DOS displaced competing OS offerings regardless of their technical merits. Yet in those early days the rest of the world still failed to understand the importance of Gates's coup. Even in 1984, *Fortune* magazine was criticizing Gates for failing to develop the management depth that would turn a temporary victory into long-term dominance. Not for the last time the media underestimated Gates's drive, ambition, and strategic vision.

When ill health forced Allen to leave Microsoft, Gates's position as leader was confirmed. Microsoft's rapid growth soon made it the darling of Wall Street. From a price of $2 per share in 1986, Microsoft stock had soared to $105 by the first half of 1996, making Gates a billionaire.

Microsoft has launched a succession of successful products. But Gates hasn't had things all his own way. When the Internet revolution took off in the early 1990s, Microsoft was momentarily caught off balance. A company called Netscape sprang up, giving away a nifty piece of software called a browser that transformed the Web from a techie's playground to a mass-market phenomenon. Microsoft responded by licensing browser technology from a company called Spyglass, tweaking it, and repackaging it as Microsoft Internet Explorer. To cover all the bases, Microsoft also bought WebTV, eShops, Hotmail, and Vermeer, the original developers of the Front Page HTML editing software.

Critics regularly deride the company for buying technology rather than developing its own solutions. Microsoft has countered that it has developed a number of important technologies and is still doing so.

Criticism has also constantly been leveled at Microsoft, alleging that it abuses its dominant market position. Matters came to a head when the U.S. Justice Department investigated Microsoft to establish whether the company was in breach of antitrust law. In June 2000, after a lengthy trial, U.S. District Judge Thomas Penfield Jackson ordered Microsoft to be split into two companies, holding that it had used monopoly power to push aside potential competitors to the detriment of consumers. Microsoft took the case to the appeals court in 2001, and the court decided to overturn part of the original decision, withdrawing the requirement for Microsoft to be broken up. Despite that, the company continues to grow and, in 2003, it passed $200 billion market capitalization.

Ultimately it may not be the antitrust ruling that poses the biggest threat to Microsoft's bottom line. Microsoft risks being sidelined by the sheer pace of technological progress. Handhelds and cellphones may be the PCs of the future, and those markets are not dominated by Microsoft. The company has also conceded that it needs to be nimbler, and to that end reorganized itself in September 2005, slimming its seven divisions down to three. It is too early to tell whether the impact of that change will be enough to preserve Microsoft's hegemony, but Gates, the architect of the world's greatest software company, won't go down without a fight.

CONTEXT AND CONCLUSIONS

Bill Gates is lauded and reviled in almost equal measure.

His charitable work, which tends to be overlooked, has grown rapidly and, in 2002, the Bill & Melinda Gates Foundation gave more than $300 million to tackle AIDS and other global health challenges. He added another $83 million to this in 2004, as a donation to help combat tuberculosis. Overall, the year 2004 was a mixed one. A highlight came early when in January he was awarded an honorary knighthood for his services to the British economy. However, the European Union put a damper on things when it instructed Microsoft to undergo a series of anti-monopoly measures, and in May Gates was fined $800,000 by the Federal Trade Commission for not reporting that he had bought more than $50 million worth of stock in Icos Corp (a drug company based in Washington State). Gates is nothing if not indefatigable, though. Whatever you think of the dominance of Microsoft, or Gates's methods, it cannot be doubted that when it comes to building and retaining a competitive advantage he has few peers. His technical skills, while not to be underrated, are not his greatest attribute. Far more important is his strategic thinking. It is this that has enabled him to outsmart his opponents at every turn. His other great attribute is the ability to hire the best talent and then motivate it to work at high tempo. He may appear awkward, geeky even, in public—but Gates is as sharp as a tack.

> Yet in those early days the rest of the world still failed to understand the importance of Gates's coup. Even in 1984, *Fortune* magazine was criticizing Gates for failing to develop the management depth that would turn a temporary victory into long-term dominance.

CLOSE BUT NO CIGAR

Ken Olsen

Olsen was once hailed by *Fortune* magazine as the "most successful entrepreneur in the history of American business." Founding Digital Equipment Corporation (DEC) in 1959, he spent the next 35 years riding the IT roller coaster at the helm of his company. Olsen, the man who pioneered the minicomputer, was heavily influenced by the writings of Alfred Sloan and organized DEC along similar lines to GM (small business units) when under Sloan's control. He left in 1992 to found Advanced Modular Solutions Inc. After a disastrous spell in the early 1990s, DEC was finally bought by Compaq in 1998.

FOR MORE INFORMATION

Book:
Gates, Bill. *Business @ the Speed of Thought*. New York: Warner Books, 1999.

Web site:
Microsoft: **www.microsoft.com**

"Take our 20 best people away, and I will tell you that Microsoft would become an unimportant company."

Bill Gates

Harold Geneen

Harold Geneen is the classic example of the C.E.O. as analyst. He joined the board of ITT in 1959 and set about turning the company into the world's greatest conglomerate. His basic organizational strategy was that diversification was a source of strength. Under Geneen, ITT's spending spree amounted to 350 companies. By 1970, ITT was composed of 400 separate companies operating in 70 countries.

By sheer force of personality, Geneen's approach worked. Between 1959 and 1977, ITT's sales went from $765 million to nearly $28 billion and earnings per share rose from $1 to $4.20. Geneen stepped down as chairman in 1979. But a company built around the drive and energy of one man will not last longer than that man's career. His followers were unable to sustain Geneen's uniquely driven working style. In the month of Harold Geneen's death, ITT was taken over.

Geneen spreads the word about ITT.

1910	Born.
1934	Obtains a degree in accounting.
1934–1959	Works for a number of firms including American Can, Bell and Howell, Jones and Laughlin Steel, and Raytheon.
1959	Joins ITT.
1966	ABC merger blocked.
1971	Acquires Hartford Insurance.
1977	Steps down as chief executive.
1979	Steps down as chairman.
1983	Resigns as director.
1997	Dies.

BACKGROUND AND RISE

Son of a Russian Jewish father and an Italian Catholic mother, Harold Geneen was born in Bournemouth, England in 1910. His family moved to the United States before his first birthday, but his parents separated soon after they arrived. As a result, Geneen's childhood was spent at boarding schools and summer camps. When Geneen started work as a runner for the New York Stock Exchange, he continued to study at night at New York University. In 1934 his hard work was rewarded with a degree in accounting.

For the next 25 years his career took in a string of companies, starting with the forerunners of Coopers & Lybrand, followed by Montgomery (an accounting firm), then the American Can Co., Bell and Howell Co., Jones and Laughlin Steel Co., and Raytheon. After Raytheon, where Geneen was vice president, came the biggest challenge of his career and the job that made him famous: the International Telegraph and Telephone Company, more commonly known as ITT.

> **Fortunately for ITT, Geneen was no slouch; on the contrary, he was a fiercely driven workaholic.**

DEFINING MOMENTS

When Geneen arrived at ITT in 1959, the corporation was a ragbag collection of businesses, loosely focused around telecommunications, with revenues of $800,000. During the 1960s the predominant organizational trend was one of diversification and conglomeration. C.E.O.s went into a purchasing frenzy, raiding the corporate aisles for any company, no matter what business it was in, so long as it turned a profit. Geneen was no exception.

Over the ensuing decade Geneen purchased over 300 companies, operating in over 60 different countries. There was no rationale to these purchases, no common thread, other than that of profit. Sheraton hotels, Avis car rental, and Continental Baking were all tucked away in ITT's roomy locker. "I never met a business that I didn't find interesting," said Geneen, and the ITT balance sheet certainly bore him out.

It was a mammoth undertaking to manage so many disparate companies. Fortunately for ITT, Geneen was no slouch; on the contrary, he was a fiercely driven workaholic. His ITT office in New York was equipped with eight telephones and a clock that showed which parts of the world were in daylight and which were in darkness. Ten suitcase-sized leather attaché cases crammed full of documents were stacked along the window ledges. Six of the cases, stuffed with reports, communiqués, and memos from over 400 reporting corporations, followed Geneen around the country and the world. "If I had enough arms and legs and time, I would do it all myself," said Geneen. Well into his eighties, long after he left ITT, Geneen was still working a ten-hour day at his office in New York's Waldorf-Astoria hotel. A typical Geneen story is recounted by an old ITT executive. Dragging a group of executives in for an evening meeting, Geneen worked them late into the night. At 11:45 p.m., the last of the executives made his way out of the office, pausing to wait for Geneen. Instead the C.E.O. peeled off his jacket, pulled on a

"Every company has two organizational structures: the formal one is written on the charts; the other is the everyday relationships of the men and women in the organization."

Harold S. Green

sweater and kept on working—the last executive in the building.

Even so, it required all his energy to control the ITT conglomerate. To keep it together, Geneen employed rigorous financial accounting methods. Each month, 50 or more executives flew to Brussels to spend several days examining the figures. "I want no surprises," was one of Geneen's mantras. Full information was paramount, as was the ability to tell real facts from details masquerading as facts. "The highest art of professional management requires the literal ability to smell a real fact from all others," asserted Geneen.

And his approach seemed to work. From 1959 to 1977, ITT sales rocketed from some $765 million to approaching $28 billion, with earnings up from $29 million to $562 million. It was a success by most people's standards, not just Geneen's. Yet the more companies he acquired, the harder it was to keep all the plates spinning in the air. In 1974 and 1975 profits fell: Geneen may have been able to keep up a relentless pace, but his followers were either unable or unwilling to match it.

Geneen's efforts to support his company's stock price sometimes strayed outside the boundaries of acceptable practice. In 1972, the Securities and Exchange Commission discovered $8.7 million had been sunk into nefarious and illegal activities around the world. This allegedly included bribery and collusion with the CIA in an attempt to undermine the Allende government in Chile.

Geneen stepped down as chief executive in 1977, as chairman in 1979, and as a director four years later—not that such a relentless man could ever retire to a life of quiet contemplation and gentle pastimes. He carried on working in a number of different companies of his own creation until his death from a heart attack in 1997.

ITT, however, was a different proposition. Without Geneen to support it, the house of cards collapsed. ITT limped on but eventually, after selling many of the companies acquired by Geneen, it was split up into three separate companies.

CONTEXT AND CONCLUSIONS

Harold Geneen was one of the last of his breed. He came to power at ITT at the height of the mania for conglomerates. Size mattered, and if size mattered then Geneen was very, very important. It is doubtful if any other C.E.O. in corporate history acquired more companies—over 300—with less rationale. Of course acquisition is one way to grow earnings, but eventually the relentless growth has to stop and increased earnings must come from existing operations. Even a man with Geneen's drive and boundless energy will struggle to keep 300 plates in the air, and so it proved. In the decade following his departure from ITT, the cry from the boardroom was "stick to the knitting." Companies slimmed down, shed noncore business, and left ITT looking like a bloated dinosaur. Yet Geneen deserves his place in the pantheon of business greats. Why? Because he was the best of his type, the paragon of his age, the king of the conglomerates.

> Harold Geneen was one of the last of his breed.

Charles G. Bludhorn
Who today remembers Charlie Bludhorn? Yet in the 1960s and 1970s, Bludhorn—then head of conglomerate Gulf and Western—was one of the most fashionable C.E.O.s of his time. Along with conglomerate kings such as James Ling, Henry Singleton, Charles "Tex" Thornton, and of course Harold Geneen, Bludhorn was fêted as a business visionary. Among the many corporate baubles he accumulated were Music Corporation of America, Madison Square Garden, and Paramount Studios. When conglomerates fell out of fashion, so did Bludhorn. Gulf and Western was whittled down to size until Paramount was pretty much all that remained.

FOR MORE INFORMATION

Books:
Sampson, Anthony. *The Sovereign State of ITT*. New York: Stein and Day, 1973.
Shoenberg, Robert J. *Geneen*. New York: Norton, 1985.

"The worst disease which can afflict business executives in their work is not, as popularly supposed, alcoholism; it's egotism."

Harold S. Geneen

King Camp Gillette

King Camp Gillette, the safety-razor entrepreneur, made his fortune by taking a mundane everyday product and improving it. So confident was he of his invention that he formed the American Safety Razor Company in 1901 and persuaded investors to back him before he even had a commercial product. In the first year of production Gillette sold 51 razor sets and 168 blades. By 1905 the figure was 250,000 razor sets and 100,000 blade packages. Part of the secret of Gillette's success was his modern attitude towards branding. With his picture on the wrappers of his disposable blades, he was soon known the world over. By the time he had moved on to improving the world through his social theories, the Gillette safety razor was a permanent fixture in the grooming habits of a large proportion of the world's male population.

Gillette was at the cutting edge of shaving technology.

1302

MANAGEMENT GIANTS

1855	Born.
1871	Gillette family hardware business burns down.
1890	Holds four patents.
1894	Writes *The Human Drift*.
1895	Works for the inventor of cork-lined bottle caps.
1901	Gillette and Nickerson form the American Safety Razor Company.
1903	Production begins on the new safety razor.
1904	The renamed Gillette company is awarded the patent for the new invention. Invents the double-edged blade—a concept still used to this day.
1906	Twelve million blades sold to date, generating revenues of $90,000.
1915	Sales of seven million blades a year.
1932	Dies.

BACKGROUND AND RISE

King Camp Gillette was born in Fond du Lac, Wisconsin, into a family of innovators. His father was a patent agent and small-time inventor. His mother wrote a cookbook based on a lifetime of culinary experimentation; the book was still in print a century later. When Gillette was four, his family moved to Chicago to start up a hardware business. Unfortunately, the business was ravaged by the Great Fire, and in 1871 the family moved once again, this time to New York City.

> His father was a patent agent and small-time inventor. His mother wrote a cookbook based on a lifetime of culinary experimentation; the book was still in print a century later.

Gillette took a job as a traveling salesman. Not content with merely selling his products, he couldn't resist improving them. By 1890 he had accumulated four patents. In 1895 he was working for the man who had invented cork-lined bottle caps. He had some simple advice for Gillette: "Invent something people use and throw away." Gillette took his words to heart and turned his attention to the safety razor.

Traditionally, men of the time used the straight razor to shave. The increasing use of the railroad, however, had prompted a rethinking of the design of this basic implement. The swaying of the carriages made it downright dangerous to use the traditional cut-throat. Safety razors had been invented—a heavy blade fitted at right angles to a short handle—but they still had major shortcomings. Gillette used a Star safety razor. This required continual sharpening on a leather strop just as the traditional razor did. Eventually the blade wore out.

Gillette had an idea. What if it were possible to take a small square of sheet steel and put a permanently sharp edge on it? Such a product would be sufficiently affordable to throw away when it became dull.

DEFINING MOMENTS

To help him in his quest for a new improved safety razor, Gillette turned to metallurgists at the Massachusetts Institute of Technology. They assured Gillette that his idea was impossible. Undaunted, Gillette continued to search for someone who shared his belief and vision. That person was William Emery Nickerson, an inventor who, ironically, had been educated at MIT.

Gillette's search had taken six years. His doggedness was rewarded in 1901 when, together with Nickerson, he formed the American Safety Razor Company. Then in 1903 production began on the new safety razor. Razor blades were bundled up and sold as a package. The razor handle was sold as a one-time purchase. In 1904 the renamed Gillette Safety Razor Company was awarded the patent for the new invention. Initial sales were disappointing. After an intensive advertising campaign in men's magazines and newspapers in the United

"An idea can turn to dust or magic, depending on the talent that rubs against it."

William Bernbach

States and Europe, however, things improved. By 1906 12 million blades had been sold, generating revenues of $90,000.

The inevitable patent battles ensued. With a large proportion of the world's population as a potential market, sharp practices were rife. Competitors came to the market with modified versions of Gillette's product. Gillette responded with litigation or, in many cases, by buying the competition. And all the while he continued to tinker with his invention. In 1904 he came up with the double-edged blade, a concept used to this day. With his face plastered over the wrappers of his razor blades, Gillette became a celebrity.

Although the Gillette razor made King Camp Gillette a millionaire, he remained unfulfilled. He had strong philosophical and political beliefs. With his newly made millions he was now a powerful figure in North American commerce. He had an idealistic vision of a utopian society based on universal cooperation, and he now had the means to attempt to make it a reality.

Gillette wrote several books outlining his vision, beginning with *The Human Drift* (1894) that predated the invention of the Gillette razor. In a reaction against the mass pollution and sprawling urban development of the Industrial Revolution, he planned pollution-free cities contained in giant glass domes. In this new utopia, one company would perform all production with the citizens as the stockholders. "Selfishness would be unknown, and war would be a barbarism of the past," he wrote.

One interesting byproduct of Gillette's obsession was his meeting with Henry Ford. In the years before World War I Gillette attempted to set the wheels of his World Corporation in motion. First he asked Teddy Roosevelt to be president. When Roosevelt unsurprisingly declined, Gillette approached the writer Sinclair Lewis, who in turn arranged a meeting between Gillette and Ford. The outcome of this meeting between two dogmatic, strong-willed millionaires should have been no surprise. At first the two merely talked over each other then, growing angrier, they began to shout at each other.

CONTEXT AND CONCLUSIONS

Gillette's attempts at social engineering came to nothing. The stock market crash of 1929, coupled with boardroom machinations and constant patent litigation, wiped out his personal fortune. He spent a lot of time during his final years trying unsuccessfully to extract oil from shale. In the end he died, unfulfilled and frustrated, in 1932. The Gillette Safety Razor Company, however, thrived, carrying on its founder's tradition of innovation and remaining at the cutting edge of safety razor development. The company introduced foam shaving cream (Foamy), anti-perspirant (Right Guard), and continued to do what Gillette had always done—improve the safety razor with twin-blade, pivoting-head, disposable, and triple-blade razors.

> The stock market crash of 1929, coupled with boardroom machinations and constant patent litigation, wiped out his personal fortune.

King Camp Gillette will be remembered for creating a product used daily by people the world over. Not only did he pioneer the market for disposable products, but he also showed an early and prescient awareness of the power of both celebrity and the brand. His image on the packaging of his product made him famous and helped reassure the consumer about the product's quality. This in turn boosted sales and helped make the Gillette Safety Razor Company the leader in its market.

1303

MANAGEMENT GIANTS

FOR MORE INFORMATION

Book:
Adams, Russell B., Jr. *King C. Gillette: The Man and His Wonderful Shaving Device*. Boston, MA: Little, Brown., 1978.

Web site:
The Gillette Company: **www.gillette.com**

"Don't study the idea to death with experts and committees. Get on with it and see if it works."
Kenneth Iverson

Andrew S. Grove

Andy Grove (1936–) managed to survive a childhood in Nazi-occupied Hungary only to find himself a victim of the Cold War. He escaped to the United States in 1957. After educating himself in New York and California, Grove joined Fairchild Semiconductor. In 1968 he followed colleagues Bob Noyce and Gordon Moore to form a new company, Intel. By 1979 he was chief operating officer.

In the 1980s Grove concentrated the company's efforts on manufacturing microprocessors. He was made C.E.O. in 1987. In 1994 he faced a crisis when a flaw was discovered in the company's flagship product, the Pentium processor. Under pressure, Grove made the decision to replace the chips rather than try to tough it out, reinforcing Intel's reputation.

Andy Grove with one of the keys to his success.

Year	Event
1936	Born.
1957	"Traitorous eight" start Fairchild Semiconductor. Grove escapes to United States.
1963	Gains Ph.D. from University of California, Berkeley.
1968	Gordon Moore and Bob Noyce start Intel.
1979	Becomes Intel's president and chief operating officer.
1981	IBM decides to use Intel microprocessors.
1985	Shifts Intel's focus to microprocessors.
1987	Becomes C.E.O. of Intel.
1994	Flawed Pentium microprocessors recalled.
1998	Steps down as Intel's C.E.O.
1999	Intel launches Pentium 3 processors.
1999	Grove, a former journalist, warns media to adapt to threat of Web publications.
2001	Intel experiences product shortages and delays. 500 job cuts.
2001	Launch of Itanium high-end processor.
2001	European Commission launches antitrust case against Intel.
2002	Intel's warning of low sales sends stock price crashing.
2004	Japanese offices raided by fair trade watchdog.

BACKGROUND AND RISE

Illness, discrimination, poverty: Andy Grove, born Andras Grof in prewar Hungary on September 2, 1936, suffered them all as a child. At the age of four he contracted scarlet fever which left him with impaired hearing. Then another, more sinister, threat cast its shadow: as the Nazis swept to power in Europe, the Jewish Grof family feared for their lives. Grof and his mother assumed false identities and were sheltered by friends. The young Grof became Andras Malesevics.

Miraculously he and his family avoided the death camps and survived the war, but they then found themselves on the wrong side of the Iron Curtain. After the failure of the Hungarian uprising in 1956, Grof decided to escape.

He fled to Austria and from there to the United States, changing his name to Andrew S. Grove along the way. In 1957 he enrolled at City College of New York, graduating in 1960 with a degree in chemical engineering. After City College, he studied at the University of California, Berkeley, receiving his Ph.D. in 1963.

His first job after graduation was at Fairchild Semiconductor, a young company formed by several research scientists including Robert Noyce and Gordon Moore.

DEFINING MOMENTS

Fairchild Semiconductor was the cradle of the computing revolution. It was formed by a disaffected group of researchers from William Shockley's research team at Shockley Semiconductor Laboratory in Palo Alto, California. Shockley had received the Nobel Prize for his work developing the transistor, and his academic reputation attracted some of the finest minds in electronics to his company, including Bob Noyce, Gordon Moore (of Moore's Law fame), Julius Blank, Victor Grinich, Eugene Kleiner, Jean Hoerni, Jay Last, and Sheldon Roberts.

Shockley's poor management style bred disaffection among his research team. The eventual exodus from his company of the so-called "traitorous eight" was one of the landmarks of computing history. The company they founded, Fairchild Semiconductor, revolutionized the world of computing with its work on the silicon transistor. The drain of talent from Shockley's lab went on after Fairchild to start up some of the best-known companies in Silicon Valley. Intel (Bob Noyce and Gordon Moore), Advanced Micro Devices (Jerry Sanders), and National Semiconductor (Charlie Sporck) were all spinoffs from Fairchild.

"Much as we talk about Internet companies today, in five years' time there won't be any Internet companies. All companies will be Internet companies or they will be dead."

Andrew S. Grove

When Gordon Moore and Bob Noyce left Fairchild in 1968 to start Intel, they asked Grove to come with them. Their original business plan involved manufacturing a new kind of computer memory using semiconductor technology, and in 1970 the first dynamic random-access memory (DRAM) for commercial use rolled off Intel's production lines. Intel had also been approached by a Japanese company, Nippon Calculating Machine Corporation (NCM), to produce logic chips. Intel had already been working on a smaller single chip and offered its own solution. A chip was eventually developed. Instead of the patent rights passing to NCM, Intel retained ownership and licensed manufacturing and selling rights. This key decision by Grove and the management team paved the way for Intel to become the microprocessor giant it is today.

Intel's success was founded not only on its innovative skills but also on its skillful repositioning of a commodity computer component into a household-name brand. TV commercials elevated the mundane microchip to an aspirational product. Encouraged by the "Intel Inside" ad campaign, consumers insisted on having an Intel chip inside their PCs. The Intel Pentium processor became as strongly associated with PCs as Microsoft's Windows operating system, another marketing success story.

Andy Grove's vision was instrumental in Intel's success. He got things done. In the early days he was the man who organized the office space and manufacturing capacity. He played a key role in the 1981 negotiations with IBM that saw Intel beat off competition from Motorola to supply the microprocessors for IBM's PCs.

In many ways Grove's childhood experiences in war-torn Europe had prepared him well for business life. He was a man who didn't avoid tough decisions. In the 1980s, when microprocessors looked as if they might be a better bet than memory, Grove made the bold and risky decision to refocus the company's efforts, which meant laying off thousands of employees. In 1987 he became the C.E.O. of Intel. The decisions didn't get any easier. Grove averted a potential crisis when a flaw was discovered in the company's flagship Pentium microprocessor. With a technical problem probably discernible only by mathematicians threatening to balloon into a public relations disaster, Grove acted decisively. He could have used Intel's muscle to pass on the burden of replacement to the retailers and consumers. Instead he offered to replace the processors. The move cost a fortune—$475 million—but it safeguarded the Intel brand. Profits went up.

Grove was a godsend to the company's stockholders. During his tenure as C.E.O. Intel's stock value increased 24-fold. In 1998 he resigned as C.E.O., remaining as chairman of the board. Since stepping down he has focused on strategic thinking. Drawing on his experience as a journalist, he advised the media in 1999 to change its approach in light of the growing strength of Web publications.

Since Grove took a back seat at Intel, the company has been wrestling with a number of difficult issues, not least a likely future decline in demand for microchips. Moore's Law (originated by Intel cofounder Gordon Moore) states that microprocessing power will double every 18 months. It has held true for over a decade, delivering revenue growth to Intel through consumer chip upgrades. Eventually, though, Moore believes that the rate of increase will slow. Grove appears to be prepared for this. He is on record as saying that "all companies will be Internet companies." Backing this view, Intel has diversified its operations to embrace the Internet. Technical innovation continued after Grove's departure with the launch of the Pentium 3 processor in 1999, Pentium 4 in 2000, and the Itanium high-end 4-bit processor in 2001.

> Fairchild Semiconductor was the cradle of the computing revolution. It was formed by a disaffected group of researchers from William Shockley's research team at Shockley Semiconductor Laboratory in Palo Alto, California.

However, supply problems hit the company hard in 2000, leading to the loss of 500 jobs that year. In 2001, the company hit further problems when the European Commission launched an antitrust case against Intel for alleged abuse of a dominant position to stifle competition. A similar specter appeared in April 2004. The company's offices in Japan were raided by the national fair trade commission following allegations that Intel had been pursuing anti-competitive practices and attempting to ask its clients to not use chips made by other companies. More positively, however, in the same month, and after several years of fluctuating fortunes, Intel was able to report an 89% increase on first quarter profits. In real terms, this meant a profit of over $1.5 billion, an increase of almost 50% on the same period in 2003. The long-vaunted upswing in computer spending may yet be upon us.

CONTEXT AND CONCLUSIONS

Just as all companies need an entrepreneur to make things happen in the formative stages of a new venture, so too they need an organizer and steady hand to help guide them from startup through the growth phase and beyond. Andy Grove is such a man. As a child in war torn Europe, Grove learned to assess a situation using all available information and then make a decision. It is a skill that has served him well throughout his life, both business and personal. Whatever his future achievements, his accomplishments at Intel alone merit a place alongside the great business leaders of the 20th century.

1305

MANAGEMENT GIANTS

FOR MORE INFORMATION

Books:
Grove, Andrew S. *Only the Paranoid Survive: How to Exploit the Crisis Points that Challenge Every Company.* New York: Doubleday, 1999.
Grove, Andrew S. *Swimming Across: A Memoir.* New York: Warner Books, 2001.
Jackson, Tim. *Inside Intel: Andy Grove and the Rise of the World's Most Powerful Chip Company.* Collingdale, PA: DIANE, 2001.

Web site:
Intel: **www.intel.com**

"Columbus didn't have a business plan when he discovered America." — Andrew S. Grove

William Randolph Hearst

Arguably the most famous media mogul of the 20th century, William Randolph Hearst (1863–1951) took the silver spoon of his inheritance and fashioned it into a gold one. Despite his patrician upbringing, he succeeded in keeping his finger on the pulse of his industry. Through a combination of media savvy and extraordinary stamina and persistence, he built an ailing newspaper, the *San Francisco Examiner*, into a billion dollar media empire. At his peak, Hearst owned over 40 major newspapers and magazines, not to mention a handful of radio stations and movie companies. In 1951 he died an immensely wealthy and powerful man, immortalized ten years previously, and much to his chagrin, in Orson Welles's movie, *Citizen Kane*.

Hearst knew how to handle the media.

1863	Born.
1887	Takes control of the *San Francisco Examiner*.
1889	The *San Francisco Examiner* makes a profit.
1895	Heads for New York to save the *New York Morning Journal*.
1896	Acquires New York's *Evening Journal*.
1902	Becomes a Democratic congressional representative for New York.
1920s	Builds a fabulous castle on San Simeon estate.
1930s	Forced to consolidate empire following the Great Depression.
1951	Dies.

BACKGROUND AND RISE

Hearst was born in San Francisco on April 29, 1863. His father was a wealthy industrialist and speculator, and his mother a socialite and philanthropist. It was a potent cocktail of wealth, commerce, and culture that was to have a profound effect on him. An only child, he spent his early years shuttling between the family's huge estate at San Simeon, California, and their home in New York.

> **An only child, he spent his early years shuttling between the family's huge estate at San Simeon, California, and their home in New York.**

The classical academic route for the privileged awaited: a first-class prep school—St. Paul's Preparatory School in Concord, New Hampshire—followed by an Ivy League university—Harvard. At Harvard, Hearst excelled in social activities. He was a member of the Hasty Pudding Theater and, more notably, business manager for the college magazine, the *Harvard Lampoon*. So much energy was put into his social life that he neglected his academic work. Hearst was eventually expelled and he never received his degree.

Shrugging off his academic failure, he took a job instead at the *New York World*. Joseph Pulitzer's newspaper was one of the leading newspapers in New York at the time. Hearst may not have paid attention in his Harvard classes, but at the *New York World* he received a first-class education in how to run a newspaper. However, he was soon summoned back to San Francisco by his father.

DEFINING MOMENTS

In contrast to media moguls like Louis B. Mayer who worked their way up from the bottom of the pile, Hearst was handed his first newspaper as a gift. The *San Francisco Examiner* had been purchased by Hearst's father to provide him with a voice when he was running for the U.S. Senate. With the senate seat secured, the paper was surplus to requirements. Neglected, its circulation dwindled. The younger Hearst was desperate to take charge of it. His father was less enthusiastic and offered him as alternative inducements a one-million-acre ranch in Chihuahua, the 275,000-acre San Simeon ranch north of San Luis Obsipo, the Anaconda copper mines in Montana, and the Homestake gold mine in South Dakota. Hearst refused them all saying: "You are very kind but I would rather have the *Examiner*." Reluctantly, his father relented.

On March 4, 1887 Hearst took up residence at the *San Francisco Examiner*. He had discovered his métier. He was a brilliant newspaper owner. Thanks to a radical overhaul, by 1889 the *Examiner* was in profit. The staid format Hearst had inherited was replaced with hard-hitting investigative reporting, coupled with sensationalist, attention grabbing headlines. Increased sports coverage, serialized stories by well-known authors, banner headlines like "Huge Frantic Flames," biographical sketches, and exposés of the seedy underbelly of Californian life all contributed to the heady populist mix.

As circulation and profits rose, Hearst expanded the business. In 1895 he returned to his old hunting ground

on the East Coast to save the *New York Morning Journal*. It was a decision that put him in direct competition with his onetime mentor, Joseph Pulitzer. Hearst pulled no punches in the ensuing circulation war. He added the *Evening Journal* to his collection in 1896 and poached some of Pulitzer's top writers. It was a period that gave rise to the term "yellow journalism," where newspapers assumed the role of opinion formers and determiners of morals. In scenes commonplace today, rival newspapers vied for scoops and used their front pages to boast of their achievements.

The most famous example of Hearst's proactive stance to newspaper reporting is the comment attributed to him when the illustrator Frederick Remington informed him that he wished to return from an uneventful Havana. Hearst supposedly responded: "Please remain. You furnish the pictures and I'll furnish the war."

His methods may have been controversial, but they worked. Hearst was unstoppable. He soon acquired newspapers in major cities throughout the United States. Following in his father's footsteps he became involved in politics. In 1902 Congress welcomed Hearst as a Democratic representative for New York. In all he served two terms in Congress and also became Mayor of New York City.

With his newspaper empire firmly established, Hearst expanded into other areas of the media. As a publisher he produced titles that included *Cosmopolitan*, *Good Housekeeping*, and *Harper's Bazaar*. He also moved into the movie business, cutting his teeth with Hearst-Metronome News. Ultimately it was the movie industry, coupled with his infatuation for the actress Marion Davies, that was to prove his downfall.

He formed W. R. Hearst's Cosmopolitan Productions as a vehicle for Davies, his Brooklyn-born mistress and a former Ziegfeld Follies girl. Abandoning his political career after failed attempts at the Senate and the presidency, Hearst focused solely on films. Of the hundred films he sanctioned over the next 20 years, half featured his mistress. As well as sinking millions of dollars into making movies, Hearst spent more millions on a Beverly Hills mansion for Davies. Finally he embarked on the folly that was to prove his undoing, the construction of the Hearst Castle estate at San Simeon. The 25,000 acres of the estate and castle contained rare and priceless works of art, antiquities, a zoo, an airfield, and guest houses which were chateaux dismantled in Europe and flown to California to be reassembled stone by stone.

Hearst might have survived such profligate extravagance had it not been for the Great Depression. During the 1930s he was forced to consolidate his empire, selling newspapers and works of art to remain afloat. By the end of the decade he had halved his business interests and

plundered the treasures at San Simeon. Marion Davies too, liquidated her personal assets and pumped $1 million into her lover's business. His final years were spent trying to prevent the release of Orson Welles's film *Citizen Kane*, a thinly disguised biopic of him. He failed. In the end, in ill health and bitter at the Welles episode, he retreated to San Simeon, handing over control of his empire to lawyers and managers. He died at the home of Marion Davies on August 14, 1951.

CONTEXT AND CONCLUSIONS

Although Hearst's final years were marred by what must have been for him a humiliating fall from grace, he will still be remembered as one of the greatest media barons of all time. While he was born with all the advantages wealth brings, Hearst turned around the *San Francisco Examiner*, invented a new style of popular journalism, and fashioned a media empire through hard-nosed determination, incredible stamina, and a common touch that belied his background. Hearst was truly a paradox. A man with wealth beyond the dreams and understanding of most, he was blessed nevertheless with the innate ability to appreciate the hopes and fears of ordinary people.

To the last he saw himself as the people's champion. He believed that the criticism and misfortunes that had befallen him were the result of his willingness to take a stand on behalf of the masses. "Any man who has the brains to think and the nerve to act for the benefit of the people of the country," he said, "is considered a radical by those who are content with stagnation and willing to endure disaster."

> His final years were spent trying to prevent the release of Orson Welles's film *Citizen Kane*, a thinly disguised biopic of him. He failed.

1307

MANAGEMENT GIANTS

FOR MORE INFORMATION

Books:
Davies, Marion. *The Times We Had: Life with William Randolph Hearst*. New York: Ballantine Books, 1975.
Nasaw, David. *The Chief: The Life of William Randolph Hearst*. Boston, MA: Houghton Mifflin Co., 2000.
Proctor, Ben. *William Randolph Hearst: The Early Years 1866–1910*. New York: Oxford University Press, 1998.

Web site:
The William Randolph Hearst Foundations:
www.hearstfdn.org

"For a politician to complain about the press is like a ship's captain complaining about the sea."

Enoch Powell

Milton Snavely Hershey

Milton Snavely Hershey (1857–1945) is the entrepreneur who brought the world the Hershey chocolate bar. He was a late starter in business, his first attempts in the confectionery industry ending in failure. Real success finally came in his late thirties with the Lancaster Caramel Company, a business he eventually sold to a rival for a large sum. The break that put Hershey in the history books came in 1893 when he stumbled across chocolate-manufacturing equipment at the World's Fair in Chicago. Hershey concentrated on chocolate, perfected a recipe for milk chocolate, introduced mass production, and built a thriving chocolate business as well as a town called Hershey.

Milton Hershey enjoyed the sweet taste of success with the innovative Hershey Kiss.

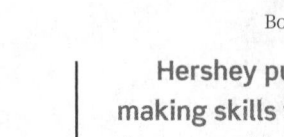
1857	Born.
1871	Drops out of school at age 13.
1872	Apprenticed at Joe Royer's Ice Cream Parlor and Garden.
1876	Opens a store making and selling candy in Philadelphia.
1882	Closes business in Philadelphia; opens and fails in Chicago.
1883	Opens candy store in New York City, which closes in 1886.
1886	Starts the Lancaster Caramel Company.
1893	Visits Chicago World's Fair and orders chocolate making equipment.
1895	Starts selling chocolate.
1900	Hershey's Chocolate Bar introduced. Lancaster Caramel Company sold for $1 million.
1906	Derry Church becomes Hershey Town.
1916	Builds sugar mill in Cuba.
1920	Loses $2.5 million on sugar futures. Forced to borrow from banks.
1942	U.S. Army asks Hershey to develop chocolate bar for field rations.
1945	Dies.

BACKGROUND AND RISE

Born on September 13, 1857, Milton Snavely Hershey was brought up in Hockersville, Pennsylvania. It was a small rural town and he was educated in a one-room schoolhouse. His parents were farmers and, from a very early age, Hershey was expected to help out on the farm tending the livestock and doing other chores.

> Hershey put his caramel making skills to work. From the outset his business was based on quality of product.

After attending a string of schools—including a private high school, the Village Academy of Green Tree, where he did not do well—Hershey gave up on education and took a position as an apprentice with a German-language newspaper based in Gap, Lancaster County. It was soon clear that his talents did not lie with either journalism or publishing. He left the paper and joined Joseph H. Royer of Lancaster as an apprentice confectioner.

He was an ambitious young man. Aged 19 he founded his own company, M. S. Hershey, Wholesale and Retail Confectioner. The business failed and was sold in 1882. Over the following few years Hershey traveled the country trying to set himself up in the candy business. In Denver, Colorado, he learned how to make caramels. In New York City he sold his candy on the street. None of these ventures prospered, so he headed back to Lancaster. It was in Lancaster, the scene of his first business failure, that Hershey finally met with some success.

DEFINING MOMENTS

Hershey put his caramel making skills to work. From the outset his business was based on quality of product. "Give them the quality, that's the best kind of advertising in the world" was his motto. The business took off when Hershey's caramels came to the attention of a candy importer who bought some to sell in England.

In 1893, however, while visiting Chicago, Hershey met the manufacturer of a German-made chocolate-making machine. He ordered one of the machines and had it shipped to Lancaster. The eventual result was a change of direction and the development of his most famous product, Hershey Chocolate.

With the caramel business, Hershey had excelled in creating a variety of candies. Now he concentrated on perfecting a single product—chocolate. In 1900 he sold his caramel business for $1 million to the American Caramel Company of Philadelphia. With the proceeds, he

---

"Give them quality. That's the best kind of advertising." Milton Snavely Hershey

invested in a new chocolate factory near his family home—he was married by now—in Derry Church.

When it came to making chocolate, Hershey had no recipe book or magic formula to rely on. Together with a few trusted colleagues he locked himself away and labored over the perfect milk chocolate recipe. "Nobody told Mr. Hershey how to make milk chocolate. He just found out the hard way," recalled one of his employees. Hard work though it was, Hershey struck chocolate gold. The result of his research—the Hershey chocolate bar—soon became a byword for quality in the United States.

Hershey continued to consolidate his chocolate business. He produced variations on the standard bar including: Mr. Goodbar, a milk chocolate and peanut candy bar, in 1925; Krackel, a chocolate bar filled with crisped rice, in 1938; and Hershey miniatures—small versions of all Hershey's chocolate bars—in 1939. To secure his sugar supply and guarantee its quality, he built a sugar mill and small town in Cuba, along the lines of Hershey, Pennsylvania.

In 1920 Hershey suffered a setback when he lost $2.5 million on the sugar futures market. He was forced to borrow from the bank, and, as a condition of the loan, the bank put a representative in Hershey's factory. It took him two years to pay the loan off and eject the overseer.

As Hershey's business grew, so too did the town surrounding the factory. Hershey wanted to build a town in keeping with his social philosophy in the same way that other chocolate philanthropists, like Joseph Rowntree and George Cadbury, had done in England. He drew up plans for an idyllic community that would not only house its inhabitants but provide for their every need, including employment at the Hershey chocolate factory. When the town was completed it contained parks, churches, a school, a hotel, a golf course, and even a zoo. Townsfolk would walk along streets such as Areba, Caracus, and Para, all named after cocoa bean-producing regions. Hershey held a competition to name the new town. The winning entry, Hersheyoko, was vetoed by the U.S. Post Office, so he settled for plain old Hershey Town. He also constructed a mansion, High Point, overlooking the chocolate factory, to house his family.

Shortly before his death, one last act assured the name of Hershey a place in business history. When the United States entered World War II, the U.S. military instructed him to develop a chocolate bar for the troops—one that wouldn't melt. He once again set about chocolate inno-vation. The resulting Field Ration D Chocolate Bar formed an essential part of the army's personal kit. Not only was it a great favorite of the U.S. personnel, but with the stationing of U.S. troops in England and the subsequent D-Day invasion of Europe, it became part of World War II folklore. Hershey died on October 13, 1945 at age 88.

CONTEXT AND CONCLUSIONS

First and foremost Hershey pioneered the mass production of food and, in particular, chocolate. It may only have been milk chocolate, but Hershey manufactured it on an unprecedented scale. Besides his single-minded approach, Hershey possessed a number of other qualities that contributed to his success. He was innovative, creating the Hershey Kiss and inventing his own recipe for milk chocolate. He was a bold risk-taker, making decisions like the one to build a sugar plant in Cuba. Perhaps his defining characteristic, however, was his enlightened attitude toward corporate social responsibility. It makes sense to keep the work force happy, but few can claim to have gone to such lengths as Hershey to do so. The business history books tell how successful the Hershey chocolate bar was and still is. Hershey Town with its schools, parks, churches, and chocolate factory is a more permanent record.

> Hershey wanted to build a town in keeping with his social philosophy in the same way that other chocolate philanthropists, like Joseph Rowntree and George Cadbury, had done in England.

1309

MANAGEMENT GIANTS

FOR MORE INFORMATION

Books:
Brenner, Joël Glenn. *The Emperors of Chocolate: Inside the Secret World of Hershey and Mars.* New York: Random House, 1999.
McMahon, James D. *Built on Chocolate: The Story of the Hershey Chocolate Company.* Santa Monica, CA: General Publishing Group, 1999.

Web site:
Hershey Foods Corporation: **www.hersheys.com**

"You have to love the products if you are going to sell them."   Barbara Thomas

Soichiro Honda

Soichiro Honda made his own way in business with no help from cronies. The Honda Company was founded in 1948 and its first motorcycle—the Dream—was produced a year later. Success followed success. In 1959 Honda became the leading motorcycle manufacturer in Japan, and the Honda sports motorcycle team won the team prize at the Isle of Man TT races. In the same year the first Honda motorcycles were sold in the United States; soon they were outselling every other brand. The company went into the automobile business in the 1960s. Until Soichiro Honda's death in 1992, the company continued to be the most popular motorcycle manufacturer in the world.

A 21st-Century Honda.

1906	Born.
1937	Founds Tokai Seiki Heavy Industry (TSHI).
1948	Cofounds Honda with Takeo Fujisawa.
1949	D Type motorcycle—the Dream—manufactured.
1952	Production of Cub begins.
1954	Honda motorcycle team is founded.
1959	Opens dealership in United States. Super Cub goes into production.
1963	Honda becomes top-selling motorcycle brand in United States.
1973	Officially retires.
1984	Ten million Honda 50s sold in United States.
1992	Dies.

BACKGROUND AND RISE

Born in the small Japanese town of Komyo in 1906, Soichiro Honda spent his early childhood helping his father with his bicycle repair business. At 15, without the benefit of a formal education, Honda traveled to Tokyo to look for work. He secured an apprenticeship at a garage, but ended up babysitting for the garage owner. Frustrated and dispirited, he returned home, only to be called back within six months. This time he stayed for six years, working as car mechanic before returning home once more to start his own car mechanic business. He was 22.

> **Born in the small Japanese town of Komyo in 1906, Soichiro Honda spent his early childhood helping his father with his bicycle repair business.**

Honda's love of cars extended to racing them, and he set a new average speed record in 1936. Unfortunately he suffered a bad crash, breaking several bones, including both wrists. His wife, fearing for his safety, persuaded him to give up his hobby. Without the distraction of racing, Honda concentrated his energies on his business, and in 1937 he expanded into piston ring manufacture, founding Tokai Seiki Heavy Industry (TSHI). He was still conscious of his lack of education, however, and enrolled at the Hamamatsu School of Technology. As it turned out, he needn't have bothered.

Honda made a poor student. The demands of his business made it difficult to keep up with his classwork. He was reluctant to pay attention to engineering lectures that didn't involve piston rings, and he refused to take notes or attend written examinations. When the school's principal warned Honda that if he did not submit to examination he would not receive his diploma, Honda was unrepentant. "I am not impressed by diplomas. They don't do the work," he later said. "My marks were not as good as those of others, and I didn't take the final examination. The principal called me in and said I should leave. I told him that I didn't want a diploma—it had less value than a cinema ticket. A ticket at least guaranteed you would get in. A diploma guaranteed nothing."

Giving up on the diploma and therefore shunning the *gakubatsa* (the Japanese old-boy networking system) the maverick Honda set out to make his fortune on his own terms.

DEFINING MOMENTS

By 1948 Honda had sold TSHI to Toyota for 450,000 yen (worth about $1 million today). He had established the Honda Technical Research Institute in 1946 and had tried to retire but found he couldn't resist the lure of engineering.

In 1948 Honda met a kindred spirit in financier Takeo Fujisawa. The two men had similar opinions on Japan's postwar industrial strategy. Both believed in long term investment, and in partnership with Honda, Fujisawa agreed to invest in a new company to manufacture engines. Honda retained responsibility for engineering, while Fujisawa dealt with marketing and sales.

By the 1950s Honda had signed a contract to sell the company's entire output of motorcycle engines to a company called Kitagawa. This wasn't as good a deal as it first appeared: Honda was geared up to produce 100 engines a month, while Kitagawa only produced 80 motorcycles at the most during the same period. Honda addressed the resulting cash flow problem by tearing up his contract

"To me success can only be achieved through repeated failure and introspection. In fact, success represents 1 percent of your work which results from the 99 percent that is called failure."

Soichiro Honda

with Kitagawa and replacing it with deals to supply complete motorcycles to distributors.

The company's first big hit was the Cub, which offered customers the choice, of either buying an engine to fit to their bicycles or buying a complete motorcycle. In less than a year the Cub was selling 6,500 units a month and had captured over 70% of the Japanese domestic motorcycle market.

While Honda's reluctance to play by the rules caused problems in some areas, particularly with the Japanese Ministry of International Trade and Industry, it served the company well in others. Honda adopted a refreshingly open recruitment policy. Although the company had problems recruiting graduate students because of Honda's unwillingness to play the *gakubatsa* game, it attracted many high caliber employees who had been rejected by other Japanese corporations.

Honda was a perfectionist when it came to product design. He traveled the world conducting market research in person. He attended motorcycle races, taking notes on the competition. By using the best of the competition as a benchmark, Honda managed to turn the Honda motorcycle from an average product into the best racing motorcycle in the world. Success in motorcycle racing (Honda launched its own motorcycle racing team in 1954) raised the public profile of the company, added to the brand value, and enabled racing technology to filter down to the standard production model.

A big year for Honda came in 1959, when the company went into large scale production of a new model that would sweep all before it, the Super Cub. To manufacture it Honda constructed the world's largest motorcycle plant in Suzuka City, which turned out 30,000 machines a month. In the same year the Honda team won first prize in the Isle of Man motorcycle races. Success on the track translated into sales.

In 1959 Honda Motorcycles opened its first dealership in the United States. Instead of selling through the existing U.S. motorcycle distributors, Honda took a more unconventional approach. He sold the small Honda motorcycles wherever he thought he might attract customers. At the time, total motorcycle sales in the United States were less than 5,000 a month. But by 1963 the company was selling 7,800 units; by 1984 Honda had sold some ten million Honda 50s. This remarkable success was due to the quality of the product and a brilliant advertising campaign. Instead of targeting its product at conventional motorcycle enthusiasts, Honda authorized a campaign with the slogan "You meet the nicest people on a Honda." The campaign targeted the family market and was a huge success.

The company Honda built went on to dominate the motorcycle market and make a big impact in the car market. At the end of the 20th century the company was still the world's number one motorcycle manufacturer. Honda retired on October 1973, taking an office in Tokyo where he busied himself with work connected with the Honda Foundation. He died in 1992.

CONTEXT AND CONCLUSIONS

Along with Konosuke Matsushita, Akio Morita, and Eiji Toyoda, Soichiro Honda was one of Japan's greatest industrialists. Notable for his independent streak, Honda spurned the traditional methods of building a business, deciding instead to go it alone. Turning a hobby into a business, he built a billion dollar company that produced the best selling motorcycle in the world. So good were their design and production quality that Honda motorcycles were soon outselling Triumph and Harley-Davidson in the U.K. and U.S. markets. To achieve this Honda used a combination of excellent engineering and clever marketing. By making a sports motorcycle that was faster than its competitors, the Honda company gained cachet for its consumer models and stayed at the cutting edge of technological development.

Above all, Soichiro Honda was determined to make his dreams a reality. "Many people dream of success," he said. "To me success can only be achieved through repeated failure and introspection. In fact, success represents 1% of your work which results from the 99% that is called failure."

> Honda was a perfectionist when it came to product design. He traveled the world conducting market research in person.

1311

MANAGEMENT GIANTS

FOR MORE INFORMATION

Web site:
Honda: **www.honda.com**

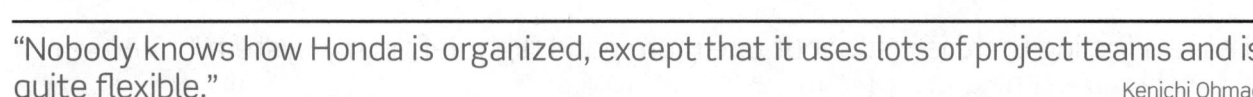
"Nobody knows how Honda is organized, except that it uses lots of project teams and is quite flexible."

Kenichi Ohmae

Howard Robard Hughes, Jr.

Howard Robard Hughes, Jr. (1905–1975) was born into wealth. His father founded a company that exploited a new design of oil drill. The Sharp-Hughes Tool Company was to provide a safety net of wealth throughout Hughes's life that made it possible for him to indulge his every whim. Indulge he did. Before the age of 25 he had moved to Hollywood and made several successful movies; founded a new drill bit company; bought over a hundred movie theaters; and learned to fly. By the time of his death in 1975, he had a built a successful airline (TWA); run a movie business; bought a piece of the gaming action on the Strip in Las Vegas; broken several airspeed records; survived three plane crashes; and become a legendary recluse. Few people have packed as much into one lifetime as Howard Hughes.

Howard Hughes on the way up.

1905	Born.
1909	Father forms Sharp-Hughes Tool Company.
1925	Hughes moves to Hollywood, California. Starts making movies.
1927	*Two Arabian Knights* wins the Academy Award for comedy.
1934	Sets up Hughes Aircraft Company.
1935	Breaks airspeed record.
1936	Aged 30, breaks U.S. transcontinental speed record in a self-built plane.
1938	Smashes record for New York–Paris flight with time of 16 hours and 35 minutes.
1939	Obtains majority stock in Transcontinental & West Airline.
1948	Saves airline (now renamed Trans World Airlines) from bankruptcy.
1954	Sells large part of RKO and concentrates on TWA.
1955	Establishes the Howard Hughes Medical Institute in Miami, Florida.
1966	Sells TWA stock for $750 million.
1975	Dies.
2001	TWA bought by American Airlines.

BACKGROUND AND RISE

There is much disagreement about the facts surrounding the life of Howard Hughes. The disagreement even extends to his birthplace. Was it the city of Houston or the oil town of Humble? But there is no argument that Hughes was born on December 24, 1905 in Texas. His father was a wealthy man with a business degree from Harvard and a law degree from Iowa State University. In 1909 Howard Sr. formed the Sharp-Hughes Tool Company, manufacturing drilling bits for the oil industry. It was his invention of a new oil drill bit that propelled his family to the kind of wealth that even Hughes Jr.'s noted profligacy could not dent.

As a boy, Howard Jr. was especially interested in engineering. He showed an impressive knack for building machines, constructing his own radio set as well as his own motorcycle. Away from engineering, Hughes's Uncle Rupert, a novelist and playwright, would take the boy to visit the Goldwyn studio where he developed a fascination with the movies.

Both Hughes's parents died before he was 20. On the death of his father, he somehow persuaded his relatives to sell him the Hughes Tool Company. Then, in 1925, he married a wealthy woman, Ella Rice, and moved to Hollywood, California.

In Hollywood Hughes began to exhibit the almost maniacal energy and drive that sustained him throughout his varied career.

DEFINING MOMENTS

By 1925 Hughes had created the Caddo Rock Drill Bit Company, bought a controlling interest in Multi-Color, Inc., moved into a house on Muirfield Road in Los Angeles, and hired Noah Dietrich, ostensibly as an assistant. Dietrich was to become the "fixer" for the Hughes empire in the coming years. Hughes also purchased over a hundred movie theaters to assist him in his latest venture—moviemaking.

Hughes's first movie, *Swell Hogan*, was a flop. His third, *Two Arabian Knights*, made money and won the 1927 Academy Award for comedy. Hughes had another hit with *Scarface* and followed it with *The Front Page*. The difficulties involved in making *Scarface*, which stemmed partly from antagonism toward his anti-Semitic beliefs, took their toll on him and he temporarily abandoned movie making. For a time he restricted his interest

> Hughes's first movie, *Swell Hogan*, was a flop. His third, *Two Arabian Knights*, made money and won the 1927 Academy Award for comedy.

"I have a feeling there is just about one more good flight left in my system." Amelia Earhart

in the movies to dating some of the most beautiful women of the time, including Ida Lupino, Katharine Hepburn, Ginger Rogers, Ava Gardner, and Lana Turner. Instead of making movies he turned his attention to the aviation business.

Hughes decided to form an aircraft company, so he hired a brilliant aeronautical engineer, Glen Odekirk, and established business in a hangar in California. In the interval between shooting *The Front Page*, and establishing the Hughes Aircraft Company in 1934, he disappeared from sight. At about the same time, however, there appeared on the scene a gangly employee of American Airways, 6 feet 3 inches tall, called Charles Howard, who, irritatingly, asked endless questions about the airline's operations. Charles Howard, it transpired, was none other than Howard Hughes himself. Hughes also spent some of this "missing" period traveling as a hobo, and as a society photographer—a business he started from scratch in Huntsville, Texas, under the name R. Wayne Rector.

In 1939 Hughes helped finance Transcontinental & West Airline, obtaining a majority share in the process. The airline was later renamed Trans World Airlines (TWA). By 1940 the dynamic Hughes was running several businesses simultaneously, in different fields. He still owned the tool manufacturing company he had bought from his father's estate, which made him $2 million a month. In addition he was back in the movie business, running an airline, and gearing up for wartime manufacturing.

In the first half of the 1940s Hughes ordered commercial aircraft from Lockheed, made and released the film *The Outlaw*, created a new starlet in Jane Russell, opened a manufacturing plant to assist the U.S. war effort, and crashed yet another aircraft. He had already crashed two planes, killing two passengers.

In 1946, after another period of absence, Hughes reappeared to test his experimental reconnaissance aircraft, the XF-11. At 400 mph the plane became unstable. To the consternation of the members, he tried to land on the Los Angeles Country Club golf course. Luckily for the club, but unluckily for him, he didn't make it, plowing into a house on the way down. He was admitted to the Cedars of Lebanon Hospital, and the doctors predicted he would not last through the night. His injuries were extensive: a crushed chest, 12 broken ribs, a collapsed left lung, fractured shoulder, crushed vertebrae, and third-degree burns. Remarkably, the apparently indestructible Hughes made a good recovery. He was left with burn scars and a deformed left hand, but very much alive.

Discharged from the hospital, he set about turning TWA around. He saved the ailing airline by obtaining a subsidy from the Civil Aeronautics Board in 1948, and a $10 million loan from the Reconstruction Finance Corporation. He also bolstered his movie business, buying the struggling RKO studio (Radio-Keith Orpheum) for $9 million. In 1954 Hughes sold most of RKO to concentrate on TWA. A year later he established the Howard Hughes Medical Institute in Miami, Florida, in an attempt to reduce his tax liabilities. On May 3, 1966 he sold 78% of his TWA stock for $750 million. It made him, temporarily, the richest man in the world.

The remainder of Hughes's career, until his death in 1975, was characterized by obsessive-neurotic behavior and flight from the IRS. Yet, despite his continual dislocation—moving from one hotel to another, and one country to another—his increasingly bizarre behavior, and his dependence on pain-killing drugs, Hughes somehow managed to control his businesses from the end of a phone line. In an incredible spending spree, he even expanded into hotels and casinos, buying the Desert Inn, Sands, Castaways, New Frontier, and Silver Slipper on the Strip in Las Vegas, as well as thousands of acres of land and over 500 mining concessions.

The fact that Hughes's disparate collection of companies fell apart within 12 years of his death is evidence, if any were needed, that his bizarre personality was the glue that bound his business empire together.

> The remainder of Hughes's career, until his death in 1975, was characterized by obsessive-neurotic behavior and flight from the IRS.

CONTEXT AND CONCLUSIONS

Of all the business leaders and entrepreneurs of the 20th century, Howard Hughes is one of the most colorful, controversial, and bizarre. An examination of his life reveals a man driven by the most basic of instincts: power, greed, lust, enmity. He ended his days a compulsive-obsessive, drug dependent hypochondriac, but consistently conducted business deals with a shrewdness beyond most of his peers. His achievements encompass movie making, aviation, and the hotel and gaming industry. In the movies Hughes notoriously pushed back the boundaries of decency and showed that it was possible to make successful movies outside the studio system. In Nevada he succeeded in loosening the Mob's grip on Las Vegas. In aviation he was among those who pioneered commercial airflight.

FOR MORE INFORMATION

Books:
Brown, Peter Harry, and Pat H. Broeske. *Howard Hughes: the Untold Story.* Brentwood, CA: Dutton, 1996.
Keats, John. *Howard Hughes.* New York: Random House, 1972.
Rummel, Robert W. *Howard Hughes and TWA.* Washington, D.C.: Smithsonian Institution Press, 1991.
Thomas, Tony. *Howard Hughes in Hollywood.* Sacramento, CA: Citadel Press, 1985.

Web site:
Howard Hughes Medical Institute: **www.hhmi.org**

1313

MANAGEMENT GIANTS

Lee Iacocca

The lionization of chief executive officers began in earnest with Lee Iacocca. The myth he helped to create culminated in the extraordinary worship of GE's Jack Welch in recent years. Arriving at the Ford Motor Corporation as a trainee engineer in 1946, Iacocca received the best education available in the industry. He worked his way up through Ford, not in engineering but in sales. Iacocca always claimed he wasn't a natural salesman, but he made a big impact at Ford with his revolutionary financing plan. He introduced the Ford Mustang, and was promoted to president of the company. After an internal power struggle, instigated by Henry Ford II, Iacocca was fired in 1978. He switched sides, joining Chrysler and becoming C.E.O. in 1979.

Iacocca was the driving force behind Chrysler's turnaround.

1924	Born.
1946	Joins Ford as a trainee engineer.
1949	Becomes sales manager.
1956	Introduces a new financing plan called the "56 for '56."
1970	Becomes president of Ford.
1978	Fired by Henry Ford II.
1979	Iacocca becomes chairman and C.E.O. of Chrysler.
1983	Writes out check for $813,487,500 to clear Chrysler's federal debt.
1992	Retires from Chrysler.
1999	Starts E.V. Global Motors.

BACKGROUND AND RISE

Lee Iacocca was born on October 15, 1924 in Allentown, Pennsylvania. Iacocca's father ran a small hot dog business. For the Iacoccas, as for many other families during the late 1920s and 1930s, times were hard. Iacocca Sr. lost all his money and nearly lost the family home. Even though Lee Iacocca was only seven at the time, the harshness of the Depression ingrained frugality so deeply that, while he may not have been risk-averse in his business dealings, he always invested money conservatively and to this day dislikes waste.

DEFINING MOMENTS

As a trainee at Ford's famous River Rouge plant, Iacocca got to see every stage of automobile production, from the extraction of coal and limestone, through the production of steel, to the manufacturing of the cars on the assembly line. It represented the best training the auto industry had to offer. Graduating from his trainee course, Iacocca decided against engineering and instead went to work in the Ford sales office in Chester, Pennsylvania. He was not a born salesman, yet through practice and experience he improved quickly, moving from a bashful, stammering sales clerk to become sales manager in 1949.

The 1950s were good years for Iacocca. In 1956, to combat poor sales of Ford automobiles, he introduced a new financing plan called the "56 for '56." Credit financing was just beginning to take hold as a way of purchasing cars. The plan allowed the cash strapped purchaser to make a modest down payment of 20% and then follow up with three further payments of $56. The plan was a success, and was adopted company-wide, making Iacocca an overnight star within the Ford ranks. One promotion quickly followed another. By 1960 he was head of the Ford division. Aged 36, Iacocca was general manager of the largest division in the world's second biggest automobile company.

He soon stamped his authority on the company, playing an influential role in the decision to abandon a proposed new model, the Cardinal, which was dropped despite the company incurring a $35 million loss. In its place, the first Ford Mustang rolled off the assembly line. The new car had been designed from scratch and was priced at an affordable level. Its launch created a wave of publicity, simultaneously being featured on the covers of *Time* and *Newsweek* magazines. The Mustang was the car the market had been waiting for. In its first year it sold a record 418,812, making a profit of $1.1 billion.

For Iacocca, who had championed the Mustang, the car's popularity had certain unwelcome side effects. There was no such thing as a private life anymore for the man who had brought Ford's most popular car to market. When Iacocca was returning from a trip to Europe on the Ford company plane, the pilot was contacted by two other pilots and a radio operator from a ship below, all of them wanting to speak to his celebrated passenger. "Is

> **Iacocca received the best education available in the industry. He worked his way up through Ford, not in engineering but in sales.**

"We at Chrysler borrow money the old-fashioned way. We pay it back."   Lee Iacocca

nothing sacred? It's Sunday morning. I am in the middle of nowhere, and I can't get away from this Mustang mania!" was Iacocca's reply. But Iacocca had much to thank the Mustang for. In January 1965 he was promoted to vice president of the corporate car/truck group, and on December 10, 1970 he became president of the Ford empire.

President he may have been, but Iacocca was not the most powerful person at Ford. That honor was reserved for the founder's grandson, Henry Ford II. Ford operated an unorthodox management style; he ruled through fear. Executives could find themselves clearing their desks for the most unlikely reasons. For several years Iacocca managed to walk the tightrope, on the one hand not seeming to threaten Ford's authority yet, on the other, doing a good enough job to avoid being fired. It is to his credit that Iacocca managed to stay in the job as long as he did.

In ill health, with his marriage strained, Ford became increasingly paranoid and his decisions increasingly bizarre. There was even an internal investigation within the company at Ford's request into Iacocca's activities which allegedly cost over $1,500,000 and came up with nothing damaging. Then, in 1977, Ford turned to the management consulting firm McKinsey & Company, calling them in to reorganize the company's management structure. McKinsey recommended a new structure with a chairman/C.E.O., vice chairman, and president at the top. Iacocca now became number three in the ruling triumvirate, and to humiliate him further, Ford insisted on parading this apparent demotion in public. Then in 1978 Ford fired Iacocca. The reason—in Ford's own words—was: "Sometimes you just don't like somebody."

Iacocca was 54. He could have retired. Yet a few months later he joined the Chrysler Motor Corporation, becoming chairman and C.E.O. in September 1979. During his time at Chrysler Iacocca executed one of the most impressive turnarounds in automobile history. When he arrived, the Detroit press was full of gloomy headlines such as "Chrysler losses are worst ever." The company was struggling, but, when he joined, Iacocca had not realized how serious its problems were. He soon found out—Chrysler was running out of money, and fast. Iacocca took swift remedial action: he eradicated excess inventory, renegotiated contracts with car rental companies Hertz and Avis, recruited a slew of top talent, and made substantial layoffs. Most important of all, he went cap in hand to the government and applied for a loan guarantee for $1.2 billion. It required new legislation. To secure government support Iacocca had to give testimony in Washington before the House of Representatives and Senate hearings. But the request was granted.

That it was granted attests to Iacocca's powers as a salesman. As he cut costs at Chrysler (he cut his own salary to $1), and the automobile market picked up, Chrysler's flagging fortunes revived. In 1983 Chrysler made a profit of $925 million and not long after a new stock offering, Iacocca wrote out a historic check for $813,487,500 to clear the balance of the debt outstanding on the government loan.

Iacocca went on to steer Chrysler to greater success. He engineered the company's $1.5 billion acquisition of American Motors, and incorporated the Jeep into Chrysler's product offering. Iacocca retired from Chrysler in 1992, but his enthusiasm for business remained undiminished. Leaving the motor giants behind him, he founded a small start-up company, E.V. Global Motors, selling electric powered bicycles. In 2001, he took "clean transportation" a stage further by launching the LIDO, an electric-powered vehicle designed for local driving, that resembled a cross between a golf cart and Chrysler's retro PT Cruiser. Critics claimed that he had spent his career putting polluting vehicles on highways and now it was payback time. Iacocca also invested in diabetes research through his support for Olivio Premium Products, a company marketing products based on olive oil. Iacocca pledged the equivalent of 25 percent of Olivio sales to research.

CONTEXT AND CONCLUSIONS

Brilliant businessmen such as Henry Ford, Walter Chrysler, and Billy Durant long ago earned their place in the auto hall of fame. But among the postwar generation, few deserve to sit alongside the founding fathers. Lee Iacocca is one of the few, successfully running not one but two of the big three U.S. motor manufacturers.

A rare combination of talented salesman and empathetic people-manager, Iacocca had an instinctive feeling for which models would sell and which would not. He introduced the Ford Mustang and revitalized Ford's prospects when the company was drifting directionless following the death of the first Henry Ford. At Chrysler Iacocca performed one of the most breathtaking turnarounds in corporate history; in the process he became a corporate icon.

CLOSE BUT NO CIGAR

Bob Lutz
Ex-Marine fighter pilot Lutz paid his dues in the motor business, working his way through General Motors, BMW, and, finally, Ford, where he was vice president. After Ford he became Iacocca's right-hand man at Chrysler and played a big part in the company's revival. Many think he should have gotten the C.E.O. job when Iacocca left. In 2001 he left Chrysler to join General Motors as vice president.

FOR MORE INFORMATION

Book:
Iacocca, Lee, with William Novak. *IACOCCA: An Autobiography*. New York: Bantam Books, 1984.

Web sites:
Chrysler: **www.chrysler.com**
EV Global: **www.evglobal.com**

1315

MANAGEMENT GIANTS

Steve Jobs

Steve Jobs, cofounder of Apple Computer, is one of the folk hero C.E.O.s. The company was started in a garage by Jobs and his colleague Steve Wozniak—and its PCs changed the face of computing. Unfortunately, it got its strategy wrong, tying the Mac operating system software to Apple hardware. Microsoft went in the other direction, licensing the MS-DOS operating system to any and every PC manufacturer. The rest is history.

In 1985, former Pepsi chairman John Sculley, enlisted to add beef to Apple, removed Jobs from the company he had founded. Sculley himself was removed in 1993, and Jobs was eventually asked to return.

Since his comeback, Jobs has breathed new life into the company. To his many fans, Apple's revival confirms Jobs's status as one of the greatest technology entrepreneurs ever.

Steve Jobs, folk-hero founder of Apple.

1955	Born.
1974	Takes a job with Atari.
1976	First product, the Apple I, marketed.
1977	Apple II. Apple incorporated; Mike Markkula buys stock in the company and becomes chairman.
1980	Apple goes public.
1982	$1 billion sales; John Sculley becomes C.E.O.
1984	Launch of Apple Macintosh.
1985	Jobs leaves Apple.
1986	Founds NeXT. Cofounds Pixar.
1993	Sculley leaves Apple.
1996	Jobs returns as consultant.
1997	Becomes "interim C.E.O."
1998	iMac launched.
2000	Drops "interim" from job title.
2001	Apple launches iPhoto.
2003	New iMac launched.
2003	Launch of world's first 17-inch portable computer.
2003	Oracle announces it may buy into Apple.
2004	iPod sales exceed computer sales.
2005	Apple drops IBM chips in favor of Intel's.

BACKGROUND AND RISE

In February 1955 Paul and Clara Jobs adopted an orphan, Stephen Jobs. Jobs was brought up in Los Altos, California.

Out of school, Jobs attended lectures at the Hewlett-Packard electronics company. It was while working at Hewlett-Packard that he met Stephen Wozniak, a University of California dropout. Wozniak was an engineering whiz kid who was continually inventing gadgets.

Jobs and Wozniak attended meetings of the "Homebrew Computer Club." Most of the members were geeks, interested only in diodes, transistors, and the electronic gadgets they built from them. Jobs was different; he had an eye for style, utility, and marketability. Jobs persuaded Wozniak to work with him to build a personal computer. The Apple I computer was designed in Jobs's bedroom and the prototype constructed in his garage.

After moderate success selling their first computer—a local electronics retailer ordered 25—some helpful advice from a retired C.E.O. of Intel inspired Jobs and Wozniak to start their own company. To do so they sold their most treasured possessions, in Jobs's case his Volkswagen microbus. For Wozniak it was his prized Hewlett-Packard calculator. With the $1,300 they raised, the two started a new company, which they named Apple.

DEFINING MOMENTS

The company's first product, the Apple I, was marketed in 1976, priced at $666. As members of the local computing fraternity, Jobs and Wozniak were well positioned to drum up interest in their new machine. Sales of the Apple I brought in $774,000 and soon the two entrepreneurs were working on the Apple II. It was a resounding success. This was not just down to its engineering, it was also due in large part to Jobs's marketing savvy. In an inspired move he brought in Regis McKenna, the best public relations man in Silicon Valley; the man who went on to popularize relationship marketing.

In 1980 Apple went public. Originally priced at $22 per share, the stock rose on the first day to $29, capitalizing the company at $1.2 billion. Between 1978 and 1983, in the absence of any real competition, Apple forged ahead in the personal computer market; its compound growth rate was over 150% per year. Then, in 1981, IBM introduced its first PC, using an operating system called MS-DOS, licensed from a small software company called Microsoft. Within two years, IBM had exceeded Apple's dollar sales of PCs. Furthermore, Microsoft was causing a stir in the PC market, even though it didn't manufacture PC hardware. Microsoft licensed its operating software to

"I'm just a guy who probably should have been a semi-talented poet on the Left Bank. I got sort of side-tracked here."

Steve Jobs

PC producers. Jobs realized that if IBM and Microsoft were allowed to dominate the market then Apple could become marginalized.

To restore Apple's fortunes, Jobs turned to John Sculley, C.E.O. at Pepsi. The result of this unlikely alliance between the corporate suit, Sculley, and the counterculture kid, Jobs, was the personal computer that cemented Apple Computer's status as the computer enthusiast's favorite computer company—the Apple Macintosh.

Rather than writing commands in computerese, Macintosh owners used a mouse to click on easily recognizable icons—a trash can and file folders, for example. Suddenly, you didn't need a degree in computer science to operate a personal computer. Other companies followed where Apple led, most significantly Microsoft. Apple became the darling of the creative world with an iconic status that Bill Gates and his crew never achieved. But what Microsoft did do was to dominate the PC software industry, commanding 80% market share as against Apple's 20%. In the end that proved critical.

The Apple fairy tale came to a sticky end in 1985 when Sculley did the unthinkable and removed Jobs from the company he had founded. A fired-up Jobs proceeded to plow $250 million of investors' money into another startup, NeXT Computer. It disappointed, selling only 50,000 units. Pixar Animation Studios, in which he invested $60 million of his own fortune, was a different story, however. This investment eventually paid out with the computer-animated blockbusters *Toy Story* and *A Bug's Life*. Back at Apple, Sculley himself was booted out in 1993 after a disastrous period that saw Apple's market share plummet from 20% to just 8%. He was replaced by Michael Spindler who lasted until 1996, by which time Apple's market share had fallen to just over 5%. Apple was staring oblivion in the face as even its long-term devotees began to switch to PCs. Spindler was shown the door; Gil Amelio took over in the hot seat. After 500 days in the job, and with Apple's market share unmoved, Amelio invited Jobs back to help in a consulting role. It wasn't long before Amelio was on his way out too, and Jobs, now Apple's self-styled interim C.E.O., was back where he started.

With Jobs back at the helm, Apple looked more like its old self. He dumped the NeXT operating system that he had sold to Apple, ditched loss-making licensing contracts, and, most significantly, launched the new iMac. The iMac was the embodiment of everything Jobs believed in: eye-catching design and simple operation. It was also the product of a different vision of the computer itself. It had no disk drive because Jobs believed they had been superseded by external storage devices such as zip drives and the Internet. The stylish Internet-ready machine was launched with the slogan "Chic Not Geek" blazed across advertising posters. A vision in translucent blue, it sold 278,000 units in the first six weeks, an achievement that had *Fortune* magazine describing it as "one of the hottest computer launches ever." Wall Street, too, recovered its confidence in Apple: the company's stock price doubled in less than a year. Fiscal 2000 revenues were some $7.98 billion, with net earnings of $786 million, and Apple has started to open a series of retail stores across the United States. Since then, Apple's stock price has been caught up in the same vortex as other technology companies. Product development has continued to follow the Steve Jobs theme of cool computing. 2001 saw the launch of iPhoto, Apple's strategy to win a strong position in digital photography. This was followed in 2003 by an even more powerful version of the iMac plus the world's first 17-inch portable, the latest version of the Powerbook. However, despite the continuing innovation, Apple's financial performance remained poor until things began to look up in 2004 thanks to the iPod, a personal music player that also allows users to download music from the Internet. iPods caught the public's imagination around the world, and over five million were sold in the first three months of 2005 alone. Their impact on Apple's balance sheet has been just as impressive. In April 2005, the company reported that its net income was up by 530% on the same period in 2004 (from $46 million to $290 million). While it is unlikely that growth is sustainable at that level, Jobs and the top team at Apple are looking to the future with confidence.

> The Apple I computer was designed in Jobs's bedroom and the prototype constructed in his garage.

CONTEXT AND CONCLUSIONS

Described by one newspaper as a "corporate Huckleberry Finn," Steve Jobs is one of a select group of IT whiz kids that includes Bill Gates, Larry Ellison, and Scott McNealy. Where Jobs differs from his peers is in his sense of style. IBM brought computers to the business world; Microsoft gave the PC its MS-DOS operating system; but Jobs made computing easy. By taking the graphical user interface that he had first seen in a Xerox PARC laboratory and incorporating it into the Apple Mac, Jobs enabled the technologically illiterate to use a computer by simply pointing and clicking.

> The iMac was the embodiment of everything Jobs believed in: eye-catching design and simple operation.

And if that wasn't a sufficient contribution to the history of IT, Jobs developed one of the first computer animation film studios, Pixar, and then returned to Apple just in time to save it from rotting. With the introduction of the iMac, he once again demonstrated the imagination and design flair that made him a multimillionaire and Apple the computer of choice for millions of devoted followers.

FOR MORE INFORMATION

Books:
Deutschman, Alan. *The Second Coming of Steve Jobs.* New York: Broadway Books, 2000.
Young, Jeffrey S. *Steve Jobs: The Greatest Second Act in the History of Business.* New York: Wiley, 2006.

Web site:
Apple: **www.apple.com**

"I want to put a ding in the universe."

Steve Jobs

Ingvar Kamprad

The flat-pack king of furniture, Kamprad is a brilliant if unorthodox businessman. Like Richard Branson, Kamprad enjoys challenging the establishment and upsetting the odds. Industrious from an early age, Kamprad took on the furniture cartel in Sweden and neatly outsmarted it. In the end, as he always predicted they would, customers got what they demanded: low prices and good quality. Kamprad continued to deliver value for money to ordinary people through innovations such as flat-pack furniture and self-service. Shopping the IKEA way became a family day out, a fun experience, long before the advent of the out-of-town supermall. When Kamprad officially took a back seat from line management at IKEA in 1986, he had changed the nature of retailing and provided inspiration for thousands of entrepreneurs.

IKEA, Kamprad's home base.

1926	Born in Sweden.
1943	Registers company, Ikéa (letters don't become uppercase until much later).
1948	Advertises furniture for the first time.
1951	Publishes first catalog. Revenue exceeds one million krona ($95,000).
1953	Opens factory combined with furniture exhibition center in Älmhult.
1956	Introduces flat packaging.
1958	Opens first store in Älmhult.
1965	Introduces self-service in stores.
1982	Ownership transferred to Dutch Foundation—Stichting INGKA.
1986	Officially retires, handing day-to-day running to Anders Moberg.
1995	Stichting INGKA buys Habitat chain.
1999	150th store opens. Turnover reaches Kr60 billion ($5.689 billion).
2002	Becomes the United Kingdom's largest furniture retailer. Announces sons will take over running of IKEA.
2002	Bombs planted outside Dutch stores.
2003	Apologizes for past involvement in Nazi activities.
2003	Opens first Russian store.
2005	Net worth estimated at $23 billion by *Forbes* magazine.

BACKGROUND AND RISE

Ingvar Kamprad was born on the family farm, Elmtaryd, in 1926, in the harsh country side of Småland, Sweden. His was a tough upbringing. Sweden in the late 1920s and early 1930s was a difficult place in which to grow up. Outside the Swedish cities, the cold unforgiving landscape of the country offered few opportunities for advancement. Yet Kamprad was resourceful and full of the enthusiasm of youth.

He began in a small way by selling matches to neighbors. He was five years old. He graduated to catching fish and selling them, as well as picking lingonberries which he dispatched by bus to a local buyer. He made his first real money selling garden seed. It was enough to buy a new racing bike and a typewriter.

DEFINING MOMENTS

Kamprad was still only 17 when, in 1943, he started his own company. He called it Ikéa: IK from his initials, E for Elmtaryd, the farm he grew up on, and A for Agunnaryd, his home village. By 1945 he was selling a hodgepodge of products. His business outgrew local delivery and he began to sell by mail order. Newspaper advertisements stimulated demand, and the local milk cart and train network solved his distribution problems. Soon pens, pencils, picture frames, wallets, watches and other assorted goods were wending their way across Sweden, courtesy of IKEA. Astonishingly Kamprad was still working full time as well. It was only after completing his national service in 1946 that he began to focus solely on his business.

Kamprad advertised furniture for the first time in 1948. His decision to sell furniture was initially a result of matching his main competitor. The furniture was sourced from local manufacturers; it was cheap, and sales were promising—so much so that four years later he abandoned his other products to concentrate on affordably-priced furniture and domestic articles.

Until 1953 the business operated as a mail order business only. The problem was that competition in the mail order industry drove down prices and product quality. Kamprad was engaged in a vicious and unsustainable price war on several fronts, and delivery of shoddy goods by competitors was also adversely affecting the industry's reputation. The solution was to allow the customers to

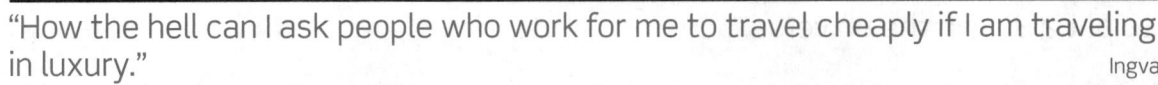

"How the hell can I ask people who work for me to travel cheaply if I am traveling in luxury."

Ingvar Kamprad

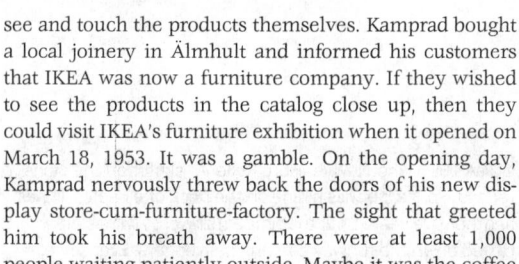

see and touch the products themselves. Kamprad bought a local joinery in Älmhult and informed his customers that IKEA was now a furniture company. If they wished to see the products in the catalog close up, then they could visit IKEA's furniture exhibition when it opened on March 18, 1953. It was a gamble. On the opening day, Kamprad nervously threw back the doors of his new display store-cum-furniture-factory. The sight that greeted him took his breath away. There were at least 1,000 people waiting patiently outside. Maybe it was the coffee and buns that he had rashly promised to all first-day visitors.

The principles that underpin IKEA's business today were developed in those early years. Cost awareness was one fundamental rule. Kamprad saved on string, boxes, paper, and whatever he could. Another feature was the provision of food. IKEA's stores may have progressed from providing buns and coffee to restaurants with extensive menus, but the idea that you can get something tasty to eat remains. For Kamprad it was always a practical decision to provide food, since people were traveling long distances to reach the Ämhult factory.

In 1955, Kamprad encountered his first major setback. IKEA was doing too well. Unable to compete fairly, competitors turned to less savory methods. Suppliers suddenly found themselves under pressure not to supply IKEA. The company was mysteriously banned from trade fairs. On one occasion, Kamprad had to enter a trade fair hidden under a carpet, in the back of a friend's Volvo. But he had the last laugh. Facing difficulties in obtaining supplies, he decided to build and design his own furniture. Banned from trade exhibitions, he bought his own exhibition centers. Whatever the competition did, Kamprad outfoxed them.

IKEA milestones followed, one after another. Flat packaging was introduced in 1956, so customers could get the furniture into their cars more easily. A 72,000 square foot IKEA store was opened in Älmhult in 1958, and the company signed on its 100th employee. Self-service was introduced in 1965. By the 1970s, IKEA was an international company with stores across Europe. By 1999 it had 150 stores in 30 countries, employing 44,000 people. Revenues were over $7 billion and the IKEA catalog's circulation was a staggering 100 million.

Although officially retired from day-to-day management, Kamprad is still seen by many as the company's totemic leader. Despite his phenomenal wealth—taxation and legal issues mean that he resides in Switzerland—he appears to be fundamentally the same person who started out selling matches all those years ago. He is still famously cost conscious—he once described himself as a "Swedish Scotsman." He flies economy, eats modestly, dresses casually, and has been known to haggle at his local market. IKEA is the same: suits are conspicuously absent; there is minimal hierarchy; the advertising is a little oddball.

IKEA's international expansion continues. In 2002, IKEA became the U.K.'s largest furniture retailer and, in 2003, Kamprad opened a shopping mall in St. Petersburg. The announcement of the planned opening of the first store in Israel in 2001 preceded Kamprad's public apology for his Nazi sympathies in early life. Controversy also hit the company in the Netherlands, with bombs found outside several stores in December 2002.

As for succession, Kamprad finally agreed that his three sons should take over the company in 2002. Earlier he had shown no signs of making way for them; statements such as "I don't think any of my sons are capable of running the company, at least not yet," reinforced the impression that he believes there is still an important role for him at IKEA. As does his biography, *Leading by Design*, in which he says, "The demon in me says that there is so much to do . . . I'm never satisfied."

CONTEXT AND CONCLUSIONS

Kamprad's unique approach to management is encapsulated in "A Furniture Dealer's Testament," the list of concepts he wrote down for his co-workers before he emigrated from Sweden. This creed says as much about Kamprad himself as about his company. It is based on some simple statements: "The product range is our identity; the IKEA spirit is a strong and living reality; profits give us resources; reaching good results with small means; simplicity is a virtue; doing it a different way; concentration is important to our success; taking responsibility is our privilege, and many things remain to be done—a glorious future." IKEA is a company made in Kamprad's own image. He has done things his way, the different way. He has taken the road less traveled. It is a lesson for all entrepreneurs.

> He flies economy, eats modestly, dresses casually, and has been known to haggle at his local market.

CLOSE BUT NO CIGAR

Terence Conran
With a similar idea at a similar time, Conran first started selling furniture from his basement in London's Notting Hill in 1952, just as Kamprad was about to open his factory store. The first in the Habitat chain opened on the Fulham Road in 1964. Conran was always strongly design-led. The Conran Design Group was founded in 1956, and he was instrumental in shaping the look and feel of London's "swinging sixties." Selling affordable, stylish furniture, Habitat stores flourished and were joined by The Conran Shop. In the early 1990s, Conran sold the Habitat chain to IKEA. He continues to control the chain of Conran Shops and has successfully branched out into restaurants.

FOR MORE INFORMATION

Book:
Lewis, Elen. *Great IKEA! A Brand for All the People*. London: Cyan Books, 2005.

Web site:
Ikea: **www.ikea.com**

"My answer is to stay close to ordinary people because at heart I am one." — Ingvar Kamprad

Herb Kelleher

It was 1966 when lawyer Herb Kelleher sketched the plans for a low-price, no frills airline on the back of a napkin. It was another five years until the first Southwest Airlines plane taxied down the runway carrying passengers. Ever since, Kelleher has been tearing up the management rule book. With singing flight attendants, practical jokes, and costumes, a Southwest ticket is worth its price just for the onboard entertainment—forget the fast turnarounds, reliability, convenience, and low cost. But what else would you expect from a Harley-riding, bourbon-drinking C.E.O. who dresses up as Elvis and arm wrestles executives from competing carriers? From nowhere, Kelleher has created a company with $5 billion in annual revenues and a record of over 25 years of profitability. Maybe it doesn't seem so crazy after all.

Kelleher and Southwest Airlines fly to success.

1932	Born.
1956	Graduates from New York University.
1960	Starts to practice law in San Antonio, Texas.
1966	Discusses plan to start airline with Rollin King.
1968	Competing airlines sue Southwest.
1971	Southwest starts flying in Texas. Has its I.P.O.
1973	Southwest turns first profit.
1978	Becomes chairman.
1982	Becomes president and C.E.O.
1989	$1 billion in revenues.
1992	Arm wrestles Kurt Herwald.
2001	Steps down as C.E.O.
2001	Donates $4 million to University of Texas Center for Entrepreneurship.
2002	Named C.E.O. of the Year.

BACKGROUND AND RISE

Born on March 12, 1932 in New Jersey, Herb Kelleher was an exceptional scholar. An undergraduate at Wesleyan University in Connecticut, he was one of those lucky students who excel at both sports and studies, and he racked up an impressive list of achievements. From Wesleyan, Kelleher went on to New York University where he studied law, graduating in 1956.

After law school, Kelleher had a stint as a clerk in the Supreme Court of New Jersey and then practiced law in San Antonio, Texas, starting in 1960. Over the next six years he built his law practice up, until in 1966 a chance conversation with one of his clients set him on an entirely new career path.

> In hindsight, the resignation of Muse was the making of Southwest: it brought Kelleher in as president.

In a downtown bar—the St. Anthony's Club—Kelleher's client Rollin King explained his idea for a budget airline service to connect three of Texas's main cities: Dallas, Houston, and San Antonio. The two of them drew up a business plan and jotted down the flight pattern on the back of a paper napkin: it was the outline for Southwest Airlines. The napkin is now framed and hanging on the wall in the company HQ. Kelleher put in $10,000 (for a stake worth over $200 million by 2001), and the company was incorporated in March, 1967.

DEFINING MOMENTS

With three airlines dominating the air traffic in Texas—Braniff, Texas International, and Continental—breaking up the cozy status quo was no easy task. Neither was it cheap. Over the next four years, Kelleher and Southwest Airlines sunk over a million dollars into fighting moves to block the company's application for airline certification. It was a bitter fight. A newspaper reported, "Don't bother spending your money on a movie or going to see a play or attending a concert. Just come over and watch Herb Kelleher and the lawyers for Braniff and Texas International cut each other into little bits and pieces." Colleagues and friends told Kelleher to give up, but Kelleher, a born fighter, won a final appeal to the Texas Supreme Court.

With Kelleher as chief legal counsel and Lamar Muse, a veteran of the airline business, as C.E.O., Southwest Airlines opened for business in 1971. Under intense pressure from the competition, Southwest toughed out the early years. Smarting from their legal defeat, the competing airlines embarked on a savage price war, which at times turned into physical violence. "We were the bar room brawlers of the airline industry," said Kelleher. It wasn't until the third year in business that the company turned a profit. But, in 1978, Southwest Airlines flew into more turbulence when Muse resigned. In hindsight, the resignation of Muse was the making of Southwest: it brought Kelleher in as president. In 1982 he became C.E.O. He was to prove one of the most unorthodox, innovative, and successful C.E.O.s of any major U.S. corporation.

"There are a hundred roads to Rome; the important thing is to get there, not to use the same road."

Herb Kelleher

Kelleher had no time for existing airline business practice unless it supported his two principal objectives: keeping the customer happy, and keeping costs down. He instigated a raft of measures designed to keep costs to a minimum. For example, customers choose seats on a first-come, first-served basis. And those hoping for a meal will be disappointed, as there are no in-flight meals—only peanuts—thus saving time and speeding up turnaround.

Kelleher's no frills service is backed up with excellent customer care, driven by even better employee care. The key to this is the corporate culture that Kelleher has inspired. As far as he is concerned, working for Southwest Airlines should, above all else, be fun. At Southwest headquarters, casual dress is the norm, practical jokes are encouraged, employee birthdays are celebrated, and any excuse to have a party is a good one. It is no different on the planes. Passengers are likely to be greeted by flight attendants dressed as leprechauns on St. Patrick's Day, have their safety instructions delivered in a Southwest Airlines version of stand up comedy, and jump when the flight attendants pop out of the overhead luggage compartments.

Nor is Kelleher above these bizarre pranks. There can be few C.E.O.s of major U.S. companies who have settled a high-level dispute with another corporation by arm wrestling their opposite number (Kelleher arm wrestled Kurt Herwald, chairman of Stevens Aviation, instead of going to court over an advertisement; he lost). Or who, when faced with a complaining customer who was clearly in the wrong, authorized a letter to the offending party advising them to fly with another airline. Or dressed up as Elvis for a recruitment ad that helpfully suggests résumés should be marked "Attention Elvis."

But despite what many may think, there is method in Kelleher's madness. The staff turnover rate at Southwest—below 7%—is one of lowest in the industry. And the company has never lost at any time because of union disputes. When Kelleher took over as C.E.O. in 1982, revenues were $270 million, there were 2,000 employees and 27 planes. By 2001, revenues had soared to over $5 billion, with 30,000 employees and 344 planes.

Kelleher's unique brand of management continues to dazzle in an intensely competitive business. There is no doubt that Southwest Airlines' success is principally down to its C.E.O. The question is, what happens when Kelleher steps down? Southwest is about to find out. In 2001, Kelleher retired as C.E.O. When asked what he would be doing with his new-found free time he replied, in his characteristic but offbeat style, "I might write about science. I might write about astronomy."

Shortly after he retired, Kelleher was named as C.E.O. of the Year. In 2002, he set out to encourage other entrepreneurs by donating $4 million dollars to the University of Texas Herb Kelleher Center for Entrepreneurial Excellence. He remained involved with Southwest Airlines as Chairman of the Board, but finally cut all links in 2005.

CONTEXT AND CONCLUSIONS

Southwest took a risk when it named a lawyer with no practical airline experience as president, and then C.E.O. The gamble paid off. Kelleher has inspired a unique corporate culture of fun and family at Southwest. Employees want to work for Southwest, and don't want to leave. Passengers want to fly Southwest because they know that, as well as a quick, on-time, low-cost flight, the likelihood is they will have a light-hearted, amusing trip.

Success didn't come overnight. Kelleher had to do battle with the competing carriers in the courts. He then had to convince the people at Southwest that the zany and offbeat can work, if it is underpinned by sound business practice. It may seem a little crazy on board, but the planes are full and the company is turning a profit every year. Along with C.E.O.s such as IKEA's Ingvar Kamprad, Kelleher has pioneered unconventional management practices and shown you can "do it different" and win.

> Kelleher's unique brand of management continues to dazzle in an intensely competitive business.

CLOSE BUT NO CIGAR

Sir Freddie Laker
Laker started the U.K. version of Southwest Airlines, Laker Airways Ltd., in 1966. He followed up with Laker Skytrain in 1977, flying across the Atlantic for rock-bottom prices. The cut-price, no frills, no reservations approach was the same as Southwest, but Sir Freddie was no Kelleher. When the competition ganged up on Southwest Airlines, Kelleher beat them off—just. Sir Freddie was less fortunate. After a vicious price war, Laker Airways was grounded in 1982 when the receivers were called in. Resolutely, Laker bounced back in 1992 with Laker Airways (Bahamas) Ltd., a small carrier that flies tourists to the Bahamas.

FOR MORE INFORMATION

Books:
Freiberg, Kevin, and Jackie Freiberg. *NUTS! Southwest Airlines' Crazy Recipe for Business and Personal Success.* Austin, TX: Bard Press, Inc., 1996.
Goddard, Larry, and David Brown. *The Turbocharged Company: Igniting Your Business to Soar Ahead of the Competition.* Collingdale, PA: DIANE, 1995.

Web site:
Southwest Airlines: www.southwest.com

1321

MANAGEMENT GIANTS

"Think small and act small, and we'll get bigger. Think big and act big, and we'll get smaller."

Herb Kelleher

Ray Kroc

Ray Kroc was looking forward to retiring after a comfortable career selling milkshake mixers. All that changed one day in 1954 when he walked into a small restaurant in San Bernardino, California. It was called McDonald's Famous Hamburgers, and Kroc's visit was the catalyst for a global food revolution. He cut himself a deal with the McDonald brothers and set about creating a franchise network. In 1961 he bought out the brothers for a bargain $2.7 million.

The company went public in 1965. By the 1970s Kroc had turned a $2.7 million investment into a $500 million fortune. The public bought McDonald's burgers by the million. By the time of Kroc's death in 1984, the McDonald's golden arches were recognized the world over as a symbol for convenient and cheap fast food.

Ray Kroc on the way to a fast food fortune.

1902	Born.
1922	Begins work as sales representative for Lily-Tulip Cup.
1954	Visits McDonald's burger restaurant in San Bernardino, California.
1955	Opens his first McDonald's in Des Plaines, Illinois.
1961	Buys out the McDonald brothers for $2.7 million.
1963	Number of hamburgers sold reaches one billion.
1965	Ronald McDonald introduced.
1967	First overseas branch opened.
1974	Buys the San Diego Padres.
1984	Dies.

BACKGROUND AND RISE

Raymond A. Kroc was born in Oak Park, Illinois, on October 5, 1902. His life and career can be divided up into two periods—before McDonald's and after it. Before McDonald's Kroc tried a variety of jobs before carving out a role as a milkshake-mixer sales rep.

At 15 he lied about his age so he could take part in World War I as a Red Cross ambulance driver. Disappointingly for him, the nearest he got to Europe was Connecticut. He was still finishing his training the day the war ended.

Having missed out on the war, Kroc looked for a job. He spent some time playing the piano for a living, and in 1922 landed a job selling paper cups for Lily-Tulip Cup Company. Kroc was good at sales and had an eye for business. When one of his customers, Earl Prince, patron of Prince Multimixers, showed Kroc the five-spindle mixer he had invented, Kroc switched companies. He got a contract to sell the mixers nationally, and for the next 17 years that was exactly

> **Kroc was convinced that fast food, McDonald's style, could be the next restaurant revolution.**

what he did. At 52 Kroc had spent most of his working life selling mixers. He was comfortably off and was thinking about his retirement—until, that is, the fateful day in 1954 when he walked into the small burger restaurant in San Bernardino run by the McDonald brothers.

DEFINING MOMENTS

What impressed Kroc about the burger restaurant run by brothers Dick and Mac McDonald, apart from the large number of mixers they ordered and the lines of customers down the street, was the way the business was run. It was as if Henry Ford had applied his mass-production formula to the food business. The brothers ran a burger assembly line. There were eight five-milkshake mixers churning out 40 milkshakes at a time. To speed up the cleaning, the brothers dispensed plastic utensils and paper napkins. So efficient was the McDonalds' operation that customers received their meal within 60 seconds. Furthermore, the brothers offered a very limited menu at extremely competitive prices. For Kroc it was commercial love at first sight. "I felt like some latter-day Newton who'd just had an Idaho potato caromed off his skull," he later wrote.

Kroc was convinced that fast food, McDonald's style, could be the next restaurant revolution. Using all the skills he had acquired in 25-plus years of selling, he sold himself to the McDonald brothers, persuading them to license their name to him. In return they would receive a percentage of the sales for each franchise he created. To the McDonald's model Kroc brought dynamism and a homespun business philosophy. "Luck is a dividend of sweat," he once observed. "The more you sweat, the luckier you get."

The four pillars on which Kroc built the McDonald's empire were quality, service, cleanliness, and value. He introduced some innovations of his own such as standardizing the size of the burger and the amount of onions served with each one. He even built a laboratory in Chi-

---

cago to research the ultimate french fry. Kroc's obsession with perfecting the McDonald's business formula cost him his marriage.

Kroc's first restaurant opened in Des Plaines, Illinois, in 1955. Several others quickly followed. Kroc insisted that franchisees run their restaurants according to his strict guidelines. Although he had little trouble convincing franchisees to open McDonald's restaurants, Kroc still encountered severe financial problems that nearly bankrupted him in the early years. In 1960 sales of $75 million translated into a profit of $139,000. His solution was to buy the land where the restaurants were to be located and then lease them to the franchisees. In this way Kroc retained closer control over the business and made more money.

Soon Kroc's financial problems were a thing of the past and he was eyeing a bigger prize. In 1961 he bought out the McDonald brothers for just $2.7 million. It was one of the best deals in business history—for Kroc at least. He then embarked on a massive advertising campaign. The McDonald's landmarks kept coming: a billion hamburgers by 1963; the five hundredth restaurant; the brilliant concept of the burger clown, Ronald McDonald, universally appealing to children. In fact, so popular was Ronald McDonald that not long after his first national ad appearance in 1965, more children knew his name than that of the U.S. president.

When the company went public in 1965, Kroc was $3 million richer. It was a fortune that grew to $500 million by the mid-1970s as McDonald's franchises sprang up everywhere. With the company firmly established in the United States, Kroc expanded overseas. In 1967 he took the golden arches to Canada, followed by Europe, Asia, and the rest of the world.

Kroc's great wealth affected him very little, since he spent much of his time ensuring that the McDonald's franchises maintained his high standards. One small in-

dulgence was his acquisition of the San Diego Padres in 1974. He died at the age of 81 in San Diego, California.

CONTEXT AND CONCLUSIONS

Few people can claim to have changed the way the world eats. Ray Kroc is one such individual. It took vision and courage to turn his back on a comfortable retirement for a new business opportunity at the age of 52. Kroc's idea was perfect for his time. The United States was suburbanizing, prospering, and depending more and more on the automobile. Kroc provided an increasingly mobile nation with fast, cheap, convenient food. His genius was not only to spot the opportunity but to package the experience carefully. Through franchises, strictly-regulated service and food production values, and innovative marketing, Kroc single-handedly invented the modern concept of fast food. He also pioneered the global brand, cooking up a McDonald's-style food revolution across the world.

> Few people can claim to have changed the way the world eats. Ray Kroc is one such individual.

FOR MORE INFORMATION

Books:
Kroc, Ray, with Robert Anderson. *Grinding it Out: The Making of McDonald's*. New York: St. Martin's Press, 1992.
Love, John F. *McDonald's: Behind the Arches*. Revised ed. New York: Bantam, 1995.

Web site:
McDonald's™: **www.mcdonalds.com**

1323

MANAGEMENT GIANTS

"The world is filled with unsuccessful men of talent."

Ray Kroc

Estée Lauder

Much of the U.S. cosmetic queen Estée Lauder's (1908–2004) early life is shrouded in mystery. What is known is that she started in the cosmetics business selling her uncle's Six-in-One cold cream in 1924. By 1944 she had acquired a husband, an office in New York City, and a cosmetics concession in Saks Fifth Avenue. Lauder formally incorporated Estée Lauder Inc. in 1947. Resisting calls to go public, she kept her company in family hands and used her formidable sales and marketing talents to drive the business forward. In 1968 revenues were an estimated $40 million with profits of $4 million. Lauder ceded control to her son, Leonard, in 1972. By 1999, Estée Lauder, Inc. was earning over $3 billion in revenue from over a hundred products.

Lauder rejuvenated the world of cosmetics.

1908	Born.
1924	Uncle founds New Way Laboratories.
1944	Lauder sets up her own office.
1947	Estée Lauder Inc. founded.
1948	First retail account at Saks Fifth Avenue, New York City.
1960	First international account at Harrods, London.
1968	Revenues of $40 million.
1972	Son Leonard made president. Lauder becomes chair.
1980s	Lauder steps back from running the company.
1995	Company I.P.O.
2004	Dies.

BACKGROUND AND RISE

Estée Lauder was born Josephine Esther Mentzer in Queens, New York City, in 1908, the youngest of nine children. Her father ran a hardware store, and Lauder went to school nearby.

The young Lauder was introduced to the cosmetics business through her uncle Dr. Schotz, a chemist. His business, New Way Laboratories, was founded in 1924. Among the various potions and lotions he made—which included a poultry-lice killer, paint stripper, varnish, and embalming fluid—were several beauty treatments. Lauder helped her uncle out by selling products with names like Six-in-One Cold Cream and Dr. Schotz Viennese Cream.

In 1930 she married Joe Lauder, but by 1939 the couple had separated. A subsequent reconciliation led to their remarriage in 1942, at which time Lauder vowed to direct all her energies to selling cosmetics products. She continued to sell her uncle's products, establishing her own office at 39 East 60th St. in February 1944.

Soon afterward Lauder won a sales concession in the Bonwit Teller department store. She then set her sights

higher. The prize concession was in Saks Fifth Avenue. When she told Bob Fiske, cosmetics buyer at Saks, that the department store should give her a concession, Fiske demurred, explaining that there was no demand for her products from his customers. Undeterred, Lauder created a demand by giving her products away at a talk at the Waldorf-Astoria Hotel. When she returned to Fiske, he relented.

In the late 1940s, with $60,000 or so at her disposal, Lauder was unable to persuade the BBD&O advertising agency to create a campaign for Estée Lauder. Instead she chose a more direct route to her customers. Using Saks's mailing list, Lauder sent out samplers and gifts as an enticement for customers to visit her store concessions.

DEFINING MOMENTS

Lauder's breakthrough came with the invention of her first fragrance, the bath oil Youth Dew. Her principal competition, firms like Arden and Rubenstein, had all started with skincare products and gravitated to fragrances.

Accounts of how Lauder created her first fragrance differ. It seems that an old friend, A. L. van Amerigan, president of van Amerigan-Haebler (which subsequently became International Flavors and Fragrances), was involved. Similarly Ernest Shiftan, an employee of IFF and one of the country's top perfumers, may well have been responsible for the development of the fragrance. Whether Amerigan gave the fragrance to Lauder is unclear. What is certain is that Youth Dew, introduced at Bonwit's as bath oil, was an instant success. For $8.50 customers got a perfume that lasted a whole day.

Shrewdly, Lauder used the demand for the new perfume to sell her other cosmetics. The Youth Dew line was eventually extended across a variety of cosmetics including a pure fragrance. With Lauder shamelessly promoting it at every opportunity, it wasn't long before Estée Lauder

was the third-largest cosmetics business in the United States behind Arden and Rubenstein.

Lauder's marketing acumen was again evident when a new breed of skincare products making dubious scientific claims began to spread from Europe to the United States. In France an emphasis on "feeding" the skin had given rise to products that made various health claims about their effects. The Food and Drug Administration, however, imposed tough regulations on products making any such claims. There were, for example, a host of placental-based products that ran afoul of the FDA and were withdrawn. Lauder, instead of making scientific claims for her new skin product, simply named it Re-Nutriv. The product's health enhancing attributes were implied in the name. She was also careful not to cross the line in her advertising. It focused instead on the high price of the product, and how a price of $115 a pound was justified by the inclusion of the "costliest" ingredients.

At the time Estée Lauder's headquarters were at 666 Fifth Avenue, on the second floor—Lauder had a fear of heights. Competitors were close at hand. Charles Revson, founder of Revlon, was on the top floor of the same building and Helena Rubenstein was across the street. As Lauder made progress commercially she was also climbing socially. Her house in Palm Beach, Florida, afforded her the opportunity to meet rich people from the upper echelons of U.S. society. Lauder's efforts at networking were not entirely without mishap. One story has it that, arriving for dinner at the home of Dorothy Munn, wife of financier Charles Munn, she gave a box of cosmetics (presumably her own) to her hostess. This was viewed as a gauche gesture as Dorothy Munn was wealthy enough to have her cosmetics made privately—a kind of haute-perfume.

By the 1970s Estée Lauder had bested its corporate competition and added the Clinique brand to its beautifying armory. Lauder herself had outlasted her personal rivals as both Elizabeth Arden and Helena Rubenstein had died within a year of each other in the 1960s. Lauder had since moved her headquarters to the new General Motors Building (with the ever-present Revlon camped on the top floors); she had also, by virtue of her friendship with the Duchess of Windsor, firmly placed herself at the pinnacle of the social scene. Her son Leonard be-

came president of the company in 1972, with Lauder becoming chair.

The "little business" that Leonard Lauder once said his mother was growing now controls over 45% of the cosmetics market in U.S. department stores. Available in 130 countries, Estée Lauder products bring in over $3 billion in revenue.

CONTEXT AND CONCLUSIONS

Estée Lauder Inc. is an astonishing example of how an international business can be built up from humble beginnings through one woman's relentless drive, networking, belief in her own products, and brilliant marketing. In particular, Lauder was responsible for a number of innovative marketing techniques for the cosmetics business, most notably the free gift with purchase.

Her strength of leadership was emphasized through her determination to keep the company in the control of her family. Estée Lauder remained an entirely private company until its I.P.O. in 1995. The Lauder family still holds a significant proportion of the stock. Although Lauder took a progressively back seat from the 1980s, her sons Leonard and Ronald, daughter-in-law Evelyn, grandson William, and great-granddaughter Aerin remain actively involved in the company. On her death in April 2004, the company was thought to be worth $10 billion.

> The "little business" that Leonard Lauder once said his mother was growing now controls over 45% of the cosmetics market in U.S. department stores.

FOR MORE INFORMATION

Books:
Israel, Lee. *Estée Lauder: Beyond the Magic: An Unauthorized Biography*. New York: Macmillan, 1985.
Lauder, Estée. *Estée: A Success Story*. New York: Random House, 1985.

Web site:
Estée Lauder: **www.esteelauder.com**

1325

MANAGEMENT GIANTS

"Observing your own and your competitor's successes and failures makes your inner business voice more sure and vivid."

Estée Lauder

Henry Robinson Luce

When Henry Robinson Luce graduated from Yale University in 1920, he had already shown a talent for editing by radically overhauling the Yale newspaper, the *Daily News*. Following a tour of Europe, he worked on the *Chicago Daily News*, and then the *Baltimore News*, where he linked up with fellow Yale alumnus Briton Hadden. Together they launched a new publication *Time: The Weekly News Magazine* in March 1923. In 1929 they followed with the launch of the business magazine *Fortune* to chronicle the ups and downs of Wall Street. After Hadden's untimely death in 1929, Luce went on to publish one successful magazine after another. *Life*, founded in 1936, broke the company's circulation records, and they were broken again by *Sports Illustrated*, launched in 1954. Luce died of a heart attack in 1967, still at the helm of his empire.

Fortune smiled on Henry Luce.

1898	Born.
1920	Graduates from Yale. Voted "most brilliant student."
1922	Leaves Baltimore for New York. Time, Inc. incorporated on November 28.
1923	The first issue of *Time* hits the stands.
1927	First profit posted—$3,860.
1928	Profits of $126,000.
1929	*Fortune* magazine launched.
1936	*Life* magazine launched.
1954	*Sports Illustrated* magazine launched.
1958	Suffers heart attack.
1967	Dies.

BACKGROUND AND RISE

Henry Robinson Luce was born on April 3, 1898 in Teng-chow, China, where his Presbyterian missionary parents were teaching at a Christian mission. His upbringing was an austere one. His daily schedule began at six in the morning with a cold bath, followed by half an hour of Bible study. With six hours of Chinese lessons a day, he was fluent in the local tongue before he was able to speak English.

Barring a brief visit to the United States in 1906, Luce was to remain in China until he was 14. A precocious scholar, he attended the British-run boarding school in Chefoo. It was a tough environment with strict discipline. Fortunately for Luce, a strong work ethic, combined with a keen mind, kept him at the top of the class and away from the master's cane. The school's pupils were predominantly English, and Luce frequently found himself sticking up for the United States. "My Anglo-Americanism is deeper than any words," he once said. "Indeed, it is written in the blood of that shameful, and futile, endless two hours one Saturday afternoon, when I rolled around the unspeakably dirty floor of the main

schoolroom with a British boy who had insulted my country."

After Chefoo came the Hotchkiss School in Connecticut. There Luce continued his excellent scholastic record: outstanding marks in his Greek exams, the honor roll, and leader of the class in most subjects. Outside his classes he discovered a new talent as editor-in-chief of the *Hotchkiss Literary Monthly* and assistant managing editor of the weekly school newspaper, the *Record*. Luce had found his vocation.

DEFINING MOMENTS

It was at Yale that Luce started his career in publishing in earnest. Together with fellow student and ex-Hotchkiss pupil Briton Hadden, he revolutionized the Yale newspaper, the *Daily News*. On graduation in 1920 Luce was voted "most brilliant" and Hadden "most likely to succeed." The combination proved irresistible. After Yale, Luce continued his tour of the world's most prestigious educational establishments, heading for Oxford, England, where he studied history. Then, after a whistle-stop tour of Europe, he returned to the United States, obtaining work first on the *Chicago Daily News* and then on the *Baltimore News*. In Baltimore Luce rejoined his old friend Hadden and together they developed a plan to launch a new weekly news magazine called *Facts*. When the magazine was finally launched it was called *Time: The Weekly News Magazine*.

The pair left Baltimore for New York in February 1922. There they rented a small one-room office, acquired a third partner in Culbrith Sudler, reportedly an expert at selling advertising, and spent the next few months seeking advice and capital. Advice was forthcoming—mostly along the lines of "don't do it"—but capital was less plentiful. Eventually, however, they managed to raise sufficient funds (partly through a stock issue) and incorporated the business on November 28, 1922, having moved to a small loft in the printing trades building on

"What I love about magazines is that an individual can change the destiny of an entire business."
Duncan Edwards

Eighth Avenue. To decide who should edit the magazine and who should manage the business side of things, Hadden and Luce tossed a coin. It was to Luce's ever-lasting chagrin that he lost and, in the three years before he took up the post of editor, Hadden had the opportunity to stamp his mark on *Time* magazine. The first issue of *Time* hit the newsstands in March 1923, with a cover price of 15 cents.

The distribution of the first issues was farcical. A string of debutante acquaintances was entrusted with the task of addressing the first three issues and dispatching them to subscribers, who could read all three before making a financial commitment. In the ensuing mix-up some subscribers received three copies of the same issue, only one issue, or no issue at all. Of the 25,000 who agreed to take a look, only 9,000 ever received a copy. And of the 5,000 sent to the newsstands, 3,000 were returned unsold.

After this inauspicious start, however, circulation grew steadily. By the third year it had reached 110,000, with advertising revenue of $283,000, yet a profit remained elusive. Indeed, it wasn't until 1927 that the new magazine made a profit, and then it was just $3,860. In 1928 a more respectable figure of $126,000 was posted, and from that point onward figures improved rapidly. By then, Luce was editor. He ensnared his readers with an array of literary devices: compound words such as "sexational" and the more successful "socialite" made their debut on the pages of *Time*. Foreign words such as "tycoon"—from the Japanese *taikun*, meaning prince and "pundit"—from the Hindu *pandit*, meaning sage—were popularized by Luce; and he also made common the use of euphemisms such as "great and good friend"—meaning mistress—to skirt around potentially libelous issues.

By 1927 *Time* had moved again, not once but twice, coming to rest eventually in Manhattan, just off Fifth Avenue. Luce's lifelong friend Hadden had always said his goal was to make one million dollars by the age of 30. As it turned out he made more than that, but in February 1929, nine days after his 31st birthday, he died. Luce was left in full charge of the magazine.

Fortune magazine was the second major venture for Time, Inc. Founded in 1929, it was Luce's idea, based on his instinct that "business is obviously the greatest single common denominator of interest among the active leading citizens of the United States—our best men are in business." *Fortune* was two years in the planning. It owes its name to Luce's wife Lila, who preferred *Fortune* to *Power*. To head the editorial staff, Luce chose Parker Lloyd Smith, a brilliant Oxford graduate who did an excellent job in the magazine's early days, until in 1931 he threw himself to his death from a hotel window, for no apparent reason.

The first issue of *Fortune*—30,000 copies in all—rolled off the presses just three months after the spectacular stock market crash of October 1929. In spite of (or perhaps because of) its timing, the first issue was well received, and the magazine managed to survive the economic depression that followed. By 1937 revenues were up to $500,000 and circulation in excess of 460,000. Through the ensuing decades *Fortune* magazine cataloged the ups and downs of U.S. business life.

Over the next 30 years, Luce built a publishing business with a worldwide circulation of over 13 million. To *Time* and *Fortune* he added the even more successful *Life* magazine in 1936. In 1954 when *Sports Illustrated* was introduced, it broke the circulation records set by *Life*. Luce successfully steered the company through World War II; adroitly negotiated the communist witch hunts that swept the United States in the postwar years; and fended off hundreds of threats to sue the company for invasion of privacy or libel each year.

In 1967 the circulation of Luce's flagship magazine was some 7,500,000. Advertising, which was twice as much as for any other magazine, brought in $170 million to Time, Inc. *Time* magazine itself sold some 3,500,000 copies, yielding $86 million in advertising revenue. The company that Luce founded on a budget of $86,000 had total revenues in excess of $500 million, with profits of $37 million. For much of his later career Luce regularly threatened to retire. "At 40 I will retire and let the young take over," he used to say. But even after his heart attack in 1958, he could not drag himself away. In February 1967, still in command of his empire, he finally succumbed to another heart attack.

CONTEXT AND CONCLUSIONS

Flamboyant media moguls such as William Randolph Hearst, Lord Beaverbrook, and Lord Thomson are better remembered today than Henry Robinson Luce, especially outside the United States. Luce, the man with a Presbyterian upbringing, was content to remain in the shadows. He neither sought political power, as Beaverbrook did, nor did he go in for ostentatious shows of wealth like Hearst's mansion in San Simeon. Yet Luce's contribution to publishing was just as important, if not more so, as that of his peers. He created a number of magazines that have survived him and gone on to become national institutions.

> Over the next 30 years, Luce built a publishing business with a worldwide circulation of over 13 million. To *Time* and *Fortune* he added the even more successful *Life* magazine in 1936.

> The first issue of *Fortune*— 30,000 copies in all—rolled off the presses just three months after the spectacular stock market crash of October 1929.

FOR MORE INFORMATION

Books:
Cort, David. *The Sin of Henry R. Luce*. Secaucus, NJ: Carol Publishing Group, 1974.
Swanberg, W. A. *Luce and His Empire*. New York: Scribner, 1972.

Web sites:
Time: **www.time.com/time**
Fortune.com: **www.fortune.com**

"The newspaper and magazine business is an intellectual brothel from which there is no escape."

Leo Tolstoy

Konosuke Matsushita

For a man who never left his native country before the age of 56, Konosuke Matsushita (1894–1989) made a big impact on the world. Matsushita started work at the age of nine. After stints as a coal worker and at an engineering company, Matsushita started his own company, Matsushita Electric Appliance (later Matsushita Electric Industrial, or MEI) in 1918. Through a combination of product innovation, clever marketing, and forward-thinking management, Matsushita developed the company into one of the largest of its kind in prewar Japan.

After a difficult postwar period, Matsushita rejoined his company in 1950. Reasserting his business values, he transformed MEI into an industrial giant that today consists of over 300 subsidiaries.

A key subsidiary of Matsushita's MEI.

MANAGEMENT GIANTS

1894	Born.
1918	Starts Matsushita Electric Appliance Factory.
1929	Formulates the "basic management objective."
1933	Introduces the "five guiding principles."
1935	Matsushita Electric Appliance renamed Matsushita Electric Industrial Company (MEI).
1937	Adds two more guiding principles.
1946	Founds the Peace and Happiness through Prosperity (PHP) Institute.
1950	Returns to the company.
1961	Becomes chairman of MEI.
1965	Introduces five-day workweek.
1973	Steps down as chairman.
1989	Dies.

BACKGROUND AND RISE

The youngest of eight children, Konosuke Matsushita was born in 1894 in the farming village of Wasa in Wakayama Prefecture, Japan. His father was a landlord who received income from the local tenant farmers, enabling the family to live in reasonable comfort. That changed in 1898 when Matsushita's father decided to speculate on the rice market. The investment was spectacularly unsuccessful and left the family in financial ruin. The changed circumstances spelled the end of Matsushita's rudimentary schooling. At the tender age of nine, he was asked by his father to go to Osaka to work in a charcoal brazier shop. This was followed by an apprenticeship in a bicycle shop.

In 1910 the young Matsushita was taken on as a wiring assistant at the Osaka Electric Light Company (OELC).

> **Matsushita's first socket design turned out to be a dud. But the next product, an electrical attachment plug, sold well, especially since Matsushita undercut the competition by up to a third.**

He was a quick learner and despite his age, just 16, his skill at wiring earned him rapid promotion. But in 1917 he decided to leave OELC, partly due to health problems. Matsushita suffered from a debilitating lung condition and frequently took days off from work to rest. He decided that if he could start his own business he would be able to accommodate his poor health. He also wanted to market a new light socket he had invented, and his employers at OELC had done little to encourage his inventiveness.

DEFINING MOMENTS

In 1918, at the age of 23, he founded Matsushita Electric Appliance Factory (the company became Matsushita Electric Industrial Company—MEI—in 1935). He had three employees, the equivalent of $50, and a prototype for a new type of electrical socket. Business was tough at first. Matsushita's first socket design turned out to be a dud. But the next product, an electrical attachment plug, sold well, especially since Matsushita undercut the competition by up to a third. The product that kept the company going, though, was a battery powered bicycle lamp shaped like a bullet. The lamp was unique in being able to run for up to 40 hours. Some Japanese even used it to light their houses.

Matsushita was a good engineer, but he was even better at marketing. He used the demand for his bicycle lamp to build a sales network throughout Japan. Once he had established countrywide distribution, he put the trademark "National" on Matsushita products and lowered prices to make his lamp a mass-market product. He also pioneered the use of national newspaper advertising, a relatively rare sight in Japan in the 1920s.

In 1929, with the company firmly established, Matsushita put into practice the management practices and philosophy for which he was to become famous. He was an extremely enlightened manager for his time. This much is evident from the slogan he adopted for the

---

"Big things and little things are my job. Middle level management can be delegated."

Konosuke Matsushita

company: "harmony between corporate profit and social justice." Matsushita followed this in 1933 with his "five guiding principles" (two more were added in 1937), which shaped the conduct of the company. The principles, still adhered to today, are service to the public, fairness and honesty, teamwork for the common cause, untiring effort for improvement, courtesy and humility, accord with natural laws, and gratitude for blessings.

During the 1930s Matsushita made a number of decisions illustrating the leadership style that was to earn him the nickname "the god of management." During the recession of 1930 Matsushita refused to make wholesale layoffs. Instead he recruited underemployed factory workers to go out and sell stockpiled inventory. Later in 1931 he bought the rights to a radio patent, which he then made freely available to the market. This was an expensive ploy, but it had the effect of stimulating the market and so ultimately profited the company. It presaged a similar move by David Sarnoff, the head of RCA, with the patent for building color television sets, and anticipated the stance taken much later by the open source movement in computing. In 1932 Matsushita declared that entrepreneurs and manufacturers should aim "to make all products as inexhaustible and as cheap as tap water."

Somehow Matsushita managed to hold the company together during World War II. In postwar Japan, MEI came under the severe restrictions imposed on certain Japanese companies by the Allies. Matsushita was almost removed as president, but was saved in part by a petition from 15,000 employees. For a time he devoted his energies to the Peace and Happiness through Prosperity Institute, which he founded in 1946, returning to his company duties only in 1950. He reinvigorated the company, reorganizing it along divisional lines. At the same time he reassessed processes to make them more efficient and refocused the company on the core values he had expressed in the 1930s.

From 1950 until his retirement as chairman in 1973, Matsushita oversaw a huge expansion of the company as its "three treasures"—washing machines, refrigerators, and televisions—as well as other electrical goods were exported around the world. The company grew to become one of the world's largest manufacturers of electrical goods, controlling a stable of global brand names including Panasonic, Technics, and JVC.

A measure of the man's attention to his business is revealed by an incident at the Matsushita Pavilion during the Osaka World's Fair in 1970. The exposition had been open for a few days when the pavilion's staff were surprised to see Matsushita waiting in line outside. When they rushed out to usher the founder of their company indoors, he told them that he had stood in line to find out how long visitors had to wait before they were admitted.

Later that day he ordered that the system be redesigned to speed up admission and that shade from the sun be provided for the people waiting outside.

From the 1970s onward Matsushita concentrated much of his time on developing and explaining his social and commercial philosophies, mainly in his 44 published books. His most popular title, *Developing a Road to Peace and Happiness Through Prosperity*, sold over four million copies. He continued to teach his unique concept of management until his chronic lung problems claimed his life. He died of pneumonia on April 27, 1989. He was 94.

CONTEXT AND CONCLUSIONS

Konosuke Matsushita founded one of Japan's greatest corporations, Matsushita Electric Industrial. Yet he is remembered for much more than the creation of an electrical goods empire. At MEI Matsushita implemented management practices that were far ahead of their time. He abandoned the conventional centralized management structure. He drew up a corporate creed and identified corporate values. He pioneered advertising in the press and competed both on price and quality.

Matsushita's philosophy can best be summed up by the "basic management objective" he formulated in 1929: "Recognizing our responsibilities as industrialists, we will devote ourselves to the progress and development of society and the well-being of people through our business activities, thereby enhancing the quality of life throughout the world." It was something Matsushita did to great effect.

> **The company grew to become one of the world's largest manufacturers of electrical goods, controlling a stable of global brand names including Panasonic, Technics, and JVC.**

1329

MANAGEMENT GIANTS

FOR MORE INFORMATION

Books:
Gould, Rowland. *The Matsushita Phenomenon.* Tokyo: Diamond Sha, 1970.
Kotter, John P. *Matsushita: Leadership Lessons from the Life of the 20th Century's Most Remarkable Entrepreneur.* New York: Free Press, 1997.
Matsushita, Konosuke. *Quest for Prosperity—The Life of a Japanese Industrialist.* Tokyo: PHP Institute, 1988.

Web site:
Panasonic USA: **www.panasonic.com**

"The mission of a manufacturer should be to overcome poverty, to relieve society as a whole from misery and bring it wealth."
Konosuke Matsushita

Louis B. Mayer

The real-life story of movie tycoon Louis B. Mayer reads like a script from one of his movies. Mayer hauled himself up from his humble beginnings as the son of an immigrant scrap-metal dealer to become a Hollywood legend. Starting in 1907 with a small chain of movie theaters, by 1924 he was vice president of Metro Goldwyn Mayer, arguably the greatest studio in Hollywood history.

Over the following decades the studio with the famous lion emblem was a roaring success as Mayer exerted his despotic influence over every aspect of the moviemaking process. Like many dictators, benign or otherwise, Mayer was ousted from MGM in 1951 after a bitter power struggle.

MGM's classic symbol.

1885	Born.
1907	Buys rundown movie theater in Haverhill, Massachusetts.
1915	Shows D. W. Griffith's *Birth of a Nation* at his theaters.
1918	Starts movie production firm in Los Angeles—Louis B. Mayer Pictures.
1924	Louis B. Mayer Productions, the Samuel Goldwyn Company, and Metro merge to form Metro Goldwyn Mayer, or MGM.
1926	*Ben Hur.*
1927	Formation of the Academy of Motion Pictures Arts and Sciences.
1932	*Grand Hotel.*
1936	Rival Irving Thalberg dies.
1951	Ousted from MGM after a power struggle with Dore Schary.
1957	Dies.

BACKGROUND AND RISE

Louis B. Mayer was born Eliezar Mayer on July 4, 1885 in Minsk, Russia (now in Belarus). In 1888 Mayer emigrated with his family to New Brunswick, Canada. In Canada Mayer's father built a small junk-dealing business into a profitable scrap-metal organization. After elementary school Mayer joined his father's business, preferring the world of commerce to that of academia. Soon he had his own scrap business in Boston.

In 1907 Mayer took his first small step on the road to Hollywood. Relinquishing his position in the family business, he bought a small dilapidated movie theater in Haverhill, Massachusetts at a knockdown price. He completely overhauled the theater and made a decision to show only quality movies. His gamble paid off. Soon he was the owner of the largest theater chain in New England. Film exhibitors fought to show new movies at Mayer's theaters. In 1915 he showed D. W. Griffith's *Birth of a Nation*, one of the most popular movies of its time. The huge profit Mayer made from showing the movie helped finance his ensuing adventures in Hollywood.

DEFINING MOMENTS

By 1918 Mayer was camped out in Los Angeles, operating as a movie promoter through his company, Louis B. Mayer Pictures. It was the start of his personal main event. At first productions were funded from the proceeds of the theater chain business. He made a star of the actress Anita Stewart and, fired up by the acclaim received for his first production, *Virtuous Wives*, continued to use her as his main attraction for the following five years.

Hollywood was still in its infancy. For aspiring moguls there remained a once-in-a-lifetime opportunity to stake a claim in the city of celluloid. Mayer may have been wealthy because of his movie theater business, but his fortune was small change in an industry dominated by fabulously rich power brokers. And the mogul of all moguls was Marcus Loew. He commanded his fiefdom from the East Coast; 3,000 miles away in his New York City office Loew pulled the strings that made Hollywood dance.

In 1924 Mayer hit the jackpot. Loew decided that he wanted his own studio, Metro, to merge with Louis B. Mayer Pictures and the Samuel Goldwyn Company. What Loew wanted, he generally got, to the point that when Samuel Goldwyn backed out of the deal, Loew retained the Goldwyn name, calling the newly-formed company Metro Goldwyn Mayer (MGM). Mayer was

> In 1907 Mayer took his first small step on the road to Hollywood. Relinquishing his position in the family business, he bought a small dilapidated movie theater in Haverhill, Massachusetts at a knockdown price.

"There's got to be some way of stopping the word of mouth on this picture."

Samuel Goldwyn

appointed vice president. With his inherited stable of stars he was finally in a position to dominate Hollywood.

At MGM Mayer ostensibly shared his power with Irving Thalberg, hired in from Universal by Loew. In reality, Mayer ruled the roost, conducting a bitter battle behind the scenes with Thalberg that ended only with Thalberg's death in 1936.

By all accounts Mayer was an autocratic, manipulative despot who ruled MGM using extreme cunning. He was described by Ephraim Katz, the late respected film scholar and author of the classic resource, *The Film Encyclopedia*, as "a ruthless, quick-tempered, paternalistically tyrannical executive." Mayer ruled MGM "as one big family, rewarding obedience, punishing insubordination, and regarding opposition as personal betrayal." His political acumen must truly have been brilliant to control the egos of movie stars such as Lon Chaney and Greta Garbo, as well as directors like King Vidor and Erich von Stroheim.

Unashamedly populist, Mayer was said to abhor intellectualism. Like many other media moguls he had an innate sense of what the masses wanted. He was also a hands-on operator. To the frequent annoyance of the studio employees, who considered themselves the true auteurs, Mayer not only constantly intervened in moviemaking but also managed to take many of the plaudits.

Inexorably MGM's power grew, and with it, Mayer's. The studio churned out a movie a week and created its own town, Culver City, where thousands of studio employees participated in the American dream. Off screen, Mayer was as ruthless as ever. He was equally adept at cutting film or cutting staff. He used the rise of the talkies as an excuse for a purge of the studio stars. Names that Mayer had helped make he now discarded: Buster Keaton, Erich von Stroheim, even Greta Garbo, were swept off the lot as Mayer and MGM marched on through the 1930s and 1940s.

Mayer cleverly managed to thwart objections to MGM's increasing dominance of the movie industry by forming an alliance of sorts under the banner of the Academy of Motion Pictures Arts and Sciences. Mayer, along with Douglas Fairbanks Sr., was a prime mover behind the Academy's creation in 1927.

Like most dictatorial leaders, however, his ruthlessness eventually caught up with him. In the 1950s, lacking the energy of the emerging generation of would-be studio executives, he was finally ground down by the behind-the-scenes scheming. Outmaneuvered, he was ejected from MGM in 1951 to be replaced by Dore Schary. Grittily determined to the last, Mayer spent his final years failing to persuade the stockholders of MGM's parent company, Loew, to reinstate him and dump Schary. He died as a result of leukemia in 1957.

CONTEXT AND CONCLUSIONS

In many ways Mayer's life was a drama in which he himself played the roles of both hero and villain. On his journey to moguldom he made countless enemies. It was said at the time of his death that the reason that half of Hollywood attended his funeral was to check that the great man was indeed dead. Mayer also earned the grudging respect of his competitors, who harbored a sneaking admiration for his commercial acumen.

At MGM Mayer presided over a golden age of moviemaking. He was responsible for a host of hits like *Ben Hur* (1926) and *Dinner at Eight* (1933). At his zenith he commanded the highest salary in the world—over a million dollars a year. Bob Hope said of Mayer that he "came out west with 28 dollars, a box camera, and an old lion. He built a monument to himself—the Bank of America."

Perhaps Mayer's most fitting epitaph is one of his own observations. Commenting on survival in the movie business, the combative son of a scrap dealer who became the most powerful man in Hollywood eloquently put it thus: "Look out for yourself or they'll pee on your grave."

1331

MANAGEMENT GIANTS

Mayer ruled MGM "as one big family, rewarding obedience, punishing insubordination, and regarding opposition as personal betrayal."

FOR MORE INFORMATION

Books:
Altman, Diana. *Hollywood East: Louis B. Mayer and the Origins of the Studio System.* Secaucus, NJ: Carol Publishing Group, 1992.
Gabler, Neal. *An Empire of Their Own: How the Jews Invented Hollywood.* New York: Doubleday, 1988.
Schulberg, Budd. *Moving Pictures.* New York: Stein and Day, 1982.
Zierold, Norman. *The Moguls: Hollywood's Merchants of Myth.* Silman-James Press, 1991.

Web site:
MGM: **www.mgm.com**

Cyrus Hall McCormick

Cyrus Hall McCormick had invention in his blood. He grew up with a father who was constantly inventing strange contraptions. On the family farm in Virginia, McCormick perfected the design of one of his father's crazy ideas—the mechanized reaping machine. Aged only 22, he started a small-scale home-manufacturing operation in Virginia Valley, producing two machines in 1840. It ended up as a massive manufacturing concern, based in Chicago. In 1884, the McCormick Harvesting Machine Company sold 54,841 harvesting machines to farmers from the United States to Australia.

A millionaire by the age of 50, McCormick paved the way for an agrarian revolution through the invention of his reaping machine and a host of innovative marketing techniques, from the installment plan to the money-back guarantee.

McCormick was a leader in his field.

1332

MANAGEMENT GIANTS

1809	Born.
1830	Given ownership of his father's prototype reaper invention.
1831	Produces viable working machine.
1834	Receives 14-year patent for the threshing machine.
1843	Head-to-head showdown with rival Obed Hussey.
1847	Moves business to Chicago.
1851	Awarded prize at Crystal Palace Grand Exhibition.
1859	Production at 4,119 machines a year.
1861	Beginning of American Civil War.
1870	Production of 10,000 machines a year.
1871	Great fire of Chicago destroys McCormick's manufacturing plant.
1873	New production plant opens.
1884	Dies.

BACKGROUND AND RISE

The son of a farmer and inventor, Cyrus Hall McCormick was the eldest of eight children. Born on February 15, 1809 in Rockbridge County, Virginia, he grew up on the 532 rolling acres of farmland belonging to the family. His father Robert, in addition to running the farm, spent a lot of time tinkering with inventions aimed at easing the burden of farming. The most significant was a horse-drawn reaping device, abandoned when he failed to perfect it. McCormick's father lacked the business sense, the will, and the drive necessary to turn any of his various inventions into a commercial venture.

> He arranged a head-to-head showdown with his rival in 1843, in which the McCormick reaper cut down 17 acres in the time it took Obed Hussey to clear just two.

The young McCormick had already demonstrated an ability for invention when, aged 15, he built a light-weight cradle for harvesting grain. At 21, his father gave him a head start in life, handing over ownership of his reaper invention. In 1831, McCormick worked six weeks non-stop to perfect the invention, to produce a viable working machine.

DEFINING MOMENTS

In the summer of 1831, the 22-year-old McCormick used his horse-drawn reaper to mow down the field of wheat at John Steele's farm in Rockbridge County, Virginia. The assembled audience—farmers, laborers, and slaves—had witnessed the beginning of the mechanization of agriculture. Quality control would come later.

McCormick wasn't the first to invent the reaper. Others, such as Obed Hussey, were also thinking along the same lines. In 1834, McCormick applied for and received a 14-year patent for his threshing machine. Hussey had patented his reaping device a year earlier. In the end it was McCormick's marketing genius that would make his product the standard for mechanical threshing.

Despite the obvious advantages of the reaper, developing the business proved difficult. McCormick set about remedying the situation by eliminating the competition in the minds of the consumer. He arranged a head-to-head showdown with his rival in 1843, in which the McCormick reaper cut down 17 acres in the time it took Obed Hussey to clear just two. Word soon traveled through the farming community about the disparity in performance between the two machines.

Next, McCormick developed a licensing system. Manufacturers close to market were granted a license to produce the McCormick reaping machine. In some cases the agreement operated like a franchise, demarcating area in return for a franchise fee; in others it was simply a question of paying McCormick $20 for each reaper produced and sold.

"Only a real lazybones can produce labor-saving inventions."   Günter Grass

To obviate the need to walk alongside his machine, McCormick designed a seat so the operator could sit above the reaper. This design, known as the "old reliable," became the standard model.

In 1840, from his Walnut Grove base, McCormick sold two machines—they both broke down. The following year, he sold seven. In 1844, still in the Virginia Valley, production had risen to 75 machines, 25 manufactured under license.

In 1847, McCormick moved to Chicago. The decision was motivated by the knowledge that, although he had manufactured 75 reapers in 1846, this was still a long way short of the demand. Devotion to his father, Robert, had kept McCormick in his hometown. When his father died in 1846, there were few reasons for him to remain in the backwoods of Walnut Grove. In Chicago, McCormick built a plant on the banks of the Chicago River. Over 7,500 square feet of factory space and river frontage, which meant completed machines could be loaded onto river transport, allowed McCormick to expand production rapidly. In 1849, before completion of the factory, his company produced 1,500 reapers. By 1859, production had rocketed to 4,119 machines a year.

By 1860, some 70% of the country's wheat harvest was gathered using McCormick's reaper. Before the reaper, it took a man 40 hours to harvest an acre of wheat. With the McCormick reaper, two people could harvest an acre of wheat in a day. In the decade leading up to 1859, U.S. production of wheat boomed from 100 million bushels to 173 million. The agricultural revolution made McCormick a millionaire. It also made him a worldwide celebrity. The machine, first described by the *London Times* as a "contraption seemingly a cross between a wheelbarrow, a chariot, and a flying machine," won the main prize at the Grand Exhibition at Crystal Palace in 1851. This award was followed by prizes at the Hamburg Exposition, the Vienna Exposition and the Paris Exposition.

McCormick continued to manage his business well into his seventies. It was quite a feat, considering some of the severe setbacks he suffered. Production was slack for the duration of the American Civil War, starting in 1861, during which time McCormick took the opportunity to promote his machine in Europe. By 1870 his factory was producing a staggering 10,000 machines year. Then in 1871, in a devastating blow to his business, the great fire of Chicago destroyed $188 million worth of property at his manufacturing plant. The resilient McCormick built an even bigger factory and production complex that sprawled over a 160-acre site. It opened in 1873.

In the final years of his life McCormick successfully promoted his business abroad, taking the reaper to the both the Pacific and South America. McCormick died in 1884, leaving the business safely in the hands of his enterprising son, Cyrus McCormick, Jr.

CONTEXT AND CONCLUSIONS

In 1831, the year that McCormick invented his mechanized reaping machine, 80% of all workers in the United States worked in farming. By the 1930s this figure was down to just 2%. That dramatic reduction, which freed up the workforce to better mankind in other ways than through the drudgery of manual agricultural work, is largely due to Cyrus Hall McCormick and his "Virginia Reaper." The effects of his achievements cannot be overstated. The commercial success of his machine accelerated the colonization of the West Coast, and allowed for the wholesale exploitation of the nation's bread basket, the Midwest, which in turn allowed for a rapid expansion in the United States population. This growth, coupled with the release of workers from work on the land, was a significant factor in the growth of the United States as the biggest economy in the world.

Would this have happened without McCormick? Possibly, but McCormick was blessed with talents that many of his competitors lacked. His inventiveness extended beyond the creation of machines. He pioneered marketing innovations such as installment plans, commission sales, and money-back guarantees, that ensured every farmer who wanted a McCormick reaper could have one.

> McCormick continued to manage his business well into his seventies. It was quite a feat, considering some of the severe setbacks he suffered.

1333

MANAGEMENT GIANTS

CLOSE BUT NO CIGAR

John Deere
Inventor and entrepreneur John Deere was a contemporary of Cyrus Hall McCormick. A blacksmith by trade, Deere invented the first self-polishing steel plow in the 1830s, just as McCormick was testing his reaping machine. In the end, McCormick's invention proved the more significant of the two. By 1855 Deere was selling 13,000 plows a year. He went on to found Deere & Company in 1868, which is still around today. He survived McCormick by two years, dying in 1886.

Obed Hussey
The "almost-ran" of agricultural invention, Obed Hussey could justifiably lay claim to the invention of the reaping machine. A former whaler, Hussey patented his device in 1833, a year before McCormick. However his big mistake was to stay in Baltimore, Maryland, miles from his market. McCormick bit the bullet and moved from Virginia to Chicago in the Midwest. Hussey also lacked McCormick's flair for marketing and was unwilling to accommodate improvements to his design suggested by others.

FOR MORE INFORMATION

Books:
Casson, Herbert N. *Cyrus Hall McCormick: His Life and Work.* Chicago, IL: A. C. McClure & Co., 1909.
McCormick, Cyrus. *The Century of the Reaper—Cyrus Hall McCormick & Business.* Boston, MA: Houghton Mifflin Co., 1931.

J. P. Morgan

J. P. Morgan was one of the greatest financiers of his age. As a child he kept a close account of the receipt and expenditure of his allowance. As an adult he parlayed his attention to cash flow into a large fortune. He saw the Civil War as an opportunity to make money, and in 1862 he founded his own company, Dabrey, Morgan, and Co. By 1871 he had teamed up with the firm of Drexel to form Drexel, Morgan, and Co. He swiftly established himself as one of the leading financiers in New York. Industrialists and governments regularly turned to him for advice, and he helped avert a U.S. financial crisis in 1895. Morgan attempted to unify the railroad bosses in opposition to the U.S. government. A powerful influence in the formation of so-called industry "trusts," his business empire was eventually cut down to size by President Theodore Roosevelt.

J. P. Morgan—the man who bankrolled the United States.

1837	Born.
1857	Joins Duncan, Sherman, and Co.
1862	Founds Dabrey, Morgan, and Co.
1871	Teams up with the firm of Drexel to form Drexel, Morgan, and Co.
1879	Puts together stock offering of $18 million for the New York Central Railroad.
1887	U.S. government passes the Interstate Commerce Act.
1895	Helps avert U.S. financial crisis.
1907	Bails out U.S. government again.
1912	Appears before Pujo Committee.
1913	Dies.

BACKGROUND AND RISE

J. P. Morgan was born in Hartford, Connecticut, on April 17, 1837. In the year of his birth the United States was plunged into financial gloom. Morgan, however, was unaffected; his father was a rich commodity broker who managed to make the most of the financial downturn. While he was still a boy, his father moved the family to Boston where he became involved in the cotton trade.

Morgan took an early interest in business. Spurning childhood games, he spent much of his time poring over his accounts (a habit he carried with him throughout his life), detailing the receipt and expenditure of his allowance. He had a bookish nature—partly a result of his interest in business and money, and partly a result of a sickly constitution. Morgan was never a popular child at school. His aloof manner failed to impress his classmates, just as it would later alienate the

> Morgan was never a popular child at school. His aloof manner failed to impress his classmates, just as it would later alienate the U.S. public.

U.S. public. His habits, such as writing to Paris in fluent French to order a pair of $900 boots, only served to reinforce the impression of arrogance.

Morgan's education was in keeping with his privileged status. When his family moved to London, he was dispatched to a private school in Switzerland. He then studied at the University of Göttingen in Germany and so impressed his tutors that he was asked to stay on as an assistant to one of the professors. The ambitious Morgan declined, insisting that he had to start out in business.

DEFINING MOMENTS

Morgan returned to the United States, and in 1857 joined Duncan, Sherman, and Co., a firm with which his father had an association.

When the Civil War broke out in 1861, Morgan treated it not as a calamity but as an opportunity. He avoided enlistment through the accepted practice among the wealthy of paying a substitute to take his place (the going rate was $300). In 1862 he left Duncan Sherman and founded his own company, Dabrey, Morgan, and Co. While the war raged, Morgan piled up the profits. By 1864 he had amassed over $50,000. The war ended, but Morgan continued to go from strength to strength. By 1871 he had teamed up with the firm of Drexel, based in Philadelphia, to form Drexel, Morgan, & Co., based on the corner of Wall Street and Broad Street in New York.

Morgan swiftly established a reputation as one of the leading financiers in the United States. His salary was more than $500,000—an astronomical amount at the time. It was during the 1870s that his association with the railroads began. The financing of the railroads required significant private capital, something that Morgan was only too happy to arrange.

His importance in the railroad business grew to the extent that leading players would turn to him to resolve disputes and offer his opinion. In an industry where companies fought increasingly hostile battles to gain

"The first thing is character . . . Money cannot buy it . . . because a man I do not trust could not get money from me on all the bonds in Christendom."
J. P. Morgan

supremacy, Morgan found himself playing the role of mediator.

When the U.S. government passed the Interstate Commerce Act in 1887, banning price-fixing collusion among railroads, the railroad companies naturally turned to Morgan again to organize a response. Obtaining a lasting consensus among the distrustful company bosses proved a task beyond even his talents. The misguided effort suggests a man whose ego was beginning to run out of control. Not only did he fail to unite the railroads against the government, he succeeded in setting himself up as the head of a conspiracy and thus an obvious target for the U.S. government, which was aiming to cut powerful business interests down to size.

By the 1890s Morgan had turned into a figure of hate among the U.S. public. Yet, despite this perception, Morgan's greatest public service lay ahead of him. In 1893 the withdrawal of funds from the United States by British investors sparked a financial crisis. As banks failed and the stock market collapsed, the U.S. government resorted to shoring up the financial system with its gold reserves. Statute prohibited the value of the reserves from falling below a prescribed level. The magic figure was $100 million in gold. In January 1895 gold reserves collapsed to $58 million and the treasury secretary John Carlisle turned to Morgan to save the day. Morgan proposed a syndicate of investors who would sell gold coin to the U.S. Treasury, paid for with newly issued bonds. It was a brilliant solution, as it provided not only an economic way out but also a politically expedient one. Morgan went further and guaranteed the plan to the then president, Grover Cleveland. The Morgan syndicate intervention succeeded in stopping the financial slide and made Morgan a considerable profit, estimated at anywhere between $250,000 and $16 million.

This episode merely reinforced Morgan's already legendary financial prowess. He followed his rescue of the U.S. financial system with a series of breathtaking deals such as the financing of United States Steel, the largest steel corporation in the world. From the 1900s onward he devoted his attention to consolidating the railroad companies through his concern the Northern Securities Corporation, and to building a shipping trust. Unfortunately for him, however, the incumbent president, Theodore Roosevelt, had decided that political advantage could be gained by cracking down on the so-called trusts. As the well-known figure of Morgan stood behind the Northern Securities Corporation, Roosevelt decided that it should be made an example of. This time Morgan had met his match. Apart from a brief respite in 1907, when a U.S. president again turned to him for salvation during a financial crisis, Morgan's power waned.

By then in his 70s, Morgan devoted more time to his hobby of collecting art and to his private life. He died in Rome at the age of 76.

CONTEXT AND CONCLUSIONS

J. P. Morgan was a remarkable businessman. His success owed much to his self-belief and opportunism, and a little to his wealthy and well-connected father. He suffered ill health throughout his life, particularly the periodic embarrassment of a large red bulbous nose, a result of eczema, the appearance of which would inevitably send him into deep melancholia. Yet despite frequent periods of illness-induced rest and recuperation, Morgan managed to build a string of business interests in the fashionable industries of the day—railroads, shipping, and electricity. He also, on more than one occasion, financed the U.S. government out of a mess.

Although not as wealthy as the likes of Carnegie or the Vanderbilts, Morgan amassed a fortune worthy of Croesus. He also accumulated a fabulous hoard of art treasures—a who's who of the old masters, including works by Vermeer, Gainsborough, Rembrandt, and da Vinci—as well as one of the finest libraries in the world. His reputation as a proud, vain, arrogant, and greedy man is justified. But he could be generous when it interested him. To a woman who offered him one of a missing pair of porcelain figures, he gave a handsome sum of money and a cottage in Wales.

> Obtaining a lasting consensus among the distrustful company bosses proved a task beyond even his talents. The misguided effort suggests a man whose ego was beginning to run out of control.

1335

MANAGEMENT GIANTS

CLOSE BUT NO CIGAR

Jay Gould

A U.S. financier born in 1836, Gould was the most despised and underhanded of the "robber barons." He started out as a mapmaker and publisher of local history, then inveigled his way into a tannery business. He gained full control when his partner committed suicide. In the 1860s he took to speculating on the railroads. There followed a period of unscrupulous dealings, bribery of officials, and dubious financial practices that would rival if not surpass the worst examples of modern times. Gould emerged from the 1860s/1870s with a fortune of some $25 million (many others lost the shirts off their backs). A neurotic man who suffered terribly from dyspepsia and took his personal chef with him wherever he traveled, Gould was the driving force behind the expansion of the railroads across vast tracts of the United States. He died from tuberculosis, aged 57.

FOR MORE INFORMATION

Books:
Wheeler, George. *Pierpont Morgan and Friends: The Anatomy of a Myth*. Englewood Cliffs, NJ: Prentice Hall, 1973.
Winkler, John. *Morgan the Magnificent: Life of J.P. Morgan*. New York: The Vanguard Press, 1932.

Web site:
JPMorgan: **www.jpmorgan.com**

Akio Morita

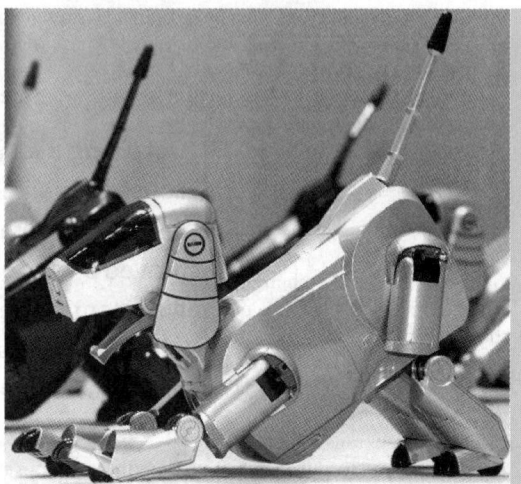

Akio Morita passed up the opportunity to lead an easy and secure life at the helm of the family sake business. Instead he chose to pursue his love of electrical engineering and start his own business, with all the risks that entailed. Starting with a prototype for a humble rice cooker, Morita's small company TTK grew into the electronic products giant Sony. In a lifetime devoted to his company, Morita gave the world a stream of innovative technologies and gadgets, from the portable transistor radio to the Sony Playstation. He was also the man responsible for making music portable, introducing the word "Walkman" into the global lexicon. In later life Morita refused to take a comfortable retirement, choosing to remain at the helm of Sony until he was forced to step down because of ill health.

Sony—always ahead of the pack.

1336

MANAGEMENT GIANTS

1921	Born.
1946	Cofounds Tokyo Tshushin Kyogu.
1953	Travels to United States to license transistor technology.
1958	Company changes name to Sony.
1960	World's first all-transistor television.
1961	First Japanese company to list on New York Stock Exchange.
1963	Moves with his family to United States to establish Sony America.
1980	Sony produces Sony Walkman.
1982	Sony produces first CD players.
1993	Suffers stroke while playing tennis.
1999	Dies.

BACKGROUND AND RISE

Akio Morita was born on January 26, 1921 in Nagoya, an industrial city in Japan. By Japanese standards, his family was affluent middle class. Morita was heir to the family rice-wine brewing business, although he showed little interest in his father's company. Instead he preferred to tinker with electronics equipment. He soon became an avid amateur electronics enthusiast, neglecting his studies to build electronic gadgets, including a radio and a record player.

> **Morita's biggest breakthrough was the transistor radio, despite the fact that the transistor was a U.S., not a Japanese, invention.**

Morita continued to pursue his interest in electronics in college by studying physics. He joined the Japanese army during World War II and rose to the rank of lieutenant.

After the war Morita passed up the easy career route of working in the family sake business. Instead, in 1946 he traveled to Tokyo, where he joined his future partner Masaru Ibuka. With a $530 loan, the two started a new company, Tokyo Tshushin Kyogu (TTK). It was housed in a bombed-out department store.

DEFINING MOMENTS

Morita eventually built one of the world's largest electronics companies, famed for its sophisticated miniaturized products. His first product prototype was a little less glamorous—a specialized rice cooker. But radio components and radio upgrades followed, and in the 1950s Morita produced his first major product, the tape recorder. It was the first in Japan.

Morita's biggest breakthrough was the transistor radio, despite the fact that the transistor was a U.S., not a Japanese, invention. Nor was the miniature radio that Morita produced using transistor technology the first of its kind. Morita had traveled to the United States in 1953 to license the technology from Bell Laboratories, but it was a joint venture between Texas Instruments and Regency Electronics that produced the world's first commercial transistor radio, the Regency TR-1, in October 1954.

TTK's first model was the TR-55, a set for which serious transistor radio collectors today would happily trade their grandmothers. Made in August 1955 in limited numbers, its production was restricted to Japan. TTK's first radio for export was the TR-63, produced in 1957.

Morita's small TR-63 was extremely successful for two main reasons. First, it was a truly innovative design, sold in a presentation box complete with a soft leather case, antistatic cloth, and earphone.

The second factor was Morita's dogged persistence. Taking the product direct to the distributors, he trekked around New York convincing electronic store owners to stock the TTK radio. He even turned down one large order because the potential purchaser didn't want the TTK company name on the product. He returned to Japan with a full order book.

"Recession isn't the fault of the workers. If management takes the risk of hiring them, we have to take the responsibility for them."

Akio Morita

In 1958 Morita pushed through a change of name for the company. A keen proponent of globalization, he was quick to realize that a name like Tokyo Tshushin Kyogu would prove an obstacle to capturing foreign markets. "We wanted a new name that could be recognized anywhere in the world, one that could be pronounced the same in any language," Morita said. He settled for Sony. This was a combination of the Latin word for sound—*sonus*—and the colloquial U.S. term "sonny." Morita's strategy clearly worked. When U.S. radio dealers were asked in a survey, "Have you ever handled Japanese radios?" they answered no. Asked whether they had ever dealt with Sony radios, they returned an unequivocal yes.

Over the years TTK/Sony produced a steady stream of innovative electronic products: the pocket radio in 1957, the world's first all-transistor television in 1960, and in 1968 the first home videotape recorder.

In 1963 Morita moved to the United States with his family and establish the Sony Corporation of America. It was a bold move for a man from a country whose businessmen were traditionally isolationist and protectionist in outlook. Morita pushed Sony's products in the United States, positioning the brand as premium quality. Soon the company's products were available nationwide.

When Morita noticed that young people liked listening to music wherever they went, he proposed that the company develop a portable tape cassette player. Morita's colleagues were unconvinced there was a market for a tape player of any size that lacked a recording facility. Morita stuck to his guns and persuaded his colleagues, and the Walkman was born in 1980. In a characteristically idiosyncratic move, there was no market research to back Morita's hunch. "The public does not know what is possible. We do," he said.

Interestingly, "Walkman" was not the product's universal name in the early days. Sony America thought the name poor English and changed it to "Soundabout" for the U.S. market. In Sweden it was known as "Freestyle" and in the United Kingdom, "Stowaway." Morita wasn't enthusiastic about this approach. As soon as he received a bad set of sales figures he used it as an excuse to change the name to Walkman throughout the world. The word has since become part of the global lexicon.

Another Sony innovation was video technology. Sony's Betamax technology lost out to VHS in the video standards war, but the company was instrumental in making home video recording a mainstream technology.

As the company's profits grew, Morita relentlessly pursued his vision of globalization. He used the expression "think globally, act locally" to describe his philosophy of corporate values that transcended national boundaries.

Management thinkers such as Theodore Levitt and later Kenichi Ohmae popularized the phrase, and it became part of the business vernacular.

Having built Sony into a multibillion dollar company, Morita, by now a billionaire himself, refused to let up. Still brimming with energy, he spent time indulging in pastimes such as scuba diving, skiing, and tennis, all of which he started when he was past 50. He pursued a relentless schedule until he suffered a stroke while playing tennis. Ill health forced him to resign as president of Sony in 1993, and he died in October 1999.

CONTEXT AND CONCLUSIONS

Akio Morita, along with entrepreneurs like Eiji Toyoda and Soichiro Honda, ranks as one of Japan's greatest business executives. Blessed with extraordinary drive, Morita was a risk-taker who would doggedly pursue his instincts. Time and again he followed his intuition, beginning with his original rejection of the safe option of working in the family business in favor of starting an electronics company with virtually no experience. The scale of his ambition was apparent in his decision to take his business to the United States at a time when Japan was not yet celebrated for its manufacturing techniques or the quality of its products.

It was Morita who helped put Japanese innovation on the world map by pushing through his globalization agenda, and, by backing his vision, he established Sony as a truly global company. He is responsible for making Japanese electronics a byword for innovative design and function.

> **As soon as he received a bad set of sales figures he used it as an excuse to change the name to Walkman throughout the world. The word has since become part of the global lexicon.**

1337

MANAGEMENT GIANTS

FOR MORE INFORMATION

Books:
Morita, Akio, with Edwin M. Reingold and Mitsuko Shimomura. *Made in Japan: Akio Morita and Sony*. New York: Dutton, 1989.
Nathan, John. *Sony: The Private Life*. Boston: Houghton Mifflin, 2001.

Web site:
Sony: **www.sony.com**

"All you need is the best product in the world, the most efficient production in the world and global marketing."

Akio Morita

Rupert Murdoch

Rupert Murdoch is one of the best-known media barons of the modern age. After finishing his education at Oxford and a stint at the *Daily Express* newspaper, Murdoch returned to his native Australia to take over from his father at the helm of the *Adelaide News*.

He moved on to expand his media empire through a spate of acquisitions across the globe. In the 1980s he branched into movies and television, acquiring 20th Century Fox and Fox TV. In the United Kingdom he bought *The Times* and *The Sunday Times*, and emerged victorious from a bitter battle with the printers' unions. By the end of the 1980s the empire was mortgaged to the hilt, but after a major debt rescheduling exercise, Murdoch marched on into the 1990s, acquiring Star TV in Asia.

Rupert Murdoch—the man behind the headlines.

Year	Event
1931	Born.
1950	Attends Oxford University, England.
1952	Works in Fleet Street on the London *Daily Express*. Returns to Australia.
1960	Buys the *Sydney Daily Mirror*.
1964	Founds the *Australian*.
1969	Buys the *News of the World* and the *Sun* in the United Kingdom.
1976	Buys the *New York Post*.
1981	Buys *The Times* of London.
1986	The "battle of Wapping."
1990	Saves business empire by restructuring debt.
1993	Buys into Star TV in Asia.
1997	Fox releases *Titanic*, biggest grossing film ever.
2002	Attempts to merge Sky TV with GM's Direct TV founder.
2002	Collapse of ITV Digital leaves Murdoch in control of 30% of U.K. media.
2002	Worldwide assets $42 billion, revenue $16 billion.
2003	U.S. regulators approve News Corp plans to move into satellite TV market.
2003	Son James elected to BSkyB board.
2004	News Corp moves stock from Australia to United States.

BACKGROUND AND RISE

> A restless child, he was more likely to be found cartwheeling across the outfield during play than participating in the school cricket match.

Now a U.S. citizen, Keith Rupert Murdoch was born in Melbourne, Australia, on March 11, 1931. His early education took place at Geelong Grammar school in Geelong, Victoria. He was not an impressive student—he admits he was "bone lazy" at school—other than in English, where his grades were above average. He also lacked sporting prowess. A restless child, he was more likely to be found cartwheeling across the outfield during play than participating in the school cricket match. His lack of interest on the athletic field led to him being disciplined on more than one occasion.

In 1950 he was sent to England to study economics at Worcester College, Oxford. While there, he ran unsuccessfully for president of the Labour Club—an interesting choice for a man whose political sympathies lay with the brand of right-wing ideology later embodied by Margaret Thatcher. His real education, however, took place on the *Daily Express* newspaper in Fleet Street, where he worked before returning home to Australia in 1952.

Back in Australia Murdoch, like the media baron William Randolph Hearst before him, was handed the opportunity to run a newspaper. On the death of his father, the Melbourne publisher Sir Keith Murdoch, he inherited the *Adelaide News*. It was the start of Murdoch's mercurial career as a news proprietor and media mogul.

DEFINING MOMENTS

To begin with the board was reluctant to hand over complete control of the newspaper to the young tyro. But Murdoch wasn't a man to take no for an answer, even at this early stage in his career. He steered the newspaper in an avowedly populist direction. Headlines like the sensationalist "Queen eats a rat" boosted its circulation and gave it a new lease on life.

Murdoch's success with the *Adelaide News* spurred him on. He bought the *Daily Mirror* in Sydney and dabbled in television. His newspaper acquisitions were driven by opportunity rather than rationale at this point. "We tended to take the sick newspapers, the ones that weren't worth much, that people thought were about to fold up," he later observed. In 1964 he made his boldest move yet, founding the *Australian*—a national newspaper. The *Australian* gave Murdoch political clout

---

"I'm not going to claim that we fought the battle of Wapping because we wanted to bring a silver age to British journalism."

Rupert Murdoch

and influence and made him a national figure, though commercially it was less successful.

Murdoch moved on from these early triumphs to expand his media empire through a spate of acquisitions across the globe. In the United Kingdom in 1969, he galloped in as an improbable white knight to save the *News of the World*, a downmarket and populist paper, from falling into enemy hands. The enemy in this case was Robert Maxwell, the Czech-born entrepreneur and budding media mogul. The owners of the paper, the Carrs, were reluctant sellers and strongly opposed a sale to a "foreigner." However when no home-grown business executive would come to their aid, they turned to the Australian Rupert Murdoch. It was the deal that gave Murdoch a toehold in the United Kingdom. Later that year he bought the newspaper the *Sun* for £500,000. In 1976 he added the *New York Post* to his growing empire. He subsequently lost, then regained, control of the newspaper. All the newspapers he acquired received the Murdoch treatment, adopting a right-wing, populist tone.

In 1981 Murdoch made an acquisition that was to have a long-lasting impact on newspapers in the United Kingdom. Fighting off fierce competition, he bought *The Times* of London. A serious newspaper, it seemed an unlikely target. Yet it was a clever purchase as it allowed him to reach a far broader cross-section of the British public. What followed was even more unexpected. Murdoch set himself on a collision course with the powerful U.K. printers' unions, challenging their inefficient working practices. He built a new printing plant at Wapping, away from Fleet Street, the traditional home of the London press, introduced computerization, and cut out the unions. The unions decided to make Wapping their Waterloo, and for most of 1986 the plant was under virtual siege, becoming the site for a pitched battle between the progressive Murdoch troops and the traditionalist unions. The outcome was a victory for Murdoch and his no-nonsense approach to business.

Wapping was a defining moment not only in union history in the United Kingdom, but in the world's perception of Murdoch. He emerged from the episode as a tough, ruthless proprietor who would go to almost any lengths to achieve his objectives. The truth was a little more prosaic. If Murdoch hadn't challenged the unions, someone else would have: Margaret Thatcher's Conservative government and the introduction of tough new antistrike legislation had provided a political context that was bound to result in such a battle. And there could be no resisting the march of technological progress—even in the printing industry.

The rest of the 1980s saw Murdoch branch into movies and television, acquiring Fox Studios in the United States in 1985, and seven Metromedia TV stations in 1986. By the end of the 1980s, however, Murdoch had overstretched himself, and a massive debt rescheduling exercise was required in 1990. This successfully shored up his empire. Murdoch then marched on through the 1990s,

one deal coming hard on the heels of another. Today his business empire is a truly global one: in all, he has over 750 businesses in over 50 countries. At the end of 2002 his holding company, News Corporation, was worth some $42 billion, with revenues of $16 billion. Companies in the News Corporation empire include Harper-Collins Publishers, BSkyB, News International, the Los Angeles Dodgers, Fox TV, and Star TV.

Murdoch made his first move into Internet business in 1999 by taking a stake in WebMD, the company established by Jim Clark as Healtheon. By 2002, News Corporation held 30% of U.K. media. BSkyB was given a boost by the demise of ITVDigital, a situation frustrating to the British Office of Fair Trading who had criticized the station just a year before for its dominant position. Murdoch attempted to build similar domination in the United States with an attempt to merge GM-owned Direct TV with his own Sky TV, but the merger was blocked by the Federal Communications Commission.

Murdoch continues to work long days at a fast pace and shows little sign of slowing down. There is endless speculation in the media about who will eventually succeed him, his children (Lachlan, James, and Elisabeth Murdoch) being the main candidates—although both Lachlan and Elisabeth have moved away from the family fold in recent years. His third wife, Wendy Deng, is another possible candidate. For now, though, as demonstrated by his recent attempts to merge GM-owned Direct TV with his own Sky TV, megabillionaire Murdoch retains an iron grip on his empire.

> Wapping was a defining moment not only in union history in the United Kingdom, but in the world's perception of Murdoch.

CONTEXT AND CONCLUSIONS

Murdoch has more than his share of critics, many of them strident. He is accused of a variety of sins from wielding too much power to "dumbing down" his media vehicles. Perhaps the criticism is overdone. Murdoch has an innate sense of what the public wants, and he makes sure he provides it. He is an astute pragmatist and brilliant entrepreneur who has built the world's first global media empire through instinct, talent, and hard work.

FOR MORE INFORMATION

Books:
Crainer, Stuart. *Business the Rupert Murdoch Way*. New York: Capstone, 2001.
Regan, Simon. *Rupert Murdoch: A Business Biography*. London: Angus & Robertson, 1976.

Web site:
News International: **www.newsinternational.com**

1339

MANAGEMENT GIANTS

David Ogilvy

It was fortunate for the world of advertising that David Ogilvy eventually found his way to its door. But he took a circuitous route. After working in Paris, he returned to England and pursued a career as an Aga cooker salesman. Next he dallied with advertising at the agency Mather & Crowther, enjoying the bright lights of London before packing his bags and heading for the United States. A job as a pollster for Dr. George Gallup was followed by a stint as a tobacco farmer with the Amish community in Pennsylvania. Finally in 1948, in his late thirties, Ogilvy started his own advertising agency. With a flair for copywriting, he was soon acknowledged by competitors and clients alike as one of the most brilliant advertising executives of his generation. He retired in 1975 after building Ogilvy & Mather into a business with annual billings of $800 million.

David Ogilvy was rarely lost for words.

1911	Born.
1938	Travels to the United States.
1948	Starts new advertising agency, Hewitt, Ogilvy, Benson, & Mather.
1960	Challenges the advertising industry practice of charging 15% commission.
1963	Publishes *Confessions of an Advertising Man*.
1965	Merges firm with Mather & Crowther to form Ogilvy & Mather.
1975	Steps down from position as creative head.
1999	Dies.

BACKGROUND AND RISE

The son of a stockbroker, David Ogilvy was born on June 23, 1911 and educated at Fettes School, a prestigious private school near Edinburgh, Scotland. What he lacked in natural academic ability he made up for in scholarly application, securing a scholarship to study history at Christ Church at Oxford University.

When he left Oxford, the young Ogilvy sought adventure abroad. In France he worked in the kitchens of the Hotel Majestic. Tiring of *la vie parisienne*, he returned to England to sell a new type of stove, the Aga. As a salesman Ogilvy proved a great success, so much so that he was asked to write a manual for the Aga salesforce on how to sell the stove. (Thirty years later, the editors of *Fortune* magazine announced that it was probably the best sales manual of all time.) Ogilvy sent his manuscript, "The Theory and Practice of Selling the Aga Cooker," to his brother, who was working at the London-based advertising agency Mather & Crowther. His winning way with words earned him a place as a trainee at the agency.

DEFINING MOMENTS

Ogilvy enjoyed the London lifestyle, partying till dawn at every opportunity. He combined his social life with hard work, showing a natural aptitude for his new vocation. Very early on he began to develop his own theories about advertising. "Concrete figures must be substituted for atmospheric claims; clichés must give way to facts, and empty exhortations to alluring offers," he wrote in a presentation to his colleagues in the early 1930s.

In 1938 he left his job and embarked on another adventure. This time the United States attracted his interest. He enjoyed himself so much that he decided to stay, moving to Princeton, New Jersey, where he worked with Dr. George Gallup, the man behind the Gallup polls. The experience he gained working for Gallup was invaluable, as it provided him with insights into U.S. consumer preferences and the way they were formed.

During World War II Ogilvy worked for British intelligence in Washington. When the war ended, he decided to try his hand at tobacco farming, acquiring several acres of land in the heart of the Amish community in Lancaster County, Pennsylvania. Exactly what possessed Ogilvy to pursue an agricultural career is unclear. What is certain is that he was most unsuited to it, and before long he was back in New York.

It is fair to say that, without the help of his brother Francis, Ogilvy might never have become one of the great advertising figures of the 20th century. Casting around for a job, the 37-year-old enlisted the help of his brother to establish his own advertising agency in the United States. His brother not only rounded up $45,000 to help finance the new venture but also persuaded another British advertising agency, S. H. Benson, to invest a further $45,000 in return for a partnership. The newly created agency, Hewitt, Ogilvy, Benson, & Mather, opened in 1948. As an Englishman, Ogilvy struggled to win U.S. clients, although the addition of former J. Walter Thompson employee Anderson Hewitt helped. Hewitt saved the day when the business threatened to run out of capital after only a few months. His uncle was

the chairman of JPMorgan and he lent the agency $100,000 with no security. And it was Hewitt who brought in the first major account, Sun Oil, worth some $3 million.

Despite the agency's diminutive size, it was clear from the beginning that Ogilvy's advertising intuition set the company apart from its competitors. His style was evident in an early campaign for shirtmakers, Hathaway. Ads featured a man with an eye patch, known as the man from Hathaway, who supported the small shirtmakers from Maine in their efforts to take on the giant shirtmaker Arrow. Ogilvy used photographs, then still a rarity in advertising, featuring a male model complete with eye patch performing a variety of unusual tasks. The Hathaway campaign made Ogilvy's reputation and was an early example of his approach to brand building and supporting brands through brand image.

He followed this success with a campaign for Schweppes, the soft drink manufacturer. Putting to good use knowledge gained with Gallup, he assuaged U.S. consumer sensibilities about class with Commander Edward Whitehead, the distinguished-looking boss of Schweppes. Schweppes sales in the United States bubbled up by 500% over the following nine years.

Ogilvy's role at the agency was to be jack of all trades, master of most. The exception was administration, for which he had little time. To his credit he realized that this weakness was hampering the firm and employed Esty Stowell, a Benson & Bowles executive, as vice president in 1957. Stowell took responsibility for managing the entire agency, with Ogilvy retaining control of the creative department only.

"At 60 miles an hour the loudest noise in this new Rolls-Royce comes from the electric clock." This was Ogilvy's slogan for his Rolls-Royce campaign. It exemplified his approach of putting the product center stage. "Make your product the hero of the commercial," he famously entreated. In 1960 he challenged one of the industry's prized but anachronistic practices—the 15% commission. As usual his stance was not merely ethical, but guaranteed to attract publicity. It succeeded, bringing in new clients such as Shell Oil who were only too happy to exchange the 15% commission for a flat fee.

The 1960s was a big decade for Ogilvy. In 1963 he published his book *Confessions of an Advertising Man*, which sold well over half a million copies and cemented his position as an advertising guru. In 1965, the year after his brother's death, his firm merged with Mather & Crowther to form Ogilvy & Mather.

By 1975 Ogilvy & Mather was one of the top five advertising agencies in the world with around a thousand clients, offices in 29 countries, and billings of some $800 million. In the same year Ogilvy stepped down from his position as creative head to spend more time at his home in the south of France. In 1989, following a wave of mergers in the industry, Ogilvy's remaining share in the business was acquired by the WPP group.

CONTEXT AND CONCLUSIONS

For Ogilvy, the secret of success was simple: "First, make a reputation for being a creative genius. Second, surround yourself with partners who are better than you are. Third, leave them to get on with it." But the most important things that Ogilvy acquired in his time on Madison Avenue were the ability and creative flair needed to lead by example. "The most important ingredient in any agency is the ability of the top man to lead his troops," he said. He was a late starter in advertising at 39. Yet he still made it to the top—and made an indelible mark there. Ogilvy died on July 21 1999.

> Ogilvy's role at the agency was to be jack of all trades, master of most. The exception was administration, for which he had little time.

1341

MANAGEMENT GIANTS

CLOSE BUT NO CIGAR

Lord Saatchi
Charles Saatchi built not one but two successful advertising agencies. First there was Saatchi & Saatchi, the U.K. agency that helped win a general election with its "Labour isn't working" posters for the Conservative party. Then, when Charles and brother Maurice got a little overambitious and were kicked out of their own company after an ill-conceived bid for a well known bank, they started up another agency. The new agency was M&C Saatchi. They took a few prestigious clients with them. Soon Maurice received a peerage, and M&C Saatchi overtook Saatchi & Saatchi in the billings rankings.

James Walter Thompson
J. Walter Thompson bought out William James Carlton, owner of advertising "broker" Carlton & Smith, for $500 in 1877. The furniture cost $800. In 1887 the JWT Company became the first agency to write advertisements for their clients rather than just sell them advertising space. By 1909 JWT had opened in London. It went on to become one of the world's most successful agencies.

FOR MORE INFORMATION

Books:
Ogilvy, David. *Confessions of an Advertising Man*. New York: Atheneum, 1963.
Ogilvy, David. *Blood, Brains & Beer*. New York: Atheneum, 1978.
Ogilvy, David. *Ogilvy on Advertising*. New York: Crown, 1983.

Web site:
Ogilvy: **www.ogilvy.com**

David Packard

From a rented garage in Palo Alto, California, David Packard and Bill Hewlett founded one of Silicon Valley's most enduring IT companies—Hewlett-Packard. When Packard met Hewlett at Stanford University in the 1930s, Palo Alto was best known for its prunes. By the time he died, it had established itself as the epicenter of the most famous high-tech cluster in the world.

Packard graduated from Stanford in 1934 and, after a stint at General Electric, teamed up with Hewlett to start a rent-an-inventor company in a garage in Palo Alto. First-year profits were $1,539. By 1942, sales were $2 million. In the 1970s the company made a tactical switch to computing, and throughout the 1980s it was consistently among the top five IT companies. In the 1990s Packard revitalized it with a back-to-basics move.

David Packard, one half of the dynamic HP duo.

1912	Born.
1934	Meets friend and future partner Bill Hewlett at Stanford University, Palo Alto.
1938	After a stint at General Electric, teams up with Bill Hewlett once more.
1939	Starts Hewlett-Packard in a garage in Palo Alto with just $538 of capital.
1942	HP turnover is $2 million.
1970	The company declines to make wholesale layoffs when the U.S. economy hits a recession.
1972	HP introduces the handheld scientific calculator, the model 35.
1980s	HP consistently in top five computer manufacturers.
1990s	Back-to-basics drive revitalizes company fortunes.
1996	Dies.
2001	HP cuts 3,000 jobs.
2002	Compaq merges with HP.
2004	HP teams up with British Telecom.

BACKGROUND AND RISE

"We figured that people will accomplish more," Packard said, "if they are given an opportunity to use their talents and abilities in the way they work best."

Born into a middle-class family on September 7, 1912, David Packard grew up in Pueblo, Colorado. At an early age he decided that he wanted to be an engineer. Unlike the millions of children whose ambitions to become an astronaut, firefighter, doctor, or nurse come to nothing, he was not be shaken from his goal. Packard studied at Stanford University. It was there that he met his friend and partner-to-be, Bill Hewlett.

When he graduated in 1934 the United States was still recovering from the Great Depression. Packard took one of the few jobs available to an electrical engineering student, working at General Electric. He also studied for a master's degree at the Massachusetts Institute of Technology. In 1938 Packard returned to Palo Alto and teamed up with Bill Hewlett. They decided to start their own company.

DEFINING MOMENTS

The company was founded in 1939 with just $538 of capital. The original location, a Palo Alto garage, was to become part of Silicon Valley folklore. It sent a message to all future entrepreneurs that great businesses could grow from small beginnings. A number of corporate giants were later to be hatched in the humble garage.

The original plan was for Packard to become a kind of rent-an-inventor. But his creativity soon ran riot, and he and Hewlett began developing their own gadgets together. The inventions were many and varied. Early designs included an electric shock machine to help people lose weight and an optical device to trigger automatic urinal flushing. But the first invention that made money was a piece of equipment designed to help sound engineers make better recordings. By the end of the first year of business, Hewlett and Packard had amassed a profit of $1,539. The garage was replaced with more substantial premises in 1940. The company, by now named Hewlett-Packard, prospered during World War II, even though Hewlett joined the Signal Corps and left Packard to run the business. By 1942 sales were $2 million. In the immediate postwar period, however, business dropped off alarmingly. Nevertheless, when Hewlett returned from the military, a number of talented staff were hired, and the business began to improve again.

In a division of duties, Packard assumed the managerial role, with Hewlett in charge of engineering and R&D. Although Packard had little theoretical knowledge of

"We have a technique at Hewlett-Packard for helping managers and supervisors know their people and understand the work their people are doing . . . Management by Walking About."

David Packard

management—his only experience was growing the company—he proved a natural. He introduced a system of management that involved walking among the employees and maintaining a visible presence. This was in contrast to the idea, prevalent among companies at the time, that the management and the workforce were breeds apart and should have little to do with each other. That philosophy was perpetuated by corporate institutions such as the management dining room, where the great and the good tucked into a three-course culinary extravaganza while the workers huddled around their workstations eating bologna sandwiches.

Packard, however, spurned the trappings of executive status. He maintained a policy of openness, making himself available to speak to employees. His accessibility and the practice of Management By Walking About (MBWA for short) endeared him to the staff. Packard repaid their respect by empowering them in their daily work. "We figured that people will accomplish more," Packard said, "if they are given an opportunity to use their talents and abilities in the way they work best." While many managers have paid lip service to worker empowerment and enlightened management practice, these are often the first casualties in times of difficulty and economic downturn. Not in the case of Hewlett-Packard, however. In 1970, when the U.S. economy slipped into recession, Packard did not make wholesale layoffs. Instead, he agreed to a new working pattern with the staff. Employees worked nine days in every two weeks instead of ten. In addition, management and workforce alike took a 10% pay cut.

Within a year, the U.S. economy was staging a recovery. Packard had avoided the unnecessary expense of layoffs followed by rehiring. Besides following forward-looking human resource policies, he took an innovative approach to organizational structure. "I've often thought that after you get organized you ought to throw the chart away", he stated. It wasn't that Packard didn't believe in organization, it was just that he believed in small agile units operating within the company. So, whenever a division grew cumbersome and unwieldy, Packard would break it up into small units.

In 1972 Hewlett-Packard introduced a handheld scientific calculator, the model 35, and during the 1970s and 1980s the company moved into the computer business.

Throughout the 1980s, HP was one of the top five computer manufacturers in the United States. In the 1990s, however, it struggled as competitors began to out-innovate it. Packard's solution was a return to basics, back to Management By Walking About. Although both Packard and Hewlett were approaching 80, they took action to reinvigorate the company. The HP hierarchy had grown unwieldy, they decided, so they took a scalpel to the organization, cutting out unnecessary layers. The philosophy of small teams and less management was restored, as was Hewlett-Packard's competitiveness, and the company reclaimed its place among the leading IT corporations in the United States.

David Packard died in 1996, knowing that his company was once more in shape to compete with the best. Today, HP's future looks less certain, but many of Packard's enlightened management principles remain etched in the company's culture.

CONTEXT AND CONCLUSIONS

From a small engineering company founded in a garage, Dave Packard, with the help of his friend and fellow student Bill Hewlett, built a multinational technology company with over 100,000 employees and annual revenues in excess of $40 billion.

Packard's key contribution to Hewlett-Packard and to business, according to Bill Hewlett (his lifelong business partner and buddy) was "the HP Way," a set of values and management principles put together by Packard in 1957. In his book of the same name, he explains that one of the objectives of the company was "to maintain an organizational environment that fosters individual motivation, initiative, and creativity, and a wide latitude of freedom in working toward established objectives and goals." It is for this enlightened attitude to worker empowerment and the other forward-looking practices enshrined in *The HP Way* that Packard will probably be best remembered.

> That philosophy was perpetuated by corporate institutions such as the management dining room, where the great and the good tucked into a three-course culinary extravaganza while the workers huddled around their workstations eating bologna sandwiches.

1343

MANAGEMENT GIANTS

CLOSE BUT NO CIGAR

Joseph C. Wilson
Wilson staked his small company, Haloid Corporation, on a new, commercially untried technology developed by a physicist called Chester Carlson. The technology was xerography. The first copier, the 914, was shipped in March 1960. It was one of the most successful single products ever. In 1959 Haloid revenue was $2 million; in 1960 it was $4 million; in 1963 it was a staggering $422 million. The company went on to become the Xerox Corporation.

FOR MORE INFORMATION

Book:
Packard, David. *The HP Way: How Bill Hewlett and I Built Our Company*. New York: HarperBusiness, 1995.

Web site:
Hewlett-Packard: **www.hp.com**

"Anyone can build market share and, if you set your prices low enough, you can get the whole damn market."

David Packard

John H. Patterson

The seeds of John H. Patterson's (1844–1922) rise to fame were sown on his family's farm. If his father hadn't constantly asked him how much he charged customers for the farm produce, he might not have been interested in the invention of a local merchant. Patterson took that invention, the automatic cash register, and turned it into a multimillion dollar business, National Cash Register. On his way to a personal fortune, Patterson redefined the art of salesmanship, introduced the idea of the corporate classroom, and saved a town from drowning. He was a pioneer in linking productivity to better working conditions.

John Patterson, NCR's chief.

1844	Born.
1867	Graduates from Dartmouth College.
1884	Purchases National Manufacturing Company and renames it National Cash Register.
1887	Company holds first annual sales convention.
1893	New, modern factory building constructed.
1913	Dayton floods.
1915	Court of Appeals overturns Patterson's conviction on antitrust charges.
1922	Dies.

BACKGROUND AND RISE

Born near Dayton, Ohio, in 1844, John Henry Patterson spent his childhood working on the 2,000-acre family farm. One of eight children, Patterson would help out when he was growing up by selling his father's farm goods. The amounts charged for the produce would frequently go unrecorded, and Patterson would be interrogated by his father, day or night, about whom he had charged and how much they paid.

Patterson attended local schools, followed by Miami University and Dartmouth College, graduating with a B.A. in 1867. In the meantime he fought in the Union army in the Civil War.

When Patterson left college he was determined to go into business for himself. He saved money from a job collecting tolls on the Miami & Erie Canal and established himself as a coal retailer back in his hometown. From selling coal he moved into coal and iron ore mining with his brother Frank. Then, again with his brother, he established a mining supply store. Here the inventory sold well, but the profits failed to materialize. Since the brothers were adding a healthy markup, something else was clearly wrong. Patterson determined to track down the discrepancy. Hearing of a machine invented by local merchant that automatically recorded sales, he bought two.

DEFINING MOMENTS

Primitive though they were, when Patterson saw the machines he immediately appreciated the possibilities they offered. If he had a use for one, wouldn't every shopkeeper in the country? In 1884, moving swiftly, he bought out inventor Jacob Ritty's business for $6,500, changing the name from the National Manufacturing Company to National Cash Register. But when he looked over the books he discovered the business was losing money and, suffering a temporary loss of faith, offered $2,000 to get out of the contract. Luckily for him, the seller wasn't interested.

Patterson was forced to make a go of the cash register business. He acquired premises in a rundown section of Dayton known as Slidertown, and began manufacturing cash registers on a commercial scale. He was by no means an enlightened employer; he saw his work force only in terms of production. In return his employees, uninspired by their work and their boss, took advantage whenever they could. The result was poor quality—$50,000 worth of faulty machinery in one year—and poor performance.

Eventually it dawned on Patterson that if he were to treat his workers a little better, he might improve the quality of his products. He started in a small way by buying a property opposite the factory where the workers could get coffee. It was the first time any provision had been made for refreshments for them. He began buying other property in the neighborhood and gradually improving conditions in the surrounding area, where most of the work force lived. Turning his attention to the factory premises, he hired architects to design a new building that would be as comfortable for the work force as it was efficient for the work performed there. When the people of Dayton saw the new building—constructed predominantly from glass and steel—they laughed at Patterson, declaring that there wouldn't be an unbroken window in the building before a week was out. But Pat-

terson had the last laugh. His modern building, with its built-in lecture rooms, air conditioning, showers, and movie theaters, instilled a sense of civic pride in Slidertown. Very few windows were broken. Patterson even opened up his private estate to the public, including his golf course and swimming pool.

Patterson's style of paternalistic leadership wasn't always successful. His insistence that workers use the baths provided by the company and attend various entertainments caused resentment. By the time he had backed down, it was too late to stop a threatened strike. But in a masterly outflanking maneuver he gathered his employees together, reassured them that he understood the reasons for their dissatisfaction, and proclaimed that everyone needed a rest. At which point he promptly shut down the factory and went traveling. The stunned workers were triumphant at first, but as the weeks passed, triumph quickly turned to concern and then to despair. The workers telegraphed Patterson, imploring him to reopen the factory. After two months he returned to a hero's welcome. His pointed comments about there being several offers on the table to relocate his factory elsewhere did not fall on deaf ears.

When Patterson returned he didn't hold a grudge against his employees, and they in turn put in extra effort. Patterson's innovative ideas on sales were beginning to reap rewards. NCR was one of the first companies in the United States to train a professional salesforce. Sales agents had to memorize a 16-page, 4,500-word sales primer. Patterson would drop in on the agents and quiz them on the contents of the primer—anyone who failed was fired. By 1894 NCR was producing half a million copies of its sales newsletter, *Hustler*. Sales conventions were held annually after 1887.

Brilliant at promoting sales of NCR cash registers, Patterson was equally effective at stifling the sales of competitors' products. In fact he was sometimes too effective. Patterson called in a promising executive from the Rochester office to coordinate the company's response to the competition. The executive was a former piano salesman, Thomas J. Watson (who was later to found IBM). With Watson's help Patterson eliminated the competition by means of acquisitions and the vigorous defense of his cash register patents. So successful was his campaign that he attracted the unwelcome attention of the U.S. government. Against a backdrop of public antitrust sentiment, he and 28 other NCR executives each received a year's jail sentence and a $5,000 fine.

Patterson's reputation might have been permanently stained by the judgment were it not for the great Dayton floods. On the night of March 25–26, 1913, Dayton was submerged under 17 feet of water. Patterson personally took control of the situation. In the hours before the flood hit he organized safety and rescue plans and constructed hundreds of makeshift boats at the company's lumberyards, building rafts at the rate of one every seven minutes. For his role in the town's relief efforts he was dubbed "the Savior of Dayton." The townsfolk petitioned President Woodrow Wilson to pardon Patterson. The petition would probably have been successful had the lower court's decision not been overturned, in any case, by the Court of Appeals in 1915.

During World War I Patterson committed his company's resources to the war effort. He insisted on carrying out contracts on a fixed-fee instead of a cost-plus basis, refusing to profit from the war. He died on May 14, 1922.

> On his way to a personal fortune, Patterson redefined the art of salesmanship, introduced the idea of the corporate classroom, and saved a town from drowning. He was a pioneer in linking productivity to better working conditions.

CONTEXT AND CONCLUSIONS

Patterson is the perfect example of a man with the right product at the right time. National Cash Register replaced the pencil behind the ear of the grocery store clerk with on-the-counter, state-of-the-art technology. In addition—after an early conversion—he turned out to be a model employer. An early exponent of classroom learning in the corporation, Patterson was one of the first of the great entrepreneurs of his time to make the connection between improved productivity and better working conditions. And unlike many of his contemporaries, his heroism was not just corporate: he was a real-life hero, too, organizing the rescue and relief of his hometown from dramatic floods.

> Brilliant at promoting sales of NCR cash registers, Patterson was equally effective at stifling the sales of competitors' products.

1345

MANAGEMENT GIANTS

FOR MORE INFORMATION

Book:
Marcosson, Isaac F. *Wherever Men Trade: The Romance of the Cash Register.* Manchester, NH: Ayer, 1972.

"With money in your pocket, you are wise and you are handsome and you sing well too."

Yiddish proverb

Arthur Rock

Arthur Rock is the man credited with coining the term "venture capital." Without the venture capital industry, there would probably have been no new economy or information revolution. Without Rock, there might not be a venture capital industry. Rock was the first venture capitalist (VC) operating on the West Coast of the United States. He organized the funding that got the computer revolution under way when he helped eight researchers break out of William Shockley's laboratories to found Fairchild Semiconductors. Then, he rounded up financing for some of the biggest companies in Silicon Valley, including Intel and Apple. It wasn't just money that Rock supplied. He also provided sage advice from his seat on the board of directors. He was still passing on the benefit of his considerable experience well into his seventies.

Arthur Rock bestrides the venture capital industry.

1926	Born.
1948	Graduates from Syracuse University.
1951	Finishes MBA at Harvard Business School. Joins Hayden Stone.
1957	"Traitorous eight" leave Shockley labs.
1959	Fairchild Semiconductors formed.
1961	Founds the firm of Davis & Rock.
1968	Davis and Rock dissolved after a seven-year life. Backs Gordon Moore and Bob Noyce, who found Intel.
1970	Forms Arthur Rock & Associates; sets up on his own as Arthur Rock & Co.
1980	Invests in Apple Computing. Joins board of directors.
1993	Steps down from Apple board because of conflict of interests.
1994–1999	Director of Air Touch Communications.
1998	Appointed to board of governors of NASD.
2002	Named Business Leader of the Year.
2003	Donates $25 million to Harvard Business School.

BACKGROUND AND RISE

The son of a candy store owner, Arthur Rock was born in the United States in 1926. After graduating with an MBA from Harvard Business School in 1951, Rock went to work for Hayden Stone, a New York investment banking firm. Hayden Stone specialized in financing companies. At the time, the venture capital industry didn't exist in a formal sense: they tended to be private family organizations, such as the one run by the Rockefellers.

Rock's lucky break came when he was shown a letter sent to one of the firm's brokers by the son of a client. The writer of the letter was Eugene Kleiner, a scientist at William Shockley's laboratory in California. Shockley was a brilliant but erratic research scientist who pioneered research on the transistor. Unfortunately his people-management skills were negligible and he was verging on the paranoid, making the atmosphere at the labs extremely unpleasant. Revolution was in the air. Key employees decided that they could no longer work with Shockley, but, before the team was split up, Kleiner wrote a speculative letter to Hayden Stone asking if anyone knew of a place where they could continue to work together. Intrigued, Rock persuaded one of Hayden Stone's partners to fly out to the West Coast with him and meet Kleiner and his associates.

DEFINING MOMENTS

Kleiner explained that the research team wanted to investigate the possibility of manufacturing transistors using silicon. If the process worked, it would revolutionize the computer industry. Rock was impressed with the young scientists and agreed to help Kleiner raise $1.5 million to establish a separate company. Rock contacted a long list of potential investors, but managed to raise nothing more than a few eyebrows. Luckily, at the last moment, he thought of Sherman Fairchild.

Sherman Fairchild was the largest stockholder in IBM; he had financed Tom Watson Sr. when he founded the predecessor company to IBM. He was also an inventor. Fairchild thought Rock's proposal was a good one, and agreed to invest $1.5 million through Fairchild Camera and Instrument. Kleiner and his associates were given an option to buy all the stock for $3 million.

The new company was named Fairchild Semiconductors. It was the technology gene pool from which, eventually, the Silicon Valley high-tech phenomenon evolved. Rock's success with the Fairchild deal spurred him on to investigate other investment opportunities on the West Coast. He made friends with Tommy Davis, who was working for Kern County Land Company, advising the firm on using surplus cash to finance other

companies. Davis left in 1961 to join Rock, and together they formed the investment partnership Davis & Rock.

Investment in Rock's first partnership fund came largely from private individuals on the East Coast who were his contacts. Institutional investors showed little enthusiasm. From an investment of roughly $3 million of the fund's capital, over $70 million was returned to the limited partners. Unlike some later VCs, Rock's approach was about much more than just investing money. He also sat on the boards of companies he invested in, working closely with them to increase their chances of success. Rock was on the board of Teledyne, one of the fund's first investments, for 33 years. Another early investment was in Scientific Data Systems. The company was sold to Xerox in 1969 for some $990 million—in Rock's words, "a humongous deal in those days."

In 1970 Rock formed a new partnership, Arthur Rock & Associates. Fairchild Semiconductors was in a state of flux. Sherman Fairchild was dead and a new C.E.O., John Carter, was in charge of the Fairchild Group. Carter's ideas about business conflicted with the ideas of Bob Noyce and Gordon Moore, two of the key researchers. Disenchanted with life at Fairchild, Moore and Noyce approached Rock and explained that they wanted to start their own company to research and produce semiconductor memory. Rock raised $2.5 million from 25 investors, including $300,000 of his own money. It took him two days. The new company was called Intel. The world's largest producer of microprocessors started with a modest $5.5 million of private funding, raised on the strength of a business plan written on one and a half pages. Rock remained on Intel's board for over 30 years.

The financing of two of the most important companies in the history of computing would have been enough to ensure Rock's place in the pantheon of venture capitalists, but he followed Intel with another seminal computing company, Apple Computers. Mike Markkula, ex-vice president of Intel, tipped Rock off about the fledgling company. Rock was not immediately persuaded and decided to pay a visit to the San José Homebrew Computer Show to see for himself. When he arrived he was unable to get anywhere near the Apple stand because of the assembled crowds, desperate to get a glimpse of the mock-up computer the two young entrepreneurs, Steve Jobs and Steve Wozniak, were demonstrating. But despite the obvious interest, Rock invested only $57,000. As usual he assumed his position on the board, a position he relinquished years later only because of a conflict of interest.

His contribution to technology business was recognized in 1998 when he was appointed to the board of governors of NASD, the technology investment governing body. In 2002, he was nominated Business Leader of the Year, and in 2003 he set out to encourage others by donating $25 million to Harvard Business School to fund the Arthur Rock Center for Entrepreneurship.

A lot has changed during Rock's time as a venture capitalist. As Rock says, "It's just a different world. It's an order of magnitude different. The pace of venture capital has changed. You don't get much time to look at the company. Sometimes you have to make up your mind that day."

One of the questions Rock is asked most often is, "What makes a good VC?" Is it luck, or perhaps a technology background? Rock says neither. According to him, being a good VC is about the ability to listen; about having a diverse variety of interests; and, above all, about being able to read people. It's a talent that takes years to develop, and Rock has it in spades. He still works in the industry he helped to create. Based in San Francisco, he is a director on a number of boards, both profit and non-profit. And he still recalls the words of his Harvard professor: "If you're interested in building a business to make money, forget it. You won't. If you're interested in building a business to make a contribution to society, then let's talk."

> The world's largest producer of microprocessors started with a modest $5.5 million of private funding, raised on the strength of a business plan written on one and a half pages.

CONTEXT AND CONCLUSIONS

Arthur Rock is an important figure in postwar economic history. Rock lit the VC match that ignited the technology industry in Silicon Valley. Through his efforts, eight of the brightest researchers were able to form Fairchild Semiconductors. Without him, the best research team in its field would have scattered across California, the United States, or even the world. Instead they worked together to give the world the silicon chip and then to found Intel, the powerhouse of the personal computer revolution. Rock also helped shape the nature of the PC by investing in Apple Computers. The fact that Eugene Kleiner, one of the original "Fairchildren," later went on to found the VC firm Kleiner Perkins means that Rock can also lay claim to having helped create the modern VC industry.

> Rock lit the VC match that ignited the technology industry in Silicon Valley.

1347

MANAGEMENT GIANTS

CLOSE BUT NO CIGAR

Tom Perkins

After a stellar career with tech companies like Spectra-Physics and Hewlett-Packard, Tom Perkins founded the venture capital firm Kleiner Perkins in 1972. Perkins's partner in the firm was Eugene Kleiner, the man who brought Arthur Rock out to the West Coast. Kleiner Perkins and its later partnership incarnation (Kleiner Perkins Caulfield & Byers) were at the heart of the IT revolution on Sand Hill Road in Menlo Park. The firm pioneered the concept of incubators and hatched companies such as Genentech, Tandem Computers, America Online, and Amazon.

FOR MORE INFORMATION

Web site:
Intel: www.intel.com

"Money speaks sense in a language all nations understand."   Aphra Behn

John D. Rockefeller

MANAGEMENT GIANTS

In the course of his long life, U.S. industrialist John D. Rockefeller (1839–1937), the son of a farmer, progressed from being an office boy earning $25 a month to being an oil tycoon worth over $900 million. Starting work aged 16, Rockefeller had his own firm within three years and by 1862 had moved into the oil business. After buying out most of the local competition, Rockefeller set his sights on building a national oil company with a national delivery network. He accomplished his vision with Standard Oil, which by 1879 controlled 90% of the oil refining in the United States. Rockefeller withdrew from active management of the company in 1897, remaining president until 1911, when the Standard Oil trust was finally dissolved by the U.S. government. Rockefeller's final years were devoted to giving away the bulk of his huge fortune.

Rockefeller's Standard Oil helped keep the United States on the move.

1839	Born.
1855	Starts work at Hewitt & Tuttle.
1862	Enters oil refining business.
1869	Rockefeller, Andrews, & Flagler becomes the Standard Oil Company of Ohio.
1882	Standard Oil businesses brought under control of the Standard Oil Company.
1890	Nationwide distribution system reaches most towns in the United States.
1892	Trust dissolved by Ohio government. Reconstitutes as Standard Oil Trust (New Jersey).
1900	Standard Oil controls over three-quarters of the U.S. petroleum industry.
1904	80% of U.S. towns served by Standard Oil delivery carts.
1911	Resigns as president. Standard Oil Trust dissolved.
1913	Establishes Rockefeller Foundation.
1937	Dies.

BACKGROUND AND RISE

John D. Rockefeller was born in 1839 in Richford, Tioga County, New York, the eldest son and second of six children. His parents were farmers, and Rockefeller, along with his brothers and sisters, was expected to help out on the farm. Even at this tender age, the young Rockefeller displayed a keen business mind. He raised turkeys, sold them for a profit, and then lent the proceeds at 7%.

> **Even at this tender age, the young Rockefeller displayed a keen business mind. He raised turkeys, sold them for a profit, and then lent the proceeds at 7%.**

By the time Rockefeller was 14, his family had moved to Cleveland, Ohio. Here, in 1855, after a year at high school and a stint at Folsom Mercantile College, Rockefeller was offered employment as an office boy and assistant bookkeeper at the firm of Hewitt & Tuttle, produce commission merchants. No salary was agreed at the outset, and Rockefeller received no payment for 14 weeks, at which point he was handed $50 and put on $25 per month.

Rockefeller stayed at Hewitt & Tuttle for three years, leaving when the firm declined to meet his wage demands of $800 a year. Having spent the previous three years paying particular attention to how a business is run, Rockefeller decided to start his own.

DEFINING MOMENTS

With his partner, Morris B. Clark, and $1,000 borrowed from his father at 10%, Rockefeller started a produce business. He visited all the local farmers, charmed them, and left his card. The response was so good that, in its first year of business in 1859, the company's revenues were $500,000.

About this time oil was just beginning to make an impact in Ohio. Several refineries had been opened near Cleveland. Rockefeller, sensing the potential of the new fuel, wasted no time forming Andrews, Clark, and Co., oil refiners, in 1862. Later he sold his produce commission interests to Clark and bought out Clark's interest in Andrews, Clark, and Co., to form Rockefeller & Andrews.

By 1869 Rockefeller's firm had acquired a number of other similar small firms and was now called Rockefeller, Andrews, & Flagler. But the oil business generally was going through a tough time. With the proliferation of firms all trying to get in on the action, the price of oil became so severely depressed that many companies went bankrupt. Undeterred, Rockefeller chose to merge Rockefeller, Andrews, & Flagler into the Standard Oil Company of Ohio in 1869, with $1 million capital and himself as president.

He then proceeded to apply to Standard Oil's business

> "I believe it is my duty to make money and still more money and to use the money I make for the good of my fellow man according to the dictates of my conscience."
>
> John D. Rockefeller

the "combination" strategy that J. P. Morgan had so successfully applied to the steel industry. The best way to ensure survival, he figured, was to spread the risk of operating in such a volatile and risky industry. The obvious way to achieve this was to buy up competitors, both locally and elsewhere in the United States. By 1872 Standard Oil had acquired all the refining firms in Cleveland. In 1882, after a prosperous decade, all the businesses belonging to Standard Oil were brought under the single umbrella of the Standard Oil Trust.

The dominance of the Standard Oil Trust soon gave rise to a barrage of criticism. In 1892 the Attorney General of Ohio won a suit to dissolve the Trust. During the court case, brought in 1890, Rockefeller was put under severe stress; he lost all his hair, including his eyebrows, and was reputed to have suffered a nervous breakdown. The effects of the court case on Standard Oil were less dramatic. The company simply reformed as the Standard Oil Company (New Jersey), because the laws of New Jersey permitted a parent company to own the stock of other companies. The Standard Oil Company (New Jersey) controlled three-quarters of the U.S. petroleum business.

Rockefeller remained president of Standard Oil until 1911. That was the year in which the U.S. Supreme Court finally ordered its dissolution, declaring the company to be in contravention of the country's antitrust laws. The 38 companies that made up the oil giant were split into separate entities.

During his lifetime Rockefeller came in for much criticism, as well as some odd mythologizing. It was claimed, for example, that he would eat only bread and milk. Another persistent story was of his phenomenal capacity for hard work and long hours, something that Rockefeller denied all knowledge of. "People persist in thinking that I was a tremendous worker, always at it, early and late, winter and summer," he said. "The real truth is that I was what would now be called a 'slacker' after I reached my middle thirties . . . I never, from the time I first entered an office, let business engross all my time and attention."

The latter years of Rockefeller's life were spent carrying out philanthropic work. He gave over $35 million to the University of Chicago, founded the Rockefeller Institute for Medical Research, the Rockefeller Foundation, and the Rockefeller Sanitary Commission, which eradicated hookworm in the southern areas of the United States. At its height Rockefeller's wealth was $900 million. When he died, aged 97, on May 23, 1937, at his home in Ormond Beach, he had given away all but $26,410,837.

CONTEXT AND CONCLUSIONS

John D. Rockefeller created the modern oil industry. The impact of Rockefeller's business on the United States may have been less immediate than that of Edison's electric light or Ford's Model T automobile, but without the cheap gasoline that Standard Oil produced, it is likely that neither the widescale electrification of the country nor the mass-marketing of the car would have happened when they did.

One of Rockefeller's greatest attributes was his understanding of the importance of hiring brilliant people. "Men, not machinery or plant, make up an organization," was one of his sayings. He assembled a team of the brightest men in business and harnessed their collective abilities to drive Standard Oil's expansion. In later years he was vilified as the head of one of the hated "trusts" dominating industry in the United States. It should be remembered, however, that, despite its controlling influence, the establishment of the Standard Oil Trust saw the oil industry through some difficult times, and ensured its strength in the United States for the following decades.

> During his lifetime Rockefeller came in for much criticism, as well as some odd mythologizing. It was claimed, for example, that he would eat only bread and milk.

1349

MANAGEMENT GIANTS

FOR MORE INFORMATION

Book:
Chernow, Ron. *Titan: The Life of John D. Rockefeller, Sr.* New York: Random House, 1998.

Anita Roddick

Anita Roddick, the British businesswoman and founder of the cosmetics phenomenon The Body Shop, might never have started her business at all. It was an unusual combination of factors that led her to open her first store in 1976. But The Body Shop concept soon outgrew her small store in Brighton. Had the company expanded in the traditional manner, it might well have lost the small-business charm that made it so successful. Instead, Roddick expanded through franchises, a relatively new concept in the United Kingdom at the time, guaranteeing that the vibrancy and enthusiasm of the concept was maintained. In 2006 The Body Shop agreed to a £652 million takeover by French beauty giant L'Oréal. Roddick plans to continue spending much of her time and energy championing the ethical causes close to her heart.

Anita Roddick—the ethical face of capitalism.

1942	Born.
1960	Attends Newton Park College of Education in Bath.
1962	Travels to Israel on a study scholarship.
1971	Opens bed and breakfast business in Littlehampton.
1976	The Body Shop opens in Brighton selling environmentally friendly cosmetics.
1976	Ian McGlinn's investment enables second store to be opened.
1978	First informal franchises open. First franchise outside the United Kingdom opens in Brussels.
1984	The Body Shop goes public.
1988	The Body Shop opens in the United States.
1989	Roddick commissions environmental audit of all company's practices.
1998	Steps down as C.E.O.
2000	Sets up Anitaroddick.com to communicate environmental issues.
2000	Publication of *Business As Unusual*.
2001	Publication of *Take It Personally*.
2002	Steps down as co-chairman of The Body Shop.
2004	The Body Shop announces plans for £100 million expansion.
2006	Agrees to takeover by L'Oréal.

BACKGROUND AND RISE

Born in Sussex, England, in 1942, Roddick was the third of four children. Her parents ran a North American-style diner in the sleepy English coastal town of Littlehampton. After secondary school, despite being offered a place at the prestigious Guildhall School of Music and Drama, Roddick attended the Newton Park College of Education in Bath.

After college Roddick flitted from one job to another. In Paris she worked for the *International Herald Tribune*; she taught in England; then she worked for the United Nations in Geneva. After the UN, Roddick followed what became known as the hippy trail to Africa, the Far East, and Australia, making her way around the globe. Her stay in South Africa was cut short when she was ejected for breaking the apartheid laws by attending a jazz club on "nonwhites" night. Her rebellious spirit may have earned her an early ticket out of Africa, but it was to stand her in good stead when she later launched The Body Shop.

Returning to Littlehampton, Roddick settled down, married, had children, and with her husband Gordon opened a hotel and then a restaurant. Running both businesses eventually became too demanding on family life. The restaurant was sold, and Roddick's husband declared that he was planning an ambitious expedition of his own—intending to ride a horse from South America to New York City.

DEFINING MOMENTS

Unable to curb her entrepreneurial instincts, Roddick looked for another enterprise on which to concentrate, one that would also earn some money in her husband's absence. After some thought she came up with the idea of a cosmetics business with a difference: the use of natural ingredients. Her husband helped arrange a bank loan using the hotel as collateral, and Roddick bought premises next to a funeral parlor in the nearby town of Brighton.

On March 27, 1976, with her husband about to leave on his travels, Roddick opened for business, selling environmentally friendly cosmetics. The idea was not just to sell socially responsible products using natural ingredients, but to sell them in convenient small sizes that would tempt customers to try them out. Thus, many of The Body Shop's defining characteristics were decided upon at this early stage, though the decisions were often

"If you think morality is a luxury business can't afford, try living in a world without it."

Anita Roddick

based on cost effectiveness rather than any grand strategic plan. The walls were painted green, not in anticipation of the Green movement, but to hide the damp patches. Product packaging was minimal and recyclable, and Roddick wrote the labels out by hand.

The Brighton store prospered, and she was soon planning another in nearby Chichester. When the bank refused to finance her, she turned to a local businessman, Ian McGlinn, who agreed to put up £4,000 for a half share of the business. Roddick agreed. For McGlinn, it proved to be the investment opportunity of his life. By the time Roddick's husband returned in 1977, The Body Shop concept was unstoppable. Her friends and family ran the first few stores, but requests to establish branches elsewhere in the country were flooding in. To cater to the demand for stores, Roddick and her husband began franchising the concept. Potential franchisees would finance the business and agree to buy their inventory from Roddick, and, in return, would be licensed to use The Body Shop name. She interviewed many of the early franchisees herself. A high proportion of them were women, and she can justifiably claim to have helped change the traditional male-dominated image of entrepreneurs in the United Kingdom.

What she had started was not a conventional cosmetics business. Roddick had little time for the beauty industry, believing that it was in the business of selling unattainable dreams. The Body Shop was different. Roddick made no special claims for her products. In fact she didn't advertise, relying mainly on word of mouth to bring customers through the store doors.

"Making products that work—that aren't part of the cosmetic industry's lies to women—is all-important," Roddick has said. "Making sure we minimize our impact in our manufacturing processes, clean up our waste, put back into the community . . . we go where businesses never want to because they don't think it is the role of business to get involved."

Roddick espouses profits with principles. Through The Body Shop she has supported campaigns by Greenpeace, Friends of the Earth, and Amnesty International, among others. Messages on shopping bags and vehicles express The Body Shop's support for these causes.

In April 1984 the company became publicly listed. The stock price shot up on the opening day, and Roddick, her husband, and Ian McGlinn all became paper millionaires overnight. From one small store next to a funeral parlor, The Body Shop network has expanded to over 1,800 stores worldwide, offering over 400 products. Roddick, now one of the richest women in England, has been showered with awards as a result of both her business endeavors and her social conscience. Besides the titles of London's Business Woman of the Year and Retailer of the Year, she has received the United Nations' "Global 500" environmental award and the Order of the British Empire (OBE).

In 1994 Roddick brought in external management help to refocus the business. Unsurprisingly she found the shift from her hands-on role difficult to adjust to. In 1998 she stepped down as C.E.O., and remained as co-chair with her husband Gordon until 2002, when she adopted a new role as creative consultant to the company. In 2006, she attracted bouquets and brickbats when L'Oréal's acquisition of The Body Shop was announced. Spending less time with The Body Shop as a result of these changes allows her more scope to champion the causes she so passionately believes in. One of her first actions was to establish AnitaRoddick.com, a Web site devoted to raising awareness of issues she cares about. She has also been busy writing books. Business As Unusual was published in 2000, followed a year later by Take it Personally, a book encouraging people to take action to change the world.

> After college Roddick flitted from one job to another. In Paris she worked for the *International Herald Tribune*; she taught in England; then she worked for the United Nations in Geneva.

CONTEXT AND CONCLUSIONS

Displayed on the side of The Body Shop vehicles is the following: "If you think you are too small to have an impact, try going to bed with a mosquito." The phrase is one of Roddick's favorite quotations—not surprisingly, considering her achievements. She has captured a large share of the market with her ethically driven approach to business. She has built a global company from a one-woman cottage industry, changed the attitude toward businesswomen through her franchise operation, and, in addition, found time to make her voice heard championing the rights of minorities and unsung causes—often through her company.

> Roddick had little time for the beauty industry, believing that it was in the business of selling unattainable dreams. The Body Shop was different.

"Today's corporations have global responsibilities because their decisions affect world problems concerning economics, poverty, security and the environment." — Anita Roddick

Julius Rosenwald

Julius Rosenwald started in the retail business at the tender age of 21, with his own clothing store in New York. He then showed an excellent nose for an opportunity, first by ditching his retail business to manufacture men's summer clothing, and then abandoning manufacturing to join Sears, Roebuck as vice president. His big break was choosing Chicago as the base for his manufacturing business. There he met the entrepreneur R. W. Sears, who made his fortune with a mail-order business. Sears needed the right person to take his business into the 20th century—he chose Rosenwald. By the time Rosenwald died in 1932, the company had revitalized its mail-order business, expanded its product range, introduced innovative work practices, and opened hundreds of retail stores throughout the United States, leaving competitors like Montgomery Ward far behind.

Rosenwald racked up a catalog of success.

Year	Event
1862	Born.
1885	Moves to Chicago.
1885–1895	Manufactures men's summer clothing as Rosenwald & Weil.
1895	Takes share of Sears, Roebuck as sleeping partner.
1896	Becomes vice president of Sears.
1900–1906	Total sales increased from $11 million to over $50 million.
1908	Sears retires. Rosenwald becomes president.
1916	Over 40 million catalogs distributed.
1925	Opens first retail store. Becomes chairman. Personal holdings worth $150 million.
1932	Dies.
1999	Sears taken over by Barclay brothers.

BACKGROUND AND RISE

Julius Rosenwald was born in Springfield, Illinois in 1862. As a child he would sell goods door to door in his hometown. He pumped the bellows on the church organ, peddled pamphlets, and sold chromolithographs, the latest consumer craze. During the summer vacation, he worked in an ornamental goods store.

At age 16, Rosenwald left school to work for his uncle's wholesale clothing business in New York. By living frugally, he saved enough money so that at the age of 21 he could afford to buy a small retail clothing store on 4th Avenue.

One day Rosenwald was in idle conversation with the owner of a nearby business. The man, who manufactured summer clothing for men, revealed that he was struggling to keep pace with orders. Rosenwald turned the statement over and over in his mind until, in the middle of the night, he dramatically resolved to abandon his retail store. Chicago was the city that Rosenwald chose to start his new business. There, with partner Ju-

lius E. Weil, he formed Rosenwald & Weil, manufacturers and wholesalers of summer clothing.

DEFINING MOMENTS

One of Rosenwald's best customers was Richard Warren Sears of Sears, Roebuck and Company. Sears's one problem was that he needed more capital to expand. He asked if Rosenwald was interested in investing in the business. Rosenwald agreed, and took a quarter interest in Sears, Roebuck for $70,000.

To begin with, Rosenwald was a silent partner. But by 1896, Sears—who ran the company single-handedly—asked Rosenwald to join him as vice president. Over the next 30 years, Rosenwald transformed Sears, Roebuck into one of the largest retailers in the United States.

Rosenwald first turned his attention to the Sears, Roebuck catalog. As Ingvar Kamprad of IKEA would find out over 50 years later, Rosenwald discovered that if mail-order companies were less than honest in the wording and illustration of their catalogs, it damaged the reputation of the entire industry. Even Sears, Roebuck was guilty of delivering products that didn't always correspond to the promises of the lavishly worded and sumptuously illustrated catalog.

Rosenwald insisted on a fastidiously precise correlation between the advertisements in the catalog and the goods supplied. First, he ensured that every illustration and description in the catalog be carefully compared with the relevant article. He established laboratories and employed scientists to examine merchandise received from suppliers. Any defective goods were immediately rejected and returned. To increase consumer confidence, he introduced a novel concept—a "money back if not satisfied" guarantee, supported by an advertising campaign. In this way Rosenwald removed the burden of risk from the consumer and placed it squarely on the shoulders of Sears, Roebuck.

Once consumer confidence was secure, Rosenwald set about broadening the range of products offered in a mail-order catalog. Soon everything from buttons to bungalows was sold by mail order. Other innovations were introduced. To secure quality supplies, Rosenwald constructed factories employing over 20,000 workers. Technological innovations such as the conveyor belt were introduced (it was said that Henry Ford "borrowed" Rosenwald's idea for his assembly lines). The catalog was expanded, and special editions were introduced for seasonal goods and special events. New goods like shoes and books were featured in the catalog. Shoes, an unlikely candidate for mail order, earned revenues of $1 million a month. The sale of Encyclopedia Britannicas alone added an incredible $5 million in revenues to the annual balance sheet. Between 1900 and 1906, total sales increased from $11 million to over $50 million. By 1914 they had reached $100 million.

Rosenwald was also making changes to the way the company's employees were treated. He spurned the trappings of status, preferring to be seen as one of the workers. Asked what it felt like to have so many people working for him he replied, "I always think of them as just working with me." When he was presented with an oriental rug to cover the floor of his executive office, it remained rolled up in the corner. Rosenwald figured if linoleum was good enough for everybody else, it was good enough for him. "I have played only a very small part in the building up of Sears, Roebuck and Company," he modestly told his admirers. To improve the lot of his workers, Rosenwald introduced recreation facilities, as well as an innovative "employee savings and profit-sharing plan." True, his management style was a little paternalistic. He was overprotective of his female employees, for example; familiarity between men and women was forbidden at social functions, and the sexes were segregated in the cafeteria.

Eternally cost-conscious in business, Rosenwald encouraged his workers to be equally parsimonious. Employees who earned below $1,500 received a bonus on the anniversary of their joining the company. The bonus was a percentage of the annual salary, equal to the number of years an employee had worked for the company. Starting in the fifth year, it rose to 10% in the tenth year, and remained at 10% thereafter. His employees, Rosenwald suggested, should save the bonus.

On Sears' retirement in 1908, Rosenwald became president and, in 1925, chairman. In the 1920s he took the company in a new direction. The mail-order catalog was still an essential element of the Sears, Roebuck retail strategy, but now Rosenwald expanded into retail stores. In 1925 Sears opened its first retail store in Chicago. By 1929 there were 324 stores with the name Sears, Roebuck above the doors.

In his final years, Rosenwald focused his attention on philanthropy. He established the Julius Rosenwald Fund, a charity for the economic, medical, and cultural advancement of African Americans, with an endowment of $30 million. He gave money to aid the Jews in the Middle East and to help German children after World War I. He also endowed the University of Chicago and helped to establish the Museum of Science and Industry in Chicago. He died in 1932.

CONTEXT AND CONCLUSIONS

Julius Rosenwald took a promising business and turned it into a great one. Without his intervention, it is arguable whether Sears, Roebuck would have become the retailing giant it did. At the time Rosenwald joined, the reputation of the mail-order industry was under a cloud because of the less-than-scrupulous practices of many of the companies involved. Through a variety of innovations, Rosenwald breathed new life into a tired format. Greater choice, better quality, and a money-back guarantee were among the features that won the customers back. Internally, Rosenwald concentrated on ensuring a quality supply of merchandise and keeping the workforce happy. Finally, he moved to secure the future of the company by extending the brand and opening a chain of retail stores.

> He spurned the trappings of status, preferring to be seen as one of the workers.

1353

MANAGEMENT GIANTS

CLOSE BUT NO CIGAR

Aaron Montgomery Ward

Montgomery Ward is said to have founded the first dry goods mail-order business in 1872. He also coined the phrase "satisfaction guaranteed or your money back." But by 1900, after Julius Rosenwald had injected new life into Sears, Roebuck, Montgomery Ward's eponymous company began to trail its main rival. Montgomery Ward died in 1913, 13 years before his company opened its first retail store. Had he been alive in 1930, he might have sanctioned a merger with Sears—proposed but declined by Ward's directors. Instead his company's fortunes subsided until, in 2001, it shut its doors for the last time.

FOR MORE INFORMATION

Books:
Harris, Leon. *Merchant Princes*. New York: Harper & Row Publishers, 1979.
Werner, M. R. *Julius Rosenwald: The Life of a Practical Humanitarian*. New York: Harper & Brothers, 1939.

Web site:
Sears.com: **www.sears.com**

"Clothes don't make the man—but they go a long way toward making a businessman."

Thomas J. Watson, Sr.

David Sarnoff

David Sarnoff (1891–1971) was a media pioneer. He was responsible for the introduction of radio and television in the United States as forms of mass media. Born in Russia, Sarnoff emigrated to the United States in 1900; by 1930 he was president of the Radio Corporation of America (RCA). He went on to develop FM radio on a commercial basis and bring color television to the people of the United States. Behind Sarnoff's public success story with RCA, however, lay the personal saga of his long-running relationship with the inventor Edwin H. Armstrong. Originally based on friendship, the relationship descended into animosity and ended with Armstrong's suicide in 1954. Sarnoff was succeeded at RCA by his son, Robert, in 1965. The remaining years of his life were spent bitterly watching his son modernize the company that he had spent his life building.

David Sarnoff—RCA's biggest star.

1891	Born.
1916	Sarnoff states his vision for radio.
1919	Radio Corporation of America (RCA) incorporated.
1920	Cuts a deal with Armstrong to secure the latter's radio technology patents.
1921	RCA begins radio broadcasting.
1930	Aged 39, Sarnoff becomes president of RCA.
1933	Has new headquarters constructed for RCA. Armstrong invents FM.
1939	Introduces television to the United States just before World War II at the World's Fair.
1954	Introduces color television.
1965	His son Robert becomes president of the company; Sarnoff becomes chairman.
1971	Dies.

BACKGROUND AND RISE

David Sarnoff was born in Uzlian in Russia. His father, Abraham, was a Jewish painter who traveled to the United States in 1896, determined to earn enough money to bring the rest of his family across the Atlantic to join him. It took him four years.

When Sarnoff arrived in Manhattan on July 2, 1900, his father was renting a squalid apartment on the lower East Side. In the four years since Abraham had arrived in the sprawling metropolis, he had been struggling to make a living. Not only was he reduced to doing menial work for little pay, but his health had deteriorated to the point where he was unable to provide for his family. At the tender age of nine, therefore, Sarnoff became the family breadwinner.

> Like several other great business leaders of his generation, Sarnoff started out on the path to success in the employ of a telegraph company—in this case, American Marconi Wireless Telegraph.

He started by selling Yiddish newspapers on street corners, earning a quarter for every 50 papers sold. To supplement his income he delivered another paper in the morning and sang at the local synagogue for a small fee. Despite the long hours—he rose at 4:00 a.m. for the morning round—Sarnoff still managed to find time to study at a local school, the Educational Alliance. Within a year he could read the English newspapers. At 14 he opened his own newspaper stand, employing his father and brothers.

Like several other great business leaders of his generation, Sarnoff started out on the path to success in the employ of a telegraph company—in this case, American Marconi Wireless Telegraph. At that time Marconi's U.S. operation was a loss-making company, unlike its British parent. Sarnoff started at Marconi as an office boy, little realizing that he would spend the next 60 years at the company and its successor, the Radio Corporation of America, rising to become president before the age of 40.

DEFINING MOMENTS

Brashly, Sarnoff introduced himself in person to Marconi as the newest employee of the company. His impudence paid off, and he was promoted to junior wireless operator, and not long after to chief inspector.

It was as chief inspector that Sarnoff met the man who was to change his life. Edwin H. Armstrong was an inventor who had been working on an improved wireless receiver. At a demonstration of his invention in front of Sarnoff and three other Marconi engineers, Armstrong received radio signals from Clifden, Ireland, and a radio station in San Francisco. Sarnoff, immediately aware of the commercial potential of the machine, advised his bosses to explore the possibility of developing a similar device.

Unfortunately for Sarnoff, his superiors were not as impressed, preferring to stick with the existing point-to-point system that had served Marconi so well. In 1916

Sarnoff, with considerable foresight, wrote a memo to the board: "I have in mind a plan of development which would make radio a household utility in the same sense as the piano or the phonograph."

During World War I the U.S. Navy made significant technical advances in radio engineering. At the end of the war companies stood in line to purchase the new technology. The U.S. government was reluctant to hand over its know-how to a British company like Marconi, so a new company, Radio Corporation of America (RCA), was incorporated in 1919. The new company held the patents of GE and Marconi; its commercial manager and second-in-command was Sarnoff. Now in a better position to lobby for his vision of ubiquitous radio, Sarnoff sent a 28-page "blueprint for success" to the chairman. Sarnoff got his way, and RCA began to churn out radio sets. The ensuing radio craze assured RCA's success, despite competition from companies like Westinghouse.

Armstrong, meanwhile, was continuing to develop radio technology. In 1920, hearing that Armstrong had come up with yet another breakthrough, Sarnoff cut out the middlemen and went straight to him to secure the technology patents. After some tough bargaining, he got the technology and Armstrong received enough stock in RCA to make him the leading stockholder—plus some cash. Armstrong also agreed to give RCA first refusal on future innovations.

The Wall Street Crash of 1929 and ensuing financial chaos hit RCA badly. This was despite the company's domination of its market, the increasing popularity of radio as a form of entertainment, and the creation of the National Broadcasting Company. In January 1930 after a boardroom shuffle, Sarnoff became president of RCA.

In December 1933 Armstrong surfaced once more with yet another invention: Frequency Modulation (FM). This time, however, Sarnoff was less interested; his focus was directed toward television rather than radio. He introduced television to the United States just before the outbreak of World War II at the 1939 World's Fair.

After the war a private conflict broke out between Armstrong and Sarnoff over FM. Eventually, after years of banging his head against the giant RCA, Armstrong was forced to agree to a settlement in court. In 1954, embittered by the outcome, Armstrong jumped to his death from a 13th-story window. Sarnoff's only comment on learning of the death of his one-time friend was, "I didn't kill Armstrong."

Sarnoff carried on business as usual. He introduced color television in 1954. To avoid damaging litigation, he placed all RCA's color television patents in the public domain and at the same time tripled spending on color programming. Any manufacturer could produce a color television set, but RCA had prime-mover advantage in color broadcasting.

Color television was Sarnoff's last throw of the dice. The protracted litigation with Armstrong may have taken more of a toll on him than he realized at the time. In 1965 his son, Robert, was made president of the company and Sarnoff became chairman.

A change of name and logo for RCA, pushed through by his son, roused Sarnoff one last time, and he fought successfully to reinstate the old name. In reality it was a hollow victory. The RCA that Sarnoff had created metamorphosed into a conglomerate containing a disparate collection of companies, including Hertz car rentals and Random House Publishing. After a lengthy illness David Sarnoff died in December 1971.

CONTEXT AND CONCLUSIONS

Sarnoff was more than just a forerunner of modern media magnates such as Rupert Murdoch and Ted Turner. He pioneered the mass-market entertainment industry of radio and television. Edwin Armstrong played a large part in creating the technology of commercial radio, but it was Sarnoff who had the vision to recognize the commercial potential of Armstrong's scientific inventions when others did not. Moreover, Sarnoff had the sense to tie up the technology patents in the case of radio and, more remarkably, to place all RCA's color television patents in the public domain. This last act alone is testimony to Sarnoff's genius and was a forerunner of the approach taken by Linus Torvalds when developing the computer operating system Linux.

> The RCA that Sarnoff had created metamorphosed into a conglomerate containing a disparate collection of companies, including Hertz car rentals and Random House Publishing.

1355

MANAGEMENT GIANTS

FOR MORE INFORMATION

Books:
Bilby, Kenneth M. *The General: David Sarnoff and the Rise of the Communications Industry.* New York: Harper & Row, 1986.
Lyons, Eugene. *David Sarnoff: A Biography.* New York: Harper & Row, 1966.
Myers, Elisabeth P. *David Sarnoff: Radio and TV Boy.* Indianapolis, IN: Bobbs-Merrill Co., 1972.
Sobel, Robert. *RCA.* New York: Stein and Day, 1986.

Web site:
RCA: **www.rca.com**

Alfred P. Sloan, Jr.

Alfred P. Sloan Jr. (1875–1966) was both a brilliant engineer and a forward-thinking manager. After transforming the fortunes of Hyatt Roller Bearing Company, Sloan became president of United Motors Corporation, which soon merged with General Motors. Sloan succeeded Pierre du Pont as president of General Motors in 1923.

From this position Sloan created one of the most influential organizational designs of the 20th century. He restructured the company along divisional lines, with an executive committee sitting above the divisions. Sloan's design became the organizational blueprint for corporations for the next 50 years. Six years after Sloan took over the GM presidency, net sales were $1.5 billion and the stock price was up by 480%. During his tenure he consistently out-thought his main competitor, Ford, turning GM into the world's greatest automobile manufacturer.

Sloan rebuilt General Motors along his own lines.

1875	Born.
1899	Buys a controlling interest in Hyatt Roller Bearing Company.
1903	Hyatt makes profits of $60 million.
1916	Sloan becomes president of the United Motors Corporation.
1918	United Motors becomes part of General Motors.
1923	Sloan becomes president of General Motors.
1937	Steps down as president, but remains chairman and C.E.O.
1946	Steps down as C.E.O.
1956	Relinquishes position as chairman.
1966	Dies.

BACKGROUND AND RISE

Alfred Pritchard Sloan Jr. was born in New Haven, Connecticut, on May 23, 1875, the first of five children in a prosperous family. His father, an engineer by training, was an importer of coffee and tea who later became a wholesale grocer.

At age ten Sloan moved with his family to Brooklyn, New York, where he attended public school and then Brooklyn Polytechnic Institute. Sloan wanted to go on to MIT. Told he was too young, he persisted with his application and eventually took his place there to study electrical engineering. The youngest member of his class, he graduated in 1895 after just three years.

Having displayed a talent for engineering, Sloan went to work at Hyatt Roller Bearing Company in Harrison, New Jersey. To his disappointment he was employed as a draftsman, salesperson, and general gofer. Sloan could see no future at the company, so he left to join a household refrigerator business. But he was not there long before he changed his mind and in 1899 returned to Hyatt. The firm was in financial difficulties and, with help from his father, Sloan bought a controlling interest.

The ambitious young man soon brought his influence to bear on his new company. Aged 24, Sloan became president of Hyatt and proposed that the company manufacture a new antifriction bearing for automobiles. With this move to manufacturing products for the rapidly growing automobile market, Sloan forged a connection with the industry that would propel him to greatness.

DEFINING MOMENTS

Until Hyatt's production of the antifriction bearing, the automobile industry had been using a well-greased axle. Immediately the Olds Motors Company, followed by Ford and the other automobile manufacturers, turned to Sloan and signed contracts for the new bearing. By 1903 Hyatt was making profits of $60 million.

As part of the drive to keep Hyatt's customers happy, Sloan organized a big party once a year. Known as "frictionless feasts" in reference to the company's auto bearings, these events drew the greatest names in the automobile industry. Sloan would mingle with luminaries such as Henry Ford and the Dodge brothers, as guests drank cocktails pumped from a 50-gallon container made to resemble a service station oil drum.

Sloan forged excellent contacts in the industry, particularly with Henry Leland, who became his mentor. Leland, one of the architects of manufacturing using interchangeable parts, had worked for Olds, Cadillac, and General Motors, and created the Lincoln. Leland's watchword was quality—a mantra that rubbed off on Sloan.

Despite Sloan's apparent success at Hyatt (people would comment on the constant emergence of new buildings as they passed the plant on the Pennsylvania Railroad), he was still concerned about the company's

> **Sloan forged excellent contacts in the industry, particularly with Henry Leland, who became his mentor.**

future prospects. Its two largest customers were Ford and GM, and either of these giants, Sloan knew, could easily build a plant to manufacture bearings.

In 1916 Sloan sealed his own and Hyatt's future by securing a deal in which William Crapo Durant, who had just regained control of GM, took a financial interest in Hyatt. Hyatt merged with several other companies to become United Motors Corporation and Sloan became president of the new company. United Motors was in turn subsumed into GM in 1918, with Sloan becoming vice president in charge of accessories and a member of GM's executive committee.

At GM Sloan worked closely with its founder, Durant. He admired Durant's tenacity while frequently disagreeing with his methods. By 1920 Sloan had risen to the position of vice president. In the same year Durant was forced by his bankers to relinquish his position in the company and was succeeded as president by Pierre S. du Pont. In 1923 du Pont was succeeded by Sloan.

As company president Sloan set about reorganizing GM. The organizational architecture he developed secured his place in business history. He structured the company into separate divisions. Under Durant's management GM cars had competed with each other in the market; Sloan ensured that each car and truck division had its own price and style categories. Each GM model was updated annually, offering greater choice to the consumer than Ford's mass-market Model T (famously available in any color—"as long as it's black").

Soon companies under the GM umbrella, such as Buick, Cadillac, and Pontiac, were semiautonomous, responsible for almost every aspect of their business. This mix of decentralization and coordinated policy control left Sloan and the senior executives free to worry about GM corporate strategy while the divisional managers ran their divisions as they saw fit—providing, of course, they made a profit.

And make a profit they did. When Sloan took over GM's presidency, net sales were $698 million. Just six years later, net sales were $1.5 billion and the stock price was up by 480%. With Sloan's new organizational structure came a new type of employee, the professional manager. Sloan took management—until then conducted largely in an amateurish, entrepreneurial way—and turned it into a serious professional discipline focusing on decision making based on facts, particularly financial facts.

Sloan remained president of GM for 14 years, from 1923 until 1937, continuing as chairman until 1956. He ran the company quietly from behind the scenes, known by his workers as "Silent Sloan" and preferring to trust in the ability of his managers. He also liked to get out of the office and visit his clients—he traveled the breadth of the country regularly.

Later in life Sloan made considerable philanthropic donations. He established the Alfred P. Sloan Foundation, to which he and his wife gave $305 million during his lifetime. Gifts from the foundation have benefited, among other institutions, the Sloan-Kettering Institute for Cancer Research in New York and Sloan's alma mater, MIT. Sloan died of a heart attack in 1966, aged 90.

CONTEXT AND CONCLUSIONS

Alfred Sloan made his name by revolutionizing the structure of the corporation and, in doing so, making General Motors the greatest automobile company in the world. Unlike his contemporaries Henry Ford and William Crapo Durant, Sloan was as comfortable with his management role as he was in the workshop. A prudent man who took measured risks, Sloan restructured GM along divisional lines and introduced rigorous financial controls. At the same time he created a new type of business executive—the professional manager. Sloan may justifiably be remembered for his contribution to the U.S. automobile industry because of his work at General Motors. He should be remembered equally for his role in the evolution of management and corporate structure.

> **As company president Sloan set about reorganizing GM. The organizational architecture he developed secured his place in business history.**

FOR MORE INFORMATION

Book:
Sloan, Alfred P., Jr. *My Years with General Motors.* Reissue. New York: Doubleday, 1996.

Web site:
General Motors: **www.gm.com**

"I have never issued an order since I have been the operating head of the corporation."

Alfred P. Sloan

Martha Stewart

A U.S. icon, Martha Stewart has fashioned a fortune from her lifestyle. She studied architectural history at college, and put the learning to good use renovating the country home that became the hub of her business empire. After careers in modeling and stockbroking, she turned to cooking, first in a small way, then in a multimillion-dollar way. Her catering business was lucrative, but it was her books that really launched her to stardom. Her first, *Entertaining*, was published in 1982. It was followed by TV shows, magazines, product endorsement, consulting, and public speaking. In the 1990s everyone in the United States wanted a piece of Stewart's life. And she was only too happy to sell them her version. Her reign as the Queen of Homemaking made her a billionaire and even her very public fall from grace has not tarnished her crown too much.

Martha Stewart—The Queen of Homemaking.

1941	Born.
1964	Graduates from Barnard College.
1967	Obtains job as a stockbroker.
1973	Moves to Westport, Connecticut, and starts a catering business.
1982	Publishes her first book, *Entertaining*.
1987	Stewart signs up to a $5 million, five-year contract with Kmart.
1988	*Time* magazine calls her "the guru of good taste."
1990	Divorces Andy Stewart.
1991	Launches *Martha Stewart Living* magazine.
1997	Forms Martha Stewart Living Omnimedia. Becomes chair and C.E.O.
1999	*Fortune* magazine names her as one of the "50 Most Powerful Women" in the United States.
2000	Ranked in the Forbes Four Hundred list of billionaires.
2003	Charged with securities fraud and the obstruction of justice.
2004	Convicted and sentenced to five months in prison plus five months' house arrest. Resigns from board of Martha Stewart Omnimedia
2004	Brand continues to grow despite Stewart's conviction and Kmart extends contract to sell Martha Stewart products until 2009.
2005	Signs exclusive four-year deal with satellite radio company.

BACKGROUND AND RISE

Martha Stewart was born Martha Kostyra in Jersey City, New Jersey, on August 3, 1941. When she was three, she moved with her family to Nutley, a New Jersey suburb of New York City. Stewart owes much of her later business success to her childhood. As a girl she would cook, bake, and sew with her mother, who was a schoolteacher by profession but stayed home to bring up six children. Her father, who was a pharmaceutical salesman, was a keen gardener and taught her about planting, garden design, and flower arranging.

There was no clue to Stewart's eventual career, however, in her choice of subjects at college. She studied history and architectural history at Barnard College, Columbia University. To pay for her tuition, she relied on modeling fees. While at college she married Yale law student Andy Stewart. She was 19.

Stewart turned to modeling for full-time work when she left college in 1964. But she was forced to give it up in 1965 when she gave birth to her daughter. A complete change of direction followed when, in 1967, with the help of her father-in-law, she got a job as a stockbroker.

Stewart excelled at her new career, her salary soon reaching $100,000 plus. However, the oil crisis of the early 1970s brought about an economic slowdown in the United States. In 1973, Stewart and her husband packed their bags and moved to Westport, Connecticut.

DEFINING MOMENTS

Stewart readily adjusted to rural life. With her husband she set about restoring the farmhouse they had purchased, known locally as "the Westport Horror." While her husband commuted to New York City, Stewart redecorated the house and began to overhaul the garden. Soon the house was completely renovated and the grounds boasted an orchard, vegetable garden, beehives, and a variety of livestock. Stewart still lives in the house today. She uses it as a base for her business.

By 1976, with the house fixed up, Stewart had turned her attention to cooking. She gave herself a crash course and swiftly moved on to teach—first children and then adults—in her own home. She opened a small gourmet food business in Westport called Market Basket. When the business began to grow, she moved out of her shared premises and into her home. When requests for her

services became too great to manage alone, she went into partnership with a friend, Norma Collier. But within a year the partnership was over. Collier said later that she didn't want to work a "128-hour week."

Stewart had no such qualms. She continued the business on her own, catering for celebrated Connecticut neighbors such as Paul Newman. She called her company Martha Stewart, Inc., and slowly raised her profile through teaching, catering, and writing articles for publications such as the *New York Times* and *Family Circle*.

What started as a cottage industry soon grew into a large business, and by 1986 was worth $1 million. She had, by this time, outgrown her house's kitchen and moved into a separate building next to the house. On the way to her first million, Stewart wrote one of the country's most successful books of its type, *Entertaining*, published in 1982. A small library of books followed, each accompanied by promotional book signing tours and each garnering plaudits and more fans, so much so that by 1988 *Time* magazine was referring to her as "the guru of good taste (and taste buds) in American entertaining, looked to by millions of American women for guidance about everything from weddings to weeding."

Stewart was not without her detractors. After the publication of *Entertaining*, there were accusations of plagiarism. *Newsweek* reported similarities between her recipes for orange almond cake and cherry pound cake with raisins and recipes in *Mastering the Art of French Cooking, Vol III* by Simone Beck and Julia Child. But the allegations were never proved. In her later books Stewart ensured that recipes were credited if necessary. But while her business life blossomed, her personal life suffered: she was divorced from her husband.

Business continued to grow at a phenomenal rate. In 1987 Stewart signed a $5 million, five-year contract as a consultant to Kmart department stores. She had her own lines of paint and linens, produced a series of commercials, and gave up the catering business to concentrate on writing.

The *Martha Stewart Living* magazine and television programs followed, as did lecturing, personal appearances, and a host of accolades. She was named among the "50 Most Powerful Women" by *Fortune* magazine in 1999, and received Emmy awards for her television shows. In 2000 she made the *Forbes* Four Hundred list of billionaires—a prime example of "the American dream" come true.

The dream turned into a nightmare in June 2003, however. That month saw the culmination of over two years' speculation about Stewart's financial affairs. In December 2001, she sold stock in a company called ImClone Systems, which at one time had been run by an acquaintance. While Stewart has consistently denied accusations of insider dealing, probes into the sale set off a chain of brand-damaging events. In October 2002 she resigned from the board of the New York Stock exchange and by the end of December 2002, Martha Stewart Living Omnimedia had lost $2 million. Worse was to come. In June 2003, Stewart was charged with securities fraud and the obstruction of justice, and ordered to face trial. In March 2004 she was found guilty of the charges and in July sentenced to a five-month prison term plus five months' house arrest.

Stewart has, however, been able to weather this very public storm. Martha Stewart Living Omnimedia took a battering as events surrounding the trial unfolded, but the stock price did not tumble cataclysmically, mainly due to the support of Stewart's faithful fans. There has been extra light at the end of the tunnel too: just as she headed off to prison, MSLO signed a new five-year deal with her, thought to be worth $900,000 annually, and in April 2005, she signed an exclusive four-year deal with a leading satellite radio company that will allow her to create a channel featuring entertainment programs for an all-female listening audience.

> Soon the house was completely renovated and the grounds boasted an orchard, vegetable garden, beehives, and a variety of livestock.

CONTEXT AND CONCLUSIONS

Martha Stewart is a symbol of modern culture, despite her recent difficulties. She is a woman who turned her life into a business, who, in the manner of the modern alchemist, transmuted cookies into cash. What better way to become both wealthy and famous than simply by living the life you would most wish to lead? As Stewart said, "My life is my work, my work is my life, and that it involves the home, the family, the gardens, everything else involved in living, is my luck . . . I can think about my work twenty-four hours a day and it's pleasant." Even when that veneer was battered by her involvement in financial irregularities, she has been able to keep moving forward.

CLOSE BUT NO CIGAR

Delia Smith

As the U.K. Martha Stewart equivalent, Smith has capitalized on her mildly old-fashioned image to cook up a small fortune. However, Smith will never quite make it to Stewart's exalted standing. Not that Smith lacks pep; she's always on the go, managing to combine her culinary empire with her directorship of Norwich City Football Club. But Smith has a different approach to the public/private mix. Her private persona is kept firmly under wraps; no holiday snaps or interior decor shots on *her* Web site! And, if the public don't have an admission ticket into her life, they're unlikely ever to aspire to be Delia Smith, or to connect with her as the U.S. public do with Martha Stewart.

FOR MORE INFORMATION

Book:
Byron, Christopher. *Martha Inc.*. New York: Wiley, 2002.

Web site:
Martha Stewart Living Omnimedia:
www.marthastewart.com

"I'm a brand."

Eiji Toyoda

If Eiji Toyoda hadn't joined his family business, the Toyota name might have been associated with the textile industry instead of automobiles.

Toyoda helped to grow a thriving automobile business from a loom manufacturing company. He joined the company in 1936 and was responsible for recruiting the best research engineers and organizing production. Toyota's breakthrough came when Toyoda visited Ford's Rouge automobile plant in the 1950s. It was a revelation to him. He returned to Japan determined to combine the best of U.S. manufacturing processes with his own innovative approach to production. The result was the Toyota Production System. Successful models—from the Corolla to the introduction of the Lexus—paved the way for the company's global success.

Eiji Toyoda engineered Toyota's global success.

1913	Born.
1933	Cousin starts automobile production.
1936	Toyoda joins the firm, which is renamed Toyota.
1950	Toyoda visits Ford River Rouge plant in Dearborn, Michigan.
1955	Crown model successful in Japan but not in United States.
1967	Becomes president of Toyota.
1968	Successfully launches Corolla in United States.
1975	Toyota replaces Volkswagen as number one imported car in United States.
1989	Launches luxury Lexus model.
1994	Resigns.

BACKGROUND AND RISE

It is no surprise that Eiji Toyoda grew up to be an industrialist. Born on September 12, 1913, Toyoda spent much of his childhood in and around his father's textile mill near Nagoya. From his earliest years he was surrounded by both business and heavy machinery.

The driving force behind the textile business was Toyoda's uncle, Rashomon Sakichi Toyoda. Sakichi was a carpenter by trade and an inventor by nature. In 1929 the British company Platt Brothers paid Sakichi £100,000 for the rights to a textile loom he had invented. Sakichi put the money to one side to invest in automobile production.

> **The driving force behind the textile business was Toyoda's uncle, Rashomon Sakichi Toyoda. Sakichi was a carpenter by trade and an inventor by nature.**

Given the nature of the family business, Eiji Toyoda's choice of an engineering degree was a natural one. He started his studies at Tokyo Imperial University in 1933. While Toyoda was taking his degree his cousin Kiichiro, Sakichi's eldest son, was establishing an automobile plant at the Toyoda Automatic Loom Works. In 1936, his degree completed, Toyoda joined his cousin at the plant. In that year the company changed its name from Toyoda Automatic Loom Works to Toyota.

DEFINING MOMENTS

Toyoda's first assignment was to organize the company's research facility, hiring talented scientists and engineers to work on research and development. Next he worked on the shop floor in production planning.

At that time Toyota was producing a car designed to be built with Chevrolet parts. Toyota's first cars rolled off the production line in 1936. The timing was unfortunate: the advent of World War II and Japan's entry into the war in December 1941 meant that Toyota's production expertise had to be redirected toward the manufacture of trucks for the war effort.

After the war Eiji Toyoda made plans to establish a chinaware business. Kiichiro Toyoda was diversifying the company, expecting the occupying forces to place limitations on the automobile business. Instead, as Japan underwent a period of reconstruction, the Toyota car plant was called upon to build vehicles to help get the country moving again.

Despite the boost in production, trading conditions were still extremely tough; Toyota was driven to the brink of bankruptcy. The company was saved only by dramatic cuts in the work force, which Toyoda had the painful task of enforcing. He also created a new company, Toyota Motor Sales, to help ease cash flow problems and satisfy his bankers' concerns.

It wasn't until the 1950s that Toyota firmly established itself as a major car manufacturer. The breakthrough came when Toyoda visited Ford's immense River Rouge plant in Dearborn, Michigan. Toyota had by then been in the car business for 13 years and had produced just over 2,500 automobiles. The River Rouge plant turned out a staggering 8,000 vehicles a day. Impressed with the scale

---

of U.S. automobile production, Toyoda realized that if he could combine the best of U.S. and Japanese production methods, Toyota could be a world leader.

With the help of his production guru Taichi Ohno, Toyoda established the Toyota Production System (TPS), also known as "lean production." It was a revolutionary approach to manufacturing comprising three main elements. The first is just-in-time production. There is no point in producing cars simply hoping that customers will buy them. Waste (Japanese muda) is bad; therefore production must be linked to the market's requirements. Second, responsibility for quality rests with everyone, and any quality defect needs to be rectified as soon as it is identified. The third element is the "value stream": instead of seeing the company as a series of unrelated products and processes, it should be seen as a continuous and uniform whole—a stream that includes suppliers as well as customers.

Toyota's first full scale production car, the Crown, proved a somewhat shaky start. Driven off the production line by Eiji Toyoda—dressed in a tuxedo—on New Year's Day, 1955, the Crown was a success in Japan, but it failed to make any impression on the U.S. market when it was introduced in 1957. Designed for Japanese roads, it was slow and prone to overheating—problems that made it ill-suited to U.S. highways.

Persistence eventually paid off and by the 1960s Toyota cars were a hit, with the Corona and Corolla both selling well. The success of the Corolla in 1968 enabled the company to make a big leap forward, and by 1975 Toyota had replaced Volkswagen as the number one imported car in the United States. In 1984 the company entered a joint venture with General Motors to build Toyota vehicles in the United States. Along the way Toyota established an unrivaled reputation for production quality. But it was the Toyota Lexus that finally secured the company's reputation in the United States.

The Lexus was a personal triumph for Toyoda. In August 1983 he had convened a top-secret meeting inside the company, asking those present, "Can we create a luxury car to challenge the very best?" The answer was a resounding "yes."

In the luxury car market Toyota faced competition from a variety of established brands, including Mercedes and BMW. Undaunted by the scale of the task, Toyota created a new brand—the Lexus—to create psychological distance from the other Toyota value-for-money models. Toyoda neutralized any concerns over the reliability and quality of the Lexus by insisting that the company should

out-engineer Mercedes and BMW. The eventual result was the Lexus LS400. It took seven years, $2 billion, 1,400 engineers, 2,300 technicians, and 450 prototypes—and generated 200 patents. The Lexus was tested in Japan on miles of carefully built highways that exactly imitated roads in the United States, Germany, and the United Kingdom. Toyota even reproduced foreign road signs.

> Persistence eventually paid off and by the 1960s Toyota cars were a hit, with the Corona and Corolla both selling well.

Toyota is now the dominant car manufacturer in Japan and the third biggest carmaker in the world (behind General Motors and Ford). It now sells nearly 1.5 million cars in the United States every year. Toyoda stepped down as president in 1994.

CONTEXT AND CONCLUSIONS

Eiji Toyoda didn't found the Toyota Motor Corporation, but he did help make it a world leader.

After an inauspicious attempt to crack the U.S. market with the Crown, Toyoda was quick to admit that Toyota would need an extra competitive edge to compete with the likes of Ford and General Motors. It was no good trying to compete on price alone; instead Toyoda concentrated on efficiency and quality.

He employed the inventive Taichi Ohno to help develop a new production system that came to be known as the Toyota Production System. Through quality and reliability, Toyoda took on the great U.S. automobile manufacturers and emerged victorious. And if imitation is the sincerest form of flattery, the modest Toyoda must be embarrassed by the number of U.S. firms that have tried to adopt Toyota's production methods.

FOR MORE INFORMATION

Books:
Braddon, Russell. *The Other 100 Years War: Japan's Bid for Supremacy 1941–2041.* London: Collins, 1983.
Toyoda, Eiji. *Toyota: Fifty Years in Motion.* Tokyo: Kodansha International, 1987.

Web site:
Toyota: **www.toyota.com**

"No other man-made device since the shields and lances of ancient knights fulfills a man's ego like an automobile."

William Rootes

Robert Edward Turner III

Robert Edward Turner III (1938–) started in business in unfortunate circumstances after his father's suicide. Showing considerable resilience, he went on to improve on his father's business and, ultimately, to help create the biggest entertainment and media company in the world—AOL Time Warner. Turner became president and chief operating officer of the Turner Advertising Company in 1963 and set out on a trail of acquisitions and channel launches. A UHF station, professional sports teams, Headline News, TNT, The Cartoon Network, Turner Classic Movies, New Line Cinema: all these and many more came under Turner's control as he built his company—the Turner Broadcasting System—into a media giant. Turner is probably best known for the creation of the news station Cable News Network, CNN, in June 1980, and the part he played in the formation of AOL Time Warner in 2000/2001.

With CNN, Turner made news broadcasting 24/7.

1938	Born.
1970	Acquires the UHF station, WTCG.
1976	WTCG becomes WTBS and goes nationwide. Transmits across the United States via satellite. Buys the major-league baseball team, the Atlanta Braves.
1977	Wins America's Cup with his yacht *Courageous*.
1980	Cable News Network launched.
1986	Acquires MGM Entertainment Company.
1991	*Time Magazine*'s "Man of the Year."
1994	Turner Broadcasting Systems merges with New Line Cinema.
1996	Turner Broadcasting Systems merges with Time Warner.
2001	Time Warner merger with AOL approved.
2001	Loses control of Turner Broadcasting.
2002	AOL Time-Warner posts $100 million loss.
2003	Turner Foundation loses value and declines fund requests.
2003	Resigns chairmanship of AOL Time-Warner.

BACKGROUND AND RISE

Robert Edward Turner III was born in Cincinnati, Ohio, in 1938. His checkered school career was notable for eccentric and unconventional behavior rather than academic excellence. At McCallie, an exclusive school for boys in Chattanooga, Tennessee, he was an unruly pupil who showed a peculiar penchant for taxidermy and for catching squirrels in pillowcases. McCallie's method of punishing offenders was to issue demerits. Each demerit required the recipient to walk a quarter of a mile. Turner earned over 1,000 demerits in his first year, further than any pupil could walk in the time available. The school was forced to reinvent its disciplinary methods especially for him.

At Brown University Turner continued to challenge authority. Eventually, having been caught with a woman in his room, he was asked to leave—but not before he had made a name for himself on the university sailing team. Sailing was to remain an abiding passion, and he later won the America's Cup in 1977 with his yacht Courageous.

After college Turner returned home to work in his father's billboard advertising business. His father made him manager of the firm's operation in Macon, Georgia. Turner married and settled down to a tough schedule, working 15 hours per day for six and a half days each week. Like his father, he was a natural salesman making fast progress in the business.

Turner's often difficult relationship with his father came to a shocking end in March 1963 when he was just 24. His father, under severe pressure at work, took a silver .38 revolver and shot himself in the head. In these terrible circumstances Turner became president and C.O.O. of the Turner Advertising Company.

DEFINING MOMENTS

Turner expanded the company into television with an audacious move to acquire the UHF station WTCG in 1970. At the time WTCG had the worst ratings of the major television channels in Atlanta. Turner engineered a deal that involved taking Turner Advertising public; acquiring the assets of WTCG; and forming a new company, Turner Communications. Determined to lift the station's fortunes, he changed the programming schedule and fed the viewers a diet of reruns—classic shows and black and white movies. It worked. Bemused critics could only watch as the viewing figures shot up and the advertising

> **At McCallie, an exclusive school for boys in Chattanooga, Tennessee, was an unruly pupil who showed a peculiar pencha for taxidermy and for catching squirrels in pillowcases.**

"If I only had a little humility, I'd be perfect."

Ted Turner

revenue flooded in. In 1976 the station went nationwide as WTBS, transmitting to cable systems across the United States via satellite—it was the start of the "superstation concept."

Turner continued to diversify and expand, and not always into obvious areas. In 1976 he bought a major league baseball team, the Atlanta Braves, and in 1977 the Atlanta Hawks of the National Basketball Association. Once again he was ahead of the game. His instincts told him that televised sports would attract a big audience.

In 1980 Turner used the profits from Turner Broadcasting System to launch CNN (Cable News Network). The critics were scathing, predicting inevitable failure for the 24/7 all-news network. But once again Turner proved that, despite his often dogmatic approach, when it came to business he knew best. "I am the right man in the right place at the right time," he said. "Not me alone, but all the people who think the world can be brought together by telecommunications."

CNN was a hit. It brought news, like the Reagan assassination attempt, to viewers as events unfurled. It revolutionized the news industry. CNN cemented its reputation with its coverage of the first Gulf War when, for the first time, a TV audience could watch a war in real time, from the comfort of their armchairs.

Turner continued to collect television stations: Headline News (1982), CNN International (1985), TNT (1988), SportsSouth (1990), The Cartoon Network (1992), Turner Classic Movies (1994), CNNfn (1995), and CNN SI (1997) were all added to the network. Shortly after Castle Rock Entertainment joined Turner Broadcasting in 1993, Turner merged TBS with New Line Cinema.

Not everything Turner touched turned to gold. Eager to purchase a film studio, he made a bid for CBS. The hostile takeover bid failed. Another Turner idea, the "Checkout Channel," providing in-store news and information, proved a disappointment. Turner also paid $1.6 billion for the MGM film library, a sum many commentators considered too generous.

In 1996 he completed the biggest deal of his career to date, when he merged TBS with Time Warner. Holding 10% of Time Warner, Turner had the largest single stockholding. It was an astute move, leaving him well positioned to profit from the development of a new communication phenomenon—the Internet. He assumed the role of vice chair in the new organization, taking responsibility for Time Warner's Cable Networks division, which included the assets of Turner Broadcasting System, Inc. (TBS, Inc.), Home Box Office, Cinemax, and Time Warner's interests in Comedy Central and Court TV. He was also responsible for New Line Cinema and the company's professional sports teams.

In 2001 Turner was involved in one of the biggest mergers of the postwar period when AOL merged with Time Warner to create the largest entertainment conglomerate in the world. Time Warner's stockholders received 45% of the new company to AOL's 55%. Turner became vice chair and senior adviser of AOL Time Warner.

It proved an ill-fated move. Almost immediately Turner found himself side-lined and he lost control of Turner Broadcasting, the company he had built. In a bad year, he was involved in a divorce with Jane Fonda and lost his World Wrestling Championship, along with its star Hulk Hogan, to long-time rival World Wrestling Federation. Worse was to follow in 2002 as AOL Time-Warner posted a record loss of $100 billion. In 2003, he resigned his chairmanship. The loss also hit the Turner Foundation badly since much of its value derived from AOL Time-Warner investments. In 1997, the Foundation hit the headlines when it made a $1 billion donation to the UN for humanitarian projects. In sharp contrast, 2003 saw the Foundation unable to meet any funding requests.

> CNN was a hit. It brought news, like the Reagan assassination attempt, to viewers as events unfurled. It revolutionized the news industry.

CONTEXT AND CONCLUSIONS

Turner's career is distinguished by relentless drive, an uncanny ability to predict consumer demand, and a supreme confidence in his own vision. Competitiveness and drive are evident in his sailing achievements, too. He could have made a good living as an international yachtsman. Probably the best illustration of Turner's qualities, though, is the founding of CNN. Critics derided the idea of a nonstop news network. Turner thought differently and pursued his vision doggedly. He was right, the critics were wrong, and CNN's coverage of the Gulf War has become part of media folklore. Turner may have made an occasional bad call, but more often than not his instincts proved successful. It is this quality of vision, and having the guts to execute it, that made him one of the world's great media magnates.

FOR MORE INFORMATION

Book:
Bibb, Porter. *It Ain't As Easy As It Looks: Ted Turner's Amazing Story.* New York: Crown Publishers, 1993.

Web site:
CNN.com: **www.cnn.com**

1363

MANAGEMENT GIANTS

Theodore Newton Vail

Most individuals would be happy with one successful career. The U.S. serial entrepreneur Theodore Newton Vail (1845–1920) enjoyed several. First Vail worked for the U.S. government reforming the mail delivery system. The next chapter of his working life was spent establishing and expanding the American Bell Telegraph Company. Vail exemplifies the truth that behind every successful great inventor is a business innovator capable of building an enterprise from scratch. Finally, after retiring to a tranquil life on his farm in Vermont, the 62-year-old Vail was persuaded to come out of retirement to save the American Telephone & Telegraph company.

Vail sent out the right signals to corporate America.

1845	Born.
1878	Joins Bell Telephone Co.
1882	Secures control of Western Electric Co.
1885	Incorporation of American Telephone & Telegraph Company.
1889	Resigns as president of AT&T, buys a 200-acre farm in Vermont.
1907	Recalled as President of AT&T.
1910	Buys control of Western Union Telegraph Company for $30 million.
1913	Forced by Justice Department to dispose of Western Union stock.
1919	Retires from AT&T.
1920	Dies.

BACKGROUND AND RISE

Theodore Newton Vail was born in 1845 in Carroll County, Ohio, where his father, who was from a Quaker family, and his Dutch mother had temporarily settled. Two years later the family returned to New Jersey. They remained there until 1866 when they moved to a farm in Iowa.

Unhappy with farming life and restless for adventure, the young Vail headed west, landing a job as an operator in a Union Pacific boxcar. Telegraphy was in the Vail genes. His uncle Alfred had helped finance F. S. B. Morse in the development of the telegraph.

Before long the restless Vail moved out of the boxcar and into the railroad mail delivery service. It was here that his talents began to shine. The railroad mail service was a shambles with no sorting system in the trains, no routing for letters other than to the major cities, and no system-

> **In 1878 Vail accepted the position of general manager at the newly founded American Bell Telephone Company.**

ized train connections. Vail set about sorting out the mess. He pored over railway timetables and train connections, calculating the quickest routes. The result was a railroad mail guide for the efficient transport of mail in the region.

DEFINING MOMENTS

Eventually Vail's endeavors came to the attention of the U.S. government, and he was summoned to Washington. If he could reform local mail deliveries, the government figured, then why not the entire country's? Vail set about the task and swiftly rose from assistant superintendent of the mail service to general superintendent. It was a difficult task, not least because he was up against the vested interests of the railroad companies. Rescheduling the entire country's delivery service cut into the revenues of some of them. Vail, however, resisted their lobbying and carried the day.

It was his indomitable nature that brought him to the attention of Gardiner G. Hubbard, the father-in-law of Alexander Graham Bell, inventor of a contraption that had been exhibited at the Centennial Exposition in Philadelphia, much to the amusement of visitors. The invention was the telephone. When they proposed creating a commercial enterprise founded on the telephone, Bell and Hubbard were ridiculed. The *Times* of London called it "the latest American humbug." Hubbard needed a man with a forceful personality and uncompromising drive to build a viable company to exploit the telephone. Vail was that man. He had the vision to see how the telephone could revolutionize communications not only on a regional, but also on a national level.

In 1878 Vail accepted the position of general manager at the newly founded American Bell Telephone Company. "I gave up a $3,500 salary for no salary," he remarked at the time. His salary at Bell was ostensibly $5,000, but he rarely collected it. Instead he devoted his entire energy and passion to rolling out the telephone

---

"Communication, whether it be in the dance, or whether it be in the spoken word, is now the great need of the world."

Martha Graham

nationwide. In 1882 he oversaw the purchase of the Western Electric Co. of Chicago, one of the premier manufacturers of telephone equipment. In 1885 the group of companies Vail presided over was incorporated as AT&T (the American Telephone and Telegraph Company). Despite attempts from competitor Western Union to seduce him away from Bell, Vail stuck to his post. He stayed with Bell until it was sufficiently well established to secure enough capital to expand across the country, city by city. When in 1889 that moment arrived, he bought himself a 200-acre farm in Vermont.

Before retiring to his farm, the nomadic Vail toured South America, replaced the horse-drawn streetcars in Buenos Aires with electric ones, opened offices in London, spent time in France and Italy, and installed electric lighting and telephone systems in numerous other cities. Finally, his wanderlust apparently sated, he became a farmer. The farm was rapidly expanded to 6,000 acres as Vail set about farming with the same intensity that he applied to his earlier careers. No comfortable slippers and armchair for him.

Little did Vail realize that, though he was retired and past 60, some of his greatest achievements still lay ahead. In 1907 confidence in big business plummeted. Companies had overextended themselves. Banks withdrew credit, capital dried up and new stock issues failed. Amid the economic turmoil dark clouds were gathering over AT&T. Its competitors had muddied the company's waters to the extent that the Federal Government was being urged to bust the "telephone trust." So, cap in hand, the directors of AT&T arrived at Vail's Lyndon ranch in Vermont and pleaded with him to help save the company. He said yes.

Using the considerable business acumen that he had acquired over the years, Vail swiftly raised $21 million of new capital, followed by a quarter of a billion over the next six years. He attacked the critics of the "telephone trust" head on by buying up competitors and consolidating telephone networks under the AT&T umbrella. At the same time he campaigned under the slogan "One system, One policy, Universal service" to persuade the public that a single telephone service was the best way. And to placate the government, he acceded to regulatory supervision. It was a masterful performance. Vail fended off the financial crisis of October–November 1907 and AT&T emerged as the unquestioned dominant force in telephony. Vail also earned the loyalty of the workforce by increasing pension, sickness, and accident benefits.

A man of vision, Vail was still pursuing new ventures into his 70s. In 1910 he bought control of the Western Union Telegraph Company for $30 million. His intention was to bring people closer together with the "tel-letter"—mail delivered over the wire at a nominal cost. Unfortunately for Vail, the Department of Justice stepped in to break up the telegraph–telephone combine and Vail was forced to sell Western Union and agree that AT&T would not buy any more independents, thus scuttling his plans for the tel-letter.

> **Little did Vail realize that, though he was retired and past 60, some of his greatest achievements still lay ahead.**

CONTEXT AND CONCLUSIONS

Vail was one of a generation of entrepreneurs who helped change the face of the United States and the world at the turn of the 20th century. It was the era of the electrical revolution. The pioneering spirit of men such as Vail sparked the transformation from the steam age to the electrical age. A serial entrepreneur, the crowning glory of his achievements survives to this day: AT&T is one of the oldest companies quoted on the New York Stock Exchange.

When asked how he managed to achieve so much in one lifetime, Vail answered "By never being unwilling when young to do another man's work, and then, when older, by never doing anything somebody else could do better for me."

FOR MORE INFORMATION

Web site:
AT&T: **www.att.com**

MANAGEMENT GIANTS

"One of the indispensable functions of informal organizations . . . is that of communication."

Chester Barnard

Cornelius Vanderbilt

Cornelius "Commodore" Vanderbilt is one of the greatest-ever businessmen in the United States. Applying the principles of economy, competition, and innovation, Vanderbilt expanded from a small-time ferry operator to a shipping and railroad magnate. In his lifetime Vanderbilt amassed fabulous wealth—some $105 million. Yet he did so by genuinely improving the lot of people. Wherever Vanderbilt opened for business, the prices came down and the services improved. He risked arrest to bust government-subsidized monopolies by running competing services illegally. By eradicating government monopolies, Vanderbilt increased the incentive to invest in improving technology to provide a competitive advantage. It was a classic case of how capitalism and competition can deliver a better deal for the consumer, and benefit a nation's economy.

Vanderbilt revolutionized the U.S. transportation industry.

Year	Event
1794	Born.
1810	Mother gives him $100 to clear and plant an eight-acre field. He buys a boat with the proceeds.
1812	U.S. war with England.
1817	Robert Fulton and Robert R. Livingston introduce steamboats.
1829	Uses savings to start a steamboat business.
1851	Forms the Accessory Transit Company.
1863	Has amassed a fortune of $40 million. Switches focus to railroads.
1869	Merges the Hudson River Railroad with the New York Central system.
1877	Dies.

BACKGROUND AND RISE

Cornelius Vanderbilt was born on May 27, 1794 on Staten Island, New York. His father was a farmer who sold produce in the markets of New York, sailing across the harbor to get there.

Vanderbilt paid little attention to school, preferring the outdoor life. As a child he could barely read and write. He did, however, take a keen interest in business. In 1810, when he was 16, Vanderbilt's mother gave him $100 to clear and plant an eight-acre field. Instead of frittering the money away, the enterprising Vanderbilt used it to buy a small flat-bottom sailing boat. He then started a ferry business, taking passengers between Staten Island and New York City. The business was almost sunk in the first few weeks when the boat hit an obstacle, but both boat and business survived.

The ferry business taught Vanderbilt some important commercial lessons. Known locally as "Cornele, the boatman," he discovered that by taking any fare, no matter how rough the weather, he obtained a reputation for both reliability and a willingness to please the customer. This in turn brought him repeat business. He also learned the simple economics of low costs, quick turnover, consistently undercutting his rivals, and filling his boat.

DEFINING MOMENTS

Like many other entrepreneurs, when war with England came in 1812 Vanderbilt saw the conflict as an opportunity to improve his business. As well as continuing to ply his normal routes, he was awarded an army contract and also made extra money ferrying food along the Hudson River to a blockaded New York City. With the profits, he bought an interest in two more boats.

By the age of 24, Vanderbilt had saved $9,000, expanded his business to ply the coastal routes between Chesapeake Bay and New York, and developed a retail business selling provisions to ships in the harbor. In addition, he owned interests in a number of boats. Things were going well for Vanderbilt when, in 1817, the steamboats arrived. Entrepreneurs Robert Fulton and Robert R. Livingston had brought their new technology to New York and were granted a monopoly on all steamboat traffic for a period of 30 years.

Realizing that sailboats were about to become obsolete, Vanderbilt sold out rather than persist with outdated technology. He went to work for a small steamboat operator, Thomas Gibbons, a wealthy attorney and plantation owner, and learned how to sail the steamboat. As soon as he was able, he began ferrying passengers from New Jersey to Manhattan in direct contravention of the monopoly. He persuaded passengers to use the service by undercutting Fulton and Livingston's $4 ticket price, charging only $1. The loss was made up on food and drink prices.

In 1824, the United States Supreme Court declared the

> **In 1824, the United States Supreme Court declared the Fulton and Livingston monopoly illegal. Now Vanderbilt could operate openly.**

"Successful entrepreneurs judge correctly the need for change, then do something about it."

James Edward Hanson

Fulton and Livingston monopoly illegal. Now Vanderbilt could operate openly. With the monopoly broken, things changed quickly in the steamboat business. Prices came down, competitors entered the market and boat technology improved. In a competitive environment where innovation was rewarded, Vanderbilt thrived. In 1829 he used his savings to start his own steamboat business. He put together a connecting service—steamboat, stagecoach, steamboat—from New York City to Philadelphia. And, in what became a classic Vanderbilt business strategy, he immediately slashed prices. The competition, fearing a price war, gathered enough money together to pay him to go away.

Vanderbilt had discovered a new way to make money. Keen to protect the market and unwilling to cut their profits to provide real value to the customer, the lazy established operators would rather pay Vanderbilt to stop operating. It was the same story in the Hudson River. Up against the Hudson River Steamboat Association, Vanderbilt cut fares savagely until he was carrying passengers for free and, as before, making the losses up on the food. It wasn't long before the Steamboat Association caved in. They gave Vanderbilt $100,000, as well as ten annual payments of $5,000, in return for him leaving the area.

Before long, Vanderbilt—now Commodore Vanderbilt—owned over 100 steamboats and was worth many millions of dollars. His next move was inspired by the discovery of gold in California in 1848. The ensuing gold rush created a demand for transportation from East Coast to West. Initially, clipper boats took passengers around Cape Horn—a journey that took 90 days. Next, an alternative route was organized that involved land travel across the Isthmus of Panama. It was at this point that the ever-innovative Vanderbilt entered the fray. Studying the maps he discovered a new route, which involved sailing inland along the San Juan River, on across Lake Nicaragua, and finally across the shortest 12-mile land gap to the Pacific Ocean.

Vanderbilt formed the Accessory Transit Company, struck a deal with the Nicaraguan government, constructed a port on the Pacific Coast and, in 1851, started sailing the new route. As usual his fares were cheaper—$400 compared to the competition's $600. And as usual, after some political wrangling and maneuvering, the competition offered Vanderbilt $672,000 not to operate a route to California. His first foray into the transatlantic and shipping routes was no less successful. Used to competing with government subsidized business by now, Vanderbilt cut fares, built volume, and used the latest technology in shipping so that, when government subsidy was finally withdrawn from the competition, he was best-placed to take advantage.

By 1863 Vanderbilt, in his sixties, had amassed a fortune of $40 million. For most people this would have been enough. Not for him. Over the next 13 years, abandoning water for land, Vanderbilt made the switch from old technology—steamboats, to new technology—the railroads.

By 1869, Vanderbilt had taken control of the Hudson River Railroad and the New York Central system. He merged the two companies, gained control of railroad lines from New York to Chicago, and created a consolidated railroad system between the two cities. Toward the end of his career, Vanderbilt continued to apply the principles of competitiveness, low costs, and innovation to the business. He upgraded iron rails with steel imported from England, doubled tracks, and built the Grand Central Depot in New York, the largest railroad terminal in the world.

By the time of his death on January 4, 1877, Vanderbilt commanded a railroad empire that extended over 740 miles of track and included 486 locomotives and 9,000 freight cars. Every year thousands of passengers were transported courtesy of Vanderbilt. When he died, he left a fortune of $105 million in his will.

> By 1869, Vanderbilt had taken control of the Hudson River Railroad and the New York Central system.

CONTEXT AND CONCLUSIONS

Cornelius Vanderbilt was simply the most brilliant businessman of his generation. He combined an innate understanding of the principles of economics with a consummate grasp of business strategy. Everything that Vanderbilt touched turned to gold. Only once was he ever bested. When he tried to corner the stock in the New York and Erie Railroad Company, notorious financiers Jay Gould and Jim Fisk merely kept on issuing new shares until finally Vanderbilt had to give up. But no one ever beat him fairly. Why? Because Vanderbilt understood that delivering a reasonable service, at a low cost, would always win out over a government-subsidized monopoly. Rather than fleece consumers by providing a substandard, outdated, expensive service, Vanderbilt gave his customers innovation and value for money. In doing so he helped drive economic growth on both the East and West Coast, and to fast-track technological innovation in transportation. And, in the process, he became fabulously wealthy.

1367

MANAGEMENT GIANTS

FOR MORE INFORMATION

Books:
Metzman, Gustav. *Commodore Vanderbilt (1794–1877): Forefather of the New York Central.* New York: The Newcomen Society of England, 1946.
Smith, Arthur D. Howden. Commodore Vanderbilt: An Epic of American Achievement. New York: Robert McBride, 1927.

"When it's time to make a decision about a person or problem . . . trust your intuition . . . act."

Bud Hadfield

Samuel Walton

Samuel Moore Walton created a retail empire after the fashion of the great Frank Woolworth. A hard upbringing in the depression-ridden Midwest was followed by college and then commerce. Having sampled the retail business courtesy of JCPenney, Walton opened a Ben Franklin store with $25,000 borrowed from his father-in-law. When he lost the lease on his first store he simply opened another, and then another. Soon he had a small collection of retail outlets. To keep tight control of them, he would fly himself from one to the other. Walton opened the first Wal-Mart in 1962 and the second in 1964. By 1987 there were over 1,000. At the time of his death in 1992, Walton had made millions from his retail business, and so had many of his stockholders. One hundred shares bought in 1970 for a mere $1,650 were, by 1992, worth a staggering $2.6 million.

Wal-mart's appeal is undiminished.

1918	Born.
1945	Gets franchise for Ben Franklin store in Newport, Arkansas.
1953	Obtains pilot's license.
1962	Opens first Wal-Mart discount store in Rogers, Arkansas.
1964	Second Wal-Mart store in the town of Harrison, Arkansas.
1970	Raises $5 million on the stock market through a public offering of Wal-Mart stock.
1970s	Builds 452 new stores.
1974	Retires for two years.
1980s	Builds 1,237 new stores.
1985	Wal-Mart stock makes him wealthiest man in the United States.
1987	1,000th store opens.
1991	Wal-Mart overtakes Sears to become biggest retailer in the United States.
1992	Dies.

BACKGROUND AND RISE

Samuel Moore Walton was born in Oklahoma on March 29, 1918. His father was employed variously as a farm loan appraiser, a real estate salesman, and an insurance salesman. Walton and his family moved from small town to small town in Missouri as his father pursued work. When they finally settled in Columbia, Missouri in 1933, Walton helped bolster the family income by taking on several jobs.

His work commitments did not prevent Walton from attending school. He was bright enough and hardworking enough to gain a place at the University of Missouri at Columbia, where he studied for a business degree, graduating in 1940. After college he decided to take a position as a management trainee in Des Moines, Iowa, at the retail store JCPenney. It was here that he learned many of the management techniques that he was to apply later—these included fostering a sense of inclusion by calling his employees "associates" and managing by walking about or, in Walton's case, by flying about.

Walton enlisted to fight in World War II. Unfit for full service because of a heart irregularity, he spent the war in the United States serving in the military police. He also married during the war, in 1943. It was a fortunate marriage. When Walton returned to civilian life at the end of the war, he decided to establish a business himself rather than return to JCPenney. He borrowed $20,000 from his father-in-law and bought a Ben Franklin store in Newport, Arkansas. It was September 1945, Walton was 27, and he was in the retail business.

DEFINING MOMENTS

Walton proved tough competition for the nearby better established businesses. One such was the Sterling Variety store, where Bud Hewitt, who would become a great friend of his, worked. In 1947, however, they were in competition, and when Hewitt had a run on rayon underwear for women (he was cleaned out of inventory), Walton was determined to outdo him. Rather than place an order, Walton went to Little Rock and bought the distributor. At a stroke, he cut the competition out of the market and secured his own store's supply of lingerie.

In 1950, despite his success, Walton was unable to renew the lease on his Newport store and was forced to sell out. He didn't quit though; he merely moved to nearby Bentonville where he bought another Ben Franklin store, calling it "Walton's Five and Dime." Before long he had added to his burgeoning retail empire by acquiring a number of other stores in the region. They were spread out over a wide area and potentially difficult to keep in

> **Rather than place an order, Walton went to Little Rock and bought the distributor.**

> "A computer can tell you down to the dime what you've sold, but it can never tell you how much you could have sold."
> Sam M. Walton

touch with and manage satisfactorily. He solved the problem imaginatively; he got his pilot's license in 1953 and acquired a decrepit prewar airplane, in which he simply flew from one store to the next.

Walton then cast his eye further afield. He began by visiting a couple of Ben Franklin "self-service" stores in Minnesota. The idea of self-service was then a new one, and the fact that it enabled the owner to pass on cheaper prices to the customer appealed to him. Back in Bentonville he opened his own self-service store. One of Walton's greatest strengths was that he was always willing to embrace innovation, whether it was self-service or, as in the early 1960s, the discount store concept.

The first Wal-Mart opened in 1962. It owed a great deal to the Kmart store in Chicago, a shop that Walton had visited to observe its operations at first hand. It was tough going initially. It wasn't easy to stock a full range of goods, since suppliers were reluctant to be associated with mass merchandising. Walton spent much of his time over the next few years experimenting with different layouts and different mixes of inventory to create the perfect discount store. All this time he continued to earn the bulk of his income from his chain of Ben Franklin stores. The second Wal-Mart opened in 1964 in Harrison, Arkansas. The first day was a disaster, primarily because of the inhospitable temperature of 115 degrees. The manure from the donkeys providing rides was trodden through the store. The watermelons outside popped in the heat. Local businessman David Glass uttered the legendary observation: "It was the worst retail store I've ever seen." Glass went on to become president of the Wal-Mart Corporation.

In 1970 Walton raised $5 million on the stock market through a public offering of Wal-Mart stock. The 1970 financing enabled Walton to construct six more stores as well as a distribution center. In fact, from the 1970s onward, the rate of construction of new Wal-Mart stores increased phenomenally; 452 were built during the 1970s and 1,237 in the 1980s.

As the Wal-Mart empire blossomed, Walton spent more and more time keeping his employees happy and up to scratch. He would still travel from store to store by plane and, where he found a store that didn't meet his high standards, he would close it on the spot and not reopen it until it was ready. Somehow Walton managed to keep in touch with his thousands of employees. He wrote a monthly column in the company newspaper, *Wal-Mart World*, he personally replied to letters from staff raising questions or suggesting ideas, and he insisted on attending the opening of new stores whenever possible. His commitment to the staff in his business was illustrated in 1983 when he promised to dance down Wall Street in a grass skirt if the company posted profit targets. It did, and Wall Street was graced with the sight of Walton dancing the hula.

By 1987 Wal-Mart had opened its 1,000th store and was an early adopter of network technology linking all the stores through a satellite system, something that, sadly, obviated the need for Walton's airborne excursions, much

to the relief of the stockholders. They profited greatly from his canny business sense. One hundred shares bought in 1970 for a mere $1,650 were, by the time of Walton's death, worth a staggering $2.6 million.

In 1986 Walton was diagnosed with bone marrow cancer. He died on April 6, 1992.

CONTEXT AND CONCLUSIONS

Frank Woolworth pioneered the concept of the five and dime store. He was also one of the first mass-market retailers with thousands of stores across the world. Sam Walton was a retailer out of the same mold, the Frank Woolworth of his generation who steadily built up a network of mass-merchandise discount stores under the Wal-Mart name. Always keen to embrace innovation, he pioneered the self-service concept, was one of the first retailers to adopt network technology via satellite to link stores, and championed hypermarkets. A stickler for high standards, he also was known to close down stores immediately if he felt they failed to come up to scratch. One of the greatest retailers of his generation, he died one of the richest men in the world, having built an empire of over 1,000 stores.

> Local businessman David Glass uttered the legendary observation: "It was the worst retail store I've ever seen." Glass went on to become president of the Wal-Mart Corporation.

1369

CLOSE BUT NO CIGAR

Sebastian Spering Kresge
Kresge was a traveling tinware salesman who founded a chain of S.S. Kresge discount retail stores in 1912. All the goods were priced at less than a dime. World War I inflation pushed the price limit up to a dollar. Kresge opened his first Kmart store in 1962. He died in 1966, the same year company sales topped $1 billion.

Richard Warren Sears
Sears was station agent for the Minnesota and St. Louis Railroad in North Redwood when he became the beneficiary of an unwanted consignment of watches. He sold them to other station agents and started the R. W. Sears Watch Company in 1886. This became Sears, Roebuck, & Co. in 1893 with the addition of Alvah C. Roebuck, a watchmaker. Sears went on to build the biggest retail business in the United States through the use of the mail-order catalog.

FOR MORE INFORMATION

Web site:
Wal-Mart: **www.walmart.com**

MANAGEMENT GIANTS

"Our best ideas come from clerks and schoolboys."   Sam M. Walton

Thomas J. Watson, Sr.

Thomas J. Watson, Sr. is reported to have made the unfortunately inaccurate prediction, "I think that there may be a world market for possibly five computers." But his misjudgment didn't prevent him from building the industrial and technological titan IBM. Watson graduated from hawking pianos to selling the cash register. He learned his trade under John Patterson, who taught him about commerce and social responsibility. When Watson was sacked by Patterson after an argument, he took with him progressive ideas about corporate culture and the working environment, and a small sign that said "THINK!" At Computing-Tabulating-Recording Co., the company that eventually became IBM, he engineered a corporate transformation, pumping money into research and development, nurturing exciting new technologies, and galvanizing the sales force.

Thomas J. Watson, Sr., champion of employee satisfaction.

1874	Born.
1893	Sells musical instruments.
1898	Joins the National Cash Register Company.
1914	Joins Computing-Tabulating-Recording Co. Revenues $4 million.
1924	Company's name changed to International Business Machines Corp.
1944	IBM builds world's first large-scale computer.
1946	IBM revenues $115 million.
1952	IBM manufactures world's first commercially available computer, the 701.
1956	Dies.

BACKGROUND AND RISE

Thomas J. Watson, Sr. was born in Campbell, New York, on February 17, 1874. Son of an upstate New York farmer, Watson's upbringing was a traditional, rural 19th-century one. Life was shaped by a strong moral code. Dignity, respect for others, self-respect, conscientious work, optimism, and loyalty were values ingrained in Watson throughout his childhood. Unlike many of his peers, he carried the values throughout his public and private life.

His first real job was as a bookkeeper at Clarence Risley's Market in Painted Post, NY. Later, when he was 18, Watson drove a horse and buggy across northern New York State, hawking an unlikely combination of pianos and sewing machines to farmers. As farmers were often short of cash, he took all manner of goods in trade. Animals, farm equipment, and produce were all exchanged and then sold again by Watson. It was invaluable training. It taught him the value of goods and that if he kept his customers happy, more people would buy his goods on recommendation.

> **His first real job was as a bookkeeper at Clarence Risley's Market in Painted Post, NY.**

DEFINING MOMENTS

In 1898, Watson went to work for the National Cash Register Company, known universally as "the cash." NCR was run by John Patterson, an eccentric, charismatic businessman and a remarkable business pioneer, who introduced many enlightened liberal working practices. Watson joined as a salesman. His first few weeks were spent calling on various prospects, without success. His manager, after giving the dispirited Watson a talking to, promised to accompany him and show him how it should be done. He was true to his word; they traveled together, and Watson finally made a number of sales. The attitude of his manager made a great impression on Watson. Later at IBM, he made sure all managers were able to work with their staff and provide them with adequate training.

With his first few sales in the bag, Watson made swift progress. In 1899 he was promoted to manager of the company's Rochester branch and then to general sales manager—Patterson's right-hand man. While at NCR he came up with the slogan that would later become firmly associated with IBM—"THINK!" Not many people know that the motto was originally conceived, and used to good effect, to pep up a dispirited NCR salesforce.

After a number of disagreements with Patterson, Watson was fired from NCR. In 1914 he moved on to the Computing-Tabulating-Recording Company (CTR), an alliance of three small companies, as general manager. When he arrived, CTR was in poor shape. Worse still, as a newcomer brought into shake things up, Watson was resented by the staff who naturally feared for their jobs. But Watson did not fire a single member of staff. Instead he determined to make the existing workforce better at their jobs. This was the foundation of IBM's famous policy of job security. This policy was even adhered to during the great depression. Despite one quarter of the United States labor force being unemployed, IBM carried on expanding, producing excess inventory and stockpiling it, a gamble which ultimately paid off.

"Business is a game, the greatest game in the world if you know how to play it."

Thomas J. Watson, Sr.

At CTR, Watson also took a lead from Patterson's liberal working practices and theories. He didn't have the resources to build a modern, forward-looking factory like NCR's in Dayton, but he did do everything in his power to create an enthusiastic atmosphere at the company. This included staging concerts, picnics, and other entertainment, as well as giving rousing speeches. This close and almost paternalistic relationship with his employees led to the "open door" policy, where Watson made himself available in person to see his employees whenever they wished and actively encouraged their visits. This policy was another key element of Watson's management strategy at IBM and only lapsed after his death, when the size of the company made it impracticable.

At IBM, Watson always went out of his way to keep his employees happy. In 1939, he took 10,000 people to IBM Day at the World's Fair, at the company's expense. The sales conventions became increasingly extravagant affairs. Waking delegates were greeted with newspapers recounting the previous day's events, and overseas visitors were provided with headphones through which they heard a translation of the proceedings. A visit by General Eisenhower in July 1948 was extended, after some persuasion by Watson, to allow Eisenhower to address workers at the IBM plant, who were all given time off work to attend.

Watson's obsession with excellent customer service is illustrated by an incident that occurred during World War II. On Good Friday in 1942, an official from the War Production Board telephoned Watson late in the afternoon. He placed an order for 150 machines and challenged Watson to deliver the equipment to Washington D.C. by the following Monday. Watson agreed. Saturday morning saw him, with his staff, phoning IBM offices across the country to organize the dispatch of 150 machines over the Easter holiday. To emphasize the effort he was making, he instructed his staff to let the War Production Board people know the minute each truck began its journey to Washington, no matter what time of day or night. Police and army officials were rounded up to escort trucks, which were driven through the night. A makeshift factory was also established in Georgetown to deal with the reception and installation of the equipment. It was a remarkable effort, typical of Watson's attitude.

Between 1914 and 1946, IBM's profits grew 38 times, giving great weight to Watson's management strategy. And even though this growth was a magnificent achievement, it was nothing compared to what happened in the postwar period, as IBM grew its revenues from $115 million in 1946 to $1.7 billion by 1961, with employee numbers growing from 17,000 in the United States to 80,000 during the same period. One hundred shares bought in 1914 would have cost $2,740. By 1962, shortly after Watson's death, they were worth $5.45 million.

Much of this was due to the success of a new breed of computer. The Mach 1 was the world's first large-scale computer, built by IBM in collaboration with Dr. Howard Aiken and presented to Harvard University in 1944. This was followed with the first commercially available IBM computer, the 701, in 1952.

Thomas J. Watson, Sr. died on June 19, 1956. A month earlier, he passed his control in the company to his eldest son, Thomas J. Watson, Jr.

CONTEXT AND CONCLUSIONS

Thomas J. Watson, Sr. achieved great things at IBM. He managed the growth of a small company with a promising technology into a billion-dollar company with a technology that changed the world. The history of computing is not just about the scientists and inventors. It is also about the men who manage creativity and innovation, and who help turn the fantastic dreams of scientists into commercial reality. Watson was one such man. He cajoled, he improved, he inspired. Many of his methods he owed to his inspirational mentor, John Patterson at NCR. Watson took Patterson's ideals forward into the 20th century and, in doing so, created one of the most enduring companies in the United States.

> At IBM, Watson always went out of his way to keep his employees happy. In 1939, he took 10,000 people to IBM Day at the World's Fair, at the company's expense.

1371

MANAGEMENT GIANTS

FOR MORE INFORMATION

Books:
Rodgers, William. *THINK. A Biography of the Watsons and IBM.* New York: Stein and Day, 1969.
Watson, Thomas J. Jr, with Peter Petre. *Father Son & Co. My Life at IBM and Beyond.* Rev. ed. New York: Bantam, 2000.

Jack Welch

One of the most renowned corporate leaders of the 20th century, Jack Welch maintained General Electric's reputation as a world leader throughout his 20-year reign as C.E.O. Under Welch the company moved into new business areas and reached new heights.

Jack Welch, named in 1999 as *Fortune*'s "manager of the century," started at General Electric as a trainee in 1960. At the age of 33 he became the youngest general manager in the company's history, and in 1981 became C.E.O. Over a 20-year period he oversaw revolution, reorganization, Six Sigma, tough targets, and a blaze of corporate acquisitions. The results were a 600% increase in profits, 100 consecutive quarters of increased earnings, and a status as one of the most profitable companies in the world. Welch stepped down as C.E.O. in September 2001.

The Giant of GE.

1935	Born.
1960	Starts at General Electric.
1961	Almost quits General Electric.
1963	Put in charge of chemical development.
1968	Becomes General Electric's youngest ever general manager.
1981	Becomes C.E.O.
1986	Buys RCA.
1995	Introduces Six Sigma
2000	Postpones retirement to oversee Honeywell Bull deal.
2000	Receives $7 million book advance.
2001	Steps down as C.E.O.
2001	Publication of *Straight from the Gut*.
2002	Public criticism of retirement settlement.

BACKGROUND AND RISE

Jack Francis Welch, Jr., one of most celebrated managers and leaders of the 20th century, was born on November 19, 1935 in Peabody, Massachusetts. He grew up in Salem, where his father worked as a railroad conductor. As a boy he suffered from a stutter that might have badly affected his confidence, had it not been for his mother's imaginative explanation. "She told me [it was] just that my brain worked too fast," Welch said.

At school he was a keen sportsman; he also was described by classmates as the "most talkative and noisiest boy" they knew. After high school he set off for the University of Massachusetts, where he studied chemistry. Then came the University of Illinois, where he obtained a Ph.D. in chemical engineer-

ing. From there he moved to Pittsfield, Massachusetts, to start his first real job at General Electric.

DEFINING MOMENTS

Welch's meteoric career at General Electric (GE) almost didn't happen. In 1961, sick of the cumbersome bureaucratic systems, Welch quit. Fortunately for GE, his boss at the time persuaded him to stay. In 1963 Welch was put in charge of chemical development, and in 1968, aged 33, he became GE's youngest general manager ever. By 1972 he had risen to the position of divisional vice president and set his sights on rising even higher. On his employee evaluation form Welch was asked to state his long-term ambitions—to become C.E.O., he wrote. By 1979 he was vice chairman and executive officer.

Along the way he built plastics into a formidable $2 billion business, turned around the medical diagnostics business, and began the development of GE Capital. In 1980 he was announced as the new C.E.O. and chairman of GE, at 45 the youngest chief the company had ever appointed and only the eighth C.E.O. in 92 years.

At the time, GE was in reasonable shape. That year *Fortune* magazine voted it the best-managed company in the United States, and Reg Jones, the C.E.O. who Welch had replaced, was ranked number one among C.E.O.s. Yet GE's stock was performing poorly. Against the backdrop of a faltering world economy, the Japanese were posing a real threat to U.S. manufacturers with new production systems such as "lean manufacturing."

During the 1980s, recognizing that GE would have to change in order to compete successfully on the world stage, Welch declared that it was going become the world's most valuable company. This meant getting rid of all unprofitable areas. The focus was shifted to service industries, creating over 1000 new businesses, and resulting in the disposal of 70 existing businesses.

But that was only a start. Next Welch turned his attention to the organizational structure. He pared down the

> On his employee evaluation form Welch was asked to state his long-term ambitions—to become C.E.O., he wrote. By 1979 he was vice chairman and executive officer.

"People always overestimate how complex business is. This isn't rocket science; we've chosen one of the world's more simple professions."

Jack Welch

    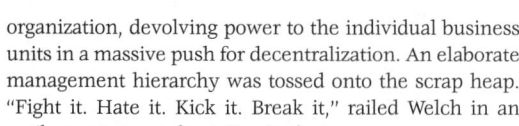

organization, devolving power to the individual business units in a massive push for decentralization. An elaborate management hierarchy was tossed onto the scrap heap. "Fight it. Hate it. Kick it. Break it," railed Welch in an antibureaucracy exhortation to the troops.

Nearly 200,000 GE employees left the company and over $6 billion was saved. The media dubbed Welch "Neutron Jack." But by the end of the 1980s, having proved that he could tear the company apart, Welch moved on to stage two: rebuilding a company fit for the 21st century. To encourage innovation and the communication of ideas, he vowed to create a "boundaryless" organization. "Knock down the walls that separate us from each other on the inside and from our key constituents on the outside," was how he put it. In the pre-Welch era, employees with a good idea would squirrel it away. Now they would be encouraged to share their ideas, and the culture would make sure they received the praise they deserved.

So that all employees were pulling in the same direction, Welch used corporate values to guide behavior. He famously carried a copy of them printed on a card.

In the mid-1990s, in a drive for quality, Welch adopted the concept of Six Sigma, developed by Motorola in 1985. A statistical term, Six Sigma refers to products with a 99.9998% perfection rate. Implementation relies on rigorous measurement and testing to deliver results. Welch made sure that the adoption of Six Sigma had 100% management backing, and attributed a 3% increase in profit margins between 1995 and 1999 to its roll out.

A stack of figures attest to the success of Jack Welch's reign: between 1981 and 1999, for example, the GE stock price rose from just over $4 to $133 (allowing for four stock splits), an increase of 3,200%. From 1980 onward, the average total return on GE stock was about 27%, and the company has returned 100 consecutive quarters of increased earnings from continuing operations. If you had bought $10,000 worth of General Electric stock in March 1981 and reinvested the dividends, by the end of 1999 they would have been worth $640,000. Over the same period GE sales rose from $27.2 billion to $173.2 billion, while profits rose from $1.6 billion to $10.7 billion. By 1999 General Electric was the second most profitable company in the world.

The only slight tarnishing of Welch's luster came in 2001. Due to retire, Welch postponed his departure for one last hurrah: a mega deal with Honeywell Bull, snatched from under the noses of intended purchasers, United Technologies. Despite Welch's best efforts, however, this deal was scuppered by European Union regulators. In some ways it was an unfortunate end to a majestic career. Commenting on the affair, Welch was his characteristic self: "GE was a great company before I took a swing at it. It's a great company after. It would have been better if we had gotten it. But as far as regrets for doing it? No way. I'd do the same thing again tomorrow." He finally handed over the baton to his successor, Jeff Immelt, on September 7, 2001. His next job—to promote his autobiography, *Jack: Straight from the Gut.*

Retirement started with promise, a $7 million advance from his publishers, and an extremely generous retirement package, but personal matters changed public attitudes. In 2002, he admitted to an affair with an editor of the *Harvard Business Review* and, during the subsequent divorce proceedings, there was public outrage when the scale of his retirement package was revealed.

CONTEXT AND CONCLUSIONS

The failed Honeywell takeover and personal revelations dominated press coverage of the end of Welch's rule at GE. The actions of the E.U. regulators briefly blotted out the achievements of an exceptional leader. But the three stages of development under Welch—destruction, creation, and quality—have reshaped GE and made Welch the C.E.O. role model of his generation. Inevitably, he also has his critics. They point to the size of corporate pay packets, GE's ecological record, high levels of layoffs, and the lack of loyalty throughout the organization. But there can be little disagreement that Welch made a difference where it mattered. History will remember him as one of the most important corporate leaders of the 20th century.

> A stack of figures attest to the success of Jack Welch's reign: between 1981 and 1999, for example, the GE stock price rose from just over $4 to $133 (allowing for four stock splits), an increase of 3,200%.

1373

MANAGEMENT GIANTS

CLOSE BUT NO CIGAR

John Marous
Concentrating on investor value worked for Welch, but it didn't work for Marous. A Westinghouse Electrical Company executive man and boy, Marous had been at the company for 40 years before he became C.E.O. in 1988. The similarities between Welch and Marous are many: both excelled at sports, were tough negotiators, and were results-driven in the extreme. "Don't just bring me bad news, bring me solutions," was a Marous motto. Under his leadership, some of Westinghouse's core businesses were sold off and Westinghouse Credit was given a free rein to lend, lend, lend. In 1990, the year Marous stepped down, the stock price was at its highest ever. But from there it was all downhill. After his departure the once great company drowned in the sea of bad debts left by its subsidiary Westinghouse Credit.

FOR MORE INFORMATION

Books:
Welch, Jack, and John A. Byrne. *Jack: Straight from the Gut.* New York: HarperBusiness, 2001.
Welch, Jack, and Suzy Welch. *Winning.* New York: HarperBusiness, 2005.

Web site:
General Electric: **www.ge.com**

Oprah Winfrey

The child of separated parents, the victim of childhood sexual abuse, teenage pregnancy, and juvenile delinquency, Oprah Winfrey (1954–) overcame a difficult start to become a U.S. icon.

Her career in broadcasting began as a teenager reading the news on the radio. By the age of 30 she had become the talk-show queen of the United States, hosting the nation's number one talk show. In 1988 she became the third woman ever to own her own film studio, Harpo Productions. At a time when talk shows seemed to be descending into the gutter, she pulled them back out again with a move to "change your life" television. Winfrey's future seems assured: she has secured her talk-show contract until 2011, she publishes a number of magazines and produces other television programs, and she's becoming more involved with social issues in the United States and beyond.

Winfrey's informal style changed television radically.

1954	Born.
1963	Moves to live with mother.
1972	Wins Miss Black Tennessee pageant.
1976	Moves to Baltimore and lands job with WJZ-TV.
1984	Achieves first major television success with AM Chicago.
1985	Plays Sofia in movie *The Color Purple*.
1986	Goes nationwide with *The Oprah Winfrey Show*.
1987	Wins first daytime Emmy for *The Oprah Winfrey Show*.
1994	Repositions her show as "change your life television."
1996	Establishes Book Club.
2000	Diversifies into publishing, brings out new magazine called *O*.
1998	Named second most admired woman in the United States.
1998	Lifetime achievement award at Emmys.
1999	Launches Oxygen cable TV network.
2003	First African-American woman billionaire.
2004	Secures deal to stay on U.S. television until 2011. Co-hosts Nobel Prize Concert with Tom Cruise.
2005	Named as world's most powerful celebrity by *Forbes* magazine.

BACKGROUND AND RISE

Oprah Winfrey had a tough start in life. Born to unmarried teenagers on July 29, 1954, she grew up in poverty on her grandmother's farm in Mississippi. The first Winfrey's father knew of her existence was when he received an instruction to send some clothes for her. Brought up initially by her grandmother, at four she moved to Milwaukee to live with her mother. After a brief but happy interlude with her father, Vernon Winfrey, a businessman in Nashville, Tennessee, she again ended up with

her mother in Milwaukee in 1963. During her time there she was raped, at the age of nine.

Her mother attempted to send her to a home for juvenile delinquents, but she was unable to wait two weeks for a place to become available. Winfrey was despatched back to live with her father. Had it not been for her father, Winfrey's life might easily have been a tale of loss and waste. Luckily for her, her father was a strict disciplinarian, and with his help Winfrey began to turn her life around.

At 16 she got her first lucky break. As the first African American girl to win a national beauty contest, she was invited on a tour of a local radio station to pick up her prize. Her talent was spotted there and she was asked to read the radio news after school. She had her next big break at 19, landing a job as a reporter for the Nashville radio station WVOL. At the same time she enrolled at Tennessee State University to study performing arts.

When she was initially offered a TV job, she turned it down until one of her professors persuaded her to change her mind. Winfrey became a news anchor on WTVF-TV in Nashville, the first African American to do so. Her star quality was evident from the moment she was put in front of the camera. On television she was a natural. Her personality lit up the screen.

DEFINING MOMENTS

In 1976 Winfrey moved to Baltimore, Maryland, and landed herself a job with WJZ-TV as a news co-anchor. The management wasn't impressed, criticizing her appearance and eventually demoting her to a morning spot. Luckily a station executive, Phil Baker, offered her an opportunity to co-host a chat show on the station. Reluctant at first, she accepted. It was a risk for the station to put an African American woman on as host of its principal talk show. And it was a risk for Winfrey, who thought her future lay in news. The show was called *People Are Talking,* and viewers were soon talking about Winfrey. They

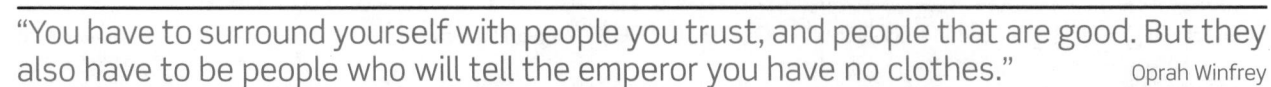

"You have to surround yourself with people you trust, and people that are good. But they also have to be people who will tell the emperor you have no clothes."
Oprah Winfrey

liked her down-to-earth style, and her Nielsen ratings began to rise. In 1984 she moved to Chicago to host WLS-TV's morning talk show, *AM Chicago*, going head-to-head with Phil Donahue, the country's top-rated talk-show host. Her show ranked number one within a month. Winfrey was just 30 years old.

Winfrey continued in her own inimitable style, being open and honest about her past and her emotions. It struck a chord with her audience. Viewers empathized with her. Her high profile began to pay dividends as she was asked to audition for the part of Sofia in Steven Spielberg's 1985 movie adaptation of Alice Walker's novel, *The Color Purple*. When she received a call telling her Steven Spielberg wanted her in his office in California the next day, she was at a health spa on one of her frequent attempts to lose weight. She was warned that if she lost as much as a pound it might jeopardize her chances of getting the part—she later joked that she stopped off at a Dairy Queen on the way to California. She got the part and was nominated for an Oscar for Best Supporting Actress.

The timing couldn't have been better for Winfrey. She was about to launch her nationally syndicated chat show, *The Oprah Winfrey Show*. It was 1986 and, despite one viewer in Iowa calling in to say he could get better ratings with a potato, Winfrey had hit the big time. Her style remained unaffected, and she soon racked up ten million viewers across the United States.

Astutely, Winfrey took control of her own destiny in 1988 by forming Harpo Productions—her name spelled backward—acquiring the rights to her show from Capital Cities/ABC. She also spent $20 million on a production facility in Chicago, a step on the way to becoming only the third woman to own a major studio (following in the footsteps of Mary Pickford and Lucille Ball).

Winfrey's professional life was blooming, but her personal life was plagued by her struggle with her weight. Her repeated and very public attempts to reduce her weight varied from exercise to a radical, four-month-long liquid diet. Eventually she managed to come to terms with herself and her weight, an achievement that helped her self-esteem and her bank balance: her 1994 book *In the Kitchen with Rosie* (Rosie was her chef) became the fastest selling book in the country.

Winfrey's immense success spawned a host of imitators. Talk shows sprang up on every station, delving into the private lives of individuals, exposing the underbelly of human existence. Appealing to the lowest common denominator, such programs can at times seem little more than a license to televise sleaze. In 1994 Winfrey decided to distance herself from the excesses of the genre by repositioning herself in the marketplace. She vowed to concentrate on more uplifting and more highbrow issues, calling her concept "change your life" TV. She has succeeded in both redefining herself and differentiating her show in the talk-show marketplace. The shift of emphasis secured another series run until 2011. The "Oprah Factor" has also begun to move beyond television in recent years. The appearance of "Oprah's Book Club" on U.S. screens in 1996 had a dramatic effect on book sales in the United States, and any title recommended by Winfrey in the on-air discussion group went on to massive success. After a short break, the book club was revived in 2003, with Steinbeck's *East of Eden* being the first to feel the benefit of Oprah's recommendation.

In 1999, she launched the Oxygen cable TV network. 2000 saw her using her influence to encourage others. She made a series of $100,000 "Use your Life" awards to people who improve the lives of others. Her contribution to broadcasting has not gone unrewarded. In 1998, she was voted second most admired woman in the United States behind Hillary Clinton, followed by a lifetime achievement award at the 1998 Emmys. The material rewards were there too when, in 2003, she became the first African-American woman to become a billionaire. The ultimate accolade came in 2005, however, when *Forbes* nominated her as the world's most powerful celebrity.

> When she was initially offered a TV job, she turned it down until one of her professors persuaded her to change her mind.

CONTEXT AND CONCLUSIONS

Oprah Winfrey's story is one of triumph over adversity. It offers a message of hope to those from disadvantaged backgrounds: that it is possible to achieve success through talent, hard work, and a little good fortune. Overcoming a childhood marked by abuse and discrimination, Winfrey has become a U.S. icon, an African American woman who has conquered television and found a place in the hearts of the public. She has succeeded by being herself, and today Winfrey is one of the most influential people in the United States. Her widely publicized comments about not eating beef, for example, were followed by a 10% drop in beef futures, an event that resulted in an unsuccessful attempt by the beef industry to sue her for millions of dollars in damages. With no sign of Winfrey's star fading, who knows what she will turn her hand to next? A growing interest in social issues suggests that her career could take on a more political direction. In his book *Dude, Where's My Country?* (Warner, 2003), the U.S. documentary-maker and political activist Michael Moore recommended that Oprah run for president in the future. Could she be the first female president of the United States?

> Winfrey's immense success spawned a host of imitators. Talk shows sprang up on every station, delving into the private lives of individuals, exposing the underbelly of human existence.

FOR MORE INFORMATION

Web site:
Oprah.com: **www.oprah.com**

1375

MANAGEMENT GIANTS

"I don't invest in anything I don't understand—it makes more sense to buy TV stations than oil wells."

Oprah Winfrey

Robert Winship Woodruff

Robert Woodruff was the natural heir to the Coca-Cola empire. His father was behind the $25 million buyout of the Candler family interests in Coca-Cola in 1919. Yet to begin with, his familial advantage did Woodruff no good at all. When he sought a job outside the family's beverage interests, his father attempted to restrict his career at every turn. Woodruff succeeded on his own terms as a sales representative for White Motor Company before bowing to the inevitable and joining Coca-Cola in 1923. For the next four decades until his official retirement in 1965, he ruled the company. He presided over a period of momentous growth that transformed Coca-Cola into a global corporation. By the time of his death in 1985 he had helped create one of the world's most valuable brands.

Robert Woodruff put the fizz back into Coca-Cola.

1889	Born.
1919	Father's syndicate buys Coca-Cola Company.
1923	Becomes president of Coca-Cola.
1926	Creates Coca-Cola's Foreign Department.
1928	Coca-Cola supplies beverages for Amsterdam Olympics.
1930	Foreign Department becomes Coca-Cola Export Corporation.
1933	Automatic Coca-Cola dispensers introduced at Chicago World's Fair.
1939	Steps down as president.
1965	Officially retires.
1985	Dies.

BACKGROUND AND RISE

Woodruff was born on December 6, 1889, in Columbus, Georgia. His father, Ernest Woodruff, was president of the Trust Company of Georgia, which was part of a syndicate that bought control of the Coca-Cola company. Ernest Woodruff became the company's president.

For the first stage of his education Woodruff was sent to the Georgia Military Academy. He proved a poor student. The school may have overlooked his disappointing grades, however, as the young Woodruff saved the academy from bankruptcy. Discovering that the Atlanta National Bank was about to foreclose on the school's mortgage, Woodruff paid a visit to the bank's vice president, and through a combination of bluffing and name-dropping he persuaded him to hold off.

Woodruff completed his education at Emory College, where he paid other students to complete his homework. When asked later in life about his tips for a being a suc-

> **Woodruff's working life also got off to an inauspicious start. He was dismissed from a series of jobs for no obvious reason.**

cessful manager, he replied, "If you can get someone to do something better than you can, it is always a good idea." Despite delegating his college work, he still failed to complete his degree.

Woodruff's working life also got off to an inauspicious start. He was dismissed from a series of jobs for no obvious reason. In fact he was not responsible for his appalling employment record: his father was. Ernest Woodruff had arranged for his son to be fired on each occasion to teach the young man that having a rich father was no guarantee of an easy life. Once, when Woodruff was refused a raise, he discovered that his father was interfering in his career and swore that he would never work for him again.

Instead he went to work as a truck sales representative at White Motor Company, but was swiftly promoted through the company, becoming vice president and then general manager.

DEFINING MOMENTS

While Woodruff was climbing the corporate ladder at White Motor Company, his father had been putting together an investment group that in 1919 paid $25 million for the Candler family's interest in the Coca-Cola Company. As part of the deal, 500,000 shares of Coca-Cola common stock were sold on the stock market for $40 a share. Asked by his father if he wished to participate in the syndicate, Woodruff agreed—picking up a large holding of the company's stock at $5 a share.

In 1923, aged 33, Woodruff achieved a business reconciliation with his father by accepting the presidency of Coca-Cola. He must have wanted the position badly because he took a substantial pay cut and turned down an offer to be president of Standard Oil at a salary of $250,000. Woodruff later said that the reason he took the job was that it was the only way he could boost the value of his stock in the company.

Over the next six decades Woodruff oversaw the transformation of Coca-Cola from a promising U.S. soft-drink

"Without the right attitude, a business with everything going for it will fail." Robert Heller

manufacturer into a global giant. His influence extended into every aspect of the company's operations and began with changing the company's marketing strategy. Only positive images were to be associated with the product: all negative connotations were banished, and Coca-Cola's medicinal roots were severed.

In production and distribution Woodruff set in motion a drive for quality. In 1928 soda fountains exceeded bottled sales, and Woodruff made sure the employees who serviced the fountains were highly trained and could pass their knowledge on to the storekeepers operating the fountains. A Fountain Training School was established where sales representatives could learn how to mix Coca-Cola properly. Woodruff also introduced a standard procedure manual. At the same time, realizing that the bottled drink was the future of the company, he introduced quality standards in the bottling plants. All employees were to wear uniforms, and hygiene and quality checks were introduced.

While all these changes were an essential part of Coca-Cola's success, Woodruff's most important contribution to the company was probably his move to open up international markets. As early as 1900 the Coca-Cola drink had been taken abroad by Asa Candler—the first international order was from England. Through the early 1900s the company built bottling plants in a number of countries from Cuba to the Philippines. But the expansion was disorganized, with no coordinated management of international product rollout.

In 1926 Woodruff changed that by creating the Foreign Department, which four years later became a full blown subsidiary, the Coca-Cola Export Corporation. Coca-Cola's march to global domination was inexorable under Woodruff. The company cleverly brokered a deal with the Olympics movement, with Coca-Cola being exported to Holland for sale at the 1928 Amsterdam Olympics. Woodruff secured Coca-Cola's beachheads abroad by investing in local economies, building bottling plants, and employing locals for the distribution. In this way the brand acquired goodwill in its export markets.

Although Woodruff resigned as president in 1939 he continued to play an active role in the company. As World War II approached he promised, "We'll see that every man in uniform gets a bottle of Coca-Cola for five cents, wherever he is and whatever it costs our company." The war helped proliferate Coca-Cola throughout the world.

In the postwar period Woodruff's efforts were increasingly concentrated on battling rival Pepsi-Cola. His influence at Coca-Cola persisted right up until and beyond his retirement in 1965. He remained a kingmaker, grooming potential C.E.O.s, including Roberto Goizueta, from behind the scenes. He died on March 7, 1985, at the age of 95.

CONTEXT AND CONCLUSIONS

Robert Woodruff the private man was an enigma. He was not a cultured man: he didn't read, nor, unlike many other wealthy executives, was he interested in collecting art or antiques. He had a fear of being alone and would often call friends and colleagues to his home in the small hours to keep him company. Yet he was also an intensely private person who installed a private elevator to his office.

Woodruff "the Boss," however, was a different story. The force behind one of the biggest corporate success stories of the last century, he was a restless, driven, controlling figurehead. Unlike many entrepreneurs, Woodruff didn't invent the product his company sold. But he was responsible for aggressively marketing Coca-Cola to a thirsty world—and for taking a caramel-based soda drink and turning it into a U.S. icon. Woodruff's personal creed was, "There is no limit to what a man can do or where he can go if he doesn't mind who gets the credit." Much of the credit for creating one of the world's most enduring products must go to him.

1377

MANAGEMENT GIANTS

> The force behind one of the biggest corporate success stories of the last century, he was a restless, driven, controlling figurehead.

FOR MORE INFORMATION

Book:
Pendergrast, Mark. *For God, Country, and Coca-Cola: The Definitive History of the Great American Soft Drink and the Company that Makes It.* 2nd ed. New York: Basic Books, 2000.

Web site:
Coca-Cola: **www.cocacola.com**

"There is no limit to what a man can do or where he can go if he doesn't mind who gets the credit."

Robert W. Woodruff

Frank Winfield Woolworth

Frank Winfield Woolworth (1852–1919) was a pioneer of the chain store. He came from a humble background, and became one of the richest men in the United States, despite many early setbacks in his career. Emerging from a small town in New York State, the farmer's boy rolled out his "five and ten cents" concept first across the United States and then around the world. From a single store in 1879 to a thousand in 1918, the growth of F. W. Woolworth & Co. was phenomenal, changing the nature of retailing and bringing its founder riches and fame. Woolworths was the original price-driven retail chain. The secret of his success he put down to delegating well.

F. W. Woolworth changed the way the world shops.

1852	Born.
1858	Family moves to 108-acre farm near Great Bend, New York.
1873	Woolworth goes to work at Augsbury & Moore's store.
1878	The five-cent table causes a stir in U.S. retailing.
1879	First Woolworth store opens in Utica, New York.
1895	28 stores and revenues of over $1 million.
1905	F. W. Woolworth & Co. incorporated.
1913	Company moves into the tallest skyscraper of its time, in New York City.
1918	In January the 1000th store opens on Fifth Avenue, New York City.
1919	Dies.

BACKGROUND AND RISE

Woolworth was born in Rodman, the eldest son of the family. In late 1858, when Woolworth was seven, the family moved to a 108-acre farm near Great Bend, New York. In a town with a population of only 125, Woolworth's opportunities for education were limited; there was only a one-room schoolhouse, which he attended along with his brother. Much of Woolworth's time, in fact, was taken up helping his father with the family's eight-cow dairy herd rather than studying.

> At Augsbury & Moore, Woolworth started at the bottom of the ladder. He swept floors, created window displays, delivered goods, and generally made himself useful.

When he was 16 Woolworth attended commercial college for a brief period before offering his services first to the stationmaster's small store, and then to Dan McNeil's general store in Great Bend as a clerk. On both occasions Woolworth worked for free. In return, Dan McNeil re-commended Woolworth to William Moore, the owner of a leading dry-goods store in Watertown, New York. In 1873 Moore agreed to take Woolworth on.

At Augsbury & Moore, Woolworth started at the bottom of the ladder. He swept floors, created window displays, delivered goods, and generally made himself useful. The hours were long—six days a week, 7:00 a.m. to 9:00 p.m.—and the pay offered little compensation. The owners initially wanted Woolworth to work for a year with no salary, but after some discussion Woolworth persuaded them to let him work for three months for nothing, rising to $3.50 for the following three months.

Two years later Woolworth moved on to another store, Bushnall's Department Store, as a senior clerk. In 1876 he married Jennie Creighton, a Canadian, and purchased a four-acre farm. Unfortunately, the tough conditions and lack of support at work meant Woolworth suffered from fever and stress-related illness, which forced him to give up his position at Bushnall's and kept him at home for a year unable to work. As he was recovering, his old employer William Moore came knocking at his door requesting him to return to work at the now renamed Moore & Smith's. Woolworth accepted on a salary of $10 a week.

DEFINING MOMENTS

In 1878 Woolworth's daughter was born and his mother died. But it was also a year of radical change in the world of retailing. In stores in the Midwest a new tactic had made its debut—the five-cent table. Surplus merchandise was marked down to a nickel by retailers and displayed on a five-cent table. Customers snapped up the bargains and were then drawn into buying other goods at full price. Moore traveled to New York City and came home with $100 worth of five-cent goods for Moore & Smith. Woolworth arranged the counter, and they were sold out in a day.

With goods supplied by Moore, Woolworth opened his own store in Utica, New York, selling only on the five-cent principle. "The Great Five Cent Store" opened for

"Retail has been described as selling things which don't come back to customers who do."

Tom Farmer

business on a Saturday evening in February 1879 with $321 worth of five-cent goods. The first ever item sold was a fire shovel. However, the store was a failure and soon closed. Undaunted, Woolworth opened another in June of the same year in Lancaster, Pennsylvania. Now he sold goods for five and ten cents. The Lancaster store was a success. In November 1880 he opened a second store in Scranton, Pennsylvania. This too was a success, and Woolworth never looked back.

Woolworth brought in family members to help expand his empire. By 1895 he had 28 stores, including that of his ex-boss William Moore, and revenues of over $1 million. The growth continued at breakneck speed. In 1900 there were 35 stores; by 1908, 189; and by 1911, 600. In January 1918 the thousandth store opened on Fifth Avenue in New York City.

Woolworth's one-man retail business had burgeoned into a global enterprise. In 1905, bowing to commercial pressures, he incorporated F. W. Woolworth & Co., issuing 50,000 shares to executives and employees. Corporate offices were first located in the Stewart Building overlooking City Hall Park in New York City. Then, in April 1913, the company moved into the Woolworth Building, the tallest skyscraper of its time. Woolworth's office was situated on the 24th floor. Thirty feet square, its design was based on Napoleon's famous Empire Room and contained the clock and other articles from the original room.

In 1916 the F. W. Woolworth stores served over 700 million customers and had revenues of over $87 million. Every town in the United States with a population of over 8,000 had a Woolworth's.

By the time Woolworth was installed in the Woolworth Building he was approaching the end of his career. With his health failing, he began taking periods of rest in Europe. His wife, Jennie, was suffering from premature senility. Woolworth's own health continued to decline steadily, partly due to a refusal to care for his teeth. On April 4, 1919 he fell desperately ill, dying four days later.

CONTEXT AND CONCLUSIONS

F. W. Woolworth & Co. was the pioneer of price-driven retail. Laying down a tradition of value for money that was later followed by companies such as Wal-Mart, Woolworth was one of the first merchants to build a retail empire founded on chain stores and volume retailing.

Working for very little or no money, enduring long periods of ill health, and with three out of his first five stores failing, no one would have blamed Woolworth for giving up his business dreams. Instead, his extraordinary persistence saw off all his five-and-ten-cents competitors and made him the most successful retailer of his time.

Woolworth's concept of a business based on bargain goods survived until the 1990s. In 1997, however, the Woolworth corporation announced that it was to close its last 400 F. W. Woolworth five-and-dime stores in the United States, finally retreating from the low-priced general merchandise business that had shaped its identity for 117 years.

> In 1916 the F. W. Woolworth stores served over 700 million customers and had revenues of over $87 million.

What was Woolworth's secret? Delegation apparently: "So long as I was obsessed with the idea that I must attend personally to everything, large-scale success was impossible. A man must select able lieutenants and/or associates and give them power and responsibility."

FOR MORE INFORMATION

Books:
Baker, Nina Brown. *Nickels and Dimes: The Story of F. W. Woolworth*. New York: Harcourt, Brace & World, 1954.
Nichols, John P. *Skyline Queen and the Merchant Prince: The Woolworth Story*. London: Trident Press, 1973.
Plunkett-Powell, Karen. *Remembering Woolworth's: A Nostalgic History of the World's Most Famous Five-and-Dime*. New York: St. Martin's Press, 1999.
Winkler, John Kennedy. *Five and Ten: The Fabulous Life of F. W. Woolworth*. Freeport, NY: Books for Libraries Press, 1970.

Web site:
Woolworths: **www.woolworths.co.uk**

1379

MANAGEMENT GIANTS

"The customer isn't king anymore. The customer is a dictator."

Anonymous

DICTIONARY

a-z Dictionary

Defining business: the most up-to-date global Business English dictionary

In a dynamic business environment, it is essential that managers keep up to date with the latest business terms and jargon.

The Dictionary provides clear definitions to more than 7,000 international business and management terms, abbreviations, and acronyms. It has been compiled by an international team of expert researchers and business information specialists, led by the Chartered Management Institute in Europe.

Special features:

World Business English terms are included to reflect the globalization of the business world

Abbreviations, acronyms, and their expansions are shown in full and cross-referred for ease of use

Mini-essays to explain more complex concepts and help you get to grips with ideas quickly

Biographical entries to detail the lives and careers of key business thinkers and leaders

Extensive listings of international stock exchanges and trade organizations

Business slang from around the world—some humorous, some serious, some baffling. If English is not your first language, these entries will help you find a **level playing field**, avoid a **seagull manager**, and make sure you avoid being implicated in **blamestorming** at work.

A

AAA *abbr* FINANCE, BANKING, AND ACCOUNTING American Accounting Association

AAD FINANCE, BANKING, AND ACCOUNTING a unit of accounting used between member states of the Arab Monetary Fund

AAIA *abbr* FINANCE, BANKING, AND ACCOUNTING Associate of the Association of International Accountants

AAMOF *abbr* GENERAL MANAGEMENT as a matter of fact (*slang*)

AARF *abbr* FINANCE, BANKING, AND ACCOUNTING Australian Accounting Research Foundation

AAS *abbr* FINANCE, BANKING, AND ACCOUNTING Australian Accounting Standard

AASB *abbr* FINANCE, BANKING, AND ACCOUNTING Australian Accounting Standards Board

AAT *abbr* (*U.K.*) FINANCE, BANKING, AND ACCOUNTING Association of Accounting Technicians

abacus FINANCE, BANKING, AND ACCOUNTING a counting device used for making basic arithmetic calculations, that consists of parallel rods strung with beads. Still widely used in education worldwide and for business and accounting in China and Japan, its origins can be traced back to early civilizations. Australia's oldest accounting journal bears the same name.

abandonment option FINANCE, BANKING, AND ACCOUNTING the option of terminating an investment before the time that it is scheduled to end

abandonment value FINANCE, BANKING, AND ACCOUNTING the value that an investment has if it is terminated at a particular time before it is scheduled to end

ABA transit number FINANCE, BANKING, AND ACCOUNTING a 9-digit number allocated to a U.S. financial institution, such as a bank. It appears on U.S. checks in the lower left-hand corner. Also known as *routing number*

ABB *abbr* FINANCE, BANKING, AND ACCOUNTING activity based budgeting

abbreviated accounts (*U.K.*) FINANCE, BANKING, AND ACCOUNTING a shortened version of a company's annual accounts that a company classified as small- or medium-sized under the

Companies Act (1989) can file with the **Registrar of Companies**, instead of having to supply a full version

ABC *abbr* FINANCE, BANKING, AND ACCOUNTING activity based costing

ABI *abbr* FINANCE, BANKING, AND ACCOUNTING Association of British Insurers

Abilene paradox GENERAL MANAGEMENT a theory stating that some decisions that seem to be based on consensus are in fact based on misperception and lead to courses of action that defeat original intentions. The Abilene paradox was proposed by management professor Jerry Harvey in 1974 following a trip made by his family to the town of Abilene. One person suggested the visit and the others agreed, each believing that everyone else wanted to go. On their return, everyone admitted that they would rather have stayed at home. Harvey used this experience to illustrate the mismanagement of agreement, and of *decision making* in organizations when apparent consensus is actually founded on poor communication. The Abilene paradox shows similarities to the **attribution theory of leadership** .

ability test HR & PERSONNEL see *aptitude test*

ability-to-pay principle FINANCE, BANKING, AND ACCOUNTING a theory which holds that taxes should be paid only by those who can best afford them

ABM *abbr* FINANCE, BANKING, AND ACCOUNTING activity-based management

ABN *abbr* FINANCE, BANKING, AND ACCOUNTING Australian Business Number: a numeric code that identifies an Australian business for the purpose of dealing with the Australian Tax Office and other government departments. ABNs are part of the new tax system that came into operation in Australia in 1998.

abnormal loss FINANCE, BANKING, AND ACCOUNTING any loss which exceeds the normal loss allowance. Abnormal losses are generally accounted for as though they were completed products.

abnormal shrinkage FINANCE, BANKING, AND ACCOUNTING the unexpectedly high level of *shrinkage* that has contributed to an *abnormal loss*

abnormal spoilage FINANCE, BANKING, AND ACCOUNTING the unexpectedly high level of shortfall that has contributed to an *abnormal loss*

abnormal waste FINANCE, BANKING, AND ACCOUNTING the unexpectedly high level of *waste* that has contributed to an *abnormal loss*

above par FINANCE, BANKING, AND ACCOUNTING used to describe a security that trades above its *nominal value*

above-the-fold E-COMMERCE relating to the portion of a Webpage that can be seen without scrolling downward. Commercially this is the most valuable portion of the page, as it is seen by everybody who calls it up. See also *below-the-fold*

above-the-line
1 MARKETING relating to marketing expenditure on advertising in media such as the press, radio, television, film, and the World Wide Web, on which a commission is usually paid to an agency
2 FINANCE, BANKING, AND ACCOUNTING used to describe entries in a company's profit and loss accounts that appear above the line separating those entries that show the origin of the funds that have contributed to the profit or loss from those that relate to its distribution. Exceptional and extraordinary items appear above the line. See also *below-the-line* **2**
3 FINANCE, BANKING, AND ACCOUNTING in macroeconomics, used to describe a country's revenue transactions. See also *below-the-line* **3**

abridged accounts (*U.K.*) FINANCE, BANKING, AND ACCOUNTING financial statements produced by a company that fall outside the requirements stipulated in the **Companies Act**. Abridged accounts are often made public through the media.

ABS *abbr* FINANCE, BANKING, AND ACCOUNTING Australian Bureau of Statistics

absenteeism HR & PERSONNEL the problem of employees taking short-term, unauthorized *leave* from work, resulting in lost *productivity* and increased costs. Absenteeism is usually sickness-related. Other causes may include a lack of *motivation*, domestic difficulties, or poor management. See checklist **Managing Absenteeism**

absorb FINANCE, BANKING, AND ACCOUNTING to assign an overhead to a particular cost center in a company's production accounts so that its identity becomes lost. See also *absorption costing*

absorbed account FINANCE, BANKING, AND ACCOUNTING an account that has lost its separate identity by being combined with related accounts in the preparation of a financial statement

absorbed business FINANCE, BANKING, AND ACCOUNTING GENERAL MANAGEMENT a company that has been merged into another company

absorbed costs FINANCE, BANKING, AND ACCOUNTING the indirect costs associated with manufacturing, for example, insurance or property taxes

absorbed overhead FINANCE, BANKING, AND ACCOUNTING an overhead attached to products or services by means of *absorption rates*

absorption costing FINANCE, BANKING, AND ACCOUNTING an accounting practice in which fixed and variable costs of production are absorbed by different cost centers. Providing all the products or services can be sold at a price that covers the allocated costs, this method ensures that both fixed and variable costs are recovered in full. However, should sales be lost because the resultant price is too high, the organization may lose revenue that would have contributed to its overhead. See also *marginal costing*

abusive tax shelter FINANCE, BANKING, AND ACCOUNTING a tax shelter that somebody claims illegally to avoid or minimize tax

ACA *abbr* FINANCE, BANKING, AND ACCOUNTING
1 Australian Communications Authority
2 Associate of the Institute of Chartered Accountants in England and Wales

Academy of Accounting Historians FINANCE, BANKING, AND ACCOUNTING a U.S. body founded in 1973 that promotes "research, publication, teaching and personal interchanges in all phases of Accounting History and its interrelation with business and economic history"

ACAS *abbr* (*U.K.*) FINANCE, BANKING, AND ACCOUNTING Advisory, Conciliation and Arbitration Service

ACAUS *abbr* FINANCE, BANKING, AND ACCOUNTING Association of Chartered Accountants in the United States

ACCA *abbr* FINANCE, BANKING, AND ACCOUNTING
1 Association of Chartered Certified Accountants
2 associate of the Association of Chartered Certified Accountants

ACCC *abbr* FINANCE, BANKING, AND ACCOUNTING Australian Competition and Consumer Commission: an independent statutory body responsible for monitoring trade practices in Australia. It was established in November 1995 as a result of the merger of the Trade Practices Commission and the Prices Surveillance Authority.

accelerated cost recovery system FINANCE, BANKING, AND ACCOUNTING a system used for computing the depreciation of some assets acquired before 1986 in a way that reduces taxes. Abbr. *ACRS*

accelerated depreciation ECONOMICS FINANCE, BANKING, AND ACCOUNTING a system used for computing the depreciation of some assets in a way that assumes that they depreciate faster in the early years of their acquisition. Also known as *declining balance method*

acceleration clause FINANCE, BANKING, AND ACCOUNTING a section of a contract which details how a loan may be required to be repaid early if the borrower defaults on other clauses of the contract

acceptable quality level OPERATIONS & PRODUCTION the level at which an output of manufactured components is considered to be of satisfactory quality. Acceptable quality level is usually expressed with the number of defective items shown as a proportion of the total output. Today, owing to a general increase in competitive pressure, the only acceptable quality level is *zero defects*, so the term is rarely used.

acceptance FINANCE, BANKING, AND ACCOUNTING the signature on a bill of exchange, indicating that the drawee (the person to whom it is addressed) will pay the face amount of the bill on the due date

acceptance bonus FINANCE, BANKING, AND ACCOUNTING HR & PERSONNEL a *bonus* paid to a new *employee* on acceptance of a job. An acceptance bonus can be a feature of a *golden hello* and is designed both to attract and to retain staff.

acceptance credit FINANCE, BANKING, AND ACCOUNTING a line of credit granted by a bank to an importer against which an exporter can draw a bill of exchange. After acceptance by the bank, the bill can either be sold in the market or held until maturity.

acceptance house (*U.K.*) ECONOMICS FINANCE, BANKING, AND ACCOUNTING an institution that accepts financial instruments and agrees to honor them should the borrower default

acceptance region STATISTICS the set of values in a test statistic for which the null hypothesis can be accepted

acceptance sampling OPERATIONS & PRODUCTION a *quality control* decision-making technique used in a manufacturing environment, in which acceptance or rejection of a batch of

parts is decided by testing a sample of the batch. The sample is checked against established standards and, if it meets those standards, the whole batch is deemed acceptable.

accepting bank FINANCE, BANKING, AND ACCOUNTING the bank that accepts a bill of exchange drawn under a *documentary credit*

acceptor FINANCE, BANKING, AND ACCOUNTING the person to whom a signed bill of exchange is addressed

access FINANCE, BANKING, AND ACCOUNTING the right to sell goods or services into a particular market without contravening related legislation

access bond (*S. Africa*) FINANCE, BANKING, AND ACCOUNTING a type of mortgage that permits borrowers to take out loans against extra capital paid into the account, home-loan interest rates being lower than interest rates on other forms of credit

access number E-COMMERCE the telephone number used to link to an Internet service provider or other network provider using a dial-up connection

access point E-COMMERCE a transceiver in a wireless local area network that connects a wired local area network to wireless devices or that connects wireless devices to each other

ACCI *abbr* FINANCE, BANKING, AND ACCOUNTING Australian Chamber of Commerce and Industry

accommodation address FINANCE, BANKING, AND ACCOUNTING an address used for receiving messages, which is not the real address of the company

accommodation bill FINANCE, BANKING, AND ACCOUNTING a bill of exchange where the drawee who signs it is helping another company (the drawer) to raise a loan. The bill is given on the basis of trade debts owed to the borrower.

account
1 FINANCE, BANKING, AND ACCOUNTING a business arrangement involving the exchange of money or credit in which payment is deferred, or a record maintained by a financial institution itemizing its dealings with a particular customer
2 MARKETING a client of an advertising or PR agency
3 FINANCE, BANKING, AND ACCOUNTING a structured record of transactions in monetary terms, kept as part of an accounting system.

This may take the form of a simple list or that of entries on a credit and debit basis, maintained either manually or as a computer record.

accountability GENERAL MANAGEMENT the allocation or acceptance of *responsibility* for actions

accountancy bodies FINANCE, BANKING, AND ACCOUNTING professional institutions and associations for accountants

accountancy profession FINANCE, BANKING, AND ACCOUNTING collectively, the professional bodies of accountants that establish and regulate training entry standards and professional examinations, as well as ethical and technical rules and guidelines. These bodies are organized on national and international levels.

accountant FINANCE, BANKING, AND ACCOUNTING a professional person who maintains and checks the business records of a person or organization and prepares forms and reports for financial purposes

accountant's letter FINANCE, BANKING, AND ACCOUNTING a written statement by an independent accountant that precedes a financial report, describing the scope of the report and giving an opinion on its validity

account day (*U.K.*) FINANCE, BANKING, AND ACCOUNTING the day on which an executed order is settled by the delivery of securities, payment to the seller, and payment by the buyer. This is the final day of the *accounting period* .

account debtor FINANCE, BANKING, AND ACCOUNTING a person or organization responsible for paying for a product or service

account director MARKETING a senior person within an advertising agency responsible for overall policy on a client's advertising account

account executive MARKETING an employee of an organization such as a bank, public relations firm, or advertising agency who is responsible for the business of a particular client

accounting FINANCE, BANKING, AND ACCOUNTING a generic term for all the activities conducted by accountants, for example, bookkeeping and financial accounting. Accounting involves the classification and recording of monetary transactions; the presentation and interpretation of the results of those transactions in order to assess performance over a period and the financial position at a given date; and the monetary projection of future activities arising from alternative planned courses of action. Account-

ing in larger businesses is typically carried out by financial accountants, who focus on formal, corporate issues such as taxation, and management accountants, who provide management reports and guidance.

Accounting and Finance Association of Australia and New Zealand FINANCE, BANKING, AND ACCOUNTING an organization for accounting and finance academics, researchers, and professionals. The Association has a variety of objectives, including the promotion of information on accounting to the public, and the provision of programs in continual professional development to both members and nonmembers. The Association's name was changed in 2002 to incorporate the Accounting Association of Australia and New Zealand (AAANZ) and the Australian Association of University Teachers in Accounting (AAUTA). Abbr. *AFAANZ*

accounting bases FINANCE, BANKING, AND ACCOUNTING the methods used for applying fundamental accounting concepts to financial transactions and items; preparing financial accounts; determining the accounting periods in which revenue and costs should be recognized in the profit and loss account; and determining the amounts at which material items should be stated in the balance sheet

accounting concept FINANCE, BANKING, AND ACCOUNTING any of the general assumptions on which accounts are prepared. The main concepts are: that the business is a going concern; that revenue and costs are noted when they are incurred and not when cash is received or paid; that the present accounts are drawn up following the same principles as the previous accounts; and that the revenue or costs are only recorded if it is certain that they will be received or incurred.

accounting cost FINANCE, BANKING, AND ACCOUNTING the cost of maintaining and checking the business records of a person or organization and the preparation of forms and reports for financial purposes

accounting cycle FINANCE, BANKING, AND ACCOUNTING the regular process of formally updating a firm's financial position by recording, analyzing, and reporting its transactions during the accounting period

accounting date FINANCE, BANKING, AND ACCOUNTING the date on which an accounting period ends

accounting department FINANCE, BANKING, AND ACCOUNTING see *accounts department*

accounting equation FINANCE, BANKING, AND ACCOUNTING a formula in which a firm's assets must be equal to the sum of its liabilities and the owners' equity. Also known as *balance sheet equation*

accounting exposure ECONOMICS FINANCE, BANKING, AND ACCOUNTING the risk that foreign currency held by a company may lose value because of exchange rate changes when it conducts overseas business

accounting fees FINANCE, BANKING, AND ACCOUNTING fees paid to an accountant for preparing accounts (such fees are tax-deductible)

accounting insolvency ECONOMICS FINANCE, BANKING, AND ACCOUNTING the condition that a company is in when its liabilities to its creditors exceed its assets

accounting manual FINANCE, BANKING, AND ACCOUNTING a collection of accounting instructions governing the responsibilities of persons, and the procedures, forms, and records relating to the preparation and use of accounting data. There can be separate manuals for the constituent parts of the accounting system, for example, budget manuals or cost accounting manuals.

accounting period FINANCE, BANKING, AND ACCOUNTING a length of time for which businesses may prepare internal accounts so as to monitor progress on a weekly, monthly, or quarterly basis. Accounts are generally prepared for external purposes on an annual basis.

accounting policies FINANCE, BANKING, AND ACCOUNTING the specific *accounting bases* selected and consistently followed by an entity as being, in the opinion of the management, appropriate to its circumstances and best suited to present fairly its results and financial position. For example, from the various possible methods of *depreciation*, the accounting policy may be to use *straight-line depreciation*.

accounting principles FINANCE, BANKING, AND ACCOUNTING the rules that apply to accounting practices and provide guidelines for dealing appropriately with complex transactions

Accounting Principles Board FINANCE, BANKING, AND ACCOUNTING the professional body which issued opinions that formed much of U.S. Generally Accepted Accounting Principles up to 1973, when the Financial Accounting Standards Board (FASB) took over that role. Abbr. *APB*

accounting procedure FINANCE, BANKING, AND ACCOUNTING an accounting method developed

by an individual or organization to deal with routine accounting tasks

accounting profit FINANCE, BANKING, AND ACCOUNTING the difference between total revenue and explicit costs

accounting rate of return FINANCE, BANKING, AND ACCOUNTING the ratio of profit before interest and taxation to the percentage of capital employed at the end of a period. Variations include using profit after interest and taxation, equity capital employed, and average capital for the period.

accounting ratio FINANCE, BANKING, AND ACCOUNTING an expression of accounting results as a ratio or percentage, for example, the ratio of *current assets* to *current liabilities*

accounting records FINANCE, BANKING, AND ACCOUNTING all documentation and books used during the preparation of financial statements

accounting reference date FINANCE, BANKING, AND ACCOUNTING the last day of a company's accounting reference period

accounting software FINANCE, BANKING, AND ACCOUNTING computer programs used to help maintain *books of account* electronically. Such software can be used for a variety of tasks, including preparing statements and recording transactions.

accounting standard FINANCE, BANKING, AND ACCOUNTING an authoritative statement of how particular types of transaction and other events should be reflected in financial statements. Compliance with accounting standards will normally be necessary for financial statements to give a true and fair view.

Accounting Standards Board FINANCE, BANKING, AND ACCOUNTING a U.K. standard-setting organization established on August 1, 1990 to develop, issue, and withdraw accounting standards. Its objectives are "to establish and improve standards of financial accounting and reporting, for the benefit of users, preparers, and auditors of financial information." Abbr. *ASB*

accounting system FINANCE, BANKING, AND ACCOUNTING the means, including staff and equipment, by which an organization produces its accounting information

accounting year (*U.K.*) FINANCE, BANKING, AND ACCOUNTING the 12-month *accounting period*

account reconciliation FINANCE, BANKING, AND ACCOUNTING

1 a procedure for ensuring the reliability of accounting records by comparing balances of transactions
2 a procedure for comparing the register of a checkbook with an associated bank statement

accounts department FINANCE, BANKING, AND ACCOUNTING the department in a company which deals with money paid, received, borrowed, or owed. Also known as *accounting department*

accounts payable FINANCE, BANKING, AND ACCOUNTING the amount that a company owes for goods or services obtained on credit. Abbr. *AP*

accounts receivable FINANCE, BANKING, AND ACCOUNTING the money that is owed to a company by those who have bought its goods or services and have not yet paid for them. Abbr. *AR*

accounts receivable aging FINANCE, BANKING, AND ACCOUNTING a periodic report that classifies outstanding receivable balances according to customer and month of the original billing date

accounts receivable factoring FINANCE, BANKING, AND ACCOUNTING the buying of accounts receivable at a discount with the goal of making a profit from collecting them

accounts receivable financing ECONOMICS FINANCE, BANKING, AND ACCOUNTING a form of borrowing in which a company uses money that it is owed as collateral for a loan it needs for business operations

accounts receivable turnover ECONOMICS FINANCE, BANKING, AND ACCOUNTING a ratio that shows how long the customers of a business wait before paying what they owe. This can cause cash flow problems for small businesses.

The formula for accounts receivable turnover is straightforward. Simply divide the average amount of receivables into annual credit sales:

Sales / Receivables = Receivables turnover

If, for example, a company's sales are $4.5 million and its average receivables are $375,000, its receivables turnover is:

4,500,000 / 375,000 = 12

A high turnover figure is desirable, because it indicates that a company collects revenues effectively, and that its customers pay bills promptly. A high figure also suggests that a firm's credit and collection policies are sound.

In addition, the measurement is a reasonably good indicator of cash flow, and of overall operating efficiency.

accreditation of prior learning HR & PERSONNEL a process through which formal recogni-tion for the achievements of past learning and experiences may be obtained. Accreditation of prior learning may be used to support the award of a vocational qualification.

accredited investor FINANCE, BANKING, AND ACCOUNTING an investor whose wealth or income is above a particular amount. It is illegal for an accredited investor to be a member of a private limited partnership.

accreted value FINANCE, BANKING, AND ACCOUNTING the value of a bond if interest rates do not change

accretion FINANCE, BANKING, AND ACCOUNTING the growth of a company through additions or purchases of plant or value-adding services

accrual FINANCE, BANKING, AND ACCOUNTING a charge that has not been paid by the end of an accounting period but must be included in the accounting results for the period. If no invoice has been received for the charge, an estimate must be included in the accounting results.

accrual basis FINANCE, BANKING, AND ACCOUNTING see *accrual method*

accrual bond FINANCE, BANKING, AND ACCOUNTING see *zero coupon bond*

accrual concept FINANCE, BANKING, AND ACCOUNTING the idea that income and expense items must be included in financial statements as they are earned or incurred. See also *cash accounting*

accrual method FINANCE, BANKING, AND ACCOUNTING an accounting method that includes income and expense items as they are earned or incurred irrespective of when money is received or paid out. Also known as *accrual basis*

accrual of discount FINANCE, BANKING, AND ACCOUNTING the annual gain in value of a bond owing to its having been bought originally for less than its *nominal value*

accrual of interest FINANCE, BANKING, AND ACCOUNTING the automatic addition of interest to capital

accruals basis FINANCE, BANKING, AND ACCOUNTING a concept that accounts are prepared with financial transactions accrued (revenue and costs are both reported during the period to which they refer and not during the period when payments are received or made). Also known as *accruals concept*

accruals concept FINANCE, BANKING, AND ACCOUNTING see *accruals basis*

accrue FINANCE, BANKING, AND ACCOUNTING
1 to include an income or expense item in transaction records at the time it is earned or incurred
2 to increase and be due for payment at a later date, for example, interest

accrued expense FINANCE, BANKING, AND ACCOUNTING an expense that has been incurred within a given accounting period but not yet paid

accrued income FINANCE, BANKING, AND ACCOUNTING income that has been earned but not yet received

accrued interest FINANCE, BANKING, AND ACCOUNTING the amount of interest earned by a bond or similar investment since the previous interest payment

accrued liabilities FINANCE, BANKING, AND ACCOUNTING liabilities which are recorded, although payment has not yet been made. This can include liabilities such as rent and utility payments.

accruing FINANCE, BANKING, AND ACCOUNTING added as a periodic gain, for example, as interest on an amount of money

accumulated depreciation FINANCE, BANKING, AND ACCOUNTING the cumulative annual depreciation of an *asset* that has been claimed as an expense since the asset was acquired. Also known as *aggregate depreciation*

accumulated dividend FINANCE, BANKING, AND ACCOUNTING the amount of money in dividends earned by a stock or similar investment since the previous dividend payment

accumulated earnings tax *or* **accumulated profits tax** FINANCE, BANKING, AND ACCOUNTING the tax that a company must pay because it chose not to pay dividends that would subject its owners to higher taxes

accumulated profit FINANCE, BANKING, AND ACCOUNTING profit which is not paid as dividend but is taken over into the accounts of the following year

accumulated reserves FINANCE, BANKING, AND ACCOUNTING reserves which a company has put aside over a period of years

accumulating shares FINANCE, BANKING, AND ACCOUNTING common stock issued by a company equivalent to and in place of the net dividend payable to holders of common stock

accumulation unit FINANCE, BANKING, AND ACCOUNTING (*U.K.*) a unit in a unit trust for which dividends accumulate and form more units, as opposed to an income unit, where the investor receives the dividends as *income*

accuracy STATISTICS the degree to which data conforms to a recognized standard value

ACH *abbr* E-COMMERCE FINANCE, BANKING, AND ACCOUNTING automated clearing house

achievement test HR & PERSONNEL a type of *psychometric test* which measures what a person already knows and can do at the time of testing. The two most common types of achievement tests are those that measure verbal reasoning and mathematical ability. There are many test preparation books available. As well as explaining how the questions are structured, they offer test strategies and sample tests. As with other psychometric tests, it has been proven that people perform better at these tests when they are well rested, in good physical shape, and slightly hungry.

acid test
1 FINANCE, BANKING, AND ACCOUNTING a test used to measure an organization's liquidity. The *acid-test ratio* is calculated by taking the business's current assets, minus its stocks, divided by its current liabilities. The higher the ratio, the better: a low ratio is usually a sign that a company is overstretched.
2 GENERAL MANAGEMENT a stringent test of the worth or reliability of something

acid-test ratio FINANCE, BANKING, AND ACCOUNTING an accounting ratio used to measure an organization's liquidity. The most common expression of the ratio is:

$$\frac{(\text{Current assets} - \text{Inventory})}{\text{Current liabilities}} = \text{Acid-test ratio}$$

If, for example, current assets total $7,700, inventory amounts to $1,200, and current liabilities total $4,500, then:

$$(7,700 - 1,200) / 4,500 = 1.44$$

A variation of this formula ignores inventories altogether, distinguishes assets as cash, receivables, and short-term investments, then divides the sum of the three by the total current liabilities, or:

$$\frac{\text{Cash} + \text{Accounts receivable} + \text{Short-term investments}}{\text{Current liabilities}}$$

$$= \text{Acid-test ratio}$$

If, for example, cash totals $2,000, receivables total $3,000, short-term investments total $1,000, and liabilities total $4,800, then:

$$(2,000 + 3,000 + 1,000) / 4,800 = 1.25$$

In general, the ratio should be 1:1 or better. It means a company has a unit's worth of easily convertible assets for each unit of its current liabilities.

Ackoff, Russell Lincoln (*b.* 1919) GENERAL MANAGEMENT U.S. academic. Pioneer of operations research and systems thinking, whose publications include *Ackoff's Fables: Irreverent Reflections on Business and Bureaucracy* (1991). See checklist *Open Systems Thinking*

ACM *abbr* GENERAL MANAGEMENT Australian Chamber of Manufacturers

acquiescence bias STATISTICS the bias produced when respondents in a survey give positive answers to two mutually conflicting questions

acquirer *or* **acquiring bank** FINANCE, BANKING, AND ACCOUNTING
1 a financial institution, commonly a bank, that processes a merchant's credit card authorizations and payments, forwarding the data to a credit card association, which in turn communicates with the issuer. Also known as *clearing house*
2 an organization or individual that buys a business or *asset*

acquisition FINANCE, BANKING, AND ACCOUNTING GENERAL MANAGEMENT see *merger*

acquisition accounting FINANCE, BANKING, AND ACCOUNTING the standard accounting procedures that must be followed when one company merges with another

acquisition rate GENERAL MANAGEMENT a measure of the ability of marketing programs to win new business

ACRS *abbr* FINANCE, BANKING, AND ACCOUNTING accelerated cost recovery system

ACT *abbr* FINANCE, BANKING, AND ACCOUNTING Advance Corporation Tax

action-centered leadership GENERAL MANAGEMENT a *leadership* model developed by *John Adair* that focuses on what leaders actually have to do in order to be effective. The action-centered leadership model is illustrated by three overlapping circles representing the three key activities undertaken by leaders: achieving the task, building and maintaining the team, and developing the individual. See thinker *John Adair*

action learning HR & PERSONNEL learning by sharing real problems with others, as opposed to theoretical classroom learning. Action learning was introduced in the mid-1940s by *Reg Revans*, who expressed it as Learning =

Programmed knowledge + the ability to ask insightful Questions, or L = P + Q. The technique works best when people in small groups tackle real work-based problems with a view to solving them. Action learning differs from *experiential learning*, which can apply to an individual alone. See thinker *Reg Revans*

action research GENERAL MANAGEMENT research in which the researcher takes an involved role as a participant in planning and implementing change. Action research was originated by *Kurt Lewin*, and it involves conducting experiments by making changes while simultaneously observing the results. See thinker *Kurt Lewin*

active E-COMMERCE describes the part of a computer screen or window that is currently in use or ready to accept input from the user

active asset FINANCE, BANKING, AND ACCOUNTING an *asset* that is used in the daily operations of a business

active fund management FINANCE, BANKING, AND ACCOUNTING the managing of a mutual fund by making judgments about market movements instead of relying on automatic adjustments such as indexation. See also *passive investment management*

active listening HR & PERSONNEL a technique for improving understanding of what is being said by taking into account how something is said and the nonverbal signs and *body language* that accompany it. This technique requires receptive awareness and response on the part of the listener. Six principles form the core of active listening: encourage people to express opinions; clarify perceptions of what is said; restate essential points and ideas; reflect the speaker's feeling and opinions; summarize the content of the message to check validity; acknowledge the opinion and contribution of the speaker. It is used particularly in counseling.

active portfolio strategy FINANCE, BANKING, AND ACCOUNTING the managing of an investment portfolio by making judgments about market movements instead of relying on automatic adjustments

activist fiscal policy FINANCE, BANKING, AND ACCOUNTING the policy of a government or national bank that tries to affect the value of its country's money by such measures as changing interest rates for loans to banks and buying or selling foreign currencies

activity based budgeting FINANCE, BANKING, AND ACCOUNTING the allocation of resources to individual activities. Activity based budgeting involves determining which activities incur costs within an organization, establishing the relationships between them, and then deciding how much of the total *budget* should be allocated to each activity. Abbr. *ABB*

activity based costing FINANCE, BANKING, AND ACCOUNTING GENERAL MANAGEMENT a method of calculating the cost of a business by focusing on the actual cost of activities, thereby producing an estimate of the cost of individual products or services.

An ABC cost-accounting system requires three preliminary steps: converting to an *accrual method* of accounting; defining cost centers and cost allocation; and determining process and procedure costs.

Businesses have traditionally relied on the cash basis of accounting, which recognizes income when received and expenses when paid. ABC's foundation is the accrual-basis income statement. The numbers this statement presents are assigned to the various procedures performed during a given period. Cost centers are a company's identifiable products and services, but also include specific and detailed tasks within these broader activities. Defining cost centers will of course vary by business and method of operation. What is critical to ABC is the inclusion of all activities and all resources.

Once cost centers are identified, management teams can begin studying the activities each one engages in and allocating the expenses each one incurs, including the cost of employee services.

The most appropriate method is developed from time studies and direct expense allocation. Management teams who choose this method will need to devote several months to data collection in order to generate sufficient information to establish the personnel components of each activity's total cost.

Time studies establish the average amount of time required to complete each task, plus best- and worst-case performances. Only those resources actually used are factored into the cost computation; unused resources are reported separately. These studies can also advise management teams how best to monitor and allocate expenses that might otherwise be expressed as part of general overheads, or go undetected altogether. Abbr. *ABC*

activity based management

1 GENERAL MANAGEMENT a management control technique that focuses on the resource costs of organizational activities and processes, and the improvement of quality, profitability, and customer value. This technique uses *activity based costing* information to identify strategies for removing resource waste from operating activities. Main tools employed include: *strategic analysis*, *value analysis*, cost analysis, *life-cycle costing*, and *activity based budgeting* .

2 FINANCE, BANKING, AND ACCOUNTING a system of management that uses activity-based cost information for a variety of purposes, including cost reduction, cost modeling, and customer profitability analysis. Abbr. *ABM*

activity cost pool FINANCE, BANKING, AND ACCOUNTING a grouping of all cost elements associated with an activity

activity driver FINANCE, BANKING, AND ACCOUNTING see *cost driver*

activity driver analysis FINANCE, BANKING, AND ACCOUNTING the identification and evaluation of the activity drivers used to trace the cost of activities to cost objects. It may also involve selecting activity drivers with potential to contribute to the cost management function, with particular reference to cost reduction.

activity indicator ECONOMICS a calculation used to measure labor productivity or manufacturing output in an economy

activity sampling OPERATIONS & PRODUCTION a *work measurement* technique used to analyze the activities of employees, machines, or business operations. Activity sampling requires random observations of the amount of time spent on a given activity to be recorded over a fixed period. The results are used to predict the total time spent on each activity and to highlight areas in need of quality, efficiency, or effectiveness improvement. Also known as *work sampling*, *ratio-delay study*, *random observation method*

act of God FINANCE, BANKING, AND ACCOUNTING an unexpected and unavoidable event or occurrence, such as a storm or a flood, that is not covered by an insurance policy

ACTU *abbr* GENERAL MANAGEMENT Australian Council of Trade Unions

actual cash value FINANCE, BANKING, AND ACCOUNTING the amount of money, less *depreciation*, that it would cost to replace something damaged beyond repair with a comparable item

actuals FINANCE, BANKING, AND ACCOUNTING earnings and expenses that have occurred rather than being only projected, or commodities that can be bought and used, as contrasted with commodities traded on a futures contract

actual to date FINANCE, BANKING, AND ACCOUNT-ING the cumulative value realized by something between an earlier date and the present

actual turnover FINANCE, BANKING, AND AC-COUNTING the number of times during a particular period that somebody spends the average amount of money that he or she has available to spend during that period

actuarial age FINANCE, BANKING, AND ACCOUNT-ING the statistically derived life expectancy for any given person's age, used, for example, to calculate the periodic payments from an annuity

actuarial analysis FINANCE, BANKING, AND AC-COUNTING a life expectancy or risk calculation carried out by an actuary

actuarial science FINANCE, BANKING, AND AC-COUNTING STATISTICS the branch of statistics used in calculating risk and life expectancy for the administration of pension funds and life insurance policies

actuarial tables FINANCE, BANKING, AND AC-COUNTING lists showing how long people of certain ages are likely to live, used to calculate life assurance premiums

actuary FINANCE, BANKING, AND ACCOUNTING STATISTICS a statistician who calculates probable life spans so that the insurance premiums to be charged for various risks can be accurately determined

ACU *abbr* FINANCE, BANKING, AND ACCOUNTING Asian Currency Unit

ad E-COMMERCE a banner, button, pop-up screen, or other on-screen device calling attention to an e-commerce product or business

Adair, John Eric (*b.* 1934) GENERAL MANAGE-MENT British academic. Best known for his three-circle model of *leadership*, which is based on overlapping circles representing the task, the team, and the individual. Adair's model, otherwise known as *action-centered leadership*, is described in the book of the same name (1973). Like *Warren Bennis*, Adair, who has a military background, believes that leadership can be taught.

Adams, Scott (*b.* 1957) GENERAL MANAGEMENT U.S. humorist. Creator of the *Dilbert principle*, he satirizes the many absurdities of business life through his cartoons and books.

adaptive control OPERATIONS & PRODUCTION a system of automatic monitoring and adjust-ment, usually by computer, of an industrial process. Adaptive control allows operating parameters to be changed continuously in response to a changing environment in order to achieve optimum performance.

adaptive learning GENERAL MANAGEMENT a style of organizational learning that focuses on prior successes and the use of these as the basis for developing future strategies and successes. Organizations use adaptive learning to make incremental improvements to existing products, services, and processes in response to the changing business environment. *Generative learning* is a contrasting approach to organizational learning.

adaptive measure STATISTICS a means of choosing the most appropriate method for a statistical analysis

ad banner E-COMMERCE see *banner*

ad click E-COMMERCE see *click-through*

ad click rate E-COMMERCE see *click-through rate*

ADDACS *abbr* FINANCE, BANKING, AND ACCOUNT-ING Automated Direct Debit Amendments and Cancellation Service

added value
1 GENERAL MANAGEMENT see *value added*
2 MARKETING an increase in the attractiveness to customers of a product or a service achieved by adding something to it

addend FINANCE, BANKING, AND ACCOUNTING the initial number added to an *augend* in order to complete an *addition*

addition FINANCE, BANKING, AND ACCOUNTING an arithmetical operation consisting of adding together two or more numbers to make a sum

additional voluntary contributions FINANCE, BANKING, AND ACCOUNTING extra money paid by an individual into a company pension plan to improve the benefits he or she will receive on retirement. Abbr. *AVCs*

address book E-COMMERCE an e-mail software facility enabling people and businesses to store and manage e-mail addresses and contact information

address verification E-COMMERCE a procedure used by the processor of a credit card to verify that a customer's ordering address matches the address in the customer's record

ADF *abbr* FINANCE, BANKING, AND ACCOUNTING Approved Deposit Fund

adhocracy GENERAL MANAGEMENT a system of organization that emphasizes informality and flexibility and does not employ fixed rules or standard procedures for dealing with problems

ad hoc research MARKETING a single, one-time piece of research designed for a particular purpose, as opposed to continuous, regularly repeated, or syndicated research

ad impression E-COMMERCE see *ad view*

adjustable rate mortgage FINANCE, BANKING, AND ACCOUNTING a mortgage where the interest rate changes according to the current market rates

adjustable rate preferred stock FINANCE, BANKING, AND ACCOUNTING preferred stocks on which dividends are paid in line with the interest rate on Treasury bills

adjusted book value FINANCE, BANKING, AND ACCOUNTING the value of a company in terms of the current market values of its assets and liabilities. Also known as *modified book value*

adjusted futures price FINANCE, BANKING, AND ACCOUNTING the current value of a futures contract to buy a commodity at a fixed future date

adjusted gross income FINANCE, BANKING, AND ACCOUNTING the amount of annual income that a person or company has after various adjustments for income or corporation tax purposes. Abbr. *AGI*

adjusted present value where the capital structure of a company is complex, or expected to vary over time, discounted cash flows may be separated into (i) those which relate to operational items, and (ii) those associated with financing. This treatment enables assessment to be made of the separate features of each area. Abbr. *APV*

adjustment credit FINANCE, BANKING, AND AC-COUNTING a short-term loan from the Federal Reserve to a commercial bank

adjustment trigger FINANCE, BANKING, AND ACCOUNTING a factor (such as a certain level of inflation) which triggers an adjustment in exchange rates

adminisphere GENERAL MANAGEMENT the part of an organization that deals with administrative matters, often perceived negatively by employees because of the apparently unnecessary nature of decisions taken by its members (*slang*)

a-z
1389

DICTIONARY

administered price FINANCE, BANKING, AND ACCOUNTING the price of a good or service which is fixed by a manufacturer and which cannot be varied by a retailer

administration GENERAL MANAGEMENT the management of the affairs of a business, especially the planning and control of its operations

administration costs FINANCE, BANKING, AND ACCOUNTING costs of management, not including production, marketing, or distribution costs

administration school GENERAL MANAGEMENT see *business administration*

administrative receiver FINANCE, BANKING, AND ACCOUNTING a receiver appointed by a *debenture* holder to liquidate the assets of a company on his or her behalf

administrivia E-COMMERCE the often tedious tasks associated with maintaining a Web site, mailing list, or any other form of Internet resource (*slang*)

admissibility STATISTICS the property of a procedure if, and only if, no other of its class exists that performs as well as it and better than it in at least one case

ADR *abbr* FINANCE, BANKING, AND ACCOUNTING American depository receipt: a document that indicates a U.S. investor's ownership of stock in a foreign corporation

Adshel™ *tdmk* MARKETING in the United Kingdom, a type of bus shelter, specifically designed to carry advertising posters

ADSL *abbr* E-COMMERCE asymmetrical digital subscriber line: a system that provides high speed, high *bandwidth* connections to the Internet. ADSL is asymmetric because it has more capacity for data received by a computer than for data to be sent from it. This uneven upload/download balance means that downloaded text and graphics appear quickly and that audiovisual elements are of better quality than when sent via a normal telephone line. ADSL was initially developed by Bellcore Labs in New Jersey in 1993 as a means of bringing bandwidth to homes and small businesses. Often it is simply called DSL.

adspend MARKETING see *advertising expenditure*

ad transfer E-COMMERCE see *click-through*

ad valorem FINANCE, BANKING, AND ACCOUNTING a tax or commission, for example, Value Added Tax, that is calculated on the value of the products or services provided, rather than on their number or size

ad valorem duty *or* **ad valorem tax** FINANCE, BANKING, AND ACCOUNTING a duty based on the value of a product or service

ad valorem tax FINANCE, BANKING, AND ACCOUNTING see *ad valorem duty*

Advance Corporation Tax FINANCE, BANKING, AND ACCOUNTING formerly, in the United Kingdom, a tax paid by a company equal to a percentage of its dividends or other distributions of profit to its stockholders. It was abolished in 1999. Abbr. *ACT*

advanced manufacturing technology GENERAL MANAGEMENT OPERATIONS & PRODUCTION a high technology development in computing and microelectronics, designed to enhance manufacturing capabilities. Advanced manufacturing technology is used in all areas of manufacturing, including design, control, fabrication, and assembly. This family of technologies includes *robotics*, *computer-aided design* (CAD), *computer-aided engineering* (CAE), *MRP II*, automated *materials handling* systems, *electronic data interchange* (EDI), computer-integrated manufacturing (CIM) systems, *flexible manufacturing systems*, and *group technology*. Abbr. *AMT*

advance payment FINANCE, BANKING, AND ACCOUNTING an amount paid before it is earned or incurred, for example, a prepayment by an importer to an exporter before goods are shipped, or a cash advance for travel expenses

advance payment guarantee *or* **advance payment bond** FINANCE, BANKING, AND ACCOUNTING a guarantee that enables a buyer to recover an advance payment made under a contract or order if the supplier fails to fulfill its contractual obligations

adventure learning HR & PERSONNEL see *adventure training*

adventure training HR & PERSONNEL activities undertaken out of doors and away from the everyday work environment with a view to developing the skills and abilities of participants. Adventure training often takes place at a residential outdoor activity center and may include physically challenging activities such as climbing and rappelling or group exercises and games. The activities are designed to promote *experiential learning* in areas such as *interpersonal communication*, *problem solving*, *decision making*, and *teamwork*, and to develop self-confidence and *leadership* skills.

Adventure training has its origins in the work of Kurt Hahn, the founder of Gordonstoun School in Scotland, who developed the Outward Bound program of outdoor activities during World War II. Adventure training programs for organizational personnel became popular during the late 1970s and 1980s, although some have doubted their value and effectiveness. Also known as *adventure learning*, *outdoor training*, *outward bound training*

adverse action FINANCE, BANKING, AND ACCOUNTING the action of refusing someone credit

adverse balance FINANCE, BANKING, AND ACCOUNTING the deficit on an account, especially a nation's balance of payments account

adverse balance of trade FINANCE, BANKING, AND ACCOUNTING a situation where a country imports more than it exports

adverse opinion FINANCE, BANKING, AND ACCOUNTING a statement in the auditor's report of a company's annual accounts indicating a fundamental disagreement with the company to such an extent that the auditor considers the accounts misleading

advertisement MARKETING a public announcement by a company in a newspaper, on television or radio, or over the Internet, intended to attract buyers for a product or service

advertising MARKETING the promotion of goods, services, or ideas, through paid announcements. Advertising aims to persuade or inform the general public and can be used to induce purchase, increase *brand awareness*, or enhance *product differentiation*. An advertisement has two main components: the message, and the medium by which it is transmitted. Advertising forms just one part of an organization's total marketing strategy.

advertising agency MARKETING an organization that, on behalf of clients, drafts and produces advertisements, places advertisements in the media, and plans *advertising campaigns*. Advertising agencies may also perform other marketing functions, including *market research* and consulting.

advertising campaign MARKETING a planned program using *advertising* aimed at a particular target market or audience over a defined period of time for the purpose of increasing sales or raising awareness of a product or service

advertising department MARKETING the department within an organization which is

responsible for advertising its products or services. The advertising department is also the name given to the section of a publishing house that coordinates the placing of advertisements in its magazines, newspapers, or other publications. It is involved in the sale of advertising space to clients.

advertising expenditure MARKETING the amount spent by an organization on advertising, usually per year. Advertising expenditure is analyzed by breaking it down into the main advertising channels used by companies, such as newspapers, magazines, television, radio, movie theaters, and outdoor advertising. Expenditure can show the total spending nationally, by sector, or by type and size of company, or may relate to one company's spend on advertising, including the proportion spent on its specific brands. Also known as *ad-spend*

advertising manager MARKETING an employee of a business who is responsible for planning and controlling its advertising activities and budgets

advertising media MARKETING the communication channels used for advertising, including television, radio, the printed press, and outdoor advertising

advertising research MARKETING research carried out before or after advertising to ensure or test its effectiveness

advertorial MARKETING a combination of an *advertisement* and an article. The content of an advertorial is significantly influenced, and may even be entirely written, by the advertisers. Examples of advertorials include travel or leisure supplements in newspapers or magazines that are designed to attract advertisements from suppliers of relevant goods or services. A criticism of advertorials is that it is sometimes difficult to distinguish between an advertising article and ordinary journalistic articles, particularly when they appear in the same typeface as the other contents of the newspaper or magazine. To overcome this, some advertorials are headed "Advertisement."

advice of fate (*U.K.*) FINANCE, BANKING, AND ACCOUNTING immediate notification from a drawer's bank as to whether a check is to be honored or not. This special presentation of a check bypasses the normal clearing system and so saves time.

advid MARKETING a video used to promote a product or service

ad view E-COMMERCE the number of times a banner or other ad is downloaded and presumably seen on a Web page. Also known as *ad impression exposure*

advisory management FINANCE, BANKING, AND ACCOUNTING an advisory service offered by some stockbrokers in which clients are able to discuss a variety of investment options with their broker and receive appropriate advice. No resulting action may be taken, however, without a client's express approval.

AFAANZ *abbr* FINANCE, BANKING, AND ACCOUNTING Accounting and Finance Association of Australia and New Zealand

AFAIK *abbr* GENERAL MANAGEMENT as far as I know (*slang*)

affiliate FINANCE, BANKING, AND ACCOUNTING GENERAL MANAGEMENT a company that is controlled by another or is a member of a group, or either of two companies that owns a minority of the voting stock of the other

affiliated enterprise FINANCE, BANKING, AND ACCOUNTING a company which is partly owned by another (though less than 50%), and in which the stock-owning company exerts some management control or has a close trading relationship with the associate. Also known as *associate company*

affiliate directory E-COMMERCE a directory that indexes sites belonging to affiliate programs. Affiliate directories offer information for companies seeking to subscribe to a program, as well as for those wanting to establish affiliate programs of their own.

affiliate marketing E-COMMERCE the use of *affiliate programs*

affiliate partner MARKETING a company that markets a product or service on the Internet for another company

affiliate program E-COMMERCE an advertising program in which one merchant induces others to place their banners and buttons on its Web site in return for a commission on purchases made by their customers. Also known as associate program.

There is no better example of the success of affiliate marketing than that of Amazon.com. The company has links on literally hundreds of thousands of external Web sites, linking through to its own site, from where it offers books and other products. It is a win-win situation: the external vendors can offer extra services to their visitors that are easy to establish, and receive revenue from Amazon. At the

same time, Amazon opens up a new channel for marketing each time a new visitor links through to its Web site.

affinity card MARKETING a credit or debit card for which the issuing bank makes a donation to a specified charity each time it is used

affirmative action HR & PERSONNEL preferential treatment, usually through a quota system, to prevent, or correct, discriminatory employment practices, particularly relating to recruitment and promotion. The term is widely used in the United States, whereas in the United Kingdom, *positive discrimination* is the preferred term.

affluent society ECONOMICS a community in which material wealth is widely distributed

affluenza GENERAL MANAGEMENT feelings of unhappiness, stress, and guilt induced by the pursuit and possession of wealth (*slang*)

AFTA *abbr* FINANCE, BANKING, AND ACCOUNTING ASEAN Free Trade Area

after-acquired collateral FINANCE, BANKING, AND ACCOUNTING collateral for a loan that a borrower obtains after making the contract for the loan

after date FINANCE, BANKING, AND ACCOUNTING see *bill of exchange*

after-hours buying FINANCE, BANKING, AND ACCOUNTING buying, selling, or dealing in stock after the Stock Exchange has officially closed for the day, such deals being subject to normal Stock Exchange rules. In this way, dealers can take advantage of the fact that, because of time differences and the various stock exchanges round the world, there is almost always at least one stock exchange open throughout the twenty-four hours.

after-sales service MARKETING customer support following the purchase of a product or service. In some cases, after-sales service can be almost as important as the initial purchase. The manufacturer, retailer, or service provider determines what is included in any warranty (or guarantee) package. This will include the duration of the warranty—traditionally one year from the date of purchase, but increasingly two or more years—maintenance and/or replacement policy, items included/excluded, labor costs, and speed of response. In the case of a service provider, after-sales service might include additional training or helpdesk availability. Of equal importance is the customer's perception of the degree of willingness with

which a supplier deals with a question or complaint, speed of response, and action taken.

after sight FINANCE, BANKING, AND ACCOUNTING see *bill of exchange*

after-tax FINANCE, BANKING, AND ACCOUNTING relating to earnings or income from which tax has already been deducted

AG *abbr* FINANCE, BANKING, AND ACCOUNTING Aktiengesellschaft: used after the title of a German, Austrian, or Swiss business to identify it as a public limited company

against actuals FINANCE, BANKING, AND ACCOUNTING relating to a trade between owners of futures contracts that allows both to reduce their positions to cash instead of commodities

aged debt FINANCE, BANKING, AND ACCOUNTING a debt that is overdue by one or more given periods, usually increments of 30 days

aged debtor FINANCE, BANKING, AND ACCOUNTING a person or organization responsible for an overdue debt

age discrimination HR & PERSONNEL unfavorable treatment in employment based on prejudice in relation to a person's age. While age discrimination affects people at all stages of their working lives, difficulties experienced in selection, development, and promotion can be particularly acute at the two extremes of the age spectrum. Countries such as Australia and the United States have passed legislation to make it unlawful to discriminate on the basis of age. Also known as *ageism*

age diversity HR & PERSONNEL the inclusion of people of all age groups, especially in the workplace

ageism HR & PERSONNEL see *age discrimination*

agency GENERAL MANAGEMENT a relationship between two people or organizations in which one is empowered to act on behalf of the other in dealings with a third party

agency bill FINANCE, BANKING, AND ACCOUNTING a bill of exchange drawn on the local branch of a foreign bank

agency broker FINANCE, BANKING, AND ACCOUNTING a dealer who acts for a client, buying and selling stock for a commission

agency commission MARKETING a percentage of advertising expenditure rebated to an advertising agency, media buyer, or client organization by a media owner

agency markup MARKETING a management fee charged by an advertising agency in addition to the cost of external services that it buys on behalf of a client

agenda GENERAL MANAGEMENT a list of topics to be discussed or business to be transacted during the course of a meeting, usually sent prior to the meeting to those invited to attend

agent GENERAL MANAGEMENT
1 a person or organization empowered to act on behalf of another when dealing with a third party
2 see *executive*

agent bank (*ANZ*) FINANCE, BANKING, AND ACCOUNTING a bank that acts on behalf of a foreign bank, or a bank that participates in another bank's credit card program, acting as a depository for merchants

age pension (*ANZ*) FINANCE, BANKING, AND ACCOUNTING a sum of money paid regularly by the government to people who have reached the age of retirement

aggregate demand ECONOMICS the sum of all expenditures in an economy that makes up its *GDP*, for example, consumers' expenditure on goods and services, investment in *capital stocks*, and government spending

aggregate depreciation FINANCE, BANKING, AND ACCOUNTING see *accumulated depreciation*

aggregate income FINANCE, BANKING, AND ACCOUNTING the total of all incomes in an economy without adjustments for inflation, taxation, or types of *double counting*

aggregate output ECONOMICS the total value of all the goods and services produced in an economy

aggregate planning OPERATIONS & PRODUCTION medium-range *capacity planning*, typically covering a period of 3 to 18 months. Aggregate planning is used in a manufacturing environment and determines not only the overall output levels planned but the appropriate resource input mix to be used for related groups of products. Generally, planners focus on overall or aggregate capacity rather than on individual products or services. Aggregate planning can be used to influence demand as well as supply, in which case variables such as price, advertising, and the product mix are taken into account.

aggregate supply ECONOMICS the total of all goods and services produced in an economy

aggregator E-COMMERCE MARKETING an organization that acts as an intermediary between producers and customers in an Internet business web. The aggregator selects products, sets prices, and ensures fulfillment of orders.

aggressive FINANCE, BANKING, AND ACCOUNTING relating to an investment strategy marked by willingness to accept high risk while trying to realize higher than average gains. Such a strategy involves investing in rapidly growing companies that promise capital appreciation but produce little or no income from dividends and de-emphasizes income-producing instruments such as bonds.

aggressive accounting FINANCE, BANKING, AND ACCOUNTING inaccurate or unlawful accounting practices used by an organization in order to make its financial position seem healthier than it is in reality (*slang*)

aggressive growth fund FINANCE, BANKING, AND ACCOUNTING a mutual fund that takes considerable risks in the hope of making large profits

AGI *abbr* FINANCE, BANKING, AND ACCOUNTING adjusted gross income

agile manufacturing OPERATIONS & PRODUCTION a manufacturing philosophy that focuses on meeting the demands of customers by adopting flexible manufacturing practices. Agile manufacturing emerged as a reaction to *lean production*. It differs by focusing on meeting the demands of customers without sacrificing quality or incurring added costs. Based on the idea of the *virtual organization*, agile manufacturing aims to develop flexible, often short-term, relationships with suppliers, as market opportunities arise. Stock control is considered less important than satisfying the customer, and so *customer satisfaction* measures become more important than output measures. Agile manufacturing requires an adaptable, innovative, and empowered work force.

agility GENERAL MANAGEMENT the organizational capability to be flexible, responsive, adaptive, and show initiative in times of change and uncertainty. Agility has origins in manufacturing and has been cited as a source of *competitive advantage* by many management gurus, including *Rosabeth Moss Kanter* and *Tom Peters*. One writer who has explored the concept of agility in greater depth is *Richard Pascale*, for whom the key to agility lies in what the organization is, as opposed to what it

does. Agility grew as a reaction against the slowness of bureaucratic organizations to respond to changing market conditions. The *virtual organization* has been quoted as one extreme example of an agile organization. See thinker **Rosabeth Moss Kanter**, **Richard Tanner Pascale**, **Tom Peters**

AGM (*U.K.*) FINANCE, BANKING, AND ACCOUNTING GENERAL MANAGEMENT = *annual meeting*

agora E-COMMERCE a marketplace on the Internet. The term comes from an ancient Greek word for "market."

agreement among underwriters FINANCE, BANKING, AND ACCOUNTING a document which forms a syndicate of underwriters, linking them to the issuer of a new stock issue

agreement of sale GENERAL MANAGEMENT a written contract specifying the terms under which the buyer agrees to buy particular real estate and the seller agrees to sell it

agreement to sell FINANCE, BANKING, AND ACCOUNTING a contract between two parties in which one agrees to sell something to the other at a date in the future

agricultural produce FINANCE, BANKING, AND ACCOUNTING see *biological assets*

AHI (*S. Africa*) GENERAL MANAGEMENT Afrikaanse Handelsinstituut, the national chamber of commerce for Afrikaans businesses

AICPA *abbr* FINANCE, BANKING, AND ACCOUNTING American Institute of Certified Public Accountants

AIFA *abbr* FINANCE, BANKING, AND ACCOUNTING Association of Independent Financial Advisers

aim GENERAL MANAGEMENT see *objective*

AIM *abbr* FINANCE, BANKING, AND ACCOUNTING Alternative Investment Market: the London market trading in stocks of emerging or small companies not eligible for listing on the London Stock Exchange. It replaced the Unlisted Securities Market (USM) in 1995.

air bill FINANCE, BANKING, AND ACCOUNTING the documentation accompanying a package sent using an express mail service

AIRC *abbr* HR & PERSONNEL Australian Industrial Relations Commission

air cover GENERAL MANAGEMENT support from a senior member of staff, usually during a time of change, upheaval, or unpopular decisions (*slang*)

airtime MARKETING the amount of time given to an advertisement on television, radio, or in movie theaters

air waybill FINANCE, BANKING, AND ACCOUNTING a U.K. term for a receipt issued by an airline for goods to be freighted

AITC *abbr* FINANCE, BANKING, AND ACCOUNTING Association of Investment Trust Companies

Aktb *abbr* FINANCE, BANKING, AND ACCOUNTING Aktiebolaget: the Swedish equivalent of Inc

alien corporation FINANCE, BANKING, AND ACCOUNTING a company which is based in one country, but registered in another

alignment GENERAL MANAGEMENT the process of building a corporate culture to achieve strategic goals

all equity rate FINANCE, BANKING, AND ACCOUNTING the interest rate that a lender charges because of the apparent risks of a project that are independent of the normal market risks of financing it

alligator spread FINANCE, BANKING, AND ACCOUNTING a *spread* which remains unprofitable even with good market conditions, usually as the result of high *commissions* paid to *brokers* or agents (*slang*)

All Industrials Index FINANCE, BANKING, AND ACCOUNTING a subindex of the Australian All Ordinaries Index which includes all the companies from that index that are not involved in resources or mining

All Mining Index FINANCE, BANKING, AND ACCOUNTING a subindex of the Australian All Ordinaries Index which includes all the companies from that index that are involved in the mining industry

allocate FINANCE, BANKING, AND ACCOUNTING to assign a whole item of *cost*, or of *revenue*, to a single cost unit, center, account, or time period

All Ordinaries Accumulation Index FINANCE, BANKING, AND ACCOUNTING a measure of the change in stock prices on the Australian Stock Exchange, based on the *All Ordinaries Index*, but assuming that all dividends are reinvested

All Ordinaries Index FINANCE, BANKING, AND ACCOUNTING the major index of Australian stocks, comprising more than 300 of the most active Australian companies listed on the Australian Stock Exchange. Abbr. *All Ords*

All Ords *abbr* FINANCE, BANKING, AND ACCOUNTING All-Ordinaries Index

all-or-none underwriting (*ANZ*) FINANCE, BANKING, AND ACCOUNTING the option of canceling a public offering of stock if the underwriting is not fully subscribed

allowable deductions FINANCE, BANKING, AND ACCOUNTING deductions from income which are allowed by the IRS, and which reduce the tax payable

allowable losses FINANCE, BANKING, AND ACCOUNTING losses (as on the sale of assets) which are allowed to be set off against gains

All Resources Index FINANCE, BANKING, AND ACCOUNTING a subindex of the Australian All Ordinaries Index which includes all the companies from that index that are involved in the resources industry

alphabet theories of management GENERAL MANAGEMENT management theories named along the lines of **Douglas McGregor**'s *Theory X* and *Theory Y*. Alphabet theories of management include *Theory E*, *Theory J*, *Theory O*, *Theory W*, and *Theory Z*. See thinker **Douglas McGregor**

alpha geek GENERAL MANAGEMENT the person who knows most about computer technology in a company or department (*slang*)

alpha rating FINANCE, BANKING, AND ACCOUNTING the return a security or a portfolio would be expected to earn if the market's rate of return were zero. Alpha expresses the difference between the return expected from a stock or mutual fund, given its beta rating, and the return actually produced. A stock or trust that returns more than its beta would predict has a positive alpha, while one that returns less than the amount predicted by beta has a negative alpha. A large positive alpha indicates a strong performance, while a large negative alpha indicates a dismal performance.

To begin with, the market itself is assigned a beta of 1.0. If a stock or trust has a beta of 1.2, this means its price is likely to rise or fall by 12% when the overall market rises or falls by 10%; a beta of 7.0 means the stock or trust price is likely to move up or down at 70% of the level of the market change.

In practice, an alpha of 0.4 means the stock or trust in question outperformed the market-based return estimate by 0.4%. An alpha of −0.6 means the return was 0.6% less than would have been predicted from the change in the market alone.

Both alpha and beta should be readily available upon request from investment firms, because the figures appear in standard performance reports. It is always best to ask for them, because calculating a stock's alpha rating re-

quires first knowing a stock's beta rating, and beta calculations can involve mathematical complexities. See also ***beta rating***

alpha test GENERAL MANAGEMENT a test of a new or upgraded piece of computer software or hardware carried out by the manufacturer before it is released to the public

alpha value (*ANZ*) FINANCE, BANKING, AND ACCOUNTING a sum paid to an employee when he or she leaves a company that can be transferred to a concessionally taxed investment account such as an ***Approved Deposit Fund***

alternate director FINANCE, BANKING, AND ACCOUNTING a person who is allowed to act for an absent named director of a company at a board meeting

alternative investment FINANCE, BANKING, AND ACCOUNTING an investment other than in bonds or stock of a large company or one listed on a stock exchange

Alternative Investment Market FINANCE, BANKING, AND ACCOUNTING see ***AIM***

alternative mortgage instrument FINANCE, BANKING, AND ACCOUNTING any form of mortgage other than a fixed-term amortizing loan

AM *abbr* FINANCE, BANKING, AND ACCOUNTING asset management

amalgamation FINANCE, BANKING, AND ACCOUNTING GENERAL MANAGEMENT the process of two or more organizations joining together for mutual benefit, either through a ***merger*** or ***consolidation***

Amazon E-COMMERCE to claim a significant portion of the market from a traditional retail business that failed to develop an effective e-business strategy. The term stems from the seemingly overnight success of online bookseller Amazon.com™. (*slang*)

AMBA GENERAL MANAGEMENT an analysis of the potential effects of a building development or a similar project on the natural environment

ambit claim (*ANZ*) FINANCE, BANKING, AND ACCOUNTING GENERAL MANAGEMENT a claim made to an arbitration authority for higher pay or improved conditions that is deliberately exaggerated because the claimants know that they will subsequently have to compromise

American Accounting Association FINANCE, BANKING, AND ACCOUNTING a voluntary organization for those with an interest in accounting research and best practice. Its mission is "to

foster worldwide excellence in the creation, dissemination and application of accounting knowledge and skills." The AAA was founded in 1916. Abbr. ***AAA***

American depository receipt FINANCE, BANKING, AND ACCOUNTING see ***ADR***

American depository share FINANCE, BANKING, AND ACCOUNTING see ***ADR***

American Institute of Certified Public Accountants FINANCE, BANKING, AND ACCOUNTING founded in New York in 1887, AICPA is the national association for certified public accountants. Abbr. ***AICPA***

American option FINANCE, BANKING, AND ACCOUNTING an option contract that can be exercised at any time up to and including the expiration date. Most exchange-traded options are of this style. See also ***European option***

American Stock Exchange FINANCE, BANKING, AND ACCOUNTING see ***AMEX***

American style option FINANCE, BANKING, AND ACCOUNTING see ***American option***

AMEX *abbr* FINANCE, BANKING, AND ACCOUNTING American Stock Exchange: a New York stock exchange listing smaller and less mature companies than those listed on the larger New York Stock Exchange (NYSE)

amortization FINANCE, BANKING, AND ACCOUNTING

1 a method of recovering (deducting or writing off) the capital costs of intangible assets over a fixed period of time.

For tax purposes, the distinction is not always made between amortization and depreciation, yet amortization remains a viable financial accounting concept in its own right.

It is computed using the straight-line method of depreciation: divide the initial cost of the intangible asset by the estimated useful life of that asset.

$$\frac{\text{Initial cost}}{\text{Useful life}} = \text{Amortization per year}$$

For example, if it costs \$10,000 to acquire a patent and it has an estimated useful life of 10 years, the amortized amount per year is \$1,000.

The amount of amortization accumulated since the asset was acquired appears on the organization's balance sheet as a deduction under the amortized asset.

While that formula is straightforward, amortization can also incorporate a variety of non-cash charges to net earnings and/or asset values, such as depletion, write-offs, prepaid expenses, and deferred charges. Accordingly,

there are many rules to regulate how these charges appear on financial statements. The rules are different in each country, and are occasionally changed, so it is necessary to stay abreast of them and rely on expert advice.

For financial reporting purposes, an intangible asset is amortized over a period of years. The amortizable life—"useful life"—of an intangible asset is the period over which it gives economic benefit.

Intangibles that can be amortized can include

Copyrights, based on the amount paid either to purchase them or to develop them internally, plus the costs incurred in producing the work (wages or materials, for example). At present, a copyright is granted to a corporation for 75 years, and to an individual for the life of the author plus 50 years. However, the estimated useful life of a copyright is usually far less than its legal life, and it is generally amortized over a fairly short period;

Cost of a ***franchise***, including any fees paid to the franchiser, as well legal costs or expenses incurred in the acquisition. A franchise granted for a limited period should be amortized over its life. If the franchise has an indefinite life, it should be amortized over a reasonable period not to exceed 40 years;

Covenants not to compete: an agreement by the seller of a business not to engage in a competing business in a certain area for a specific period of time. The cost of the not-to-compete covenant should be amortized over the period covered by the covenant unless its estimated economic life is expected to be less;

Easement costs that grant a right of way may be amortized if there is a limited and specified life;

Organization costs incurred when forming a corporation or a partnership, including legal fees, accounting services, incorporation fees, and other related services. Organization costs are usually amortized over 60 months;

Patents, both those developed internally and those purchased. If developed internally, a patent's "amortizable basis" includes legal fees incurred during the application process. A patent should be amortized over its legal life or its economic life, whichever is the shorter;

Trademarks, ***brands***, and ***trade names***, which should be written off over a period not to exceed 40 years;

Other types of property that may be amortized include certain intangible drilling costs, circulation costs, mine development costs, pollution control facilities, and reforestation expenditures;

Certain intangibles cannot be amortized, but may be depreciated using a straight-line approach if they have "determinable" useful life. Because the rules are different in each country

and are subject to change, it is essential to rely on specialist advice.

2 the payment of the principal and interest on a loan in equal amounts over a period of time

amortize FINANCE, BANKING, AND ACCOUNTING to reduce the value of an *asset* gradually by systematically writing off its cost over a period of time, or to repay a *debt* in a series of regular installments or transfers

amortized mortgage FINANCE, BANKING, AND ACCOUNTING a long-term loan, usually for the purchase of real estate, in which the borrower makes monthly payments, part of which cover the interest on the loan and part of which cover the repayment of the principal. In the early years, the greater proportion of the payment is used to cover the interest charged but, as the principal is gradually repaid, the interest portion diminishes and the repayment portion increases. See also *mortgage*

amortized value FINANCE, BANKING, AND ACCOUNTING the value at a particular time of a financial instrument that is being amortized

AMPS *abbr* FINANCE, BANKING, AND ACCOUNTING auction market preferred stock

AMT *abbr* OPERATIONS & PRODUCTION advanced manufacturing technology

analysis of variance STATISTICS the process of separating the statistical variance caused by a particular factor from that caused by other factors

analysis of variance table STATISTICS a table that shows the total variation in the observations in a statistical data set

analytical review FINANCE, BANKING, AND ACCOUNTING the examination of ratios, trends, and changes in balances from one period to the next, to obtain a broad understanding of the financial position and results of operations and to identify any items requiring further investigation

angel investor E-COMMERCE FINANCE, BANKING, AND ACCOUNTING an individual or group of individuals willing to invest in an unproven but well-researched e-business idea. Angel investors are typically the first port of call for Internet startups looking for financial backing, because they are more inclined to provide early funding than *venture capital* firms are. After investing in a company, angel investors take an advisory role without making demands.

angel network FINANCE, BANKING, AND ACCOUNTING a network of backers, organized through a central office which keeps a database of suitable investors and puts them in touch with entrepreneurs who need financial backing

angry fruit salad E-COMMERCE a garish and unattractive visual interface on a computer (*slang*)

angular histogram STATISTICS a histogram that represents data in a circular form

announcement FINANCE, BANKING, AND ACCOUNTING a statement that a company makes to provide information on its trading prospects, which will be of interest to its existing and potential investors

announcement date FINANCE, BANKING, AND ACCOUNTING see *declaration date*

annoyware E-COMMERCE a shareware program that repeatedly interrupts normal functioning to remind users they are using an unregistered copy and will have to pay in order to continue (*slang*)

annual accounts (*U.K.*) FINANCE, BANKING, AND ACCOUNTING see *annual report*

annual charge FINANCE, BANKING, AND ACCOUNTING a management fee paid yearly to a stockbroker or collective fund manager by a client to cover a variety of administrative costs and *commission*

annual depreciation provision FINANCE, BANKING, AND ACCOUNTING the allocation of the cost of an asset to a single year of the asset's expected lifetime

annual general meeting (*U.K.*) FINANCE, BANKING, AND ACCOUNTING GENERAL MANAGEMENT = *annual meeting*

annual hours HR & PERSONNEL a *flexible working hours* practice in which working hours are averaged over a year. Employees are contracted to work a given number of hours per year rather than the traditional number of hours per week. Earnings are determined on a similar basis, but usually a fixed weekly or monthly salary is paid regardless of the number of hours worked. Hours are worked when demand dictates and therefore the need for *overtime* diminishes. Annual hours systems usually cover manual *shiftworkers*, rather than other parts of the workforce.

annualized percentage rate FINANCE, BANKING, AND ACCOUNTING yearly percentage rate, calculated by multiplying the monthly rate by

twelve. It is not as accurate as the *APR*, which includes fees and other charges.

annual meeting FINANCE, BANKING, AND ACCOUNTING GENERAL MANAGEMENT a yearly meeting at which a company's management reports the year's results and stockholders have the opportunity to vote on company business, for example, the appointment of directors and auditors. Other business, for example, voting on dividend payments and board, and stockholder-sponsored resolutions, may also be transacted. U.K. term *AGM*

annual percentage rate *or* **annualized percentage rate** FINANCE, BANKING, AND ACCOUNTING see *APR*

annual percentage yield FINANCE, BANKING, AND ACCOUNTING the effective or true annual rate of return on an investment, taking into account the effect of *compounding*. For example, an annual percentage rate of 6% compounded monthly translates into an annual percentage yield of 6.17%. Abbr. *APY*

annual report FINANCE, BANKING, AND ACCOUNTING a document prepared each year to give a true and fair view of a company's state of affairs.

Annual reports are issued to shareholders and filed at the Securities and Exchange Commission in accordance with the provisions of company legislation. Contents include a profit and loss account and *balance sheet*, a *cash flow statement*, directors' report, *auditor's report*, and, where a company has subsidiaries, the company's group accounts.

The *financial statements* are the main purpose of the annual report, and usually include notes to the accounts. These amplify numerous points contained in the figures and are critical for anyone wishing to study the accounts in detail.

annual report and accounts FINANCE, BANKING, AND ACCOUNTING a report from the directors on the company's financial situation at the end of a fiscal year, together with the balance sheet, profit and loss account, statement of source and application of funds, and the auditor's report, all prepared for the stockholders of the company each year

annual rest system FINANCE, BANKING, AND ACCOUNTING a system in which extra payments or overpayments made to reduce the amount borrowed on a mortgage are credited to the account only once a year

annuity FINANCE, BANKING, AND ACCOUNTING a contract in which a person pays a lump-sum premium to an insurance company and in

return receives periodic payments, usually yearly, often beginning on retirement.

There are several types of annuity. They vary both in the ways they accumulate funds and in the ways they dispense earnings. A *fixed annuity* guarantees fixed payments to the individual receiving it for the term of the contract, usually until death; a *variable annuity* offers no guarantee but has potential for a greater return, usually based on the performance of a stock or mutual fund; a deferred annuity delays payments until the individual chooses to receive them; a *hybrid annuity*, also called a *combination annuity*, combines features of both the fixed and variable annuity.

annuity contract FINANCE, BANKING, AND ACCOUNTING a contract under which a person is paid a fixed sum regularly for life

annuity in arrears FINANCE, BANKING, AND ACCOUNTING an *annuity* whose first payment is due at least one payment period after the start date of the annuity's contract

anonymizer E-COMMERCE a website through which a person browsing can visit the World Wide Web without leaving any identity traces

anorexic organization GENERAL MANAGEMENT an organization that has become so small that it has lost the strength and depth to compete effectively. An anorexic organization may have been through the process of extreme *downsizing* or *delayering*, probably with accompanying *layoffs*. (*slang*)

ANSI X.12 standard E-COMMERCE an American National Standards Institute-supported protocol for the electronic interchange of business transactions. Also known as *X.12*

Ansoff , H. Igor (*b.* 1918–2002) GENERAL MANAGEMENT Russian-born manager and academic. Established *strategic planning* (see *planning*) as a management activity, developing a framework of tools and techniques by which strategic planning decisions could be made. He explained his approach in *Corporate Strategy* (1965). One of his most well-known models is the *three Ss*. He later introduced the concept of *strategic management*. See checklist *Strategic Planning* and thinker *Igor Ansoff*

anticipation note FINANCE, BANKING, AND ACCOUNTING a bond that a borrower intends to pay off with money from taxes due or money to be borrowed in a later and larger transaction

anticipatory hedging FINANCE, BANKING, AND ACCOUNTING hedging conducted before the transaction occurs to which the hedge applies

anticipointment GENERAL MANAGEMENT high public expectations of a new product, entertainment, or service that are subsequently disappointed (*slang*)

anti-dumping ECONOMICS intended to prevent the sale of goods on a foreign market at a price below their *marginal cost*

anti-site E-COMMERCE a Web site devoted to attacking a company or organization. Typically, an anti-site is established by an aggrieved customer who has been unable to contribute his or her opinion to the company's Web site. Anti-sites are often intended to parody or replicate the site they are targeting. In some instances, an anti-site can beat the official site in the search engine rankings by generating more site visits. Also known as *hate site*

antitrust FINANCE, BANKING, AND ACCOUNTING GENERAL MANAGEMENT relating to legislative initiatives aimed at protecting trade and commerce from monopolistic business practices that restrict or eliminate competition. Antitrust laws also attempt to curb trusts and cartels and to keep them from employing monopolistic practices to make unfair profits.

anti-trust laws FINANCE, BANKING, AND ACCOUNTING laws in the United States which prevent the formation of monopolies

ANZCERTA *abbr* FINANCE, BANKING, AND ACCOUNTING Australia and New Zealand Closer Economic Relations Trade Agreement

AP *abbr* FINANCE, BANKING, AND ACCOUNTING accounts payable

APB *abbr* FINANCE, BANKING, AND ACCOUNTING
1 (*U.K.*) Auditing Practices Board
2 Accounting Principles Board

APEC FINANCE, BANKING, AND ACCOUNTING Asia-Pacific Economic Cooperation, a forum designed to promote trade and economic cooperation among countries bordering the Pacific Ocean. It was established in 1989. Members include Australia, Indonesia, Thailand, the Philippines, Singapore, Brunei, and Japan.

applet E-COMMERCE a small application, usually written in *Java*™. Owing to their miniature size, applets can be set to download automatically when an Internet user visits a Web page.

application form HR & PERSONNEL a form used in the *recruitment* process to enable a job candidate to supply information about his or her qualifications, skills, and experience. Employers may ask a candidate to complete an application form instead of, or as well as,

providing a *résumé*. Application forms should be reviewed regularly to ensure that questions asked take account of current legislation, accepted good practice, and internal organizational developments. These questions should be job-related and avoid unjustifiable intrusion into a candidate's personal life.

application program interface GENERAL MANAGEMENT a computer program or piece of software designed to perform a function directly for a user, for example, a word processor, spell checker, or spreadsheet

application server E-COMMERCE an advanced type of server used to run programming languages that help Web sites to deliver dynamic information such as the latest news headlines, stock quotes, personalized information, or shopping carts

application service provider E-COMMERCE see *ASP*

applied economics ECONOMICS the practical application of theoretical economic principles, especially in formulating national and international economic policies

appointment
1 GENERAL MANAGEMENT an engagement to meet at a particular place and time for a particular purpose
2 HR & PERSONNEL the selection of somebody for a position or job

appraisal HR & PERSONNEL see *performance appraisal*

appreciation FINANCE, BANKING, AND ACCOUNTING
1 the value that certain assets, particularly land and buildings, accrue over time. Directors of companies are obliged to reflect this in their accounts.
2 the increase in value of one currency relative to another

appreciative inquiry GENERAL MANAGEMENT an approach to organizational change that focuses and builds on the strengths and potential of an organization. The concept of appreciative inquiry was developed by David L. Cooperrider and Suresh Srivastva in the course of research into organizational behavior at Case Western Reserve University, Cleveland Ohio, in the 1980s. They maintain that a change of perspective, such as focusing on and asking questions about the positive characteristics of an organization rather than focusing on negative aspects such as problems, needs, and deficits, can inspire an image of what the future could be, mobilize positive creative energy and initi-

ate a process of discovery and change within an organization. Appreciative inquiry has its roots in **action research** and focuses on organizations as social systems.

appropriation FINANCE, BANKING, AND ACCOUNTING a sum of money that has been allocated for a particular purpose

approved accounts FINANCE, BANKING, AND ACCOUNTING accounts that have been formally accepted by a company's board of directors

Approved Deposit Fund (*ANZ*) FINANCE, BANKING, AND ACCOUNTING a concessionally taxed fund managed by a financial institution into which **Eligible Termination Payments** can be transferred from a superannuation fund. Abbr. **ADF**

APR *abbr* FINANCE, BANKING, AND ACCOUNTING annual or annualized percentage rate of interest: the interest rate that would exist if it were calculated as simple rather than compound interest.

Different investments typically offer different compounding periods, usually quarterly or monthly. The APR allows them to be compared over a common period of time: one year. This enables an investor or borrower to compare like with like, providing an excellent basis for comparing mortgage or other loan rates.

APR is calculated by applying the formula:

$$APR = [1 + i/m]m - 1.0$$

In the formula, **i** is the interest rate quoted, expressed as a decimal, and **m** is the number of compounding periods per year.

The APR is usually slightly higher than the quoted rate, and should be expressed as a decimal, that is, 6% becomes 0.06. When expressed as the cost of credit, other costs should be included in addition to interest, such as loan closing costs and financial fees. Also known as **nominal annual rate**

APRA *abbr* FINANCE, BANKING, AND ACCOUNTING Australian Prudential Regulation Authority

aptitude test HR & PERSONNEL a measure of a person's natural ability or potential to learn a skill or set of skills. Abilities that are typically measured by aptitude tests include abstract, verbal, and numerical reasoning, because these give a rounded view of a person's general ability in relation to the workplace. Aptitude tests are a form of **psychometric test** and are administered by trained users.

APV *abbr* FINANCE, BANKING, AND ACCOUNTING adjusted present value

APY *abbr* FINANCE, BANKING, AND ACCOUNTING annual percentage yield

AR *abbr* FINANCE, BANKING, AND ACCOUNTING accounts receivable

arb GENERAL MANAGEMENT an **arbitrageur** (*slang*)

arbitrage FINANCE, BANKING, AND ACCOUNTING the buying and selling of foreign currencies, products, or financial securities between two or more markets in order to make an immediate profit by exploiting the differences in market prices quoted

arbitrage fund FINANCE, BANKING, AND ACCOUNTING a fund which tries to take advantage of price discrepancies for the same **asset** in different **markets**

arbitrage pricing theory FINANCE, BANKING, AND ACCOUNTING a model of financial instrument and portfolio behavior that provides a benchmark of return and risk for capital budgeting and securities analysis. It can be used to create portfolios that track a market index, estimate the risk of an asset allocation strategy, or estimate the response of a portfolio to economic developments.

arbitrage syndicate FINANCE, BANKING, AND ACCOUNTING a group of people formed to raise the capital to invest in arbitrage deals

arbitrageur FINANCE, BANKING, AND ACCOUNTING a firm or individual who purchases stock or financial securities to make a windfall profit

arbitration GENERAL MANAGEMENT HR & PERSONNEL the settlement of a dispute by an independent third person, rather than by a court of law. Arbitration allows for claims or grievances to be settled quickly, cost-effectively, privately, and by somebody who is suitably qualified. A contract may include an arbitration clause to be invoked in the case of a dispute. **Mediation** is a related term.

arbitrator GENERAL MANAGEMENT an impartial person accepted by both parties in a dispute to hear both sides and make a judgment

area sampling STATISTICS a form of sampling in which a region is subdivided and some of the divisions are then selected at random for a complete survey

area under a curve STATISTICS a means of summarizing the information from a series of statistical measurements made over a period of time such as a month

Argyris, Christopher (*b.* 1923) GENERAL MANAGEMENT U.S. academic and consultant. Known for his work on **training** and **organizational**

learning, specifically **T-Groups** (see **sensitivity training**), and single-loop and double-loop learning. Argyris's research is set out in *Organizational Learning* (1978), cowritten with **Donald Schön**. Their work also produced the idea of a **learning organization**, later developed by **Peter Senge** .

Argyris argues that organizations depend fundamentally on people, but too often stand in the way of people fulfilling their potential. The main thrust of his work has been to explore the relations between personality and the organization and to suggest how these relations can best be made mutually beneficial. See thinker **Chris Argyris**, **Peter Senge**

arithmetic mean FINANCE, BANKING, AND ACCOUNTING a simple average calculated by dividing the sum of two or more items by the number of items

Arizmendietta, José Maria (1915–77) GENERAL MANAGEMENT Basque priest, more commonly known as Father Arizmendi. Cofounder of the **Mondragon cooperative** movement.

armchair economics FINANCE, BANKING, AND ACCOUNTING GENERAL MANAGEMENT economic forecasting or theorizing based on insufficient data or knowledge of a subject (*slang*)

arm's-length price FINANCE, BANKING, AND ACCOUNTING a price at which an unrelated seller and buyer agree to deal on an **asset** or a product

ARPAnet E-COMMERCE the precursor to the Internet, an experimental network that linked scientists engaged in military research. It was developed by the U.S. Defense Department in the late 1960s, and was originally intended to link together different computers spread out throughout the world.

arrow shooter GENERAL MANAGEMENT a person within an organization who produces visionary new ideas (*slang*)

art director MARKETING a person who is responsible for planning and designing the creative element for advertisements and other communications material

articles of association (*U.K.*) FINANCE, BANKING, AND ACCOUNTING an official document governing the running of a company, that is placed with the **Registrar of Companies**. The articles of association constitute a contract between the company and its members, set out the voting rights of stockholders and the conduct of stockholders' and directors' meetings, and detail the powers of management of the

company. A memorandum of association is a related document. = **bylaws**

articles of incorporation FINANCE, BANKING, AND ACCOUNTING a legal document that creates a corporation and sets forth its purpose and structure according to the laws of the state in which it is established

articles of partnership FINANCE, BANKING, AND ACCOUNTING see **partnership agreement**

artificial intelligence GENERAL MANAGEMENT a branch of computer science concerned with the development of computer systems capable of performing functions that normally require human intelligence, for example, reasoning, problem solving, learning from experience, and speech recognition. Artificial intelligence research combines elements of computer science and cognitive psychology. It is a controversial field because of the difficulty of defining its goals and disagreement over whether these goals are attainable. Much research has been done since World War II, beginning with the theoretical work of Alan Turing during the 1940s. The term became known with the publication in 1961 of the paper *Steps Toward Artificial Intelligence* by Marvin Minsky, cofounder with John McCarthy of the Artificial Intelligence Laboratory at Massachusetts Institute of Technology. Branches of artificial intelligence with applications in business and management include **expert systems** and **robotics**.

artificial neural network E-COMMERCE an information processing system with interconnected components analogous to neurons, based on mathematical models that mimic some features of biological nervous systems and the ability to learn through experience. Abbr. **ANN**

ASAP abbr GENERAL MANAGEMENT as soon as possible (*slang*)

ASB abbr FINANCE, BANKING, AND ACCOUNTING Accounting Standards Board

ASC abbr FINANCE, BANKING, AND ACCOUNTING Accounting Standards Committee

ASEAN Free Trade Area FINANCE, BANKING, AND ACCOUNTING a conceptual regional free trade agreement supported by Singapore to foster trade within the region. Abbr. **AFTA**

A share FINANCE, BANKING, AND ACCOUNTING
1 a type of mutual fund share that has a sales charge associated with it
2 (*U.K.*) a **nonvoting share** of stock in a company issued to raise additional capital without diluting control of the company

3 a class of mutual fund share that is front-end loaded (has a sales charge associated with it). U.K. term **nonvoting share**

Asian Currency Unit FINANCE, BANKING, AND ACCOUNTING a bookkeeping unit used for recording transactions made by approved financial institutions operating in the Asian Dollar market. Abbr. **ACU**

ASIC abbr FINANCE, BANKING, AND ACCOUNTING Australian Securities and Investments Commission

ask FINANCE, BANKING, AND ACCOUNTING
1 the **bid price** at which a dealer in stocks, commodities, or financial securities is prepared to buy
2 the price that a security is offered for sale, or the net asset value of a mutual fund plus any sales charges. Also known as **asked price offering price**

asked price FINANCE, BANKING, AND ACCOUNTING see **ask 2**

asking price FINANCE, BANKING, AND ACCOUNTING the price that a seller puts on something before any negotiation

ASP abbr E-COMMERCE application service provider: a hosting service that will operate, support, manage, and maintain a company's software applications for a fee.

The advantages to an organization of using an ASP are several. It can save time and money: rented applications can be cost-effective and (in theory) can be up and running more quickly than buying an application. It gives them access to the best and latest software without worrying about upgrades and costly installations. It can fill any IT skills shortage.

However, there are disadvantages too, including considerable risk: the ASP industry is still young, and many ASPs have gone out of business. Problems may also arise because many applications are simply not designed to be accessed over a network, especially the Internet, and speed of access is often slow.

assembly OPERATIONS & PRODUCTION the joining together of components to make a complete product

assembly line OPERATIONS & PRODUCTION a line of production in which a number of assembly operations are performed in a set sequence. The speed of movement of an assembly line has to be matched with the skills and abilities of the **workforce** and the complexity of the assembly process to be performed. The assembly

line emerged from the ideas of **scientific management** and was popularized by a number of entrepreneurs, including **Henry Ford** in the car production industry.

assembly plant OPERATIONS & PRODUCTION the building in which an **assembly line** is housed

assessed loss FINANCE, BANKING, AND ACCOUNTING the excess of tax-deductible expenses over taxable income as confirmed by the South African Revenue Service. It may be carried forward and deducted in determining the taxpayer's taxable income in subsequent years of assessment.

assessed value FINANCE, BANKING, AND ACCOUNTING a value for something that is calculated by a person such as an investment advisor

assessment center HR & PERSONNEL a process whereby a group of participants undertakes a series of job-related exercises under observation, so that skills, competencies, and character traits can be assessed. Specially trained assessors evaluate each participant against predetermined criteria. Various methods of assessment may be used, including interviews, **psychometric tests**, group discussions, group problem solving exercises, individual job-simulated tasks, and role-plays. Assessment centers are used in selection for recruitment and promotion and in training and development, and aim to provide an organization with an assessment process that is consistent, free of prejudice, and fair.

assessment of competence HR & PERSONNEL the measurement of an employee's performance against an agreed set of standards for work-based activities. There are four dimensions to assessment: the knowledge and understanding required to carry out a task; the **performance indicators** to be looked for; the scope or range of situations across which an employee is expected to perform; and any particular evidence requirements. **Vocational qualifications** for a wide range of jobs in the United Kingdom are based on a set of occupational standards that contain these elements. A wide variety of techniques or instruments exists to assess **competence**. These include specific work-based ability and **aptitude tests**, as well as traditional methods of **performance appraisal** and evaluation. Recent years have seen a dramatic rise in the use of direct observation at work by trained assessors, the collection of personal portfolios, and peer assessment techniques such as **360 degree appraisal**. All require the careful review of work behavior against a set of indicators that

have been clearly shown to be associated with successful performance.

asset FINANCE, BANKING, AND ACCOUNTING GENERAL MANAGEMENT any tangible or intangible item to which a value can be assigned. Assets can be physical, such as machinery and consumer durables, or financial, such as cash and accounts receivable.

Assets are typically broken down into five different categories. *Current assets* include cash, cash equivalents, marketable securities, inventories, and prepaid expenses that are expected to be used within one year or a normal operating cycle. All cash items and inventories are reported at historical value. Securities are reported at market value. Noncurrent assets, or long-term investments, are resources that are expected to be held for more than one year. They are reported at the lower of cost and current market value, which means that their values will vary. *Fixed assets* include property, plant and facilities, and equipment used to conduct business. These items are reported at their original value, even though current values might well be much higher. *Intangible assets* include legal claims, patents, franchise rights, and accounts receivable. These values can be more difficult to determine. *Accounts receivable*, for example, reflect the amount a business expects to collect, such as, say, $9,000 of the $10,000 owed by customers. Deferred charges include prepaid costs and other expenditures that will produce future revenue or benefits.

asset allocation (*ANZ*) FINANCE, BANKING, AND ACCOUNTING an investment strategy that distributes investments in a portfolio so as to achieve the highest investment return while minimizing risk. Such a strategy usually apportions investments among cash equivalents, stock in domestic and foreign companies, fixed-income investments, and real estate.

asset-backed security ECONOMICS FINANCE, BANKING, AND ACCOUNTING a security for which the collateral is neither land nor a land-based financial instrument

asset backing FINANCE, BANKING, AND ACCOUNTING support for a stock price provided by the value of the company's assets

asset-based lending FINANCE, BANKING, AND ACCOUNTING the lending of money with the expectation that the proceeds from an asset or assets will allow the borrower to repay the loan

asset conversion loan FINANCE, BANKING, AND ACCOUNTING a loan that the borrower will repay with money raised by selling an asset

asset coverage FINANCE, BANKING, AND ACCOUNTING the ratio measuring a company's solvency and consisting of its net assets divided by its debt

asset demand ECONOMICS the amount of assets held as money, which will be low when interest rates are high and high when interest rates are low

asset financing FINANCE, BANKING, AND ACCOUNTING the borrowing of money by a company using its assets as collateral

asset for asset swap FINANCE, BANKING, AND ACCOUNTING an exchange of one bankrupt debtor's debt for that of another

asset management FINANCE, BANKING, AND ACCOUNTING an investment service offered by some financial institutions that combines banking and brokerage services. Abbr. *AM*

asset play FINANCE, BANKING, AND ACCOUNTING the purchase of a company's stock in the belief that it has assets that are not properly documented and therefore unknown to others

asset pricing model FINANCE, BANKING, AND ACCOUNTING a pricing model used to determine the profit that an asset will yield

asset protection trust FINANCE, BANKING, AND ACCOUNTING a trust, often established in a foreign country, used to make the trust's principal inaccessible to creditors

asset restructuring FINANCE, BANKING, AND ACCOUNTING the purchase or sale of assets worth more than 50% of a listed company's total or net assets

asset side FINANCE, BANKING, AND ACCOUNTING the side of a balance sheet that shows the economic resources a firm owns, for example, cash in hand or in bank deposits, products, or buildings and fixtures

assets requirements FINANCE, BANKING, AND ACCOUNTING the assets needed for a business to continue trading

asset-stripper FINANCE, BANKING, AND ACCOUNTING a company that acquires another company and sells its assets to make a profit without regard for the acquired company's future business success

asset-stripping FINANCE, BANKING, AND ACCOUNTING the purchase of a company whose market value is below its asset value, usually so that the buyer can sell the assets for immediate gain. The buyer usually has little or

no concern for the purchased company's employees or other *stakeholders*, so the practice is generally frowned upon.

asset substitution FINANCE, BANKING, AND ACCOUNTING the purchase of assets that involve more risk than those a lender expected the borrower to buy

asset swap FINANCE, BANKING, AND ACCOUNTING an exchange of assets between companies so that they may divest parts no longer required and enter another product area

asset turnover FINANCE, BANKING, AND ACCOUNTING the ratio of a firm's sales revenue to its total assets, used as a measure of the firm's business efficiency

asset valuation FINANCE, BANKING, AND ACCOUNTING the aggregated value of the assets of a firm, usually the capital assets, as entered on its balance sheet

assign FINANCE, BANKING, AND ACCOUNTING to transfer ownership of an *asset* to another person or organization

assignable cause of variation OPERATIONS & PRODUCTION an evident reason for deviation from the norm. An assignable cause exists when variation within a process can be attributed to a particular cause that is a fundamental part of the process. Once identified, the assignable cause of the errors must be investigated and the process adjusted before other possible causes of variation are examined. Using the technique of *statistical process control*, control charts can be used to distinguish causes that are assignable from those that are random.

assigned risk FINANCE, BANKING, AND ACCOUNTING a poor insurance risk that a company is required by law to insure against

associate (*ANZ*) FINANCE, BANKING, AND ACCOUNTING a member of a stock exchange who does not have a seat on it

associate company FINANCE, BANKING, AND ACCOUNTING see *affiliated enterprise*

Associate of the Association of International Accountants FINANCE, BANKING, AND ACCOUNTING abbr. *AAIA*

associate program E-COMMERCE see *affiliate program*

Association of British Insurers FINANCE, BANKING, AND ACCOUNTING an association that represents over 400 U.K. insurance companies

to the government, the regulators, and other agencies, as well as providing a wide range of services to its members. Abbr. **ABI**

Association of Chartered Accountants in the United States FINANCE, BANKING, AND ACCOUNTING a nonprofit professional and educational organization that represents over 5,000 chartered accountants based in the United States. The Association was founded in 1985. Abbr. **ACAUS**

Association of Chartered Certified Accountants FINANCE, BANKING, AND ACCOUNTING an international accounting organization with over 300,000 members in more than 160 countries. It was formed in 1904 as the London Association of Accountants. Abbr. **ACCA**

Association of Independent Financial Advisers (*U.K.*) FINANCE, BANKING, AND ACCOUNTING a trade association that represents the interests of independent financial advisers. Abbr. **AIFA**

Association of Unit Trusts and Investment Funds FINANCE, BANKING, AND ACCOUNTING abbr. **AUTIF**

assumable mortgage FINANCE, BANKING, AND ACCOUNTING a mortgage that the buyer of a property can take over from the seller

assumed bond FINANCE, BANKING, AND ACCOUNTING a bond for which a company other than the issuer takes over responsibility

assumption STATISTICS the conditions under which valid results can be obtained from a statistical technique

assured shorthold tenancy (*U.K.*) FINANCE, BANKING, AND ACCOUNTING a tenancy for a fixed period of at least six months during which the tenant cannot be evicted other than by court order. Any new tenancy without a written agreement is an assured shorthold tenancy.

assured tenancy (*U.K.*) FINANCE, BANKING, AND ACCOUNTING a tenancy for an indefinite period in which the tenant cannot be evicted other than by court order

ASX *abbr* FINANCE, BANKING, AND ACCOUNTING Australian Stock Exchange

ASX 100 FINANCE, BANKING, AND ACCOUNTING a measure of the change in stock prices on the *Australian Stock Exchange* based on changes in the stocks of the top 100 companies. Similar indexes include the ASX 20, ASX 50, ASX 200, and ASX 300.

asymmetrical digital subscriber line E-COMMERCE see *ADSL*

asymmetrical distribution STATISTICS a frequency or probability distribution of statistical data that is not symmetrical about a central value in the data

asymmetric taxation FINANCE, BANKING, AND ACCOUNTING a difference in tax status between parties to a transaction, typically making the transaction attractive to both parties because of taxes that one or both can avoid

asynchronous transmission E-COMMERCE the transmission of data in which the end of the transmission of one unit denotes the start of the next, rather than transmission at fixed intervals

at best FINANCE, BANKING, AND ACCOUNTING an instruction to a stockbroker to buy or sell securities immediately at the best possible current price in the market, regardless of adverse price movements. It is also applicable to the commodity or currency markets. See also *at limit*

at call FINANCE, BANKING, AND ACCOUNTING used to describe a short-term loan that is repayable immediately upon demand

Athos, Anthony G. (*b.* 1934) GENERAL MANAGEMENT U.S. academic. See also *Pascale, Richard Tanner*

at limit FINANCE, BANKING, AND ACCOUNTING an instruction to a stockbroker to buy or sell a security within certain limits, usually not to sell below or to buy above a set price. A time limit is stipulated by the investor, and, if there has been no transaction within that period, the instruction lapses. It is also applicable to the commodity or currency markets. See also *at best*

ATM FINANCE, BANKING, AND ACCOUNTING automated teller machine: an electronic machine from which bank customers can withdraw paper money using an encoded plastic card

ATO *abbr* FINANCE, BANKING, AND ACCOUNTING Australian Taxation Office

atom MARKETING any traditional nondigital means of delivering information, such as a newspaper, book, or magazine

atomize GENERAL MANAGEMENT to split a large organization into smaller operating units

at sight FINANCE, BANKING, AND ACCOUNTING see *bill of exchange*

attachment

1 E-COMMERCE a file that is attached to a standard text e-mail message

2 FINANCE, BANKING, AND ACCOUNTING a process that enables a judgment creditor to secure dues from a debtor. A debtor's earnings and/or funds held at his or her bankers may be attached.

attendance HR & PERSONNEL presence at work, normally noted in an attendance register. The phenomenon of irregular attendance is referred to as *absenteeism*. One method of improving attendance is by paying an *attendance bonus* .

attendance bonus HR & PERSONNEL a financial or nonfinancial incentive offered to employees by an employer to arrive for work on time

attention economy ECONOMICS a view of the economy in the late 20th century that suggests that people's attention to Web sites is a valuable and tradable commodity

attention management GENERAL MANAGEMENT a method of ensuring that employees are focused on their work and on organizational goals. Attention management is similar to *time management*, as inattentiveness results in wasted time. An important factor in winning and sustaining attention is tapping into people's emotions.

attestation clause FINANCE, BANKING, AND ACCOUNTING a clause showing that the signature of the person signing a legal document has been witnessed

at-the-money FINANCE, BANKING, AND ACCOUNTING used to describe an option with a strike price roughly equivalent to the price of the underlying stock

attitude GENERAL MANAGEMENT a mental position consisting of a feeling, emotion, or opinion evolved in response to an external situation. An attitude can be momentary or can develop into a habitual position that has a long-term influence on an individual's behavior. Attempts can be made to modify attitudes that have a negative effect in the workplace, for example, through education and training. The *employee attitude survey* is one tool used to assess prevalent attitudes in the workforce.

attitude research GENERAL MANAGEMENT an investigation into people's beliefs regarding an organization, its products or services, or its activities. Attitude research is used in marketing

to ascertain opinions among consumers and the public in general. It is also used within organizations when **employee attitude surveys** are conducted.

attitude survey MARKETING a piece of research carried out to assess the feelings of a target audience toward a product, brand, or organization

attribute sampling OPERATIONS & PRODUCTION a random testing method for determining the quality of a finished product by inspecting a sample number of the items in each batch. The items selected are examined for a particular attribute, which is usually an abnormal or negative characteristic—for example, a sample of cars from one production run might be inspected for poor paintwork, and the number of sampled cars found with this attribute used to calculate the number of defective items in the whole batch.

attribution theory of leadership GENERAL MANAGEMENT the theory that leaders observe their followers' behavior, attribute it to particular causes, and as a result respond in a particular way

auction E-COMMERCE FINANCE, BANKING, AND ACCOUNTING a sale of goods or property by competitive bidding on the spot, by mail, by telecommunications, or over the Internet

auction market preferred stock FINANCE, BANKING, AND ACCOUNTING stock in a company owned in the United Kingdom that pays dividends which track a money-market index. Abbr. **AMPS**

AUD abbr FINANCE, BANKING, AND ACCOUNTING Australian dollar

audience MARKETING the total number of readers, viewers, or listeners who are exposed to an advertisement

audience research MARKETING research carried out to measure the size or composition of the target audience for a piece of advertising

audit FINANCE, BANKING, AND ACCOUNTING a systematic examination of the activities and status of an entity, based primarily on investigation and analysis of its systems, controls, and records

audit committee FINANCE, BANKING, AND ACCOUNTING a committee of a company's board of directors, from which the company's executives are excluded, that monitors the company's finances

audited accounts FINANCE, BANKING, AND ACCOUNTING a set of accounts that have been thoroughly scrutinized, checked, and approved by a team of auditors

audit of management GENERAL MANAGEMENT see **operational audit**

Auditor-General (ANZ) FINANCE, BANKING, AND ACCOUNTING an officer of a state or territory government who is responsible for ensuring that government expenditure is made in accordance with legislation

auditors' fees FINANCE, BANKING, AND ACCOUNTING fees paid to a company's auditors, which are approved by the stockholders at an **annual meeting**

auditor's report FINANCE, BANKING, AND ACCOUNTING a certification by an auditor that a firm's financial records give a true and fair view of its profit and loss for the period

audit report FINANCE, BANKING, AND ACCOUNTING the summary submission made by auditors of the findings of an **audit**. An audit report is usually of the financial records and accounts of a company. An auditor's report normally takes one of the forms approved by the accountancy professional organizations to cover all requirements imposed by law on the auditor. If reports do not support the company's records, they may be termed "qualified." A report is qualified if it contains any indication that the auditor has failed to satisfy himself or herself on any of the points that the law requires. The qualification may, for example, add a rider stating that the appointed auditor has had to rely on secondary information supplied by other auditors under circumstances in which it has been inappropriate to do otherwise. Qualifications may also refer to the inadequacy of information or explanations supplied, or to the fact that the auditor is not satisfied that proper books or other records are being kept.

audit risk FINANCE, BANKING, AND ACCOUNTING the risk that auditors may give an inappropriate audit opinion on financial statements

audit trail FINANCE, BANKING, AND ACCOUNTING the records of all the sequential stages of a transaction. An audit trail may trace the process of a purchase, a sale, a customer complaint, or the supply of goods. Tracing what happened at each stage through the records can be a useful method of problem solving. In financial markets, audit trails may be used to ensure fairness and accuracy on the part of the dealers.

augend FINANCE, BANKING, AND ACCOUNTING the number added to an **addend** in order to complete an addition

aural signature MARKETING a musical theme that is part of a company or product's brand identity

Aussie Mac FINANCE, BANKING, AND ACCOUNTING an informal name for a mortgage-backed certificate issued in Australia by the National Mortgage Market Corporation. The corporation has been issuing such certificates since 1985.

austerity budget FINANCE, BANKING, AND ACCOUNTING a budget imposed on a country by its government with the goal of reducing the national deficit by way of cutting consumer spending

Austrade FINANCE, BANKING, AND ACCOUNTING Australian Trade Commission, a federal government body responsible for promoting Australian products abroad and attracting business to Australia. It currently has 108 offices in 63 countries.

Australia and New Zealand Closer Economic Relations Trade Agreement FINANCE, BANKING, AND ACCOUNTING an accord between Australia and New Zealand designed to facilitate the exchange of goods between the two countries. It was signed on January 1, 1983. Abbr. **ANZCERTA**

Australian Accounting Standards Board FINANCE, BANKING, AND ACCOUNTING the body that is responsible for setting and monitoring accounting standards in Australia. It was established under Corporations Law in 1988, replacing the Accounting Standards Review Board. Abbr. **AASB**

Australian Bureau of Statistics STATISTICS an Australian federal government body responsible for compiling national statistics and conducting regular censuses. It was established in 1906. Abbr. **ABS**

Australian Chamber of Commerce and Industry FINANCE, BANKING, AND ACCOUNTING a national council of business organizations in Australia. It represents around 350,000 businesses and its members include state chambers of commerce as well as major national employer and industry associations. Abbr. **ACCI**

Australian Chamber of Manufacturers GENERAL MANAGEMENT a body representing Australian manufacturers, established in 1878. Abbr. **ACM**

Australian Communications Authority FI-NANCE, BANKING, AND ACCOUNTING the government body responsible for regulating practices in the communications industries. It was established in 1997 as a result of the merger of the Australian Telecommunications Authority and the Spectrum Management Agency. Abbr. *ACA*

Australian Council of Trade Unions GENERAL MANAGEMENT Australia's national labor union organization. It was founded in 1927 and is based in Melbourne. Abbr. *ACTU*

Australian Industrial Relations Commission HR & PERSONNEL an administrative tribunal responsible for settling industrial disputes by conciliation and for setting and modifying industrial awards. It was established in 1988 to replace the Arbitration Commission and other specialist tribunals. Abbr. *AIRC*

Australian Prudential Regulation Authority FINANCE, BANKING, AND ACCOUNTING a federal government body responsible for ensuring that financial institutions are able to meet their commitments

Australian Securities and Investments Commission FINANCE, BANKING, AND ACCOUNTING an Australian federal government body responsible for regulating Australian businesses and the provision of financial products and services to consumers. It was established in 1989, replacing the Australian Securities Commission. Abbr. *ASIC*

Australian Stock Exchange FINANCE, BANKING, AND ACCOUNTING the principal market for trading stock and other securities in Australia. It was formed in 1987 as a result of the amalgamation of six state stock exchanges and has offices in most state capitals. Abbr. *ASX*

Australian Taxation Office FINANCE, BANKING, AND ACCOUNTING a statutory body responsible for the administration of the Australian federal government's taxation system. It is based in Canberra and is also responsible for the country's superannuation system. Abbr. *ATO*

authentication E-COMMERCE a software security verification procedure to acknowledge or validate the source, uniqueness, and integrity of an e-commerce message to make sure data is not being tampered with. The verification is typically achieved through the use of an electronic signature in the form of a key or algorithm that is shared by the trading partners.

authority GENERAL MANAGEMENT the right to act or command. People willingly obey a person in authority, because they believe he or she has a legitimate entitlement to exercise power. *Max Weber* distinguishes three types of legitimate authority: rational-legal, derived from the office held; traditional, from custom, an ancient tradition of obedience; and charismatic, exerted by those whose exceptional abilities confer the right to lead. The third form is the basis for the *charismatic authority* leadership theory. See thinker *Max Weber*

authority chart GENERAL MANAGEMENT a diagram showing the hierarchical lines of *authority* and reporting within an organization. *Organization charts* are similar.

authority-compliance management GENERAL MANAGEMENT see *Managerial Grid™*

authority to purchase FINANCE, BANKING, AND ACCOUNTING a bill drawn up and presented with shipping documentation to the purchaser's bank, allowing the bank to purchase the bill

authorization FINANCE, BANKING, AND ACCOUNTING the process of assessing a financial transaction, confirming that it does not raise the account's debt above its limit, and allowing the transaction to proceed. This would be undertaken, for example, by a credit card issuer. A positive authorization results in an authorization code being generated and the relevant funds being set aside. The available credit limit is reduced by the amount authorized.

authorized capital FINANCE, BANKING, AND ACCOUNTING the money made by a company from the sale of authorized shares of common and preferred stock. It is measured by multiplying the number of authorized shares by their par value.

authorized share FINANCE, BANKING, AND ACCOUNTING a share that a company is authorized to issue

authorized share capital FINANCE, BANKING, AND ACCOUNTING the type, class, number, and amount of the shares which a company may issue, as empowered by its memorandum of association. Also known as *nominal share capital*, *registered share capital*

authorized signatory FINANCE, BANKING, AND ACCOUNTING the most senior issuer of authorization certificates in an organization, recognized by a signatory authority and designated in a signatory certificate

AUTIF *abbr* FINANCE, BANKING, AND ACCOUNTING Association of Unit Trusts and Investment Funds

automated clearing house E-COMMERCE FINANCE, BANKING, AND ACCOUNTING ATM systems for interbank clearing and settlement of financial transactions. The network is also used for electronic fund transfers from a checking or savings account. Abbr. *ACH*

Automated Direct Debit Amendments and Cancellation Service FINANCE, BANKING, AND ACCOUNTING in the United Kingdom, a *BACS* service that allows paying banks to inform direct debit payees of a change of instruction, for example, an amendment to the customer's account details or a request to cancel the instructions. Abbr. *ADDACS*

automated handling OPERATIONS & PRODUCTION the use of computers to control the moving and positioning of materials in a warehouse or factory. Automated handling may involve the use of robots.

Automated Order Entry System FINANCE, BANKING, AND ACCOUNTING in the United States, a system that allows small orders to bypass the floor brokers and go straight to the specialists on the exchange floor

automated screen trading FINANCE, BANKING, AND ACCOUNTING an electronic trading system for the sale and purchase of securities. Customers' orders are entered via a keyboard; a computer system matches and executes the deals; and prices and deals are shown on monitors, thus dispensing with the need for face-to-face contact on a trading floor.

automated storage and retrieval systems OPERATIONS & PRODUCTION the use of computerized vehicles to store, select, and move pallets around a large warehouse

automated teller machine FINANCE, BANKING, AND ACCOUNTING see *ATM*

automatic assembly OPERATIONS & PRODUCTION a computerized *production control* technique used in the production of manufactured goods to balance output of production with demand. All factors affecting production performance are input when setting the operating parameters of an automatic assembly system, including sales information and production *capacity*.

automatic debit FINANCE, BANKING, AND ACCOUNTING an instruction given by an account holder to a bank to make regular payments on given dates to the same payee. U.K. term *standing order*

automatic guided vehicle system OPERATIONS & PRODUCTION a transportation system

consisting of driverless electric vehicles that follow a predetermined track, used for the distribution of materials around a plant

automatic rollover FINANCE, BANKING, AND ACCOUNTING on the London Money Market, the automatic reinvestment of a maturing fixed term deposit for a further identical fixed term, an arrangement that can be canceled at any time

automation OPERATIONS & PRODUCTION the self-controlling operation of machinery that reduces or dispenses with human communication or control when used in normal conditions. Automation was first introduced in the late 1940s by the Ford Motor Company. Also known as *mechanization*

autonomation OPERATIONS & PRODUCTION a production system in which workers are allowed, and machines are equipped with a mechanism, to stop production if a defect in a product is detected during the production process. Autonomation became known through the *Toyota production system*. The concept evolved from braking devices on machines that automatically stop if a problem occurs. Within Toyota, the concept has been carried forward so that all machines are equipped with various safety devices to prevent defective products, and production workers are allowed to stop the production line if a problem occurs. The problem is then properly explored in order to find a solution and to ensure that everyone understands the underlying reasons for it. In the long term, this creates a more efficient production line.

autonomous work group HR & PERSONNEL a small group of people who are empowered to manage themselves and the work they do on a day-to-day basis. The members of an autonomous work group are usually responsible for a whole process, product, or service, and not only perform the work but also design and manage it. Also known as *self-directed team*, *self-managed team*, *self-managed work team*, *self-managing team*

Auto Pact FINANCE, BANKING, AND ACCOUNTING the informal name for the Agreement Concerning Automotive Products between Canada and the United States, by which duties were reduced on imported cars for U.S. automakers assembling vehicles in Canada. Subsequent provisions of the North American Free Trade Agreement reduced its effect.

autopoiesis E-COMMERCE a process whereby a system, organization, or organism produces and replaces its own components and distinguishes itself from its environment

autoresponder E-COMMERCE an e-mail software application that enables Internet users to send automated e-mails when they are not able to respond to incoming e-mail. Some autoresponse software enables a degree of personalization, for example, by incorporating the recipient's name in the responding message.

availability float FINANCE, BANKING, AND ACCOUNTING money that is available to a company because checks that it has written have not yet been charged against its accounts

AVCs *abbr* FINANCE, BANKING, AND ACCOUNTING additional voluntary contributions

average STATISTICS the arithmetic mean of a sample of observations

average accounting return FINANCE, BANKING, AND ACCOUNTING the percentage return realized on an asset, as measured by its book value, after taxes and depreciation

average adjuster FINANCE, BANKING, AND ACCOUNTING a person who calculates how much of an insurance is to be borne by each party

average adjustment FINANCE, BANKING, AND ACCOUNTING the calculation of the share of cost of damage to or loss of a ship

average collection period FINANCE, BANKING, AND ACCOUNTING the mean time required for a firm to liquidate its accounts receivable, measured from the date each receivable is posted until the last payment is received.

Its formula is:

$$\frac{\text{Accounts receivable}}{\text{Average daily sales}} = \text{Average collection period}$$

For example, if accounts receivable are $280,000, and average daily sales are 7,000, then:

$$\frac{280,000}{7,000} = 40$$

average cost of capital FINANCE, BANKING, AND ACCOUNTING the average of what a company is paying for the money it borrows or raises by selling stock

average deviation STATISTICS the spread of a sample of observations

average nominal maturity FINANCE, BANKING, AND ACCOUNTING the average length of time until a mutual fund's financial instruments mature

average option FINANCE, BANKING, AND ACCOUNTING an option whose value depends on

the average price of a commodity during a particular period of time

Average Weekly Earnings STATISTICS a measure of wage levels in the Australian workforce that is calculated regularly by the *Australian Bureau of Statistics*. The measure is considered one of Australia's key economic indicators. Abbr. *AWE*

Average Weekly Ordinary Time Earnings STATISTICS a measure of wage levels in the Australian workforce that excludes overtime payments, published by the *Australian Bureau of Statistics*

award HR & PERSONNEL
1 the terms of employment set by an industrial court or tribunal for a particular occupation
2 (*ANZ*) a decision handed down by a court of arbitration

award wage (*ANZ*) HR & PERSONNEL a rate of pay set by an industrial court or tribunal for a particular occupation

AWE *abbr* STATISTICS Average Weekly Earnings

"aw shucks" FINANCE, BANKING, AND ACCOUNTING see *Sarbanes-Oxley*

axis STATISTICS a reference line used in geometry to locate a point in space or in a plane

B

B2B *abbr* E-COMMERCE business-to-business: relating to an advertising or marketing program aimed at businesses doing business with other businesses as opposed to consumers. The term is most commonly used in reference to commerce or business that is conducted over the Internet between commercial enterprises.

B2B advertising MARKETING advertising that is aimed at buyers for organizations rather than domestic consumers

B2B agency MARKETING an advertising agency that specializes in planning, creating, and buying advertising aimed at buyers for organizations rather than domestic consumers

B2B auction E-COMMERCE a Web marketplace that provides a mechanism for negotiating prices and bidding for services. Web-based B2B auctions reverse the traditional auction formula in which the goal is to help the seller get the best price. B2B Web auctions involve suppliers competing with one another by bidding down the price of their service. This inevitably benefits the buyer, as, instead of having to bid

higher for a particular service or product, he or she can wait until the suppliers have bid themselves down to a reasonable price. Typically, online auctions require companies to follow a registration process in order to take part. During this process, users have to provide their credit card information and shipping preferences as well as agree to the site's code of conduct. Some sites (for example, BusinessAuctions.com) also manage secure auctions, which restrict potential bidders to specific firms or individuals.

B2B commerce E-COMMERCE the business conducted between companies, rather than between a company and individual consumers

B2B marketing
1 E-COMMERCE the planning, promotion, and distribution of goods or services for use by businesses rather than individual consumers
2 MARKETING marketing activities aimed at buyers for organizations rather than domestic consumers

B2C *abbr* E-COMMERCE business-to-consumer: relating to an advertising or marketing program aimed at businesses doing business directly with consumers as opposed to other businesses. The term is most commonly used in reference to commerce or business that is conducted over the Internet between a commercial enterprise and a consumer.

B4N *abbr* GENERAL MANAGEMENT bye for now (*slang*)

BAA *abbr* FINANCE, BANKING, AND ACCOUNTING British Accounting Association

Baby Bell FINANCE, BANKING, AND ACCOUNTING one of the regional phone companies that was established after the demise of AT&T in 1984. Most Baby Bells have since merged with other telephone companies, including SBC with AT & T. (*slang*)

back duty FINANCE, BANKING, AND ACCOUNTING tax relating to a past period that has not been paid because of the taxpayer's failure to disclose relevant information through negligence or fraud. If back duty is found to be payable, the relevant authorities may instigate an investigation and penalties or interest may be charged on the amount.

back-end loading FINANCE, BANKING, AND ACCOUNTING the practice of charging a redemption fee or deferred sales charge if the holder of an investment decides to sell it. This is used as a discouragement to selling. See also *front-end loading*

backlink checking E-COMMERCE a means of finding out which Web pages are linking to a specific Web site. Many *search engines* enable users to conduct backlink searches by entering the name of a Web site into the search box preceded by a special command (for example, "link":). AltaVista and HotBot are two of the most popular search engines to offer this facility. The backlink checking process can be automated by using a service such as LinkPopularity.com, which enables users to search for linking sites at various search engines at once. Backlink checking enables e-business and Web site managers to keep track of their own and their competitors' online popularity.

backlog OPERATIONS & PRODUCTION the buildup of unfulfilled orders for a product or process that is behind schedule. A backlog can result from bad scheduling, production delays, an unanticipated demand for a product or process, or where the capacity of the process is not able to keep up with demand. Some large products, for example, aircraft and ships, have to be built to a backlog of orders, as it is not feasible to supply them on demand.

backlog depreciation FINANCE, BANKING, AND ACCOUNTING the additional depreciation required when an asset is revalued to make up for the fact that previous depreciation had been calculated on a now out-of-date valuation

back office FINANCE, BANKING, AND ACCOUNTING GENERAL MANAGEMENT the administrative staff of a company who do not have face-to-face contact with the company's customers

back pay HR & PERSONNEL pay that is owed to an employee for work carried out before the current payment period and is either overdue or results from a backdated pay increase

back-to-back loan FINANCE, BANKING, AND ACCOUNTING an arrangement in which two companies in different countries borrow offsetting amounts in each other's currency and each repays it at a specified future date in its domestic currency. Such a loan, often between a company and its foreign subsidiary, eliminates the risk of loss from exchange rate fluctuations.

back-to-school sale GENERAL MANAGEMENT a store sale that is timed to coincide with the return of children to school after the summer vacation (*slang*)

backup FINANCE, BANKING, AND ACCOUNTING a period in which bond yields rise and prices fall, or a sudden reversal in a stock market trend

back-up credit FINANCE, BANKING, AND ACCOUNTING credit provided by banks for a Eurocurrency note

backup facility GENERAL MANAGEMENT a secondary system, record, or contract intended to take the place of another that fails

backup withholding FINANCE, BANKING, AND ACCOUNTING a withholding tax that a payer sends to the Internal Revenue Service so that somebody receiving income cannot avoid all taxes on that income

backward compatible E-COMMERCE describes a computer hardware or software product that is compatible with its predecessors to the extent that it can use interfaces and data from earlier versions

backward integration OPERATIONS & PRODUCTION the building of relationships with *suppliers* in order to secure the supply of *raw materials*. Backward integration can involve taking control of supply companies and is a feature of Japanese *keiretsu*. It is the opposite of *forward integration*.

backward scheduling OPERATIONS & PRODUCTION a *production scheduling* (see *production smoothing*) technique for planning work on the basis of when the completed work is due. By using backward scheduling, managers are able to assign work to particular workstations so that the overall task is completed exactly when it is due. The technique allows potential bottlenecks and idle time for particular workstations to be identified in advance.

BACS FINANCE, BANKING, AND ACCOUNTING in the United Kingdom, an electronic bulk clearing system generally used by banks and building societies for low-value and/or repetitive items such as standing orders, direct debits, and automated credits such as salary payments. It was formerly known as the Bankers Automated Clearing Service.

BADC *abbr* FINANCE, BANKING, AND ACCOUNTING Business Accounting Deliberation Council of Japan

bad debt FINANCE, BANKING, AND ACCOUNTING a debt which is or is considered to be uncollectable and is, therefore, written off either as a charge to the profit and loss account or against an existing doubtful debt provision

bad debt provision FINANCE, BANKING, AND ACCOUNTING an accounting estimate of the amount of debts thought likely to have to be written off

bad debt reserve FINANCE, BANKING, AND ACCOUNTING an amount of money that a company sets aside to cover bad debts

bad debts recovered FINANCE, BANKING, AND ACCOUNTING money formerly classified as *bad debts* and therefore written off that has since been recovered either wholly or in part

badwill FINANCE, BANKING, AND ACCOUNTING negative goodwill (*slang*)

bailment FINANCE, BANKING, AND ACCOUNTING the delivery of goods from the owner to another person on the condition that they will eventually be returned

bait and switch MARKETING a marketing practice whereby customers are encouraged to enter a store by an advertisement for one product and are then persuaded to buy another more expensive product (*slang*)

balance FINANCE, BANKING, AND ACCOUNTING
1 the state of an account, indicating whether money is owed or owing, i.e. a debit or a credit balance
2 in double-entry bookkeeping, the amount required to make the debit and credit figures in the books equal each other
3 the difference between the totals of the debit and credit entries in an account

balance billing FINANCE, BANKING, AND ACCOUNTING the practice of requesting payment from a receiver of a service such as medical treatment for the part of the cost not covered by the person's insurance

balance brought down FINANCE, BANKING, AND ACCOUNTING an amount entered in an account at the end of a period to balance income and expenditure

balanced budget ECONOMICS a budget in which planned expenditure on goods and services and debt income can be met by current income from taxation and other central government receipts

balanced design STATISTICS an experimental design in which the same number of observations is used for each combination of the experimental factors

balanced fund FINANCE, BANKING, AND ACCOUNTING a mutual fund that invests in a variety of types of companies and financial instruments to reduce the risk of loss through poor performance of any one type

balanced investment strategy FINANCE, BANKING, AND ACCOUNTING the practice of invest-ing in a variety of types of companies and financial instruments to reduce the risk of loss through poor performance of any one type

balanced line OPERATIONS & PRODUCTION an *assembly line* in which the cycle time for all the workstations is equal. A balanced line is achieved by allocating the right amount of work and the correct amount of operators and machinery to produce a given flow of product over a set period, taking into account the fact that each workstation will have a different capacity and that each process involved has a different cycle time.

balanced quantity OPERATIONS & PRODUCTION an *inventory* measure of the quantity of materials and parts required by a workstation to achieve a planned level of output

balanced scorecard FINANCE, BANKING, AND ACCOUNTING GENERAL MANAGEMENT a system that measures and manages an organization's progress toward strategic objectives. Introduced by *Robert Kaplan* and *David Norton* in 1992, the balanced scorecard incorporates not only financial indicators but also three other perspectives: customer, internal business, and learning/innovation. The scorecard shows how these measures are interlinked and affect each other, enabling an organization's past, present, and potential performance to be tracked and managed. See thinker *Robert S. Kaplan*

balanced scorecard approach FINANCE, BANKING, AND ACCOUNTING an approach to the provision of information to management in order to assist strategic policy formulation and implementation to build the long-term value of the business. It emphasizes the need to provide the user with a set of information that addresses all relevant areas of performance in an objective and unbiased fashion. The information provided may include financial and non-financial elements and cover areas such as profitability, customer satisfaction, internal efficiency, and innovation. The term originates from the best-selling business book *The Balanced Scorecard*, written by Robert Kaplan and David Norton and published by Harvard Business School Press in 1996. Their approach applies the concept of stockholder value analysis, and is based on the premise that the traditional measures used by managers to see how well their organizations are performing, such as business ratios, productivity, unit costs, growth, and profitability, are only a part of the picture. Traditional measures are seen as providing a narrowly focused snapshot of how an organization performed in the past, and give little indication of likely future perform-ance. In contrast, the Balanced Scorecard (BSC) offers a measurement and management system that links strategic objectives to comprehensive performance indicators.

balance off FINANCE, BANKING, AND ACCOUNTING to add up and enter the totals for both sides of an account at the end of an accounting period in order to determine the balance

balance of payments ECONOMICS a list of a country's credit and debit transactions with international financial institutions and foreign countries over a specific period. Abbr. *BOP*

balance of payments capital account FINANCE, BANKING, AND ACCOUNTING items in a country's balance of payments which refer to capital investments made in or by other countries

balance of payments current account FINANCE, BANKING, AND ACCOUNTING a record of imports and exports of goods and services and the flow of money between countries arising from investments

balance of payments deficit FINANCE, BANKING, AND ACCOUNTING a situation where a country buys more from other countries than it sells as exports

balance of payments on capital account FINANCE, BANKING, AND ACCOUNTING a system of recording a country's investment transactions with the rest of the world during a given period, usually one year. Among the included transactions are the purchase of physical and financial assets, intergovernmental transfers, and the provision of economic aid to developing nations.

balance of payments on current account FINANCE, BANKING, AND ACCOUNTING a system of recording a country's imports and exports of goods and services during a period, usually one year

balance of payments surplus FINANCE, BANKING, AND ACCOUNTING a situation where a country sells more to other countries than it buys from them

balance of trade ECONOMICS FINANCE, BANKING, AND ACCOUNTING the difference between a country's exports and imports of goods and services. Abbr. *BOT*

balance sheet FINANCE, BANKING, AND ACCOUNTING a financial report stating the total assets, liabilities, and owners' equity of an organization at a given date, usually the last day of the accounting period. The debit side of the bal-

ance sheet states assets, while the credit side states liabilities and equity, and the two sides must be equal, or balance.

Assets include cash in hand and cash anticipated (receivables), inventories of supplies and materials, properties, facilities, equipment, and whatever else the company uses to conduct business. Assets also need to reflect depreciation in the value of equipment such as machinery that has a limited expected useful life.

Liabilities include pending payments to suppliers and creditors, outstanding current and long-term debts, taxes, interest payments, and other unpaid expenses that the company has incurred.

Subtracting the value of aggregate liabilities from the value of aggregate assets reveals the value of owners' equity. Ideally, it should be positive. Owners' equity consists of capital invested by owners over the years and profits (net income) or internally generated capital, which is referred to as "retained earnings"; these are funds to be used in future operations. See actionlist **Creating a Balance Sheet**. Abbr. **B/S**

balance sheet audit FINANCE, BANKING, AND ACCOUNTING a limited audit of the items on a company's balance sheet in order to confirm that it complies with the relevant standards and requirements. Such an audit involves checking the value, ownership, and existence of assets and liabilities and ensuring that they are correctly recorded.

balance sheet date FINANCE, BANKING, AND ACCOUNTING the date, usually the end of a financial or accounting year, when a company's balance sheet is drawn up

balance sheet equation FINANCE, BANKING, AND ACCOUNTING see **accounting equation**

balance sheet total FINANCE, BANKING, AND ACCOUNTING in the United Kingdom, the total of assets shown at the bottom of a balance sheet and used to classify a company according to size

balancing figure FINANCE, BANKING, AND ACCOUNTING a number added to a series of numbers to make the total the same as another total. For example, if a debit total is higher than the credit total in the accounts, the balancing figure is the amount of extra credit required to make the two totals equal.

ball
carry the ball GENERAL MANAGEMENT to have responsibility for a project (*slang*)
drop the ball GENERAL MANAGEMENT to avoid your responsibilities (*slang*)

take the ball and run with it GENERAL MANAGEMENT to take an idea and implement it (*slang*)

balloon loan FINANCE, BANKING, AND ACCOUNTING a loan repaid in regular installments with a single larger final payment

balloon payment FINANCE, BANKING, AND ACCOUNTING the final larger payment on a balloon loan

ballpark FINANCE, BANKING, AND ACCOUNTING GENERAL MANAGEMENT an informal term for a rough, estimated figure. The term was derived from the approximate assessment of the number of spectators at a sporting event that might be made on the basis of a glance around.

BALO FINANCE, BANKING, AND ACCOUNTING Bulletin des Annonces Légales Obligatoires: a French government publication that includes financial statements of public companies

BAN *abbr* FINANCE, BANKING, AND ACCOUNTING bond anticipation note

banded pack MARKETING a product pack that has an additional product or promotional offer attached to it

bandwidth E-COMMERCE the capacity of fiber-optic cables that carry information to and from the Internet. The higher the bandwidth, the faster information will pass through a cable, and therefore the faster information can be downloaded or uploaded via the Internet.

bang for the buck FINANCE, BANKING, AND ACCOUNTING GENERAL MANAGEMENT a return on investment (*slang*)

bangtail MARKETING an order form for a new product that is attached by a perforated join to an envelope flap (*slang*)

bank FINANCE, BANKING, AND ACCOUNTING a commercial institution that keeps money in accounts for individuals or organizations, makes loans, exchanges currencies, provides credit to businesses, and offers other financial services

bank base rate FINANCE, BANKING, AND ACCOUNTING the basic rate of interest on which the actual rate a bank charges on loans to its customers is calculated

bank bill FINANCE, BANKING, AND ACCOUNTING
1 a piece of paper currency
2 (*U.K.*) a bill of exchange issued or accepted by a bank

bank card FINANCE, BANKING, AND ACCOUNTING a plastic card issued by a bank and accepted by merchants in payment for transactions. The most common types are **credit cards** and **debit cards**. Bank cards are governed by an internationally recognized set of rules for the authorization of their use and the clearing and settlement of transactions.

bank certificate FINANCE, BANKING, AND ACCOUNTING a document, often requested during an audit, that is signed by a bank official and confirms the balances due to or from a company on a specific date

bank confirmation FINANCE, BANKING, AND ACCOUNTING verification of a company's balances requested by an auditor from a bank

bank credit FINANCE, BANKING, AND ACCOUNTING the maximum credit available to an individual from a particular bank

bank discount FINANCE, BANKING, AND ACCOUNTING the charge made by a bank to a company or customer who pays a note before it is due

bank discount basis FINANCE, BANKING, AND ACCOUNTING the expression of yield that is used for treasury bills, based on a 360-day year

bank draft FINANCE, BANKING, AND ACCOUNTING see **banker's draft**

bank-eligible issue FINANCE, BANKING, AND ACCOUNTING U.S. Treasury obligations that commercial banks may buy

banker FINANCE, BANKING, AND ACCOUNTING somebody who owns or is a senior executive of a bank

banker's acceptance FINANCE, BANKING, AND ACCOUNTING see **banker's credit**

banker's check FINANCE, BANKING, AND ACCOUNTING see **banker's draft**

banker's credit FINANCE, BANKING, AND ACCOUNTING a financial instrument, typically issued by an exporter or importer for a short term, that a bank guarantees. Also known as **banker's acceptance**

banker's draft FINANCE, BANKING, AND ACCOUNTING a bill of exchange payable on demand and drawn by one bank on another. Regarded as being equivalent to cash, the draft cannot be returned unpaid. Also known as **bank draft**, **banker's check**. Abbr. **B/D**

bankers' hours FINANCE, BANKING, AND ACCOUNTING short hours of work. The term refers

to the relatively short time that a bank is open in some countries. (*slang*)

banker's order FINANCE, BANKING, AND ACCOUNTING an instruction by a customer to a bank to pay a specific amount at regular intervals, usually monthly or annually, until the order is canceled

banker's reference FINANCE, BANKING, AND ACCOUNTING a written report issued by a bank regarding a particular customer's creditworthiness

bank fee FINANCE, BANKING, AND ACCOUNTING a charge included in most lease transactions that is either paid in advance or is included in the gross capitalized cost. The fee usually covers administrative costs such as the costs of obtaining a credit report, verifying insurance coverage, and checking the lease documentation.

Bank for International Settlements FINANCE, BANKING, AND ACCOUNTING see *BIS*

bank giro FINANCE, BANKING, AND ACCOUNTING see *giro* 1

bank guarantee FINANCE, BANKING, AND ACCOUNTING a commitment made by a bank to a foreign buyer that the bank will pay an exporter for goods shipped if the buyer defaults

bank holding company FINANCE, BANKING, AND ACCOUNTING a company that owns one or more banks as part of its assets

Banking Code FINANCE, BANKING, AND ACCOUNTING a voluntary code of best practice for the banking and financial services industry, which is developed and revised by the *British Bankers' Association*

banking insurance fund FINANCE, BANKING, AND ACCOUNTING a fund maintained by the Federal Deposit Insurance Corporation to provide deposit insurance for banks other than savings and savings and loan banks

Banking Ombudsman FINANCE, BANKING, AND ACCOUNTING an official of the Australian or New Zealand government responsible for dealing with complaints relating to banking practices

banking passport FINANCE, BANKING, AND ACCOUNTING a document used to provide somebody with a false identity for banking transactions in another country

banking products FINANCE, BANKING, AND ACCOUNTING goods and services produced by

banks for customers, such as statements, direct debits, and standing orders

banking syndicate FINANCE, BANKING, AND ACCOUNTING a group of investment banks that jointly underwrite and distribute a new security offering

banking system FINANCE, BANKING, AND ACCOUNTING a network of commercial, savings, and specialized banks that provide financial services, including accepting deposits and providing loans and credit, money transmission and investment facilities

bank investment contract FINANCE, BANKING, AND ACCOUNTING a contract that specifies what a bank will pay its investors

bankmail FINANCE, BANKING, AND ACCOUNTING an agreement by a bank not to finance any rival's attempt to take over the same company that a particular customer is trying to buy (*slang*)

bank mandate FINANCE, BANKING, AND ACCOUNTING a written order to a bank which asks the bank to open an account, names the person(s) allowed to sign checks on behalf of the account holder, and provides specimen signatures etc.

Bank of England FINANCE, BANKING, AND ACCOUNTING the central bank of the United Kingdom, established in 1694. Originally a private bank, it became public in 1946 and increased its independence from government in 1997, when it was granted sole responsibility for setting base interest rates.

bank reserve ratio FINANCE, BANKING, AND ACCOUNTING a standard established by a central bank governing the relationship between the amount of money that other banks must keep on hand and the amount that they can loan out. By raising and lowering the ratio, the central bank can decrease or increase the money supply.

bank reserves FINANCE, BANKING, AND ACCOUNTING the money that a bank has available to meet the demands of its depositors

bankroll FINANCE, BANKING, AND ACCOUNTING the money used as financing for a project

bankrupt FINANCE, BANKING, AND ACCOUNTING a person or corporation that has been declared by a court of law as unable to meet their financial obligations

bankruptcy FINANCE, BANKING, AND ACCOUNTING the condition of being unable to pay debts, with liabilities greater than assets. There are two types of bankruptcy: involuntary bank-

ruptcy, where one or more creditors bring a petition against the debtor; and voluntary bankruptcy, where the debtor files a petition claiming inability to meet his or her debts.

bank term loan FINANCE, BANKING, AND ACCOUNTING a loan from a bank that has a term of at least one year

banner *or* **banner ad** E-COMMERCE an online interactive ad, often using graphic images and sound as well as text, placed on a Web page that is linked to an external advertiser's Web site. The banner typically is sized so as to appear at the top or bottom of the Web page. Also known as *ad banner*

banner advertising MARKETING the use of rectangular advertisements or logos across the width of a page on a Web site. Organizations place such ads on a third party's Web site in order to attract users to visit their own.

Debate still continues on whether banner advertising is an efficient and cost-effective way of promoting a Web site. However, prices for banner advertising have dropped significantly in recent years, and it can be effective if the Web site is visited by people whose profile accurately matches the advertiser's target market. Banner ads are particularly useful for raising awareness when a new Web site, product, or service is being launched.

banner exchange E-COMMERCE an advertising program in which one merchant induces others to place his or her banners and buttons on their Web sites in return for similarly displaying theirs

bar
outside the bar (*U.K.*) FINANCE, BANKING, AND ACCOUNTING one million pounds sterling (*slang*)

bar-bell FINANCE, BANKING, AND ACCOUNTING a portfolio which concentrates on very long-term and very short-term bonds only

bar chart GENERAL MANAGEMENT the presentation of data in the form of a graph using blocks or bars of color or shading. A bar chart is especially useful for showing the impact of one factor against another, for example, income over time, or customer calls against sales.

bar coding OPERATIONS & PRODUCTION the process of attaching a machine-readable code to a product, package, container, or subassembly, and using a scanner to relate its location to the product characteristics. Bar codes have uses in *stock control* and *order picking* and are used to validate every single

transaction from packaging through to customer delivery.

barefoot pilgrim FINANCE, BANKING, AND ACCOUNTING an unsophisticated investor who has lost everything trading in securities (*slang*)

bargain (*U.K.*) FINANCE, BANKING, AND ACCOUNTING a transaction on a stock market (*slang*)

bargaining chip FINANCE, BANKING, AND ACCOUNTING something that can be used as a concession or inducement in negotiation

bargain tax date (*U.K.*) FINANCE, BANKING, AND ACCOUNTING the date of a transaction on a stock market

Barnard, Chester (1886–1961) GENERAL MANAGEMENT U.S. business executive. President of the New Jersey Bell Telephone Company, whose book, *The Functions of the Executive* (1938), looked at the relationship of the individual to the organization and at *organization structure*. Barnard's observations also covered the topics of *communication*, *authority*, and organizational *core values*.

Barnevik, Percy (*b.* 1941) GENERAL MANAGEMENT Swedish business executive. Formerly chief executive, and now chairman, of Asea Brown Boveri, where he reduced *bureaucracy*, decentralized resources and *authority*, introduced a *matrix management* structure, and ran a global expansion strategy.

barometer stock FINANCE, BANKING, AND ACCOUNTING a widely held security such as a blue chip that is regarded as an indicator of the state of the market

barren money FINANCE, BANKING, AND ACCOUNTING money that is unproductive because it is not invested

barrier option FINANCE, BANKING, AND ACCOUNTING an option that includes automatic trading in other options when a commodity reaches a specified price

barrier to entry FINANCE, BANKING, AND ACCOUNTING any impediment to the free entry of new competitors into a market

barrier to exit FINANCE, BANKING, AND ACCOUNTING any impediment to the exit of existing competitors from a market

barter ECONOMICS FINANCE, BANKING, AND ACCOUNTING the direct exchange of goods or services between two parties without the use of money as a medium

Bartlett, Christopher A. (*b.* 1943) GENERAL MANAGEMENT Australian-born academic. Professor at Harvard Business School, and coauthor with **Sumantra Ghoshal** of *Managing Across Borders* (1989).

BAS *abbr* GENERAL MANAGEMENT Business Activity Statement

base currency FINANCE, BANKING, AND ACCOUNTING the currency used for measuring the return on an investment

base date ECONOMICS the reference date from which an index number such as the *retail price index* is calculated

base interest rate FINANCE, BANKING, AND ACCOUNTING the minimum interest rate that investors will expect for investing in a non-Treasury security. Also known as *benchmark interest rate*

base pay HR & PERSONNEL a guaranteed sum of money given to an employee in payment for work, disregarding any fringe benefits, allowances, or extra rewards from an *incentive plan*. U.K. term *basic pay*

base rate FINANCE, BANKING, AND ACCOUNTING the interest rate set by the Federal Reserve that dictates the rate at which money is lent to other banks and which they in turn charge their customers

base rate tracker mortgage FINANCE, BANKING, AND ACCOUNTING a mortgage whose interest rate varies periodically, usually annually, so as to remain a specified percentage above a particular standard rate

base year ECONOMICS the year from which an index is calculated

basic balance FINANCE, BANKING, AND ACCOUNTING the balance of current and long-term capital accounts in a country's balance of payments

basic pay (*U.K.*) HR & PERSONNEL FINANCE, BANKING, AND ACCOUNTING = *base pay*

basic rate FINANCE, BANKING, AND ACCOUNTING the percentage of income that the majority of workers in the United Kingdom pay to HM Revenue & Customs

basic rate tax FINANCE, BANKING, AND ACCOUNTING the main or first rate of income tax, currently 22%, levied on taxable in the United Kingdom, income after the lowest, or starting, rate, and running until the higher rate threshold is reached

basic wage (*U.K.*) HR & PERSONNEL the minimum rate of pay set by an industrial court or tribunal for a particular occupation

basic wage rate FINANCE, BANKING, AND ACCOUNTING in the United Kingdom, the wages paid for a specific number of hours' work per week, excluding overtime payments and any other incentives

basis of assessment FINANCE, BANKING, AND ACCOUNTING a method of deciding in which year financial transactions should be assessed for taxation

basis period FINANCE, BANKING, AND ACCOUNTING the period during which transactions occur, used for the purpose of deciding when they should be assessed for taxation

basis point FINANCE, BANKING, AND ACCOUNTING one hundredth of 1%, used in relation to changes in bond interest rates. Thus a change from 7.5% to 7.4% is 10 basis points.

basis risk FINANCE, BANKING, AND ACCOUNTING the risk that price variations in the cash or futures market will diminish revenue when a futures contract is liquidated, or the risk that changes in interest rates will affect repricing interest-bearing liabilities

basis swap FINANCE, BANKING, AND ACCOUNTING the exchange of two financial instruments, each with a variable interest calculated at a different rate

basket case FINANCE, BANKING, AND ACCOUNTING a company or individual considered to be in such dire circumstances as to be beyond help (*slang*)

basket of currencies FINANCE, BANKING, AND ACCOUNTING a group of selected currencies used in establishing a standard of value for another unit of currency

batch E-COMMERCE a collection of credit card transactions including authorizations, payments, and credits saved for electronic submission to an *acquirer* for settlement. The merchant is encouraged to submit one large batch rather than several small ones by being charged a fee for each batch submitted.

batch production OPERATIONS & PRODUCTION a production system in which a process is broken down into distinct operations that are completed on a batch or group of products before moving to the next production stage. As batch sizes can vary from very small to extremely large quantities, batch production offers greater flexibility than other production systems.

bath

take a bath FINANCE, BANKING, AND ACCOUNTING to suffer a serious financial loss (*slang*)

baud E-COMMERCE FINANCE, BANKING, AND ACCOUNTING a unit used to measure speed of data transmission, equal to one data unit per second

Bayesian theory STATISTICS a statistical theory and method for drawing conclusions about the future occurrence of a given parameter of a statistical distribution by calculating from prior data on its frequency of occurrence. The theory is useful in the solution of theoretical and applied problems in science, industry, and government, for example, in econometrics and finance.

Bayes' theorem STATISTICS a probability theorem that allows statisticians continually to revise the probability of an event according to new evidence

BBA *abbr* FINANCE, BANKING, AND ACCOUNTING British Bankers' Association

BBS *abbr* E-COMMERCE bulletin board system: a system enabling Internet users to read and post messages in newsgroups

BC *abbr* FINANCE, BANKING, AND ACCOUNTING budgetary control

BCA *abbr* GENERAL MANAGEMENT Business Council of Australia

bcc *abbr* E-COMMERCE blind carbon copy: a function that enables a user to send an e-mail message to any number of e-mail addresses while concealing each recipient's e-mail address. The bcc box is widely used for distributing press releases, newsletters, and other mass mailings via e-mail. If there is no desire to conceal names, the *cc* address line can be used.

BCC *abbr* FINANCE, BANKING, AND ACCOUNTING British Chambers of Commerce

BCCS *abbr* FINANCE, BANKING, AND ACCOUNTING Board of Currency Commissioners

BCNU *abbr* GENERAL MANAGEMENT be seeing you (*slang*)

B/D *abbr* FINANCE, BANKING, AND ACCOUNTING banker's draft

bean counter (*slang*)
1 FINANCE, BANKING, AND ACCOUNTING a derogatory term for an accountant, especially one who works in a large organization

2 (*U.K.*) GENERAL MANAGEMENT a person of low rank within an organization who has no real influence on the decision-making process

bear FINANCE, BANKING, AND ACCOUNTING somebody who anticipates unfavorable business conditions, especially somebody who sells stocks or commodities expecting their prices to fall, often with the intention of buying them back cheaply later. See also *bull*

bear covering FINANCE, BANKING, AND ACCOUNTING the point in a market at which dealers who sold stock short now buy back (at lower prices) to cover their positions

bearer bond FINANCE, BANKING, AND ACCOUNTING a negotiable bond or security whose ownership is not registered by the issuer, but is presumed to lie with whoever has physical possession of the bond

bearer instrument FINANCE, BANKING, AND ACCOUNTING a financial instrument such as a check or bill of exchange that entitles the person who presents it to receive payment

bearer security FINANCE, BANKING, AND ACCOUNTING a stock or bond that is owned by the person who possesses it

bear hug GENERAL MANAGEMENT an attempt to get the board of a company that is a target acquisition to recommend an offer to its shareholders. A bear hug may include the acquiring company offering to buy shares in the target at a premium. In a *reverse bear hug*, the board of the company to be acquired demonstrates its willingness to recommend an offer, usually on particular conditions. (*slang*)

bearish FINANCE, BANKING, AND ACCOUNTING relating to unfavorable business conditions or selling activity in anticipation of falling prices. See also *bullish*

bear market FINANCE, BANKING, AND ACCOUNTING a market in which prices are falling and in which a dealer is more likely to sell securities than to buy them. See also *bull market*

bear raid FINANCE, BANKING, AND ACCOUNTING see *raid*

bear spread FINANCE, BANKING, AND ACCOUNTING a combination of purchases and sales of options for the same commodity or stock with the intention of making a profit when the price falls. See also *bull spread*

bear tack FINANCE, BANKING, AND ACCOUNTING a downward movement in the value of a stock, a part of the market, or the market as a whole

beauty parade GENERAL MANAGEMENT a situation in which several organizations in turn compete in order to persuade another organization to use their services

bed

get into bed with somebody HR & PERSONNEL to begin a business association with an individual or organization (*slang*)
put something to bed GENERAL MANAGEMENT to dismiss an idea or put an end to a project (*slang*)

bed and breakfast deal FINANCE, BANKING, AND ACCOUNTING a transaction in which somebody sells a security at the end of one trading day and repurchases it at the beginning of the next. This is usually done to formally establish the profit or loss accrued to this security for tax or reporting purposes.

Beer, Stafford (1926–2002) GENERAL MANAGEMENT British industrialist. Organization systems thinker associated with cybernetics. Also a writer, his approach was first laid out in *Cybernetics and Management* (1959).

before-tax profit margin FINANCE, BANKING, AND ACCOUNTING the amount by which net income before tax exceeds expenditure

beginning inventory FINANCE, BANKING, AND ACCOUNTING the closing inventory at the end of the balance sheet from one accounting period that is transferred forward and becomes the opening stock in the one that follows. U.K. term *opening stock*

behavioral accounting FINANCE, BANKING, AND ACCOUNTING an approach to the study of accounting that emphasizes the psychological and social aspects of the profession in addition to the more technical areas

behavioral interview HR & PERSONNEL see *interviewing*

behavioral modeling HR & PERSONNEL
1 a process of capturing and encoding unconscious human expertise to make it transferable to others
2 a skills training technique that seeks to imitate models and maintain learned behaviors

behavioral science HR & PERSONNEL academic disciplines such as sociology and psychology that relate to the study of the way in which humans conduct themselves. In the field of management, the behavioral sciences are used to study *organization behavior*.

behaviorist theories of leadership GENERAL MANAGEMENT a school of thought that defines *leadership* by leaders' actions, rather than by their personality characteristics or their sources of *power*. Behaviorist theories were developed in the 1970s as disillusionment with situational theory grew. There are many different behaviorist theories. One of the most prominent—the *Managerial Grid*™—was developed by *Robert Blake* and *Jane Mouton* as a tool to enable leaders to understand their own behavior patterns. *Rensis Likert* also conducted research in this area, focusing on how behavior adapts to take account of people and situations.

Behn, Hernand (1880–1933) GENERAL MANAGEMENT U.S. industrialist. Founder, with his brother *Sosthenes Behn*, of the conglomerate International Telephone and Telegraph (ITT) in 1920.

Behn, Sosthenes (1882–1957) GENERAL MANAGEMENT U.S. industrialist. Founder, with his brother *Hernand Behn*, of the conglomerate International Telephone and Telegraph (ITT) in 1920. Under Behn's leadership, ITT expanded from the United States into Europe and South America. When Behn retired from ITT in 1956, most of its turnover came from its overseas interests. Under the leadership of *Harold Geneen*, ITT then developed into a massive diverse multinational incorporating hotels, car rental, frozen foods, potato chips, and candy. The history of ITT is detailed in *Sovereign State—The Secret History of ITT* (1973).

Belbin, R. Meredith (*b.* 1926) GENERAL MANAGEMENT British academic and consultant. Acknowledged as the father of team-role theory, which identifies nine useful roles necessary for a successful team of managers. Belbin's approach to *team building* and *teamwork* was described in *Management Teams: Why They Succeed or Fail* (1981). Other models of team relationships include the Team Management System, developed by *Charles Margerison* and *Dick McCann*. See thinker *R. Meredith Belbin*

bell cow FINANCE, BANKING, AND ACCOUNTING a product that sells well and makes a reasonable profit (*slang*)

bells and whistles (*slang*)
1 MARKETING unnecessary but desirable peripheral features of a product
2 FINANCE, BANKING, AND ACCOUNTING special features attached to a derivatives instrument or securities issue that are intended to attract investors or reduce issue costs

bellwether FINANCE, BANKING, AND ACCOUNTING a security whose price is viewed by investors as an indicator of future developments or trends

belly
go belly up FINANCE, BANKING, AND ACCOUNTING to fail financially or go bankrupt (*slang*)

below-the-fold E-COMMERCE relating to the portion of a webpage that is seen only by scrolling down to the middle or bottom of the page and is therefore less commercially valuable. See also *above-the-fold*

below-the-line
1 MARKETING relating to the proportion of marketing expenditure allocated to nonadvertising activities such as public relations, sales promotion, printing, presentations, sponsorship, and sales force support
2 FINANCE, BANKING, AND ACCOUNTING used to describe entries in a company's profit and loss account that show how the profit is distributed, or where the funds to finance the loss originate. See also *above-the-line 2*
3 FINANCE, BANKING, AND ACCOUNTING in macroeconomics, used to describe a country's capital transactions. See also *above-the-line 3*

belt and braces man FINANCE, BANKING, AND ACCOUNTING a very cautious lender who asks for extra collateral as well as guarantees for a loan (*slang*)

benchmark GENERAL MANAGEMENT a point of reference or standard against which to measure performance. Originally used for a set of computer programs to measure the performance of a computer against similar models, benchmark is now used more generally to describe a measure identified in the context of a *benchmarking* program against which to evaluate an organization's performance in a specific area.

benchmark accounting policy FINANCE, BANKING, AND ACCOUNTING one of a choice of two possible policies within an International Accounting Standard. The other policy is marked as an "allowed alternative," although there is no indication of preference.

benchmark index FINANCE, BANKING, AND ACCOUNTING an influential index for a particular market or activity

benchmarking
1 MARKETING a systematic process of comparing the activities and work processes of an organization or department with those of outstanding organizations or departments in order to identify ways to improve performance.

Benchmarking was first developed by the Xerox Corporation in the late 1970s in order to learn from the achievements of Japanese competitors and was described by a Xerox manager, Robert C. Camp, in his book *Benchmarking: The Search for Industry Best Practices That Lead to Superior Performance* (1989). The use of benchmarking has become widespread and individual organizations have developed distinct approaches toward it. Benchmarking programs commonly include the following stages: identifying the area requiring benchmarking and the process to use, collecting and analyzing the data, implementing changes, and monitoring and reviewing improvements. Benchmarking is used in business appraisal, often as part of a *total quality management* or *business process reengineering* program.

Types of benchmarking include internal benchmarking, a method of comparing one operating unit or function with another within the same industry; functional benchmarking, in which internal functions are compared with those of the best external practitioners of those functions, regardless of the industry they are in; competitive benchmarking, in which information is gathered about direct competitors, through techniques such as reverse engineering; and strategic benchmarking, a type of competitive benchmarking aimed at strategic action and organizational change.
2 the establishment, through data gathering, of targets and comparators, through whose use relative levels of performance (and particularly areas of underperformance) can be identified. By the adoption of identified best practices it is hoped that performance will improve.

There are various types of benchmarking. *Internal benchmarking* is a method of comparing one operating unit or function with another within the same industry. *Functional benchmarking* compares internal functions with those of the best external practitioners of those functions, regardless of the industry they are in (also known as operational benchmarking or generic benchmarking). *Competitive benchmarking* gathers information about direct competitors, through techniques such as reverse engineering. *Strategic benchmarking* is a type of competitive benchmarking aimed at strategic action and organizational change.

benchmark interest rate FINANCE, BANKING, AND ACCOUNTING the lowest interest rate that U.S. investors will accept on securities other than Treasury bills

beneficial interest FINANCE, BANKING, AND ACCOUNTING an arrangement whereby someone is allowed to occupy or receive rent from a house without owning it

beneficial owner FINANCE, BANKING, AND AC-COUNTING somebody who receives all the benefits of a stock, such as dividends, rights, and proceeds of any sale, but is not the registered owner of the stock

beneficiary bank FINANCE, BANKING, AND AC-COUNTING a bank that handles a gift such as a bequest

benefit FINANCE, BANKING, AND ACCOUNTING something that improves the profitability or efficiency of an organization or reduces its risk, or any nonmonetary reward given to employees, for example, paid vacations or employer contributions to pensions

benefit-cost ratio FINANCE, BANKING, AND ACCOUNTING = *cost-benefit analysis*

benefit in kind (*U.K.*) HR & PERSONNEL a *benefit* other than cash received by employees as part of their total *compensation package*

benefits plan HR & PERSONNEL a Canadian government program for the employment of Canadian citizens and for providing Canadian manufacturers, consultants, contractors, and service companies with opportunities to compete for projects

Benford's Law FINANCE, BANKING, AND ACCOUNT-ING a law proposed in 1938 by Dr. Frank Benford, a physicist at the General Electric Company, which shows that in sets of random numbers it is more likely that the set will begin with the number 1 than with any other number.

Bennis, Warren G. (*b.* 1925) GENERAL MANAGE-MENT U.S. academic. Guru of *leadership* theory, who has also carried out work in the areas of small *group dynamics*, change in social systems, and *T-Groups* (see *sensitivity training*). Bennis wrote his first article on leadership in 1959, and subsequently carried out extensive research in the United States into common leadership factors. His findings are reported in *Leaders: The Strategies for Taking Charge* (1985). He was influenced by the theories of *Douglas McGregor*. See thinker *Warren Bennis*, *Douglas McGregor*

bequest FINANCE, BANKING, AND ACCOUNTING a gift that has been left to somebody in a will

Berhad FINANCE, BANKING, AND ACCOUNTING a Malay term for "private." Companies can use "Sendirian Berhad" or "Sdn Bhd" in their name instead of "plc." Abbr. *Bhd*

Berners-Lee, Tim (*b.* 1955) GENERAL MANAGE-MENT British computer scientist. Creator of the World Wide Web and director of the World Wide Web Consortium, the world coordinating body for developing the Web. Berners-Lee is concerned that the growth of the Web should benefit all, rather than make money for the few. His experiences and thoughts are recorded in *Weaving the Web: The Original Design and Ultimate Destiny of the World Wide Web* (1999).

Berne Union FINANCE, BANKING, AND ACCOUNTING see *International Union of Credit and Investment Insurers*

best-in-class GENERAL MANAGEMENT leading a market or industrial sector in efficiency. A best-in-class organization exhibits exemplary *best practice*. Such an organization is clearly singled out from the pack and is recognized as a leader for its procedures for dealing with the acquisition and processing of materials and the delivery of end products or services to its customers. The concept of best in class is closely allied with *total quality management*, and one tool that can help in achieving this status is *benchmarking*.

best-of-breed MARKETING in marketing, sales, and competitive analysis, describes a computer product that is the best available software, hardware, or system in its class

best practice GENERAL MANAGEMENT the most effective and efficient method of achieving any objective or task. What constitutes best practice can be determined through a process of *benchmarking*. An organization can move toward achieving best practice, either across the whole organization or in a specific area, through *continuous improvement*. In production-based organizations, *world class manufacturing* is a related concept. More generally, a market or sector leader may be described as *best-in-class*.

beta FINANCE, BANKING, AND ACCOUNTING a numerical measure of the change in value of something such as a stock

beta coefficient FINANCE, BANKING, AND AC-COUNTING an indication of the level of risk attached to a stock. A high beta coefficient indicates that a stock is likely to be more sensitive to market movements.

beta rating FINANCE, BANKING, AND ACCOUNTING a means of measuring the volatility (or risk) of a stock or fund in comparison with the market as a whole.

The beta of a stock or fund can be of any value, positive or negative, but usually is between +0.25 and +1.75. Stocks of many utilities have a beta of less than 1. Conversely, most high-tech NASDAQ-based stocks have a beta greater than 1; they offer a higher rate of return but are also risky.

Both alpha and beta ratings should be readily available upon request from investment firms, because the figures appear in standard performance reports. It is always best to ask for them, because beta calculations can involve mathematical complexities. See also *alpha rating*

beta software E-COMMERCE a version of a software product that is almost ready for release but needs more testing. It is possible to download beta software on the Internet free, as software companies like to test their products on members of the public before they are put on the market.

beta test E-COMMERCE a test of a new or upgraded piece of computer software or hardware carried out by a few chosen customers before it is released to the public

BFH FINANCE, BANKING, AND ACCOUNTING Bundesfinanzhof: in Germany, the supreme court for issues concerning taxation

Bhd *abbr* FINANCE, BANKING, AND ACCOUNTING Berhad

BHP *abbr* GENERAL MANAGEMENT Broken Hill Proprietary Company Ltd.: Australia's largest manufacturing company. Also known as Big Australian.

bias STATISTICS inaccuracy or deviation in inferences, results, or a statistical method

bid FINANCE, BANKING, AND ACCOUNTING
1 an offer to buy all or the majority of the capital shares of a company in an attempted takeover
2 the highest price a prospective buyer for a good or service is prepared to pay

bid-ask quote FINANCE, BANKING, AND ACCOUNT-ING a statement of the prices that are being offered and asked for a security or option contract

bid bond FINANCE, BANKING, AND ACCOUNTING a guarantee by a financial institution of the fulfillment of an international tender offer

bid costs FINANCE, BANKING, AND ACCOUNTING costs incurred during the takeover of a company as a result of professional advice to the purchasing company from, for example, lawyers, accountants, and bankers

bidding war FINANCE, BANKING, AND ACCOUNTING a competition between prospective buyers for the same stock or security

bid form FINANCE, BANKING, AND ACCOUNTING a form containing details of an offer to underwrite municipal bonds

bid market FINANCE, BANKING, AND ACCOUNTING a market for bids (the price at which a dealer will buy stocks)

bid-offer spread FINANCE, BANKING, AND ACCOUNTING the difference between the highest price that a buyer is prepared to offer and the lowest price that a seller is prepared to accept

bid price FINANCE, BANKING, AND ACCOUNTING the price a stock exchange dealer will pay for a security or option contract

bid-to-cover ratio FINANCE, BANKING, AND ACCOUNTING a number that shows how many more people wanted to buy Treasury bills than actually did buy them

bid up
1 FINANCE, BANKING, AND ACCOUNTING to bid for something merely to increase its price
2 to make successive increases to the *bid price* for a security so that unopened orders do not remain unexecuted

Big Australian (*ANZ*) GENERAL MANAGEMENT see *BHP*

Big Bang FINANCE, BANKING, AND ACCOUNTING radical changes to practices on the London Stock Exchange implemented in October 1986. Fixed commission charges were abolished, leading to an alteration in the structure of the market, and the right of member firms to act as market makers as well as agents was also abolished. (*slang*)

big bath FINANCE, BANKING, AND ACCOUNTING the practice of making a particular year's poor income statement look even worse by increasing expenses and selling assets. Subsequent years will then appear much better in comparison. (*slang*)

Big Board FINANCE, BANKING, AND ACCOUNTING the New York Stock Exchange (*slang*). See also *Little Board*

big business GENERAL MANAGEMENT powerful business interests or companies in general. The term is particularly used when referring to *large-sized businesses* or *multinational businesses*.

Big Four (*ANZ*) FINANCE, BANKING, AND ACCOUNTING Australia's four largest banks: the Commonwealth Bank of Australia, Westpac Banking Corporation, National Australia Bank, and ANZ Bank

Big GAAP FINANCE, BANKING, AND ACCOUNTING the Generally Accepted Accounting Principles that apply to large companies (*slang*)

big picture GENERAL MANAGEMENT an informal term for a broad perspective on an issue that encompasses its surrounding context and long-term implications

Big Three FINANCE, BANKING, AND ACCOUNTING before the merger of Chrysler and Mercedes in 1998, a phrase used to refer to the three largest automobile manufacturers in the United States: Chrysler, Ford, and General Motors

bilateral clearing FINANCE, BANKING, AND ACCOUNTING the system of annual settlements of accounts between certain countries, where accounts are settled by the central banks

bilateral credit FINANCE, BANKING, AND ACCOUNTING credit allowed by banks to other banks in a clearing system to cover the period while checks are being cleared

bilateral facility FINANCE, BANKING, AND ACCOUNTING a loan by one bank to one borrower

bilateral monopoly ECONOMICS a market in which there is a single seller and a single buyer

bilateral netting FINANCE, BANKING, AND ACCOUNTING the settling of contracts between two banks to give a new position

bilateral trade ECONOMICS trade between two countries which give each other specific privileges such as favorable import quotas that are denied to other trading partners

bill broker FINANCE, BANKING, AND ACCOUNTING somebody who buys and sells promissory notes and bills of exchange

bill discount FINANCE, BANKING, AND ACCOUNTING the interest rate that the Federal Reserve charges banks for short-term loans. This establishes a de facto floor for the interest rate that banks charge their customers, usually a fraction above the discount rate.

bill discounting rate FINANCE, BANKING, AND ACCOUNTING the amount by which the price of a Treasury bill is reduced to reflect expected changes in interest rates

billing cycle FINANCE, BANKING, AND ACCOUNTING the period of time, often one month, between successive requests for payment

bill of entry FINANCE, BANKING, AND ACCOUNTING a statement of the nature and value of goods to be imported or exported, prepared by the shipper and presented to a customhouse

bill of exchange FINANCE, BANKING, AND ACCOUNTING

1 an unconditional order in writing from one person (the drawer) to another (the drawee and signatory), requiring the drawee to pay on demand a sum to a specified person (the payee) or bearer. It is now usually used in overseas trade and the drawee may be a bank as opposed to an importer.

The supplier or drawer usually submits the bill with the related shipping documents. It is then accepted by the drawee either as the agreed or implied method of payment. On receipt, the drawee either makes the required payment, or, if payment is to be made at a future date, indicates acceptance by signing it.

Wording on the bill will state when payment has to be made, for example, "60 days after date, we promise to pay >" means 60 days after the date of the bill; "60 days after sight, we promise to pay >" means 60 days after acceptance; and "at sight" means the bill is payable upon presentation.

Once accepted, a bill of exchange is a negotiable instrument. The drawer can therefore obtain the money it represents by selling it to a financial institution at a discount. In the United States, the law relating to these instruments is found in the *Uniform Commercial Code*.

2 a negotiable instrument, drawn by one party on another, for example, by a supplier of goods on a customer, who, by accepting (signing) the bill, acknowledges the debt, which may be payable immediately (a *sight draft*) or at some future date (a *time draft*). The holder of the bill can thereafter use an accepted time draft to pay a bill to a third party, or can discount it to raise cash.

bill of goods FINANCE, BANKING, AND ACCOUNTING a consignment of goods, or a statement of their nature and value (*slang*)

bill of lading FINANCE, BANKING, AND ACCOUNTING a document prepared by a consignor by which a carrier acknowledges the receipt of goods and which serves as a document of title to the goods consigned

bill of sale FINANCE, BANKING, AND ACCOUNTING a document confirming the transfer of goods or services from a seller to a buyer

binary thinker GENERAL MANAGEMENT somebody who thinks only in absolute, black-and-white terms (*slang*)

binder FINANCE, BANKING, AND ACCOUNTING a document that an insurance company issues to a customer to serve as a temporary insurance certificate until the issue of the policy itself

bingo card MARKETING a postcard advertisement for a product that is bound into a publication and can be returned to the manufacturer for additional information on the product (*slang*)

biodata HR & PERSONNEL
1 information taken from an ***application form***, *résumé*, or questionnaire concerning an employee's or potential employee's background and experience that is objectively scored by recruiters to predict job performance
2 a canned biography placed in a periodical article or conference paper

biological assets FINANCE, BANKING, AND ACCOUNTING farm animals and plants classified as assets. International Accounting Standards require that they are recorded on balance sheets at market value. Once they have been slaughtered or harvested, the assets become ***agricultural produce***.

biometrics E-COMMERCE the study of measurable biological characteristics, or, in computer security, authentication techniques that use characteristics such as speech, fingerprints, or scans of the human eye

biomimicry GENERAL MANAGEMENT the use in business of processes that imitate natural ones to reduce waste and limit impact on the environment

bionomics ECONOMICS a theory suggesting that economics can usefully be thought of as similar to an evolving ecosystem

biopiracy E-COMMERCE the commercial development of genetic resources such as plants with medicinal properties or genes for resistance to disease without compensating the inhabitants or government of the area where the substances or materials were originally discovered

biorhythm HR & PERSONNEL any recurring biological cycle thought to affect the physical or mental state of a person, particularly patterns of digestion, sleep, and fatigue

BiRiLiG FINANCE, BANKING, AND ACCOUNTING Bilanzrichtlinien iengesetz: the 1985 German accounting directives law

birth-death ratio STATISTICS the ratio of the number of births to the number of deaths in a population over a period of time such as ten years

BIS *abbr* FINANCE, BANKING, AND ACCOUNTING Bank for International Settlements: a bank that promotes cooperation between central banks, provides facilities for international financial operations, and acts as agent or trustee in international financial settlements. The 17-member board of directors consists of the governors of the central banks of Belgium, Canada, France, Germany, Italy, Japan, the Netherlands, Sweden, Switzerland, the United Kingdom, and the United States.

bit E-COMMERCE
1 a binary digit number (0 or 1), the smallest unit of computerized data
2 an item of information or knowledge

bit bucket E-COMMERCE an imaginary electronic trash can in cyberspace into which all lost e-mail and news messages disappear

bivariate data STATISTICS data in which two variables are involved in each subject

bivariate distribution STATISTICS a form of distribution involving two random variables

black
in the black FINANCE, BANKING, AND ACCOUNTING making a profit, or having more assets than debt (*slang*)

BlackBerry E-COMMERCE an electronic device that allows users to pick up their e-mail messages when they are away from their computer. Although very useful for employees who are often out of the office or those taking advantage of ***flexible working*** practices, some employees have found it hard to switch off from work during their leisure time and constantly check their BlackBerries for messages. This addictive aspect of the devices has led to their being referred to as "Crackberries" by some commentators.

blackbox engineering OPERATIONS & PRODUCTION the manufacturing of a component in which the supplier has total control over the design and content of the component and the purchaser knows only its external and physical specifications. The term blackbox engineering is derived from the fact that the component in question appears as a black box on the design drawings for the purchaser.

Black chip (*S. Africa*) GENERAL MANAGEMENT a company that is owned or managed by black people, or is controlled by black shareholders

black economic empowerment (*S. Africa*) GENERAL MANAGEMENT the promotion of black ownership and control of South Africa's economic assets

black economy ECONOMICS economic activity that is not declared for tax purposes and is usually carried out in exchange for cash

Black Friday FINANCE, BANKING, AND ACCOUNTING any precipitous one-day drop in a financial market, originally September 24, 1869, when prospectors attempting to corner the gold market caused a business panic followed by a depression

black hole GENERAL MANAGEMENT a project that consumes unlimited amounts of resources without yielding any profit (*slang*)

black knight GENERAL MANAGEMENT see ***knight***

blacklist E-COMMERCE a list of e-mail addresses, for example, of unknown senders, to which somebody does not want to permit access

black market FINANCE, BANKING, AND ACCOUNTING GENERAL MANAGEMENT an illegal ***market***, usually for goods that are in short supply. Black market trading breaks government regulations or legislation and is particularly prevalent during times of shortage, such as rationing, or in industries that are very highly regulated, such as pharmaceuticals or armaments. Also known as ***shadow market***

black market economy FINANCE, BANKING, AND ACCOUNTING
1 a system of illegal trading in officially controlled goods
2 an illicit secondary currency market that has rates markedly different from those in the official market

Black Monday FINANCE, BANKING, AND ACCOUNTING either of two Mondays, October 28, 1929 or October 19, 1987, that were marked by the largest stock market declines of the 20th century. Although both market crashes originated in the United States, they were immediately followed by similar market crashes around the world.

black money ECONOMICS money circulating in the ***black economy*** in payment for goods and services

Black Tuesday FINANCE, BANKING, AND ACCOUNTING October 29, 1929, when values of stocks fell precipitously

Blake, Robert R. (1918–2004) GENERAL MANAGEMENT U.S. psychologist. Collaborated with ***Jane Mouton*** on the development of *The Managerial Grid*™ (1964), a framework for understanding managerial behavior.

blame culture GENERAL MANAGEMENT a set of attitudes, for example, within a business or

organization, characterized by an unwillingness to take risks or accept responsibility for mistakes because of a fear of criticism or prosecution

blamestorming GENERAL MANAGEMENT group discussion as to the reasons why a project has failed or is late and who is to blame for it. The term is modeled on "brainstorming." (*slang*)

blame-time GENERAL MANAGEMENT the moment in an organization when blame for the failure of a project or task is publicly allocated (*slang*)

Blanchard , **Kenneth** (*b.* 1939) GENERAL MANAGEMENT U.S. academic. Best known for his concept of one-minute management. *The One Minute Manager* (1982), cowritten with **Spencer Johnson**, became a bestseller in the tradition of management self-help books alongside those by **Dale Carnegie** and **Stephen Covey**. See thinker *Kenneth Blanchard*

blanket bond FINANCE, BANKING, AND ACCOUNTING an insurance policy that covers a financial institution for losses caused by the actions of its employees

bleed MARKETING an area of a piece of printed material that extends beyond given margins or its edges

blended learning GENERAL MANAGEMENT the combination of traditional and online learning methods to maximize the effectiveness of training programs. In blended learning the training program is broken down into modules and the most appropriate delivery methods are selected for each and tailored to individual needs. The objective is to take advantage of the best features of each method while avoiding the drawbacks. A variety of media may be used, ranging from traditional workshops, classroom-based teaching, books and other support materials, *computer-based training*, CD-ROM, and e-learning.

blended rate FINANCE, BANKING, AND ACCOUNTING an interest rate charged by a lender that is between an old rate and a new one

blind carbon copy GENERAL MANAGEMENT see *bcc*

blind certificate E-COMMERCE a *cookie* from which the user's name is omitted so as to protect his or her privacy while making collected data available for marketing studies

blind entry FINANCE, BANKING, AND ACCOUNTING
1 a bookkeeping entry that records a debit or

credit but fails to show other essential information
2 (*ANZ*) a document issued by a supplier that stipulates the amount charged for goods or services as well as the amount of **Goods and Services Tax** (GST) payable

blind offer MARKETING an inconspicuous offer buried in the body copy of a print advertisement, often used to determine the degree of reader attention to the advertisement

blind pool FINANCE, BANKING, AND ACCOUNTING a limited partnership in which the investment opportunities the general partner plans to pursue are not specified

blindside MARKETING to attack somebody in a way that he or she cannot anticipate (*slang*)

blind trust FINANCE, BANKING, AND ACCOUNTING a trust that manages somebody's business interests, with contents that are unknown to the beneficiary. People assuming public office use such trusts to avoid conflicts of interest.

block diagram STATISTICS a diagram that represents statistical data by rectangular blocks

blocked account FINANCE, BANKING, AND ACCOUNTING a bank account from which funds cannot be withdrawn for any of a number of reasons, for example, bankruptcy proceedings, liquidation of a company, or government order when freezing foreign assets

blocked currency FINANCE, BANKING, AND ACCOUNTING a currency that people cannot easily trade for other currencies because of foreign exchange control

blocked funds FINANCE, BANKING, AND ACCOUNTING money that cannot be transferred from one place to another, usually because of **exchange controls** imposed by the government of the country in which the funds are held

block grant FINANCE, BANKING, AND ACCOUNTING money that the federal government gives to a local government to spend in ways that the recipient determines

blockholder FINANCE, BANKING, AND ACCOUNTING an individual or institutional investor who holds a large number of shares of stock or a large dollar amount of bonds in a given company

block investment (*ANZ*) FINANCE, BANKING, AND ACCOUNTING the purchase or holding of a large number of shares of stock or a large dollar amount of bonds in a given company

block release HR & PERSONNEL an arrangement whereby an employer permits an employee to be away from work to attend an educational institution for a period of time, usually several weeks

block trade FINANCE, BANKING, AND ACCOUNTING the sale of a large round number of stocks or large amount of bonds

blog E-COMMERCE
1 a personal online journal that can be accessed by visitors to the host Web site. Blogs have developed massively in a very short space of time, so much so that *Fortune* ranked them as the most important tech trend for 2005. Used initially to record the thoughts and views of private individuals, blogs are beginning to be used by corporate organizations as a means of communicating with staff and customers. Also called *weblog*
2 to create or run a blog

blogosphere E-COMMERCE the World Wide Web environment in which bloggers communicate with each other

blogware E-COMMERCE computer software tools for creating a weblog

blow-in MARKETING advertising in the form of cards bound inside magazines or newspapers (*slang*)

blow-off top FINANCE, BANKING, AND ACCOUNTING a rapid increase in the price of a financial stock followed by an equally rapid drop in price (*slang*)

blowout FINANCE, BANKING, AND ACCOUNTING the rapid sale of the whole of a new stock issue

bludge (*ANZ*) GENERAL MANAGEMENT to shirk work or responsibility, or to live off the earnings of others

Blue Book FINANCE, BANKING, AND ACCOUNTING national statistics of personal incomes and spending patterns in the United Kingdom, published annually

blue chip FINANCE, BANKING, AND ACCOUNTING a description of an equity or company which is of the highest quality and in which an investment would be considered as low risk with regard to both dividend payments and capital values

blue-chip stocks FINANCE, BANKING, AND ACCOUNTING common stock in a company that is considered to be well established, highly successful, and reliable, and is traded on a stock market

blue-collar job HR & PERSONNEL a position that involves mainly physical labor. With the decline in manufacturing and an increase in harmonization agreements, the term blue collar is now rarely used. Blue collar refers to the blue overalls traditionally worn in factories in contrast to the white shirt and tie supposedly worn by an office worker, known as a *white-collar worker* .

blue-collar worker HR & PERSONNEL somebody whose job involves mainly physical labor

blue hair MARKETING used in advertising and marketing to refer to women customers of advanced years (*slang*)

Blue List FINANCE, BANKING, AND ACCOUNTING a daily list of municipal bonds and their ratings, published by Standard & Poor's

blueshirt GENERAL MANAGEMENT an employee of the computer company IBM (*slang*)

blue-sky ideas GENERAL MANAGEMENT extremely ambitious, idealistic, or unrealistic proposals, apparently unconfined by conventional thinking (*slang*)

blue-sky law FINANCE, BANKING, AND ACCOUNTING a state law that regulates investments to prevent investors from being defrauded

blue-sky securities FINANCE, BANKING, AND ACCOUNTING stocks and bonds that have no value, being worth the same as a piece of "blue sky" (*slang*)

blur GENERAL MANAGEMENT a period of transition for a business in which changes occur at great speed and on a large scale

BO *abbr* FINANCE, BANKING, AND ACCOUNTING branch office

board GENERAL MANAGEMENT see *board of directors*

board dismissal FINANCE, BANKING, AND ACCOUNTING GENERAL MANAGEMENT the dismissal and removal from power of an entire board or *board of directors*

Board of Currency Commissioners FINANCE, BANKING, AND ACCOUNTING the sole currency issuing authority in Singapore, established in 1967. Abbr. *BCCS*

Board of Customs and Excise FINANCE, BANKING, AND ACCOUNTING see *Her Majesty's Revenue & Customs*

board of directors FINANCE, BANKING, AND ACCOUNTING GENERAL MANAGEMENT the people se-lected to sit on an authoritative standing committee or governing body, taking responsibility for the management of an organization. Members of the board of directors are officially chosen by stockholders, but in practice they are usually selected on the basis of the current board's recommendations. The board usually includes major stockholders as well as directors of the company. Also known as *board*

Board of Inland Revenue FINANCE, BANKING, AND ACCOUNTING see *Her Majesty's Revenue & Customs*

board of trustees FINANCE, BANKING, AND ACCOUNTING GENERAL MANAGEMENT a committee or governing body that takes responsibility for managing—and holds in trust—funds, assets, or property belonging to others, for example, charitable or pension funds or assets

boardroom GENERAL MANAGEMENT a room in which board meetings are held. A boardroom may be a room used only for board meetings or can be a multiuse room that becomes a board-room for the duration of a board meeting.

boardroom battle GENERAL MANAGEMENT a conflict or power struggle between individual board members or between groups of board members

board seat FINANCE, BANKING, AND ACCOUNTING GENERAL MANAGEMENT a position of membership of a board, especially a *board of directors*

board secretary FINANCE, BANKING, AND ACCOUNTING GENERAL MANAGEMENT see *company secretary*

body corporate FINANCE, BANKING, AND ACCOUNTING an association, such as a company or institution, that is legally authorized to act as if it were one person

body language HR & PERSONNEL the combination of often subconscious gestures, postures, and facial expressions that send out messages about a person's feelings and emotions. Body language is an important aspect of *nonverbal communication* .

body of creditors FINANCE, BANKING, AND ACCOUNTING the creditors of a company or individual treated as a single creditor in dealing with the debtor

body of shareholders FINANCE, BANKING, AND ACCOUNTING the stockholders of a company treated as a single stockholder in dealing with the company

bogey FINANCE, BANKING, AND ACCOUNTING a benchmark, often the Standard and Poor's 500 Index, against which mutual fund managers or portfolio managers measure their performance (*slang*)

BOGOF MARKETING buy one get one free, a sales promotion technique in which consumers are offered two products for the price of one

bogus degree HR & PERSONNEL a degree award-ed by an organization of questionable or un-recognized standing, usually capitalizing on the naiveté of overseas students and the repu-tation of the education system of the host country. A bogus degree is normally offered by an organization with a similar sounding name to a university of good standing.

boilerplate FINANCE, BANKING, AND ACCOUNTING GENERAL MANAGEMENT a standard version of a contract that can be used interchangeably from contract to contract (*slang*)

boiler room HR & PERSONNEL a room from which telemarketers using high-pressure sales tactics, usually by telephone and often using illegal tactics, try to sell financial products or real estate of questionable value

bona fide FINANCE, BANKING, AND ACCOUNTING used to describe a sale or purchase that has been conducted in good faith, without collu-sion or fraud

bona vacantia FINANCE, BANKING, AND ACCOUNTING the goods of a person who has died intes-tate and has no traceable living relatives. In the United Kingdom, these goods become the property of the state.

bond FINANCE, BANKING, AND ACCOUNTING
1 a promise to repay with interest on specified dates money that an investor lends a company or government
2 a certificate issued by a company or govern-ment that promises repayment of borrowed money at a set rate of interest on a particular date
3 (*ANZ*) a sum of money paid as a deposit, especially on rented premises
4 (*S. Africa*) a mortgage bond

bond anticipation note FINANCE, BANKING, AND ACCOUNTING a loan that a government agency receives to provide capital that will be repaid from the proceeds of bonds that the agency will issue later. Abbr. *BAN*

bond covenant FINANCE, BANKING, AND ACCOUNTING part of a bond contract whereby the lender promises not to do certain things, for example, borrow beyond a particular limit

bond discount FINANCE, BANKING, AND ACCOUNTING the difference between the face value of a bond and the lower price at which it is issued

bonded warehouse FINANCE, BANKING, AND ACCOUNTING a warehouse that holds goods awaiting duty or tax to be paid on them

bond equivalent yield FINANCE, BANKING, AND ACCOUNTING the interest rate that an investor would have to receive on a bond to profit as much as from investment in another type of security. Also known as *equivalent bond yield*

bond fund FINANCE, BANKING, AND ACCOUNTING a mutual fund that invests in bonds

bondholder FINANCE, BANKING, AND ACCOUNTING an individual or institution owning bonds issued by a government or company. Bondholders are entitled to payments of the interest as due and the return of the *principal* when the bond matures.

bond indenture FINANCE, BANKING, AND ACCOUNTING a document that specifies the terms of a bond

bond indexing FINANCE, BANKING, AND ACCOUNTING the practice of investing in bonds in such a way as to match the yield of a designated index

bond market FINANCE, BANKING, AND ACCOUNTING a market in which government or municipal bonds are traded

bond premium FINANCE, BANKING, AND ACCOUNTING the difference between the face value of a bond and a higher price at which it is issued

bond quote FINANCE, BANKING, AND ACCOUNTING a statement of the current market price of a bond

bond rating FINANCE, BANKING, AND ACCOUNTING the rating of the reliability of a company, government, or local authority which has issued a bond. The highest rating is AAA.

bond swap FINANCE, BANKING, AND ACCOUNTING an exchange of some bonds for others, usually to gain a tax advantage or to diversify a portfolio

bond value FINANCE, BANKING, AND ACCOUNTING the value of an *asset* or *liability* as recorded in the accounts of an individual or organization

bond-washing FINANCE, BANKING, AND ACCOUNTING the practice of selling a bond before its dividend is due and buying it back later in order to avoid paying tax

bond yield FINANCE, BANKING, AND ACCOUNTING the annual return on a bond (the rate of interest) expressed as a percentage of the current market price of the bond. Bonds can tie up investors' money for periods of up to 30 years, so knowing their yield is a critical investment consideration.

Bond yield is calculated by multiplying the face value of the bond by its stated annual rate of interest, expressed as a decimal. For example, buying a new ten-year $1,000 bond that pays 6% interest will produce an annual yield amount of $60:

$$1,000 \times 0.060 = 60$$

The $60 will be paid as $30 every six months. At the end of ten years, the purchaser will have earned $600, and will also be repaid the original $1,000. Because the bond was purchased when it was first issued, the 6% is also called the *yield to maturity*.

This basic formula is complicated by other factors. First is the "time-value of money" theory: money paid in the future is worth less than money paid today. A more detailed computation of total bond yield requires the calculation of the present value of the interest earned each year. Second, changing interest rates have an impact on bond trading and, ultimately, on yield. Changes in interest rates cannot affect the interest paid by bonds already issued, but they do affect the prices of new bonds.

bonus HR & PERSONNEL a financial incentive given to employees in addition to their *base pay* in the form of a one-time payment or as part of a *bonus plan*

bonus dividend FINANCE, BANKING, AND ACCOUNTING a one-time extra dividend in addition to the usual payment

bonus issue FINANCE, BANKING, AND ACCOUNTING the capitalization of the reserves of a company by the issue of additional shares to existing stockholders, in proportion to their holdings. Such shares are normally fully paid up with no cash called for from the stockholders.

bonus offer MARKETING a sales promotion technique offering consumers an additional amount of product for the basic price

bonus plan HR & PERSONNEL a form of *incentive program* under which a *bonus* is paid to employees in accordance with rules concerning eligibility, performance targets, time period, and size and form of payments. A bonus plan may apply to some or all employees and may be determined on organization, business unit, or individual performance, or on a combination of these. A bonus payment may be expressed as a percentage of salary or as a flat-rate sum.

bonus shares FINANCE, BANKING, AND ACCOUNTING

1 see *stock split*

2 in the United Kingdom, extra shares paid by the government as a reward to founding stockholders who did not sell their initial holding within a certain number of years

book-building FINANCE, BANKING, AND ACCOUNTING the research done among potential institutional investors to determine the optimum offering price for a new issue of stock

book cost FINANCE, BANKING, AND ACCOUNTING the price paid for a stock, including any commissions

book entry FINANCE, BANKING, AND ACCOUNTING an accounting entry indicated in a record somewhere but not represented by any document

book inventory FINANCE, BANKING, AND ACCOUNTING the number of items in stock according to accounting records. This number can be validated only by a physical count of the items.

bookkeeper FINANCE, BANKING, AND ACCOUNTING a person who is responsible for maintaining the financial records of a business

bookkeeping FINANCE, BANKING, AND ACCOUNTING the activity or profession of recording the money received and spent by an individual, business, or organization

bookkeeping barter FINANCE, BANKING, AND ACCOUNTING the direct exchange of goods between two parties without the use of money as a medium, but using monetary measures to record the transaction

bookmark

1 E-COMMERCE a Web browser software tool that enables users to select and store pages they are likely to return to, so that they can be accessed quickly and conveniently. On Microsoft Internet Explorer (the most popular Web browser) this function is referred to as "Favorites."

2 GENERAL MANAGEMENT to make a mental note to remember somebody or something for future reference (*slang*)

book of original entry FINANCE, BANKING, AND ACCOUNTING see *book of prime entry*

book of prime entry FINANCE, BANKING, AND ACCOUNTING a chronological record of a business's transactions arranged according to type, for example, cash or sales. The books are then

used to generate entries in a double-entry bookkeeping system. Also called **book of original entry**

books of account FINANCE, BANKING, AND ACCOUNTING collectively, the ledgers and journals used in the preparation of financial statements

book-to-bill ratio FINANCE, BANKING, AND ACCOUNTING the ratio of the value of orders that a company has received to the amount for which it has billed its customers

book transfer FINANCE, BANKING, AND ACCOUNTING a transfer of ownership of a security without physical transfer of any document that represents the instrument

book value FINANCE, BANKING, AND ACCOUNTING the value of a company's stock according to the company itself, which may differ considerably from the market value.

It is calculated by subtracting a company's liabilities and the value of its debt and preferred stock from its total assets. All of these figures appear on a company's balance sheet. For example:

	$
Total assets	1,300
Current liabilities	- 400
Long-term liabilities, preference shares	- 250
Book value	**= 650**

Book value per share is calculated by dividing the book value by the number of shares in issue. If our example is expressed in millions of dollars and the company has 35 million shares outstanding, the book value per share would be $650 million divided by 35 million:

650 / 35 = $18.57 book value per share

Book value represents a company's net worth to its shareholders. When compared with its market value, book value helps reveal how a company is regarded by the investment community. A market value that is notably higher than the book value indicates that investors have a high regard for the company. A market value that is, for example, a multiple of book value suggests that investors' regard may be unreasonably high. Also known as **carrying value**

book value per share FINANCE, BANKING, AND ACCOUNTING the value of one share of a stock according to the company itself, which may differ considerably from the market value

Boolean search E-COMMERCE a search allowing the inclusion or exclusion of documents containing certain words through the use of operators such as AND, NOT, and OR

boom ECONOMICS FINANCE, BANKING, AND ACCOUNTING a period of time during which business activity increases significantly, with the result that demand for products grows, as do prices, salaries, and employment

boomerang worker HR & PERSONNEL an employee who returns to work for a previous employer (*slang*)

boot camp HR & PERSONNEL an induction or orientation program for new employees, designed to push recruits to their limits. Boot camps are modeled on the basic training of the U.S. Marine Corps and aim to immerse new employees in the **corporate culture** of the employer, as well as transferring knowledge about technical skills.

bootstrapping GENERAL MANAGEMENT the early stages of setting up a new business, when a lot of effort is required (*slang*)

BOP *abbr* ECONOMICS balance of payments

border crosser HR & PERSONNEL a multiskilled employee who is able to move from job to job within a company (*slang*)

borderless world E-COMMERCE the global economy considered as having had barriers to international trade removed by use of the Internet

border tax adjustment FINANCE, BANKING, AND ACCOUNTING the application of a domestic tax on imported goods while exempting exported goods from the tax in an effort to make the exported goods' price competitive both nationally and internationally

borrowing costs FINANCE, BANKING, AND ACCOUNTING expenses, for example, interest payments, incurred from taking out a loan or any other form of borrowing. In the United States, such costs are included in the total cost of the asset whereas in the United Kingdom, and in International Accounting Standards, this is optional.

bosberaad (*S Africa*) GENERAL MANAGEMENT
1 a **think tank**, **strategy**, or long-term planning meeting. Also known as **lekgotla**
2 a meeting of leaders at a remote place to avoid distractions. The word means literally "bush summit."

boss GENERAL MANAGEMENT the person in charge of a job, process, department, or organization, more formally known as a **manager** or **supervisor**

Boston Box FINANCE, BANKING, AND ACCOUNTING GENERAL MANAGEMENT a model used for analyzing a company's potential by plotting **market share** against growth rate. The Boston Box was conceived by the Boston Consulting Group in the 1970s to help in the process of assessing in which businesses a company should invest and of which it should divest itself. A business with a high market share and high growth rate is a **star**, and one with a low market share and low growth rate is a **dog**. A high market share with low growth rate is characteristic of a **cash cow**, which could yield significant but short-term gain, and a low market share coupled with high growth rate produces a **question mark company**, which offers a doubtful return on investment. To be useful, this model requires accurate assessment of a business's strengths and weaknesses, which may be difficult to obtain.

Boston matrix MARKETING a management technique developed by the Boston Consulting Group for assessing the long-term viability or profitability of products and market sectors. Categories include **cash cows**, dogs, stars, **problem children**, and question mark companies. See also **Boston Box**

BOT *abbr* ECONOMICS balance of trade

bottleneck
1 FINANCE, BANKING, AND ACCOUNTING an activity within an organization which has a lower capacity than preceding or subsequent activities, thereby limiting throughput. Bottlenecks are often the cause of a build-up of work in progress and of idle time.
2 OPERATIONS & PRODUCTION a limiting factor on the rate of an operation. A workstation operating at its maximum **capacity** becomes a bottleneck if the rate of production elsewhere in the plant increases but throughput at that workstation cannot be increased to meet demand. An understanding of bottlenecks is important if the efficiency and capacity of an **assembly line** are to be increased. The techniques of **fishbone charts**, **Pareto charts**, and **flow charts** can be used to identify where and why bottlenecks occur.

bottom fisher FINANCE, BANKING, AND ACCOUNTING an investor who searches for bargains among stocks that have recently dropped in price (*slang*)

bottom line
1 FINANCE, BANKING, AND ACCOUNTING the net profit or loss that a company makes at the end of a given period of time, used in the calculation of the earnings-per-share business ratio
2 GENERAL MANAGEMENT work that produces net gain for an organization

bottom-of-the-harbor scheme (ANZ) FINANCE, BANKING, AND ACCOUNTING a tax avoidance strategy that involves stripping a company of assets and then selling it a number of times so that it is hard to trace

bottom out FINANCE, BANKING, AND ACCOUNTING to reach the lowest level in the downward trend of the market price of securities or commodities before the price begins an upward trend again

bottom-up FINANCE, BANKING, AND ACCOUNTING relating to an approach to investing that seeks to identify individual companies that are fundamentally sound and whose stock will perform well regardless of general economic or industry-group trends

bottom-up approach GENERAL MANAGEMENT a consultative *leadership* style that promotes *employee participation* at all levels in *decision making* and *problem solving*. A bottom-up approach to leadership is associated with *flat organizations* and the *empowerment* of employees. It can encourage *creativity* and flexibility and is the opposite of a *top-down approach*.

bottom-up budgeting FINANCE, BANKING, AND ACCOUNTING see *participative budgeting*

bought day book FINANCE, BANKING, AND ACCOUNTING a book used to record purchases made on credit, that is, for which cash is not paid immediately

bought-in goods FINANCE, BANKING, AND ACCOUNTING OPERATIONS & PRODUCTION components and subassemblies that are purchased from an outside supplier instead of being made within the organization

bought ledger FINANCE, BANKING, AND ACCOUNTING a book in which all of a company's expenditure is logged

bounce FINANCE, BANKING, AND ACCOUNTING to refuse payment of a check because the account for which it is written holds insufficient money (*slang*). Also known as *dishonor*

bounced check FINANCE, BANKING, AND ACCOUNTING a draft on an account that a bank will not honor, usually because there are insufficient funds in the account

bounce off GENERAL MANAGEMENT to discuss a new idea with somebody in order to find out what his or her reaction to it is (*slang*)

boundaryless organization GENERAL MANAGEMENT a model that views organizations as having permeable boundaries. An organization has external boundaries that separate it from its suppliers and customers, and internal boundaries that provide demarcation to departments. This rigidity is removed in boundaryless organizations, where the goal is to develop greater flexibility and responsiveness to change and to facilitate the free exchange of information and ideas. The boundaryless organization behaves more like an organism encouraging better integration between departments and closer partnerships with suppliers and customers. The concept was developed at General Electric and described in the book *The Boundaryless Organization: Breaking the Chains of Organizational Structure* by Ron Ashkenas and others, which was published in 1995.

bourse FINANCE, BANKING, AND ACCOUNTING a European stock exchange, especially the one in Paris

boutique investment house FINANCE, BANKING, AND ACCOUNTING see *niche player*

box
think outside the box GENERAL MANAGEMENT to think imaginatively about a problem (*slang*)

box spread FINANCE, BANKING, AND ACCOUNTING an arbitrage strategy that eliminates risk by buying and selling the same thing

Boyatzis, **Richard Eleftherios** (b. 1946) GENERAL MANAGEMENT U.S. academic. One of the key movers of the *competence* movement. His book, *The Competent Manager* (1982), acknowledged *David McClelland*'s earlier work.

BPR *abbr* GENERAL MANAGEMENT business process reengineering

bracket creep FINANCE, BANKING, AND ACCOUNTING the way in which a gradual increase in income moves somebody into a higher tax bracket

Brady bond FINANCE, BANKING, AND ACCOUNTING a bond issued by an emerging nation that has U.S. Treasury bonds as collateral. It is named for Nicholas Brady, banking reformer and former Secretary of the Treasury.

brain drain GENERAL MANAGEMENT the overseas migration of specialists, usually highly qualified scientists, engineers, or technical experts, in pursuit of higher salaries, better research funding, and a perceived higher quality of working life

brainiac HR & PERSONNEL a highly intelligent and creative employee who is also unpredictable and eccentric (*slang*)

brainsketching GENERAL MANAGEMENT a technique for idea generation and problem solving in groups that uses sketching as the primary means of recording ideas. Individuals start to sketch their ideas on a sheet. After a few minutes these are exchanged and they continue on a sheet already started by someone else. These sheets are then placed on a flip chart and used as the inspiration for the generation of new ideas. *Brainstorming* is a related technique.

brainstorming GENERAL MANAGEMENT a technique for generating ideas, developing *creativity*, or *problem solving* in small groups, through the free-flowing contributions of participants. The concept of brainstorming was originated by A. F. Osborn and described in his book *Applied Imagination: Principles and Practices of Creative Thinking* (1957). To encourage the free flow of ideas, brainstorming sessions operate according to a set of guidelines, and the production and evaluation of ideas are kept separate. Several variations of brainstorming and related techniques have emerged such as *brainwriting*, where ideas are written down by individuals, and *buzz groups*. See checklist *Brainstorming*

brainwriting GENERAL MANAGEMENT see *brainstorming*

branch accounts FINANCE, BANKING, AND ACCOUNTING the *books of account* or *financial statements* for the component parts of a business, especially those that are located in a different region or country from the main enterprise

branch office FINANCE, BANKING, AND ACCOUNTING a bank or other financial institution that is part of a larger group and is located in a different geographic area from the parent organization. Abbr. *BO*

branch tax FINANCE, BANKING, AND ACCOUNTING a South African tax imposed on nonresident companies that register a branch rather than a separate company

brand MARKETING the distinguishing proprietary name, symbol, or *trademark* that differentiates a particular product, or service, from others of a similar nature

brand architecture MARKETING the naming and structuring of *brands* within the product portfolio of an organization. Brand architectures may be monolithic (the corporate name is used on all products and services), endorsed (sub-brands are linked to the corporate brand by means of either a verbal or visual endorsement), or freestanding (each product or service is individually branded for its target

market). Brand architecture is influenced by the overall brand management and brand positioning strategy of the organization.

brand awareness MARKETING the level of *brand recognition* that consumers have of a particular brand and its specific product category. Brand awareness examines three levels of recognition: whether the brand name is the first to come to mind when a consumer is questioned about a particular product category; whether the brand name is one of several that come to mind when a consumer is questioned about a particular product category; and whether or not a consumer has heard of a particular brand name.

brand building MARKETING the establishment and improvement of a brand's identity, including giving the brand a set of values that the consumer wants, recognizes, identifies with, and trusts. Values developed in the process of brand building include psychological, physical, and functional properties that consumers desire and should always identify a property that is unique to that brand.

brand champion MARKETING an employee of an organization who is responsible for the development, performance, and communication of a particular brand

brand equity MARKETING the estimated value of a *brand*

brand extension MARKETING the exploitation, diversification, or stretching of a brand to revive or reinvigorate it in the marketplace. Products developed in the brand extension process may be directly recognizable derivatives or may look and feel completely different.

brand image MARKETING the perception that consumers have of a brand. Brand image is usually carefully developed by the brand owner through marketing campaigns or product positioning. Occasionally, the image of a brand may develop spontaneously through customer responses to a product. The image of a brand can be seriously tarnished through inappropriate advertising or association with somebody or something that has fallen from public favor.

branding MARKETING a means of distinguishing one firm's products or services from another's and of creating and maintaining an image that encourages confidence in the quality and performance of that firm's products or services

brand leader MARKETING the brand with the largest *market share*

brand life cycle MARKETING the three phases through which brands pass as they are introduced, grow, and then decline. The three stages of the brand life cycle are the introductory period, during which the brand is developed and is introduced to the market; the growth period, when the brand faces competition from other products of a similar nature; and, finally, the maturity period, in which the brand either extends to other products or its image is constantly updated. Without careful *brand management*, the maturity period can lead to decline and result in the brand being withdrawn. Similar stages can be observed in the *product life cycle*.

brand loyalty MARKETING a long-term customer preference for a particular product or service. Brand loyalty can be produced by factors such as customer satisfaction with the performance or price of a specific product or service, or through identifying with a *brand image*. It can be encouraged by *advertising*.

brand management MARKETING the marketing of one or more proprietary products. *Brand managers* (see *product management*) have responsibility for the promotion and marketing of one or more commercial brands. This includes setting targets, advertising, and retailing, and coordinating all related activities to achieve those targets. In the case of multiple brand management, consideration needs be given to questions relating to the treatment of the brands as equal or as having some differentiating value. This may affect the amount of resources committed to each brand. See also *product management*

brand manager MARKETING see *brand management*

brand positioning MARKETING the development of a brand's position in the market by heightening customer perception of the brand's superiority over other brands of a similar nature. Brand positioning relies on the identification of a real strength or value that has a clear advantage over the nearest competitor and is easily communicated to the consumer.

brand recognition MARKETING a measurement of the ability of consumers to recall their experience or knowledge of a particular brand. Brand recognition forms part of *brand awareness*.

brand value MARKETING the amount that a brand is worth in terms of income, potential income, reputation, prestige, and market value. Brands with a high value are regarded as considerable assets to a company, so that when a company is sold a brand with a high value may be worth more than any other consideration.

brand wagon MARKETING the trend toward using branding in marketing concepts and techniques (*slang*)

brandwidth MARKETING the degree to which a brand of product or service is recognized (*slang*)

Branson, Sir Richard (*b*. 1950) GENERAL MANAGEMENT British entrepreneur. Chairman of the Virgin Group, whose dominant *corporate strategy* has been to enter a variety of industries and challenge the existing leaders, using Branson's flair for publicity. This *diversification* strategy is balanced by that of limiting *risk*. Branson's approach is explained in *Losing My Virginity: The Autobiography* (1998).

BRB *abbr* GENERAL MANAGEMENT be right back

breach of contract GENERAL MANAGEMENT a refusal or failure to fulfill an obligation imposed by a *contract*

breadth-of-market theory FINANCE, BANKING, AND ACCOUNTING the theory that the health of a market is measured by the relative volume of items traded that are going up or down in price

break-even MARKETING the point at which revenue equals costs

break-even analysis FINANCE, BANKING, AND ACCOUNTING GENERAL MANAGEMENT a method for determining the point at which fixed and variable production costs are equaled by sales revenue and where neither a profit nor a loss is made. Usually illustrated graphically through the use of a *break-even chart*, break-even analysis can be used to aid decision making, set product prices, and determine the effects of changes in production or sales volume on costs and profits.

break-even chart

1 GENERAL MANAGEMENT a management aid used in conjunction with *break-even analysis* to calculate the point at which fixed and variable production costs are met by incoming revenue. Lines are plotted to indicate expected sales revenue and production costs. The point at which the lines intersect marks the *break-even point*, where no profit or loss is made.
2 FINANCE, BANKING, AND ACCOUNTING a chart which indicates approximate profit or loss at different levels of sales volume within a limited range

break-even point FINANCE, BANKING, AND ACCOUNTING the point or level of financial activity at which expenditure equals income, or the value of an investment equals its cost, so that the result is neither a profit nor a loss. Abbr. **BEP**

breakout
1 GENERAL MANAGEMENT a summary or breakdown of data that has been collected
2 FINANCE, BANKING, AND ACCOUNTING a rise in a security's price above its previous highest price, or a drop below its former lowest price, taken by technical analysts to signal a continuing move in that direction

breakthrough strategy GENERAL MANAGEMENT a strategy that achieves significant new results

break-up value FINANCE, BANKING, AND ACCOUNTING the combined market value of a firm's assets if each were sold separately, as contrasted with selling the firm as an ongoing business. Analysts look for companies with a large break-up value relative to their market value to identify potential takeover targets.

Brech, Edward Francis Leopold (*b.* 1909) GENERAL MANAGEMENT British manager, writer, and historian. A publicizer and developer of the theories of *Henri Fayol* and *Frederick Winslow Taylor*, in common with *Lyndall Urwick*. Brech's *Principles and Practice of Management* (1953), sets down a structural and functional approach to management. In the 1990s, Brech completed a history of British management. See thinker *Henri Fayol*, *Frederick Winslow Taylor*

Bretton Woods ECONOMICS an agreement signed at a conference at Bretton Woods in July 1944 that established the *IMF* and the *IBRD*

bribery HR & PERSONNEL the act of persuading somebody to exercise his or her business judgment in your favor by offering cash or a gift and thereby gaining an unfair advantage. Many organizations have *codes of conduct* that expressly forbid the soliciting or payment of bribes.

brick
hit the bricks GENERAL MANAGEMENT to go out on strike (*slang*)

bricks-and-mortar E-COMMERCE relating to a traditional business not involved in e-commerce and incurring the cost of physical structures such as warehouses

bricolage E-COMMERCE the opportunistic way in which the Web is put together, with Web designers being able to take *GIFs*, formats, and links from elsewhere on the Web to create new pages

bridge financing FINANCE, BANKING, AND ACCOUNTING borrowing that the borrower expects to repay with the proceeds of later, larger loans. See also *takeout financing*

bridge loan FINANCE, BANKING, AND ACCOUNTING a temporary loan providing funds until further money is received, for example, for buying one property while trying to sell another. U.K. term *bridging loan*

bridging FINANCE, BANKING, AND ACCOUNTING the obtaining of a short-term loan to provide a continuing source of financing in anticipation of receiving an intermediate- or long-term loan. Bridging is routinely employed to finance the purchase or construction of a new building or property until an old one is sold.

bridging loan (*U.K.*) FINANCE, BANKING, AND ACCOUNTING = *bridge loan*

briefing group HR & PERSONNEL see *team briefing*

Briggs, Katherine Cook (1875–1968) GENERAL MANAGEMENT U.S. researcher. Inventor, together with her daughter, *Isabel Briggs-Myers*, of the *Myers-Briggs type indicator*.

Briggs-Myers, Isabel (1897–1980) GENERAL MANAGEMENT U.S. researcher. Inventor, together with her mother, *Katherine Cook Briggs*, of the *Myers-Briggs type indicator*.

brightsizing HR & PERSONNEL the reduction of staff numbers within a company by letting go the most recently hired employees, an unintentional byproduct of which being that often the most highly capable or qualified employees are lost (*slang*)

bring forward FINANCE, BANKING, AND ACCOUNTING to carry a sum from one column or page to the next

Brisch system OPERATIONS & PRODUCTION a coding system, developed principally for the engineering industry by E. G. Brisch and Partners, in which a code is assigned to every item of resources, including materials, labor, and equipment.

British Accounting Association FINANCE, BANKING, AND ACCOUNTING an organization whose goal is to promote accounting education and research in the United Kingdom. Abbr. **BAA**

British Bankers' Association FINANCE, BANKING, AND ACCOUNTING a not-for-profit trading association for the financial services and banking industry. The Association was established in 1919 and has 295 members as well as numerous associate members. It aims to address a variety of industry issues, including the development and revision of the voluntary *Banking Code*, which aims to set standards of best practice. Abbr. **BBA**

British Chambers of Commerce FINANCE, BANKING, AND ACCOUNTING a national network of accredited *chambers of commerce*. The BCC represents over 135,000 in the United Kingdom. Abbr. **BCC**

broadband E-COMMERCE a class of transmission system that allows large amounts of data to be transferred at high speed

broadbanding HR & PERSONNEL the reworking of the pay hierarchy into fewer, wider *pay scales*. Pioneered by GEC in the United States, broadbanding provides a more flexible reward structure that is more in tune with the *flat organization*. The introduction of broadbanding can provide a method for pay increases and *career development*, even without a formal career ladder, and consequently can help improve *motivation*.

brochure FINANCE, BANKING, AND ACCOUNTING a booklet or pamphlet that contains descriptive information or advertising, for example, in relation to a product or real estate for sale, or an available service

brochure site E-COMMERCE a simple, often one-page Web site advertising a company's products and giving contact details

brochureware E-COMMERCE a Web site that is the online equivalent of a printed brochure, providing information about products and services. The term is most often used in a derogatory way to refer to electronic advertising for planned but nonexistent products.

broker GENERAL MANAGEMENT to act as an agent in arranging a deal, sale, or contract

brokerage FINANCE, BANKING, AND ACCOUNTING
1 a company whose business is buying and selling stocks and bonds for its clients. Also known as *brokerage firm*, *brokerage house*
2 the business of being a broker
3 a fee paid to somebody who acts as a financial agent for somebody else

brokerage firm *or* **brokerage house** FINANCE, BANKING, AND ACCOUNTING see *brokerage*

brokered market FINANCE, BANKING, AND ACCOUNTING a market in which brokers bring buyers and sellers together

broker loan rate FINANCE, BANKING, AND ACCOUNTING the interest rate that banks charge brokers on money that they lend for purchases on margin

Brown, Wilfred (1908–85) GENERAL MANAGEMENT British business executive. Chairman and managing director of the Glacier Metal Company, who introduced works councils as an attempt at *industrial democracy*. During Brown's leadership, the Glacier Metal Company was used as the basis for the *Glacier studies*, carried out by *Elliot Jaques* of the Tavistock Institute of Human Relations.

brownfield GENERAL MANAGEMENT see *brownfield site*

brownfield site GENERAL MANAGEMENT an urban development site that has been previously built on but is currently unused

brown goods (*U.K.*) MARKETING electrical consumer goods used primarily for home entertainment, for example, televisions, radios, and hi-fis

browser E-COMMERCE a piece of software that allows people to access the Internet and World Wide Web. Internet Explorer and Netscape Navigator are the most commonly used browsers.

B/S *abbr* FINANCE, BANKING, AND ACCOUNTING balance sheet

B share (*ANZ*) FINANCE, BANKING, AND ACCOUNTING a share in a mutual fund that has no front-end sales charge but carries a redemption fee, or back-end load, payable only if the share is redeemed. This load, called a CDSC, or contingent deferred sales charge, declines every year until it disappears, usually after six years.

BTI *abbr* FINANCE, BANKING, AND ACCOUNTING Business Times Industrial index

BTW *abbr* GENERAL MANAGEMENT by the way

bubble economy ECONOMICS an unstable boom based on speculation in stocks, often followed by a financial crash. This happened, for example, in the 1630s in the Netherlands and in the 1720s in England.

bucket shop FINANCE, BANKING, AND ACCOUNTING a firm of brokers or dealers that sells stocks of questionable value

bucket trading FINANCE, BANKING, AND ACCOUNTING an illegal practice in which a stockbroker accepts a customer's order but does not execute the transaction until it is financially

advantageous to the broker but at the customer's expense

budget FINANCE, BANKING, AND ACCOUNTING a quantitative statement, for a defined period of time, which may include planned revenues, expenses, assets, liabilities, and cash flows. A budget provides a focus for an organization, as it aids the coordination of activities, allocation of resources, and direction of activity, and facilitates control. Planning is achieved by means of a fixed master budget, whereas control is generally exercised through the comparison of actual costs with a flexible budget.

Budget FINANCE, BANKING, AND ACCOUNTING the U.K. Government's annual spending plan, which is announced to the House of Commons by the Chancellor of the Exchequer. The Government is legally obliged to present economic forecasts twice a year, and since the 1997 general election the main Budget has been presented in the Spring while a Pre-Budget Report is given in the Autumn. This outlines government spending plans prior to the main Budget, and also reports on progress since the last Budget.

budget account (*U.K.*) FINANCE, BANKING, AND ACCOUNTING a bank account established to control a person's regular expenditure, for example, the payment of insurance premiums, mortgage, utilities, or telephone bills. The annual expenditure for each item is paid into the account in equal monthly installments, bills being paid from the budget account as they become due.

budgetary FINANCE, BANKING, AND ACCOUNTING relating to a detailed plan of financial operations, with estimates of both revenue and expenditure for a specific future period

budget committee FINANCE, BANKING, AND ACCOUNTING the group within an organization responsible for drawing up budgets that meet departmental requirements, ensuring they comply with policy, and then submitting them to the board of directors

budget deficit FINANCE, BANKING, AND ACCOUNTING the extent by which expenditure exceeds revenue. Also known as *deficit*

budget director FINANCE, BANKING, AND ACCOUNTING the person in an organization who is responsible for running the budget system

budgeted capacity FINANCE, BANKING, AND ACCOUNTING an organization's available output level for a budget period according to the

budget. It may be expressed in different ways, for example, in machine hours or standard hours.

budgeted revenue FINANCE, BANKING, AND ACCOUNTING the income that an organization expects to receive in a budget period according to the budget

budget management FINANCE, BANKING, AND ACCOUNTING the comparison of actual financial results with the estimated expenditures and revenues for the given time period of a budget and the taking of corrective action as necessary

budget surplus FINANCE, BANKING, AND ACCOUNTING the extent by which revenue exceeds expenditure. Also known as *surplus*

budget variance FINANCE, BANKING, AND ACCOUNTING the difference between the financial value of something (such as cost or revenue) as estimated for in the budget, and the actual financial value

buffer inventory FINANCE, BANKING, AND ACCOUNTING OPERATIONS & PRODUCTION the products or supplies of an organization maintained on hand or in transit to stabilize variations in supply, demand, production, or lead time

buffer stock FINANCE, BANKING, AND ACCOUNTING a stock of materials, or of work in progress, maintained in order to protect user departments from the effect of possible interruptions to supply

Buffett, Warren (*b.* 1930) GENERAL MANAGEMENT U.S. investment banker. Chairman and C.E.O. of Berkshire Hathaway, a vehicle for investing his vast wealth realized from a unique and successful stock-purchase strategy. Buffett, dubbed the "sage of Omaha," is much admired by *Bill Gates*.

Building Societies Ombudsman FINANCE, BANKING, AND ACCOUNTING a U.K. official whose duty is to investigate complaints by members of the public against building societies. All building societies belong to the Building Societies Ombudsman Scheme.

building society FINANCE, BANKING, AND ACCOUNTING in the United Kingdom, a financial institution that offers interest-bearing savings accounts, the deposits being reinvested by the society in long-term loans, primarily mortgage loans for the purchase of real estate

bulk handling FINANCE, BANKING, AND ACCOUNTING the financing of receivables in bulk to reduce processing costs

bull FINANCE, BANKING, AND ACCOUNTING somebody who anticipates favorable business conditions, in particular somebody who buys particular stocks or commodities in anticipation that their prices will rise, often with the expectation of selling them at a large profit at a later time. See also *bear*

bulldog GENERAL MANAGEMENT to attack a problem relentlessly (*slang*)

bulldog bond FINANCE, BANKING, AND ACCOUNTING a bond issued in sterling in the U.K. market by a non-British corporation

bullet bond FINANCE, BANKING, AND ACCOUNTING a Eurobond which is redeemed only when it is mature. A bullet bond is used in payments between central banks and also acts as currency backing.

bulletin board E-COMMERCE a computer-based forum used by an interest group to allow members to exchange e-mails, chat online, and access software. Also known as *newsgroup*

bulletin board system E-COMMERCE see *BBS*

bullet loan FINANCE, BANKING, AND ACCOUNTING a loan that involves specified payments of interest until maturity, when the principal is repaid

bullish
1 GENERAL MANAGEMENT anticipating favorable business conditions
2 FINANCE, BANKING, AND ACCOUNTING conducive to or characterized by buying stocks or commodities in anticipation of rising prices. See also *bearish*

bull market FINANCE, BANKING, AND ACCOUNTING a market in which prices are rising and in which a dealer is more likely to be a buyer than a seller. See also *bear market*

bullshit bingo GENERAL MANAGEMENT a game that involves counting how frequently words of incomprehensible jargon are used (*slang*)

bull spread FINANCE, BANKING, AND ACCOUNTING a combination of purchases and sales of options for the same commodity or stock, intended to produce a profit when the price rises. See also *bear spread*

bullying HR & PERSONNEL see *workplace bullying*

bump up GENERAL MANAGEMENT to upgrade somebody to a higher class of service than has been paid for, for example, in an airplane or hotel (*slang*)

bundle
1 MARKETING to group together two or more products or services into a single package that is then offered to the consumer at one price, for example, providing software with a personal computer
2 FINANCE, BANKING, AND ACCOUNTING a package of financial products or services offered to a customer

bundling MARKETING the practice of grouping together two or more products or services into a single package that is then offered to the consumer at one price

Bundy (*ANZ*) HR & PERSONNEL a timing system that records the arrival and departure of employees at their place of work

Bundy off (*ANZ*) HR & PERSONNEL to punch out from work

Bundy on (*ANZ*) HR & PERSONNEL to punch in for work

buoyant market FINANCE, BANKING, AND ACCOUNTING a market which sees plenty of trading activity and on which prices are rising, rather than falling

bureaucracy GENERAL MANAGEMENT an *organization structure* with a rigid hierarchy of *personnel*, regulated by set rules and procedures. *Max Weber* believed that a bureaucracy was technically the most efficient form of organization, one structured around official functions that are bound by rules, each function having its own specified competence. The functions are structured into offices, which are organized into a hierarchy that follows technical rules and norms. Managers in a bureaucracy possess a rational-legal type of *authority* derived from the office they hold. Bureaucracies have been criticized for eradicating inspiration and *creativity* in favor of impersonality and the mundaneness and regularity of corporate life. This was best described in *William H. Whyte*'s *The Organization Man,* published in 1956, in which the individual was taken over by the bureaucratic machine in the name of efficiency. A more recent and humorous interpretation of life in a bureaucracy has been depicted by *Scott Adams* in *The Dilbert Principle* (1996). The term bureaucracy has gradually become a pejorative synonym for excessive and time-consuming paperwork and administration. Bureaucracies fell subject to *delayering* and *downsizing* from the 1980s onward, as the flatter organization became the target structure to ensure swifter market response and organizational flexibility.

Burns, **James MacGregor** (*b.* 1918) GENERAL MANAGEMENT U.S. political scientist. Noted in the business sphere for identifying two approaches to leadership, the *transactional theory of leadership* and the *transformational theory of leadership*, described in his book *Leadership* (1978), which has a historical, social, and political perspective.

bush telegraph GENERAL MANAGEMENT a method of communicating information or rumors swiftly and unofficially by word of mouth or other means

Business Accounting Deliberation Council FINANCE, BANKING, AND ACCOUNTING in Japan, a committee controlled by the Ministry of Finance that is responsible for drawing up regulations regarding the consolidated financial statements of listed companies

Business Activity Statement FINANCE, BANKING, AND ACCOUNTING a standard document used in Australia to report the amount of *GST* and other taxes paid and collected by a business. Abbr. *BAS*

business administration GENERAL MANAGEMENT
1 the establishment and maintenance of *procedures*, records, and regulations in the pursuit of a commercial activity. Business administration involves the conduct of activities leading to, and resulting from, the delivery of a product or service to the customer. Administration is often seen as paperwork and form-filling, but it reaches more widely than that to encompass the coordination of all the procedures that enable a product or service to be delivered, together with the keeping of records that can be checked to identify errors or opportunities for improvement.
2 a form of *management*. Business administration is used as a synonym for management, notably in government or the public sector. This use has developed from the *administration school* of thought established by *Henri Fayol*, which defines management activities as a set of processes. He argued that to manage was to plan, organize, coordinate, command, and control. These principles were put into exemplary practice by *Alfred P. Sloan, Jr.* at General Motors and are often seen as characteristic of large *bureaucracies*.

business angel FINANCE, BANKING, AND ACCOUNTING an individual who is prepared to invest money in a startup company. The amount offered by angels is typically much less than that offered by venture capitalists, but angels are often willing to take greater risks.

business card FINANCE, BANKING, AND ACCOUNT-ING a small card printed with somebody's name, job title, business address, and contact numbers or e-mail address

business case (*U.K.*) GENERAL MANAGEMENT the essential value to an organization of a proposal. A business case is made through the preparation and presentation of a business plan and is used to prevent *blue-sky ideas* taking root without justifiable or provable value to an organization.

business cluster FINANCE, BANKING, AND AC-COUNTING GENERAL MANAGEMENT a group of small firms from similar industries that team up and act as one body. Creating a business cluster enables firms to enjoy economies of scale usually only available to bigger competitors. Marketing costs can be shared and goods can be bought more cheaply. There are also networking advantages, which small firms can share experiences and discuss business strategies.

business combinations FINANCE, BANKING, AND ACCOUNTING acquisitions or mergers involving two or more enterprises

business continuity GENERAL MANAGEMENT the uninterrupted maintenance of business activities. Ensuring business continuity requires a proactive process of identifying essential business functions within an organization and threats to those functions. Plans and procedures may then be put in place to ensure that key functions can continue whatever the circumstances. Plans may be drawn up, for example, for *contingency*, *disaster*, and *risk management*, or for *total loss control*.

Business Council of Australia FINANCE, BANK-ING, AND ACCOUNTING GENERAL MANAGEMENT a national association of chief executives, designed as a forum for the discussion of matters pertaining to business leadership in Australia. Abbr. *BCA*

business cycle ECONOMICS a regular pattern of fluctuation in national income, moving from upturn to downturn in about five years

business efficiency GENERAL MANAGEMENT a situation in which an organization maximizes benefit and profit, while minimizing effort and expenditure. Maximization of business efficiency is a balance between two extremes. Managed correctly, it reduces costs, waste, and duplication. *Max Weber*, who developed the concept of the *bureaucracy*, believed that efficiency was the goal of all bureaucratic organizations, which were designed to run like smooth machines. The greater the efficiency, the more impersonal, rational, and emotionally detached a bureaucracy becomes. The flatter organizations more prevalent today attempt to be more customer-responsive than efficient in this sense, and the notion of such an ordered and impersonal efficiency has lost favor in an era when *creativity* and *innovation* are valued as a *competitive advantage*.

business ethics GENERAL MANAGEMENT a system of moral principles applied in the commercial world. Business ethics provide guidelines for acceptable behavior by organizations in both their strategy formulation and day-to-day operations. An ethical approach is becoming necessary both for corporate success and a positive *corporate image*. Following pressure from consumers for more ethical and responsible business practices, many organizations are choosing to make a public commitment to ethical business by formulating *codes of conduct* and operating principles. In doing so, they must translate into action the concepts of personal and corporate accountability, *corporate giving*, corporate governance, and *whistleblowing*. Also known as *morality in business*

business excellence GENERAL MANAGEMENT see *excellence*

business excellence model GENERAL MAN-AGEMENT see *EFQM Excellence Model*

business failure GENERAL MANAGEMENT an organization that has gone bankrupt. A business that is at risk of failure may be saved by *turnaround management*, which identifies and deals with the reasons for decline. Also known as *failure*

business game GENERAL MANAGEMENT a type of *simulation game* in which a model of a business situation is explored competitively for the purpose of learning

business gift MARKETING a present, usually from a supplier to a customer, often used to maintain good relations. Business gifts may range from a pen to a hamper and are often a form of *merchandising*. The acceptance of a business gift is often governed by an organization's *code of conduct* and is often forbidden on the grounds that business gifts, particularly high value ones, may be seen as an attempt to bribe.

business intelligence GENERAL MANAGEMENT any information that can be of strategic use to a business

business interruption insurance FINANCE, BANKING, AND ACCOUNTING a policy indemnifying an organization for loss of profits and continuing fixed expenses when some insurable disaster, for example, a fire, causes the organization to stop or reduce its activities. Also known as *consequential loss policy*

business name FINANCE, BANKING, AND AC-COUNTING in the United Kingdom, the legal term for the name under which an organization operates

business objective GENERAL MANAGEMENT a goal that an organization sets for itself, for example, profitability, sales growth, or return on investment. These goals are the foundation upon which the strategic and operational policies adopted by the organization are based.

business plan FINANCE, BANKING, AND ACCOUNT-ING GENERAL MANAGEMENT a document describing the current activities of a business, setting out its goals and objectives and how they are to be achieved over a set period of time. A business plan may cover the activities of an organization or a group of companies, or it may deal with a single department within the organization. In the former case, it is sometimes referred to as a corporate plan. The sections of a business plan usually include a market analysis describing the target market, customers, and competitors, an operations plan describing how products and services will be developed and produced, and a financial section providing profit, budget, and cash flow forecasts, annual accounts, and financial requirements. Businesses may use a business plan internally as a framework for implementing strategy and improving performance or externally to attract investment or raise capital for development plans. A business plan may form part of the overall planning process, or corporate planning, within an organization and be used for the implementation of corporate strategy.

business process reengineering GENERAL MANAGEMENT OPERATIONS & PRODUCTION the initiation and control of the change of *processes* within an organization, in order to derive *competitive advantage* from improvement in the quality of products. Business process reengineering was popularized by *Michael Hammer*. It requires a review and imaginative analysis of the processes currently used by the organization. BPR, therefore, has similarities to *benchmarking*, as this review of processes can reveal critical points where significant improvements in *quality* can be made. Business process reengineering was at the height of its popularity in the early to mid-1990s. It has been criticized as one of the root causes of the bouts of *downsizing* and *delayering* that have affected many parts of industry. It has also received a negative press because few BPR

projects have delivered the benefits expected of them. Abbr. **BPR**

business property relief FINANCE, BANKING, AND ACCOUNTING in the United Kingdom, a reduction in the amount liable to inheritance tax on certain types of business property

business rate FINANCE, BANKING, AND ACCOUNTING in the United Kingdom, a tax on businesses calculated on the value of the property occupied. Although the rate of tax is set by central government, the tax is collected the local authority.

business risk FINANCE, BANKING, AND ACCOUNTING the uncertainty associated with the unique circumstances of a particular company, for example, the introduction of a superior technology, as it might affect the price of that company's securities

business school GENERAL MANAGEMENT
1 a higher education institution that offers undergraduate and graduate courses in business-related subjects. Business schools provide courses of varying length and level, up to Master of Business Administration. They cater to full-time students, but also offer part-time and *distance learning* to those already in employment. Subject coverage is broad, and courses cover all areas of business administration, management, technology, finance, and interpersonal skills.
2 in the United States, a department of a university or college that provides similar types of courses

business segment FINANCE, BANKING, AND ACCOUNTING a distinguishable part of a business or enterprise that is subject to a different set of risks and returns from any other part. Listed companies are required to declare in their annual reports certain information, for example, sales, profits, and assets, for each segment of an enterprise.

business strategy FINANCE, BANKING, AND ACCOUNTING a long-term approach to implementing a firm's business plans in order to achieve its business objectives

business theory GENERAL MANAGEMENT see *organization theory*

Business Times Industrial index FINANCE, BANKING, AND ACCOUNTING an index of 40 Singapore and Malaysian stocks. Abbr. **BTI**

business-to-business E-COMMERCE see **B2B**

business-to-consumer E-COMMERCE see **B2C**

business transfer relief FINANCE, BANKING, AND ACCOUNTING the U.K. tax advantage gained when selling a business for shares of stock in the company that buys it

business unit FINANCE, BANKING, AND ACCOUNTING a part of an organization that operates as a distinct function, department, division, or stand-alone business. Business units are usually treated as a separate *profit center* within the overall, owning business.

business web E-COMMERCE see *b-web*

bust up FINANCE, BANKING, AND ACCOUNTING to split up a company or a division of a company into smaller units

bust-up proxy proposal FINANCE, BANKING, AND ACCOUNTING an overture to a company's stockholders for a leveraged buy-out in which the acquirer will sell some of the company's assets in order to repay the debt used to finance the takeover

busymeet GENERAL MANAGEMENT a business meeting (*slang*)

butterfly spread FINANCE, BANKING, AND ACCOUNTING a complex option strategy based on simultaneously purchasing and selling calls at different exercise prices and maturity dates, the profit being the premium collected when the options are sold. Such a strategy is most profitable when the price of the underlying security is relatively stable.

button E-COMMERCE an online interactive ad, smaller than the traditional *banner*, placed on a Web page and linked to an external advertiser's site. Buttons are usually square in shape, represented to look like a push button, and located down the left or right edge of the page.

buy and hold FINANCE, BANKING, AND ACCOUNTING an investment strategy based on retaining securities for a long time

buy and write FINANCE, BANKING, AND ACCOUNTING an investment strategy involving buying stock and selling options to eliminate the possibility of loss if the value of the stock goes down

buyback
1 FINANCE, BANKING, AND ACCOUNTING an arrangement whereby a company buys its own stock on the stock market. Also known as *stock buyback*
2 ECONOMICS FINANCE, BANKING, AND ACCOUNTING the repurchase of bonds or stock, as agreed by contract

buydown FINANCE, BANKING, AND ACCOUNTING the payment of principal amounts that reduce the monthly payments due on a mortgage

buyer FINANCE, BANKING, AND ACCOUNTING
1 somebody who is in the process of buying something or who intends to buy something
2 somebody whose job is to choose and buy goods, merchandise, services, or media time or space for a company, factory, store, or advertiser

buyer expectation GENERAL MANAGEMENT see *customer expectation*

buyer's guide MARKETING a document that offers information on a variety of related products, usually from a number of different organizations

buyer's market FINANCE, BANKING, AND ACCOUNTING a situation in which supply exceeds demand, prices are relatively low, and buyers therefore have an advantage

buy in FINANCE, BANKING, AND ACCOUNTING to buy stock in a company so as to have a controlling interest. This is often done by or for executives from outside the company.

buying economies of scale FINANCE, BANKING, AND ACCOUNTING a reduction in the cost of purchasing raw materials and components or of borrowing money due to the increased size of the purchase

buying manager FINANCE, BANKING, AND ACCOUNTING OPERATIONS & PRODUCTION see *purchasing manager*

buy on close FINANCE, BANKING, AND ACCOUNTING a purchase at the end of the trading day

buy one get one free MARKETING see *BOGOF*

buy on opening FINANCE, BANKING, AND ACCOUNTING a purchase at the beginning of the trading day

buy or make OPERATIONS & PRODUCTION see *purchasing versus production*

buy out FINANCE, BANKING, AND ACCOUNTING GENERAL MANAGEMENT
1 to purchase the entire stock of, or controlling financial interest in, a company
2 to pay somebody to relinquish his or her interest in a property or other enterprise

buyout
1 FINANCE, BANKING, AND ACCOUNTING GENERAL MANAGEMENT the purchase and *takeover* of an ongoing business. It is more formally known as

an *acquisition* (see *merger*). If a business is purchased by managers or staff, it is known as a *management buy-out*.

2 FINANCE, BANKING, AND ACCOUNTING GENERAL MANAGEMENT the purchase of somebody else's entire stock ownership in a firm. It is more formally known as an *acquisition* (see *merger*).

3 FINANCE, BANKING, AND ACCOUNTING HR & PERSONNEL an option to transfer benefits of a pension plan on leaving a company

buy stop order FINANCE, BANKING, AND ACCOUNTING an order to buy stock when its price reaches a specified level

Buzan, Tony (*b.* 1942) GENERAL MANAGEMENT British writer. Originator of the *Mind Map*™, a technique he explained in *Use Your Head* (1974).

buzz group GENERAL MANAGEMENT a small discussion group formed for a specific task such as generating ideas, solving problems, or reaching a common viewpoint on a topic within a specific period of time. The use of buzz groups was first associated with J. D. Phillips and is sometimes known as the Phillips 66 technique. Large groups may be divided into buzz groups after an initial presentation in order to cover different aspects of a topic or maximize participation. Each group appoints a spokesperson to report the results of the discussion to the larger group. Buzz groups are a form of *brainstorming*.

buzz marketing MARKETING see *word of mouth marketing*

buzzword-compliant E-COMMERCE familiar with the latest Internet jargon (*slang*)

BV *abbr* FINANCE, BANKING, AND ACCOUNTING besloten venootschap: the Dutch term for a limited liability company

b-web E-COMMERCE a business web, a group of complementary businesses that come together over the Internet. While each company retains its autonomous identity, the businesses work in unison to generate more income than they could do individually. Characteristics of b-webs include *extranets*, *viral marketing*, online marketplaces, and affiliate programs. The term was originally used by Don Tapscott, David Ticoll, and Alex Lowry in an article published by *eCompany Now* magazine.

by-bidder FINANCE, BANKING, AND ACCOUNTING somebody who bids at an auction solely to raise the price for the seller

Byham, William C. GENERAL MANAGEMENT U.S. consultant and writer. Coauthor of *Zapp! The Lightning of Empowerment* (1987), a modern fable in an industrial setting that popularized the benefits that *empowerment* can bring to the workplace.

bylaws FINANCE, BANKING, AND ACCOUNTING rules governing the internal running of a corporation, such as the number of meetings, the appointment of officers, and so on

bypass trust FINANCE, BANKING, AND ACCOUNTING a trust that leaves money in a will in trust to people other than the prime beneficiary in order to gain tax advantage

byte E-COMMERCE a unit of computer memory equal to that needed to store a single character, now commonly a group of eight adjacent *bits*

C

CA *abbr* FINANCE, BANKING, AND ACCOUNTING chartered accountant *or* certified accountant

c/a *abbr* FINANCE, BANKING, AND ACCOUNTING current account

C/A *abbr* FINANCE, BANKING, AND ACCOUNTING capital account

cache E-COMMERCE a small memory bank inside a computer that stores all the images and text from every Web site visited. This speeds up the download time when an Internet user revisits a site.

CAD *abbr* OPERATIONS & PRODUCTION computer-aided design

Cadbury, Sir George Adrian Hayhurst (*b.* 1929) GENERAL MANAGEMENT British business executive. Former chairman of Cadbury Schweppes and, in the 1990s, chairman of the Committee on the Financial Aspects of *Corporate Governance*.

Cadbury, Sir Nicholas Dominic (*b.* 1940) GENERAL MANAGEMENT British industrialist. Chair of the Wellcome Trust, and past chair of Cadbury Schweppes. Sir Dominic Cadbury is celebrated for his often-quoted dictum "There is no such thing as a career path; it is crazy-paving and you have to lay it yourself."

CAD/CAM GENERAL MANAGEMENT the integration of data and technologies from *computer-aided manufacturing* and *computer-aided design* into the entire design-to-manufacture cycle. Data from a combined CAD/CAM database can be used for the control of a totally automated computer-integrated manufacturing system.

CAE *abbr* OPERATIONS & PRODUCTION computer-aided engineering

cage FINANCE, BANKING, AND ACCOUNTING the part of a brokerage firm where the paperwork involved in the buying and selling of stock is processed (*slang*)

calendar variance FINANCE, BANKING, AND ACCOUNTING a variance which occurs if a company uses calendar months for the financial accounts but uses the number of actual working days to calculate overhead expenses in the cost accounts

call FINANCE, BANKING, AND ACCOUNTING
1 an option to buy stock. Also known as *call option*
2 a request made to the holders of partly paid-up share capital for the payment of a predetermined sum due on the share capital, under the terms of the original subscription agreement. Failure on the part of the stockholder to pay a call may result in the forfeiture of the relevant holding of partly paid shares. Also known as *call up*

callable FINANCE, BANKING, AND ACCOUNTING a financial instrument with a call provision in its indenture

callable bond FINANCE, BANKING, AND ACCOUNTING a bond that may be bought back by the issuer prior to its maturity. Also known as *redeemable bond*

callable preferred stock FINANCE, BANKING, AND ACCOUNTING preferred stock that may be bought back by the issuing corporation at a certain date and for a certain price. Also known as *redeemable preferred stock*

call center GENERAL MANAGEMENT a department or business wholly focused on telephone inquiries. Call centers usually provide a centralized point of contact for an organization and support *telephone selling*, *after-sales service*, telephone helplines, or information services, either for a parent organization or on a contract basis for other businesses.

called-up share capital FINANCE, BANKING, AND ACCOUNTING the amount which a company has required stockholders to pay on stock issued

caller identification *or* **caller ID** GENERAL MANAGEMENT see *computer telephony integration*

a-z

1426

DICTIONARY

calling line identification GENERAL MANAGE-MENT see *computer telephony integration*

call money FINANCE, BANKING, AND ACCOUNTING money that brokers use for their own purchases or to help their customers to buy on margin

call option FINANCE, BANKING, AND ACCOUNTING see *call*

call payment FINANCE, BANKING, AND ACCOUNTING an amount that a company demands in partial payment for stock such as a rights issue that is not paid for at one time

call provision FINANCE, BANKING, AND ACCOUNTING a clause in an indenture that lets the issuer of a bond redeem it before the date of its maturity

call purchase FINANCE, BANKING, AND ACCOUNTING a transaction where either the seller or purchaser can fix the price for future delivery

calls in arrears FINANCE, BANKING, AND ACCOUNTING money called up for shares, but not paid at the correct time. The shares may be forfeited or a special calls in arrears account is established to debit the sums owing.

call up FINANCE, BANKING, AND ACCOUNTING see *call*

CAM *abbr* OPERATIONS & PRODUCTION computer-aided manufacturing

campaign MARKETING a program of advertising and marketing activities with a specific objective

camp on the line GENERAL MANAGEMENT to wait on hold for a long time on the telephone (*slang*)

can HR & PERSONNEL to dismiss somebody from employment (*slang*)

Canadian Institute of Chartered Accountants FINANCE, BANKING, AND ACCOUNTING in Canada, the principal professional accountancy body that is responsible for setting accounting standards. Abbr. *CICA*

cancellation price (*U.K.*) FINANCE, BANKING, AND ACCOUNTING the lowest value possible in any one day of a unit trust

canned E-COMMERCE describes a Web site or its features that are designed according to a standard template rather than to somebody's personal specifications

cap FINANCE, BANKING, AND ACCOUNTING an upper limit such as on a rate of interest for a loan

CAPA *abbr* FINANCE, BANKING, AND ACCOUNTING Confederation of Asian and Pacific Accountants: an umbrella organization for a number of Asia-Pacific accountancy bodies

capacity OPERATIONS & PRODUCTION the measure of the capability of a workstation or a plant to produce output. Capacity measures can focus on a variety of factors, which typically include quantity, for example, the number of items produced over a given period; and scope, for example, the range of items produced by type or size.

capacity planning OPERATIONS & PRODUCTION the process of measuring the amount of work that can be completed within a given time and determining the necessary physical and human resources needed to accomplish it. Capacity planning uses *capacity utilization* to ensure that the maximum amount of product is made and sold. The planning involves a regulation process that identifies deviations from the plan, allowing corrective action to be taken. A *capacity requirements planning* program can aid in the process of capacity planning.

capacity requirements planning GENERAL MANAGEMENT OPERATIONS & PRODUCTION a computerized tracking process that translates production requirements into practical implications for manufacturing resources. Capacity requirements planning is part of manufacturing resource planning and is carried out after a manufacturing resource planning program has been run. This produces an *infinite capacity plan*, as it does not take account of the capacity constraints of each workstation. Where the process is extended to cover capacity requirements, a *finite capacity plan* is produced. This enables *loading* at each workstation to be smoothed and determines the need for additional resources.

capacity usage variance FINANCE, BANKING, AND ACCOUNTING the difference in gain or loss in a given period compared to budgeted expectations, caused because the hours worked were longer or shorter than planned

capacity utilization

1 OPERATIONS & PRODUCTION a measure of the plant and equipment of a company or an industry that is actually being used to produce goods or services. Capacity utilization is usually measured over a specific period of time, for example, the average for a month, or at a

given point in time. It can be expressed as a ratio, where utilization = actual output divided by design capacity. This measure is used in both *capacity planning* and *capacity requirements planning* processes.

2 ECONOMICS the output of an economy, firm, or plant divided by its output when working at full capacity

Caparo case FINANCE, BANKING, AND ACCOUNTING in England, a court decision taken by the House of Lords in 1990 that auditors owe a duty of care to present (not prospective) stockholders as a body but not as individuals

CAPEX *abbr* FINANCE, BANKING, AND ACCOUNTING capital expenditure

capital FINANCE, BANKING, AND ACCOUNTING money that can be invested by an individual or organization in order to make a profit

capital account FINANCE, BANKING, AND ACCOUNTING the sum of a company's capital at a particular time. Abbr. *C/A*

capital adequacy ratio FINANCE, BANKING, AND ACCOUNTING an amount of money which a bank has to have in the form of stockholders' capital, shown as a percentage of its assets. This has been agreed internationally at 8%.

capital allowances FINANCE, BANKING, AND ACCOUNTING in the United Kingdom and Ireland, an allowance against income or corporation tax available to businesses or sole traders who have purchased plant and machinery for business use. The rates are set annually and vary according to the type of fixed asset purchased, for example, whether it is machinery or buildings. This system effectively removes subjectivity from the calculation of depreciation for tax purposes.

capital appreciation FINANCE, BANKING, AND ACCOUNTING the increase in a company's or individual's wealth

capital appreciation fund FINANCE, BANKING, AND ACCOUNTING a mutual fund that aims to increase the value of its holdings without regard to the provision of income to its owners

capital asset FINANCE, BANKING, AND ACCOUNTING real estate that a company owns and uses but that the company does not buy or sell as part of its regular trade

capital asset pricing model

1 ECONOMICS a model of the market used to assess the cost of capital for a company based on the rate of return on its assets.

The capital asset pricing model holds that the expected return on a security or portfolio equals the rate on a risk-free security plus a risk premium. If this expected return does not meet or beat a theoretical required return, the investment should not be undertaken. The formula used for the model is

Risk-free rate + (Market return –
Risk-free rate) × Beta value =
Expected return

The risk-free rate is the quoted rate on an asset that has virtually no risk. In practice, it is the rate quoted for 90-day U.S. Treasury bills. The market return is the percentage return expected of the overall market, typically a published index such as Standard & Poor's. The beta value is a figure that measures the volatility of a security or portfolio of securities compared with the market as a whole. A beta of 1, for example, indicates that a security's price will move with the market. A beta greater than 1 indicates higher volatility, while a beta less than 1 indicates less volatility.

Say, for instance, that the current risk-free rate is 4%, and the S&P 500 index is expected to return 11% next year. An investment club is interested in determining next year's return for XYZ Software Ltd., a prospective investment. The club has determined that the company's beta value is 1.8. The overall stock market always has a beta of 1, so XYZ Software's beta of 1.8 signals that it is a more risky investment than the overall market represents. This added risk means that the club should expect a higher rate of return than the 11% for the S&P 500. The CAPM calculation, then, would be

4% + (11% – 4%) × 1.8 =
16.6% Expected Return

What the results tell the club is that, given the risk, XYZ Software Ltd. has a required rate of return of 16.6%, or the minimum return that an investment in XYZ should generate. If the investment club does not think that XYZ will produce that kind of return, it should probably consider investing in a different company.

2 FINANCE, BANKING, AND ACCOUNTING a theory which predicts that the expected risk premium for an individual stock will be proportional to its beta, such that expected risk premium on a stock = beta × expected risk premium in the market. Risk premium is defined as the expected incremental return for making a risky investment rather than a safe one. Abbr. *CAPM*

capital bonus FINANCE, BANKING, AND ACCOUNTING a bonus payment by an insurance company which is produced by capital gain

capital budget FINANCE, BANKING, AND ACCOUNTING a subsection of a company's master budget that deals with expected capital expenditure within a defined period. Also known as *capital expenditure budget*, *capital investment budget*

capital budgeting FINANCE, BANKING, AND ACCOUNTING the process concerned with decision making with respect to the following issues: the choice of specific investment projects; the total amount of capital expenditure to commit; and the method of financing the investment portfolio

capital commitments FINANCE, BANKING, AND ACCOUNTING expenditure on assets which has been authorized by directors, but not yet spent at the end of a financial period

capital consumption FINANCE, BANKING, AND ACCOUNTING in a given period, the total depreciation of a national economy's fixed assets, based on replacement costs

capital controls ECONOMICS regulations placed by a government on the amount of capital residents may hold

capital cost allowance FINANCE, BANKING, AND ACCOUNTING a tax advantage in Canada for the depreciation in value of capital assets

capital costs FINANCE, BANKING, AND ACCOUNTING expenses on the purchase of fixed assets

capital deepening ECONOMICS the process whereby increasingly capital-intensive production results when a country's *capital stock* increases but the numbers employed fall or remain constant

capital expenditure FINANCE, BANKING, AND ACCOUNTING the cost of acquiring, producing, or enhancing fixed assets. Abbr. *CAPEX*. Also known as *capital investment*

capital expenditure budget FINANCE, BANKING, AND ACCOUNTING see *capital budget*

capital expenditure proposal FINANCE, BANKING, AND ACCOUNTING a formal request for authority to undertake capital expenditure. This is usually supported by the case for expenditure in accordance with capital investment appraisal criteria. Levels of authority must be clearly defined and the reporting structure of actual expenditure must be to the equivalent authority level.

capital flight FINANCE, BANKING, AND ACCOUNTING the transfer of large sums of money between countries to seek higher rates of return or to escape a political or economic disturbance

capital formation ECONOMICS the process of adding to the stock of a country's *real capital* by investment in fixed assets

capital funding planning FINANCE, BANKING, AND ACCOUNTING the process of selecting suitable funds to finance long-term assets and working capital

capital gain FINANCE, BANKING, AND ACCOUNTING the financial gain made upon the disposal of an asset. The gain is the difference between the cost of its acquisition and the net proceeds upon its sale.

capital gains distribution FINANCE, BANKING, AND ACCOUNTING a sum of money that, for example, a mutual fund pays to its owners in proportion to the owners' share of the organization's capital gains for the year

capital gains expenses FINANCE, BANKING, AND ACCOUNTING expenses incurred in buying or selling assets, which can be deducted when calculating a capital gain or loss

capital gains reserve FINANCE, BANKING, AND ACCOUNTING a tax advantage in Canada for money not yet received in payment for something that has been sold

capital gearing FINANCE, BANKING, AND ACCOUNTING the amount of fixed-cost debt that a company has for each share of its common stock

capital goods ECONOMICS stocks of physical or financial assets that are capable of generating income

capital growth FINANCE, BANKING, AND ACCOUNTING an increase in the value of assets in a fund, or of the value of stock

capital inflow ECONOMICS the amount of capital that flows into an economy from services rendered abroad

capital instruments FINANCE, BANKING, AND ACCOUNTING the means that an organization uses to raise finance, for example, the issue of stocks or debentures

capital-intensive FINANCE, BANKING, AND ACCOUNTING using a greater proportion of capital, as opposed to labor

capital investment FINANCE, BANKING, AND ACCOUNTING see *capital expenditure*

capital investment budget FINANCE, BANKING, AND ACCOUNTING see *capital budget*

capitalism ECONOMICS an economic and social system in which individuals can maximize profits because they own the means of production

capitalist FINANCE, BANKING, AND ACCOUNTING an investor of capital in a business

capitalization FINANCE, BANKING, AND ACCOUNTING

1 the amount of money invested in a company, or the worth of the bonds and stocks of a company

2 the conversion of a company's reserves into capital through a stock split

3 see *market capitalization*

capitalization issue (*U.K.*) FINANCE, BANKING, AND ACCOUNTING a proportional issue of free shares to existing owners of a company's stock. = *stock split*

capitalization rate FINANCE, BANKING, AND ACCOUNTING the rate at which a company's *reserves* are converted into capital by way of a *stock split*

capitalization ratio FINANCE, BANKING, AND ACCOUNTING the proportion of a company's value represented by debt, stock, assets, and other items.

By comparing debt to total capitalization, these ratios provide a glimpse of a company's long-term stability and ability to withstand losses and business downturns.

A company's capitalization ratio can be expressed in two ways:

$$= \frac{\text{Long-term Debt}}{\text{Long-term Debt} + \text{Owners' Equity}}$$

and

$$= \frac{\text{Total Debt}}{\text{Total Debt} + \text{Preferred} + \text{Common Equity}}$$

For example, a company whose long-term debt totals $5,000 and whose owners hold equity worth $3,000 would have a capitalization ratio of

$$\frac{5,000}{(5,000 + 3,000)} = \frac{5,000}{8,000} =$$

625 capitalization ratio

Both expressions of the ratio are also referred to as component percentages, since they compare a firm's debt with either its total capital (debt plus equity) or its equity capital. They readily indicate how reliant a firm is on debt financing.

Capitalization ratios need to be evaluated over time, and compared with other data and standards. Care should be taken when comparing companies in different industries or sectors. The same figures that appear to be low in one industry can be very high in another.

capitalize FINANCE, BANKING, AND ACCOUNTING

1 to provide *capital* for a business

2 to include money spent on the purchase of an *asset* as an element in a *balance sheet*

capital lease GENERAL MANAGEMENT

a lease that is treated as though the lessee had borrowed money and bought the leased assets.

If a lease agreement does not meet any of the criteria below, the lessee treats it as an *operating lease* for accounting purposes. If, however, the agreement meets one of the following criteria, it is treated as a capital lease:

1. The lease agreement transfers ownership of the assets to the lessee during the term of lease.

2. The lessee can purchase the assets leased at a bargain price (also called a bargain purchase option), such as $1, at the end of the lease term.

3. The lease term is at least 75% of the economic life of the leased asset.

4. The present value of the minimum lease payments is 90% or greater of the asset's value.

capital leases are reported by the lessee as if the assets being leased were acquired and the monthly rental payments as if they were payments of principal and interest on a debt obligation. Specifically, the lessee capitalizes the lease by recognizing an asset and a liability at the lower of the present value of the minimum lease payments or the value of the assets under lease. As the monthly rental payments are made, the corresponding liability decreases. At the same time, the leased asset is depreciated in a manner that is consistent with other owned assets having the same use and economic life.

capital levy FINANCE, BANKING, AND ACCOUNTING a tax on fixed assets or property

capital loss FINANCE, BANKING, AND ACCOUNTING a loss made through selling a *capital asset* for less than its market price

capital maintenance concept FINANCE, BANKING, AND ACCOUNTING a concept used to determine the definition of profit, that provides the basis for different systems of inflation accounting

capital market FINANCE, BANKING, AND ACCOUNTING a financial market dealing with securities that have a life of more than one year

capital project OPERATIONS & PRODUCTION see *capital project management*

capital project management FINANCE, BANKING, AND ACCOUNTING GENERAL MANAGEMENT control of a project that involves expenditure of an organization's monetary resources for the purpose of creating capacity for production. Capital project management often involves the organization of major construction or engineering work. *Capital projects* are usually large scale, complex, need to be completed quickly, and involve capital investment. Different techniques have evolved for capital project management from those used for normal *project management*, including methods for managing the complexity of such projects and for analyzing return on investment afterward.

capital property FINANCE, BANKING, AND ACCOUNTING under Canadian tax law, assets that can depreciate in value or be sold for a capital gain or loss

capital ratio FINANCE, BANKING, AND ACCOUNTING a company's income expressed as a fraction of its tangible assets

capital rationing FINANCE, BANKING, AND ACCOUNTING

1 the restriction of new investment by a company

2 a restriction on an organization's ability to invest capital funds, caused by an internal budget ceiling being imposed by management (*soft capital rationing*), or by external limitations being applied to the company, as when additional borrowed funds cannot be obtained (*hard capital rationing*)

capital reconstruction FINANCE, BANKING, AND ACCOUNTING the act of placing a company into voluntary liquidation and then selling its assets to another company with the same name and same stockholders, but with a larger capital base

capital reduction FINANCE, BANKING, AND ACCOUNTING the retirement or redemption of capital funds by a company

capital reorganization FINANCE, BANKING, AND ACCOUNTING the act of changing the capital structure of a company by amalgamating or dividing existing shares to form shares of a higher or lower nominal value

capital reserves (*U.K.*) FINANCE, BANKING, AND ACCOUNTING a former name for *undistributable reserves*

capital resource planning FINANCE, BANKING, AND ACCOUNTING the process of evaluating and selecting long-term assets to meet strategies

capital shares FINANCE, BANKING, AND ACCOUNTING shares in a mutual fund which rise in value

as the capital value of the individual stocks rises, but do not receive any income

capital stock ECONOMICS FINANCE, BANKING, AND ACCOUNTING the stock authorized by a company's charter, representing no ownership rights

capital structure FINANCE, BANKING, AND ACCOUNTING the relative proportions of equity capital and debt capital in a company's balance sheet

capital sum FINANCE, BANKING, AND ACCOUNTING a lump sum of money that an insurer pays, for example, on the death of the insured person

capital surplus FINANCE, BANKING, AND ACCOUNTING the value of all of the stock in a company that exceeds the nominal value of the stock

capital tax FINANCE, BANKING, AND ACCOUNTING a tax levied on the *capital* owned by a company, rather than on its spending

capital transactions FINANCE, BANKING, AND ACCOUNTING transactions affecting non-current items such as fixed assets, long-term debt, or share capital, rather than revenue transactions

capital transfer tax FINANCE, BANKING, AND ACCOUNTING in the United Kingdom, a tax on the transfer of assets that was replaced in 1986 by inheritance tax

capital turnover FINANCE, BANKING, AND ACCOUNTING the value of annual sales as a multiple of the value of the company's stock

capital widening ECONOMICS the process whereby capital-intensive production is reduced as a result of an increase in a country's *capital stock* and the number of people employed

CAPM *abbr* FINANCE, BANKING, AND ACCOUNTING capital asset pricing model

capped rate FINANCE, BANKING, AND ACCOUNTING an interest rate on a loan that may change, but cannot be greater than an amount fixed at the time when the loan is taken out by a borrower

captive finance company FINANCE, BANKING, AND ACCOUNTING an organization that provides credit and is owned or controlled by a commercial or manufacturing company, for example, a retailer that owns its store card operation or a car manufacturer that owns a company for financing the vehicles it produces

captive insurance company FINANCE, BANKING, AND ACCOUNTING an insurance company that has been established by a parent company to underwrite all its insurance risks and those of its subsidiaries. The benefit is that the premiums paid do not leave the organization. Many captive insurance companies are established offshore for tax purposes.

capture E-COMMERCE the submission of a credit card transaction for processing and settlement. Capture initiates the process of moving funds from the *issuer* to the *acquirer*.

carbon copy E-COMMERCE see *cc*

cardholder E-COMMERCE FINANCE, BANKING, AND ACCOUNTING an individual or company that has an active credit card account with an *issuer* with which transactions can be initiated

card-issuing bank E-COMMERCE FINANCE, BANKING, AND ACCOUNTING see *issuer*

card-not-present merchant account E-COMMERCE an account that permits e-merchants to process credit card transactions without the purchaser being physically present for the transaction

career anchor HR & PERSONNEL a guiding force that influences people's career choices, based on self-perception of their own skills, *motivation*, and values. The term was coined by *Edgar Schein* in *Career Anchors: Discovering Your Real Values*, published in 1985. He believed that people develop one underlying anchor, perhaps subconsciously, that they are unwilling to give up when faced with different pressures. Schein distinguishes several career anchor groups such as technical/functional competence, managerial *competence*, *creativity*, security or stability, and autonomy. See thinker *Edgar Schein*

career break HR & PERSONNEL a planned interruption to working life, usually for a predetermined period of time. A career break is usually designed either to aid *career development* or to enable somebody to balance work and family life. It may take the form of parental leave, or a *sabbatical* for study, research, or exploring alternative activities. A career break may be sanctioned by an employer or taken without the support of an employer.

career change HR & PERSONNEL a switch in profession or in type of job, often to a different employer. Career change may be planned as part of the continuing professional development (CPD) or *career development* processes, or it may be forced on an employee by *down-*

sizing, ill-health, or a change in personal circumstance.

career development HR & PERSONNEL progression through a sequence of jobs, involving continually more advanced or diverse activities and resulting in wider or improved skills, greater responsibility and prestige, and higher income. Formerly, career development was seen as the responsibility of the employer, and many organizations had formal career development programs that marked an employee's advancement through the levels of management. It is now more usually held to be the responsibility of the employee, sometimes as part of the *CPD* process.

career ladder HR & PERSONNEL a sequence of posts from most junior to most senior within an organization or department. A career ladder provides a structure for an employee to climb up through an organization. It is most typical of *bureaucracies*, as *flat organization* structures tend not to be hierarchical to the same extent.

career-limiting move HR & PERSONNEL see *CLM*

career path HR & PERSONNEL a planned, logical progression of jobs within one or more professions throughout working life. A career path can be planned with greater assurance in market conditions of stability and little change. In times of great change and uncertainty, some people, such as *Dominic Cadbury*, have argued that there is no longer such a thing as a planned career path and instead place greater emphasis on the importance of *CPD* in order to maintain *employability*.

career pattern HR & PERSONNEL the sequence of jobs undertaken by somebody during his or her working life. A career pattern can be structured in advance as part of *career development* planning, and may allow for *career breaks* or *career changes*. Career patterns can also be discerned more generally as trends in employee development within particular sectors of the *labor force*.

careline MARKETING a telephone service allowing customers to obtain information, advice, or assistance from retailers

caring economy ECONOMICS an economy based on amicable and helpful relationships between businesses and people

Carnegie, Dale Breckinridge (1888–1955) GENERAL MANAGEMENT U.S. writer and trainer. Best known for his advice on self-improvement, which focused on *inter-*

personal communication and effective *communication skills*, including public speaking. Carnegie's bestseller, *How to Win Friends and Influence People* (1936), included guidance on never criticizing, complaining about, or condemning another person, giving sincere appreciation to others, and stimulating in others a specific desire in order to motivate them.

carriage inward FINANCE, BANKING, AND ACCOUNTING delivery expenses incurred through the purchase of goods

carriage outward FINANCE, BANKING, AND ACCOUNTING delivery expenses incurred through the sale of goods

carrier GENERAL MANAGEMENT a telecommunications company that provides network infrastructure services and charges customers for carrying their communications over the network. Carriers do not necessarily own their own network, but may rent time on a number of networks.

carrying amount FINANCE, BANKING, AND ACCOUNTING see *book value*

carrying cost FINANCE, BANKING, AND ACCOUNTING any expense associated with holding stock for a given period, for example, from the time of delivery to the time of dispatch. Carrying costs will include storage and insurance.

carrying value FINANCE, BANKING, AND ACCOUNTING see *book value*

carryover FINANCE, BANKING, AND ACCOUNTING the stock of a commodity held at the beginning of a new fiscal year

cartel FINANCE, BANKING, AND ACCOUNTING an alliance of business companies formed to control production, competition, and prices

cartogram STATISTICS a diagrammatic map on which statistical information is represented by shading and symbols

cash

1 FINANCE, BANKING, AND ACCOUNTING to exchange a check for cash
2 ECONOMICS FINANCE, BANKING, AND ACCOUNTING *money* in the form of bank bills and coins that are legal tender. This includes cash in hand, deposits repayable on demand with any bank or other financial institution, and deposits denominated in foreign currencies.

cash account FINANCE, BANKING, AND ACCOUNTING
1 a brokerage account that permits no buying on margin

2 a record of receipts and payments of cash, checks, or other forms of money transfer

cash accounting FINANCE, BANKING, AND ACCOUNTING
1 an accounting method in which receipts and expenses are recorded in the accounting books in the period when they actually occur. See also *accrual concept*
2 in the United Kingdom, a system for Value Added Tax that enables the taxpayer to account for tax paid and received during a given period, thus allowing automatic relief for bad debts

cash advance FINANCE, BANKING, AND ACCOUNTING a loan on a credit card account

cash and carry GENERAL MANAGEMENT see *wholesaler*

cash at bank FINANCE, BANKING, AND ACCOUNTING the total amount of money held at the bank by an individual or company

cash available to invest FINANCE, BANKING, AND ACCOUNTING the amount, including cash on account and balances due soon for outstanding transactions, that a client has available for investment with a broker

cashback FINANCE, BANKING, AND ACCOUNTING MARKETING a sales promotion technique offering customers a cash refund after they buy a product

cash basis FINANCE, BANKING, AND ACCOUNTING the bookkeeping practice of accounting for money only when it is actually received or spent

cash bonus FINANCE, BANKING, AND ACCOUNTING an unscheduled dividend that a company declares because of unexpected income

cashbook FINANCE, BANKING, AND ACCOUNTING a book in which all cash payments and receipts are recorded. In a double-entry bookkeeping system, the balance at the end of a given period is included in the trial balance and then transferred to the balance sheet itself.

cash budget FINANCE, BANKING, AND ACCOUNTING a detailed budget of estimated cash inflows and outflows incorporating both revenue and capital items. Also known as *cash flow projection*

cash contract FINANCE, BANKING, AND ACCOUNTING a contract for actual delivery of a commodity

cash conversion cycle FINANCE, BANKING, AND ACCOUNTING the time between the acquisition of a raw material and the receipt of payment for the finished product. Also known as *cash cycle*

cash cow
1 MARKETING a product that sells well and makes a substantial profit without requiring much advertising or investment (*slang*)
2 FINANCE, BANKING, AND ACCOUNTING a product characterized by a high market share but low sales growth, whose function is seen as generating cash for use elsewhere within the organization
3 GENERAL MANAGEMENT see *Boston Box*

cash crop ECONOMICS a crop, for example, tobacco, that can be sold for cash, usually by a developing country

cash cycle FINANCE, BANKING, AND ACCOUNTING see *cash conversion cycle*

cash deficiency agreement FINANCE, BANKING, AND ACCOUNTING a commitment to supply whatever additional cash is needed to complete the financing of a project

cash discount FINANCE, BANKING, AND ACCOUNTING a discount offered to a customer who pays for goods or services with cash, or who pays an invoice within a particular period

cash dividend FINANCE, BANKING, AND ACCOUNTING a share of a company's current earnings or accumulated profits distributed to stockholders

cash equivalents FINANCE, BANKING, AND ACCOUNTING short-term investments that can be converted into cash immediately and that are subject to only a limited risk. There is usually a limit on their duration, for example, three months.

cash float FINANCE, BANKING, AND ACCOUNTING notes and coins held by a retailer for the purpose of supplying customers with change

cash flow FINANCE, BANKING, AND ACCOUNTING the movement through an organization of money that is generated by its own operations, as opposed to borrowing. It is the money that a business actually receives from sales (the cash inflow) and the money that it pays out (the cash outflow).

cash flow accounting FINANCE, BANKING, AND ACCOUNTING see *cash flow statement*

cash flow coverage ratio FINANCE, BANKING, AND ACCOUNTING the ratio of income to cash obligations

cash flow forecast FINANCE, BANKING, AND ACCOUNTING a prediction of the amount of money that will move through an organization. This is an important tool for monitoring its solvency. See also *cash budget*

cash flow life HR & PERSONNEL a lifestyle characterized by working for individual project fees rather than a regular salary

cash flow per common share FINANCE, BANKING, AND ACCOUNTING the amount of cash that a company has for each share of its common stock

cash flow projection FINANCE, BANKING, AND ACCOUNTING see *cash budget*

cash flow risk FINANCE, BANKING, AND ACCOUNTING the risk that a company's available cash will not be sufficient to meet its financial obligations

cash flow statement FINANCE, BANKING, AND ACCOUNTING a record of a company's cash inflows and cash outflows over a specific period of time, typically a year.

It reports funds on hand at the beginning of the period, funds received, funds spent, and funds remaining at the end of the period. Cash flows are divided into three categories: cash from operations; cash-investment activities; and cash-financing activities. Companies with holdings in foreign currencies use a fourth classification: effects of changes in currency rates on cash.

cash fraction FINANCE, BANKING, AND ACCOUNTING a small amount of cash paid to a stockholder to make up the full amount of part of a share which has been allocated in a *stock split*

cash-generating unit FINANCE, BANKING, AND ACCOUNTING the smallest identifiable group of assets that generates cash inflows and outflows that can be measured

cashier's check FINANCE, BANKING, AND ACCOUNTING a bank's own check, drawn on itself and signed by the cashier or other bank official

cashless pay HR & PERSONNEL the payment of a weekly or monthly wage through the electronic transfer of funds directly into the bank account of an employee

cashless society ECONOMICS a society in which all bills and debits are paid by electronic money media, for example, bank and credit cards, direct debits, and online payments

cash loan company (*S. Africa*) FINANCE, BANKING, AND ACCOUNTING a microlending busi-ness that provides short-term loans without collateral, usually at high interest rates

cash market FINANCE, BANKING, AND ACCOUNTING the gilt-edged securities market where purchases are paid for almost immediately, as opposed to the futures market

cash offer FINANCE, BANKING, AND ACCOUNTING an offer to buy a company for cash rather than for stock

cash payments journal FINANCE, BANKING, AND ACCOUNTING a chronological record of all the payments that have been made from a company's bank account

cash ratio FINANCE, BANKING, AND ACCOUNTING the ratio of a company's liquid assets such as cash and securities divided by total liabilities. Also known as *liquidity ratio*

cash receipts journal FINANCE, BANKING, AND ACCOUNTING a chronological record of all the receipts that have been paid into a company's bank account

cash sale FINANCE, BANKING, AND ACCOUNTING a sale in which payment is made immediately in cash rather than put on credit

cash settlement FINANCE, BANKING, AND ACCOUNTING
1 an immediate payment on an options contract without waiting for expiration of the normal, usually five-day, settlement period
2 the completion of a transaction by paying for securities

cash surrender value FINANCE, BANKING, AND ACCOUNTING the amount of money that an insurance company will pay to terminate a policy at a particular time if the policy does not continue until its normal expiration date

casual worker HR & PERSONNEL somebody who provides labor or services under an irregular or informal working arrangement. A casual worker is usually considered as an independent contractor rather than as an *employee*. Consequently, there is no obligation on the part of an employer to provide work, and there is no obligation on the part of the casual worker to accept all offers of work made by an employer.

catastrophe bond FINANCE, BANKING, AND ACCOUNTING a bond with a very high interest rate which may be worth less or give a lower rate of interest if a disaster occurs, whether it be natural or otherwise

category killer FINANCE, BANKING, AND ACCOUNTING a major organization that puts out of business smaller or more specialized companies in a given field by offering goods or services at a lower price, or by using its brand to attract more consumer interest (*slang*)

category management MARKETING the process of manufacturers and retailers working together to maximize profits and enhance customer value in any given product category. Category management has developed from *brand management* and the techniques of efficient consumer response, and is most prevalent in the fast moving consumer goods sector. It is founded on the assumption that consumer purchase decisions are made from a variety of products within a category and not merely by *brand*. It has gained in prominence, as it is believed to meet customer needs better than standard brand management. Abbr. *CM*

cats and dogs FINANCE, BANKING, AND ACCOUNTING stocks with dubious sale histories (*slang*)

causality STATISTICS the relation of events to the effects they produce

cause and effect diagram
1 GENERAL MANAGEMENT see *fishbone chart*
2 FINANCE, BANKING, AND ACCOUNTING a diagram that aids the generation and sorting of the potential causes of variation in an activity or process

CBD *abbr* GENERAL MANAGEMENT central business district: the area of a city where most company offices are located

CBI *abbr* FINANCE, BANKING, AND ACCOUNTING Confederation of British Industry

cc *abbr* E-COMMERCE carbon copy: a function included on most e-mail programs that enables Internet users to send a copy of the same message to as many people as they choose. All they need to do is place the e-mail addresses of intended recipients in the cc address line. Recipients see all other names. To conceal names, the *bcc* address line can be used.

CC *abbr* (*S. Africa*) FINANCE, BANKING, AND ACCOUNTING close corporation

CCA *abbr* FINANCE, BANKING, AND ACCOUNTING current cost accounting

CCAB *abbr* (*U.K.*) FINANCE, BANKING, AND ACCOUNTING Consultative Committee of Accountancy Bodies

ccc *abbr* (*U.K.*) FINANCE, BANKING, AND ACCOUNTING cwmni cyfyngedig cyhoeddus: the Welsh term for a public limited company

CD *abbr* FINANCE, BANKING, AND ACCOUNTING certificate of deposit

CDSC *abbr* FINANCE, BANKING, AND ACCOUNTING contingent deferred sales charge

CEIC *abbr* FINANCE, BANKING, AND ACCOUNTING closed-end investment company

ceiling effect STATISTICS the occurrence of clusters of scores near the upper limit of the data in a statistical study

cellular manufacturing OPERATIONS & PRODUCTION see *group technology*

cellular organization OPERATIONS & PRODUCTION a form of organization consisting of a collection of self-managing firms or cells held together by mutual interest. A cellular organization is built on the principles of self-organization, member ownership, and entrepreneurship. Each cell within the organization shares common features and purposes with its sister cells but is also able to function independently. The idea is an extension of the principles of *group technology*, or cellular manufacturing.

cellular production OPERATIONS & PRODUCTION see *group technology*

census STATISTICS a study in which every member of a population is observed

center FINANCE, BANKING, AND ACCOUNTING a department, area, or function to which costs and/or revenues are charged

central bank ECONOMICS the bank of a country that controls its credit system and its money supply

central business district GENERAL MANAGEMENT see *CBD*

centralization FINANCE, BANKING, AND ACCOUNTING GENERAL MANAGEMENT the gathering together, at a corporate headquarters, of specialist functions such as finance, personnel, *centralized purchasing*, and information technology. Centralization is usually undertaken in order to effect economies of scale and to standardize operating procedures throughout the organization. Centralized management can become cumbersome and inefficient, and may produce communications problems. Some organizations have shifted toward *decentralization* to try to avoid this.

centralized purchasing FINANCE, BANKING, AND ACCOUNTING OPERATIONS & PRODUCTION the control by a central department of all the purchasing undertaken within an organization. In a large organization centralized purchasing is often located in the headquarters. Centralization has the advantages of reducing duplication of effort, pooling volume purchases for discounts, enabling more effective inventory control, consolidating transport loads to achieve lower costs, increasing skills development in purchasing personnel, and enhancing relationships with *suppliers*.

Central Provident Fund HR & PERSONNEL in Singapore, a retirement benefit plan. All employees and employers make compulsory contributions each month. Abbr. *CPF*

central purchasing FINANCE, BANKING, AND ACCOUNTING purchasing organized by a company's main office on behalf of all its departments or branches

Centrelink (*ANZ*) GENERAL MANAGEMENT an Australian government authority responsible for providing access to government services, including social security allowances and employment plans. Established in 1997, it maintains a network of around 1,000 outlets.

C.E.O. *abbr* GENERAL MANAGEMENT chief executive officer

C.E.O. churning GENERAL MANAGEMENT the rapid rate at which chief executive officers are often removed from their positions (*slang*)

CER GENERAL MANAGEMENT see *Australia and New Zealand Closer Economic Relations Trade Agreement*

certificate authority E-COMMERCE an independent organization that verifies the identity of a purchaser or merchant and issues a *digital certificate* attesting to this for use in e-commerce transactions

certificate of incorporation FINANCE, BANKING, AND ACCOUNTING in the United Kingdom, a written statement by the Registrar of Companies confirming that a new company has fulfilled the necessary legal requirements for incorporation and is now legally constituted

certificate of tax deducted FINANCE, BANKING, AND ACCOUNTING in the United Kingdom, a document issued by a financial institution showing that tax has been deducted from interest payments on an account

certificate to commence business FINANCE, BANKING, AND ACCOUNTING in the United Kingdom, a written statement issued by the Registrar of Companies confirming that a public limited company has fulfilled the necessary legal requirements regarding its authorized minimum share capital

certified accountant (*U.K.*) FINANCE, BANKING, AND ACCOUNTING an accountant trained in industry, the public service, or in the offices of practicing accountants, who is a member of the *Association of Chartered Certified Accountants*. Although they are not *chartered accountants*, they fulfill much the same role and they are qualified to audit company records. Abbr. *CA*

certified public accountant FINANCE, BANKING, AND ACCOUNTING an accountant trained in industry, the public service, or in the offices of practicing accountants, who is a member of the American Institute of Certified Public Accountants. Although they are not *chartered accountants*, they fulfill much the same role and they are qualified to audit company records. Abbr. *CPA*

cessation FINANCE, BANKING, AND ACCOUNTING the discontinuation of a business for tax purposes or of its trading on the stock market

C.F.O. *abbr* GENERAL MANAGEMENT chief financial officer

CFR *abbr* E-COMMERCE cost and freight

CGI Joe HR & PERSONNEL a computer programmer who lacks social skills and charisma. The term is modeled on "GI Joe," a word for a U.S. soldier that dates from World War II; its first part is an abbreviation of computer generated imagery. (*slang*)

CGT *abbr* FINANCE, BANKING, AND ACCOUNTING capital gains tax

CH *abbr* FINANCE, BANKING, AND ACCOUNTING Companies House

chaebol GENERAL MANAGEMENT see *keiretsu*

chain of command HR & PERSONNEL the line of authority in a hierarchical organization through which instructions pass. The chain of command usually runs from the most senior personnel, through all reporting links in an organization's or department's structure, to a targeted person or to front-line employees. *Line management* relies on the chain of command in order for instructions to pass throughout an organization.

chainsaw consultant HR & PERSONNEL an outside expert brought into a company to reduce staff levels (*slang*)

chair GENERAL MANAGEMENT the most senior executive in an organization. The chair of an organization is responsible for running the **annual meeting**, and meetings of the **board of directors**. He or she may be a figurehead, appointed for prestige or power, and may have no role in the day-to-day running of the organization. Sometimes the roles of chair and **chief executive** are combined, and the chair then has more control over daily operations; sometimes the chair is a retired chief executive. In the United States, the person who performs this function is often called a **president**. Historically, the term **chairman** was more common. The terms **chairwoman** or **chairperson** are later developments, although chair is now the most generally acceptable. Chairman, however, remains in common use, especially in the corporate sector.

chairman GENERAL MANAGEMENT see **chair**

chairman's report _or_ **chairman's statement** FINANCE, BANKING, AND ACCOUNTING a statement included in the annual report of most large companies in which the chair of the board of directors gives an often favorable overview of the company's performance and prospects

chairperson GENERAL MANAGEMENT see **chair**

chairwoman GENERAL MANAGEMENT see **chair**

chamber of commerce FINANCE, BANKING, AND ACCOUNTING an organization of local businesspeople who work together to promote trade in their area and protect common interests

Champy, James (_b._ 1942) GENERAL MANAGEMENT U.S. consultant. See also **Hammer, Michael**

Chancellor of the Exchequer FINANCE, BANKING, AND ACCOUNTING the United Kingdom's chief finance minister, based at **HM Treasury** in London. The office of Chancellor dates back to the 13th century. Some of the most famous names in British politics have served in this very senior government position, including William Gladstone and Lloyd George.

Chandler, Alfred D. (_b._ 1918) GENERAL MANAGEMENT U.S. academic. Pioneer of business history who established a framework and rationale for the subject and suggested that the main function of an organization is to implement **strategy**. In _Strategy and Structure_ (1962), he argued that the optimum use of resources stemmed not merely from the way they were organized but, more importantly, from the organization's strategic goals. He concluded that organizational structures are driven by the changing demands and pressures of the

marketplace, and that market-driven organizations favor a loosely coupled divisional structure. See thinker **Alfred D. Chandler, Jr.**

change agent GENERAL MANAGEMENT see **change management**

change management GENERAL MANAGEMENT the coordination of a structured period of transition from situation A to situation B in order to achieve lasting change within an organization. Change management can be of varying scope, from **continuous improvement**, which involves small ongoing changes to existing processes, to radical and substantial change involving organizational strategy. Change management can be reactive or proactive. It can be instigated in reaction to something in an organization's external environment, for example, in the realms of economics, politics, legislation, or competition, or in reaction to something within the processes, structures, people, and events of the organization's internal environment. It may also be instigated as a proactive measure, for example, in anticipation of unfavorable economic conditions in the future. Change management usually follows five steps: recognition of a trigger indicating that change is needed; clarification of the end point, or "where we want to be"; planning how to achieve the change; accomplishment of the transition; and maintenance to ensure the change is lasting. Effective change management involves alterations on a personal level, for example, a shift in attitudes or work routines, and thus personnel management skills such as **motivation** are vital to successful change. Other important influences on the success of change management include leadership style, communication, and a unified positive attitude to the change among the workforce. **Business process reengineering** is one type of change management, involving the redesign of processes within an organization to raise performance. **Change agents** are those people within an organization who are leaders and champions of the change process. With the accelerating pace of change in the business environment in the 1990s and 2000s, change has become accepted as a fact of business life and is the subject of books on management. See checklist **Motivating Your Staff in a Time of Change**

changeover time FINANCE, BANKING, AND ACCOUNTING the period required to change a workstation from a state of readiness for one operation to a state of readiness for another

channel MARKETING a method of selling and distributing products to customers, directly or through intermediaries. Channels include

direct sales, retail outlets, the Internet, and wholesalers.

channel communications MARKETING communications aimed at organizations that sell and distribute products to customers, for example, retailers, sales teams, or wholesalers

channel management MARKETING the organization of the ways in which companies reach and satisfy their customers. Channel management involves more than just distribution, and has been described as management of how and where a product is used and of how the customer and the product interact. Channel management covers processes for identifying key customers, communicating with them, and continuing to create value after the first contact.

channel strategy MARKETING a management technique for determining the most effective method of selling and distributing products to customers

channel stuffing FINANCE, BANKING, AND ACCOUNTING the artificial boosting of sales at the end of a fiscal year by offering distributors and dealers incentives to buy a greater quantity of goods than they actually need (_slang_)

channel support MARKETING marketing or financial support aimed at improving the performance of organizations that sell and distribute products to customers, for example, retailers, sales teams, or wholesalers

chaos

1 GENERAL MANAGEMENT a situation of unpredictability and rapid change. **Chaos theory** emerged in the 1970s as a mathematical concept that defied the theory of cause and effect to assert that behavior is essentially random. Such writers as **Tom Peters**, who wrote _Thriving on Chaos_ in 1987, have applied the theory to management, arguing that attempts to plan and control management processes are fundamentally doomed to failure and that, instead, managers should embrace change and flexibility in order to cope with an environment that is altering at an ever-increasing rate. **2** STATISTICS a situation in which a deterministic model displays behavior that appears to be random

chaos theory GENERAL MANAGEMENT see **chaos**

CHAPS _abbr_ FINANCE, BANKING, AND ACCOUNTING Clearing House Automated Payment System: a method for the rapid electronic transfer of funds between participating banks on behalf of large commercial customers, where transfers tend to be of significant value

Chapter 11 FINANCE, BANKING, AND ACCOUNTING the U.S. Bankruptcy Reform Act (1978) that entitles enterprises experiencing financial difficulties to apply for protection from creditors and thus have an opportunity to avoid bankruptcy

charge FINANCE, BANKING, AND ACCOUNTING a legal interest in land or real estate created in favor of a creditor to ensure that the amount owing is paid off

chargeable asset FINANCE, BANKING, AND ACCOUNTING an asset which will produce a capital gain when sold. Assets which are not chargeable include family homes, cars, and some types of investments, such as government stocks.

chargeable gain (*U.K.*) FINANCE, BANKING, AND ACCOUNTING a *profit* from the sale of an *asset* that is subject to capital gains tax

chargeable transfer FINANCE, BANKING, AND ACCOUNTING in the United Kingdom, gifts that are liable to inheritance tax

charge account FINANCE, BANKING, AND ACCOUNTING a facility with a retailer that enables the customer to buy goods or services on credit rather than pay in cash. The customer may be required to settle the account within a month to avoid incurring interest on the credit. Also known as *credit account*

charge and discharge accounting FINANCE, BANKING, AND ACCOUNTING formerly, a bookkeeping system in which a person charges himself or herself with receipts and credits himself or herself with payments. This system was used extensively in medieval times before the advent of double-entry bookkeeping.

chargee FINANCE, BANKING, AND ACCOUNTING
1 a person who holds a charge over a property
2 a person who has the right to force a debtor to pay

charismatic authority GENERAL MANAGEMENT a style of *leadership* based on the leader's exceptional personal qualities. Charismatic authority is one of *Max Weber*'s three types of legitimate *authority*. A charismatic leader is set apart from others by special qualities that inspire employees to follow and obey of their own free will. This is similar to the *great man theory* of leadership. See thinker *Max Weber*

charitable contribution FINANCE, BANKING, AND ACCOUNTING a donation by a company to a charity

charity accounts FINANCE, BANKING, AND ACCOUNTING the accounting records of a charitable institution, that include a statement of financial activities rather than a profit and loss account. In the United Kingdom, the accounts should conform to the requirements stipulated in the Charities Act (1993).

chartered accountant FINANCE, BANKING, AND ACCOUNTING in the United Kingdom, a qualified professional accountant who is a member of an Institute of Chartered Accountants. Chartered accountants are qualified to audit company accounts and some hold management positions in companies. Abbr *CA*

Chartered Association of Certified Accountants (*U.K.*) FINANCE, BANKING, AND ACCOUNTING the former name of the Association of Chartered Certified Accountants

chartered company or **chartered entity** FINANCE, BANKING, AND ACCOUNTING in the United Kingdom, an organization formed by the grant of a royal charter. The charter authorizes the entity to operate and states the powers specifically granted.

Chartered Institute of Management Accountants FINANCE, BANKING, AND ACCOUNTING see *CIMA*

Chartered Institute of Public Finance and Accountancy FINANCE, BANKING, AND ACCOUNTING see *CIPFA*

Chartered Institute of Taxation FINANCE, BANKING, AND ACCOUNTING in the United Kingdom, an organization for professionals in the field of taxation, formerly the Institute of Taxation

charter value FINANCE, BANKING, AND ACCOUNTING the value of a bank being able to continue to do business in the future, reflected as part of its share price

charting FINANCE, BANKING, AND ACCOUNTING the use of charts to analyze stock market trends and to forecast future rises or falls

chartist FINANCE, BANKING, AND ACCOUNTING an analyst who studies past stock market trends, the movement of stock prices, and changes in the accounting ratios of individual companies. The chartist's philosophy is that history repeats itself: using charts and graphs, he or she uses past trends and repetitive patterns to forecast the future. Although the chartist approach is considered narrower than that of a traditional analyst, it nevertheless has a good following.

chase demand plan OPERATIONS & PRODUCTION a *production control* plan that attempts to match *capacity* to the varying levels of forecast demand. Chase demand plans require *flexible working* practices and place varying demands on equipment requirements. Pure chase demand plans are difficult to achieve and are most commonly found in operations where output cannot be stored or where the organization is seeking to eliminate stores of finished goods.

chat system E-COMMERCE a system that enables Internet users to engage in text-based communication in real time. Messages posted via a chat system will be seen by every member of the participating group. It is a useful means for an organization to take the pulse of consumers to find out what they are thinking, and to generate unique content.

Online chat can be particularly effective when there is a specific event occurring that is of interest to people, or when an expert can be made available to talk about a subject or product. To be productive, online chat needs to be well moderated, and is really only suited to small groups of people (2 to 20) at any one time.

cheap money FINANCE, BANKING, AND ACCOUNTING low interest rates, used as a government strategy to stimulate an economy either at the initial signs of, or during, a recession

check FINANCE, BANKING, AND ACCOUNTING an order in writing requiring the banker to pay on demand a certain sum in money to a specified person or bearer. Although a check can theoretically be written on anything—in a P.G. Woodhouse story, one was written on the side of a cow—banks issue preprinted, customized forms for completion by an account holder who inserts the date, the name of the person to be paid (the payee), the amount in both words and figures, and his or her signature. The customer is the drawer. U.K. term *cheque*

check digit FINANCE, BANKING, AND ACCOUNTING the last digit of a string of computerized reference numbers, used to validate a transaction

checking account FINANCE, BANKING, AND ACCOUNTING a bank account in which deposits can be withdrawn at any time, but do not usually earn interest, except in the case of some online accounts. It is the most common type of bank account. U.K. term *current account*

check register FINANCE, BANKING, AND ACCOUNTING a control record of checks issued or received

cheque FINANCE, BANKING, AND ACCOUNTING = *check*

cherry picking GENERAL MANAGEMENT the selection of what is perceived to be the best or most valuable from a series of ideas or options

CHESS GENERAL MANAGEMENT Clearing House Electronic Subregister System: a centralized electronic stock transfer and settlement system operated by the Australian Stock Exchange. It issues stockholders with regular holding statements.

chief executive GENERAL MANAGEMENT the person with overall responsibility for ensuring that the daily operations of an organization run efficiently and for carrying out strategic plans. The chief executive of an organization normally sits on the **board of directors**. In a limited company, he or she is usually known as a **managing director**.

chief executive officer GENERAL MANAGEMENT the highest ranking executive officer within a company or corporation, who has responsibility for overall management of its day-to-day affairs under the supervision of the board of directors. Abbr. **C.E.O.**

chief financial officer GENERAL MANAGEMENT the officer in an organization responsible for handling funds, signing checks, the keeping of financial records, and financial planning for the company. Abbr. **C.F.O.**

chief information officer GENERAL MANAGEMENT the officer in an organization responsible for its internal information systems and sometimes for its e-business infrastructure. Abbr. **C.I.O.**

chief operating officer GENERAL MANAGEMENT the officer in a corporation responsible for its day-to-day management, usually reporting to the chief executive officer. Abbr. **C.O.O.**

chief technology officer *or* **chief technical officer** GENERAL MANAGEMENT the officer in an organization responsible for research and development and possibly for new product plans. Abbr. **C.T.O.**

childcare provision HR & PERSONNEL a **personnel policy** to supply or to help toward the cost of care for the children of employees during working hours. The goal of childcare provision is to enable primary caregivers to return to work despite childcare responsibilities. It may apply to children of all ages and can be implemented in a single program or as a combination of options, for example, by setting up a workplace nursery or giving childcare vouchers or allowances. To comply with **equal opportunities** legislation, childcare provision has to be made available to both male and female employees.

Chinese wall FINANCE, BANKING, AND ACCOUNTING GENERAL MANAGEMENT the procedures enforced within a securities firm to prevent the exchange of confidential information between the firm's departments so as to avoid the illegal use of inside information

chit
call in chits GENERAL MANAGEMENT to ask favors from people indebted to you (*slang*)

chose in action FINANCE, BANKING, AND ACCOUNTING a personal right which can be enforced or claimed as if it were property, such as a patent, copyright, debt, or check

chose in possession FINANCE, BANKING, AND ACCOUNTING a physical item which can be owned, such as a piece of furniture

churn
1 FINANCE, BANKING, AND ACCOUNTING to encourage an investor to change stock frequently because the broker is paid every time there is a change in the investor's portfolio (*slang*)
2 GENERAL MANAGEMENT to suffer a high labor turnover rate, especially in areas such as call centers or at chief executive level in large companies
3 GENERAL MANAGEMENT to purchase a quick succession of products or services without displaying loyalty to any of them, often as a result of competitive marketing strategies that continually undercut rival prices, thus encouraging customers to switch brands constantly in order to take advantage of the cheapest or most attractive offers

churn rate
1 FINANCE, BANKING, AND ACCOUNTING a measure of the frequency and volume of trading of stocks and bonds in a brokerage account
2 GENERAL MANAGEMENT the rate at which new customers try a product or service and then stop using it

chute
right out of the chute HR & PERSONNEL extremely inexperienced (*slang*)

CICA *abbr* FINANCE, BANKING, AND ACCOUNTING Canadian Institute of Chartered Accountants

CIF *abbr* E-COMMERCE cost, insurance, and freight

cigar
close, but no cigar GENERAL MANAGEMENT almost correct, but not quite. The term refers to the fact that cigar smoking is seen by many businesspeople as a symbol of the celebration of a success. (*slang*)

CIMA *abbr* (*U.K.*) FINANCE, BANKING, AND ACCOUNTING Chartered Institute of Management Accountants: an organization that is internationally recognized as offering a financial degree for business, focusing on strategic business management. Founded in 1919 as the Institute of Cost and Works Accountants, it has offices worldwide, supporting over 128,000 members and students in 156 countries.

C.I.O. *abbr* GENERAL MANAGEMENT chief information officer

CIPFA *abbr* FINANCE, BANKING, AND ACCOUNTING Chartered Institute of Public Finance and Accountancy: in the United Kingdom, one of the leading professional accountancy bodies and the only one that specializes in the public services, for example, local government, public service bodies, and national audit agencies, as well as major accounting firms. It is responsible for the education and training of professional accountants and for their regulation through the setting and monitoring of professional standards. CIPFA also provides a variety of advisory, information, and consulting services to public service organizations. It is the leading independent commentator on managing accounting for public money.

circle the drain GENERAL MANAGEMENT to be on the brink of complete failure (*slang*)

circuit breaker FINANCE, BANKING, AND ACCOUNTING a rule created by the major U.S. stock exchanges and the **Securities and Exchange Commission** by which trading is halted during times of extreme price fluctuations (*slang*)

circular file GENERAL MANAGEMENT a wastebasket in an office (*slang*)

circular flow of income ECONOMICS a model of a country's economy showing the flow of resources when consumers' wages and salaries are used to buy goods and so generate income for manufacturing firms

circularization of debtors FINANCE, BANKING, AND ACCOUNTING the sending of letters by a company's auditors to debtors in order to verify the existence and extent of the company's assets

circular letter of credit FINANCE, BANKING, AND ACCOUNTING a letter of credit sent to all branches of the bank which issues it

circular merger GENERAL MANAGEMENT see *merger*

circulating capital FINANCE, BANKING, AND ACCOUNTING = *working capital*

circulation MARKETING the number of copies sold or distributed of a single issue of a newspaper or magazine

circulation of capital FINANCE, BANKING, AND ACCOUNTING the movement of capital from one investment to another

City Code on Takeovers and Mergers FINANCE, BANKING, AND ACCOUNTING in the United Kingdom, a code issued on behalf of the Panel on Takeovers and Mergers that is designed principally to ensure fair and equal treatment of all stockholders in relation to takeovers. The Code also provides an orderly framework within which takeovers are conducted. It is not concerned with the financial or commercial advantages or disadvantages of a takeover, nor with those issues, such as competition policy, which are the responsibility of the government. The Code represents the collective opinion of those professionally involved in the field of takeovers on how fairness to stockholders can be achieved in practice.

claim FINANCE, BANKING, AND ACCOUNTING an official request for money, usually in the form of compensation, from an individual or organization

claims adjuster FINANCE, BANKING, AND ACCOUNTING somebody who determines the value of a claim made under an insurance policy. U.K. term *loss adjuster*

class action FINANCE, BANKING, AND ACCOUNTING a civil law action taken by a group of individuals who have a common grievance against an individual, organization, or legal entity

classical economics ECONOMICS a theory focusing on the functioning of a market economy and providing a rudimentary explanation of consumer and producer behavior in particular markets. The theory postulates that, over time, the economy would tend to operate at full employment because increases in supply would create corresponding increases in demand.

classical system of corporation tax FINANCE, BANKING, AND ACCOUNTING a system in which companies and their owners are liable for corporation tax as separate entities. A company's taxed income is therefore paid out to stockholders, who are in turn taxed again. This system operates in the United States and the Netherlands. It was replaced in the United Kingdom in 1973 by an *imputation system*.

classified advertising MARKETING advertising placed in newspapers or magazines under specific categories, for example, cars or real estate

classified stock FINANCE, BANKING, AND ACCOUNTING a company's *common stock* divided into classes such as Class A and Class B

class interval STATISTICS any of the intervals of the frequency distribution in a set of statistical observations

class of assets FINANCE, BANKING, AND ACCOUNTING the grouping of similar assets into categories. This is done because, under International Accounting Standards Committee rules, *tangible assets* and *intangible assets* cannot be revalued on an individual basis, only in a class of assets.

clean float ECONOMICS a floating exchange rate that is allowed to vary without any intervention from the country's monetary authorities

clean opinion *or* **clean report** FINANCE, BANKING, AND ACCOUNTING an auditor's report that is not qualified

clean surplus concept FINANCE, BANKING, AND ACCOUNTING the idea that a company's income statement should show the totality of gains and losses, without any of them being taken directly to equity

clearing bank FINANCE, BANKING, AND ACCOUNTING a bank that deals with other banks through a clearing house in the United Kingdom

clearing house
1 E-COMMERCE see *acquirer*
2 FINANCE, BANKING, AND ACCOUNTING an institution that settles accounts between banks

Clearing House Automated Payment System FINANCE, BANKING, AND ACCOUNTING see *CHAPS*

clearing system FINANCE, BANKING, AND ACCOUNTING the system of settling accounts among banks

clear title FINANCE, BANKING, AND ACCOUNTING see *good title*

clerical work improvement program GENERAL MANAGEMENT a *clerical work measurement* technique that applies *standard time* data to clerical and administrative jobs, the objective of which is to ensure higher productivity and greater efficiency

clerical work measurement GENERAL MANAGEMENT an umbrella term for a collection of methods for measuring administrative and clerical work activities. Clerical work measurement is a variation on conventional *work measurement* practices. The main clerical work measurement techniques include *clerical work improvement programs* and *group capacity assessment*.

CLI *abbr* GENERAL MANAGEMENT calling line identification

clickable corporation E-COMMERCE a company that operates on the Internet

click rate E-COMMERCE see *click-through rate*

clicks-and-bricks *or* **clicks-and-mortar**
1 GENERAL MANAGEMENT a business strategy that involves combining traditional retail outlets with online commerce
2 E-COMMERCE combining a traditional *bricks-and-mortar* organization with the click technology of the Internet. Such an organization has both a virtual and a physical presence. Examples include retailers with physical shops and also Web sites where their goods can be bought online.

clickstream E-COMMERCE the virtual trail that a user leaves behind while surfing the Internet. A clickstream is a record of a user's activity on the Internet, including every Web page visited, how long each page is visited for, and the order in which the pages are visited. Both *ISPs* and individual Web sites are able to track an Internet user's clickstream.

click-through E-COMMERCE the selection of an ad by clicking on the banner or other on-screen device to take the user to the advertiser's Web site. The number of times users click on an ad can be counted, the total number of click-throughs being a measure of the success of the ad. Also known as *ad click*, *ad transfer*

click-through rate E-COMMERCE the percentage of ad views that result in a click-through, a measure of the success of the ad in enticing users to the advertiser's Web site. Also known as *ad click rate*, *click rate*

click wrap agreement *or* **click wrap license** E-COMMERCE a contract presented entirely over

the Internet, the purchaser indicating assent to be bound by the terms of the contract by clicking on an "I agree" button. The term stems from "shrink wrap" agreements, licenses that become enforceable when the user removes designated packaging containing a copy of the agreement. Also known as *point and click agreement*

client
1 E-COMMERCE see *server*
2 MARKETING a person or organization that employs the services of a professional person or organization

client base MARKETING the regular *clients* of a professional person or organization

clientele effect FINANCE, BANKING, AND AC-COUNTING the preference of an investor or group of investors for buying a particular type of security

clinical trial STATISTICS a statistical study of human subjects to determine the effectiveness of a medical treatment

Clintonomics ECONOMICS the policy of former President Clinton's Council of Economic Advisors to intervene in the economy to correct market failures and redistribute income

CLM *abbr* HR & PERSONNEL career-limiting move: an action that could endanger your career prospects, for example, criticizing your boss publicly (*slang*)

CLOB International FINANCE, BANKING, AND ACCOUNTING in Singapore, a mechanism for buying and selling foreign stocks, especially Malaysian stocks

clock in
1 (*U.K.*) GENERAL MANAGEMENT to register arrival at work without actually inserting a card into a time clock (*slang*)
2 (*U.K.*) HR & PERSONNEL to register your arrival for work by inserting a card into a machine to record the time. Clocking in is a method of officially monitoring employees' *time keeping*.

close company *or* **closed company** (*U.K.*) FI-NANCE, BANKING, AND ACCOUNTING GENERAL MAN-AGEMENT a company in which five or fewer people control more than half the voting shares, or in which such control is exercised by any number of people who are also directors

close corporation *or* **closed corporation**
1 FINANCE, BANKING, AND ACCOUNTING GENERAL MANAGEMENT a public corporation in which all of the voting shares are held by a few stock-

holders, for example, management or family members. Although it is a public company, shares would not normally be available for trading because of a lack of liquidity.
2 (*S. Africa*) FINANCE, BANKING, AND ACCOUNTING a business registered in terms of the Close Corporations Act of 1984, consisting of not more than 10 members who share its ownership and management. Abbr. *CC*

closed-door policy GENERAL MANAGEMENT see *open-door policy*

closed economy ECONOMICS an economic system in which little or no external trade takes place

closed-end credit FINANCE, BANKING, AND AC-COUNTING GENERAL MANAGEMENT a loan, plus any interest and finance charges, that is to be repaid in full by a specified future date. Loans that have real estate or motor vehicles as collateral are usually closed-end. See also *open-end credit*

closed-end fund *or* **closed-end investment company** FINANCE, BANKING, AND ACCOUNTING an investment company such as an investment trust that has a fixed number of shares. See also *open-end fund*

closed-end investment company FINANCE, BANKING, AND ACCOUNTING see *closed-end fund* Abbr. *CEIC*

closed-end mortgage FINANCE, BANKING, AND ACCOUNTING a mortgage in which no prepayment is allowed. See also *open-end mortgage*

closed-loop production system OPERATIONS & PRODUCTION an environmentally friendly production system in which any industrial output is capable of being recycled to create another product

closed-loop system FINANCE, BANKING, AND AC-COUNTING a management control system which includes a provision for corrective action, taken on either a feedforward or a feedback basis

closed mortgage FINANCE, BANKING, AND ACCOUNTING see *closed-end mortgage*

closed shop HR & PERSONNEL an agreement requiring members of a particular group of employees to be or to become members of a specified *labor union*

closely held corporation FINANCE, BANKING, AND ACCOUNTING a company whose stock is publicly traded but held by very few people

closely held shares FINANCE, BANKING, AND ACCOUNTING shares that are publicly traded but held by very few people

Closer Economic Relations agreement FINANCE, BANKING, AND ACCOUNTING see *Australia and New Zealand Closer Economic Relations Trade Agreement*

closing balance FINANCE, BANKING, AND AC-COUNTING
1 the amount in credit or debit in a bank account at the end of a business day
2 the difference between credits and debits in a ledger at the end of one accounting period that is carried forward to the next

closing bell FINANCE, BANKING, AND ACCOUNTING the end of a trading session at a stock or commodities exchange

closing entries FINANCE, BANKING, AND AC-COUNTING in a double-entry bookkeeping system, entries made at the very end of an accounting period to balance the expense and revenue ledgers

closing price FINANCE, BANKING, AND ACCOUNT-ING the price of the last transaction for a particular security or commodity at the end of a trading session

closing quote FINANCE, BANKING, AND ACCOUNT-ING the last bid and offer prices recorded at the close of a trading session

closing rate FINANCE, BANKING, AND ACCOUNTING the exchange rate of two or more currencies at the close of business of a balance sheet date, for example, at the end of the fiscal year

closing rate method (*U.K.*) FINANCE, BANKING, AND ACCOUNTING a technique for translating the figures from a set of financial statements into a different currency using the *closing rate*. This method is often used for the accounts of a foreign subsidiary of a parent company.

closing sale FINANCE, BANKING, AND ACCOUNTING a sale that reduces the risk that the seller has through holding a greater number of shares or a longer term contract

closing stock FINANCE, BANKING, AND ACCOUNT-ING a business's remaining stock at the end of an accounting period. It includes finished products, raw materials, or work in progress and is deducted from the period's costs in the balance sheets.

club culture GENERAL MANAGEMENT a *corporate culture* in which all lines of communication

lead formally or informally to the leader. Club culture was identified by **Charles Handy**. See thinker **Charles Handy**

cluster analysis GENERAL MANAGEMENT a statistical method used to analyze complex data and identify groupings that share common features. Cluster analysis is a form of **multivariate analysis** that attempts to explain variability in a set of data. It involves finding unifying elements that enable identification of groups or clusters displaying common characteristics. It could be used, for example, to analyze results of **attitude research** and delineate groups of respondents that share certain attitudes.

clustered data STATISTICS data in which sampling units in a study are grouped into clusters sharing a common feature, or longitudinal data in which clusters are defined by repeated measures on the unit

cluster sampling OPERATIONS & PRODUCTION see **random sampling**

Clutterbuck, David (*b.* 1947) GENERAL MANAGEMENT British academic. Best known for his work on **mentoring**, and his research, with Walter Goldsmith, on consistently high-performing companies. Their findings were published in *The Winning Streak* (1984), which was viewed as the British equivalent of **Tom Peters**'s and **Robert Waterman**'s *In Search of Excellence* (1982).

CM *abbr* GENERAL MANAGEMENT category management

CN *abbr* FINANCE, BANKING, AND ACCOUNTING credit note

CNC *abbr* FINANCE, BANKING, AND ACCOUNTING Conseil National de la Comptabilité

CNCC *abbr* FINANCE, BANKING, AND ACCOUNTING Compagnie Nationale des Commissaires aux Comptes

coaching HR & PERSONNEL the development of somebody's skills and knowledge through one-to-one **training**. Coaching is usually conducted by a more senior and experienced colleague. It involves planned training activities that have measurable outcomes and is designed to facilitate learning by providing guidance and support as well as tutoring. **Executive coaching** is a form of coaching used with senior managers.

COAG *abbr* GENERAL MANAGEMENT Council of Australian Governments

COB *abbr* FINANCE, BANKING, AND ACCOUNTING Commission des Opérations de Bourse

cobrowsing E-COMMERCE a facility that enables two or more Web users to synchronize their **browsers**, so that they can see the same Web pages at the same time.

Frequently employed by customer support services, cobrowsing means that a customer service representative, using **live chat** or the telephone, can take a customer through a process, changing the customer's Web page as they change their own. It is a particularly valuable feature if complex processes and information have to be delivered. Also known as **page pushing**

cobweb site E-COMMERCE an Internet site that has not been updated for a long time (*slang*)

codec E-COMMERCE either a hardware or a software component, used in **videoconferencing**, that compresses and decompresses the audio and video signals. Hardware codecs are generally faster.

code of conduct GENERAL MANAGEMENT a statement and description of required behaviors, responsibilities, and actions expected of employees of an organization or of members of a professional body. A code of conduct usually focuses on ethical and socially responsible issues and applies to individuals, providing guidance on how to act in cases of doubt or confusion.

code of practice GENERAL MANAGEMENT a policy statement and description of preferred methods for organizational **procedures**.

Codes of practice may govern procedures for industrial relations, health and safety, and, more recently, customer service and professional development. An agreed code of practice enables activities to be carried out to a required organizational standard and provides a basis for dispute resolution.

coefficient of variation STATISTICS a measure of the spread of a set of statistical data, calculated as the mean or standard deviation of the data multiplied by 100

co-financing FINANCE, BANKING, AND ACCOUNTING the joint provision of money for a project by two or more parties

COGS *abbr* FINANCE, BANKING, AND ACCOUNTING cost of goods sold

coherence STATISTICS a measure of the strength of association between two time series

cohesion fund FINANCE, BANKING, AND ACCOUNTING GENERAL MANAGEMENT the main financial instrument for reducing economic and social disparities within the European Union by providing financial help for projects in the fields of the environment and transport infrastructure

cohort STATISTICS a group of individuals in a statistical study that have a common characteristic

cohort study STATISTICS a study in which a group of individuals, such as children with the same birth date, are observed over several years

coincidence STATISTICS the occurrence of events that are related but have no apparent common cause

COLA *abbr* FINANCE, BANKING, AND ACCOUNTING cost-of-living adjustment

cold calling MARKETING the practice of making unsolicited calls to customers or consumers in an attempt to sell products or services. Cold calling is disliked, particularly by individual consumers, and is an inefficient way of selling, as the take-up rate is very low.

cold transfer GENERAL MANAGEMENT an incoming phone call that is transferred by an operator without giving any notice or explanation to the caller or to the recipient of the call (*slang*)

collaborative working HR & PERSONNEL a method of working in which people at different locations or from different organizations work together electronically using **videoconferencing**, **e-mail**, networks, and other communication tools

collar FINANCE, BANKING, AND ACCOUNTING a contractually imposed lower limit on a financial instrument

collateral FINANCE, BANKING, AND ACCOUNTING property or goods used as security against a loan and forfeited to the lender if the borrower defaults

collateralize FINANCE, BANKING, AND ACCOUNTING to secure a loan by pledging assets. If the borrower defaults on loan payments, the pledged assets can be taken by the lender.

collateral trust certificate FINANCE, BANKING, AND ACCOUNTING a bond for which stock in another company, usually a subsidiary, is used as collateral

collecting bank FINANCE, BANKING, AND ACCOUNTING a bank into which a person has deposited a check, and which has the duty to collect the money from the account of the writer of the check

collection agency FINANCE, BANKING, AND ACCOUNTING a business that collects payments on unpaid loans or on bills

collection ratio FINANCE, BANKING, AND ACCOUNTING the average number of days it takes a firm to convert its accounts receivable into cash.

Ideally, this period should be decreasing or constant. A low figure means the company collects its outstanding receivables quickly. Collection ratios are usually reviewed quarterly or yearly.

Calculating the collection ratio requires three figures: total accounts receivable, total credit sales for the period analyzed, and the number of days in the period (annual, 365; six months, 182; quarter, 91). The formula is:

Accounts receivable / Total credit sales for the period × Number of days in the period

For example: if total receivables are $4,500,000, total credit sales in a quarter are $9,000,000, and number of days is 91, then:

4,500,000 / 9,000,000 × 91 = 45.5

Thus, it takes an average of 45.5 days to collect receivables.

Properly evaluating a collection ratio requires a standard for comparison. A traditional rule of thumb is that it should not exceed a third to a half of selling terms. For instance, if terms are 30 days, an acceptable collection ratio would be 40 to 45 days.

Companies use collection ratio information with an *accounts receivable aging* report. This lists four categories of receivables: 0–30 days, 30–60 days, 60–90 days, and over 90 days. The report also shows the percentage of total accounts receivable that each group represents, allowing for an analysis of delinquencies and potential bad debts. Also known as *days' sales outstanding*

collective agreement HR & PERSONNEL a contract between a *labor union* and an employer, resulting from *collective bargaining* and covering *conditions of employment* and procedural arrangements for resolving disputes. In the United Kingdom, a collective agreement is not legally binding unless it is in writing and specifically states the parties' intention to be bound. An agreement can become legally binding by being incorporated into an employee's personal *contract of employment*. Agreements may be concluded at organization or industry level.

collective bargaining HR & PERSONNEL negotiations about *conditions of employment* between an employer, a group of employers or their representatives, and employees' representatives such as a *labor union* with a view to reaching a *collective agreement*

collocation hosting E-COMMERCE a *hosting option* which involves a customer placing their own servers with a hosting vendor. The customer manages everything that happens on their servers: content, software, and the hardware itself. The hosting provider supplies an agreed speed of access to the Internet and amount of *data transfer*, and usually some minimum service, such as ensuring that the customer's server is up and running, and rebooting it if necessary.

collusive tendering FINANCE, BANKING, AND ACCOUNTING the illegal practice among companies making tenders for a job of sharing inside information between themselves, with the objective of fixing the end result

colocation E-COMMERCE the sharing of the facilities of a hosting center with other Internet clients

combat pay FINANCE, BANKING, AND ACCOUNTING extra tax-free pay that members of the United States armed forces are awarded while on duty in combat zones

combination annuity FINANCE, BANKING, AND ACCOUNTING see *annuity*

combination bond FINANCE, BANKING, AND ACCOUNTING a government bond for which the collateral is both revenue from the financed project and the government's credit

combined financial statement FINANCE, BANKING, AND ACCOUNTING a written record covering the assets, liabilities, net worth, and operating statement of two or more related or affiliated companies

COMEX *abbr* FINANCE, BANKING, AND ACCOUNTING commodity exchange

comfort letter FINANCE, BANKING, AND ACCOUNTING

1 in the United States, a statement from an accounting firm provided to a company preparing for a public offering, that confirms that the unaudited financial information in the prospectus follows Generally Accepted Accounting Principles

2 a letter from the parent company of a subsidiary that is applying for a loan, stating the intention that the subsidiary should remain in business

command and control approach GENERAL MANAGEMENT a style of leadership that uses standards, *procedures*, and output statistics to regulate the organization. A command and control approach to leadership is authoritative in nature and uses a *top-down approach*, which fits well in bureaucratic organizations in which privilege and power are vested in *senior management*. It is founded on, and emphasizes a distinction between, executives on the one hand and workers on the other. It stems from the principles of *Frederick Winslow Taylor*, and the applications of *Henry Ford* and *Alfred P. Sloan, Jr.* As more empowered, *flat organizations* have come to the fore, command and control leaders have been increasingly criticized for stifling creativity and limiting flexibility. See thinker *Frederick Winslow Taylor*

command economy ECONOMICS an economy in which all economic activity is regulated by the government, as in the former Soviet Union or China

commerce FINANCE, BANKING, AND ACCOUNTING the large-scale buying and selling of goods and services, usually applied to trading between different states or countries

commerce integration FINANCE, BANKING, AND ACCOUNTING the blending of Internet-based commerce capabilities with the *legacy systems* of a traditional business to create a seamless transparent process

commerce server E-COMMERCE

1 a computer in a network that maintains all transactional and backend data for an e-commerce Web site

2 a networked computer that contains the programs required to process transactions via the Internet, including dynamic inventory databases, shopping cart software, and online payment systems

commerce service provider E-COMMERCE an organization or company that provides a service to a company to facilitate some aspect of electronic commerce, for example, by functioning as an Internet *payment gateway*. Abbr. *CSP*

commercial

1 FINANCE, BANKING, AND ACCOUNTING relating to the buying and selling of goods and services

2 MARKETING an advertising message that is broadcast on television or radio

commercial bank FINANCE, BANKING, AND ACCOUNTING a bank that provides financial services to individuals and businesses, for example checking and savings accounts and loans. See also *investment bank*

commercial exposure potential MARKETING the estimated number of possible recipients of a commercial message

commercial hedger FINANCE, BANKING, AND ACCOUNTING a company that holds options in the commodities it produces

commercialization FINANCE, BANKING, AND ACCOUNTING the application of business principles to something in order to run it as a business

commercial law FINANCE, BANKING, AND ACCOUNTING GENERAL MANAGEMENT the body of law that deals with the rules and institutions of commercial transactions, including banking, commerce, contracts, copyrights, insolvency, insurance, patents, trademarks, shipping, storage, transportation, and warehousing

commercial loan FINANCE, BANKING, AND ACCOUNTING a short-term renewable loan or line of credit used to finance the seasonal or cyclical working capital needs of a company

commercial mortgage-backed securities FINANCE, BANKING, AND ACCOUNTING stocks which are backed by the security of a commercial mortgage

commercial paper FINANCE, BANKING, AND ACCOUNTING an unsecured short-term loan note issued by companies and generally maturing within nine months

commercial property FINANCE, BANKING, AND ACCOUNTING buildings and land used for the performance of business activities. Commercial property can include single offices, buildings, factories, and hotels.

commercial report FINANCE, BANKING, AND ACCOUNTING an investigative report made by an organization such as a credit bureau that specializes in obtaining information regarding a person or organization applying for something such as credit or employment

commercial substance FINANCE, BANKING, AND ACCOUNTING the economic reality that underlies a transaction or arrangement, regardless of its legal or technical denomination. For example, a company may sell an office block and then immediately lease it back: the commercial substance may be that it has not been sold.

commercial time MARKETING an interval of time, usually measured in multiples of 15 seconds, during a radio or television broadcast available for purchase by an advertiser to broadcast its commercial message

commercial version GENERAL MANAGEMENT a version of a software program that is released for sale to customers. Earlier versions, called test versions or beta versions, are used to develop and test the software.

commercial year FINANCE, BANKING, AND ACCOUNTING an artificial year treated as having 12 months of 30 days each, used for calculating such things as monthly sales data and inventory levels

commission FINANCE, BANKING, AND ACCOUNTING HR & PERSONNEL a payment made to an intermediary, often calculated as a percentage of the value of goods or services provided. Commission is most often paid to sales staff, brokers, or agents.

Commission des Opérations de Bourse FINANCE, BANKING, AND ACCOUNTING the body, established by the French government in 1968, that is responsible for supervising France's stock exchanges. Abbr. *COB*

commitment document FINANCE, BANKING, AND ACCOUNTING a contract, change order, purchase order, or letter of intent pertaining to the supply of goods and services that commits an organization to legal, financial, and other obligations

commitment fee FINANCE, BANKING, AND ACCOUNTING a fee that a lender charges to guarantee a rate of interest on a loan a borrower is soon to make. Also known as *establishment fee*

commitment letter FINANCE, BANKING, AND ACCOUNTING an official notice from a lender to a borrower that the borrower's application has been approved and confirming the terms and conditions of the loan

commitments basis FINANCE, BANKING, AND ACCOUNTING the method of recording the expenditure of a public sector organization at the time when it commits itself to it rather than when it actually pays for it

commitments for capital expenditure FINANCE, BANKING, AND ACCOUNTING the amount a company has committed to spend on fixed assets in the future. In the United Kingdom, companies are legally obliged to disclose this amount, and any additional commitments, in their *annual report*.

committee GENERAL MANAGEMENT a group of people appointed and authorized to study, investigate, or make recommendations on a particular matter

Committee on Accounting Procedure FINANCE, BANKING, AND ACCOUNTING in the United States, a committee of the American Institute of Certified Public Accountants that was responsible between 1939 and 1959 for issuing accounting principles, some of which are still part of the Generally Accepted Accounting Principles

commodities exchange FINANCE, BANKING, AND ACCOUNTING a market in which raw materials are bought and sold in large quantities as *actuals* or *futures*

commodity ECONOMICS a good or service, for example, cotton, wool, or a laptop computer, resulting from a production process

commodity-backed bond FINANCE, BANKING, AND ACCOUNTING a bond tied to the price of an underlying commodity, for example, gold or silver, often used as a hedge against inflation

commodity contract FINANCE, BANKING, AND ACCOUNTING a legal document for the delivery or receipt of a commodity

commodity exchange FINANCE, BANKING, AND ACCOUNTING an exchange where futures are traded, for example, the commodity exchange for metals. Abbr. *COMEX*

commodity future FINANCE, BANKING, AND ACCOUNTING a contract to buy or sell a commodity at a predetermined price and on a particular delivery date

commodity paper FINANCE, BANKING, AND ACCOUNTING loans for which commodities are collateral

commodity pool FINANCE, BANKING, AND ACCOUNTING a group of people who join together to trade in options

commodity-product spread FINANCE, BANKING, AND ACCOUNTING coordinated trades in both a commodity and a product made from it

common cost FINANCE, BANKING, AND ACCOUNTING
1 cost relating to more than one product or service
2 a cost which is allocated to two or more cost centers within a company

common market ECONOMICS an economic association, typically between nations, with the goal of removing or reducing trade barriers

common pricing FINANCE, BANKING, AND ACCOUNTING the illegal fixing of the price of a good or service by several businesses so that they all charge the same price

common seal FINANCE, BANKING, AND ACCOUNTING see *company seal*

common-size financial statements FINANCE, BANKING, AND ACCOUNTING statements in which all the elements are expressed as percentages of the total. Such statements are often used for making performance comparisons between companies.

common stock FINANCE, BANKING, AND ACCOUNTING a stock that provides voting rights but only pays a dividend after dividends for preferred stock have been paid

common stock ratio FINANCE, BANKING, AND ACCOUNTING a measure of the interest each stockholder has in the company's capital

Commonwealth of Australia GENERAL MANAGEMENT the full, official name of the country of Australia

Commonwealth of Australia Gazette GENERAL MANAGEMENT a journal that reports the actions and decisions of the Australian federal government. It has been published since 1901.

Commonwealth Scientific and Industrial Research Organization (*ANZ*) GENERAL MANAGEMENT see *CSIRO*

commorientes FINANCE, BANKING, AND ACCOUNTING the legal term for two or more people who die at the same time. For the purposes of inheritance law, in the event of two people dying at the same time, it is assumed that the older person died first.

communication GENERAL MANAGEMENT the exchange of messages conveying information, ideas, attitudes, emotions, opinions, or instructions between individuals or groups with the objective of creating, understanding, or coordinating activities. Communication is essential to the effective operation of an organization. It may be conducted informally through a *grapevine* or formally by means of letters, reports, briefings, and *meetings*. Communication may be verbal or *nonverbal* and include spoken, written, and visual elements.

communications GENERAL MANAGEMENT
1 systems or technologies used for the communication of messages, such as postal and telephone networks, or for communicating within an organization
2 messages exchanged in the process of *communication*

communications channel GENERAL MANAGEMENT a medium through which a message is passed in the process of *communication*. Communications channels include the spoken, written, and printed word, and electronic or computer-based media such as radio and television, telephones, videoconferencing, and electronic mail. The most effective channel for a specific message depends on the nature of the message and the audience to be reached, as well as the context in which the message is to be transmitted.

communications envelope E-COMMERCE see *electronic envelope*

communication skills HR & PERSONNEL skills that enable people to communicate effectively with one another. Effective communication involves the choice of the best *communications channel* for a specific purpose, the technical knowledge to use the channel appropriately, the presentation of information in an appropriate manner for the target audience, and the ability to understand messages and responses received from others. The ability to establish and develop mutual understanding, trust, and cooperation is also important. More specifically, communication skills include the ability to speak in public, make presentations, write letters and reports, chair committees and meetings, and conduct negotiations.

communications management MARKETING the management, measurement, and control activities undertaken to ensure the effectiveness of communications

communications strategy MARKETING a management technique for determining the most effective method of communicating with the marketplace

communication technology GENERAL MANAGEMENT electronic systems used for communication between individuals or groups. Communication technology facilitates communication between individuals or groups who are not physically present at the same location. Systems such as telephones, telex, fax, radio, television, and video are included, as well as more recent computer-based technologies, including *electronic data interchange* and *e-mail*.

Communism ECONOMICS a classless society where private ownership of goods is abolished and the means of production belong to the community

community E-COMMERCE a group of Internet users with a shared interest or concept who interact with each other in newsgroups, mailing-list discussion groups, and other online interactive forums

community initiative GENERAL MANAGEMENT see *community involvement*

community involvement GENERAL MANAGEMENT programs through which organizations aim to make a positive contribution to the local community by identifying problems and initiating practical action in order to address them in partnership with local people. Community involvement programs developed through the growing emphasis on the social responsibility of business in the 1960s and 1970s. Such *community initiatives* often seek to promote economic and social regeneration in urban or rural areas and include activities such as the involvement of employees with appropriate skills, educational and training initiatives, *sponsorship* of arts and sports programs, and *corporate giving* programs.

community of interest a group of diverse people or organizations with a shared concern who have united to campaign for a common cause

Compagnie Nationale des Commissaires aux Comptes FINANCE, BANKING, AND ACCOUNTING in France, an organization that regulates external audit. Abbr. *CNCC*

Companies Act (*U.K.*) FINANCE, BANKING, AND ACCOUNTING an Act of Parliament that regulates the working of companies. Although the first one was passed in 1844, the Acts of 1985 and 1989 consolidated previous legislation and incorporated directives from the European Union.

Companies House FINANCE, BANKING, AND ACCOUNTING in the United Kingdom, the office of the *Registrar of Companies*. It has three main functions: the incorporation, re-registration, and striking-off of companies; the registration of documents that must be filed under company, insolvency, and related legislation; and the provision of company information to the public. Abbr. *CH*

companion bond FINANCE, BANKING, AND ACCOUNTING a class of a collateral mortgage obligation that is paid off first when interest rates

fall, leading to the underlying mortgages being prepaid. Conversely, the principal on these bonds will be repaid more slowly when interest rates rise and fewer mortgages are prepaid.

company law FINANCE, BANKING, AND ACCOUNTING GENERAL MANAGEMENT the body of legislation that relates to the formation, status, conduct, and *corporate governance* of companies as legal entities

company limited by guarantee FINANCE, BANKING, AND ACCOUNTING a type of organization, normally formed for nonprofit purposes, in which each member of the company agrees to be liable for a specific sum in the event of liquidation

company limited by shares FINANCE, BANKING, AND ACCOUNTING a type of organization in which each member of the company is liable only for the fully paid value of the shares they own. Also known as *limited liability company*

company policy GENERAL MANAGEMENT a statement of desired standards of behavior or procedure applicable across an organization. Company policy defines ways of acting for staff in areas where there appears to be latitude in deciding how best to operate. This may concern areas such as time off for special circumstances, drug or alcohol abuse, *workplace bullying*, personal use of *Internet* facilities, or business travel. Company policy may also apply to customers, for example, policy on *complaints*, *customer retention*, or *disclosure of information*. Sometimes a company policy may develop into a *code of practice*.

company report FINANCE, BANKING, AND ACCOUNTING GENERAL MANAGEMENT a document giving details of the activities and performance of a company. Companies are legally required to produce particular reports and submit them to the competent authorities in the country of their registration. These include *annual reports* and financial reports. Other reports may cover specific aspects of an organization's activities, for example, environmental or social impact.

company seal FINANCE, BANKING, AND ACCOUNTING the impression of a company's official signature on paper or wax. Certain documents, such as stock certificates, have to bear this seal.

company secretary (*U.K.*) HR & PERSONNEL FINANCE, BANKING, AND ACCOUNTING a senior employee in an organization with director status and administrative and legal authority. The appointment of a company secretary is a legal requirement for all limited companies. A company secretary can also be a board secretary with appropriate qualifications.

comparative advantage FINANCE, BANKING, AND ACCOUNTING GENERAL MANAGEMENT an instance of higher, more efficient production in a particular area. A country that produces far more cars than another, for example, is said to have the comparative advantage in car production. *David Ricardo* originally argued that specialization in activities in which individuals or groups have a comparative advantage will result in gains in trade.

comparative advertising MARKETING a form of advertising that gives carefully selected details of competitor products for comparison with a company's own product, usually to the detriment of competitors. Comparative advertising is frequently used to advertise cars, where the availability of features such as a sun roof, air conditioning, advanced braking systems, fuel efficiency, safety features, and warranty terms in similarly priced cars is given.

comparative balance sheet FINANCE, BANKING, AND ACCOUNTING one of two or more financial statements prepared on different dates that lend themselves to a comparative analysis of the financial condition of an organization

comparative credit analysis FINANCE, BANKING, AND ACCOUNTING an analysis of the risk associated with lending to different companies

comparative management GENERAL MANAGEMENT the simultaneous study of management or business practice in two or more different cultures, countries, companies, or departments

compassionate leave HR & PERSONNEL exceptional leave that may be granted to an employee on the death or serious illness of a close relative

compensating balance FINANCE, BANKING, AND ACCOUNTING
1 the amount of money a bank requires a customer to maintain in a non-interest-bearing account, in exchange for which the bank provides free services
2 the amount of money a bank requires a customer to maintain in an account in return for holding credit available, thereby increasing the true rate of interest on the loan

compensating errors FINANCE, BANKING, AND ACCOUNTING two or more errors which are set against each other so that the accounts still balance

compensation HR & PERSONNEL
1 *pay* given in recompense for work performed
2 money paid by an employer on the order of an employment tribunal to an employee who has been unfairly dismissed

compensation package HR & PERSONNEL a bundle of rewards including *pay*, financial incentives, and fringe benefits offered to, or negotiated by, an employee

compensatory financing FINANCE, BANKING, AND ACCOUNTING finance from the International Monetary Fund to help a country in economic difficulty

competence GENERAL MANAGEMENT HR & PERSONNEL an acquired personal skill that is demonstrated in an employee's ability to provide a consistently adequate or high level of performance in a specific job function. Competence should be distinguished from *competency*, although in general usage the terms are used interchangeably. Early attempts to define the qualities of effective managers were based on lists of the personality traits and skills of the ideal manager. This is an input model approach, focusing on the skills that are needed to do the job. These skills are competencies and reflect potential ability to do something. With the advent of scientific management, people turned their attention more to the behavior of effective managers and to the outcomes of successful management. This approach is an output model, in which a manager's effectiveness is defined in terms of actual achievement. This achievement manifests itself in competences, which demonstrate that somebody has learned to do something well. There tends to be a focus in the United Kingdom on competence, whereas in the United States, the concept of competency is more popular. Competences are used in the workplace in a variety of ways. Competences are also used in reward management, for example, in competence-based pay. The *assessment of competence* is a necessary process for underpinning these initiatives by determining what competences an employee shows. At an organizational level, the idea of *core competence* is gaining in popularity.

competency GENERAL MANAGEMENT HR & PERSONNEL an innate personal skill or ability. See also *competence*

competition ECONOMICS GENERAL MANAGEMENT rivalry between companies to achieve greater *market share*. Competition between companies for customers will lead to product innovation and improvement, and ultimately,

lower prices. The opposite of market competition is either a **monopoly** or a **controlled economy**, where production is governed by quotas. A company that is leading the market is said to have achieved **competitive advantage**.

competitive advantage ECONOMICS FINANCE, BANKING, AND ACCOUNTING GENERAL MANAGEMENT a factor giving an advantage to a nation, company, group, or individual in competitive terms. Used by **Michael Porter** for the title of his classic text on international corporate strategy, *The Competitive Advantage of Nations* (1990), the concept of competitive advantage derives from the ideas on **comparative advantage** of the 19th-century economist **David Ricardo**. See thinker **Michael Porter**

competitive analysis GENERAL MANAGEMENT analysis carried out for marketing purposes that can include industry, customer, and **competitor analysis**. A thorough competitive analysis done within a strategic framework can provide in-depth evaluation of the capabilities of key competitors.

competitive bid FINANCE, BANKING, AND ACCOUNTING a method of auctioning new securities whereby various underwriters offer the stock at competing prices or terms

competitive devaluation FINANCE, BANKING, AND ACCOUNTING the devaluation of a currency to make a country's goods more competitive on the international markets

competitive equilibrium price ECONOMICS the price at which the number of buyers willing to buy a good equals the number of sellers prepared to sell it

competitive forces GENERAL MANAGEMENT the external business and economic factors that compel an organization to improve its competitiveness

competitive intelligence GENERAL MANAGEMENT data gathered to improve an organization's competitive capacity. Competitive intelligence may include, for example, information about competitors' plans, activities, or products, and may sometimes be gained through **industrial espionage**. Such information can have a significant impact on a company's own plans: it could potentially limit the effectiveness of a new product launch, or identify growing threats to important accounts, for example. Unless organizations monitor competitor activity and take appropriate action, their business faces risk.

competitive local exchange carrier GENERAL MANAGEMENT a company that offers an alternate service to the established telephone service provider in a particular area

competitiveness index GENERAL MANAGEMENT an international ranking of states which uses economic and other information to list countries in order of their competitive performance. A competitiveness index can show which countries have overall or industry sector **competitive advantage** .

competitive position FINANCE, BANKING, AND ACCOUNTING the market share, costs, prices, quality, and accumulated experience of an entity or product relative to competition

competitive pricing FINANCE, BANKING, AND ACCOUNTING setting a price by reference to the prices of comparable competitive products

competitor analysis *or* **competitor profiling** GENERAL MANAGEMENT the identification and quantification of the relative strengths and weaknesses of a product or service (compared with those of competitors or potential competitors) which could be of significance in the development of a successful competitive strategy

competitor profiling GENERAL MANAGEMENT see **competitor analysis**

complaint GENERAL MANAGEMENT an expression of dissatisfaction with a product or service, either orally or in writing, from an internal or external customer. A customer may have a genuine cause for complaint, although some complaints may be made as a result of a misunderstanding or an unreasonable expectation of a product or service. How a complaint is handled will affect the overall level of **customer satisfaction** and may affect long-term customer loyalty. It is important for providers to have clear procedures for dealing rapidly with any complaints, to come to a fair conclusion, and to explain the reasons for what may be perceived by the customer as a negative response. Also known as **customer complaint**. See checklist **Handling Complaints**

complaints management MARKETING a management technique for assessing, analyzing, and responding to customer complaints

complementary goods MARKETING goods sold separately, but dependent on each other for sales. Examples of complementary goods include toothbrushes and toothpaste or computers and computer desks.

complementor GENERAL MANAGEMENT a company that supplies a product that complements a product supplied by another company, for example, computers and software

complex adaptive system GENERAL MANAGEMENT a system that overrides conventional human controls because those controls will subdue inevitable change and development within that system. Complex adaptive systems are a product of the application of **chaos theory** (see **chaos**) and **complexity theory** to the world of organizations. According to writers such as **Richard Pascale**, organizations that are subject to too much control are at risk of failure. The **bureaucracy** has been cited as an example of extreme control, and the **top down approach** to management. However, if a bureaucracy is left to adapt naturally, it could become capable of self-organization and of creating new methods of operating.

complexity theory GENERAL MANAGEMENT the theory that random events, if left to happen without interference, will settle into a complicated pattern rather than a simple one. Complexity theory is a development of **chaos theory**. In a business context, it suggests that events within organizations and in the wider economic and social spheres cannot be predicted by simple models but will develop in a seemingly random and complex manner.

compliance audit FINANCE, BANKING, AND ACCOUNTING an audit of specific activities in order to determine whether performance conforms with a predetermined contractual, regulatory, or statutory requirement

compliance documentation FINANCE, BANKING, AND ACCOUNTING documents that a stock-issuing company publishes in line with regulations on stock issues

compliance officer FINANCE, BANKING, AND ACCOUNTING an employee of a financial organization who ensures that regulations governing its business are observed

componentize E-COMMERCE to divide a large software application into smaller independently functioning parts

component percentage FINANCE, BANKING, AND ACCOUNTING see **capitalization ratio**

compounded annual return FINANCE, BANKING, AND ACCOUNTING the net return on an investment, calculated after adding interest and deducting tax

compounding FINANCE, BANKING, AND ACCOUNT-ING the calculation, payment, or receipt of *compound interest*

compound interest FINANCE, BANKING, AND ACCOUNTING interest calculated on the sum of the original borrowed amount and the accrued interest. See also *simple interest*

compound rate FINANCE, BANKING, AND ACCOUNTING an interest rate of a loan based on its *principal*, the amount remaining to be paid, or any interest payments already received

comprehensive auditing FINANCE, BANKING, AND ACCOUNTING see *value for money audit*

compressed workweek HR & PERSONNEL a standard number of working hours squeezed into fewer than five days. Common models of the compressed workweek include four ten-hour days or three twelve-hour days each week. An alternative variation is to lengthen the normal workday to a lesser extent, for example, by 45 minutes, to allow an extra day off every two or three weeks. The minimum modification is to work a slightly longer day for four days in return for a shorter Friday. A compressed workweek is often introduced as an employee benefit to provide an extended weekend through shorter Friday working.

compression E-COMMERCE a technique for reducing the number of bits required to represent text, data, or images so as to save storage space or reduce transmission time

Comptroller of the Currency FINANCE, BANKING, AND ACCOUNTING an official of the government responsible for the regulation of banks which are members of the Federal Reserve

compulsory acquisition FINANCE, BANKING, AND ACCOUNTING the purchase, by right, of the last 10% of stocks in an issue in the United Kingdom by a bidder at the offer price

computer-aided design OPERATIONS & PRODUCTION the use of a computer to assist with the design of a product. Computer graphics, modeling, and simulation are used to represent a product on screen, so that designers can produce more accurate drawings than is possible on paper alone, and to perform calculations easily, thereby optimizing designs for production. Abbr. *CAD* Also known as *computer-assisted design*

computer-aided diagnosis STATISTICS the use of a computer program that presents a patient with a series of diagnostic questions designed to produce a diagnosis of a health problem

computer-aided engineering OPERATIONS & PRODUCTION the application of computers to the generation of the engineering specifications of a product. Computer-aided engineering fits into the production process between *computer-aided design* and *computer-aided manufacturing*. It is similar to *CAD/CAM* software, but with a focus on the engineering processes required for converting a design to a manufacturable product. The software package can include aspects of design, analysis, process planning, numerical control, mold and tool design, and *quality control*. Abbr. *CAE*

computer-aided manufacturing OPERATIONS & PRODUCTION a system in which the manufacture and assembly of a product are directed by a computer. Computer-aided manufacturing can be integrated with *computer-aided design* to create a *CAD/CAM* system. Abbr. *CAM*. Also known as *computer-assisted manufacturing*

computer-aided production management OPERATIONS & PRODUCTION a system that enables all functions within an organization that are associated with production management to be directed by computer. *MRP II* is a well-known form of computer-aided production management. Abbr. *CAPM*

computer-assisted design OPERATIONS & PRODUCTION see *computer-aided design*

computer-assisted interview STATISTICS an interview in which the interviewee keys in answers to questions displayed on screen by a computer program

computer-assisted manufacturing OPERATIONS & PRODUCTION see *computer-aided manufacturing*

computer-based training HR & PERSONNEL training carried out via a stand-alone or networked computer. Programs are usually interactive, so that students can select from multiple-choice options or key in their own answers. A popular medium for computer-based training is CD-ROM, although there is a growing trend toward *online training*, where computer-based training is delivered over the Internet or through company intranets. Computer-based training is a form of *e-learning*.

computer model FINANCE, BANKING, AND ACCOUNTING a system for calculating investment opportunities, used by fund managers to see the right moment to buy or sell

computer telephony integration GENERAL MANAGEMENT the combining of computer and telephone technology to allow a computer to dial telephone numbers, route calls, and send and receive messages. One product of computer telephony integration is the process of *caller identification*, or caller ID. Caller ID identifies the telephone number a customer is calling from, searches the customer database to identify the caller, and pops up the customer account on the receiver's computer screen, using the facility known as *screen popping*, before the call is answered. Abbr. *CTI*

computer worm E-COMMERCE a computer *virus* that does not try to damage the files it infects. Its objective is instead to replicate itself as quickly and as often as possible. Computer worms are a major drain on the Internet because they clog up *bandwidth*.

concentration services FINANCE, BANKING, AND ACCOUNTING the placing of money from various accounts into a single account

concept board MARKETING a board used for presenting creative advertising ideas

concept product MARKETING a highly advanced and innovative product that is not yet in commercial production

concepts FINANCE, BANKING, AND ACCOUNTING principles underpinning the preparation of accounting information. See also *fundamental accounting concepts*

concept search E-COMMERCE an online search for documents related conceptually to a word, rather than specifically containing the word itself

concept statement MARKETING an explanation or summary of the overall goals or nature of a project

concept testing MARKETING research carried out to test the effectiveness of a creative advertising idea

concession
1 GENERAL MANAGEMENT a compromise in opinion or action by a party to a dispute
2 FINANCE, BANKING, AND ACCOUNTING GENERAL MANAGEMENT a reduction in price for a particular group of people
3 FINANCE, BANKING, AND ACCOUNTING GENERAL MANAGEMENT the right of a retail outlet to operate within another establishment
4 GENERAL MANAGEMENT an agreement to ignore the failure of a product or service to conform to its specification, with a possible resultant

deterioration in the quality of the product or service

conciliation HR & PERSONNEL action taken by an independent negotiator to bring disputing sides together with the goal of restoring trust or goodwill and reaching an agreement or bringing about a reconciliation

concurrent engineering
1 FINANCE, BANKING, AND ACCOUNTING a means of reducing product development time and cost by managing development processes so that they can be implemented simultaneously, rather than sequentially
2 OPERATIONS & PRODUCTION a team-based co-operative approach to product design and development, in which all parties are involved in *new product development* work in parallel. Concurrent engineering reduces or removes the time lag between the different stages of a product's development, and earlier entry into a market is therefore possible. Product quality is improved, development and product costs are minimized, and competitiveness is increased. Also known as *parallel engineering*, *simultaneous engineering*

conditional distribution STATISTICS the probability distribution of a random variable while the values of one or more random variables are fixed

conditions of employment GENERAL MANAGEMENT HR & PERSONNEL terms agreed between an employer and employee that are legally enforceable through a *contract of employment*. Conditions of employment include conditions that may be unique to the individual, for example, *notice periods*, remuneration, fringe benefits, and *hours of work*, as well as those that form organization-wide policies, such as discipline and *grievance procedures* and those dictated by legislation. See checklist *Drawing Up a Contract of Employment*

conditions of sale FINANCE, BANKING, AND ACCOUNTING agreed ways in which a sale takes place (such as discounts and credit terms)

Confederation of British Industry FINANCE, BANKING, AND ACCOUNTING a corporate membership organization which aims to promote the interests of U.K. business. The CBI's headquarters are in London, but it has regional offices throughout the United Kingdom, a European office in Brussels, and a U.S. base in Washington DC. Abbr. *CBI*

conference GENERAL MANAGEMENT a type of *meeting* held between members of often disparate organizations to discuss matters of

mutual interest. Conferences are held for a variety of reasons, including resolving problems, making decisions, developing co-operation, and publicizing ideas, products, and services. They may take place within an organization but often draw people together regionally, nationally, or internationally, and involve a large number of speakers and delegates. Many conferences are organized for commercial profit.

conference call GENERAL MANAGEMENT a telephone call that connects three or more lines so that people in different locations can communicate and exchange information by voice. Conference calls reduce the cost of *meetings* by eliminating travel time and expenditure. Public switched telephone networks or dedicated private networks and a centrally located device called a bridge are used to connect the participants. Microphones and loudspeakers may also be used to make group-to-group communication possible. Conference calls are a type of *teleconferencing*.

confidence indicator FINANCE, BANKING, AND ACCOUNTING a number that gives an indication of how well a market or an economy will fare

confidence interval STATISTICS the range of values of sample observations in a statistical study that contain the true parameter value within a given probability

confidentiality agreement GENERAL MANAGEMENT an agreement whereby an organization that has access to information about the affairs of another organization makes an undertaking to treat the information as private and confidential. A potential buyer of a company who requires further information in the process of due diligence may be asked to sign a confidentiality agreement stating that the information will only be used for the purpose of deciding whether to go ahead with the deal and will only be disclosed to employees involved in the negotiations. Such agreements are also used where information is shared in the context of a partnership or *benchmarking* program.

conflict management GENERAL MANAGEMENT HR & PERSONNEL the identification and control of conflict within an organization. There are three main philosophies of conflict management: all conflict is bad and potentially destructive; conflict is inevitable and managers should attempt to harness it positively; conflict is essential to the survival of an organization and should be encouraged. See checklist *Handling Conflict Situations*

conflict of interests GENERAL MANAGEMENT a situation in which a person or institution is caught between opposing concerns, loyalties, or objectives that prejudice impartiality. A conflict of interests may be between self-advantage and the benefit of an organization for which somebody works, or it could arise when somebody is connected with two or more companies that are competing. The correct course of action in such cases is for the person concerned to declare any interests, to make known the way in which those interests conflict, and to abstain from participating in the decision-making process involving those interests. A conflict of interests may also arise when an institution acts for parties on both sides of a transaction and could derive an advantage from a particular outcome.

confusion matrix GENERAL MANAGEMENT see *discriminant analysis*

conglomerate company FINANCE, BANKING, AND ACCOUNTING GENERAL MANAGEMENT an organization that owns a diverse range of companies in different industries. Conglomerates are usually *holding companies* with subsidiaries in wide-ranging business areas, often built up through mergers and takeovers and operating on an international scale.

conglomerate diversification FINANCE, BANKING, AND ACCOUNTING GENERAL MANAGEMENT the *diversification* of a *conglomerate company* through the setting-up of *subsidiary companies* with activities in various areas

conjoint analysis GENERAL MANAGEMENT a research method aimed at discovering the most attractive combination of attributes, including price, package style, and size, for a product or service. In conjoint analysis, respondents express their preferences by filling in a questionnaire and ranking a number of contrasting combinations of attributes from the most to the least preferred. This enables values to be assigned to the range of features that customers consider when making a decision to purchase. Also known as *tradeoff analysis*

connectivity GENERAL MANAGEMENT the ability of electronic products to connect with others, or of individuals, companies, and countries to be connected with one another electronically

connexity GENERAL MANAGEMENT the condition of being closely and intricately connected by worldwide communications networks

consensual relationship agreement HR & PERSONNEL an agreement signed by employer and employees confirming that a romantic or

sexual relationship between employees is voluntary and consensual. A consensual relationship agreement may be used where an employer actively discourages, or requires notification of such relationships, especially between supervisors and junior employees. They have been introduced, primarily in the United States, as an alternative to no-dating policies and to protect the employer against liability in possible claims of sexual harassment should the relationship break down. The agreement may also stipulate that the relationship will not affect or interfere with the work of those involved. Also called *love contract*, *cupid contract*

consequential loss policy FINANCE, BANKING, AND ACCOUNTING see *business interruption insurance*

consignment stock FINANCE, BANKING, AND ACCOUNTING stock held by one party (the "dealer") but legally owned by another (the "manufacturer") on terms that give the dealer the right to sell the stock in the normal course of its business, or, at its option, to return it unsold to the legal owner

consistency FINANCE, BANKING, AND ACCOUNTING the idea that a company should apply the same rules and standards to its accounting procedures from year to year. In the United Kingdom, any changes to the rules of recognition, presentation, and measurement must be disclosed in the annual report.

consolidated accounts (*U.K.*) FINANCE, BANKING, AND ACCOUNTING see *consolidated financial statement*

consolidated balance sheet FINANCE, BANKING, AND ACCOUNTING a listing of the most significant details of a company's finances

consolidated debt FINANCE, BANKING, AND ACCOUNTING the use of a large loan to eliminate smaller ones

consolidated financial statement FINANCE, BANKING, AND ACCOUNTING a listing of the most significant details of the finances of a company and of all its subsidiaries. Also known as *consolidated accounts*

consolidated fund FINANCE, BANKING, AND ACCOUNTING a fund of public money, especially from taxes, used by the government to make interest payments on the national debt and other regular payments

consolidated invoice FINANCE, BANKING, AND ACCOUNTING an invoice that covers all items shipped by one seller to one buyer during a particular period

consolidated loan FINANCE, BANKING, AND ACCOUNTING a large loan, the proceeds of which are used to eliminate smaller ones

consolidated tape FINANCE, BANKING, AND ACCOUNTING a ticker tape that lists all transactions of the New York and other U.S. stock exchanges

consolidated tax return FINANCE, BANKING, AND ACCOUNTING a tax return that covers several companies, typically a parent company and all of its subsidiaries

consolidation FINANCE, BANKING, AND ACCOUNTING

1 the uniting of two or more businesses into one company

2 the combination of several lower-priced shares into one higher-priced one

consolidation accounting FINANCE, BANKING, AND ACCOUNTING the process of adjusting and combining financial information from the individual financial statements of a parent undertaking and its subsidiary undertakings to prepare consolidated financial statements that present financial information for the group as a single economic entity

consortium

1 GENERAL MANAGEMENT a group of independent organizations that join forces to achieve a particular goal, for example, to bid for a project or to conduct cooperative purchasing. A consortium goes on to complete the project if its bid is successful and is often dissolved on completion. This form of temporary alliance allows diverse skills, capabilities, and knowledge to be brought together.

2 FINANCE, BANKING, AND ACCOUNTING an association of several entities with a view to carrying out a joint venture. See also *joint venture*

Constable, **John** (*b.* 1936) GENERAL MANAGEMENT British educator and consultant. Best known for the report *The Making of British Managers* (1987), with **Roger McCormick**, which led to major changes in the structure of *management development* in the United Kingdom. The publication of the report coincided with the equally influential *The Making of Managers: A Report on Management Education, Training, and Development in the USA, West Germany, France, Japan, and the U.K.* (1987) by **Charles Handy** and others. See thinker **Charles Handy**

constitutional strike HR & PERSONNEL a form of *industrial action* that takes place after all dispute procedures or other provisions for the avoidance of strikes agreed between labor union and employer representatives have been exhausted. A *no-strike agreement* effectively precludes constitutional strikes because it generally provides for automatic *arbitration*.

constructive dismissal (*U.K.*) HR & PERSONNEL a form of *dismissal* that occurs when an employee leaves a job and his or her claim of *breach of contract* or overbearing conduct by the employer is proven

constructive engagement GENERAL MANAGEMENT the policy of maintaining limited political and business links with a country while continuing to demand political or social reform in that country

consultant GENERAL MANAGEMENT an expert in a specialized field brought in to provide independent professional advice to an organization on some aspect of its activities. A consultant may advise on the overall management of an organization or on a specific project, such as the introduction of a new computer system. Consultants are usually retained by a client for a set period of time, during which they will investigate the matter in hand and produce a report detailing their recommendations. Consultants may be established in business independently or be employed by a large consulting firm. Specific types of consultants include *management consultants* and *internal consultants*.

consultative committee HR & PERSONNEL a meeting of representatives of management and staff, convened for the purposes of joint consultation

consultative management GENERAL MANAGEMENT a style of management that takes employees' views into account for decision-making purposes

consulting actuary FINANCE, BANKING, AND ACCOUNTING an independent actuary who advises large pension funds

consumer ECONOMICS MARKETING somebody who uses a product or service. A consumer may not be the purchaser of a product or service and should be distinguished from a customer, who is the person or organization that purchased the product or service.

consumer advertising MARKETING advertising aimed at individuals and the domestic and

family market as opposed to *industrial advertising*, which is aimed at businesses

consumer behavior MARKETING see *consumer demand*

consumer confidence FINANCE, BANKING, AND ACCOUNTING a measure of how people feel about the future of the economy and their own financial situation, obtained through polling

consumer demand MARKETING the patterns of *consumer behavior* that affect their buying decisions. Consumer demand is influenced in various ways. Psychologists and marketers have identified three important factors affecting buying decisions: needs, which are things we must have, such as food; wants, which are nice to have but not essential, such as a new car; and motives, such as keeping up appearances. These factors form part of a profile that includes motivations, personality, perceptions, cognition, attitudes, and values. Other factors that influence demand include gender, age, social grouping, education, location, income, culture, and the seasons. Consumers can therefore be divided into discrete segments, each of which has a particular pattern of buying behavior. Products and services can then be targeted at specific segments of the market.

consumer-facing GENERAL MANAGEMENT involving direct contact with, or able to be directly accessed by, consumers

consumer goods marketing MARKETING the promotion of products to members of the public. Consumer goods marketing is aimed at individuals rather than organizations and promotes products directly to the end user rather than to intermediaries. Marketing strategies will be different from those used in *industrial goods marketing*.

consumerism MARKETING the influence of the general public, as end users of products and services, on the way companies manufacture and sell their goods. Consumers exert considerable power over companies as organizations become more customer-focused. Demand is rising for products that are of high quality, ethically produced, well priced, and safe, and consumerism pressurizes companies to operate and produce goods and services in accordance with the public's wishes. In fact, the goals of consumerism are not at odds with those of *marketing* (see *marketing management*), as both have the end goal of pleasing the consumer. In practice, however, marketing does not always succeed, and there is still a need for legislation to back up the right of consumers to demand products that are of good quality and for consumer protection bodies that influence the commercial world on consumers' behalf. A particular form of consumer pressure, motivated by environmental concerns, is *green consumerism*, which campaigns for environmentally friendly goods, services, and means of production.

consumer market research MARKETING *market research* that focuses on gathering and analyzing data on individual or domestic consumers, as opposed to industrial or business customers. Also known as *consumer research*

consumer panel MARKETING a carefully selected group of people whose purchasing habits are regularly monitored. A consumer panel usually consists of a large cross-section of the population so as to provide meaningful data. There are two types of panel: *diary panels*, where members fill in a regular detailed diary of purchases, and, less commonly, *home audit panels*, where visits are made to the homes of members to check purchases, packaging, and used cartons. These panels run over a period of time to gain a broad overview of purchasing habits. A *focus group* is similar to a consumer panel, but is usually used to determine customers' views of a specific product or range of products. Members of a group meet together under the guidance of a facilitator to discuss their opinions on a face-to-face basis.

consumer price index ECONOMICS an index of the prices of goods and services that consumers purchase, used to measure the cost of living or the rate of inflation in an economy. Abbr. *CPI*

consumer profile MARKETING a detailed analysis of a group of like *consumers*, covering influences on their purchasing habits such as age, gender, education, occupation, income, and personal and psychological characteristics. Consumer profiles are built up from extensive *market research* and are used for market segmentation purposes.

consumer protection MARKETING the safeguarding of *consumer* interests in terms of quality, price, and safety, usually within a statutory framework. The growing purchasing power of consumers and the rise in *consumerism* from the late 1950s onward led to increased demands for protection against unsafe goods and services and unscrupulous trading practices.

consumer research MARKETING see *consumer market research*

consumer services marketing MARKETING the marketing of services to domestic consumers. Consumer services marketing may promote such services as banking, insurance, travel and tourism, leisure, telecommunications, and services provided by local authorities. Strategies to market these services to business constitute *industrial services marketing*.

consumer spending MARKETING the total value of household and personal expenditure measured at macro and micro levels. At the macro level, consumer confidence can be measured by the overall levels of consumer spending and from a demonstration that earnings have increased at a faster rate than prices, which indicates that spending power, or disposable income, has increased. At a micro level, there are innumerable market reports on the value of actual and predicted spend on a vast range of consumer goods, including food, pharmaceuticals, clothing, cars, and vacations. *Consumer demand* is a related concept.

consumer-to-consumer commerce E-COMMERCE e-business transactions conducted between two individuals

consumption ECONOMICS the quantity of resources that consumers use to satisfy their current needs and wants, measured by the sum of the current expenditure of the government and individual consumers

consumption tax FINANCE, BANKING, AND ACCOUNTING a tax used to encourage people to buy less of a particular good or service by increasing its price. This type of tax is often levied in times of national hardship.

contact card E-COMMERCE a *smart card* in which the microprocessor chip is visible and can make physical contact with the reading device

contactless card E-COMMERCE a *smart card* in which the microprocessor chip is not visible and is accessed by the reading device by radio signals rather than by physical contact. An increasingly common use of this technology is in such applications as toll collection, where the card is accessed as the motorist displays it to the reading device in passing.

contact list HR & PERSONNEL a list of people created for the purpose of networking, job searching, and marketing and selling products and services.

Someone wanting to expand and develop their contact list should seek to do so both inside and outside the organization they work for. Joining professional associations and vol-

unteering for committees are good ways of doing this. Building relationships can take time, and it is better to do this before going to someone for help. It is also important that the relationships are reciprocal; someone building a contact list should think about what they can offer to their contacts, as well as what their contacts can do for them.

A contact list should cover three basic types of network: the personal (friends, family, church, local community); the professional (current and former colleagues, supervisors, teachers, customers, consultants, members of professional organizations); and the work life network (executive recruiters, college placement officers, career counselors). A good system is needed for keeping track of these contacts, their details (including personal information), and any correspondence with them. Keeping in regular contact with them is vital, and finding ways to thank them for their help will ensure good future relations.

a-z

1448

DICTIONARY

contango FINANCE, BANKING, AND ACCOUNTING a situation where the price of commodities is higher for future delivery than it is for immediate delivery

content E-COMMERCE the textual, graphical, and multimedia material that constitutes a Web page or Web site

content management E-COMMERCE the means and methods of managing the textual and graphical content of a Web site. For large sites with thousands of pages and many interchangeable words and images, it pays to invest in a content management application system that facilitates the creation and organization of Web content. Some content management systems also offer caching (where a server stores frequently requested information) and analysis of site traffic.

Recent years have seen a vast growth in the quantity of content produced by organizations, particularly in digital form. In 2001, it was estimated that there were over 550 billion documents on Internet, intranet, and extranet Web sites—making professional content management vital. Without it, it becomes almost impossible for a user to find the information they are looking for.

However, excellent content management is expensive, and organizations need to establish a solid business case in order to justify it. The initial point for consideration is that content is not a low-level commodity that merely needs to be stored—it is a critical resource, and its value lies in it being read. So an understanding of who will read it is essential. Decisions need to be taken over what languages the material needs to be published in, and in what media

(Web or e-mail, for example). The form of the content—text, audio, video—is also important, as is the sensitivity of the material and the consequent security required.

Simply storing content is data management, but content management should have publication as its main focus, with the intention of informing or entertaining readers. There is a big difference in approach between the two.

content provider E-COMMERCE a Web site containing mainly news or information rather than commercial facilities such as shopping or banking, or a business supplying the information for such a Web site

contestable market ECONOMICS a market in which there are no barriers to entry, as when there is *perfect competition*

context E-COMMERCE information about a product made available on an Internet site that is seen as adding value for the consumer, for example, book reviews on a book site

contingency allowance GENERAL MANAGEMENT see *standard time*

contingency management GENERAL MANAGEMENT the capacity for flexibility in varying responses and attitudes to meet the needs of different situations. Contingency management may be practiced by both individuals and organizations. Within the latter, it may be formalized through a *contingency plan* linked to *risk* or *crisis management* strategies, or be derived from the results of *scenario planning*.

contingency plan
1 GENERAL MANAGEMENT a plan, drawn up in advance, to ensure a positive and rapid response to a changing situation. A contingency plan often results from *scenario planning* and may form part of an organization's *disaster management* strategy.
2 FINANCE, BANKING, AND ACCOUNTING action to be implemented only upon the occurrence of anticipated future events other than those in the accepted forward plan

contingency planning GENERAL MANAGEMENT see *FMEA*

contingency table STATISTICS a table in which observations on several categorical variables are cross-classified

contingency tax ECONOMICS a one-off tax levied by a government to deal with a particular economic problem, for example, too high a level of imports coming into the country

contingency theory GENERAL MANAGEMENT
1 in management, the theory that there is no single best way to organize or manage and that each firm should be organized and structured to suit the technology used and the environment around it. Contingency theory is particularly attributed to *Joan Woodward*, whose extensive company research during the 1950s found that different types of production processes were linked to different structures and spans of control. During the 1960s, contingency theory was further extended, especially by Tom Burns.
2 in leadership, the theory that different *management styles* will be more effective in different situations. In this context, contingency theory developed from situational leadership theory and is usually linked to the 1970s' work of Fred Fiedler.

contingent deferred sales charge FINANCE, BANKING, AND ACCOUNTING abbr. *CDSC*

continuing professional development HR & PERSONNEL see *CPD*

continuous disclosure FINANCE, BANKING, AND ACCOUNTING in Canada, the practice of ensuring that complete, timely, accurate, and balanced information about a public company is made available to stockholders

continuous improvement FINANCE, BANKING, AND ACCOUNTING GENERAL MANAGEMENT OPERATIONS & PRODUCTION the seeking of small improvements in processes and products, with the objective of increasing quality and reducing waste. Continuous improvement is one of the tools that underpin the philosophies of *total quality management* and *lean production*. Through constant study and revision of processes, a better product can result at reduced cost. *Kaizen* has become a foundation for many continuous improvement strategies, and for many employees it is synonymous with continuous improvement.

continuous inventory *or* **continuous stocktaking** FINANCE, BANKING, AND ACCOUNTING regular and consistent stocktaking throughout the fiscal year in order to ensure that the physical reality of the stock situation at any given time tallies with the accounting records such as bin cards. Any discrepancies will highlight errors or losses of stock and the accounts are adjusted to reflect this. Continuous inventory may preclude the need for an annual inventory.

continuous operation costing *or* **continuous process costing** FINANCE, BANKING, AND ACCOUNTING the costing method applicable where goods or services result from a

sequence of continuous or repetitive operations or processes. Costs are averaged over the units produced during the period, being initially charged to the operation or process.

continuous relationship marketing GENERAL MANAGEMENT see *pyramid selling*

continuous service HR & PERSONNEL a period of employment with one *employer*, which begins with the day on which the *employee* starts work and ends with the date of *resignation* or *dismissal*. All service, regardless of hours worked, counts toward calculating continuous service. The length of continuous service may affect the length of *notice period* and is taken into account when calculating redundancy pay.

continuous shift work HR & PERSONNEL a pattern of work designed to provide cover seven days a week, 24 hours a day, comprising three eight-hour or two twelve-hour *shifts*, or a mix of the two. Continuous shift work may be necessary to make full use of expensive capital equipment or to provide round-the-clock customer service. It may be confined to one group of employees, such as computer or security staff, while other parts of the organization use different shift patterns.

contour plot STATISTICS a graphical representation of data in which three variables are plotted on a topographical map

contract FINANCE, BANKING, AND ACCOUNTING **1** the buying and selling of securities and other financial instruments **2** a mutually-agreed, legally binding agreement between two or more parties

contract broker FINANCE, BANKING, AND ACCOUNTING a broker who fills an order placed by somebody else

contract costing FINANCE, BANKING, AND ACCOUNTING a form of specific order costing in which costs are attributed to individual contracts

contract distribution GENERAL MANAGEMENT the *outsourcing* of a company's distribution requirement to a third party under contract. Contract distribution can help a company drive down costs, reduce stockholdings, and achieve increased flexibility of delivery.

contract hire (*U.K.*) GENERAL MANAGEMENT an arrangement whereby an organization enters into a *contract* for the use of assets owned by another organization, as an alternative to purchasing the assets itself. Contract hire

agreements normally cover a period shorter that the useful economic life of the assets concerned and often include arrangements for maintenance and replacement. Organizations frequently use contract hire arrangements for the provision of company cars or office equipment.

contracting GENERAL MANAGEMENT the process of making an agreement governed by a *contract* for the provision of goods or services to an organization

contracting out
1 GENERAL MANAGEMENT see *outsourcing*
2 (*U.K.*) HR & PERSONNEL the withdrawal of employees by an employer from the State Earnings-Related Pension Scheme and their enrollment in an occupational pension scheme that meets specified standards
3 (*U.K.*) HR & PERSONNEL the withdrawal by an employee from the State Earnings-Related Pension Scheme and the purchase by the employee of an appropriate *personal pension*

contract manufacturing OPERATIONS & PRODUCTION the *outsourcing* of a requirement to manufacture a particular product or component to a third party. Contract manufacturing enables companies to reduce the level of investment in their own capabilities to manufacture, while retaining a product produced to a high quality, at a reasonable price, and delivered to a flexible schedule.

contract month FINANCE, BANKING, AND ACCOUNTING the month in which an option expires and goods covered by it must be delivered. Also known as *delivery month*

contract note FINANCE, BANKING, AND ACCOUNTING a document with the complete description of a stock transaction

contract of employment GENERAL MANAGEMENT HR & PERSONNEL a legally enforceable agreement, either oral or written, between an employer and an employee that defines terms and *conditions of employment* to which both parties must adhere. Express terms of the contract are agreed between the two parties and include the organization's normal terms and conditions in addition to those that relate specifically to the individual. These terms can only be changed by employee agreement, if the contract itself allows for variation, or by terminating the contract. Terms are also implied in the contract by custom and practice or by common law.

contract purchasing OPERATIONS & PRODUCTION a mechanism for buying leased goods. In

contract purchasing, a purchaser agrees to buy goods or equipment to be paid for in a series of installments, each comprising a proportion of the capital and an interest element. After a final payment, legal ownership passes to the user.

contractual obligation HR & PERSONNEL the legal duty to take a stated course of action, as imposed by a commercial *contract* or a *contract of employment*

contractual savings FINANCE, BANKING, AND ACCOUNTING savings in the form of regular payments into long-term investments, such as pension schemes

contrarian research FINANCE, BANKING, AND ACCOUNTING research that advises potential purchasers to buy stocks against the current trend

contrarian stockpicking FINANCE, BANKING, AND ACCOUNTING the choosing of stocks against the trend of the market

contributed content Web site E-COMMERCE a Web site which allows visitors to contribute content, such as information about their identity, or postings on message boards. A good example is Amazon.com, which encourages users to publish reviews of the books they have read.

contributed surplus FINANCE, BANKING, AND ACCOUNTING the portion of stockholders' equity that comes from sources other than earnings, for example, from the initial sale of stock above its nominal value

contribution center FINANCE, BANKING, AND ACCOUNTING a profit center in which marginal or direct costs are matched against revenue

contribution margin FINANCE, BANKING, AND ACCOUNTING a way of showing how much individual products or services contribute to net profit

contributions holiday FINANCE, BANKING, AND ACCOUNTING a period during which a company stops making contributions to its pension plan because the plan is sufficiently well funded

contributory pension scheme FINANCE, BANKING, AND ACCOUNTING a pension scheme where the worker has to pay a proportion of his or her salary

control FINANCE, BANKING, AND ACCOUNTING the ability to direct the financial and operating policies of an entity with a view to gaining economic benefits from its activities

control environment FINANCE, BANKING, AND ACCOUNTING the overall attitude, awareness, and actions of directors and management regarding internal *controls* and their importance to the organization

controlled circulation MARKETING the distribution, usually free of charge, of a newspaper or magazine exclusively to a selected target audience

controlled company FINANCE, BANKING, AND ACCOUNTING a company where more than 50% (or, in the United States, 25%) of the stock belongs to one owner

controlled disbursement FINANCE, BANKING, AND ACCOUNTING the presentation of checks only once each day

controlled economy GENERAL MANAGEMENT see *competition*

control procedures FINANCE, BANKING, AND ACCOUNTING the policies and procedures in addition to the *control environment* which are established to achieve an organization's specific objectives. They include in particular procedures designed to prevent or to detect and correct errors.

control risk FINANCE, BANKING, AND ACCOUNTING the part of an audit risk that relates to a client's internal control system

conversion FINANCE, BANKING, AND ACCOUNTING
1 a trade of one convertible financial instrument for another, for example, a bond for shares of stock
2 a trade of shares of one mutual fund for shares of another in the same family

conversion costs FINANCE, BANKING, AND ACCOUNTING the cost of changing raw materials into finished or semi-finished products. Conversion costs include wages, other direct production costs, and the production overhead.

conversion issue FINANCE, BANKING, AND ACCOUNTING the issue of new bonds, timed to coincide with the date of maturity of older bonds, with the intention of persuading investors to reinvest

conversion rate MARKETING
1 the percentage of inquiries or sales calls resulting in sales
2 the percentage of potential customers who actually make a purchase

conversion ratio *or* **conversion price**
FINANCE, BANKING, AND ACCOUNTING

1 an expression of the quantity of one security that can be obtained for another, for example, shares for a *convertible bond* .

The conversion ratio may be established when the convertible is issued. If that is the case, the ratio will appear in the indenture, the binding agreement that details the convertible's terms.

If the conversion ratio is not set, it can be calculated quickly: divide the nominal value of the convertible security (typically $1,000) by its conversion price.

$$\frac{\$1,000}{\$40\ \text{per share}} = 25$$

In this example, the conversion ratio is 25:1, which means that every bond held with a $1,000 nominal value can be exchanged for 25 shares of common stock.

Knowing the conversion ratio enables an investor to decide whether convertibles (or a group of them) are more valuable than the shares of common stock they represent. If the stock is currently trading at 30, the conversion value is $750, or $250 less than the nominal value of the convertible. It would therefore be unwise to convert.

A convertible's indenture can sometimes contain a provision stating that the conversion ratio will change over the years.
2 the number of shares of one common stock to be issued for each outstanding ordinary share of a different type when a merger takes place

conversion value FINANCE, BANKING, AND ACCOUNTING the value a security would have if converted into another security

convertible ARM FINANCE, BANKING, AND ACCOUNTING an adjustable-rate mortgage that the borrower can convert into a fixed-rate mortgage under specified terms

convertible bond FINANCE, BANKING, AND ACCOUNTING a bond that the owner can convert into another asset, especially common stock

convertible preferred stock FINANCE, BANKING, AND ACCOUNTING stocks that give the holder the right to exchange them at a fixed price for another security, usually common stock.

Preferred stocks and other convertible securities offer investors a hedge: fixed-interest income without sacrificing the chance to participate in a company's capital appreciation.

When a company does well, investors can convert their holdings into common stock that is more valuable. When a company is less successful, they can still receive interest and principal payments, and also recover their investment and preserve their capital if a more favorable investment appears.

Conversion ratios and prices are important facts to know about preferred stocks. This information is found on the indenture statement that accompanies all issues. Occasionally the indenture will state that the conversion ratio will change over time. For example, the conversion price might be $50 for the first five years, $55 for the next five years, and so forth. Stock splits can affect conversion considerations.

In theory, convertible preferred stocks (and convertible exchangeable preferred stocks) are usually perpetual. However, issuers tend to force conversion or induce voluntary conversion for convertible preferred stocks within ten years. Steadily increasing common stock dividends is one inducement tactic used. As a result, the conversion feature for preferred stocks often resembles that of debt securities. Call protection for the investor is usually about three years, and a 30- to 60-day call notice is typical.

About 50% of convertible equity issues also have a "soft call provision." If the common stock price reaches a specified ratio, the issuer is permitted to force conversion before the end of the normal protection period.

convertibles FINANCE, BANKING, AND ACCOUNTING corporate bonds or preferred stocks which can be converted into common stock at a set price on set dates

convertible security FINANCE, BANKING, AND ACCOUNTING a convertible bond, warrant, or share of preferred stock

convertible term insurance FINANCE, BANKING, AND ACCOUNTING term insurance that the policyholder can convert to fixed life insurance under particular conditions

conveyance FINANCE, BANKING, AND ACCOUNTING the legal transfer of a property from the seller to the buyer

C.O.O. *abbr* GENERAL MANAGEMENT chief operating officer

cookie E-COMMERCE a file written to a computer's hard disk by an Internet application to store small amounts of information that can be accessed to identify users and customize interactions with them. Cookies contain such data as registration or login information, user preferences, shopping cart items, and credit card numbers and expiration dates. The name is derived from UNIX objects called "magic cookies."

cooling-off period
1 HR & PERSONNEL an agreed pause in a dispute, especially a labor dispute, to allow the tempers

of the negotiating parties to cool before the resumption of negotiations

2 FINANCE, BANKING, AND ACCOUNTING a period during which someone who is about to enter into an agreement may reflect on all aspects of the arrangement and change his or her mind if necessary

3 (*U.K.*) FINANCE, BANKING, AND ACCOUNTING in insurance, a period of ten days during which a person who has signed a life assurance policy may cancel it

Cooper, Cary L. (*b.* 1940) GENERAL MANAGEMENT U.S.-born academic. Based at Lancaster University Management School, United Kingdom, Cooper focuses on *occupational psychology*, particularly *stress* management issues. His biggest-selling book is *Living with Stress* (1988, coauthor). See checklist **Stress Management: Self First**

cooperative MARKETING a business that is jointly owned by the people who operate it, with all profits shared equally

cooperative advertising MARKETING a joint advertising campaign between groups with a shared objective, for example, retailer groups, or manufacturer and retailer

cooperative movement GENERAL MANAGEMENT a movement that aims to share profits and benefits from jointly owned commercial enterprises among members. The movement was begun in Rochdale, Lancashire, England, in 1844 by 28 weavers and developed to include manufacturing and wholesale businesses as well as insurance and financial services. The Co-op in the United Kingdom and the *Mondragon cooperative* in Spain are two of the best-known examples.

coopetition GENERAL MANAGEMENT cooperation between competing companies (*slang*)

coproprietor FINANCE, BANKING, AND ACCOUNTING a person who owns a property with one other person or more

copyright MARKETING the legal protection for creative ideas, trademarks, and other brand-related material

copy testing MARKETING research carried out to test the effectiveness of creative advertising copy

copywriter MARKETING a person who devises the wording of an advertisement or promotional material. A copywriter may be employed by an advertising agency or, in scientific or technical areas, directly by a

manufacturing or distribution company. Many copywriters also work *freelance* .

core business GENERAL MANAGEMENT the central, and usually the original, focus of an organization's activities that differentiates it from others and makes a vital contribution to its success. The concept of core business became prominent in the 1980s when *diversification* by large companies failed to generate the anticipated degree of commercial success. In 1982, *Tom Peters*'s and *Robert Waterman*'s book *In Search of Excellence* suggested that organizations should *stick to the knitting* and avoid diversifying into areas beyond their field of expertise. An organization's core business should be defined by its *core competences*.

core capability GENERAL MANAGEMENT see *core competence*

core competence GENERAL MANAGEMENT HR & PERSONNEL a key ability or strength that an organization has acquired that differentiates it from others, gives it *competitive advantage*, and contributes to its long-term success. The concept of core competence is most closely associated with the work of *Gary Hamel* and *C. K. Prahalad*, notably in their book *Competing for the Future* (1994). They describe core competences as bundles of skills and technologies resulting from *organizational learning*. These provide access to markets, contribute to customer value, and are difficult for competitors to imitate. Core competence is a resource-based approach to *corporate strategy*. The terms core competence and *core capability* are often used interchangeably, but some writers make varying distinctions between the two concepts. See thinker *C. K. Prahalad*

core values

1 GENERAL MANAGEMENT the guiding principles of an organization, espoused by senior management, and accepted by employees, often reflected in the *mission statement* of the organization. Core values often influence the culture of an organization and are normally long-standing beliefs. As *shared values*, they are included in the *McKinsey 7-S framework*, and are reported in *Richard Pascale* and *Anthony Athos*'s *The Art of Japanese Management* in their analysis of the rise of *Konosuke Matsushita*. See giant *Konosuke Matsushita* See thinker *Richard Tanner Pascale*

2 HR & PERSONNEL a small set of key concepts and ideals that guide a person's life and help him or her to make important decisions

corpocracy GENERAL MANAGEMENT excessive or unwieldy corporate management resulting from the merger of several companies (*slang*)

corporate action FINANCE, BANKING, AND ACCOUNTING a measure that a company takes that has an effect on the number of shares outstanding or the rights that apply to shares

corporate amnesia GENERAL MANAGEMENT loss of organizational history and memory. Corporate amnesia occurs when senior or long-standing members of staff leave and their personal knowledge, built up from years of experience in the company, goes with them. This is occurring more frequently with the rise in *downsizing* and *delayering*, and the phenomenon goes hand in hand with the *anorexic organization*. Amnesia can be a significant disadvantage to an organization, causing it to forget the lessons it has learned and to waste time and effort in doing things again.

corporate anorexia GENERAL MANAGEMENT see *anorexic organization*

corporate bond FINANCE, BANKING, AND ACCOUNTING a long-term bond with fixed interest issued by a corporation

corporate brand GENERAL MANAGEMENT the coherent outward expression projected by an organization. A corporate brand is a product of an organization's *corporate strategy*, mission, image, and activities. Corporate brands distinguish organizations from their competitors, orient the organization in the minds of customers and employees, and create a perception of what an organization stands for. There is much debate about the precise nature of corporate brands, and about their depth. Corporate branding has been seen as a superficial quick fix to restore a company's tarnished image or revitalize an ailing company. It requires board level coordination, however, and rather than being arbitrarily imposed on an organization, it is actually a product of the sum of its activities. Changing a corporate brand, or rebranding a company, can only be accomplished by changing strategy and activity within the company.

corporate climate GENERAL MANAGEMENT the environment created by the managerial style and attitudes that pervade an organization. Corporate climate is strongly linked to *corporate culture* in creating the general feeling and atmosphere of an organization. The climate within an organization can affect aspects such as *productivity*, *creativity*, and *customer focus*, and each organization needs to create a climate that will facilitate organizational success.

corporate communication GENERAL MANAGEMENT the activities undertaken by an organiza-

tion to communicate both internally with employees and externally with existing and prospective customers and the wider public. Corporate communication is sometimes used to refer principally to external communication and sometimes to internal communication, but strictly speaking covers both. The term implies an emphasis on promoting a sense of *corporate identity* and presenting a consistent and coherent *corporate image*.

corporate concierge GENERAL MANAGEMENT an employee whose job involves doing personal tasks such as booking hotels or collecting shopping on behalf of other employees who have little time for these tasks (*slang*)

corporate culture GENERAL MANAGEMENT the combined beliefs, values, ethics, procedures, and atmosphere of an organization. The culture of an organization is often expressed as "the way we do things around here" and consists of largely unspoken values, norms, and behaviors that become the natural way of doing things. An organization's culture may be more apparent to an external observer than an internal practitioner. The first person to attempt a definition of corporate culture was *Edgar Schein*, who said that it consisted of rules, procedures, and processes that governed how things were done, as well as the philosophy that guides the attitude of senior management toward staff and customers. The difficulty in identifying the traits of culture and changing them is borne out by the fact that culture is not merely climate, power, and politics, but all those things and more. There can be several subcultures within an organization, for example, defined by hierarchy—shop floor or executive—or by function—sales, design, or production. Changing or renewing corporate culture in order to achieve the organization's strategy is considered one of the major tasks of organization *leadership*, as it is recognized that such a change is hard to achieve without the will of the leader. Also known as *organizational culture*. See thinker *Charles Handy*

corporate evolution GENERAL MANAGEMENT the way in which organizations are transformed through the use of information technology

corporate fraud FINANCE, BANKING, AND ACCOUNTING *fraud* committed by large organizations, rather than individuals. Auditing practice around the world, but especially in the United States, has come under much scrutiny since the collapse of Enron and WorldCom in 2001 and 2002 respectively. Both companies had overstated their profits, but the auditors, Arthur Andersen, had approved accounts in each case.

corporate giving GENERAL MANAGEMENT monetary or in-kind donations by organizations as part of the process of *community involvement*

corporate governance FINANCE, BANKING, AND ACCOUNTING the system by which companies are directed and controlled. Boards of directors are responsible for the governance of their companies. The stockholders' role in governance is to appoint the directors and the auditors and to satisfy themselves that an appropriate governance structure is in place. The responsibilities of the board include setting the company's strategic goals, providing the leadership to put them into effect, supervising the management of the business, and reporting to the stockholders on their stewardship. The board's actions are subject to laws, regulations, and the wishes of the stockholders in the general meeting.

corporate hospitality GENERAL MANAGEMENT entertainment provided by an organization. Corporate hospitality was originally designed to help sales people build relationships with customers, but it is now increasingly used as a staff incentive and in employee *team building* and training exercises.

corporate identity GENERAL MANAGEMENT the distinctive characteristics or personality of an organization, including *corporate culture*, values, and philosophy as perceived by those within the organization and presented to those outside. Corporate identity is expressed through the name, symbols, and logos used by the organization, and the design of communication materials, and is a factor influencing the *corporate image* of an organization. The creation of a strong corporate identity also involves consistency in the organization's actions, behavior, products, and brands, and often reflects the *mission statement* of an organization. A positive corporate identity can promote a sense of purpose and belonging within the organization and encourage *employee commitment* and involvement.

corporate image GENERAL MANAGEMENT the perceptions and impressions of an organization by the public as a result of interaction with the organization and the way the organization presents itself. Organizations have traditionally focused on the design of communication and advertising materials, using logos, symbols, text, and color to create a favorable impression on target groups, but a variety of additional activities contribute to a positive corporate image. These include *PR* programs such as *community involvement*, *sponsorship*, and environmental projects, participa-

tion in quality improvement schemes, and good practice in industrial relations.

corporate planning GENERAL MANAGEMENT the process of drawing up detailed action plans to achieve an organization's goals and objectives, taking into account the resources of the organization and the environment within which it operates. Corporate planning represents a formal, structured approach to achieving objectives and to implementing the *corporate strategy* of an organization. It has traditionally been seen as the responsibility of senior management. The use of the term became predominant during the 1960s but has now been largely superseded by the concept of *strategic management*.

corporate portal GENERAL MANAGEMENT a single gateway to information and software applications held within an organization that also allows links to information outside the organization. A corporate portal is a development of *intranet* technology. Ideally, it should allow users to access groupware, e-mail, and desktop applications, and to customize both the way information is presented and the way it is used. It should also provide dynamic access to data held within an *MIS*, *decision support system*, or other corporate database, and enable *virtual team* working across an organization. Like many purely technological solutions, a corporate portal still relies on good *internal communication* and a *corporate culture* that embraces openness and information sharing.

corporate resolution FINANCE, BANKING, AND ACCOUNTING a document signed by the officers of a corporation naming those persons who can sign checks, withdraw cash, and have access to the corporation's bank account

corporate restructuring GENERAL MANAGEMENT a fundamental change in direction and strategy for an organization that affects the way in which the organization is structured. Corporate restructuring may involve increasing or decreasing the layers of personnel between the top and the bottom of an organization, or reassigning roles and responsibilities. Invariably, corporate restructuring has come to mean reorganizing after a period of unsatisfactory performance and poor results, and is often manifested in the *divestment* or closure of parts of the business and the *outplacement*, or shedding, of personnel. In this case, corporate restructuring is used as a euphemism for *delayering*, *rationalization*, *downsizing*, or *rightsizing*.

corporate social responsibility GENERAL MANAGEMENT a voluntary approach that a

business enterprise takes to meet or exceed stakeholder expectations by integrating social, ethical, and environmental concerns together with the usual measures of revenue, profit, and legal obligation. Abbr. **CSR**

corporate spinoff FINANCE, BANKING, AND ACCOUNTING a small company which has been split off from a larger, parent organization

corporate strategy GENERAL MANAGEMENT the direction an organization takes with the objective of achieving business success in the long term. A number of models such as **Michael Porter**'s Five Forces model and **Gary Hamel** and **C. K. Prahalad**'s model of **core competencies** have been used to develop corporate strategy. More recent approaches have focused on the need for companies to adapt to and anticipate changes in the business environment. The formulation of corporate strategy involves establishing the purpose and scope of the organization's activities and the nature of the business it is in, taking the environment in which it operates, its position in the marketplace, and the competition it faces into consideration. **Corporate planning** and **business plans** are used to implement corporate strategy.

corporate tribes GENERAL MANAGEMENT a group of **employees** who develop their own languages, traditions, values (**core values**), and culture. Tribes are broadly classified as generalists (such as sales people) or specialists (such as engineers). The different values and languages of the tribes means that communication between them may be disrupted. It is therefore important for organizations to understand the differences between its tribes and devise ways to enable them to work effectively together.

corporate university HR & PERSONNEL a centralized training and education facility within an organization offering **training** and development only to employees of that organization. Traditionally, corporate universities only offered internal accreditation and were used as a means of channeling **employee development** toward meeting corporate goals, sharing corporate information or knowledge, and disseminating **corporate culture**. More recently, some corporate universities have established links with academic institutions in order to offer formal degrees.

corporate veil GENERAL MANAGEMENT immunity granted to stockholders to protect them from legal action in the event of the failure of a business

corporate venturing GENERAL MANAGEMENT the undertaking of an investment initiative by a commercial organization to gain experience of a new technology or an unfamiliar market

corporate vision GENERAL MANAGEMENT the overall goal of an organization that all business activities and processes should contribute toward achieving. Ideally, the workforce should be committed to, and driven by, the vision, because it is they who make it happen. As the vision nears achievement, a new corporate vision or an evolution of the existing one should be established. Corporate vision is usually summed up in a formal **vision statement**.

corporation FINANCE, BANKING, AND ACCOUNTING an organization in which a number of people provide finance in return for stock. The principle of **limited liability** limits the maximum loss a stockholder can make if the company fails. U.K. term **limited liability company**

correlation STATISTICS the interdependence between pairs of variables in data

correlation coefficient STATISTICS an index of the linear relationship between two variables in data

cosmeceuticals GENERAL MANAGEMENT pharmaceuticals such as anti-aging creams that have a cosmetic rather than a health-related purpose (*slang*)

cost FINANCE, BANKING, AND ACCOUNTING
1 the amount of money that is paid to secure a good or service. Cost is the amount paid from the purchaser's standpoint, whereas the price is the amount paid from the vendor's standpoint.
2 to ascertain the cost of a specific thing or activity

cost, insurance, and freight E-COMMERCE indicates that a quoted price includes the costs of the merchandise, transportation, and insurance. Abbr. **CIF**

cost account FINANCE, BANKING, AND ACCOUNTING a record of revenue and/or expenditure of a cost center or cost unit

cost and freight E-COMMERCE indicates that a quoted price includes the costs of the merchandise and the transportation but not the cost of insurance. Abbr. **CFR**

cost audit FINANCE, BANKING, AND ACCOUNTING the verification of cost records and accounts, and a check on adherence to prescribed **cost accounting** procedures and their continuing relevance

cost-benefit analysis FINANCE, BANKING, AND ACCOUNTING a comparison between the cost of the resources used, plus any other costs imposed by an activity (for example, pollution, environmental damage) and the value of the financial and non-financial benefits derived

cost center FINANCE, BANKING, AND ACCOUNTING GENERAL MANAGEMENT a department, function, section, or individual whose cost, overall or in part, is an accepted overhead of a business in return for services provided to other parts of the organization. A cost center is usually an **indirect cost** of an organization's products or services.

cost-cutting FINANCE, BANKING, AND ACCOUNTING GENERAL MANAGEMENT the reduction of the amount of money spent on the operations of an organization or on the provision of products and services. Cost-cutting measures such as budget reductions, salary freezes, and staff layoffs may be taken by an organization at a time of **recession** or financial difficulty or in situations where inefficiency has been identified. Alternative approaches to cost-cutting include modifying organizational structures and redesigning organizational processes for greater efficiency. Excessive cost-cutting may affect **productivity** and quality or the organization's ability to add value.

cost driver FINANCE, BANKING, AND ACCOUNTING GENERAL MANAGEMENT a factor that determines the cost of an activity. Cost drivers are analyzed as part of **activity based costing** and can be used in **continuous improvement** programs. They are usually assessed together as multiple drivers rather than singly. There are two main types of cost driver: the first is a **resource driver**, which refers to the contribution of the quantity of resources used to the cost of an activity; the second is an **activity driver**, which refers to the costs incurred by the activities required to complete a particular task or project.

cost-effective FINANCE, BANKING, AND ACCOUNTING GENERAL MANAGEMENT offering the maximum benefit for a given level of expenditure. When limited resources are available to meet specific objectives, the cost-effective solution is the best that can be achieved for that level of expenditure and the one that provides good value for money. The term is also used to refer to a level of expenditure that is perceived to be commercially viable.

cost-effectiveness analysis FINANCE, BANKING, AND ACCOUNTING a method for measuring the benefits and effectiveness of a particular item of expenditure. Cost-effectiveness analy-

sis requires an examination of expenditure to determine whether the money spent could have been used more effectively or whether the resulting benefits could have been attained through less financial outlay.

cost function ECONOMICS a mathematical function relating a firm's or an industry's total cost to its output and factor costs

costing GENERAL MANAGEMENT the determination of the total cost of a product, from the purchase of *raw materials* to delivery to the consumer. There are a large number of costing techniques, including *life-cycle costing*, *activity based costing*, and *operating costing*.

cost of appraisal FINANCE, BANKING, AND ACCOUNTING costs incurred in order to ensure that outputs produced meet required quality standards

cost of conformance FINANCE, BANKING, AND ACCOUNTING the cost of achieving specified quality standards. See also *cost of appraisal*, *cost of prevention*

cost of entry MARKETING the cost of introducing a new product to the market. Cost of entry calculations include the cost of all research, development, production, testing, marketing, advertising, and distribution of the new product.

cost of external failure FINANCE, BANKING, AND ACCOUNTING the cost arising from inadequate quality discovered after the transfer of ownership from supplier to purchaser

cost of goods sold FINANCE, BANKING, AND ACCOUNTING
1 for a retailer, the cost of buying and acquiring the goods it sells to its customers
2 for a service firm, the cost of the employee services it supplies
3 for a manufacturer, the cost of buying the raw materials and manufacturing its finished products Abbr. *COGS*

cost of internal failure FINANCE, BANKING, AND ACCOUNTING the costs arising from inadequate quality which are identified before the transfer of ownership from supplier to purchaser

cost of living FINANCE, BANKING, AND ACCOUNTING the average amount spent by an individual on accommodations, food, and other basic necessities. Salaries are usually increased annually to cover rises in the cost of living.

cost-of-living adjustment FINANCE, BANKING, AND ACCOUNTING a small increase to salaries

made to account for rises in the *cost of living* . Abbr. *COLA*

cost-of-living allowance FINANCE, BANKING, AND ACCOUNTING a salary supplement paid to some employees to cover rises in the *cost of living*. The specific amount of the supplement is dictated by the *cost of living index*.

cost of living index FINANCE, BANKING, AND ACCOUNTING an index which indicates changes in the cost of living by comparing current prices for a variety of goods with the prices paid for them in previous years

cost of nonconformance FINANCE, BANKING, AND ACCOUNTING the cost of failure to deliver the required standard of quality. See also *cost of external failure*, *cost of internal failure*

cost of prevention FINANCE, BANKING, AND ACCOUNTING the costs incurred prior to or during production in order to prevent substandard or defective products or services from being produced

cost per action E-COMMERCE see *CPA*

cost per click-through E-COMMERCE a pricing model for online advertising, where the seller gets paid whenever a visitor clicks on an ad

cost-plus pricing
1 MARKETING a standard *markup* added to the cost of a product or service to establish a selling price. Many companies simply add a percentage of production costs to arrive at a selling price. The degree of markup depends on the level of anticipated sales. Low volume luxury goods may have a high markup; high volume goods may have a relatively lower markup.
2 FINANCE, BANKING, AND ACCOUNTING the determination of price by adding a markup, which may incorporate a desired return on investment, to a measure of the cost of the product or service

cost-push FINANCE, BANKING, AND ACCOUNTING inflation in which price rises result from increased production costs or similar factors rather than from customer demand

cottage industry FINANCE, BANKING, AND ACCOUNTING an industry made up of small businesses, often run from the home of the proprietor

Council of Australian Governments GENERAL MANAGEMENT a body consisting of the heads of the Australian federal, state, and territory governments that meets to discuss matters of national importance. Abbr. *COAG*

Council of Trade Unions (ANZ) GENERAL MANAGEMENT see *CTU*

council tax (U.K.) FINANCE, BANKING, AND ACCOUNTING a tax paid by individuals or companies to a local authority, Introduced in April 1993 as a replacement for the much maligned community charge, or "poll tax," council tax depends on the value of the residential or commercial property occupied

counseling HR & PERSONNEL the provision of help by a trained person to permit somebody to clarify concerns, come to terms with feelings, and take responsibility for and begin to resolve difficulties. Counseling is a technique inherent to the *mentoring* process.

counterfactual GENERAL MANAGEMENT untrue (*slang*)

counterfeit GENERAL MANAGEMENT to produce forged or imitation goods or money intended to deceive or defraud. Counterfeited goods of inferior quality are often sold at substantially lower prices than genuine products and may bear the *brand* or *trade name* of the company. Counterfeiting violates *trademark* and *intellectual property* rights and may damage the reputation of producers of authentic goods. National and international legislation provides some recourse to companies against counterfeiters, but strategies such as consumer warnings and labeling methods are also used to minimize the impact of counterfeiting. Efforts to eliminate counterfeiting are coordinated by the International Anti-Counterfeiting Coalition.

counterparty FINANCE, BANKING, AND ACCOUNTING a person with whom somebody is entering into a contract

counterpurchase ECONOMICS see *countertrade*

countertrade ECONOMICS a variety of reciprocal trading practices. This umbrella term encompasses the direct exchange of goods for goods (or *barter*), where no cash changes hands, to more complex variations: *counterpurchase*, which involves a traditional export transaction plus the commitment of the exporter to buy additional goods or services from that country; and *buyback*, in which the supplier of plant or equipment is paid from the future proceeds resulting from the use of the plant. Countertrade conditions vary widely from country to country and can be costly and administratively cumbersome.

country club management GENERAL MANAGEMENT see *Managerial Grid*™

country risk FINANCE, BANKING, AND ACCOUNTING the risk associated with undertaking transactions with, or holding assets in, a particular country. Sources of risk might be political, economic, or regulatory instability affecting overseas taxation, repatriation of profits, nationalization, currency stability, etc.

coupon FINANCE, BANKING, AND ACCOUNTING
1 a piece of paper attached to a government bond certificate that a bondholder presents to request payment
2 the rate of interest on a bond
3 an interest payment made to a bondholder
clip coupons to collect periodic interest on a bond (*slang*)

coupon rate FINANCE, BANKING, AND ACCOUNTING the rate of interest paid on a *bond*

covariance STATISTICS the value that is predicted from the product of the deviations of two variables from each of their means

covariate STATISTICS a variable that is not crucial in an investigation but may affect the crucial variables from which a model is being built

covenant FINANCE, BANKING, AND ACCOUNTING to agree to pay annually a specified sum of money to a person or an organization by contract

coverage MARKETING the percentage of a target audience reached by different media

Coverdale training HR & PERSONNEL a system of training that concentrates on improving *teamwork* and methods of getting a job done. Coverdale training is concerned with management behavior, including setting *objectives*, briefing subordinates, and tackling a job. Groups of people are put into *scenarios* reproducing everyday situations and encouraged to experiment and build up successful working practices.

covered option FINANCE, BANKING, AND ACCOUNTING an option whose owner has the stock for the option

covered warrant FINANCE, BANKING, AND ACCOUNTING a futures contract for stock in a company

cover letter HR & PERSONNEL a letter sent to a potential employer together with a résumé. It is used when a jobseeker knows the exact position he or she is applying for, and the name of the person to whom the résumé is being sent.
A cover letter is important because it is the first thing the hiring manager will read, and is

key to them forming their first impression of the jobseeker. It must, therefore, be well-presented, well-informed, concise, professional, and yet enthusiastic.

cover note (*U.K.*) FINANCE, BANKING, AND ACCOUNTING a document that an insurance company issues to a customer to serve as a temporary insurance certificate until the issue of the policy itself. = *binder*

Covey, Stephen R. (*b.* 1932) GENERAL MANAGEMENT U.S. writer and consultant. Offers a holistic approach to life and work, based on Mormon principles, the self-drive philosophy of *Dale Carnegie*, and the self-help advice of Samuel Smiles. His message is enshrined in *The Seven Habits of Highly Effective People* (1989), which calls for a rethink of many fundamental assumptions and attitudes. See thinker *Stephen R. Covey*

CPA *abbr*
1 E-COMMERCE cost per action: a pricing model for online advertising based on the number of times an Internet user clicks on a banner ad that is linked to a particular Web site
2 FINANCE, BANKING, AND ACCOUNTING customer profitability analysis
3 FINANCE, BANKING, AND ACCOUNTING certified public accountant

CPD *abbr* HR & PERSONNEL continuing professional development: ongoing training and education throughout a career to improve the skills and knowledge used to perform a job or succession of jobs. CPD should be a planned, structured process, involving the assessment of development needs and the tailoring of training to meet those needs. CPD is founded on the belief that the development of professionals should not finish after initial qualification, especially in a fast changing business environment in which skills are likely to obsolesce quickly. CPD requires commitment and resources from the employee, the employer, and supportive agencies such as professional bodies. Advocates of CPD argue that it can enhance *employability* and *career development* by keeping skills up to date and broadening a person's skill base. *Dominic Cadbury* has said that CPD should be centered on the individual, who must take responsibility for the continuing assessment and satisfaction of his or her own development needs. Much can be found in support of the principle of CPD in the concepts of *David Kolb*'s *experiential learning* cycle, *Peter Honey* and *Alan Mumford*'s learning types, the *personal development* cycle, and *lifelong learning*.

CPF *abbr* HR & PERSONNEL Central Provident Fund

CPI *abbr* ECONOMICS consumer price index

CPIX (*ANZ*) ECONOMICS the *consumer price index* excluding interest costs, on the basis that these are a direct outcome of monetary policy

CPM *abbr* E-COMMERCE cost per thousand impressions: a pricing model for online advertising. The M represents the Roman numeral for 1,000.

crack E-COMMERCE
1 to defeat the copy protection that is intended to prevent somebody from illegally copying and distributing a software product, music CD, or DVD
2 to gain unauthorized access to a computer system with the intention of doing damage or committing a crime

cracker E-COMMERCE
1 somebody who defeats the copy protection of a software product, music CD, or DVD
2 somebody who gains unauthorized access to a computer system with the intention of doing damage or committing a crime

crash
1 FINANCE, BANKING, AND ACCOUNTING a precipitous drop in value, especially of the stocks traded in a market
2 ECONOMICS a sudden and catastrophic downturn in an economy. The crash in the United States in 1929 is one of the most famous.

creative accounting FINANCE, BANKING, AND ACCOUNTING the use of accounting methods to hide aspects of a company's financial dealings in order to make the company appear more or less successful than it is in reality (*slang*). See also *corporate fraud*

creative consultant MARKETING a person or organization that plans and creates advertising on behalf of a client

creative destruction GENERAL MANAGEMENT FINANCE, BANKING, AND ACCOUNTING a way of describing the endless cycle of innovation which results in established goods, services, or organizations being replaced by new models. The term was first mentioned by Joseph Schumpeter in *Capitalism, Socialism and Democracy* (1942), but used heavily during the dot-com boom of the late 1990s and early 2000s.

creative director MARKETING an employee of an advertising agency who is responsible for planning and managing the creative work of a campaign

a-z

1455

DICTIONARY

creative strategy MARKETING a technique for determining the most effective creative approach to reach a target audience

creative thinking GENERAL MANAGEMENT see *creativity*

creativity GENERAL MANAGEMENT the generation of new ideas by approaching problems or existing practices in innovative or imaginative ways. Psychologists have disagreed on the nature of creativity. Until about 1980, research concentrated on identifying the personality traits of creative people, but more recently psychologists have focused on the mental processes involved. Creativity involves reexamining assumptions and reinterpreting facts, ideas, and past experience. A growing interest in creativity as a source of *competitive advantage* has developed in recent years, and creativity is considered important, not just for the development of new products and services, but also for its role in organizational *decision making* and *problem solving*. Many organizations actively seek a *corporate culture* that encourages creativity. There are a number of techniques used to foster *creative thinking*, including *brainstorming* and *lateral thinking*. Creativity is linked to *innovation*, the process of taking a new idea and turning it into a market offering. See best practice *Creating Corporate Creativity*

credit FINANCE, BANKING, AND ACCOUNTING
1 the amount of money left over when an individual or organization has more *assets* than *liabilities*, and those liabilities are subtracted from the total of the assets
2 the trust that a lender has in a borrower's ability to repay a loan, or a loan itself
3 a financial arrangement between the vendor and the purchaser of a good or service by which the purchaser may buy what he or she requires, but pay for it at a later date

credit account FINANCE, BANKING, AND ACCOUNTING see *charge account*

credit availability *or* **credit available** FINANCE, BANKING, AND ACCOUNTING the amount of money that can be borrowed at a given time

credit balance FINANCE, BANKING, AND ACCOUNTING the amount of money that somebody owes on a credit account

credit bureau FINANCE, BANKING, AND ACCOUNTING a company that assesses the creditworthiness of people for businesses or banks. See also *mercantile agency*

credit capacity FINANCE, BANKING, AND ACCOUNTING the amount of money that a person

or organization can borrow and be expected to repay

credit card E-COMMERCE FINANCE, BANKING, AND ACCOUNTING a card issued by a bank or financial institution and accepted by a merchant in payment for a transaction for which the cardholder must subsequently reimburse the issuer

credit ceiling FINANCE, BANKING, AND ACCOUNTING see *credit limit*

credit committee FINANCE, BANKING, AND ACCOUNTING a committee that evaluates a potential borrower's creditworthiness

credit company FINANCE, BANKING, AND ACCOUNTING a company that extends credit to people

credit controller FINANCE, BANKING, AND ACCOUNTING a member of staff whose job is to expedite the payment of overdue invoices

credit cooperative FINANCE, BANKING, AND ACCOUNTING an organization of people who join together to gain advantage in borrowing

credit creation FINANCE, BANKING, AND ACCOUNTING the collective ability of lenders to make money available to borrowers

credit crunch FINANCE, BANKING, AND ACCOUNTING a situation in which money for borrowing is unavailable (*slang*)

credit deposit E-COMMERCE the value of the credit card purchases deposited in a merchant's bank account after the acquirer's fees are deducted

credit derivative FINANCE, BANKING, AND ACCOUNTING a financial instrument that transfers a lender's risk to a third party

credit entity FINANCE, BANKING, AND ACCOUNTING a borrower or lender

credit entry FINANCE, BANKING, AND ACCOUNTING an item on the asset side of a financial statement

credit exposure FINANCE, BANKING, AND ACCOUNTING the risk to a lender of a borrower defaulting

credit freeze FINANCE, BANKING, AND ACCOUNTING a period during which lending by banks is restricted by the government

credit granter FINANCE, BANKING, AND ACCOUNTING a person or organization that lends money

credit history FINANCE, BANKING, AND ACCOUNTING a potential borrower's record of debt repayment. Individuals or organizations with a poor credit history may find it difficult to find lenders who are willing to risk their taking out a loan.

crediting rate FINANCE, BANKING, AND ACCOUNTING the interest rate paid on an insurance policy that is an investment

credit limit FINANCE, BANKING, AND ACCOUNTING the highest amount that a lender will allow somebody to borrow, for example, on a credit card. Also known as *credit ceiling*

credit line FINANCE, BANKING, AND ACCOUNTING see *line of credit*

credit note (*U.K.*) FINANCE, BANKING, AND ACCOUNTING a document stating that a store owes somebody an amount of money and entitling the person to goods to the specified value. Abbr. *CN*

creditor FINANCE, BANKING, AND ACCOUNTING a person or an entity to whom money is owed as a consequence of the receipt of goods or services in advance of payment

creditor days FINANCE, BANKING, AND ACCOUNTING the number of days on average that a company requires to pay its creditors.

To determine creditor days, divide the cumulative amount of unpaid suppliers' bills (also called trade creditors) by sales, then multiply by 365. If suppliers' bills total $800,000 and sales are $9,000,000, the calculation is

$$\frac{800,000}{9,000,000} \times 365 = 32.44 \text{ days}$$

The company takes 32.44 days on average to pay its bills.

Creditor days is an indication of a company's creditworthiness in the eyes of its suppliers and creditors, since it shows how long they are willing to wait for payment. Within reason, the higher the number the better, because all companies want to conserve cash. At the same time, a company that is especially slow to pay its bills (100 or more days, for example) may be a company having trouble generating cash, or one trying to finance its operations with its suppliers' funds. See also *debtor days*

creditor nation ECONOMICS a country that has a balance of payments surplus

creditors' committee FINANCE, BANKING, AND ACCOUNTING a group that directs the efforts of creditors to receive partial repayment from a

bankrupt person or organization. Also known as **creditors' steering committee**

creditors' meeting FINANCE, BANKING, AND ACCOUNTING a meeting of those to whom a bankrupt person or organization owes money

creditors' settlement FINANCE, BANKING, AND ACCOUNTING an agreement on partial repayment to those to whom a bankrupt person or organization owes money

creditors' steering committee FINANCE, BANKING, AND ACCOUNTING see **creditors' committee**

credit rating *or* **credit ranking** FINANCE, BANKING, AND ACCOUNTING
1 an assessment of somebody's creditworthiness
2 the process of assessing somebody's creditworthiness

credit rating agency FINANCE, BANKING, AND ACCOUNTING a company that assesses the creditworthiness of people on behalf of businesses or banks. U.K. term **credit-reference agency**

credit rationing FINANCE, BANKING, AND ACCOUNTING the process of making credit less easily available or subject to high interest rates

credit receipt FINANCE, BANKING, AND ACCOUNTING a document stating that a store owes somebody an amount of money and entitling the person to goods to the specified value

credit-reference agency *(U.K.)* FINANCE, BANKING, AND ACCOUNTING = **credit rating agency**

credit references FINANCE, BANKING, AND ACCOUNTING details of individuals, companies, or banks who have given credit to a person or company in the past, supplied as references when opening a credit account with a new supplier

credit risk FINANCE, BANKING, AND ACCOUNTING the possibility that a loss may occur from the failure of another party to perform according to the terms of a contract

credit sale FINANCE, BANKING, AND ACCOUNTING a sale for which the buyer need not pay immediately

credit scoring FINANCE, BANKING, AND ACCOUNTING a calculation done in the process of credit rating

credit side FINANCE, BANKING, AND ACCOUNTING the part of a financial statement that lists assets. In **double-entry bookkeeping**, the right-hand side of each account is designated as the credit side.

credit squeeze FINANCE, BANKING, AND ACCOUNTING a situation in which credit is not easily available or is subject to high interest rates

credit standing FINANCE, BANKING, AND ACCOUNTING the reputation that somebody has with regard to meeting financial obligations

credit system FINANCE, BANKING, AND ACCOUNTING a set of rules and organizations involved in making loans

credit union FINANCE, BANKING, AND ACCOUNTING a cooperative financial organization that provides banking services, including loans, to its members at low rates of interest

creditworthy FINANCE, BANKING, AND ACCOUNTING regarded as being reliable in terms of meeting financial obligations

creeping takeover FINANCE, BANKING, AND ACCOUNTING a takeover achieved by the gradual acquisition of small amounts of stock over an extended period of time *(slang)*

creeping tender offer FINANCE, BANKING, AND ACCOUNTING an acquisition of many shares in a company by purchase, especially to avoid restrictions on tender offers

CREST FINANCE, BANKING, AND ACCOUNTING the paperless system used for settling stock transactions electronically in the United Kingdom

crisis management MARKETING actions taken by an organization in response to unexpected events or situations with potentially negative effects that threaten resources and people or the success and continued operation of the organization. Crisis management includes the development of plans to reduce the risk of a crisis occurring and to deal with any crises that do arise, and the implementation of these plans so as to minimize the impact of crises and assist the organization to recover from them. Crisis situations may occur as a result of external factors such as the development of a new product by a competitor or changes in legislation, or internal factors such as a product failure or faulty **decision making**, and often involve the need to make quick decisions on the basis of uncertain or incomplete information. See also **risk management disaster management**

critical mass GENERAL MANAGEMENT the point at which an organization or **project** has gained sufficient momentum or **market share** to be either self-sustaining or worth the input of extra investment or resources

critical-path analysis GENERAL MANAGEMENT OPERATIONS & PRODUCTION see **critical-path method**

critical-path method GENERAL MANAGEMENT OPERATIONS & PRODUCTION a **network analysis** planning technique used especially in **project management** to identify the activities within a project that are critical for its success. In critical-path method, individual activities within a project and their duration are recorded in a diagram or flow chart. A critical path is plotted through the diagram, showing the sequence in which activities must be completed in order to complete the project in the shortest amount of time, incurring the least cost. Also known as **critical-path analysis**

critical-ratio analysis GENERAL MANAGEMENT a technique used in inventory control to calculate comparative priorities for the reordering of inventory. Critical-ratio analysis requires the division of remaining stock items by the likely daily demand for them. This figure is then divided by the time taken to process an order, to derive the critical ratio. The smaller the ratio, the greater the reorder priority. A ratio of less than 1 indicates an imminent shortage. Critical ratios are also used in conjunction with **MRP II** systems to determine the sequence in which orders should be processed. In this case, a ratio of less than 1 indicates that the order is behind schedule.

critical region STATISTICS the range of values of a test statistic that lead a researcher to reject the null hypothesis

critical restructuring GENERAL MANAGEMENT major economic or social changes that fundamentally reshape traditional patterns of organization

critical success factor
1 FINANCE, BANKING, AND ACCOUNTING an element of organizational activity which is central to its future success. Critical success factors may change over time, and may include items such as product quality, employee attitudes, manufacturing flexibility, and brand awareness.
2 GENERAL MANAGEMENT any of the aspects of a business that are identified as vital for successful targets to be reached and maintained. Critical success factors are normally identified in such areas as production processes, employee

and organization skills, functions, techniques, and technologies. The identification and strengthening of such factors may be similar to identifying **core competences**, and is considered an essential element in achieving and maintaining **competitive advantage**.

critical value STATISTICS the value with which a researcher compares a statistic from sample data in order to determine whether or not the null hypothesis should be rejected

CRM *abbr* MARKETING customer relationship management

crony capitalism ECONOMICS a form of capitalism in which business contracts are awarded to the family and friends of the government in power rather than by open-market tender

Crosby, **Philip B.** (1926–2001) GENERAL MANAGEMENT U.S. business executive and consultant **quality** guru who introduced and popularized catchphrases such as "zero defects," "get it right first time," and "quality is free." Crosby summarized his approach toward quality improvement as the Fourteen Steps, set down in *Quality is Free* (1979). See thinker **Philip Crosby**

cross FINANCE, BANKING, AND ACCOUNTING a transaction in securities in which one broker acts for both parties

crossborder services FINANCE, BANKING, AND ACCOUNTING accounting services provided by an accounting firm in one country on behalf of a client based in another country

crossborder trade ECONOMICS trade between two countries that have a common frontier

crossed cheque (*U.K.*) FINANCE, BANKING, AND ACCOUNTING a check with two lines across it showing that it can only be deposited at a bank and not exchanged for cash

cross-hedging FINANCE, BANKING, AND ACCOUNTING a form of hedging using an option on a different but related commodity, especially a currency

cross listing FINANCE, BANKING, AND ACCOUNTING the practice of offering the same item for sale in more than one place

cross-post E-COMMERCE to post a single electronic message or article simultaneously to multiple news or discussion groups, an action generally considered a serious breach of netiquette

cross-rate ECONOMICS the rate of exchange between two currencies expressed in terms of the rate of exchange between them and a third currency, for example, sterling and the peso in relation to the dollar

cross-sectional study STATISTICS a statistical study in which a variety of information is collected at the same time, for example, in a single telephone call

cross sell FINANCE, BANKING, AND ACCOUNTING MARKETING to sell customers a variety of products or services offered by an organization at the same time, for example, offering insurance services while selling someone a mortgage

crowding out FINANCE, BANKING, AND ACCOUNTING the effect on markets of credit produced by extraordinarily large borrowing by a national government

crown jewels FINANCE, BANKING, AND ACCOUNTING an organization's most valuable **assets**, often the motivation behind **takeover** bids

crude annual death rate STATISTICS the total number of deaths in a population in one year divided by the total population at the midpoint of the year

cryptography E-COMMERCE a powerful means of restricting access to part or all of a Web site, whereby only a user with an assigned "key" can request and read the information

CSIRO *abbr* (*ANZ*) GENERAL MANAGEMENT Commonwealth Scientific and Industrial Research Organization: an Australian federal government body in charge of scientific research, established in 1949

CSP *abbr* E-COMMERCE commerce service provider

CTO *abbr* GENERAL MANAGEMENT chief technical officer

CTU *abbr* GENERAL MANAGEMENT Council of Trade Unions: New Zealand's national labor union organization. It has 19 affiliated unions and represents approximately 200,000 workers.

cube farm GENERAL MANAGEMENT an office that is divided into cubicles (*slang*)

cue GENERAL MANAGEMENT a factor that differentiates a high-value product from an ordinary commodity

CUL *abbr* GENERAL MANAGEMENT see you later (*slang*)

cultural creative HR & PERSONNEL somebody who values personal and spiritual development, enjoys change, likes learning about new cultures, and typically desires to live a simpler way of life

cultural synergy GENERAL MANAGEMENT the harmonization of the direction and operation of separate organizations into a whole. Whether cultural synergy can be achieved lies in the degree to which there is congruence of vision, mission, values, strategy, and operational processes in the different organizations. The lack of cultural and **strategic fit** is the main cause of failure of **mergers**, sometimes because of the major partner imposing its own **corporate culture**, rather than developing a shared culture. Cultural integration, therefore, needs to be carefully analyzed, planned, and implemented.

culture shock GENERAL MANAGEMENT the effects on an employee or organization when faced with new, unfamiliar, or rapidly changing circumstances. Symptoms of culture shock include uncertainty, **stress**, confusion, disorientation, or simply not knowing how to act in the circumstances. Culture shock can occur in a number of scenarios, for example, when **expatriates** come across new cultures and customs in a foreign country; when new staff are thrown into the deep end of a busy department; when two organizations merge with poor strategic, operational, or **cultural synergy**; or when public sector organizations adopt private sector practices. The degree of shock can be reduced through careful analysis, planning, training, and consequent preparedness.

cum FINANCE, BANKING, AND ACCOUNTING Latin, meaning "with"

cum rights FINANCE, BANKING, AND ACCOUNTING an indication that the buyer of the shares is entitled to participate in a forthcoming rights issue

cumulative interest FINANCE, BANKING, AND ACCOUNTING interest which is added annually to **capital** originally invested

cumulative method FINANCE, BANKING, AND ACCOUNTING a system in which items are added together

cumulative preferred stock FINANCE, BANKING, AND ACCOUNTING preferred stock for which dividends accrue even if they are not paid when due

cupid contract HR & PERSONNEL see **consensual relationship agreement**

currency FINANCE, BANKING, AND ACCOUNTING the money in circulation in a particular country

currency band FINANCE, BANKING, AND ACCOUNTING exchange rate levels between which a *currency* is allowed to move without full revaluation or devaluation

currency clause FINANCE, BANKING, AND ACCOUNTING a clause in a contract which avoids problems of payment caused by exchange rate changes by fixing in advance the exchange rate for the various transactions covered by the contract

currency future FINANCE, BANKING, AND ACCOUNTING an option on currency

currency hedging FINANCE, BANKING, AND ACCOUNTING a method of reducing *exchange rate risk* by diversifying currency holdings and adjusting them according to changes in exchange rates

currency mismatching FINANCE, BANKING, AND ACCOUNTING the practice of borrowing money in the currency of a country where interest rates are low and depositing it in the currency of a country with higher interest rates. The potential profit from the interest rate margin may be offset by changes in the exchange rates which increase the value of the loan in the company's balance sheet.

currency note FINANCE, BANKING, AND ACCOUNTING a banknote

currency risk FINANCE, BANKING, AND ACCOUNTING the possibility of a loss or gain due to future changes in exchange rates

currency swap FINANCE, BANKING, AND ACCOUNTING
1 an agreement to use a certain currency for payments under a contract in exchange for another currency. The organizations bound by the contract may buy one of the currencies at a more favorable rate than the other.
2 the buying or selling of a fixed amount of a foreign currency on the *spot market*, and the selling or buying of the same amount of the same currency on the *forward market*

currency unit ECONOMICS each of the notes and coins that are the medium of exchange in a country

current account FINANCE, BANKING, AND ACCOUNTING
1 a record of transactions between two parties, for example, between a bank and its customer, or a branch and head office. Abbr. *c/a*
2 (*U.K.*) = *checking account*

current account equilibrium ECONOMICS a country's economic circumstances when its expenditure equals its income from trade and invisible earnings

current asset FINANCE, BANKING, AND ACCOUNTING cash or other assets, such as stock, debtors, and long-term investments, held for conversion into cash in the normal course of trading

current assets financing FINANCE, BANKING, AND ACCOUNTING the use of current assets as collateral for a loan

current cash balance FINANCE, BANKING, AND ACCOUNTING the amount, which excludes balances due soon for outstanding transactions, that a client has available for investment with a broker

current cost accounting FINANCE, BANKING, AND ACCOUNTING a method of accounting which notes the cost of replacing assets at current prices, rather than valuing assets at their original cost. Abbr. *CCA*

current earnings FINANCE, BANKING, AND ACCOUNTING the annual earnings most recently reported by a company

current liabilities FINANCE, BANKING, AND ACCOUNTING liabilities which fall due for payment within one year. They include that part of any long-term loan due for repayment within one year.

current principal factor FINANCE, BANKING, AND ACCOUNTING the portion of the initial amount of a loan that remains to be paid

current ratio FINANCE, BANKING, AND ACCOUNTING a ratio of *current assets* to *current liabilities*, used to measure a company's liquidity and its ability to meet its short-term debt obligations.

The current ratio formula is a simple one:

$$\frac{\text{Current assets}}{\text{Current liabilities}} = \text{Current ratio}$$

Current assets are the ones that a company can turn into cash within 12 months during the ordinary course of business. Current liabilities are bills due to be paid within the coming 12 months.

For example, if a company's current assets are \$300,000 and its current liabilities are \$200,000, its current ratio would be

$$\frac{300,000}{200,000} = 1.5$$

As a rule of thumb, the 1.5 figure means that a company should be able to get hold of \$1.50 for every \$1.00 it owes.

The higher the ratio, the more liquid the company. Prospective lenders expect a positive current ratio, often of at least 1.5. However, too high a ratio is cause for alarm too, because it indicates declining receivables and/or inventory—which may mean declining liquidity.

current stock value FINANCE, BANKING, AND ACCOUNTING the value of all stock in a portfolio, including stock in transactions that have not yet been settled

current value FINANCE, BANKING, AND ACCOUNTING a ratio indicating the amount by which *current assets* exceed *current liabilities*

current yield FINANCE, BANKING, AND ACCOUNTING the interest being paid on a bond divided by its current market price, expressed as a percentage

cushion FINANCE, BANKING, AND ACCOUNTING money which allows an organization to pay interest on its borrowings or to survive a loss of some type

cushion bond FINANCE, BANKING, AND ACCOUNTING a bond that pays a high rate of interest but sells at a low premium because of the risk of its being called soon

custodial account FINANCE, BANKING, AND ACCOUNTING a bank account opened, normally by a parent or guardian, in the name of a minor who is too young to control it

custodian FINANCE, BANKING, AND ACCOUNTING a *bank* whose principal function is to maintain and grow the assets contained in a trust

customer MARKETING a purchaser of a product or service. A customer is a person or organization that purchases or obtains goods or services from other organizations such as manufacturers, retailers, wholesalers, or service providers. A customer is not necessarily the same person as the *consumer*, as a product or service can be paid for by one party, the customer, and used by another, the consumer.

customer capital GENERAL MANAGEMENT the value of an organization's relationships with its customers, which involves factors such as market share, customer retention rates, and profitability of customers

customer care MARKETING see *customer relations*

customer-centric model GENERAL MANAGE-MENT a business model organized around the needs of the customer

customer complaint GENERAL MANAGEMENT see *complaint*

customer equity MARKETING the total asset value of the relationships which an organization has with its customers. The term was coined by Robert C. Blattberg and John Deighton in their article, "Manage Marketing by the Customer Equity Test," *Harvard Business Review*, Jul/Aug, vol. 74 no. 4, pp. 136–144. Customer equity is based on *customer lifetime value*, and an understanding of customer equity can be used to optimize the balance of investment in the acquisition and retention of customers. It is also known as customer capital and forms one component of the *intellectual capital* of an organization.

customer expectation GENERAL MANAGEMENT the needs, wants, and preconceived ideas of a customer about a product or service. Customer expectation will be influenced by a customer's perception of the product or service and can be created by previous experience, advertising, hearsay, awareness of competitors, and *brand image*. The level of *customer service* is also a factor, and a customer might expect to encounter efficiency, helpfulness, reliability, confidence in the staff, and a personal interest in his or her patronage. If customer expectations are met, then *customer satisfaction* results. Also known as *buyer expectation*

customer flow MARKETING the number and pattern of customers coming into a store or passing through a railway or bus station, airport, or other large service, retail, or leisure area. Customer flow can be monitored by observation, time lapse or normal closed circuit television, or, less satisfactorily, by analysis of purchase data. This provides useful information about the number of customers, flow patterns, bottlenecks, areas not visited, and other aspects of consumer behavior.

customer focus MARKETING an organizational orientation toward satisfying the needs of potential and actual *customers*. Customer focus is considered to be one of the keys to business success. Achieving customer focus involves ensuring that the whole organization, and not just frontline service staff, puts its customers first. All activities, from the planning of a new product to its production, marketing, and after-sales care, should be built around the customer. Every department and every employee should share the same customer-focused vision. This can be aided by practicing good

customer relationship management and maintaining a *customer relations* program.

customer knowledge management MARKETING the acquisition and use of customer-related knowledge to create value for both the organization and the purchasers of its products and services. Customer knowledge management is a form of *knowledge management* which focuses on the human aspects of customer knowledge acquired through direct interaction with the customer as well as quantitative transactional data. Some writers restrict the concept to the use of knowledge residing in, or acquired from, customers as opposed to information *about* customers collected by *customer relationship management* systems. Interactive technologies, conversations with customers and user groups may be used to create knowledge-sharing and partnership between the organization and its customers.

customer lifetime value MARKETING the *net present value* of the profit an organization expects to realize from a *customer* for the duration of their relationship. Customer lifetime value focuses on customers as *assets* rather than sources of revenue. The volume of purchases made, customer retention rates, and profit margins are factors taken into account in calculating customer lifetime value. Strategies for increasing customer lifetime value aim to improve customer retention and lengthen the life of the relationship with the customer. Customer lifetime value is a key factor in the customer equity of an organization.

customer profitability MARKETING the degree to which a *customer* or segment of customers contributes toward an organization's profits. Customer profitability has been shown to be produced primarily by a small proportion of customers, perhaps 10% to 20%, who generate up to 80% of a company's profits. Up to 40% of customers may generate only moderate profits, and the other 40% may be loss making. Such data enables companies to focus efforts on the most profitable segments.

customer rage HR & PERSONNEL extreme frustration and anger on the part of a consumer-caller with the quality of a product or service, exhibited by aggressive behavior toward a customer-service representative, for example, over the telephone

customer recovery MARKETING activities intended to win back customers who no longer buy from an organization

customer relations MARKETING the approach of an organization to winning and retaining

customers. The most critical activity of any organization wishing to stay in business is its approach to dealing with its customers. Putting customers at the center of all activities is seen by many as an integral part of quality, pricing, and product differentiation. On one level, customer relations means keeping customers fully informed, turning complaints into opportunities, and genuinely listening to customers. On another level, being a customer-focused organization means ensuring that all activities relating to trading—for example, planning, design, production, marketing, and after-sales of a product or service—are built around the customer, and that every department and individual employee understands and shares the same vision. Only then can a company deliver continuous *customer satisfaction* and experience good customer relations. Also known as *customer care*

customer relationship management MARKETING the cultivation of meaningful relationships with actual or potential purchasers of goods or services. Customer relationship management aims to increase an organization's sales by promoting customer satisfaction, and can be achieved using tools such as relationship marketing.

CRM is particularly important in the sphere of e-commerce, as there is no personal interaction between the vendor and the customer. A Web site therefore has to work hard to develop the relationship with customers and demonstrate that their business is valued. A CRM system generally includes some or all of the following components: customer information systems, *personalization* systems, *content management* systems, *call center* automation, *data warehousing*, *data mining*, sales force automation, and campaign management systems. All these elements combine to provide the essentials of CRM: understanding customer needs; anticipating their information requirements; answering their questions promptly and comprehensively; delivering exactly what they order; making deliveries on time; and suggesting new products that they will be genuinely interested in. Abbr. *CRM*

customer retention MARKETING the maintenance of the patronage of people who have purchased a company's goods or services once and the gaining of repeat purchases. Customer retention occurs when a customer is loyal to a company, *brand*, or to a specific product or service, expressing long-term commitment and refusing to purchase from competitors. A company can adopt a number of strategies to retain its customers. Of critical importance to such strategies are the wider concepts of *customer service*, *customer relations*, and

relationship marketing. Companies can build loyalty and retention through the use of a number of techniques, including **database marketing**, the issue of loyalty cards, redeemable against a variety of goods or services, preferential **discounts**, free gifts, special promotions, newsletters or magazines, members' clubs, or customized products in limited editions. It has been argued that customer retention is linked to employee loyalty, since loyal employees build up long-term relationships with customers.

customer satisfaction MARKETING the degree to which customer expectations of a product or service are met or exceeded. Corporate and individual customers may have widely differing reasons for purchasing a product or service and therefore any measurement of satisfaction will need to be able to take into account such differences. The quality of **after-sales service** can also be a crucial factor in influencing any purchasing decision. More and more companies are striving, not just for customer satisfaction, but for customer delight, that extra bit of added value that may lead to increased customer loyalty. Any extra added value, however, will need to be carefully costed.

customer service MARKETING the way in which an organization deals with its **customers**. Customer service is most evident in sales and **after-sales service**, but should infuse all the processes in the **value chain**. Good customer service is the result of adopting **customer focus**. Poor customer service can be a product of poor **customer relations**.

customization GENERAL MANAGEMENT the process of modifying products or services to meet the requirements of individual customers

customized service GENERAL MANAGEMENT a service tailored to the requirements of an individual customer

customs broker FINANCE, BANKING, AND ACCOUNTING a person or company that takes goods through customs for a shipping company

customs declaration FINANCE, BANKING, AND ACCOUNTING a statement showing goods being imported on which duty will have to be paid

customs duty FINANCE, BANKING, AND ACCOUNTING tax paid on goods brought into or taken out of a country

customs formalities FINANCE, BANKING, AND ACCOUNTING a declaration of goods by the shipper and examination of them by the customs authorities

customs union FINANCE, BANKING, AND ACCOUNTING an agreement between several countries that goods can travel between them without paying duty while goods from other countries have to pay duties

cutthroat MARKETING aggressively ruthless, especially in dealing with competitors

cutting-edge GENERAL MANAGEMENT at the forefront of new technologies or markets

CV (*U.K.*) HR & PERSONNEL = *résumé*

cyberbole E-COMMERCE hype about the Internet and the online world (*slang*)

cybercast E-COMMERCE a broadcast of an event transmitted via the Internet, in either sound or vision or in both

cyberchondriac E-COMMERCE someone who feels physically unwell if he or she spends too much time away from an Internet connection (*slang*)

cybercrud E-COMMERCE confusing and useless computer jargon (*slang*)

cyber mall E-COMMERCE a Web site shared by two or more commercial organizations, usually with some similarity in appearance, function, product, or service. Also known as **e-commerce mall**, **electronic mall**, **online shopping mall**

cybermarketing E-COMMERCE the use of Internet-based promotions of any kind. This may involve targeted e-mail, bulletin boards, Web sites, or sites from which the customer can download files.

cybersales E-COMMERCE FINANCE, BANKING, AND ACCOUNTING sales made electronically through computers and information systems

cyberslacker GENERAL MANAGEMENT somebody who spends time surfing the Internet for personal purposes during office hours (*slang*)

cyberspace E-COMMERCE the online world and its communication networks

cyberterrorism E-COMMERCE the use of techniques that disrupt or damage computer-based information systems to cause fear, injury, or economic loss

cyberwar E-COMMERCE the use of information systems such as the Internet to exploit or damage an adversary's computer-based network processes

cycle plot STATISTICS a graphical representation of the behavior of seasonal time series

cycle time
1 OPERATIONS & PRODUCTION see **lead time**
2 FINANCE, BANKING, AND ACCOUNTING the total time taken from the start of the production of a product or service to its completion. Cycle time includes processing time, move time, wait time, and inspection time, only the first of which creates value.

cyclical stock FINANCE, BANKING, AND ACCOUNTING a stock whose value rises and falls periodically, for example, according to the seasons of the year or economic cycles

cyclical unemployment ECONOMICS unemployment, usually temporary, caused by a lack of **aggregate demand**, for example, during a downswing in the business cycle

cyclic variation STATISTICS the repeatable systematic variation of a variable over time

D

D/A *abbr* FINANCE, BANKING, AND ACCOUNTING deposit account

daemon E-COMMERCE a piece of software that carries out background tasks such as filtering or debugging, at fixed intervals or in response to specific events

daily price limit FINANCE, BANKING, AND ACCOUNTING the amount by which the price of an **option** can rise or fall within one trading day

Daimyo bond FINANCE, BANKING, AND ACCOUNTING a Japanese bearer bond that can be cleared through European clearing houses

daisy chaining FINANCE, BANKING, AND ACCOUNTING an illegal financial practice whereby traders create artificial transactions in order to make a particular security appear more active than it is in reality (*slang*)

dancing frog E-COMMERCE a problem or image on somebody's computer screen that disappears when shown to somebody else (*slang*)

D&B *abbr* FINANCE, BANKING, AND ACCOUNTING Dun and Bradstreet

Darwin Trade Development Zone GENERAL MANAGEMENT a free trade zone in the city of Darwin in the Northern Territory of Australia. Companies operating within the zone, which is intended to facilitate trade with Asia, are exempt from certain state taxes and customs duties.

a-z

1462

DICTIONARY

data STATISTICS the measurements and observations collected during a statistical investigation

database GENERAL MANAGEMENT a structured collection of related information held in any form, especially on a computer. The creation of a database assists organizations in keeping records and facilitates the retrieval of specific facts or different categories of information as and when required. Databases of various kinds may form part of an organization's *MIS*.

database management system STATISTICS a dedicated computer program designed to manipulate a collection of information

database marketing MARKETING the collection and analysis of information about customers and their buying habits, lifestyles, and other such data. Database marketing is used to build profiles of individual customers, who are then targeted with customized mailings, special offers, and other incentives to encourage spending. Database marketing is a form of relationship marketing.

data capture MARKETING the acquisition of information through advertisement coupons, inquiry forms, or other response mechanisms

data cholesterol E-COMMERCE the clogging up of a computer system with files or traffic to the extent that software programs can no longer run effectively on it (*slang*)

data cleansing MARKETING the process of ensuring that data is up to date and free of duplication or error

data dredging STATISTICS the process of making comparisons with and drawing conclusions from data that was not part of the original basis of a study

data editing STATISTICS the removal of keying or format errors from data

Data Encryption Standard E-COMMERCE see *DES*

data fusion E-COMMERCE the integration of data and knowledge collected from disparate sources by different methods into a consistent, accurate, and useful whole

dataholic GENERAL MANAGEMENT somebody who is obsessed with obtaining information, especially on the Internet (*slang*)

data mining
1 E-COMMERCE the process of using sophisticated software to identify commercially useful statistical patterns or relationships in online databases
2 MARKETING extraction of information from a *data warehouse* to assist managerial *decision making*. The information obtained in this way helps organizations gain a better understanding of their customers and can be used to improve customer support and marketing activities.

dataport E-COMMERCE a socket for connecting a laptop computer to the Internet

data protection MARKETING the safeguards that govern the storage and use of personal data held on computer systems and in paper-based filing systems. The growing use of computers to store information about individuals has led to the enactment of legislation in many countries designed to protect the privacy of individuals and prevent the disclosure of information to unauthorized persons.

data reduction STATISTICS the process of summarizing large data sets into histograms or frequency distributions so that calculations such as means can be made

data screening STATISTICS the process of assessing a set of observations to detect significant deviations such as *outliers*

data set STATISTICS all of the measurements or observations collected in a statistical investigation

data smoothing algorithm STATISTICS a procedure for removing meaningless data from a sequence of observations so that a pattern can be detected

data transfer E-COMMERCE the amount of data downloaded from a Web site. This information can be useful, particularly for measuring the number of visitors to a Web site.

data warehouse
1 GENERAL MANAGEMENT a collection of subject-orientated data collected over a period of time and stored on a computer to provide information in support of managerial *decision making*. A data warehouse contains a large volume of information selected from different sources, including operational systems and organizational databases, and brought together in a standard format to facilitate retrieval and analysis. Like *EIS*s, data warehouses can be used to support decision making, but the ways in which they can be searched are not predetermined. Organizations often use data warehouses for marketing purposes, for example, the analysis of customer information, or for market segmentation. *Data mining* tech-niques are used to access the information in a data warehouse.
2 FINANCE, BANKING, AND ACCOUNTING a database in which information is held not for operational purposes, but to assist in analytical tasks such as the identification of new market segments. Data warehouses provide a repository for historical data and collect, integrate, and organize data from unintegrated application systems. The data stored in a data warehouse almost certainly comes from the operational environment, but is always physically separate from it.

dawn raid FINANCE, BANKING, AND ACCOUNTING a sudden, planned purchase of a large amount of a company's stocks at the beginning of a day's trading. Up to 15% of a company's stocks can be bought in this way, and the purchaser must wait for seven days before buying more. A dawn raid may sometimes be the first step toward a *takeover*.

DAX *abbr* FINANCE, BANKING, AND ACCOUNTING Deutscher Aktienindex: the principal German stock exchange, based in Frankfurt

day in the sun GENERAL MANAGEMENT the period of time during which a product is successful in the marketplace

day order FINANCE, BANKING, AND ACCOUNTING an order that is valid only during one trading day

day release (*U.K.*) HR & PERSONNEL the discharge of an employee from normal work to take part in education or training. Day release is normally for one day each week, fortnight, or month, and it enables an employee to study for further education or vocational degrees on a part-time basis.

days' sales outstanding FINANCE, BANKING, AND ACCOUNTING see *collection ratio*

day trader FINANCE, BANKING, AND ACCOUNTING somebody who makes trades with very close dates of maturity

day trading FINANCE, BANKING, AND ACCOUNTING the making of trades that have very close dates of maturity

DCF *abbr* FINANCE, BANKING, AND ACCOUNTING discounted cash flow

DCM *abbr* (*S. Africa*) FINANCE, BANKING, AND ACCOUNTING Development Capital Market

DD *abbr* FINANCE, BANKING, AND ACCOUNTING
1 direct debit
2 due diligence

D.D. *abbr* GENERAL MANAGEMENT demand draft

dead cat bounce FINANCE, BANKING, AND AC-COUNTING a short-term increase in the value of a stock following a precipitous drop in value (*slang*)

dead ringer MARKETING an automatically dialed telemarketing call that cuts off when answered because there is nobody at the sender's end available to deal with it

dead tree edition E-COMMERCE the print version of a publication that is also available in electronic form (*slang*)

dead wood HR & PERSONNEL employees who are no longer considered to be useful to a company (*slang*)

dead zone GENERAL MANAGEMENT area in which cell phone users are unable to receive signals

deal
cut somebody a deal GENERAL MANAGEMENT to agree on terms for a business arrangement with somebody (*slang*)

dealership MARKETING a retail outlet distributing, selling, and servicing products such as cars or construction plant on behalf of a manufacturer

dealing room FINANCE, BANKING, AND ACCOUNT-ING a room at a stock exchange where the buying and selling of stocks takes place

dear money FINANCE, BANKING, AND ACCOUNTING money which has to be borrowed at a high interest rate, thus restricting the borrower's expenditure

death by committee GENERAL MANAGEMENT the prevention of serious consideration of a proposal by assigning a committee to look at it

Death Valley curve GENERAL MANAGEMENT a point in the development of a new business when losses begin to erode the company's equity base, so that it becomes difficult to raise new equity (*slang*)

debenture FINANCE, BANKING, AND ACCOUNTING the written acknowledgment of a debt by a company, usually given under its seal, and normally containing provisions as to payment of interest and principal. A debenture may be secured on some or all of the assets of the company or its subsidiaries.

debenture bond FINANCE, BANKING, AND ACCOUNTING
1 a certificate showing that a *debenture* has been issued
2 a long-term unsecured loan

debit FINANCE, BANKING, AND ACCOUNTING an entry in accounts which shows an increase in *assets* or expenses or a decrease in liabilities, revenue, or capital. It is entered in the left-hand side of an account in *double-entry bookkeeping* .

debit balance FINANCE, BANKING, AND ACCOUNT-ING the difference between debits and credits in an account where the value of *debits* is greater

debit card FINANCE, BANKING, AND ACCOUNTING a card issued by a bank or financial institution and accepted by a merchant in payment for a transaction. Unlike the procedure with a *credit card*, purchases are deducted from the cardholder's account, as with a check, when the transaction takes place.

debit column FINANCE, BANKING, AND ACCOUNT-ING the left-hand side of an account, showing increases in a company's assets or decreases in its liabilities

debit entry FINANCE, BANKING, AND ACCOUNTING an entry on the debit side of an account

debits and credits FINANCE, BANKING, AND ACCOUNTING figures entered in a company's accounts to record increases and decreases in *assets*, expenses, liabilities, revenues, or capital

de Bono, Edward (*b.* 1933) GENERAL MANAGE-MENT Maltese-born academic and consultant. Creator of the concept of *lateral thinking*, which was introduced in *Lateral Thinking: A Textbook of Creativity* (1970).

debt FINANCE, BANKING, AND ACCOUNTING
1 an amount of money owed to a person or organization
2 money borrowed by a person or organization to finance personal or business activities

debt collection agency FINANCE, BANKING, AND ACCOUNTING a business that secures the repayment of debts for third parties on a commission or fee basis

debt counseling FINANCE, BANKING, AND AC-COUNTING a service offering advice and support to individuals who are financially stretched

debt/equity ratio FINANCE, BANKING, AND ACCOUNTING the ratio of what a company owes to the value of all of its outstanding shares of stock

debt factoring FINANCE, BANKING, AND ACCOUNT-ING the business of buying debts at a discount. A factor collects a company's debts when

due, and pays the creditor in advance part of the sum to be collected, thus "buying" the debt.

debt forgiveness FINANCE, BANKING, AND ACCOUNTING the writing off of all or part of a nation's debt by a lender

debt instrument FINANCE, BANKING, AND AC-COUNTING any document used or issued for raising money, for example, a bill of exchange, bond, or promissory note

debtnocrat FINANCE, BANKING, AND ACCOUNTING a senior bank official who specializes in lending extremely large sums, for example, to developing nations (*slang*)

debtor FINANCE, BANKING, AND ACCOUNTING a person or entity owing money

debtor days FINANCE, BANKING, AND ACCOUNTING the number of days on average that it takes a company to receive payment for what it sells.
To determine debtor days, divide the cumulative amount of accounts receivable by sales, then multiply by 365. If accounts receivable total $600,000 and sales are $9,000,000, the calculation is

$$\frac{600{,}000}{9{,}000{,}000} \times 365 = 24.33 \text{ days}$$

The company takes 24.33 days on average to collect its debts.
Debtor days is an indication of a company's efficiency in collecting monies owed. Obviously, the lower the number the better. An especially high number is a telltale sign of inefficiency or worse. See also *creditor days*

debtors' control FINANCE, BANKING, AND AC-COUNTING strategies used to ensure that borrowers pay back loans on time

debt ratio FINANCE, BANKING, AND ACCOUNTING the debts of a company shown as a percentage of its equity plus loan capital

debt rescheduling FINANCE, BANKING, AND AC-COUNTING GENERAL MANAGEMENT the renegotiation of debt repayments. Debt rescheduling is necessary when a company can no longer meet its debt payments. It can involve deferring debt payments, deferring payment of interest, or negotiating a new loan. It is usually undertaken as part of *turnaround management* to avoid *business failure*. Debt rescheduling is also undertaken in less developed countries that encounter national debt difficulties. Such arrangements are usually overseen by the International Monetary Fund.

debt/service ratio ECONOMICS the ratio of a country's or company's borrowing to its equity or *venture capital*

debugging STATISTICS the identification and removal of errors in a computer program or system

decentralization GENERAL MANAGEMENT the dispersal of decision-making control. Decentralization involves moving power, authority, and decision-making control within an organization from a central headquarters or from high managerial levels to subsidiaries, branches, divisions, or departments. As an organizational concept, decentralization implies *delegation* of both power and responsibility by top management in order to promote flexibility through faster decision making and improved response times. Decentralization is, therefore, strongly related to the concept of *empowerment*, though the latter is perhaps more focused on direct working front-line staff.

decision lozenge GENERAL MANAGEMENT see *flow chart*

decision maker GENERAL MANAGEMENT somebody with the responsibility and authority to make decisions within an organization, especially those that determine future direction and strategy. *Decision theory* is used to assist decision makers in the process of *decision making*.

decision making GENERAL MANAGEMENT the process of choosing between alternative courses of action. Decision making may take place at an individual or organizational level. The process may involve establishing objectives, gathering relevant information, identifying alternatives, setting criteria for the decision, and selecting the best option. The nature of the decision-making process within an organization is influenced by its culture and structure, and a number of theoretical models have been developed. One well-known method for individual decision making was developed by *Charles Kepner* and *Benjamin Tregoe* in their book *The New Rational Manager* (1981). *Decision theory* can be used to assist in the process of decision making. Specific techniques used in decision making include *heuristics* and *decision trees*. Computer systems designed to assist managerial decision making are known as *decision support systems*.

decision-making unit MARKETING a group of people who directly or indirectly influence the purchase of a product or service

decision support system GENERAL MANAGEMENT a computer system designed to collect, store, process, and provide access to information to support managerial *decision making*. Decision support systems were developed in the 1970s to facilitate unstructured and one-off decision making, as the standard reporting capabilities of *MIS*s were perceived to be more suitable for routine day-to-day decisions. Data on an organization's external operating environment, as well as internal operational information, is included and an interactive interface allows managers to retrieve and manipulate data. Modeling techniques are used to examine the results of alternative courses of action.

decision theory *or* **decision analysis** GENERAL MANAGEMENT a body of knowledge that attempts to describe, analyze, and model the process of *decision making* and the factors influencing it. Decision theory encompasses both formal mathematical and statistical approaches to solving decision problems, using quantitative techniques, such as probability and *game theory*, and more informal behavioral approaches. It is used to inform and assist decision making in organizations.

decision tree GENERAL MANAGEMENT a diagram designed to help decision-makers by representing available options and possible outcomes as branches of a tree. Decision trees provide an overview of multiple-stage *decision making* by showing successive decision points arising from previous choices. Values representing the relative probability of individual outcomes may be assigned to each branch of the tree in order to compare strategies and select the most favorable.

declaration date FINANCE, BANKING, AND ACCOUNTING the date when the directors of a company meet to announce the proposed dividend per share that they recommend be paid

declaration of dividend FINANCE, BANKING, AND ACCOUNTING a formal announcement by a company's directors of the proposed dividend per share that they recommend be paid. It is subsequently put to a stockholders' vote at the company's annual meeting.

declaration of solvency *(U.K.)* FINANCE, BANKING, AND ACCOUNTING a document, filed with the Registrar of Companies, that lists the assets and liabilities of a company seeking voluntary liquidation to show that the company is capable of repaying its debts within 12 months

declared value FINANCE, BANKING, AND ACCOUNTING the value of goods as entered on a customs declaration

declining balance method ECONOMICS FINANCE, BANKING, AND ACCOUNTING see *accelerated depreciation*

decompilation OPERATIONS & PRODUCTION see *reverse engineering*

deconstruction GENERAL MANAGEMENT the breaking up of traditional business structures to meet the requirements of the modern economy

dedicated line E-COMMERCE a telephone line assigned to a designated user, usually to provide a permanent connection to the Internet

de-diversify FINANCE, BANKING, AND ACCOUNTING to sell off parts of a company or group that are not considered directly relevant to its main area of interest

deductible FINANCE, BANKING, AND ACCOUNTING the part of a commercial insurance claim that has to be met by the policyholder rather than the insurance company. A deductible of $1,000 means that the company pays all but $1,000 of the claim for loss or damage. See also *excess*

deduction at source FINANCE, BANKING, AND ACCOUNTING a U.K. term for the collection of taxes from an organization or individual paying an income rather than from the recipient, for example, from an employer paying wages, a bank paying interest, or a company paying dividends

deed FINANCE, BANKING, AND ACCOUNTING a legal document, most commonly one that details the transfer or sale of real estate

deed of arrangement FINANCE, BANKING, AND ACCOUNTING a legal document which sets out the agreement between an insolvent person and his or her *creditors*

deed of assignment *(U.K.)* FINANCE, BANKING, AND ACCOUNTING a legal document detailing the transfer of real estate from a *debtor* to a *creditor*

deed of covenant *(U.K.)* FINANCE, BANKING, AND ACCOUNTING a legal document in which a person or organization promises to pay a third party a sum of money on an annual basis. In certain countries this arrangement may have tax advantages. For example, in the United Kingdom, it is often used for making regular payments to a charity.

deed of partnership *(U.K.)* FINANCE, BANKING, AND ACCOUNTING a legal document formalizing the agreement and financial arrangements between the parties that make up a partnership

deed of transfer (*U.K.*) FINANCE, BANKING, AND ACCOUNTING a legal document which attests to the transfer of stock ownership

deed of variation FINANCE, BANKING, AND ACCOUNTING in the United Kingdom, an arrangement that allows the will of a deceased person to be amended, provided certain conditions are met and the amendment is signed by all the original beneficiaries

deep-discount bond FINANCE, BANKING, AND ACCOUNTING a bond offered at a large discount on the face value of the debt so that a significant proportion of the return to the investor comes by way of a capital gain on redemption, rather than through interest payments

deep-in-the-money call option FINANCE, BANKING, AND ACCOUNTING a call option that has become very profitable and is likely to remain so

deep-in-the-money put option FINANCE, BANKING, AND ACCOUNTING a put option that has become very profitable and is likely to remain so

deep market FINANCE, BANKING, AND ACCOUNTING a commodity, currency, or stock market in which the volume of trade is such that a considerable number of transactions will not influence the market price

deep pocket FINANCE, BANKING, AND ACCOUNTING a term used to refer to a company which provides much-needed funds for another company (*slang*)

de facto standard GENERAL MANAGEMENT a standard set in a given market by a highly successful product or service

defalcation FINANCE, BANKING, AND ACCOUNTING the improper and illegal use of funds by someone who does not own them, but who has been charged with their care

default FINANCE, BANKING, AND ACCOUNTING to fail to comply with the terms of a contract, especially to fail to pay back a debt

default notice (*U.K.*) FINANCE, BANKING, AND ACCOUNTING = *notice of default*

defended takeover bid FINANCE, BANKING, AND ACCOUNTING a bid for a company takeover in which the directors of the target company oppose the action of the bidder

defensive stock FINANCE, BANKING, AND ACCOUNTING stock that prospers predictably, regardless of external circumstances such as an economic slowdown, for example, the stock of a company that markets a product everyone must have

deferred consideration FINANCE, BANKING, AND ACCOUNTING installment payments for the acquisition of new subsidiaries, usually made in the form of cash and stock, where the balance due after the initial deposit depends on the performance of the business acquired

deferred coupon FINANCE, BANKING, AND ACCOUNTING a *coupon* that pays no interest at first, but pays relatively high interest after a specified date

deferred credit *or* **deferred income** FINANCE, BANKING, AND ACCOUNTING revenue received but not yet reported as income in the profit and loss account, for example, payment for goods to be delivered or services provided at a later date, or government grants received for the purchase of assets. The deferred credit is treated as a credit balance on the balance sheet while waiting to be treated as income. See also *accrual concept*

deferred income FINANCE, BANKING, AND ACCOUNTING see *deferred credit*

deferred month FINANCE, BANKING, AND ACCOUNTING a month relatively late in the term of an option

deferred share FINANCE, BANKING, AND ACCOUNTING
1 a type of share, usually held by founding members of a company, often with a higher dividend that is only paid after other stockholders have received their dividends and, in some cases, only when a certain level of profit has been achieved
2 (*U.K.*) a stock that pays no dividend for a certain number of years after its issue date but that then ranks with the company's common stock

deficit FINANCE, BANKING, AND ACCOUNTING see *budget deficit*

deficit financing FINANCE, BANKING, AND ACCOUNTING the borrowing of money because expenditure will exceed receipts

deficit spending FINANCE, BANKING, AND ACCOUNTING government spending financed through borrowing rather than taxation

deflation ECONOMICS a reduction in the general level of prices sustained over several months, usually accompanied by declining employment and output

deflationary fiscal policy ECONOMICS a government policy that raises taxes and reduces public expenditure in order to reduce the level of *aggregate demand* in the economy

deflationary gap ECONOMICS a gap between *GDP* and the potential output of the economy

deflator ECONOMICS the amount by which a country's *GDP* is reduced to take into account *inflation*

degearing FINANCE, BANKING, AND ACCOUNTING a reduction in a company's loan capital in relation to the value of its common stock plus reserves

de Geus, **Arie P.** (*b.* 1930) GENERAL MANAGEMENT Dutch business executive, adviser, and consultant. Former strategist for Royal Dutch Shell, who, in *The Living Company* (1997), identified the characteristics of long-lived companies: financial conservatism, sensitivity to their environment, cohesiveness, and tolerance of unconventional thinking.

degree mill HR & PERSONNEL an establishment that offers to award a degree for little or no work, often on payment of a large sum of money. Degree mills mostly operate on the edge of the law, often being unaccredited or unregistered as educational institutions. Most degree mills fail to offer any worthwhile education, and those that do lack the appropriate accreditation that makes their degrees acceptable by employers, with the result that they award *bogus degree* certificates.

degressive tax FINANCE, BANKING, AND ACCOUNTING a tax whose payments depend on an individual's salary. Those on smaller salaries pay a lower percentage of their income than those with larger salaries.

delayed settlement processing E-COMMERCE a procedure for storing authorized transaction settlements online until after the merchant has shipped the goods to the purchaser

delayering GENERAL MANAGEMENT the removal of supposedly unproductive layers of middle management to make organizations more efficient and customer-responsive. The term came into vogue during the 1980s. When taken to extremes, delayering can lead to an *anorexic organization*.

del credere agent FINANCE, BANKING, AND ACCOUNTING an agent who agrees to sell goods on commission and pay the principal even if the buyer defaults on payment. To cover the risk of default, the commission is marginally higher than that of a general agent.

delegation HR & PERSONNEL the process of entrusting somebody else with the appropriate responsibility and authority for the accomplishment of a particular activity. Delegation involves briefing somebody else to perform a task for which the delegator holds individual responsibility, but which need not be executed by him or her. There are various degrees of delegation: for example, a manager may delegate responsibility, but not necessarily full authority, and continue to supervise the activity. Delegation should be a positive activity, for example, as an aid to *employee development*, rather than a negative one, for example, passing on an unpopular task. It should be accompanied by support and encouragement from the delegator to the delegatee. An extension of delegation is *empowerment*, in which complete authority for a task is passed to somebody else, who takes full responsibility for its objectives, execution, and results.

delinquent FINANCE, BANKING, AND ACCOUNTING used to refer to an individual who or an organization which is late in paying an account

delist FINANCE, BANKING, AND ACCOUNTING to remove a company from the list of companies whose stocks are traded on an exchange

delivery month FINANCE, BANKING, AND ACCOUNTING see *contract month*

Dell, Michael S. (*b*. 1965) GENERAL MANAGEMENT U.S. business executive. Founder of Dell Computer Corporation and youngest C.E.O. to run a *Fortune 500* company, whose business achieved success through building to order, *direct selling*, minimizing *inventory*, and using *Internet* technology.

Delphi technique GENERAL MANAGEMENT a qualitative *forecasting* method in which a panel of experts respond individually to a questionnaire or series of questionnaires, before reaching a consensus. The Delphi technique requires individual submission of, and response to, the questionnaire on the topic under investigation, in order to avoid the effect of a dominant personality influencing a group discussion. A summary of the written replies is then distributed so that responses can be revised in the light of the views expressed. This cycle is repeated until the coordinator of the group is satisfied that the best possible consensus has been reached. The Delphi technique was developed at the Rand Corporation during the late 1940s and 1950s and owes its name to the Greek oracle at Delphi, which was believed to make predictions about the future.

demand forecasting FINANCE, BANKING, AND ACCOUNTING GENERAL MANAGEMENT the activity of estimating the quantity of a product or service that consumers will purchase. Demand forecasting involves techniques including both informal methods, such as educated guesses, and quantitative methods, such as the use of historical sales data or current data from test markets. Demand forecasting may be used in making pricing decisions, in assessing future capacity requirements, or in making decisions on whether to enter a new market.

demarcation dispute HR & PERSONNEL an industrial *dispute* between *labor unions*, or between members of the same union, regarding the allocation of work between different types of workers. Demarcation disputes are much less prevalent than in the past because of *multiskilling* agreements between employers and unions and the greater use of *teamwork*.

demassifying GENERAL MANAGEMENT the process of changing a mass medium to a medium that is customized to meet the requirements of individual consumers

demerge FINANCE, BANKING, AND ACCOUNTING to split up an organization into a number of separate parts

Deming, W. Edwards (1900–93) GENERAL MANAGEMENT U.S. academic and statistician. A leading champion of the *quality* movement and the most influential catalyst for the economic resurgence of postwar Japan, Deming's approach is summarized in his 14 points, which form the central thesis to his book *Out of the Crisis* (1986). See thinker *W. Edwards Deming*

Deming Prize GENERAL MANAGEMENT an annual award to a company that has achieved significant performance improvement through the successful application of company-wide *quality control*. The Deming Prize was established in recognition of the work carried out by *W. Edwards Deming* in postwar Japan to improve manufacturing quality by reducing the potential for error. The Deming Prize has been awarded annually since 1951 by the Union of Japanese Scientists and Engineers. Contenders have to be able to demonstrate that, by applying the disciplines outlined by the assessment components, the productivity, growth, and financial performance of the organization have been improved. Entrants require substantial resources in order to be able to submit their entry, which can take years to prepare. The focus of the Deming Prize reflects a rigor for the identification and elimination of defects through teamwork. The prize was also the first

to apply the process of self-assessment, which has been adopted by other models such as the *Malcolm Baldrige National Quality Award* and the *EFQM Excellence Model*. See thinker *W. Edwards Deming*

democracy GENERAL MANAGEMENT see *industrial democracy*

demographics STATISTICS the characteristics of the size and structure of a human population, such as its distribution and age range

demography STATISTICS the study of the size and structural characteristics of human populations

demonetize FINANCE, BANKING, AND ACCOUNTING to withdraw a coin or note from a country's currency

demurrage FINANCE, BANKING, AND ACCOUNTING compensation paid to a customer when shipment of a good is delayed at a port or by customs

denial of service attack E-COMMERCE an attack on a computer system by a *hacker* or *virus* that does not seek to break into the system, but rather to crash a Web site by deluging it with phony traffic. Such attacks are difficult to defend against, but *firewall*s can be designed to block repeated traffic from a particular source.

department GENERAL MANAGEMENT a section of an organization, usually centered on a specialized function, under the responsibility of a head of department or team leader

departmental budget FINANCE, BANKING, AND ACCOUNTING see *functional budget*

departmentalization GENERAL MANAGEMENT the division of an organization into sections. Departmentalization is usually based on operating function, and organizations will commonly have departments for, for example, finance, personnel, or marketing. Such organizational structure is typical of a *bureaucracy*. It may be used in *centralization*, when a particular activity is undertaken by one department in one location on behalf of the whole organization, but may equally be a feature of a *decentralized* organization, in which departments are used as individual operating units responsible for their own management.

depositary FINANCE, BANKING, AND ACCOUNTING a person who or organization which has placed money or documents for safekeeping with a *depository*

depository FINANCE, BANKING, AND ACCOUNTING a bank or organization with whom money or documents can be left for safekeeping

deposit protection FINANCE, BANKING, AND ACCOUNTING insurance that depositors have against loss. In the United States, the Federal Deposit Insurance Corporation (FDIC) provides this.

deposit receipt FINANCE, BANKING, AND ACCOUNTING see *deposit slip*

deposit slip FINANCE, BANKING, AND ACCOUNTING a U.S. term for the slip of paper that accompanies money or checks being paid into a bank account. Also called *deposit receipt*

depreciable cost FINANCE, BANKING, AND ACCOUNTING an expense which may be set against the profits of more than one accounting period

depreciation FINANCE, BANKING, AND ACCOUNTING
1 an allocation of the *cost* of an *asset* over a period of time for accounting and tax purposes. Depreciation is charged against earnings, on the basis that the use of capital assets is a legitimate cost of doing business. Depreciation is also a non-cash expense that is added into net income to determine cash flow in a given accounting period.

To qualify for depreciation, assets must be items used in the business that wear out, become obsolete, or lose value over time from natural causes or circumstances, and they must have a useful life beyond a single tax year. Examples include vehicles, machines, equipment, furnishings, and buildings, plus major additions or improvements to such assets. Some intangible assets also can be included under certain conditions. Land, personal assets, stock, leased or rented property, and a company's employees cannot be depreciated.

Straight-line depreciation is the most straightforward method. It assumes that the net cost of an asset should be written off in equal amounts over its life. The formula used is

$$\frac{\text{Original cost} - \text{Scrap value}}{\text{Useful life (years)}}$$

For example, if a vehicle cost $30,000 and can be expected to serve the business for seven years, its original cost would be divided by its useful life:

$$\frac{(30,000 - 2,000)}{7} = 4,000 \text{ per year}$$

The $4,000 becomes a depreciation expense that is reported on the company's year-end income statement under "operation expenses."

In theory, an asset should be depreciated over the actual number of years that it will be used, according to its actual drop in value each year. At the end of each year, all the depreciation claimed to date is subtracted from its cost in order to arrive at its *book value*, which would equal its market value. At the end of its useful business life, any undepreciated portion would represent the salvage value for which it could be sold or scrapped.

For tax purposes, some accountants prefer to use *accelerated depreciation* to record larger amounts of depreciation in the asset's early years in order to reduce tax bills as soon as possible. In contrast to the straight-line method, the declining balance method assumes that the asset depreciates more in its earlier years of use. The table below compares the depreciation amounts that would be available, under these two methods, for a $1,000 asset that is expected to be used for five years and then sold for $100 as scrap.

Straight-line Method

Year	Annual Depreciation	Year-end Book Value
1	$900 × 20% = $180	$1,000 - $180 = $820
2	$900 × 20% = $180	$820 - $180 = $640
3	$900 × 20% = $180	$640 - $180 = $460
4	$900 × 20% = $180	$460 - $180 = $280
5	$900 × 20% = $180	$280 - $180 = $100

Declining-balance Method

Year	Annual Depreciation	Year-end Book Value
1	$1,000 × 40% = $400	$1,000 - $400 = $600
2	$600 × 40% = $240	$600 - $240 = $360
3	$360 × 40% = $144	$360 - $144 = $216
4	$216 × 40% = $86.40	$216 - $86.40 = $129.60
5	$129.60 × 40% = $51.84	$129.60 - $51.84 = $77.76

The depreciation method to be used for a particular asset is fixed at the time that the asset is first placed in service. Whatever rules or tables are in effect for that year must be followed as long as the asset is owned.

Depreciation laws and regulations change frequently over the years as a result of government policy changes, so a company owning property over a long period may have to use several different depreciation methods.
2 a reduction of a currency's value in relation to the value of other currencies

depression ECONOMICS a prolonged slump or downturn in the business cycle, marked by a high level of unemployment

deregulation GENERAL MANAGEMENT the process of removing government regulations from an industry

derivative FINANCE, BANKING, AND ACCOUNTING a security, such as an option, the price of which has a strong correlation with an underlying financial instrument

Derivative Trading Facility FINANCE, BANKING, AND ACCOUNTING a computer system and associated network operated by the Australian Stock Exchange to facilitate the purchase and sale of exchange-traded options. Abbr. *DTF*

DES *abbr* E-COMMERCE Data Encryption Standard: the most widely used standard for encrypting sensitive business information

designated account FINANCE, BANKING, AND ACCOUNTING an account opened and held in one person's name, but which also features another person's name for extra identification purposes

design audit MARKETING an examination of the branding, style, and design of an organization's marketing material. A design agency may conduct a design audit free of charge in the hope that an organization will accept their recommendations and place design of material with them.

design consultancy MARKETING an organization that plans and carries out design work for clients, including packaging, corporate identity, products, and publication graphics

design for manufacturability *or* **design for assembly** *or* **design for production** GENERAL MANAGEMENT the process of designing a product for best-fit with the manufacturing system of an organization in order to reduce the problems of bringing a product to market. Design for manufacturability is a team approach to manufacturing that pairs those responsible for the design of a product with those who build it. The manufacturing issues that need to be taken into account in the design process may include using the minimum number of parts, selecting appropriate materials, ease of assembly, and minimizing the number of machine set-ups. Design for manufacturability is one of the elements of *concurrent engineering* and is sometimes used as a synonym for it. Also known as *engineering for excellence, manufacturing for excellence, producibility engineering*

design protection MARKETING see *copyright*

desk dining GENERAL MANAGEMENT eating lunch at your desk at your place of work, in order to save time

deskfast GENERAL MANAGEMENT breakfast eaten in the office at a desk (*slang*)

de-skilling HR & PERSONNEL the removal of the need for skill or judgment in the performance of a task, often because of new technologies. While it can be argued that de-skilling has adversely affected some *manual workers* in trad-

itional manufacturing industries, the technologies used in modern production systems require a wider range and higher level of skill among the workforce as a whole.

desk jockey GENERAL MANAGEMENT somebody who works at a desk (*slang*)

desk research MARKETING research carried out using documents, telephone interviews, or the Internet

Deutscher Aktienindex FINANCE, BANKING, AND ACCOUNTING see *DAX*

devaluation ECONOMICS a reduction in the official fixed rate at which one currency exchanges for another under a fixed-rate regime, usually to correct a balance of payments deficit

developing country ECONOMICS a country, often a producer of primary goods such as cotton or rubber, which cannot generate investment income to stimulate growth and which possesses a national income that is vulnerable to change in commodity prices

development capital GENERAL MANAGEMENT finance for the expansion of an established business

Development Capital Market (*S. Africa*) FINANCE, BANKING, AND ACCOUNTING a sector on the JSE Securities Exchange for listing smaller developing companies. Criteria for listing in the Development Capital Market sector are less stringent than for the main board listing. Abbr. *DCM*

development cycle MARKETING see *new product development*

Diagonal Street (*S. Africa*) FINANCE, BANKING, AND ACCOUNTING an informal term for the financial center of Johannesburg or, by extension, South Africa

dial and smile MARKETING to cold call potential customers of a product or service (*slang*)

dicing and slicing MARKETING the analysis of raw data to extract information under different categories (*slang*)

differential costing FINANCE, BANKING, AND ACCOUNTING a costing method which shows the difference in costs which results from different levels of activity, such as the cost of making one thousand or ten thousand extra units of a product

differential pricing MARKETING a method of pricing that offers the same product at different prices, for example, in different markets, countries, or retail outlets

differential tariff FINANCE, BANKING, AND ACCOUNTING a tariff on goods or services which varies according to their class or source

differentiation MARKETING see *product differentiation*

digerati E-COMMERCE people who have or claim to have a sophisticated understanding of Internet or computer technology (*slang*)

digital cash E-COMMERCE an anonymous form of *digital money* that can be linked directly to a bank account or exchanged for physical money. As with physical cash, there is no way to obtain information about the buyer from it, and it can be transferred by the seller to pay for subsequent purchases. Also known as *e-cash*

digital certificate E-COMMERCE an electronic document issued by a recognized authority that validates a purchaser. It is used much as a driver's license or passport is used for identification purposes in a traditional business transaction.

digital coins E-COMMERCE a form of electronic payment authorized for instant transactions that facilitates the purchase of items priced in small denominations of *digital cash*. Digital coins are transferred from customer to merchant for a transaction such as the purchase of a newspaper using a *smart card* for payment.

digital coupon E-COMMERCE a voucher or similar form that exists electronically, for example, on a Web site, and can be used to reduce the price of goods or services

digital Darwinism E-COMMERCE the idea that the development of Internet companies is governed by rules similar to Darwin's theory of evolution, and that those that adapt best to their environment will be the most successful

digital divide E-COMMERCE the difference in opportunities available to people who have access to modern information technology and those who do not

digital economy ECONOMICS an economy in which the main productive functions are in electronic commerce, for example, trade on the Internet

digital goods E-COMMERCE merchandise that is sold and delivered electronically, for example, over the Internet

digital hygienist GENERAL MANAGEMENT somebody within a company who is responsible for checking employees' e-mails and surfing habits for non-work-related activity (*slang*)

digital money E-COMMERCE a series of numbers with an intrinsic value in some physical currency. Online digital money requires electronic interaction with a bank to conduct a transaction; offline digital money does not. Anonymous digital money is synonymous with *digital cash*. Identified digital money carries with it information revealing the identities of those involved in the transaction. Also known as *e-money*, *electronic money*

digital nervous system GENERAL MANAGEMENT an information system that allows an organization to respond to external events through the accumulation, management, and distribution of knowledge

digital strategy GENERAL MANAGEMENT a business strategy that is based on the use of information technology

digital wallet
1 E-COMMERCE software on the hard drive of an online shopper from which the purchaser can pay for the transaction electronically. The wallet can hold in encrypted form such items as credit card information, digital cash or coins, a digital certificate to identify the user, and standardized shipping information. Also known as *electronic wallet*
2 FINANCE, BANKING, AND ACCOUNTING a fund of digital cash

digithead GENERAL MANAGEMENT somebody who is very knowledgeable about technology and mathematics but has poor social skills (*slang*)

digitizable E-COMMERCE capable of being converted to digital form for distribution via the Internet or other networks

dilberted HR & PERSONNEL badly treated by your boss. The term derives from the same fictional character who gave his name to the *Dilbert principle*. (*slang*)

Dilbert principle HR & PERSONNEL the principle that the most inefficient employees are moved to the place where they can do the least damage. Dilbert is the main character in a comic strip and cartoon series by Scott Adams that satirizes office and corporate life.

dilution levy FINANCE, BANKING, AND ACCOUNTING an extra charge levied by fund managers on investors buying or selling units in a fund,

designed to offset any potential effect on the value of the fund of such purchases or sales

dilution of equity FINANCE, BANKING, AND ACCOUNTING a situation in which a company makes more shares of common stock available without an increase in its assets, with the end result that each share is worth less than before

DINKY GENERAL MANAGEMENT dual income, no kids (*slang*)

direct action marketing MARKETING see *direct response marketing*

direct channel MARKETING a method of selling and distributing products direct to customers. Direct channels include direct sales, mail order, and the Internet.

direct connection E-COMMERCE a permanent connection between a computer system and the Internet

direct cost FINANCE, BANKING, AND ACCOUNTING GENERAL MANAGEMENT OPERATIONS & PRODUCTION a variable cost directly attributable to production. Items that are classed as direct costs include materials used, labor deployed, and marketing budget. Amounts spent will vary with output. See also *indirect cost*

direct labor HR & PERSONNEL personnel directly involved in the manufacturing of products or the provision of services. Direct labor includes *blue-collar workers*.

direct labor cost percentage rate FINANCE, BANKING, AND ACCOUNTING an *overhead absorption rate* based on direct labor cost

direct labor hour rate FINANCE, BANKING, AND ACCOUNTING an *overhead absorption rate* based on direct labor hours

direct mail MARKETING the sending by mail, fax, or e-mail of *advertising* communications addressed to specific prospective customers. Direct mail is one tool that can be used as part of a marketing strategy. The use of direct mail is often administered by third-party companies that own databases containing not only names and addresses, but also social, economic, and lifestyle information. It is sometimes seen as an invasion of personal privacy, and there is some public resentment of this form of advertising. This is particularly true of e-mailed direct mail, known derogatively as *spam*. By enabling advertisers to target a specific type of potential customer, however, direct mail can be more cost-efficient than other *advertising media*. It is frequently used as part of a relationship marketing strategy.

direct mail preference scheme MARKETING an arrangement that allows individuals and organizations to refuse direct mail by having participating organizations remove them from their mailing lists

direct marketing MARKETING see *direct response marketing*

directorate GENERAL MANAGEMENT the governing or controlling body of an organization responsible for the organization's *corporate strategy* and accountable to its *stakeholders* for business results. A directorate may also be known as a *board of directors* or council, or, at an inner level, the executive or management committee.

director's dealing FINANCE, BANKING, AND ACCOUNTING the purchase or sale of a company's stock by one of its directors

direct response marketing *or* **direct response advertising** MARKETING the use of direct forms of *advertising* to elicit inquiries or sales from potential customers directly to producers or service providers. Direct response marketing aims to bypass intermediaries such as retailers or wholesalers. Forms of communication used include *direct mail*, home shopping channels, and television and press advertisements. Also known as *direct action marketing*, *direct marketing*

direct selling MARKETING the selling of products or services directly to customers without the use of intermediaries such as wholesalers, retailers, or brokers. Direct selling offers many advantages to the customer, including lower prices and shopping from home. Potential disadvantages include lack of *after-sales service*, an inability to inspect products prior to purchase, lack of specialist advice, and difficulties in returning or exchanging goods. Methods of direct selling include mail order catalogs and door-to-door and telephone sales. Direct selling has increased with the growth of the Internet, which enables producers to make direct contact with potential customers.

direct tax FINANCE, BANKING, AND ACCOUNTING a tax on income or capital that is paid directly rather than added to the price of goods or services

dirty float ECONOMICS a floating exchange rate that cannot float freely because a country's central bank intervenes on foreign exchange markets to alter its level

dirty price FINANCE, BANKING, AND ACCOUNTING the price of a debt instrument that includes the

amount of accrued interest that has not yet been paid

disaggregation GENERAL MANAGEMENT the breaking apart of an alliance of companies to review their strengths and contributions as a basis for rebuilding an effective business web

disaster management GENERAL MANAGEMENT the actions taken by an organization in response to unexpected events that are adversely affecting people or resources and threatening the continued operation of the organization. Disaster management includes the development of *disaster recovery plans*, for minimizing the risk of disasters and for handling them when they do occur, and the implementation of such plans. Disaster management usually refers to the management of natural catastrophes such as fire, flooding, or earthquakes. Related techniques include *crisis management*, *contingency management*, and *risk management*.

disaster recovery plan GENERAL MANAGEMENT see *disaster management*

disbursing agent FINANCE, BANKING, AND ACCOUNTING see *paying agent*

disciplinary procedure HR & PERSONNEL see *discipline*

discipline HR & PERSONNEL standards of required behavior or performance. Good practice requires an organization to establish a *disciplinary procedure* in order to ensure just decisions. A disciplinary procedure should consist of a formal system of documented warnings and hearings, with rights of representation and appeal at each stage.

disclosure of information GENERAL MANAGEMENT the release of information to a third party or parties that may be considered confidential. The disclosure of information in the public interest may be prohibited, permitted, or required, by legislation in a variety of contexts. For example: *data protection* legislation restricts the disclosure of personal data held by organizations; *company law* requires the publication of certain financial and company data; and *whistleblowing* legislation entitles employees to divulge information relating to unethical or illegal conduct in the workplace. Restrictive covenants and *confidentiality agreements* also regulate the information that may be disclosed to third parties.

discount
1 FINANCE, BANKING, AND ACCOUNTING GENERAL MANAGEMENT a reduction in the price of goods or services in relation to the standard price. A discount is a selling technique that is used, for

example, to encourage customers to buy in large quantities or to make payments in cash. It can also be used to improve sales of a slow-moving line. The greater the purchasing power of the buyer, the greater the discounts that can be negotiated. Some companies inflate original list prices to give the impression that discounts offer value for money; conversely too many genuine discounts may harm profitability.

2 FINANCE, BANKING, AND ACCOUNTING the difference between the share price of an investment trust and its *net asset value*

discount allowed FINANCE, BANKING, AND ACCOUNTING the amount by which the seller agrees to reduce his or her price to the customer

discount broker FINANCE, BANKING, AND ACCOUNTING a broker who charges relatively low fees because he or she provides restricted services

discounted bond FINANCE, BANKING, AND ACCOUNTING a bond that is sold for less than its face value because its yield is not as high as that of other bonds

discounted dividend model FINANCE, BANKING, AND ACCOUNTING a method of calculating a stock's value by reducing future dividends to the present value. Also known as *dividend discount model*

discounted value FINANCE, BANKING, AND ACCOUNTING the difference between the face value of a stock and its lower market price

discount loan FINANCE, BANKING, AND ACCOUNTING a loan that amounts to less than its face value because payment of interest has been subtracted

discount rate

1 FINANCE, BANKING, AND ACCOUNTING the rate charged by a central bank on any loans it makes to other banks

2 E-COMMERCE a percentage fee that an e-commerce merchant pays to an account provider or independent sales organization for settling an electronic transaction

discount received FINANCE, BANKING, AND ACCOUNTING the amount by which the purchaser receives a reduction in price from the seller

discount security FINANCE, BANKING, AND ACCOUNTING a security that is sold for less than its face value in lieu of bearing interest

discrete variable STATISTICS a variable in a statistical study that has only a whole number

value, such as the number of deaths in a population

discretionary account FINANCE, BANKING, AND ACCOUNTING a securities account in which the broker has the authority to make decisions about buying and selling without the customer's prior permission

discretionary management FINANCE, BANKING, AND ACCOUNTING an arrangement between a stockbroker and his or her client whereby the stockbroker makes all investment decisions. It is the opposite of an *advisory management* arrangement.

discretionary order FINANCE, BANKING, AND ACCOUNTING a security transaction in which a broker controls the details, such as the time of execution

discretionary trust FINANCE, BANKING, AND ACCOUNTING a trust where the trustees decide how to invest the income and when and how much income should be paid to the beneficiaries

discriminant analysis GENERAL MANAGEMENT a statistical technique designed to predict the groups or categories into which individual cases will fall on the basis of a number of independent variables. Discriminant analysis attempts to identify which variables or combinations of variables accurately discriminate between groups or categories by means of a scatter diagram or classification table called a *confusion matrix*. Discriminant analysis has applications in finance, for example, credit risk analysis, or in the prediction of company failure, and in the field of marketing, for market segmentation purposes.

discriminating monopoly ECONOMICS a company able to charge different prices for its output in different markets because it has power to influence prices for its goods

discrimination HR & PERSONNEL unfavorable treatment in employment based on prejudice. Major forms of outlawed discrimination include sex discrimination, *racial discrimination*, disability discrimination, and, in some countries, *age discrimination*. Discrimination may also be practiced through *indirect discrimination*.

discussion board E-COMMERCE an area on a Web site that allows people to contribute opinions, ideas, and announcements. It is particularly suitable for casual, one-off interactions, because little commitment is required from participants. They can generally review a discussion topic without subscribing, although

they do have to subscribe if they want to contribute something themselves.

It is not essential for the Web site owner to moderate discussion boards, although it is important to watch out for the emergence of "off-topic" subjects—contributions that are unnecessarily negative or perhaps libelous—and copyright infringement.

A prime example of the success of the discussion board approach is the way Amazon.com uses it to allow its consumers to publish book reviews.

discussion list E-COMMERCE an arrangement for sending e-mail messages to a number of people that also allows recipients to respond and everyone else on the list to see these responses. A discussion list is similar to a distribution list except that it is based on a two-way model. Discussion lists can be moderated or unmoderated. In a moderated list, all mail is screened by an intermediary, typically the individual or organization that established the list. Unmoderated lists involve no editorial process, so any subscriber can contribute anything he or she wants to the e-mail discussion. Unlike newsgroups, discussion lists do not provide a consolidated record of responses.

diseconomies of scale FINANCE, BANKING, AND ACCOUNTING a situation in which increased production increases, rather than decreases, unit costs

disequilibrium price ECONOMICS the price of a good set at a level at which demand and supply are not in balance

dishonor FINANCE, BANKING, AND ACCOUNTING to refuse payment of a check because the account for which it is written holds insufficient money. Also known as *bounce*

disinflation ECONOMICS the elimination or reduction of inflation or inflationary pressures in an economy by fiscal or monetary policies

disintermediation E-COMMERCE the elimination of intermediaries, for example, the wholesalers found in traditional retail channels, in favor of direct selling to the consumer. See also *reintermediation*

dismissal HR & PERSONNEL the termination of an *employee's* employment by his or her *employer*

dispensation (*U.K.*) FINANCE, BANKING, AND ACCOUNTING an arrangement between an employer and HM Revenue & Customs in which business expenses paid to an employee are not declared for tax

dispersion STATISTICS the amount by which a set of observations deviates from its mean

display advertising MARKETING newspaper or magazine advertisements that use eye-catching typography and graphic images

disposable income FINANCE, BANKING, AND ACCOUNTING income that is left for spending after tax and other deductions

dispute HR & PERSONNEL a disagreement. An *industrial dispute* is a disagreement between an *employer* and an employees' representative, usually a *labor union*, over pay and conditions and can result in *industrial action*. A *commercial dispute* is a disagreement between two businesses, usually over a contract. There are three main types of dispute resolution: litigation, *arbitration*, and alternative dispute resolution.

dispute benefit HR & PERSONNEL see *strike pay*

disqualification FINANCE, BANKING, AND ACCOUNTING a court order which forbids a person from being a director of a company. A variety of offenses, even those termed as "administrative," can result in some people being disqualified for up to five years.

distance learning GENERAL MANAGEMENT a course of study that involves minimal or no attendance at an academic institution, but relies instead on personal study, using books, audiovisual materials, and computer-based materials. Tutorial support may be available via the telephone or Internet, and attendance at weekend or summer schools may be required. Distance learning is similar to *open learning*.

distance sampling STATISTICS a method of sampling in ecological statistics used to determine the number of animals that feed or plants that grow in a particular habitat

distrain FINANCE, BANKING, AND ACCOUNTING to seize *assets* belonging to a person or organization in order to pay off a debt

distressed property FINANCE, BANKING, AND ACCOUNTING property purchased with the aid of a loan on which payments have stopped and the borrower has defaulted

distribution center OPERATIONS & PRODUCTION a warehouse or storage facility where the emphasis is on processing and moving goods on to wholesalers, retailers, or consumers rather than on storage

distribution channel OPERATIONS & PRODUCTION the route by which a product or service is moved from a producer or supplier to customers. A distribution channel usually consists of a chain of intermediaries, including *wholesalers*, *retailers*, and distributors, that is designed to transport goods from the point of production to the point of consumption in the most efficient way.

distribution list E-COMMERCE a list of e-mail addresses given one collective name. Internet users can send a message to all the addresses on the list simultaneously by referring to the list name.

distribution management OPERATIONS & PRODUCTION the management of the efficient transfer of goods from the place of manufacture to the point of sale or consumption. Distribution management encompasses such activities as *warehousing*, *materials handling*, packaging, stock control, order processing, and transportation.

distribution resource planning OPERATIONS & PRODUCTION a computerized system that integrates distribution with manufacturing by identifying requirements for finished goods and producing schedules for *inventory* and its movement within the distribution process. Distribution resource planning systems receive data on sales forecasts, customer order and delivery requirements, available inventory, *logistics*, and manufacturing and purchasing *lead times*. This data is analyzed to produce a time-phased schedule of resource requirements that is matched against existing supply sources and production schedules to identify the actions that must be taken to synchronize supply and demand. The effective integration of material requirements planning and distribution resource planning systems leads to the more effective and timely delivery of finished goods to the customer, and to reduced inventory levels and lower material costs. Abbr. *DRP*

distributions FINANCE, BANKING, AND ACCOUNTING any income arising from a bond fund or an equity

distributive network E-COMMERCE a system or infrastructure that enables products and services to move around. Offline distributive networks include roads, telephone companies, electrical power grids, and the mail service. In the new economy, distributive networks include online banks and Web-enabled mobile telephones.

distributor MARKETING an organization that distributes products to retailers on behalf of a manufacturer

distributor support MARKETING marketing or financial support by manufacturers aimed at improving the performance of organizations that distribute their products

District Bank FINANCE, BANKING, AND ACCOUNTING one of the 12 banks that make up the *Federal Reserve System*. Each District Bank is responsible for all banking activity in its area.

diversification FINANCE, BANKING, AND ACCOUNTING GENERAL MANAGEMENT a strategy to increase the variety of business, service, or product types within an organization. Diversification can be a growth strategy, taking advantage of market opportunities, or it may be aimed at reducing risk by spreading interests over different areas. It can be achieved through *acquisition* or through internal research and development, and it can involve managing two, a few, or many different areas of interest. Diversification can also be a *corporate strategy* of investment in acquisitions within a broad portfolio range by a large *holding company*. One distinct type is *horizontal diversification*, which involves expansion into a similar product area, for example, a domestic furniture manufacturer producing office furniture. Another is *vertical diversification*, in which a company moves into a different level of the *supply chain*, for example, a manufacturing company becoming a retailer. A well-known example of diversification is the move of BIC, the ballpoint pen manufacturer, into the production of disposable razors.

diversified investment company FINANCE, BANKING, AND ACCOUNTING a mutual fund with a variety of types of investments

diversity GENERAL MANAGEMENT a difference between people, for example, in race, age, gender, disability, geographic origin, family status, education, or personality, that can affect workplace relationships and achievement. Diversity management aims to value these differences and encourage each person to fulfill his or her potential in terms of organizational objectives. The approach goes beyond *equal opportunities*, which stresses the rights of particular disadvantaged groups rather than those of the individual.

divestment
1 GENERAL MANAGEMENT the sale or closure of one or several businesses, or parts of a business. Divestment often takes place as part of a *rationalization* effort to cut costs or to enable

an organization to concentrate on core business or competences, and may take the form of a *management buy-out* .

2 FINANCE, BANKING, AND ACCOUNTING the proportional or complete reduction in an ownership stake in an organization

dividend clawback FINANCE, BANKING, AND ACCOUNTING an agreement that dividends will be reinvested as part of the financing of a project

dividend cover FINANCE, BANKING, AND ACCOUNTING the number of times a company's dividends to ordinary stockholders could be paid out of its net after-tax profits. This measures the likelihood of dividend payments being sustained, and is a useful indication of sustained profitability.

If the figure is 3, a firm's profits are three times the level of the dividend paid to shareholders.

Dividend cover is calculated by dividing earnings per share by the dividend per share:

$$\frac{\text{Earnings per share}}{\text{Dividend per share}} = \text{Dividend cover}$$

If a company has earnings per share of $8, and it pays out a dividend of 2.1, dividend cover is

$$\frac{8}{2.1} = 3.80$$

An alternative formula divides a company's net profit by the total amount allocated for dividends. So a company that earns $10 million in net profit and allocates $1 million for dividends has a dividend cover of 10, while a company that earns $25 million and pays out $10 million in dividends has a dividend cover of 2.5:

$$\frac{10,000,000}{1,000,000} = 10$$

and

$$\frac{25,000,000}{10,000,000} = 2.5$$

A dividend cover ratio of 2 or higher is usually adequate, and indicates that the dividend is affordable. A dividend cover ratio below 1.5 is risky, and a ratio below 1 indicates a company is paying the current year's dividend with retained earnings from a previous years—a practice that cannot continue indefinitely. On the other hand, a high dividend cover figure may disappoint an investor looking for income, since the figure suggests directors could have declared a larger dividend. See also *payout ratio*

dividend discount model FINANCE, BANKING, AND ACCOUNTING see *discounted dividend model*

dividend limitation FINANCE, BANKING, AND ACCOUNTING a provision in a bond limiting the dividends that may be paid

dividend mandate FINANCE, BANKING, AND ACCOUNTING an authorization by a stockholder to the company in which he or she has a holding to pay dividends directly into his or her bank account

dividend reinvestment plan FINANCE, BANKING, AND ACCOUNTING a plan that provides for the reinvestment of dividends in the stock of the company paying the dividends. Abbr. **DRIP**

dividend rights FINANCE, BANKING, AND ACCOUNTING rights to receive dividends

dividends-received deduction FINANCE, BANKING, AND ACCOUNTING a tax advantage on dividends that a company receives from a company it owns

dividend yield FINANCE, BANKING, AND ACCOUNTING dividends expressed as a percentage of a stock's price

division of labor OPERATIONS & PRODUCTION the allocation of each task in a process to a different worker. Division of labor is a concept originated by **Adam Smith** in order to increase output. It enables workers to become highly skilled at one job, but they may lack transferable skills and find their work monotonous. To a certain extent, division of labor has been superseded by *multiskilling*. See thinker **Adam Smith**

D/N *abbr* FINANCE, BANKING, AND ACCOUNTING debit note

document E-COMMERCE an electronic file containing text, graphics, multimedia, or hyperlinks

documentary credit FINANCE, BANKING, AND ACCOUNTING an arrangement, used in the finance of international transactions, whereby a bank undertakes to make a payment to a third party on behalf of a customer

dog GENERAL MANAGEMENT see **Boston Box**

that dog won't hunt GENERAL MANAGEMENT that idea will not work (*slang*)

dog and pony show GENERAL MANAGEMENT a national tour by the top staff of a company aimed at persuading investors to invest in the company (*slang*)

dog-eat-dog MARKETING ruthless, especially in the marketplace (*slang*)

dogfood E-COMMERCE temporary software used by an organization for testing purposes

dogs of the Dow FINANCE, BANKING, AND ACCOUNTING the stocks in the Dow Jones Industrial Average that pay the smallest dividends as a percentage of their prices (*slang*)

dole bludger (*ANZ*) GENERAL MANAGEMENT somebody who lives off social security payments and makes no attempt to find work (*slang*)

dollar area FINANCE, BANKING, AND ACCOUNTING an area of the world where the U.S. dollar is the main trading currency

dollar cost averaging FINANCE, BANKING, AND ACCOUNTING the regular periodic purchase of the same amount in dollars of the same security regardless of its price. U.K. term *pound cost averaging*

dollar roll FINANCE, BANKING, AND ACCOUNTING an agreement to sell a stock and buy it back later for a specified price

dollars-and-cents FINANCE, BANKING, AND ACCOUNTING considering money as the determining factor

domain name E-COMMERCE the officially registered address of a Web site. Domain names typically contain two or more parts separated from each other by a dot, for example, www.yahoo.com. The domain name suffix (following the final dot) is intended to indicate either the nature or location of the Web site, for example, com for a commercial Web site and co.uk for a British Web site.

domicilium citandi et executandi (*S. Africa*) FINANCE, BANKING, AND ACCOUNTING the address where a summons or other official notice should be served if necessary, which must be supplied by somebody applying for credit or entering into a contract

dominant influence FINANCE, BANKING, AND ACCOUNTING influence that can be exercised to achieve the operating and financial policies designed by the holder of the influence, notwithstanding the rights or influence of any other party

donut MARKETING the middle section of a commercial where the product information is usually placed (*slang*)

dormant account FINANCE, BANKING, AND ACCOUNTING a bank account which is no longer used by the account holder

dormant company FINANCE, BANKING, AND ACCOUNTING a company which has not made any transactions during a specified accounting period

dot bam E-COMMERCE a real-world business with a strong Web presence. The "bam" stands for "bricks and mortar."

dot-com *or* **dot.com** E-COMMERCE an e-commerce enterprise. It markets its products through the Internet, rather than through traditional channels.

dotted-line relationships HR & PERSONNEL the links, as shown on an organizational chart, that exist between managers and staff whom they oversee indirectly rather than on a day-to-day basis (*slang*)

double-blind STATISTICS relating to an experiment, usually a medical one, in which neither the experimenter nor the subject knows whether the treatment being administered is genuine or a control procedure

double counting GENERAL MANAGEMENT the counting of a cost or benefit element twice when doing analysis. This can happen when calculating the total sales in a market as the sum of all sales made by firms, without deducting the purchases firms make from other firms in the market.

double dipping GENERAL MANAGEMENT the practice of receiving income from a government pension as well as social security payments

double-entry bookkeeping FINANCE, BANKING, AND ACCOUNTING the most commonly used system of *bookkeeping*, based on the principle that every financial transaction involves the simultaneous receiving and giving of value, and is therefore recorded twice

double indemnity FINANCE, BANKING, AND ACCOUNTING a provision in an insurance policy that guarantees payment of double its face value on the accidental death of the holder

double opt-in E-COMMERCE a type of *subscription process* for users wanting to sign up to receive specific information or services via a Web site. The double opt-in approach is emerging as the industry standard for subscription management, as it protects the user from being maliciously subscribed to a service by a third party.

The user requests a subscription, via e-mail or Web form. The vendor's system replies with a verification message, requesting an affirmative reply to the message. Only when an affirmative reply is received from the user is the subscription completed.

double taxation FINANCE, BANKING, AND ACCOUNTING the taxing of something twice, usually the combination of corporation tax and tax on the dividends that stockholders earn

double taxation relief FINANCE, BANKING, AND ACCOUNTING a reduction of tax payable in one country by the amount of tax on income, profits, or capital gains already paid in another country

doughnut principle GENERAL MANAGEMENT a concept that likens an organization to an *inverted doughnut* with a center of dough—the core activities—surrounded by a hole—a flexible area containing the organization's partners. The doughnut principle was originated by *Charles Handy* in *The Age of Paradox* (1994). He saw organizations as having an essential core of jobs and people, surrounded by a space filled with flexible workers and flexible supply contracts. He maintained that organizations often neglect the core, developing the surrounding hole instead. The doughnut analogy is a way of helping a balance to be achieved between what has to be done and what could be done, by analyzing the dough and the hole of a particular organization. The principle has also been applied to personal life. See thinker *Charles Handy*

Dow Jones Averages FINANCE, BANKING, AND ACCOUNTING an index of the prices of selected stocks on the New York Stock Exchange compiled by Dow Jones & Company, Inc

downgrade FINANCE, BANKING, AND ACCOUNTING
1 to reduce the forecast for a stock
2 to reduce the credit rating for a *bond*

downshifting GENERAL MANAGEMENT the concept of giving up all or part of your work commitment and income in exchange for improved quality of life. The term was coined by *Charles Handy*. Downshifting has increased in popularity because of rising *stress* in the workplace caused partly by the *downsizing* trend of the late 20th century, and may be contrasted with the concept of the *organization man*. Downshifting is integral to the idea of *portfolio working*, in which individuals opt out of a formal employee relationship to sell their services at a pace and at a price to suit themselves.

Most people consider downshifting because of family demands, or because they have been asked to do something by their organization that goes strongly against their values, pushing them to question why they are working so hard for that organization. Others downshift as they approach retirement, in order to smooth the transition. People who downshift need to be very sure that that is what they really want and know why they want it, as it can be hard to reverse the decision.

Someone wanting to take the risk of downshifting should make a thorough assessment of his or her short-term and long-term financial situation by way of preparation. They will need to have a good bed of savings to rely on in the first year. It may be necessary to consider moving to a smaller, cheaper place. Deciding what to keep of the old life and what to let go is another important part of the preparation. Some downshifters will want to completely leave their old work life behind them, start a new job in a slower-paced organization, or set up on their own. Others will want to stay with their organization but perhaps move to a less demanding job. Once these things have been considered and decided upon, it is time for the downshifter to make an action plan with a schedule which includes regular re-assessment periods. See thinker *Charles Handy*

downsizing
1 FINANCE, BANKING, AND ACCOUNTING organizational restructuring involving outsourcing activities, replacing permanent staff with contract employees, and reducing the number of levels within the organizational hierarchy, with the intention of making the organization more flexible, efficient, and responsive to its environment
2 HR & PERSONNEL the reduction of the size of a business, especially by laying staff off. Downsizing may be part of a *rationalization* process, or *corporate restructuring*, with the removal of hierarchies or the closure of departments or functions either after a period of unsatisfactory results or as a consequence of strategic review. The terms *upsizing* and *resizing* are applied when an organization increases the number of staff employed.

downstream OPERATIONS & PRODUCTION later in the production process

downstream progress GENERAL MANAGEMENT movement by a company toward achieving its objectives that is easy because it involves riding a wave or trend and benefiting from favorable conditions. See also *upstream progress*

downtime OPERATIONS & PRODUCTION a period of time during which a machine is not available for use because of maintenance or breakdown

Dow Theory FINANCE, BANKING, AND ACCOUNTING the theory that stock market prices can be forecast on the basis of the movements of selected industrial and transportation stocks

Doz, Yves L. (*b.* 1947) GENERAL MANAGEMENT French academic. Collaborator with *C. K. Prahalad* and *Gary Hamel* in researching *strategic models* to tackle the complexities

a-z
1473

DICTIONARY

and *globalization* of markets. His *Alliance Advantage* (1998, coauthor), focuses on *strategic partnering*. See thinker *Gary Hamel, C. K. Prahalad*. See checklist *Strategic Partnering*

draft FINANCE, BANKING, AND ACCOUNTING a written order to pay a particular sum from one account to another, or to a person. See also *sight draft, time draft*

drawee FINANCE, BANKING, AND ACCOUNTING the individual or institution to whom a bill of exchange or check is addressed

drawing account FINANCE, BANKING, AND ACCOUNTING an account that permits the tracking of withdrawals

dress-down day HR & PERSONNEL a day on which employees are allowed to wear informal clothes to work

drill down E-COMMERCE to access data or information organized in hierarchical form by starting from general information and moving through increasingly detailed data

drilling down MARKETING a technique for managing data by arranging it in hierarchies that provide increasing levels of detail

DRIP FINANCE, BANKING, AND ACCOUNTING see *dividend reinvestment plan*

drip method MARKETING a marketing method that involves calling potential customers at regular intervals until they agree to make a purchase (*slang*)

drive time MARKETING the time of the day when most people are likely to be in their cars, usually early in the morning or late in the afternoon, considered to be the optimum time to broadcast a radio commercial (*slang*)

drop a bundle FINANCE, BANKING, AND ACCOUNTING to spend or lose a lot of money, especially on the stock market (*slang*)

drop-down menu E-COMMERCE a vertical list of options that appears on clicking on an item on a computer screen. It remains visible until one of the options has been selected by clicking on it.

drop lock FINANCE, BANKING, AND ACCOUNTING the automatic conversion of a debt instrument with a floating rate to one with a fixed rate when interest rates fall to an agreed percentage

downloading E-COMMERCE the act of simultaneously downloading so many files that a computer crashes (*slang*)

DRP *abbr* OPERATIONS & PRODUCTION distribution resource planning

Drucker, Peter (1909–2005) GENERAL MANAGEMENT U.S. academic. Recognized as the father of management thinking. His earlier works studied management practice, while later he tackled the complexities and the management implications of the post-industrial world. *The Practice of Management* (1954), best known perhaps for the introduction of *management by objectives*, remains a classic. He also anticipated other management themes such as the importance of *marketing* and the rise of the *knowledge worker*.

DSL E-COMMERCE see *ADSL*

DSO *abbr* FINANCE, BANKING, AND ACCOUNTING days' sales outstanding. See also *collection ratio*

DTF *abbr* (ANZ) FINANCE, BANKING, AND ACCOUNTING Derivative Trading Facility

dual currency bond FINANCE, BANKING, AND ACCOUNTING a bond that pays interest in a currency other than the one used to buy it

dual economy ECONOMICS an economy in which the manufacturing and service sectors are growing at different rates

dual trading FINANCE, BANKING, AND ACCOUNTING the practice of acting as agent for both a broker's firm and its customers

duck
get your ducks in a row *or* **line up your ducks** GENERAL MANAGEMENT (*slang*)
1 to get everything properly organized
2 to get all concerned parties to agree to a plan of action

due diligence
1 FINANCE, BANKING, AND ACCOUNTING the examination of a company's accounts prior to a potential *takeover* by another organization. This assessment is often undertaken by an independent third party. Abbr. *DD*
2 GENERAL MANAGEMENT the collection, verification, analysis, and assessment of information about the operations and management of a company undertaken by a potential purchaser or investor. Due diligence aims to confirm that the purchaser or investor has an accurate picture of the target company and to identify risks and benefits associated with the prospective deal. Due diligence normally starts after the signing of a letter of intent by both parties and information disclosed during the process is normally protected by the signing of a *confidentiality agreement*. Due diligence often

leads on to negotiations on the detailed terms of the agreement. The process may cover the financial, legal, commercial, technical, cultural, and environmental aspects of the organization's operations as well as its *assets* and *liabilities*, and may be conducted with the assistance of professional advisers.

due-on-sale clause FINANCE, BANKING, AND ACCOUNTING a provision requiring a homeowner to pay off a mortgage upon sale of the property

dumbsizing GENERAL MANAGEMENT the process of reducing the size of a company to such an extent that it is no longer profitable or efficient (*slang*)

dumb terminal E-COMMERCE a terminal without an internal microprocessor and therefore without independent processing capability that can enter, transmit, and display alphanumeric data

dumping ECONOMICS the selling of a commodity on a foreign market at a price below its *marginal cost*, either to dispose of a temporary surplus or to achieve a monopoly by eliminating competition

Dun and Bradstreet FINANCE, BANKING, AND ACCOUNTING an international organization that sources credit information from companies and their creditors which it then makes available to subscribers. Abbr. *D&B*

Dunlap, Albert J. (*b.* 1937) GENERAL MANAGEMENT U.S. business executive. He is noted for his *turnaround management* capabilities, based on *downsizing* and *cost-cutting*, which earned him the nickname "Chainsaw Al" and which are described in his book *Mean Business* (1996).

duopoly ECONOMICS a market in which only two sellers of a good exist. If one decides to alter the price, the other will respond and influence the market's response to the first decision.

Dutch auction FINANCE, BANKING, AND ACCOUNTING an auction in which the lot for sale is offered at an initial price which, if there are no takers, is then reduced until there is a bid

Dynamic HTML E-COMMERCE a relatively limited animation tool for creating Web site graphics which, if properly designed, can be viewed by most *browsers*. Its major advantage is that it does not require a *plug-in* to view. Abbr. *DHTML*

dynamic pricing FINANCE, BANKING, AND ACCOUNTING GENERAL MANAGEMENT pricing that changes in line with patterns of demand

dynamic programming GENERAL MANAGEMENT a mathematical technique used in *management science* to solve complex problems in the fields of production planning and inventory control. Dynamic programming divides the problem into subproblems or decision stages that can be addressed sequentially, normally by working backward from the last stage. Applications of the technique include maintenance and replacement of equipment, resource allocation, and process design and control. The term comes from the work of Richard Bellman published in the late 1950s and early 1960s.

E

E2E *abbr* E-COMMERCE exchange

EAA *abbr* FINANCE, BANKING, AND ACCOUNTING European Accounting Association

EAI *abbr* E-COMMERCE enterprise application integration

e-alliance E-COMMERCE a partnership forged between organizations in order to achieve business objectives for enterprises conducted over the Web. There has been a surge in such alliances since the Internet took off in the mid-1990s, and studies show that the most successful have been those involving traditional offline businesses and online entities—the *clicks-and-mortar* strategy—such as that between Amazon.com and Toys 'R' Us. Toys 'R' Us had the physical infrastructure and brand, while Amazon.com had the online infrastructure and experience of making e-commerce work.

E&O *abbr* FINANCE, BANKING, AND ACCOUNTING errors and omissions

E&OE *abbr* FINANCE, BANKING, AND ACCOUNTING errors and omissions excepted

EAP *abbr* HR & PERSONNEL employee assistance program

early adopter GENERAL MANAGEMENT an individual or organization that is among the first to make use of a new technology

early retirement HR & PERSONNEL *retirement* from work before the statutory retirement age or before the normal retirement age set by an employer. Early retirement may be taken because of poor health or at the request of the employee or employer. An employer may offer opportunities for early retirement on ad-

vantageous financial terms as a way of reducing staff numbers without *layoffs*. Also known as *premature retirement*

early withdrawal FINANCE, BANKING, AND ACCOUNTING the removal of money from a deposit account before the due dates. Early withdrawal often incurs a penalty that the account holder must pay.

earned income FINANCE, BANKING, AND ACCOUNTING money generated by an individual's or an organization's labor, for example, wages, salaries, fees, royalties, and business profits. See also *unearned income*

earning potential FINANCE, BANKING, AND ACCOUNTING
1 the amount of money somebody should be able to earn in his or her professional capacity
2 the amount of dividend that a share potentially can produce

earnings
1 HR & PERSONNEL a sum of money gained from paid employment, usually quoted before tax, including any extra rewards such as allowances or incentives. Also known as *pay*
2 FINANCE, BANKING, AND ACCOUNTING income or profit from a business, quoted gross or net of tax, which may be retained and distributed in part to the stockholders

earnings before interest, tax, depreciation, and amortization FINANCE, BANKING, AND ACCOUNTING see *EBITDA*

earnings before interest and taxes FINANCE, BANKING, AND ACCOUNTING abbr. *EBIT*

earnings cap FINANCE, BANKING, AND ACCOUNTING the top limit of earnings which can be used in calculating a retirement pension paid from an occupational pension plan

earnings credit FINANCE, BANKING, AND ACCOUNTING an allowance which reduces bank charges on checking accounts

earnings per share FINANCE, BANKING, AND ACCOUNTING a financial ratio that measures the portion of a company's profit allocated to each outstanding share of common stock. It is the most basic measure of the value of a share, and also is the basis for calculating several other important investment ratios.
EPS is calculated by subtracting the total value of any preferred stock from net income (earnings) for the period in question, then dividing the resulting figure by the number of shares outstanding during that period.

Net income –
Dividends on any preferred stock

Average number of shares outstanding
Companies usually use a weighted average number of shares outstanding over the reporting period, but shares outstanding can either be "primary" or "fully diluted." Primary EPS is calculated using the number of shares that are currently held by investors in the market and able to be traded. Diluted EPS is the result of a complex calculation that determines how many shares would be outstanding if all exercisable warrants and options were converted into shares at the end of a quarter.

Suppose, for example, that a company has granted a large number of stock options to employees. If these options are capable of being exercised in the near future, that could significantly alter the number of shares in issue and thus the EPS, even though the net income is the same. Often in such cases, the company might quote the EPS on the existing shares and the fully diluted version. Abbr. *EPS*

earnings-related contributions FINANCE, BANKING, AND ACCOUNTING contributions to social security which rise as the worker's earnings rise

earnings report FINANCE, BANKING, AND ACCOUNTING a company's financial statements that must by law be published. U.K. term *published accounts*

earnings retained FINANCE, BANKING, AND ACCOUNTING see *retained profits*

earnings surprise FINANCE, BANKING, AND ACCOUNTING a considerable difference in size between a company's actual and anticipated earnings

earnings yield FINANCE, BANKING, AND ACCOUNTING money earned by a company during a year, expressed as a percentage of the price of one of its shares

EASDAQ *abbr* FINANCE, BANKING, AND ACCOUNTING European Association of Securities Dealers Automated Quotations: a stock exchange for technology and growth companies based in Europe and modeled on *NASDAQ* in the United States

eased (*U.K.*) FINANCE, BANKING, AND ACCOUNTING used in stock market reports to describe a market that has experienced a slight fall in prices

easy market FINANCE, BANKING, AND ACCOUNTING a market in which fewer people are buying, with the effect that prices are lower than hoped

easy money FINANCE, BANKING, AND ACCOUNTING see *cheap money*

easy money policy FINANCE, BANKING, AND ACCOUNTING a government policy which aims to expand the economy by making money more easily accessible to the public. This is done by strategies such as lowering interest rates and offering easy access to credit.

EBIT *abbr* FINANCE, BANKING, AND ACCOUNTING earnings before interest and taxes. See also *operating income*

EBITDA *abbr* FINANCE, BANKING, AND ACCOUNTING earnings before interest, tax, depreciation, and amortization: the earnings generated by a business's fundamental operating performance, frequently used in accounting ratios for comparison with other companies. Interest on borrowings, tax payable on those profits, depreciation, and amortization are excluded on the basis that they can distort the underlying performance.

It is calculated as follows:

Revenue – Expenses (excluding tax and interest, depreciation, etc.) = EBITDA

It is important to note that EBITDA ignores many factors that impact on true cash flow, such as working capital, debt payments, and other fixed expenses. Even so, it may be useful for evaluating firms in the same industry with widely different capital structures, tax rates, and depreciation policies.

EBQ *abbr* OPERATIONS & PRODUCTION economic batch quantity: the optimum batch size for the manufacture of an item or component, at the lowest cost. The batch size is a tradeoff between unit costs that increase with batch size and those that decrease. The point of lowest combined or total cost indicates the most economic batch size for production. Also known as *economic lot quantity*. See also *economic order quantity*

EBRD *abbr* FINANCE, BANKING, AND ACCOUNTING European Bank for Reconstruction and Development: the bank, which was established in 1991, developed programs to tackle a variety of issues. These included the creation and strengthening of infrastructure; industry privatization; the reform of the financial sector, including the development of capital markets and the privatization of commercial banks; the development of productive competitive private sectors of small and medium-sized enterprises in industry, agriculture, and services; the restructuring of industrial sectors to put them on a competitive basis; and encouraging foreign investment and cleaning up the environment. The EBRD had 41 original members: the European Commission, the European Investment Bank, all the then EU countries, and all the countries of Eastern Europe except Albania, which finally became a member in October 1991, followed by all the republics of the former USSR in March 1992.

e-business E-COMMERCE
1 the conduct of business on the Internet, including the electronic purchasing and selling of goods and services, servicing customers, and communications with business partners. Also known as *electronic business*
2 a company that conducts business on the Internet

e-cash E-COMMERCE see *digital cash*

ECB *abbr* FINANCE, BANKING, AND ACCOUNTING European Central Bank: the financial institution which replaced the European Monetary Institute (EMI) in 1998 and which is responsible for carrying out EU monetary policy and administering the Euro

ECML *abbr* E-COMMERCE electronic commerce modeling language

ecoconsumer GENERAL MANAGEMENT a customer who will only select from, or subscribe to, goods that meet environmentally sound considerations

ecolabel GENERAL MANAGEMENT a label used to characterize products that satisfy particular *environmental management* considerations with regard to their production, usage, or disposal

e-collaboration E-COMMERCE collaboration among people or organizations made possible by means of electronic technologies such as the Internet, videoconferencing, and wireless devices

ecological priority GENERAL MANAGEMENT the priority for organizations and governments to put as much emphasis on environmental protection as economic performance

ecological statistics STATISTICS statistical studies in the field of ecology using such techniques as *distance sampling*

ECO-Management Audit Scheme GENERAL MANAGEMENT abbr. *EMAS*

e-commerce E-COMMERCE FINANCE, BANKING, AND ACCOUNTING the exchange of goods, information products, or services via an electronic medium such as the Internet. Originally limited to buying and selling, it has evolved to include such functions as customer service, marketing, and advertising. Also known as *electronic commerce web commerce*

e-commerce mall E-COMMERCE see *cyber mall*

e-commerce processes E-COMMERCE the flow of information through planning, design, manufacture, sales, order processing, distribution, and quality in an e-business

e-company E-COMMERCE an e-commerce enterprise (*slang*)

econometric model ECONOMICS a way of representing the relationship between economic variables as an equation or set of equations with statistically precise parameters linking the variables

econometrics ECONOMICS the branch of economics concerned with using mathematical models to describe relationships in an economy, for example, between wage rates and levels of employment

Economic and Monetary Union FINANCE, BANKING, AND ACCOUNTING see *EMU*

economic assumption ECONOMICS an assumption built into an economic model, for example, that output will grow at 2.5% in the next tax year

economic batch quantity OPERATIONS & PRODUCTION see *EBQ*

Economic Development Board FINANCE, BANKING, AND ACCOUNTING an organization established in 1961 that works to promote investment in Singapore by providing various services and assistance programs to foreign and local companies. Abbr. *EDB*

economic goods ECONOMICS services or physical objects that can command a price in the market

economic growth ECONOMICS an increase in the national income of a country created by the long-term productive potential of its economy

economic indicator ECONOMICS a statistic that may be important for a country's long-term economic health, for example, rising prices or falling exports

economic life ECONOMICS the conditions of trade and manufacture in a country that contribute to its prosperity or poverty

economic lot quantity OPERATIONS & PRODUCTION see *EBQ*

economic miracle ECONOMICS the rapid growth after 1945 in countries such as Germany and Japan, where in ten years economies shattered by World War II were regenerated

economic order quantity

1 OPERATIONS & PRODUCTION a reorder method that attempts to estimate the best order quantity by balancing the conflicting costs of holding stock and of placing replenishment orders. For large orders, the unit cost may be lower, but storage costs will be higher, because the average storage time will increase. For small orders, the cost of order processing and unit cost may be higher, but storage costs will be lower, because the average storage time is less. **2** FINANCE, BANKING, AND ACCOUNTING the most economic stock replenishment order size, which minimizes the sum of stock ordering costs and stockholding costs. EOQ is used in an "optimizing" stock control system. Abbr. *EOQ*

economic paradigm ECONOMICS a basic unchanging economic principle

Economic Planning and Advisory Council FINANCE, BANKING, AND ACCOUNTING a committee of businesspeople and politicians appointed to advise the Australian government on economic issues

economic pressure ECONOMICS a condition in a country's economy in which economic indicators are unfavorable

economics ECONOMICS the study of the consumption, distribution, and production of wealth in a society

economic sanctions FINANCE, BANKING, AND ACCOUNTING restrictions on trade with a country in order to influence its political situation or to make its government change its policy

economic surplus ECONOMICS the difference between an economy's output and the costs incurred, for example, wages, raw material costs, and depreciation

economic theory of the firm FINANCE, BANKING, AND ACCOUNTING GENERAL MANAGEMENT the theory that states that the only duty that a company has to those external to it is financial. The economic theory of the firm holds that stockholders should be the prime beneficiaries of an organization's activities. The theory is associated with *top-down leadership* and *cost-cutting* through rationalization and *downsizing*. With immediate stock price dominating management activities, economic theory has been criticized as being too short-term,

as opposed to the longer-term thinking behind *stakeholder theory*.

economic value added FINANCE, BANKING, AND ACCOUNTING a way of judging financial performance by measuring the amount by which the earnings of a project, an operation, or a corporation exceed or fall short of the total amount of capital that was originally invested by its owners.

EVA is conceptually simple: from net operating profit, subtract an appropriate charge for the opportunity cost of all capital invested in an enterprise—the amount that could have been invested elsewhere. It is calculated using this formula:

Net operating profit less applicable taxes –
Cost of capital = EVA

If a company is considering building a new plant, and its total weighted cost over ten years is $80 million, while the expected annual incremental return on the new operation is $10 million, or $100 million over ten years, then the plant's EVA would be positive, in this case $20 million:

$100 million – $80 million = $20 million

An alternative but more complex formula for EVA is:

(% Return on invested capital –
% Cost of capital) ×
Original capital invested = EVA

EVA is frequently linked with shareholder value analysis, and an objective of EVA is to determine which business units best utilize their assets to generate returns and maximize shareholder value; it can be used to assess a company, a business unit, a single plant, office, or even an assembly line. This same technique is equally helpful in evaluating new business opportunities. Abbr. *EVA*

economic welfare ECONOMICS the level of prosperity in an economy, as measured by employment and wage levels

economist ECONOMICS somebody who studies the consumption, distribution, and production of wealth in a society

economy ECONOMICS the distribution of wealth in a society and the means by which that wealth is produced and consumed

economy efficiency principle ECONOMICS the principle that if an economy is efficient, no one can be made better off without somebody else being made worse off

e-consulting E-COMMERCE the business of providing services such as webpage design and

marketing advice to companies doing business on the Internet

ecopreneur FINANCE, BANKING, AND ACCOUNTING GENERAL MANAGEMENT an entrepreneur who is concerned with environmental issues

EDB *abbr* FINANCE, BANKING, AND ACCOUNTING Economic Development Board

EDC *abbr* E-COMMERCE electronic data capture

EDI *abbr* E-COMMERCE electronic data interchange

EDI envelope E-COMMERCE see *electronic envelope*

EDIFACT E-COMMERCE see *UN/EDIFACT*

EDI for Administration, Commerce, and Trade E-COMMERCE see *UN/EDIFACT*

educational leave HR & PERSONNEL *special leave* granted to assist those undertaking a course of study

Edwardes, Sir Michael (*b.* 1930) GENERAL MANAGEMENT South African-born business executive. Chairman of British Leyland from 1977 to 1982, he was appointed to rescue the company from financial difficulties and industrial disruption. His reassertion of the manager's right to manage led to the coining of the term *macho management*. He recorded his experiences in *Back from the Brink* (1983).

e-economy ECONOMICS an economy that is characterized by extensive use of the Internet and information technology

effect STATISTICS the change in a response that is created by a change in one or more of the explanatory *variables* in a statistical study

effective annual interest rate FINANCE, BANKING, AND ACCOUNTING the average interest rate paid on a deposit for a period of a year. It is the total interest received over 12 months expressed as a percentage of the principal at the beginning of the period.

effective capacity OPERATIONS & PRODUCTION the volume that a workstation or process can produce in a given period under normal operating conditions. Effective capacity can be influenced by the age and condition of the machine, the skills, training, and flexibility of the workforce, and the availability of *raw materials*.

effective date FINANCE, BANKING, AND ACCOUNTING the date when an action, such as the issuing of new stock, is effective

effective price (*U.K.*) FINANCE, BANKING, AND ACCOUNTING the price of a stock adjusted to take into account the effects of a rights issue. See also *rights issue*

effective sample size STATISTICS the remaining size of a sample after irrelevant or excluded factors have been removed

effective spread FINANCE, BANKING, AND ACCOUNTING the difference between the price of a newly issued stock and what the underwriter pays, adjusted for the effect of the announcement of the offering

effective strike price FINANCE, BANKING, AND ACCOUNTING the price of an option at a specified time, adjusted for fluctuation since the initial offering

effective tax rate FINANCE, BANKING, AND ACCOUNTING the average tax rate applicable to a given transaction, whether it is income from work undertaken, the sale of an asset, or a gift, taking into account personal allowances and scales of tax. It is the amount of money generated by the transaction divided by the additional tax payable because of it.

efficiency FINANCE, BANKING, AND ACCOUNTING GENERAL MANAGEMENT the achievement of goals in an economic way. Efficiency involves seeking a good balance between economy in terms of resources such as time, money, space, or materials, and the achievement of an organization's goals and objectives. A distinction is often made between technical and economic efficiency. *Technical efficiency* means producing maximum output with minimum input, while economic efficiency means the production and distribution of goods at the lowest possible cost. In management, a further distinction is often made between efficiency and effectiveness, with the latter denoting performance in terms of achieving objectives.

efficiency ratio FINANCE, BANKING, AND ACCOUNTING a way of measuring the proportion of operating revenues or fee income spent on overhead expenses.

Often identified with banking and financial sectors, the efficiency ratio indicates a management's ability to keep overhead costs low. In banking, an acceptable efficiency ratio was once in the low 60s. Now the goal is 50, while better-performing banks boast ratios in the mid-40s. Low ratings usually indicate a higher return on equity and earnings.

This measurement is also used by mature industries, such as steel manufacture, chemicals, or car production, that must focus on tight cost controls to boost profitability because growth prospects are modest.

The efficiency ratio is defined as operating overhead expenses divided by turnover. If operating expenses are $100,000, and turnover is $230,000, then

$$\frac{100,000}{230,000} = 0.43 \text{ efficiency ratio}$$

However, not everyone calculates the ratio in the same way. Some institutions include all non-interest expenses, while others exclude certain charges and intangible asset amortization.

A different method measures efficiency simply by tracking three other measures: accounts payable to sales, days' sales outstanding, and stock turnover. This indicates how fast a company is able to move its merchandise. A general guide is that if the first two of these measures are low and the third is high, efficiency is probably high; the reverse is likewise true.

To find the stock turnover ratio, divide total sales by total stock. If net sales are $300,000, and stock is $140,000, then

$$\frac{300,000}{140,000} = 2.14 \text{ stock turnover ratio}$$

To find the accounts payable to sales ratio, divide a company's accounts payable by its annual net sales. A high ratio suggests that a company is using its suppliers' funds as a source of cheap financing because it is not operating efficiently enough to generate its own funds. If accounts payable are $50,000, and total sales are $300,000, then

$$\frac{50,000}{300,000} = 0.14 \times 100 =$$

14% Accounts payable to sales ratio

efficiency variance FINANCE, BANKING, AND ACCOUNTING the difference between the standard cost of making a product and actual costs of production. A separate variance can be calculated for materials, labor, and overhead.

efficient capital market FINANCE, BANKING, AND ACCOUNTING a market in which stock prices reflect all the information available to the market about future economic trends and company profitability

EFQM Excellence Model *or* **EFQM European Excellence Award** GENERAL MANAGEMENT a framework that can be used to assess a company's achievement of business *excellence*. The European Foundation for Quality Management (EFQM) was founded in the late 1980s by leading companies in Western Europe that saw a need for the implementation of a *quality award* in Europe. EFQM launched the *European Quality Award* in 1991. In the United Kingdom, the British Quality Founda-

tion promoted the model, now often referred to as the *Business Excellence Model*. The model was revised in 1999 and renamed the EFQM European Excellence Model. The model focuses on all the key elements that sustain business success, and incorporates nine criteria that cover all aspects of business.

EFT *abbr* FINANCE, BANKING, AND ACCOUNTING electronic funds transfer

EGM *abbr* GENERAL MANAGEMENT extraordinary general meeting

egosurfing GENERAL MANAGEMENT the practice of surfing the Internet in search of references to yourself (*slang*)

EIB *abbr* FINANCE, BANKING, AND ACCOUNTING European Investment Bank: a financial institution whose main task is to further regional development within the EU by financing capital projects, modernizing or converting undertakings, and developing new activities

eighty-twenty rule GENERAL MANAGEMENT the principle that explores the natural balance between the causes and effects of business activities, and holds that all business activities display an 80%/20% split. Developed by *Vilfredo Pareto*, the eighty-twenty rule can be used to concentrate management control and identify problem areas. Examples of the eighty-twenty rule in practice might include 20% of the workforce accounting for 80% of the salary bill; 80% of a company's profits coming from 20% of its products; 80% of the stock value being tied up in 20% of the inventory. The rule can be represented graphically in the form of a Pareto chart, which is a bar chart identifying the relationships between causes and effects of activities. Also known as *Pareto analysis*, *Pareto's principle*. See also *Pareto's Law*

EIS *abbr* GENERAL MANAGEMENT
1 environmental impact statement
2 environmental impact study
3 executive information system: a computer system designed to collect, store, process, and provide access to information appropriate to the needs of senior management. Executive information systems combine internal organizational information with data from external sources. The emphasis of executive information systems is on supporting strategic *decision making* by presenting information in accessible formats and enabling users to get an overview of trends, often through the use of advanced graphical capabilities. Decision making at managerial levels is supported by *decision support systems*.

Eisner, Michael (*b.* 1942) GENERAL MANAGE-MENT U.S. business executive. Former C.E.O. and chairman of Disney, who *turned around* the company by encouraging *creativity* while maintaining financial control and discipline. His autobiography *Work in Progress* (1998) explains his *leadership* philosophy.

either-way market FINANCE, BANKING, AND ACCOUNTING a currency market with identical prices for buying and selling, especially for the Euro

e-lance GENERAL MANAGEMENT a type of *freelance* work that makes use of the *Internet*. It enables a freelancer to accept work opportunities anywhere in the world.

elasticity FINANCE, BANKING, AND ACCOUNTING the measure of the sensitivity of one variable to another.

In practical terms, elasticity indicates the degree to which consumers respond to changes in price. It is obviously important for companies to consider such relationships when contemplating changes in price, demand, and supply.

Demand elasticity measures how much the quantity demanded by a customer changes when the price of a product or service is increased or lowered. This measurement helps companies to find out whether demand will remain constant despite price changes. Supply elasticity measures the impact on supply when a price is changed.

The general formula for elasticity is

$$\text{Elasticity} = \frac{\% \text{ change in x}}{\text{change in y}}$$

In theory, x and y can be any variable. However, the most common application measures price and demand. If the price of a product is increased from \$20 to \$25, or 25%, and demand in turn falls from 6,000 to 3,000, elasticity would be calculated as

$$\frac{50\%}{25\%} = -2$$

A value greater than 1 means that demand is strongly sensitive to price, while a value of less than 1 means that demand is not price-sensitive.

eldercare HR & PERSONNEL an organization's approach toward care for employees' elderly relatives in the form of an *employee assistance program*

e-learning HR & PERSONNEL the facilitation of learning through the *Internet* or an *intranet*. E-learning is a development from *computer-based training* and consists of self-contained learning materials and resources that can be used at the pace and convenience of the learner. An e-learning package normally incorporates some form of test that can demonstrate how much an e-learner has assimilated from a course, as well as some form of monitoring to enable managers to check the use of the system of e-learning. Successful e-learning depends largely on the self-motivation of individuals to study effectively. Because it is Internet-based, it has excellent potential to respond to a company's rapidly changing needs and offer new learning opportunities relevant to a company's new position very quickly. Also known as *electronic learning*

elected officers HR & PERSONNEL officials such as directors or union representatives who are chosen by a vote of the members or shareholders of an organization and who hold a *decision making* position on a committee or board

electronic business E-COMMERCE see *e-business*

electronic cash E-COMMERCE see *digital cash*

electronic catalog E-COMMERCE a listing of available products that can be viewed in an electronic format, for example, on a Web site, and can include information such as illustrations, prices, and product descriptions

electronic check E-COMMERCE a payment system in which fund transfers are made electronically from the buyer's checking account to the seller's bank account. U.K. term *electronic cheque*

electronic commerce E-COMMERCE see *e-commerce*

electronic commerce modeling language E-COMMERCE a standardization of field names to streamline the process by which e-merchants electronically collect information from consumers about order shipping, billing, and payment. Abbr. *ECML*

electronic data capture E-COMMERCE the use of a point-of-sale terminal or other data-processing equipment to validate and submit credit or debit card transactions. Abbr. *EDC*

electronic data interchange E-COMMERCE a standard for exchanging business documents, such as invoices and purchase orders, in a standard form between computers through the use of electronic networks such as the Internet. Abbr. *EDI*

electronic envelope E-COMMERCE the header and trailer information that precedes and follows the data in an electronic transmission to provide routing information and security. Also known as *communications envelope, EDI envelope, envelope*

electronic funds transfer E-COMMERCE a payment system that processes financial transactions between two or more parties or institutions. Abbr. *EFT*

electronic funds transfer at point of sale FINANCE, BANKING, AND ACCOUNTING the payment for goods or services by a bank customer using a card that is swiped through an electronic reader on the register, thereby transferring the cash from the customer's account to the retailer's or service provider's account. See also *debit card*

electronic learning HR & PERSONNEL see *e-learning*

electronic mail E-COMMERCE see *e-mail*

electronic mall E-COMMERCE see *cyber mall*

electronic money E-COMMERCE see *digital money*

electronic office GENERAL MANAGEMENT see *paperless office*

electronic payment system E-COMMERCE a means of making payments over an electronic network such as the Internet

electronic procurement E-COMMERCE see *e-procurement*

electronic retailer E-COMMERCE see *e-retailer*

electronic shopping E-COMMERCE the process of selecting, ordering, and paying for goods or services over an electronic network such as the Internet. Also known as *online shopping*

electronic software distribution E-COMMERCE a form of electronic shopping in which computer programs can be purchased and downloaded directly from the Internet

electronic store E-COMMERCE a Web site that is specifically designed to provide product information and handle transactions, including accepting payments

electronic trading FINANCE, BANKING, AND ACCOUNTING the buying and selling of investment instruments using computers

electronic wallet E-COMMERCE see *digital wallet*

elephant (*slang*)

1 GENERAL MANAGEMENT a large corporate institution

2 FINANCE, BANKING, AND ACCOUNTING a very large financial institution, such as a bank, which makes trades in high volumes, thereby increasing prices

elevator pitch GENERAL MANAGEMENT the practice of pitching business plans to investors in a short space of time

eligible paper FINANCE, BANKING, AND ACCOUNTING

1 in the United States, first class paper (such as a bill of exchange or a check) acceptable for rediscounting by the Federal Reserve System. See also *lender of last resort*

2 in the United Kingdom, bills of exchange or securities accepted by the Bank of England as security for loans to discount houses

eligible reserves FINANCE, BANKING, AND ACCOUNTING the sum of the cash held by a bank plus the money it holds at its local Federal Reserve Bank

eligible service period GENERAL MANAGEMENT the amount of time an employee works for one employer or contributes to a particular retirement plan. Abbr. *ESP*

eligible termination payment FINANCE, BANKING, AND ACCOUNTING a sum paid to an employee when he or she leaves a company, that can be transferred to a concessionally taxed investment account, such as an Approved Deposit Fund. Abbr. *ETP*

Elvis year GENERAL MANAGEMENT the year in which the popularity of a product, service, or individual is at its peak (*slang*)

e-mail E-COMMERCE electronic mail, a message sent across the Internet, or a system for transferring messages between computers, cell phones, or other communications attached to the Internet

e-mail address E-COMMERCE somebody's electronic address on the Internet or an intranet. An e-mail address is commonly formed by joining the user name and the mail server name, separating the two by an @ symbol.

e-mail mailing list E-COMMERCE a marketing technique particularly suited to discussing complex topics over a period of time. Members can be drawn from anywhere in the world, and come together to share information and experience on a particular theme or subject area. It works as follows: a *moderator* compiles a list of e-mail addresses for possible members, and mails them with the theme for discussion. People then join up, via e-mail or *Web form*. The moderator invites contributions, which are duly published by e-mail; subscribers then react to the initial publication with their opinions and feedback. A selection of these reactions is published in the next e-mail sent out—and so on. If successful, a feedback and opinion loop is created, with new topics being introduced as older topics have received sufficient discussion.

e-mail shorthand E-COMMERCE the set of acronyms and abbreviations for common phrases originally used in e-mail and subsequently in chat rooms, instant messaging, and newsgroup postings

e-mail signature E-COMMERCE the text at the bottom of an e-mail that contains information about the sender.

In general, the signature should be no longer than five lines, but it can be used in marketing to place a short, two-line ad. E-mail signature promotion was used very effectively when Andersen Consulting changed its name to Accenture. Every time one of its 60,000 employees sent an e-mail, there was a short e-mail signature ad notifying the recipient of the change of name.

e-mail system E-COMMERCE the collective e-mail software that allows somebody to create, send, receive, and store e-mail messages

e-marketplace E-COMMERCE an Internet-based environment that brings together business-to-business buyers and sellers so that they can trade more efficiently online.

The key benefits for users of an e-marketplace are reduced purchasing costs, greater flexibility, saved time, better information, and better collaboration. However, the drawbacks include costs in changing procurement processes, cost of applications, set-up, and integration with internal systems, and transaction/subscription fees.

There are three distinct types of e-marketplace: independent, in which public environments seek simply to attract buyers and sellers to trade together; consortium-based, in which sites are established on an industry-wide basis, typically when a number of key buyers in a particular industry get together; and private, in which e-marketplaces are established by a particular organization to manage its purchasing alone.

EMAS *abbr* GENERAL MANAGEMENT ECO-Management Audit Scheme

embargo FINANCE, BANKING, AND ACCOUNTING a government order which stops a type of trade, such as exports to, or imports from, a specified country

embezzlement FINANCE, BANKING, AND ACCOUNTING the illegal practice of using money entrusted to an individual's care by a third party for personal benefit

emergency credit FINANCE, BANKING, AND ACCOUNTING credit given by the Federal Reserve to an organization which has no other means of borrowing capital

emerging market FINANCE, BANKING, AND ACCOUNTING a country that is becoming industrialized

Emery, Frederick Edmund (1928–97) GENERAL MANAGEMENT Australian psychologist and sociologist. Contributor to the development of theories of *industrial democracy* in collaboration with *Einar Thorsrud* at the Tavistock Institute of Human Relations.

EMH *abbr* FINANCE, BANKING, AND ACCOUNTING efficient markets hypothesis

emoluments FINANCE, BANKING, AND ACCOUNTING wages, salaries, fees, or any other monetary benefit derived from employment

e-money E-COMMERCE see *digital money*

emotag E-COMMERCE a tag such as < smile > or < growl > used in an e-mail instead of an emoticon (*slang*)

emoticon E-COMMERCE a symbol commonly used in e-mail and newsgroup messages to denote a particular emotion by representing a face on its side. For example, :-) indicates happiness by representing a smiley face. The word is a combination of "emotion" and "icon."

emotional capital GENERAL MANAGEMENT the intangible organizational asset created by employees' cumulative emotional experiences, which give them the ability to successfully communicate and form interpersonal relationships. Emotional capital is increasingly being seen as an important factor in company performance. Low emotional capital can result in conflict between staff, poor *teamwork*, and poor *customer relations*. By contrast, high emotional capital is evidence of *emotional intelligence* and an ability to think and feel in a positive way that results in good *interpersonal communication* and self-motivation. Related concepts are *intellectual capital* and *social capital*.

emotional intelligence HR & PERSONNEL the ability to perceive and understand personal

feelings and those of others. Emotional intelligence means recognizing emotions and acting on them in a reflective and rational manner. It involves self-awareness, empathy, and self-restraint. In the workplace, this ability can greatly enhance **interpersonal communication** and people skills. Emotional intelligence was first broadly discussed by **Daniel Goleman**. See thinker **Daniel Goleman**

employability HR & PERSONNEL the potential for obtaining and keeping fulfilling work through the development of skills that are transferable from one employer to another. Employability is affected by market demand for a particular set of skills and by personal circumstances. Employees may take responsibility for developing their own employability through learning and training, or, as part of the **psychological contract**, employers may assist their employees in enhancing their employability. An important factor in employability is the concept of **lifelong learning**.

employee HR & PERSONNEL someone hired by an employer under a **contract of employment** to perform work on a regular basis at the employer's behest. An employee works either at the employer's premises or at a place otherwise agreed, is paid regularly, and enjoys **fringe benefits** and **employment protection**.

employee assistance program HR & PERSONNEL a structured and integrated support service that identifies and resolves the concerns of employees that may affect performance. Employee assistance programs can range from support for staff during periods of intensive change, **counseling** to tackle the problem of **stress**, return-to-work, and **eldercare** initiatives, to defined organizational policies on substance abuse and bullying. Employee assistance programs are established by employers who recognize that providing professional support for their staff makes good business sense. Some organizations find it cost-effective to **outsource** the program, depending on the nature of the problem and on the size of the organization. Abbr. **EAP**

employee association (*U.K.*) HR & PERSONNEL a professional or social body of employees who work for the same organization

employee attitude survey HR & PERSONNEL a systematic investigation of the views and opinions of those employed by an organization on issues relating to the work of that organization or their role within it. Employee attitude surveys may be conducted by means of questionnaires or interviews. They may be undertaken occasionally or at regular intervals and may be used to make a general assessment of employee morale or focus on a specific issue such as the introduction of a new policy. Goals may be to identify or gain an understanding of problems so that action to resolve them can be taken, to encourage employee involvement and commitment, or to assist in planning, implementing, and evaluating new initiatives.

employee commitment HR & PERSONNEL the psychological bond of an employee to an organization, the strength of which depends on the degree of **employee involvement**, employee loyalty, and belief in the values of the organization. Employee commitment was badly damaged in the late 20th century during corporate reorganizations and **downsizing**, which undermined job security and resulted in fewer **promotion** opportunities. This led to the renegotiation of the **psychological contract** and the need to develop strategies for increasing commitment. These included **flexible working** and **work-life balance** policies, **teamwork**, **training** and development, **employee participation**, and **empowerment**.

employee development HR & PERSONNEL the enhancement of the skills, knowledge, and experience of employees with the purpose of improving performance. Employee development, unlike **personal development**, is usually coordinated by the employing organization. It can use a variety of **training** methods, and is usually conducted on a planned basis, perhaps as a result of a **performance appraisal**.

employee discount HR & PERSONNEL a reduction in the price of company goods or services offered to employees as one of their **fringe benefits**

employee handbook HR & PERSONNEL a reference document containing information on what an employee should know about his or her organization or employment. Employee handbooks typically include information on terms and **conditions of employment**, organizational policies and procedures, and **fringe benefits**.

employee involvement HR & PERSONNEL a variety of management practices centered on **empowerment** and trust that are designed to increase **employee commitment** to organizational objectives and performance improvement. The term employee involvement is often used interchangeably with **employee participation**, but employee involvement practices tend to take place at individual or workgroup level, rather than at higher **decision making** levels.

employee ownership HR & PERSONNEL the possession of stock in a company, in whole or in part, by the workers. There are various forms of employee ownership that give employees a greater or lesser stake in the business. These include: **employee stock ownership plans**, employee **buyouts**, cooperatives, and employee trusts. Ownership does not necessarily lead to greater **employee participation** in **decision making**, although the evidence suggests that where employees are involved in this, the company is more successful.

employee participation HR & PERSONNEL the involvement of workers in **decision making**. Employee participation can take either a representational or direct form. Representation takes place through bodies such as consultative committees. Direct participation can be achieved through communication methods such as newsletters, **employee attitude surveys**, **team briefing**, and **open-book management**, or through involvement initiatives such as self-managed teams, **suggestion programs**, and **quality circles**.

employee referral program HR & PERSONNEL a policy, popular in the United States, for encouraging employees, usually through cash incentives, to nominate potential job candidates as part of the recruiting process. Employee referral programs have been developed in an attempt to address the recruitment difficulties experienced by organizations in times of full employment. Although they can be very successful, there is a danger that if a referral program is relied on too heavily, only limited sectors of the potential labor force will be available for recruitment, which might lead to a reduction in the **diversity** of the workforce.

employee stock fund FINANCE, BANKING, AND ACCOUNTING a fund from which money is taken to buy shares of a company's stock for its employees

employee stock option FINANCE, BANKING, AND ACCOUNTING a type of **stock incentive plan** in which an employee is given the option to buy a specified number of stock at a future date, at an agreed price. Stock options provide a financial benefit to the recipient only if the stock price rises over the period the option is available. If the stock price falls over the period, the employee is under no obligation to buy the stock. There may be a tax advantage to the employees who participate in such a program. Share options may be available to all employees or operated on a discretionary basis.

employee stock ownership plan HR & PERSONNEL a plan sponsored by a company by

which a trust holds stock in the company on behalf of *employees* and distributes that stock to employees. In the United States, stock can only be sold when an employee leaves the organization, and is thus thought of as a form of pension provision. In the United Kingdom, stock can be disposed of at any time. There are two types of employee stock ownership plans in the United Kingdom: the case-law employee stock ownership plan, which can benefit all or some employees but may not qualify for tax benefits; and the employee stock ownership trust. Abbr. *ESOP*

employer HR & PERSONNEL a person or organization that pays people to perform specified activities. An employer usually contracts an *employee* to fill a permanent or temporary position to perform work on a regularly paid basis within the relevant legal framework of the country of residence.

employers' association (*U.K.*) HR & PERSONNEL a body that regulates relations between employers and employees, represents members' views on public policy issues affecting their business to national and international policy-makers, and supplies support and advice. An employers' association represents companies within one or many sectors at regional, national, or international level and is usually a nonprofit, nonparty political organization, funded by subscriptions paid by its members.

employer's contribution FINANCE, BANKING, AND ACCOUNTING money paid by an employer towards a worker's pension

employment contract GENERAL MANAGEMENT HR & PERSONNEL see *contract of employment*

Employment Court (*ANZ*) HR & PERSONNEL a higher court in New Zealand responsible for arbitrating in industrial relations disputes. It hears cases relating to disputes between employers and employees or unions as well as appeals referred to the court by *employment tribunals*.

employment equity (*S. Africa*) HR & PERSONNEL the policy of giving preference in employment opportunities to qualified people from sectors of society that were previously discriminated against, for example, black people, women, and physically challenged people

employment law HR & PERSONNEL the collection of statutes, common law rules, and decisions in court or employment tribunal cases that govern the rights and duties of employers and employees. The *contract of employment* forms the cornerstone of employment law,

which also embraces *discrimination* and termination rights, *collective bargaining*, health and safety, union membership, and *industrial action*.

employment pass (*S. Africa*) GENERAL MANAGEMENT a visa issued to a foreign national who is a professional earning in excess of R1,500 per month

employment protection HR & PERSONNEL the legal framework for establishing and defending the rights of employees

employment tribunal HR & PERSONNEL a government body responsible for hearing and adjudicating in disputes between employees and employers

empowerment GENERAL MANAGEMENT the redistribution of *power* and *decision making* responsibilities, usually to *employees*, where such *authority* was previously a management prerogative. Empowerment is based on the recognition that employee abilities are frequently underused, and that, given the chance, most employees can contribute more. Empowered workplaces are characterized by managers who focus on energizing, supporting, and *coaching* their staff in a blame-free environment of trust. See thinker *Rosabeth Moss Kanter*, *Douglas McGregor*

empty suit GENERAL MANAGEMENT a corporate executive who dresses very smartly and follows all procedures exactly without actually contributing anything of significance to the company (*slang*)

EMS *abbr*
1 FINANCE, BANKING, AND ACCOUNTING European Monetary System: the first stage of economic and monetary union of the EU, which came into force in March 1979, giving stable, but adjustable, exchange rates
2 GENERAL MANAGEMENT environmental management system

EMU *abbr* FINANCE, BANKING, AND ACCOUNTING Economic and Monetary Union, or European Monetary Union: the timetable for EMU was outlined in the Maastricht Treaty in 1991. The criteria were that national debt must not exceed 60% of GDP; budget deficit should be 3% or less of GDP; inflation should be no more than 1.5% above the average rate of the three best performing economies of the EU in the previous 12 months; and applicants must have been members of the *ERM* for two years without having realigned or devalued their currency.

encash FINANCE, BANKING, AND ACCOUNTING to exchange a check for cash

encryption E-COMMERCE a means of encoding information, especially financial data, so that it can be transmitted over the Internet without being read by unauthorized parties.

Within an Internet security system, a secure server uses encryption when transferring or receiving data from the Web. Credit card information, for example, which could be targeted by a *hacker*, is encrypted by the server, turning it into special code that will then be decrypted only when it is safely within the server environment. Once the information has been acted on, it is either deleted or stored in encrypted form.

encryption key E-COMMERCE a sequence of characters known to both or all parties to a communication, used to initiate the *encryption* process

encumbrance FINANCE, BANKING, AND ACCOUNTING a liability, such as a mortgage or charge, which is attached to a property or piece of land

end-around GENERAL MANAGEMENT an approach to a problem that does not attack it directly but rather tries to avoid it

end consumer MARKETING see *consumer*

endogenous variable STATISTICS the dependent variable in an econometric study

endorse FINANCE, BANKING, AND ACCOUNTING to sign a bill or check on the back to show that its ownership is being passed to another person or company

endorsement GENERAL MANAGEMENT the public approval of a product by a person or organization. The endorsement can be used to promote the product to other organizations that may be more cautious in their approach to adopting new products.

endowment fund FINANCE, BANKING, AND ACCOUNTING a mutual fund that supports a nonprofit institution

endowment insurance FINANCE, BANKING, AND ACCOUNTING life coverage that pays a specific sum of money on a specified date, or earlier in the event of the policyholder's death. Part of the premium paid is for the life coverage element, while the remainder is invested in real estate and stocks (either a "with-profits" or "without-profits" policy) or, in the case of a share-linked policy, is used to purchase shares in a life fund. The sum the policyholder receives at the end of the term depends on the

size of the premiums and the performance of the investments.

endowment policy FINANCE, BANKING, AND AC-COUNTING an insurance policy of a type popular in the United Kingdom that pays a set amount to the policyholder when the policy matures, or to a beneficiary if the policyholder dies before it matures

endpoint STATISTICS a point at which a definable event in a study takes place, for example, the recovery of a patient in a medical study

energy audit GENERAL MANAGEMENT a review, inspection, and evaluation of sources and uses of energy within an organization to ensure efficiency and lack of waste

energy conservation GENERAL MANAGEMENT the minimization of fuel consumption. Energy conservation, through the monitoring and control of the amounts of electricity, gas, and other fuels used in the workplace, can help reduce costs and damage to the environment. An energy management plan provides a systematic method of assessing, evaluating, and improving an organization's energy usage. This forms part of an organization's approach to *environmental management*.

e-network E-COMMERCE an Internet forum, usually of a professional nature and requiring a subscription to participate

engagement letter FINANCE, BANKING, AND AC-COUNTING a letter, usually required by professional standards, sent by a professional, such as an accountant, to a client setting out the work the accountant is to do and further administrative matters, such as any limit on the accountant's liability

engineering for excellence OPERATIONS & PRODUCTION see *design for manufacturability*

English disease GENERAL MANAGEMENT the supposed predilection of British workers to opt for *strike* action. In the United Kingdom in the 1960s and 1970s, strikes were commonly used by workers for *dispute* resolution. Government legislation in the 1980s, however, made striking more difficult for workers.

entail FINANCE, BANKING, AND ACCOUNTING a legal condition which passes ownership of a property to specified persons only

enterprise GENERAL MANAGEMENT
1 a venture characterized by *innovation*, *creativity*, dynamism, and risk. An enterprise can consist of one project, or may refer to an entire organization. It usually requires several of

the following attributes: flexibility, initiative, *problem solving* ability, independence, and imagination. Enterprises flourish in the environment of *delayered*, nonhierarchical organizations but can be stifled by *bureaucracy*. Enterprises are often created by *entrepreneurs* .
2 a business or company

enterprise application integration E-COMMERCE the unrestricted sharing of data and business processes via integrated and compatible software programs. As businesses expand and recognize the need for their information and applications to be shared between systems, they are investing in enterprise application integration in order to streamline processes and keep all the elements of their organizations, for example, human resources and inventory control, connected. Abbr. *EAI*

enterprise culture GENERAL MANAGEMENT an organizational or social environment that encourages and makes possible initiative and *innovation*. An organization with an enterprise culture is usually more competitive and more profitable than a *bureaucracy*. Such an organization is believed to be more rewarding and stimulating to work in. A society with an enterprise culture facilitates individuality and requires people to take responsibility for their own welfare. Conservative governments in the United Kingdom during the 1980s and 1990s promoted an enterprise culture by introducing market principles into all areas of economic and social life. These included policies of deregulation of financial services, *privatization* of utilities and national monopolies, and commercialization of the public sector.

enterprise investment scheme FINANCE, BANKING, AND ACCOUNTING a U.K. plan to promote investment in unquoted companies by which qualifying gains are exempt from capital gains tax

enterprise portal E-COMMERCE a Web site that assembles a wide range of content and services for employees of a particular organization, with the goal of bringing together all the key information they need to do a better job. The key difference between an enterprise portal and an *intranet* is that an enterprise portal contains not just internal content, but also external content that may be useful—such as specialized news feeds, or access to industry research reports. Ensuring that content is relevant, current, and frequently refreshed is essential for such sites to succeed, and enterprise portals are thus expensive to maintain.

enterprise resource planning GENERAL MANAGEMENT see *ERP*

enterprise zone FINANCE, BANKING, AND ACCOUNTING GENERAL MANAGEMENT an area in which the government offers financial incentives, such as tax relief, to encourage new business activities. Abbr. *EZ*

entertainment expenses HR & PERSONNEL costs, reimbursable by an employer, that are incurred by an employee in hosting social events for clients or suppliers in order to obtain or maintain their patronage or goodwill

entitlement GENERAL MANAGEMENT the expectation that an organization or individual will make large profits regardless of their contribution to the economy or company

entitlement offer FINANCE, BANKING, AND AC-COUNTING an offer that cannot be transferred to anyone else

entreprenerd GENERAL MANAGEMENT an entrepreneur with computing skills, especially one who starts up an Internet business (*slang*)

entrepreneur FINANCE, BANKING, AND ACCOUNT-ING GENERAL MANAGEMENT somebody who sets up a business or enterprise. An entrepreneur typically demonstrates effective application of a number of enterprising attributes, such as creativity, initiative, risk taking, problem solving ability, and autonomy, and will often risk his or her own capital to establish a business.

entropy STATISTICS a measure of the rate of transfer of the information that a system such as a computer program or factory machine receives or outputs

entry barrier MARKETING a perceived or real obstacle preventing a competitor from entering a market

envelope E-COMMERCE see *electronic envelope*

environment E-COMMERCE the different computers, *browsers*, or *bandwidth* access points from which a user may access a Web site. Web pages may download at very different speeds according to the environment, so when building a Web site, it is important to test its performance within as many different environments as possible.

environmental accounting FINANCE, BANKING, AND ACCOUNTING the practice of including the indirect costs and benefits of a product or activity, for example, its environmental effects on health and the economy, along with its direct costs when making business decisions

environmental analysis GENERAL MANAGEMENT see *environmental scanning*

environmental audit GENERAL MANAGEMENT the regular systematic gathering of information to monitor the effectiveness of environmental policies. An environmental audit now often forms part of an organization's *environmental management systems*, and is concerned with checking conformity with legislative requirements and environmental standards such as *ISO 14001* (see *ISO 14000*), as well as with company policy. The audit may also cover potential improvements in environmental performance and systems.

environmental impact assessment FINANCE, BANKING, AND ACCOUNTING a study, undertaken during the planning phase before an investment is made or an operation started, to consider any potential environmental effects

environmental impact statement GENERAL MANAGEMENT a report on the results of an Environmental Impact Study. Abbr. *EIS*

environmental impact study GENERAL MANAGEMENT an analysis of the potential effects on the natural environment of a project such as a building development, mining operation, or factory. Abbr. *EIS*

environmental management GENERAL MANAGEMENT a systematic approach to minimizing the damage created by an organization to the environment in which it operates. Environmental management has become an issue in organizations because consumers now expect them to be environmentally aware, if not environmentally friendly. Senior managers and directors are increasingly being held liable for their organizations' environmental performance, and the onus is on them to adopt a *corporate strategy* that balances economic growth with environmental protection.

Environmental management involves reducing pollution, waste, and the consumption of natural resources by implementing an environmental action plan. This plan brings together the key elements of environmental management, including an organization's *environmental policy* statement, an *environmental audit*, *environmental management system*, and standards such as the EC *ECO-Management Audit Scheme* and *ISO 14000*.

environmental management system GENERAL MANAGEMENT a procedure to manage and control an organization's impact on the environment. An environmental management system is part of an organization's *environmental management* practice. It includes creation of an *environmental policy*, which sets objectives and targets a program of implementation, effectiveness monitoring, problem correction, and system review. An environmental management system should also identify key resources and holders of responsibility for determining and implementing environmental policy. Systems for environmental management have been formalized in the *ISO 14000* quality standards. Abbr. *EMS*

environmental policy GENERAL MANAGEMENT a statement of organizational intentions regarding the safeguarding of the environment. Clause 4.2 of the *ISO 14001* (see *ISO 14000*) series of environmental management standards, which many organizations now either apply in full or make use of for guidance on environmental management, focuses on environmental policy and states the necessary themes and commitments for an environmental policy that conforms to ISO 14001 requirements.

environmental scanning GENERAL MANAGEMENT the monitoring of changes in the external environment in which an organization operates in order to identify threats and opportunities for the future and maintain *competitive advantage*. The process of environmental scanning includes gathering information on an organization's competitors, markets, customers, and suppliers; carrying out a *PEST analysis* of social, economic, technological, and political factors that may affect the organization; and analyzing the implications of this research. Environmental scanning may be undertaken systematically by a dedicated department or unit within an organization or more informally by project groups and may be used in the planning and development of *corporate strategy*. Also known as *environmental analysis*

environmental statistics STATISTICS statistical studies concerning environmental matters such as pollution

EOQ *abbr* OPERATIONS & PRODUCTION economic order quantity

e-procurement E-COMMERCE the business-to-business sale and purchase of goods and services over an electronic network such as the Internet. Also known as *electronic procurement*

EPS *abbr* GENERAL MANAGEMENT earnings per share

equal opportunities HR & PERSONNEL the granting of equal rights, privileges, and status regardless of gender, age, race, religion, disability, or sexual orientation. Equality in employment is regulated by law in most Western countries. An organizational equal opportunities policy works to go further than the regulatory framework demands. Such a policy should focus on preventing discriminatory or harassing behavior in the workplace and achieving equal access to training, job, and promotion opportunities. *Affirmative action*, which is referred to as positive discrimination in the United Kingdom, is a controversial approach to encouraging the advancement of minorities. *Diversity* management builds on and goes beyond equal opportunities by looking at the rights of individuals rather than groups.

equal pay HR & PERSONNEL the principle and practice of paying men and women in the same organization at the same rate for like work, or work that is rated as of equal value. Work is assessed either through an organization's job evaluation plan or by the judgment of an independent expert appointed by an industrial committee. Although many countries have legislation on equal pay, a gap still exists between men's pay and women's pay and is attributed to sexual discrimination in job evaluation and payment systems.

equal treatment HR & PERSONNEL a principle of the European Union that requires member states to ensure that there is no *discrimination* with regard to employment, vocational training, and working conditions. The principle of equal treatment is applied through Europe-wide directives and national legislation of the member states.

equilibrium price ECONOMICS the price at which the supply of and the demand for a good are equal. Suppliers increase prices when demand is high and reduce prices when demand is low.

equilibrium quantity ECONOMICS the quantity that regulates supply and demand. Suppliers increase quantity when demand is high and reduce quantity when demand is low.

equilibrium rate of interest ECONOMICS the rate at which the expected interest rate in a market equals the actual rate prevailing

equipment trust certificate FINANCE, BANKING, AND ACCOUNTING a bond in the United Kingdom sold for a 20% down payment and collateralized by the equipment purchased with its proceeds

equity claim FINANCE, BANKING, AND ACCOUNTING a claim on earnings that remain after debts are satisfied

equity contribution agreement FINANCE, BANKING, AND ACCOUNTING an agreement to provide equity under specified circumstances

equity dilution FINANCE, BANKING, AND ACCOUNTING the reduction in the percentage of a company represented by each share for an existing stockholder who has not increased his or her holding in the issue of new common stock

equity dividend cover (*U.K.*) FINANCE, BANKING, AND ACCOUNTING an accounting ratio, calculated by dividing the distributable profits during a given period by the actual dividend paid in that period, that indicates the likelihood of the dividend being maintained in future years

equity floor FINANCE, BANKING, AND ACCOUNTING an agreement for one party to pay another whenever some indicator of a stock market's value falls below a specified limit

equity gearing FINANCE, BANKING, AND ACCOUNTING the ratio between a company's borrowings and its equity

equity multiplier FINANCE, BANKING, AND ACCOUNTING a measure of a company's worth, expressed as a multiple of each dollar of its stock's price

equity sweetener (*U.K.*) FINANCE, BANKING, AND ACCOUNTING an incentive to encourage people to lend a company money. The sweetener takes the form of a warrant that gives the lender the right to buy stock at a later date and at a specified price.

equivalent annual cash flow FINANCE, BANKING, AND ACCOUNTING the value of an annuity required to provide an investor with the same return as some other form of investment

equivalent bond yield FINANCE, BANKING, AND ACCOUNTING see *bond equivalent yield*

equivalent taxable yield FINANCE, BANKING, AND ACCOUNTING the value of a taxable investment required to provide an investor with the same return as some other form of investment

e-retailer E-COMMERCE a business that uses an electronic network such as the Internet to sell its goods or services. Also known as *electronic retailer*, *e-tailer*

erf (*S. Africa*) FINANCE, BANKING, AND ACCOUNTING a plot of rural or urban land, usually no larger than a smallholding

ergonomics GENERAL MANAGEMENT HR & PERSONNEL the study of workplace design and the physical and psychological impact it has on workers. Ergonomics is about the fit between people, their work activities, equipment, work systems, and environment to ensure that workplaces are safe, comfortable, efficient, and that *productivity* is not compromised. Ergonomics may examine the design and layout of buildings, machines, and equipment, as well as aspects such as lighting, temperature, ventilation, noise, color, and texture. Ergonomic principles also apply to working methods such as systems and *procedures*, and the allocation and scheduling of work.

ERM *abbr* FINANCE, BANKING, AND ACCOUNTING Exchange Rate Mechanism: a system to maintain exchange rate stability used in the past by member states of the European Community

ERP *abbr* GENERAL MANAGEMENT enterprise resource planning: a software system that coordinates every important aspect of an organization's production into one seamless process so that maximum efficiency can be achieved

ERR *abbr* FINANCE, BANKING, AND ACCOUNTING expected rate of return

error account FINANCE, BANKING, AND ACCOUNTING an account for the temporary placement of funds involved in a financial transaction known to have been executed in error

error rate FINANCE, BANKING, AND ACCOUNTING the number of mistakes per thousand entries or per page

errors and omissions FINANCE, BANKING, AND ACCOUNTING mistakes from incorrect record keeping or accounting. Abbr. *E&O*

ESC *abbr* FINANCE, BANKING, AND ACCOUNTING European Social Charter: a charter adopted by the European Council of the EU in 1989. The 12 rights it contains are: freedom of movement, employment, and remuneration; social protection; improvement of living and working conditions; freedom of association and collective bargaining; worker information; consultation and participation; vocational training; equal treatment of men and women; health and safety protection in the workplace; pension rights; integration of those with disabilities; and protection of young people.

escalator clause FINANCE, BANKING, AND ACCOUNTING a clause in a contract which allows for regular price increases for a product or service to cover projected cost increases

escrow FINANCE, BANKING, AND ACCOUNTING an agreement between two parties which holds that something, such as a good, document, or amount of money should be held for safekeeping by a third party until certain conditions are fulfilled

escrow account FINANCE, BANKING, AND ACCOUNTING an account where money is held in *escrow* until certain conditions are met, for example, a contract is signed, or a consignment of goods safely delivered

e-shock E-COMMERCE the forward momentum of electronic commerce, considered as irresistible

ESOP *abbr* HR & PERSONNEL employee stock ownership plan

ESP *abbr* GENERAL MANAGEMENT eligible service period

essential industry FINANCE, BANKING, AND ACCOUNTING an industry regarded as crucial to a country's economy and often supported financially by a government by way of tariff protection and tax breaks

establishment fee FINANCE, BANKING, AND ACCOUNTING see *commitment fee*

estate FINANCE, BANKING, AND ACCOUNTING
1 a substantial area of land that normally includes a large house
2 a deceased person's net assets

estimate FINANCE, BANKING, AND ACCOUNTING
1 an approximate calculation of an uncertain value. An estimate may be a reasonable guess based on knowledge and experience or it may be calculated using more sophisticated techniques designed to forecast projected costs, profits, losses, or value.
2 an approximate price quoted for work to be undertaken by a business

estimation STATISTICS the provision of a numerical value for a parameter of a population that has been sampled

estoppel FINANCE, BANKING, AND ACCOUNTING a rule of evidence whereby someone is prevented from denying or asserting a fact in legal proceedings

e-tailer E-COMMERCE see *e-retailer*

e-tailing E-COMMERCE the practice of doing business over an electronic network such as the Internet

ethical fund FINANCE, BANKING, AND ACCOUNTING a fund which invests in companies that follow certain moral standards, for example, companies that do not manufacture weapons, do

not trade with certain countries, or use only environmentally acceptable sources of raw materials

ethical index FINANCE, BANKING, AND ACCOUNTING an index of stocks in companies which follow certain moral standards

ethical investment FINANCE, BANKING, AND ACCOUNTING investment only in companies whose policies meet the ethical criteria of the investor. Also known as *socially conscious investing*

Ethical Investment Research Service FINANCE, BANKING, AND ACCOUNTING an organization which does research into companies and recommends those which follow certain ethical standards

ethnic monitoring HR & PERSONNEL the recording and evaluation of the racial origins of employees or customers with the goal of ensuring that all parts of the population are represented. When ethnic monitoring is conducted as a part of the *recruitment* process, candidates are asked to indicate their ethnic origin on an anonymous basis. Information thus supplied is removed from the application as soon as it is received by the prospective employer.

ETP *abbr* FINANCE, BANKING, AND ACCOUNTING eligible termination payment

EU *abbr* FINANCE, BANKING, AND ACCOUNTING European Union: a social, economic, and political organization of European countries whose goal is integration for all member nations. It has been so called since November 1993 under the Maastricht Treaty, before which it was known as the European Community (EC), and before that as the European Economic Community. Also called *single market*

EUREX *abbr* FINANCE, BANKING, AND ACCOUNTING Eureka Research Expert System: EUREX was established by Eureka (European Research and Coordination Agency) in 1985 on a French initiative for nonmilitary industrial research in advanced technologies in Europe

Euro FINANCE, BANKING, AND ACCOUNTING the currency of 12 member nations of the European Union. The Euro was introduced in 1999, when the first 11 countries to adopt it joined together in an Economic and Monetary Union and tied their currencies' exchange rate to the Euro. Notes and coins were brought into general circulation in January 2002, although banks and other financial institutions had before that time carried out transactions in Euros.

Eurobank FINANCE, BANKING, AND ACCOUNTING a bank that handles transactions in European currencies

Eurobond FINANCE, BANKING, AND ACCOUNTING a bond specified in the currency of one country and sold to investors from another country. Also known as *global bond*

Euro-commercial paper FINANCE, BANKING, AND ACCOUNTING short-term uncollateralized loans obtained by companies in foreign countries

Eurocredit FINANCE, BANKING, AND ACCOUNTING intermediate-term notes used by banks to lend money to governments and companies

Eurocurrency FINANCE, BANKING, AND ACCOUNTING money deposited in one country but denominated in the currency of another country

Eurodeposit FINANCE, BANKING, AND ACCOUNTING a short-term deposit of Eurocurrency

Eurodollar FINANCE, BANKING, AND ACCOUNTING a dollar deposited in a European bank or other bank outside the United States

Euroequity issue FINANCE, BANKING, AND ACCOUNTING a note issued by banks in several countries

Euroland FINANCE, BANKING, AND ACCOUNTING the area of Europe comprising those countries that have adopted the Euro

Euro-note FINANCE, BANKING, AND ACCOUNTING a note in the Eurocurrency market

European Accounting Association FINANCE, BANKING, AND ACCOUNTING an organization for accounting academics. Founded in 1977 and based in Brussels, the EAA aims to be a forum for European research in the subject. It holds an annual congress and since 1992 has published a journal, *European Accounting Review*. Abbr. *EAA*

European Association of Securities Dealers Automated Quotations FINANCE, BANKING, AND ACCOUNTING see *EASDAQ*

European Bank for Reconstruction and Development FINANCE, BANKING, AND ACCOUNTING see *EBRD*

European Central Bank FINANCE, BANKING, AND ACCOUNTING see *ECB*

European Economic Community *or* **European Community** FINANCE, BANKING, AND ACCOUNTING see *EU*

European Investment Bank FINANCE, BANKING, AND ACCOUNTING see *EIB*

European Monetary System FINANCE, BANKING, AND ACCOUNTING see *EMS*

European Monetary Union FINANCE, BANKING, AND ACCOUNTING see *EMU*

European option FINANCE, BANKING, AND ACCOUNTING an option that the buyer can exercise only on the day that it expires. See also *American option*

European Quality Award GENERAL MANAGEMENT see *EFQM Excellence Model*

European Social Charter FINANCE, BANKING, AND ACCOUNTING see *ESC*

European Union FINANCE, BANKING, AND ACCOUNTING see *EU*

Euroyen bond FINANCE, BANKING, AND ACCOUNTING a Eurobond denominated in yen

EVA *abbr* FINANCE, BANKING, AND ACCOUNTING economic value added

evaluation of training HR & PERSONNEL a continuous cycle consisting of defining training objectives, carrying out *training needs analysis*, delivering training, assessing reactions to training, and measuring the bottom-line effects of training

event marketing MARKETING the promotion and marketing of a specific event such as a conference, seminar, exhibition, or trade fair. Event marketing may encompass *corporate hospitality* activities, business or charity functions, or sporting occasions. The planning, marketing, and managing of the function on the day are sometimes entirely *outsourced* to companies specializing in event management.

evergreen loan (*U.K.*) FINANCE, BANKING, AND ACCOUNTING a series of loans providing a continuing stream of capital for a project

ex-all (*U.K.*) FINANCE, BANKING, AND ACCOUNTING having no right in any transaction that is pending with respect to stocks, such as a split, or the issuance of dividends

excellence GENERAL MANAGEMENT OPERATIONS & PRODUCTION a state of organizational performance achieved through the successful integration of a variety of operational and strategic elements that enables an organization to become one of the best in its field. Excellence is initially evident when an organization rises above its competitors, and it is usually

measured by the ability to sustain a leading or significant market share. The strategic and operational elements contributing to excellence include the organization's approach to **total quality management**, **quality assurance**, **quality awards** and **quality standards**, core competency, **benchmarking**, **customer service**, the **balanced scorecard**, and **leadership**. Taken altogether, these components should produce an organizational approach to the generation, development, and delivery of products and services that is better, cheaper, and smarter than that of the competition. Attempts at becoming an excellent organization have spawned terms such as **best practice**, **best-in-class**, and **world class manufacturing** and are usually associated with a holistic approach to **competitive advantage**. See thinker **W. Edwards Deming**, **Tom Peters**

exception reporting GENERAL MANAGEMENT the passing on of information only when it breaches or transcends agreed norms. Exception reporting is intended to reduce **information overload** by minimizing the circulation of repetitive or old information. Under this system, only information that is new and out of the ordinary will be transmitted. See also **management by exception**

excess FINANCE, BANKING, AND ACCOUNTING
1 the part of an insurance claim that has to be met by the policyholder rather than the insurance company. An excess of $100 means that the company pays all but $100 of the claim for loss or damage. See also **deductible**
2 in a financial institution, the amount by which assets exceed liabilities

excess liquidity FINANCE, BANKING, AND ACCOUNTING cash held by a bank above the normal requirement for that bank

excess profits tax FINANCE, BANKING, AND ACCOUNTING a tax levied by a government on a company that makes extraordinarily large profits in times of unusual circumstances, for example, during a war. An excess profits tax was imposed in both the United States and the United Kingdom during World War II.

excess reserves FINANCE, BANKING, AND ACCOUNTING reserves held by a financial institution that are higher than those required by the regulatory authorities. As such reserves may indicate that demand for loans is low, banks often sell their excess reserves to other institutions.

exchange¹
1 E-COMMERCE the main type of business-to-business marketplace. The **B2B exchange**

enables suppliers, buyers, and intermediaries to come together and offer products to each other according to a set of criteria. **B2B Web exchanges** provide constant price adjustments in line with fluctuations of supply and demand. In E2E or "exchange-to-exchange" e-commerce, buyers and sellers conduct transactions not only within exchanges but also between them.
2 FINANCE, BANKING, AND ACCOUNTING the conversion of one type of security for another, for example, the exchange of a bond for stock
3 FINANCE, BANKING, AND ACCOUNTING a **market** where goods, services, or financial instruments are bought and sold

exchange² FINANCE, BANKING, AND ACCOUNTING
1 to trade one currency for another
2 to barter

exchange controls ECONOMICS the regulations by which a country's banking system controls its residents' or resident companies' dealings in foreign currencies and gold

exchange equalization account ECONOMICS the Bank of England account that sells and buys sterling for gold and foreign currencies to smooth out fluctuations in the exchange rate of the British pound

exchange offer FINANCE, BANKING, AND ACCOUNTING an offer to trade one security for another

exchange rate FINANCE, BANKING, AND ACCOUNTING the rate at which one country's currency can be exchanged for that of another country

Exchange Rate Mechanism FINANCE, BANKING, AND ACCOUNTING see **ERM**

exchange rate parity FINANCE, BANKING, AND ACCOUNTING the relationship between the value of one currency and another

exchange rate risk FINANCE, BANKING, AND ACCOUNTING the risk of suffering loss on converting another currency to the currency of a company's own country.
Exchange rate risks can be arranged into three primary categories. (1) Economic exposure: operating costs will rise due to changes in rates and make a product uncompetitive in the world market. Little can be done to reduce this routine business risk that every enterprise must endure. (2) Translation exposure: the impact of currency exchange rates will reduce a company's earnings and weaken its balance sheet. To reduce translation exposure, experienced corporate fund managers use a variety of techniques known as **currency hedging**. (3)

Transaction exposure: there will be an unfavorable move in a specific currency between the time when a contract is agreed and the time it is completed, or between the time when a lending or borrowing is initiated and the time the funds are repaid. Transaction exposure can be eased by **factoring**—transferring title to foreign accounts receivable to a third-party factoring house.
Although there is no definitive way of forecasting exchange rates, largely because the world's economies and financial markets are evolving so rapidly, the relationships between exchange rates, interest rates, and inflation rates can serve as leading indicators of changes in risk. These relationships are as follows. Purchasing Power Parity theory (PPP): while it can be expressed differently, the most common expression links the changes in exchange rates to those in relative price indices in two countries:

Rate of change of exchange rate = Difference in inflation rates

International Fisher Effect (IFE): this holds that an interest-rate differential will exist only if the exchange rate is expected to change in such a way that the advantage of the higher interest rate is offset by the loss on the foreign exchange transactions. Practically speaking, the IFE implies that while an investor in a low-interest country can convert funds into the currency of a high-interest country and earn a higher rate, the gain (the interest rate differential) will be offset by the expected loss due to foreign exchange rate changes. The relationship is stated as

Expected rate of change of the exchange rate = Interest-rate differential

Unbiased Forward Rate Theory: this holds that the forward exchange rate is the best unbiased estimate of the expected future spot exchange rate.

Expected exchange rate = Forward exchange rate

exchange rate spread (*U.K.*) FINANCE, BANKING, AND ACCOUNTING the difference between the price at which a broker or other intermediary buys and sells foreign currency

Exchequer FINANCE, BANKING, AND ACCOUNTING in the United Kingdom, the government's account at the Bank of England into which all revenues from taxes and other sources are paid

Exchequer stocks FINANCE, BANKING, AND ACCOUNTING U.K. government stocks used to finance government expenditure

excise duty FINANCE, BANKING, AND ACCOUNTING a tax on goods such as alcohol or tobacco produced and sold within a particular country

exclusive economic zone ECONOMICS a zone in a country in which particular economic conditions apply. The Special Economic Zone (SEZ) in China, where trade is conducted free of state control, is an example.

ex dividend FINANCE, BANKING, AND ACCOUNTING used to refer to bonds or stocks which, when they are sold, do not provide the buyer with the right to a dividend

execution only FINANCE, BANKING, AND ACCOUNTING used to describe a stock market transaction undertaken by an intermediary who acts on behalf of a client without providing advice. See also *active fund management*, *discretionary management*

executive GENERAL MANAGEMENT an employee in a position of senior responsibility in an organization. An executive is involved in planning, strategy, policy making, and *line management*. The term executive can also be used as an alternative to *manager*, *consultant*, executive officer, or *agent*.

executive chairman GENERAL MANAGEMENT see *chair*

executive coaching HR & PERSONNEL regular one-to-one *coaching* for leaders, designed as part of a *management development* program to provide knowledge and skills in a particular area. Executive coaching involves giving *feedback* to a leader and assisting in the creation of a development plan, often using *360 degree appraisal*. It can include in-depth development coaching conducted by colleagues, superiors, or specialist trainers, lasting perhaps six to twelve months.

executive director GENERAL MANAGEMENT a senior employee of an organization, usually with line responsibility for a particular function and usually, but not always, a member of the *board of directors*

executive information system GENERAL MANAGEMENT see *EIS*

executive officer GENERAL MANAGEMENT see *executive*

executive pension plan FINANCE, BANKING, AND ACCOUNTING in the United Kingdom, a pension plan for senior executives of a company. The company's contributions are a tax-deductible expense but are subject to a cap. The plan does not prevent the executive from being a member of the company's group pension plan although the executive's total contributions must not exceed a certain percentage of his or her salary.

executive search HR & PERSONNEL the identification, by recruitment agents or consultants on behalf of an organization, of suitable external candidates for senior positions, often by means of *headhunting* techniques. Executive search consultants work from personal recommendation and lists of their own contacts, and monitor rising stars or key personnel in particular organizations or professions. The number of potential candidates is usually limited because of the specialty or seniority of the post, so that the search takes place within upper salary ranges. Executive search consultants rarely advertise because the publicity may be unfruitful or detrimental to the organization for which they are working, and they do not find posts for individual job hunters.

executive share option scheme FINANCE, BANKING, AND ACCOUNTING a U.K. term for an arrangement whereby certain directors and employees are given the opportunity to purchase stock in the company at a fixed price at a future date. In certain jurisdictions, such arrangements can be tax efficient if certain local tax authority conditions are met.

executor FINANCE, BANKING, AND ACCOUNTING a person appointed under a will to ensure the deceased's estate is distributed according to the terms of the will

exempt gift FINANCE, BANKING, AND ACCOUNTING a gift that is not subject to gift tax

exempt investment fund FINANCE, BANKING, AND ACCOUNTING in the United Kingdom, a collective investment, usually a mutual fund, for investors who have certain tax privileges, for example, charities or contributors to pension plans

exemption FINANCE, BANKING, AND ACCOUNTING an amount per family member that an individual can subtract when reporting income to be taxed

exempt purchaser FINANCE, BANKING, AND ACCOUNTING an institutional investor who may buy newly issued securities without filing a prospectus with a securities commission

exempt security FINANCE, BANKING, AND ACCOUNTING a security that is not subject to a provision of law such as margin or registration requirements

exempt supply (*U.K.*) FINANCE, BANKING, AND ACCOUNTING an item or service on which VAT (Value Added Tax) is not levied, for example, the purchase of, or rent on, real estate and financial services

exercise notice FINANCE, BANKING, AND ACCOUNTING an option holder's notification to the option's writer of his or her desire to exercise the option

exercise of warrants FINANCE, BANKING, AND ACCOUNTING the use of a warrant to purchase stock

exercise value FINANCE, BANKING, AND ACCOUNTING the amount of profit that can be realized by cashing in an option

ex-gratia payment HR & PERSONNEL a one-time extra payment in addition to normal *pay*, made out of gratitude or courtesy, or in recognition of a special contribution

exhibition MARKETING an event organized to bring together buyers and sellers at a single venue

Eximbank *abbr* FINANCE, BANKING, AND ACCOUNTING Export-Import Bank: a bank founded in 1934 that provides loans direct to foreign importers of U.S. goods and services

existential culture GENERAL MANAGEMENT a form of *corporate culture* in which the organization exists to serve the individual, rather than individuals being servants of the organization. Existential culture was identified by *Charles Handy*. It typically consists of a group of professionals who work together, but have no leader. See thinker *Charles Handy*

exit interview HR & PERSONNEL a meeting between an employee and a management representative on the employee's departure from an organization. An exit interview is conducted in order to ascertain why an employee is leaving, either because of pull factors, such as better pay and conditions, or push factors, such as poor training or management. Another purpose of the exit interview is to capture information relating to the departing employee's knowledge and experience.

exit P/E ratio FINANCE, BANKING, AND ACCOUNTING the *price/earnings ratio* when a company changes hands

exit strategy FINANCE, BANKING, AND ACCOUNTING a plan for disposing of a business and realizing the value of the investment made in it. The development of an exit strategy involves establishing the value of the business, identify-

ing and selecting exit options, identifying and removing obstacles, and preparing and implementing a plan. Exit options include the sale of the business, **merger**, flotation or public listing, **management buy-out**, **franchising**, family succession, ceasing to trade, or **liquidation** .

exogenous variable STATISTICS any variable in an econometric study that has an impact on it from outside

expatriate HR & PERSONNEL somebody who has left his or her home country to live or work abroad, either for a long period of time or permanently

expectancy theory HR & PERSONNEL a view that people will be motivated to behave in particular ways if they believe that doing so will bring them rewards they both seek and value. Expectancy theory was first applied in the context of the workplace by **Victor Vroom** in the 1960s. He defined the concepts of valence and expectancy to explain how people decide to act. Valence refers to somebody's perception of the value of the reward or outcome that might be obtained if he or she performs a task successfully.

expected rate of return FINANCE, BANKING, AND ACCOUNTING the projected percentage return on an investment, based on the weighted probability of all possible rates of return.

It is calculated by the following formula:

$$E[r] = \Sigma s P(s) rs$$

where $E[r]$ is the expected return, $P(s)$ is the probability that the rate rs occurs, and rs is the return at s level.

The following example illustrates the principle which the formula expresses.

The current price of ABC Inc. stock is trading at \$10. At the end of the year, ABC shares are projected to be traded:

25% higher if economic growth exceeds expectations—a probability of 30%;

12% higher if economic growth equals expectations—a probability of 50%;

5% lower if economic growth falls short of expectations—a probability of 20%.

To find the expected rate of return, simply multiply the percentages by their respective probabilities and add the results:

(30% × 25%) + (50% × 12%) + (25% × −5%)
    = 7.5 + 6 + −1.25 = 12.25% ERR

A second example:

if economic growth remains robust (a 20% probability), investments will return 25%;

if economic growth ebbs, but still performs adequately (a 40% probability), investments will return 15%;

if economic growth slows significantly (a 30% probability), investments will return 5%;

if the economy declines outright (a 10% probability), investments will return 0%.

Therefore:

(20% × 25%) + (40% × 15%) +
(30% × 5%) + (10% × 0%) =
5% + 6% + 1.5% + 0% = 12.5% ERR.

Abbr. **ERR**

expenditure switching ECONOMICS government action to divert domestic spending from one sector to another, for example, from imports to home-produced goods

expense FINANCE, BANKING, AND ACCOUNTING
1 a cost incurred in buying goods or services
2 a charge against a company's profit

expense account
1 FINANCE, BANKING, AND ACCOUNTING money which businesspeople are allowed by their companies to spend on traveling and entertaining clients in connection with business
2 HR & PERSONNEL an amount of money that an employee or group of employees can draw on to reclaim personal **expenses** incurred in carrying out activities for an organization

expenses HR & PERSONNEL personal costs incurred by an employee in carrying out activities for an organization that are reimbursed by the employer

experience curve GENERAL MANAGEMENT see **learning curve**

experience economy GENERAL MANAGEMENT an economy in which products are differentiated through the quality of the "consumer experience" or level of added value (*slang*)

experiential learning HR & PERSONNEL a model that views learning as a cyclical process in four stages: concrete experience, reflective observation, abstract conceptualization, and active experimentation. Experiential learning relates to participants' activities and reactions to a training event, in contrast to passive learning. Proposed by **David Kolb** in 1971, the model was later expanded by other practitioners including **Peter Honey** and **Alan Mumford**. Experiential learning differs from **action learning** in that it can apply to an individual working alone while action learning is seen essentially as a group activity.

experimental design STATISTICS the planning of the procedures to be used in an **experimental study**

experimental study STATISTICS a statistical investigation in which the researcher can influence events in the study

expert system GENERAL MANAGEMENT a computer program that emulates the reasoning and **decision making** of a human expert in a particular field. The main components of an expert system are the knowledge base, which consists of facts and rules about appropriate courses of action based on the knowledge and experience of human experts; the inference engine, which simulates the inductive reasoning of a human expert; and the user interface, which enables users to interact with the system. Expert systems may be used by nonexperts to solve well-defined problems when human expertise is unavailable or expensive, or by experts seeking to find solutions to complex questions. They are used for a wide variety of tasks, including medical diagnostics and financial decision making, and are an application of **artificial intelligence**.

explicit knowledge GENERAL MANAGEMENT see **knowledge**

exploding bonus HR & PERSONNEL a bonus offered to recent graduates that encourages them to sign for a job as quickly as possible as it reduces in value with every day of delay (*slang*)

exponent FINANCE, BANKING, AND ACCOUNTING the number indicating the power to which a base number is to be raised

exponential smoothing GENERAL MANAGEMENT a statistical technique used in quantitative **forecasting**, particularly in the areas of inventory control and **sales forecasting**, that adjusts data to give a clearer view of trends in the long term. In exponential smoothing, values are calculated using a formula that takes all previous values into account but assigns greatest weight to the most recent data.

exponential trend STATISTICS a statistical trend that is revealed in a **time series**

export agent GENERAL MANAGEMENT an intermediary who acts on behalf of a company to open up or develop a market in a foreign country. Export agents are often paid a commission on all sales and may have exclusive rights in a particular geographic area. A good agent will know or get to know local market conditions and will have other valuable information that can be used to mutual benefit.

Export-Import Bank FINANCE, BANKING, AND ACCOUNTING see **Eximbank**

exporting MARKETING the process of selling goods to other countries. Exporting provides access to nondomestic markets and can be co-

ordinated by an export manager. As with all business activities, careful market research needs to be undertaken. This can be conducted by the company itself or through an experienced export agent. Many companies produce goods almost entirely for export. Services also can be exported, but require different delivery mechanisms through subsidiary offices, or local *franchise* or *licensing agreements*.

export-led growth ECONOMICS growth in which a country's main source of income is from its export trade

exposure E-COMMERCE see *ad view*

ex-rights FINANCE, BANKING, AND ACCOUNTING for sale without rights, for example, voting or conversion rights. The term can be applied to transactions such as the purchase of new shares.

ex-rights date FINANCE, BANKING, AND ACCOUNTING the date when a stock first trades ex-rights

extendable bond FINANCE, BANKING, AND ACCOUNTING a bond whose maturity can be delayed by either the issuer or the holder

extendable note FINANCE, BANKING, AND ACCOUNTING a note whose maturity can be delayed by either the issuer or the holder

extended fund facility ECONOMICS a credit facility of the *IMF* that allows a country up to eight years to repay money it has borrowed from the fund

Extensible Business Reporting Language FINANCE, BANKING, AND ACCOUNTING abbr. *XBRL*

external account FINANCE, BANKING, AND ACCOUNTING an account held at a United Kingdom-based bank by a customer who is an overseas resident

external audit FINANCE, BANKING, AND ACCOUNTING a periodic examination of the books of account and records of an entity conducted by an independent third party (an auditor) to ensure that they have been properly maintained, are accurate and comply with established concepts, principles, and accounting standards, and give a true and fair view of the financial state of the entity. See also *internal audit*

external communication GENERAL MANAGEMENT the exchange of information and messages between an organization and other organizations, groups, or individuals outside its formal structure. The goals of external

communication are to facilitate cooperation with groups such as suppliers, investors, and shareholders, and to present a favorable image of an organization and its products or services to potential and actual customers and to society at large. A variety of channels may be used for external communication, including face-to-face meetings, print or broadcast media, and electronic communication technologies such as the Internet. External communication includes the fields of *PR*, media relations, *advertising*, and *marketing management*.

external debt ECONOMICS the part of a country's debt that is owed to creditors who are not residents of the country

external finance FINANCE, BANKING, AND ACCOUNTING money that a company obtains from investors, for example, by loans or by issuing stock

external funds FINANCE, BANKING, AND ACCOUNTING money that a business obtains from a third party rather than from its own resources

external growth FINANCE, BANKING, AND ACCOUNTING business growth as a result of a merger, a takeover, or through a partnership with another organization

extranet E-COMMERCE a closed network of Web sites and e-mail systems that is open to people outside as well as inside an organization. An extranet enables third-party access to internal applications or information—usually subject to some kind of signed agreement. This is useful for organizations that need to share internal systems and information with potential partners. As with *intranets*, extranets provide all the benefits of Internet technology (browsers, Web servers, HTML, etc.) with the added benefit of security, being confined to an isolated network.

Because this is a work environment and partners enter it to access information as quickly as possible, extranet design generally focuses on minimal graphics and maximum content. Security being a key issue, it is generally password-protected in order to maintain confidentiality. *Content management* is also essential, as the extranet is only as useful as the information it contains. Many extranets fall down because the content is not updated and managed properly.

extraordinary general meeting GENERAL MANAGEMENT any general meeting of an organization other than the *annual meeting*. Directors can usually call an extraordinary

general meeting at their discretion, as can company members who either hold not less than 10% of the paid-up voting shares, or who represent not less than 10% of the voting rights. Directors are obliged to call an EGM if there is a substantial loss of capital. Fourteen days' written notice must be given, or 21 days' written notice if a special resolution is to be proposed. Only special business can be transacted at the meeting, the general nature of which must be specified in the convening notice. Abbr. *EGM*

extraordinary item FINANCE, BANKING, AND ACCOUNTING an *item* included in a company's accounts that is not likely to occur again, such as an acquisition or a sale of assets. These items are not taken into account when a company's operating profit is calculated.

extraordinary resolution FINANCE, BANKING, AND ACCOUNTING in the United Kingdom, an exceptional issue that is put to the vote at a company's general meeting, for example, a change to the company's articles of association. Also known as *special resolution*

extrapolate STATISTICS to estimate from a data set values that lie beyond the range of the data collected

extreme value STATISTICS either of the smallest or largest variate values in a sample of observations from a statistical study

eyeballing STATISTICS the process of informally inspecting statistical data by simply looking at it to assess results (*slang*)

eyeballs E-COMMERCE a measure of the number of visits made to a Web site (*slang*)

eyebrow management GENERAL MANAGEMENT a management style whereby a manager or top executive can change a course of action simply by implying his or her disapproval (*slang*)

eye candy GENERAL MANAGEMENT visually attractive material (*slang*)

eye service GENERAL MANAGEMENT the practice of working only when a supervisor is present and able to see you (*slang*)

EZ *abbr* FINANCE, BANKING, AND ACCOUNTING enterprise zone

e-zine E-COMMERCE a regular publication on a particular topic distributed in digital form, mainly via the Web but also by e-mail

F

F2F *abbr* GENERAL MANAGEMENT face-to-face (*slang*)

face time HR & PERSONNEL time spent in face-to-face communication as opposed to time spent communicating electronically (*slang*)

face value FINANCE, BANKING, AND ACCOUNTING the value written on a financial instrument

facilitation HR & PERSONNEL the process of helping groups, or individuals, to learn, find a solution, or reach a consensus, without imposing or dictating an outcome. Facilitation works to *empower* individuals or groups to learn for themselves or find their own answers to problems without control or manipulation. Facilitators need good *communication skills*, including listening, questioning, and reflecting. Facilitation is used in a variety of contexts including *training*, *experiential learning*, conflict resolution, and *negotiation*.

facilities management GENERAL MANAGEMENT
1 the management of an organization's property
2 the provision of equipment or services such as information technology, systems, and electronic data services to an organization by an agent company

facing matter MARKETING advertisements printed opposite editorial material in newspapers or magazines

factor STATISTICS a variable investigated in a statistical study

factor analysis STATISTICS the examination of the covariances, correlations, or relationships between the variables observed in a statistical study

factor four OPERATIONS & PRODUCTION a concept of environmentally friendly production based on increasing the productivity of resources by a factor of four to reduce waste

factoring FINANCE, BANKING, AND ACCOUNTING
1 the practice of transferring title to foreign accounts receivable to a third-party factoring house that assumes responsibility for collections, administrative services, and any other services requested. Major exporters use factoring as a way of reducing exchange rate risk. The fee for this service is a percentage of the value of the receivables, anywhere from 5% to 10% or higher, depending on the currencies

involved. Companies often include this percentage in selling prices to recoup the cost.
2 the sale of debts to a third party (the factor) at a discount, in return for prompt cash. A factoring service may be with recourse, in which case the supplier takes the risk of the debt not being paid, or without recourse, when the factor takes the risk. See also *invoice discounting*

factor market ECONOMICS a market in which factors of production are bought and sold, for example, the capital market or the labor market

factory GENERAL MANAGEMENT a building or set of buildings housing workers and equipment for the sole purpose of manufacturing goods, often on a large scale

factory gate price OPERATIONS & PRODUCTION the actual cost of manufacturing goods before any *markup* is added to give profit. The factory gate price includes direct costs such as labor, *raw materials*, and energy, and indirect costs such as interest on loans, plant maintenance, or rent.

failure GENERAL MANAGEMENT see *business failure*

failure mode effects analysis GENERAL MANAGEMENT see *FMEA*

fair value FINANCE, BANKING, AND ACCOUNTING the amount for which an *asset* (or liability) could be exchanged in an arm's length transaction between informed and willing parties, other than in a forced or liquidation sale

fallen angel FINANCE, BANKING, AND ACCOUNTING a stock that was once very desirable but has now dropped in value (*slang*)

falling knife FINANCE, BANKING, AND ACCOUNTING a stock whose price has fallen at an alarming rate over a short time period

false accounting FINANCE, BANKING, AND ACCOUNTING the criminal offense of changing, destroying, or hiding accounting records for a dishonest purpose, such as to gain money

false market FINANCE, BANKING, AND ACCOUNTING a market in stocks caused by persons or companies conspiring to buy or sell and so influence the stock price to their advantage

family business GENERAL MANAGEMENT a *small* or *medium-sized business* that is controlled and operated by members of a family. It may

be organized as a sole proprietorship, partnership, corporation, or limited liability company.

family friendly policy HR & PERSONNEL a variety of working practices designed to enable employees to achieve a satisfactory *work-life balance*. A family friendly policy is often introduced by an organization to facilitate the reintroduction of women with children into the workplace. *Equal opportunities* legislation and corporate good practice, however, require that such a policy is open to all employees. Typically, a family friendly policy will allow for a variety of *flexible working* practices and may go further by providing childcare, eldercare facilities, or paid time off for participation in community activities as part of a *community involvement* program. Although the introduction of a family friendly policy may initially be expensive, benefits to the organization, including improved employee retention and higher *motivation* and *job satisfaction* levels, are believed to offset these costs.

Fannie Mae FINANCE, BANKING, AND ACCOUNTING see *FNMA*

FAO *abbr* GENERAL MANAGEMENT the Food and Agriculture Organization of the United Nations: the FAO's priority objectives include encouraging sustainable agriculture and rural development and ensuring the availability of adequate food supplies

FAQ *abbr* E-COMMERCE frequently asked question: FAQ pages are often included on Web sites to provide first-time visitors with answers to the most likely questions they may have. FAQ pages are also used in newsgroups and software applications.

far month FINANCE, BANKING, AND ACCOUNTING the latest month for which there is a futures contract for a particular commodity. See also *nearby month*

FASB *abbr* FINANCE, BANKING, AND ACCOUNTING Financial Accounting Standards Board: a body responsible for establishing the standards of financial reporting and accounting for companies in the private sector. The Securities and Exchange Commission (SEC) performs a comparable role for public companies.

FASTER FINANCE, BANKING, AND ACCOUNTING a computer-based clearing, settlement, registration, and information system operated by the New Zealand Stock Exchange. Abbr of *Fully Automated Screen Trading and Electronic Registration*

fast track GENERAL MANAGEMENT a rapid route to success or advancement. The fast track in-

volves competition and a race to get ahead, and is associated with high ambition and great activity. An employee can be on a fast track, for example, to **promotion**, but an activity also can be said to take the fast track, for example, to rapid **product development**. The **horizontal fast track** is a variation on the idea of the fast track in which advancement is not upward but sideways.

fat

trim the fat GENERAL MANAGEMENT to lay off unnecessary staff in an organization during a time of economic difficulty (*slang*)

fat cat FINANCE, BANKING, AND ACCOUNTING a derogatory term used to describe a chief executive of a large company or organization who secures extremely large pay, pension, and termination packages, often causing concern among stockholders

faxback MARKETING a method of distributing information in which customers dial a dedicated fax machine that automatically sends information back to the customer's fax machine

Fayol, Henri Louis (1841–1925) GENERAL MANAGEMENT French engineer and industrialist. The first European to define **management** as a process, consisting, he argued, of five activities—planning, organizing, coordinating, commanding, and controlling—with further detail contained in 14 general principles. Fayol's ideas were published in *Administration Industrielle et Générale* (1916), and were practiced by others, notably **Alfred P. Sloan, Jr.** See thinker **Henri Fayol**

FCA *abbr* FINANCE, BANKING, AND ACCOUNTING Fellow of the Institute of Chartered Accountants in England and Wales

FCCA *abbr* FINANCE, BANKING, AND ACCOUNTING Fellow of the Association of Chartered Certified Accountants

FCM *abbr* FINANCE, BANKING, AND ACCOUNTING futures commission merchant

FCMA *abbr* FINANCE, BANKING, AND ACCOUNTING Fellow of the Chartered Institute of Management Accountants

FCOL *abbr* GENERAL MANAGEMENT for crying out loud (*slang*)

feasibility study GENERAL MANAGEMENT an investigation into a proposed plan or project to determine whether and how it can be successfully and profitably carried out. Frequently used in **project management**, a feasibility study may examine alternative methods of

reaching objectives or be used to define or redefine the proposed project. The information gathered must be sufficient to make a decision on whether to go ahead with the project, or to enable an investor to decide whether to commit finances to it. This will normally require analysis of technical, financial, and market issues, including an estimate of resources required in terms of materials, time, personnel, and finance, and the expected return on investment.

Fed FINANCE, BANKING, AND ACCOUNTING see **Federal Reserve System**

Federal Funds FINANCE, BANKING, AND ACCOUNTING deposits held in reserve by the Federal Reserve System

Federal income tax FINANCE, BANKING, AND ACCOUNTING money deducted from employees' salaries in order to fund Federal services and projects

Federal National Mortgage Association FINANCE, BANKING, AND ACCOUNTING see **FNMA**

federal organization GENERAL MANAGEMENT a form of **organization structure**, identified by **Charles Handy**, in which subsidiaries federate to gain benefits of scale. In a federal organization, the leader provides coordination and vision, and initiatives are generated from the component subsidiary organizations. Federal organization is one of the many ways in which organizations **restructure** in order to deal with the dilemmas of power and control. According to Handy, federal organization offers an enabling framework for autonomy to release corporate energy for people to do things in their own way, provided that it is in the common interest, and for people to be well informed so as to be able to interpret that common interest. Handy cites Royal Dutch Shell, Unilever, and ABB as exemplars of federalism.

Federal Reserve bank FINANCE, BANKING, AND ACCOUNTING a bank that is a member of the **Federal Reserve System**

Federal Reserve Board FINANCE, BANKING, AND ACCOUNTING a body of seven governors appointed by Congress on the nomination of the President that supervises the U.S. Federal Reserve System and formulates monetary policy. Appointees to the Board of Governors serve for 14 years. Abbr. **FRB**

Federal Reserve note FINANCE, BANKING, AND ACCOUNTING a note issued by the Federal Reserve System to increase the availability of money temporarily

Federal Reserve System FINANCE, BANKING, AND ACCOUNTING the central banking system of the United States, founded in 1913 by an Act of Congress. The board of governors, made up of seven members, is based in Washington, D.C. and 12 Reserve Banks are located in major cities across the United States. Also known as **Fed**

Fed pass FINANCE, BANKING, AND ACCOUNTING the addition of reserves to the **Federal Reserve System** in order to increase credit availability

FEDUSA *abbr* GENERAL MANAGEMENT Federation of Unions of South Africa

Fedwire FINANCE, BANKING, AND ACCOUNTING the U.S. **Federal Reserve System**'s electronic system for transferring funds

feedback GENERAL MANAGEMENT the communication of responses and reactions to proposals and changes, or of the findings of **performance appraisals**, with the goal of enabling improvements to be made. Feedback can be either positive or negative. In the context of performance evaluation, or performance appraisal, positive feedback should be delivered to reinforce good performance, whereas negative feedback should be intended to correct or improve poor performance. Feedback that is delivered inappropriately can be very demotivating, so good communication skills are a prerequisite.

feedback control FINANCE, BANKING, AND ACCOUNTING the measurement of differences between planned outputs and actual outputs achieved, and the modification of subsequent action and/or plans to achieve future required results

feeding frenzy FINANCE, BANKING, AND ACCOUNTING a period of frantic buyer activity in a market (*slang*)

feet

get your feet wet GENERAL MANAGEMENT to begin a new project or activity (*slang*)

fee work FINANCE, BANKING, AND ACCOUNTING GENERAL MANAGEMENT work on a project carried out by independent workers or contractors, rather than employees of an organization

Feigenbaum, Armand Vallin (*b.* 1920) GENERAL MANAGEMENT U.S. manager and author. Originator of the concept of total **quality control**, the forerunner of **total quality management**. In *Quality Control* (1951), Feigenbaum argued that quality should be a companywide process.

Fellow of the Association of Chartered Certified Accountants FINANCE, BANKING, AND ACCOUNTING abbr. *FCCA*

Fellow of the Chartered Institute of Management Accountants FINANCE, BANKING, AND ACCOUNTING abbr. *FCMA*

Fellow of the Institute of Chartered Accountants in England and Wales FINANCE, BANKING, AND ACCOUNTING abbr. *FCA*

Ferguson, **Sir Alex** (*b.* 1941) GENERAL MANAGEMENT British soccer manager. Considered to be one of the most successful club managers of all time, whose management methods, particularly in the area of *motivation*, are studied by other business leaders. His approach is set out in *Managing My Life: My Autobiography* (1999). See checklist *Motivating Your Staff in a Time of Change*

fiat money FINANCE, BANKING, AND ACCOUNTING coins or notes which are not worth much as paper or metal but which are said by the government to have some value

fictitious assets FINANCE, BANKING, AND ACCOUNTING assets, such as prepayments, which do not have a resale value, but which are entered as assets on a company's balance sheet

FID *abbr* (*ANZ*) FINANCE, BANKING, AND ACCOUNTING Financial Institutions Duty

fiduciary deposit FINANCE, BANKING, AND ACCOUNTING a bank deposit which is managed for the depositor by the bank

field a call GENERAL MANAGEMENT to take a difficult phone call from somebody (*slang*)

field plot STATISTICS a statistical study, usually in agriculture, of the results of an operation such as planting genetically modified crops

field research MARKETING the collection of data directly from contact with customers and potential customers through surveys, interviews, and other forms of *market research*

field staff HR & PERSONNEL sales staff who cover a specific geographic region and who travel regularly to meet customers. The term field staff may also be applied to professional and technical staff who operate mainly on site, such as conservationists and archaeologists.

field trial MARKETING a limited pilot test of a product under real conditions. A field trial is undertaken to test the physical or engineering properties of a product in order to identify and iron out any technical shortcomings prior to

marketing. Customers may be involved in some trials, for example, in testing a new laundry detergent. Field trials should not be confused with *test marketing*, which is used to determine the likely market for, and likely consumer response to, a new product or service.

field work MARKETING practical work, study, or research carried out in the real world away from the desk. In a marketing context, field work forms primary *market research* and involves obtaining customers' views and opinions on a face-to-face basis or through mail questionnaires or telephone surveys.

FIFO *abbr* FINANCE, BANKING, AND ACCOUNTING first in first out: a method of inventory control in which the stock of a given product first placed in store is used before more recently produced or acquired goods or materials

FIF Tax *abbr* (*ANZ*) FINANCE, BANKING, AND ACCOUNTING Foreign Investment Funds Tax

file server E-COMMERCE a computer that stores and makes software programs and data available to other computers on a network

file transfer protocol E-COMMERCE see *FTP*

filter GENERAL MANAGEMENT a process for analyzing large amounts of incoming information to identify any material that might be of interest to an organization

Filthy Five GENERAL MANAGEMENT a list of companies with a poor environmental record, compiled annually by *Mother Jones Magazine*

final average monthly salary FINANCE, BANKING, AND ACCOUNTING a U.S. term for the earnings on which most defined benefit pensions are based. U.K. term *pensionable earnings*

final closing date FINANCE, BANKING, AND ACCOUNTING the last date for the acceptance of a *takeover* bid, when the bidder has to announce how many stockholders have accepted his or her offer

final demand FINANCE, BANKING, AND ACCOUNTING a last reminder from a supplier to a customer to pay an outstanding debt. Suppliers often begin legal proceedings if a final demand is ignored.

final discharge FINANCE, BANKING, AND ACCOUNTING the final payment on the amount outstanding on a debt

final dividend FINANCE, BANKING, AND ACCOUNTING the dividend paid at the end of a year's trading. The final dividend must be approved by a company's stockholders.

final sale FINANCE, BANKING, AND ACCOUNTING a sale which does not allow the purchaser to return the goods

finance (*U.K.*) FINANCE, BANKING, AND ACCOUNTING the money needed by an individual or company to pay for something, for example, a project or stocks

Finance and Leasing Association FINANCE, BANKING, AND ACCOUNTING an organization representing firms engaged in business finance and the leasing of equipment and cars

finance bill FINANCE, BANKING, AND ACCOUNTING an act passed by a legislature to provide money for public spending

finance company FINANCE, BANKING, AND ACCOUNTING a business that lends money to people or companies against collateral of some kind

finance house (*U.K.*) FINANCE, BANKING, AND ACCOUNTING a financial institution

finance lease FINANCE, BANKING, AND ACCOUNTING a lease that is treated as though the leassee had borrowed money and bought the leased assets. Also known as *capital lease*

financial FINANCE, BANKING, AND ACCOUNTING relating to finance

financial accountant FINANCE, BANKING, AND ACCOUNTING a qualified accountant, a member of the Institute of Financial Accountants, who advises on accounting matters or who works as the financial director of a company

Financial Accounting Standards Board FINANCE, BANKING, AND ACCOUNTING see *FASB*

financial adviser FINANCE, BANKING, AND ACCOUNTING somebody whose job is to give advice about investments

financial aid FINANCE, BANKING, AND ACCOUNTING monetary assistance given to an individual, organization, or nation. International financial aid, that is from one country to another, is often used to fund educational, health-related, or other humanitarian activities.

financial analyst FINANCE, BANKING, AND ACCOUNTING see *investment analyst*

financial distress FINANCE, BANKING, AND ACCOUNTING the condition of being in severe

difficulties over money, especially being close to bankruptcy

financial economies of scale FINANCE, BANKING, AND ACCOUNTING financial advantages gained by being able to do things on a large scale

financial engineering FINANCE, BANKING, AND ACCOUNTING the conversion of one form of financial instrument into another, such as the swap of a fixed-rate instrument for a floating-rate one

financial institution FINANCE, BANKING, AND ACCOUNTING an organization such as a bank, savings and loan, pension fund, or insurance company which invests large amounts of money in securities

Financial Institutions Duty (*ANZ*) FINANCE, BANKING, AND ACCOUNTING a tax on monies paid into financial institutions imposed by all state governments in Australia except for Queensland. Financial institutions usually pass the tax on to customers. Abbr. *FID*

financial instrument FINANCE, BANKING, AND ACCOUNTING any contract that gives rise to both a financial asset of one entity and a financial liability or equity instrument of another entity. Financial instruments include both primary financial instruments, such as bonds, currency, and stocks, and derivative financial instruments, whose value derives from the underlying assets.

financial intermediary FINANCE, BANKING, AND ACCOUNTING an institution which accepts deposits or loans from individuals and lends money to clients. Banks, building societies, and hire purchase companies are all financial intermediaries.

financial planning FINANCE, BANKING, AND ACCOUNTING planning the acquisition of funds to finance planned activities

Financial Planning Association of Australia (*ANZ*) FINANCE, BANKING, AND ACCOUNTING a national organization representing companies and individuals working in the Australian financial planning industry. Established in 1992, the Association is responsible for monitoring standards among its members. Abbr. *FPA*

Financial Reporting Review Panel FINANCE, BANKING, AND ACCOUNTING a U.K. review panel established to examine contentious departures from accounting standards by large companies

Financial Reporting Standards Board (*ANZ*) FINANCE, BANKING, AND ACCOUNTING a body that is responsible for setting and monitoring accounting standards in New Zealand. Abbr. *FRSB*

financial risk FINANCE, BANKING, AND ACCOUNTING the possibility of loss in an investment or speculation

Financial Services Authority FINANCE, BANKING, AND ACCOUNTING an independent nongovernmental body formed in the United Kingdom in 1997 following reforms in the regulation of financial services. The FSA's four statutory objectives were specified by the Financial Services and Markets Act 2000: maintaining market confidence; increasing public knowledge of the finance system; ensuring appropriate protection for consumers; and reducing financial crime. Abbr. *FSA*

financial statements FINANCE, BANKING, AND ACCOUNTING summaries of accounts to provide information for interested parties. The most common financial statements are trading and profit and loss account; profit and loss appropriation account; balance sheet; cash flow statement; report of the auditors; statement of total recognized gains and losses; and reconciliation of movements in shareholders' funds. See also *annual report*

financial supermarket FINANCE, BANKING, AND ACCOUNTING a company which offers a variety of financial services. For example, a bank may offer loans, mortgages, pensions, and insurance alongside its existing range of normal banking services.

financial year FINANCE, BANKING, AND ACCOUNTING
1 see *final year*
2 (*U.K.*) for corporation tax purposes, the period from 1 April of a given year to 31 March of the following year

financier FINANCE, BANKING, AND ACCOUNTING a person who specializes in the provision of finance to other people or organizations

financing FINANCE, BANKING, AND ACCOUNTING the money needed by an individual or company to pay for something, for example, a project or inventory.

financing gap ECONOMICS a gap in funding for institutions such as the *IMF* caused by canceling the debts of poorer countries such as those in West Africa

finder's fee FINANCE, BANKING, AND ACCOUNTING a fee paid to a person who finds a client for another person or company, for example,

someone who introduces a new client to a brokerage firm

find time MARKETING the time it takes a consumer to locate a company's product among other products on the shelf (*slang*)

finished goods OPERATIONS & PRODUCTION completed goods that are available for sale to customers

finite capacity plan OPERATIONS & PRODUCTION see *capacity requirements planning*

finite loading OPERATIONS & PRODUCTION the scheduling or *loading* of jobs onto a workstation so that the number of jobs matches the *effective capacity* of that station over a given time period. Finite loading is often used in a computerized operation of *loading*. See also *infinite loading*

finite population STATISTICS a statistical population that has a limited size

FIRB *abbr* (*ANZ*) FINANCE, BANKING, AND ACCOUNTING Foreign Investment Review Board

firewall E-COMMERCE a combination of hardware, software, and procedures that controls access to an *intranet*. Firewalls help to control the information that passes between an intranet and the Internet. A firewall can be simple or complex, depending on how an organization decides to control its Internet traffic. It may, for example, be established to limit Internet access to e-mail only, so that no other types of information can pass between the intranet and the Internet.

firm GENERAL MANAGEMENT a *partnership* business. A firm is strictly the name for a business run by partners, but it is often used more generally as a synonym for a *company*, or *organization*.

firm sale (*U.K.*) FINANCE, BANKING, AND ACCOUNTING see *final sale*

first in first out FINANCE, BANKING, AND ACCOUNTING see *FIFO*

first-line management HR & PERSONNEL see *supervisory management*

first mover MARKETING the company that first introduces a new type of product or service to a market. Those organizations that follow a first mover to market are known as *followers* or *laggards*—terms that also describe companies that are not the recognized leaders in a sector.

first mover advantage GENERAL MANAGEMENT the benefit produced by being the first to enter a market with a new product or service. First mover advantages include becoming a market leader in a new area, establishing a new leading **brand**; being able to charge a premium until competitor products appear; enhanced reputation, design, and copyright protection; and possibly setting an industry standard to which other competitors may have to aspire. Disadvantages include cheaper, and possibly better, **follower** products; the possibility of having to reduce prices or continuously having to add value to stay ahead; first mover development costs; a possible shift in consumer tastes away from the product; obsolescence; and a follower product being accepted as the industry standard.

first-round financing FINANCE, BANKING, AND ACCOUNTING the first infusion of capital into a project

fiscal FINANCE, BANKING, AND ACCOUNTING relating to financial matters, especially in respect of governmental collection, use, and regulation of money through taxation

fiscal balance ECONOMICS a taxation policy that keeps a country's employment and taxation levels in balance

fiscal drag (*U.K.*) FINANCE, BANKING, AND ACCOUNTING the effect that inflation has on taxation in that, as earnings rise, the amount of tax collected increases without a rise in tax rates

fiscal policy ECONOMICS the central government's policy on lowering or raising taxation or increasing or decreasing public expenditure in order to stimulate or depress *aggregate demand*

fiscal year FINANCE, BANKING, AND ACCOUNTING the twelve-month period for which a company produces accounts. A fiscal year is not necessarily the same as a calendar year. Abbr. **FY**

fishbone chart GENERAL MANAGEMENT a diagram resembling the skeleton of a fish that is used to identify and categorize the possible causes of problems. Within a fishbone chart, the topic or problem to be discussed is placed in a box at the right-hand side that corresponds to the fish's head, and the major elements to be investigated are shown as branches at an angle to the horizontal spine. Questions are asked to identify possible causes of problems in each area and the results are added to the diagram as additional layers of branches. This ensures that all aspects of the problem are considered systematically. The fishbone chart is also

known as a *cause and effect diagram* or an *Ishikawa diagram* (after the originator, Professor *Kaoru Ishikawa* of Tokyo University), and is frequently used in **brainstorming** and *problem solving*.

fixed annuity FINANCE, BANKING, AND ACCOUNTING see *annuity*

fixed asset FINANCE, BANKING, AND ACCOUNTING a long-term asset of a business such as a machine or building that will not usually be traded

fixed assets register FINANCE, BANKING, AND ACCOUNTING a record of individual tangible fixed assets

fixed-asset turnover ratio FINANCE, BANKING, AND ACCOUNTING a measure of the use a business makes of its capital assets. It is calculated by dividing sales by net fixed assets.

fixed cost FINANCE, BANKING, AND ACCOUNTING a cost that does not change according to sales volumes, unlike variable costs. Fixed costs are usually overheads, such as rent and utility payments.

fixed deduction FINANCE, BANKING, AND ACCOUNTING a deduction agreed by HM Revenue & Customs and a group of employees which covers general expenditure on clothes or tools used in the course of employment

fixed exchange rate system FINANCE, BANKING, AND ACCOUNTING a system of currency exchange in which there is no change of rate

fixed-interest loan FINANCE, BANKING, AND ACCOUNTING a loan whose rate of interest does not change

fixed interval re-order system OPERATIONS & PRODUCTION see *periodic inventory review system*

fixed-price agreement FINANCE, BANKING, AND ACCOUNTING an agreement whereby a company provides a service or a product at a price which stays the same for the whole period of the agreement

fixed rate GENERAL MANAGEMENT an interest rate for loans that does not change with fluctuating conditions in the market

fixed-rate loan FINANCE, BANKING, AND ACCOUNTING a loan with an interest rate that is set at the beginning of the term and remains the same throughout

fixtures and fittings FINANCE, BANKING, AND ACCOUNTING the objects in a property which are sold with the property, both those which cannot be removed and those which can. Fixtures and fittings are a category of *fixed assets*.

flagpole
let's run it up a flagpole and see who salutes GENERAL MANAGEMENT let's try this idea and see what level of support or popularity it commands (*slang*)

flame E-COMMERCE a hostile or aggressive message sent via e-mail or posted into an online newsgroup. Typically, flame messages are sent in response to *spam* or unsolicited commercial e-mail. If a flame message is responded to in a similarly hostile manner, it can lead to a *flame war*.

flash drive E-COMMERCE a small plastic device functioning as a disk drive, containing memory chips that retain their contents without electrical power and that have a capacity of between 16 megabytes and 4 gigabytes of data.
   On the end is a standard USB connector that fits into USB ports.

flat organization GENERAL MANAGEMENT HR & PERSONNEL a slimmed-down *organization structure*, with fewer levels between top and bottom than a traditional *bureaucracy*, that is supposedly more responsive and better able to cope with fast-moving change. A flat organization can be the result of *delayering*. Also known as *horizontal organization*

flat panel E-COMMERCE a very thin computer screen with a flat viewing surface that employs liquid-crystal display technology, commonly used in portable personal computers

flat tax FINANCE, BANKING, AND ACCOUNTING a tax levied at one fixed rate whatever an individual's income

flat yield curve FINANCE, BANKING, AND ACCOUNTING a *yield curve* with the same interest rates for long-term bonds as for short-term bonds

flexecutive HR & PERSONNEL a multiskilled executive able to switch jobs or tasks easily (*slang*)

flexed budget FINANCE, BANKING, AND ACCOUNTING a budget which changes in response to changes in sales turnover and output

flexible exchange rate system FINANCE, BANKING, AND ACCOUNTING a system of currency exchange in which rates change from time to time

flexible manufacturing system OPERATIONS & PRODUCTION

1 an integrated system of computer-controlled machine tools and transport and handling systems under the control of a larger computer. Flexibility is achieved by having an overall method of control that coordinates the functions of both the machine tools and the handling systems. A flexible manufacturing system is a type of *advanced manufacturing technology*.

2 an integrated, computer-controlled production system which is capable of producing any of a variety of parts, and of switching quickly and economically between them Abbr. *FMS*

flexible working HR & PERSONNEL a generic term for employment practices that differ from the traditional norm in terms of the hours worked, the length of contract, or the place of work. Flexible working practices can be divided into three categories: those that give flexibility in the management of time through *flexible working hours* programs such as *flextime* or shift work; those that allow employers to adapt to peaks or troughs in demand through numerical flexibility, for example, by employing temporary staff; and those that give flexibility regarding the place of work, for example, teleworking.

flexible working hours HR & PERSONNEL flexibility in the management of working time. Flexible working hours are achieved through systems such as *annual hours*, *part-time work*, *flextime*, or jobsharing, that are arranged to meet organizational requirements or to help employees reconcile the demands of work and personal circumstances.

flexilagger (*U.K.*) HR & PERSONNEL a company or organization considered to put too little emphasis on flexibility in its employment practices (*slang*)

flexileader (*U.K.*) HR & PERSONNEL a company or organization considered to put a great deal of emphasis on flexibility in its employment practices (*slang*)

flextime HR & PERSONNEL a system of *flexible working hours* based on a set number of hours to be worked per week. Employees are able to determine their precise hours of work, provided business demands are met and attendance at work during core periods is achieved. A debit or credit of hours can be carried forward into the next accounting period.

flight of capital FINANCE, BANKING, AND ACCOUNTING the rapid movement of *capital* out of one country because of lack of confidence in that country's economic future

flight risk HR & PERSONNEL an employee who may be planning to leave a company in the near future (*slang*)

flip GENERAL MANAGEMENT a startup company that works to build market share quickly and generate short-term personal wealth for its founders through flotation or sell-off

float FINANCE, BANKING, AND ACCOUNTING

1 (*U.K.*) to sell stocks or bonds, for example, to finance a project

2 the period between the presentation of a check as payment and the actual payment to the payee or the financial advantage provided by this period to the drawer of a check

3 a small cash balance maintained to facilitate low-value cash transactions. Records of these transactions should be maintained as evidence of expenditure, and periodically a float or petty cash balance will be replenished to a predetermined level.

floating asset FINANCE, BANKING, AND ACCOUNTING an asset which it is assumed will be consumed during the company's normal trading cycle and then replaced by the same type of asset

floating debenture FINANCE, BANKING, AND ACCOUNTING a debenture secured on all of a company's *assets* which runs until the company is wound up

floating debt FINANCE, BANKING, AND ACCOUNTING a short-term borrowing that is repeatedly refinanced

floating rate FINANCE, BANKING, AND ACCOUNTING an interest rate that is not fixed and which changes according to fluctuations in the market

floor FINANCE, BANKING, AND ACCOUNTING a lower limit on an interest rate, price, or the value of an asset

floor broker FINANCE, BANKING, AND ACCOUNTING see *pit broker*

floor effect STATISTICS the occurrence of clusters of scores near the lower limit of the data in a statistical study

floor limit FINANCE, BANKING, AND ACCOUNTING the highest sale through a credit card that a retailer can accept without having to obtain authorization from the issuing bank

flotation FINANCE, BANKING, AND ACCOUNTING the financing of a company by selling stock in it or a new debt issue, or the offering of stock

and bonds for sale on the stock exchange. See also *initial public offering*

flow chart *or* **flow diagram** GENERAL MANAGEMENT a graphic representation of the stages in a process or system, or of the steps required to solve a problem. A flow chart is commonly used to represent the sequence of functions in a computer program or to model the movement of materials, money, or people in a complex process. Two primary symbols used in flow charts are the *process box*, indicating a process or action taking place, and the *decision lozenge*, indicating the need for a decision.

flow line production *or* **flow lines** OPERATIONS & PRODUCTION see *flow production*

flow on FINANCE, BANKING, AND ACCOUNTING GENERAL MANAGEMENT a pay increase awarded to one group of workers as a result of a pay raise awarded to another group working in the same field

flow production OPERATIONS & PRODUCTION a production method in which successive operations are carried out on a product in such a way that it moves through the factory in a single direction. Flow production is most widely used in *mass production* on production lines. More recently, it has been linked with *batch production*. Under flow production, inventory is often kept to the minimum necessary to ensure continued activity. Stoppages and interruptions to the flow indicate a fault, and corrective action can be taken. *Assembly line* production is an extreme version of flow production. Also known as *flow line production*

flow theory GENERAL MANAGEMENT a theory of the way in which people become engaged with, or disengaged from, change. Flow theory suggests that people harmonize in change situations, and open, honest, trusting relationships emerge. The theory recognizes the unpredictability and rigidity of human nature when faced with change. See also *change management*

fluff it and fly it MARKETING to make a product look good and then sell it (*slang*)

FMA *abbr* FINANCE, BANKING, AND ACCOUNTING Fund Managers' Association. See also *Investment Management Association*

FMCG *abbr* GENERAL MANAGEMENT fast moving consumer goods

FMEA *abbr* GENERAL MANAGEMENT failure mode effects analysis: a technique for analyzing the causes, risks, and effects of potential systems

or component failures that is used as a basis for prevention and contingency planning. FMEA was developed by engineers primarily to prevent defects in electrical and mechanical systems. All possible failures and their potential effects are listed and ranked according to severity of impact and probability of occurrence so that prevention efforts can be focused on the most critical issues.

FMS *abbr* FINANCE, BANKING, AND ACCOUNTING OPERATIONS & PRODUCTION flexible manufacturing system

FNMA *abbr* FINANCE, BANKING, AND ACCOUNTING Federal National Mortgage Association: the largest source of housing finance in the United States, the FNMA trades in mortgages guaranteed by the Federal Housing Finance Board. Created in 1938, the FNMA is a stockholder-owned private company and its stock is traded on the New York Stock Exchange. It has two principal regulators; the Department for Housing and Urban Development (HUD) aims to make sure that liquidity in the residential mortgage finance market is increased, while the Office of Federal Housing Enterprise Oversight (OFHEO) monitors soundness of accounting practice and financial safety. Also known as *Fannie Mae*

focus group MARKETING a carefully selected representative variety of consumers or employees used for the purposes of providing feedback on consumer preferences and responses to a selected range of products or marketing issues. A focus group usually operates with a facilitator to guide discussion. Although primarily used for marketing purposes, focus groups are also being more widely used to obtain employee feedback on a wide range of employment and other issues within an organization.

FOK *abbr* FINANCE, BANKING, AND ACCOUNTING fill or kill

followback survey STATISTICS a further survey of a statistical population carried out a period of years after an original survey

follower MARKETING see *first mover*

Fong Kong (*S. Africa*) GENERAL MANAGEMENT a product with a fake designer label, especially sports shoes (*slang*)

Food and Agriculture Organization GENERAL MANAGEMENT see *FAO*

footer E-COMMERCE an information section at the bottom of a Web page, usually containing a copy of the essential links, contact informa-

tion, and links to copyright and privacy policy information

footfall MARKETING a measure of the number of people who walk past a store (*slang*)

Forbes 500 FINANCE, BANKING, AND ACCOUNTING a list of the 500 largest public companies in the United States, ranked according to various criteria by *Forbes* magazine

forced sale FINANCE, BANKING, AND ACCOUNTING a sale which takes place as the result of a court order or because it represents the only reasonable way for a company or individual to avoid a financial crisis

force field analysis GENERAL MANAGEMENT a technique for promoting change by identifying positive and negative factors and by working to lessen the negative forces while developing the positive ones. Force field analysis was developed by *Kurt Lewin* as an aid to *decision making*, *problem solving*, and conflict prevention.

Ford, Henry (1863–1947) GENERAL MANAGEMENT U.S. industrialist. Founder of the Ford Motor Company, who organized the *assembly line* along the scientific management principles of *Frederick Winslow Taylor* and recorded his philosophy in *My Life and Work* (1922).

After spending time as a machinist's apprentice, a watch repairer, and a mechanic, Ford built his first car in 1896. He quickly became convinced of the vehicle's commercial potential and started his own company in 1903. His first car was the Model A. After a year in business he was selling 600 a month.

In 1907 Ford professed that his aim was to build a motor car for the masses. In 1908 his Model T was born. Through innovative use of new mass-production techniques, 15 million Model Ts were produced between 1908 and 1927.

At that time, Ford's factory at Highland Park, Michigan, was the biggest in the world. Over 14,000 people worked on the 57-acre site. He was quick to establish international operations as well. Ford's first overseas sales branch was opened in France in 1908 and, in 1911, Ford began making cars in the United Kingdom.

In 1919 Henry Ford resigned as the company's president, letting his son, Edsel, take over. By then the Ford company was making a car a minute and Ford's market share was in excess of 57%. See thinker *Frederick Winslow Taylor*

forecast STATISTICS a prediction of the value of a variable in a statistical study

forecasting GENERAL MANAGEMENT the prediction of outcomes, trends, or expected future behavior of a business, industry sector, or the economy through the use of statistics. Forecasting is an *operational research* technique used as a basis for management planning and decision making. Common types of forecasting include trend analysis, *regression analysis*, *Delphi technique*, time series analysis, *correlation*, *exponential smoothing*, and input-output analysis.

foreign bill FINANCE, BANKING, AND ACCOUNTING a bill of exchange that is not payable in the country where it is issued

foreign currency ECONOMICS the currency or interest-bearing bonds of a foreign country

foreign debt FINANCE, BANKING, AND ACCOUNTING hard-currency debt owed to a foreign country in payment for goods and services

foreign dividend FINANCE, BANKING, AND ACCOUNTING in the United Kingdom, a dividend paid by another country, possibly subject to special rules under U.K. tax codes

foreign draft FINANCE, BANKING, AND ACCOUNTING a check that is not both drawn and payable in the same country

foreign equity market FINANCE, BANKING, AND ACCOUNTING the market in one country for equities of companies in other countries

foreign exchange FINANCE, BANKING, AND ACCOUNTING the currencies of other countries, or dealings in these

foreign exchange option FINANCE, BANKING, AND ACCOUNTING a contract which, for a fee, guarantees a worst-case exchange rate for the future purchase of one currency for another. Unlike a *forward transaction*, the option does not obligate the buyer to deliver a currency on the settlement date unless the buyer chooses to. These options protect against unfavorable currency movements while preserving the ability to participate in favorable movements.

foreign income dividend FINANCE, BANKING, AND ACCOUNTING a dividend paid from earnings in other countries

Foreign Investment Funds Tax (*ANZ*) FINANCE, BANKING, AND ACCOUNTING a tax imposed by the Australian government on unrealized gains made by Australian residents from offshore investments. It was introduced in 1992 to prevent overseas earnings from being taxed at

low rates and never brought to Australia. Abbr. *FIF Tax*

Foreign Investment Review Board (*ANZ*) FINANCE, BANKING, AND ACCOUNTING a non-statutory body that regulates and advises the federal government on foreign investment in Australia. It was established in 1976. Abbr. *FIRB*

foreign reserve FINANCE, BANKING, AND ACCOUNTING the currency of other countries held by an organization, especially a country's central bank

foreign subsidiary company GENERAL MANAGEMENT see *subsidiary company*

foreign tax credit FINANCE, BANKING, AND ACCOUNTING a tax advantage for taxes that are paid to or in another country

forensic accounting FINANCE, BANKING, AND ACCOUNTING the use of accounting records and documents in order to determine the legality or otherwise of past activities

forfeit clause FINANCE, BANKING, AND ACCOUNTING a clause in a contract which states that goods or a deposit will be taken away if the contract is not fulfilled by one of the signers

formica parachute HR & PERSONNEL unemployment insurance (*slang*)

Fortune 500 FINANCE, BANKING, AND ACCOUNTING a list of the 500 largest industrial companies in the United States, compiled annually by *Fortune* magazine

forum E-COMMERCE a newsgroup, mailing-list discussion group, chat room, or other online area that enables Internet users to read, post, and respond to messages

forward contract FINANCE, BANKING, AND ACCOUNTING a private futures contract for delivery of a commodity

forward cover FINANCE, BANKING, AND ACCOUNTING the purchase for cash of the quantity of a commodity needed to fulfill a futures contract

forwarding agent FINANCE, BANKING, AND ACCOUNTING a person or company that arranges shipping and customs documents for clients

forward integration OPERATIONS & PRODUCTION a means of guaranteeing *distribution channels* for products and services by building relationships with, or taking control of, *distributors*. Forward integration can free the supplier from the threat or influence of major buyers

and can also provide a barrier to market entry by potential rivals. *Backward integration* can provide similar guarantees on the supply side. Forward integration is a feature of Japanese *keiretsu* .

forward interest rate FINANCE, BANKING, AND ACCOUNTING an interest rate specified for a loan to be made at a future date

forward-looking study STATISTICS a survey of a statistical population carried out for a period such as a year after an original survey

forward margin FINANCE, BANKING, AND ACCOUNTING the difference between the current (or spot) price and the forward price

forward market FINANCE, BANKING, AND ACCOUNTING a market for the buying of foreign currency, stocks, or commodities for delivery at a later date at a certain price

forward pricing FINANCE, BANKING, AND ACCOUNTING the establishment of the price of a share in a mutual fund based on the next asset valuation

forward rate FINANCE, BANKING, AND ACCOUNTING an estimate of what an interest rate will be at a specified future time

forward scheduling OPERATIONS & PRODUCTION a method for determining the start times for the various operations involved in a particular *job*. Forward scheduling is most often used when the operations department sets the delivery date for a job, rather than the sales or marketing departments. Jobs are scheduled for the various operations as the workstations are expected to become available. The customer can then be informed of the projected delivery date. See also *backward scheduling*

forward transaction FINANCE, BANKING, AND ACCOUNTING an agreement to buy one currency and sell another on a date some time beyond two business days. This allows an exchange rate on a given day to be locked in for a future payment or receipt, thereby eliminating exchange rate risk.

fourth level of service GENERAL MANAGEMENT a very high rating in a system of measuring the added value in a product or service

fourth market FINANCE, BANKING, AND ACCOUNTING trading conducted directly without brokers, usually by large institutions

FPA *abbr* FINANCE, BANKING, AND ACCOUNTING Financial Planning Association of Australia

fractional certificate FINANCE, BANKING, AND ACCOUNTING a certificate for part of a *share*

fractional currency FINANCE, BANKING, AND ACCOUNTING the paper money that is in denominations smaller than one unit of a standard national currency

frames E-COMMERCE a feature of *HTML* that allows different Web pages to be displayed in one window simultaneously. Frames enable Web sites to keep a standard navigation bar on the screen regardless of the Web page a visitor decides to access. However, there are a number of problems with frames. For instance, pages can be more difficult to print and bookmark because browsers can often only recognize one frame at a time.

franchise MARKETING an agreement enabling a third party to sell or provide products or services owned by a manufacturer or supplier. A franchise is granted by the manufacturer, or *franchisor*, to a *franchisee*, who then retails the product. The franchise is regulated by a *franchise contract*, or *franchise agreement*, that specifies the terms and conditions of the franchise. These may include an obligation for the franchisor to provide national advertising or training for sales staff in return for the meeting of agreed sales targets by the franchisee. The franchisee normally retains a percentage of sales income. In other cases, a franchise may involve the *licensing* of a franchisee to manufacture a product to the franchisor's specification, and the sale of this product to retailers. Franchises can also be organized by issue of a *master franchise*.

franchise agreement MARKETING see *franchise*

franchise chain MARKETING a number of retail outlets operating the same *franchise*. A franchise chain may vary in size from a few to many thousands of outlets and in coverage from a small local area to worldwide.

franchise contract MARKETING see *franchise*

franchisee MARKETING see *franchise*

franchisor MARKETING see *franchise*

franked payment FINANCE, BANKING, AND ACCOUNTING dividends plus tax credits paid by a company to stockholders

fraud FINANCE, BANKING, AND ACCOUNTING GENERAL MANAGEMENT the use of dishonesty, deception, or false representation in order to gain a material advantage or to injure the interests of others. Types of fraud include false accounting,

theft, third party or investment fraud, employee collusion, and computer fraud. See also **corporate fraud**

FRB *abbr* FINANCE, BANKING, AND ACCOUNTING Federal Reserve Board

free agent HR & PERSONNEL a worker who operates on a *freelance* or *e-lance* basis, offering skills and expertise to companies anywhere in the world. A free agent works independently and may follow a pattern of *portfolio working*.

freebie MARKETING a product or service that is given away, often as a business promotion

free coinage FINANCE, BANKING, AND ACCOUNTING a government's minting of coins from precious metals provided by citizens

free enterprise ECONOMICS the trade carried on in a free-market economy, where resources are allocated on the basis of supply and demand

free gold FINANCE, BANKING, AND ACCOUNTING gold held by a government but not pledged as a reserve for the government's currency

freelance GENERAL MANAGEMENT working on the basis of being self-employed, and possibly working for several employers at the same time, perhaps on a temporary basis. Freelance workers have been described by **Charles Handy** as ideally suited to *portfolio working*.

Freelancers must be good at *multitasking*; they require the skills of a manager, bookkeeper, and a promoter. People thinking about becoming freelance should conduct plenty of research, not only into the industry in which they will be offering their services, but also into their own motivation for freelancing, and into whether their character is suited to the freelance life. Before leaving their day job, they should put together a business plan plotting the first year's goals and activity, perhaps considering the possibility of starting their freelance business on a part-time basis, so that they can initially rely on their current income.

An important part of this first year will be in marketing and promoting the business. Freelancers should develop a target list of companies they wish to work for, learning all they can about each company before approaching them with marketing and proposals. Good customer service could be the thing to make or break their career. Being liked is as valuable as being prompt and doing a professional job, and will encourage future business. It is, though, inevitable that a set of clients will change as time goes by. To protect themselves against this, freelancers should try to plan six months

ahead and create diversity in their client base. See thinker **Charles Handy**

free market ECONOMICS a market in which supply and demand are unregulated, except by the country's competition policy, and rights in physical and intellectual property are upheld

free period FINANCE, BANKING, AND ACCOUNTING the period of grace allowed to credit card holders before payment for credit card purchases is demanded

freephone (*U.K.*) MARKETING a telephone service in which the cost of calls to an organization is borne by the organization rather than the caller

freepost (*U.K.*) MARKETING a postal service in which the cost of postage to an organization is borne by the organization rather than the sender

free reserves FINANCE, BANKING, AND ACCOUNTING the part of a bank's reserves which are above the statutory level and so can be used for various purposes as the bank wishes

freeware E-COMMERCE free software programs

free worker HR & PERSONNEL somebody who frequently moves from one job or project to another, transferring skills and ideas. The term free worker was coined by the Industrial Society in the United Kingdom in 2000. Free workers have knowledge or skills that organizations value. They do not subscribe to the idea of a job for life or long-term loyalty to any one organization but instead work on short-term *personal contracts*. They depend largely on networking to find new assignments. They may be *freelance* or *e-lance* workers and may follow a pattern of *portfolio working*.

freeze-out FINANCE, BANKING, AND ACCOUNTING GENERAL MANAGEMENT the exclusion of minority stockholders in a company that has been taken over. A freeze-out provision may exist in a *takeover* agreement, which permits the acquiring organization to buy the noncontrolling shares held by small shareholders. A fair price is usually set, and the freeze-out may take place at a specified time, perhaps two to five years after the takeover. A freeze-out can still take place, even if provision for it is not made in a corporate charter, by applying pressure to minority stockholders to sell their shares to the acquiring company.

freight OPERATIONS & PRODUCTION goods loaded for onward transport, most often by sea or by air

freight forwarder OPERATIONS & PRODUCTION an organization that collects shipments from a number of businesses and consolidates them into larger shipments for economies of scale. A freight forwarder often also deals with route selection, price negotiation, and documentation of distribution, and can act as a distribution agent for a business. By consolidating loads, a freight forwarder can negotiate cheaper rates of transportation than the individual businesses and can prebook space to ensure a more rapid delivery schedule.

frequency analysis MARKETING a technique for comparing the number of opportunities to reach the same target audience in different media

frequency distribution STATISTICS the process of dividing a sample of observations in a statistical study into classes and listing the number of observations in each class

frequency polygon STATISTICS a diagrammatic representation showing the values in a *frequency distribution*

frequently asked question E-COMMERCE see *FAQ*

frictional unemployment ECONOMICS a situation in which people are temporarily out of the labor market. They could be seeking a new job, incurring search delays as they apply, attending interviews, and relocating.

friction-free market FINANCE, BANKING, AND ACCOUNTING GENERAL MANAGEMENT a market in which there is little differentiation between competing products, so that the customer has exceptional choice

fringe benefits HR & PERSONNEL rewards given or offered to employees in addition to their wages or salaries and included in their employment contract. Fringe benefits range from share options, company cars, expense accounts, cheap loans, medical insurance, and other types of *incentive plan* to discounts on company products, subsidized meals, and membership of social and health clubs. Many of these benefits are liable for tax. A *cafeteria benefits* plan permits employees to select from a variety of such benefits, although usually some are deemed to be core and not exchangeable for others. Minor benefits, sometimes appropriated rather than given, are known as *perks*.

front end GENERAL MANAGEMENT the part of an organization that deals with customers on a face-to-face basis

front-end loading FINANCE, BANKING, AND ACCOUNTING the practice of taking the commission and administrative expenses from the early payments made to an investment or insurance plan. See also *back-end loading*

frozen account FINANCE, BANKING, AND ACCOUNTING a bank account whose funds cannot be used or withdrawn because of a court order

FRSB *abbr* (ANZ) FINANCE, BANKING, AND ACCOUNTING Financial Reporting Standards Board

FSA *abbr* FINANCE, BANKING, AND ACCOUNTING Financial Services Authority

FSB *abbr* FINANCE, BANKING, AND ACCOUNTING Federation of Small Businesses

FTP *abbr* E-COMMERCE file transfer protocol: a set of communication rules that allow data or files to be transferred between computers over a network

FTSE 30 *abbr* FINANCE, BANKING, AND ACCOUNTING FTSE 30 Share Index

FTSE 30 Share Index FINANCE, BANKING, AND ACCOUNTING an index showing the stock prices of 30 influential companies on the London Stock Exchange. Although in existence since 1935, the 30 Share Index is now one of the less popular indices. Abbr. *FTSE 30*

FTSE 100 *abbr* FINANCE, BANKING, AND ACCOUNTING FTSE 100 Share Index

FTSE 100 Share Index FINANCE, BANKING, AND ACCOUNTING an index, established in 1984, that is based on the stock prices of the 100 most highly capitalized public companies in the United Kingdom. Abbr. *FTSE 100*

FTSE 250 *abbr* FINANCE, BANKING, AND ACCOUNTING FTSE 250 Index

FTSE 250 Index FINANCE, BANKING, AND ACCOUNTING an index of medium-capitalized companies not included in the FTSE 100 Index. It represents over 17% of U.K. market capitalization. Abbr. *FTSE 250*

FTSE All-Share *abbr* FINANCE, BANKING, AND ACCOUNTING FTSE All-Share Index

FTSE All-Share Index FINANCE, BANKING, AND ACCOUNTING an average of the stock prices of all the companies listed on the London Stock Exchange. As this encompasses over 1,000 companies, this index is often used as a reliable barometer of the performance of different companies. This index aggregates the FTSE 100, FTSE 250, and FTSE Small Cap indices. Abbr. *FTSE All-Share*

FTSE Small Cap *abbr* FTSE Small Cap Index

FTSE Small Cap Index FINANCE, BANKING, AND ACCOUNTING an index which indicates the performance of companies with the smallest market capitalization, representing roughly 2% of market capitalization in the United Kingdom. Abbr. *FTSE Small Cap*

FTSE TMT *abbr* FINANCE, BANKING, AND ACCOUNTING FTSE TMT Index

FTSE TMT Index FINANCE, BANKING, AND ACCOUNTING an index which indicates the performance of companies in three key business areas: technology, media, and telecommunications. Abbr. *FTSE TMT*

fulfillment MARKETING the process of responding to customer inquiries, orders, or sales promotion offers

fulfillment house MARKETING an organization that specializes in responding to inquiries, orders, or sales promotion offers on behalf of a client

full bank FINANCE, BANKING, AND ACCOUNTING a local or foreign bank permitted to engage in the full range of domestic and international services

full coupon bond FINANCE, BANKING, AND ACCOUNTING a bond whose interest rate is competitive in the current market

full nine yards
go the full nine yards to follow something through completely or do something to its greatest extent (*slang*)

full-service banking FINANCE, BANKING, AND ACCOUNTING a type of banking that offers a whole range of services including mortgages, loans, and pension plans

full-service broker FINANCE, BANKING, AND ACCOUNTING a broker who manages portfolios for clients, and gives advice on stocks and financial questions in general

full-text index E-COMMERCE an index consisting of every single word of every document cataloged

full-time HR & PERSONNEL standard hours of *attendance* in an organization, on the basis of a permanent *contract of employment*, for example, 9a.m.–5p.m., five days a week

full-time job HR & PERSONNEL a position of paid employment that occupies all somebody's normal working hours

Fully Automated Screen Trading and Electronic Registration (ANZ) GENERAL MANAGEMENT see *FASTER*

fully connected world GENERAL MANAGEMENT a world in which most people and organizations are linked by networks such as the Internet

fully diluted earnings per share FINANCE, BANKING, AND ACCOUNTING *earnings per share* calculated over the whole number of shares on the assumption that convertible shares have been converted to ordinary shares

fully diluted earnings per (common) share FINANCE, BANKING, AND ACCOUNTING earnings on a share that take into account commitments to issue more shares, for example, as a result of convertibles, stock options, or warrants

fully distributed issue FINANCE, BANKING, AND ACCOUNTING an issue of stock sold entirely to investors rather than held by dealers

functional budget FINANCE, BANKING, AND ACCOUNTING a budget of income and/or expenditure applicable to a particular function. A function may refer to a department or a process. Functional budgets frequently include the following: production cost budget (based on a forecast of production and plant utilization); marketing cost budget; sales budget; personnel budget; purchasing budget; and research and development budget. Also known as *departmental budget*

functional relationship STATISTICS the relationship between the variables in a study, in which there is no bias or any other distorting factor

fundamental accounting concepts FINANCE, BANKING, AND ACCOUNTING broad basic assumptions that underlie the periodic financial accounts of business enterprises. See also *concepts*

funded debt FINANCE, BANKING, AND ACCOUNTING long-term debt or debt that has a maturity date in excess of one year. Funded debt is usually issued in the public markets or in the form of a private placement to qualified institutional investors.

funding risk FINANCE, BANKING, AND ACCOUNTING the risk that an entity will encounter difficulty in realizing assets or otherwise raising funds to meet commitments associated with financial instruments. See also *liquidity risk*

fund manager FINANCE, BANKING, AND ACCOUNTING somebody who manages the investments of a mutual fund or large financial institution

Fund Managers' Association FINANCE, BANKING, AND ACCOUNTING an association which represents the interests of U.K.-based institutional fund managers. Abbr. *FMA*

fund of funds (*S. Africa*) FINANCE, BANKING, AND ACCOUNTING a registered mutual fund that invests in a variety of underlying mutual funds; subscribers own units in the fund of funds, not in the underlying mutual funds

fungible FINANCE, BANKING, AND ACCOUNTING interchangeable and indistinguishable for business purposes from other items of the same type

funny money FINANCE, BANKING, AND ACCOUNTING
1 counterfeit or forged currency
2 money obtained from a legally or morally suspect source

future FINANCE, BANKING, AND ACCOUNTING a contract to deliver a commodity at a future date. Also known as *futures contract*

future option FINANCE, BANKING, AND ACCOUNTING a contract in which somebody agrees to buy or sell a commodity, currency, or security at an agreed price for delivery in the future. Also known as *futures option*

futures commission merchant FINANCE, BANKING, AND ACCOUNTING somebody who acts as a broker for futures contracts. Abbr. *FCM*

futures contract FINANCE, BANKING, AND ACCOUNTING see *future*

futures exchange FINANCE, BANKING, AND ACCOUNTING an exchange on which futures contracts are traded

futures market FINANCE, BANKING, AND ACCOUNTING a market for buying and selling securities, commodities, or currencies that tend to fluctuate in price over a period of time. The market's goal is to reduce the risk of uncertainty about future prices.

futures option FINANCE, BANKING, AND ACCOUNTING see *future option*

futures research GENERAL MANAGEMENT the identification of possible future *scenarios* with the goal of anticipating and perhaps influencing what the future holds. Futures research is important to the process of *issues management*. It normally identifies several possible

scenarios for any particular set of circumstances, and enables an informed decision to be made.

future value FINANCE, BANKING, AND ACCOUNTING the value that a sum of money will have in the future, taking into account the effects of inflation, interest rates, or currency values.

Future value calculations require three figures: the sum in question, the percentage by which it will increase or decrease, and the period of time. In this example, these figures are $1,000, 11%, and two years.

At an interest rate of 11%, the sum of $1,000 will grow to $1,232 in two years:

$1,000 × 1.11 = $1,110 (first year) × 1.11 = $1,232 (second year, rounded to whole dollars)

Note that the interest earned in the first year generates additional interest in the second year, a practice known as compounding. When large sums are in question, the effect of compounding can be significant.

At an inflation rate of 11%, by comparison, the sum of $1,000 will shrink to $812 in two years:

$$\frac{\dfrac{\$1,000}{1.11} = \$901 \text{ (first year)}}{1.11} = \$812 \text{ (second year)}$$

(rounded to whole dollars)

In order to avoid errors, it is important to express the percentage as 1.11 and multiply and divide by that figure, instead of using 11%; and to calculate each year, quarter, or month separately. See also *present value*

futuristic planning FINANCE, BANKING, AND ACCOUNTING planning for that period which extends beyond the planning horizon in the form of future expected conditions which may exist in respect of the entity, products/services, and environment, but which cannot usefully be expressed in quantified terms. An example would be working out the actions needed in a future with no automobiles.

futurize GENERAL MANAGEMENT to ensure that an organization is taking full advantage of the latest technologies

fuzzword GENERAL MANAGEMENT a piece of jargon that is obscure or difficult to understand (*slang*)

fuzzy search E-COMMERCE a computer search that returns not only exact matches to the search request, but also close matches that include possibilities and allow for such things as spelling errors

FWIW *abbr* GENERAL MANAGEMENT for what it's worth (*slang*)

FY *abbr* FINANCE, BANKING, AND ACCOUNTING fiscal year

FYI *abbr* GENERAL MANAGEMENT for your information (*slang*)

G

G7 FINANCE, BANKING, AND ACCOUNTING the group of seven major industrial nations established in 1985 to discuss the world economy, consisting of Canada, France, Germany, Italy, Japan, the United Kingdom, and the United States

G8 FINANCE, BANKING, AND ACCOUNTING the group of eight major industrial nations consisting of the *G7* plus Russia

G10 *abbr* FINANCE, BANKING, AND ACCOUNTING Group of Ten

GAB *abbr* FINANCE, BANKING, AND ACCOUNTING General Arrangements to Borrow: a fund financed by the *Group of Ten* that is used when the IMF's own resources are insufficient, for example, when there is a need for large loans to one or more industrialized countries

gain sharing HR & PERSONNEL a group-based *bonus plan* to share profits from improvements in production efficiency between employees and the company. There are many variants of gain sharing, the *Rucker* and *Scanlon plans* being the best known.

game plan GENERAL MANAGEMENT a strategy worked out in advance. The term game plan derives from sports terminology.

game theory GENERAL MANAGEMENT a mathematical technique used in *operational research* to analyze and predict the outcomes of games of strategy and conflicts of interest. Game theory is used to represent conflicts and problems involved in formulating marketing and organizational strategy, with the goal of identifying and implementing optimal strategies. It involves assessing likely strategies to be adopted by players in a given situation under a particular set of rules. It was initially developed by John Von Neumann, who later developed the theory further with Oskar Morgenstern to apply it to economics.

Gantt, Henry Laurence (1861–1919) GENERAL MANAGEMENT U.S. mechanical engineer and consultant. Originated the *Gantt chart*, which was popularized by Wallace Clark in *The Gantt Chart: a Working Tool of Management* (1952). See thinker *Henry Laurence Gantt*. See checklist *Managing Projects*

Gantt chart GENERAL MANAGEMENT a graphic tool widely used in **project management** for planning and scheduling work, setting out tasks and the time periods within which they should be completed. The Gantt chart looks like a lateral bar chart and was initially developed by **Henry Gantt** during the 1900s. It is still used both in its traditional form and in the evolved form of program evaluation and review technique.

gap analysis
1 MARKETING a marketing technique used to identify gaps in market or product coverage. In gap analysis, consumer information or requirements are tabulated and matched to product categories in order to identify product or service opportunities or gaps in product planning.
2 FINANCE, BANKING, AND ACCOUNTING a method of improving a company's financial performance by reducing the gap between current results and long-term objectives

garage FINANCE, BANKING, AND ACCOUNTING
1 a U.K. term meaning to transfer assets or liabilities from one financial center to another to take advantage of a tax benefit
2 the annex to the main floor of the New York Stock Exchange

garbatrage FINANCE, BANKING, AND ACCOUNTING stocks that rise because of a takeover but are not connected to the target company (*slang*)

GAS *abbr* FINANCE, BANKING, AND ACCOUNTING Government Accountancy Service

gatekeeper GENERAL MANAGEMENT somebody within an organization who controls the flow of information and therefore influences policy

Gates, **Bill** (*b.* 1955) GENERAL MANAGEMENT U.S. entrepreneur. Founder of the Microsoft™ Corporation, which led the information technology revolution and still dominates the world software market through the Windows™ operating system and the Web browser Internet Explorer. Microsoft has made Gates one of the richest men in the world, although antitrust proceedings have forced him to step down as C.E.O. His book *Business@the Speed of Thought* (1999) focuses on the impact of technology on business.

gateway E-COMMERCE a point where two or more computer networks meet and can exchange data

gateway page E-COMMERCE a Web page customized to each search engine with specific meta-tags and keywords. These pages are intended to appeal to search engine robots and are not always visible to customers who visit the Web site.

GATT *abbr* FINANCE, BANKING, AND ACCOUNTING General Agreement on Tariffs and Trade: a treaty signed in Geneva in 1947 that aimed to foster multilateral trade and settle trading disputes between adherent countries. Initially signed by 23 nations, it started to reduce trade tariffs and, as it was accepted by more and more countries, tackled other barriers to trade. It was replaced on January 1, 1995 by the World Trade Organization.

gazelle GENERAL MANAGEMENT a fast-growing and volatile new company (*slang*)

gazump (*U.K.*) FINANCE, BANKING, AND ACCOUNTING in the period between agreeing verbally to sell to one buyer but before the agreement becomes legally binding, to accept a higher offer from another buyer. Gazumping is normally associated with the real estate market, although it can occur in any market where the prices are rising rapidly.

gazunder (*U.K.*) FINANCE, BANKING, AND ACCOUNTING in the period between agreeing verbally to buy at one price but before the agreement is legally binding, to offer a lower price. Gazundering is normally associated with the real estate market, although it can occur in any market where the prices are falling rapidly.

GBE *abbr* (*ANZ*) GENERAL MANAGEMENT Government Business Enterprise

GDP *abbr* ECONOMICS gross domestic product: the total flow of services and goods produced by an economy over a quarter or a year, measured by the aggregate value of services and goods at market prices

GDP per capita ECONOMICS *GDP* divided by the country's population so as to achieve a figure per head of population

GEAR *abbr* (*S Africa*) FINANCE, BANKING, AND ACCOUNTING Growth, Employment, and Redistribution: the macroeconomic reform program of the South African government, intended to foster economic growth, create employment, and redistribute income and opportunities in favor of the poor

geared investment trust (*U.K.*) FINANCE, BANKING, AND ACCOUNTING an investment trust that borrows money in order to increase its portfolio. When the market is rising, stocks in a geared investment trust rise faster than those in an ungeared trust, but they fall faster when the market is falling.

gearing *or* **leverage** FINANCE, BANKING, AND ACCOUNTING This relates to financial gearing, the relationship between a company's borrowings (which includes both prior charge capital and long-term debt) and its stockholders' funds (common share capital plus reserves). Gearing calculations can be made in a number of ways, and may be based on capital values or on earnings/interest relationships. Overdrafts and interest paid thereon may also be included:

$$\frac{\text{Profit before interest and tax}}{\text{Profit before tax}}$$

shows the effect of interest on the operating profit.

$$\frac{\text{Profit before interest and tax}}{\text{Interest expense}}$$

shows the number of times that profit will cover interest expense.

$$\frac{\text{Total long-term debt}}{\text{Shareholders' funds + long-term debt}}$$

shows the proportion of long-term financing which is being supplied by debt.

$$\frac{\text{Total long-term debt}}{\text{Total assets}}$$

a measure of the capacity to redeem debt obligations by the sale of assets.

$$\frac{\text{Operating cash flows – Taxation paid –}}{\text{returns on investment and servicing of finance}}$$
repayments of debt due within one year

measures ability to redeem debt.

A company with a high proportion of prior charge capital to shareholders' funds is high geared, and is low geared if the reverse situation applies.

geisha bond FINANCE, BANKING, AND ACCOUNTING see **shogun bond**

Geneen, **Harold** (1910–97) GENERAL MANAGEMENT British-born business executive. C.E.O. of International Telephone and Telegraph (ITT) in the 1960s and 1970s, who turned a moderately successful U.S. company into a massive, international conglomerate. Geneen built a business machine that was almost without parallel in terms of its systematic efficiency. He explained his approach in *Managing* (1985). ITT was broken up following antitrust proceedings during the 1980s and **taken over** in 1997.

General Agreement on Tariffs and Trade FINANCE, BANKING, AND ACCOUNTING see **GATT**

General Arrangements to Borrow FINANCE, BANKING, AND ACCOUNTING see *GAB*

general audit FINANCE, BANKING, AND ACCOUNTING an examination of all books and accounts belonging to a company

General Commissioners FINANCE, BANKING, AND ACCOUNTING a body of unpaid individuals appointed by the Lord Chancellor in England, Wales, and Northern Ireland, and the Secretary of State for Scotland in Scotland, to hear appeals on tax matters

general fund FINANCE, BANKING, AND ACCOUNTING a mutual fund with investments in a variety of stocks

general ledger FINANCE, BANKING, AND ACCOUNTING a book that lists all of the financial transactions of a company

general manager GENERAL MANAGEMENT HR & PERSONNEL a *manager* whose work encompasses all areas of an organization. A general manager is traditionally a nonspecialist, has a working knowledge of all aspects of an organization's activities, and oversees all operating functions. In large companies and the public sector, specialist managers with expert knowledge may control departments, while a general manager provides unifying *leadership* from the top.

general undertaking FINANCE, BANKING, AND ACCOUNTING an agreement signed by all the directors of a company applying for Stock Exchange listing, which promises that they will work within the regulations of the Stock Exchange

Generation X GENERAL MANAGEMENT HR & PERSONNEL the generation of people born between 1963 and 1981 who entered the workplace from the 1980s onward, bringing new attitudes to working life that run contrary to traditional corporate expectations. The term was popularized by the writing of Douglas Coupland and also by *Bruce Tulgan* in *Managing Generation X* (1995). Those who belong to Generation X are said to be not solely motivated by money, but they look for a *work-life balance*, favor *flexible working*, embrace the concept of *employability*, and value opportunities for learning, self-advancement, and new challenges. Human resource management practices are increasingly being adapted to accommodate new ways of working.

generative learning GENERAL MANAGEMENT a style of *organizational learning* that encourages experimentation, risk-taking, openness, and system-wide thinking. Organizations have

successfully used this style of learning to transform themselves in the face of technological, social, and market change. *Adaptive learning* is a contrasting approach to organizational learning.

generic strategy GENERAL MANAGEMENT a strategy for marketing products or services. Generic strategy is a term introduced by *Michael Porter*. He suggested there are three generic strategies for marketing products or services: cost leadership, differentiation, and focus. The first implies supplying products in a more cost-effective way than competitors; the second refers to adding value to products or services; and the third focuses on a specific product market segment with the goal of establishing a *monopoly*. See thinker *Michael Porter*

gensaki FINANCE, BANKING, AND ACCOUNTING the Japanese term for a bond sale incorporating a repurchase agreement at a later date

gentleman's agreement GENERAL MANAGEMENT a verbal agreement between two parties who trust each other

geographical information systems MARKETING technology used to integrate maps and data to provide multidimensional marketing information. Abbr. *GIS*

Ghoshal, Sumantra (1946–2004) GENERAL MANAGEMENT Indian-born academic. Author of work that has shifted its focus from international *strategy* to the importance of people and *creativity*. Ghoshal put forward a new model of transnational enterprise to cope with the complexities of *competition* and the growing global marketplace. He also suggested the *three Ps* of Purpose, Process, and People to replace the old model of Strategy, Structure, and Systems and proposed a new moral contract. He first came to prominence with *Managing Across Borders* (1989), co-authored with *Christopher Bartlett*.

ghost rider GENERAL MANAGEMENT somebody who claims to have been in a vehicle that was involved in an accident in order to claim compensation (*slang*)

giant-killer GENERAL MANAGEMENT somebody or something that defeats a superior or better-known opponent, especially in sports, business, or politics

GIF *abbr* E-COMMERCE Graphics Interchange Format: a type of file used to compress and store images for transfer via the Internet. The major advantage of GIF files is that you do not need a *plug-in* to view them, so almost any

browser can display them. GIF is ideal for small, simple icons and basic images. More complex images, including photographs, can be compressed using *JPEG* files.

gift-leaseback FINANCE, BANKING, AND ACCOUNTING the practice of giving somebody a property and then leasing it back, usually for tax advantage or charitable purposes

gift with reservation (*U.K.*) FINANCE, BANKING, AND ACCOUNTING a gift with some benefit retained for the donor, for example, the legal transfer of a dwelling when the donor continues in residence

gig GENERAL MANAGEMENT an individual project or assignment, typical of a working pattern made up of a series of one-time projects rather than a career with a single employer

gigabyte GENERAL MANAGEMENT a measure of the memory capacity of a computer. One gigabyte equals 1024 megabytes.

Gilbreth, Frank (1868–1924) GENERAL MANAGEMENT U.S. consulting engineer. Formed a husband-and-wife team with *Lillian Gilbreth* and pioneered the principles of *motion study*, which embraced *work simplification*, and took a strong interest in *occupational psychology*. Their work, which straddled the *scientific management* and *human relations* schools of management, is recorded in *Writings of the Gilbreths* (1953), edited by William R. Spriegel and Clark E. Myers.

Gilbreth, Lillian (1878–1972) GENERAL MANAGEMENT U.S. consulting engineer

gilt FINANCE, BANKING, AND ACCOUNTING see *gilt-edged security*

gilt-edged security FINANCE, BANKING, AND ACCOUNTING
1 a security issued by the U.K. government that pays a fixed rate of interest on a regular basis for a specific period of time until the redemption date, when the principal is returned. Their names, for example, Exchequer 10½% 2005 (abbreviated to Ex 10½% '05) or Treasury 11¾% 2003–07 (abbreviated to Tr 11¾% '03–'07) indicate the rate and redemption date. Thought to have originated in the 17th century to help fund the war with France, today they form a large part of the National Debt. Also known as *gilt*. See also *index-linked gilt*
2 a U.S. term used to describe a security issued by a blue-chip company, which is therefore considered very secure

gilt repos (*U.K.*) FINANCE, BANKING, AND ACCOUNTING the market in agreed sales and

repurchase of gilt-edged securities, launched in 1996 by the Bank of England to make gilts more attractive to overseas investors

gilt strip (*U.K.*) FINANCE, BANKING, AND ACCOUNTING a zero-coupon bond created by unbundling the interest payments from a gilt-edged security so that it produces a single cash payment at maturity

gilt unit trust FINANCE, BANKING, AND ACCOUNTING in the United Kingdom, a mutual fund where the underlying investments are gilt-edged securities

Ginnie Mae FINANCE, BANKING, AND ACCOUNTING see *GNMA*

giro FINANCE, BANKING, AND ACCOUNTING
1 a European term for the transfer of money from one bank account to another. Also known as *bank giro*
2 (*U.K.*) a benefit paid by the state (*slang*)

GIS *abbr* MARKETING geographical information systems

Glacier studies GENERAL MANAGEMENT research experiments conducted at the Glacier Metal Company in London from 1948 to 1965 to investigate the development of group relations, the effects of *change*, and employee roles and responsibilities. The Glacier studies were conducted by the Tavistock Institute of Human Relations, with the research being headed by *Elliot Jaques* and *Frederick Emery*. Findings from the initial study came from a methodology called "working-through," which examined possible social and personal factors at play in any potential dispute. From this arose an early form of works council, where employees could participate in setting policy for their department. It was also discovered that employees felt the need to have their role and status defined in a way acceptable to both themselves and their colleagues. This research into job roles led Jaques to come up with the notion of the *time span of discretion*, according to which all jobs, no matter how strictly defined, have some level of content that requires judgment and therefore discretion by the jobholder. Jaques then examined this phenomenon in bureaucratic organizations. In defining a *bureaucracy* as a hierarchical system in which employees are accountable to their bosses for the work they do, he took a different stance from *Max Weber*. Much like the *Hawthorne experiments*, the Glacier studies had far-reaching implications for the way organizations were managed. The initial findings were written up by Jaques in *The Changing Culture of a Factory* (1951). In 1965, Jaques

published the *Glacier Project Papers* with *Wilfred Brown*, the managing director of Glacier. See thinker *Max Weber*

glad-hand GENERAL MANAGEMENT to shake hands with and greet people at a business party or meeting (*slang*)

glamour stock FINANCE, BANKING, AND ACCOUNTING a fashionable security with an investment following

glass ceiling (*U.K.*) GENERAL MANAGEMENT = *lead ceiling*

Glass-Steagall Act FINANCE, BANKING, AND ACCOUNTING a law (enacted in 1933) that enforces the separation of the banking and brokerage industries

glaze GENERAL MANAGEMENT to doze or sleep with your eyes open during a business meeting (*slang*)

global bank FINANCE, BANKING, AND ACCOUNTING a bank that is active in the international markets and that has a presence in several continents

global bond FINANCE, BANKING, AND ACCOUNTING see *Eurobond*

global bond issue FINANCE, BANKING, AND ACCOUNTING an issue of bonds that incorporates a settlement mechanism allowing for the transfer of titles between markets

global brand MARKETING the brand name of a product that has worldwide recognition. A global brand has the advantage of economies of scale in terms of production, recognition, and packaging. While the product or brand itself remains the same, the marketing must take into account the local market conditions and the resulting marketing campaign must be tailored accordingly. Care must also be taken to ensure that there is nothing offensive in terms of the name or packaging in the various cultures and languages. A problem with global branding is that, if problems are experienced in one country, there could be worldwide repercussions for the brand. Also known as *global product*

global coordinator FINANCE, BANKING, AND ACCOUNTING the lead manager of a global offering who is responsible for overseeing the entire issue and is usually supported by regional and national coordinators

global custody FINANCE, BANKING, AND ACCOUNTING a financial service, usually available to institutional investors only, that includes

the safekeeping of securities certificates issued in markets across the world, the collection of dividends, dealing with tax, valuation of investments, foreign exchange, and the settlement of transactions

global hedge FINANCE, BANKING, AND ACCOUNTING see *macrohedge*

globalization GENERAL MANAGEMENT the creation of international strategies by organizations for overseas expansion and operation on a worldwide level. The process of globalization has been precipitated by a number of factors, including rapid technology developments that make global communications possible, political developments such as the fall of communism, and transportation developments that make traveling faster and more frequent. These produce greater development opportunities for companies with the opening up of additional markets, allow greater customer harmonization as a result of the increase in shared cultural values, and provide a superior competitive position with lower operating costs in other countries and access to new raw materials, resources, and investment opportunities.

global marketing MARKETING a marketing strategy used mainly by multinational companies to sell goods or services internationally. Global marketing requires that there be harmonization between the marketing policies for different countries and that the *marketing mix* for the different countries can be adapted to the local market conditions. Global marketing is sometimes used to refer to overseas expansion efforts through *licensing*, *franchises*, and *joint ventures*.

global offering FINANCE, BANKING, AND ACCOUNTING the offering of securities in several markets simultaneously, for example, in Europe, the Far East, and North America

global pricing contract OPERATIONS & PRODUCTION a contract between a customer and a supplier whereby the supplier agrees to charge the customer the same price for the delivery of parts or services anywhere in the world. As *globalization* increases, more customers are likely to press their suppliers for global pricing contracts. Through such contracts suppliers can benefit by gaining access to new markets and growing their business, achieving economies of scale, developing strong relationships with customers, and thereby gaining a *competitive advantage* that is difficult for competitors to break. There are risks involved, too, for example, being in the middle of a conflict between a customer's head office and its local business units, or being tied to one customer

when there are more attractive customers to serve.

global product MARKETING see *global brand*

glocalization GENERAL MANAGEMENT the process of tailoring products or services to different local markets around the world. Glocalization is a combination of globalization and localization. Improved communication and advancements in technology have made worldwide markets accessible to even small companies but, rather than being homogenous, the global market is in fact made up of many different localities. Success in a globalized environment is more likely if products are not globalized or *mass marketed*, but glocalized and customized for individual local communities that have different needs and different cultural approaches.

glue GENERAL MANAGEMENT something such as information that unifies organizations, supply chains, and other commercial groups

GM *abbr* FINANCE, BANKING, AND ACCOUNTING gross margin

GmbH *abbr* GENERAL MANAGEMENT Gesellschaft mit beschränkter Haftung: the German term for a corporation

GNMA *abbr* FINANCE, BANKING, AND ACCOUNTING Government National Mortgage Association: a U.S.-owned corporation that issues mortgage-backed bonds. Also known as *Ginnie Mae*

gnomes of Zurich FINANCE, BANKING, AND ACCOUNTING a derogatory term for Swiss bankers and currency dealers (who have a reputation for secrecy), often used when unknown currency speculators cause havoc in the currency markets (*slang*)

GNP *abbr* ECONOMICS gross national product: GDP plus domestic residents' income from investment abroad less income earned in the domestic market accruing to noncitizens abroad

GNP per capita ECONOMICS *GNP* divided by the country's population so as to achieve a figure per head of population

goal GENERAL MANAGEMENT see *objective*

gofer GENERAL MANAGEMENT an employee who carries out menial duties for a manager or another employee (*slang*)

go-go fund FINANCE, BANKING, AND ACCOUNTING a mutual fund that trades heavily and predominantly in high-return, high-risk investments

going concern FINANCE, BANKING, AND ACCOUNTING an actively trading company

going plural HR & PERSONNEL giving up a full time position in order to take on a variety of part-time roles. The term was coined by Allan Leighton, former chief executive of Asda, a leading chain of U.K. supermarkets, in September 2000 when he resigned from a full-time position at Wal-Mart to take over a number of boardroom roles. Going plural has similarities with *portfolio working*.

going short FINANCE, BANKING, AND ACCOUNTING selling an asset one does not own with the intention of acquiring it at a later date at a lower price for delivery to the purchaser. See also *bear*

gold bond FINANCE, BANKING, AND ACCOUNTING a bond for which gold is collateral, often issued by mining companies

goldbricker or **gold brick** HR & PERSONNEL a lazy employee who attempts to get away with doing the least possible amount of work (*slang*)

gold card FINANCE, BANKING, AND ACCOUNTING a gold-colored credit card, generally issued to customers with above average incomes, that may include additional benefits, for example, an overdraft at an advantageous interest rate, and may have an annual fee

gold certificate FINANCE, BANKING, AND ACCOUNTING a document that shows ownership of gold

golden handcuffs FINANCE, BANKING, AND ACCOUNTING a financial incentive paid to encourage employees to remain in an organization and dissuade them from leaving for a rival business or to start their own company (*slang*)

golden handshake or **golden goodbye** FINANCE, BANKING, AND ACCOUNTING HR & PERSONNEL a sum of money given to a senior executive on his or her involuntary departure from an employing organization as a form of severance pay. A golden handshake can be offered when an executive is required to leave before the expiration of his or her contract, for example, because of a *merger* or corporate restructuring. It is intended as compensation for loss of office. It can be a very large sum of money, but often it is not related to the perceived performance of the executive concerned. (*slang*)

golden hello FINANCE, BANKING, AND ACCOUNTING HR & PERSONNEL a welcome package for a new employee that may include a *bonus* and stock options. A golden hello is designed as an incen-

tive to attract employees. Some of the contents of the welcome package may be contingent on the performance of the employee.

golden parachute FINANCE, BANKING, AND ACCOUNTING HR & PERSONNEL a clause inserted in the contract of employment of a senior employee that details a financial package payable if the employee is dismissed. A golden parachute provides an executive with a measure of financial security and may be payable if the employee leaves the organization following a *takeover* or *merger*, or is dismissed as a result of poor performance. Also known as *golden umbrella*

golden rolodex GENERAL MANAGEMENT the small group of experts who are most frequently quoted in news stories or asked to appear on television to give an opinion. "Rolodex" is a trademark for a desktop card index. (*slang*)

golden share FINANCE, BANKING, AND ACCOUNTING a controlling interest retained by a government in a company that has been privatized after having been in public ownership

golden umbrella HR & PERSONNEL FINANCE, BANKING, AND ACCOUNTING see *golden parachute*

gold fix or **gold fixing** FINANCE, BANKING, AND ACCOUNTING the twice-daily setting of the gold price in London, Paris, and Zurich

Goldratt, Eliyahu M. (*b.* 1948) GENERAL MANAGEMENT Israeli author and educator. Disseminator of theories, through the medium of novels, on optimizing *production* methods and *project management*. Goldratt explained the technique of *optimized production technology* in *The Goal* (1993, coauthored), and his theory later broadened into the *Theory of Constraints* (see *optimized production technology*). His third book applies the concept of the theory of constraints to *project management*.

gold reserve FINANCE, BANKING, AND ACCOUNTING gold coins or bullion held by a central bank to support a paper currency and provide security for borrowing

gold standard FINANCE, BANKING, AND ACCOUNTING a system in which a currency unit is defined in terms of its value in gold

Goleman, Daniel (*b.* 1946) GENERAL MANAGEMENT U.S. psychologist and journalist. Popularized the concept of *emotional intelligence*, and credited with making it generally accessible, initially through the book of the same

name (1995). He was influenced by **Richard E. Boyatzis**. See thinker **Daniel Goleman**. See best practice **Emotional Intelligence**

good for the day FINANCE, BANKING, AND ACCOUNTING used to describe instructions to a broker that are valid only for the day given

Goods and Services Tax FINANCE, BANKING, AND ACCOUNTING
1 a government-imposed consumption tax, currently of 10%, added to the retail cost of goods and services in Australia
2 a former Canadian tax on goods and services. It was a value-added tax and was replaced by the **harmonized sales tax**. Abbr. **GST**

goods received note FINANCE, BANKING, AND ACCOUNTING a record of goods at the point of receipt

good this week/month FINANCE, BANKING, AND ACCOUNTING used to describe instructions to a broker that are valid only for the duration of the week/month given. Abbr. **GTW/GTM**

good 'til cancel FINANCE, BANKING, AND ACCOUNTING relating to an order to buy or sell a security that is effective until an investor cancels it, up to a maximum of 60 days. Abbr. **GTC**

good title FINANCE, BANKING, AND ACCOUNTING the legally unquestionable title to property. Also known as **clear title**

goodwill FINANCE, BANKING, AND ACCOUNTING an intangible asset of a company that includes factors such as reputation, contacts, and expertise, for which a buyer of the company may have to pay a premium.
Goodwill becomes an intangible asset when a company has been acquired by another. It then appears on a balance sheet in the amount by which the price paid by the acquiring company exceeds the net tangible assets of the acquired company. In other words
   Purchase price – Net assets = Goodwill
If an airline is bought for $12 billion and its net assets are valued at $9 billion, $3 billion of the purchase would be allocated to goodwill on the balance sheet.

gopher an employee who carries out menial duties for a manager or another employee. (*slang*) Also known as **gofer**

go plural GENERAL MANAGEMENT see **going plural** (*slang*)

go private FINANCE, BANKING, AND ACCOUNTING to revert from being a public limited company

quoted on a stock exchange to a private company without a stock market listing

go public FINANCE, BANKING, AND ACCOUNTING to offer the stock in a privately held company for sale to the public for the first time either as a means of raising funds or in order to become a publicly traded company. See also **initial public offering**

go-slow HR & PERSONNEL a protest in which employees demonstrate their dissatisfaction by carrying out their work slowly. A go-slow is a form of **industrial action** designed to inconvenience an employer without the more serious effects of an all-out **strike**.

Government Accountancy Service (*U.K.*) FINANCE, BANKING, AND ACCOUNTING part of **HM Treasury**, a service whose duty is to ensure that best accounting practice is observed and conducted across the whole of the Civil Service. Abbr. **GAS**

Government Business Enterprise (*ANZ*) GENERAL MANAGEMENT an Australian business that is fully or partly owned by the state. Abbr. **GBE**

government gazette (*ANZ*) GENERAL MANAGEMENT a journal published by the Australian federal government or a state or territory government that reports all actions and decisions made by that body

Government National Mortgage Association FINANCE, BANKING, AND ACCOUNTING see **GNMA**

government securities/stock FINANCE, BANKING, AND ACCOUNTING securities or stock issued by a government, for example, U.S. Treasury bonds or U.K. gilt-edged securities

gradual retirement HR & PERSONNEL see **phased retirement**

graduated payments mortgage FINANCE, BANKING, AND ACCOUNTING a mortgage with a fixed interest rate but with low payments that gradually increase over the first few years. Abbr. **GPM**

graduated tax FINANCE, BANKING, AND ACCOUNTING a tax that increases in line with an individual's income

granny bond FINANCE, BANKING, AND ACCOUNTING see **index-linked savings certificate**

grant of probate FINANCE, BANKING, AND ACCOUNTING in the United Kingdom, a document issued by a probate office that pronounces the

validity of a will and upholds the appointment of the executor(s)

grantor FINANCE, BANKING, AND ACCOUNTING a person who sells an option

grapevine GENERAL MANAGEMENT an informal communication network within an organization that conveys information through unofficial channels independent of management control. Information travels much more quickly through the grapevine than through formal channels and may become distorted. A grapevine may reinterpret official corporate messages or spread gossip and rumor in the absence of effective organization channels. It can, however, also complement official communication, provide feedback, and strengthen social relationships within the organization.

graph GENERAL MANAGEMENT a diagram depicting the relationship between dependent and independent variables through the use of lines, curves, or figures on horizontal and vertical axes. Time is the most common independent variable, showing how the dependent variable has altered over a defined period.

graphical user interface E-COMMERCE an easy-to-use interface or operating system that allows a user to give a computer instructions by using icons, menus, and windows. Abbr. **GUI**

Graphics Interchange Format E-COMMERCE see **GIF**

graphology HR & PERSONNEL the study of handwriting styles in an attempt to identify personality traits and to predict how somebody may react in particular situations. Graphology is sometimes used as part of the **recruitment** process. Because it cannot be substantiated, it is not recommended as a formal test and tends to be used informally.

grass ceiling GENERAL MANAGEMENT the set of social and cultural factors that discourage or prevent women from using golf to conduct business (*slang*)

graveyard market FINANCE, BANKING, AND ACCOUNTING
1 a U.K. term for a market for stocks that are infrequently traded either through lack of interest or because they are of little or no value
2 a bear market where investors who dispose of their holdings are faced with large losses, as potential investors prefer to stay liquid until the market shows signs of improving

gravy train FINANCE, BANKING, AND ACCOUNTING any type of business activity in which an

individual or an organization makes a large *profit* without much effort

graybar-land GENERAL MANAGEMENT a state of vagueness induced by staring at the gray bar that appears on a computer screen when the computer is processing something (*slang*)

gray knight FINANCE, BANKING, AND ACCOUNTING GENERAL MANAGEMENT see *knight*

gray market MARKETING
1 a *market* in which goods are sold that have been manufactured abroad and imported. A gray market product is one that has been imported legally, in contrast to one on the *black market*, which is illegal. Such markets arise when there is a supply shortage, usually for exclusive goods, and the goods are offered for sale at lower prices than the equivalent goods manufactured in the home country.
2 the market segment occupied by older members of a population
3 the unofficial trading of securities that have not yet been formally issued

gray marketing MARKETING marketing aimed at older age groups

gray matter GENERAL MANAGEMENT older and more experienced business experts who are hired by young companies to give an impression of seriousness and reliability (*slang*)

gray wave (*U.K.*) FINANCE, BANKING, AND AC-COUNTING used to describe a company that is thought likely to have good prospects in the distant future. It gets its name from the fact that investors are likely to have gray hair before they see their expectations fulfilled. (*slang*)

greater fool theory FINANCE, BANKING, AND AC-COUNTING the investing strategy that assumes it is wise to buy a stock that is not worth its current price. The assumption is that somebody will buy it from you later for an even greater price.

great man theory GENERAL MANAGEMENT the idea that *leaders* possess innately superior qualities that distinguish them from other people, including the ability to capture the imagination and loyalty of the masses

green ban (*ANZ*) GENERAL MANAGEMENT a ban imposed by unions on work that is perceived to pose a threat to the natural environment or an area of historical significance

green chips FINANCE, BANKING, AND ACCOUNTING small companies with potential for growth

green issues GENERAL MANAGEMENT see *environmental management*

greenmail FINANCE, BANKING, AND ACCOUNTING GENERAL MANAGEMENT the purchase of enough of a company's stock to threaten it with take-over, so that the company is forced to buy back the stock at a higher price to avoid the takeover (*slang*)

green marketing MARKETING marketing that highlights an organization's environmentally friendly policies or achievements

green pound ECONOMICS the fixed European currency unit (ECU) in which prices of agricultural goods in the European Union are set

green shoe *or* **greenshoe option** FINANCE, BANKING, AND ACCOUNTING an option offered by a company raising the capital for the issue of further shares of stock to cover a shortfall in the event of overallocation. It gets its name from the Green Shoe Manufacturing Company, which was the first to include the feature in a public offering. (*slang*)

green taxes FINANCE, BANKING, AND ACCOUNTING taxes levied to discourage behavior that will be harmful to the environment

greenwash GENERAL MANAGEMENT information produced by an organization to present an environmentally responsible public image (*slang*)

grievance procedure HR & PERSONNEL a process for settling or redressing employee complaints. A grievance procedure is part of an organization's *personnel policy* and sets out how an employee with a work-related griev-ance can bring up the issue and how it may be addressed and resolved. Such a procedure should focus on settling the matter as soon as possible, so as to promote employee satisfac-tion and prevent the issue escalating into a *dispute*. See checklist *Setting Up a Grievance Procedure*

gross FINANCE, BANKING, AND ACCOUNTING total, before consideration of taxes

gross borrowings FINANCE, BANKING, AND AC-COUNTING the total of all monies borrowed by a company, such as overdrafts and long-term loans, but without deducting cash in bank ac-counts and on deposit

gross domestic product ECONOMICS see *GDP*

gross earnings FINANCE, BANKING, AND AC-COUNTING total earnings before tax and other deductions

gross income yield FINANCE, BANKING, AND AC-COUNTING the yield of an investment before tax is deducted

gross interest FINANCE, BANKING, AND ACCOUNT-ING the interest earned on a deposit or security before the deduction of tax. See also *net interest*

gross lease FINANCE, BANKING, AND ACCOUNTING a lease that does not require the lessee to pay for things the owner usually pays for. See also *net lease*

gross margin FINANCE, BANKING, AND AC-COUNTING
1 the differential between the interest rate paid by a borrower and the cost of the funds to the lender. Abbr. *GM*
2 the differential between the manufacturing cost of a unit of output and the price at which it is sold

gross misconduct HR & PERSONNEL behavior in the workplace that may lead to a warning or to dismissal in extreme cases. Most contracts of employment provide guidelines on the type of behavior that constitutes gross misconduct.

gross national product ECONOMICS see *GNP*

gross negligence GENERAL MANAGEMENT see *negligence*

gross profit FINANCE, BANKING, AND ACCOUNTING the difference between an organization's sales revenue and the cost of goods sold. Unlike *net profit*, gross profit does not include distribu-tion, administration, or financing costs. Also known as *trading profit*

gross profit margin FINANCE, BANKING, AND ACCOUNTING GENERAL MANAGEMENT see *profit margin*

gross receipts FINANCE, BANKING, AND ACCOUNT-ING the total revenue received by a business

gross sales FINANCE, BANKING, AND ACCOUNTING the total of all sales before discounts

gross turnover FINANCE, BANKING, AND AC-COUNTING total *turnover* including discounts, such as VAT

gross yield FINANCE, BANKING, AND ACCOUNTING the share of income return derived from securities before the deduction of tax

gross yield to redemption (*U.K.*) FINANCE, BANKING, AND ACCOUNTING also known as *gross redemption yield*. See *yield to maturity*

group FINANCE, BANKING, AND ACCOUNTING a parent company and all its subsidiaries

group capacity assessment GENERAL MANAGEMENT the application of *work measurement* techniques such as *activity sampling* and *standard time* data to clerical, administrative, and indirect staff to measure group effort and establish optimum performance levels. Group capacity assessment is used to plan and control payroll costs for groups of clerical and administrative workers.

group certificate (*ANZ*) HR & PERSONNEL a document provided by an employer that records an employee's income, income tax payments, and superannuation contributions during the previous fiscal year

group discussion MARKETING a research technique in which groups of people discuss attitudes to a product or organization

group dynamics HR & PERSONNEL the interaction and interpersonal relationships between members of a group and the ways in which groups form, function, and dissolve. Group dynamics is an important aspect of successful *teamwork* and is a factor influencing the outcome of any form of group activity, including *training* courses. Issues of power, influence, and interpersonal conflict all affect dynamics and group performance. One means of helping people to create positive group dynamics is *sensitivity training* .

group incentive plan HR & PERSONNEL a reward system giving *bonuses* to workers in a team. A group incentive scheme is designed to promote effective *teamwork*, as the bonus is dependent on the performance and output of the team as a whole.

group interview HR & PERSONNEL see *group selection*

group investment FINANCE, BANKING, AND ACCOUNTING an investment made by more than one person

group life insurance FINANCE, BANKING, AND ACCOUNTING a life insurance policy that covers a number of people, for example, members of an association or club, or a group of employees at a company

Group of Seven FINANCE, BANKING, AND ACCOUNTING see *G7*

Group of Ten FINANCE, BANKING, AND ACCOUNTING the group of ten countries who contribute to the General Arrangements to Borrow fund: Belgium, Canada, France, Germany, Italy,

Japan, the Netherlands, Sweden, the United States, and the United Kingdom. Switzerland joined in 1984. Also known as *Paris Club*. See also *GAB*. Abbr. *G10*

group selection HR & PERSONNEL a method of *recruitment* in which candidates are assessed in groups rather than individually. Group selection can take place in an *assessment center*. It should not be confused with a *panel interview*, which involves one candidate but several interviewers. Also known as *group interview*

group technology OPERATIONS & PRODUCTION the practice of gathering operations and resources for the manufacture of specific components or products into groups or cells with the goal of simplifying manufacturing operations. Group technology is an attempt to take advantage of the benefits of both *batch production* and *flow production*. Similar tasks or products are identified and are grouped into families. This requires a robust coding or classification system. The manufacturing resources, including workers, for each family are then grouped together into cells. The sense of ownership encouraged by such organization has resulted in benefits including improved quality, *productivity*, and *motivation* of employees, as well as reductions in work in progress, inventory, and materials movement. Also known as *cellular manufacturing cellular production*

groupthink GENERAL MANAGEMENT a phenomenon that occurs during *decision making* or *problem solving* when a team's desire to reach an agreement overrides its ability to appraise the problem properly. It is similar to the *Abilene paradox* in that it is based on people's desire to conform and please others.

group tool GENERAL MANAGEMENT an electronic tool such as videoconferencing, networking, or electronic mail that allows people in different locations to collaborate on a project

groupware GENERAL MANAGEMENT software that enables a group whose members are based in different locations to work together and share information. Groupware enables collective working by providing communal diaries, address books, work planners, bulletin boards, newsletters, and so on, in electronic format on a closed network. This network may take the form of an *intranet*. Groupware can be used to facilitate collaborative *project management* or to coordinate any kind of work involving input from more than one person, and is particularly useful to those working in a *virtual team*.

Grove, **Andrew S.** (*b.* 1936) GENERAL MANAGEMENT U.S. business executive. Former chairman of Intel Corporation, which became the world's largest semiconductor manufacturer. He coined the term *strategic inflection point*, which he discusses in *Only the Paranoid Survive* (1996).

Growth, Employment, and Redistribution FINANCE, BANKING, AND ACCOUNTING see *GEAR*

growth and income fund FINANCE, BANKING, AND ACCOUNTING a mutual fund that tries to maximize growth of capital while paying significant dividends

growth capital FINANCE, BANKING, AND ACCOUNTING funding that allows a company to accelerate its growth. For new startup companies, growth capital is the second stage of funding after *seed money*.

growth company ECONOMICS a company whose contribution to the economy is growing because it is increasing its workforce or earning increased foreign exchange for its exported goods

growth curve STATISTICS a line plotted on a graph that shows statistically an increase over a period of time

growth equity FINANCE, BANKING, AND ACCOUNTING an equity that is thought to have good investment prospects

growth fund FINANCE, BANKING, AND ACCOUNTING a mutual fund that tries to maximize growth of capital without regard to dividends

growth industry FINANCE, BANKING, AND ACCOUNTING an industry that has the potential to expand at a faster rate than other industries

growth rate ECONOMICS the rate of an economy's growth as measured by its technical progress, the growth of its labor force, and the increase in its *capital stock*

growth stock *or* **growth share**
1 FINANCE, BANKING, AND ACCOUNTING a stock or share that offers investors the prospect of longer-term earnings, rather than a quick return
2 GENERAL MANAGEMENT a stock that has been rising greatly in value, relative to its industry or to the market as a whole

grunt work GENERAL MANAGEMENT time and labor intensive work, often carried out by junior members of staff (*slang*)

grupo GENERAL MANAGEMENT a group of companies in Mexico, based on a parent company or central family. Grupos may be involved in a cross-section of industries, much like a **conglomerate company**. Some grupos are integrated financially, legally, and administratively, while others have a looser structure, with stockholding interests and interrelated directorates.

GST *abbr* FINANCE, BANKING, AND ACCOUNTING Goods and Services Tax

GTC *abbr* FINANCE, BANKING, AND ACCOUNTING good 'til cancel

guan xi GENERAL MANAGEMENT a Mandarin term for "connections," used to describe the level of personal trust required between business partners

guarantee FINANCE, BANKING, AND ACCOUNTING a promise made by a third party, or guarantor, that he or she will be liable if one of the parties to a contract fails to fulfill their contractual obligations. A guarantee may be acceptable to a bank as security for borrowing, provided the guarantor has sufficient financial means to cover his or her potential liability.

guaranteed bond FINANCE, BANKING, AND ACCOUNTING in the United States, a bond on which the principal and interest are guaranteed by a company other than the one that issues them, or a stock in which the dividends are similarly guaranteed. See also **guaranteed stocks**

guaranteed fund FINANCE, BANKING, AND ACCOUNTING a fixed term investment where a third party promises to repay the investors' principal in full should the investment fall below the initial sum invested

guaranteed income bond FINANCE, BANKING, AND ACCOUNTING a bond issued by a U.K. life insurance company designed to provide an investor with a fixed rate of income for a specified period of time. Changes to the regulations now permit only those policies with an independent third party guarantee to receive this denomination.

guaranteed investment contract FINANCE, BANKING, AND ACCOUNTING an investment instrument issued by an insurance company that guarantees interest but not principal

guaranteed stocks FINANCE, BANKING, AND ACCOUNTING in the United Kingdom, bonds issued by nationalized industries that incorporate an explicit guarantee from the government. See also **guaranteed bond**

guaranteed wage HR & PERSONNEL see **guaranteed employment**

guaranteed week HR & PERSONNEL see **guaranteed employment**

guarantor FINANCE, BANKING, AND ACCOUNTING a person or organization that guarantees repayment of a loan if the borrower defaults or is unable to pay

guard book MARKETING a book or folder for storing copies of published advertisements

guardian ad litem FINANCE, BANKING, AND ACCOUNTING a person who acts on behalf of a minor who is a defendant in a court case

guerrilla marketing MARKETING a variety of low-cost, high-impact marketing techniques that allow small companies and/or individuals to act like big companies. The concept was popularized by Jay Conrad Levinson.

GUI *abbr* E-COMMERCE graphical user interface

Gulick, Luther (1892–1993) GENERAL MANAGEMENT U.S. academic. Member of President Roosevelt's Committee on Administrative Management (1936–38), who, following the earlier work of **Henri Fayol**, coined the acronym **POSDCORB** to describe the functions of management.

gun jumping FINANCE, BANKING, AND ACCOUNTING an informal alternative name for **insider trading**

GW *abbr* E-COMMERCE payment gateway

gweeping GENERAL MANAGEMENT the activity of spending many hours at a time surfing the Internet (*slang*)

H

hacker E-COMMERCE somebody who gains unauthorized access to computer systems, often to corrupt or steal stored data

hacker ethic E-COMMERCE the belief that all technical information should be freely shared and that gaining unauthorized access to computer systems is acceptable if there is no injury or expense to others

haggle FINANCE, BANKING, AND ACCOUNTING to negotiate a price with a buyer or seller by the gradual raising of offers and lowering of asking prices until a mutually agreeable price is reached

half-normal plot STATISTICS a plot of statistical data used to check for the presence of **outliers** in the data

Hamel, Gary (*b.* 1954) GENERAL MANAGEMENT U.S. academic and consultant. With **C. K. Prahalad**, introduced the concept of **core competences** and argued for an innovative approach to **corporate strategy** creation, based on emotion as well as analysis. They coauthored *Competing for the Future* (1994), which set out their revolutionary but well-respected view of strategy.

Hamel believes that too many managers operate essentially on a hand-to-mouth basis, not devoting sufficient time to thinking about and planning for the future. He argues that developing strategy ('strategizing' in his terminology) should be an ongoing, radical, and inclusive process that habitually challenges existing assumptions, involves as many people as possible, and looks for its inspiration as often outside the organization as within it. See thinker **C. K. Prahalad**

Hammer, Michael (*b.* 1948) GENERAL MANAGEMENT U.S. academic and consultant. Advocate of reengineering, a concept he explained in the book *Reengineering the Corporation* (1993), coauthored with **James Champy**. See checklist *Implementing Business Process Reengineering*

hammering the market FINANCE, BANKING, AND ACCOUNTING used to describe a situation where there is intense selling (*slang*)

Hampel, Sir Ronald Claus (*b.* 1932) GENERAL MANAGEMENT British business executive. Former chairman of ICI and chairman of the Committee on **Corporate Governance** (1995–98).

hand-hold HR & PERSONNEL to reassure a nervous client or colleague (*slang*)

handling charge FINANCE, BANKING, AND ACCOUNTING money to be paid for packing, invoicing, or dealing with goods which are being shipped

hand off GENERAL MANAGEMENT to transfer responsibility for a project

hand signals FINANCE, BANKING, AND ACCOUNTING the signs used by traders on the trading floors at exchanges for futures and options to overcome the problem of noise

hands-off GENERAL MANAGEMENT without continuing management attention

hands-on GENERAL MANAGEMENT favoring firsthand personal involvement in a task

Handy, Charles (*b.* 1932) GENERAL MANAGEMENT Irish-born academic, writer, and social commentator. Known for his work on *organization structures*, the future of work, and the implications of change for people. Since his landmark book *Understanding Organizations* (1976), he has originated concepts such as the *shamrock organization*, the *federal organization*, the *doughnut principle*, and *portfolio working*.

After graduating from Oxford, Handy worked for Shell until 1972, when he left to teach at the London Business School. He also spent time at MIT, where he came into contact with many of the leading lights in the human relations school of thinking, including *Ed Schein*. See thinker *Charles Handy*

hang out loan FINANCE, BANKING, AND ACCOUNTING the amount of a loan that is still outstanding after the termination of the loan

Hang Seng index FINANCE, BANKING, AND ACCOUNTING an index of the prices of selected stocks on the Hong Kong Stock Exchange

happy camper GENERAL MANAGEMENT somebody who has no grievances against his or her employer (*slang*)

hara-kiri swap FINANCE, BANKING, AND ACCOUNTING an interest rate swap made without a profit margin

hard capital rationing FINANCE, BANKING, AND ACCOUNTING see *capital rationing*

hard commodities FINANCE, BANKING, AND ACCOUNTING metals and other solid raw materials. See also *commodity soft commodities*

hard currency ECONOMICS a currency that is traded in a foreign exchange market and for which demand is persistently high relative to its supply. See also *soft currency*

hard disk E-COMMERCE a thin rigid magnetized disk inside a computer, used for storing data and programs

hard landing ECONOMICS the rapid decline of an economy into recession and business stagnation after a sustained period of growth

hard sell MARKETING a heavily persuasive and highly pressured approach used to sell a product or service. In a hard sell situation, salespeople may use incentives such as a limited special offer or a discount to encourage people to buy, or to sign an agreement to buy on the spot.

hard systems GENERAL MANAGEMENT see *systems method*

hardware E-COMMERCE the physical components of a computer system, such as the processor, keyboard, and monitor. "Software" is the name given to operating systems and applications.

harmonization GENERAL MANAGEMENT
1 the resolution of inequalities in the *pay* and *conditions of employment* between different categories of workers
2 the alignment of the systems of pay and benefits of two companies upon *merger*, acquisition, or takeover
3 the removal of discrimination between full- and part-time workers
4 the convergence of social regulation in the European Union

harmonized sales tax FINANCE, BANKING, AND ACCOUNTING a Canadian tax on goods and services. It is a value-added tax that replaced the Goods and Services Tax. Abbr. *HST*

Harrigan, Kathryn Mary Rudie (*b.* 1951) GENERAL MANAGEMENT U.S. academic. Known for her work on mature and declining industries, and on *strategic alliances*.

harvesting strategy FINANCE, BANKING, AND ACCOUNTING a reduction in or cessation of marketing for a product prior to it being withdrawn from sale, resulting in an increase in profits on the back of previous marketing and advertising campaigns

Harvey-Jones, Sir John (*b.* 1924) GENERAL MANAGEMENT British business executive. Chairman of ICI (1982–87), who recorded his reflections on leadership in *Making It Happen* (1987). After his retirement, he advised a number of ailing British companies in a television series, "Troubleshooter."

hate site GENERAL MANAGEMENT see *anti-site*

Hawthorne effect GENERAL MANAGEMENT see *Hawthorne experiments*

Hawthorne experiments GENERAL MANAGEMENT a series of studies undertaken at the Hawthorne plant of Western Electric in the United States from which *Elton Mayo* concluded that an approach emphasizing *employee participation* can improve *productivity*. The Hawthorne experiments began in 1924 as a study conducted by the National Research Council into the relationship between workplace lighting and employee efficiency, and was then extended to include *wage incentives* and *rest periods*. It was found that

whatever variations were applied upward or downward, output rose, and this was termed the *Hawthorne effect*. The increased productivity was attributed to several causes, including small group size, earnings, the novelty of being part of an experiment, and the increased attention given to the employees being studied. The style of the supervisor, which was relaxed and friendly, in contrast to the then standard practice, was found to be particularly important. In a second group of employees, however, it was observed that, as the experiments progressed, output was restricted, and that whatever the incentive the group showed a resistance to it. In 1929 and 1930, Elton Mayo visited Hawthorne. He linked supervisory style and levels of morale with productivity. High productivity resulted from an engaged supervisory style that encouraged participation. Low productivity resulted when a supervisor remained remote and retained a traditional supervisory role. The Hawthorne experiments established the importance of management style and interpersonal skills to organizational success. See thinker *Elton Mayo*

Hayes, Robert H. (*b.* 1936) GENERAL MANAGEMENT U.S. academic. Harvard professor who came to prominence following the publication in 1981 of his coauthored *Harvard Business Review* article, "Managing Our Way to Economic Decline." Hayes argued that U.S. manufacturing companies were at a competitive disadvantage as a result of a too heavy reliance on detached, precisely structured analysis. A more positive future was foreseen by Hayes in the cowritten *Restoring Our Competitive Edge* (1984), which examines the structural changes required of manufacturing in order to succeed and provides some guidance on how management practices need to change.

hazardous substance GENERAL MANAGEMENT a substance that creates a potential danger to people in the workplace. Employers have a duty to assess the risks from hazardous substances to personnel and customers, and to ensure that no one is endangered. Substances classed as hazards could be raw materials used in production, fumes, or other byproducts resulting from workplace activities. They may also be substances linked to seemingly innocuous activities, for example, cleaning fluids and toner for photocopiers. *Health and safety* policies must cover this area, and *risk assessments* must be carried out to ascertain the potential dangers.

head
be in over your head GENERAL MANAGEMENT to be attempting more, or more difficult, work than you can really do (*slang*)

head and shoulders FINANCE, BANKING, AND ACCOUNTING used to describe a graph plotting a company's stock price that resembles the silhouette of a person's head and shoulders. Analysts see this as an early indication of a market fall.

headcount HR & PERSONNEL the total number of *employees* in an organization

headhunting HR & PERSONNEL the practice of approaching people already working for one company with an offer of a job at another. Headhunting is usually carried out by a recruiter—either an employee within a company or an employment agency—who keeps an eye on the performance of targeted personnel. The recruiter then matches high-performing personnel with job vacancies, contacting individuals directly, without the knowledge of the employer, with a job offer. Headhunters most often perform *executive searches*, but they may also work at lower levels with the intention of picking out those with management potential. Headhunting is often seen as poaching, and it can create employee retention problems, since a company's best staff can be tempted to leave by better job offers.

headline rate of inflation ECONOMICS a measure of inflation that takes account of homeowners' mortgage costs

heads of agreement GENERAL MANAGEMENT the most important elements of a commercial agreement

head tax FINANCE, BANKING, AND ACCOUNTING a tax paid by all inhabitants of a country, regardless of their income

health and safety GENERAL MANAGEMENT HR & PERSONNEL the area of policy and legislation covering employee wellbeing. Health and safety within an organization is often coordinated by a particular person, but it is the responsibility of all employees. Maintaining a safe working environment and safe working practices and ensuring that employees' health is not detrimentally affected by their work is a statutory duty of organizations.

health screening HR & PERSONNEL the checking of employees' health to ensure they are fit for work. Health screening can take the form of *pre-employment screening*, which takes place after a new employee has been appointed, but before employment commences. It also is a feature of *occupational health* programs and involves the monitoring of employee health at work. This is particularly important if the work involves hazardous substances or strenuous physical conditions.

Health screening can also be used, for example, to detect substance abuse or to test the eyesight of users of VDUs.

health warning FINANCE, BANKING, AND ACCOUNTING a warning message printed on advertisements for investments, stating that the value of investments can fall as well as rise. This is a legal requirement in the United Kingdom. (*slang*)

heatseeker E-COMMERCE somebody who always buys the latest version of a software product as soon as it comes on the market (*slang*)

heavy hitter GENERAL MANAGEMENT an executive or company that performs extremely well (*slang*)

heavy share price FINANCE, BANKING, AND ACCOUNTING a price on the London Stock Exchange which is over £10.00 per share, and so discourages the small investor from buying. If the company wants to encourage more people to buy its stock, it may take steps to reduce the share price by splitting or issuing bonus shares.

heavy site E-COMMERCE see *sticky site* (*slang*)

hedge fund FINANCE, BANKING, AND ACCOUNTING a mutual fund that takes considerable risks, including heavy investment in unconventional instruments, in the hope of generating great profits

hedging against inflation FINANCE, BANKING, AND ACCOUNTING investing in order to avoid the impact of inflation, thus protecting the purchasing power of capital. Historically, equities have generally outperformed returns from savings accounts in the long term and beaten the Retail Price Index. They are thus considered as one of the best hedges against inflation, although it is important to bear in mind that no stock market investment is without risk.

held order FINANCE, BANKING, AND ACCOUNTING an order that a dealer does not process immediately, often because of its great size

Helgeson, Sally (*b.* 1948) GENERAL MANAGEMENT U.S. consultant and author. Researcher on the effects of changing technology, demographics, and the knowledge economy on organizations and *leadership*. Her book *The Female Advantage* (1990) considers women's *management styles*.

helicopter view GENERAL MANAGEMENT an overview of a problem (*slang*)

helpline MARKETING a telephone service operated by a company that offers customers product information, advice, or technical support

Henderson, Bruce (1915–92) GENERAL MANAGEMENT Australian engineer and consultant. Founder of the Boston Consulting Group (1963), a firm that has specialized in *corporate strategy* and conceived the *experience curve* and the *Boston Box*.

heritage industry GENERAL MANAGEMENT an industry centered on the efficient business management of a country's historical monuments, with the goal of encouraging tourism and boosting the local economy

Her Majesty's Revenue & Customs *or* **HM Revenue & Customs** FINANCE, BANKING, AND ACCOUNTING in the United Kingdom, the government department responsible for the administration and collection of all forms of tax, including VAT, income tax, and excise duties. HMRC combines the duties of two formerly separate departments, the Inland Revenue and HM Customs and Excise. Abbr. *HMRC*

Herzberg, Frederick (*b.* 1923) GENERAL MANAGEMENT U.S. psychologist and academic. Took a particular interest in *motivation* and put forward the "hygiene-motivation theory" of *job satisfaction*. Herzberg was a coauthor of *The Motivation to Work* (1959) and the author of "One More Time: How Do You Motivate Employees?" (1968), one of the most requested reprints of all time from *Harvard Business Review*. Through his work for the U.S. Public Health Service, Herzberg became an influential figure in the human relations school of the 1950s. See thinker *Frederick Herzberg*. See checklist *Motivating Your Staff in a Time of Change*

heuristics GENERAL MANAGEMENT a method for *problem solving* or *decision making* that arrives at solutions through exploratory means such as experimentation, trial and error, or evaluation

HHOK *abbr* GENERAL MANAGEMENT ha ha, only kidding (*slang*)

hidden asset FINANCE, BANKING, AND ACCOUNTING an *asset* which is shown in a company's accounts as being worth much less than its true market value

hidden reserves FINANCE, BANKING, AND ACCOUNTING illegal reserves which are not declared in the company's balance sheet

hidden tax FINANCE, BANKING, AND ACCOUNTING a tax that is not immediately apparent. For

example, while a consumer may be aware of a tax on retail purchases, a tax imposed at the wholesale level, which consequently increases the cost of items to the retailer, will not be apparent.

high concept GENERAL MANAGEMENT a compelling idea expressed clearly and economically

highdome GENERAL MANAGEMENT a scientist. This term stems from the stereotype of scientists, who are often depicted as having high foreheads that are supposed to be a sign of intelligence. (*slang*)

high-end GENERAL MANAGEMENT relating to the most expensive, most advanced, or most powerful in a variety of things, for example, computers

higher-rate tax FINANCE, BANKING, AND ACCOUNTING the highest of three income tax brackets in the United Kingdom. Most countries have income tax brackets with different rates applicable to income within each bracket.

high finance FINANCE, BANKING, AND ACCOUNTING the lending, investing, and borrowing of very large sums of money organized by financiers

high-flier *or* **high-flyer** FINANCE, BANKING, AND ACCOUNTING a heavily traded stock that increases in value quickly over a short period

high gearing FINANCE, BANKING, AND ACCOUNTING a situation in which a company has a high level of borrowing compared to its stock price

high-performance work organization GENERAL MANAGEMENT an organization which has adopted a set of working practices deemed to enhance individual and organizational performance. The concept of the HPWO has evolved from research into the link between *human resource management* and organizational performance. The characteristics commonly associated with HPWOs and identified in the *OECD*'s definition are: moves toward a flatter and less hierarchical organization structure; a willingness to adopt new working practices; an emphasis on *empowerment* and *teamwork*; and high levels of *employee participation* and learning. These characteristics are believed to foster *motivation*, trust, *communication*, knowledge sharing, and *innovation* within the organization. They are also thought to lead to an ability to adapt to the changing business environment and to improvements in performance and quality of working life. Abbr. *HPWO* Also called *high-performance workplace*. See also *high-performance work system*

high-performance workplace GENERAL MANAGEMENT see *high-performance work organization*

high-performance work system GENERAL MANAGEMENT a set of working practices adopted by a *high-performance work organization*

high-powered GENERAL MANAGEMENT having great dynamism and ability

high-premium convertible debenture FINANCE, BANKING, AND ACCOUNTING a convertible bond sold at a high premium that offers a competitive rate of interest and has a long term

high-pressure MARKETING a selling technique in which the sales representative attempts to persuade a buyer forcefully and persistently

high-risk company GENERAL MANAGEMENT a company that is exposed to high levels of business risk

high street (*U.K.*) GENERAL MANAGEMENT a main street considered as an important retail area

high yielder FINANCE, BANKING, AND ACCOUNTING a security that has a higher than average yield and is consequently often a higher risk investment

hip shooter GENERAL MANAGEMENT an executive who follows his or her immediate instinct when responding to a question or problem rather than considering it rationally (*slang*)

hired gun (*slang*)
1 HR & PERSONNEL somebody who works for whoever will contract for his or her services for as long as he or she is needed for a particular project
2 GENERAL MANAGEMENT an adviser, lawyer, or accountant brought into a company during a takeover battle

hire purchase (*U.K.*) FINANCE, BANKING, AND ACCOUNTING = *installment plan*. Abbr. *HP*

historical summary FINANCE, BANKING, AND ACCOUNTING in the United Kingdom, an optional synopsis of a company's results over a period of time, often five or ten years, featured in the annual accounts

historic pricing FINANCE, BANKING, AND ACCOUNTING the establishment of the price of a share in a mutual fund on the basis of the most recent values of its holdings

hit E-COMMERCE a measure of the number of files or images that are sent to a browser from a Web site in response to a single request.

The measure is one of the most abused statistics on the Internet, as hits do not provide an accurate picture of Web site visitor activity. Every Web page is made up of a number of components—graphics, text, programming elements—and many have anything from 10 to 20 components. Each component is counted as a hit. Therefore, the total number of hits is generally very high and bears little or no relation to the number of people visiting.

hit squad GENERAL MANAGEMENT a company's acquisitions team (*slang*)

HMCE *abbr* FINANCE, BANKING, AND ACCOUNTING HM Customs and Excise. See also *Her Majesty's Revenue & Customs*

HM Customs and Excise FINANCE, BANKING, AND ACCOUNTING abbr. *HMCE*

HMRC *abbr* FINANCE, BANKING, AND ACCOUNTING Her Majesty's Revenue & Customs

HMT *abbr* FINANCE, BANKING, AND ACCOUNTING HM Treasury

HM Treasury FINANCE, BANKING, AND ACCOUNTING the U.K. government department responsible for managing the country's public revenues. While the incumbent prime minister holds the title of First Lord of the Treasury, the department is run on a day-to-day basis by the *Chancellor of the Exchequer*.

hockey stick FINANCE, BANKING, AND ACCOUNTING a performance curve typical of businesses in their early stages that descends then rises sharply in a straight line, creating a shape similar to that of a hockey stick (*slang*)

Hofstede, Geert H. (*b.* 1928) GENERAL MANAGEMENT Dutch academic and business executive. Identified four work-related dimensions of national culture, thus providing a framework for understanding cultural differences within business. His work, first published in *Culture's Consequences* (1980), has been extended by *Fons Trompenaars*.

After spending time working in factories as a foreman and plant manager, Hofstede became chief psychologist on the international staff of IBM, and then joined IMEDE, the Swiss business school, in 1971. He has also worked at the European Institute for Advanced Studies in Management in Brussels and at the University of Limburg in Maastricht, where he is now emeritus professor of organizational

anthropology and international management. See thinker **Geert Hofstede**

holdback E-COMMERCE funds from a merchant's credit card transactions held in reserve for a predetermined time by the merchant account provider to cover possible disputed charges. Also known as **reserve account**

holder FINANCE, BANKING, AND ACCOUNTING the person who is in possession of a bill of exchange or promissory note

holding company GENERAL MANAGEMENT FINANCE, BANKING, AND ACCOUNTING a parent organization that owns the majority of share capital in other companies in order to gain control of them. A holding company may have no other business than the holding of stock in other companies.

holiday (U.K.) HR & PERSONNEL = **vacation**

home loan FINANCE, BANKING, AND ACCOUNTING a mortgage

homepage E-COMMERCE the first and/or main page on a Web site

home run
1 FINANCE, BANKING, AND ACCOUNTING GENERAL MANAGEMENT a very great achievement
2 FINANCE, BANKING, AND ACCOUNTING GENERAL MANAGEMENT an investment that produces a high rate of return in a short time
3 GENERAL MANAGEMENT the journey home at the end of the working day (slang)

home shopping MARKETING the ordering of goods from home by telephone, Internet, mail order, or direct-response television

homeworker HR & PERSONNEL somebody who carries out paid work in his or her home for one or more businesses, but who is not **self-employed**. The method of working can be a permanent or occasional arrangement, or may involve a split of work between an employer's premises and home. See also **teleworker**

homogenization GENERAL MANAGEMENT the removal of characteristic differences between separate markets and cultures. Globalization is frequently blamed for homogenization.

Honey, Peter GENERAL MANAGEMENT British psychologist and consultant. With **Alan Mumford**, he identified four types of **learning styles** and devised an instrument to determine somebody's predominant style in their book, *The Manual of Learning Styles* (1982).

honeypot E-COMMERCE a server connected to the Internet that is used as a decoy to attract potential hackers in order to study their activities and techniques

honorarium HR & PERSONNEL a token sum given in recognition of the recipient's performance of specific, nononerous duties. An honorarium may take the form of an annual retainer.

hook
by hook or by crook GENERAL MANAGEMENT in any way possible, whether or not moral, honest, or legal (slang)

HOPEFUL abbr GENERAL MANAGEMENT hard-up older person expecting full useful life (slang)

HOQ abbr OPERATIONS & PRODUCTION house of quality

horizontal diversification GENERAL MANAGEMENT see **diversification**

horizontal fast track GENERAL MANAGEMENT a variation of **fast track** developed by **Charles Handy**, in which talented people are moved around from task to task to test and develop their capability in different working situations. See thinker **Charles Handy**

horizontal integration GENERAL MANAGEMENT the merging of functions or organizations that operate on a similar level. Horizontal integration involves the union of companies producing the same kinds of goods or operating at the same stage of the **supply chain**. It may also describe the merging of departments within an organization that perform similar tasks. See also **vertical integration**

horizontal keiretsu GENERAL MANAGEMENT see **keiretsu**

horizontal merger GENERAL MANAGEMENT FINANCE, BANKING, AND ACCOUNTING see **merger**

horizontal organization GENERAL MANAGEMENT see **flat organization**

horizontal spread FINANCE, BANKING, AND ACCOUNTING a purchase of two options that are identical except for their dates of maturity

horse-trading FINANCE, BANKING, AND ACCOUNTING hard bargaining that results in one party giving the other a concession

hostile bid FINANCE, BANKING, AND ACCOUNTING a takeover bid that is opposed by the target company. See also **greenmail knight**

hostile takeover FINANCE, BANKING, AND ACCOUNTING see **takeover**

hosting E-COMMERCE the process of putting a Web site on the Internet so that people can visit it.

There are two basic options: internal or external hosting. Internal hosting is often the option when dealing with an intranet, because most of the access to the intranet will be from within the organization. For most public Web sites, it makes sense to use a third-party hosting company. Such companies have mastered the complexities of Web site hosting and can offer excellent service. Issues that need to be considered when deciding whether to outsource include whether you need a **domain name**; how many visitors you expect each month; how much space and what access speeds are needed; whether you require **e-commerce** or special programming facilities; whether you need to deal with **e-mail**; what support is offered, and price and payment options. See also **hosting options**

hosting options E-COMMERCE the different kinds of **hosting**, usually offered by third-party hosting companies. There are several options: **non-virtual hosting**, **virtual hosting**, **collocation hosting**, and **managed hosting**.

hot button MARKETING a sales or marketing offer that particularly appeals to a buyer (slang)

hot card FINANCE, BANKING, AND ACCOUNTING a credit card that has been stolen

hot-desking GENERAL MANAGEMENT a flexible working practice enabling employees to occupy any vacant workspace instead of sitting at a permanent personalized desk. Organizations using a hot-desking system may have a set of standardized workspaces equipped with **information and communications technologies**, and employees may sit at a different desk each day. Alternatively, the majority of employees may have their own desks, but some employees, such as consultants or part-time workers, may sit at any desk that happens to be free that day. Most conventional offices are only full for a fraction of the time they are open because of sickness, vacations, or **teleworking** and this results in empty desks and wasted resources. Hot-desking enables expensive office space to be fully utilized and forms part of the concept of the **virtual office**. Although employees practicing hot-desking may have limited storage space in the form of a filing cabinet or locker, most of their work and information will be stored electronically.

hoteling GENERAL MANAGEMENT the practice of occupying a desk or workspace in another employer's premises. Hoteling is normally carried out by employees such as consultants or salespeople, who spend more time with customers than at their employers' offices and rely on their clients to provide desk space. Hoteling has developed through improved *information and communications technologies* and is an extension of the *virtual office*.

hot file FINANCE, BANKING, AND ACCOUNTING a list of stolen credit cards

hot issue FINANCE, BANKING, AND ACCOUNTING a new security that is expected to trade at a significant premium to its issue price. See also *hot stock*

hot money FINANCE, BANKING, AND ACCOUNTING
1 money that has been obtained by dishonest means. See also *money laundering*
2 money that is moved at short notice from one financial center to another to secure the best possible return

hot spot E-COMMERCE a building or locale in which wireless Internet users can access a high-speed Internet connection

hot stock FINANCE, BANKING, AND ACCOUNTING a stock, usually a new issue, that rises quickly on the stock market. See also *hot issue*

hours of work
1 GENERAL MANAGEMENT the actual hours worked by an employee, often well in excess of those stated in the *contract of employment* and sometimes without the payment of *overtime*
2 HR & PERSONNEL the hours agreed between an employer and employee for which the employee is paid

house journal GENERAL MANAGEMENT see *newsletter*

house of quality OPERATIONS & PRODUCTION a *decision making* and planning tool that brings customers and engineers together in the product design process. House of quality is one of the four houses or phases of *quality function deployment*. House of quality provides a structure for the design and development cycle. The name is derived from the use of matrices that explore the relationship between customer needs and design attributes. The matrices used in the analysis fit together to form a houselike structure. Abbr. *HOQ* Also known as *quality table*

HP *abbr* (*U.K.*) FINANCE, BANKING, AND ACCOUNTING hire purchase

HPWO *abbr* GENERAL MANAGEMENT high-performance work organization

HR *abbr* HR & PERSONNEL human resources

HREOC *abbr* (*ANZ*) HR & PERSONNEL Human Rights and Equal Opportunities Commission

HRIS *abbr* HR & PERSONNEL human resource information system

HRM *abbr* HR & PERSONNEL human resource management

HR scorecard HR & PERSONNEL a tool for measuring the contribution of human resource management practices to the financial performance of an organization. The HR scorecard was developed by academics Bryan E. Becker, Mark A. Huselid, and Dave Ulrich and presented in their book *The HR Scorecard: Linking People, Strategy, and Performance* (Harvard Business School Press, 2001). It was intended as a supplementary tool to Kaplan and Norton's *balanced scorecard*, which does not focus on HR practice. The HR scorecard sees human resource management practices as a strategic *asset* and provides a road map of six steps designed to help organizations integrate human resource systems with organizational strategy.

HR service center HR & PERSONNEL a *centralized* office that handles routine administration and answers inquiries from managers and staff throughout an organization on *human resources*-related matters

HST *abbr* FINANCE, BANKING, AND ACCOUNTING harmonized sales tax

HTH *abbr* GENERAL MANAGEMENT hope this helps (*slang*)

HTML *abbr* E-COMMERCE hypertext markup language: a computer code used to build and develop Web pages. It is used to format the text of a document and indicate *hyperlinks* to other Web pages, and describes the layout of the Web page.

HTTP *abbr* E-COMMERCE hypertext transport (or transfer) protocol: the communications mechanism used to exchange information on the Internet

hub and spoke GENERAL MANAGEMENT any arrangement of component parts resembling a wheel, with a central hub and a series of spokes radiating outward. The metaphor of the hub and spoke arrangement can be applied to any area. Examples include *organization structure*, computer network design, work processes, service delivery methods, and transportation systems.

humanagement GENERAL MANAGEMENT a style of management that emphasizes the *empowerment* of people

human asset accounting HR & PERSONNEL see *human capital accounting*

human capital HR & PERSONNEL the *employees* of an organization. The term builds on the concept of capital as an asset of an organization, implying recognition of the importance and monetary worth of the skills and experience of its employees. It is measured through *human capital accounting*.

human capital accounting HR & PERSONNEL an attempt to place a financial figure on the knowledge and skills of an organization's *employees* or *human capital*. Also known as *human asset accounting*, *human resource accounting*

human factors engineering GENERAL MANAGEMENT the analysis of human needs and abilities in the design of workplace activities, facilities, and systems in order to optimize employee performance. Human factors engineering uses *ergonomics* in the design of the workplace and strives to offer a better choice of computer software by obtaining a fit between human operators and the equipment or technology that they are using. In this way, human factors engineering tries to reduce risk by raising safety levels, and to produce cost savings by improving performance.

human relations HR & PERSONNEL an interdisciplinary study of social relations in the workplace that embraces sociology, social anthropology, and social psychology. The human relations movement presents a counterpoint to the scientific management view that focuses on maximizing the productivity and income of individual manual workers and on the separation of mental and physical work between management and workers. In contrast, supporters of the human relations movement believe that workers want to feel part of a team with socially supportive relationships and to grow and develop. *Motivation*, communication, *employee participation*, and *leadership* are significant issues. See thinker *Mary Parker Follett*

human resource accounting
1 GENERAL MANAGEMENT see *human capital accounting*

2 FINANCE, BANKING, AND ACCOUNTING the identification, recording, and reporting of the investment in, and return from the employment of, the personnel of an organization

human resource information system HR & PERSONNEL a data *MIS*, usually computerized, that facilitates strategic and operational *decision making* for *human resource management*. Abbr. *HRIS*

human resource management HR & PERSONNEL a model of *personnel management* that focuses on the individual rather than taking a collective approach. Responsibility for human resource management is often devolved to *line management*. It is characterized by an emphasis on strategic integration, *employee commitment*, workforce flexibility, and quality of goods and services. Abbr. *HRM*

human resource planning HR & PERSONNEL the development of strategies for matching the size and skills of the workforce to organizational needs. Human resource planning assists organizations to recruit, retain, and optimize the deployment of the personnel needed to meet business objectives and to respond to changes in the external environment. The process involves carrying out a *skills analysis* of the existing workforce, carrying out *manpower forecasting*, and taking action to ensure that supply meets demand. This may include the development of training and retraining strategies. Also known as *manpower planning*

human resources HR & PERSONNEL
1 the discipline of managing people in an organization. Abbr. *HR*
2 the employees of an organization

Human Rights and Equal Opportunities Commission (*ANZ*) HR & PERSONNEL an Australian federal government body that administers legislation relating to human rights, antidiscrimination, privacy, and social justice. It was established in 1986, replacing the Human Rights Commission. Abbr. *HREOC*

Humble, John William (*b*. 1925) GENERAL MANAGEMENT British consultant. Popularized *Peter Drucker*'s concept of *management by objectives*, which he explained in *Improving Business Results* (1967). See thinker *Peter Drucker*

hunch marketing MARKETING marketing based on instinct rather than research (*slang*)

hurry sickness GENERAL MANAGEMENT a state of anxiety caused by the feeling of not having enough time in the day to achieve everything that is required (*slang*)

hybrid FINANCE, BANKING, AND ACCOUNTING a combination of financial instruments, for example, a bond with warrants attached, or a variety of cash and derivative instruments designed to mirror the performance of a financial market

hybrid annuity FINANCE, BANKING, AND ACCOUNTING see *annuity*

hybrid financial instrument FINANCE, BANKING, AND ACCOUNTING a financial instrument such as a convertible bond that has characteristics of multiple types of instruments, often convertible from one to another

hygiene factors GENERAL MANAGEMENT see *job satisfaction*

hymn sheet
sing from the same hymn sheet HR & PERSONNEL to be in agreement about something with another person or group of people (*slang*)

hyperinflation ECONOMICS a very rapid growth in the rate of inflation so that money loses value and physical goods replace currency as a medium of exchange. This happened in Latin America in the early 1990s, for example.

hyperlink E-COMMERCE an image or piece of text that enables the user, by clicking on it, to move directly to other Web pages. Hyperlinks are most commonly found on Web pages, and can be used to connect Web pages within the same site, as well as to link to other Web sites. Hyperlinks can be added to Web pages by using simple *HTML* commands. They can also be used in e-mail messages, for example, to include the address of a company's Web site. Also known as *hypertext link*

hyperpartnering E-COMMERCE a form of commerce in which companies use Internet technology to form partnerships and execute transactions at high speed and low cost in order to take advantage of business opportunities as soon as they appear

hypertext link E-COMMERCE see *hyperlink*

hypertext markup language E-COMMERCE see *HTML*

hypertext transport protocol *or* **hypertext transfer protocol** E-COMMERCE see *HTTP*

hyper time E-COMMERCE the apparent fast pace and decentralized nature of Internet time

hypothecate FINANCE, BANKING, AND ACCOUNTING to use a property as collateral for a loan

hypothesis testing STATISTICS the process of testing sample data from a statistical study to determine whether it is consistent with what is known about the sample population

---

I

Iacocca, Lee A. (*b*. 1924) GENERAL MANAGEMENT U.S. business executive. President of the Ford Motor Company and subsequently Chairman and Chief Executive of the Chrysler Corporation. His experiences are described in *Iacocca: An Autobiography* (1985).

IANAL *abbr* GENERAL MANAGEMENT I am not a lawyer (*slang*)

IAP *abbr* E-COMMERCE Internet access provider

IAS *abbr* (*ANZ*) FINANCE, BANKING, AND ACCOUNTING installment activity statement

IASC *abbr* FINANCE, BANKING, AND ACCOUNTING International Accounting Standards Committee

IB *abbr* FINANCE, BANKING, AND ACCOUNTING investment bank

IBOR *abbr* FINANCE, BANKING, AND ACCOUNTING Inter Bank Offered Rate: the rate of interest at which banks lend to each other on the interbank market

IBR *abbr* FINANCE, BANKING, AND ACCOUNTING Inter Bank Rate. See also *IBOR*

IBRC *abbr* FINANCE, BANKING, AND ACCOUNTING Insurance Brokers Registration Council: in the United Kingdom, a statutory body established under the Insurance Brokers Registration Act of 1977 that was deregulated following the establishment of the Financial Services Authority and the General Insurance Services Council. Its complaints and administration functions passed to the Institute of Insurance Brokers.

IBRD *abbr* ECONOMICS FINANCE, BANKING, AND ACCOUNTING International Bank for Reconstruction and Development: a United Nations organization that provides funds, policy guidance, and technical assistance to facilitate economic development in its poorer member countries

ICAEW *abbr* FINANCE, BANKING, AND ACCOUNTING Institute of Chartered Accountants in England and Wales

ICAI *abbr* FINANCE, BANKING, AND ACCOUNTING Institute of Chartered Accountants in Ireland

ICANZ *abbr* FINANCE, BANKING, AND ACCOUNTING Institute of Chartered Accountants of New Zealand

Icarus factor GENERAL MANAGEMENT the tendency of managers or executives to embark on overambitious projects which then fail. In Greek mythology, Icarus made himself wings of wax and feathers to attempt to escape from Crete, but flew too near the sun and drowned in the sea after the wax melted. (*slang*)

ICAS *abbr* FINANCE, BANKING, AND ACCOUNTING Institute of Chartered Accountants of Scotland

ICC *abbr* FINANCE, BANKING, AND ACCOUNTING International Chamber of Commerce: an organization that represents business interests to governments, working to improve trading conditions and foster private enterprise

iceing GENERAL MANAGEMENT dismissal from employment. The first part of the word is derived from "involuntary career event." (*slang*)

ICSA *abbr* (*U.K.*) FINANCE, BANKING, AND ACCOUNTING Institute of Chartered Secretaries and Administrators: an organization that works to promote the efficient administration of commerce, industry, and public affairs. Founded in 1891 and granted a royal charter in 1902, it represents the interests of its members to government, publishes journals and other materials, promotes the standing of its members, and provides educational support and qualifying programs.

ICT *abbr* GENERAL MANAGEMENT information and communications technologies

IDA *abbr*
1 FINANCE, BANKING, AND ACCOUNTING International Development Association: an agency administered by the IBRD to provide assistance on concessionary terms to the poorest developing countries. Its resources consist of subscriptions and general replenishments from its more industrialized and developed members, special contributions, and transfers from the net earnings of the IBRD.
2 GENERAL MANAGEMENT Infocomm Development Authority

idea
let's put some ideas on the ground and see if any of them walk GENERAL MANAGEMENT let's try some of these ideas and see whether any of them is successful (*slang*)

idea hamster GENERAL MANAGEMENT somebody who appears to have an endless supply of new ideas (*slang*)

idea practitioner GENERAL MANAGEMENT an individual who specializes in identifying, developing, and implementing business and management ideas. Idea practitioners contribute to the success of an organization by facilitating innovation, especially with regard to business performance and management. They have the ability to select the most appropriate and timely ideas and to translate the ideas of management theorists into practice in their own organizations. The term was introduced by Thomas H. Davenport and Laurence Prusak in their book *What's the Big Idea?* (Harvard Business School Press, 2003).

ideation GENERAL MANAGEMENT MARKETING the thought processes involved in apprehending and expressing a new concept, often in a graphical format. Ideation involves the use of imagination to form new ideas and may be used in an organizational context for problem-solving or in the conceptual phase of *new product development*.

Identrus E-COMMERCE a consortium of financial institutions engaged in developing a standard for a network over which business-to-business e-commerce can be conducted securely

idle time GENERAL MANAGEMENT time spent waiting to continue working on a task while there is a delay (*slang*)

IDR *abbr* FINANCE, BANKING, AND ACCOUNTING International Depository Receipt

IEA *abbr* GENERAL MANAGEMENT International Energy Authority: an autonomous agency within the OECD whose objectives include improving global energy cooperation, developing alternative energy sources, and promoting relations between oil-producing and oil-consuming countries

IFA *abbr* FINANCE, BANKING, AND ACCOUNTING Institute of Financial Accountants

IFC *abbr* FINANCE, BANKING, AND ACCOUNTING International Finance Corporation: a United Nations organization promoting private sector investment in developing countries to reduce poverty and improve the quality of people's lives. It finances private sector projects that are profit-oriented and environmentally and socially sound, and helps to foster development. The IFC has a staff of 2,000 professionals around the world who seek profitable and creative solutions to complex business issues.

IHT *abbr* FINANCE, BANKING, AND ACCOUNTING inheritance tax

IIB *abbr* FINANCE, BANKING, AND ACCOUNTING Institute of Insurance Brokers: in the United Kingdom, the professional body for insurance brokers and the caretaker for the deregulated Insurance Brokers Registration Council's complaints program

ILG *abbr* FINANCE, BANKING, AND ACCOUNTING index-linked gilt

illegal parking FINANCE, BANKING, AND ACCOUNTING a stock market practice that involves a broker or company purchasing securities in another company's name though they are guaranteed by the real investor (*slang*)

illiquid FINANCE, BANKING, AND ACCOUNTING
1 used to describe a person or business that lacks cash or assets such as securities that can readily be converted into cash
2 used to refer to an asset that cannot be easily converted into cash

IMA *abbr* FINANCE, BANKING, AND ACCOUNTING
1 (*ANZ*) investment management agreement
2 Investment Management Association

image advertising MARKETING a form of advertising that attempts to create a positive attitude to a product, brand, or company

imaginization GENERAL MANAGEMENT an approach to *creativity* originated by **Gareth Morgan** in 1993. Imaginization is concerned with improving our ability to see and understand situations in new ways, with finding new ways of organizing, with creating shared understanding and personal *empowerment*, and with developing a capability for continuing self-organization.

IMAP *abbr* E-COMMERCE internet message access protocol: a protocol that enables e-mails to be received from any computer

IMF *abbr* ECONOMICS FINANCE, BANKING, AND ACCOUNTING International Monetary Fund: the organization that industrialized nations have established to reduce trade barriers and stabilize currencies, especially those of less industrialized nations

IMHO *abbr* GENERAL MANAGEMENT in my humble opinion (*slang*)

immediate holding company (*U.K.*) FINANCE, BANKING, AND ACCOUNTING a company with one or more subsidiaries but which is itself a subsidiary of another company (the holding company)

IMNSHO *abbr* GENERAL MANAGEMENT in my not so humble opinion (*slang*)

IMO *abbr* GENERAL MANAGEMENT in my opinion (*slang*)

impact day FINANCE, BANKING, AND ACCOUNTING the day when the terms of a new issue of stock are announced

impaired capital FINANCE, BANKING, AND ACCOUNTING a company's capital that is worth less than the nominal value of its stock

impairment of capital FINANCE, BANKING, AND ACCOUNTING the extent to which the value of a company is less than the nominal value of its stock

imperfect competition FINANCE, BANKING, AND ACCOUNTING a situation that exists in a market when there are strong barriers to the entry of new competitors

implicit knowledge GENERAL MANAGEMENT see *knowledge*

import MARKETING a product or service brought into another country from its country of origin either for sale or for use in manufacturing

import duty FINANCE, BANKING, AND ACCOUNTING a tax on goods imported into a country. Although it may simply be a measure for raising revenue, it can also be used to protect domestic manufacturers from overseas competition.

import penetration ECONOMICS the situation in which one country's imports dominate the market share of those from other industrialized countries. This is the case, for example, with high-tech imports to the United States from Japan.

import surcharge FINANCE, BANKING, AND ACCOUNTING an extra duty levied on imported goods in an attempt to limit imports in general and to encourage local manufacture

impression E-COMMERCE a measure of the number of times an online advertisement is viewed. One impression is equal to one *click-through*.

imprest account FINANCE, BANKING, AND ACCOUNTING a U.K. term for a record of the transactions of a type of petty cash system. An employee is given an advance of money, an imprest, for incidental expenses and, when most of it has been spent, he or she presents receipts for the expenses to the accounts department and is then reimbursed with cash to the total value of the receipts.

improvement curve GENERAL MANAGEMENT see *learning curve*

imputation system FINANCE, BANKING, AND ACCOUNTING a system in which recipients of dividends gain tax advantage for taxes paid by the company that paid the dividends

in box GENERAL MANAGEMENT HR & PERSONNEL a receptacle for documents and other items requiring the attention of an individual. An in box is normally placed on the desk or in the office of the person responsible for dealing with the contents. The phrase "in the in box" is also used figuratively to describe items that have not yet been dealt with. U.K. term *in tray*

in-box learning HR & PERSONNEL a training exercise in which the trainee plays the role of a manager dealing with the contents of an *in box* within a set period of time. In-box training is a form of *simulation* used to develop the *decision making*, prioritizing, and *time management* skills of managers and supervisors in the context of the normal working day.

inc. *abbr* GENERAL MANAGEMENT incorporated

incentive plan HR & PERSONNEL a program established to give benefits to employees to reward them for improved commitment and performance and as a means of motivation. An incentive plan is designed to supplement *base pay* and *fringe benefits*. A *financial incentive plan* may offer stock options or a cash bonus, whereas a *nonfinancial incentive plan* offers benefits such as additional paid vacations. Awards from incentive plans may be made on an individual or team basis.

incentive program MARKETING an award or reward program designed to improve sales force or retail performance

incentive stock option FINANCE, BANKING, AND ACCOUNTING in the United States, an employee stock option plan that gives each qualifying employee the right to purchase a specific number of the corporation's shares at a set price during a specific time period. Tax is only payable when the shares are sold.

incestuous share dealing FINANCE, BANKING, AND ACCOUNTING stock trading by companies within a group in the stock of the other companies within that group. The legality of such transactions depends on the objective of the deals.

inchoate instrument FINANCE, BANKING, AND ACCOUNTING a negotiable instrument that is incomplete because, for example, the date or amount is missing. The person to whom it is delivered has the prima facie authority to complete it in any way he or she considers fit.

incidence of tax FINANCE, BANKING, AND ACCOUNTING used to indicate where the final burden of a tax lies. For example, although a retailer pays any sales tax to the tax collecting authority, the tax itself is ultimately paid by the customer.

income FINANCE, BANKING, AND ACCOUNTING
1 money received by a company or individual
2 money received from savings or investments, for example, interest on a bank account or dividends from stock. This is also known as unearned income.
3 money generated by a business

income bond FINANCE, BANKING, AND ACCOUNTING a bond that a company repays only from its profits

income distribution FINANCE, BANKING, AND ACCOUNTING
1 (*U.K.*) = *income dividend*
2 the distribution of income across a particular group, such as a company, region, or country. It shows the various wage levels and gives the percentage of individuals earning at each level.

income dividend FINANCE, BANKING, AND ACCOUNTING the U.S. term for payment to investors of the income generated by a collective investment, less management charges, tax, and expenses. It is distributed in proportion to the number of shares held by each investor. U.K. term *income distribution*

income gearing FINANCE, BANKING, AND ACCOUNTING the ratio of the interest a company pays on its borrowing shown as a percentage of its pre-tax profits

income-linked gilt FINANCE, BANKING, AND ACCOUNTING a bond whose principal and interest track the retail price index

income redistribution ECONOMICS a government policy to redirect income to a targeted sector of a country's population, for example, by lowering the rate of tax paid by low-income earners

income shares FINANCE, BANKING, AND ACCOUNTING shares in an investment trust which receive income from the investments, but do not benefit from the rise in capital value of the investments. The other form of shares in a split-level investment trust is capital shares, which increase in value as the value of the investments rises, but do not receive any income.

income smoothing FINANCE, BANKING, AND ACCOUNTING a U.K. term for a form of creative accounting that involves the manipulation of a company's financial statements to show steady annual profits rather than large fluctuations

incomes policy (*U.K.*) ECONOMICS a government policy that seeks to restrain increases in wages or prices by regulating the permitted level of increase

income stock FINANCE, BANKING, AND ACCOUNTING
1 common stock sought because of their relatively high yield as opposed to their potential to produce capital growth
2 certain funds, for example, investment trusts, that issue split level funds where holders of the income element receive all the income (less expenses, charges, and tax), while holders of the capital element receive only the capital gains (less expenses, charges, and tax)

income stream FINANCE, BANKING, AND ACCOUNTING the income received by a company from a particular product or activity

income tax FINANCE, BANKING, AND ACCOUNTING a tax levied directly on the income of a person or a company and paid to the local, state, or federal government. Abbr. *IT*

income tax allowance FINANCE, BANKING, AND ACCOUNTING a proportion of a person's income that is not subject to tax. Allowances are announced each year by the *Chancellor of the Exchequer* in the *Budget*. See also *income tax*

income tax return FINANCE, BANKING, AND ACCOUNTING a form used for reporting income and computing the tax due on it

income unit FINANCE, BANKING, AND ACCOUNTING a share in a mutual fund that makes regular dividend payments to its shareholders

income yield FINANCE, BANKING, AND ACCOUNTING the actual percentage yield of government stocks, the fixed interest being shown as a percentage of the market price

incorporation FINANCE, BANKING, AND ACCOUNTING the legal process of creating a corporation or company. Incorporated entities have a legal status distinct from that of their owners, and limited liability.

incorporeal chattels FINANCE, BANKING, AND ACCOUNTING intangible properties, such as patents or copyrights

incrementalism GENERAL MANAGEMENT a collective term for the many initiatives of the 1980s and 1990s that took a small-step approach to improving quality and productivity and reducing costs. Incrementalism encompasses initiatives such as *total quality management*, *continuous improvement*, and *benchmarking*. Although incrementalism originally provided a source of *competitive advantage*, it is generally recognized today that a more radical approach is required.

indaba (*S. Africa*) GENERAL MANAGEMENT a meeting or conference

indemnity FINANCE, BANKING, AND ACCOUNTING an agreement by one party to make good the losses suffered by another. See also *indemnity insurance*, *letter of indemnity*

indemnity insurance FINANCE, BANKING, AND ACCOUNTING an insurance contract in which the insurer agrees to cover the cost of losses suffered by the insured party. Most insurance contracts take this form except personal accident and life insurance policies, where fixed sums are paid as compensation, rather than reimbursement, for a loss that cannot be quantified in monetary terms.

indenture FINANCE, BANKING, AND ACCOUNTING a formal agreement showing the terms of a *bond issue*

independent authenticator FINANCE, BANKING, AND ACCOUNTING a company that has the authority, either from the government or a controlling body, to issue certificates of authentication when they are sure that a company is who it claims to be

independent service organization E-COMMERCE see *ISO*

index FINANCE, BANKING, AND ACCOUNTING
1 a standard that represents the value of stocks in a market, particularly a figure such as the Hang Seng, Dow Jones, or Nikkei average
2 an amount calculated to represent the relative value of a group of things

index arbitrage FINANCE, BANKING, AND ACCOUNTING the buying or selling of a basket of stocks against an index option or future

indexation FINANCE, BANKING, AND ACCOUNTING the linking of a rate to a standard index of prices, interest rates, stock prices, or similar items

indexed portfolio FINANCE, BANKING, AND ACCOUNTING a portfolio of stocks in all the

companies which form the basis of a stock exchange index

index fund FINANCE, BANKING, AND ACCOUNTING a mutual fund composed of companies listed in an important stock market index in order to match the market's overall performance. See also *managed fund*. Also known as *tracker fund*

index futures FINANCE, BANKING, AND ACCOUNTING a futures contract trading in one of the major stock market indices, such as the *Standard & Poor's 500*. See also *Dow Jones Averages*

index-linked bond FINANCE, BANKING, AND ACCOUNTING a security where the income is linked to an index, such as a financial index. See also *index-linked gilt*, *index-linked savings certificate*

index-linked gilt FINANCE, BANKING, AND ACCOUNTING an inflation-proof U.K. government bond, first introduced for institutional investors in 1981 and then made available to the general public in 1982. It is inflation-proof in two ways: the dividend is raised every six months in line with the Retail Price Index and the original capital is repaid in real terms at redemption, when the indexing of the repayment is undertaken. The nominal value of the stock, however, does not increase with inflation. Like other gilts, ILGs are traded on the market. Price changes are principally dependent on investors' changing perceptions of inflation and real yields. Abbr. *ILG*

index-linked savings certificate FINANCE, BANKING, AND ACCOUNTING a certificate issued by the U.K. National Savings & Investments organization, with a return linked to the rate of inflation. Also known as *granny bond*

index number ECONOMICS a weighted average of a number of observations of an economic attribute, such as retail prices expressed as a percentage of a similar weighted average calculated at an earlier period

index tracker FINANCE, BANKING, AND ACCOUNTING a fund which follows closely one of the stock market indices, such as the *Standard & Poor's 500*. See also *index fund*

index tracking FINANCE, BANKING, AND ACCOUNTING an investment technique whereby a portfolio is maintained in such a way as to match the growth in a stock market index

indicated dividend FINANCE, BANKING, AND ACCOUNTING the forecast total of all dividends in

a year if the amount of each dividend remains as it is

indicated yield FINANCE, BANKING, AND ACCOUNTING the yield that an indicated dividend represents

indication price (*U.K.*) FINANCE, BANKING, AND ACCOUNTING an approximation of the price of a security as opposed to its firm price

indicative price FINANCE, BANKING, AND ACCOUNTING the price shown on a screen-based system for trading securities such as the U.K. Stock Exchange Automated Quotations system. The price is not firm, as the size of the bargain will determine the final price at which market makers will actually deal.

indirect channel MARKETING the selling and distribution of products to customers through intermediaries such as wholesalers, distributors, agents, dealers, or retailers

indirect cost FINANCE, BANKING, AND ACCOUNTING GENERAL MANAGEMENT a fixed or overhead cost that cannot be attributed directly to the production of a particular item and is incurred even when there is no output. Indirect costs may include the *cost center* functions of finance and accounting, information technology, administration, and personnel. See also *direct cost*

indirect discrimination HR & PERSONNEL apparently *equal treatment* that in fact *discriminates* because the employment requirement can be met only by a proportion of those in the relevant group and cannot be justified on nondiscriminatory grounds

indirect labor HR & PERSONNEL personnel not directly engaged in the manufacturing of products or the provision of services. Indirect labor includes *white-collar workers* and office and support staff.

individual retirement account FINANCE, BANKING, AND ACCOUNTING see *IRA*

Individual Savings Account FINANCE, BANKING, AND ACCOUNTING see *ISA*

induction (*U.K.*) HR & PERSONNEL = *orientation*

industrial action HR & PERSONNEL concerted action taken by employees to pressure an employer to accede to a demand, usually work-related, but sometimes of a political or social nature. Examples of industrial action include *strikes*, overtime bans, *go-slows*, and extended coffee breaks.

industrial advertising MARKETING the advertising of technical products and services to the industrial or business sectors

Industrial Arbitration Court HR & PERSONNEL an organization which arbitrates in industrial disputes

industrial award GENERAL MANAGEMENT see *award*

industrial cooperative GENERAL MANAGEMENT a group of individuals who together produce goods or provide services and share any profits that are made. Industrial cooperatives are an extension of the *cooperative movement* that developed during the 1800s.

industrial court (*ANZ*) HR & PERSONNEL a state body in Australia responsible for arbitrating in industrial disputes and setting wage awards

industrial democracy (*U.K.*) GENERAL MANAGEMENT a way of running an organization that involves employees in strategy and *decision making*. Industrial democracy involves *employee participation* in management, which encourages *empowerment* and aids *motivation*. It can be facilitated by such setups as consultation committees. In an industrial democracy, workers should not only share in inputs to the running of the organization but also in its outputs, for example, by taking part in a profit-sharing plan.

industrial dispute GENERAL MANAGEMENT see *dispute*

industrial engineering GENERAL MANAGEMENT an applied science discipline concerned with the prediction, planning, evaluation, and improvement of company effectiveness. The purpose of industrial engineering is to maximize efficiency, quality, and production through the best use of personnel, materials, facilities, and equipment.

industrial espionage GENERAL MANAGEMENT the practice of spying on a business competitor in order to obtain its trade or commercial secrets. Information sought through industrial espionage will often refer to new products, designs, formulas, manufacturing processes, marketing surveys, research, or future plans. The goal of industrial espionage is either to injure the business prospects or market share of the target company, or to use the secrets discovered for another organization's commercial benefit.

industrial goods OPERATIONS & PRODUCTION goods produced for industry, which include

processed or *raw materials*, and goods used to produce other goods, machinery, components, and equipment

industrial goods marketing MARKETING the *industrial marketing* of products. Industrial goods marketing is different from the marketing of consumer goods in that it is directed at organizations, businesses, and other institutions, rather than at the individual end user of a product. It may require different marketing strategies from those used in *consumer goods marketing* to be effective.

industrial housekeeping GENERAL MANAGEMENT the process of ensuring that the workplace is kept clean and tidy. Industrial housekeeping forms part of the general responsibility of managers. It includes the provision of adequate workspace, adequate storage arrangements, both around the workstation and within the unit, and the development of effective administration and procedures to ensure a culture of tidiness and cleanliness within the workforce. A lack of concern with housekeeping can result in an increase in accidents and machine failure and in a reduction in the overall efficiency of the unit. The introduction of the Japanese 5-S concept into Western companies has renewed management interest in industrial housekeeping.

industrialization GENERAL MANAGEMENT the change from a society based on agriculture to one based on manufacturing. Industrialization is the process undergone in much of the developed world during the Industrial Revolution. Features of the process include *automation*, scientific development, the introduction of factories, the *division of labor*, the replacement of barter with a money-based economy, a more mobile workforce, and the growth of urban centers. The phase of development following industrialization is the *postindustrial society*.

industrial marketing MARKETING the marketing of goods or services to companies, as opposed to individual consumers. Industrial marketing involves a number of key differences from selling to consumers. These include a smaller customer base with higher value or larger unit purchases, more technically complex or specially tailored products, professionally qualified purchasers, closer buyer-seller relationships, and possible group-purchasing decision making. Also known as *B2B marketing*

industrial market research MARKETING *market research* into the marketing of services and goods to industry, businesses, and other in-

stitutions. Industrial market research is used as an aid to **decision making** and concerns the manufacture, selling, and distribution of products with the goal of reducing costs and increasing profits. It considers factors such as the available labor force, location of the firm, export market potential, and use of resources.

industrial production ECONOMICS the output of a country's productive industries. Until the 1960s, this commonly related to iron and steel or coal, but since then lighter engineering in automobile or robotics manufacture has taken over.

industrial psychology HR & PERSONNEL see *occupational psychology*

Industrial Relations Commission GENERAL MANAGEMENT see *Australian Industrial Relations Commission*

Industrial Relations Court of Australia HR & PERSONNEL an Australian superior court responsible for enforcing industrial awards, hearing and ruling on claims for unfair dismissal, and ruling on points of industrial law. Abbr. *IRCA*

industrial revenue bond FINANCE, BANKING, AND ACCOUNTING a bond that a private company uses to finance construction

industrial-sector cycle ECONOMICS a business cycle that reflects patterns of an old economy rather than the new electronic economy

industrial services marketing MARKETING the *industrial marketing* of services. Industrial services marketing may promote services such as maintenance contracts, insurance, training, transportation, office cleaning, and advertising to industry, businesses, and other institutions. Many services offered to industry are also offered to the consumer, but promoting them to consumers requires strategies derived from *consumer services marketing*.

industry rules GENERAL MANAGEMENT the unwritten conventions that are considered to govern the interactions of organizations within an industry

ineligible bills FINANCE, BANKING, AND ACCOUNTING bills of exchange which cannot be discounted by a central bank

inertia selling (*U.K.*) MARKETING a method of selling that involves the sending of unsolicited goods on a sale or return policy. Inertia selling relies on the passive reaction of a potential purchaser to choose to pay for the goods received rather than undertake the effort to send them back. The receiver of the goods is not bound by law to pay for them but must keep them in good condition until they are collected or returned. Regarded by some as unethical, inertia selling is the principle by which many mail-order book, record, and video clubs operate.

infant industry FINANCE, BANKING, AND ACCOUNTING an industry in the early stages of development

inference STATISTICS a conclusion drawn by a researcher about a statistical population after observing individuals in the population

infinite capacity plan OPERATIONS & PRODUCTION see *capacity requirements planning*

infinite loading OPERATIONS & PRODUCTION the scheduling or loading of jobs onto a workstation as if it had a limitless capacity to handle them. See also *finite loading*

inflation ECONOMICS a sustained increase in a country's general level of prices that devalues its currency, often caused by excess demand in the economy

inflation accounting FINANCE, BANKING, AND ACCOUNTING the adjustment of a company's accounts to reflect the effect of inflation and provide a more realistic view of the company's position

inflationary ECONOMICS characterized by excess demand or high costs creating an excessive increase in the country's money supply

inflationary gap ECONOMICS a gap that exists when an economy's resources are utilized and *aggregate demand* is more than the full-employment level of output. Prices will rise to remove the excess demand.

inflationary spiral ECONOMICS a situation in which, repeatedly, in inflationary conditions, excess demand causes producers to raise prices and workers to demand wage rises to sustain their living standards

inflation-proof pension FINANCE, BANKING, AND ACCOUNTING a pension which will rise to keep pace with inflation

inflation-proof security FINANCE, BANKING, AND ACCOUNTING a security that is indexed to inflation

inflation rate ECONOMICS the rate at which general price levels increase over a period of time

inflation tax ECONOMICS an income policy that taxes companies that grant pay raises above a particular level

Infocomm Development Authority GENERAL MANAGEMENT a statutory board responsible for developing the information and communications sector in Singapore. It was formed in 1999 as a result of the merger of the Telecommunications Authority of Singapore and the National Computer Board. Abbr. *IDA*

infoholic GENERAL MANAGEMENT somebody who is obsessed with obtaining information, especially on the Internet (*slang*)

infomatics GENERAL MANAGEMENT the process of automation using information systems

infomediary E-COMMERCE a Web site that provides and aggregates relevant customer or industry information for other companies

infomercial MARKETING a television or cinema commercial that includes helpful information about a product as well as advertising content

info rate FINANCE, BANKING, AND ACCOUNTING a money market rate quoted by dealers for information only

informal economy ECONOMICS the economy that runs in parallel to the formal economy but outside the reach of the tax system, most transactions being paid for in cash or goods

information and communications technologies GENERAL MANAGEMENT computer and telecommunications technologies considered collectively. Information and communications technology convergence has given rise to technologies such as the *Internet*, *videoconferencing*, *groupware*, *intranets*, and third-generation cellphones. Information and communications technologies enable organizations to be more flexible in the way they are structured and in the way they work, and this has given rise to both the *virtual organization* and the *virtual office*. Abbr. *ICT*

information architecture E-COMMERCE the means and methods of designing metadata, navigation, search, and content layout for a Web site

information management GENERAL MANAGEMENT the acquisition, recording, organizing, storage, dissemination, and retrieval of information. Good information management has been described as getting the right information to the right person in the right format at the right time.

information overload E-COMMERCE the problem caused by the excessive quantity of Web and e-mail-based information and the Internet's inability to discriminate between useful and useless material. In 1997, the problem of information overload was identified in an influential report from the British MCA (Marketing and Communication Agency). The report concluded that "information overload is not simply the problem of too much information. It is the problem of too much *irrelevant* information caused by the heavy reliance on one medium (the Internet) to distribute information."

information space E-COMMERCE the abstract concept of all the knowledge, expertise, and information accessible on the Web

infotainment GENERAL MANAGEMENT television programs that deal with serious issues or current affairs in an entertaining way

infrastructure GENERAL MANAGEMENT the basic elements that together support something, for example, the network and systems that support computing or the public services and facilities that support business activity

in-house newsletter GENERAL MANAGEMENT see *newsletter*

initial offer FINANCE, BANKING, AND ACCOUNTING the first offer that a company makes to buy the stock of another company in the United Kingdom

initial public offering FINANCE, BANKING, AND ACCOUNTING the first instance of making particular stock available for sale to the public. Abbr. *IPO*

initial yield GENERAL MANAGEMENT the estimated yield at the launch of an investment fund

injunction FINANCE, BANKING, AND ACCOUNTING a court order forbidding an individual or organization from doing something

inland bill FINANCE, BANKING, AND ACCOUNTING a U.K. term for a bill of exchange that is payable and drawn in the same country

Inland Revenue FINANCE, BANKING, AND ACCOUNTING see *Her Majesty's Revenue & Customs*

Inland Revenue Department (*ANZ*) FINANCE, BANKING, AND ACCOUNTING the New Zealand government body responsible for the administration of the national taxation system. Abbr. *IRD*

innovation GENERAL MANAGEMENT the creation, development, and implementation of a new product, process, or service with the goal of improving efficiency, effectiveness, or *competitive advantage*. Innovation may apply to products, services, manufacturing processes, managerial processes, or the design of an organization. It is most often viewed at a product or process level, where product innovation satisfies a customer's needs, and process innovation improves efficiency and effectiveness. Innovation is linked with *creativity*, and involves taking new ideas and turning them into reality through invention, research, and *new product development*.

inpatriation GENERAL MANAGEMENT HR & PERSONNEL the transfer of foreign employees to work in the home country of an international organization on a temporary or permanent basis. Inpatriation often involves the relocation of employees of a foreign *subsidiary company* in a developing country to the home base or headquarters of a *multinational business* in the developed world. The objective may be to fill a *skills shortage* or to develop a global, multicultural perspective in the organization. The use of the term has developed by analogy with the term "expatriate."

input tax FINANCE, BANKING, AND ACCOUNTING see *VAT*

input tax credit (*ANZ*) FINANCE, BANKING, AND ACCOUNTING an amount paid as *Goods and Services Tax* on supplies purchased for business purposes, which can be offset against Goods and Services Tax collected

insert MARKETING a loose piece of advertising material, for example, a card or brochure, placed inside a newspaper or magazine

insertion rate MARKETING the cost of a single appearance of an advertisement

in-service training HR & PERSONNEL programs of *employee development* that are delivered within an organization by external training providers. In-service training allows programs to be tailored to a company's specific needs. It is the opposite of *public training programs*, which have a set syllabus and are open to employees of any organization.

inside information FINANCE, BANKING, AND ACCOUNTING information that is of advantage to investors but is only available to people who have personal contact with a company

inside quote FINANCE, BANKING, AND ACCOUNTING a variety of prices for a security, from the highest offer to buy to the lowest offer to sell

insider FINANCE, BANKING, AND ACCOUNTING GENERAL MANAGEMENT somebody who has access to information that is privileged and unavailable to most members of the public

insider trading *or* **insider dealing** FINANCE, BANKING, AND ACCOUNTING profitable, usually illegal, trading in securities carried out using information not available to the public

insolvency FINANCE, BANKING, AND ACCOUNTING GENERAL MANAGEMENT the inability to pay debts when they become due. Insolvency will apply even if total assets exceed total liabilities, if those assets cannot be readily converted into cash to meet debts as they mature. Even then, insolvency may not necessarily mean *business failure*. *Bankruptcy* may be avoided through *debt rescheduling* or *turnaround management*.

insourcing GENERAL MANAGEMENT the use of in-house personnel or an internal department to meet an organization's need for specific services. Insourcing is seen as a reaction to the growing popularity of *outsourcing*, that has not always met expectations. An insourcing strategy is chosen where it appears that a better service can be provided from internal resources than from an external supplier. In some cases, organizations opt for a combination of outsourcing and insourcing, in which external service providers work in cooperation with in-house personnel.

installment FINANCE, BANKING, AND ACCOUNTING one of two or more payments for the purchase of an initial public offering

installment activity statement (*ANZ*) FINANCE, BANKING, AND ACCOUNTING a standard form used in Australia to report *pay-as-you-go* installment payments on investment income. Abbr. *IAS*

installment credit (*U.K.*) FINANCE, BANKING, AND ACCOUNTING = *installment loan*

installment loan FINANCE, BANKING, AND ACCOUNTING the U.S. term for a loan that is repaid with fixed regular installments, and with a rate of interest fixed for the duration of the loan. U.K. term *installment credit*

installment plan *or* **installment purchase** FINANCE, BANKING, AND ACCOUNTING a method of buying something by paying for it in regular equal amounts over a period of time

instant access account FINANCE, BANKING, AND ACCOUNTING an account which pays interest, but from which the account holder can withdraw money when he or she needs it

a-z

1521

DICTIONARY

instant messaging E-COMMERCE see *live chat*

Institute of Chartered Accountants in England and Wales FINANCE, BANKING, AND ACCOUNTING the largest professional accounting body in Europe, providing certification by examinations, ensuring high standards of education and training, and supervising professional conduct. Abbr. *ICAEW*

Institute of Chartered Accountants in Ireland FINANCE, BANKING, AND ACCOUNTING the oldest and largest professional body for accountants in Ireland, the ICAI was founded in 1888. Its many objectives include promoting best practice in chartered accountancy and maintaining high standards of professionalism among its members. It publishes a journal, *Accountancy Ireland*, and has offices in Dublin and Belfast. Abbr. *ICAI*

Institute of Chartered Accountants of New Zealand FINANCE, BANKING, AND ACCOUNTING the only professional accounting body in New Zealand, representing over 26,000 members in that country and abroad. ICANZ has overseas branch offices in Fiji, London, Melbourne, and Sydney. Abbr. *ICANZ*

Institute of Chartered Accountants of Scotland FINANCE, BANKING, AND ACCOUNTING the world's oldest professional body for accountants, based in Edinburgh. Abbr. *ICAS*

Institute of Chartered Secretaries and Administrators FINANCE, BANKING, AND ACCOUNTING see *ICSA*

Institute of Directors FINANCE, BANKING, AND ACCOUNTING an individual membership association whose stated objective is to "serve, support, represent, and set standards for directors." Founded in 1903 by Royal Charter, the IoD has approximately 55,000 members and is an independent, nonpolitical body. It is based in London, but also has offices in Belfast, Birmingham, Bristol, Edinburgh, Manchester, and Nottingham. Abbr. *IoD*

Institute of Financial Accountants FINANCE, BANKING, AND ACCOUNTING a professional body, established in 1916, which aims to set technical and ethical standards in U.K. financial accounting. Abbr. *IFA*

Institute of Financial Services FINANCE, BANKING, AND ACCOUNTING the trading name of the Chartered Institute of Bankers

Institute of Insurance Brokers FINANCE, BANKING, AND ACCOUNTING see *IIB*

institutional buyout FINANCE, BANKING, AND ACCOUNTING the takeover of a company by a financial institution, which backs a group of managers who will run it

institutional investor FINANCE, BANKING, AND ACCOUNTING an institution that makes investments

institutional survey STATISTICS a statistical investigation in which an institution such as a company is the unit of analysis

instrument
1 HR & PERSONNEL see *psychometric test*
2 FINANCE, BANKING, AND ACCOUNTING a generic term for either securities or derivatives. See also *financial instrument*
3 FINANCE, BANKING, AND ACCOUNTING an official or legal document
4 FINANCE, BANKING, AND ACCOUNTING a means to an end, for example, a government's expenditure and taxation in its quest for reducing unemployment

insurable risk FINANCE, BANKING, AND ACCOUNTING see *risk*

insurance
1 FINANCE, BANKING, AND ACCOUNTING GENERAL MANAGEMENT an arrangement in which individuals or companies pay another company to guarantee them compensation if they suffer loss resulting from risks such as fire, theft, or accidental damage
2 FINANCE, BANKING, AND ACCOUNTING in financial markets, hedging or any other strategy that reduces risk while permitting participation in potential gains

Insurance and Superannuation Commission (*ANZ*) FINANCE, BANKING, AND ACCOUNTING GENERAL MANAGEMENT an Australian federal government body responsible for regulating the superannuation and insurance industries. Abbr. *ISC*

insurance broker FINANCE, BANKING, AND ACCOUNTING a person or company that acts as an intermediary between companies providing insurance and individuals or companies who need insurance

Insurance Brokers Registration Council FINANCE, BANKING, AND ACCOUNTING see *IBRC*

Insurance Council of Australia FINANCE, BANKING, AND ACCOUNTING GENERAL MANAGEMENT an independent body representing the interests of businesses involved in the insurance industry. It was established in 1975 and currently represents around 110 companies. Abbr. *ICA*

insurance intermediary FINANCE, BANKING, AND ACCOUNTING an individual or firm that provides advice on insurance and can arrange policies. See also *IIB IBRC*

insurance policy FINANCE, BANKING, AND ACCOUNTING GENERAL MANAGEMENT a document that sets out the terms and conditions for providing insurance coverage against specified risks

insurance premium tax (*U.K.*) FINANCE, BANKING, AND ACCOUNTING a tax on household, motor vehicle, travel, and other general insurance

insured FINANCE, BANKING, AND ACCOUNTING covered by a contract of insurance

insured account FINANCE, BANKING, AND ACCOUNTING an account with a bank or savings institution that belongs to a federal or private insurance organization

insurer FINANCE, BANKING, AND ACCOUNTING the underwriter of an insurance risk

intangible asset FINANCE, BANKING, AND ACCOUNTING an asset, such as intellectual property or *goodwill*, that is not physical. Also known as *invisible asset*

integrated implementation model GENERAL MANAGEMENT see *new product development*

Integrated Services Digital Network E-COMMERCE see *ISDN*

intellectual assets GENERAL MANAGEMENT the knowledge, experience, and skills of its staff that an organization can make use of

intellectual capital GENERAL MANAGEMENT the combined intangible assets owned or controlled by a company or organization that provide *competitive advantage*. Intellectual capital assets can include the knowledge and expertise of employees, brands, customer information and relationships, contracts, *intellectual property* such as patents and copyright, and organizational technologies, processes, and methods. Intellectual capital can be implicit and intangible—stored in people's heads—or explicit and documented in written or electronic format.

intellectual property GENERAL MANAGEMENT the ownership of rights to ideas, designs, and inventions, including *copyrights*, *patents*, and *trademarks*. Intellectual property is protected by law in most countries, and the World Intellectual Property Organization is responsible

for harmonizing the law across different countries and promoting the protection of intellectual property rights.

intelligence test HR & PERSONNEL see *aptitude test*

intelligent e-mail E-COMMERCE an e-mail system that is automatically able to analyze incoming messages without the need for criteria preset by each user

interactive E-COMMERCE relating to a facility of an online service or software program that allows the user to enter data or issue commands

interactive planning GENERAL MANAGEMENT a process that promotes participation in both the design of a desirable future and the developments that enable this future to be achieved rather than waiting for it to happen. Interactive planning is associated with *Russell Ackoff*, and was outlined in *Creating the Corporate Future* (1981).

Inter Bank Offered Rate FINANCE, BANKING, AND ACCOUNTING see *IBOR*

Inter Bank Rate FINANCE, BANKING, AND ACCOUNTING abbr. *IBR*

interchange E-COMMERCE a transaction between the acquiring bank and the issuing bank

interchangeable bond FINANCE, BANKING, AND ACCOUNTING a bond whose owner can change it at will between registered and coupon form, sometimes for a fee

interchange fee E-COMMERCE the charge on a transaction between the acquiring bank and the issuing bank, paid by the acquirer to the issuer

intercommodity spread FINANCE, BANKING, AND ACCOUNTING a combination of purchase and sale of options for related commodities with the same delivery date

intercompany pricing FINANCE, BANKING, AND ACCOUNTING the setting of prices by companies within a group to sell products or services to each other, rather than to external customers

interest FINANCE, BANKING, AND ACCOUNTING the rate that a lender charges for the use of money that is a loan

interest arbitrage (*U.K.*) FINANCE, BANKING, AND ACCOUNTING transactions in two or more financial centers in order to make an immediate profit by exploiting differences in interest rates. See also *arbitrage*

interest assumption FINANCE, BANKING, AND ACCOUNTING the expected rate of return on a portfolio

interest cover FINANCE, BANKING, AND ACCOUNTING the amount of earnings available to make interest payments after all operating and non-operating income and expenses—except interest and income taxes—have been accounted for.

Interest cover is regarded as a measure of a company's creditworthiness because it shows how much income there is to cover interest payments on outstanding debt.

It is expressed as a ratio, comparing the funds available to pay interest—earnings before interest and taxes, or EBIT—with the interest expense. The basic formula is

$$\frac{\text{EBIT}}{\text{Interest expense}} = \text{Interest coverage ratio}$$

If interest expense for a year is \$9 million, and the company's EBIT is \$45 million, the interest coverage would be

$$\frac{45 \text{ million}}{9 \text{ million}} = 5:1$$

The higher the number, the stronger a company is likely to be. A ratio of less than 1 indicates that a company is having problems generating enough cash flow to pay its interest expenses, and that either a modest decline in operating profits or a sudden rise in borrowing costs could eliminate profitability entirely. Ideally, interest coverage should at least exceed 1.5; in some sectors, 2.0 or higher is desirable.

Variations of this basic formula also exist. For example, there is

$$\frac{\text{Operating cash flow} + \text{Interest} + \text{Taxes}}{\text{Interest}}$$

= Cash flow interest coverage ratio

This ratio indicates the firm's ability to use its cash flow to satisfy its fixed financing obligations. Finally, there is the fixed-charge coverage ratio, which compares EBIT with fixed charges:

$$\frac{\text{EBIT} + \text{Lease expenses}}{\text{LOWER}}$$

= Fixed-charge coverage ratio

"Fixed charges" can be interpreted in many ways, however. It could mean, for example, the funds that a company is obliged to set aside to retire debt, or dividends on preferred stock.

interest-elastic investment FINANCE, BANKING, AND ACCOUNTING an investment with a rate of return that varies with interest rates

interest-inelastic investment FINANCE, BANKING, AND ACCOUNTING an investment with a rate of return that does not vary with interest rates

interest in possession trust (*U.K.*) FINANCE, BANKING, AND ACCOUNTING a trust that gives one or more beneficiaries an immediate right to receive any income generated by the trust's assets. It can be used for real estate, enabling the beneficiary either to enjoy the rent generated by the property or to reside there, or as a life policy, a common arrangement for Inheritance Tax planning.

interest-only mortgage FINANCE, BANKING, AND ACCOUNTING a long-term loan, usually for the purchase of real estate, in which the borrower only pays interest to the lender during the term of the mortgage, with the principal being repaid at the end of the term. It is thus the borrower's responsibility to make provisions to accumulate the required capital during the period of the mortgage, usually by contributing to tax efficient investment plans. See also *mortgage*

interest rate FINANCE, BANKING, AND ACCOUNTING the amount of interest charged for borrowing a sum of money over a specified period of time

interest rate cap FINANCE, BANKING, AND ACCOUNTING an upper limit on a rate of interest, for example, in an adjustable-rate mortgage

interest rate effect ECONOMICS the mechanism by which interest rates adjust so that investment is equal to savings in an economy

interest rate exposure (*U.K.*) FINANCE, BANKING, AND ACCOUNTING the risk of a loss associated with movements in the level of interest rates. See also *bond*

interest rate floor FINANCE, BANKING, AND ACCOUNTING a lower limit on a rate of interest, for example, in an adjustable-rate mortgage

interest rate future FINANCE, BANKING, AND ACCOUNTING see *future*

interest rate guarantee (*U.K.*) FINANCE, BANKING, AND ACCOUNTING
1 an interest rate cap, collar, or cap and collar
2 a tailored indemnity protecting the purchaser against future changes in interest rates

interest rate option FINANCE, BANKING, AND ACCOUNTING see *option*

interest rate swap FINANCE, BANKING, AND ACCOUNTING an exchange of two debt instruments with different rates of interest, made to tailor cash flows to the participants' different requirements

interest sensitive FINANCE, BANKING, AND ACCOUNTING used to describe assets, generally purchased with credit, that are in demand when interest rates fall but considered less attractive when interest rates rise

interface GENERAL MANAGEMENT
1 the point of contact between two or more things, for example, between a computer and user, or customer and seller
2 a face-to-face meeting (*slang*)

interfirm cooperation GENERAL MANAGEMENT a formal or informal agreement between organizations to collaborate in achieving common or new goals more efficiently or effectively. Interfirm cooperation usually takes the form of a *joint venture*, *strategic alliance*, or *strategic partnering* arrangement.

interim certificate FINANCE, BANKING, AND ACCOUNTING a document certifying partial ownership of stock that is not totally paid for at one time

interim dividend FINANCE, BANKING, AND ACCOUNTING a dividend whose value is determined on the basis of a period of time of less than a full fiscal year

interim financial statement FINANCE, BANKING, AND ACCOUNTING a financial statement that covers a period other than a full fiscal year. Although U.K. companies are not legally obliged to publish interim financial statements, those listed on the London Stock Exchange are obliged to publish a half-yearly report of their activities and a profit and loss account which may either be sent to stockholders or published in a national newspaper. In the United States, the practice is to issue quarterly financial statements.

interim financing FINANCE, BANKING, AND ACCOUNTING financing by means of bridge loans

interim manager GENERAL MANAGEMENT see *interim management*

interim statement FINANCE, BANKING, AND ACCOUNTING a financial statement relating to a period of time of less than a full fiscal year

intermarket spread FINANCE, BANKING, AND ACCOUNTING a combination of purchase and sale of options for the same commodity with the same delivery date on different markets

intermediary FINANCE, BANKING, AND ACCOUNTING somebody who makes investments for others

intermediate goods OPERATIONS & PRODUCTION goods bought for use in the production of other products

intern HR & PERSONNEL a trainee working in a low-ranking position in a company

internal audit FINANCE, BANKING, AND ACCOUNTING an audit of a company undertaken by its employees. See also *external audit*

internal communication GENERAL MANAGEMENT communication between employees or departments across all levels or divisions of an organization. Internal communication is a form of *corporate communication* and can be formal or informal, upward, downward, or horizontal. It can take various forms such as *team briefing*, *interviewing*, employee or works councils, *meetings*, *memos*, an *intranet*, *newsletters*, the *grapevine*, and reports.

internal consultant GENERAL MANAGEMENT an employee who uses knowledge and expertise to offer advice or business solutions to another department or business unit within an organization. *Internal consulting* is one aspect of work carried out by a *management services* department.

internal consulting GENERAL MANAGEMENT see *internal consultant*

internal cost analysis FINANCE, BANKING, AND ACCOUNTING an examination of an organization's value-creating activities to determine sources of profitability and to identify the relative costs of different processes. Internal cost analysis is a tool for analyzing the *value chain*. Principal steps include identifying those processes that create value for the organization, calculating the cost of each value-creating process against the overall cost of the product or service, identifying the cost components for each process, establishing the links between the processes, and working out the opportunities for achieving relative cost advantage.

internal differentiation analysis GENERAL MANAGEMENT an examination of processes in the *value chain* to determine which of them create differentiation of the product or service in the customer's eyes, and thus enhance its value. Internal differentiation analysis enables an organization to focus on improving the identified processes to maximize *competitive advantage*. Steps involve identification of value-creating activities, evaluation of strategies that can enhance value for the customer, and assessment of which differentiation strategies are the most sustainable.

internal growth FINANCE, BANKING, AND ACCOUNTING organic growth created within a business, for example, by inventing new products and so increasing its market share, producing products that are more reliable, offering a more efficient service than its competitors, or being more aggressive in its marketing. See also *external growth*

internal marketing MARKETING the application of the principles of marketing within an organization. Internal marketing involves the creation of an internal market by dividing departments into *business units*, with control over their own operations and expenditure, with attendant impacts on *corporate culture*, politics, and power. Internal marketing also involves treating employees as internal customers with the goal of increasing employees' motivation and *customer focus*.

internal rate of return FINANCE, BANKING, AND ACCOUNTING in a discounted cash flow calculation, the rate of interest that reduces future income streams to the cost of the investment; practically speaking, the rate that indicates whether or not an investment is worth pursuing.

Let's assume that a project under consideration costs $7,500 and is expected to return $2,000 per year for five years, or $10,000. The IRR calculated for the project would be about 10%. If the cost of borrowing money for the project, or the return on investing the funds elsewhere, is less than 10%, the project is probably worthwhile. If the alternative use of the money will return 10% or more, the project should be rejected, since from a financial perspective it will break even at best.

Typically, managements require an IRR equal to or higher than the cost of capital, depending on relative risk and other factors.

The best way to compute an IRR is by using a spreadsheet (such as Excel) or financial calculator.

If using Excel, for example, select the IRR function. This requires the annual cash flows to be set out in columns and the first part of the IRR formula requires the cell reference range of these cash flows to be entered. Then a guess of the IRR is required. The default is 10%, written 0.1.

If a project has the following expected cash flows, then guessing IRR at 30% returns an accurate IRR of 27%, indicating that if the next best way of investing the money gives a return of –20%, the project should go ahead.

Now	-2,500
Year 1	1,200
Year 2	1,300
Year 3	1,500

IRR can be misleading, especially as significant costs will occur late in the project. The rule of thumb "the higher the IRR the better" does not always apply. For the most thorough analysis of a project's investment potential, some experts urge using both IRR and net present value calculations, and comparing their results. Abbr. *IRR*

internal recruitment HR & PERSONNEL *recruitment* carried out within the existing workforce. Internal recruitment gives employees opportunities for *promotion* and to develop new skills.

Internal Revenue Code FINANCE, BANKING, AND ACCOUNTING the complex series of federal tax laws

Internal Revenue Service FINANCE, BANKING, AND ACCOUNTING see *IRS*

internal versus external sourcing GENERAL MANAGEMENT see *purchasing versus production*

International Accounting Standards Board FINANCE, BANKING, AND ACCOUNTING an independent and privately funded accounting standards setting organization, based in London. The Board, whose members come from nine countries and a variety of backgrounds, is committed to developing a single set of high quality, understandable, and enforceable global standards that require transparent and comparable information in general purpose financial statements. It also works with national accounting standard setters to achieve convergence in accounting standards around the world. Abbr. *IASB*

International Accounting Standards Committee FINANCE, BANKING, AND ACCOUNTING an organization based in London that works toward achieving global agreement on accounting standards. Abbr. *IASC*

International Bank for Reconstruction and Development FINANCE, BANKING, AND ACCOUNTING see *IBRD*

International Centre for Settlement of Investment Disputes FINANCE, BANKING, AND ACCOUNTING one of the five institutions that comprises the World Bank Group. It was established in 1966 to undertake the role previously undertaken in a personal capacity by the President of the World Bank in assisting in mediation or conciliation of investment disputes between governments and private foreign investors. The overriding consideration in its establishment was that a specialist institution

could help to promote increased flows of international investment. Although ICSID has close links to the World Bank, it is an autonomous organization. Abbr. *ICSID*

International Chamber of Commerce FINANCE, BANKING, AND ACCOUNTING see *ICC*

International Depository Receipt FINANCE, BANKING, AND ACCOUNTING the equivalent of an *American depository receipt* in the rest of the world, an IDR is a negotiable certificate issued by a bank that indicates ownership of stock. Abbr. *IDR*

International Development Association FINANCE, BANKING, AND ACCOUNTING see *IDA*

International Energy Authority FINANCE, BANKING, AND ACCOUNTING see *IEA*

International Finance Corporation FINANCE, BANKING, AND ACCOUNTING see *IFC*

international fund FINANCE, BANKING, AND ACCOUNTING a mutual fund that invests in securities both inside and outside a country

International Fund for Agricultural Development FINANCE, BANKING, AND ACCOUNTING a specialized United Nations agency with a mandate to combat hunger and rural poverty in developing countries. Established as an international financial institution in 1977 following the 1974 World Food Conference, it has financed projects in over 100 countries and independent territories, to which it has committed U.S.$7.7 billion in grants and loans. It has three sources of finance (contributions from members, loan payments, and investment income) and an annual commitment level of approximately U.S.$450 million.

international management GENERAL MANAGEMENT
1 the maintenance and development of an organization's *production* or market interests across national borders with either local or *expatriate* staff
2 the process of running a *multinational business* made up of formerly independent organizations
3 the body of skills, knowledge, and understanding required to manage cross-cultural operations

International Monetary Fund FINANCE, BANKING, AND ACCOUNTING see *IMF*

International Organization of Securities Commissions FINANCE, BANKING, AND ACCOUNTING an organization of securities commissions

from around the world, based in Madrid. Its objectives are to promote high standards of regulation, exchange information, and establish standards for and effective surveillance of international securities transactions. Abbr. *IOSCO*

International Securities Market Association FINANCE, BANKING, AND ACCOUNTING the self-regulatory organization and trade association for the international securities market. Its primary role is to oversee the fast-changing marketplace through the issuing of rules and recommendations relating to trading and settlement practices. Established in 1969, the organization has over 600 members from 51 countries. Abbr. *ISMA*

International Union of Credit and Investment Insurers FINANCE, BANKING, AND ACCOUNTING an organization that works for international acceptance of sound principles of export credit and foreign investment insurance. Founded in 1934, the London-based Union has 51 members in 42 countries that play a role of central importance in world trade, both as regards exports and foreign direct investments. Also known as *Berne Union*

Internesia E-COMMERCE the tendency to find interesting Web sites on the Internet and then forget how to locate them again (*slang*)

Internet E-COMMERCE the global network of computers accessed with the aid of a modem. The Internet includes Web sites, e-mail, newsgroups, and other forums. It is a public network, although many of the computers connected to it are also part of *intranets*. It uses the *Internet Protocol* (IP) as a communication standard.

Internet access provider E-COMMERCE a company or organization that provides its customers with an entry point to the Internet via a dial-up connection, cable modem, or wireless application. Abbr. *IAP*

Internet commerce E-COMMERCE the part of *e-commerce* that consists of commercial transactions conducted over the Internet

Internet marketing E-COMMERCE marketing of products or services over the Web.
    Although similar in many ways to traditional marketing, Internet marketing is best suited to several particular purposes. It is ideal for marketing products and services that require a lot of information to sell, such as travel and books; products and services that people feel strongly

about, such as music and films (much of the success of *The Blair Witch Project* was credited to fans getting together on the Internet and promoting it through enthusiastic reviews and dialogue); and products and services that are bought by the Internet demographic.

In terms of advertising, online advertisements do not have the same impact as television or glossy media, as consumers are generally unwilling to download them. However, due to extensive *personalization* capabilities, Internet marketing has a unique ability to reach niche markets and target just the right consumer with just the right product.

Internet marketing is thus best used as an adjunct to a traditional offline marketing strategy. Offline marketing is used to raise consumer awareness and arouse interest; Internet marketing educates and answers questions by having comprehensive information on offer.

Internet merchant E-COMMERCE a businessperson who sells a product or service over the Internet

Internet message access protocol E-COMMERCE see *IMAP*

Internet payment system E-COMMERCE any mechanism for fund transfer from customer to merchant or business to business via the Internet. There are many payment options available, including credit card payment, credit transfer, electronic checks, direct debit, smart cards, prepaid plans, loyalty plan points-based approaches, person-to-person payments, and cellphone plans.

Getting the online payment system right is critical to the success of e-commerce. Currently, the most common form of online consumer payment is by credit card (90% in the United States; 70% in Europe). The most common business-to-business payments, however, are still offline—probably because such transactions often involve large sums of money.

Good online payment systems share key characteristics: ease of use; robustness and reliability; proper authentication (to combat fraud); efficient integration with the vendor's own internal systems; and security and assurance procedures which check that the seller gets the money and the buyer gets the goods.

Internet protocol E-COMMERCE see *Internet*. Abbr. *IP*

Internet security E-COMMERCE the means used to protect Web sites and other electronic files from attack by *hacker*s and *virus*es. The Internet is, by definition, a network; networks

are open, and are thus open to attack. A poor Internet security policy can result in a substantial loss of productivity and a drop in consumer confidence.

The essential elements of Internet security are constant vigilance—the perfect Internet security system will be out of date the next day; a combination of software and human expertise—security software can only do so much, it must be combined with human experience; and internal as well as external security—many security breaches come from within an organization.

Internet service provider E-COMMERCE see *ISP*

interoperability GENERAL MANAGEMENT the ability of products from different manufacturers to be used in conjunction with each other

interpersonal communication HR & PERSONNEL all aspects of personal interaction, contact, and communication between individuals or members of a group. Effective interpersonal communication depends on a variety of *interpersonal skills* including listening, asserting, influencing, persuading, empathizing, sensitivity, and diplomacy. Important aspects of communication between people include *body language* and other forms of *nonverbal communication*.

interpersonal skills HR & PERSONNEL see *interpersonal communication*

interquartile range STATISTICS the difference between the first and third quartiles of a statistical sample, used to measure the spread of variables in the data

interstate commerce FINANCE, BANKING, AND ACCOUNTING commerce that involves more than one state and is therefore subject to regulation by Congress. See also *intrastate commerce*

interstitial E-COMMERCE a Web advertisement that appears on its own page. This can either be sandwiched between content pages on a Web site, in a similar way to that used in traditional magazine advertising, or appear on its own before the actual Web page loads. The latter gets visitors' attention, but can be very frustrating.

intervention ECONOMICS government action to manipulate market forces for political or economic purposes

intervention mechanism FINANCE, BANKING, AND ACCOUNTING any of the methods used by central banks in maintaining exchange rate

parities, such as buying or selling of foreign currency

interviewer bias STATISTICS distortion in the results of a statistical survey caused by actions of the interviewer such as cues given to the interviewee

interviewing HR & PERSONNEL the practice of asking questions of another person in order to gain information and make an assessment. Interviewing is a selection tool used in recruitment to assess somebody's suitability for a job. A *structured interview* relies on asking the same job-related questions of all candidates and systematically evaluating their responses. There are two principal models: the *behavioral interview*, which strives to find out how applicants have behaved in the past in similar situations; and the *situational interview*, in which they are asked hypothetical questions to determine how they might act in the future. Interviewing is a technique also used in *counseling*, *performance appraisal*, and as part of a disciplinary procedure. See also *discipline*

in the money FINANCE, BANKING, AND ACCOUNTING used to refer to an option with *intrinsic value*

intranet E-COMMERCE a corporate network of computers utilizing Internet tools and technology for the purpose of communication and information sharing. Intranets have been introduced by many organizations as an aid to *internal communication*. Where an intranet is extended beyond the employees of an organization, perhaps to suppliers, customers, or distributors, it is called an *extranet*.

At their best, intranets can combine internal and external information resources in a one-stop information shop, and become the intellectual capital library of an organization, capturing staff knowledge, facilitating teamwork and collaboration, and providing an excellent induction vehicle for new employees. However, if not managed properly, intranets can easily evolve in a haphazard way with no clear objectives, and simply become information dumps. Consequently, staff do not use them and their potential is lost.

intrapreneur GENERAL MANAGEMENT an *employee* who uses the approach of an *entrepreneur* within an organizational setting. An intrapreneur must have freedom of action to explore and implement ideas, although the outcome of such work will be owned by the organization rather than the intrapreneur, and it is the organization that will take the associated risk. Managers of organizations in which

intrapreneurs are allowed to operate subscribe to the view that **innovation** can be achieved by encouraging **creative** and exploratory activity in semiautonomous units.

intrastate commerce FINANCE, BANKING, AND ACCOUNTING commerce that occurs within a single state. See also **interstate commerce**

in tray (*U.K.*) GENERAL MANAGEMENT = **in box**

intrinsic value FINANCE, BANKING, AND ACCOUNTING the difference between the exercise price of an option and its market value

introducing broker FINANCE, BANKING, AND ACCOUNTING a broker who cannot accept payment from customers

intuitive management GENERAL MANAGEMENT a **management style** that relies on gut feeling or a sixth sense, rather than on analytical or objective reasoning. Intuitive management exploits the holistic, imaginative, spiritual skills of the right side of the brain, whereas the conventional school of management favors the skills of the left side of the brain, which are logical, rational, linear, and mathematical in nature. Intuitive management is closely linked to a style of **decision making** that encourages **creativity** and **innovation**. Because this style of decision making has no rational basis, however, it can be difficult to justify decisions that turn out to be wrong.

inventory
1 GENERAL MANAGEMENT the stock of finished goods, raw materials, and work in progress held by a company
2 FINANCE, BANKING, AND ACCOUNTING the total of an organization's commercial assets

inventory record OPERATIONS & PRODUCTION a record of the **inventory** held by an organization. An inventory record forms an important part of material requirements planning systems. Such records usually make use of some form of part numbering or classification system, and include a description of the part, the quantity held, and the location of all the holdings. A **transaction file** keeps track of inventory use and replenishment.

inventory turnover FINANCE, BANKING, AND ACCOUNTING an accounting ratio of the number of times **inventory** is replaced during a given period. The ratio is calculated by dividing net sales by average inventory over a given period. Values are expressed as times per period, most often a year, and a higher figure indicates a more efficient manufacturing operation.

It is calculated as follows:

$$\frac{\text{Cost of goods sold}}{\text{Inventory}}$$

If COGS is $2 million, and inventory at the end of the period is $500,000, then

$$\frac{2,000,000}{500,000} = 4$$

Also known as **stock turns**

inverse floating rate note FINANCE, BANKING, AND ACCOUNTING a note whose interest rate varies inversely with a **benchmark interest rate**

inverted doughnut GENERAL MANAGEMENT see **doughnut principle**

inverted market FINANCE, BANKING, AND ACCOUNTING a situation in which near-term futures cost more than long-term futures for the same commodity

inverted yield curve FINANCE, BANKING, AND ACCOUNTING a yield curve with lower interest rates for long-term bonds than for short-term bonds. See also **yield curve**

investment GENERAL MANAGEMENT the spending of money on stocks and other securities, or on assets such as plant and machinery

investment analyst FINANCE, BANKING, AND ACCOUNTING an employee of a stock exchange company who researches other companies and identifies investment opportunities for clients. Also known as **financial analyst**

investment appraisal FINANCE, BANKING, AND ACCOUNTING analysis of the future profitability of capital purchases as an aid to good management

investment bank FINANCE, BANKING, AND ACCOUNTING
1 a bank that specializes in providing funds to corporate borrowers for start-up or expansion
2 a bank that does not accept deposits but provides services to those who offer securities to investors, and to those investors. U.K. term **merchant bank**. See also **commercial bank**. Abbr. **IB**

investment bill FINANCE, BANKING, AND ACCOUNTING a bill of exchange that is an investment

investment bond FINANCE, BANKING, AND ACCOUNTING in the United Kingdom, a product where the investment is paid as a single premium into a life insurance policy with an underlying asset-backed fund. The bondholder receives a regular income until the end of the bond's term when the investment—the current

value of the fund—is returned to the bondholder.

investment borrowing ECONOMICS the borrowing of funds intended to encourage a country's economic growth or to support the development of particular industries or regions by adding to physical or human capital

investment center FINANCE, BANKING, AND ACCOUNTING a profit center with additional responsibilities for capital investment, and possibly for financing, whose performance is measured by its return on investment

investment club FINANCE, BANKING, AND ACCOUNTING a group of people who join together to make investments in securities

investment committee FINANCE, BANKING, AND ACCOUNTING a group of employees of an investment bank who evaluate investment proposals

investment company FINANCE, BANKING, AND ACCOUNTING a company that pools for investment the money of several investors. See also **investment fund**

investment dealer (*Canada*) FINANCE, BANKING, AND ACCOUNTING a securities broker

investment fund FINANCE, BANKING, AND ACCOUNTING a savings plan that invests its clients' funds in corporate start-up or expansion projects. See also **investment company**

investment management agreement (*ANZ*) FINANCE, BANKING, AND ACCOUNTING a contract between an investor and an investment manager required under SIS legislation. Abbr. **IMA**

Investment Management Association FINANCE, BANKING, AND ACCOUNTING the trade body for the U.K. investment industry, formed in February 2002 following the merger of the Association of Unit Trusts and Investment Funds (AUTIF) and the Fund Managers' Association. Abbr. **IMA**

investment manager FINANCE, BANKING, AND ACCOUNTING see **fund manager**

investment portfolio FINANCE, BANKING, AND ACCOUNTING see **portfolio**

investment properties FINANCE, BANKING, AND ACCOUNTING either commercial buildings (for example, stores, factories, or offices) or residential dwellings (for example, houses or apartments) that are purchased by businesses or individuals for renting to third parties

a-z
1527

DICTIONARY

investment revaluation reserve (U.K.) FINANCE, BANKING, AND ACCOUNTING the capital reserve where changes in the value of a business's investment properties are disclosed when they are revalued

investment tax credit FINANCE, BANKING, AND ACCOUNTING a tax advantage for investment, available until 1986

investment trust FINANCE, BANKING, AND ACCOUNTING an investment company with a fixed number of shares available. Investment trusts trade like stocks.

investomer FINANCE, BANKING, AND ACCOUNTING a customer of a business who is also an investor (slang)

investor FINANCE, BANKING, AND ACCOUNTING a person or organization that invests money in something, especially in the stock of publicly owned corporations

investor relations research MARKETING research carried out on behalf of an organization in order to gain an understanding of how financial markets regard the organization, its stock, and its sector

invisible asset FINANCE, BANKING, AND ACCOUNTING see *intangible asset*

invisible earnings FINANCE, BANKING, AND ACCOUNTING foreign currency earned by a country in providing services, such as banking and tourism, rather than in selling goods

invisible exports ECONOMICS the profits, dividends, interest, and royalties received from selling a country's services abroad

invisible imports ECONOMICS the profits, dividends, interest, and royalties paid to foreign service companies based in a country

invisibles ECONOMICS items such as financial and leisure services, as opposed to physical goods, that are traded by a country

invisible trade ECONOMICS trade in items such as financial and other services that are listed in the current account of the balance of payments

invitation to tender GENERAL MANAGEMENT a formal statement of requirements sent to shortlisted suppliers, inviting the submission of a formal proposal for completing a particular piece of work. An invitation to tender should provide background information on the organization and identify the key areas that suppliers need to address such as functionality and operating requirements. A timetable for the tendering process should also be included.

invoice FINANCE, BANKING, AND ACCOUNTING a document that a supplier sends to a customer detailing the cost of products or services supplied and requesting payment

invoice date FINANCE, BANKING, AND ACCOUNTING the date on which an invoice is issued. The invoice date may be different from the delivery date.

invoice discounting FINANCE, BANKING, AND ACCOUNTING the selling of invoices at a discount for collection by the buyer

invoice register FINANCE, BANKING, AND ACCOUNTING a list of purchase invoices recording the date of receipt of the invoice, the supplier, the invoice value, and the person to whom the invoice has been passed to ensure that all invoices are processed by the accounting system

invoicing FINANCE, BANKING, AND ACCOUNTING the process of issuing invoices

involuntary liquidation preference FINANCE, BANKING, AND ACCOUNTING a payment that a company must make to holders of its preferred stock if it is forced to sell its assets when facing bankruptcy

inward investment FINANCE, BANKING, AND ACCOUNTING investment by a government or company in its own country or region, often to stimulate employment or develop a business infrastructure

IOD abbr FINANCE, BANKING, AND ACCOUNTING Institute of Directors

IOSCO abbr FINANCE, BANKING, AND ACCOUNTING International Organization of Securities Commissions

IOU FINANCE, BANKING, AND ACCOUNTING a rebus representing "I owe you" that can be used as legal evidence of a debt, although it is most commonly used by an individual as a reminder that small change has been taken, for example, from a float

IOW abbr GENERAL MANAGEMENT in other words (slang)

IP E-COMMERCE Internet protocol. See also *Internet*

IP address E-COMMERCE Internet Protocol address, an identifier for a computer or other Internet-enabled device on the Internet and other *TCP/IP* networks. The format of an IP address is a numeric address written as four groups of numbers separated by dots. For example, 1.542.20.350 could be an IP address.

IPO abbr FINANCE, BANKING, AND ACCOUNTING initial public offering

IRA abbr FINANCE, BANKING, AND ACCOUNTING individual retirement account: a pension plan, designed for individuals without a company pension plan, that allows annual sums, subject to limits dependent upon employment income, to be set aside from earnings tax-free. Individuals with a company pension may invest in an IRA, but only from their net income. IRAs, including the Education IRA, designed as a way of saving for children's education, may invest in almost any financial security except real estate.

IRCA (ANZ) HR & PERSONNEL see *Industrial Relations Court of Australia*

IRD (ANZ) FINANCE, BANKING, AND ACCOUNTING full form *Inland Revenue Department*

IRD number (ANZ) FINANCE, BANKING, AND ACCOUNTING a numeric code assigned to all members of the New Zealand workforce for the purpose of paying income tax

IRL abbr GENERAL MANAGEMENT in real life (slang)

IRR abbr FINANCE, BANKING, AND ACCOUNTING internal rate of return

irredeemable bond FINANCE, BANKING, AND ACCOUNTING a government bond which has no date of maturity and which therefore provides interest but can never be redeemed at full value

irrevocable letter of credit FINANCE, BANKING, AND ACCOUNTING see *letter of credit*

irritainment GENERAL MANAGEMENT television programs or other forms of entertainment that are irritating but nevertheless compulsive viewing (slang)

IRS abbr FINANCE, BANKING, AND ACCOUNTING Internal Revenue Service: in the United States, the branch of the federal government charged with collecting the majority of federal taxes

ISA abbr FINANCE, BANKING, AND ACCOUNTING Individual Savings Account: an equivalent in the United Kingdom of a Roth Individual Retirement Account in the United States

ISC (ANZ) GENERAL MANAGEMENT see *Insurance and Superannuation Commission*

ISCID *abbr* International Centre for Settlement of Investment Disputes

ISDA *abbr* FINANCE, BANKING, AND ACCOUNTING International Swaps and Derivatives Association

ISDN *abbr* E-COMMERCE Integrated Services Digital Network: a digital telephone network supporting advanced communications services and used for high-speed data transmission

ISDN line E-COMMERCE a digital telephone line supporting advanced communications services and used for high-speed data transmission

Ishikawa, Kaoru (1915–89) GENERAL MANAGEMENT Japanese academic. Originator of *fishbone charts* and champion of other *quality control* tools such as *Pareto charts*, as explained in *Guide to Quality Control* (1976).

Ishikawa diagram GENERAL MANAGEMENT see *fishbone chart*

ISMA *abbr* FINANCE, BANKING, AND ACCOUNTING International Securities Market Association

ISO *abbr*
1 E-COMMERCE independent service organization: a company that processes online credit card transactions for small businesses, usually in exchange for a fee or percentage of sales
2 GENERAL MANAGEMENT International Standards Organization: an organization responsible for determining and managing common standards for products and for business and manufacturing processes

ISO 9000 GENERAL MANAGEMENT a series of international quality management system *standards*. ISO 9000 provides a framework that can be used by any size or type of organization to develop a quality system. It lays down a general set of principles about good management practice, which identify the basic disciplines and specify criteria to ensure that products and services meet customers' requirements. The framework enables the measurement of consistency of an organization's systems for dealing with customer orders, purchasing, stock control, service provision, and service delivery. Requirements for certification include written quality procedures, regular management reviews, control of documentation, traceability, internal auditing, and the provision of training.

ISO 14000 GENERAL MANAGEMENT a series of internationally recognized *quality standards* providing a framework that organizations can use to regulate the environmental impact of their activities. ISO 14000 is a management system standard rather than a performance standard and can be applied to organizations of all shapes and sizes, wherever they may be located. The standard does not identify specific goals but presents a framework for carrying out environmental management. *ISO 14001* is the part of the standard that specifies the requirements that organizations must meet if they are to obtain certification. ISO 14001 gives a framework for identifying operations, processes, and products that impact the environment, for evaluating these impacts, for setting objectives and targets for reducing any negative impacts that have been identified, and for implementing activities to achieve targets. ISO 14000 provides a certified standard that can be seen as a reflection of an organization's ethical achievements. It pays no attention, however, to cultural or human dimensions and disregards the fact that organizations will need to perceive bottom-line cost benefits if they are to implement the standard.

ISO 14001 GENERAL MANAGEMENT see *ISO 14000*

ISP *abbr* E-COMMERCE Internet service provider: a company or organization that not only provides an entry point to the Internet, like an *Internet access provider*, but also additional services such as Web site hosting and Web page development

issuance costs FINANCE, BANKING, AND ACCOUNTING the underwriting, legal, and administrative fees required to issue a debt. These fees are significant when issuing debt in the public markets, such as bonds. However, other types of debt, such as private placements or bank loans, are cheaper to issue because they require less underwriting, legal, and administrative support.

issue FINANCE, BANKING, AND ACCOUNTING a set of stocks or bonds that a company offers for sale at one time

issue by tender FINANCE, BANKING, AND ACCOUNTING see *sale by tender*

issued capital FINANCE, BANKING, AND ACCOUNTING an amount of capital which is formed of money paid for shares issued to stockholders

Issue Department FINANCE, BANKING, AND ACCOUNTING the department of the Bank of England that is responsible for issuing currency

issued price FINANCE, BANKING, AND ACCOUNTING the price of stocks in a new company when they are offered for sale for the first time

issued share capital FINANCE, BANKING, AND ACCOUNTING the type, class, number, and amount of the shares held by stockholders

issued shares FINANCE, BANKING, AND ACCOUNTING those shares that comprise a company's authorized capital that has been distributed to investors. They may be either fully paid or partly paid shares.

issue price FINANCE, BANKING, AND ACCOUNTING the price at which securities are first offered for sale

issuer E-COMMERCE FINANCE, BANKING, AND ACCOUNTING a financial institution that issues payment cards such as credit or debit cards, pays out to the merchant's account, and bills the customer or debits the customer's account. The issuer guarantees payment for authorized transactions using the payment card. Also known as *card-issuing bank*, *issuing bank*

issuer bid FINANCE, BANKING, AND ACCOUNTING an offer made by an issuer for its own securities when it is disappointed by the offers of others

issues management GENERAL MANAGEMENT the anticipation and assessment of key trends and themes of the next decade, and the relation of these to the organization. Issues management is informed by *futures research* in order to formulate strategic plans and actions.

issuing bank E-COMMERCE FINANCE, BANKING, AND ACCOUNTING see *issuer*

issuing house FINANCE, BANKING, AND ACCOUNTING in the United Kingdom, a financial institution that specializes in the flotation of private companies. See also *investment bank*, *merchant bank*

IT *abbr* FINANCE, BANKING, AND ACCOUNTING income tax

itchy finger syndrome E-COMMERCE the Internet user's need for interactivity. Sites can combat this by adding interactive elements such as *hyperlinks* and online *forums*.

item
1 FINANCE, BANKING, AND ACCOUNTING a single piece of information included in a company's accounts
2 GENERAL MANAGEMENT one of the subjects selected for discussion during a meeting and listed on an *agenda*

item non-response STATISTICS a refusal to respond to a question in a statistical survey or a response that cannot be fitted into the given response design

J

jack in GENERAL MANAGEMENT to connect to something electronically, especially to a network via a modem or other communication device

Japanese management GENERAL MANAGEMENT HR & PERSONNEL a *management style* with particular emphasis on employees and manufacturing techniques, to which the Japanese economic miracle that began in the 1960s is attributed. Japanese management practices have been studied in the rest of the world in the hope that the economic success they brought to Japan can be recreated elsewhere. These practices emphasize forming collaborations, particularly in times of uncertainty, human resources, closer superior-subordinate relationships, and consensus as a means of facilitating implementation. *Richard Pascale* and *Anthony Athos* suggested that the Japanese *competitive advantage* stemmed from skills, staff, and superordinate goals, the softer features identified by the *McKinsey 7-S framework*. Other dominant characteristics include people-centered management, loyalty to employees, *just-in-time*, *kaizen*, *continuous improvement*, *quality control*, *total quality management*, and the ideas of *W. Edwards Deming*. *William Ouchi* expounded *Theory J* and *Theory Z*, which demonstrated the differences between U.S. and Japanese styles of management. With the downturn in the Japanese economy in the 1990s, management practices were reappraised, and there emerged a focus on radical change as opposed to incremental improvement. Customers were offered less variety, there was a shift toward simplicity, and an alternative to consensus-based decision making was adopted, with individuals making decisions based on high-tech information systems. See thinker *W. Edwards Deming*, *Richard Tanner Pascale*

Japanese payment option E-COMMERCE a series of extensions to the *SET* protocol to facilitate handling features unique to the Japanese market. Abbr *JPO*

Jaques, Elliot (1917–2003) GENERAL MANAGEMENT Canadian psychologist and writer. Best known for his participation in the *Glacier studies*, and for originating the *time span of discretion* theory.

Java™ E-COMMERCE a programming language developed in the mid-1990s to enhance the visual appearance and interactive elements of Web documents. Java™ is automatically translated using a Java™-compatible Web browser.

For example, an Internet user can connect to a Java™ *applet* on the Web, download it, and run it, all at the click of a mouse.

jelly

like nailing jelly to a tree GENERAL MANAGEMENT used for describing a task that is considered impossible, especially when the difficulty arises from poor or sloppy specifications (*slang*)

Jensen's measure FINANCE, BANKING, AND ACCOUNTING see *risk-adjusted return on capital*

JEPI *abbr* E-COMMERCE joint electronic payment initiative

jikan FINANCE, BANKING, AND ACCOUNTING in Japan, the priority rule relating to transactions on the Tokyo Stock Exchange whereby the earlier of two buy or sell orders received at the same price prevails

JIT *abbr* OPERATIONS & PRODUCTION just-in-time

job

1 FINANCE, BANKING, AND ACCOUNTING a customer order or task of a relatively short duration
2 HR & PERSONNEL a position of employment
3 OPERATIONS & PRODUCTION a batch of work that undergoes a specific action through a workstation or workshop

jobber's turn FINANCE, BANKING, AND ACCOUNTING formerly, a term used on the London Stock Exchange for a *spread*

jobbing OPERATIONS & PRODUCTION see *job production*

jobbing backward FINANCE, BANKING, AND ACCOUNTING a U.K. term for the analysis of an investment transaction with a view to learning from mistakes rather than apportioning blame

job classification HR & PERSONNEL the listing of jobs in groups according to areas of similarity. At an organizational level, job classification is often referred to as *job grading* and is used for *job evaluation* purposes.

job design HR & PERSONNEL the process of putting together various elements to form a job, bearing in mind organizational and individual worker requirements, as well as considerations of health, safety, and *ergonomics*. The *scientific management* approach of *Frederick Winslow Taylor* viewed job design as purely mechanistic, but the later *human relations* movement rediscovered the importance of workers' relationship to their work and stressed the importance of *job satisfaction*.

job enlargement HR & PERSONNEL the addition of extra similar tasks to a job. In job enlargement, the job itself remains essentially unchanged, the employee rarely needs to acquire new skills to perform the additional task, and the motivational benefits of job enrichment are not experienced. Job enlargement is sometimes viewed by employees as a requirement to perform more work for the same amount of pay.

job evaluation HR & PERSONNEL a technique that strives to provide a systematic, rational, and consistent approach to defining the relative worth of jobs within an organization. Job evaluation is a system for analyzing and comparing different jobs and placing them in a ranking order according to the overall demands of each one. It is not concerned with the volume of work, or with the person doing it, or with determining pay. It is used in order to provide the basis for an equitable and defensible pay structure, particularly in determining *equal pay* for equal value. Job evaluation programs can be divided into two main categories: nonanalytical and analytical. In nonanalytical programs a job is compared with others as a whole, but such programs have a limited use, because they are unlikely to succeed as a defense against an equal value claim. In an analytical program, a job is split up into a number of different aspects and each factor is measured separately. The main types of analytical programs are factor comparison, point-factor rating, competency-based programs, and the *profile method*.

job family HR & PERSONNEL a category of jobs in a similar area. Examples of job families might be engineering, agriculture, health, and sports and leisure. Job families are also found within an organization, for example, clerical, sales, information technology, and so on. Such families are sometimes used when determining *pay scales* or for statistical analysis of the *workforce*.

job grading HR & PERSONNEL see *job classification*

job lock GENERAL MANAGEMENT the inability to leave a job because of a fear of losing the benefits associated with it (*slang*)

job lot (*U.K.*) FINANCE, BANKING, AND ACCOUNTING a miscellaneous assortment of items, including securities, that are offered as a single deal

job process system OPERATIONS & PRODUCTION see *job production*

job production OPERATIONS & PRODUCTION the manufacture of different products in unit quantities or in very small numbers. In job production, a complete task may be handled by one worker and is often carried out in a *job shop*. A company may operate under a *job process system*, producing small batches of sometimes unique products and so becoming a job shop in itself. Job production is characterized by a functional grouping of equipment and staff and by the considerable variation in the time it takes to complete a given job. Also known as *jobbing*

job rotation HR & PERSONNEL the movement of employees through a variety of jobs in order to increase interest and *motivation*. Job rotation can improve *multiskilling* but involves the need for greater *training*.

job satisfaction HR & PERSONNEL the sense of fulfillment and pride felt by people who enjoy their work and do it well. Various factors influence job satisfaction, and our understanding of the significance of these stems in part from *Frederick Herzberg*. He called elements such as remuneration, working relationships, status, and job security "*hygiene factors*" because they concern the context in which somebody works. Hygiene factors do not in themselves promote job satisfaction, but serve primarily to prevent job dissatisfaction. *Motivators* contribute to job satisfaction and include achievement, recognition, the work itself, responsibility, advancement, and growth. An absence of job satisfaction can lead to poor *motivation*, *stress*, *absenteeism*, and high labor turnover.

job-share HR & PERSONNEL a form of employment in which two or more people occupy a single job. Each person works on a part-time basis and is paid pro-rata for the number of hours they work in the job.

job shop OPERATIONS & PRODUCTION a manufacturing facility designed to work on a *job production* basis, producing small quantities of what are often specialized or expensive items. A job shop can be a special facility within a factory, or a whole company can be run as a job shop. Job shops often have the ability to produce a wide variety of products.

job vacuum GENERAL MANAGEMENT an employee who voluntarily takes on extra duties (*slang*)

Johari window HR & PERSONNEL a *communication* model that facilitates analysis of both how someone gives and receives information and the dynamics of *interpersonal communica-*

tion. The Johari window was developed by Joseph Luft and Henry Ingram. It is normally represented in the form of a grid divided into four sections, each of which represents a type of communication exchange. First, there is the open self: you have awareness of the impact you have on the other and the impact they have on you, so that the risk of interpersonal conflict is minimized. The second sector covers the hidden self: you have awareness of your impact on others, but not of their impact on you. This leads to defensive behavior in which you seek to hide what you want and increases the possibility of interpersonal conflict. In the third sector, or blind self, you have awareness of what the other wants, but you lack self-awareness of the impact of your communication or actions. Finally, there is the undiscovered self: you lack self-awareness and are either unaware of or cannot understand the other. Although the Johari window can be used in a number of situations, it is most frequently used as a tool for *training* or *coaching* purposes, in order to provide feedback on communication skills.

Johnson, Spencer GENERAL MANAGEMENT U.S. writer and consultant. Collaborated with *Kenneth Blanchard* on the concept of one minute management, but is also known for *Who Moved My Cheese?* (1998), a parable on *change management*. See thinker *Kenneth Blanchard*

joined-up (*U.K.*) GENERAL MANAGEMENT relating to an idea or initiative that involves both the community and government in an effort to improve the quality of life for everyone (*slang*)

joint account FINANCE, BANKING, AND ACCOUNTING an account, for example, one held at a bank or by a broker, that two or more people own in common and have access to

joint and several liability FINANCE, BANKING, AND ACCOUNTING a legal liability that applies to a group of individuals as a whole and each member individually, so that if one member does not meet his or her liability, the shortfall is the shared responsibility of the others. Most guarantees given by two or more individuals to secure borrowing are joint and several. It is a typical feature of most partnership agreements.

joint electronic payment initiative E-COMMERCE a proposed industry standard protocol for electronic payment in e-commerce transactions. Abbr. *JEPI*

joint float ECONOMICS a group of currencies which maintains a fixed internal relationship and moves jointly in relation to another currency

joint life annuity FINANCE, BANKING, AND ACCOUNTING an annuity that continues until both parties have died. They are attractive to married couples as they ensure that the survivor has an income for the rest of his or her life.

joint ownership GENERAL MANAGEMENT ownership by more than one party, each with equal rights in the item owned. Joint ownership is often applied to property or other assets.

Joint Photographics Experts Group E-COMMERCE see *JPEG*

joint return FINANCE, BANKING, AND ACCOUNTING a tax return filed jointly by a husband and wife

joint stock bank FINANCE, BANKING, AND ACCOUNTING a term that was formerly used for a commercial bank (one that is a partnership), as opposed to a bank that is a public limited company

joint venture FINANCE, BANKING, AND ACCOUNTING a business project in which two or more independent companies collaborate and share the risks and rewards. Abbr. *JV*

journal FINANCE, BANKING, AND ACCOUNTING a record of original entry, into which transactions are normally transferred from source documents. The journal may be subdivided into: sales journal/day book for credit sales; purchases journal/day book for credit purchases; cash book for cash receipts and payments; and the journal proper for transactions which could not appropriately be recorded in any of the other journals.

JPEG *abbr* E-COMMERCE joint photographics experts group: a file format used to compress and store photographic images for transfer over the Internet

JPO *abbr* E-COMMERCE Japanese payment option

JSE *abbr* FINANCE, BANKING, AND ACCOUNTING Johannesburg Stock Exchange: the former unofficial name of the JSE Securities Exchange

judgment creditor FINANCE, BANKING, AND ACCOUNTING in a legal action, the individual or business who has brought the action and to whom the court orders the judgment debtor to pay the money owed. In the event of the judgment debtor not conforming to the court order, the judgment creditor must return to the court to request that the judgment be enforced.

judgment debtor FINANCE, BANKING, AND ACCOUNTING in a legal action, the individual or business ordered to pay the judgment creditor the money owed

jumbo mortgage FINANCE, BANKING, AND ACCOUNTING a mortgage that is too large to qualify for favorable treatment by a government agency

junior capital FINANCE, BANKING, AND ACCOUNTING capital in the form of stockholders' equity, which is repaid only after secured loans (or senior capital) have been paid if the firm goes into liquidation

junior debt FINANCE, BANKING, AND ACCOUNTING a debt that has no claim on a debtor's assets, or less claim than another debt. See also *senior debt*

junior mortgage FINANCE, BANKING, AND ACCOUNTING a mortgage whose holder has less claim on a debtor's assets than the holder of another mortgage. See also *senior mortgage*

junk bond FINANCE, BANKING, AND ACCOUNTING a high-yielding bond issued on a low-grade security. The issue of junk bonds has most commonly been linked with takeover activity.

Juran, **Joseph Moses** (*b*. 1904) GENERAL MANAGEMENT Romanian-born engineer and consultant. Introduced ideas on *total quality management* to Japan and later, like *W. Edwards Deming*, to the West. Juran's methods, first published in *Quality Control Handbook* (1951), center on building a customer-focused organization through planning, control and improvement, and good people management.

Juran trained as an electrical engineer, worked for Western Electric in the 1920s, becoming quality manager at their Chicago plant, and later went to work for AT&T. In 1953, he made his first visit to Japan, where he spent two months observing Japanese practices and training managers and engineers in what he called managing for quality. For the next quarter of a century, Juran continued to give seminars on the subject of quality throughout the world. In 1979 he founded the Juran Institute to spread and facilitate the implementation of quality-management programs worldwide. See thinker *W. Edwards Deming*

just-in-time OPERATIONS & PRODUCTION GENERAL MANAGEMENT a manufacturing philosophy involving the total elimination of waste. Just-in-time is a system of supplying to each process what is needed, at the time it is needed, and in the quantity it is needed. Production *lead time* is minimized and significant savings can be made from reduced *inventory*. Just-in-time requires all activities in the production process to be geared to adding value for the customer. Critical components of the system include *total quality management* and *employee*

involvement. The concept was invented by Kiichiro Toyoda and developed further by *Taiichi Ohno* at the Toyota Motor Company following World War II. *Kanban* is part of this system but is aimed solely at the elimination of waste. Abbr. *JIT*

JV *abbr* FINANCE, BANKING, AND ACCOUNTING joint venture

K

K *abbr* FINANCE, BANKING, AND ACCOUNTING a thousand

kaizen GENERAL MANAGEMENT OPERATIONS & PRODUCTION the Japanese term for the *continuous improvement* of current processes. Kaizen is derived from the words "kai," meaning "change," and "zen," meaning "good" or "for the better." It is a philosophy that can be applied to any area of life, but its application has been most famously developed at the Toyota Motor Company, and it underlies the philosophy of *total quality management*. Under kaizen, continuous improvement can mean waste elimination, innovation, or working to new standards. The kaizen process makes use of a variety of techniques, including small-group *problem solving*, statistical techniques, *brainstorming*, and *work study*. Although kaizen forms only part of a strategy of continuous improvement, for many employees it is the element that most closely affects them and is therefore synonymous with continuous improvement.

kakaku yusen FINANCE, BANKING, AND ACCOUNTING in Japan, the price priority system operated on the Tokyo Stock Exchange whereby a lower price takes precedence over a higher price for a sell order, and vice versa for a buy order. See also *jikan*

kanban OPERATIONS & PRODUCTION a Japanese production management technique that uses cards attached to components to monitor and control workflow in a factory. The kanban system was first developed by the car manufacturer Toyota.

kanbrain GENERAL MANAGEMENT relating to the technology that is used in the transmission of knowledge (*slang*)

kangaroo FINANCE, BANKING, AND ACCOUNTING an Australian stock traded on the London Stock Exchange (*slang*)

Kansas City Board of Trade FINANCE, BANKING, AND ACCOUNTING a commodities exchange, established in 1856, that specializes in futures

and options contracts for red winter wheat, the Value Line™ Index, natural gas, and the ISDEX™ Internet Stock Index

Kanter, **Rosabeth Moss** (*b*. 1943) GENERAL MANAGEMENT U.S. academic. Known for her interest in new *organization structures*, with a focus on harnessing *change*, encouraging *innovation*, and increasing *empowerment* among employees. Her research has also embraced *globalization*. Among her many books is *The Change Masters* (1988). See thinker *Rosabeth Moss Kanter*

Kaplan, **Robert S.** GENERAL MANAGEMENT U.S. academic. Codeveloper, with *David P. Norton*, of the *balanced scorecard*, which looks at intangible assets such as *customer satisfaction* alongside traditional financial measures. This concept, introduced in a *Harvard Business Review* article of 1992 with the saying "What you measure is what you get," was explained in *The Balanced Scorecard* (1996). See thinker *Robert S. Kaplan*

KBG GENERAL MANAGEMENT OPERATIONS & PRODUCTION see *keiretsu*

Keidanren FINANCE, BANKING, AND ACCOUNTING the Japanese abbreviation for the Japan Federation of Economic Organizations. Established in 1946, it strives to work toward a resolution of the major problems facing the Japanese and international business communities and to contribute to the sound development of their economies. Its members include over 1,000 of Japan's leading corporations (including over 50 foreign companies) and over 100 industry-wide groups representing such major sectors as manufacturing, trade, distribution, finance, and energy.

keiretsu *or* **Keiretsu Business Group** GENERAL MANAGEMENT OPERATIONS & PRODUCTION a Japanese loose *conglomerate company* that promotes interdependencies between firms with interlocking interests in each other and is characterized by close internal control, policy coordination, and cohesiveness. Keiretsu business groups are alliances between firms that share close buyer-supplier relationships. The issue of interlocking stocks by group affiliated companies to member companies of the group keeps ownership in friendly hands, helps prevent foreign *takeovers*, and aids a company's long-term survival and growth. There are two sorts of keiretsu operation: *horizontal keiretsu*, in which member firms are involved in different industries, and *vertical keiretsu*, in which member firms in one industry form themselves into a hierarchy with a lead company. Vertical KBGs consist largely of manufacturing companies and their subcontractors.

Some keiretsu are 350 years old, but most developed from the prewar *zaibatsu*. The Korean equivalent of the keiretsu is the *chaebol*, and a Mexican equivalent is the *grupo*. Abbr. *KBG*

Keough Plan FINANCE, BANKING, AND ACCOUNTING a pension subject to tax advantage for somebody who is self-employed or has an interest in a small company. See also *stakeholder pension*

Kepner, **Charles Higgins** (*b.* 1922) GENERAL MANAGEMENT U.S. manager and consultant. Originator with *Benjamin Tregoe* of a methodological approach to *decision making* based on information gathering, organization, and analysis, which was first explained in *The Rational Manager* (1965).

kerb market (*U.K.*) FINANCE, BANKING, AND ACCOUNTING a stock market that exists outside the stock exchange. The term originates from markets held in the street.

Kets de Vries, **Manfred Florian Robert** (*b.* 1942) GENERAL MANAGEMENT Dutch psychoanalyst and academic. His principal academic interests focus on the interface between psychoanalysis/dynamic psychiatry and *management*, *leadership*, *entrepreneurship*, and *family business*.

key account management MARKETING the management of the customer relationships that are most important to a company. Key accounts are those held by customers who produce most *profit* for a company or have the potential to do so, or those who are of strategic importance. Development of these *customer relations* and *customer retention* is important to business success. Particular emphasis is placed on analyzing which accounts are key to a company at any one time, determining the needs of these particular customers, and implementing procedures to ensure that they receive premium *customer service* and to increase *customer satisfaction*.

keyboard plaque GENERAL MANAGEMENT the buildup of dirt that becomes ingrained in computer keyboards (*slang*)

key-man insurance GENERAL MANAGEMENT see *key-person insurance*

Keynesian economics ECONOMICS the economic teachings and doctrines associated with John Maynard Keynes

key-person insurance GENERAL MANAGEMENT an insurance policy taken out to cover the costs of replacing a key *employee*. Key-person insurance comes into play in the case of an employee's medium- to long-term sickness or death. Also known as *key-man insurance*

keyword E-COMMERCE a word used by a search engine to help locate and register a Web site. Companies need to think very carefully about the keywords they place in their *meta-tags* and in Web pages in order to attract relevant search-engine traffic.

keyword search E-COMMERCE a search for documents containing one or more words that are specified by a search-engine user

kiasu GENERAL MANAGEMENT a Hokkien word, used to describe the "must win, never lose" mentality of Singaporeans

kickback FINANCE, BANKING, AND ACCOUNTING a sum of money paid illegally in order to gain concessions or favors (*slang*)

kicker FINANCE, BANKING, AND ACCOUNTING an addition to a standard security that makes it more attractive, for example, options and warrants. (*slang*) See also *bells and whistles* *sweetener*

kill FINANCE, BANKING, AND ACCOUNTING to stop, as in the request "kill that order" (*slang*)

killer app E-COMMERCE a computer application that is extremely effective or commercially successful

killer bee FINANCE, BANKING, AND ACCOUNTING somebody, especially a banker, who helps a company avoid being taken over

killfile E-COMMERCE a list on an Internet newsreader of undesirable authors or threads that can be filtered out by the user (*slang*)

killing FINANCE, BANKING, AND ACCOUNTING a considerable profit on a transaction (*slang*)

Kim, **W. Chan** GENERAL MANAGEMENT Koreanborn academic. INSEAD professor, Fellow of the World Economic Forum, writer on the knowledge economy and collaborator with *Renée Mauborgne* on research into *corporate strategy* and *value innovation*.

kimono
open the kimono GENERAL MANAGEMENT to inspect something that has not been open for examination before, especially a company's accounts (*slang*)

KISS *abbr* GENERAL MANAGEMENT keep it simple stupid (*slang*)

kiss up to somebody GENERAL MANAGEMENT to attempt to ingratiate yourself with somebody who is in a position of power (*slang*)

kite FINANCE, BANKING, AND ACCOUNTING
1 a fraudulent financial transaction, for example, a bad check that is dated to take advantage of the time interval required for clearing
2 to write bad checks in order to take advantage of the time interval required for clearing
fly a kite 1 GENERAL MANAGEMENT to make a suggestion in order to test people's opinion of it
2 FINANCE, BANKING, AND ACCOUNTING to use a fraudulent financial document such as a bad check

kiwibond FINANCE, BANKING, AND ACCOUNTING a Eurobond denominated in New Zealand dollars

knight FINANCE, BANKING, AND ACCOUNTING GENERAL MANAGEMENT a term borrowed from chess strategy to describe a company involved in the politics of a *takeover* bid. There are three main types of knights. A *white knight* is a company that is friendly to the board of the company to be acquired. If the white knight gains control, it may retain the existing *board of directors*. A *black knight* is a former white knight that has disagreed with the board of the company to be acquired and has established its own hostile bid. A *gray knight* is a white knight that does not have the confidence of the company to be acquired.

Knight, **Phil** (*b.* 1938) GENERAL MANAGEMENT U.S. entrepreneur. Founder of Nike Inc., whose worldwide success is based on strong *brand building*, aggressive marketing, and the *outsourcing* of production to Asia.

knock-for-knock (*U.K.*) FINANCE, BANKING, AND ACCOUNTING used to describe a practice between insurance companies whereby each will pay for the repairs to the vehicle it insures in the event of an accident

knocking copy GENERAL MANAGEMENT advertising copy that consists of criticism of a competitor's product or company

knockout option FINANCE, BANKING, AND ACCOUNTING an option to which a condition relating to the underlying security's or commodity's present price is attached so that it effectively expires when it goes out of the money

know-how GENERAL MANAGEMENT practical knowledge and experience of a particular product, market, or technology

know-how fund FINANCE, BANKING, AND ACCOUNTING a fund created by the U.S.

government to provide technical training and advice to countries of Eastern Europe

knowledge GENERAL MANAGEMENT information acquired by the interpretation of experience. Knowledge is built up from interaction with the world and organized and stored in each individual's mind. It is also stored on an organizational level within the minds of employees and in paper and electronic records. Two forms of knowledge can be distinguished: *tacit knowledge* or *implicit knowledge*, which is held in a person's mind and is instinctively known without being formulated into words; and *explicit knowledge*, which has been communicated to others and is contained in written documents and procedures. Organizations are increasingly recognizing the value of knowledge, and many employees are now recognized as *knowledge workers*. A major writer in this area is *Ikujiro Nonaka*, coauthor of *The Knowledge-creating Company* (1995), who asserted that knowledge is the greatest *core capability* (see *core competence*) that an organization can have.

knowledge capital GENERAL MANAGEMENT knowledge that a company possesses and can put to profitable use

knowledge management GENERAL MANAGEMENT
1 the process of acquiring, storing, distributing, and using information within a company. The information is generally held on a powerful database and distributed via a communications network.
2 the coordination and exploitation of an organization's *knowledge* resources, in order to create benefit and *competitive advantage*. See thinker *Peter Drucker*

knowledge worker GENERAL MANAGEMENT an *employee* who deals in information, ideas, and expertise. Knowledge workers are products of the so-called information age, in which the emphasis is on *creativity* and *innovation* rather than on maintaining the status quo. According to *Peter Drucker*, in the new economy every employee is becoming a knowledge worker.

Kolb, David A. (*b.* 1939) GENERAL MANAGEMENT U.S. academic. Originator of the concept of *experiential learning*, a model describing how adults learn, which he explained in his book of the same name (1984).

Kotler, Philip (*b.* 1931) GENERAL MANAGEMENT U.S. academic. Acknowledged as an expert in marketing theory, which he has made a major business function and academic discipline,

and which he explained in *Marketing Management* (first published 1980).

Krugerrand FINANCE, BANKING, AND ACCOUNTING a South African coin consisting of one ounce of gold, first minted in 1967, bearing the portrait of 19th-century statesman and South African president Paul Kruger on the obverse

L

laboratory training GENERAL MANAGEMENT see *sensitivity training*

labor dispute HR & PERSONNEL
1 a disagreement or conflict between an *employer* and *employees* or between the *employers' association* and *labor union*
2 see *strike*

labor force HR & PERSONNEL people of working age who are available for paid employment, including the unemployed looking for work, but excluding categories such as full-time students, caregivers, and the long-term sick and disabled

labor force survey STATISTICS a survey carried out every quarter in the United Kingdom, covering such topics as unemployment and hours of work

labor-intensive FINANCE, BANKING, AND ACCOUNTING involving large numbers of workers or high labor costs

labor market HR & PERSONNEL a market that brings together employers and people who are looking for employment

labor shortage HR & PERSONNEL
1 a lack of workers or potential workers to fill the jobs available
2 a lack of suitably qualified and skilled workers to fill particular vacancies. This is more correctly described as a *skills shortage*.

labor tourist HR & PERSONNEL somebody who lives in one country but works in another (*slang*)

labor union GENERAL MANAGEMENT HR & PERSONNEL an organization of *employees* within a trade or profession that has the objective of representing its members' interests, primarily through improving pay and conditions, and provides a variety of services. U.K. term *trade union*

Lady Macbeth strategy GENERAL MANAGEMENT a change of approach on the part of a

presumed white knight, in which it becomes a black knight. A Lady Macbeth strategy is usually associated with *takeover* battles and has connotations of treachery.

laggard MARKETING see *first mover*

lagging indicator ECONOMICS a measurable economic factor, for example, corporate profits or unemployment, that changes after the economy has already moved to a new trend, which it can confirm but not predict

LAN E-COMMERCE see *network*

land bank (*U.K.*) FINANCE, BANKING, AND ACCOUNTING the land that a builder or developer has that is available for development

land banking FINANCE, BANKING, AND ACCOUNTING the practice of buying land that is not needed immediately, but with the expectation of using it in the future

landed costs FINANCE, BANKING, AND ACCOUNTING costs of goods which have been delivered to a port, unloaded, and passed through customs

landing order FINANCE, BANKING, AND ACCOUNTING a permit which allows goods to be unloaded into a bonded warehouse without paying customs duty

land tax FINANCE, BANKING, AND ACCOUNTING a form of wealth tax imposed in Australia on the value of residential land. The level and conditions of the tax vary from state to state.

lapping FINANCE, BANKING, AND ACCOUNTING an attempt to hide missing funds by delaying the recording of cash receipts in a business's books

lapse FINANCE, BANKING, AND ACCOUNTING the termination of an option without trade in the underlying security or commodity

lapse rights FINANCE, BANKING, AND ACCOUNTING rights, such as those to a specified premium, owned by the person who allows an offer to lapse

laptop GENERAL MANAGEMENT a compact portable computer

large-sized business GENERAL MANAGEMENT an organization that has grown beyond the limits of a *medium-sized business* and has 500 or more employees. It is usually from the ranks of large-sized businesses that *multinational businesses* arise.

last-in first-out HR & PERSONNEL see *LIFO*

last survivor policy FINANCE, BANKING, AND ACCOUNTING an insurance policy covering the lives of two or more people. The sum insured is not paid out until all the policyholders are deceased. See also *joint life annuity*

latent market MARKETING a group of people who have been identified as potential consumers of a product that does not yet exist

lateral thinking GENERAL MANAGEMENT a creative method of problem solving that ignores traditional logic and approaches problems from unorthodox perspectives. Lateral thinking was developed by *Edward de Bono*, who distinguished two forms of thinking: vertical thinking, which is based on logic; and lateral thinking, which disregards apparently rational trains of thought and branches out at tangents. Lateral thinking involves the examination of a problem and its possible solutions from all angles. Seemingly intractable problems often can be solved in this manner, and it is a technique used in *brainstorming*, or to help generate *creativity* and *innovation* within organizations.

launch MARKETING the process of introducing a new product to the market

launder FINANCE, BANKING, AND ACCOUNTING to pass the profits of illegal activities, such as tax evasion, into the normal banking system via apparently legitimate businesses

laundering FINANCE, BANKING, AND ACCOUNTING the process of making money obtained illegally appear legitimate by passing it through banks or businesses

law of diminishing returns FINANCE, BANKING, AND ACCOUNTING GENERAL MANAGEMENT a rule stating that as one factor of production is increased, while others remain constant, the extra output generated by the additional input will eventually fall. The law of diminishing returns therefore means that extra workers, extra capital, extra machinery, or extra land may not necessarily raise output as much as expected. For example, increasing the supply of raw materials to a production line may allow additional output to be produced by using any spare capacity workers have. Once this capacity is fully used, however, continually increasing the amount of raw material without a corresponding increase in the number of workers will not result in an increase of output.

law of supply and demand ECONOMICS see *supply and demand*

lay-away GENERAL MANAGEMENT the reservation of an article for purchase by the payment of an initial deposit followed by regular interest-free installments, on completion of which the article is claimed by the buyer

lay off HR & PERSONNEL
1 to dismiss workers permanently
2 to suspend workers temporarily because of lack of work

layoff GENERAL MANAGEMENT dismissal, often temporarily, from work because a job ceases to exist or because of lack of work. Employees who are laid off may qualify for *unemployment compensation*. If the layoff process is handled incorrectly, the employer may be faced with claims for unfair dismissal. U.K. term *redundancy*

layout by function OPERATIONS & PRODUCTION see *process layout*

LBO *abbr* FINANCE, BANKING, AND ACCOUNTING leveraged buyout

L/C *abbr* FINANCE, BANKING, AND ACCOUNTING letter of credit

LCH *abbr* FINANCE, BANKING, AND ACCOUNTING London Clearing House

LCM *abbr* FINANCE, BANKING, AND ACCOUNTING lower of cost or market

LDC *abbr* ECONOMICS less developed country

lead FINANCE, BANKING, AND ACCOUNTING in an insurance policy from Lloyd's, the first named underwriting syndicate

lead bank FINANCE, BANKING, AND ACCOUNTING the main bank in a loan syndicate

lead ceiling GENERAL MANAGEMENT the level in an organization beyond which women are supposedly unable to gain *promotion*. A lead ceiling often exists at *senior management* level and is perceived as an invisible barrier to career progression for women. *Equal opportunities* policies and legislation work to break such ceilings to make equal career advancement opportunities available to both men and women.

leader
1 GENERAL MANAGEMENT HR & PERSONNEL a business executive who possesses exceptional leadership qualities as well as management skills
2 MARKETING the most successful product or company in a marketplace

leadership GENERAL MANAGEMENT HR & PERSONNEL the capacity to establish direction and to influence and align others toward a common goal, motivating and committing them to action and making them responsible for their performance. Leadership theory is one of the most discussed areas of management, and many different approaches are taken to the topic. Some notions of leadership are related to types of *authority* delineated by *Max Weber*. It is often suggested that leaders possess innate personal qualities that distinguish them from others: *great man theory* and *trait theory* express this idea. Other theories, such as *Behaviorist theories of leadership*, suggest that leadership is defined by action and behavior, rather than by personality. A related idea is that leadership style is not fixed but should be adapted to different situations, and this is explored in *contingency theory* and situational theory. A further branch of research that examines relationships between leaders and followers is found in *transactional*, *transformational*, *attribution*, and *power and influence theories of leadership*. Perhaps the most simple model of leadership is *action-centered leadership*, which focuses on what an effective leader actually does. These many approaches and differences of opinion illustrate the complexity of the leadership role and the intangibility of the essence of good leadership. See thinker *Max Weber*

leading economic indicator *or* **leading indicator** ECONOMICS an economic variable, such as private-sector wages, that tends to show the direction of future economic activity

leading edge GENERAL MANAGEMENT situated at the forefront of *innovation*. A leading edge company is ahead of others in such areas as inventing or implementing new technologies, and in entering new markets.

lead manager (*U.K.*) FINANCE, BANKING, AND ACCOUNTING a lead underwriter

lead partner GENERAL MANAGEMENT the organization that takes the lead role in an alliance

leads and lags FINANCE, BANKING, AND ACCOUNTING in businesses that deal in foreign currencies, the practice of speeding up the receipt of payments (leads) if a currency is going to weaken, and slowing down the payment of costs (lags) if a currency is thought to be about to strengthen, in order to maximize gains and reduce losses

lead time
1 FINANCE, BANKING, AND ACCOUNTING the time interval between the start of an activity or

process and its completion, for example, the time between ordering goods and their receipt, or between starting manufacturing of a product and its completion

2 OPERATIONS & PRODUCTION in inventory control, the time between placing an order and its arrival on site. Lead time differs from delivery time in that it also includes the time required to place an order and the time it takes to inspect the goods and receive them into the appropriate store. Inventory levels can afford to be lower and orders smaller when purchasing lead times are short.

3 OPERATIONS & PRODUCTION in *new product development* and manufacturing, the time required to develop a product from concept to market delivery. Lead time increases as a result of the poor sequencing of dependent activities, the lack of availability of resources, poor quality in the component parts, and poor plant layout. The technique of *concurrent engineering* focuses on the entire concept-to-customer process with the goal of reducing lead time. Companies can gain a *competitive advantage* by achieving a lead time reduction and so getting products to market faster. Also known as *cycle time*

lead underwriter FINANCE, BANKING, AND ACCOUNTING the financial institution with overall responsibility for a new issue including its coordination, distribution, and related administration

leaky reply E-COMMERCE an e-mail response that is accidentally sent to the wrong recipient and causes embarrassment to the sender (*slang*)

lean enterprise OPERATIONS & PRODUCTION an organizational model that strategically applies the key ideas behind *lean production*. The concept of the lean enterprise was proposed by J. P. Womack and D. T. Jones in their 1994 *Harvard Business Review* article "From Lean Production to the Lean Enterprise." They view the lean enterprise as a group of separate individuals, functions, or organizations that operate as one entity. The goal is to apply lean techniques that create individual breakthroughs in companies and to link these up and down the *supply chain* to form a continuous value stream to raise the whole chain to a higher level.

lean manufacturing OPERATIONS & PRODUCTION see *lean production*

lean operation OPERATIONS & PRODUCTION see *lean production*

lean production OPERATIONS & PRODUCTION a methodology aimed at reducing waste in the form of overproduction, excessive *lead time*, or product defects in order to make a business more effective and more competitive. Lean production originates in the production systems established by Toyota in Japan in the 1950s. In the early 1980s there was a significant increase in the application of lean production in Western companies. Lean production is characterized by *lean operations* with low *inventories*, *quality management* through prevention of errors, small batch runs, *just-in-time* production, high commitment human resource policies, team-based working, and close relations with suppliers. The term was popularized by researchers on the International Motor Vehicle Program of the Massachusetts Institute of Technology in their book *The Machine That Changed the World*. Concepts that can help an organization move toward lean production include *continuous improvement* and *world class manufacturing*. Also known as *lean manufacturing*

LEAPS *abbr* FINANCE, BANKING, AND ACCOUNTING long-term equity anticipation securities: options that expire between one and three years in the future

learning by doing GENERAL MANAGEMENT the acquisition of knowledge or skills through direct experience of carrying out a task. Learning by doing often happens under supervision, as part of a training or *orientation* process, and is closely associated with the practical experience picked up by "*sitting with Nellie*." It is an outcome of the research into learning of *David Kolb* and *Reg Revans*. A more formalized approach to learning by doing is *experiential learning*. See thinker *Reg Revans*

learning curve
1 GENERAL MANAGEMENT a graphic representation of the acquisition of knowledge or experience over time. A steep learning curve reflects a substantial amount of learning in a short time, and a shallow curve reflects a slower learning process. The curve eventually levels out to a plateau, during which time the knowledge gained is being consolidated.
2 GENERAL MANAGEMENT the proportional decrease in effort when production is doubled. The learning curve has its origin in *productivity* research in the airplane industry of the 1930s, when *T. P. Wright* discovered that in assembling an aircraft, the time and effort decreased by 20% each time the cumulative number of planes produced doubled. *Bruce Henderson* of the Boston Consulting Group formulated the learning curve as a strategic

planning device in the 1960s by plotting product costs against cumulative volume.
3 FINANCE, BANKING, AND ACCOUNTING the mathematical expression of the phenomenon that when complex and labor intensive procedures are repeated, unit labor times tend to decrease at a constant rate. The learning curve models mathematically this reduction in unit production time.

learning opportunity GENERAL MANAGEMENT a positive way of referring to a mistake that someone has made at work

learning organization GENERAL MANAGEMENT an organizational model characterized by a *flat* structure and *customer-focused* teams, that engenders the collective ability to develop shared visions by capturing and exploiting employees' willingness, commitment, and curiosity. The concept of the learning organization was proposed by *Chris Argyris* and *Donald Schön* as part of their work on *organizational learning*, but was brought back to public attention in the 1990s by *Peter Senge*. For Senge, a learning organization is one with the capacity to shift away from views inherent in a traditional hierarchical organization, toward the ability of all employees to challenge prevailing thinking and gain a balanced perspective. Senge believes the five major elements of a learning organization are mental models, personal mastery, *systems thinking*, shared vision, and team learning. Because of the requirement for an open, risk-tolerant culture (which is the opposite of the *corporate culture* of most organizations today) the learning organization remains, for many, an unattainable ideal. See thinker *Chris Argyris*, *Peter Senge*

learning relationship GENERAL MANAGEMENT a relationship between a supplier and a customer in which the supplier modifies or customizes a product as it learns more about the customer's requirements

learning style GENERAL MANAGEMENT the way in which somebody approaches the acquisition of knowledge and skills. Learning styles have been divided into four main types by *Peter Honey* and *Alan Mumford*, in their *Manual of Learning Styles* (1982). The types of learners are the activist, who likes to get involved in new experiences and enjoys the challenges of change; the theorist, who likes to question assumptions and methodologies and learns best when there is time to explore links between ideas and situations; the pragmatist, who prefers practicality and learns best when there is a link between the subject matter and the job in hand and when he or she can try out what he

or she has learned; and the reflector, who likes to take his or her time and think things through, and who learns best from activities where he or she can observe and conduct research. One person can demonstrate more than one learning style, and the category or categories that best describe somebody can be determined through use of a learning styles questionnaire.

leaseback FINANCE, BANKING, AND ACCOUNTING see *sale and leaseback*

leave HR & PERSONNEL work time when an employee is paid, but is not required to be at work. Leave takes several forms and includes time off for *vacation*. The number of days of vacation is agreed in the *contract of employment* and may be dependent on the employee's length of service. It may also take the form of *sick leave*, *educational leave*, or *maternity* or *paternity leave* .

Leavitt, Harold J. (*b.* 1922) GENERAL MANAGEMENT U.S. psychologist and academic. Researcher with an interest in *organization behavior* and psychology, and originator of *Leavitt's Diamond* and author of *Managerial Psychology* (1958).

Leavitt's Diamond GENERAL MANAGEMENT a model for analyzing management change, developed by *Harold J. Leavitt*. Leavitt's Diamond is based on the idea that it is rare for any change to occur in isolation. Leavitt sees technology, tasks, people, and the organizational structure in which they function as four interdependent variables, visualized as the four points of a diamond. Change at any one point of the diamond will impact some or all of the others. Thus, a changed task will necessarily affect the people involved in it, the structure in which they work, and the technology that they use. Failure to manage these interdependencies at critical times of change can create problems. See also *change management*

ledger FINANCE, BANKING, AND ACCOUNTING
1 a book in which account transactions are recorded
2 a collection of accounts, or book of accounts. Credit sales information is recorded, for example, by debtor, in the sales ledger.
3 a collection of accounts, maintained by transfers from the books of original entry. The ledger may be subdivided as follows: the sales ledger/debtors' ledger contains all the personal accounts of customers; the purchases ledger-/creditors' ledger contains all the personal accounts of suppliers; the private ledger contains accounts relating to the proprietor's interest in the business such as capital and drawings; the

general ledger/nominal ledger contains all other accounts relating to assets, expenses, revenue, and liabilities.

legacy system E-COMMERCE FINANCE, BANKING, AND ACCOUNTING an existing computer system that provides a strategic function for a specific part of a business. Inventory management systems, for example, are legacy systems.

legal loophole GENERAL MANAGEMENT an area in the law that is insufficiently explicit or comprehensive and allows the law to be circumvented

legal tender FINANCE, BANKING, AND ACCOUNTING paper money and coins that have to be accepted within a given jurisdiction when offered as payment of a debt. See also *limited legal tender*

legs GENERAL MANAGEMENT a longer-than-usual life for an advertising campaign, movie, book, or other short-lived product (*slang*)

lekgotla (*S. Africa*) GENERAL MANAGEMENT see *bosberaad*

lemon FINANCE, BANKING, AND ACCOUNTING GENERAL MANAGEMENT a product that is defective in some way, for example, an investment that is performing poorly (*slang*)

lender of last resort FINANCE, BANKING, AND ACCOUNTING a central bank that lends money to banks that cannot borrow elsewhere

length of service HR & PERSONNEL the period in which a person has been continually employed in an organization, without breaks in the *contract of employment*. Length of service may determine entitlement to employment rights or *fringe benefits*, for example, the amount of annual leave allocated.

less developed countries FINANCE, BANKING, AND ACCOUNTING countries which are not economically advanced and borrowed heavily from commercial banks in the 1970s and 1980s to finance their industrial development, and so created an international debt crisis

less developed country ECONOMICS a country whose economic development is held back by the lack of natural resources to produce goods demanded on world markets. Abbr. *LDC*

lessee FINANCE, BANKING, AND ACCOUNTING the person who has the use of a leased asset

lessor FINANCE, BANKING, AND ACCOUNTING the person who provides the asset being leased

letter of acceptance FINANCE, BANKING, AND ACCOUNTING a document that says how many shares have been allotted to a stockholder

letter of agreement GENERAL MANAGEMENT a document that constitutes a simple form of contract

letter of comfort (*U.K.*) FINANCE, BANKING, AND ACCOUNTING = *letter of moral intent*

letter of credit FINANCE, BANKING, AND ACCOUNTING a letter issued by a bank that can be presented to another bank to authorize the issue of credit or money. Abbr. *L/C* Also known as *irrevocable letter of credit*

letter of indemnity FINANCE, BANKING, AND ACCOUNTING a statement that a stock certificate has been lost, destroyed, or stolen and that the stockholder will indemnify the company for any loss that might result from its reappearance after the company has issued a replacement to the shareholder

letter of intent FINANCE, BANKING, AND ACCOUNTING a document in which an individual or organization indicates an intention to do something, for example, buy a business, grant somebody a loan, or participate in a project. The intention may or may not depend on certain conditions being met and the document is not legally binding. See also *letter of moral intent*

letter of license FINANCE, BANKING, AND ACCOUNTING a letter from a creditor to a debtor who is having problems repaying money owed, giving the debtor a certain period of time to raise the money and an undertaking not to bring legal proceedings to recover the debt during that period

letter of moral intent FINANCE, BANKING, AND ACCOUNTING a letter from a holding company addressed to a bank where one of its subsidiaries wishes to borrow money. The purpose of the letter is to support the subsidiary's application to borrow funds and offer reassurance—although not a guarantee—to the bank that the subsidiary will remain in business for the foreseeable future, often with an undertaking to advise the bank if the subsidiary is likely to be sold. U.K. term *letter of comfort*

letter of renunciation FINANCE, BANKING, AND ACCOUNTING a form used to transfer an allotment

letters patent FINANCE, BANKING, AND ACCOUNTING an official document which gives someone the exclusive right to make and sell something which he or she has invented

level playing field GENERAL MANAGEMENT a situation in which all competitors are in a position of equal strength or weakness

level production GENERAL MANAGEMENT see *production smoothing*

level term insurance FINANCE, BANKING, AND ACCOUNTING a life insurance policy in which an agreed lump sum is paid if the policyholder dies before a certain date. A joint form of this life coverage is popular with couples who have children.

leverage FINANCE, BANKING, AND ACCOUNTING a method of corporate funding in which a higher proportion of funds is raised through borrowing than stock issue

leveraged bid FINANCE, BANKING, AND ACCOUNTING a takeover bid financed by borrowed money, rather than by a stock issue

leveraged buyout FINANCE, BANKING, AND ACCOUNTING a takeover using borrowed money, with the purchased company's assets as collateral. Abbr. *LBO*

leveraged required return FINANCE, BANKING, AND ACCOUNTING the rate of return from an investment of borrowed money needed to make the investment worthwhile

leverage ratios FINANCE, BANKING, AND ACCOUNTING ratios that indicate the level of risk taken by a company as a result of its capital structure. A number of different ratios may be calculated, for example, debt ratio (total debt divided by total assets), debt-to-equity or leverage ratio (total debt divided by total equity), or interest cover (earnings before interest and tax divided by interest paid).

Levitt, Theodore (b. 1925) GENERAL MANAGEMENT German-born academic. Harvard professor, who wrote the landmark article "Marketing Myopia," *Harvard Business Review* (July/August 1960). In this article, which has sold over 500,000 reprints and genuinely changed basic perceptions of business practice, Levitt argued that the central preoccupation of corporations should be with satisfying their customers, rather than simply producing goods. According to Levitt, production-led thinking inevitably led to narrow perspectives, the ultimate result of which would be that customers would be overlooked. See thinker *Theodore Levitt*

Lewin, Kurt (1890–1947) GENERAL MANAGEMENT German-born social psychologist. Known for studies of *leadership* styles and group *decision making*, developer of *force field analysis*

with a linked *change management* model, pioneer of *action research* and the *T-Group* (see *sensitivity training*) approach.

Lewin was a professor of philosophy and psychology at Berlin University until 1932 when he fled from the Nazis to the United States. He was professor of child psychology at the Child Welfare Research Station in Iowa until 1944. After leaving Iowa, Lewin worked at MIT, with *Douglas McGregor* among others, founding a research center for group dynamics. See thinker *Kurt Lewin*

liability FINANCE, BANKING, AND ACCOUNTING a debt that has no claim on a debtor's assets, or less claim than another debt

liability insurance FINANCE, BANKING, AND ACCOUNTING insurance against legal liability that the insured might incur, for example, from causing an accident

liability management FINANCE, BANKING, AND ACCOUNTING any exercise carried out by a business with the objective of controlling the effect of liabilities on its profitability. This will typically involve controlling the amount of risk undertaken, and ensuring that there is sufficient liquidity and that the best terms are obtained for any funding needs.

LIBID *abbr* FINANCE, BANKING, AND ACCOUNTING London Inter Bank Bid Rate

LIBOR *abbr* FINANCE, BANKING, AND ACCOUNTING London Inter Bank Offered Rate

license FINANCE, BANKING, AND ACCOUNTING GENERAL MANAGEMENT a contractual arrangement, or a document representing this, in which one organization gives another the rights to produce, sell, or use something in return for payment

licensing FINANCE, BANKING, AND ACCOUNTING MARKETING the transfer of rights to manufacture or market a particular product to another individual or organization through a legal arrangement or contract. Licensing usually requires that a fee, commission, or royalty is paid to the licensor.

licensing agreement FINANCE, BANKING, AND ACCOUNTING MARKETING an agreement permitting a company to market or produce a product or service owned by another company. A licensing agreement grants a license in return for a fee or royalty payment. Items licensed for use can include patents, trademarks, techniques, designs, and expertise. This kind of agreement is one way for a company to penetrate overseas markets in that it provides a

middle path between direct export and investment overseas.

life annuity FINANCE, BANKING, AND ACCOUNTING an annuity that pays a fixed amount per month until the holder's death

life assurance (U.K.) FINANCE, BANKING, AND ACCOUNTING = *life insurance*

lifeboat (S. Africa) FINANCE, BANKING, AND ACCOUNTING a low-interest emergency loan made by a central bank to rescue a commercial bank in danger of becoming insolvent

life cover FINANCE, BANKING, AND ACCOUNTING see *life insurance*

life cycle GENERAL MANAGEMENT the sales pattern of a product or service over a period of time. Typically, a life cycle falls into four stages: introduction, growth, maturity, and decline.

life-cycle costing OPERATIONS & PRODUCTION a method of calculating the total cost of a physical asset throughout its life. Life-cycle costing is concerned with all costs of ownership and takes account of the costs incurred by an asset from its acquisition to its disposal, including design, installation, operating, and maintenance costs.

life-cycle savings motive ECONOMICS a reason that a household or individual has for saving or spending during the course of their life, as, for example, spending when starting a family or saving when near retirement

life expectancy STATISTICS the number of years that somebody of a given age is expected to live

life insurance FINANCE, BANKING, AND ACCOUNTING insurance that pays a specified sum to the insured person's beneficiaries after the person's death. U.K. term *life assurance*. Also known as *life coverage*

life insured FINANCE, BANKING, AND ACCOUNTING the person or persons covered by a life insurance policy. The insurance company pays out on the death of the policyholder.

life interest FINANCE, BANKING, AND ACCOUNTING a situation where someone benefits from a property for the entirety of his or her lifetime

lifelong learning GENERAL MANAGEMENT the continual acquisition of knowledge and skills throughout somebody's life. Lifelong learning occurs in preparation for, and in response to,

the different roles, situations, and environments that somebody will encounter in the course of a lifetime. It is supported by formal and informal education systems, both within and outside the workplace, through which somebody can both learn and receive guidance and encouragement. The adoption of lifelong learning is seen as a key element in **CPD**, and as an important tool in maintaining **employability**.

life office (*U.K.*) FINANCE, BANKING, AND ACCOUNTING a company that provides life insurance

life policy FINANCE, BANKING, AND ACCOUNTING a life insurance contract

lifestyle business FINANCE, BANKING, AND ACCOUNTING a typically small business run by individuals who have a strong interest in the product or service offered, for example, handmade greeting cards or jewelry, antique dealing or restoring. Such businesses tend to operate during hours that suit the owners, and generally provide them with a comfortable living.

life table STATISTICS a table that shows the probabilities of death, survival, and remaining years of life for people of given ages

lifetime customer value FINANCE, BANKING, AND ACCOUNTING MARKETING see **lifetime value**

lifetime value FINANCE, BANKING, AND ACCOUNTING MARKETING a measure of the total value to a supplier of a customer's business over the duration of their transactions.

In a consumer business, customer lifetime value is calculated by analyzing the behavior of a group of customers who have the same recruitment date. The revenue and cost for this group of customers is recorded, by campaign or season, and the overall contribution for that period can then be worked out. Industry experience has shown that the benefits to a business of increasing lifetime value can be enormous. A 5% increase in customer retention can create a 125% increase in profits; a 10% increase in retailer retention can translate to a 20% increase in sales; and extending customer life cycles by three years can treble profits per customer.

LIFFE *abbr* FINANCE, BANKING, AND ACCOUNTING London International Financial Futures and Options Exchange

LIFO *abbr* HR & PERSONNEL last in first out: a technique used when selecting employees for **layoffs**, where the most recent recruits are the first to be laid off. The LIFO technique has the

benefits of reducing layoff costs and of being seen as fair by some employees. Its disadvantages, however, are increasingly being recognized. It can result in a serious imbalance in the age profile of the workforce and can remove recently acquired skills. It may also be discriminatory, as men are more likely to have built up periods of **continuous service** than women.

lift
let's put it in a lift and see what floor it stops at (*U.K.*) GENERAL MANAGEMENT let's try this idea and see what happens (*slang*)

lightning strike (*U.K.*) HR & PERSONNEL a *strike* that occurs at very short notice. It may be of short duration and may not be sanctioned by a **labor union**.

light pages E-COMMERCE Web pages that are under 50KB in size, enabling them to download quickly

Likert, Rensis (1903–81) GENERAL MANAGEMENT U.S. psychologist and academic. Known for situational leadership research and in particular for establishing four systems of management to interpret the way managers behave toward others. In *New Patterns of Management* (1961), Likert described these systems as exploitive/authoritative, benevolent/authoritative, consultative, and participative. He later suggested a fifth system in which the authority of hierarchy disappears.

LIMEAN *abbr* FINANCE, BANKING, AND ACCOUNTING London Inter Bank Mean Rate

limit FINANCE, BANKING, AND ACCOUNTING an amount above or below which a broker is not to conclude the purchase or sale of a security for the client who specifies it

limit down FINANCE, BANKING, AND ACCOUNTING the most that the price of an option may fall in one day on a particular market

Limited FINANCE, BANKING, AND ACCOUNTING when placed at the end of the company's name, used to indicate that a U.K. company is a limited company

limited by guarantee FINANCE, BANKING, AND ACCOUNTING see **public limited company**

limited company FINANCE, BANKING, AND ACCOUNTING a British-registered company in which each stockholder is responsible for the company's debts only to the amount that he or she has invested in the company. Limited companies must be formed by at least two

directors. See also **private company public limited company**. Abbr. **Ltd**

limited legal tender FINANCE, BANKING, AND ACCOUNTING in some jurisdictions, low denomination bills and all coins that may only be submitted up to a certain sum as legal tender in any one transaction

limited liability FINANCE, BANKING, AND ACCOUNTING the restriction of an owner's loss in a business to the amount of capital he or she has invested in it

limited market FINANCE, BANKING, AND ACCOUNTING a market in which dealings for a specific security are difficult to transact, for example, because it has only limited appeal to investors or, in the case of stock, because institutions or family members are unlikely to sell it

limited partnership FINANCE, BANKING, AND ACCOUNTING a registered business in which the liability of the partners is limited to the amount of capital they have each provided for the business, and in the running of which the partners may not take part

limit up FINANCE, BANKING, AND ACCOUNTING the most that the price of an option may rise in one day on a particular market

linear programming
1 GENERAL MANAGEMENT a mathematical technique used to identify an optimal solution for the deployment of resources to meet organizational objectives. Linear programming uses graphic and algebraic means to calculate which combination of resources, subject to predicted constraints, is most likely to fulfill a given objective. It was developed during the 1940s for use in military planning.
2 FINANCE, BANKING, AND ACCOUNTING the use of a series of linear equations to construct a mathematical model. The objective is to obtain an optimal solution to a complex operational problem, which may involve the production of a number of products in an environment in which there are many constraints.

line management (*U.K.*) GENERAL MANAGEMENT HR & PERSONNEL a hierarchical **chain of command** from executive to front-line level. Line management is the oldest and least complex management structure, in which top management have total and direct authority and employees report to only one **supervisor**. Managers in this type of **organization structure** have direct responsibility for giving orders to their subordinates. Line management structures are usually organized along functional

lines, although they increasingly undertake a variety of cross-functional duties such as *employee development* or strategic direction. The lowest managerial level in an organization following a line management structure is *supervisory management*.

line manager (*U.K.*) HR & PERSONNEL an employee's immediate superior, who oversees and has responsibility for the employee's work. A line manager at the lowest level of a large organization is a *supervisor*, but a manager at any level with direct responsibility for employees' work can be described as a line manager.

line of credit FINANCE, BANKING, AND ACCOUNTING an agreed finance facility that allows a company or individual to borrow money. Also known as *credit line*

line organization GENERAL MANAGEMENT an *organization structure* based on *line management*

link E-COMMERCE a pointer to another record, embedded in a document. One or more documents can be connected by inserting links. On the Internet, a link is a reference either to another Web site or to another document.

linking E-COMMERCE connecting two Web sites or documents by inserting *links*.

Linking is one of the simplest, yet most effective, Internet marketing devices available. It is like embedded word of mouth: if another Web site links to yours, it is essentially recommending you to its own visitors. Likewise, it is important to be certain that any other Web sites that you place links to within your own site are likely to be of interest to your own visitors.

liquid asset ratio FINANCE, BANKING, AND ACCOUNTING the ratio of liquid assets to total assets

liquid assets FINANCE, BANKING, AND ACCOUNTING ECONOMICS cash, and other assets readily convertible into cash

liquidate FINANCE, BANKING, AND ACCOUNTING to close a company by selling its assets, paying off any outstanding debts, distributing any remaining profits to the stockholders, and then ceasing trading

liquidated damages FINANCE, BANKING, AND ACCOUNTING an amount of money somebody pays for breaching a contract

liquidated damages clause FINANCE, BANKING, AND ACCOUNTING GENERAL MANAGEMENT a clause in a *contract* which sets out the compensation to be paid in the event of a breach or a default of the terms of the contract. The compensation set out in a liquidated damages clause should be a genuine preestimate of the loss suffered as a result of the noncompletion of the contract. An example would be an amount payable per day in the event of the noncompletion of a building project. If the amount specified is not considered a genuine estimate of the losses incurred, and the clause is perceived to be solely an incentive for the completion of the contract, the clause is deemed a penalty clause and is not legally enforceable. However, liquidated damages clauses are often inaccurately referred to as penalty clauses. See also *breach of contract*

liquidation FINANCE, BANKING, AND ACCOUNTING the winding-up of a company, a process during which assets are sold, liabilities settled as far as possible, and any remaining cash returned to the members. Liquidation may be voluntary or compulsory.

liquidation value FINANCE, BANKING, AND ACCOUNTING the amount of money that a quick sale of all of a company's assets would yield

liquidator FINANCE, BANKING, AND ACCOUNTING the person appointed by a company, its creditors, or its stockholders to sell the assets of an insolvent company. The proceeds of the sale are used to discharge debts to creditors, with any surplus distributed to stockholders.

liquidity FINANCE, BANKING, AND ACCOUNTING a condition in which assets are held in a cash or near cash form

liquidity agreement FINANCE, BANKING, AND ACCOUNTING an agreement to allow conversion of an asset into cash

liquidity preference ECONOMICS a choice made by people to hold their wealth in the form of cash rather than bonds or stocks

liquidity ratio FINANCE, BANKING, AND ACCOUNTING see *cash ratio*

liquidity risk FINANCE, BANKING, AND ACCOUNTING the risk that an entity will encounter difficulty in realizing assets or otherwise raising funds to meet commitments associated with financial instruments. Also called *funding risk*

liquidity trap FINANCE, BANKING, AND ACCOUNTING a central bank's inability to lower interest rates once investors believe rates can go no lower

liquid market FINANCE, BANKING, AND ACCOUNTING a market in which a large number of trades are being made

list broker FINANCE, BANKING, AND ACCOUNTING GENERAL MANAGEMENT a person or organization that makes the arrangements for one company to use another company's direct mail list

listed company FINANCE, BANKING, AND ACCOUNTING a company whose stock trades on an exchange

listed securities FINANCE, BANKING, AND ACCOUNTING stock which can be bought or sold on the Stock Exchange and which appear on its official list

listed security FINANCE, BANKING, AND ACCOUNTING a security listed on an exchange

listing FINANCE, BANKING, AND ACCOUNTING see *listed company*, *listing requirements*

Listing Agreement FINANCE, BANKING, AND ACCOUNTING a document which a company signs when being listed on the Stock Exchange, in which the company promises to abide by stock exchange regulations

listing requirements FINANCE, BANKING, AND ACCOUNTING the conditions that have to be met before a security can be traded on a recognized stock exchange. Although exact requirements vary from one exchange to another, the two main ones are that the issuing company's assets should exceed a minimum amount and that the required information about its finances and business should have been published.

list price OPERATIONS & PRODUCTION the price of goods or services published by a supplier. The list price of an item may be discounted to regular customers or for bulk purchases.

list renting GENERAL MANAGEMENT an arrangement in which a company that owns a direct mail list lets another company use it for a fee

litigation GENERAL MANAGEMENT the process of bringing a lawsuit against an individual or organization

Little Board FINANCE, BANKING, AND ACCOUNTING the American Stock Exchange (*slang*)

live chat E-COMMERCE a facility that enables two or more Web users to communicate with each other in real time, using text.

Live chat is frequently employed in customer support services. This is because one of its main benefits is that a customer does not

need to disconnect from the Internet in order to telephone a support line: live chat means they can receive text-based support without having to disconnect. This is more appropriate for people with dial-up access rather than broadband. Also called *instant messaging*

lively market FINANCE, BANKING, AND ACCOUNTING an active stock market which sees many stocks being bought or sold

livery MARKETING a mark of corporate identity used on a company vehicle

living wage HR & PERSONNEL a level of *pay* that provides just enough income for normal day-to-day subsistence

LLC *abbr* GENERAL MANAGEMENT limited liability company

Lloyd's broker FINANCE, BANKING, AND ACCOUNTING an agent who represents a client who wants insurance, and who arranges this insurance for him through a Lloyd's underwriting syndicate

LME *abbr* FINANCE, BANKING, AND ACCOUNTING London Metal Exchange

load FINANCE, BANKING, AND ACCOUNTING an initial charge in some investment funds. See also *load fund*

load fund FINANCE, BANKING, AND ACCOUNTING a mutual fund that charges a fee for the purchase or sale of shares. See also *no-load fund*

loading
1 OPERATIONS & PRODUCTION the assignment of tasks or jobs to a workstation. The loading of jobs is worked out through the use of *master production scheduling*. Workstations may be loaded to *finite* or *infinite loading* levels.
2 (*ANZ*) HR & PERSONNEL a payment made to workers over and above the basic wage in recognition of special skills or unfavorable conditions, for example, for overtime or shiftwork

loan FINANCE, BANKING, AND ACCOUNTING a borrowing either by a business or a consumer where the amount borrowed is repaid according to an agreed schedule at an agreed interest rate, typically by regular installments over a set period of years. However, the principal may be repayable in one installment. See also *balloon loan*, *fixed-rate loan*, *interest-only mortgage*, *variable interest rate*

loanable funds theory FINANCE, BANKING, AND ACCOUNTING the theory that interest rates are determined solely by supply and demand

loanback FINANCE, BANKING, AND ACCOUNTING the return to somebody of a loan money that has been given, often as a way of illegally masking the money's true owner

loan committee FINANCE, BANKING, AND ACCOUNTING a committee which examines applications for special loans, such as higher loans than normally allowed by a bank

loan constant ratio FINANCE, BANKING, AND ACCOUNTING the total of annual payments due on a loan as a fraction of the amount of the principal

Loan Council (*ANZ*) FINANCE, BANKING, AND ACCOUNTING an Australian federal body, made up of treasurers from the states and the Commonwealth of Australia that monitors borrowing by state governments

loan loss reserves FINANCE, BANKING, AND ACCOUNTING the money a bank holds to cover losses through defaults on loans that it makes

loan participation FINANCE, BANKING, AND ACCOUNTING the grouping together by several banks to share a very large loan to one single customer

loan production cycle FINANCE, BANKING, AND ACCOUNTING the period that begins with an application for a loan and ends with the lending of money

loan schedule FINANCE, BANKING, AND ACCOUNTING a list of the payments due on a loan and the balance outstanding after each has been made

loan shark FINANCE, BANKING, AND ACCOUNTING somebody who lends money at excessively, often illegally, high rates of interest

loan stock FINANCE, BANKING, AND ACCOUNTING bonds and debentures

loan to value ratio FINANCE, BANKING, AND ACCOUNTING the ratio of the amount of a loan to the value of the collateral for it

loan value FINANCE, BANKING, AND ACCOUNTING the amount that a lender is willing to lend a borrower

lobby GENERAL MANAGEMENT a pressure group that seeks to influence government or legislators on behalf of a particular cause or interest

local authority bond FINANCE, BANKING, AND ACCOUNTING a loan raised by a local authority in the form of a fixed-interest bond, repayable at a certain date. Local authority bonds are similar to *Treasury bonds*.

local authority deposits FINANCE, BANKING, AND ACCOUNTING money deposited with a local authority to earn interest for the depositor

localization E-COMMERCE the translation of a Web site into the language or idiom of the target user.
   Studies have shown that if a vendor is serious about selling to foreign marketplaces, localizing their Web site is essential; without it, sales will be minimal and returns very high because of misunderstanding by people who are purchasing in a foreign language.

lock-out HR & PERSONNEL a form of industrial action taken by an employer during a dispute in which employees are prevented from entering the business premises

logistics OPERATIONS & PRODUCTION the management of the movement, storage, and processing of materials and information in the *supply chain*. Logistics encompasses the acquisition of raw materials and components, manufacturing or processing, and the distribution of finished products to the end user. Each organization focuses on a different aspect of logistics, depending on its area of interest. For example, one might apply logistics to find a way of linking *physical distribution management* with earlier events in the supply chain, another to plan its acquisition and storage, while a third might use logistics as a support operation.

logistics management OPERATIONS & PRODUCTION the management of the distribution of products to the market

logo GENERAL MANAGEMENT a graphic device or symbol used by an organization as part of its corporate identity. A logo is used to facilitate instant recognition of an organization and to reinforce *brand* expectations and public image.

log of claims (*ANZ*) HR & PERSONNEL a document listing the demands made by employees on an employer or vice versa, often submitted during industrial negotiations

LOL *abbr* GENERAL MANAGEMENT laugh out loud (*slang*)

London Bullion Market FINANCE, BANKING, AND ACCOUNTING the world's largest market for gold, where silver is also traded. It is a wholesale market, where the minimum trades are generally 1,000 ounces for gold and 50,000 ounces for silver. Members typically trade with each other and their clients on a principal-to-principal basis so that all risks, including those

of credit, are between the two parties to the transaction.

London Chamber of Commerce and Industry FINANCE, BANKING, AND ACCOUNTING in the United Kingdom, the largest chamber of commerce, that strives "to help London businesses succeed by promoting their interests and expanding their opportunities as members of a worldwide business network." See also **ICC**

London Clearing House FINANCE, BANKING, AND ACCOUNTING an organization that acts on behalf of its members as a central counterparty for contracts traded on the London International Financial Futures and Options Exchange, the International Petroleum Exchange, and the London Metal Exchange. When the LCH has registered a trade, it becomes the buyer to every member who sells and the seller to every member who buys, ensuring good financial performance. To protect it against the risks assumed as central counterparty, the LCH establishes margin requirements. See also *margining*. Abbr. **LCH**

London Commodity Exchange FINANCE, BANKING, AND ACCOUNTING see *London International Financial Futures and Options Exchange*

London Inter Bank Bid Rate FINANCE, BANKING, AND ACCOUNTING on the U.K. money markets, the rate at which banks will bid to take deposits in Eurocurrency from each other. The deposits are for terms from overnight up to five years. Abbr. **LIBID**

London Inter Bank Mean Rate FINANCE, BANKING, AND ACCOUNTING the average of the London Inter Bank Offered Rate and the London Inter Bank Bid Rate, occasionally used as a reference rate. Abbr. **LIMEAN**

London Inter Bank Offered Rate FINANCE, BANKING, AND ACCOUNTING on the U.K. money markets, the rate at which banks will offer to make deposits in Eurocurrency from each other, often used as a reference rate. The deposits are for terms from overnight up to five years. Abbr. **LIBOR**

London International Financial Futures and Options Exchange FINANCE, BANKING, AND ACCOUNTING an exchange for trading financial futures and options. Established in 1982, it offered contracts on interest rates denominated in most of the world's major currencies until 1992, when it merged with the London Traded Options Market, adding equity options to its product range. In 1996 it merged with the London Commodity Exchange, adding a variety of soft commodity and

agricultural commodity contracts to its financial portfolio. From November 1998, trading gradually migrated from the floor of the exchange to screen-based trading. Abbr. **LIFFE**

London Metal Exchange FINANCE, BANKING, AND ACCOUNTING one of the world's largest nonferrous metal exchanges, that deals in aluminum, tin, and nickel. The primary roles of the exchange are hedging, providing official international reference prices, and appropriate storage facilities. Its origins can be traced back to 1571, though in its present form it dates from 1877. Abbr. **LME**

London Traded Options Market FINANCE, BANKING, AND ACCOUNTING see *London International Financial Futures and Options Exchange*

long FINANCE, BANKING, AND ACCOUNTING having more shares than are promised for sale

long-dated bond FINANCE, BANKING, AND ACCOUNTING a bond issued by the United Kingdom with a maturity at least 15 years in the future

long-dated gilt FINANCE, BANKING, AND ACCOUNTING see *gilt-edged security*

longitudinal study STATISTICS a statistical study that produces data gathered over a period of time

long position FINANCE, BANKING, AND ACCOUNTING a situation in which dealers hold securities, commodities, or contracts, expecting prices to rise

longs FINANCE, BANKING, AND ACCOUNTING government stocks which will mature more than15 years after the date of purchase

long-service award HR & PERSONNEL a gift to recognize the *length of service* of an employee within an organization. A long-service award may be cash or may take the form of something an employee will value. The tradition of a clock or watch for 25 or 40 years of service is being replaced by awards recognizing shorter durations of employment and the greater mobility of employees.

long-service leave (*ANZ*) HR & PERSONNEL a period of paid leave awarded by some employers to staff who have completed several years of service

long-term GENERAL MANAGEMENT involving a long period of time, for example, years rather than weeks or months

long-term balance of payments FINANCE, BANKING, AND ACCOUNTING a record of movements of capital relating to overseas investments and the purchase of companies overseas

long-term bond FINANCE, BANKING, AND ACCOUNTING a bond that has at least ten years before its redemption date, or, in some markets, a bond with more than seven years until its redemption date

long-term debt FINANCE, BANKING, AND ACCOUNTING loans that are due after at least one year

long-term equity anticipation securities FINANCE, BANKING, AND ACCOUNTING see **LEAPS**

long-term financing FINANCE, BANKING, AND ACCOUNTING forms of funding such as loans or stock issue that do not have to be repaid immediately

long-term lease FINANCE, BANKING, AND ACCOUNTING a lease of at least ten years

long-term liabilities FINANCE, BANKING, AND ACCOUNTING forms of debt such as loans that do not have to be repaid immediately

lookback option FINANCE, BANKING, AND ACCOUNTING an option whose price the buyer chooses from all of the prices that have existed during the option's life

loop
in the loop GENERAL MANAGEMENT up to date with what is happening currently (*slang*)

loss FINANCE, BANKING, AND ACCOUNTING a financial position in which the *costs* of an activity exceed the *income* derived from it

loss adjuster (*U.K.*) FINANCE, BANKING, AND ACCOUNTING GENERAL MANAGEMENT see *claims adjuster*

loss assessor FINANCE, BANKING, AND ACCOUNTING in the United Kingdom, a person appointed by an insurance policyholder to assist with his or her claim. See also *claims adjuster*

loss control GENERAL MANAGEMENT see *total loss control*

loss leader FINANCE, BANKING, AND ACCOUNTING MARKETING a product or service that is sold at a *loss* in order to attract more customers to an organization

lossmaker GENERAL MANAGEMENT a product or company that fails to make a profit or break even

lot FINANCE, BANKING, AND ACCOUNTING
1 the minimum quantity of a commodity that may be purchased on an exchange, for example, 1,000 ounces of gold on the London Bullion Market
2 an item or a collection of related items being offered for sale at an auction
3 a group of shares held or traded together, usually in units of 100
4 a piece of land that can be sold

lottery FINANCE, BANKING, AND ACCOUNTING the random method of selecting successful applicants for something, occasionally used when a new stock issue is oversubscribed

lowball GENERAL MANAGEMENT to begin a sales negotiation by quoting low prices, and then raise them once a buyer appears interested (*slang*)

lower level domain E-COMMERCE the main part of a domain name. For most e-business sites this is usually the company or brand name.

lower of cost or market FINANCE, BANKING, AND ACCOUNTING a method used by manufacturing and supply firms when accounting for their homogeneous stocks that involves valuing them either at their original cost or the current market price, whichever is lower. Abbr. *LCM*

low-hanging fruit (*slang*)
1 MARKETING people who are easy marketing targets because they are already thinking about buying a product or signing up for a service
2 GENERAL MANAGEMENT something that is easy to obtain. Low-hanging fruit is highly visible, easily obtained, and provides good short-term opportunities for profit. Such fruit must be taken advantage of quickly, because it is accessible to anyone and there might be considerable competition. Picking low-hanging fruit may involve, for example, taking over a company or choosing the easiest tasks to do first, in order to achieve a quick result.

low start mortgage FINANCE, BANKING, AND ACCOUNTING a long-term loan, usually for the purchase of real estate, in which the borrower only pays the interest on the loan for the first few years, usually three. After that, the payments increase to cover the interest and part of the original loan, as in an *amortized mortgage*. Low start mortgages are popular with first-time buyers, as the lower initial costs may free up funds for furnishings or home improvements. See also *mortgage*

loyalty bonus FINANCE, BANKING, AND ACCOUNTING in the United Kingdom in the 1980s, a number of extra shares, calculated as a propor-

tion of the shares originally subscribed, given to original subscribers of privatization issues providing the shares were held continuously for a given period of time

loyalty plan MARKETING a sales promotion technique to encourage customers to continue buying a product or using an organization's services. It works by rewarding customers who spend more and/or stay longer with an organization. Examples include a shopper card that gives discounts on purchases over a period of time.

There are several other loyalty plan approaches: points systems—which give points to customers based on what they purchase; premium customer programs—where customers who spend certain amounts of money and are repeat purchasers gain special status and receive benefits such as discounts, exclusive offers, and gifts; buyers' clubs—where a certain number of customers can club together to buy a particular product, at a special volume discount.

If implementing a loyalty plan, it is important to remember that it must be there for the long term, and the level of incentive must be right. Offering too much will hurt your profits; offering too little will not attract members. Customers also need to be able to check up on their status easily—to see, for example, how many points they have currently accumulated.

lump sum FINANCE, BANKING, AND ACCOUNTING
1 used to describe a loan that is repayable with one installment at the end of its term. See also *balloon loan interest-only mortgage*
2 an amount of money received in one payment, for example, the sum payable to the beneficiary of a life insurance policy on the death of the policyholder

lunch
do lunch GENERAL MANAGEMENT to have a lunch meeting with somebody (*slang*)

lurk E-COMMERCE to visit an Internet newsgroup without taking part. People wishing to promote their company's products or services within a newsgroup lurk to see whether the group accepts commercial messages or whether there are any questions they could answer. Lurking is important because inappropriate messages are likely to receive a hostile response from newsgroup members and may even be considered as *spam*. Lurking in relevant newsgroups can also be an effective means of online market research.

luxury tax FINANCE, BANKING, AND ACCOUNTING a tax on goods or services that are considered nonessential

M

Ma and Pa shop (*U.K.*) GENERAL MANAGEMENT a small family-run business (*slang*)

Machiavelli, Niccolò (1469–1527) GENERAL MANAGEMENT Italian politician. Machiavelli's *The Prince* (1532) is one of the earliest works on political theory, embracing the concepts of *power*, *authority*, and *leadership*. In *Management and Machiavelli* (1967), Antony Jay sought to show the relevance of Machiavelli's philosophy to modern society.

Machiavelli was born in Florence, Italy, and served as an official in the Florentine government. His work brought him into contact with some of Europe's most influential ministers and government representatives. His chief diplomatic triumph occurred when Florence obtained the surrender of Pisa. But in 1512 when the Medicis returned to power, his career came to an abrupt end. He was accused of being involved in a plot against the government. For this he was imprisoned, tortured, and finally exiled.

He retired to a farm outside Florence and began a successful writing career, producing plays and a history of Florence as well as the books on politics for which he is now chiefly remembered. See thinker *Niccolò Machiavelli*

machine code E-COMMERCE a set of instructions to a computer in the form of a binary code

machine hour rate FINANCE, BANKING, AND ACCOUNTING an *overhead absorption rate* based on machine hours

macho management GENERAL MANAGEMENT an authoritarian management style that asserts a manager's right to manage. Macho management is a term coined by *Michael Edwardes*, and it was adopted by the media in the 1980s. Macho managers tend to take a tough approach to improving *productivity* and efficiency, and are unsympathetic to *labor unions*.

macroeconomics ECONOMICS the study of national income and the economic systems of national economies

macroeconomy ECONOMICS the broad sectors of a country's economic activity, for example, the financial or industrial sectors, that are aggregated to form its economic system as a whole

macrohedge FINANCE, BANKING, AND ACCOUNTING a hedge that pertains to an entire portfolio. See also *microhedge*

Macromedia Flash™ *tdmk* E-COMMERCE a type of Web animation software. Its small file sizes and easy *scalability* make Flash one of the more flexible animation packages, and it uses *streaming* technology so that animations can be viewed more quickly. Flash also allows sound to be added to an animation effectively.

magnet employer HR & PERSONNEL a popular organization which attracts many job applicants (*slang*)

mail form E-COMMERCE a Web page that requires the user to input data, for example, name, address, or order or shipping information, that is transmitted to an e-merchant via e-mail

mailing house MARKETING an organization that specializes in planning, creating, and implementing direct mail campaigns for clients

mailing list MARKETING the names and addresses of a particular group of people compiled for marketing purposes. A mailing list may be compiled internally or bought or rented from an outside agency, and can be used for advertising, fundraising, news releases, or for *direct mail* or a *mailshot*. A mailing list is usually compiled for a selected group using one or more criteria, such as men between the ages of 25 and 30.

mail order MARKETING a form of retailing in which consumers order products from a catalog for delivery to their home

mail-out GENERAL MANAGEMENT a single instance of using direct mail

mail server E-COMMERCE a remote computer enabling people and organizations to send and receive e-mail

mailshot MARKETING the speculative targeting of a particular or specified group of people by mail. A mailshot normally contains *advertising*, fundraising requests, or *press releases*.

mailsort MARKETING a sorting service offered to organizations by the Post Office, intended to reduce the cost and time spent on direct mail

mail survey MARKETING a research technique in which questionnaires are sent and returned by mail. U.K. term *postal survey*

mainframe E-COMMERCE a powerful computer capable of supporting hundreds of thousands of users simultaneously

mainstream corporation tax FINANCE, BANKING, AND ACCOUNTING the principal U.K. tax on corporations

maintenance OPERATIONS & PRODUCTION the process of keeping physical assets in working order to ensure their availability and to reduce the chance of failure. An effective maintenance program can enhance safety, increase reliability, reduce quality errors, lower operating costs, and increase the life span of assets. There are different maintenance approaches, including *reactive maintenance*, *predictive maintenance*, and *preventive maintenance*. Two strategies that have more recently become prominent are *reliability centered maintenance* and *total productive maintenance*.

maintenance bond FINANCE, BANKING, AND ACCOUNTING a bond that provides a guarantee against defects for some time after a contract has been fulfilled

majority shareholder FINANCE, BANKING, AND ACCOUNTING a stockholder with a controlling interest in a company

make or buy GENERAL MANAGEMENT see *purchasing versus production*

make-to-order OPERATIONS & PRODUCTION the production of goods or components to meet an existing order. Make-to-order products are made to the customer's specification, and are often processed in small batches.

Malcolm Baldrige National Quality Award GENERAL MANAGEMENT an award recognizing achievements in quality and business performance. The Malcolm Baldrige National Quality Award was launched by the U.S. government in 1987 to encourage U.S. companies to publicize successful quality and improvement strategies, to adopt *total quality management*, and to encourage competitiveness. In assessing companies for the Award, examiners allocate points in seven major areas: leadership, information and analysis, strategic planning, human resource development, process management, customer focus and satisfaction, and business results. The Award also involves evaluation of companies according to three main factors: 1. What is the organization's approach to achieving its goals: how does it attempt to achieve top-class performance? 2. How is this approach put into practice in the organization, what resources are being brought to bear, and how widespread is this action throughout the organization? 3. What evidence is there to demonstrate that improvements are really taking place?

malware E-COMMERCE software such as viruses or Trojans designed to cause damage or disruption to a computer system

managed currency fund FINANCE, BANKING, AND ACCOUNTING a mutual fund that makes considered investments in currencies

managed derivatives fund FINANCE, BANKING, AND ACCOUNTING a fund which uses mainly futures and options instead of investing in the underlying securities

managed economy FINANCE, BANKING, AND ACCOUNTING an economy directed by a government rather than the free market

managed float ECONOMICS the position when the exchange rate of a country's currency is influenced by government action in the foreign exchange market

managed fund FINANCE, BANKING, AND ACCOUNTING a mutual fund that makes considered investments. See also *index fund*

managed hosting E-COMMERCE a *hosting option* in which the hosting provider is principally responsible for a client's servers. This role can range from the vendor supplying and managing the hardware only, to supplying the software as well. This type of vendor is called an *ASP* (application service provider).

managed rate (*U.K.*) FINANCE, BANKING, AND ACCOUNTING a rate of interest charged by a financial institution for borrowing that is not prescribed as a margin over base rate but is set from time to time by the institution

management GENERAL MANAGEMENT HR & PERSONNEL the use of professional skills for identifying and achieving organizational objectives through the deployment of appropriate resources. Management involves identifying what needs to be done, and organizing and supporting others to perform the necessary tasks. A manager has complex and ever-changing responsibilities, the focus of which shifts to reflect the issues, trends, and preoccupations of the time. At the beginning of the 20th century, the emphasis was both on supporting the organization's administration and managing *productivity* through increased efficiency. Organizations following the models of *Henri Fayol* and *Max Weber* built the functional divisions of personnel management, production management, marketing management, operations management, and financial management. At the beginning of the 21st century, those original drivers are still much in evidence, although the emphasis has moved to

the key areas of **competence** such as people management. Although management is a profession in its own right, its skill-set often applies to professionals of other disciplines. See thinker *Henri Fayol*, *Max Weber*

management accountant FINANCE, BANKING, AND ACCOUNTING a person who contributes to management's decision-making processes by, for example, collecting and processing data relating to a business's costs, sales, and the profitability of individual activities

management accounting FINANCE, BANKING, AND ACCOUNTING the application of the principles of accounting and financial management to create, protect, preserve, and increase value so as to deliver that value to the stakeholders of profit and nonprofit enterprises, both public and private. Management accounting is an integral part of management, requiring the identification, generation, presentation, interpretation, and use of information relevant to formulating business strategy; planning and controlling activities; decision making; efficient resource usage; performance improvement and value enhancement; safeguarding tangible and intangible assets; and corporate governance and internal control.

management audit GENERAL MANAGEMENT see *operational audit*

management buy-in GENERAL MANAGEMENT the purchase of an existing business by an individual manager or management group outside that business. In the United Kingdom, the company 3i is often involved in supporting management buy-ins. 3i has also promoted a hybrid form of management buy-in and *management buy-out*, given the acronym *BIMBO*, which involves an incoming chief executive sharing his or her investment with the company's existing management team. Abbr. *MBI*

management buy-out FINANCE, BANKING, AND ACCOUNTING GENERAL MANAGEMENT the purchase of an existing business by an individual manager or management group from within that business. Abbr. *MBO*

management by exception GENERAL MANAGEMENT a system of management in which only deviations from the plan or the norm are to be reported to the manager, ensuring management attention is only given when necessary

management by objectives *or* **management by results** GENERAL MANAGEMENT a method of managing an organization by setting a series of *objectives* that contribute toward

the achievement of its goals. Abbr. *MBO*. See thinker *Peter Drucker*

management by walking around GENERAL MANAGEMENT a hands-on style of management based on regularly walking around to speak to, question, and listen to employees, and to learn more about work processes

management company GENERAL MANAGEMENT a company that takes over responsibility from internal staff for managing facilities such as computer systems, telecommunications, or maintenance. The process is known as *outsourcing*.

management consultant GENERAL MANAGEMENT a person professionally engaged in advising on, and providing, a detached, external view of a company's management techniques and practices. A management consultant may be self-employed, a partner, or employed in a firm. Consultants can be called in for many reasons, but are employed particularly for projects involving business improvement, *change management*, information technology, and long-term planning.

management consulting GENERAL MANAGEMENT
1 the activity of advising on management techniques and practices. Management consulting usually involves the identification of a problem, or the analysis of a specific area of one organization, and the reporting of any resulting findings. The consulting process can sometimes be extended to help put into effect the recommendations made.
2 a firm of *management consultants*

management control systems GENERAL MANAGEMENT measures, procedures, *performance indicators*, and other instruments used to check and regulate operations systematically. Management control systems are established to maintain management *control* on a routine basis, and can include *budgets* and budgetary controls, credit control, working procedures, inventory control, production processes, and quality measures or controls.

management development HR & PERSONNEL the process of creating and enhancing the *competences* of *managers* and potential managers. Management development is usually thought of as a planned process, focusing on a long-term development program to increase managerial effectiveness, but it also incorporates informal and unplanned elements such as learning from day-to-day experience. Management development programs within an organization work to identify and recruit

potential managers, and develop their knowledge and skills to meet organizational needs. They also equip managers for more senior posts. Management development activities include short courses, *management education* programs, *management training*, *coaching*, and *mentoring*.

management education HR & PERSONNEL formal instruction in the principles and techniques of *management*, and in related subjects, leading to a degree. Management education strives to develop management knowledge, understanding, and *competence* through classroom or distance-based methods. Management education is a main component of *management development*, and differs from *management training* in that the latter may exploit any one of a variety of formal or informal methods, tends to be focused on a specific skill, and does not result directly in a formal degree.

management guru GENERAL MANAGEMENT an informal term for a *management theorist*

management information system GENERAL MANAGEMENT see *MIS*

management science GENERAL MANAGEMENT the application of scientific methods and principles to management *decision making* and *problem solving*. Management science encompasses the use of quantitative, mathematical, and statistical techniques. The term can be used to denote scientific management, which has origins in the work of *Frederick Winslow Taylor*, *Henry Gantt*, and *Frank* and *Lillian Gilbreth*. Management science lies at the opposite end of the spectrum to the *human relations* school. See thinker *Henry Laurence Gantt*, *Frederick Winslow Taylor*

management services GENERAL MANAGEMENT a department or team of internally employed technical and professional specialists offering services or advice to management. Management services can cover areas such as work study, legal, computer, information, economic intelligence, and similar specialist support services.

management standards GENERAL MANAGEMENT published guidelines to best practice, outlining the knowledge, understanding, and personal *competences* that managers need to develop and demonstrate if they are to be effective

management style GENERAL MANAGEMENT the general manner, outlook, attitude, and behavior of a manager in his or her dealings with

subordinates. Organizations may have, or seek to have, distinctive management styles, and sometimes train employees to try to ensure that a preferred style, fitting in with the desired **corporate culture**, is always used. Management styles can vary widely between extremes of control and consultation. The latter are generally thought to encourage degrees of **employee participation** in management with consequently improved **employee commitment**, **employee involvement**, and **empowerment**. More participatory styles are also usually related to more open organizational cultures and flatter organizational structures. One well-known instrument for distinguishing individual management styles is **Robert Blake**'s and **Jane Mouton**'s **Managerial Grid™**.

management succession GENERAL MANAGEMENT see **succession planning**

management team GENERAL MANAGEMENT see **senior management**

management theorist GENERAL MANAGEMENT somebody who puts forward original ideas and theories about management. The work of a management theorist is usually presented through books or articles, and often has its base in practical or academic research, and consulting or practical work experience.

management threshold GENERAL MANAGEMENT an outmoded term for a level of seniority in an organization which somebody cannot surmount. The management threshold is reached by an **employee** who has risen to a certain level in an organization and seems unable to rise any further. It can lead to plateauing, where an employee is unable to gain **promotion** and stays in the same role for many years. Failure to surmount the management threshold can be caused by lack of opportunities for advancement, lack of ambition, or lack of skills or ability.

management trainee HR & PERSONNEL an employee who holds a low-level management position while undergoing formal training in management techniques

management training HR & PERSONNEL planned activities for **management development**. Management training methods include public or **in-company training** courses and **on-the-job training** designed to improve managerial **competences**. Management training tends to be practical and to focus on specific management techniques. Unlike **management education**, it does not result in a formal degree.

manager GENERAL MANAGEMENT a person who identifies and achieves organizational objectives through the deployment of appropriate resources. A manager can have responsibilities in one or more of five key areas: managing activities; managing resources; managing information; managing people; and managing him- or herself at the same time as working within the context of the organizational, political, and economic business environments. There are managers in all disciplines and activities, although some may not bear the title of manager. Some specialize in areas such as personnel, marketing, production, finance, or project management, while others are **general managers**, applying **management** skills across all business areas. Very few jobs are entirely managerial, and very few exist without any management responsibilities. It is the capability to harness resources that largely distinguishes a manager from a non-manager.

Managerial Grid™ *tdmk* GENERAL MANAGEMENT a tool to measure and understand managerial behavior which places concern for task and concern for people on two matrices against which a manager's style can be plotted. The Managerial Grid™ grades each matrix 1 to 9, and identifies five different managerial behavior patterns: 1–1, or impoverished management, in which a minimum of concern for either people or task is displayed; 9–1, or **authority-compliance management**, in which a preoccupation with task is displayed; 5–5, or **middle-of-the-road management**, in which a balance between task and people is striven for; 1–9, or **country club management**, which is concerned with human relations to the detriment of output; and 9–9, or **team management**, the ideal, in which production and human requirements are integrated in a team approach to achieving results.

managerialism GENERAL MANAGEMENT emphasis on efficient management, and the use of systems, planning, and management practice. Managerialism is often used in a critical sense, especially from the perspective of the public sector, to imply overenthusiasm for efficiency, or private sector management techniques and systems, possibly at the expense of service or quality considerations. The term is also used to describe confrontational attitudes, or actions displayed by management toward labor unions.

managing agent FINANCE, BANKING, AND ACCOUNTING a person who runs the day-to-day activities of a Lloyd's syndicate

managing director GENERAL MANAGEMENT a director of a company who has overall responsibility for its day-to-day operations. Abbr **MD**

managing for value FINANCE, BANKING, AND ACCOUNTING an approach to building the long-term value of a business. The term is most frequently used by businesses that are implementing the **balanced scorecard** and emphasizes the need to make financial and commercial decisions that build the value of the business for its stockholders.

M&A *abbr* FINANCE, BANKING, AND ACCOUNTING mergers and acquisitions

mandarin GENERAL MANAGEMENT a high-ranking and influential adviser, especially in government circles

mandatory quote period (*U.K.*) FINANCE, BANKING, AND ACCOUNTING a period of time during which prices of securities must be displayed in a market

manpower forecasting GENERAL MANAGEMENT the prediction of future levels of demand for, and supply of, workers and skills at organizational, regional, or national level. A variety of techniques are used in manpower forecasting, including the statistical analysis of current trends and the use of mathematical models. At national level, these include the analysis of census statistics; at organizational level, projections of future requirements may be made from sales and production figures. Manpower forecasting forms part of the **manpower planning** process.

manpower planning GENERAL MANAGEMENT the development of strategies to match the supply of workers to the availability of jobs at organizational, regional, or national level. Manpower planning involves reviewing current manpower resources, forecasting future requirements and availability, and taking steps to ensure that the supply of people and skills meets demand. At a national level, this may be conducted by government or industry bodies, and at an organizational level, by human resource managers. A more current term for manpower planning at organizational level is **human resource planning**.

manual worker HR & PERSONNEL an employee who performs physical work, especially in a factory or outdoors. Also known as **blue-collar worker**

manufacture OPERATIONS & PRODUCTION the large-scale production of goods from raw materials or constituent parts

manufacturer OPERATIONS & PRODUCTION a person or organization involved in *production*

manufacturer's agent OPERATIONS & PRODUCTION a person or organization with authority to act for a *manufacturer* in obtaining a *contract* with a third party

manufacturing GENERAL MANAGEMENT see *production*

manufacturing account FINANCE, BANKING, AND ACCOUNTING a financial statement which shows production costs only, as opposed to a trading account, which shows sales and costs of sales. A manufacturing account will include direct materials and labor costs and the production overhead.

manufacturing cost OPERATIONS & PRODUCTION the expenditure incurred in carrying out the *production* processes of an organization. The manufacturing cost includes *direct costs*, for example, labor, materials, and expenses, and indirect costs, for example, *subcontracting* and overheads.

manufacturing for excellence GENERAL MANAGEMENT see *design for manufacturability*

manufacturing information system OPERATIONS & PRODUCTION an *MIS* designed specifically for use in a *production* environment

manufacturing management GENERAL MANAGEMENT see *production management*

manufacturing resource planning OPERATIONS & PRODUCTION see *MRP II*

manufacturing system OPERATIONS & PRODUCTION a method of organizing *production*. Manufacturing systems include assembly and *batch production*, *flexible manufacturing systems*, *lean production*, *group technology*, *job production*, *kanban*, and *mass production*.

manufacturing to order OPERATIONS & PRODUCTION a production management technique in which goods are produced to meet firm orders, rather than being produced for stock

MAPS *abbr* E-COMMERCE Mail Abuse Prevention System: the leading organization campaigning against unsolicited commercial e-mail messages, or "spam"

Marché des Options Négotiables de Paris FINANCE, BANKING, AND ACCOUNTING in France, the traded options market. Abbr. *MONEP*

Marché International de France FINANCE, BANKING, AND ACCOUNTING in France, the international futures and options exchange

Margerison, Charles J. (*b.* 1940) GENERAL MANAGEMENT U.K. business researcher and writer. See also *McCann, Dick*

margin
1 FINANCE, BANKING, AND ACCOUNTING GENERAL MANAGEMENT the difference between the cost and the selling price of a product or service
2 (*ANZ*) HR & PERSONNEL a payment made to workers over and above the basic wage in recognition of special skills

margin account FINANCE, BANKING, AND ACCOUNTING an account with a broker who lends money for investments

marginal analysis ECONOMICS the study of how small changes in an economic variable will affect an economy

marginal cost
1 ECONOMICS the amount by which the costs of a firm will be increased if its output is increased by one more unit, or if one more customer is served.

If the price charged is greater than the marginal cost, then the revenue gain will be greater than the added cost. That, in turn, will increase profit, so the expansion in production or service makes economic sense and should proceed. The reverse is also true: if the price charged is less than the marginal cost, expansion should not go ahead.

The formula for marginal cost is:

$$\frac{\text{Change in cost}}{\text{Change in quantity}}$$

If it costs a company $260,000 to produce 3,000 items, and $325,000 to produce 3,800 items, the change in cost would be:

$$\$325,000 - \$260,000 = \$65,000$$

The change in quantity would be:

$$3,800 - 3,000 = 800$$

When the formula to calculate marginal cost is applied, the result is:

$$\frac{\$65,000}{800} = \$81.25$$

If the price of the item in question were $99.95, expansion should proceed.

Relying on marginal cost is not fail-safe, however; putting more products on a market can drive down prices and thus cut margins. Moreover, committing idle capacity to long-term production may tie up resources that could be directed to a new and more profitable opportunity. An important related principle is contribution: the cash gained (or lost) from selling an additional unit.

2 FINANCE, BANKING, AND ACCOUNTING the part of the cost of one unit of product or service which would be avoided if that unit were not produced, or which would increase if one extra unit were produced

marginal costing FINANCE, BANKING, AND ACCOUNTING the accounting system in which variable costs are charged to cost units and fixed costs of the period are written off in full against the aggregate contribution. Its special value is in recognizing cost behavior, and hence assisting in decision making. Also known as *variable costing*

marginal costs and benefits ECONOMICS the losses or gains to an individual or household arising from a small change in a variable, such as food consumption or income received

marginalization GENERAL MANAGEMENT the process by which countries lose importance and status because they are unable to participate in mainstream activities such as industrialization or the Internet economy

marginal lender FINANCE, BANKING, AND ACCOUNTING a lender who will make a loan only at or above a particular rate of interest

marginal private cost ECONOMICS the cost to an individual of a small change in the price of a variable, for example, gas

marginal revenue FINANCE, BANKING, AND ACCOUNTING the revenue generated by additional units of production

marginal tax rate FINANCE, BANKING, AND ACCOUNTING the rate of tax payable on a person's income after business expenses have been deducted

margining FINANCE, BANKING, AND ACCOUNTING the system by which the London Clearing House (LCH) controls the risk associated with a London International Financial Futures and Options Exchange clearing member's position on a daily basis. To achieve this, clearing members deposit cash or collateral with the LCH in the form of initial and variation margins. The initial margin is the deposit required on all open positions (long or short) to cover short-term price movements and is returned to members by the LCH when the position is closed. The variation margin is the members' profits or losses, calculated daily from the marked-to-market-close value of their position (whereby contracts are revalued daily for the calculation of variation margin), and credited to or debited from their accounts.

margin of error OPERATIONS & PRODUCTION an allowance made for the possibility of miscalculation

margin of safety OPERATIONS & PRODUCTION the difference between the level of activity at which an organization breaks even and the level of activity greater than this point. For example, a margin of safety of $300,000 is achieved when the break-even point is $900,000 and sales reach $1,200,000. This measure can be expressed as a proportion of sales value, as a number of units sold, or as a percentage of *capacity*.

marital deductions FINANCE, BANKING, AND ACCOUNTING the part of an estate which, after a death, is not subject to estate tax because it goes to the spouse of the deceased

marked cheque (*U.K.*) FINANCE, BANKING, AND ACCOUNTING a certified check (*slang*)

marked price FINANCE, BANKING, AND ACCOUNTING the original displayed price of a product in a store. In a sale, customers may be offered a savings on the marked price.

market
1 ECONOMICS GENERAL MANAGEMENT a group of people or organizations unified by a common need
2 ECONOMICS GENERAL MANAGEMENT a gathering of sellers and purchasers to exchange commodities
3 ECONOMICS FINANCE, BANKING, AND ACCOUNTING the rate at which financial commodities or securities are being sold

marketable MARKETING possessing the potential to be commercially viable. To determine whether a new product or service is marketable, an assessment needs to be conducted to see if it is likely to make a profit. The assessment is often based on detailed *market research* analyzing the potential market, and the projected financial returns and any other benefits for the company.

market analysis MARKETING the study of a market to identify and quantify business opportunities

market area MARKETING the geographic location of a market

market based pricing FINANCE, BANKING, AND ACCOUNTING setting a price based on the value of the product in the perception of the customer. Also known as *perceived value pricing*

market bubble FINANCE, BANKING, AND ACCOUNTING a stock market phenomenon in which

values in a particular sector become inflated for a short period. If the bubble bursts, stock prices in that sector collapse.

market cap *abbr* FINANCE, BANKING, AND ACCOUNTING market capitalization

market capitalization FINANCE, BANKING, AND ACCOUNTING the total market value of a company, calculated by multiplying the price of its shares on the Stock Exchange by the number of shares outstanding. Abbr. *market cap*

market coverage GENERAL MANAGEMENT the degree to which a product or service meets the needs of a market

market development MARKETING marketing activities designed to increase the overall size of a market through education and awareness

market driven MARKETING using market knowledge to determine the *corporate strategy* of an organization. A market driven organization has a *customer focus*, together with awareness of competitors, and an understanding of the *market*.

market economist FINANCE, BANKING, AND ACCOUNTING a person who specializes in the study of financial structures and the return on investments in the stock market

market economy ECONOMICS an economy in which a *free market* in goods and services operates

marketeer MARKETING a small company that competes in the same market as larger companies. Examples of marketeers are restaurants, travel agents, computer software providers, garages, and insurance brokers.

marketer MARKETING somebody who is responsible for developing and implementing marketing policy

marketface GENERAL MANAGEMENT the interface between suppliers and customers

market-facing enterprise GENERAL MANAGEMENT an organization that aligns itself with its markets and customers

market-focused organization MARKETING an organization whose strategies are determined by market requirements rather than organizational demands

market forces FINANCE, BANKING, AND ACCOUNTING influences on sales which bring about a change in prices

market fragmentation MARKETING a situation in which the buyers or sellers in a market consist of a large number of small organizations

market gap MARKETING an opportunity in a market where no supplier provides a product or service that buyers need

market if touched FINANCE, BANKING, AND ACCOUNTING an order to trade a security if it reaches a specified price. Abbr. *MIT*

marketing MARKETING see *marketing management*

4 Ps of marketing GENERAL MANAGEMENT see *marketing mix*

marketing audit MARKETING an analysis of either the external marketing environment or a company's internal marketing goals, objectives, operations, and efficiency. An external marketing audit covers issues such as economic, political, infrastructure, technological, and consumer perspectives; *market size* and *structure*; and competitors, suppliers, and distributors. An internal marketing audit covers aspects such as the company's *mission statement*, goals, and objectives; its structure, corporate culture, systems, operations, and processes; *product development* and pricing; profitability and efficiency; *advertising*; and deployment of the *sales force*.

marketing consultancy MARKETING an organization that plans and develops marketing strategies and programs on behalf of clients

marketing information system MARKETING an information system concerned with the collection, storage, and analysis of information and data for marketing *decision making* purposes. Information for use in marketing information systems is gathered from customers, competitors and their products, and from the market itself.

marketing management MARKETING one of the main management disciplines, encompassing all the strategic planning, operations, activities, and processes involved in achieving organizational objectives by delivering value to customers. Marketing management focuses on satisfying customer requirements by identifying needs and wants, and developing products and services to meet them. In seeking to satisfy customer requirements, *marketing* goals to build long-term relationships with customers and with other interested parties and to provide value to them. This begins with *market research*, which analyzes needs and wants in society, and continues with attracting customers and

the cultivation of mutually beneficial exchange processes with them. Tools used in this process are diverse and include market segmentation, **brand management**, **PR**, **logistics**, **direct response marketing**, **sales promotion**, and **advertising**.

marketing manager MARKETING an employee of a client organization who is responsible for planning and controlling its marketing activities and budgets

marketing mix MARKETING the variety of integrated decisions made by a marketing manager to ensure successful marketing. These decisions are made in four key areas known as the **4 Ps of marketing** —product, price, place, and promotion—and cover issues such as the type of product to be marketed, brand name, pricing, advertising, publicity, geographic coverage, retailing, and distribution.

marketing myopia MARKETING the name given to the theory that some organizations ignore the fact that to be successful, the wants of customers must be their central consideration. First promoted by **Theodore Levitt** in "Marketing Myopia," published in the *Harvard Business Review* during 1960, the theory has gained such widespread acceptance that it now appears commonplace.

marketing plan MARKETING overall marketing objectives and the strategies and programs of action designed to achieve those objectives

marketing planning MARKETING the process of producing a **marketing plan**. Marketing planning requires a careful examination of all strategic issues, including the business environment, the markets themselves, competitors, the corporate **mission statement**, and organizational capabilities. The resulting marketing plan should be communicated to appropriate staff through an oral briefing to ensure it is fully understood.

market intelligence MARKETING a collection of internal and external data on a given market. Market intelligence focuses particularly on competitors, customers, consumer spending, market trends, and suppliers.

market leader MARKETING FINANCE, BANKING, AND ACCOUNTING see **market share**

market logic FINANCE, BANKING, AND ACCOUNTING the prevailing forces or attitudes that determine a company's success or failure on the stock market

market maker FINANCE, BANKING, AND ACCOUNTING

1 (*U.K.*) somebody who works in a stock exchange to facilitate trades in one particular company

2 a broker or bank that maintains a market for a security that does not trade on any exchange

market neutral funds FINANCE, BANKING, AND ACCOUNTING hedge funds which are not related to general market movements but which are used to find opportunities to arbitrage temporary slight changes in the relative values of particular financial assets

market order FINANCE, BANKING, AND ACCOUNTING an order to trade a security at the best price the broker can obtain

market penetration HR & PERSONNEL a measure of the percentage or potential percentage of the market that a product or company is able to capture, expressed in terms of total sales or turnover. Market penetration is often used to measure the level of success a new product or service has achieved.

market penetration pricing MARKETING the policy of pricing a product or service very competitively, and sometimes at a loss to the producer, in order to increase its **market share**

market position MARKETING the place held by a product or service in a **market**, usually determined by its percentage of total sales. An ideal market position is often predefined for a product or service. Analysis of potential customers and competing products can be used with product differentiation techniques to formulate a product to fill the desired market position.

market potential MARKETING a forecast of the size of a market in terms of revenue, numbers of buyers, or other factors

market power MARKETING the dominance of a market either by customers, who create a buyer's market, or by a particular company, which creates a seller's market. Individuals or companies retain control of the market by fixing the pricing and number of products available.

market price ECONOMICS in economics, the theoretical price at which supply equals demand

market research MARKETING research conducted to assess the size and nature of a market

market risk FINANCE, BANKING, AND ACCOUNTING risk that cannot be diversified away, also known as systematic risk. **Non-systematic** or

unsystematic risk applies to a single investment or class of investments, and can be reduced or eliminated by diversification.

market sector or **market segment** MARKETING a subdivision of a **market** with distinctive characteristics. Market sectors are usually determined by market segmentation, which divides a market into different categories. Car buyers, for example, could be put into sectors such as car fleet buyers, private buyers, buyers under 20 years old, and so on. The smaller the sector, the more its members will have in common. Sellers may decide to compete in the whole market or only in segments that are attractive to them or where they have an advantage.

market sentiment FINANCE, BANKING, AND ACCOUNTING the mood of those participating in exchange dealings that can range from absolute euphoria to downright gloom and despondency and tends to reflect recent company results, economic indicators, and comments by politicians, analysts, or opinion formers. Optimism increases demand and therefore prices, while pessimism has the opposite effect.

market share

1 MARKETING the proportion of the total market value of a product or group of products or services that a company, service, or product holds. Market share is shown as a percentage of the total value or output of a market, usually expressed in sterling or U.S. dollars, by weight (tons or tonnes), or as individual units, depending on the commodity. The product, service, or company with a dominant market share is referred to as the **market leader**.

2 FINANCE, BANKING, AND ACCOUNTING one entity's sales of a product or service in a specified market expressed as a proportion of total sales by all entities offering that product or service to the market. It can be viewed as a planning tool and a performance assessment ratio.

market site E-COMMERCE a Web site shared by multiple e-commerce vendors, each having a different specialty, to conduct business over the Internet

market size FINANCE, BANKING, AND ACCOUNTING the largest number of shares that a market will handle in one trade of a particular security

market structure MARKETING the makeup of a particular **market**. Market structure can be described with reference to different characteristics of a market, including its size and value, the number of providers and their **market share**, consumer and business purchasing behavior, and growth forecasts. The description

may also include a demographic and regional breakdown of providers and customers and an analysis of pricing structures, likely technological impacts, and domestic and overseas sales.

market targeting MARKETING the selection of a particular market segment toward which all marketing effort is directed. Market targeting enables the characteristics of the chosen segment to be taken into account when formulating a product or service and its advertising.

market valuation FINANCE, BANKING, AND ACCOUNTING

1 see *market capitalization*

2 the value of a portfolio at market prices

3 the opinion of an expert professional as to the current worth of a piece of real estate

market value FINANCE, BANKING, AND ACCOUNTING the price that buyers are willing to pay for a good or service

market value added FINANCE, BANKING, AND ACCOUNTING the difference between a company's market value (derived from the stock price), and its economic book value (the amount of capital that stockholders have committed to the firm throughout its existence, including any retained earnings). Abbr. *MVA*

marking down FINANCE, BANKING, AND ACCOUNTING the reduction by market makers in the price at which they are prepared to deal in a security, for example, because of an adverse report by an analyst, or the announcement or anticipated announcement of a profit warning by a company

markup FINANCE, BANKING, AND ACCOUNTING the addition to the cost of goods or services which results in a selling price. The markup may be expressed as a percentage or as an absolute monetary amount.

marzipan HR & PERSONNEL belonging to the level of management immediately below the top executives (*slang*)

Maslow, Abraham (1908–70) GENERAL MANAGEMENT U.S. psychologist and behavioral scientist. Known for his work on *motivation*, principally the hierarchy of needs, which was set out in his book *Motivation and Personality* (1954). Maslow's concepts were originally offered as general explanations of human behavior but are now seen as a significant contribution to workplace motivation theory. He is often mentioned in connection with his contemporaries *Douglas McGregor* and *Frederick Herzberg*, all part of the *human relations*

movement in management. See thinker *Frederick Herzberg*, *Douglas McGregor*, *Abraham Maslow*. See checklist *Motivating Your Staff in a Time of Change*

massaging FINANCE, BANKING, AND ACCOUNTING the adjustment of financial figures to create the impression of better performance (*slang*)

mass customization OPERATIONS & PRODUCTION a process that allows a standard, mass-produced item, for example, a bicycle, to be individually tailored to specific customer requirements

mass market MARKETING a market that covers substantial numbers of the population. A mass market may consist of a whole population or just a segment of that population. *Mass customization* of products has allowed a greater number of single products to satisfy a mass market.

mass medium MARKETING an advertising medium such as television or national newspapers which reaches a very large audience

mass meeting HR & PERSONNEL the assembling of most or all of the members of a *labor union* in order to reach a decision on workforce policy. Mass meetings were frequently called during the 1960s and 1970s to determine whether or not *industrial action* would take place. In the United Kingdom, the most memorable examples occurred at British Leyland.

mass production OPERATIONS & PRODUCTION large-scale manufacturing, often designed to meet the demand for a particular product. Mass production methods were developed by *Henry Ford*, founder of the Ford Motor Company. Mass production involves using a moving production or assembly line on which the product moves while operators remain at their stations carrying out their work on each passing product. Mass production is now challenged by methods including *just-in-time* and *lean production*.

master franchise MARKETING a license issued by the owner of a product or service to another party or master franchisee allowing them to issue further *franchise* licenses. A master franchise can benefit the original franchisor, as the master franchisee effectively develops the *franchise chain* on their behalf. A master franchise usually grants further licenses within a defined geographic area, and several master franchises may cover a country.

master limited partnership FINANCE, BANKING, AND ACCOUNTING a partnership of a type that combines tax advantages and advantages of liquidity

Master of Business Administration GENERAL MANAGEMENT see *MBA*

master production scheduling OPERATIONS & PRODUCTION a technique used in material requirements planning systems to develop a detailed plan for product manufacturing. The master production schedule, compiled by a master scheduler, takes account of the requirements of various departments, including sales (delivery dates), finance (inventory minimization), and manufacturing (minimization of setup times), and it schedules production and the purchasing of materials within the capacity of and resources available to the production system.

masthead E-COMMERCE the area at the top of a Web page, usually containing the logo of the organization, often with a *search* box and a set of essential links to important areas of the Web site

matador bond FINANCE, BANKING, AND ACCOUNTING a foreign bond in the Spanish domestic market (*slang*)

matched bargain (*U.K.*) FINANCE, BANKING, AND ACCOUNTING the linked sale and repurchase of the same security. See also *bed and breakfast deal*

matching convention FINANCE, BANKING, AND ACCOUNTING the basis for preparing accounts which says that profits can only be recognized if sales are fully matched with costs accrued during the same period

material cost OPERATIONS & PRODUCTION the cost of the raw materials that go into a product. The material cost of a product excludes any *indirect costs*, for example, overheads or wages, associated with producing the item.

material facts FINANCE, BANKING, AND ACCOUNTING

1 information that has to be disclosed in a prospectus. See also *listing requirements*

2 in an insurance contract, information that the insured has to reveal at the time that the policy is taken out, for example, that a house is located on the edge of a crumbling cliff. Failure to reveal material facts can result in the contract being declared void.

material information FINANCE, BANKING, AND ACCOUNTING price sensitive developments in a company, for example, proposed acquisitions, mergers, profit warnings, and the resignation of directors, that most stock exchanges require a company to announce immediately to the exchange

material news FINANCE, BANKING, AND ACCOUNT-ING = *material information*

materials handling OPERATIONS & PRODUCTION the techniques employed to move, transport, store, and distribute materials, with or without the aid of mechanical equipment

materials management OPERATIONS & PRO-DUCTION an approach for planning, organizing, and controlling all those activities principally concerned with the flow of materials into an organization. The scope of materials management varies greatly from company to company and may include materials planning and control, *production planning*, *purchasing*, inventory control and stores, in-plant materials movement, and *waste management*.

materials testing OPERATIONS & PRODUCTION the process of analyzing the physical and chemical characteristics of materials against a specification

maternity leave HR & PERSONNEL time off work because of pregnancy and childbirth. All female *employees*, regardless of *length of service* and *hours of work*, are legally entitled to statutory maternity leave and to statutory *maternity pay*. Many *employers* offer improved maternity arrangements but these vary from organization to organization and often depend on length of service.

matrix management GENERAL MANAGEMENT management based on two or more reporting systems that are linked to the vertical organization hierarchy, and to horizontal relationships based on geographic, product, or project requirements

matrix organization GENERAL MANAGEMENT organization by both vertical administrative functions and horizontal tasks, areas, processes, or projects. Matrix organization originated in the 1960s and 1970s, particularly within the U.S. aerospace industry, when *organization charts* showing how the management of a given *project* would relate to *senior management* were often required to win government contracts. A two-dimensional matrix chart best illustrates the dual horizontal, and vertical, reporting relationships. Matrix organization is closely linked to *matrix management*.

matrix structure GENERAL MANAGEMENT a form of *organization structure* based on horizontal and vertical relationships. The matrix structure is linked closely to *matrix management*, and is related to *project management*. It emerged on an improvised rather than a planned basis as a way of showing how people

work with or report to others in their organization, project, geographic region, process, or team.

Matsushita, **Konosuke** (1894–1989) GEN-ERAL MANAGEMENT Japanese entrepreneur, business executive, and philanthropist. Founder of Matsushita Electric, and owner of the Panasonic brand, noted for his humanistic approach to business, which was described by John P. Kotter in *Matsushita Leadership* (1997).

mature economy FINANCE, BANKING, AND ACCOUNTING an economy that is no longer developing or growing rapidly

maturity FINANCE, BANKING, AND ACCOUNTING the stage at which a financial instrument, such as a bond, is due for repayment

maturity date FINANCE, BANKING, AND ACCOUNT-ING the date when an *option* expires

maturity yield FINANCE, BANKING, AND ACCOUNT-ING see *yield*

Mauborgne, **Renée** GENERAL MANAGEMENT French academic. INSEAD professor, Fellow of the World Economic Forum, and collaborator of *W. Chan Kim* on research into *corporate strategy* and *value innovation*.

maximum stock level FINANCE, BANKING, AND ACCOUNTING a stock level, set for control purposes, which actual stockholding should never exceed. It is calculated as follows:

((Reorder level + Economic order quantity) –
(Minimum rate of usage ×
Minimum lead time))

Mayo, **Elton** (1880–1949) GENERAL MANAGE-MENT Australian psychologist and academic. Responsible for finding, through the *Hawthorne experiments*, that *job satisfaction* increases through employee participation in decision making, rather than through short-term incentives. The results of the Hawthorne studies were published in Mayo's *The Human Problems of an Industrial Civilization* (1933), and were further publicized by one of his collaborators, *Fritz Jules Roethlisberger*. Mayo is recognized as the founder of the *human relations* school of management.

In the early part of his career, Mayo studied in London and Edinburgh and taught at Queensland University. He arrived in the United States in 1923 and worked at the University of Pennsylvania before moving to Harvard. It was while he was at Harvard that Mayo became involved in the Hawthorne Studies. See thinker *Elton Mayo*

MBA *abbr* GENERAL MANAGEMENT Master of Business Administration: a postgraduate qualification awarded after a period of study of topics relating to the strategic management of businesses. A Master of Business Administration course can be taken at a *business school* or university, and covers areas such as finance, personnel, and resource management, as well as the wider business environment and skills such as information technology use. The course is mostly taken by people with experience of managerial work, and is offered by universities worldwide. Part-time or distance learning MBAs are available, so that students can study while still working. There is an increasing number of MBA graduates, as an MBA is seen as a passport to a better job and higher salary. For many positions at a higher level within organizations, an MBA is now a prerequisite.

MBI *abbr* GENERAL MANAGEMENT management buy-in

MBIA *abbr* FINANCE, BANKING, AND ACCOUNTING Municipal Bond Insurance Association: a group of insurance companies that insure high-rated municipal bonds

MBO *abbr* GENERAL MANAGEMENT
1 management buy-out
2 management by objectives

McCann, **Dick** (*b.* 1943) GENERAL MANAGEMENT Australian business researcher and writer. Developer, with *Charles Margerison*, of the *Team Management Wheel*™, and the team management index/questionnaire, as originally reported in *How to Lead a Winning Team* (1985). Their work on team roles and work preferences compares with that of Carl Jung and *R. Meredith Belbin*. See thinker *R. Meredith Belbin*

McClelland, **David Clarence** (1917–98) GEN-ERAL MANAGEMENT U.S. academic. Initiator of research into the use of *competences* to predict effective job performance, later developed by *Richard Boyatzis*. Author of "Testing for Competence Rather than For Intelligence," *American Psychologist* (1973).

McGregor, **Douglas** (1906–64) GENERAL MANAGEMENT U.S. social psychologist and academic. Developer of *Theory X* and *Theory Y*, which describe two views of people at work and two opposing *management styles*. McGregor's writings on *motivation* and *leadership*, first published in *The Human Side of Enterprise* (1960), have been very influential. *William G. Ouchi* later developed the idea of *Theory Z*.

The son of a clergyman, McGregor graduated from the City College of Detroit (now Wayne University) in 1932. He then went on to Harvard to study for a PhD. After working at Harvard, MIT, and Antioch College in Ohio, McGregor returned to MIT in 1954 as a professor of management. At MIT he attracted some of the stars of the emerging generation of thinkers to work with him, including **Warren Bennis** and **Ed Schein**. See thinker **Douglas McGregor**. See checklist **Motivating Your Staff in a Time of Change**

McKinsey 7-S framework GENERAL MANAGEMENT a model for identifying and exploiting an organization's **human resources** in order to create **competitive advantage**. The McKinsey 7-S framework was developed by McKinsey consultants, including **Tom Peters** and **Robert H. Waterman**, with the academic partnership of **Richard Pascale** and **Anthony G. Athos** in the early 1980s. It sought to present an emphasis on human resources, rather than the traditional mass production tangibles of capital, infrastructure, and equipment. The 7-Ss are: Structure, Strategy, Skills, Staff, Style, Systems, and **Shared values** (see **core values**).

m-commerce E-COMMERCE electronic transactions between buyers and sellers using mobile communications devices such as cellphones, personal digital assistants (PDAs), or laptop computers

MD GENERAL MANAGEMENT see **managing director**

mean STATISTICS a central value or location for a continuous variable in a statistical study

mean reversion FINANCE, BANKING, AND ACCOUNTING the tendency of a variable such as price to return toward its average value after approaching an extreme position

measurement error STATISTICS an error in the recording, calculating, or reading of a numerical value in a statistical study

mechanical handling OPERATIONS & PRODUCTION the use of machines for moving and positioning materials in a warehouse or factory

mechanization GENERAL MANAGEMENT see **automation**

medallion E-COMMERCE the microprocessor chip in a **smart card**

media independent MARKETING an organization that specializes in planning and buying advertising for clients or advertising agencies

median STATISTICS the value that divides a set of ranked observations into two parts of equal size

media plan MARKETING an assessment and outline of the various **advertising media** to be used for a campaign

media planner MARKETING an employee of an advertising agency or media independent who chooses the media, timing, and frequency of advertising

media schedule MARKETING a document that sets out the choice of media, timing, and frequency of advertising

mediation HR & PERSONNEL intervention by a third party in a dispute in order to try to reach agreement between the disputing parties. Where a commitment or award is imposed on either party the process is known as **arbitration**. Also known as **conciliation**

Medicare
1 FINANCE, BANKING, AND ACCOUNTING a health insurance program in which the government pays part of the cost of medical care and hospital treatment for people over 65
2 (*ANZ*) GENERAL MANAGEMENT the Australian public health insurance system. It was created in 1983 and is funded by a levy on income.

medium FINANCE, BANKING, AND ACCOUNTING see **gilt-edged security**

medium-dated gilt FINANCE, BANKING, AND ACCOUNTING see **gilt-edged security**

medium of exchange FINANCE, BANKING, AND ACCOUNTING anything that is used to pay for goods. Nowadays, this usually takes the form of money (bills and coins), but in ancient societies, it included anything from cattle to shells.

medium-sized business GENERAL MANAGEMENT an organization with between 100 and 500 employees. See also **small business large-sized business**

medium-term bond FINANCE, BANKING, AND ACCOUNTING a bond that has at least five but no more than ten years before its redemption date. See also **long-term bond**

meeting GENERAL MANAGEMENT a gathering of two or more people for a particular purpose. Meetings are convened for a variety of purposes, including planning, **decision making**, **problem solving**, communication, and the exchange of information. They may be informal, for example, a few people getting together to discuss ideas, or they may be formal, following

strict procedures. Formal meetings are conducted by a chairperson according to an **agenda** set in advance, and the proceedings are recorded in **minutes**. Some meetings, such as company board meetings and **annual meetings**, are a legal requirement, and take place on a regular basis. See also **chair**

megacity GENERAL MANAGEMENT a very large city in which media and political power is concentrated because of its key role in global information networks

megacorporation or **megacorp** GENERAL MANAGEMENT an informal term for an extremely large and powerful business organization

megatrend GENERAL MANAGEMENT a general shift in thinking or approach affecting countries, industries, and organizations. The term was made popular by **John Naisbitt** in his bestseller *Megatrends* (1982).

MEGO *abbr* GENERAL MANAGEMENT my eyes glaze over: an often sarcastic exclamation of wonder at the complexity of what a person has just said (*slang*)

meltdown FINANCE, BANKING, AND ACCOUNTING an incidence of substantial losses on the stock market. Black Monday (October 19, 1987) was described as Meltdown Monday in the press the following day.

member bank FINANCE, BANKING, AND ACCOUNTING a bank that is a member of the Federal Reserve System

member firm FINANCE, BANKING, AND ACCOUNTING a firm of brokers or market makers that is a member of the London Stock Exchange

member of a company FINANCE, BANKING, AND ACCOUNTING in the United Kingdom, a stockholder whose name is recorded in the register of members

members' voluntary liquidation FINANCE, BANKING, AND ACCOUNTING in the United Kingdom, a special resolution passed by the members of a solvent company for the winding-up of the organization. Prior to the resolution the directors of the company must make a declaration of solvency. Should the appointed liquidator have grounds for believing that the company is not solvent, the winding-up will be treated as compulsory liquidation. See also **voluntary liquidation**

memo GENERAL MANAGEMENT a documented note that acts as a reminder and is used for conveying and recording information. The

memo has to some extent been displaced by e-mail, although it is still sometimes used for important communications.

memory E-COMMERCE the facility that enables a computer to store data and programs

mentoring HR & PERSONNEL a form of *employee development* whereby a trusted and respected person—the mentor—uses their experience to offer guidance, encouragement, career advice, and support to another person—the mentee. The aim of mentoring is to facilitate the mentee's learning and development and to enable them to discover more about their potential. Mentoring can occur informally or it can be arranged by means of an organizational program.

Mentor/mentee relationships can take any form that suits the individuals involved, but in practice there are a few rules that apply to most such arrangements—the most important of which is that anything discussed remains confidential. The relationship also needs to be based on trust and candid communication. A mentor does not have to belong to the same organization as the mentee, but can come from any sphere of the mentee's life—professional association, a community center, your alumni organization, for example—just as long as he or she is not the mentee's direct supervisor or working in the same department. Mentoring does not have to be paid for; in fact it is usually seen as an honor by the mentor. Many accomplished individuals consider it good professional citizenship to participate in the process of helping those coming up after them. It can also frequently be beneficial to volunteer to be a mentor, as many organizations consider mentoring a valuable hallmark of leadership material. See checklist *Mentoring in Practice*

mercantile ECONOMICS relating to trade or commercial activity

mercantile agency FINANCE, BANKING, AND ACCOUNTING a company that evaluates the creditworthiness of potential corporate borrowers. See also *credit bureau*

mercantile paper FINANCE, BANKING, AND ACCOUNTING see *commercial paper*

mercantilism ECONOMICS the body of economic thought developed between the 1650s and 1750s, based on the belief that a country's wealth depended on the strength of its foreign trade

merchandising MARKETING
1 the process of increasing the market share

of a product in retail outlets using display, stocking, and sales promotion techniques
2 the promotion and display of goods associated with a particular *brand*, movie, or celebrity. Merchandising based on a specific movie, for example, may significantly add to its total revenues through appropriate *licensing* opportunities. Merchandising may include clothing, toys, food products, or music and often extends well beyond the *core business* of the producer of the original product.

merchant account E-COMMERCE an account established by an e-merchant at a financial institution or *merchant bank* to receive the proceeds of credit card transactions

merchant bank
1 E-COMMERCE a financial institution at which an e-merchant has opened a merchant account into which the proceeds of credit card transactions are credited after the institution has subtracted its fee
2 (*U.K.*) FINANCE, BANKING, AND ACCOUNTING = *investment bank*

merger FINANCE, BANKING, AND ACCOUNTING GENERAL MANAGEMENT the union of two or more organizations under single ownership, through the direct *acquisition* by one organization of the net assets or liabilities of the other. A merger can be the result of a friendly *takeover*, which results in the combining of companies on an equal footing. After a merger, the legal existence of the acquired organization is terminated. There is no standard definition of a merger, as each union is different, depending on what is expected from the merger, and on the negotiations, strategy, stock and assets, human resources, and stockholders of the players. Four broad types of mergers are recognized. A *horizontal merger* involves firms from the same industry, while a *vertical merger* involves firms from the same supply chain. A *circular merger* involves firms with different products but similar distribution channels. A *conglomerate company* is produced by the union of firms with few or no similarities in production or marketing but that come together to create a larger economic base and greater profit potential. Also known as *acquisition one-to-one merger*. See also *consolidation joint venture partnership*

merger accounting FINANCE, BANKING, AND ACCOUNTING a method of accounting which regards the business combination as the acquisition of one company by another. The identifiable assets and liabilities of the company acquired are included in the consolidated balance sheet at their fair value at the date of acquisition, and its results included in the

profit and loss account from the date of acquisition. The difference between the fair value of the consideration given and the fair values of the net assets of the entity acquired is accounted for as *goodwill*.

mergers and acquisitions FINANCE, BANKING, AND ACCOUNTING a blanket term covering the main ways in which organizations change hands. Abbr. *M&A*

merit rating *or* **merit pay** HR & PERSONNEL a payment system in which the personal qualities of an employee are rated according to organizational requirements, and a pay increase or bonus is made against the results of this rating. Merit rating has been in use since the 1950s. Unlike new *performance-related pay* systems, which focus rewards on the output of an employee, merit rating examines an employee's input to the organization—for example, their attendance, adaptability, or aptitude—as well as the quality or quantity of work produced. In merit rating programs, these factors may be weighted to reflect their relative importance and the resultant points score determines whether the employee earns a bonus or pay increase.

metadata E-COMMERCE essential information on a document or Web page, such as publication date, author, keywords, title, and summary. This information is used by search engines to find relevant Web sites when a user requests a search.

When designing metadata, there are several rules to keep in mind. Always remember the type of person who will be looking for the content—how would they like the content classified? Only collect metadata that is genuinely useful—someone has to fill in all the metadata, and if you ask for too much, it will slow down the publishing process and make it more expensive. Make sure that all essential information is collected—if copyright information is needed, make certain that copyright is part of the metadata list. Check that people are not abusing metadata—some will put popular keywords in their metadata just to increase the chance of their documents coming up in a search, whether relevant or not. Remember that metadata should be strongly linked with advanced search—the metadata forms the parameters for refining an advanced search. See also *meta-tag*

meta-tag E-COMMERCE any of the keyword and description commands used in a Web page code that are used to help search engines index the Web site

Metcalfe's law E-COMMERCE the proposition that networks dramatically increase in value with each additional user. Metcalfe's law was formulated by Robert Metcalfe, founder of 3Com, and has been instrumental in developing the concept of *viral marketing*.

methods-time measurement GENERAL MANAGEMENT a system of *standard times* for movements made by people in the performance of work tasks. Methods-time measurement was developed in the 1940s and is the most widely used of *predetermined motion-time systems* of *work measurement* designed to increase efficiency and consistency in work operations. Work operations are broken down into a set of basic motions such as reach, grasp, position, and release and standard times for each motion are calculated by analyzing films of industrial operations. Simplified versions of the system called MTM2 and MTM3, approved in 1965 and 1970 respectively, use combinations of the basic motions, such as get and put. Abbr. *MTM*

method study GENERAL MANAGEMENT the systematic recording, examination, and analysis of existing and proposed ways of conducting work tasks in order to discover the most efficient and economical methods of performing them. The basic procedure followed in method study is as follows: select the area to be studied; record the data; examine the data; develop alternative approaches; install the new method; maintain the new method. Method study forms part of *work study* and is normally conducted prior to *work measurement*. The technique was initially developed to evaluate manufacturing processes but has been used more widely to evaluate alternative courses of action. It is based on research into *motion study* conducted by *Frank* and *Lillian Gilbreth* during the 1920s and 1930s.

Mickey Mouse GENERAL MANAGEMENT so simple as to appear silly or trivial (*slang*)

microbusiness GENERAL MANAGEMENT a very *small business* with fewer than ten employees

microcash E-COMMERCE a form of electronic money with no denominations, permitting sub-denomination transactions of a fraction of a cent or penny

microcredit FINANCE, BANKING, AND ACCOUNTING the extension of credit to entrepreneurs and *microbusinesses* too poor to qualify for conventional bank loans. Also known as *microlending*

microeconomic incentive ECONOMICS a tax benefit or subsidy given to a business to achieve a particular objective such as increased sales overseas

microeconomics ECONOMICS the branch of economics that studies the contribution of groups of consumers or firms, or of individual consumers, to a country's economy

microeconomy ECONOMICS the narrow sectors of a country's economic activity that influence the behavior of the economy as a whole, for example, consumer choices

microhedge FINANCE, BANKING, AND ACCOUNTING a hedge that relates to a single asset or liability. See also *macrohedge*

microlending FINANCE, BANKING, AND ACCOUNTING see *microcredit*

micromanagement GENERAL MANAGEMENT a style of management where a manager becomes over-involved in the details of the work of subordinates, resulting in the manager making every decision in an organization, no matter how trivial. Micromanagement is a euphemism for meddling, and has the opposite effect to *empowerment*. Micromanagement can retard the progress of *organizational development*, as it robs employees of their self-respect.

micromarketing MARKETING marketing to individuals or very small groups. Micromarketing contrasts with mass marketing and targets the specific interests and needs of individuals by offering customized products or services. It is similar to niche marketing, but rather than targeting one large niche, a micromarketing company targets a large number of very small niches.

micromerchant E-COMMERCE a provider of goods or services on the Internet in exchange for electronic money

micropayment E-COMMERCE FINANCE, BANKING, AND ACCOUNTING a payment protocol for small amounts of electronic money, ranging from a fraction of a cent or penny to no more than ten U.S. dollars or Euros

middleman GENERAL MANAGEMENT an intermediary in a transaction. With direct sales models, manufacturers cut out the middleman by dealing directly with end customers.

middle management HR & PERSONNEL the position held by managers who are considered neither senior nor junior in an organization. Middle managers were subject to *delayering* and *downsizing* in the 1980s as organizations sought to reduce costs by removing the layer of managers between those who had direct interface with customers and senior decision-makers.

middle price (*U.K.*) FINANCE, BANKING, AND ACCOUNTING a price, halfway between the bid price and the offer price, that is generally quoted in the press and on information screens

mid-range STATISTICS the mean of the largest and smallest values in a statistical sample

MIGA *abbr* FINANCE, BANKING, AND ACCOUNTING Multilateral Investment Guarantee Agency

migrate GENERAL MANAGEMENT to transfer data and applications from an existing computer system to a new one

millennium bug GENERAL MANAGEMENT the inability of some computer systems to recognize the year 2000 as a date. The millennium bug arose from the computer programming practice of using two digits to represent a year. It was thought that this could cause great problems when digital clocks turned from 1999 to 2000, because computers would read 00 and cease to function. The millennium bug was thought to affect any business system that used electronically generated date information. Speculation on what would happen sparked fears of global disaster. Much work was conducted in the late 1990s in order to correct the problem, and systems that did not have the bug were referred to as *Y2K-compliant*, Y2K being shorthand for Year 2000. In the end, the anticipated disaster did not occur.

Miller's rule of seven GENERAL MANAGEMENT see *rule of seven*

millionerd E-COMMERCE somebody who has become a millionaire through working in a high-tech business (*slang*)

MIME *abbr* E-COMMERCE multipurpose Internet mail extension: a standard Internet protocol enabling users to send binary files as e-mail attachments

Mind Map™ *tdmk* GENERAL MANAGEMENT a graphic tool that can be used to visualize and clarify thoughts or ideas. In a Mind Map, the central image or idea is drawn in the middle of a piece of paper with major branches radiating from it to denote related themes. Second and third levels of thought are connected by thinner branches. Mind Maps can include the use of color or pictures. Developed by *Tony Buzan*, the Mind Mapping technique can be used to introduce order and rationality to thought processes, and develop the creative,

artistic, logical, and mathematical elements of the brain.

mindshare MARKETING the process of fostering favorable attitudes toward a product or organization

minimax regret criterion FINANCE, BANKING, AND ACCOUNTING an approach to decision making under uncertainty in which the opportunity cost (regret) associated with each possible course of action is measured, and the decision-maker selects the activity which minimizes the maximum regret, or loss. Regret is measured as the difference between the best and worst possible payoff for each option.

minimum lending rate FINANCE, BANKING, AND ACCOUNTING an interest rate charged by a central bank, which serves as a floor for loans in a country

minimum quote size FINANCE, BANKING, AND ACCOUNTING the smallest number of shares that a market must handle in one trade of a particular security

minimum stock level FINANCE, BANKING, AND ACCOUNTING a stock level, set for control purposes, below which stockholding should not fall without being highlighted. It is calculated as follows:

(Re-order level –
    (Average rate of usage × Average lead time))

minimum subscription (*U.K.*) FINANCE, BANKING, AND ACCOUNTING the smallest number of shares or securities that may be applied for in a new issue

minimum wage HR & PERSONNEL an hourly rate of pay, usually set by government, to which all *employees* are legally entitled

minority ownership FINANCE, BANKING, AND ACCOUNTING ownership of less than 50% of a company's common stock, which is not enough to control the company

Mintzberg, Henry (*b.* 1939) GENERAL MANAGEMENT Canadian academic. Known for his views on *strategic management* and *strategic planning* (see *planning*), and for analyzing managerial work. In *The Nature of Managerial Work* (1973), he showed that the work done by managers was substantially different from the way it was described in business theory.

Mintzberg graduated in mechanical engineering from McGill University in 1961 and later obtained a PhD in management from MIT. He is currently professor of management

at McGill University, Montreal, and professor of organization at INSEAD in Fontainebleau, France. See thinker **Henry Mintzberg**. See checklist **Strategic Planning**

minutes GENERAL MANAGEMENT an official written record of the proceedings of a *meeting*. Minutes normally record points for action, and indicate who is responsible for implementing decisions. Good practice requires that the minutes of a meeting be circulated well in advance of the next meeting, and that those attending that meeting read the minutes in advance. Registered companies are required to keep minutes of meetings and make them available at their registered offices for inspection by company members and shareholders.

mirror E-COMMERCE a copy of a Web site held on a different server and therefore available at a different location. Mirror sites can be used to accelerate download times by alleviating Web site congestion. Sites offering software downloads are the most common form of mirror site.

mirror fund FINANCE, BANKING, AND ACCOUNTING an investment trust where the manager also runs a mutual fund with the same objectives

mirror site E-COMMERCE a copy of a Web site maintained on a different file server in order to spread the distribution load or to back up data

MIS *abbr* OPERATIONS & PRODUCTION management information system: a computer-based system for collecting, storing, processing, and providing access to information used in the management of an organization. Management information systems evolved from early electronic data processing systems. They support managerial *decision making* by providing regular structured reports on organizational operations. Management information systems may support the functional areas of an organization such as finance, marketing, or production. *Decision support systems* and *EISs* are types of MIS developed for more specific purposes.

mismanagement GENERAL MANAGEMENT functional or ethical dereliction of duty due to ignorance, negligence, incompetence, avoidance, or criminality

missing value STATISTICS an observation that is absent from a set of statistical data, for example, because a member of a population to be sampled was not at home when the researcher called

mission statement GENERAL MANAGEMENT a short memorable statement of the reasons for

the existence of an organization. See also *vision statement*

MIT *abbr* FINANCE, BANKING, AND ACCOUNTING market if touched

Mittelstand GENERAL MANAGEMENT a German term which incorporates the meaning of *small and medium-sized enterprises*

mixed economy ECONOMICS an economy in which both public and private enterprises participate in the production and supply of goods and services

MMC *abbr* FINANCE, BANKING, AND ACCOUNTING Monopolies and Mergers Commission

MMDA *abbr* FINANCE, BANKING, AND ACCOUNTING money market deposit account

mobile office GENERAL MANAGEMENT the practice of working on the move. Mobile office equipment would typically include a cellphone, laptop computer, and a modem to link the computer to the Internet or a company's main office.

mobile worker HR & PERSONNEL an employee who does not have one fixed place of work. Mobile workers are linked to a central base by telephone and sometimes by computer technology. A *teleworker* is a form of mobile worker.

moblogging E-COMMERCE the use of a cell phone or other handheld digital device to post text and images to a weblog

mode STATISTICS the most frequently occurring value in a set of ranked observations

model building STATISTICS the process of providing an adequate fit to the data in a set of observations in a statistical study

model risk FINANCE, BANKING, AND ACCOUNTING the possibility that a computer model used when investing may have a flaw which makes it function badly in extreme market conditions

modem E-COMMERCE a device that transforms computer data into signals that can be sent over telephone lines. The modem enables computers to transmit and receive data. The speed at which it can send and receive data is measured in BPS (bits per second).

moderator E-COMMERCE somebody in charge of a newsgroup, mailing list discussion group, or similar forum

modernization GENERAL MANAGEMENT investing in new equipment or upgrading existing

equipment to bring resources up to date or improve efficiency

modified accounts (*U.K.*) FINANCE, BANKING, AND ACCOUNTING see *abbreviated accounts*

modified ACRS FINANCE, BANKING, AND ACCOUNTING a system used for computing the depreciation of some assets acquired after 1985 in a way that reduces taxes. The ACRS applies to older assets. See also *accelerated cost recovery system*

modified book value FINANCE, BANKING, AND ACCOUNTING see *adjusted book value*

modified cash basis FINANCE, BANKING, AND ACCOUNTING the bookkeeping practice of accounting for short-term assets on a cash basis and for long-term assets on an accrual basis

Moller, **Claus** (*b.* 1942) GENERAL MANAGEMENT Danish consultant. Founder of Time Manager International™ (1975), advocate of the theory that effective *customer service* is achieved through employees' personal development, he is the originator of the concepts "Time Manager" and "Putting People First."

mom-and-pop operation (*U.S. & Canada*) GENERAL MANAGEMENT a business owned and run by a couple (*slang*) U.K. term **Ma and Pa shop**

moment of conception GENERAL MANAGEMENT the point at which a new organization takes shape in the mind of its founder

momentum investor FINANCE, BANKING, AND ACCOUNTING an investor who buys stock which seem to be moving upward

Monday-morning quarterback (*U.S. & Canada*) GENERAL MANAGEMENT somebody who criticizes a decision only when it is too late to change it (*slang*)

Mondex E-COMMERCE an electronic cash system that uses a smart card for both traditional shopping and e-commerce transactions

Mondragon cooperative GENERAL MANAGEMENT a large, worker-ownership movement based in the town of Mondragon, in the Basque region of northwest Spain. The Mondragon cooperative movement started in 1956, and was founded on the teachings of *José Maria Arizmendietta*. It consists of worker-owned businesses, supported by a savings bank that raises money for the cooperative enterprises. Mondragon is not part of the traditional *cooperative movement*, and is instead based on

ten principles: equality of opportunity; the democratic election of managers; sovereignty of labor; a requirement for capital to be used by labor rather than labor used by capital; participative management; low pay differentials; cooperation with other cooperative movements; social change; solidarity with those working for peace, justice, and development; and education.

MONEP *abbr* FINANCE, BANKING, AND ACCOUNTING Marché des Options Négotiables de Paris

monetarism ECONOMICS an economic theory that states that inflation is caused by increases in a country's money supply

monetary FINANCE, BANKING, AND ACCOUNTING relating to or involving money, cash, or assets

monetary assets FINANCE, BANKING, AND ACCOUNTING a generic term for accounts receivable, cash, and bank balances—assets that are realizable at the amount stated in the accounts. Other assets, for example, facilities and machinery, inventories, and marketable securities will not necessarily realize the sum stated in a business's balance sheet.

monetary base ECONOMICS the stock of a country's coins, notes, and bank deposits with the central bank

monetary base control ECONOMICS the restricting of the amount of *liquid assets* in an economy through government control

monetary items FINANCE, BANKING, AND ACCOUNTING monetary assets (such as cash and debtors) and monetary liabilities (such as overdraft and creditors) whose values stay the same in spite of inflation

monetary policy ECONOMICS FINANCE, BANKING, AND ACCOUNTING government economic policy concerning a country's rate of interest, its exchange rate, and the amount of money in the economy

monetary reserve FINANCE, BANKING, AND ACCOUNTING the foreign currency and precious metals that a country holds, usually in a central bank

monetary system ECONOMICS the set of government regulations concerning a country's monetary reserves and its holdings of notes and coins

monetary targets FINANCE, BANKING, AND ACCOUNTING figures which are given as targets by

the government when setting out its budget for the forthcoming year

monetary unit FINANCE, BANKING, AND ACCOUNTING the standard unit of a country's currency

monetary working capital adjustment FINANCE, BANKING, AND ACCOUNTING an adjustment in current cost accounting to the historical cost balance sheet to take account of the effect of inflation on the value of debtors, creditors, and stocks of finished goods. Abbr. *MWCA*

monetize ECONOMICS to establish a currency as a country's legal tender

money ECONOMICS FINANCE, BANKING, AND ACCOUNTING a medium of exchange that is accepted throughout a country as payment for services and goods and as a means of settling debts

money at call FINANCE, BANKING, AND ACCOUNTING money loaned for which repayment can be demanded without notice. It is used by commercial banks placing money on very short-term deposit with discount houses.

money at call and short notice FINANCE, BANKING, AND ACCOUNTING
1 in the United Kingdom, advances made by banks to other financial institutions, or corporate and personal customers, that are repayable either upon demand (call) or within 14 days (short notice)
2 in the United Kingdom, balances in an account that are either available upon demand (call) or within 14 days (short notice)

money broker FINANCE, BANKING, AND ACCOUNTING an intermediary who works on the money market

moneyer FINANCE, BANKING, AND ACCOUNTING somebody who is authorized to coin money

money laundering FINANCE, BANKING, AND ACCOUNTING the process of making money obtained illegally appear legitimate by passing it through banks or businesses

moneylender FINANCE, BANKING, AND ACCOUNTING a person who lends money for interest

money market
1 ECONOMICS a country's financial center, where foreign currency and domestic and foreign bills are bought and sold
2 FINANCE, BANKING, AND ACCOUNTING the wholesale market for short-term debt instruments and money market instruments. New York is the major money market center followed by London and Tokyo.

money market account FINANCE, BANKING, AND ACCOUNTING an account with a financial institution that requires a high minimum deposit and pays a rate of interest related to the wholesale money market rates and so is generally higher than retail rates. Most institutions offer a variety of term accounts, with either a fixed rate or variable rate, and notice accounts, with a variety of notice periods at variable rates.

money market fund FINANCE, BANKING, AND ACCOUNTING a mutual fund that invests in short-term debt securities

money market instruments FINANCE, BANKING, AND ACCOUNTING short-term (usually under 12 months) assets and securities, such as certificates of deposit, and commercial paper and Treasury bills, that are traded on money markets

money national income ECONOMICS GDP measured using money value, not adjusted for the effect of inflation

money of account FINANCE, BANKING, AND ACCOUNTING a monetary unit that is used in keeping accounts but is not necessarily an actual currency unit

money order FINANCE, BANKING, AND ACCOUNTING a written order to pay somebody a sum of money, issued by a bank or post office

money purchase pension HR & PERSONNEL a pension plan to which both employer and employee make contributions

money purchase pension scheme FINANCE, BANKING, AND ACCOUNTING in the United Kingdom, a pension plan where the fund that is built up is used to purchase an annuity. The retirement income that the beneficiary receives therefore depends on his or her contributions, the performance of the investments those contributions are used to buy, the annuity rates, and the type of annuity purchased at retirement.

money-purchase plan FINANCE, BANKING, AND ACCOUNTING in the United States, a pension plan (a defined benefit plan) in which the participant contributes part and the firm contributes at the same or a different rate

money substitute ECONOMICS any goods used as a medium of exchange because of the degree of devaluation of a country's currency

money supply ECONOMICS the stock of *liquid assets* in a country's economy that can be given in exchange for services or goods

Monopolies and Mergers Commission FINANCE, BANKING, AND ACCOUNTING in the United Kingdom, a commission that was replaced by the Competition Commission in April 1999. Abbr *MMC*

monopoly GENERAL MANAGEMENT a *market* in which there is only one producer or one seller. A company establishes a monopoly by entering a new market or eliminating all competitors from an existing market. A company that holds a monopoly has control of a market and is able to fix prices. For this reason, governments usually try to avoid monopoly situations. Some monopolies, however, such as government-owned utilities, are seen as beneficial to *consumers*.

Monte Carlo method GENERAL MANAGEMENT a statistical technique used in business *decision making* that involves a number of uncertain variables, such as capital investment and resource allocation. The name of the Monte Carlo method derives from the use of random numbers as generated by a roulette wheel. The numbers are used in repeated simulations, often performed by spreadsheet programs on computers, to calculate a variety of possible outcomes. The technique was developed by mathematicians in the early 1960s for use in nuclear physics and *operational research* but has since been used more widely.

moonlighting HR & PERSONNEL undertaking a second job, often for cash and in the evenings, in addition to a full-time permanent job

Moore's law E-COMMERCE the proposition that every 18 months computer chip density (and hence computer power) will double while costs remain constant, creating ever more powerful computers without raising their price. Moore's law was formulated by Intel founder Gordon Moore in the 1960s. IBM and Intel research published in 1997 corroborates it.

moral hazard FINANCE, BANKING, AND ACCOUNTING a risk that somebody will behave immorally because insurance, the law, or some other agency protects them against loss that the immoral behavior might otherwise cause

moratorium FINANCE, BANKING, AND ACCOUNTING a period of delay, for example, additional time agreed by a creditor and a debtor for recovery of a debt

more bang for your buck FINANCE, BANKING, AND ACCOUNTING a better return on your investment (*slang*)

Morgan, Gareth (*b.* 1943) GENERAL MANAGEMENT Canadian academic. Originator of the term *imaginization*, which he described in the book of the same name (1993).

Morita, Akio (1921–99) GENERAL MANAGEMENT Japanese business executive. Cofounder and chairman of the electronics company Sony, whose global success has been based on product innovation, most famously the Walkman. The phrase "Think global, act local" has been attributed to Morita. His experiences are recorded in his autobiography *Made in Japan* (1986).

mortgage FINANCE, BANKING, AND ACCOUNTING
1 a financial lending arrangement whereby an individual borrows money from a bank or another lending institution in order to buy property or land. The original amount borrowed, the *principal*, is then repaid with interest to the lender over a fixed number of years.
2 a borrowing arrangement whereby the lender is granted a legal right to an asset, usually a piece of real estate, should the borrower default on the payments. Mortgages are usually taken out by individuals who wish to secure a long-term loan to buy a home. See also *interest-only mortgage*, *low start mortgage*, *amortized mortgage*

mortgage-backed security FINANCE, BANKING, AND ACCOUNTING a security for which a mortgage is collateral

mortgage bond FINANCE, BANKING, AND ACCOUNTING a debt secured by real estate

mortgage broker FINANCE, BANKING, AND ACCOUNTING a person or company that acts as an agent between people seeking mortgages and organizations that offer them

mortgage debenture FINANCE, BANKING, AND ACCOUNTING a debenture in which the loan is secured against a company's *fixed assets*

mortgagee FINANCE, BANKING, AND ACCOUNTING a person or organization that lends money to a borrower under a mortgage agreement. See also *mortgagor*

mortgage equity analysis FINANCE, BANKING, AND ACCOUNTING a computation of the difference between the value of a property and the amount owed on it in the form of mortgages

mortgage famine FINANCE, BANKING, AND ACCOUNTING a situation where there is not enough money available to offer mortgages to house buyers

mortgage insurance FINANCE, BANKING, AND ACCOUNTING insurance that provides somebody holding a mortgage with protection against default

mortgage lien FINANCE, BANKING, AND ACCOUNTING a claim against a property that is mortgaged

mortgage note FINANCE, BANKING, AND ACCOUNTING a note that documents the existence and terms of a mortgage

mortgage pool FINANCE, BANKING, AND ACCOUNTING a group of mortgages with similar characteristics packaged together for sale

mortgage portfolio FINANCE, BANKING, AND ACCOUNTING a group of mortgages held by a mortgage banker

mortgage rate FINANCE, BANKING, AND ACCOUNTING the interest rate charged on a mortgage by a lender

mortgage tax FINANCE, BANKING, AND ACCOUNTING a tax on mortgages

mortgagor FINANCE, BANKING, AND ACCOUNTING somebody who has taken out a mortgage to borrow money. See also *mortgagee*

Mosaic E-COMMERCE the first Web browser made available for Macintosh and Windows. It was developed by Netscape founder Marc Andreessen.

most distant futures contract FINANCE, BANKING, AND ACCOUNTING a futures option with the latest delivery date. See also *nearby futures contract*

MOTAS *abbr* GENERAL MANAGEMENT member of the appropriate sex (*slang*)

motion study GENERAL MANAGEMENT the observation of physical movements involved in the performance of work, and investigation of how these can be made more effective and cost efficient. Motion study was originally developed by *Frank* and *Lillian Gilbreth*, and is now often grouped with *time study*, to form *time and motion study*.

motion-time analysis GENERAL MANAGEMENT see *predetermined motion-time system*

motivate (*S. Africa*) GENERAL MANAGEMENT to argue for a position or request, especially in a proposal

motivation GENERAL MANAGEMENT
1 the creation of stimuli, incentives, and working environments which enable people to perform to the best of their ability in pursuit of organizational success. Motivation is commonly viewed as the magic driver that enables managers to get others to achieve their targets. In the 20th century, there was a shift, at least in theory, away from motivation by dictation and discipline, exemplified by *Frederick Winslow Taylor*'s scientific management, toward motivation by creating an appropriate corporate climate and addressing the needs of individual employees. Although it is widely agreed to be one of the key management tasks, it has frequently been argued that one person cannot motivate others but can only create conditions for others to self-motivate. Many *management theorists* have provided insights into motivation. *Elton Mayo*'s *Hawthorne experiments* identify some root causes of self-motivation, and *Abraham Maslow*'s hierarchy of needs provides insight into personal behavior patterns. Other influential research has been conducted by *Frederick Herzberg*, who looked at *job satisfaction*, and *Douglas McGregor* whose *Theory X* and *Theory Y* suggest management styles that motivate and demotivate employees. See checklist *Motivating Your Staff in a Time of Change*. See thinker *Elton Mayo*, *Douglas McGregor*
2 (*S. Africa*) a formal written proposal

motivators HR & PERSONNEL see *job satisfaction*

MOTOS *abbr* GENERAL MANAGEMENT member of the opposite sex (*slang*)

MOTSS *abbr* GENERAL MANAGEMENT member of the same sex (*slang*)

mouse milk GENERAL MANAGEMENT to do a disproportionately large amount of work on a project that yields very little return (*slang*)

mouse potato E-COMMERCE a person who spends an excessive amount of time using a computer (*slang*)

mousetrap
build a better mousetrap MARKETING to create a new or better product (*slang*)

Mouton, Jane S. (1930–87) GENERAL MANAGEMENT U.S. psychologist. See also *Blake, Robert R.*

mover and shaker GENERAL MANAGEMENT an influential and dynamic person within an organization or group of people (*slang*)

MRP II *abbr* FINANCE, BANKING, AND ACCOUNTING OPERATIONS & PRODUCTION manufacturing resource planning: a computer-based manufacturing, inventory planning and control system that broadens the scope of production planning by involving other functional areas that influence production decisions. Manufacturing resource planning evolved from material requirements planning to integrate other functions in the planning process. These functions may include engineering, marketing, purchasing, production scheduling, business planning, and finance.

MSB *abbr* FINANCE, BANKING, AND ACCOUNTING mutual savings bank

MTM *abbr* GENERAL MANAGEMENT methods-time measurement

multichannel E-COMMERCE using a combination of online and offline communication methods to conduct business

multicurrency FINANCE, BANKING, AND ACCOUNTING relating to a loan that gives the borrower a choice of currencies

multiemployer bargaining HR & PERSONNEL the centralization of *pay* negotiations at industry level, either nationally or regionally, usually conducted by *employers' associations* and *labor unions*. Multiemployer bargaining is a form of *collective bargaining* that declined in the United Kingdom in the 1980s. Seen as having a moderating influence on pay rises, it hinders flexibility to link pay awards to company or individual employee performance.

multifunctional card FINANCE, BANKING, AND ACCOUNTING a plastic card that may be used for two or more purposes, for example, as an ATM card, a check card, and a debit card

Multilateral Investment Guarantee Agency FINANCE, BANKING, AND ACCOUNTING one of the five institutions that comprise the World Bank Group. MIGA was created in 1988 to promote foreign direct investment into emerging economies with the objective of improving people's lives and to reduce poverty. This is fulfilled by the Agency by offering political risk insurance to investors and lenders and by assisting developing countries to attract and retain private investment. Abbr *MIGA*

multilevel marketing GENERAL MANAGEMENT see *network marketing*

multimedia GENERAL MANAGEMENT a method of presenting information on a computer, CD-ROM, television, or games console. The presentation combines different media such as sound, graphics, video, and text.

Multimedia has had problems on the Web,

due mainly to limited **bandwidth**. Web browsers are not designed to view most multimedia so extra software is required—a **plug-in**.

multimedia document GENERAL MANAGEMENT an electronic document that incorporates interactive material from a variety of different media such as text, video, sound, graphics, and animation. Such documents can be viewed on a multimedia computer or transmitted via the Internet.

multinational business *or* **multinational company** *or* **multinational corporation** FINANCE, BANKING, AND ACCOUNTING GENERAL MANAGEMENT a company that operates internationally, usually with subsidiaries, offices, or production facilities in more than one country

multinational corporation FINANCE, BANKING, AND ACCOUNTING see **multinational business**

multiparty auction E-COMMERCE a method of buying and selling on the Internet in which prospective buyers make electronic bids

multiple exchange rate FINANCE, BANKING, AND ACCOUNTING a two-tier rate of exchange used in certain countries where the more advantageous rate may be for tourists or for businesses proposing to build a factory

multiple regression analysis GENERAL MANAGEMENT see **regression analysis**

multiple sourcing OPERATIONS & PRODUCTION a **purchasing** policy of using two or more suppliers for products or services. Multiple sourcing prevents reliance on any one supplier, as is the case in **single sourcing**. It encourages competition between suppliers, and ensures access to a wide variety of goods or services. Dealing with more than one supplier can improve access to market information but can also entail more administration.

multiple time series STATISTICS two or more **time series** that are observed simultaneously

multiskilling HR & PERSONNEL OPERATIONS & PRODUCTION a process by which employees acquire new skills. Multiskilling is a form of **flexible working** in which employees are available to undertake a number of different jobs. It has led to a reduction in **demarcation disputes** and greater **employability** for employees.

multitasking
1 GENERAL MANAGEMENT the practice of performing several different tasks simultaneously (*slang*)

2 E-COMMERCE the ability to execute more than one task at a time. In a computing context, a task is a program that is running on a computer.

multivariate analysis GENERAL MANAGEMENT any of a number of statistical techniques used in **operational research** to examine the characteristics and relationships between multiple variables. Multivariate analysis techniques include **cluster analysis**, **discriminant analysis**, and multiple **regression analysis** .

multivariate data STATISTICS data for which each observation involves values for more than one random variable

Mumford, **Alan** GENERAL MANAGEMENT British academic. See also **Honey, Peter**

Mumford, **Enid** (*b.* 1924) GENERAL MANAGEMENT British academic. She adopted the sociotechnical approach of the Tavistock Institute of Human Relations, applying it to the design and implementation of information technology. Mumford termed her method ETHICS (Effective Technical and Human Implementation of Computer-based Systems), which is explained in *Effective Systems Design and Requirements Analysis: The ETHICS Approach* (1995).

municipal bond *or* **muni** *or* **muni-bond** FINANCE, BANKING, AND ACCOUNTING in the United States, a security issued by states, local governments, and municipalities to pay for special projects such as highways

Municipal Bond Insurance Association FINANCE, BANKING, AND ACCOUNTING full form of **MBIA**

municipals FINANCE, BANKING, AND ACCOUNTING see **municipal bond**

Murphy's Law GENERAL MANAGEMENT the principle that if something can go wrong, it will

mushroom job GENERAL MANAGEMENT a job that is unpleasant (*slang*)

mutual FINANCE, BANKING, AND ACCOUNTING used to describe an organization that is run in the interests of its members and that does not have to pay dividends to its stockholders, so surplus profits can be plowed back into the business. In the United Kingdom, building societies and friendly societies were formed as mutual organizations, although in recent years many have demutualized, either by becoming public limited companies or by being bought by other financial organizations, resulting in members receiving cash or share windfall payments. In

the United States, **mutual associations**, a type of savings and loan association, and state-chartered mutual savings banks are organized in this way.

mutual association FINANCE, BANKING, AND ACCOUNTING see **mutual**

mutual company FINANCE, BANKING, AND ACCOUNTING a company that is owned by its customers who share in the profits

mutual fund FINANCE, BANKING, AND ACCOUNTING an investment company that sells shares to investors and invests for their benefit. U.K. term **unit trust**

mutual insurance FINANCE, BANKING, AND ACCOUNTING an insurance company that is owned by its policyholders who share the profits and cover claims with their pooled premiums

mutual savings bank FINANCE, BANKING, AND ACCOUNTING in the United States, a state-chartered savings bank run in the interests of its members. It is governed by a local board of trustees, not the legal owners. Most of these banks offer accounts and services that are typical of full-service banks. Abbr. **MSB**

MVA *abbr* FINANCE, BANKING, AND ACCOUNTING market value added

MWCA *abbr* FINANCE, BANKING, AND ACCOUNTING monetary working capital adjustment

Myers-Briggs type indicator HR & PERSONNEL a **psychometric test** that identifies four basic preferences in people's behavior. The indicator was created in the 1940s by **Katherine Cook Briggs** and her daughter **Isabel Briggs-Myers**. It is based largely on the Jungian theory of personality types. The four preferences identified are made up of pairs of opposites: extraversion and introversion; sensing and intuition; thinking and feeling; and judgment and perception. The indicator provides a framework allowing people to understand themselves and others more fully, as well as encouraging the appreciation of different styles and perceptions. It is often used in **team building** and in the **recruitment** process.

MYOB *abbr* GENERAL MANAGEMENT mind your own business (*slang*)

mystery shopping MARKETING the use of employees or agents to visit a store or use a service anonymously and assess its quality. Mystery shopping is used to assess such factors as the quality of customer service, including general and technical efficiency, and

friendliness of staff, layout, and appearance of the premises, and quality and variety of goods or services on offer. Mystery shoppers fill in a questionnaire based on their impressions and this information is then used to identify possible areas for business or service improvement.

N

Naisbitt, **John** (*b*. 1930) GENERAL MANAGEMENT U.S. business executive and forecaster. Known for the publication of *Megatrends* (1982) in which he predicted ten main patterns of change that would shape the world.

naked debenture FINANCE, BANKING, AND ACCOUNTING see *debenture*

naked option FINANCE, BANKING, AND ACCOUNTING an option in which the underlying asset is not owned by the seller, who risks considerable loss if the price of the asset falls

naked position FINANCE, BANKING, AND ACCOUNTING a holding of unhedged securities

naked writer FINANCE, BANKING, AND ACCOUNTING a writer of an option who does not own the underlying shares

name FINANCE, BANKING, AND ACCOUNTING an individual who is a member of Lloyd's of London

NAO *abbr* FINANCE, BANKING, AND ACCOUNTING National Audit Office

Napsterize E-COMMERCE
1 to distribute without charge something that somebody else owns. The term stems from the peer-to-peer business model pioneered by Napster, a software package for electronically distributing copies of copyrighted music without charge or payment of royalties. (*slang*)
2 to have something that you own distributed without charge and without your consent
3 to be legally prevented from giving away without charge something that is owned by somebody else

narrowcasting E-COMMERCE targeting information to a niche audience. Owing to its ability to personalize information to the requirements of individual users, the Internet is generally viewed as a narrowcast (rather than broadcast) medium.

narrow market FINANCE, BANKING, AND ACCOUNTING a market where the trading volume is low. A characteristic of such a market is a wide spread of bid and offer prices.

narrow range securities FINANCE, BANKING, AND ACCOUNTING see *trustee investment*

NASD *abbr* FINANCE, BANKING, AND ACCOUNTING National Association of Securities Dealers

NASDAQ *or* **Nasdaq** *abbr* FINANCE, BANKING, AND ACCOUNTING a computerized quotation system that supports market making in over-the-counter and listed securities. It was established by the *National Association of Securities Dealers* in 1971. NASDAQ International has operated from London since 1992.

NASDAQ Composite Index FINANCE, BANKING, AND ACCOUNTING a specialist U.S. stock price index covering stocks of high-technology companies

National Association of Investors Corporation FINANCE, BANKING, AND ACCOUNTING an organization that fosters investment clubs

National Association of Securities Dealers FINANCE, BANKING, AND ACCOUNTING in the United States, the self-regulatory organization for securities dealers that develops rules and regulations, conducts regulatory reviews of members' business activities, and designs and operates marketplace services facilities. It is responsible for the regulation of the NASDAQ securities market. Established in 1938, it operates subject to the Securities Exchange Commission oversight and has a membership that includes virtually every U.S. broker or dealer doing securities business with the public. Abbr. *NASD*

national bank FINANCE, BANKING, AND ACCOUNTING
1 a bank that operates under federal charter and is legally required to be a member of the Federal Reserve System
2 a bank owned or controlled by the state that acts as a bank for the government and implements its monetary policies

national debt ECONOMICS the total borrowing of a country's central government that is unpaid

national demand ECONOMICS the total demand of consumers in an economy

National Guarantee Fund (*ANZ*) FINANCE, BANKING, AND ACCOUNTING a supply of money held by the Australian Stock Exchange which is used to compensate investors for losses incurred when an exchange member fails to meet its obligations

national income ECONOMICS the total earnings from a country's production of services and goods in a particular year

national income accounts FINANCE, BANKING, AND ACCOUNTING economic statistics that show the state of a nation's economy over a given period of time, usually a year

National Insurance (*U.K.*) FINANCE, BANKING, AND ACCOUNTING a compulsory state social insurance plan to which employees and employers contribute. Abbr. *NI*

National Insurance contributions (*U.K.*) FINANCE, BANKING, AND ACCOUNTING payments made by both employers and employees to the government. The contributions, together with other government receipts, are used to finance state pensions and other benefits such as welfare. Abbr. *NIC*

National Insurance number FINANCE, BANKING, AND ACCOUNTING a unique number allocated to each U.K. citizen at the age of 16. It allows HM Revenue & Customs and the Department for Work and Pensions to record contributions and credit to each person's national insurance account.

nationalization GENERAL MANAGEMENT the taking over of privately owned companies by government. Nationalization has strong political connotations. Recent global political trends have moved away from nationalization by introducing more competition and liberalization into markets. See also *privatization*

National Market System FINANCE, BANKING, AND ACCOUNTING in the United States, an inter-exchange network system designed to foster greater competition between domestic stock exchanges. Legislated for in 1975, it was implemented in 1978 with the Intermarket Trading System that electronically links eight markets: American, Boston, Cincinnati, Chicago, New York, Pacific, Philadelphia, and the NASD over-the-counter market. It allows traders at any exchange to seek the best available price on all other exchanges that a particular security is eligible to trade on. Abbr. *NMS*

National Occupational Health and Safety Commission (*ANZ*) GENERAL MANAGEMENT an Australian statutory body responsible for coordinating efforts to prevent injury, disease, and deaths occurring in the workplace. Abbr. *NOHSC*. Also known as *Worksafe Australia*

National Savings & Investments FINANCE, BANKING, AND ACCOUNTING in the United Kingdom, a government agency accountable to the

Treasury that offers a variety of savings and investment products directly to the public or through post offices. The funds raised finance the national debt.

National Savings Bank FINANCE, BANKING, AND ACCOUNTING in the United Kingdom, a savings plan established in 1861 as the Post Office Savings Bank and now operated by National Savings & Investments. Abbr. **NSB**

National Savings Certificate FINANCE, BANKING, AND ACCOUNTING in the United Kingdom, either a fixed-interest or an index-linked certificate issued for two- or five-year terms by National Savings & Investments with returns that are free of income tax. Abbr. **NSC**

National Society of Accountants FINANCE, BANKING, AND ACCOUNTING a non-profit organization of some 30,000 professionals who provide accounting, tax preparation, financial and estate planning, and management advisory services to an estimated 19 million individuals and business clients. Most of the NSA's members are individual practitioners or partners in small to mid-size accounting and tax firms. Abbr. **NSA**

natural capitalism GENERAL MANAGEMENT an approach to capitalism in which protection of the earth's resources is a strategic priority

NAV *abbr* FINANCE, BANKING, AND ACCOUNTING net asset value

navigate E-COMMERCE to find your way around the Internet, a Web site, or an **HTML** document.

Research has shown that people navigate in a certain way when reading content in a Web site, and certain standards and conventions of navigation are emerging for Web site design. More important than anything else is functionality—visitors want to find the information they are seeking quickly and easily, and are not particularly interested in style.

The most basic design convention, termed "essential" or "global" navigation, holds that every Web page should have a set of essential navigation tools that are visible when the first screen loads, linking to key areas within the Web site. Essential navigation should contain links such as Home, About, Products, Customers, and Contact.

It is also important to let visitors know where they are on a Web site, with each page clearly displaying what part of the overall classification it represents. If it is the home page, for example, this should be made clear; or if it is a page dealing with pricing information, the heading at the top of the page should say so.

Users also find it useful to know where they have been on a Web site—usually done by changing the color of **hyperlink**s that have been clicked on from blue to purple.

NBFI *abbr* (*ANZ*) FINANCE, BANKING, AND ACCOUNTING nonbank financial institution

NBV *abbr* FINANCE, BANKING, AND ACCOUNTING net book value

NCUA *abbr* FINANCE, BANKING, AND ACCOUNTING National Credit Union Administration

NDA *abbr* GENERAL MANAGEMENT nondisclosure agreement *or* nondisparagement agreement

NDP *abbr* ECONOMICS net domestic product

nearby futures contract FINANCE, BANKING, AND ACCOUNTING a futures option with the earliest delivery date. See also **most distant futures contract**

nearby month FINANCE, BANKING, AND ACCOUNTING the earliest month for which there is a futures contract for a particular commodity. Also known as **spot month**. See also **far month**

near money FINANCE, BANKING, AND ACCOUNTING assets that can quickly be turned into cash, for example, some types of bank deposit, short-dated bonds, and certificates of deposit

negative amortization FINANCE, BANKING, AND ACCOUNTING an increase in the **principal** of a loan due to the inadequacy of payments to cover the interest

negative carry FINANCE, BANKING, AND ACCOUNTING interest that is so high that the borrowed money does not return enough profit to cover the cost of borrowing

negative cash flow FINANCE, BANKING, AND ACCOUNTING a cash flow with higher expenditures than income

negative equity FINANCE, BANKING, AND ACCOUNTING a situation in which a fall in prices leads to a property being worth less than was paid for it

negative gearing FINANCE, BANKING, AND ACCOUNTING the practice of borrowing money to invest in property or stocks and claiming a tax deduction on the difference between the income and the interest payments

negative income tax ECONOMICS payments such as tax credits made to households or individuals to make their income up to a guaranteed minimum level

negative pledge clause FINANCE, BANKING, AND ACCOUNTING a provision in a bond that prohibits the issuer from doing something that would give an advantage to holders of other bonds

negative yield curve FINANCE, BANKING, AND ACCOUNTING a representation of interest rates that are higher for short-term bonds than they are for long-term bonds

negligence GENERAL MANAGEMENT the breach of a duty of care, resulting in harm to one or more people. Negligence occurs when an organization causes harm or injury through carelessness or inattention to the needs of the groups to which it owes a duty of care. These can include its customers, consumers of its product or service, shareholders, or the local community. Victims of negligence are entitled to claim compensation. Negligence is considered to be **gross negligence** if it is the result of excessively careless behavior.

negotiable certificate of deposit FINANCE, BANKING, AND ACCOUNTING a certificate of deposit with a very high value that can be freely traded

negotiable order of withdrawal FINANCE, BANKING, AND ACCOUNTING a check drawn on an account that bears interest

negotiable security FINANCE, BANKING, AND ACCOUNTING a security that can be freely traded

negotiate FINANCE, BANKING, AND ACCOUNTING to transfer financial instruments such as bearer securities, bills of exchange, checks, and promissory notes, for consideration to another person

negotiated commissions FINANCE, BANKING, AND ACCOUNTING commissions that result from bargaining between brokers and their customers, typically large institutions

negotiated issue FINANCE, BANKING, AND ACCOUNTING see **negotiated offering**

negotiated market FINANCE, BANKING, AND ACCOUNTING a market in which each transaction results from negotiation between a buyer and a seller

negotiated offering FINANCE, BANKING, AND ACCOUNTING a public offering, the price of which is determined by negotiations between the issuer and a syndicate of underwriters. Also known as **negotiated issue**

negotiated sale FINANCE, BANKING, AND ACCOUNTING a public offering, the price of which is determined by negotiations between the issuer and a single underwriter

negotiation GENERAL MANAGEMENT a discussion with the goal of resolving a difference of opinion or dispute, or to settle the terms of an agreement or transaction

nest egg FINANCE, BANKING, AND ACCOUNTING assets, usually other than a pension plan or retirement account, that have been set aside by an individual for his or her retirement (*slang*)

nester MARKETING in advertising or marketing, a consumer who is not influenced by advertising hype but prefers value for money and traditional products (*slang*)

net advantage of refunding FINANCE, BANKING, AND ACCOUNTING the amount realized by refunding debt

net advantage to leasing FINANCE, BANKING, AND ACCOUNTING the amount by which leasing something is financially better than borrowing money and purchasing it

net advantage to merging FINANCE, BANKING, AND ACCOUNTING the amount by which the value of a merged enterprise exceeds the value of the preexisting companies, minus the cost of the merger

net assets FINANCE, BANKING, AND ACCOUNTING the amount by which the value of a company's assets exceeds its liabilities

net asset value FINANCE, BANKING, AND ACCOUNTING a sum of the values of all that a mutual fund owns at the end of a trading day. Abbr. *NAV*

NetBill E-COMMERCE a micropayment system developed at Carnegie Mellon University for purchasing digital goods over the Internet. After the goods are delivered in encrypted form to the purchaser's computer, the money is debited from the purchaser's prefunded account and the goods are decrypted for the purchaser's use.

net borrowings FINANCE, BANKING, AND ACCOUNTING the total of all borrowings less the cash in bank accounts and on deposit

net capital FINANCE, BANKING, AND ACCOUNTING the amount by which net assets exceed the value of assets not easily converted to cash

net cash balance FINANCE, BANKING, AND ACCOUNTING the amount of cash that is on hand

net change on the day FINANCE, BANKING, AND ACCOUNTING the difference between the opening price of a stock at the beginning of a day's trading and the closing price at the end

NetCheque™ *tdmk* E-COMMERCE a trademark for an electronic payment system developed at the University of Southern California to allow users to write electronic checks to one another

net current assets FINANCE, BANKING, AND ACCOUNTING the amount by which the value of a company's current assets exceeds its current liabilities

net dividend FINANCE, BANKING, AND ACCOUNTING the value of a dividend after the recipient has paid tax on it

net domestic product ECONOMICS the figure produced after factors such as depreciation have been deducted from *GDP*

net errors and omissions FINANCE, BANKING, AND ACCOUNTING the net amount of the discrepancies that arise in calculations of balances of payments

net fixed assets FINANCE, BANKING, AND ACCOUNTING the value of fixed assets after depreciation

net foreign factor income FINANCE, BANKING, AND ACCOUNTING income from outside a country, constituting the amount by which a country's gross national product exceeds its gross domestic product

nethead E-COMMERCE somebody who is obsessed with the Internet (*slang*)

Net imperative E-COMMERCE the idea that Internet business processes must be adopted by organizations for future success

net income FINANCE, BANKING, AND ACCOUNTING **1** an organization's income less the costs incurred to generate it **2** gross income less tax **3** a salary or wage less tax and other statutory deductions, for example, Social Security contributions

net interest FINANCE, BANKING, AND ACCOUNTING gross interest less tax

netiquette E-COMMERCE the etiquette of the Internet. The term is used mainly in the context of e-mail and newsgroup communication.

netizen E-COMMERCE a regular user of the Internet

net lease FINANCE, BANKING, AND ACCOUNTING a lease that requires the lessee to pay for things that the owner usually pays for. See also *gross lease*

net liquid funds FINANCE, BANKING, AND ACCOUNTING an organization's cash plus its marketable investments less its short-term borrowings, such as overdrafts and loans

net margin FINANCE, BANKING, AND ACCOUNTING the percentage of revenues that is profit

net operating income FINANCE, BANKING, AND ACCOUNTING the amount by which income exceeds expenses, before considering taxes and interest

net operating margin FINANCE, BANKING, AND ACCOUNTING net operating income as a percentage of revenues

net pay HR & PERSONNEL see *take-home pay*

net position FINANCE, BANKING, AND ACCOUNTING the difference between an investor's long and short positions in the same security

net present value FINANCE, BANKING, AND ACCOUNTING the value of an investment calculated as the sum of its initial cost and the *present value* of expected future cash flows

A positive NPV indicates that the project should be profitable, assuming that the estimated cash flows are reasonably accurate. A negative NPV indicates that the project will probably be unprofitable and therefore should be adjusted, if not abandoned altogether.

NPV enables a management to consider the time-value of money it will invest. This concept holds that the value of money increases with time because it can always earn interest in a savings account. When the time-value-of-money concept is incorporated in the calculation of NPV, the value of a project's future net cash receipts in "today's money" can be determined. This enables proper comparisons between different projects.

For example, if Global Manufacturing Inc. is considering the acquisition of a new machine, its management will consider all the factors: initial purchase and installation costs; additional revenues generated by sales of the new machine's products, plus the taxes on these new revenues. Having accounted for these factors in its calculations, the cash flows that Global Manufacturing projects will generate from the new machine are:

Year 1:   -100,000 (initial cost of investment)
Year 2:   30,000
Year 3:   40,000
Year 4:   40,000
Year 5:   35,000
Net Total: 145,000

At first glance, it appears that cash flows total 45% more than the $100,000 initial cost, a

sound investment indeed. But the time-value of money shrinks the return on the project considerably, since future dollars are worth less than present dollars in hand. NPV accounts for these differences with the help of present-value tables, which list the ratios that express the present value of expected cash flow dollars, based on the applicable interest rate and the number of years in question.

In the example, Global Manufacturing's cost of capital is 9%. Using this figure to find the corresponding ratios on the present value table, the $100,000 investment cost and expected annual revenues during the five years in question, the NPV calculation looks like this:

Year	Cash flow	Table factor (at 9%)		Present value
1	($100,000)	× 1.000000	=	($100,000)
2	$30,000	× 0.917431	=	$27,522.93
3	$40,000	× 0.841680	=	$33,667.20
4	$40,000	× 0.772183	=	$30,887.32
5	$35,000	× 0.708425	=	$24,794.88

NPV = $16,873.33

NPV is still positive. So, on this basis at least, the investment should proceed. Abbr. **NPV**

net price FINANCE, BANKING, AND ACCOUNTING the price paid for goods or services after all relevant discounts have been deducted

net proceeds FINANCE, BANKING, AND ACCOUNTING the amount realized from a transaction minus the cost of making it

net profit FINANCE, BANKING, AND ACCOUNTING an organization's income as shown in a *profit and loss account* after all relevant expenses have been deducted

net profit margin FINANCE, BANKING, AND ACCOUNTING see *profit margin*

net profit ratio FINANCE, BANKING, AND ACCOUNTING the ratio of an organization's net profit to its total net sales. Comparing the net profit ratios of companies in the same sector shows which are the most efficient.

net realizable value FINANCE, BANKING, AND ACCOUNTING the value of an asset if sold, allowing for costs

net relevant earnings FINANCE, BANKING, AND ACCOUNTING earnings which qualify for calculating pension contributions and against which relief against tax can be claimed. Such earnings can be income from employment which is not pensionable, for example, the profits of a self-employed sole proprietor.

net residual value FINANCE, BANKING, AND ACCOUNTING the anticipated proceeds of an asset at the end of its useful life, less the costs of selling it, for example, transportation and commission. It is used when calculating the annual charge for the straight-line method of depreciation. Abbr. **NRV**

net return FINANCE, BANKING, AND ACCOUNTING the amount realized on an investment, taking taxes and transaction costs into account

net sales FINANCE, BANKING, AND ACCOUNTING a company's total sales less any relevant discounts, such as those given to retailers

net salvage value FINANCE, BANKING, AND ACCOUNTING the amount expected to result from terminating a project, taking tax consequences into consideration

network

1 HR & PERSONNEL to build up and maintain relationships with people whose interests are similar or whose friendship could bring advantages such as job or business opportunities.

It is important to network for the good of the organization and the professional field in which the networker operates. The networker should know what they hope to accomplish by networking, and what they have to offer other people: it is a two-way process, as the more someone has to offer other people, the more those people will want to do things for them.

In order to network effectively, it is useful to make a list of organizations and events for networking, a *contact list*, and an action plan with a schedule. The organizations and events list helps the networker identify and target places and situations where they are likely to meet with people who may be of assistance to them in their career or with a particular project. The contact list allows the networker to keep track of the people they have met, or want to meet. It is a good idea to prioritize this list according to who is most likely to be helpful. Using these two lists, the networker can then put together a schedule for making or maintaining connections.

2 E-COMMERCE a group of computers that are able to communicate with each other. There are two types of computer networks: *LAN* (a local area network) and *WAN* (a wide area network). LANs are typically used by organizations that have a large number of computers based in one location and connected to a single computer server. They are often used as the basis for private networks such as *intranets*. WANs are slower than LANs because they use telephone cables as well as computer servers. The Internet is the main WAN in existence.

network analysis GENERAL MANAGEMENT OPERATIONS & PRODUCTION any of a set of techniques developed to aid the planning, monitoring, and controlling of complex *projects* and project resources. Network analysis is a tool of *project management* that involves breaking down a project into component parts or individual activities and recording them on a network diagram or *flow chart*. The resulting chart shows the interaction and interrelations between activities and can be used to determine project duration, time and resource limitations, and cost estimates. Constituent techniques include the *critical-path method* and the program evaluation and review technique. Also known as *network flow analysis*

network culture GENERAL MANAGEMENT forms of culture that are heavily influenced by communication using global networks

network flow analysis GENERAL MANAGEMENT see *network analysis*

network management GENERAL MANAGEMENT the coordinated control of computer systems and programs to allow access to and delivery of information to a number of users. Network management enables users to connect by means of cabling within a *LAN* (see *network*) or via telecommunications lines in a wide area network.

network marketing MARKETING the selling of goods or services through a network of self-employed agents or representatives. Network marketing usually involves several levels of agents, each level on a different commission rate. Each agent is encouraged to recruit other agents. In genuine network marketing, in contrast to *pyramid selling*, there is an end product or service sold to customers. Another version of network marketing is the loose cooperative relationship between a company, its competitors, collaborators, suppliers, and other organizations affecting the overall marketing function. Also known as *multilevel marketing*

network organization GENERAL MANAGEMENT a company or group of companies that has a minimum of formal structures and relies instead on the formation and dissolution of teams to meet specific objectives. A network organization utilizes *information and communications technologies* extensively, and makes use of know-how across and within companies along the *value chain*. See also *virtual organization*

network revolution GENERAL MANAGEMENT the fundamental change in business practices triggered by the growth of global networks

a-z

1563

DICTIONARY

network society GENERAL MANAGEMENT a society in which patterns of work, communication, and government are characterized by the use of global networks

net worth FINANCE, BANKING, AND ACCOUNTING the difference between the assets and liabilities of a person or company

net yield FINANCE, BANKING, AND ACCOUNTING the rate of return on an investment after considering all costs and taxes

neural network STATISTICS a computer system designed to mimic the neural patterns of the human brain

neurolinguistic programming GENERAL MANAGEMENT an approach to recognizing, applying, developing, and reproducing behavior, thought processes, and ways of communicating that contribute to success. Neurolinguistic programming was developed by Richard Bandler and John Grinder through their observations of how therapists achieved excellent results with clients. It is popular in the business environment, where its influencing techniques can help firms implement change initiatives, improve communication and management skills, and develop training techniques. Abbr. *NLP*

new economy ECONOMICS a term used in the late 1990s and 2000s to describe the e-commerce sector and the *digital economy*, in which firms mostly trade online rather than in the bricks and mortar of physical premises in the main

new entrants MARKETING organizations or products that have recently come into a market or sector

new issue FINANCE, BANKING, AND ACCOUNTING
1 a new security, for example, a bond or stock, being offered to the public for the first time. See also *float*, *initial public offering*
2 a rights issue, or any further issue of an existing security

new issue market FINANCE, BANKING, AND ACCOUNTING a market where companies can raise funds by issuing new shares or by a flotation

new issues market FINANCE, BANKING, AND ACCOUNTING the part of the market in which securities are first offered to investors by the issuers. See also *float*, *initial public offering*, *primary market*

newly industrialized economy ECONOMICS a country whose industrialization has reached a level beyond that of a developing country.

Mexico and Malaysia are examples of newly industrialized economies.

new product development MARKETING the processes involved in getting a new product or service to market. The traditional *product development cycle*, the *stage-gate model*, embraces the conception, generation, analysis, development, testing, marketing, and commercialization of new products or services. Alternative models of new product development fall into two broad categories: *accelerating time to market models* and *integrated implementation models*. These strive to achieve both flexibility and acceleration of development. All activities such as design, production planning, and test marketing are performed in parallel rather than going through a sequential linear progression. Abbr. *NPD*

newsgroup E-COMMERCE see *bulletin board*

newsletter GENERAL MANAGEMENT an informal publication, issued periodically by an organization or agency to provide information to a particular audience. A newsletter may be issued externally or it may take the form of an *in-house newsletter*, or *house journal*, used to aid the *internal communication* process. It is becoming more common for newsletters to be issued in electronic format.

newsreader E-COMMERCE a program that enables Internet users to send and access newsgroup messages. Newsreader programs are contained within e-mail software available as independent programs.

new time FINANCE, BANKING, AND ACCOUNTING the next account on a stock exchange where sales in the last few days of the previous account are credited to the following account

New York Mercantile Exchange FINANCE, BANKING, AND ACCOUNTING the world's largest physical commodity exchange and North America's most important trading exchange for energy and precious metals. It deals in crude oil, gasoline, heating oil, natural gas, propane, gold, silver, platinum, palladium, and copper. Abbr. *NYMEX*

New Zealand Stock Exchange FINANCE, BANKING, AND ACCOUNTING the principal market in New Zealand for trading in securities. It was established in 1981, replacing the Stock Exchange Association of New Zealand and a number of regional trading floors. Abbr. *NZSE*

New Zealand Trade Development Board FINANCE, BANKING, AND ACCOUNTING a government body responsible for promoting New Zealand

exports and facilitating foreign investment in New Zealand. Also known as *TRADENZ*

next futures contract FINANCE, BANKING, AND ACCOUNTING an option for the month after the current month

NI *abbr* FINANCE, BANKING, AND ACCOUNTING National Insurance

NIC *abbr* FINANCE, BANKING, AND ACCOUNTING National Insurance contribution

nice guys finish last GENERAL MANAGEMENT an axiom used in business to suggest that people should think about themselves first (*slang*)

nice-to-haves HR & PERSONNEL benefits of a job, such as free parking or subsidized meals, that are good to have but not essential (*slang*)

niche company FINANCE, BANKING, AND ACCOUNTING a company specializing in a particular type of product or service, which occupies a market niche

niche market MARKETING a very specific market segment within a broader segment. A niche market involves specialist goods or services with relatively few or no competitors. Niche consumers often look for exclusiveness or some other differentiating factor such as high status. Alternatively, they may have a specific requirement not satisfied by standard products. Allergy sufferers, for example, may require specially formulated soaps and detergents. Niche markets are often targeted by small companies that produce specialized goods and services. See also *micromarketing*

niche player FINANCE, BANKING, AND ACCOUNTING
1 an investment banker specializing in a particular field, for example, management buyouts
2 a brokerage that deals in securities of only one industry. Also known as *boutique investment house*

nickel FINANCE, BANKING, AND ACCOUNTING five basis points (*slang*)

Nifty Fifty FINANCE, BANKING, AND ACCOUNTING on Wall Street, the 50 most popular stocks among institutional investors (*slang*)

night shift HR & PERSONNEL a *shift* within a *shiftwork* pattern that takes place during the evening and overnight. Night shifts involve particular health and social issues, and the antisocial hours usually incur a pay premium.

NIH syndrome GENERAL MANAGEMENT a problem afflicting large old-fashioned companies

which reject ideas that come from outside the company simply because they were "not invented here" (*slang*)

Nikkei 225 *or* **Nikkei Index** FINANCE, BANKING, AND ACCOUNTING the Japanese stock price index

nil paid (*U.K.*) FINANCE, BANKING, AND ACCOUNTING with no money yet paid. This term is used in reference to the purchase of newly issued stocks, or to the stocks themselves, when the stockholder entitled to buy new stocks has not yet made a commitment to do so and may sell the rights instead.

NLP *abbr* GENERAL MANAGEMENT neurolinguistic programming

NMS *abbr* FINANCE, BANKING, AND ACCOUNTING National Market System

NNP *abbr* FINANCE, BANKING, AND ACCOUNTING net national product

no-brainer FINANCE, BANKING, AND ACCOUNTING a transaction so favorable that no intelligence is required when deciding whether to enter into it (*slang*)

no-dating policy HR & PERSONNEL a policy introduced by an employer to prohibit or discourage consensual romantic or sexual relationships between employees. No-dating policies are intended to prevent problems arising from employee relationships in the workplace, such as preferential treatment, or claims of *sexual harassment* in the case of relationship breakdown. The policy defines what constitutes acceptable and unacceptable behavior and what sanctions will be enforced if the terms of the policy are violated. No-dating policies are not widely used and may raise concerns about employees' rights to privacy. An alternative option is the use of *consensual relationship agreements*.

node E-COMMERCE any single computer connected to a network

NOHSC *abbr* GENERAL MANAGEMENT National Occupational Health and Safety Commission

noise FINANCE, BANKING, AND ACCOUNTING irrelevant or insignificant data which overload a feedback process. The presence of noise can confuse or divert attention from relevant information; efficiency in a system is enhanced as the ratio of information to noise increases.

noise traders FINANCE, BANKING, AND ACCOUNTING uninformed market participants (*slang*)

Nolan, **Lord Michael Patrick, Baron of Brasted** (*b.* 1928) GENERAL MANAGEMENT British

lawyer. Chairman of the Committee on Standards in Public Life 1994–97.

no-load fund FINANCE, BANKING, AND ACCOUNTING a mutual fund that does not charge a fee for the purchase or sale of shares. See also *load fund*

nomadic worker HR & PERSONNEL see *mobile worker*

nominal account FINANCE, BANKING, AND ACCOUNTING a record of revenues and expenditures, liabilities and assets classified by their nature, for example, sales, rent, rates, electricity, wages, or share capital

nominal annual rate FINANCE, BANKING, AND ACCOUNTING see *APR*

nominal capital FINANCE, BANKING, AND ACCOUNTING the total value of all of a corporation's stock

nominal cash flow FINANCE, BANKING, AND ACCOUNTING cash flow in terms of currency, without adjustment for inflation

nominal exchange rate FINANCE, BANKING, AND ACCOUNTING the exchange rate as specified, without adjustment for transaction costs or differences in purchasing power

nominal interest rate FINANCE, BANKING, AND ACCOUNTING the interest rate as specified, without adjustment for compounding or inflation

nominal ledger FINANCE, BANKING, AND ACCOUNTING in the United Kingdom, a ledger listing revenue, operating expenses, assets, and capital

nominal price FINANCE, BANKING, AND ACCOUNTING the price of an item being sold when consideration does not reflect the value

nominal share capital FINANCE, BANKING, AND ACCOUNTING see *authorized share capital*

nominal value FINANCE, BANKING, AND ACCOUNTING the value of a newly issued share. Also known as *par value*

nominee FINANCE, BANKING, AND ACCOUNTING a financial institution, or an individual employed by such an institution, that holds a security on behalf of the actual owner. While this may be to hide the owner's identity, for example, in the case of a celebrity, it is also to allow an institution managing any individual's portfolio to conduct transactions without the need for the owner to sign the required paperwork.

nominee account FINANCE, BANKING, AND ACCOUNTING an account held not in the name of the real owner of the account, but instead in the name of another person, organization, or *financial institution*. Stocks can be bought and held in nominee accounts so that the owner's identity is not disclosed.

nonacceptance FINANCE, BANKING, AND ACCOUNTING on the presentation of a bill of exchange, the refusal by the person on whom it is drawn to accept it

Nonaka, **Ikujiro** (*b.* 1935) GENERAL MANAGEMENT Japanese academic. Focuses on the creation of organizational *knowledge*, believing this to be the most meaningful *core competence* for a company, particularly because it leads to *innovation* and *competitive advantage*. His ideas on knowledge management, published in *The Knowledge-creating Company* (1995, coauthored by Hirotaka Takeuchi) draw on *Peter Drucker*'s earlier ideas of the *knowledge worker* and the knowledge society.

nonbranded goods MARKETING generic goods that are not linked to a particular *brand* name, manufacturer, or producer, such as food produce, pharmaceuticals, floor coverings, furniture, computer keyboards, or hand tools. Nonbranded goods are often widely available in street markets or by mail order and are often perceived to be of low quality.

nonbusiness days FINANCE, BANKING, AND ACCOUNTING those days when banks are not open for business, for example, in the West, Saturdays, Sundays, and public holidays

noncash item FINANCE, BANKING, AND ACCOUNTING an item in an income statement that is not *cash*, such as *depreciation* expenses, and gains or losses from investments

nonconformance costs GENERAL MANAGEMENT see *quality costs*

nonconforming loan FINANCE, BANKING, AND ACCOUNTING a loan that does not conform to the lender's standards, especially those of a U.S. government agency

noncontributory pension plan FINANCE, BANKING, AND ACCOUNTING a pension plan to which the employee makes no contribution

non-contributory pension scheme (*U.K.*) FINANCE, BANKING, AND ACCOUNTING = *noncontributory pension plan*

nondeductible FINANCE, BANKING, AND ACCOUNTING not allowed to be deducted, especially as an allowance against income taxes

nondisclosure agreement HR & PERSONNEL a legally enforceable agreement preventing present or past *employees* from disclosing commercially sensitive information belonging to the employer to any other party. A nondisclosure agreement can remain in force for several years after an employee leaves a company. In the event of a dispute, a company may be required to prove that the information in question belongs to the company itself, is not in the public domain, or cannot be obtained elsewhere. Abbr. *NDA*

nondisparagement agreement HR & PERSONNEL an agreement that prevents present or past *employees* from criticizing an employing organization in public. Nondisparagement agreements are a relatively new type of agreement and have arisen primarily to prevent employees putting comments about their employing organization onto the Internet. Case law has yet to determine whether such agreements are legally binding. Abbr. *NDA*

nonexecutive director GENERAL MANAGEMENT a part-time, nonsalaried member of the *board of directors*, involved in the planning, strategy, and policy making of an organization but not in its day-to-day operations. The appointment of a nonexecutive director to a board is normally made in order to provide independence and balance to that board, and to ensure that good *corporate governance* is practiced. A nonexecutive director may be selected for the prestige they bring or for their experience, contacts, or specialist knowledge. Also known as *part-time director outside director*

nonfinancial asset FINANCE, BANKING, AND ACCOUNTING an asset that is neither money nor a financial instrument, for example, real or personal property

nonfinancial incentive plan HR & PERSONNEL see *incentive plan*

noninterest-bearing bond FINANCE, BANKING, AND ACCOUNTING a bond that is sold at a discount instead of with a promise to pay interest

nonjudicial foreclosure FINANCE, BANKING, AND ACCOUNTING a foreclosure on property without recourse to a court

nonlinear programming FINANCE, BANKING, AND ACCOUNTING a process in which the equations expressing the interactions of variables are not all linear but may, for example, be in proportion to the square of a variable

nonnegotiable instrument FINANCE, BANKING, AND ACCOUNTING a financial instrument that cannot be signed over to anyone else

nonoperational balances FINANCE, BANKING, AND ACCOUNTING accounts that banks maintain at the Bank of England without the power of withdrawal

nonoptional FINANCE, BANKING, AND ACCOUNTING not subject to approval by stockholders

nonparticipating preferred stock FINANCE, BANKING, AND ACCOUNTING the most common type of preferred stock that pays a fixed dividend regardless of the profitability of the company. See also *participating preferred stock*

nonperforming asset FINANCE, BANKING, AND ACCOUNTING an asset that is not producing income

nonprofit organization GENERAL MANAGEMENT HR & PERSONNEL an *organization* that does not have financial profit as a main strategic objective. Nonprofit organizations include charities, professional associations, labor unions, and religious, arts, community, research, and campaigning bodies. These organizations are not situated in either the *public* or *private sectors*, but in what has been called the *third sector*. Many have paid staff and working capital but, according to *Peter Drucker*, their fundamental purpose is not to provide a product or service, but to change people. They are led by values rather than financial commitments to stockholders.

nonrandom sampling OPERATIONS & PRODUCTION a *sampling* technique which is used when it cannot be ensured that each item has an equal chance of being selected, or when selection is based on expert knowledge of the population. See also *random sampling*

nonrecourse debt FINANCE, BANKING, AND ACCOUNTING a debt for which the borrower has no personal responsibility, typically a debt of a limited partnership

nonrecoverable FINANCE, BANKING, AND ACCOUNTING relating to a debt that will never be paid, for example, because of the borrower's bankruptcy

nonrecurring charge FINANCE, BANKING, AND ACCOUNTING a charge that is made only once

nonrecurring items FINANCE, BANKING, AND ACCOUNTING special items in a set of accounts which appear only once

nonresident FINANCE, BANKING, AND ACCOUNTING used to describe an individual who has left his or her native country to work overseas for a period. Nonresidency has tax implications, for example, while a U.S. citizen is working overseas for a period of 11 out of 12 months, a limited amount of his or her earned income generated overseas is exempt from U.S. income tax. During a period of nonresidency, many expatriates choose to bank offshore.

Non-Resident Withholding Tax FINANCE, BANKING, AND ACCOUNTING a duty imposed by the New Zealand government on interest and dividends earned by a nonresident from investments. Abbr. *NRWT*

nonstore retailing E-COMMERCE the selling of goods and services electronically without establishing a physical store

nontariff barrier ECONOMICS see *NTB*

nontaxable FINANCE, BANKING, AND ACCOUNTING not subject to tax

nonverbal communication GENERAL MANAGEMENT any form of *communication* that is not expressed in words. Nonverbal communication is estimated to make up 65–90% of all communication, and understanding, interpreting, and using it are essential skills. Forms of nonverbal communication include actions and behavior such as silence, failure or slowness to respond to a message, and lateness in arriving for a meeting. *Body language* is also an important part of nonverbal communication. Nonverbal elements of communication may reinforce or contradict a verbal message.

non-virtual hosting E-COMMERCE the most basic *hosting option*, which is often provided free, and is advisable only for very small businesses. The client does not have their own domain name; instead, their address would be: www.hostingcompany.com/clientname. The most serious drawback of this kind of package is the lack of flexibility: the client cannot change their hosting company without changing their Web address.

nonvoting share FINANCE, BANKING, AND ACCOUNTING common stock that is paid a dividend from the company's profits, but that does not entitle the stockholder to vote at any meeting of stockholders. Such stock is unpopular with institutional investors.

Nordstrom, Kjell (*b.* 1958) GENERAL MANAGEMENT Swedish academic. Known for a focus on *globalization*, *innovation*, *agility*, and *product differentiation*. Coauthor of *Funky Business* (2000), with *Jonas Ridderstråle*.

norm STATISTICS a variety of statistics that are normal for a population

normal distribution STATISTICS the probability distribution of a random variable

normal profit ECONOMICS the minimum level of profit that will attract an entrepreneur to begin a business or remain trading

normal yield curve FINANCE, BANKING, AND ACCOUNTING a yield curve with higher interest rates for long-term bonds than for short-term bonds. See also *yield curve*

Norton, David P. (*b.* 1941) GENERAL MANAGEMENT U.S. consultant. See also *Kaplan, Robert S.*

no-strike agreement HR & PERSONNEL a formal understanding between an *employer* and a *labor union* that the union will not call its members out on *strike*. A no-strike agreement is usually won by the employer in exchange for improved terms and *conditions of employment*, including pay, and sometimes *guaranteed employment*.

nostro account FINANCE, BANKING, AND ACCOUNTING an account which a bank has with a correspondent bank in another country

notch (*S. Africa*) HR & PERSONNEL an increment on a salary scale

notes to the accounts FINANCE, BANKING, AND ACCOUNTING an explanation of particular items in a set of accounts

notes to the financial statements FINANCE, BANKING, AND ACCOUNTING an explanation of particular items in a set of financial statements

notice of coding FINANCE, BANKING, AND ACCOUNTING a notice which informs a third party of the code number given to indicate the amount of tax allowances a person has

notice of default FINANCE, BANKING, AND ACCOUNTING a formal document issued by a lender to a borrower who is in default. U.K. term *default notice*

notice period HR & PERSONNEL the amount of time specified in the terms and *conditions of employment* that an *employee* must work between resigning from an organization and leaving the employment of that organization

notional income FINANCE, BANKING, AND ACCOUNTING invisible benefit which is not money or goods and services

notional principal amount FINANCE, BANKING, AND ACCOUNTING the value used to represent a loan in calculating *interest rate swaps*

notional rent FINANCE, BANKING, AND ACCOUNTING an amount of money noted in accounts as rent where the company owns the building it is occupying and so does not pay an actual rent

not negotiable FINANCE, BANKING, AND ACCOUNTING wording on a check or bill of exchange to denote that it is deprived of its inherent quality of negotiability. When such a document is transferred from one person to another, the recipient obtains no better title to it than the signatory.

novation FINANCE, BANKING, AND ACCOUNTING an agreement to change a contract by substituting a third party for one of the two original parties

NPD *abbr* MARKETING new product development

NPV *abbr* FINANCE, BANKING, AND ACCOUNTING net present value

NRWT *abbr* FINANCE, BANKING, AND ACCOUNTING Non-Resident Withholding Tax

NSA *abbr* FINANCE, BANKING, AND ACCOUNTING National Society of Accountants

NSB *abbr* FINANCE, BANKING, AND ACCOUNTING National Savings Bank

NSC *abbr* FINANCE, BANKING, AND ACCOUNTING National Savings Certificate

NTB *abbr* ECONOMICS nontariff barrier: a country's economic regulation on something such as safety standards that impedes imports, often from developing countries

nuisance parameter STATISTICS a parameter in a statistical model that is insignificant in itself but whose unknown value is needed to make inferences about significant variables in a study

numbered account FINANCE, BANKING, AND ACCOUNTING a bank account identified by a number to allow the holder to remain anonymous

numerical control OPERATIONS & PRODUCTION the use of numerical data to influence the operation of equipment. It allows the operation of machinery to be automated and usually involves the use of computer systems. Data is generated, stored, manipulated, and retrieved while a process is in operation.

nuncupative will FINANCE, BANKING, AND ACCOUNTING a will that is made orally in the presence of a witness, rather than in writing

NYMEX *abbr* FINANCE, BANKING, AND ACCOUNTING New York Mercantile Exchange

NYSE *abbr* FINANCE, BANKING, AND ACCOUNTING New York Stock Exchange: the leading stock exchange in New York, which is self-regulatory but has to comply with the regulations of the U.S. Securities and Exchange Commission

NZSE *abbr* FINANCE, BANKING, AND ACCOUNTING New Zealand Stock Exchange

NZSE10 *abbr* FINANCE, BANKING, AND ACCOUNTING NZSE10 Index

NZSE10 Index FINANCE, BANKING, AND ACCOUNTING a measure of changes in stock prices on the New Zealand Stock Exchange, based on the change in value of the stocks of the ten largest companies. Abbr. *NZSE10*

NZSE30 Selection Index FINANCE, BANKING, AND ACCOUNTING a measure of changes in stock prices on the New Zealand Stock Exchange, based on the change in value of the stocks of the 30 largest companies. Abbr. *NZSE30*

NZSE40 Index FINANCE, BANKING, AND ACCOUNTING the principal measure of changes in stock prices on the New Zealand Stock Exchange, based on the change in value of the stocks of the 40 largest companies. The composition of the index is reviewed every three months.

O

Obeng, Eddie (*b.* 1959) GENERAL MANAGEMENT Ghanaian-born academic and consultant. Pioneer of the first virtual business school. Obeng founded the school, named Pentacle, in 1994, to assist managers and organizations facing the pressures and challenges of the global economy, a situation described in his book *New Rules for the New World* (1997).

OBI *abbr* E-COMMERCE FINANCE, BANKING, AND ACCOUNTING open buying on the Internet

object and task technique GENERAL MANAGEMENT a method of budgeting that involves assessing a project's objectives, determining the tasks required for their accomplishment, and then estimating the cost of each task

objective GENERAL MANAGEMENT HR & PERSONNEL an end toward which effort is directed and on which resources are focused, usually to achieve an organization's *strategy*. There is endless discussion on whether objective, *goal*, *target*, and *aim* are the same. In general usage, the terms are often interchangeable, so it is

important that, if an organization has a particular meaning for one of these terms, it must define it in its documentation. Sometimes an objective is seen as the desired final end result, while a goal is a smaller step on the road to it. Objective setting is given a practical application in *management by objectives*.

obscuranto GENERAL MANAGEMENT incomprehensible jargon used by large international organizations such as the European Commission (*slang*)

OBSF *abbr* FINANCE, BANKING, AND ACCOUNTING off-balance-sheet financing

obsolescence
1 MARKETING the decline of products in a market due to the introduction of better competitor products or rapid technology developments. Obsolescence of products can be a planned process, controlled by introducing deliberate minor cosmetic changes to a product every few years to encourage new purchases. It can also be unplanned, however, and in some sectors the pace of technological change is so rapid that the rate of obsolescence is high. This is the case particularly in consumer and industrial electronics, affecting computers, Internet-related products, telecommunications, and television, audio, and car technology. Obsolescence is part of the product *life cycle*, and if a product cannot be turned around, it may lead to *product abandonment*.
2 FINANCE, BANKING, AND ACCOUNTING the loss of value of a fixed asset due to advances in technology or changes in market conditions

occupational health HR & PERSONNEL the wellbeing of *employees* at work. An occupational health service is concerned with reacting to and preventing work-related illness and injury, and with maintaining and improving employees' health. Occupational health may involve some or all of these elements: health screening, including *pre-employment screening* (see *health screening*); monitoring compliance with health and safety legislation; health promotion activities; and initiating and maintaining health-related policies. There may be some overlap with *employee assistance programs*. An occupational health service strives to reduce *absenteeism* and improve employee morale and performance.

occupational illness HR & PERSONNEL an illness associated with a particular job. Occupational illnesses include lung disease, which can affect miners, *repetitive strain injury*, which can be suffered by keyboard users, and asbestosis, caused by working with asbestos. *Occupational health* policies must take all

hazards into account and minimize the potential for these diseases to develop. Government benefits are sometimes available to people who are disadvantaged because of occupational illness.

occupational psychology HR & PERSONNEL the branch of psychology concerned with the assessment of the well-being of *employees* within their work environment in order to improve performance and efficiency, *job satisfaction*, and *occupational health*. The eight main areas of occupational psychology include: human-machine interaction; design of working environment; *health and safety*; personnel *recruitment* and assessment; *performance appraisal* and career development; *counseling* and *personal development*; *training*; *motivation*; industrial relations; and organization change and development. Also known as *industrial psychology*

OCF *abbr* FINANCE, BANKING, AND ACCOUNTING operating cash flow

OCR *abbr* FINANCE, BANKING, AND ACCOUNTING official cash rate

O/D *abbr* FINANCE, BANKING, AND ACCOUNTING overdraft

Odiorne, George Stanley GENERAL MANAGEMENT U.S. academic. Known for his popularization in the United States of *Peter Drucker*'s *Management by Objectives*. Odiorne is said to have coined the saying "If you can't measure it, you can't manage it."

OECD *abbr* FINANCE, BANKING, AND ACCOUNTING Organisation for Economic Co-operation and Development: a group of 30 member countries, with a shared commitment to democratic government and the market economy, that has active relationships with some 70 other countries via nongovernmental organizations. Formed in 1961, its work covers economic and social issues from macroeconomics to trade, education, development, and scientific innovation. Its goals are to promote economic growth and employment in member countries in a climate of stability; to assist the sustainable economic expansion of both member and nonmember countries; and to support a balanced and even-handed expansion of world trade.

OEIC *abbr* FINANCE, BANKING, AND ACCOUNTING open-ended investment company

OEM *abbr* OPERATIONS & PRODUCTION original equipment manufacturer

off-balance-sheet financing FINANCE, BANKING, AND ACCOUNTING financing obtained by means other than debt and equity instruments, for example, partnerships, joint ventures, and leases. Abbr. *OBSF*

offer FINANCE, BANKING, AND ACCOUNTING the price at which a market maker will sell a security, or a unit trust manager in the United Kingdom will sell units. It is also the net asset value of a mutual fund plus any sales charges in the United States. It is the price investors pay when they buy a security. Also known as *ask*, *offering price*, *offer price*

offer by prospectus FINANCE, BANKING, AND ACCOUNTING in the United Kingdom, one of the ways available to a lead manager of offering securities to the public. See also *float initial public offering*, *new issue offer for sale*

offer document FINANCE, BANKING, AND ACCOUNTING a description of the loan a lender is offering to provide

offer for sale FINANCE, BANKING, AND ACCOUNTING an invitation by a party other than the company itself to apply for stock in a company based on information contained in a prospectus

offering circular FINANCE, BANKING, AND ACCOUNTING a document which gives information about a company whose stock is being sold to the public for the first time

offering memorandum FINANCE, BANKING, AND ACCOUNTING a description of an offer to sell securities privately

offering price FINANCE, BANKING, AND ACCOUNTING the price at which somebody offers a share of a stock for sale. Also known as *offer price*

offeror FINANCE, BANKING, AND ACCOUNTING somebody who makes a bid

offer price FINANCE, BANKING, AND ACCOUNTING see *offering price*

office design GENERAL MANAGEMENT the arrangement of workspace so that work can be performed in the most efficient way. Office design incorporates both *ergonomics* and *work flow*, which examine the way in which work is performed in order to optimize layout. Office design is an important factor in *job satisfaction*. It affects the way in which employees work, and many organizations have implemented open-plan offices to encourage *teamwork*. The development of *information and communications technologies* has led to changes in traditional layouts and some offices

are designed to facilitate **hot-desking** or **hotel-ing**. The design of workspaces must conform to health and safety legislation.

office-free HR & PERSONNEL used to refer to employees whose jobs do not require them to work in an office (*slang*)

office junior HR & PERSONNEL an employee with no responsibilities who carries out mundane or routine tasks in an office

office politics GENERAL MANAGEMENT interpersonal dynamics within a workplace. Office politics involves the complex network of power and status that exists within any group of people.

officer GENERAL MANAGEMENT see *executive*

officer of a company HR & PERSONNEL an individual who acts in an official capacity in a company, for example, the company secretary, a director, or a manager. Officers share legal liability for the actions of their company.

official bank FINANCE, BANKING, AND ACCOUNTING a bank that has a charter from a government

official books of account FINANCE, BANKING, AND ACCOUNTING the official financial records of an institution

official cash rate FINANCE, BANKING, AND ACCOUNTING the current interest rate as set by a central bank. Abbr. **OCR**

official development assistance FINANCE, BANKING, AND ACCOUNTING money that the Organization for Economic Cooperation and Development's Development Assistance Committee gives or lends to a developing country

official intervention FINANCE, BANKING, AND ACCOUNTING an attempt by a government to influence the exchange rate by buying or selling foreign currency

official list FINANCE, BANKING, AND ACCOUNTING in the United Kingdom, the list maintained by the Financial Services Authority of all the securities traded on the London Stock Exchange

official receiver FINANCE, BANKING, AND ACCOUNTING an officer of the court who is appointed to wind up the affairs of an organization that goes bankrupt. In the United Kingdom, an official receiver is appointed by the Department of Trade and Industry and often

acts as a *liquidator*. The job involves realizing any assets that remain to repay debts, for example, by selling property. Abbr. **OR**

off-line transaction processing E-COMMERCE the receipt and storage of order and credit or debit card information through a computer network or point-of-sale terminal for subsequent authorization and processing

offset FINANCE, BANKING, AND ACCOUNTING a transaction that balances all or part of an earlier transaction in the same security

offset clause FINANCE, BANKING, AND ACCOUNTING a provision in an insurance policy that permits the balancing of credits against debits so that, for example, a party can reduce or omit payments to another party that owes it money and is bankrupt

offshore account FINANCE, BANKING, AND ACCOUNTING an account in a *tax haven*

offshore bank FINANCE, BANKING, AND ACCOUNTING a bank that offers only limited wholesale banking services to nonresidents

offshore company FINANCE, BANKING, AND ACCOUNTING a company that is registered in a country other than the one in which it conducts most of its business, usually for tax purposes. For example, many captive insurance companies are registered in the Cayman Islands.

offshore finance subsidiary (*U.K.*) FINANCE, BANKING, AND ACCOUNTING = *offshore financial subsidiary*

offshore financial center FINANCE, BANKING, AND ACCOUNTING a country or other political unit that has banking laws intended to attract business from industrialized nations

offshore financial subsidiary FINANCE, BANKING, AND ACCOUNTING a company created in another country to handle financial transactions, giving the owning company certain tax and legal advantages in its home country. U.K. term *offshore finance subsidiary*

offshore holding company FINANCE, BANKING, AND ACCOUNTING a company created in another country to own other companies, giving the owning company certain legal advantages in its home country

offshore production OPERATIONS & PRODUCTION the manufacture of goods abroad for import to the domestic market

offshore trading company FINANCE, BANKING, AND ACCOUNTING a company created in another

country to handle commercial transactions, giving the owning company certain legal advantages in its home country

offshoring HR & PERSONNEL the transfer of service operations to foreign countries in order to take advantage of a supply of skilled but relatively cheap labor. Services may be outsourced to a foreign company or a wholly owned foreign *subsidiary company* may be established. The main benefit of offshoring is the reduction of costs but concerns about redundancies and job losses in the home countries have been raised.

off-the-shelf company (*U.K.*) FINANCE, BANKING, AND ACCOUNTING a company for which all the legal formalities, except the appointment of directors, have been completed so that a purchaser can transform it into a new company with relative ease and low cost

off-topic GENERAL MANAGEMENT irrelevant or off the subject (*slang*)

Ohmae, Kenichi (*b.* 1943) GENERAL MANAGEMENT Japanese consultant, writer, and politician. Herald of Japanese management techniques in the West, arguing that the success of Japanese companies could be attributed to Japanese strategic thinking based on *creativity* and *innovation*. In *The Mind of the Strategist* (1982), Ohmae identified key differences between the strategies adopted by Japanese managers and their Western counterparts. He later challenged all companies to take account of *globalization* in their *strategic planning* (see *planning*) and to focus on the relationship between business and the nation state. His recent work examines the relationship between old economy and *new economy* companies and identifies the basic forces influencing the new economy.

Ohmae is a graduate of Waseda University and the Tokyo Institute of Technology, and has a PhD in nuclear engineering from the Massachusetts Institute of Technology. He joined McKinsey in 1972, becoming managing director of its Tokyo office. See thinker *Kenichi Ohmae*

Ohno, Taiichi (1912–90) GENERAL MANAGEMENT Japanese business executive. Responsible for much of the background work and thinking that created the *Toyota production system*, explained in the book of the same name (1988). See thinker *Taiichi Ohno*

ohnosecond GENERAL MANAGEMENT the short time required to realize that you have made a serious mistake (*slang*)

OI *abbr* FINANCE, BANKING, AND ACCOUNTING operating income

oil

the good oil (*ANZ*) GENERAL MANAGEMENT accurate and useful information (*slang*)

OINK GENERAL MANAGEMENT one income, no kids (*slang*)

older worker HR & PERSONNEL generally considered to mean an employee aged 50 or over but in some industries, such as IT, an older worker is somebody over 30. Older workers can be subject to *age discrimination*.

Old Lady of Threadneedle Street FINANCE, BANKING, AND ACCOUNTING the Bank of England, which is located in Threadneedle Street in the City of London (*slang*)

old old MARKETING the oldest age group, consisting of people over the age of 75

oligarchy GENERAL MANAGEMENT an organization in which a small group of managers exercises control. Within an oligarchy, the controlling group often directs the organization for its own purposes, or for purposes other than the best interests of the organization.

oligopoly ECONOMICS a market in which there are only a few, very large, suppliers

ombudsman GENERAL MANAGEMENT someone who investigates complaints against public departments, large organizations, or business sectors

omitted dividend FINANCE, BANKING, AND ACCOUNTING a regularly scheduled dividend that a company does not pay

omnibus account FINANCE, BANKING, AND ACCOUNTING an account of one broker with another that combines the transactions of multiple investors for the convenience of the brokers

omnibus survey MARKETING a survey covering a number of topics, usually undertaken on behalf of several clients who share the cost of conducting the survey. It is a cost-effective means of researching several subjects at the same time, and is also suitable for measuring attitudes and behavior toward different types of products and services, or monitoring changes in attitude among groups of consumers.

on account FINANCE, BANKING, AND ACCOUNTING paid in advance against all or part of money due in the future

on demand FINANCE, BANKING, AND ACCOUNTING
1 used to describe an account from which withdrawals may be made without giving a period of notice
2 used to describe a loan, usually an overdraft, that the lender can request the borrower to repay immediately
3 used to describe a bill of exchange that is paid upon presentation

one-stop shopping FINANCE, BANKING, AND ACCOUNTING the ability of a single financial institution to offer a full variety of financial services

one-to-one marketing MARKETING a marketing technique using detailed data, personalized communications, and customized products or services to match the requirements of individual customers

one-to-one merger GENERAL MANAGEMENT FINANCE, BANKING, AND ACCOUNTING see *merger*

one-way trade FINANCE, BANKING, AND ACCOUNTING an economic situation in which one country sells to another, but does not buy anything in return

one-year money FINANCE, BANKING, AND ACCOUNTING money placed on a money market for a fixed period of one year, with either a fixed or variable rate of interest. It can be removed during the fixed term only upon payment of a penalty.

on-hold advertising MARKETING telephone advertising aimed at consumers who are being kept on hold while waiting to speak to somebody (*slang*)

online capture E-COMMERCE a payment transaction generated after goods have been shipped, in which funds are transferred from issuer to acquirer to merchant account

online catalog E-COMMERCE a business-to-business marketplace that collects the catalog data of every supplier in a particular industry and places it on one central Web resource. Catalogs are important to companies for marketing purposes because they are one of the main ways to distribute product information to public marketplaces and private exchanges. Also known as *procurement portal*

online community E-COMMERCE a means of allowing Web users to engage with one another and with an organization through use of interactive tools such as e-mail, *discussion boards*, and *chat systems*.

They are a means by which a Web site owner can take the pulse of consumers to find out what they are thinking, and to generate unique content. As stand-alone businesses, online communities have been found to be weak; they work best when they are supporting the need for an organization to collect ongoing feedback.

online shopping E-COMMERCE see *electronic shopping*

online shopping mall E-COMMERCE see *cyber mall*

online training HR & PERSONNEL see *computer-based training*

on-pack offer MARKETING a sales promotion technique in which customers are offered a premium on the pack

on-target earnings HR & PERSONNEL the amount earned by a person working on *commission* who has achieved the targets set. Abbr. **OTE**

on-the-job training HR & PERSONNEL *training* given to employees in the workplace as they perform everyday work activities. On-the-job training is based on the principle of *learning by doing* and includes demonstration and explanation by a more experienced employee, supervisor, or manager; performance of tasks under supervision; and the provision of appropriate *feedback*. Types of on-the-job training include *coaching*, *delegation*, *job rotation*, *secondment*, and participation in special projects. In the United Kingdom, on-the-job training is sometimes informally referred to as *sitting with Nellie*.

ooda loop GENERAL MANAGEMENT a model of the strategic decision-making process, whose elements (observation, orientation, decision, and action) succeed each other in a continuous cycle, each informing and shaping the next. The model was developed by Colonel John Boyd (1927–97) of the United States Air Force, building on the work of military strategists such as Sun Tzu and Karl von Clausewitz. Boyd suggested that it was possible to outthink and outmaneuver the enemy by moving through the cycle with variety, rapidity, harmony, and initiative and by thinking inside the enemy's ooda loop. The concept has been applied to organizational decision making and corporate strategy as a means of gaining competitive advantage in changing environments.

OPEC *abbr* FINANCE, BANKING, AND ACCOUNTING Organization of the Petroleum Exporting Countries: an international organization of 11 developing countries, each one largely reliant on oil revenues as its main source of income,

that tries to ensure there is a balance between supply and demand by adjusting the members' oil output. OPEC's headquarters are in Vienna. The current members, Algeria, Indonesia, Iran, Iraq, Kuwait, Libya, Nigeria, Qatar, Saudi Arabia, the United Arab Emirates, and Venezuela, meet at least twice a year to decide on output levels and discuss recent and anticipated oil market developments.

open-book management GENERAL MANAGEMENT a *management style* in which everything is revealed to employees and there are no secrets. Open-book management involves not only revealing a company's full financial information to its employees but also making transparent all of the workings of the company. Open-book management has been viewed as enabling the *empowerment* and *involvement* of the workforce, increasing employee *motivation* and organizational efficiency.

open buying on the Internet E-COMMERCE FINANCE, BANKING, AND ACCOUNTING a standard built around a common set of business requirements for electronic communication between buyers and sellers that, when implemented, allows different e-commerce systems to talk to one another. Abbr. *OBI*

open check FINANCE, BANKING, AND ACCOUNTING **1** (*U.K.*) a check that is not crossed and so may be cashed by the payee at the branch of the bank where it is drawn
2 a signed check where the amount payable has not been indicated

open-collar worker HR & PERSONNEL a person who works from home (*slang*)

open communication GENERAL MANAGEMENT a communications policy intended to ensure that employees have full information about their organization

open-door policy GENERAL MANAGEMENT a receptive, listening approach to management characterized by a ready, informal availability on the part of the manager toward employees. Open-door management removes the need to make appointments or to show the deference traditionally associated with relationships between superiors and subordinates in hierarchies. The opposite management style is a *closed-door policy*, which is more formal. Open- and closed-door policies can reflect different kinds of *corporate culture*.

open economy ECONOMICS an economy that places no restrictions on the movement of capital, labor, foreign trade, and payments into and out of the country

open-end credit FINANCE, BANKING, AND ACCOUNTING a form of credit that does not have an upper limit on the amount that can be borrowed or a time limit before repayment is due

open-ended credit (*U.K.*) FINANCE, BANKING, AND ACCOUNTING = *open-end credit*

open-ended fund *or* **open-ended investment company** (*U.K.*) FINANCE, BANKING, AND ACCOUNTING = *open-end fund*

open-ended management company (*U.K.*) FINANCE, BANKING, AND ACCOUNTING = *open-end management company*

open-ended mortgage (*U.K.*) FINANCE, BANKING, AND ACCOUNTING = *open-end mortgage*

open-end fund *or* **open-end investment company** FINANCE, BANKING, AND ACCOUNTING a mutual fund that has a variable number of shares. U.K. term *open-ended fund*. See also *closed-end fund*

open-end management company FINANCE, BANKING, AND ACCOUNTING a company that sells mutual funds. U.K. term *open-ended management company*

open-end mortgage FINANCE, BANKING, AND ACCOUNTING a mortgage in which prepayment is allowed. U.K. term *open-ended mortgage*

opening balance FINANCE, BANKING, AND ACCOUNTING the value of a financial quantity at the beginning of a period of time, such as a day or a year

opening balance sheet FINANCE, BANKING, AND ACCOUNTING an account showing an organization's opening balances

opening bell FINANCE, BANKING, AND ACCOUNTING the beginning of a day of trading on a market

opening price FINANCE, BANKING, AND ACCOUNTING a price for a security at the beginning of a day of trading on a market

opening purchase FINANCE, BANKING, AND ACCOUNTING a first purchase of a series to be made in options of a particular type for a particular commodity or security

opening stock (*U.K.*) FINANCE, BANKING, AND ACCOUNTING = *beginning inventory*

open interest FINANCE, BANKING, AND ACCOUNTING options that have not yet been closed

open learning HR & PERSONNEL a flexible approach to a course of study that allows

individuals to learn at a time, place, and pace to suit their needs. A typical open learning program might offer the student a variety of delivery methods, including tutorials, workshops, formal lectures, and the Internet, supported by a variety of learning materials such as textbooks, workbooks, and video, audio, and computer-based materials. See also *distance learning*

open loop system FINANCE, BANKING, AND ACCOUNTING a management control system which includes no provision for corrective action to be applied to the sequence of activities

open market operation FINANCE, BANKING, AND ACCOUNTING a transaction by a central bank in a public market

open market value FINANCE, BANKING, AND ACCOUNTING the price that an asset or security would realize if it was offered on a market open to all

open standard GENERAL MANAGEMENT a standard for computers and related products that allows pieces of equipment from different manufacturers to operate with each other

open system E-COMMERCE an operating system whose developer encourages the development of applications that use it

open systems thinking GENERAL MANAGEMENT a learning and *problem solving* approach that involves describing the behavior of a system, then exploring possibilities for improving it. Open systems thinking encourages *creativity* and is used by *learning organizations*.

open trading protocol E-COMMERCE FINANCE, BANKING, AND ACCOUNTING a standard designed to support Internet-based retail transactions, that allows different systems to communicate with each other for a variety of payment-related activities. The *open buying on the Internet* protocol is a competing standard. Abbr. *OTP*

operating cash flow FINANCE, BANKING, AND ACCOUNTING the amount used to represent the money moving through a company as a result of its operations, as distinct from its purely financial transactions. Abbr. *OCF*

operating costing OPERATIONS & PRODUCTION a costing system that is applied to continuous operations in mass production or in the service industries. In the simplest form of operating costing, the costing period is set at a specific length of time, usually a calendar month or four weeks. The costs incurred over the period

are related to the number of units produced, and the division of the first by the second gives the average unit cost for the period. Also known as **batch costing**

operating cycle OPERATIONS & PRODUCTION the cycle of business activity in which cash is used to buy resources which are converted into products or services and then sold for cash

operating income FINANCE, BANKING, AND ACCOUNTING revenue minus the cost of goods sold and normal operating expenses. Also known as **earnings before interest and taxes**. Abbr. **OI**

operating lease GENERAL MANAGEMENT a lease that is regarded by accountants as rental rather than as a **capital lease**. The monthly lease payments are simply treated as rental expenses and recognized on the income statement as they are incurred. There is no recognition of a leased asset or liability.

operating leverage FINANCE, BANKING, AND ACCOUNTING the ratio of a business's fixed costs to its total costs. As the fixed costs have to be paid regardless of output, the higher the ratio, the higher the risk of losses in an economic downturn.

operating margin FINANCE, BANKING, AND ACCOUNTING see **profit margin**

operating profit FINANCE, BANKING, AND ACCOUNTING the difference between a company's revenues and any related costs and expenses, not including income or expenses from any sources other than its normal methods of providing a good or a service

operating risk FINANCE, BANKING, AND ACCOUNTING the risk of a high operating leverage

operating system OPERATIONS & PRODUCTION a program that controls the basic operation of a computer and its communication with devices such as the keyboard, printer, and mouse

operational audit GENERAL MANAGEMENT a structured review of the systems and procedures of an organization in order to evaluate whether they are being conducted efficiently and effectively. An operational audit involves establishing performance **objectives**, agreeing the standards and criteria for assessment, and evaluating actual performance against targeted performance. Also known as **management audit operations audit**

operational gearing FINANCE, BANKING, AND ACCOUNTING the ongoing financial operations of a company

operational research GENERAL MANAGEMENT the application of scientific methods to the solution of managerial and administrative problems, involving complex systems or processes. Operational research strives to find the optimum plan for the control and operation of a system or process. It was originally used during World War II as a means of solving logistical problems. It has since developed into a planning, scheduling, and **problem solving** technique applied across the industrial, commercial, and public sectors.

operation planning OPERATIONS & PRODUCTION see **planning**

operations OPERATIONS & PRODUCTION see **operations management**

operations audit GENERAL MANAGEMENT see **operational audit**

operations management OPERATIONS & PRODUCTION the maintenance, control, and improvement of organizational activities that are required to produce goods or services for consumers. Operations management has traditionally been associated with manufacturing activities but can also be applied to the service sector. The measurement and evaluation of operations is usually undertaken through a process of business appraisal. Efficiency and effectiveness may be monitored by the application of **ISO** 9001 quality systems, or **total quality management** techniques.

operation time OPERATIONS & PRODUCTION the period required to perform an operation on a complete batch exclusive of set-up and breaking-down times

opinion leader MARKETING a high-profile person or organization that can significantly influence public opinion. An opinion leader can be a politician, religious, business or community leader, journalist, or educator. Show business and sports personalities can exert a great deal of influence on young people's leisure lifestyles and buying habits and are consequently frequently used in **advertising campaigns**.

opinion leader research MARKETING the investigation of the perceptions of **corporate image** and reputation among the people at the top of a company, industry, or profession

opinion shopping GENERAL MANAGEMENT the practice of searching for an auditor whose views are in line with those of a company being audited. Opinion shopping can take place when a company is about to be audited

and has recently undertaken questionable dealings. Auditors are sought whose interpretation of the law matches the company's own, and who will approve the company's financial statements.

opinion survey STATISTICS a survey conducted to determine what members of a population think about a given topic

opportunity cost ECONOMICS FINANCE, BANKING, AND ACCOUNTING GENERAL MANAGEMENT an amount of money lost as a result of choosing one investment rather than another

OPT *abbr* OPERATIONS & PRODUCTION optimized production technology

optimal portfolio FINANCE, BANKING, AND ACCOUNTING a theoretical set of investments that would be the most profitable for an investor

optimal redemption provision FINANCE, BANKING, AND ACCOUNTING a provision that specifies when an issuer can call a bond

optimize FINANCE, BANKING, AND ACCOUNTING to allocate such things as resources or capital as efficiently as possible

optimized production technology OPERATIONS & PRODUCTION a sophisticated **production planning** and **control** system, based on **finite loading** procedures, that concentrates on reducing **bottlenecks** in the system in order to improve efficiency. The key task of OPT is to increase total systems throughput by realizing existing capacity in other parts of the system. OPT is a practical application of the **theory of constraints**. Abbr. **OPT**

optimum capacity OPERATIONS & PRODUCTION the level of output at which the minimum cost per unit is incurred

opt-in E-COMMERCE a type of **subscription process** for users of a Web site wanting to sign up to receive specific information or services. An opt-in approach is where a user actively decides to provide their e-mail address, so the Web site owner can send them e-mail. However, the emerging convention is **double opt-in**.

option FINANCE, BANKING, AND ACCOUNTING
1 a contract for the right to buy or sell an asset, typically a commodity, under certain terms. Also known as **option contract**
2 the right of an option holder to buy or sell a specific asset on predetermined terms on, or before, a future date

option account FINANCE, BANKING, AND ACCOUNTING a brokerage account used for trading in options

optionaire FINANCE, BANKING, AND ACCOUNTING a millionaire whose wealth consists of stock options (*slang*)

option buyer FINANCE, BANKING, AND ACCOUNTING an investor who buys an option

option class FINANCE, BANKING, AND ACCOUNTING a set of options that are identical with respect to type and underlying asset

option contract FINANCE, BANKING, AND ACCOUNTING see *option*

option elasticity FINANCE, BANKING, AND ACCOUNTING the relative change in the value of an option as a function of a change in the value of the underlying asset

option income fund FINANCE, BANKING, AND ACCOUNTING a mutual fund that invests in options

option premium FINANCE, BANKING, AND ACCOUNTING the amount per share that a buyer pays for an option

option price FINANCE, BANKING, AND ACCOUNTING the price of an option

option pricing model FINANCE, BANKING, AND ACCOUNTING a model that is used to determine the fair value of options

options clearing corporation FINANCE, BANKING, AND ACCOUNTING an organization responsible for the listing of options and clearing trades in them

option seller FINANCE, BANKING, AND ACCOUNTING see *option writer*

option series FINANCE, BANKING, AND ACCOUNTING a collection of options that are identical in terms of what they represent

options market FINANCE, BANKING, AND ACCOUNTING the trading in options, or a place where options trading occurs

options on physicals FINANCE, BANKING, AND ACCOUNTING options on securities with fixed interest rates

option writer FINANCE, BANKING, AND ACCOUNTING a person or institution that sells an option. Also known as *option seller*

OR *abbr* FINANCE, BANKING, AND ACCOUNTING official receiver

order
1 OPERATIONS & PRODUCTION a *contract* made between a customer and a supplier for the supply of a variety of goods or services in a determined quantity and quality, at an agreed price, and for delivery at or by a specified time
2 FINANCE, BANKING, AND ACCOUNTING an occasion when a broker is told to buy or sell something for an investor's own account

order book OPERATIONS & PRODUCTION a record of the outstanding orders that an organization has received. An order book may be physical, with the specifications and delivery times of orders recorded in it, or the term may be used generally to describe the health of a company. A full order book implies a successful company, while an empty order book can indicate an organization at risk of *business failure*.

order confirmation E-COMMERCE an e-mail message informing a purchaser that an order has been received

order picking OPERATIONS & PRODUCTION selecting and withdrawing goods or components from a store or warehouse to meet production requirements or to satisfy customer orders

order point FINANCE, BANKING, AND ACCOUNTING the quantity of an item that is on hand when more units of the item are to be ordered

order processing OPERATIONS & PRODUCTION the tracking of *orders* with suppliers and from customers

orders pending FINANCE, BANKING, AND ACCOUNTING orders that have not yet resulted in transactions

ordinary interest FINANCE, BANKING, AND ACCOUNTING interest calculated on the basis of a year having only 360 days

ordinary shares FINANCE, BANKING, AND ACCOUNTING stocks bought by investors in the United States in foreign companies that are traded on their home markets, as opposed to stocks that trade in the United States. Ordinary shares are equivalent to common stock traded on U.S. markets.

organigram GENERAL MANAGEMENT see *organization chart*

Organisation for Economic Co-operation and Development FINANCE, BANKING, AND ACCOUNTING see *OECD*

organization GENERAL MANAGEMENT an arrangement of people and resources working in a planned manner toward specified strategic goals. An organization can be any structured body such as a business, company, or firm in the private or public sector, or in a nonprofit association. See also *organization structure*, *organization theory*

organizational analysis GENERAL MANAGEMENT a type of internal business appraisal aimed at identifying areas of inefficiency and opportunities for streamlining and reorganization

organizational change GENERAL MANAGEMENT see *change management*

organizational chart GENERAL MANAGEMENT see *organization chart*

organizational commitment GENERAL MANAGEMENT
1 the commitment of an organization to given goals and objectives, as demonstrated through its stated goals and policies, and its actions and allocation of resources
2 the degree of *employee commitment* within an organizational workforce

organizational culture GENERAL MANAGEMENT see *corporate culture*

organizational design GENERAL MANAGEMENT see *organization structure*

organizational development GENERAL MANAGEMENT a planned approach to far-reaching organizational change designed to enable an organization to respond and adapt to changing market conditions and to set a new agenda. Organizational development is frequently linked to *organization structure*, which can act either as an enabling or restrictive mechanism for change. For organizational development to succeed, any policies or strategies introduced must fit with the *corporate culture*

organizational federalism GENERAL MANAGEMENT see *federal organization*

organizational learning GENERAL MANAGEMENT a culture of change and improvement within an organization, characterized by employee enthusiasm, energy, and high levels of *creativity* and *innovation*. In their book *Organizational Learning* (1978), *Chris Argyris* and *Donald Schön* suggest that if a number of employee development activities are in progress within an organization, a sense of organizational movement and development can be achieved, and that, with the right encouragement, support, and reward, this can become self-perpetuating. The concept of organizational learning was further developed by *Peter*

a-z
1573

DICTIONARY

Senge, and repopularized as the *learning organization*. See thinker *Chris Argyris*, *Peter Senge*

organization behavior GENERAL MANAGEMENT the study of human and group behavior within organizational settings. The study of organization behavior involves looking at the attitudes, interpersonal relationships, performance, *productivity*, *job satisfaction*, and commitment of employees, as well as levels of *organizational commitment* and industrial relations. Organization behavior can be affected by *corporate culture*, *leadership*, and *management style*. Organization behavior emerged as a distinct specialty from *organization theory* in the late 1950s and early 1960s through attempts to integrate different perspectives on human and management problems and develop an understanding of behavioral dynamics within organizations. See thinker *Chris Argyris*, *Douglas McGregor*

organization chart GENERAL MANAGEMENT a graphic illustration of an *organization's structure*, showing hierarchical authority and relationships between departments and jobs. The horizontal dimension of an organization chart shows the nature of job function and responsibility and the vertical dimension shows how jobs are coordinated in reporting or authority relationships. Some charts include managers' names, others only job titles. Organization charts are widely used to bring order and clarity to the way the organization is structured. Despite this, they reflect little of the way organizations actually work and can appear complex, especially in highly *bureaucratic* organizations. The first recorded organization chart was produced in the United States by David C. McCallum for the New York and Erie Railroad. Also known as *organigram*, *organizational chart*, *org chart*

organization hierarchy GENERAL MANAGEMENT the vertical layers of ranks of personnel within an organization, each layer subordinate to the one above it. Organization hierarchy is often shown in the form of an *organization chart*. An extended hierarchy is typical of a *bureaucracy*, but during the later 20th and early 21st centuries the layers of hierarchical positions within large organizations have often been reduced as part of *downsizing* exercises. These result in the shallow or nonexistent hierarchies of flexible, *flat organizations*, within which there is greater employee *empowerment* and autonomy.

organization man GENERAL MANAGEMENT somebody who fully accepts and may be absorbed by organizational objectives and values.

The Organization Man, a bestselling novel by *William Whyte*, is the source of the phrase.

Organization of the Petroleum Exporting Countries FINANCE, BANKING, AND ACCOUNTING see *OPEC*

organization structure GENERAL MANAGEMENT the form of an organization that is evident in the way divisions, departments, functions, and people link together and interact. Organization structure reveals vertical operational responsibilities, and horizontal linkages, and may be represented by an *organization chart*. The complexity of an organization's structure is often proportional to its size and its geographic dispersal. The traditional organization structure for many businesses in the 20th century was the *bureaucracy*, originally defined by *Max Weber*. More recent forms include the *flat*, *network*, *matrix* (see *matrix organization*), and *virtual organizations*. These forms became more prevalent during the last decades of the 20th century as a result of the trend toward restructuring and downsizing and developments in telecommunications technology. According to *Harold J. Leavitt*, organization structure is inextricably linked to the technology and people who perform the tasks. *Charles Handy* has shown that it is also directly linked to *corporate culture*. See thinker *Charles Handy*, *Max Weber*

organization theory GENERAL MANAGEMENT the body of research and knowledge concerning organizations. Organization theory originally focused primarily on the organization as a unit, as opposed to *organization behavior*, which explored individual and group behavior within the organization. Organization behavior emerged as a separate discipline in the late 1950s and early 1960s but there remains a large amount of overlap between the two. Organization theory covers a variety of areas including *organization structure* and organizational psychology. See thinker *Charles Handy*, *Henry Mintzberg*

org chart GENERAL MANAGEMENT see *organization chart*

orientation HR & PERSONNEL a process through which a new employee is integrated into an organization, learning about its *corporate culture*, policies and *procedures*, and the specific practicalities of his or her job. An orientation program should not consist of a one-day introduction, but should be planned and paced over a few days or weeks. There is a growing use of *boot camps*, which work to assimilate a new employee rapidly into the culture of the employing organization. U.K. term *induction*

original equipment manufacturer
1 OPERATIONS & PRODUCTION a company that assembles components from other suppliers or subcontractors to produce a complete product such as a car or aircraft. Abbr. *OEM*
2 GENERAL MANAGEMENT a company that makes a product that works with a basic and common product, for example, a computer

original face value FINANCE, BANKING, AND ACCOUNTING the amount of the principal of a mortgage on the day it is created

original issue discount FINANCE, BANKING, AND ACCOUNTING the discount offered on the day of sale of a debt instrument

original maturity FINANCE, BANKING, AND ACCOUNTING a date on which a debt instrument is due to mature

origination fee FINANCE, BANKING, AND ACCOUNTING a fee charged by a lender for providing a mortgage, usually expressed as a percentage of the principal

orthogonal STATISTICS statistically independent

OTC market *abbr* FINANCE, BANKING, AND ACCOUNTING over-the-counter market

OTE *abbr* HR & PERSONNEL on-target earnings

other capital FINANCE, BANKING, AND ACCOUNTING capital that is not listed in specific categories

other current assets FINANCE, BANKING, AND ACCOUNTING assets that are not cash and are due to mature within a year

other long-term capital FINANCE, BANKING, AND ACCOUNTING long-term capital that is not listed in specific categories

other prices FINANCE, BANKING, AND ACCOUNTING prices that are not listed in a catalog

other short-term capital FINANCE, BANKING, AND ACCOUNTING short-term capital that is not listed in specific categories

OTOH *abbr* GENERAL MANAGEMENT on the other hand (*slang*)

OTP *abbr* E-COMMERCE FINANCE, BANKING, AND ACCOUNTING open trading protocol

Ouchi, William G. (*b.* 1943) GENERAL MANAGEMENT Japanese-U.S. academic. Best known for *Theory Z* (1981), which developed the work of

Douglas McGregor. See thinker *Douglas Mc-Gregor*

out box GENERAL MANAGEMENT a receptacle for documents and other items that have been dealt with. An out box is normally placed in the office or on the desk of the person responsible for dealing with the contents. Items are placed in the out box before being filed or delivered to another person. U.K. term *out tray*

outdoor advertising MARKETING the use of outdoor advertising media in venues such as airports, shopping malls, bus shelters, and railway stations

outdoor training HR & PERSONNEL see *adventure training*

outlier STATISTICS a statistical observation that deviates significantly from other members of a sample

out of the loop GENERAL MANAGEMENT excluded from communication within a group. Somebody who is out of the loop may have been deliberately or inadvertently excluded from the decision-making process or the information flow around an organization. That person is likely to feel isolated and will be unable to contribute fully to the organization. Effective networking may help to prevent this from happening. (*slang*)

outplacement HR & PERSONNEL a program of resources, information, and advice provided by an employing organization for employees who are about to be laid off. Outplacement agencies typically help by drafting résumés, offering career guidance, providing practice interviews, and placing laid-off employees in new jobs. Outplacement programs are often put into place well before the laid-off employees leave the employer and, in the case of large-scale layoff programs, may remain in place for several years.

output ECONOMICS FINANCE, BANKING, AND ACCOUNTING anything produced by a company, usually physical products

output gap ECONOMICS the difference between the amount of activity that is sustainable in an economy and the amount of activity actually taking place

output method ECONOMICS an accounting system that classifies costs according to the *outputs* for which they are incurred, not the inputs they have bought

output tax (*ANZ*) FINANCE, BANKING, AND ACCOUNTING the amount of Goods and Services Tax paid to the tax office after the deduction of *input tax credits*

outside director GENERAL MANAGEMENT a member of a company's *board of directors* neither currently nor formerly in the company's employment. An outside director is sometimes described as being synonymous with a *nonexecutive director*, and as usually being employed by a holding or associated company. In the United States, an outside director is somebody who has no relationships at all to a company. In U.S. public companies, compensation and audit committees are generally made up of outside directors, and use of outside directors to select board directors is becoming more common.

outsourcing
1 GENERAL MANAGEMENT the transfer of the provision of services previously performed by in-house personnel to an external organization, usually under a *contract* with agreed standards, costs, and conditions. Areas traditionally outsourced include legal services, transport, catering, and security. An increasing variety of activities, including IT services, training, and public relations are now being outsourced. Outsourcing, or *contracting out*, is often introduced with the goal of increasing efficiency and reducing costs, or to enable the organization to develop greater flexibility or to concentrate on *core business* activities. The term *subcontracting* is sometimes used to refer to outsourcing.
2 FINANCE, BANKING, AND ACCOUNTING the use of external suppliers as a source of finished products, components, or services

outstanding check FINANCE, BANKING, AND ACCOUNTING a check which has been written and therefore has been entered in the company's ledgers, but which has not been presented for payment and so has not been debited from the company's bank account

outstanding share FINANCE, BANKING, AND ACCOUNTING a share that a company has issued and somebody has bought

outstanding share capital FINANCE, BANKING, AND ACCOUNTING the value of all of the stock of a company minus the value of retained shares

out tray (*U.K.*) GENERAL MANAGEMENT = *out box*

outward bound training HR & PERSONNEL see *adventure training*

outwork FINANCE, BANKING, AND ACCOUNTING GENERAL MANAGEMENT work performed for a company away from its premises, for example, by subcontractors or employees working from home

outworker FINANCE, BANKING, AND ACCOUNTING GENERAL MANAGEMENT a subcontractor or employee carrying out work for a company away from its premises

overall capitalization rate FINANCE, BANKING, AND ACCOUNTING net operating income other than debt service divided by value

overall market capacity ECONOMICS the amount of a service or good that can be absorbed in a market without affecting the price

overall rate of return FINANCE, BANKING, AND ACCOUNTING the yield of a bond held to maturity, expressed as a percentage

overall return FINANCE, BANKING, AND ACCOUNTING the aggregate of all the dividends received over an investment's life together with its capital gain or loss at the date of its realization, calculated either before or after tax. It is one of the ways an investor can look at the performance of an investment.

overbid FINANCE, BANKING, AND ACCOUNTING
1 to bid more than necessary
2 an amount that is bid that is unnecessarily high

overbought FINANCE, BANKING, AND ACCOUNTING used to describe a market or security considered to have risen too rapidly as a result of excessive buying

overbought market FINANCE, BANKING, AND ACCOUNTING a market where prices have risen beyond levels that can be supported by fundamental analysis. The market for Internet companies in 2001 was overbought and subsequently collapsed when it became clear that their trading performance could not support such price levels.

overcapacity OPERATIONS & PRODUCTION an excess of capability to produce goods or provide a service over the level of demand

overcapitalize FINANCE, BANKING, AND ACCOUNTING to supply a company with more capital than it needs or should have with the result that it is liable for unnecessary interest charges or dividend payments

overcapitalized FINANCE, BANKING, AND ACCOUNTING used to describe a business that has more capital than can profitably be employed. An overcapitalized company could buy back some of its own stock in the market; if it has significant debt capital it could repurchase its

bonds in the market; or it could make a large one-time dividend to stockholders.

overdraft FINANCE, BANKING, AND ACCOUNTING the amount by which the money withdrawn from a bank account exceeds the balance in the account. Abbr. *O/D*

overdraft facility FINANCE, BANKING, AND AC-COUNTING a credit arrangement with a bank, allowing a person or company with an account to use borrowed money up to an agreed limit when nothing is left in the account

overdraft line FINANCE, BANKING, AND ACCOUNT-ING an amount in excess of the balance in an account that a bank agrees to pay in honoring checks on the account

overdraft protection FINANCE, BANKING, AND ACCOUNTING the bank service, amounting to a line of credit, that assures that the bank will honor overdrafts, up to a limit and for a fee

overdraw FINANCE, BANKING, AND ACCOUNTING to withdraw more money from a bank account than it contains, thereby exceeding an agreed credit limit

overdrawn FINANCE, BANKING, AND ACCOUNTING in debt to a bank because the amount withdrawn from an account exceeds its balance

overdue FINANCE, BANKING, AND ACCOUNTING an amount still owed after the date due

overgeared FINANCE, BANKING, AND ACCOUNTING used to describe a company with debt capital and preferred stock that outweigh its common stock capital

overhanging FINANCE, BANKING, AND ACCOUNT-ING large amounts of commodities or securities that have not been sold and therefore have a negative effect on prices, for example, that part of a new issue left in the hands of the under-writers

overhead absorption rate FINANCE, BANKING, AND ACCOUNTING a means of attributing over-head to a product or service, based for example on direct labor hours, direct labor cost, or ma-chine hours. The choice of overhead absorp-tion base may be made with the objective of obtaining "accurate" product costs, or of influ-encing managerial behavior, for example, overhead applied to labor hours or part num-bers appears to make the use of these re-sources more costly, thus discouraging their use.

overhead capacity variance FINANCE, BANK-ING, AND ACCOUNTING the difference between the

overhead absorbed, based on budgeted hours, and actual hours worked

overhead costs FINANCE, BANKING, AND AC-COUNTING the indirect recurring costs of run-ning a business that are not linked directly to the goods or service produced and sold. Over-head costs can include payments for the rent of premises, utility bills, and employees' salar-ies. Also called *overheads*

overhead expenditure variance FINANCE, BANKING, AND ACCOUNTING the difference be-tween the budgeted *overhead costs* and the ac-tual expenditure

overheads FINANCE, BANKING, AND ACCOUNTING see *overhead costs*

overinsuring FINANCE, BANKING, AND ACCOUNT-ING insuring an asset for a sum in excess of its market or replacement value. However, it is unlikely that an insurance company will pay out more in a claim for loss than the asset is worth or the cost of replacing it.

overinvested FINANCE, BANKING, AND ACCOUNT-ING used to describe a business that invests heavily during an economic boom only to find that when it starts to produce an income, the demand for the product or service has fallen

overlap profit FINANCE, BANKING, AND ACCOUNT-ING *profit* which occurs in two overlapping ac-counting periods and on which overlap relief can be claimed

overnight position FINANCE, BANKING, AND ACCOUNTING a trader's position in a security or option at the end of a trading day

overnight repo FINANCE, BANKING, AND AC-COUNTING a repurchase agreement where banks sell securities for cash and repurchase them the next day at a higher price. This type of agreement is used by central banks as a means of regulating the money markets.

overprice MARKETING to set the price of a prod-uct or service too high, with the result that it is unacceptable to the market

overrated FINANCE, BANKING, AND ACCOUNTING used to describe something that is valued more highly than it should be

overseas company FINANCE, BANKING, AND AC-COUNTING a branch or subsidiary of a business that is incorporated in another country

Overseas Investment Commission FINANCE, BANKING, AND ACCOUNTING an independent body reporting to the New Zealand government that

regulates foreign investment in New Zealand. It was established in 1973 and is funded by the Reserve Bank of New Zealand.

overseas taxation FINANCE, BANKING, AND AC-COUNTING see *double taxation*

oversold FINANCE, BANKING, AND ACCOUNTING used to describe a market or security that is considered to have fallen too rapidly as a result of excessive selling. See also *bear market*

overstocked FINANCE, BANKING, AND ACCOUNT-ING used to describe a business that has more inventory than it needs

over-the-counter market FINANCE, BANKING, AND ACCOUNTING a market in which trading takes place directly between licensed dealers, rather than through an auction system as used in most organized exchanges. Abbr. *OTC market*

overtime HR & PERSONNEL extra time worked beyond normal *hours of work*. Overtime is a traditional form of *flexible working*, often used by employers to cover periods of peak demand without incurring a permanent increase in costs. Some workers are entitled to a higher rate of *overtime pay* for the extra hours, but salaried workers in particular can be expected to work overtime with no additional reward.

overtime pay HR & PERSONNEL remuneration for *overtime* worked. Overtime pay often comes at a premium rate but in some occupa-tions overtime is paid at a lower rate than the standard rate of pay.

Owen, Robert (1771–1858) GENERAL MAN-AGEMENT British industrialist, and social re-former. Owner of a factory at New Lanark, that he ran on model lines, pioneering improved working and living conditions for his em-ployees. Author of *A New View of Society* (1813). See thinker *Robert Owen*

own brand (*U.K.*) MARKETING a product or range of products offered by a retailer under their own name in competition with branded goods. Own brand products, like *nonbranded goods*, are normally cheaper than branded items but can be perceived to be of a lower quality. = *private label*

owner GENERAL MANAGEMENT
1 a person or organization that has legal title to products or services
2 the person who controls a private company

owner-operator GENERAL MANAGEMENT see *sole proprietor*

owners' equity FINANCE, BANKING, AND AC-COUNTING a business's total assets less its total liabilities. See also *capital common stock*

ownership of companies GENERAL MANAGE-MENT the possession of stock in companies. Company ownership structures can differ widely. Owners of public companies may be institutions, or individuals, or a mixture of both. Directors are often offered company stock as incentives and more participative companies may offer stock to employees through *employee ownership* plans. Private companies are usually owned by individuals, families, or groups of individual stockholders. Nationalized industries are publicly owned. Cooperatives are wholly owned by employees. A separation between the ownership and control of companies became a widely discussed issue during the 20th century, especially in the United States and the United Kingdom where stockholders have tended to be more passive. Managers were viewed as having come to occupy controlling positions as the scale of industry grew. From the 1980s, this position changed to some extent as *privatization*, *management buy-outs*, restructuring, and *stock incentive plans* led to greater stock ownership among managers and produced less passive stockholders.

own-label MARKETING see *private label*

P

P2P *abbr* E-COMMERCE peer-to-peer: a means of optimizing the networking capabilities of the Internet among groups of computers. Effectively it puts every computer on an equal footing, in that each can be both a publisher and consumer of information. The traditional model on the Web is the client-server one: the client is a computer that is able only to receive information; the server, on the other hand, publishes information on a Web site. Peer-to-peer makes a computer both a server and a client. Perhaps the best-known example of peer-to-peer is Napster, which enabled person A to search for and download music from person B's computer, while person B could search for and download music from person A's computer.

There are several options for the use of peer-to-peer technologies. Information/content: where the content on your computer becomes accessible to everyone else in the peer-to-peer environment, and vice versa; processing sharing: where computers with spare processing capacity network together in order to combine resources. Using a large number of computers, this can create very significant processing

capabilities; services: a computer user can offer services to other people in the peer-to-peer network; file sharing: if person A downloads a file from a central server (an e-learning course from the Internet, for example), other people can use it from person A's machine instead of having to download it again, significantly reducing strain on *bandwidth*.

The main problem with peer-to-peer is the issue of security, and therefore it is essential to authenticate users. Many peer-to-peer interactions also use *encryption*, which ensures that the communication is secure as it is being passed from computer to computer.

paced line OPERATIONS & PRODUCTION a production line that moves at a constant speed. A paced line, such as a car *assembly line*, moves partly finished products past a *workstation* or zone at a constant speed. Work is performed on products within each work zone as the line continues to move. The speed of movement of the line is set to match worker proficiency or machine processing speed.

packaging
1 OPERATIONS & PRODUCTION materials used for containing, protecting, and presenting goods during the delivery process from the producer to the consumer. Packaging has evolved from the basic function of protection to become an important marketing tool for communicating brand values.
2 FINANCE, BANKING, AND ACCOUNTING the practice of combining securities in a single trade

Packard, David (1912–96) GENERAL MAN-AGEMENT U.S. entrepreneur and business executive. Co-founder of Hewlett-Packard. Hewlett-Packard was noted for its *corporate culture* and *management style* based on openness and respect for its employees. See Packard's book *The HP Way* (1995).

Pac Man defense FINANCE, BANKING, AND ACCOUNTING a strategy to avoid the purchase of a company by making an offer to buy the prospective buyer

padrino E-COMMERCE a senior patron or adviser who assists non-Mexican businesspeople in starting and running commercial operations in Mexico

page counter E-COMMERCE a utility program that registers the number of times a Web page is visited, for example, by means of a *click-through*

page impressions E-COMMERCE the number of customers who land on a Web page, as in an *ad view*. Also known as *page views*

page pushing E-COMMERCE see *cobrowsing*

page views E-COMMERCE see *page impressions*

paid circulation MARKETING the number of copies of a newspaper or magazine that are actually bought

paid-up policy FINANCE, BANKING, AND ACCOUNT-ING
1 (*U.K.*) an endowment insurance policy that continues to provide life insurance while the cost of the premiums is covered by the underlying fund after the policyholder has decided not to continue paying premiums. If the fund is sufficient to pay the premiums for the remainder of the term, the remaining funds will be paid to the policyholder at maturity.
2 an insurance policy on which all the premiums have been paid

paid-up share FINANCE, BANKING, AND ACCOUNT-ING a stock for which stockholders have paid the full contractual amount. See also *call*, *called-up share capital*, *paid-up share capital*, *share capital*

paid-up share capital FINANCE, BANKING, AND ACCOUNTING the amount which stockholders are deemed to have paid on the shares issued and called up

painting the tape FINANCE, BANKING, AND AC-COUNTING an illegal practice in which traders break large orders into smaller units in order to give the illusion of heavy buying activity. This encourages investors to buy, and the traders then sell as the price of the stock goes up. (*slang*)

palmtop GENERAL MANAGEMENT a very small portable computer. Compared to a personal computer or laptop, the functionality of a palmtop is currently limited but it is increasing.

panda FINANCE, BANKING, AND ACCOUNTING one of a series of Chinese gold and silver bullion/collector coins, each featuring a panda, that were first issued in 1982. Struck with a highly polished surface, the smallest gold coin weighs 0.05 ounces, the largest 12 ounces.

P&L FINANCE, BANKING, AND ACCOUNTING see *profit and loss account*

panel interview HR & PERSONNEL an interview that takes place before two or more interviewers, who may be from different parts of the interviewing organization or external to it.

Organizations tend to use panel interviews, as they save time by bringing all the interviewers together rather than shuffling the applicant

around from one office to the next. They are also used for their consistency of information: from the applicant and from the organization.

As with any job interview, it is important beforehand for the applicant to find out not only about the position they are applying for, but the organization to which they are applying. It may also help them to mentally rehearse the panel interview situation. With several interviewers, the applicant may feel bombarded by questions. He or she should attempt to answer all the questions, taking one at a time and, if necessary, ask for clarification where a question is not clear.

The interview is an opportunity for the applicant to showcase his or her strengths to several interviewers at once, and so while it is not wise to interrupt the interviewers, he or she should resist the temptation to let them do most of the talking. Making meaningful eye contact with all members of the panel when talking is a good way for the applicant to convey a sense of confidence and calm—the key to success in the panel interview.

Panel on Takeovers and Mergers FINANCE, BANKING, AND ACCOUNTING see *City Code on Takeovers and Mergers*

panel study STATISTICS a study that surveys a selected group of people over a period of time

panic buying FINANCE, BANKING, AND ACCOUNTING an abnormal level of buying caused by fear or rumors of product shortages or by severe price rises

panic dumping of sterling FINANCE, BANKING, AND ACCOUNTING a rush to sell sterling at any price because of possible devaluation

PANSE GENERAL MANAGEMENT politically active and not seeking employment (*slang*)

pants
drop your pants MARKETING to lower the price of a product in order to sell it (*slang*)
put some pants on something GENERAL MANAGEMENT to supply the missing details of a plan or idea (*slang*)

paper FINANCE, BANKING, AND ACCOUNTING
1 a certificate of deposits and other securities
2 a rights issue or an issue of bonds launched by a company to raise additional capital (*slang*)
3 all debt issued by a company (*slang*)

paper architecture GENERAL MANAGEMENT an ambitious business project that never gets beyond the planning stage, because of lack of funding or because it is not feasible (*slang*)

paper company FINANCE, BANKING, AND ACCOUNTING a company that only exists on paper and has no physical assets

paperless office GENERAL MANAGEMENT a workplace in which as much communication and as many procedures as possible have been computerized. The paperless office was predicted in the 1960s. The recent widespread availability of *e-mail*, the *Internet*, and word processing, file transfer, and *intranet* systems means that it is beginning to become achievable for those organizations that wish to pursue it. In a truly paperless office, document storage is on computer rather than in filing cabinets and written communication is not circulated in hard copy but e-mailed. This is largely unattainable, as most people still prefer paper to electronic copy, especially when faced with reading more than one page. Encouraging employees to cut down on paper usage can help achieve *environmental management* targets, and storing information electronically can lead to greater communication efficiency, which may result in *competitive advantage*.

paper millionaire FINANCE, BANKING, AND ACCOUNTING an individual who owns stocks that are worth in excess of a million in currency, but which may fall in value. In 2001, many of the founders of dot-com companies were paper millionaires. See also *paper profit*

paper money FINANCE, BANKING, AND ACCOUNTING
1 currency that is not coins
2 payments in paper form, for example, checks

paper profit FINANCE, BANKING, AND ACCOUNTING an increase in the value of an investment that the investor has no immediate intention of realizing

paper trail GENERAL MANAGEMENT all of the documentation of an event, especially a decision (*slang*)

PAR *abbr* FINANCE, BANKING, AND ACCOUNTING prime assets ratio

paradigm shift GENERAL MANAGEMENT a change in an accepted pattern of thought or behavior

paradox management GENERAL MANAGEMENT the holding together in tension of conflicting and contradictory ideas and the balancing of polar opposites in order to achieve a creative synergy which enhances organizational effectiveness. The concept of paradox is based in philosophy. Charles Handy identified nine principal paradoxes inherent in modern society in his book, *The Empty Raincoat* (Hutchin-

son, 1994), and put forward principles for living with paradox. The idea has also been discussed by writers such as Professor Paul Evans of INSEAD, who argues that many contradictions and dilemmas are not problems which can be solved but paradoxes that need to be managed. An organization which focuses exclusively on a strategy which has brought success in the past runs the risk of subsequent failure.

parallel engineering OPERATIONS & PRODUCTION see *concurrent engineering*

parallel pricing FINANCE, BANKING, AND ACCOUNTING the practice of varying prices in a similar way and at the same time as competitors, which may be done by agreement with them

paralysis by analysis GENERAL MANAGEMENT the inability of managers to make decisions as a result of a preoccupation with attending meetings, writing reports, and collecting statistics and analyses. Paralysis of effective *decision making* in organizations can occur in situations where there is horizontal conflict, disagreement between different hierarchical levels, or unclear objectives.

parameter STATISTICS a quantity that is numerically characteristic of a whole model or population

parameter design STATISTICS a process aimed at reducing variation in processes or products

parent company FINANCE, BANKING, AND ACCOUNTING a company with one or more subsidiary undertakings

Pareto, Vilfredo Frederico Damaso (1848–1923) GENERAL MANAGEMENT Italian economist, mathematician, and sociologist. Originator of the *eighty-twenty rule*, and of the law of income distribution known as *Pareto's Law*, which he explained in *Cours d'économie Politique* (1896–97).

Pareto analysis GENERAL MANAGEMENT see *eighty-twenty rule*

Pareto chart GENERAL MANAGEMENT see *eighty-twenty rule*

Pareto's Law ECONOMICS a theory of income distribution. Developed by *Vilfredo Pareto*, Pareto's Law states that regardless of political or taxation conditions, income will be distributed in the same way across all countries.

Pareto's principle GENERAL MANAGEMENT see *eighty-twenty rule*

pari passu FINANCE, BANKING, AND ACCOUNTING ranking equally

Paris Club FINANCE, BANKING, AND ACCOUNTING see *Group of Ten*

Paris Inter Bank Offered Rate FINANCE, BANKING, AND ACCOUNTING the French equivalent of the London Inter Bank Offered Rate. Abbr. *PIBOR*

parity FINANCE, BANKING, AND ACCOUNTING a situation when the price of a commodity, foreign currency, or security is the same in different markets. See also *arbitrage*

parity bit E-COMMERCE an odd or even digit used to check binary computer data for errors

parity value FINANCE, BANKING, AND ACCOUNTING see *conversion value*

park FINANCE, BANKING, AND ACCOUNTING to place owned stocks with third parties to disguise their ownership, usually illegally

Parker Follett, Mary (1868–1933) GENERAL MANAGEMENT U.S. academic. Applied psychological and social science insights to the study of industrial organization at a time when the *scientific management* methods of *Frederick Winslow Taylor* were predominant. Recent interest in her work owes much to Pauline Graham's writings, including *Mary Parker Follett: Prophet of Management* (1995). Follett's career was largely spent in social work, though her books appeared regularly—*The New State* (1918) was an influential description of her own brand of dynamic democracy, and *Creative Experience* (1924) was her first business-oriented book. In her later years she was in great demand as a lecturer. See thinker *Mary Parker Follett*, *Frederick Winslow Taylor*

parking FINANCE, BANKING, AND ACCOUNTING
1 the transfer of stock in a company to a nominee or the name of an associate, often for non-legitimate or illegal reasons (*slang*)
2 putting money into safe investments while deciding where to invest the money

Parkinson, C. Northcote (1909–93) GENERAL MANAGEMENT British academic. Known for *Parkinson's Law* (1957).

Parkinson's Law HR & PERSONNEL the facetious assertion that work will expand to fill the time available

Parquet FINANCE, BANKING, AND ACCOUNTING an informal name for the Paris Bourse (*slang*)

partial retirement HR & PERSONNEL see *phased retirement*

participating bond FINANCE, BANKING, AND ACCOUNTING a bond that pays the holder dividends as well as interest

participating insurance FINANCE, BANKING, AND ACCOUNTING a form of insurance in which policy-holders receive a dividend from the insurer's profits

participating preferred stock FINANCE, BANKING, AND ACCOUNTING a type of preferred stock that entitles the holder to a fixed dividend and, in addition, to the right to participate in any surplus profits after payment of agreed levels of dividends to holders of common stock has been made. See also *nonparticipating preferred stock*

participative budgeting FINANCE, BANKING, AND ACCOUNTING a budgeting system in which all budget holders are given the opportunity to participate in setting their own budgets. Also known as *bottom-up budgeting*

partly-paid share FINANCE, BANKING, AND ACCOUNTING a stock for which stockholders have not paid the full contractual amount. See also *call share capital*

partnering GENERAL MANAGEMENT see *strategic partnering*

partnership FINANCE, BANKING, AND ACCOUNTING according to the Partnership Act 1890, the relationship which exists between persons carrying on business in common with a view to profit. The liability of the individual partners is unlimited unless provided for by the partnership agreement. The Limited Partnership Act 1907 allows a partnership to contain one or more partners with limited liability so long as there is at least one partner with unlimited liability. A partnership consists of not more than 20 persons.

partnership accounts FINANCE, BANKING, AND ACCOUNTING the capital and checking accounts of each partner in a partnership, or the accounts recording the partnership's business activities

partnership agreement FINANCE, BANKING, AND ACCOUNTING the document that establishes a partnership, detailing the capital contributed by each partner; whether an individual partner's liability is limited; the apportionment of the profit; salaries; and possibly procedures to be followed, for example, in the event of a partner retiring or a new partner joining. Also known as *articles of partnership*

part-time director GENERAL MANAGEMENT see *nonexecutive director*

part-time work GENERAL MANAGEMENT work that occupies fewer hours than *full-time* work. Traditionally, part-time simply meant working fewer hours a day, or fewer days a week, than a full-time employee, but part-time working is now seen as one of several *flexible working hours* alternatives to the 9–5 working day.

party plan MARKETING a sales technique in which local agents host parties to demonstrate or sell products to customers

par value FINANCE, BANKING, AND ACCOUNTING see *nominal value*

Pascale, Richard Tanner (*b.* 1938) GENERAL MANAGEMENT U.S. academic and consultant. Co-developer of the *McKinsey 7-S framework* of corporate success, and coauthor, with *Anthony Athos*, of *The Art of Japanese Management* (1982). Pascale also originated the concept of organizational *agility*. Pascale and Athos collaborated with *Tom Peters* and *Bob Waterman* on the 7-S model at the management consulting company McKinsey. Peters and Waterman cited U.S. examples of success in *In Search of Excellence*, but it was Pascale and Athos who explored the model in greater depth, tracing many of its origins to working practices in Japanese organizations. See thinker *Richard Tanner Pascale*, *Tom Peters*

passbook FINANCE, BANKING, AND ACCOUNTING a small booklet issued by banks, building societies, and other financial institutions to record deposits, withdrawals, interest paid, and the balance on savings and deposit accounts. In all but the smaller institutions, it has now largely been replaced by statements.

passing off FINANCE, BANKING, AND ACCOUNTING a form of fraud in which a company tries to sell its own product by deceiving buyers into thinking it is another product

passive investment management FINANCE, BANKING, AND ACCOUNTING the managing of a mutual fund or other investment portfolio by relying on automatic adjustments such as indexation instead of making personal judgments. See also *active fund management*

passive portfolio strategy FINANCE, BANKING, AND ACCOUNTING the managing of an investment portfolio by relying on automatic adjustments or tracking an index

password E-COMMERCE a series of characters that enables a user to access a private file, Web site, computer, or application

patent MARKETING a type of *copyright* granted as a fixed-term monopoly to an inventor by the

state to prevent others copying an invention or improvement to a product or process.

The granting of a patent requires the publication of full details of the invention or improvement. The use of the patented information is restricted to the patent holder or any organizations licensed by them.

A patent's value is usually the sum of its development costs, or its purchase price if acquired from someone else. It is generally to a company's advantage to spread the patent's value over several years. If this is the case, the critical time period to consider is not the full life of the patent (17 years in the United States), but its estimated useful life.

For example, in January 2000 a company acquired a patent issued in January 1995 at a cost of $100,000. It concludes that the patent's useful commercial life is ten years, not the 12 remaining before the patent expires. In turn, patent value would be $100,000, and it would be spread (or amortized in accounting terms) over 10 years, or $10,000 each year.

patent attorney GENERAL MANAGEMENT a lawyer who specializes in the type of *intellectual property* called a patent

paternity leave HR & PERSONNEL time off work given to a new father on the birth of his child. Paternity leave is a form of *special leave*, and is granted at an organization's discretion. It may be paid, or unpaid. Paternity leave forms an important part of an organization's *family friendly policies*.

path analysis STATISTICS a means of showing the correlation between variables in a statistical study

path diagram STATISTICS a diagram that shows the correlation between variables in a statistical study

pathfinder prospectus (*U.K.*) FINANCE, BANKING, AND ACCOUNTING a preliminary prospectus used in initial public offerings to gauge the reaction of investors. Also known as *red eye*

pawnbroker FINANCE, BANKING, AND ACCOUNTING a person who lends money against the security of a wide variety of chattels, from jewelry to cars. The borrower may recover the goods by repaying the loan and interest by a certain date. Otherwise, the items pawned are sold and any surplus after the deduction of expenses, the loan, and interest is returned to the borrower.

pay HR & PERSONNEL a sum of money given in return for work done or services provided. Pay, in the form of *salary* or *wages*, is generally provided in weekly or monthly fixed amounts,

and is usually expressed in terms of the total sum earned per year. It may also be allocated using a *piece-rate system*, where workers are paid for each unit of work they perform.

payable to order FINANCE, BANKING, AND ACCOUNTING the legend on a bill of exchange or check, used to indicate that it may be transferred

Pay As You Earn HR & PERSONNEL in the United Kingdom, a system for collecting direct taxes that requires employers to deduct taxes from employees' *pay* before payment is made. Abbr. *PAYE*

pay-as-you-go (*Canada*) HR & PERSONNEL a means of financing a pension system whereby benefits of current retirees are financed by current workers

Pay-As-You-Go (*ANZ*) FINANCE, BANKING, AND ACCOUNTING a system used in Australia for paying income tax installments on business and investment income. PAYG is part of the new tax system introduced by the Australian government on July 1, 2000. Abbr. *PAYG*

payback period FINANCE, BANKING, AND ACCOUNTING the length of time it will take to earn back the money invested in a project.

The straight payback period method is the simplest way of determining the investment potential of a major project. Expressed in time, it tells a management how many months or years it will take to recover the original cash cost of the project. It is calculated using the formula:

$$\frac{\text{Cost of project}}{\text{Annual cash revenues}} = \text{Payback period}$$

Thus, if a project cost $100,000 and was expected to generate $28,000 annually, the payback period would be:

$$\frac{100,000}{28,000} = 3.57 \text{ years}$$

If the revenues generated by the project are expected to vary from year to year, add the revenues expected for each succeeding year until you arrive at the total cost of the project.

For example, say the revenues expected to be generated by the $100,000 project are:

Revenue	Total	Cum. Total
Year 1	$19,000	$19,000
Year 2	$25,000	$44,000
Year 3	$30,000	$74,000
Year 4	$30,000	$104,000
Year 5	$30,000	$134,000

Thus, the project would be fully paid for in Year 4, since it is in that year the total revenue reaches the initial cost of $100,000. The precise payback period would be calculated as:

$$\frac{100,000 - 74,000}{1,000,000 - 74,000} \times 365 = 316 \text{ days} + 3 \text{ years}$$

The picture becomes complex when the time-value-of-money principle is introduced into the calculations. Some experts insist this is essential to determine the most accurate payback period. Accordingly, the annual revenues have to be discounted by the applicable interest rate, 10% in this example. Doing so produces significantly different results:

Revenue	Present value	Total	Cum. Total
Year 1	$19,000	$17,271	$17,271
Year 2	$25,000	$20,650	$37,921
Year 3	$30,000	$22,530	$60,451
Year 4	$30,000	$20,490	$80,941
Year 5	$30,000	$18,630	$99,571

This method shows that payback would not occur even after five years.

Generally, a payback period of three years or less is desirable; if a project's payback period is less than a year, some contend it should be judged essential.

PAYE *abbr* HR & PERSONNEL Pay As You Earn

payee FINANCE, BANKING, AND ACCOUNTING
1 the person or organization to whom a check is payable. See also *drawee*
2 the person to whom a payment has to be made

payer FINANCE, BANKING, AND ACCOUNTING the person making a payment

PAYG *abbr* (*ANZ*) FINANCE, BANKING, AND ACCOUNTING Pay-As-You-Go

paying agent FINANCE, BANKING, AND ACCOUNTING the institution responsible for making interest payments on a security and repaying capital at redemption. Also known as *disbursing agent*

paying banker (*U.K.*) FINANCE, BANKING, AND ACCOUNTING the bank on which a bill of exchange or check is drawn

paying-in book (*U.K.*) FINANCE, BANKING, AND ACCOUNTING a book of detachable slips that accompany money or checks being paid into a bank account

payload FINANCE, BANKING, AND ACCOUNTING the amount of cargo that a vessel can carry

paymaster FINANCE, BANKING, AND ACCOUNTING the person responsible for paying an organization's employees

payment by results HR & PERSONNEL a system of *pay* that directly links an employee's salary

to his or her work output. The system is based on the view put forward by **Frederick Winslow Taylor** that payment by results will increase workers' productivity by appealing to their materialism. The concept is closely related to **performance-related pay** which rewards employees for behavior and skills rather than quantifiable productivity measures. See thinker **Frederick Winslow Taylor**

payment gateway E-COMMERCE a company or organization that provides an interface between a merchant's point-of-sale system, **acquirer** payment systems, and **issuer** payment systems. Abbr. **GW**

payment in advance FINANCE, BANKING, AND ACCOUNTING a payment made for goods when they are ordered and before they are delivered. See also **prepayment**

payment in due course FINANCE, BANKING, AND ACCOUNTING the payment of a bill of exchange on a fixed date in the future

payment-in-kind HR & PERSONNEL an alternative form of **pay** given to employees in place of monetary reward but considered to be of equivalent value. A payment in kind may take the form of use of a car, purchase of goods at cost price, or other nonfinancial exchange that benefits the employee. It forms part of the total pay package rather than being an extra benefit.

payment-in-lieu HR & PERSONNEL payment that is given in place of an entitlement

payment terms FINANCE, BANKING, AND ACCOUNTING the stipulation by a business as to when it should be paid for goods or services supplied, for example, cash with order, payment on delivery, or within a particular number of days of the invoice date

payout ratio FINANCE, BANKING, AND ACCOUNTING an expression of the total dividends paid to stockholders as a percentage of a company's net profit in a given period of time. This measures the likelihood of dividend payments being sustained, and is a useful indication of sustained profitability. The lower the ratio, the more secure the dividend, and the company's future.

The payout ratio is calculated by dividing annual dividends paid on common stock by earnings per share:

$$\frac{\text{Annual dividend}}{\text{Earnings per share}} = \text{Payout ratio}$$

Take the company whose earnings per share is $8 and its dividend payout is 2.1. Its payout ratio would be:

$$\frac{2.1}{8} = 0.263 \text{ or } 26.3\%$$

A high payout ratio clearly appeals to conservative investors seeking income. When coupled with weak or falling earnings, however, it could suggest an imminent dividend cut, or that the company is short-changing reinvestment to maintain its payout. A payout ratio above 75% is a warning. It suggests the company is failing to reinvest sufficient profits in its business, that the company's earnings are faltering, or that it is trying to attract investors who otherwise would not be interested. See also **dividend cover**

PayPal™ E-COMMERCE a Web-based service that enables Internet users to send and receive payments electronically. To open a PayPal™ account, users register and provide their credit card or checking account details. When they decide to make a transaction via PayPal™, their card or account is charged for the transfer.

pay-per-click E-COMMERCE see **pay-per-view**

pay-per-play E-COMMERCE a Web site that charges a **micropayment** to play an interactive game over the Internet

pay-per-view E-COMMERCE a Web site that charges a **micropayment** to see digital information, for example, an e-book or e-magazine. Also known as **pay-per-click**

payroll FINANCE, BANKING, AND ACCOUNTING a record showing for each employee his or her gross pay, deductions, and net pay. The payroll may also include details of the employer's associated employment costs.

payroll giving plan FINANCE, BANKING, AND ACCOUNTING a plan by which an employee pays money to a charity directly out of his or her salary. The money is deducted by the employer and paid to the charity, and the employee gets tax relief on such donations.

payslip HR & PERSONNEL a document given to employees when they are paid, providing a statement of **pay** for that period. A payslip includes details of deductions such as **income tax**, social security contributions, pension contributions, and labor union dues.

P/C *abbr* FINANCE, BANKING, AND ACCOUNTING petty cash

PDA *abbr* E-COMMERCE personal digital assistant: a handheld mobile device that can access the Internet and act as a personal organizer

PDF GENERAL MANAGEMENT MARKETING an electronic document format that allows all elements of a document, including page layout, text, photographs, and colors to be viewed on different computers or systems. Abbr of **portable document format**

PDR *abbr* FINANCE, BANKING, AND ACCOUNTING price/dividend ratio

peer-to-peer E-COMMERCE see **P2P**

peg FINANCE, BANKING, AND ACCOUNTING
1 to fix the exchange rate of one currency against that of another or of a basket of other currencies
2 (*U.K.*) to fix wages and salaries during a period of inflation to help prevent an inflationary spiral

P/E multiple *abbr* FINANCE, BANKING, AND ACCOUNTING price/earnings multiple

penalty FINANCE, BANKING, AND ACCOUNTING an arbitrary prearranged sum that becomes payable if one party breaks a term of a contract or an undertaking. The most common penalty is a high rate of interest on an unauthorized overdraft. See also **overdraft**

penalty clause GENERAL MANAGEMENT see **liquidated damages clause**

penalty rate (*ANZ*) HR & PERSONNEL a higher than normal rate of pay awarded for work performed outside normal working hours

pencil-whip GENERAL MANAGEMENT to criticize somebody in writing (*slang*)

penetrated market MARKETING the existing customers within a market

penetration pricing FINANCE, BANKING, AND ACCOUNTING setting prices low, especially for new products, in order to maximize market penetration

penny stock FINANCE, BANKING, AND ACCOUNTING very low-priced stock, typically under one dollar, that is a speculative investment

pension FINANCE, BANKING, AND ACCOUNTING money received regularly after **retirement**, from a **personal pension** plan or state pension plan. Also known as **retirement pension**

pensionable earnings (*U.K.*) FINANCE, BANKING, AND ACCOUNTING = **final average monthly salary**

pension entitlement FINANCE, BANKING, AND ACCOUNTING the amount of pension which someone has the right to receive when he or she retires

people churner HR & PERSONNEL a bad boss with a reputation for losing talented staff (*slang*)

PEP *abbr* FINANCE, BANKING, AND ACCOUNTING personal equity plan

P/E ratio *abbr* FINANCE, BANKING, AND ACCOUNTING price/earnings ratio

per capita income ECONOMICS the average income of each of a particular group of people, for example, citizens of a country

perceived value pricing FINANCE, BANKING, AND ACCOUNTING see *market based pricing*

percussive maintenance GENERAL MANAGEMENT the practice of hitting or shaking an electronic device in order to make it work (*slang*)

per diem HR & PERSONNEL a rate paid per day, for example, for expenses when an employee is working away from the office

perfect capital market ECONOMICS a capital market in which the decisions of buyers and sellers have no effect on market price

perfect competition ECONOMICS the condition in which no buyer or seller can influence prices. In practice, perfect markets are characterized by few or no barriers to entry and by many buyers and sellers.

perfect hedge FINANCE, BANKING, AND ACCOUNTING a hedge that exactly balances the risk of another investment

performance appraisal HR & PERSONNEL a face-to-face discussion in which one employee's work is discussed, reviewed, and appraised by another, using an agreed and understood framework. Usually, line managers conduct the appraisals of their staff, although peers can appraise each other, and line managers can themselves be appraised by their staff through *360 degree appraisal*. The appraisal process focuses on behaviors and outcomes, and strives to improve *motivation*, growth, and performance of the appraisee. Performance appraisals should be conducted at least once a year. Also known as *performance evaluation*, *performance review*

performance bond FINANCE, BANKING, AND ACCOUNTING a guarantee given by a bank or insurance company to a third party stating that it will pay a sum of money if its customer, the account holder, fails to complete a specified contract

performance criteria FINANCE, BANKING, AND ACCOUNTING the standards used to evaluate a product, service, or employee

performance evaluation HR & PERSONNEL see *performance appraisal*

performance fund FINANCE, BANKING, AND ACCOUNTING an investment fund designed to produce a high return, reflected in the higher risk involved

performance indicator HR & PERSONNEL a key measure designed to assess an aspect of the qualitative or quantitative performance of a company. Performance indicators can relate to operational, strategic, confidence, behavioral, and ethical aspects of a company's operation and can help to pinpoint its strengths and weaknesses. They are periodically monitored to ensure the company's long-term success.

performance management GENERAL MANAGEMENT the facilitation of high achievement by employees. Performance management involves enabling people to perform their work to the best of their ability, meeting and perhaps exceeding targets and standards. Performance management can be coordinated by an interrelated framework between manager and employee. Key areas of the framework to be agreed are *objectives*, *human resource management*, standards and *performance indicators*, and means of reward. For successful performance management, a culture of collective and individual responsibility for the continuing improvement of business processes needs to be established, and individual skills and contributions need to be encouraged and nurtured. One tool for monitoring performance management is *performance appraisal*. For organizations, performance management is usually known as company performance and is monitored through business appraisal.

performance prism GENERAL MANAGEMENT a framework for measuring company performance which takes account of the two-way relationships between an organization and all its stakeholders. The performance prism was developed by researchers from the Centre for Business Performance at Cranfield School of Management in England and Accenture. The model takes a similar approach to the balanced scorecard in that nonfinancial measures of performance are analyzed, but it takes account of a wider range of stakeholders including investors, customers, employees, suppliers, regulators, and communities. The factors to be analyzed are represented as the five faces of a prism: stakeholder wants and stakeholder contribution at the ends, and strategies, processes, and capabilities as the three internal facets.

performance review HR & PERSONNEL see *performance appraisal*

performance share FINANCE, BANKING, AND ACCOUNTING see *performance stock*

performance stock FINANCE, BANKING, AND ACCOUNTING a stock which is likely to show capital growth rather than income, which is normally provided by stocks with a higher risk

period bill (*U.K.*) FINANCE, BANKING, AND ACCOUNTING a bill of exchange payable on a certain date rather than on demand. Also known as *term bill*

periodic inventory review system OPERATIONS & PRODUCTION a system for placing orders of varying sizes at regular intervals to replenish *inventory* up to a specified or target inventory level. A periodic inventory review system sets a specific re-order period, but the re-order quantity can vary according to need. The quantity re-ordered is calculated by subtracting existing inventory and on-order inventory from the target inventory level. Also known as *fixed interval re-order system*

perk HR & PERSONNEL see *fringe benefits*

permalancer HR & PERSONNEL a freelance worker who has worked in one company for so long that he or she is virtually a permanent member of staff (*slang*)

permanent interest-bearing shares FINANCE, BANKING, AND ACCOUNTING stock issued by the U.K. equivalent of a credit union to raise capital because the law prohibits it from raising capital in more conventional ways. Abbr. *PIBS*

permission marketing E-COMMERCE any form of online direct marketing that involves gaining each recipient's permission. This type of marketing typically involves sending promotional material via e-mail to an opt-in list of subscribers. The term was popularized by business author Seth Godin, who has written a book on the subject, *Permission Marketing* (1999).

Perot GENERAL MANAGEMENT to leave, fail, or give up something unexpectedly. The term comes from the sudden withdrawal from the U.S. presidential race of candidate Ross Perot in the 1990s. (*slang*)

perpetual bond FINANCE, BANKING, AND ACCOUNTING a bond that has no date of maturity

perpetual debenture FINANCE, BANKING, AND ACCOUNTING a debenture that pays interest in perpetuity, having no date of maturity

perpetual inventory FINANCE, BANKING, AND ACCOUNTING the daily tracking of inventory

per se GENERAL MANAGEMENT by itself or in itself

personal account FINANCE, BANKING, AND AC-COUNTING a record of amounts receivable from or payable to a person or an entity. A collection of these accounts is known as a sales/debtor ledger, or a purchases/creditors ledger. The terms sales and purchases ledger are preferred.

personal brand GENERAL MANAGEMENT the public expression and projection of an individual's identity, personality, values, skills, and abilities. The idea of personal branding has evolved by applying the concept of a product brand or a corporate brand to an individual person. The creation of a personal brand can be used as a tool for personal development as described by Thomas Gad and Anette Rozencreutz in their book, *Managing Brand Me* (Momentum, 2002). It also aims to influence the perceptions of others, emphasizing personal strengths and differentiating the individual from others. However, a personal brand should be based on an individual's real identity—who they are and what they stand for, rather than an external image they wish to project.

personal contract HR & PERSONNEL a *contract of employment* that is negotiated on an employee by employee basis, rather than using a traditional structured system that gives identical contracts to groups of workers

personal day GENERAL MANAGEMENT a day when an employee may be absent from work for any reason. In the United States, personal days are usually part of written employment policy and are frequently not distinguished from sick days or vacation days.

personal development HR & PERSONNEL the acquisition of knowledge, skills, and experience for the purpose of enhancing individual performance and self-perception. Personal development is led by the individual, in contrast to *employee development*, which is initiated by an employing organization. To be effective, it should follow a personal development cycle: establish the purpose or the reason for development; identify the skills or knowledge areas that need developing; look at development opportunities; formulate an action plan; undertake the development; record the outcomes of the development activity; review and evaluate the outputs and benefits. Personal development is an important aspect of *CPD*. See checklist *Personal Development Planning*

personal digital assistant GENERAL MANAGE-MENT see *PDA*

personal exemption FINANCE, BANKING, AND ACCOUNTING the amount of money that an individual can earn without having to pay income tax. Taxpayers can claim one exemption for every person in the household.

personal financial planning FINANCE, BANKING, AND ACCOUNTING short- and long-term financial planning by an individual, either independently or with the assistance of a professional adviser. It will include the use of tax efficient plans such as Individual Retirement Accounts, ensuring adequate provisions are being made for retirement, and examining short- and long-term borrowing requirements such as overdrafts and mortgages.

Personal Identification Number FINANCE, BANKING, AND ACCOUNTING abbr. *PIN*

personality test HR & PERSONNEL see *psychometric test*

personalization E-COMMERCE the process by which a Web site presents customers with selected information on their specific needs. To do this, personal information is collected on the individual user and employed to customize the Web site for that person. Used properly, personalization is a powerful tool that allows customers to access the right content more quickly, thus saving them valuable time. Personalization is particularly useful if a Web site contains a very large quantity of material, meaning that a visitor is slow in finding the information they seek. It also requires a large number of visitors to the Web site, because personalization systems are complex and expensive to install.

Information on the customer is usually collected in one of two ways. Either the individual is asked to fill out a personal profile, perhaps informing the organization of the type of product and service he or she is interested in, or the organization uses software that tracks the way a customer uses the Web site. For example, a customer interested in Product X last week, might receive details of an update for Product X upon their next visit to the Web site. A popular method by which such tracking is carried out is the use of *cookies*, which reside on an individual's browser and collect information on that person's Web behavior. Because it requires the collection of personal information, personalization raises key privacy policy issues.

personal pension HR & PERSONNEL a pension taken out by an individual with a private sector insurance company or bank. A personal pension usually takes the form of a program in which an individual regularly contributes money to a pension provider, who invests it in a pension fund. On retirement, a lump sum is available for the purchase of an annuity that provides weekly or monthly payments.

personal pension plan FINANCE, BANKING, AND ACCOUNTING a pension plan which applies to one worker only, usually a self-employed person or a person not in a company pension plan, rather than a group of employees

personnel HR & PERSONNEL
1 the people employed in an organization, considered collectively
2 the department of an organization that deals with the employment of staff and staffing issues

personnel management HR & PERSONNEL the part of management that is concerned with people and their relationships at work. Personnel management is the responsibility of all those who manage people, as well as a description of the work of specialists. *Personnel managers* advise on, formulate, and implement *personnel policies* such as *recruitment, conditions of employment, performance appraisal, training,* industrial relations, and *health and safety*. There are various models of personnel management, of which *human resource management* is the most recent.

personnel manager HR & PERSONNEL a professional specialist and manager responsible for advising on, formulating, and implementing personnel or human resources strategy and personnel policies. The nature of the personnel manager's job is dependent on the size of the organization and the extent to which personnel responsibilities are devolved to *line managers*.

personnel planning HR & PERSONNEL see *human resource planning*

personnel policy HR & PERSONNEL a set of rules that define the manner in which an organization deals with a *human resources* or *personnel*-related matter. A personnel policy should reflect good practice, be written down, be communicated across the organization, and should adapt to changing circumstances.

PEST analysis GENERAL MANAGEMENT a management technique that enables an analysis of four external factors that may impact the performance of the organization. These factors are: Political, Economic, Social, and Technological. PEST analysis is often conducted using *brainstorming* techniques. It offers an environment-to-organization perspective as opposed to the organization-to-environment perspective offered by *SWOT analysis*.

a-z

1583

DICTIONARY

PESTLE MARKETING an acronym that describes the six influences to which a market is subject, namely, Political, Economic, Social, Technological, Legal, and Environmental

Peter, **Laurence J.** (1919–90) GENERAL MANAGEMENT Canadian academic. Creator of the *Peter Principle*, described in the book of the same name (coauthored with Raymond Hull, 1970).

Peter Principle HR & PERSONNEL a tenet holding that all employees tend to rise to their level of incompetence within an organization, at which point it is too late to move them down or sideways

Peters, **Tom** (*b.* 1942) GENERAL MANAGEMENT U.S. consultant, writer, and lecturer. Codeveloper of the *McKinsey 7-S framework* of corporate success, and coauthor, with *Bob Waterman*, of *In Search of Excellence* (1982), which identified eight characteristics of successful companies. Peters moved the discussion of *management* away from the established structure of *bureaucracy* toward a more innovative, intuitive, and people-centered approach in which change is to be embraced, not resisted. *In Search of Excellence* was one of the first books to make management ideas generally accessible and his seminar presentations have earned Peters a reputation as an energetic, entertaining performer.

petites et moyennes entreprises GENERAL MANAGEMENT French for small and medium-sized businesses. Abbr. *PME*

petty cash FINANCE, BANKING, AND ACCOUNTING a small store of cash used for minor business expenses. Abbr. *P/C*

petty cash account FINANCE, BANKING, AND ACCOUNTING a record of relatively small cash receipts and payments, the balance representing the cash in the control of an individual, usually dealt with under a voucher system

petty cash voucher FINANCE, BANKING, AND ACCOUNTING a document supporting payments under a petty cash system

PFI *abbr* FINANCE, BANKING, AND ACCOUNTING Private Finance Initiative

phantom bid FINANCE, BANKING, AND ACCOUNTING a reported but nonexistent attempt to buy a company

phantom income FINANCE, BANKING, AND ACCOUNTING income that is subject to tax even though the recipient never actually gets control of it, for example, income from a limited partnership

phased retirement HR & PERSONNEL a gradual reduction in hours of work, typically through working a three- or four-day week in the last six months leading up to *retirement*. Phased retirement is a *personnel policy* introduced by organizations to try to ease the transition between employment and retirement, which for many employees can prove to be a traumatic change. Also known as *gradual retirement*

Phillips curve STATISTICS a graphical representation of the relationship between unemployment and the rate of inflation

phish E-COMMERCE to trick someone into providing bank or credit card details by sending a fraudulent e-mail purporting to be from a bank, Internet service provider, or similar, asking for verification of an account number or password

phone lag GENERAL MANAGEMENT tiredness caused by having to conduct business on the telephone with people who are based in different time zones (*slang*)

physical asset FINANCE, BANKING, AND ACCOUNTING an asset that has a physical embodiment, as opposed to cash or securities

physical distribution management OPERATIONS & PRODUCTION the planning, monitoring, and control of the distribution and delivery of manufactured goods

physical market FINANCE, BANKING, AND ACCOUNTING a market in futures that involves physical delivery of the commodities involved, instead of simple cash transactions

physical price FINANCE, BANKING, AND ACCOUNTING the price of a commodity for immediate delivery

physical retail shopping GENERAL MANAGEMENT shopping conducted by visiting high-street shops rather than buying online

physicals FINANCE, BANKING, AND ACCOUNTING commodities that can be bought and used, as contrasted with commodities traded on a futures contract

physical stocktaking FINANCE, BANKING, AND ACCOUNTING the ascertainment of stocks held (by counting physical objects) for comparison with accounting records. Modern practice is to count different items with different frequencies, classifying items according to the degree of control required. *Periodic stocktaking* is a process whereby all stock items are counted and valued at a set point in time, usually the end of an accounting period. *Continuous stocktaking* is the process of counting and valuing selected items at different times, on a rotating basis.

physical working conditions HR & PERSONNEL the surroundings within which somebody works, taking into account aspects such as temperature, air quality, lighting, safety, cleanliness, and noise

PIBOR *abbr* FINANCE, BANKING, AND ACCOUNTING Paris Inter Bank Offered Rate

PIBS *abbr* FINANCE, BANKING, AND ACCOUNTING permanent interest-bearing shares

pick and shovel work GENERAL MANAGEMENT boring and detailed work such as the examination of documents for mistakes (*slang*)

picture FINANCE, BANKING, AND ACCOUNTING the price and trading quantity of a particular stock on Wall Street used, for example, in the question to a specialist dealer "What's the picture on ABC?". The response would give the bid and offer price and number of shares for which there would be a buyer and seller. (*slang*)

piece-rate system *or* **piece work** HR & PERSONNEL a system of payment through which an employee is paid a predetermined amount for each unit of output. The rate of *pay*, or piece rate, is usually fixed subjectively, rather than by a more objective technique such as *work study*. Rates are said to be tight when it is difficult for an employee to earn a bonus and loose when bonuses are easily earned. Piece-rate systems, or piece work, are a form of *payment by results* or *performance-related pay*.

pie chart STATISTICS a chart drawn as a circle divided into proportional sections like portions of a pie

piggyback advertising MARKETING an offer or promotion that runs in parallel with another campaign and incurs no costs

piggyback loan FINANCE, BANKING, AND ACCOUNTING a loan that is raised against the same security as an existing loan

piggyback rights FINANCE, BANKING, AND ACCOUNTING the permission to sell existing shares in conjunction with the sale of like shares in a new offering

pig in a python GENERAL MANAGEMENT the large increase in the birth rate between 1946 and 1964 (*slang*)

pilot fish HR & PERSONNEL a junior executive who follows close behind a more senior executive (*slang*)

pilot survey MARKETING a preliminary piece of research conducted before a complete survey to test the effectiveness of the research methodology

PIN *abbr* FINANCE, BANKING, AND ACCOUNTING personal identification number

pin-drop syndrome HR & PERSONNEL stress induced by extreme quietness in a working environment (*slang*)

ping E-COMMERCE to send a packet of data to an intranet, Internet, or Web address to check whether it is accessible or is responding

pink advertising MARKETING advertising aimed at the gay and lesbian community

pink-collar job HR & PERSONNEL a sexist term for a position normally held by a woman, especially a young one (*slang*)

pink dollar FINANCE, BANKING, AND ACCOUNTING money spent by gays and lesbians. U.K. term *pink pound*

pink pound (*U.K.*) FINANCE, BANKING, AND ACCOUNTING = *pink dollar*

pink slip
get your pink slip HR & PERSONNEL to be dismissed from employment (*slang*)

pink slipper HR & PERSONNEL a person who has been dismissed from employment (*slang*)

piracy GENERAL MANAGEMENT illegal copying of a product such as software or music

pit FINANCE, BANKING, AND ACCOUNTING the area of an exchange where trading takes place. It was traditionally an octagonal stepped area with terracing so as to give everyone a good view of the proceedings during open outcry.

pit broker FINANCE, BANKING, AND ACCOUNTING a broker who transacts business in the pit of a futures or options exchange. Also known as *floor broker*

pitch GENERAL MANAGEMENT an attempt to win business from a customer, especially a *sales presentation*

placement FINANCE, BANKING, AND ACCOUNTING see *private placement*

placement fee FINANCE, BANKING, AND ACCOUNTING see *commission*

plain text e-mail E-COMMERCE a basic format option for e-mails, which is simple and cheap to produce. The advantage is that even older e-mail systems will be able to read plain text, whereas they may be unable to receive more heavily designed *HTML* messages.

If conducting an e-mail marketing campaign, the appearance of the e-mail is important. With plain text layout, it is best to keep the line length to between 65 and 70 characters (to avoid lines breaking), and to keep paragraphs short—five or six lines at most. Because plain text does not allow the use of bold type or font sizing, capitalizing is the only way to add emphasis.

plain vanilla FINANCE, BANKING, AND ACCOUNTING a financial instrument in its simplest form (*slang*)

plank
make somebody walk the plank HR & PERSONNEL to dismiss somebody from employment (*slang*)

planned maintenance OPERATIONS & PRODUCTION see *preventive maintenance*

planned obsolescence OPERATIONS & PRODUCTION a policy of designing products to have a limited life span so that customers will have to buy replacements

plan of arrangement FINANCE, BANKING, AND ACCOUNTING a plan drawn up by an individual or company to offer ways of paying debts, so as to avoid bankruptcy proceedings

plant OPERATIONS & PRODUCTION the capital assets used to produce goods, typically factories, production lines, and large equipment

plant layout OPERATIONS & PRODUCTION the grouping of equipment and operations in a factory for the greatest degree of efficiency. See also *process layout product layout*

plastic *or* **plastic money** FINANCE, BANKING, AND ACCOUNTING a payment system using a plastic card (*slang*). See also *credit card*, *debit card*, *multifunctional card*

plateauing HR & PERSONNEL the process of reaching a phase where performance is stable. Plateauing may be experienced by an employee due to a lack of ambition or ability or a lack of opportunity for *promotion* within the organizational hierarchy. One form of plateau is the *management threshold*.

platform GENERAL MANAGEMENT a product used as a basis for building more complex products or delivering services. For example, a com-

munications network is a platform for delivering knowledge or data.

plc *or* **PLC** *abbr* FINANCE, BANKING, AND ACCOUNTING public limited company

plenitude ECONOMICS a hypothetical condition of an economy in which manufacturing technology has been perfected and scarcity is replaced by an abundance of products

plough back FINANCE, BANKING, AND ACCOUNTING to reinvest a company's earnings in the business instead of paying them out as dividends

plowed-back profits FINANCE, BANKING, AND ACCOUNTING retained profits

plug and play HR & PERSONNEL relating to a new member of staff who does not require training (*slang*)

plug-in E-COMMERCE a software application that can be added to a Web browser to enable added functionality, for example, the receipt of audio or multimedia files

plum (*U.K.*) FINANCE, BANKING, AND ACCOUNTING a successful investment (*slang*)

PME *abbr* GENERAL MANAGEMENT petites et moyennes entreprises

PMTS *abbr* GENERAL MANAGEMENT predetermined motion-time system

PN *abbr* FINANCE, BANKING, AND ACCOUNTING promissory note

PO *abbr* FINANCE, BANKING, AND ACCOUNTING purchase order

poaching HR & PERSONNEL the practice of recruiting people from other companies by offering inducements

point FINANCE, BANKING, AND ACCOUNTING a unit used for calculation of a value, such as a hundredth of a percentage point for interest rates

point and click agreement E-COMMERCE see *click wrap agreement*

point-factor system HR & PERSONNEL see *points plan*

point of presence E-COMMERCE an access point to the *Internet*. A point of presence is usually controlled by an Internet service provider. Subscribers can use this to gain access to the Internet, normally by dialing a local number, and thereby saving the cost of a national phone call. A point of presence has a unique *IP address*.

point of purchase GENERAL MANAGEMENT see *point of sale*

point-of-purchase display GENERAL MANAGEMENT the physical arrangement of products and marketing material at the place where an item is bought. A point-of-purchase display is designed to encourage sales. It can include posters, leaflets, and dispensers to attract customers.

point of sale GENERAL MANAGEMENT the place at which a product is purchased by the customer. The point of sale can be a retail outlet, a display case, or even a particular shelf. Retailers refer to both point of sale and to *point of purchase*. The distinction is a fine one, but a sale and a purchase do not always take place at the same time. The difference becomes relevant where they are clearly separate, for example, with *mail order* and *Internet* shopping. Abbr. *POS*

points plan HR & PERSONNEL a method of *job evaluation* that uses a points scale for rating different criteria. Also known as *point-factor system*

poison pill FINANCE, BANKING, AND ACCOUNTING a measure taken by a company to avoid a hostile takeover, for example, the purchase of a business interest that will make the company unattractive to the potential buyer (*slang*). Also known as *show stopper*

policyholder FINANCE, BANKING, AND ACCOUNTING a person or business covered by an insurance policy

political economy ECONOMICS a country's economic organization

political price GENERAL MANAGEMENT the negative impact on a government of a business or economic decision such as raising interest rates

political risk GENERAL MANAGEMENT the potential negative impact on a government of a business or economic decision

politics GENERAL MANAGEMENT the theory of government, the making of policy, or the power struggles within an organization

poop FINANCE, BANKING, AND ACCOUNTING a person who has *inside information* on a financial deal (*slang*)

pooping and scooping FINANCE, BANKING, AND ACCOUNTING an illegal financial practice in which a person or group of individuals attempts to drive down the price of a stock by spreading false unfavorable information. The advent of the Internet has allowed pooping and scooping to become more widespread. (*slang*)

POP *abbr* E-COMMERCE Post Office protocol: the most common Internet standard for e-mail. Once POP is in use, all new incoming messages are downloaded from the server as soon as the e-mail account is accessed. All POP e-mails are stored on the server until the user removes them.

population STATISTICS the entire collection of units such as events or people from which a sample may be observed in a statistical study

population pyramid STATISTICS a graphical presentation of data in the form of two histograms with a common base, showing a comparison of a human population in terms of sex and age

pop-under ad E-COMMERCE a Web advertisement that launches in a separate browser window from the rest of a Web site

portable document format GENERAL MANAGEMENT MARKETING see *PDF*

portable pension (*U.K.*) FINANCE, BANKING, AND ACCOUNTING a pension plan that moves with an employee when he or she changes employer. See also *stakeholder pension*

portal E-COMMERCE a Web site that provides access and links to other sites and pages on the Web. *Search engines* and directories are the most common portal sites.

Porter, Michael E. (*b.* 1947) GENERAL MANAGEMENT U.S. academic and consultant. Known for his theories such as the *value chain* designed to help businesses examine their competitive capabilities. In *Competitive Strategy* (1980), Porter argued that to gain *competitive advantage*, an organization needs to perform the activities in the value chain more cheaply or in a better way than its competitors. More recently, in response to thinkers such as *Gary Hamel*, he advised on using the value chain to achieve differentiation from other players in a market.

Porter studied at Harvard, and at the age of 26 he became one of the youngest tenured professors in the school's history. He has served as a counselor on competitive strategy to many leading U.S. and international companies and plays an active role in economic policy with the U.S. Congress, business groups, and as an advisor to foreign governments.

portfolio FINANCE, BANKING, AND ACCOUNTING the variety of investments, such as stocks and bonds, owned by an individual or an organization

portfolio career HR & PERSONNEL a career based on a series of varied shorter-term jobs—either concurrently or consecutively—as opposed to one based on a progression up the ranks of a particular profession. The portfolio worker is frequently self-employed, offering his or her services on a *freelance* or consulting basis to one or more employers at the same time. However, a portfolio approach can also be taken to full-time employment with a single employer, if the employee chooses to expand his or her experience and responsibilities through taking different roles within the organization.

To critics, the portfolio approach to career development may appear unfocused and directionless. However, it is an excellent opportunity to experience the many different avenues available in modern life. It is important, in general, for the portfolio worker to maintain some overall sense of purpose or strategic direction in the work they undertake, and to view their portfolio career as a unified whole rather than a collection of "odd jobs." See thinker *Charles Handy*

portfolio immunization FINANCE, BANKING, AND ACCOUNTING measures taken by traders to protect their stock portfolios (*slang*)

portfolio insurance FINANCE, BANKING, AND ACCOUNTING options that provide hedges against stock in a portfolio

portfolio investment FINANCE, BANKING, AND ACCOUNTING a form of investment that attempts to achieve a mixture of income and capital growth

portfolio manager FINANCE, BANKING, AND ACCOUNTING a person or company that specializes in managing an investment portfolio on behalf of investors

portfolio working HR & PERSONNEL the working pattern of following several simultaneous career pursuits at any one time. Portfolio working was coined by *Charles Handy* to describe a style of working life which no longer involves working full-time for one employer. See thinker *Charles Handy*. Also known as *portfolio career*

POS *abbr* GENERAL MANAGEMENT point of sale

POSDCORB *abbr* GENERAL MANAGEMENT Planning, Organizing, Staffing, Directing, Coordinating, Reporting, and Budgeting: coined in 1935 by *Luther Gulick* to describe the functional elements of the work of a *chief*

executive. It is based on the functional analysis of management of **Henri Fayol**.

position FINANCE, BANKING, AND ACCOUNTING the number of shares of a security that are owned by an individual or company

position limit FINANCE, BANKING, AND ACCOUNTING the largest amount of a security that any group or individual may own

positive economics ECONOMICS the study of economic propositions that can be verified by observing the real economy

possessor in bad faith FINANCE, BANKING, AND ACCOUNTING somebody who occupies land even though they do not believe they have a legal right to do so

possessor in good faith FINANCE, BANKING, AND ACCOUNTING somebody who occupies land believing they have a legal right to do so

possessory action FINANCE, BANKING, AND ACCOUNTING a lawsuit over the right to own a piece of land

post a credit FINANCE, BANKING, AND ACCOUNTING to enter a credit item in a ledger

postal survey MARKETING = **mail survey**

postal vote FINANCE, BANKING, AND ACCOUNTING an election in which the voters send in their ballot papers by post

Post Big Bang FINANCE, BANKING, AND ACCOUNTING used to describe the trading mechanism on the London Stock Exchange after the market liberalization changes effected in October 1986. See also **Big Bang**

post-completion audit FINANCE, BANKING, AND ACCOUNTING an objective and independent appraisal of the measure of success of a capital expenditure project in progressing the business as planned. The appraisal should cover the implementation of the project from authorization to commissioning and its technical and commercial performance after commissioning. The information provided is also used by management as feedback, which helps the implementation and control of future projects.

postdate FINANCE, BANKING, AND ACCOUNTING to put a later date on a document or check than the date when it is signed, with the effect that it is not valid until the later date

postdated FINANCE, BANKING, AND ACCOUNTING see **postdate**

postindustrial society GENERAL MANAGEMENT a society in which the resources of labor and capital are replaced by those of knowledge and information as the main sources of wealth creation. The postindustrial society involves a shift in focus from manufacturing industries to service industries and is enabled by technological advances. The idea is associated with sociologist Daniel Bell, who wrote *The Coming of Post-Industrial Society: A Venture in Social Forecasting* (1973).

potential GDP ECONOMICS a measure of the real value of the services and goods that can be produced when a country's factors of production are fully employed

potentially exempt transfer FINANCE, BANKING, AND ACCOUNTING see **chargeable transfer**

pot trust FINANCE, BANKING, AND ACCOUNTING a trust, typically created in a will, for a group of beneficiaries

pound cost averaging (*U.K.*) FINANCE, BANKING, AND ACCOUNTING = **dollar cost averaging**

poverty trap FINANCE, BANKING, AND ACCOUNTING a situation whereby low income families are penalized by a progressive tax system: an increase in income is either counteracted by a loss of social benefit payments or by an increase in taxation

power GENERAL MANAGEMENT the ability to compel others to obey. Power refers to an authority or influence over others which, in an organizational context, may be derived from the holder's rank or status, or from their personality. According to **Max Weber**, power refers to the probability of imposing your own will despite resistance. It is closely linked to, but not the same as, **leadership**, **authority**, and **responsibility**. Organizational power is linked to **organization structure** and is an inherent part of any hierarchy or **bureaucracy**.

power and influence theory of leadership GENERAL MANAGEMENT the idea that **leadership** is based on the form of relationships between people rather than on the abilities of a single person. The power and influence theory of leadership sees a network of interaction between people, shaped by the power and influence emanating from the leader. Leadership and followership are products of the flow of power between individuals.

power center GENERAL MANAGEMENT the part of an organization that has the strongest influence on policy

power lunch GENERAL MANAGEMENT see **working lunch**

power of appointment FINANCE, BANKING, AND ACCOUNTING the power of a trustee to dispose of interests in real estate to another person

power of attorney FINANCE, BANKING, AND ACCOUNTING a legal document granting one person the right to act on behalf of another

power structure GENERAL MANAGEMENT the way in which power is distributed among different groups or individuals in an organization

pp FINANCE, BANKING, AND ACCOUNTING derived from the Latin "per pro," used beside a signature at the end of a letter, meaning "on behalf of"

PPP *abbr* ECONOMICS FINANCE, BANKING, AND ACCOUNTING purchasing power parity

PR *abbr* MARKETING public relations: the presentation of an organization and its activities to target audiences with the goal of gaining awareness and understanding, influencing public opinion, generating support, and developing trust and cooperation. Public relations programs work to create and maintain a positive **corporate image** and enhance an organization's reputation. The work of a public relations department includes research into current perceptions of the organization, the production of publicity material, the organization of events and **sponsorship** programs, and the evaluation of responses to these activities. Target audiences include the media, government bodies, customers and suppliers, investors, the wider community, or an organization's own employees. Public relations practice originated in the United States in the mid-19th century. Public relations forms part of an organization's overall **external communication** strategy.

Prahalad, C. K. (*b.* 1941) GENERAL MANAGEMENT Indian-born academic. Developer with **Gary Hamel** of a new view of competitiveness, **strategy**, and **organizations** in reaction to traditional strategic thinking. Prahalad and Hamel originated the ideas of strategic intent, **core competences**, and strategy as stretch, and published them in *Competing for the Future* (1994). See thinker **C. K. Prahalad**

prairie dogging GENERAL MANAGEMENT in an office that is divided into cubicles, the sudden appearance of people's heads over the top of the cubicle walls when something interesting or noisy happens (*slang*)

preauthorized electronic debit FINANCE, BANKING, AND ACCOUNTING a program in which a

payer agrees to let a bank make payments from an account to somebody else's account

prebilling FINANCE, BANKING, AND ACCOUNTING the practice of submitting a bill for a product or service before it has actually been delivered

preceding year FINANCE, BANKING, AND ACCOUNTING the year before the accounting year in question

precious metals FINANCE, BANKING, AND ACCOUNTING gold, silver, platinum, and palladium

predatory pricing FINANCE, BANKING, AND ACCOUNTING the practice of setting prices for products that are designed to win business from competitors or to damage competitors. This may involve dumping, which is selling a product in a foreign market at below cost or below the domestic market price (subject to adjustments for taxation differences, transportation costs, specification differences, etc.).

predetermined motion-time system GENERAL MANAGEMENT a *work measurement* technique that uses a set of established times for basic human motions to build up *standard times* for jobs and processes at a specific level of performance. The predetermined motion-time system is based on the idea, first conceived by *Frederick Winslow Taylor* and later developed by *Frank* and *Lillian Gilbreth*, that the same length of time is required for basic human motions in whatever context they are performed. These standard times are established using *time study* techniques and can then be combined to provide a standard time for specific work tasks. The first PMTS, called *motion time analysis*, was developed in 1927, and others appeared in the United States during the 1930s. Interest in the use of PMTS increased during and after World War II. The most widely used system is *methods-time measurement*. Abbr. **PMTS**

predictive maintenance OPERATIONS & PRODUCTION a set of techniques used to manage the *maintenance* of high-cost equipment that experiences extremely low failure rates. Statistical techniques for predicting service before failure are not effective for equipment with extremely low failure rates. Predictive maintenance uses the techniques of surveillance, diagnosis, and remedy to manage the maintenance of such equipment. It is based on the premise that most equipment will give indications of impending failure well in advance of it actually happening.

pre-employment screening HR & PERSONNEL see *health screening*

pre-emptive right FINANCE, BANKING, AND ACCOUNTING the right of a stockholder to maintain proportional ownership in a corporation by purchasing newly issued stock

preference share FINANCE, BANKING, AND ACCOUNTING = *preferred stock*

preferential creditor FINANCE, BANKING, AND ACCOUNTING a creditor who is entitled to payment, especially from a bankrupt, before other creditors

preferential issue FINANCE, BANKING, AND ACCOUNTING an issue of stock available only to designated buyers

preferential payment FINANCE, BANKING, AND ACCOUNTING a payment to a preferential creditor

preferred ordinary shares FINANCE, BANKING, AND ACCOUNTING ordinary shares of *preferred stock*

preferred position MARKETING the position in which an advertiser wants an advertisement to appear, for example, in a publication or on a Web site

preferred risk FINANCE, BANKING, AND ACCOUNTING somebody considered by an insurance company to be less likely to collect on a policy than the average person, for example, a non-smoker

preferred stock FINANCE, BANKING, AND ACCOUNTING stock that entitles the owner to preference in the distribution of dividends and the proceeds of liquidation in the event of bankruptcy. U.K. term *preference shares*

pre-financing FINANCE, BANKING, AND ACCOUNTING the practice of arranging funding for a project before the project begins

prelaunch MARKETING the activities that precede the launch of a new product

preliminary prospectus FINANCE, BANKING, AND ACCOUNTING a document issued prior to an initial public offering that gives details about the company and its financial situation

premarket FINANCE, BANKING, AND ACCOUNTING used to describe transactions between market members conducted prior to the official opening of the market. Also known as *pretrading*

premature retirement HR & PERSONNEL see *early retirement*

Premiers' Conference GENERAL MANAGEMENT an annual meeting at which the premiers of the states and territories of Australia meet with the federal government to discuss their funding allocations

premium

1 GENERAL MANAGEMENT a higher price paid for a scarce product or service

2 GENERAL MANAGEMENT a pricing method that uses high price to indicate high quality

3 FINANCE, BANKING, AND ACCOUNTING the price a purchaser of an option pays to its writer

4 FINANCE, BANKING, AND ACCOUNTING the difference between the futures price and the cash price of an underlying asset

5 FINANCE, BANKING, AND ACCOUNTING the consideration for an insurance contract

at a premium FINANCE, BANKING, AND ACCOUNTING

1 of a fixed interest security, at an issue price above its nominal value

2 of a new issue, at a trading price above the one offered to investors

3 at a price that is considered expensive in relation to others

premium bond FINANCE, BANKING, AND ACCOUNTING in the United States, a bond with a selling price above its face or redemption value

premium income FINANCE, BANKING, AND ACCOUNTING the income earned by an insurance company from premiums

premium offer MARKETING a sales promotion technique in which customers are offered a free gift

premium pay plan HR & PERSONNEL an enhanced pay scale for high performing employees. A premium pay plan can be offered as an incentive to motivate employees, rewarding such achievements as high productivity, long service, or completion of training with an increased pay package.

premium pricing MARKETING the deliberate setting of high prices for a product or service to emphasize its quality or exclusiveness. Also known as *prestige pricing*

prepackaged choice GENERAL MANAGEMENT a package of multimedia computer material that cannot be customized by the user

prepaid interest FINANCE, BANKING, AND ACCOUNTING interest paid in advance of its due date

prepayment FINANCE, BANKING, AND ACCOUNTING the payment of a debt before it is due to be paid

prepayment penalty FINANCE, BANKING, AND ACCOUNTING a charge that may be levied against somebody who makes a payment before its

due date. The penalty compensates the lender or seller for potential lost interest.

prepayment privilege FINANCE, BANKING, AND ACCOUNTING the right to make a prepayment, for example, on a loan or mortgage, without penalty

prepayment risk FINANCE, BANKING, AND ACCOUNTING the risk that a debtor will avoid interest charges by making partial or total prepayments, especially when interest rates fall

prequalification MARKETING a sales technique in which the potential value of a prospect is carefully evaluated through research

prescribed payments system (*ANZ*) FINANCE, BANKING, AND ACCOUNTING a system under which employers are obliged to deduct a certain amount of tax from cash payments made to casual workers. The system was introduced in Australia in 1983.

presentation GENERAL MANAGEMENT an event at which preplanned material is shown to an audience for a specific purpose. Although a presentation is a verbal form of communication, it is often supported by other media, such as computer software, slides, printed handouts, and so on and to be successful, appropriate *body language* and good *interpersonal communication* skills are required. A presentation is normally intended to introduce something new to the audience, to persuade them of a viewpoint, or to inform them of something. *Sales representatives* use presentations when introducing a product to a potential customer. Presentations are also used in *team briefing* and other business contexts.

presenteeism HR & PERSONNEL an employee or organization subscribing to the view that the hours spent at work have more value than *productivity* or results. Presenteeism is often displayed by *workaholics*. At its most extreme, presenteeism can be seen in a worker who reports for work even when sick, for fear of letting the company down or of losing their job. (*slang*) See also *absenteeism*

present value FINANCE, BANKING, AND ACCOUNTING
1 the amount that a future interest in a financial asset is currently worth, discounted for inflation
2 the value now of an amount of money that somebody expects to receive at a future date, calculated by subtracting any interest that will accrue in the interim

preservation of capital FINANCE, BANKING, AND ACCOUNTING an approach to financial manage-ment that protects a person's or company's capital by arranging additional forms of finance

press advertising MARKETING advertising in newspapers or magazines

press clipping GENERAL MANAGEMENT a copy of a news item kept by a company because it contains important business information or is a record of news published about the company. U.K. term *press cutting*

press communications MARKETING communications activities designed to improve press awareness and .attitudes to a product or an organization

press conference MARKETING a meeting to which journalists are invited to hear about a new product or other news about an organization

press cutting (*U.K.*) GENERAL MANAGEMENT = *press clipping*

press date MARKETING the date on which a newspaper or magazine is printed

press release MARKETING an item of news about an organization, its staff, products, or services that is sent to selected members of the press

press the flesh GENERAL MANAGEMENT to shake hands with people at a business function (*slang*)

pressure group GENERAL MANAGEMENT a body of people who have banded together to campaign on one or more issues of importance to them. A pressure group usually has a formal constitution and coordinates its activities to influence the attitudes or activities of business or government. One area in which pressure groups operate is the environment and some large companies that have failed to practice good *environmental management* have been targeted by campaigners. Pressure groups often represent widespread views, so it is important for a company to maintain good relations with them.

prestige pricing MARKETING see *premium pricing*

pre-syndicate bid FINANCE, BANKING, AND ACCOUNTING a bid made before a group of buyers can offer blocks of shares in an offering to the public

pretax FINANCE, BANKING, AND ACCOUNTING before tax is considered or paid

pretax profit FINANCE, BANKING, AND ACCOUNTING the amount of profit a company makes before taxes are deducted

pretax profit margin FINANCE, BANKING, AND ACCOUNTING the profit made by a company, calculated as a percentage of sales, before taxes are considered

pretesting MARKETING the practice of assessing the effectiveness of an advertising campaign or marketing activity in a small sector or single region before running the full campaign

pretrading FINANCE, BANKING, AND ACCOUNTING see *premarket*

prevalence STATISTICS a measure of the number of people with a particular quality in a statistical population

preventive maintenance *or* **preventative maintenance** OPERATIONS & PRODUCTION the scheduling of a program of planned *maintenance* services or equipment overhauls. The goal of preventive maintenance is to reduce equipment failure and the need for corrective maintenance. It can be performed at regular time intervals, after a specified amount of equipment use, when the opportunity arises, for example, at a factory's annual shutdown, or when certain preset conditions occur to trigger the need for action. Also known as *planned maintenance*. See also *reactive maintenance*

price FINANCE, BANKING, AND ACCOUNTING an amount of money that a vendor charges a customer for a good or service

price-book ratio FINANCE, BANKING, AND ACCOUNTING see *price-to-book ratio*

price ceiling FINANCE, BANKING, AND ACCOUNTING the highest price that a buyer is willing to pay

price competition FINANCE, BANKING, AND ACCOUNTING a form of competition based on price rather than factors such as quality or design

price control ECONOMICS a government regulation that sets maximum prices for commodities or controls price levels by means of credit controls

price differentiation FINANCE, BANKING, AND ACCOUNTING a pricing strategy in which a company sells the same product at different prices in different markets

price discovery FINANCE, BANKING, AND ACCOUNTING the process by which price is determined by negotiation in a free market

a-z

1590

DICTIONARY

price discrimination ECONOMICS the practice of selling the same product to different buyers at different prices

price/dividend ratio FINANCE, BANKING, AND ACCOUNTING the price of a stock divided by the annual dividend paid on a share. Abbr. *PDR*

price/earnings multiple FINANCE, BANKING, AND ACCOUNTING see *price/earnings ratio*. Abbr. *P/E multiple*

price/earnings ratio FINANCE, BANKING, AND ACCOUNTING a company's stock price divided by earnings per share (EPS).

While EPS is an actual amount of money, usually expressed in cents per share, the P/E ratio has no units, it is just a number. Thus if a quoted company has a stock price of $100 and EPS of $12 for the last published year, then it has a historical P/E ratio of 8.3. If analysts are forecasting for the next year EPS of, say, $14, then the forecast P/E ratio is 7.1.

The P/E ratio is predominantly useful in comparisons with other stocks rather than in isolation. For example, if the average P/E ratio in the market is 20, there will be many stocks with P/E ratios well above and well below this, for a variety of reasons. Similarly, in a particular sector, the P/E ratios will frequently vary from the sector average, even though the constituent companies may all be engaged in similar businesses. The reason is that even two businesses doing the same thing will not always be doing it as profitably as each other. One may be far more efficient, as demonstrated by a history of rising EPS compared with the flat EPS picture of the other over a series of years, and the market might recognize this by awarding the more profitable stock a higher P/E ratio. Abbr. *P/E ratio*

price effect ECONOMICS the impact of price changes on a market or economy

price elasticity of demand ECONOMICS the percentage change in demand divided by the percentage change in price of a good

price elasticity of supply ECONOMICS the percentage change in supply divided by the percentage change in price of a good

price escalation clause FINANCE, BANKING, AND ACCOUNTING a contract provision that permits the seller to raise prices in response to increased costs

price fixing FINANCE, BANKING, AND ACCOUNTING an often illegal agreement between producers of a good or service in order to maintain prices at a particular level

price floor FINANCE, BANKING, AND ACCOUNTING the lowest price at which a seller is prepared to do business

price index FINANCE, BANKING, AND ACCOUNTING an index, such as the consumer price index, that measures inflation

price indicator ECONOMICS a price that is a measurable variable and can be used, for example, as an index of the cost of living

price-insensitive FINANCE, BANKING, AND ACCOUNTING used to describe a good or service for which sales remain constant no matter what its price because it is essential to buyers

price instability ECONOMICS a situation in which the prices of goods alter daily or even hourly

price leadership MARKETING the establishment of price levels in a market by a dominant company or brand

price list GENERAL MANAGEMENT a document that sets out the prices of different products or services

price range GENERAL MANAGEMENT the variety of prices at which competitive products or services are available in the market

price ring FINANCE, BANKING, AND ACCOUNTING a group of traders who make an agreement, often illegally, to maintain prices at a particular level

prices and incomes policy ECONOMICS a policy limiting price or wage increases through government regulations

price-sensitive FINANCE, BANKING, AND ACCOUNTING used to describe a good or service for which sales fluctuate depending on its price, often because it is a nonessential item

price-sensitive information FINANCE, BANKING, AND ACCOUNTING as yet unpublished information that will affect a company's stock price. For example, the implementation of a new manufacturing process that will substantially cut production costs would have a positive impact, whereas the discovery of harmful side effects from a recently launched drug would have a negative impact.

price stability FINANCE, BANKING, AND ACCOUNTING a situation in which there is little change in the price of goods or services

price support ECONOMICS government assistance in keeping market prices from falling below a minimum level

price tag GENERAL MANAGEMENT
1 a label attached to an item being sold that shows its price
2 the value of a person or thing

price-to-book ratio FINANCE, BANKING, AND ACCOUNTING the ratio of the value of all of a company's stock to its *book value*. Also known as *price-book ratio*

price-to-cash-flow ratio FINANCE, BANKING, AND ACCOUNTING the ratio of the value of all of a company's stock to its cash flow for the most recent complete fiscal year

price-to-sales ratio FINANCE, BANKING, AND ACCOUNTING the ratio of the value of all of a company's stock to its sales for the previous twelve months, a way of measuring the relative value of a stock when compared with others.

The P/S ratio is obtained by dividing the market capitalization by the latest published annual sales figure. So a company with a capitalization of $1 billion and sales of $3 billion would have a P/S ratio of 0.33.

P/S will vary with the type of industry. You would expect, for example, that many retailers and other large-scale distributors of goods would have very high sales in relation to their market capitalizations—in other words, a very low P/S. Equally, manufacturers of high-value items would generally have much lower sales figures and thus higher P/S ratios.

A company with a lower P/S is cheaper than one with a higher ratio, particularly if they are in the same sector so that a direct comparison is more appropriate. It means that each share of the lower P/S company is buying more of its sales than those of the higher P/S company.

It is important to note that a stock which is cheaper only on P/S grounds is not necessarily the more attractive stock. There will frequently be reasons why it has a lower ratio than another similar company, most commonly because it is less profitable.

price war MARKETING a situation in which two or more companies each try to increase their own share of the market by lowering prices. A price war involves companies undercutting each other in an attempt to encourage more customers to buy their goods or services. In the long term, this can devalue a market and lead to loss of profits, but it can sometimes have short-term success.

price-weighted index FINANCE, BANKING, AND ACCOUNTING an index of production or market value that is adjusted for price changes

pricing model FINANCE, BANKING, AND ACCOUNTING a computerized system for calculating

prices, based on a variety of factors including costs and anticipated margins

pricing policy MARKETING the method of *decision making* used for setting the prices for a company's products or services. A pricing policy is usually based on the costs of production or provision with a margin for profit, such as, for example, *cost-plus pricing*.

primary account number FINANCE, BANKING, AND ACCOUNTING an identifier for a credit card used in secure electronic transactions

primary commodities FINANCE, BANKING, AND ACCOUNTING farm produce grown in large quantities, such as corn, rice, or cotton

primary data *or* **primary information** MARKETING original data derived from a new research study and collected at source, as opposed to previously published material

primary earnings per (common) share FINANCE, BANKING, AND ACCOUNTING see *earnings per share*

primary liability FINANCE, BANKING, AND ACCOUNTING a responsibility to pay before anyone else, for example, for damages covered by insurance

primary market FINANCE, BANKING, AND ACCOUNTING the part of the market on which securities are first offered to investors by the issuer. The money from this sale goes to the issuer, rather than to traders or investors as it does in the secondary market. See also *secondary market*

primary sector ECONOMICS the firms and corporations of the productive sector of a country's economy

prime FINANCE, BANKING, AND ACCOUNTING see *prime rate*

prime assets ratio (*ANZ*) FINANCE, BANKING, AND ACCOUNTING the proportion of total liabilities which Australian banks are obliged by the Reserve Bank to hold in secure assets such as cash and government securities. Abbr. *PAR*

prime rate *or* **prime interest rate** FINANCE, BANKING, AND ACCOUNTING the lowest interest rate that commercial banks offer on loans. Also known as *prime*

principal FINANCE, BANKING, AND ACCOUNTING the original amount of a loan, not including any *interest*. See also *mortgage*

principal shareholders *or* **principal stockholders** FINANCE, BANKING, AND ACCOUNTING the stockholders who own the largest percentage of stock in an organization

print farming MARKETING the management of an organization's print requirements, including choosing printers and overseeing production

prior charge percentage FINANCE, BANKING, AND ACCOUNTING see *priority percentage*

priority percentage FINANCE, BANKING, AND ACCOUNTING the proportion of a business's net profit that is paid in interest to holders of debt capital and preferred stock. Also known as *prior charge percentage*

prior lien bond FINANCE, BANKING, AND ACCOUNTING a bond whose holder has more claim on a debtor's assets than holders of other types of bonds

prior year adjustment FINANCE, BANKING, AND ACCOUNTING an adjustment made to accounts for previous years, because of changes in accounting policies or because of errors

private bank FINANCE, BANKING, AND ACCOUNTING
1 a bank that is owned by a single person or a limited number of private stockholders
2 a bank that provides banking facilities to high net worth individuals. See also *private banking*
3 a bank that is not state-owned in a country where most banks are owned by the government

private banking FINANCE, BANKING, AND ACCOUNTING a service offered by certain financial institutions to high net worth individuals. In addition to standard banking services, it will typically include portfolio management and advisory services on taxation, including estate planning.

private cost ECONOMICS the cost incurred by individuals when they use scarce resources such as gas

private debt FINANCE, BANKING, AND ACCOUNTING money owed by individuals and organizations other than governments

private enterprise ECONOMICS business or industry that is controlled by companies or individuals rather than the government

private label MARKETING a product or variety of products offered by a retailer under their own name in competition with branded goods. Private label products, like *nonbranded goods*, are normally cheaper than branded items but are often perceived to be of lower quality. Also known as *own-label*. U.K. term *own brand*

private placement FINANCE, BANKING, AND ACCOUNTING the sale of securities directly to institutions for investment rather than resale

private placing (*U.K.*) FINANCE, BANKING, AND ACCOUNTING = *private placement*

private sector ECONOMICS the section of the economy that is financed and controlled by individuals or private institutions, such as companies, stockholders, or investment groups. See also *public sector*

private sector investment ECONOMICS investment by the private enterprise sector of an economy

private treaty FINANCE, BANKING, AND ACCOUNTING the sale of land without an auction

privatization FINANCE, BANKING, AND ACCOUNTING the transfer of a company from ownership by either a government or a few individuals to the public via the issuance of stock

probability STATISTICS the quantitative measure of the likelihood that a given event will occur

probability distribution STATISTICS a mathematical formula showing the probability for each value of a variable in a statistical study

probability plot STATISTICS a graphic plot of data that compares two probability distributions

probability sample STATISTICS a sample in which every individual in a finite statistical *population* has a known chance, but not necessarily an equal chance, of being included

probability sampling STATISTICS sampling in which every individual in a finite *population* has a known but not necessarily equal chance of being included in the sample

probation HR & PERSONNEL a trial period in the first months of employment when an employer checks the suitability and capability of a person in a certain role, and takes any necessary corrective action. An employee's performance during a probation period may be evaluated informally, for example, by means of conversations with a supervisor. If a probationary period is included in a *contract of employment*, formal documented assessment is required.

problem child

1 FINANCE, BANKING, AND ACCOUNTING a subsidiary company that is not performing well or is damaging the **parent company** in some way **2** MARKETING a product with a low market share but high growth potential. Problem children often have good long-term prospects, but high levels of investment may be needed to realize the potential, thereby draining funds that may be needed elsewhere.

problem solving GENERAL MANAGEMENT a systematic approach to overcoming obstacles or problems in the management process. Problems occur when something is not behaving as it should, when something deviates from the norm, or when something goes wrong. A number of problem-solving methodologies exist, but the most widely used is that proposed by **Charles H. Kepner** and **Benjamin B. Tregoe**. Steps in their problem solving process include: recognizing a problem exists and defining it; generating a variety of solutions; evaluating the possible solutions and choosing the best one; implementing the solution and evaluating its effectiveness in solving the problem. Various techniques can aid problem solving, such as **brainstorming**, **fishbone charts**, and **Pareto charts** (see **bottleneck**).

procedure GENERAL MANAGEMENT a set of step-by-step instructions designed to ensure that a task is efficiently and consistently performed. Procedures regulate the conduct of an organization's activities and ensure that **decision making** is undertaken fairly and with due consideration, as, for example, in the case of disciplinary and complaints procedures. In the context of formal quality management systems, procedures are used to control and monitor work processes and to ensure that standards are met.

procedure manual GENERAL MANAGEMENT a document containing written rules and regulations that govern the conduct of **procedures** within an organization. Procedure manuals are often used in the orientation and training of new recruits.

proceeds FINANCE, BANKING, AND ACCOUNTING the income from a transaction

process GENERAL MANAGEMENT a structured and managed set of work activities designed to produce a particular output

process box GENERAL MANAGEMENT see **flow chart**

process chart GENERAL MANAGEMENT a diagrammatic representation of the sequence of work and the nature of events in a **process**.

This breaks down a process into a series of steps and provides the basis for visualizing the different stages for evaluation and possible improvement. The development of a process chart is also known as **process mapping**. Process mapping is a valuable tool used in **process management** and business process re-engineering.

process control OPERATIONS & PRODUCTION the inspection of work-in-progress to provide feedback on, and correct, a production process. First developed as a mechanical feedback mechanism, process control is now widely used to monitor and maintain the quality of output. See also **statistical process control**

process costing FINANCE, BANKING, AND ACCOUNTING a method of costing something which is manufactured from a series of continuous processes, where the total costs of those processes are divided by the number of units produced

process layout OPERATIONS & PRODUCTION a type of office or **plant layout** that groups together workstations or equipment that undertake similar processes. Within a process layout organization, the partly finished product moves from process to process and each batch may follow a different route. Also known as **process-oriented layout**, **layout by function**. See also **product layout**

process management OPERATIONS & PRODUCTION the operation, **control**, evaluation, and improvement of interconnected tasks, with the goal of maximizing effectiveness and efficiency

process mapping GENERAL MANAGEMENT see **process chart**

processor E-COMMERCE see **acquirer**

process-oriented layout OPERATIONS & PRODUCTION see **process layout**

process production OPERATIONS & PRODUCTION the continuous production of a product in bulk, often by a chemical rather than mechanical **process**

process time GENERAL MANAGEMENT the period which elapses between the start and finish of one process or stage of a process

procurement GENERAL MANAGEMENT see **purchasing**

procurement exchange E-COMMERCE a group of companies that act together to buy products or services they need at lower prices

procurement manager GENERAL MANAGEMENT see **purchasing manager**

procurement portal E-COMMERCE see **online catalog**

producer price index ECONOMICS a statistical measure, the weighted average of the prices of commodities that firms buy from other firms

producibility engineering OPERATIONS & PRODUCTION see **design for manufacturability**

product MARKETING anything that is offered to a market that customers can acquire, use, interact with, experience, or consume, to satisfy a want or need. Early **marketing** tended to focus on tangible physical goods and these were distinguished from **services**. More recently, however, the distinction between products and services has blurred, and the concept of the product has been expanded so that in its widest sense it can now be said to cover any tangible or intangible thing that satisfies the consumer. Products that are marketed can include services, people, places, and ideas.

product abandonment MARKETING the ending of the manufacture and sale of a product. Products are abandoned for many reasons. The market may be saturated or declining, the product may be superseded by another, costs of production may become too high, or a product may simply become unprofitable. Product abandonment usually occurs during the decline phase of the **product life cycle**.

product assortment MARKETING see **product mix**

product churning GENERAL MANAGEMENT the flooding of a market with new products in the hope that one of them will become successful. Product churning is especially prevalent in Japan, where prelaunch **test marketing** is often replaced by multiple product launches. Most of these products will decline and disappear, but one or more of the new products churned out may become profitable.

product development MARKETING the revitalization of a product through the introduction of a new concept or consumer benefit. Product development is part of the **product life cycle**. The concepts or benefits that can be implemented range from modification of the product to simply introducing new packaging.

product development cycle MARKETING see **new product development**

product differentiation MARKETING a marketing technique that promotes and emphasizes a

product's difference from other products of a similar nature. Product differentiation is one of the aspects of **Michael Porter**'s *generic strategy* theory and it has been described by *Anita Roddick* as being the key to the success of the Body Shop. See actionlist *Better Communication with Resellers*

product family MARKETING a group of products or services that meet a similar need in the market

production OPERATIONS & PRODUCTION the processes and techniques used in making a product. Also known as *manufacturing*

production control OPERATIONS & PRODUCTION the control of all aspects of *production* according to a predetermined production plan. *Production planning* and production control are closely linked, and sometimes the terms are used interchangeably. Nevertheless, they differ in focus: production planning focuses on the scheduling of the production process; production control focuses on the application of the plan which results from the production planning. Computerized techniques, such as material requirements planning and *optimized production technology*, combine elements of planning and control.

production leveling OPERATIONS & PRODUCTION see *production smoothing*

production management OPERATIONS & PRODUCTION the management of those resources and activities of a business that are required to produce goods for sale to consumers or to other organizations. Production management is concerned with the manufacturing industry. The growing interest in the production management task in service industries has led to the use of *operations management* as a more general term. Also known as *manufacturing management*

production planning *or* **production scheduling** OPERATIONS & PRODUCTION the process of producing a specification or chart of the manufacturing operations to be performed by different functions and workstations over a particular time period. Production scheduling takes account of factors such as the availability of plant and materials, customer delivery requirements, and maintenance schedules.

production smoothing OPERATIONS & PRODUCTION the smoothing, or leveling, of *production planning* so that mix and volume are even over time. Production smoothing is an important condition for production by *kanban*, and is key to the *Toyota production system*. The goal

is to minimize idle time. Also known as *production leveling*

production versus purchasing OPERATIONS & PRODUCTION see *purchasing versus production*

productive capacity OPERATIONS & PRODUCTION the maximum amount of output that an organization or company can generate at any one time

productivity FINANCE, BANKING, AND ACCOUNTING, GENERAL MANAGEMENT, OPERATIONS & PRODUCTION a measurement of the efficiency of production, taking the form of a ratio of the output of goods and services to the input of factors of production. *Labor productivity* takes account of inputs of employee hours worked; *capital productivity* takes account of inputs of machines or land; and *marginal productivity* measures the additional output gained from an additional unit of input. Techniques to improve productivity include greater use of new technology, altered working practices, and improved training of the workforce.

productivity agreement HR & PERSONNEL see *productivity bargaining*

productivity bargaining HR & PERSONNEL a form of *collective bargaining* leading to a *productivity agreement* in which management offers a pay raise in exchange for alterations to employee working practices designed to increase *productivity*

productivity measurement HR & PERSONNEL see *productivity*

product launch MARKETING the introduction of a new product to a market. A product launch progresses through a number of important stages: internal communication, which encourages high levels of awareness and commitment to the new product; pre-launch activity, which secures distribution and makes sure that retailers have the resources and knowledge to market the product; launch events at national, regional, or local level; post-event activity, which helps salesforces and retailers make the most of the event; and launch advertising and other forms of customer communication.

product layout OPERATIONS & PRODUCTION the organization of a factory or office so that the position of the *workstations* is optimized to suit the product. Product layout ensures that products follow an *assembly line* where the different operations are undertaken in a logical sequence. Also known as *product-oriented layout*. See also *process layout*

product leader MARKETING see *brand leader*

product liability MARKETING a manufacturer's, producer's, or service provider's obligation to accept responsibility for defects in their products or services. Faulty products may result in personal injury or damage to property, in which case product liability may result in the payment of compensation to the purchaser.

product life cycle
1 FINANCE, BANKING, AND ACCOUNTING the period which begins with the initial product specification and ends with the withdrawal from the market of both the product and its support. It is characterized by defined stages, including research, development, introduction, maturity, decline, and abandonment.
2 MARKETING the life span of a product from development, through testing, promotion, growth, and maturity, to decline and perhaps regeneration. A new product is first developed and then introduced to the market. Once the introduction is successful, a growth period follows with wider awareness of the product and increasing sales. The product enters maturity when sales stop growing and demand stabilizes. Eventually, sales may decline until the product is finally withdrawn from the market or redeveloped.

product line MARKETING a family of related products. Products within a line may be the same type of product, they may be sold to the same type of customer or through similar outlets, or they may all be within a certain price range.

product management MARKETING a system for the coordination of all the stages through which a product passes during its life cycle. Product management involves control of a product from its innovation and development to its decline. The process is coordinated by a *product manager*, who focuses on the marketing of the product but may also be responsible for pricing, packaging, branding, research and development, production, distribution, sales targets, and product performance appraisal. This cross-departmental approach is based on the theory that a dedicated product management system will lead to tighter control over the product, and thus higher sales and profits. A *brand manager* fulfills a similar function to a product manager, concentrating on products within one brand.

product manager MARKETING see *product management*

product market MARKETING the *market* in which products are sold, usually to organizations rather than consumers. The product

market is concerned with **purchasing** by organizations for their own use, and includes such items as raw materials, machinery, and equipment, which may in turn be used to manufacture items for the consumer market.

product mix MARKETING the variety of product lines that a company produces, or that a retailer stocks. Product mix usually refers to the length (the number of products in the product line), breadth (the number of product lines that a company offers), depth (the different varieties of product in the product line), and consistency (the relationship between products in their final destination) of product lines. Product mix is sometimes called **product assortment**.

product-oriented layout OPERATIONS & PRODUCTION see **product layout**

product placement MARKETING a form of advertising in which an identifiable branded product is seen by the audience during a movie or television program

product portfolio MARKETING the variety of products manufactured or supplied by an organization

product positioning MARKETING see **brand positioning**

product range MARKETING all of the types of products made by one company

product recall OPERATIONS & PRODUCTION the removal from sale of products that may constitute a risk to consumers because of contamination, **sabotage**, or faults in the production process. A product recall usually originates from the product manufacturer but retailers may act autonomously, especially if they believe their outlets are at particular risk. See also **brand positioning**

profession HR & PERSONNEL an occupational group characterized by extensive education and specialized training, the use of skills based on theoretical knowledge, a **code of conduct**, and an association that organizes its members. Members of a profession are normally well paid and derive social status and prestige from their occupation. They have substantial autonomy and tend to be highly resistant to control or interference in their affairs by outside groups. As many professionals now work within organizations rather than independently, there may be a conflict of interests between professional and corporate values, and between professional autonomy and bureaucratic direction.

professional
1 HR & PERSONNEL a member of a particular **profession**
2 HR & PERSONNEL somebody paid to do a job, rather than working as a volunteer or pursuing a hobby
3 GENERAL MANAGEMENT somebody who shows a high level of skill or **competence**
4 GENERAL MANAGEMENT somebody who habitually indulges in a particular activity, fanatically and annoyingly (slang)

professionalism HR & PERSONNEL the skill, **competence**, or standards expected of a member of a **profession**

profile FINANCE, BANKING, AND ACCOUNTING a description of a company, including its products and finances

profile method HR & PERSONNEL an analytical form of **job evaluation** used by management consultants. The most well-known version of the profile method is the Hay Guide Chart and Profile Methodology.

profit FINANCE, BANKING, AND ACCOUNTING the difference between the selling price and the purchase price of a security or financial instrument when the selling price is higher

profitability FINANCE, BANKING, AND ACCOUNTING
1 the degree to which an individual, company, or single activity makes a **profit**
2 the condition of making a **profit**

profitability index FINANCE, BANKING, AND ACCOUNTING the present value of the money an investment will earn divided by the amount of the investment

profitability threshold FINANCE, BANKING, AND ACCOUNTING the point at which a business begins to make profits

profitable FINANCE, BANKING, AND ACCOUNTING used to refer to a product, service, or organization which makes money

profit and loss FINANCE, BANKING, AND ACCOUNTING the difference between a company's income and its costs

profit and loss account or **profit and loss statement** FINANCE, BANKING, AND ACCOUNTING the summary record of a company's sales revenues and expenses over a period, providing a calculation of profits or losses during that time. Abbr. **P&L**

profit before tax FINANCE, BANKING, AND ACCOUNTING the amount that a company or investor has made, without taking taxes into account

profit center
1 FINANCE, BANKING, AND ACCOUNTING a part of a business accountable for both costs and revenues
2 GENERAL MANAGEMENT a person, unit, or department within an organization that is considered separately when calculating profit. Profit centers are used as part of **management control systems**. They operate with a degree of autonomy with regard to marketing and pricing, and have responsibility for their own costs, revenues, and profits.

profit distribution FINANCE, BANKING, AND ACCOUNTING the allocation of profits to different recipients such as stockholders and owners, or for different purposes such as research or investment

profiteer FINANCE, BANKING, AND ACCOUNTING an individual or organization who aims to make excessive profits, often with a detrimental effect on others

profit from ordinary activities FINANCE, BANKING, AND ACCOUNTING profits earned in the normal course of business, as opposed to profits from extraordinary sources such as windfall payments

profit margin
1 GENERAL MANAGEMENT the amount by which income exceeds expenditure. The profit margin of an individual product is the sale price minus the cost of production and associated costs such as **distribution** and **advertising**. On a larger scale, the profit margin is an accounting ratio of company income compared with sales. The profit margin ratio can be used to compare the efficiency and profitability of a company over a number of years, or to compare different companies. The **gross profit margin** or **operating margin** of a company is its operating, or gross, profit divided by total sales. The **net profit margin** or **return on sales** is net income after taxes divided by total sales.
2 FINANCE, BANKING, AND ACCOUNTING sales less cost of sales, expressed either as a value or as a percentage of sales value. The profit margin may be calculated at different stages, hence the terms **gross profit margin** and **net profit margin**. The level of profit reported is also influenced by the extent of the application of accounting conventions, and by the method of product costing used, for example, marginal or **absorption costing**.

profit motive FINANCE, BANKING, AND ACCOUNTING the desire of a business or service provider to make a profit

profit sharing FINANCE, BANKING, AND ACCOUNTING the allocation of a proportion of company

profit to employees by an issue of stock or other means

profit-sharing debenture FINANCE, BANKING, AND ACCOUNTING a debenture held by an employee, the payouts from which depend on the employing company's financial success

profit squeeze FINANCE, BANKING, AND ACCOUNTING the inability to maintain an individual or an organization's profit in a venture, in comparison to previous ventures

profits tax (*U.K.*) FINANCE, BANKING, AND ACCOUNTING a tax on profits, for example, corporation tax (*slang*)

profits warning FINANCE, BANKING, AND ACCOUNTING an announcement by a company of lower than expected profits for a particular period. Also known as *profit warning*

profit warning FINANCE, BANKING, AND ACCOUNTING see *profits warning*

pro-forma GENERAL MANAGEMENT a document issued before all relevant details are known, usually followed by a final version

pro forma balance sheet FINANCE, BANKING, AND ACCOUNTING a projection showing a business's financial statements after the completion of a planned transaction

pro-forma invoice FINANCE, BANKING, AND ACCOUNTING an invoice that does not include all the details of a transaction, often sent before goods are supplied and followed by a final detailed invoice

program E-COMMERCE a set of instructions for a computer to act upon

program trading FINANCE, BANKING, AND ACCOUNTING the trading of securities electronically, by sending messages from the investor's computer to a market

progressive tax FINANCE, BANKING, AND ACCOUNTING a tax with a rate that increases proportionately with taxable income. See also *proportional tax*, *regressive tax*

project GENERAL MANAGEMENT a set of activities designed to achieve a specified goal, within a given period of time. Projects focus on activities outside the routine operations of an organization. They vary immensely in size, scope, and complexity; and often involve drawing together resources from different parts of an organization for the duration of the project. The process of planning and completing projects is known as *project management*.

project creep GENERAL MANAGEMENT the gradual slippage of deadlines and targets during a project

project finance FINANCE, BANKING, AND ACCOUNTING money, usually non-recourse finance, raised for a specific self-contained venture, usually a construction or development project

project management FINANCE, BANKING, AND ACCOUNTING the integration of all aspects of a project in order to ensure that the proper knowledge and resources are available when and where needed, and above all to ensure that the expected outcome is produced in a timely, cost-effective manner. The primary function of a project manager is to manage the trade-offs between performance, timeliness, and cost.

project risk analysis *or* **project risk assessment** GENERAL MANAGEMENT the identification of *risks* to which a *project* is exposed, and the assessment of the potential impact of those risks on the project. Project risk analysis forms part of the process of *project management* and is a specialized type of *risk analysis*.

promissory note FINANCE, BANKING, AND ACCOUNTING a contract to pay money to a person or organization for a good or service received. Abbr. *PN*

promotion
1 HR & PERSONNEL the award to an employee of a job at a higher grade, usually offering greater responsibility and more money
2 MARKETING see *sales promotion*

proof-of-purchase MARKETING a sales receipt or other document that can be used to show that someone has bought a product

property FINANCE, BANKING, AND ACCOUNTING *assets*, such as real estate or goods, that an individual or organization owns

property bond FINANCE, BANKING, AND ACCOUNTING a bond, especially a bail bond, for which a property is collateral

property damage insurance FINANCE, BANKING, AND ACCOUNTING insurance against the risk of damage to property

proportional tax FINANCE, BANKING, AND ACCOUNTING a tax which is strictly proportional in amount to the value of the item being taxed, especially income. See also *progressive tax*, *regressive tax*

proprietary ordering system E-COMMERCE a family of computer programs, usually inter-

active and online, that is developed and owned by a supplier and made available to its customers to facilitate ordering

proprietors' interest FINANCE, BANKING, AND ACCOUNTING an amount of money which the owners of a business have invested in the business

ProShare FINANCE, BANKING, AND ACCOUNTING a group that acts in the interests of private investors in securities of the London Stock Exchange

prospect MARKETING a person or organization considered likely to buy a product or service

prospecting MARKETING the process of identifying people or organizations that are likely to buy a product or service

prospect theory GENERAL MANAGEMENT a branch of decision theory which attempts to explain why individuals make decisions that deviate from rational decision making by examining how the expected outcomes of alternative choices are perceived. Prospect theory was developed by Daniel Kahneman and Amos Tversky in 1979, in their article "Prospect Theory: An Analysis of Decision Making under Risk," *Econometrica XX*, pp. 263–291. The theory is based on the premise that people treat risks associated with perceived losses differently from risks associated with perceived gains. Prospect theory has applications in a wide range of fields, including marketing management, where it is relevant to the way in which choices are presented to the consumer.

prospectus FINANCE, BANKING, AND ACCOUNTING a description of a company's operations, financial background, prospects, and the detailed terms and conditions relating to an offer for sale or placing of its stock by notice, circular, advertisement, or any form of invitation which offers securities to the public

prosuming GENERAL MANAGEMENT acting both as producer and consumer, as, for example, when a person plays an interactive computer game (*slang*)

protected class HR & PERSONNEL an employee with skills that are currently in short supply (*slang*)

protectionism ECONOMICS a government economic policy of restricting the level of imports by using measures such as tariffs and *NTBs* in order to protect a country's domestic industries

protective put buying FINANCE, BANKING, AND ACCOUNTING the purchase of *puts* for stocks already owned

protective tariff ECONOMICS a tariff imposed to restrict imports into a country

protirement HR & PERSONNEL leaving or retiring from a stressful professional job to focus on a new blend of work and other activities. Protirement is similar to *downshifting* but is seen as a more positive approach to retirement. It is a lifestyle option increasingly taken by successful people in mid-life or later, sometimes including a new career or educational activities, but most importantly involving a plan for self-enrichment and fulfillment. It may also involve portfolio working. The term was first used in the book *The Adult Years: Mastering the Art of Self Renewal* by F. M. Hudson (Jossey-Bass, 1991).

protocol FINANCE, BANKING, AND ACCOUNTING a set of rules that govern and regulate a process

prototype GENERAL MANAGEMENT an initial version or working model of a new product or invention. A prototype is constructed and tested in order to evaluate the feasibility of a design and to identify problems that need to be corrected. Building a prototype is a key stage in *new product development*.

provision FINANCE, BANKING, AND ACCOUNTING a sum set aside in the accounts of an organization in anticipation of a future expense, often for doubtful debts. See also *bad debt*

provisional tax FINANCE, BANKING, AND ACCOUNTING tax paid in advance on the following year's income, the amount being based on the actual income from the preceding year

proxy GENERAL MANAGEMENT somebody who votes on behalf of another person at a company meeting

proxy fight FINANCE, BANKING, AND ACCOUNTING the use of proxy votes to settle a contentious issue at a company meeting

proxy server E-COMMERCE a program added to an intranet to provide one-way (outward) access to the Internet. In addition to providing Internet access for those within the intranet, the proxy server creates a *firewall* to prevent external users from accessing the private network.

proxy statement FINANCE, BANKING, AND ACCOUNTING a notice that a company sends to stockholders, allowing them to vote and giving them all the information they need to vote in an informed way

prudence FINANCE, BANKING, AND ACCOUNTING see *prudence concept*

prudence concept FINANCE, BANKING, AND AC-COUNTING the principle that revenue and profits are not anticipated but are included in the *profit and loss account* only when realized in the form either of *cash* or of other assets, the ultimate cash realization of which can be assessed with reasonable certainty. Provision is made for all known liabilities (expenses and losses) whether the amount of these is known with certainty, or is a best estimate in the light of the information available.

prudential ratio FINANCE, BANKING, AND AC-COUNTING the ratio of capital to assets which, according to European Union regulations, a bank feels it is prudent to have

prudent man rule FINANCE, BANKING, AND ACCOUNTING the rule that trustees who make financial decisions on behalf of other people should act carefully (as a normal prudent person would)

psychic income HR & PERSONNEL the level of satisfaction derived from a job rather than the salary earned doing it (*slang*)

psychological contract HR & PERSONNEL the set of unwritten expectations concerning the relationship between an *employee* and an *employer*. The psychological contract addresses factors that are not defined in a written *contract of employment* such as levels of *employee commitment*, *productivity*, *quality of working life*, *job satisfaction*, attitudes to *flexible working*, and the provision and take-up of suitable training. Expectations of both employer and employee can change, so the psychological contract must be reevaluated at intervals to minimize misunderstandings.

psychological test HR & PERSONNEL see *psychometric test*

psychometric test HR & PERSONNEL a series of questions, problems, or practical tasks that provide a measurement of aspects of somebody's personality, knowledge, ability, or experience. There are three main categories of psychometric test: ability or *aptitude tests*, *achievement tests*, and *personality tests*. A test should be both valid—it should measure what it says it measures—and reliable—it should give consistent scores. However, no test can ever be 100% accurate, and should be viewed more as a useful indicator than a definitive verdict on a person's skills or potential. Tests are used in *recruitment*, to ascertain whether or not a candidate is likely to be a good fit for a job, and in *employee development*, and their administration and interpretation must be carried out by qualified people.

Tests are increasingly taken, scored, and interpreted with the aid of computer-based systems. A test may also be referred to as an *instrument*, and tests can be grouped into a *test battery*.

Pty *abbr* (*S. Africa*) FINANCE, BANKING, AND AC-COUNTING used in company names to indicate a private limited liability company. Abbr of *proprietary*

Public Accounts Committee FINANCE, BANK-ING, AND ACCOUNTING a committee of the House of Commons which examines the spending of each department and ministry

public corporation FINANCE, BANKING, AND ACCOUNTING a state owned organization established to provide a particular service, for example, the British Broadcasting Corporation

public debt ECONOMICS the money that a government or a set of governments owes

public deposits FINANCE, BANKING, AND AC-COUNTING in the United Kingdom, the government's credit monies held at the Bank of England

public expenditure ECONOMICS spending by the government of a country on things such as pension provision and infrastructure enhancement

public finance law FINANCE, BANKING, AND AC-COUNTING legislation relating to the financial activities of government or public sector organizations

public issue FINANCE, BANKING, AND ACCOUNTING a way of making a new issue of stock by offering it for sale to the public. An issue of this type is often advertised in the press. See also *offer for sale offer by prospectus*

public-liability insurance FINANCE, BANKING, AND ACCOUNTING insurance against the risk of being held financially liable for injury to somebody

public limited company FINANCE, BANKING, AND ACCOUNTING a company in the United Kingdom that is required to have a minimum authorized capital of £50,000 and to offer its stock to the public. A public limited company has the letters "plc" after its name. In the United Kingdom, only public limited companies can be listed on the London Stock Exchange. = *publicly held corporation*. Abbr. *plc*, *PLC*

publicly held corporation FINANCE, BANKING, AND ACCOUNTING an organization with common

stock listed on a stock exchange. U.K. term **public limited company**

public monopoly ECONOMICS a situation of limited competition in the public sector, usually relating to nationalized industries

public offering FINANCE, BANKING, AND ACCOUNTING a method of raising money used by a company in which it invites the public to buy stock

public private partnership FINANCE, BANKING, AND ACCOUNTING a partnership between government and the private sector for the purpose of more effectively providing services and infrastructure traditionally provided by the public sector. Abbr. **PPP**

public relations MARKETING see **PR**

public relations consulting firm MARKETING an organization specializing in planning and implementing public relations strategies

public sector ECONOMICS FINANCE, BANKING, AND ACCOUNTING the organizations in the section of the economy that is financed and controlled by central government, local authorities, and publicly funded corporations. See also **private sector**

public servant GENERAL MANAGEMENT a person employed by a government department or agency

public service GENERAL MANAGEMENT the various departments and agencies that administer government policies and provide government-funded services

public spending ECONOMICS spending by the government of a country on publicly provided goods and services

public training program HR & PERSONNEL see **in-company training**

published accounts (*U.K.*) FINANCE, BANKING, AND ACCOUNTING = **earnings report**

puff FINANCE, BANKING, AND ACCOUNTING to overstate the virtues of a product, especially a stock (*slang*)

puffery MARKETING exaggerated claims made for a product or service. In general, puffery does not constitute false advertising under law. (*slang*)

puff piece MARKETING an article in a news-

paper or magazine promoting a product, person, or service (*slang*)

pull factor E-COMMERCE a measure of the strength of the retail trade in an area, based on a comparison of local spending in relation to that of a wider geographic area, for example, a state

pull strategy MARKETING see **push and pull strategies**

pull system OPERATIONS & PRODUCTION a production planning and control system in which the specification and pace of output of a delivery, or supplier, **workstation** is set by the receiving, or customer, workstation. In pull systems, the customer acts as the only trigger for movement. The supplier workstation can only produce output on the instructions of the customer for delivery when the customer is ready to receive it. Demand is therefore transferred down through the stages of production from the order placed by an end customer. Pull systems are far less likely to result in work-in-progress inventory, and are favored by just-in-time or **lean production** systems. See also **push system**

pull technology E-COMMERCE technology that enables users to seek out and then pull in information, rather than having it pushed in their way. Understanding the "pull" nature of the Internet is often considered to be one of the key factors in determining a Web site's success. The Internet is essentially a pull technology, though direct outbound e-mail can be classified as a **push technology**.

pull the plug on something GENERAL MANAGEMENT to bring something such as a business project to an end, especially by cutting off its financial support (*slang*)

pump-and-dump E-COMMERCE describes a fraudulent scheme in which unscrupulous stockbrokers, analysts, or stockholders highly recommend their own stocks in order to drive up the price before selling for a quick profit

pump priming FINANCE, BANKING, AND ACCOUNTING the injection of further investment in order to revitalize a company in stagnation, or to help a **startup** over a critical period. Pump priming has a similar effect to the provision of **seed money**.

punch in HR & PERSONNEL see **clock in**

punt GENERAL MANAGEMENT to stop trying to accomplish something and just try to avoid losing any more resources (*slang*)

purchase contract FINANCE, BANKING, AND ACCOUNTING a form of agreement to buy specified products at an agreed price

purchase history MARKETING a record of a customer's transactions with an organization

purchase ledger GENERAL MANAGEMENT a record of all purchases made by an organization

purchase money mortgage FINANCE, BANKING, AND ACCOUNTING a mortgage whose proceeds the borrower uses to buy the property that is collateral for the loan

purchase order FINANCE, BANKING, AND ACCOUNTING a written order for goods or services specifying quantities, prices, delivery dates, and contract terms

purchase price FINANCE, BANKING, AND ACCOUNTING the price that somebody pays to buy a good or service

purchase requisition GENERAL MANAGEMENT an internal instruction to a buying office to purchase goods or services, stating their quantity and description and generating a purchase order

purchasing GENERAL MANAGEMENT the acquisition of goods and services needed to support the various activities of an organization, at the optimum cost and from reliable suppliers. Purchasing involves defining the need for goods and services; identifying and comparing available supplies and suppliers; negotiating terms for price, quantity, and delivery; agreeing contracts and placing orders; receiving and accepting delivery; and authorizing the payment for goods and services. Also known as **procurement**

purchasing by contract OPERATIONS & PRODUCTION see **contract purchasing**

purchasing manager FINANCE, BANKING, AND ACCOUNTING an individual with responsibility for all activities concerned with purchasing. The responsibilities of a purchasing manager can include ordering, commercial negotiations, and delivery chasing. Also known as **buying manager**

purchasing power FINANCE, BANKING, AND ACCOUNTING a measure of the ability of a person, organization, or sector to buy goods and services

purchasing power parity FINANCE, BANKING, AND ACCOUNTING a theory that the exchange rate between two currencies is in equilibrium when the purchasing power of currency is the same in each country. If a basket of goods costs

£100 in the United Kingdom and $150 for an equivalent in the United States, for equilibrium to exist, the exchange rate would be expected to be £1 = $1.50. If this were not the case, *arbitrage* would be expected to take place until equilibrium was restored. Abbr. **PPP**

purchasing routine FINANCE, BANKING, AND ACCOUNTING the various stages involved in organizing the purchase of a product or service

purchasing versus production OPERATIONS & PRODUCTION a decision on whether to produce goods internally or to buy them in from outside the organization. The goal of purchasing versus production is to secure needed items at the best possible cost, while making optimum use of the resources of the organization. Factors influencing the decision may include: cost, spare *capacity* within the organization, the need for tight quality and scheduling control, flexibility, the enhancement of skills that can then be used in other ways, volume and economies of scale, utilization of existing personnel, the need for secrecy, capital and financing requirements, and the potential reliability of supply. Also known as *buy or make*, *make or buy*, *internal versus external sourcing*

pure competition FINANCE, BANKING, AND ACCOUNTING a situation in which there are many sellers in a market and there is free flow of information

pure endowment FINANCE, BANKING, AND ACCOUNTING a gift whose use is fully prescribed by the donor

pure play E-COMMERCE a company that conducts business only over the Internet, provides only Internet services, or sells only to other Internet companies (*slang*)

purpose credit FINANCE, BANKING, AND ACCOUNTING credit used for trade in securities

push and pull strategies MARKETING approaches used as part of a marketing strategy to encourage customers to purchase a product or service. Push and pull strategies are contrasting approaches and tend to target different types of consumers. A *pull strategy* targets the end consumer, using *advertising*, *sales promotions*, and *direct response marketing* to pull the customer in. This approach is common in consumer markets. A *push strategy* targets members of the *distribution channel*, such as *wholesalers* and *retailers*, to push the promotion up through the channel to the consumers. This approach is more common in industrial markets.

push system OPERATIONS & PRODUCTION a *production control* and planning system in which demand is predicted centrally and each *workstation* pushes work out without considering if the next station is ready for it. While the central control aspect of a push system can achieve a balance across workstations, in practice a particular station can suffer from any one of a number of problems that delays work flow, so affecting the whole system. Push systems are characterized by work-in-progress inventory, lines, and idle time. See also *pull system*

push technology E-COMMERCE see *pull technology*

push the envelope GENERAL MANAGEMENT to exceed normal limits. Pushing the envelope is a term adapted from aviation. The term implies a sense of risk at transcending the normal safe limits of operation.

put *or* **put option** FINANCE, BANKING, AND ACCOUNTING an option to sell stock within a specified time at a specified price

PYB *abbr* FINANCE, BANKING, AND ACCOUNTING preceding year basis

pyramid selling MARKETING the sale of the right to sell products or services to distributors who in turn recruit other distributors. Sometimes ending with no final buyer, pyramid selling is a form of multilevel marketing, and often involves a system of franchises. It is similar to *network marketing*, but in many cases no end products are actually sold. Unscrupulous instigators of a pyramid marketing plan profit from the initial fees paid to them by distributors in advance of promised sales income.

Q

QFD *abbr* OPERATIONS & PRODUCTION quality function deployment

qualification payment (*ANZ*) FINANCE, BANKING, AND ACCOUNTING an additional payment sometimes made to employees of New Zealand companies, who have gained an academic degree relevant to their job

qualified auditor's report FINANCE, BANKING, AND ACCOUNTING see *adverse opinion*

qualified domestic trust FINANCE, BANKING, AND ACCOUNTING a trust for the noncitizen spouse of a U.S. citizen, affording tax advantages at the time of the citizen's death

qualified lead FINANCE, BANKING, AND ACCOUNTING a sales prospect whose potential value has been carefully researched

qualified listed security FINANCE, BANKING, AND ACCOUNTING a security that is eligible for purchase by a regulated entity such as a trust

qualifying distribution FINANCE, BANKING, AND ACCOUNTING the payment to a stockholder of a dividend, on which *Advance Corporation Tax* is paid

qualifying ratio FINANCE, BANKING, AND ACCOUNTING a calculation of how much mortgage a borrower can afford, by comparing his or her monthly income against monthly outgoings

qualitative analysis FINANCE, BANKING, AND ACCOUNTING the subjective appraisal of a project or investment for which there is no quantifiable data. See also *chartist*, *quantitative analysis*, *technical analysis*

qualitative lending guideline FINANCE, BANKING, AND ACCOUNTING a rule for evaluating creditworthiness that is not objective

qualitative research MARKETING FINANCE, BANKING, AND ACCOUNTING research that focuses on "soft" data, for example, attitude research or focus groups. See also *quantitative research*

quality GENERAL MANAGEMENT all the features and characteristics of a product or service that affect its ability to meet stated or implied needs. Quality can be assessed in terms of conforming to specification, being fit for purpose, having zero defects, and producing *customer satisfaction*. Quality can be managed through *total quality management*, *quality standards*, and *performance indicators*.

quality assurance GENERAL MANAGEMENT all the methods used to ensure compliance with a *quality standard*. Quality assurance is recognized by the international standard *ISO 9000*.

quality audit GENERAL MANAGEMENT an independent and systematic examination to establish whether quality activities and related results comply with planned arrangements. A quality audit is a form of internal *audit*, useful in the maintenance of *quality control*. A quality audit needs to look at effective implementation of quality arrangements and whether they are suitable for the achievement of objectives. It is an integral part of working toward a *quality standard* or a *quality award*.

quality award GENERAL MANAGEMENT a formal recognition of quality and business *excellence*. The best known quality awards include the

Malcolm Baldrige National Quality Award, the *Deming Prize*, and the *EFQM Excellence Model*.

quality bond FINANCE, BANKING, AND ACCOUNTING a bond issued by an organization that has an excellent credit rating

quality circle GENERAL MANAGEMENT a group of employees who meet voluntarily and on a regular basis to discuss performance and problems evident in their working environment. A quality circle is usually made up of employees from the shop floor, led by a supervisor. The group has responsibility for implementing solutions to identified problems. Participants are trained in the necessary leadership, *problem solving*, and *decision making* skills to enable them to contribute fully to the group. The quality circle is a form of *employee involvement* derived from a Japanese idea.

quality control GENERAL MANAGEMENT an inspection system for ensuring that predetermined *quality standards* are being met. Quality control measures the progress of an activity by means of a *quality inspection*, checking for and identifying non-conformance. See thinker *Philip Crosby*

quality control plan OPERATIONS & PRODUCTION a means of setting out practices, resources, and sequences of activities relevant to the *quality control* of a particular product, service, contract, or project

quality costs GENERAL MANAGEMENT costs associated with the failure to achieve conformance to requirements. Quality costs accrue when organizations waste large sums of money because of carrying out the wrong tasks, or failing to perform the right tasks *right first time*. Also known as *nonconformance costs*

quality equity FINANCE, BANKING, AND ACCOUNTING an equity with a good track record of earnings and dividends. See also *blue chip*

quality function deployment OPERATIONS & PRODUCTION a *quality* technique used to design services or products based on customer expectations. Quality function deployment is an approach that sees quality as something that can be designed into a product or service at an early stage. It involves converting customers' demands into quality characteristics of the finished product. The four phases of the approach are design or *house of quality*, detail, process, and production. Each phase helps to steer a design team toward *customer satisfaction*. Quality function deployment is based on

methods developed by *Genichi Taguchi*. Abbr. *QFD*

quality inspection GENERAL MANAGEMENT see *quality control*

quality loss OPERATIONS & PRODUCTION see *Taguchi methods*

quality management GENERAL MANAGEMENT the use of a program to ensure the production of high-quality products. See also *total quality management*

quality manual GENERAL MANAGEMENT a document containing the quality policy, quality objectives, structure chart, and description of the quality system of an organization. A quality manual often explains how the requirements of a *quality standard* are to be met and identifies the person responsible for *quality management* functions.

quality of design OPERATIONS & PRODUCTION the degree to which the design of a product or service meets its purpose. Quality of design is an important factor in *customer satisfaction*.

quality of life HR & PERSONNEL
1 at a personal level, the degree of enjoyment and satisfaction experienced in everyday life, embracing health, personal relationships, the environment, *quality of working life*, social life, and leisure time
2 at community level, a set of social indicators such as nutrition, air quality, incidence of disease, crime rates, health care, educational services, and divorce rates

quality of working life HR & PERSONNEL the degree of personal satisfaction experienced at work. Quality of working life is dependent on the extent to which an employee feels valued, rewarded, motivated, consulted, and empowered. It is also influenced by factors such as job security, opportunities for *career development*, work patterns, and *work-life balance*.

quality standard GENERAL MANAGEMENT a framework for achieving a recognized level of *quality* within an organization. Achievement of a quality standard demonstrates that an organization has met the requirements laid out by a certifying body. Quality standards recognized on an international basis include *ISO 9000* and *ISO 14000*.

quality table OPERATIONS & PRODUCTION see *house of quality*

quality time GENERAL MANAGEMENT time that is set aside for activities which you consider

important, for example, time spent with your family (*slang*)

quango (*U.K.*) GENERAL MANAGEMENT an acronym derived from quasi-autonomous non-governmental organization. Established by the government and answerable to a government minister, some, but not all quangos are staffed by civil servants and some have statutory powers in a specified field.

quantitative analysis FINANCE, BANKING, AND ACCOUNTING the appraisal of a project or investment using econometric, mathematical, and statistical techniques. See also *chartist*, *qualitative analysis*, *technical analysis*

quantitative research FINANCE, BANKING, AND ACCOUNTING the gathering and analysis of data that can be expressed in numerical form. Quantitative research involves data that is measurable and can include statistical results, financial data, or demographic data. See also *qualitative research*

quantum meruit FINANCE, BANKING, AND ACCOUNTING a Latin phrase meaning "as much as has been earned"

quarterback GENERAL MANAGEMENT to give directions on a project (*slang*)

quarterly report FINANCE, BANKING, AND ACCOUNTING see *interim statement*

quartile STATISTICS any of the values in a frequency or probability distribution that divide it into four equal parts

quasi-contract FINANCE, BANKING, AND ACCOUNTING a decree by a U.K. court stipulating that one party has a legal obligation to another, even though there is no legally binding contract between the two parties

quasi-loan FINANCE, BANKING, AND ACCOUNTING an arrangement whereby one party pays the debts of another, on the condition that the sum of the debts will be reimbursed by the indebted party at some later date

quasi-money (*U.K.*) FINANCE, BANKING, AND ACCOUNTING see *near money*

quasi-public corporation FINANCE, BANKING, AND ACCOUNTING an organization that is owned partly by private or public stockholders and partly by the government

quasi-rent ECONOMICS the short-run excess earnings made by a firm: the difference between production cost (the cost of labor and materials) and selling cost

question mark company GENERAL MANAGEMENT see *Boston Box*

questionnaire GENERAL MANAGEMENT a collection of structured questions designed to elicit information for a specific purpose. Questionnaires are commonly used in *market research* and make use of two types of questions: multiple choice questions, which are designed to produce a limited response, and open questions, which allow respondents the opportunity to air their views freely.

queuing theory GENERAL MANAGEMENT techniques developed by the study of people standing in line to determine the optimum level of service provision. In queuing theory, mathematical formulae, or *simulations*, are used to calculate variables such as length of time spent standing in line and average service time, which depend on the frequency and number of arrivals and the facilities available. The results enable decisions to be made on the most cost-effective level of facilities and the most efficient organization of the process. Early developments in queuing theory were applied to the provision of telephone switching equipment but the techniques are now used in a wide variety of contexts, including machine maintenance, production lines, and air transportation.

queuing time OPERATIONS & PRODUCTION the time between the arrival of material at a workstation and the start of work on it

quick asset FINANCE, BANKING, AND ACCOUNTING see *near money*

quick ratio FINANCE, BANKING, AND ACCOUNTING **1** a measure of the amount of cash a potential borrower can acquire in a short time, used in evaluating creditworthiness **2** the ratio of liquid assets to current debts

quid pro quo FINANCE, BANKING, AND ACCOUNTING a Latin phrase meaning "something for something"

quorum FINANCE, BANKING, AND ACCOUNTING the minimum number of people required in a meeting for it to be able to make decisions that are binding on the organization

quota FINANCE, BANKING, AND ACCOUNTING **1** the maximum sum to be contributed by each party in a joint venture or joint business undertaking **2** the maximum number of investments that may be purchased and sold in a given situation or market, for example, at U.S. Treasury auctions, bidders may not apply for more than a certain percentage of the securities being offered **3** the maximum amount of a particular commodity, product, or service that can be imported into or exported out of a country

quote FINANCE, BANKING, AND ACCOUNTING a statement of what a person is willing to accept when selling a product or service

quoted company FINANCE, BANKING, AND ACCOUNTING a company whose stock is listed on a stock exchange

quote driven FINANCE, BANKING, AND ACCOUNTING used to describe a stock dealing system where prices are initially generated by dealers' and market makers' quotes before market forces come into play and prices are determined by the interaction of supply and demand. The London Stock Exchange's dealing system, as well as those of many over-the-counter markets, have quote driven systems.

quoted securities FINANCE, BANKING, AND ACCOUNTING securities or stocks that are listed on a stock exchange

R

R150 Bond FINANCE, BANKING, AND ACCOUNTING the benchmark South African government bond which has a fixed interest rate of 12% and matures in 2005

racial discrimination HR & PERSONNEL the practice of making unfavorable distinctions between the members of different groups of people on the grounds of color, race, nationality, or ethnic origin. See also *indirect discrimination*

radio button GENERAL MANAGEMENT a device on a computer screen that can be used to select an option from a list

raid FINANCE, BANKING, AND ACCOUNTING the illegal practice of selling stocks short to drive the price down. Also known as *bear raid*

raider FINANCE, BANKING, AND ACCOUNTING a person or company that makes hostile takeover bids

rainmaker HR & PERSONNEL somebody, especially a lawyer, who procures clients who spend a lot of money on their firm's business

rake it in FINANCE, BANKING, AND ACCOUNTING to make a great deal of money (*slang*)

rake-off FINANCE, BANKING, AND ACCOUNTING commission (*slang*)

rally FINANCE, BANKING, AND ACCOUNTING a rise in stock prices after a fall

ramp FINANCE, BANKING, AND ACCOUNTING to buy stocks with the objective of raising their price. See also *rigged market*

ramp up GENERAL MANAGEMENT to increase significantly your interest or efforts in a particular area

rand FINANCE, BANKING, AND ACCOUNTING the South African unit of currency, equal to 100 cents

R&D *abbr* OPERATIONS & PRODUCTION research and development

Randlord FINANCE, BANKING, AND ACCOUNTING originally a Johannesburg-based mining magnate or tycoon of the late 19th or early 20th-centuries, now used informally for any wealthy or powerful Johannesburg businessman

random STATISTICS not part of a pattern but governed by chance

random observation method GENERAL MANAGEMENT see *activity sampling*

random sampling OPERATIONS & PRODUCTION an unbiased *sampling* technique in which every member of a population has an equal chance of being included in the sample. Based on probability theory, random sampling is the process of selecting and canvassing a representative group of individuals from a particular population in order to identify the attributes or attitudes of the population as a whole. Related sampling techniques include: *stratified sampling*, in which the population is divided into classes, and random samples are taken from each class; *cluster sampling*, in which a unit of the sample is a group such as a household; and *systematic sampling*, which refers to samples chosen by any system other than random selection. See also *nonrandom sampling*

range STATISTICS the difference between the smallest and the largest observations in a data set

range pricing FINANCE, BANKING, AND ACCOUNTING the pricing of individual products so that their prices fit logically within a variety of connected products offered by one supplier, and differentiated by a factor such as weight of pack or number of product attributes offered

rank and yank E-COMMERCE a system of reviewing employee performance by which top performers are slated for promotion and compensation increases and low performers are slated for reassignment or termination

ranking STATISTICS the ordered arrangement of a set of variable values

ratchet effect ECONOMICS the result when households adjust more easily to rising incomes than to falling incomes, as, for example, when their consumption drops by less than their income in a recession

rateable value FINANCE, BANKING, AND ACCOUNTING the value of something as calculated with reference to a rule, such as the value of a commercial property as a basis for calculating local taxes

rate cap FINANCE, BANKING, AND ACCOUNTING see *cap*

rate of exchange FINANCE, BANKING, AND ACCOUNTING see *exchange rate*

rate of interest FINANCE, BANKING, AND ACCOUNTING a percentage charged on a loan or paid on an investment for the use of the money

rate of return FINANCE, BANKING, AND ACCOUNTING an accounting ratio of the income from an investment to the amount of the investment, used to measure financial performance.

There is a basic formula that will serve most needs, at least initially:

$$\frac{[(\text{Current value of amount invested} - \text{Original value of amount invested})}{\text{Original value of amount invested}]} \times 100\%$$
$$= \text{Rate of return}$$

If $1,000 in capital is invested in stock, and one year later the investment yields $1,100, the rate of return of the investment is calculated like this:

$$\frac{(1100 - 1000)}{1000} \times 100\% = \frac{100}{1000} \times 100\%$$
$$= 10\% \text{ Rate of return}$$

Now, assume $1,000 is invested again. One year later, the investment grows to $2,000 in value, but after another year the value of the investment falls to $1,200. The rate of return after the first year is:

$$\frac{(2000 - 1000)}{1000} \times 100\% = 100\%$$

The rate of return after the second year is:

$$\frac{(1200 - 2000)}{2000} \times 100\% = -40\%$$

The average annual return for the two years (also known as average annual arithmetic return) can be calculated using this formula:

$$\frac{(\text{Rate of return for Year 1} + \text{Rate of return for Year 2})}{2} = \text{Average annual return}$$

Accordingly:

$$\frac{(100\% + -40\%)}{2} = 30\%$$

The average annual rate of return is a percentage, but one that is accurate over only a short period, so this method should be used accordingly.

The geometric or compound rate of return is a better yardstick for measuring investments over the long term, and takes into account the effects of compounding. This formula is more complex and technical.

The real rate of return is the annual return realized on an investment, adjusted for changes in the price due to inflation. If 10% is earned on an investment but inflation is 2%, then the real rate of return is actually 8%. Also known as *return*

rating agency FINANCE, BANKING, AND ACCOUNTING an organization which gives a rating to companies or other organizations issuing bonds

ratings MARKETING the proportion of a target audience who are exposed to a television or radio commercial

ratio analysis FINANCE, BANKING, AND ACCOUNTING the use of ratios to measure financial performance

ratio-delay study GENERAL MANAGEMENT see *activity sampling*

rationalization GENERAL MANAGEMENT the application of efficiency or effectiveness measures to an organization. Rationalization can occur at the onset of a downturn in an organization's performance or results. It usually takes the form of cutbacks intended to bring the organization back to profitability and may involve layoffs, plant closures, and cutbacks in supplies and resources. It often involves changes in *organization structure*, particularly in the form of *downsizing*. The term is also used in a cynical way as a euphemism for mass layoffs.

raw materials OPERATIONS & PRODUCTION items bought for use in the manufacturing or development processes of an organization. While most often referring to bulk materials, raw materials can also include components, sub-assemblies, and complete products.

RBA *abbr* FINANCE, BANKING, AND ACCOUNTING Reserve Bank of Australia

RBNZ *abbr* FINANCE, BANKING, AND ACCOUNTING Reserve Bank of New Zealand

RD *abbr* FINANCE, BANKING, AND ACCOUNTING refer to drawer

RDO *abbr* (ANZ) HR & PERSONNEL rostered day off: a day of leave allocated under certain employment agreements to staff in lieu of accumulated overtime

RDP *abbr* (S. Africa) FINANCE, BANKING, AND ACCOUNTING Reconstruction and Development Program: a policy framework by means of which the South African government intends to correct the socioeconomic imbalances caused by apartheid

RDPR *abbr* FINANCE, BANKING, AND ACCOUNTING refer to drawer please represent

reactive maintenance OPERATIONS & PRODUCTION a form of *maintenance* in which equipment and facilities are repaired only in response to a breakdown or a fault. Because of the potential for loss of production, reactive maintenance is at odds with *just-in-time*. See also *preventive maintenance*

readership MARKETING a detailed profile of the readers of a newspaper or magazine

Reaganomics ECONOMICS the economic policy of former U.S. President Reagan in the 1980s, who reduced taxes and social security support and increased the national budget deficit to an unprecedented level

real FINANCE, BANKING, AND ACCOUNTING after the effects of inflation are taken into consideration

real asset FINANCE, BANKING, AND ACCOUNTING a nonmovable asset such as land or a building

real balance effect ECONOMICS the effect on income and employment when prices fall and consumption increases

real capital ECONOMICS FINANCE, BANKING, AND ACCOUNTING assets that can be assigned a monetary value

real estate GENERAL MANAGEMENT property consisting of land or buildings

real estate developer GENERAL MANAGEMENT a person or company that develops land or buildings to increase their value

real exchange rate FINANCE, BANKING, AND ACCOUNTING an exchange rate that has been adjusted for inflation

real GDP ECONOMICS *GDP* adjusted for changes in prices

real growth ECONOMICS the growth of a country or a household adjusted for changes in prices

real investment FINANCE, BANKING, AND ACCOUNTING the purchase of assets such as land, real estate, and plant and machinery as opposed to the acquisition of securities

realize FINANCE, BANKING, AND ACCOUNTING to change an *asset* into cash by selling it

real purchasing power ECONOMICS the purchasing power of a country or a household adjusted for changes in prices

real time company GENERAL MANAGEMENT a company that uses the Internet and other technologies to respond immediately to customer demands

real time credit card processing E-COMMERCE the online authorization of a credit card indicating that the credit card has been approved or rejected during the transaction

real time EDI E-COMMERCE online *electronic data interchange*: the online transfer and processing of business data, for example, purchase orders, customer invoices, and payment receipts, between suppliers and their customers

real time manager GENERAL MANAGEMENT a manager who is responsible for delivering the immediate service that customers expect, using the Internet and other technologies

real time transaction E-COMMERCE an Internet payment transaction that is approved or rejected immediately when the customer completes the online order form

rebadge MARKETING to buy a product or service from another company and sell it as part of your own product range

rebate FINANCE, BANKING, AND ACCOUNTING
1 money returned because a payment exceeded the amount required, for example, a tax rebate
2 a discount
3 of a broker, to reduce part of the commission charged to the client as a promotional offer

rebating MARKETING a sales promotion technique in which the customer is offered a rebate for reaching volume targets

recapitalize FINANCE, BANKING, AND ACCOUNTING
1 to increase the *capital* owned by an individual, company, or industry
2 to change the organization of a company's *capital*, usually in response to a major financial problem, such as *bankruptcy*

recd. *abbr* FINANCE, BANKING, AND ACCOUNTING received

receipt FINANCE, BANKING, AND ACCOUNTING a document acknowledging that something—for example, a payment—has been received

receiver FINANCE, BANKING, AND ACCOUNTING a person appointed to sell the assets of a company that is insolvent. The proceeds of the sale are used to discharge debts to creditors, with any surplus distributed to *shareholders*.

Receiver of Revenue FINANCE, BANKING, AND ACCOUNTING
1 (*S. Africa*) a local office of the South African Revenue Service
2 an informal term for the South African Revenue Service as a whole

receivership GENERAL MANAGEMENT a state of *insolvency* prior to *liquidation*, and *bankruptcy*. During receivership, receivers may attempt to undertake *turnaround management* or decide that the company must go into liquidation.

recession ECONOMICS a stage of the *business cycle* in which economic activity is in slow decline. Recession usually follows a boom, and precedes a *depression*. It is characterized by rising unemployment and falling levels of output and investment.

recessionary gap ECONOMICS a shortfall in the amount of *aggregate demand* in an economy needed to create full employment

reciprocal link E-COMMERCE a link in both directions from one Web site to another as a form of bartering for advertising space

recognized investment exchange FINANCE, BANKING, AND ACCOUNTING a stock exchange, futures exchange, or commodity exchange recognized by the *Financial Services Authority*

reconciliation FINANCE, BANKING, AND ACCOUNTING adjustment of an account, such as an individual's own record of a bank account, to match more authoritative information

record date GENERAL MANAGEMENT the date when a computer data entry or record is made

recourse agreement FINANCE, BANKING, AND ACCOUNTING an agreement in an installment plan whereby the retailer repossesses the goods being purchased in the event of the purchaser failing to make regular payments

recoverable ACT FINANCE, BANKING, AND ACCOUNTING *Advance Corporation Tax* which can be set against the corporation tax payable for the period

recoverable amount FINANCE, BANKING, AND ACCOUNTING the value of an asset, either the price it would fetch if sold, or its value to the company when used, whichever is the larger figure

recovery ECONOMICS the return of a country to economic health after a crash or a depression

recovery fund FINANCE, BANKING, AND ACCOUNTING a fund that invests in recovery stock

recovery stock FINANCE, BANKING, AND ACCOUNTING a stock that has fallen in price because of poor business performance, but is now expected to climb as a result of an improvement in the company's prospects

recruitment HR & PERSONNEL the activity of employing workers to fill vacancies or enrolling new members. Employment recruitment is composed of several stages: verifying that a vacancy exists; drawing up a job specification; finding candidates; selecting them by *interviewing* and other means such as conducting a *psychometric test*; and making a job offer. Effective recruitment is important in achieving high organizational performance and minimizing labor turnover. Employees may be recruited either externally or internally.

rectification note FINANCE, BANKING, AND ACCOUNTING the authorization for more work to be done to improve a product which did not originally meet the required standard

recurring billing transaction E-COMMERCE an electronic payment facility based on the automatic charging of a customer's credit card in each payment period

recurring payments E-COMMERCE an electronic payment facility that permits a merchant to process multiple authorizations by the same customer either as multiple payments for a fixed amount or recurring billings for varying amounts

red FINANCE, BANKING, AND ACCOUNTING the color of debit or overdrawn balances in some bank statements

in the red FINANCE, BANKING, AND ACCOUNTING in debt, or losing money (*slang*)

Red Book (*U.K.*) FINANCE, BANKING, AND ACCOUNTING a copy of the Chancellor of the Exchequer's speech published on the day of the Budget. It can be regarded as the country's financial statement and report.

Red chips FINANCE, BANKING, AND ACCOUNTING good risk-free Chinese companies

red day FINANCE, BANKING, AND ACCOUNTING an unprofitable day (*slang*)

Reddin, **William James** (*b.* 1930) GENERAL MANAGEMENT British-born Canadian academic. Best known for his research on ***three-dimensional management***, a development of the work of ***Robert Blake*** and ***Jane Mouton*** explained in *Managerial Effectiveness* (1970).

redeemable bond FINANCE, BANKING, AND ACCOUNTING see ***callable bond***

redeemable gilt FINANCE, BANKING, AND ACCOUNTING see ***gilt-edged security***

redeemable government stock FINANCE, BANKING, AND ACCOUNTING stock which can be redeemed for cash at some time in the future

redeemable preferred stock FINANCE, BANKING, AND ACCOUNTING see ***callable preferred stock***

redeemable security FINANCE, BANKING, AND ACCOUNTING a security which can be redeemed at its face value at a certain date in the future

redemption FINANCE, BANKING, AND ACCOUNTING repayment, this term being most frequently used in connection with preferred stock, bonds, and debentures

redemption date FINANCE, BANKING, AND ACCOUNTING the date on which a redeemable security is due to be repaid

redeployment HR & PERSONNEL the movement of employees by their employer from one location or task to another. Redeployment is often used to minimize layoffs, ensure the fulfillment of a specific order, or ensure the most cost-effective use of employees.

red eye FINANCE, BANKING, AND ACCOUNTING see ***pathfinder prospectus*** (*slang*)

redistributive effect FINANCE, BANKING, AND ACCOUNTING the tendency toward equalization of people's wealth that results from a progressive tax or benefit

red screen market FINANCE, BANKING, AND ACCOUNTING in the United Kingdom, a market where the prices are down and are being shown as red on the dealing screens

red tape GENERAL MANAGEMENT excessive bureaucracy

reducing balance depreciation FINANCE, BANKING, AND ACCOUNTING see ***depreciation***

redundancy (*U.K.*) HR & PERSONNEL = ***severance***

redundancy package (*U.K.*) HR & PERSONNEL = ***severance package***

redundant capacity OPERATIONS & PRODUCTION see ***surplus capacity***

reengineering GENERAL MANAGEMENT see ***business process reengineering***

reference
1 HR & PERSONNEL a statement of facts and opinions concerning the qualifications, skills, capabilities, personal qualities, conduct, and attitudes of a person, usually a job applicant. Employers supplying references have a legal obligation to take reasonable care that the information provided is accurate.
2 FINANCE, BANKING, AND ACCOUNTING see ***banker's reference***

reference population STATISTICS a standard against which a statistical population under study can be compared

reference rate FINANCE, BANKING, AND ACCOUNTING a benchmark rate, for example, a bank's own base rate or LIBOR. Lending rates are often expressed as a margin over a reference rate.

reference site E-COMMERCE a customer site where a new technology is being used successfully

referred share FINANCE, BANKING, AND ACCOUNTING a stock that is ***ex dividend***

refer to drawer (*U.K.*) FINANCE, BANKING, AND ACCOUNTING to refuse to pay a check because the account from which it is drawn has too little money in it. Abbr. **RD**

refer to drawer please represent FINANCE, BANKING, AND ACCOUNTING in the United Kingdom, written on a check by the paying banker to indicate that there are currently insufficient funds to meet the payment, but that the bank believes sufficient funds will be available shortly. See also ***refer to drawer***. Abbr. **RDPR**

refinance FINANCE, BANKING, AND ACCOUNTING to replace one loan with another, especially at a lower rate of interest

refinancing FINANCE, BANKING, AND ACCOUNTING
1 the process of taking out a loan to pay off other loans
2 a loan taken out for the purpose of repaying another loan or loans

reflation ECONOMICS a method of reducing unemployment by increasing an economy's ***aggregate demand***. See also ***recession***

refugee capital FINANCE, BANKING, AND ACCOUNTING people and resources that come into a country because they have been forced to leave their own country for economic or political reasons

refund MARKETING the reimbursement of the purchase price of a good or service, for reasons such as manufacturing flaws or dissatisfaction with the service provided

regeneration GENERAL MANAGEMENT the redevelopment of industrial or business areas that have suffered decline, in order to increase employment and business activity

regional fund FINANCE, BANKING, AND ACCOUNTING a mutual fund that invests in the markets of a geographic region

registered bond FINANCE, BANKING, AND ACCOUNTING a bond, the ownership of which is recorded on the books of the issuer

registered broker FINANCE, BANKING, AND ACCOUNTING a broker registered on a particular exchange

registered capital FINANCE, BANKING, AND ACCOUNTING see ***authorized capital***

registered name FINANCE, BANKING, AND ACCOUNTING in the United Kingdom, the name of a company as it is registered at Companies House. It must appear, along with the company's registered number and office, on all its letterheads and orders. See also ***company corporation***

registered number FINANCE, BANKING, AND ACCOUNTING in the United Kingdom, a unique number assigned to a company registered at Companies House. It must appear, along with the company's registered name and office on all its letterheads and orders. See also ***company corporation***

registered security FINANCE, BANKING, AND ACCOUNTING a security where the holder's name

is recorded in the books of the issuer. See also *nominee*

registered share FINANCE, BANKING, AND ACCOUNTING a stock, the ownership of which is recorded on the books of the issuer

registered share capital FINANCE, BANKING, AND ACCOUNTING see *authorized share capital*

registered trademark GENERAL MANAGEMENT see *trademark*

register of companies FINANCE, BANKING, AND ACCOUNTING in the United Kingdom, the list of companies maintained at Companies House. See also *company corporation*

register of directors and secretaries FINANCE, BANKING, AND ACCOUNTING a record that every *registered company* in the United Kingdom must maintain of the names and residential addresses of directors and the company secretary together with their nationality, occupation, and details of other directorships held. Public companies must also record the date of birth of their directors. The record must be kept at the company's registered office and be available for inspection by stockholders without charge and by members of the public for a nominal fee.

register of directors' interests FINANCE, BANKING, AND ACCOUNTING a record that every *registered company* in the United Kingdom must maintain of the stocks and other *securities* that have been issued by the company and are held by its directors. It has to be made available for inspection during the company's *annual meeting*.

register of stockholders FINANCE, BANKING, AND ACCOUNTING a list of the stockholders in a particular company

Registrar of Companies (*U.K.*) FINANCE, BANKING, AND ACCOUNTING GENERAL MANAGEMENT the person charged with the duty of holding and registering the official startup and constitutional documents of all *registered companies* in the United Kingdom

registration statement FINANCE, BANKING, AND ACCOUNTING in the United States, a document that corporations planning to issue securities to the public have to submit to the Securities and Exchange Commission. It features details of the issuer's management, financial status, and activities, and the purpose of the issue. See also *shelf registration*

registration sticker FINANCE, BANKING, AND ACCOUNTING a prominent sticker displayed inside the window of a motor vehicle to prove that the owner has paid road tax on it. U.K. term *tax disc*

regression analysis STATISTICS a *forecasting* technique used to establish the relationship between quantifiable variables. In regression analysis, data on dependent and independent variables is plotted on a scatter graph or diagram, and trends are indicated through a line of best fit. The use of a single independent variable is known as *simple regression analysis*, while the use of two or more independent variables is called *multiple regression analysis*.

regressive tax FINANCE, BANKING, AND ACCOUNTING a tax with a rate that decreases proportionally as the value of the item being taxed, especially income, rises. Social security taxes are regressive. See also *progressive tax*, *proportional tax*

regulated superannuation fund (*ANZ*) FINANCE, BANKING, AND ACCOUNTING an Australian superannuation fund that is regulated by legislation and therefore qualifies for tax concessions. To attain this status, a fund must either show that its main function is the provision of pensions, or adopt a corporate trustee structure.

regulation FINANCE, BANKING, AND ACCOUNTING the use of laws or rules stipulated by a government or regulatory body, such as the Securities and Exchange Commission, to provide orderly procedures and to protect consumers and investors

regulator GENERAL MANAGEMENT an official or body that monitors the behavior of companies and the level of competition in particular markets, for example, telecommunications or energy

regulatory body FINANCE, BANKING, AND ACCOUNTING GENERAL MANAGEMENT an independent organization, usually established by government, that regulates the activities of companies in an industry

regulatory pricing risk FINANCE, BANKING, AND ACCOUNTING the risk an insurance company faces that a government will regulate the prices it can charge

reinsurance FINANCE, BANKING, AND ACCOUNTING a method of reducing risk by transferring all or part of an insurance policy to another insurer

reinsurer FINANCE, BANKING, AND ACCOUNTING see *reinsurance*

reintermediation E-COMMERCE the reintroduction of intermediaries found in traditional retail channels. See also *disintermediation*

reinvestment rate FINANCE, BANKING, AND ACCOUNTING the interest rate at which an investor is able to reinvest income received from another investment

reinvestment risk FINANCE, BANKING, AND ACCOUNTING the risk that it will not be possible to invest the proceeds of an investment at as high a rate as they earned

reinvestment unit trust FINANCE, BANKING, AND ACCOUNTING a mutual fund in the United Kingdom that uses dividends to buy more shares in the company issuing them

rejects FINANCE, BANKING, AND ACCOUNTING OPERATIONS & PRODUCTION units of output which fail a set quality standard and are subsequently rectified, sold as substandard, or disposed of as scrap

relational database GENERAL MANAGEMENT a computer database in which different types of data are linked for analysis

relationship management MARKETING the process of fostering good relations with customers to build loyalty and increase sales

relationship marketing MARKETING see *pyramid selling*

relative income hypothesis ECONOMICS the theory that consumers are concerned less with their absolute living standards than with consumption relative to other consumers

relaxation allowance GENERAL MANAGEMENT see *standard time*

release E-COMMERCE a version of a software program that has been modified. Release 1.0 would be followed by release 1.1 after minor modification, or release 2.0 after major changes to the program.

relevant interest (*ANZ*) FINANCE, BANKING, AND ACCOUNTING the legal status held by stock investors who can legally dispose of, or influence the disposal of, stocks

reliability GENERAL MANAGEMENT the quality of being fit for an intended purpose over a continued period of time

reliability centered maintenance OPERATIONS & PRODUCTION a *maintenance* system that focuses on ensuring equipment is always functioning reliably. Reliability centered main-

tenance involves assessing each piece of equipment or other asset individually and in the context of how it is being used—for example, frequency of use and volume of output. Analysis is made of its weak points and a *preventive maintenance* schedule is drawn up taking them into account.

relocation GENERAL MANAGEMENT the transfer of a business from one location to another. Relocation occurs for a variety of reasons, including the need for more space, the desire to centralize operations, or to be nearer to suppliers, customers, or raw materials.

relocation package FINANCE, BANKING, AND ACCOUNTING payments made by an employer to an employee when the employee is asked to move to a new area in order to work. Some of these payments may be exempt from tax if they are below the minimum level.

remitting bank FINANCE, BANKING, AND ACCOUNTING see *collecting bank*

remuneration HR & PERSONNEL see *earnings*

remuneration package HR & PERSONNEL the salary, pension contributions, bonuses, and other forms of payment or benefits that an employer gives a member of staff

renounceable document FINANCE, BANKING, AND ACCOUNTING written proof of ownership for a limited period, for example, a letter of allotment. See also *letter of renunciation*

renting back FINANCE, BANKING, AND ACCOUNTING see *sale and leaseback*

renunciation FINANCE, BANKING, AND ACCOUNTING see *letter of renunciation*

reorder level FINANCE, BANKING, AND ACCOUNTING a level of stock at which a replenishment order should be placed. Traditional "optimizing" systems use a variation on the computation of maximum usage multiplied by maximum lead, which builds in a measure of safety stock and minimizes the likelihood of a stock out.

reorganization bond FINANCE, BANKING, AND ACCOUNTING in the United States, a bond issued to creditors of a business that is undergoing a Chapter 11 form of reorganization. Interest is normally only paid when the company can make the payments from its earnings.

repayment mortgage FINANCE, BANKING, AND ACCOUNTING see *mortgage*, *amortized mortgage*

repeat business MARKETING the placing of order after order with the same supplier. Repeat business can be implemented by an agreement between the customer and supplier for purchase on a regular basis. It is often used where there are small numbers of customers, or high volumes per product and low product variety. There is market competition for the first order only, and customization is usually available for the initial purchase only. Sales and marketing have a diminished role once the business has been gained.

repertory grid GENERAL MANAGEMENT a technique for gathering information on an individual's personal constructs or perceptions of their environment through mapping interview responses to a matrix. The repertory grid was initially used and developed by clinical psychologists in the 1930s. It has business applications in job analysis, performance measurement, *evaluation of training*, questionnaire design, and *market research*.

repetitive strain injury HR & PERSONNEL damage caused to muscles or tendons as the result of prolonged repetitive movements or actions. Repetitive strain injury is most commonly associated with injury to the wrist or arms through the use of computer keyboards. Abbr. *RSI*

replacement cost FINANCE, BANKING, AND ACCOUNTING the cost of replacing an asset or service with its current equivalent

replacement cost accounting FINANCE, BANKING, AND ACCOUNTING a method of valuing company assets based on their replacement cost

replacement ratio ECONOMICS the ratio of the total resources received when unemployed to those received when in employment

replenishment system OPERATIONS & PRODUCTION an inventory control system that relies on accurate estimates of usage rates and delivery lead times to allow orders to be completed and to ensure stock does not run out. The timing of a replenishment order is crucial, as *buffer stock* should not be allowed to run out during the time it takes for a delivery to arrive.

repo FINANCE, BANKING, AND ACCOUNTING
1 repurchase agreement (*slang*)
2 an open market operation undertaken by the Federal Reserve to purchase securities and agree to sell them back at a stated price on a future date
3 (*U.K.*) a Bank of England repurchase agreement with market makers in gilt-edged securities. It is used to provide securities for short positions.

report GENERAL MANAGEMENT a written or verbal statement analyzing a particular issue, incident, or state of affairs, usually with some form of recommendations for future action

reporting entity FINANCE, BANKING, AND ACCOUNTING any organization, such as a limited company, which reports its accounts to its stockholders

repositioning MARKETING a marketing strategy that changes aspects of a product or brand in order to change *market position* and alter consumer perceptions

repossession FINANCE, BANKING, AND ACCOUNTING the return of goods purchased through an installment plan when the purchaser fails to make the required regular payments. See also *recourse agreement*

repudiation FINANCE, BANKING, AND ACCOUNTING a refusal to pay or acknowledge a debt

repurchase FINANCE, BANKING, AND ACCOUNTING of a fund manager, to buy the shares in a mutual fund when an investor sells

repurchase agreement FINANCE, BANKING, AND ACCOUNTING in the bond and money markets, a spot sale of a security combined with its repurchase at a later date and pre-agreed price. In effect, the buyer is lending money to the seller for the duration of the transaction and using the security as collateral. Dealers finance their positions by using repurchase agreements. Also known as *repo*

request form E-COMMERCE an interactive Web page that accepts user-provided data—for example, name, address, or shipping information—that can be saved for recurring use or sent by e-mail to the page owner

required rate of return FINANCE, BANKING, AND ACCOUNTING the minimum return for a proposed project investment to be acceptable

required reserves FINANCE, BANKING, AND ACCOUNTING the minimum reserves that member banks of the Federal Reserve System have to maintain

requisition FINANCE, BANKING, AND ACCOUNTING an official order form used by companies when purchasing a product or service

resale price maintenance (*U.K.*) MARKETING an agreement between suppliers or manufacturers and retailers, restricting the price that retailers can ask for a product or service. Resale price maintenance was designed to enable all retailers to make a profit. The Resale Prices

Act now prevents this practice on the grounds that it is uncompetitive. Now, unless they can prove that resale price maintenance is in the public interest, manufacturers can only recommend a retail price. Abbr. *RPM*

research FINANCE, BANKING, AND ACCOUNTING the examination of statistics and other information regarding past, present, and future trends or performance that enables analysts to recommend to investors which stocks to buy or sell in order to maximize their return and minimize their risk. It may be used either in the top-down approach (where the investor evaluates a market, then an industry, and finally a specific company) or the bottom-up approach (where the investor selects a company and confirms his or her findings by evaluating the company's sector and then its market). Careful research is likely to help investors find the best deals, in particular *value shares* or *growth equities*. See also *technical analysis*

research and development OPERATIONS & PRODUCTION the pursuit of new knowledge and ideas and the application of that knowledge to exploit new opportunities to the commercial advantage of a business. The research and development functions are often grouped together to form a division or department within an organization. Abbr. *R&D*

research park GENERAL MANAGEMENT an area developed as a location for high-tech or research-based companies. Usually developed by a university or local government, a research park is often in the same locality as a higher education establishment. U.K. term *science park*

reserve account E-COMMERCE see *holdback*

reserve bank FINANCE, BANKING, AND ACCOUNTING a bank such as a Federal Reserve bank that holds the reserves of other banks

Reserve Bank of Australia FINANCE, BANKING, AND ACCOUNTING Australia's central bank, which is responsible for managing the Commonwealth's monetary policy, ensuring financial stability, and printing and distributing currency. Abbr. *RBA*

Reserve Bank of New Zealand FINANCE, BANKING, AND ACCOUNTING New Zealand's central bank, which is responsible for managing the government's monetary policy, ensuring financial stability, and printing and distributing currency. Abbr. *RBNZ*

reserve currency FINANCE, BANKING, AND ACCOUNTING foreign currency that a central bank holds for use in international trade

reserve for fluctuations FINANCE, BANKING, AND ACCOUNTING money set aside to allow for changes in the values of currencies

reserve price FINANCE, BANKING, AND ACCOUNTING a price for a particular lot, set by the vendor, below which an auctioneer may not sell

reserve ratio FINANCE, BANKING, AND ACCOUNTING the proportion of a bank's deposits that must be kept in reserve.

In the United Kingdom and in certain European countries, there is no compulsory ratio, although banks will have their own internal measures and targets to be able to repay customer deposits as they forecast they will be required. In the United States, specified percentages of deposits—established by the Federal Reserve Board—must be kept by banks in a non-interest-bearing account at one of the twelve Federal Reserve Banks located throughout the country.

In Europe, the reserve requirement of an institution is calculated by multiplying the reserve ratio for each category of items in the reserve base, set by the European Central Bank, with the amount of those items in the institution's balance sheets. These figures vary according to the institution.

The required reserve ratio in the United States is set by federal law, and depends on the amount of checkable deposits a bank holds. The first $44.3 million of deposits are subject to a 3% reserve requirement. Deposits in excess of $44.3 million are subject to 10% reserve requirement. These breakpoints are reviewed annually in accordance with money supply growth. No reserves are required against certificates of deposit or savings accounts.

The reserve ratio requirement limits a bank's lending to a certain fraction of its demand deposits. The current rule allows a bank to issue loans in an amount equal to 90% of such deposits, holding 10% in reserve. The reserves can be held in any combination of till money and deposit at a Federal Reserve Bank.

reserve requirements FINANCE, BANKING, AND ACCOUNTING the requirements an agency levies on a nation's banks to hold reserves

reserves FINANCE, BANKING, AND ACCOUNTING
1 the money that a bank holds to ensure that it can satisfy its depositors' demands for withdrawals
2 profits made by a company in previous accounting periods that have not yet been made available to stockholders
3 a sum of money held by an individual or company to finance unexpected business opportunities. See also *war chest*

residuary legatee FINANCE, BANKING, AND ACCOUNTING the person to whom a testator's estate is left after specific bequests have been made

resignation HR & PERSONNEL the act of voluntarily leaving a job. Resignation is normally signaled by a formal letter of resignation. On acceptance, a *notice period* is usually served before the employee can leave.

resizing HR & PERSONNEL see *downsizing*

resolution GENERAL MANAGEMENT a proposal put to a meeting, for example, an Annual Meeting of shareholders, on which those present and eligible can vote. See also *extraordinary resolution*

resource allocation OPERATIONS & PRODUCTION the process of assigning human and material resources to projects to ensure that they are used in the optimum way. Resource allocation is used in conjunction with *network analysis* techniques such as *critical-path method*. Basic data assembled for a project is displayed as a *bar chart* with start and finish times and resources required for each day of the project being easily identifiable. If there is a mismatch between planned resources and those available, resources can be reallocated or smoothed by manipulating start and finish times, or changing activities around. Resource allocation is usually computerized.

resource driver
1 GENERAL MANAGEMENT see *cost driver*
2 FINANCE, BANKING, AND ACCOUNTING a measurement unit which is used to assign resource costs to activity cost pools based on some measures of usage. For example, it may be used to assign office occupancy costs to purchasing or accounting services within a company.

resource productivity GENERAL MANAGEMENT an environmentally friendly approach to production based on increasing the productivity of resources to reduce waste

resources OPERATIONS & PRODUCTION anything that is available to an organization to help it achieve its purpose. Resources are often categorized into finance, property, premises, equipment, people, and raw materials.

response bias STATISTICS the disparity between information that a survey respondent provides and data analysis, for example, a person claiming to watch little television but giving answers showing 30 hours' weekly viewing

response level MARKETING a measurement of response to an advertising or marketing campaign

response marketing E-COMMERCE in e-marketing, the process of managing responses or leads from the time they are received through to conversion to sale

response mechanism MARKETING a means of reply such as a coupon or reply card in an advertisement or mail shot by which customers can request further information

response rate STATISTICS the proportion of subjects in a statistical study who respond to a researcher's questionnaire

response surface methodology STATISTICS mathematical and statistical techniques that are used to improve product design systems

responsibility GENERAL MANAGEMENT the duty to conduct certain activities and be accountable for them to others

responsibility accounting FINANCE, BANKING, AND ACCOUNTING the keeping of financial records with an emphasis on who is responsible for each item

responsibility center FINANCE, BANKING, AND ACCOUNTING a department or organizational function whose performance is the direct responsibility of a specific manager

restated balance sheet FINANCE, BANKING, AND ACCOUNTING a balance sheet reframed to serve a particular purpose, such as highlighting depreciation on assets

rest break HR & PERSONNEL a period of time during the working day when an employee is allowed to be away from their workstation for a rest or meal break. Many countries have statutory regulations governing the frequency and length of rest breaks related to the hours worked in a day. Regulations also may cover the requirement for a *rest period* over a working week or month.

rest period HR & PERSONNEL the length of time between periods of work that an employee is entitled to have for rest. Many countries have statutory regulations governing the rights of employees to periods of rest over daily, weekly, and, sometimes, monthly timescales. Different allowances may be given to younger workers. In addition, employees may be entitled to *rest breaks* during the working day.

restraint of trade GENERAL MANAGEMENT HR & PERSONNEL a term in a contract of employment that restricts a person from carrying on their trade or profession if they leave an organization. Generally illegal, it is usually intended to prevent key employees from leaving an organization to establish a competing organization.

restricted tender FINANCE, BANKING, AND ACCOUNTING an offer to buy stock only under specified conditions

restrictive covenant FINANCE, BANKING, AND ACCOUNTING an agreement by a borrower not to sell an asset which he or she has used as collateral for a loan

restructuring GENERAL MANAGEMENT see *corporate restructuring*

result-driven GENERAL MANAGEMENT relating to a form of *corporate strategy* focused on outcomes and achievements. A result-driven organization concentrates on meeting objectives, delivering to the required time, cost, and quality, and holds performance to be more important than *procedures*.

résumé HR & PERSONNEL a document that provides a summary of personal career history, skills, and experience. A résumé is usually prepared to aid in a job application. A job advertisement may ask either for a résumé or instead may require a candidate to complete an *application form*.

Every résumé should include the following: the jobseeker's name and contact details; a clear and concise description of his or her career objective; some kind of outline of work experience; and a list of education and degrees. It is important to customize a résumé to the type of job or career being applied for, and to make sure it has impact: a hiring manager receives an average of over 120 résumés for every job opening.

There are four basic types of résumé: the chronological, the functional, the targeted, and the capabilities résumé. A chronological résumé is useful for people who stay in the same field and do not make major career changes. They should start with and focus on the most recent positions held. A functional résumé is the preferred choice for those seeking their first professional job, or those making a major career change. It is based around 3–5 paragraphs, each emphasizing and illustrating a particular skill or accomplishment. A targeted résumé is useful for jobseekers who are very clear about their job direction and need to make an impressive case for a specific job. Like a functional résumé, it should be based around several capabilities and accomplishments that are relevant to the target job, focusing on action and results. A capabilities résumé is used for people applying for a specific job within their current organization. It should focus on 5–8 skills and accomplishments achieved with the company.

The format of a résumé should also be considered—whether it is to be printed out, incorporated into an e-mail, posted on a Web site, or burned onto a CD-ROM. Different layout and design elements, such as the choice of fonts or inclusion of multimedia, are suitable for each medium, and should be thought through carefully. U.K. term *CV*

retail banking FINANCE, BANKING, AND ACCOUNTING services provided by commercial banks to individuals (as opposed to business customers) that include current accounts, deposit and savings accounts, as well as credit cards, mortgages, and investments. In the United Kingdom, although this service was traditionally provided by high street banks, separate organizations, albeit offshoots of established financial institutions, are now providing Internet and telephone banking services.

retail cooperative GENERAL MANAGEMENT a concern for the collective purchase and sale of goods by a group who share profits or benefits. Retail cooperatives were the first offshoot of the *cooperative movement* and profits were originally shared among members through dividend payments proportionate to a member's purchases.

retailer MARKETING OPERATIONS & PRODUCTION an outlet through which products or services are sold to customers. Retailers can be put into three broad groups: independent traders, multiple stores, or *retail cooperatives*.

retail investor FINANCE, BANKING, AND ACCOUNTING an investor who buys and sells stock in retail organizations

retail management MARKETING marketing or financial support aimed at improving the performance of retail outlets

retail price MARKETING a price charged to customers who buy in limited quantities

retail price index ECONOMICS a listing of the average levels of prices charged by retailers for goods or services. The retail price index is calculated on a set variety of items, and usually excludes luxury goods. It is updated monthly, and provides a running indicator of changing costs. Abbr *RPI*

retained earnings FINANCE, BANKING, AND ACCOUNTING the share of a company's profits remaining after the distribution of dividends that

is kept as capital. U.K. term *earnings retained*

retained profits FINANCE, BANKING, AND ACCOUNTING the amount of profit remaining after tax and distribution to stockholders that is retained in a business and used as a reserve or as a means of financing expansion or investment. Also known as *earnings retained*

retirement HR & PERSONNEL the voluntary or forced termination of employment because of age, illness, or disability. *Retirement age* is often stipulated in the *contract of employment*. Differences between the retirement ages of men and women are no longer allowed in many countries. Employees may take *early retirement* from their employer, or may, with the agreement of their employer, take gradual, or *phased retirement*. A *pension* may be drawn on reaching retirement age.

retirement age HR & PERSONNEL see *retirement*

retirement annuity FINANCE, BANKING, AND ACCOUNTING an annuity paid to a person when they reach a certain age, from funds paid into a retirement annuity contract

retirement benefits FINANCE, BANKING, AND ACCOUNTING benefits which are payable by a pension plan to a person on retirement

retirement pension FINANCE, BANKING, AND ACCOUNTING see *pension*

retraining HR & PERSONNEL *training* designed to enable employees to perform a job that their previous training has not equipped them for or to adapt to changes in the workplace. Retraining may be needed when new methods or equipment are introduced or when jobs for which employees have trained are phased out. It may also be provided by employers or governments for employees who have been laid off and are no longer able to find employment using the skills they already possess. The need for retraining may arise because of a decline in a particular industry sector or because of rapid technological change.

retrenchment FINANCE, BANKING, AND ACCOUNTING the reduction of costs in order to improve profitability

retro logistics OPERATIONS & PRODUCTION see *reverse logistics*

retrospective study STATISTICS a study that examines data collected before it began, for example, to measure the risk factors that predispose people to disease

return FINANCE, BANKING, AND ACCOUNTING
1 the income derived from an activity
2 see *rate of return*
3 see *tax return*

return logistics OPERATIONS & PRODUCTION see *reverse logistics*

return on assets FINANCE, BANKING, AND ACCOUNTING a measure of profitability calculated by expressing a company's net income as a percentage of total assets. Abbr. *ROA*

return on capital employed *or* **return on capital** FINANCE, BANKING, AND ACCOUNTING in the United Kingdom, a ratio of the net profit made in a fiscal year in relation to the capital employed, in a formulation similar to that of ROE. It is used as a measure of business profitability. Abbr. *ROCE, ROC*

return on equity FINANCE, BANKING, AND ACCOUNTING the ratio of a company's net income as a percentage of shareholders' funds.

Return on equity is easy to calculate and is applicable to the majority of industries. It is probably the most widely used measure of how well a company is performing for its shareholders.

It is calculated by dividing the net income shown on the income statement (usually of the past year) by shareholders' equity, which appears on the balance sheet:

$$\frac{\text{Net income}}{\text{Owners' equity}} \times 100\% = \text{Return on equity}$$

For example, if net income is \$450 and equity is \$2,500, then:

$$\frac{450}{2{,}500} = 0.18 \times 100\% = 18\% \text{ return on equity}$$

Return on equity for most companies should be in double figures; investors often look for 15% or higher, while a return of 20% or more is considered excellent. Seasoned investors also review five-year average ROE, to gauge consistency. Abbr. *ROE*

return on investment FINANCE, BANKING, AND ACCOUNTING a ratio of the profit made in a financial year as a percentage of an investment. Abbr. *ROI*

return on net assets FINANCE, BANKING, AND ACCOUNTING a ratio of the profit made in a fiscal year as a percentage of the assets of a company. Abbr. *RONA*

return on sales FINANCE, BANKING, AND ACCOUNTING a company's operating profit or loss as a percentage of total sales for a given period, typically a year. See also *profit margin*. Abbr. *ROS*

returns to scale ECONOMICS the proportionate increase in a country's or firm's output as a result of increases in all its inputs

revaluation ECONOMICS a rise in the value of a country's currency in relation to other currencies

revaluation method FINANCE, BANKING, AND ACCOUNTING a method of calculating the depreciation of assets by which the asset is depreciated by the difference in its value at the end of the year over its value at the beginning of the year

revaluation of assets FINANCE, BANKING, AND ACCOUNTING the revaluation of a company's *assets* to take account of inflation or changes in value since the assets were acquired. The change in value is credited to the revaluation reserve account.

revaluation of currency FINANCE, BANKING, AND ACCOUNTING an increase in the value of a currency in relation to others. In situations where there is a floating exchange rate, a currency will normally find its own level automatically but this will not happen if there is a fixed exchange rate. Should a government have persistent balance of payment surpluses, it may exceptionally decide to revalue its currency, making imports cheaper but its exports more expensive.

revaluation reserve FINANCE, BANKING, AND ACCOUNTING money set aside to account for the fact that the value of assets may vary as a result of accounting in different currencies

revaluation reserve account FINANCE, BANKING, AND ACCOUNTING see *revaluation of assets*

Revans, Reginald William (1907–2003) GENERAL MANAGEMENT British educator and academic. Originator of *action learning*, explained in the book of the same name (1980), which rejected the traditional approach to *management education* in favor of learning from sharing problems with others. See thinker *Reg Revans*

revenue FINANCE, BANKING, AND ACCOUNTING the income generated by a product or service over a period of time

revenue account FINANCE, BANKING, AND ACCOUNTING an accounting system which records the revenue and expenditure incurred by a company during its normal business

revenue anticipation note FINANCE, BANKING, AND ACCOUNTING a government-issued debt instrument for which expected income from taxation is collateral

revenue bond FINANCE, BANKING, AND ACCOUNTING a bond that a government issues, to be repaid from the money made from the project financed with it

revenue center FINANCE, BANKING, AND ACCOUNTING a center devoted to raising revenue but with no responsibility for costs, for example, a sales center

revenue expenditure FINANCE, BANKING, AND ACCOUNTING expenditure on purchasing stock (but not on capital items) which is then sold during the current accounting period

revenue ledger FINANCE, BANKING, AND ACCOUNTING a record of all the income received by an organization

revenue reserves FINANCE, BANKING, AND ACCOUNTING retained earnings which are shown in the company's balance sheet as part of the stockholders' funds

revenue sharing FINANCE, BANKING, AND ACCOUNTING
1 distribution to states by the federal government of money that it collects in taxes
2 the distribution of income within limited partnerships

revenue stamp FINANCE, BANKING, AND ACCOUNTING a stamp that a government issues to certify that somebody has paid a tax

revenue tariff FINANCE, BANKING, AND ACCOUNTING a tax levied on imports or exports to raise revenue for a national government

reversal stop FINANCE, BANKING, AND ACCOUNTING a price at which a trader stops buying and starts selling a security, or vice versa

reverse bear hug GENERAL MANAGEMENT see *bear hug*

reverse commuter GENERAL MANAGEMENT a commuter who travels to work in the opposite direction to the majority of people (*slang*)

reverse distribution OPERATIONS & PRODUCTION see *reverse logistics*

reverse engineering OPERATIONS & PRODUCTION the decomposition and analysis of a product to establish how it was put together, and the costs of production. Reverse engineering enables a company to redesign or otherwise develop a product. It also enables competitors to analyze the composition, technology, and development of rival products. Also known as *decompilation*

reverse leverage FINANCE, BANKING, AND ACCOUNTING
1 the negative flow of cash
2 the borrowing of money at a rate of interest higher than the expected rate of return on investing the money borrowed

reverse logistics OPERATIONS & PRODUCTION the flow of goods in the opposite direction to the traditional flow of the *supply chain*, from producer to consumer, back to a point of recovery or disposal. Reverse logistics is a branch of *logistics* which involves the collection, transportation and redistribution or disposal of returned, unwanted, damaged, or surplus goods. This may be through reuse, resale, repair, or refurbishment. The term also covers the management of products at the end of their life which contain a hazardous substance needing special treatment for environmental reasons. However, it differs from waste management in that the emphasis is on recapturing value through redistribution, cannibalization, or recycling, rather than safe disposal. Also called *retro logistics*, *return logistics*, *reverse distribution*

reverse mentoring HR & PERSONNEL the *mentoring* of senior personnel by younger people. Reverse mentoring aims to help older, more senior people learn from the knowledge of younger people, usually in the field of information technology, computing, and Internet communications.

reverse mortgage FINANCE, BANKING, AND ACCOUNTING a financial arrangement in which a lender such as a bank takes over a mortgage and then pays an annuity to the homeowner

reverse split FINANCE, BANKING, AND ACCOUNTING the issuing to stockholders of a fraction of one share for every share that they own. See also *split*. Also known as *consolidation*

reverse takeover GENERAL MANAGEMENT the *takeover* of a large company by a smaller one, or the takeover of a public company by a private one

reversionary annuity FINANCE, BANKING, AND ACCOUNTING an annuity paid to someone on the death of another person

revolving charge account FINANCE, BANKING, AND ACCOUNTING a charge account with a company for use in buying that company's goods with *revolving credit*

revolving credit FINANCE, BANKING, AND ACCOUNTING a credit facility which allows the borrower, within an overall credit limit and for a set period, to borrow or repay debt as required

revolving fund FINANCE, BANKING, AND ACCOUNTING a fund the resources of which are replenished from the revenue of the projects that it finances

revolving loan FINANCE, BANKING, AND ACCOUNTING a loan facility whereby the borrower can choose the number and timing of withdrawals against their bank loan and any money repaid may be reborrowed at a future date. Such loans are available both to businesses and personal customers.

reward management HR & PERSONNEL the establishment, maintenance, and development of a system that rewards the work done by employees. Reward management involves offering not only *base pay*, but also an *incentive plan* and *fringe benefits*. Levels of reward may be based on different criteria. Some involve *performance appraisal* to determine whether an employee merits a certain reward, while others may be dependent on length of service, type of job, or team or company performance. The notion of a reward system is gradually replacing the traditional idea of a standard pay system, as it incorporates all aspects of employee compensation into one package.

Ricardo, David (1772–1823) GENERAL MANAGEMENT British economist. Developer of the concept of *comparative advantage*, as explained in his book *Principles of Political Economy* (1820).

rich media E-COMMERCE technology that can integrate audio, video, and high-resolution graphics

Ridderstråle, Jonas (1966) GENERAL MANAGEMENT Swedish academic. See also *Nordstrom, Kjell*

ride the curve E-COMMERCE to take advantage of rapid growth in demand for a new technology as it becomes widely adopted (*slang*)

rigged market FINANCE, BANKING, AND ACCOUNTING a market where two or more parties are buying and selling securities among themselves to give the impression of active trading with the intention of attracting investors to purchase the stocks. This practice is illegal in most jurisdictions.

right first time OPERATIONS & PRODUCTION a concept integral to *total quality management*, where there is a commitment to customers not to make mistakes. The approach requires

employees at all levels to commit to, and take responsibility for, achieving this goal. *Quality circles* are sometimes used as a method to help in this process.

rights issue FINANCE, BANKING, AND ACCOUNTING the raising of new capital by giving existing stockholders the right to purchase new shares or *debentures* in proportion to their current holdings. These stocks are normally issued at a discount to market price. A stockholder not wishing to take up a rights issue may sell the rights. Also known as *rights offer*

rightsizing GENERAL MANAGEMENT *corporate restructuring*, or *rationalization*, with the goal of reducing costs and improving efficiency and effectiveness. Rightsizing is often used as a euphemism for *downsizing*, or *delayering*, with the suggestion that it is not as far-reaching. Rightsizing can also be used to describe increasing the size of an organization, perhaps as an attempt to correct a previous downsizing, or delayering, exercise.

rights offer FINANCE, BANKING, AND ACCOUNTING see *rights issue*

rights offering FINANCE, BANKING, AND ACCOUNTING an offering for sale of a *rights issue*

ring FINANCE, BANKING, AND ACCOUNTING
1 a trading pit
2 a trading session on the London Metal Exchange

ring-fence FINANCE, BANKING, AND ACCOUNTING
1 to set aside a sum of money for a specific project
2 to allow one company within a group to go into liquidation without affecting the viability of the group as a whole or any other company within it

ring member FINANCE, BANKING, AND ACCOUNTING a member of the London Metal Exchange

ring trading FINANCE, BANKING, AND ACCOUNTING business conducted in a trading pit

rising bottoms FINANCE, BANKING, AND ACCOUNTING a pattern on a graph of the price of a security or commodity against time that shows an upward price movement following a period of low prices. (*slang*) See also *chartist*

risk
1 GENERAL MANAGEMENT the possibility of suffering damage or loss in the face of uncertainty about the outcome of actions, future events, or circumstances. Organizations are exposed to various types of risk, including damage to property, injury to personnel, financial loss, and legal liability. These may affect profitability, hinder the achievement of objectives, or lead to business interruption or failure. Risk may be deemed high or low, depending on the probability of an adverse outcome. Risks that can be quantified on the basis of past experience are insurable and those that cannot be calculated are uninsurable.
2 FINANCE, BANKING, AND ACCOUNTING a condition in which there exists a quantifiable dispersion in the possible outcomes from any activity

risk-adjusted return on capital FINANCE, BANKING, AND ACCOUNTING return on capital calculated in a way that takes into account the risks associated with income

risk analysis GENERAL MANAGEMENT the identification of risks to which an organization is exposed and the assessment of the potential impact of those risks on the organization. The goal of risk analysis is to identify and measure the risks associated with different courses of action in order to inform the *decision making* process. In the context of business decision making, risk analysis is especially used in investment decisions and capital investment appraisal. Techniques used in risk analysis include sensitivity analysis, probability analysis, *simulation*, and modeling. Risk analysis may be used to develop an organizational *risk profile*, and also may be the first stage in a *risk management* program.

risk arbitrage FINANCE, BANKING, AND ACCOUNTING *arbitrage* without certainty of profit

risk assessment GENERAL MANAGEMENT the determination of the level of risk in a particular course of action. Risk assessments are an important tool in areas such as *health and safety* management and *environmental management*. Results of a risk assessment can be used, for example, to identify areas in which safety can be improved. Risk assessment can also be used to determine more intangible forms of risk, including economic and social risk, and can inform the *scenario planning* process. The amount of risk involved in a particular course of action is compared to its expected benefits to provide evidence for decision making.

risk-based capital assessment FINANCE, BANKING, AND ACCOUNTING an internationally approved system of calculating a bank's capital value by assessing the risk attached to its assets. Cash deposits and gold, for example, have no risk, while loans to less-developed countries have a high risk.

risk-bearing economy of scale FINANCE, BANKING, AND ACCOUNTING conducting business on such a large scale that the risk of loss is reduced because it is spread over so many independent events, as in the issuance of insurance policies

risk capital FINANCE, BANKING, AND ACCOUNTING see *venture capital*

risk factor GENERAL MANAGEMENT the degree of risk in a project or other business activity

risk-free return FINANCE, BANKING, AND ACCOUNTING the profit made from an investment that involves no risk

risk management
1 GENERAL MANAGEMENT the variety of activities undertaken by an organization to control and minimize threats to the continuing efficiency, profitability, and success of its operations. The process of risk management includes the identification and analysis of risks to which the organization is exposed, the assessment of potential impacts on the business, and deciding what action can be taken to eliminate or reduce risk and deal with the impact of unpredictable events causing loss or damage. Risk management strategies include taking out insurance against financial loss or legal liability and introducing safety or security measures.
2 FINANCE, BANKING, AND ACCOUNTING the process of understanding and managing the risks that an organization is inevitably subject to in attempting to achieve its corporate objectives. For management purposes, risks are usually divided into categories such as operational, financial, legal compliance, information, and personnel.

risk profile GENERAL MANAGEMENT
1 an outline of the risks to which an organization is exposed. An organizational risk profile may be developed in the course of *risk analysis* and used for *risk management*. It examines the nature of the threats faced by an organization, the likelihood of adverse effects occurring, and the level of disruption and costs associated with each type of risk.
2 an analysis of the willingness of individuals or organizations to take risks. A risk profile describes the level of risk considered acceptable by an individual or by the leaders of an organization, and considers how this will affect *decision making* and *corporate strategy*.

ROA *abbr* FINANCE, BANKING, AND ACCOUNTING return on assets

robot OPERATIONS & PRODUCTION a programmable machine equipped with sensing capabil-

ities used in **production** environments. Robots are used in automatic assembly and **automated handling** situations.

robotics GENERAL MANAGEMENT the industrial use of robots to perform repetitive tasks. Robotics is an application of artificial intelligence.

ROC *abbr* return on capital

rocket scientist FINANCE, BANKING, AND ACCOUNTING an employee of a financial institution who creates innovative securities that usually include derivatives (*slang*)

Roddick, **Anita Lucia** (*b.* 1942) GENERAL MANAGEMENT British business executive. Founder of the Body Shop, whose principles, reflected in the company's **core values** of **social responsibility** and care for the environment, are explained in her autobiography *Business As Unusual* (2000). See giant **Anita Roddick**

rodo kinko FINANCE, BANKING, AND ACCOUNTING in Japan, a financial institution specializing in providing credit for small businesses

ROE *abbr* FINANCE, BANKING, AND ACCOUNTING return on equity

Roethlisberger, **Fritz Jules** (1898–1974) GENERAL MANAGEMENT U.S. academic. Collaborated with **Elton Mayo** in the **Hawthorne experiments**, leading the research and data analysis and publicizing the findings in *Management and the Worker* (1939). See thinker **Elton Mayo**

rogue trader FINANCE, BANKING, AND ACCOUNTING a dealer in stocks who uses illegal methods to make profits

ROI *abbr* FINANCE, BANKING, AND ACCOUNTING return on investment

role ambiguity GENERAL MANAGEMENT a lack of clarity on the part of an employee about the expectations of colleagues concerning his or her role within an organization. Role ambiguity may occur in newly created posts or in positions that are undergoing change. When role ambiguity extends to responsibilities or priorities it can lead to **role conflict**.

role conflict GENERAL MANAGEMENT a situation in which two or more job requirements are incompatible. Role conflict can arise from others' misperceptions of what the priorities of a role holder should be. It may also be caused by a division of loyalties between departmental peers and the organization, or between personal professional ethics and those of the organization.

role culture GENERAL MANAGEMENT a style of **corporate culture**, identified by **Charles Handy**, which assumes that employees are rational and that roles can be defined and discharged within clearly defined procedures. An organization with a role culture is believed to be generally very stable but poor at implementing **change management**. See thinker **Charles Handy**

role playing HR & PERSONNEL performing either as yourself in a contrived situation, in order to analyze how you react, or in the manner expected of another person. The role playing technique is a useful tool in **training**, as it enables trainees to gain a better understanding of themselves, other people, new situations, and different jobs.

roll-out MARKETING the full-scale implementation of an advertising campaign or marketing program

roll up (*U.K.*) FINANCE, BANKING, AND ACCOUNTING the addition of interest amounts to principal in loan payments

RONA *abbr* FINANCE, BANKING, AND ACCOUNTING return on net assets

root cause analysis GENERAL MANAGEMENT a technique used in **problem solving** to identify the underlying reason why something has gone wrong or why a difficulty has arisen. The root cause of a problem may be identified by repeatedly asking the question "Why?", by examining relationships of cause and effect, or by defining the distinctive features of the problem and developing a number of hypotheses that can be tested. Root cause analysis has been criticized on the grounds that it presupposes a single source for a problem, while in reality the situation may be more complex.

rootless capitalism GENERAL MANAGEMENT a form of capitalism that is not tied to a specific country or economy

rort (*ANZ*) GENERAL MANAGEMENT
1 an illegal or underhand strategy
2 to manipulate or break the rules of a system for personal gain

ROS *abbr* FINANCE, BANKING, AND ACCOUNTING return on sales

RosettaNet E-COMMERCE a consortium focusing on the development of e-business interfaces and a common global business language that would permit sharing of efficient e-business processes, for example, manufacturing, distribution, and sales

ROTFL *abbr* GENERAL MANAGEMENT rolling on the floor laughing (*slang*)

round figures FINANCE, BANKING, AND ACCOUNTING figures that have been adjusted up or down to the nearest 10, 100, 1,000, and so on

rounding STATISTICS the practice of reducing the number of significant digits in a number, for example, expressing a figure that has four decimal places with only two decimal places

router GENERAL MANAGEMENT a telecommunications device used to transfer calls to an alternative network that may offer cheaper rates

routing number FINANCE, BANKING, AND ACCOUNTING U.K. term **sort code**. See **ABA transit number**

royalties FINANCE, BANKING, AND ACCOUNTING a proportion of the income from the sale of a product paid to its creator, for example, an inventor, author, or composer

RPI *abbr* ECONOMICS retail price index

RPIX FINANCE, BANKING, AND ACCOUNTING an index based on the Retail Price Index that excludes mortgage interest payments and is commonly referred to as the underlying rate of inflation

RPIY FINANCE, BANKING, AND ACCOUNTING an index based on the Retail Price Index that excludes mortgage interest payments and indirect taxation

RPM *abbr* MARKETING resale price maintenance

RSI *abbr* GENERAL MANAGEMENT repetitive strain injury

RTM *abbr* GENERAL MANAGEMENT read the manual (*slang*)

RTSC *abbr* GENERAL MANAGEMENT read the source code (*slang*)

RUBBY MARKETING Rich Urban Biker (*slang*)

Rucker plan OPERATIONS & PRODUCTION a type of **gain sharing** program that is concerned with the value added by labor. The Rucker plan was developed in the 1950s by Allen W. Rucker. A typical Rucker plan includes a **suggestion program**, a committee system, and a **bonus** formula, based on **value added**. It assesses the relationship between the value added to goods as they pass through the manufacturing process, and the total labor costs. Bonuses are earned when the current ratio is better than the base ratio over a given time period. A Rucker plan usually has a far less elaborate structure than the similar **Scanlon plan**.

a-z
1611

DICTIONARY

rule of 78 FINANCE, BANKING, AND ACCOUNTING a method used to calculate the rebate on a loan with front-loaded interest that has been repaid early. It takes into account the fact that as the loan is repaid, the share of each monthly payment related to interest decreases, while the share related to principal increases.

rule of seven GENERAL MANAGEMENT the generally accepted claim that people can hold approximately seven chunks or units of information in their short-term memory at a time. Sometimes also known as Miller's rule of seven, as G. A. Miller was the first to suggest this memory range in an article entitled "The Magic Number Seven, Plus or Minus Two: Some Limits on Our Capacity for Processing Information" in the *Psychological Review* (Vol. 63, 1956).

rumortrage FINANCE, BANKING, AND ACCOUNTING speculation in securities issued by companies that are rumored to be the target of an imminent takeover attempt (*slang*)

run
1 STATISTICS an uninterrupted sequence of the same value in a statistical series
2 FINANCE, BANKING, AND ACCOUNTING an incidence of bank customers or owners of holdings in a particular currency simultaneously withdrawing their entire funds because of a lack of confidence in the institution

running account credit FINANCE, BANKING, AND ACCOUNTING an overdraft facility, credit card, or similar system that allows customers to borrow up to a specific limit and reborrow sums previously repaid by either writing a check or using their card

running total FINANCE, BANKING, AND ACCOUNTING a total carried from one column of figures to the next

running yield FINANCE, BANKING, AND ACCOUNTING see *yield*

run with something GENERAL MANAGEMENT to pursue an idea or project (*slang*)

rust belt GENERAL MANAGEMENT the manufacturing areas in the Midwest that have experienced severe decline following the move away from manufacturing to service industries (*slang*)

S

SA *abbr* FINANCE, BANKING, AND ACCOUNTING Société Anonyme *or* Sociedad Anónima *or* Sociedade Anónima

sabbatical HR & PERSONNEL a period of *special leave*, traditionally a year, granted to an employee for the purpose of study, work experience, or travel

sabotage GENERAL MANAGEMENT a deliberate action to damage property or equipment. In an industrial context, sabotage may be undertaken by employees who have a grievance against an employer in order to halt production or undermine the efficiency of an organization. Sabotage of this type may include time wasting or other measures designed to reduce *productivity*. Sabotage against organizations is also undertaken by terrorist or political groups in protest against their actions or policies. Security measures may be necessary to prevent sabotage.

SADC *abbr* FINANCE, BANKING, AND ACCOUNTING Southern African Development Community: an organization that aims to harmonize economic development in Southern Africa. The member countries are Angola, Botswana, Democratic Republic of Congo, Lesotho, Malawi, Mauritius, Mozambique, Namibia, Seychelles, South Africa, Swaziland, Tanzania, Zambia, and Zimbabwe.

safe custody FINANCE, BANKING, AND ACCOUNTING see *safe keeping*

safe hands FINANCE, BANKING, AND ACCOUNTING
1 investors who buy securities and are unlikely to sell in the short- to medium-term
2 securities held by friendly investors

safe keeping FINANCE, BANKING, AND ACCOUNTING the holding of stock certificates, deeds, wills, or a locked deed box on behalf of customers by a financial institution. Securities are often held under the customer's name in a locked cabinet in the vault so that if the customer wishes to sell, the bank can forward the relevant certificate to the broker. A will is also normally held in this way so that it may be handed to the executor on the customer's death. Deed boxes are always described as "contents unknown to the bank." Most institutions charge a fee for this service. Also known as *safe custody*

salad
let's toss it around and see if it makes a salad GENERAL MANAGEMENT let's try this idea and see if it is successful (*slang*)

salaried partner FINANCE, BANKING, AND ACCOUNTING a partner, often a junior one, who receives a regular salary, detailed in the partnership agreement

salary HR & PERSONNEL a form of *pay* given to employees at regular intervals in exchange for the work they have done. Traditionally, a salary is a form of remuneration given to professional employees on a monthly basis. In modern usage, the word refers to any form of pay that employees receive on a regular basis. A salary is normally paid straight into an employee's account.

salary ceiling HR & PERSONNEL
1 the highest level on a *pay scale* that a particular employee can achieve under his or her contract
2 an upper limit on *pay* imposed by government or according to *labor union* and employer agreements

salary review HR & PERSONNEL a reassessment of an individual employee's rate of *pay*, usually conducted on an annual basis

salary sacrifice plan HR & PERSONNEL an agreement between *employer* and employees by which the employees relinquish a right to future cash in exchange for a noncash benefit of some sort

salary scale HR & PERSONNEL see *pay scale*

sale and leaseback FINANCE, BANKING, AND ACCOUNTING the sale of an asset, usually buildings, to a third party that then leases it back to the owner. It is used by a company as a way of raising finance. Also known as *renting back*

sale by installments FINANCE, BANKING, AND ACCOUNTING see *installment plan*

sale by tender FINANCE, BANKING, AND ACCOUNTING the sale of an asset to interested parties who have been invited to make an offer. The asset is sold to the party that makes the highest offer.

sales MARKETING the activity of selling a company's products or services, the income generated by this, or the department that deals with selling

sales channel GENERAL MANAGEMENT a means of distributing products to the marketplace, either directly to the end customer, or indirectly through intermediaries such as retailers or dealers

sales conference MARKETING a conference at which the members of a sales team are brought together for a review or a significant announcement, such as a product launch.
Sales conferences are also useful for making sure that sales representatives are fully aware

of company policies, products, and support; without these, time spent with customers may be unproductive. They also play a key role in motivating sales teams and building team spirit, an important factor for people who spend most of their time working alone. In addition, conferences can be used to reward high achievement. Many organizations run annual incentive and recognition programs for sales employees, and using a national conference as the occasion for the award ceremony can confer real status on the winner and raise the profile of the program among the whole sales force, encouraging high levels of participation and effort.

sales contest MARKETING a prize competition for salespeople, often part of an *incentive program*, designed to increase sales. A sales contest winner is usually the person who has achieved the most sales for a particular time period.

sales force MARKETING a group of salespeople or sales representatives responsible for the sales of either a single product or the entire range of an organization's products. A sales force normally reports to a *sales manager*. Also known as *sales team*

sales force communications MARKETING communications aimed at improving the performance and market awareness of a sales force

sales forecast MARKETING a prediction of future sales, based mainly on past sales performance. Sales forecasting takes into account the economic climate, current sales trends, company capacity for production, *company policy*, and *market research*. A sales forecast can be a good indicator of future sales in stable market conditions, but may be less reliable in times of rapid market change.

sales manager MARKETING the manager directly responsible for the planning, organization, and performance of the *sales force*

sales network MARKETING the distribution network by which goods and services are sold. A sales network will include both independent agents and retailers.

sales office MARKETING the department responsible for selling a company's products or services, or the office in the company's premises that this department occupies

sales outlet MARKETING a company's office that deals with customers in a particular region or country

sales plan GENERAL MANAGEMENT the development of the future objectives of a sales department in order to improve performance and increase sales. A sales plan is a form of *business plan* that sets out the short- and long-term opportunities for the sales department, concentrating on building on the department's strengths and analyzing and avoiding weaknesses. It also includes the setting of future sales objectives, based on realistic projections, looking at future costs, and taking into account the objectives of other departments.

sales presentation MARKETING a structured product presentation using a binder, flipchart, or laptop computer

sales promotion MARKETING activities, usually short-term, designed to attract attention to a particular product and to increase its sales, using *advertising* and publicity. Sales promotion usually runs in conjunction with an advertising campaign that offers free samples or money-off coupons. During the period of a sales promotion, the product may be offered at a reduced price and the campaign may be supported by additional telephone or door-to-door selling or by competitions. Also known as *promotion*

sales promotion agency MARKETING an organization that specializes in planning, creating, and implementing sales promotion activities

sales quota GENERAL MANAGEMENT a target set for the *sales force* stating the number and range of products or services that should be sold

sales representative MARKETING a salesperson selling the products or services of a particular organization or manufacturer. Sales representatives are sometimes employed directly by a company as part of the *sales force*, or they may work independently and be employed by contract. Sales representatives are often paid on a commission basis.

sales resistance MARKETING a potential customer's refusal to allow a *sales representative's* sales pitch to persuade them to buy. Sales resistance may be caused, for example, by lack of interest in, or determined dislike of, the product or service offered, or a dislike of the sales technique.

sales statistics MARKETING data relating to the sales of a particular *product*, service, or *brand*. Sales statistics include numbers and types of products sold, areas where they are sold, calls and visits made, contacts established, categories of customers, costs and time spent on sales

activities, and administration. These statistics are often used in conjunction with the *sales plan* and for sales forecasting. They can also be used to identify areas of weakness in sales support staff and to identify areas for training. Statistics can also contribute to the identification of profitable product lines or products to *abandon*.

sales team MARKETING see *sales force*

sales territory MARKETING a defined area within which a designated salesperson is responsible for selling a product or service. A sales territory is usually organized along geographic lines (for example, counties or regions) but it can also be defined by *market sector* or by product group.

sales turnover MARKETING the total amount sold within a specified time period, usually a year. Sales turnover is often expressed in monetary terms but can also be expressed in terms of the total amount of stock or products sold.

salmon day GENERAL MANAGEMENT a day spent making a great deal of effort to achieve something but getting nowhere (*slang*)

sample STATISTICS a subset of a population in a statistical study chosen so that selected properties of the overall population can be investigated

sample size STATISTICS the number of individuals included in a statistical survey

sample survey STATISTICS a statistical study of a sample of individuals designed to collect information on specific subjects, such as buying habits or voting behavior

sampling
1 MARKETING a sales promotion technique in which customers and prospects are offered a free sample of a product
2 STATISTICS the selection of a small proportion of a set of items being studied, from which valid inferences about the whole set or population can be made. Sampling makes it possible to obtain valid research results when it is impracticable to survey the whole population. The size of the sample needed for valid results depends on a number of factors, including the uniformity of the population being studied and the level of accuracy required. The technique is based on the laws of probability, and a number of different sampling methods can be used, including *random sampling* and *nonrandom sampling*. Specialized applications of sampling include *activity sampling*, *acceptance sampling*, and *attribute sampling*.

sampling design STATISTICS the procedure by which a particular sample is chosen from a population

sampling error STATISTICS the difference between the population characteristic being estimated in a statistical study and the result produced by the sample investigated

sampling units STATISTICS the elements chosen to be sampled by a sampling design

sampling variation STATISTICS variation between different samples of the same size taken from the same population

samurai bond FINANCE, BANKING, AND ACCOUNTING a bond issue denominated in yen and issued in Japan by a foreign institution

sandbag FINANCE, BANKING, AND ACCOUNTING in a hostile *takeover* situation, to enter into talks with the bidder and attempt to prolong them as long as possible, in the hope that a white *knight* will appear and rescue the target company (*slang*)

S&L *abbr* FINANCE, BANKING, AND ACCOUNTING savings and loan association

S&P 500 *abbr* FINANCE, BANKING, AND ACCOUNTING Standard & Poor's 500 Index

S&P Index *abbr* FINANCE, BANKING, AND ACCOUNTING Standard & Poor's 500 Index

sanity check GENERAL MANAGEMENT a check to verify that no obvious mistakes have been made (*slang*)

Santa Claus rally FINANCE, BANKING, AND ACCOUNTING a rise in stock prices in the last week of the year

Sarbanes-Oxley FINANCE, BANKING, AND ACCOUNTING a corporate governance law which came into effect in 2005. Created in the aftermath of a raft of high-profile financial scandals, including Enron and Worldcom, Sarbanes-Oxley aims to overhaul corporate financial reporting by improving its accuracy and reliability. Accountability standards have also been considerably tightened, and chief executives are to take full responsibility for the accuracy of all financial results by signing a statement to that effect. This latter aspect effectively dismisses the so-called "aw shucks" defense strategy adopted by senior executives involved in earlier financial scandals. Under this strategy, the accused maintained that they were simply not aware of the distortion of financial reporting that took place on their watch.

SARS *abbr* FINANCE, BANKING, AND ACCOUNTING South African Revenue Service

satellite center GENERAL MANAGEMENT a *telecenter* that houses employees from a single organization

savings FINANCE, BANKING, AND ACCOUNTING money set aside by consumers for a particular purpose, to meet contingencies, or to provide an income during retirement. Savings (money in deposit and savings accounts) differ from investments—for example, on the stock market—in that they are not subject to price fluctuations and are thus considered safer.

savings account FINANCE, BANKING, AND ACCOUNTING an account with a financial institution that pays interest. See also *fixed rate gross interest net interest*

savings and loan association FINANCE, BANKING, AND ACCOUNTING a chartered bank that offers savings accounts, pays dividends, and invests in new mortgages. See also *thrift institution*. Abbr. *S&L*

savings bank FINANCE, BANKING, AND ACCOUNTING a bank that specializes in managing small investments. See also *thrift institution*

savings bond FINANCE, BANKING, AND ACCOUNTING a U.S. bond that an individual buys from the federal government

savings certificate FINANCE, BANKING, AND ACCOUNTING see *National Savings Certificate*

savings function ECONOMICS an expression of the extent to which people save money instead of spending it

savings ratio ECONOMICS the proportion of the income of a country or household that is saved in a particular period

SC *abbr* FINANCE, BANKING, AND ACCOUNTING Securities Commission

scalability E-COMMERCE the capability of the hardware and software that support an e-business to grow in capacity as transaction demand increases

Scanlon plan HR & PERSONNEL a type of *gain sharing* plan that pays a *bonus* to employees for incremental improvements. The Scanlon plan was developed by Joseph N. Scanlon in the 1930s. A typical Scanlon plan includes an employee *suggestion program*, a committee system, and a formula-based bonus system. The simplest formula is: base ratio = HR payroll costs divided by net sales or production

value. A Scanlon organization is characterized by *teamwork* and *employee participation*. A bonus is paid when the current ratio is better than that of the base period. A Scanlon plan focuses attention on the variables over which the organization and its employees have some control. See also *Rucker plan*

scatter STATISTICS the amount by which a set of observations deviates from its mean

scatter chart *or* **scatter diagram** STATISTICS a chart or diagram that plots a sample of bivariate observations in two dimensions

scenario GENERAL MANAGEMENT a possible future state of affairs or sequence of events. Scenarios are imagined or projected on the basis of current circumstances and trends and expectations of change in the future.

scenario planning GENERAL MANAGEMENT a technique that requires the use of a scenario in the process of *strategic planning* (see *planning*) to aid the development of *corporate strategy* in the face of uncertainty about the future. Scenario planning was developed in a military context during the 1940s. Its use in a business context was pioneered at Royal Dutch Shell during the 1960s and increased after the 1972 oil crisis. The process of identifying alternative scenarios of the future, based on a variety of differing assumptions, can help managers anticipate changes in the business environment and raise awareness of the frame of reference within which they are operating. The scenarios are then used to assist in both the development of strategies for dealing with unexpected events and the choice between alternative strategic options.

Schedule C (*U.K.*) FINANCE, BANKING, AND ACCOUNTING a schedule to the Finance Acts under which tax was charged on income from public sources, such as government stock

Schein, Edgar H. (*b.* 1928) GENERAL MANAGEMENT U.S. academic. The first to define *corporate culture* in *Organizational Culture and Leadership* (1985), and the developer of the notion of the *psychological contract*, originated by *Chris Argyris*.

Schein completed a PhD in social psychology at Harvard and, after graduating in 1952, conducted research into leadership as part of the Army Program. He joined MIT in 1956 and has remained there ever since. At MIT Schein researched the similarities between the brainwashing of POWs and the techniques of indoctrination used by corporations. Out of this came Schein's book *Coercive Persuasion*. His subsequent work and writing has mainly been

on organizational culture, organization development, and career development. See thinker **Edgar Schein**, **Chris Argyris**

schmooze GENERAL MANAGEMENT to behave flatteringly during a social event toward somebody who might be in a position to benefit your career (*slang*)

Schön, Donald A. (1931–97) GENERAL MANAGEMENT U.S. academic. Co-author, with Chris Argyris, of *Organizational Learning* (1978). See thinker **Chris Argyris**

Schonberger, Richard J. (*b.* 1937) GENERAL MANAGEMENT U.S. industrial engineer and writer. Known for showing how techniques such as **total quality management** and **just-in-time** can be used to achieve **world class manufacturing**. Author of *World Class Manufacturing* (1986).

Schumacher, Ernst Friedrich (1911–77) GENERAL MANAGEMENT German economist. Author of *Small is Beautiful* (1973), a counterblast to the dominance of big companies. Schumacher developed his people-centered approach to life and business working alongside **Reg Revans**.

science park (*U.K.*) GENERAL MANAGEMENT = **research park**

scientific management GENERAL MANAGEMENT HR & PERSONNEL an analytical approach to managing activities by optimizing efficiency and **productivity** through measurement and control. Scientific management theories, attributed to **Frederick Winslow Taylor**, dominated the 20th century, and many management techniques such as **benchmarking**, **total quality management**, and **business process reengineering** result from a scientific management approach. Other figures such as **Henry Gantt** and **Frank** and **Lillian Gilbreth** were firmly in the scientific school and furthered its influence, particularly through the **time and motion study**. Such was the dominance of Taylor's influence that scientific management is also known as Taylorism. The main criticism of Taylorism is that it degenerated into an inhumane and mechanistic approach to working, treating people like machines.

scorched earth policy GENERAL MANAGEMENT destructive actions taken by an organization in defense against a hostile **takeover**. Extreme actions under a scorched earth policy may include voluntary liquidation or selling off critical assets. A scorched earth policy may come into play if the value of the company to

be acquired exceeds the value of the company making a hostile bid. (*slang*)

S Corporation FINANCE, BANKING, AND ACCOUNTING a corporation that is restricted to no more than 100 stockholders. It enjoys the legal rights of a corporation but is taxed like a partnership. Also known as **Subchapter S Corporation**

screen-based activity GENERAL MANAGEMENT a task that requires access to a computer

screening study STATISTICS a medical statistical study of a population conducted to investigate the prevalence of a disease

screen popping GENERAL MANAGEMENT see **computer telephony integration** (*slang*)

screensaver E-COMMERCE a program that displays a series of moving images, designed to prevent a static image being burned into the phosphor monitor screen when a computer is idle

scrip dividend FINANCE, BANKING, AND ACCOUNTING a dividend paid by the issue of additional company shares, rather than by cash

scrip issue (*U.K.*) FINANCE, BANKING, AND ACCOUNTING = **stock split**

scripophily FINANCE, BANKING, AND ACCOUNTING the collecting of valueless stock or bond certificates

scroll bar E-COMMERCE a bar at the right-hand side and/or bottom of a window that enables users to view more information on a Web page

SCUM *abbr* GENERAL MANAGEMENT self-centered urban male (*slang*)

Sdn *abbr* FINANCE, BANKING, AND ACCOUNTING Sendirian

seagull manager HR & PERSONNEL a manager who is brought in to deal with a project, makes a lot of fuss, achieves nothing, and then leaves (*slang*)

SEAQ *abbr* FINANCE, BANKING, AND ACCOUNTING Stock Exchange Automated Quotations system: the London Stock Exchange's system for U.K. securities. It is a continuously updated computer database containing quotations that also records prices at which transactions have been struck.

SEAQ International *abbr* FINANCE, BANKING, AND ACCOUNTING Stock Exchange Automated Quotations system International: the London Stock Exchange's system for overseas secur-

ities. It is a continuously updated computer database containing quotations that also records prices at which transactions have been struck.

search E-COMMERCE the facility that enables visitors to a Web site to look for the information they want.

Search is one of the most common activities that people perform on a Web site, and therefore needs to be prominently displayed—preferably on every page, near the top. There are essentially two approaches to Web site search: basic search, suitable for small Web sites of 50 pages or under, and advanced search, for larger Web sites, which allows a user to refine their search on the basis of various parameters.

In either case, because search is an exclusively functional activity, the search results should be very clear and contain no distractions. Each set of results should include the title of the Web page that it refers to, shown in bold type and hyperlinked to that page; a two-line summary describing the content on that page; the URL for the page, and its date of publication.

search directory E-COMMERCE a Web site in which links to information are organized into a categorical, alphabetical hierarchy to provide the broadest response to a query

search engine E-COMMERCE a Web site that enables users to conduct **keyword** searches of indexed information on its database

search engine registration E-COMMERCE the process of enlisting a Web site with a **search engine**, so that the Web site is selected when a user requests a search. The process involves choosing the right **keywords** and **metadata** for the documents, in order for them to be selected in as many appropriate circumstances as possible.

When registering a Web site with search engines, it is important to consider which will be of most benefit. Of the hundreds of search engines and directories, only a few really matter in terms of mass appeal—such as Yahoo, Google, and Alta Vista. However, there may well be specialist search engines for your particular industry, which should be on your list. All search engines used to be free to register with, but many are now charging, so consider whether they are worth the fee. An increasing number sell special placements in their search results: you choose a keyword, and when that keyword is input by a searcher, a short promotion for your Web site will appear. Search engines also need to be monitored regularly, as they can change the rules by which search results are presented. If your Web site is

dropping down the results page, you may need to re-register.

seasonal adjustment FINANCE, BANKING, AND ACCOUNTING an adjustment made to accounts to allow for any short-term seasonal factors, such as Christmas sales, that may distort the figures

seasonal business FINANCE, BANKING, AND ACCOUNTING trade that is affected by seasonal factors, for example, trade in goods such as suntan products or Christmas trees

seasonal products MARKETING products that are only marketed at particular times of the year, for example, Christmas trees or fireworks

seasonal variation STATISTICS the variation of data according to particular times of the year such as winter months or a tourist season

seasoned equity FINANCE, BANKING, AND ACCOUNTING stocks that have traded long enough to have a well-established value

seasoned issue FINANCE, BANKING, AND ACCOUNTING an issue for which there is a preexisting market. See also *unseasoned issue*

SEATS *abbr* FINANCE, BANKING, AND ACCOUNTING Stock Exchange Automatic Trading System: the electronic screen-trading system operated by the Australian Stock Exchange. It was introduced in 1987.

SEC *abbr* FINANCE, BANKING, AND ACCOUNTING Securities and Exchange Commission

secondary issue FINANCE, BANKING, AND ACCOUNTING an offer of listed stocks that have not previously been publicly traded

secondary market FINANCE, BANKING, AND ACCOUNTING a market that trades in existing stocks rather than new stock issues, for example, a stock exchange. The money earned from these sales goes to the dealer or investor, not to the issuer.

secondary offering FINANCE, BANKING, AND ACCOUNTING an offering of securities of a kind that is already on the market

secondment (*U.K.*) HR & PERSONNEL the temporary transfer of a member of staff to another organization for a defined length of time, usually for a specific purpose. Secondment has grown in popularity in recent years, primarily for *career development* purposes. Secondments between the public and private sectors have been used as a mechanism to share management techniques and to disseminate *best practice*.

second mortgage FINANCE, BANKING, AND ACCOUNTING a loan that uses the equity on a mortgaged property as security and is taken out with a different lender from the first mortgage. The second mortgagee has to record its interest and cannot be paid off on foreclosure until the first mortgagee is paid off.

second-tier market FINANCE, BANKING, AND ACCOUNTING a market in stocks where the listing requirements are less onerous than for the main market, as in, for example, London's Alternative Investment Market

secretary of the board GENERAL MANAGEMENT see *company secretary*

secret reserves FINANCE, BANKING, AND ACCOUNTING see *hidden reserves*

Section 21 company (*S. Africa*) FINANCE, BANKING, AND ACCOUNTING a company established as a *nonprofit organization*

sector index FINANCE, BANKING, AND ACCOUNTING an index of companies in certain parts of a market whose stocks are listed on a general or specialist stock exchange

secular trend STATISTICS the underlying smooth movement of a *time series* over a time period of several years

secured FINANCE, BANKING, AND ACCOUNTING
1 used to describe borrowing when the lender has a charge over an asset or assets of the borrower, for example, a mortgage or floating charge
2 used to describe a creditor who has a charge over an asset or assets of the borrower, for example, a mortgage or floating charge. See also *collateral security*

secured bond FINANCE, BANKING, AND ACCOUNTING a collateralized bond

secure electronic transaction E-COMMERCE see *SET*

secure server E-COMMERCE a combination of hardware and software that secures e-commerce credit card transactions so that there is no risk of unauthorized people gaining access to credit card details online

secure sockets layer E-COMMERCE see *SSL*

securities account FINANCE, BANKING, AND ACCOUNTING an account that shows the value of financial assets held by a person or organization

securities analyst FINANCE, BANKING, AND ACCOUNTING a professional person who studies the performance of securities and the companies that issue them

Securities and Exchange Commission FINANCE, BANKING, AND ACCOUNTING the government agency responsible for establishing standards of financial reporting and accounting for public companies. Abbr **SEC**

Securities and Futures Authority FINANCE, BANKING, AND ACCOUNTING a self-regulatory organization responsible for supervising the activities of institutions advising on corporate finance activity, or dealing or facilitating deals in securities or derivatives. Abbr **SFA**

Securities Commission FINANCE, BANKING, AND ACCOUNTING a statutory body responsible for monitoring standards in the New Zealand securities markets and for promoting investment in New Zealand. Abbr **SC**

securities deposit account FINANCE, BANKING, AND ACCOUNTING a brokerage account into which securities are deposited electronically

Securities Institute of Australia FINANCE, BANKING, AND ACCOUNTING a national professional body that represents people involved in the Australian securities and financial services industry. Abbr **SIA**

Securities Investor Protection Corporation FINANCE, BANKING, AND ACCOUNTING in the United States, a corporation created by Congress in 1970 that is a mutual insurance fund established to protect clients of securities firms. In the event of a firm being closed because of bankruptcy or financial difficulties, the SIPC will step in to recover clients' cash and securities held by the firm. The corporation's reserves are available to satisfy cash and securities that cannot be recovered up to a maximum of $500,000, including a maximum of $100,000 on cash claims. Abbr **SIPC**

securities lending FINANCE, BANKING, AND ACCOUNTING the loan of securities to those who have **sold short**

securitization FINANCE, BANKING, AND ACCOUNTING the process of changing financial *assets* such as mortgages and loans into *securities*

securitized mortgage FINANCE, BANKING, AND ACCOUNTING see *securitization*

securitized paper FINANCE, BANKING, AND ACCOUNTING the *bond* or *promissory note* resulting from securitization

security FINANCE, BANKING, AND ACCOUNTING
1 a tradable financial asset, for example, a bond, stock, or a warrant
2 the collateral for a loan or other borrowing

security deposit FINANCE, BANKING, AND ACCOUNTING an amount of money paid before a transaction occurs to compensate the seller in the event that the transaction is not concluded and this is the buyer's fault

security investment company FINANCE, BANKING, AND ACCOUNTING a financial institution that specializes in the analysis and trading of securities

security of tenure FINANCE, BANKING, AND ACCOUNTING the right to keep a job or rented accommodations, provided that certain conditions are met

security printer FINANCE, BANKING, AND ACCOUNTING a printer who prints paper money, stock prospectuses, and confidential government documents

seed capital (*U.K.*) FINANCE, BANKING, AND ACCOUNTING a usually modest amount of money used to convert an idea into a viable business. Seed capital is a form of *venture capital*. = *seed money*

seed money GENERAL MANAGEMENT a usually modest amount of money used to convert an idea into a viable business. Seed money is a form of *venture capital*. U.K. term *seed capital*

segmentation STATISTICS the division of the data in a study into regions

selection bias STATISTICS the effect on a statistical or clinical trial of unmeasured variables that are unknown to the researcher

selection board HR & PERSONNEL see *panel interview*

selection instrument HR & PERSONNEL see *psychometric test*

selection interviewing HR & PERSONNEL see *interviewing*

selection of personnel HR & PERSONNEL see *recruitment*

selection test HR & PERSONNEL see *psychometric test*

selective pricing FINANCE, BANKING, AND ACCOUNTING setting different prices for the same product or service in different markets. This practice can be broken down as follows: category pricing, which involves cosmetically modifying a product such that the variations allow it to sell in a number of price categories, as where a variety of brands are based on a common product; customer group pricing, which involves modifying the price of a product or service so that different groups of consumers pay different prices; peak pricing, setting a price which varies according to the level of demand; and service level pricing, setting a price based on the particular level of service chosen from a range.

self-actualization HR & PERSONNEL the maximization of your skills and talents. Self-actualization was considered by *Abraham Maslow* as the pinnacle of his hierarchy of needs. Also known as *self-fulfillment*

self-appraisal HR & PERSONNEL an assessment by an individual of his or her own ability or understanding. Self-appraisal is sometimes part of the *performance appraisal* process, but is also conducted as part of *continuing professional development* or *career development*.

self-assessment
1 OPERATIONS & PRODUCTION a systematic and regular review of the activities of an organization and the referencing of the results against a model of *excellence* that is conducted by the organization itself. Self-assessment allows an organization to identify its strengths and weaknesses and to plan improvement activities. The technique came to prominence with the spread of the *EFQM Excellence Model*.
2 FINANCE, BANKING, AND ACCOUNTING in the United Kingdom, a system that enables taxpayers to assess their own income tax and capital gains tax payments for the fiscal year

self-certification HR & PERSONNEL in the United Kingdom, the notification and recording of the first seven days of an employee's *sick leave*. Self-certification requires the completion of a form by the employee on their return to work, indicating the nature and duration of their illness and countersigned by a manager.

self-development HR & PERSONNEL see *personal development*

self-directed team HR & PERSONNEL see *autonomous work group*

self-employment HR & PERSONNEL being in business on one's own account, either on a *freelance* basis, or by reason of owning a business, and not being engaged as an *employee* under a *contract of employment*. The distinction between the self-employed and the employed is not always clear in law, but has a crucial bearing on matters such as the tax treatment of pay and the applicability of *employment protection*. A self-employed person may be an *employer* of others.

self-fulfillment HR & PERSONNEL see *self-actualization*

self-insurance FINANCE, BANKING, AND ACCOUNTING the practice of saving money to pay for a possible loss rather than taking out an insurance policy against it

self-liquidating FINANCE, BANKING, AND ACCOUNTING providing enough income to pay off the amount borrowed for financing

self-liquidating premium MARKETING a sales promotion technique that pays for itself, in which customers send money and vouchers or proof of purchase to obtain a premium gift

self-liquidating promotion MARKETING a sales promotion in which the cost of the campaign is covered by the incremental revenue generated by the promotion

self-managed team *or* **self-managing team** HR & PERSONNEL see *autonomous work group*

self-regulatory organization GENERAL MANAGEMENT an organization that polices its members, for example, an exchange. Abbr *SRO*

self-tender FINANCE, BANKING, AND ACCOUNTING in the United States, the repurchase by a corporation of its stock by way of a tender

sell and build GENERAL MANAGEMENT an approach to manufacturing in which the producer builds only when a customer has placed an order and paid for it, rather than building products for stock

seller's market FINANCE, BANKING, AND ACCOUNTING a market in which sellers can dictate prices, typically because demand is high or there is a product shortage

selling season FINANCE, BANKING, AND ACCOUNTING a period in which market conditions are favorable to sellers

sell short FINANCE, BANKING, AND ACCOUNTING to sell commodities, currencies, or securities that one does not own in the expectation that prices will fall before delivery to the seller's profit

seminar GENERAL MANAGEMENT a small business meeting at which participants present information or exchange ideas

Semler, Ricardo (*b.* 1957) GENERAL MANAGEMENT Brazilian business executive. Owner of Semco, which he **turned around**, using three main strategies: **employee democracy**, **open-book management**, and self-setting salaries. His methods were written up in *Maverick!* (1993).

Sendirian FINANCE, BANKING, AND ACCOUNTING Malay term for "limited." Companies can use "Sendirian Berhad" or "Sdn Bhd" in their name instead of "plc." Abbr. **Sdn**

Senge, Peter (*b.* 1947) GENERAL MANAGEMENT U.S. academic. Popularized the theory of the **learning organization**, first suggested by **Chris Argyris** and **Donald Schön**. Senge studied how organizations develop adaptive capabilities in a world of increasing complexity and change. His work culminated in the publication of *The Fifth Discipline: The Art and Practice of the Learning Organization* (1990).

Senge studied engineering at Stanford before completing a PhD on social systems modeling at the Massachusetts Institute of Technology. He is currently director of the Center for Organizational Learning at MIT, and is also a founding partner of the training and consulting company, Innovation Associates, now part of Arthur D. Little. See thinker **Chris Argyris**, **Peter Senge**

senior capital FINANCE, BANKING, AND ACCOUNTING capital in the form of secured loans to a company which, in the event of liquidation, is repaid before junior capital, such as stockholders' equity

senior debt FINANCE, BANKING, AND ACCOUNTING a debt whose holder has more claim on the debtor's assets than the holder of another debt. See also **junior debt**

senior management GENERAL MANAGEMENT the managers and executives at the highest level of an organization. Senior management includes the **board of directors**. Senior management has responsibility for **corporate governance**, **corporate strategy**, and the interests of all the organization's **stakeholders**. Also known as **management team**

senior mortgage FINANCE, BANKING, AND ACCOUNTING a mortgage whose holder has more claim on the debtor's assets than the holder of another mortgage with the same mortgagee. See also **junior mortgage**

sensitivity training HR & PERSONNEL group-based training designed to help participants develop **interpersonal skills** (see **interpersonal communication**). Sensitivity train-

ing is a form of human relations training, and was developed by **Kurt Lewin** and others at the National Training Laboratory in the United States during the 1940s. The format most commonly used is a **training group**, or **T-group**, consisting of between 7 and 12 people who meet together over a period of about two weeks, normally at a residential training center. The objectives are to develop sensitivity and awareness of participants' own feelings and reactions, to increase their understanding of **group dynamics**, and to help them learn to adapt their behavior in appropriate ways. Group activities may include discussion, games, and exercises but may also be relatively unstructured. The provision of **feedback** is a key feature. This type of training has been controversial, as the group interactions can be confrontational, and some have suggested that participants could suffer emotional harm. The popularity of T-groups has declined since the 1960s and 1970s. Sensitivity training is also known as **laboratory training**. This term emphasizes the way participants are placed in an environment in which different ways of interacting can be tried out. See thinker **Kurt Lewin**

separation HR & PERSONNEL a term used to refer to **termination of service** or **resignation**

serial entrepreneur GENERAL MANAGEMENT an **entrepreneur** who sets up a string of new ventures, one after the other

seriation STATISTICS the process of arranging a set of objects in a series on the basis of similarities or dissimilarities

SERPS *abbr* FINANCE, BANKING, AND ACCOUNTING State Earnings-Related Pension Scheme: in the United Kingdom, a state program designed to pay retired employees an additional pension to the standard state pension. Contributions are collected through National Insurance payments, and benefits are related to earnings. Individuals may opt out of SERPS and have their contributions directed to an occupational or personal pension.

server E-COMMERCE a computer that provides services to another computer. Typically, a server stores data to be shared over a computer network. The computers receiving services are called **clients**.

server farm E-COMMERCE a place where a number of server computers are located, usually providing server functions for a number of different organizations

server log E-COMMERCE see **Web log**

service MARKETING any activity with a mix of tangible and intangible outcomes that is offered to a market with the goal of satisfying a customer's need or desire. Early **marketing** tended to distinguish a service from a physical good, but more recently these two have been seen as interrelated because service delivery frequently has physical aspects. For example, in a restaurant, service is provided by a waiter but physical goods, such as the food and the dining room, are also involved. In modern marketing, all forms of services and goods can be seen as **products**.

service charge
1 MARKETING a gratuity usually paid in restaurants and hotels. A service charge may be voluntary or may be added as a percentage to the bill.
2 FINANCE, BANKING, AND ACCOUNTING a fee for any service provided, or an additional fee for any enhancements to an existing service. For example, banks may charge a fee for obtaining foreign currency for customers. Residents in apartment buildings may pay an annual maintenance fee that is also referred to as a service charge.

service contract HR & PERSONNEL a **contract of employment** for **executive directors** which lays down the **conditions of employment** and details of any **bonus** which may be paid, and outlines the procedure for **termination of service**

service cost center FINANCE, BANKING, AND ACCOUNTING a cost center providing services to other cost centers. When the output of an organization is a service, rather than goods, an alternative name is normally used, for example, support cost center or utility cost center.

service/function costing FINANCE, BANKING, AND ACCOUNTING cost accounting for services or functions, for example, canteens, maintenance, or personnel

service industry FINANCE, BANKING, AND ACCOUNTING an industry which does not make products, but instead offers a service such as banking, insurance, or transport

service level agreement
1 MARKETING an agreement drawn up between a customer or client and the provider of a service or product. A service level agreement can cover a straightforward provision of a service—for example, office cleaning—or the provision of a complete function such as the **outsourcing** of the administration of a payroll or the maintenance of plant and equipment for a large

company. The agreement lays down the detailed specification for the level and quality of the service to be provided. The agreement is essentially a legally binding contract.

2 FINANCE, BANKING, AND ACCOUNTING a contract between service provider and customer which specifies in detail the level of service to be provided over the contract period (quality, frequency, flexibility, charges, etc) as well as the procedures to implement in the case of default

servicing borrowing FINANCE, BANKING, AND ACCOUNTING paying the interest due on a loan

SET *abbr* E-COMMERCE secure electronic transaction: a payment protocol that permits secure credit card transactions over open networks such as the Internet, developed by Visa and MasterCard

set-aside FINANCE, BANKING, AND ACCOUNTING see *reserves*

set-off FINANCE, BANKING, AND ACCOUNTING an agreement between two parties to balance one debt against another or a loss against a gain

set the bar HR & PERSONNEL to motivate staff by setting targets that are above their current level of achievement

settlement
1 E-COMMERCE the portion of an electronic transaction during which the customer's credit card is charged for the transaction and the proceeds are deposited into the merchant account
2 FINANCE, BANKING, AND ACCOUNTING the payment of a debt or charge

settlement date FINANCE, BANKING, AND ACCOUNTING the date on which an outstanding debt or charge is due to be paid

setup costs GENERAL MANAGEMENT the costs associated with making a workstation or equipment available for use. Setup costs include the personnel needed to set up the equipment, the cost of down time during a new setup, and the resources and time needed to test the new setup to achieve the specification of the parts or materials produced.

setup fees E-COMMERCE the costs associated with establishing a *merchant account*, for example, application and software licensing fees and point-of-sale equipment purchases

setup time OPERATIONS & PRODUCTION the time it takes to prepare, calibrate, and test a piece of equipment to produce a required output

setup time reduction OPERATIONS & PRODUCTION see *single minute exchange of dies*

seven-day money FINANCE, BANKING, AND ACCOUNTING funds that have been placed on the money market for a term of seven days

severance HR & PERSONNEL dismissal from employment because the job or worker is considered no longer necessary. U.K. term *redundancy*

severance package HR & PERSONNEL a package of benefits that an employer gives to an employee who is dismissed. U.K. term *redundancy package*

severance pay HR & PERSONNEL a lump-sum payment made by an employer to an employee at the point at which the employee leaves the organization. U.K. term *redundancy payment*. See also *unemployment compensation*

sexual discrimination HR & PERSONNEL unfavorable treatment or *discrimination*, especially in employment, based on prejudice against a person's sex. Legislation against sexual discrimination is in place in many countries and many organizations have specific *personnel policies* to prevent sexual discrimination in the workplace.

sexual harassment HR & PERSONNEL a form of *discrimination* through the unwelcome and unwanted sexual conduct of one employee toward another. Most of the victims of sexual harassment are women, and the most common forms are physical, verbal, suggestive gesturing, written messages, graphic or pictorial displays, or the emotional isolation of an individual. The effective promotion of a policy to protect employees and customers from such harassment is good organizational practice.

SFA *abbr* FINANCE, BANKING, AND ACCOUNTING Securities and Futures Authority

SFAS *abbr* FINANCE, BANKING, AND ACCOUNTING Statement of Financial Accounting Standards

SFE *abbr* FINANCE, BANKING, AND ACCOUNTING Sydney Futures Exchange

SGX *abbr* FINANCE, BANKING, AND ACCOUNTING Singapore Exchange

shadow market FINANCE, BANKING, AND ACCOUNTING GENERAL MANAGEMENT see *black market*

shadow price ECONOMICS the *opportunity cost* to an individual or economy of engaging in an economic activity

shakeout FINANCE, BANKING, AND ACCOUNTING the elimination of weak or cautious investors during a crisis in the financial market (*slang*)

shamrock organization GENERAL MANAGEMENT a form of *organization structure* with three bases on which people can be employed and on which organizations can be linked to each other. The shamrock organization was identified by *Charles Handy*. The three bases or groups are professional managers; contracted specialists such as advertising, computing, or catering personnel; and a flexible labor force discharging part-time, temporary, or seasonal roles. See also *Handy, Charles*

shape up or ship out HR & PERSONNEL an order to improve your performance at work or else be fired (*slang*)

share FINANCE, BANKING, AND ACCOUNTING a fixed identifiable unit of capital which has a fixed nominal or face value, which may be quite different from the market price of the share

share account FINANCE, BANKING, AND ACCOUNTING
1 an account with a credit union that pays dividends rather than interest
2 (*U.K.*) an account at a building society where the account holder is a member of the society

share buyback FINANCE, BANKING, AND ACCOUNTING an arrangement whereby a company buys its own shares on the stock market

share capital FINANCE, BANKING, AND ACCOUNTING the amount of capital that a company raises by issuing shares

share certificate (*U.K.*) FINANCE, BANKING, AND ACCOUNTING = *stock certificate*

shared drop MARKETING a sales promotion technique in which a number of promotional offers are delivered by hand to *prospects* at the same time

shared values GENERAL MANAGEMENT see *core values*

share exchange FINANCE, BANKING, AND ACCOUNTING a service provided by certain collective investment plans whereby they exchange investors' existing individual shareholdings for shares in their funds. This saves the investor the expense of selling holdings, which can be uneconomical when dealing with small shareholdings.

shareholder FINANCE, BANKING, AND ACCOUNTING
1 = *stockholder*
2 a person who owns shares of a fund or investment trust

a-z
1619

DICTIONARY

shareholders' perks FINANCE, BANKING, AND ACCOUNTING benefits offered to stockholders in addition to dividends, often in the form of discounts on the company's products and services. Also known as *stockholder perks*

shareholder value FINANCE, BANKING, AND ACCOUNTING the. Also known see *stockholder value*

shareholder value analysis FINANCE, BANKING, AND ACCOUNTING a calculation of the value of a company made by looking at the returns it gives to its stockholders. Abbr. *SVA*. Also known as *stockholder value analysis*. See checklist *Shareholder Value Analysis (SVA)*

share incentive scheme HR & PERSONNEL in the United Kingdom, a type of financial *incentive plan* in which employees can acquire shares in the company in which they work and so have an interest in its financial performance. A share incentive scheme is a type of *employee stock ownership plan*, in which employees may be given shares by their employer, or shares may be offered for purchase at an advantageous price, as a reward for personal or group performance. A *share option* is a type of share incentive scheme.

share index (*U.K.*) FINANCE, BANKING, AND ACCOUNTING see *index*

share issue FINANCE, BANKING, AND ACCOUNTING the offering for sale of shares in a business. The *capital* derived from share issues can be used for investment in the core business or for expansion into new commercial ventures.

share of voice MARKETING an individual company's proportion of the total advertising expenditure in a sector

shareowner FINANCE, BANKING, AND ACCOUNTING somebody who owns a share of stock

share premium FINANCE, BANKING, AND ACCOUNTING
1 the amount by which the price at which a company sells a share exceeds its par value
2 the amount payable for a share above its nominal value. Most shares are issued at a premium to their nominal value. Share premiums are credited to the company's *share premium account*.

share premium account FINANCE, BANKING, AND ACCOUNTING the special reserve in a company's balance sheet to which *share premiums* are credited. Expenses associated with the issue of shares may be written off to this account.

shares of negligible value FINANCE, BANKING, AND ACCOUNTING shares which are considered in income tax terms as having no value because the company has ceased to exist. The shares of companies in receivership are not deemed to be of negligible value, although they may eventually end up as such.

share split FINANCE, BANKING, AND ACCOUNTING see *stock split*

shareware E-COMMERCE software distributed free of charge, but usually with a request that users pay a small fee if they like the program

shark repellent GENERAL MANAGEMENT provisions in a company's bylaws that make it more difficult for a proposition such as a change of status or the acceptance of a hostile *takeover* bid to succeed. Elements of shark repellent may include requiring a vote that is substantially higher than that required by law; creating different voting rights attached to different stocks; very long notice for special business meetings; or requiring certain stockholders to waive rights to any capital gains resulting from a takeover. (*slang*)

shark watcher FINANCE, BANKING, AND ACCOUNTING in the United States, a firm specializing in monitoring the stock market for potential takeover activity (*slang*)

shelf registration FINANCE, BANKING, AND ACCOUNTING a registration statement, filed with the Securities and Exchange Commission two years before a corporation issues securities to the public. The statement, which has to be updated periodically, allows the corporation to act quickly when it considers that the market conditions are right without having to start the registration procedure from scratch.

shelfspace MARKETING the amount of space allocated to a product in a retail outlet

shell company FINANCE, BANKING, AND ACCOUNTING a company that has ceased to trade but is still registered, especially one sold to enable the buyer to begin trading without having to establish a new company

Shewhart, Walter Andrew (1891–1967) GENERAL MANAGEMENT U.S. statistician. Pioneer of the development and application of statistical techniques for the control of variation in industrial production, in particular *statistical process control*. Mentor of *W. Edwards Deming*. See thinker *W. Edwards Deming*

shibosai FINANCE, BANKING, AND ACCOUNTING the Japanese term for a private placing

shibosai bond FINANCE, BANKING, AND ACCOUNTING a *samurai bond* sold direct to investors by the issuing company as opposed to a financial institution

shift HR & PERSONNEL
1 a designated period during a working day when a group of employees work continuously. Shifts are arranged in a variety of different patterns during a day or over a week or month, to enable a business to make more effective use of its equipment, and to enable a greater level of output to be achieved.
2 a group of employees working for a designated period during a working day. Where a shift pattern changes, the hours of work for the whole group of employees alters.

shift differential HR & PERSONNEL payment made to employees over and above their basic rate to compensate them for the inconvenience of the pattern of *shiftwork*. A shift differential usually takes account of the time of day when the shift is worked, the duration of the shift, the extent to which weekend working is involved, and the speed of rotation within the shift.

shiftwork HR & PERSONNEL an arrangement whereby the working day is divided into a number of *shifts* and a separate group of employees works for each period

shingle
hang out your shingle GENERAL MANAGEMENT to start a business or announce the startup of a new business (*slang*)

Shingo, Shigeo (1909–90) GENERAL MANAGEMENT Japanese researcher and consultant. Inventor of the *single minute exchange of dies* and a developer of the *Toyota production system*. Methods to achieve *zero defects* were explained in *Zero Quality Control* (1985).

shinyo kinku FINANCE, BANKING, AND ACCOUNTING in Japan, a financial institution that provides financing for small businesses

shinyo kumiai FINANCE, BANKING, AND ACCOUNTING in Japan, a credit union that provides financing for small businesses

shipping confirmation E-COMMERCE an e-mail message informing the purchaser that an order has been shipped

shogun bond FINANCE, BANKING, AND ACCOUNTING a bond denominated in a currency other than the yen that is sold on the Japanese market by a non-Japanese financial institution. Also known as *geisha bond*. See also *samurai bond*

shopbot E-COMMERCE an automated means of searching the Internet for particular products or services, allowing the user to compare prices or specifications

shopping cart *or* **shopping basket** E-COMMERCE a software package that collects and records items selected for purchase along with associated data, for example, item price and quantity desired, during shopping at an electronic store

shopping experience E-COMMERCE the virtual environment in which a customer visits an e-merchant's Web site, selects items and places them in an electronic *shopping cart*, and notifies the merchant of the order. The experience does not include a payment transaction, which is initiated by a message generated to the point-of-sale program when the customer signals the experience is completed.

shopping trolley E-COMMERCE see *shopping cart*

shop steward HR & PERSONNEL a representative elected by *labor union* members within an office or factory to represent their feelings, wishes, and grievances to management. A shop steward is often the first point of contact for supervisors and personnel officers in their industrial relations dealings with an outside labor union.

shop window Web site E-COMMERCE a Web site which provides information about an organization and its products, but without encouraging any significant visitor interaction—rather like an online company brochure

short FINANCE, BANKING, AND ACCOUNTING
1 a short-dated gilt (*slang*)
2 an asset in which a dealer has a short position

short covering FINANCE, BANKING, AND ACCOUNTING the purchase of foreign exchange, commodities, or securities by a firm or individual that has been *selling short*. Such purchases are undertaken when the market has begun to move upward, or when it is thought to be about to do so.

short-dated gilt FINANCE, BANKING, AND ACCOUNTING see *gilt-edged security*

short-dated gilts FINANCE, BANKING, AND ACCOUNTING government stocks which mature in less than five years from the date of purchase

shorthand GENERAL MANAGEMENT a system of rapid note-taking, using abbreviations and symbols to represent words and phrases

shorting FINANCE, BANKING, AND ACCOUNTING the act of *selling short*

short-interval scheduling OPERATIONS & PRODUCTION a technique for assigning a planned quantity of work to a workstation, to be completed in a specific time. Short-interval scheduling was pioneered during the 1930s by large mail-order houses in the United States. It was widely used in the 1950s to provide greater control of routine and semi-routine processes, through regular checks on individual performance over short spans of time. Short-interval scheduling enables *productivity* to be improved, as all delays can be identified and corrected at an early stage.

short-run production OPERATIONS & PRODUCTION a production system designed to produce unique or small batches of a product

short selling FINANCE, BANKING, AND ACCOUNTING see *sell short*

short-term bond FINANCE, BANKING, AND ACCOUNTING a bond on the corporate bond market that has an initial maturity of less than two years

short-term capital FINANCE, BANKING, AND ACCOUNTING funds raised for a period of less than 12 months. See also *working capital*

short-term debt FINANCE, BANKING, AND ACCOUNTING debt with a term of one year or less

short-term economic policy FINANCE, BANKING, AND ACCOUNTING an economic policy with objectives that can be met within a period of months or a few years

short-termism GENERAL MANAGEMENT an approach to business that concentrates on short-term results rather than long-term objectives

shout E-COMMERCE to type a sentence or paragraph entirely in capital letters—the netiquette equivalent of raising the voice in anger or for emphasis

shovelware E-COMMERCE a derogatory term for materials produced by converting existing materials from a traditional medium (for example, a catalog) without taking advantage of the digital medium's audiovisual and linking possibilities (*slang*)

show stopper FINANCE, BANKING, AND ACCOUNTING see *poison pill*

shrinkage FINANCE, BANKING, AND ACCOUNTING
1 a reduction in the amount of a company's inventories, often caused by production processes
2 a term used to describe goods that leave a retail outlet but are not logged as sales. Shrinkage can include goods that are stolen by shoplifters, or are damaged or broken.

shrink wrap agreement *or* **shrink wrap license** E-COMMERCE see *click wrap agreement*

shutdown of production OPERATIONS & PRODUCTION the action of stopping production due to a lack of resources or components, equipment failure or installation, or *industrial action* by workers. Shutdown of production may also be instigated by management to reduce output. A shutdown can be a temporary measure (for example, in holiday periods) but it can also be permanent—for example, when a manufacturing company closes down after *business failure*.

SIA *abbr* FINANCE, BANKING, AND ACCOUNTING Securities Institute of Australia

sickie (*U.K.*) (*ANZ*) HR & PERSONNEL a day of sick leave, often implying that the sickness is not genuine (*slang*)

sick leave *or* **sickness absence** HR & PERSONNEL absence from work caused by illness

sickness and accident insurance FINANCE, BANKING, AND ACCOUNTING a form of permanent health insurance that may be sold with some form of credit, for example a credit card or personal loan. In the event of the borrower being unable to work because of accident or illness, the policy covers the regular payments to the credit card company or lender.

sickout HR & PERSONNEL a form of protest by a group of employees who attempt to achieve their demands by absenting themselves from work on the grounds of ill-health (*slang*)

sight bill FINANCE, BANKING, AND ACCOUNTING a bill of exchange payable on sight

sight deposit FINANCE, BANKING, AND ACCOUNTING a bank deposit against which the depositor can immediately draw

sight draft FINANCE, BANKING, AND ACCOUNTING a bill of exchange that is payable on delivery. See also *time draft*

signature E-COMMERCE the name, position, and full contact details of the sender of an e-mail, added to the end of a business message. Some e-mail programs enable users to automatically add a signature to all sent messages.

signature guarantee FINANCE, BANKING, AND ACCOUNTING a stamp or seal, usually from a bank or a broker, that vouches for the authenticity of a signature

signature loan FINANCE, BANKING, AND ACCOUNTING see *unsecured loan*

silent partner FINANCE, BANKING, AND ACCOUNTING a person or organization that invests money in a company but takes no active part in the management of the business. Although a silent partner is inactive in the operation of the business, they have legal obligations and benefits of ownership, and are therefore fully liable for any debts. U.K. term *sleeping partner*

silver ceiling E-COMMERCE discrimination in the workplace against employees and job applicants who are no longer considered young

silversurfer E-COMMERCE an Internet user aged between 45 and 65 (*slang*)

silvertail (*ANZ*) GENERAL MANAGEMENT a wealthy person of high social standing (*slang*)

Simon, Herbert A. (1916–2001) GENERAL MANAGEMENT U.S. economist, and political and social scientist. Respected for his work on *problem solving*, *decision making*, and *artificial intelligence*. He began developing his ideas in *Administrative Behavior* (1946).

simple interest FINANCE, BANKING, AND ACCOUNTING interest charged simply as a constant percentage of principal and not compounded. See also *compound interest*

simple moving average STATISTICS the selection of units from a population in such a way that every possible combination of selected units is equally likely to be in the sample chosen

simple regression analysis GENERAL MANAGEMENT see *regression analysis*

simulation GENERAL MANAGEMENT the construction of a mathematical model to imitate the behavior of a real-world situation or system in order to test the outcomes of alternative courses of action. Simulation was used in a military context by the Chinese as many as 5,000 years ago and has applications in the fields of science, research and development, economics, and business systems. The use of simulation has become more widespread since the development of computers in the 1950s, which facilitated the manipulation of large quantities of data and made it possible to model more complex systems. Simulation techniques are used in situations where real-life experimentation would be impossible, costly, or dangerous, and for training purposes.

simulation game GENERAL MANAGEMENT an interactive game based on a simulation of a real-life situation, where participants role-play, make decisions, and receive *feedback* on the results of their actions. A simulation game is used for training purposes and enables trainees to put theory into practice in a risk-free environment. Simulation games are used to increase business awareness and develop management skills such as *decision making*, *problem solving*, and team working. An element of competition between individuals or teams of players is normally involved. Formats used include board games and computer-based simulations of the running of a business.

simulation model GENERAL MANAGEMENT a mathematical representation of the essential characteristics of a real-world system or situation, which can be used to predict future behavior under a variety of different conditions. The process of developing a simulation model involves defining the situation or system to be analyzed, identifying the associated variables, and describing the relationships between them as accurately as possible.

simultaneous engineering FINANCE, BANKING, AND ACCOUNTING OPERATIONS & PRODUCTION see *concurrent engineering*

simultaneous management GENERAL MANAGEMENT a *management style* in which managers organize competing demands in an integrated way, rather than sequentially. Simultaneous management reflects the increasingly rapid changes of the business environment, which create conflicting demands on a manager's attention. It involves integrating tasks, people, and procedures and handling them in an interactive way, rather than tackling problems individually.

SINBAD *abbr* MARKETING Single Income, No Boyfriend, And Absolutely Desperate: one of many humorous acronyms used in advertising to help define the market of a product or service (*slang*)

Singapore dollar FINANCE, BANKING, AND ACCOUNTING Singapore's unit of currency, whose exchange rate is quoted as S$ per U.S.$

Singapore Exchange FINANCE, BANKING, AND ACCOUNTING a merger of the Stock Exchange of Singapore and the Singapore International Monetary Exchange, established in 1999. It provides securities and derivatives trading, securities clearing and depository, and derivatives clearing services. Abbr. *SGX*

Singapore Immigration and Registration GENERAL MANAGEMENT the department responsible for all entry and immigration issues relating to Singapore. Abbr. *SIR*

single currency FINANCE, BANKING, AND ACCOUNTING denominated entirely in one currency

single customs document FINANCE, BANKING, AND ACCOUNTING a standard, universally-used form for the passage of goods through customs

single-employer bargaining HR & PERSONNEL see *collective bargaining*

single entry FINANCE, BANKING, AND ACCOUNTING a type of bookkeeping where only one entry, reflecting both a credit to one account and a debit to another, is made for each transaction

single market FINANCE, BANKING, AND ACCOUNTING see *EU*

single minute exchange of dies OPERATIONS & PRODUCTION a technique for reducing the *setup times* of equipment. Single minute exchange of dies was developed by *Shigeo Shingo* to improve setup times in the *Toyota production system*. It is a simple technique that divides the elements of a setup task into internal activities (those that can be performed only when the machine is stopped) and external activities (those that can be performed in advance). Single minute refers to making the changes in less than ten minutes, while exchange of dies comes from the steel presses that were the focus of Shingo's attention. By converting as many internal activities to external activities as possible, Shingo was able to reduce a four-hour setup time on a large press to less than ten minutes. Abbr. *SMED*

single-payment bond FINANCE, BANKING, AND ACCOUNTING a bond redeemed with a single payment combining principal and interest at maturity

single premium deferred annuity FINANCE, BANKING, AND ACCOUNTING an annuity that is paid for with a single payment at inception and pays returns regularly after a set date. It gives a tax advantage.

single premium insurance FINANCE, BANKING, AND ACCOUNTING life cover where the premium is paid in one lump sum when the policy is taken out, rather than in monthly installments

single sourcing OPERATIONS & PRODUCTION the *purchasing* policy of using one supplier for a particular component or service. Single sourcing can result in higher quality and a greater level of cooperation in *product development* than the traditional Western approach of *multiple sourcing*. Single sourcing has risen in prominence in the West following the introduction of Japanese production techniques, particularly *just-in-time*, which encourage manufacturers to establish closer relationships with a smaller number of suppliers.

single tax FINANCE, BANKING, AND ACCOUNTING a tax that supplies all revenue, especially on land

SINK *abbr* MARKETING Single, Independent, No Kids (*slang*)

sinking fund FINANCE, BANKING, AND ACCOUNTING money put aside periodically to settle a liability or replace an *asset*. The money is invested to produce a required sum at an appropriate time.

SIPC *abbr* FINANCE, BANKING, AND ACCOUNTING Securities Investor Protection Corporation

SIR *abbr* GENERAL MANAGEMENT Singapore Immigration and Registration

SIS *abbr* GENERAL MANAGEMENT strategic information systems

site analysis E-COMMERCE analysis of information about a Web site stored on Web servers. Typically, this information details how many page views they serve, as well as more specific data about the site's performance such as how long visitors stayed on the site and which pages they looked at when they were there.

situational interview HR & PERSONNEL see *interviewing*

six-month money FINANCE, BANKING, AND ACCOUNTING funds invested on the money market for a period of six months

Six Sigma OPERATIONS & PRODUCTION a data-driven method for achieving near perfect quality. Sigma is the Greek letter used to denote *standard deviation*, or the measure of variation from the mean, which in production terms is used to imply a defect. The greater the number of sigmas, the fewer the defects. In true Six Sigma environments, companies operate at a quality level of six standard deviations from the mean, or at a defect level of 3.4 per million. Six Sigma analysis can be focused upon any part of production or service activities, and has a strong emphasis on statistical

analysis in design, manufacturing, and customer-oriented activities. It is based on statistical tools and techniques of quality management developed by *Joseph Juran*. It was pioneered in the United States by Motorola, and subsequently became much more popular in the 1990s after its adoption by General Electric under Jack Welch.

size of firm GENERAL MANAGEMENT a method of categorizing companies according to size for the purposes of government statistics. Divisions are typically *microbusiness*, *small business*, *medium-sized business*, and *large-sized business*.

skeleton staff HR & PERSONNEL the minimum number of employees needed to keep a business running, for example, during a holiday period

skewness STATISTICS a lack of symmetry in a probability distribution

skill HR & PERSONNEL the ability to do something well, gained through training and experience. See also *competence*

skills analysis *or* **skills mapping** HR & PERSONNEL the process of obtaining information on employees' technical and behavioral *skills*. Skills analysis is used to define the skills or *competencies* required in a particular job. It is also used to identify those skills that are not being deployed at all or could be utilized by another part of the organization.

skills shortage HR & PERSONNEL a shortfall in the number of workers with the *skills* needed to fill the jobs currently available. A skills shortage may be caused by a lack of education and *vocational training*, or by wider social and economic factors such as new technological developments. A skills shortage may affect a region, an industry, or a whole country. Skills shortages of this type need to be addressed at national level through effective *manpower planning* and the development of strategies for adult education and vocational training. An organization may suffer from a skills shortage as a result of poor *recruitment* and employee retention policies, or through inadequate provision of training and employee development opportunities.

skimming FINANCE, BANKING, AND ACCOUNTING the unethical and usually illegal practice of taking small amounts of money from accounts that belong to other individuals or organizations

skunkworks GENERAL MANAGEMENT a fast-moving group, working at the edge of the *or-*

ganization structure, which aims to accelerate the *innovation* process without the restrictions of organizational policies and procedures. Skunkworks can operate unknown to an organization, or with its tacit acceptance. With the organization's acceptance, skunkworks are an extreme form of *intrapreneurialism*. The term skunkworks was popularized by *Tom Peters* and *Bob Waterman* in *A Passion for Excellence* (1984).

sleeping partner (*U.K.*) FINANCE, BANKING, AND ACCOUNTING GENERAL MANAGEMENT = *silent partner*

Sloan, Alfred Pritchard (1875–1966) GENERAL MANAGEMENT U.S. industrialist. Chairman and C.E.O. of General Motors, which he built into the largest company in the world by developing *decentralized organization structure* and adopting the theories of *Henri Fayol*. Sloan's divisional structure, which became the model for organizing large business, is described in *My Years with General Motors* (1963).

slowdown ECONOMICS a fall in demand that causes a lowering of economic activity, less severe than a *recession* or *slump*

slump ECONOMICS a severe downturn phase in the business cycle

slumpflation ECONOMICS a collapse in all economic activity accompanied by wage and price inflation. This happened, for example, in the United States and Europe in 1929. (*slang*)

slush fund FINANCE, BANKING, AND ACCOUNTING a fund used by a company for illegal purposes such as bribing officials to obtain preferential treatment for planned work or expansion

small and medium-sized enterprises GENERAL MANAGEMENT organizations that are in the *startup* or growth phase of development and have fewer than 500 employees. Abbr *SME*

small business GENERAL MANAGEMENT an organization that is small in relation to the potential market size, managed by its owners, and not part of a larger organization. There is no single official definition of what constitutes a small business. A standard definition for the size of small business is one having fewer than 100 employees.

small change FINANCE, BANKING, AND ACCOUNTING a quantity of coins that a person might carry with them

Small Order Execution System FINANCE, BANKING, AND ACCOUNTING on the NASDAQ, an automated execution system for bypassing

brokers when processing small order agency executions of NASDAQ securities up to 1,000 shares

small print GENERAL MANAGEMENT details in an official document such as a contract that are usually printed in a smaller size than the rest of the text and, while often important, may be overlooked. Items often referred to as "small print" can include deliberately hidden charges, unfavorable terms, or loopholes.

smart card E-COMMERCE a small plastic card containing a microprocessor that can store and process transactions and maintain a bank balance, thus providing a secure, portable medium for electronic money. Financial details and personal data stored on the card can be updated each time the card is used.

smart market E-COMMERCE a market in which all transactions are performed electronically using network communications

smartsizing HR & PERSONNEL the process of reducing the size of a company by laying off employees on the basis of incompetence and inefficiency (*slang*)

SME *abbr* GENERAL MANAGEMENT small and medium-sized enterprises

SMED *abbr* OPERATIONS & PRODUCTION single minute exchange of dies

Smith, **Adam** (1723–90) GENERAL MANAGEMENT Scottish political economist and philosopher. Author of *The Wealth of Nations* (1776), one of the most influential books written on political economy, Smith did much to promulgate the theory of free trade in a society based on *mercantilism*. He is recognized for his use of the expression "the invisible hand," which he used to describe the important role of self-interest in a free market.

smoking memo GENERAL MANAGEMENT a memo, letter, or e-mail message containing evidence of a corporate crime (*slang*)

smoko (*ANZ*) GENERAL MANAGEMENT a break taken by employees during working hours, traditionally to smoke cigarettes but often to take tea or other refreshments (*slang*)

smoothing methods STATISTICS procedures used in fitting a model to a set of statistical observations in a study, often by graphing the data to highlight its characteristics

SMS *abbr* E-COMMERCE short messaging service: the system used to send text messages via cellphone networks

SMTP *abbr* E-COMMERCE simple mail transfer protocol: an e-mail protocol used to help pass messages along their route. SMTP is understood by e-mail software and by the server computers that each e-mail message passes.

snail mail E-COMMERCE a derogatory term for the mail service, viewed as slow in comparison to e-mail (*slang*)

snowball sampling STATISTICS a form of sampling in which existing sample members suggest potential new sample members, for example, personal acquaintances

snowflake STATISTICS a graph that shows *multivariate data*

SO *abbr* GENERAL MANAGEMENT significant other (*slang*)

social audit GENERAL MANAGEMENT a process for evaluating, reporting on, and improving an organization's performance and behavior, and for measuring its effects on society. The social audit can be used to produce a measure of the *social responsibility* of an organization. It takes into account any internal *code of conduct* as well as the views of all *stakeholders* and draws on *best practice* factors of *total quality management* and human resource development. Like *internal auditing*, social auditing requires an organization to identify what it is seeking to achieve, who the stakeholders are, and how it wants to measure performance.

social capital GENERAL MANAGEMENT the asset to an organization produced by the cumulative social skills of its employees. Social capital, like *intellectual* and *emotional capital*, is intangible and resides in the employees of the organization. It is a form of capital produced by good *interpersonal skills* (see *interpersonal communication*), which can be considered an asset as they are an important factor in organizational success. Key components of social capital include trust; a sense of community and belonging; unrestricted and participative communication; democratic decision making; and a sense of collective responsibility. Evidence of social capital can be seen, for example, in trust relationships, in the establishment of effective personal networks, in efficient *teamwork*, and in an organization's exercise of *social responsibility*.

socially conscious investing FINANCE, BANKING, AND ACCOUNTING see *ethical investment*

social marginal cost ECONOMICS the additional cost to a society of a change in an economic variable, for example, the price of gas or bread

social responsibility GENERAL MANAGEMENT the approach of an organization to managing the impact it has on society. Social responsibility involves behaving within certain socially acceptable limits. These limits may not always take the form of written laws or regulations, but they amount to an accepted organization-wide moral or ethical code. Organizations that transgress this code are viewed as irresponsible. In order to determine levels of social responsibility, organizations may choose to undertake a *social audit*, or more specifically an *environmental audit*. Social responsibility, along with *business ethics*, has grown as a strategic issue: *empowerment* and the *flat organization* have opened up decision making to a wider range of employees, and at the same time, "green" or caring consumers are becoming a more powerful market segment.

Sociedad Anónima FINANCE, BANKING, AND ACCOUNTING the Spanish equivalent of a U.K. private limited company. Abbr. *SA*

Sociedade Anónima FINANCE, BANKING, AND ACCOUNTING the Portuguese equivalent of a U.K. private limited company. Abbr. *SA*

Società a responsabilità limitata FINANCE, BANKING, AND ACCOUNTING an Italian limited liability company that is unlisted. Abbr. *Srl*

Società per Azioni FINANCE, BANKING, AND ACCOUNTING an Italian public limited company. Abbr. *SpA*

Société Anonyme FINANCE, BANKING, AND ACCOUNTING the French equivalent of a U.K. private limited company. Abbr. *SA*

société à responsabilité limitée FINANCE, BANKING, AND ACCOUNTING a French limited liability company that is unlisted. Abbr. *SARL*

société d'investissement à capital variable FINANCE, BANKING, AND ACCOUNTING the French term for collective investment. Abbr. *SICAV*

Society for Worldwide Interbank Financial Telecommunication FINANCE, BANKING, AND ACCOUNTING see *SWIFT*

sociocultural research MARKETING exploration of social and cultural trends which identifies how they are likely to impact on different *market sectors*

socioeconomic ECONOMICS involving both social and economic factors. Structural unemployment, for example, has socioeconomic causes.

socioeconomic environment GENERAL MANAGEMENT the combination of external social and economic conditions that influence the operation and performance of an organization. The socioeconomic environment is part of the overall business environment.

socioeconomic segmentation MARKETING the division of a market by socioeconomic categories

soft benefits HR & PERSONNEL nonmonetary benefits offered to employees (*slang*)

soft capital rationing FINANCE, BANKING, AND ACCOUNTING see *capital rationing*

soft commissions FINANCE, BANKING, AND ACCOUNTING brokerage commissions that are rebated to an institutional customer in the form of, or to pay for, research or other services

soft commodities FINANCE, BANKING, AND ACCOUNTING commodities, such as foodstuffs, that are neither metals nor other solid raw materials. Also known as *softs*. See also *future*, *hard commodities*

soft-core radicalism MARKETING a marketing technique that plays on people's concerns about environmental and ethical issues in order to sell them a product (*slang*)

soft currency FINANCE, BANKING, AND ACCOUNTING ECONOMICS a currency that is weak, usually because there is an excess of supply and a belief that its value will fall in relation to others. See also *hard currency*

soft landing ECONOMICS the situation when a country's economic activity has slowed down but demand has not fallen far enough or rapidly enough to cause a recession

soft loan FINANCE, BANKING, AND ACCOUNTING a loan on exceptionally favorable terms, for example, for a project that a government considers worthy

soft market FINANCE, BANKING, AND ACCOUNTING a market in which prices are falling

softs FINANCE, BANKING, AND ACCOUNTING see *soft commodities*

soft systems GENERAL MANAGEMENT see *systems method*

sold short FINANCE, BANKING, AND ACCOUNTING see *sell short*

sole distributor FINANCE, BANKING, AND ACCOUNTING a retailer who is the only one in an area who is allowed by the manufacturer to sell a certain product or service

sole proprietor GENERAL MANAGEMENT somebody who owns and runs an unincorporated business by himself or herself. Sole proprietors are taxed at the personal income level and are personally liable for all business losses or debts and in the event of bankruptcy personal possessions may be forfeited.

sole proprietorship GENERAL MANAGEMENT a business operated by a sole proprietor

sole trader (*U.K.*) GENERAL MANAGEMENT a person conducting business with total legal responsibility for his/her actions, neither in partnership nor as a company. See also *sole proprietor*

solicit FINANCE, BANKING, AND ACCOUNTING to ask another person or company for money

solus position MARKETING the condition of being the only advertisement to appear on a page

solution brand MARKETING a combination of products and related services, for example, a computer system with presales consulting, installation, and maintenance, that meets a customer's needs more effectively than a product alone

solvency margin FINANCE, BANKING, AND ACCOUNTING
1 a business's liquid assets that exceed the amount required to meet its liabilities
2 (*U.K.*) the extent to which an insurance company's assets exceed its liabilities

solvency ratio FINANCE, BANKING, AND ACCOUNTING
1 a ratio of assets to liabilities, used to measure a company's ability to meet its debts
2 in the United Kingdom, the ratio of an insurance company's net assets to its non-life premium income

solvent FINANCE, BANKING, AND ACCOUNTING used to refer to a situation in which the *assets* of an individual or organization are worth more than their *liabilities*

sort code (*U.K.*) FINANCE, BANKING, AND ACCOUNTING see *ABA transit number*

sort field E-COMMERCE a computer field used to identify data in such a way that it can be easily categorized and arranged in sequence

source and application of funds statement FINANCE, BANKING, AND ACCOUNTING see *cash flow statement*

sources and uses of funds statement FINANCE, BANKING, AND ACCOUNTING see *cash flow statement*

sovereign loan FINANCE, BANKING, AND ACCOUNTING a loan by a financial institution to an overseas government, usually of a developing country. See also *sovereign risk*

sovereign risk FINANCE, BANKING, AND ACCOUNTING the risk that an overseas government may refuse to repay or may default on a *sovereign loan*

SpA *abbr* FINANCE, BANKING, AND ACCOUNTING Società per Azioni

spam
1 E-COMMERCE unsolicited bulk e-mail, usually sent for commercial purposes. Spam is used by some companies as a cheap form of advertising, although it is generally considered offensive and unwelcome by the Internet community. Sending spam is regarded as unethical because the cost is paid by the recipient's site or server, not the sender's. Various Internet bodies campaign against spam and those individuals or organizations accused of spamming. The term may originate from a sketch in the U.K. comedy program *Monty Python* in which customers at a "greasy spoon" café are served the canned meat Spam with everything, regardless of whether it was part of their order, or may simply derive from the pre-existing use of the word to represent something, like the rations available to soldiers in World War II, that is plentiful and unappetizing.
2 MARKETING see *direct mail*

spam filter E-COMMERCE software available from an Internet service provider which blocks e-mails that contain certain terms or other attributes that identify the message as potential spam

spam killer E-COMMERCE a piece of software that automatically identifies and deals with spam in incoming e-mail

span of control GENERAL MANAGEMENT the number and range of subordinates for whom a manager is responsible. The span of control can be calculated by various methods which take into account such factors as whether those supervised are doing the same or different jobs and their levels of seniority, *empowerment*, experience, and qualification.

spare parts OPERATIONS & PRODUCTION a stock of components of machinery or plant held in store in case of breakdown

spatial data STATISTICS variables that are measured at different locations to illustrate the spatial organization of data

SPC *abbr* OPERATIONS & PRODUCTION statistical process control

speako GENERAL MANAGEMENT a mistake made by a computer while using a speech-recognition program (*slang*)

spear carrier HR & PERSONNEL somebody who is in the second tier of command in an organization and is responsible for carrying out the commands and communicating the messages of the top-level executives (*slang*)

Special Commissioner FINANCE, BANKING, AND ACCOUNTING an official appointed by the U.K. Treasury to hear cases where a taxpayer is appealing against an income tax assessment

special damages FINANCE, BANKING, AND ACCOUNTING damages awarded by a court to compensate for a loss which can be calculated, such as the expense of repairing something

special deposit (*U.K.*)
1 FINANCE, BANKING, AND ACCOUNTING an amount of money set aside for the rehabilitation of a mortgaged house
2 a large sum of money which a commercial bank has to deposit with the Bank of England

special leave HR & PERSONNEL exceptional *leave* that may be granted to an *employee*. Special leave includes *sabbaticals*, leave granted for study (also known as *educational leave*), leave for jury service or for volunteer forces training, leave granted to candidates for local or national elections, or for labor union duties and activities, and for *community involvement* purposes. Special leave can also refer to *maternity leave* and *paternity leave*.

special notice FINANCE, BANKING, AND ACCOUNTING notice of a proposal to be put before a meeting of the stockholders of a company which is issued less than 28 days before the meeting

special presentation FINANCE, BANKING, AND ACCOUNTING the sending of a check directly to the paying banker rather than through the clearing system. Also known as *special clearing*. See also *advice of fate*

special purpose bond FINANCE, BANKING, AND ACCOUNTING a bond for one particular project, financed by levies on the people who benefit from the project

special resolution FINANCE, BANKING, AND ACCOUNTING see *extraordinary resolution*

specie FINANCE, BANKING, AND ACCOUNTING coins, as opposed to banknotes, that are legal tender

specification OPERATIONS & PRODUCTION documentation relating to the required quantity and quality of materials, and the order of the work to be done to complete a task

specific charge FINANCE, BANKING, AND ACCOUNTING a fixed charge as opposed to a floating charge

specific order costing FINANCE, BANKING, AND ACCOUNTING the basic cost accounting method applicable where work consists of separately identifiable contracts, jobs, or batches

speculation FINANCE, BANKING, AND ACCOUNTING a purchase made solely to make a profit when the price or value increases

speech GENERAL MANAGEMENT a formal spoken address made to an audience by a speaker. Speeches are made in the context of a meeting or conference or on other occasions such as after a business dinner. The goal of a speech may be to motivate, inspire, or entertain as well as to inform. In contrast to *presentations*, speeches are a form of public speaking normally made without the assistance of audio-visual aids, and may be wide ranging rather than focusing on a well-defined topic or proposal. Jokes, humorous anecdotes, and quotations are frequently used in speeches. To give a speech successfully requires good *communication skills*.

spider food E-COMMERCE words that are embedded in a Web page to attract search engines

spiffs MARKETING gifts or money offered to store managers in exchange for promoting a product (*slang*)

spim E-COMMERCE unsolicited e-mail that arrives on a personal computer screen in the form of an instant message

spin-off GENERAL MANAGEMENT a company or subsidiary formed by splitting away from a parent company. A spin-off company can, for example, be created when research and development yields a new product that does not fit into the company's current portfolio, or when a company wants to explore a new venture related to its current activities. It can also be formed from a demerger, in which acquired companies or parts of a business are separated in order to create a more streamlined parent organization. A spin-off is often entrepreneurial in spirit, but the backing of the parent company can provide financial stability.

splash page E-COMMERCE an introductory or initial page, usually containing advertisements, presented to visitors to a Web site before they get to the *homepage*

split FINANCE, BANKING, AND ACCOUNTING an issuance to stockholders of more than one share for every share owned. See also *reverse split*

split commission FINANCE, BANKING, AND ACCOUNTING *commission* that is divided between two or more parties in a transaction

split coupon bond FINANCE, BANKING, AND ACCOUNTING see *zero coupon bond*

splitter E-COMMERCE an electronic or other device that divides something into parts, for example, a software device that enables a long file to be divided into sections or a device that splits a telephone signal so that it can carry voice and data transmissions simultaneously

sponsorship MARKETING a form of advertising in which an organization provides funds for something such as a television program or sports event in return for exposure to a target audience

Spoornet GENERAL MANAGEMENT the rail division of the state-owned South African transport company, Transnet Ltd

spot MARKETING a TV or radio commercial (*slang*)

spot color MARKETING single color overprinted on a black-and-white advertisement

spot currency market FINANCE, BANKING, AND ACCOUNTING see *spot market*

spot exchange rate FINANCE, BANKING, AND ACCOUNTING the exchange rate used for immediate currency transactions

spot goods FINANCE, BANKING, AND ACCOUNTING a commodity traded on the spot market

spot interest rate FINANCE, BANKING, AND ACCOUNTING an interest rate that is determined when a loan is made

spot market FINANCE, BANKING, AND ACCOUNTING a market that deals in commodities or foreign exchange for immediate rather than future delivery

spot month FINANCE, BANKING, AND ACCOUNTING see *nearby month*

spot price FINANCE, BANKING, AND ACCOUNTING the price for immediate delivery of a commodity or foreign exchange

spot rate FINANCE, BANKING, AND ACCOUNTING the rate of interest to maturity currently offered on a particular type of security

spot transaction FINANCE, BANKING, AND ACCOUNTING a transaction in commodities or foreign exchange for immediate delivery

spread FINANCE, BANKING, AND ACCOUNTING
1 the difference between the buying and selling price of a stock on a stock exchange
2 the range of investments in a portfolio

spreadsheet GENERAL MANAGEMENT a computer program that provides a series of ruled columns in which data can be entered and analyzed

sprinkling trust FINANCE, BANKING, AND ACCOUNTING a trust with multiple beneficiaries whose distributions occur at the trustees' discretion

spruik (*ANZ*) GENERAL MANAGEMENT to publicize goods or services, typically by standing at the door of a shop and addressing passers-by using a microphone (*slang*)

spyware E-COMMERCE software surreptitiously installed on a hard disk without the user's knowledge that relays encoded information on his or her identity and Internet use via an Internet connection

squatter (*ANZ*) GENERAL MANAGEMENT a wealthy landowner (*slang*)

squattocracy (*ANZ*) GENERAL MANAGEMENT a derogatory term for wealthy landowners, who are considered a powerful social class (*slang*)

squeaky wheel GENERAL MANAGEMENT somebody who gets good results by being extremely assertive in their dealings with other people (*slang*)

squeeze ECONOMICS a government policy of restriction, commonly affecting the availability of credit in an economy

squirt the bird GENERAL MANAGEMENT to transmit a signal to a satellite (*slang*)

Srl *abbr* FINANCE, BANKING, AND ACCOUNTING Società a responsabilità limitata

SSADM *abbr* GENERAL MANAGEMENT structured systems analysis and design method

SSL *abbr* E-COMMERCE secure sockets layer: a widely used protocol for encrypting data that permits the transmission of credit card transactions in a secure fashion

stabilization fund ECONOMICS a fund created by a government as an emergency savings account for international financial support

staffing level HR & PERSONNEL the number and type of personnel employed by an organization for the performance of a given workload. The ideal staffing level for an organization depends on the amount of work to be done and the skills required to do it. If the number and quality of staff employed are greater than necessary for the workload, an organization may be deemed to be overstaffed; if the number of staff is insufficient for the workload, an organization is deemed to be understaffed. Effective **human resource planning** will determine the appropriate staffing level for an organization at any given point in time.

stage-gate model MARKETING see *new product development*

stagflation ECONOMICS the result when both inflation and unemployment exist at the same time in an economy. There was stagflation in the United Kingdom and the United States in the 1970s, for example.

stakeholder FINANCE, BANKING, AND ACCOUNTING GENERAL MANAGEMENT a person or organization with a vested interest in the successful operation of a company or organization. A stakeholder may be an employee, customer, supplier, partner, or even the local community within which an organization operates.

stakeholder pension (*U.K.*) FINANCE, BANKING, AND ACCOUNTING HR & PERSONNEL a pension, bought from a private company, in which the retirement income depends on the level of contributions made during a person's working life. Stakeholder pensions are designed for people without access to an occupational pension plan, and are intended to provide a low-cost supplement to the state earnings related pension plan. A stakeholder pension plan can either be trust-based, like an occupational pension plan, or contract-based, similar to a personal pension. Subject to certain exceptions, employers must provide access to a stakeholder pension plan for employees, although they are not required to establish a stakeholder pension plan themselves. Membership of a stakeholder pension plan is voluntary. See also *Keough Plan*

stakeholders FINANCE, BANKING, AND ACCOUNTING groups or individuals having a legitimate interest in the activities of an organization, generally comprising customers, employees, the community, stockholders, suppliers, and lenders

stakeholder theory FINANCE, BANKING, AND ACCOUNTING GENERAL MANAGEMENT the theory that an organization can enhance the interests of its stockholders without damaging the interests of its wider *stakeholders*. Stakeholder theory grew in response to the *economic theory of the firm*, and contrasts with *Theory E*. One of the difficulties of stakeholder theory is allocating importance to the values of different groups of stakeholders, and a solution to this is proposed by *stakeholder value analysis*.

stakeholder value analysis FINANCE, BANKING, AND ACCOUNTING GENERAL MANAGEMENT a method of determining the values of the *stakeholders* in an organization for the purposes of making strategic and operational decisions. Stakeholder value analysis is one method of justifying an approach based on *stakeholder theory* rather than the *economic theory of the firm*. It involves identifying groups of stakeholders and eliciting their views on particular issues in order that these views may be taken into account when making decisions.

stale bull FINANCE, BANKING, AND ACCOUNTING an investor who bought stocks hoping that they would rise, and now finds that they have not risen and wants to sell them

stamp duty FINANCE, BANKING, AND ACCOUNTING in the United Kingdom, a duty that is payable on some legal documents and is shown to have been paid by a stamp being affixed to the document

standard FINANCE, BANKING, AND ACCOUNTING a benchmark measurement of resource usage, set in defined conditions.

Standards can be set on the following bases: on an ex ante estimate of expected performance; on an ex post estimate of attainable performance; on a prior period level of performance by the same organization; on the level of performance achieved by comparable organizations; and on the level of performance required to meet organizational objectives.

Standards may also be set at attainable levels, which assume efficient levels of operation, but which include allowances for normal loss, waste, and machine downtime, or at ideal levels, which make no allowance for the above losses and are only attainable under the most favorable conditions.

Standard & Poor's 500 Index FINANCE, BANKING, AND ACCOUNTING a U.S. index of 500 general stock prices selected by the Standard & Poor agency. Abbr. *S&P 500*, *S&P Index*

Standard & Poor's rating FINANCE, BANKING, AND ACCOUNTING a stock rating service provided by the U.S. agency Standard & Poor

standard business transaction E-COMMERCE any business procedure conducted between trading partners, characterized by a paper document or its equivalent EDI transaction set or message

standard costing FINANCE, BANKING, AND ACCOUNTING a control technique which compares standard costs and revenues with actual results to obtain variances which are used to stimulate improved performance

standard deviation OPERATIONS & PRODUCTION a measure of how dispersed a set of numbers are around their mean

standard hour FINANCE, BANKING, AND ACCOUNTING the amount of work achievable, at standard efficiency levels, in an hour

standard of living ECONOMICS a measure of economic well-being based on the ability of people to buy the goods and services they desire

standard time GENERAL MANAGEMENT
1 the length of time taken by a worker to complete a particular motion, such as reaching or grasping
2 the total time required to complete a specific task for an employee working at the expected rate. The standard time for any particular task is derived through *work measurement* and *time study* techniques, and takes into account *relaxation allowances*, which allow employees time to recover from the psychological or physiological effects of performing a task, and *contingency allowances*, which recognize that there may be legitimate causes of delay before a task can be completed. *Predetermined motion-time systems* may be used to help determine a standard time.

standby credit ECONOMICS credit drawing rights given to a developing country by an international financial institution to fund industrialization or other growth policies

standby loan ECONOMICS a loan given to a developing country by an international financial institution, to fund technology hardware purchase or other growth policies

stand down (*ANZ*) HR & PERSONNEL to suspend an employee without pay (*slang*)

standing instructions FINANCE, BANKING, AND ACCOUNTING instructions, that may be revoked at any time, for a particular procedure to be

undertaken in the event of a certain occurrence, for example, for the monies from a fixed term account that has just matured to be placed on deposit for a further fixed period

standing order (*U.K.*) FINANCE, BANKING, AND ACCOUNTING = *automatic debit*

standing room only MARKETING a sales technique whereby customers are given the impression that there are many other people waiting to buy the same product at the same time (*slang*)

staple commodity FINANCE, BANKING, AND ACCOUNTING any basic food or a raw material which is important in a country's economy

star
1 GENERAL MANAGEMENT see *Boston Box*
2 FINANCE, BANKING, AND ACCOUNTING an investment that is performing extremely well (*slang*)

startup GENERAL MANAGEMENT FINANCE, BANKING, AND ACCOUNTING a relatively new, usually small business, particularly one supported by venture capital and within those sectors closely linked to new technologies

startup costs FINANCE, BANKING, AND ACCOUNTING the initial sum required to establish a business or to get a project underway. The costs will include the capital expenditure and related expenses before the business or project generates revenue.

startup model GENERAL MANAGEMENT a business model based on rapid short-term success. Typically, the objective is to acquire venture capital, grow rapidly, and go public or sell off quickly, generating profit for the founders but not necessarily for the business.

state bank FINANCE, BANKING, AND ACCOUNTING a bank chartered by a state

state capitalism ECONOMICS a way of organizing society in which the state controls most of a country's means of production and capital

State Earnings-Related Pension Scheme FINANCE, BANKING, AND ACCOUNTING see *SERPS*

state enterprise GENERAL MANAGEMENT an organization in which the government or state has a controlling interest

statement FINANCE, BANKING, AND ACCOUNTING a summary of all transactions, such as deposits or withdrawals, that have occurred in an account over a given period of time

statement of account FINANCE, BANKING, AND ACCOUNTING
1 a summary of recent transactions between two parties
2 a list of sums due, usually relating to unpaid invoices, items paid on account but not offset against particular invoices, credit notes, debit notes, and discounts

statement of affairs FINANCE, BANKING, AND ACCOUNTING a statement, usually prepared by a receiver, in a prescribed form, showing the estimated financial position of a debtor or of a company which may be unable to meet its debts. It contains a summary of the debtor's assets and liabilities. The assets are shown at their estimated realizable values. The various classes of creditors, such as preferential, secured, partly secured, and unsecured, are shown separately.

statement of cash flows FINANCE, BANKING, AND ACCOUNTING a statement that documents actual receipts and expenditures of cash

statement-of-cash-flows method FINANCE, BANKING, AND ACCOUNTING a method of accounting that is based on flows of cash rather than balances on accounts

statement of changes in financial position FINANCE, BANKING, AND ACCOUNTING a financial report of a company's incomes and outflows during a period, usually a year or a quarter

Statement of Financial Accounting Standards FINANCE, BANKING, AND ACCOUNTING in the United States, a statement detailing the standards to be adopted for the preparation of financial statements. Abbr *SFAS*

statement of source and application of funds FINANCE, BANKING, AND ACCOUNTING see *cash flow statement*

statement of total recognized gains and losses FINANCE, BANKING, AND ACCOUNTING a financial statement showing changes in stockholders' equity during an accounting period

state of balance GENERAL MANAGEMENT an approach to capitalism that balances ecological and economic priorities

statistic FINANCE, BANKING, AND ACCOUNTING a piece of information in numerical form

statistical expert system STATISTICS a computer program used to conduct a statistical analysis of a set of data

statistical model STATISTICS the particular methods used to investigate the data in a statistical study

statistical process control OPERATIONS & PRODUCTION a means of monitoring a *process* to assist in identifying causes of variation with the goal of improving process performance. Statistical process control consists of three elements: data gathering; determining control limits; and variation reduction. The tools used include process *flow charts*, tally charts, histograms, graphs, *fishbone charts*, and control charts. The thinking behind SPC has been attributed to *Walter Shewhart* in the 1920s. Abbr. *SPC*

statistical quality control STATISTICS the process of inspecting samples of a product to check for consistent quality according to given parameters

statistical significance FINANCE, BANKING, AND ACCOUNTING the level of importance at which an event influences a set of *statistics*

statistics FINANCE, BANKING, AND ACCOUNTING information in numerical form and its collection, analysis, and presentation

statute-barred debt FINANCE, BANKING, AND ACCOUNTING a debt that cannot be pursued as the time limit laid down by law has expired

statutory auditor (*U.K.*) FINANCE, BANKING, AND ACCOUNTING a professional person qualified to conduct an audit required by the U.K. Companies Act

statutory body FINANCE, BANKING, AND ACCOUNTING an entity formed by government legislation

STC *abbr* (*S. Africa*) FINANCE, BANKING, AND ACCOUNTING Secondary Tax on Companies: a secondary tax levied on corporate dividends

steg analysis E-COMMERCE the process of searching through computer files to find slight deviations in expected patterns that may reveal the presence of hidden messages

steganography E-COMMERCE the production and placing in computer files of secret messages so small as to be detectable only by special software

STEP analysis GENERAL MANAGEMENT see *PEST analysis*

Stewart, Rosemary Gordon GENERAL MANAGEMENT British academic. Respected for her research on managerial work and behavior, including the essential aspects of becoming an effective manager, published in *The Reality of Management* (1963).

Stewart, Thomas A. (*b.* 1948) GENERAL MANAGEMENT U.S. publisher and writer. A leader in the *knowledge management* debate who, in *Intellectual Capital: The New Wealth of Organizations* (1997), encouraged organizations to exploit their untapped knowledge.

stickiness E-COMMERCE a Web site's ability to hold visitors and to keep them coming back (*slang*)

stick to the knitting GENERAL MANAGEMENT an exhortation to organizations to concentrate on the activities, products, and services that are key to their *core business* and consequently to their success. Stick to the knitting was popularized by *Tom Peters* and *Bob Waterman* in their book *In Search of Excellence* (1984).

sticky floor HR & PERSONNEL the factors which keep women in low level, nonmanagerial and support roles and prevent them from seeking or gaining promotion or career development. This term may refer to barriers to the advancement of women such as family commitments, attitudes, stereotyping, and organizational structures but has also been used to focus on circumstances where women are promoted but do not receive commensurate wage rises. It is most likely to be used with reference to women, though it may also apply to other groups of employees. The *lead ceiling* is a similar concept.

sticky site E-COMMERCE a Web site that holds the interest of visitors for a substantial amount of time, and is therefore effective as a marketing vehicle. (*slang*) Also known as *heavy site*

stipend HR & PERSONNEL a regular remuneration or allowance paid to an individual holding a particular office

stock FINANCE, BANKING, AND ACCOUNTING **1** equity in a company measured in shares **2** (*U.K.*) the *capital* made available to an organization after a stock issue

stockalypse FINANCE, BANKING, AND ACCOUNTING a dramatic drop in stock price

stockbroker FINANCE, BANKING, AND ACCOUNTING somebody who arranges the sale and purchase of stocks

stock capital FINANCE, BANKING, AND ACCOUNTING an amount of fully paid-up capital, any part of which can be transferred, for example, a block of $1,000 of stock out of a total holding of $15,000

stock certificate FINANCE, BANKING, AND ACCOUNTING a document that certifies ownership of a stock in a company. U.K. term *share certificate*

stock control GENERAL MANAGEMENT see *inventory*

stockcount FINANCE, BANKING, AND ACCOUNTING profit gained from ownership of a stock

stock exchange FINANCE, BANKING, AND ACCOUNTING a registered market in securities

Stock Exchange Automated Quotations system FINANCE, BANKING, AND ACCOUNTING see *SEAQ*

Stock Exchange Automated Quotations system International FINANCE, BANKING, AND ACCOUNTING see *SEAQ International*

Stock Exchange Automatic Trading System FINANCE, BANKING, AND ACCOUNTING see *SEATS*

stock-for-stock offer FINANCE, BANKING, AND ACCOUNTING a takeover bid where the bidder offers its own stock, or a combination of cash and stock, for the target company

stockholder FINANCE, BANKING, AND ACCOUNTING a person or organization that owns one or more shares of stock in a corporation. Also known as *shareholder*

stockholders' equity FINANCE, BANKING, AND ACCOUNTING a company's share capital and reserves. Also known as *shareholders' equity*

stockholder value FINANCE, BANKING, AND ACCOUNTING total return to the stockholders in terms of both dividends and share price growth, calculated as the present value of future free cash flows of the business discounted at the weighted average cost of the capital of the business less the market value of its debt. Also known as *shareholder value*

stockholder value analysis FINANCE, BANKING, AND ACCOUNTING see *shareholder value analysis*

stockholding FINANCE, BANKING, AND ACCOUNTING the stock in a limited company owned by a stockholder

stock incentive plan a type of financial *incentive plan* in which employees can acquire shares in the company in which they work and so have an interest in its financial performance. A stock incentive plan is a type of *employee stock ownership plan*, in which employees may be given stock by their employer, or stock may be offered for purchase at

a-z

1630

DICTIONARY

an advantageous price, as a reward for personal or group performance.

stock index FINANCE, BANKING, AND ACCOUNTING see *index*

stock issue FINANCE, BANKING, AND ACCOUNTING the offering for sale of stock in a company. The *capital* derived from stock issues can be used for investment in the core business or for expansion into new commercial ventures.

stockjobber (*India*) FINANCE, BANKING, AND ACCOUNTING see *market maker*

stock market FINANCE, BANKING, AND ACCOUNTING the trading of stocks, or a place where this occurs

stock market index FINANCE, BANKING, AND ACCOUNTING see *index*

stock market manipulation FINANCE, BANKING, AND ACCOUNTING an attempt or series of attempts to influence the price of stocks by buying or selling in order to give the impression that the stocks are widely traded

stock market rating FINANCE, BANKING, AND ACCOUNTING the price of a stock on the stock market, which shows how investors and financial advisers generally consider the value of the company

stock option FINANCE, BANKING, AND ACCOUNTING see *option*

stockout (*U.K.*) OPERATIONS & PRODUCTION the situation where the stock of a particular component or part has been used up and has not yet been replenished. Stockouts result from poor inventory control or the failure of a *just-in-time* supply system. They can result in delays in the delivery of customer orders and can damage the reputation of the business.

stock split FINANCE, BANKING, AND ACCOUNTING a proportional issue of free stocks to existing owners of a company's stock. Also known as *bonus shares*, *share split*. U.K. term *scrip issue*

stock symbol FINANCE, BANKING, AND ACCOUNTING a shortened version of a company's name, usually made up of two to four letters, used in screen-based trading systems

stocktaking OPERATIONS & PRODUCTION the process of measuring the quantities of stock held by an organization. Stock, or *inventory*, can be held both in stores and within the processes of the operation. Better *materials management* and inventory systems have made annual stocktaking less important.

stock transfer form FINANCE, BANKING, AND ACCOUNTING a form used to transfer stock between parties, for example, from an individual to a charitable organization or university

stock turnover FINANCE, BANKING, AND ACCOUNTING the total value of stock sold in a year divided by the average value of goods held in stock. This checks that cash is not tied up in stock for too long, losing its value over time.

stock turns or **stock turnover** FINANCE, BANKING, AND ACCOUNTING see *inventory turnover*

stokvel (*S. Africa*) FINANCE, BANKING, AND ACCOUNTING an informal, widely used cooperative savings program that provides small-scale loans

stop-go ECONOMICS the alternate tightening and loosening of fiscal and monetary policies. This characterized the U.K. economy in the 1960s and 1970s.

stop limit order FINANCE, BANKING, AND ACCOUNTING an order to trade only if and when a security reaches a specified price

stop loss FINANCE, BANKING, AND ACCOUNTING an order to trade only if and when a security falls to a specified price

stop order FINANCE, BANKING, AND ACCOUNTING an order to trade only if and when a security rises above or falls below its current price

stop-work meeting (*ANZ*) HR & PERSONNEL a meeting held by employees during working hours to discuss issues such as wage claims and working conditions with union representatives or management

story stock FINANCE, BANKING, AND ACCOUNTING a stock that is the subject of a press or financial community story that may affect its price

stovepiping GENERAL MANAGEMENT a rigidly vertical management style that discourages lateral lines of responsibility and hinders communication among individual groups within an organization

straight-line depreciation FINANCE, BANKING, AND ACCOUNTING a form of depreciation in which the cost of a fixed asset is spread equally over each year of its anticipated lifetime

Straits Times Industrial Index FINANCE, BANKING, AND ACCOUNTING an index of 30 Singapore stocks, the most commonly quoted indicator of stock market activity in Singapore

strata title (*ANZ*) GENERAL MANAGEMENT a system for registering ownership of space within a

multilevel building, under which a title applies to the space and a proportion of the common property

strata unit (*ANZ*) GENERAL MANAGEMENT an apartment or office within a multilevel building that has been registered under the *strata title* system

STRATE *abbr* (*S. Africa*) FINANCE, BANKING, AND ACCOUNTING Share Transactions Totally Electronic: the electronic stock transactions system of the Johannesburg Stock Exchange

strategic alignment GENERAL MANAGEMENT see *strategic fit*

strategic alliance GENERAL MANAGEMENT an agreement between two or more organizations to cooperate in a specific business activity, so that each benefits from the strengths of the other, and gains *competitive advantage*. The formation of strategic alliances has been seen as a response to *globalization* and increasing uncertainty and complexity in the business environment. Strategic alliances involve the sharing of knowledge and expertise between partners as well as the reduction of risk and costs in areas such as relationships with suppliers and the development of new products and technologies. A strategic alliance is sometimes equated with a *joint venture*, but an alliance may involve competitors, and generally has a shorter life span. *Strategic partnering* is a closely related concept.

strategic analysis GENERAL MANAGEMENT the process of conducting research on the business environment within which an organization operates and on the organization itself, in order to formulate *strategy*. A number of tools are used in the process of strategic analysis, including *PEST*, *SWOT analysis*, and *Michael Porter*'s five forces model.

strategic business unit GENERAL MANAGEMENT a division within a large organization that shares the organization's market and customer focus but has responsibility for development of its own marketing strategy. The establishment of a structure based on a strategic business unit recognizes that a single strategic approach is often inappropriate in large diversified organizations or multinational companies.

strategic capability GENERAL MANAGEMENT the competencies, knowledge, and skills that an organization can apply to achieve success in a competitive environment. The concept is thought to be derived from the core competencies approach to corporate strategy. It is viewed as one of the main pillars of strategic management and focuses on the ability to

provide products that customers value or will value in the future. This involves the need to adjust and change in order to "fit" the changing environment and the need to "stretch" to exploit organizational resources in ways that are innovative, or that other organizations will find it hard to match.

strategic financial management FINANCE, BANKING, AND ACCOUNTING the identification of the possible strategies capable of maximizing an organization's net present value, the allocation of scarce capital resources among the competing opportunities, and the implementation and monitoring of the chosen strategy so as to achieve stated objectives

strategic fit GENERAL MANAGEMENT the extent to which the activities of a single organization or of organizations working in partnership complement each other in such a way as to contribute to *competitive advantage*. The benefits of good strategic fit include cost reduction, due to economies of scale, and the transfer of knowledge and skills. The success of a *merger*, *joint venture*, or *strategic alliance* may be affected by the degree of strategic fit between the organizations involved. Similarly, the strategic fit of one organization with another is often a factor in decisions about acquisitions, mergers, *diversification*, or *divestment*. Also known as *strategic alignment*

strategic goal GENERAL MANAGEMENT the overall goal of an organization in terms of its market position in the medium or long-term. A strategic goal forms part of an organization's *corporate strategy*, and should act as a motivating force as well as a measure of performance and achievement for those working in an organization.

strategic inflection point GENERAL MANAGEMENT the time at which an organization takes a decision to change its *corporate strategy* to pursue a different direction and avoid the risk of decline. The term was coined by *Andy Grove* of Intel to describe the period of change that affects an organization's competitive position. It also concerns the ability of organizations to recognize and adapt to change factors of major significance.

strategic information systems GENERAL MANAGEMENT an information system established with the goal of creating *competitive advantage* and improving the competitive position of an organization. A strategic information system supports and shapes the *corporate strategy* of an organization, often leading to innovation in the way the organization conducts its business, the creation of new

business opportunities, or the development of products and services based on information technology. Strategic information systems represent a development in organizational use of information systems, following in the wake of *MIS*s, *EIS*s, and *decision support systems*. Abbr. **SIS**

strategic management GENERAL MANAGEMENT the development of *corporate strategy*, and the management of an organization according to that strategy. Strategic management focuses on achieving and maintaining a strong *competitive advantage*. It involves the application of corporate strategy to all aspects of the organization, and especially to *decision making*. As a discipline, strategic management developed in the 1970s, but it has evolved in response to changes in *organization structure* and *corporate culture*. With greater *empowerment*, strategy has become the concern not just of directors but also of employees at all levels of the organization.

strategic marketing MARKETING a method of selling products directly to customers, bypassing traditional retailers or distributors

strategic partnering GENERAL MANAGEMENT structured collaboration between organizations to take joint advantage of market opportunities, or to respond to customers more effectively than could be achieved in isolation. Strategic partnering occurs both in and between the public and private sectors. Besides allowing information, skills, and resources to be shared, a strategic partnership also permits the partners to share risk. See also *strategic alliance*

strategic planning GENERAL MANAGEMENT see *planning*

strategy
1 FINANCE, BANKING, AND ACCOUNTING a course of action, including the specification of resources required, to achieve a specific objective
2 GENERAL MANAGEMENT HR & PERSONNEL a planned course of action undertaken to achieve the goals and objectives of an organization. The term was originally used in the context of warfare to describe the overall planning of a campaign as opposed to tactics, which enable the achievement of specific short-term objectives. The overall strategy of an organization is known as *corporate strategy*, but strategy may also be developed for any aspect of an organization's activities such as *environmental management* or manufacturing strategy.

strategy mapping GENERAL MANAGEMENT the visual representation of an organization's plans

to turn its resources and *assets*, including intangibles such as knowledge and culture, into tangible outcomes linked to organizational objectives. Strategy maps provide a detailed picture of organizational objectives and the relationships between them. They are used to help organizations manage corporate strategy and realize objectives through improvements in specific areas such as customer retention or faster cycle times. The concept of strategy mapping was developed by Robert Kaplan and David Norton as part of their work on the *balanced scorecard*.

stratified random sampling STATISTICS sampling carried out at random from each stratum of a stratified population

stratified sampling OPERATIONS & PRODUCTION see *random sampling*

straw man GENERAL MANAGEMENT a first proposal for a solution to a problem, offered more as a place to start looking for a solution than as a serious suggestion for final action

streaming E-COMMERCE Web technology used for simultaneous downloading and viewing of large amounts of material. For example, with a *multimedia* file, the user can download just enough of the file to start viewing or listening to it, while the rest of the file is downloaded in the background—reducing, but not eliminating, download time.

street FINANCE, BANKING, AND ACCOUNTING used to describe somebody who is considered to be well informed about the market (*slang*)

street name FINANCE, BANKING, AND ACCOUNTING a broker who holds a customer's security in the brokerage house's name to facilitate transactions

stress HR & PERSONNEL the psychological and physical state that results when perceived demands exceed an individual's ability to cope with them

stress puppy HR & PERSONNEL somebody who complains a lot and seems to enjoy being stressed (*slang*)

strike HR & PERSONNEL a concerted refusal to work by employees, with the goal of improving wages or employment conditions, voicing a grievance, making a protest, or supporting other workers in such an endeavor. A strike is a form of *industrial action*.

strike pay *or* **strike benefit** HR & PERSONNEL a benefit or allowance paid by a *labor union* to its members during the course of official *strike*

action to help offset loss of earnings. Also known as **dispute benefit**

strike price FINANCE, BANKING, AND ACCOUNTING the price for a security or commodity that underlies an option

stripped bond FINANCE, BANKING, AND ACCOUNTING a bond that can be divided into separate zero-coupon bonds to represent its principal and interest payments

stripped stock FINANCE, BANKING, AND ACCOUNTING stock whose rights to dividends have been separated and sold

strips FINANCE, BANKING, AND ACCOUNTING the parts of a bond that entitle the owner to only interest payments or to only the payment of principal

structural adjustment ECONOMICS the reallocation of resources in response to a change in the output composition of an economy. Also known as **structural change**

structural change ECONOMICS see **structural adjustment**

structural fund FINANCE, BANKING, AND ACCOUNTING a mutual fund that invests in projects that contribute to the economic development of poorer nations in the European Union

structural inflation FINANCE, BANKING, AND ACCOUNTING inflation that naturally occurs in an economy, without any particular triggering event

structural unemployment ECONOMICS unemployment resulting from a change in demand or technology changes so that there is a surplus of labor in a particular location or skills area

structured interview HR & PERSONNEL see **interviewing**

structured systems analysis and design method GENERAL MANAGEMENT a technique for the analysis and design of computer systems. The structured systems analysis and design method was developed by the Central Computer and Telecommunications Agency in the United Kingdom in the early 1980s. The technique adopts a structured methodology toward systems development through the use of data flow, logical data, and entity event modeling. Core development stages include **feasibility study**; requirements analysis; requirements specification; logical system specification; and physical design. All the steps and tasks within each stage must be complete before subsequent stages can begin. Abbr. **SSADM**

stub equity FINANCE, BANKING, AND ACCOUNTING the money raised through the sale of high risk bonds in large amounts or quantities, as in a leveraged takeover or a leveraged buyout

Subchapter S Corporation FINANCE, BANKING, AND ACCOUNTING see **S Corporation**

subcontract GENERAL MANAGEMENT a **contract** under which all, or part, of the work specified in an existing contract is delegated to another person or organization

subcontracting GENERAL MANAGEMENT OPERATIONS & PRODUCTION the delegation to a third party of some, or all, of the work that one has **contracted** to do. Subcontracting usually occurs where the contracted work (for example, the construction of a building) requires a variety of skills. Responsibility for the fulfillment of the original **contract** remains with the original contracting party. Where the fulfillment of a contract depends on the skills of the person who has entered into the contract (for example, in the painting of a portrait), then the work cannot be subcontracted to a third party. The term subcontracting is sometimes used to describe **outsourcing** arrangements.

subject line E-COMMERCE the field at the top of an e-mail template in which the title or subject of the e-mail can be typed. The subject line is the only part of the e-mail—apart from the name of the sender—which can be read immediately by the recipient. It is important to have a strong subject line, particularly if using e-mail for advertising or promotional purposes, or the recipient may simply delete the e-mail.

subject to collection FINANCE, BANKING, AND ACCOUNTING dependent upon the ability to collect the amount owed

subliminal advertising MARKETING advertising intended to influence an audience subconsciously, especially through images shown very briefly on a movie or television screen

subordinated debt FINANCE, BANKING, AND ACCOUNTING see **junior debt**

subordinated loan FINANCE, BANKING, AND ACCOUNTING a loan that ranks below all other borrowings with regard to both the payment of interest and principal. See also **pari passu**

subscribed share capital FINANCE, BANKING, AND ACCOUNTING see **issued share capital**

subscriber
1 E-COMMERCE a Web site user who chooses to receive information, content, or services on a regular basis

2 FINANCE, BANKING, AND ACCOUNTING a buyer, especially one who buys stocks in a new company or new issues
3 FINANCE, BANKING, AND ACCOUNTING a person who signs a company's Memorandum of Association

subscription-based publishing E-COMMERCE content or a selection of content from a Web site, magazine, book, or other publication, delivered regularly by e-mail or other means to a group of people who have subscribed to received this content

subscription process E-COMMERCE the means by which users of a Web site sign up to receive specific information, content, or services via that Web site. Someone may become a subscriber as a result of giving personal information such as an e-mail address, or of making a payment if the subscription service is directly revenue-generating.

The early Internet promoted a culture that encouraged the free transfer of information, so subscription processes were relatively rare. However, it is becoming clear that in general Web sites must pay for themselves—either directly through subscription or advertising revenues, or indirectly by delivering valuable information that will further the organization's objectives. As the Internet evolves, many more Web sites will become subscription-based.

Subscription processes are also used to limit access to certain information. An extranet, for example, may contain confidential material, and a subscription process will be required to make sure that the right people have access to the right information.

subscription share FINANCE, BANKING, AND ACCOUNTING a stock purchased by a subscriber when a new company is formed

subsidiary account FINANCE, BANKING, AND ACCOUNTING an account for one of the individual people or organizations that jointly hold another account

subsidiary company GENERAL MANAGEMENT a company that is controlled by another. A subsidiary company operates under the control of a parent or **holding company**, which may have a majority on the subsidiary's **board of directors**, or a majority shareholding in the subsidiary—giving it majority voting rights—or it may be named in a contract as having control of the subsidiary. If all of the stock in a company is owned by its parent, it is known as a **wholly-owned subsidiary**. A subsidiary that is located in a different country from the parent is a **foreign subsidiary company**.

subsistence allowance HR & PERSONNEL *expenses* paid by an *employer*, usually within pre-set limits, to cover the cost of accommodations, meals, and incidental expenses incurred by employees when away on business

subtreasury FINANCE, BANKING, AND ACCOUNTING a place where some of a nation's money is held

succession planning GENERAL MANAGEMENT the preparation for the replacement of one jobholder by another, usually prompted by *retirement* or *resignation*. Succession planning involves preparing the new jobholder before the old one leaves, possibly with training or through work shadowing. At a senior level, *management succession* should be accomplished as smoothly as possible in order to avoid organizational crises caused by absent or inadequate top management. General Electric is held to be an exemplar of succession planning for its successful transition following the retirement of *Jack Welch*.

suggestion program HR & PERSONNEL a policy designed to encourage employees to generate ideas or proposals that improve work processes, for which they receive a gift or cash reward. The objective of a suggestion program is to promote *employee involvement*, creative thinking, and continuous improvement. Its success can be evaluated in terms of the participation rate or by the level of cost savings, but there may be an incalculable beneficial effect on sales, customer loyalty, retention of employees, and *motivation*.

suit GENERAL MANAGEMENT somebody who works for a large corporation and is required to wear a suit for work (*slang*)

sum FINANCE, BANKING, AND ACCOUNTING
1 an amount of money
2 the total amount of any given item, such as stocks or securities
3 the total arising from the addition of two or more numbers

sum at risk FINANCE, BANKING, AND ACCOUNTING an amount of any given item, such as money, stocks, or securities that an investor may lose

sum insured FINANCE, BANKING, AND ACCOUNTING the maximum amount that an insurance company will pay out in the event of a claim

sum of digits method FINANCE, BANKING, AND ACCOUNTING a method of depreciating a fixed asset where the cost of the asset (less its residual value) is multiplied by a fraction based on the number of years of its expected useful life. The fraction changes each year and charges the highest costs to the earliest years.

sum-of-the-year's-digits depreciation FINANCE, BANKING, AND ACCOUNTING accelerated depreciation, conferring tax advantage by assuming more rapid depreciation when an asset is new

Sunday night syndrome GENERAL MANAGEMENT feelings of depression experienced by employees when they consider their return to work on Monday morning (*slang*)

sunk cost FINANCE, BANKING, AND ACCOUNTING a cost which has been irreversibly incurred or committed prior to a decision point, and which cannot therefore be considered relevant to subsequent decisions

sunshine law FINANCE, BANKING, AND ACCOUNTING a law that requires public disclosure of a government act

superannuation plan HR & PERSONNEL a pension plan in Australia

superannuation scheme HR & PERSONNEL a pension plan in New Zealand

superindustrial society GENERAL MANAGEMENT a society in which technology dominates both the personal and working lives of its members

superstitial E-COMMERCE a form of Web-based advertisement that is run while new Web pages are loading onto a user's computer. Unlike *interstitials*, superstitials are loaded onto the computer using a "cache-and-play" delivery system that works while the Internet user is browsing the Web. Superstitials are mainly used during business-to-consumer advertising campaigns.

supervisor GENERAL MANAGEMENT HR & PERSONNEL an employee who is given authority and responsibility for planning and controlling the work of a group through close contact. A supervisor is the first level of management in an organization. The subordinates he or she controls are usually at a nonmanagerial level, and the supervisor is wholly responsible for their work.

supervisory management GENERAL MANAGEMENT HR & PERSONNEL the most junior level of management within an organization. Supervisory management activities include staff *recruitment*, handling day-to-day grievances and staff discipline, and ensuring that quality and production targets are met. Also known as *first-line management*

supplier OPERATIONS & PRODUCTION an organization that delivers materials, components, goods, or services to another organization

supplier appraisal OPERATIONS & PRODUCTION see *vendor rating*

supplier evaluation OPERATIONS & PRODUCTION the process of screening and evaluating potential suppliers of materials, goods, or services. Supplier evaluation involves establishing a set of requirements, which may include basic business robustness, performance elements specific to the product or service, and the key order winning criteria for final selection. Existing and potential suppliers are screened against these criteria, prior to placing a new order. When this process is undertaken after the fulfillment of an order, it is known as *vendor rating*.

supplier rating OPERATIONS & PRODUCTION see *vendor rating*

supply and demand ECONOMICS the quantity of goods available for sale at a given price, and the level of consumer need for those goods. The balance of supply and demand fluctuates as external economic factors (such as the cost of materials and the level of competition in the marketplace) influence the level of demand from consumers and the desire and ability of producers to supply the goods. Supply and demand is recognized as an economic force, and is often referred to as the *law of supply and demand*.

supply chain GENERAL MANAGEMENT OPERATIONS & PRODUCTION the network of *manufacturers*, *wholesalers*, distributors, and *retailers*, who turn *raw materials* into *finished goods* and services and deliver them to *consumers*. Supply chains are increasingly being seen as integrated entities, and closer relationships between the organizations throughout the chain can bring *competitive advantage*, reduce costs, and help to maintain a loyal customer base.

supply chain management OPERATIONS & PRODUCTION the management of the movement of goods and flow of information between an organization and its *suppliers* and *customers*, to achieve strategic advantage. Supply chain management covers the processes of *materials management*, *logistics*, *physical distribution management*, *purchasing*, and *information management*.

supply-side economics ECONOMICS the study of how economic agents behave when supply is affected by changes in price

support MARKETING help, advice, and services offered to customers by a seller after a sale

support price ECONOMICS the price of a product that is fixed or stabilized by a government so that it cannot fall below a certain level

surety FINANCE, BANKING, AND ACCOUNTING
1 a guarantor
2 the collateral given as security when borrowing

surplus FINANCE, BANKING, AND ACCOUNTING see *budget surplus*

surplus capacity OPERATIONS & PRODUCTION the capability of a factory or workstation to produce output over and above the level required by consumers or subsequent processes. Surplus capacity is a product of materials, personnel, and equipment that are superfluous, or not working to maximum *capacity*. Some surplus capacity is required in any production system to deal with fluctuations in demand, and as a backup in case of failure. Excessive surplus capacity, however, adds to the cost of the production process as work-in-process inventory or finished-goods storage increases, and can result in *overcapacity*. If a workstation has no surplus capacity its workloads cannot be increased, so it is at risk of becoming a *bottleneck*. Also known as *redundant capacity*

surrender value FINANCE, BANKING, AND ACCOUNTING the sum of money offered by an insurance company to somebody who cancels a policy before it has completed its full term

surtax FINANCE, BANKING, AND ACCOUNTING a tax paid in addition to another tax, typically levied on a corporation with very high income

survey MARKETING STATISTICS the collection of data from a given population for the purpose of analysis of a particular issue. Data is often collected from only a sample of a population, and this is known as a *sample survey*. Surveys are used widely in research, especially in *market research*.

survivalist enterprise (S. Africa) FINANCE, BANKING, AND ACCOUNTING a business that has no paid employees, generates income below the poverty line, and is considered the lowest level of microenterprise

sushi bond FINANCE, BANKING, AND ACCOUNTING a bond that is not denominated in yen and is issued in any market by a Japanese financial institution. This type of bond is often bought by Japanese institutional investors. (*slang*)

suspense account FINANCE, BANKING, AND ACCOUNTING an account in which debits or credits are held temporarily until sufficient information is available for them to be posted to the correct accounts

sustainable advantage GENERAL MANAGEMENT a competitive advantage that can be maintained over the long term, as opposed to one resulting from a short-term tactical promotion

sustainable development GENERAL MANAGEMENT development that meets the needs of the present without compromising the ability of future generations to meet their own needs. The concept of sustainable development was introduced by the Brundtland Report, the first report of the World Commission on Environment and Development, established by the United Nations in 1983. It advocates the integration of social, economic, and environmental considerations into policy decisions by business and government. Particular emphasis is given to social, cultural, and ethical implications of development. Sustainable development can be achieved through *environmental management* and is a feature of a socially responsible business.

SVA *abbr* FINANCE, BANKING, AND ACCOUNTING shareholder value analysis

swap FINANCE, BANKING, AND ACCOUNTING
1 an exchange of *credits* or *liabilities*. See also *asset swap*, *bond swap*, *interest rate swap*
2 an arrangement whereby two organizations contractually agree to exchange payments on different terms, for example, in different currencies, or one at a fixed rate and the other at a floating rate

swap book FINANCE, BANKING, AND ACCOUNTING a broker's list of stocks or securities that clients wish to swap

swaption FINANCE, BANKING, AND ACCOUNTING an option to enter into a *swap* contract (*slang*)

sweat equity GENERAL MANAGEMENT an investment of labor rather than cash in a business enterprise (*slang*)

sweep facility FINANCE, BANKING, AND ACCOUNTING the automatic transfer of sums from a checking account to a deposit account, or from any low interest account to a higher one. For example, a personal customer may have the balance transferred just before receipt of their monthly salary, or a business may stipulate that when a balance exceeds a certain sum, the excess is to be transferred.

sweetener
1 GENERAL MANAGEMENT an incentive offered to somebody to take a particular course of action

2 FINANCE, BANKING, AND ACCOUNTING a feature added to a security to make it more attractive to investors
3 FINANCE, BANKING, AND ACCOUNTING a security with a high yield that has been added to a portfolio to improve its overall return. See also *kicker*

sweetheart agreement (ANZ) HR & PERSONNEL an agreement reached between employees and their employer without recourse to arbitration

SWIFT *abbr* FINANCE, BANKING, AND ACCOUNTING Society for Worldwide Interbank Financial Telecommunication: a nonprofit cooperative organization with the mission of creating a shared worldwide data processing and communications link and a common language for international financial transactions. Established in Brussels in 1973 with the support of 239 banks in 15 countries, it now has over 7,000 live users in 192 countries, exchanging millions of messages valued in trillions of dollars every business day.

swing trading FINANCE, BANKING, AND ACCOUNTING the trading of stock by individuals that takes advantage of sudden price movements that occur especially when large numbers of traders have to cover short sales

swipe box E-COMMERCE an electronic device used for reading the magnetic data on a credit card during a card-present transaction

switch FINANCE, BANKING, AND ACCOUNTING
1 to exchange a specific security with another within a portfolio, usually because the investor's objectives have changed
2 a swap exchange rate. See also *swap*
3 to move a commodity from one location to another

Switch FINANCE, BANKING, AND ACCOUNTING a debit card widely used in the United Kingdom

switching FINANCE, BANKING, AND ACCOUNTING the simultaneous sale and purchase of contracts in futures with different expiration dates, as for example, when a business decides that it would like to take delivery of a commodity earlier or later than originally contracted

switching discount FINANCE, BANKING, AND ACCOUNTING the discount available to holders of collective investments who move from one fund to another offered by the same fund manager. This is usually a lower initial charge compared to the one made to new investors or when existing investors make a further investment.

SWOT analysis GENERAL MANAGEMENT MARKETING an assessment of Strengths, Weaknesses, Opportunities, and Threats. SWOT analysis is used within organizations in the early stages of strategic and *marketing planning*. It is also used in *problem solving*, *decision making*, or for making staff aware of the need for change. It can be used at a personal level when examining your *career path* or determining possible *career development*.

Sydney Futures Exchange FINANCE, BANKING, AND ACCOUNTING the principal market in Australia for trading financial and commodity futures. It was established in 1962 as a wool futures market, the Sydney Greasy Wool Futures Exchange, but adopted its current name in 1972 to reflect its widening role. Abbr. *SFE*

symmetrical distribution STATISTICS a distribution of statistical data that is symmetrical about a central value

syndicated research MARKETING trend data supplied by research agencies from their regularly operated retail audits or consumer panels

sysop E-COMMERCE systems operator; somebody who manages a Web site or bulletin board (*slang*)

systematic sampling OPERATIONS & PRODUCTION see *random sampling*

system attack E-COMMERCE a deliberate attack on an e-mail system, usually in the form of a barrage of messages sent to one address simultaneously

systems administrator E-COMMERCE the person responsible for the management of an e-mail system

systems analysis GENERAL MANAGEMENT the examination and evaluation of an operation or task in order to identify and implement more efficient methods, usually through the use of computers. Systems analysis can be broken down into three main areas: the production of a statement of objectives; determination of the methods of best achieving these objectives in a cost-effective and efficient way; and the preparation of a *feasibility study*. Also known as *systems planning*

systems approach GENERAL MANAGEMENT a technique employed for organizational *decision making* and *problem solving* involving the use of computer systems. The systems approach uses *systems analysis* to examine the interdependency, interconnections, and interrelations of a system's components. When working in synergy, these components produce an effect greater than the sum of the parts. System components might comprise departments or functions of an organization or business which work together for an overall objective.

systems audit GENERAL MANAGEMENT an approach to *auditing* which utilizes the *systems method*. By using a systems audit to assess the internal control system of an organization, it is possible to assess the quality of the accounting system and the level of testing required from the financial statements. One shortcoming of systems audit is that it does not consider audit *risk*. Consequently, risk-based audit is now considered more effective.

systems design GENERAL MANAGEMENT the creation of a computer program to meet predetermined functional, operational, and personnel specifications. The systems design process involves the use of *systems analysis* and flow-charting of organizational functions and operations. It can be split into four stages: definition of the system's goals; preparation of a conceptual model of how these goals will be achieved; development of a physical design; and preparation of a system specification.

systems dynamics GENERAL MANAGEMENT a computer-based tool, developed at the Massachusetts Institute of Technology, designed to model the behavior of constantly changing systems. Systems dynamics investigates the combined effects of individual changes made at different points in a system, and uses *simulation* to design information feedback structures.

systems engineering GENERAL MANAGEMENT the process of planning, designing, creating, testing, and operating complex systems. Systems engineering can be viewed as a continuous cycle, aimed at developing alternative strategies for effective systems utilization. It is concerned with the definition, planning, and deployment of future systems.

systems method GENERAL MANAGEMENT a widely-used group of methodologies which explore the nature of complex business situations by mapping activities in a model. The systems method can be applied to systems that are either *hard systems*, where precise objectives are expressed in mathematical terms, or *soft systems*, where a human factor is involved and situations often do not involve such precise objectives. A variety of *systems approaches* are available including *operational research*, *systems analysis*, and *systems dynamics*.

systems planning GENERAL MANAGEMENT see *systems analysis*

T

T+ FINANCE, BANKING, AND ACCOUNTING an expression of the number of days allowed for settlement of a transaction

TA *abbr* GENERAL MANAGEMENT transactional analysis

tacit knowledge GENERAL MANAGEMENT see *knowledge*

tactical campaign MARKETING a series of marketing activities designed to achieve short-term targets

tactical plan FINANCE, BANKING, AND ACCOUNTING a short-term plan for achieving an entity's objectives

TAFN *abbr* GENERAL MANAGEMENT that's all for now (*slang*)

Taguchi, Genichi (*b.* 1924) GENERAL MANAGEMENT Japanese academic and consultant. Known for his contribution to quality engineering and founder of the *Taguchi method*, which seeks to integrate *quality control* into product design, using experiment and statistical analysis. His concepts, including *quality loss* (see *Taguchi methods*), are explained in publications such as *Introduction to Quality Engineering* (1986).

Taguchi methods OPERATIONS & PRODUCTION the pioneering techniques of *quality control* developed by *Genichi Taguchi*, which focus on improving the quality of a product or process at the design stage rather than after manufacture or delivery. Taguchi's philosophy is that a quality approach that focuses on the parameters or factors of design produces a design that is more robust and is capable of withstanding variations from unwanted sources in the production or delivery process. He developed methods for both offline (design) and online (production) quality control. He developed the concepts of *quality loss* and the signal-to-noise ratio, and a product design improvement process based on three steps: system design, parameter design, and tolerance design.

tailgating FINANCE, BANKING, AND ACCOUNTING the practice by a broker of buying or selling a security immediately after a client's transaction, in order to take advantage of the impact of the client's deal

tailormade promotion MARKETING a promotional campaign that is customized for a particular customer

take a flier FINANCE, BANKING, AND ACCOUNTING to speculate (slang)

take a hit FINANCE, BANKING, AND ACCOUNTING to make a loss on an investment (slang)

take a view FINANCE, BANKING, AND ACCOUNTING to form an opinion on the likely direction a market will take, and to take a position to benefit if the opinion proves correct

takeaway GENERAL MANAGEMENT the impressions that a consumer forms about a product or service

take-home pay HR & PERSONNEL the amount of **pay** an employee receives after all deductions, such as income tax, social security, or pension contributions. Also known as **net pay**

takeout financing FINANCE, BANKING, AND ACCOUNTING loans used to replace bridge financing

takeover FINANCE, BANKING, AND ACCOUNTING the acquisition by a company of a controlling interest in the voting share capital of another company, usually achieved by the purchase of a majority of the voting stocks

takeover battle FINANCE, BANKING, AND ACCOUNTING the result of a hostile takeover bid. The bidder may raise the offer price and write to the stockholders extolling the benefits of the takeover. The board may contact other companies in the same line of business, hoping that a **white knight** may appear. It could also take action to make the company less desirable to the bidder. See also **poison pill**

takeover bid MARKETING an attempt by one company to acquire another. A takeover bid can be made either by a person or an organization, and usually takes the form of an approach to **shareholders** with an offer to purchase. The bidding stage is often difficult and fraught with politics, and various forms of **knight** may be involved.

takeover ratio (U.K.) FINANCE, BANKING, AND ACCOUNTING the book value of a company divided by its market capitalization. If the resulting figure is greater than one, then the company is a candidate for a takeover. See also **appreciation asset-stripping**

taker FINANCE, BANKING, AND ACCOUNTING
1 the buyer of an option
2 a borrower

takings FINANCE, BANKING, AND ACCOUNTING a retailer's net receipts

talent HR & PERSONNEL people with exceptional abilities, especially a company's most valued employees (slang)

talent management HR & PERSONNEL the recruitment, selection, identification, retention, management, and development of personnel considered to have the potential for high performance. Talent management is a model of personnel management. It focuses on the skills and abilities of the individual and on his or her potential for promotion to senior management roles. It also assesses how much of a contribution the individual can make to the success of the organization.

talk offline GENERAL MANAGEMENT
1 to continue a particular line of discussion outside the original context. A person may wish to talk offline about an issue tangential to the current discussion, or may carry on that branch of the conversation at a later time, using different media. (slang)
2 to express an opinion in opposition to an employing organization's official position

tall organization GENERAL MANAGEMENT an **organization structure** with many levels of management. A tall organization contrasts with a **flat organization**, since it has an extended vertical structure with well-defined but long reporting lines. The number of different levels may cause **communication** problems and slow **decision making**. It is for this reason that many companies are converting to flatter structures more suited to the fast responses needed in a rapidly-changing business environment.

tall poppy (ANZ) GENERAL MANAGEMENT a prominent member of society (slang)

tall poppy syndrome (ANZ) GENERAL MANAGEMENT an inclination in the media and among the general public to belittle the achievements of prominent people (slang)

talon (U.K.) FINANCE, BANKING, AND ACCOUNTING a form attached to a bearer bond that the holder of the bond uses to order new coupons when those attached to the bond have been depleted

tangible assets FINANCE, BANKING, AND ACCOUNTING assets that are physical, such as buildings, cash and stock. Leases and securities, although not physical in themselves, are classed as tangible assets because the underlying assets are physical.

tangible book value FINANCE, BANKING, AND ACCOUNTING the book value of a company after intangible assets, patents, trademarks, and the value of research and development have been subtracted

tank FINANCE, BANKING, AND ACCOUNTING to fall precipitously. This term is used especially with reference to stock prices. (slang)

tap CD FINANCE, BANKING, AND ACCOUNTING the issue of certificates of deposit, normally in large denominations, when required by a specific investor

tape
don't fight the tape FINANCE, BANKING, AND ACCOUNTING don't go against the direction of the market (slang)

target GENERAL MANAGEMENT see **objective**

target audience MARKETING a group of people considered likely to buy a product or service

target cash balance FINANCE, BANKING, AND ACCOUNTING the amount of cash that a company would like to have in hand

target company FINANCE, BANKING, AND ACCOUNTING a company that is the object of a takeover bid

targeted repurchase FINANCE, BANKING, AND ACCOUNTING a company's purchase of its own stock from somebody attempting to buy the company

target population STATISTICS the collection of individuals or regions that are to be investigated in a statistical study

target savings motive ECONOMICS the tendency of people not to save when their families are growing up but to save when they are in middle age and trying to build up a pension

target stock level OPERATIONS & PRODUCTION the level of **inventory** that is needed to satisfy all demand for a product or component over a specified period

tariff
1 ECONOMICS a government duty imposed on imports or exports to stimulate or dampen economic activity
2 FINANCE, BANKING, AND ACCOUNTING a list of prices at which goods or services are supplied

Tariff Concession Scheme FINANCE, BANKING, AND ACCOUNTING a system operated by the Australian government in which imported goods that have no locally produced equivalent attract reduced duties. Abbr. **TCS**

tariff office (*U.K.*) FINANCE, BANKING, AND ACCOUNTING an insurance company whose premiums are determined according to a scale set collectively by several companies

task analysis HR & PERSONNEL a methodology for identifying and examining the jobs performed by users when interacting with computerized, or noncomputerized, systems. Task analysis employs a variety of techniques to help analysts collect information, organize it, and use it to integrate the human element in systems. It assists in the achievement of higher safety, *productivity*, and maintenance standards.

task culture GENERAL MANAGEMENT a form of *corporate culture* based on individual projects completed by small teams. Task culture was identified by *Charles Handy*. It draws resources from different parts of the organization to form study groups, working parties, and ad hoc committees to take on problems, projects, and initiatives as they arise. See thinker *Charles Handy*

task group HR & PERSONNEL a group of employees temporarily brought together to complete a specific project or task. A task group can take the form of an *autonomous work group* if it is responsible for its own management.

taste space MARKETING a community of consumers identified as having similar tastes or interests, for example, in music or books, enabling companies to recommend purchases or to target advertising at them (*slang*)

tax FINANCE, BANKING, AND ACCOUNTING a charge levied by a government on individuals and companies to pay for public services. The amount of money required from a person or organization depends on their income and assets.

taxability FINANCE, BANKING, AND ACCOUNTING the extent to which a good or individual is subject to a tax

taxable FINANCE, BANKING, AND ACCOUNTING subject to a tax

taxable base FINANCE, BANKING, AND ACCOUNTING the amount subject to taxation

taxable income FINANCE, BANKING, AND ACCOUNTING income that is subject to taxes

taxable matters FINANCE, BANKING, AND ACCOUNTING goods or services that can be taxed

tax and price index (*U.K.*) ECONOMICS an index number showing the percentage change in gross income that taxpayers need if they are to maintain their real disposable income

tax auditor FINANCE, BANKING, AND ACCOUNTING a government employee who investigates taxpayers' returns

tax avoidance FINANCE, BANKING, AND ACCOUNTING the organization of a taxpayer's affairs so that the minimum tax liability is incurred. Tax avoidance involves making the maximum use of all legal means of minimizing liability to taxation.

tax bracket FINANCE, BANKING, AND ACCOUNTING a variety of income levels subject to marginal tax at the same rate

tax break FINANCE, BANKING, AND ACCOUNTING an investment that is tax efficient or a legal arrangement that reduces the liability to tax. See also *tax avoidance tax shelter*

tax consultant FINANCE, BANKING, AND ACCOUNTING a professional who advises on all aspects of taxation from tax avoidance to estate planning

tax-deductible FINANCE, BANKING, AND ACCOUNTING allowed to be subtracted from taxable income before tax is paid

tax-deductible public debt FINANCE, BANKING, AND ACCOUNTING any debt instrument that is exempt from federal income tax

tax-deferred FINANCE, BANKING, AND ACCOUNTING not to be taxed until a later time

tax dodge FINANCE, BANKING, AND ACCOUNTING an illegal method of paying less tax than an individual or company is obliged to pay

tax domicile FINANCE, BANKING, AND ACCOUNTING a place that a government levying a tax considers to be a person's home

tax-efficient FINANCE, BANKING, AND ACCOUNTING financially advantageous by leading to a reduction of taxes to be paid

tax evasion FINANCE, BANKING, AND ACCOUNTING the illegal practice of paying less money in taxes than is due. See also *tax avoidance*

tax evasion amnesty FINANCE, BANKING, AND ACCOUNTING a governmental measure that affords those who have evaded a tax in some specified way freedom from punishment for their violation of the tax law

tax-exempt FINANCE, BANKING, AND ACCOUNTING not subject to tax

Tax Exempt Special Savings Account FINANCE, BANKING, AND ACCOUNTING a U.K. savings account in which investors could save up to £9,000 over a period of five years and not pay any tax, provided they made no withdrawals over that time. The advent of the ISA in 1999 meant that no new accounts of this type could be opened. Abbr. *TESSA*

tax exile FINANCE, BANKING, AND ACCOUNTING a person or business that leaves a country to avoid paying taxes, or the condition of having done this

tax-favored asset FINANCE, BANKING, AND ACCOUNTING an asset that receives more favorable tax treatment than some other asset

tax file number (*ANZ*) FINANCE, BANKING, AND ACCOUNTING an identification number assigned to each taxpayer in Australia. Abbr. *TFN*

tax-free FINANCE, BANKING, AND ACCOUNTING not subject to tax

tax harmonization FINANCE, BANKING, AND ACCOUNTING the enactment of taxation laws in different jurisdictions, such as neighboring countries, provinces, or states of the United States, that are consistent with one another

tax haven FINANCE, BANKING, AND ACCOUNTING a country that has generous tax laws, especially one that encourages noncitizens to base operations in the country to avoid higher taxes in their home countries

tax holiday (*U.K.*) FINANCE, BANKING, AND ACCOUNTING an exemption from tax granted for a specified period of time

taxi industry (*S. Africa*) FINANCE, BANKING, AND ACCOUNTING the privately owned minibus taxi services in South Africa, which constitute the largest sector of public transport in that country

tax incentive FINANCE, BANKING, AND ACCOUNTING a tax reduction afforded to people for particular purposes, for example, sending their children to college

tax inspector FINANCE, BANKING, AND ACCOUNTING see *tax auditor*

tax invoice (*ANZ*) FINANCE, BANKING, AND ACCOUNTING a document issued by a supplier which stipulates the amount charged for goods or services as well as the amount of *Goods and Services Tax* payable

tax law FINANCE, BANKING, AND ACCOUNTING the body of laws on taxation, or one such law

tax loophole FINANCE, BANKING, AND ACCOUNTING an ambiguity in a tax law that enables some individuals or companies to avoid or reduce taxes

tax loss FINANCE, BANKING, AND ACCOUNTING a loss of money that can serve to reduce tax liabilities

tax loss carry back FINANCE, BANKING, AND ACCOUNTING the reduction of taxes in a previous year, by subtraction from income for that year of losses suffered in the current year

tax loss carry forward FINANCE, BANKING, AND ACCOUNTING the reduction of taxes in a future year, by subtraction from income for that year of losses suffered in the current year

tax obligation FINANCE, BANKING, AND ACCOUNTING the amount of tax a person or company owes

tax on capital income FINANCE, BANKING, AND ACCOUNTING a tax on the income from sales of capital assets

tax payable FINANCE, BANKING, AND ACCOUNTING the amount of tax a person or company has to pay

taxpayer FINANCE, BANKING, AND ACCOUNTING an individual or corporation who pays a tax

tax rate FINANCE, BANKING, AND ACCOUNTING the rate at which a tax is payable, usually expressed as a percentage

tax refund FINANCE, BANKING, AND ACCOUNTING an amount that a government gives back to a taxpayer who has paid more taxes than were due

tax relief FINANCE, BANKING, AND ACCOUNTING
1 money given to a certain group of people by a government in the form of a reduction of taxes
2 (*U.K.*) the reduction in the amount of taxes payable, as for example, on capital goods a company has purchased

tax return FINANCE, BANKING, AND ACCOUNTING an official form on which a company or individual enters details of income and expenses, used to assess tax liability. Also known as *return*

tax revenue FINANCE, BANKING, AND ACCOUNTING money that a government receives in taxes

tax sale FINANCE, BANKING, AND ACCOUNTING a sale of an item by a government to recover overdue taxes on a taxable item

tax shelter FINANCE, BANKING, AND ACCOUNTING a financial arrangement designed to reduce tax liability. See also *abusive tax shelter*

tax subsidy FINANCE, BANKING, AND ACCOUNTING a tax reduction that a government gives a business for a particular purpose, usually to create jobs

tax system FINANCE, BANKING, AND ACCOUNTING a schema for imposing and collecting taxes

tax treaty FINANCE, BANKING, AND ACCOUNTING an international agreement that deals with taxes, especially taxes by several countries on the same individuals

tax year FINANCE, BANKING, AND ACCOUNTING a period covered by a statement about taxes

Taylor, Frederick Winslow (1856–1917) GENERAL MANAGEMENT U.S. engineer. Acknowledged as the father of *scientific management*, which is sometimes referred to as "Taylorism." Taylor's methods, recorded in *The Principles of Scientific Management* (1911), have been criticized as too mechanistic, treating people like machines rather than human beings needing to be motivated. They were later counterbalanced by the *human relations* school of management.

Taylor grew up in an affluent Philadelphia family. He worked as chief engineer at the Midvale Steel Company, and later became general manager of the Manufacturing Investment Company's paper mills in Maine. In 1893 he moved to New York and began business as a consulting engineer. See thinker *Frederick Winslow Taylor*

T-bill *abbr* FINANCE, BANKING, AND ACCOUNTING Treasury bill

TCO *abbr* GENERAL MANAGEMENT total cost of ownership

T-commerce E-COMMERCE business that is conducted by means of interactive television (*slang*)

TCP/IP *abbr* E-COMMERCE transmission control protocol/Internet protocol: the combination of protocols that enables the Internet to function. TCP deals with the process of sending packets of information from one computer to another. IP is the process of passing each packet between computers until it reaches its intended destination.

TCS *abbr* FINANCE, BANKING, AND ACCOUNTING Tariff Concession Scheme

TDB *abbr* FINANCE, BANKING, AND ACCOUNTING Trade Development Board

team briefing HR & PERSONNEL a regular meeting between managers or supervisors and their teams to exchange information and ideas. The idea of team briefing evolved from the concept of *briefing groups*, which was developed in the United Kingdom in the 1960s and promoted by the Industrial Society as a means of communicating systematically with managers and employees throughout an organization. The goal was to reduce misunderstandings and rumors and increase cooperation, *employee commitment*, and *team building*. Team briefings are characterized as being regular face-to-face meetings of small teams which are led by a team leader and are relevant to the work of the group, providing an opportunity for questions.

team building GENERAL MANAGEMENT the selection and grouping of a mix of people and the development of skills required within the group to achieve agreed objectives. Effective team building can be achieved through a number of models, one of the most established of which was created by *R. Meredith Belbin*.

team management GENERAL MANAGEMENT see *Managerial Grid*™

Team Management Wheel™ *tdmk* GENERAL MANAGEMENT a visual aid for the efficient coordination of *teamwork*, which can be used to analyze how teams work together, assist in *team building*, and aid self-development and training. The Team Management Wheel outlines eight main team roles. Team members can determine the main functions of their jobs (what they have to do), by using the "Types of Work Index," and can determine their own work preferences (what they want to do), using the "Team Management Index." They are then assigned one major role and two minor roles on the Team Management Wheel. At the center of the Wheel are the linking skills common to all team members. The Team Management Wheel was developed by *Charles Margerison* and *Dick McCann* in 1984.

team player GENERAL MANAGEMENT somebody who works well within a team (*slang*)

teamwork GENERAL MANAGEMENT collaboration by a group of people to achieve a common purpose. Teamwork is often a feature of day-to-day working, and is increasingly used to accomplish specific projects, in which case it may bring together people from different

functions, departments, or disciplines. A team should ideally consist of people with complementary skills. **R. Meredith Belbin** has established nine personality types that are needed in every team. One tool aimed at effective **team building** is the **Team Management Wheel**™. There are various types of teamworking, including the **autonomous work group** and the **virtual team**.

teaser e-mail MARKETING an e-mail message sent to a group of existing or potential customers (who have already given their permission to be contacted) which trails a special offer or piece of news that they will be told about fully at a later date. Teaser e-mails are used to increase the effectiveness of direct marketing campaigns. See also **opt-in**

teaser rate FINANCE, BANKING, AND ACCOUNTING a temporary concessionary interest rate offered on mortgages or credit cards in order to attract new customers

technical analysis FINANCE, BANKING, AND ACCOUNTING the analysis of past movements in the prices of financial instruments, currencies, commodities, etc., with a view to predicting future price movements by applying analytical techniques

technical correction FINANCE, BANKING, AND ACCOUNTING a situation where a stock price or a currency moves up or down because it was previously too low or too high, because of technical factors

technical rally FINANCE, BANKING, AND ACCOUNTING a temporary rise in security or commodity prices while the market is in a general decline. This may be because investors are seeking bargains, or because analysts have noted a support level.

technical reserves (U.K.) FINANCE, BANKING, AND ACCOUNTING the assets that an insurance company maintains to meet future claims

technocracy GENERAL MANAGEMENT an organization controlled by technical experts. See also **bureaucracy**

techno-determinist GENERAL MANAGEMENT somebody who believes that technological progress is inevitable

technographics GENERAL MANAGEMENT a research process that evaluates the attitudes of consumers toward technology. The process was introduced by Forrester Research.

technological risk OPERATIONS & PRODUCTION the risk that a newly-designed plant will not operate to specification

technology adoption life cycle GENERAL MANAGEMENT a model used to describe the adoption of new technologies, typically including the stages of innovators, early adopters, early majority, late majority, and **technology laggards**

Technology and Human Resources for Industry Programme (S Africa) FINANCE, BANKING, AND ACCOUNTING see **THRIP**

technology laggard GENERAL MANAGEMENT an organization that is very slow or reluctant to adopt new technology

technology stock FINANCE, BANKING, AND ACCOUNTING stock issued by a company that is involved in new technology

telcos (ANZ) GENERAL MANAGEMENT telecommunications companies (slang)

telebanking FINANCE, BANKING, AND ACCOUNTING electronic banking conducted by using a telephone line to communicate with a bank

telecenter GENERAL MANAGEMENT a building offering office space and facilities outside the home but away from the main workplace to enable remote working. A telecenter may be owned by one employer—in which case it is known as a **satellite center** —or may be independently-run on behalf of a number of organizations. Employees avoid long commuting times, but work in an office rather than at home; employers avoid having to equip several homes with expensive office equipment.

telecommute GENERAL MANAGEMENT to work without leaving your home by using telephone lines to carry data between your home and your employer's place of business

telecommuter GENERAL MANAGEMENT see **teleworker**

telecommuting GENERAL MANAGEMENT see **teleworking**

teleconferencing GENERAL MANAGEMENT the use of telephone or television channels to connect people in different locations in order to conduct group discussions, meetings, conferences, or courses

telegraphic transfer FINANCE, BANKING, AND ACCOUNTING a method using telegraphs of transferring funds from a bank to a financial institution overseas. Abbr. **TT**

teleimmersion E-COMMERCE an enhanced teleconferencing technology that uses banks of video cameras linked to computers, enabling users in remote locations to collaborate as if they were in the same room

telemarketing MARKETING see **telephone selling**

telementoring E-COMMERCE the practice of conducting a mentoring relationship remotely, usually by e-mail

teleoperation E-COMMERCE the operation of systems or equipment in a physically remote location, carried out using specialized electronic communication and robotic engineering

telephone banking FINANCE, BANKING, AND ACCOUNTING a system in which customers can access their accounts and a variety of banking services up to 24 hours a day by telephone. Apart from convenience, customers usually benefit from higher interest rates on savings accounts and lower interest when borrowing, as providers of telephone banking have lower overheads than traditional banks.

telephone interview survey STATISTICS a method of sampling a population by telephoning its members

telephone number salary HR & PERSONNEL a six- or seven-figure salary (slang)

telephone selling MARKETING the sale of products or services to customers over the telephone. Telephone selling may be used as an alternative, cheaper, method than door-to-door selling, or may be used to obtain an initial appointment for a salesperson to visit a potential customer. Also known as **telemarketing**, **telesales**

telephone survey MARKETING a research technique in which members of the public are asked a series of questions on the telephone

telephone switching GENERAL MANAGEMENT the process of connecting telephones to one another

telephone tag GENERAL MANAGEMENT the reciprocal calling and leaving of messages by two people who wish to speak to each other, but who are never available when the other calls (slang)

telepresence E-COMMERCE the virtual presence of somebody whose actions are transmitted by electronic signals to a physically remote site, for example, in telesurgery

telesales MARKETING see *telephone selling*

teleshopping E-COMMERCE the use of telecommunications and computers to shop for and purchase goods and services

television audience measurement MARKETING the recording of the viewing patterns of a sample of the population, used as the basis for estimating national viewing figures for individual programs

teleworker GENERAL MANAGEMENT an employee who spends a substantial amount of working time away from the employer's main premises and communicates with the organization through the use of computing and telecommunications equipment. A teleworker may be based at home, in which case the worker is known as a *homeworker*, or in a *telecenter*, or on a variety of sites, in which case he or she may be known as a *mobile worker*. Also known as *telecommuter*

teller FINANCE, BANKING, AND ACCOUNTING a bank cashier

tender
1 GENERAL MANAGEMENT to make or submit a bid to undertake work or supply goods at a stated price. A tender is usually submitted in response to an invitation to bid for a work contract in competition with other suppliers.
2 FINANCE, BANKING, AND ACCOUNTING to bid for securities at auction. The securities are allocated according to the method adopted by the issuer. In the standard auction style, the investor receives the security at the price they tendered. In a Dutch style auction, the issuer announces a strike price after all the tenders have been examined. This is set at a level where all the issue is sold. Investors who submitted a tender above the strike price just pay the strike price. The Dutch style of auction is increasingly being adopted in the United Kingdom. U.S. Treasury Bills are also sold using the Dutch system. See also *offer for sale*, *sale by tender*

tender offer FINANCE, BANKING, AND ACCOUNTING the price at which a suitor offers to buy a corporation's stock

10-K FINANCE, BANKING, AND ACCOUNTING the filing of a company's annual accounts with the New York Stock Exchange

tenor (*U.K.*) FINANCE, BANKING, AND ACCOUNTING the period of time that has to elapse before a bill of exchange becomes payable

10-Q FINANCE, BANKING, AND ACCOUNTING the filing of a company's quarterly accounts with the New York Stock Exchange

term FINANCE, BANKING, AND ACCOUNTING the period of time that has to elapse from the date of the initial investment before a security or other investment (such as a term deposit or endowment insurance) becomes redeemable or reaches its maturity date

term bill FINANCE, BANKING, AND ACCOUNTING see *period bill*

term deposit (*U.K.*) FINANCE, BANKING, AND ACCOUNTING a deposit account held for a fixed period. Withdrawals are either not allowed during this period, or they involve a fee payable by the depositor.

terminal date (*U.K.*) FINANCE, BANKING, AND ACCOUNTING the day on which a futures contract expires

terminal identification number E-COMMERCE see *TIN*

terminal market FINANCE, BANKING, AND ACCOUNTING an exchange on which futures contracts or spot deals for commodities are traded

termination interview HR & PERSONNEL a meeting between an employee and a management representative in order to *dismiss* the employee. A termination interview should be brief, explaining the reasons for the dismissal, and giving details of whether a *notice period* should be worked and whether—especially in the case of a *layoff*—additional assistance will be forthcoming from the employer.

termination of service HR & PERSONNEL the ending of an employee's *contract of employment* for a reason such as employer *insolvency* or *dismissal*

term insurance[1] (*U.K.*) FINANCE, BANKING, AND ACCOUNTING a life insurance policy that will pay out upon the death of the life insured, or in the event of the death of the first life insured (with a joint life insurance)

term insurance[2] FINANCE, BANKING, AND ACCOUNTING insurance, especially life insurance, that is in effect for a specified period of time

term loan FINANCE, BANKING, AND ACCOUNTING a loan for a fixed period, usually called a personal loan when it is for non-business purposes. While a personal loan is normally at a fixed rate of interest, a term loan to a business may be at either a fixed or variable rate. Term loans may be either secured or

unsecured. An early payment fee is usually payable when such a loan is repaid before the end of the term. See also *balloon loan*, *bullet loan*

term share (*U.K.*) FINANCE, BANKING, AND ACCOUNTING a share account in a building society that is for a fixed period of time. Withdrawals are usually not allowed during this period. However, if they are, then a fee is normally payable by the account holder.

terotechnology OPERATIONS & PRODUCTION a multidisciplinary technique that combines the areas of management, finance, and engineering with the goal of optimizing life-cycle costs for physical assets and technologies. Terotechnology is concerned with acquiring and caring for physical assets. It covers the specification and design for the reliability and maintainability of plant, machinery, equipment, buildings, and structures, including the installation, commissioning, maintenance, and replacement of this plant, and also incorporates the feedback of information on design, performance, and costs.

tertiary sector ECONOMICS the part of the economy made up of nonprofit organizations such as consumer associations and self-help groups

TESSA *abbr* FINANCE, BANKING, AND ACCOUNTING Tax Exempt Special Savings Account

testacy FINANCE, BANKING, AND ACCOUNTING the legal position of a person who has died leaving a valid will

testate FINANCE, BANKING, AND ACCOUNTING used to refer to a person who has died leaving a valid will

testator FINANCE, BANKING, AND ACCOUNTING a man who has made a valid will

testatrix FINANCE, BANKING, AND ACCOUNTING a woman who has made a valid will

test battery HR & PERSONNEL see *psychometric test*

testimonial advertising MARKETING advertising in which customers or celebrities recommend the product

test marketing MARKETING the use of a small-scale version of a *marketing plan*, usually in a restricted area or with a small group, to test the marketing strategy for a new product. Test marketing gauges both the success of the marketing strategy and the reactions of consumers to a new product by giving an indication of the

potential response to a product nationwide. Test marketing avoids the costs of a full-scale launch of an untested product, but a drawback is that both the product and marketing plan are exposed to competitors.

TFN *abbr* (*ANZ*) FINANCE, BANKING, AND ACCOUNTING tax file number

TFN Withholding Tax *abbr* (*ANZ*) FINANCE, BANKING, AND ACCOUNTING Tax File Number Withholding Tax: a levy imposed on financial transactions involving an individual who has not disclosed his or her tax file number

TGIF *abbr* GENERAL MANAGEMENT thank God it's Friday (*slang*)

T-Group HR & PERSONNEL see *sensitivity training*

Theory J GENERAL MANAGEMENT the *Japanese* form of management. Theory J is closely related to *Theory Z*, and was expounded by *William Ouchi*. See also *alphabet theories of management*

Theory O GENERAL MANAGEMENT a mechanism for organizational *change* based on developing *corporate culture* and human capability through personal and *organizational learning*. Theory O involves fostering a culture that encourages employees to find their own solutions to problems through *empowerment* and participative *leadership*. Theory O contrasts with *Theory E*, which involves a *top-down approach* style of leadership rather than *employee participation*. See also *alphabet theories of management*

theory of constraints OPERATIONS & PRODUCTION see *optimized production technology*

theory of the horizontal fast track GENERAL MANAGEMENT a variation of *fast track* coined by *Charles Handy*. The theory of the horizontal fast track describes the development of talented people who are moved around from task to task to test and develop their capability in different working situations. See thinker *Charles Handy*

Theory W GENERAL MANAGEMENT an extreme extension of *Douglas McGregor's Theory X*, which proposes that not only should employees be coerced into action, but that force is often required. Theory W is a humorous contribution to the *alphabet theories of management*. Theory W stands for Theory Whiplash.

Theory X GENERAL MANAGEMENT a management theory based on the assumption that most people are naturally reluctant to work and need discipline, direction, and close control if they are to meet work requirements. Theory X was coined by *Douglas McGregor* in *The Human Side of Enterprise* (1960), and it was considered by him to be an implicit basis for traditional hierarchical management. McGregor rejected Theory X as an appropriate management style, and favored instead his proposed alternative, *Theory Y*. See also *alphabet theories of management*. See thinker *Douglas McGregor*

Theory Y GENERAL MANAGEMENT a management theory based on the assumption that employees want to work, achieve, and take responsibility for meeting their work requirements. Theory Y was coined by *Douglas McGregor* in *The Human Side of Enterprise* (1960). Although he recognized that Theory Y could not solve all *human resource management* problems, McGregor favored it over his *Theory X*, which required an autocratic management style. See also *alphabet theories of management*. See thinker *Douglas McGregor*

Theory Z GENERAL MANAGEMENT a management theory based on the assumption that greater employee involvement leads to greater productivity. Theory Z was proposed by *Douglas McGregor* shortly before his death, in an attempt to address the criticisms of his *Theory X* and *Theory Y*. McGregor's ideas were expanded by *William Ouchi* in his book *Theory Z* (1981), reflecting the Japanese approach to *human resource management*. Theory Z advocates greater *employee participation* in management, greater recognition of employees' contributions, better career prospects and security of employment, and greater mutual respect between employees and managers. See also *alphabet theories of management*. See thinker *Douglas McGregor*

think tank GENERAL MANAGEMENT an organization or group of experts researching and advising on issues of society, science, technology, industry, or business

thin market FINANCE, BANKING, AND ACCOUNTING a market where the trading volume is low. A characteristic of such a market is a wide spread of bid and offer prices.

third market FINANCE, BANKING, AND ACCOUNTING a market other than the main stock exchange in which stocks are traded

third-party network *or* **third-party service provider** E-COMMERCE see *value-added network*

third sector HR & PERSONNEL see *nonprofit organization*

Thorsrud, Einar (1923–85) GENERAL MANAGEMENT Norwegian academic. Researcher at the Tavistock Institute of Human Relations and collaborator with *Fred Emery*. Thorsrud established an institute in Oslo which became the center of Scandinavian exploration of the concept of *industrial democracy*.

three-dimensional management *or* **3-D management** GENERAL MANAGEMENT a theory outlining eight *management styles* that differ in effectiveness. Three-dimensional management was coined by *Bill Reddin* and was a development of the work of *Robert Blake* and *Jane Mouton*. Reddin described four managerial styles that he considered effective, and four that he considered less effective. These can be plotted in grids, showing how each style approaches relationships and tasks. The least effective type of manager is called the Deserter, the most effective is the Executive. Reddin believed that different styles are used in different types of work settings and that managers modify their style to suit different circumstances.

three martini lunch GENERAL MANAGEMENT a business lunch involving a lot of alcohol to relax the client (*slang*)

three Ps GENERAL MANAGEMENT a model proposed by *Sumantra Ghoshal* to succeed the *three Ss*, which refers to the three foundations of today's leading companies: purpose, process, and people

360 degree appraisal HR & PERSONNEL on the *Managerial Grid*™, the *management style* indicating a preference for focusing on the task or people side of management

three Ss GENERAL MANAGEMENT a classification of *decision making* relating to strategy, structure, and systems. *Sumantra Ghoshal* suggested replacing the three Ss model with the *three Ps*.

three steps and a stumble FINANCE, BANKING, AND ACCOUNTING a rule of thumb used on the stock market that if the Federal Reserve increases interest rates three times consecutively, stock market prices will go down (*slang*)

threshold company GENERAL MANAGEMENT a company that is on the verge of becoming well-established in the business world (*slang*)

thrift institution *or* **thrift** FINANCE, BANKING, AND ACCOUNTING a bank that offers savings accounts. See also *savings and loan association*, *savings bank*

THRIP *abbr* (*S. Africa*) FINANCE, BANKING, AND ACCOUNTING Technology and Human Resources

for Industry Programme: a collaborative program involving industry, government, and educational and research institutions that supports research and development in technology, science, and engineering

throw somebody a curve ball GENERAL MANAGEMENT to do or say something unexpected, for example, during a meeting or a project (*slang*)

TIBOR *abbr* FINANCE, BANKING, AND ACCOUNTING Tokyo Inter Bank Offered Rate

Tichy, **Noel M.** GENERAL MANAGEMENT U.S. academic. Known for his research on the *transformational theory of leadership*, which developed the work of *James Burns*.

tick FINANCE, BANKING, AND ACCOUNTING the least amount by which a value such as the price of a stock or a rate of interest can rise or fall. This could be, for example, an eighth of a dollar or a hundredth of a percentage point.
have ticks in all the right boxes GENERAL MANAGEMENT to be on course to meet a series of objectives (*slang*)

tied loan FINANCE, BANKING, AND ACCOUNTING a loan made by one national government to another on the condition that the funds are used to purchase goods from the lending nation

tie-in MARKETING an advertising campaign in which two or more companies share the costs by combining their products or services (*slang*)

tiger FINANCE, BANKING, AND ACCOUNTING any of the key markets in the Pacific Basin region, except Japan: Hong Kong, South Korea, Singapore, and Taiwan

tight money ECONOMICS a situation where it is expensive to borrow because of restrictive government policy or high demand

TILA *abbr* FINANCE, BANKING, AND ACCOUNTING Truth in Lending Act

time and material pricing FINANCE, BANKING, AND ACCOUNTING a form of cost plus pricing in which price is determined by reference to the cost of the labor and material inputs to the product/service

time and motion study HR & PERSONNEL the measurement and analysis of the motions or steps involved in a particular task and the time taken to complete each one. Time and motion study can be broken down into two distinct techniques: *method study*, the analysis of how people work and how jobs are performed, and *work measurement*, the time taken to

complete each job. It can be used to set job standards, simplify work, and check and improve the efficiency of workers. Time and motion study is similar to the broader concept of *work study*.

time bargain FINANCE, BANKING, AND ACCOUNTING a stock market transaction in which the securities are deliverable at a future date beyond the exchange's normal settlement day

time deposit FINANCE, BANKING, AND ACCOUNTING a U.S. savings account or a certificate of deposit, issued by a financial institution. While the savings account is for a fixed term, deposits are accepted with the understanding that withdrawals may be made subject to a period of notice. Banks are authorized to require at least 30 days' notice. While a certificate of deposit is equivalent to a term account, passbook accounts are generally regarded as funds readily available to the account holder.

time draft FINANCE, BANKING, AND ACCOUNTING a bill of exchange drawn on and accepted by a U.S. bank. It is either an after date or after sight bill.

time keeping HR & PERSONNEL the activity of recording the amount of time an employee works. Time keeping may involve a formal *clock in* system or it may be an informal arrangement based on trust.

time management GENERAL MANAGEMENT conscious control of the amount of time spent on work activities, in order to maximize personal efficiency. Time management involves analyzing how time is spent, and then prioritizing different work tasks. Activities can be reorganized to concentrate on those that are most important. Various techniques can be of help in performing tasks more quickly and efficiently: information handling skills; verbal and written communication skills; *delegation*; and daily time planning. Time management is an important tool in avoiding *information overload-*

time off in lieu HR & PERSONNEL *leave* given to compensate an employee for additional hours worked. Time off in lieu is often given instead of a payment for *overtime*. Abbr. *TOIL*

timeous (*S. Africa*) GENERAL MANAGEMENT done or happening in good time

time series GENERAL MANAGEMENT a series of measurements, observations, and recordings of a set of variables at successive points in time. The time series forecasting technique is commonly used to track long-term trends and seasonal fluctuations and variations in data or

statistics. It can be applied in an economic context in the review of sales, production, and investment performance, or in a sociological context in the compilation of census or panel study statistics. It can include the use of input-output analysis and *exponential smoothing*.

time sheet FINANCE, BANKING, AND ACCOUNTING a record of how a person's time has been spent. It is used to calculate pay, assess the efficient use of time, or charge for work done.

time sovereignty GENERAL MANAGEMENT control over the way you spend your time. Time sovereignty gives employees the ability to arrange their working lives to suit their own situations. It involves handing decisions on working hours to employees, enabling them to work flexibly, so that they can better juggle the *work-life balance*. Time sovereignty is more than just good *time management*, as it gives people control over the way they arrange their lives, rather than having to manage time within the decreed hours. It has been argued that rather than viewing work and home as separate lives, employees should see that they are living just one life that integrates both parts. Time sovereignty gives mastery over managing life as a whole.

time span of discretion HR & PERSONNEL the time between starting and completing the longest task within a job, used as a measure of the level of a job within an organization. The time span of discretion was originated by *Elliot Jaques* as part of the *Glacier studies*. He saw two components to any job: prescribed and discretionary. The time span of the discretionary component refers to the longest span of time that employees spend working on a task on their own initiative, and often unsupervised. This reflects the amount of responsibility an individual has, and Jaques found that the time span of discretion rises steadily with the position of an employee in the company hierarchy. An hourly worker may have a time span of discretion of one hour, a middle manager of one year, and a chief executive of a large company of 20 years.

time spread FINANCE, BANKING, AND ACCOUNTING the purchase and sale of options in the same commodity or security with the same price and different maturities

time study GENERAL MANAGEMENT a *work measurement* technique designed to establish the time taken to complete work tasks in order to set a *standard time* for each task

time value FINANCE, BANKING, AND ACCOUNTING the premium at which an option is trading relative to its *intrinsic value*

TIN *abbr* E-COMMERCE terminal identification number: a bank-provided identification number that uniquely identifies a merchant for point-of-sale transactions

tip FINANCE, BANKING, AND ACCOUNTING a piece of useful expert information. Used in the sense of a "stock tip," it is a stock recommendation published in the financial press, usually based on research published by a financial institution.

tip-off FINANCE, BANKING, AND ACCOUNTING a warning based on confidential information. See also *insider trading*, *money laundering*

tipping point GENERAL MANAGEMENT the moment in time at which an emerging trend or idea achieves the critical mass which enables it to gain momentum, spread rapidly, and become dominant. The term was introduced by Malcolm Gladwell in his book *The Tipping Point* (Abacus, 2001), which compares the development of trends and fashions to the sudden spread of epidemics and suggests that change is not a gradual process, but takes place in sudden dramatic shifts. In the same way as a small weight will tip the balance of a pair of scales in equilibrium, a small change in organizational strategy may have major effects. The concept has been applied to *leadership* and *change management*. A related concept is *strategic inflection point*.

tirekicker MARKETING a prospective customer who asks for a lot of information and requires a lot of attention but does not actually buy anything (*slang*)

title FINANCE, BANKING, AND ACCOUNTING a legal term meaning ownership. Deeds to land are sometimes referred to as title deeds. If a person has good title to a property, their proof of ownership is beyond doubt.

title inflation HR & PERSONNEL the practice of giving an employee a job title that implies status and importance. Title inflation renames an employee's job with a title that sounds more elevated or grand than the old one, even though the nature of the job has not changed. This is sometimes used as a form of *motivation* or incentive to make employees feel rewarded and more valued. See also *uptitling*

TLS *abbr* E-COMMERCE transaction layer security: a payment protocol based on *SSL* that offers improved security for credit card transactions

TNA *abbr* HR & PERSONNEL training needs analysis

toasted FINANCE, BANKING, AND ACCOUNTING used to refer to someone or something that has lost money (*slang*)

toehold FINANCE, BANKING, AND ACCOUNTING a stake in a corporation built up by a potential bidder which is less than 5% of the corporation's stock. It is only when a 5% stake is reached that the holder has to make a declaration to the Securities and Exchange Commission.

Toffler, Alvin (*b.* 1928) GENERAL MANAGEMENT U.S. futurist and social commentator. Known for his analyses of the future which embraced the impact of the Information Society and the wired age, and the knowledge economy. His first book was *Future Shock* (1970).

Toffler studied English at New York University. In the early stages of his journalistic career, he was commissioned by IBM to write a report on the long-term social and organizational implications of the computer. He worked as Washington correspondent for a Pennsylvania newspaper and as associate editor of *Fortune* before being employed as a visiting professor at Cornell University, a visiting scholar at the Russell Sage Foundation, and a teacher at the New School for Social Research. See thinker *Alvin Toffler*

TOIL *abbr* HR & PERSONNEL time off in lieu

Tokyo Inter Bank Offered Rate FINANCE, BANKING, AND ACCOUNTING on the Japanese money markets, the rate at which banks will offer to make deposits in yen with each other, often used as a reference rate. The deposits are for terms from overnight up to five years. Abbr. *TIBOR*

tombstone FINANCE, BANKING, AND ACCOUNTING a notice in the financial press giving details of a large lending facility to a business. It may relate to a management buyout or to a package that may include an interest rate cap and collars to finance a specific package. More than one bank may be involved. Although it may appear to be an advertisement, technically in most jurisdictions it is regarded as a statement of fact and therefore falls outside the advertisement regulations. The borrower generally pays for the advertisement, though it is the financial institutions that derive the most benefit.

tool up GENERAL MANAGEMENT to provide a person, company, or organization with the resources or equipment needed to do something

top-down approach GENERAL MANAGEMENT an autocratic style of *leadership* in which strategies and solutions are identified by *senior management* and then cascaded down through the organization. The top-down approach can be considered a feature of large *bureaucracies* and is associated with a *command and control approach* to management. A number of management gurus, particularly *Gary Hamel*, have criticized it as an out-of-date style that leads to stagnation and *business failure*. It is the opposite of a *bottom-up approach*.

top level domain E-COMMERCE the concluding part of a domain name, for example, the .com, .net, or .co.uk suffixes.

top management HR & PERSONNEL an informal term for *senior management* or a *board of directors*

top slicing FINANCE, BANKING, AND ACCOUNTING
1 selling part of a stockholding that will realize a sum that is equal to the original cost of the investment. What remains therefore represents potential pure profit.
2 in the United Kingdom, a complex method used by HM Revenue & Customs for assessing what tax, if any, is paid when certain investment bonds or endowment policies mature or are cashed in early

total absorption costing FINANCE, BANKING, AND ACCOUNTING a method used by a cost accountant to price goods and services, allocating both direct and indirect costs. Although this method is designed so that all of an organization's costs are covered, it may result in opportunities being missed because of high prices. Consequently sales may be lost that could contribute to overheads. See also *marginal costing*

total cost of ownership GENERAL MANAGEMENT a structured approach to calculating the *costs* associated with buying and using a product or service. Total cost of ownership takes the purchase cost of an item into account but also considers related costs such as ordering, delivery, subsequent usage and maintenance, supplier costs, and after-delivery costs. Originally designed as a process for measuring IT expense after implementation, total cost of ownership considers only financial expenses and excludes any *cost-benefit analysis*. Abbr. *TCO*

total-debt-to-total-assets FINANCE, BANKING, AND ACCOUNTING the premium at which an option is trading relative to its *intrinsic value*

total environmental management GENERAL MANAGEMENT see *environmental management*

total loss control GENERAL MANAGEMENT the implementation of safety procedures to prevent or limit the impact of a complete or partial loss of an organization's physical assets. Total loss control is based on safety audit and prevention techniques. It is concerned with reduction or elimination of losses caused by accidents and occupational ill health. The extent to which it is implemented is usually decided by calculating the total organizational asset cost and weighing this against the likelihood of failure and its worst possible effects on the organization. Total loss control was developed in the 1960s as an approach to *risk management*.

total overhead cost variance FINANCE, BANKING, AND ACCOUNTING the difference between the overhead cost absorbed and the actual overhead costs incurred (both fixed and variable)

total productive maintenance OPERATIONS & PRODUCTION a Japanese approach to maximizing the effectiveness of facilities used within a business. Total productive maintenance, or TPM, aims to improve the condition and performance of particular facilities through simple, repetitive maintenance activities. Based on a culture of teamwork and consensus, TPM teams are encouraged to take a proactive approach to maintenance. A team is made up of operators and those involved in the setting up and maintenance of the facilities. TPM can be compared to *reliability centered maintenance*.

total quality management

1 GENERAL MANAGEMENT a philosophy and style of management that gives everyone in an organization responsibility for delivering quality to the customer. Total quality management views each task in the organization as a process that is in a customer/supplier relationship with the next process. The objective at each stage is to define and meet the customer's requirements in order to maximize the satisfaction of the final consumer at the lowest possible cost. Total quality management constitutes a challenge to organizations that have to manage the conflict between *cost-cutting* and the commitment of employees to *continuous improvement*. Achievement of quality can be assessed by *quality awards* and *quality standards*. See thinker *Philip Crosby*, *W. Edwards Deming*

2 FINANCE, BANKING, AND ACCOUNTING an integrated and comprehensive system of planning and controlling all business functions so that products or services are produced which meet or exceed customer expectations. TQM is a philosophy of business behavior, embracing principles such as employee involvement, continuous improvement at all levels, and customer focus, as well as being a collection of related techniques aimed at improving quality, such as full documentation of activities, clear goal-setting, and performance measurement from the customer perspective. Abbr. *TQM*

total responsibility management GENERAL MANAGEMENT systems and procedures to ensure responsible business practices and management. The term was introduced by Waddock, Bodwell, and Graves in their article "Responsibility: The New Business Imperative," published in the *Academy of Management Executive* in May 2002. It is used to describe the codes of practice and systems that organizations are developing to manage their social, environmental, and ethical responsibilities in response to pressures from stakeholders, emerging global standards, general social trends, and institutional expectations. Some issues, linked to labor, ecology, and community are included because they are subject to increasing assessment or regulation, while others are raised intermittently as a result of public controversies.

total return FINANCE, BANKING, AND ACCOUNTING the total percentage change in the value of an investment over a specified time period, including capital gains, dividends, and the investment's appreciation or depreciation.

The total return formula reflects all the ways in which an investment can earn or lose money, resulting in an increase or decrease in the investment's net asset value (NAV):

$$\frac{(\text{Dividends} + \text{Capital gains distributions} \pm \text{Change in NAV})}{\text{Beginning NAV}}$$

= Total return × 100%

If, for instance, you buy a stock with an initial NAV of $40, and after one year it pays an income dividend of $2 per share and a capital gains distribution of $1, and its NAV has increased to $42, then the stock's total return would be:

$$\frac{(2 + 1 + 2)}{40} = \frac{5}{40} = 0.125 \times 100\% = 12.5\%$$

The total return time frame is usually one year, and it assumes that dividends have been reinvested. It does not take into account any sales charges that an investor paid to invest in a fund, or taxes they might owe on the income dividends and capital gains distributions received.

touch FINANCE, BANKING, AND ACCOUNTING the difference between the best bid and the best offer price quoted by all market makers for a particular security

touchdown GENERAL MANAGEMENT offering computer and telephone connections and Internet access to visitors and business travelers

touchdown center GENERAL MANAGEMENT a center where business people can make calls and use computers and the Internet while traveling (*slang*)

touch price FINANCE, BANKING, AND ACCOUNTING the best bid and offer price available

tourist HR & PERSONNEL somebody who takes a training course in order to get away from his or her job (*slang*)

Townsend, Robert (1920–1998) GENERAL MANAGEMENT U.S. business executive. One-time chairman of Avis Rent-a-car, who built up the company into an international organization. Best known for his book *Up the Organization* (1970), a humorous A–Z of management practices.

toxic employee HR & PERSONNEL a disgruntled and resentful employee who spreads discontent within a company or department (*slang*)

Toyota production system OPERATIONS & PRODUCTION a *manufacturing system*, developed by Toyota in Japan after World War II, which aims to increase production efficiency by the elimination of waste in all its forms. The Toyota production system was invented, and made to work, by *Taiichi Ohno*. Japan's fledgling car-making industry was suffering from poor *productivity*, and Ohno was brought into Toyota with an initial assignment of catching up with the productivity levels of Ford's car plants. In analyzing the problem, he decided that although Japanese workers must be working at the same rate as their American counterparts, waste and inefficiency were the main causes of their different productivity levels. Ohno identified waste in a number of forms, including overproduction, waiting time, transportation problems, inefficient processing, *inventory*, and defective products. The philosophy of TPS is to remove or minimize the influence of all these elements. In order to achieve this, TPS evolved to operate under *lean production* conditions. It is made up of soft or cultural aspects, such as automation with the human touch—*autonomation*—and hard, or technical, aspects, which include *just-in-time*, *kanban*, and *production smoothing*. Each aspect is equally important and complementary. TPS has proven itself to be one of the most efficient manufacturing systems in the world but although leading companies have adopted it in one form or another, few have

been able to replicate the success of Toyota. Abbr. **TPS**

TPM *abbr* OPERATIONS & PRODUCTION total productive maintenance

TPS *abbr* OPERATIONS & PRODUCTION Toyota production system

TQM *abbr* GENERAL MANAGEMENT total quality management

tracker fund FINANCE, BANKING, AND ACCOUNTING see *index fund*

tracking MARKETING research designed to monitor changes in the public perception of a product or organization over a period of time

tracking error FINANCE, BANKING, AND ACCOUNTING the deviation by which an index fund fails to replicate the index it is aiming to mirror

tracking stock FINANCE, BANKING, AND ACCOUNTING a stock whose dividends are tied to the performance of a subsidiary of the corporation that owns it

trade agreement FINANCE, BANKING, AND ACCOUNTING an international agreement between countries over general terms of trade

trade balance FINANCE, BANKING, AND ACCOUNTING see *balance of trade*

trade barrier ECONOMICS a condition imposed by a government to limit free exchange of goods internationally. *NTB*s, safety standards, and tariffs are typical trade barriers.

trade bill FINANCE, BANKING, AND ACCOUNTING a bill of exchange between two businesses that trade with each other. See also *acceptance credit*

trade credit FINANCE, BANKING, AND ACCOUNTING credit offered by one business when trading with another. Typically this is for one month from the date of the invoice, but it could be for a shorter or longer period.

trade debt FINANCE, BANKING, AND ACCOUNTING a debt that originates during the normal course of trade

trade debtors FINANCE, BANKING, AND ACCOUNTING debtors who owe money to a company in the normal course of that company's trading

trade delegation MARKETING a group of manufacturers or suppliers who visit another country to increase export business

Trade Development Board FINANCE, BANKING, AND ACCOUNTING a government agency that was established in 1983 to promote trade and explore new markets for Singapore products, and offers various programs of assistance to companies. Abbr. **TDB**

traded option FINANCE, BANKING, AND ACCOUNTING an option that is traded on an exchange that is different from the one on which the asset underlying the option is traded

trade fair MARKETING a commercial exhibition designed to bring together buyers and sellers from a particular market sector. For the publishing industry, for example, the annual Frankfurt Book Fair is a key trade fair.

trade gap FINANCE, BANKING, AND ACCOUNTING a balance of payments deficit

trade investment FINANCE, BANKING, AND ACCOUNTING the action or process of one business making a loan to another, or buying stock in another. The latter may be the first stages of a friendly takeover.

trademark GENERAL MANAGEMENT an identifiable mark on a product that may be a symbol, words, or both, that connects the product to the trader or producer of that product. In the United Kingdom, a trademark can be registered at the Register of Trademarks, giving the producer or trader protection from fraudulent use. Any use of the trademark without permission gives the owner the right to sue for damages.

trade mission FINANCE, BANKING, AND ACCOUNTING a visit by businessmen from one country to another for the purpose of discussing trade between their respective nations

trade name MARKETING the proprietary name given by the producer or manufacturer to a product or service. A trade name occasionally becomes the generic name for products of a similar nature, for example, "Thermos" is often applied to all insulated flasks, and "Kleenex" to all tissues.

Tradenet GENERAL MANAGEMENT an electronic system for applying for import or export licenses from *Trade Development Boards*

TRADENZ *abbr* FINANCE, BANKING, AND ACCOUNTING New Zealand Trade Development Board

tradeoff analysis GENERAL MANAGEMENT see *conjoint analysis*

trade point FINANCE, BANKING, AND ACCOUNTING a stock exchange that is less formal than the major exchanges

trade press MARKETING specialist publications aimed at people in particular industries or business sectors

trades and labour council (*ANZ*) HR & PERSONNEL a collective organization that represents unions at a level such as that of a state or territory

trade union (*U.K.*) GENERAL MANAGEMENT HR & PERSONNEL = *labor union*

trade war ECONOMICS a competition between two or more countries for a share of international or domestic trade

trade-weighted index ECONOMICS an index that measures the value of a country's currency in relation to the currencies of its trading partners

trading account FINANCE, BANKING, AND ACCOUNTING see *profit and loss account*

trading floor FINANCE, BANKING, AND ACCOUNTING see *floor*

trading halt FINANCE, BANKING, AND ACCOUNTING a stoppage of trading in a stock on an exchange, usually in response to information about a company, or concern about rapid movement of the stock price

trading loss FINANCE, BANKING, AND ACCOUNTING a situation in which the amount of money an organization takes in sales is less than its expenditure

trading partner E-COMMERCE the merchant, customer, or financial institution with whom an EDI (*electronic data interchange*) transaction takes place. Transactions can be either between senders and receivers of EDI messages or within distribution channels in an industry, for example, financial institutions or wholesalers.

trading pit FINANCE, BANKING, AND ACCOUNTING see *pit*

trading profit FINANCE, BANKING, AND ACCOUNTING see *gross profit*

traffic E-COMMERCE the number of visitors to a Web site measured in any of several ways, for example, *click-throughs*, hits, or page views

traffic builder MARKETING a marketing promotion that is designed to generate an increase in customers (*slang*)

training HR & PERSONNEL activities designed to facilitate the learning and development of new and existing skills, and to improve the

performance of specific tasks or roles. Training may involve structured programs or more informal and interactive activities—such as group discussion or *role playing*—which promote *experiential learning*. A wide variety of activities, including classroom-based courses, *on-the-job training*, and business or *simulation games*, are used for training. Audio-visual and multimedia aids such as videos and CD-ROMs may also be employed. Training may be provided by an internal training officer or department, or by external training organizations. The effectiveness of training can be maximized by conducting a *training needs analysis* beforehand, and following up with *evaluation of training*. Training should result in individual learning and enhanced organizational performance.

training group HR & PERSONNEL see *sensitivity training*

training needs HR & PERSONNEL a shortage of skills or abilities which could be reduced or eliminated by means of training and development. Training needs hinder employees in the fulfillment of their job responsibilities and prevent an organization from achieving its objectives. They may be caused by a lack of skills, knowledge, or understanding, or arise from changes in the workplace. Training needs are identified through *training needs analysis*.

training needs analysis HR & PERSONNEL the identification of *training needs* at employee, departmental, or organizational level, in order for the organization to perform effectively. The aim of training needs analysis is to ensure that training addresses existing problems, is tailored to organizational objectives, and is delivered in an effective and cost-efficient manner. Training needs analysis involves monitoring current performance using techniques such as observation, interviews, and questionnaires; anticipating future shortfalls or problems; identifying the type and level of training required; and analyzing how this can best be provided. Abbr. *TNA*

trait theory GENERAL MANAGEMENT the belief that all leaders display the same key personality traits. Trait theory developed from the *great man theory* of leadership as researchers attempted to identify universally applicable characteristics that distinguish leaders from other people. During the 1920s and 1930s, theorists compiled lists of traits, but these were often contradictory and no single trait was consistently identified with good leadership.

tranche CD FINANCE, BANKING, AND ACCOUNTING one of a series of certificates of deposit that are

sold by the issuing bank over time. Each of the CDs in a tranche has the same maturity date.

transaction
1 E-COMMERCE any item or collection of sequential items of business that are enclosed in encrypted form in an electronic envelope and transmitted between trading partners
2 FINANCE, BANKING, AND ACCOUNTING a trade of a security

transactional analysis GENERAL MANAGEMENT a theory that describes sets of feelings, thoughts, and behavior or ego states that influence how individuals interact, communicate, and relate with each other. The theories of transactional analysis were developed between the 1950s and 1970s by Eric Berne, a U.S. psychiatrist who studied the behavior patterns of his patients. Berne identified three ego states, parent, adult, and child, and examined how these affected interactions or transactions between individuals. Transactional analysis is used in psychotherapy but also has applications in education and training. In *human relations* training, transactional analysis is used to help people understand and adapt their behavior and develop more effective ways of communicating. Abbr. *TA*

transactional theory of leadership GENERAL MANAGEMENT the idea that effective *leadership* is based on a reciprocal exchange between leaders and followers. Transactional leadership involves giving employees something in return for their compliance and acceptance of authority, usually in the form of incentives such as pay raises or an increase in status. The theory was propounded by *James MacGregor Burns*, and is closely linked with his *transformational theory of leadership*, which involves moral, rather than tangible, rewards for compliance.

transaction e-commerce E-COMMERCE the electronic sale of goods and services, either business-to-business or business-to-customer

transaction file OPERATIONS & PRODUCTION see *inventory record*

transaction history FINANCE, BANKING, AND ACCOUNTING a record of all of an investor's transactions with a broker

transaction layer security E-COMMERCE see *TLS*

transaction message *or* **transaction set** E-COMMERCE the EDI (*electronic data interchange*) equivalent of a paper document, exchanged as part of an e-commerce transaction,

comprising at least one data segment representing the document sandwiched between a header and a trailer. It is called a transaction message in the *UN/EDIFACT* protocol and a transaction set in the ANSI X.12 protocol.

transactions motive ECONOMICS the motive that consumers have to hold money for their likely purchases in the immediate future

transfer FINANCE, BANKING, AND ACCOUNTING
1 the movement of money through the domestic or international banking system. See also *BACS Fedwire SWIFT*
2 the change of ownership of an asset

transferable skill HR & PERSONNEL a skill typically considered as not specifically related to a particular job or task. Transferable skills are usually those related to relationship, leadership, communication, critical thinking, analysis, and organization. See actionlist *Staying Marketable: Identifying Your Transferable Skills*

transfer of training HR & PERSONNEL the appropriate and continued application of skills learned during a training course to the working environment. A measure of the transfer of training should form part of any *evaluation of training* conducted, as it can help demonstrate the cost-effectiveness of a training program. It is normally measured between three to six months after the training course in order to allow trainees time to apply their newly-learned skills in the workplace.

transfer of value FINANCE, BANKING, AND ACCOUNTING see *chargeable transfer*

transferor FINANCE, BANKING, AND ACCOUNTING a person who transfers an asset to another person

transfer out fee FINANCE, BANKING, AND ACCOUNTING a fee for closing an account with a broker

transfer price FINANCE, BANKING, AND ACCOUNTING the price at which goods or services are transferred between different units of the same company. If those units are located in different countries, the term *international transfer pricing* is used.

The extent to which the transfer price covers costs and contributes to (internal) profit is a matter of policy. A transfer price may, for example, be based upon marginal cost, full cost, market price or negotiation. Where the transferred products cross national boundaries, the transfer prices used may have to be agreed with the governments of the countries concerned.

transfer pricing MARKETING a pricing method used when supplying products or services from one part of an organization to another. The transfer pricing method can be used to supply goods either at cost or at profit if profit targets are to be achieved. This can cause difficulties if an internal customer can buy more cheaply outside the organization. Multinational businesses have been known to take advantage of this pricing policy by transferring products from one country to another in order for profits to be higher in the country where corporation tax is lower.

transfer stamp (*U.K.*) FINANCE, BANKING, AND ACCOUNTING the mark embossed onto transfer deeds to signify that stamp duty has been paid

transformational theory of leadership GENERAL MANAGEMENT the idea that effective *leadership* is based on inspiring and enthusing subordinates with a *corporate vision* in order to gain their commitment. Transformational leadership theory was developed by *James MacGregor Burns*, and is similar to his *transactional theory of leadership*. Both involve an exchange between leaders and followers, but while the transactional leader offers tangible rewards for compliance, the transformational leader offers moral rewards.

transformative potential GENERAL MANAGEMENT the ability of a force such as information technology to transform the economy, society, and business

transit time FINANCE, BANKING, AND ACCOUNTING the period between the completion of an operation and the availability of the material at the next workstation

transmission E-COMMERCE digital data sent electronically from one trading partner to another, or from a trading partner to a *value-added network*

transmission control standards E-COMMERCE the defined format by which to address the *electronic envelopes* used by trading partners to exchange business data

Transnet (*S Africa*) GENERAL MANAGEMENT a state-owned holding company that controls the main South African transport networks

transparency FINANCE, BANKING, AND ACCOUNTING the condition in which nothing is hidden. This is an essential condition for a free market in securities. Prices, the volume of trading, and factual information must be available to all.

travel accident insurance FINANCE, BANKING, AND ACCOUNTING a form of insurance coverage offered by some credit card companies when the whole or part of a travel arrangement is paid for with the card. In the event of death resulting from an accident in the course of travel, or the loss of eyesight or a limb, the credit card company will pay the cardholder (or his or her estate) a pre-stipulated sum. See also *travel insurance*

travel insurance FINANCE, BANKING, AND ACCOUNTING a form of insurance coverage that provides medical cover while abroad as well as covering the policyholder's possessions and money while traveling. Many travel insurance policies also reimburse the policyholder if a vacation has to be canceled and pay compensation for delayed journeys. See also *travel accident insurance*

treasurer FINANCE, BANKING, AND ACCOUNTING somebody who is responsible for an organization's funds

Treasurer (*ANZ*) FINANCE, BANKING, AND ACCOUNTING the minister responsible for financial and economic matters in a national, state, or territory government

treasuries FINANCE, BANKING, AND ACCOUNTING the generic name for negotiable debt instruments issued by the U.S. government. See also *Treasury bill*, *treasury bond*, *treasury note*

treasury FINANCE, BANKING, AND ACCOUNTING the department of a company or corporation that deals with all financial matters

Treasury FINANCE, BANKING, AND ACCOUNTING in some countries, the government department responsible for the nation's financial policies as well as the management of the economy

Treasury bill FINANCE, BANKING, AND ACCOUNTING a short-term security issued by the government. Abbr. *T-bill*

Treasury bill rate FINANCE, BANKING, AND ACCOUNTING the rate of interest obtainable by holding a Treasury bill. Although Treasury bills are non-interest bearing, by purchasing them at a discount and holding them to redemption, the discount is effectively the interest earned by holding these instruments. The Treasury bill rate is the discount expressed as a percentage of the issue price. It is annualized to give a rate per annum.

treasury bond FINANCE, BANKING, AND ACCOUNTING a long-term bond issued by the U.S. government that bears interest

treasury management FINANCE, BANKING, AND ACCOUNTING the corporate handling of all financial matters, the generation of external and internal funds for business, the management of currencies and cash flows, and the complex strategies, policies, and procedures of corporate finance

treasury note FINANCE, BANKING, AND ACCOUNTING
1 a note issued by the U.S. government
2 a short-term debt instrument issued by the Australian federal government. Treasury notes are issued on a tender basis for periods of 13 and 26 weeks.

treasury stock *or* **treasury shares** FINANCE, BANKING, AND ACCOUNTING shares of a company's stock that have been bought back by the company and not canceled. In the United States, these shares are shown as deductions from equity, in the United Kingdom, they are shown as *assets* in the *balance sheet*.

treaty FINANCE, BANKING, AND ACCOUNTING
1 a written agreement between nations, such as the Treaty of Rome (1957), that was the foundation of the European Union
2 a contract between an insurer and the reinsurer whereby the latter is to accept risks from the insurer
3 see *private treaty*

Tregoe, Benjamin Bainbridge (*b.* 1927) GENERAL MANAGEMENT U.S. manager and consultant. See also *Kepner, Charles Higgins*

trend STATISTICS the movement in a particular direction of the values of a variable in a statistical study over a period of time

trendline STATISTICS the tendency to move in a particular direction, shown by data variables over a period of time such as a month or year

Treynor ratio FINANCE, BANKING, AND ACCOUNTING see *risk-adjusted return on capital*

trickle-down theory ECONOMICS the theory that if markets are open and programs exist to improve basic health and education, growth will extend from successful parts of a developing country's economy to the rest

triple bottom line FINANCE, BANKING, AND ACCOUNTING environmental sustainability and social responsibility used as criteria when judging the overall performance of a company, in addition to purely financial considerations

triple I organization GENERAL MANAGEMENT a type of *corporate culture* identified by *Charles Handy* in which the focus is on three areas: Information, Intelligence, and Ideas. The triple I organization recognizes the value

of information and learning. It minimizes the distinction between managers and workers, concentrating instead on people and the need to pursue learning, including personal, *life-long learning*, and *organizational learning*, in order to keep up with the pace of change.

triple tax exempt FINANCE, BANKING, AND ACCOUNTING exempt from federal, state, and local income taxes

triple witching hour FINANCE, BANKING, AND ACCOUNTING a time when stock options, stock index futures, and options on such futures all mature at once. Triple witching hours occur quarterly and are usually marked by highly volatile trading.

Trist, **Eric Lansdown** (1909–93) GENERAL MANAGEMENT British social psychologist. Known for research into sociotechnical systems, particularly in the U.K. coal-mining industry, with associates such as *Fred Emery*, at the Tavistock Institute of Human Relations.

Trojan horse E-COMMERCE a computer *virus* that pretends to serve a useful function, such as a screen saver. However, as soon as it is run, it fulfills its true purpose, which can be anything from using the computer as a host to infect other computers to wiping the entire hard drive of the computer.

troll E-COMMERCE
1 to lure other Internet users into sending responses to carefully designed incorrect statements
2 a carefully worded but incorrect statement that is designed to lure other Internet users into sending responses

trolling MARKETING making cold calls in an effort to solicit new business (*slang*)

Trompenaars, **Fons** (*b.* 1952) GENERAL MANAGEMENT Dutch academic. Known for his research into how national cultures influence *corporate cultures*. His work owes much to that of *Geert Hofstede*, and is published in *Riding the Waves of Culture* (1993). See thinker *Geert Hofstede*. See *Viewpoint: Fons Trompenaars*

trophy wife GENERAL MANAGEMENT the young wife of an older executive (*slang*)

troubleshooter FINANCE, BANKING, AND ACCOUNTING an independent person, often a consultant, who is called in by a company in difficulties to help formulate a strategy for recovery

troy ounce FINANCE, BANKING, AND ACCOUNTING the traditional unit used when weighing precious metals such as gold or silver. It is equal to approximately 1.097 ounces avoirdupois or 31.22 grams.

true interest cost FINANCE, BANKING, AND ACCOUNTING the effective rate of interest paid by the issuer on a debt security that is sold at a discount

trump MARKETING to make something such as a competitor's product appear useless because what you have is so much better (*slang*)

trust
1 FINANCE, BANKING, AND ACCOUNTING a collection of assets held by somebody for another person's benefit
2 ECONOMICS a company that has a *monopoly*

trust account FINANCE, BANKING, AND ACCOUNTING a bank account that is held in trust for somebody else

trust bank FINANCE, BANKING, AND ACCOUNTING a Japanese bank that acts commercially in the sense of accepting deposits and making loans and also in the capacity of a trustee

trust company FINANCE, BANKING, AND ACCOUNTING a company whose business is administering trusts

trust corporation FINANCE, BANKING, AND ACCOUNTING a U.S. state-chartered institution that may undertake banking activities. A trust corporation is sometimes known as a non-bank bank.

trustee FINANCE, BANKING, AND ACCOUNTING somebody who holds assets in trust

trustee in bankruptcy FINANCE, BANKING, AND ACCOUNTING somebody appointed by a court to manage the finances of a bankrupt person or company

trustee investment FINANCE, BANKING, AND ACCOUNTING an investment that is made by a trustee and is subject to legal restrictions

trusteeship FINANCE, BANKING, AND ACCOUNTING the holding of a trust, or the term of such a holding

trust fund FINANCE, BANKING, AND ACCOUNTING assets held in trust by a trustee for the trust's beneficiaries

trust officer FINANCE, BANKING, AND ACCOUNTING somebody who manages the assets of a trust, especially for a bank that is acting as a trustee

Truth in Lending Act FINANCE, BANKING, AND ACCOUNTING in the United States, a law requiring lenders to disclose the terms of their credit offers accurately so that consumers are not misled and are able to compare the various credit terms available. The Truth in Lending Act requires lenders to disclose the terms and costs of all loan plans, including the following: annual percentage rate, points and fees; the total of the principal amount being financed; payment due date and terms, including any balloon payment where applicable and late payment fees; features of variable-rate loans, including the highest rate the lender would charge, how it is calculated and the resulting monthly payment; total finance charges; whether the loan is assumable; application fee; annual or one-time service fees; pre-payment penalties; and, where applicable, confirm the address of the property securing the loan. Abbr. *TILA*

tshayile time (*S. Africa*) GENERAL MANAGEMENT an informal term for the end of the working day

TT *abbr* FINANCE, BANKING, AND ACCOUNTING telegraphic transfer

TTFN *abbr* GENERAL MANAGEMENT ta ta for now (*slang*)

TTP *abbr* E-COMMERCE Trusted Third Party: an independent, trustworthy organization that verifies individuals, companies, and organizations over the Internet

Tulgan, **Bruce Lorin** (*b.* 1967) GENERAL MANAGEMENT U.S. lawyer, writer, and consultant. Pioneer of the concept that young people have a different attitude to work from their forebears and need to be managed differently. He explores this in *Managing Generation X* (1995).

turbulence GENERAL MANAGEMENT unpredictable and swift changes in an organization's external or internal environments which affect its performance. The late 20th century was considered a turbulent environment for business because of the rapid growth in technology and globalization, and the frequency of restructuring and merger activity.

turkey FINANCE, BANKING, AND ACCOUNTING a poorly performing investment or business (*slang*)

turkey trot HR & PERSONNEL the practice of transferring a difficult, incompetent, or nonessential employee from one department to another (*slang*)

turn FINANCE, BANKING, AND ACCOUNTING the difference between a market maker's bid and offer prices

turn a profit GENERAL MANAGEMENT to make a profit (*slang*)

turnaround management FINANCE, BANKING, AND ACCOUNTING GENERAL MANAGEMENT the implementation of a set of actions required to save an organization from *business failure* and return it to operational normality and financial solvency. Turnaround management usually requires strong *leadership* and can include *corporate restructuring* and redundancies, an investigation of the root causes of failure, and long-term programs to revitalize the organization.

turnkey contract GENERAL MANAGEMENT an agreement in which a contractor designs, constructs, and manages a *project* until it is ready to be handed over to the client and operation can begin immediately

turnover
1 GENERAL MANAGEMENT The total of value transactions in a specific period, either for the stock market as a whole or for a specific company
2 (*U.K.*) FINANCE, BANKING, AND ACCOUNTING the total sales *revenue* of an organization for an accounting period. This is shown net of *VAT*, trade discounts, and any other taxes based on the revenue in a *profit and loss account*.
3 HR & PERSONNEL the rate at which staff leave and are replaced in an organization

turnover of shares FINANCE, BANKING, AND ACCOUNTING total value of stocks bought and sold on the Stock Exchange during the year. This covers both sales and purchases, so each transaction is counted twice.

turnover ratio FINANCE, BANKING, AND ACCOUNTING a measure of the number of times in a year that a business's stock or inventory is turned over. It is calculated as the cost of sales divided by the average book value of inventory/stock.

twenty-four hour trading FINANCE, BANKING, AND ACCOUNTING the possibility of trading in currencies or securities at any time of day or night, because there are always trading floors open at different locations in different time zones. A financial institution with offices in the Far East, Europe, and the United States can offer its clients 24-hour trading—either by the client contacting their offices in each area, or by the customer's local office passing the orders on to another center.

20-F FINANCE, BANKING, AND ACCOUNTING a document compiled by non-U.S. companies listed on the New York Stock Exchange for the SEC that gives detailed corporate information

two-tier tender offer FINANCE, BANKING, AND ACCOUNTING in the United States, a takeover bid in which the acquirer offers to pay more for shares bought in order to gain control than for those acquired at a later date. The ploy is to encourage stockholders to accept the offer. This form of bidding is outlawed in some jurisdictions, including the United Kingdom.

type I error STATISTICS an error arising from incorrectly rejecting the null hypothesis in a statistical study

type II error STATISTICS an error arising from incorrectly accepting the null hypothesis in a statistical study

Tzu, Sun (*b.* uncertain) GENERAL MANAGEMENT Chinese general. Although he lived over 2,400 years ago, he is said to have an influence on modern business thinking, based on his thoughts on *strategy* recorded in *The Art of War* (various translations). See thinker *Sun Tzu*

U

UBR *abbr* FINANCE, BANKING, AND ACCOUNTING uniform business rate

UCC *abbr* FINANCE, BANKING, AND ACCOUNTING Uniform Commercial Code

UCE *abbr* E-COMMERCE unsolicited commercial e-mail: the official term for *spam*

UIF *abbr* (*S. Africa*) FINANCE, BANKING, AND ACCOUNTING Unemployment Insurance Fund: a system, administered through payroll deductions, that insures employees against loss of earnings through being made unemployed by such causes as retrenchment, illness, or maternity

ultra vires FINANCE, BANKING, AND ACCOUNTING the Latin for "beyond the powers," used to refer to an activity that normally falls beyond the scope of the instrument from which an organization's authority is derived, and thus may be challenged by the courts. A company's powers are limited by the objectives in its memorandum of association. Most company's objectives are wide-ranging, but, should it act outside of these objectives, any resulting agreement may be unenforceable.

ultra vires activity FINANCE, BANKING, AND ACCOUNTING an act that is not permitted by applicable rules, such as a corporate charter. Such acts may lead to contracts being void.

umbrella fund FINANCE, BANKING, AND ACCOUNTING a collective investment based offshore that invests in other offshore collective investments

unbalanced growth ECONOMICS the situation when not all sectors of an economy can grow at the same rate

unbundling FINANCE, BANKING, AND ACCOUNTING the dividing of a company into separate constituent companies, often to sell all or some of them after a takeover

uncalled share capital FINANCE, BANKING, AND ACCOUNTING the amount of the nominal value of a share which is unpaid and has not been called up by the company

uncertainty analysis STATISTICS a study designed to assess the extent to which the variability in an outcome variable is caused by uncertainty at the time of estimating the input parameters of the study

uncollected funds FINANCE, BANKING, AND ACCOUNTING money deriving from the deposit of an instrument that a bank has not been able to negotiate

uncollected trade bill FINANCE, BANKING, AND ACCOUNTING an account with an outstanding balance for purchases made from the company that holds it

unconditional bid FINANCE, BANKING, AND ACCOUNTING in a takeover battle, a situation in which a bidder will pay the offered price irrespective of how many shares are acquired

unconsolidated FINANCE, BANKING, AND ACCOUNTING not grouped together, as of shares or holdings

uncontested bid FINANCE, BANKING, AND ACCOUNTING an offering of a contract by a government or other organization to one bidder only, without competition

uncovered bear FINANCE, BANKING, AND ACCOUNTING a person who sells stock which he or she does not hold, hoping to be able to buy stock later at a lower price when he needs to settle

UNCTAD *abbr* FINANCE, BANKING, AND ACCOUNTING United Nations Conference on Trade and Development: the focal point within the UN system for the integrated treatment of development and interrelated issues in trade, finance, technology, and investment

underbanked FINANCE, BANKING, AND ACCOUNTING without enough brokers to sell a new issue

underlying asset FINANCE, BANKING, AND ACCOUNTING an asset that is the subject of an option

underlying inflation FINANCE, BANKING, AND ACCOUNTING the rate of inflation that does not take mortgage costs into account

underlying security FINANCE, BANKING, AND ACCOUNTING a security that is the subject of an option

undermargined account FINANCE, BANKING, AND ACCOUNTING an account that does not have enough money to cover its margin requirements, resulting in a margin call

undervalued FINANCE, BANKING, AND ACCOUNTING used to describe an asset that is available for purchase at a price lower than its worth

undervalued currency FINANCE, BANKING, AND ACCOUNTING a currency that costs less to buy with another currency than its worth in goods

underwrite FINANCE, BANKING, AND ACCOUNTING to assume risk, especially for a new issue or an insurance policy

underwriter FINANCE, BANKING, AND ACCOUNTING a person or organization that buys an issue from a corporation and sells it to investors

underwriters' syndicate FINANCE, BANKING, AND ACCOUNTING a group of organizations that buys an issue from a corporation and sells it to investors

underwriting FINANCE, BANKING, AND ACCOUNTING the buying of an issue from a corporation for the purpose of selling it to investors

underwriting income FINANCE, BANKING, AND ACCOUNTING the money that an insurance company makes because the premiums it collects exceed the claims it pays out

underwriting spread FINANCE, BANKING, AND ACCOUNTING an amount that is the difference between what an organization pays for an issue and what it receives when it sells the issue to investors

undistributable reserves FINANCE, BANKING, AND ACCOUNTING in the United Kingdom, reserves that are not legally available for distribution to stockholders as dividends according to the Companies Act (1985)

UNDP *abbr* ECONOMICS United Nations Development Program: the world's largest source of grants for sustainable human development. Its goals include the elimination of poverty, environmental regeneration, job creation, and advancement of women.

unearned income FINANCE, BANKING, AND ACCOUNTING income received from sources other than employment

unearned increment FINANCE, BANKING, AND ACCOUNTING an increase in the value of a property that arises from causes other than the owner's improvements or expenditure

unearned premium FINANCE, BANKING, AND ACCOUNTING the amount repaid by an insurance company when a policy is terminated

uneconomic ECONOMICS not profitable for a country, firm, or investor in the short or long term

UN/EDIFACT E-COMMERCE a standard for *electronic data interchange* widely used in Western Europe and very similar to the *ANSI X.12 standard*. Also known as *EDIFACT EDI For Administration, Commerce, and Trade*

unemployment ECONOMICS the situation in which some members of a country's labor force are willing to work but cannot find employment

unemployment compensation HR & PERSONNEL regular payments made to someone who has been dismissed or laid off from work from a government insurance fund contributed to by employers

uneven playing field MARKETING a situation in which some competitors have an unfair advantage over others (*slang*)

unfunded debt FINANCE, BANKING, AND ACCOUNTING short-term debt requiring repayment within a year from issuance

ungluing GENERAL MANAGEMENT the process of breaking up traditional supply chains or groups of cooperating organizations by taking control of the element of mutual interest that holds the partners together

unhappy camper HR & PERSONNEL somebody who has grievances against his or her employer (*slang*)

uniform business rate (*U.K.*) FINANCE, BANKING, AND ACCOUNTING the rate of tax set by the central government that is to be collected from businesses by the local authority. Abbr. *UBR*

Uniform Commercial Code FINANCE, BANKING, AND ACCOUNTING a set of laws that govern commercial transactions in the United States. The Code has been adopted totally or in part by all 50 states. Abbr. *UCC*

uniform costing FINANCE, BANKING, AND ACCOUNTING the use by several undertakings of the same costing methods, principles, and techniques

unimodal STATISTICS describes a frequency or probability distribution that has only one mode

uninstalled HR & PERSONNEL dismissed from employment (*slang*)

uninsurable FINANCE, BANKING, AND ACCOUNTING considered unsuitable for insurance, especially because of being a poor risk

unique selling point *or* **unique selling proposition** MARKETING OPERATIONS & PRODUCTION a specific feature that differentiates a product from similar products. Abbr. *USP*

unique visitor E-COMMERCE somebody who visits a Web site more than once within a specified period of time. Tracking software that monitors site traffic can distinguish between visitors who only visit the site once and unique visitors who return to the site. Unique visitor statistics are considered to be the most accurate measurement of a Web site's popularity because they reflect the number of people who want to be there rather than those who have arrived there by accident. Furthermore, unlike hits (which are measured by the number of files that are requested from a site) unique visitors are measured according to their unique *IP addresses*. This means that no matter how many times they visit the site, they are only counted once.

unissued share capital (*U.K.*) FINANCE, BANKING, AND ACCOUNTING = *unissued stock*

unissued stock FINANCE, BANKING, AND ACCOUNTING stock that is authorized but has not been issued. U.K. term *unissued share capital*

unit FINANCE, BANKING, AND ACCOUNTING a collection of securities traded together as one item

unit cost FINANCE, BANKING, AND ACCOUNTING the cost to a company of producing one item that it markets

United Nations Conference on Trade and Development FINANCE, BANKING, AND ACCOUNTING see *UNCTAD*

unit of account ECONOMICS a unit of a country's currency that can be used in payment for goods or in a firm's accounting

unit of trade FINANCE, BANKING, AND ACCOUNTING the smallest amount that can be bought or sold of a share of stock, or a contract included in an option

unit trust (*U.K.*) FINANCE, BANKING, AND ACCOUNTING = *mutual fund*

universe MARKETING the total market for a product or service

unlimited liability FINANCE, BANKING, AND ACCOUNTING full responsibility for the obligations of a general partnership

unlimited risk FINANCE, BANKING, AND ACCOUNTING a risk whose potential loss is unlimited, such as futures trading

unlisted FINANCE, BANKING, AND ACCOUNTING used to refer to a security that is not traded on an exchange

unlisted securities market FINANCE, BANKING, AND ACCOUNTING a market for stocks that are not listed on an exchange. Abbr. *USM*

unofficial strike HR & PERSONNEL a *strike* that is called without the approval or recognition of a labor union. An unofficial strike, also known as a *wildcat strike*, is a form of *industrial action* often associated with the activities of shop stewards. Any workers involved do not receive *strike pay*.

unquoted FINANCE, BANKING, AND ACCOUNTING having no publicly stated price, usually referring to an unlisted security

unquoted investments FINANCE, BANKING, AND ACCOUNTING investments which are difficult to value, such as stocks which have no stock exchange listing, or land of which the asset value is difficult to estimate

unrealized capital gain *or* **unrealized gain** FINANCE, BANKING, AND ACCOUNTING a profit from the holding of an asset worth more than its purchase price, but not yet sold

unrealized profit/loss FINANCE, BANKING, AND ACCOUNTING a profit or loss that need not be reported as income, for example, deriving from the holding of an asset worth more/less than its purchase price, but not yet sold

unreason GENERAL MANAGEMENT the process of thinking the unlikely and doing the unreasonable that can be a means by which an organization or individual achieves success

unremittable gain (*U.K.*) FINANCE, BANKING, AND ACCOUNTING in the United Kingdom, a capital gain that cannot be imported into the taxpayer's country, especially because of currency restrictions

unseasoned issue FINANCE, BANKING, AND ACCOUNTING an issue of stocks or bonds for which there is no existing market. See also *seasoned issue*

unsecured FINANCE, BANKING, AND ACCOUNTING without collateral

unsecured debt FINANCE, BANKING, AND ACCOUNTING money borrowed without supplying collateral

unsecured loan FINANCE, BANKING, AND ACCOUNTING a loan made with no collateral. Also known as *signature loan*

unsocial hours HR & PERSONNEL the working hours of an employee outside the socially recognized working day, for which an additional payment is sometimes made

unstable equilibrium ECONOMICS a market situation in which, if there is a movement (of price or quantity) away from the equilibrium, existing forces will push the price even further away

upsell MARKETING to sell customers a higher-priced version of a product they have bought previously

upsizing HR & PERSONNEL see *downsizing*

upstairs market FINANCE, BANKING, AND ACCOUNTING the place where traders for major brokerages and institutions do business at an exchange

upstream progress GENERAL MANAGEMENT advancement against opposition or in difficult conditions. A company or project can make upstream progress if it moves toward achieving its objectives despite impediments. See also *downstream progress*

uptitling HR & PERSONNEL the change of a job title to make it sound more important, although the job content and level of responsibility remain the same. Uptitling has been seen by some as an attempt by employers to improve job satisfaction without increasing pay. See also *title inflation*

URL *abbr* E-COMMERCE uniform resource locator: a full Web address, for example, http://www.mysite.com.

Urwick, Lyndall Fownes (1891–1983) GENERAL MANAGEMENT British educator and consultant. Promulgator of the theories of *Frederick Winslow Taylor* and *Henri Fayol*, which he developed in *Elements of Administration* (1944). Urwick was a founder of the British Institute of Management (1947), and of the management consulting firm Urwick Orr (1934). See thinker *Henri Fayol*, *Frederick Winslow Taylor*

usability E-COMMERCE the suitability of a Web site design from the user's perspective. The term has been popularized by Web design guru Jakob Nielsen who has stressed that a Web site must be simple to use. One of the main points of usability relates to download times. For Nielsen, "fast response times are the most important criterion for Web pages." Nielsen also believes usability involves a human approach. He states that "what constitutes a good site relates to the core basis of human nature and not to technology."

used credit FINANCE, BANKING, AND ACCOUNTING the portion of a line of *credit* that is no longer available for use

usenet E-COMMERCE the vast information space encompassed by the thousands of publicly available newsgroups

USM *abbr* FINANCE, BANKING, AND ACCOUNTING unlisted securities market

USP MARKETING OPERATIONS & PRODUCTION see *unique selling point*

utopian socialism ECONOMICS a form of socialism in which the use and production of all services and goods are held collectively by the group or community, rather than by a central government

V

vacation HR & PERSONNEL a day of work on which an employee is not required to be at work but is paid by the employer. The number of days of vacation is agreed in the *contract of employment* and may be dependent on the employee's length of service. U.K. term *holiday*

valence HR & PERSONNEL see *expectancy theory*

value added GENERAL MANAGEMENT
1 originally, the difference between the cost of bought-in materials and the eventual selling price of the finished product
2 loosely, the features that differentiate one product or service from another, and thus

create value for the customer. Value added is a customer perception of what makes a product or service desirable over others and worth a higher price. Value added is more difficult to measure without a physical end product, but value can be added to services as well as physical goods, through the process of *value engineering*. Also known as *added value*

value-added network E-COMMERCE an organization that provides messaging-related functions and EDI communications services, for example, protocol matching and line-speed conversion, between trading partners. Abbr. *VAN*. Also known as *third-party network*, *third-party service provider*

value-added reseller FINANCE, BANKING, AND ACCOUNTING a merchant who buys products at retail and packages them with additional items for sale to customers. Abbr. *VAR*

value-added services MARKETING services that enhance a basic product, such as the design in engineering components or technical support for software

value-added tax FINANCE, BANKING, AND ACCOUNTING see *VAT*

value-adding intermediary GENERAL MANAGEMENT a distributor who adds value to a product before selling it to a customer, for example, by installing software or a modem in a computer

value analysis OPERATIONS & PRODUCTION a cost reduction and *problem solving* technique that analyzes an existing product or service in order to reduce or eliminate any costs that do not contribute to value or performance. Value analysis usually focuses on design issues relating to the function of a product or service, looking at the properties that make it work, or which are *unique selling points*.

value chain
1 FINANCE, BANKING, AND ACCOUNTING the sequence of business activities by which, in the perspective of the end user, value is added to products or services produced by an organization
2 GENERAL MANAGEMENT the sequence of activities a company performs in order to design, produce, market, deliver, and support its product or service. The concept of the value chain was first suggested by *Michael Porter* in 1985, to demonstrate how value for the customer accumulates along the chain of organizational activities that make up the final customer product or service. Porter describes two different types of business activity: primary and

secondary. Primary activities are concerned principally with transforming inputs, such as raw materials, into outputs, in the form of products or services, delivery, and after-sales support. Secondary activities support the primary activities and include procurement, technology development, and human resource management. All of these activities form part of the value chain and can be analyzed to assess where opportunities for *competitive advantage* may lie. To survive competition and supply what customers want to buy, the firm has to ensure that all value chain activities link together, even if some of the activities take place outside the organization.
3 HR & PERSONNEL the most traditional approach to exploring career prospects, which involves identifying the next—most obvious—move in a career path. The next step is usually assumed to be the role occupied by a manager.

value driver FINANCE, BANKING, AND ACCOUNTING an activity or organizational focus which enhances the perceived value of a product or service in the perception of the consumer and which therefore creates value for the producer. Advanced technology, reliability, or reputation for customer relations can all be value drivers.

value engineering
1 FINANCE, BANKING, AND ACCOUNTING an activity which helps to design products which meet customer needs at the lowest cost while assuring the required standards of quality and reliability
2 OPERATIONS & PRODUCTION the practice of designing a product or service so that it gives as much value as possible to the consumer. Value engineering analyses a developing product so that the focus is on those attributes that make the product appeal to the consumer over competing items and produce *customer satisfaction*. Value engineering also concentrates on eliminating costs that do not contribute to the creation of customer value.

value for customs purposes only FINANCE, BANKING, AND ACCOUNTING what somebody importing something into the United States declares that it is worth

value for money audit FINANCE, BANKING, AND ACCOUNTING an investigation into whether proper arrangements have been made for securing economy, efficiency, and effectiveness in the use of resources. Abbr. *VFM* Also known as *comprehensive auditing*

value innovation GENERAL MANAGEMENT a strategic approach to business growth, involving a shift away from a focus on the existing competition to one of trying to create entirely new

markets. Value innovation can be achieved by implementing a focus on *innovation* and creation of new marketspace. The term was coined by *W. Chan Kim* and *Renée Mauborgne* in 1997.

value map GENERAL MANAGEMENT the level of value that the market recognizes in a product or service and that helps to differentiate it from competitors

value mesh HR & PERSONNEL an expanded look at the positioning of a job in the overall marketplace. Seen as a way of helping employees identify their next move, a value mesh encourages them to consider all opportunities within their organization and others.

value proposition
1 FINANCE, BANKING, AND ACCOUNTING a proposed plan for making a profit (*slang*)
2 MARKETING a statement by an organization of the way in which it can provide value for a prospective customer. A value proposition is a marketing tool that explains why customers can benefit from a company's products or services. It can also be created for *recruitment* purposes, to show applicants the value of becoming an employee of the company.

value share *or* **value stock** FINANCE, BANKING, AND ACCOUNTING a stock that is considered to be currently underpriced by the market, and therefore an attractive investment prospect

VAN *abbr* E-COMMERCE value-added network

vanilla E-COMMERCE relating to the most basic version of a hardware device or a software program that does not have the refinements of the full-featured version

VAR *abbr* FINANCE, BANKING, AND ACCOUNTING value-added reseller

variable STATISTICS an element of data whose changes are the object of a statistical study

variable annuity FINANCE, BANKING, AND ACCOUNTING see *annuity*

variable costing FINANCE, BANKING, AND ACCOUNTING see *marginal costing*

variable interest rate FINANCE, BANKING, AND ACCOUNTING an interest rate that changes, usually in relation to a standard index, during the period of a loan

variable rate note FINANCE, BANKING, AND ACCOUNTING a note the interest rate of which is tied to an index, such as the prime rate in the United States or the London InterBank

Offering Rate (LIBOR) in the United Kingdom. Abbr. **VRN**

variance

1 OPERATIONS & PRODUCTION the square of a standard deviation

2 OPERATIONS & PRODUCTION a measure of the difference between actual performance and forecast, or standard, performance. Variance is a key measure in *statistical process control*.

3 FINANCE, BANKING, AND ACCOUNTING the difference between a planned, budgeted, or standard cost and the actual cost incurred. The same comparisons may be made for revenues.

variance analysis FINANCE, BANKING, AND ACCOUNTING the evaluation of performance by means of variances, whose timely reporting should maximize the opportunity for managerial action

variance components STATISTICS the changes in random effect terms, such as error terms, in a linear statistical model

variety reduction OPERATIONS & PRODUCTION the process of controlling and minimizing the range of new parts, equipment, materials, methods, and procedures that are used to produce goods or services. Variety reduction aims to minimize the variety of all elements in the production or service delivery process. Variety adds costs to any organization and variety management and reduction can immediately benefit profitability. The main techniques of variety reduction are simplification, standardization, and specialization.

VAT *abbr* FINANCE, BANKING, AND ACCOUNTING value added tax: a tax added at each stage in the manufacture of a product. It acts as a replacement for a sales tax in almost every industrialized country outside North America. It is levied on selected goods and services, paid by organizations on items they buy, and then charged to customers.

VAT inspector FINANCE, BANKING, AND ACCOUNTING a U.K. government official who examines VAT returns and checks that VAT is being paid

VAT paid FINANCE, BANKING, AND ACCOUNTING with the VAT already paid

VAT receivable FINANCE, BANKING, AND ACCOUNTING with the VAT for an item not yet collected by a taxing authority

VAT registration FINANCE, BANKING, AND ACCOUNTING the process of listing with a European government as a company eligible for return of VAT in certain cases

VCM *abbr* FINANCE, BANKING, AND ACCOUNTING Venture Capital Market

velocity management OPERATIONS & PRODUCTION the management of processes, people, and systems so that they operate reliably and accurately at high speeds to enable fast responses to orders and inquiries. The development of information and communications technologies has led to faster delivery of value chain information, and velocity management is used to develop the strategies, processes, people, and organizational discipline to fully support and exploit this advantage. Velocity management is a form of *process management* which has been used in the context of military *logistics* as well as in business.

velocity of circulation of money ECONOMICS the rate at which money circulates in an economy

vendor placing FINANCE, BANKING, AND ACCOUNTING the practice of issuing stock to acquire a business, where an agreement has been made to allow the vendor of the business to place the stock with investors for cash

vendor rating OPERATIONS & PRODUCTION a system for recording and ranking the performance of a supplier in terms of a variety of issues, which may include delivery performance and the quality of the items. A process of vendor rating is essential to effective *purchasing*. When conducted before an order is placed, it is known as *supplier evaluation*. When undertaken after the fulfillment of an order, it is called *supplier rating*, or *supplier appraisal*.

Venn diagram STATISTICS a diagram in which overlapping circles are used to show how two or more items in a statistical study are mutually inclusive or exclusive

venture capital FINANCE, BANKING, AND ACCOUNTING ECONOMICS

1 money used to finance new companies or projects, especially those with high earning potential and high risk. Also known as *risk capital*

2 the money invested in a new company or business venture

venture capital fund FINANCE, BANKING, AND ACCOUNTING a fund which invests in finance houses providing *venture capital*

Venture Capital Market FINANCE, BANKING, AND ACCOUNTING a sector on the *JSE* Securities Exchange for listing smaller developing companies. The criteria for listing in the VCM

sector are less stringent than for the DCM (*Development Capital Market*) sector. See also *Development Capital Market*. Abbr. **VCM**

venture funding FINANCE, BANKING, AND ACCOUNTING the round of funding for a new company that follows seed funding, provided by venture capitalists

venture management GENERAL MANAGEMENT the collaboration of various sections within an organization to encourage an *entrepreneurial* spirit, increase *innovation*, and produce successful *new products* more quickly. Venture management is used within large organizations to create a small-firm, entrepreneurial atmosphere, releasing innovation and talent from promising employees. It cuts out *bureaucracy* and bypasses traditional management systems. The collaboration is generally between research and development, corporate planning, marketing, finance, and purchasing functions.

venturer FINANCE, BANKING, AND ACCOUNTING one of the parties involved in a *joint venture*

verbal contract GENERAL MANAGEMENT an agreement that is oral and not written down. It remains legally enforceable by the parties who have agreed to it.

verification FINANCE, BANKING, AND ACCOUNTING in an audit, a substantive test of the existence, ownership, and valuation of a company's assets and liabilities

versioning GENERAL MANAGEMENT MARKETING the practice of offering products or information to customers in different versions to suit particular customer groups. Publishers, for example, may produce branded versions of their books. (*slang*)

vertical diversification GENERAL MANAGEMENT see *diversification*

vertical equity FINANCE, BANKING, AND ACCOUNTING the principle that people with different incomes should pay different rates of tax

vertical form FINANCE, BANKING, AND ACCOUNTING the presentation of a financial statement in which the debits and credits are shown in one column of figures

vertical integration GENERAL MANAGEMENT the practice of combining some or all of the sequential operations of the *supply chain* between the sourcing of *raw materials* and sale of the final product. Vertical integration can be pursued as a strategy through the acquisition of *suppliers*, *wholesalers*, and *retailers* to

increase control and reliability. It can also be achieved when a company gains strong control over suppliers or distributors, usually by exercising purchasing power.

vertical keiretsu GENERAL MANAGEMENT see *keiretsu*

vertical linkage analysis GENERAL MANAGE-MENT a tool that enables analysis of the *value chain* in order to determine where opportunities for enhancing *competitive advantage* may lie. Vertical linkage analysis extends the value chain beyond the organization to incorporate the suppliers and users who are at either end of the chain. This maximizes the number of locations where value can be created for customers. Vertical linkage analysis incorporates three steps: working out the value chain for the industry and costing value-creating activities; determining cost drivers for each of these activities; and evaluating opportunities for competitive advantage.

vertical market E-COMMERCE a market that is oriented to one particular specialty, for example, plastics manufacturing or transportation engineering

vertical merger GENERAL MANAGEMENT FINANCE, BANKING, AND ACCOUNTING see *merger*

vertical thinking GENERAL MANAGEMENT see *lateral thinking*

vested employee benefits FINANCE, BANKING, AND ACCOUNTING employee benefits that are not conditional on future employment

vested rights FINANCE, BANKING, AND ACCOUNT-ING the value of somebody's rights in a pension if he or she leaves a job

VFM *abbr* FINANCE, BANKING, AND ACCOUNTING value for money audit

v-form FINANCE, BANKING, AND ACCOUNTING a graphic representation of something that had been falling in value and is now rising

videoconferencing GENERAL MANAGEMENT the use of a live video link to connect people in different locations so that they can see and hear one another and conduct real-time *meetings*. Videoconferencing is a useful tool for managing *communication* with remote workers, between staff at geographically dispersed offices, including those who form a *virtual team*, or with clients at remote locations. It is also used in *distance learning* courses.

There are two basic options for videoconferencing. The more expensive option is full-blown videoconferencing using *ISDN* lines,

dedicated equipment, and large screens, which guarantee a higher quality experience. Cheaper and more common is the PC/Web-based videoconferencing, which piggybacks on existing PC and Internet technology, and occupies a small box window on a PC. However, it is less reliable, and still requires an ISDN line to achieve any degree of quality.

viewing figures MARKETING the number of people who watch a particular television program or channel

viewtime E-COMMERCE the length of time an advertising banner is visible on a Web page

viral marketing MARKETING the rapid spread of a message about a new product or service, in a similar way to the spread of a virus. Viral marketing can be by word of mouth, but it is particularly common on the Internet, where messages can be spread easily and quickly to reach millions of people. Products can become household names in this way with very little advertising expenditure.

Viral marketing works well in the following circumstances: when a product is genuinely new and different, and it is something that opinion leaders want to associate with; when the benefits of the product are real; when the product is relevant to a large number of people, and the benefits are easy to communicate.

Some viral marketing campaigns use an incentive-based approach, rewarding people if, for example, they inform their friends and a percentage of these friends make a purchase. Because the Internet is perceived as an information resource, it is also useful to publish on a Web site information that users are allowed to quote and redistribute, perhaps by means of an "e-mail-to-a-friend" button. *Linking* is also an effective viral marketing tool, as is the provision of free products or services. The Hotmail™ free e-mail service, for example, grew quickly with little marketing investment.

virtual hosting E-COMMERCE a type of *hosting option*, suitable for small and medium-sized businesses, in which the customer uses space on a network vendor's server that is also used by other organizations. The hosting company agrees to deliver minimum access speeds and *data transfer* rates, and to conduct basic hardware maintenance, but the customer is responsible for managing the content and software.

virtualization GENERAL MANAGEMENT the creation of a product, service, or organization that has an electronic rather than a physical existence

virtual office GENERAL MANAGEMENT a workplace that is not based in one physical location but consists of employees working remotely by using *information and communications technologies*. A virtual office is characterized by the use of *teleworkers*, *telecenters*, *mobile workers*, *hot-desking*, and *hoteling*, and promotes the use of *virtual teams*. A virtual office can increase an organization's flexibility, cost effectiveness, and efficiency.

virtual organization E-COMMERCE OPERATIONS & PRODUCTION a temporary network of companies, suppliers, customers, or employees, linked by *information and communications technologies*, with the purpose of delivering a service or product. A virtual organization can bring together companies in *strategic partnering* or *outsourcing* arrangements, enabling them to share expertise, resources, and cost savings until objectives are met and the network is dissolved. Such organizations are virtual not only in the sense that they exist largely in cyberspace, but also in that they are unconstrained by the traditional barriers of time and place. A greater level of trust is required between employer and employee or coworkers, or partner organizations, because they will be working out of one another's sight for most of the time. See also *network organization*

virtual team GENERAL MANAGEMENT a group of employees using *information and communications technologies* to collaborate from different work bases. Members of a virtual team may work in different parts of the same building or may be scattered across a country or around the world. The team can be connected by technology such as *groupware*, e-mail, an *intranet*, or *videoconferencing* and can be said to inhabit a *virtual office*. Although virtual teams can work efficiently, occasional face-to-face meetings can be important to avoid feelings of isolation and to enable *team building*.

virus E-COMMERCE a computer program designed to damage or destroy computer systems and the information contained within them. The fact that extremely destructive viruses can be attached to, and even embedded in, e-mail messages means that anyone with an e-mail account is a potential target. Although there is no single foolproof way to eradicate the risk of viruses, the threat they pose can be reduced in a number of ways. The main precaution that should be taken is to invest in antivirus software that can check e-mail messages and attachments automatically.

visible trade ECONOMICS trade in physical goods and merchandise

vision statement GENERAL MANAGEMENT a statement giving a broad, aspirational image of the future that an organization is aiming to achieve. Vision statements express *corporate vision*. They are related to *mission statements*.

visit E-COMMERCE the first entry in a given time period into a Web site by a Web user, as identified by a unique Web address. A visit is considered to be concluded when the user has not viewed any page at the Web site in a given time period.

vocational degree HR & PERSONNEL a degree awarded after a period of *vocational training* has been successfully completed. Vocational degrees provide the knowledge and skills for a particular trade or profession, and may lead to full membership of a professional body.

vocational training HR & PERSONNEL *training* that equips somebody for a specific trade or profession. Vocational training may lead to a recognized *vocational degree*, or it may form part of in-company *employee development*. It might take the form of a short course, practical training, or part-time or full-time study at a college or university.

voetstoots (*S. Africa*) FINANCE, BANKING, AND ACCOUNTING purchased at the buyer's risk or without warranty

volume of retail sales ECONOMICS the amount of trade in goods conducted in the retail sector of an economy in a particular period

volume of trade FINANCE, BANKING, AND ACCOUNTING the number of shares sold on the Stock Exchange during a day's trading

volume variances FINANCE, BANKING, AND ACCOUNTING differences in costs or revenues compared with budgeted amounts, caused by differences between the actual and budgeted levels of activity

voluntary arrangement FINANCE, BANKING, AND ACCOUNTING an agreement the terms of which are not legally binding on the parties

voluntary bankruptcy GENERAL MANAGEMENT see *bankruptcy*

voluntary liquidation FINANCE, BANKING, AND ACCOUNTING liquidation of a solvent company that is supported by the stockholders

voluntary registration FINANCE, BANKING, AND ACCOUNTING in the United Kingdom, registration for *VAT* by a trader whose turnover is

below the registration threshold. This is usually done in order to reclaim tax on inputs.

vortal E-COMMERCE a portal Web site devoted to one specific industry. These sites enable business-to-business e-commerce transactions by bringing businesses at different points of the supply chain together. Vortal is formed from "vertical portal."

vostro account FINANCE, BANKING, AND ACCOUNTING an account held by a local bank on behalf of a foreign bank

votes on account FINANCE, BANKING, AND ACCOUNTING in the United Kingdom, money granted by Parliament in order to continue spending in a fiscal year before final authorization of the totals for the year

voting shares (*U.K.*) FINANCE, BANKING, AND ACCOUNTING = *voting stock*

voting stock FINANCE, BANKING, AND ACCOUNTING stocks whose owners have voting rights. U.K. term *voting shares*

voting trust FINANCE, BANKING, AND ACCOUNTING a group of individuals who have collectively received voting rights from stockholders

voucher FINANCE, BANKING, AND ACCOUNTING a document supporting an accounting entry

vouching FINANCE, BANKING, AND ACCOUNTING an auditing process in which documentary evidence is matched with the details recorded in an accounting record in order to check for validity and accuracy

Vredeling Directive FINANCE, BANKING, AND ACCOUNTING a proposal, presented to the European Council of Ministers in 1980, for obligatory information, consultation, and participation of workers at headquarters level in multinational enterprises

Vroom, Victor Harold (1932) GENERAL MANAGEMENT Canadian academic. An authority on the psychological analysis of behavior in organizations, whose work includes contributions on *motivation*, *leadership* styles, and *decision making*. He described his *expectancy theory* in *Work and Motivation* (1964).

Vulcan nerve pinch GENERAL MANAGEMENT the uncomfortable hand position required to reach all the keys for certain computer commands (*slang*)

vulture capitalist FINANCE, BANKING, AND ACCOUNTING a venture capitalist who structures deals on behalf of an entrepreneur in such a

way that the investors benefit rather than the entrepreneur (*slang*)

W

wage drift FINANCE, BANKING, AND ACCOUNTING the difference between wages and money actually earned, the difference being made up by bonus or overtime payments

wage earner HR & PERSONNEL a person in paid employment

wage freeze HR & PERSONNEL government policy of preventing *pay* rises in order to combat inflation

wage incentive HR & PERSONNEL a monetary benefit offered as a reward to those employees who perform well in a specified area

wage-price spiral FINANCE, BANKING, AND ACCOUNTING a situation where price rises encourage higher wage demands, which in turn make prices rise

wages HR & PERSONNEL a form of *pay* given to employees in exchange for the work they have done. Traditionally, the term wages applied to the weekly pay of manual, or nonprofessional workers. In modern usage, the term is often used interchangeably with *salary*.

wage scale HR & PERSONNEL see *pay scale*

wages costs FINANCE, BANKING, AND ACCOUNTING the costs of paying employees' salaries. Along with other costs such as pension contributions and salaries, these costs typically form the largest single cost item for a business.

wages payable account (*U.K.*) FINANCE, BANKING, AND ACCOUNTING an account showing the gross wages and employer's *National Insurance contributions* paid during a certain period

waiting time FINANCE, BANKING, AND ACCOUNTING the period for which an operator is available for production but is prevented from working by shortage of material or tooling, or by machine breakdown

waiver of premium FINANCE, BANKING, AND ACCOUNTING a provision of an insurance policy that suspends payment of premiums, for example, if the insured suffers a disabling injury

walk GENERAL MANAGEMENT to resign from a job (*slang*)

wall

let's throw it at the wall and see if it sticks GENERAL MANAGEMENT let's try this idea and see if it is successful (*slang*)

walled garden E-COMMERCE an environment on the Internet in which customers can access only e-merchants selected by the owner of the environment (*slang*)

wallet technology E-COMMERCE a software package providing *digital wallets* or purses on the computers of merchants and customers to facilitate payment by digital cash

wallflower FINANCE, BANKING, AND ACCOUNTING an investment that does not attract a lot of interest from potential investors because it has not been profitable enough

wallpaper FINANCE, BANKING, AND ACCOUNTING a disparaging term used to describe a situation where a company issues and sells many new shares in order to finance a series of takeovers

Wall Street FINANCE, BANKING, AND ACCOUNTING **1** a collective name for the U.S. financial industry **2** the area of New York City where the financial industry is based and does much of its business

WAN E-COMMERCE see *network*

WAP *abbr* E-COMMERCE wireless application protocol: the mobile equivalent of *HTML*, enabling Web sites to be accessed via mobile devices

war chest FINANCE, BANKING, AND ACCOUNTING a large amount of money held by a person or a company in *reserves* that can be used to finance the *takeover* of other companies (*slang*)

warehousing OPERATIONS & PRODUCTION the storage and protection of *raw materials* and *finished goods* in a dedicated building or room

war for talent GENERAL MANAGEMENT competition between organizations to attract and retain the most able employees

war loan FINANCE, BANKING, AND ACCOUNTING a U. K. government bond that pays a fixed rate of *interest* and has no *redemption date*. War loans were originally issued to finance military expenditure.

warrant FINANCE, BANKING, AND ACCOUNTING a contract that gives the right to buy a predetermined number of shares of stock in the future

warrants risk warning notice FINANCE, BANKING, AND ACCOUNTING a statement that a broker in the United Kingdom gives to clients to alert them to the risks inherent in trading in options

waste FINANCE, BANKING, AND ACCOUNTING discarded material having no value

waste management *or* **waste control** GENERAL MANAGEMENT a sustainable process for reducing the environmental impact of the disposal of all types of materials used by businesses. Waste management aims to avoid excessive use of resources and damage to the environment and may be achieved through processes such as recycling. It focuses on efficiency in the use of materials and on disposing of rubbish in the least harmful way. Waste management also involves compliance with the legislation and regulations covering this area.

wasting asset FINANCE, BANKING, AND ACCOUNTING a fixed asset which is consumed or exhausted in the process of earning income, such as a mine or a quarry

watchdog FINANCE, BANKING, AND ACCOUNTING an independent organization whose duty it is to police a particular industry, ensuring that member companies do not act illegally

water

let's put it in the water and see if it floats GENERAL MANAGEMENT let's try this idea and see if it is successful (*slang*)

watered stock FINANCE, BANKING, AND ACCOUNTING stock in a company that is worth less than the total *capital* invested

Waterman, Robert H. (*b.* 1936) GENERAL MANAGEMENT U.S. consultant. Former McKinsey consultant, who, with *Tom Peters*, wrote the best-selling work *In Search of Excellence* (1984).

watermark FINANCE, BANKING, AND ACCOUNTING a design inserted into documents to prove their authenticity. For example, banknotes all carry watermarks to prevent forgery.

Watson, Jr., Thomas J. (1914–93) GENERAL MANAGEMENT U.S. industrialist. C.E.O. of IBM, 1956–70, who gave the company a strong core philosophy and led it through a period of complete domination of the computer industry. His beliefs, which centered on consideration for the employee, care for the customer, and taking time to get things right, are described in *A Business and its Beliefs: The Ideas that Helped Build IBM* (1963).

WDA *abbr* FINANCE, BANKING, AND ACCOUNTING writing down allowances

WDV *abbr* FINANCE, BANKING, AND ACCOUNTING written down value

weak market FINANCE, BANKING, AND ACCOUNTING a stock market in which prices tend to fall because there are no buyers

wealth ECONOMICS physical assets such as a house or financial assets such as stocks and bonds that can yield an income for their holder

wealth tax FINANCE, BANKING, AND ACCOUNTING a tax on somebody's accumulated wealth, as opposed to their income

wear a hat GENERAL MANAGEMENT to fulfill a specified role at a particular time. Somebody may be required to wear several hats within the same company. (*slang*)

wear and tear FINANCE, BANKING, AND ACCOUNTING the deterioration of a tangible fixed asset as a result of normal use. This is recognized for accounting purposes by *depreciation*.

Web bug E-COMMERCE a small file sent to reside in a Web site user's browser, in order to track that consumer the next time he or she visits the Web site—in much the same manner as a *cookie*.

Web bugs, however, are not generally detectable by standard browsers, although there is software that can be downloaded to spot them. They are therefore controversial, as their very design reflects a desire not to let a person know that they are being tracked, and they have sometimes been used in a surreptitious manner. This has added fuel to the fear that people's privacy rights are being abused on the Internet.

Web cast E-COMMERCE use of the Web to broadcast information. A Web cast event is intended to be viewed simultaneously by numerous people connecting to the same Web site. Web cast events often use *rich media* technology.

Web commerce E-COMMERCE see *e-commerce*

Weber, Max (1864–1920) GENERAL MANAGEMENT German sociologist. Remembered for his work on *power* and *authority*, published in *Theory of Social and Economic Organization* (1924), where he proposed *bureaucracy* as the most efficient form of *organization*.

After studying legal and economic history, Weber was a law professor at the University of Freiburg and later at the University of Heidelberg. He studied the sociology of religion and in this area he produced his best-known work, *The Protestant Work Ethic and the Spirit of Capitalism* (1904). In political sociology he examined the relationship between social and

economic organizations. Toward the end of his life, Weber developed his political interests and was on the committee that drafted the constitution of the Weimar Republic in 1918.

Web form E-COMMERCE a means of collecting information from a visitor to a Web site in a structured manner. Once the consumer has filled in the form, it is usually returned to the owner of the Web site via e-mail.

There are several golden rules to follow when designing a Web form. It should be short or, if necessary, split into clear sections. Mandatory fields—such as e-mail addresses—should be clearly marked, conventionally with red type or red asterisks. Consumers should be given an alternative for information they cannot give—for example: "If you don't have a ZIP code, please write 'None.'" Errors should be isolated: if the consumer makes an error in the form, they should be asked to correct that specific error, not simply have the form returned to them. Fields should be of sufficient size for all the requested information. Alternative means of providing the information should be made available for people with disabilities.

Webinar GENERAL MANAGEMENT a seminar held on the Internet, linking participants via conference calls and PCs with access to the Internet

Web log E-COMMERCE
1 a means of tracking activity on a Web site or computer system. It can provide important marketing information such as how many users are visiting the site, how they behave, and what they are interested in, as well as highlighting useful technical issues such as whether there are page errors occurring, or whether spikes in visitor behavior are causing *bandwidth* shortages. Also called *server log*
2 an increasingly popular form of public journal using the Internet to post entries and encourage commentaries. It is commonly referred to as a *blog*. See also *blog*

Web marketing E-COMMERCE the process of creating, developing, and enhancing a Web site in order to increase the number of visits by potential customers

Web marketplace E-COMMERCE a business-to-business Web community that brings business buyers and sellers together. Although their exact nature can vary considerably, there are essentially three types of Web-based B2B marketplace: *online catalogs*, *auctions*, and *exchanges*.

Web master E-COMMERCE the person responsible for managing the content of a Web site and monitoring traffic through the site. The role of Web master may be shared between numerous individuals within an organization.

Web response form E-COMMERCE see *WRF*

Web server E-COMMERCE
1 the physical computer that supports a Web site
2 the software that runs on Web servers. Web server software delivers Web pages to browsers on Internet-based computers.

Web site classification E-COMMERCE the organization of content on a Web site into different categories, so that it can be identified and found easily by a user. Classification is a particularly important form of *metadata*, as a Web site with poor classification will be difficult to navigate and of little use to the visitor.

The top-level classification of a Web site expresses (in the fewest and simplest words possible) the nature of the business. For example, is it selling "products," "services," or "solutions?" Are its customers "home users," "small businesses," "large businesses?" It is important, if possible, to avoid going more than five levels deep in further classification. The more levels there are, the more clicks will be required from visitors to find what they are looking for. It is also best to avoid having too many documents under one classification: more than 50 becomes confusing, and it would probably be better to break down the classification further.

WEF *abbr* FINANCE, BANKING, AND ACCOUNTING World Economic Forum

weighted average STATISTICS an average of quantities that have been adjusted by the addition of a statistical value to allow for their relative importance in a data set

weighted average cost FINANCE, BANKING, AND ACCOUNTING a method of unit cost determination often applied to stocks. When a new purchase quantity is received, an average unit cost is calculated by dividing the sum of the cost of the opening stock plus the cost of the acquisitions by the total number of units in stock.

weighted average cost of capital FINANCE, BANKING, AND ACCOUNTING The average cost of the company's finance (equity, debentures, bank loans) weighted according to the proportion each element bears to the total pool of capital. Weighting is usually based on market valuations, current yields, and costs after tax.

The weighted average cost of capital is often used as the hurdle rate for investment decisions, and as the measure to be minimized in order to find the optimal capital structure for the company.

weighted average cost price FINANCE, BANKING, AND ACCOUNTING a value for the cost of each item of a specific type in an inventory, taking into account what quantities were bought at what prices

weighted average number of shares outstanding FINANCE, BANKING, AND ACCOUNTING the number of shares of common stock at the beginning of a period, adjusted for shares canceled, bought back, or issued during the period, multiplied by a time-weighting factor. This number is used in the calculation of *earnings per share*.

weighting STATISTICS the assigning of greater importance to particular items in a data set

weightlessness GENERAL MANAGEMENT a quality considered to characterize an economy that is based on knowledge or other intangibles rather than on physical assets

Welch, Jack (*b.* 1935) GENERAL MANAGEMENT U.S. business executive. Turned around General Electric in the 1980s by making redundancies, *divesting* and *acquiring* businesses, and introducing "Work-Out," a program centered on *communication* and *innovation*.

welfare HR & PERSONNEL the physical and mental well-being of employees, and the provision of help for those in need of assistance. Welfare embraces: *physical working conditions*, such as hygiene, sanitation, temperature, humidity, ventilation, lighting, physical comfort, and refreshments; *occupational health* or wellness promotion; *counseling* and advice on personal problems, such as bereavement, drug abuse, or *stress*; and working time, covering matters such as *hours of work*, rest periods, paid vacation, and *shiftwork*. *Employee assistance programs* are a modern form of welfare policy, although not common outside the United States.

well
let's drop it down the well and see what kind of splash it makes GENERAL MANAGEMENT let's try this idea and see if it is successful (*slang*)

wellness program HR & PERSONNEL a company program offering benefits, activities, or training, to improve and promote employees' health and fitness. A wellness program can include *wellness benefits* such as fitness training, company sponsored athletics and sports teams, health education, and life improvement

classes. It also includes prevention of mental health problems by **stress** management.

wet signature GENERAL MANAGEMENT a signature on paper rather than a faxed or e-mailed copy (*slang*)

wharfie (*ANZ*) GENERAL MANAGEMENT a dockworker (*slang*)

Wheat Report FINANCE, BANKING, AND ACCOUNTING a report produced by a committee in 1972 that set out to examine the principles and methods of accounting in the United States. Its publication led to the establishment of the **FASB**.

whisper number or **whisper estimate** FINANCE, BANKING, AND ACCOUNTING an estimate of a company's earnings that is based on rumors

whisper stock FINANCE, BANKING, AND ACCOUNTING a stock about which there is talk of a likely change in value, usually upward and often related to a takeover

whistle
blow the whistle on somebody or something GENERAL MANAGEMENT see **whistleblowing**

whistleblowing GENERAL MANAGEMENT speaking out to the media or the public on malpractice, misconduct, corruption, or mismanagement witnessed in an organization. Whistleblowing is usually undertaken on the grounds of morality or conscience, or because of a failure of **business ethics** on the part of the organization being reported.

white coat rule FINANCE, BANKING, AND ACCOUNTING MARKETING a Federal Trade Commission rule prohibiting the use of actors dressed as doctors to promote a product in TV commercials (*slang*)

white-collar crime GENERAL MANAGEMENT a crime committed by somebody doing a white-collar job

white-collar job HR & PERSONNEL a position that does not involve physical labor. See also **blue-collar job**

white-collar worker HR & PERSONNEL an office worker. Office workers traditionally wore a white shirt and a tie.

white elephant FINANCE, BANKING, AND ACCOUNTING a product or service that has not sold well, despite large amounts of money being pumped into its development

white goods MARKETING large household electrical appliances such as ranges, refrigerators, and freezers

white knight FINANCE, BANKING, AND ACCOUNTING a person or company liked by a company's management, who buys the company when a hostile company is trying to buy it. See also **knight**

white squire GENERAL MANAGEMENT a **shareholder** who purchases a significant, but not controlling, number of shares in order to prevent a **takeover bid** from succeeding. A white squire is often invited to purchase the shares by the company to be acquired, and may be required to sign an agreement to prevent them from later becoming a black **knight**.

whiz kid FINANCE, BANKING, AND ACCOUNTING a young, exceptionally successful person—especially one who makes a lot of money in large financial transactions, including takeovers

wholesale price FINANCE, BANKING, AND ACCOUNTING a price charged to customers who buy large quantities of an item for resale in smaller quantities to others

wholesale price index FINANCE, BANKING, AND ACCOUNTING a government-calculated index of wholesale prices, indicative of inflation in an economy

wholesaler MARKETING OPERATIONS & PRODUCTION an intermediary who buys in bulk from manufacturers for resale to **retailers** or other traders. Some wholesalers sell directly to the public. One type of wholesaler is a **cash and carry**, which offers discounted prices for bulk purchases that are paid for and taken away at the time of sale. Cash and carries traditionally serve the business community, but many now allow the general public to buy from them.

wholesale trade MARKETING trade at wholesale prices

wholly-owned subsidiary FINANCE, BANKING, AND ACCOUNTING a company that is completely owned by another company. A wholly-owned subsidiary is a **registered company** with board members who all represent one **holding company** or corporation. Board members may be directly from the holding company or acting as its nominees, or they may be from other wholly-owned subsidiaries of the holding company.

Whyte, **William Hollingsworth** (1917–99) GENERAL MANAGEMENT U.S. urban theorist. Author of *The Organization Man* (1956), a study of the impact of the power of **corporate**

culture on individuals from the suburban middle class.

Wickens, **Peter D.** (*b.* 1938) GENERAL MANAGEMENT British business executive. Personnel director at Nissan U.K., where he helped to introduce Japanese working practices, such as **continuous improvement**, into the U.K. car industry. Wickens's employee relations philosophy at Nissan was based on job flexibility, **single status**, and a single union deal. His book, *The Ascendant Organisation* (1995), brings together his experience and knowledge of **best practice**.

widow-and-orphan stock FINANCE, BANKING, AND ACCOUNTING a stock considered extremely safe as an investment

wiggle room GENERAL MANAGEMENT flexibility in matters relating to contracts or deadlines (*slang*)

Willie Sutton rule GENERAL MANAGEMENT the maxim that it is most logical to concentrate on areas that yield most profit. The Willie Sutton rule is based on an alleged remark made by bank robber Willie Sutton. He was reputedly asked why he robbed banks and replied "Because that's where the money is." A person or organization following this rule will focus their effort on those activities that give the greatest return.

windfall gains and losses FINANCE, BANKING, AND ACCOUNTING unexpected gains and losses

windfall profit FINANCE, BANKING, AND ACCOUNTING a sudden large profit, subject to extra tax

windfall tax FINANCE, BANKING, AND ACCOUNTING excess profits tax

winding-up FINANCE, BANKING, AND ACCOUNTING the legal process of closing down a company

winding-up petition FINANCE, BANKING, AND ACCOUNTING a formal request to a court for the compulsory liquidation of a company

win win situation GENERAL MANAGEMENT a business situation in which all parties stand to gain something (*slang*)

WIP *abbr* FINANCE, BANKING, AND ACCOUNTING work in process

wired company GENERAL MANAGEMENT a company that makes full use of information technology to run its business (*slang*)

wireless application protocol E-COMMERCE see **WAP**

witching hour FINANCE, BANKING, AND ACCOUNTING the time when a type of derivative financial instrument such as a *put*, a *call*, or a contract for advance sale becomes due (*slang*)

withdrawal FINANCE, BANKING, AND ACCOUNTING the regular disbursements of dividend or capital gain income from an open-end mutual fund

withholding tax FINANCE, BANKING, AND ACCOUNTING
1 in the United States, the money that an employer pays directly to the government as a payment of the income tax on the employee
2 the money deducted from a dividend or interest payment that a financial institution pays directly to the government as a payment of the income tax on the recipient

WOMBAT *abbr* GENERAL MANAGEMENT waste of money, brains, and time (*slang*)

wood
put wood behind the arrow GENERAL MANAGEMENT to provide resources or money for a project or enterprise (*slang*)

Woodward, Joan (1916–71) GENERAL MANAGEMENT British academic. Originator of what subsequently became known as the *contingency theory* of organizations, based on research inspired by *Elton Mayo* and written up in *Industrial Organization* (1965). See thinker *Elton Mayo*

word of mouse E-COMMERCE word-of-mouth publicity on the Internet. Owing to the fast-paced and interactive nature of online markets, word of mouse can spread much faster than its offline counterpart. (*slang*)

word of mouth marketing MARKETING a marketing strategy which uses the person-to-person communication of satisfied customers to raise awareness of an organization's products and services and generate sales. Word of mouth communication spreads through social and business networks and communities, and is regarded as a particularly influential, cost-effective, and speedy means of disseminating information about an organization's products. Various methods are adopted to promote this process, including customer partnerships and customer referral plans. *Viral marketing* and *buzz marketing* are similar concepts, the latter focusing particularly on the creation of an atmosphere of excitement or "buzz" about a new product, often within a specific social group.

work GENERAL MANAGEMENT the expenditure of physical or mental energy to achieve a pur-

poseful task. Work is usually performed by *employees* within organizations, where it involves completion of a particular activity that contributes to the achievement of organizational goals.

workaholic HR & PERSONNEL somebody who is addicted to working. A workaholic spends long hours in the workplace and probably suffers from *presenteeism*. While workaholics may be very productive, workaholism is sometimes a sign of *stress* or personal problems. The term was coined in the 1960s.

worker control GENERAL MANAGEMENT participation by employees in the management of an organization. Worker control can involve *worker directors* or a *management buy-out*.

worker director HR & PERSONNEL an *employee* raised to executive status within an organization, usually as part of a structured program of *employee participation* in management. A worker director usually represents the views of staff at board level.

workers' cooperative GENERAL MANAGEMENT see *industrial cooperative*

work ethic GENERAL MANAGEMENT the belief that *work* itself is as important and fulfilling as the end result. The work ethic originated among Protestants and was central to the views of Martin Luther and John Calvin. It played an important role in the achievements of the Industrial Revolution.

work experience HR & PERSONNEL the temporary placement of young people in organizations to give them a taste of the work environment. Successful work experience programs require adequate preparation by schools and employing organizations, together with follow-up activities to monitor the outcomes of a placement.

work flow GENERAL MANAGEMENT see *office design*

workforce HR & PERSONNEL the whole body of employees, either in an organization or across an industry

working capital FINANCE, BANKING, AND ACCOUNTING the funds that are readily available to operate a business.
Working capital comprises the total net current assets of a business minus its liabilities.
Current assets – current liabilities
Current assets are cash and assets that can be converted to cash within one year or a normal operating cycle; current liabilities are monies owed that are due within one year.

If a company's current assets total $300,000 and its current liabilities total $160,000, its working capital is:
$$\$300,000 - \$160,000 = \$140,000$$

working capital productivity a way of measuring a company's efficiency by comparing working capital with sales or turnover.
It is calculated by first subtracting current liabilities from current assets, which is the formula for working capital, then dividing this figure into sales for the period.

$$\frac{Sales}{(Current\ assets - Current\ liabilities)} = Working\ capital\ productivity$$

If sales are $3,250, current assets are $900 and current liabilities are $650, then:

$$\frac{3250}{(900 - 650)} = \frac{3250}{250} = 13 \text{ working capital productivity}$$

In this case, the higher the number the better. Sales growing faster than the resources required to generate them is a clear sign of efficiency and, by definition, productivity.
The working capital to sales ratio uses the same figures, but in reverse:

$$\frac{Working\ capital}{Sales} \times 100\% = Working\ capital\ to\ sales\ ratio$$

Using the same figures in the example above, this ratio would be calculated:

$$\frac{250}{3250} = 0.077 \times 100\% = 7.7\%$$

For this ratio, obviously, the lower the number the better.
Some experts recommend doing quarterly calculations and averaging them for a given year to arrive at the most reliable number.

working capital ratio FINANCE, BANKING, AND ACCOUNTING see *current ratio*

working hours HR & PERSONNEL see *hours of work*

working hours directive (*U.K.*) HR & PERSONNEL government regulations that aim to protect employees' health and safety at work by making sure that they do not work for too long, have too little rest, or have disrupted patterns of work. According to the directive, employees must not work more than an average of 48 hours per week, although they may opt out and work longer if they so choose. They must not be forced to work for more than eight hours a night on average. Employees are also legally entitled to one day off each week; 11 hours rest a day; an in-work rest break if they work for more than six hours per day; and four weeks' paid leave annually.

working lunch GENERAL MANAGEMENT a lunchtime meal during which business is transacted. A working lunch can occur either when an employee continues to work through their lunch hour, or when clients or colleagues are entertained and business is conducted at the same time. This is also known as a *power lunch*.

work in process FINANCE, BANKING, AND ACCOUNTING products that are in the process of being made. They are included in inventories and usually valued according to their production costs. U.K. term *work in progress*. Abbr. *WIP*

work in progress (*U.K.*) FINANCE, BANKING, AND ACCOUNTING = *work in process*. Abbr. *WIP*

work-life balance HR & PERSONNEL the equilibrium between the amount of time and effort somebody devotes to work and that given to other aspects of life. Work-life balance is the subject of widespread public debate on how to allow *employees* more control over their working arrangements in order to better accommodate other aspects of their lives, while still benefiting their organizations. The agenda consists primarily of *flexible working* practices and *family friendly policies*, although good practice demonstrates that flexibility should be open to all, including those without caring responsibilities. The work-life balance debate has arisen through social and economic changes, such as greater numbers of women in the workforce, the expectations of the younger *Generation X*, a growing reluctance to accept the longer hours culture, the rise of the 24/7 society, and technological advancements. It has been supported by government and by organizations which see it as a means of aiding *recruitment* and employee retention.

work measurement GENERAL MANAGEMENT the establishment of *standard times* for the completion of particular work tasks to a particular level of performance. In work measurement, tasks are broken down into elements. The time required for each is established and an assessment of relaxation and contingency allowances is made. Work measurement forms part of *work study* and is normally conducted subsequent to *method study* with the goal of increasing efficiency and *productivity*. Work measurement was developed in the context of industrial *production management* but has recently become more widely used. *Time study* and *predetermined motion-time systems* are used in work measurement.

work permit HR & PERSONNEL a license granted to a foreign national in order that they may perform a specific job for a limited period. A work permit program is intended to safeguard the interests of the resident labor force while enabling employers to recruit or transfer skilled workers from abroad. It is the responsibility of the employing organization to obtain permits from its national government.

workplace bullying HR & PERSONNEL persistent intimidation or harassment at work which demoralizes and humiliates a person or group. There are no universally agreed definitions of what constitutes workplace bullying, as there are many kinds of bullying behaviors or tactics. As a general guideline to distinguish between workplace bullying and legitimate criticism, comments should follow the principles for offering *feedback*: it should be properly conducted, nonpersonal, and constructive, and should not be abusive, aiming to help people to improve their behavior or performance rather than cause them anxiety or distress.

work profiling HR & PERSONNEL see *profile method*

work rage GENERAL MANAGEMENT an expression of irrational anger felt by an employee in the workplace (*slang*)

work sampling GENERAL MANAGEMENT see *activity sampling*

work shadow HR & PERSONNEL somebody who observes a jobholder in action with the goal of learning something about how that role is performed. Work shadowing has traditionally been seen as a way of giving *work experience* to school students or graduates but it is also a means of offering employees the opportunity to find out more about other jobs within their own or other organizations.

work simplification GENERAL MANAGEMENT an idea pioneered by *Frank* and *Lillian Gilbreth* and favored by practitioners of *scientific management*. Any work that does not add value to an idea or process is seen as reducible waste. Tasks in a procedure are analyzed to see if unnecessary steps can be eliminated, thereby reducing complexity as much as possible. This should enable workers to complete tasks more quickly. Work simplification is most suited to manufacturing processes and low-skilled jobs. It can lead to cost savings and better use of resources but it has been criticized for resulting in workers specializing in only one task and for making work repetitive and monotonous.

works manager HR & PERSONNEL the person in charge of a factory, plant, or area of operations in a manufacturing company. A works manager is usually a *general manager*, with responsibility not just for the manufacturing operation but also for personnel, finance, marketing, etc.

workstation

1 E-COMMERCE a powerful, single-user computer. A workstation is like a personal computer, but it has a more powerful microprocessor and a higher-quality monitor.

2 GENERAL MANAGEMENT the place where a person or small group performs their particular work tasks. A workstation might take the form of an individual unit where a stage of the manufacturing process is completed. A factory may contain many workstations, organized to optimize the production process. In an office environment, a workstation may refer to a desk with a computer, telephone, and other equipment at which one person sits.

work structuring HR & PERSONNEL the design of work processes. Work structuring involves arranging the factors that make up employees' jobs in the most efficient way. Factors to be engineered include *hours of work*, duties performed, and level of *empowerment*. Work structuring can make use of practices such as *flexible working*, *teamwork*, job enrichment, *job enlargement*, and *job rotation*. It is similar to *job design*.

work study GENERAL MANAGEMENT HR & PERSONNEL OPERATIONS & PRODUCTION the analysis of activities of employees within an organizational context. Work study comprises a set of techniques that are used to examine a work process and determine where improvements can be made. It usually involves *method study* followed by *work measurement*, and is an important tool in *total quality management*. It is similar to *time and motion study*.

work-to-rule HR & PERSONNEL a form of *industrial action* in which employees work strictly according to the terms of their *contract of employment*. A work-to-rule usually involves refusal to do any extra tasks and an overtime ban, causing production to slow down.

World Bank FINANCE, BANKING, AND ACCOUNTING one of the largest sources of funding for less developed countries in the world. It is made up of five organizations: the International Bank for Reconstruction and Development, the International Development Association, the International Finance Corporation, the Multilateral Investment Guarantee Agency, and the International Centre for Settlement of Investment Disputes. The World Bank was founded at the 1944 Bretton Woods Conference and has over 180 member countries. Its head office is based in Washington, D.C., but the Bank has field offices in over 100 countries. Its focus has

shifted dramatically since the 1980s, when over one-fifth of its lending was made up of investment in the power industry. Its current priorities are education, health, and nutrition in the most economically-challenged countries of the world.

world class manufacturing
1 FINANCE, BANKING, AND ACCOUNTING a position of international manufacturing excellence, achieved by developing a culture based on factors such as continuous improvement, problem prevention, zero defect tolerance, customer-driven *just-in-time* production, and *total quality management*
2 OPERATIONS & PRODUCTION the capability of a manufacturer to compete with any other manufacturing organization in a chosen market, with the aspiration of achieving world-beating standards in all organizational aspects. World class manufacturing encompasses the practices of *total quality management, continuous improvement*, international *benchmarking*, and *flexible working*.

World Economic Forum FINANCE, BANKING, AND ACCOUNTING an independent economic organization whose stated mission is to "improve the state of the world." Based in Switzerland, the WEF was formed in the 1970s by Professor Klaus Schwab, who set out to bring together the C.E.O.s of leading European companies in order to discuss strategies that would enable Europe to compete in the global marketplace. Since then, over 1,000 companies around the world have become members of the WEF and its interests have diversified to cover health, corporate citizenship, and peace-building activities. However, it has attracted criticism from some quarters, and antiglobalization protestors gather regularly at its meetings. Abbr. *WEF*

world economy ECONOMICS the global marketplace that has grown up since the 1970s, in which goods can be produced wherever the production costs are cheapest

wrap fund (*S. Africa*) FINANCE, BANKING, AND ACCOUNTING a registered fund, not itself a mutual fund but with similar status to that of a stockbroker's portfolio, which invests in a variety of underlying mutual funds, each of which is treated as a discrete holding

WRF *abbr* E-COMMERCE Web response form: a Web-based form designed to collect site-visitor contact and other information. A WRF often forms part of a landing page or termination point of a Web site address intended to funnel response not just from a Web site but also from traditional direct marketing material.

Wright , **T. P.** GENERAL MANAGEMENT originator of a mathematical model describing a *learning curve*, introduced in an article entitled "Factors Affecting the Cost of Airplanes" in *the Journal of Aeronautical Science* (February 1936)

write off FINANCE, BANKING, AND ACCOUNTING a reduction in the recorded value of an asset, usually to zero

writing-down allowance FINANCE, BANKING, AND ACCOUNTING in the United Kingdom, a form of capital allowance giving tax relief to companies acquiring fixed assets which are then depreciated. This allowance forms part of the system of *capital allowances*. Abbr. **WDA**

wrongful trading (*U.K.*) FINANCE, BANKING, AND ACCOUNTING the continuation of trading when a company's directors know that it cannot avoid insolvent liquidation

WRT *abbr* GENERAL MANAGEMENT with respect to (*slang*)

WYSIWYG *abbr* E-COMMERCE what you see is what you get: refers to Web creation software that enables users to design content on their computer that will look exactly the same when transferred to the Web. Before the advent of the Internet, the term was also used in reference to word processing software that allowed the user to see exactly how a document would look when it was printed.

X

XBRL *abbr* E-COMMERCE FINANCE, BANKING, AND ACCOUNTING Extensible Business Reporting Language: a computer language for financial reporting. It allows companies to publish, extract, and exchange financial information through the Internet and other electronic means.

XML *abbr* E-COMMERCE extensible markup language: a meta-language that describes rules for defining tagged mark-up languages. XML is similar to *HTML*, except that it is intended to deliver data to a variety of applications and is designed to be read by the applications run by a system, whereas HTML is intended to be read from a Web browser by a person.

XML is an emerging world standard for *metadata*, delivering a common approach by which metadata for content is collected. So in order to achieve a common standard, organizations in a particular industry would agree to structure their documents in the same way. For example, finance companies would agree to use the same methods of creating documen-

tation such as morning notes, which are short analyses issued daily. The morning notes would all use the same layout structure, and have the same metadata such as author name, date, ticker symbols, buy and sell rating. Because of this common structure, anyone receiving these morning notes would be able to search and interrogate them in a far more comprehensive manner.

Y

Y2K-compliant GENERAL MANAGEMENT see *millennium bug*

yakka (*ANZ*) HR & PERSONNEL an informal term for work

Yankee bond FINANCE, BANKING, AND ACCOUNTING a bond issued in the U.S. domestic market by a non-U.S. company

YAPPY *abbr* MARKETING young affluent parent (*slang*)

year-end FINANCE, BANKING, AND ACCOUNTING relating to the end of a financial or fiscal (tax) year

year-end closing FINANCE, BANKING, AND ACCOUNTING the financial statements issued at the end of a company's fiscal (tax) year

year to date FINANCE, BANKING, AND ACCOUNTING the period from the start of specified fiscal year to the current time. A variety of financial information, such as a company's profits, losses, or sales, may be displayed in this way. Abbr. *YTD*

yield FINANCE, BANKING, AND ACCOUNTING a percentage of the amount invested that is the annual income from an investment.

Yield is calculated by dividing the annual cash return by the current share price and expressing that as a percentage.

Yields can be compared against the market average or against a sector average, which in turn gives an idea of the relative value of the share against its peers. Other things being equal, a higher yield share is preferable to that of an identical company with a lower yield.

An additional feature of the yield (unlike many of the other share analysis ratios), is that it enables comparison with cash. Cash placed in an interest-bearing source like a bank account or a government stock, produces a yield—the annual interest payable. This is usually a safe investment. The yield from this cash investment can be compared with the

DICTIONARY

yield on shares, which are far riskier. This produces a valuable basis for share evaluation.

Share yield is less reliable than bank interest or government stock interest yield, because, unlike banks paying interest, companies are under no obligation at all to pay dividends. Frequently, if they go through a bad patch, even the largest companies will cut dividends or abandon paying them altogether.

yield curve FINANCE, BANKING, AND ACCOUNTING a visual representation of relative interest rates of short- and long-term bonds. It can be normal, flat, or inverted.

yield gap FINANCE, BANKING, AND ACCOUNTING an amount representing the difference between the yield on a very safe investment and the yield on a riskier one

yield management FINANCE, BANKING, AND ACCOUNTING securing maximum profits from available capacity by manipulating pricing to gain business at different times, and from differing market segments. Yield management is used particularly in service industries such as the airline, hotel, and equipment rental industries, where there are heavy fixed overheads and additional *revenue* has a big impact on bottom line profitability. Increasing computing power has enabled organizations to integrate complex information from different sources (for example, customer travel histories and current information on bookings) and use mathematical models to analyze the possibility of increasing profitability. Hotel businesses, for example, can use price offers to increase "revenue per available room," or "RevPAR," on the basis of yield management analysis.

yield to call FINANCE, BANKING, AND ACCOUNTING the yield on a bond at a date when the bond can be called

yield to maturity FINANCE, BANKING, AND ACCOUNTING the total return to an investor if a fixed interest security is held to maturity, in other words, the aggregate of gross interest received and the capital gain or loss at redemption, annualized. Abbr. *YTM*. U.K. term ***gross yield to redemption***

YK *abbr* FINANCE, BANKING, AND ACCOUNTING yugen kaisha

young old MARKETING the group of people aged between 55 and 75

youth-centric MARKETING specifically focused on and directed toward the interests of young people

YTD *abbr* FINANCE, BANKING, AND ACCOUNTING year to date

YTM *abbr* GENERAL MANAGEMENT yield to maturity

yugen kaisha FINANCE, BANKING, AND ACCOUNTING in Japan, a private limited liability corporation. Usually, the number of stockholders must be less than 50. The minimum capital of a limited liability corporation is 3 million yen. The nominal value of each share must be 50,000 yen or more. Abbr. *YK*

YUPPY *abbr* MARKETING young urban professional (*slang*)

Z

zaibatsu GENERAL MANAGEMENT Japanese mining-to-manufacture conglomerates dating from before World War II. At the end of World War II, zaibatsu were disbanded because of their involvement in the war effort. When postwar restrictions were relaxed, these groups of companies reformed as *keiretsu*.

Zaleznik, Abraham (*b*. 1924) GENERAL MANAGEMENT U.S. academic. Author of the landmark article "Managers and Leaders: Are They Different?" published in the *Harvard Business Review* (1977), which influenced the ideas of *Warren Bennis* on the key elements found in effective *leaders*.

ZBB *abbr* FINANCE, BANKING, AND ACCOUNTING zero-based budgeting

Z bond FINANCE, BANKING, AND ACCOUNTING a bond whose holder receives no accrued interest until all of the holders of other bonds in the same series have received theirs

zero-balance account FINANCE, BANKING, AND ACCOUNTING a bank account that does not hold funds continuously, but has money automatically transferred into it from another account when claims arise against it

zero-based budgeting FINANCE, BANKING, AND ACCOUNTING a method of budgeting which requires each cost element to be specifically justified, as though the activities to which the budget relates were being undertaken for the first time. Without approval, the budget allowance is zero. Abbr. *ZBB*

zero coupon bond FINANCE, BANKING, AND ACCOUNTING a bond that pays no interest and is sold at a large discount. Also known as ***accrual bond***

zero defects OPERATIONS & PRODUCTION a *quality* philosophy according to which organizations aim to produce goods that are 100% perfect. Zero defects was developed during the early 1960s in the United States by *Philip Crosby* while he was working for the Martin-Marietta Corporation. The goal is to eliminate the smallest defects at each process stage. It requires a high level of *employee participation*. When introduced in Japan it merged with *quality circle* concepts.

zero-fund FINANCE, BANKING, AND ACCOUNTING to assign no money to a business project without actually canceling it (*slang*)

zero growth ECONOMICS a fall in output for two successive quarters

zero out GENERAL MANAGEMENT to dial zero when using an automated call system in the hope of finding a live person to speak to (*slang*)

zero-rated supplies *or* **zero-rated goods and services** (*U.K.*) FINANCE, BANKING, AND ACCOUNTING taxable items or services on which *VAT* (Value Added Tax) is charged at zero rate, such as food, books, public transport, and children's clothes

zombie FINANCE, BANKING, AND ACCOUNTING a business that continues to trade even though it is officially insolvent (*slang*)

BUSINESS
INFORMATION
SOURCES

Business Information Sources

Providing the quickest and easiest route to the best business information available

Sometimes it's easy to grasp the basics about a topic, such as business plans, marketing, or budgeting. More often than not, it's difficult to know where to start—or where to go next. There is plenty of free world-class business advice out there—but where is it?

Business Information Sources is a highly selective collection of sources: it's designed to give you the quickest and easiest route to the information you need, in a variety of media.

We cite thousands of sources of the best business information from around the world, divided up into over 100 subject areas. These include the best management Web Sites, the most informative books, magazines, and journals, and the most authoritative organizations.

Contents

BUSINESS INFORMATION SOURCES

BUSINESS INFORMATION SOURCES

Accounting

BOOKS

2005 FASB (Financial Accounting Standards Board) Current Text

Financial Accounting Standards Board
Hoboken, New Jersey: Wiley, 2005
1400pp ISBN: 0471737895
This book is a collection of generally accepted accounting principles (GAAP) organized by topic. Material in the book is drawn from the Financial Accounting Standards Board's Statements on Financial Accounting Standards and Interpretations, the AICPA's Accounting Research Bulletins, and APB Opinions. Volume 1 is a collection of GAAP that has general applicability to all businesses. Volume 2 contains standards that apply to specific industries and nonprofit organizations. The book is updated annually to reflect new standards promulgated during the year.

After the Merger: Seven Strategies for Successful Post-merger Integration

Max M. Habeck, Fritz Kröger,
Michael R. Träm
Upper Saddle River, New Jersey: Financial Times Prentice Hall, 2003
192pp ISBN: 0273643541
Drawing on their experience as management consultants, the authors offer seven rules for merger success—vision, leadership, growth, early wins, cultural differences, communication, and risk management—with a focus on the integration process. An assessment of future trends in mergers and acquisitions is also made.

Cost and Effect

Robert S. Kaplan, Robin Cooper
Boston, Massachusetts: Harvard Business School Press, 1997
357pp ISBN: 0875847889
This book demonstrates how the principles of activity-based costing and other advanced cost management techniques can drive business performance. It includes examples from a variety of leading companies worldwide.

Essentials of Credit, Collections and Accounts Receivable

Mary S. Schaeffer
Hoboken, New Jersey: Wiley, 2002
272pp ISBN: 0471220744
This paperback will help the reader stay up to date with the latest strategies, developments, and technologies in credit, collections, and accounts receivable. With tips, techniques, and real-world examples, the book offers practical solutions for the credit and collection professional.

Excel 2003 for Dummies

Greg Harvey
Hoboken, New Jersey: Wiley, 2003
408pp ISBN: 0764537563
This book gives the reader key advice and help on how to get to grips with this useful computer package. It covers the basics of setting up a worksheet to creating formulas, charts, graphs, and spreadsheets so that all your essential business information can be safely and effectively stored.

Finance and Accounting for Nonfinancial Managers: All the Basics You Need to Know 5th ed.

William G. Droms
Cambridge, Massachusetts: Perseus Books Group, 2003
304pp ISBN: 0738208183
This helpful book demystifies the complex world of finance and accounting and makes it accessible to managers of all levels.

How to Collect Debts (and Still Keep Your Customers)

David Sher, Martin Sher
New York: AMACOM, 1999
173pp ISBN: 0814404871
This book provides a comprehensive step-by-step system that should minimize difficulties with accounts receivable. Encouraging a reevaluation of current policies and procedures, it proposes a new system—ASK (Attitude, Speed, and Knowledge)—and a dignified approach which will strengthen relationships with customers.

How to Read a Financial Report 6th ed.

John A. Tracey
Hoboken, New Jersey: Wiley, 2004
216pp ISBN: 0471478679
Tracey provides guidance on interpreting company accounts (with relation to U.S. practice), paying particular attention to the three essential parts of every financial report—the balance sheet, the income statement, and the cash-flow statement. His explanations are illustrated with many examples.

Intermediate Accounting 11th ed.

Donald E. Keiso, Jerry J. Weygandt,
Terry D. Warfield
Hoboken, New Jersey: Wiley, 2003
1392pp ISBN: 0471072087
The book covers the conceptual framework underlying financial accounting, financial reporting standards and statements, and more complex topics and transactions that are encountered in today's business environment. Specific guidance is provided for numerous topics, including accounting for cash and receivables, inventory, intangible assets, current and long-term liabilities, income taxes, leases, shareholders' equity, and revenue recognition.

Managerial Accounting 2nd ed.

James Jiambalvo
Hoboken, New Jersey: Wiley, 2000
448pp ISBN: 0471238236
The author presents the fundamental concepts of managerial accounting including job-order and process costing, cost-volume-profit analysis, cost allocation and activity-based costing, capital budgeting decisions, and standard cost and variance analysis. Unlike many cost and managerial accounting texts that focus on accounting skills, the book approaches the subject matter from a manager's perspective.

Relevance Lost: The Rise and Fall of Management Accounting

H. Thomas Johnson, Robert S. Kaplan
Boston, Massachusetts: Harvard Business School Press, 1991
269pp ISBN: 0875842542
First published in 1987, this book has won two major awards from the accounting profession, and has become a manifesto for managers in accounting and control. It explores the evolution of management accounting in U.S. business and how this relates to modern corporations.

Teach Yourself Book Keeping

Andrew G. Piper, Andrew Lymer
London: Hodder Arnold, 2003
356pp (Teach Yourself)
ISBN: 0340859423
This book aims to demystify the areas of bookkeeping that are essential for small business owners and managers. Offering plenty of examples to help explain key

1667

BUSINESS INFORMATION SOURCES

"Balance sheets are meaningless. Our accounting system is still based on the assumption that 80 percent of costs are manual labor."

Peter F. Drucker

terms and concepts, it covers the double-entry system and the processes of recording purchases and different types of transactions. Profit and loss accounts and balance sheets are also explained, and the book includes helpful completed exam pages with worked examples.

Teach Yourself Small Business Accounting
Mike Truman
London: Hodder Arnold, 2003
176pp (Teach Yourself)
ISBN: 0340859415
This practical guide is for the small business owner with no aptitude for figures or interest in bookkeeping or accountancy. It provides jargon-free step-by-step instructions, using the examples of real businesses, how to record each transaction, as well as advice on pricing goods and services. It also offers an alternative, easier, and less time-consuming system to that of double-entry bookkeeping.

Unlocking Company Reports and Accounts
Wendy McKenzie
Upper Saddle River, New Jersey: Financial Times Pitman, 1998
484pp ISBN: 0273632507
McKenzie provides a key to understanding company reports and accounts from first principles, explaining every point through the use of worked examples. She takes extracts from published accounts, including those of overseas companies, to illustrate accounting presentation, and enables the reader to understand and analyze a company's accounts and so build a comprehensive picture of its financial state.

MAGAZINES
Accounting Horizons
ISSN: 0888–7993
American Accounting Association (AAA)
5717 Bessie Drive, Sarasota, Florida, 34233–2399
T: +1 941 921 7747
F: +1 941 923 4093
http://aaahq.org
Published quarterly, this reviewed magazine thoroughly covers all aspects of banking and finance, business, and accounting. The theory and application of business finance is paramount in this journal.

The Accounting Review
ISSN: 0001–4826
American Accounting Association (AAA)

5717 Bessie Drive, Sarasota, Florida, 34233–2399
T: +1 941 921 7747
F: +1 941 923 4093
http://aaahq.org
The *Review* contains news and articles on all aspects of teaching and research in the field of accounting.

Accounting Technician
ISSN: 1358–6297
McMillan-Scott
9 Savoy Street, London, WC2E 7HR, U.K.
T: + 44 (0) 207 878 2300
F: + 44 (0) 207 379 7118
www.accountingtechnician.co.uk
Aimed at members and students of the Association of Accounting Technicians, the magazine covers all aspects of business and accounting of interest to accounting professionals.

Accounting Today
ISSN: 1044–5714
Accountants Media Group/Thomson
P.O. Box 966, Fort Worth, Texas, 76101
T: +1 800 260 2793
F: +1 817 252 4400
www.electronicaccountant.com
Published bimonthly, this magazine is an essential resource for accounting professionals. Covering the latest trends in finance, it is a useful source of current information.

Journal of Accountancy
ISSN: 0021–8448
AICPA
1211 Avenue of the Americas, New York, 10036
T: +1 212 596 6200
F: +1 212 596 6213
www.aicpa.org/pubs/jofa
Published monthly, this journal provides articles, interviews, and legislative updates on all aspects of accounting. The magazine is the publication of the American Institute of Certified Public Accountants.

INTERNET
Accountants World
www.accountantsworld.com
This is an extensive portal based in the United States with links to a wide range of Web sites of interest to accountants. It relates mainly to U.S. accounting practice.

American Institute of Certified Public Accountants
www.aicpa.org
With over 328,000 members, this

organization and its Web site provide information, continuing education, accreditation, advocacy, and leadership to certified public accountants in the United States. The AICPA publishes Accounting Trends and Techniques, Statements of Position, Practice Bulletins, Accounting Interpretations, and other guidance for financial accounting and reporting, including an extensive section on Sarbanes-Oxley.

Financial Accounting Standards Board
www.fasb.org
This is the Web site for the Financial Accounting Standards Board, the independent private-sector entity that establishes generally accepted accounting principles (GAAP). The Board issues formal accounting guidance on the treatment and reporting of financial transactions and performance.

Internal Revenue Service
www.irs.gov
One of the best-known American institutions, the Internal Revenue Service (IRS) is the main body in charge of U.S. taxes. It oversees tax laws and their enforcement, and tax collection. It also has numerous resources available online, from helpful agencies to forms for download.

Tax and Accounting Sites Directory
www.taxsites.com
Created by Dennis Schmidt, Professor of Accounting at the University of Northern Iowa, this site has numerous links to additional accounting and tax information across a broad spectrum. Easy to navigate and simple to make sense of, the directory helps businesses and individuals to find what they need quickly.

ORGANIZATIONS
USA
American Institute of Certified Public Accountants (AICPA)
1211 Avenue of the Americas, New York, 10036–8775
T: +1 212 596 6200
F: +1 212 596 6213
www.aicpa.org
This organization provides information, continuing education, accreditation, advocacy, and leadership to certified public accountants in the United States. The AICPA's Audit and Attest Standards team directs and develops standards for audit, attestation, and review services performed by CPAs.

"Economics is as much a study in fantasy and aspiration as in hard numbers—maybe more so."
Theodore Roszak

National Society of Accountants

1010 North Fairfax Street, Alexandria, Virginia, 22314
T: +1 703 549 6400
F: +1 703 549 2984
E: *members@nsacct.org*
www.nsacct.org
The National Society of Accountants is a nonprofit organization of some 30,000 professionals which provides accounting, tax preparation, financial and estate planning, and management advisory services to an estimated 19 million individuals and business clients. Most of the Society's members are independent practitioners or partners in small- to mid-size accounting and tax firms.

Europe

Association of Chartered Certified Accountants (ACCA)

2 Central Park Quay, 89 Hydepark Street, Glasgow, G3 8BW, U.K.
T: +44 (0) 141 582 2000
F: +44 (0) 141 582 2222
E: *info@accaglobal.com*
www.acca.co.uk
The Association is a professional

and examining body in accountancy, recognized under the Companies Act 1989 by the U.K. Department of Trade and Industry.

Chartered Institute of Management Accountants (CIMA)

26 Chapter Street, London, SW1P 4NP, U.K.
T: + 44 (0) 20 8849 2251
www.cimaglobal.com
CIMA is the leading U.K. professional organization for management accountants, but it also has a global reach: it represents more than 85,000 students and 65,000 members in more than 150 countries.

Institute of Chartered Accountants in England and Wales (ICAEW)

Chartered Accountants' Hall, P.O. Box 433, Moorgate Place, London, EC2P 2BJ, U.K.
T: +44 (0) 20 7920 8100
F: +44 (0) 20 7920 0547
www.icaew.co.uk
This, the largest professional accountancy organization in Europe with over 120,000 members, is responsible for educating and training chartered accountants and

maintaining standards of professional conduct among its members.

Institute of Chartered Accountants of Scotland (ICAS)

CA House, 21 Haymarket Yards, Edinburgh, Scotland, EH12 5BH, U.K.
T: +44 (0) 131 347 0100
F: +44 (0) 131 347 0105
E: *enquiries@icas.org.uk*
www.icas.org.uk
The ICAS is the leading professional accounting body in Scotland, and the oldest professional body of accountants in the world.

1669

BUSINESS INFORMATION SOURCES

"Accounting issues did not cause Enron's stock price to fall—its failed business model did."

Joseph Berardino

Acquisitions, Takeovers, and Mergers

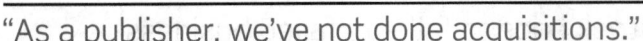

BOOKS

Acquisition: Strategy and Implementation 2nd ed.

Nancy Hubbard
Basingstoke, United Kingdom: Palgrave Macmillan, 2000
320pp ISBN: 0333945484
The process of acquisition is explored through an in-depth look at its key stages: preacquisition planning, communication during the deal, and implementation. The book also gives an overview of the history of acquisitions, global trends, and the reasons for success and failure. Case studies demonstrate different approaches and degrees of success. The new edition includes a chapter on new technology and e-commerce acquisitions.

The Art of M and A Integration: A Guide to Merging Resources, Processes and Responsibilities

Alexandra Reed Lajoux
New York: McGraw-Hill, 1998
448pp ISBN: 0786311274
A comprehensive treatment of post-merger integration is provided, covering the following areas: planning and communications; integration of resources; processes and management systems; technology and innovation; and commitments to customers, suppliers, shareholders, and employees.

Barbarians at the Gate

Bryan Burrough, John Helyar
New York: HarperCollins, 2003
592pp ISBN: 0060536357
This is a classic tale of corporate greed based on the merger of RJR and Nabisco. It is as gripping a read as any work of fiction.

Capitalize on Merger Chaos: Six Ways to Profit from Your Competitors' Consolidation and Your Own

Thomas M. Grubb, Robert B. Lamb
New York: Free Press, 2001
218pp ISBN: 068486777X
The authors suggest that, although merger mania is at an all-time high, up to 80% of mergers fail because of culture clashes, mismanagement, and the chaos that ensues. They examine the growth and profit opportunities that can arise from

competitors' merger chaos, and identify strategies which managers can adopt to exploit them. They further illustrate their argument by considering the winning strategies devised by companies such as AOL, General Electric, Dell, and Vodafone, and the failures at Coca-Cola, Boeing, and Compaq.

Complete Guide to Mergers and Acquisitions: Process Tools to Support M and A Integration at Every Level

Timothy J. Galpin, Mark Herndon
San Francisco, California: Jossey-Bass, 1999
272pp (Jossey-Bass Business and Management)
ISBN: 0787947865
The authors provide a guide to the process of managing a merger, focusing on due diligence, change management, integration task forces, communication, retaining key people, structure and staffing decisions, cultural factors, and human resources.

Due Diligence: Definitive Steps to Successful Business Combinations

Denzil Rankine, Graham Stedman, Mark Bomer
Upper Saddle River, New Jersey: Financial Times Prentice Hall, 2003
256pp ISBN: 0273661019
Due diligence is a key part of the (often fraught) acquisitions process in business. Done properly, it means that potential risks are reduced and chances of success increased. This book is a useful guide to the process and offers advice, cases studies, and analysis.

HR Know-how in Mergers and Acquisitions

Sue Cartwright, Cary L. Cooper
London: Chartered Institute of Personnel and Development (CIPD), 2000
230pp (Developing Practice)
ISBN: 0846451751
The authors offer guidance on the human factors involved in mergers and acquisitions. The topics they cover include: influencing the decision to merge; establishing effective communication; handling job insecurity; pay and benefits; downsizing, early retirement, and relocation; support systems and counseling;

creating a new corporate culture; and establishing new roles and training. Case studies are included.

The Morning After: Making Corporate Mergers Work After the Deal Is Sealed

Stephen J. Wall, Shannon Rye Wall
Cambridge, Massachusetts: Perseus Books Group, 2002
288pp ISBN: 0738205230
This book deals with merger management. It offers insights for recognizing when a merger is in danger, and advice on issues such as communicating effectively with stakeholders. It includes several case studies.

MAGAZINES

Acquisitions Monthly

ISSN: 0592–3618
Thomson Financial (U.K.)
Aldgate House, 33 Aldgate High Street, London, EC3N 1DL, U.K.
T: +44 (0) 20 7369 7000
F: +44 (0) 20 7369 7373
www.acquisitions-monthly.com
This monthly journal for financial executives, directors, bankers, and accountants provides information on international mergers, acquisitions, and management buyouts.

Mergers and Acquisitions: The Dealmaker's Journal

ISSN: 0026–1101
Source Media
One State Street Plaza, New York 10004, USA
T: + 1 212 803 8200
www.majournal.com
This monthly journal offers complete listings of all M&A deals, including pricing, deal structure, and the sales and profit levels of merger partners. In-depth feature articles cover trends in the industry and provide practical advice.

INTERNET

Acquisitions Monthly

www.acquisitions-monthly.com
The site provides M&A news and data worldwide and information on trends, industries, and sectors. Some services are subscription-based.

"As a publisher, we've not done acquisitions."   Duncan Edwards

Antitrust Division Department of Justice
www.usdoj.gov/atr
This U.S. government site provides information on antitrust enforcement, case filings, and links to competition authorities worldwide.

BizBuySell
www.bizbuysell.com
As well as databases of businesses for sale and e-mail notification of listings, this U.S.-based site includes articles on how to go about buying or selling a business. Users may search for their target company by category or location.

@brint.com
www.brint.com
This extensive portal and community network for e-business, information, technology, and knowledge management contains news, articles, book reviews, and links to relevant Web sites in the featured areas.

Company Mergers and Acquisitions
www.ventureeconomics.com
Containing details of over 1,900 deals in the United States from 1970 onwards, this database is drawn from quarterly and annual fund reports, news sources, and telegrams. It is produced by Venture Economics, a Thomson Financial Company.

MergerNetwork
www.mergernetwork.com
This site acts as a marketplace for buyers and sellers of companies, predominantly in North America but increasingly also in Europe, Asia, and South America. Users may search the databases of buyer profiles and businesses for sale free of charge but must pay for contact information.

ORGANIZATIONS
USA
Alliance of Merger and Acquisition Advisors (AMAA)
150 North Michigan Avenue, Suite 2700, Chicago, Illinois, 60601
T: +1 877 844 2535
F: +1 312 729 9800
www.amaaonline.org/amHome.asp
This association was formed to bring together all professionals who work with mergers and acquisitions. AMAA provides national certification for members, as well as various opportunities for networking with other organization members.

M&A Source
401 North Michigan Avenue, Suite 2200, Chicago, Illinois, 60611
T: +1 888 686 4222
F: +1 312 673 6599
E: *admin@masource.org*
www.masource.org
Founded in 1991, M&A Source proclaims itself to be the world's largest organization of middle market intermediaries. With a focus on the enhancement of member skills and abilities, this body provides members with the guidance needed to assist clients. M&A Source keeps its members current on the latest issues and trends in mergers and acquisitions, and strives to enhance their professional development.

International
International Network of M&A Partners (IMAP)
525 SW Fifth Street, Des Moines, Iowa, 50309
T: +1 515 282 8192
F: +1 515 282 9117
E: *info@imap.com*
www.imap.com
Founded in 1971 and formerly called the International Association of Merger and Acquisition Consultants, the IMAP is a global networking organization with over 50 members. It is dedicated to helping middle-market companies obtain confidential business information on available merger and acquisition prospects. It also assists individuals in a variety of financial transactions, such as the sale of private or public companies, the purchase of product lines, leveraged buyouts, financing and investment banking services, and mezzanine financing.

1671

FOR MORE INFORMATION
- Corporate Strategy (pp. 1721–1723)
- Interfirm Cooperation, Strategic Alliances, Joint Ventures (pp. 1780–1781)
- Organic Growth Versus Acquisition (pp. 106–107)
- Organization and Organization Structure (pp. 1847–1850)
- Venture Capital (pp. 1927–1929)
- Why Mergers Fail and How to Prevent It (pp. 108–109)

BUSINESS INFORMATION SOURCES

"I learned then what a bunch of gangsters the banks are. They *really* are gangsters."
Alan Sugar

Advertising

BOOKS

Advertising Management 5th ed.

David A. Aaker, Rajeev Batra, John G. Myers

Upper Saddle River, New Jersey: Prentice Hall, 1995

754pp ISBN: 0133057151

This is a comprehensive and detailed book on advertising management for both advertising students and those working in the field. Case studies are included.

Advertising: What It Is and How to Do It 3rd ed.

Roderick White

Maidenhead, United Kingdom: McGraw-Hill, 1999

320pp ISBN: 0077094581

This informative and detailed introduction to all aspects of advertising is aimed at organizations new to advertising, as well as people training in the area. It discusses the necessity and cost of advertising, the use of agents, the definitions and theories of advertising, planning advertisements, the media, and international and multinational advertising. Further sources of information are also listed.

Brand Failures: The Truth about the Biggest Branding Mistakes of All Time

Matt Haig

London: Kogan Page, 2003

256pp ISBN: 0749439270

Some brands just don't work. Many companies around the world have been affected by branding disasters, from Coke to Ford, Sony to Harley Davidson. Some have lived to fight another day, some not. In this book, Matt Haig looks at the stories behind brand failures and the key lessons that can be learned from them. Useful for advertisers as well as brand managers, the book looks at several types of marketing malfunction including: idea failures, PR failures, culture failures, and people failures.

Disruption: Overturning Conventions and Shaking Up the Marketplace

Jean-Marie Dru

Hoboken, New Jersey: Wiley, 1996

256pp ISBN: 0471165654

This book aims to enable advertising and marketing professionals to break the usual conventions in their field and produce a new vision of a product, brand, or service. It examines advertising across the globe and highlights examples of especially effective and ineffective advertising campaigns.

The Elements of Copywriting: The Essential Guide to Creating Copy That Gets the Results You Want

Gary Blake, Robert W. Bly

Upper Saddle River, New Jersey: Longman, 1997

184pp ISBN: 0028626303

A tightly written overview of copywriting, this book concentrates on the use of words that have exceptional impact on consumers. It is an especially useful text because it addresses several direct-marketing forms that are still comparatively new—press releases, e-mails, and Web advertising. It also deals with traditional marketing forms such as brochures, catalogs, and print ads.

Gabay's Copywriting Compendium

Jonathan J. Gabay

Woburn, Massachusetts: Butterworth-Heinemann, 2005

704pp ISBN: 0750664029

The author offers a comprehensive guide to writing powerful copy, and includes tips, ideas, and descriptions to help the creative process. All aspects of creative advertising and promotion are covered, including direct mail, the Internet, radio and TV, business-to-business, the press, PR, charities, and posters. The book is written for both the beginner and the more experienced copywriter.

How Not to Come Second: The Art of Winning Business Pitches

David Kean

London: Cyan Books, 2006

160pp ISBN: 1904879624

The commercial world has never been more competitive, and most companies today will need to pitch for new clients or new business. Written by·an author with over 20 years' experience in advertising, this book is a powerful guide to coming out on top. *How Not to Come Second* offers methods that have been tested on more than 200 companies around the world. It includes information on what potential clients are looking for,.what will put them off, and the seven secrets of the ultimate pitch.

My Life in Advertising and Scientific Advertising

Claude C. Hopkins

Maidenhead, United Kingdom: McGraw-Hill, 1966

318pp (Classic Reprint Edition)

ISBN: 0844231010

This book is a reprint of two classic works on advertising originally published some 80 years ago. Their succinct advice on reaching customers effectively has never been bettered—which accounts for their continuing pre-eminence in the field. *Scientific Advertising* is the more important of the two reprints here: it details methods for copywriting and test marketing, and introduces many more ideas that have come to be accepted as the building blocks of successful advertising campaigns. Hopkins coined the phrase "Advertising is salesmanship"; these texts are the touchstone for all advertising texts that followed.

Ogilvy on Advertising

David Ogilvy

New York: Vintage, 1987

224pp ISBN: 039472903X

David Ogilvy's firm, Ogilvy and Mather, changed the way advertising firms work. His advertising ideas became cultural icons. The text is written in a conversational way, making it an easy read—yet it contains profound truths about advertising as a business, as an art form, and as a creative outlet.

SPIN Selling

Neil Rackham

Aldershot, United Kingdom: Gower Publishing, 1988

208pp ISBN: 0070511136

Practical, easy-to-use and easy-to-understand information on how to make selling easier for the salesperson. Based on extensive research, its direct and helpful advice may also be helpful in all other work situations.

Tested Advertising Methods 5th ed.

John Caples, Fred E. Hahn

Upper Saddle River, New Jersey: Prentice Hall, 1998

320pp ISBN: 0130957011

This classic text has been reissued because its influence has been so far-reaching. Caples has had some 60 years of experience

"A good ad should be like a good sermon: It must not only comfort the afflicted—it must *afflict the comfortable*!"

Bernice Fitz-Gibbon

in advertising and gives clear, easy-to-understand examples of advertising that works and advertising that fails. Fred Hahn, the listed coauthor, has updated the book to reflect some more current trends in advertising, but still adheres to the basic principles set forth by Caples, which remain very sound.

We, Me, Them & IT: How to Write Powerfully for Business Revised ed.
John Simmons
London: Cyan Books, 2006
256pp ISBN: 1904879683

A revised edition of this popular business book aims to get readers using words more powerfully at work. A key question lies at heart of the book: what good is it to have a fantastic idea if you can't communicate it to anyone? Simmons offers practical, inspirational advice for anyone feeling stuck in this situation and demonstrates how words and writing can be powerfully employed to gain competitive advantage.

MAGAZINES
Advertising Age
ISSN: 0001–8899
Crain Communications, Inc.
711 Third Avenue, New York, 10017–4036
T: +1 212 210 0100
F: +1 212 210 0200

This is the flagship magazine of the Ad Age Group. Widely regarded as the authoritative source for articles on national and international marketing, *Advertising Age* is the premier U.S. weekly journal for in-depth information and current trends regarding marketing news, and is a must read for individuals working in advertising and marketing.

AdWeek
ISSN: 0199–2864
VNU Business Publications
770 Broadway, New York, 10003–9595
T: +1 646 654 4500
F: +1 646 654 4480
www.vnubusinessmedia.com

Accompanied by regional Web sites, this magazine provides specialized information for industry professionals. It includes feature articles, trend analysis, and news about industry events. The publishing company is responsible for *AdWeek*, *BrandWeek*, and *MediaWeek*, all of which cover aspects of advertising and are aimed at advertising executives. As a result, the information is often a little arcane for the layperson, but invaluable for those familiar

enough with methods, layout, and advertising jargon to decipher the text.

American Demographics
ISSN: 0163–4089
Brill's Media Ventures, L.P.
521 Fifth Avenue, 11th Floor, New York, 10175
T: +1 800 529 7502
www.demographics.com/Publications/AD

Formerly called *Marketing Tools*, this monthly magazine is a key title for marketing executives wanting credible and timely information regarding the latest consumer trends. The journal is dedicated to demographical studies in the United States. Each issue offers in-depth analysis of the latest events and how they influence the public consumer. This magazine is filled with up to the minute techniques for advertising and marketing research.

Journal of Advertising Research
ISSN: 0021–8499
Advertising Research Foundation
641 Lexington Avenue, New York, 10022
T: +1 212 751 5656
F: +1 212 319 5265
www.arfsite.org/Webpages/JAR_pages/jarhome.htm

This is the quarterly journal of the Advertising Research Foundation, featuring reports of field or laboratory research and case studies.

Marketing Management
ISSN: 1061–3846
American Marketing Association
311 S. Wacker Drive, Suite 5800, Chicago, Illinois, 60606–5819
T: +1 312 542 9000
F: +1 312 542 9001
www.marketingpower.com

Published by the American Marketing Association, this bimonthly journal was developed with the purpose of providing middle- to senior-level marketing executives with thought provoking discussions on emerging issues in the marketing profession. It provides in-depth coverage of many aspects of the profession, including national and international strategies.

INTERNET
AdForum
www.adforum.com

This gateway Web site offers links to advertising agencies, press releases, videos of ads in production, advocacy agencies, consultants, the trade press, and more.

Advertising Age
www.adage.com

Adage.com is the official Web site of the 73-year-old magazine, Advertising Age, from the Ad Age Group and is a wonderful resource for the industry.

Advertising Educational Foundation
www.aef.com

This is an advertising resource that includes information on careers, academic courses, industry news and events. Users may register to receive a free newsletter by e-mail.

Advertising World
http://advertising.utexas.edu/world

Extensive resources for advertising and marketing professors, students, and teachers are to be found on this site which is maintained by the Department of Advertising, University of Texas at Austin.

B to B: The Magazine for Marketing and E-Commerce Strategists
www.Btobonline.com

This is the electronic counterpart to the print magazine. It provides a good overview of online marketing strategies and news on developing issues in this area. The site features polls, surveys, and lists of top advertisers and top advertising venues. It is recommended for those trying to target advertising and for those interested in ad analysis.

ORGANIZATIONS
USA
The Advertising Council
261 Madison Avenue, 11th Floor, New York, 10016
T: +1 212 922 1500
F: +1 212 922 1676
E: *info@adcouncil.org*
www.adcouncil.org

The foremost creator of public service announcements in the United States, The Advertising Council is a nonprofit organization that was created in 1942 out of the remnants of the War Advertising Council. Its work focuses primarily on issues concerning quality of life, health, and community. Some of the most influential ad campaigns in the United States originated from this organization.

Advertising Research Foundation
641 Lexington Avenue, New York, 10022
T: +1 212 751 5656
F: +1 212 319 5265
E: *info@thearf.org*
www.arfsite.org

1673

BUSINESS INFORMATION SOURCES

A nonprofit corporate membership association which arranges conferences, workshops, and other events, and promotes research and development in the field of advertising.

American Advertising Federation

1101 Vermont Avenue, NW, Suite 500, Washington, D.C., 20005–6306
T: +1 202 898 0089
F: +1 202 898 0159
E: *aaf@aaf.org*
www.aaf.org
The Federation has a network of local chapters and clubs. It administers a prestigious award, the Advertising Hall of Fame, as well as other awards, conferences, and exhibitions.

American Association of Advertising Agencies (AAAA)

405 Lexington Avenue, 18th Floor, New York, 10174–1801
T: +1 212 682 2500
F: +1 212 682 8391
www.aaaa.org
This is an industry organization for advertising agencies. Lobbyists under AAAA auspices work for the industry on Capitol Hill. The Web site features upcoming events, news, tutorials, and the programs and publications of the group.

American Marketing Association

311 S. Wacker Drive, Suite 5800, Chicago, Illinois, 60606
T: +1 312 542 9000
F: +1 312 542 9001
E: *info@ama.org*
www.marketingpower.com
This association is an advocacy group providing resources to marketing professionals. Its site gives access to a job directory, provides courses for skill upgrades, and permits the tracking of trends in the industry. It also includes articles and tutorials for registrants.

Direct Marketing Association (DMA)

1120 Avenue of the Americas, New York, 10036–6700
T: +1 212 768 7277
F: +1 212 302 6714
E: *lrc@the-dma.org*
www.the-dma.org
This group is the largest trade organization for companies involved in direct marketing, database marketing, and interactive global marketing. It is involved in promoting direct marketing, and lobbying and disseminating trade information on Capitol Hill, working with government agencies,

and within all U.S. states. It is also expanding to include international trade issues. It is well known for its work on telemarketing and is spearheading the national campaign to remove disgruntled customers from telemarketer call lists.

Europe
Advertising Standards Authority Ltd. (ASA)

Mid City Place, 71 High Holborn, London, WC1V 6QT, U.K.
T: +44 (0) 20 7492 2222
F: +44 (0) 20 7242 3696
E: *enquiries@asa.org.uk*
www.asa.org.uk
The ASA exists to protect the public by ensuring that the rules contained in the British Codes of Advertising and Sales Promotion are followed by everyone who prepares and publishes advertisements. Its declared aim is to promote the highest standards in advertising.

European Advertising Standards Alliance

10a rue de la Pépinière, Brussels, B-1000, Belgium
T: +32 2 513 78 06
F: +32 2 513 28 61
www.easa-alliance.org
The Alliance is a coordinating body for self-regulatory organizations within Europe. Its main task is to administer a cross-border complaints procedure.

Institute of Practitioners in Advertising (IPA)

44 Belgrave Square, London, SW1X 8QS, U.K.
T: +44 (0) 20 7235 7020
F: +44 (0) 20 7245 9904
E: *info@ipa.co.uk*
www.ipa.co.uk
The mission of the IPA is to serve, promote, and anticipate the collective interests of advertising agencies, and, at the same time, to define, develop, and help maintain the highest possible standards of professional practice within the advertising business.

International Advertising Association (U.K. Chapter) Ltd. (IAA)

12 Rickett Street, London, SW6 1RU, U.K.
T: +44 (0) 20 7381 8777
F: +44 (0) 20 7610 0541
www.iaauk.com
The Association promotes the role and benefits of advertising as the vital force behind all healthy economies and the foundation of diverse, independent, and affordable media in an open society.

Outdoor Advertising Association of Great Britain Ltd. (OAA)

Summit House, 27 Sale Place, London, W2 1YR, U.K.
T: +44 (0) 20 7973 0315
F: +44 (0) 20 7973 0318
E: *enquiries@oaa.org.uk*
www.oaa.org.uk
The OAA is the central reference point for the outdoor advertising industry. It seeks to advance and protect the interests of its members, promote standards of best practice in the industry, and encourage the growth of business.

International
Interactive Advertising Bureau

116 East 27th Street, 17th Floor, New York, 10016
T: +1 212 380 4700
F: +1 212 380 4702
www.iab.net
This association undertakes a variety of activities. These include: evaluating and recommending guidelines and best practice; funding research to document the effectiveness of interactive media; and educating the advertising industry about the use of interactive advertising and marketing.

International Advertising Association (IAA)

521 Fifth Avenue, Suite 1807, New York, 10175
T: +1 212 557 1133
F: +1 212 983 0455
E: *iaa@iaaglobal.org*
www.iaaglobal.org
The IAA is a strategic partnership between advertisers, media companies, agencies, direct marketing firms, and individual practitioners, formed to advocate responsible marketing and free choice for advertisers and marketers. In addition to acting as a legislative advocate for commercial free speech, the IAA sponsors conferences and offers networking opportunities.

FOR MORE INFORMATION

- Customer Relations/Customer Service (pp. 1725–1726)
- Direct Marketing (pp. 1730–1731)
- Marketing Management (pp. 1827–1832)
- Market Research and Competitor Intelligence (pp. 1824–1826)
- Product and Brand Management (pp. 1870–1872)

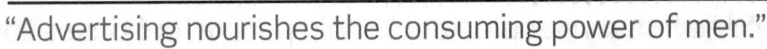
"Advertising nourishes the consuming power of men."   Winston Churchill

Analytical Techniques and Statistics

BOOKS

Applied Statistical Decision Theory

Howard Raiffa, Robert Schlaifer
Hoboken, New Jersey: Wiley, 2000
356pp (Wiley Classics Library)
ISBN: 047138349X
This book is aimed at people who are interested in using statistics as a tool in practical decision making under conditions of uncertainty, and who also have the necessary training in mathematics and statistics to employ the relevant analytical techniques. It focuses on experimentation and decision, general theory, extensive-form analysis, and distribution theory.

Basic Business Statistics: Concepts and Applications 10th ed.

Mark L. Berenson, David M. Levine
Upper Saddle River, New Jersey: Prentice Hall, 2005
1114pp ISBN: 0131678310
This textbook deals with the techniques of analyzing and presenting business data. The authors explain probability, normal distribution, estimation, hypothesis testing, analysis of variance, and linear and multiple regression models. A CD-ROM is included with the book.

Dictionary of Economics

Jae K. Shim, Joel G. Siegel
Hoboken, New Jersey: Wiley, 1995
373pp ISBN: 0471013145
This is an economic forecasting and analysis textbook that is geared to the lay reader. It is remarkably jargon-free and features paraphrased basic English descriptions of complex economic terms. It is also notable both for its inclusion of slang terms and for its extremely clear graphics: there are many charts and diagrams that are very useful in understanding complicated concepts. While not exactly a guide to performing statistical analysis, this book is essential for nonspecialists who wish to understand reports they have commissioned on economic subjects.

Doing Research in Business and Management: An Introduction to Process and Method

Dan Remenyi et al.
London: Sage Publications, 1998
336pp ISBN: 0761959505
After first highlighting the different contexts and purposes, strategies and tactics, and programs and processes of management research, the authors then move on to a more detailed review of the relevant research approaches and methods. They discuss the interrelationship of theoretical and empirical research and examine how these different approaches are used in practice. The implications of using quantitative and qualitative methods are reviewed, and the book also contains practical advice on available analysis techniques and software packages.

Effective Use of Statistics: A Practical Guide for Managers 2nd ed.

Tim Hannagan
London: Kogan Page, 1999
160pp (Business Skills)
ISBN: 0749429690
Hannagan provides a statistical foundation for managers, focusing on integrating statistical information into everyday work and presenting it effectively. An appendix offers basic math for managers, and the book comes with an accompanying computer disk with a data file in Microsoft Word for Windows.

Essential Quantitative Methods for Business Management and Finance 3rd ed.

Les Oakshott
New York: Palgrave, 2006
512pp ISBN: 1403949913
This is a student guide to the major topics likely to be taught on a quantitative methods course. Excel and SPSS software is included, along with extra support for lecturers.

Implementing Global Performance Measurement Systems: A Cookbook Approach to Evaluation

Ferdinand Tesoro, Jack Tootson
San Francisco, California: Jossey-Bass, 1999
256pp ISBN: 078794744X
This practical guide presents a step-by-step approach to evaluating and measuring ongoing business performance. Following an overview of performance measurement, the areas covered include establishing the business case, identifying the right performance metrics, implementing the performance measurement system, and leveraging results to improve performance. Guidance is offered on constructing a line graph, a cause–effect diagram, and a scatter diagram. A CD-ROM is included.

Practical Business Statistics 5th ed.

Andrew Siegel
Maidenhead, United Kingdom: McGraw-Hill, 2002
730pp ISBN: 0072821256
Though this is a college textbook, it is not simply filled with formulas and equations. It offers a less theoretical approach to statistics, focusing on examples using real data, on applications, and on the underlying reasons for using statistical analysis in business. It is especially useful because the text acknowledges that much of what is done in business statistics and analysis is now done by computer programs, rather than by unhappy, squinting workers in visors with scientific calculators.

Quantitative Approaches in Business Studies 6th ed.

Claire Morris
Upper Saddle River, New Jersey: Financial Times Prentice Hall, 2002
512pp ISBN: 0273657593
Using a problem-driven approach, this textbook for students on business courses aims to demonstrate the effectiveness of quantitative methods. The four parts cover: handling numbers; numbers as a means of communication; numbers as a basis for deduction; and numbers as a tool of planning. This edition includes a chapter on multiple regression and the use of statistical methods for a substantial student project or dissertation.

Root Cause Failure Analysis

R. Keith Mobley
Woburn, Massachusetts: Newnes, 1999
360pp (Plant Engineering Maintenance)
ISBN: 0750671580
The author outlines the tools needed to carry out industrial troubleshooting investigations effectively and explains the principles of Root Cause Failure Analysis (RCFA). He also provides extensive information on equipment design and equipment troubleshooting.

Time Series Models for Business and Economic Forecasting

Philip Hans Franses
New York: Cambridge University Press, 1998
280pp ISBN: 0521586410

1675

BUSINESS INFORMATION SOURCES

"There should be some professional exam for these analysts. Most of the time they talk through their backsides."

Alan Sugar

Generally regarded as one of the best introductory texts on economic forecasting, this book nonetheless requires a bit more background in business and economics than the average lay-person usually possesses. Its focus is on economic time series analysis—in other words, it explains statistical analyses of trends, seasonality, and other nonlinear series. The book uses real market examples, rather than simulated data and simple equations. There is also an emphasis on model identification and diagnostics, which baffle many business forecasters. This book is definitely skewed to the academic, yet is far easier for most readers to use than standard econometrics texts.

MAGAZINES
Journal of the American Statistical Association (JASA)
ISSN: 0162–1459
American Statistical Association (ASA)
1429 Duke Street, Alexandria, Virginia, 22314–3415
T: +1 703 684 1221
F: +1 703 684 2037
www.amstat.org/publications/jasa
JASA was established in 1888 and is published in March, June, September, and December. Subjects covered include statistical applications and statistical education.

Journal of the Royal Statistical Society
Blackwell Publishing
350 Main Street, Malden, Massachusetts, 02148
T: +1 781 388 8200
F: +1 781 388 8232

www.blackwellpublishing.com
The *Journal* was established in 1838. It is divided into Series A: Statistics in Society (ISSN: 0964–1998); Series B: Statistical Methodology (ISSN: 1369–7412); and Series C: Applied Statistics (ISSN: 0035–9254). Each is available as a separate journal. Series A is produced quarterly; B and C five times a year.

INTERNET
Milner Library, Illinois State University
www.mlb.ilstu.edu/learn/stat
This is an online tutorial called "Finding Statistics." Via a series of Internet pages, it covers (a) finding statistics, (b) understanding them, and (c) evaluating their usefulness. A self-assessment tool, or quiz, is included in each section. On this site, the reader can find answers to a number of basic questions, such as what the general definitions and terminology are in statistical research, how to locate statistics easily, how to determine whether statistics are reliably relevant, and what statistical databases are available. This is an excellent primer on the subject.

ORGANIZATIONS
USA
American Statistical Association (ASA)
1429 Duke Street, Alexandria, Virginia, 22314–3415
T: +1 703 684 1221
F: +1 703 684 2037
E: *asainfo@amstat.org*
www.amstat.org
Founded in 1839, this is an educational society for professional statisticians that

boasts Florence Nightingale, Alexander Graham Bell, and Andrew Carnegie among its former members. It now has some 16,000 members in the United States, Canada, and throughout the world. The ASA publishes or copublishes a number of journals, including the Journal of the American Statistical Association. The Association's Web site has a searchable database of relevant events.

Europe
Royal Statistical Society (RSS)
12 Errol Street, London, EC1Y 8LX, U.K.
T: +44 (0) 20 7638 8998
F: +44 (0) 20 7614 3905
E: *rss@rss.org.uk*
www.rss.org.uk
Founded in 1834, the RSS has 6,500 members in the United Kingdom and internationally. It holds a number of meetings annually, including an annual international conference, and offers several professional qualifications to members. The society also publishes the *Journal of the Royal Statistical Society* (in four series), and a monthly news magazine, *RSS News*.

FOR MORE INFORMATION

☆ Benchmarking (pp. 381–382)
🖰 Business Process Reengineering (pp. 1694–1695)
☆ Lean Manufacturing (pp. 218–219)
🖰 Market Research and Competitor Intelligence (pp. 1824–1826)
🖰 Process Control and Statistical Process Control (pp. 1868–1869)

"There are two kinds of statistics, the kind you look up and the kind you make up."
Rex Stout

Auditing and Management Audit

BOOKS

The Internal Auditing Handbook 2nd ed.
K. H. Spencer Pickett
Hoboken, New Jersey: Wiley, 2003
802pp ISBN: 0470848634
The book is a comprehensive guide to audit standards, internal controls, planning and risk analysis, statistical sampling, client interviews and flowcharting. It provides many examples of the application of audit theory by means of case studies and assignments with suggested solutions. *The Internal Auditing Handbook* also deals with special engagements and topics including computer audits, fraud investigations, establishing an audit function, and training audit staff. It is organized in four major parts that cover theory, techniques, internal audit management, and specialist auditing.

Montgomery's Auditing 12th ed.
Vincent M. O'Reilly et al.
Hoboken, New Jersey: Wiley, 2001
336pp ISBN: 0471327425
The book outlines all the information needed to understand and apply generally accepted auditing standards. It assists auditors in developing an enterprise plan, testing specific accounting cycles and accounts, and producing the final audit report. The book is organized in five parts that cover the audit environment, theory and concepts, auditing specific accounts, completing the audit and reporting results, and auditing specialized industries.

Quantitative Analysis for Management 9th ed.
Barry Render, Ralph M. Stair, Michael E. Hanna
Upper Saddle River, New Jersey: Prentice Hall, 2005
731pp ISBN: 0131857029
This textbook for students combines coverage of traditional management science techniques with modern technology solutions. It includes a CD-ROM.

The Smartest Guys in the Room: The Amazing Rise and Scandalous Fall of Enron
Bethany McLean, Peter Elkind
New York: Portfolio, 2004
464pp ISBN: 1591840538
Written by two *Fortune* journalists, this book attempts to lay bare the extraordinary story behind Enron's collapse in 2001. A tale of jaw-dropping corporate arrogance, it shows the impact of incompetence and greed on the notion of corporate governance.

MAGAZINES

ABI Journal
American Bankruptcy Institute (ABI)
44 Canal Center Plaza, Suite 404, Alexandria, Virginia, 22314
T: +1 703 739 0800
F: +1 703 739 1060
www.abiworld.org
The *ABI Journal* is published ten times a year. It is written by experts from the insolvency community and addresses issues such as consumer bankruptcy, the intersection of state laws and the Bankruptcy Code, valuation, turnaround management concerns, and recent legislative developments.

Internal Auditing and Business Risk
Institute of Internal Auditors—United Kingdom & Ireland (IIA-U.K.)
13 Abbeville Mews, 88 Clapham Park Road, London, SW4 7BX, U.K.
T: +44 (0) 20 7498 0101
F: +44 (0) 20 7978 2492
www.iia.org.uk
This magazine, the journal of the IIA-U.K., covers all aspects of internal auditing and of risk assessment and risk management.

Internal Auditor
ISSN: 0020–5745
Institute of Internal Auditors, Inc.
247 Maitland Avenue, Altamonte Springs, Florida, 32701–4201
T: +1 407 937 1100
F: +1 407 937 1101
www.theiia.org
This magazine, the journal of the IIA in the United States, covers auditing techniques and applications, internal control systems, and corporate governance, besides containing practical case studies.

Managerial Auditing Journal
ISSN: 0268–6902
Emerald
44 Brattle Street, 4th Floor, Cambridge, Massachusetts, 02138
T: +1 888 622 0075
F: +1 617 354 6875
www.emeraldinsight.com

The *Managerial Auditing Journal* addresses the changing function of the auditor and examines both the professional and the managerial aspects of the role. Its articles are mainly concerned with the latest developments in auditing theory and practice, research, and case studies.

INTERNET

The American Institute of Certified Public Accountants (AICPA)
www.aicpa.org
This is the Web site of a large membership organization that provides information, continuing education, accreditation, advocacy, and leadership to certified public accountants in the United States. The AICPA's Audit and Attest Standards team directs and develops standards for audit, attestation, and review services performed by CPAs.

Information Systems Audit and Control Association (ISACA)
www.isaca.org
This is the Web site of the Information Systems Audit and Control Association, a recognized leader in information technology assurance, control, and governance. With 50,000 members in more than 140 countries, the organization provides CISA (Certified Information Systems Auditor) certification and develops worldwide standards for information systems auditing and control.

The Institute of Internal Auditors (IIA)
www.theiia.org
This is the Web site of a nonprofit organization with more than 117,000 members from all over the world. Its purpose is to serve as the profession's international watchdog and primary resource for certification, continuing education, research, and technological issues related to internal audits.

ORGANIZATIONS
USA
American Accounting Association (AAA)
5717 Bessie Drive, Sarasota, Florida, 34233–2399
T: +1 941 921 7747
F: +1 941 923 4093
E: *office@aaahq.org*
http://aaahq.org

1677

BUSINESS INFORMATION SOURCES

"The most important thing American industry needs to do is reduce the number of management layers."

Kenneth Iverson

The AAA is a professional body with a particular interest in developments in the teaching of accountancy.

American Institute of Certified Public Accountants (AICPA)

1211 Avenue of the Americas, New York, NY 10036–8775
T: +1 212 596 6200
F: +1 212 596 6213
www.aicpa.org
This is the Web site of an organization with 328,000 members that provides information, continuing education, accreditation, advocacy, and leadership to certified public accountants in the United States. The AICPA's Audit and Attest Standards team directs and develops standards for audit, attestation, and review services performed by CPAs.

Association to Advance Collegiate Schools of Business (AACSB International)

777 South Harbour Island Boulevard, Suite 750, Tampa, Florida, 33602–5730
T: +1 813 769 6560
F: +1 813 769 6559
www.aacsb.edu
Founded in 1916, AACSB International acts as an accrediting agency for bachelor's, master's, and doctoral degree programs in business administration and accounting.

Europe
Institute of Internal Auditors—United Kingdom & Ireland (IIA-U.K.)

13 Abbeville Mews, 88 Clapham Park Road, London, SW4 7BX, U.K.
T: +44 (0) 20 7498 0101
F: +44 (0) 20 7978 2492
E: *info@iia.org.uk*
www.iia.org.uk

The IIA-U.K. is the U.K. professional body for internal auditors. It offers its members information and advice on all aspects of internal auditing, and presents their views to the government and other national and international bodies.

BUSINESS INFORMATION SOURCES

"It seems to me that there must be an ecological limit to the number of paper pushers the earth can sustain."

Barbara Ehrenreich

Bankruptcy and Business Failure

BOOKS

Corporate Bankruptcy: Tools, Strategies and Alternatives

Grant A. Newton
Hoboken, New Jersey: Wiley, 2003
256pp ISBN: 0471332682
In its examination of the complexities of restructuring and bankruptcy, this book provides a working knowledge of the bankruptcy process and of its benefits and challenges for both companies and their creditors. Supported by actual case studies, it assesses the legal and practical problems facing both debtors and creditors. It is a useful reference tool for every bankruptcy practitioner.

Corporate Failure by Design: Why Organizations Are Built to Fail

Jonathan I. Klein
Westport, Connecticut: Quorum Books, 2000
328pp ISBN: 1567202977
Despite all that has been written on the subject of making organizations succeed, the reality is that an overwhelming majority of businesses fail within five years and almost all fail within ten years. The author suggests that this tendency is inherent in the organization and explains his theory of organizational self-destruction. Besides analyzing the causes and processes of failure, however, he also points out the lessons that can be learned from it.

Corporate Financial Distress and Bankruptcy: A Complete Guide to Predicting and Avoiding Distress and Profiting from Bankruptcy 2nd ed.

Edward I. Altman
Hoboken, New Jersey: Wiley, 1993
356pp (Wiley Finance Edition)
ISBN: 0471552534
A leading expert on bankruptcy examines the trends in this field, reflecting the atmosphere in corporate America. He also presents models that can be used to analyze companies and their financial options and includes a number of relevant case studies.

Corporate Turnaround: How Managers Turn Losers into Winners

Donald B. Bibeault
Frederick, Maryland: Beard Group, 1998
482pp ISBN: 1893122026
This is a reprint of a classic book that

remains a source of effective advice on financial crisis management. It distills the experiences of close to 100 managers who successfully restored companies to profitability and constitutes a practical guide to management strategies to prevent bankruptcy.

Creating Value through Corporate Restructuring: Case Studies in Bankruptcies, Buyouts, and Breakups

Stuart C. Gilson
Hoboken, New Jersey: Wiley, 2001
528pp ISBN: 0471405590
Management buyouts are a common form of business restructuring. This collection of recent case studies from the United States and several other countries illustrates the real-world techniques and strategies that are common to all types of restructuring. It demystifies the complex financial issues surrounding business valuation and gives the reader a better understanding of the possibilities when dealing with corporate restructuring.

Elements of Bankruptcy 3rd ed.

Douglas G. Baird
New York: Foundation Press, 2000
304pp ISBN: 1566628687
Baird's book gives an overview of current law and practice in the United States. Recent changes in the law and topical issues are discussed and placed in context.

The Executive Guide to Corporate Bankruptcy

Thomas J. Salerno, Jordan A. Kroop, Craig D. Hansen
Frederick, Maryland: Beard Group, 2001
736pp ISBN: 1587980266
This book was written to provide a comprehensive resource for managers of financially troubled companies facing Chapter 11 bankruptcy proceedings. The authors outline the history of American bankruptcy law and explain bankruptcy terminology for the lay person, then provide a step-by-step guide to the bankruptcy and reorganization process, including sample documents.

The Turnaround Manager's Handbook

Richard S. Sloma
Frederick, Maryland: Beard Group, 2000
244pp ISBN: 1893122409
Designed for the corporate manager, this

book provides specific details of the actions to be taken to achieve a turnaround in a failing business. The author addresses operational issues and provides recommendations and tools to restore a business to profitability.

MAGAZINES

Insolvency Intelligence

ISSN: 0950–2645
Sweet & Maxwell
100 Avenue Road, Swiss Cottage, London, NW3 3PF, U.K.
T: +44 (0) 20 7393 7000
F: +44 (0) 20 7393 7010
www.smlawpub.co.uk
This magazine, published ten times a year, contains news and views on insolvency law for lawyers and accountants.

Insolvency Law and Practice

ISSN: 0267–0771
LexisNexis
Tolley House, 2 Addiscombe Road, Croydon, CR9 5AF, U.K.
T: +44 (0) 20 8662 2000
F: +44 (0) 20 8662 2012
www.lexisnexis.co.uk
Aimed at legal practitioners, students, and accountants, this magazine covers all aspects of insolvency law and accountancy. It appears six times a year.

International Insolvency Review (IIR)

ISSN: 1180–0518
Wiley
111 River St, Hoboken, New Jersey, 07030–5774
T: +1 201 748–6000
F: +1 212 850 6021
www.wiley.com
The *IIR* is published three times a year, in association with INSOL, and provides an international perspective on developments in insolvency law and practice, in addition to covering issues relating to cross-border insolvency.

INTERNET

ABIWorld

www.abiworld.org
ABIWorld is sponsored by the American Bankruptcy Institute and is a major source of U.S. bankruptcy information. The site includes news and statistics, information and opinions on bankruptcy cases, information on international bankruptcy

BUSINESS INFORMATION SOURCES

"If we are to be more prosperous we need more millionaires and more bankrupts."

Keith Joseph

legislation, an interactive newsletter, and information on how to find a bankruptcy professional. Some sections are restricted to ABI members.

American Bankruptcy Institute
www.abiworld.org
The American Bankruptcy Institute is a nonprofit, nonpartisan organization promoting education, research, and the analysis of bankruptcy issues. Its Web site provides access to current news and legislation pertaining to bankruptcy and business failures, an interactive newsletter, and research and analysis.

Business Bankruptcy Info
www.creditworthy.com/topics/bankruptcy.html
Hosted by Creditworthy Co., this Web site provides links to business bankruptcy information covering the United States, Canada, and the United Kingdom. It includes information on, and links to, a U.S. bankruptcy dictionary, an overview of the U.S. Bankruptcy Code, and statistics and research on bankruptcy filings.

InsolvencyAsia
www.insolvencyasia.com
This site, based in Hong Kong, provides insolvency-related news together with information on bankruptcy legislation and listings of consultants, associations, and regulatory authorities in Asian countries.

InterNet Bankruptcy Library
www.bankrupt.com
Sponsored by the Bankruptcy Creditors' Service and the Beard Group, this site is aimed particularly at creditors. It includes a

news archive, a database of bankruptcy professionals, information on legal rules in American states, and details of publications, as well as providing access to discussion groups.

United States Bankruptcy Courts
www.uscourts.gov/bankruptcycourts.html
Since there are specialized courts that settle bankruptcy claims in America, this site offers information about the courts themselves, offers downloadable forms, has an F.A.Q. section, and has links to the individual courts for a particular area.

ORGANIZATIONS
USA
American Bankruptcy Institute (ABI)
44 Canal Center Plaza, Suite 404, Alexandria, Virginia, 22314
T: +1 703 739 0800
F: +1 703 739 1060
E: *info@abiworld.org*
www.abiworld.org
The ABI was founded in 1982 to provide the U.S. Congress and public with unbiased information on bankruptcy issues. Its interests include research, conferences, training programs, and publications. Opportunities for the exchange of information and ideas are also provided. The membership of more than 11,000 includes attorneys, auctioneers, bankers, judges, accountants, and other professionals.

Europe
Bankruptcy Association of England and Wales
4 Johnson Close, Abraham Heights,

Lancaster, Lancashire, LA1 5EU, U.K.
T: +44 (0) 1524 64305
E: *bankruptcyassociation@gbandi.freeserve.co.uk*
www.theba.org.uk
The Association was founded by John McQueen in 1983 to provide information and advice to debtors and bankrupts in the United Kingdom and to campaign for reform of insolvency legislation.

International
INSOL International—International Federation of Insolvency Professionals
2–3 Philpot Lane, London, EC3M 8AQ, U.K.
T: +44 (0) 20 7929 6679
F: +44 (0) 20 7929 6678
E: *heather@insol.ision.co.uk*
www.insol.org
INSOL is a grouping of member associations that aims to facilitate the exchange of information and ideas and to encourage international cooperation within the insolvency profession. It participates in governmental advisory groups, supports research, and promotes the development of international guidelines and codes of practice. Its activities include the organization of seminars and conferences and the publication of newsletters, reports, and a journal.

FOR MORE INFORMATION
- Accounting (pp. 1667–1669)
- Auditing and Management Audit (pp. 1677–1678)

1680

BUSINESS INFORMATION SOURCES

"Through the fat years, the bankers were always right there by our side. But in bad times they backed off in a hurry."

Lee Iacocca

Benchmarking

BOOKS

Benchmarking: A Practitioner's Guide for Becoming and Staying Best of the Best

Gerald Balm
Schaumberg, Illinois: QPMA Press, 1992
178pp ISBN: 0963216708
This book is a practical guide for understanding benchmarking strategies, and applying them in an efficient, effective way to various types of organizations, such as industry, healthcare and government. It explains the benchmarking process used at award-winning IBM-Rochester, and includes bibliographical references and an index.

Benchmarking for Best Practices: Winning through Innovative Adaptation

Christopher Bogan, Michael English
Maidenhead, United Kingdom: McGraw-Hill, 1994
312pp ISBN: 0070063753
With its nine-step benchmarking model for management, this book aims to tailor benchmarking to a firm's unique identity. It features timesaving tips, evaluation charts, graphs, ethics, and antitrust guidelines, and includes bibliographical references and indexes.

Benchmarking Strategies: A Tool for Profit Improvement

Rob Reider, Harry Reider
Hoboken, New Jersey: Wiley, 2000
276pp ISBN: 0471344648
This is a practical manual covering benchmarking principles, techniques, and implementation. It examines how corporations perform various tasks in identifying and implementing internal and external best practices in a program of continuous improvement. It includes an index.

Best Practices: Building Up Your Business with Customer-Focused Solutions

R. Hiebeler, T. B. Kelly, C. Ketteman
Carmichael, California: Touchstone Books, 2000
240pp ISBN: 068484804X
From case studies of over 40 best practice companies, this book draws lessons on how to focus on customers, create growth, reduce costs, and increase profits. The topics it discusses are: new insights beyond

benchmarking; best practices auditing; understanding markets and customers; involving customers in the design of products and services; selling products and services; how best to serve customers; managing customer information; and putting best practices to work.

Best Practices in Planning and Management Reporting: From Data to Decisions

David A. J. Axson
New York: Wiley, 2003
304pp ISBN: 0471224081
This book examines the process of improving business performance through the adoption of best practices. The author introduces the technique of best practice benchmarking and explains how best practices may be used to drive change. The issues of strategic planning, operational and financial planning, management reporting, forecasting, and the use of technology are discussed and the use of benchmarking as a starting point is also explained.

Effective Management of Benchmarking Projects: Practical Guidelines and Examples of Best Practice

Mohamed Zairi
Woburn, Massachusetts: Butterworth-Heinemann, 1998
348pp ISBN: 0750639873
This book begins with a profile of Rank Xerox—where the benchmarking story started. It examines the strategic application of benchmarking for best practice, as well as such topics as partner selection, the ethics of benchmarking, and the value of industrial visits and benchmarking awards. It also describes the process of benchmarking in practice.

High Performance Benchmarking: 20 Steps to Success

H. James Harrington, James S. Harrington
Maidenhead, United Kingdom: McGraw-Hill, 1995
173pp ISBN: 007026774X
The aim of this book is to provide a complete understanding of how the total benchmarking process in any organization ought to be managed. It explains the process of benchmarking, data collection and analysis, organizing for benchmarking, and the five phases of benchmarking,

presenting helpful hints and tips along the way. Case studies and checklists illustrate the key issues.

Winning Business: How to Use Financial Analysis and Benchmarks to Outscore Your Competition

Rich Gildersleeve
Houston: Gulf Professional Publishing Company, 1999
334pp ISBN: 0884158985
Financial analysis, with all its detailed measurements and calculations, is often overlooked as a benchmarking tool. Gildersleeve provides clear explanations of the fundamental terms used to analyze and understand financial statements and demonstrates their value in benchmarking companies. The benchmarking indicators in this book can be used to track key measurements or as a metric by which to measure your company against others.

MAGAZINES

Benchmarking: An International Journal

ISSN: 1463–5771
Emerald
44 Brattle Street, 4th Floor, Cambridge, Massachusetts, 02138
T: +1 888 622 0075
F: +1 617 354 6875
www.emeraldinsight.com
The journal focuses on the theory and practice of benchmarking, with articles on recent academic research as well as real-life case studies of benchmarking activities by companies. Contributors are from a wide range of countries.

INTERNET

APQC's Benchmarking and Best Practice
www.apqc.org/best
This site summarizes the benefits of benchmarking, outlines a methodology, and lists the keys to success in the area. The "free resources" section includes articles, case studies, and white papers to guide you through the benchmarking process.

Avoid These Ten Benchmarking Mistakes
www.benchmarkingplus.com.au/mistakes.htm
Many sites tell you how to benchmark. This site lists the ten most common mistakes in benchmarking so that you can avoid making them yourself.

1681

BUSINESS INFORMATION SOURCES

"You are always going to have people who copy things that work."   Jay S. Walker

Benchmarking Exchange
www.benchnet.com

This is an extremely comprehensive site with a lot of information on benchmarking practices for both members and nonmembers. Members can conduct benchmark surveys online and have the information collected and returned through the Exchange as replies are received.

Benchmarking Network
www.benchmarkingnetwork.com

This is another comprehensive site. Members share information about best practice in a wide range of operations across all industry sectors.

Best-Practice.com
www.Best-Practice.com

Providing a range of information on benchmarking, this site has links to more detailed research and tools that can be purchased direct from the various partners in the network. Membership is free.

Global Benchmarking Council
www3.best-in-class.com/gbc

Members have access to a benchmarking database, regular meetings, and research reports, plus a range of other services and detailed information.

ORGANIZATIONS
USA
American Productivity and Quality Center (APQC)

123 North Post Oak Lane, 3rd Floor, Houston, Texas, 77024
T: +1 800 776 9676
F: +1 713 681 1182
E: *apqcinfo@apqc.org*
www.apqc.org

This nonprofit organization works with people and organizations around the world to improve productivity and quality. Nearly 500 companies, government organizations, and educational institutions support it. It provides the tools, information, expertise, and support needed to discover and implement best practices in a variety of areas, including knowledge management, benchmarking, and performance measurement.

Europe
Best Practice Club

The Atrium, Curtis Road, Dorking, Surrey, RH4 1XA, U.K.
T: +44 (0) 1306 646 555
F: +44 (0) 1306 646 556
E: *enquiries@bpclub.com*
www.bpclub.com

With an international membership, this organization promotes organizational excellence through members networking

and comparing their practice. Member companies come from both the manufacturing and the service sectors and pool their experience.

Centre for Interfirm Comparison (CIFC)

CIFC Ltd, 32 Thomas Street, Winchester, Hampshire, SO23 9HJ, U.K.
T: +44 (0) 1962 844 144
F: +44 (0) 1962 843 180
E: *enquiries@cifc.co.uk*
www.cifc.co.uk

The Centre helps businesses of all types and in all sectors to assess their performance through confidential, detailed comparison of their financial ratios and other data with those of similar businesses, and to target improvements in specific areas of their operations. It provides a wide range of benchmarking and related consulting services.

FOR MORE INFORMATION

✔ A Program for Benchmarking (pp. 540–541)
∽ Business Appraisal and Performance Measurement (pp. 1685–1688)
∽ Quality and Total Quality Management (pp. 1886–1889)
☆ The Balanced Scorecard (pp. 389–390)

BUSINESS INFORMATION SOURCES

"Copying other organizations' activities sounds like industrial espionage to some people, but the truth is that benchmarking is perfectly legal and ethical."
Warren Bennis

Budgeting

BOOKS

Beyond Budgeting: How Managers Can Break Free from the Annual Performance Trap

Jeremy Hope, Robin Fraser
Boston, Massachusetts: Harvard Business School Press, 2003
272pp ISBN: 1578518660
An enlightening read for all managers, not just finance specialists, this book posits that traditional budgeting processes are unproductive. Recognizing the fact that many executives are forced to spend their time "making the numbers work" rather than making the most of their company's potential, the book offers an alternative way forward. Case studies and findings from the "Beyond Budgeting Roundtable" are also included.

Budgeting Basics and Beyond: A Complete Step-by-Step Guide for Nonfinancial Managers 2nd ed.

Jae K. Shim, Joel G. Siegel
Englewood Cliffs, New Jersey: Prentice Hall, 2005
416pp ISBN: 0471725021
This book is a guide to effective budgeting, that takes the reader through every step from preparing and presenting budgets to handling budgeting difficulties. Extra features include case studies, illustrations, and checklists, together with suggestions for getting the most out of accounting software packages and spreadsheet applications.

Budgeting: Technology, Trends, Software Selection and Implementation

Nils H. Rasmussen, Christopher J. Eichorn
New York: Wiley, 2000
290pp ISBN: 0471392073
Describing itself as a guide to "essential budget planning for the 21st century corporation," this practically oriented book introduces and explains new trends in budgeting and budgeting software. By means of various report and contract samples, questionnaires, and interviews with leading managers, it guides the reader through the range of considerations that are crucial to streamlining the budget-planning process.

Capital Budgeting: Theory and Practice

Pamela P. Peterson, Frank J. Fabozzi
New York: Wiley, 2002
243pp ISBN: 0471218332

The book covers the underlying principles of capital budgeting, including discounted net cash-flows, risk assessment, and leases. It explains the importance of making wise decisions when investing in long-lived assets, and provides quantitative decision-making tools that assist managers in choosing between options.

Cashflow Reengineering: How to Optimize the Cashflow Timeline and Improve Financial Efficiency

James Sagner
New York: AMACOM, 1997
256pp ISBN: 0814403611
Sagner shows how to diagnose a company's cash flow situation accurately and prescribe the correct treatment. He presents ten management principles and procedures, which, he suggests, have saved many companies large amounts of money.

Cash Flows and Budgeting Made Easy: How to Set and Monitor Financial Targets in Any Organization 4th ed.

Peter Taylor
Oxford, United Kingdom: How To Books, 2002
160pp ISBN: 1857038037
This practical guide aims to cover the whole budgeting process, and contains information on planning financial requirements, forecasting, VAT, managing cash-flows, and using IT to help make your financial life easier.

Credit Risk Management: A Guide to Sound Business Decisions

H. A. Schaeffer, Jr.
Hoboken, New Jersey: Wiley, 2000
288pp ISBN: 0471350206
This book examines the steps leading to a sound business credit decision. It is divided into four main sections: analysis for creative credit management; building up essential business credit information; considering all factors that affect the business credit decision; and making a decision or recommendation. Twelve detailed case studies are provided, illustrating common problems along with their solutions.

Driving Value Using Activity-based Budgeting

James A. Brimson, John Antos, R. Steven Player, Jay Collins
Hoboken, New Jersey: Wiley, 1998
288pp ISBN: 0471086312

The book introduces activity-based budgeting (ABB) and feature costing as methods to create value and establish linkage between daily operations and strategic objectives. It covers the essentials of ABB including its fundamental concepts, methods of forecasting revenue based on activities, gap analysis, and capacity management. Using examples, case studies, and target-setting techniques. It also illustrates the shortcomings of the traditional budget approach and provides guidance on implementing ABB effectively.

Managing by the Numbers

Chuck Kremer, Ron Rizzuto, John Case
Cambridge, Massachusetts: Perseus Books Group, 2000
224pp ISBN: 0738202568
This is a handy and practical guide to reading and using balance sheets, income statements, and cash-flow statements to drive business growth and profitability.

Mastering Spreadsheet Budgets and Forecasts: How to Save Time and Gain Control of Your Business

Malcolm Secrett
Upper Saddle River, New Jersey: Financial Times Prentice Hall, 1999
260pp (Smarter Solutions)
ISBN: 0273644912
This step-by-step, jargon-free guide demonstrates the advantages and potential of using spreadsheets to prepare and present budgets and forecasts. It includes examples of budgets and forecasts, followed through completely from beginning to end.

Total Business Budgeting: A Step-by-Step Guide with Forms 2nd ed.

Robert Rachlin
Hoboken, New Jersey: Wiley, 1999
321pp ISBN: 0471351032
Rachlin provides an introduction to a wide range of budgetary techniques and applications and shows how to analyze outside influences, develop performance targets and budgeting segments, and administer the right budgeting processes. He includes detailed instructions, forms, examples, schedules, and formats.

INTERNET

Accountants World
www.accountantsworld.com
This is an extensive portal based in the

1683

BUSINESS INFORMATION SOURCES

"If I confess to you why I was so far behind you in these examples, you'd know why we have a budget deficit."

Ronald Reagan

United States with links to a wide range of Web sites of interest to accountants. It relates mainly to U.S. accounting practice.

CFO.com—Tools and Resources for Financial Executives
www.cfo.com

CFO.com is a great resource for anyone in a business financial setting. With multiple articles to read, CFO.com also has a newsletter, webcasts, and a magazine, which was named Magazine of the Year by the American Society of Business Publication Editors (ASBPE).

Credit to Cash
www.credit-to-cash.com

This U.K. portal provides a wide range of financial information and advice, specifically on credit management and policy, debt recovery, cash flow control, and other issues of interest to small businesses.

Institute of Management Accountants
www.imanet.org

This is the Web site of the Institute of Management Accountants (IMA), a professional organization that promotes management accounting and financial management. The IMA is responsible for the education and certification of professionals involved in management accounting, including operational and capital budgeting responsibilities. Members of the IMA receive information and educational materials on financial budgeting and control, capital budgeting, and management accounting topics.

ORGANIZATIONS
USA
American Accounting Association (AAA)
5717 Bessie Drive, Sarasota, Florida, 34233–2399
T: +1 941 921 7747
F: +1 941 923 4093
E: *office@aaahq.org*
www.aaahq.org

The AAA is a professional body with particular interest in developments in the teaching of accountancy.

American Institute of Certified Public Accountants (AICPA)
1211 Avenue of the Americas, New York, 10036–8775
T: +1 212 596 6200
F: +1 212 596 6213
www.aicpa.org

This organization provides information, continuing education, accreditation, advocacy, and leadership to certified public accountants in the United States. The AICPA's Audit and Attest Standards team directs and develops standards for audit, attestation, and review services performed by CPAs.

National Society of Accountants
1010 North Fairfax Street, Alexandria, Virginia, 22314
T: +1 703 549 6400
F: +1 703 549 2984
E: *members@nsacct.org*
www.nsacct.org

The National Society of Accountants is a nonprofit organization of some 30,000 professionals which provides accounting, tax preparation, financial and estate planning, and management advisory services to an estimated 19 million individuals and business clients. Most of the Society's members are independent practitioners or partners in small to midsize accounting and tax firms.

Europe
Chartered Institute of Management Accountants (CIMA)
26 Chapter Street, London, SW1P 4NP, U.K.
T: + 44 (0) 20 8849 2251
www.cimaglobal.com

CIMA is the leading U.K. professional organization for management accountants, but it also has a global reach: it represents more than 85,000 students and 65,000 members in more than 150 countries.

Institute of Credit Management (ICM)
The Water Mill, Station Road, South Luffenham, Oakham, Leicestershire, LE15 8NB, U.K.
T: +44 (0) 1780 722 900
F: +44 (0) 1780 721 333
E: *info@icm.org.uk*
www.icm.org.uk

The Institute of Credit Management (ICM) is the largest organization of credit professionals in Europe, and the focal point in the United Kingdom for all matters relating to credit management and its ancillary functions. The ICM sets professional standards and tests and assesses those who wish to gain its professional qualification. It also provides advice to government and other national bodies.

Institute of Financial Accountants (IFA)
Burford House, 44 London Road, Sevenoaks, Kent, TN13 1AS, U.K.
T: +44 (0) 1732 458 080
F: +44 (0) 1732 455 848
E: *mail@ifa.org.uk*
www.ifa.org.uk

The Institute of Financial Accountants, established in 1916, is the largest professional body of its type in the world. It represents members and students in more than 80 countries around the world and provides a qualification and continuing professional development for those who want to become financial accountants. It also sets both technical and ethical standards within the profession.

FOR MORE INFORMATION

"Whenever I think about the budgetary problems, I think about the problems of Errol Flynn . . . reconciling net income with gross habits."

Malcolm Rifkind

Business Appraisal and Performance Measurement

BOOKS

Assessing Business Excellence: A Guide to Self Assessment 2nd ed.

Les Porter, Steve Tanner
Oxford: Elsevier Butterworth-Heinemann, 2002
472pp ISBN: 0750655178
A strategic framework to help companies achieve business excellence and total quality management is presented in this well-informed guide. The main quality frameworks are introduced and compared, before the self-assessment process is examined.

The Balanced Scorecard

Robert S. Kaplan, David P. Norton
Boston, Massachusetts: Harvard Business School Press, 1996
322pp ISBN: 0875846513
This book demonstrates to managers how to utilize their people to fulfill the company's mission. It shows how to channel the energies, abilities, and specific knowledge belonging to each individual into the achievement of long-term strategic goals for the company. The "balanced scorecard" is a measurement tool, but it is also a management tool for investing in the long term in customers, employees, new product development, and systems.

Balanced Scorecard in a Week 2nd ed.

Mike Bourne, Pippa Bourne
London: Hodder & Stoughton, 2002
96pp (Business in a Week)
ISBN: 0340849452
This book introduces the balanced scorecard, a framework for measuring and improving business performance developed by Kaplan and Norton, and gives practical guidance on applying it in an organizational context. The processes involved in creating the right environment, identifying important factors to measure, designing performance measures, and using tools and techniques are all outlined. Potential pitfalls and setbacks are also described, and the authors give examples of how companies have adapted the model to their own needs. Finally a new stakeholder-oriented framework called the Performance Prism is briefly outlined.

The Balanced Scorecard Step-by-Step: Maximising Performance and Maintaining Results

Paul R. Niven
Hoboken, New Jersey: Wiley, 2002
336pp ISBN: 0471078727
This book gives valuable advice on developing a performance management system. Areas covered in this text include: the development of performance objectives and measures; the finalizing of cause and effect links; methods of embedding the balanced scorecard in the organization and sustaining its implementation; and procedures for implementing the balanced scorecard in nonprofit and public sector organizations.

Corporate Valuation: Tools for Effective Appraisal and Decision Making

Bradford Cornell
Maidenhead, United Kingdom: McGraw-Hill, 1993
303pp (Business One)
ISBN: 1556237308
This book illustrates the best practices for measuring and predicting value by combining the science of business appraisal with the art of perceived value. It provides a tool for comparing various valuation techniques, and shows how to rethink the investment process into the future.

Determining Value: Valuation Models and Financial Statements

Richard Barker
Upper Saddle River, New Jersey: Financial Times Prentice Hall, 2001
232pp ISBN: 027363979X
This book is designed for members of the professional and private investment community such as stockbrokers, fund managers, corporate financiers and bankers, and advanced students of finance and accounting. It provides a comprehensive overview of valuation methods such as price-earnings ratio, dividend yield and EVA (economic value added) and analyzes the quality and availability of the financial data used in these models. Topics covered include: stock market valuation; dividends and stock prices; price-earnings ratio; measuring earnings; measuring return on capital, and

cash-flow models from stockholder value analysis to cash-flow return on investment (CFROI).

Essentials of Balanced Scorecard

Mohan Nair
Hoboken, New Jersey: Wiley, 2004
248pp (Essentials)
ISBN: 0471569739
Taking simplicity as a guiding principle, the author sets out to help managers understand the fundamentals of the balanced scorecard. In this book, the concept is introduced and the four perspectives that make up the methodology are outlined. The relationship of the balanced scorecard to strategy and performance management is also examined. The book also identifies and describes six factors that make for success in implementing the balanced scorecard and discusses the eleven deadly sins that can lead to failure.

Essentials of Corporate Performance Measurement

George T. Friedlob, Lydia L. F. Schleifer, Franklin J. Plewa
New York: Wiley, 2002
216pp (Essentials)
ISBN: 0471203750
The most common way to evaluate the success of investment is by measuring the return on investment (ROI). This practical guide explains the importance of ROI and examines its use to analyze performance. Different forms of ROI are described and its use in analyzing sales revenues, costs, and profits is considered. The techniques of return on technology investment (ROTI and ROIT) are also covered, as are residual performance measures (RI and EVA).

The EVA Challenge: Implementing Value Added Change in Organisations

Joel M. Stern, John S. Shiely, Irwin Ross
New York: Wiley, 2001
256pp ISBN: 0471405558
The authors outline how to implement EVA and customize it for individual organizations. EVA, which encompasses measurement, incentives, and a financial management system, aims to measure a

BUSINESS INFORMATION SOURCES

"The pursuit of alibis for poor industry performance is one of the great Australian art forms."
John Button

company's time economic performance and wealth-creating strategy. Case studies are also included.

Evaluation in Organizations: A Systematic Approach to Enhancing Learning, Performance, and Change

Darlene Russ-Eft, Hallie Preskill
Cambridge, Massachusetts: Perseus Books Group, 2001
416pp ISBN: 0738202681
This book is a guide to the context of evaluation and to its implementation in a three-phase system. It includes an audit mechanism and comprehensive resources.

EVA: The Real Key to Creating Wealth

Al Ehrbar
New York: Wiley, 1998
240pp ISBN: 0471298603
This book provides a complete, accessible overview of how EVA (Economic Value Added) works, how it is measured, and what it can do to structure incentives for employees. It presents case histories of EVA success stories, including those of Briggs and Stratton, the U.S. Postal Service, and Coca Cola, to demonstrate real-world practice.

Harvard Business Review on Measuring Corporate Performance

Boston, Massachusetts: Harvard Business School Press, 1998
224pp (Harvard Business Review Paperbacks) ISBN: 0875848826
A collection of articles from leading management thinkers, this book shows how to evaluate performance measures and discusses the importance of aligning corporate strategy with them. It includes discussion of the balanced scorecard, customer relationships, internal business processes, and employee learning.

Implementing Global Performance Measurement Systems: A Cookbook Approach to Evaluation

Ferdinand Tesoro, Jack Tootson
San Francisco, California: Jossey-Bass, 1999
256pp ISBN: 078794744X
This practical guide presents a step-by-step approach to evaluating and measuring ongoing business performance. Following an overview of performance measurement, the areas covered include establishing the business case, identifying the right performance metrics, implementing the performance measurement system, and leveraging results to improve performance. Guidance is offered on constructing a line

graph, a cause–effect diagram, and a scatter diagram. A CD-ROM is included.

Making Scorecards Actionable: Balancing Strategy and Control

Nils-Goran Olve et al.
Hoboken, New Jersey: Wiley, 2003
304pp ISBN: 0470848715
Focusing on the experiences of a broad range of companies and looks at the challenges and key design issues that emerge as scorecards are put into operation. Practical guidance on operational issues is provided, which covers assigning roles and responsibilities, balancing the incentive system, and using IT. Case studies of a number of well-known companies such as Skandia, British Airways, Ericsson, Xerox, Volvo, and Hewlett Packard are included.

Measuring Business Performance 2nd ed.

Andy Neely
London: Profile Economist Books, 2003
256pp ISBN: 1861973802
The author looks at why businesses should measure their performance, what should be measured, and how measurements should be made.

Natural Capitalism: Creating the Next Industrial Revolution

Paul Hawken, Amory Lovins, L. Hunter Lovins
Boston, Massachusetts: Back Bay Books, 2000
396pp ISBN: 0316353000
In this title, the coauthors discuss how top companies are carrying out a modern form of industrialism which runs more smoothly, increases profits, lessens damage to the environment, and creates more jobs. They call this system "natural capitalism" and give several examples of organizations which have benefited the environment.

Oliver Wight ABCD Checklist for Operational Excellence 5th ed.

Oliver Wight International
New York: Wiley, 2000
167pp ISBN: 047138819X
The Oliver Wight ABCD Checklists are a widely recognized tool used by organizations as part of an appraisal of their performance. The aim of this checklist is to become an industry standard for operational performance measurement. Beginning with an explanation of the use of the performance measures, the assessment tool then focuses on the following areas: strategic planning; people and teams; total quality and continuous improvement; new

product development; and planning and control.

Operational Performance Measurement: Increasing Total Productivity

Will Kaydos
Boca Raton, Florida: St. Lucie Press, 1998
272pp ISBN: 1574440993
A practical approach to performance measurement, this book makes the case for implementing measurement in all business activities. It describes measurement methods, standards, and techniques, enumerates requirements for successful measurement, outlines how to implement, analyze, and interpret measures, and gives examples from leading companies. It is targeted at managers at all levels.

The Organizational Measurement Manual

David Wealleans
Aldershot, United Kingdom: Gower Publishing, 2001
178pp ISBN: 0566083493
Divided into three parts—the concept of measurement, establishing a process measurement program, and looking beyond the basics—this book gives a guide to performance measurements at the working level. It identifies procedures for using measurements and shows how to relate them to organizational objectives and initiatives. Wealleans demonstrates a best-practice approach, and illustrates his text with figures and tables throughout.

Performance Scorecards

Richard Y. Chang, Mark W. Morgan
San Francisco, California: Jossey-Bass, 2000
224pp ISBN: 0787952729
The authors contend that many corporations have too many performance measurements, which causes them to lose sight of the ones that are really important. They advocate customizing performance scorecards to suit an organization's strategy. The book uses a fictional storyline to illustrate the six steps that go into performance scorecards: collect, create, cultivate, cascade, connect, and confirm.

Strategy-focused Organization: How Balanced Scorecard Companies Thrive in the New Business Environment

Robert S. Kaplan, David P. Norton
Boston, Massachusetts: Harvard Business School Press, 2001
400pp ISBN: 1578512506
This book presents case studies of over twenty companies that have adopted the balanced scorecard approach. Five

"It is not only by the questions we have answered that progress will be measured, but also by those we are still asking."

Freda Adler

principles for strategy-focused organizations, drawn from their experiences, are outlined in this text. These are: translating the strategy into operational terms; aligning the organization to strategy; making strategy everyone's everyday job; making strategy a continual process, and mobilizing change through effective leadership.

Strategy Maps: Converting Intangible Assets into Tangible Outcomes

Robert S. Kaplan, David P. Norton
Boston, Massachusetts: Harvard Business School Press, 2004
454pp ISBN: 1591391342
This book explores what a strategy map is—a tool that can provide the missing link between strategy formulation and implementation. Derived from the balanced scorecard technique devised by the authors, *Strategy Maps* provides a blueprint for describing, measuring, and aligning tangible assets for superior performance. Through numerous examples of private, public, and nonprofit organizations, the process of creating customized strategy maps is explained.

Total Performance Scorecard: Redefining Management to Achieve Performance with Integrity

Hubert K. Rampersad
New York: Butterworth-Heinemann, 2003
336pp ISBN: 0750677147
Rampersad introduces a new concept of improvement and change management called the Total Performance Scorecard (TPS). This model integrates aspects of the balanced scorecard, total quality management and competence management. It is based around a cyclical process of continuous improvement, development, and learning and also takes account of the connections between personal and organizational development. The book draws on the author's experience as a management consultant in the field of organizational behavior and development for its case studies, examples, and exercises. Model appraisal forms and scorecard questions are included in appendices.

The Value Mindset: Returning to the First Principles of Capitalist Enterprise

Erik Stern, Mike Hutchinson
Hoboken, New Jersey: Wiley, 2004
456pp ISBN: 0471650293
In *The Value Mindset* the authors present their ideas as to how companies can transform themselves to deliver value and returns to shareholders. Building on their

experience of EVA (Economic Value Added) programs at Stern Stewart, they explain the development of the WAI (Wealth Added Index) performance metric and illustrate the concept of the value mindset through real-world success stories, such as those of Isadore Sharp at the Four Seasons hotel chain and Roberto Goizueta at Coca-Cola. The theory and practice of strategic reconfiguration is described, and a number of related issues including financial architecture and the motivation of managers and employees are explored.

Valuing a Business: The Analysis and Appraisal of Closely-held Companies 4th ed.

Shannon P. Pratt, Robert F. Reilly, Robert P. Schweihs
Maidenhead, United Kingdom: McGraw-Hill, 2000
1296pp ISBN: 0071356150
This latest edition, originally published in 1981, includes significant revisions and ten new chapters. Its coverage now extends to topics such as credentials and standards, analyzing financial statements, control and acquisition premiums, valuing debt securities and litigation support. The book is a standard reference for defining the methodology of business valuation—for businesses of all sizes—and then arriving at an accurate and supportable estimation of value.

MAGAZINES

Balanced Scorecard Report

ISSN: 1526–145X
Harvard Business School Publishing and Balanced Scorecard Collaborative
PO Box 257, Shrub Oak, New York, 10588–0257
T: +1 800 668 6705
F: +1 914 962 1338
www.hbsp.harvard.edu
This monthly newsletter, developed in conjunction with David S. Kaplan and David P. Norton, creators of the balanced scorecard, provides the latest research and implementation news from companies using the balanced scorecard management system.

Business Valuation Review

ISSN: 0882–2875
American Society of Appraisers (ASA)
555 Herndon Parkway, Suite 125, Herndon, Virginia, 20170
T: +1 703 478 2228
F: +1 703 742 8471
www.appraisers.org

This quarterly journal features articles on the practice and theory of appraisal. The articles present various opinions on the latest trends in business. The journal will be beneficial for any business valuation professional.

Financial Management

ISSN: 1471–9185
Chartered Institute of Management Accountants (CIMA)
26 Chapter Street, London, SW1P 4NP, U.K.
T: +44 (0) 20 8849 2313
www.cimaglobal.com/main/about/financial
This monthly magazine provides practical articles on a wide range of issues of interest to management accountants, including business performance and appraisal.

The Valuation Examiner

National Association of Valuation Analysts
1111 Brickyard Road, Suite 200, Salt Lake City, Utah, 84106–5401
T: +1 801 486 0600
F: +1 801 486 7500
www.nacva.com
This bimonthly magazine focuses on the latest developments regarding industry issues. It covers a variety of industry related topics, such as trends, forecasts and the latest technology resources, and provides the resources needed for business appraisal professionals.

INTERNET

Balanced Scorecard Collaborative
www.bscol.com

The website of Robert Kaplan and David Norton, creators of the balanced scorecard. Their professional services company provides training, networking events, and BSC software certification. The bimonthly *Balanced Scorecard Report* magazine is also available to members through the Web site.

College of Performance Management
www.pmi-cpm.org

Sponsored by a nonprofit professional organization, the site offers news, information about events and conferences, and links.

Interthink Consulting, Inc.
www.interthink.ca

Sponsored by a Canadian consulting firm, the site includes research on topics including assessment, processes, training, and implementation, and a newsletter of industry events.

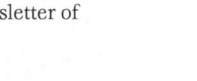

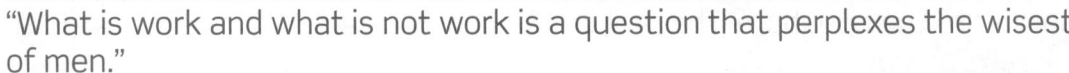

"What is work and what is not work is a question that perplexes the wisest of men."

Bhagavad Gita

ORGANIZATIONS
USA
American Society of Appraisers (ASA)
555 Herndon Parkway, Suite125, Herndon, Virginia, 20170

T: +1 703 478 2228 or 1 800 272 8258

F: +1 703 742 8471

E: *asainfo@appraisers.org*

www.appraisers.org

Founded in 1952, this organization has more than 6,000 members. ASA is a professional appraisal educator and represents all the disciplines of appraisal specialists. The society requires a mandatory certification program for all of its members, including the ASA Ethics Exam and the Uniform Standards of Professional Appraisal Practice Examination.

Institute of Business Appraisers (IBA)
P.O. Box 17410, Plantation, Florida, 33318

T: +1 954 584 1144

F: +1 954 584 1184

E: *ibahq@go-iba-org*

www.instbusapp.org

Established in 1978, the Institute of Business Appraisers is the oldest professional society devoted to the appraisal of closely-held businesses. This nationally recognized organization has a membership of over 3,000. The IBA seeks to educate the public in all aspects of business valuation and appraisal and is involved in monitoring and supporting national legislation that affects the business valuation community.

Measure.net
2115 West Lawn Ave, Madison, Wisconsin, 53711

T: +1 608 256 9993

F: +1 435 304 8452

E: *greg@measure.net*

www.measure.net

This organization is concerned with extending and improving corporate performance measurement strategies. It provides information for measuring performance within a company, and for managing a business. To this end, it is involved in research, education and consulting services, and also conducts various seminars and courses.

Europe
Best Practice Club
The Atrium, Curtis Road, Dorking, Surrey, RH4 1XA, U.K.

T: +44 (0) 1306 646 555

F: +44 (0) 1306 646 556

E: *enquiries@bpclub.com*

www.bpclub.com

With an international membership, this organization promotes organizational excellence through members networking and comparing their practice. Member companies come from both the manufacturing and the service sectors and pool their experience.

British Chambers of Commerce
65 Petty France, London, SW1H 9EU, U.K.

T: +44 (0) 20 7654 5800

F: +44 (0) 20 7654 5819

E: *info@britishchambers.org.uk*

www.chamberonline.co.uk

This is an umbrella body for a national network of chambers of commerce serving local businesses and providing advice on exporting and export services to member companies.

British Quality Foundation (BQF)
32–34 Great Peter Street, London, SW1P 2QX, U.K.

T: +44 (0) 20 7654 5000

F: +44 (0) 20 7654 5001

www.quality-foundation.co.uk

The BQF is a nonprofit membership organization that promotes business excellence to other public and private sector organizations in the United Kingdom. It undertakes numerous activities in pursuit of this aim, most of which have the Business Excellence Model at their core. It also sponsors the U.K. Business Excellence Award.

Centre for Interfirm Comparison (CIFC)
CIFC Ltd, 32 Thomas Street, Winchester, Hampshire, SO23 9HJ, U.K.

T: +44 (0) 1962 844 144

F: +44 (0) 1962 843 180

E: *enquiries@cifc.co.uk*

www.cifc.co.uk

The Centre helps businesses of all types and in all sectors to assess their performance through confidential, detailed comparison of their financial ratios and other data with those of similar businesses, and to target improvements in specific areas of their operations. It provides a wide range of benchmarking and related consulting services.

European Foundation for Quality Management (EFQM)
Avenue des Pléiades 15, B-1200 Brussels, Belgium

T: +33 2 775 35 11

F: +33 2 775 35 35

E: *info@efqm.org*

www.efqm.org

The EFQM introduced the European Excellence Model in the early 1990s to help businesses assess and improve their performance.

FOR MORE INFORMATION
- Benchmarking (pp. 1681–1682)
- ✔ Establishing a Performance Measurement System (pp. 548–549)
- ✔ Implementing the Balanced Scorecard (pp. 566–567)
- ✔ Shareholder Value Analysis (SVA) (pp. 602–603)
- ☆ The Balanced Scorecard (pp. 389–390)

"What is the answer to the question? The problem."

Michel Foucault

Business Ethics and Codes of Practice

BOOKS

Absolute Honesty: Building a Corporate Culture That Values Straight Talk and Rewards Integrity

Larry Johnson, Bob Phillips
New York: AMACOM, 2003
304pp ISBN: 0814407811
This book examines the crisis of ethics in business, which has had an impact on economic performance and public trust. It suggests that honesty can produce rewards in both these areas as well as in terms of integrity, productivity, competitive advantage, and morale. It emphasizes the need to re-establish a culture of openness and truth in communication methods and presents a framework of six laws of absolute honesty, with advice on implementing them. The book is written in short, easy-to-read sections with checklists and diagrams.

Business Ethics: The Ethical Revolution of Minority Shareholders

Jacques Cory
Dordrecht, The Netherlands: Springer, 2001
272pp ISBN: 0792373006
This book deals with the relationships between companies and minority stockholders, from the perspective of business ethics. It highlights the inefficiency of traditional safeguards of the rights of small stockholders and discusses the new "vehicles" that can bring about an ethical revolution for minority shareholders and tilt the balance in their favor. It provides four cases of companies in the United States, France, and Israel to show how minority stockholders can lose their investments.

Business Ethics: The State of the Art

R. Edward Freeman, ed.
New York: Oxford University Press, Inc., 1993
225pp ISBN: 0195081986
This volume contains a series of essays by such leading thinkers as Kenneth Goodpaster, Norman Bowie, and Joanne Ciulla, which explore the myriad facets of the role of ethics in business. The essays cover such areas as ethical imperatives, corporate leadership, corporate rights and responsibilities, and the complexity of ethics in multinational and multicultural

settings. They also deal with broader subjects such as the role of businesses with respect to literacy.

Defining Moments: When Managers Must Choose Between Right and Right

Joseph L. Badaracco, Jr.
Boston, Massachusetts: Harvard Business School Press, 1997
176pp ISBN: 0875848036
This book outlines a realistic approach to ethics in management. It offers advice and guidelines for managers at all levels on how to deal with morally sensitive issues in a way that is satisfactory on both a professional level and on a personal one. It provides useful examples, actionable steps, and a flexible framework that managers can use to make the choices that will affect their careers and their characters.

Just Business: Business Ethics in Action 2nd ed.

Elaine Sternberg
New York: Oxford University Press, Inc., 2000
320pp ISBN: 0198296630
The author presents an ethical decision model that can be used as a conceptual framework for resolving questions of business ethics and corporate governance in all their variety and complexity. While the book is intended for active businessmen and presupposes no knowledge of philosophy, it provides a reasoned philosophical approach to determining what constitutes ethical conduct in business.

Leading with Soul 2nd ed.

Lee G. Bolman, Terrence E. Deal
Hoboken, New Jersey: Wiley, 2001
224pp ISBN: 0787955477
This is a contemporary parable about an executive's quest for passion and purpose in work and in life. The authors draw upon many spiritual traditions, poetry, philosophy, and social science teachings on leadership and organizations. They demonstrate how to lead with soul and how to ignite the soul of an organization. This second edition has a new introduction, new material, and includes letters written by readers of the first edition.

Managing Values and Beliefs in Organizations

Tom McEwan
Upper Saddle River, New Jersey: Financial Times Prentice Hall, 2001
560pp ISBN: 0273643401
This is book written as a student text that summarizes the origins of corporate responsibility, business ethics, and corporate governance, and reviews the similarities and differences between them. The specific issues covered include: moral meaning and applied ethics; values, beliefs, and ideologies; individual morality in organizations; unethical behavior by individuals; international business and the developing world; ethical investment; organization culture and stakeholder theory; and corporate social performance, ethical leadership, and reputation management.

Perspectives on Corporate Social Responsibility

David Crowther, Lez Rayman-Bacchus, eds
Aldershot, Hampshire: Ashgate Publishing Ltd, 2004
256pp ISBN: 0754638863
This book aims to explore different perspectives on what is meant by corporate social responsibility (CSR), based on the experiences of people in different parts of the world. Contributors investigate the theoretical aspects of socially responsible behavior, its application in practice, and its ethical dimension. Specific topics covered include: assessing trust in, and the legitimacy of, the Corporate; limited liability or limited responsibility; the power of networks—organizing versus organization; social performance in government; exploration inside experience and practice at the European level; corporate social reporting; the impact of socially responsible investment upon CSR; bioengineering and CSR; the ethics of CSR; and the future.

Trust or Consequences: Build Trust Today or Lose Your Market Tomorrow

Al Golin
New York: AMACOM, 2003
256pp ISBN: 0814472087
In a climate of public skepticism toward

business there is a need for organization to create a trust bank of goodwill to communicate that they are trustworthy, it is claimed. This book deals with the creation of trust strategies using the author's tried-and-tested methods in various international organizations. The book's three sections cover, respectively, an assessment of external and internal trends that have contributed to the debate; the steps organizations can take; and a framework of strategies and scenarios for action. Case studies are also included.

Value Shift: Why Companies Must Merge Social and Financial Imperatives to Achieve Superior Performance

Lynn Sharp Paine
New York: McGraw-Hill, 2003
304pp ISBN: 0071382399
It is argued that there is now a dichotomy between traditional management and the expectations of business in contemporary society. In acknowledging that it is no longer enough simply to produce goods and services and create wealth, today's corporate leaders need to make a shift in management values to incorporate high ethical standards along with strong financial results. This book argues the case for a new style of management that will align company performance with today's ethical standards.

What Matters Most? Business Social Responsibility and the End of the Era of Greed

Jeffrey Hollender, Stephen Fenichell
London: Random House Business Books, 2004
320pp ISBN: 1844133966
Jeffrey Hollender, C.E.O. of Seventh Generation, a world leader in manufacturing environmentally friendly household products, is a frequent commentator on corporate responsibility. This book, coauthored with Stephen Fenichell, puts forward an approach to corporate strategy that is said to help integrate concerns related to social responsibility into an organization's culture, systems, and activities.

When Good Companies Do Bad Things: Responsibility and Risk in an Age of Globalization

Peter Schwartz, Blair Gibb
Hoboken, New Jersey: Wiley, 1999
208pp ISBN: 0471323322
This book sets out to show how essential social responsibility is to the success of corporations in today's globalized economy.

Illustrating their argument with case studies of large multinationals, the authors demonstrate how corporations make poor choices, exposing themselves to huge financial risks and potential loss of reputation. They also explain, however, how corporations can learn from their mistakes and turn social value into business value.

Working Ethics: Strategies for Decision Making and Organizational Responsibility

Marvin T. Brown
San Francisco, California: Jossey-Bass, 2000
219pp ISBN: 1889059552
This book explores the role of ethics as a tool in decision-making, showing how ethical behavior can improve organizational effectiveness by fostering open communications, resolving disputes, and enhancing employee–management relations. It highlights the fact that arguments centering on an open expression of disagreements can lead to better relations, and provides examples and practical exercises for building an organization that makes morally and socially responsible decisions.

MAGAZINES

Business & Professional Ethics Journal

ISSN: 0277–2027
Public Interest Enterprises Inc.
P.O. Box 15017, Gainesville, Florida, 32604
T: +1 325 392 2084
F: +1 325 392 0057
www.ethics.ufl.edu/BPEJ/index.html
Published four times per year, this journal contains articles that focus on the ethical issues encountered by business professionals working in large organizations.

Business and Society Review

ISSN: 0045–3609
Blackwell Publishing
350 Main Street, Malden, Massachusetts, 02148
T: +44 (0) 1865 778315
F: +44 (0) 1865 471775
www.blackwellpublishers.co.uk/listofj.asp
This quarterly publication covers the debate on the role of business in society and covers a wide range of ethical issues relating to business, society, and the public good. Contributors include business professionals, researchers, government administrators, and legal experts.

Business Ethics: A European Review

ISSN: 0962–8770
Blackwell Publishing
350 Main Street, Malden, Massachusetts, 02148
T: +1 781 388 8200
F: +1 781 388 8232
www.blackwellpublishing.com
Offering rigorous analysis of ethical issues faced by business worldwide, this quarterly is primarily an academic research journal. However, it is readable and user-friendly, and its focus is not exclusively European.

Business Ethics Quarterly: The Journal of the Society for Business Ethics

ISSN: 1052–150X
Philosophy Documentation Center
Society for Business Ethics, Philosophy Documentation Center, P.O. Box 7147, Charlottesville, Virginia, 22906–7147
T: +1 434 220 3300 or 800 444 2419
F: +1 434 220 3301
www.pdcnet.org/beq.html
This learned peer-reviewed journal explores the application of ethics to international business. It focuses on theoretical and methodological questions that can advance ethical inquiry and enhance the ethical performance of business organizations.

Journal of Business Ethics

ISSN: 0167–4544
Springer
Customer Service Department, P.O. Box 358, Dordrecht, 3300 AA, The Netherlands
T: +31 78 657 6392
F: +31 78 657 6474
www.springerlink.com
From 2004 this monthly journal has incorporated *The International Journal of Value-Based Management* and *Teaching Business Ethics*. It covers a wide range of ethical issues related to business and includes empirical research reports. The use of specialist jargon is avoided as the publication is intended for a wide constituency including the business community, universities, government, and consumer groups.

INTERNET

Business Impact

www.bitc.org.uk/index.html
This site contains information from Business in the Community's Business Impact task force, including a news directory and general information on corporate social responsibility.

"It's possible to live in this country and create wealth legally and ethically." Narayana Murthy

Center for the Study of Ethics in the Professions
http://ethics.iit.edu/codes
This site makes available 850 codes of ethics from professional societies, corporations, government, and academic institutions, as well as a literature review and a user guide.

Ethics Connection
www.scu.edu/SCU/Centers/Ethics
This site, run by the Markkula Center for Applied Ethics at Santa Clara University, offers case briefings, articles, and dialogue in all fields of applied ethics, including business and technology.

Ethics Resource Center
www.ethics.org
A range of resources from this Washington-based ethics education organization can be accessed here. These include articles from *Ethics Today* magazine, useful links, book reviews, and details of training resources and events.

Global Business Society Resource Center
www.bsr.org/CSRResources/index.cfm
Business for Social Responsibility offers an introduction to issues of social responsibility and business ethics on this site. The site also includes a news archive, information about company practices and policies, award and recognition programs, and publications. A special feature is the facility it provides for creating reports on selected topics.

ORGANIZATIONS
USA
Business for Social Responsibility (BSR)
111 Sutter Street, 11th floor, San Francisco, California, 94104

T: +1 415 984 3200
F: +1 415 984 3201
www.bsr.org
Founded in 1992, this organization provides resources—including information, news, publications, training, and consulting—designed to help member companies succeed in business while respecting ethical values. Based in the United States, BSR has developed regional networks and alliances with similar organizations worldwide.

Society for Business Ethics (SBE)
School of Business Administration, Loyola University Chicago, 25 E. Pearson Avenue, Chicago, Illinois, 60611–2196
T: +1 312 915 6112
F: +1 312 915 7207
http://sba.luc.edu
The SBE is an international association of scholars and professionals that aims to promote the study of business ethics, to improve the way they are taught, and to provide a forum for the exchange of ideas in the field.

Europe
Business in the Community
137 Shepherdess Walk, London, N1 7RQ, U.K.
T: +44 (0) 870 600 2482
E: *information@bitc.org.uk*
www.bitc.org.uk
Business in the Community was set up as a partnership between business, government, local authorities, and labor unions to promote corporate community involvement. It has a support network aimed particularly at helping new and developing businesses to become involved in the community.

Institute of Business Ethics (IBE)
24 Greencoat Place, London, SW1P 1BE, U.K.

T: +44 (0) 20 7798 6040
F: +44 (0) 20 7798 6044
E: *info@ibe.org.uk*
www.ibe.org.uk
Launched in 1986 by the then Lord Mayor of London, Alderman Sir Allan Davis, the Institute aims to emphasize the essentially ethical nature of wealth creation, to encourage the highest standards of behavior by companies, and to publicize the best ethical practices. Its activities include research, conferences, seminars, and the development of codes of practice and resource material.

International
Institute for Global Ethics
P.O. Box 563, Camden, Maine, 04843
T: +1 207 236 6658
F: +1 207 236 4014
E: *webethics@globalethics.org*
www.globalethics.org
A nonsectarian membership organization funded by private foundations, sponsors, and members, the Institute fosters public discussion of and practical action on ethical issues and promotes the teaching of "Ethical Fitness." It has an international board of directors, an international advisory council, and branch offices in the United Kingdom and Canada. Its activities are centered on three areas: corporate services, educational programs, and public policy. Visitors to IBE's online site may register free for the weekly *Ethics Newsline* e-newsletter.

1691

FOR MORE INFORMATION
☆ Business Ethics (pp. 279–281)
✔ Codes of Ethics (pp. 510–511)
🐭 Social Responsibility of Management (pp. 1910–1912)
☆ Viewpoint: Charles Handy (pp. 97–98)

BUSINESS INFORMATION SOURCES

"The greater the wealth, the thicker will be the dirt."   J. K. Galbraith

Business Plans and Planning

BOOKS

The Complete Book of Business Plans: Simple Steps to Writing a Powerful Business Plan
Joseph A. Covello, Brian J. Hazelgren
Naperville, Illinois: Sourcebooks, 1994
320pp ISBN: 0942061411
This classic presents the key questions to bear in mind when writing a plan for a new business, and encourages the reader to look for answers to the kinds of questions that investors ask, to develop marketing strategies and financial presentations, and to find ways to stay ahead of the competition.

The Definitive Business Plan: The Fast Track to Intelligent Business Planning for Executives and Entrepreneurs 2nd ed.
Richard Stutley
Upper Saddle River, New Jersey: Financial Times Prentice Hall, 2002
288pp ISBN: 0273659219
Written for both the newcomer and the experienced planner, this text provides a concise guide to the business planning process, and focuses attention on strategic planning and strategic and operational controls. The practical aspects of constructing various types of business plan are explained in some detail.

Fast Forward MBA in Business Planning for Growth
Philip Walcoff
Hoboken, New Jersey: Wiley, 1999
212pp (Fast Forward MBA)
ISBN: 0471345482
Walcoff's step-by-step guide to the process of creating a business plan that ensures growth and profitability identifies and resolves key issues that block a company's growth and develops strategies and tactics that foster it.

How to Prepare a Business Plan 4th ed.
Edward Blackwell
London: Kogan Page, 2004
192pp (Sunday Times Business Enterprise Guide)
ISBN: 0749441917
This highly-recommended title takes the owner/manager through the process of developing a business plan for start-up or expansion. This book covers financial forecasting and planning and gives useful

case studies of businesses preparing and following business plans.

How to Really Create a Successful Business Plan 4th ed.
David E. Gumpert
Boston, Massachusetts: Inc. Publishing, 2003
236pp ISBN: 0970118171
This book provides a step-by-step method for completing a high-quality business plan. It also provides models of business plans from a number of highly successful U.S. companies.

The Mission-driven Organization: From Mission Statement to a Thriving Enterprise, Here's Your Blueprint for Building an Inspired, Cohesive, Customer-oriented Team
Bob Wall, Mark R. Sobol, Robert S. Solum
Roseville, California: Prima Publishing, 1999
256pp ISBN: 0761518819
This book examines the move towards a more streamlined, horizontal power structure, showing how a company can be remotivated by this new way of thinking. It outlines the problems and associated laws, and creates a clear, concise solution to the complications involved in managing change and making cultural improvements.

The Mission Primer: Four Steps to an Effective Mission Statement
Richard O'Halloran, David O'Halloran
Richmond, Virginia: Mission Incorporated, 2000
130pp ISBN: 0967663504
Including an easy-to-use guide, examples of model mission statements, and a glossary of useful terms, this book will enable you to analyze your situation and create your own mission statement.

Morrisey on Planning: A Guide to Long-range Planning: Creating Your Strategic Journey
George L. Morrisey
San Francisco, California: Jossey-Bass, 1995
109pp ISBN: 0787901695
This, the second in a three-volume series, follows Morrisey's exploration of strategic thinking and precedes his work on tactical planning. It is aimed at organizations that are willing to embark on a three-to-five-year planning process, and focuses on long-term objectives and how to place them in the

context of the organization's vision and mission.

Plan to Win: A Definitive Guide to Business Processes
John Garside
West Lafayette, Indiana: Purdue University Press, 1999
304pp ISBN: 1557531633
The author provides a clear and practical approach to creating and implementing cost-effective business processes. Focusing on the key elements of a robust business plan, he defines and describes the core business processes needed in a successful process-driven organization, supporting his descriptions with diagrams and checklists of essential criteria for process design. Garside brings to this work an extensive experience of business planning with various major companies, including Dunlop, GKN Technology, and Lucas Aerospace.

The Successful Business Plan: Secrets and Strategies 4th ed.
Rhonda M. Abrams
Palo Alto, California: Running R Media, 2003
409pp ISBN: 0966963563
This book is designed to help readers create a business plan that will attract the funding they need to get started. It presents insights from some 200 business owners, venture capitalists, and C.E.O.s, but, in addition, contains worksheets and sample business plans, provides tools to help in number-crunching, and offers guidance on the length of an ideal plan and the way it should be worded and formatted.

Your First Business Plan: A Simple Question and Answer Format Designed to Help You Write Your Own Plan 3rd ed.
Joseph Covello
Naperville, Illinois: Sourcebooks, 1998
149pp ISBN: 1570712190
With little or no company history, the first business plan can be the most difficult. By outlining each part of the business plan and making suggestions for what to focus on and what to avoid, this book will help your writing. Also included are a glossary and a sample business plan.

INTERNET
Business Plan Guide
www.business-plans.co.uk
Sponsored by Miller Consultancy, this site

"A lot of companies . . . find planning more interesting than getting out a saleable product."
Ed Wrapp

provides information on business planning resources. It includes books, links to Web sites, and articles.

Business Plans
www.bplans.com

This site, created by Palo Alto Software, offers planning advice for small businesses and a substantial range of sample plans, which subscribers to bplans' software can download and edit. It also includes a resource center with links to other Web sites, as well as an "ask the experts" section.

More Business
www.morebusiness.com

This site has a lengthy business and marketing plans section and provides some useful sample business plans.

United States Small Business Administration
www.sba.gov

This Web site, run by the U.S. government organization dedicated to helping small business owners, provides sources for technical, managerial, and financial advice and assistance.

U.S. Small Business Administration
www.sba.gov/starting_business/ planning/basic.html

The SBA's site provides a model business plan, addresses relevant FAQs, and offers general information on startups.

Venture Capital Resource Library
www.vfinance.com

This site provides a business plan template, general articles, and texts of SEC and UCC rules and regulations, as well as leads to sources of venture capital.

ORGANIZATIONS
USA
American Management Association (AMA)

1601 Broadway, New York, 10019
T: +1 212 586 8100
F: +1 212 903 8168
E: *customerservice@amanet.org*
www.amanet.org

Founded in 1923, this association has over 80,000 members. With a focus on practical training, the AMA provides business forums and seminars worldwide. Members can enhance their business skills and develop successful planning strategies by studying the best practices of various world-class organizations. Seminars are geared to every professional level, from C.E.O. to administrative assistant. The AMA also publishes valuable print resources that cover a wide range of topics including business plans, career building, and technology.

Chief Executive Officers' Club

47 West Street, New York, 10013
T: +1 212 925 7911
F: +1 212 925 7463
E: *main@ceoclubs.org*
http://ceoclubs.org/main/default.htm

Established in 1978, this association serves as a management resource for entrepreneurs and their professional advisers. Membership is by invitation only. Membership is restricted to C.E.O.s of businesses that have over $2m in annual sales. The organization selects publications on developing business plans and conducts seminars on the entrepreneurial process.

United States Small Business Administration

409 Third Street, SW, Washington, D.C., 20416

T: 1–800-U-ASK-SBA
www.sba.gov

Providing multiple resources for the small business covering a wide range of topics, such as Starting Your Business, Financing Your Business, Managing Your Business, and Business Opportunities, this link, provided by the United States government, is a handy stop for anyone interested in business planning.

Europe
Chartered Management Institute (CMI)

Management House, Cottingham Road, Corby, Northamptonshire, NN17 1TT, U.K.
T: +44 (0) 1536 204 222
F: +44 (0) 1536 201 651
E: *enquiries@managers.org.uk*
www.managers.org.uk

Formed in 1992, the CMI is the largest organization for professional management in the United Kingdom, representing almost 89,000 individual members and embracing 560 corporate partners. It exists to promote the art and science of management through research, publications, the provision of information services, networking opportunities, education and training, and the objective presentation of managers' views and opinions.

1693

> ### FOR MORE INFORMATION
>
> 🐭 Budgeting (pp. 1683–1684)
> 🐭 Corporate Strategy (pp. 1721–1723)
> 🐭 Forecasting and Scenario Planning (pp. 1759–1760)
> ☆ How to Plan Marketing (pp. 67–68)
> ☆ Scenario Planning (pp. 334–335)
> 🐭 Small and Growing Businesses (pp. 1905–1909)
> ✔ Writing a Business Plan (pp. 538–539)

BUSINESS INFORMATION SOURCES

"Planning is good, but not if it excludes the opportunity to be able to take chances when they come up."
Chris Wright

     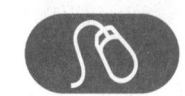

Business Process Reengineering

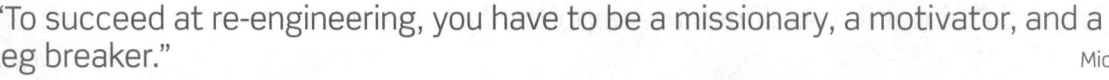
BOOKS

The Aftermath of Reengineering: Downsizing and Corporate Performance

Tony Carter

Binghamton, New York: The Haworth Press, 1999

165pp ISBN: 0789007207

Carter takes a much needed, thorough look at the effectiveness of reengineering and both its positive and negative human, strategic, and societal consequences. Every chapter concludes with a case study that illustrates the topic, and the final chapter of the book provides an evaluation of reengineering best practices from a variety of companies and industries.

Beyond Reengineering: How the Process-centered Organization Is Changing

Michael Hammer

London: HarperCollins Business, 1997

304pp ISBN: 0887308805

This book explores the strategy and structure of the process-centred organisation, and the consequences of re-engineering.

The Process Edge: Creating Value Where It Counts

Peter G. W. Keen

Boston, Massachusetts: Harvard Business School Press, 1997

185pp ISBN: 0875845886

The author takes a multidisciplinary approach to reengineering and stresses the need to focus on those processes that add value. He also includes a description of a salience/worth matrix model designed to help companies determine their most critical processes, as well as a number of company case studies.

Process Mapping: How to Reengineer Your Business Process

V. Daniel Hunt

Hoboken, New Jersey: Wiley, 1996

274pp ISBN: 0471132810

This book provides a detailed guide to the techniques of process mapping and its role in reengineering. The contents include: assessing the need for process improvement; deciding if is right for you; creating a process mapping team; selecting the best software tools for the job; using the data to build process maps; and using the maps to improve business performance.

The Reengineering Alternative: A Plan for Making Your Current Culture Work

William E. Schneider

Maidenhead, United Kingdom: McGraw-Hill, 1999

173pp ISBN: 0071359818

Reengineering has virtually become business dogma, yet there are viable, and perhaps even preferable, alternatives. Mechanistic approaches to reengineering often fail to take into account one of a company's most vital and enduring resources—its culture. This book describes an approach to change management that focuses on a company's unique existing strengths and corporate objectives, and shows how to work effectively to foster improvement according to four basic corporate culture types.

Reengineering Business for Success in the Internet Age: Business-to-Business E-commerce Strategies

Debra Cameron

Charleston, South Carolina: Computer Technology Research Corporation, 2000

197pp ISBN: 1566070848

The publisher is now out of business—another casualty of the e-commerce nosedive—but this report may still be purchased through online booksellers. It applies reengineering strategies to the dynamic e-business environment. Topics range from integrating legacy systems to implementing B2B security strategies, with special emphasis on the unique role of XML in reengineering for e-business.

Reengineering the Corporation: A Manifesto for Business Revolution

Michael Hammer, James A. Champy

New York: HarperCollins, 2001

257pp ISBN: 0066621127

Hammer and Champy have updated their classic—and controversial—text on reengineering to deal with the challenges of the new millennium. The reengineering process requires a reinvention of the post-industrial organization through visionary leadership, optimization by means of information technologies, working in close consultation with suppliers to reduce inventories, and integrating decision-making into the nature work of all employees.

MAGAZINES

Business Process Management Journal

ISSN: 1463–7154

Emerald

44 Brattle Street, 4th Floor, Cambridge, Massachusetts, 02138

T: +1 888 622 0075

F: +1 617 354 6875

www.emeraldinsight.com

This journal is published in association with the European Centre for Total Quality Management. Contributions from both academics and practitioners are included, and the focus is on the management of business processes for efficiency and competitive success.

Knowledge and Process Management

ISSN: 1092–4604

Wiley

111 River St, Hoboken, New Jersey, 07030–5774

T: +1 201 748–6000

F: +1 212 850 6021

www.wiley.com

Formerly called *Business Change and Reengineering: Journal of Corporate Transformation*, this quarterly journal aims to meet the needs of executives responsible for organizational performance improvement. Articles focus on the areas of knowledge management, organizational learning, core competences, and process management. Emphasis is placed on the practical lessons learned from the experience of organizations.

INTERNET

Brint.com Business Process Reengineering

www.brint.com/BPR.htm

A comprehensive collection of links to BPR resources.

Business Process Reengineering (BPR) Online Learning Center

www.prosci.com

This online learning center features seven series of multiple online tutorials on various aspects of business process reengineering, together with best practice benchmarking studies, a change management resource library, a project trouble shooter, and much more.

National Center for Public Productivity

www.andromeda.rutgers.edu/~ncpp

Affiliated with Rutgers University, the Web

"To succeed at re-engineering, you have to be a missionary, a motivator, and a leg breaker."

Michael Hammer

site for this center is a gateway to federal, state, and international resources on productivity in the public sector, and for "citizen-driven government performance."

ORGANIZATIONS
International
Business Process Management Group (BPMG)

Burlington Center, 35 Corporate Drive, Burlington, Massachusetts, 01803
T: + 1 781 685 4993
F: + 1 1 781 998 5346
E: *editor@bpmg.org*
www.bpmg.org
The BPMG is a business interest group, established in the United Kingdom in 1992,

which now has over 15,000 members worldwide. Its aims are to advance the understanding and application of business process management, to raise business awareness of BPM, and to provide a forum for the exchange of information relevant to BPM.

Workflow and Reengineering International Association (WARIA)

2436 North Federal Highway 374, Lighthouse Point, Florida, 33064
T: +1 954 782 3376
F: +1 954 782 6365
E: *waria04@waria.com*
www.waria.com
WARIA is a nonprofit organization

concerned with issues that arise at the intersection between BPR, knowledge management, electronic commerce, and workflow management. It encourages the sharing of information on issues common to these fields by providing networking opportunities.

FOR MORE INFORMATION

- ℘ Business Appraisal and Performance Measurement (pp. 1685–1688)
- ℘ Corporate Strategy (pp. 1721–1723)
- ✔ Implementing Business Process Reengineering (pp. 558–559)

BUSINESS INFORMATION SOURCES

"An important technology first creates a problem and then solves it."   Alan Kay

Change Management

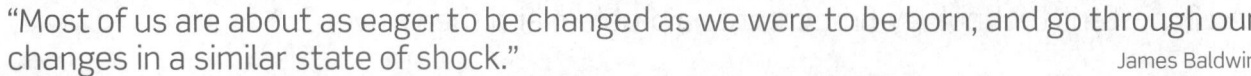
BOOKS

All Hat and No Cattle

Chris Turner

Cambridge, Massachusetts: Perseus Books Group, 2000

272pp ISBN: 0738203661

This book takes a humorous look at current corporate wisdom. It is a critique of total quality management that offers anecdotes of managerial incompetence and challenges the status quo.

Change without Pain: How Managers Can Overcome Initiative Overload Organizational Chaos and Employee Burnout

Eric Abrahamson

Boston, Massachusetts: Harvard Business School Press, 2004

224pp ISBN: 157851827X

This book outlines a new approach to change—creative recombination—that stands in sharp contrast to the creative destruction advocated for the last two decades. Drawing on research and using examples it presents a range of hands-on tools and techniques for identifying and reusing five key organizational assets: people, processes, structures, culture, and social networks. The author also guides managers in determining when, and how often, to initiate change to ensure the greatest chance of success.

The Dance of Change: The Challenges to Sustaining Momentum in Learning Organizations

Peter M. Senge et al.

New York: Doubleday, 1999

224pp ISBN: 0385493223

Written for managers at all levels, this book addresses ways in which the challenges brought by profound change can be met. In a clear and practical format, it describes methods for building personal and organizational capabilities to accomplish long-term change initiatives. Exercises, practical advice, and case studies are included.

Exploring Strategic Change 2nd ed.

Julia Balogun, Veronica Hope Hailey

Upper Saddle River, New Jersey: Prentice Hall, 2003

288pp (Exploring Corporate Strategy)

ISBN: 0273683276

This textbook focuses on the implementation of strategic change. It presents a framework, the change kaleidoscope, that can be used to consider the most appropriate implementation approach, and offers guidance on the management of transition. It brings together a range of human resource management and strategic management techniques and includes case studies.

The Heart of Change: Real Life Stories of How People Change Their Organizations

John P. Kotter, Dan S. Kotter

Boston, Massachusetts: Harvard Business School Press, 2002

196pp ISBN: 1578512549

Based on interviews with over 100 organizations of different types, all engaged in large-scale change, this book aims to describe how change actually happens and how behavior is actually altered. The authors maintain that the key to behavioral change lies in making people feel differently, rather than in merely trying to influence the way they think. The book describes and is structured around the eight key steps in the process of successful change management. It also includes many case studies.

Leader's Change Handbook: An Essential Guide to Setting Direction and Taking Action

Jay A. Conger, Gretchen M. Spreitzer, Edward E. Lawler, eds

San Francisco, California: Jossey-Bass, 1998

320pp ISBN: 0787943517

This handbook contains chapters by various leading contributors to the field, introducing new thinking on ways in which leaders, managers, consultants, and human resource specialists can implement change within their organizations. It outlines the main elements of effective change management, expands traditional ideas of leadership, and discusses the future of organizational change.

Leading Change

John Kotter

Boston, Massachusetts: Harvard Business School Press, 1996

187pp ISBN: 0875847471

This book identifies the most common mistakes in effecting organizational change, and offers an eight-step process to overcoming such obstacles.

Leading in Turbulent Times: Managing in the New World of Work

Ronald J. Burke, Cary L. Cooper

London: Kogan Page, 2004

336pp ISBN: 140511522X

This collection of papers highlights the crucial role of organizational leadership in responding to new challenges in an increasingly turbulent environment. The four sections in the text cover: leading self; leading others; leading on issues; and leading change. Topics explored in the book include: teamwork; generation Xers; managing contingent workers; corporate governance; business and the environment; work-family integration; and employee health and well being, including stress.

Making Sense of Change Management: A Complete Guide to the Models, Tools, and Techniques

Esther Cameron, Mike Green

London: Kogan Page, 2004

288pp ISBN: 0749440872

This book aims to explain why and how change happens and what needs to be done to make change a welcome rather than a dreaded concept. It explores the theory behind individual, team and organizational change together with the concept of leading change. Specific change scenarios are also covered within the text with a view to providing guidelines, hints, and tips to those involved in change processes. The applications discussed are restructuring, mergers and acquisitions, cultural change, and IT-based process change. Case studies are also provided for the different applications.

The Manager As Change Agent

Jerry W. Gilley et al.

Cambridge, Massachusetts: Perseus Books Group, 2001

208pp ISBN: 0738204625

The authors offer a practical approach to developing the skills necessary for leading change in an organization, including motivating people who are resistant to change, resolving conflict, and building consensus.

Managing Change in the Workplace: A 12-Step Program for Success

Ralph L. Kliem, Irwin S. Ludin

New York: HNB Publishing, 1999

139pp ISBN: 0966428617

"Most of us are about as eager to be changed as we were to be born, and go through our changes in a similar state of shock."

James Baldwin

One chapter of this book is devoted to each of the 12 steps involved in accomplishing change. The book provides a practical approach for managers who are planning or implementing organizational change.

Productive Workplaces Revisited: Dignity Meaning and Community in the 21st Century

Marvin R. Weisbord
San Francisco, California: Jossey-Bass, 2004
512pp ISBN: 0787971170
Building on an earlier book, *Productive Workplaces*, Weisbord takes the next step in exploring effective strategies for improving productivity in the workplace through dignity, meaning, and community. Part One provides a review of management theory in the search for productive workplaces, drawing upon the ideas of Taylor and scientific management, Lewin and learning organizations, and McGregor and the roots of organizational development. Part Two focuses on transforming theory into practice and practice into theory, and Part Three looks at learning and applying new practice theories. The author also reinterprets his systems work and explains how Future Search—his method for getting everybody involved in improving whole systems—has crossed cultures. Also included in the text are updated case studies from the first edition, which provide a valuable insight for academics and practitioners.

Revival of the Fittest: Why Good Companies Go Bad and How Great Managers Remake Them

Donald N. Sull
Boston, Massachusetts: Harvard Business School Press, 2003
208pp ISBN: 1578519934
Based on the author's research, this text discusses the reasons why corporate collapses often follow initial success. It also explores the concept of active inertia, explained as the continued application by managers of formulae that brought success in the past, despite changes in the competitive environment. The book presents a practical three-step model for making transformational commitments that will help managers to avoid reinforcing past behaviors and to develop new strategies for organizational transformation.

MAGAZINES
Industrial and Corporate Change
ISSN: 0960-6491
Oxford University Press, Inc.
198 Madison Avenue, New York, 10016

T: +1 212 726 6000
F: +1 212 726 6440
www.oup-usa.org
This academic quarterly journal presents and interprets evidence on corporate and industrial change, drawing from interdisciplinary approaches.

Journal of Organizational Change Management
ISSN: 0953-4814
Emerald (North America)
4th Floor, 44 Brattle Street, Cambridge, Massachusetts, 02138
T: +1 888 622 0075
www.emeraldinsight.com/ccm.htm
The articles in this journal set out for managers the agenda for organizational change and development. They analyze new approaches and present new research theories.

Strategic Change
ISSN: 1086-1718
Wiley
111 River St, Hoboken, New Jersey, 07030-5774
T: +1 201 748-6000
F: +1 212 850 6021
www.wiley.com
The journal has international scope. It aims to publish authoritative and topical papers on sources of change, options for responding to change, and the implementation and management of change processes.

Strategic Management Journal
ISSN: 0143-2095
Wiley
111 River St, Hoboken, New Jersey, 07030-5774
T: +1 201 748-6000
F: +1 212 850 6021
www.wiley.com
Published 13 times per year, this journal covers all aspects of business and management. Articles focus on advances in strategic management and communications. Major topics of interest include entrepreneurship, business environments, organization structure, and strategic business processes.

T+D
ISSN: 1535-7740
American Society for Training and Development (ASTD)
1640 King Street, Box 1443, Alexandria, Virginia, 22313
T: +1 703 683 8100
F: +1 703 683 1523
www.astd.org

Published 12 times per year, this magazine is the publication for the American Society of Training and Development. Articles are written with an emphasis on business professionals involved in the training, development skills, and management guidance of their employees.

INTERNET
Change Management 101: A Primer
http://home.att.net/~nickols/change.htm
Fred Nickols, a consultant based in New Jersey, provides a broad overview of the concept of change management. Coverage is given to definitions of change, the problem of change, skill requirements, four change strategies, and ways of managing change.

Change Management Learning Center
http://change-management.com
Sponsored by ProSci, this site includes a collection of articles posted by consultants, a book store, benchmarking tools, and links.

Management First
www.managementfirst.com
This membership site from Emerald includes a section devoted to full-text articles on change management.

ORGANIZATIONS
USA
Center for Management Effectiveness (CME)
15332 Antioch Street, Suite #46, Pacific Palisades, California, 90272
T: +1 310 459 6052
F: +1 310 459 9307
E: *info@cmeinc.org*
www.cmeinc.org
Specializing in training programs, this education and research center is dedicated to helping organizations of all sizes improve output and performance. With a unique focus on change and the management of change, the programs offered are geared toward current topics such as strategic decision-making, stress management, and managing change. Programs utilize books, audio cassettes, and active participation. The Center provides training for commercial business, nonprofit organizations, and government agencies.

1697

BUSINESS INFORMATION SOURCES

> **FOR MORE INFORMATION**
>
> ✔ Implementing an Effective Change Program (pp. 556–557)

     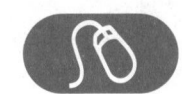

Coaching, Counseling, and Mentoring

BOOKS

Coaching for Leadership: How the World's Greatest Coaches Help Leaders Learn

Marshall Goldsmith, Laurence Lyons, Alyssa Freas, eds
San Francisco, California: Jossey-Bass, 2000
392pp ISBN: 0787955175

This book brings together the thinking of a number of experienced coaches with the aim of giving both an insight into the importance of coaching as a route to leadership and an understanding of what can be achieved through coaching. It is intended for those who provide or receive coaching and those who sponsor or design coaching programs. It explains the foundations of coaching, the roles adopted by those who participate in it, and coaching situations that arise from moments of transition, besides examining the practice and techniques involved. A number of case studies are included.

Coaching with NLP: How to Be a Master Coach

Joseph O'Connor, Andrea Lages
London: Element Books, 2004
240pp ISBN: 0007151225

Written by NLP experts, this book is a practical guide to using it as part of business and life coaching. Suitable for those giving and receiving coaching, it aims to boost all-round performance at work. As NLP helps improve communication, it is an excellent way of making coaching more effective; also, fewer meetings are needed, which can be a boon for time-poor managers.

Developing High-performance People

Oscar G. Mink, Keith Owen, Barbara Mink
Cambridge, Massachusetts: Perseus Books Group, 1993
271pp ISBN: 0201563134

This book addresses the changing role of managers in today's business world. It deals with emerging management challenges, including self-managed work teams, empowerment of employees, and organizational learning.

Executive Coaching with Backbone and Heart: A Systems Approach to Engaging Leaders with their Challenges

Mary Beth O'Neill
San Francisco, California: Jossey-Bass, 2000
224pp (Jossey-Bass Business and Management)
ISBN: 0787950165

Drawing on her own experience of coaching high-powered executives, the author outlines a systems approach to coaching which takes account of "force fields"—the political and emotional climate within organizations that affects decision making. The book provides both a way of thinking about coaching and a methodology for it.

Handbook of Coaching: A Comprehensive Resource Guide for Managers, Executives, Consultants, and Human Resource Professionals

Frederic M. Hudson
San Francisco, California: Jossey-Bass, 1999
264pp ISBN: 0787947954

Coaching is viewed as a fundamental element of any successful organization. This handbook offers coaches a complete guide to the emerging field of professional adult coaching. The author introduces the concept of coaching, reviews its theoretical roots, develops a conceptual model for it, and explains how it can be applied throughout the adult years. A "basic library for coaches" is provided at the end of each chapter.

Handbook of Counselling in Organizations

Michael Carroll, Michael Walton, eds
London: Sage Publications, 1997
363pp ISBN: 0761950877

This handbook presents a collection of articles covering all aspects of counseling in an organizational context. It provides a thorough examination of the key issues and concerns within the field, includes models of counseling in organizations, and deals with understanding counseling provision and its introduction into an organization.

The Heart of Coaching: Using Transformational Coaching to Create a High-Performance Culture

Thomas G. Crane
San Diego, California: FTA Press, 2002
224pp ISBN: 0966087437

The Heart of Coaching is a comprehensive overview of the practice of executive coaching derived from Tom Crane's 15 years of experience as an executive coach. His message advocates a move from a hierarchical organization of bosses and subordinates to a collaborative organization of coaches and learners.

Improving On-the-job Training and Coaching

Karen Lawson
Alexandria, Virginia: American Society for Training and Development (ASTD), 1997
96pp ISBN: 1562860623

This is a comprehensive and usable manual on how to provide on-the-job training. Practical advice and guidance are offered on training adults, selecting the trainer, developing a training plan, conducting and evaluating training, and on-the-job coaching.

Masterful Coaching: Extraordinary Results by Impacting People and the Way They Think and Work Together 2nd ed.

Robert Hargrove
San Francisco, California: Jossey-Bass, 2002
304pp ISBN: 0787960845

This book shows how to reach breakthrough goals and implement transformational change in the workplace. It emphasizes the core coaching skills of sponsoring, counseling, acknowledging, teaching, and confronting. It provides ideas, methods, and tools for implementing the model, and examples from leading companies.

Masterful Coaching Fieldbook

Robert Hargrove
San Francisco, California: Jossey-Bass, 1999
372pp ISBN: 0787947555

Providing how-to guidelines for becoming a successful coach and mentor, this fieldbook can be used alone or alongside Hargrove's *Masterful Coaching* as a practical, hands-on guide for coaching individuals and groups through multiple media.

Mentoring Executives and Directors

David Clutterbuck, David Megginson
Woburn, Massachusetts: Butterworth-Heinemann, 1999
167pp ISBN: 0750636955

This is one of the few books to focus specifically on the role of mentoring in the development of senior managers and

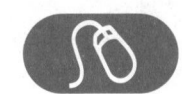

1698

BUSINESS INFORMATION SOURCES

"The information age is one in which workers give way to professionals and managers are replaced by coaches."

Michael Hammer

directors. The authors explore the issue of mentoring for executives and present 22 case study examples. The lessons to be learned from the case studies are discussed.

Mentoring Manager: Strategies for Fostering Talent and Spreading Knowledge

Gareth Lewis
Philadelphia, Pennsylvania: Trans-Atlantic Publications, 2000
192pp (Smarter Solutions)
ISBN: 027364484X
The author reviews the history and purposes of mentoring and describes the attributes and skills needed by mentors in order to help others to learn. He also provides a practical guide to getting started in mentoring and developing mentoring relationships and programs.

Mentoring Manual

Mike Whittaker, Ann Cartwright
Aldershot, United Kingdom: Gower Publishing, 2000
202pp ISBN: 0566081474
This book includes eight related OHP slides, questionnaires, forms, and a mentoring workshop outline, and offers the theories and materials needed for providing a mentoring scheme or for improving an existing one.

The Tao of Coaching: Boost Your Effectiveness at Work by Inspiring and Developing Those Around You

Revised ed.
Max Landsberg
London: Profile Books, 2003
144pp ISBN: 186197650X
This book is a good introduction to those new to the concept of coaching. Ideal for beginners, it uses the character of the hapless Alex as the medium for its useful examples and advice on how to tap into the potential of others and be a good coach.

Techniques for Coaching and Mentoring

David Clutterbuck, David Megginson
Oxford: Butterworth-Heinemann, 2004
224pp ISBN: 075065287X
This book aims to complement coaching and mentoring skills that employees may have gained from experience or by attending courses. It draws on the authors' own experiences as well as those of other professionals and will help readers prepare for both general and specific issues.

Workplace Counselling: A Systematic Approach to Employee Care

Michael Carroll

London: Sage Publications, 1996
247pp ISBN: 0761950214
Carroll provides a practical introduction to the whole area of providing counseling in the workplace. The topics he covers include: understanding, setting up, and supervising workplace counseling; and models of workplace counseling.

MAGAZINES
Therapy Today
ISSN: 0264–9977
British Association for Counselling and Psychotherapy (BACP)
35–37 Albert Street, Rugby, Warwickshire, CV21 2SG, U.K.
T: +44 (0) 870 443 5252
F: +44 (0) 870 443 5161
www.bacp.co.uk
The monthly professional journal for U.K. counselors is sent to members free of charge ten times a year. Users may search for articles by subject. The index includes articles from *Counselling* and *CPJ*.

INTERNET
Coach Universe
www.coachuniverse.com
Coach Universe is a comprehensive guide to resources for corporate coaches. It offers links to training services, profiling services, discussion groups, articles on coaching, and coaching-related businesses.

European Mentoring and Coaching Council
www.emccouncil.org
Members have access to the EMC library, while nonmembers can download copies of recent research reports as PDF files. Details of the annual European Mentoring Conference can also be viewed.

The Knowledge Base of Coachville.com
www.topten.org
This site offers an interesting and large collection of knowledge "nuggets" on coaching and business life in general. The "nuggets" are short articles and can be easily located through topic lists.

The Mentoring Group
www.mentoringgroup.com
The Group is a division of the nonprofit corporation, the Coalition of Counseling Centers, and was founded in 1980. Besides promoting various products and services, the site also provides freely available information on starting a program, best practice, ethics in mentoring, and the reasons for being a mentor.

MentorsForum
http://www.exemplas.com/employers/ leadership_management/ insights_our_research_into_mentoring. asp
This site offers a range of good quality material on mentoring. Users must register to access it, but registration is free.

ORGANIZATIONS
USA
American Counseling Association (ACA)
5999 Stevenson Avenue, Alexandria, Virginia, 22304
T: +1 703 823 6862
F: +1 703 823 0252
E: *webmaster@counseling.org*
www.counseling.org
The American Counseling Association is a nonprofit professional and educational organization that is dedicated to the growth and enhancement of the counseling profession. Founded in 1952, the ACA is the world's largest association exclusively representing professional counselors in various practice settings. By providing leadership training, publications, continuing education opportunities, and advocacy services to nearly 55,000 members, the ACA helps counseling professionals develop their skills and expand their knowledge base.

Europe
British Association for Counselling and Psychotherapy (BACP)
35–37 Albert Street, Rugby, Warwickshire, CV21 2SG, U.K.
T: +44 (0) 870 443 5252
F: +44 (0) 870 443 5161
E: *bacp@bacp.co.uk*
www.bacp.co.uk
The BACP has been the United Kingdom's leading representative organization for counseling professionals since 1977. It provides a range of member services, including training and development, and accredited professional recognition. The BACP also maintains the United Kingdom Register of Counsellors.

Employee Assistance Professionals Association (EAPA)
3 Moors Close, Ducklington, Witney, Oxfordshire, OX29 7TW, U.K.
T: +44 (0) 800 783 7616 (U.K. only)
F: +44 (0) 1993 772 765
E: *info@eapa.org.uk*
www.eapa.org.uk
The EAPA is the professional body for Employee Assistance Programs (EAPs).

1699

BUSINESS INFORMATION SOURCES

"I have often heard that the outstanding man is he who thinks deeply about a problem, and the next is he who listens carefully to advice."

Livy

It represents the interests of professionals concerned with employee assistance, and with the psychological health and the well-being of employees in the United Kingdom. It exists to provide leadership in promoting and developing EAPs in the United Kingdom, to set national standards of practice and professional guidelines, and to provide support and stimulation for the professional development of its members. It has close links with Employee Assistance Programs International.

European Mentoring & Coaching Council (EMC)

Sherwood House, 7 Oxhey Road, Watford, Hertfordshire, WD19 4QF, U.K.
T: + 44 (0) 7000 234 683
www.emccouncil.org
The European Mentoring Centre aims to promote mentoring in business, education, and the community at large. It brings together practitioners, researchers, and institutions internationally to explore and foster best practice. The EMC also undertakes a research program, maintains a library, and runs the annual European Mentoring Conference. David Clutterbuck is one of its directors.

The Work Foundation

Peter Runge House, 3 Carlton House Terrace, London, SW1Y 5DG, U.K.
T: + 44 (0) 870 165 6700
F: + 44 (0) 870 165 6701
E: *customercentre@theworkfoundation.com*
www.theworkfoundation.com
Established in 2002, The Work Foundation is a new incarnation of The Industrial Society, an independent body with over 80 years' experience in management development and training. The Work Foundation operates under the belief that business success goes hand-in-hand with fair management practices. The services offered to members include an information service and employment law helpline; a publishing program of books, research reports, and videos; plus a training and consulting service, which includes the School of Coaching.

International
Canadian Counselling Association (CCA)
16 Concourse Gate, Suite 600, Ottawa, Ontario, K2E 7SS, Canada
T: + 1 613 237 1099
F: + 1 613 237 9786

E: *info@ccacc.ca*
www.ccacc.ca
The Canadian Counselling Association, founded in 1965, is a national association of professionally trained counselors. Its members work in many diverse fields—education, employment and career development, social work, business, industry, mental health, public service agencies, government, and private practice.

FOR MORE INFORMATION

☆ Coaching (pp. 416–417)
✔ Coaching for Better Performance (pp. 434–435)
✔ Counseling Your Colleagues (pp. 440–441)
☆ Creating Fun in the Workplace (pp. 37–38)
☆ Driving Fear from the Workplace (pp. 420–421)
☆ Mentoring (pp. 414–415)
✔ Mentoring in Practice (pp. 436–437)
🐁 Motivation (pp. 1835–1837)
🐁 Performance Appraisal (pp. 1854–1855)
🐁 Personnel Management and HR Management (pp. 1856–1859)

Competences

BOOKS

Art and Science of Competency Models: Pinpointing Critical Success Factors in Organizations

Antoinette D. Lucia, Richard Lepsinger
San Francisco, California: Jossey-Bass, 1999
197pp ISBN: 0787946028
Lucia and Lepsinger examine the what, why, and how of competency models. They look at how competency models can enhance HRM systems, and discuss developing a competency model from scratch, finalizing and validating it, integrating it into an HRM system, and gaining support for it within the organization.

Building Robust Competencies: Linking Human Resource Systems to Organizational Strategies

Paul C. Green
San Francisco, California: Jossey-Bass, 1999
213pp ISBN: 0787946494
Building Robust Competencies offers a practical guide to tying organizational competencies to human resource development and hiring practices. The book outlines a method for determining the strategic core competencies of an organization and then focuses on hiring to enhance them.

Competency-based Recruitment and Selection

Robert Wood, Tim Payne
Hoboken, New Jersey: Wiley, 1998
214pp (Wiley Series in Strategic Human Resource Management)
ISBN: 0471974730

This guide is one of the few works to examine the place of competency in recruitment, and it offers a comprehensive approach to its subject. It considers application forms, competency-based interviewing, psychometric tests, and the use of assessment centers.

Developing Managerial Competence

Jonathan Winterton, Ruth Winterton
New York: Routledge, 1999
336pp ISBN: 0415183464
The Wintertons take a comprehensive and analytical look at the field of modern management development, discussing, among other questions, how to measure development and how it can benefit corporate strategy. Their aim is to demonstrate the value of the occupational standards for managers developed by the Management Charter Initiative, and also the value of Investors in People. The book offers a conceptual framework for evaluating the business advantages of management development and gives 16 detailed case studies of organizations, across different sectors, to show how this works in practice. The overview approach makes it suitable for both practicing managers and students.

Sustaining Corporate Growth: Harnessing Your Strategic Strengths

A. T. Kearney
New York: CRC Press, 2000
120pp ISBN: 1574442899
Sustaining Corporate Growth highlights eight global corporations with case studies

that clearly demonstrate a common theme of sustained growth and success. Corporate strategists can use this book to learn how to identify the core competencies their company possesses and those that they need to develop for the future.

MAGAZINES

Competency and Emotional Intelligence

ISSN: 1351–5802
LexisNexis
Tolley House, 2 Addiscombe Road, Croydon, CR9 5AF, U.K.
T: + 44 (0) 20 7354 6746
F: + 44 (0) 20 7354 8106
www.lexisnexis.co.uk
Published quarterly, this journal was launched to meet the need for information in the practical application of competency and emotional intelligence and to create an interactive forum for discussion. It is business-focused, concentrating on how real organizations are implementing competency and EQ programs, and provides an Annual Benchmarking Survey of employers' use of competency frameworks, the results being published as a special supplement to the journal, completely free of charge to subscribers. The service is also available online at no extra charge for subscribers.

FOR MORE INFORMATION

⌕ Personnel Management and HR Management (pp. 1856–1859)

1701

BUSINESS INFORMATION SOURCES

Competition

BOOKS

The Agenda: What Every Business Must Do to Dominate the Decade

Michael Hammer
New York: Crown Publishing, 2001
288pp ISBN: 0609609661
This book is more of an outline of what companies need to do to remain competitive than a complete specification. Nevertheless, it is a valuable tool for keeping track of the important things and the reasons why they are important. The book focuses on customer service, but it also covers the more recent strategies of virtual organizations and collaboration with other companies.

Blue Ocean Strategy

W. Chan Kim, Renée Mauborgne
Boston, Massachusetts: Harvard Business School Press, 2005
272pp ISBN: 1591396190
Challenging the age-old notion of "battling" with competitors for customers, this well-received book argues that new customers are won by organizations that create "blue oceans": untapped markets which offer excellent growth potential. Kim and Mauborgne draw on their extensive academic expertise to create a compelling argument for this new approach to strategy.

Competitive Advantage through People: Unleashing the Power of the Work Force

Jeffrey Pfeffer
Boston, Massachusetts: Harvard Business School Press, 1996
304pp ISBN: 087584717X
This book explores the extent to which a genuine commitment to the workforce can provide companies with competitive advantage. It considers the implications of this shift in competitive focus, discusses potential barriers to its success, and examines strategies for overcoming these barriers and implementing change.

Differentiate or Die: Survival in Our Era of Killer Competition

Jack Trout, Steve Rivkin
Hoboken, New Jersey: Wiley, 2001
230pp ISBN: 0471028924
Differentiate or Die focuses on the specific attributes of a company and its products or services that set it apart from the competition. It is a book, aimed at all business readers, about becoming known for being different and better in the eyes of customers. It starts off with several chapters describing strategies that do not lead to differentiation and then moves on to discuss the many ways to differentiate, including globally.

The Discipline of Market Leaders: Choose Your Customers, Narrow Your Focus, Dominate Your Market

Michael Treacy, Fred Wiersema
Cambridge, Massachusetts: Perseus Books Group, 1997
210pp ISBN: 0201407191
The rules for market leadership are constantly changing, but this best-selling book offers suggestions on how to become a leader in your market, and how to sustain your lead in a competitive field.

Gaining and Sustaining Competitive Advantage 2nd ed.

Jay B. Barney
Upper Saddle River, New Jersey: Prentice Hall, 2001
600pp ISBN: 0130307947
Barney's book is focused on the strategic aspects of competition. It covers both the external and internal strategies that are needed to remain competitive. It does this from both a "what to do" and a "what to avoid" perspective, offering good coverage of the topic for both advanced business students and current managers.

Getting Everything You Can Out of All You've Got: 21 Ways You Can Out-think, Out-perform, and Out-earn the Competition

Jay Abraham
New York: St. Martin's Press, 2001
384pp ISBN: 0312284543
This book by marketing guru Jay Abraham presents sound competitive strategies for creating and capturing market share. It focuses on how to implement these strategies, illustrating each point with plenty of real-life stories. Any small to medium-size business that wants to be truly competitive can learn from this book. Larger companies that want to revitalize their competitiveness may find useful information here as well.

Mission Critical: Realizing the Promise of Enterprise Systems

Thomas H. Davenport
Boston, Massachusetts: Harvard Business School Press, 2000
352pp ISBN: 0875849067
This book presents an authoritative and no-nonsense view of the opportunities and challenges presented by Enterprise Systems, and provides a set of guidelines to help managers evaluate the benefits and risks for their organizations. The author describes in detail the changes that should be formulated in advance of ES adoption and monitored throughout its implementation—changes in an organization's information systems, business processes, and business strategy—and gives extensive real-world examples.

The New Market Leaders: Who's Winning and How to Battle for Customers

Fred Wiersema
New York: Free Press, 2002
272pp ISBN: 0743204662
A detailed analysis, based on six years of research of 100 companies, this book offers insights into successful customer service strategies. Managers and customer service executives should find Wiersema's book a practical reference tool.

On Competition

Michael E. Porter
Boston, Massachusetts: Harvard Business School Press, 1998
320pp (Harvard Business Review Book Series)
ISBN: 0875847951
This book brings together 11 of Michael Porter's landmark articles on competition and complements them with two entirely new ones. The articles are grouped under three headings: competition and strategy—the core concepts; the competitiveness of locations; and competitive solutions to societal problems.

Wharton on Dynamic Competitive Strategy

George S. Day, David J. Reibstein, eds
Hoboken, New Jersey: Wiley, 2004
464pp ISBN: 0471689572
A comprehensive guide to handling competitive situations, this book covers a range of strategies that can be used to assess and challenge your organization's competitors. The book provides guidelines culled from a history of research into competitive strategy.

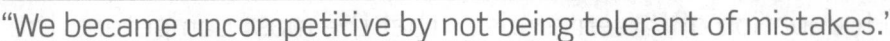
"We became uncompetitive by not being tolerant of mistakes." — Roberto Goizueta

     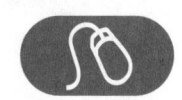

MAGAZINES

Advances in Competitiveness Research
ISSN: 1077–0097
American Society for Competitiveness (ASC)
P.O. Box 1658, Indiana, Pennsylvania, 15705
T: +1 724 357 5928
F: +1 724 357 7768
http://ecobweb.ecob.iup.edu/asc
The annual research journal of the American Society for Competitiveness, this publication considers conceptual, theoretical, and empirical advances in competitiveness and their effects on global economic and management issues.

Butterworth's Competition Law
LexisNexis
Tolley House, 2 Addiscombe Road, Croydon, CR9 5AF, U.K.
T: +44 (0) 20 8662 2000
F: +44 (0) 20 8662 2012
www.lexisnexis.co.uk
This publication consists of a five-volume loose-leaf base, with quarterly updates. Written by an expert legal team, it focuses on facets of competition law and legislation in the European Community and the United Kingdom, viewed both from a national and an industry sector perspective.

Competition and Change: The Journal of Global Business and Political Economy
ISSN: 1024–5294
Maney Publishing
1 Carlton House Terrace, London, SW1Y 5DB, U.K.
T: +44 (0)20 7451 7300
F: +44 (0)20 7451 7307
www.tandf.co.uk/journals/titles/10245294.asp
This quarterly journal examines the changing nature of global business and competition processes and their relationship to economic, political, and social forces.

Competitiveness Review
ISSN: 1059–5422
American Society for Competitiveness (ASC)
P.O. Box 1658, Indiana, Pennsylvania, 15705
T: +1 724 357 5928
F: +1 724 357 7768
http://ecobweb.ecob.iup.edu/asc
This journal is published biannually and is devoted to exploring, developing, and understanding global competitiveness and related issues, from national competitiveness and strategic management to innovation and business intelligence.

OECD Journal of Competition Law and Policy
ISSN: 1560–7771
Organisation for Economic Cooperation and Development (OECD)
2 rue André Pascal, Paris, 75775, France
T: +33 1 45 24 82 00
F: +33 1 45 24 85 00
www.oecd.org
This is a quarterly journal written for competition experts in business, the law, economics, consulting, and academia. It provides insight into the thinking of competition law enforcers while also focusing on the practical application of competition law and policy.

World Competition
ISSN: 1011–4548
Aspen Publishers
1185 Avenue of the Americas, New York, 10036
T: +1 212 597 0200
F: +1 212 597 0338
www.aspenpublishers.com
Drawing on both legal and economic disciplines, this quarterly journal publishes articles on the latest developments in international competition legislation and presents a rounded view of the global implications of competition issues.

INTERNET

ESRC Centre for Research on Innovation and Competition
http://les.man.ac.uk/cric
Funded by the ESRC and run by the University of Manchester, the CRIC draws from the knowledge of staff members to study competition and how innovation truly helps an organization to get ahead in business. The CRIC has a mailing list, a PhD program, and research papers, and is open for seminars and workshops.

European Union—Competition Directorate General
www.europa.eu.int/comm/dgs/competition
This is the official Web site of the European Union Competition Directorate, whose role is to establish a coherent competition policy across E.U. member countries. The site includes links to relevant competition bodies throughout the world.

MarketingProfs.com
www.marketingprofs.com
This Web site is aimed at marketing professionals and professors. It is a membership site, but a good deal of the information is free. Members must pay for

premium content material, but registering is hassle-free. There are a variety of articles on competition that can be accessed through the site's search engine.

Your Success Store
www.yoursuccessstore.com
This is a commercial site with some good free content in its "Resource Center." It offers a number of articles related to competition and business success in its resource section. The articles are organized by author, and the author list includes some well-known business experts.

ORGANIZATIONS
USA

American Society for Competitiveness (ASC)
P.O. Box 1658, Indiana, Pennsylvania, 15705
T: +1 724 357 5928
F: +1 724 357 7768
E: *ASC@iup.edu*
http://ecobweb.ecob.iup.edu/asc
The Society's main aim is to encourage education in and knowledge of the theory and practice of competitiveness. It seeks to achieve this aim through the exchange of information and ideas by assisting in research activities and by providing teaching and practice materials.

U.S. Department of Justice—Antitrust Division
950 Pennsylvania Avenue NW, Washington, D.C., 20530
T: +1 202 514 2481
F: +1 202 514 3763
E: *antitrust.atr@usdoj.gov*
www.usdoj.gov/atr
The role of the Antitrust Division of the U.S. Department of Justice is to promote and protect the U.S. economy and its competitive processes through the enforcement of antitrust laws. It is committed to preserving the rights of both company and consumer, and provides information and guidance on competition issues.

Europe

Competition Directorate General—European Union
European Commission, Directorate-General for Competition, Brussels, B-1049, Belgium
E: *infocomp@cec.eu.int*
www.europa.eu.int/comm/dgs/competition
The mission of the Competition Directorate General is to establish and implement a coherent competition policy across the

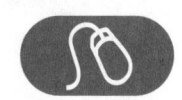

1703

BUSINESS INFORMATION SOURCES

"We need to re-establish the blue water between ourselves and the competition."

Roger Holmes

countries of the European Union. Its main focus is on antitrust activity, merger control, liberalization and state intervention, and state aid.

Office of Fair Trading

Fleetbank House, 2–6 Salisbury Square, London, EC4Y 8JX, U.K.
T: +44 (0) 20 7211 8000
F: +44 (0) 20 7211 8800
E: *enquiries@oft.gov.uk*
www.oft.gov.uk
The Office of Fair Trading is a U.K. government body whose various divisions are responsible for monitoring and investigating competition policy and consumer affairs, and for regulating and enforcing legislation in these areas.

Organisation for Economic Cooperation and Development (OECD)

2 rue André Pascal, Paris, 75775, France

T: +33 1 45 24 82 00
F: +33 1 45 24 85 00
E: *webmaster@oecd.org*
www.oecd.org
Made up of 30 member countries, all of which are committed to the market economy and pluralistic democracy, the OECD provides governments with a forum in which to discuss and develop economic and social policy, and with the information, data, and analysis needed to support these discussions. It includes a division and committee assigned to competition law and policy.

International

World Trade Organization (WTO)

Centre William Rappard, Rue de Lausanne 154, Geneva, CH-1211, Switzerland
T: +41 22 739 51 11
F: +41 22 731 42 06
E: *enquiries@wto.org*

www.wto.org
The WTO is an international member-based organization, whose role is to deal with the rules of trade between member nations. It aims to help producers of goods and services, and exporters and importers, to conduct their business effectively. It includes the Working Group on the Interaction between Trade and Competition Policy.

FOR MORE INFORMATION

🐭 Corporate Strategy (pp. 1721–1723)
★ Globalization and Regional Business Strategy (pp. 128–129)
🐭 Marketing Management (pp. 1827–1832)
★ Marketing: The Importance of Being First (pp. 69–70)

"A prosperous competitor is often less dangerous than a desperate one." Barry Nalebuff

     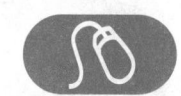

Computers, Information Technology, and E-commerce

BOOKS

Absolute Beginner's Guide to Computer Basics 3rd ed.

Michael Miller

Indianapolis, Indiana: Que, 2005
480pp (Absolute Beginner's Guide)
ISBN: 0789734303

Designed to equip readers with the knowledge they need to set up and learn more about their PC, this book includes advice on maintenance, adding new hardware and devices, using the Internet, shopping online, and buying and selling on eBay. Readers' basic skills are developed so that they can be applied in more specialist or business-related areas.

Blogwild! A Guide for Small Business Blogging

Andy Wibbels

New York: Portfolio, 2006
192pp ISBN: 1591841178

Blogging was named the "tech trend of 2005 and beyond" by Fortune Magazine, and this book taps into this concept and explains how it can benefit businesses. Of particular use to small and growing companies, *Blogwild!* tells readers all they need to know to get blogging, explains where blogging came from, where it's going, and how it can be used to "humanize" a corporate brand.

The Change Function: Why Some Technologies Take Off and Others Crash and Burn

Pip Coburn

New York: Portfolio, 2006
240pp ISBN: 1591841321

Pip Coburn is a former global strategist in the technology group at UBS Warburg, and in this book he draws on his considerable experience to explain why some technologies take off and others never leave the launch pad. Coburn's theory is that consumers are only ready to change when the "pain" of their current position is outweighs the potential pain of trying something new. Although of particular use to investors in new technology, the principles outlined in the book will be of interest anyone involved in new product development.

E-Business for the Small Business

John G. Fisher

London: Kogan Page, 2001
192pp (Business Enterprise Guide)
ISBN: 0749434791

E-business presents many new opportunities for businesses of all sizes. This guide takes owner-managers through the necessary steps for building a successful and sustainable e-business. It deals with finding the funds, getting the right equipment, setting up a Web site, legal issues, online marketing and advertising, business-to-business opportunities, and developing an e-business plan.

E-Commerce Law for Business Managers

Charles Chatterjee

Canterbury, United Kingdom: Financial World Publishing, 2002
338pp ISBN: 0852975643

Aimed specifically at smaller businesses, this is a guide to the legal issues of launching a commercial Internet site. Those issues include e-commerce security; corporate identity; service provision; intellectual property rights; domain names; and e-mail marketing. Many well-established businesses have been caught out by the requirements of the Data Protection Act, and so this book seeks to help readers to understand the legal status of electronic money, signatures, privacy, and consumer rights. It provides this advice in a clear, practical, and user-friendly format, so that all types of manager can gain an understanding of key U.K. legislation and EU directives.

E-mail Etiquette: How to Get the Best Results from Your E-mails

London: A & C Black Publishers Ltd, 2004
96pp (Steps to Success)
ISBN: 0747573530

E-mail has revolutionised the modern business, but at times it can feel like too much of a good thing. Ideal for busy managers, this book offers practical advice on a range of e-mail-related issues, such as managing your inbox, responding to tricky messages, using e-mail responsibly, and understanding related legal issues.

Information Rules: A Strategic Guide to the Network Economy

Carl Shapiro, Hal R. Varian

Boston, Massachusetts: Harvard Business School Press, 1998
352pp ISBN: 087584863X

The advent of technological advances is not a new phenomenon—it has happened before, say the authors, who also note that when such advances occur economic rules and cycles do not disappear, thus making it critical for managers to avoid focusing on technology to the exclusion of all else. What managers need to do, they suggest, is to find ways to deal with such issues as the distribution and marketing of goods in a networked economy and to resolve problems such as compatibility and standards to ease an organization's road to the information age.

IT Investment: Making a Business Case

Dan Remenyi

Oxford, United Kingdom: Digital Equipment Corp., 1999
210pp (Computer Weekly)
ISBN: 0750645040

The author presents clear arguments for preparing an IT business case and includes model questionnaires and forms that managers can use in preparing a case of their own. He stresses in particular the importance of demonstrating the improvements an IT project can make to business processes, practice, and efficiency, and introduces a five-factor model which ties the project into an organization's corporate strategy.

Learning Web Design 2nd ed.

Jennifer Niederst

Farnham, United Kingdom: O'Reilly U.K., 2003
496pp ISBN: 0596004842

Aimed at those new to web design, this book is a comprehensive introduction to the fundamentals. The book is accessible in both tone and layout and is split into four sections: an overview of the web design process; an introduction to HTML, the coding that makes up the background of web pages; a guide to web graphics; and advice on design. Jargon-free and full of practical tips, this book is ideal for beginners.

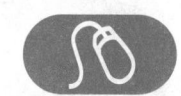

1705

BUSINESS INFORMATION SOURCES

"The one thing computers have done is let us make bigger mistakes. We have to be careful not to depend on our machines."

Michael Bloomberg

Leveraging the New Infrastructure: How Market Leaders Capitalize on Information Technology
Peter Weill, Marianne Broadbent
Boston, Massachusetts: Harvard Business School Press, 1998
294pp ISBN: 0875848303
This book, which is based on research at more than 100 major multinational corporations, shows how various information technology strategies have brought these organizations huge rewards. Promoting the idea that information technology must be treated as another asset for success, it offers guidelines to follow, questions to resolve, and ways to measure results when dealing with your information investment.

Mission Critical: Realizing the Promise of Enterprise Systems
Thomas H. Davenport
Boston, Massachusetts: Harvard Business School Press, 2000
352pp ISBN: 0875849067
This book presents an authoritative and no-nonsense view of the opportunities and challenges presented by Enterprise Systems, and provides a set of guidelines to help managers evaluate the benefits and risks for their organizations. The author describes in detail the changes that should be formulated in advance of ES adoption and monitored throughout its implementation—changes in an organization's information systems, business processes, and business strategy—and gives extensive real-world examples.

The Valuation of Information Technology: A Guide for Strategy Development, Valuation, and Financial Planning
Christopher Gardner
New York: Wiley, 2000
297pp (Wiley Financial Management)
ISBN: 0471378313
Written for practicing managers, but from a stakeholder's perspective, this book presents a way of analyzing and quantifying whether an IT system will add value to an organization. It stresses the importance of seeking the opinion of the end-customer and includes real-world examples of the process in action.

MAGAZINES
Computerworld
ISSN: 0010–4841
Computerworld, Inc.
500 Old Connecticut Path, Framingham, Massachusetts, 01701–9171

T: +1 508 879 0700
www.computerworld.com
Written for professionals working with computers, business executives, and managers of information systems, this magazine focuses on the very latest developments in the advanced technologies of desktop and workgroup computing. Features include reviews of the latest developments in computer products and services.

Information Resources Management Journal
ISSN: 1040–1628
Idea Group, Inc.
701 East Chocolate Avenue, Suite 200, Hershey, Philadelphia, 17033
T: +1 717 533 8845
F: +1 717 533 8661
www.idea-group.com/journals
Intended for both researchers and practitioners in the field of information technology management, the *Information Resources Management Journal* includes applied research findings, case studies, and interviews, and covers subjects such as the success and failure of IT projects and the strategy, policy, and application of IT within organizations.

Information Systems Management
Auerbach Publications
29 West 35th Street, New York, 10001
T: +44 (0) 1264 342 932
F: +44 (0) 1264 342 788
www.auerbach-publications.com
Published four times per year, this magazine focuses on problem-solving strategies and techniques for managers of corporate information systems. This magazine is a must-have for all information technology professionals.

Journal of Information Technology Management
ISSN: 1042–1319
Maximilian Press Publishers
P.O. Box 64841, Virginia Beach, Virginia, 23467–4841
T: +1 757 482 2273
Aimed at a nontechnical audience, the *Journal of Information Technology Management* is concerned with the application of information technology to areas such as information systems planning, network management, database design and administration, and with the human resources aspects of IT. Case study material is included, as well as surveys, research, and reviews.

Wall Street & Technology
ISSN: 1060–989X
CMP Media LLC
3 Park Avenue, New York, 10016
T: +1 212 600 3000
F: +1 212 600 3045
www.wallstreetandtech.com
This journal is published 12 times per year and is written for those working in the financial technology marketplace. IT professional, traders, investment advisers, and analysts can quickly and easily track the latest developments and trends in information technology. The magazine also offers detailed product information.

INTERNET
Beginners.co.uk
www.beginners.co.uk
This Web site offers advice for both absolute beginners and those with some IT knowledge. The site offers a range of free tutorials and online training courses to help those who would like to gain or expand their IT knowledge for work or personal use, and also offers packages of courses that may be purchased. The site is easy to navigate even for Internet novices.

@brint.com
www.brint.com
This extensive portal and community network for e-business, information, technology, and knowledge management contains news, articles, book reviews, and links to relevant Web sites in the featured areas.

CMC Information Sources
www.december.com/cmc/info
This site, which focuses on computer-mediated communications, offers a set of links to essential Web sites concerned with computer training, applications, technology, and culture.

Which? Online
www.which.net
A subscription website, *Which?* Online offers access via the Internet to the wide range of information contained in the range of *Which?* magazines, including *Computing Which?*. The site offers a tour and a 30-day free trial. Subscribers gain access to thousands of reports contained in the print versions of all *Which?* magazines, searchable guides, and interactive features.

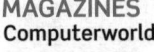
"We couldn't afford to miss the computer revolution."

Stan Shih

ORGANIZATIONS
USA
Association of Information Technology Professionals (AITP)

401 North Michigan Avenue, Suite 2400, Chicago, Illinois, 60611–4267
T: +1 800 224 9371
F: +1 312 527 6636
E: *aitp_hq@aitp.org*
www.aitp.org

This association is the founder of the Certificate in Data Processing examination. The management of information resources is a vital aspect of today's business world, and the AITP provides various resource materials, such as self-study and videotape management development courses, to aid managers and support staff in developing an information resource department.

Association of the Institute for Certification of Computing Professionals

2350 East Devon Avenue, Suite 115, Des Plaines, Illinois, 60018–4610
T: +1 847 299 4227 or 800 843 8227
F: +1 847 299 4280
E: *office@iccp.org*
www.iccp.org

Founded in 1973, this association has over 50,000 members. The prestigious Certified Computing Professional (CCP) designation from the Institute for Certification of Computing Professionals (ICCP) is the only internationally recognized certification program in the profession. Employers value CCP certification as the highest standard of computer knowledge and professional competence. ICCP certifications indicate a precise knowledge and understanding of industry fundamentals.

Information Technology Association of America (ITAA)

1401 Wilson Boulevard, Suite 1100, Arlington, Virginia, 22209
T: +1 703 522 5055
F: +1 703 525 2279
E: *webmaster@itaa.org*
www.itaa.org

This organization, founded in 1982, is the United States' leading trade association for the information technology industry. With a special focus on computers and communications, the ITAA has developed numerous resources for anyone in the information technology field, and its information is timely and relevant in this fast-paced and ever-changing area.

Europe
British Computer Society

1st floor, block D, North Star House, North Star Avenue, Swindon, Wiltshire, SN2 1FA, U.K.
T: +44 (0) 1793 417 417
F: +44 (0) 1793 480 270
E: *bcshq@hq.bcs.org.uk*
www.bcs.org.uk

Founded in 1957, the British Computer Society is a professional and learned society with members from both the United Kingdom and overseas. It aims to provide a voice for the IT industry in discussions with the U.K. government. In addition, it offers both its own certifications and others accredited by the Engineering Council that can lead to Chartered Engineer status.

National Computing Centre Limited

Oxford House, Oxford Road, Manchester, M1 7ED, U.K.
T: +44 (0) 161 228 6333
F: +44 (0) 161 242 2499
E: *info@ncc.co.uk*

www.ncc.co.uk

Founded in 1966, the National Computing Centre is an international, membership-based organization that aims to promote the effective use of IT and computers. Its areas of particular interest include systems design, computer security, communications, and training.

International
Information Resources Management Association (IRMA)

701 East Chocolate Avenue, Suite 200, Hershey, Philadelphia, 17033–1240
T: +1 717 533 8879
F: +1 717 533 8661
E: *member@irma-international.org*
www.irma-international.org

IRMA is a nonprofit, independent, professional body that aims to develop the practices of information technology management within organizations. It also publishes a number of journals, organizes seminars, conventions, and training programs on subjects relating to IT and information resources, and hosts an annual international conference.

1707

FOR MORE INFORMATION

☆ Enterprise Information Systems (pp. 176–177)
🐭 Information Management (pp. 1772–1773)
🐭 Knowledge Management (pp. 1794–1797)
☆ Marketspaces (pp. 189–191)
✔ Planning the Replacement of Software Systems (pp. 598–599)
☆ Viewpoint: Jeffrey F. Rayport (pp. 184–186)

BUSINESS INFORMATION SOURCES

Conditions of Employment

BOOKS

101 Salary Secrets: How to Negotiate Like a Pro
Daniel Porot, Frances Bolles Haynes
Berkeley, California: Ten Speed Press, 2001
240pp ISBN: 1580082300
This is a pocket-sized guide to getting a better salary. It shows how to tackle all types of salary-related negotiations, including starting salaries and benefits packages, future advancement, and raises and changes in benefits for the already employed. It provides sample language for saying the things that are hardest to say in salary negotiations.

Competing for Talent: Key Recruitment and Retention Strategies for Becoming an Employer of Choice
Nancy S. Ahlrichs
Palo Alto, California: Davies-Black, 2000
254pp ISBN: 0891061487
Drawing on the author's 20 years' experience in HR roles, this book sets out to help companies become magnet organizations, or employers of choice. Based on the principle that your people are your key asset, this book examines how you can target, recruit, and retain the staff who can improve your bottom line.

Drawing Up Employment Contracts 3rd ed.
Olga Aikin
New York: Beekman, 2001
336pp (Developing Practice)
ISBN: 0846452324
This comprehensive book deals with creating contracts of employment that will promote professional relationships, meet business needs, and retain enough flexibility to cope with change. In all, it covers 18 different types of contract, including contracts for self-employed workers. It also addresses issues such as confidentiality, working hours, and intellectual property, and discusses how to change contracts and deal with breaches.

Get Paid What You're Worth: The Expert Negotiator's Guide to Salary and Compensation
Robin L. Pinkley, Gregory B. Northcraft
New York: St. Martin's Press, 2003
208pp ISBN: 031230269X
This book offers advice on how and why to negotiate salary and job issues. It explains which kind of job issues can be negotiated, and advises how to prepare for and conduct a negotiation and how to close the deal. It also advises ways to respond to various offers and how to avoid "deal killers."

Keeping Your Valuable Employees: Retention Strategies for Your Organization's Most Important Resource
Suzanne Dibble
Hoboken, New Jersey: Wiley, 1999
284pp ISBN: 0471320536
Based on extensive research and experience, the author discusses various strategies for retaining employees. The topics covered include: identifying your company's unique selling points; looking at the recruitment package; incentive schemes; and career development plans. Performance management, counter offers, and exit interviews are also discussed.

The Workplace Law Advisor
Anne Covey
Cambridge, Massachusetts: Perseus Books Group, 2000
256pp ISBN: 0738203742
This is a useful, comprehensive resource for managers and executives. It offers sound advice on the legal rights and responsibilities of both employers and employees in the workplace. It shows the various reasons why employers often get sued, and advises on how to avoid such situations. It discusses relevant Acts such as the Americans with Disabilities Act and the Family and Medical Leave Act.

MAGAZINES

Employee Rights and Employment Policy Journal
Chicago-Kent College of Law
Illinois Institute of Technology, 565 West Adams Street, Chicago, Illinois, 60661–3691
T: +1 312 906 5000
F: +1 312 906 5280
www.kentlaw.edu/ilw/erepj
Published jointly by Chicago-Kent College and Workplace Fairness, this journal includes articles on legal and law-related issues that affect the well-being of employees in the workplace. It has a multidisciplinary approach, and its articles are peer-reviewed.

INTERNET

American Federation of Labor and the Congress of Industrial Organizations
www.aflcio.org
This official Web site of the AFL-CIO has links to dozens of pages, all concerning the right for American workers to have their opinions heard by businesses and the federal government.

elaws
www.dol.gov/elaws
Employment law assistance for workers and small businesses is given by the U.S. Department of Labor in a question and answer format on this site. The information provided by virtual advisers can be searched in a variety of ways, including by topic.

ORGANIZATIONS
USA
Workplace Fairness
44 Montgomery Street, Suite 2080, San Francisco, California, 94104
T: +1 415 362 7373
F: + 1 415 677 9445
www.workplacefairness.org
Workplace Fairness, founded in 1994 as the National Employee Rights Institute (NERI), is a nonprofit organization that promotes employee rights and provides information to workers and their advocates. The name was changed in 2001 to reflect wider concerns and efforts to link the work of legal and nonlegal organizations in this field. The NERI continues as the publishing arm of Workplace Fairness, producing books and journals on employee rights.

Europe
Advisory Conciliation and Arbitration Service (ACAS)
Euston Tower, 286 Euston Road, London, NW1 3JJ, U.K.
T: +44 (0) 20 7396 0022
www.acas.org.uk
ACAS is a national organization (with its head office in London) of employment relations experts. It has been working with employers, employees, trade unions, and other representatives for more than 25 years. The organization has a network of telephone helplines giving free help and information, and the Advisory Service works with hundreds of companies every year to develop a joint approach to problem

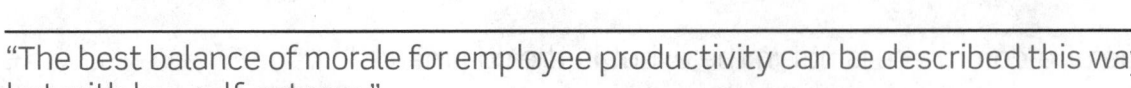
"The best balance of morale for employee productivity can be described this way: happy, but with low self-esteem."
Scott Adams

solving. Most cases going to an employment tribunal are first referred to ACAS to see if there is a less damaging and expensive way of sorting the problem out. The organization also runs workshops and seminars around the country, targeting small businesses without specialist personnel sections.

European Foundation for the Improvement of Living and Working Conditions

Wyattville Road, Loughlinstown, Dublin, 18, Republic of Ireland

T: +353 1 204 3100

F: +353 1 282 6456

E: *postmaster@eurofound.eu.int*

www.eurofound.eu.int

The Foundation was set up in 1975 to provide information to European institutions and social partners that would support the improvement of living and working conditions. It promotes and coordinates research projects, including the European Surveys of Working Conditions.

Labour Research Department (LRD)

78 Blackfriars Road, London, SE1 8HF, U.K.

T: +44 (0) 20 7928 3649

F: +44 (0) 20 7928 0621

E: *info@lrd.org.uk*

www.lrd.org.uk

The LRD is an independent, trade-union-based research organization, founded over 80 years ago. Its function is to provide information to support negotiations and campaigns, and around 2,000 labor union organizations are affiliated to it. Its publications include journals, advice booklets, and an online pay database.

International

International Labour Organization (ILO)

Juan Somavia

4, route des Morillons, CH-1211, Geneva 22, Switzerland

T: +41 22 799 61 11

F: +41 22 798 86 85

E: *ilo@ilo.org*

www.ilo.org

The ILO is a UN specialized agency, founded in 1919 to promote social justice

and human and labor rights. It formulates international labor standards, sets minimum standards for basic workers' rights, provides technical assistance in related areas, and supports the development of employers' and workers' organizations.

1709

BUSINESS INFORMATION SOURCES

"Had the employers of past generations all of them dealt fairly with their employees there would have been no unions."

Stanley Baldwin

Conferences and Exhibitions

BOOKS

The Business of Event Planning: Behind-the-scenes Secrets of Successful Special Events
Judy Allen
Hoboken, New Jersey: Wiley, 2002
340pp ISBN: 047083188X
This book provides a practical toolkit for anyone who has to plan and execute a truly special event. It includes information on choosing the venue, preparing and managing the budget, scheduling and staffing, coordinating food and beverages, arranging decor and entertainment, and working with professionals such as public relations firms and creative directors.

Event Management in Leisure and Tourism
David C. Watt
Upper Saddle River, New Jersey: Longman, 1998
211pp ISBN: 0582357063
Written by an experienced industry practitioner, this book is designed for students studying event management. It considers a wide variety of events, including exhibitions. The text covers planning and administration, fundraising and budgeting, marketing and advertising, and features case studies of good practice. Sources of further information and assistance are also listed.

Guerrilla Trade Show Selling
Jay Conrad Levinson, Mark S. A. Smith, Orvel Ray Wilson
Hoboken, New Jersey: Wiley, 1997
320pp ISBN: 0471165689
This book applies guerrilla sales and marketing tactics to the high-pressure environment of the trade show floor. It contains lots of insider secrets, tips, and techniques on how to use trade shows as an effective marketing weapon.

How to Run a Successful Conference: Proven Management Techniques for Delivering a Successful Event on Budget 2nd ed.
John G. Fisher
London: Kogan Page, 2000
129pp ISBN: 0749434066
This is a practical, user-friendly guide that will take you step by step through the process of organizing a conference or event.

It includes expert advice on: finding the right venue; event management and logistics; accommodation and catering; and constructing and sticking to a budget.

Open Space Technology: A User's Guide 2nd ed.
Harrison Owen
San Francisco, California: Berrett-Koehler, 1997
173pp ISBN: 1576750248
This is a guide for organizing meetings for between five and 1,000 participants. Owen is the originator of a technique called Open Space Technology, which many managers find useful for organizing large groups of people, especially when these groups are being called upon to think about complex issues. The text includes descriptions of how to set up large rooms, how to break up participants into smaller groups, and how to organize space physically during conferences.

MAGAZINES

Exhibitor Magazine
Exhibitor Magazine
Rochester, Minnesota, 559040–6565, USA
T: +1 507 289 6556 (+1 888 235 6155)
F: +1 507 289 5253
www.exhibitoronline.com/exhibitormagazine
A monthly magazine covering best practice in trade show and corporate event marketing.

Journal of Convention and Event Tourism
ISSN: 1547–0148
Haworth Press
Binghamton, New York, 13904, USA
T: +1 800 429 6784
F: +1 800 895 0582
www.haworthpress.com
This quarterly journal, formerly the *Journal of Convention and Exhibition Management, Meetings and Conventions*, provides a forum for the exchange of ideas in the field of convention and exhibition management. Articles cover research studies, management practice, business, and government policies. Book reviews and industry trends are also included.

Meetings and Conventions
ISSN: 0025–8652
Reed Business Information

8878 Barrons Boulevard, Highlands Ranch, Colorado, 80129–2345
T: +1 800 446 6551
F: +1 303 470 4280
www.reedbusiness.com
This monthly magazine is aimed at meetings professionals and covers news, trends, and issues in the meetings industry. It also provides practical hints and tips and destination guides.

INTERNET

Expo24-7.Com
www.expo24-7.com
This site provides comprehensive online business information and Internet solutions for people who visit, organize, and exhibit at trade shows worldwide.

TSNN: The Ultimate Trade Show Directory
www.tsnn.com
This extensive resource is ideal for trade show professionals. Users may search for suppliers and make use of the research center, which contains information on industry profiiles, customer recommendations, and indepth reports. Users must register to use some sections of the site, but registration is free.

ORGANIZATIONS
USA
Exhibit Designers and Producers Association (EDPA)
5775 Peachtree-Dunwoody Road, Suite 500, Atlanta, Georgia, 30342
T: +1 404 303 7310
F: +1 404 252 0774
E: *edpa@edpa.com*
www.edpa.com
Formed in 1955, this organization has over 370 members. The EDPA is an internationally recognized trade association, designed to provide networking opportunities for workers involved in the design, manufacture, and installation of displays and exhibits.

Exposition Operations Society (EOS)
P.O. Box 949, Framingham, Massachusetts, 01701–1949
T: +1 508 544 1527
F: +1 508 435 0280
E: *info@ExpoOps.com*
www.expoops.com

"Never dump a good idea on a conference table. It will belong to the conference."

Jane Trahey

Formed in 2000, EOS is a professional network where members can share ideas, experiences, challenges, and solutions relating to the exhibition industry.

International Association for Exhibition Management

8111 LBJ Freeway, Suite 750, Dallas, Texas, 75251–1313
T: +1 972 458 8002
F: +1 972 458 8119
www.iaem.org
The Association is open to all individuals with business interests in the exhibition industry. It offers a range of products and services.

National Association of Consumer Shows (NACS)

147 SE 102nd St, Portland, Oregon, 97216
T: +1 503 253 0832 or 800 728 6227
F: +1 503 253 9172
E: *info@publicshows.com*
www.publicshows.com

The National Association of Consumer Shows (NACS) was founded in 1987 for the advancement of the consumer (public) show industry and to further the growth and professionalism of those involved in the production of consumer shows.

Europe

Association for Conferences and Events

Riverside House, High Street, Huntingdon, Cambridgeshire, PE18 6SG, U.K.
T: +44 (0) 1480 457 595
F: +44 (0) 1480 412 863
E: *ace@martex.co.uk*
www.martex.co.uk/ace
The benefits of membership of ACE include social and networking events, seminars, inspection visits, a monthly newsletter, a job vacancy list, a calendar of industry events, and free entry to the ACE Internet site. The Association's other services are a confidential helpline and the Aceplan Insurance Scheme.

Meetings Industry Association

P.O. Box 6984, Wellingborough, Northamptonshire, NN29 7WU, U.K.
T: +44 (0) 845 230 5508
F: +44 (0) 845 230 7708
E: *info@mia-uk.org*
www.mia-uk.org
The aims of this body are to strengthen the position of members' businesses in an increasingly competitive environment and to raise the profile of the United Kingdom as an international conference destination. It pursues the best interests of members and meeting buyers alike by encouraging excellence and ethical standards.

FOR MORE INFORMATION

- Direct Marketing (pp. 1730–1731)
- Marketing Management (pp. 1827–1832)
- ✔ Planning a Conference (pp. 522–523)

1711

BUSINESS INFORMATION SOURCES

"A conference is a gathering of important people who, singly, can do nothing but together can decide that nothing can be done."

Fred Allen

Consulting Services/Management Consultants

BOOKS

Business Consulting
Gilbert Toppin, Fiona Czerniawska
New York: Bloomberg Press, 2005
256pp ISBN: 1861977026
Business consulting is a billion-dollar industry. Not all consulting is worth the money, however. Drawing on examples from both the public and private sectors, this book sets out to help readers make sure that their hard-won budgets are well spent on consulting that really delivers.

The Business of Consulting: The Basics and Beyond
Elaine Biech
San Francisco, California: Jossey-Bass/ Pfeiffer, 1999
256pp ISBN: 0787940216
This practical manual covers all aspects of starting, developing, and growing a small consultancy, including marketing, charging for services, building client relationships, personal and professional development, and making money. The accompanying disk provides worksheets and forms for a range of business activities such as marketing plans and cash-flow management.

Clients for Life: Evolving from an Expert-for-Hire to an Extraordinary Adviser
Jagdish N. Sheth, Andrew Sobel
Columbus, Ohio: Fireside, 2002
272pp ISBN: 0684870304
This title uses the results of over 100 case studies and numerous interviews with chief executives to reveal what clients really want and how those who serve them can gain the skills needed to be successful in a challenging, modern society.

Concise Guide to Becoming an Independent Consultant
Herman Holtz
Hoboken, New Jersey: Wiley, 1999
320pp ISBN: 0471315737
This abridged version of *How to Succeed as an Independent Consultant* is packed with expert advice, helpful tips, and industry secrets that can lead to successful self-marketing. It provides the crucial tools and techniques needed to survive and thrive in this highly competitive field. It also

includes material on founding the business, writing proposals, negotiating fees, and vital consulting skills.

The Consultant's Scorecard: Tracking Results and Bottom-line Impact of Consulting Projects
Jack Phillips
Maidenhead, United Kingdom: McGraw-Hill, 1999
400pp ISBN: 0071348166
You want to know that the money you pay a management consultant will bring measurable success to your company. You want the same return on this investment as on any other. Good consultants are just as interested in demonstrating that ROI to you. This book is a general overview of the metrics both sides can use to evaluate the business impact—and return on investment—of any consulting project.

Consulting Demons: Inside the Unscrupulous World of Global Corporate Consulting
Lewis Pinault, Stephen M. Pollan
New York: HarperCollins, 2001
320pp ISBN: 006661998X
This tale of Pinault's 12-year career as a management consultant is a stunning exposé of some of the most prestigious and respected names in the business. An intriguing story, it is an alarming reflection on the major consulting firms and contains a wealth of information on how best to deal with them. This rare insider's view of global management consulting is useful information that the reader needs to evaluate critically.

Developing Knowledge-based Client Relationships: Leadership in Professional Services 2nd ed.
Ross Dawson
Woburn, Massachusetts: Butterworth-Heinemann, 2005
416pp ISBN: 0750678712
This book provides consulting and other professional services firms with a new model for doing business. In essence, it encourages such firms to focus on adding value to the client through the transfer of knowledge. This is not a particularly radical shift, since knowledge is the trade of

professional services firms—but they need to be aware of the consequences of not fully sharing that knowledge.

Flawless Consulting: A Guide to Getting Your Expertise Used 2nd ed.
Peter Block
San Francisco, California: Jossey-Bass, 1999
400pp ISBN: 0787948039
Flawless Consulting is essentially a how-to book on the subject of consulting from the perspective of a successful management consultant. It covers every aspect of the consultancy process, from defining what it is to be a consultant through to disengaging from the client. It offers sound, theoretically grounded advice in a simple and friendly manner. This book is extremely useful for consultants, both internal and external.

High Impact Consulting: How Clients and Consultants Can Work Together to Achieve Extraordinary Results
Robert H. Schaffer
New York: Jossey-Bass, 2002
272pp ISBN: 0787960497
The author examines the idea that consultant-based solutions often fail and that there is often a big gap between what clients should do to make a project succeed and what they are actually willing to do. Five "fatal flaws" of conventional consulting are identified in the text: psychological barriers within the organization; wasteful work patterns; low performance goals; poor management practices, and cultural weaknesses. The text offers a field-tested approach to support effective results-based project design, together with practical new tools to assist in project planning.

High Income Consulting: How to Build and Market Your Professional Practice 2nd ed.
Tom Lambert
Naperville, Illinois: Nicholas Brealey Publishing, 1997
324pp ISBN: 1857881699
This practical workbook is designed to help consultants build and sustain a high-quality, profitable professional practice. It contains guides for action, summaries of key information, an extensive resource glossary

"Get the advice of everybody whose advice is worth having—they are very few—and then do what you think best yourself."

Charles Stewart Parnell

of business ideas and terms, and an equally extensive bibliography of books about consulting.

How to Succeed as an Independent Consultant 4th ed.

Herman Holtz, David Zahn
Hoboken, New Jersey: Wiley, 2004
432pp ISBN: 0471469106
This book is considered by many to be a classic on the subject of consulting. In it Holtz essentially presents his ideas on what an independent consultant should do, how the various tasks should be approached, and, in particular, how the work of consulting should be marketed to different business sectors.

Management Consultancy: A Handbook of Best Practice 2nd ed.

Philip Sadler, ed.
London: Kogan Page, 2001
496pp ISBN: 0749436530
This handbook explores the principles behind the application of specialized management techniques to the consultancy process. It also seeks to promote an understanding of the dynamics of the client-consultant relationship. Sections focus on management consultancy today and in the future, the consulting process, and managing the business of management consultancy. Change management concepts and tools and the different fields of consulting activity are also covered.

The McKinsey Mind: Understanding and Implementing the Problem-Solving Tools and Management Techniques of the World's Top Strategic Consulting Firm

Ethan M. Rasiel, Paul Friga
San Francisco, California: Jossey-Bass/ Pfeiffer, 2001
272pp ISBN: 0071374299
McKinsey & Company is one of the most respected consulting firms in the world. This book is a manual for putting McKinsey concepts and skills into action. It describes the step-by-step techniques and strategies used to solve core business problems. Real-world examples and exercises are designed to help the reader begin to think in McKinsey's rigorous, structured manner.

The McKinsey Way: Using the Techniques of the World's Top Strategic Consultants to Help You and Your Business

Ethan M. Rasiel
Maidenhead, United Kingdom: McGraw-Hill, 1999
187pp ISBN: 0070534489

McKinsey & Company is one of the best-known management consultancies in the world, with a reputation for recruiting and developing some of the world's greatest management thinkers and business leaders. The author, a former McKinsey analyst, introduces some of the tools and techniques used by the company to approach and solve many business problems, as well as providing an insight into the working life of a McKinsey consultant.

Relationships That Enable Enterprise Change: Leveraging the Client/ Consultant Connection

Ron A. Carucci et al.
San Francisco, California: Jossey-Bass/ Pfeiffer, 2002
256pp ISBN: 0787960802
This is a practical resource for management consultants who want to enhance their relationships with senior managers in order to drive organizational change. It includes self-assessments, tools, and models intended to help consultants develop the skills needed for successful collaborative relationships. The authors show how to build trust, demonstrate the courage needed to address the tough issues, and act as an advocate for your client.

The Trusted Advisor

David H. Maister, Charles H. Green, Robert M. Galford
Carmichael, California: Touchstone Books, 2001
256pp ISBN: 0743212347
The Trusted Advisor is a guide for consulting professionals on how to establish effective relationships with clients through building trust. That trust comes from delivering skilled, quality services in line with the client's needs and wants. The book is filled with practical advice for the consultant, but is an equally valuable tool for those who contract consulting services.

Ultimate Consultant: Powerful Techniques for the Successful Practitioner

Alan Weiss
San Francisco, California: Jossey-Bass/ Pfeiffer, 2001
272pp (Ultimate Consultant)
ISBN: 0787955086
Successful consultants, it is suggested, often become the victims of their own success and fail to develop their business, raise performance, and attract new clients from a wider range of organizations. The author offers practical advice and tips on acquiring *Fortune* 1,000 clients, developing

international business, forming partnerships and alliances, and working with family-owned businesses. The text also addresses the ways to increase income through fee-setting. Promotional activities are described and practical issues, such as managing time and maintaining work-life balance, are discussed. Interviews and brief case studies of successful consultants are also included.

Vault Guide to the Top 50 Consulting Firms 8th ed.

Marcy Lerner
New York: Vault Reports, 2005
512pp ISBN: 1581313578
This is an annually updated guidebook that includes a wealth of information for those seeking to join or engage a large consulting firm. It offers insights on everything from what firms do well and not so well, to what it is like to work for the firms listed. This is not a resource for gaining theoretical or operational knowledge, but it has very great practical value.

MAGAZINES
Management Consultancy

ISSN: 1351–0924
VNU Business Media
VNU House, 32–34 Broadwick Street, London, W1A 2HG, U.K.
T: +44 (0) 20 7316 9000
F: +44 (0) 20 7316 9250
News, surveys, and reports from the field of management consulting are the mainstay of this magazine, which also carries feature articles on issues connected with management and consulting.

Management Consultant International

Kennedy Information
One Phoenix Mill Lane, 3rd Floor, Peterborough, New Hampshire, 03458
T: +1 800 531 0007 or +1 603 924 1006
F: +1 603 924 4460
www.kennedyinfo.com/mci/mci.html
This monthly newsletter provides current information on management consulting in an international context. Its coverage includes trends in charging, new business areas, and contracts, mergers, and acquisitions.

INTERNET
Institute of Management Consultants of the United States of America
www.imcusa.org
This is the site of the national professional association representing management consultants. It certifies and awards the designation of Certified Management

---

"The consultants are the thinkers and the strategists. And the managers have the most bizarre job."

Eileen C. Shapiro

Consultant (CMC). The site features a consultant search page that lets you search by type of consulting practice, specialty, or type of industry.

Skidmore College, Saratoga Springs, NY
www.skidmore.edu/administration/career/consulting.htm
This URL will take you to a resource guide on consulting services. It is geared to those interested in pursuing a career with a consulting firm, but also offers links of a more general nature.

ORGANIZATIONS
USA
Association of Internal Management Consultants (AIMC)
824 Caribbean Court, Marco Island, Florida, 34145
T: +1 239 642 0580
F: +1 239 642 1119
E: *info@aimc.org*
www.aimc.org
The AIMC promotes internal consulting as a profession and gives formal recognition to the internal consultant's role. Their Web site provides a place for members to support each other through the exchange of ideas and information.

Association of Management Consulting Firms (AMCF)
380 Lexington Avenue, Suite 1700, New York, 10168
T: +1 212 551 7887
F: +1 212 551 7934

E: *info@amcf.org*
www.amcf.org
The AMCF was established in 1929 to foster an understanding of the management consulting profession's scope and purposes. It provides a forum for the exchange of ideas and to confront common challenges. It also serves as a voice of the industry on major issues and represents the profession before government and regulatory bodies.

Institute of Management Consultants of the United States of America (IMCUSA)
2025 M Street NW, Suite 800, Washington, D.C., 20036–3309
T: +1 202 367 1134
F: +1 202 367 2134
E: *office@imcusa.org*
www.imcusa.org
The Institute was founded in 1968 as a nonprofit, national, professional association to set standards of professionalism and ethics for management consulting. It certifies and awards the designation of Certified Management Consultant (CMC). It also sponsors workshops, seminars, and conferences at national and regional level and is a member of the International Council of Management Consulting Institutes.

Europe
Institute of Management Consultancy (IMC)
3rd Floor, 17–18 Hayward's Place, London, EC1R 0EQ, U.K.
T: +44 (0) 20 7566 5220
F: +44 (0) 20 7566 5230

E: *consult@imc.co.uk*
www.imc.co.uk
Founded in 1962 as a professional institute for management consultants in the United Kingdom, the IMC became a member of the International Council of Management Consulting Institutes in 1993 and is involved in developing the Certified Management Consultant qualification. It organizes social and learning networks and special interest groups as part of its service to members.

Management Consultancies Association (MCA)
49 Whitehall, London, SW1A 2BX, U.K.
T: +44 (0) 20 7321 3990
F: +44 (0) 20 7321 3991
www.mca.org.uk
Formed in 1956, this association acts as a kind of trade body for leading management consulting firms in the United Kingdom. The criteria for membership are high, and there is a rigid code of practice to which members have to adhere. The MCA uses these routes to enhance the standing of the profession and to increase public awareness of the value of bringing in outside advisers.

FOR MORE INFORMATION

☆ Using Management Consultants Effectively (pp. 368–369)
✔ Using Management Consulting Services Effectively (pp. 578–579)

BUSINESS INFORMATION SOURCES

"Effective visions are lived in details, not broad strokes."   Tom Peters

Contingency, Crisis, Disaster Management

BOOKS

Business Continuity Planning: A Step-by-step Guide with Planning Forms on CD-ROM 3rd ed.
Kenneth L. Fulmer
Brookfield, Connecticut: Rothstein Associates, 2004
190pp ISBN: 1931332215
This detailed workbook will help you build a corporate disaster plan. It covers factors such as choosing an alternate location and selecting vendors to enable your organization to resume business as soon as possible. It reviews how to choose a planning coordinator and recovery team and how to write a planning document and stresses the importance of testing the plan to be sure it works.

Business Continuity Planning: Protecting Your Organization's Life
Ken Doughty, ed.
Boca Raton, Florida: CRC Press, 2000
408pp (Best Practices)
ISBN: 0849309077
Contributions from a range of experts provide a comprehensive overview of business continuity planning. They indicate the importance of analyzing the risks to which an organization is exposed and of developing a plan for the resumption of business after a crisis. They also give detailed guidance on building, testing, maintaining, and updating a business continuity plan.

The Definitive Handbook of Business Continuity Management
Andrew Hiles, Peter Barnes, eds
Hoboken, New Jersey: Wiley, 2001
410pp ISBN: 0471485594
This book tackles business continuity from two perspectives: the first part discusses the key concepts and provides an overview of the type of events which can interrupt business; the second takes the form of a practical how-to guide. A variety of further resources, including case studies and standards for business continuity practitioners, are listed in the appendices at the back of the book.

Disaster Recovery Planning: Preparing for the Unthinkable 3rd ed.
Jon William Toigo
Upper Saddle River, New Jersey: Prentice Hall, 2002
512pp ISBN: 0130462829
This volume provides the information needed to develop a plan to protect your company's data in case of an emergency. Filled with interviews with vendors and practitioners, it walks the reader through the steps that those responsible for an organization's information technology must take to ensure that organizational data will be available in the aftermath of a disaster.

Manager's Guide to Contingency Planning for Disasters: Protecting Vital Facilities and Critical Operations 2nd ed.
Kenneth N. Myers
Hoboken, New Jersey: Wiley, 1999
252pp ISBN: 047135838X
Following a proven methodology, this guide shows how to establish a corporate contingency plan to ensure minimal disruption to operations in the event of a disaster. The author devotes particular attention to ways of minimizing development time and costs by avoiding extensive information gathering, and to the importance of conducting briefings to communicate aims and objectives before commencing the development process.

Managing Communications in a Crisis
Peter Ruff, Khalid Aziz
Brookfield, Vermont: Gower Publishing, 2003
176pp ISBN: 0566082942
This book details how crisis situations can be identified and dealt with to ensure that risks to an organization's financial well-being and reputation are minimized. Part I considers the definitions of a crisis and the theory behind dealing with crisis communications, both externally and internally. Practicalities of crisis management communications dealt with in Part II include the identification of audiences and how and by whom each should be dealt with. Checklists and supporting information on the key aspects of the communication process are also supplied, together with brief case studies.

Managing Crises Before They Happen
Ian I. Mitroff, Gus Anagnos
New York: AMACOM, 2000
172pp ISBN: 0814405630
Having explained the specific features of corporate culture that enable crises to happen, the authors present a framework for preventing such crises happening and for controlling the damage they cause.

Risk Issues and Crisis Management: A Casebook of Best Practice 3rd ed.
Michael Regester, Judy Larkin
London: Kogan Page, 2005
240pp (PR in Practice)
ISBN: 0749423935
This book deals with the successful handling of crisis situations so that damage and disruption are minimized. Case studies and models are included and illustrate how complex crises have been handled in practice, both successfully and unsuccessfully.

Secure Online Business Handbook: E-Commerce, IT Functionality, and Business Continuity 2nd ed.
Jonathan Reuvid
London: Kogan Page, 2004
224pp ISBN: 0749442212
This practical handbook, divided into five sections, contains a collection of contributions from a range of experts in the field of information technology and e-commerce and addresses the need for effective management of business risk. Information at risk and the business case for security are considered first. Points of exposure and the range of threats to privacy and integrity are explored, and methods of software protection such as firewalls, encryption, digital signatures and biometrics are covered. In the operational management section, the need for a culture of workplace security is also discussed, and data recovery, disaster management, and forensics are covered under the heading of contingency planning.

MAGAZINES
Continuity
ISSN: 1460–1451
Business Continuity Institute
10 Southview Park, Marsack Street, Caversham, Berkshire, RG4 5AF, U.K.

1715

BUSINESS INFORMATION SOURCES

"I believe that crisis really tends to help develop the character of an organization."

John Sculley

T: +44 (0) 870 603 8783
F: +44 (0) 870 603 8761
www.thebci.org
Continuity is the official journal of the Business Continuity Institute. It appears quarterly and includes articles, news, and reports of research projects.

Disaster Prevention and Management
ISSN: 0965–3562
Emerald (North America)
4th Floor, 44 Brattle Street, Cambridge, Massachusetts, 02138
T: +1 888 622 0075
www.emeraldinsight.com/ccm.htm
This journal appears five times a year and focuses on the latest research into the prevention and mitigation of natural and man-made disasters. Each issue includes articles by international experts in the field, news, product reviews, case studies, and details of events, conferences, and resources.

Disaster Recovery Journal
ISSN: 1079–736X
Richard L. Arnold
P.O. Box 510110, St. Louis, Missouri, 63151
T: +1 314 894 0276
F: +1 314 894 7474
www.drj.com
The *DRJ* was founded in 1987 and is published quarterly. It covers the field of business continuity and disaster recovery.

Journal of Contingencies and Crisis Management
ISSN: 0966–0879
Blackwell Publishing
350 Main Street, Malden, Massachusetts, 02148
T: +1 781 388 8200
F: +1 781 388 8232
www.blackwellpublishing.com
This is a quarterly journal for managers with responsibilities in the area of risk and crisis management.

INTERNET
Crisis Management and Disaster Recovery Group
www.crisis-management-and-disaster-recovery.com
This site provides information on how to create and maintain a disaster recovery or crisis management plan and provides access to leading support resources.

Disaster Recovery Journal
www.drj.com
This journal's Web site provides access to a great deal of free material and resources

including articles, a vendor directory, and chat groups.

Federal Emergency Management Agency
www.fema.gov
This U.S. federal government site features GEMS (Global Emergency Management System), a searchable database of reviewed Web sites in fields related to emergency management, and a virtual library including practical guides and checklists.

globalcontinuity.com
www.globalcontinuity.com
This is a portal site for business recovery and continuity planning information, featuring a database of suppliers and including news, articles, surveys, and related links.

ORGANIZATIONS
USA
Contingency Planning Exchange, Inc. (CPE)
11 Hanover Square, Suite 501, New York, 10176–3099
T: +1 212 344 4003
F: +1 212 344 2016
E: *headquarters@cpeworld.org*
www.cpeworld.org
The CPE is a professional organization for disaster recovery specialists which provides a forum for members to exchange information and represents the views of members to government agencies and the wider business community.

Federal Emergency Management Agency (FEMA)
500 C Street S.W., Washington, D.C., 20472
T: +1 800 621 3362
www.fema.gov
An independent agency of the federal government of the United States, FEMA was founded in 1979, but can trace its origins back to the Congressional Act of 1803. The mission of the agency is to reduce loss of life and property and to protect the national infrastructure from all types of hazard through an emergency management program that includes preparation, mitigation, response, and recovery.

Europe
Emergency Planning Society
The Media Centre, Culverhouse Cross, Cardiff, CF6 6XJ, U.K.
T: +44 (0) 845 600 9587
F: +44 (0) 29 2059 0396
www.emergplansoc.org.uk
The Society was formed in 1993 through the

merger of the Emergency Planning Association and the County Emergency Planning Officers Society. Its aims are to foster effective emergency planning and management in the United Kingdom and to promote the professional interests of its members, who include representatives of the emergency services, local and central government, the health services, industry, consultants, and voluntary organizations. It is active in the areas of training, professional development, networking, representation, and publications.

International
Association of Contingency Planners (ACP)
Technical Enterprises, Inc., 7044 S. 13th Street, Oak Creek, Wisconsin, 53154
T: +1 414 768 8000
E: *ACP_Membership@techenterprises.net*
www.acp-international.com
The ACP is a nonprofit trade association for contingency planners, business continuity professionals, and emergency managers. The organization, which began informally in 1983 and was incorporated in 1985, provides an international forum for networking and information exchange. Activities include a branch network, a quarterly newsletter, and an annual international symposium.

Business Continuity Institute (BCI)
10 Southview Park, Marsack Street, Caversham, RG4 5AF, U.K.
T: +44 (0) 870 603 8783
F: +44 (0) 870 603 8761
E: *bci@thebci.org*
www.thebci.org
The BCI is a professional organization founded in 1994 to promote high standards of professional competence and ethics in the provision of business continuity planning and services. It has developed standards of competence, a code of ethics, and an accreditation scheme for continuity practitioners. Additional activities include seminars, conferences, and the Business Continuity Awards. The organization has over 1,100 members in 32 countries.

Disaster Preparedness and Emergency Response Association (DERA)
P.O. Box 280795, Denver, Colorado, 80228
E: *dera@disasters.org*
www.disasters.org
DERA is a nonprofit professional association, established in 1962, whose members include emergency management specialists, government officials, consultants, business managers, volunteers,

researchers, and educators. It sponsors research projects in the field and publishes a newsletter, *DisasterCom*.

DRI International

1400 Eye Street, NW, Suite 1050, Washington D.C., 20005
T: +1 202 962 3979
F: +1 202 962 3939
www.drii.org
Formerly the Disaster Recovery Institute, DRI International was formed in 1988 by a group of professionals in St. Louis, Missouri, who saw a need for education in business continuity. The organization is a nonprofit one; it sets standards of competence for business continuity and has developed a certification program.

Emergency Preparedness for Industry and Commerce Council (EPICC)

9800–140 Street, Surrey, British Columbia, V3T 4M5, Canada
T: +1 604 580 7373
F: +1 604 586 4334
E: *epicc@telus.net*
www.epicc.org
The aim of this organization is to help

businesses and communities prepare to survive disasters through education and representation. It organizes workshops and forums, and publishes a newsletter.

International Association of Emergency Managers (IAEM)

201 Park Washington Court, Falls Church, Virginia, 22046–4527
T: +1 703 538 1795
F: +1 703 241 5603
E: *info@iaem.com*
www.iaem.com
The IAEM is a nonprofit educational organization; it created the Certified Emergency Manager program to maintain professional standards in emergency management. Members receive a monthly newsletter and can participate in Internet discussion groups.

Survive International

Lloyd's Avenue House, 6 Lloyd's Avenue, London, EC3N 3AX, U.K.
T: +44 (0) 20 7265 2030
E: *survive@survive.com*
www.survive.com

Survive is a membership group for business continuity management. Founded in 1989, it aims to raise awareness of the need for and value of effective business continuity management, to encourage excellence in the disaster recovery, contingency planning, and business continuity industry, and to support networking and information sharing within this constituency. Survive publishes a magazine and organizes conferences and training events.

1717

BUSINESS INFORMATION SOURCES

Contracts and Contracting

BOOKS

Business Contracts Kit for Dummies Book/CD-ROM ed.
Richard D. Harroch
New York: Hungry Minds, 2000
330pp ISBN: 0764552368
This kit comprises a book and a CD-ROM providing a reference guide to business contracts and 200 sample documents.

Contract Law 6th ed.
Catherine Elliott, Frances Quinn
Upper Saddle River, New Jersey: Longman, 2005
400pp ISBN: 1405807105
This is a popular student textbook on U.K. contract law. The authors present a clear explanation of the law of contract, and make reference to contemporary cases and topical issues in the media. They also present guidelines on answering typical examination questions, together with more general advice.

Contract Negotiation Handbook 3rd ed.
P. D. V. Marsh
Aldershot, United Kingdom: Gower Publishing, 2001
320pp ISBN: 0566080214
This textbook sets out a structured approach to all stages of contract negotiation. It covers the entire process: preparing to negotiate, the opening and development of negotiations, and the closing and recording of the bargain.

Essentials of Contract Law
Martin A. Frey, Phyllis Hurley Frey, Terry H. Bitting

Albany, New York: Delmar Publishing, 2000
303pp ISBN: 0766821455
This textbook uses a "road map" format to present contract law. It discusses each rule of law first conceptually, then follows with an example and a concrete problem.

MAGAZINES

Contract Management
Emerald Group Publishing Ltd
60/62 Toller Lane, Bradford, West Yorkshire, BD8 9BY, U.K.
T: +44 (0) 1274 777700
F: +44 (0) 1274 785200
www.emeraldinsight.com
This is a monthly publication for government and industry contract managers which is also aimed at other readers such as executives, lawyers, and owners of small businesses. It covers many aspects of government and business contract management, and contains news and features.

INTERNET

Contracting and Organizations Research Initiative (CORI)
http://cori.missouri.edu
CORI is a research initiative at the University of Missouri. Its mission is to improve understanding of how the economic system works by facilitating empirical research on contracting and organizational structure. It has created an extensive collection of contracts that researchers can use, which can be accessed via a free online database.

Where in Federal Contracting?
www.wifcon.com
This nonprofit site is a free resource to help individuals and businesses find information about such areas of interest as federal assistance sites, associations, grants and cooperative agreements, contracting laws, courts and boards of contract appeals, and current legislation.

ORGANIZATIONS

USA
National Contract Management Association (NCMA)
8260 Greensboro Drive, Suite 200, McLean, Virginia, 22102
T: +1 571 382 0082
F: +1 703 448 0939
E: *info@ncmahq.org*
www.ncmahq.org
Formed in 1959, the NCMA aims to foster the professional growth and educational advancement of contract managers in order to promote business excellence. It is a professional society with individual members. It includes the Contract Management Institute, a nonprofit foundation set up in 1991 to extend NCMA's education and research activities.

FOR MORE INFORMATION
- Conditions of Employment (pp. 1708–1709)
- ✔ Deciding Whether to Outsource (pp. 542–543)
- Employment Law (pp. 1743–1744)
- Outsourcing (p. 1851)

1718

BUSINESS INFORMATION SOURCES

Corporate Culture

BOOKS

Absolute Honesty: Building a Corporate Culture that Values Straight Talk and Rewards Integrity

Larry Johnson, Bob Phillips
New York: AMACOM, 2003
304pp ISBN: 0814407811
This book starts out from the belief that honesty can produce economic as well as moral rewards, in terms of improved productivity, competitive advantage, morale, and public trust. It asserts the need to reestablish a culture of openness and truth in communication methods, grounded in absolute honesty, setting out a framework of six laws of absolute honesty and gives advice on implementing them within an ethical infrastructure.

Balancing Individual and Organizational Values: Walking the Tightrope to Success

Ken Hultman, Bill Gellermann
San Francisco, California: Jossey-Bass/ Pfeiffer, 2002
240pp ISBN: 0787957208
This book is designed to help organization development practitioners create the conditions for organizational effectiveness by balancing individual and organizational values. It explores the nature and importance of beliefs, values, and norms and their relationship with behavior, and presents the Motivational System Model, a tool which can be used with individuals, teams, and organizations.

Built to Last: Successful Habits of Visionary Companies

Jim Collins, Jerry I. Porras
New York: HarperCollins, 2004
368pp ISBN: 0060566108
This book draws upon a six-year research project at the Stanford University Graduate School of Business, in which 18 truly exceptional and long-lasting companies were examined in depth to see what makes them so successful. It highlights factors such as their flexibility, ideology, and strong purpose. The authors then give practical guidance to those who would like to build similar landmark companies.

Business Across Cultures

Fons Trompenaars, Peter Wooliams
Chichester, United Kingdom: Capstone, 2003
368pp (Culture for Business)
ISBN: 1841124745

Geared towards companies or individuals working with those from other cultures, this book is a useful overview of key issues in cross-cultural business. Accessible and engaging, it sets out to show readers how everyone working in or with a company in this situation can benefit from it.

Corporate Culture and Performance

John P. Kotter, James L. Heskett
New York: Free Press, 1992
214pp ISBN: 0029184673
The authors describe their research into the effects of corporate culture on economic performance in international companies. They challenge the belief that strong corporate cultures automatically create excellent business performance, arguing instead for an "adaptive" culture that takes into account the interests of stakeholders such as customers and employees to produce better results. Case studies are included.

Corporate Culture Survival Guide

Edgar H. Schein
San Francisco, California: Jossey-Bass, 1999
224pp ISBN: 0787946990
This book provides practical advice for for front-line managers and change agents. It examines business on three levels: behaviours, values, and shared assumptions. It shows how corporations can assess their own atmosphere to determine if they have the right culture for their product and organizational structure and then proceed to make real changes.

Creating the Innovation Culture: Leveraging Visionaries, Dissenters and other Useful Troublemakers in Your Organization

Frances Horibe
Hoboken, New Jersey: Wiley, 2001
256pp ISBN: 0471646288
This book offers practical strategies for managing creative people or dissenters and for developing processes and mechanisms to support and sustain innovation within the organization. The author emphasizes the distinction between healthy dissent and undesirable troublemaking.

Cultures and Organizations: Software for the Mind 2nd ed.

Geert Hofstede, Gert Jan Hofstede
Maidenhead, United Kingdom: McGraw-Hill, 2004
300pp ISBN: 0071439595

The book, first published in 1991, aims to give practicing managers and students an understanding of cultural differences which will assist them in intercultural communication and cooperation in business and society. It examines the nature of culture and cultural differences and considers their implications.

Diagnosing and Changing Organizational Culture: Based on the Competing Values Framework

Kim S. Cameron, Robert E. Quinn
Cambridge, Massachusetts: Longman, 1998
221pp ISBN: 0201338718
Written with the aim of helping managers, change agents, and scholars to understand and facilitate cultural and behavioral change within organizations, this book provides a theoretical framework for organizational culture, validated instruments for diagnosing it, and a systematic methodology for changing it.

Evolve! Succeeding in the Digital Culture of Tomorrow

Rosabeth Moss Kanter
Boston, Massachusetts: Harvard Business School Press, 2001
304pp ISBN: 1578514398
An exploration of "e-culture"—a new way of living and working that will transform every aspect of today's organizations—this book is for anyone who wants to realize the potential and avoid the pitfalls of the Internet age. It draws on over 300 interviews and a global-scale company survey to provide a framework for adopting the core principles of e-culture.

Harvard Business Review on Culture and Change

Boston, Massachusetts: Harvard Business School Press, 2002
179pp (Harvard Business Review Paperbacks)
ISBN: 1578518369
This text brings together a collection of articles from Harvard Business Review. It provides insights into the confusing and challenging process of changing workplace culture. The different authors examine a range of issues, including why people resist change on both the individual and corporate level and how passive aversion to cultural problems affects company performance, and provide an actionable framework for transforming corporate culture.

1719

BUSINESS INFORMATION SOURCES

"The decision to do that extra bit must be embedded in the company's culture."

Tom Farmer

The Naked Corporation: How the Age of Transparency Will Revolutionize Business
Don Tapscott, David Ticoll
New York: Free Press, 2003
352pp ISBN: 0743246500
Transparency is a new global business issue and one of the forces of change that is revolutionizing the way business is done. Drawing on case studies such as Chiquita and Shell, the authors of this text offer a way to lead in and manage transparency as a new opportunity for business, rather than simply reacting to its requirements. The nature of transparency is discussed and the subject is explored in the contexts of the employee, business partner, customer, community, and owner. The text also considers the power of openness and leadership issues.

The New Corporate Cultures: Revitalizing the Workplace after Downsizing, Mergers, and Reengineering
Terrence E. Deal, Allan A. Kennedy
Cambridge, Massachusetts: Perseus, 2000
312pp ISBN: 0738203807
This book examines how changes brought about by economic forces and management trends, such as downsizing, outsourcing, new technology, and globalization, have affected company cultures. The authors consider how companies can approach the task of rebuilding cohesive organizational cultures for greater effectiveness following the fragmentation that many have experienced.

Organizational Culture and Leadership 3rd ed.
Edgar H. Schein
San Francisco, California: Jossey-Bass, 2004
464pp ISBN: 0787968455
This third edition of a classic work on the dynamics of organizational culture draws on contemporary research to show how leaders can apply the principles of culture change in order to achieve organizational goals.

Organizational Culture: Mapping the Terrain
Joanne Martin
Thousand Oaks, California: Sage Publications, 2002
400pp ISBN: 0803972954
An elegant introduction to a complex topic, this book describes the main relevant theories and definitions of the subject, and the disputes that have arisen concerning them. The various methods

that have evolved for studying the subject, and the ways in which these studies might develop, are also discussed. Examples and case studies are included.

Riding the Waves of Culture: Understanding Cultural Diversity in Business 2nd ed.
Fons Trompenaars,
Charles Hampden-Turner
New York: McGraw-Hill, 1997
416pp ISBN: 0786311258
This book is written by leading authorities on cultural diversity, and based on research and experience gained in cross-cultural training programs in 18 countries. The authors contest the view that there is one best way of managing and attempt to give readers a better understanding of their own business culture. The cultural dilemmas facing international organizations are also examined.

Understanding Organizational Culture
Mats Alvesson
Thousand Oaks, California: Sage Publications, 2002
224pp ISBN: 0761970061
This text examines the concept of culture from various perspectives, and discusses key research issues. It provides a new framework for understanding organizational culture and describes the range of advances in the area. Illustrative examples are included.

MAGAZINES
Cross Cultural Management
ISSN: 1352–7606
Emerald
44 Brattle Street, 4th Floor, Cambridge, Massachusetts, 02138
T: +1 888 622 0075
F: +1 617 354 6875
www.emeraldinsight.com
This quarterly journal focuses on all aspects of cross-cultural relationships at work.

International Journal of Cross-cultural Management
ISSN: 1470–5958
Sage Publications
1 Oliver's Yard, 55 City Road, London, EC1Y 1SP, U.K.
T: +44 (0) 20 7324 8500
F: +44 (0) 20 7324 8600
www.sagepub.co.uk
Published three times a year, this is an academic journal that acts as a medium for

the dissemination of research on the cross-cultural aspects of management, work, and organization. It promotes understanding of the role of culture in management theory and practice.

Organization Studies
ISSN: 0170–8406
Walter de Gruyter, Inc.
200 Saw Mill River Road, Hawthorne, New York, 10532
T: +1 914 747 0110
F: +1 914 747 1326
www.degruyter.de/journals/os
An international multidisciplinary journal devoted to the study of organizations, organizing, and the organized in and between societies.

INTERNET
Business.com
www.business.com
The section on "Management Theory" under the "Management" tab in the business directory includes links to sites covering leading writers and researchers in the field of organizational development theory.

Culture in the Workplace Questionnaire
www.itapintl.com
This questionnaire is based on the work of Geert Hofstede and is provided by ITAP International, a consulting company offering crosscultural services for business.

Intermundo
www.intermundo.net
This is the site for an online journal of intercultural communication.

Official Ed Schein Website
http://web.mit.edu/scheine/www/home.html
The site gives information about publications and presentations by Edgar Schein.

Onepine
www.onepine.info
Theories and works of major thinkers are examined under the "People & Theories" option, which users can find when they click through on "Site contents."

FOR MORE INFORMATION
☆ Keeping Control in Nonhierarchical Organizations (pp. 231–232)
☆ Making Cultures Behave (pp. 51–52)

"We need a can-do, vibrant, innovation-driven culture. Not wearing a tie is just a snippet of that."
Paul Walsh

Corporate Strategy

BOOKS

The Alchemy of Growth: Practical Insights for Building the Enduring Enterprise
Muhrdad Baghai, Stephen Coley
Cambridge, Massachusetts: Perseus Books Group, 1999
250pp ISBN: 0738201006
Using a range of real examples of companies that have turned themselves around, this is a comprehensive guide on how to maintain a business by means of sustainable growth. The book cites three points that must be addressed if a business is to keep on growing: entrepreneurial ventures; the very basics of a particular business; and the ideas that are most likely to bring profits.

The Art of the Long View: Planning for the Future in an Uncertain World
Peter Schwartz
New York: Wiley, 1996
288pp ISBN: 0385267320
The author gives practical guidance on the use of scenarios in business, drawn from his experience in a range of contexts from a small-business start-up to multinational companies and government institutions. The history of scenario planning, in particular the pioneering work of Pierre Wack at Royal Dutch/Shell, is reviewed, and its continuing relevance explained.

Business Strategy: A Guide to Effective Decision Making
Jeremy Kourdi
London: Economist Books, 2003
256pp ISBN: 1861974590
This practical guide provides help for those involved in making strategic decisions. The text also examines the decision making process in detail. The forces shaping major decisions, including social, cultural, and commercial, are explained, and various rational and intuitive frameworks are introduced. Practical insights and techniques for handling decisions are also outlined.

Competing for the Future
Gary Hamel, C. K. Prahalad
Boston, Massachusetts: Harvard Business School Press, 1996
352pp ISBN: 0875847161
In this book the authors put forward a radically new approach to strategy. They introduce the concept of organizational core competencies, suggesting that organizations should examine what it is they do better than others. They particularly highlight the danger of losing competitive advantage by sticking with past achievements, and the importance of unleashing the corporate imagination and developing a dynamic view of the future.

Competitive Strategy: Techniques for Analyzing Industries and Competitors
Michael E. Porter
New York: Free Press, 1998
432pp ISBN: 0684841487
This work, researched by Porter during the 1970s, is regarded as a management classic and has shaped and influenced mainstream thinking on competition and strategy. The author argues that in order to retain competitive capability companies need to choose from three generic strategies (cost leadership, differentiation, and focus), which are driven by five competitive forces (customers, suppliers, the threat of similar products, existing competition, and the threat of new market entrants).

Contemporary Strategy Analysis: Concepts, Techniques, Applications 5th ed.
Robert M. Grant
Cambridge, Massachusetts: Blackwell Publishing, 2004
560pp ISBN: 1405119993
This text reflects current academic thinking and management practice and presents the tools required to formulate and implement strategies. In this edition, extra coverage is given to value creation in electronic commerce, the new economy, complexity and self-organization, and strategic innovation.

The Discipline of Market Leaders: Choose Your Customers, Narrow Your Focus, Dominate Your Market
Michael Treacy, Fred Wiersema
Cambridge, Massachusetts: Perseus, 1997
224pp ISBN: 0201407191
This book reveals how altering and increasing the value expectations of your customers can cause severe problems for those who are trying to compete with you. Several examples of companies who are pursuing such a policy are given, including Intel, Walmart, Charles Schwab, and Southwest Airlines.

Essentials of Strategic Management 3rd ed.
J. David Hunger, Thomas L. Wheelen
Harlow, United Kingdom: Pearson Education, 2003
192pp ISBN: 0131227882
This text provides the essentials of the most important concepts and techniques in strategic management. The topics covered by the authors are: basics of strategic management; corporate governance and social responsibility; environmental scanning and industry analysis; internal scanning; strategy formulation; strategy implementation; evaluation and control; and suggestions for analysis.

Every Business Is a Growth Business
Noel M. Tichy, R. Charan
Hoboken, New Jersey: Wiley, 2000
352pp ISBN: 0812933052
In this title, the authors outline how to turn an ordinary company into one that grows. The book gives two main pointers for successful growth; first, to redefine your market and increase demand by seeing things from your customers' point of view, and, second, to reinvigorate the corporate culture to enable growth. The authors give many real-life examples to support these central points.

Exploring Corporate Strategy 7th ed.
Gerry Johnson, Kevan Scholes
Upper Saddle River, New Jersey: Prentice Hall, 2005
1072pp (Exploring Corporate Strategy)
ISBN: 0273687344
This classic textbook provides an overview of the principles and practice of corporate strategy in a variety of contexts. The areas of strategic analysis, resource allocation, strategic choice, strategy implementation, and managing strategic change are covered. Recent developments in the field of strategy, including core competence knowledge and learning, have been incorporated into the seventh edition, which also includes a list of recommended key reading and work assignments for students.

1721

BUSINESS INFORMATION SOURCES

"Strategic planning can neither provide creativity nor deal with it when it emerges by other means."

Henry Mintzberg

Financial Times Guide to Strategy 2nd ed.

Richard Koch

Upper Saddle River, New Jersey: Financial Times Prentice Hall, 2000
288pp ISBN: 027365022X

This title offers executives the help needed to build a strategic structure for a business, to organise a marketplace, and to create a business model. The book also reveals how strategy can help to raise profits and analyses the views on strategic thinking that have emerged over the last 40 years.

Good to Great: Why Some Companies Make the Leap . . . and Others Don't

Jim Collins

London: Random House Business Books, 2001
320pp ISBN: 0066620996

Written by one of the world's bestselling business writers and based on extensive research of over 1,000 businesses, this book focuses on eleven of the world's leading corporations and analyzes their successes. Concluding that an excellent corporate culture is the way forward, this book offers advice and useful tactics for all aspiring business builders.

The Mind of the Strategist

Kenichi Ohmae

New York: McGraw-Hill, 1991
304pp ISBN: 0070479046

This work, first published in Japan in 1975, was instrumental in introducing the Japanese approach to strategic thinking to the West during the early 1980s and laid the foundation for more radical approaches to management thinking, including Gary Hamel's work on strategy innovation. The author analyzes strategy in terms of the strategic triangle—corporation, customer, and competition—and sees vision and dynamic leadership as key features of successful business strategy.

On the Fly: Executive Strategy in a Changing World

Stephen J. Wall

Hoboken, New Jersey: Wiley, 2004
240pp ISBN: 0471464848

Businesses operate in a volatile external environment where rapid change is the norm, and it is always difficult for them to formulate a clear sense of sustained strategic direction for the future. While emphasizing the case for strong corporate identity grounded in strategic focus, this book offers a model for combining a flexible response to external factors with the analytical tools of strategic planning.

The Portable MBA in Strategy 2nd ed.

Liam Fahey, Robert M. Randall

Hoboken, New Jersey: Wiley, 2000
414pp ISBN: 0471197084

This comprehensive guide features contributions from internationally recognized leaders in strategic thought and practice. Topics covered include: strategic management practices; analysis of customers, markets, and competitors; identification and assessment of strategic alternatives; and threats and opportunities facing business.

The Rise and Fall of Strategic Planning

Henry Mintzberg

New York: Free Press, 1994
464pp ISBN: 0029216052

Mintzberg traces the history of strategic planning since the 1960s and gives his own perspective on past failures. The various planning models are reviewed and analyzed, the pitfalls identified, and a new approach is put forward.

Strategic Management and Organisational Dynamics: The Challenge of Complexity 4th ed.

Ralph D. Stacey

Upper Saddle River, New Jersey: Financial Times Prentice Hall, 2003
496pp ISBN: 0273658980

The author of this work takes a radically different approach to strategic management. He is concerned with unpredictability and the limitations of control, factors that militate against the rational models of planning and control presented by other authors. The book explores strategy and organizational dynamics, and includes European case studies.

The Strategy-focused Organization: How Balanced Scorecard Companies Thrive in the New Business Environment

Robert S. Kaplan, David P. Norton

Boston, Massachusetts: Harvard Business School Press, 2000
416pp ISBN: 1578512506

The originators of the balanced scorecard examine how 20 companies have implemented and adapted the model and draw out five principles for strategy-focused organizations.

Strategy Process: Concepts, Contexts and Cases 4th ed.

Henry Mintzberg, James Brian Quinn

Upper Saddle River, New Jersey: Prentice Hall, 2002
1040pp ISBN: 027365120X

This book is designed to support the teaching and practice of strategy formulation. A collection of readings covers the concepts and contexts of strategy and is supplemented by U.S. and international case studies. Discussion questions for students are included.

Strategy Safari: A Guided Tour through the Wilds of Strategic Management

Henry Mintzberg, Bruce Ahlstrand, Joseph Lampel

New York: Simon & Schuster, 1998
304pp ISBN: 0684847434

This book provides a thorough critique of the contributions and limitations of ten different approaches to strategic planning. These include such schools of thought as entrepreneurial, cognitive, cultural, and environmental. The book then goes on to show how these alternative schools can be merged and shaped to produce one coherent approach to strategy formation.

MAGAZINES

Business Strategy Review

ISSN: 0955–6419
Blackwell Publishing
350 Main Street, Malden, Massachusetts, 02148
T: +1 781 388 8200
F: +1 781 388 8232
www.blackwellpublishing.com

Business Strategy Review is a quarterly journal published on behalf of the London Business School. It includes articles on strategic issues relevant to modern business, taking a multi-disciplinary approach, and aiming for accessibility to a wide audience, including students and academics.

Harvard Business Review

ISSN: 0017–8012
Harvard Business School Press
60 Harvard Way, Boston, Massachusetts, 02163
T: +1 800 988 0886
F: +1 617 783 7555
www.hbr.org

HBR is a leading magazine for business leaders and senior executives, which emphasizes current best practice and the application of leading-edge research to business problems. Coverage is wide-ranging with a strong focus on strategy. Each issue includes feature articles written by experts and an interview with a business leader.

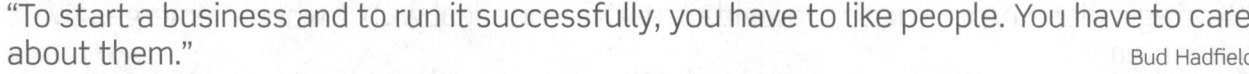
"To start a business and to run it successfully, you have to like people. You have to care about them."

Bud Hadfield

Journal of Business Strategy

ISSN: 0275–6668

EC Media Group, Thomson Financial

Corporate Communications, 195 Broadway, New York, 10007

T: +1 642 822 2000

www.ecmediagroup.com

This is a bimonthly magazine featuring practical articles on current business topics written by senior executives and strategists.

Long Range Planning

ISSN: 0024–6301

Elsevier Science

Customer Service Department, 6277 Sea Harbor Drive, Orlando, Florida, 32887–4800

T: +1 877 839 7126 or +1 407 345 4020

F: +1 407 363 1354

www.elsevier.com

LRP, published in association with the Strategic Planning Society and the European Strategic Planning Federation, is a leading international journal in the field of strategic management. Aimed at senior managers, administrators, and academics, it includes articles from academics and practitioners.

MIT Sloan Management Review

ISSN: 1532–9194

MIT Sloan School of Management

77 Massachusetts Avenue, Cambridge, Massachusetts, 02139–4307

T: +1 617 253 7170

F: +1 617 258 9739

www.sloanreview.mit.edu

Founded in 1959, this quarterly publication aims to provide senior managers with the best of current management theory and practice. It has a strong focus on corporate strategy and leadership.

Strategic Change

ISSN: 1086–1718

Wiley

111 River St, Hoboken, New Jersey, 07030–5774

T: +1 201 748 6000

F: +1 212 850 6021

www.wiley.com

Eight issues of *Strategic Change* are published annually. The journal aims to provide authoritative and topical research papers addressing the strategic management of change and its implementation in an increasingly globalized business environment.

Strategic Management Journal

ISSN: 0143–2095

Wiley

111 River St, Hoboken, New Jersey, 07030–5774

T: +1 201 748 6000

F: +1 212 850 6021

www.wiley.com

SMJ is a monthly journal devoted to the theory and practice of strategic management. It is aimed at academics and practicing managers and has a strong emphasis on research.

INTERNET

Business.com Strategic Planning

www.business.com

The strategic planning section (in the business directory) under "Management" includes a comprehensive collection of links to Web sites, associations, and publications.

Knowledge@Wharton

http://knowledge.wharton.upenn.edu

The section on Strategic Management on this site, sponsored by the Wharton School at the University of Pennsylvania, includes articles and useful links.

Strategic Management Club Online

www.strategyclub.com

This Web site, developed by Dr. Fred David for graduate and undergraduate students, provides links, templates, a discussion forum, and a chat facility.

ORGANIZATIONS
USA

Association for Strategic Planning

12021 Wilshire Boulevard, Suite 286, Los Angeles, California, 90025–1200

T: +1 877 816 2080

F: +1 323 954 0507

E: *executivedirector@strategyplus.org*

www.strategyplus.org

This professional association aims to promote effective strategic thinking, planning, and action in public and private organizations.

Europe

Strategic Planning Society (SPS)

Buxton House, 7 Highbury Hill, London, N5 1SU, U.K.

T: +44 (0) 845 056 3663

F: +44 (0) 870 751 8216

E: *membership@sps.org.uk*

www.sps.org.uk

The SPS is a professional organization, founded in 1967, which aims to promote knowledge and understanding of strategic management through publications, training events, conferences, and special interest groups.

International

Global Business Network (GBN)

5900-X Hollis Street, Emeryville, California, 94608

T: +1 510 547 6822

F: +1 510 547 8510

E: *info@gbn.com*

www.gbn.com

The GBN was founded in 1987 by Peter Schwartz, Jay Ogilvy, Napier Collyns, and Stewart Brand, with the collaboration of European colleagues Kees van der Heijden, Arie de Geus, and Bo Ekman. The founders' aim was to develop a worldwide community of individual members and subscribing organizations interested in increasing their understanding of change in the business environment and in developing ideas and tools for planning and innovation. The organization has a strong focus on the use of scenarios.

Strategic Management Society (SMS)

Purdue University, Krannert Center, 425 West State Street, West Lafayette, Indiana, 47907–2056

T: +1 765 494 6984

F: +1 765 494 1533

E: *sms@exchange.purdue.edu*

www.smsweb.org

The Strategic Management Society is an international organization founded in 1981 with members in more than 50 countries. It focuses on the development and dissemination of insights into strategic management, combining the contributions of practitioners and academics. It holds an international conference and smaller special interest conferences annually, and supports publications such as the *Strategic Management Journal* and a book series.

Strategos Institute

820 West Jackson Blvd, Suite 450, Chicago, Illinois, 60607

T: +1 312 655 0826

F: +1 312 655 8334

E: *contact@strategos.com*

http://institute.strategos.com

The Strategos Institute is a consortium of world-class companies working on the development of tools, processes, and metrics for strategy innovation. Business practitioners, consultants, and business school professors are involved, and the writer and thinker Gary Hamel is the chairman.

> ### FOR MORE INFORMATION
>
> ✔ Developing a Strategy for World-Class Business (pp. 514–515)
> ✔ Strategic Planning (pp. 536–537)

1723

BUSINESS INFORMATION SOURCES

"For many businesses, the Internet is still a technology in search of a strategy."

Mary J. Cronin

Creating a Résumé

BUSINESS INFORMATION SOURCES

BOOKS

Global Résumé and CV Guide

Mary Anne Thompson
Hoboken, New Jersey: Wiley, 2000
288pp ISBN: 0471380768
This international approach will be of interest to managers seeking to work overseas and to multinational organizations. Experts from over 40 countries provide cultural dos and don'ts, information on business practices, and job hunting tips that will help create a résumé tailored to the specific requirements of a target country. Standard coverage for each country includes a country overview, résumé specifics, résumé presentation, cover letters, job-information sources, Web sites, and interview advice.

I Don't Know What I Want, But I Know It's Not This: A Step-by-step Guide to Finding Gratifying Work

Julie Jansen
New York: Penguin USA, 2003
288pp ISBN: 0142002488
A useful resource for anyone unhappy at work, this book is full of exercises to assess the reader's personality and skills and will help people understand their present situation and come up with ways to find the job or career they really want to embark on.

The Perfect Cover Letter 3rd ed.

Richard H. Beatty
Hoboken, New Jersey: Wiley, 2004
224pp ISBN: 047147374X
The Perfect Cover Letter provides an introduction to the purpose of cover letters and describes how employers read and use them. Guidance is given on how to write an effective cover letter for a number of different situations. Example letters are included.

The Résumé Handbook 4th ed.

Arthur D. Rosenberg, David Hizer
Holbrook, Massachusetts: Adams Media Corporation, 2003
160pp ISBN: 1580628540
This is a concise guide to the principles of writing an effective résumé. It includes examples of cover letters and both well-written and poorly written résumés. Such examples are used to highlight important changes in today's job market.

Résumé Kit 5th ed.

Richard H. Beatty
Hoboken, New Jersey: Wiley, 2003

368pp ISBN: 0471449261
The author adopts a step-by-step workbook approach that identifies 12 myths of résumé writing. The "electronic résumé" is covered, complete with instructions on the recommended format for online databases. There are over 80 sample résumés and cover letters to cater for a wide range of jobs and a section on jobhunting techniques for the information age, which includes listings and descriptions of the "top 20" career sites on the Web.

Résumés That Knock 'Em Dead 6th ed.

Martin Yate
Holbrook, Massachusetts: Adams Media Corporation, 2004
320pp ISBN: 159337108X
A comprehensive guide to creating résumés designed to make a job applicant stand out from all the other applicants. The contents include types of résumés and how to choose the right format for your field, the ingredients for a basic résumé, creating a scannable résumé for electronic databases, and examples of successful résumés for a variety of careers.

What Color Is Your Parachute? A Practical Manual for Job-hunters and Career-changers

Richard Nelson Bolles
Berkeley, California: Ten Speed Press, 2005
432pp ISBN: 1580087272
Revised and updated annually, this edition of the classic job-hunting reference guide works in conjunction with its Web site. The book covers areas such as Internet job hunting, the alternative job-hunting approach, dealing with rejection, interviews, negotiating a salary, and choosing a career counselor.

INTERNET

The CV-Index Directory
www.cvindex.com
The CV-Index Directory is a searchable directory of CVs and résumés, which covers every major profession and provides listings in several countries.

GetMYonlineCV.com
www.getmyonlinecv.com
This site focuses on giving you a place and a means to create your online CV. It offers numerous tips and links to other sites for more information and services (paid and/or free). Members of this site have their own personal URL to showcase their résumé.

JobHuntersBible.com: Job Hunting Online
www.jobhuntersbible.com
Designed as a companion to the book *What Color Is Your Parachute?*, this Web site includes comprehensive links to information on such topics as building a résumé, polishing the quality of a résumé, and posting a résumé online.

Monster Career Center
www.monster.com
Monster.Com provides online job-searching services, including job postings and company information. Its Résumé Center is available to subscribers and offers a variety of services for job seekers, including résumé writing information such as the elements of a good résumé, how to address potential problem areas such as lack of experience, and career-specific résumés.

Résumé.com
www.resume.com
This site offers samples of résumés and services for preparing your résumé (with a link to products and prices). Contact can be made via e-mail or phone.

Rebecca Smith's eRésumés & Resources
www.eresumes.com
Subtitled the "Ultimate Online eRésumé Guide for Winners," Rebecca Smith's site provides step-by-step advice on how to convert paper-based résumés for the Web. There is a gallery of online résumés and a book list, as well as links to job search and résumé sites. The site offers free and fee-based material.

Workthing.com
www.workthing.com
This site offers articles and advice on résumés, interviews, and job hunting, tailored to different industry sectors. It also provides access to a database of on- and offline courses. The Career Advice section offers a wide variety of high-quality advice for all jobseekers, whether they are looking for their first job or looking for a new senior management role.

FOR MORE INFORMATION

☆ Taking Charge of Your Career (pp. 412–413)

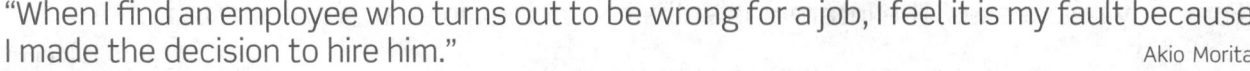
"When I find an employee who turns out to be wrong for a job, I feel it is my fault because I made the decision to hire him."

Akio Morita

Customer Relations/Customer Service

BOOKS

Chief Customer Officer : Getting Past Lip Service to Passionate Action

Jeanne Bliss
San Francisco, California: Jossey-Bass, 2006
320pp ISBN: 0787980943
Based on the author's own experience at leading international firms, this book explains what companies need to do to give their customers exactly what they want. It offers advice and strategies on how to improve communication, overcome inertia, and work out what organizational challenges need to be made to build exceptional customers relationships.

Customer Relationship Management: A Strategic Imperative in the World of E-Business

Stanley A. Brown, ed.
Hoboken, New Jersey: Wiley, 2000
345pp ISBN: 0471644099
This book asserts that CRM is the key to competitive advantage. It describes the leading trends and best practices in CRM, the successes and failures of organizations around the globe that have implemented it, the 20 key steps in its implementation, and how to define strategies for customers, channels, and products. Case studies are included.

Customer Relationship Management: How to Turn a Good Business into a Great One!

Graham Roberts-Phelps
Hoboken, New Jersey: Wiley, 2001
230pp ISBN: 185418119X
This book sets out the essential features of CRM. It examines why customers defect and the economics of customer care, and shows how to define and achieve customer service excellence, manage for customer satisfaction, develop customer-focused selling and marketing skills, and connect with customers in the digital age. It sums everything up in ten keys to outstanding customer service.

Customer Service: A Practical Approach 3rd ed.

Elaine K. Harris
Upper Saddle River, New Jersey: Prentice Hall, 2002
304pp ISBN: 0130978531

Harris takes a practical approach to explaining the dynamics of customer service, covering areas such as barriers to customer service, problem solving, strategy, empowerment, and communications. She also has chapters on coping with challenging customers, motivation, leadership, and customer retention, and includes self-development exercises.

Discovering the Soul of Service

Leonard L. Berry
New York: Free Press, 1999
269pp ISBN: 0684845113
This book is based on a study of 14 mature, highly successful service companies. It presents the concept that the single most important factor in building a lasting service business is not a matter of business practice know-how, but of humane values.

Harvard Business Review on Customer Relationship Management

various authors
Boston, Massachusetts: Harvard Business School Press, 2002
224pp (Harvard Business Review Paperbacks) ISBN: 1578516994
In this anthology of eight articles the focus is on building a strong, positive customer relationship. Partnering and personalizing the marketing relationship, branding, and providing outstanding customer service and support are outlined as the means to establishing a relationship that fosters customer loyalty.

How to Measure Customer Satisfaction 2nd ed.

Nigel Hill, John Brierley, Rob MacDougall
Aldershot, United Kingdom: Gower Publishing, 2003
160pp ISBN: 056608595X
The authors take you through the whole process of measuring customer satisfaction. Starting with setting objectives and project planning, they go on to deal with everything involved in successful exploratory research—questionnaire design, introducing the survey, maximizing response rates, analyzing the results, and benchmarking your performance—that will assist you in ensuring the continued satisfaction, delight, and loyalty of your customers.

The Life Belt: The Definitive Guide to Managing Customer Retention

John A. Murphy
Hoboken, New Jersey: Wiley, 2001
304pp ISBN: 0471498181
Research provides evidence that the most sustainable levels of customer loyalty and retention are achieved through consistent excellence in service delivery. This book introduces the Customer Service Integration Framework—the lifebelt—based on four years of research. The author suggests that, while many organizations have some good practices in place, most appear to lack synchronization. He gives a detailed case study of N. G. Bailey and Co. to illustrate his argument.

Loyalty.com: Customer Relationship Management in the New Era of Internet Marketing

Frederick Newell
Maidenhead, United Kingdom: McGraw-Hill, 2002
320pp ISBN: 007138782X
This book outlines what the new technology means for marketers in every field and provides techniques for creating and implementing CRM strategies. It shows how to give customers what they want to buy, as opposed to what you want to sell them, and how to win customer share, as opposed to market share.

The Loyalty Effect

Frederick F. Reichheld
Boston, Massachusetts: Harvard Business School Press, 2001
352pp ISBN: 1578516870
Revealed in this book are the secrets of successful companies which base their business strategies on loyal relationships, with employees, investors, and customers. It demonstrates the measurable results that strong loyalties have on corporate profits.

Loyalty Rules! How Today's Leaders Build Lasting Relationships

Frederick F. Reichheld
Boston, Massachusetts: Harvard Business School Press, 2003
240pp ISBN: 1591393248
Based on extensive research into companies from online start-ups to established institutions, this book looks at the issue of

1725

"A manufacturer is not through with his customer when a sale is completed. He has then only started with his customer."

Henry Ford

loyalty in industry. It is a practical guidebook, showing how employee and customer loyalty is necessary for lasting success.

Monitoring, Measuring, & Managing Customer Service
Gary S. Goodman
San Francisco, California: Jossey-Bass, 2000
240pp (Jossey-Bass Business and Management)
ISBN: 0787951390
Goodman explains how to produce great customer service consistently and identifies the 18 communication factors that promote it. He deals with monitoring customer service, measuring the performance of representatives, team leaders, supervisors, and managers, recruiting, motivating and retaining quality customer service staff, and making a corporate commitment to first-class customer care.

On Great Service: A Framework for Action
Leonard L. Berry
New York: Free Press, 1995
292pp ISBN: 0029185556
This book offers a dynamic framework for improving service quality, based on the author's on-site observations in a two-year study of dozens of companies of all sizes renowned for their service excellence. It contains a number of compelling examples of the strategies and practices that these companies implement in delivering great service.

Relationship Marketing: Successful Strategies for the Age of the Customer
Regis McKenna
Cambridge, Massachusetts: Perseus, 1993
242pp ISBN: 0201622408
This book offers advice to organizations on how to dominate and control the market through the construction of significant relationships with customers.

The Service Profit Chain
James L. Heskett, W. Earl Sasser, Jr., Leonard A. Schlesinger
New York: Free Press, 1997
320pp ISBN: 0684832569
The authors provide service industry business leaders with practical guidelines on how to manage, market, hire, and deliver services and how to assess results. They use detailed case studies to demonstrate how

successful companies already use these principles.

Total Relationship Marketing: Rethinking Marketing Management 2nd ed.
Evert Gummesson
Woburn, Massachusetts: Butterworth-Heinemann, 2002
320pp ISBN: 0750654074
As an alternative to the 4Ps of traditional marketing management (product, price, promotion, and place), the author offers 30 relationships, the 30Rs, that are fundamental to the marketing activities of every business. He covers the key relationships in which businesses are involved, from those with customers and competitors to those with government and the media.

MAGAZINES
Managing Service Quality
ISSN: 0960-4529
Emerald
60/62 Toller Lane, Bradford, West Yorkshire, BD8 9BY, U.K.
T: +44 (0) 1274 777 700
F: +44 (0) 1274 785 200
www.emeraldinsight.com
This magazine aims to bring ideas, case studies, reviews, and techniques primarily to working managers but also to the scholars and researchers who assist them in helping organizations to improve the quality of their service.

INTERNET
CRM guru
www.crmguru.com
This site carries information on customer relationship management and the CRM industry, and provides a discussion forum and e-mail newsletter. Registration is required.

crmindustry
www.crmindustry.com
This free service provides a weekly e-newsletter, industry research, a resource center, and links to other sites.

eCustomerServiceWorld
www.ecustomerserviceworld.com
Sponsored by an international membership organization, the site offers free news, articles, surveys and results, conference

information, research articles, and products and services sites.

International Customer Service Association
www.icsa.com
Sponsored by a membership organization, the site offers recent publications, case histories, conference information, merchandise, reports on industry activities, and links to other resources.

ORGANIZATIONS
USA
Customer Care Institute (CCI)
17 Dean Overlook, NW, Atlanta, Georgia, 30318
T: +1 404 352 9291
F: +1 404 355 5059
E: *info@customercare.com*
www.customercare.com
The CCI provides customer care professionals with information, research, advisory services, benchmarking, training, and networking opportunities. In addition, it conducts studies, organizes forums, workshops, and conferences, and offers other programs and services that will enhance the delivery of customer care.

Europe
Institute of Customer Service (ICS)
2 Castle Court, St. Peter's Street, Colchester, Essex, CO1 1EW, U.K.
T: +44 (0) 120 657 1716
F: +44 (0) 120 654 6688
E: *enquiries@icsmail.co.uk*
www.instituteofcustomerservice.com
The Institute of Customer Service was formed in 1997 primarily to help people and organizations raise customer service standards. It is recognized by the U.K. government as the national training organization for customer service.

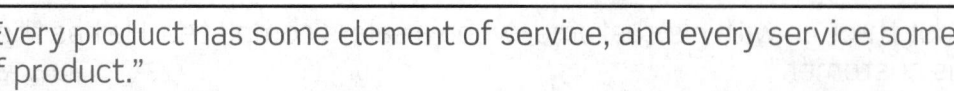
"Every product has some element of service, and every service some element of product."
Aubrey Wilson

Decision Making and Problem Solving

BOOKS

Applied Statistical Decision Theory
Howard Raiffa, Robert Schlaifer
Hoboken, New Jersey: Wiley, 2000
356pp (Wiley Classics Library)
ISBN: 047138349X
This book is aimed at people who are interested in using statistics as a tool in practical decision making under conditions of uncertainty, and who also have the necessary training in mathematics and statistics to employ the relevant analytical techniques. It focuses on experimentation and decision, general theory, extensive-form analysis, and distribution theory.

Creative Problem Solving for Managers 2nd ed.
Tony Proctor
New York: Routledge, 2005
288pp ISBN: 0415345421
This book focuses on the role of creativity and creative thinking in problem solving. It describes a range of methods and techniques including morphological analysis, brainstorming and its variants, and lateral thinking. The text is illustrated with case studies and case histories.

Decision Analysis for Management Judgment 3rd ed.
Paul Goodwin, George Wright
Hoboken, New Jersey: Wiley, 2003
480pp ISBN: 0470861088
This book assumes no prior knowledge of decision analysis, and makes the concept accessible to students, managers, and administrators. Written in a user-friendly textual style, it explains the dangers of unaided decision making and demonstrates a structured process. The 17 chapters that make up the text include an introduction to probability, decision making under uncertainty, decision trees and influence diagrams, risk and uncertainty management, and scenario planning.

Decision Making: An Integrated Approach 2nd ed.
David Jennings, Stuart Wattam
Upper Saddle River, New Jersey: Financial Times Pitman, 1998
364pp ISBN: 0273628593
This textbook is suitable for business studies students. It provides a comprehensive overview of various approaches to decision making, including systems thinking, simulation, model building, and management science techniques. There is also a strong focus on the factors influencing decision making within groups and organizations. Summaries, case study exercises, glossaries of terms, and suggestions for further reading are included.

Essential Managers: Making Decisions
Robert Heller
New York: DK Publishing, 1999
72pp ISBN: 078942889X
This compact resource offers a quick overview of the essentials of effective managerial decision making. Topics include defining decisions, identifying decision-making styles, knowing your corporate culture, analyzing your responsibility, being decisive, identifying issues, and deciding whom to involve in a decision. The book covers both the formal and informal aspects of decision making, and includes practical techniques, checklists, flowcharts, and other illustrations to aid the decision maker.

The Paradox of Choice: Why More Is Less
Barry Schwartz
New York: HarperCollins, 2005
288pp ISBN: 0060005688
Addressing one of the ironies of modern life (namely that our decision-making capabilities are severely hampered by having too much choice), this book is an engaging read. A balm to any reader who has been bewildered by the choices to be made in everyday life and in business, it offers suggestions for ways to whittle down potential outcomes to a more manageable— and less stressful—number.

The Problem Solving Journey: Your Guide for Making Decisions and Getting Results
Christopher W. Hoenig
Cambridge, Massachusetts: Perseus Books Group, 2000
283pp ISBN: 0738202800
This book is a thorough guide to the art of problem-solving that uses examples as varied as NASA and VISA to illustrate how best this can be achieved. Having helped the reader to create a problem-solving profile, the author then presents problem-solving as a journey made up of six stages, each of which needs to be successfully negotiated. The journey culminates in "Delivering the results."

Smart Choices: A Practical Guide to Making Better Decisions
John S. Hammond, Ralph L. Keeney, Howard Raiffa
Boston, Massachusetts: Harvard Business School Press, 2002
256pp ISBN: 0767908864
Three world-renowned experts on complex decision making join forces to craft a practical approach to making better decisions in our business, professional, and personal lives. They offer a simple, flexible technique based on a solid triumvirate of research, practical experience, and common sense that supports the decision maker in clearly and effectively assessing options, specifying objectives, identifying creative alternatives, making reasoned tradeoffs, clarifying uncertainties, and evaluating associated risks. Their approach integrates the intuitive and rational analytic approaches.

The Thinking Manager's Toolbox: Effective Processes for Problem Solving and Decision Making
William J. Altier
New York: Oxford University Press, Inc., 1999
219pp ISBN: 0195131967
The author argues that an understanding of the processes that are being employed in a particular business, and the experience of going through those processes repeatedly over a long period of time, will determine who is a successful leader. He also reveals ways of preventing problems before they occur, and teaches the reader how to create "thinking tools" to help make choices.

The Wisdom of Crowds: Why the Many Are Smarter Than the Few
James Surowiecki
Boston, Massachusetts: Back Bay Books, 2004
320pp ISBN: 0385503865
This book presents the challenging notion that the wisdom of the many (that is, a

1727

BUSINESS INFORMATION SOURCES

"Every solution of a problem raises new unsolved problems."   Karl Raimund Popper

crowd) is preferable to a specialist's thoughts on a given topic or issue—if certain conditions are met. Illustrating his points with case studies and writing in an accessible style, the author contends that collective wisdom can exist if four key elements are in place: independence, diversity, decentralization, and aggregation.

MAGAZINES
Decision Sciences Journal
ISSN: 0011-7315
Decision Sciences Institute
J. Mack Robinson College of Business, Georgia State University, 35 Broad Street, Atlanta, Georgia, 30303
T: +1 404 651 4073
F: +1 404 651 2804
www.decisionsciences.org
The *DSJ* is a quarterly journal that focuses on the use of behavioral, economic, and quantitative methods of analysis in decision making in public and private organizations.

Decision Support Systems
ISSN: 0167-9236
Elsevier Science
Customer Service Department, 6277 Sea Harbor Drive, Orlando, Florida, 32887–4800
T: +1 877 839 7126 or +1 407 345 4020
F: +1 407 363 1354
www.elsevier.com
DSS is an academic journal that appears eight times a year and covers the concept, implementation, and evaluation of decision support systems, together with related studies.

Journal of Behavioral Decision Making
ISSN: 0894-3257
Wiley
111 River St, Hoboken, New Jersey, 07030–5774
T: +1 201 748 6000
F: +1 212 850 6021
www.wiley.com
This is a multidisciplinary journal, broad-based in content and style, that publishes reports, critical review papers, theoretical analyses, and methodological contributions. It presents behavioral research on decision making and provides a forum for the evaluation of complementary, contrasting, and conflicting perspectives.

Journal of Multi-Criteria Decision Analysis
ISSN: 1057-9214
Wiley
111 River St, Hoboken, New Jersey, 07030–5774

T: +1 201 748 6000
F: +1 212 850 6021
www.wiley.com
The *JMCDA* is published in association with the International Society on Multiple-Criteria Decision Making. The journal appears six times a year and provides an international forum for the presentation and discussion of all aspects of research into, and the application and evaluation of, multi-criteria decision analysis, covering its mathematical, theoretical, and behavioral aspects.

Theory and Decision
ISSN: 0040-5833
Springer
Customer Service Department, P.O. Box 358, Dordrecht, 3300 AA, The Netherlands
T: +31 78 657 6392
F: +31 78 657 6474
www.springerlink.com
This academic, cross-discipline journal on the mechanics of decision making focuses on preference and uncertainty modeling, multi-criteria decision making, social choice, negotiation and group decisions, game theory, and gaming and conflict analysis.

INTERNET
Brainstorming.co.uk
www.brainstorming.co.uk
This site offers an introduction to brainstorming, plus information on brainstorming software, a list of recommended books, and a mailing list provided by Infinite Innovation.

The Data Warehousing Information Center
www.dwinfocenter.org
This targeted-knowledge portal provides information and education for the layperson on data warehousing and decision support. Primarily an informational site, it does not market any particular product or service. It offers instead a series of essays on this theme plus a useful search facility.

DAWeb
http://faculty.fuqua.duke.edu/daweb
The Web site of the Decision Analysis Society provides a range of information in the field of decision analysis, related links, newsletter abstracts, a calendar of events, and information on courses and syllabuses.

Decision Support Systems Resources
www.dssresources.com
With everything you ever wanted to know

about computerized decision support systems, this knowledge portal, established and maintained by Professor Daniel J. Power, provides case studies, a glossary of terms, extensive links, and a "Web-tour" for newcomers.

MindTools
www.mindtools.com
This site includes introductions to a number of problem-solving techniques, such as brainstorming and decision trees.

Society for Judgment and Decision Making
www.sjdm.org/index.shtml
At this interdisciplinary academic society Web site, nonmembers can access a searchable database of references to books and book chapters on judgment and decision making. The site also provides links to journals, academic programs, and other organizations related to the field, as well as syllabuses for an extensive series of courses ranging from managerial decision making to decision making in government and administration.

ORGANIZATIONS
USA
Decision Analysis Society (DAS)
c/o INFORMS, 7240 Parkway Drive, Suite 400, Hanover, Maryland, 21076
T: +1 443 757 3500
F: +1 443 757 3515
E: *informs@mail.informs.org*
http://faculty.fuqua.duke.edu/daweb
The DAS started life in 1980 as a special interest group of ORSA (Operations Research Society of America) and became a section of INFORMS (Institute for Operations Research and the Management Sciences) following a merger with the Institute for Management Sciences in 1995. The Society promotes the development and use of logical methods for the improvement of decision making in public and private enterprise. Members include practitioners, educators, and researchers.

Europe
European Association for Decision Making (EADM)
A. John Maule, Leeds University Business School, Leeds, U.K.
www2.fmg.uva.nl/eadm/home.html
EADM was founded in 1969 as SPUDM (Subjective Probability and Utility Decision Making) and changed to its current name in 1993. The organization is based in Leiden in the Netherlands. Membership is open to academics and students in the field of

1728

"If businessmen always made the right decisions, business wouldn't be business."

J. Paul Getty

human judgment and decision making. EADM promotes the advancement and dissemination of knowledge in this area through meetings, workshops, and conferences, publication of a bulletin, and sponsorship of the Bruno de Finetti prize for promising researchers.

International
Decision Sciences Institute

J. Mack Robinson College of Business, Georgia State University, 35 Broad Street, Atlanta, Georgia, 30303
T: +1 404 651 4073
F: +1 404 651 2804
E: *dsi@gsu.edu*
www.decisionsciences.org
The Institute's aims are to develop and apply methodologies for solving

multiple-criteria decision making problems and to encourage interaction, cooperation, and research in the field. In pursuit of these aims it organizes workshops, conferences, and student exchanges, and publishes *Decision Sciences Journal*.

International Society on Multiple Criteria Decision Making

Terry College of Business at the University of Georgia, Athens, Georgia, 30602–6253
T: +1 706 542 3782
F: +1 706 542 9434
E: *rsteuer@uga.edu*
www.terry.uga.edu/mcdm
The Society is an interdisciplinary organization concerned with the methods and procedures by which a concern for

multiple conflicting criteria can be formally incorporated into managerial decision making. The organization was founded in 1969 and has a membership of over 1,400 in over 90 countries. Publications, conferences, and other services are organized with the needs of academics and students in mind.

FOR MORE INFORMATION

∽ Analytical Techniques and Statistics (pp. 1675–1676)
☆ Developing Exceptional Problem-solving Skills (pp. 428–429)
✔ Open Systems Thinking (pp. 596–597)
✔ Solving Problems (pp. 840–841)

1729

BUSINESS INFORMATION SOURCES

Direct Marketing

BOOKS

2,239 Tested Secrets for Direct Marketing Success

Denny Hatch, Don Jackson
Maidenhead, United Kingdom: McGraw-Hill, 1999
368pp ISBN: 0844203491
Divided in topic sections for easy reference, this book is an excellent source of direct marketing advice drawn from the experience of experts.

Commonsense Direct Marketing 4th ed.

Drayton Bird
London: Kogan Page, 2000
352pp ISBN: 0749431210
This practical textbook introducing direct marketing is packed with international case studies and demonstrations of successful strategies. It covers the following topics: the role of the marketing department; how to acquire and keep customers; how to achieve objectives and evaluate results; what you should sell; how to position products effectively; how to choose an agency and how to do without one; and the Internet, the direct marketer's newest and potentially most effective tool.

Direct and Database Marketing

Graeme McCorkell
London: Institute of Direct Marketing/Kogan Page, 1997
320pp ISBN: 0749419601
The best U.K. introduction to direct marketing, this book was written to be read from cover to cover and contains some good small-business examples. The text is also useful to dip into for examples of how direct marketing campaigns are measured and evaluated. Case studies and illuminating examples are included.

Direct Marketing: A Step-by-step Guide to Effective Planning and Targeting

Roddy Mullin
London: Kogan Page, 2002
192pp ISBN: 0749436778
Aimed at both practicing managers and students of marketing, this guide looks at ways to use direct marketing as an effective marketing tool, and provides information to support the drawing up and running of a direct marketing campaign. Mullin discusses when to use direct marketing and which direct marketing method to choose, also covering electronic methods such as

e-mail, text messaging, and the Internet. Other techniques dealt with include direct response advertising, catalogs, leaflets or handouts, mail order, call centers, and field marketing.

Direct Marketing: Strategy, Planning, Execution 4th ed.

Edward L. Nash
Maidenhead, United Kingdom: McGraw-Hill, 2000
600pp ISBN: 0071352872
This is an updated edition of a classic of the direct marketing industry. The author, a direct marketing company executive, presents a thorough overview of all aspects of direct marketing, including strategic planning, media-specific marketing techniques, the economics of direct marketing, and direct marketing considerations for Internet and global marketing.

E-mail Marketing: Using E-mail to Reach Your Target Audience and Build Customer Relationships

Jim Sterne, Anthony Priore
Hoboken, New Jersey: Wiley, 2000
304pp ISBN: 0471383090
This book gives guidance on the stages involved in creating a successful permission-based e-mail marketing campaign. It covers the development of a campaign strategy and writing an e-mail masterpiece, and also offers advice on targeting your audience. Other areas discussed include monitoring and improving response rates, advertising on other people's electronic newsletters, and hosting your own discussion group.

The Engaged Customer: The New Rules of Internet Direct Marketing

Hans Peter Brondmo
London: Piatkus Books, 2001
256pp ISBN: 0749922370
This book discusses e-mail strategies for creating profitable customer relationships. The main areas it covers are: ways in which e-mail may be used to engage customers; the many applications of e-mail marketing, emphasizing the importance of taking a strategic approach; ways of establishing and developing customer relationship marketing, and of getting a marketing program up and running; and various future possibilities in electronic marketing and

communication, and their general implications for business. The book considers the significance of customer data, together with the difficulties of handling it, and also lists some important organizations in the field, such as service providers and portals, online agencies and system integrators. Examples and case studies are included.

Enterprise One-to-One: Tools for Competing in the Interactive Age

Don Peppers, Martha Rogers
New York: Currency/Doubleday, 1999
464pp ISBN: 038548755X
Written by the champions of customer relationship marketing, this is a best-selling guide to using new technology in your quest to get ahead, and stay ahead, of the field.

Making It Personal: How to Profit from Personalization without Invading Privacy

Bruce Kasanoff, Don Peppers, Martha Rogers
Cambridge, Massachusetts: Perseus Books Group, 2001
240pp ISBN: 0738205362
This book is a study of how the forthcoming growth in the use of personal information will affect the corporate world. Using research carried out in real life, the authors investigate the conflict that can arise between increasing profits through personal interaction and not invading privacy.

The One to One Fieldbook: The Complete Toolkit for Implementing a 1 To 1 Marketing Program

Don Peppers, Martha Rogers, Bob Dorf
New York: Bantam Books, 1999
288pp ISBN: 038549369X
A practical resource designed for use with *Enterprise One to One*, full of information on how to identify and develop a loyal customer base for your business.

The One to One Future: Building Relationships One Customer at a Time

Don Peppers, Martha Rogers
New York: Currency/Doubleday, 1996
464pp ISBN: 0385485662
Mass marketing has had its day. This is the era of relationship marketing, where firms expend their energy trying to develop

customer loyalty in order to sell more products to fewer people. This milestone work looks to strategies for the future in one to one marketing.

Relationship Marketing: Successful Strategies for the Age of the Customer

Regis McKenna

Cambridge, Massachusetts: Perseus Books Group, 1993

256pp ISBN: 0201622408

This book offers advice to organizations on how to dominate and control the market through the construction of significant relationships with customers.

Successful Direct Marketing Methods 7th ed.

Bob Stone, Ron Jacobs

Maidenhead, United Kingdom: McGraw-Hill, 2001

608pp ISBN: 0658001450

This updated edition provides a classic guide to direct marketing, combining new media with traditional marketing strategies to provide effective direct marketing to consumers. The content includes identifying and meeting consumers' needs, business-to-business marketing, and e-commerce techniques such as powerful branding strategies for Internet sites. An eight edition is planned for 2007.

MAGAZINES

Journal of Direct, Data and Digital Marketing Practice

ISSN: 1463–5178

Institute of Direct Marketing in association with Henry Stewart Publications

Russell House, 28–30, Little Russell Street, London, WC1A 2HN, U.K.

T: +44 (0) 20 7404 3040

F: +44 (0) 20 7404 2081

www.henrystewart.com

Previously known as *Interactive Marketing*, this international journal provides a forum for up-and-coming stars of marketing to share their experience, ideas, research, and case studies. A legal and regulatory update is also included.

Marketing Direct

Haymarket Publishing

174 Hammersmith Road, London, W6 7JP, U.K.

T: +44 (0) 20 8267 5000

F: +44 (0) 20 8267 4157

www.haymarketgroup.com

Targeted at direct marketers, this magazine

contains news, case studies, a think tank, features, personality profiles, and letters.

INTERNET
Direct
www.directmag.com

This is the site of an American-based online magazine for senior direct marketers that covers all aspects of direct marketing.

The Direct Marketing Association
www.the-dma.org

The Direct Marketing Association is a trade association serving the needs of direct marketing users and suppliers. Its Web site provides comprehensive information on direct marketing. This includes: conferences and seminars; professional development; industry guidelines; directories of direct marketers listed by name and type of service; a job bank; privacy information; research; and legislative issues.

Direct Marketing Linked Resources
www.dmlr.org/guide.htm

Many links to useful sites connected with marketing on the Internet are to be found at this address.

DM News
www.dmnews.com

DM News is an online newspaper covering the direct marketing industry. Its Web site provides the latest information on legislative, business, and postal news affecting the industry. This site includes registration for free e-mail newsletters, searchable lists and databases, and privacy information.

International Chamber of Commerce
www.iccwbo.org/policy/marketing/ id920/index.html

The International Chamber of Commerce sets out its code for direct marketing on this site. The code is intended to promote high standards of ethics within marketing.

MarketingProfs.com
www.marketingprofs.com

This Web site is aimed at marketing professionals and professors. It is a membership site, but a good deal of the information is free. Members must pay for premium content material, but registering is hassle-free. There are a variety of articles on competition that can be accessed through the site's search engine.

Target Marketing
www.targetonline.com

This site houses an America-based online magazine with articles and information on direct marketing.

ORGANIZATIONS
USA
Direct Marketing Association (DMA)

1120 Avenue of the Americas, New York, 10036–6700

T: +1 212 768 7277

F: +1 212 302 6714

E: *customerservice@the-dma.org*

www.the-dma.org

The DMA is a trade association for users and suppliers in the fields of direct, database, and interactive marketing. Founded in 1917, it now has over 5,000 members. Membership services include events, professional development, representation to government and in public affairs, and a library.

Europe
Federation of European Direct Marketing (FEDMA)

Tervurenlaan, Avenue de Tervuren 439, Brussels, B-1150, Belgium

T: +32 2779 42 68

F: +32 2779 42 69

E: *info@fedma.org*

www.fedma.org

A membership organization for national direct marketing associations, FEDMA aims to promote, protect, and provide information about the European direct-marketing industry.

Institute of Direct Marketing (IDM)

1 Park Road, Teddington, Middlesex, TW11 0AR, U.K.

T: +44 (0) 20 8614 0277

E: *enquiries@theidm.com*

www.theidm.co.uk

Founded in 1987, the IDM describes itself as "Europe's leading professional development body for direct, data, and digital marketing." The Institute has trained more than 67,000 marketing practitioners.

1731

BUSINESS INFORMATION SOURCES

FOR MORE INFORMATION

- ☆ Managing 1:1 Marketing (pp. 63–64)
- ☆ Marketing in the Internet Age (pp. 94–96)
- ᔕ Marketing Management (pp. 1827–1832)

"We don't so much have a marketing department, as anthropologists working for us."

Anita Roddick

Diversity

BOOKS

Beyond Race and Gender: Unleashing the Power of Your Total Work Force by Managing Diversity

R. Roosevelt Thomas, Jr.
New York: AMACOM, 1992
189pp ISBN: 0814478077
The author of this classic and groundbreaking book explores the problems facing managers trying to offer equal opportunities to all in order to take advantage of needed talents and skills. He presents an action plan for changing corporate cultures as well as case studies that highlight the problems that emerge once an organization recruits a diverse workforce, especially the failure of those recruited to move up the corporate ladder.

Creating the Multicultural Organization: A Strategy for Capturing the Power of Diversity

Taylor Cox
New York: Jossey-Bass, 2001
168pp (University of Michigan Business School Management Series)
ISBN: 0787955841
Cox outlines the challenges that the management of diversity presents to organizations. He presents a model designed to help chief executives, steering committees, human resource professionals, and team leaders develop a cultural environment in which every individual is respected and enabled to reach their potential. The text also describes methods that can be used to implement the five stages of the model and develop a diversity-competent organization. Each of the book's chapters ends with a set of thought-provoking questions.

Cultural Diversity in Organizations

Taylor Cox
San Francisco, California: Berrett-Koehler, 1994
ISBN: 1881052435
The author comprehensively covers all aspects of cultural diversity and its relation to business, including organizational performance, individual and group factors, and guidelines for leadership in managing diversity.

Diversity Consciousness: Opening Our Minds to People, Cultures, and Opportunities 2nd ed.

Richard D. Bucher
Upper Saddle River, New Jersey: Prentice Hall, 2003
272pp ISBN: 013049111X
This book is aimed at helping readers value diversity so that they can understand others' viewpoints and thus deal better with issues in the workplace such as conflict management, teamwork, prejudice, and communications. Its goal is to show how workplace success comes with employees' ability to accept differences. The book provides material such as interactive exercises that could be of great use to managers and human relations professionals.

The Diversity Directive: Why Some Initiatives Fail and What to Do about It

Robert Hayles, Armida Mendez Russell
New York: McGraw-Hill in association with the American Society for Training and Development, 1997
150pp ISBN: 0786308192
This practical text offers a step-by-step process that will help managers to initiate corporate diversity efforts, or to revitalize their existing diversity initiatives. Models, recommended actions, and real-world examples are presented to help organizations to diagnose problems and develop tactical action plans for the diversity change process. Appendices give a sample process outline and schedule for a diversity audit.

Diversity Scorecard: Evaluating the Impact of Diversity on Organizational Performance

Edward E. Hubbard
Oxford: Elsevier Butterworth-Heinemann, 2004
348pp ISBN: 0750674571
This book presents practical strategies for assessing and measuring the contribution of diversity management to organizational performance and strategy implementation. The first section puts forward the business case for diversity and explains the need for diversity measurement; the second applies the return on investment (ROI) process to diversity management producing the diversity return on investment (DROI) model; the third outlines how to build a

diversity scorecard, adding the dimension of diversity to the scorecard developed by Kaplan and Norton; and the final section addresses key implementation issues. Extra tools and additional resources are listed in an appendix.

The Equal Opportunities Guide: How to Deal with Everyday Issues of Unfairness 2nd ed.

Phil Clements, Tony Spinks
Sterling, Virginia: Stylus Publishing, 1997
192pp ISBN: 0749421037
This is a plainly written resource for students, managers, trainers, human resource management staff, teachers, and all those with an interest in equality of opportunity. The text sets out straightforward procedures to guide fair, courteous, and sensitive behavior to others, and includes a summary of recent U.K. legislation and agencies, self-assessment sections, and ways of identifying and preventing institutional discrimination.

Harvard Business Review on Managing Diversity

Boston, Massachusetts: Harvard Business School Press, 2001
240pp ISBN: 1578517001
This collection draws together both classic and more recent writings on this theme. Care has been taken to include both case studies and first-person accounts to provide a wide perspective on diversity.

A Peacock in the Land of Penguins: A Fable About Creativity and Courage

B. J. Hateley, Warren H. Schmidt
San Francisco, California: Berrett-Koehler, 2001
158pp ISBN: 1576751732
Using the metaphor of a peacock living in the midst of penguins, this book offers a different perspective on valuing and building a diverse workplace. The authors include tips on creating organizational change and training materials to assist in implementing diversity.

When Generations Collide

David Stillman, Lynne C. Lancaster
New York: HarperCollins, 2003
384pp ISBN: 0066621070
Addressing issues of generational differences as part of workplace diversity, the authors describe the potential problems

"Diversity raises the intelligence of groups."   Nancy Kline

involved in managing the four generational groups they have identified among members of the workforce. The contents include recommendations for bringing each group together as a unified team.

MAGAZINES

Black EOE Journal

National Women's Business Council
6845 Indiana Avenue, Suite 200, Riverside, California, 92506
T: +1 800 487 5099
F: +1 714 974 3978
www.blackeoejournal.com
This magazine contains articles about all minorities and provides valuable information regarding career opportunities. The journal focuses on the needs of employers in relation to workplace diversity. A section on career planning and advancement is particularly valuable to readers.

Cross Cultural Management

ISSN: 1352–7606
Emerald
60/62 Toller Lane, Bradford, West Yorkshire, BD8 9BY, U.K.
T: +44 (0) 1274 777 700
F: +44 (0) 1274 785 201
www.emeraldinsight.com/dpm.htm
This quarterly journal focuses on all aspects of cross-cultural relationships at work.

Diversity Digest

Association of American Colleges and Universities
1818 R Street NW, Washington, D.C., 20009
T: +1 202 387 3760
F: +1 202 265 9532
www.diversityweb.org/digest
Available in both online and print versions, this quarterly newsletter is targeted at campus practitioners in colleges and universities. It aims to support the facilitation of diversity and is supported as part of the Diversity Works initiative, financed by grants from the Ford Foundation to AAC&U and the University of Maryland at College Park.

Equal Opportunities International

ISSN: 0261–0159
Barmarick Publications
Enholmes Hall, Patrington, East Riding of Yorkshire, HU12 0PR, U.K.
T: +44 (0) 1964 630 033
F: +44 (0) 1964 631 716
www.emeraldinsight.com
This is a high-priced subscription journal

carrying articles by academics involved in equal opportunities teaching or research. The number of issues per year is variable, but four were published in 2005.

Equal Opportunities Review

ISSN: 0268–7143
Industrial Relations Services
Tolley House, 2 Addiscombe Road, Croydon, CR9 5AF, U.K.
T: +44 (0) 20 8686 2000
F: +44 (0) 20 8686 3155
Issued six times a year, this publication focuses on U.K. equal opportunities legislation and employment practice.

INTERNET

American Institute for Managing Diversity
www.aimd.org
This site provides a wealth of resources on managing diversity provided by a nonprofit organization dedicated to promoting research and education in this field.

Diversity Central
www.diversitycentral.com
This site provides an array of resources for managers and consultants addressing the issue of workplace diversity. The resources include articles and research on current topics, reports on employment law, online learning activities and tutorials, a directory of consultants, and a fee-based online journal.

European Institute for Managing Diversity (EIMD)
www.iegd.org
This is an international network of local consulting organizations in various countries, specializing in diversity management and offering services to address the diversity needs of European organizations. The site offers information in both English and Spanish.

Society for Human Resource Management (SHRM) Diversity Initiative
www.shrm.org/diversity
This site gives access to articles about diversity, and information on tools and resources. Parts of the site, including the online text of the *Mosaics* journal on diversity, are accessible to SHRM members only.

University of Maryland Diversity Database
www.inform.umd.edu/EdRes/Topic/Diversity

This site provides an index of multicultural and diversity resources, and of academic material, from local, national, and international sources.

Workplace Diversity for African, Hispanic (Latino), and Asian Americans
www.ethnicmajority.com/workplace.htm
This Web site addresses workplace diversity issues targeting African Americans, Hispanic Americans, and Asian Americans. Its resources include information about and links to current employment laws, understanding affirmative action, and indicators measuring corporate diversity.

ORGANIZATIONS
USA

American Institute for Managing Diversity (AIMD)
1155 Peachtree Road, Suite 6B, Atlanta, Georgia, 30303
T: +1 404 575 2131
F: +1 404 575 2139
www.aimd.org
The American Institute for Managing Diversity is a nonprofit organization dedicated to promoting research and education regarding the value of implementing workplace diversity. Its site provides a wealth of resources, including research and information on managing diversity.

Equal Employment Opportunity Commission
P. O. Box 7033, Lawrence, Kansas, 66044, USA
T: +1 800 669 4000
F: + 703 997 4890
E: *info@ask.eeoc.gov*
www.eeoc.gov
This body was established by Title VII of the Civil Rights Act of 1964 to enforce federal statutes prohibiting employment discrimination. It began operating on July 2, 1965.

1733

FOR MORE INFORMATION

☆ Boosting Business Success through Diversity (pp. 28–29)
☆ Generation Veneration (pp. 39–40)
✔ Implementing a Diversity Management Program (pp. 496–497)
✑ Social Responsibility of Management (pp. 1910–1912)

BUSINESS INFORMATION SOURCES

"Make your employers understand that you are in their service as workers, not as women."

Susan B. Anthony

Education Management

BOOKS

Human Resource Management in Schools and Colleges
David Middlewood, Jacky Lumby
Thousand Oaks, California: Paul Chapman, 1999
104pp ISBN: 1853964018
This textbook is designed for those taking courses in education management. It explains the importance of human resource management in education, addresses key issues in the application of HRM principles in the context of educational institutions, and provides practical activities and details of background reading.

Making Managers in Universities and Colleges
Craig Prichard
Buckingham, United Kingdom: Open University Press/Society for Research into Higher Education, 2000
224pp ISBN: 0335204856
The book draws on interviews with over 70 senior managers to illustrate contemporary issues and problems in educational management. It pays particular attention to the role of managers in universities and colleges in the light of moves to operate post-compulsory education in the United Kingdom on a more commercial basis.

Managing Schools
Patrick Whitaker
Woburn, Massachusetts: Butterworth-Heinemann, 1997
221pp (IM Diploma in Management)
ISBN: 075062194X
This book is one of a series designed for managers wishing to develop their capabilities and is suitable for those undertaking courses leading to the Certificate and Diploma in Management. Written by an educational consultant, it provides a strategic approach to educational management and focuses on the application of best practice to the management of schools in the context of rapid change. It defines the role of management in education and gives guidance on developing vision and making and reviewing progress toward objectives.

Reflecting on School Management
Anne Gold, Jennifer Evans
New York: Routledge/Falmer, 1998
160pp (Master Classes in Education)
ISBN: 0750708050

Written in a style that is practical and interactive, and including thought-provoking readings and activities, this book is for schoolteachers, at all levels of responsibility, who wish to reflect on and develop the management aspects of their job. The topics covered include philosophy and values in education management, management and leadership styles, working with people, managing finance and resources, and managing the curriculum.

MAGAZINES

Educational Management and Leadership
ISSN: 0263–211X
Sage Publications
1 Oliver's Yard, 55 City Road, London, EC1Y 1SP, U.K.
T: +44 (0) 20 7324 8500
F: +44 (0) 20 7324 8600
www.sagepub.co.uk
Educational Management and Leadership is the quarterly journal of the British Educational Management and Administration Society. It provides a forum for analysis of all aspects of management, administration, and policy in education, and publishes original research on educational management, administration, and policy in all its forms, including the management of schools and the administration of institutions of further and higher education.

International Journal of Educational Management
ISSN: 0951–354X
Emerald (North America)
4th Floor, 44 Brattle Street, Cambridge, Massachusetts, 02138
T: +1 888 622 0075
www.emeraldinsight.com/ccm.htm
This journal addresses the role of managers in the field of education against a background of changes in structures and philosophy, and diminishing resources. Seven issues appear each year covering topics such as resource allocation, the management and development of professional staff, and the government of educational institutions.

Journal of Educational Administration
ISSN: 0957–8234
Emerald (North America)
4th Floor, 44 Brattle Street, Cambridge, Massachusetts, 02138

T: +1 888 622 0075
www.emeraldinsight.com/ccm.htm
This academic journal is published five times a year. It focuses on the challenges facing educational administrators and reports on relevant research in this field. Coverage includes leadership styles, policy formulation, quality and evaluation, performance measurement, and organizational processes in schools.

The School Administrator
ISSN: 0036–6439
American Association of School Administrators
1801 North Moore Street, Arlington, Virginia, 22209–1813
T: +1 703 528 0700
F: +1 703 841 1543
www.aasa.org
The official magazine of the AASA is published 12 times a year and aims to provide practical information for district level school administrators in the United States. Each issue focuses on a theme from the area of school system practices, policies, and programs, and includes feature articles, news items, personal profiles, book reviews, and information on resources for school management.

School Leadership and Management
ISSN: 1363–2434
Carfax
Suite 800, 325 Chestnut Street, Philadelphia, Pennsylvania, 19106
T: +1 215 625 8900
F: +1 215 625 8914
www.tandf.co.uk/journals/carfax/13632434.html
This journal that addresses issues relating to school management. Its content consists of articles, research news, and book reviews. It is published five times a year.

ORGANIZATIONS
USA
American Association of University Administrators (AAUA)
Roberts Hall 407, Rhode Island College, Providence, Rhode Island, 02908–1991
T: +1 401 456 2808
F: +1 401 456 8287
www.aaua.org
The AAUA is a professional organization, founded in 1970, whose aims are to promote the professional development of those

> "In the early days, it was easy to lead by example. Now it has to be done by structured education and training."
>
> Tom Farmer

responsible for the administration of higher education, to encourage cooperation, and to represent the interests of its members. The AAUA has developed ethical and professional standards for administrators in higher education. It also publishes a quarterly newsletter and annually sponsors a national assembly.

Europe
Association of University Administrators

Manchester

AUA National Office, University of Manchester, Oxford Road, Manchester, M13 9PL, U.K.
T: +44 (0) 161 275 2063
F: +44 (0) 161 275 2036
E: *aua@man.ac.uk*
www.aua.ac.uk

The AUA is a professional body for higher education administrators and managers which promotes excellence in higher education management in the United Kingdom and the Republic of Ireland. It was formed in 1993 through the merger of the Meeting of University Academic Administrative Staff (MUAAS) and the Association of Polytechnic Administrators (APA). Currently the AUA has over 4,000 members, offers a range of networking and professional development activities including conferences, and operates a branch network.

British Educational Leadership, Management and Administration Society (BELMAS)

BELMAS Office, Sheffield Hallam University, 36 Collegiate Crescent, Sheffield, South Yorkshire, S10 2BP, U.K.
T: +44 (0) 114 225 2328
F: +44 (0) 114 225 5649
E: *info@belmas.org.uk*
www.shu.ac.uk/bemas

The Society seeks to promote the practice, teaching, and study of educational management in the United Kingdom and internationally. Founded in 1971, it brings together practitioners, researchers, and

providers of training and consulting in the field. Its activities include publications, conferences, and special interest groups.

Quality Assurance Agency for Higher Education (QAA)

Southgate House, Southgate Street, Gloucester, Gloucestershire, GL1 1UB, U.K.
T: +44 (0) 1452 577 000
F: +44 (0) 1452 557 070
E: *comms@qaa.ac.uk*
www.qaa.ac.uk

The QAA is an independent body established in 1997 to promote public confidence in the quality and standard of educational provision. It conducts reviews and publishes reports on the performance of higher education institutions in the United Kingdom. A code of practice for quality and standards in education has been developed and the QAA is working with the higher education sector to introduce an integrated system of review.

Staff and Educational Development Association (SEDA)

Selly Wick House, 59/61 Selly Wick Road, Birmingham, B29 7JE, U.K.
T: +44 (0) 121 415 6801
F: +44 (0) 121 415 6802
E: *office@seda.ac.co.uk*
www.seda.ac.uk

SEDA is a professional association for staff and educational developers in the United Kingdom, promoting innovation and good practice in higher education. It was formed in 1993 by the merger of the Standing Conference on Educational Development (SCED) and the Staff Development Group of the Society for Research into Higher Education (SRHE). The Association for Education and Training Technology merged with SEDA in 1996. Activities include the accreditation of professional development, conferences and similar events, and the award of SEDA Research and Development grants. The results of former rounds have been published in various journals and papers.

International
OECD Programme on Institutional Management in Higher Education (IMHE)

2 rue André Pascal, Paris, 75775 Paris 16, France
T: +33 1 45 24 82 00
F: +33 1 42 24 85 00
E: *imhe@oecd.org*
www.oecd.org/els/education/higher

Founded in 1969, IMHE forms part of the OECD's Directorate for Education, Employment, Labour, and Social Affairs. It provides an international forum for administrators, researchers, and policymakers in higher education. Membership is open to institutions of higher education in OECD member countries. Activities include publications, seminars, study visits, training courses, and a biennial general conference.

Society for Research into Higher Education (SRHE)

76 Portland Place, London, W1B 1NT, U.K.
T: +44 (0) 20 7637 2766
F: +44 (0) 20 7637 2781
E: *srheoffice@srhe.ac.uk*
www.srhe.ac.uk

Established in 1965, the SRHE is an independent society that aims to improve the quality of higher education by stimulating and coordinating research in addition to encouraging debate on issues of policy, the organization and management of educational institutions, the curriculum, and teaching and learning methods. The individual members are researchers, teachers, and managers, while corporate members include higher educational institutions, research institutes, and professional and governmental bodies. Activities include an annual conference, publications, and special interest networks.

FOR MORE INFORMATION

- Nonprofit Organizations (pp. 1844–1846)
- Public Sector Management (pp. 1881–1882)

BUSINESS INFORMATION SOURCES

"Perhaps one of the greatest advantages I have is that I am not educated in the academic sense."

Jack Petchey

Employee Benefits/Compensation

BOOKS

The Compensation Handbook: A State of the Art Guide to Compensation Strategy and Design 4th ed.

Lance A. Berger, Dorothy R. Berger, eds
Maidenhead, United Kingdom: McGraw-Hill, 1999
656pp ISBN: 0071343091

This updated and expanded edition is one of the classic books covering the field of employee compensation. The authors provide authoritative information written by experts in employee benefits and compensation. Topics covered include: base, variable, and executive compensation; measuring performance and compensation; and compensation trends and surveys.

The HR Book: Human Resources Management for Small Business

Lin Grensing Prophal
Naperville, Illinois: Sourcebooks, 1999
280pp ISBN: 1551802414

This is a "complete guide" to human resource management for the small business.

MAGAZINES

Benefits and Compensation International

ISSN: 0268–764X
Pension Publications Ltd.
East Wing, 4th Floor, Hope House, 45 Great Peter Street, London, SW1P 3LT, U.K.
T: +44 (0) 20 7222 0288
F: +44 (0) 20 7799 2163
www.benecompintl.com

This monthly magazine, aimed at multinational companies, provides up-to-date information and analysis concerning employee benefits and remuneration trends. A detailed country report is published twice a year.

Benefits Quarterly

ISSN: 8756–1263
International Society of Certified Employee Benefit Specialists (ISCEBS)
P.O. Box 209, Brookfield, Wisconsin, 53008
T: +1 262 786 8771
F: +1 262 786 8650
www.iscebs.org

This journal provides an overview of the major issues facing benefits professionals. It covers areas such as employee communication, healthcare cost management, flexible benefits, work and family issues, and post-retirement benefits. Each issue includes a legal update and book reviews.

Compensation and Benefits Review

ISSN: 0886–3687
Sage Publications
1 Oliver's Yard, 55 City Road, London, EC1Y 1SP, U.K.
T: +44 (0) 20 7324 8500
F: +44 (0) 20 7324 8600
www.sagepub.co.uk

This bimonthly journal focuses on compensation and benefits and how they affect, and are affected by, the changing nature of the workplace and the way companies do business. It is available online at http://cbr.sagepub.com.

Employee Benefit News

ISSN: 1044–6265
Thomson Financial & IMG Media
11 Penn Plaza, 17th Floor, New York, 10001
T: +1 888 280 4820
F: +1 301 545 4836
www.benefitnews.com

This magazine is the preeminent source of information on employee benefits. It provides coverage invaluable to employee benefits executives through comprehensive and useful articles that highlight the trends in all aspects of the subject.

Employee Benefits

ISSN: 1366–8722
Centaur Holdings
St. Giles House, 50 Poland Street, London, W1F 7AX, U.K.
T: +44 (0) 20 7970 4000
F: +44 (0) 20 7943 8172
www.centaur.co.uk

This monthly magazine aims to provide information to help companies align benefits with corporate objectives. The full spectrum of benefits is covered with news of new ideas and research.

Employer's Handbook: Complying with IRS Employee Benefits Rules

Thompson Publishing Group
1725 K Street NW, Suite 700, Washington, D.C., 20006
T: +1 800 964 5815
F: +1 800 999 5661
www.thompson.com

This is a comprehensive and authoritative guide to help administrators ensure that benefits comply with federal regulations. Sample forms and documents are provided. The subscription includes a loose-leaf manual and monthly updates and newsletters.

Flex Plan Handbook

Thompson Publishing Group
1725 K Street NW, Suite 700, Washington, D.C., 20006
T: +1 800 964 5815
F: +1 800 999 5661
www.thompson.com

This guide shows how to introduce and administer flexible benefits programs. Model plan documents and forms are included. The subscription includes a loose-leaf manual and quarterly updates and newsletters.

INTERNET

AHI Employment Law Resource Center
www.ahipubs.com

This site provides an array of information on employee compensation and benefits issues. The site includes free reports useful to employers, covering topics such as employee benefits, benefits forms, research, information on benefits laws written for the layperson, discussion areas, e-mail newsletters, and alerts.

BenefitsLink
www.benefitslink.com

This U.S. site is aimed at employers and provides news, compliance information, a question and answer service, free e-mail nesletters, links to articles, a bookstore, job listings, and a database of speakers.

Employee Benefit News
www.benefitnews.com

Registration is required for this site, which provides news and analysis of benefits issues and an e-mail newsletter.

Employee Benefits Survey
www.bls.gov/ncs/ebs

This site provides access to data from the U.S. Bureau of Labor Statistics Employee Benefits Survey in PDF format.

National Employee Benefits Web Site
www.benefitslink.com

This site provides comprehensive information and links related to employee benefits plans and compliance

"The most un-American phrase in our modern vocabulary is 'take-home pay.'"

Vivien Kellems

issues for businesses of any size, as well as for employee benefits specialists. The resources include articles with current information, discussion areas involving compensation experts, links to government publications and regulations, conferences, directories of service providers, and a search engine dedicated to employee compensation issues.

ORGANIZATIONS
USA
American Benefits Council
1212 New York Avenue NW, Suite 1250, Washington, D.C., 20005
T: +1 202 289 6700
F: +1 202 289 4582
E: *info@abcstaff.org*
www.americanbenefitscouncil.org
The American Benefits Council serves as the business community's lobbying arm on employee benefits policy. Professionals in the benefits field can keep abreast of changes through the organization's weekly e-mail updates on the latest legislative and regulatory developments.

Council on Employee Benefits (CEB)
4910 Moorland Lane, Bethesda, Maryland, 20814
T: +1 301 664 5940
F: +1 301 664 5944
E: *vschieber@ceb.org*
www.ceb.org
CEB, founded in 1946, is an association of companies with an interest in the management of employee benefits programs. It provides opportunities for the exchange of ideas, information, and statistics, sponsors research, and runs an annual conference.

Employee Benefit Research Institute (EBRI)
2121 K Street NW, Washington, D.C., 20037–1896
T: +1 202 659 0670
F: +1 202 775 6312
E: *info@ebri.org*
www.ebri.org
The EBRI was founded in 1978 with the aim

of encouraging and contributing to the development of employee benefits programs through education and research on a nonprofit and nonpartisan basis. It conducts research, collects and disseminates information, and sponsors lectures, debates, discussions, and study groups on employee benefit plans. Publications include the *EBRI Databook on Employee Benefits*, *Fundamentals of Employee Benefit Programs*, and monthly *Notes* and *Issue Brief* studies.

Employers' Council on Flexible Compensation (ECFC)
927 15th Street NW, Suite 1000, Washington, D.C., 20005
T: +1 202 659 4300
F: +1 202 371 1467
E: *info@ecfc.org*
www.ecfc.org
The ECFC was founded in 1981 by a group of Fortune 500 companies to promote a favorable regulatory climate and public opinion for flexible compensation. The organization engages in lobbying activities and provides up-to-date information for its 3,000 members.

International
International Employee Benefits Association (IEBA)
U.K.
T: +44 (0) 20 7902 0491
F: +44 (0) 20 7802 3786
www.ieba.org.uk
Founded in 1994 to promote professionalism among those involved in the management of international employee benefits, the IEBA facilitates the exchange of information as well as providing information on employee benefits issues to governments and other organizations. It holds four meetings a year, including an AGM, and each focuses on a specific issue in the field.

International Foundation of Employee Benefit Plans (IFEBP)
18700 West Bluemound Road, P.O. Box 69,

Brookfield, Wisconsin, 53008–0069
T: +1 262 786 6700
F: +1 262 786 8780
E: *webmaster@ifebp.org*
www.ifebp.org
The IFEBP is a nonprofit educational association that provides training and information for the employee benefits and compensation industry in the United States and Canada. Its membership comprises 35,000 individuals from multiemployer trust funds, corporations, public employee groups, and advisory firms.

International Society of Certified Employee Benefit Specialists (ISCEBS)
18700 West Bluemound Road, P.O. Box 209, Brookfield, Wisconsin, 53008–0209
T: +1 262 786 8771
F: +1 262 786 8650
E: *iscebs@iscebs.org*
www.iscebs.org
Employee benefits specialists who have successfully completed the CEBS program of the International Foundation of Employee Benefit Plans are eligible for membership of the ISCEBS. The organization, founded in 1981, provides professional development, networking opportunities, and information resources for its 4,000 members.

FOR MORE INFORMATION

1737

BUSINESS INFORMATION SOURCES

Employee Participation in Management

BOOKS

The American Workplace: Skills, Compensation, and Employee Involvement

Casey Ichniowski, David I. Levine, Craig Olson, George Strauss
Basingstoke, United Kingdom: Taylor & Francis Journals (U.K.), 2000
304pp ISBN: 0521650283
This book is a summary of studies aimed at identifying the best practices to date for effective work environments. The authors look at specific industries (for example, the automotive, machine tools, and apparel industries) as well as cross-industry studies of financial performance. The research and discussion focuses on three particular areas: the "modular" production approach as against the traditional assembly line, employee involvement practices, and TQM programs and their impact on financial performance.

Flight of the Buffalo: Soaring to Excellence, Learning to Let Employees Lead

James A. Belasco, Ralph C. Stayer
New York: Warner Books, 1994
355pp ISBN: 0446670081
This popular book uses the analogies of buffalos and geese to explain different ways of viewing leadership and followership. In so doing, the authors explore some of the shifts that are necessary to move from a traditional, hierarchical mode of running your business to one that is primarily employee-driven. Topics covered include leadership as a personal choice, what a "transfer of ownership" looks like, and how employees need to redefine their role with their bosses.

Leading Self-directed Work Teams

Kimball Fisher
Maidenhead, United Kingdom: McGraw-Hill, 2000
339pp ISBN: 0071349243
In this book Fisher describes the change in roles between management and employees that must occur for self-directed work teams (SDWTs) to succeed. Fisher discusses how SDWTs can be perceived as a threat to current management and how supervisors need to rethink their role. He offers results from situations where SDWTs are being used and also explains how technology is helping the movement toward SDWTs.

Managing Employee Involvement and Participation

Jeff Hyman, Bob Mason
London: Sage Publications, 1995
222pp ISBN: 0803987277
This textbook for students and others interested in management, HRM, and industrial relations offers an introduction to the complex topic of employee involvement and participation. The different ways in which employee influence can be articulated at work are examined, and two main strands of evolution are identified.

The Open-Book Experience: Lessons from Over 100 Companies Who Successfully Transformed Themselves

John Case
Cambridge, Massachusetts: Perseus Books Group, 1999
256pp ISBN: 0738200409
This extremely practical, how-to book for business owners and managers reviews the principles of open-book management and explains it as a system, focusing on the implementation process in some detail. The experiences of companies that have implemented open-book management provide much of the basic material on implementation tools.

Open Space Technology: A User's Guide

Harrison Owen
San Francisco, California: Berrett-Koehler, 1997
173pp ISBN: 1576750248
This manual describes the author's "Open Space Technology" process and the concepts behind it. It is actually a lot simpler than it sounds and is based on the premise that when you bring together large groups of employees to problem-solve, it is better to give them an overall theme, then let them generate the topics of importance within that theme. Finally, instead of forcing them toward a particular topic, you should let them choose which ones they wish to pursue. By these means, the author would argue, you enable employee commitment to come forth naturally.

Trends in Organizational Behaviour: Volume 8, Employee Versus Owner Issues in Organizations

Cary L. Cooper, Denise M. Rousseau, eds.
Hoboken, New Jersey: Wiley, 2001
158pp ISBN: 0471498548
This volume of *Trends in Organizational Behaviour*, written for students, academics, and HR or management practitioners, explores employee versus owner issues, focusing particularly on employee involvement and ownership. The areas covered include employee equity and share ownership, the psychological consequences of ownership, employee loyalty, and open-book management.

MAGAZINES

Ideas Express

Ideas Management
4216 77th Avenue Court NW, Gig Harbour, Washington, D.C., 98335–6542
T: +1 253 265 2137
F: +1 253 265 2138
www.ideasmanagement.com/public.htm
This bimonthly magazine for suggestion plan and recognition professionals reviews the latest practices and trends and offers expert advice and ideas for implementing successful suggestion plans.

IPA Bulletin

Involvement and Participation Association (IPA)
42 Colebrooke Row, London, N1 8AF, U.K.
T: +44 (0) 20 7354 8040
F: +44 (0) 20 7354 8041
www.ipa-involve.com
This is a monthly bulletin for IPA member companies on developments in partnership and employee involvement.

New Horizons

Employee Involvement Association (EIA)
P.O. Box 2307, Dayton, Ohio, 45401–2307
T: +1 937 586 3224
F: +1 937 586 3699
www.eianet.org
As well as articles on aspects of the administration, maintenance, and promotion of employee involvement programs, this quarterly journal also provides information about the activities of

"Many companies say they want to change, but they need to empower people below."
Marvin Bower

the Employee Involvement Association and its branches.

INTERNET
Australian Employee Ownership Association
www.aeoa.org.au

This site is run by the Australian Employee Ownership Association. Some of it is open to nonmember visitors interested in employee ownership issues and related policy.

Employee Ownership Options
www.employee-ownership.org.uk

The site belongs to a regional consortium network called Employee Ownership Options, and was set up with assistance from the EU ADAPT program to provide information on employee ownership options for all those involved with organizations facing closure due to financial or succession problems.

European Federation of Employee Shareownership
www.efesonline.org

This site organizes the international exchange of information on employee ownership and participation. Its content is available in a variety of European languages and covers news, case studies, a forum, and a synopsis of the Federation's recent activities.

Ideas Management
www.ideasmanagement.com

This site belongs to an organization providing specialist consulting, training, and software advice on all aspects of company suggestion plans. The site is suitable for visitors from both the United States and the rest of the world.

Involvement and Participation Association
www.ipa-involve.com

This membership site gives a basic overview of IPA services. IPA case studies are available for download free of charge.

The Teamwork & Participation Forum
www.asq.org/teamwork

The Teamwork & Participation Forum was formed in 2004 when the Association for Quality and Participation merged with the American Society for Quality. The Forum focuses on the "people" side of quality, and provides human resource-focused services, with the aim of helping individuals, teams, and organizations to attain performance excellence. Their site has information about educational programs and seminars, as well as information on books and other publications.

ORGANIZATIONS
USA
Employee Involvement Association (EIA)
P.O. Box 2307, Dayton, Ohio, 45401–2307

T: +1 937 586 3224

F: +1 937 586 3699

E: *eia@eianet.org*

www.eianet.org

Founded in 1948 as the National Association of Suggestion Schemes, this nonprofit professional body became the Employee Involvement Association in 1992. It aims to promote the use of employee suggestion plans and other processes that encourage networking and the exchange of ideas.

National Center for Employee Ownership (NCEO)
1736 Franklin Street, Oakland, California, 94612

T: +1 510 208 1300

F: +1 510 272 9510

E: *nceo@nceo.org*

www.nceo.org

A nonprofit, private membership and research organization that seeks to act as a source of unbiased information on employee stock-ownership plans (ESOPs), employee stock options, and employee participation. It offers a library, newsletters, and links from its Web site to related sites.

Europe
Employee Share Ownership (Esop) Centre Ltd.
2 Ridgmount Street, London, WC1E 7AA, U.K.

T: +44 (0) 20 7436 9936

F: +44 (0) 20 7580 0016

E: *esop@hurlstons.com*

www.mhcc.co.uk/esop

The Centre is a nonprofit, membership organization that supports employee share ownership development in the United Kingdom and Europe. It produces publications, organizes events and research, and offers support in starting and operating all forms of broad-based employee share schemes, including SAYE-Sharesave or profit-share schemes, and all-employee share-option or ownership plans (AESOPs).

European Study Group
Building 2, Brunel Science Park, Kingston Lane, Uxbridge, Middlesex, UB8 3PQ, U.K.

T: +44 (0) 1895 812 993

F: +44 (0) 1895 812 991

E: *ask@esg.eu.com*

http://esg.eu.com

This nonprofit association of multinational employers was formed originally as the European Works Council Study Group by eight senior HR executives. Now with a wider membership, it has become a broader forum for considering aspects of employee information and consultation linked to European social policy and legislation.

ideasUK
52 Peveril Bank, Dawley Bank, Telford, Shropshire, TF4 2BZ, U.K.

T: +44 (0) 870 902 1658

E: *enquiries@ideasUK.com*

www.ideasuk.com

This nonprofit membership organization is dedicated to supporting and developing the growth of suggestion and employee involvement programs through networking and the exchange of knowledge and best practice. Founded in 1986 as the United Kingdom Association of Suggestion Schemes, it adopted ideasUK as its trading name in 1998.

Industrial Common Ownership Movement Ltd. (ICOM)
Holyoake House, Hanover Street, Manchester, M60 0AS, U.K.

T: +44 (0) 161 246 2959

E: *icom@icom.org.uk*

www.icof.co.uk/icom

A national, nonprofit membership organization for cooperatives and other businesses democratically controlled by employees, ICOM provides legal and registration services, training programs, publications, and information. Its aim is to promote the democratic control and ownership of enterprises by those who work within them.

Involvement and Participation Association (IPA)
42 Colebrooke Row, London, N1 8AF, U.K.

T: +44 (0) 20 7354 8040

F: +44 (0) 20 7354 8041

www.ipa-involve.com

The Association is a nonprofit organization with charitable status that aims to help organizations to develop working practices and strategies for employee involvement and partnership. It acts as a focal point for best practice, and offers advice and support to members, as well as a monthly bulletin on new developments in the field.

Mondragon Cooperative Corporation (Mondragon Corporación Cooperativa)
Pa José Maria Arizmendiarrieta, No. 5, 20500 Mondragón, Guipúzcoa, Spain

"When participation is suggested in terms of control over overall goals, it is usually a sham."

Frederick Herzberg

T: +34 943 779 300
F: +34 943 796 632
E: *wm@mcc.coop*
www.mondragon.mcc.es
MCC is a large-scale, cooperative business corporation in the Basque country of Spain that also provides education and social welfare for its members.

Tomorrow's Company
235 Blackfriar's Road, London, SE1 8NW, U.K.
T: +44 (0) 20 7021 0550
F: +44 (0) 20 7021 0549
E: *info@tomorrowscompany.com*
www.tomorrowscompany.com
A research and policy-focused organization founded in 1996, Tomorrow's Company aims to enable businesses to achieve success through a more inclusive approach to management.

International
International Co-operative Alliance (ICA)
15, route des Morillons, 1218 Grand-Saconnex, Geneva, Switzerland
T: +41 22 929 88 88
F: +41 22 798 41 22
E: *ica@coop.org*
www.ica.coop
The ICA is an international, nongovernmental organization which unites, represents, and serves cooperatives worldwide. Details of members from Europe and elsewhere are available from the ICA Web site, together with information on the cooperative movement, the development of cooperatives, and related issues.

"I felt the only way to turn things round was to get people to think like owners."

Jack Stack

Employee Relations

BOOKS

The Changing Nature of Work
Frank Ackerman, Neva R. Goodwin, Laurie Dougherty, Kevin Gallagher, eds
Washington, D.C.: Island Press, 1998
417pp ISBN: 1559636653
This volume presents summaries of 86 articles on almost every aspect of work. It has sections devoted to emerging industrial relations issues such as alternative forms of work organization and works councils. It also covers globalization and labor, new technologies and work organization, diversity in the workplace, and flexibility versus security.

The Employment Relationship: A Psychological Perspective
Peter Herriot
New York: Routledge, 2001
256pp ISBN: 1841692395
This book, aimed particularly at managers and occupational psychologists, gives an unusual, psychologist's perspective on employment relations. It discusses some complex ideas, using metaphors to help the understanding of organizational employment relations and to highlight features of the employment relationship and its psychology.

Exploring Employee Relations
Mike Leat
Woburn, Massachusetts: Butterworth-Heinemann, 2001
320pp ISBN: 075064396X
This is a student textbook, aimed at those on undergraduate, postgraduate, and professional courses, which provides a grounding in the theory and practice of employee relations. It focuses on the employment relationship, the nature of work, globalization and employee relations, and the political and legal aspects. Each chapter includes student activities, with answers and feedback, and summaries of key points.

Love 'Em or Lose 'Em: Getting Good People to Stay 2nd ed.
Beverly L. Kaye, Sharon Jordan-Evans
San Francisco, California: Berrett-Koehler, 2005
277pp ISBN: 1576753271
This book explores a major problem facing employers: the fact that the best employees, the ones you simply cannot afford to lose, are the ones who find it easiest to move on. The book presents strategies for retaining the best and brightest, including creating connections, providing recognition, telling the truth, sharing information, reconsidering rules, enhancing rewards, yielding responsibility, and listening.

Mediation for Managers: Resolving Conflict and Rebuilding Relationships at Work
John Crawley, Katherine Graham
Naperville, Illinois: Nicholas Brealey Publishing, 2002
224pp ISBN: 1857883152
Mediation is increasingly being recognized as an effective way to reduce conflict, resolve disputes, and build a productive workplace. This text provides a practical toolkit of exercises, case studies, and examples to help managers become effective mediators at work. This text also explains the process of mediation, looks at the practicalities, and describes day-to-day mediation skills.

Securing Prosperity: The American Labor Market: How It Has Changed and What to Do about It
Paul Osterman
Princeton, New Jersey: Princeton University Press, 2001
240pp ISBN: 0691086885
Osterman examines the forces that have impacted on the American workplace over the past decade—especially globalization and the new market economy—and have shifted the balance of power between workers and managers. It looks at the effects of restructuring organizations to increase productivity, the advent of new technologies, and the effects of these changes on the employment contract. The author recommends new policies for a workforce that is becoming increasingly mobile.

What's Next for Organized Labor? The Report of The Century Foundation Task Force on the Future of Unions
Nelson Lichtenstein
New York: Century Foundation Press, 1998
120pp ISBN: 0870784188
This book contains a report by a task force of business, labor, and political leaders who examined the need for and the future of unions. They found that unions are the only mechanism that has proved effective in helping workers gain influence in the workplace over the long term, and made recommendations for rebuilding them, including changes to make them more popular and combat their falling membership. The book includes a background paper that analyzes the history of the labor movement, highlighting its successes and failures.

MAGAZINES

Employee Relations
ISSN: 0142–5455
Emerald Group Publishing Ltd.
60/62 Toller Lane, Bradford, West Yorkshire, BD8 9BY, U.K.
T: +44 (0) 1274 777 700
F: +44 (0) 1274 785 200
www.emeraldinsight.com
This journal, aimed at academics and key HR practitioners, focuses on the importance of understanding and merging corporate, management and employee needs to achieve optimum performance, commitment and effectiveness. It takes an international perspective and its coverage draws on current ideas, research and best practice in the field.

European Industrial Relations Review
ISSN: 0309–7234
Lexis Nexis Customer Services
U.K.
T: +44 (0) 20 8662 2000
F: +44 (0) 20 8662 2012
This monthly journal provides coverage of employment relations and practice across Europe for those interested in the field. It provides special features, reports, surveys, recent news from 20 countries, and legal reviews.

Industrial Relations Journal
ISSN: 0019–8692
Blackwell Publishing
350 Main Street, Malden, Massachusetts, 02148
T: +1 781 388 8200
F: +1 781 388 8232
www.blackwellpublishing.com
Intended for academics and practitioners, this journal is published six times a year. It reports on research and practice in industrial relations, management and law worldwide.

1741

BUSINESS INFORMATION SOURCES

"A chairman who never wanders about his agency becomes a hermit, out of touch with his staff."

David Ogilvy

International Labour Review

ISSN: 0020–7780

International Labour Organization (ILO)
4, route des Morillons, CH-1211, Geneva 22,
Switzerland
T: +41 22 799 61 11
F: +41 22 798 86 85
www.ilo.org/public/english/support/
publ/revue
This quarterly journal, aimed at
policymakers and academic and other
researchers, contains academic papers on
the international labor market and labor
issues.

INTERNET
Bureau of Labor Statistics
www.bls.gov
This U.S. government site is a rich source of
statistics and data about labor and
employment as well as publications and
press releases. It provides information
about such topics as wages and benefits,
productivity, health and safety, the state of
the economy, and demographics.

ILR Catherwood Library
www.ilr.cornell.edu/library
This U.S.-based site links to a number of
informative sites concerned with labor
unions, labor law and labor history,
industrial action, and online newsletters
and magazines related to these issues.

ORGANIZATIONS
USA
American Benefits Council
1212 New York Avenue NW, Suite 1250,
Washington, D.C., 20005
T: +1 202 289 6700

F: +1 202 289 4582
E: *info@abcstaff.org*
www.americanbenefitscouncil.org
The American Benefits Council serves as
the business community's lobbying arm on
employee benefits policy. Professionals in
the benefits field can keep abreast of
changes through the organization's weekly
e-mail updates on the latest legislative and
regulatory developments.

International Society of Certified Employee Benefit Specialists (ISCEBS)
P.O. Box 209, Brookfield, Wisconsin, 53008
T: +1 262 786 8771
F: +1 262 786 8650
E: *iscebs@iscebs.org*
www.iscebs.org
This society of over 3,500 members
encourages the professional development
of employee benefit practitioners. The
society prides itself on providing career-
specific materials that cover all areas of
employee benefits. This exclusive
organization requires members to be
graduates of one or more specialized
programs.

Europe
Institute of Employment Rights
177 Abbeville Road, London, SW4 9RL, U.K.
T: +44 (0) 20 7498 6919
F: +44 (0) 20 7498 9080
E: *ier@gn.apc.org*
www.ier.org.uk
The Institute is an independent think-tank
aiming to provide a center for
disseminating ideas related to the labor
movement and labor law. It is involved in
research, conferences, meetings, and

seminars, and produces pamphlets on
various aspects of labor and employment.

Trades Union Congress (TUC)
Congress House, Great Russell Street,
London, WC1B 3LS, U.K.
T: +44 (0) 20 7636 4030
F: +44 (0) 20 7636 0632
www.tuc.org.uk
The TUC is the representative organization
for the U.K. trade union movement.

International
International Labour Organization (ILO)
Juan Somavia
4, route des Morillons, CH-1211, Geneva 22,
Switzerland
T: +41 22 799 6111
F: +41 22 798 8685
E: *ilo@ilo.org*
www.ilo.org
The central role of the ILO is to generate
and disseminate knowledge about the world
of work, and it has offices in many
countries in addition to its headquarters in
Switzerland.

FOR MORE INFORMATION

- Conditions of Employment
  (pp. 1708–1709)
- Employee Benefits/Compensation
  (pp. 1736–1737)
- Employee Participation in Management
  (pp. 1738–1740)
- Employment Law (pp. 1743–1744)
- ☆ Making Loyalty Work (pp. 370–371)
- Recruitment and Selection
  (pp. 1890–1892)

BUSINESS INFORMATION SOURCES

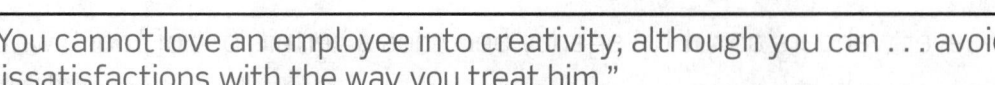
"You cannot love an employee into creativity, although you can . . . avoid his
dissatisfactions with the way you treat him."

Frederick Herzberg

Employment Law

BOOKS

ADA Compliance Guide

Charles D. Goldman, ed.

Tampa, Florida: Thompson Publishing Group

Updated monthly, the *Americans With Disabilities Act Compliance Guide* is a handy reference source for understanding the complexities of the employment provisions of the ADA. Written in plain English, the Guide explains the meaning of "disability," "reasonable accommodation," and "undue hardship." It also contains information on the nonemployment provision accessibility standards.

Covenants Not to Compete: A State-by-State Survey 2nd ed.

Brian M. Malsberger, ed.

Washington, D.C.: BNA Books, 1996

(Supp. 2001)

1275pp ISBN: 157018030X

Written for attorneys, this supplemented volume covers a growing practice area in U.S. law—the protection of an employer's trade secrets and other confidential information. Organized by the state, it covers state statutes governing restrictive covenants and the extent to which a covenant may be forced against an employee.

Employment, Disability, and the Americans with Disabilities Act: Issues in Law, Public Policy, and Research

Peter Blanck, ed.

Evanston, Illinois: Northwestern University Press, 2000

488pp (Psychological Issues)

ISBN: 081011688X

This is a collection of scholarly essays on employment law, especially as it relates to the Americans with Disabilities Act (ADA). It includes bibliographical references and indexes.

Employment Law: New Challenges in the Business Environment 3rd ed.

John Jude Moran

Upper Saddle River, New Jersey: Prentice Hall, 2005

512pp ISBN: 0131477358

Aimed at Human Resource managers and those in the legal profession, this book takes a simple approach to employment law with a foundation of legal principles explained in language that is easy to understand. The text discusses the overall employment

relationship and discrimination topics such as sex, race, age, gender, religion, and AIDS. It looks at the regulatory aspects of employment and in every chapter presents several sample cases and hypothetical situations to illustrate the employment law problems faced by small businesses.

Foundations of Employment Discrimination Law 2nd ed.

John J. Donohue III

New York: Foundation Press, 2002

551pp (Interdisciplinary Readers in Law)

ISBN: 1587780968

This book presents a broad collection of edited readings covering the general development of the law from the perspectives of history, philosophy, economy, sociology, politics, and psychology among others. The two sections—one on race discrimination and the other on sex discrimination—consider the theoretical and empirical foundations of the law, its operation, and its impact.

MAGAZINES

HR Magazine

ISSN: 1047–3149

Society for Human Resource Management (SHRM)

1800 Duke Street, Alexandria, Virginia, 22314

T: +1 703 548 3440

F: +1 703 535 6490

www.shrm.org

HR Magazine is published by SHRM, the world's largest human resource management association. The magazine is a monthly subscription publication that provides in-depth coverage and feature articles on all aspects of the HR profession.

Human Resource Executive

LRP Publications

747 Dreshers Road, Suite 500, Horsham, Pennsylvania, 19044–0980

T: +1 215 784 0860

F: +1 215 784 9639

www.hrexecutive.com

Human Resource Executive is a monthly subscription magazine focusing on strategic issues in human resources. Its articles cover all elements of human resource management including personnel, benefits, training and development, HR information systems, relocation, retirement planning, workplace security, and healthcare.

Workforce

ACC Communications, Inc.

245 Fischer Avenue B-2, Costa Mesa, California, 92626

T: +1 714 751 1883

F: +1 714 751 4106

www.workforce.com

A monthly magazine, *Workforce* targets HR practitioners with content on a variety of topics, including performance appraisal. It offers case studies, trend analysis, and commentary on the social and economic effects of HR practices.

INTERNET

Alexander Hamilton Institute (AHI) Employment Law Resource Center

www.ahipubs.com

With newsletters and multiple publications, AHI aims to keep business leaders and executives on top of what's new in employment law, to avoid future legal issues.

BenefitsLink

www.benefitslink.com

BenefitsLink is one of the oldest law sites on the Web. It offers compliance information and tools about employee benefit plans sponsored by private or governmental employers in the United States. The site contains recent articles on employee benefits, links to key government documents, and an "ask the experts" Q&A forum.

Employment Law Information Network

www.elinfonet.com

The Employment Law Information Network is a portal site containing thousands of links to employment law content on the Web. Links to U.S. employment law statutes and regulations, employment law articles, and example human resource policies, forms, and contracts can be found here. The site also offers an "Ask the Experts" feature, and users can sign up for daily or weekly newsletters.

Findlaw

www.findlaw.com

Findlaw, the legal media site (owned by Thomson Business) contains information and links to information on virtually every

1743

BUSINESS INFORMATION SOURCES

aspect of U.S. law, including employment law. The employment law section is focused on small businesses and includes useful articles, forms and contracts, and links to relevant federal advice.

U.S. Department of Labor
www.dol.gov
The U.S. Department of Labor is responsible for the administration and enforcement of a vast range of federal statutes, covering areas from wages and hours to family and medical leave. The DOL's Web site contains a extensive array of legal compliance information, online forms, and useful statistics.

U.S. Equal Employment Opportunity Commission (EEOC)
www.eeoc.gov
The EEOC is the primary federal agency that enforces the U.S. employment discrimination statutes (protecting employees from discrimination on the basis of protected traits like race, sex, age, and disability status). The Commission's site includes a wide variety of primary source documents on U.S. employment laws, including statutory and regulation text, enforcement guidance, and the Commission's compliance manual. Information is available for both employees and employers, much of which is written in non-technical terms for the layman.

WorkIndex
www.workindex.com
WorkIndex.com provides a comprehensive index of workplace related Web sites (over 5,000) as well as human resource tools and information. The site is produced and maintained by the publishers of *Human Resource Executive* magazine, in cooperation with Cornell University's School of Industrial Labor Relations. It offers articles, a salary calculator, and HR news. Users can consult a legal clinic, post and search jobs, and sign up for a weekly newsletter.

ORGANIZATIONS
USA
American Management Association (AMA)
1601 Broadway, New York, 10019
T: +1 212 586 8100
F: +1 212 903 8168
www.amanet.org
One of the world's leading nonprofit membership-based educational organizations, the AMA offers a range of business education and management development programs for individuals and enterprises in the Americas, Europe, and Asia. It identifies best management practices worldwide to provide assessment, design, development, self-development, and instruction services through a variety of print and electronic media and learning methodologies, including conferences and seminars, all designed to enhance the growth of individuals and organizations.

Society for Human Resource Management (SHRM)
1800 Duke Street, Alexandria, Virginia, 22314
T: +1 703 548 3440
F: +1 703 535 6490
www.shrm.org
SHRM is the world's largest human resource management association. It provides education and information services, conferences and seminars, government and media representation, online services, and publications to more than 200,000 professional and student members around the world.

Europe
Advisory Conciliation and Arbitration Service (ACAS)
Euston Tower, 286 Euston Road, London, NW1 3JJ, U.K.
T: + 44 (0) 20 7396 0022
www.acas.org.uk
ACAS is a nationwide organization (with its head office in London) of employment relations experts. It has been working with

employers, employees, trade unions, and other representatives for more than 25 years. The organization has a network of telephone helplines giving free help and information, and the Advisory Service works with hundreds of companies every year to develop a joint approach to problem solving. Most cases going to an employment tribunal are first of all referred to ACAS to see if there is a less damaging and expensive way of sorting the problem out. The organization also runs workshops and seminars around the country, targeting small businesses without specialist personnel sections.

International
International Labour Organization (ILO)
Juan Somavia
4, route des Morillons, CH-1211, Geneva 22, Switzerland
T: +41 22 799 6111
F: +41 22 798 8685
E: *ilo@ilo.org*
www.ilo.org
The ILO is the United Nations specialized agency with international responsibilities for work and employment issues. Governments, employers and trade unions all participate in its work and decision making processes. The primary goal of the ILO today is to promote opportunities for men and women to obtain decent work and income, in conditions of freedom, equity, security, and human dignity.

FOR MORE INFORMATION

"Where the people possess no authority, their rights obtain no respect."   George Bancroft

Entrepreneurs

BOOKS

Against the Odds: An Autobiography 2nd ed.

James Dyson

New York: Texere Publishing, 2003
320pp ISBN: 1587991705

The story of man and machine, this book charts the path to the shops of James Dyson's innovative vacuum cleaner.

The Age of Enterprise: The Emergence and Evolution of Entrepreneurial Management

Patricia Carr

Dublin, Republic of Ireland: Silver Lake Publishing, 2001
256pp ISBN: 1563437627

This book sets out to analyze the nature of enterprise culture and explores its impact on small business owners, entrepreneurs, and business advisers. It describes the evolution of enterprise culture and considers contemporary issues.

Anyone Can Do It

Sahar Hashemi, Bobby Hashemi

Chichester: Capstone, 2004
224pp ISBN: 1841125792

Written by the brother and sister team behind the successful Coffee Republic chain, this book offers the reader "57 real-life laws on entrepreneurship." An accessible and inspirational read, the book is a truthful, no-holds-barred description of getting a great idea off the ground.

The E-Myth Revisited: Why Most Small Businesses Still Don't Work and What You Can Do About Yours 2nd ed.

Michael E. Gerber

New York: HarperCollins, 2005
288pp ISBN: 0060766611

First published in 1986, this best-selling book provides information and guidance on starting and maintaining a small business or franchise. "E-myth" stands for "entrepreneurial myth" and refers to Gerber's belief that entrepreneurs do not necessarily make good business people. The book shows the reader how to simplify the systems involved in running a business, and instead create an incredibly organized and regimented plan, so that the systems can more or less run themselves, freeing the entrepreneur's mind to focus on long-term strategy.

The Entrepreneurial Spirit: Learning to Unlock Value

David Rae

Dublin, Republic of Ireland: Silver Lake Publishing, 2001
210pp ISBN: 1563437589

This book is designed to help those who see themselves as potential entrepreneurs. It is suitable for students on entrepreneurship courses and aims to help develop the practical skills, habits, and mindset vital to entrepreneurial success. It also addresses fundamental questions about the nature and history of entrepreneurship, covering each stage in the entrepreneurial process. It provides advice on recognizing and exploiting opportunities and on developing an entrepreneurial career.

Entrepreneurship in the Global Firm

Julian Birkinshaw

London: Sage Publications, 2000
256pp (Sage Strategy)
ISBN: 0761958096

Birkinshaw examines the dynamics affecting the growth and position of international firms, and shows that many changes result from the initiatives of subsidiary managers.

European Casebook on Entrepreneurship and New Ventures

David Molian, Benoit Leleux

Upper Saddle River, New Jersey: Prentice Hall, 1996
256pp (European Casebook Series)
ISBN: 0133106810

This collection of case studies explores the development of the entrepreneur, the acquisition of resources, taking the business to market, managing the post-startup phase, and valuing and selling the business. The companies featured include Motivation Ltd., Robinson Instruments, Prestel and Minitel, Isis Scientific Software, MTL Instruments Group, Dockspeed Ltd., Advanced Business Computers Ltd., Pizza Pomodoro, and Naf-Naf.

Fostering Entrepreneurship

Organisation for Economic Co-operation and Development

Paris, France: The Brookings Institution, 1999
286pp ISBN: 9264161392

This book explains the importance of entrepreneurship and its benefits in terms of job creation and economic growth. It looks at ways of removing impediments and developing the conditions that enable entrepreneurs to flourish. A second section provides country-by-country information on the entrepreneurial climate, and summarizes the lessons that can be learned from entrepreneurs' experience.

Generation Entrepreneur

Stuart Crainer, Des Dearlove

London: Financial Times Business, 2000
266pp ISBN: 0273649205

This title looks at the future of business in the hands of "Generation X." This inspirational book suggests that entrepreneurship is now a "lifestyle choice" for young people wise in the ways of e-commerce, but there are also lessons here for more traditional businesses.

Good to Great: Why Some Companies Make the Leap . . . and Others Don't

Jim Collins

London: Random House Business Books, 2001
320pp ISBN: 0066620996

Written by one of the world's bestselling business writers and based on extensive research of over 1,000 businesses, this book focuses on eleven of the world's leading corporations and analyzes their successes. Concluding that an excellent corporate culture is the way forward, this book offers advice and useful tactics for all aspiring business builders.

The Guru Guide to Entrepreneurship: A Concise Guide to the Best Ideas from the World's Top Entrepreneurs

Joseph H. Boyett, Jimmie T. Boyett

Hoboken, New Jersey: Wiley, 2000
400pp ISBN: 0471390844

Drawing on the wisdom and experience of 70 of the world's leading entrepreneurs, this book examines the personal qualities of the successful entrepreneur, and considers what it takes to succeed in business.

How I Made It: 40 Successful Entrepreneurs Reveal All

Rachel Bridge

London: Kogan Page, 2004
192pp ISBN: 0749443111

This book features the inspiring stories behind 40 successful businesses. Adapted from interviews conducted by the author in her columns in the *Sunday Times*. Each piece looks at the early life and career of the

1745

BUSINESS INFORMATION SOURCES

"I want Britain to be a nation of entrepreneurs, a nation where talent and ability flourish."

Tony Blair

person in focus, and the motivation behind their achievements. Those profiled include Rosemary Conley, Prue Leith, and Mark Ellingham (founder of the Rough Guides series).

The HP Way
David Packard
New York: HarperCollins, 1996
224pp ISBN: 0887308171
In this book, Packard charts the emergence of his technology business: Hewlett Packard. He attributes the company's success to the unique outlook of the firm, "The HP Way," which promotes a combination of openness, honesty, and flexibility. The book should interest both entrepreneurs and technologists alike, in demonstrating the growth of a major contemporary technology company.

Management and Entrepreneurism
John C. Chicken
Stamford, Connecticut: International Thomson Publishing, 2000
192pp (Smart Strategies)
ISBN: 1861526393
This book examines the nature of constraints and the role of management in securing maximum benefit from entrepreneurism in both the private and public sectors. It considers the nature of activities requiring management, the forms of entrepreneurism, and the reality of management in the public and private sectors, and suggests how management efficiency can be improved. The book is suitable for students on MBA courses.

Marketing and Entrepreneurship in SMEs: An Innovative Approach
David Carson, Stanley Cromie, Pauric McGowan, Jimmy Hill
Upper Saddle River, New Jersey: Prentice Hall, 1996
296pp ISBN: 0131509705
Combining entrepreneurial theory and research with marketing knowledge to give a new perspective on the small business, this book is useful as both a reference book and as a support to general business education.

The MouseDriver Chronicles
John Lusk, Kyle Harrison
Cambridge, Massachusetts: Perseus Books Group, 2003
272pp ISBN: 0738208019
Lusk and Harrison, MBA graduates, narrate their experiences of starting their own company, and the problems they encountered along the way. Their product

was the MouseDriver, a computer mouse fashioned as a golf club head, which experienced mixed fortunes in a volatile technology market. Lusk and Harrison describe the events leading up to the product's conception, and how they managed to support it in a continually changing marketplace.

The Origin and Evolution of New Businesses
Amar V. Bhide
New York: Oxford University Press, Inc., 1999
432pp ISBN: 0195131444
This book develops a comprehensive framework for understanding entrepreneurship by drawing upon anecdote and folklore, intensive research, and modern theories of business and economics. It examines the concept of entrepreneurship, beginning with the improvised business start-up, through the radical shifts required to compete in niche markets, to the pursuit of entrepreneurship in large organizations.

Winning: The Ultimate Business How-to Book
Jack Welch, Suzy Welch
New York: HarperCollins, 2005
384pp ISBN: 0007197691
Written by a giant of 20th century business in the United States, *Winning* is Jack Welch's boot camp (in print form) for aspiring entrepreneurs. Aimed at people who, in Welch's own words are "in the trenches," the book is divided into three key sections: working within an organization, dealing with competitors, and handling work-life balance.

MAGAZINES
Entrepreneur
ISSN: 0163-3341
Entrepreneur Media, Inc.
2445 McCabe Way, Irvine, California, 92614
T: +1 415 433 2325
www.EntrepreneurMag.com
This magazine, established in 1978, contains articles, interviews, business profiles, financing, marketing, advertising, and legislative news written for the small business owner or those planning to start a new business.

Entrepreneurship and Regional Development
ISSN: 0898-5626
Routledge
29 West 35th Street, New York, NY, 10001
T: +1 212 216 7800
F: +1 212 564 7854

This quarterly journal provides a multidisciplinary forum for researchers and practitioners in the field of entrepreneurship and small-business development. It focuses on local and national factors which encourage entrepreneurial vitality.

Inc.
Gruner & Jahr U.S.A. Publishing
38 Commercial Wharf, Boston, Massachusetts, 02110-3883
T: +1 617 248 8000
F: +1 617 248 8090
www.inc.com
Published 12 times per year, this magazine is a premier journal on entrepreneurship. Each issue includes articles on financial and personnel management, marketing, administration, sales, and operations from the unique perspective of small businesses. It is a valuable publication for any executive or manager.

International Journal of Entrepreneurship and Innovation Management
ISSN: 1368-275X
Inderscience Enterprises Ltd.
World Trade Center Building, 29 route de Pre-Bois, Case Postale 896, CH-1215, Geneva, 15, Switzerland
T: +44 (0) 1234 240515
F: +41 22 791 08 85
www.inderscience.com
This journal publishes original, empirical, and review papers, case studies, and conference reports. It covers the areas of corporate venturing and intrapreneurship, the international aspects of entrepreneurship, the role of entrepreneurship in economic development, and government policies toward entrepreneurship. It is published quarterly.

International Journal of Management and Enterprise Development
ISSN: 1468-4330
Inderscience Enterprises Ltd.
World Trade Center Building, 29 route de Pre-Bois, Case Postale 896, CH-1215, Geneva, 15, Switzerland
T: +44 (0) 1234 240515
F: +41 22 791 08 85
www.inderscience.com
This bimonthly jounral, aimed at professionals, academics, and managers, covers the area of SME start-up, and development and related issues.

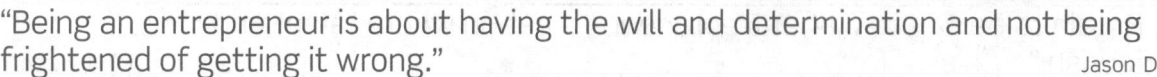
"Being an entrepreneur is about having the will and determination and not being frightened of getting it wrong."
Jason Drummond

Journal of Business Venturing
ISSN: 0883–9026
Elsevier Science
Customer Service Department, 6277 Sea
Harbor Drive, Orlando, Florida, 32887–4800
T: +1 877 839 7126 or +1 407 345 4020
F: +1 407 363 1354
www.elsevier.com
This bimonthly research journal publishes
articles by leading scholars and
practitioners, reporting theoretical findings
in the areas of entrepreneurship, new
business development, industry evolution,
and technology management.

INTERNET
CELCEE (Center for Entrepreneurial Leadership Clearinghouse on Entrepreneurship Education)
www.celcee.com
This site provides free access to an
extensive database of information relating
to entrepreneurship education. The
information is drawn from a wide range of
sources including articles, books, Web sites,
and conferences and updated weekly. Items
are indexed and abstracted, and include
details of availability.

Entrepreneur.com
www.entrepreneur.com
This is a magazine site sponsored by
Entrepreneur Media, Inc., offering a
comprehensive range of practical
information for owners of small businesses.
The information includes a search engine,
databases, blogs, and links to free business
tools.

Entrepreneurial Edge
www.lowe.org
The Michigan-based Edward Lowe
Foundation provides information and
resources for entrepreneurs including news
and relevant articles.

The Entrepreneurs' Help Page
www.tannedfeet.com
Written by young professionals for other
professionals and entrepreneurs,
tannedfeet.com has numerous pages of
simple business information that help
individuals save time and money. Instead of
hiring a professional for a fee, try finding
what you need at this site instead.

EntreWorld
www.entreworld.org
This is a collection of resources for
entrepreneurs provided by the Kauffman
Center for Entrepreneurial Leadership in

Kansas City. Three sections focus on
starting, growing, and finding support for a
business. The site includes articles, a
glossary, practical advice, an e-mail
newsletter, an events calendar, and a
bookstore.

eWeb
http://eweb.slu.edu/eweb.htm
This Web site is provided by St. Louis
University, and provides information on
entrepreneurial education programs,
organizations, research centers, and
assistance for entrepreneurs, including
advice on business planning.

Global Entrepreneurship Institute
www.gcase.org
The site sponsored by this nonprofit,
nongovernmental organization provides
open source material for entrepreneurs
and managers of small businesses, and
includes articles, book lists, and useful
links.

ORGANIZATIONS
USA
Kauffman Center for Entrepreneurial Leadership
Ewing Marion Kauffman Foundation, 4801
Rockhill Road, Kansas City, Missouri, 64110
T: +1 816 932 1000
www.emkf.org
The Kauffman Center promotes
entrepreneurship in the United States
through education, training, research, and a
program of grants. The Center is involved in
a wide range of initiatives to develop the
concepts and skills of entrepreneurship in
young people, and to promote the
contribution entrepreneurship can
make to community and economic
development.

National Business Incubation Association (NBIA)
20 East Circle Drive, #37198, Athens, Ohio,
45701–3571
T: +1 740 593 4331
F: +1 740 593 1996
E: *info@nbia.org*
www.nbia.org
The NBIA provides information, education,
advocacy, and networking opportunities for
those involved or interested in business
incubation programs. The organization
conducts research, produces statistics and
publications on this subject, and runs a
referral service. Members include directors
of incubator firms, business advisers,
consultants, and investors.

Europe
National Federation of Enterprise Agencies (NFEA)
12 Stephenson Court, Fraser Road, Priory
Business Park, Bedford, Bedfordshire,
MK44 3WH, U.K.
T: +44 (0) 1234 831 623
F: +44 (0) 1234 831 625
E: *enquiries@nfea.com*
www.nfea.com
The NFEA is a network of independent,
nonprofit local enterprise agencies for the
support of small and growing businesses,
especially start-ups and microbusinesses.
The organization aims to identify the needs
of such businesses, encourage the
government and others to provide the
conditions for them to flourish, and provide
a forum for members to share best practice.
The British Volunteer Mentor Programme is
an initiative of the NFEA.

International
Entrepreneurs' Organization (EO)
Suite 500, 500 Montgomery Street,
Alexandria, Virginia, 22314
T: +1 703 519 6700
F: +1 703 519 1864
www.eonetwork.org
EO is a membership organization designed
to help international business owners to
achieve greater business and personal
fulfilment. Members must be the founder,
co-founder, owner or controlling
stockholder of a business that exceeds
U.S.$1 million in annual gross sales.
Founded in 1987, EO now has 6,000
members in over 120 chapters.

National Foundation for Teaching Entrepreneurship (NFTE)
29th Floor, 120 Wall Street, New York, 10005
T: +1 212 232 3333
www.nfte.com
NFTE was founded in 1987 as a program for
students to prevent dropouts and improve
academic performance. Now an
international nonprofit organization, it
aims to help low-income young people by
strengthening academic skills and teaching
the basics of how to start and run a small
business. This is achieved through the
development of curricula, training
teachers, and the provision of services to
alumni.

1747

BUSINESS INFORMATION SOURCES

FOR MORE INFORMATION

☆ Avoiding the Mistakes of the Past:
  Lessons from the Startup World
  (pp. 164–165)

"Enough of talking—it is now time to do."

Tony Blair

Environmental Management

BUSINESS INFORMATION SOURCES

BOOKS

Corporate Environmental Management 3: Towards Sustainable Development
Richard Welford, ed.
Sterling, Virginia: Stylus Publishing, 2000
184pp (Corporate Environmental Management 3)
ISBN: 1853836419
The author reviews the environmental responsibilities that businesses and organizations must carry in order to ensure a sustainable future. He considers strategies for achieving operations consistent with this goal, focusing on societal, ethical, and social issues.

The Ecology of Commerce: A Declaration of Sustainability
Paul Hawken
New York: HarperCollins, 1994
320pp ISBN: 0887307043
The author asserts that powerful, modern companies need to lessen the amount of energy and resources they use. He also suggests that the aims of business should be altered so as to ensure that the natural world benefits and the needs of the planet are catered for.

Environmental Management and Business Strategy: Leadership Skills for the 21st Century
Bruce W. Piasecki, Kevin A. Fletcher, Frank J. Mendelson
Hoboken, New Jersey: Wiley, 1998
368pp ISBN: 0471169722
The authors explore the factors influencing the development of corporate environmental strategies. The topics covered include: regulatory requirements; environmental policy; environmental accounting; new product development; the use of environmental management systems; and stakeholder expectations. Case studies and further sources of information are appended.

Lean and Green: Profit for Your Workplace and the Environment
Pamela Gordon
San Francisco, California: Berrett-Koehler, 2001
250pp ISBN: 1576751708
This book shows, through over a hundred examples, how companies can save money by following environmentally sound policies. The author provides a detailed

plan of action and discusses procedures such as questioning wasteful practices, setting goals to make facilities more energy- and cost-efficient, gaining management's endorsement for environmentally sound policies by introducing them in business terms, and tracking progress.

Managing Environmental Risks and Liabilities
Paul Pritchard
London: Earthscan, 2000
240pp (Business and Environmental Practitioner)
ISBN: 1853835986
Recent developments in environmental risk management are discussed in this book, which focuses on the nature of environmental risks and their relation to property, financial risk transfer, decision making, risk-management integration, and risk-management frameworks.

Managing Green Issues
Tom Curtin, Jacqueline Jones
New York: St. Martin's Press, 2001
205pp ISBN: 0312237162
The authors explore the potential and the pitfalls of environmental management and analyze green issues to give an insight into why many companies fail to manage them successfully. The book includes strategies, advice, and case studies.

Measuring Corporate and Environmental Performance: Best Practices for Costing and Managing an Effective Environment
Marc Epstein
Maidenhead, United Kingdom: McGraw-Hill, 1996
319pp ISBN: 0786302305
This book provides information and suggestions on how to develop and implement a corporate environmental strategy. It describes the best and the most up-to-date practices of corporate environmental performance, and includes the results of the largest field study to be conducted in this area.

The Natural Step for Business: Wealth, Ecology, and the Evolutionary Corporation
Brian Nattrass, Mary Altomare
Gabriola Island, British Columbia: New Society Publishers, 1999
222pp ISBN: 0865713847

The book explains the Natural Step Process, a framework for creating environmentally aware companies that are successful enterprises. It is filled with case studies of such companies as IKEA, Scandic Hotels, Electrolux, and Mitsubishi, highlighting how businesses can change to a new model of operations.

Principles of Environmental Management: The Greening of Business 2nd ed.
Rogene A. Bucholz
Upper Saddle River, New Jersey: Prentice Hall, 1998
448pp ISBN: 0136848958
This updated edition focuses on the management of the environment as a business concern. The book provides examples of corporate efforts to respond to specific environmental issues and offers strategic approaches to issues such as ozone depletion, acid rain, air and water pollution, and disposal of hazardous wastes. It examines the regulations corporations must deal with and the public pressure they face as well as highlighting the responsibilities of business for helping create a sustainable society.

Sustainability Strategies for the Industry: The Future of Corporate Practice
Nigel Roome, ed.
Washington, D.C.: Island Press, 1998
322pp (Greening of Industry Network)
ISBN: 1559635983
This book contains essays by members of the Greening of Industry Network. The essays examine the emerging picture of sustainability and its implications for industry, as well as for the relationship between industry and consumers, employees, and the community at large.

MAGAZINES
Business and the Environment
ISSN: 1052–7206
Cutter Information Corporation
37 Broadway, Suite 1, Arlington, Massachusetts, 02474
T: +1 800 964 5118 or 781 648 8700
F: +1 800 888 1816 or 781 648 1950
www.cutter.com
This monthly publication enables worldwide environmental professionals to learn about and debate environmental

---

"It is not until a creature begins to manage its environment that nature is thrown into disorder."

Clifford Simak

management issues. It contains case studies, news coverage, and helpful contact information. Each issue also includes the supplemental service BATE's ISO 14000 Update, including news on the status of the ISO 14000 standards and case studies of companies that have implemented the environmental management systems (EMS) standards.

Business Strategy and the Environment

ISSN: 0964–4733
ERP Environment and Wiley
111 River St, Hoboken, New Jersey, 07030–5774
T: +1 800 825 7550
F: +1 212 850 6021
www.wiley.com
Aimed at environmental managers and strategic planners, this bimonthly journal addresses key environmental issues facing managers and industry.

The ENDS Report

ISSN: 0966–4076
Environmental Data Services Ltd.
Finsbury Business Centre, 40 Bowling Green Lane, London, EC1R 0NE, U.K.
T: +44 (0) 20 7814 5300
F: +44 (0) 20 7415 0106
www.ends.co.uk
This is a monthly digest of U.K. and European environmental developments, news, and legislation, aimed at environmental professionals.

Environmental Quality Management

ISSN: 1088–1913
Wiley
111 River St, Hoboken, New Jersey, 07030–5774
T: +1 201 748 6000
F: +1 212 850 6021
www.wiley.com
Published four times per year, this magazine covers the growing application of total quality management to environmental programs. The magazine highlights such issues as how to improve environmental performance and how to apply TQM to environmental practice. It also features case studies of successful environmental quality programs and includes implementation guidelines.

Environment Business Magazine

ISSN: 1352–8882
GEE Publishing Ltd.
100 Avenue Road, Swiss Cottage, London, NW3 3PG, U.K.
T: +44 (0) 20 7393 7400
F: +44 (0) 20 7393 7915

www.gee.co.uk
A magazine for senior managers that focuses on environmental management and technology across business and industry.

International Journal of Environmental Studies

ISSN: 0020–7233
Taylor & Francis
325 Chestnut St., Suite 800, Philadelphia, Pennsylvania 19106
T: +1 800 354 1420
F: +1 215 625 2940
www.tandf.co.uk
This bimonthly journal for academics, researchers, and environmentalists publishes original papers, review articles, and research on environmental problems and their solutions.

INTERNET
SustainableBusiness.com
www.sustainablebusiness.com
This site features news about environmental issues and industry, along with a newsletter, and gives access to information about resources and events, as well as posting press releases from organizations involved in this subject.

Sustainable Enterprise Program—World Resources Institute
www.wri.org
The SEP section of the World Resources Institute site provides information about programs, publications, and projects focusing on business and the environment. To reach this section's page, click on "Business and Economics" under the "Research Topics" tab.

U.S. Environmental Protection Association (EPA)
www.epa.gov
This content-rich site includes information on current issues, legislation, government programs, regional links, regulatory guidance, and publications. Visitors can check their region's air quality at a glance and also test their own "EnviroQ." The site may also be viewed in Spanish.

ORGANIZATIONS
USA
National Association for Environmental Management (NAEM)
1612 K Street NW, Suite 1102, Washington, D.C., 20006
T: +1 202 986 6616 or 800 391 6236
F: +1 202 530 4408

E: *programs@naem.org*
www.naem.org
The NAEM has over 1,000 members and is the leading organization for the advancement of professional environmental management. The association was created specifically to unite environmental managers from a wide range of industries. NAEM provides professional development opportunities for workers in both the private and public sector.

National Registry of Environmental Professionals (NREP)
P.O. Box 2099, Glenview, Illinois, 60025–6090
T: +1 847 724 6631
F: +1 847 724 4223
E: *nrep@nrep.org*
www.nrep.org
The NREP has over 27,000 members. This association certifies property assessors, indoor air quality specialists, hazardous and chemical material managers, ISO 14000 program administrators, and environmental managers. The NREP also promotes the benefits of their accreditation to the public and private sector and provides lists of qualified environmental professionals to governmental agencies.

U.S. Environmental Protection Association (EPA)
Ariel Rios Building, 1200 Pennsylvania Avenue NW, Washington, D.C., 20460
T: +1 202 272 0167
www.epa.gov
Formed in 1970, this is the U.S. government body concerned with the enforcement and protection of environmental standards consistent with national environmental goals. The U.S. EPA is involved in environmental research and the collation of environmental information, and also offers technical and policy advice.

1749

BUSINESS INFORMATION SOURCES

"Accuse not Nature, she hath done her part; Do thou but thine."

John Milton

Equal Opportunities

BOOKS

Beyond Race and Gender: Unleashing the Power of Your Total Work Force by Managing Diversity

R. Roosevelt Thomas, Jr.
New York: AMACOM, 1991
189pp ISBN: 0814478077
Looking ahead to a time when the U.S. workforce will be truly diverse, the author of this classic and groundbreaking book explores the problems facing managers trying to offer equal opportunities to all in order to take advantage of needed talents and skills. He presents an action plan for changing corporate cultures as well as case studies that highlight the problems that emerge once an organization recruits a diverse work force, especially the failure of those recruited to move up the corporate ladder.

Breaking through the Glass Ceiling: Women in Management

Linda Wirth
Washington, D.C.: Brookings Institution, 2001
144pp ISBN: 9221108457
This ILO report is an international study of the changing position of women in the labor market, in professional and managerial jobs, and in politics. It gives figures and statistical information from many sources, and focuses on issues such as discrimination, equal pay, gender mainstreaming, career building strategies, and actions to improve women's opportunities, thus giving an international overview of the effects of the glass ceiling on women.

The Equal Opportunities Guide: How to Deal with Everyday Issues of Unfairness 2nd ed.

Phil Clements, Tony Spinks
Sterling, Virginia: Stylus Publishing, 1997
192pp ISBN: 0749421037
This is a plainly written resource for students, managers, trainers, human resource management staff, teachers, and all those with an interest in equality of opportunity. The text sets out straightforward procedures to guide fair, courteous, and sensitive behavior to others, and includes a summary of recent U.K. legislation and agencies, self-assessment sections, and ways of identifying and preventing institutional discrimination.

Federal Law of Employment Discrimination in a Nutshell 5th ed.

Mack A. Player
Saint Paul, Minnesota: West Publishing Company, 2004
352pp ISBN: 0314150021
Issues of workplace discrimination based on race, sex, national origin, religion, age, and disability are examined in this book, and placed in a legal and regulatory context. The author also explores the history of such relevant statutes as the Equal Employment Opportunity Act and the Age Discrimination in Employment Act and considers the enforcement procedures in place, as well as dealing with difficult subjects such as liability in the absence of motive, retaliation, and remedies.

Investigating Harassment and Discrimination Complaints: A Practical Guide

Jan C. Salisbury, Bobbi Killian Dominick
New York: Wiley, 2004
320pp ISBN: 0787967849
This manual provides practical guidance for human resource professionals who deal with harassment, discrimination, or retaliation complaints and is accessible to both novices and the experienced. It provides tools for the development of skills and competencies within a framework for investigation, following the process in logical order. It begins with information essential for the understanding of complaints. This book then proceeds to deal with pre-investigation, followed by an exploration of the strengths and characteristics of investigators and of an organization's systems. The investigation process itself is then discussed, focusing on issues of planning, documentation, tips and techniques for carrying out an investigation, and the conclusions that can be drawn.

Job Discrimination in the Workplace II: How to Fight . . . How to Win!

Jeffrey M. Bernbach
Englewood Cliffs, New Jersey: Voir Dire Press, 1998
173pp ISBN: 0965375315
This book, a legal expert's guide to employees who believe they are the victims of discrimination in the workplace on the basis of their race, age, sex, disability, or religion, explains how to determine whether you have a real case and how to wage a court battle to prove it. Bernbach offers case histories, job bias rulings, including rulings by the Supreme Court, and information that proves it is possible to make such a case successfully.

Organizational Behaviour and Gender 2nd ed.

Fiona M. Wilson
Aldershot, Hampshire: Ashgate Publishing Ltd, 2003
256pp ISBN: 0754609006
This text examines some of the assumptions that have been made about women at work and considers the key topics in organizational behavior (OB) to test such assumptions. This book describes the reality of working life for women and asks whether inequality of opportunity comes about because of actual gender or from prejudicial expectations and thinking. Topics covered include men's and women's place at work and home; perceiving men and women in organizations; learning and socialization; motivation; leadership; personality and sex, and the body and sexuality in organizations. This last chapter describes the masculine and heterosexual business environment and examines the issues of work romances and sexual harassment.

Powerful Women: Dancing on the Glass Ceiling

Sam Parkhouse
Hoboken, New Jersey: Wiley, 2001
256pp ISBN: 0471499056
A very readable book, written in a popular magazine style, it focuses on the individual stories behind the successes of several unusual women. It is aimed at a very general audience and takes neither an academic nor an equal opportunities perspective but attempts to get to grips with the real experiences of case study women, such as Barbara Cassani, Belinda Earl, Nicola Horlick, Anita Roddick, and Margaret Jay.

MAGAZINES

Black EOE Journal

National Women's Business Council
6845 Indiana Avenue, Suite 200, Riverside, California, 92506
T: +1 800 487 5099
F: +1 714 974 3978

"Saying that a person cannot be kept out doesn't ensure that that person can get in, and more important, stay in."

Margaret Hennig

www.blackeoejournal.com

This magazine contains articles about all minorities and provides valuable information regarding career opportunities. The journal focuses on the needs of employers in relation to workplace diversity. A section on career planning and advancement is particularly valuable to readers.

Careers & the Disabled

ISSN: 1056–277X
Equal Opportunities Publications, Inc.
445 Broad Hollow Road, Suite 425, Melville, New York, 11747
T: +1 631 421 9421
F: +1 631 421 0359
www.eop.com

This magazine is the premier U. S. career guidance and recruitment magazine for people with disabilities. Unique to this publication is the inclusion of a special braille section.

The Diversity Factor

ISSN: 1067-7194
Elsie Y. Cross Associates, Inc.
7627 Germantown Avenue, Philadelphia, Pennsylvania, 19118
T: +1 215 248 8100
F: +1 215 242 3328
www.eyca.com/diversity.html

This quarterly journal, founded in 1992, is a must-read for any business professional working with equal opportunity issues. Cutting-edge strategies are detailed to provide the latest developments in handling workplace discrimination. The magazine provides updates to the latest legislative action regarding discrimination and EOE/AA, and also reviews current literature.

Equal Opportunities International

ISSN: 0261-0159
Barmarick Publications
Enholmes Hall, Patrington, East Riding of Yorkshire, HU12 0PR, U.K.
T: +44 (0) 1964 630 033
F: +44 (0) 1964 631 716
www.emeraldinsight.com

This is a high-priced subscription journal carrying articles by academics involved in equal opportunities teaching or research. The number of issues per year is variable, but four were published in 2005.

INTERNET
Equal Opportunity Employment Commission
www.eeoc.gov

This U.S. government-sponsored Web site provides a vast amount of material on

equal opportunities, ranging from statistics to federal laws to information about technical assistance and training programs.

ORGANIZATIONS
USA
American Association for Affirmative Action (AAAA)
888 16th Street, NW, Suite 800, Washington, D.C., 20006
T: +1 800 252 8952
F: +1 202 355 1399
www.affirmativeaction.org

This association focuses on managing affirmative action, equal opportunity, diversity, and related human resource issues. The association is committed to the advancement of affirmative action at the local, state and national level. Members are also involved in creating and implementing strategies for maintaining equal employment opportunities. The AAAA will provide individualized assessments of EOE/AA compliance concerns.

Center for Equal Opportunity (C.E.O.)
14 Pidgeon Hill Drive, Suite 500, Sterling, Virginia, 20165
T: +1 703 421 5443
F: +1 703 421 6401
E: *comment@ceousa.org*
www.ceousa.org

Founded in 1995, the C.E.O. promotes the assimilation of immigrants into American society. It demands that local, state and national governments stop public policies that divide Americans by national origin, and provides research showing the harmful effects of dividing the American workplace by race, sex, and ethnic background.

Employment Policy Foundation (EPF)
1015 15th Street NW, Suite 1200, Washington, D.C., 20005
T: +1 202 789 8685
F: +1 202 789 8684
E: *info@epf.org*
www.epf.org

Founded in 1983, the EPF is a nonpartisan public policy research foundation focused on workforce trends. This organization conducts studies and provides U.S. policymakers with economic analyses of employment policies, revealing how these policies affect the goals of American industry and workers. The EPF is regarded as one of the best sources for unbiased, reliable and thorough research on employment issues.

Equal Employment Opportunity Commission (EEOC)
P.O. Box 7033, Lawrence, Kansas, 66044
T: +1 800 669 4000
F: +1 703 997 4890
E: *info@ask.eeoc.gov*
www.eeoc.gov

This body was established by Title VII of the Civil Rights Act of 1964 to enforce federal statutes prohibiting employment discrimination. It began operating on July 2, 1965.

Europe
Commission for Racial Equality (CRE)
St. Dunstan's House, 201–211 Borough High Street, London, SE1 1GZ, U.K.
T: +44 (0) 20 7939 0000
F: +44 (0) 20 7939 0001
E: *info@cre.gov.uk*
www.cre.gov.uk

This is a publicly funded but nongovernmental body set up under the Race Relations Act 1976 to deal with racial discord and promote racial equality. It provides information and advice, seeks to raise awareness of relevant issues, and promotes policies and practices to ensure equality of treatment for all.

Disability Rights Commission (DRC)
DRC Helpline, Freepost MID 02164, Stratford-upon-Avon, Warwickshire, CV37 9BR, U.K.
T: +44 (0) 8457 622 633
F: +44 (0) 8457 778 878
www.drc-gb.org

Established by an Act of Parliament, the Commission came into operation in April 2000 to ensure that the Disability Discrimination Act 1995 takes effect, to keep disability legislation under review, and to publicize and promote good practice.

1751

BUSINESS INFORMATION SOURCES

FOR MORE INFORMATION

- ☆ Boosting Business Success through Diversity (pp. 28–29)
- ℘ Conditions of Employment (pp. 1708–1709)
- ℘ Diversity (pp. 1732–1733)
- ℘ Employee Relations (pp. 1741–1742)
- ℘ Employment Law (pp. 1743–1744)
- ☆ Improving Company Performance with an Older Work Force (pp. 23–24)
- ✔ Introducing an Equal Opportunities Policy (pp. 494–495)
- ☆ Tackling Sexual Harassment in the Workplace (pp. 47–48)
- ☆ Transcending the Glass Ceiling (pp. 289–291)

"Equal opportunity means everyone will have a fair chance at becoming incompetent."

Laurence J. Peter

Exporting

BOOKS

Building an Import/Export Business 3rd ed.
Kenneth D. Weiss
Hoboken, New Jersey: Wiley, 2002
320pp ISBN: 0471202495
This is a user-friendly guide to starting and building a successful import or export business. It gives guidance on potential areas of concern, such as operational procedures, trade agreements, and marketing techniques. It also provides practical advice on how best to tap into the lucrative global markets. It includes bibliographical references and an index.

Export Savvy: From Basics to Strategy
Zak Karamally
New York: International Business Press/The Haworth Press, 1998
198pp ISBN: 0789005778
This book deals with export management from the concepts of international trade to the key elements that influence and comprise its effectiveness. It relates the export experience to the commercial experience as a whole. This involves breaking down the complicated process of exporting into simple and familiar terms. It includes bibliographical references and an index.

Global Jumpstart: The Complete Resource for Expanding Small and Midsized Businesses
Ruth Stanat, Chris West
Cambridge, Massachusetts: Perseus Books Group, 2000
198pp ISBN: 073820160X
This book is a useful resource guide for companies of the size mentioned in the title who have reached any stage of the expansion process. It provides in-depth analysis of business opportunities around the world, while also giving a valuable insight into the pitfalls in international markets for small companies.

MAGAZINES

Export and Freight
4 square media
12 Main Street, Hillsborough, Northern Ireland, U.K.
T: +44 (0) 289268 8888
F: +44 (0) 289268 8866
This journal covers all aspects of exporting, including freight, handling, and storage.

The Exporter
The Exporter
26 Broadway, Suite 776, New York, 10004
T: +1 212 269 2016
F: +1 212 269 2740
www.exporter.com
This journal is aimed at government, financial institutions, and trade brokers, as well as manufacturers and large exporters.

Foreign Affairs
ISSN: 0015–7120
Council on Foreign Relations
58 East 68th Street, New York, 10021
T: +1 386 246 3386 or 800 829 5539
www.foreignaffairs.org
Published six times a year, this influential journal covers American foreign policy and international affairs and acts as a forum for debate on current world issues.

International Business Review
ISSN: 0969–5931
Elsevier Science
Customer Service Department, 6277 Sea Harbor Drive, Orlando, Florida, 32887–4800
T: +1 877 839 7126 or +1 407 345 4020
F: +1 407 363 1354
www.elsevier.com
Published six times per year, this magazine is vital for any business professional working in international business. With an emphasis on marketing and management issues, the magazine has an international list of authors and aims to keep senior management abreast of the most recent thinking and developments in the field of international business.

INTERNET

American Countertrade Association
www.countertrade.org
The objects of the American Countertrade Association are to promote trade and commerce between companies and their foreign customers who engage in countertrade as a form of doing business. This site does not include a great deal of content, but would be a useful starting point for those beginning research in this area.

Customs & Border Protection, U.S. Department of Homeland Security
www.customs.gov/xp/cgov/export
This site has information regarding exporting from the United States. Features include a list of export requirements and licenses, info about blocked or denied persons, fees, and links to other government sites.

Exportinfo.org
www.exportinfo.org
Produced by students at the University of Washington Business School, exportinfo.org provides basic information for anyone new to the exportation process.

Kompass
www.kompass.com
This online searchable database lists some 1.9 million companies in about 70 countries, under 53,000 product headings. The databases for individual countries may also be purchased in printed format. CDs are also available.

Market Access Database
http://mkaccdb.eu.int/mkaccdb2/indexPubli.htm
The Market Access Database is provided by the DG Trade, European Commission. Certain parts of the site are open only to people having an ISP connection located in Europe, but the section on trade barriers is open to all Internet users. The site contains details about trade barriers by market sector and country, import formalities by country, and import duties by product code and by country.

Thomas Global Register
www.tgrnet.com
Formerly the American Export Register, this comprehensive Web-based directory run by Thomas Publishing gives details of some 700,000 manufacturers and distributors across 28 countries, divided into 11,000 product and service classifications.

Trade Information Center
www.trade.gov/td/tic
The Trade Information Center (TIC) is a comprehensive resource for information and advice on all U.S. Federal Government export assistance programs. It is operated by the International Trade Administration of the U.S. Department of Commerce for the federal agencies comprising the Trade Promotion Coordinating Committee (TPCC). These agencies are responsible for managing the U.S. Government's export promotion programs and activities.

"There is nothing Japan really wants to buy from foreign countries except, possibly, neckties with unusual designs."

Yoshihiro Inayama

     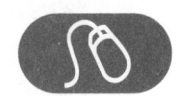

ORGANIZATIONS
USA
Bureau of Export Administration, U.S. Department of Commerce (BXA)

1401 Constitution Avenue, NW, Washington, D.C., 20230

T: +1 202 482 0097

F: +1 202 482 2421

http://bxa.fedworld.gov

The Bureau of Export Administration is concerned with advancing U.S. national security, foreign policy, and economic interests. Its key activities include regulating the export of sensitive goods and technologies in an effective and efficient manner, cooperating with and assisting other countries on export control and strategic trade issues, and promoting federal initiatives and public-private partnerships across industry sectors to protect national infrastructures.

Federation of International Trade Associations (FITA)

11800 Sunrise Valley Drive, Suite 210, Reston, Virginia, 20190

T: +1 800 969 3482

F: +1 703 620 4922

E: *info@fita.org*

www.fita.org

The Federation fosters international trade by strengthening the role of local, regional, and national associations throughout the United States, Mexico, and Canada. Its Web site includes a directory of 8,000 Trade and Import/Export Web sites.

International Trade Administration, U.S. Department of Commerce (ITA)

1401 Constitution Avenue, NW, Room 3414, Washington, D.C., 20230

T: +1 202 482 3809

F: +1 282 482 5819

www.ita.doc.gov

This organization is the lead unit for trade in the Department of Commerce. It participates in formulating and implementing U.S. foreign trade and economic policies, and monitors market access and compliance of U.S. international trade agreements.

Europe
Institute of Export

Export House, Minerva Business Park, Lynch Wood, Peterborough, Cambridgeshire, PE2 6FT, U.K.

T: +44 (0) 1733 404 400

F: +44 (0) 1733 404 444

E: *institute@export.org.uk*

www.export.org.uk

This body of professional members aims to raise standards in international trade management and export practice. It offers training programs and other education to members.

U.K. Trade and Investment

Kingsgate House, 66–74 Victoria Street, London, SW1E 6SW, U.K.

T: +44 (0) 20 7215 8200

F: +44 (0) 20 7215 4699

www.uktradeinvest.gov.uk

Created in 2003 and taking the place of Trade Partners U.K., this government service supports British companies aiming to do business internationally as well as overseas organizations wishing to establish operations in the United Kingdom.

World Trade and International Trade Rules

Bay 4141, 1 Victoria Street, London, SW1E 0ET, U.K.

T: +44 (0) 20 7215 5000

E: *dti.enquiries@dti.gsi.gov.uk*

www.dti.gov.uk/ewt/import.htm

The Department of Trade and Industry is responsible for U.K. trade policy at international, European, and national levels, and for harmonizing customs tariff levels with European Union member states. It is also responsible, in conjunction with several other government departments, for policy on all U.K. export and import prohibitions and restrictions.

International
International Chamber of Commerce (ICC)

38 Cours Albert 1er, Paris, 75008, France

T: +33 1 49 53 28 28

F: +33 1 49 53 28 59

E: *webmaster@iccwbo.org*

www.iccwbo.org

The ICC is the only representative body that speaks out with authority on behalf of enterprises from all sectors in every part of the world. The ICC provides a number of international services and publications.

World Trade Organization (WTO)

Centre William Rappard, Rue de Lausanne 154, CH-1211 Geneva 21, Switzerland

T: +41 22 739 51 11

F: +41 22 731 42 06

E: *enquiries@wto.org*

www.wto.org

The WTO is an international member-based organization, whose role is to deal with the rules of trade between member nations. It aims to help producers of goods and services, and exporters and importers, to conduct their business effectively. It includes the Working Group on the Interaction between Trade and Competition Policy.

FOR MORE INFORMATION

☆ Globalization and Regional Business Strategy (pp. 128–129)

꙰ Importing (p. 1771)

꙰ International Management, Cross Cultural Management (pp. 1784–1786)

✔ Preparing for Business Abroad (pp. 570–571)

☆ Viewpoint: Fons Trompenaars (pp. 25–27)

1753

BUSINESS INFORMATION SOURCES

"You can always buy something in English, you can't always sell something in English."

Rosabeth Moss Kanter

Facilities Management

BOOKS

Facility Design and Management Handbook

Eric Teicholz

Maidenhead, United Kingdom: McGraw-Hill, 2001

752pp ISBN: 0071353941

This handbook contains tips and case studies for several industries. It discusses the tools and technologies needed to develop cost-effective solutions to common problems like space planning, environmental sensitivity, technology integration, and disaster planning. It also shows how to automate most tasks and apply benchmarking for measurable improvements in productivity. The CD-ROM included with the book contains sample forms and links to additional resources.

Manager's Guide to Contingency Planning for Disasters: Protecting Vital Facilities and Critical Operations 2nd ed.

Kenneth N. Myers

Hoboken, New Jersey: Wiley, 1999

252pp ISBN: 047135838X

This book is designed to help you either avoid a disaster or recover from one quickly with a minimum of expense and lost time. It provides a structured approach to contingency planning that aims to minimize plan development costs. It helps the reader define the problem, increase awareness, conduct a business impact analysis, and develop an implementation strategy.

Work Transformation: Planning and Implementing the New Workplace

Ken Robertson

New York: HNB Publishing, 1998

286pp ISBN: 0966428609

The author shows how the integration of human resources, facilities management, and information technology strategies creates ways of delivering work transformation. The chapter on facilities management looks at how to investigate, design, and implement alternative space arrangements such as space sharing, hoteling, team spaces, casual meeting areas, and meditation zones. It then reports on how this can reduce costs, utilize space effectively, and help to create a community environment.

INTERNET

British Institute of Facilities Management
www.bifm.org.uk

The Institute's Web site provides information on membership benefits, industry news and events listings, education and professional development, and the BIFM awards. Users can also gain access to an online bookshop. Some content is available to members only.

FMLink
www.fmlink.com

If this site doesn't have the facilities management information you need, it will tell you where to find it. It features news and an events calendar, survey and benchmarking data, access to the FM job market, a marketplace, and an ideas exchange, where facility managers can discuss issues.

I-FM
www.i-fm.net

This site offers a wide selection of facilities management resources, including news items and articles, and company and job listings. Users must register, however, to read the most up-to-date features, which are updated daily. A discussion group is also featured.

International Facility Management Association
www.ifma.org

Through this site, the IFMA provides professional development courses, access to the job market, facility management certification, and benchmarking and best practices metrics. The site includes details of membership benefits and a bookstore.

ORGANIZATIONS
Europe
British Institute of Facilities Management (BIFM)

67 High Street, Saffron Walden, Essex, CB10 1AA, U.K.

T: +44 (0) 1799 598 606

E: *admin@bifm.org.uk*

www.bifm.org.uk

The Institute is a professional membership body, founded in 1993, for managers responsible for facilities management of office premises, including planning, design, and equipment purchasing. It is also for people working in organizations that supply facilities management goods and services.

Facilities Management Association (FMA)

Charter House, 13–15 Carteret Street, London, SW1H 9DJ, U.K.

T: +44 (0) 7960 428 146

E: *mtaffler@fmassociation.org.uk*

www.fmassociation.org.uk

This is a trade organization, established in 1995, representing organizations that are suppliers of facilities services. The FMA promotes and represents members' interests at government level, and is affiliated with the International Facility Management Association.

International
International Facility Management Association (IFMA)

1 E. Greenway Plaza, Suite 1100, Houston, Texas, 77046–0194

T: +1 713 623 4362

F: +1 713 623 6124

E: *ifma@ifma.org*

www.ifma.org

This is a nonprofit incorporated association, established in 1980, that is dedicated to providing excellence in the management of facilities. The IFMA has members throughout the world.

FOR MORE INFORMATION

☆ Outsourcing (pp. 120–121)
℘ Outsourcing (p. 1851)

"Just look at him. He runs his company with five people in an office the size of a closet."

Katharine Graham

     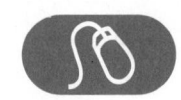

Finding Out What You Are Worth: Remuneration/Salaries

MAGAZINES

Kiplinger's Personal Finance Magazine
ISSN: 1056–697X
Kiplinger
1729 H Street, Washington, D.C., 20006
T: +1 888 419 0424
www.kiplinger.com
Formerly entitled *Changing Times*, this magazine is published 12 times per year. With a concentration on banking, accounting, and general financial information, this publication will appeal to both professionals and the general public. It provides concise yet informative articles on salaries, spending, and saving.

Labour Force Survey Quarterly Supplement
ISSN: 0967–5876
Office for National Statistics
1 Drummond Gate, London, SW1V 2QQ, U.K.
T: +44 (0) 1633 812 973
F: +44 (0) 1633 652 747
www.statistics.gov.uk
This Labour Market Trends supplement contains tables of labor market statistics for the United Kingdom, including average gross weekly earnings by region, occupation, and industry sector.

Money
Time, Inc.
P.O. Box 60001, Tampa, Florida, 33660
T: +1 800 633 9970
http://money.cnn.com
This magazine is designed to help individuals with personal and family finance. Articles provide guidance on making, investing, and spending money.

INTERNET

HayPayNet
www.haypaynet.com
Access to Hay's PayNet databases of pay rates in 55 countries worldwide is by subscription. The site also provides links to related sites within the Hay Group and free access to its "Quick Poll" feature.

Job Star Central Salary Information
http://jobstar.org/tools/salary
This site contains a collection of links to over 300 Web-based salary surveys, as well as articles and advice.

Monster.com's Salary Center
http://content.salary.monster.com
On this portion of the Monster.com site, users who want to know their worth can take advantage of the Salary Wizard. You can choose by job category and/or region. An initial report is free, but users may also purchase a more detailed, personalized report.

National Compensation Survey
www.bls.gov/ncs
This site gives access to data from the U.S. Bureau of Labor Statistics.

SalariesReview.com
www.salariesreview.com
This site offers access to salary and cost-of-living information from the Economic Research Institute on thousands of jobs in Canada and the United States and internationally on a pay-per-view basis.

Salary.com
www.salary.com
This U.S. site provides a range of resources, including the Salary Wizard, news, and advice. It contains useful information for small businesses as well as individuals and larger enterprises.

ORGANIZATIONS
USA
Hay Group
101 Hudson Street, Jersey City, New Jersey, 07302
T: +1 201 557 8400
F: +1 201 557 8444
E: *maria_sasso@haygroup.com*
www.haygroup.com
This organization provides a full spectrum of business information. Offering comprehensive analysis of best practices, it can aid in organizing work, developing careers, determining reasonable benefits, and providing innovative ways to retain top employees.

Institute of Management and Administration (IOMA)
3 Park Avenue, 30th Floor, New York, 10001–5902
T: +1 212 244 0360
F: +1 212 564 0465

E: *info@ioma.com*
www.ioma.com
IOMA publishes a monthly *Report on Salary Surveys* and makes selected information from it available in the Salary Zone section of its Web site.

U.S. Department of Labor
200 Constitution Avenue NW, Washington, D.C., 20210
T: +1 866 487 2365
www.dol.gov/dol/topic/wages
This organization provides information on legislation governing salaries in the United States, including the Fair Labor Standards Act, the Family and Medical Leave Act, and the Equal Pay Act.

WorldatWork
14040 North Northsight Boulevard, Scottsdale, Arizona, 85260
T: +1 480 951 9191
F: +1 480 483 8352
E: *customerrelations@worldatwork.org*
www.worldatwork.org
WorldatWork is a professional organization for those working in the field of compensation, benefits, and HR. It was founded in 1995, was previously known as the American Compensation Association, and has a current membership of over 26,000. Its activities include education and accreditation programs, workshops and conferences, research, publications, and networking opportunities.

Europe
Croner Reward
145 London Road, Kingston upon Thames, Surrey, KT2 6SR, U.K.
T: +44 (0) 1785 813566
F: +44 (0) 1785 817007
E: *enquiries@croner-reward.co.uk*
www.croner.co.uk
Croner Reward publishes about 50 regional, national, and specialist salary surveys. Access to the Salary Search database of pay data for over 50,000 job records is available by subscription on the Web site.

Hay Group
101 Hudson Street, Jersey City, New Jersey, 07302
T: +1 201 557 8400
F: +1 201 557 8444

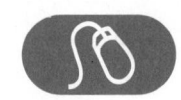

1755

BUSINESS INFORMATION SOURCES

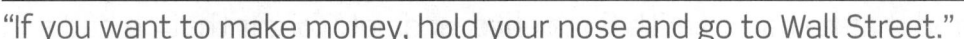

"If you want to make money, hold your nose and go to Wall Street."   Warren Buffett

E: *maria_sasso@haygroup.com*
www.haygroup.com
This organization provides full-spectrum business information. Offering comprehensive analysis on best practices, this group can aid in organizing work, developing careers, determining reasonable benefits, and providing innovative ways to retain top employees.

Incomes Data Services (IDS)

77 Bastwick Street, London, EC1V 3TT, U.K.
T: +44 (0) 20 7250 3434
F: +44 (0) 20 7324 2510
E: *ids@incomesdata.co.uk*
www.incomesdata.co.uk
This is an independent U.K.-based research organization whose publications focus on the employment field. IDS publications and information services are used by those responsible for personnel and related issues in thousands of companies, voluntary associations, and public sector organizations. They are also extensively used by consulting firms, trade unions, lawyers and specialist advisers of many types, academics, and economic commentators.

LexisNexis

Subscriptions, Customer Services, Tolley House, 2 Addiscombe Road, Croydon,

CR9 5AF, U.K.
T: +44 (0) 20 8662 2000
F: +44 (0) 20 8662 2012
E: *publications@irseclipse.co.uk*
www.irsonline.co.uk
The IRS (a member of the LexisNexis Group) publishes the biweekly *Pay and Benefits Bulletin* and the *Pay Intelligence* database which is available on paper and online.

Remuneration Economics

Survey House, 51 Portland Road, Kingston-upon-Thames, Surrey, KT1 2SH, U.K.
T: +44 (0) 20 8549 8726
F: +44 (0) 20 8541 5705
E: *cel@celre.co.uk*
www.celre.co.uk
Remuneration Economics publishes the *National Management Salary Survey* in association with the Chartered Management Institute, and surveys of other professional groups such as engineers, sales and marketing staff, personnel staff, and financial staff.

International
Watson Wyatt Data Services

1717 H Street NW, Washington, D.C., 20006–3900
T: +1 202 715 7000
F: +1 202 715 7700

E: *survey_service@watsonwyatt.com*
www.wwdssurveys.com
This company produces a wide range of industry- and geography-based compensation and benefits surveys for the United States and other countries.

William M. Mercer

Global Information Services, Mercer House, Thames Side, Windsor, Berkshire, SL4 1QN, U.K.
T: +44 (0) 1753 842 188
F: +44 (0) 1753 854 990
E: *richard.j.smith@uk.wmmercer.com*
www.wmmercer.com
This global consulting company publishes a wide range of compensation and benefits surveys covering the United States, the United Kingdom, and the Far East.

FOR MORE INFORMATION

- Conditions of Employment (pp. 1708–1709)
- Employee Benefits/Compensation (pp. 1736–1737)
- Remuneration (pp. 1894–1895)
- Taking Charge of Your Career (pp. 412–413)

BUSINESS INFORMATION SOURCES

"Dr __ well remembered that he had a salary to receive, and only forgot that he had a duty to perform."
Edward Gibbon

Flexible Working/Teleworking/ Homeworking

BOOKS

101 Tips for Telecommuters
Debra A. Dinnocenzo
San Francisco, California: Berrett-Koehler, 1999
250pp ISBN: 1576750698
This book is for telecommuters and their managers and contains many practical ways of getting the most out of this method of working.

The Distance Manager: A Hands-on Guide to Managing Off-site Employees and Virtual Teams
Kimball Fisher, Mareen Duncan Fisher
Maidenhead, United Kingdom: McGraw-Hill, 2000
252pp ISBN: 0071360654
This volume is designed to help the manager with a far-flung workforce develop the kinds of relationships needed to keep employees connected and motivated. It provides tips on how to stay connected through frequent use of e-mails and videoconferencing. It also stresses the need for distance managers to enhance their human relations skills.

The Flexible Workplace: A Sourcebook of Information and Research
Christine Avery, Diane Zabel
Westport, Connecticut: Quorum Books, 2000
224pp ISBN: 156720189X
A handbook on flexible working and the changing nature of work, this guide is international in scope and offers a review of existing research together with a summary of existing resources. A range of flexible options are covered and the future of workplace flexibility is assessed.

The Home Office Solution: How to Balance Your Professional and Personal Lives While Working at Home
Alice Bredin, Kirsten M. Lagatree
Hoboken, New Jersey: Wiley, 1998
224pp ISBN: 0471192090
This book explores the advantages and disadvantages of homeworking, acknowledging the invaluable flexibility it provides as well as the dangers. It offers tips to help home workers manage such problems as isolation, interruptions, and burnout and suggests ways to keep motivated and connected with those at the office.

Managing Telework: Strategies for Managing the Virtual Workforce
Jack M. Nilles
Hoboken, New Jersey: Wiley, 1998
352pp ISBN: 0471293164
This volume begins by looking at the rationale for a decentralized work style, providing data to show the differences between the kinds of work done in the information age and those done in a manufacturing environment. It considers the different forms of teleworking, the personalities suited to this form of work, the problems of managing teleworkers, and the legal and regulatory issues relevant to home offices and the provision of equipment.

Telecommute! Go to Work without Leaving Home
Lisa Shaw
Hoboken, New Jersey: Wiley, 1996
224pp ISBN: 0471118206
The book views telecommuting from the employee's perspective, revealing who is likely to be successful in this area and the type of jobs that work best with telecommunication. According to the author, the culture that exists within a particular business and the supervisor's manner have important parts to play, but ultimately it is down to the individual telecommuter and the way they perform.

Teleworking in Brief
Mike Johnson
Woburn, Massachusetts: Butterworth-Heinemann, 1997
208pp (In Brief)
ISBN: 0750628758
This practical guide presents an overview of teleworking and looks at the key benefits and disadvantages for both the individual and for the company. It includes the Teleworking Toolkit, a set of practical guidelines, documentation, and checklists that can be adapted for use in any organization.

The Virtual Office Survival Handbook
Alice Bredin
Hoboken, New Jersey: Wiley, 1996
259pp ISBN: 0471120596

This is a comprehensive guide aimed at those working at home, on the road, or with other nontraditional arrangements. It examines both setting up your own business and telecommuting, and covers the following topics: organizing the office and selecting the appropriate technology; communication with colleagues; generating business; and publicity. Balancing work and private life, time management, structure of work, and self-management are also reviewed.

INTERNET

About.com—Telecommuting
www.about.com
A search for "telecommuting" on the about.com site offers good information and connections to resources, including a newsletter.

All Freelance
www.allfreelance.com
This rich site for freelance workers presents information about managing time, finances, payment, and legal issues. It also provides pages devoted to job listings.

Flexibility
www.flexibility.co.uk
This is a nonprofit online journal on flexible working. It includes an archive of articles, an interactive forum, case studies, issues, and links to other sites.

Gil Gordon Associates
www.gilgordon.com
This site provided by a New Jersey consulting and training organization includes articles, links to journals and newsletters, and links to other websites.

Homeworking
www.homeworking.com
Homeworking is a general information site for those already working and those wanting to work at home. It includes information on how to get started, how to find work, and how to avoid scams.

International Telework Association and Council
www.workingfromanywhere.org
This site offers free web seminars and a free monthly newsletter as well as articles and

1757

"Perfect freedom is reserved for the man who lives by his own work and, in that work, does what he wants to do."
R. G. Collingwood

information about various aspects of teleworking.

Internet Homeworking Directory
www.homeworkinguk.com

This site offers advice and information on U.K. opportunities for working from home. It includes a link to an international site.

Telework Association
www.tca.org.uk

This site is dedicated to the promotion of teleworking and aims to benefit people by improving both quality of life and access to work. It offers useful links, a library of relevant articles, membership information, and access to *Teleworker* magazine.

ORGANIZATIONS
USA
9 to 5 National Association of Working Women

207 E Buffalo Street, Milwaukee, Wisconsin, 53202
T: +1 414 274 0925
E: *naww9to5@execpc.com*
www.9to5.org

Established in 1973, this group conducts research on the concerns of women office workers. In addition to compiling current employment statistics, the association has conducted and published research on health and safety issues, the Family and Medical Leave Act, and the importance of

flexible time scheduling. 9to5 will also conduct seminars for corporations.

Labor Project for Working Families

2521 Channing Way, No 5555, Berkeley, California, 94720
T: +1 510 643 7088
F: +1 510 642 6432
E: *lpwf@berkeley.edu*
www.laborproject.org

This group works with labor unions to develop work and family policies related to all aspects of flexible work schedules. It provides research facts and statistics to employers and workers and has set up a series of training seminars on various work and family topics, including the Family and Medical Leave Act.

Europe
Working Families

1–3 Berry Street, London, EC1V 0AA, U.K.
T: +44 (0) 20 7253 7243
F: +44 (0) 20 7253 6253
E: *office@workingfamilies.org.uk*
www.workingfamilies.org.uk

Working Families works with parents, carers, and businesses to find a better balance between work and family life. It provides information and advice on the full range of flexible working arrangements, training, consulting services, and research case studies, and contributes to public and government policy.

International
International Telework Association and Council (ITAC)

401 Edgewater Place, Suite 600, Wakefield, Massachusetts, 01880
T: +1 202 547 6157
F: +1 202 546 3289
E: *info@telecommute.org*
www.workingfromanywhere.org

ITAC is a nonprofit organization that promotes the benefits of telework, and studies, develops, and recommends tools, techniques, and processes for teleworking. Activities include an annual international conference, local groups, and public policy and legislative forums.

FOR MORE INFORMATION

"When work is a pleasure, life is a joy! When work is a duty, life is slavery." Maksim Gorky

Forecasting and Scenario Planning

BOOKS

20-20 Foresight: Crafting Strategy in an Uncertain World

Hugh Courtney

Boston, Massachusetts: Harvard Business School Press, 2001

207pp ISBN: 1578512662

This book sets out to help managers understand the concept of "residual uncertainty" in today's business environment—that is, the difference between what can be known and what *can't* be known—so that they can develop 20/20 foresight and create competitive advantage. A five-piece management toolkit of scenario planning, game theory, decision analysis, system dynamics models, and management flight simulators can be used to plot strategy against uncertainty.

The Art of the Long View: Planning for the Future in an Uncertain World

Peter Schwartz

New York: Currency, 1996

272pp ISBN: 0385267320

The author argues that the only way to plan successfully for the future is to take a long view, taking into account technological, social, political, and economic developments. He then shows the reader how to write scenarios, based on understanding the forces that drive events and signposts that suggest how things may play out in the long term.

Building Financial Models: A Guide to Creating and Interpreting Financial Statements

John S. Tjia

Maidenhead: McGraw-Hill, 2004

340pp ISBN: 0071402101

This book provides step-by-step instructions for the design and development of financial projection models according to Generally Accepted Accounting Principles (GAAP) using Microsoft Excel software. In-depth explanations of the principles of accounting, including income statements, balance sheets, and cash-flow statements, and the concepts of model building are given. The book also describes the use of spreadsheet functions and tools and offers guidelines for making useful business forecasts.

The Change Game: How Today's Global Trends are Shaping Tomorrow's Companies

Peter Lawrence

London: Kogan Page, 2002

272pp ISBN: 0749439262

Based on interviews with managers from around the world, this book is an account of change in business in the West. The text provides insights into the major global trends and issues that are influencing organizations today, and what they mean for the future. The new management consensus is examined, including the gains it has made and some of the blind spots to which it has given rise. The text also addresses the ideas of competitive advantage and the unique business proposition.

How to Forecast: A Guide for Business

James Morrell

Aldershot: Gower Publishing, 2001

208pp ISBN: 0566084929

Drawing on his experience as a forecaster, the author considers the key areas that affect businesses. These are divided into those that lie *beyond* the control of an organization and those that are *under* its control. The former include the national economy, government policy, the global market, population and social trends, and technological change. The latter include long-term strategy and investment, costs and prices, and profits and share prices. Each section of this book provides a set of practical conclusions and a listing of key sources of information. The book closes with a set of simple rules and guidelines for successful forecasting.

Learning from the Future: Competitive Foresight Scenarios

Liam Fahey, Robert Randall

New York: Wiley, 1997

288pp ISBN: 0471303526

Aimed at managers, consultants, and leaders, this book comprises a selection of articles that explain how to construct and model the outcomes of a variety of strategic decisions. Four key areas are addressed: the basics of scenario learning; approaches to constructing scenarios; scenario application in diverse contexts; and managing scenario learning in the organizational context.

The Living Company: Habits for Survival in a Turbulent Business Environment

Arie de Geus

Boston, Massachusetts: Harvard Business School Press, 2002

240pp ISBN: 1578518202

This book by one of the gurus of scenario planning focuses on his belief that businesses are like living organisms and must be managed as such if they are to survive over time and become what he calls "living companies."

Quantitative Analysis for Management 9th ed.

Barry Render, Ralph M. Stair, Michael E. Hanna

Upper Saddle River, New Jersey: Allyn & Bacon, 2005

736pp ISBN: 0131857029

This is a general textbook that introduces the principal techniques of quantitative analysis for organizational decision making. The chapter on forecasting explores different forecasting models and methods, effective monitoring techniques, and the use of computers in the forecasting process. The package also includes a CD.

Scenario Planning 2nd ed.

Gill Ringland

Hoboken, New Jersey: Wiley, 2006

490pp ISBN: 047001881X

Updated for this new edition, this book focuses on how scenarios can be used effectively to manage the future. It is aimed at practicing managers. The book includes extensive case studies, checklists, and practical advice.

Scenarios: The Art of Strategic Conversation 2nd ed.

Kees van der Heijden

Hoboken, New Jersey: Wiley, 2005

384pp ISBN: 0470023686

Aimed at strategic managers, this book explores the relationship between the strategy process and scenario planning in order to facilitate effective decisions. Drawing on his own experiences while working for Shell, and on the experiences of the company as a whole, the author explores the principles, practices, implementation, and applications of scenario planning.

"The further ahead you forecast, the less well you do." C. W. J. Granger

The Sixth Sense: Accelerating Organizational Learning with Scenarios

Kees van der Heijden et al.
Hoboken, New Jersey: Wiley, 2002
304pp ISBN: 0470844914

The key issue of this book revolves around addressing the flaws at individual, organizational, and community levels that inhibit organizational change. The text highlights a link between organizational learning and scenario planning in order to overcome these flaws. It suggests that by motivating learners to develop a deeper perspective on the long-term business environment, and scenario planners to see their work in the context of organizational survival and development, creative limitations can be overcome and a favorable environment for multiple futures developed.

Trajectory Management: Leading a Business Over Time

Paul Strebel
New York: Wiley, 2003
208pp ISBN: 0470862904

Paul Strebel believes that the search for universal best practice has given rise to the impression that there is "one true way" to business success. To work effectively, however, best practice must be adapted to the particular conditions facing the organization at the time. The author aims to help business leaders succeed over time by identifying and adapting internal business drivers to exploit changing conditions. This is the art of trajectory management, which will enable organizations to succeed in differing conditions.

MAGAZINES

International Journal of Forecasting

ISSN: 0169–2070
Elsevier Science
Customer Service Department, 6277 Sea Harbor Drive, Orlando, Florida, 32887–4800
T: +1 877 839 7126 or +1 407 345 4020
F: +1 407 363 1354
www.elsevier.com

This is the official journal of the International Institute of Forecasters, whose aims and scope it shares: to unify the field of forecasting; to bridge the gap between theory and practice; and to make forecasting useful and relevant for decision and policy makers. It publishes high-quality refereed papers on all aspects of forecasting.

Journal of Business Forecasting

ISSN: 0278–6087
Graceway Publishing Company Inc.
P.O. Box 670159, Station C, Flushing, New York, 11367–0159

T: +1 516 504 7576
F: +1 516 498 2029
www.ibforecast.com

This is a quarterly journal aimed at business executives and managers which provides practical forecasting ideas plus guidance on recognizing and using effective forecasting models for key business decisions. The *Journal* also includes forecasts on the international economic outlook and corporate earnings.

Journal of Forecasting

ISSN: 0277–6693
Wiley
111 River St, Hoboken, New Jersey, 07030–5774
T: +1 201 748 6000
F: +1 212 850 6021
www.wiley.com

This international journal, published eight times a year, presents papers on theoretical, practical, and computational approaches to forecasting across a range of sectors including business, technology, and government. Individual issues include research reports, review articles, and book and software reviews.

INTERNET

Forecasting: Methods and Applications
www.robhyndman.info/forecasting

This site is based on the book of the same name and offers hundreds of forecasting data sets plus links to forecasting resources and software on the Internet.

Global Business Network
www.gbn.org

This is the premier site for those interested in scenario planning, including among its founders and members some of those who were involved in Royal Dutch/Shell's groundbreaking work in this area.

International Institute of Forecasters
www.forecasters.org

The organization is dedicated to the research and development of forecasting techniques, with the aim of bridging the gap between forecasting theory and practice and contributing to the professional development of forecasters. Its site includes information on events and conferences, information on its journal, *Foresight*, time series data, and links to other forecasting sites.

Principles of Forecasting
http://morris.wharton.upenn.edu/forecast

Useful for practitioners and academics

alike, this site offers useful information on the subject of forecasting. Its features include a dictionary of key related terms, frequently asked questions, links, and targeted pages for special interest groups.

World Future Society
www.wfs.org

This nonprofit educational and scientific organization provides information about the technological and social forces that shape the future—and are fundamental to scenario planning and forecasting.

ORGANIZATIONS
USA
Institute of Business Forecasting

P.O. Box 670159, Flushing, New York, 11367–0159
T: +1 516 504 7576
E: *info@ibf.org*
www.ibforecast.com

The aims of this member-based organization are to disseminate knowledge about business forecasting and planning, and to provide products and services to help business executives in their planning and forecasting efforts.

Europe
Lancaster University Centre for Forecasting

Lancaster University, Lancaster, Lancashire, LA1 4YX, U.K.
T: +44 (0) 1524 593 879
F: +44 (0) 1524 844 885
E: *r.fildes@lancaster.ac.uk*
www.lums.lancs.ac.uk/research/forecast.htm

This center is part of the Management School at Lancaster University. It aims to promote the development of new approaches to forecasting and business models, supports the integration of forecasting theory and practice, and offers research and consultancy services to industry, commerce, and government. Its services corporate research, courses for practitioners, and consultancy services. The site also offers advice for special interest groups.

FOR MORE INFORMATION

🐭 Business Plans and Planning (pp. 1692–1693)
🐭 Contingency, Crisis, Disaster Management (pp. 1715–1717)
☆ Scenario Planning (pp. 334–335)

Franchising

BOOKS

Franchise Bible: How to Buy a Franchise or Franchise Your Own Business 5th ed.
Erwin J. Keup
Central Point, Oregon: PSI Research/Oasis Press, 2004
288pp ISBN: 1932156623
This practical guide to franchising includes sample documents and checklists aimed at helping newcomers to this form of business by providing discussion of the kinds of agreements involved, the advantages and disadvantages of franchising, how to rate potential opportunities, and how to decide if this is the right road to success for them.

Franchise Opportunities Guide
International Franchise Association
Washington, D.C.: International Franchise Association (IFA), 2005
301pp ISBN: 9990031231
This seasonal directory provides a comprehensive listing of franchise companies.

Franchise Organizations
Jeffrey L. Bradach
Boston, Massachusetts: Harvard Business School Press, 1998
238pp ISBN: 087584832X
Using examples primarily from the restaurant business, the book examines the attributes of a successful franchise chain. It also describes the plural-form model (where franchise outlets are merged into a corporate structure) and sets out a framework for managing and expanding plural-form organizations.

Franchising & Licensing: Two Ways to Build Your Business 3rd ed.
Andrew J. Sherman
New York: AMACOM, 2004
448pp ISBN: 0814472222
The third edition of a guide to franchising as a growth strategy for business, this book is geared to helping those who decide to franchise or leverage intellectual property in order to expand their market share and wish to avoid pitfalls such as disputes with franchisees. It explores the legal, operational, and management issues that arise when developing partnering relationships.

Franchising for Dummies
Michael Seid, Dave Thomas
New York: Hungry Minds, 2000
378pp ISBN: 0764551604
This simple-to-follow but detailed guide to entering the world of franchises presents the basics, ranging from initial research, selecting locations, and training employees, to running and growing the business. One of the authors is the late Dave Thomas, founder of the ultra-successful *Wendy's International*; the other is a consultant with more than 20 years of hands-on experience. They provide practical advice on the major issues facing those who decide to follow this route to self-employment.

The Guide to Franchising 7th ed.
Martin Mendelsohn
London: Cassell, 2004
416pp ISBN: 1844801624
The author introduces franchising by describing its history and development and deals with fundamental questions such as "Why franchise your business?" "Why acquire a franchise?" and "What can be franchised?" He also provides essential information on the legal aspects of the franchise contract. Profiles of the British Franchise Association and the Franchise Consultants Association are included.

Tips and Traps When Buying a Franchise 2nd ed.
Mary E. Tomzack
Oakland, California: Source Book Publications, 1999
236pp ISBN: 1887137122
The second, revised edition of this guide provides those new to franchising with information on the right questions to ask at the outset, how to find the right location, where to get loans, how to find and train employees, and the ins and outs of buying equipment. It contains "war stories" and success secrets from a wide variety of franchisees.

MAGAZINES

Franchise International
ISSN: 1363–7274
Franchise Development Services Ltd.
Franchise House, 56 Surrey Street, Norwich, Norfolk, NR1 3FD, U.K.
T: +44 (0) 1603 620 301
F: +44 (0) 1603 630 174
www.franchise-international.net

Franchise International promotes the availability of franchise rights worldwide and is aimed at both companies and individuals seeking to take out a master franchise.

Franchise Times
Franchise Times
2500 Cleveland Avenue N, Suite D So, Roseville, Minnesota, 55113
T: +1 651 631 4995
F: +1 651 633 8749
www.franchisetimes.com
This is a news and information source for franchising. It is published ten times per year and includes information that is related to franchising in areas such as business life, analyst reports, finance, and real estate.

Franchising World
International Franchise Association (IFA)
1350 New York Avenue NW, Suite 900, Washington, D.C., 20005–4709
T: +1 202 628 8000
F: +1 202 628 0812
www.franchise.org
Published six times per year, this magazine produced by the International Franchise Association highlights all areas of franchise business. Featuring current articles by franchising experts, it focuses on topics of interest such as legislative developments, educational programs, and current franchise news. A must-read for anyone working in the franchise industry.

INTERNET

Business Opportunities Handbook Online
www.franchise1.com
This online directory provides comprehensive information about franchising opportunities and franchising companies. Contact information is provided as well as a description of the operation, franchising fee, capital requirements, and financing options. The site also contains franchise industry news, articles, trade show information, a list of franchises for sale, and links to other franchise resources.

Entrepreneur.com
www.entrepreneur.com
This is a magazine site sponsored by Entrepreneur Media, Inc., offering a comprehensive range of practical

1761

BUSINESS INFORMATION SOURCES

"In business for yourself, not by yourself."

Ray Kroc

information for owners of small businesses. The information includes a search engine, databases, blogs, and links to free business tools.

Franchise.com
www.franchise.com
Built for both franchisers and franchisees, this site has information on a broad range of topics and includes tools such as an alphabetical directory, newsletter, global search, industry events, and a blog.

Franchising.org
www.franchising.org
This is a useful site with links to many other franchise organizations. Articles, advice, and information are also provided.

Franinfo
www.franinfo.com
This site provides an overview of franchising as well as advice and guidance. It contains two self-tests to determine whether you are suited to being a franchisee and what type of franchise would suit you best.

International Franchising
www.franchiseintl.com
This is a guide to international franchising and offers news, articles, and a bookstore among its resources. Its many listings include franchise attorneys, consultants, and the top 100 franchises in the United States, split across three key sectors: food, retail, and service.

Nolo—Law for All
www.nolo.com
This is a good source of legal information, some of which is specifically related to franchising.

Small Business Administration
www.sba.gov
This U.S. government site provides information about resources available to those who need help with their entrepreneurial efforts, including finding financing and locating workshops and training.

World Franchising—The Definitive Guide to the World of Franchising
www.worldfranchising.com
This directory has links to over 1,000 franchises in North America and is kept up-to-date with the franchise field.

ORGANIZATIONS
USA
American Association of Franchisees and Dealers
P.O. Box 81887, San Diego, California, 92138–1887
T: +1 800 733 9858
F: +1 619 209 3777
E: *benefits@aafd.org*
www.aafd.org
The Association is a nonprofit trade organization representing the rights of independent dealers and franchisees in the United States. It provides guidance and advice on how to take out a franchise.

International Franchise Association (IFA)
1350 New York Avenue NW, Suite 900, Washington, D.C., 20005–4709
T: +1 202 628 8000
F: +1 202 628 0812
E: *ifa@franchise.org*
www.franchise.org
The IFA is a membership organization with a heavy bias toward American franchisers, franchisees, and suppliers, although other countries are represented. It is a useful

contact for existing or prospective franchisers and franchisees.

Europe
British Franchise Association (BFA)
Thames View, Newtown Road, Henley-on-Thames, Oxfordshire, RG9 1HG, U.K.
T: +44 (0) 1491 578 050
F: +44 (0) 1491 573 517
E: *mailroom@british-franchise.org.uk*
www.british-franchise.org
The BFA was formed in 1977 to promote high standards of practice in franchising; member companies adhere to a code of ethics drawn up by the Association. It also provides a range of information to both member and nonmember organizations through its extensive Web site and publications. It is affiliated with the World Franchise Council and the European Franchise Federation.

European Franchise Federation
Avenue Louise 179/15, Brussels, 10750, Belgium
T: +32 2 520 16 07
F: +32 2 520 17 35
E: *info@eff-franchise.com*
www.eff-franchise.com
The Federation is an international nonprofit organization, founded in 1972, that aims to promote franchising in Europe and the interests of the national franchise associations or federations that make up its membership.

FOR MORE INFORMATION
✔ Franchising Your Business
(pp. 969–970)
 Small and Growing Businesses
(pp. 1905–1909)

1762

BUSINESS INFORMATION SOURCES

Online Business Newspapers (General Business Information)

INTERNET

China Daily
www.chinadaily.com.cn/english/home/
biznews.html
This site delivers daily news from China in the English language. It covers Chinese and international business.

Daily Telegraph
www.telegraph.co.uk
This is the site for the daily U.K. newspaper providing national and international coverage.

Daily Yomiuri Online
www.yomiuri.co.jp
An online Japanese daily paper containing national and international news. It covers political and economic topics in English under "The Daily Yomiuri."

Financial Times
www.ft.com
The online version of the U.K. daily newspaper, which provides international business and financial news and analysis. International markets and industries and company information are covered. Some articles are free, but others are available only to subscribers.

The Guardian
www.guardian.co.uk
This online version of the U.K. daily newspaper contains in-depth coverage of national and international news including politics, finance, social issues, and education.

Handelsblatt
www.handelsblatt.com
The online version of the German-language daily newspaper providing in-depth economic and corporate news.

The Independent
www.independent.co.uk
This online version of the U.K. daily newspaper provides national and international news.

International Herald Tribune
www.iht.com
The site of the English-language daily paper published in Paris, it provides news, analysis, and commentary on international business affairs.

Le Monde
www.lemonde.fr
This online version of the French-language daily paper covers politics, economics, and current affairs generally. It provides information on the Francophone world.

Los Angeles Times
www.latimes.com
This is the online version of the U.S. daily paper with national and international news covering business and finance.

New York Times
www.nytimes.com
This online version of the U.S. daily paper covers national and international news. The business section includes U.S. and international market news and company research tools.

The Times
www.timesonline.co.uk
This online version of the U.K. daily newspaper provides national and international coverage.

USA Today
www.usatoday.com
This U.S. daily paper features financial news, stock reports and business articles under the "Money" tab online.

Wall Street Journal Online
http://online.wsj.com/public/us
This is the paper of record for most financial news in the United States. Unless you take the print edition of the paper, you will need to subscribe to access full articles, but the site features items by many columnists and news from around the world. Many people uninterested in business still read this paper and Web site for its uncluttered style and low-jargon articles.

Washington Post
www.washingtonpost.com
This is the online version of the U.S. daily paper, containing national and international news. It has a strong business section that covers a range of information and resources including market news, stock quotes, and a glossary of business terms.

1763

BUSINESS INFORMATION SOURCES

"All great change in business has come from outside the firm, not from inside."

Peter F. Drucker

Online Financial Information (General Business Information)

INTERNET
Accounting Web
www.accountingweb.co.uk
This is an online community site for accountants providing news, online discussions, reviews of accountancy products and services, a database of training courses, job listings, and access to external services such as ICC company information.

Bloomberg
www.bloomberg.com
This site provides a range of business, market, and financial news. Its comprehensive coverage includes news, commentary, and analysis.

The Economist
www.economist.com
This is the Web site of *The Economist* magazine. It contains news of global business and politics, with an archive of articles and book reviews.

FinanceWise
www.financewise.com
This is a U.K.-based search engine for financial information sites, which can be searched by company name, sector, or keyword. The site also contains special reports, news on financial books, and links to appropriate career resources.

Financial Times
www.ft.com
The online version of the U.K. daily newspaper, which provides international business and financial news and analysis. International markets and industries and company information are covered. Some articles are free, but others are available only to subscribers.

FIND Financial Information Net Directory
www.find.co.uk
FIND is an independent gateway to U.K. financial Web sites covering banking and savings, investment, insurance, pensions, and financial information services.

Global Investor
www.global-investor.com
Global Investor offers information for investors with news and access to a range of free resources, including a glossary of financial terms and details of financial books and periodicals.

HM Treasury
www.hm-treasury.gov.uk
This site offers economic and financial information from the U.K. government, including press releases and speeches, regulatory information, policy statements, budget documentation, and information on the Euro.

Interactive Investor International
www.iii.co.uk
This site provides information for investors including share tracking, market news, and advice on personal finance.

Nasdaq
www.nasdaq.com
This is the Web site of the world's largest electronic stock market, with stock quotes, news and articles, annual reports, overviews, and global market information.

OSU Virtual Finance Library
http://fisher.osu.edu/fin/overview.htm
This is an index of financial sites for investors, executives, researchers, and students provided by Ohio State University's Department of Finance. It covers a range of areas including banks, exchanges, market news, and insurers.

SEC U.S. Securities and Exchange Commission
www.sec.gov
The SEC Web site offers news and reports from the U.S. government body and access to the database of company filings.

Standard & Poor's
www.standardpoor.com
Standard & Poor's provides financial information and services. The Web site features stock quotes, ratings, and indices, along with global financial news, and analyses.

Wachowicz's Web World
http://web.utk.edu/~jwachowi/wacho_world.html
Listing financial management sites aimed at students, this index is based on the chapters of a financial management textbook.

Wall Street Journal Online
http://online.wsj.com/public/us
This is the paper of record for most financial news in the United States. Unless you take the print edition of the paper, you will need to subscribe to access full articles, but the site features items by many columnists and news from around the world. Many people uninterested in business still read this paper and Web site for its uncluttered style and low-jargon articles.

"Business is all about putting out money today to get a whole lot back later."

Warren Buffett

     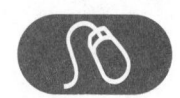

Online Human Resources Sources (General Business Information)

INTERNET

American Society for Training and Development (ASTD)
www.astd.org

ASTD is a professional association for training personnel. The site provides an online magazine, news, virtual communities, a free e-mail newsletter, and a buyer's guide listing training suppliers and consultants. Many of the services are for members only.

Chartered Institute of Personnel and Development
www.cipd.co.uk

The CIPD is a professional association for personnel managers in the United Kingdom. Registration is required and some services are available only to members. The site provides *People Management* magazine, news, summaries of research reports, fact sheets, and information on publications, training courses, and events.

HR Guide
www.hr-guide.com

This site provides definitions and basic introductions to a range of human resource subjects linked to a collection of Web site listings with ratings and brief descriptions. It has a strong focus on HR software and includes a demo of an online 360-degree feedback questionnaire.

HR Tools.com
www.hrtools.com

As its name would suggest, this site focuses on online tools, including forms and training resources. Registration is required for all users.

HRZone
www.hrzone.com

This site, based in the United States, provides information on the basics of human resource management. In addition, users will find articles, news, legal information including case summaries, Web site reviews, and a directory of suppliers.

Nottingham Trent University
www.ntu.ac.uk/nbs/school/acad/hrm/6831gp.html

This online directory provides a comprehensive collection of links to HR sites. It is compiled at Nottingham Business School Department of Human Resource Management and is arranged in broad categories.

Online Recruitment
www.onrec.com

This site provides a database of online recruitment sites, and offers the facility to search for sites that cover all or specific sectors. It also gives information on the sites offered, including services, charges, strengths, and weaknesses.

Personnel Today
www.personneltoday.com

This is a comprehensive site including information from a leading U.K. magazine. Covering HR news and events, legal developments, and career advice, the site also provides book reviews, a conference calendar, and links to HR-related Web sites.

Society for Human Resources Management
www.shrm.org

The society is a professional organization for HR managers in the United States. The site contains a range of resources including news, a magazine, chatrooms, bulletin boards, an information center, and an extensive set of links. Some resources are for members only.

Training Zone
www.trainingzone.co.uk

A portal site for training professionals, its resources include a sales success toolkit, a document centre, and a library. Registration is required for users.

U.K.-HRD
www.ukhrd.com

This is a site is for training and HR specialists and is sponsored by Fenman. Users may subscribe to receive a comprehensive daily newsletter, while some free articles are available on the site itself.

Workforce Online
www.workforce.com

This site is an online HR magazine with feature articles, news, discussion forums, and a free e-mail newsletter.

Workindex
www.workindex.com

Sponsored by the publishers of *Human Resource Executive* and featuring an index from Cornell University School of Labor and Industrial Relations, this site provides a comprehensive set of links to HR Web sites. Book extracts and reviews, a salary calculator, a jobs database, legal questions and answers, HR news, and magazine articles are also available.

WorldatWork
www.worldatwork.org

Formerly the American Compensation Association, this site offers information for human resource managers including news, topic briefings, a free e-mail newsletter, a glossary of terms, magazine articles, and a buyer's guide. Information on training courses, seminars, accredited programs, publications, and research surveys produced by the organization are also available.

BUSINESS INFORMATION SOURCES

"I find it rather easy to portray a businessman. Being bland, rather cruel and incompetent comes naturally to me."

John Cleese

Online Sources for Marketing (General Business Information)

INTERNET
American Marketing Association
www.marketingpower.com
Online resources for marketing professionals are provided by the American Marketing Association, including best practice information and articles, a directory of suppliers, links to business information and marketing tools, as well as job and career information.

Business Day
www.businessday.co.za
Covering South African and international business, this site provides news, information, and analysis and includes company and market information.

Business Marketing Association
www.marketing.org
This site offers a directory of marketing communications and advertising agencies. The members' library contains industry surveys, articles, white papers, and book reviews. Visitors may also view articles from *Business to Business Marketer*.

Ed Osworth's Internet Marketing Index
www.internetmarketingindex.com
This collection of links to marketing sites has a strong focus on using the Web for marketing but also includes sections on new marketing products, discussion boards, e-zines, and marketing news.

Larry Chase's Web Digest for Marketers
www.wdfm.com
Writer and consultant, Larry Chase, offers a free weekly e-mail newsletter with reviews of marketing Web sites and a searchable archive of previous editions.

Marketing and International Business Links
http://wtfaculty.wtamu.edu/ ~sanwar.bus/otherlinks.htm
This site offers an extensive list of links to journals, sources of company, market, and industry information, international marketing sites, and many others connected with international business and trade. Syed Tariq Anwar, the compiler of the list, is Professor of Marketing and International Business at West Texas A & M University.

Marketing Terms.com
www.marketingterms.com
Included on this site are an Internet marketing dictionary and links to a number of marketing dictionaries and glossaries on the Web.

Marketing Virtual Library
www.knowthis.com
This is an excellent collection of well organized and evaluated links to general marketing sites and related areas.

Marketing Week
www.marketingweek.co.uk
This site provides news, articles, and analysis from *Marketing Week* magazine.

Wilson Internet Web Marketing and E-commerce
www.wilsonweb.com
This extensive site, sponsored by Wilson Internet Services, features the Web Marketing Info Center and the E-Commerce Research Room with links to thousands of articles, and offers a free e-mail newsletter.

"All the great work comes from people's obsession and imagination, not from focus groups."

Michael Grade

Health and Safety

BOOKS

Health and Safety in Brief 3rd ed.
John Ridley
Woburn, Massachusetts: Butterworth-Heinemann, 2004
288pp ISBN: 0750662115
Aimed at students and managers with responsibility for workplace health and safety, the book provides practical and succinct guidance on day-to-day health and safety considerations in the workplace. The issues covered include U.K. health and safety law, management responsibilities, accidents, health protection, chemicals, noise and hearing protection, construction, manual handling, and the safe use of electricity.

Workplace Health and Safety Sourcebook
Helene Henderson
Detroit, Michigan: Omnigraphics, 2001
624pp ISBN: 0780802314
This book identifies a number of hazards associated with the workplace, and suggests ways in which these hazards can be avoided. It also offers steps toward recovery for those who suffer from workplace-related disorders. Issues discussed include child labor, stress, workplace violence, and the use of hazardous chemicals. It includes a glossary and lists of resources.

MAGAZINES

Industrial Safety & Hygiene News
ISSN: 8755–2566
BNP Media
755 West Big Beaver Road, Suite 1000, Troy, Michigan, 48084
T: +1 248 244 6498
F: +1 248 244 6439
www.ishn.com
Published monthly, this magazine is targeted at health and safety managers at high-hazard worksites in manufacturing, construction, health facilities and service industries. It provides the latest developments in industry news and legislation.

Occupational Hazards
ISSN: 0029–7909
Penton Publishing
1300 East 9th Street, Cleveland, Ohio, 44114
T: +1 216 696 7000
F: +1 216 696 7658
www.occupationalhazards.com

Published 12 times per year, this magazine focuses on occupational hazards in industry and manufacturing. The articles in the magazine provide updates on the latest in national and regional legislative action, as well as insight into current news headlines in this field. Environmental professionals will find this to be an informative resource.

Occupational Health and Safety
ISSN: 0362–4064
Stevens Publishing Corporation
5151 Beltline Road, 10th Floor, Dallas, Texas, 75254
T: +1 972 687 6700
F: +1 972 687 6770
www.ohsonline.com
This journal covers occupational health and safety in a range of industries and is aimed at professional health and safety advisers and consultants.

Professional Safety
ISSN: 0099–0027
American Society of Safety Engineers
1800 E. Oakton Street, Des Plaines, Illinois, 60018
T: +1 847 699 2929
F: +1 847 768 3434
www.asse.org
This monthly journal delivers information and in-depth articles aimed at promoting the advancement of the safety profession. Articles focus on innovative research and analysis of successful real-world applications. The journal also contains timely news sections and information on relevant governmental regulations.

Safety + Health
ISSN: 0891–1797
National Safety Council
1121 Spring Lake Drive, Itasca, Illinois, 60143–3201
T: +1 630 285 1121
F: +1 630 285 1315
www.nsc.org
Safety + Health covers the subject from an international perspective, providing practical information to employers responsible for safety and health issues.

World Safety Journal
ISSN: 1015–5589
World Safety Organization (WSO)
WSO World Management Center, 106 W. Young Avenue, Suite G, P.O. Box 518, Warrensburg, Missouri, 64093

T: +1 660 747 3132
F: +1 660 747 2647
www.worldsafety.org
The official journal of the WSO (World Safety Organization), this is a biannual publication for safety professionals around the world. Disciplines covered are safety, environment, security, public health, transportation, and construction.

INTERNET

The American College of Healthcare Executives
www.ache.org
ACHE is an international professional society of 30,000 healthcare executives. It is known for its credentialing and educational programs and for its publications. This site provides useful resources for 13 areas of special interest, career services, governmental news, and an events calendar.

American Society for Industrial Security
www.asisonline.org
ASIS is an organization for professionals responsible for security and for others who need a better understanding of the constant changes in security issues and solutions. The site provides its members and the security community with access to a full range of industrial security programs and services.

European Agency for Health and Safety at Work
http://europe.osha.eu.int
The EAHSW was set up by member states of the European Union to provide a wide range of information promoting good health and safety practices.

ORGANIZATIONS
USA
National Institute for Occupational Safety and Health (NIOSH)
Room 715H, Hubert Humphrey Building, 200 Independence Avenue SW, Washington, D.C., 20201
T: +1 513 533 8328 or 800 356 4674
F: +1 513 533 8573
www.cdc.gov/niosh
NIOSH is the U.S. federal agency responsible for conducting research into, and making recommendations for, the prevention of work-related disease and

1767

BUSINESS INFORMATION SOURCES

injury under the Occupational Safety and Health Act of 1970. It is part of the Centers for Disease Control and Prevention. NIOSH offers free access to a number of databases containing a wide range of information.

Occupational Safety & Health Administration (OSHA)
T: +1 800 321 6742
www.osha.gov
OSHA is responsible for overseeing compliance with all health and safety legislation in the United States and for workplace inspections.

Europe
British Safety Council (BSC)
70 Chancellors Road, London, W6 7RS, U.K.
T: +44 (0) 20 8741 1231
F: +44 (0) 20 8741 4555
www.britishsafetycouncil.co.uk

The BSC is an independent membership organization with 10,000 corporate members who receive a range of research and information services aimed at improving safety in the workplace.

Health and Safety Executive (HSE)
Rose Court, 2 Southwark Bridge, London, SE1 9HS, U.K.
T: +44 (0) 20 7717 6000
F: +44 (0) 20 7717 6717
E: *hseinformationservices@natbrit.com*
www.hse.gov.uk
The HSE is the executive arm of the U.K. government's Health and Safety Commission. It is responsible for advising the HSC on formulating policy, overseeing the implementation of all health and safety legislation in the United Kingdom, carrying out inspections required by the legislation, and providing advice and guidance on all occupational health and safety matters. It has a number of regional offices.

International
World Safety Organization (WSO)
WSO World Management Center, 106 W. Young Avenue, Suite G, P.O. Box 518, Warrensburg, Missouri, 64093
T: +1 660 747 3132
F: +1 660 747 2647
E: *wsowmc@sockert.net*
www.worldsafety.org
The WSO has offices all over the world, including Australia, Taiwan, and Russia. It holds international conferences, publishes newsletters and the biannual *World Safety Journal*, develops training programs, and administers a number of awards.

FOR MORE INFORMATION

"There is no right to strike against the public safety by anybody, anywhere, any time."

Calvin Coolidge

Health Services Management

BOOKS

Financial Management of Hospitals and Healthcare Organizations 3rd ed.

Michael Nowicki
Chicago, Illinois: Health Administration Press, 2004
368pp ISBN: 1567932266
This book uses a practical and nontechnical approach to introduce the basic concepts of healthcare financial management. Capital management, strategic planning, budgeting, resource allocation, and financial analysis are all covered.

The Global Challenge of Healthcare Rationing

Angela Coulter, Chris Ham, eds
Philadelphia, Pennsylvania: Taylor & Francis, 2000
288pp (State of Health)
ISBN: 0335204635
This book offers an overview of current thinking in the area of resource allocation and priority setting in health services. The contributors are decision makers and researchers from around the world who provide an insight into the factors that influence decision making, such as medical research and cost-effectiveness studies.

Health Care Management: Organization Design & Behavior 5th ed.

Arnold D. Kaluzny, Stephen M. Shortell
Albany, New York: Delmar, 2005
448pp ISBN: 1418001899
This textbook, for students in health services administration, management, and policy programs, reviews the application of management and organizational thinking and research to healthcare organizations. It includes sections on organizations and managers, on motivating, leading, and negotiating, on operating the technical systems, on renewing the organization, and on charting the future.

Health Services Management: Readings and Commentary 7th ed.

Anthony R. Kovner, Duncan Neuhasuer, eds
Chicago, Illinois: Health Administration Press, 2001
525pp ISBN: 1567931456
This compilation of recent readings from leading scholars and writers in the field of healthcare management covers a wide spectrum of management functions, including organizational issues and the role of the manager.

Market-Driven Healthcare: Who Wins, Who Loses in the Transformation of America's Largest Service Industry

Regina Herzlinger
Cambridge, Massachusetts: Perseus Books Group, 1999
416pp ISBN: 0738201367
A well-received work on how the healthcare industry in the United States copes with the demands of the modern consumer.

Risk Management Handbook For Health Care Organizations 4th ed.

Roberta Carroll
San Francisco, California: Jossey-Bass, 2003
976pp ISBN: 0787967971
This handbook for health facility risk managers is a collection of ideas from 40 risk management professionals. It identifies some of the problem areas in healthcare, and offers current information on risk management treatments and techniques, regulatory and legal updates, and tools for assessing risk in this field.

MAGAZINES

European Journal of Public Health (EJPH)

ISSN: 1101–1262
Oxford University Press, Inc.
198 Madison Avenue, New York, 10016
T: +1 212 726 6000
F: +1 212 726 6440
www.oup-usa.org
The *EJPH* is a multidisciplinary journal providing a forum for discussion and debate on current public health issues. Coverage is international but with a focus on the European region. Original scientific articles, policy articles, reviews on major themes, editorials, commentaries, book reviews, and news are all included.

International Journal for Quality in Health Care (IJQHC)

ISSN: 1353–4505
Oxford University Press, Inc.
198 Madison Avenue, New York, 10016
T: +1 212 726 6000
F: +1 212 726 6440
www.oup-usa.org
The *IJQHC* is the official journal of the International Society for Quality in Health

Care. It is an interdisciplinary peer-reviewed bimonthly journal that includes contributions from health professionals and researchers. Articles cover health services research, healthcare evaluation, technology issues, and health economics.

International Journal of Health Care Quality Assurance

ISSN: 0952–6862
Emerald (North America)
4th Floor, 44 Brattle Street, Cambridge, Massachusetts, 02138
T: +1 888 622 0075
www.emeraldinsight.com/ccm.htm
This journal appears seven times a year and is aimed at those involved in developing and monitoring quality assurance programs in the healthcare sector. Issues relating to healthcare quality and standards are covered from both practical and theoretical perspectives.

Journal for Healthcare Quality (JHQ)

ISSN: 1062–2551
National Association for Healthcare Quality (NAHQ)
4700 West Lake Avenue, Glenview, Illinois, 60025
T: +1 800 966 9392 or 847 375 4720
www.nahq.org
The *JHQ* is published by the National Association for Healthcare Quality in the United States and is aimed at professionals responsible for promoting and monitoring the quality of health care. Articles focus on such areas as improvement, risk management, and payment systems. Book reviews and legislative updates are also provided. Extra resources are available online at www.nahq.org/journal/online.

Journal of Healthcare Management (JHM)

ISSN: 1096–9012
American College of Healthcare Executives (ACHE)
1 North Franklin, Suite 1700, Chicago, Illinois, 60606–4425
T: +1 312 424 2800
F: +1 312 424 0023
www.ache.org
The *JHM* is the official journal of the American College of Healthcare Executives. It is a bimonthly peer-reviewed publication for executives, practicing healthcare managers, academics, and policymakers.

"The manifest picture of bureaucratic organization is a confusing one."
Elliot Jacques

Articles cover strategic issues in the provision and delivery of healthcare services.

Modern Healthcare

ISSN: 0160–7480
Crain Communications, Inc.
711 Third Avenue, New York, 10017–4036
T: +1 212 210 0100
F: +1 212 210 0200
www.modernhealthcare.com
Modern Healthcare is a weekly magazine designed to provide news and information on current trends for healthcare executives, principally those responsible for finance and purchasing. Major areas of coverage include finance, managed care, marketing, technology, information systems, and regulatory developments.

INTERNET

National Information Center on Health Services Research and Health Care Technology

www.nlm.nih.gov/nichsr/nichsr.html
This site, which is part of the U.S. National Library of Medicine, provides information on databases, training, and research programs.

ORGANIZATIONS
USA
American College of Healthcare Executives (ACHE)

1 North Franklin, Suite 1700, Chicago, Illinois, 60606–4425
T: +1 312 424 2800
F: +1 312 424 0023
E: *geninfo@ache.org*
www.ache.org
ACHE is a professional organization for healthcare executives that aims to meet its members' professional and educational needs, and to promote high ethical standards and advance management excellence in health care. Its activities include training and career development programs, research, and an annual congress on healthcare management. ACHE produces the magazine, *Healthcare*

Executive, the *Journal of Healthcare Management*, and books published by the Health Administration Press.

National Association for Healthcare Quality (NAHQ)

4700 West Lake Avenue, Glenview, Illinois, 60025
T: +1 800 966 9392 or 847 375 4720
www.nahq.org
The NAHQ has the goal of improving the quality of health care and supporting the development of those working in healthcare quality. Founded in 1976, it currently has over 5,000 individual and 100 institutional members.

Europe
European Health Management Association (EHMA)

Vergemount Hall, Clonskeagh, Dublin, 6, Republic of Ireland
T: +353 1 283 9299
F: +353 1 283 8653
E: *info@ehma.org*
www.ehma.org
The EHMA acts as a forum for policy makers and senior managers, personnel directors and training officers, and academic and research organizations in the health sector. Its aim is to build bridges between them.

Institute of Healthcare Management (IHM)

18 Morley Street, London, SE1 7QZ, U.K.
T: +44 (0) 20 7620 1030
F: +44 (0) 20 7620 1040
E: *enquiries@ihm.org.uk*
www.ihm.org.uk
The IHM is a professional body for managers working in all areas of healthcare. The organization was formed by the merger of the Institute of Health Services Management and the Association of Managers in General Practice and incorporated in 1999. Its aims are to promote high standards of professional healthcare management, to represent the views and interests of healthcare managers,

to influence policy, to advance research, and to encourage networking. Its activities include publications, education and training, and an annual conference.

King's Fund

11–13 Cavendish Square, London, W1G 0AN, U.K.
T: +44 (0) 20 7307 2400
F: +44 (0) 20 7307 2801
E: *library@kingsfund.org.uk*
www.kingsfund.org.uk
The King's Fund is a London-based independent healthcare charity that works at national and international levels for better health policies and services. The organization awards grants, carries out research and development projects, and offers conference facilities, a bookshop, library and information services, and training courses.

International
International Society for Quality in Health Care (ISQHC)

Clarendon Terrace, 212 Clarendon Street, East Melbourne, Victoria, 3002, Australia
T: +61 3 9417 6971
F: +61 3 9417 6851
E: *isqua@isqua.org*
www.isqua.org.au
The ISQHC provides a multidisciplinary forum for the exchange of information and expertise in the field of healthcare. The organization promotes quality improvement in the healthcare sector, and its activities include the development of an internationally agreed method of assessing healthcare standards, research and education, meetings, and the publication of a journal. The membership includes individuals and institutions from over 70 countries.

FOR MORE INFORMATION

 Public Sector Management (pp. 1881–1882)

 1770

BUSINESS INFORMATION SOURCES

Importing

BOOKS

Building an Import/Export Business 3rd ed.
Kenneth D. Weiss
Hoboken, New Jersey: Wiley, 2002
320pp ISBN: 0471202495
This is a user-friendly guide to starting and building a successful import or export business. It gives guidance on potential areas of concern, such as operational procedures, trade agreements, and marketing techniques. It also provides practical advice on how best to tap into the lucrative global markets. It includes bibliographical references and an index.

Import/Export: How to Get Started in International Trade 3rd ed.
Carl A. Nelson
Maidenhead, United Kingdom: McGraw-Hill, 2000
340pp ISBN: 0071358714
This book is aimed at those wanting to make a start in international trade. Fully revised and including a section on e-commerce, it sets out to guide beginners through the myriad challenges of importing and exporting.

MAGAZINES

International Trade Today
The Hemming Group
32 Vauxhall Bridge Road, London, SW1V 2SS, U.K.
T: +44 (0) 20 7973 6400
F: +44 (0) 20 7233 5056
www.hgluk.com
International Trade Today is the official journal of the Institute of Export and is published ten times per year in the United Kingdom. The magazine contains useful articles about all facets of importing and exporting.

INTERNET

Kompass
www.kompass.com
This online searchable database lists some 1.9 million companies in about 70 countries, under 53,000 product headings. The databases for individual countries may also be purchased in printed format. CDs are also available.

Market Access Database
http://mkaccdb.eu.int/mkaccdb2/indexPubli.htm
The Market Access Database is provided by the DG Trade, European Commission. Certain parts of the site are open only to people having an ISP connection located in Europe, but the section on trade barriers is open to all Internet users. The site contains details about trade barriers by market sector and country, import formalities by country, and import duties by product code and by country.

Thomas Global Register
www.tgrnet.com
Formerly the American Export Register, this comprehensive Web-based directory run by Thomas Publishing gives details of some 700,000 manufacturers and distributors across 28 countries, divided into 11,000 product and service classifications.

Thomas Register of American Manufacturers
www.thomasregister.com
This online searchable database includes information on 165,000 American and Canadian manufacturing companies. Products are listed across more than 60,000 product categories and about 130,000 brand names.

World Trade Organization (WTO)
www.wto.org
The WTO site gives comprehensive details about inter-governmental actions on trade issues. The site offers statistics about world trade and downloadable documents.

ORGANIZATIONS
USA
American Association of Exporters and Importers (AAEI)
1050 17th Street, Washington, D.C., 20036
T: +1 202 857 8009
F: +1 202 857 7843
www.aaei.org
The AAEI is a trade association promoting fair and open trade for the benefit of its members and has close links with all relevant U.S. government departments and regulatory bodies. It publishes a Web-based newsletter giving details of trade matters of interest to members.

Bolero International
Centre Point Tower, 103 New Oxford Street, London, WC1A 1DD, U.K.
T: +1 212 735 0002
F: +44 (0) 20 7759 7001
www.bolero.net
Bolero has offices in New York, London, Hong Kong, Tokyo, Johannesburg, Santiago, Dubai, and Amman. Through bolero.net it offers an XML Web-based electronic document transfer system. Four grades of membership are available for global, large, medium, and small exporters/importers.

International
World Trade Organization (WTO)
Centre William Rappard, Rue de Lausanne 154, CH-1211 Geneva 21, Switzerland
T: +41 22 739 51 11
F: +41 22 731 42 06
E: *enquiries@wto.org*
www.wto.org
The WTO is an international member-based organization, whose role is to deal with the rules of trade between member nations. It aims to help producers of goods and services, and exporters and importers, to conduct their business effectively. It includes the Working Group on the Interaction between Trade and Competition Policy.

1771

BUSINESS INFORMATION SOURCES

FOR MORE INFORMATION
Exporting (pp. 1752–1753)

"My style of dealmaking is quite simple and straightforward. I just keep pushing and pushing to get what I'm after."
Donald J. Trump

Information Management

BOOKS

The Art of Strategic Planning for Information Technology 2nd ed.
Bernard H. Boar
Hoboken, New Jersey: Wiley, 2000
416pp ISBN: 0471376558
The second edition of this book provides strategy frameworks for information management, offering advice on how to choose the most appropriate strategy and how to deploy IT resources to suit that strategy. It analyzes information systems management in relation to competitive advantage, execution, quality control, and administration and discusses technologies including e-commerce, data warehousing, and architectures.

Assessing Information Needs: Tools, Techniques, and Concepts for the Internet Age 2nd ed.
David Nicholas
London: Aslib, The Association for Information Management, 2000
160pp (Aslib Know How Guides)
ISBN: 0851424333
This know-how guide is aimed at those working or teaching in library and information services and covers a range of basic techniques, concepts, and activities in the field. These include: understanding information needs; undertaking an assessment of them; developing a framework for evaluating them; determining the factors involved in the meeting them; and collecting the relevant data.

Business in a Virtual World: Exploiting Information for Competitive Advantage
Fiona Czerniawska, Gavin Potter
West Lafayette, Indiana: Purdue University Press, 2002
272pp ISBN: 1557531943
A big change is currently taking place in the world of business as companies shift their assets from the physical to the virtual domain. This book explains the new economic laws of the virtual environment, gives examples of companies already exploiting virtual opportunities, and provides a practical toolkit for succeeding in the virtual world.

Corporate Information Strategy and Management: Text and Cases
Lynda M. Applegate, F. Warren McFarlan,

Robert D. Austin
Maidenhead, United Kingdom: McGraw-Hill, 2005
672pp ISBN: 0072947756
Targeted at either students or managers with some IT experience, the book offers an overview of information systems technology management. It offers case studies to illustrate how to put theories into practice and contains a good discussion of the people issues involved in information systems management.

Information Strategy in Practice
Elizabeth Orna
Aldershot, Hampshire: Ashgate Publishing Ltd, 2004
163pp ISBN: 0566085798
This book, designed for students of information management and information managers, sets out a practical step-by-step approach to implementing information management strategies in organizations. The process starts by showing how to conduct an information audit and interpret the results, then goes on to discuss the development of information policies and strategies. The book offers definitions of information, knowledge, and information management and explains the ways in which they complement each other. Advice on overcoming difficulties is drawn from the author's own experience as an information manager and consultant.

The Knowing Organization: How Organizations Use Information to Construct Meaning, Create Knowledge, and Make Decisions
Chun Wei Choo
New York: Oxford University Press, Inc., 1998
256pp ISBN: 0195110129
The book looks at the relationship between organizational behavior and information management, detailing the ways in which information acts in various organizational-behavior models. It is divided into three sections: analyzing the ways in which organizations use information; comparing the dynamics of different models; and proposing a new framework for organizations to make sense of information, create knowledge, and make decisions.

Organizing Knowledge: An Introduction to Managing Access to Information 3rd ed.
Jennifer Rowley, John Farrow
Aldershot, United Kingdom: Gower Publishing, 2000
424pp ISBN: 0566080478
This is a comprehensive text on knowledge organization and retrieval, aimed mainly at students. It looks at the nature of information and knowledge and their incorporation into documents. It deals with records, focusing particularly on the use of electronic databases and the range of tools available for accessing information resources. Finally, it examines knowledge storage systems, including CD-ROMs, online services, OPACs, and the Internet.

Practical Information Policies 2nd ed.
Elizabeth Orna
Aldershot, United Kingdom: Gower Publishing, 1999
375pp ISBN: 0566076934
Aimed at managers, information managers, and information students, Orna's book looks at why information should be managed, and includes an information audit, before focusing on the formation and implementation of information policies. It considers in particular the areas of people, systems, cost measurement, and change management, and presents many case studies.

The Social Life of Information
John Seely Brown, Paul Duguid
Boston, Massachusetts: Harvard Business School Press, 2002
336pp ISBN: 1578517087
The book presents a picture of information management separated from technology, arguing that a focus on technology obscures the issues of how people work and learn. By emphasizing the practice of knowledge rather than the processes of managing information, this book puts information into a social context.

MAGAZINES
C.I.O. Magazine
CXO Media
492 Old Connecticut Path, P.O. Box 9208, Framingham, Massachusetts, 0170–9208
T: +1 508 872 0080
www.cio.com
This magazine, written for Chief

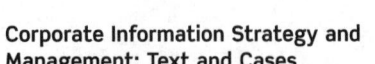
"There is a strong tendency among European managers to be selective about sharing information."

Percy Barnevik

Information Officers and other information executives, provides valuable research and insights using a case-study approach. It also features opinion and current topic columns.

International Journal of Information Management

ISSN: 0268-4012
Elsevier Science
Customer Service Department, 6277 Sea Harbor Drive, Orlando, Florida, 32887–4800
T: +1 877 839 7126 or +1 407 345 4020
F: +1 407 363 1354
www.elsevier.com
The Journal aims to provide the very best analysis and discussion in the developing field of information management and is written for senior managers and others in that field. It contains major papers, reports and reviews and is highly topical.

Journal of Information Science

ISSN: 0165-5515
Sage Publications
1 Oliver's Yard, 55 City Road, London, EC1Y 1SP, U.K.
T: +44 (0) 20 7324 8500
F: +44 (0) 20 7324 8600
www.sagepub.co.uk
Published in association with the Chartered Institute of Library and Information Professionals, this international journal seeks to achieve a better understanding of the principles that underpin the effective creation, organization, storage, communication and utilization of information and knowledge resources.

Managing Information

ISSN: 1352-0229
Aslib, The Association for Information Management
Holywell Centre, 1 Phipp Street, London, EC2A 4PS, U.K.
T: +44 (0) 20 7613 3031
F: +44 (0) 20 7613 5058
www.aslib.co.uk
Written for everyone who uses or manages information, this journal combines interviews, analysis, and practical solutions with in-depth news and trends analysis. There is a website at www.managinginformation.com.

INTERNET
The Information Management Forum
www.theimf.com
Aimed at senior IT and HR managers, this membership site offers reports, an events calendar, and a networking service.

InformationR.net supported by University of Sheffield, U.K.
http://informationr.net
This site offers an online journal, a world list of departments and schools specializing in information research, a guide to journals and newsletters on the subject, and details of electronic resources for information research methods.

Society for Information Management
www.simnet.org
Sponsored by a nonprofit organization of technology experts, this site offers white papers and publications, information on upcoming events, discussions of current issues, and regional leadership forums. Registration is needed to access certain areas of the site.

ORGANIZATIONS
USA
Association for Information and Image Management (AIIM)
1100 Wayne Avenue, Suite 1100, Silver Spring, Maryland, 20910
T: +1 301 587 8202
F: +1 301 587 2711
www.aiim.org
Founded in 1943, this association has over 10,000 members. Professionals in the manufacturing, vending and information/image management equipment business will find the statistical information compiled by this group invaluable. Chapters of this association meet across the United States. The group also maintains a resource center.

Society for Information Management (SIM)
401 N. Michigan Avenue, Chicago, Illinois, 60611
T: +1 312 527 6734 or 800 387 9746
F: +1 312 245 1081
E: *info@simnet.org*
www.simnet.org
Founded in 1968, SIM is a nonprofit organization for information technology experts, including C.I.O.s, C.T.O.s, and IT professionals, with over 2,500 members. It aims to keep its members abreast of advances in information technology worldwide and opportunities in continuing education, and to maintain a network of peer resources through programs designed for information management professionals.

Europe
Aslib, The Association for Information Management
Holywell Centre, 1 Phipp Street, London, EC2A 4PS, U.K.
T: +44 (0) 20 7613 3031
F: +44 (0) 20 7613 5058
E: *aslib@aslib.co.uk*
www.aslib.co.uk
Aslib is a charity, registered in 1924, whose 2,000 members are private- and public-sector companies and organizations throughout the world concerned with managing information resources efficiently. Its key roles are: to stimulate awareness of the value and benefits of good management of information resources; to represent and lobby for the interests of the information sector on matters of national and international importance; and to provide a range of information-related products and services to meet the needs of the information society.

International
ARMA International—The Information Management Professionals
4200 Somerset, Suite 215, Prairie Village, Kansas, 66208
T: +1 913 341 3808
F: +1 913 341 3742
E: *hq@arma.org*
www.arma.org
Founded in 1975, this association has over 10,500 members. ARMA provides research and networking opportunities for anyone involved in the information management world. The mission of ARMA is to enhance the skills and experience of information management professionals.

1773

FOR MORE INFORMATION

BUSINESS INFORMATION SOURCES

"The information highway will transform our culture as dramatically as Gutenberg's press did the Middle Ages."

Bill Gates

Innovation and Creativity

BOOKS

The Artist's Way: A Spiritual Path to Higher Creativity 2nd ed.

Julia Cameron, Mark Bryan
New York: J.P. Tarcher, 2002
272pp ISBN: 1585421464
The book contains a thorough 12-week program on how to rediscover creativity after suffering mental blocks. The authors suggest that people try to get in tune with their creative energies, thereby finding a connection between spirituality and creativity.

The Art of Innovation: Lessons in Creativity from IDEO, America's Leading Design Firm

Tom Kelley
London: Currency, 2001
320pp ISBN: 0385499841
This book is the story of IDEO, the beliefs of its founders, and their process for achieving innovation. The authors examine why many manufacturing companies have difficulty in innovating. They then describe the IDEO process, which is characterized by brainstorming techniques, and a focus on fast prototyping for immediate feedback. Finally, they detail the thinking necessary to develop an overall environment for innovation.

Big Ideas: Putting the Zest into Creativity and Innovation at Work

Jonne Ceserani
London: Kogan Page, 2003
208pp ISBN: 0749438789
This collection of thoughts and ideas has been brought together by a partner in the innovation and change management consultancy Synectics. It aims to help readers develop both their own creativity and their ability to stimulate and encourage innovation and change in their organizations. The book includes tools for problem-solving and collaborative working, guidance on developing leadership qualities that will promote creativity, and suggestions on how to work with groups to maximize successful creativity.

Building the Innovative Organization: Management Systems That Encourage Innovation

James A. Christiansen
Basingstoke, United Kingdom: Macmillan Business, 2000
320pp ISBN: 0312232837

This textbook, based on research undertaken at INSEAD, explains how highly innovative large companies have learned to manage differently. It presents an overview of the innovation process, and sets out the ways in which corporate managers can influence it. From there it proceeds to show how the more innovative companies can differ in such fundamental areas as organization structure, communication systems, incentives, and project funding and management.

Conceptual Blockbusting: A Guide to Creative Ideas 4th ed.

James L. Adams
Cambridge, Massachusetts: Perseus Books Group, 2001
224pp ISBN: 0738205370
The author of this book uses examples from areas such as engineering, philosophy, and psychology to help people overcome writing blocks and to generate ideas. He also discusses in detail the major types of block and provides exercises to help tackle them.

Corporate Creativity: How Innovation and Improvement Actually Happen

Alan G. Robinson, Sam Stern
San Francisco, California: Berrett-Koehler, 1998
300pp ISBN: 1576750493
Robinson and Stern propose a way of managing for creativity that allows companies to realize their creative potential and improve their competitive position and profitability. Having investigated hundreds of creative acts in organizations around the world, they make some surprising discoveries about how innovation and improvement actually happen. In a text enlivened with plenty of detailed examples, they reveal six essential elements that individuals and companies can use to turn their creativity from a hit-or-miss proposition into something consistent they can count on.

Creativity in Virtual Teams: Key Components for Success

Jill E. Nemiro
New York: Pfeiffer & Co., 2004
320pp (Collaborative Work Systems)
ISBN: 0787971146
This book looks at how creativity can be

promoted in the context of virtual teamworking. The first section outlines how to develop an effective creative process and work structure for the team. The vital ingredients of climate—attitudes, feelings, and behaviors, the development of a sense of connection or community, and the process of establishing norms and protocols—are then addressed. The book also presents a range of tools and techniques for assessing and promoting communication and creativity, including force field analysis, mind mapping, brainwriting, electronic meetings, and electronic brainstorming. A final section underlines the importance of ongoing assessment and learning.

Innovation: Driving Product Process and Market Change

Edward B. Roberts, ed.
San Francisco, California: Jossey-Bass, 2002
352pp (MIT Sloan Management Review)
ISBN: 0787962139
This book explores the key managerial issues of the innovation process. Part one covers innovating from the inside, including strategic innovation, creativity versus structure, integrating the fuzzy front end of new product development, the product family and the dynamics of core capability, and planning for product platforms. Part two looks at innovating from the outside, exploring whether to ally or acquire, outsourcing, making strategic alliances work, and location. Part three investigates new dimensions for innovation, such as software-based innovation, user innovation communities or creating complex products with limited manufacturer involvement, and weird ideas that spark innovation.

The Innovator's Dilemma: The Revolutionary National Bestseller That Will Change the Way You Do Business

Clayton M. Christensen
London: HarperCollins Business, 2003
320pp ISBN: 0060521996
Christensen looks at products that have redefined their own particular markets by entering the marketplace at the bottom end of the scale, making a niche for themselves, and then, over a period of time, removing competitors from the top. He also includes suggestions on how to prevent such an occurrence.

"You can innovate by not doing anything, if it's a conscious decision."   Herb Kelleher

The Innovator's Solution: Creating and Sustaining Successful Growth

Clayton M. Christensen, Michael E. Raynor
Boston, Massachusetts: Harvard Business School Press, 2003
304pp ISBN: 1578518520

This book shows how to create a disruptive growth engine that fuels ongoing success. The authors consider how to tell if an idea has disruptive potential, which competitive situations favor incumbents and which favor entrants, which customer segments are primed to embrace a new offering, and which activities should be outsourced and which kept in-house. They also explore how to structure and find a new venture, how to choose the right managers to lead it, and how to position the organization so that profits will be made in the future.

Jamming: The Art and Discipline of Business Creativity

John Kao
New York: HarperCollins, 1997
224pp ISBN: 0887308643

The emphasis of this title is on creativity and how top companies get ahead of the field by nurturing this important element of their businesses. The book covers all aspects of creativity, from weighing up the creativity of a company to overcoming possible pitfalls.

Leading for Innovation: And Organizing for Results

Frances Hesselbein, Marshall Goldsmith, Iain Somerville, eds
San Francisco, California: Jossey-Bass, 2001
190pp ISBN: 0787953598

This book is a collection of articles and essays by some noted thinkers and speakers on innovation and leadership. The editors have compiled the writings into four categories: leading the people who make innovation happen; creating an environment that encourages innovation; changing the way you think about leadership and innovation; and the practice of innovation. Contributors include William Bratton (former Chief of Police in New York City), who outlines his thoughts on "leading for innovation and results," and Dave Ulrich (an HR professor and practitioner), who offers an "innovation protocol."

Leading the Revolution

Gary Hamel
Boston, Massachusetts: Harvard Business School Press, 2002
352pp ISBN: 0452283248

Hamel argues that companies must adopt a radical new innovation agenda and

continually reinvent themselves. He explains the underlying principles of radical innovation, explores where revolutionary new business concepts come from, identifies the key design criteria for building companies that are activist friendly and revolution ready, and details, with case study illustrations, the steps a company must take to make innovation an enduring capability.

Managing Creativity: The Dynamics of Work and Organisation

Howard Davis, Richard Scase
Buckingham, United Kingdom: Open University Press, 2001
160pp (Managing Work and Organisations)
ISBN: 033520693X

The authors investigate the organizational dynamics of creative companies on the basis of research into firms in publishing, advertising, television, radio, the performing arts, and the music industry. Chapters focus on: managing creative organizational cultures; trends in creative organizations; creative employees—their attitudes and values; and the creative challenge.

Managing Strategic Innovation and Change: A Collection of Readings 2nd ed.

Michael L. Tushman, Philip Anderson
New York: Oxford University Press USA, 2004
640pp ISBN: 0195135784

This book is a collection of 42 articles, written by leading industry and academic experts. It aims to create an overall framework for thinking about how technologies evolve and drive the need for organizational change and adaptation. The papers are grouped under the headings of: innovation over time and in a historical context; organizational architectures and managing innovation; innovation and business strategy; knowledge, learning, and intellectual capital; managing linkages; and executive leadership and managing innovation and change.

Mastering the Dynamics of Innovation

James M. Utterback
Boston, Massachusetts: Harvard Business School Press, 1996
288pp ISBN: 0875847404

The author discusses the way in which innovation can affect industries and firms, and how innovation begins in an industry. He also gives examples of new product development and provides valuable insights into how to encourage innovation.

Orbiting the Giant Hairball: A Corporate Fool's Guide to Surviving with Grace

Gordon MacKenzie
New York: Penguin, 1998
224pp ISBN: 0670879835

This is a fun book that shares some of the wisdom MacKenzie acquired in his 30 years as a creative talent working at Hallmark Cards. It even looks different from most business works because MacKenzie uses crude drawings and pictures as well as different type fonts to make the point that creativity is about going outside the lines. The text is full of humorous stories about MacKenzie's fight to stay non-traditional and his battles against the forces inside organizations that inhibit creativity.

Organizing Genius: The Secrets of Creative Collaboration

Warren Bennis, Patricia Ward Biederman
Cambridge, Massachusetts: Addison-Wesley, 1998
239pp ISBN: 0201339897

Bennis and Biederman explore the forces that foster creative collaboration by analyzing the histories of six "Great Groups" in order to uncover the secrets of collective genius. The "Great Groups" are: the Walt Disney Studio; Xerox's Palo Alto Research Center and Apple; the 1992 Clinton campaign; Lockheed's Skunk Works; Black Mountain College; and the Manhattan Project.

The Power of Strategy Innovation: A New Way of Linking Creativity and Strategic Planning to Discover Great Business Opportunities

Robert E. Johnson Jr., J. Douglas Bate
New York: AMACOM, 2003
286pp ISBN: 0814407684

This book aims to show you how to connect analytical, day-to-day planning with the market-centric, discovery-driven innovation that focuses on the future. This text also outlines what strategy is, what it is not, and how to integrate it into an organization. It provides specific guidance for implementing a strategy innovation initiative called the Discovery Process, and also discusses an example of how the process worked in a real company, including details of the five phases of its implementation: staging, aligning, exploring, creating, and mapping.

Releasing Creativity: How Leaders Develop Creative Potential in Their Teams

John Whatmore
London: Kogan Page, 1999
224pp ISBN: 0749430109

BUSINESS INFORMATION SOURCES

"Creativity is thinking new things. Innovation is doing new things."   Theodore Levitt

Organizations of all types are under increasing pressure to develop climates and cultures that nurture creativity, innovation, and change. The work of the creative leader and the creative team is explored in this book through the experiences of a range of leading organizations. The author also considers the importance of recognizing, nurturing, controlling, and developing individual skills and talents, and discusses such questions as how to identify the kind of creativity needed, how to match the right task to the right leader, and how to develop and support teams for the chosen tasks.

Seeing What's Next: Using the Theories of Innovation to Predict Industry Change

Clayton M. Christensen, Scott D. Anthony, Erik A. Roth
Boston, Massachusetts: Harvard Business School Press, 2004
336pp ISBN: 1591391857
In this book, Christensen and his fellow authors attempt to take the guesswork out of innovation and new product development by suggesting a framework via which outcomes in any industry can be predicted. Drawing on key theories developed in Christensen's bestselling books *The Innovator's Dilemma* and *The Innovator's Solution*, this book focuses on three main phases: spotting the signs of change, working out the potential end result of competitive battles, and analyzing whether corporate decisions will boost the company's chance of success, or endanger it.

Serious Play

Michael Schrage, Tom Peters
Boston, Massachusetts: Harvard Business School Press, 1999
244pp ISBN: 0875848141
The authors suggest that in order to create innovative products, top companies need play. Their book describes the type of environment that creates innovation and studies the methods of successful prototyping at companies like Boeing and Microsoft.

Six Thinking Hats

Edward De Bono
New York: Little, Brown, 1999
192pp ISBN: 0316178314
De Bono represents six different approaches to decision-making and problem-solving by six "thinking hats" of different colors: white, factual; red, emotional; yellow, positive; black, critical

and negative; green, intuitive; and blue, seeing the big picture. He suggests that by knowing that there are different approaches, and through role play in which each member of a group literally or metaphorically wears a different hat, communication can be improved and the overall effectiveness of the group as a generator of new ideas can be enhanced.

Strategic Innovation: Embedding Innovation as a Core Competency in Your Organization

Nancy Tennant Snyder, Deborah L. Duarte
New York: Jossey-Bass, 2003
224pp ISBN: 0787964050
The authors argues that strategic innovation should be a core competency throughout an organization to ensure a continuous pipeline of innovation from everywhere and everyone. The authors offer a flexible template to achieve this objective. Using corporate examples, they describe and explain the tools and techniques needed to become a customer-focused organization, where innovation is strategically embedded.

Weird Ideas that Work: 11½ Practices for Promoting, Managing, and Sustaining Innovation

Robert I. Sutton
New York: Free Press, 2001
224pp ISBN: 0743212126
In a work that will challenge many of the current practices of organizations, Sutton argues that organizing for innovation is very different from organizing for routine and that many companies are currently organized for routine. Six Sigma and TQM processes push companies to drive out variation, which is, Sutton argues, necessary for innovation. He suggests some thought-provoking and challenging practices to help companies break from this "reduce variation" mantra. He advocates, for example, holding onto the "slow learner of the organizational code," because it is this type of person who tends to find innovative solutions faster than anyone else.

Wellsprings of Knowledge: Building and Sustaining the Sources of Innovation

Dorothy Leonard-Barton
Boston, Massachusetts: Harvard Business School Press, 1998
334pp ISBN: 0875848591
This book raises the question of why some organizations are better at creating new products than other ones, using interviews

with those who have failed and those who have succeeded in the manufacturing industries to help find an answer.

A Whack on the Side of the Head: How You Can Be More Creative

Roger Von Oech
New York: Warner Books, 1998
232pp ISBN: 0446674559
Containing a range of exercises and useful ideas, this title is designed to increase creativity and innovation.

When Sparks Fly: Harnessing the Power of Group Creativity

Dorothy Leonard, Walter Swap
Boston, Massachusetts: Harvard Business School Press, 2005
256pp ISBN: 1591397936
The basic premise of this book is that the creative process is the same, whatever the size or type of company. The coauthors describe a five-stage process of creativity that includes developing alternatives, choosing the right blend of people, and taking time to consider choices. Their ideas are supported by true examples of creativity from the corporate world.

MAGAZINES
Creativity and Innovation Management

ISSN: 0963–1690
Blackwell Publishing
350 Main Street, Malden, Massachusetts, 02148
T: +1 781 388 8200
F: +1 781 388 8232
www.blackwellpublishing.com
The aim of this journal is to enable an international community of practitioners and academics to share and extend their understanding of creativity and innovation management.

International Journal of Innovation Management (IJIM)

ISSN: 1363–9196
World Scientific Publishing Co., Ltd.
1060 Main Street, River Edge, New Jersey, 07661
T: +1 800 227 7562
F: +1 888 977 2665
www.worldscinet.com/ijim/ijim.shtml
Published quarterly, the IJIM is dedicated to the advancement of academic research and management practice in the field of innovation management. It aims to provide a forum for the insights of academics, practicing managers and consultants, and to integrate the theory and practice of innovation management.

"To invent, you need a good imagination and a pile of junk."   Thomas Edison

Journal of Innovative Management
ISSN: 1081–0714
Goal QPC
12B Manor Parkway, Salem, New
Hampshire, 03079–2841
T: +1 603 890 8800
F: +1 603 870 9122
www.goalqpc.com
This quarterly journal is written for
managers who are responsible for leading
or implementing improvement initiatives.
Articles describe best practices in the field
and offer new ideas and tools.

INTERNET
CreativityPool.com
www.creativitypool.com
This site contains a database that allows
people to submit creative ideas to solve
problems. Users can search for solutions
already posted. There is no cost to use the
site, and ideas are freely shared as part of
the rules for use.

Creativity Unleashed Limited
www.cul.co.uk
Developed to assist in the development of
business creativity, this site includes free
and shareware software to download, book
and software reviews, a mailing list, and
links to other creativity sites.

Directed Creativity
www.directedcreativity.com
A site based around the theory of "directed
creativity," as developed by Paul Plsek, it
includes a creativity bookstore and a toolkit
of techniques.

Innovation Tools
www.innovationtools.com
This site is designed for the busy executive
as a place to get some quick ideas. It
includes information about idea-generating
software and up-to-date news items related
to innovation.

ORGANIZATIONS
USA
American Creativity Association (ACA)
P.O. Box 5856, Philadelphia, Pennsylvania,
19128
T: +1 888 837 1409
F: +1 502 254 5746
E: *ACAinformation@aol.com*
www.amcreativityassoc.org
Founded in 1989, this organization has over
350 members. The ACA seeks to promote
and develop creativity on personal and
professional levels, and to increase
awareness of the importance of creativity in
society. It also works with business to
illustrate the importance of employee
creativity and how this employee asset
helps organizations remain competitive.

American Society for Technical Innovation (ASTI)
P.O. Box 1242, Arlington, Virginia, 22210
www.washacadsci.org

Comprising professionals from industry,
government, and educational institutions,
ASTI aims to establish a dialogue among
different disciplines that share the
common problem of effective
management of innovation. ASTI
encourages members to share ideas,
information, and experiences found among
diverse communities. The association
works to improve the management of
innovation.

Innovation Network
451 E. 58th Avenue, No. 4625, Denver,
Colorado, 80216
T: +1 303 308 1088
F: +1 303 295 6108
E: *staff@thinksmart.com*
www.thinksmart.com
Founded in 1993, this organization
comprises individuals and companies who
are committed to innovative thinking and
processes.

FOR MORE INFORMATION

☆ Brainstorming (pp. 408–409)
✔ Brainstorming (pp. 584–585)
☆ Creating Corporate Creativity
  (pp. 341–342)
✔ Developing Your Creativity
  (pp. 941–943)
✔ Open Systems Thinking (pp. 596–597)

1777

BUSINESS INFORMATION SOURCES

"The first rule of intelligent tinkering is to save all the parts."   Paul Ehrlich

Intellectual Property

BOOKS

Copyright: Interpreting the Law for Libraries, Archives and Information Services 4th ed.

Graham Cornish

London: Library Association Publishing, 2004

208pp ISBN: 1856045080

Cornish's book explains the provisions of the Copyright, Designs, and Patents Act 1988 and supporting legislation in quick and easy question and answer form. New sections cover licensing schemes and developments in electronic copyright issues, including the legal deposit of electronic materials.

Essentials of Intellectual Property

Alexander I. Poltorak, Paul J. Lerner

Hoboken, New Jersey: Wiley, 2002

260pp ISBN: 0471209422

Poltorak and Lerner have compiled a concise and useful primer for professionals who need answers fast and novices who would like to learn more about this subject. The book goes from the basics of the intellectual property field to copyright laws and to strategies and technologies that are in place today.

From Ideas to Assets: Investing Wisely in Intellectual Property

Bruce M. Berman, ed.

Hoboken, New Jersey: Wiley, 2002

624pp ISBN: 0471400688

Based on the experience of expert contributors, the book argues that corporations need to understand what their intellectual property assets are and how to protect their rights to them. It covers such topics as maximizing returns on intellectual property assets, valuing those assets, and discerning performance variables.

Patent It Yourself 11th ed.

David Pressman

Berkeley, California: Nolo Press, 2005

512pp ISBN: 1413301800

As an experienced patent attorney and former patent examiner of the U.S. Patent and Trademark Office, David Pressman has developed a very useful guide containing all the instructions and forms necessary to patent an invention in the United States. The book offers comprehensive and up-to-date advice for obtaining a high-quality patent and presents the information in a user-friendly, jargon-free, and well-illustrated way.

Protecting Your #1 Asset: Creating Fortunes from Your Ideas: An Intellectual Property Handbook

Michael A. Lechter

Boston, Massachusetts: Back Bay Books, 2001

320pp ISBN: 0446678317

Placing its emphasis on protecting intellectual property (IP), this book makes the case for understanding developments in this arena. It covers topics including identifying and benefiting from IP assets, using IP assets to build barriers to competition, licensing IP assets, and using IP assets to raise capital.

Rembrandts in the Attic: Unlocking the Hidden Value of Patents

Kevin G. Rivette, David Kline

Boston, Massachusetts: Harvard Business School Press, 1999

220pp ISBN: 0875848990

This is a practical book full of strategic advice on how to protect your ideas and inventions. Aimed at C.E.O.s as well as managers, the book contains essential information and case studies that can help readers release the power of their "hidden" portfolio.

The Strategic Management of Intellectual Capital

David A. Klein

Woburn, Massachusetts: Butterworth-Heinemann, 1997

246pp (Resources for the Knowledge-based Economy)

ISBN: 0750698500

This collection of articles addresses central themes in the strategic management of intellectual capital. It is designed to assist organizations in understanding the strategic and operational roles of intellectual property and in developing organizational infrastructures and cultures that foster the creation, development, sharing, and mentoring of intellectual capital.

Valuation of Intellectual Property and Intangible Assets 3rd ed.

Gordon V. Smith, Russell L. Parr

Hoboken, New Jersey: Wiley, 2000

638pp (Intellectual Property)

ISBN: 0471362816

Smith and Parr argue that intellectual property and intangible assets represent the core of most corporations' value, and offer advice on how to identify, define, and exploit these assets. They also include a discussion of setting royalty rates based on rates of return. This third edition of the book offers analysis of recent developments in the field.

Value Driven Intellectual Capital: How to Convert Intangible Corporate Assets into Market Value

Patrick H. Sullivan

Hoboken, New Jersey: Wiley, 2000

240pp (Intellectual Property)

ISBN: 0471351040

This book explores the expanding world of intellectual assets, where translating an innovative idea into bottom-line profits involves a tightly focused strategy. It offers suggestions for turning corporate knowledge, know-how, and intellectual property into a sustainable competitive weapon that will build reputation and market share.

MAGAZINES

Copyright World

ISSN: 0950–2505

Informa Law

30–32 Mortimer Street, London, W1W 7RE, U.K.

T: +44 (0) 20 7017 4046

F: +44 (0) 20 7453 2221

www.ipworldonline.com

This publication contains international news and updates on copyright and intellectual property matters, covering both legal and practical issues.

INTERNET

Copyright and Fair Use: Stanford University Libraries

http://fairuse.stanford.edu

The site provides a quick search facility and overview of copyright law, with links to Internet resources, current legislation, cases, judicial opinions, regulations, treaties, and conventions.

Copyright Clearance Center

www.copyright.com

Copyright Clearance Center, Inc., the largest licenser of text reproduction rights in the world, was formed in 1978 to facilitate compliance with U.S. copyright law. It provides licensing systems for the

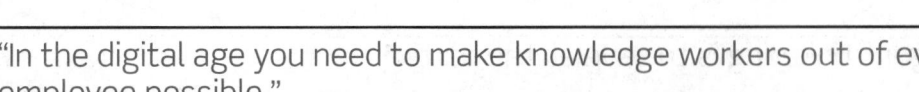

"In the digital age you need to make knowledge workers out of every employee possible."

Bill Gates

reproduction and distribution of copyrighted materials in print and electronic formats throughout the world.

The Copyright Licensing Agency
www.cla.co.uk
The Agency is the United Kingdom's reproduction rights organization—the U.K. equivalent of the U.S. Copyright Clearance Center.

Franklin Pierce Law Center
www.fplc.edu
Sponsored by a law school, the site offers an extensive list of articles relating to intellectual property.

Intellectual Property
www.intellectual-property.gov.uk
This site gives information and advice on patents, trademarks, design, and copyright with links to the relevant government departments. It also addresses key questions on protection, permissions, and enforcing rights.

International Intellectual Property Alliance
www.iipa.com
Sponsored by a private-sector coalition formed to protect U.S. copyrighted material around the world, the site offers articles on a variety of IP topics and country-specific copyright information.

U.K. Patent Office
www.patent.gov.uk
The Web site of the U.K. government department responsible for intellectual property—copyright, patents, designs, and trademarks—has a section of links to government, academic, and general IP sites.

United States Copyright Office
www.loc.gov/copyright
The U.S. Copyright Office is located in the Library of Congress. The site has a section for FAQs and another for requests relating to the Freedom of Information Act, besides material on copyright legislation and an international section with links to the WIPO.

ORGANIZATIONS
USA
American Intellectual Property Law Association (AIPLA)
2001 Jefferson Davis Highway, Suite 203, Arlington, Virginia, 22202
T: +1 703 415 0780
F: +1 703 415 0786
E: *aipla@aipla.org*
www.aipla.org
Founded in 1897 and having more than 16,000 members, this association is composed of national bar association lawyers practicing in the fields of patents, trademarks, and copyrights. AIPLA works to promote the improvement of U.S. intellectual property systems.

Intellectual Property Owners Association (IPO)
1255 23rd St. NW, Suite 200, Washington, D.C., 20037
T: +1 202 466 2396
F: +1 202 466 2893
E: *info@ipo.org*
www.ipo.org
This group comprises over 400 major corporations and lawyers that deal with intellectual property issues and concerns. The IPO works to support and strengthen the patent, trademark, copyright, and trade secret laws of the United States. It also monitors legislative activities.

United States Patent and Trademark Office (USPTO)
P. O. Box 1450, Alexandria, VA, 22313–1450
E: *usptoinfo@uspto.gov*
www.uspto.gov
The PTO promotes industrial and technological progress in the United States and strengthens the national economy by administering the laws relating to patents and trademarks, and advising the U.S. government on patent, trademark, and copyright protection, and on trade-related aspects of intellectual property.

International
World Intellectual Property Organization (WIPO)
34, chemin des Colombettes, Geneva, Switzerland, Switzerland
www.wipo.org
WIPO is a Geneva-based specialized agency of the United Nations whose mandate is to promote the protection of intellectual property worldwide. Counting 182 countries among its member states, WIPO administers 23 treaties in the field of intellectual property. The first general group of treaties defines internationally agreed basic standards of intellectual property in each of the member states.

1779

FOR MORE INFORMATION

☆ Intellectual Capital (pp. 198–199)
📖 Intellectual Capital (p. 1104)
🐭 Knowledge Management (pp. 1794–1797)
☆ Managing Intellectual Capital (pp. 49–50)

BUSINESS INFORMATION SOURCES

"To engage in the learning cycle, some firms move their employees instead of their knowledge."

Anthony DiBella

     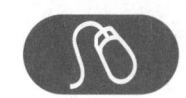

Interfirm Cooperation, Strategic Alliances, Joint Ventures

BOOKS

Alliance Competence: Maximizing the Value of Your Partnerships

Robert E. Spekman, Lynn A. Isabella, Thomas C. MacAvoy
Hoboken, New Jersey: Wiley, 2000
256pp ISBN: 0471330639
This text combines research and case studies to explore the key aspects of successful alliances. The authors focus on building alliance competence, balancing business and relationships, managing the alliance over time, and conflict resolution. The concept of the "no blame review" is outlined.

The Alliance Revolution: The New Shape of Business Rivalry

Benjamin Gomes-Casseres
Cambridge, Massachusetts: Harvard University Press, 1998
320pp ISBN: 0674016483
The author examines business alliances and intercompany collaborations that change the way business is conducted. Case studies are used to explore the implications of the increasing use of alliances, and the book provides recommendations for organizations considering collaboration.

Building Strategic Relationships: How to Extend Your Organization's Reach Through Partnerships, Alliances, and Joint Ventures

William Bergquist, Juli Betwee, David Meuel
San Francisco, California: Jossey-Bass, 1995
246pp ISBN: 0787900923
Providing a macro view of strategic partnerships, the book draws on interviews and case studies to look at the process from launch through development to conclusion. Rather than exploring the logistics of partnerships, the book focuses on the reasons for creating them and addresses "soft" issues such as trust and communication.

The Collaboration Challenge: How Nonprofits and Businesses Succeed Through Strategic Alliances

James E. Austin, The Drucker Foundation
San Francisco, California: Jossey-Bass, 2000
272pp ISBN: 0787952206
This book offers insights into the process of creating and sustaining strategic partnerships between businesses and nonprofit organizations. Its contents include the strategic benefits of alliances, understanding strategic collaboration, making the connection, generating value, managing the relationship, and guidelines for collaborating successfully.

The Collaborative Enterprise: Why Links across the Corporation Often Fail and How to Make Them Work

Andrew Campbell, Michael Goold
Cambridge, Massachusetts: Perseus Books Group, 2000
224pp ISBN: 0738203106
Using examples from real life, this book reports on the growing need for businesses to work together in order to achieve success in the future. The book also looks at the problems that can occur in such dealings and offers ways of overcoming them from the varying perspectives of people in different management positions.

Cooperative Strategy: Competing Successfully through Strategic Alliances

Pierre Dussauge, Bernard Garrette
Hoboken, New Jersey: Wiley, 1999
236pp ISBN: 0471974927
Aimed at managers, this book gives a framework for analyzing strategic alliances and dealing with the issues of intercompany cooperation. Using case studies, it considers the global perspective and offers flexible approaches, operational recommendations, and guidance for alliances between competitors.

Developing Strategic Partnerships: How to Leverage More Business from Major Customers

Chris Steward
Aldershot, United Kingdom: Gower Publishing, 1999
197pp ISBN: 0566081016
This text uses a step-by-step methodology to explain the planning, implementation, and evaluation processes of building a partnership. It looks at many important issues, including identification of potential alliances, gaining customer commitment, building the partnership team, and evaluating progress.

Effective International Joint Venture Management: Practical Legal Insights for Successful Organization and Implementation

Ronald Charles Wolf
New York: M.E. Sharpe, Inc., 2001
500pp ISBN: 0765605473
The essential steps toward the creation of an international joint venture are described in this book. It covers the commercial aspects, capital structure, due diligence, ownership rights, dispute resolution, and termination, among other topics. Though the text deals with complex subjects in detail, it is written in language that is easy to understand and is appropriate for managers, lawyers, and business students.

Inter-firm Collaboration, Learning and Networks: An Integrated Approach

Bart Nooteboom
New York: Routledge, 2003
256pp ISBN: 041532954X
Looking at the key questions of who should collaborate, why, and how, this book offers an integrated approach to this issue. There is a particular emphasis on learning and innovation.

International Joint Venture Management: Learning to Cooperate and Cooperating to Learn

Bettina S. T. Buchel et al.
Hoboken, New Jersey: Wiley, 1998
300pp ISBN: 0471828947
The book provides an overview of the history of joint ventures and of recent trends, identifying four key areas to address if a joint venture is to be successfully created: strategy, structure, culture, and human resources. It also offers a chapter on negotiation in joint ventures.

International Joint Ventures: Theory and Practice

Aimin Yan, Yadong Luo
New York: M.E. Sharpe, Inc., 2000
323pp ISBN: 0765604736
This book integrates theory and practice to address issues critical to international joint ventures, including culture, human

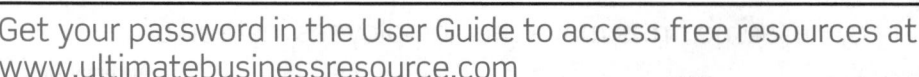

resources, learning, legal issues, management, and research and development. It also includes guidelines for the formation and management of such ventures, and contains more than 30 case studies to benefit both students and practitioners.

Multinational Strategic Alliances
Robert J. Mockler
Hoboken, New Jersey: Wiley, 1999
266pp ISBN: 0471987751
This book takes a practical approach, presenting decision-making models that cover issues such as strategic fit, negotiating alliances, selection of partners, formulating the type and structure of alliances, and ensuring alliance success. It also considers alternatives to alliances and includes case studies.

Partnering Intelligence: Creating Value for Your Business by Building Strong Alliances 2nd ed.
Stephen M. Dent
Palo Alto, California: Davies-Black, 2004
304pp ISBN: 0891061819
Dent focuses on the skills necessary for creating successful strategic alliances and details the interpersonal skills needed in partnerships. He offers self-assessments and case studies, a model for partnerships, exercises designed to enhance partnering skills, and an analysis of how skillful leaders can foster an alliance mentality throughout an organization.

The Power of Two: How Companies of All Sizes Can Build Alliance Networks that Generate Business Opportunities
John K. Conlon, Melissa Giovagnoli
San Francisco, California: Jossey-Bass, 1998
256pp ISBN: 0787909467
This text shows how companies must respond quickly to market opportunities and presents ways of forming business alliances for speed and agility. The authors give a framework for knowledge-based networks, outline conditions for productive alliances, and present a process for developing the networks through alliance managers.

Smart Alliances: A Practical Guide to Repeatable Success
John R. Harbison, Peter Pekar, Jr.
San Francisco, California: Jossey-Bass, 1998
167pp ISBN: 0787943266
This text is of benefit to practitioners, showing ways to identify opportunities for alliances and presenting a road map with eight stages for setting up and managing alliances. It includes a section on best practice, focusing on European, Asian, and Latin American alliances.

Strategic Alliances: An Entrepreneurial Approach to Globalization
Michael Y. Yoshino, U. Srinivasa Rangan
Boston, Massachusetts: Harvard Business School Press, 1995
259pp ISBN: 0875845843
The book is a thorough guide to modern alliances, viewing them not as a means of protection, but as tools that can be used to help gain advantages over competitors.

Strategies of Co-operation: Managing Alliances, Networks, and Joint Ventures
John Child, David Faulkner
New York: Oxford University Press, Inc., 1998
350pp ISBN: 0198774850
In this book alliances, networks, and joint ventures are examined from the perspectives of economics, strategy, and organization theory. The four parts respectively cover the nature of cooperation; establishing cooperation; managing cooperation; and maturing relationships.

INTERNET
Alliance Strategy
www.alliancestrategy.com
This site offers resources and literature on alliance strategy and management. It is maintained by Ben Gomes-Casseres, author of *The Alliance Revolution*. Some sections of the site have restricted access, but most of it is accessible free of charge.

Joint Venture: Silicon Valley
www.jointventure.org
This site represents what it calls a "nonprofit dynamic model." While this has a West Coast U.S. high-tech focus, it does capture the spirit of what is possible in a joint venture.

smartalliances.com
www.smartalliances.com
Established by Booz, Allen & Hamilton (international consultants), this site provides information on the world of strategic alliances. It focuses on practical advice on how alliance companies raise profitability, best practice in alliances, and institutional alliance learning, and contains details of relevant books, articles, and links.

Think Joint Venture
www.thinkjointventure.com
This is a site that tries to make profitable joint ventures happen. It also commends itself by focusing on the prospect of joint ventures between smaller businesses instead of concentrating solely large international corporations.

ORGANIZATIONS
USA
Association of Strategic Alliance Professionals
Massachusetts
P.O. Box 812–027, Wellesley, Massachusetts, 02482
T: +1 781 263 0066
F: +1 781 263 0027
E: *bill@strategic-alliances.org*
www.strategic-alliances.org
This membership organization raises awareness of strategic-alliance issues, acts as a forum for strategic-alliance professionals, organizes conferences, and identifies best practices. It aims to establish a distinct professional identity for strategic-alliance practitioners. Members receive discounts on conferences and publications, a directory of strategic-alliance professionals, and other benefits.

FOR MORE INFORMATION
- Acquisitions, Takeovers, and Mergers (pp. 1670–1671)
- Maximizing a New Strategic Alliance (pp. 116–117)
- Organic Growth Versus Acquisition (pp. 106–107)
- Strategic Partnering (pp. 534–535)
- Why Mergers Fail and How to Prevent It (pp. 108–109)

1781

BUSINESS INFORMATION SOURCES

"Cooperative capitalism does not spontaneously emerge from free markets—it needs to be designed."
Will Hutton

Internal Communication

BOOKS

Beyond Spin: The Power of Strategic Corporate Journalism

Markos Kounalakis, Drew Banks, Kim Daus

San Francisco, California: Jossey-Bass, 1999

256pp ISBN: 0787945501

This book covers issues relating to internal and external communication for the corporate world. It focuses on the purpose of effective communication and the strategic value it brings to a company. It includes discussion of current practice in corporate and general media journalism and presents typical situations.

Communicating across Cultures at Work 2nd ed.

Maureen Guirdham

West Lafayette, Indiana: Purdue University Press, 2005

352pp ISBN: 1403913498

Guirdham's book explores the need for improved intercultural communication skills in the workplace and discusses strategies for improving understanding of cultures and diversity at work. It contains sections on diversity at work, how cultures differ, subcultural communication at work, barriers to communicating across cultures, intercultural communication theories, and the skills required for working abroad.

Corporate Communication 3rd ed.

Paul A. Argenti

Maidenhead, United Kingdom: McGraw-Hill, 2003

256pp ISBN: 0072314028

Corporate Communication is a handbook for everyone in the business world on how to communicate with those inside and outside your company. This is a comprehensive text that focuses on the basics of good communication and places a strong emphasis on the political and social consequences of poor communication.

Guide to Managerial Communication: Effective Business Writing and Speaking 7th ed.

Mary Munter

Upper Saddle River, New Jersey: Prentice Hall, 2005

208pp ISBN: 0131467042

The book is a guide for managers and others wanting to develop their communications skills. It covers all the usual forms of business communication in a detailed manner with clear examples.

Handbook of Communication Audits for Organisations

Owen Hargie, Dennis Tourish, eds

New York: Routledge, 2000

312pp (International Series on Communication Skills)

ISBN: 0415186420

The contributors to this handbook offer practical guidance on the design, implementation, and assessment of communication audits within organizations. They discuss the main options confronting organizations that embark on an audit and consider the merits of all available approaches. Case studies of the communication audit process are presented along the way, and guidance is also given on how to interpret audit findings, how to construct reports, and how to make recommendations based on an audit.

In Good Company: How Social Capital Makes Organizations Work

Don Cohen, Laurence Prusak

Boston, Massachusetts: Harvard Business School Press, 2001

224pp ISBN: 087584913X

In Good Company focuses on the positive effects of informal connections within large corporations. The authors argue that informal connections such as elevator conversations build trust and result in an exchange of useful information. This book does not focus on theory but is filled with real-life examples from well-respected companies.

MAGAZINES

Business Communication Quarterly

ISSN: 1080–5699

Association for Business Communication (ABC)

Box G 1326, Baruch College, 17 Lexington Avenue, New York, 10010

T: +1 212 387 1620

F: +1 212 387 1655

www.bcq.theabc.org

The *Quarterly* is an international journal devoted to the teaching of business communication. A subscription to this journal is included in membership of the Association for Business Communication.

CiB News

ISSN: 1360–4678

British Association of Communicators in Business

42 Borough High Street, London, SE1 1XW, U.K.

T: +44 (0) 20 7378 7139

F: +44 (0) 20 7378 7140

www.abraca.net/cib_enews

CiB News is the journal of the British Association of Communicators in Business and is published ten times a year. It largely concentrates on membership news.

Corporate Communications: An International Journal

ISSN: 1356–3289

Emerald Group Publishing Ltd

60/62 Toller Lane, Bradford, West Yorkshire, BD8 9BY, U.K.

T: +44 (0) 1274 777700

F: +44 (0) 1274 785200

www.emeraldinsight.com

This quarterly journal covers communications within organizations, and between organizations and the public, as well as strategic communications planning.

Internal Communication

ISSN: 0965–5999

Informa Publishing Group

19 Portland Place, London, W1B 1PX, U.K.

T: +44 (0) 20 7553 1000

F: +44 (0) 20 7553 1100

www.informa.com

This journal acts as a forum for all those interested in employee communications. It is published ten times a year and contains academic articles, together with case studies and surveys.

Journal of Business Communication

ISSN: 0021–9436

Association for Business Communication (ABC)

Box G 1326, Baruch College, 17 Lexington Avenue, New York, 10010

T: +1 212 387 1620

F: +1 212 387 1655

www.businesscommunication.org/publications/jbc/about_jbc.html

Subscription to this quarterly journal is included in membership of the Association for Business Communication. It seeks to publish a broad and diverse range of research, focusing on business communication and covering business

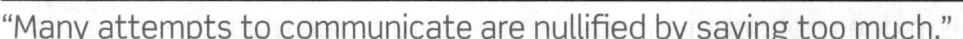

composition and technical writing, information systems, international business communication, management communication, and organizational and corporate communication. It is aimed primarily at the academic community.

Journal of Communication Management
ISSN: 1363–254X
Emerald Group Publishing Ltd
60/62 Toller Lane, Bradford, West Yorkshire, BD8 9BY, U.K.
T: +44 (0) 1274 777700
F: +44 (0) 1274 785200
www.emeraldinsight.com
This quarterly journal contains the latest developments, thinking, and practice in the management of internal and external communications. It is aimed at senior management, academics, consultants, and researchers.

Journal of Employee Communication Management
Ragan Communications
Suite 300, 316 N. Michigan Avenue, Chicago, Illinois, 60601
T: +1 800 878 5331
F: +1 312 960 4106
www.ragan.com
In this magazine, leaders in the communication field provide in-depth coverage of how their organizations' communication needs are satisfied. A sample from the magazine is provided on the Web site.

Strategic Communication Management
ISSN: 1363-9064
Melcrum
First Floor, Chelsea Reach, 79–89 Lots Road, London, SW10 0RN, U.K.
T: +44 (0) 20 7795 2205
F: +44 (0) 20 7795 2156
www.melcrum.com
This international journal, published six times a year, aims to cover the latest ideas and concepts in communication strategy, offering the sort of practical solutions and information that will enable professionals to tackle their jobs more successfully.

INTERNET
American Communication Association
www.uark.edu/~aca
This is the site of a virtual professional association created to promote academic and professional research, criticism, teaching, practice, and the exchange of principles and theories of human

communication. It contains a communication studies center that provides listings of related links, associations, and journals, and has a special section on business communication.

Association for Business Communication
www.businesscommunication.org
The Association for Business Communication's site contains information on membership, on the history of the Association, on the awards and publications it makes available, and on its conventions, as well as providing news items and other resources.

International Association of Business Communicators
www.iabc.com
This site provides information resources and a journal, besides giving details of member services and events, the accreditation program, awards, and professional development opportunities.

Lawrence Ragan Communications, Inc.
www.ragan.com
Belonging to a corporate communication consultancy for internal communicators, trainers, and speechwriters, this site offers newsletters and other products and services in the fields of employee communication, management strategy, and public relations. Some resources are available only to subscribers.

Melcrum
www.melcrum.com
This site provides ideas and solutions of use to corporate communication and knowledge management professionals. A selection of free articles is available, while other resources may be purchased online.

Work911/Bacal & Associates
www.work911.com/articles.htm
This commercial Web site offers a selection of free, easy-to-access articles on a variety of useful topics, including how to engage employees and how to align internal and external communication. Visitors may also subscribe to a free e-mail newsletter.

ORGANIZATIONS
Europe
British Association of Communicators in Business
42 Borough High Street, London, SE1 1XW, U.K.

T: +44 (0) 20 7378 7139
F: +44 (0) 20 7378 7140
www.cib.uk.com
This organization was founded in 1949 to promote the importance of effective communications, facilitate the exchange of ideas and experience between members, and improve standards. It also aims to develop members' management and related skills and offers education and training in all areas of corporate communication.

International Association for Business Communication (ABC)
Box G 1326, Baruch College, 17 Lexington Avenue, New York, 10010
T: +1 212 387 1620
F: +1 212 387 1655
E: *myers@theabc.org*
www.businesscommunication.org
ABC is an international organization committed to fostering excellence in scholarship, research, education, and practice relating to business communication. Its membership is interdisciplinary.

International Association of Business Communicators
Suite 600, One Hallidie Plaza, San Francisco, California, 94102–2818
T: +1 415 544 4700
F: +1 415 544 4747
E: *iabccustomerservicecentre. service_centre@iabc.com*
www.iabc.com
Formed in 1970, the Association is a nonprofit international network of professionals committed to improving the effectiveness of organizations through strategic, interactive, and integrated business communication management. It provides a range of member benefits.

FOR MORE INFORMATION

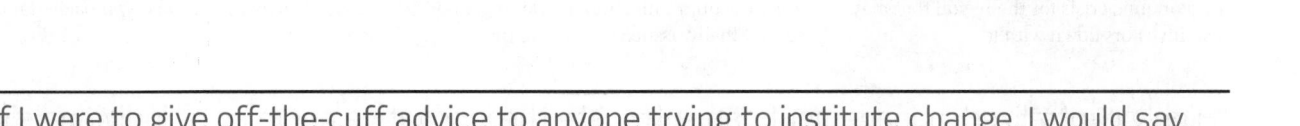

International Management, Cross Cultural Management

BOOKS

Breaking through Culture Shock: What You Need to Succeed in International Business

Elizabeth Marx

Naperville, Illinois: Nicholas Brealey Publishing, 2001

233pp ISBN: 1857882202

This book explores the issue of culture shock, and the extent to which it affects success in today's global business environment. It stresses the importance of understanding the different motivations, behaviors, and ways of making decisions, found in other cultures. The author puts forward the culture shock triangle model as a way of helping managers to behave differently and manage their emotions so as to become truly cross-culturally effective.

Building Cross-cultural Competence: How to Create Wealth from Conflicting Values

Charles M. Hampden-Turner, Fons Trompenaars

New Haven, Connecticut: Yale University Press, 2000

388pp ISBN: 0300084978

Drawing on the results of 14 years of research, the authors examine the different cultural values of more than 40 nations and explore how managers can become successful in the global economy by being able to think in both directions and to gain cross-cultural competence. The text is illustrated with stories, cartoons, and case histories throughout.

China Dream: The Elusive Quest for the Last Great Untapped Market on Earth 3rd ed.

Joe Studwell

London: Profile Books, 2005

416pp ISBN: 1861979487

Many Western companies are desperate to get into China and tap into what is generally seen as the biggest potential marketplace of the 21st century. This book sees that rush to profit from and in China, but warns that it may just be too good to be true. It forecasts an economic crisis for the region that may take investors down with it.

China, Inc.: How the Rise of the Next Superpower Challenges America and the World

Ted Fishman

New York: Simon & Schuster, 2006

368pp ISBN: 0743257529

Featuring interviews with workers and managers in China, the United States, and elsewhere, this book paints a vivid picture of China, its economy, and its role in the rest of the commercial world. It provides a useful overview of China's resurgence and what that might mean for businesses elsewhere.

Cultural Dimension of International Business 5th ed.

Gary P. Ferraro

Upper Saddle River, New Jersey: Prentice Hall, 2005

224pp ISBN: 0131927671

This book explores the contribution that cultural anthropology can make to the conduct of international business. It outlines a conceptual approach to culture and international business and examines the nature of verbal and nonverbal communication patterns, as well as contrasting cultural values, cross-cultural negotiation, culture shock, and the development of global managers. Advice on sources of cultural information is appended.

Doing Business Internationally: The Guide to Cross-cultural Success 2nd ed.

Danielle Walker, Thomas Walker

Maidenhead, United Kingdom: McGraw-Hill, 2002

288pp ISBN: 0071378324

The authors aim to raise awareness of the importance of cross-cultural knowledge and understanding for the effective management of international business in the context of rapid globalization. The cultural orientations model, a framework for understanding how cultural forces influence and underpin decision-making and strategy planning, is presented and illustrated through an overview of worldwide cultural patterns. The cultural orientations approach is applied to the areas of communication, marketing, and sales. Finally, issues relevant to the

management of global, multicultural teams are discussed.

Global Literacies: Lessons on Business Leadership and National Cultures

Robert H. Rosen et al.

New York: Simon & Schuster, 2000

416pp ISBN: 0684859025

In this title, the author makes a comparison between the way a child learns how to speak and the redefinition of the way top businesses work due to the arrival of a global marketplace. The authors assert that in order to achieve success, organizations must educate themselves in this new language, and use numerous surveys, interviews, and studies to reveal how top companies and individuals approach both this and other challenges.

Global Smarts: The Art of Communicating and Deal Making Anywhere in the World

Sheida Hodge

Hoboken, New Jersey: Wiley, 2000

256pp ISBN: 0471382469

The author focuses on the underlying values that inform culture in different countries, asserting that "tips" on correct international behavior do not provide the strategic insight necessary for managers. She illustrates her points by analyzing common American business practices to make readers question assumptions before contrasting these with practices overseas. The book addresses how corporate training programs can better prepare executives for cross-cultural assignments.

International Management: An Essential Guide to International Business 3rd ed.

John Mattock, ed.

London: Kogan Page, 2003

224pp (Professional Paperbacks)

ISBN: 074943922X

The author explores the problems and issues surrounding international and cross-cultural management, focusing on the six key steps to effective communication and negotiation: culture, company, character, tactics, timing, and talk. Each of these areas is discussed, with quizzes and exercises to illustrate how they can be approached most effectively.

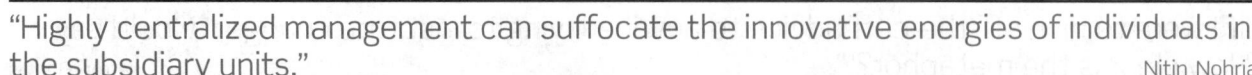

"Highly centralized management can suffocate the innovative energies of individuals in the subsidiary units."

Nitin Nohria

International Management: Cross-cultural Dimensions 3rd ed.
Richard Mead
Cambridge, Massachusetts: Blackwell, 2004
464pp ISBN: 0631231773
Written for management students, this book examines how cultural factors and differences affect behavior in the workplace and the boardroom. The key skills demanded by international management are identified and discussed, their practical application is shown, and the influence and effects of culture are investigated from four viewpoints: national, organizational, strategic, and personnel.

Made in China: What Western Managers Can Learn from Trailblazing Chinese Entrepreneurs
Donald Sull, Yong Wang
Boston, Massachusetts: Harvard Business School Press, 2005
256pp ISBN: 1591397154
Profiling eight of China's leading firms, this book looks at the secrets of Chinese commercial success in the 21st century. An enlightening read for any business operating in that region, hoping to begin operations there, or simply trying to keep afloat in turbulent times, the book describes the tactics of leading Chinese entrepreneurs and their key strategies.

Managing across Borders 2nd ed.
Christopher A. Bartlett, Sumantra Ghoshal
Boston, Massachusetts: Harvard Business School Press, 2002
416pp ISBN: 1578517079
Two of the leading writers in the field offer valuable lessons on running transnational companies.

Managing Cultural Differences: Leadership Strategies for a New World of Business 6th ed.
Philip R. Harris, Robert T. Moran
Houston: Gulf Professional Publishing Company, 2004
600pp ISBN: 0750677368
The book is divided into three sections: addressing the need for multicultural managerial skills, the characteristics that make up a culture, and the specifics of cultures from countries on every continent. The fifth edition contains a new chapter on women in global business.

Riding the Waves of Culture: Understanding Cultural Diversity in Business 2nd ed.
Fons Trompenaars,
Charles Hampden-Turner

New York: McGraw-Hill, 1997
416pp ISBN: 0786311258
The authors explore cultural extremes and the incomprehension that can arise when doing business across cultures, even within the same organization. They identify five key orientations that affect how people deal with each other, do business, and manage, and propose strategies for reconciling these orientations across different cultures. They also review the concept of the "Trans-national Corporation," in which companies take from each culture what is best.

The World Is Flat: A Brief History of the Twenty-first Century
Thomas L. Friedman
New York: Farrar, Straus and Giroux, 2005
496pp ISBN: 0374292884
The World Is Flat central argument is that the world has "flattened" with the rise of globalization. It looks at how other events on the world stage (from 9/11, to the war in Iraq, and the democratization of technology) will impact on individuals, companies, and nations alike.

MAGAZINES
Cross-cultural Research
ISSN: 1069–3971
Sage Publications
1 Oliver's Yard, 55 City Road, London, EC1Y 1SP, U.K.
T: +44 (0) 20 7324 8500
F: +44 (0) 20 7324 8600
www.sagepub.co.uk
This is the official journal of the Society for Cross-cultural Research, published quarterly. It is a key source for peer-reviewed articles, research reports, bibliographies, and discussion pieces on all aspects of cross-cultural and comparative studies in the fields of social and behavioral science.

Foreign Affairs
ISSN: 0015–7120
Council on Foreign Relations
58 East 68th Street, New York, 10021
T: +1 386 246 3386 or 800 829 5539
www.foreignaffairs.org
Published six times per year, this magazine covers current events and how they affect U.S. relations worldwide. With a focus on international, political, commercial, and cultural relations, it has often been described as the premier journal of world affairs. This is a must-read for any corporate executive involved with international business.

Global Finance
ISSN: 0896–4181
Global Finance
411 Fifth Avenue, New York, 10018
T: +1 212 447 7900
F: +1 212 447 7750
www.gfmag.com
This monthly magazine provides news and analysis of companies and financial institutions around the world. Coverage aimed at an international corporate audience includes corporate finance, joint ventures and M&A, country profiles, capital markets, investor relations, currencies, banking, risk management, custody, direct investment, and money management.

International Business Review
ISSN: 0969–5931
Elsevier Science
Customer Service Department, 6277 Sea Harbor Drive, Orlando, Florida, 32887–4800
T: +1 877 839 7126 or +1 407 345 4020
F: +1 407 363 1354
www.elsevier.com
This bimonthly magazine provides a forum for the latest developments and advances in the practice of international business and includes contributions from professionals and academics. Theoretical and practical articles are included, as well as literature reviews.

International Journal of Commerce and Management
ISSN: 1056–9219
International Academy of Business Disciplines
P.O. Box 1659, Indiana, Pennsylvania, 15705
T: +1 724 357 5928
F: +1 724 357 7768
http://ecoweb.ecob.iup.edu/asc/ internationaljournalof3.htm
Intended for business practitioners, academics, policy makers, and nonprofit organizations, this quarterly publication aims to promote understanding among mangers and organizations internationally and publishes articles on management theory and practice.

International Journal of Cross-cultural Management
ISSN: 1470–5958
Sage Publications
1 Oliver's Yard, 55 City Road, London, EC1Y 1SP, U.K.
T: +44 (0) 20 7324 8500
F: +44 (0) 20 7324 8600
www.sagepub.co.uk

"Management—the collective effort of intelligence, experience, and imagination."

Alfred P. Sloan

Published three times a year, this journal is aimed at academics working in the fields of organizational behavior, HRM, international and comparative management, and international industrial relations. Its contents cover both the theoretical and conceptual aspects of cross-cultural management and aim to promote an understanding of the role of culture in management, work, and throughout the organization. It is available electronically at http://ccm.sagepub.com.

Journal of International Business Studies

ISSN: 0047–2506
3240 Prospect Street NW, Washington, D.C., 20007–3214
T: +1 202 944 3755
F: +1 202 944 3762
www.aibworld.net
This bimonthly journal is the official publication of the Academy of International Business at the Eli Broad College of Business, Michigan State University. The journal has a broad scope, encompassing the whole range of international business studies and encouraging an inter-disciplinary approach. It includes research on a wide variety of topics, including: multinational business activities; strategies and managerial processes that cross national boundaries; joint ventures; strategic alliances; mergers and acquisitions; cross-national research involving innovation entrepreneurship; knowledge-based competition; judgment and decision making; bargaining; leadership; corporate governance; and new organizational forms.

Journal of International Management

ISSN: 1075–4253
Elsevier Science
Customer Service Department, 6277 Sea Harbor Drive, Orlando, Florida, 32887–4800
T: +1 877 839 7126 or +1 407 345 4020
F: +1 407 363 1354
www.elsevier.com
This is a quarterly journal devoted to advancing the understanding of issues involved in the theory and practice of global management and focusing on international strategic management. It is aimed at business professionals working in the fields of risk management, organizational behavior, human resources, and cross-cultural management.

Journal of World Business

ISSN: 1090–9516
Elsevier Science
Customer Service Department, 6277 Sea Harbor Drive, Orlando, Florida, 32887–4800
T: +1 877 839 7126 or +1 407 345 4020
F: +1 407 363 1354
www.elsevier.com
This is a quarterly journal committed to developing discussion of groundbreaking practices in international management, marketing, and strategy. It was formerly published as the *Columbia Journal of World Business*.

INTERNET
Learn about Cultures
www.learnaboutcultures.com
Sponsored by a consulting firm, the site offers abstracts on the cultures of different countries (for which users must pay) and free articles on aspects of cross-cultural management, including training, technology, and gender.

ORGANIZATIONS
USA
Academy of International Business (AIB)
College of Business Administration, University of Hawaii at Manoa, 2404 Maile Way, Honolulu, Hawaii, 96822
T: +1 808 956 3665
F: +1 808 956 3261
E: *aib@cba.hawaii.edu*
www.aibworld.net
A leading body for scholars and specialists in the field of international business, this association aims to disseminate knowledge and understanding of international business issues across the globe through the exchange of information, ideas, and research, and through business cooperation.

International Association of Management (IAoM)
P.O. Box 64841, Virginia Beach, Virginia, 23467–4841
T: +1 757 482 2273
F: +1 757 482 0325
E: *aomgt@infi.net*
www.aom-iaom.org
A nonprofit professional organization for students, teachers, and practitioners of management, the IAoM is dedicated to advancing the international practice of management across professional fields through the provision of support, information, products, and services.

FOR MORE INFORMATION
☆ Viewpoint: Christopher Bartlett (pp. 45–46)
☆ Viewpoint: Fons Trompenaars (pp. 25–27)
∽ Working Abroad (pp. 1930–1931)

1786

BUSINESS INFORMATION SOURCES

     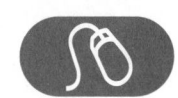

Interpersonal Communication/ Relations

BOOKS

The Anatomy of Persuasion
Norbert Aubuchon
New York: AMACOM, 1997
208pp ISBN: 0814479529
The author examines the use and importance of persuasion as a personal skill when communicating. He describes processes for applying persuasive techniques to improve communication, decision making, and creativity, at both personal and managerial levels. Case study examples illustrate how the process can be adapted to different business situations.

The Art of Speedreading People: How to Size People Up and Speak Their Language
Paul D. Tieger, Barbara Barron-Tieger, Marly A. Swick
Boston, Massachusetts: Back Bay Books, 1999
208pp ISBN: 0316845183
This is a comprehensive layperson's guide to the application of the Myers-Briggs personality types. It is valuable as a celebration of individual differences and of the particular strengths each type can bring to a working relationship. Though people seldom fit nicely into the little boxes we try to put them in, the authors here strive to help readers quickly assess others.

Body Language at Work
Adrian Furnham
London: Chartered Institute of Personnel and Development (CIPD), 1999
96pp (Management Shapers)
ISBN: 0852927711
This book offers an introduction to the significance of body language and what it reveals about attitudes and emotions. It also presents techniques for interpreting nonverbal gestures and expressions and considers how they might be used in work situations.

Effective Communication Skills for Scientific and Technical Professionals
Harry E. Chambers
Cambridge, Massachusetts: Perseus Books Group, 2000
272pp ISBN: 0738202878
This book is a guide to improving interpersonal, communication, and managerial skills by means of a huge range of methods designed for developing such talents. The book also highlights the difficulties encountered in real life by people in the workplace, and suggests ways of improving communication skills.

Loud and Clear: How to Prepare and Deliver Effective Business and Technical Presentations 4th ed.
George L. Morrisey, Thomas L. Sechrest, Wendy B. Warman
Cambridge, Massachusetts: Perseus Books Group, 1997
208pp ISBN: 0201127938
This title is a comprehensive guide on how to deliver a presentation effectively. The book covers all the main points from visuals to delivery, but places the greatest emphasis on preparation, which the coauthors say is the most important factor of all.

The Story Factor: Inspiration, Influence, and Persuasion Through the Art of Storytelling
Annette Simmons
Cambridge, Massachusetts: Perseus Books Group, 2002
272pp ISBN: 0738206717
The author suggests that the unique way in which storytelling can influence people makes it one of the most useful management techniques available. The book includes six varieties of story that can be used in any situation and emphasizes the importance of bringing together all the various components that make up a good presentation, such as tone and body language.

True Partnership: Revolutionary Thinking about Relating to Others
Carl D. Zaiss
San Francisco, California: Berrett-Koehler, 2002
150pp ISBN: 157675166X
This book is designed to change the way we look at interactions in order to form better relationships. The author's intention is to challenge the assumptions and standard behavior that most of us use, for the sake of expedience, when interacting with others. Connecting at a deeper level of understanding can improve the quality of our relationships, and the end result is more productive and fulfilling interactions.

What to Say to Get What You Want: Strong Words for 44 Challenging Types of Bosses, Employees, Co-workers, and Customers
Samuel D. Deep, Lyle Sussman
Cambridge, Massachusetts: Perseus Books Group, 1992
316pp ISBN: 0201577127
This book describes how to get on the right side of colleagues at work. In order to achieve this goal, the authors guide the reader through the 44 varieties of difficult people and how to handle them, advocating, above all, a considerate attitude.

Working with Emotional Intelligence
Daniel P. Goleman
New York: Bantam, 2000
400pp ISBN: 0553378589
Daniel Goleman is the foremost proponent of the concept of emotional intelligence—the capacity to work well with emotions, our own and those of others. In this book he applies his theories to the work environment with definitions of the concepts and the reasons they are important. According to Goleman, interpersonal skills are the most important part of sustaining career success, and this book will help anyone begin the process of increasing those skills.

MAGAZINES
Communication Research
ISSN: 0093–6502
Sage Publications
1 Oliver's Yard, 55 City Road, London, EC1Y 1SP, U.K.
T: +44 (0) 20 7324 8500
F: +44 (0) 20 7324 8600
www.sagepub.co.uk
This bimonthly publication, aimed at academics and professionals, explores the processes involved in, and the consequences of, different types of communication, whether interpersonal, mass media, political, organizational, or intercultural.

European Journal of Communication
ISSN: 0267–3231
Sage Publications
1 Oliver's Yard, 55 City Road, London, EC1Y 1SP, U.K.

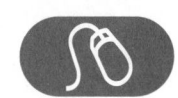

1787

BUSINESS INFORMATION SOURCES

"Even the frankest and bravest of subordinates do not talk with their boss the same way they talk with colleagues."

Robert Greenleaf

T: +44 (0) 20 7324 8500
F: +44 (0) 20 7324 8600
www.sagepub.co.uk
Published quarterly, this is a leading international journal that provides information on the latest international communications research, practice, and policy developments. It also promotes information exchange between European scholars and publishes occasional special issues on key communication topics.

Journal of Communication Management
ISSN: 1363–254X
Emerald Group Publishing Ltd
60/62 Toller Lane, Bradford, West Yorkshire, BD8 9BY, U.K.
T: +44 (0) 1274 777700
F: +44 (0) 1274 785200
www.emeraldinsight.com
A quarterly journal available both in paper copy and online, this title is published in association with the Institute of Public Relations and the International Association of Business Communicators. It provides in-depth, peer-reviewed articles and papers on communications practice and theory.

Management Communication Quarterly
ISSN: 0893–3189
Sage Publications
1 Oliver's Yard, 55 City Road, London, EC1Y 1SP, U.K.
T: +44 (0) 20 7324 8500
F: +44 (0) 20 7324 8600
www.sagepub.co.uk
A quarterly journal aimed at managers, researchers, professionals, consultants, and trainers, this publication presents the latest theory, research, and practice in management and organizational communication. The topics it covers include: intercultural communication, corporate culture, TQM applications,

emotional intelligence, group decision-making, organizational commitment, and power and control issues.

INTERNET
American Communication Association
www.uark.edu/~aca
The Association is a nonprofit organization concerned with academic and professional research into the principles and theories of human communication. Services provided include free membership, a collection of online resources, and an online journal.

Communication Briefings
www.briefings.com/cb
This Internet address leads to a commercial site that offers a number of communication-related publications on issues such as communicating with employees, giving speeches and presentations, and dealing with difficult people. Each one offers advice, tips, articles, and techniques for handling each situation.

EQ.org—Emotional Intelligence
www.eq.org
This is a free Web site with links to over 215 online resources concerning emotional intelligence. Many of the links are to commercial sites, but this is nonetheless a good place to start a search.

Pertinent Information—Interpersonal Communication Articles
www.pertinent.com/articles/ communication/index.asp
The site contains a selection of articles relating to all aspects of interpersonal communication, from improving influencing skills and communicating across cultures to developing interaction techniques.

ORGANIZATIONS
USA
International Communication Association (ICA)
Suite 300, 1730 Rhode Island Avenue NW, Washington, D.C., 20036
T: +1 202 530 9855
F: +1 202 530 9851
E: *ica@icahdq.org*
www.icahdq.org
ICA is a members organization that promotes the systematic study of communication theories, processes, and skills. It provides a range of services including interest groups, journals, publications, a network forum, and annual conferences, and has a specific division concerned with interpersonal communication.

National Communication Association
1765 N. Street NW, Washington, D.C., 20036
T: +1 202 464 4622
F: +1 202 464 4600
www.natcom.org
The Association is a nonprofit scholarly society of practitioners, educators, and students whose aim is to promote the study, research, teaching, and application of scientific and humanistic aspects of communication. It publishes a range of journals and books, a newsletter, and an electronic bulletin, and also organizes events, conferences, and an annual convention.

1788

FOR MORE INFORMATION

✔ Developing Passive People
  (pp. 442–443)
🐭 Internal Communication
  (pp. 1782–1783)
🐭 Management Styles (p. 1819)
🐭 Presentation/Speaking
  (pp. 1865–1866)

BUSINESS INFORMATION SOURCES

"Society cannot share a common communication system so long as it is split into warring factions."
Bertolt Brecht

ISO 9000

BOOKS

Achieving Quality Through Continual Improvement
Claude Burrill, Johannes Ledolter
Hoboken, New Jersey: Wiley, 1999
630pp ISBN: 0471092207
This book addresses the managerial aspects involved in improving the quality of all processes in order to stay competitive in today's marketplace. The text combines both managerial and statistical coverage, with an emphasis on processes and discussion of quality tools. Case studies and extensive examples complement the text. It includes bibliographical references and an index.

How to Make Money with ISO 9000: A Guide to Profitable Quality Management
James Highlands
Maidenhead, United Kingdom: McGraw-Hill, 1999
177pp ISBN: 0071359699
Aimed at those who have adopted ISO 9000 quality management systems, this book provides a practical guide to gaining profits through these new processes. It also gives detailed instructions for putting ISO 9000 quality standards to work throughout the organization, which is, in the author's view, the key to increasing market share and profitability.

Interpreting ISO 9001:2000 with Statistical Methodology
James L. Lamprecht
Milwaukee, Wisconsin: ASQ Quality Press, 2001
205pp ISBN: 0873895177
This book provides statistical information relating to the most recent revision of the ISO standard, the ISO 9001:2000 standard, intended to help the reader design the questionnaires needed. The book also contains non-statistical material, including tables and sample forms and questionnaires. In addition to many case studies, tables, and graphics, Lamprecht provides information on the sequence of changes from the 1994 to the 2000 version.

ISO 9000:2000 in a Nutshell: A Concise Guide to the Revisions 2nd ed.
Jeanne Ketola, Kathy Roberts
Chico, California: Paton Press, 2001
140pp ISBN: 0965044599
A simple, clear, and concise guide to the ISO 9000:2000 revisions, this book analyzes the differences from the process management approach in the ISO 9000:1994 version in order to explain what professionals charged with implementing the new standards need to know to meet the new requirements for certification.

ISO 9000:2000 New Requirements: 28 New Requirements Checklist and Compliance Guide 3rd ed.
Jack Kanholm
Los Angeles, California: AQA Press, 2001
64pp ISBN: 1882711076
This book contains in-depth information for interpreting, understanding, and implementing all new ISO 9000:2000 standards and requirements. Every requirement is systematically explained with regard to interpretation, procedures and records, the way certification auditors will verify conformance, and the specific actions that need to be taken to achieve compliance.

ISO 9001:2000 for Small Businesses 3rd ed.
Ray Tricker
Woburn, Massachusetts: Butterworth-Heinemann, 2005
480pp ISBN: 075066617X
This book explains the new requirements of ISO 9001:2000 and looks at how smaller companies can benefit from it and set up their own quality management systems. Written for engineers and managers in small and medium-sized companies, it examines the background of ISO 9000, the structure of ISO 9000:2000, the importance of quality control and quality assurance, quality management systems, and quality organizational structure. It includes an example quality manual, along with a number of checklists and an extensive glossary.

The Quality Audit for ISO 9001:2000: A Practical Guide 2nd ed.
David Wealleans
Aldershot, United Kingdom: Gower Publishing, 2005
304pp ISBN: 0566085984
This is a wide-ranging and detailed explanation of the entire range of quality audits associated with maintaining compliance to ISO 9001 and similar international standards. The book covers all aspects of auditing, including certification assessment, supplier investigation, and internal auditing. It also provides a detailed analysis of the requirements of ISO 9001:2000.

MAGAZINES
Quality World
ISSN: 1352–8769
Institute of Quality Assurance
12 Grosvenor Crescent, London, SW1X 7EE, U.K.
T: +44 (0) 20 7245 6722
F: +44 (0) 20 7245 6755
www.iqa.org
Quality World is the journal of the Institute of Quality Assurance. It reviews recent news and issues in the field of quality and includes feature articles for practicing managers.

INTERNET
ISO 9000
www.praxiom.com
This Web site, compiled by Praxiom Research Group Ltd., which is based in Edmonton, Canada, provides a broad introduction to ISO 9000:2000 and interprets the standard in plain English. Much of the information is available free of charge, while the company also offers guidance to its additional range of products and services.

ISO Online
www.iso.ch
An electronic information service provided by the International Organization for Standardization (ISO), this site provides a detailed explanation of the work of ISO, a directory of its member organizations, and access to its technical work. Information on the ISO 9000 and ISO 14000 standards can be accessed. The site's collection of frequently asked questions about standards and standards-related topics is a useful tool for anyone starting to work with these standards.

Quality Digest Online
www.qualitydigest.com
An online journal for news, tips, and techniques to do with quality and for articles on quality-related issues, the site also includes a searchable ISO 9000 and QS 9000 registered company database.

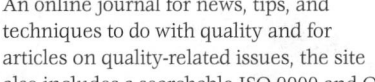

1789

BUSINESS INFORMATION SOURCES

"What the hell is quality? What is it ... need we ask anyone to tell us these things?"

Robert M. Pirsig

Simply Quality
www.isoeasy.org
This site is dedicated to helping organizations understand and implement the ISO 9000 and 9001 standards.

Underwriter's Laboratories
www.ul.com
This site of the Underwriter's Laboratories, Inc., an independent, nonprofit product safety testing and certification organization, provides links to companies that adhere to various quality and management system standards, including ISO 9000 and ISO 9001.

ORGANIZATIONS
USA
American Society for Quality (ASQ)
600 North Plankinton Avenue, Milwaukee, Wisconsin, 53203–3005
T: +1 414 272 8575
F: +1 414 272 1734
E: *cs@asq.org*
www.asq.org
ASQ is the leading quality-improvement member organization in the United States. It has 117,000 individual and 1,100 corporate members, in 247 local sections and 22 industry divisions. The Society focuses on issues including statistical process control, quality cost measurement and control, total quality management,

failure analysis, and zero defects. It offers continuing education, certification programs, conferences, and reference, referral, and research services. The ASQ publishes widely under its Quality Press imprint, and produces the monthly magazines *Quality Progress* and *Six Sigma Forum Magazine*, and the quarterly *Quality Management Journal*.

Europe
British Standards Institution (BSI)
389 Chiswick High Road, London, W4 4AL, U.K.
T: +44 (0) 20 8996 9000
F: +44 (0) 20 8996 7400
E: *info@bsi-global.com*
www.bsi-global.com
The BSI was founded in 1901 and received a royal charter in 1929. It is an independent body whose objectives include setting quality standards and promoting the adoption of British Standard specifications. The BSI provides copies of, and information on, the new ISO 9000:2000 standard and offers training and consulting services.

International
International Organization for Standardization (ISO)
1 rue de Varembé, Case postale 56, CH 1211, Geneva, 20, Switzerland

T: +41 22 749 01 11
F: +41 22 733 34 30
E: *central@iso.org*
www.iso.ch
The ISO is a worldwide federation of the national standards bodies of some 130 countries, each represented by one organization. A nongovernmental institution established in 1947, the ISO aims to promote the development of standardization and related activities in the world in order to facilitate the international exchange of goods and services and to develop cooperation in the spheres of intellectual, scientific, technological, and economic activity. The ISO's work results in international agreements that are published as International Standards. It is also actively involved in consultation and training services and produces a range of publications.

FOR MORE INFORMATION

- Benchmarking (pp. 1681–1682)
- Manufacturing Systems (pp. 1821–1823)
- Process Control and Statistical Process Control (pp. 1868–1869)
- Quality and Total Quality Management (pp. 1886–1889)
- The True Total Quality (pp. 208–209)

"Alignment is not about the management of quality. It is about the quality of management."

George Labovitz

Japanese Management Techniques

BOOKS

Can Japan Compete?

Michael E. Porter, Mariko Sakakibara, Hirotaka Takeuchi
Cambridge, Massachusetts: Perseus Books Group, 2000
208pp ISBN: 0465059899
This title questions why Japan's economy slumped for so long and asks what the problems it encountered have to teach the world about the modern global marketplace.

Gemba Kaizen: A Commonsense, Low-cost Approach to Management

Masaaki Imai
Maidenhead, United Kingdom: McGraw-Hill, 1997
384pp ISBN: 0070314462
Gemba Kaizen is the focusing of the techniques of Kaizen on the place where they will do the most good—Gemba being the critical area, the place where things are really happening. In business, Gemba is where products are developed and made or where services are delivered. The author introduces the idea of the "house of Gemba" and explains how to manage quality, cost, and delivery. He also discusses related issues, such as the 5Ss (the five steps of housekeeping), Muda (waste), the roles and accountability of Gemba managers, and the just-in-time production system, and presents 21 case studies of, for the most part, Japanese companies.

The Hybrid Factory in Europe: The Japanese Management and Production System Transferred

Hiroshi Kumon, Tetsuo Abo, eds
New York: Oxford University Press, Inc., 2005
320pp ISBN: 1403917213
The authors explore the potential for the effective transfer of Japanese management and production systems, credited with giving Japanese firms their competitive superiority, to other countries. The management factors that give strength to Japanese production systems are, in their view, however, related to the sociocultural background, and they question whether a radically different cultural environment makes such a transfer possible.

Inside the Kaisha: Demystifying Japanese Business Behavior

Noboru Yoshimura, Philip Anderson
Boston, Massachusetts: Harvard Business School Press, 1997
272pp ISBN: 0875844154
This book attempts to explain six aspects of Japanese business behavior that seem to be contradictory, contains valuable insights into the world of the Japanese salaryman that Western managers could learn from in their own business practice, and offers useful advice to people who do business with them.

The Kaizen Blitz: Accelerating Breakthroughs in Productivity and Performance

Anthony C. Laraia, Patricia E. Moody, Robert W. Hall
Hoboken, New Jersey: Wiley, 1999
304pp ISBN: 0471246484
A new version of Kaizen, called the Kaizen Blitz and pioneered by the Association for Manufacturing Excellence, is the subject of this guide. The authors introduce the process, which is designed to achieve continuous improvement, and describe the benefits it can offer an organization. Their aim is to teach any individual how to use the Kaizen Blitz tool to deliver breakthrough improvements in an organization in areas such as productivity, inventory reduction, and capacity expansion.

Kaizen: The Key to Japan's Competitive Success

Masaaki Imai
Maidenhead, United Kingdom: McGraw-Hill, 1986
260pp ISBN: 007554332X
Written with the aim of helping Western managers to develop a Kaizen strategy, this book provides a comprehensive introduction to the concept and its implementation.

The Knowledge-creating Company: How Japanese Companies Create the Dynamics of Innovation

Ikujiro Nonaka, Hirotaka Takeuchi
New York: Oxford University Press, Inc., 1995
304pp ISBN: 0195092694
This title looks at how Japanese businesses discover new knowledge organizationally and suggests that the reason for the success of such businesses is linked to this ability.

The coauthors also discuss the two types of knowledge that exist; explicit (gained from books) and tacit (gained empirically), and say the key to the success of the Japanese has been their ability to change from the latter to the former, while the U.S. approach concentrates only on the former. The book uses examples from firms including Honda, Canon, and NEC to explain the theory of organizational knowledge.

The Machine That Changed the World

James P. Womack, Daniel T. Jones, Daniel Roos
New York: Rawson Associates, 1991
336pp ISBN: 0060974176
The authors present the findings of a five-year research project undertaken by the Massachusetts Institute of Technology to look at Japanese manufacturing techniques in the motor vehicle industry and the lessons that can be learned from them. The text includes the rise and fall of mass production; the rise of lean production; running the factory; designing the car; coordinating the supply chain; dealing with customers; and managing the lean enterprise.

The Mind of the Strategist: The Art of Japanese Business

Kenichi Ohmae
Maidenhead, United Kingdom: McGraw-Hill, 1991
304pp ISBN: 0070479046
This title is a guide to Japanese strategic thinking with examples of how it can be applied. The book explains how readers can create successful strategies by liberating their creative strength.

A Revolution in Manufacturing: The SMED System

Shigeo Shingo (Andrew P. Dillon, trans.)
Cambridge, Massachusetts: Productivity Press, 1985
383pp ISBN: 0915299038
In this book Shingo describes the development of the SMED (Single Minute Exchange of Die) system, which he invented for Toyota, explains the techniques for applying it, and considers the effects of its introduction—notably claiming to reduce changeovers by 98%. He also presents 12 case studies of the application of SMED.

1791

BUSINESS INFORMATION SOURCES

"For us to get out of a business would involve firing people and that cannot be done easily in Japan."
Tsutomu Kanai

Toyota Production System: Beyond Large-Scale Production

Taiichi Ohno

Cambridge, Massachusetts: Productivity Press, 1988

163pp ISBN: 0915299143

This introduction to the Toyota Production System by one of its founders explains how it evolved and describes a range of techniques, including just-in-time and *kanban*.

INTERNET

Kaizen Institute

www.kaizen-institute.com

The Kaizen Institute (KI) is a global management consulting company, founded by Masaaki Imai, that specializes in helping companies implement Kaizen tools and strategies. This site offers introductory explanations of Kaizen and Gemba and outlines the workshops and consultancy service available from the Institute.

FOR MORE INFORMATION

"Most Japanese corporations lack even an approximation of an organization chart."

Kenichi Ohmae

Job Hunting

BOOKS

60 Seconds & You're Hired
Robin Ryan
New York: Penguin USA, 2000
160pp ISBN: 0140289038
This book places an emphasis on getting an interviewer's attention and summarizing each aspect of the agenda you want to communicate in 60 seconds or less. It lists questions that you should ask and gives advice on learning about a company's culture, unlawful questions, salary negotiation, different types of interviews, and pitfalls to avoid.

Don't Send a Résumé: And Other Contrarian Rules to Help Land a Great Job
Jeffrey J. Fox
New York: Hyperion, 2001
192pp ISBN: 0786865962
This book focuses on networking and self-promotion, emphasizing that developing contacts with executives leads to more job offers than sending résumés to HR departments. The author's advice includes unorthodox places to look for job leads, calculating what a given position is worth to a company, and writing "boomerang" letters in response to job ads.

I Don't Know What I Want, But I Know It's Not This: A Step-by-step Guide to Finding Gratifying Work
Julie Jansen
New York: Penguin USA, 2003
288pp ISBN: 0142002488
A useful resource for anyone unhappy at work, this book is full of exercises to assess the reader's personality and skills and will help people understand their present situation and come up with ways to find the job or career they really want to embark on.

Landing the Job You Want: How to Have the Best Job Interview of Your Life
William C. Byham
New York: Three Rivers Press (Random House), 1999
195pp ISBN: 0609804081
Appropriate for job hunters at various career levels, this book deals with interview preparation, the interview itself, and post-interview assessment. Topics covered include deciding whether a job is right for you, presenting your skills, handling a badly prepared interviewer, and closing the interview on a positive note.

The Monster Guide to Jobhunting: Winning That Job with Internet Savvy
Andrew Chapman
Upper Saddle River, New Jersey: Financial Times Prentice Hall, 2001
184pp ISBN: 0273654098
Aimed at anyone relatively new to the world of jobhunting online, this book sets out to help readers get the best from this vast resource. It offers advice on using the Internet for research, creating an online résumé, and networking via chatrooms and mailing lists.

What Color Is Your Parachute? A Practical Manual for Job-hunters and Career-changers
Richard Nelson Bolles
Berkeley, California: Ten Speed Press, 2006
432pp ISBN: 1580087949
Revised and updated annually, this edition of the classic job-hunting reference guide works in conjunction with its Web site. The book covers areas such as Internet job hunting, the alternative job-hunting approach, dealing with rejection, interviews, negotiating a salary, and choosing a career counselor.

INTERNET

CareerMag
www.careermag.com
The comprehensive site offers an extensive range of useful content for jobseekers. Visitors to the site will find a wealth of information and tools, including articles, information on career strategies, job listings, a résumé-posting facility, and a personality test.

Careerpath International
www.careerpath.co.uk
This site for executives offers services covering career guidance, résumé and cover letter writing, career planning, employment outplacement, and job search. There is also a database of job vacancies in the United States, Europe, and Asia. Initial information is free, but additional services are charged for.

Monster
www.monster.com
Primarily a job board, the site also offers extensive information on producing résumés and cover letters, salary negotiation, and interviews.

Online Recruitment
www.onrec.com
This site provides a database of online recruitment sites, and offers the facility to search for sites that cover all or specific sectors. It also gives information on the sites offered, including services, charges, strengths, and weaknesses.

Vault
www.vault.com
In addition to job listings, this site offers a résumé distribution service, salary information articles on job-hunting issues, message boards, and a research center.

Yahoo Careers and Jobs
http://dir.yahoo.com/Business_and_Economy/Employment_and_Work/Careers_and_Jobs
The search engine Yahoo provides a comprehensive listing of recruitment Web sites.

1793

FOR MORE INFORMATION

☆ Avoiding Your Worst Career Nightmare (pp. 404–405)
🐁 Finding Out What You Are Worth: Remuneration/Salaries (pp. 1755–1756)
🐁 Planning Your Career (pp. 1863–1864)
🐁 Remuneration (pp. 1894–1895)
☆ Taking Charge of Your Career (pp. 412–413)

BUSINESS INFORMATION SOURCES

"You must accept that if the computer is a tool, it is the job of the tool user to know what to use it for."

Peter F. Drucker

     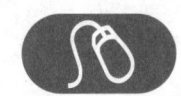

Knowledge Management

BOOKS

Beyond Knowledge Management: Dialogue, Creativity, and the Corporate Curriculum

Bob Garvey, Bill Williamson
Upper Saddle River, New Jersey: Financial Times Prentice Hall, 2002
224pp ISBN: 0273655175
In this book the authors explore the ways in which learning and knowledge processes link to the success of an organization. They encourage managers to think critically and offer useful frameworks for identifying and releasing tacit knowledge. They draw on a unique triad framework of strategic capability, knowledge productivity, and corporate curriculum, and stress the use of critical dialogue, learning histories, narratives, and metaphors. The implications of the knowledge economy on corporations today are explored and debated.

Building a Knowledge-driven Organization

Robert H. Buckman
New York: McGraw-Hill, 2004
272pp ISBN: 0071384715
The author, chairman and C.E.O. emeritus of Buckman Laboratories, describes how the company pioneered the development of a knowledge sharing culture as opposed to a knowledge hoarding one. The lessons learned in the process are presented with the aim of assisting others to change organizational culture and develop a knowledge-based strategy. There is a strong focus on the people aspects of implementing a knowledge system, breaking down organizational hierarchies and motivating employees to share their expertise. Aspects of knowledge management also covered include: the choice between customized and off-the-shelf information systems: the creation of communities and virtual teams; the importance of customer centricity; the development of new knowledge based products and services; and the measurement of outcomes.

Capitalizing On Knowledge: From e-business to k-business

David J. Skyrme
New York: Butterworth-Heinemann, 2001
336pp ISBN: 0750650117
Knowledge management and e-business are rapidly converging into the emerging field of k-business. A k-business is one that turns an organization's knowledge assets into knowledge products and services, and uses the Internet to market and deliver them. The book provides models and frameworks with checklists and case examples to help unravel the next phase of the knowledge and dot-com economy. Sections cover the nature of knowledge and e-business, new markets and models for conducting k-business, knowledge markets, and the 10 Ps of using the Internet for marketing. Assessment tools and checklists are provided that cover readiness for k-business, online market evaluation, Web site evaluation, and Web site project planning.

Common Knowledge: How Companies Thrive by Sharing What They Know

Nancy M. Dixon
Boston, Massachusetts: Harvard Business School Press, 2000
188pp ISBN: 0875849040
Creating successful knowledge transfer systems requires matching the type of knowledge to be shared to the method best suited for transferring it effectively. Based on an in-depth study of several organizations that are leading the field in successful knowledge transfer (including Ernst & Young, Bechtel, Ford, Chevron, British Petroleum, Texas Instruments, and the U.S. Army), *Common Knowledge* reveals groundbreaking insights into how organizational knowledge is created, how it can be effectively shared, and why transfer systems work when they do.

Cross-cultural Management: A Knowledge Management Perspective

Nigel Holden
Upper Saddle River, New Jersey: Financial Times Prentice Hall, 2002
336pp ISBN: 027364680X
The author treats culture as an object of knowledge management, and as an organizational knowledge resource. Previous writing on cross-cultural management is discussed, and the idea of knowledge management is described. The two are linked through four case studies, of Novo Nordisk, Matsushita Electric, LEGO, and Sulzer Infra. The final part of the book is concerned with the redesign of cross-cultural management as a knowledge domain.

Cultivating Communities of Practice: A Guide to Managing Knowledge

Etienne Wenger, Richard McDermott, William M. Snyder
Boston, Massachusetts: Harvard Business School Press, 2002
288pp ISBN: 1578513308
It is argued that while knowledge drives today's marketplace, leveraging knowledge remains a challenge. Leading companies are adopting communities of practice as a keystone of an effective knowledge strategy. Such communities may form naturally, but organizations need to become proactive to develop and integrate them into their strategy. Practical methods and models for nurturing communities of practice to their full potential are described.

Effective Knowledge Management: A Best Practice Blueprint

Sultan Kermally
Hoboken, New Jersey: Wiley, 2002
208pp ISBN: 0470844493
Kermally discusses best practice transfer and benchmarking and the creation of organizational knowledge of external changes. He also deals with the importance of managing knowledge, the creation and transfer of knowledge within the organization, the role of new technology, and leadership, together with intangible assets and their management. The book includes many case studies.

Enabling Knowledge Creation: How to Unlock the Mystery of Tacit Knowledge and Release the Power of Innovation

Georg von Krogh, Kazuo Ichijo, Ikujiro Nonaka
New York: Oxford University Press, Inc., 2000
192pp ISBN: 0195126165
Written as a sequel to the authors' work *The Knowledge-Creating Company*, this book examines how organizations can encourage and enable the creation of knowledge and the generation of ideas. Knowledge management, it suggests, has overemphasized information technology and measurement tools and focused on controlling rather than supporting knowledge. The authors then introduce five

activities that they term "knowledge enablers": instilling a knowledge vision; managing conversations; mobilizing knowledge activists; creating the right context; and globalizing local knowledge. A case study of Gemini Consulting is included in the text.

From Know-how to Knowledge: The Essential Guide to Understanding and Implementing Knowledge Management
Bryan Gladstone
London: Industrial Society, 2000
224pp ISBN: 1858358809
The concept of knowledge management is defined and explored under the headings: knowledge management; better information management is not enough; knowledge creation cycle; why knowledge management is important now; process of knowledge management; being a knowledge manager; and the future of knowledge management.

Intellectual Capital: Core Asset for the Third Millennium
Annie Brooking
Boston, Massachusetts: International Thomson Business Press, 1996
224pp ISBN: 1861524080
Brooking identifies and analyzes four primary categories of intellectual capital: market assets, intellectual property assets, human-centered assets, and infrastructure assets. This book is particularly suitable for corporations evaluating these assets prior to reengineering or downsizing, or for corporations looking to acquire a knowledge-intensive organization.

Key Issues in the New Knowledge Management
Joseph M. Firestone, Mark W. McElroy
New York: Butterworth-Heinemann, 2003
352pp ISBN: 0750676558
The authors present their concept of The New Knowledge Management (TNKM) as a broadening of the scope of knowledge management from a concern with the sharing, dissemination and retrieval of knowledge to a concern with its creation or production. They discuss definitions of information, data, and knowledge, introduce the knowledge life cycle, and describe its applications. They also explore the relationships between knowledge management concepts and the practical management issues of organizational learning, culture, and strategy.

The Knowing–Doing Gap: How Smart Companies Turn Knowledge into Action
Jeffrey Pfeffer, Robert I. Sutton
Boston, Massachusetts: Harvard Business School Press, 2000
320pp ISBN: 1578511240
This book is all about turning knowledge to practical account. The subject headings of its main sections give a good idea of its content and approach: knowing what to do is not enough; when talk substitutes for action; when memory is a substitute for thinking; when fear prevents acting on knowledge; when measurement obstructs good judgment; when internal competition turns friends into enemies; firms that surmount the knowing–doing gap; turning knowledge into action.

The Knowledge Activist's Handbook: Adventures from the Knowledge Trenches
Victor Newman
Chichester: Capstone, 2002
176pp ISBN: 184112320X
The author's own consulting experiences are used to demonstrate how emotion and reflection can effectively combine to create knowledge. Rejecting an academic approach, the style is discursive and entertaining, indeed openly critical of the "tedium" of knowledge management literature. Generally structured around a collection of easy-to-read, thematically connected anecdotes of between 700 to 1500 words, each section ends with a series of punchlines or implications for the reader to consider.

Knowledge Entrepreneur: How Your Business Can Create, Manage, and Profit from Intellectual Property
Colin Coulson-Thomas
London: Kogan Page, 2003
240pp ISBN: 0749439467
This book goes beyond the management of existing knowledge assets and intellectual property to examine how companies can create knowledge and develop new information and knowledge-based products to increase revenues and boost profits. It discusses the process of creating an enterprise culture and becoming a knowledge entrepreneur, describes the qualities needed by entrepreneurs, and outlines routes to entrepreneurship. Additional issues such as information overload and protecting intellectual property are also covered. Practical advice with checklists and exercises is provided throughout.

Knowledge Management and Organizational Competence
Ron Sanchez, ed.
New York: Oxford University Press, 2001
256pp ISBN: 0199240280
A collection of papers from notable management scholars offers a framework for understanding organizational knowledge and its role in building and leveraging competences. New insights into various kinds of knowledge that are of value to organizations are discussed.

Knowledge Management Casebook: Siemens Best Practices 2nd ed.
Thomas H. Davenport, Gilbert J. B. Probst
Munich: Publicis, 2002
336pp ISBN: 3895781819
Siemens has been recognized as one of the top ten knowledge management companies worldwide. This case study describes the best of the corporation's practical applications and experiences. The six sections cover: knowledge strategy, knowledge transfer, communities of practice, added value of knowledge management, learning and knowledge management, and visualizing more of the value creation.

Knowledge Networking: Creating the Collaborative Enterprise
David J. Skyrme
Woburn, Massachusetts: Butterworth-Heinemann, 1999
311pp ISBN: 0750639768
This book offers a comprehensive overview of the strategic application of knowledge management within global corporations. With an emphasis on good leadership practice, it shows how companies have successfully leveraged the knowledge dispersed and fragmented throughout their companies to deliver organizational benefits and create new opportunities. It gives guidance on how to innovate quickly and exploit human networks, wherever they are based, and provides examples of how global companies can harness employees' accumulated knowledge and apply it to specific problems. It also contains toolkits and checklists for individual, team, organizational, and collaborative enterprises.

Leading Organizational Learning: Harnessing the Power of Knowledge
Marshall Goldsmith, Howard Morgan, Alexander J. Ogg, eds
New York: Jossey-Bass, 2004
368pp ISBN: 0787972185
This book brings together contributions

1795

BUSINESS INFORMATION SOURCES

"The art of being wise is the art of knowing what to overlook."   William James

from experts in the field of organizational learning and knowledge management including Fons Trompenaars, Jon Katzenbach, Margaret J. Wheatley, and many others. These are grouped in five sections covering: the challenges and dilemmas of knowledge management; processes for managing knowledge and learning; the role of leaders in the knowledge organization; changes for the future, including the development of new ideas and case studies and examples.

Learning to Fly: Practical Lessons From One of the World's Leading Knowledge Companies 2nd ed.

Chris Collinson, Geoff Parcell
Chichester: Capstone, 2004
332pp ISBN: 184112509
Based on the authors' experiences at BP, as a detailed case study, the book sets out to provide a practical, jargon-free overview of what knowledge is, how it can be harnessed, stored, and—most importantly—shared throughout any organization. This updated edition includes a CD.

Managing Knowledge: An Essential Reader

Stephen Little, Paul Quintas, Tim Ray, eds
New York: Palgrave, 2002
400pp ISBN: 0761972137
This book provides general background on the major themes in the field. A critical overview of the theories is offered, and the four parts cover: creating knowledge; resources and capabilities; communicating and sharing knowledge; and knowledge, innovation and human resources. Some reprints of significant articles and papers are collected together to give key theoretical work, and critical case studies are included as well as newly written chapters.

Managing Knowledge: Building Blocks for Success

Gilbert Probst, Steffen Raub, Kai Romhardt
Hoboken, New Jersey: Wiley, 1999
368pp ISBN: 0471997684
Based on many years of research and experience, the ideas put forward in *Managing Knowledge* result from intensive collaboration with many major organizations. The book provides a road map of the most important stages of the knowledge management process; it presents a wide range of knowledge techniques, assesses their possible effects, and addresses key questions faced by managers. It is illustrated throughout with examples from managerial practice and is designed to prompt critical thinking and

assist practitioners to chart their own path through the knowledge jungle.

Managing Knowledge Work

Sue Newell et al.
New York: Palgrave, 2002
208pp ISBN: 0333962990
This textbook looks at the nature and management of knowledge work in a wide range of organizational contexts. The introduction examines the nature of knowledge and the shifts in society that have made knowledge work central to wealth creation. The book covers the knowledge intensive organization, the importance of teamworking in knowledge creation, the impact of HRM policies in knowledge work, the relationship between knowledge and information and communication technologies (ICT), the value and management of communities of practice and the link between knowledge management and innovation. A final section draws conclusions about the key challenges in the management of knowledge work. Case studies are included.

Organizing Knowledge: An Introduction to Managing Access to Information 3rd ed.

Jennifer Rowley, John Farrow
Aldershot, United Kingdom: Gower Publishing, 2000
424pp ISBN: 0566080478
This is a standard text on knowledge organization and retrieval. The different sections focus on: the nature of information and knowledge and their incorporation into documents; the use of electronic databases; the range of tools for accessing information resources, including indexing, classification, and catalogs; and the electronic contexts in which knowledge can be stored.

Profiting from Intellectual Capital: Extracting Value from Innovation

Patrick H. Sullivan
Hoboken, New Jersey: Wiley, 2001
384pp ISBN: 0471417475
This volume provides examples from companies' best practices in knowledge management, with a focus on getting value from intellectual capital. The book offers an overview of essential knowledge-management concepts and detailed coverage of strategies for measuring, monitoring, and assigning value to existing knowledge assets. It provides practical advice for those familiar with the basics of knowledge generation and information sharing.

Sharing Expertise: Beyond Knowledge Management

Mark S. Akerman, Volkmar Pipek, Volker Wulf, eds
Cambridge, Massachusetts: MIT Press, 2003
432pp ISBN: 0262011956
A new approach to knowledge management (KM), "expertise sharing," focuses on what can be gained from the cognitive, social and organizational, or human expertise aspect in knowledge work. A literature review, overview, and background are provided, and expertise sharing in organizational settings is explored empirically. The tools, technology, and architectures designed for expertise management are also discussed.

Smart Things to Know about Knowledge Management

Thomas M. Koulopoulos, Carl Frappaolo
Chichester: Capstone, 2001
240pp (Smart Series)
ISBN: 1841120413
In the new economy, say the authors, knowledge management is vital. It allows companies to leverage their most precious assets, collective know-how, talent, and experience, and only by focusing on these valuable resources can companies handle new market challenges and opportunities. The aim of this book, therefore, is to provide a framework for practical action, helping people to understand knowledge management and how it can benefit their organization, to position it at the heart of their business, to measure success in a knowledge-based economy, and to become the knowledge management champions in their organizations.

The Wealth of Knowledge: Intellectual Capital and the Twenty-First Century Organization

Thomas A. Stewart
New York: Currency/Doubleday, 2003
400pp ISBN: 0385500726
This book builds on Stewart's 1997 book *Intellectual Capital*, which outlined organizational assets in a knowledge economy. It analyzes corporate practices in managing intellectual capital, providing the basics of knowledge organization theory and real-world examples. A four-step process is used to describe the day-to-day management of knowledge and how it can improve productivity and profitability.

Working Knowledge: How Organizations Manage What They Know

Thomas H. Davenport, Laurence Prusak
Boston, Massachusetts: Harvard Business School Press, 2000
240pp ISBN: 1578513014

BUSINESS INFORMATION SOURCES

"Inequality of knowledge is the key to a sale."

Deil O. Gustafson

The authors break down knowledge management into four activities—accessing, generating, embedding, and transferring—and identify the key processes involved in each. They discuss skills and techniques, knowledge-management technologies, and best practices from their work with leading companies. They also emphasize the importance of corporate culture in fostering knowledge creation and sharing.

MAGAZINES

Journal of Knowledge Management

ISSN: 1367-3270
Emerald Group Publishing Ltd.
60/62 Toller Lane, Bradford, West Yorkshire, BD8 9BY, U.K.
T: +44 (0) 1274 777 700
F: +44 (0) 1274 785 200
www.emeraldinsight.com
This quarterly, peer-reviewed publication includes original research and case studies on strategies, tools, and techniques and technologies for knowledge management. It focuses on the identification of innovative knowledge management strategies and the application of theoretical concepts to real-world situations.

Knowledge and Process Management

ISSN: 1092-4604
Wiley
111 River St, Hoboken, New Jersey, 07030-5774
T: +1 201 748 6000
F: +1 212 850 6021
www.wiley.com
Covering theory, practice, research, and case studies relating to knowledge management, organizational learning, core competences, and process management, this journal is aimed at managers responsible for driving performance improvement or introducing new ideas into their organizations.

Knowledge Management Review

ISSN: 1369-7633
Melcrum
First Floor, Chelsea Reach, 79–89 Lots Road, London, SW10 0RN, U.K.
T: +44 (0) 20 7795 2205
F: +44 (0) 20 7795 2156
www.melcrum.com

This journal provides the latest trends, techniques, and ideas in knowledge management through corporate case studies, practitioners' insights, and practical articles.

INTERNET

International Knowledge Management Network
www.cibit.com
This site offers news, conference and seminar details, a discussion forum, an archive of literature resources, and Weblinks. Visitors need to register to use parts of the site.

Knowledge Management Research Center
www.cio.com/research/knowledge
The online presence of *C.I.O. Magazine*, this site offers a series of articles on key knowledge management topics along with a newsletter, conference information, blogs, and access to the C.I.O. store.

The KNOW Network
www.knowledgebusiness.com
This site contains a knowledge management library consisting of news, summaries of trends, market research, a diary, links, and a KM resources guide to publications, reviews, and Web sites. It also acts as the gateway to the KNOW Network—a group of leading knowledge organizations dedicated to the identification and exchange of best practice. Some of the site can only be accessed by joining the KNOW Network.

WWW Virtual Library on Knowledge Management
www.brint.com/km
This site provided by @brint.com offers full-text articles, book reviews, Weblinks, and a discussion forum on various issues relating to knowledge management.

ORGANIZATIONS

USA

American Productivity and Quality Center (APQC)
123 North Post Oak Lane, 3rd Floor, Houston, Texas, 77024
T: +1 713 681 4020
F: +1 713 681 1182
E: *apqcinfo@apqc.org*

www.apqc.org
Founded in 1977, APQC works with organizations of all sizes to improve productivity and quality. Its aim is to research and understand both emerging improvement methods and methods whose effectiveness is already proven, and it distributes its findings through education, advice, and information services. In 1992 it set up the International Benchmarking Clearinghouse to promote and facilitate the process of learning from best practice.

Europe

International Knowledge Management Network
Secretariat, Kenniscentrum CIBIT, Arthur van Schendelstraat 570, P.O. Box 19210, Utrecht, 3501 AD, The Netherlands
T: +31 30 230 8900
F: +31 30 230 8999
E: *info@cibit.nl*
www.cibit.com
Set up in 1994, the Network evolved from the experiences of the Dutch Knowledge Management Network and is now a worldwide organization for exchanging ideas and experiences in the knowledge management field.

The KNOW Network
4 St. George's Road, Bedford, Bedfordshire, MK40 2LS, U.K.
T: +44 (0) 1234 314 197
F: +44 (0) 1234 308 824
E: *info@knowledgebusiness.com*
www.knowledgebusiness.com
A Web-based network of some of the world's foremost knowledge-based organizations, the Network is dedicated to the identification and exchange of best practice for competitive advantage.

1797

BUSINESS INFORMATION SOURCES

Leadership

BOOKS

21 Leaders for the 21st Century: How Innovative Leaders Manage in the Digital Age

Fons Trompenaars,
Charles Hampden-Turner
Chichester: Capstone, 2001
480pp ISBN: 1900961660
Leaders of global corporations, it is argued, are beset by a series of dilemmas, pairs of conflicting propositions that clamor for their attention. Successful leadership depends on the capacity to integrate these demands and create powerful strategies that unite them. 21 corporate giants reveal their personal experiences of business dilemmas and these are used to show how managers understand and use the seven dilemmas of leadership.

The Accidental Leader: What to Do When You're Suddenly in Charge

Harvey Robbins, Michael Finley
New York: Jossey-Bass, 2004
192pp ISBN: 0787968552
Written in an easy to read anecdotal style, this practical toolkit can act as a resource book and inspiration for those who have been thrust suddenly into a position of responsibility. Part one addresses self-management and areas such as coping with responsibility and meeting the team. Part two deals with technical issues such as planning and creating a learning environment; and part three explores people management.

Alpha Leadership: Tools for Business Leaders Who Want More from Life

Anne Deering, Robert Dilts, Julian Russell
Hoboken, New Jersey: Wiley, 2002
240pp ISBN: 0470844833
This "how to" book is based on the authors' research that shows that the successful leader has three related strengths: anticipation, alignment, and action. Each of these areas is covered, and tools and frameworks are provided.

Arc of Ambition: Defining the Leadership Journey

James Champy, Nitin Nohria
Hoboken, New Jersey: Wiley, 2001
282pp ISBN: 0471530204
Champy and Nohria explore the fascinating dimensions of ambition through the stories of dozens of achievers, past and present, who exemplify both its positive and negative qualities. From the quest of Giuseppe Garibaldi for a unified Italy to the vision of Alfred Sloan for General Motors, which changed management practice forever, and the boyhood dream of Michael Dell to have a building with a flag out front, ambition comes in many guises. Champy and Nohria outline how it can be channeled toward creative and enriching endeavors at the personal, organizational, and even national levels.

Are Leaders Born or Are They Made? The Case of Alexander the Great

Manfred F. R. Kets de Vries, Elisabet Engellau
London, United Kingdom: Karnac Books, 2004
128pp ISBN: 1855753154
In this text, the life story of Alexander the Great and how he created and administered an empire that spanned most of the ancient world is examined. The authors go on to analyze his personality and behavior from a clinical perspective, examining the psychological forces that shaped his character, the leadership qualities that brought him success, and his strengths and weaknesses as a leader. Finally, the key leadership lessons that contemporary leaders in business and politics can learn from his life are identified.

The Art and Science of Leadership 3rd ed.

Afsaneh Nahavandi
Upper Saddle River, New Jersey: Prentice Hall, 2002
272pp ISBN: 0130458120
The author presents a broad overview of the field of leadership, focusing on the history of leadership theory, popular current trends, and prospects for the future. This edition includes expanded coverage of personality traits, abilities, values, and skills. Contingency models of leadership are also examined, and separate chapters cover participative management and team leadership, change-oriented leadership, and strategic leadership. The book is intended for students of leadership and each chapter includes details of relevant research, examples of innovative practices, ethical dilemmas faced by leaders, and case studies of real-life leaders.

Building Leaders: How Successful Companies Develop the Next Generation

Jay A. Conger, Beth Benjamin
San Francisco, California: Jossey-Bass, 1999
278pp (Jossey-Bass Business and Management)
ISBN: 0787944696
The successes and failures of the leadership development initiatives of over a dozen organizations including Federal Express, Motorola, and Ernst & Young are examined in this book. The authors identify three dominant approaches to leadership education: individual skill development, instilling organization values that promote leadership, and strategic intervention. They also present their own model for successful leadership development.

The Center for Creative Leadership Handbook of Leadership Development 2nd ed.

Cynthia D. McCauley, Ellen van Velsor, eds
New York: Jossey-Bass, 2004
528pp ISBN: 0787965294
This handbook explores the essence of leadership development, reveals how individuals can effectively enhance their leadership skills, and demonstrates what organizations can do to help build leaders and leadership capacity. Part one focuses on individual leader development. Part two explores leader development across gender and race, cross-cultural issues, global roles, and lifelong adult development. Part three looks at organizational capacity for leadership and development.

Complete Leadership: A Practical Guide for Developing Your Leadership Talents

Susan Bloch, Philip Whiteley
Harlow, United Kingdom: Pearson Education, 2003
192pp ISBN: 1843040255
This book is a personal coaching manual with questionnaires, guides and case studies for readers to evaluate and improve their leadership style. The book covers the following: how your style affects your staff, how it affects the organization, looking at your leadership type, how your team views you, self-awareness, personal development and progress.

"I think leadership is valuing the time you spend with your people more than anything else you do."

Herb Kelleher

     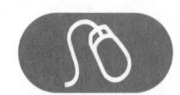

Connective Leadership: Managing in a Changing World

Jean Lipman-Blumen

New York: Oxford University Press, Inc., 2000
432pp ISBN: 0195134699

A new form of leadership is needed in an era of increasing interdependence and diversity, the author suggests. She reviews the psychological and historical foundations of leadership and develops a new model of connective leadership based around nine behavioral facets. The book draws on the results of qualitative interview research and quantitative survey research on achieving styles, conducted among over 5,000 leaders. A final section examines how the connective leadership model relates to new organizational structures and the wider social context.

Effective Strategic Leadership

John Adair

Indianapolis, Indiana: Macmillan, 2002
352pp ISBN: 0333906446

This readable and practical analysis of the nature of strategic leadership starts from a historical (ancient world) and military perspective, defining the different types of leadership with specific reference to the strategic variety. The second part of the book looks at the practical aspects of becoming a strategic leader, with many suggestions, exercises and a large number of short case studies of leaders through the ages from all walks of life.

First, Break All the Rules

Marcus Buckingham, Curt Coffman

New York: Simon & Schuster, 1999
256pp ISBN: 0684852861

This book is based directly on a huge research project into the behavior of managers and how they conduct business matters to achieve success. Acknowledging that good managers are pivotal to realizing a company's potential, the authors cite instances of successful employee selection and development techniques that reflect the quality of excellent management.

Focus on Leadership: Servant-Leadership for the 21st Century

Larry C. Spears, Michele Lawrence, eds

Hoboken, New Jersey: Wiley, 2002
400pp ISBN: 0471411620

Focus on Leadership expands on Robert K. Greenleaf's idea of a servant-leader, an individual who seeks to improve and enhance the workplace and the community rather than focusing on company profit. This book offers writings from some of the leading thinkers on management and

leadership, including Margaret Wheatley, Danah Zohar, Warren Bennis, and Stephen Covey.

The Future of Leadership: Today's Top Leadership Thinkers Speak to Tomorrow's Leaders

Warren Bennis, Gretchen M. Spreitzer, Thomas G. Cummings, eds

New York: Jossey-Bass, 2001
320pp ISBN: 0787955671

Nineteen essays are written by some of the leading thinkers in management today. The essays are arranged in the sections: including the leader of the future; how leaders stay on top of their game; insights from young leaders; and some closing thoughts. Contributors include Warren Bennis, Edward E. Lawler III, Charles Handy, Thomas H. Davenport, Tom Peters, Jeffrey Sonnenfeld, Philip Slater, and James O'Toole.

Geeks and Geezers: How Era Values and Defining Moments Shape Leaders

Warren G. Bennis, Robert J. Thomas

Boston, Massachusetts: Harvard Business School Press, 2002
224pp ISBN: 1578515823

A study of two groups of leaders is presented: geeks—young leaders under 35 —and geezers—older leaders over 70. The authors interviewed both groups on their experiences of leadership and success to gain an insight into how they were shaped by the times in which they grew up and to identify the qualities that enabled them to become successful leaders. Brief biographies of geezers and geeks are included.

Improving Leadership in Nonprofit Organizations

Ronald E. Riggio, Sarah Smith Orr, eds

New York: Jossey-Bass, 2004
304pp ISBN: 0787968307

Leadership issues and challenges for nonprofit organizations are discussed by various authors, including Jay Conger. Areas covered include future challenges, ethical challenges, board leadership, pay in nonprofit organizations, succession, and assessment.

In Search of Leaders

Hilarie Owen

Hoboken, New Jersey: Wiley, 2000
192pp ISBN: 0471491977

Leadership is discussed as a potential that all individuals have and can develop, rather than as a phenomenon based on hierarchical authority or a heroic chairman.

The author offers a three-stage model for a journey of self-discovery. She outlines the "seven essences" of leadership and explores transformational ideas about leadership to help individuals develop their own inner leadership potential.

The Inspirational Leader: How to Motivate, Encourage, and Achieve Success

John Adair

London: Kogan Page, 2003
208pp ISBN: 0749440465

This book explores the nature and practice of leadership and reinforces the author's argument that leaders are not born but made. It takes the form of conversations between a young chief executive and the author. Each aspect of leadership is studied and discussed so that the key skills are revealed for anyone to adopt and use.

Inspiring Leadership: Learning from Great Leaders

John Adair

London: Thorogood, 2002
368pp ISBN: 1854182072

This book discusses some of the great leaders in history, aiming to identify the main lessons of leadership that can be learnt from them. Each section takes a particular theme, illustrated by one or more individuals. Amongst the many individuals described are Socrates, Lao Tzu, Jesus Christ, Alexander the Great, Churchill, Machiavelli, Nelson, Shackleton, Margaret Thatcher, and Nelson Mandela.

John Adair's 100 Greatest Ideas for Effective Leadership and Management

John Adair

Chichester: Capstone, 2002
192pp ISBN: 1841121401

Adair offers accessible advice relating leadership to areas including time management, leadership functions, skills and team management, creativity and innovation and communication. These are organized under the headings: getting your act together; understanding leadership; performing as a leader; thinking as a leader; power through the people; and getting the message across.

John P. Kotter On What Leaders Really Do

John P. Kotter

Boston, Massachusetts: Harvard Business School Press, 1999
184pp ISBN: 0875848974

In this book, John P. Kotter argues that many companies lack the leadership they

"Leadership is not about being nice. It's about being right and being strong." Paul Keating

require at all hierarchical levels. The title is a collection of the author's most influential articles for the *Harvard Business Review* and includes his more recent essay containing "Ten Observations About Management Behavior."

Leader's Change Handbook: An Essential Guide to Setting Direction and Taking Action

Jay A. Conger, Gretchen M. Spreitzer, Edward E. Lawler, eds
San Francisco, California: Jossey-Bass, 1998
320pp ISBN: 0787943517
This handbook contains chapters by various leading contributors to the field, introducing new thinking on ways in which leaders, managers, consultants, and human resource specialists can implement change within their organizations. It outlines the main elements of effective change management, expands traditional ideas of leadership, and discusses the future of organizational change.

Leadership—The Inner Side of Greatness: A Philosophy for Leaders

Peter Koestenbaum
New York: Jossey-Bass, 2002
384pp ISBN: 0787959561
The author explores how to be an exceptional and passionate leader in today's complex world. He presents his Leadership Diamond Model that challenges managers to transform their thinking and approach everything with fresh effectiveness. Insights into the characteristics great leaders have in common—vision, reality, ethics, and courage—are presented and strategies that all managers can use are described.

Leadership and the New Science

Margaret J. Wheatley
San Francisco, California: Berrett-Koehler, 2001
208pp ISBN: 1576751198
This updated version of the original 1992 title discusses the effect of quantum physics on the way we organize our lives, how biology and chemistry influence the way we live, and how leadership is affected by science and chaos theory.

The Leadership Challenge 3rd ed.

James M. Kouzes, Barry Z. Posner
San Francisco, California: Jossey-Bass, 2003
496pp ISBN: 0787968331
This key title aims to help people to further their abilities to lead others to get "extraordinary" things done, presenting principles and practices that are based in solid research. It describes the five practices of exemplary leadership, discussing the characteristics that people most admire in leaders, the motives of leaders, how leaders foster collaboration and create a climate for high performance, and how leadership practices can be learnt by anyone.

The Leadership Crash Course: How to Create Personal Leadership Value 2nd ed.

Paul Taffinder
London: Kogan Page, 2006
192pp ISBN: 0749446382
The Leadership Crash Course is designed to help readers develop their skills and effectiveness. Split into seven sections, this book aims to build personal capability.

Leadership in Organizations: Current Issues and Key Trends

John Storey, ed.
New York: Routledge, 2004
352pp ISBN: 0415310334
This study not only strongly criticizes many currently available leadership training and development approaches, but also suggests alternatives. Areas covered include post-transformational leadership, leadership competencies, leader integrity, leadership learning, corporate university solutions, public sector leadership development, leadership and business strategy, and leadership career development.

The Leadership Moment: Nine True Stories of Triumph and Disaster and Their Lessons for Us All

Michael Useem
New York: Times Books, 2000
336pp ISBN: 0812932307
The author uses a variety of real examples of people in highly pressured situations to show the different ways one can react in adversity. These examples provide valuable lessons in how to cope with the same high levels of stress endured in the world of business.

Leadership on the Line: Staying Alive through the Dangers of Leading

Ronald A. Heifetz, Marty Linsky
Boston, Massachusetts: Harvard Business School Press, 2002
256pp ISBN: 1578514371
The book describes the difficulties, risks and rewards of leadership, and discusses some strategies for surviving the dangers. It also shows how a leader may manage his or her own personal needs and vulnerabilities, and how the spirit may be sustained during difficult times. Examples are drawn from politics, business, and family life.

The Leadership Pipeline: How to Build the Leadership-powered Company

Ram Charan, Stephen Drotter, James Noel
New York: Jossey-Bass, 2001
256pp ISBN: 0787951722
The authors show how to identify future leaders, assess their competence, plan their development, and measure the results. They also show how this process may be integrated with succession planning, so that the supply of leaders at all levels may be constantly renewed. Six critical stages in the leadership development pipeline are identified and separately addressed.

Leadership: Theory, Application, Skill Development 2nd ed.

Robert N. Lussier, Christopher F. Achua
Cincinnati, Ohio: South-Western College Publishing, 2003
544pp ISBN: 0324155565
By providing new, engaging ways to learn, including role-playing and using the Internet for readings and exercises, this textbook seeks to expand the user's knowledge about leadership. It is divided into three sections that focus on individual, team, and organizational leadership.

Leader to Leader: Enduring Insights on Leadership from the Drucker Foundation's Award-winning Journal

Frances Hesselbein, Paul M. Cohen, eds
San Francisco, California: Jossey-Bass, 1999
400pp ISBN: 0787947261
This collection of articles, taken from the journal *Leader to Leader*, brings together the wisdom of world renowned leaders, bestselling writers, leading thinkers, and business philosophers. These include Peter Drucker, Herb Kelleher, John P. Kotter, Rosabeth Moss Kanter, Peter Senge, and Charles Handy.

Leading at the Edge: Leadership Lessons from the Extraordinary Saga of Shackleton's Antarctic Expedition

Dennis N. T. Perkins et al.
New York: AMACOM, 2000
268pp ISBN: 0814405436
This book records the adventures of Sir Ernest Shackleton on his Antarctic expedition and examines through the lens of business the extraordinary leadership skills he displayed. Ten lessons on what it takes to be a great leader are drawn from the account. Contemporary business case studies further illustrate leadership at the edge, and the behaviors, attitudes, and ways

of thinking about life that help individuals to realize their full potential as leaders are discussed.

Leading Beyond the Walls

Frances Hesselbein, Marshall Goldsmith, Iain Somerville, eds
San Francisco, California: Jossey-Bass, 2001
320pp ISBN: 0787955558
Twenty-nine of the world's leading management thinkers explore the need for a new paradigm in leadership. In today's fast-paced global society, leaders must be adept at establishing diverse partnerships, alliances, and networks by building and maintaining relationships both within and outside their own organization. *Leading Beyond the Walls* brings together Peter Drucker, Stephen Covey, Peter Senge, Jim Collins, Noel Tichy, Regina Herzlinger, C. K. Prahalad, Sally Helgesen, and other thought leaders to describe new ways of building relationships, new approaches to strategy and marketing, new models of employee relations, and other innovative ways of thinking and acting.

Leading the Professionals: How to Inspire and Motivate Professional Service Teams

Geoff Smith
London: Kogan Page, 2004
256pp ISBN: 0749439963
This book supplies practical advice for those who lead professionals. It suggests an encouraging and supportive approach to meet the challenges of managing highly qualified or creative individuals and of developing high performing teams. Smith reviews keys to success such as objectives and values, and communication and coaching, and suggests ways to resolve performance problems and conflicts.

Leading the Way: Three Truths from the Top Companies for Leaders

Robert Gandossy, Marc Effron
Hoboken, New Jersey: Wiley, 2004
224pp ISBN: 047148301X
Three leadership truths are identified and these are said to be the fundamental building blocks used by top companies to build a sustainable pipeline of great leaders. Advice is given on identifying the leadership capabilities necessary for your organization and the process for building them, as well as considering the challenges, opportunities, and solutions that lie ahead.

Lead to Succeed: Creating Entrepreneurial Organisations

Colin Turner
New York: Texere Publishing, 2002
240pp ISBN: 1587991241
In this book the author puts forward his ideas on creating an entrepreneurial culture in established organizations. Part one examines the essential attributes of entrepreneurial leaders and how the OILS (opportunity, innovation, leadership, and service) of entrepreneurship can be applied. In part two the principles and practices of entrepreneurial leadership are outlined. Finally it looks at creating entrepreneurial people, culture, customer ethos and opportunities.

A Manager's Guide to Leadership

Mike Pedler, John Burgoyne, Tom Boydell
New York: McGraw-Hill, 2004
288pp ISBN: 0077104234
This is a practical self-development guide that is designed to help managers meet key leadership tasks and challenges. Part one helps you establish your leadership strengths and weaknesses and consider personal goals. Part two examines the leadership practices of power, risk taking, critical questioning, facilitation, and networking. Part three helps you develop your leadership skills by addressing the challenges to be found in the workplace.

Managing the Dream: Reflections on Leadership and Change

Warren G. Bennis
Cambridge, Massachusetts: Perseus Books Group, 2000
317pp ISBN: 0738203327
This book contains over ten of the author's most significant essays on leadership. The majority of the essays concentrate on how to make leadership possible and how to cope with change, while others discuss the character and ethics of a good leader.

On Becoming a Leader 2nd ed.

Warren Bennis
Cambridge, Massachusetts: Perseus Books Group, 2003
256pp ISBN: 0738208175
In this key title, updated for the new millennium, the author outlines the characteristics that determine whether a person will become a leader and, using key figures from a range of business areas as examples, the various ways companies treat such people.

Primal Leadership: Realizing the Power of Emotional Intelligence

Daniel Goleman, Annie McKee, Richard E. Boyatzis
Boston, Massachusetts: Harvard Business School Press, 2004
336pp ISBN: 1591391849
This title centres round the authors' assertion that in order to have good leadership, society needs to develop the emotional intelligence of its leaders. The book lists the four areas of emotional intelligence—self-awareness, self-management, social awareness, and relationship management—and discusses how these various abilities create different types of leadership. The authors use extensive research to give examples of these leadership styles.

Results-based Leadership

Dave Ulrich, Jack Zenger, Norm Smallwood
Boston, Massachusetts: Harvard Business School Press, 1999
234pp ISBN: 0875848710
According to the authors of this book, becoming a results-based leader involves the following: defining desired results; connecting leadership attributes to results; investing in people for employee results; creating capabilities for organizational and customer results; and building firm equity and stockholder value for investor results.

Ruthless Leader: Three Classics of Strategy and Power

Alistair McAlpine, ed.
Hoboken, New Jersey: Wiley, 2000
272pp ISBN: 0471372471
The texts of three classic works on leadership make up this compilation: *The Prince* by Nicolò Machiavelli, *The Servant* by Alistair McAlpine, and *The Art of War* by Sun Tzu. The introduction places these texts in their contemporary contexts, and compares and contrasts them, drawing out their major themes and demonstrating their application to modern business organizations.

The Smartest Guys in the Room: The Amazing Rise and Scandalous Fall of Enron

Bethany McLean, Peter Elkind
New York: Portfolio, 2004
464pp ISBN: 1591840538
Written by two *Fortune* journalists, this book attempts to lay bare the extraordinary story behind Enron's collapse in 2001. A tale of jaw-dropping corporate arrogance, it shows

1801

BUSINESS INFORMATION SOURCES

"All leadership, management, or vision will be useless if it becomes static." Paul Corrigan

the impact of incompetence and greed on the notion of corporate governance.

The Transparency Edge: How Credibility Can Make or Break You in Business

Barbara Pagano, Elizabeth Pagano
New York: McGraw-Hill, 2004
224pp ISBN: 0071422544
This text argues that, in line with a growing culture of transparency in business, the demand for clear and transparent leadership is becoming a priority. The authors demonstrate the benefits of clear and open business policy and transparent leadership practices. This book helps leaders to develop the "transparent edge" through nine key behavioral patterns that build and enhance credibility for leaders and consequently for business.

The Trusted Leader: Bringing Out the Best in Your People and Your Company

Robert Galford, Anne Seibold Drapeau
New York: Free Press, 2002
272pp ISBN: 0743235398
The importance of trust within organizations is outlined, and the difference between being trustworthy and building trust is explained. The characteristics and competencies of the trusted leader are established, and the identification and application of the tools of trusted leaders are examined through a series of interactive exercises and diagnostic tools.

Up Your Business: 7 Steps to Fix, Build, or Stretch Your Organization

Dave Anderson
Hoboken, New Jersey: Wiley, 2003
272pp ISBN: 0471445460
Achieving the highest organizational performance is about quality leadership; and without the right team, vision, strategy, and values are worthless. This book encourages reflection on leadership style and strategy and discusses areas such as recruitment, culture, employee development, goal setting, and growth. Written from a nonacademic, anti-intellectual stance, it is based on real-world experience.

Why Most Things Fail: Evolution, Extinction and Economics

Paul Ormerod
London: Faber & Faber, 2005
254pp ISBN: 0571220126
In what could be a wake-up call for many senior leaders, this book tackles one of the great unspoken truths of the business world: most things do not work. Drawing on the author's experience as a professor of economics and reflecting on the raft of scandals witnessed since the fall of Enron, this book sets out to equip readers with the knowledge they need to avoid a similar fate.

The Will to Lead: Running a Business with a Network of Leaders

Marvin Bower
Boston, Massachusetts: Harvard Business School Press, 1997
208pp ISBN: 0875847587
In this key work, the author uses his considerable experience in management to suggest how best to teach people how to work together. Bowers's theory is that organizations should be based on groups of leaders rather than a system of "command and control" leadership.

MAGAZINES

Harvard Business Review (HBR)

ISSN: 0017–8012
Harvard Business School Press
60 Harvard Way, Boston, Massachusetts, 02163
T: +1 800 988 0886
F: +1 617 783 7555
www.hbr.org
The *HBR* is a leading magazine for business leaders and senior executives that emphasizes current best practice and the application of leading edge research to business problems. Coverage is wide-ranging with a strong focus on leadership and strategy. Each issue includes feature articles written by experts and an interview with a business leader.

Leadership Quarterly

ISSN: 1048–9843
Elsevier Science
Customer Service Department, 6277 Sea Harbor Drive, Orlando, Florida, 32887–4800
T: +1 877 839 7126 or +1 407 345 4020
F: +1 407 363 1354
www.elsevier.com
Published four times per year, this journal analyzes the many factors that contribute to outstanding leadership. Executive managers and upper-level administrators will find the information presented in this journal will enhance and improve their leadership skills. It provides current information on the latest in leadership research. There is also an annual review of leadership topics.

Long Range Planning

ISSN: 0024–6301
Elsevier Science
Customer Service Department, 6277 Sea Harbor Drive, Orlando, Florida, 32887–4800
T: +1 877 839 7126 or +1 407 345 4020
F: +1 407 363 1354
www.elsevier.com
LRP, published in association with the Strategic Planning Society and the European Strategic Planning Federation, is a leading international journal in the field of strategic management. Aimed at senior managers, administrators, and academics, it includes articles from academics and practitioners.

MIT Sloan Management Review

ISSN: 1532–9194
MIT Sloan School of Management
77 Massachusetts Avenue, Cambridge, Massachusetts, 02139–4307
T: +1 617 253 7170
F: +1 617 258 9739
www.sloanreview.mit.edu
Founded in 1959, this quarterly journal aims to provide senior managers with the best of current management theory and practice. It has a strong focus on corporate strategy and leadership.

Strategic Change

ISSN: 1086–1718
Wiley
111 River St, Hoboken, New Jersey, 07030–5774
T: +1 201 748 6000
F: +1 212 850 6021
www.wiley.com
Eight issues of *Strategic Change* are published annually. The journal aims to provide authoritative and topical research papers addressing the strategic management of change and its implementation in an increasingly globalized business environment.

Strategy and Leadership

ISSN: 1087–8572
Emerald Group Publishing Ltd.
60/62 Toller Lane, Bradford, West Yorkshire, BD8 9BY, U.K.
T: +44 (0) 1274 777 700
F: +44 (0) 1274 785 200
www.emeraldinsight.com
This bimonthly journal for business leaders publishes articles describing effective practice in strategy and leadership and new theories that have the potential to advance

1802

BUSINESS INFORMATION SOURCES

"Isolation deprives leaders of new ideas."   Don Goodwin

the art of strategy development and its implementation.

INTERNET
Leaders Direct
www.leadersdirect.com
Offering extensive tips for managers and leaders, this site focuses on the nature and development of leadership.

Leader to Leader
www.pfdf.org/leaderbooks
This site offers access to a contents listing from the *Drucker Foundation Journal* and selected articles written by today's leading thinkers from the private, public, and social sectors.

weLEAD, Incorporated
www.leadingtoday.org
weLEAD is a nonprofit organization that believes that everyone is capable of being a great leader. The site includes an online magazine, tips, and book reviews. Extra services, including access to an article archive and related useful links, are available for members.

ORGANIZATIONS
USA
Center for Creative Leadership
1 Leadership Place, P.O. Box 26300, Greensboro, North Carolina, 27438–6300
T: +1 336 545 2810
F: +1 336 282 3284
E: *info@leaders.ccl.org*
www.ccl.org
The Center for Creative Leadership is a nonprofit educational institution that is an internationally recognized resource for understanding and expanding the leadership capabilities of individuals and organizations.

Europe
The Leadership Trust Foundation
Weston-under-Penyard, Ross-on-Wye, Herefordshire, HR9 7YH, U.K.
T: +44 (0) 1989 767 667
F: +44 (0) 1989 768 133
www.leadership.org.uk
The Foundation provides courses, postgraduate education, grants, and bursaries for those in pursuit of excellence in leadership.

International
Association for Corporate Growth (ACG)
International Headquarters, Suite 1, 1926 Waukegan Road, Glenview, Illinois, 60025–1770
T: +1 847 657 6730
F: +1 847 657 6819
E: *acghq@tcag.com*
www.acg.org
The ACG was founded in 1954 for professional managers involved in corporate growth and development in middle-market companies. The organization now has 5,000 members in the United States, Mexico, Canada, and the United Kingdom, and undertakes a range of activities including conferences. It also publishes a newsletter and offers networking opportunities.

FOR MORE INFORMATION

1803

Learning Organization

BOOKS

Beyond the Learning Organization: Creating a Culture of Continuous Growth and Development through State-of-the-Art Human Resource Practices

Jerry W. Gilley, Ann Maycunich
Cambridge, Massachusetts: Perseus Books Group, 1999
362pp ISBN: 0738200735

This title advises business executives and those working in human resources on how to use the theories behind organizational development to create corporate growth. The book also shows the reader how to create an organizational environment that can cope with a variety of possible problems and reveals how organizational aims are evaluated.

Creating a Learning Culture: Strategy, Technology, and Practice

Marcia L. Conner, James G. Clawson
New York: Cambridge University Press, 2004
352pp ISBN: 0521537177

This book focuses on creating an environment where learning takes place each day, all day. Three key aspects of a learning culture are addressed: the modern business context and the importance of learning at every juncture; the organic and adaptive approaches organizational leaders can take to design enduring success; and the expanding role of individuals within organizations, and its implications for business leaders, educators, technologists, and learners.

Facilitating Learning Organizations: Making Learning Count

Victoria J. Marsick, Karen E. Watkins
Aldershot, United Kingdom: Gower Publishing, 1999
240pp ISBN: 0566080397

Building learning into organizations is a strategic task requiring complex change interventions in most cases. The authors of this book offer managers their insights, experiences, and the lessons they have learned, suggesting essential steps that will help the change process and make it more effective, and advising on the processes of facilitation used by themselves and others when leading the learning journey.

The Fifth Discipline Fieldbook: Strategies and Tools for Building a Learning Organization

Peter M. Senge et al.
New York: Doubleday, 1994
608pp ISBN: 0385472560

Aimed particularly at managers, but of interest to all who want to learn and to make their organizations more effective, this book includes contributions from many people committed to building learning organizations who seek to share the strategies and tools they find useful. Designed to encourage a browsing, participatory approach, the text is built around brief, focused entries and includes practical exercises and techniques.

The Fifth Discipline: The Art and Practice of the Learning Organization

Peter M. Senge
New York: Currency/Doubleday, 1994
424pp ISBN: 0385260954

This seminal work sets out Senge's argument that successful organizations of the future will know how to tap their people's commitment and learning capacity. It draws on a variety of disciplines to illustrate the importance of being able to respond to change. It utilizes a framework based around personal mastery, mental models, shared vision, and team learning to remove obstacles to learning, recognize new opportunities, and achieve competitive advantage.

Fifty Ways towards a Learning Organization

Andrew Forrest
London: Industrial Society, 2000
192pp ISBN: 1858355990

This clearly written book is intended primarily for managers who can influence activities and expenditure within organizations, but is also of interest to anyone who wants to know more about practical options to make the learning organization a reality. It contains summaries of key issues, practical steps and guidance, and examples of best practice.

Handbook of Organisational Learning and Knowledge

Meinolf Dierkes et al.
New York: Oxford University Press, 2001
1008pp ISBN: 0198295839

A comprehensive overview of how the concept of organizational learning emerged, how it has been used and debated, and where it may be going is provided. An international team of authors examine both the central themes and the key emerging issues. The nine parts include, amongst other topics, insights from major social science disciplines; external triggers for learning; the factors and conditions shaping organizational learning; and the processes of organizational learning and knowledge creation.

How Organizations Learn: An Integrated Strategy for Building Learning Capability

Anthony J. Dibella, Edwin C. Nevis
San Francisco, California: Jossey-Bass, 1997
300pp ISBN: 0787911070

This book is a comprehensive synthesis of previously published thinking on learning organizations, with additional input from the authors' experience. It emphasizes that learning strategies will differ in different corporate cultures and that those differences are a source of competitive advantage.

The Infinite Resource: Creating and Leading the Knowledge Enterprise

William E. Halal, ed.
San Francisco, California: Jossey-Bass, 1998
300pp ISBN: 0787910155

A collection of essays from executives and management thinkers, this book offers a multidiscipline approach to creating the learning organization. It addresses the need for entrepreneurial freedom and nonhierarchical structures in the knowledge era, the importance of collaborative relationships within corporations, and the structures necessary to share knowledge.

Knowledge Management and Organizational Competence

Ron Sanchez, ed.
New York: Oxford University Press, 2001
256pp ISBN: 0199240280

A collection of papers from notable management scholars offers a framework for understanding organizational knowledge and its role in building and leveraging competences. New insights into various kinds of knowledge that are of value to organizations are discussed.

"Often the most effective facilitators in learning processes are not professional trainers but line managers themselves."

Peter Senge

Leading Organizational Learning: Harnessing the Power of Knowledge

Marshall Goldsmith, Howard Morgan, Alexander J. Ogg, eds
New York: Jossey-Bass, 2004
368pp ISBN: 0787972185

This book brings together contributions from experts in the field of organizational learning and knowledge management including Fons Trompenaars, Jon Katzenbach, Margaret J. Wheatley and many others. These are grouped in five sections covering: the challenges and dilemmas of knowledge management; processes for managing knowledge and learning; the role of leaders in the knowledge organization; changes for the future, including the development of new ideas; and case studies and examples.

Learning in Action: A Guide to Putting the Learning Organization to Work

David A. Garvin
Boston, Massachusetts: Harvard Business School Press, 2003
256pp ISBN: 1591391903

The author suggests that, while the idea of learning organizations is now generally accepted, it has proved difficult to create them in practice. This well-written text, intended for those involved in organizational learning, aims to give practical answers to practical questions and turn theory into reality. It presents a set of processes that can be used to enable employees to acquire, interpret, and apply knowledge, and, having identified three modes of learning (intelligence gathering, experience, and experimentation), suggests strategies to capitalize on each.

The Organizational Learning Cycle: How We Can Learn Collectively 2nd ed.

Nancy M. Dixon
Aldershot, United Kingdom: Gower Publishing, 1999
264pp ISBN: 0566080583

Dixon's very readable book was first published in 1994 by McGraw-Hill. Its aim is to clarify organizational learning sufficiently to allow managers to pursue it in ways that will integrate with other business objectives, such as competitiveness and productivity. She covers both theory and practice and uses layman's language throughout, giving explanations of any technical terms that she uses.

Organizational Learning from Performance Feedback: A Behavioural Perspective on Innovation and Change

Henrich R. Greve
New York: Cambridge University Press, 2003
224pp ISBN: 0521534917

Greve offers an analysis of how firms evolve in response to feedback about their own performance. Basing his work on ideas from organizational theory, social psychology, and economics, he explains how managers set goals, evaluate performance, and determine strategic changes. He reports on how theory fits current evidence, drawing on a range of recent studies, and on issues such as organizational change and risk-taking, research and development expenditures, innovativeness, facility investment, and strategic change. The practical implications of, and future directions for, this research are discussed.

Organizational Learning, Performance, and Change: An Introduction to Strategic Human Resource Development

Jerry W. Gilley, Ann Maycunich
Cambridge, Massachusetts: Perseus Books Group, 2000
408pp ISBN: 0738202487

The co-authors of this title have created a thorough guide to human resource development. They use numerous examples to illustrate their ideas and give clear methods for turning those ideas into programmes that will achieve the desired results.

Rethinking the Fifth Discipline: Learning within the Unknowable

Robert Louis Flood
New York: Routledge, 1999
213pp ISBN: 0415185300

This is an academic book. It offers a review and account of Senge's *The Fifth Discipline*, compares it to the concepts and approaches of Ludwig von Bertalanffy, Stafford Beer, Russell L. Ackoff, Peter B. Checkland, and C. West Churchman, and includes a critique of Senge's ideas. This opens the way to a discussion in Part Two of complexity theory and the concepts and approaches involved in it.

Supporting Workplace Learning for High Performance Working

David N. Ashton, Johnny Sung
Geneva, Switzerland: International Labour Office, 2002
192pp ISBN: 9221128016

Based on the results of the ILO InFocus program on Skills, Knowledge, and Employability, which focused on the role of workplace learning and training in high performance work organizations (HPWOs), the authors suggest that high performance work practices (HPWPs) can increase productivity and improve quality of working life. The growing importance of workplace learning is underlined and research evidence on the characteristics of HPWOs and the implementation of HPWPs is outlined. The theory of how learning contributes to performance improvement is set out in an appendix.

Ten Steps to a Learning Organization

Peter Kline, Bernard Saunders
Arlington, Virginia: Great Ocean Publishers, 1998
271pp ISBN: 0915556324

This book integrates a number of topics related to organizational learning, including systems thinking, communication, organizational and cultural change, and multiple intelligences. It consolidates these different approaches into ten concrete steps, applicable to most organizations, to creating a learning organization.

The Web Learning Fieldbook: Using the World Wide Web to Build Workplace Learning Environments

Valorie Beer
San Francisco, California: Jossey-Bass, 2000
304pp ISBN: 0787950238

This "how-to" book for those concerned with company training deals with using the Internet for workplace learning. It focuses on defining learners' needs and then using the Web to help them, rather than choosing Web possibilities first. An idea of the scope of Web learning possibilities is given in the form of snapshots, and access to sample learning environments, advice, links, and customizable templates are also provided.

MAGAZINES

Journal of Workplace Learning

ISSN: 1366–5626
Emerald
44 Brattle Street, 4th Floor, Cambridge, Massachusetts, 02138
T: +1 888 622 0075
F: +1 617 354 6875
www.emeraldinsight.com

This journal concentrates on the growth of the individual within the enterprise and aims to help researchers, practitioners, and consultants gain insights into workplace learning and development from theory, research findings, and organizational practice. Subscribers receive eight printed issues a year.

1805

BUSINESS INFORMATION SOURCES

"Shared vision is vital for the learning organization because it provides the focus and energy for learning."

Peter Senge

The Learning Organization: An International Journal

ISSN: 0969–6474

Emerald

44 Brattle Street, 4th Floor, Cambridge, Massachusetts, 02138

T: +1 888 622 0075

F: +1 617 354 6875

www.emeraldinsight.com

Five printed issues of this journal are published a year; access to current and previous volumes is also available over the Internet to subscribers via MCB's Emerald Fulltext. The journal focuses on the basic question of what a learning organization is, practices within learning organizations, and ways in which learning strategies can be adopted and applied.

Management Learning

ISSN: 1350–5076

Sage Publications

1 Oliver's Yard, 55 City Road, London, EC1Y 1SP, U.K.

T: +44 (0) 20 7324 8500

F: +44 (0) 20 7324 8600

www.sagepub.co.uk

This quarterly journal is aimed at human resource specialists, educators, and others in the field, *Management Learning* focuses on organizational behavior, organizational psychology, and change, development, and learning within the organization. There is a Web edition available over the Internet as well as the print version.

INTERNET

Brint.com

www.brint.com/papers/orglrng.htm

Contained on this site is a working paper giving an overview of the theoretical background and the meaning of organizational learning and learning organizations.

Fieldbook.com

www.fieldbook.com

This site gives details of *The Fifth Discipline Fieldbook*, a book of practice following up on Senge's more theoretical *Fifth Discipline* and aiming to answer the question, What can be done differently at work? It also contains information on books, links, and events, and details of authors and contributors.

Peter Honey Learning

www.peterhoneylearning.com

This resources site is accessed by registering details to benchmark your learning styles with comparable others (users must pay a one time fee to use this service). It features the Learning Series

modules, which are concerned with learning styles, motivation, environment, and skills, and each of which includes a questionnaire with the analysis and planning to create a learner-needs analysis. The other resources offered include a library of Peter Honey's articles.

Society for Organizational Learning

www.solonline.org

Sponsored by a nonprofit members' organization, the site offers publications, an events calendar, course information, and articles.

ORGANIZATIONS
USA

Society for Organizational Learning (SOL)

Suite 201, 955 Massachusetts Avenue, Cambridge, Massachusetts, 02139

T: +1 617 300 9500

F: +1 617 354 2093

E: *info@solonline.org*

www.solonline.org

Originally founded at MIT, SOL describes itself as a global learning community dedicated to building knowledge about basic institutional change. It offers courses for members and invited nonmembers, and also publications and various events or forums.

Europe

Campaign For Learning

19 Buckingham Street, London, WC2N 6EF, U.K.

T: +44 (0) 20 7930 1111

F: +44 (0) 20 7930 1551

E: *gphyall@cflearning.org.uk*

www.campaign-for-learning.org.uk

The Campaign for Learning is a national charity working to create an appetite for learning in individuals. It focuses on the three main themes: learning at work, family learning, and learning through school/ learning to learn. Its newsletter includes coverage relevant to learning at work. The organization also encompasses The Talent Foundation (see below).

ECLO—European Consortium for the Learning Organisation

Venelle des Lauriers, Wavre, 8 B-1300, Belgium

T: +32 (0) 10 24 16 00

E: *info@eclo.org*

www.eclo.org

The ECLO draws its members from business, academia, the public sector, and consultancies, bringing together people

involved with learning organizations from across Europe.

The Talent Foundation

19 Buckingham Street, London, WC2N 6EF, U.K.

T: +44 (0) 20 7930 1524

F: +44 (0) 20 7930 1551

E: *info@talentfoundation.org*

www.talentfoundation.org

The Foundation is a nonprofit initiative, set up with the support of various organizations to provide solutions for businesses that need to attract, retain, and develop talent. It offers a range of tools to help unlock workforce talent and is involved in large-scale research investigating the link between innovation and adaptability in organizations.

International

The 21st Century Learning Initiative (U.S.)

1329 B South Main Street, Harrisonburg, Virginia, 22801

T: +1 540 438 5653

F: +1 540 437 4832

This transnational initiative, established in 1995 by a group of British and American businessmen and organizations, aims to synthesize the best research and development in the field of human learning and examine its implications for work, education, and communities.

SEAL—The International Learning Community

37 Park Hall Road, East Finchley, London, N2 9PT, U.K.

T: +44 (0) 20 8365 3869

F: +44 (0) 20 8444 0339

E: *seal@seal.org.uk*

www.seal.org.uk

SEAL—the Society for Effective Affective Learning, based in the United Kingdom—is an international networking association of people interested in the dynamics of learning. It was originally founded in 1983 to promote the ideas of Suggestopedia (Lozanov), and has now been broadened to include all learning methods with similar principles. Members are usually individuals or parents committed to lifelong learning or involved in teaching, business and management training or education, counseling, therapy, or care work. SEAL aims to empower individuals to discover their learning potential and to transform attitudes to learning in educational institutions, families, and wider society.

"Control and learning are deeply embedded in the specific cultural and institutional ethos of an organization."

Yanni Yan

Logistics and Distribution

BOOKS

Contemporary Logistics 8th ed.
Paul R. Murphy, Jr., Donald F. Wood
Upper Saddle River, New Jersey: Prentice Hall, 2003
586pp ISBN: 0130352802
Often used as a college textbook, this volume provides clear descriptions of supply channel systems from freight movement to materials management and end-point distribution to customers. This edition also covers customer service, packaging, and traffic and inventory management. Clear writing and real-world examples make the book more understandable than many others in the field.

Fundamentals of Logistics
Douglas M. Lambert, James R. Stock, Lisa M. Ellram
Maidenhead, United Kingdom: McGraw-Hill, 1997
640pp ISBN: 0256141177
This book offers a unique take on the area of logistics, approaching the topic from both a marketing and customer service perspective. The text emphasizes concept and context over actual system design proposals. The book is considered noteworthy for its insistence that logistics is much more than solving transportation problems—it is a fully integrated science demanding customer service and internal organizational attention.

The Handbook of Logistics and Distribution Management 2nd ed.
Alan Rushton, John Oxley, Phil Croucher
London: Kogan Page, 2000
582pp ISBN: 0749433655
Written to appeal to both students and experienced managers, this handbook explains the basics of modern logistics and distribution. The authors explain the fundamental concepts of logistics and include discussions of warehousing, transportation, and information and control systems.

Logistics and Supply Chain Management: Creating Value-Adding Networks 3rd ed.
Martin Christopher
Upper Saddle River, New Jersey: Financial Times Prentice Hall, 2005
320pp ISBN: 0273681761

The goal of supply chain management is to link the marketplace, the distribution network, the manufacturing process, and procurement activity in such a way that customers are serviced at higher levels and yet at lower total cost. The author explores the role of logistics in achieving these goals. He examines the relationship between logistics and competitive strategy, the customer service dimension, methods of measuring logistics costs and performance, benchmarking, and the task of managing the supply chain.

Logistics and the Extended Enterprise: Benchmarks and Best Practices for the Manufacturing Professional
Sandor Boyson et al.
New York: Wiley, 1999
230pp ISBN: 0471314307
This book answers the question "How can organizations best apply logistics and supply chain management practices in order to break down internal and external walls and to become more effective extended enterprises?" The authors have gained first-hand insights into their subject through interviews, site visits, focus groups, and targeted surveys. Their core research findings and conclusions are summarized here, using case studies of major companies including Amoco, DuPont, Johnson & Johnson, and UPS.

A Practical Guide to Transportation and Logistics
Michael B. Stroh
Dumont, New Jersey: The Logistics Network, 2001
184pp ISBN: 0970811500
This book provides the logistics manager with a guide to purchasing, traffic and transportation, warehousing, and inventory control. It includes a long chapter on computers with discussion of various software packages.

Strategic Logistics Management 4th ed.
James R. Stock, Douglas Lambert
Maidenhead, United Kingdom: McGraw-Hill, 2000
896pp ISBN: 0256136874
The fourth edition of this book examines the subject of logistics from the perspective of customer satisfaction and marketing. The authors have incorporated large amounts of new material, including chapters on supply

chain management and measuring, and selling the value of logistics, aimed at making the book more managerial, integrative, and globally focused. The book shows the importance of integrating all the functional areas of a business and putting logistics in its proper place in the supply chain.

Supercharging Supply Chains: New Ways to Increase Value through Global Operational Excellence
G. Tyndall et al.
New York: Wiley, 1998
272pp ISBN: 0471254371
The authors of this innovative view of supply chain excellence are key partners and leaders of the Ernst & Young Global Supply Chain Management Team. They explain why and how operational excellence helps companies sell more products, examine its impact on shareholder value, describe the new ideas being implemented to achieve excellence, and consider how leading companies can effectively introduce new products into global supply chains.

MAGAZINES

The International Journal of Logistics Management
ISSN: 0957–4903
Emerald
60/62 Toller Lane, Bradford, West Yorkshire, BD8 9BY, U.K.
T: +44 (0) 1274 777 700
F: +44 (0) 1274 785 201
www.ijlm.org
A collection of refereed articles for executives, researchers, and teachers, this journal focuses on current developments and new thinking in the field of logistics.

Logistics and Transport Focus
ISSN: 1466–836X
Chartered Institute of Logistics and Transport
Earlstrees Court, Earlstrees Road, Corby, Northamptonshire, NN17 4AX, U.K.
T: +44 (0) 1536 740 100
F: +44 (0) 1536 740 101
www.ciltuk.org.uk
Published ten times a year, this journal reviews recent news and developments in the logistics and transport sectors. It contains a range of articles exploring various developments in techniques and

1807

BUSINESS INFORMATION SOURCES

"Order and simplification are the first steps toward the mastery of a subject."

Thomas Mann

processes within the sector. The emphasis is on U.K. and European case studies.

INTERNET
The Logistics Network
www.logisticsnetwork.com
This site offers information for the logistics manager, including news, recommended reads, and Vinny the "Virtual Logistics Manager."

Logistics World
www.logisticsworld.com
This site provides a directory of logistics resources, including subsites devoted to freight, transportation, supply chain management, warehousing, and distribution. It is also home of the WWW Virtual Library of Logistics.

Loglink
www.loglink.com
This is a gateway Web site featuring hundreds of links to providers of logistics support, from freight, air, and rail transport, to straight logistics, to providers of logistical software, to warehousing and distribution services.

ORGANIZATIONS
USA
American Purchasing Society (APS)
N. Island Center, Suite 203, 8 E. Galena Boulevard, Aurora, Illinois, 60506
T: +1 630 859 0250
F: +1 630 859 0270
E: *propurch@aol.com*
www.american-purchasing.com
This organization certifies qualified purchasing personnel. The APS conducts research and compiles business statistical data, including tracking salary surveys. APS can also provide consulting services for materials management.

Council of Supply Chain Management Professionals (CSCMP)
Suite 200, 2805 Butterfield Road, Oak Brook, Illinois, 60523
T: +1 630 574 0985
F: +1 630 574 0989
E: *cscmpadmin@cscmp.com*
www.cscmp.org
The Council of Supply Chain Management Professionals is a nonprofit organization of business personnel who are interested in improving their logistics management skills. It works in cooperation with private industry and various other organizations to further the understanding and development of the logistics concept. It was founded in

1963 as the National Council of Physical Distribution Management, changing to its present name in 1985. The CLM organizes activities, research, and meetings, all designed to develop the theory and understanding of the logistics process, to promote the art and science of managing logistics systems, and to foster professional dialog and development within the profession.

National Association of Purchasing Management (NAPM)
2055 East Centennial Cir., P.O. Box 22160, Tempe, Arizona, 85285
T: +1 480 752 6276 or 800 888 6276
F: +1 480 752 7890
E: *rlatondr@napm.org*
www.napm.org
The more than 46,000 members of this association are supply management personnel involved in industrial, commercial, and utility firms. NAPM members work to develop efficient supply management.

Procurement and Supply Chain Benchmarking Association (PASBA)
4606 FM 1960 W, Suite 250, Houston, Texas, 77069
T: +1 281 440 5044
F: +1 281 440 6677
E: *info@pasba.com*
www.pasba.com
Founded in 1998 and with over 800 members, this association targets the procurement and supply chain managers of corporations with an interest in benchmarking. PASBA promotes the use of benchmarking to improve corporate efficiency and profitability.

Europe
Chartered Institute of Logistics and Transport
Earlstrees Court, Earlstrees Road, Corby, Northamptonshire, NN17 4AX, U.K.
T: +44 (0) 1536 740 100
F: +44 (0) 1536 740 101
E: *membership@ciltuk.org.uk*
www.ciltuk.org.uk
The Institute exists to promote professional excellence and social responsibility in the fields of transportation and supply chain management. Formed in 1999 from the integration of the Institute of Logistics and the Chartered Institute of Transport, it offers members a range of activities and benefits, including development programs and information services. A number of special interest groups enable members to

network and share experiences with like minded individuals.

European Logistics Association (ELA)
Avenue des Arts 19/ Kunstlaan 19, Brussels, B-1210, Belgium
T: +32 2 230 02 11
F: +32 2 230 81 23
E: *ela@elalog.org*
www.elalog.org
ELA is a federation of 36 Western European national logistics associations. It aims to provide a link and an open forum for any individual or society concerned with logistics. ELA formulates European logistics education standards and has established a vocational qualification procedure to enable the standards to be accepted on a pan-European basis.

International
Canadian Association of Supply Chain and Logistics Management
590 Alden Road, Suite 211, Markham, Ontario, L3R 8N2, Canada
T: +1 905 513 7300
F: +1 905 513 1248
E: *members@infochain.org*
www.sclcanada.org
Established in 1967, the Association is a nonprofit, membership organization which aims to advance the logistics and supply chain profession in Canada. Through a range of activities, research, and informal discussion, members are encouraged to further their understanding of logistics and the art and science of its management.

Logistics Association of Australia (LAA)
P.O. Box W154, Parramatta, New South Wales, 2150, Australia
T: +61 2 9635 3422
F: +61 2 9635 3466
E: *admin@laa.asn.au*
www.laa.asn.au
The LAA represents the interests of professionals involved in logistics and the supply chain in Australia. It is primarily an educational body which aims to provide a forum for Australian managers to expand and develop their understanding and skills in the practical implementation of the operational and strategic aspects of logistics.

FOR MORE INFORMATION
☆ Managing the Challenge of E-service (pp. 223–224)
♋ Purchasing and Supply Chain Management (pp. 1883–1885)

"If you are having as much fun running a big corporation as you did running a piece of it, then you are probably interfering too much with the people who really make it happen."

James Burke

Maintenance

BOOKS

Planning and Control of Maintenance Systems: Modeling and Analysis

Salih O. Duffuaa, A. Raouf, John Dixon Campbell

Hoboken, New Jersey: Wiley, 1998
400pp ISBN: 0471197817

Using the concept of total productive maintenance, the authors outline a technique for planning a maintenance system using statistical and optimization techniques in order to avert equipment failure. Written for students and practicing engineers and managers, it covers statistical models for load forecasting and capacity planning, productivity measurement, maintenance materials control, designing a maintenance training program, maintenance audits, computerized maintenance systems, monitoring equipment using diagnostic technology, and fitting preventive maintenance into a busy production schedule.

Reliability-centred Maintenance 2nd ed.

John Moubray

Woburn, Massachusetts: Butterworth-Heinemann, 1999
440pp ISBN: 0750633581

Moubray provides an introduction to the theory and practice of reliability-centered maintenance (RCM). He describes the main elements of RCM and offers a practical explanation of how it can be applied to the manufacturing operation.

Total Productive Maintenance 2nd ed.

Terry Wireman

New York: Industrial Press, Inc., 2004
208pp ISBN: 0831131721

Behind every world class manufacturing company there is a world class maintenance department. This textbook, based on a five-year global study of Japanese, European, and American companies, develops a viable strategy for total productive maintenance (TPM). New features include case studies, advice on presenting the financial terms, a clarification of the goals and objectives of TPM, and explanations of the pitfalls that may be encountered.

MAGAZINES

IMI News

International Maintenance Institute
P.O. Box 751896, Houston, Texas, 77275

T: +1 281 481 0869
F: +1 281 481 8337
www.imionline.org
This is a bimonthly publication that features news and technical feature articles. One issue per year provides a buyer's guide of members' products and services. It highlights the activities of the International Maintenance Institute.

Reliability Magazine

ISSN: 1090–3259
Reliability Magazine
6500 Papermill Road, Knoxville, Tennessee, 37919

T: +1 865 531 2193
F: +1 865 531 2459
www.reliability-magazine.com
Reliability Magazine claims to be the first trade journal dedicated specifically to machinery reliability, the predictive maintenance industry, root cause failure analysis, and reliability centered maintenance. It is published bimonthly. Some articles can be read online at its Web site.

INTERNET

Maintenance Resources.com

www.maintenanceresources.com
This Web site is dedicated to plant engineering, maintenance, and reliability resources. It includes a reference library with extensive abstracts of a range of publications from TWI Press.

MaintenanceWorld.com

www.maintenanceworld.com
This is a selection of book abstracts and links to articles and Web sites on a range of maintenance-related topics.

ORGANIZATIONS

USA

ASME International

3 Park Avenue, New York, 10016–5990
T: +1 973 882 1167
F: +1 973 882 1717
E: *infocentral@asme.org*
www.asme.org
ASME was founded in 1880 as the American Society of Mechanical Engineers. It is a nonprofit educational and technical organization with a worldwide membership of 120,000. ASME aims to be the premier organization for promoting the art, science, and practice of mechanical engineering by promoting and enhancing the technical competency of its members. It runs and promotes training courses, meetings, and online discussion groups and produces a range of publications.

Institute of Industrial Engineers (IIE)

3577 Parkway Lane, Suite 200, Norcross, Georgia, 30092
T: +1 770 449 0460
F: +1 770 441 3295
E: *cs@iienet.org*
www.iienet.org
The IIE was founded in 1948 and is the only international, nonprofit, professional society dedicated to advancing the technical and managerial excellence of industrial engineers. The IIE sees industrial engineering as being concerned with the design, improvement, and installation of integrated systems.

International Maintenance Institute (IMI)

P.O. Box 751896, Houston, Texas, 77275
T: +1 281 481 0869
F: +1 281 481 8337
E: *iminst@swbell.net*
www.imionline.org
The IMI was chartered as a nonprofit corporation in 1960. The philosophy of the organization is to professionalize the maintenance function by helping managers to work more effectively through education and the exchange of ideas. Its Web site provides information on training options and job vacancies in the profession.

Society for Maintenance and Reliability Professionals (SMRP)

PO Box 51787, Knoxville, Tennessee, 37950–1787
T: +1 865 212 0111
F: +1 865 558 3060
E: *info@smrp.org*
www.smrp.org
The SMRP is an independent, nonprofit society run by and for practitioners in the maintenance and reliability profession. The Society was formed and chartered in 1992 and is dedicated to promoting excellence in maintenance and reliability in all types of manufacturing.

BUSINESS INFORMATION SOURCES

"The spark-gap is mightier than the pen. This is not the age of the pamphleteers, it is the age of the engineers."

Lancelot Hogben

Europe
Institution of Mechanical Engineers (IMechE)

1 Birdcage Walk, London, SW1H 9JJ, U.K.
T: +44 (0) 20 7222 7899
F: +44 (0) 20 7222 4557
E: *membership@imeche.org.uk*
www.imeche.org.uk
The IMechE was founded in 1847 by George Stephenson, of "Rocket" railroad locomotive fame. It holds a royal charter and is the United Kingdom's certifying body for mechanical engineers. The Institution operates under a number of specialist divisions and interest groups and offers a range of professional development services, conferences, and events, and has a library and information service.

FOR MORE INFORMATION

☆ Facilities Management (pp. 214–215)
🐭 Facilities Management (p. 1754)
🐭 Manufacturing Systems (pp. 1821–1823)
☆ Outsourcing (pp. 120–121)
🐭 Process Control and Statistical Process Control (pp. 1868–1869)

"The possible use of automated equipment in the over-the-counter marketplace has become an increasingly important subject."
Robert W. Haack

Management Buyouts

BOOKS

The Art of M&A: A Merger Acquisition Buyout Guide 3rd ed.

Stanley Foster Reed, Alexandra Reed Lajoux
Maidenhead, United Kingdom: McGraw-Hill, 1999
1008pp ISBN: 0070526605
Presented in a question-and-answer format, this book looks at over 1,000 aspects of mergers, acquisitions, and buyouts. Questions covered range from locating a suitable target to closing and post-merger integration. The book gives real-world insights through synopses of dozens of landmark cases and includes sample forms and checklists.

Barbarians at the Gate

Bryan Burrough, John Helyar
New York: HarperCollins, 2003
592pp ISBN: 0060536357
This is a classic tale of corporate greed based on the merger of RJR and Nabisco. It is as gripping a read as any work of fiction.

Big Deal: Mergers and Acquisitions in the Digital Age

Bruce Wasserstein
New York: Warner Books, 2001
960pp ISBN: 0446675210
The legendary Bruce Wasserstein uses his own experience to describe what happens during an M&A deal. The book starts with an account of how the M&A trend developed and then focuses on how to get the deal done.

Buyout: The Insider's Guide to Buying Your Own Company

Rick Rickersten et al.
New York: AMACOM, 2001
304pp ISBN: 0814406262
This book gives you the tools and strategies you need to lead a successful management buyout. It includes everything from how to select the company you want to buy, through due diligence issues and finding equity partners, to running the company when you succeed in your buyout.

Creating Value through Corporate Restructuring: Case Studies in Bankruptcies, Buyouts, and Breakups

Stuart C. Gilson
Hoboken, New Jersey: Wiley, 2001
528pp ISBN: 0471405590
Management buyouts are a common form of business restructuring. This collection of recent case studies from the United States and several other countries illustrates the real-world techniques and strategies that are common to all types of restructuring. It demystifies complex financial issues surrounding business valuation and gives the reader a better understanding of the possibilities when dealing with corporate restructuring.

Management Buyout: A Guide for the Prospective Entrepreneur 2nd ed.

Ian Webb
Aldershot, United Kingdom: Gower Publishing, 1990
176pp ISBN: 0566028107
This book provides an introduction to the process of achieving a successful buyout and considers the financial and legal issues involved. It reviews the development of the buyout market in the United Kingdom and considers the relevance of an entrepreneurial mindset to buyout situations. Five case studies are included.

MAGAZINES

Buyouts Newsletter

ISSN: 1040–0990
Thomson Financial
195 Broadway, 10th Floor, New York, 10007
T: +1 646 822 2000
F: +1 646 822 3230
www.buyoutsnewsletter.com
Buyouts is a biweekly newsletter offering news, data, and analysis relating to the buyout industry. Listings of deals and funds in the United States are published quarterly. Readers can sign up for the newsletter on the Web site.

European Management Buyout Review

Centre for Management Buyout Research (CMBOR)
Nottingham University Business School, Jubilee Campus, Wollaton Road, Nottingham, NG8 1BB, U.K.
T: +44 (0) 115 951 5493
F: +44 (0) 115 951 5204
www.nottingham.ac.uk/business/Cmbor
The *Review* focuses on trends in the European buyout market and covers 14 Western European countries.

INTERNET

Are You Management Buyout Material?

www.cfo.com/Article?article=2117
Management buyouts are not for everyone. This checklist can help you determine whether you have what it takes to be successful.

Is a Management Buyout in Your Future?

www.imakenews.com/rcwmirus/e_article000017429.cfm
This article from the Mirus Online Newsletter describes management buyouts and identifies the characteristics of typical candidate companies. It outlines what each side is looking for and presents financing options that can be used.

Orchestrating a Management Buyout

www.southflorida.bizjournals.com/milwaukee/stories/1996/12/09/focus1.html
Describing the management buyout experience as a roller coaster ride, this article points out that perseverance is often a key element in completing the buyout successfully. It provides real-world examples of how obstacles can be overcome.

ORGANIZATIONS

Europe

Centre for Management Buyout Research (CMBOR)

Nottingham University Business School, Jubilee Campus, Wollaton Road, Nottingham, NG8 1BB, U.K.
T: +44 (0) 115 951 5493
F: +44 (0) 115 951 5204
E: *margaret.burdett@nottingham.ac.uk*
www.nottingham.ac.uk/business/Cmbor
CMBOR was founded by Barclays Private Equity Limited and Deloitte & Touche at the Nottingham University Business School in March 1986 to monitor and analyze management buyouts in a comprehensive and objective way. A database of MBOs in the United Kingdom and Europe has been developed, and quarterly reviews and research papers are published.

FOR MORE INFORMATION

- Acquisitions, Takeovers, and Mergers (pp. 1670–1671)
- Venture Capital (pp. 1927–1929)

1811

BUSINESS INFORMATION SOURCES

"Sometimes you have to pay a high price for an opportunity."   Rupert Murdoch

Management Development

BOOKS

Building Leaders: How Successful Companies Develop the Next Generation

Jay A. Conger, Beth Benjamin
San Francisco, California: Jossey-Bass, 1999
278pp (Jossey-Bass Business and Management)
ISBN: 0787944696
The successes and failures of the leadership development initiatives of over a dozen organizations including Federal Express, Motorola, and Ernst & Young are examined in this book. The authors identify three dominant approaches to leadership education: individual skill development, instilling organization values that promote leadership, and strategic intervention. They also present their own model for building a successful leadership development program.

Changing Patterns of Management Development

Andrew Thomson et al.
Malden, Massachusetts: Blackwell Business, 2001
288pp ISBN: 0631209980
An examination is made of where management development in Britain stands at the start of the 21st century, focusing primarily on the way in which organizations develop their managers, and on how managers themselves view this development. The historical background to management development is described, along with models of management development.

Developing and Managing Talent: A Blueprint for Business Survival

Sultan Kermally
London: Thorogood, 2004
112pp ISBN: 1854182293
The importance of developing talent is explained with particular reference to the key role of knowledge and knowledge management in developing and sustaining competitive advantage in the modern economy. The author explains how organizations can develop strategies for the recruitment, development, and retention of talented employees. Separate sections focus on the e-dimension—the use of the Internet and e-learning, the global dimension, and the development of leadership talent. The perspectives of key thinkers such as John Kotter, Peter Drucker, Peter Senge, Tom

Peters, and Steven Covey are outlined and the key messages to be learned from them are drawn out.

Developing Managers: A European Perspective

Chris Mabey, Matias Ramirez
Corby, Northamptonshire: Chartered Management Institute (CMI), 2004
80pp ISBN: 0859463311
The findings of a research program that investigated management development and training in seven European countries (Germany, Denmark, France, Spain, United Kingdom, Norway, and Romania) are presented. The research looked at the amount of development carried out, management development policy and systems, links to business, how training evaluation is carried out, the impact of development on organizational performance, and the existence of a management development ethos. The results are analyzed and recommendations are made.

Developing Managers for Business Performance: What Your Board Needs to Know Today

Chartered Institute of Personnel and Development
London, United Kingdom: Chartered Institute of Personnel and Development (CIPD), 2002
48pp ISBN: 0852929609
A practical framework for strengthening the connection between corporate performance and business, this book presents organization and management development strategies derived from the experience of senior executives. Also included are: a process framework for engaging colleagues; and case studies showing how others are integrating management development with business plans.

A Guide to Management Development Techniques: What to Use When

Kenneth Fee
London: Kogan Page, 2001
192pp ISBN: 0749436204
This is a detailed guide to the various techniques used in management development. Offering both underpinning theory and practical advice, the book looks in detail at each technique described, analyzing and evaluating its strengths and

weaknesses and providing examples of the technique in use.

The Leader in You: How to Win Friends, Influence People and Succeed in a Changing World

Dale Carnegie et al.
New York: Pocket Books, 1995
245pp ISBN: 0671519980
This is a step-by-step guide to strategies intended to help individuals unlock their inner potential and become leaders. Using anecdotes and advice from a variety of people, including famous names such as Margaret Thatcher, it offers its readers assistance in identifying their leadership strengths, achieving their goals, and increasing their self-confidence, while at the same time showing them how to become team players and strengthen cooperation among associates. It also contains advice on balancing work and leisure and energizing one's life generally.

Learning and Development 4th ed.

Rosemary Harrison
London, United Kingdom: Chartered Institute of Personnel and Development (CIPD), 2005
416pp ISBN: 18439805509
This book offers a clear and detailed exposition of learning and development, equipping students and practitioners alike with the tools to perform at both an operational and a strategic level. It has been thoroughly revised to take into account the CIPD professional standard in learning and development.

Management Development Strategies for Action 4th ed.

Alan Mumford, Jeff Gold
London, United Kingdom: Chartered Institute of Personnel and Development (CIPD), 2004
272pp ISBN: 0852929846
This text discusses the purpose, benefits, and value of management development and provides an overview of practical issues in the field, covering strategic management development, theories and models of managerial learning, the assessment of development needs, the measurement of competence, and the evaluation of management development. The text also looks at management development for particular groups such as women managers and ethnic managers, and considers the supply of future managers and future

"The learning person looks forward to failure or mistakes. The worst problem in leadership is basically early success."

Warren Bennis

trends in management development. This edition, originally intended for practitioners, now incorporates resources designed for students at degree and masters level and includes chapter outlines, questions for discussion and reflection, group activities, and Weblinks.

MAGAZINES
British Journal of Management
ISSN: 1045–3172
Blackwell Publishing
350 Main Street, Malden, Massachusetts, 02148
T: +44 (0) 1865 791 100
F: +44 (0) 1865 791 347
www.blackwellpublishing.com/ journal.asp?ref=1045–3172
The *Journal* publishes articles from the full range of business and management disciplines, priding itself on combining scholarly merit with readability.

Business Horizons
ISSN: 0007–6813
Elsevier Science
Customer Service Department, 6277 Sea Harbor Drive, Orlando, Florida, 32887–4800
T: +1 877 839 7126 or +1 407 345 4020
F: +1 407 363 1354
www.elsevier.com
Of interest to both practicing managers and academics, *Business Horizons* covers a wide range of business and management subjects, often with a broad economic or social content. Issues relating to cultural values in the context of business are often featured. It aims to strike a balance between the practical and the theoretical, and presents material in readable and nontechnical language.

efmd Forum
European Foundation for Management Development (EFMD)
88 Rue de Gachard, Brussels, B-1050, Belgium
T: +32 2 629 08 10
F: +32 2 629 08 11
www.efmd.be
efmd Forum is the journal of the European Foundation for Management Development. Its focus is on senior-level management development processes, innovations, and techniques. Its contributors are from Europe's business schools and consulting organizations.

Harvard Business Review
ISSN: 0017–8012
Harvard Business School Press
60 Harvard Way, Boston, Massachusetts, 02163

T: +1 800 988 0886
F: +1 617 783 7555
www.hbr.org
HBR is a magazine for business leaders and senior executives which emphasizes current best practice and the application of leading edge research to business problems. Coverage is wide ranging with a strong focus on leadership, strategy, and all aspects of management development. Each issue includes feature articles written by experts and an interview with a business leader.

Human Resource Development Quarterly
ISSN: 1044–8004
Jossey-Bass
989 Market Street, San Francisco, California, 94103–1741
T: +1 415 433 1740
F: +1 415 433 0499
www.josseybass.com
Sponsored by the American Society for Training and Development and the Academy of Human Resource Development, this publication provides a focus for research on human resource development issues and fully recognizes their interdisciplinary nature. The emphasis is on the theory, research, and evaluation of HRD practices.

Journal of Management Development
ISSN: 0262–1711
Emerald
44 Brattle Street, 4th Floor, Cambridge, Massachusetts, 02138
T: +1 888 622 0075
F: +1 617 354 6875
www.emeraldinsight.com
The *Journal of Management Development* provides an international communications medium for all those working in management development, whether in industry, consulting, or academia. Its focus is on competence-based management development, developing leadership skills, developing women in management, global management, the new technology of management development, team building, organizational development and change, and performance appraisal.

Management Decision
ISSN: 0025–1747
Emerald
44 Brattle Street, 4th Floor, Cambridge, Massachusetts, 02138
T: +1 888 622 0075
F: +1 617 354 6875
www.emeraldinsight.com

Management Decision provides insights into current management practice from leading management thinkers and practitioners. The issues it covers include strategy and policy, management training and development, crisis management, problem solving, motivation, and entrepreneurship.

Organisations and People
ISSN: 1350–6269
Association for Management Education and Development
12 Station Road, St. Ives, Huntingdon, Cambridgeshire, PE27 5BH, U.K.
T: +44 (0) 1480 493 253
F: +44 (0) 1480 493 259
www.amed.org.uk
Organisations and People is the journal of the Association of Management Education and Development (AMED). Its target readership includes managers with responsibility for the development of organizations and individuals. It aims to form a link between academic advance and the practitioner whose results may be influenced by the success, or otherwise, of development activities. It combines intellectual rigor with readability, producing material which is also accessible to those do not specialize in development.

People Management
ISSN: 1358–6297
Personnel Publications Ltd.
17 Britton Street, London, EC1M 5TP, U.K.
T: +44 (0) 20 7880 6200
F: +44 (0) 20 7336 7637
www.peoplemanagement.co.uk
People Management is the official journal of the Chartered Institute of Personnel and Development. It reports on current issues in the personnel and human resources fields, including legislation and pay. Articles focus on a variety of subjects, for example industrial relations, training and development, and personnel techniques. Case studies and profiles of leading practitioners are also a regular feature.

ORGANIZATIONS
USA
American Management Association (AMA)
1601 Broadway, New York, 10019
T: +1 212 586 8100
F: +1 212 903 8168
www.amanet.org
One of the world's leading nonprofit membership-based educational organizations, the AMA offers a range of business education and management development programs for individuals and

BUSINESS INFORMATION SOURCES

enterprises in the Americas, Europe, and Asia. It identifies best management practices worldwide to provide assessment, design, development, self-development, and instruction services through a variety of print and electronic media and learning methodologies, including conferences and seminars, all designed to enhance the growth of individuals and organizations.

Europe
Chartered Management Institute (CMI)
Management House, Cottingham Road, Corby, Northamptonshire, NN17 1TT, U.K.
T: +44 (0) 1536 204 222
F: +44 (0) 1536 201 651
E: *enquiries@managers.org.uk*
www.managers.org.uk
Formed in 1992, the CMI is the largest organization for professional management

in the United Kingdom, representing almost 89,000 individual members and embracing 560 corporate partners. It exists to promote the art and science of management through research, publications, the provision of information services, networking opportunities, education and training, and the objective presentation of managers' views and opinions.

European Foundation for Management Development (EFMD)
Rue Gachard 88, B-1050, Brussels, Belgium
T: +32 2 62 90 810
F: +32 2 62 90 811
E: *info@efmd.be*
www.efmd.org
The European Foundation for Management Development (EFMD) has set itself a mission: to promote the development of

people and organizations through learning and leadership. It is Europe's forum for information, research, networking, and dialog on innovation and best practice in management development, and its network includes some 400 member organizations in over 40 countries.

"Helping someone personally is a better measure of success than picking a hot stock."

Grace Fey

Management Education: Executive Training

BOOKS

Developing Global Executives
Morgan McCall, George P. Hollenbeck
Boston, Massachusetts: Harvard Business School Press, 2002
272pp ISBN: 1578513367
This book makes the distinction between a domestic leader and a global executive, and focuses on the best career path to follow in order to become a global executive. Using insights from business leaders around the world, the authors outline the various decisions and career changes that can help lead to successfully managing a global career. The book also offers guidelines for anticipating potential challenges or pitfalls that may arise as a job progresses.

E-learning: Strategies for Delivering Knowledge in the Digital Age
Marc J. Rosenberg
Maidenhead, United Kingdom: McGraw-Hill, 2000
344pp ISBN: 0071362681
The most recent trend in management development has been to turn to e-learning options. This book provides a comprehensive look at what is available.

The Leadership Investment: How the World's Best Organizations Gain Strategic Advantage through Leadership Development
Robert M. Fulmer, Marshall Goldsmith
New York: AMACOM, 2000
334pp ISBN: 0814405584
The Leadership Investment highlights innovative practices in the area of management education. The practices of seven global corporations, including GE and Johnson & Johnson, are reviewed in detail. A chapter on university-based programs explains how institutions like Harvard are working to better meet the educational needs of business leaders. Another chapter is devoted to management development firms that offer specialized learning opportunities.

The Leadership Pipeline: How to Build the Leadership-powered Company
Ram Charan, Steve Drotter, Jim Noel
San Francisco, California: Jossey-Bass, 2000
224pp ISBN: 0787951722

The Leadership Pipeline presents six steps for moving from managing yourself to managing an enterprise and includes chapters on developing and troubleshooting a leadership pipeline. This book should help organizations avoid the "Peter Principle" by making sure managers are selected for promotion based on objective standards of readiness.

Linkage Inc.'s Best Practices in Leadership Development Handbook: Case Studies, Instruments, Training
David J. Giber, Louis Carter, Marshall Goldsmith, eds
San Francisco, California: Jossey-Bass, 2000
432pp ISBN: 0787952370
This handbook is a collection of the practices in management and leadership development of 15 large corporations. BP Amoco, Colgate Palmolive, and Motorola are among the companies who contributed to this book. It is a practical guide written by practitioners for practitioners.

MAGAZINES

Journal of Management Education
ISSN: 1052–5629
Sage Publications
1 Oliver's Yard, 55 City Road, London, EC1Y 1SP, U.K.
T: +44 (0) 20 7324 8500
F: +44 (0) 20 7324 8600
www.sagepub.co.uk
This bimonthly journal focuses on the methods and theories used in management and organizational behavior education in both classroom and corporate settings, and on how these can be improved.

Management Learning
ISSN: 1350–5076
Sage Publications
1 Oliver's Yard, 55 City Road, London, EC1Y 1SP, U.K.
T: +44 (0) 20 7324 8500
F: +44 (0) 20 7324 8600
www.sagepub.co.uk
This quarterly journal explores the fundamental issues, nature, processes, and outcomes of management and organizational learning across cultures by reviewing the results of research, theory, methods, and practice in the field.

INTERNET

The Association to Advance Collegiate Schools of Business
www.aacsb.edu
This site lists hundreds of accredited management education programs worldwide. Management education articles can be found in "eNewsline," which is listed under "Publications" on the home page.

Hobsons
www.hobsons.com
The site gives access to educational and vocational databases which cover first degrees, postgraduate education, MBAs, executive programs, international education, and distance learning.

Leader to Leader Institute
www.pfdf.org
Formerly the Peter F. Drucker Foundation, the Institute is committed to improving the way people work together in businesses, governments, and communities. Although not specifically a management education site, it contains a great deal of useful information.

Management Courses Information Site
www.managementcourses.com
A database of more than 2,000 executive education and development courses worldwide can be found on this site. The courses cover a wide range of subjects and are relevant to specific regions, business sectors, types of organization, and levels of manager. The site also includes advice on choosing a course or provider and a glossary of terms.

Training Pages
www.trainingpages.com
This site contains a database of U.K. training courses in business, management, and information technology.

ORGANIZATIONS
USA
American Management Association (AMA)
1601 Broadway, New York, 10019
T: +1 212 586 8100
F: +1 212 903 8168

1815

BUSINESS INFORMATION SOURCES

"For tired and harried executives, books are a balm for their worries." Stuart Crainer

E: *cust_serv@amanet.org*

www.amanet.org

One of the world's leading nonprofit membership-based educational organizations, the AMA offers a range of business education and management development programs for individuals and enterprises in the Americas, Europe, and Asia. It identifies best management practices worldwide to provide assessment, design, development, self-development, and instruction services through a variety of print and electronic media and learning methodologies, including conferences and seminars, all designed to enhance the growth of individuals and organizations.

American Society for Training and Development (ASTD)

1640 King Street, Box 1443, Alexandria, Virginia, 22313–2043

T: +1 800 628 2783 or +1 703 683 8100

F: +1 703 683 1523

E: *customercare@astd.org*

www.astd.org

An association of workplace learning and performance professionals, ASTD's members come from multinational corporations, medium-sized and small businesses, government, academia, consultancy firms, and product and service suppliers. It offers research and analysis, conferences, expositions, seminars, and publications. Though its primary focus is

training and development, it also addresses issues of performance appraisal.

Europe

Association of Management Education and Development (AMED)

12 Station Road, St Ives, Huntingdon, Cambridgeshire, PE29 5BH, U.K.

T: +44 (0) 1480 493253

F: +44 (0) 1480 493259

E: *office@amed.org.uk*

www.amed.org.uk

The Association is a member-based organization that provides a professional network for people involved in individual or organizational development and aims to promote innovation and good practice in the working environment.

Chartered Institute of Personnel and Development (CIPD)

151 The Broadway, Wimbledon, London, SW19 1JQ, U.K.

T: +44 (0) 20 8612 6200

F: +44 (0) 20 8012 6201

www.cipd.co.uk

Formed in 1995 from the amalgamation of the Institute of Personnel Management and the Institute of Training and Development, the CIPD is a professional body for personnel and training professionals that aims to promote good practice in the management and development of people— a company's core strength.

Chartered Management Institute (CMI)

Management House, Cottingham Road, Corby, Northamptonshire, NN17 1TT, U.K.

T: +44 (0) 1536 204 222

F: +44 (0) 1536 201 651

E: *enquiries@managers.org.uk*

www.managers.org.uk

Formed in 1992, the CMI is the largest organization for professional management in the United Kingdom, representing almost 89,000 individual members and embracing 560 corporate partners. It exists to promote the art and science of management through research, publications, the provision of information services, networking opportunities, education and training, and the objective presentation of managers' views and opinions.

FOR MORE INFORMATION

☆ Choosing the Best Training Curriculum for You (pp. 426–427)

🐁 Management Development (pp. 1812–1814)

🐁 Management Education: MBAs (pp. 1817–1818)

🐁 Training and Development (pp. 1922–1924)

✔ Training Needs Analysis (pp. 476–477)

1816

BUSINESS INFORMATION SOURCES

Management Education: MBAs

BOOKS

Bricker's International Directory 2006: University-based Executive Programs 37th ed.
Princeton, New Jersey: Peterson's, 2005
1664pp ISBN: 0768918928
Published annually, *Bricker's International Directory* contains information on over 900 university-based management development programs from around the world. The details it provides include the content and length of programs and the costs associated with them.

How to Get into the Top MBA Programs 3rd ed.
Richard Montauk
New York: Prentice Hall, 2005
672pp ISBN: 0735203903
A useful aid to anyone thinking of applying for an MBA program, this book takes readers through the process step by step. It begins within looking at the decision to apply in the first place before moving through to how to cope with the schedule once your application has been accepted. The book will help readers pick the right program for them, perform to their best in interviews and prepare well before the course begins.

The MBA Jungle B-School Survival Guide
Jon Housman
Cambridge, Massachusetts: Perseus Books Group, 2001
224pp ISBN: 0738205117
This title is a very useful guide for those hoping to become business student. It covers a wide variety of key issues, from selecting a business school to the types of questions asked at interviews, to advice on how to network successfully. A typical week in the life of an MBA student and other important areas are also covered in detail in the guide.

MBA Programs 2005 10th ed.
Princeton, New Jersey: Peterson's, 2004
1072pp ISBN: 0768913969
This is a guide to degree and MBA programs offered by Canadian, international, and United States business schools. A wealth of information, including details of the length and type of program, the admission criteria, and any financial assistance available, is included.

Official MBA Handbook 2005–2006 21st ed.
Michael Pilgrim, Association of MBAs
Upper Saddle River, New Jersey: Financial Times Prentice Hall, 2005
512pp ISBN: 027370608X
In addition to giving details of all major U.K. and international business schools, the *Official MBA Handbook* offers guidance on choosing the right business school, making an application and taking the GMAT, financing an MBA, and the impact an MBA may have on a career.

Which MBA? Making the Right Choice of Executive Education 16th ed.
George Bickerstaffe, ed.
Upper Saddle River, New Jersey: Financial Times Prentice Hall, 2005
528pp ISBN: 0273695363
This book gives details of full-time, part-time, and distance learning courses in the United Kingdom, the rest of Europe, North America, and the rest of the world. Further sections examine entry requirements, applications details, and how to finance an MBA.

MAGAZINES

European Executive Education Directory
ISSN: 1383–6218
European Management Development Centre
Naarderstraat 296, Huizen, 1272 NT, The Netherlands
T: +31 35 695 1111
F: +31 35 695 1900
www.emdcentre.com
Published annually since 1986, the *European Executive Education Directory* contains details of MBA and other management programs from the major business schools in Europe. The contents of the directory are also available to subscribers via the EMD Web site.

INTERNET

BSchool.com
www.bschool.com
This site aims to provide links to business school Web sites, and lists hundreds of schools in the United States and worldwide in alphabetical order. Links to news and articles on business education, and information on selecting and applying for courses are also available; these have a strong U.S. focus. A particular feature of this site is the Best B-Schools section which

contains a host of useful comparative tables and links.

MBA Program Information Site
www.mbainfo.com
A database of more than 2,700 programs worldwide can be found on this site, which can be searched by course structure, subject focus, location, duration, and start date. There is also a good advice section with information on selecting a school, making applications, and funding.

MBAZone
www.mbazone.com
This is a large site that aims to function as an online community for MBAs. Three separate sections cater for the needs of prospective MBAs, current students, and alumni. Advice is given on choosing a school and making applications, surviving as a student, and developing a career.

Online Business and Management Course Directory
www.abs.bized.ac.uk
This online directory of management and business qualifications is offered by members of the Association of Business Schools (ABS). The Directory was developed by Biz/ed in conjunction with the ABS and provides details of the institutions and courses available. The contents are limited to business schools in the United Kingdom.

ORGANIZATIONS

USA

Graduate Management Admission Council
1750 Tysons Boulevard, Suite 1100, McLean, Virginia, 22102
T: +1 703 749 0131
F: +1 703 749 0169
E: *gmacmail@gmac.com*
www.gmac.com
Graduate business and management schools make up the Council's membership. It produces the GMAT (Graduate Management Admission Test) which is used to assess candidates' suitability for MBA programs.

Europe

Association of Business Schools
137 Euston Road, London, NW1 2AA, U.K.

1817

BUSINESS INFORMATION SOURCES

"One useful starting point for all managers is to look at their time for thinking."

Peter Senge

T: +44 (0) 20 7388 0007
F: +44 (0) 20 7388 0009
E: *abs@the-abs.org.uk*
www.the-abs.org.uk
Formed in 1992 by the merger of the Council of University Management Schools and the Association for Management and Business Education, the ABS is the representative body of business schools in the United Kingdom. It has 102 members, all of whom are providers of business and management education at the tertiary level.

Association of MBAs (AMBA)

25 Hosier Lane, London, EC1A 9LQ, U.K.
T: +44 (0) 20 7246 2686
F: +44 (0) 20 7246 2687
www.mbaworld.com

The AMBA was formed in 1967 as the Business Graduates Association. It runs an accreditation scheme for MBA courses, besides offering a number of member benefits. Links to a number of useful organizations are available via its Web site. AMBA is the administrator of the U.K. MBA Loan Scheme in partnership with the Bank of Scotland and NatWest Bank.

European Foundation for Management Development (EFMD)

Rue Gachard 88, B-1050 Brussels, Belgium
T: +32 2 629 08 10
F: +32 2 629 08 11
E: *info@efmd.be*
www.efmd.be
The EFMD is a European network of organizations and individuals involved in management development, and has 390 members including business schools and executive development centers. It was founded in 1971 and promotes research, networking, and dialogue on innovation and best practice in management development. It was also responsible for developing EQUIS (European Quality Improvement System), an accreditation scheme for business schools.

FOR MORE INFORMATION

- Management Development (pp. 1812–1814)
- Training and Development (pp. 1922–1924)
- Viewpoint: Henry Mintzberg (pp. 292–293)

1818

BUSINESS INFORMATION SOURCES

"Managerial skill cannot be painted on the outside of executives—it has to go deeper than that."

Mary Parker Follett

Management Styles

BOOKS

Brainstyles: Change Your Life Without Changing Who You Are

Marlane Miller

New York: Simon & Schuster, 1997
384pp ISBN: 0684807572

This book offers a method of assessment which sorts people into four categories (deliberators, conceptors, knowers, and conciliators) and includes tips on dealing with each of the styles presented. Miller makes a strong case for people to focus on their strengths instead of working on their "non-strengths."

Douglas McGregor, Revisited: Managing the Human Side of the Enterprise

Gary Heil, Warren Bennis,
Deborah C. Stephens

Hoboken, New Jersey: Wiley, 2000
224pp ISBN: 0471314625

Paying tribute to the influence of Douglas McGregor, this book updates his thinking with new concepts, fresh strategies, and modern methods of implementation. It indicates how his original thinking has reemerged in current approaches that stress distributed leadership, open-minded appraisal techniques, and employee-customer commitment. Highlighted throughout with gems of wisdom in McGregor's own words, the book emphasizes the value of his theories for the managers of today.

Jack: Straight from the Gut

Jack Welch, John A. Byrne

New York: Warner Books, 2003
496pp ISBN: 0446690686

In this title, Welch discusses the method of management he adopted in order to turn General Electric into the hugely successful company that it has become. The book also contains a brief look at Welch's childhood and charts a career that started with him working in the plastics division of General Electric and ended with him becoming Chief Executive Officer.

Management in the USA

Peter Lawrence

London: Sage Publications, 1996
160pp ISBN: 0803978332

The author draws on interviews and observations from a range of organizations across the United States in order to identify and analyze the defining aspects of management styles, practice, and values in this country. There are a number of factors, he argues, that are central to understanding management in the United States. These include differentiated individualism, free speech, self-interest, and proactivity.

The New Imperialists

Mark Leibovich, Paul Saffo

Upper Saddle River, New Jersey: Prentice Hall, 2002
320pp ISBN: 0735203172

This title profiles five leaders of the digital age: Bill Gates of Microsoft, AOL-Time Warner's Steve Case, Amazon.com's Jeff Bezos, Oracle's Larry Ellison, and John Chambers at Cisco. Using hundreds of interviews with friends, family, and rivals, the book charts the most significant events in these revolutionary figures' lives and reveals how they dealt with such experiences.

Primal Leadership: Realizing the Power of Emotional Intelligence

Daniel Goleman, Richard Boyatzis,
Annie McKee

Boston, Massachusetts: Harvard Business School Press, 2004
336pp ISBN: 1591391849

The authors describe six styles that account for all critical management behavior: visionary, coaching, affiliative, democratic, pace-setting, and commanding. Good leaders use different styles according to the situation. They explain that the importance of these styles is that the right style used with the right team will generate "good feelings" and that style is a critical factor, not only in managing and leading but also in generating organizational profits. The book is based on studies of nearly 4,000 executives.

The Way We Work: What You Know About Working Styles Can Increase Your Efficiency, Productivity, and Job Satisfaction

Cynthia Ulrich Tobias

Nashville, Tennessee: Broadman & Holman Publishers, 1999
157pp ISBN: 0805418334

This book provides insight into the different learning and work styles that people bring to their workplaces, and suggests commonsense ways of responding to those differences. The author provides information and an assessment to understand your preferred learning style and a discussion of the different types of intelligence each style offers.

Where Egos Dare: The Untold Truth about Narcissistic Leaders—and How to Survive Them

Dean B. McFarlin, Paul D. Sweeney

London: Kogan Page, 2002
272pp ISBN: 0749437731

This book explores the seamier side of leadership. Much has been written about the dynamic, focused leader, but what about the obsessive and egocentric leader? The authors investigate the psyche of such leaders and the devastating effect it can have on both individual and organizational performance. They also suggest proactive measures that can be taken to curb the excesses of a narcissistic leader.

INTERNET

The Consortium for Research on Emotional Intelligence in Organizations
www.eiconsortium.org

This site has a comprehensive listing of topics related to the field of emotional intelligence. It provides downloadable reports on academic research and programs in organizations where emotional intelligence is the focus of training. It is also a useful source of information on instruments for measuring emotional intelligence.

Institute for Management Excellence
www.itstime.com

This site has many areas of information relating to management practices. It offers a number of articles on personality styles and management, an online personality test, and a monthly newsletter on various people-management topics.

1819

FOR MORE INFORMATION

- Entrepreneurs (pp. 1745–1747)
- Leadership (p. 1108)
- Leadership (pp. 1798–1803)
- Leading from the Middle (pp. 452–453)
- Management Development (pp. 1812–1814)

BUSINESS INFORMATION SOURCES

"A major reason for the superiority of the Japanese is their managerial skill." Richard Pascale

Management Theorists

BOOKS

The Best Business Books Ever
Cambridge, Massachusetts: Perseus Books Group, 2003
256pp ISBN: 0738208493
Contained in this volume are incisive, time-saving digests of more than 100 of the finest and most influential books on business and management.

The Essential Drucker: The Best of Sixty Years of Peter Drucker's Essential Writings on Management
Peter F. Drucker
New York: HarperCollins, 2003
368pp ISBN: 006093574X
When it comes to American management theorists, Peter Drucker tops almost everyone's list. This book is a compilation of Drucker's most important writings over the course of his lengthy and still very active career. Each article has been chosen by virtue of its contemporary relevance or its historical significance.

The Guru Guide: The Best Ideas of the Top Management Thinkers
Joseph H. Boyett, Jimmie T. Boyett
Hoboken, New Jersey: Wiley, 2000
400pp ISBN: 0471380547
The key ideas of 79 of the world's leading management experts are examined here. Presenting the gurus' works in seven subject-oriented chapters, the authors cross-link their ideas and provide critical commentaries and case study examples of the ideas in practice.

Leader to Leader: Enduring Insights on Leadership from the Drucker Foundation's Award-winning Journal
Frances Hesselbein, Paul M. Cohen, eds
San Francisco, California: Jossey-Bass, 1999
400pp ISBN: 0787947261
This collection of articles, taken from the journal *Leader to Leader*, brings together the wisdom of world renowned leaders, bestselling writers, leading thinkers, and

business philosophers. These include Peter Drucker, Herb Kelleher, John P. Kotter, Rosabeth Moss Kanter, Peter Senge, and Charles Handy.

Management Gurus: What Makes Them and How to Become One
Andrzej A. Huczynski
Boston, Massachusetts: International Thomson Business Press, 1996
352pp ISBN: 1861520212
Placing management guruship in its historical context, the author identifies the essential ingredients of the few popular management ideas of the 20th century. He argues that winning guru ideas meet enduring managerial needs, are launched at the most opportune time, and are promoted by the zeal of their developers.

Management of Organizational Behavior: Leading Human Resources 8th ed.
Paul Hersey, Kenneth H. Blanchard, Dewey E. Johnson
Upper Saddle River, New Jersey: Prentice Hall, 2000
550pp ISBN: 0130175986
This book is primarily concerned with what many consider the soft side of management: dealing with people. The book provides a good overview of contemporary management theorists before tying their theories into Hersey and Blanchard's "situational leadership" theory. Overall, this is a lengthy but valuable book for anyone wishing to learn more about leading theories on management.

Ruthless Leader: Three Classics of Strategy and Power
Alistair McAlpine, ed.
Hoboken, New Jersey: Wiley, 2000
272pp ISBN: 0471372471
The texts of three classic works on leadership make up this compilation: *The Prince* by Nicolò Machiavelli, *The Servant* by Alistair McAlpine, and *The Art of War* by

Sun Tzu. The introduction places these texts in their contemporary contexts, and compares and contrasts them, drawing out their major themes and demonstrating their application to modern business organizations.

The Ultimate Business Guru Book: 50 Thinkers Who Made Management 2nd ed.
Stuart Crainer, Des Dearlove
Chichester: Capstone, 2002
320pp ISBN: 1841120758
Crainer discusses the ideas of 50 leading management thinkers in detail and lists their key publications. He also provides brief summaries of the work of other thinkers.

INTERNET
Business.com
www.business.com/directory/ management/management_theory/ management_theorists
This Web site offers a comprehensive list of modern management theorists in the form of links to articles by and about those theorists. With over 65 primary links and several articles in every secondary link, the coverage is extensive.

Thinkers50
www.thinkers50.com
This management guru Web site was set up by guru-spotters Stuart Crainer and Des Dearlove in 2001. The Thinkers 50 tends to appear every two years, and visitors to the page are able to vote for their favorite guru and give their reasons. The results of the most recent poll appear on the site, with concise biographies of the relevant management thinker.

FOR MORE INFORMATION

Management Styles (p. 1819)

"Businessmen will have to learn to build and manage innovative organizations."
Peter F. Drucker

     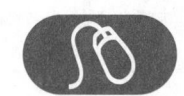

Manufacturing Systems

BOOKS

America's Best: IndustryWeek's Guide to World-class Manufacturing Plants

Theodore B. Kinni
Hoboken, New Jersey: Wiley, 1996
429pp ISBN: 0471160024
A reference of award-winning plants including Hewlett-Packard, Sony Electronics, and Xerox, *America's Best* looks at manufacturing practices, offering guidelines to help managers make strategic decisions within their own organizations. The book details nine manufacturing components, and describes how they interact with each other. It includes profiles of each of the 62 Best Plant winners and reports by editors from *IndustryWeek*, which list techniques and tools being used at the plants and contact information for them. It also includes a set of the winners' statistical measurements for use in benchmarking and a plant assessment survey.

Finite Capacity Scheduling: Management, Selection, and Implementation

Gerhard Plenert, Bill Kirchmier
New York: Wiley, 2000
304pp (Oliver Wight Manufacturing)
ISBN: 0471352640
The authors provide a comprehensive guide to finite capacity scheduling (FCS), focusing on understanding, implementing, and making the most of FCS and powerful, modern systems.

High Performance Manufacturing: Global Perspectives

Roger G. Schroeder, Barbara B. Flynn, eds
New York: Wiley, 2001
320pp (Wiley Operations Management Series for Professionals)
ISBN: 0471388149
This book is the result of extensive research undertaken in 164 factories in the United States, Japan, Germany, Italy, and the United Kingdom. It identifies and describes a range of specific high-performance manufacturing practices and compares manufacturing in each of these five countries.

Lean Thinking 2nd ed.

James P. Womack, Daniel T. Jones
New York: Simon & Schuster, 2003
384pp ISBN: 0743249275
Lean Thinking explores the idea that companies can improve their overall performance through Toyota's "lean production" approach. The book is aimed at corporate leaders and shows how managers can specify value to improve performance. It provides an action plan based on a broad range of industries worldwide (this includes Porsche and Toyota).

The Machine That Changed the World

James P. Womack, Daniel T. Jones, Daniel Roos
New York: Harper Perennial, 1991
336pp ISBN: 0060974176
The authors present the findings of a five-year research project undertaken by the Massachusetts Institute of Technology to look at Japanese manufacturing techniques in the motor vehicle industry and the lessons that can be learned from them. The text includes the rise and fall of mass production; the rise of lean production; running the factory; designing the car; coordinating the supply chain; dealing with customers; and managing the lean enterprise.

Manufacturing Planning and Control Systems for Supply Chain Management 5th ed.

Thomas E. Vollmann, William L. Berry, D. Clay Whybark, F. Robert Jacobs
Maidenhead, United Kingdom: McGraw-Hill, 2004
608pp ISBN: 007144033X
This book describes in detail the key functions and processes of the manufacturing planning and control system.

Manufacturing Strategy: Text and Cases 3rd ed.

Terry Hill
New York: McGraw-Hill, 1999
600pp ISBN: 0256230722
This text is written for both students and practitioners; it demonstrates how decisions relating to manufacturing should form part of the strategic direction of a company as a whole. Individual chapters focus on the principles and concepts of developing a manufacturing strategy, process choice, product profiling, making or buying and the supply chain, and manufacturing infrastructure development. Twenty-two case studies are included.

Next Generation Manufacturing: Methods and Techniques

James A. Jordan, Frederick J. Michel
New York: Wiley, 2000
464pp ISBN: 0471360066
During the 1990s a three-year research program—the Next Generation Manufacturing Project—sought to present a vision of the future of manufacturing and to put together a framework for action. This book reviews its reported recommendations. It describes how manufacturing is continuing to evolve and what significant changes companies must make to remain competitive. It also emphasizes the importance of understanding the roles played by innovation, knowledge, and people.

The Technology Machine

Patricia E. Moody, Richard E. Morley
New York: Free Press, 1999
256pp ISBN: 0684837099
Details drivers of growth and discusses why these should be fully taken on in industry. Offers a guide to the growth of an organization by introducing software that may change the face of manufacturing.

World Class Manufacturing: The Lessons of Simplicity Applied

Richard J. Schonberger
New York: Free Press, 1986
252pp ISBN: 0029292700
The author describes how the use of techniques such as just-in-time and total quality control has enabled almost 100 successful American corporations to achieve world class manufacturing standards. He uses them as examples to illustrate the theory, concepts, and implementation of world class manufacturing. Furthermore, he shows how the steps taken by these top companies can be implemented in any factory and in all industries so as to bring any operation up to world class status.

MAGAZINES
Control

ISSN: 0266-1713
Institute of Operations Management (IOM)
The University of Warwick, Science Park, Sir William Lyons Road, Coventry, Warwickshire, CV4 7EZ, U.K.
T: +44 (0) 2476 692 266
F: +44 (0) 2476 692 305

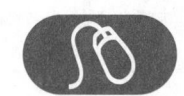
1821

BUSINESS INFORMATION SOURCES

"The modern corporation must manufacture not only goods but the desire for the goods it manufactures."

J. K. Galbraith

www.iomnet.org.uk

Control, the journal of the Institute of Operations Management, provides news of its current events and activities, and contains feature articles on a range of subjects related to production. A full archive can be found online.

International Journal of Manufacturing Technology and Management

ISSN: 1368–2148

Inderscience Enterprises Ltd.

World Trade Center Building, 29 route de Pre-Bois, Case Postale 896, CH-1215, Geneva, 15, Switzerland

T: +44 (0) 1234 240515

F: +41 22 791 08 85

www.inderscience.com

The *IJMTM* publishes original empirical and review papers, case studies, and various reports on a broad range of issues related to manufacturing processes and techniques. Published eight times a year, it has a wide target audience among academics, researchers, and consultants and managers in manufacturing and related industries.

International Journal of Operations and Production Management

ISSN: 0144–3577

Emerald

44 Brattle Street, 4th Floor, Cambridge, Massachusetts, 02138

T: +1 888 622 0075

F: +1 617 354 6875

www.emeraldinsight.com

This monthly journal is targeted at everyone in the operations and production field, whether in academic institutions, industry, or consulting. The articles tend to have a substantial managerial, as opposed to technical, content.

Journal of Manufacturing Technology Management.

ISSN: 0957–6061

Emerald

44 Brattle Street, 4th Floor, Cambridge, Massachusetts, 02138

T: +1 888 622 0075

F: +1 617 354 6875

www.emeraldinsight.com

This journal aims to provide international coverage of subjects relating to the management of manufacturing technology and the integration of the production, design, supply, and marketing functions of manufacturing businesses. It is published eight times a year and is also available online. The journal was previously called *Integrated Manufacturing Systems*.

Manufacturing Business Technology

ISSN: 1533–7758

Reed Business Information

This journal, published 12 times per year, is dedicated to innovative information technologies, focusing on enterprise management and data collection, and is vital for staying abreast of the latest trends in manufacturing systems. It was previously called *MSI*.

INTERNET
Best Manufacturing Practices
www.bmpcoe.org

The BMP Program is a unique cooperative effort between industry and government in technology transfer that aims to improve the global competitiveness of the U.S. industrial base. The primary objective toward this goal is simple: to identify and validate best practices, to document them, and to encourage industry, government, and academia to share information about them. This site gives details of current news, seminars and conferences, and best practice surveys, and also contains a glossary and links to related sites.

Intelligent Manufacturing Systems
www.ims.org

IMS is an industry-led, international research and development program, established to develop the next generation of manufacturing and processing technologies. Companies and research institutions from Australia, Canada, the European Union, Norway, Switzerland, Japan, Korea, and the United States participate in it, and other regions are being encouraged to join. This site reports on current events, activities, and progress.

ORGANIZATIONS
USA
Association of Manufacturing Excellence (AME)

3115 No. Wilke Road, Suite G, Arlington Heights, Illinois, 60004

T: +1 224 232 5980

F: +1 224 232 5981

E: *info@ame.org*

www.ame.org

The 6,000 plus members of AME are manufacturing executives, united in their pursuit of excellence in manufacturing. AME members strive to develop a deeper understanding of productivity methods.

Institute of Industrial Engineers

3577 Parkway Lane, Suite 200, Norcross, Georgia, 30092–2988

T: +1 770 449 0460

F: +1 770 441 3295

E: *cs@iienet.org*

www.iienet.org

IIE was founded in 1948 and is the only international, nonprofit, professional society dedicated to advancing the technical and managerial excellence of industrial engineers. It sees industrial engineering as being concerned with the design, improvement, and installation of integrated systems.

Manufacturers Alliance (MAPI Inc.)

1600 Wilson Blvd., Suite 1100, Arlington, Virginia, 22209

T: +1 703 841 9000

F: +1 703 841 9514

E: *info@mapi.net*

www.mapi.net

This organization is composed of executives in manufacturing and related business service companies. MAPI conducts research on all management and economic issues that affect U.S. industry. They are advocates for legislative policies that will advance technological and economic progress.

National Association of Manufacturers (NAM)

1331 Pennsylvania Avenue, NW Washington, D.C., 20004

T: +1 202 637 3000

F: +1 202 637 3182

E: *manufacturing@nam.org*

www.nam.org

Founded in 1895, NAM has over 14,000 members. The association maintains a public affairs and public relations program. NAM members are also involved in proposing current legislation and offering advice on legal matters affecting the manufacturing industry.

Europe
Institute of Operations Management (IOM)

The University of Warwick, Science Park, Sir William Lyons Road, Coventry, Warwickshire, CV4 7EZ, U.K.

T: +44 (0) 2476 692 266

F: +44 (0) 2476 692 305

E: *iom@iomnet.org.uk*

www.iomnet.org.uk

The IOM is a professional body for individuals involved in manufacturing and service industries. It was founded in 1963 as the British Production and Inventory Control Society, and changed to its present name in 1996. It offers its members a range of services, including a qualifications

program and a variety of training courses and development seminars.

International
Manufacturing Society of Australia
P.O. Box 19, Parkville, Victoria, 3052, Australia
T: +61 3 9328 3664
F: +61 3 0326 7272

E: *mansa@immanet.asn.au*
www.mansa.ieust.org.au
The Manufacturing Society of Australia (ManSA) is the national focus on manufacturing for the Institution of Engineers, Australia, and aims to provide authoritative leadership and foster excellence in Australian manufacturing practice.

"Any engineer that doesn't need to wash his hands at least three times a day is a failure."

Shoichiro Toyoda

Market Research and Competitor Intelligence

BOOKS

Competitive Intelligence: How to Gather, Analyze, and Use Information to Move Your Business to the Top

Larry Kahaner
Carmichael, California: Touchstone Books, 1998
300pp (Pocket Books)
ISBN: 0684844044
Kahaner presents examples to show corporations how they can create their own competitive intelligence units, and fully understand the collected data so that it can be used to their advantage.

Competitor Intelligence: Turning Analysis into Success

David Hussey, Per Jenster
Hoboken, New Jersey: Wiley, 1999
296pp (Wiley Series in Practical Strategy)
ISBN: 0471984078
This book, written for managers, aims to give practical advice on how to identify and analyze intelligence relating to competitors for the purpose of gaining a competitive advantage. The authors also discuss, again in practical terms, the critical success factors involved in planning, in understanding competitors, and in sourcing information. Case studies are included.

How Customers Think: Essential Insights into the Mind of the Market

Jerry Zaltman
Boston, Massachusetts: Harvard Business School Press, 2003
352pp ISBN: 1578518261
This book offers a unique perspective on tapping into what it is exactly that your customers want. Using as a base key themes from psychology, sociology, and other sciences, it sets out to help marketers ask the right questions (and work out the right answers) so that the innovation and production cycle benefits.

Managing Frontiers in Competitive Intelligence

Craig S. Fleisher, David Blenkhorn
Westport, Connecticut: Quorum Books, 2000
328pp ISBN: 1567203841
This book is a nice balance of the theoretical and the practical aspects of Competitive Intelligence (CI). While describing the best

practices in the industry, the authors present the steps necessary to counter CI. They provide information on how to improve your intelligence collection process, methods, and tools. Significantly, they tie CI back to the needs of the business and point out its interface with finance, research and development, and product development.

Marketing Research 8th ed.

David A. Aaker, V. Kumar, George S. Day
Hoboken, New Jersey: Wiley, 2003
800pp ISBN: 047123057X
The authors adopt a "macro-micro-macro" approach toward marketing research and its uses within organizations. They initially explore the uses and place of marketing research in managerial decision making, as well as the industry itself (briefly examining both suppliers and users) at macro level. They also examine the processes of marketing research in more depth, including industry examples to fulfill the micro phase of the text, and provide coverage of the most recent research techniques.

Marketing Research: An Integrated Approach

Alan Wilson
Upper Saddle River, New Jersey: Financial Times Prentice Hall, 2002
488pp ISBN: 0273651137
This book looks at market research within the context of marketing as a whole, and argues that it is a process that should not be split off from all other related activity. Full of useful references, cases studies, and summaries, the book is partciularlly useful for students but may also serve as a primer for managers new to this area.

Marketing Research Essentials 6th ed.

Carl McDaniel, Roger Gates
Hoboken, New Jersey: Wiley, 2004
704pp ISBN: 0471455199
This comprehensive manual surveys the whole process of modern market research. It deals with the role of market research in management decision making, sources of data and primary data collection techniques, sampling and statistical analysis, and how to communicate results

through effective reports. It backs up its account with many worked examples, illustrations, and case studies.

Marketing Research for Managers 3rd ed.

Sunny Crouch, Matt Housden
Woburn, Massachusetts: Butterworth-Heinemann, 2003
352pp ISBN: 0750654538
This is one of the leading U.K. texts for managers seeking to understand market research. Rather than proffering over-detailed explanations of how to undertake research, this book explains enough for managers to be able to commission worthwhile research from professionals.

Market Research Matters: Tools and Techniques for Aligning Your Business

Robert Duboff, Jim Spaeth
New York: Wiley, 2000
320pp ISBN: 0471360058
The authors explain the value of market research and forecasting techniques to successful business strategies. They describe the tools and techniques that enable analysts to anticipate marketplace shifts and the methods of using them. Among other topics, they discuss customer loyalty, brand management, competition, distribution channels, employee performance and loyalty, and the Internet. Diagnostic material to allow readers to assess the progress of their business in each area is also included.

The Market Research Toolbox: A Concise Guide for Beginners 2nd ed.

Edward F. McQuarrie
London: Sage Publications, 2005
224pp ISBN: 1412913195
Aimed at giving a basic understanding of market research tools, this book looks at market research in the context of making a business decision. Beginning with an explanation of market research, the author goes on to describe how each of the six traditional market research techniques works, along with its costs and uses, and tips for success. Also examined are the nontraditional methods that have evolved in recent years.

"Market research can be not just misleading, but disastrous for people who work on instinct."

Terence Conran

Proven Strategies in Competitive Intelligence: Lessons from the Trenches
John E. Prescott, Stephen H. Miller, eds
Hoboken, New Jersey: Wiley, 2001
288pp ISBN: 0471401781
The editors have assembled a collection of articles that identify and explore proven practicable approaches to competitive intelligence that can be applied across a variety of business areas. Once the concept of competitive intelligence has been introduced and its legal and ethical boundaries have been explored, further contributions from leading executives and market leaders highlight the best techniques that can be used to outwit and outperform current, emerging, and potential competitors.

MAGAZINES
Competitive Intelligence Review
ISSN: 1058–0247
Wiley
111 River St, Hoboken, New Jersey, 07030–5774
T: +1 201 748 6000
F: +1 212 850 6021
www.wiley.com
The *Review* is the journal of the competitive intelligence (CI) profession and covers all aspects of the field, with its main emphasis on practical applications. Its target readership includes CI practitioners, managers, vendors, government organizations, and academics.

Journal of Marketing Research
ISSN: 0022–2437
American Marketing Association
311 S. Wacker Drive, Suite 5800, Chicago, Illinois, 60606–5819
T: +1 312 542 9000
F: +1 312 542 9001
www.marketingpower.com
JMR is a quarterly publication aimed at academics and practitioners in the marketing profession, providing cutting-edge information on research techniques, methods, and applications.

Marketing Research
ISSN: 1040–8460
American Marketing Association
311 S. Wacker Drive, Suite 5800, Chicago, Illinois, 60606–5819
T: +1 312 542 9000
F: +1 312 542 9001
www.marketingpower.com
This quarterly magazine aims to help companies build a strategy for success. Articles are written by practitioners and have a practical bias. Issues covered are

legislation and regulation, demographic and social change, research methods, and management tools.

Marketing Surveys Index
ISSN: 0964–0142
Midnight Crocquet Ltd
Units A5 and A6, Dunkeswell Airport, Honiton, Devon, EX14 4LE, U.K.
T: +44 (0) 1404 891 528
F: +44 (0) 1404 891 717
www.worldmarketresearch.com
Now managed by Midnight Crocquet, the *MSI* contains details of published market research from more than 1,000 organizations around the world.

Market Research Europe
ISSN: 0308–3446
Euromonitor
60–61 Britton Street, London, EC1M 5UX, U.K.
T: +44 (0) 20 7251 8024
F: +44 (0) 20 7608 3149
www.euromonitor.com
Each issue of this monthly journal contains five or six market reports providing in-depth analysis of consumer markets in European countries. Coverage includes key trends, market background, key players, market share, and company profiles.

Market Research International
ISSN: 1352–1101
Euromonitor
60–61 Britton Street, London, EC1M 5UX, U.K.
T: +44 (0) 20 7251 8024
F: +44 (0) 20 7608 3149
www.euromonitor.com
Each issue of this monthly journal contains five or six market reports providing in-depth analysis of international consumer markets. Coverage includes key trends, market background, key players, market share, and company profiles.

INTERNET
ECNext
www.ecnext.com
This is a site offering online access to a database of business and market intelligence from global publishers.

Esomar Glossary
www.esomar.org
This section of the useful Esomar site contains a glossary of market research terms. It seeks to explain frequently-used marketing research terms in language that someone new to the industry can easily understand.

Euromonitor International
www.euromonitor.com
In-depth strategic analysis and up-to-date market statistics and market reports are all available to purchase online from this site.

Forrester
www.forrester.com
Forrester is a leading independent research firm that conducts technology research for its clients. Its expertise is in analyzing the research results and synthesizing the critical information. Some free information is available to nonclients on its site.

Key Note Market Information Centre
www.keynote.co.uk
This site is run by suppliers of market research reports, which are available for purchase, and provides free executive summaries.

Market Research.com
www.marketresearch.com
Collecting reports from all over the world, marketresearch.com is one of the largest sources of published research on the Web. Reports can be bought and managed with a personal account, and the site has other features, such as an e-mail update service.

@ResearchInfo.com
www.researchinfo.com
This site is a remarkable collection of information on the market research industry. It includes the Market Research Roundtable, a directory of research companies, software reviews, and market research calculators.

ORGANIZATIONS
USA
American Marketing Association
311 S. Wacker Drive, Suite 5800, Chicago, Illinois, 60606–5819
T: +1 312 542 9000
F: +1 312 542 9001
E: *info@ama.org*
www.marketingpower.com
The American Marketing Association (AMA) has over 40,000 members worldwide, with nearly 400 chapters throughout the United States and Canada. It is an international professional organization for people involved in the practice, study, and teaching of marketing. As well as setting standards of best practice in the industry, the AMA seeks to help marketers by providing them with products, services, information, education, and resources. It has a large, informative Web site and publishes a wide range of journals.

1825

BUSINESS INFORMATION SOURCES

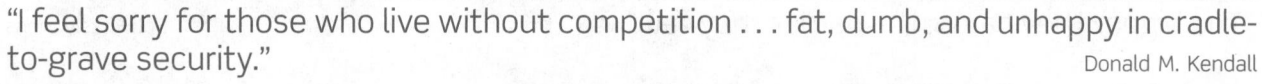
"I feel sorry for those who live without competition . . . fat, dumb, and unhappy in cradle-to-grave security."
Donald M. Kendall

Council for Marketing and Opinion Research

4147U Crossgate Drive, Cincinnati, Ohio, 45236

T: +1 513 985 0001

F: +1 513 985 0119

E: *info@cmor.org*

www.cmor.org

CMOR is a nonprofit trade association formed to protect the interests of the marketing and opinion research industry. Its members are research companies and their clients.

Marketing Research Association (MRA)

1344 Silas Deane Highway, Suite 306, P.O. Box 230, Rocky Hill, Connecticut, 06067–0230

T: +1 860 257 4008

F: +1 860 257 3990

E: *email@mra-net.org*

www.mra-net.org

Founded in 1954, MRA is dedicated to promoting excellence in opinion and marketing research. It provides training and development opportunities for members, and acts as an advocate with government bodies and the public. Its activities include two annual national conferences and the publication of an official monthly newsletter and a directory of research services.

The Society of Competitive Intelligence Professionals

1700 Diagonal Road, Suite 600, Alexandria, Virginia, 22314

T: +1 703 739 0696

F: +1 703 739 2524

E: *info@scip.org*

www.scip.org

The Society is dedicated to helping professionals develop expertise in creating, collecting, and analyzing information, in disseminating competitive intelligence, and in engaging decision makers in a productive dialogue that creates organizational competitive advantage.

Europe
Association of European Market Research Institutes

26 Granard Avenue, London, SW15 6HJ, U.K.

T: +44 (0) 20 8780 3343

F: +44 (0) 20 7246 6893

E: *info@aemri.org*

www.aemri.org

The Association is a representative organization for market research institutes in Europe and other parts of the world.

British Market Research Association

Devonshire House, 60 Goswell Road, London, EC1M 7AD, U.K.

T: +44 (0) 20 7566 3636

F: +44 (0) 20 7689 6220

E: *admin@bmra.org.uk*

www.bmra.org.uk

The BMRA aims to represent and promote the professional and commercial interests of its members, to increase the professionalism of market research, and to promote confidence in the market research industry generally.

Market Research Society

15 Northburgh Street, London, EC1V 0JR, U.K.

T: +44 (0) 20 7490 4911

F: +44 (0) 20 7490 0608

E: *info@mrs.org.uk*

www.mrs.org.uk

MRS sets and enforces the ethical standards to be observed by research practitioners. Its framework of qualifications and membership grades reflects the education, knowledge, and competence required for the effective conduct of market research.

International
EFAMRO

Hoek van Hollandlaan 13, 2554 EA Den Haag, The Netherlands, U.K.

T: +44 (0) 20 7224 3873

www.efamro.org

EFAMRO is a federation of market research agency associations in the European Union, founded in 1992. Its aims are to represent the interests of its members and to maintain high standards in the industry. Members adhere to the ICC/ESOMAR International Code of Marketing and Social Research Practice.

FOR MORE INFORMATION

☆ Competitor Analysis: From Data to Insight (pp. 328–329)

☆ Viewpoint: Philip Kotler (pp. 61–62)

 1826

BUSINESS INFORMATION SOURCES

"The bigger they came, the harder they fall." — Bob Fitzsimmons

Marketing Management

BOOKS

The 22 Immutable Laws of Marketing: Violate Them at Your Own Risk!
Al Ries, Jack Trout
New York: HarperCollins, 1994
160pp ISBN: 0887306667
Designed by marketing strategists for marketing strategists, this perennially popular illustrated book contains 22 practical rules aimed at promoting readers' success in global marketing of products and services.

101 Ways to Market Your Business
Andrew Griffiths
Crow's Nest, New South Wales: Allen & Unwin, 2001
272pp ISBN: 1865083860
Packed full of practical yet simple marketing ideas for business owners, this book will be a huge help to anyone thinking of setting up or running a small business. With suggestions of ways to attract new customers—and keep them—and how to develop a strong corporate image, the book also features quick marketing strategies that take less than 30 minutes. The author steers clear of theory and concentrates instead on easy-to-follow advice that should reap rewards.

The Anatomy of Buzz: How to Create Word-of-mouth Marketing
Emanuel Rosen
New York: HarperCollins, 2002
320pp ISBN: 0385496680
Rosen discusses the benefits of "word-of-mouth" marketing, and explores the capacity of large companies to exploit this strategy.

Auditing Markets, Products and Marketing Plans
David Parmerlee
Lincolnwood, Illinois: McGraw-Hill Trade, 2000
240pp ISBN: 0658001337
A source of information and ideas for anyone who is building an effective marketing campaign or interested in improving existing marketing activities. This book provides you with the tools you need for every critical task—checklists, document templates, forms, and tables—to enable you to complete those tasks quickly and effectively. Perfect for beginning marketers, small business owners, and entrepreneurs.

Crossing the Chasm: Marketing and Selling High-tech Products to Mainstream Customers 2nd ed.
Geoffrey A. Moore
New York: HarperCollins, 2002
256pp ISBN: 0060517123
This practical approach to modern marketing techniques, with emphasis on the special realities of today's marketplace, aims to advise the reader with a wide range of insights and strategic guidelines for marketing technology products.

Customer Experience Management: A Revolutionary Approach to Connecting With Your Customers
Bernd H. Schmitt
Hoboken, New Jersey: Wiley, 2003
256pp ISBN: 0471237744
This marketing guide introduces a straightforward five-step process for managing your customer's experience. Case studies of successful customer experience management (CEM) implementations in a variety of industries are provided. Topics covered include: an overview of the CEM framework; analyzing the experiential world of the customer; building the experiential platform; designing the brand experience; structuring the customer interface; engaging in continuous innovation; delivering a seamlessly integrated customer experience; organizing for CEM.

The End of Marketing As We Know It
Sergio Zyman
New York: HarperCollins, 2000
272pp ISBN: 0887309836
In this title, the author argues that for marketing to be truly efficient, it must sell the product and not merely focus on advertising image. The book contains several stories concerning campaigns at Coca-Cola, where Zyman was chief marketing officer.

Getting Business to Come to You 2nd ed.
Paul Edwards, Sarah Edwards, Laura Clampitt Douglas
New York: J.P. Tarcher, 1998
688pp ISBN: 087477845X
A popular book aimed at helping businesses expand their customer base. Although written from a U.S. perspective, the tips and examples offered work well wherever your business is located.

Gonzo Marketing: Winning through Worst Practices
Christopher Locke
Cambridge, Massachusetts: Perseus Books Group, 2002
256pp ISBN: 0738207691
This book is a knuckle-whitening ride to the place where social criticism, biting satire, and serious commerce meet . . . and where the outdated ideals of mass marketing and broadcast media are being left in the dust. As master of ceremonies at the wake for traditional one-size-fits-all marketing, Locke has assembled a unique guest list, from Geoffrey Chaucer to Hunter S. Thompson, to guide us through the revolution that is rocking business today, as people connect on the Web to form powerful micromarkets. These networked communities, based on candor, trust, passion, and a general disdain for anything that smacks of corporate smugness, reflect much deeper trends in our culture, which Locke illuminates with his characteristic wit.

Guerrilla Marketing with Technology: Unleashing the Full Potential of Your Small Business
Jay Conrad Levinson
Cambridge, Massachusetts: Perseus Books Group, 1997
224pp ISBN: 0201328046
A good introduction to the "guerrilla" concept for SMEs, this book takes a simple question-and-answer approach to implementing innovative and exciting ideas.

Gurus on Marketing
Sultan Kermally
London: Thorogood, 2003
160pp ISBN: 1845182439
A book on marketing gurus which describes their key ideas and explains their meaning and application. As an "insider" who has worked with many of the people covered, the author is able to compare and comment on the key concepts with considerable knowledge. People covered include Theodore Levitt, Philip Kotler, Jagdish Sheth and Thomas Nagle. The ideas of other gurus not always related directly to marketing, such as Michael Porter and Peter Drucker, are analyzed from a marketing perspective.

1827

BUSINESS INFORMATION SOURCES

"A product is anything that can be offered to a market for attention, acquisition, use, or consumption."

Philip Kotler

Handbook of Marketing

Barton A. Weitz, Robin Wensley, eds
Thousand Oaks, California: Sage Publications, 2002
592pp ISBN: 0761956824
This handbook brings together contributions from leading scholars and academics in the field of marketing to provide an overview of research on marketing management issues, both looking back at the history of the discipline and analyzing prospects for the future. A wide range of marketing activities is covered including strategy, branding, product development, channel management, pricing, communication, sales promotion and the allocation of resources. Specialist areas such as global marketing, service marketing, and marketing and the Internet are also considered in the text.

The Highly Effective Marketing Plan

Peter Knight
Englewood Cliffs, New Jersey: Prentice Hall, 2004
176pp ISBN: 0273687867
In this practical guide the author describes the 15 steps to producing a HEMP (highly effective marketing plan). He helps managers to understand their business and what makes people buy from it, to learn from the successes of others, and to identify the real obstacles to their plan and how to overcome them.

Inside the Tornado 2nd ed.

Geoffrey A. Moore
New York: HarperCollins, 2004
272pp (HarperBusiness Essentials)
ISBN: 0060745819
This book addresses the ever-changing face of market-focused business, aiming to highlight the importance of adapting to keep up with competitors. Moore uses examples from inside the industry to discuss a range of managerial strategies, and how they can be usefully applied in today's marketing world.

International Retail Marketing: A Case Study Approach

Margaret Bruce, Christopher M. Moore, Grete Birtwistle, eds
New York: Butterworth-Heinemann, 2004
256pp ISBN: 0750657480
A broad thematic overview of the key issues concerning international retail marketing is provided, with a series of case studies giving examples of industry practice from various organizations and sectors including fashion, food, banking, and healthcare.

Introduction to Marketing: Theory and Practice

Adrian Palmer
New York: Oxford University Press, 2004
656pp ISBN: 0199266271
In a book offering both critical analysis of theory and applied case studies, the author provides a concise overview of the principles of marketing, understanding the customer, and developing the marketing mix.

Kotler on Marketing: How to Create, Win, and Dominate Markets

Philip Kotler
New York: Free Press, 1999
272pp ISBN: 0684850338
Kotler discusses his ideas on how marketing programs should be approached by executives. The book is divided into several sections addressing strategy, tactics, administrative issues, and transformational marketing. The latter is a term that the author uses to describe the effect of new technology, such as the Internet and cable TV, on marketing practice.

The Market-driven Organization

George S. Day
New York: Free Press, 1999
304pp ISBN: 0684864673
This is a straightforward approach to marketing, directed at managers who want to improve performance within their organizations. It discusses the importance of understanding customers and advises on dealing with the competition.

The Market-driven Strategy

George S. Day
New York: Free Press, 1999
432pp ISBN: 068486536X
In this practical guide, Day aims to widen his readers' understanding of the term "market-driven." The plan follows five major steps covering major strategic issues.

Marketing and Selling Professional Services: Practical Approaches to Practice Development 3rd ed.

Patrick Forsyth
London: Kogan Page, 2003
320pp ISBN: 0749440902
With the aim of helping professionals of all kinds to develop successful strategies for marketing what are essentially intangible services, the author starts by explaining the importance and role of marketing in professional service businesses, and goes on to explore a range of practical issues,

including marketing planning, promotional mix, advertising, and postal promotion. A second section deals with professional personal selling, and covers persuasive writing and communication, and systematic client development.

Marketing Communications: A European Perspective 2nd ed.

Patrick De Pelsmacker, Maggie Geuens, Joeri Van den Bergh
Upper Saddle River, New Jersey: Financial Times Prentice Hall, 2004
592pp ISBN: 0273685007
This comprehensive textbook, for both students and marketing communication professionals, covers the key aspects of marketing communications including objectives, planning and budgets, target groups, and branding. The main instruments of advertising and public relations, sales promotion, direct marketing and personal selling, sponsorships, point-of-purchase, exhibitions and trade fairs, and business-to-business and international communications are introduced. The use of the Internet for e-communications is also considered.

Marketing Genius

Peter Fisk
New York: Wiley, 2006
498pp ISBN: 1841126810
Billed as "the little black book of marketing," this book aims to help readers tap into the massive potential of marketing so that their businesses stand out from the crowd. Full of examples of real-life excellence from companies such as Alessi, Innocent, and Google, it is full of inspiration for marketers who know that the consumer is in the driving seat.

Marketing Management 12th ed.

Philip Kotler, Kevin Lane Keller
Upper Saddle River, New Jersey: Prentice Hall, 2005
816pp ISBN: 0131457578
In their exploration of the latest developments in worldwide marketing, the authors approach strategic market planning from a new angle and highlight the need for effective teamwork in a marketing environment. They discuss the practices of modern marketing strategies and examine a range of topics from consumer markets to competitors. The book aims to widen managerial knowledge and understanding of marketing issues, while preparing managers for the future of the marketplace.

"Every company should work hard to obsolete its own product line before its competitors do."

Philip Kotler

Marketing Plans: How to Prepare Them, How to Use Them 5th ed.

Malcolm McDonald

New York: Butterworth-Heinemann, 2002
640pp ISBN: 0750656255

The fifth edition of this work has been thoroughly revised and updated, with particular reference to developments in e-marketing, CRM (customer relationship management), and new integrated marketing and planning practices. Exercises and case studies are also included.

Marketing Plans That Work 2nd ed.

Malcolm H. B. McDonald, Warren J. Keegan

Woburn, Massachusetts: Butterworth-Heinemann, 2001
264pp ISBN: 0750673079

With discussions of new product development, market extension and diversification strategies and a step-by-step planning system, this book offers a comprehensive guide to preparing a strategic marketing program.

Marketing Strategies: A Twenty-first Century Approach

Ashok Ranchhod

Upper Saddle River, New Jersey: Financial Times Prentice Hall, 2004
240pp ISBN: 0273651927

The changing nature of marketing is examined in this text from the perspective of issues and norms that characterize the 21st century. From a predominantly European perspective, this book addresses cultural issues through case studies and explores marketing from a range of angles. The role of branding and philosophy of marketing is dealt with, and sustainability, ethics, market orientation, technology, and globalization are also covered.

Marketing Strategy and Competitive Positioning 3rd ed.

Graham J. Hooley, John A. Saunders, Nigel F. Piercy

Upper Saddle River, New Jersey: Financial Times Prentice Hall, 2004
624pp ISBN: 0273655167

This updated edition deals with the process of developing and implementing a marketing strategy. It focuses on competitive positioning at the centre of marketing strategy and explores the processes used in marketing to achieve competitive advantage. The main sections of the book deal with marketing strategy, competitive market analysis, identifying current and future competitive positions,

and competitive positioning strategies. Case studies and discussion questions are also included.

Marketing Warfare Revised ed.

Al Ries, Jack Trout

Maidenhead, United Kingdom: McGraw-Hill, 2005
224pp ISBN: 0071460829

In a "military" approach to the world of marketing, Ries and Trout aim to teach marketers tough strategies, both defensive and offensive, to deal with the competition.

Mastering Marketing Management

Roger Cartwright

New York: Palgrave, 2002
336pp ISBN: 0333948971

This practical guide to the role of marketing in modern organizations, produced in association with St. Anthony's College, Oxford, focuses particularly on the product or service itself and the value placed upon it by the customer. Prices and costs, promotion and communication, and distribution and delivery are also covered, and examples from a variety of sectors are included.

Meeting of the Minds: Creating the Market-based Enterprise

Vincent P. Barabba

Boston, Massachusetts: Harvard Business School Press, 1995
272pp ISBN: 0875845770

Barabba expounds his theory that working with customer-oriented information is a more effective method of achieving organizational success than simply restructuring within a corporation. The author offers practical guidelines for creating market-based mechanisms leading to competitive advantage, and demonstrates how this can be achieved through combining a focused market and customer-based approach.

The New Marketing: Transforming the Corporate Future

Malcolm McDonald, Hugh Wilson

New York: Butterworth-Heinemann, 2002
240pp ISBN: 0750653876

This work addresses the changes brought about by technological development and the digital information revolution, and describes how these changes may be incorporated effectively into marketing practice. The text also focuses on the concept of a value exchange between suppliers and customers, and describes how today's consumer revolution also is having a major impact on services and marketing.

Permission Marketing: Turning Strangers into Friends, and Friends into Customers

Seth Godin, Don Peppers

New York: Free Press, 2002
256pp ISBN: 0743221427

In this title, the authors claim that traditional forms of advertising such as magazines and radio are no longer sufficient in themselves. They assert that what is most important is to find a way of luring the customer into giving some of their time, and then creating a lasting relationship with them. The book backs up this theory of permission marketing by discussing the techniques of some of the companies who use it.

Positioning: The Battle for Your Mind 2nd ed.

Al Ries, Jack Trout

Maidenhead, United Kingdom: McGraw-Hill, 2001
224pp ISBN: 0071373586

This book discusses the notion that a market strategist can achieve better results in business by "positioning" his or her company in the marketplace. Ries and Trout explore the ways in which this goal can be achieved, and offer cautionary advice about the hazards of advertising.

Precision Marketing: The New Rules for Attracting, Retaining, and Leveraging Profitable Customers

Jeff Zabin, Gresh Brebach

Hoboken, New Jersey: Wiley, 2004
256pp ISBN: 0471467618

Within the context of an increasing need for marketers to show a return on marketing investment, the authors propose that precision marketing tools and techniques can increase the effectiveness of marketing. The topics covered include the precision marketing cycle, exploiting the data with new technology-enabled processes, using outsourcing to improve effectiveness, and using modeling and scoring techniques to predict future customer requirements and to create messages more likely to encourage favorable responses.

Principles and Practice of Marketing 4th ed.

David Jobber

New York: McGraw-Hill, 2004
944pp ISBN: 007710708X

This student textbook looks at marketing concepts and principles supported by examples of international practice. The various sections of the book cover the

1829

BUSINESS INFORMATION SOURCES

fundamentals of modern marketing thought, marketing mix decisions, competition and marketing, and the implementation and application of marketing.

Rand McNally 2005 Commercial Atlas and Marketing Guide 136th ed.

Chicago, Illinois: Rand McNally & Co., 2005
ISBN: 0528934651
Containing population, economic, and geographic data for more than 124,000 U.S. places, and large-scale maps that are detailed and thoroughly indexed for easy cross-referencing, this "big book" should be the first point of reference for up-to-date business planning data. The many raw data listings include: 2000 census information and Year 2007 projections; latest estimations on population for the U.S. states, counties, cities, MSAs, and trading areas; information on income, buying power, and sales; and corporate economic profiles.

Real Time: Preparing for the Age of the Never Satisfied Customer

Regis McKenna
Boston, Massachusetts: Harvard Business School Press, 1999
224pp ISBN: 0875847943
McKenna addresses the issue of what customers expect from the modern world. In order to fulfill customer expectations, he argues, companies must be prepared to adapt to the increasingly rapid modes of global communication (e-mail, fax, etc.). McKenna aims to clarify the abstract notion of collecting and using "real time," with the view that this can lead to greater organizational success and consumer satisfaction.

Relationship Marketing: Successful Strategies for the Age of the Customer

Regis McKenna
Cambridge, Massachusetts: Perseus, 1993
242pp ISBN: 0201622408
This book offers advice to organizations on how to dominate and control the market through the construction of significant relationships with customers.

Selling the Invisible

Harry Beckwith
New York: Warner Books, 1997
252pp ISBN: 0446520942
Selling the Invisible is aimed at marketers who work to promote a service ("the invisible") rather than a tangible product. The book contains a large range of practical suggestions and ideas, addressing some

new developments in marketing, and discussing how an organization can use them to best effect.

Successful Direct Marketing Methods 7th ed.

Bob Stone, Ron Jacobs
Maidenhead, United Kingdom: McGraw-Hill, 2001
608pp ISBN: 0658001450
This updated edition provides a classic guide to direct marketing, combining new media with traditional marketing strategies to provide effective direct marketing to consumers. The content includes identifying and meeting consumers' needs, business-to-business marketing, and e-commerce techniques such as powerful branding strategies for Internet sites. An eight edition is planned for 2007.

The Tipping Point: How Little Things Can Make a Big Difference

Malcolm Gladwell
Boston, Massachusetts: Back Bay Books, 2002
304pp ISBN: 0316346624
Although no standard marketing textbook, this extremely popular title may help many a marketer understand more about how and why some products or services take off while others languish in the doldrums. Tying together multiple strands of social history, business, and psychology, it offers an engaging insight into mass behavior.

Total Access

Regis McKenna
Boston, Massachusetts: Harvard Business School Press, 2002
240pp ISBN: 1578512441
In *Total Access* McKenna suggests that traditional marketing is being overtaken by advances in technology. He argues that modern marketers have a double role to play, fully understanding and anticipating new technology and also managing it. The book aims to characterize success in today's market climate.

MAGAZINES
Advertising Age

ISSN: 0001–8899
Crain Communications, Inc.
711 Third Avenue, New York, 10017–4036
T: +1 212 210 0100
F: +1 212 210 0200
www.adage.com
This is the flagship magazine of the Ad Age Group. Widely regarded as the authoritative source for articles on national and international marketing, *Advertising Age* is

a premier journal for news, in-depth information, and current trends in marketing.

AdWeek

ISSN: 0199–2864
VNU Business Publications
770 Broadway, New York, 10003–9595
T: +1 646 654 4500
F: +1 646 654 4480
www.vnubusinessmedia.com
Accompanied by regional Web sites, this magazine provides specialized information for industry professionals. It includes feature articles, trend analysis, and news about industry events. The publishing company is responsible for *AdWeek*, *BrandWeek*, and *MediaWeek*, all of which cover aspects of advertising and are aimed at advertising executives. As a result, the information is often a little arcane for the layperson, but invaluable for those familiar enough with methods, layout, and advertising jargon to decipher the text.

American Demographics

ISSN: 0163–4089
Crain Communications, Inc.
711 Third Avenue, New York, 10017–4036
T: +1 212 210 0100
F: +1 212 210 0200
www.adage.com/section.cms?sectionId=195
Formerly called *Marketing Tools*, this monthly magazine is aimed at marketing executives who want credible and timely information regarding the latest consumer trends. It is dedicated to demographical studies in the United States, and each issue offers in-depth analysis of the latest current events and how these influence the consuming public. This magazine is filled with the latest techniques for advertising and marketing research.

Brandweek

ISSN: 1064–4318
VNU Business Publications
770 Broadway, New York, 10003–9595
T: +1 646 654 4500
F: +1 646 654 4480
www.vnubusinessmedia.com
Brandweek is a weekly magazine for brand-marketing executives, offering feature articles, trend analysis, and news about industry events.

Direct Marketing

ISSN: 0012–3188
Hoke Communications, Inc.
224 7th Street, Garden City, New York, 11530

"The meek shall inherit the earth, but they'll never increase market share." William McGowan

T: +1 516 746 6700 or 800 229 6700
F: +1 516 294 8141

http://hoke.micronpcweb.com

Published 12 times per year, this magazine focuses on sales and marketing techniques. Features include the best methods of direct response advertising. The magazine is a helpful resource for any advertising executive wanting to increase their marketing reach.

The Hub Magazine

David X. Manners Company, Inc.
107 Post Road East, Westport, Connecticut, 06880
T: +1 203 227 7060
F: +1 203 227 7067

www.hubmagazine.com

The Hub features roundtable discussions between industry thought-leaders on marketing challenges and issues. Each issue is hosted by a sponsor.

Logistics Management & Distribution Report

ISSN: 1098–7355
Cahners Business Information
275 Washington Street, Newton, Massachusetts, 02458
T: +1 617 558 4473
F: +1 617 558 4480

www.cahners.com

Published 12 times per year, this magazine features articles on production and operations management, industry, and manufacturing. This magazine also tracks the latest information regarding national legislation changes.

Marketing Management

ISSN: 1061–3846
American Marketing Association
311 S. Wacker Drive, Suite 5800, Chicago, Illinois, 60606–5819
T: +1 312 542 9000
F: +1 312 542 9001

www.marketingpower.com

This journal, published every other month by the American Marketing Association, was developed with the purpose of providing middle- to senior-level marketing executives with thought provoking discussions on emerging issues in the marketing profession. It provides in-depth coverage of many aspects of the profession, including national and international strategies.

Marketing News

ISSN: 0025–3790
American Marketing Association
311 S. Wacker Drive, Suite 5800, Chicago, Illinois, 60606–5819

T: +1 312 542 9000
F: +1 312 542 9001

www.marketingpower.com

This is a biweekly journal, one of many magazines published by the American Marketing Association. It covers the latest trends in marketing strategies, communications and technology, as well as giving examples of how the industry's best practices have been implemented, and insights into career and management issues. It follows the regulatory and legislative developments that marketers need to know, delves into how technology affects the practice of marketing, and covers global marketing trends and issues. *Marketing News* also publishes special directories: *Focus Group Facilities and Moderators, Marketing Research Services, Consultants and Consulting Services, International Research Firms, Interactive Marketing Services, Multicultural Marketing Agencies, Customer Satisfaction Firms,* and *Direct Marketing Services.*

Point of Purchase: The Journal of Marketing Communications at Retail

ISSN: 1085–5009
VNU Business Publications
770 Broadway, New York, 10003–9595
T: +1 646 654 4500
F: +1 646 654 4480

www.vnubusinessmedia.com

Point of Purchase covers retail marketing from the point of view of brand marketers and retailers, presenting feature stories, industry news, case studies, and guest opinions.

Quirk's Marketing Research Review

Quirk's Marketing Research Review
8030 Cedar Avenue South, Suite 229, Minneapolis, Minnesota, 55425
T: +1 952 854 5101
F: +1 952 854 8191

www.quirks.com

Published 11 times per year, the magazine provides case histories, techniques, trend analysis, industry news, and product and service updates for the marketing research industry.

Sales and Marketing Management

ISSN: 0163–7517
VNU Business Publications
770 Broadway, New York, 10003–9595
T: +1 646 654 4500
F: +1 646 654 4480

www.vnubusinessmedia.com

This monthly magazine features articles, profiles, and interviews written for top executives who have direct responsibility

for all aspects of sales, marketing, and management. Featured topics include case studies and marketing strategies from the world's most successful companies.

INTERNET
American Marketing Association
www.marketingpower.com

The American Marketing Association (AMA) is an international professional organization for people involved in the practice, study, and teaching of marketing. As well as setting industry standards, the AMA seeks to help marketers by providing them with information, products, and services, many of which are available online, including a career center, best practice articles, a marketer's toolkit, and newsletter. Registration is free.

Guerrilla Marketing
www.gmarketing.com

This is the online home of the very successful "Guerrilla Marketing" series of books. Users can subscribe to a free weekly newsletter offering marketing tips.

MarketingProfs.com
www.marketingprofs.com

This Web site is aimed at marketing professionals and professors. It is a membership site, but a good deal of the information is free. Members must pay for premium content material, but registering is hassle-free. There are a variety of articles on competition that can be accessed through the site's search engine.

ORGANIZATIONS
USA
American Advertising Federation (AAF)

1101 Vermont Avenue NW, Suite 500, Washington D.C., 20005–6306
T: +1 202 898 0089
F: +1 202 898 0159
E: *aaf@aaf.org*

www.aaf.org

AAF is a network of advertisers, ad agencies, media companies, local advertising clubs, and college chapters. Membership benefits include a membership directory, networking opportunities, updates on relevant legislation, professional development, and recruitment services.

American Marketing Association

311 S. Wacker Drive, Suite 5800, Chicago, Illinois, 60606–5819
T: +1 312 542 9000
F: +1 312 542 9001
E: *info@ama.org*

1831

BUSINESS INFORMATION SOURCES

www.marketingpower.com

The American Marketing Association (AMA) has over 38,000 members worldwide, with chapters throughout the United States and Canada. It is an international professional organization for people involved in the practice, study, and teaching of marketing. As well as setting standards of best practice in the industry, the AMA seeks to help marketers by providing them with products, services, information, education, and resources. It has a large, informative Web site and publishes a wide range of journals.

Association of National Advertisers

708 Third Avenue, New York, 10017–4270
T: +1 212 697 5950
F: +1 212 661 8057
E: *info@ana.net*
www.ana.net
ANA is a trade association dedicated to marketing and brand-building. It offers its members conferences, regional meetings, training seminars, benchmarking studies, industry analysis, research services, and publications.

Direct Marketing Association

1120 Avenue of the Americas, New York, 10036–6700
T: +1 212 768 7277
F: +1 212 302 6714
E: *customerservice@the-dma.org*
www.the-dma.org
The DMA is a trade association for users and suppliers in the fields of direct, database, and interactive marketing. Founded in 1917, it now has over 5,000 members. Membership services include events, professional development, representation to government and in public affairs, and a library.

Marketing Research Association (MRA)

110 National Drive, 2nd Floor, Glastonbury, Connecticut, 06033
T: +1 860 682 1000
F: +1 860 682 1000
E: *email@mra-net.org*
www.mra-net.org
MRA is a membership organization for the marketing research industry; its members

include data collectors, full service research companies, users of research, and related service providers. Membership benefits include educational programs, training, networking opportunities, publications, and conferences.

Marketing Science Institute

1000 Massachusetts Avenue, Cambridge, Massachusetts, 02138–5396
T: +1 617 491 2060
F: +1 617 491 2065
E: *msi@msi.org*
www.msi.org
MSI is a nonprofit institute, established in 1961 as a bridge between business and academia. Its mission is to support and circulate studies by academic scholars that address research issues specified by member companies. MSI functions as a working sponsorship, and brings executives and leading international researchers together.

Society of Competitive Intelligence Professionals

1700 Diagonal Road, Suite 600, Alexandria, Virginia, 22314
T: +1 703 739 0696
F: +1 703 739 2524
E: *info@scip.org*
www.scip.org
SCIP is a nonprofit membership organization for professionals in the competitive intelligence industry. In addition to advocating ethical standards for the industry, SCIP provides seminars, networking opportunities, and publications.

Europe

Chartered Institute of Marketing (CIM)

Moor Hall, Cookham, Maidenhead, Berkshire, SL6 9QH, U.K.
T: +44 (0) 1628 427 500
F: +44 (0) 1628 427 499
E: *marketing@cim.co.uk*
www.cim.co.uk
The CIM is the main organization for professional marketers in the United Kingdom. It runs courses, holds examinations, produces publications, and offers information services covering all aspects of marketing.

Direct Marketing Association (DMA) (U.K.)

DMA House, 70 Margaret Street, London, W1W 8SS, U.K.
T: +44 (0) 20 7291 3300
F: +44 (0) 20 7323 4426
E: *info@dma.org.uk*
www.dma.org.uk
Founded in 1992, the DMA (U.K.) is Europe's largest trade association in this sector. Committed to the promotion of best practice and the raising of industry standards, it aims to raise the stature of the direct marketing industry and to give the consumer trust in direct marketing.

International

International Advertising Association (IAA)

521 Fifth Avenue, Suite 1807, New York, 10175
T: +1 212 557 1133
F: +1 212 983 0455
E: *iaa@iaaglobal.org*
www.iaaglobal.org
The IAA is a strategic partnership between advertisers, media companies, agencies, direct marketing firms, and individual practitioners, formed to advocate responsible marketing and free choice for advertisers and marketers. In addition to acting as a legislative advocate for commercial free speech, the IAA sponsors conferences and offers networking opportunities.

"Music is spiritual. The music business is not."   Van Morrison

     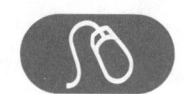

Meetings

BOOKS

101 Ways to Make Meetings Active: Surefire Ideas to Engage Your Group

Mel Silberman
San Francisco, California: Jossey-Bass, 1999
336pp ISBN: 0787946079
This book provides 101 tools, tips, and techniques for successful meetings. The topics that the author covers include preparing for meetings, obtaining group participation, stimulating discussion, the roles and responsibilities of chairpersons and other officers, timesavers, managing conflict, problem-solving, using flip charts, and closing the meeting. All are illustrated with a number of practical examples.

First Aid for Meetings: Quick Fixes and Major Repairs for Running Effective Meetings

Charlie Hawkins
Newberg, Oregon: Bookpartners, Inc., 1997
190pp ISBN: 1885221614
This book provides concrete ideas for running effective meetings, including planning, managing the flow of the meeting, moving groups to consensus and closure, and dealing with disruptive behavior. The author also discusses how to manage meetings in which electronic media are being used and how to apply meeting management concepts to one-on-one meetings.

How to Make Meetings Work!

Michael Doyle
New York: Berkeley Publishing Group, 1993
320pp ISBN: 0425138704
This is a pragmatic approach to troubleshooting the problems of interaction in meetings. Doyle offers a range of techniques aimed at both management and staff, and advises on ways to make company meetings clear and productive.

Meeting Management

Taggart Smith
Upper Saddle River, New Jersey: Prentice Hall, 2001
166pp (NetEffect)

ISBN: 0130173916
Offering a practical framework for managing meetings, this book demonstrates how to lead them effectively and make them as time-efficient as possible. It outlines three types of meetings: information-giving, interactive, and problem solving, and covers areas such as structuring a topic and organizing the message, audiences, visuals, disruptions, and asking and answering questions.

Meetings That Work: A Practical Guide to Shorter and More Productive Meetings

Richard Y. Chang, Kevin R. Kehoe
San Francisco, California: Jossey-Bass, 1994
112pp ISBN: 0787950793
With a wealth of practical examples, this guidebook offers proven methods of running more productive meetings which can be applied immediately on the job. It covers preparation, the meeting itself, and evaluating the meeting, and includes many checklists and worksheets.

Robert's Rules of Order 10th ed.

Henry M. Robert III et al.
Cambridge, Massachusetts: Perseus Books Group, 2000
704pp ISBN: 0738203076
This is the classic guide to conducting well-ordered, structured, and productive meetings.

MAGAZINES

The Facilitator

The Bagheri Group
P.O. Box 670705, Dallas, Texas, 75367–0705
T: +1 972 243 1356
F: +1 972 243 1357
www.thefacilitator.com
The Facilitator provides meeting facilitators with tips, case studies, and discussion items on running effective meetings. Techniques for managing meetings are explained in detail.

INTERNET

The Facilitator.Com

www.thefacilitator.com

This site provides meeting management tips, a quarterly newsletter, information on chat groups and conferences, and links.

Meetings.net

www.meetingsnet.com
This site is a resource for those needing to find information on planning meetings and events. It has links to their separate magazines specifically for the association, corporate, insurance/financial, religious, and medical areas.

Midwest Facilitators' Network

www.midwest-facilitators.net
This site for professional facilitators operating in the Midwest of the United States provides information on workshops, conferences, and facilitators. There is also a selection of archived presentations.

ORGANIZATIONS

International

ESOMAR (World Association of Research Professionals)

John Kelly, President
Vondelstraat 172, Amsterdam, 1054 GV, The Netherlands
T: +31 20 664 2141
F: +31 20 664 2922
E: *email@esomar.nl*
www.esomar.nl
ESOMAR was founded in 1948 as the European Society for Opinion and Marketing Research and now has over 4,000 members in 100 countries. The organization promotes the use of opinion and marketing research in business and society through seminars and conferences, professional publications, and training and education, and represents its membership on international bodies.

FOR MORE INFORMATION

☆ Boardroom Roles (pp. 296–297)
⟋⟍ Interpersonal Communication/ Relations (pp. 1787–1788)

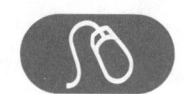
1833

BUSINESS INFORMATION SOURCES

"Don't try to manage from any board of directors—or any other kind of meeting."

Robert Heller

Mission Statements

BOOKS

Make Your Mission Statement Work: How to Identify and Promote the Values of Your Organisation 2nd ed.

Marianne Talbot
Oxford, United Kingdom: How To Books, 2003
176pp ISBN: 1857038207

This book explains the importance of clarifying an organization's purpose and identifying its values as a foundation for the development of a mission statement. It offers a step-by-step guide to writing a mission statement, which emphasizes the importance of consulting and involving everyone in the organization. Advice on monitoring progress, evaluating success, and rewarding achievement is also provided, and examples of value statements are given in an appendix.

The Mission Primer: Four Steps to an Effective Mission Statement

Richard O'Hallaron, David O'Hallaron
Richmond, Virginia: Mission Incorporated, 2000
144pp ISBN: 0967663504

In this primer the authors present a clear and simple guide to writing a mission statement tailored to the reader's organization or department. They lead the reader through a series of steps that will help those involved to develop a collective vision by uncovering their assumptions about and conflicting perceptions of the organization, forcing them to resolve those differences.

The Mission Statement Book: 301 Corporate Mission Statements from America's Top Companies 2nd ed.

Jeffrey Abrahams
Berkeley, California: Ten Speed Press, 1999
512pp ISBN: 1580081320

This book provides an extensive selection of mission statements from America's top companies, ranging from Ben & Jerry's to Federal Express to General Motors. It gives detailed information on how mission statements are used and on how to write one that incorporates your organization's vision and values. It also offers an index that allows you to compare one company's statement with another's.

Say It and Live It: The 50 Corporate Mission Statements That Hit the Mark

Patricia Jones, Larry Kahaner
New York: Currency/Doubleday, 1995
272pp ISBN: 0385476302

This volume presents mission statements from diverse organizations such as Avis, Ben & Jerry's, IBM, and Southwest Airlines, in each case adding a commentary to give life to the statement. The authors begin the book with an exploration of commonalities in the statements and close it with tips on how to prepare your own mission statement.

Success in Sight: Visioning

Andrew P. Kakabadse, Frederic Nortier, Nello-Bernard Abramovici
Boston, Massachusetts: International Thomson Business Press, 1998
224pp (Smart Strategies)
ISBN: 186152160X

The authors explore the concept of visioning as a crucial strategic tool and show how effective visioning can map the way ahead for the success of an organization. They discuss the history of leadership and the nature of visionary leadership, as well as providing practical guidance on promoting a shared perspective and generating a corporate vision. Global case studies are included.

INTERNET

U.S. Charter Schools
www.uscharterschools.org

This section of a Web site devoted to the development of mission statements for charter schools provides information that could easily be applied by other organizations.

FOR MORE INFORMATION

✔ Producing a Corporate Mission (pp. 526–527)

BUSINESS INFORMATION SOURCES

"To be mission-based means that those in positions of authority are not the source of authority."

Peter Senge

Motivation

BOOKS

1001 Ways to Energize Employees

Bob Nelson

New York: Workman Publishing, 1997

224pp ISBN: 0761101608

This book follows *1001 Ways to Reward Employees*, Nelson's previous title in the series. Aimed at managers, the book suggests strategies for inspiring and motivating staff. Nelson's research includes case studies as well as feedback from large corporations to help illustrate his suggestions.

Becoming an Employee of Choice: Make Your Organisation a Place Where People Want to Do Great Work

Judith Leary-Joyce

London, United Kingdom: Chartered Institute of Personnel and Development (CIPD), 2004

224pp ISBN: 1843980576

The author identifies the lessons to be learned from the results of the *Sunday Times 100 Best Companies to Work For* awards and explains how organizations can create a working environment that attracts employees and inspires them to give of their best. The benefits of a company culture in which staff feel valued and respected and in which they can flourish are described in terms of recruitment, retention, high levels of creativity and innovation, and improved customer service. Slides designed for a company presentation that provide evidence of the business case for becoming an employer of choice are included.

The Daily Drucker: 366 Days of Insight and Motivation for Getting the Right Things Done

Peter F. Drucker

New York: HarperCollins, 2004

448pp ISBN: 0060742445

This book distils many of Peter Drucker's key thoughts into an unusual calendar style format that managers can draw on for inspiration in everyday life. Each thought is linked to an action point. The subjects covered include enterepreneurship, decision making, innovation, and management.

Fish! A Remarkable Way to Boost Morale and Improve Results

Stephen C. Lundin, Harry Paul, John Christensen

London: Hyperion, 2000

112pp ISBN: 0786866020

Written as a parable, this book charts the progress of a fictional manager as he aims to turn his unmotivated team into a productive one. The authors present examples from "Seattle's Pike Place Fish," a "world famous market," to demonstrate the positive effects of a happy, energized workplace.

Gung Ho! Turn On the People in Any Organization

Ken Blanchard, Sheldon Bowles

New York: William Morrow, 1997

256pp ISBN: 068815428X

Using his experience of large corporations (such as General Motors and Microsoft), Blanchard suggests a strategy by which employers can boost motivation among their employees in order to inspire greater productivity at work. The author discusses the three core elements of this strategy, and discusses how they can be put into practice.

Harvard Business Review on Motivating People

Boston, Massachusetts: Harvard Business School Press, 2003

224pp (Harvard Business Review Paperbacks) ISBN: 1591391326

A collection of "evergreen" HBR articles featuring both new and classic writings on leadership, performance measurement, compensation and other aspects of motivation. The articles included are: "Beyond empowerment—building a company of citizens," by Brook Manville and Josiah Ober; "How to motivate your problem people," by Nigel Nicholson; "One more time—how do you motivate employees," by Frederick Hertzberg; "Management by whose objectives," by Harry Levinson; "Power of the great motivator," by David McClelland and David H. Burnham; "The best-laid incentive plans," by Steve Kerr; "Moving mountains," by Bronwyn Fryer; and "Pygmalion is management," by J. Sterling Livingston.

How to Build a Great Team

Ros Jay

Englewood Cliffs, New Jersey: Prentice Hall, 2002

146pp ISBN: 0273663232

A practical guide designed to help managers select the right people for the right roles, and build a winning team. Issues considered include team roles, motivation, dealing with problem people and difficult situations, and handling team meetings.

How to Run Successful Incentive Schemes: A Manager's Guide 3rd ed.

John G. Fisher

London: Kogan Page, 2005

192pp ISBN: 0749443960

The revised edition of this book offers practical advice for any manager wishing to construct a motivational scheme or formulate best practice in the use of incentives for performance improvement. Topics covered include: profit potential; human audit; constructing a program; building the budget; cash or non-cash schemes; flexible benefits; incentive travel; measure, monitor, mirror; recognition systems.

Intrinsic Motivation at Work: Building Energy and Commitment 2nd ed.

Kenneth W. Thomas

San Francisco, California: Berrett-Koehler, 2002

160pp ISBN: 1576752380

Intrinsic Motivation at Work presents a new model for motivating the worker in the new economy. The knowledge worker looks for intrinsically motivating factors as opposed to the generally effective extrinsic factors of the earlier industrial worker. The four intrinsic motivators for this new worker are a sense of purpose, autonomy concerning how to do the work, an increasing sense of competence, and a sense of accomplishment. Overall this book can help organizational leaders challenge their assumptions and create a more positive and rewarding work environment.

The Living Dead: Switched Off, Zoned Out—The Shocking Truth About Office Life

David Bolchover

Oxford, Oxfordshire: Capstone, 2005

160pp ISBN: 184112656X

If you are a manager and you have to

1835

"Striving for excellence motivates you; striving for perfection is demoralizing."

Harriet Beryl Braiker

motivate others, this book may be a salutary read. It argues that millions of workers around the world do everything at the office other than work. The good news is that there is something managers can do to break this type of cycle, and the book includes information on how to turn things round as well as diverting nuggets of information.

Love 'Em or Lose 'Em: Getting Good People to Stay 3rd ed.

Beverly L. Kaye, Sharon Jordan-Evans
San Francisco, California: Berrett-Koehler, 2005
288pp ISBN: 1576753271
Love 'Em or Lose 'Em looks at motivation from a whole-workplace perspective and considers how the systems, policies, and procedures in a work environment can either motivate and inspire or demotivate and demoralize.

Maslow on Management

Abraham H. Maslow
Hoboken, New Jersey: Wiley, 1998
320pp ISBN: 0471247804
This is a new edition of Maslow's work *Eupsychian Management*, with a foreword by Warren Bennis. The work was written in 1962 as a journal kept by Maslow while at a factory in Southern California. He addresses self-actualization (the freedom to put into effect one's own ideas), synergy (the alignment of goals between individuals and of personal and organizational goals), enlightened management policy, and many other topics.

Motivate and Reward: Performance Appraisal and Incentive Systems for Business Success

Herwig W Kressler
Basingstoke, United Kingdom: Palgrave Macmillan, 2003
176pp ISBN: 1403903786
This book provides an overview of the relationships between motivation, performance appraisal, evaluation of potential, and pay and reward systems. The first section of the book discusses motivation and, in particular, motivation to work. The main theories and models of motivation are described, and general principles for dealing with motivational issues are outlined. The second section deals with the evaluation of performance and potential, and the final section looks at reward strategies and incentive systems.

Motivating People in Lean Organizations

Linda Holbeche
Woburn, Massachusetts: Butterworth-Heinemann, 1997
256pp ISBN: 0750633751
The core themes in this guide for managers in lean organizations who need to motivate employees and promote new forms of career development include: how to implement motivational strategies; the importance of good internal communications; how to develop new career development structures; and how to recognize and reward achievement. Case studies of Thresher and General Electric are used to illustrate the text, which also includes examples of cross-cultural lean organizations.

Motivational Styles in Everyday Life: A Guide to Reversal Theory

Michael J. Apter, ed.
Washington, D.C.: American Psychological Association, 2001
384pp ISBN: 1557987394
This book provides an introduction to a complex theory with broad implications for understanding both normal and pathological human behavior. Topics covered include: reversal theory as a set of propositions; reversal theory measures; basic research on reversal theory; the psychophysiology of metamotivation; and the challenge of reversal theory.

Motivation Handbook

Sarah Hollyforde, Steve Whiddett
London, United Kingdom: Chartered Institute of Personnel and Development (CIPD), 2002
288pp ISBN: 0852929250
A comprehensive overview of the study of motivation and its applications in the workplace. The main theories of motivation are described, with critical commentary and practical illustrations. Key organizational terms such as job design, reward, communication, team management, objective setting, and performance are discussed in the light of the relevant theories, with a wide range of examples and character profiles.

Peak Performance: Aligning the Hearts and Minds of Your Employees

Jon R. Katzenbach
Boston, Massachusetts: Harvard Business School Press, 2000
304pp ISBN: 0875849369
This text draws on research involving leaders in a range of industries that examines how to move from merely motivating employees to gaining the emotional commitment that yields consistently high performance. Five balanced paths to success in this area are identified, and the ways in which leading companies pursue one or more of them are investigated. The author then reviews the key lessons to be learned.

Punished by Rewards: The Trouble with Gold Stars, Incentive Plans, A's, Praise, and Other Bribes

Alfie Kohn
Boston, Massachusetts: Houghton Mifflin, 2000
416pp ISBN: 0618001816
Punished by Rewards is a controversial book which attacks the established beliefs of the Skinner school of behavioral science. The book highlights the difficulties of using rewards in the workplace and the classroom, and offers suggestions for enhancing intrinsic motivation.

Transforming Work

Michael Kroth, Patricia Boverie
Cambridge, Massachusetts: Perseus Books Group, 2002
256pp ISBN: 0738205060
Aimed at management and executive level, this book works on the premise that organizations should be more aware of staff needs and requirements. The authors use their extensive research to show professionals how to cultivate a happy and motivated office environment, with a view to "transforming" the outlook of the entire company.

We Are All Self-employed: How to Take Control of Your Career 2nd ed.

Cliff Hakim
San Francisco, California: Berrett-Koehler, 2003
256pp ISBN: 1576752674
Hakim discusses the possibility of changing our approach to work, by taking on a "self-employed" attitude. He describes the notion of actively engaging with the workplace, rather than passively "fitting in," and examines the practical applications of this notion.

INTERNET

Accel-team.com
www.accel-team.com/motivation
This commercial Web site has a good, multi-page article on theories of workplace motivation. The article is available for download for a fee but can be read in its entirety online.

1836

BUSINESS INFORMATION SOURCES

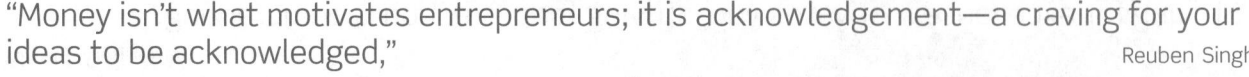
"Money isn't what motivates entrepreneurs; it is acknowledgement—a craving for your ideas to be acknowledged,"
Reuben Singh

ORGANIZATIONS
USA
Academy of Human Resource Development

College of Technology, Bowling Green State University, Bowling Green, Ohio, 43403
T: +1 419 372 9155
F: +1 419 372 8385
E: *office@ahrd.org*
www.ahrd.org

The Academy is a global organization devoted to the study of human resource theories, processes, and techniques. As part of this research, it publishes a range of journals, holds conferences, establishes partnerships, conducts a number of educational programs, and presents awards to scholars in the field of human resources.

American Society for Training and Development (ASTD)

1640 King Street, Box 1443, Alexandria, Virginia, 22313–2043
T: +1 703 683 8100
F: +1 703 683 8103
www.astd.org

An association of workplace learning and performance professionals, ASTD's members come from multinational corporations, medium-sized and small businesses, government, academia, consultancy firms, and product and service suppliers. It offers research and analysis, conferences, expositions, seminars, and publications. Though its primary focus is training and development, it also addresses issues of performance appraisal.

Society for Human Resource Management (SHRM)

1800 Duke Street, Alexandria, Virginia, 22314
T: +1 703 548 3440
F: +1 703 535 6490
E: *shrm@shrm.org*
www.shrm.org

SHRM is the world's largest human resource management association. It provides education and information services, conferences and seminars, government and media representation, online services, and publications to more than 200,000 professional and student members around the world.

Europe
Chartered Institute of Personnel and Development (CIPD)

151 The Broadway, Wimbledon, London, SW19 1JQ, U.K.
T: +44 (0) 20 8612 6200
F: +44 (0) 20 8012 6201
www.cipd.co.uk

Formed in 1995 from the amalgamation of the Institute of Personnel Management and the Institute of Training and Development, the CIPD is a professional body for personnel and training professionals that aims to promote good practice in the management and development of people— a company's core strength.

Chartered Management Institute (CMI)

Management House, Cottingham Road, Corby, Northamptonshire, NN17 1TT, U.K.

T: +44 (0) 1536 204 222
F: +44 (0) 1536 201 651
E: *enquiries@managers.org.uk*
www.managers.org.uk

Formed in 1992, the CMI is the largest organization for professional management in the United Kingdom, representing almost 89,000 individual members and embracing 560 corporate partners. It exists to promote the art and science of management through research, publications, the provision of information services, networking opportunities, education and training, and the objective presentation of managers' views and opinions.

FOR MORE INFORMATION

- Coaching, Counseling, and Mentoring (pp. 1698–1700)
- Creating Fun in the Workplace (pp. 37–38)
- Employee Benefits/Compensation (pp. 1736–1737)
- Finding and Keeping Top Talent (pp. 33–34)
- Making Loyalty Work (pp. 370–371)
- Making Recognition and Rewards a "Whole-Person" Experience (pp. 12–13)
- Management Development (pp. 1812–1814)
- Motivating Your Staff in a Time of Change (pp. 458–459)
- Snapping Managerial Inertia (pp. 322–323)

1837

BUSINESS INFORMATION SOURCES

"If you don't undrestand what makes people tick, they won't tick." Robert Swan

Negotiation

BOOKS

Bargaining for Advantage: Negotiation Strategies for Reasonable People

G. Richard Shell

New York: Penguin USA, 2000

304pp ISBN: 0140281916

Based on an executive training program that gets its message across through storytelling, this is a practical guide to negotiations. With useful checklists, it highlights the value of communication and covers such issues in negotiating as bargaining style, making concessions, gaining commitment, understanding each party's goals and expectations, and making sure there is clear information on the table, including standards and norms.

Beyond Winning

Robert H. Mnookin, Scott R. Peppet, Andrew S. Tulumello

Cambridge, Massachusetts: Harvard University Press, 2004

368pp ISBN: 0674012313

In this book, the authors offer advice on overcoming the difficulties faced in legal negotiations. A step-by-step guide, *Beyond Winning* describes a range of ways in which lawyers can seek to improve their negotiating skills. By enhancing communication and using troubleshooting techniques, the authors argue, "disputes can be turned into deals."

Breakthrough Business Negotiation: A Toolbox for Managers

Michael Watkins

New York: Wiley, 2002

304pp ISBN: 0787960128

Real-world negotiations, it is suggested, are rarely simple, and over-simplified models of negotiation will not equip business people for the complexities they may face. The author of this book outlines the breakthrough approach to analyzing complex negotiations that is based on systems thinking. Techniques for overcoming power imbalances, building coalitions, resolving conflicts, and handling crises are described.

Complete Guide to Selling Your Business 2nd ed.

Paul S. Sperry, Beatrice H. Mitchell

London: Kogan Page, 2004

192pp ISBN: 0749441615

This practical guide covers the process of selling a business—from taking the decision to sell, knowing the right time to sell, and valuing the business, to negotiating and completing the deal. Case studies and sample documents such as a confidentiality agreement, a due diligence checklist, and contents of share sale and asset purchase agreements are provided. A glossary of relevant terms is also included.

Difficult Conversations

Douglas Stone, Bruce Patton, Sheila Heen

New York: Penguin Putnam, Inc., 2000

272pp ISBN: 014028852X

Designed to help readers to become calm and assertive in difficult situations (such as asking for a pay rise, or experiencing problems with colleagues), this book discusses the different emotions and requirements that arise from such conversations and pinpoints ways of managing them more effectively.

Essential Negotiation

Gavin Kennedy

London: Profile Economist Books, 2004

240pp ISBN: 1861975708

This book is a guide to the essentials of negotiation, helping you to understand and manage the process. An overview is provided followed by an A to Z of topics, terms, and jargon. Appendices cover negotiation training resources, specialized consultants and trainers, and further reading.

Essentials of Negotiation 3rd ed.

Roy J. Lewicki, David M. Saunders, John W. Minton

Maidenhead, United Kingdom: McGraw-Hill, 2003

288pp ISBN: 0072545828

This book looks at the psychology of bargaining and negotiation and the dynamics involved in conflict and its resolution. It provides an in-depth discussion of aspects of negotiation such as communication, strategy and tactics, dealing with breakdowns in negotiations, social context, ethics, third party roles, and power.

Fast Forward MBA in Negotiating and Deal Making

Roy J. Lewicki, Alexander Hiam

Hoboken, New Jersey: Wiley, 1998

288pp (Fast Forward MBA)

ISBN: 0471256986

The authors explore cutting edge ideas on negotiation and deal making through real-world examples. Key concepts are introduced and illustrated, and warnings provided on how to avoid pitfalls.

Getting Past No: Negotiating Your Way from Confrontation to Cooperation

William Ury

New York: Bantam Doubleday Dell, 1993

208pp ISBN: 0553371312

This book provides a step-by-step method for negotiation that aims to ensure that satisfactory agreement is reached with even the most intransigent people. It contains advice, hints and tips, useful strategies, and plenty of real examples.

Getting to Resolution: Turning Conflict into Collaboration

Stewart Levine

San Francisco, California: Berrett-Koehler, 2000

208pp ISBN: 1576751155

This book examines the nature of conflicts, finding that they most often result from a breakdown in communications. It then describes a process for negotiation that is useful for both mediators and individuals. The book provides a detailed roadmap to resolve disputes, including believing in abundance, relying on feelings and intuition, being creative, and disclosing information.

Getting to Yes 2nd ed.

Roger Fisher, William Ury, Bruce Patton

New York: Penguin Putnam, 1991

208pp ISBN: 0140157352

By working around four main principles of effective negotiation and discussing some of the difficulties that can arise, the authors show the reader how to pursue his or her own interests while keeping adversaries happy at the same time. A few principles will guide the reader no matter what the other side does, or whatever what tricks they may resort to.

Lateral Leadership: Getting It Done When You Are Not the Boss 2nd ed.

Roger Fisher, Alan Sharp

London: Profile Books, 2004

240pp ISBN: 1861977239

The authors have written a guide to improving collaboration so that everyone benefits. They look at detailed strategies

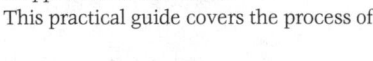
"Never wrestle with a pig. You get dirty and only the pig enjoys himself." Mark McCormack

required to work effectively with others and to get people to work effectively with you. They also consider how best to help a group formulate a clear common vision of the results to be achieved, overcome clashes of multiple views and work styles, and develop agreed courses of action.

Negotiate Successfully: How to Get Your Way and Find Win-win Solutions

New York: Perseus Books Group, 2004
96pp (Steps to Success)
ISBN: 0747572097
A short, action-packed guide to the world of negotiating, this book offers advice on negotiation basics and planning tips as well as on how to negotiate over the phone or via e-mail. There are also special sections on coping with difficult negotiations and negotiating with people from other cultures.

Negotiating in a Week 3rd ed.

Peter Fleming
London: Hodder & Stoughton, 2003
96pp (in a Week)
ISBN: 0340849541
This practical guide to negotiating covers ten steps. These include creating the right environment, preparation and planning, opening the meeting, talking and listening, making proposals, and closing and confirming the deal. Also included is advice on developing personal negotiating skills.

The Negotiation Toolkit: How to Get Exactly What You Want in Any Business or Personal Situation

Roger J. Volkema
New York: AMACOM, 1999
208pp ISBN: 081448008X
This is a guide to negotiation, aimed at helping people build the skills and self-confidence to become good negotiators. It explores the golden rule of negotiation, explains when not to negotiate, discusses the issue of tough negotiators and how to deal with them, describes the tactics, skills, and behavior of star negotiators, looks at cross-cultural negotiations, and provides ways to measure your own skills.

The Power of Nice: How to Negotiate So Everyone Wins—Especially You!

Ronald M. Shapiro, Mark A. Jankowski, James Dale
Hoboken, New Jersey: Wiley, 2001
304pp ISBN: 0471080721
This book is based on Shapiro's belief that negotiation works best if two negotiators can build a common bond between them. In

exploring this theory, Shapiro offers advice on various types of negotiation, and on creating effective proposals.

Six Weeks to Professional Excellence

Chartered Management Institute
London: Hodder & Stoughton, 2003
560pp ISBN: 0340812621
This volume gathers together six titles in the Business in a Week series, covering: project management, negotiating, time management, dealing with difficult people, presentation, and memory techniques. Each section provides a practical introduction to the subject.

Skilled Negotiator: Mastering the Language of Engagement

Kathleen Kelley Reardon
New York: Jossey-Bass, 2004
272pp ISBN: 078796655X
This practical book explains how to expand on negotiation strategies and develop language skills to enhance success in negotiation. The processes of identifying your negotiation style and understanding its limitations, using language strategically, recognizing deception and managing it, using positioning and persuasion, and effectively negotiating one-to-one and in teams, are all examined.

When I Say No, I Feel Guilty

Manuel J. Smith
New York: Bantam Books, 1985
352pp ISBN: 0553263900
This best-selling book offers a range of strategies to help people feel comfortable when they assert their needs at work and at home. It also offers advice on how to combat manipulation and emotional game-playing by others.

MAGAZINES

International Negotiation: A Journal of Theory and Practice

ISSN: 1382–340X
Brill Academic Publishers
Blackhorse Road, Letchworth Garden City, Hertfordshire, SG6 1HN, U.K.
T: +44 (0) 1462 687528
F: +44 (0) 1462 480947
This journal, published three times a year, explores the theoretical issues and practical applications of negotiation; it aims to identify, analyze, and explain effective and efficient international negotiation and mediation processes through research articles and case study examples. The journal is available in printed form and via the Internet.

Negotiation Journal

ISSN: 0748–4526
Blackwell Publishing
108 Cowley Road, Oxford, Oxfordshire, OX4 1JF, U.K.
T: +44 (0) 1865 791100
F: +44 (0) 1865 791347
www.blackwellpublishing.com
Aimed at planning, economic, and public policy professionals and published in association with the inter-university consortium Program on Negotiation, this quarterly journal aims to promote the development of better techniques for resolving conflict. It is available in printed form and via the Internet.

INTERNET
Batna.com—The Negotiation Resource Center
www.batna.com
Created by Eric C. Gould, this site has negotiation tips and analysis, with examples that help make the points more easily understood. Areas include powerful tips, communication, difficult negotiations, training, and a list of the author's favorite resources.

Interneg—For and About Negotiation
http://interneg.org/interneg/links/learning.html
This site is a directory of resources for the negotiation field, with links to numerous other sites covering areas from training and teaching materials to games to programs and seminars.

Mediate.com
www.mediate.com
This site provides articles and news on mediation, conflict resolution, and arbitration. It also includes information about training, events, organizations, and academic programs in this field.

The Negotiating Edge
www.negotiatingedge.com
This site provides information about seminars, Negotiating Edge white papers, links to other negotiating sites, and lists of recommended readings on negotiation and conflict resolution.

The Negotiation Skills Company, Inc.
www.negotiationskills.com
This site is provided by a consulting company that specializes in negotiation training and consultancy. It offers free information and articles, and an occasional newsletter on all aspects of the negotiation process.

BUSINESS INFORMATION SOURCES

"This is about negotiations, but the answer to that question is 'No.'"   David Andrews

ORGANIZATIONS
USA
Institute for Operations Research and the Management Sciences

901 Elkridge Landing Road, Suite 400, Linthicum, Maryland, 21090–2909
T: +1 410 850 0300
F: +1 410 684 2963
E: *informs@informs.org*
www.informs.org

The Institute represents professionals within the operations research and management sciences fields. It has a section dedicated to group decision and negotiation that provides online discussions, organizes conferences, and publishes articles through its journal, *Group Decision and Negotiation*.

National Contract Management Association (NCMA)

8260 Greensboro Drive, Suite 200, McLean, Virginia, 22102
T: +1 571 382 0082
F: +1 703 448 0939
E: *info@ncmahq.org*
www.ncmahq.org

This Association comprises professionals concerned with all aspects of contract management. NCMA also has developed training materials and offers certification in contract management.

International
International Association of Facilitators

7630 West 145th Street, Suite 202, St. Paul, Minnesota, 55124

T: +1 952 891 3541
F: +1 952 891 1800
E: *office@iaf-world.org*
www.iaf-world.org

The IAF was founded in 1994 and now has over 1,300 members in more than 20 countries. It aims to promote professional facilitation through information exchange and regional and global networking.

FOR MORE INFORMATION

- Decision Making and Problem Solving (pp. 1727–1729)
- Interpersonal Communication/ Relations (pp. 1787–1788)
- Pricing (p. 1867)

BUSINESS INFORMATION SOURCES

New Product Development

BOOKS

The Change Function: Why Some Technologies Take Off and Others Crash and Burn

Pip Coburn

New York: Portfolio, 2006

240pp ISBN: 1591841321

Pip Coburn is a former global strategist in the technology group at UBS Warburg, and in this book he draws on his considerable experience to explain why some technologies take off and others never leave the launch pad. Coburn's theory is that consumers are only ready to change when the "pain" of their current position is outweighs the potential pain of trying something new. Although of particular use to investors in new technology, the principles outlined in the book will be of interest anyone involved in new product development.

Managing the Design Factory: The Product Developer's Toolkit

Donald Reinertsen

New York: Free Press, 1997

256pp ISBN: 0684839911

This book applies product development principles and integrates them with management theories. In short, it shows how the two sides of the coin must work together for successful product launching. Management theories and principles are not always incorporated well in practice with a design team. Reinertsen has practical ideas about how to make sure the entire creative team is "speaking the same language" as a product launch moves from idea to reality.

Marketing the Unknown: Developing Market Strategies for Technical Innovations

Paul Millier

Hoboken, New Jersey: Wiley, 1999

256pp ISBN: 0471986216

How do you make a product successful? This is one of the basic questions that this practical book sets out to answer. It also discusses what is the best process to follow, and how you choose or transform markets so as to ensure a successful launch. It paves the way for marketing, for R & D, and for project managers in industrial organizations to launch and market innovations successfully in a very competitive field,

and outlines strategies for further development.

The PDMA Handbook of New Product Development 2nd ed.

Milton D. Rosenau, ed.

Hoboken, New Jersey: Wiley, 2004

640pp ISBN: 0471485241

Over the last decade, the theory and practice of new product development has been radically transformed. This volume, produced by the Product Development & Management Association (PDMA), combines the best aspects of product development practice in both consumer and industrial markets. Written by academic experts and industry professionals from Fortune 1,000 companies, the book offers authoritative practical information on every stage of the product development process from concept creation, through development and design, to the final assembled product and marketing campaigns.

Portfolio Management for New Products 2nd ed.

Robert G. Cooper, Scott J. Edgett, Elko J. Kleinschmidt

Cambridge, Massachusetts: Perseus Books Group, 2001

288pp ISBN: 0738205141

This book shows readers how to manage their company's product portfolio for maximum long-term growth. Its approach is pragmatic, detailing various techniques for managing a portfolio, unlocking its maximum potential, and dealing with any problems that may arise. It provides an excellent resource for any company whose profitability relies on the products it chooses to develop, and the speed with which it brings them to market.

Product Design and Development 3rd ed.

Karl T. Ulrich, Steven D. Eppinger

Maidenhead, United Kingdom: McGraw-Hill, 2003

384pp ISBN: 0072471468

This text lays out an integrative framework for product design, showing the interconnection of marketing, design, and manufacturing. The authors focus as much on aesthetics as engineering in the analysis of production and manufacturing methods, making this book unusual in the field.

Product Innovation: Leading Change Through Integrated Product Development

David Rainey

New York: Cambridge University Press, 2005

640pp ISBN: 0521842751

Product Innovation focuses on new techniques and strategies in new product development that have arisen as a result of companies seeking every-quicker routes to market. Useful for students, managers, and practitioners, this book offers advice on how to make the design and development of new products more effective, and ultimately, more profitable.

Product Juggernauts: How Companies Mobilize to Generate a Stream of Market Winners

Jean-Philippe Deschamps, P. Ranganath Nayak

Boston, Massachusetts: Harvard Business School Press, 1995

480pp ISBN: 0875843417

The authors cite stories from real companies around the world to illustrate guidelines for determining the products customers want and designing the products they want to buy. Examples used to demonstrate the importance of company-wide focus on product include (among others) Ford, Canon, and Toshiba. Using these case studies, the authors demonstrate how organizations can achieve high market performance and improve their current strategies.

Product Leadership: Pathways to Profitable Innovation 2nd ed.

Robert G. Cooper

Cambridge, Massachusetts: Perseus Books Group, 2005

288pp ISBN: 046501433X

Over a third of new products fail at launch, and many never gain a profitable return. So how do companies like 3M, Merck, and Procter & Gamble continually lead the way with exceptional new products? Cooper reveals the winners' secrets, and offers valuable advice on implementing and overseeing new product processes and strategies, managing product portfolios, determining which products to develop, and fostering ingenuity to outperform the competition.

"Everything that can be invented has been invented."   Charles H. Duell

The Product Manager's Handbook 3rd ed.
Linda Gorchels
New York: McGraw-Hill/NTC, 2005
304pp ISBN: 0071459383
This book focuses on skills acquisition, making it suitable for new product managers or people interested in moving into that line of work. The text is written as an overview and introduction to the skill set necessary for product managers, but segments of the book are also devoted to product development and launch. Useful and practical checklists are also included.

Revolutionizing Product Development
Steven C. Wheelwright, Kim B. Clark
New York: Free Press, 1992
400pp ISBN: 0029055156
This book asserts that a company's capability to design quality prototypes and bring a product to market more quickly than its competitor is increasingly the focal point of competition. The authors argue that a successful new product launch is dependent upon management's ability to integrate the marketing, manufacturing, and design functions for problem solving and fast action, particularly during the critical design-build-test cycles of prototype creation. Companies that consistently "design it right the first time" therefore have a crucial advantage.

Seeing What's Next: Using the Theories of Innovation to Predict Industry Change
Clayton M. Christensen, Scott D. Anthony, Erik A. Roth
Boston, Massachusetts: Harvard Business School Press, 2004
ISBN: 1591391857
In this book, Christensen and his fellow authors attempt to take the guesswork out of innovation and new product development by suggesting a framework via which outcomes in any industry can be predicted. Drawing on key theories developed in Christensen's bestselling books *The Innovator's Dilemma* and *The Innovator's Solution*, this book focuses on three main phases: spot the signs of change, work out the potential end result of competitive battles, and analyzing whether corporate decisions will boost the company's chance of success, or endanger it.

Successful Product Development: Speeding from Opportunity to Profit
Milton D. Rosenau, Jr.
Hoboken, New Jersey: Wiley, 1999
208pp ISBN: 047131532X

The authors set out the process of product development from beginning to end, starting with the formation of ideas and moving through design and engineering to the finished product. It is intended for all practitioners involved with any aspect of developing new products and services.

Winning at New Products: Accelerating the Process from Idea to Launch 3rd ed.
Robert G. Cooper
Cambridge, Massachusetts: Perseus Books Group, 2001
416pp ISBN: 0738204633
This book cites research and gives examples of innovative practices used by industry leaders such as 3M, Exxon Chemical, and Guinness, to present a tried-and-tested game plan for achieving product leadership. Cooper outlines specific strategies for: assessing risk; getting the necessary resources together; involving customers in the pre-development discovery phase; evaluating a project portfolio; ensuring cross-functional collaboration; and, most importantly, applying a rigorous method for making sound business decisions at every step of the process.

MAGAZINES
Journal of Product Innovation Management
ISSN: 0737–6782
Product Development and Management Association
15000 Commerce Parkway, Suite C, Mount Laurel, New Jersey, 08054
T: +1 856 439 9052
F: +1 856 439 0525
www.pdma.org
The *Journal* publishes the research, experiences, and insights of academics and practicing managers from all over the world. It is dedicated to the advancement of management practice in all aspects of product innovation, and is aimed at both practitioners and students in the field.

Visions
Product Development and Management Association
15000 Commerce Parkway, Suite C, Mount Laurel, New Jersey, 08054
T: +1 856 439 9052
F: +1 856 439 0525
www.pdma.org
This is a quarterly publication for new product development professionals which provides news, analysis, and case histories. Contributors are practitioners as well as theoreticians.

INTERNET
American Productivity and Quality Center
www.apqc.org
This site features articles on training, conferences, case studies, executive summaries, and makes available several white papers on product development. APQC is essentially a group working toward corporate organizational improvement. They sponsor conferences on product development as well as providing resources online.

Experts on New Product Development
www.expertson.com/ New_Product_Development
The resources on which information is available from this site include new product development associations, new product development centers, directories, newsgroups, mailing lists, new product development publications, and new product development reference tools.

Global New Products Database
www.gnpd.com
This site can be used to access a comprehensive database that monitors worldwide product innovation in the packaged goods market, offering coverage of new product activity for both competitor monitoring and product idea generation. Users must register to gain access to the database, but registration is free.

Product Development and Management Association
www.pdma.org
This site is everyone's first stop when trolling the Internet for information on product development. It features articles, a job bank, conference listings, a bookstore, and more.

ORGANIZATIONS
USA
Product Development and Management Association
15000 Commerce Parkway, Suite C, Mount Laurel, New Jersey, 08054
T: +1 856 439 9052
F: +1 856 439 0525
E: *pdma@pdma.org*
www.pdma.org
This professional nonprofit organization is dedicated to serving people with an interest in new products and services. It is a recognized provider of knowledge and tools intended to improve the effectiveness of the development and management of new products and services. It also arranges

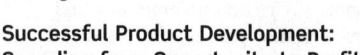

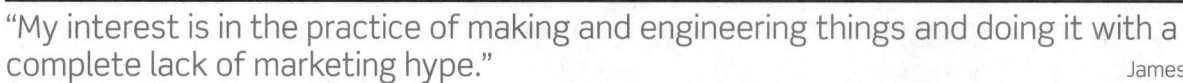
"My interest is in the practice of making and engineering things and doing it with a complete lack of marketing hype."
James Dyson

     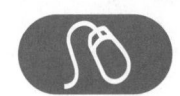

conferences, publications, awards, meetings, and workshops, and sponsors research.

Europe
Product Development and Management Association, U.K. and Ireland
Helen Perks
Manchester Business School, Booth Street West, Manchester, M15 6PB, U.K.

E: *h.perks@manchester.ac.uk*
www.pdma.org.uk
This is the U.K. and Ireland branch of the PDMA of America, a professional nonprofit organization dedicated to serving people with an interest in new products and services. In addition to providing knowledge and tools intended to improve the effectiveness of new product development and management, it arranges

conferences, publications, awards, meetings, and workshops, and sponsors research.

FOR MORE INFORMATION

- Innovation and Creativity (pp. 1774–1777)
- Research and Development (R&D) Management (pp. 1896–1897)

1843

BUSINESS INFORMATION SOURCES

Nonprofit Organizations

BOOKS

Beyond the Bottom Line: How to Do More with Less in Nonprofit and Public Organizations

Martin W. Sandler, Deborah A. Hudson
New York: Oxford University Press USA, 1998
224pp ISBN: 0195116127
This book reviews the social and economic pressures that are forcing the United States' nonprofit and public sector organizations to do more with less money. Following an investigation of nonprofit agencies that are successfully meeting these challenges, the authors present a list of competencies and strategies that other agencies should adopt.

CPR for Nonprofits: Creative Strategies for Successful Fundraising, Marketing, Communications, and Management

Alvin H. Reiss
New York: Jossey-Bass, 2000
176pp ISBN: 0787952419
A book of case studies illustrating how nonprofit organizations have met various challenges. The cases follow a common format that provides background, challenge, plan, result, questions to ask and lessons learned for each case. Areas covered include: getting your message heard; making your event special; asking for money; involving your board; reaching your audience; and maximizing your grass roots potential.

Enterprising Nonprofits: A Toolkit for Social Entrepreneurs

J. Gregory Dees, Jed Emerson, Peter Economy
New York: Wiley, 2001
336pp ISBN: 0471397350
The nature of social entrepreneurship is examined and factors leading to success are analyzed. A toolkit of techniques for social entrepreneurs is presented, covering mission and business planning, recognizing opportunities, mobilizing resources, risk management, innovation, and financial management. A brief guide to U.S. legislation relating to nonprofit organizations and suggestions for further reading are included.

Give and Take: A Candid Account of Corporate Philanthropy

Reynold Levy
Boston, Massachusetts: Harvard Business School Press, 1999
240pp ISBN: 0875848931

In this book, Levy discusses corporate giving from the perspective of both the donor and the solicitor. He points out that successful corporate philanthropy lies in business values and business interests, citing examples of large corporations who have become involved with philanthropic events. He also offers advice to fundraisers, analyzing the elements that make a successful nonprofit organization, and suggesting insider techniques for securing funds from large companies.

Going Global for the Greater Good: Succeeding as a Nonprofit in the International Community

Bonnie L. Koenig
New York: Jossey-Bass, 2004
160pp ISBN: 0787966762
The author provides practical guidance for organizations wanting to develop international partnerships and strategic alliances. Ways in which an organization can develop a global mindset and start to access international networks while remaining true to its mission and goals are outlined. The book also looks at operational, logistical and legal issues involved in developing international programs, and lessons that can be learned from the experience of international organizations are described.

The Good Employment Guide for the Voluntary Sector 4th ed.

National Council for Voluntary Organisations
London: National Council for Voluntary Organisations, 2005
192pp ISBN: 0719916569
This guide examines all aspects of employment law in the United Kingdom and its practical application within the voluntary sector. Amongst the topics discussed are equal opportunities, salaries, contracts, and selecting the right candidate in the first place.

Harvard Business Review on Nonprofits

Boston, Massachusetts: Harvard Business School Press, 1999
224pp (Harvard Business Review Paperbacks)
ISBN: 0875849091
Comprising eight essays originally published in the *Harvard Business Review*, this book explores aspects of the work of

modern nonprofit organizations. Topics include earning public trust, the work of the board, employing business leaders, learning lessons from venture capitalists, and developing profits through corporate partnerships.

High Performance Board: Principles of Nonprofit Organization Governance

Dennis D. Pointer, James E. Orlikoff
New York: Jossey-Bass, 2002
192pp ISBN: 078795697X
In this book the authors examine the functionality of boards in nonprofit organizations, and offer advice on what boards must do to maximize performance and contribution. They identify 64 principles to help a board achieve peak performance, and describe best practice and practical applications for each. Illustrative board policies, committee charters, board chair job descriptions, and governance principles are also provided.

How to Manage a Voluntary Organization: The Complete Guide for the Not-for-profit Sector

David Hussey, Robert Perrin
London: Kogan Page, 2003
320pp ISBN: 0749437804
This is a comprehensive guide to key management issues covering the importance of vision, strategy and policy, structure and governance, people management, finance, marketing and fundraising, mergers, and preparing for the future. There is practical advice on day-to-day matters and case studies. The book also includes a free CD-ROM containing useful information, templates, and other documents.

Improving Leadership in Nonprofit Organizations

Ronald E. Riggio, Sarah Smith Orr, eds
New York: Jossey-Bass, 2004
304pp ISBN: 0787968307
Leadership issues and challenges for nonprofit organizations are discussed by various authors, including Jay Conger. Areas covered include future challenges, ethical challenges, board leadership, pay in nonprofit organizations, succession, and assessment.

"There was worlds of reputation in it, but no money."   Mark Twain

Jossey-Bass Guide to Strategic Communications for Nonprofits: A Step-by-step Guide to Working with the Media to Generate Publicity, Enhance Fundraising, Build Membership, Change Public Policy, Handle Crises, and More

Kathleen Bonk, Henry Griggs, Emily Tynes
New York: Jossey-Bass, 1999
192pp ISBN: 0787943738

Designed as a tool for organizations that want to create communication strategies that work, this book discusses how to deal successfully with the media, increase public awareness, raise money, gain members, and influence changes in public policy.

Leaders Who Make a Difference: Essential Strategies for Meeting the Nonprofit Challenge

Burt Nanus, Stephen M. Dobbs
New York: Jossey-Bass, 1999
288pp ISBN: 0787946656

The authors describe the necessary leadership skills that are crucial to the success of nonprofit organizations, and give examples of how leaders' actions have made a difference to their organization.

Made Possible by: Succeeding with Sponsorship

Patricia Martin
New York: Jossey-Bass, 2004
144pp ISBN: 0787965022

A guide offering step-by-step help for nonprofit organizations on securing sponsorship that will raise their profile and give greater stability through a mutually beneficial relationship with a corporate partner. It covers in detail understanding sponsorship and engaging with sponsors, along with legal and tax concerns (United States); selling, negotiating and closing the deal; and delivering the deal and communicating the results.

ManagingNonprofits.org: Dynamic Management for the Digital Age

Ben Hecht, Rey Ramsey
Hoboken, New Jersey: Wiley, 2002
288pp ISBN: 0471395277

The authors explore potential ways in which nonprofit organizations can harness new technology to help them to change and adapt while improving their services. They advocate "Dynamic management" (described as a continual process of organizational self-reflection and repositioning) as an approach for nonprofit organizations, and link it to operating in new ways aligned to the digital age.

Managing Risk in Nonprofit Organizations: A Comprehensive Guide

Melanie L. Herman et al.
Hoboken, New Jersey: Wiley, 2004
320pp ISBN: 0471236748

This practical guide shows managers in nonprofit making organizations how to implement sound risk management procedures. It is divided into three sections: the nature and purposes of risk management; recognizing the context for risk management; and risk financing for nonprofits. Potential risks covered include: human resource issues; fundraising; Internet use; mergers; and volunteer management.

Managing the Non-Profit Organization: Principles and Practices

Peter F. Drucker
New York: HarperCollins, 1992
256pp ISBN: 0887306012

This title outlines the importance of good management in the nonprofit sector, an area that is rapidly expanding and that consequently has a workforce which includes over 80 million volunteers. The book details every aspect of nonprofit organizations, from resources to decision making, and gives several examples to support this information.

Marketing Management for Nonprofit Organizations

Adrian Sargeant
New York: Oxford University Press, 1999
304pp ISBN: 0198775660

Together with a comprehensive overview of the theory behind nonprofit marketing, this textbook provides an introduction to marketing, market planning, and market orientation, and addresses the specific application of marketing to the key nonprofit subsectors of fundraising; the arts, education, healthcare, and social ideas.

The Nonprofit Membership Toolkit

Ellis M. M. Robinson
New York: Jossey-Bass, 2003
304pp ISBN: 0787965065

In a step-by-step format, this book shows how to create, manage, and sustain a dynamic membership program. It gives managers and directors the information and tools needed to understand their current members and attract new ones. It also walks organizations through the process of linking program goals with membership goals. Illustrative examples, sample membership publications, schedules for typical tasks, worksheets, and checklists are included. Sources of information are largely U.S.-oriented.

Relationship Fundraising: A Donor-based Approach to the Business of Raising Money 2nd ed.

Ken Burnett
New York: Jossey-Bass, 2002
368pp ISBN: 0787960896

This text presents a guide to the benefits of applying relationship marketing methods in the fundraising arena. It examines the techniques for marketing to donors and emphasizes the need to establish mutually rewarding relationships with contributors. Creative approaches to relationship building are discussed.

Strategic Marketing for Nonprofit Organizations 6th ed.

Philip Kotler, Alan Andreasen
Upper Saddle River, New Jersey: Prentice Hall, 2002
544pp ISBN: 013041977X

This title provides a valuable overview of the marketing process in non-profit organisations. The co-authors discuss a range of key marketing issues in this area which include creating a greater customer focus, producing and organising resources, handling a marketing strategy, and strategic planning.

Strategic Planning for Nonprofit Organizations 2nd ed.

Michael Allison, Jude Kaye
Hoboken, New Jersey: Wiley, 2003
320pp ISBN: 0471445819

Based on a seven-stage plan of effective strategy, this book aims to help readers pinpoint the processes needed to create a successful organization. Including assessment tools such as checklists, worksheets, and an example of a strategic plan, this book/disk is suitable for a range of outfits, at whatever financial or social level. It includes advice on compiling mission statements, and sustaining all factors of the strategic plan.

Transformational Boards: A Practical Guide to Engaging your Board and Embracing Change

Byron L. Tweeten
New York: Jossey-Bass, 2002
208pp ISBN: 0787959138

The author presents an engagement model for board leadership to help directors lead their organization through times of change. The chapters focus on key issues facing the board of directors, including effective recruitment, formulating and reviewing policy, planning, managing public relations, generating financial resources, and evaluating performance.

BUSINESS INFORMATION SOURCES

"In all the ages, three-fourths of the support of the great charities has been conscience money."

Mark Twain

MAGAZINES
Nonprofit World
ISSN: 8755-7614
Society for Nonprofit Organizations
5820 Canton Center Road, Suite 165,
Canton, Michigan, 48187
T: +1 734 451 3582
F: +1 734 451 5935
www.snpo.org
The only comprehensive national leadership and management magazine in the nonprofit world, this publication is written for senior management as well as volunteers and will appeal to anyone working with a nonprofit agency. It is filled with timely information regarding current nonprofit topics.

INTERNET
BBB Wise Giving Alliance
www.give.org
The Web site for the BBB Wise Giving Alliance collects, disseminates, and distributes information on nationally soliciting charitable organizations across the United States.

GuideStar: The National Database of Nonprofit Organizations
www.guidestar.org
This Web site is run by Philanthropic Research, Inc. and allows access to a database of over 850,000 nonprofit organizations recognized by the Internal Revenue Service. The site will be useful to both donors to and founders of nonprofit organizations. Users must register to access the complete range of databases available, but registration is free.

Idealist
www.idealist.org
This is a body that offers information for and about nonprofit organizations in the United States. The site includes frequently asked questions, a nonprofit locator, a regular bulletin, and a library of related literature.

Institute for Nonprofit Organization Management
www.inom.org
Sponsored by the University of San Francisco College of Professional Studies, this Web site provides a teaching resource center and a newsletter, and lists publications and available research that will aid nonprofit organizations.

Internal Revenue Service
www.irs.gov/charities/index.html
This U.S. government Web site has a section for charities and nonprofit organizations, providing tax information and advice.

NonProfit Gateway
www.firstgov.gov
The "Businesses and Nonprofits" tab links to United States government information and services, covering areas such as fundraising, laws and regulations, and tax.

ORGANIZATIONS
USA
Alliance for Nonprofit Management
1899 L Street NW, 6th Floor, Washington, D.C., 20036
T: +1 202 955 8406
F: +1 202 721 0086
E: *alliance@allianceonline.org*
www.allianceonline.org
Founded in 1997, the organizations and individuals belonging to the Alliance are devoted to building nonprofit organizations. This association works to increase the effectiveness of nonprofits and offers support services for nonprofit agencies.

National Council for Nonprofit Organizations
1030 15th Street, NW, Suite 870, Washington, D.C., 20005
T: +1 202 962 0322
F: +1 202 962 0321
E: *ncna@ncna.org*
www.ncna.org
Representing over 22,000 members, the association works toward advancing the role of the nonprofit organizations found in local communities. It supports both state and regional associations and is involved with legislation concerning nonprofit organizations.

Society for Nonprofit Organizations
5820 Canton Center Road, Suite165, Canton, Michigan, 48187
T: +1 734 451 3582 or 800 424 7367
F: +1 734 451 5935
E: *snpo@danenet.org*
www.snpo.org
This organization, founded in 1983, has more than 3,500 members. It is dedicated to bringing together those who serve in the nonprofit world. Its mission is to provide an international forum for the exchange of information and ideas based on increasing awareness of and productivity within nonprofit organizations.

Europe
Charities Aid Foundation
25 Kings Hill Avenue, Kings Hill, West Malling, Kent, ME19 4TA, U.K.
T: +44 (0) 1732 520 000
F: +44 (0) 1732 520 001
E: *enquiries@caf.charitynet.org*
www.cafonline.org
The Foundation is an organization dedicated to helping build a robust, well-resourced, nonprofit sector and increase funding for nonprofit organizations. The Foundation provides charitable and financial support and advice to organizations, and works to help donors invest their resources in the United Kingdom and overseas.

Charity Commission
Harmsworth House, 13–15 Bouverie Street, London, EC4Y 8DP, U.K.
T: +44 (0) 870 333 0123
F: +44 (0) 20 7674 2300
E: *feedback@charity-commission.gov.uk*
www.charity-commission.gov.uk
The Charity Commission is a governmental department that exists to support, supervise, and regulate the operation of charities registered in the United Kingdom. The Commission's aims are to help charities exploit their resources more effectively through the provision of advice and information, and to maintain public confidence in the integrity of registered charities.

International
Imagine Canada
425 University Avenue, Suite 900, Toronto, Ontario, M5G 1T6, Canada
T: +1 416 597 2293
F: +1 416 597 2294
E: *info@imaginecanada.ca*
www.imaginecanada.ca
Formed in 2005 by the merger of the Canadian Centre for Philanthropy (CCP) and the Coalition of National Voluntary Organizations (NVO), this nonprofit organization provides support and resources for Canada's charitable and voluntary sector. Its main activities are conducting and funding research, lobbying organizations and the government, sharing knowledge, and promoting ethical conduct.

FOR MORE INFORMATION
☆ Converting Anonymity into Participation in a Membership Organization (pp. 239–240)
〽 Public Sector Management (pp. 1881–1882)

1846

BUSINESS INFORMATION SOURCES

"Money's a horrid thing to follow but a charming thing to meet."   Mark Twain

Organization and Organization Structure

BOOKS

Adaptive Enterprise: Creating and Leading Sense-and-Respond Organizations
Stephen H. Haeckel
Boston, Massachusetts: Harvard Business School Press, 1999
304pp ISBN: 0875848745
The author argues that in the Information Age, organizations must be able to adapt quickly to change. He outlines a "sense-and-respond" business model that can help companies cope with the unexpected by sensing changes in individual customer needs early and responding to them quickly. A step-by-step plan is mapped out, with examples and illustrations, for transforming organizations in accordance with this new model.

The Boundaryless Organization: Breaking the Chains of Organizational Structure 2nd ed.
Ron Ashkenas et al.
New York: Jossey-Bass, 2002
352pp ISBN: 078795943X
It has been argued that organizations need to sweep away the artificial obstacles that stand in the way of business performance and become boundaryless. This revised edition presents a comprehensive guide to help an organization become boundaryless and develop the ability to quickly, proactively, and creatively adjust to changes in the environment.

Corporate Failure by Design: Why Organizations are Built to Fail
Jonathan I. Klein
Westport, Connecticut: Quorum Books, 2000
304pp ISBN: 1567202977
Despite all that has been written on the subject of making organizations succeed, the reality is that an overwhelming majority of businesses fail within five years and almost all within ten years. The author suggests that this tendency is inherent within the organization and that organizations are in fact built to fail. An analysis of the causes and processes of failure, focusing on the psychopathology of leadership and the training and evaluation of incompetence, is presented and a theory of organizational self-destruction is

developed. Lessons that can be learned from failure are drawn from this analysis.

Corporate Tides: The Inescapable Laws of Organizational Structure
Robert Fritz
San Francisco, California: Berrett-Koehler, 1996
272pp ISBN: 1881052885
The failure of so many organizational change programs, it is suggested, is due to a lack of understanding of the basic laws of organizational structure. The author examines the structural dynamics of organizations and the causes of structural conflict and oscillation. He outlines a structural approach to organization design, and describes techniques that can be used for strategic planning, also giving consideration to the issues of vision, leadership, motivation, and the learning organization.

Crisis & Renewal: Meeting the Challenge of Organizational Change
David K. Hurst
Boston, Massachusetts: Harvard Business School Press, 2002
272pp (Management of Innovation and Change)
ISBN: 1578518709
This title concerns the restrictive nature of success and the way in which top companies, and those within them in management positions, must develop and refresh their ideas in order for transition to take place.

Designing Dynamic Organizations: A Hands-on Guide for Leaders at All Levels
Joy Galbraith, Diane Downey, Amy Kates
New York: AMACOM, 2002
288pp ISBN: 0814471196
Organization design is defined as the process of integrating the five major components of strategy, structure, processes, reward systems, and people practices to create an effective organization. The "star" model of organization design is introduced and used as a framework for the process of designing or reconfiguring an organization. Each component is examined in detail and the process of designing a

structure and implementing it within the organization is described.

Designing Effective Organizations: How to Create Structured Networks
Michael Goold, Andrew Campbell
New York: Jossey-Bass, 2002
368pp ISBN: 0787960640
The authors provide a rigorous, practical approach to organizational design, using nine tests including a people test, market advantage test, feasibility test, flexibility test, accountability test, and difficult links tests. General design principles of both simple and complex structures are examined, and a taxonomy of business unit roles and relationships is proposed. The role of the head office (or parent company) in complex structures is examined, and there are case studies, examples, and illustrations.

The End of Management and the Rise of Organizational Democracy
Kenneth Cloke, Joan Goldsmith
New York: Jossey-Bass, 2002
320pp ISBN: 078795912X
The authors put forward a case for putting an end to management in its traditional, authoritarian and paternalistic forms, and present their vision of the organization of the future. Practical strategies for developing collaborative, democratic, and self-managing organizations are outlined. These include: developing a values based organizational culture; encouraging democracy and webs of association; developing ubiquitous linking leadership, building innovative self-managed teams and implementing open and collaborative processes.

An Experiential Approach to Organization Development 7th ed.
Don Harvey, Donald R. Brown
Upper Saddle River, New Jersey: Prentice Hall, 2005
528pp ISBN: 013144168X
This text offers a practical and realistic approach to the study of organization development (OD). Through the application of a new paradigm—the OD Process Model—each of the stages of OD is described from the standpoint of its relationship to an overall program of

1847

BUSINESS INFORMATION SOURCES

"Corporate insiders . . . can seldom transform an organization beset by inertia."

John P. Kotter

change. The book is written primarily for students who are learning about organization development for the first time. The text relates the student to the real world through the use of numerous illustrations and company examples showing how OD is being applied in organizations today.

The Flexible Firm: Capability Management in Network Organizations
Julian Birkinshaw, Peter Hagstrom, eds
New York: Oxford University Press USA, 2000
256pp ISBN: 0198296517
The Flexible Firm is based on research into five large Swedish organizations and a number of international firms. It discusses issues affecting capability development within the networked firm. Contents include: network relationships inside and outside the company; the development of capabilities; managing relationships in the external network; innovation in the external network; and managing the internal network.

Generation to Generation: Life Cycles of the Family Business
Kelin E. Gersick, John A. Davis, et al.
Boston, Massachusetts: Harvard Business School Press, 1997
224pp ISBN: 087584555X
Intended as a comprehensive study of family businesses, this book examines the special dynamics and challenges facing these organizations in detail. It highlights the differences between family firms and public companies, and discusses issues specific to family businesses such as succession planning, managing relatives, and understanding the interactions between family, business, and ownership.

The Healthy Organization: A Revolutionary Approach to People and Management 2nd ed.
Brian Dive
London: Kogan Page, 2004
288pp ISBN: 0749442522
It is argued that most organizations remain profoundly unhealthy, due to poor design, faulty strategy, unclear links to strategy, diffuse company culture, and unhappy employees, which all stem from the same source—a lack of transparent decision-making and accountability. The author provides insights into commonly recurring issues including: how many people should there be in an organization; how many layers of hierarchy are necessary; how to effectively reward employees; what are the logical steps for employee development; what career paths

employees should follow, using extensive case studies of Unilever and Tesco. A Decision-Making Accountability (DMA) model is introduced, and pay banding is critically reassessed.

The Horizontal Organization: What the Organization of the Future Looks Like and How It Delivers Value to Customers
Frank Ostroff
New York: Oxford University Press USA, 1999
360pp ISBN: 0195121384
This book introduces the concept of the horizontal organization. It explains the way horizontal organizations operate around a core process, reviews the organizing of a horizontal operating unit, a division around a sales and service delivery process, and an entire company. The author includes case studies of the supply management organization of Motorola's Space and Systems Technology Group, G. E. Salisbury, Barclays Bank's Home Finance Division, and Xerox.

Inventing the Organizations of the 21st Century
Thomas W. Malone, Robert Laubacher, Michael S. Scott Morton, eds
Cambridge, Massachusetts: MIT Press, 2003
448pp ISBN: 0262134314
Many factors, particularly the IT revolution, have disrupted the structure and methods of the modern corporation, it is claimed. Based on a five-year study into new ways of working, twenty articles contained in this book are structured around three fundamental questions. The first—What is changing?—examines the drivers and outcomes of change, including the issue of empowerment and the impact of IT. The second question—What can you do about it?—looks at new strategies and forms, including the "delta model" and "X-Teams." The third question—What do you want in the first place?—explores possible directions that go beyond the economic model, a new "manifesto," and a new "social contract" that encompasses issues such as employer-worker relationships and the environment.

The Living Company: Habits for Survival in a Turbulent Business Environment
Arie de Geus
Boston, Massachusetts: Harvard Business School Press, 2002
240pp ISBN: 1578518202
De Geus discusses the success elements of the few organizations that survive both long time periods and big changes, and aims to pinpoint the reasons for this achievement.

A guide for managing companies over a long period of time, the book explores ideas from the angles of both profitability and survival.

Managing in Virtual Organizations
Malcolm Warner, Morgen Witzel
Florence, KY: Thomson Learning, 2004
160pp ISBN: 1861529848
"Virtual organizations" are a new form of business organization that allows teams to work together and customers to purchase goods and services across great distances. In three parts, this book takes a cross-disciplinary and questioning approach to the analysis of the virtual space, the concept of intangible capital, the knowledge transformation process, and aspects of managing in virtual organizations. Case studies of Reuters and the World Bank and examples of virtual management in practice are included.

Organising for Success in the Twenty-first Century: A Starting Point for Change
Richard Whittington, Michael Mayer
London, United Kingdom: Chartered Institute of Personnel and Development (CIPD), 2002
48pp ISBN: 0852929730
This report arises from a research project focusing on organizational design for the 21st century. The emphasis is on the skills and capabilities needed in the process of organizing rather than reliance on any specific organizational structure. The importance of integrating the hard elements of systems and structure and the soft elements of culture and behavior is underlined. It highlights tools which can be used for organizing, and outlines the implications for practitioners and further research.

The Organization in Crisis: Downsizing, Restructuring, and Privatization
Ronald J. Burke, Cary L. Cooper, eds
Cambridge, Massachusetts: Blackwell, 2000
320pp ISBN: 0631212310
This study by international researchers and practitioners examines the implementation and impact of organizational change. Drawing on a mixture of research, theory, and practice, it explores key issues such as the new employment relationship, organization restructuring, the effects of downsizing, the role of privatization, and the revitalization of best practice, and proposes and discusses strategies for managing these changes better in the future.

1848

BUSINESS INFORMATION SOURCES

"We talk about organizations in terms not unlike those used by an Ubongi medicine man to discuss diseases."

Herbert A. Simon

     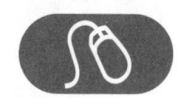

Organization Modeling: Innovative Architectures for the 21st Century

Joseph Morabito, Ira Sack, Anilkumar Bhate

Upper Saddle River, New Jersey: Prentice Hall, 1999

304pp ISBN: 0132575523

This book shows how the object-oriented modeling approach used in computer systems design can be used in conjunction with more traditional theories of organization design. The aim of the authors is to show IT professionals how to be better business people and show business people how to better marry technology and people systems.

Organization Theory and Design 8th ed.

Richard L. Daft

Cincinnati, Ohio: South-Western College Publishing, 2003

672pp ISBN: 032415691X

This book provides an overview of the field of organization theory, discusses the basics of how well an organization's design matches its purpose, and looks at how technology influences design, the difference between manufacturing and service company designs, and the impact of ethical values and company culture on design.

Organization Theory: Modern, Symbolic, and Postmodern Perspectives 2nd ed.

Mary Jo Hatch

New York: Oxford University Press USA, 2006

416pp ISBN: 0199260214

Organization Theory offers a clear and comprehensive introduction to the study of organizations and an appreciation of the different perspectives that have contributed to our knowledge of them.

Organization Theory: Selected Readings 4th ed.

Derek S. Pugh

London: Penguin, 1997

576pp ISBN: 0140250247

This resource book brings together the selected writings of leading authorities on the cutting edge of thinking, practice and research of organization theory. It spans 70 years, from Max Weber's seminal writings on bureaucratic organizations to the latest management thinking by Charles Handy and Tom Peters.

The Path of Least Resistance for Managers: Designing Organizations to Succeed

Robert Fritz

San Francisco, California: Publishers' Group West, 1999

240pp ISBN: 1576750655

Drawing upon ideas of energy flow in science, the author explains how to redesign an organization or team for success. He argues that managers are far more likely to succeed when introducing structural changes if they take structural laws into account. He examines four critical elements: moving the organization from wasteful oscillating patterns to successful advancement; managing strategy to support business; "composing" the organization to support business; and aligning people to the spiritual purpose of the organization.

Re-creating the Corporation: A Design of Organizations for the 21st Century

Russell Lincoln Ackoff

New York: Oxford University Press, Inc., 1999

352pp ISBN: 0195123875

Ackoff makes a case for developing a systems view of organizations, and underlines the importance of using systems thinking skills when re-creating a company. The book includes discussion of how to make sense of the chaos that is a part of any system, how to determine aims, and how to achieve them. The author emphasizes the need for incorporating as much democracy and flexibility as possible and warns against the quick-fix mentality.

Reframing Organizations: Artistry, Choice and Leadership 3rd ed.

Lee G. Bolman, Terrence E. Deal

Hoboken, New Jersey: Wiley, 2003

496pp ISBN: 0787964263

This text outlines a tool (called "reframing") for finding new opportunities and options in confusing and troubling organizational situations. The authors have identified four frames: the structural frame, the human resource frame, the political frame, and the symbolic frame. These multiple frames are seen as giving leaders an edge in decoding organizational complexity. This new edition highlights current development in organizational and leadership research and presents new case studies from organizations such as eBay.

Surfing the Edge of Chaos: The Laws of Nature and the New Laws of Business

Richard T. Pascale, Mark Millemann, Linda Gioja

New York: Crown Publishing, 2001

336pp ISBN: 0609808834

Starting from the thesis that business, like nature, is a living system, the authors proceed to apply four principles of the life sciences to business organizations: equilibrium is death; innovation takes place on the edge of chaos; self-organization and emergence occur naturally; organizations can only be disturbed, not directed. These principles are illustrated through in-depth case studies of Sears, Roebuck & Co., Monsanto, Hewlett Packard, Sun Microsystems, Royal Dutch Steel, and the U.S. Army. Ultimately, they suggest, businesses, like species, either respond to change and evolve or get left behind and become extinct.

A Theory of the Firm: Governance, Residual Claims, and Organizational Forms

Michael C. Jensen

Cambridge, Massachusetts: Harvard University Press, 2000

320pp ISBN: 0674002954

This presents eight articles written by the author and various co-authors between 1970 and 2000. They address aspects of the theory of the firm. The three articles in Part One examine the effects of internal governance systems and the market for corporate control on the behavior and value of corporations. The five articles in Part Two analyze various aspects of the internal organizational rules of the game, looking at agency costs, residual claims, and incentives.

Who Really Matters? The Core Group Theory of Power, Privilege and Success

Art Kleiner

Naperville, Illinois: Nicholas Brealey Publishing, 2003

288pp ISBN: 1857883357

This introduces the concept of the core group within an organization. How core groups can unconsciously guide and control organizations is explained. How to learn about your organization, understand your own position and prospects, and how to react to privileges, power, and rank around you are subjects also discussed.

Winning through Innovation: A Practical Guide to Leading Organizational Change and Renewal

Michael L. Tushman, Charles A. O'Reilly III

Boston, Massachusetts: Harvard Business School Press, 2002

272pp ISBN: 1578518210

This book examines how leadership, culture, and organizational architectures can both facilitate and, at times, impede

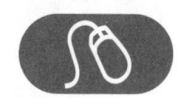

1849

BUSINESS INFORMATION SOURCES

"Real commitment is rare in today's organization. 90 percent of the time, what passes for commitment is competence."

Peter Senge

innovation. The authors demonstrate how to identify today's critical managerial problems, how to use culture and commitment to promote innovation and implement strategy, and how to deal with changing innovation requirements as organizations evolve.

Writers on Organizations 5th ed.

Derek S. Pugh, David J. Hickson
London: Penguin, 1996
224pp ISBN: 0140250239
A compendium to the principal ideas of the leading authorities on organizations. Brief résumés bring out the main thrust of each management thinker. The six sections cover the structure of organizations, the organization in its environment, the management of organizations, decision making in organizations, people in organizations, and organizational change and learning.

Zero Space: Moving beyond Organisational Limits

Frank Lekanne Deprez, Rene Tissen
San Francisco, California: Berrett-Koehler, 2002
224pp ISBN: 1576751821
In order to create organizations for the knowledge economy business, leaders are reaching for the management tools that evolved in the industrial age. The authors see this as a backward step and propose an alternative approach for creating organizational success. The "zero space" concept is introduced, and the eight key features of this model are explained. The use of these tools to create the organizations needed for today's economy is examined.

MAGAZINES

International Journal of Organization Theory and Behavior

ISSN: 1093-4537
PrAcademics Press
21760 Mountain Sugar Lane, Boca Raton, Florida, 33433
T: +1 561 362 9183
http://pracademicspress.com/ about-ijotb.html
The journal aims to bring together researchers and practitioners, both inside and outside the United States, who are in the areas of organization theory, management, development, and behavior. It covers all private, public, and nonprofit organizations' theories and behavior.

Journal of Organizational Change Management

ISSN: 0953-4814
Emerald

44 Brattle Street, 4th Floor, Cambridge, Massachusetts, 02138
T: +1 888 622 0075
F: +1 617 354 6875
www.emeraldinsight.com
International in scope and aimed at both academics and practicing managers, the *Journal of Organizational Change Management* covers areas such as organizational learning, the psychology of change, and entrepreneurship within organizations.

Journal of Organizational Excellence

ISSN: 1531-1864
Wiley
111 River St, Hoboken, New Jersey, 07030-5774
T: +1 201 748 6000
F: +1 212 850 6021
www.wiley.com
Formerly called *National Productivity Review*, this journal is published four times per year. It provides readers with the latest information on new organizational techniques, trends, and strategies, and will aid any business professional looking to find innovative ways to make their organization succeed.

Organizational Dynamics

ISSN: 0090-2616
Elsevier Science
Customer Service Department, 6277 Sea Harbor Drive, Orlando, Florida, 32887-4800
T: +1 877 839 7126 or +1 407 345 4020
F: +1 407 363 1354
www.elsevier.com
Organizational Dynamics is an international journal that aims to link academic research with management practice. It examines both organizational behavior and the strategic management and human resources management practices that influence organizations.

Organization—Critical Journal of Organization Theory and Society

ISSN: 1350-5084
Sage Publications
1 Oliver's Yard, 55 City Road, London, EC1Y 1SP, U.K.
T: +44 (0) 20 7324 8500
F: +44 (0) 20 7324 8600
www.sagepub.co.uk
This international journal is intended for those with a professional or academic interest in organization studies. Its contents typically cover areas such as organization theory, human resource management and organizational behavior, organizational psychology, the virtual organization, and globalization.

INTERNET
Organization Development Network
www.odnetwork.org
Thi is a professional association of organization development practitioners working in the fields of business and education. The site provides information on educational opportunities, job listings, conferences, and events.

ORGANIZATIONS
USA
Academy of Management
P.O. Box 3020, Briarcliff Manor, New York, 10510-8020
T: +1 914 923 2607
F: +1 914 923 2615
E: *academy@aom.pace.edu*
www.aomonline.org
The Academy of Management is a professional association of scholars dedicated to knowing more about management and organizations. Its key aim is to enhance the profession by advancing the scholarship of management and encouraging the professional progress of its members. Its membership comprises scholars and practitioners with scholarly interests from business, government, and nonprofit organizations.

Association of Management/ International Association of Management
P.O. Box 64841, Virginia Beach, Virginia, 23469-4841
T: +1 757 482 2273
F: +1 757 482 0325
E: *AoMgt@infi.net*
www.aom-iaom.org
This is a nonprofit professional association dedicated to advancing management theory in a variety of fields, including organizational theory. It offers conferences, journals, and online publications on topics including organizational behavior, structure
change and
development,
communication,
organizations as political systems, and
organizational management applications.

FOR MORE INFORMATION

🖱 Corporate Strategy (pp. 1721-1723)
🖱 Learning Organization (pp. 1804-1806)
⭐ Making the Workplace Flex, Not Break (pp. 30-32)

"In the new organization, power flows from expertise, not position." — Thomas Stewart

Outsourcing

BOOKS

The Black Book of Outsourcing: How to Manage the Changes, Challenges, and Opportunities
Douglas Brown, Scott Wilson
New York: Wiley, 2005
386pp ISBN: 0471718890
This useful and comprehensive introduction to outsourcing is an essential guide to this growing (and often controversial) area. This book is as useful for those trying to carve out a career in this industry as it is for those who need to know the nuts and bolts, such as how to manage an outsourcing program.

Business Process Outsourcing: Process, Strategies, and Contracts
John K. Halvey, Barbara Murphy Melby
New York: Wiley, 1999
416pp ISBN: 047134821X
In this guide for businesses looking to outsource some of their business functions, the topics dealt with address the process involved in contracting out key services, including the request for proposal (RFP) and selecting and contracting with an outsourcing vendor.

Outsourcing IT: The Legal Aspects
Rachel Burnett
Aldershot, United Kingdom: Gower Publishing, 1998
256pp ISBN: 0566076985
This comprehensive guide to outsourcing the information technology function focuses on the need to obtain a properly negotiated formal contract. It discusses the structure of such a contract, and then goes on to cover the provisions that relate to staffing, location, software, costs, management liaison, allowing for change, security, duration, termination, and other matters. It also gives advice on public procurement and choosing a supplier.

Strategic Outsourcing: A Structured Approach to Outsourcing Decisions and Initiatives
Maurice F. Greaver II
New York: AMACOM, 1999
320pp ISBN: 0814404340
This book provides a thorough guide for managers who face the task of outsourcing

business functions. Contents include the rationale for outsourcing, identifying functions that can be outsourced versus those key services that should remain in-house, and the process of requesting proposals. The book also covers how to select and contract with vendors for outsourced services.

What's This India Business? Offshoring, Outsourcing and the Global Services Revolution
Paul Davies
Naperville, Illinois: Nicholas Brealey Publishing, 2004
240pp ISBN: 1904838006
Many businesses have outsourced some of their operations to India, and this book is a practical guide for anyone planning or simply investigating such a route. Packed with advice on how to gain competitive advantage from outsourcing to India, the books also has helful hints on etiquette and Indian business culture.

INTERNET

Outsourcing Center
www.outsourcing-center.com
This Web site provides comprehensive information and links regarding outsourcing. Its content includes industry-specific outsourcing information, research, outsourcing processes, and an online journal. It also provides material on suppliers and legal issues.

The Outsourcing Institute
www.outsourcing.com
The Outsourcing Institute is a professional association providing information and networking resources related to outsourcing. Its Web site offers information on the outsourcing process, including needs assessment and the selection of service providers. It also has information targeted at buyers and sellers of outsourcing services. Registration is required for some information; online membership is free.

Outsourcing Research Center
www.cio.com/forums/outsourcing
The site provides online access to recent articles and gives details of forthcoming events.

TechWeb Business Technology Network
www.techweb.com
This site focuses on recent news and articles on IT outsourcing, plus links to events in its "Tech Calendar."

Virtual Corporations and Outsourcing
www.brint.com
A selection of articles on outsourcing can be sourced from this site.

ORGANIZATIONS
USA
The Outsourcing Institute
Jericho Atrium, 500 N. Broadway, Suite 141, Jericho, New York, 11753
T: +1 516 681 0066
F: +1 516 938 1839
E: *customerservice@outsourcing.com*
www.outsourcing.com
This professional body, founded in 1993, provides outsourcing professionals worldwide with access to a business-to-business marketplace and an independent advisory network, as well as with information and education on outsourcing best practice. Membership is free.

Europe
Network Outsourcing Association
Martyn Hart, Chair
Keswick House, 207 Anerley Road, London, SE20 8ER, U.K.
T: +44 (0) 20 8778 9449
F: +44 (0) 20 8778 8402
E: *admin@noa.co.uk*
www.noa.co.uk
The Association is an independent body, formed in the early 1990s, that acts as a forum for the business technology outsourcing community. Its membership is made up of U.K. and other companies with experience in outsourcing, and suppliers and consultants who support the industry.

1851

FOR MORE INFORMATION
✓ Deciding Whether to Outsource (pp. 542–543)
☆ Facilities Management (pp. 214–215)
☍ Facilities Management (p. 1754)
☆ Outsourcing (pp. 120–121)

"The personnel in India are more versatile. They're simply more hungry for work."
Lycourgos Kyprianou

Packaging

BOOKS

50 Trade Secrets of Great Design Packaging 2nd ed.
Stafford Cliff
Gloucester, Massachusetts: Rockport, 2002
224pp ISBN: 1564968723
Fifty outstanding packaging designs, covering a broad selection of products and approaches, are featured in this book. Each of the designs is individually profiled, outlining the challenges and problems each designer faced with the particular product. The case studies document the packaging design process and include discussion of new materials and methods of construction.

Forms, Folds and Sizes
Poppy Evans
Gloucester, Massachusetts: Rockport, 2004
256pp ISBN: 1592530540
Eminently practical, this book gathers together essential advice for graphic designers into one helpful resource. It includes information on typefaces, printing processes, and paper sizes (in both metric and imperial), as well as more technical advice about good design practice.

The Marketer's Guide to Successful Package Design
Herbert M. Meyers, Murray J. Lubliner
New York: McGraw-Hill/NTC, 1998
320pp ISBN: 0844234389
A guide for product marketers, this book analyzes and explores the elements of marketing and design that can lead to successful packaging results, including discussions on the research and planning involved in launching a new design.

What Is Packaging Design?
Giles Calver
Hove, United Kingdom: Rotovision, 2003
256pp (Essential Design Handbooks)
ISBN: 2880466180
Fully illustrated and highly readable, this book is an excellent guide to the state of the art in packaging design. It offers examples of the best quality work, includes essays based on them, and discusses challenges facing designers in this field. The book looks at the role of type, layout, and format within the packaging context and also covers relevant legislation, branding, and marketing.

MAGAZINES

Advanced Packaging
ISSN: 1521–3323
PennWell
P.O. Box 3425, Northbrook, Illinois, 60065–3425
T: +1 847 559 7500
F: +1 847 291 4816
http://ap.pennnet.com
AP is a monthly magazine with news and features about packaging materials, technology, and processes. Much of the information is available from the Web site.

Packaging Digest
ISSN: 0030–9117
Reed Business Information
8878 Barrons Boulevard, Highlands Ranch, Colorado, 80129–2345
T: +1 800 446 6551
F: +1 303 470 4280
www.packagingdigest.com
This U.S.-based monthly magazine covers a wide range of packaging-related issues, with a focus on packaging operations. The Web site has number of sections, including an archive of past issues; a database of machinery, materials, suppliers, and contract packagers; a calendar of industry events; and lists of relevant industry contacts.

Packaging Innovation
ISSN: 1365–5663
CMP Information Ltd.
Sovereign Way, Tonbridge, Kent, TN9 1RW, U.K.
T: +44 (0) 1732 377 486
F: +44 (0) 1732 353 328
www.dotpackaging.com
Produced for packaging development personnel, packaging technologists, consultants, and research and development institutes, this newsletter focuses on innovative developments in technology, materials, and processes.

Packaging Magazine
ISSN: 1461–4200
CMP Information Ltd.
Sovereign Way, Tonbridge, Kent, TN9 1RW, U.K.
T: +44 (0) 1732 377 486
F: +44 (0) 1732 353 328
www.dotpackaging.com
This journal provides regular coverage of the issues facing professionals and decision makers in the packaging industry today. It

contains news from the United Kingdom, Europe, and the rest of the world relating to business, market trends, product and machinery developments, and environmental issues.

Packaging Today International
ISSN: 1470–6008
Wilmington Media
Maidstone Road, Sidcup Kent, DA14 5HZ, U.K.
This is a European journal focusing on all aspects of the packaging industry, including legislation, the influence of consolidation, cost-effective production methods, and the changing face of retailing in the packaging industry.

INTERNET

Environmental Packaging International
www.enviro-pac.com
Sponsored by a consulting firm specializing in compliance with state and international environmental packaging and product laws, the site provides a list of services, industry news, and links to other sites.

Packaging Business
www.packagingbusiness.com
Sponsored by a private company in the packaging industry, the site offers industry news, discussions, classifieds, job fair information, and links to other sites.

Packaging Digest
www.packagingdigest.com
This site contains articles from current and past issues of *Packaging Digest*, together with other information resources including news and reports of developments in packaging materials, machinery, and technology, and market trends from around the world.

Packaging Network
www.packagingnetwork.com
Primarily a marketplace, the site also provides news, access to a library, a discussion forum, trade publications, and a job search. Site visitors may buy, sell, and advertise online. A free e-newsletter is also available.

Packaging Strategies
www.packstrat.com
This site provides a newsletter, articles, news, a product guide, and a calendar of events.

"Any color you like as long as it's black."   Henry Ford

Packaging World
www.packworld.com
This online U.S.-based packaging magazine has databases of topical articles on machinery, products, companies, design, materials, and regulations, along with information about jobs, events, and associations connected with the packaging industry.

ORGANIZATIONS
USA
Institute of Packaging Professionals
1601 North Bond Street, Suite 101, Naperville, Illinois, 60563
T: +1 630 544 5050
F: +1 630 544 5055
E: *info@iopp.net*
www.iopp.org
This membership organization for the packaging industry offers its members a range of benefits, including events, education, career development, and publications.

Women in Packaging, Inc.
4290 Bells Ferry Road, Suite 106–17, Kennesaw, Georgia, 30144–1300

T: + 1 678 594 6872
E: *wpstaff@womeninpackaging.org*
www.womeninpackaging.org
This organization helps provide a network of support for women who are involved in the packaging industry. Membership provides access to their magazine, forums, hotline, Speakers Bureau, and news.

Europe
Institute of Packaging
Willoughby House, Broad Street, Stamford, Lincolnshire, PE9 1PB, U.K.
T: +44 (0)1780 759200
F: +44 (0)1780 759220
E: *iop@pi2.org.uk*
www.pi2.org.uk
The aim of the Institute is to advance public education in, and improve the technology of, packaging in all its aspects, in particular by promoting the education and training of persons engaged or interested in packaging as an occupation.

The Packaging Federation
1 Warwick Row, London, SW1E 5ER, U.K.
T: +44 (0) 20 7808 7217
F: +44 (0) 20 7808 7218

E: *iandent@packagingfedn.co.uk*
www.packagingfedn.co.uk
The Federation is a trade organization representing all the material streams within the industry. Its aims are to improve significantly the way in which the industry is perceived and to protect the interests of packaging manufacturers through properly managed lobbying and public relations programs.

International
World Packaging Organisation
STFI-Packforsk, Box 5604, S-114 86 Stockholm, Sweden
F: + 46 8 411 55 18
www.packaging-technology.com
The aims of the WPO include: promoting the development of packaging technology, science, and engineering; stimulating the development of packaging skills and expertise; advising on the formation and operation of national packaging organizations and institutes; and providing information on sources of packaging knowledge, education, and training.

1853

BUSINESS INFORMATION SOURCES

"I do not want the company to become a mass production line."

Sayyid Khalid bin Hamad bin Hamoud Al Bu Said

Performance Appraisal

BOOKS

Appraisal and Feedback: Making Performance Review Work 3rd ed.
Clive Fletcher
London: Chartered Institute of Personnel and Development (CIPD), 2004
190pp ISBN: 1843980290
Both managers and employees dread appraisals, but if they are handled properly they can a be an excellent way of celebrating success, identifying areas for improvement, and working out how individuals contribute to the business's success overall. This new edition of Clive Fletcher's book offers practical advice for managers and includes a new chapter on 360 degree appraisals.

The Complete Guide to Performance Appraisal
Dick Grote
New York: AMACOM, 1996
400pp ISBN: 0814403131
From his personal knowledge of performance appraisals, Grote has compiled this reference for managers in both large and small businesses, whether they are highly experienced or relative beginners. The book provides practical guidelines for initiating successful performance appraisals, starting with the basics.

How to Do a Superior Performance Appraisal
William S. Swan
Hoboken, New Jersey: Wiley, 1991
224pp ISBN: 0471514683
This is a helpful guide for managers and appraisees on how to get the best out of appraisals.

Performance Appraisal: One More Time
John D. Drake
Menlo Park, California: Crisp Publications, 1998
80pp ISBN: 1560524421
The author addresses the need to consider performance appraisal as an ongoing process rather than an isolated activity. The book emphasizes that communication and trust are more important elements of the process than rating mechanisms or scoring methods.

Performance Appraisal: State of the Art in Practice
James W. Smither, ed.
San Francisco, California: Jossey-Bass, 1998
576pp ISBN: 0787909459
This book provides an overview of the performance appraisal process, dealing with appraisals at a strategic level and analyzing the latest research and illustrating it with examples of how the theories work in practice. It examines performance appraisals in the context of pay and performance plans, organizational culture, and motivational strategies.

Performance Management
Robert Bacal
Maidenhead, United Kingdom: McGraw-Hill, 1998
160pp ISBN: 0070718660
Designed to help managers get top performance and value from employees, this book emphasizes the importance of creating relationships and ensuring effective communication. Its chapters focus on preparation, planning, communication, data gathering, appraisal and review processes, diagnosis, and improvement. Some innovative variations are discussed and a case study helps to pull ideas together at the end.

Powerful Performance Appraisals: How to Set Expectations and Work Together to Improve Performance
Karen McKirchy
Franklin Lakes, New Jersey: Career Press, 1998
128pp ISBN: 1564143678
The author sets out to clarify the key elements that make a successful performance appraisal. She provides simple guidelines combined with genuine appraisal examples to help an employer pinpoint any potential issues and motivate his or her employees to greater goal focus.

MAGAZINES

Human Resource Executive
LRP Publications
747 Dreshers Road, Suite 500, Horsham, Pennsylvania, 19044–0980
T: +1 215 784 0860
F: +1 215 784 9639
www.hrexecutive.com
Targeted at upper-level HR practitioners, *Human Resource Executive* is published 16 times per year. It offers case studies, profiles of successful HR managers, and news, covering a number of HR topics, including performance appraisal.

Team Performance Management
ISSN: 1352–7592
Emerald
44 Brattle Street, 4th Floor, Cambridge, Massachusetts, 02138
T: +1 888 622 0075
F: +1 617 354 6875
www.emeraldinsight.com
Subscriptions to *Team Performance Management* cover eight printed issues a year and online access to current and previous volumes via Emerald Fulltext. The journal aims to support managers, HR or quality professionals, consultants, and academics in implementing and developing work team performance. Its articles include case studies, application papers, and reviews of theories and techniques.

Workforce Management
ISSN: 1092–8332
Crain Communications, Inc.
711 Third Avenue, New York, NY 10017–4036
T: +1 212 210 0100
F: +1 212 210 0200
www.adage.com
A monthly magazine, *Workforce Management* targets HR practitioners with content on a variety of topics, including performance appraisal. It offers case studies, trend analysis, and commentary on the social and economic effects of HR practices.

INTERNET

Performance Measurement Association
www.som.cranfield.ac.uk/som/ research/centres/cbp/pma
This site is the discussion forum for the Performance Measurement Association, on which anyone can post PM-related questions and utilize networking opportunities.

Zigon Performance Measurement Resources
www.zigonperf.com/performance.html
This Zigon site offers resources for free online viewing that include sample performance measures, links to related

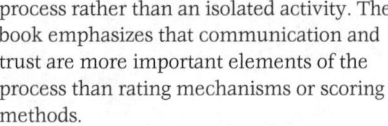
"Everyone has peak performance potential. You just need to know where they are coming from and meet them there."

Kenneth Blanchard

sites, bibliographies, a free newsletter, and articles by Jack Zigon on performance measures and management. Registration is required for some of these services.

ORGANIZATIONS
USA
American Society for Training and Development (ASTD)
1640 King Street, Box 1443, Alexandria, Virginia, 22313–2043
T: +1 703 683 8100
F: +1 703 683 1523
E: *customercare@astd.org*
www.astd.org
An association of workplace learning and performance professionals, ASTD's members come from multinational corporations, medium-sized and small businesses, government, academia, consulting firms, and product and service suppliers. It offers research and analysis, conferences, expositions, seminars, and publications. Though its primary focus is training and development, it also addresses issues of performance appraisal.

International Society for Performance Improvement (ISPI)
Suite 260, 1400 Spring Street, Silver Spring, Maryland, 20910
T: +1 301 587 8570
F: +1 301 587 8573
E: *info@ispi.org*
www.ispi.org
ISPI is an international association for improving workplace productivity and performance; it has members throughout the United States, Canada, and 40 other countries. It aims to develop and recognize members' proficiency, and advocates the use of Human Performance Technology, a systematic approach that can be applied to individuals, small groups, and large organizations.

Society for Human Resource Management (SHRM)
1800 Duke Street, Alexandria, Virginia, 22314
T: +1 703 548 3440
F: +1 703 535 6490
E: *custsvc@shrm.org*
www.shrm.org

SHRM is a leading voice of the human resource profession, offering members education and information services, conferences and seminars, government and media representation, online services, and publications. The Society, the world's largest human resource management association, is a founding member of both the North American Human Resource Management Association (NAHRMA) and the World Federation of Personnel Management Associations (WFPMA).

Europe
Centre for Business Performance
Cranfield School of Management, Cranfield, Bedfordshire, MK42 0AL, U.K.
T: +44 (0) 1234 751 122 ext 2433
F: +44 (0) 1234 757 409
E: *cbp@cranfield.ac.uk*
www.cranfield.ac.uk/som/cbp
The Centre focuses on applied research and knowledge transfer involving practical tools and concepts underpinned by high-quality academic research. It organizes courses in business performance measurement, produces publications, offers a forum and networking opportunities, and initiates research projects. It also runs the Performance Measurement Association (see below).

Institute for Employment Studies
Mantell Building, Falmer, Brighton, East Sussex, BN1 9RF, U.K.
T: +44 (0) 1273 686751
F: +44 (0) 1273 690430
E: *enquiries@employment-studies.co.uk*
www.employment-studies.co.uk
The Institute is an independent, nonprofit, international center for research and consulting that focuses on HR issues and works closely with government departments, employers in the manufacturing, public, and service sectors, agencies, professional and employee bodies, and foundations. Its work also covers performance management.

Performance Measurement Association
Centre for Business Performance, Cranfield School of Management, Cranfield, Bedfordshire, MK42 0AL, U.K.

T: +44 (0) 1234 751 122
F: +44 (0) 1234 757 409
www.performanceportal.org
The Performance Measurement Association (PMA) is a voluntary global network organized by the Centre for Business Performance at Cranfield School of Management. It has a multi-disciplinary constituency, led by a board of academics from the performance measurement and management fields. Its Web site is a valuable resource that contains a database of researchers, key references, links, the PMA's *Perspectives on Performance* newsletter, a discussion forum, and details of planned conferences.

The Work Foundation
Peter Runge House, 3 Carlton House Terrace, London, SW1Y 5DG, U.K.
T: +44 (0) 870 165 6700
F: +44 (0) 870 165 6701
E: *customercentre@theworkfoundation.com*
www.theworkfoundation.com
Established in 2002, The Work Foundation is a new incarnation of The Industrial Society, an independent body with over 80 years' experience in management development and training. The Work Foundation operates under the belief that business success goes hand-in-hand with fair management practices. The services offered to members include an information service and employment law helpline; a publishing program of books, research reports, and videos; plus a training and consulting service, which includes the School of Coaching.

FOR MORE INFORMATION

- Coaching, Counseling, and Mentoring (pp. 1698–1700)
- Coaching for Better Performance (pp. 434–435)
- Conducting a Performance Appraisal (pp. 438–439)
- Making Performance Appraisals a Win-win Experience (pp. 21–22)
- Motivation (pp. 1835–1837)
- Personnel Management and HR Management (pp. 1856–1859)

1855

BUSINESS INFORMATION SOURCES

"Resolve to perform what you ought. Perform without fail what you resolve."

Benjamin Franklin

     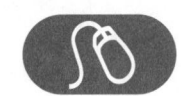

Personnel Management and HR Management

BOOKS

Aligning Human Resources and Business Strategy

Linda Holbeche

Woburn, Massachusetts: Butterworth-Heinemann, 2001
496pp ISBN: 0750653620

With tools and case studies, this book is designed to help HR planners deliver key business objectives and quantify the benefits of an effective people strategy. Profiles of top strategies and companies are included.

Handbook of Human Resource Management Practice 9th ed.

Michael Armstrong

London: Kogan Page, 2004
976pp ISBN: 0749441054

This comprehensive textbook provides an overview of current trends in human resource management and includes sections on organizational behavior, work and employment, employee resourcing, performance management, human resource development, reward management, employee relations, and health and safety. New chapters focus on the psychological contract, selection interviewing and organizational culture.

The HR Value Proposition

Dave Ulrich, Wayne Brockbank

Boston, Massachusetts: Harvard Business School Press, 2005
304pp ISBN: 1591397073

The arguments found in this book are based on a massive resarch project conducted by the authors: 29,000 HR professionals and managers were studied over 16 years. The result? That creating value through HR lies in understanding all the challenges faced by the business, and understanding what key members of staff and other stakeholders mean by "value." Offering practical advice and tools (such as worksheets), this book is ideal for anyone who needs to think about HR resources, strategy, and deliverables.

Human Resource Management 10th ed.

Gary Dessler

Upper Saddle River, New Jersey: Prentice Hall, 2004
752pp ISBN: 0131440977

This is a textbook for students on personnel and human resource management courses and for practicing managers with a need for a comprehensive review of personnel management concepts and techniques. The broad areas covered include recruitment and placement, training and development, compensation, labor relations and employee security, and international HRM.

Human Resource Strategy: Formulation, Implementation, and Impact

Peter Bamberger, Ilan Meshoulam

London: Sage Publications, 2000
224pp ISBN: 0761914250

In this text exploring the history, development and impact of human resource strategy, research on the subject is reviewed and its implications for management and for HR practice are discussed. Chapters focusing on strategies and their effectiveness include best practice cases and illustrations.

International HRM: Contemporary Issues in Europe

Chris Brewster, Hilary Harris, eds

New York: Routledge, 1998
320pp ISBN: 0415194903

This collection of edited papers from European experts in the field covers all aspects of international human resource management. A detailed introduction is followed by articles addressing key issues including the strategic role of HRM in staffing, reward management and performance management, and the dynamics of culture and gender in international management.

Introduction to Human Resource Management

Ashly Pinnington, Tony Edwards

New York: Oxford University Press, Inc., 2000
304pp ISBN: 0198775431

This textbook provides a comprehensive introduction to human resource management (HRM). The four parts cover definitions, the context of HRM, managing human resources, and future developments. It is intended for undergraduate business students and MBA students.

Managing Human Resources Through Strategic Partnerships 9th ed.

Randall Schuler, Susan Jackson

Cincinnati, Ohio: South-Western College Publishing, 2005
720pp ISBN: 032428991X

Written by experts, this is a higher-level text which covers such themes as strategy, teams, diversity, global issues, and change. The structure of the text emphasizes the HR triad (employee, line manager, HR manager), with the understanding that effective human resource management requires mutual understanding and collaboration among HR professionals, managers, and employees.

Strategic Human Resource Management: A Guide to Action 3rd ed.

Michael Armstrong

London: Kogan Page, 2006
208pp ISBN: 0749445114

This revised edition has been updated to include latest developments in the field. This book sets out to be the bridge between theory and practice, and contains checklists, examples, and case studies.

Strategic Human Resource Management: Corporate Rhetoric and Human Reality

Lynda Gratton et al.

New York: Oxford University Press, Inc., 1999
256pp ISBN: 0198782039

Based on close collaboration with a number of high profile organizations—BT, Citibank, Glaxo Wellcome, Hewlett Packard, Kraft Jacobs, Suchard, Lloyds-TSB Group, the NHS, and WH Smith—this book sheds light on the organizational responses to large-scale changes and details the changing demands made of employees in the process. It goes beyond fashionable management rhetoric to uncover the reality of human resource management.

Strategic Human Resources: Frameworks for General Managers

James N. Baron, David M. Kreps

Hoboken, New Jersey: Wiley, 1999
608pp ISBN: 0471072532

This is a comprehensive textbook for MBA students and managers, covering a wide

"Show me a man who enjoys firing people and I'll show you a charlatan or a sadist."

Tony O'Reilly

range of issues concerning human resource and personnel management.

The Workplace Scorecard: Managing Human Capital to Execute Strategy

Mark Huselid, Brian E. Becker, Richard W. Beatty

Boston, Massachusetts: Harvard Business School Press, 2005

288pp ISBN: 1591392454

This book argues that most managment and human resources-related processes actually hinder employees from perfoming to the best of their ability. As a result, the authors argue, businesses cannot achieve their strategic goals. As an alternative, they offer a scorecard that identifies and measures all the elements needed to make a workforce productive and successful.

MAGAZINES

Asia Pacific Journal of Human Resources

ISSN: 1038–4111

Australian Human Resources Institute

Level 10, 601 Bourke St, Melbourne, Victoria, 3000, Australia

T: +61 3 9918 9200

F: +61 3 9918 9201

www.ahri.com.au

This is a peer-reviewed journal which aims to reflect the development of and practice in the field of human resources in the Asia Pacific region. Articles focus on the results of research and examples of current practice.

Employee Benefit News

ISSN: 1044–6265

Thomson Financial Partners

1290 Avenue of the Americas, New York, 10104

T: +1 888 280 4820

www.tfimg.com/IMG_Media/IMGhome.html

Published 15 times per year, this magazine is the preeminent source of information on employee benefits. The magazine provides comprehensive and useful articles that highlight the trends in all areas of employee benefits. The coverage provided in this magazine is invaluable to employee benefits executives.

HRfocus

ISSN: 1059–6038

Institute of Management and Administration (IOMA)

3 Park Avenue, 30th Floor, New York, 10001–5902

T: +1 212 244 0360

F: +1 212 564 0465

www.ioma.com

A monthly newsletter, it provides a collection of news items, practical articles, and case studies on issues relating to HR.

HR Magazine

ISSN: 1047–3149

Society for Human Resource Management (SHRM)

1800 Duke Street, Alexandria, Virginia, 22314

T: +1 703 548 3440

F: +1 703 535 6490

www.shrm.org

This monthly magazine, a leading source of current information for human resource professionals, features cutting-edge articles that provide insight into and innovative approaches to solving human resource problems. Features include segments on legislation and other news of interest to those in the field.

Human Resource Development Quarterly

ISSN: 1044–8004

Wiley

111 River St, Hoboken, New Jersey, 07030–5774

T: +1 201 748 6000

F: +1 212 850 6021

www.wiley.com

Sponsored by the American Society for Training and Development and the Academy of Human Resource Development, this quarterly provides a focus for research on human resource development issues and recognizes the interdisciplinary nature of such issues. The emphasis is on the theory, research, and evaluation of HRD practices.

Human Resource Management

ISSN: 0090–4848

Wiley

111 River St, Hoboken, New Jersey, 07030–5774

T: +1 201 748 6000

F: +1 212 850 6021

www.wiley.com

Designed for executive business professionals, this quarterly magazine features articles that highlight the latest theories in human resource management. Features include case studies, business solutions, and proven management techniques.

Human Resources

Haymarket Publishing

174 Hammersmith Road, London, W6 7JP, U.K.

T: +44 (0) 20 8267 5000

F: +44 (0) 20 8267 4157

www.haymarketgroup.com

This journal offers news, profiles, case studies, and feature articles on a wide range of issues of interest to the HR professional and general managers.

Pensions & Investments

ISSN: 1050–4974

Crain Communications, Inc.

711 Third Avenue, New York, 10017–4036

T: +1 212 210 0100

F: +1 212 210 0200

Subtitled *The International Newspaper of Money Management*, this magazine is published twenty-six times a year. Containing feature articles, business profiles, and current issue news, it is a must-read for any investment or financial executive. Special reporting emphasis is placed on corporate and institutional investing.

Personnel Today

ISSN: 0959–5848

Reed Business Information

Windsor Court, East Grinstead, West Sussex, RH19 1XA, U.K.

T: +44 (0) 1342 335 876

F: +44 (0) 1342 335 998

www.personneltoday.co.uk

This is a weekly news magazine for HR and training professionals.

Workforce Management

ISSN: 1092–8332

Crain Communications, Inc.

711 Third Avenue, New York, NY 10017–4036

T: +1 212 210 0100

F: +1 212 210 0200

www.adage.com

A monthly magazine, *Workforce* targets HR practitioners with content on a variety of topics, including performance appraisal. It offers case studies, trend analysis, and commentary on the social and economic effects of HR practices.

INTERNET

American Society for Training and Development (ASTD)

www.astd.org

ASTD is a professional association for training personnel. The site provides an online magazine, news, virtual communities, a free e-mail newsletter, and a buyer's guide listing training suppliers and consultants. Many of the services are for members only.

"Chief executives repeatedly fail to recognize that for communication to be effective, it must be two-way."

Robert N. McMurry

HR Guide
www.hr-guide.com

This site provides definitions and basic introductions to a range of human resource subjects linked to a collection of Web site listings with ratings and brief descriptions. It has a strong focus on HR software and includes a demo of an online 360-degree feedback questionnaire.

HR Tools.com
www.hrtools.com

As its name would suggest, this site focuses on online tools, including forms and training resources. Registration is required for all users.

HRZone
www.hrzone.com

This site, based in the United States, provides information on the basics of human resource management. In addition, users will find articles, news, legal information including case summaries, Web site reviews, and a directory of suppliers.

Online Recruitment
www.onrec.com

This site provides a database of online recruitment sites, and offers the facility to search for sites that cover all or specific sectors. It also gives information on the sites offered, including services, charges, strengths, and weaknesses.

Personnel Today
www.personneltoday.com

This is a comprehensive site including information from a leading U.K. magazine. Covering HR news and events, legal developments, and career advice, the site also provides book reviews, a conference calendar, and links to HR-related Web sites.

Society for Human Resource Management
www.shrm.org

The Society for Human Resource Management is a professional organization for HR managers in the United States. The site contains a range of resources including news, an online magazine, discussion forums, collections of company practices and policies, mission statements, job descriptions, and an extensive set of links. Some resources are for members only.

Training Zone
www.trainingzone.co.uk

A portal site for training professionals, its resources include a sales success toolkit, a

document centre, and a library. Registration is required for users.

U.K.-HRD
www.ukhrd.com

This is a site is for training and HR specialists and is sponsored by Fenman. Users may subscribe to receive a comprehensive daily newsletter, while some free articles are available on the site itself.

Workforce Online
www.workforce.com

This site is an online HR magazine with feature articles, news, discussion forums, and a free e-mail newsletter.

Workindex
www.workindex.com

Sponsored by the publishers of *Human Resource Executive* and featuring an index from Cornell University School of Labor and Industrial Relations, this site provides a comprehensive set of links to HR Web sites. Book extracts and reviews, a salary calculator, a jobs database, legal questions and answers, HR news, and magazine articles are also available.

WorldatWork
www.worldatwork.org

Formerly the American Compensation Association, this site offers information for human resource managers including news, topic briefings, a free e-mail newsletter, a glossary of terms, magazine articles, and a buyer's guide. Information on training courses, seminars, accredited programs, publications, and research surveys produced by the organization are also available.

ORGANIZATIONS
USA
Academy of Human Resource Development

College of Technology, Bowling Green State University, Bowling Green, Ohio, 43403
T: +1 419 372 9155
F: +1 419 372 8385
E: *office@ahrd.org*
www.ahrd.org

The Academy is a global organization devoted to the study of human resource theories, processes, and techniques. It publishes a range of journals, holds conferences, establishes partnerships, conducts a number of educational programs, and presents awards to scholars in the field of human resources.

The Human Resource Planning Society

317 Madison Avenue, Suite 1509, New York, 10017
T: +1 212 490 6387
F: +1 212 682 6851
E: *info@hrps.orh*
www.hrps.org

HRPS is a unique and dynamic association of more than 3,000 human resource and business executives. The Society is committed to improving organizational performance by creating a global network of individuals who function as business partners in the application of strategic human resource management practices to their organizations.

International Personnel Management Association

1617 Duke Street, Alexandria, Virginia, 22314
T: +1 703 549 7100
F: +1 703 684 0948
E: *training@ipma-hr.org*
www.ipma.org

The International Personnel Management Association (IPMA) was established in 1973, through the consolidation of the Public Personnel Association, founded in Chicago in 1906, and the Society for Personnel Administration, founded in Washington, DC in 1937. IPMA is a nonprofit membership organization for agencies and individuals in the public sector human resources field, and others interested in the Association's objectives.

Society for Human Resource Management (SHRM)

1800 Duke Street, Alexandria, Virginia, 22314
T: +1 703 548 3440
F: +1 703 535 6490
E: *custsvc@shrm.org*
www.shrm.org

SHRM is a leading voice of the human resource profession, offering members education and information services, conferences and seminars, government and media representation, online services, and publications. The Society, the world's largest human resource management association, is a founding member of both the North American Human Resource Management Association (NAHRMA) and the World Federation of Personnel Management Associations (WFPMA).

Europe
Chartered Institute of Personnel and Development (CIPD)

151 The Broadway, Wimbledon, London, SW19 1JQ, U.K.

1858

BUSINESS INFORMATION SOURCES

     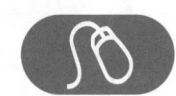

T: +44 (0) 20 8612 6200
F: +44 (0) 20 8012 6201
www.cipd.co.uk
Formed in 1995 from the amalgamation of the Institute of Personnel Management and the Institute of Training and Development, the CIPD is a professional body for personnel and training professionals which aims to promote good practice in the management and development of people—a company's core strength.

The Work Foundation
Peter Runge House, 3 Carlton House Terrace, London, SW1Y 5DG, U.K.
T: +44 (0) 870 165 6700
F: +44 (0) 870 165 6701
E: *customercentre@theworkfoundation.com*
www.theworkfoundation.com
Established in 2002, The Work Foundation is a new incarnation of The Industrial Society, an independent body with over 80 years' experience in management development and training. The Work Foundation operates under the belief that

business success goes hand-in-hand with fair management practices. The services offered to members include an information service and employment law helpline; a publishing program of books, research reports, and videos; plus a training and consulting service, which includes the School of Coaching.

International
Australian Human Resources Institute
Level 10, 601 Bourke St, Melbourne, Victoria, 3000, Australia
T: +61 3 9918 9200
F: +61 3 9918 9201
www.ahri.com.au
AHRI is recognized today as Australia's leading HR professional body, providing professional development at the leading edge of HR practice, knowledge, research, and development.

World Federation of Personnel Management Associations
1800 Duke Street, Alexandria, Virginia, 22314

T: + 1 703 548 3440
F: + 1 703 535 6490
www.wfpma.com
Founded in 1976, the WFPMA is a global network of professionals working in the area of people management. Its aim is to internationally aid the development and improve the effectiveness of professional people management. The association holds regular meetings and conferences, and commissions research projects. It also publishes a quarterly newsletter called *WorldLink*.

FOR MORE INFORMATION

- Employee Benefits/Compensation (pp. 1736–1737)
- Employee Participation in Management (pp. 1738–1740)
- Employee Relations (pp. 1741–1742)
- Employment Law (pp. 1743–1744)
- Training and Development (pp. 1922–1924)

BUSINESS INFORMATION SOURCES

"Basic assumptions about reality are the paradigms of a social science, such as management."

Peter F. Drucker

Physical Working Conditions/ Ergonomics

BOOKS

The Distributed Workplace: Sustainable Work Environments

Andrew Harrison, Paul Wheeler, Carolyn Whitehead, eds
Taylor & Francis, 2004
196pp ISBN: 0415318904
This text posits that the evolution of the knowledge economy, the continuing development of telecommunications and computer technologies, globalization, and the built environment have created the conditions for the evolution of the workplace. It makes the case for the distributed workplace and includes workplace evaluation, space environment, and cost and implementation strategies. Appendices include a glossary, case studies, an outline of CSR initiatives, and sustainability information.

Ergonomics for Beginners: A Quick Reference Guide 2nd ed.

Jan Dul, Bernard Weerdmeester
Taylor & Francis, 2001
160pp ISBN: 0748408258
An excellent first stop for anyone new to this topic, this book explains the key concepts of ergnomics: to design tasks and the working environment so that people are comfortable and perform well. Full of practical advice on how to achieve this balance, this book is useful for managers, health and safety officials, and small business owners alike.

Ergonomics: How to Design for Ease and Efficiency 2nd ed.

Karl Kroemer, Henrike Kroemer, Karin Kroemer-Elbert
Upper Saddle River, New Jersey: Prentice Hall, 2000
720pp ISBN: 0137524781
The authors, who are ergonomics engineers, have produced a reference book designed to provide comprehensive information for readers of all knowledge levels seeking to gain understanding of ergonomics and workplace safety issues. In it, they address all aspects of workplace conditions, including posture, equipment design, effective training, disabled employees, and avoiding repetitive strain injuries.

Excellence by Design

Turid Horgen et al.
Hoboken, New Jersey: Wiley, 1998
320pp ISBN: 0471246476
This text recognizes the link between well-designed office space and a productive workforce. Revolving around four years of research by the Space Organization Research Group of MIT's School of Architecture and Planning, the book examines this notion, and how it can be applied within company culture.

The Occupational Ergonomics Handbook

Waldemar Karwowski, William S. Marras, eds
New York: CRC Press, 1999
2096pp ISBN: 0849326419
This handbook presents an exhaustive array of in-depth information pertaining to workplace ergonomics written by international experts. Topics include developing ergonomic programs, workplace- and injury-specific research, managing for ergonomics, injury prevention, and workplace design and employee safety.

Office Space Planning: Designing for Tomorrow's Workplace

Alexi Marmot, Joanna Eley
Maidenhead, United Kingdom: McGraw-Hill, 2000
480pp ISBN: 0071341994
Aimed at designers (or anybody concerned with office facility management), this book provides advice on how to create an excellent work environment by using space wisely. It covers topics such as lighting and office furniture, discusses the relative merits of enclosed and open-plan office spaces, and also includes studies of well-designed workplaces.

Physical Hazards of the Workplace

Larry R. Collins, Thomas D. Schneid
Boca Raton, Florida: Lewis Publishers, 2001
336pp ISBN: 1566703395
Primarily designed for business professionals, this book presents information on federal, state, and local regulations dealing with workplace safety. The authors stress the importance of understanding and implementing these regulations, outline occupational and environmental hazards present in the workplace, and describe methods of facilitating compliance with regulatory codes.

MAGAZINES

Behaviour & Information Technology

ISSN: 0144–929X
Taylor & Francis
325 Chestnut St., Suite 800, Philadelphia, Pennsylvania 19106
T: +1 800 354 1420
F: +1 215 625 2940
www.tandf.co.uk
This publication aims to provide a focused, abstracting service mainly concerned with the human aspects of technology, including telecommunications, office systems, industrial automation, robotics, and consumer products. Its readership is international, and ranges from researchers and systems designers to personnel specialists and planners.

CWC Online

ISSN: 1059–0722
U.S. Bureau of Labor Statistics
U.S. Department of Labor, 2 Massachusetts Avenue NE, Room 2860, Washington, D.C., 20212–0001
T: +1 202 691 5200
F: +1 202 691 7890
www.bls.gov/opub/cwc
CWC Online is a monthly electronic journal that covers topics including wages and benefits, safety and health, and labor-management relations. It offers articles, summaries of major studies, and data tables and charts. It is targeted primarily at HR managers.

Ergonomics

ISSN: 0014–0139
Taylor & Francis
325 Chestnut St., Suite 800, Philadelphia, Pennsylvania 19106
T: +1 800 354 1420
F: +1 215 625 2940
www.tandf.co.uk
An international, multi-disciplinary journal concerned with all aspects of the interaction of human beings with their work and leisure, it includes a news section, research data, media reviews, and peer-reviewed scientific papers.

"American managers are too little concerned about their workers." — Akio Morita

Ergonomics Abstracts

ISSN: 0046–2446
Taylor & Francis
325 Chestnut St., Suite 800, Philadelphia,
Pennsylvania 19106
T: +1 800 354 1420
F: +1 215 625 2940
www.tandf.co.uk
This online reference resource offers a
focused, comprehensive, and international
abstracting service spanning the whole
world of ergonomics and human factors. It
covers a variety of useful subject areas
including work design, health and safety,
human characteristics, and environment.

Job Safety & Health Quarterly

ISSN: 1057–5820
*Occupational Safety & Health Administration
(OSHA)*
U.S. Department of Labor, 200 Constitution
Avenue, Washington, D.C., 20210
T: +1 202 693 1999
F: +1 202 512 2233
www.osha.gov/html/jshq-index.html
Published quarterly, the *JSHQ* is the official
magazine of OSHA, dealing with current
trends in worker safety. It offers
information on changes, developments, and
new rulings made by OSHA.

INTERNET

Cornell University Egonomics Web
http://ergo.human.cornell.edu
This site presents information on research
studies and classwork in ergonomics
undertaken by the students and faculty at
Cornell. It also gives details of general
ergonomics news, information, research,
and tools.

Ergonomics Information Analysis Centre
www.eee.bham.ac.uk/eiac

This site, run by the University of
Birmingham in the United Kingdom,
provides an information service for
ergonomics and human factors, offering
Ergonomics Abstracts online as well as a
payment-based search and delivery service.

Ergonomics (Occupational Safety & Health Administration)
www.osha-slc.gov/SLTC/ergonomics
This U.S. government Web site offers a
wealth of ergonomics information on
subjects including methods for recognizing
ergonomics problems in the workplace and
possible solutions to ergonomics problems.

Ergoweb
www.ergoweb.com/index.cfm
Providing information on workplace
ergonomics, this site covers current news
on ergonomics, recent legislation, a
glossary of terms, discussion lists, case
studies, and information on establishing
ergonomics programs.

Human Factors/Ergonomics
www.usernomics.com/hf.html
This site provides a list of links to other
Internet sites on these topics.

ORGANIZATIONS
USA
Human Factors and Ergonomics Society
P.O. Box 1369, Santa Monica, California,
90406–1369
T: +1 310 394 1811
F: +1 310 394 2410
E: *info@hfes.org*
www.hfes.org
The Society's mission is to promote the
discovery and exchange of information
about the characteristics of human beings

that are applicable to the design of systems
and devices of all kinds. It also encourages
education and training for those entering
the human factors and ergonomics
profession and for those who conceive, test,
manage, and participate in systems.

Europe
The Ergonomics Society
Elms Court, Elms Grove, Loughborough,
Leicestershire, LE11 IRG, U.K.
T: +44 (0) 1509 234 904
F: +44 (0) 1509 235 666
E: *ergsoc@ergonomics.org.uk*
www.ergonomics.org.uk
This organization is a forum for
professionals who use scientific
information about humans to design for
comfort, efficiency, and safety.

International
International Ergonomics Association
Prof. Sebastiano Bagnara, ISTC-CNR, Via
San Martino della Battaglia 44, Rome, 00185,
Italy
T: +39 06 44362366
F: +39 06 44595243
E: *iea.secr@istc.cnr.it*
www.iea.cc
The IEA is a federation of ergonomics and
human factors societies from around the
world. Its mission is to advance the science
and practice of ergonomics, expanding the
scope of its application and contribution to
society and thereby improving the quality
of life for all.

FOR MORE INFORMATION

Employment Law (pp. 1743–1744)
Facilities Management (p. 1754)
Health and Safety (pp. 1767–1768)

1861

BUSINESS INFORMATION SOURCES

"I am I plus my surroundings, and, if I do not preserve the latter, I do not
preserve myself."
Jose Ortega y Gasset

Planning for Retirement

BOOKS

The Procrastinator's Guide to Financial Security
David Teitelbaum
New York: AMACOM, 2001
304pp ISBN: 0814406211
Aimed at those who need help saving for retirement and got started later in life, this book supplies information on the fundamentals of money management, and teaches the knowledge, skills, and discipline needed to secure a comfortable retirement. It includes bibliographical references and an index.

Retire Rich: The Baby Boomer's Guide to a Secure Future
Bambi Holzer, Elaine Floyd
Hoboken, New Jersey: Wiley, 1999
240pp ISBN: 0471358487
The authors present practical and easy ways to plan, save, and invest in order to secure a comfortable retirement. Workers are encouraged to address the retirement issue while they still have a steady income. Clear, non-technical language, and charts, tables, and worksheets enhance the text.

The Wall Street Journal Guide to Planning your Financial Future: The Easy-to-read Guide to Planning for Retirement 3rd ed.
Kenneth Morris et al.
New York: Lightbulb Press, 2002
160pp ISBN: 0743225376
This book provides an overview of the important considerations and decisions that need to be made in securing a comfortable retirement. It covers the advantages of salary reduction plans, clarifies the difference between Roth and traditional IRAs and describes the benefits of effective

tax planning. It provides practical, helpful ideas on how to get started.

MAGAZINES

Goodtimes
AMS Ltd.
119 Cholmley Gardens, London, NW6 1AA, U.K.
T: +44 (0) 20 7431 2259
F: +44 (0) 20 7431 7411
www.arp050.org.uk/asp/goodtimes/index.asp
Goodtimes is the magazine of the Association of Retired and Persons over 50. It covers topics such as health, fitness, travel, and gardening.

Kiplinger's Retirement Report
ISSN: 1075–6671
Kiplinger
1729 H Street, Washington, D.C., 20006
T: +1 888 419 0424
www.kiplinger.com
This is a retirement newsletter from the respected publishers of personal finance and business forecasting information. It provides information on retirement issues, such as managing finances, retirement living, and estate planning.

Pensions & Investments
ISSN: 1050–4974
Crain Communications, Inc.
711 Third Avenue, New York, 10017–4036
T: +1 212 210 0100
F: +1 212 210 0200
Subtitled *The International Newspaper of Money Management*, this magazine is published twenty-six times a year. Containing feature articles, business profiles, and current issue news, it is a must-read for any investment or financial executive. Special reporting emphasis is

placed on corporate and institutional investing.

INTERNET

American Association of Retired Persons (AARP)
www.aarp.org
This association is one of the world's largest nonprofit, nonpartisan membership organizations for people over fifty. The site provides a wealth of data on such subjects as travel, health, learning opportunities, politics, and finance, and has links to discussion groups.

Center for Retirement Research at Boston College
www.bc.edu/centers/crr
The Center aims to promote research on retirement issues, transmit findings to the policy community and the public, and broaden access to data sources. It offers research and publications on retirement issues as well as information about upcoming events on its website.

ORGANIZATIONS

USA

American Association of Retired Persons (AARP)
601 E. Street, NW, Washington, D.C., 20049
T: +1 800 424 3410
E: *member@aarp.org*
www.aarp.org
This is a nonprofit, membership organization for people aged 50 and over. It has an enormous membership of around 32 million. It provides information and support; advocates on legislative, consumer, and legal issues; helps members to serve their communities; and offers a number of unique benefits, products, and services. Benefits include the AARP Web site, which features an online magazine.

1862

BUSINESS INFORMATION SOURCES

"Absence of occupation is not rest, A mind quite vacant is a mind distressed."

William Cowper

Planning Your Career

BOOKS

Career Intelligence: The 12 New Rules for Work and Life Success
Barbara Moses
San Francisco, California: Berrett-Koehler, 1998
304pp ISBN: 1576750485
This book offers advice on building a career in today's ruthless and rapidly changing business environment. It lists 12 essential rules for success. These include ensuring your marketability, thinking globally, continuing to learn, and preparing four areas of competence.

Career Planning & Networking
Aggie White
Cincinnati, Ohio: South-Western College Publishing, 2001
96pp ISBN: 0538724749
White walks readers through the career-planning and networking process so vital to advancement in today's rapidly shifting job markets. In addition to discussing the basics like self-assessment and researching various careers, White shows how to build an effective career network and to plan for career changes. The book concludes with case studies that illustrate career planning and advancement.

Changing Directions without Losing Your Way: Managing the Six Stages of Change at Work and in Life
Paul Edwards, Sarah Edwards
New York: J.P. Tarcher, 2001
240pp ISBN: 158542076X
Although this book is not about career planning per se, it provides valuable guidance on effectively managing significant life-change processes, including career changes. While the authors espouse finding and following one's passion, they advise readers to approach it in a grounded, well-researched, and practical way. The book includes suggested tasks, self-quizzes, a change journal, and other features that encourage introspection, self-discipline, and self-education.

Discovering Your Career in Business
Timothy Butler, James Waldroop
Cambridge, Massachusetts: Perseus Books Group, 1997
272pp ISBN: 0201461358
This career guide aims to help readers find work that fulfills their potential and suits

their character. Containing an inventory and user exercises which point an individual toward finding a range of activities appropriate to their needs, the book also gives advice on how these can be linked to employment in the business sector. There is an emphasis on self-assessment and pinpointing career goals.

The Future of Career
Audrey Collin, Richard A. Young, eds
New York: Cambridge University Press, 2000
336pp ISBN: 052164965X
The basic argument of this book is that the fragmented nature of modern working life has led to fundamental changes in our understanding of the term "career." It offers a collection of articles presenting a global view of the concept of a career, reviewing its past, and considering its future. Psychologists, sociologists, and HR managers offer a multilayered examination of career theories and practice, identifying the major changes taking place in the world, and discussing the future of "career" in the newly emerging network society of the 21st century.

Getting Promoted: Real Strategies for Advancing Your Career
Harry E. Chambers
Cambridge, Massachusetts: Perseus Books Group, 1999
256pp ISBN: 0738201022
In this guide to getting promoted, Chambers argues that good critical skills and an understanding of the problems and opportunities that may arise when looking for promotion are key. He gives practical advice on how to develop this analytical capacity, and uses research from a range of companies to help the reader assess his or her strengths in the workplace.

I Don't Know What I Want, But I Know It's Not This: A Step-by-step Guide to Finding Gratifying Work
Julie Jansen
New York: Penguin USA, 2003
288pp ISBN: 0142002488
A useful resource for anyone unhappy at work, this book is full of exercises to assess the reader's personality and skills and will help people understand their present situation and come up with ways to find the job or career they really want to embark on.

Who Do You Think You Are? Understanding Your Motives and Maximising Your Abilities
Nick Isbister, Martin Robinson
North Pomfret, Vermont: Trafalgar Square, 1999
192pp ISBN: 0551031700
In this book the authors unveil a process known as SIMA (System for Identifying Motivated Abilities). This self-assessment system aims to help individuals to understand their motivation, develop their abilities, and maximize their effectiveness. The book includes exercises to support self-evaluation and planning for the future.

Winning the Talent War: A Strategic Approach to Attracting, Developing and Retaining the Best People
Charles Woodruffe
Hoboken, New Jersey: Wiley, 1999
208pp ISBN: 0471987530
How to attract the best people and retain them in an environment of constant change is a dilemma facing all organizations. A framework for attracting, motivating, and retaining senior management, and for creating a strategy for the sustainable development of high-fliers, is presented here. Case studies from various organizations are also included.

MAGAZINES
Occupational Outlook Quarterly
ISSN: 0199–4786
U.S. Bureau of Labor Statistics
U.S. Department of Labor, 2 Massachusetts Avenue NE, Room 2860, Washington, D.C., 20212–0001
T: +1 202 691 5200
F: +1 202 691 7890
www.bls.gov/opub/ooq/ooqhome.htm
OOQ covers a variety of career topics, including training opportunities, salary trends, new and emerging occupations, and results of new studies from the Bureau of Labor Statistics. It also offers career-related data from the BLS in chart form.

INTERNET
CareerBuilder
www.careerbuilder.com
This site offers a combination of free resources and services for which users must pay. You can post your résumé, search the job database, and take advantage of helpful tools including a job search for freelancers.

1863

BUSINESS INFORMATION SOURCES

"The man who has the largest capacity for work and thought is the man who is bound to succeed."

Henry Ford

Practical guidance is offered on many aspects of job hunting, including tailoring your application to your target company and negotiating a good starting salary.

Career World
www.career-world.com

Career World provides career development programs to individuals as well as a full range of outplacement services to corporate clients throughout the United Kingdom. New visitors have to register before entering the site, which contains many example résumés, speculative letters, cover letters, and post-interview follow-up letters.

Fast Company
www.fastcompany.com

Fastcompany.com is based on the magazine of the same name, which was founded in 1995. The Web site serves people's individual career needs with six custom-built "Career Zones," each of which contains stories, career advice, interactive tools, opinions, and links to other useful sites.

Monster Career Center
www.monster.com

As well as over one million job listings, this excellent resource offers a career center that provides customized information by industry or profession, together with resources on cover letters, résumés, interviews, salaries, seasonal jobs, company profiles, and more.

WetFeet
www.wetfeet.com

Unlike Monster.com, WetFeet is not a résumé-posting site. It complements Monster by providing detailed information on companies, careers, industries, and salary benchmarks that can be used throughout one's career. Other free features include expert advice and interviews with professionals. WetFeet also publishes detailed insider's guides to dozens of companies and industries that site visitors may purchase.

Yahoo! Hotjobs
http://hotjobs.yahoo.com/careertools

The Yahoo! Hotjobs site aims to supply a dynamic exchange between job seekers and prospective employers. For those seeking employment, this site is a one-stop career resource center, offering career tools such as hints on preparing for interview and networking, a résumé posting service, and job search facilities. For recruiters, the site provides an efficient way to hire staff by cutting the time and costs associated with traditional recruiting.

ORGANIZATIONS
USA
National Career Development Association

305 N. Beech Circle, Broken Arrow, Oklahoma, 74012
T: +1 918 663 7060
F: +1 918 663 7058
www.ncda.org

NCDA is a trade association for professionals providing career-development services, acting to develop standards for career counseling and evaluating career-information materials. Membership benefits include a journal and newsletter, conferences, continuing education, and networking opportunities.

FOR MORE INFORMATION

☆ Avoiding Your Worst Career Nightmare (pp. 404–405)
ᔥ Creating a Résumé (p. 1724)
ᔥ Job Hunting (p. 1793)
ᔥ Management Education: MBAs (pp. 1817–1818)
✔ Managing the Plateaued Performer (pp. 456–457)
☆ Taking Charge of Your Career (pp. 412–413)

BUSINESS INFORMATION SOURCES

"I am a young executive. No cuffs than mine are cleaner;
I have a Slimline brief-case and I use the firm's Cortina."

John Betjeman

     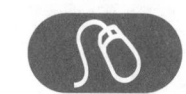

Presentation/Speaking

BOOKS

Effective Presentation: How To Create and Deliver a Winning Presentation 2nd ed.
Antony Jay, Ros Jay
London: Financial Times Management, 2004
144pp ISBN: 0273688030
Drawing on their own experience and on tips from experts and trainers in presentation and communication skills, the authors offer a step-by-step guide to planning, designing, and delivering successful presentations. They give advice on scheduling and staging the presentation, choosing appropriate visual aids, and engaging the audience.

Effective Presentation Skills: A Practical Guide for Better Speaking 3rd ed.
Steve Mandel
Menlo Park, California: Crisp Publications, 2000
96pp ISBN: 1560525266
This basic overview of presentations offers advice on topics including skill assessment, presentation planning, visual aids, teleconferencing and videoconferencing, the presentation environment, and dealing with hostile questions. It contains an especially useful section for nervous presenters on dealing with anxiety and projecting confidence.

Give Great Presentations: How to Speak Confidently and Make Your Point
New York: Perseus Books Group, 2005
96pp (Steps to Success)
ISBN: 0747577358
Full of advice on how to prepare and deliver a knockout speech, this practical book is ideal for anyone who suffers from pre-presentation nerves. Opening with essential sections on how to prepare and structure a good presentation, the book also tackles coping with nerves, boosting your message with your body language, creating online or virtual presentations, and coping with worst-case scenarios.

Knockout Presentations: How to Deliver Your Message with Power, Punch, and Pizzazz
Diane Diresta
Madison, Wisconsin: Chandler House, 1998
304pp ISBN: 1886284253
This experienced coach presents a clear and precise method of approaching public speaking. Her suggestions are easy to implement, and many readers have found this book an invaluable reference tool.

Point, Click and Wow! A Quick Guide to Brilliant Laptop Presentations 2nd ed.
Claudyne Wilder, Jennifer Rotondo
San Francisco, California: Jossey-Bass, 2002
240pp ISBN: 0787956694
Aimed at business people of all levels, this book offers a practical guide to using technology in effective presentations. The authors explore how to balance on-screen activity and human interaction, how to deal with software and hardware issues, and how, when, and where to practice. The book includes checklists and illustrations.

Presentation Skills for Managers
Jennifer Rotondo, Mike Rotondo, Jr.
Maidenhead, United Kingdom: McGraw-Hill, 2001
192pp ISBN: 0071379304
Targeted at managers at all levels, this book offers practical advice on presentation skills. It stresses the three main aspects of any presentation—content, design, and delivery—and deals with issues such as stumbling blocks and follow-up Q&A sessions. It also provides a good overview of using PowerPoint for effective presentations.

Say It with Presentations: How to Design and Deliver Successful Business Presentations Revised ed.
Gene Zelazny
Maidenhead, United Kingdom: McGraw-Hill, 2006
160pp ISBN: 0071472894
Useful for beginners as well as experienced presenters, this book will help your message pack a punch. The topics it covers include defining the purpose of the presentation, keeping the audience in mind, designing charts, and using humor. Its main focus is on how to deliver presentations with confidence and conviction.

Speaking for Impact: Connecting with Every Audience
Shirley E. Nice
Boston, Massachusetts: Allyn and Bacon, 1998
176pp (Essence of Public Speaking)
ISBN: 0205270255

Whether speaking to a small or a large group, chairing a sales meeting or giving a formal presentation, this book offers tips on how to get your message across effectively. The text suggests how you can identify the similarities and differences within audiences so you can connect with everyone in an audience made up of a diverse range of people.

Wooing and Winning Business: The Foolproof Formula for Making Persuasive Business Presentations
Spring Asher, Wicke Chambers
New York: Wiley, 1998
240pp ISBN: 0471253707
Introducing the "Speechworks Formula" for increasing your powers of persuasion and giving effective presentations, this guide explains how to look and sound like a born leader, organize your thoughts for maximum clarity, and use the most compelling evidence and anecdotes to hook even the toughest audience. Speechworks is an internationally known firm, specializing in speech and media training.

INTERNET

Advanced Public Speaking Institute
www.public-speaking.org
This site offers free advice and articles on all aspects of public speaking, including performance and storytelling techniques, how to develop a topic, the use of props and handouts, humor, tricks, gimmicks, and stage fright.

National Speakers Association
www.nsaspeaker.org
Sponsored by a professional speakers' organization, the site gives access to *Professional Speaker* magazine's article archive, reference lists, and conference and event information. Members may register to gain extra advice on how to run a profitable business.

PowerPointers
www.powerpointers.com
This site has many articles on making and creating effective presentations. Areas of interest include communicating effectively, building and planning a presentation, and communicating in your specialty.

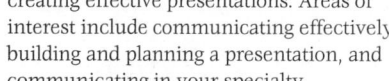

1865

BUSINESS INFORMATION SOURCES

"All the great speakers were bad speakers at first."   Ralph Waldo Emerson

Presentations.com
www.presentations.com
The online counterpart to *Presentations* magazine, the site offers news, articles, information on upcoming conferences and events, technological information, and resources.

Professional Edge
www.proedgeskills.com
Sponsored by a consulting firm, the site offers articles on presentation skills, a monthly e-zine, books and resources, and an online ask-the-expert option.

School for Champions
www.school-for-champions.com/ speaking.htm
This selection of free online lessons is designed to improve speaking skills and overcome the fear of speaking in public or to a group.

Virtual Presentation Assistant – University of Kansas
www.ku.edu/~coms/virtual_assistant/ vpa/vpa.htm

Created by the Communication Studies Department at the University of Kansas, this Web site uses material by Diana Carlin to give an outline of what a good presentation should incorporate and what the speaker should think about when presenting.

ORGANIZATIONS
USA
Toastmasters International
23182 Arroyo Vista, Rancho Santa Margarita, California, 92688
T: +1 949 858 8255
F: +1 949 858 1207
E: *tmembers@toastmasters.org*
www.toastmasters.org
A nonprofit, member-based organization, Toastmasters International was established in 1924 with the aim of helping people to speak more effectively in public. It provides members with manuals on effective speaking and other resources, as well as a subscription to its monthly magazine, *The Toastmaster*. Toastmaster clubs offer members the opportunity to develop presentation and leadership skills through chairing meetings, presenting impromptu and prepared speeches, and offering constructive evaluation.

Europe
The Speakers Trust
19 Waterer Rise, Wallington, Surrey, SM6 9DN, U.K.
T: +44 (0) 20 8669 2300
www.speakerstrust.org.uk
The Trust promotes the work of speakers' clubs across the United Kingdom with a view to making them better known and understood and increasing their membership. It offers support to existing clubs by organizing competitions, sponsoring new members, providing funds, and producing educational materials.

FOR MORE INFORMATION

- Internal Communication (pp. 1782–1783)
- Interpersonal Communication/ Relations (pp. 1787–1788)

1866

 — note: the vertical label at left:

BUSINESS INFORMATION SOURCES

"An orator is the worst person to tell a plain fact."

Maria Edgeworth

Pricing

BOOKS

Power Pricing: How Managing Price Transforms the Bottom Line
Robert J. Dolan, Hermann Simon
New York: Free Press, 1997
416pp ISBN: 068483443X
This book for managers and strategy-makers explains how a proactive, strategic approach to pricing—called "power pricing" by the authors—can have dramatic effects on profitability. Written in simple language, the book uses practical examples throughout to illustrate the attitudes, thought processes, actions, and strategies of "power pricers."

Price Advantage
Michael V. Marn, Eric V. Roegner, Craig C. Zawada
Hoboken, New Jersey: Wiley, 2004
288pp (Wiley Finance)
ISBN: 0471466697
Price advantage suggests that many companies neglect the opportunities offered by pricing strategy for increasing profitability and outperforming the competition. Drawing on their experience of advising businesses, the authors offer a practical pricing guide for managers. A three-level framework for identifying and exploiting pricing opportunities, covering industry strategy, product and market strategy and transaction level, is set out. Pricing issues in specific contexts such as the introduction of new products, packaged offerings, price wars, post-merger pricing and practical issues such as the use of technology and the regulatory framework are also addressed. These are then placed within overall organizational strategy. The text is illustrated throughout with case studies.

Pricing for Profitability: Activity-based Pricing for Competitive Advantage
John L. Daly
Hoboken, New Jersey: Wiley, 2001
288pp ISBN: 0471415359
The authors suggest that activity-based pricing helps companies set appropriate prices which both generate sales and result in a profit. Activity-based pricing analyzes the interdependence between price, cost

and sales volume, resulting in a disciplined approach to the process of price development. Other topics included in the book are estimating customer demand, pricing law in the United States, the ethics of pricing, planning profit, and tips for successful price negotiations.

Professional's Guide to Value Pricing 6th ed.
Ronald J. Baker
Riverwoods, IL: CCH, Inc., 2005
640pp ISBN: 0735548064
This book lets readers see how pricing by the hour, instead of pricing by the value, can have a negative effect on your business. Through examples and clear and powerful writing, Baker leads the businessperson to achieve a better system of charging by the services rendered to the client.

The Strategy and Tactics of Pricing: A Guide to Growing More Profitably 4th ed.
Thomas T. Nagle, Reed K. Holden
Upper Saddle River, New Jersey: Prentice Hall, 2005
349pp ISBN: 0131856774
Ideal for MBA students, this book is a practical guide to pricing strategy. Concepts are fully illustrated with examples, and this new edition features many drawn from the world of e-commerce.

Transfer Pricing Methods: An Applications Guide
Robert Feinscreiber
Hoboken, New Jersey: Wiley, 2004
320pp ISBN: 0471573604
This practical guide is designed to assist managers in mid-sized businesses with the techniques of transfer pricing. The subject is introduced and the application of specific transfer pricing techniques is explained. Also explored are various international transfer pricing issues.

Winning the Profit Game: Smarter Pricing and Smarter Branding
Robert G. Docters et al.
New York: McGraw-Hill, 2004
320pp ISBN: 0071434720
In order to improve profitability, it is argued that organizations now need to focus on the

top line, and that the two fundamental tools for doing this are price and brand. The need to take a fresh look at price and brand is explained, and the process of developing an integrated price brand strategy is examined. This focuses on setting price and creating revenue, managing ongoing revenues, and building revenue capabilities.

INTERNET
Professional Pricing Society
www.pricingsociety.com
Sponsored by a professional society dedicated to pricing management, the site offers forums, mailing list archives, products for purchase, Webinars, and a bookstore for related books. Membership services are also available, as is a free newsletter.

Strategic Pricing Group
www.strategicpricinggroup.com
Sponsored by a consulting firm that specializes in strategic pricing, this site provides articles, recommended reading, a calendar of events, and information on educational services and consulting.

ORGANIZATIONS
USA
Professional Pricing Society
3535 Roswell Road, Suite 59, Marietta, Georgia, 30062
T: +1 770 509 9933
F: +1 770 509 1963
E: *contactus@pricingsociety.com*
www.pricingsociety.com
PPS is an association for price decision makers and price management personnel; its members are primarily pricing and marketing executives. It offers its members conferences and workshops, monthly and quarterly publications, consulting services, and pricing workbooks.

1867

BUSINESS INFORMATION SOURCES

FOR MORE INFORMATION
- Marketing Management (pp. 1827–1832)
- Packaging (pp. 1852–1853)
- Profiting From Prices (pp. 395–396)

"The first law of economics is that when the price goes up, consumption comes down. This is a divine law."
— Ahmed Zaki Yamani

Process Control and Statistical Process Control

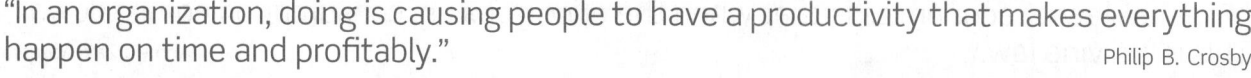
BOOKS

Managing Six Sigma: A Practical Guide to Understanding, Assessing, and Implementing the Strategy That Yields Bottom-line Success

Forrest W. Breyfogle, III, James M. Cupello, Becki Meadows
Hoboken, New Jersey: Wiley, 2000
288pp ISBN: 0471396737
This book provides detailed coverage of the Six Sigma techniques. Case studies describe some of the successes and pitfalls encountered in their successful implementation at Motorola and General Electric. Plans, checklists, and other materials are presented to help managers achieve a smooth and successful implementation.

The Six Sigma Handbook 2nd ed.

Thomas Pyzdek
Maidenhead, United Kingdom: McGraw-Hill, 2002
848pp ISBN: 0071410155
If improving the quality of your manufacturing processes is your goal, and the extraordinarily successful Six Sigma program at GE is one you want to emulate, this book will help you implement that approach. The author examines the philosophy underlying the program and explores the management and organization of Six Sigma, then explains the statistical tools and problem-solving techniques needed to implement it.

Six Sigma Revolution: How General Electric and Others Turned Process into Profits

George Eckes
Hoboken, New Jersey: Wiley, 2000
272pp ISBN: 047138822X
Presenting Six Sigma as a quantitative approach to quality that has boosted productivity and increased profits for a number of large businesses, the author explains how and why it is superior to other quality improvement methods and describes how to create and sustain a Six Sigma initiative in an organization.

Six Sigma: The Breakthrough Management Strategy Revolutionizing the World's Top Corporations

Mikel Harry, Richard Schroeder
New York: Bantam Doubleday Dell Books, Random House, 1999
320pp ISBN: 0385494378
This is an explanation of Six Sigma, in which the authors cite examples of companies (such as Polaroid) where the concept is currently in practice. Essentially, Six Sigma is a process that "guides companies into making fewer mistakes in everything they do—from filling out a purchase order to manufacturing airplane engines." A guide to achieving cost-effective quality within large corporations, this book is especially pertinent to managers and investors.

SPC Essentials and Productivity Improvement: A Manufacturing Approach

William A. Levinson, Frank Tumbelty
Milwaukee, Wisconsin: ASQ Quality Press, 1996
272pp ISBN: 0873893727
Written for quality professionals, this text presents the essentials of SPC in a way that avoids the necessity of understanding lengthy calculations. It describes the general tools for improving productivity and quality, the specific tools and techniques of SPC, and the use of attribute control charts.

Statistical Methods for Quality Improvement 2nd ed.

Thomas P. Ryan
Hoboken, New Jersey: Wiley, 2000
592pp (Wiley Series in Probability and Mathematical Statistics)
ISBN: 0471197750
Ryan provides a detailed introduction to the mathematics and statistics that form the basis of a range of fundamental quality control and statistical methods.

Statistical Process Control 5th ed.

John S. Oakland
Woburn, Massachusetts: Butterworth-Heinemann, 2003
464pp ISBN: 0750657669
This new edition of a leading text reflects recent thinking in the field and provides a reliable reference source for statistical process control. The broad issues covered include understanding processes, process variability, process control, process capability, and process improvement.

Statistical Process Control for Quality Improvement: The Deming Paradigm and Beyond 2nd ed.

James R. Thompson, Jacek Koronacki
New York: CRC Press, 2001
464pp ISBN: 1584882425
The authors draw upon their experience of presenting short seminars to workers, foremen, and managers to create this introduction to SPC. They provide an overview of the subject for those with little knowledge of statistics, but the remaining, more detailed explanations of the analytical techniques of SPC are written for statisticians and production engineers with a higher level of mathematical understanding.

Understanding Statistical Process Control 2nd ed.

Donald J. Wheeler, David S. Chambers
Knoxville, Tennessee: SPC Press, 1992
416pp ISBN: 0945320132
This textbook explains the techniques of statistical process control, including approaches to variance, summarizing data, and effective use of control charts. Glossaries of terms and symbols, lists of examples, and answers to exercises are included as appendices.

MAGAZINES

Six Sigma Forum Magazine

Six Sigma Forum, American Society for Quality
600 North Plankinton Avenue, Milwaukee, Wisconsin, 53203
T: +1 414 272 8575
F: +1 414 272 1734
www.sixsigmaforum.com
This quarterly magazine offers feature articles focusing on companies such as Motorola and GE that have benefited from the practice of Six Sigma, and is aimed at Six Sigma professionals at all levels of experience.

INTERNET

American Society for Quality

www.asq.org

"In an organization, doing is causing people to have a productivity that makes everything happen on time and profitably."

Philip B. Crosby

This ASQ site includes a profile of Walter A. Shewhart, the first honorary member of the Society and acclaimed father of modern quality control.

Six Sigma Forum
www.sixsigmaforum.com

The site of this recently formed Forum provides some introductory information on Six Sigma and its application. There are links to related informative case studies and news, but you have to become a member to access these items.

ORGANIZATIONS
USA
American Productivity and Quality Center (APQC)

123 North Post Oak Lane, 3rd Floor, Houston, Texas, 77024

T: +1 713 681 4020
F: +1 713 681 1182
E: *apqcinfo@apqc.org*
www.apqc.org

Founded in 1977, APQC works with organizations of all sizes to improve productivity and quality. Its aim is to research and understand both emerging improvement methods and methods whose effectiveness is already proven, and it distributes its findings through education, advice, and information services. In 1992 it set up the International Benchmarking Clearinghouse to promote and facilitate the process of learning from best practice.

American Society for Quality (ASQ)

600 North Plankinton Avenue, Milwaukee, Wisconsin, 53203

T: +1 414 272 8575
F: +1 414 272 1734
E: *cs@asq.org*
www.asq.org

Founded in 1946, the ASQ is a society of individual and organizational members dedicated to the development and promotion of the concepts, principles, and techniques of quality. It has recently launched the Six Sigma Forum.

FOR MORE INFORMATION

- ✔ Implementing Statistical Process Control (SPC) (pp. 592–593)
- ☆ Lean Manufacturing (pp. 218–219)
- ℘ Manufacturing Systems (pp. 1821–1823)
- ℘ Quality and Total Quality Management (pp. 1886–1889)
- ☆ X-engineering Success (pp. 300–301)

1869

"Treating processes holistically means that much more is being included under the umbrella of product development."

Dan Dimancescu

Product and Brand Management

BOOKS

The 22 Immutable Laws of Branding: How to Build a Product or Service into a World-class Brand

Al Ries, Laura Ries
London: Profile Books, 2002
272pp ISBN: 0060007737
In this title, the authors argue that branding is the basis of a strong marketing programme. If it is not possible to create a strong brand, then nothing a company does, including advertising campaigns and public relations events, will help. The book looks at both successful brands and those that have failed, providing coherent explanations of the various factors involved.

Brand Asset Management: Driving Profitable Growth through Your Brands 2nd ed.

Scott M. Davis
San Francisco, California: Jossey-Bass, 2002
288pp (Jossey-Bass Business and Management)
ISBN: 0787963941
This book suggests that brands should be seen as vehicles for company growth, and presents an 11-step strategy to help managers manage their brands as valuable assets.

Brand Failures: The Truth about the Biggest Branding Mistakes of All Time

Matt Haig
London: Kogan Page, 2003
256pp ISBN: 0749439270
Some brands just don't work. Many companies around the world have been affected by branding disasters, from Coke to Ford, Sony to Harley Davidson. Some have lived to fight another day, some not. In this book, Matt Haig looks at the stories behind brand failures and the key lessons that can be learned from them. Useful for advertisers as well as brand managers, the book looks at several types of marketing malfunction including: idea failures, PR failures, culture failures, and people failures.

Brand It Like Beckham: Building a Brand with Balls

Andy Milligan
London: Cyan Books, 2005
208pp ISBN: 1904879292
Part of the growing "Brand It Like . . ." series, this book explains how success in one arena (in this case, sport) can translate into commercial pulling power in many other areas. Explaining the key concepts behind building an international brand, this book is an entertaining take on the nature of celebrity, image, and marketing.

Brand Leadership

David A. Aaker, Erich Joachimsthaler
New York: Free Press, 2002
368pp ISBN: 074320767X
A reference tool for brand managers, this text analyzes brand management in today's world. Using case studies taken from a wide spectrum of companies (including Ralph Lauren, Swatch, and Adidas) the authors suggest that the world of brand management is undergoing structural and systematic change. The book offers guidance on accessing vital links between brands, and using these to company advantage.

Brand Warfare: 10 Rules for Building the Killer Brand

David F. D'Alessandro, Michele Owens
Maidenhead, United Kingdom: McGraw-Hill, 2001
240pp ISBN: 0071362932
The authors consider ways in which companies often mishandle their brands. They offer advice, based on their own experience and on company examples, to those wishing to build a successful brand in any market.

Building Strong Brands

David A. Aaker
San Francisco, California: Jossey-Bass, 2002
384pp ISBN: 0743232135
Aaker discusses the varying elements of a brand, and emphasizes the need for managers to be aware of the importance of strong brands in today's marketplace. In discussing various large corporations (such as McDonald's and Kodak), Aaker demonstrates the process of managing a hugely successful brand. The author also explores ways of retaining a certain brand while under some pressure to alter it. A reference tool for anybody involved in brand management.

Creating Passionbrands: Getting to the Heart of Branding

Helen Edwards, Derek Day
London: Kogan Page, 2005
320pp ISBN: 0749443707
Practical, inspiring, and rooted in the real world, this book explains how the world's most successful brands benefit from building strong emotional connections with consumers. Emphasising the difference between passion and passivity, the book explains the rise of "belief-led" brands. Its findings are based on interviews with, and research on, people behind those brands, such as Google, Camper, and Emirates.

Differentiate or Die: Survival in Our Era of Killer Competition

Jack Trout, Steve Rivkin
Hoboken, New Jersey: Wiley, 2001
240pp ISBN: 0471028924
This title is a useful guide on how to make ones product differ from those of everyone else and lists several ways to achieve this. These include being the first person to do something, being the latest person to do a version of something, and becoming the first choice of a certain type of consumer group.

The Infinite Asset: Managing Brands to Build New Value

Sam Hill, Chris Lederer, Kevin Lane Keller
Boston, Massachusetts: Harvard Business School Press, 2001
240pp ISBN: 1578512492
In a new approach to brand management, the authors argue that, instead of dealing with brands on an individual basis, a "portfolio" approach should be adopted. Brands should be grouped into actively-managed collections, regardless of ownership. The authors look at case studies of 3M and Miller Beer, among others, which help readers visualize the relationships that tie their brands to each other and to the outside world. They also put together an eight-part toolkit that covers brand extensions and repositioning, as well as an organizational design for implementing brand portfolio management.

The Invisible Grail: How Brands Can Use Words to Captivate Audiences New ed.

John Simmons
London: Cyan Books, 2006
256pp ISBN: 1904879691
The Invisible Grail takes a hard look at how language and storytelling help build compelling brands. The author is a former director of Interbrand and he draws on his considerable experience to examine how

"I think it's quite clear that in the information age, the brand is what you compete on."
Andrew Neil

the world's biggest brands, such as Guinness, connect with their customers by means of the language they use. Practical and inspiration, this book will help businesses of all sizes find their "grail": benefiting from their hidden creative resources.

Managing Brand Equity: Capitalizing on the Value of a Brand Name

David A. Aaker

San Francisco, California: Jossey-Bass, 1991
224pp ISBN: 0029001013

In this book, Aaker emphasizes the importance of understanding exactly what makes a brand so successful. For example, being in touch with your customer base and recognizing the subconscious associations that are linked to a brand name are essential. The author points out the lack of managerial understanding that prevails in branding, and aims to minimize this with practical guidelines for understanding the value of brand equity within a company.

Marketing Genius

Peter Fisk

New York: Wiley, 2006
498pp ISBN: 1841126810

Billed as "the little black book of marketing," this book aims to help readers tap into the massive potential of marketing so that their businesses stand out from the crowd. Full of examples of real-life excellence from companies such as Alessi, Innocent, and Google, it is full of inspiration for marketers who know that the consumer is in the driving seat.

Strategic Brand Management: Building, Measuring, and Managing Brand Equity 2nd ed.

Kevin Lane Keller

Upper Saddle River, New Jersey: Prentice Hall, 2003
640pp ISBN: 0131216112

In its discussion of the role of brands in our society, this book offers a pragmatic approach to brand management, discussing the creation, assessment, and use of brand equity within an organization. Aimed at a wide spectrum of different businesses (not simply large corporations) *Strategic Brand Management* is a resource for almost anybody involved in brand management.

We, Me, Them & IT: How to Write Powerfully for Business Revised ed.

John Simmons

London: Cyan Books, 2006
256pp ISBN: 1904879683

A revised edition of this popular business book aims to get readers using words more powerfully at work. A key question lies at heart of the book: what good is it to have a fantastic idea if you can't communicate it to anyone? Simmons offers practical, inspirational advice for anyone feeling stuck in this situation and demonstrates how words and writing can be powerfully employed to gain competitive advantage.

What Makes Winning Brands Different: The Hidden Method behind the World's Most Successful Brands

Andreas Buchholz, Wolfram Wordemann

Hoboken, New Jersey: Wiley, 2000
224pp ISBN: 0471720259

The authors analyze the results of a research study of over 1,000 winning brands in order to establish a blueprint for brand growth and development. They argue that brands can achieve outstanding growth by adhering to specific laws or "growth codes," of which they identify 27. Putting these "codes" into effect is explored through case studies and best practice examples.

MAGAZINES

Brand Strategy

ISSN: 0965-9390
Centaur Holdings
St. Giles House, 50 Poland Street, London, W1F 7AX, U.K.
T: +44 (0) 20 7970 4000
F: +44 (0) 20 7943 8172
www.centaur.co.uk

Aimed at marketing directors and senior managers, this monthly publication contains comment, analysis, and business intelligence on issues relating to brand management.

Brandweek

ISSN: 1064-4318
VNU Business Publications
770 Broadway, New York, 10003-9595
T: +1 646 654 4500
F: +1 646 654 4480
www.vnubusinessmedia.com

Brandweek is a weekly print and online publication aimed at top brand marketing executives in the United States. Its coverage includes marketing strategies, trends, new product news, and general news. It is aimed at all industries.

Journal of Brand Management

ISSN: 1350-231X
Henry Stewart Publications
Subscriptions Office, P.O. Box 10812, Birmingham, Alabama, 35202-0812
T: +1 800 633 4931
F: +1 205 995 1588

www.henrystewart.com/journals/jcm

This journal, published six times a year, is aimed at a wide readership of marketing directors, managers, academics, and consultants. Its content takes in all aspects of the management of brands, from their launch to their development and evaluation.

Journal of Product and Brand Management

ISSN: 1061-0421
Emerald
44 Brattle Street, 4th Floor, Cambridge, Massachusetts, 02138
T: +1 888 622 0075
F: +1 617 354 6875
www.emeraldinsight.com

Issued seven times a year; this journal covers topics such as brand management, consumer behavior, pricing strategies, marketing research, new product development, international pricing, and brand equity. Its target readership includes both practitioners and academics. The subscription includes online access via Emerald Fulltext.

INTERNET

Allaboutbranding.com
www.allaboutbranding.com

This site has multiple articles concerned with branding's role in the marketplace and what it takes to create and maintain a brand name. Site features include an "Analyze Your Brand" test, free e-mail updates, quotes, definitions of useful terms, and sections that accurately cover the field.

brandchannel.com
www.brandchannel.com

This site, produced by Interbrand, provides for an online exchange about branding. It contains a debate area, features, papers, and details of books and training.

BrandingAsia.com
www.brandingasia.com

This site focuses on branding issues in Asia, and includes brand news, tips, case studies, articles, and a discussion board. A free monthly e-mail newsletter is available.

Building Brands—Unlocking Your Potential
www.buildingbrands.com

Both free content—in the form of articles, definitions, and did-you-knows, and premium services, which include training, web seminars, student mentoring—and executive coaching are available on this site.

1871

BUSINESS INFORMATION SOURCES

"Every advertisement should be thought of as a contribution to the complex symbol which is the brand image."

David Ogilvy

Knowledge Roundtable
www.knowledge-roundtable.com
This membership-based service aims to connect people around the world and provide information to aid product development and collaboration. Members gain access to news, networking opportunities, an ask the expert facility, and audio conferences.

KnowThis.com
www.knowthis.com
This section of the Virtual Library contains articles and links to resources for successful product management, branding, and packaging.

ORGANIZATIONS
USA
Product Development and Management Association
15000 Commerce Parkway, Suite C, Mount Laurel, New Jersey, 08054
T: +1 856 439 9052
F: +1 856 439 0525
E: *pdma@pdma.org*
www.pdma.org
This professional nonprofit organization is dedicated to serving people with an interest in new products and services. It is a recognized provider of knowledge and tools intended to improve the effectiveness of the development and management of new products and services. It also arranges conferences, publications, awards, meetings, and workshops, and sponsors research.

Europe
Product Development and Management Association, U.K. and Ireland
Helen Perks
Manchester Business School, The University of Manchester, Booth Street West, Manchester, M15 6PB, U.K.
E: *h.perks@manchester.ac.uk*
www.pdma.org.uk
This is the U.K. and Ireland branch of the PDMA, a professional nonprofit organization dedicated to serving people with an interest in new products and services (see above).

International
Association of International Product Marketing and Management
PO Box 1113, Palo Cedro, California, 96073
T: +1 877 275 5500
F: +1 866 731 8421
E: *office@aipmm.com*
www.aipmm.com
AIPMM is a membership organization that aims to provide focused and strategic information, training, and networking opportunities for professional product and marketing managers and their employers.

The Product-Life Institute, Geneva
9 Chemin des Vignettes, Conches, CH-1231, Switzerland
T: +41 22 346 35 04
F: +41 22 346 04 18
E: *wrstahel@vtx.ch*
www.product-life.org
A nonprofit independent organization formed in 1982 in Geneva, the Institute is financed solely by contract research. It is involved in consulting and research in the area of optimization of the product life of goods and services, and focuses on issues of sustainability.

FOR MORE INFORMATION

- Advertising (pp. 1672–1674)
- ☆ Creating Powerful Brands (pp. 76–77)
- ☆ Managing New-product Portfolios (pp. 349–350)
- Marketing Management (pp. 1827–1832)
- New Product Development (pp. 1841–1843)
- Online Sources for Marketing (General Business Information) (p. 1766)

1872

BUSINESS INFORMATION SOURCES

"How is a legend different from a brand? An alternative spelling of legend is 'g-u-t-s'."

Harriet Rubin

Project Management

BOOKS

5-Phase Project Management
Joseph W. Weiss, Robert K. Wysocki
Cambridge, Massachusetts: Perseus Books Group, 1992
128pp ISBN: 0201563169
5-Phase Project Management offers the best project management practices in a simple, easy-to-use format. In this practical, step-by-step book, Weiss and Wysocki walk the reader through each phase of a complex project: definition, planning, implementation, management, and maintenance.

The Accidental Project Manager: Surviving the Transition from Techie to Manager
Patricia Ensworth
Hoboken, New Jersey: Wiley, 2001
272pp ISBN: 047141011X
When projects fail it is often because the person in charge has no idea how to manage projects. This no-nonsense guide provides basic project management information including project planning, the roles of team members, the tools of the trade, and project control metrics. It also supplies templates, checklists, and sample forms for the beginner to use.

Effective Project Management 3rd ed.
Robert Wysocki et al.
Hoboken, New Jersey: Wiley, 2003
512pp ISBN: 0471432210
This book and CD-ROM package provides novices with a complete introduction to the principles of project management, and offers experienced project managers an opportunity to fine-tune their skills. It describes the management tools and techniques you need to stay on schedule and within budget without compromising quality. It adheres to the Project Management Institute's curriculum outline (PMBOK), and follows the necessary course requirements for professional certification. The CD-ROM provides a simulated environment in which to apply the principles, tools, and techniques described in the book.

A Guide to the Project Management Body of Knowledge 3rd ed.
Project Management Institute
Newtown Square, Pennsylvania: Project Management Institute, 2004
384pp ISBN: 193069945X

This is the basic project management reference book and the accepted standard for the profession. It details the nine knowledge areas and 39 processes essential to a project management model that will work in any industry. By establishing a standard, the guide also provides a common language for talking about project management. It is a key resource for those seeking Project Management Professional (PMP) certification.

Managing Successful Projects with PRINCE2
APM Group Ltd.
London: The Stationery Office, 2002
432pp ISBN: 0113308914
This reference manual describes the PRINCE2 project management method, one of the most popular project management methodologies. It provides detailed guidance on how to set up, organize, manage, control, and deliver projects on time, within budget, and with high quality. The processes and techniques of PRINCE2 are said to help any project team cope with the risks, challenges, and opportunities in today's rapidly changing environment.

Project Management 8th ed.
Dennis Lock
Aldershot, United Kingdom: Gower Publishing, 2003
704pp ISBN: 0566085518
Lock provides comprehensive coverage of the subject of project management. The topics he focuses on include the nature and purpose of project management, defining the project, estimating costs, commercial management, project planning and scheduling, network analysis in practice, resource scheduling, purchasing, implementing the program, managing progress, and cost management. Case studies, graphs, and illustrations are included.

Project Management for Dummies
Stanley Portny
Hoboken, New Jersey: Wiley, 2000
288pp ISBN: 076455283X
Highly recommended by professional project managers, this book explains what project management is and then goes on to offer advice on how best to do it. It includes information on scheduling, assembling teams, and assessing resources.

Project Management: Planning and Control Techniques 4th ed.
Rory Burke
Hoboken, New Jersey: Wiley, 2003
684pp ISBN: 0958239150
This book is a step-by-step guide to the latest project management planning and control techniques. The topics it covers include the project life cycle, feasibility studies, project selection, work breakdown structures, the critical path method, resource planning, project accounts, quality management, risk management, and leadership.

Project Management: The Managerial Process 2nd ed.
Clifford Gray
New York: Irwin/McGraw-Hill, 2002
592pp ISBN: 0072833483
This book presents a balanced view of the technical and sociocultural dimensions of managing projects. It is suitable for a course in project management, and for individuals seeking a project management handbook. The text is application-oriented for managing any type of project, and includes advice on discovering the strategic role of projects in contemporary organizations, prioritizing, planning and scheduling projects, and orchestrating the complex network of relationships. It includes a CD-ROM, bibliographical references, and an index.

The Project Manager's Desk Reference 2nd ed.
James P. Lewis
Maidenhead, United Kingdom: McGraw-Hill, 1999
560pp ISBN: 007134750X
In a comprehensive guide to project planning, scheduling, evaluation, control, and systems, the author provides the reader with a template for managing projects of any size from start to finish. He discusses topics such as how to develop project plans using work breakdown structures, PERT, CPM, and Gantt schedules; how to conduct risk analysis; how to design a project control system; how to use earned value analysis to track projects; and how to communicate effectively with your team. In this edition there are updated examples, illustrations and figures, and checklists for every stage, plus lists of associations and Web sites.

"One worthwhile task carried to a successful conclusion is better than 50 half-finished tasks."
Bertie Charles Forbes

The Project Manager's MBA: How to Translate Project Decisions into Business Success

Dennis J. Cohen, Robert J. Graham
San Francisco, California: Jossey-Bass, 2000
336pp (Jossey-Bass Business and Management)
ISBN: 0787952567

This text aims to provide an introduction to the business basics that every project manager needs to understand. These include value creation, accounting and finance strategy, and marketing. These concepts are related to the decisions project managers face every day. The aim is to develop the skills of project managers so that they can meet both their technical and their business objectives.

Project Planning, Scheduling, and Control 4th ed.

James P. Lewis
Maidenhead, United Kingdom: McGraw-Hill, 2005
352pp ISBN: 0071460373

This latest edition of this well-regard text offers an applications-oriented, non-theoretical understanding of the flexibility required in day-to-day management situations, and provides guidelines that apply to every phase of steering a project to its successful conclusion.

The Project Workout 3rd ed.

Robert Buttrick
Upper Saddle River, New Jersey: Financial Times Prentice Hall, 2005
544pp ISBN: 0273681818

A best selling guide to project management, this book provides an illustrated approach to the practical theory behind best practice in the field. The package includes a CD-ROM to allow interactive practice.

Web Project Management: Delivering Successful Commercial Web Sites

Ashley Friedlein
San Francisco, California: Morgan Kaufmann, 2000
336pp ISBN: 1558606785

This book covers the usual project management subjects of organizing teams, developing goals, and managing schedules and budgets, but from the unique perspective of the requirements of Web site development. This is not a conventional project management approach, nor is it a software engineering approach. Friedlein has focused on the essentials for delivering successful commercial sites by managing to deliverables, rather than to schedules, and

balancing the often conflicting commercial, creative, content, and technical requirements.

The World Class Project Manager

Robert K. Wysocki, James P. Lewis
Cambridge, Massachusetts: Perseus Books Group, 2001
272pp ISBN: 0738202371

Wysocki and Lewis offer a practical handbook for anyone who aspires to achieve superior project-management skills. Featuring self-assessment tools, showcasing best practice examples from the field, and drawing on their own experience in training project managers around the world, the authors provide a comprehensive program for crafting a career development plan and putting it into action.

MAGAZINES

International Journal of Project Management

ISSN: 0263-7863
Elsevier Science
Customer Service Department, 6277 Sea Harbor Drive, Orlando, Florida, 32887-4800
T: +1 877 839 7126 or +1 407 345 4020
F: +1 407 363 1354
www.elsevier.com

In eight issues per year, the journal of the International Project Management Association publishes papers which cover both practical and theoretical aspects of project management. Case studies help to link theory with practice, and the latest important areas of concern are covered in special issues.

Project

ISSN: 0957-7033
Impact!
Media House, 55 Old Road, Leighton Buzzard, Bedfordshire, LU7 2RB, U.K.
T: +44 (0) 1525 370 013
F: +44 (0) 1525 382 487
www.apm.org.uk/ProjectMagazine.asp
Project, the magazine of the U.K.'s Association for Project Management, aims to cover all aspects of project management across all industries.

Project Management Journal

ISSN: 0147-5363
Project Management Institute
4 Campus Boulevard, Newtown Square, Pennsylvania, 19073
T: +1 610 356 4600
F: +1 610 356 4647
www.pmi.org/info/PIR_PMJournal.asp

Published quarterly, this journal provides comprehensive coverage of program and project management issues. Articles discuss problems and solutions in various aspects of project management.

Project Manager Today

ISSN: 1366-6851
Larchdrift Projects Ltd.
Unit 12, Moor Place Farm, Plough Lane, Bramshill, Hook, Hampshire, RG27 0RF, U.K.
T: +44 (0) 118 932 6665
F: +44 (0) 118 932 6663
www.projectnet.co.uk

This journal covers all aspects of project control, planning, costing, and management. Case studies and software reviews are included.

INTERNET

AllPM.com—The Project Manager's Homepage

www.allpm.com

This site offers free membership which allows users access to a forum, event calendar, articles and tips, and a project management template library.

Association for Project Management

www.apm.org.uk

Details of news, events, qualifications, services, and publications in the field of project management are available to visitors to this site, which also has information on member benefits and links to related organizations. It provides short reading lists, and its resources section includes a glossary and bookshop.

International Project Management Association

www.ipma.ch

This site introduces the services available from the IPMA. It lists conferences, seminars, and training courses, and also provides information on research and development activity, affiliates listing, and services for young project managers.

PMFORUM

www.pmforum.org

This information, dissemination, and exchange forum includes a portal to information, resources, and working groups associated with project manager accreditation, certification, education, research, and standards. It also contains listings of software, consulting services, and training resources, plus a calendar of events.

BUSINESS INFORMATION SOURCES

"Involve people in meaningful projects."

Stephen Covey

Project Management
www.projectmagazine.com

A "magazine" that's free to anyone, this audience-oriented resource for the project manager offers meaningful articles, book reviews, software reviews, and access to a free newsletter.

Project Management Institute
www.pmi.org

The Project Management Institute (PMI) has over 200,000 members worldwide and is the leading nonprofit professional association in this field. The site offers information on member services, including careers and awards programs, a bookshop, links to other project management organizations, and information on project management standards. It also provides opportunities for organizations to contribute to a corporate council and lists PMI seminars.

Project Management Library
www.mapnp.org/library/plan_dec/ project/project.htm

Part of the Management Assistance Program for Nonprofits, this site's resources include a project management overview, information on team building and group leadership, general resources, and online discussion groups.

Wideman Comparative Glossary of Common Project Management Terms
www.maxwideman.com/pmglossary/ index.htm

This site is a searchable glossary of hundreds of common project management terms. In many cases multiple definitions are listed, reflecting existing variations in usage within the industry.

ORGANIZATIONS
USA
Project Management Institute

Four Campus Boulevard, Newtown Square, Pennsylvania, 19073–3299
T: +1 610 356 4600
F: +1 610 356 4647
E: *pmihq@pmi.org*
www.pmi.org

A nonprofit professional association founded in 1969, PMI sets project management standards, offers educational programs and professional certification, and is a publisher.

Europe
Association for Project Management

Thornton House, 150 West Wycombe Road, High Wycombe, Buckinghamshire, HP12 3AE, U.K.
T: +44 (0) 845 458 1944
F: +44 (0) 1494 528 937
E: *info@apm.org.uk*
www.apm.org.uk

A professional body founded in 1970, the APM aims to be the U.K. national authority on project management. It promotes project management skills and training, and develops standards and certification for project managers. Services are delivered through joint ventures or through its members. The association is affiliated to the International Project Management Association.

International
International Project Management Association

P.O. Box 1167, 3860 BD, Nijkerk, The Netherlands
T: +31 33 247 3430
F: +31 33 246 0470
E: *info@ipma.ch*
www.ipma.ch

The IPMA is a nonprofit organization, founded in 1965, promoting the advancement of project management methods, systems, and practical application techniques via its network of national project management associations in 26 countries. Individual participation is possible where there is no national society.

1875

FOR MORE INFORMATION

✔ Managing Projects (pp. 568–569)
☆ Project Management (pp. 200–202)

"Project management is the furnace in which successful careers are made."

Thomas Stewart

Psychological Tests

BOOKS

Career Tests: 25 Revealing Self-tests to Help You Find and Succeed at the Perfect Career
Louis H. Janda
Holbrook, Massachusetts: Adams Media Corporation, 1999
256pp ISBN: 1580621422
Career tests used to be the exclusive—and expensive—domain of psychologists. Advances in recent years have put a variety of useful self-assessment tools directly into the hands of the individual. This book provides a collection of these self-administered psychological tests to assist you in your career search. There are scales and surveys on everything from creativity, fear of success, and procrastination, to integrity, neuroticism, and agreeableness.

Essentials of Myers-Briggs Type Indicator Assessment
Naomi L. Quenk
Hoboken, New Jersey: Wiley, 1999
208pp (Essentials of Psychological Assessment)
ISBN: 0471332399
This book provides guidance on how to interpret and administer the Myers-Briggs Type Indicator (MBTI®) test. The test classifies participants by broad personality types in order to gain an insight into how they gather information, make decisions, and orient themselves to their surroundings. This book also provides an appraisal of the test's relative strengths and weaknesses, advice on its clinical applications, and several case reports.

How to Master Personality Questionnaires 2nd ed.
Mark Parkinson
London: Kogan Page, 2001
128pp ISBN: 0749434198
This practical guide aims to help readers explore their own personalities and prepare for personality questionnaires. It explains what personality is and how it is measured, the reasons why personality questionnaires are used, why different jobs require different personalities, and what employers do with questionnaire results. In addition, it identifies and describes the personality questionnaires most used in the United

Kingdom, and provides a list of publishers with contact details.

How to Master Psychometric Tests 3rd ed.
Mark Parkinson
London: Kogan Page, 2005
192pp ISBN: 0749442794
This introduction to psychometric tests provides an overview of the different types of tests, including ability, intelligence, attainment, and aptitude tests, and explains how test results are used. It also gives practical advice on coping with anxiety and preparing for tests as well as printing practice tests supplied by Saville and Holdsworth Ltd. (SHL).

Individual Psychological Assessment: Predicting Behavior in Organizational Settings
Richard Jeanneret, Robert F. Silzer, eds
San Francisco, California: Jossey-Bass, 1998
448pp ISBN: 0787908614
This is a definitive volume on the state of the art of a practice fraught with legal, scientific, sociopolitical, and certainly managerial complexity. Topics are arranged in four sections: frameworks, processes, strategies, and perspectives. They cover: theoretical frameworks; ethical, legal, professional, and cross-cultural issues; designing the assessment process; assessing and changing managers for new organizational roles; shaping organizational leadership; and more.

IQ and Psychometric Test Workbook
Philip Carter
London: Kogan Page, 2005
272pp ISBN: 0749443782
This practical self-test resource is ideal for anyone preparing for an interview or any those seeking to improve their IQ ratings. The tests included in the book cover a range of key skill areas, including: verbal, numerical, and spatial aptitude; personality tests; and IQ tests.

Now, Discover Your Strengths: How to Develop Your Talents and Those of the People You Manage
Marcus Buckingham, Donald O. Clifton
New York: Free Press, 2001
272pp ISBN: 0743201140
This book suggests a unique path to

managerial success: focusing on the enhancement of people's strengths rather than the elimination of their weaknesses. In addition to showing how to capitalize on 34 positive personality themes in building a "strengths-based organization," the book provides an online questionnaire so that readers can instantly discover their own top five inborn talents. This interactive feature encourages introspection and provides a context for practical, real-time application.

Psychological Testing and Assessment 12th ed.
Lewis R. Aiken
Boston, Massachusetts: Allyn and Bacon, 2005
552pp ISBN: 0205457428
This book provides a comprehensive analysis of the theory and practice of psychometric testing, including the design and reliability of tests, assessment of abilities and personality, criticisms, and key issues. It is aimed both at psychometric practitioners and users of tests.

Psychological Testing: A Practical Approach to Design and Evaluation
Theresa J. B. Kline
Sage Publications, 2005
406pp ISBN: 1412905443
If you are responsible for creating or evalating psychological testing, this book offers a clear and practical approach. Full of useful examples and stressing the importance of best practice, the book covers many issues, including: classical and modern test theories; reliability; validation; and professional and ethical issues.

Psychometric Testing: 1000 Ways to Assess Your Personality, Creativity, Intelligence, and Lateral Thinking
Philip Carter, Ken Russell
Hoboken, New Jersey: Wiley, 2001
240pp (IQ Workout)
ISBN: 0471523763
This book contains 40 new psychometric tests covering such subjects as risk taking, leadership, positivity, aggression, tact, ambition, tolerance, and imagination. To these are added two intelligence tests that use word and number puzzles, math, and diagrams to test spatial, verbal, numerical, and logical ability. Scores and answers to all the tests are included.

"Blameless people are always the most exasperating." — George Eliot

Tests That Work: Designing and Delivering Fair and Practical Measurement Tools in the Workplace

Odin Westgaard
San Francisco, California: Jossey-Bass, 1999
352pp ISBN: 078794596X
This comprehensive guide to the use of tests in the assessment of people is aimed at managers and human resources professionals who require an understanding of the way tests are used and the care needed in planning, designing, and interpreting test results.

Test Your Aptitude 3rd ed.

Jim Barrett
London: Kogan Page, 2003
256pp (Test Yourself)
ISBN: 0749438878
This book aims to help job applicants prepare for selection tests and to develop personal awareness of their attributes and skills. It includes examples of a range of different types of aptitude test to help you plan your career as well as an index of over 400 jobs.

Using Psychometrics: A Practical Guide to Testing and Assessment 2nd ed.

Robert Edenborough
London: Kogan Page, 1999
240pp ISBN: 0749431261
This book provides a detailed and practical guide to the use of tests in staff selection and recruitment. The author attempts to demystify testing, while pointing out the pitfalls of ill-considered use, and shows how to understand the different types of test and choose the most appropriate one. The legal, regulatory, and commercial framework is also considered.

What Type Am I? Discover Who You Really Are

Renee Baron
New York: Penguin USA, 1998
208pp ISBN: 014026941X
This book takes on the complexity of the 16 personality types, which are derived from the Myers-Briggs Type Indicator tests, and makes them accessible to the general reader. The aim of this book is to give individuals the opportunity to comprehend the different personality types, find their own type, and use this knowledge to advance their lives, both on a professional and personal level.

MAGAZINES
Assessment Journal

ISSN: 0731–0277
International Association of Assessing Officers
130 East Randolph, Suite 850, Chicago, Illinois, 60601
T: +1 312 819 6100
F: +1 312 819 6149
www.iaao.org
A bimonthly journal containing articles on assessment techniques and practices, property taxation, assessment administration, related research, recent legislation and court decisions, assessment and appraisal literature, and other topics of interest to assessment personnel.

European Journal of Psychological Assessment

ISSN: 1015–5759
Hogrefe and Huber Publishers
Seattle Office, P.O. Box 2487, Kirkland, Washington, D.C., 98083–2487
T: +1 425 820 1500
F: +1 425 823 8324
www.hhpub.com/journals/ejpa
This journal, which is the official journal of the European Association of Psychological Assessment, is directed at both researchers and practitioners, and provides a forum for scholarly communication in the field of psychological assessment. It covers assessment in clinical, educational, and organizational contexts and addresses legal, ethical, and professional issues.

International Journal of Selection and Assessment

ISSN: 0965–075X
Blackwell Publishing
350 Main Street, Malden, Massachusetts, 02148
T: +1 781 388 8200
F: +1 781 388 8232
www.blackwellpublishing.com
This quarterly journal covers selection, performance appraisal, assessment methodology, the theory and practice of psychometric measurement, and employment legislation.

International Journal of Testing

ISSN: 1530–5058
Lawrence Erlbaum Associates, Inc.
10 Industrial Avenue, Mahwah, New Jersey, 07430–2262
T: +1 800 926 6579
F: +1 201 760 3735
www.erlbaum.com/journals/journals/ IJT/ijt.htm
This quarterly journal is dedicated to the advancement of the theory, research, and practice of testing and assessment in psychology, education, counseling, human resources management, and related disciplines. It is aimed at scholars, professionals, and students, and is the official journal of the International Test Commission.

INTERNET
ASE

www.ase-solutions.co.uk
Advice on assessments and practice tests are accessible on this site, as well as product information from a test publisher based in the United Kingdom. The site also features useful articles, which users may view for free.

Center for Applications of Psychological Type

www.capt.org
CAPT is a research and educational organization sustaining the work of Isabel Briggs Myers. The Web site offers free searches of a bibliography of psychological type.

The Keirsey Temperament Sorter II

www.advisorteam.com/user/ ktsintro.asp
Keirsey's 70-question personality assessment can be taken online (free, but you must register to proceed) to learn which of the four "temperament" types (an extension of the 16 Myers-Briggs personality types) you are. This test is used in career development programs at *Fortune* 500 companies as well as in counseling and career placement centers at major universities.

The Personality Page

www.personalitypage.com
Obtain a relatively reliable personality profile on the Internet for a mere five dollars. This test, validated with over 100,000 users, comprises 60 questions that yield 16 personality types, based on the work of Carl Jung, Isabel Myers, and Catherine Briggs. The site also offers information on personality types and careers, relationships, and personal growth.

SHLDirect

www.shldirect.com
This site, provided by a well-known test publisher, offers practice tests and advice aimed primarily at students.

Sussex University Career Development Unit Psychometric Tests

www.sussex.ac.uk/cdec/ psycho_tests.php
This simple but content-rich site offers advice for students on taking tests, links to test publishers, and tests on the Web.

1877

BUSINESS INFORMATION SOURCES

ORGANIZATIONS
USA
American Psychological Association
750 First Street NE, Washington, D.C., 20002–4242
T: +1 202 336 5580
F: +1 202 336 5568
E: *membership@apa.org*
www.apa.org
With over 150,000 members, including researchers, educators, clinicians, consultants, and students, the APA is the largest professional organization representing psychology in the United States. It works to advance psychology as a science and as a profession through divisions in 49 sub-fields of psychology and affiliation with local associations.

Association of Test Publishers
1201 Pennsylvania Avenue NW, Suite 300, Washington, D.C., 20004
T: +1 202 857 8444
E: *lauren@testpublishers.org*
www.testpublishers.org
The ATP is a nonprofit organization established in 1992 with the aims of fostering good working relationships between test publishers, and promoting integrity and professionalism in the industry. It monitors legislative and regulatory developments in the field of testing, carries out networking and advocacy activities, and publishes a newsletter and an online journal.

Buros Institute of Mental Measurements
University of Nebraska-Lincoln, 21 Teachers College Hall, Lincoln, Nebraska, 68588–0348
T: +1 402 472 6203
F: +1 403 472 6203
E: *bplake1@unl.edu*
www.unl.edu/buros/bimm/index.html
The Buros Institute provides information and assistance in the selection of appropriate tests, and encourages test development and measurement research. Its publications include the *Mental Measurements Yearbook*, *Tests in Print*, and the Buros Desk Reference series.

Fair Access Coalition on Testing (FACT)
3 Terrace Way, Suite D, Greensboro, North Carolina, 27403–3660
T: +1 336 547 0607
F: +1 336 547 0558
www.fairaccess.org
FACT was formed in 1996 to protect the rights of counseling and mental health professionals not qualified as psychologists to use psychological, educational, vocational, and industrial tests, and to promote high standards of testing practice in member organizations.

Society for Personality Assessment
6109H Arlington Boulevard, Falls Church, Virginia, 22044
T: +1 703 534 4772
E: *manager@SPAonline.org*
www.personality.org
The SPA was founded by Bruno Klopfer, incorporated as the Rorschach Institute in 1938, and renamed in 1971 to reflect a wider interest in the field. It is dedicated to the advancement of professional personality assessment, the development of procedures for personality assessment, and the ethical use of such techniques. Activities include meetings, and the publication of a newsletter and the *Journal of Personality Assessment*.

Europe
British Psychological Society
St. Andrews House, 48 Princess Road East, Leicester, Leicestershire, LE1 7DR, U.K.
T: +44 (0) 116 254 9568
F: +44 (0) 116 247 0787
E: *enquiry@bps.org.uk*
www.bps.org.uk
With over 40,000 members, the BPS is the representative body for psychologists in the United Kingdom. It was founded in 1901 under the name The Psychological Society, renamed in 1906, and granted a royal charter in 1965. The Society's aims are to encourage the development of psychology as a scientific discipline and a profession, to raise standards of training and practice in the field, and to raise public awareness of psychology. It sets standards for occupational testing and publishes reviews of ability and aptitude tests and personality assessment instruments. The Certificate of Competence in Occupational Testing is accredited by the BPS.

European Association of Psychological Assessment
Universidad de Barcelona, Facultad de Psicología, Dept. Personalidad, Evaluación y Tratamiento Psicológico, Paseo Vall d'Hebrón 171 (Edificio Ponent), Barcelona, 8035, Spain
E: *mforns@psi.ub.es*
www.uam.es/centros/psicologia/paginas/eapa
The EAPA, formerly the Spanish Association of Psychological Assessment, was founded in 1990 in Madrid. Those with a university degree or the equivalent who have contributed to the development of psychological assessment are eligible to become members. The organization aims to increase scientific interest in psychological assessment in Europe, develop research in the field, improve the practice of assessment, and create opportunities for the exchange of information among scholars in the field.

International
Association for Psychological Type
P. O. Box No. 10058, Gathersbury, Maryland, 20898–10058
T: +1 301 840 3870
F: +1 301 840 3878
E: *info@aptinternational.org*
www.aptinternational.org/index.cfm
This is an international membership organization, founded in 1979, whose members come from a variety of backgrounds in business, organization development, education, psychology, and counseling. Its activities include training programs, workshops, and conferences; it has local groups and produces publications.

Australian Association for Psychological Type
182 Keele St, Collingwood, Victoria, 3066, Australia
E: *info@aapt.org.au*
www.aapt.org.au
Founded in 1992, AusAPT promotes the knowledge and use of psychological type in Australia. Members include psychologists, consultants, academics, teachers, trainers, and managers. The Association publishes the *Australian Psychological Type Review*, supports research in this area, and organizes biennial conferences.

"Middle is the extra unknown personality in any committee."   Anthony Sampson

     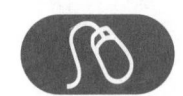

Public Relations

BOOKS

Effective Writing Skills for Public Relations 3rd ed.
John Foster
London: Kogan Page, 2005
256pp (PR in Practice)
ISBN: 0749443812
This is a practical guide to writing style for students and PR practitioners. It looks at grammar, developing a house style, headlines and captions, press releases, and speeches and public speaking.

Free Publicity for Your Business in a Week
Guy Clapperton
London: Hodder & Stoughton, 2002
96pp (Business in a Week)
ISBN: 0340858273
This book is aimed at cash-strapped small business owners and managers who need to make a splash. It covers a range of issues including how to handle the press, writing effective press releases, responding to feedback, and crisis management if things do not go to plan.

Guerrilla PR Wired: Waging a Successful Publicity Campaign Online, Offline, and Everywhere In Between
Michael Levine
Maidenhead, United Kingdom: McGraw-Hill, 2003
288pp ISBN: 0071382321
The principles of "Guerrilla PR"—the technique for creating cost-effective publicity, introduced in the author's book *Guerrilla PR*, HarperCollins, 1993—are reexamined in the age of the Web. The book explains how the key tenets have changed with developments in technology, and introduces new tactics for conveying online messages. Readers will learn how the pros use the Web efficiently for publicity, how to focus on a target to get superior results, and how to avoid all the pitfalls that lie in wait for the Web PR novice. The book also features a wide variety of empirical examples.

Harvard Business Review on Corporate Responsibility
Boston, Massachusetts: Harvard Business School Press, 2003
208pp (Harvard Business Review Paperbacks)
ISBN: 1591392748
This collection of articles answers questions

and offers ideas concerning the strategic significance of corporate social responsibility, considering the needs of both the business and the wider community.

Planning and Managing a Public Relations Campaign 2nd ed.
Anne Gregory
London: Kogan Page, 2001
160pp ISBN: 0749429917
Gregory presents a step-by-step guide to the stages of a PR campaign, covering all the important aspects, and including instructional case studies and a ten-point action plan.

Public Relations: An Introduction 2nd ed.
Shirley Harrison
Boston, Massachusetts: International Thomson Business Press, 2000
224pp ISBN: 1861525478
Aimed at students, this is a textbook covering the theory and practice of PR. It describes theoretical frameworks and applies them to the real world, and also covers recent developments in the field.

Public Relations: A Practical Guide to the Basics 2nd ed.
Philip Henslowe
London: Kogan Page, 2003
160pp (PR in Practice)
ISBN: 0749440724
This is an introduction to the basic principles of public relations. It is an easy to read, effective reference guide that provides an overview of the main areas, and is suitable for people who are not PR experts but who need to do some public relations work.

The Public Relations Handbook 2nd ed.
Alison Theaker
New York: Routledge, 2004
368pp ISBN: 0415317932
A detailed introduction to the theory and practice of public relations is provided by this comprehensive handbook, which includes illustrative case studies. It looks at all aspects of the subject, including training and entry into the profession, ethical issues, and the use of new technology.

Public Relations Kit for Dummies
Eric Yaverbaum, Robert Bly
New York: Hungry Minds, 2000
352pp ISBN: 0764552775

Part of a series offering concise, practical information on a variety of topics, this book addresses what all business owners and managers need to know about effective public relations. Presented in an easy to understand style, this title offers specific strategies and eminently practical techniques for public relations, along with information on utilizing new technologies, such as the Internet, in PR campaigns. Also included is a CD-ROM with lists of PR firms and media contacts.

Public Relations: Strategies and Tactics 8th ed.
Dennis L. Wilcox, Glen T. Cameron
Upper Saddle River, New Jersey: Longman, 2005
640pp ISBN: 0205449441
Presenting a comprehensive outline of the principles, concepts, and methods of public relations, this latest edition focuses specifically on global issues, use of the Internet and other new technologies, and ethical issues in public relations. The text differs from similar texts in the field through the inclusion of a series of up-to-date case studies.

Risk Issues and Crisis Management: A Casebook of Best Practice 3rd ed.
Michael Regester, Judy Larkin
London: Kogan Page, 2005
240pp (PR in Practice)
ISBN: 0749423935
This book deals with the successful handling of crisis situations so that damage and disruption are minimized. Case studies and models are included and illustrate how complex crises have been handled in practice, both successfully and unsuccessfully.

Running a Public Relations Department 2nd ed.
Mike Beard
London: Kogan Page, 2001
160pp (PR in Practice)
ISBN: 0749434244
This book contains a step-by-step guide to the different aspects of operating a successful public relations unit. It describes the main areas of activity and examines such issues as the departmental plan, budgets, selecting personnel and building a team, and working with PR consultants.

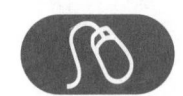
1879

BUSINESS INFORMATION SOURCES

MAGAZINES

FrontLine
ISSN: 0269–0357
International Public Relations Association
1 Dunley Hill Court, Ranmore Common,
Dorking, Surrey, RH5 6SX, U.K.
T: +44 (0) 1483 280 130
F: +44 (0) 1483 280 131
www.ipra.org
A bimonthly magazine on public relations
issues, published by the International
Public Relations Association. It is aimed at
international PR professionals and
considers topics of worldwide interest
through articles and comment.

PR Week
ISSN: 0267–6087
PR Publications Ltd.
220 Fifth Avenue, New York, 10001
T: +1 877 389 3862
www.prweekus.com/us
This is a weekly newspaper with coverage
of all areas of public relations. It is written
for public relations professionals in
consulting organizations and in-house PR
departments.

Public Relations Quarterly
ISSN: 0033–3700
44 West Market Street, P.O. Box 311,
Rhinebeck, New York, 12572–0311
T: +1 845 876 2081
F: +1 845 876 2561
www.newsletter-clearinghse.com
Aimed at PR professionals, this quarterly
publication contains items on research and
education and the theory and practice of
PR, case studies, advice, and survey results.

Public Relations Strategist
ISSN: 1082–9113
Public Relations Society of America
33 Maiden Lane, New York, 10038–5150
T: +1 212 460 1400
F: +1 212 995 0757
www.prsa.org
This quarterly journal presents new
perspectives and ideas related to the
strategic importance of effective public
relations at management level.

Public Relations Tactics
ISSN: 1080–6792
Public Relations Society of America
33 Maiden Lane, New York, 10038–5150
T: +1 212 460 1400
F: +1 212 995 0757
www.prsa.org
This monthly newspaper covers the latest

trends in public relations and is designed to
meet the current needs of public relations
professionals. The timely information it
contains should help any professional
improve his or her PR skills and remain
competitive in the field.

INTERNET

Managing Public Relations
www.workz.com/content/
view_content.html?section_id=465
This Web site serves as a resource for small
business owners. It offers comprehensive
information on public relations techniques,
including guides for creating an effective PR
plan, giving your company a PR makeover,
and avoiding bad PR.

Online Public Relations
www.online-pr.com
Online Public Relations provides links to
other sites containing public relations
resources.

PR Place
www.prplace.com
This site contains a listing of Internet
resources on public relations. The
categories it covers include organizations in
PR, publications, news sources, and
databases.

PRWeb
www.prweb.com
PRWeb is a U.S. company, based in
Ferndale, Washington, that offers a free
service distributing press releases over the
Internet.

ORGANIZATIONS
USA

Institute for Public Relations
PO Box 118400, 2096 Weimer Hall,
Gainesville, Florida, 32611–8400
T: +1 352 392 0280
F: +1 352 846 1122
www.instituteforpr.com
The mission of the IPR is to improve the
effectiveness of organizations by advancing
the professional knowledge and practice of
public relations through research and
education. It provides publications,
lectures, awards, and professional
development forums, and conducts
research projects. Within the IPR is the
Commission on Public Relations
Measurement and Evaluation. IPR services
are aimed at students, academics, and
practitioners.

Public Relations Society of America
33 Maiden Lane, New York, 10038–5150
T: +1 212 460 1400
F: +1 212 995 0757
www.prsa.org
PRSA is a membership body for public
relations professionals. Its aim is to unify,
strengthen, and advance the profession. It
conducts education and research, advances
members' professional development, and
offers other membership services. It also
produces the magazines *Public Relations
Strategist* and *Public Relations Tactics*

Women Executives in Public Relations
FDR Station, P.O. Box 7657, New York,
10150–7657
T: +1 212 750 7375
F: +1 212 750 7375
www.wepr.org
This is an organization for senior women in
the public relations field. Its mission is to
support the career advancement of female
practitioners and to foster the use of public
relations to benefit the goals of business and
society. It is an individual membership
body that is involved in influencing and
lobbying, and provides a forum for the
exchange of career, management, and
practitioner issues.

International

**International Public Relations
Association**
1 Dunley Hill Court, Ranmore Common,
Dorking, Surrey, RH5 6SX, U.K.
T: +44 (0) 1483 280 130
F: +44 (0) 1483 280 131
E: *iprasec@btconnect.com*
www.ipra.org
IPRA aims to provide professional
development and personal networking
opportunities for its worldwide
membership, and to promote the practice of
public relations on a global level. It was
founded in 1955 and now has members in
96 countries.

FOR MORE INFORMATION

- Contingency, Crisis, Disaster
  Management (pp. 1715–1717)
- Internal Communication
  (pp. 1782–1783)
- Interpersonal Communication/
  Relations (pp. 1787–1788)
- Online Sources for Marketing (General
  Business Information) (p. 1766)
- Public Relations Planning (pp. 528–529)
- Relating to the Public (pp. 65–66)

"I enjoy the fact that I am creating a climate of opinion."   Jan Brown

Public Sector Management

BOOKS

The Governance of Public and Nonprofit Organisations: What Do Boards Do?
Chris Cornforth, ed.
New York: Routledge, 2003
256pp ISBN: 0415258189
This text brings together recent studies and analyzes the effectiveness of boards in the public and nonprofit sectors. Using a new theoretical framework, the authors examine the conflicting requirements that are inherent in corporate governance in these sectors. Issues raised include the accountability of appointed, non-elected boards; how effective are they; the tensions between the views of the boards and the "parent" departments; the role of chairs of governing bodies; and the changing needs of society.

Private Sector Strategies for Social Sector Success: The Guide to Strategy and Planning for Public and Nonprofit Organizations
Kevin P. Kearns
San Francisco, California: Jossey-Bass, 2000
288pp ISBN: 0787941891
While there is a great deal of information available on strategic planning processes for government and nonprofit organizations, Kearns breaks new ground by providing them with guidelines on the selection and use of specific, real-world strategic options. Strategies discussed include vertical integration, diversification, concentration, and collaboration. Kearns tailors these business sector concepts to the unique missions, contexts, and constituencies of government and nonprofit entities.

Public Sector Management 4th ed.
Norman Flynn
Upper Saddle River, New Jersey: Financial Times Prentice Hall, 2002
288pp ISBN: 0273646346
Flynn focuses on the institutional and political context in which public sector managers work. He assesses the historical background of the last century along with the evolution of public spending and the effects of changes in social policy on the management of public services. He covers aspects of management practice in the public sector including: modes of control; the role of markets; contracting, auditing and inspection; customer orientation; people management; and financial management.

Reinventing Government: How the Entrepreneurial Spirit Is Transforming the Public Sector
David Osborne, Ted Gaebler
New York: Plume Books, 1993
416pp ISBN: 0452269423
In this book, the authors strike at the growing public apathy toward government, and suggest ways in which business people can work toward creating a better alternative. The book cites and analyzes several case studies and, using these, the authors provide a plan for "entrepreneurial government."

Seamless Government: A Practical Guide to Re-engineering in the Public Sector
Russell M. Linden
San Francisco, California: Jossey-Bass, 1994
320pp ISBN: 078790015X
This book explains how to reengineer government agencies to meet the needs of its customers "seamlessly"—that is, in as smooth and simple a way as possible. The book includes a step-by-step approach for reengineering in all levels of government, explaining how to assess, design, and execute alterations in the way government does business, and how to overcome opposition along the way.

Strategy in the Public Sector: A Guide to Effective Change Management
Paul Joyce
Hoboken, New Jersey: Wiley, 2000
256pp (Wiley Series in Practical Strategy)
ISBN: 0471895253
The public sector is experiencing pressure and strategic change with government requirements for greater responsiveness to public demand. The role of top managers in carrying through strategic change is explored, demonstrating how to prepare an organization for strategic change, how to lead strategic change, how to make changes in an organization's activities and resources, and how to involve the public and other partners to create a more open organization.

MAGAZINES

International Journal of Public Sector Management
ISSN: 0951–3558
Emerald Group Publishing Ltd.
60/62 Toller Lane, Bradford, West Yorkshire, BD8 9BY, U.K.

T: +44 (0) 1274 777 700
F: +44 (0) 1274 785 200
www.emeraldinsight.com
This journal is published seven times a year, and includes a wide range of research and practical papers on all aspects of managing in the public sector.

Public Administration and Management: An Interactive Journal
ISSN: 1087–0091
School of Public Affairs, Pennsylvania State University
Public Administration Quarterly, 2103 Fairway Lane, Harrisburg, Pennsylvania, 17112
T: +1 717 948 6363
F: +1 215 893 1763
www.spaef.com/paq.html
This online-only journal is run by academics at Pennsylvania State University (Harrisburg). It is peer-reviewed in the same way as other printed academic journals and four issues are produced annually. The scope is wide so as to include as many topics of interest to as wide an audience as possible. Articles can be read online or downloaded as PDF files.

Public Administration Quarterly
ISSN: 07349149
School of Public Affairs, Pennsylvania State University
Public Administration Quarterly, 2103 Fairway Lane, Harrisburg, Pennsylvania, 17112
T: +1 717 948 6363
F: +1 215 893 1763
www.spaef.com/paq.html
Formerly the *Southern Review of Public Administration*, this journal publishes articles on a range of public administration topics, such as budgeting, education, technology, ethics, and decision making. The American Society for Public Administration is a cosponsor.

Public Administration Review
ISSN: 00333352
Blackwell Publishing
350 Main Street, Malden, Massachusetts, 02148
T: +1 781 388 8200
F: +1 781 388 8232
www.blackwellpublishing.com
PAR is the journal of the American Society

1881

BUSINESS INFORMATION SOURCES

for Public Administration and is published six times a year. Articles focus on current trends, legislation, new publications, and a wide range of other topics, making the journal required reading for practitioners, scholars, teachers, and trainers interested in public sector management. Tables of contents are available at www.aspanet.org/publications/par.

Staffing Success
American Staffing Association
277 South Washington Street, Suite 200, Alexandria, Virginia, 22314
T: +1 703 253 2020
F: +1 703 253 2053
www.staffingtoday.net/memberserv/staffsuccessarchive.htm
Formerly known as Contemporary Times, this journal is published six times a year and is the official organ of the American Staffing Association. It provides a useful business resource for those working in the recruitment and selection field.

INTERNET
Gateways to Public Sector Resources
www.aom.pace.edu/pn/public.html
A service of the public and the nonprofit division of the Academy of Management, this page links to 15 major gateways to information related to public sector management, and provides a helpful overview of the nature of the resources available through each of those links.

Great Leaders for Great Government
www.leadership.opm.gov
This is the official site for the Federal Executive Institute and Management Development Centers with course listings in leadership and management available at three regional centers for federal government personnel.

National Association of Schools of Public Affairs and Administration
www.naspaa.org

This Washington, D.C.-based association promotes excellence in public service education. The site provides easy-to-access information on accredited educational institutions at the associate, bachelor, masters, and doctoral degree levels throughout the United States.

ORGANIZATIONS
USA
American Society for Public Administration
1120 G Street NW, Suite 700, Washington, D.C., 20005
T: + 1 202 393 7878
F: + 1 202 638 4952
E: *info@aspa.net*
www.aspanet.org
ASPA is a professional association for public administrators that acts to improve government management and ethics and as an advocate for public service; its more than 10,000 members include non-profit administrators, academics, teachers, and students. It offers conferences, publications, research, and online resources dealing with various issues related to public sector management. Local chapters enable members to meet and network, and attend talks and conferences. Members receive the *Public Administration Review* and *PA Times*, APSA's monthly newspaper.

International City/County Management Association
777 North Capitol Street NE, Suite 500, Washington, District of Columbia, 20002
T: + 1 202 289 4262
F: + 1 202 962 3500
E: *membership@icma.org*
www.icma.org
ICMA is a professional and educational organization representing managers and administrators in local governments. With a focus on local government management

issues, it offers its members research and analysis, an annual conference, publications, and professional development resources.

Europe
Office for Public Management
252b Grays Inn Road, London, WC1X 8XG, U.K.
T: +44 (0) 20 7239 7800
F: +44 (0) 20 7837 5800
E: *office@opm.co.uk*
www.opm.co.uk
OPM is a nonprofit consulting organization offering management development programs tailored specifically for public sector organizations, with a focus on the delivery of public services and the exercise of corporate responsibility.

International
International Public Management Network
Atkinson Graduate School of Management, Willamette University, 900 State Street, Salem, Oregon, 97301–3922
T: +1 503 370 6228
F: +1 503 370 3011
E: *fthompso@willamette.edu*
www.inpuma.net
IPMN is a forum for discussion of ideas and information in the field of public sector management. It holds an annual conference and workshops, and publishes the biannual *International Public Management Journal*.

"The new mixed economy looks . . . for a synergy between public and private sectors."
Anthony Giddens

Purchasing and Supply Chain Management

BOOKS

B2B: How to Build a Profitable E-commerce Strategy
Michael Cunningham
Cambridge, Massachusetts: Perseus Books Group, 2002
224pp ISBN: 0738205222
This book presents a definitive blueprint for creating a profitable business-to-business e-commerce strategy. Showcasing successful initiatives designed by industry leaders such as Cisco Systems and Dell Computers, as well as lesser-known trailblazers such as VerticalNet and eCredit.com, the author clearly identifies the key issues in assessing opportunities, building technological and organizational capabilities, and designing a successful business-to-business strategy using the full power of the Internet.

Logistics and Supply Chain Management: Strategies for Reducing Cost and Improving Service 3rd ed.
Martin Christopher
Upper Saddle River, New Jersey: Financial Times Prentice Hall, 2005
320pp ISBN: 0273681761
The goal of supply chain management is to link the marketplace, the distribution network, the manufacturing process, and the procurement activity in such a way that customers are serviced at higher levels and yet at lower total cost. The author explores the role of logistics in achieving these goals. He examines the relationship between logistics and competitive strategy, the customer service dimension, measuring logistics costs and performance, and benchmarking and managing the supply chain.

Managing the Global Supply Chain 2nd ed.
Philip B Schary, Tage Skjott-Larsen
Copenhagen, Denmark: Copenhagen Business School Press, 2001
544pp ISBN: 8763000814
The book shows how structure, process, and organization may build a supply network comprising distribution, production, and procurement within one integrated system. The importance of the supply chain in corporate strategy is also emphasized. This new edition stresses customer relationships and reflects recent changes in technology and practice.

Managing the Supply Chain: The Definitive Guide for the Business Professional
David Simchi-Levi, Philip Kaminsky, Edith Simchi-Levi
New York: McGraw-Hill, 2004
320pp ISBN: 0071410317
Interest in supply chain management has grown rapidly over past years and continues to increase. To meet this interest the authors introduce a range of state-of-the-art concepts and techniques that are important for the design, control, operation and management of supply chain systems. They focus on supply chain integration network planning, supply chain alliances, outsourcing and supply contracts, product design, customer value, and global issues in supply chain management. Numerous examples illustrate the key issues.

New Directions in Supply Chain Management: Technology Strategy and Implementation
Tonya Boone, Ram Ganeshan
New York: AMACOM, 2002
384pp ISBN: 0814406378
This collection of 18 original essays examines the efficiencies new technology has brought to supply chain management and how new strategies and solutions based on these changes can be implemented. They are grouped into three sections covering the integration of new technologies into supply chain operations, technology-based product and service development, and knowledge management and supply-chain integration issues.

Partners.com
Michael Cunningham
Cambridge, Massachusetts: Perseus, 2002
256pp ISBN: 0738206873
Partners.com shows businesses how to forge leading-edge Internet partnerships fast with competitors, customers, employees, and other businesses. The book reveals the specifics of these new and better ways of doing business. It presents a clear picture of companies such as eBay, Altra, GoFish, Egghead, VerticalNet, and Yahoo, that are utilizing technology-driven partnerships.

Profitable Purchasing Strategies: A Manager's Guide for Improving Organizational Competitiveness through the Skills of Purchasing
Paul T. Steele, Brian Court
Maidenhead, United Kingdom: McGraw-Hill, 1996
240pp ISBN: 0077092147
Purchasing is portrayed as an essential business process, and it is argued that an effective purchasing process can play a significant role in the fight for corporate survival and prosperity. This textbook explains the process of building a purchasing strategy and provides an understanding of the basics of purchasing, the buying–supplier interface, and partnership sourcing.

Purchasing and Supply Chain Management 7th ed.
Kenneth Lysons
Upper Saddle River, New Jersey: Financial Times Prentice Hall, 2003
800pp ISBN: 0273694383
A much revised and enlarged version of a successful textbook, this edition meets the requirements for an integrated approach to supply chain management, drawing on the many disciplines, from ethics and human resources to suppliers, sourcing, and strategy, that contribute to a full knowledge of purchasing practice and techniques.

The Sourcing Solution: A Step-by-step Guide to Creating a Successful Purchasing Program
Larry Paquette
New York: AMACOM, 2004
224pp ISBN: 0814471919
Larry Paquette believes that, as purchasing options and technologies become more plentiful, they also become more complex. In this text, he sets out to help managers sort through alternatives, identify the strategies that make sense, and implement them in ways that complement the overall business strategy. He explains how to make the most of vendor relationships and partnerships, opportunities for cost reduction, electronic and paperless

1883

BUSINESS INFORMATION SOURCES

"Watch the costs and the profits will take care of themselves."   Andrew Carnegie

inventory management, product knowledge and company information, different production models, global sourcing opportunities, scheduling, and contracts and negotiations.

Strategic Purchasing and Supply Chain Management 2nd ed.

Malcolm Saunders
Philadelphia, Pennsylvania: Trans-Atlantic Publications, 1997
368pp ISBN: 0273623826
This textbook aims to provide students with an understanding of the scope and potential of purchasing and supply chain management strategy in a variety of international organizations.

Supercharging Supply Chains: New Ways to Increase Value through Global Operational Excellence

G. Tyndall et al.
Hoboken, New Jersey: Wiley, 1998
288pp ISBN: 0471254371
The authors, who are key partners and leaders of the Ernst & Young Global Supply Chain Management Team, present an innovative view of supply chain excellence and examine its impact on stockholder value. They explain why and how operational excellence helps companies sell more products and describe the new ideas being implemented to achieve excellence, as well as considering how leading companies effectively introduce new products into global supply chains.

Supply Chain Excellence: A Handbook for Dramatic Improvement Using the SCOR Model

Peter Bolstorff, Robert Rosenbaum
New York: AMACOM, 2003
288pp ISBN: 0814407307
The SCOR (Supply Chain Operations Reference) model, developed by the Supply-Chain Council in the U.S., is introduced in this handbook, which also examines in detail the process of applying the model and describes the achieving of supply chain excellence over a 17-week period.

Supply Chain Management

John T. Mentzer, ed.
Thousand Oaks, California: Sage Publications, 2001
512pp ISBN: 0761921117
A group of collaborating authors present a comprehensive definition and model of supply chain management (SCM) on the basis of their interviews with top supply chain managers from 20 companies. The

book distinguishes types of chain, and discusses SCM as a management philosophy and in terms of its prerequisites and its potential effects on business and channel performance.

MAGAZINES

Journal of Purchasing and Supply Chain Management

ISSN: 1478–4092
Elsevier Science
Customer Service Department, 6277 Sea Harbor Drive, Orlando, Florida, 32887–4800
T: +1 877 839 7126 or +1 407 345 4020
F: +1 407 363 1354
www.elsevier.com
This is a refereed journal that aims to encourage the development of conceptual thinking and practical approaches within the profession. Articles cover every aspect of the purchasing of goods and services in all contexts, including industry and commerce, local and regional government, health, and transportation.

Journal of Supply Chain Management: A Global Review of Purchasing and Supply

ISSN: 1055–6001
Institute for Supply Management
P.O. Box 22160, Tempe, Arizona, 85285–2160
T: +1 480 752 6276
F: +1 480 752 7890
www.ism.ws
A quarterly publication produced specifically for purchasing professionals, this journal provides coverage and analysis of key management issues, leading research, one-to-one interviews, and supplier relationship applications. Abstracts of the articles and the one-to-one interviews can be accessed on the Web.

Purchasing

ISSN: 0033–4448
Reed Business Information
8878 Barrons Boulevard, Highlands Ranch, Colorado, 80129–2345
T: +1 800 446 6551
F: +1 303 470 4280
www.reedbusiness.com
This is a bimonthly magazine which focuses on total supply management. It has served 93,500 professionals working in manufacturing, process, and service companies throughout the full spectrum of business for 85 years. The magazine makes available the information required by purchasing professionals to do their jobs. It provides news, identifies trends, interprets events, makes forecasts, and presents exclusive information and data sources.

Supply Chain & Logistics Journal

Supply Chain & Logistics Canada
590 Alden Road, Suite 211, Markham, Ontario, L3R 8N2, Canada
T: +1 905 513 7300
F: +1 905 513 1248
www.infochain.org/quarterly/journald.html
This is a quarterly journal published for the Canadian Association of Supply Chain & Logistics Management.

INTERNET

CAPS Research
www.capsresearch.org
This site is offered by the Center for Advanced Purchasing Studies, a nonprofit independent research organization cosponsored by Arizona State University and the National Association of Purchasing and Supply. It provides full access to a range of recent research and benchmarking reports and their journal *Practix*. Access is free, but you must register to view articles. There are also links to related sites.

Chartered Institute of Purchasing and Supply
www.cips.org
While this site is designed to promote the training and research services and activities of CIPS, it does allow nonmembers access to its comprehensive bookstore with details of over 350 specialist publications.

Institute for Supply Management
www.ism.ws
This is the home site of the Institute for Supply Management. The amount of information available to nonmembers is limited, but there is access to selected articles or abstracts of recent articles in the Institute's journals.

International Purchasing and Supply Education and Research Association
www.ipsera.com
IPSERA is an active network of academics and practitioners dedicated to the development of understanding on matters concerning the future of purchasing and supply management. The site provides general information about the association, details about membership, and advice on applying for funding.

ORGANIZATIONS
USA
Institute for Supply Management
P.O. Box 22160, Tempe, Arizona, 85285–2160
T: +1 480 752 6276
F: +1 480 752 7890

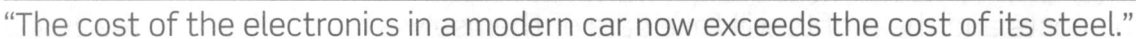

1884

BUSINESS INFORMATION SOURCES

"The cost of the electronics in a modern car now exceeds the cost of its steel."

Nicholas Negroponte

www.ism.ws

Founded in 1915, the ISM is a widely respected educational association in the United States. It aims to provide national and international leadership in purchasing and materials management through research and a program of conferences, seminars, and online learning.

Europe
Chartered Institute of Purchasing and Supply

1 Easton House, Easton-on-the-Hill, Stamford, Lincolnshire, PE9 3NZ, U.K.

T: +44 (0) 1780 756 777

F: +44 (0) 1780 751 610

www.cips.org

Based in the United Kingdom, CIPS is an international education and qualification organization serving the international purchasing and supply profession. It is dedicated to promoting best practice through the provision of a wide range of services for the benefit of members and the

wider business community. These include a program of continuous improvement in professional standards, and raising awareness of the contribution that purchasing and supply makes to corporate, national, and international prosperity. CIPS gained a Royal Charter in 1992.

International
Canadian Association of Supply Chain and Logistics Management

590 Alden Road, Suite 211, Markham, Ontario, L3R 8N2, Canada

T: +1 905 513 7300

F: +1 905 513 1248

E: *members@infochain.org*

www.sclcanada.org

Established in 1967, SCL is a nonprofit membership organization which aims to advance the logistics and supply chain profession in Canada. Through a range of activities, research, and informal discussion, members are encouraged to

further their understanding of logistics and the art and science of its management.

Purchasing Management Association of Canada

2 Carlton Street, Suite 1414, Toronto, Ontario, M5B 2J3, Canada

T: +1 416 977 7111

F: +1 416 977 8886

E: *info@pmac.ca*

www.pmac.ca

PMAC is a national, nonprofit association and is a leading source of education, training, and development in the purchasing and supply management field in Canada. The association operates with ten provincial institutes, which can be contacted through the Web site.

FOR MORE INFORMATION

✔ Effective Purchasing (pp. 546–547)

᧖ Logistics and Distribution (pp. 1807–1808)

1885

BUSINESS INFORMATION SOURCES

"The price of ability does not depend on merit but on supply and demand."

George Bernard Shaw

Quality and Total Quality Management

BOOKS

The Essence of Total Quality Management 2nd ed.

John Bank
Upper Saddle River, New Jersey: Financial Times Prentice Hall, 2000
272pp ISBN: 0135731143
John Bank suggests that customer focus represents the essence of total quality management (TQM). He outlines the core concepts of TQM and summarizes the ideas of the leading quality gurus. The book provides case studies of TQM in large and small organizations including the Body Shop, British Airways, IBM, Xerox 2000, and Paul Revere Insurance Group, and describes the tools and techniques for implementing and evaluating total quality management.

Four Days with Dr. Deming: A Strategy for Modern Methods of Management

William J. Latzko, David M. Saunders
Cambridge, Massachusetts: Addison-Wesley, 1995
256pp (Engineering Process Improvement) ISBN: 0201633663
This book recreates the experience of attending a four-day quality management workshop held by the late Dr. Deming. Aimed at a range of businesspeople from the executives, managers, and engineers of an organization to its stockholders, the authors discuss and explain Deming's theories and ideas on quality management.

A History of Managing for Quality: The Evolution, Trends, and Future Directions of Managing for Quality

J. M. Juran, ed.
Milwaukee, Wisconsin: ASQ Quality Press, 1995
608pp ISBN: 0873893417
This book, edited by a respected author in the field, focuses on the elements of quality management common to all industries and illustrates the immense effect that quality and its evolution have had on civilization over the centuries. Juran summarizes the historical profile in a chapter on worldwide trends and the lessons learned from history. Other contributors suggest the directions that managing for quality may take in the new century.

Integrating Lean Six Sigma and High Performance Organizations: Leading the Charge Toward Dramatic Rapid and Sustainable Improvement

Tom Devane
New York: Pfeiffer & Co., 2004
416pp ISBN: 0787969737
Tom Devane suggests that the seamless integration of leading improvement methods represents the next wave of performance improvement. He provides a reference to help leaders integrate the best practices of lean manufacturing, Six Sigma and high-performance organizations. The principles, tools and guidance needed to solve problems and create an environment that fosters high performance are described. This is a stage-by-stage guide that covers initiation, direction setting, design, and implementation. Stories from a wide range of organizations illustrate the key points and lessons.

Juran's Quality Handbook 5th ed.

Joseph M. Juran, A. Blanton Godfrey, eds
Maidenhead, United Kingdom: McGraw-Hill, 1998
1872pp ISBN: 007034003X
A comprehensive guide to quality engineering and management, this revised reference text covers the trilogy of essential processes—quality planning, quality control, and quality results. This edition also contains details of the most recent developments, as well as plenty of practical advice. Supported by quality research, containing new ideas and strategies, this book aims to appeal to a wide spectrum of businesses.

Juran on Leadership for Quality: An Executive Handbook

Jospeh M. Juran
New York: Free Press, 2003
384pp ISBN: 0743255771
This classic volume looks at the subject of quality as a competitive tool and shows that unless the effort to improve quality is led by committed leaders and permeates from the top down, it will fail. Juran sets forth the actions that managers must take to make quality improvement an annual goal, and gives step-by-step advice on how to lead such efforts, drawing on the experiences of thousands of chief executives from around the world.

Lean Six Sigma for Service: How to Use Lean Speed and Six Sigma Quality to Improve Services and Transactions

Michael L. George
New York: McGraw-Hill, 2003
368pp ISBN: 0071418210
The author sets out to explain how relatively simple statistical and lean tools can be applied in a service environment to reduce costs and speed up service processes and transactions. The three sections provide chapters that focus on using lean Six Sigma for strategic advantage, deploying lean Six Sigma in service organizations, and improving services. Success stories of Lockheed Martin, Bank One, City of Fort Wayne, and Stanford Hospital are included.

Managing Quality 4th ed.

Barrie G. Dale, ed.
Cambridge, Massachusetts: Blackwell Publishing, 2003
528pp ISBN: 0631236147
A broad overview of total quality management (TQM) is presented in five parts, covering the development of TQM; its business context; methods of introducing TQM quality management systems, tools, and techniques and TQM through continuous improvement. Chapters contributed by leading academics and practitioners cover specific topics and techniques, including failure mode and effects analysis and statistical process control.

Managing Six Sigma: A Practical Guide to Understanding, Assessing, and Implementing the Strategy That Yields Bottom-line Success

Forrest W. Breyfogle III, James M. Cupello, Becki Meadows
Hoboken, New Jersey: Wiley, 2000
304pp ISBN: 0471396737
Written in order to help managers decide whether or not they should implement the strategy, this book provides in-depth information on Six Sigma techniques. Case studies of how Motorola and General Electric introduced Six Sigma are included in order to demonstrate the successes

"Quality is characteristic of a product or service that helps somebody and which has a market."

W. Edwards Deming

achieved and pitfalls encountered in the process.

Out of the Crisis

W. Edwards Deming
Cambridge, Massachusetts: MIT Press, 2000
512pp ISBN: 0262541157
This book is a reprint of the 1986 classic in which the guru of quality presented his theory of management, based on his 14 points for management. Deming brings to light the failures of management that need to be corrected if manufacturing is to produce products of quality successfully and in such a way as to retain competitiveness.

The Power of Six Sigma

Subir Chowdhury
Upper Saddle River, New Jersey: Financial Times Prentice Hall, 2001
128pp ISBN: 027365621X
The principles of Six Sigma are explained through a fictional account designed to make the system accessible to everyone from entrepreneurs and chief executives to managers and assembly line workers. The process of implementing Six Sigma to attain increased profits and improved efficiency is outlined.

Quality: A Critical Introduction 2nd ed.

John Beckford
New York: Routledge, 2002
336pp ISBN: 0415259193
Examines the quality movement within the context of management thinking over the twentieth century and provides a handbook of quality tools, methods and techniques. Contributions of the quality gurus are examined and details are included on ISO9000: 2000, the Business Excellence Model, skills-based quality management, and sustainable organization. International case studies are included.

Quality Beyond Six Sigma

Ron Basu, Nevan Wright
New York: Butterworth-Heinemann, 2003
192pp ISBN: 0750655615
The authors offer a brief history of the quality movement and present case studies of Six Sigma in practice. Having described their approach to total quality management and Six Sigma, they introduce "Fit Sigma," which offers a holistic approach to fit different organizations. They describe the methodology of Fit Sigma, together with its application in projects and its implementation generally, and go on to consider lean enterprises and "Lean Sigma."

Six Sigma Continual Improvement for Businesses: A Practical Guide

William T. Truscott
New York: Butterworth-Heinemann, 2003
256pp ISBN: 0750657650
The Six Sigma approach based on statistical thinking and knowledge of processes is described and guidance is given upon its practical application and tailoring to differing organizational needs. Its comparison with other improvement initiatives is discussed, together with how it can best impact upon business performance.

The Six Sigma Handbook 2nd ed.

Thomas Pyzdek
Maidenhead, United Kingdom: McGraw-Hill, 2002
848pp ISBN: 0071410155
If improving the quality of your manufacturing processes is your goal, and the extraordinarily successful Six Sigma program at GE is one you want to emulate, this book will help you implement that approach. The author examines the philosophy underlying the program and explores the management and organization of Six Sigma, then explains the statistical tools and problem-solving techniques needed to implement it.

Six Sigma Revolution: How General Electric and Others Turned Process into Profits

George Eckes
Hoboken, New Jersey: Wiley, 2001
288pp ISBN: 047138822X
Six Sigma is introduced as a quantitative approach to quality that has boosted productivity and increased profits for a number of large businesses. This text explains how and why Six Sigma is superior to other quality improvement methods and describes how to create and sustain a Six Sigma initiative in an organization.

The Six Sigma Way: How GE, Motorola, and Other Top Companies Are Honing Their Performance

Peter S. Pande, Robert P. Neuman, Roland R. Cavanagh
New York: McGraw-Hill, 2000
432pp ISBN: 0071358064
A comprehensive guide to the application of Six Sigma across all industries. The book introduces the essentials of Six Sigma and outlines its advantages over TQM. It describes the process of adopting Six Sigma to your business and explores the Six Sigma Roadmap, a five-phase model for building the Six Sigma organization. The

experiences of top companies illustrate the key issues.

The Six Sigma Way Team Fieldbook: An Implementation Guide for Project Improvement Teams

Peter S. Pande, Robert P. Neuman, Roland R. Cavanagh
New York: McGraw-Hill, 2002
416pp ISBN: 0071373144
This practical manual explains the tools and procedures a project leader or team needs to implement a Six Sigma improvement project. It describes the Six Sigma methods that help to identify products and processes that need improvement, and explains how to adopt a proactive approach to either improve or redesign them.

Total Quality Management in a Week 3rd ed.

John Macdonald
London: Hodder & Stoughton, 2003
96pp (Business in a Week)
ISBN: 0340849460
This booklet provides a practical introduction to the principles and practice of total quality management (TQM). Readers are taken through the processes of identifying the need for change, planning change, implementing change, using tools and techniques, and maintaining the impetus.

MAGAZINES

Managing Service Quality

ISSN: 0960–4259
Emerald Group Publishing Ltd.
60/62 Toller Lane, Bradford, West Yorkshire, BD8 9BY, U.K.
T: +44 (0) 1274 777 700
F: +44 (0) 1274 785 200
www.emeraldinsight.com
Written in an accessible style, this journal is primarily practical in focus. Its contents typically include case studies and articles outlining quality techniques and new research.

Public Relations Review

ISSN: 0363–8111
Elsevier Science
Customer Service Department, 6277 Sea Harbor Drive, Orlando, Florida, 32887–4800
T: +1 877 839 7126 or +1 407 345 4020
F: +1 407 363 1354
www.elsevier.com
The *Review* is a quarterly publication containing articles that provide in-depth analysis of public relations issues. Most of these are based on research by professionals and academics.

1887

BUSINESS INFORMATION SOURCES

"Quality is a direct experience independent of and prior to intellectual abstraction."

Robert M. Pirsig

Quality Management Journal
ISSN: 10686967
American Society for Quality (ASQ)
600 North Plankinton Avenue, Milwaukee, Wisconsin, 53203–3005
T: +1 414 272 8575
F: +1 414 272 1734
www.asq.org
This is a quarterly journal that links researchers with practitioners by communicating and discussing research findings. Articles are not technical in nature, but accessible to those working in quality management.

Quality Progress
ISSN: 0033524X
American Society for Quality (ASQ)
600 North Plankinton Avenue, Milwaukee, Wisconsin, 53203–3005
T: +1 414 272 8575
F: +1 414 272 1734
www.asq.org
This is a monthly magazine of the leading quality improvement organization in the U.S. It focuses on standards and the implementation of quality methods in the fields of knowledge management, process improvement, organizational behavior, and related fields.

1888

Quality World
ISSN: 1352–8769
Institute of Quality Assurance
12 Grosvenor Crescent, London, SW1X 7EE, U.K.
T: +44 (0) 20 7245 6722
F: +44 (0) 20 7245 6755
www.iqa.org
Quality World, the journal of the Institute of Quality Assurance, is a practical publication covering all aspects of, and developments in, quality and quality management.

Six Sigma Forum Magazine
American Society for Quality (ASQ)
600 North Plankinton Avenue, Milwaukee, Wisconsin, 53203–3005
T: +1 414 272 8575
F: +1 414 272 1734
www.asq.org/pub/sixsigma
This monthly magazine was founded in January 2002 to look at Six Sigma practice in different companies and to review the literature about Six Sigma methods. For instance, Issue 2 included articles about financial services quality implementation, careers, program design, corporate culture, and information technology.

Total Quality Magazine
ISSN: 09544127
Routledge
29 West 35th Street, New York, NY, 10001
T: +1 212 216 7800
F: +1 212 564 7854
TQM is published eight times a year and covers business excellence, the Six Sigma concept, ISO 9000, customer satisfaction, quality management systems, the Balanced Scorecard, and many other topics of interest to quality managers.

TQM Magazine
ISSN: 0954–478X
Emerald Group Publishing Ltd.
60/62 Toller Lane, Bradford, West Yorkshire, BD8 9BY, U.K.
T: +44 (0) 1274 777 700
F: +44 (0) 1274 785 200
www.emeraldinsight.com
TQM Magazine is aimed primarily at practicing managers. Each issue typically contains details of research, explores quality techniques, and includes a number of case studies of quality in practice.

INTERNET
American Society for Quality
www.asq.org
This site, run by the major quality association in the United States, provides news, links to its publications, and information on the Baldrige Award.

Baldrige National Quality Program
www.baldrige.gov
This site provides information on every aspect of the Malcolm Baldrige National Quality Award and on how to obtain material and information about applying for the award and doing the assessment.

European Quality Online
www.european-quality.co.uk
Online access to articles, FAQs, discussion forums, and links can be gained via this site.

Quality Network
www.quality.co.uk
This site provides information on quality management and ISO 9000, as well as on environmental and safety management.

ORGANIZATIONS
USA
American Productivity and Quality Center (APQC)
123 North Post Oak Lane, 3rd Floor, Houston, Texas, 77024
T: +1 713 681 4020
F: +1 713 681 1182

E: *apqcinfo@apqc.org*
www.apqc.org
Founded in 1977, APQC works with organizations of all sizes to improve productivity and quality. Its aim is to research and understand both emerging improvement methods and methods whose effectiveness is already proven, and it distributes its findings through education, advice, and information services. In 1992 it set up the International Benchmarking Clearinghouse to promote and facilitate the process of learning from best practice.

American Society for Quality (ASQ)
600 North Plankinton Avenue, Milwaukee, Wisconsin, 53203–3005
T: +1 414 272 8575
F: +1 414 272 1734
E: *cs@asq.org*
www.asq.org
ASQ is the leading quality-improvement member organization in the United States. It has 117,000 individual and 1,100 corporate members, in 247 local sections and 22 industry divisions. The Society focuses on issues including statistical process control, quality cost measurement and control, total quality management, failure analysis, and zero defects. It offers continuing education; certification programs; conferences; and reference, referral, and research services. The ASQ publishes widely under its Quality Press imprint, its monthly magazines Quality Progress and Six Sigma Forum Magazine, and the quarterly Quality Management Journal.

The W. Edwards Deming Institute
P.O. Box 59511, Potomac, Maryland, 20859–9511
T: +1 301 294 8405
F: +1 301 294 8406
E: *staff@deming.org*
www.deming.org
A nonprofit organization founded in 1993, the Institute aims to foster an understanding of the Deming System of Profound Knowledge to advance commerce, prosperity, and peace.

Europe
British Quality Foundation (BQF)
32–34 Great Peter Street, London, SW1P 2QX, U.K.
T: +44 (0) 20 7654 5000
F: +44 (0) 20 7654 5001
www.quality-foundation.co.uk
The BQF is a nonprofit membership organization that promotes business excellence to other public and private sector

---

"Standards are always out of date. That's what makes them standards."   Alan Bennett

organizations in the United Kingdom. It undertakes numerous activities in pursuit of this aim, most of which have the Business Excellence Model at their core. It also sponsors the U.K. Business Excellence Award.

European Foundation for Quality Management (EFQM)

Avenue des Pléiades 15, Brussels, B-1200, Belgium
T: +32 2 775 35 11
F: +32 2 775 35 35
E: *info@efqm.org*
www.efqm.org
Founded in 1988 by the presidents of 14 major European companies, with the endorsement of the European Commission, the EFQM aims to support the managers of European organizations in efforts to accelerate the process of making TQM a decisive factor in achieving global competitive advantage. The Foundation provides information on the Business

Excellence Model/EFQM Excellence Model and the European Quality Award. It also offers various training courses and produces its own publications.

European Organisation for Quality

3 rue du Luxembourg, Brussels, B-1000, Belgium
T: +32 2 501 07 35
F: +32 2 501 07 36
www.eoq.org
An autonomous nonprofit organization established in 1956, the EOQ is the European interdisciplinary body concerned with bringing about effective improvement in the area of quality management. Its Web site provides access to the European Quality Week site and the *European Quality Journal*, besides giving details of EOQ activities.

Institute of Quality Assurance

12 Grosvenor Crescent, London, SW1X 7EE, U.K.

T: +44 (0) 20 7245 6722
F: +44 (0) 20 7245 6755
E: *iqa@iqa.org*
www.iqa.org
The IQA is a professional body for those with responsibilities for quality assurance. Founded in 1919, it aims to foster quality practices and advance national policy issues in the area of quality.

FOR MORE INFORMATION

1889

BUSINESS INFORMATION SOURCES

Recruitment and Selection

BOOKS

45 Effective Ways for Hiring Smart! How to Predict Winners & Losers in the Incredibly Expensive People-reading Game 2nd ed.
Pierre Mornell
Berkeley, California: Ten Speed Press, 2003
240pp ISBN: 1580085148
This is a practical guide to help employers cut through the complexities of hiring and select the best candidate for a particular job. As the title suggests, this text presents 45 techniques designed to take the measure of potential recruits, emphasizing behavior not words.

101 Hiring Mistakes Employers Make ... and How to Avoid Them
Richard Fein
Manassas Park, Virginia: Impact Publications, 2000
144pp ISBN: 157023129X
An analytical study of interviewing techniques, based on material from genuine interviews, it outlines some of the main hiring errors that can eventually burden an organization with an unsatisfactory employee. The author aims to help minimize "hiring mistakes" and increase the employer's understanding of interview questioning.

Competency Based Recruitment and Selection: A Practical Guide
Robert Wood, Tim Payne
Hoboken, New Jersey: Wiley, 1998
224pp (Strategic Human Resource Management)
ISBN: 0471974730
Step-by-step guidance is given to recruiters on how competencies can be used for selecting and assessing job candidates. Each of the ten chapters is written to stand alone in its area, and the book focuses on the recruitment and selection context, attracting and sifting candidates, assessment, decision making, and evaluation.

Competing for Talent: Key Recruitment and Retention Strategies for Becoming an Employer of Choice
Nancy S. Ahlrichs
Palo Alto, California: Davies-Black, 2000
256pp ISBN: 0891061487
Ahlrichs recognizes "human capital" as the key to business success. She says that the only way to attract and keep the top employees you need is by becoming an employer of choice. This book presents her strategy for achieving that. Part One looks at what other companies have done to become employers of choice. Part Two examines specific recruiting strategies. Part Three focuses on the equally important issue of retention.

The Directory of Executive Recruiters
Kennedy Information
Peterborough, New Hampshire: Kennedy Information, 2005
1104pp ISBN: 1932079491
Published since 1971 and updated annually, this famous "Red Book" lists 14,200 recruiters at 5,700 search firms in the United States, Canada, and Mexico. Indexed by function, industry, geography, and specialty, the book makes it simple to find the best recruiter for you. Although the book provides extensive contact information, the CD-ROM of the database, available at an additional cost, is really required for effective searching.

High Impact Hiring: How to Interview and Select Outstanding Employees 2nd ed.
Del J. Still
Dana Point, California: Management Development Systems, 2001
304pp ISBN: 0965465985
A "must-read" for anyone responsible for interviewing and hiring, this book will help you discover the pertinent information about a candidate. The author presents his seven-step interview model which will lead you to a successful hiring decision.

Hiring the Best: A Manager's Guide to Effective Recruitment 5th ed.
Martin Yate
Holbrook, Massachusetts: Adams Media Corporation, 2006
272pp ISBN: 1593374038
A guide for managers, this book suggests strategies for recognizing a good employee in terms of competence, willingness, and personality. It also explores a range of issues that can arise for an employer when hiring different types of employee (temporary, consultancy, and so on).

Interviewing and Selecting High Performers
Larry R. Smalley
San Francisco, California: Jossey-Bass, 1999
112pp (Management Skills)
ISBN: 0787951099
As Vice President and Principal Consultant for Richard Chang Associates, Inc. the author has plenty of expertise to offer managers, supervisors, or team leaders responsible for selecting and interviewing candidates. This text is orientated towards the practical, and includes work sheets, a continuous case study, and key tips. Appendices give reproducible documentation, a checklist, and examples of performance-based questions.

A Manager's Guide to Hiring the Best Person for Every Job
DeAnne Rosenberg
Hoboken, New Jersey: Wiley, 2000
320pp ISBN: 0471380741
This book on recruitment and selection interviewing is written in simple language and gives detailed help with structuring the dialogue and questioning in interviews in such a way as to retain control and focus on the job requirements involved. A matrix designed by the author for identifying trade-offs among competing candidates is included.

Recruit & Retain the Best
John McCarter, Ray Schreyer
Manassas Park, Virginia: Impact Publications, 2000
128pp ISBN: 1570231346
The authors claim that, to remain competitive, you must create a talent-powered company. Their solution begins with recruiting new employees based on competencies from education or previous employment. They discuss innovative recruiting tools such as the Internet and employee referral programs. However, the focus of this book is on the retention of the top employees. The last third of the book addresses ways to make your company a place where the best want to stay.

Recruiting, Interviewing, Selecting, and Orienting New Employees 3rd ed.
Diane Arthur
New York: AMACOM, 2006
400pp ISBN: 0814408613
This book is designed to give

"You must make use of people according to their abilities and realize that absolutely no one is perfect."

Françoise d'Aubigné Maintenon

comprehensive guidance through the four stages of the employment process to HR specialists and others whose work involves recruitment and selection. Besides describing methods and techniques applicable to the basic task of hiring new employees, this revised edition takes in new material dealing with areas such as additional interviewing approaches, workplace diversity, the retention of new employees, and online recruitment.

Smart Hiring: The Complete Guide to Finding and Hiring the Best Employees 3rd ed.
Robert W. Wendover
Naperville, Illinois: Sourcebooks, 2002
240pp ISBN: 140220003X
This book offers practical advice to employers on improving their employee selection skills. Examining various topics such as hiring errors, telephone interviews, and the assessment of a potential employee, Wendover's approach is pragmatic. Also included in the book are step-by-step guides to job advertising and analyzing résumés.

The War for Talent
Ed Michaels, Helen Handfield-Jones, Beth Axelrod
Boston, Massachusetts: Harvard Business School Press, 2001
208pp ISBN: 1578514592
In acknowledgment of today's increasingly competitive market for talented business individuals, this book offers guidance to managers, executives, and team leaders on ways to attract an excellent workforce to their organization. It also advises on developing the full potential of talented individuals.

MAGAZINES
Recruiting Trends
ISSN: 0163–5611
Kennedy Information
One Phoenix Mill Lane, 3rd Floor, Peterborough, New Hampshire, 03458
T: +1 800 531 0007 or +1 603 924 1006
F: +1 603 924 4460
www.kennedyinfo.com/mci/mci.html
This is a monthly loose-leaf publication for recruitment executives.

Recruitment International
Recruitment Publications Ltd.
13 High Road, West Byfleet, Surrey, KT14 7QH, U.K.
T: +44 (0) 1932 351 144
F: +44 (0) 1932 351 166
www.recruitment-intl.com
This monthly magazine is intended for

those concerned with recruitment and selection, covering issues relevant to the field and including articles on career development and training.

Recruitment Matters
Recruitment and Employment Confederation
36–38 Mortimer Street, London, W1W 7RG, U.K.
T: +44 (0) 20 7462 3260
F: +44 (0) 20 7255 2878
www.rec.uk.com
This bimonthly magazine is free to members of the Recruitment and Employment Federation. It covers all issues concerned with recruitment and employment.

Selection and Development Review
ISSN: 0963–2638
British Psychological Society
St. Andrews House, 48 Princess Road East, Leicester, Leicestershire, LE1 7DR, U.K.
T: +44 (0) 116 254 9568
F: +44 (0) 116 247 0787
www.bps.org.uk
A bimonthly publication for HR specialists and recruiters, it has a strong focus on psychometric testing.

INTERNET
Monster.com
www.monster.com
This is a global online careers network, aiming to connect companies and qualified individuals. It offers member-employers various services, including job postings, résumé screening, a résumé database, and résumé routing. Job seekers can use it to access vacancies, and can take advantage of features and services such as résumé management, a job-search agent, and a careers network.

Recruiters Network
www.recruitersnetwork.com
Recruiters Network is a free association for HR professionals, recruiters, and hiring managers. Its goal is to provide leading resources and information on the recruiting and Internet recruiting industry. Members receive a monthly newsletter, access to a resource directory, and links to related blogs.

Recruiters Online Network
www.recruitersonline.com
Recruiters Online Network is a global community of recruiters, headhunters, and staffing firms. It features separate sections for job seekers to post résumés and search for jobs, for recruiters to post jobs and

search résumé databases, and for employers to find talent or a recruiting firm.

Society for Human Resource Management
www.shrm.org
This Web site is the online presence of the leading voice of the human resource profession, providing education and information services, conferences and seminars, government and media representation, online services, and publications, to more than 190,000 professional and student members throughout the world.

ORGANIZATIONS
USA
American Staffing Association
277 South Washington Street, Suite 200, Alexandria, Virginia, 22314
T: +1 703 253 2020
F: +1 703 253 2053
E: *asa@staffingtoday.net*
www.staffingtoday.net
ASA represents the U.S. recruiting industry. Among other things, it provides job-seeking and staff-seeking services. Membership benefits include access to information and research concerned with employment, payroll, employee turnover rates, industry compensation, and other associated matters.

International Association of Corporate and Professional Recruitment
20 North Wacker Drive, #2262, Chicago, Illinois, 60606
T: +1 312 630 9881
E: *iacpr@iacpr.org*
www.iacpr.org
Formerly the National Association of Corporate and Professional Recruiters, IACPR was founded in 1978. This association boasts a membership of over 300 individuals who focus on providing research to human resource executives and search professionals in the recruitment field. IACPR strives to disseminate the latest information and problem-solving strategies found in the corporate recruiting industry.

National Association of Personnel Services
3133 Mount Vernon Avenue, Alexandria, Virginia, 22305
T: +1 703 684 0180
F: +1 703 684 0071
E: *info@napsweb.org*
http://napsweb.org
NAPS seeks to inform and represent the personnel services industry by providing

1891

BUSINESS INFORMATION SOURCES

education, certification, and member services. It has been educating and training those in the staffing industry since 1961, and now represents over 100,000 individuals and 30 state associations. A selection of articles from NAPS newsletters (InsideNAPS) is available from www.napsweb.org/newsletters, and news of pending legislation relevant to personnel from www.napsweb.org/napstrack.htm.

Europe
Chartered Institute of Personnel and Development (CIPD)

151 The Broadway, Wimbledon, London, SW19 1JQ, U.K.

T: +44 (0) 20 8612 6200
F: +44 (0) 20 8012 6201
www.cipd.co.uk

Formed in 1995 from the amalgamation of the Institute of Personnel Management and the Institute of Training and Development, the CIPD is a professional body for personnel and training professionals which aims to promote good practice in the

management and development of people—a company's core strength.

Recruitment and Employment Confederation

36–38 Mortimer Street, London, W1W 7RG, U.K.

T: +44 (0) 20 7462 3260
F: +44 (0) 20 7255 2878
E: *info@rec.co.uk*
www.rec.uk.com

The Confederation is an organization for recruitment and employment agencies and consulting firms operating in most fields of employment. Its activities include conferences, meetings, research, and the provision of information.

International
Association of Executive Search Consultants

500 Fifth Avenue, Suite 930, New York, 10110

T: +1 212 398 9556
E: *aesc@aesc.org*
www.aesc.org

The AESC is a professional association for retained executive search consulting firms worldwide. It has regional councils for Europe and the United States and an international board of directors. It defines the activity of retained executive search consulting as helping clients to find and recruit senior executives.

FOR MORE INFORMATION

- ✔ Attracting and Retaining People Reentering the Workplace (pp. 498–499)
- ☆ Finding and Keeping Top Talent (pp. 33–34)
- ℘ Management Development (pp. 1812–1814)
- ℘ Online Sources for Marketing (General Business Information) (p. 1766)
- ℘ Personnel Management and HR Management (pp. 1856–1859)
- ✔ Planning the Recruitment Process (pp. 484–485)
- ✔ Preparing and Using Job Descriptions (pp. 486–487)

BUSINESS INFORMATION SOURCES

"Modern heretics are not burned at the stake. They are relegated to backwaters or pressured to resign."

Art Kleiner

     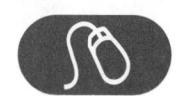

Relocation

BOOKS

Office Relocation Planner

Karen Chessler, Christopher Carmen
Vision Publications, 2001
64pp ISBN: 1928742033
Office relocation consultants and commercial real estate experts have defined the tasks associated with an office move and, using action steps and checklists, have put them into a logical sequence, making the relocation process manageable. The book also includes detailed information on issues such as facility selection, selecting a moving company, and moving computers and office equipment.

The Office Relocation Sourcebook: A Guide to Managing Staff Throughout the Move

Dennis Attwood
Hoboken, New Jersey: Wiley, 1996
288pp ISBN: 0471130168
This resource provides the corporate relocation team at firms of all sizes with the information it needs to relocate successfully, cost-efficiently, and with minimal disruption to employees. It includes checklists, survey tools, and summaries forms and access to valuable relocation tools, including a comprehensive relocation template.

Relocating Your Workplace: A User's Guide to Acquiring and Preparing Business Facilities

Wadman Daly
Menlo Park, California: Crisp Publications, 1994
368pp ISBN: 1560521864
This is a user's guide to facility relocation, from finding a new location to developing it and moving in. It includes charts, graphs, and checklists, as well as detailed explanations of lease agreements and relocation costs.

Smart Moves: Your Guide through the Emotional Maze of Relocation

Nadia Jensen, Audrey T. McCollum
Lyme, New Hampshire: Smith & Kraus, 1996
256pp ISBN: 1575250799
In this publication, the authors aim to help minimize the stress caused by important life changes. By exploring the emotional aspects of relocation, the book offers guidance on how, through increased communication and assertiveness, to turn your anxieties into positive action.

Smooth Moves: The Relocation Guide for Families on the Move

Ellen Carlisle
Charlotte, North Carolina: Teacup Press, 1999
112pp ISBN: 0966782704
The author addresses every aspect of moving a household, providing tips and checklists that cover moving basics, including selling your house, researching new schools, selecting a neighborhood that meets your needs, and easing the family trauma that results from moving.

INTERNET

123Relocation.com
www.relo-usa.com
This site is a U.S.-based relocation information resource that is searchable by state and city.

Employee Relocation Council
www.erc.org
The Employee Relocation Council is a nonprofit association providing resources addressing the issues of corporate, government, and military employee relocation. Its Web site provides details of events and conferences held by the Council as well as of its news and press releases. Links to newsletters, "Webinars," conferences, and the ERC's Global Workforce Services Directory are also given.

Relocation Central
www.relocationcentral.com
This site is a relocation directory, providing contacts for products and services and searchable by city. Relocation news and helpful advice about panic-free moving are also available.

ORGANIZATIONS
USA
Employee Relocation Council
1717 Pennsylvania Avenue NW, Washington, D.C., 20006
T: +1 202 857 0857
F: +1 202 659 8631
www.erc.org
ERC is a membership organization, founded in 1964, for professionals who manage or support U.S. and international employee relocation.

Relocation Appraisers and Consultants
1540 South Holly, #5, Denver, Colorado, 80222
T: +1 800 368 7717
www.rac.net
This national organization of independent professionals is dedicated to the promotion and recognition of relocation training, education, and general advancement in the best methods of employee relocation.

Europe
Association of Relocation Professionals (ARP)
P.O. Box 189, Diss, Norfolk, IP22 1PE, U.K.
T: +44 (0) 8700 737 475
F: +44 (0) 8700 718 719
E: *info@relocationagents.com*
www.relocationagents.com
The Association of Relocation Professionals, formerly called the Association of Relocation Agents, is a membership organization that was founded in 1986 to encourage and promote companies and individuals offering relocation services within the United Kingdom and overseas. It is affiliated with the European Relocation Association.

European Relocation Association
P.O. Box 189, Diss, Norfolk, IP22 1PE, U.K.
T: +44 (0) 8700 726 727
F: +44 (0) 1359 251 508
E: *info@eura-relocation.com*
www.eura-relocation.com
A professional membership body, launched in 1998, for relocation professionals in Europe and worldwide, EuRA aims to spread knowledge and understanding of the issues surrounding corporate mobility and to promote high industry standards. Members are required to abide by EuRA's rules of conduct.

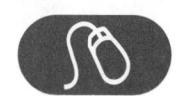

1893

FOR MORE INFORMATION

- Conditions of Employment (pp. 1708–1709)
- International Management, Cross Cultural Management (pp. 1784–1786)
- Working Abroad (pp. 1930–1931)

BUSINESS INFORMATION SOURCES

"Passion for change drives great business people. It moves them restlessly from industry to industry."

Paul Corrigan

Remuneration

BOOKS

Disciplined Minds: A Critical Look at Salaried Professionals and the Soul-battering System that Shapes Their Lives
Jeff Schmidt
Lanham, Maryland: Rowman and Littlefield, 2000
336pp ISBN: 0847693643
Schmidt takes a critical look at the U.S. system of education and professional employment. He gets to the basics of a professional's job and the dissatisfaction that many experience. Schmidt offers a different perspective on employment, and on how we can change our thinking and bring new understanding to our work and our lives.

Get Paid What You're Worth: The Expert Negotiator's Guide to Salary and Compensation
Robin L. Pinkley, Gregory B. Northcraft
New York: St. Martin's Press, 2003
208pp ISBN: 031230269X
Pinkley and Northcraft offer advice on which issues to negotiate, how to prepare and conduct interviews and negotiations, and how to close a new job package. They also include advice from experts on proven strategies, proper thinking, and how to take action.

Interview for Success: A Practical Guide to Increasing Job Interviews, Offers, and Salaries 8th ed.
Ronald L. Krannich, Caryl Rae Krannich
Manassas Park, Virginia: Impact Publications, 2002
224pp ISBN: 1570231907
Interview for Success is a "how-to" book on preparing for interviews, researching information, presenting yourself, and handling all of the details of interviewing. It is an excellent resource for the job seeker looking to negotiate a better position and compensation package.

Pay People Right!: Breakthrough Reward Strategies to Create Great Companies
Patricia K. Zingheim, Jay R. Schuster
San Francisco, California: Jossey-Bass, 2000
416pp ISBN: 078794016X
Pay People Right! is a guide to the basic issues in compensation. It deals with the topic from a strategic viewpoint and discusses compensation as a total reward as opposed to simple cash remuneration. Performance issues and group considerations are given extensive coverage. This is a good resource for executives of small-to-medium size organizations and HR professionals branching into the field of compensation.

Rewarding Excellence: Pay Strategies for the New Economy 2nd ed.
Edward E. Lawler
San Francisco, California: Jossey-Bass, 2000
352pp (Jossey-Bass Business and Management)
ISBN: 0787950742
The author suggests that in today's competitive environment organizations need to focus on rewarding excellence in all areas, and that old reward systems focused on jobs and merit pay are inadequate to motivate and develop either individuals or the organizations themselves. Drawing on research literature, he outlines a new approach to designing reward systems and makes practical suggestions for restructuring the way employees are paid.

Reward Management: A Critical Text
Geoff White, Janet Druker, eds
New York: Routledge, 2000
240pp (Routledge Studies in Employment Relations)
ISBN: 0415196809
This work offers a critical and theoretical review of changes in remuneration practice in the United Kingdom over the last 20 years. Methods of determining pay, the role of trade unions, grading systems, salary progression systems, benefits, financial participation schemes, and international reward management are covered.

Strategic Compensation: A Human Resource Management Approach 4th ed.
Joseph J. Martocchio
Upper Saddle River, New Jersey: Prentice Hall, 2005
528pp ISBN: 0131868772
This guide to the practical aspects of employee compensation covers the topic in depth but in an easy-to-follow manner. Aspects of the subject covered range from how to determine compensation levels to compensation management systems. Overall, this is a valuable resource for HR professionals in an organization of any size.

MAGAZINES

Pay for Performance Report
ISSN: 1086–9581
Institute of Management and Administration (IOMA)
3 Park Avenue, 30th Floor, New York, 10001–5902
T: +1 212 244 0360
F: +1 212 564 0465
www.ioma.com
This is a monthly newsletter providing information on how to implement variable pay and bonus programs.

workspan
ISSN: 1529–9465
WorldatWork
14040 North Northsight Boulevard, Scottsdale, Arizona, 85260
T: +1 480 951 9191
F: +1 480 483 8352
www.worldatwork.org
Formerly known as *ACA News*, this publication comes out 11 times a year and is aimed at compensation, benefits, and human resource professionals. *workspan* provides information on current trends in remuneration and covers contemporary thinking on issues in compensation and benefits design, implementation, and management.

WorldatWork Journal
ISSN: 1529–9457
WorldatWork
14040 North Northsight Boulevard, Scottsdale, Arizona, 85260
T: +1 480 951 9191
F: +1 480 483 8352
www.worldatwork.org
This quarterly journal, formerly called the *ACA Journal*, is aimed at middle and senior level managers and covers the theory and practice of compensation and benefits management.

INTERNET

College Grad Job Hunter
www.collegegrad.com
College Grad Job Hunter has a salary calculator (listed on the left-hand option menu) for new college graduates based on job type, locality, and profession. The site gives low, median, and high salaries as well as base and total compensation calculations. It also offers very useful tips on salary negotiations, relocation, and career

"Men work but slowly, that have poor wages."   Thomas Fuller

research. This is a great site for newly graduated students to find their first position.

The Minimum Wage
www.dol.gov/dol/topic/wages/minimumwage.htm
This site contains information on the minimum wage in the United States from the U.S. Department of Labor.

Salary.com
www.salary.com
One of the features of this free Web site is the salary search, that provides salary ranges for specific positions within a geographic area—information useful to job shoppers as well as HR professionals. A great deal of additional information on the subject of salaries is also available.

True Careers
www.careercity.com
The True Careers site has links to various salary surveys. Page down to the Salary Calculator, and then add in your own job title and location. An extensive series of links addresses many types of profession.

United States Department of Labor
www.dol.gov
This government Web site contains a large amount of information that is organized for easy access. It provides useful information on the legal aspects of compensation and results of large-scale studies and surveys.

U.S. Office of Personnel Management
www.opm.gov/oca/payrates
This site lists pay rates by position for government employees in the year 2005. It includes notes for adjustments made for locality, special rate, and relative memorandums.

WorldatWork—Professional Association for Compensation, Benefits, and Total Rewards
www.worldatwork.org
Designed for HR professionals, this site has a wealth of online resources including

articles, press releases, news items, a bookstore, and survey results. Although much of the site is for members only, there is good information which is accessible to the casual browser.

ORGANIZATIONS
USA
American Payroll Association (APA)
660 North Main Avenue, Suite 100, San Antonio, Texas, 78205–1217
T: +1 210 226 4600
F: +1 210 226 4027
E: *apa@americanpayroll.org*
www.americanpayroll.org
APA is a professional association for payroll managers with a membership of over 20,000. Its activities include seminars, accreditation programs, publications (including a journal), and an annual congress.

American Society for Payroll Management (ASPM)
P.O. Box 117, Stormville, New York, 12582
T: +1 800 684 4024
F: +1 845 227 9246
E: *info@aspm.org*
www.aspm.org
The ASPM, founded in 1988, provides information, resources (including an online newsletter), advocacy, and a forum for the exchange of ideas for payroll, tax, and human resources managers. It organizes a symposium and a trade show annually.

Europe
Institute of Payroll and Pensions Management
Shelly House, Farmhouse Way, Monkspath, Solihull, West Midlands, B90 4EH, U.K.
T: +44 (0) 121 712 1000
F: +44 (0) 121 712 1090
E: *info@ippm.org*
www.ippm.org
The IPPM was formed in 1997 and incorporates the former Institute of British Payroll Management and the Association of Payroll and Superannuation Administrators. It promotes good practice within payroll and pension management through

educational programs, advice and support services for members, and representation.

Low Pay Commission
5th Floor, 151 Buckingham Palace Road, London, SW1W 9SS, U.K.
T: +44 (0) 20 7215 3646
F: +44 (0) 20 7215 1560
E: *lpc@gtnet.gov.uk*
www.lowpay.gov.uk
The Low Pay Commission is a nondepartmental public body that was set up in 1998 to monitor and evaluate the introduction and impact of the National Minimum Wage in the United Kingdom.

International
WorldatWork
14040 N. Northsight Boulevard, Scottsdale, Arizona, 85260
T: +1 480 951 9191
F: +1 480 483 8352
E: *customerrelations@worldatwork.org*
www.worldatwork.org
WorldatWork is a professional organization for those working in the fields of compensation, benefits, and HR. It was founded in 1995, was previously known as the American Compensation Association, and has a current membership of over 26,000. Its activities include education and accreditation programs, workshops and conferences, research, publications, and networking opportunities.

1895

FOR MORE INFORMATION

- Conditions of Employment (pp. 1708–1709)
- Employee Benefits/Compensation (pp. 1736–1737)
- Finding and Keeping Top Talent (pp. 33–34)
- Finding Out What You Are Worth: Remuneration/Salaries (pp. 1755–1756)
- Implementing Job Evaluation (pp. 490–491)
- Implementing Performance-Related Pay (PRP) (pp. 492–493)
- Making Recognition and Rewards a "Whole-Person" Experience (pp. 12–13)

BUSINESS INFORMATION SOURCES

Research and Development (R&D) Management

BOOKS

The Development Factory: Unlocking the Potential of Process Innovation

Gary P. Pisano
Boston, Massachusetts: Harvard Business School Press, 1996
336pp ISBN: 0875846505

Gary Pisano proves that process innovation—not just product innovation—can be the key to competitive advantage. In a multiyear study of pharmaceutical and biotechnology firms, he shows that developing distinctive and superior process technologies can lower costs, improve quality, and increase flexibility. *The Development Factory* is designed to help companies unlock the potential of process development and create and implement new capabilities.

From Alchemy to IPO: The Business of Biotechnology

Cynthia Robbins-Roth
Cambridge, Massachusetts: Perseus Books Group, 2001
256pp ISBN: 073820482X

Written by an industry insider, this title addresses the coming of age of biotech products and companies and traces the history of biotechnology from its inception in the 1970s to 2001's torrent of new solutions and breakthrough treatments. It also describes the entrepreneurial trail of product development, novel business models, and critical trials, and records the inner workings of an industry which is promising to change the world as we know it.

Product Design and Development 3rd ed.

Karl T. Ulrich, Steven D. Eppinger
Maidenhead, United Kingdom: McGraw-Hill, 2003
384pp ISBN: 0072471468

This is a practical guide to the business of innovation and R&D. It covers everything from the steps necessary to design a successful product to budget management for the R&D. It should be a useful tool for anyone who is embarking on a career in R&D or who is new to its management.

The Smart Organization: Creating Value through Strategic R&D

David Matheson, Jim Matheson
Boston, Massachusetts: Harvard Business School Press, 1997
304pp ISBN: 087584765X

Designed to help managers improve their research and development management and decision making, the text discusses best practices, as well as nine principles of "smart R&D," and includes a section on testing how good an organization's R&D is.

The Valuation of Technology: Business and Financial Issues in R&D

F. Peter Boer
Hoboken, New Jersey: Wiley, 1999
400pp ISBN: 0471316385

This book is a thorough guide to the business and financial aspects of R&D. It begins with chapters devoted to the definition of and rationale behind the R&D function, but the bulk of the book is devoted to financial considerations. It is useful for detailed coverage of such topics as developing business plans, determining profit and loss, and understanding and calculating discounted cash flow.

MAGAZINES

International Journal of Technology Management

ISSN: 0267–5730
Inderscience Enterprises Ltd.
World Trade Center Building, 29 route de Pre-Bois, Case Postale 896, CH-1215, Geneva, 15, Switzerland
T: +44 (0) 1234 240515
F: +41 22 791 08 85
www.inderscience.com
International in scope, the journal tends toward the academic, and primarily covers the management of technology and engineering. However, it also has a large number of items and occasional special issues which are specific to research and development. The journal is aimed at anyone responsible for managing technology.

R&D Management

ISSN: 0033–6807
Blackwell Publishing
350 Main Street, Malden, Massachusetts, 02148

T: +1 781 388 8200
F: +1 781 388 8232
www.blackwellpublishing.com
This is an international journal for both practitioners and scholars. It covers all areas of research and development, including innovation and design, and also examines human resources and strategic issues that affect research and development management.

INTERNET

National Science Foundation
www.nsf.gov
This government-hosted Web site contains a wealth of information for anyone involved in advancing science and technology. It offers everything from statistical data to technology-specific information.

R&D Alliance Network
www.atp.nist.gov/alliance/welcome.htm
This government Web site is specifically dedicated to the needs of the research and development community. It contains useful information and services as well as links to additional resources.

R&D—Research & Development
www.rdmag.com
This Web site is a free online journal for the research and development professional. Each issue features technical and general-interest articles and provides other information and a number of useful services. The archives are easily accessed.

ORGANIZATIONS
USA
Industrial Research Institute, Inc.
Suite 1100, 1550 M Street, NW, Washington, D.C., 20005–1712
T: +1 202 296 8811
F: +1 202 776 0756
E: *information@iriinc.org*
www.iriinc.org
This is a nonprofit organization of over 260 leading industrial companies, whose aim is to enhance the effectiveness of technological innovation in industry. These member companies—representing a range of industries such as aerospace, automotive, chemical, computer, and electronics—carry

"The real measure of success is the number of experiments that can be crowded into 24 hours."

Thomas Edison

out over 80% of the industrial research effort in the United States' manufacturing sector, and account for at least 30% of its gross national product.

Product Development and Management Association

15000 Commerce Parkway, Suite C, Mount Laurel, New Jersey, 08054
T: +1 856 439 9052
F: +1 856 439 0525
E: *pdma@pdma.org*
www.pdma.org
This professional nonprofit organization is dedicated to serving people with an interest in new products and services. It provider knowledge and tools intended to improve the effectiveness of the development and management of new products and services.

It also arranges conferences, publications, awards, meetings, and workshops, and sponsors research.

Europe
Product Development and Management Association, U.K. and Ireland

Innovaro, 78 Belsize Gardens, London, NW3 4NG, U.K.
T: +44 (0) 7801 755 054
E: *timjones@innovaro.com*
www.pdma.org.uk
This is the U.K. and Ireland branch of PDMA of America, a professional nonprofit organization, which is a recognized provider of knowledge and tools intended to improve the development and management of new products and services. The Association's activities include arranging conferences,

awards, meetings and workshops; producing publications; and sponsoring research.

International
Society of Research Administrators International

1901 North Moore Street, Suite 1004, Arlington, Virginia, 22209
T: +1 703 741 0140
E: *info@srainternational.org*
www.srainternational.org
The Society is a nonprofit international association, founded in 1967 for those providing administrative support to corporate, academic, or medical researchers. An extensive Web site is available to members, with details of grants, resources, and training.

1897

BUSINESS INFORMATION SOURCES

Risk Management

BOOKS

Against the Gods: The Remarkable Story of Risk

Peter L. Bernstein
Hoboken, New Jersey: Wiley, 1998
400pp ISBN: 0471295639
A study of risk history, in which Bernstein eventually brings the reader back to the modern day and "chaos theory." The book discusses the elements of risk that appear in various life situations (with reference to the origins of the risk concept) and aims to increase the reader's understanding of them.

The Book of Risk

Dan Borge
Hoboken, New Jersey: Wiley, 2001
240pp ISBN: 0471323780
Dan Borge breaks down the concept and application of risk management into basic ideas to facilitate a more thorough understanding. He describes the techniques professional risk managers use for determining probabilities and personal preferences, and explores their use for more effective actions. The book explains how we are all already risk managers, and the aim is to help managers become better risk managers.

Managing Business Risk: An Organization-wide Approach to Risk Management

Peter C. Young, Steven C. Tippins
New York: AMACOM, 2001
448pp ISBN: 0814404618
This is a practical textbook that explains to managers the essentials of risk management. A model, called "organizational risk management," is presented to facilitate a cost saving, company-wide approach to risk management. The techniques covered include risk assessment, risk control, asset and liability exposures to risk, risk financing principles, and insurance.

Managing Corporate Reputation and Risk: Developing a Strategic Approach to Corporate Integrity Using Knowledge Management

Dale Neef
Oxford: Elsevier Butterworth-Heinemann, 2003
156pp ISBN: 0750677155
Looking at best practice techniques in risk management, this title explores the management of corporate integrity through the establishment of ethical policies, risk management through knowledge management techniques, and bottom line reporting.

Managing Environmental Risks and Liabilities

Paul Pritchard
London: Earthscan, 2000
240pp (Business and Environmental Practitioner)
ISBN: 1853835986
Recent developments in environmental risk management are discussed in this book, which focuses on the nature of environmental risks and their relation to property, financial risk transfer, decision making, risk-management integration, and risk-management frameworks.

Managing Risk in Nonprofit Organizations: A Comprehensive Guide

Melanie L. Herman et al.
Hoboken, New Jersey: Wiley, 2004
336pp ISBN: 0471236748
This practical guide shows managers in nonprofit organizations how to implement sound risk management procedures. It is divided into three sections: the nature and purposes of risk management; recognizing the context for risk management; and risk financing for nonprofits. Potential risks covered include human resource issues, fundraising, internet use, mergers, and volunteer management.

Operational Risk: Measurement and Modelling

Jack L. King
Hoboken, New Jersey: Wiley, 2001
272pp ISBN: 0471852090
Operational risk, it is reported, is concerned with the risk to the performance of a firm, due to how the firm is operated as opposed to how it is financed. The authors present a new approach to measuring operational risk. This enables firms to better control the variability or risk of earnings in their operations.

Practical Risk Management: An Executive Guide to Avoiding Surprises and Losses

Erik Banks, Richard Dunn
Hoboken, New Jersey: Wiley, 2003
176pp ISBN: 0470849673

This book looks at the world of financial risk management and offers practical approaches to managing financial risk based on the authors' experiences. It explores the challenges of risk management and how these can be overcome by focusing on governance and accountability. The book aims to provide an understanding of the different financial risks, the various measurement tools available, and how to construct a practical risk process that is consistent with corporate strategy.

Project Risk Assessment in a Week 2nd ed.

Donald Teale
London: Hodder & Stoughton, 2003
96pp (Business in a Week)
ISBN: 034084972X
This book guides you step by step through the process of identifying and analyzing the key risks to a project. Guidelines are provided for identifying the risks, assessing the impact of each risk, analyzing the combined impact of the risks on the project objectives, assigning adequate contingency to the project budget and schedule, and producing a risk management plan to assist in risk mitigation.

Risk from the C.E.O. and Board Perspective

Mary Pat McCarthy, Timothy P. Flynn
New York: McGraw-Hill, 2004
304pp ISBN: 0071434712
Corporate decision making is about navigating the business environment with one eye on the present and the other on the risks associated with each action. This text sets out to explain how corporate leaders are confronting and controlling risk in their organizations. Drawing upon their wealth of experience, the authors explore how to uncover and address sources of risk within an organization, manage risk without undermining ongoing initiatives, and link governance and risk management initiatives.

Risk Management

Michel Crouhy, Dan Galai, Robert Mark
Maidenhead, United Kingdom: McGraw-Hill, 2000
512pp ISBN: 0071357319
This book suggests ways to implement a risk management system to effectively

"In skating over thin ice, our safety is in our speed."   Ralph Waldo Emerson

     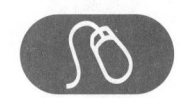

manage financial and economic risk as well as regulatory capital. It analyzes developments in risk management techniques used in the financial world and provides an up-to-date look at modern risk management tools.

Risk Management: Helping Directors to Identify and Control Business Risks Effectively

Institute of Directors and AXA Insurance
London: Kogan Page, 2003
80pp ISBN: 1901580997
This guide will assist senior decision-makers to develop a practical risk management strategy, to identify possible threats, and to introduce appropriate measures. The main areas of risk in any business are reviewed, and a wide range of advice and information provided. Case studies are included.

Risk Management: Ten Principles

Jacqueline Jeynes
New York: Butterworth-Heinemann, 2002
128pp ISBN: 0750650362
The ten main risk areas of a business are identified at the outset as premises, product, purchasing, people, procedures, protection, processes, performance, planning, and policy. The following sections identify and evaluate the risks and hazards relevant to each of these ten areas, and discuss ways in which the risks can be controlled. Case studies from service-based and production-based industries are included. Overall risk management strategies and policies are then described.

Risky Business: Corruption, Fraud, Terrorism, and Other Threats to Global Business 2nd ed.

Stuart Poole-Robb, Alan Bailey
London: Kogan Page, 2003
304pp ISBN: 0749440317
Organizations in today's world are subject to a range of risks over and above the standard expectations of terrorism and fraud, including organized crime, corruption and civil unrest. The authors' company has significant experience of these risks and the forces behind them and the book includes many case studies in areas such as Indonesia, Russia, and Asia and the Far East. Part One deals with the implications of risk for investment; Part Two looks at renowned trouble spots; and Part Three considers threats and defenses.

The Road to Audacity: Being Adventurous in Life and Work

Stephen Carter, Jeremy Kourdi
Basingstoke, United Kingdom: Palgrave Macmillan, 2003
160pp ISBN: 1403906173
The authors argue that risk-taking is an inevitable part of life and work, and that responding to uncertainty and risk is not just a matter of calculation and an attempt at objective prediction. The audacity factor is what makes the difference between caution and action. Drawing upon various examples, the book explores the way audacity can be developed and explains its importance to any individual or organization that wants to change, explore, or be different.

Secure Online Business Handbook: E-Commerce, IT Functionality, and Business Continuity 2nd ed.

Jonathan Reuvid
London: Kogan Page, 2004
224pp ISBN: 0749442212
This practical handbook, divided into five sections, contains a collection of contributions from a range of experts in the field of information technology and e-commerce and addresses the need for effective management of business risk. Information at risk and the business case for security are considered first. Points of exposure and the range of threats to privacy and integrity are explored, and methods of software protection such as firewalls, encryption, digital signatures and biometrics are covered. In the operational management section, the need for a culture of workplace security is also discussed, and data recovery, disaster management, and forensics are covered under the heading of contingency planning.

Seeing Tomorrow: Rewriting the Rules of Risk

Ron S. Dembo, Andrew Freeman
Hoboken, New Jersey: Wiley, 1998
272pp ISBN: 0471247367
This book presents a framework for forward-looking risk management. The authors assess the basic building blocks of risk management and explain their own rules for risk. These include the importance of choosing an appropriate time horizon as well as of selecting scenarios, computing Value at Risk, assessing the up- and downsides of potential deals, calculating Regret, and compiling a reliable Regret matrix.

Value at Risk: The Benchmark for Controlling Market Risk 2nd ed.

Philippe Jorion
Maidenhead, United Kingdom: McGraw-Hill, 2000
544pp ISBN: 0071355022
This book is aimed at helping professional risk managers understand and operate within today's dynamic new risk environment. This edition updates the original book, which focused on "Value at Risk" as a financial technique to measure risks run by trading and investment operations. New developments include a chapter on liquidity risk, and information on the latest risk instruments and the expanded derivatives market.

MAGAZINES

Risk

ISSN: 0952–8776
Risk Waters Group
270 Lafayette Street, Suite 700, New York, 10012
T: +1 212 925 6990
F: +1 212 925 7585
www.riskwaters.com/risk
This monthly magazine covers news, analysis, and developments in financial risk management. It is aimed at financial managers, academics, bankers, and investment bankers.

Risk Analysis—An International Journal

ISSN: 0272–4332
Blackwell Publishing
350 Main Street, Malden, Massachusetts, 02148
T: +1 781 388 8200
F: +1 781 388 8232
www.blackwellpublishing.com
The journal is an official publication of the Society for Risk Analysis. It covers new developments in risk analysis and other topics which should be of interest to scientists and managers from a wide range of disciplines.

Risk and Continuity

ISSN: 1463–1628
CHI Publishing Ltd.
17a Everard Road, Birkdale, Southport, Merseyside, PR8 6NN, U.K.
T: +44 (0) 1704 512 512
F: +44 (0) 1704 512 212
www.chi-publishing.com
This journal provides best practice information on risk and continuity management strategies. It also covers IT security, disaster management, related human factors, and legal issues, together with company and product news.

1899

BUSINESS INFORMATION SOURCES

Risk, Decision and Policy

ISSN: 1357–5309

Taylor & Francis Journals (U.K.)

Rankine Road, Basingstoke, Hampshire, RG24 8PR, U.K.

T: +44 (0) 1256 3813000

F: +44 (0) 1256 330245

www.tandf.co.uk/journals

Published three times a year, this is the official journal of the Decision and Policy Network. It specializes in the areas of economics, social science, and management, as applied to problems of interest to decision makers in business and government, and also includes information on risk communication.

Risk Management

Risk Management Society Publishing, Inc.

655 Third Avenue, Second Floor, New York, 10017–5637

T: +1 212 286 9364

F: +1 212 922 0716

www.rmmag.com

Published 12 times per year this magazine features articles, interviews, and special reports, written for executives and managers working in risk management. Recognized as the premier source of information for corporate risk managers, this is an invaluable resource for today's workplace.

Risk Management—An International Journal

ISSN: 1460–3799

Perpetuity Press Ltd.

P.O. Box 376, Leicester, Leicestershire, LE2 1UP, U.K.

T: +44 (0) 116 221 7778

F: +44 (0) 116 221 7171

www.perpetuitypress.co.uk

The purpose of this quarterly journal is to generate ideas and promote good practice for all those involved in managing risk. It takes a multidisciplinary approach and aims to facilitate the exchange of information and expertise across the world.

Risk Management Bulletin

ISSN: 3363–9498

Ark Publishing Ltd.

3000 Atrium Way, 295 Mt. Laurel, New Jersey, 08054–3911

T: +1 877 295 3967

F: +1 877 260 2918

www.ark-interactive.com

This journal provides practical examples of risk management best practice, together with innovative solutions to common problems and benchmarking opportunities.

RMA Journal

ISSN: 1531–0558

Risk Management Association

One Liberty Place, 1650 Market Street, Suite 2300, Philadelphia, Pennsylvania, 19103–7301

T: +1 215 446 4096

F: +1 215 446 4101

www.rmahq.org

Published ten times a year, this, the official journal of the Risk Management Association of the United States, covers the latest trends, techniques, and challenges that lending, credit, and risk management professionals have to deal with.

INTERNET

The Association of Insurance and Risk Managers
www.airmic.com

This site contains membership information, details of the AIRMIC conference, a newsletter, a press release index, and a members-only section.

Business Continuity Institute
www.thebci.org

This site provides free access to various guides to continuity management, which themselves include further sources of information on business continuity and risk management. It also offers recent news items, press releases, details of conferences and training courses, and a members-only area offering networking opportunities, a worldwide contact list, details of the BCI standards, a bookstore, and the BCI forum.

Global Association of Risk Professionals
www.garp.com

Specific to financial risk management, this site offers current news items, membership information, access to detailed risk technology applications, examination information, an events calendar, a newsletter, free access to articles and other reference sources, a bookstore, and useful industry links.

Institute of Risk Management
www.theirm.org

This site provides information on the membership benefits of the IRM, gives details of its courses, certificates, and examinations, and features a careers page.

Risk and Insurance Management Society, Inc.
www.rims.org

In addition to providing information about

Society membership and conferences, this site also offers access to recent government-related news, a risk management newsbrief service, a job bank, education and research activities, a bookstore, an education center, a calendar of events, and related links.

RMISWEB, the Internet Resource for Risk Management Information Systems
www.rmisweb.com

This site provides access to journal and review articles and press releases on risk management. It also contains recent news items, a directory of software providers, a list of consultants, and links to other risk and insurance sites.

Society for Risk Analysis
www.sra.org

This site provides information on membership and events, recent news, a newsletter, a section on employment opportunities in this field, a journal, and related links.

ORGANIZATIONS
USA
Global Association of Risk Professionals

28 East 18th Street, 2nd Floor, New York, 10003

T: +1 212 995 0930

F: +1 212 995 0835

E: *membership@garp.com*

www.garp.com

Originally an independent organization of risk management practitioners and researchers, founded by a group of risk managers from the finance industry, GARP is now a diverse association of over 15,000 professionals sharing a common interest in risk management. Its activities include facilitating the exchange of information, developing educational programs, and promoting standards in the area of financial risk management.

Risk and Insurance Management Society, Inc.

655 Third Avenue, 2nd Floor, New York, 10017

T: +1 212 286 9292

www.rims.org

This is a nonprofit organization dedicated to advancing the practice of risk management. It serves its members by providing quality products, services, and information designed to manage all forms of business risk. It also offers educational opportunities and aims to develop a responsive and productive network.

1900

BUSINESS INFORMATION SOURCES

Risk Management Association (RMA)

One Liberty Place, 1650 Market Street, Suite 2300, Philadelphia, Pennsylvania, 19103–7301
T: +1 215 446 4096
F: +1 215 446 4101
E: *customers@rmahq.org*
www.rmahq.org
RMA is a membership organization for lending, credit, and risk management professionals in the financial services industry. Members have access to a number of benefits including professional development and networking opportunities, benchmarking tools, RMA products, and a journal. It was formerly known as Robert Morris Associates.

Society for Risk Analysis

1313 Dolley Madison Boulevard, Suite 402, McLean, Virginia, 22101
T: +1 703 790 1745
E: *sra@burkinc.com*
www.sra.org
Providing an open forum for those interested in risk analysis in its broadest sense, this organization devotes itself to risks of concern to individuals, the public and private sectors, and society in general. Membership is multidisciplinary and international.

Europe
Association of Insurance and Risk Managers

Lloyd's Avenue House, 6 Lloyd's Avenue, London, EC3N 3AX, U.K.
T: +44 (0) 20 7480 7610
F: +44 (0) 20 7702 3752
E: *enquiries@airmic.co.uk*
www.airmic.com
This membership organization, founded in 1963, brings together over 900 U.K. and overseas risk managers within industry, commerce, and the public sector. It offers a valuable source of contacts and practical operational support to its members, as well as assisting their self-development, technical awareness, and internal working relationships.

Business Continuity Institute

10 Southview Park, Marsack Street, Caversham, Berkshire, RG4 5AF, U.K.
T: +44 (0) 870 603 8783
F: +44 (0) 870 603 8761
E: *bci@thebci.org*
www.thebci.org
The BCI is a professional organization founded in 1994 to promote high standards of professional competence and ethics in the provision of business continuity planning and services. It has developed standards of competence, a code of ethics,

and an accreditation scheme for continuity practitioners. Additional activities include seminars, conferences, and the Business Continuity Awards. The organization has over 1,100 members in 32 countries.

Institute of Risk Management

David Ovenden, Acting Chief Executive
Lloyd's Avenue House, 6 Lloyd's Avenue, London, EC3N 3AX, U.K.
T: +44 (0) 20 7709 9808
F: +44 (0) 20 7709 0716
E: *enquiries@irmgt.co.uk*
www.theirm.org
Besides providing advice and consultation, this membership organization, founded in 1986, also runs educational courses and examinations in risk management, and undertakes research.

FOR MORE INFORMATION

- ℘ Contingency, Crisis, Disaster Management (pp. 1715–1717)
- ☆ Scenario Planning (pp. 334–335)
- ☆ Viewpoint: Peter L. Bernstein (pp. 168–169)
- ☆ Walking on the Leading Edge without Falling off the Cliff (pp. 277–278)
- ✔ Workplace Health : Undertaking a Risk Assessment (pp. 552–553)

"I am cautious about going against the herd. I am liable to be trampled on." George Soros

Selling and Salesmanship

BOOKS

Advanced Selling Strategies: The Proven System of Sales Ideas, Methods, and Techniques Used by Top Salespeople Everywhere

Brian Tracy
New York: Simon & Schuster, 1996
432pp ISBN: 0684824744
Based on the author's own career lessons, this book sets out to equip the reader with the attitude, techniques, and tactics needed to succeed in sales.

Clients Forever: How Your Clients Can Build Your Business for You

Doug Carter, Jenni Green
New York: McGraw-Hill, 2003
256pp ISBN: 007140256X
This book shows you how to build your business through solid, long-term relationships with your favorite kind of clients. It provides the know-how and confidence to focus your efforts on the people you most enjoy working with, generate better results with less effort, build relationships with clients, and develop an approach that accentuates your personal strengths.

Fast Forward MBA in Selling: Become a Self-motivated Profit Center—and Prosper

Joy J. D. Baldridge
Hoboken, New Jersey: Wiley, 2000
224pp (Fast Forward MBA)
ISBN: 0471348546
This is a comprehensive guide to becoming a successful salesperson. It explores a wide range of topics, including setting the standards for success, self-motivation, time management, getting and staying connected, preparation, technology, and successful sales calls.

Global Account Management: Creating Value

H. David Hennessey, Jean-Pierre Jeannet
Hoboken, New Jersey: Wiley, 2003
272pp ISBN: 0470848928
The globalization of many industries, it is suggested, has created a unique opportunity to interact with a client on a coordinated global basis. The handling of large global customers requires special expertise, systems, and organizational alignment. This book examines the key aspects of the practice of global account management and of developing and managing global customers, and illustrates these with case studies.

How to Become a Rainmaker: The Rules for Getting and Keeping Customers and Clients

Jeffrey J. Fox
New York: Hyperion, 2000
192pp ISBN: 0786865954
This book is written to assist in identifying, attracting and keeping customers. It identifies "rainmakers" (people who bring revenue into organizations), who may be C.E.O.s, owners, partners, sales representatives, or fundraisers. Jeffrey J. Fox explains how the reader can become a rainmaker, enabling him or her to attract more customers and rise above the competition in any company.

Improving Customer Satisfaction, Loyalty, and Profit: An Integrated Measurement and Management System

Michael D. Johnson, Anders Gustafsson
San Francisco, California: Jossey-Bass, 2000
144pp ISBN: 0787953105
By outlining in detail five key areas, this book offers ways to improve customer loyalty. By outlining key measures of customer satisfaction and giving suggestions for marketing strategy and product development, the book enables a more cohesive measurement and management system.

Key Account Management: A Complete Action Kit of Tools and Techniques for Achieving Profitable Key Supplier Status 3rd ed.

Peter Cheverton
London: Kogan Page, 2004
368pp ISBN: 0749441690
This comprehensive textbook takes a broad perspective on key account management (KAM), starting from the premise that it is not just to do with selling but with developing profitable relationships between customers and suppliers. Peter Cheverton starts by defining KAM and explains how to understand the customer's perspective, put in place the organizational systems and processes required, identify key accounts, develop management strategies, and meet customer needs. Advice on developing key account plans and keeping track of progress and examples of good and bad practice are provided throughout.

Key Account Management and Planning: The Comprehensive Handbook for Managing Your Company's Most Important Strategic Asset

Noel Capon
New York: Free Press, 2001
480pp ISBN: 074321188X
With a greater level of competition and increased costs of selling, the nature of the selling process has changed. Using research, real-life stories of successes and failures, and clarifying figures, the author presents his four-part "congruence model" of key account management. He explains: how to select the key account portfolio; how to manage key accounts; how to recruit, select, train, reward and retain key account managers, and how to formulate and execute key account strategies.

Marketing and Selling Professional Services: Practical Approaches to Practice Development 3rd ed.

Patrick Forsyth
London: Kogan Page, 2003
320pp ISBN: 0749440902
With the aim of helping professionals of all kinds to develop successful strategies for marketing what are essentially intangible services, the author starts by explaining the importance and role of marketing in professional service businesses, and goes on to explore a range of practical issues, including marketing planning, promotional mix, advertising, and postal promotion. A second section deals with professional personal selling, and covers persuasive writing and communication, and systematic client development.

The New Strategic Selling: The Unique Sales System Proven Successful by the World's Best Companies 2nd ed.

Stephen E. Heiman et al.
New York: Warner Books, 2005
448pp ISBN: 044669519X
Following the strategic selling process outlined in this book, the authors lay out an effective plan that leverages the key benefits of the sellers/buyers solution, and minimizes price as the principal buying criterion. The book provides a process for what successful sales people do consistently—plan.

"Be suspicious of your sincerity when you are the advocate of that upon which your livelihood depends."

John Lancaster Spalding

Rethinking the Sales Force: Redefining Selling to Create and Capture Customer Value

Neil Rackham, John R. De Vincentis
Maidenhead, United Kingdom: McGraw-Hill, 1999
320pp ISBN: 0071342532
Rackham and De Vincentis use real-world examples such as Microsoft, IBM, and Charles Schwab to demonstrate how the commercial viability of various products and services can be improved through determining the real needs of three different buyers—identified as "intrinsic value customers," "extrinsic value customers," and "strategic value customers"—and then developing the appropriate sales strategies to meet them.

The Sales Bible: The Ultimate Sales Resource 2nd ed.

Jeffrey H. Gitomer
London: William Morrow & Company, 2003
368pp ISBN: 0471456292
Designed as a book to be read by those within the sales industry, this book targets aspiring salesmen/women and gives them practical advice on how to reconsider and reevaluate the whole selling process. Fundamentally challenging prevailing perceptions, this text offers a comprehensive range of new ideas and strategies.

Sales Genius: A Master Class in Successful Selling

Tony Buzan, Richard Israel
Aldershot, United Kingdom: Gower Publishing, 2000
272pp ISBN: 0566082098
The authors present 12 traits that can be found in professional salespeople and 12 strategies that they deploy. They then create a program of activities based on these traits.

Sales Management: Concepts and Cases 8th ed.

Douglas J. Dalrymple, William L. Cron, Thomas E. DeCarlo
Hoboken, New Jersey: Wiley, 2003
624pp ISBN: 047123060X
This book includes theoretical discussions and case studies covering all aspects of sales management. The topics dealt with in its various sections are strategic planning and budgeting, personal selling, territory management, estimating potentials and forecasting sales, recruiting and selecting personnel, sales training, leadership, motivating salespeople, compensating salespeople, and evaluating performance.

Selling Dreams: How to Make Any Product Irresistible

Gian Luigi Longinotti-Buitoni
New York: Simon & Schuster, 1999
336pp ISBN: 0684850192
The author, who is president and C.E.O. of Ferrari North America, describes how companies can market their products and services by connecting with the imagination and aspirations of their customers. The principles of "dreamketing," or selling dreams, are outlined as they relate to the most unlikely products.

Selling from the Heart: The Total Success System for Mastering Business Relationships

Steven Lloyd
Arlington, Texas: Sterling & Pope, 2000
240pp ISBN: 0967861608
The main focus of the book is "emotional selling" but it also provides practical, hands-on advice on salesmanship. It covers topics including prospecting, sales presentations, customer relationships, follow-up, and building a career in sales.

Selling in a Week 3rd ed.

Christine Harvey
London: Hodder & Stoughton, 2002
96pp (Business in a Week)
ISBN: 0340849827
This is an introductory guide to both the skills and systems of selling. It covers organizational preparation, gaining product expertise, finding emotional motives, a three-part objection process, prospect action systems, overcoming roadblocks and price objections, and self-motivation.

The Seven Keys to Managing Strategic Accounts

Sallie Sherman, Joseph Sperry, Samuel Reese
Maidenhead, United Kingdom: McGraw-Hill, 2003
256pp ISBN: 0071417524
Offering market-proven strategies for generating competitive advantage by identifying and looking after your best customers, this book provides decision makers with a strategy for profitably managing their largest and most critical accounts.

Solution Selling: Creating Buyers in Difficult Selling Markets

Michael T. Bosworth
Maidenhead, United Kingdom: McGraw-Hill, 1994
224pp ISBN: 0786303158

This book describes a coherent framework for selling in almost any situation and is useful to anyone involved with sales at any level. As well as discussing strategies, situations, cases, and so on, it examines the role of the "seller" and tries to position him or her as the "buying facilitator."

SPIN Selling

Neil Rackham
Aldershot, United Kingdom: Gower Publishing, 1988
208pp ISBN: 0070511136
Practical, easy-to-use and easy-to-understand information on how to make selling easier for the salesperson. Based on extensive research, its direct and helpful advice may also be helpful in all other work situations.

The SPIN Selling Fieldbook: Practical Tools, Methods, Exercises and Resources

Neil Rackham
Maidenhead, United Kingdom: McGraw-Hill, 1996
208pp ISBN: 0070522359
Full of case studies and practical information, this book shows the reader how to put into practice the help and advice given in *SPIN Selling*.

Tough Calls: Selling Strategies to Win Over Your Most Difficult Customers

Josh Gordon
New York: AMACOM, 1997
224pp ISBN: 0814479251
Focusing on the challenges of difficult customers, the book outlines 20 different "tough sells" and strategies to counteract them. It provides advice on what to do and what not to do with customers who, for example, are incompetent, do not have buying authority, will not see you, buy elsewhere because of company politics, or like what you say but still don't buy.

The Ultimate Sales Letter: Boost Your Sales with Powerful Sales Letters 2nd ed.

Dan S. Kennedy, Daniel Kennedy
Holbrook, Massachusetts: Adams Media Corporation, 2000
224pp ISBN: 1580622577
This text provides clear examples to assist in writing focused sales letters that target specific customer bases. Tips and features include creating powerful headlines, improving readability, when to use bullet points, which font to use, and which demographics to target. All this is performed within 28 structured steps, and

"The only people in the whole world who can change things are those who can sell ideas."

Lois Wyse

should interest sales reps, business owners, and advertising people.

Why People Don't Buy Things: Five Proven Steps to Connect with Your Customers and Dramatically Increase Your Sales
Harry Washburn, Kim Wallace
Cambridge, Massachusetts: Perseus Books Group, 2000
208pp ISBN: 073820157X
The authors provide a methodical approach to understanding customers' motivations and show how to customize an entire sales strategy to customers' shopping patterns. In identifying different sales profiles, they reveal strategies to break out of unproductive patterns, create fresh relationships, and gain a loyal customer base.

Why We Buy: The Science of Shopping
Paco Underhill
New York: Touchstone Books, 2000
256pp ISBN: 0684849143
This book is filled with retail insights, revealing, for example, how men are starting to shop like women and how women have changed the way supermarkets are designed. Looking to the future, Underhill predicts huge retail opportunities concomitant with an ageing baby-boom population, and shows how online retailing will change shopping malls.

MAGAZINES
Sales and Marketing Management
ISSN: 0163–7517
VNU Business Publications
770 Broadway, New York, 10003–9595
T: +1 646 654 4500
F: +1 646 654 4480
www.vnubusinessmedia.com
This monthly magazine features articles, profiles, and interviews written for top executives who have direct responsibility for all aspects of sales, marketing, and management. Featured topics include case studies and marketing strategies from the world's most successful companies.

Sell!ng
Dartnell Corporation
Accounting Department, 360 Hiatt Drive, Palm Beach Gardens, Florida, 33418
T: +1 800 621 5463
F: +1 561 622 2423
www.dartnellcorp.com
This newsletter is published 12 times per year. Written for novice and experienced sales personnel, it offers tips and advice on

how to capture sales. The articles are written by expert salesmen with years of experience in closing the deal on buying decisions. Sales tactics in a variety of major industries are covered.

INTERNET
BestOfSales.com
www.bestofsales.com
A list of links to sales resources on the Internet is given on this site.

Just Sell
www.justsell.com
This site offers a selection of useful sales checklists and evaluation tools for sales professionals. Users must register to access the information, but registration is free.

Salesmanship
www.dmoz.org/Business/ Marketing_and_Advertising
Maintained as part of the Open Directory Project, this site contains a large list of other Web sites, each with a brief description, relating to all aspects of salesmanship.

SalesVault
www.salesvault.com
This site is aimed at professional salespeople. It also includes articles, news, and advice, and also advertises courses that users may wish to take up for a fee.

Selling Power
www.sellingpower.com
The online counterpart to *Selling Power* magazine, the site offers archived issues of the magazine, electronic newsletters on several sales-related topics, and advice on motivation and management. Much of the information on the site can be viewed by non-members, but to access other areas you will need to register. Registration is free.

ORGANIZATIONS
USA
Direct Selling Association (DSA)
1275 Pennsylvania Avenue NW, Suite 800, Washington, D.C., 20004
T: +1 202 347 8866
F: +1 202 347 0055
E: *info@dsa.org*
www.dsa.org
DSA is a trade association for firms that manufacture and distribute goods and services sold directly to consumers. It offers its members research services, a monthly newsletter, a resource guide, conferences, networking councils, legislative lobbying, and salesforce support.

National Association of Sales Professionals
8300 North Hayden Road, Suite 207, Scottsdale, Arizona, 85258
T: +1 480 951 4311
F: +1 480 483 2860
E: *info@nasp.cpm*
www.nasp.com
Founded in 1991, NASP states that its mission is to cater for the needs of salespersons, to help in their professional development in a changing field, and to upgrade the career status of those working in sales. It runs the Certified Professional SalesPerson program, and administers the International Registry of Accredited Salespersons.

Europe
Chartered Institute of Marketing (CIM)
Moor Hall, Cookham, Maidenhead, Berkshire, SL6 9QH, U.K.
T: +44 (0) 1628 427 370
F: +44 (0) 1628 427 369
www.cim.co.uk
The Institute of Professional Sales shares the same facilities, values, and objectives as the Chartered Institute of Marketing. Its vision is to raise the profile of sales professionals, gain recognition for them, and promote their interests, as well as to offer training, develop best practice, promote sales qualifications, and provide networking opportunities.

International
Sales and Marketing Executives International, Inc.
P.O. Box 1390, Sumas, Washington, D.C., 98295–1390
T: +1 312 893 0751
F: +1 604 855 0165
E: *smeihq@smei.org*
www.smei.org
SME International is a worldwide association of sales and marketing managers whose members are top executives. Founded in 1935, it provides education in both sales and management, along with workshops, newsletters, meetings, and discussions.

FOR MORE INFORMATION
☆ Managing the Customer (pp. 85–86)
୨୦ Marketing Management (pp. 1827–1832)
☆ Viewpoint: Patty Seybold (pp. 87–88)
☆ Viewpoint: Philip Kotler (pp. 61–62)

Small and Growing Businesses

BOOKS

101 Best Businesses to Start 3rd ed.
Philip Lief Group, Russell D. Roberts, Sharon Kahn
New York: Random House, 2000
720pp ISBN: 0767906594
This popular book offers helpful, practical advice on where to start if you are looking for a new business opportunity. Each of the businesses listed is described fully and entries include profit projections, information on costs, strategies for success, and assistance on planning staff requirements.

Beating the Odds in Small Business
Tom Culley
Upper Saddle River, New Jersey: Prentice Hall, 1998
320pp ISBN: 0684841835
This book is a survival manual for new businesses, and systematically explains and analyzes every key "survival priority" upon which the sustainability of a new business is dependent in the critical first years. The author shows how the odds can be turned in your favor by avoiding the distractions of chasing easy success in order to get rich quick, and instead focusing only on the harsh realities of the business jungle.

Business Development: A Guide to Small Business Strategy
David Butler
Woburn, Massachusetts: Butterworth-Heinemann, 2001
192pp ISBN: 0750652470
This book aims to help owner-managers of small businesses draw up a plan for the long-term future. The subjects covered include: reviewing performance, resource implications, sales and marketing strategy, market expansion, staffing, and financial performance. The standards for business development established by the Small Firms Enterprise Development Institute (SFEDI) are appended.

Business Planning: A Guide to Business Start-Up
David Butler
Woburn, Massachusetts: Butterworth-Heinemann, 2000
272pp ISBN: 075064706X
This book contains all the factual information required to produce a successful business plan for presentation to a potential source of finance or for use in an NVQ portfolio. It is in line with the major syllabuses for business start-up and can be used as a course guide for anyone completing a formal NVQ level 3 qualification in this area.

Capitalizing on Success
Neil Coade
Stamford, Connecticut: International Thomson Publishing, 2000
240pp (Smart Strategies)
ISBN: 1861527659
This book takes a practical approach to the process of business development. After discussing the stages of business growth, it considers the challenges that face emerging businesses that may prevent them from reaching their potential. As means of meeting those challenges, it stresses the importance of effective leadership, good management practice, and creative people able to move the business forward.

E-Business for the Small Business
John G. Fisher
London: Kogan Page, 2001
192pp (Business Enterprise Guide)
ISBN: 0749434791
E-business presents many new opportunities for businesses of all sizes. This guide takes owner-managers through the necessary steps for building a successful and sustainable e-business. It deals with finding the funds, getting the right equipment, setting up a Web site, legal issues, online marketing and advertising, business-to-business opportunities, and developing an e-business plan.

The E-Myth Revisited: Why Most Small Businesses Still Don't Work and What You Can Do About Yours 2nd ed.
Michael E. Gerber
New York: HarperCollins, 2005
288pp ISBN: 0060766611
First published in 1986, this best-selling book provides information and guidance on starting and maintaining a small business or franchise. "E-myth" stands for "entrepreneurial myth" and refers to Gerber's belief that entrepreneurs do not necessarily make good business people. The book shows the reader how to simplify the systems involved in running a business, and instead create an incredibly organized and regimented plan, so that the systems can more or less run themselves, freeing the entrepreneur's mind to focus on long-term strategy.

Enterprise and Small Business: Principles, Practice and Policy
Sara Carter, Dylan Jones-Evans
Upper Saddle River, New Jersey: Financial Times Prentice Hall, 2000
528pp ISBN: 0201398524
This book provides a comprehensive introduction to small businesses, covering the environment in which they operate, the nature of entrepreneurship, and the techniques of practical management. Its authors draw on the work of leading academics in the United Kingdom and Europe, and cover the latest thinking and research in the field.

Entrepreneur's Ultimate Start-up Directory
James Stephenson
Irvine, California: Entrepreneur Media, Inc., 2002
432pp ISBN: 1891984330
This book offers an extensive listing of business ideas, covering more than 1,300 potential start-ups across over 30 industries. It covers new and traditional business areas, including working from home and working via the Internet. Each entry is rated according to the following criteria: ease of start-up; estimated cost and potential income; possibility of exploiting the idea online; skills required; whether the start-up could be run part-time; and licensing/franchising opportunities.

Finding Your Perfect Work: The New Career Guide for Making a Living, Creating a Life
Paul Edwards, Sarah Edwards
New York: Penguin Putnam, Inc., 2003
480pp ISBN: 1585422169
This book is aimed at those in the crucial first phase of setting up a business: assessing yourself. Considering what you really want to do and get from your own business is explored in depth here, and the book contains worksheets to help readers pinpoint their own strengths, weaknesses, and goals.

1905

BUSINESS INFORMATION SOURCES

"It can take just as much effort to run a small company as a much larger one."

Barbara Thomas

Go It Alone: The Streetwise Secrets of Success

Geoff Burch
Chichester: Capstone, 2003
336pp ISBN: 1841124702
This easy-to-read, practical guide for those thinking of starting their own business is packed with anecdotal advice drawn from the author's wealth of experience in entrepreneurship and sales and conveyed in a style that is both original and humorous.

Growing a Private Company: Commercial Strategies for Building a Business Worth Millions

Ian Smith
London: Kogan Page, 2001
192pp ISBN: 0749432802
This book is aimed at owners of private companies and provides guidance on strategy, operational efficiency, growth techniques, venture capital, acquisitions, and exit options.

Growing Business Handbook 7th ed.

Richard Willsher, Adam Jolly, eds
London: Kogan Page, 2005
448pp ISBN: 074944424X
Designed to help businesses with an established market position, this handbook presents a range of practical strategies for managing growth. The contributors, who come from a variety of backgrounds, provide advice in areas including funding options, competition, managing the risks, making the most of IT, external relations, and competitive purchasing.

Growing Your Own Business: Growth Strategies for Meeting New Challenges and Maximizing Success

Gregory F. Kishel, Patricia Gunter Kishel
Lincoln, Nebraska: iUniverse, 2000
256pp ISBN: 0595147925
Focusing on the key decisions needed for creating and maintaining your business from start-up to maturity, this book offers information and guidance in areas such as planning, financing, team building, marketing, expansion, taxation, and transition.

ISO 9001:2000 for Small Businesses 3rd ed.

Ray Tricker
Woburn, Massachusetts: Butterworth-Heinemann, 2005
480pp ISBN: 075066617X
This book explains the requirements of the new ISO 9000:2000 standard and looks at how smaller companies can benefit from it

and set up their own quality management systems. Background information on ISO 9000 and the importance of quality control and quality assurance is provided.

Kick Start Your Dream Business: Getting It Started and Keeping You Going

Romanus Wolter
Berkeley, California: Ten Speed Press, 2001
304pp ISBN: 1580082513
This book contains practical advice for anyone thinking about starting a small business as well as supportive real-life examples of successful entrepreneurship.

Limited Company Guide

London: Law Pack, 2000
96pp ISBN: 1902646584
This guide aims to explain how to set up your own limited company. Valid in England, Scotland, and Wales, it describes the essential procedures and incorporates examples of forms from Companies House, Articles and Memoranda of Association, and directors' resolutions.

The Loyalty Effect: The Hidden Force Behind Growth, Profits, and Lasting Value

Frederick F. Reichheld
Boston, Massachusetts: Harvard Business School Press, 2001
352pp ISBN: 1578516870
Loyalty is not dead, and this book explains why, demonstrating the power of loyalty-based management as a profitable alternative to a constant flux of employees, investors, and customers.

Managing by the Numbers

Chuck Kremer, Ron Rizzuto, John Case
Cambridge, Massachusetts: Perseus Books Group, 2000
224pp ISBN: 0738202568
In this text, Chuck Kremer and Ron Rizzuto present a practical approach to reading financial statements and to managing the three core issues of business financial performance: net profit, operating cash-flow, and return on assets. The book features numerous exercises and examples (with associated templates available on the Web), a powerful new management tool known as "The Financial Scoreboard," and an extensive glossary.

Managing Difficult People: A Survival Guide for Handling Any Employee

Marilyn Pincus
Holbrook, Massachusetts: Adams Media Corporation, 2004
224pp ISBN: 1593371861

While you may have a marvelous business idea, you may not be the world's most confident manager, and as your business grows, that's something you'll need to work on. If you work with someone with a challenging personality, this book will help you find practical ways of dealing with them so that you can both get on with your job. Offering practical help on how to get a tricky situation back on track, this book profiles several different types of awkward colleagues, including the Bully, the Complainer, the Procrastinator, the Know-it-All, and the Silent Type.

The MouseDriver Chronicles

John Lusk, Kyle Harrison
Cambridge, Massachusetts: Perseus Books Group, 2003
272pp ISBN: 0738208019
Lusk and Harrison, MBA graduates, narrate their experiences of starting their own company, and the problems they encountered along the way. Their product was the MouseDriver, a computer mouse fashioned as a golf club head, which experienced mixed fortunes in a volatile technology market. Lusk and Harrison describe the events leading up to the product's conception, and how they managed to support it in a continually changing marketplace.

New Venture Adventure: Succeed with Professional Business Planning

Ueli Looser, Bruno Schlapfer, eds
New York: Texere Publishing, 2001
224pp ISBN: 1587990032
This manual, written by consultants from McKinsey, offers professional advice on starting up a business. The book opens with an overview of the stages a typical start-up company will go through and a consideration of what constitutes an attractive business idea. The main focus is on the preparation of a professional business plan, and an example of a business plan is provided. The book also covers the questions of how to value a start-up business and how to raise equity.

The Next Level: Essential Strategies for Achieving Breakthrough Growth

James B. Wood
Cambridge, Massachusetts: Perseus Books Group, 2000
224pp ISBN: 0738201596
An accessible guide to planning and managing the stages of company growth, *The Next Level* centers around the use of a powerful, field-tested diagnostic tool, the Inc. Growth Strategy Analysis. James Wood

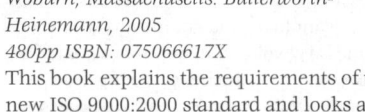

BUSINESS · INFORMATION SOURCES

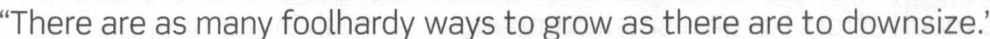
"There are as many foolhardy ways to grow as there are to downsize."   Gary Hamel

carefully shows entrepreneurs and established business leaders alike how to analyze their organization's growth potential, identify the key constraints to future growth, and put into practice the strategies that will enable them to arrive at new levels of expansion and profit generation.

The On-Purpose Business: Doing More of What You Do Best More Profitably

Kevin W. McCarthy

Colorado Springs, Colorado: Navpress Publishing Group, 2002

192pp ISBN: 1576833216

Written in a story format and with a spiritual backdrop, this book examines the principles of management and introduces the "On-Purpose" model, which focuses on all areas where each individual joins, belongs, and contributes to an organization.

Outsmarting Goliath: How to Achieve Equal Footing with Companies That Are Bigger, Richer, Older and Better Known

Debra Koontz Traverso

London: Kogan Page, 2000

224pp ISBN: 0749432985

The author presents practical advice on how to help small businesses present a professional image, produce high quality marketing materials, and win contracts that may seem out of reach for a small company. The book also outlines innovative ways to enhance company profile.

Patent It Yourself 11th ed.

David Pressman

Berkeley, California: Nolo Press, 2005

512pp ISBN: 1413301800

As an experienced patent attorney and former patent examiner of the U.S. Patent and Trademark Office, David Pressman has developed a very useful guide containing all the instructions and forms necessary to patent an invention in the United States. The book offers comprehensive and up-to-date advice for obtaining a high-quality patent and presents the information in a user-friendly, jargon-free, and well-illustrated way.

Setting Up a Limited Company 2nd ed.

Mark Fairweather, Rosy Border

London: The Stationery Office, 2004

160pp (Pocket Lawyer)

ISBN: 1859418570

This is a practical guide to the procedures for setting up a limited company in the United Kingdom. The text covers considering the options, roles and responsibilities, and completing the required forms. Sample letters, minutes, resolutions, and articles of association are included in the text and on disk. Listings of frequently asked questions and useful contacts are also provided.

Small Business Management 4th ed.

David Stokes

London: Thomson Financial (U.K.), 2002

432pp ISBN: 0826456790

This is a practical textbook, written by one of the most respected writers on small business in the United Kingdom.

Small Business Marketing Management

Ian Chaston, Terry Mangles

New York: Palgrave, 2002

272pp ISBN: 0333980751

This book is designed to give undergraduate and postgraduate students an understanding of the small business marketing process, including positioning, competitive advantage, product management, pricing, and distribution. The impact of e-commerce and the Internet, the marketing of services, and international marketing are also covered. The text is supported by real-life case studies and published research findings.

Small Time Operator: How to Start Your Own Business, Keep Your Books, Pay Your Taxes, and Stay Out of Trouble 7th ed.

Bernard B. Kamoroff

Willits, California: Bell Springs Publishing, 2004

208pp ISBN: 0917510224

Kamoroff presents the reader with the essentials of building a business, from obtaining initial permits and licenses, to seeking financing, locating the right business area, establishing an accounts and bookkeeping system, and taking on new staff. The text is continually updated in order to reflect the very latest thinking in tax and business management.

Spare Room Tycoon: Succeeding Independently—The 70 Lessons of Sane Self-Employment

James Chan

Naperville, Illinois: Nicholas Brealey Publishing, 2000

224pp ISBN: 1857882474

Written by a entrepreneur with over 20 years' experience of working from home, this book is aimed at anyone thinking of setting up a home-based business. It offers support and tips on how to avoid isolation and to spread the word about your business. The book focuses on "soft" skills, such as work–life balance, building confidence, and coping with the emotional demands of being your own boss, and offers reassuring anecdotal advice.

Start Up: An Entrepreneur's Guide to Launching and Managing a New Business 5th ed.

William J. Stolze

Franklin Lakes, New Jersey: Career Press, 1999

288pp ISBN: 1564144231

This book is aimed at those setting up or expanding a business, and is a practical guide to launching and managing a new enterprise. It includes various case studies and sample business plans.

Understanding the Small Family Business

Denise Fletcher, ed.

New York: Routledge, 2002

224pp ISBN: 0415250536

This book offers an overview of current research in the small family business sector, with the main focus on the relationship between work and family and the tensions and contradictions that can arise. The contributions are organized in three sections relating to rationality discourse, resource-based discourse, and critical discourse.

Unlocking the Value of Your Business: How to Increase It, Measure It, and Negotiate an Actual Sale Price–in Easy Step-by-step Terms

Thomas W. Horn

Fort Collins, Colorado: Charter Oak Press, 1999

272pp ISBN: 0875210163

This easy-to-follow book explains the factors that establish business value and how they fit together. It provides insights into the route your business should be taking in order to increase in value. The book also includes a glossary of terms which may be unfamiliar to some readers.

What No One Ever Tells You about Starting Your Own Business: Real Life Start-up Advice from 101 Successful Entrepreneurs

Jan Norman

Chicago, Illinois: Upstart Publishing, 2004

256pp ISBN: 0793185726

Drawing on the experience of, and mistakes made by, 100 businesspeople, this book contains helpful and practical advice on how to start your own business without headaches.

"A solid business must build on justice, fairness, and transparency."   Gaston Vizcarra

1907

BUSINESS INFORMATION SOURCES

Your First Business Plan: A Simple Question and Answer Format Designed to Help You Write Your Own Plan 4th ed.
Joseph Covello, Brian Hazelgren
Naperville, Illinois: Sourcebooks, 2002
160pp ISBN: 1402200021
This popular book contains practical advice on writing an impressive business plan, including useful information on the constituent parts of a business.

MAGAZINES

Entrepreneur
ISSN: 0163–3341
Entrepreneur Incorporated
2445 McCabe Way, Irvine, California, 92614
T: +1 949 261 2325
F: +1 949 261 0222
www.entrepreneur.com
This monthly magazine aims to give practical information to prospective entrepreneurs. It offers readers hands-on advice on many aspects of entrepreneurship, and covers the latest developments in technology, finance, management, and marketing. Products, services, and strategies are highlighted in order to help individuals run a better business, and readers can also learn from other entrepreneurs who have successfully improved their businesses.

Inc.
ISSN: 0162–8968
Gruner & Jahr U.S.A. Publishing
38 Commercial Wharf, Boston, Massachusetts, 02110–3883
T: +1 617 248 8000
F: +1 617 248 8090
www.inc.com
Inc. is a U.S. publication for entrepreneurs, and is published 14 times a year. The magazine provides advice, case studies, and overviews on the subject of small business in the United States, and also provides prospective entrepreneurs with resources and road-tested strategies for managing people, finance, sales, marketing, and technology. The magazine also looks at the personal aspects of the entrepreneurial lifestyle.

International Small Business Journal
ISSN: 0266–2426
Sage Publications
1 Oliver's Yard, 55 City Road, London, EC1Y 1SP, U.K.
T: +44 (0) 20 7324 8500
F: +44 (0) 20 7324 8600
www.sagepub.co.uk
The *ISBJ* is a quarterly journal that aims to provide a forum for the discussion and dissemination of views and research on the small business sector. It is intended for academics, policymakers, trade and business associations, and planning and development authorities.

Journal of Small Business and Enterprise Development
ISSN: 1462–6004
Emerald
44 Brattle Street, 4th Floor, Cambridge, Massachusetts, 02138
T: +1 888 622 0075
F: +1 617 354 6875
www.emeraldinsight.com
The *JSBED* is a peer-reviewed journal that disseminates research findings and best practice and aims to bridge the gap between theory and practice in the field of small business and enterprise development. The journal contains articles, case studies, and book reviews, and is aimed at those responsible for the management of SMEs, those who provide support and assistance to entrepreneurs and owner-managers, and those involved in the development of enterprise policy.

Journal of Small Business Management
ISSN: 0047–2778
Blackwell Publishing
350 Main Street, Malden, Massachusetts, 02148
T: +1 781 388 8200
F: +1 781 388 8232
www.blackwellpublishing.com
The *JSBM* is published for the International Council for Small Business and the Bureau of Business and Economic Research at West Virginia University College of Business and Economics. It is a quarterly refereed journal covering topics of interest to researchers and academics as well as practitioners. The journal is available on the Web at www.be.wvu.edu/serve/bureau/jsbm.

The Small Business Journal
Synergy Publishing Ltd.
407 Vine Street, Dept.189, Cincinnati, Ohio, 45202
T: +1 513 253 3332
F: +1 508 629 0599
www.tsbj.com
The *Journal* is a monthly magazine offering practical advice for small business owners.

INTERNET

Benchmark Index
www.benchmarkindex.com
Affiliated to Business Link, this Web site offers help and advice on benchmarking to businesses, advisors, and networks. It aims to help businesses understand their current position and effectively plan for the future.

BizMove.com
www.bizmove.com
This site, based in the United States, features the Small Business Knowledge Base, a range of free information resources for small businesses.

Business.com
www.business.com
This is an extensive and helpful search engine and directory site. The home page offers over 20 topics for users to research, including small businesses, accounting, law and computing. Search results are presented as a series of useful click-through links.

Business Owner's Toolkit
www.toolkit.cch.com
This site is packed with information for budding small business owners. Offering a series of brief guides to key aspects of starting up your own company, the site also features a selection of downloadable document templates, official government forms, and spreadsheet templates.

Inc.com
www.inc.com
Inc.com is the online version of the magazine *Inc*. The Web site provides information, products, services, and online tools—accumulated from a variety of sources—for many business or management tasks. This information has also been organized into categories to help users quickly find what they need.

IRS Small Business One Stop Resource
www.irs.gov/businesses/small/index.html
The U.S. government's Internal Revenue Service offers a broad range of tax resources for the self-employed and those running small businesses, including online workshops, forms, and publications. In addition to this, the IRS provides more general advice to those starting, operating, or closing a business, in the form of articles, checklists, tips, and extensive Web links to other sources of information and help.

SCORE
www.score.org
This site bills itself as "Counselors to America's Small Business," and is a nonprofit organization that aims to give free support and advice to entrepreneurs, both face-to-face and remotely (via e-mail).

"We learned from everyone else's book and added a few pages of our own." — Sam Walton

SCORE has a team of more than 10,500 retired and working volunteer advisors who offer guidance on a wide variety of issues, passing on the benefit of their business experience.

Welcome Business USA
www.welcomebiz.com

This site is an extensive online resource for entrepreneurs and those thinking of starting their own business. It has an alliance with SCORE, who provide a team of advisors that users can contact free. The Welcome Business site offers a variety of services, including a start-up checklist, free business counseling, information on business plans, and information on tax issues for small businesses.

ORGANIZATIONS
USA
National Business Association
Tom Sailors
P.O. Box 700728, Dallas, Texas, 75370
T: +1 800 456 0440 or 972 458 0900
F: +1 972 960 9149
E: *info@nationalbusiness.org*
www.nationalbusiness.org

Established in 1982, the National Business Association (NBA) is a nonprofit organization, designed and managed to assist the self-employed and small business community in achieving their professional goals. The NBA uses its group buying power to provide its members with support programs, cost- and time-saving products, services, and valuable small business resource materials.

National Federation of Independent Business
53 Century Boulevard, Suite 300, Nashville, Tennessee, 37214
T: +1 615 872 5800
F: +1 615 872 5353
www.nfib.org

The NFIB was founded by Wilson Harder in 1942. With 600,000 members it is the largest and probably the most influential small business lobbying group in the United States. It represents the interests of small business owners at national and state government levels and provides a range of services for its members.

Small Business Administration
200 North College Street, Suite A-2015, Charlotte, North Carolina, 28202
T: +1 704 344 6563
F: +1 704 344 6769
E: *answerdesk@sba.gov*
www.sbaonline.sba.gov

The Small Business Administration was set up by the U.S. government in 1953 to provide assistance to those starting and running their own businesses. It provides training, financial support, and advice through a network of offices in every state.

Europe
British Chambers of Commerce
65 Petty France, London, SW1H 9EU, U.K.
T: +44 (0) 20 7654 5800
F: +44 (0) 20 7654 5819
E: *info@britishchambers.org.uk*
www.chamberonline.co.uk

This is an umbrella body for a national network of chambers of commerce serving local businesses and providing advice on exporting and export services to member companies.

Institute of Business Advisers
Response House, Queen Street North, Chesterfield, S41 9AB, U.K.
T: +44 (0) 1246 453 322
F: +44 (0) 1246 453 300
E: *info@iba.org.uk*
www.iba.org.uk

The IBA is a nonprofit organization which aims to help small firms throughout the United Kingdom and Ireland. It has over 2,000 members who provide advice, training, and counseling for clients so that their businesses become more effective and thus more profitable.

International
International Council for Small Business
Jefferson Smurfit Center for Entrepreneurial Studies, St. Louis University, 3674 Lindell Boulevard, St. Louis, Missouri, 63108
T: +1 314 977 3628
F: +1 314 977 3627
E: *icsb@slu.edu*
www.icsb.org

The ICSB works to increase awareness and understanding of the role of small and medium businesses worldwide through education, research, publications, management development programs, conferences, and an international exchange program. Its membership includes educators, small business owners, consultants and advisers, government officials, and trade and business associations. It also publishes the *Journal of Small Business Management*, a bulletin, a newsletter, research papers, and conference proceedings.

World Association for Small and Medium Enterprises
Plot No. 4, Sector 16A, Noida, Uttar Pradesh, 201301, India
T: +91 118 451 5238
F: +91 118 451 5243
E: *wasme@vsnl.com*
www.wasmeinfo.org

WASME was founded in 1980 in New Delhi, India with the aim of providing support and advice to SMEs internationally and has members and associates in 112 countries. The organization promotes technology transfer, joint ventures and cooperation between SMEs in industrialized, developing, and least-developed countries. It has set up a Technology and Trade Promotion Exchange Center (TPX) and an International Committee for Rural Industrialization (ICRI). WASME has consultative status with the Economic and Social Council of the United Nations and other UN bodies.

1909

FOR MORE INFORMATION
☆ Avoiding the Mistakes of the Past: Lessons from the Startup World (pp. 164–165)
✓ Cash flow for the Small Business (pp. 582–583)
🐭 Entrepreneurs (pp. 1745–1747)

BUSINESS INFORMATION SOURCES

"Success in more a function of consistent common sense than it is of genius." — An Wang

Social Responsibility of Management

BOOKS

The Answer to How Is Yes: Acting on What Matters

Peter Block
San Francisco, California: Berrett-Koehler, 2003
208pp ISBN: 1576752712

The preponderance of the "how?" question in society, Block claims, is symptomatic of people living in accordance with an ethic of defense. We must strive to reclaim both our liberty and autonomy that have been radically sequestered from us. This position is to be attained for workers and managers by encouraging them to act on what they know, confronting passivity, and promoting a life where we can choose accountability and demand more compelling purpose from our work.

Beyond the Bottom Line: Putting Social Responsibility to Work for Your Business and the World

Joel Makower
Carmichael, California: Touchstone Books, 1995
336pp ISBN: 0684813106

Using case studies as examples, the book offers practical advice on socially responsible actions companies can take that will improve their bottom line. Based on the experiences of the organization called Business for Social Responsibility, it covers topics including workplace diversity, community involvement, work-family balance, employee empowerment and training, and environmental issues.

Building Public Trust: The Future of Corporate Reporting

Samuel A. Di Piazza, Robert G. Eccles
Hoboken, New Jersey: Wiley, 2002
192pp ISBN: 0471261513

In response to the global crisis in corporate reporting and its associated fallout, the authors offer their recommendations for addressing the increased levels of accountability, transparency, and integrity that are necessary in order to rebuild public trust. A three-tier model for corporate reporting is proposed that encompasses GAAP, industry standards, and company-specific information into a framework, which in turn feeds into new enabling technologies such as the Internet that will assist and accelerate the process.

Business and Society: Ethics and Stakeholder Management 6th ed.

Archie B. Carroll
Cincinnati, Ohio: South-Western College Publishing, 2005
768pp ISBN: 0324225814

Though the book is intended as a textbook, its managerial perspective makes it relevant for businesspeople as well. It uses case studies to illustrate relationships between business and society stakeholders and emphasizes ethical considerations in decision making.

Business as Unusual

Anita Roddick
Anita Roddick Publishing, 2005
304pp ISBN: 0954395956

This book contains the ideas for the philosophy of Anita Roddick's Body Shop chain, detailing the unique ethos of the company, which is to maintain an operation that can be at once profitable whilst not harming the environment or violating human rights.

Citizen Brands: Putting Society at the Heart of Your Business 2nd ed.

Michael Willmott
Hoboken, New Jersey: Wiley, 2003
272pp ISBN: 0470853581

"Citizen Brands" reflects on the need for organizations to demonstrate corporate social responsibility. The book develops this concept further, evolving the idea of corporate citizenship, the practice of which should make a business more successful.

Corporate Community Relations: The Principle of the Neighbor of Choice

Edmund M. Burke
Westport, Connecticut: Praeger, 1999
208pp ISBN: 027596471X

The author argues that businesses must be socially aware and gain the trust and respect of the community in which they operate. Positive strategies and policies with respect to environmental awareness and community relations can offer greater economic opportunities and attract both consumers and employees. He considers the key goals and steps required for these strategies.

Counting What Counts: Turning Corporate Accountability to Competitive Advantage

Bill Birchard, Marc J. Epstein
Cambridge, Massachusetts: Perseus Books Group, 2000
320pp ISBN: 0738203130

Fraud, tax evasion etc. are what the authors of this book identify as practices which obstruct managers from working efficiently. The text argues that managers should adopt the ethic of accountability, and succeed by becoming responsive and responsible. Using over 25 years of research and the experiences of a number of managers, Epstein and Birchard show that managers frequently overlook accountability and are in need of reform.

The Emperor's Nightingale

Robert A. G. Monks
Cambridge, Massachusetts: Perseus Books Group, 1999
288pp ISBN: 0738201332

Monks points to the need for a social conscience in a society eaten up by public companies, management consultants, and short-term thinking. Lamenting corporate lawlessness manifest in waste dumps to tax evasion, Monks vocalizes the other side of capitalist society, pointing to a more controlled, tamed market model.

The End of Shareholder Value

Allan Kennedy
New York: Texere Publishing, 2001
256pp ISBN: 0738204846

The main premise of Kennedy's argument is that the shareholder value ethic has signally failed to produce anything of lasting value, with the result that the future of the company as we know it is under threat. The book outlines three eras of business evolution, from the family enterprises of the 19th century to the entrepreneurs of high technology, often unfavorably, and ends with Kennedy's proposed remedies to create real, sustainable wealth for all of a company's stakeholder groups, not just the stockholders.

1910

BUSINESS INFORMATION SOURCES

"Companies have to be socially responsible or the shareholders pay eventually."

Warren Shaw

     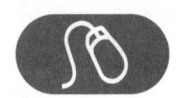

The Heroic Enterprise: Business and the Common Good

John Hood
New York: Free Press, 2005
272pp ISBN: 1587982463
Attacking the common assertion that businesses necessarily neglect the public good at the expense of short-term profits, Hood demonstrates numerous examples of how business works to enhance the wider social good. Detailing actual examples of this happening in today's world, Hood reveals how inner-city areas have been regenerated, and how the environment, workplace, and education have all been reformed in line with business initiatives.

Perspectives on Corporate Citizenship

Jorg Andriof, Malcolm McIntosh
Sheffield, United Kingdom: Greenleaf Publishing, 2001
336pp ISBN: 187471939X
Corporate citizenship is seen as one of the big issues of the 21st century. This book introduces the concept of corporate citizenship and explains the need for a fuller understanding of its impact. This collection of articles on corporate citizenship is divided into three broad sections: the evolution, context and concepts of corporate citizens; stakeholder engagement; and social accountability.

The Sustainable Company

Chris Laszlo
Washington, D.C.: Island Press, 2003
224pp ISBN: 1559638362
Leading corporations are recognizing the changing role and expectations of business in the 21st century and the competitive advantage that can be gained in addressing the problems and challenges concerned. The gap between the interests of business and those of society and the environment have created a "triple bottom line" within organizations, resulting from associated yet conflicting sets of performance measures. This book aims to go beyond the triple bottom line. It aims to bridge the gap between shareholder concerns and stakeholder expectations, and presents an integrative business paradigm for both.

Take It Personally: How to Make Conscious Choices to Change the World

Anita Roddick
Berkeley, California: Publishers Group West, 2001
224pp ISBN: 1573247073
Like Naomi Klein, Roddick points to the need to concentrate on business

accountability, focusing on human rights violations, environmental issues, the treatment of the developing world, and the growth of global markets. She forces her reader to ask the question: Who really controls the world—business or government?

Value Shift: Why Companies Must Merge Social and Financial Imperatives to Achieve Superior Performance

Lynn Sharp Paine
New York: McGraw-Hill, 2003
304pp ISBN: 0071382399
This book argues the case for a new style of management that will align company performance with today's ethical standards. It argues that there is now a dichotomy between traditional management and the expectations of business in contemporary society. Acknowledging it is no longer enough simply to produce goods and services and create wealth, the author discusses today's corporate leaders' need to make a shift in management values to incorporate high ethical standards along with strong financial results.

What Matters Most: Business, Social Responsibility and the End of the Era of Greed

Jeffrey Hollender, Stephen Fenichell
London: Random House, 2004
320pp ISBN: 1844133966
Jeffrey Hollender, C.E.O. of Seventh Generation, a world leader in manufacturing environmentally friendly household products, is a frequent commentator on corporate responsibility. This book, which he has co-authored with Stephen Fenichell, puts forward an approach to corporate strategy that is designed to help integrate concerns related to social responsibility into an organization's culture, systems, and activities.

When Good Companies Do Bad Things: Responsibility and Risk in an Age of Globalization

Peter Schwartz, Blair Gibb
Hoboken, New Jersey: Wiley, 1999
208pp ISBN: 0471323322
This book sets out to show how essential social responsibility is to the success of corporations in today's globalized economy. Illustrating their argument with case studies of large multinationals, the authors demonstrate how corporations make poor choices, exposing themselves to huge

financial risks and potential loss of reputation. They also explain, however, how corporations can learn from their mistakes and turn social value into business value.

INTERNET
Business Ethics
www.business-ethics.com
The online counterpart to *Business Ethics* magazine, the site offers articles, news, an events calendar, a marketplace, and a free e-mail newsletter.

Business for Social Responsibility
www.bsr.org
Sponsored by a membership organization, the site offers news, articles, a membership directory, conference and events information, and job listings.

The Corporate Social Responsibility Newswire
www.csrwire.com
This content-rich site bills itself as "the leading source of corporate responsibility and sustainability, press releases, reports, and news." It features CSR press releases, reports, an events calendar, useful resources (including an organization directory), and book recommendations.

ORGANIZATIONS
USA
Center for Corporate Citizenship at Boston College
Wallace E. Carroll School of Management, 55 Lee Road, Chestnut Hill, Massachusetts, 02467–3942
T: +1 617 552 4545
F: +1 617 552 8499
E: *ccc@bc.edu*
www.bc.edu/bc_org/avp/csom/ccc
This membership organization was founded in 1985 to establish corporate citizenship as a business essential. It offers executive education, particularly the certificate program in community relations. It arranges conferences, meetings, and discussions, encourages research, oversees the standards of excellence and their companion diagnostic tools, and provides consulting services.

Europe
AccountAbility
Unit A, 137 Shepherdess Walk, London, N1 7RQ, U.K.
T: +44 (0) 20 7549 0400
F: +44 (0) 20 7253 7440
E: *secretariat@accountability.org.uk*
www.accountability.org.uk

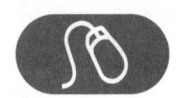
1911

BUSINESS INFORMATION SOURCES

"Ambivalence about family responsibilities has a long history in the corporate world."

Rosabeth Moss Kanter

Founded in 1996 as an international membership organization with the aim of improving the accountability and performance of organizations worldwide, AccountAbility (full name: the Institute of Social and Ethical Accountability) promotes best practice and ethical accounting, auditing, and reporting, and develops standards and certification for professionals in the field.

Corporate Social Responsibility (CSR) Europe
78–80 rue Defacqz, Brussels, B-1050, Belgium
T: +32 2 502 83 54
F: +32 2 502 84 58
E: *info@csreurope.org*
www.csreurope.org
CSR Europe helps companies achieve profitability, sustainable growth, and human progress by placing corporate social responsibility in the mainstream of business practice. It provides printed and online publications, best practices and tools, learning, benchmarking, and tailored capacity building programs.

The Prince of Wales International Business Leaders Forum (IBLF)
15–16 Cornwall Terrace, Regent's Park, London, NW1 4QP, U.K.
T: +44 (0) 20 7467 3600
F: +44 (0) 20 7467 3610
E: *info@iblf.org*
www.csrforum.com
This nonprofit membership organization was established in 1990 by HRH The Prince of Wales and a group of C.E.O.s from international companies to promote corporate social responsibility (CSR). CSR business practices are based on ethical values to help achieve socially, economically, and environmentally sustainable development.

International
Business for Social Responsibility (BSR)
609 Mission Street, 2nd Floor, San Francisco, California, 94105–3506
T: +1 415 537 0888
F: +1 415 537 0889
www.bsr.org
BSR is a global resource for companies seeking to sustain commercial success in ways that demonstrate respect for ethical values, people, communities, and the environment. It offers products and services that address the full range of corporate social responsibility issues, including audits and accountability, community economic development, community involvement, the environment, ethics, governance, human rights, the marketplace, and the workplace.

1912

BUSINESS INFORMATION SOURCES

FOR MORE INFORMATION

"You can eat an elephant one bit at a time ."

Mary-Kay Ash

     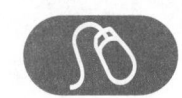

Stress and Stress Management

BOOKS

Getting Things Done: The Art of Stress-free Productivity
David Allen
New York: Penguin, 2002
288pp ISBN: 0142000280
Based on the notion that productivity is proportional to your ability to handle projects in a relaxed manner, the author offers solutions to self-management that minimize stress and enhance one's focus and efficiency. *Getting Things Done* offers a system which consigns all those must-dos clogging your brain into a framework of files and action lists—all with the intention of freeing your mind to focus on whatever you're working on now.

How to Stop Worrying and Start Living
Dale Carnegie
New York: Pocket Books, 1990
368pp ISBN: 0671733354
A classic title geared to helping people cut down on the stress and worry in their lives. The book is full of examples of how individuals can combat worry in a number of situations and ultimately gain more confidence and peace of mind.

Instant Stress Management
Brian Clegg
London: Kogan Page, 2000
128pp ISBN: 0749431164
A book of quick, easy-to-use exercises to help individuals to reduce their stress. Three introductory sections discuss stress, where it comes from, medical aspects of stress, and controlling stress. A brief exercise section then focuses on assessment, before the main part of the book concentrates on de-stressing exercises. A final section gives further reading and examples of relaxational music.

The One-minute Meditator: Relieving Stress and Finding Meaning in Everyday Life
Bill Birchard, David A. Nichol
Cambridge, Massachusetts: Perseus Books Group, 2001
176pp ISBN: 0738203785
This is a guide to why and how to meditate in short periods of time. Instead of relieving stress through temporary distractions, *The One-minute Meditator* teaches readers how to quiet their thoughts from within, reaping considerable physical and emotional benefits. The authors demonstrate that it's possible to meditate at any time and in any place—while walking to the office, waiting in queues, holding on the phone, or attempting to go to sleep.

Strategic Stress Management: An Organizational Approach
Valerie J. Sutherland, Cary L. Cooper
Basingstoke, United Kingdom: Palgrave Macmillan, 2000
272pp ISBN: 0333774876
Written for senior managers and personnel or occupational health strategists, this text addresses ways to maximise performance and workforce health by using an integrated strategy for managing stress. Areas covered include the stress litigation process at work, the nature of stress, "hot spot" stressors within specific occupational groups, the roles of change and new technology as potential sources of stress, stress auditing, and proactive stress management intervention options.

Time Management from the Inside Out 2nd ed.
Julie Morgenstern
New York: Henry Holt and Company, 2004
304pp ISBN: 0805075909
A thorough, accessible guide to creating a time management system that works for you and your personal situation. The author sets out to give sound advice that can be customized across a range of lifestyles.

MAGAZINES

International Journal of Stress and Stress Management
ISSN: 1072–5245
Springer
Customer Service Department, P.O. Box 358, Dordrecht, 3300 AA, The Netherlands
T: +31 78 657 6392
F: +31 78 657 6474
www.springerlink.com
The *International Journal of Stress and Stress Management*, a quarterly, publishes studies and theoretical essays from the broad field of stress management. and aims to give information about recent developments and innovations in the field. It is the official publication of the International Stress Management Association.

Stress News
International Stress Management Association, U.K. (ISMA U.K.)
P.O. Box 348, Waltham Cross, London, EN8 8ZL, U.K.
T: +44 (0) 7000 780 430
F: +44 (0) 1992 426 673
www.isma.org.uk
Stress News is published four times a year and is the journal of the U.K. branch of the International Stress Management Association. It is free to members and available on subscription to others. Sample articles can be viewed on the ISMA U.K. Web site.

Work and Stress
Taylor & Francis
325 Chestnut St., Suite 800, Philadelphia, Pennsylvania 19106
T: +1 800 354 1420
F: +1 215 625 2940
www.tandf.co.uk
Work and Stress, published in association with the European Academy of Occupational Health Psychology, is an international, multi-disciplinary quarterly journal. It offers refereed academic papers relating to stress, health and safety, and performance. It aims to cover psychological, social, organizational, and policy issues in relation to the nature of stress and its management.

INTERNET
Mind Tools
www.mindtools.com/smpage.html
This site offers practical advice for many people affected by stress, including sufferers, professional carers, and HR departments. It offers useful information on how to identify the causes of stress, understand it, and tackle it. There are also links to other sources of help.

Stress Cure
www.stresscure.com
Together with information relating to the specific stress coping methods of Dr. Mort Orman, this site also provides general information and resources relating to stress management. There are requests for registration linked to access for various parts of this site.

Stress Inc.—The Commerce of Coping
www.jrn.columbia.edu/stress
Created by the Columbia University

"For workaholics, all the eggs of self-esteem are in the basket of work." Judith M. Bardwick

Graduate School of Journalism, this site describes how stress has changed over the years and what it means today. Set up like a game board, viewers progress through such areas as ergonomics, publishing, consulting, a stress quiz, and more.

ORGANIZATIONS
USA
American Academy of Experts in Traumatic Stress

308 Veterans Memorial Highway, Commack, New York, 11725
T: +1 631 543 2217
F: +1 631 543 6977
www.aaets.org
A multidisciplinary network of international professionals that aims to increase awareness of the effects of traumatic events and improve the quality of interventions to support survivors. It holds an international register of stress management and traumatic stress experts, and offers membership and related publications, courses, and qualifications for over 200 professions in the health, emergency, criminal justice, forensics, law, and educational fields.

American Institute of Stress

124 Park Avenue, Yonkers, New York, 10703
T: +1 914 963 1200
F: +1 914 965 6267
E: *stress124@earthlink.net*
www.stress.org

This nonprofit organization was founded in 1978 as a clearing house for information on stress and related subjects. It maintains a library of information, coconducts an annual International Montreux Congress on Stress, provides a consultancy referral service, and produces a monthly newsletter, *Health and Stress*, reporting on stress research and linked health matters.

Europe
Centre for Stress Management

156 Westcombe Hill, Blackheath, London, SE3 7DH, U.K.
T: +44 (0) 20 8318 5653
F: +44 (0) 20 8297 5656
www.managingstress.com
A commercial training center and consultancy offering courses, counseling, coaching, and workplace stress audits and interventions. The center produces an online newsletter from which free articles and books can be downloaded.

European Academy of Occupational Health Psychology (EA-OHP)

c/o Institute of Work, Health & Organisations (I-WHO), Nottingham University Business School, Nottingham, Nottinghamshire, NG8 1BB, U.K.
T: +44 (0) 115 846 6664
F: +44 (0) 115 846 6625
E: *membership:ea-ohp.org*
www.ea-ohp.org

A membership organization established to develop and promote occupational health psychology in Europe. Members receive a discounted subscription to the *Work and Stress* quarterly journal, an Academy newsletter, and reduced registration rates for EA-OHP conferences and meetings.

International Stress Management Association, U.K. (ISMA U.K.)

P.O. Box 348, Waltham Cross, London, EN8 8ZL, U.K.
T: +44 (0) 7000 780 430
F: +44 (0) 1992 426 673
E: *stress@isma.org.uk*
www.isma.org.uk
This U.K. branch of the Internet-linked International Stress Management Association is a registered charity which aims to promote knowledge and best practice in the prevention and reduction of human stress. It has a multi-disciplinary professional membership, it sets professional standards for those using the services of members, and its provisions include conferences and events, publications, Web links, information, and a newsletter called *Stress News*.

FOR MORE INFORMATION

☆ Preventing Your Work Problems from Causing You Stress (pp. 402–403)

1914

BUSINESS INFORMATION SOURCES

Taxation

BOOKS

The Encyclopedia of Taxation and Tax Policy
Joseph J. Cordes et al.
Washington, D.C.: Urban Institute Press, 1999
468pp ISBN: 0877666822
A compilation of 200 essays on a broad array of topics including tax administration, evasion and avoidance, and the fundamentals of equity and efficiency. The primary emphasis is on issues relating to the development, administration, and evaluation of tax policy.

Zurich Tax Handbook 2005/2006
Tony Foreman, ed.
Englewood Cliffs, New Jersey: Prentice Hall, 2005
720pp ISBN: 027370592X
This comprehensive guide to the tax system in the United Kingdom offers practical advice to the individual on managing his or her tax affairs, including self-assessment and completion of the tax return, dealing with HM Revenue and Customs, stakeholder pensions, and employee share schemes.

MAGAZINES

National Tax Journal
ISSN: 0028–0283
National Tax Association
725 15th Street NW, Suite 600, Washington, D.C., 20005–2109
T: +1 202 737 3325
F: +1 202 737 7308
www.ntanet.org
The quarterly journal of the National Tax Association.

State Tax Notes
ISSN: 1057–8404
Tax Analysts
6830 North Fairfax Drive, Arlington, Virginia, 22213
T: +1 800 955 3444
F: +1 703 533 4484
This newsletter is similar to *Tax Notes*, but with a state-level focus.

State Tax Review
ISSN: 0162–1750
CCH, Inc.
4025 West Peterson Avenue, Chicago, Illinois, 60646–6085
T: +1 800 525 3353
F: +1 773 866 3895
www.cch.com
A weekly newsletter, the periodical companion to the yearly CCH state tax handbooks, it features up-to-date information on state tax policy developments.

Tax Administrators News
ISSN: 0039–9949
Federation of Tax Administrators
444 North Capitol Street NW, Suite 348, Washington, D.C., 20001
T: +1 202 624 5890
F: +1 202 624 7888
www.taxadmin.org
This is a monthly compendium of information and analysis focused on state taxation.

Taxes: The Tax Magazine
ISSN: 0040–0181
CCH, Inc.
4025 West Peterson Avenue, Chicago, Illinois, 60646–6085
T: +1 800 525 3353
F: +1 773 866 3895
www.cch.com
Covers state and federal taxation in legal, accounting, and economic terms.

Tax Notes
ISSN: 0270–5494
Tax Analysts
6830 North Fairfax Drive, Arlington, Virginia, 22213
T: +1 800 955 3444
F: +1 703 533 4484
This is a weekly newsletter providing late-breaking information on all aspects of federal taxation in the United States. Its features include in-depth economic analysis and reports from the executive, legislative, and judicial branches regarding U.S. tax policy.

INTERNET

1040.com
www.1040.com
Self-billed as the "one-stop tax source", this site provides links to finding state and federal tax forms. It also has a newsroom containing the latest tax news stories.

CCH Incorporated
www.cch.com
CCH are the publishers of numerous books

and journals on taxation, including the *Journal of Taxation of Global Transactions*. Their Web site provides links to numerous CCH information sources, mostly available for a fee.

Internal Revenue Service
www.irs.com
The IRS Web site offers downloadable income tax forms, instructions on filing taxes, and information on U.S. regulations and laws. It also features an electronic filing center.

Tax Analysts
www.tax.org
Tax Analysts, publishers of *Tax Notes Today* and *State Tax Today*, provide continuously updated tax news wire, a variety of interesting links, and weekly federal, state, and international feature articles on their Web site.

Tax and Accounting Sites Directory
www.taxsites.com
This site provides an international gateway to country-specific tax and accounting resources on the Web. It has a U.S. bias.

ORGANIZATIONS
USA

Federation of Tax Administrators
444 North Capitol Street NW, Suite 348, Washington, D.C., 20001
T: +1 202 624 5890
F: +1 202 624 7888
E: *webmaster@taxadmin.org*
www.taxadmin.org
This is the primary organization for state-level tax policy administrators. Its Web site provides links to each state's tax department.

Institute for Professionals in Taxation
3350 Peachtree Road NE, Suite 280, Atlanta, Georgia, 30326
T: +1 404 240 2300
F: +1 404 240 2315
E: *ipt@ipt.org*
www.ipt.org
This is a business organization focusing on property taxes and sales and use taxes.

Internal Revenue Service
1111 Constitution Avenue NW, Washington, D.C., 20224
T: +1 800 829 1040
www.irs.gov

1915

BUSINESS INFORMATION SOURCES

"The hardest thing in the world to understand is income tax."   Albert Einstein

The Internal Revenue Service is the official source for information on U.S. federal taxation. It offers downloadable income tax forms, instructions on filing taxes, and information on U.S. regulations and laws. It also features an electronic filing center.

Multistate Tax Commission

444 North Capitol Street NW, Suite 425, Washington, D.C., 20001
T: +1 202 624 8699
F: +1 202 624 8819
E: *mtc@mtc.gov*
www.mtc.gov
This organization consists of an alliance of representatives from 45 states dedicated, among other things, to the adoption of uniform state tax policies toward multinational firms.

National Association of Tax Professionals

720 Association Drive, Appleton, Wisconsin, 54914–1483
T: +1 800 558 3402
F: +1 800 747 0001
E: *natp@natptax.com*
www.natptax.com
This organization provides continuing professional education for tax professionals. It consists primarily of accountants, tax agents, lawyers, and financial planners.

National Tax Association

725 15th Street NW, Suite 600, Washington, D.C., 20005–2109
T: +1 202 737 3325
F: +1 202 737 7308

E: *natltax@aol.com*
www.ntanet.org
NTA was founded in 1907 and is the leading association of tax professionals in the United States. It aims to promote the study and discussion of tax theory, practice, and policy. Members of NTA come from the public, government, corporate, and academic sectors. The Association runs a national conference and a spring symposium and publishes the *National Tax Journal* and a newsletter called *NTA Forum*.

Europe
Chartered Institute of Taxation

12 Upper Belgrave Street, London, SW1X 8BB, U.K.
T: +44 (0) 20 7235 9381
F: +44 (0) 20 7235 2562
E: *post@ciot.org.uk*
www.tax.org.uk
As the senior professional body in the United Kingdom concerned solely with all aspects of taxation, the Chartered Institute of Taxation aims to advance public education in, and promote the study of, the administration and practice of taxation. It has nearly 12,000 members encompassing the professions and many occupations in industry, commerce, the public sector, and the taxation authorities. Membership is by examination and members have the practicing title of "Chartered Tax Adviser."

Institute of Chartered Accountants in England and Wales (ICAEW)

Chartered Accountants' Hall, P.O. Box 433,

Moorgate Place, London, EC2P 2BJ, U.K.
T: +44 (0) 20 7920 8100
F: +44 (0) 20 7920 0547
www.icaew.co.uk
This, the largest professional accountancy organization in Europe with over 120,000 members, is responsible for educating and training chartered accountants and maintaining standards of professional conduct among its members.

International
International Bureau for Fiscal Documentation (IBFD)

P.O. Box 20237, Amsterdam, 1000 HE, The Netherlands
T: +31 20 554 0100
F: +31 20 622 8658
E: *info@ibfd.com*
www.ibfd.nl
IBFD is an independent nonprofit research and educational foundation, established in the Netherlands in 1938 by the founders of the International Fiscal Association. It aims to research and disseminate information in the fields of international and comparative taxation.

FOR MORE INFORMATION

"Taxes are a barrier to progress, and they punish rather than reward success."

Steve Forbes

Teams and Team Building

BOOKS

The 17 Indisputable Laws of Teamwork
John C. Maxwell
New York: Thomas Nelson, 2003
256pp ISBN: 0785274340
A prescriptive popular guide to teambuilding, with lots of practical anecdotes.

Beyond the Team
R. Meredith Belbin
Woburn, Massachusetts: Butterworth-Heinemann, 2000
128pp ISBN: 0750646411
The author develops his thinking on teams and teamwork, taking a broader view of the place of the team within the organization. He defines the differences between teams and groups, and outlines a system of color coding to describe work tasks and roles. The book also considers ways in which more effective teamworking can be developed within organizations.

The Discipline of Teams: A Mindbook-Workbook for Delivering Small Group Performance
Jon R. Katzenbach, Douglas K. Smith
Hoboken, New Jersey: Wiley, 2001
256pp ISBN: 047138254X
This book is an indispensable guide to how to build effective teams and when to use them. It offers a detailed explanation of what is necessary to transform a group of people working together into a cohesive team. It also divides work groups into two basic types, the single-leader discipline and the team discipline, and explains how and why the two types should be balanced.

How to Build a Great Team 3rd ed.
Ros Jay
Upper Saddle River, New Jersey: Financial Times Prentice Hall, 2002
176pp ISBN: 0273663232
This practical guide is designed to help managers to select the right people for the right roles and to build a winning team. It covers issues relating to team roles, motivation, dealing with problem people, dealing with difficult situations, and handling team meetings.

Mastering Virtual Teams: Strategies, Tools, and Techniques That Succeed 2nd ed.
Deborah L. Duarte, Nancy Tennant Snyder
San Francisco, California: Jossey-Bass, 2001
256pp ISBN: 0787955892
A theoretical and conceptual introduction to working in and leading virtual teams, this book addresses the difficulties that can surround virtual teamworking. It covers issues relating to differences in company, country, and culture, team dynamics, virtual team facilitation, and virtual team skills and strategies. The second edition comes with a CD-ROM, and also includes practical tools, checklists, tables, and worksheets.

The New Why Teams Don't Work: What Goes Wrong and How to Make It Right
Harvey A. Robbins, Michael Finley
San Francisco, California: Berrett-Koehler, 2000
272pp ISBN: 1576751104
This is a useful guide for anyone working with teams or contemplating the formation of teams. The focus on what can go wrong will help team designers avoid problems and help team facilitators solve them. There is also a good section on various "myths" concerning teams that should prove especially valuable in deciding when and how to use teams to meet business objectives.

Organizing Genius: The Secrets of Creative Collaboration
Warren Bennis, Patricia Ward Biederman
Cambridge, Massachusetts: Perseus, 1998
256pp ISBN: 0201339897
The authors of this text have carefully researched a number of today's large corporations in order to reveal how corporate leaders interact with teams and group leaders to achieve market-leading results. The text argues that people are today's most important resource and collective collaboration is the way to secure corporate success.

The Pfeiffer Book of Successful Team-building Tools: Best of the Annuals
Elaine Biech, ed.
Hoboken, New Jersey: Wiley, 2001
432pp ISBN: 0787956937
This book of team building tools combines practical exercises with a solid theoretical foundation. Biech uses a ten-block model of team building and bases exercises on each block. The practitioner learns both the "why" and the "how" of building effective

teams. Additionally, the book provides plenty of team building games, evaluation forms, and checklists to make a trainer's work easier.

Smart Things to Know about Teams
Annemarie Caracciolo
Chichester: Capstone, 2001
240pp (Smart Series)
ISBN: 1841120367
This book provides an introduction to the fundamentals of team building in business. Drawing on the author's experiences, it offers tips and advice on managing team issues and dynamics, including how teams work, effective team communication, measuring team success, and leading the team.

Team Roles at Work
R. Meredith Belbin
Woburn, Massachusetts: Butterworth-Heinemann, 1996
160pp ISBN: 0750626755
The author charts the changing nature of team roles in a work environment and addresses issues surrounding team management and the use of team role theory and data. The resulting implications for solo and team leaders, and for the future of the team-based organization, are considered.

Teams at the Top
Jon R. Katzenbach
Boston, Massachusetts: Harvard Business School Press, 1998
240pp ISBN: 0875847897
Designed to demonstrate how executive groups can be made to work as a functional team without sacrificing the individual autonomy of its members, the text focuses on team building skills, with practical examples taken from a range of companies that include Avon and Ben & Jerry's.

When Teams Work Best: 6,000 Team Members and Leaders Tell What It Takes to Succeed
Frank M. J. Lafasto, Carl E. Larson
London: Sage Publications, 2001
224pp ISBN: 0761923667
When Teams Work Best is a book for everyone who works with teams. It provides good insights into what does and doesn't work, based on the real experiences of team members and their leaders. The

1917

BUSINESS INFORMATION SOURCES

book is well organized, easy to read, and contains useful tools and information for evaluating and building effective teams.

The Wisdom of Teams: Creating the High-performance Organization

Jon R. Katzenbach, Douglas K. Smith
Maidenhead, United Kingdom: McGraw-Hill, 2003
352pp ISBN: 0060522003
This book is the result of research into why teams are important, what distinguishes effective from ineffective teams, and how organizations can utilize the effectiveness of teams to become strong performing companies. Citing research results from 47 organizations, Katzenbach and Smith impart their views as to what makes teams work, and how this can be transferred to the reader's own workplace.

World Class Teams: Working across Borders

Lynda C. McDermott, Nolan Brawley, William W. Waite
Hoboken, New Jersey: Wiley, 1998
336pp ISBN: 0471292656
Multinational organizations are increasingly implementing team structures which cross functions, nations, and cultures. This book examines the key issues involved, including world class team launch and development; team leadership; measuring, managing, and rewarding world-class teams; and managing team functional and cultural borders.

MAGAZINES

Team Performance Management

ISSN: 1352–7592
Emerald
44 Brattle Street, 4th Floor, Cambridge, Massachusetts, 02138
T: +1 888 622 0075
F: +1 617 354 6875
www.emeraldinsight.com

This quarterly journal features articles on all aspects of work teams, including their implementation, management, organization, and development. Drawing on a mix of case studies, research articles, technical reviews, and application papers, it is aimed at HR and quality professionals, managers, and consultants.

INTERNET

Center for the Study of Work Teams— University of North Texas
www.workteams.unt.edu/links.htm
This page of links to other sites covers almost any topic that would be of interest to a person who works with teams. Most of the links are to non-commercial sites and have a brief explanation to make selection easier.

Team Technology
www.teamtechnology.co.uk
This is a consulting firm providing information on team building, MTR-I management team roles, and the Myers-Briggs Type Indicator.

United States Office of Personnel Management
www.opm.gov/perform/teams.htm
This subsite of the U.S. Office of Personnel Management has a wealth of links to articles, case studies, tools, and measures for teams, which should prove useful to anyone who works with teams.

ORGANIZATIONS
USA
Center for Collaborative Organizations
University of North Texas, Terrill Hall 343, P.O. Box 311280, Denton, Texas, 76203–1280
T: +1 940 565 3096
F: +1 940 565 4806
E: *workteam@unt.edu*
www.workteams.unt.edu
This organization is dedicated to providing education, information, and research in all

areas of collaborative work systems. The services offered include annual conferences and workshops exploring best practice teamwork, courses, and events, an online bulletin board and discussion groups, books, research papers, free articles, and a free newsletter.

Europe
The Work Foundation
Peter Runge House, 3 Carlton House Terrace, London, SW1Y 5DG, U.K.
T: +44 (0) 870 165 6700
F: +44 (0) 870 165 6701
E: *customercentre@theworkfoundation.com*
www.theworkfoundation.com
Established in 2002, The Work Foundation is a new incarnation of The Industrial Society, an independent body with over 80 years' experience in management development and training. The Work Foundation operates under the belief that business success goes hand-in-hand with fair management practices. The services offered to members include an information service and employment law helpline; a publishing program of books, research reports, and videos; plus a training and consulting service, which includes the School of Coaching.

FOR MORE INFORMATION

- Organization and Organization Structure (pp. 1847–1850)
- Self-managed Teams: How They Succeed or Fail (pp. 235–236)
- Steps in Successful Team Building (pp. 462–463)
- The Critical Factors That Build or Break Teams (pp. 225–226)
- Workers without Borders: Creating Bonds When Workers Have No Loyalty (pp. 237–238)

"Talent wins games, but teamwork wins championships."
Michael Jordan

The Top Twenty Business Magazines

MAGAZINES

Academy of Management Perspectives
ISSN: 0896–3789
Academy of Management
P.O. Box 3020, Briarcliff Manor, New York, 10510–8020
T: +1 914 923 2607
F: +1 914 923 2615
www.aomonline.org
Frequency: quarterly. A journal for professionals in the management field, *AME* aims to foster the general advancement of research, learning, teaching, and practice in management. The published articles provide managers with relevant management tools and information based on recent advances in management theory and research.

British Journal of Management
ISSN: 1045–3172
Blackwell Publishing
350 Main Street, Malden, Massachusetts, 02148
T: +1 781 388 8200
F: +1 781 388 8232
www.blackwellpublishing.com
Frequency: quarterly. This journal publishes articles from the full range of business and management disciplines. Its selection criteria should ensure that scholarly merit is combined with readability.

BusinessWeek
ISSN: 0007–7135
McGraw-Hill Companies
BusinessWeek, P.O. Box 53235, Boulder, Colorado, 80322–3235
T: +1 800 635 1200
F: +1 641 842 6101
www.businessweek.com
Frequency: weekly. The leading U.S. business weekly, supported by an excellent Web site. Essential reading for anyone doing business in the United States.

California Management Review
ISSN: 0008–1256
University of California
F501 Haas School of Business #1900, Berkeley, California, 94720–1900
T: +1 510 642 7159
F: +1 510 642 1318
www.haas.berkeley.edu/cmr
Frequency: quarterly. *CMR* publishes in-depth articles on a range of management issues. It aims to serve as a bridge between those who study management and those who practice it.

European Management Journal
ISSN: 0263–2373
Elsevier Science
Customer Service Department, 6277 Sea Harbor Drive, Orlando, Florida, 32887–4800
T: +1 877 839 7126 or +1 407 345 4020
F: +1 407 363 1354
www.elsevier.com
Frequency: bimonthly. The articles in this magazine are based on up-to-date research and recent experience in management policies and procedures, and are aimed at both practicing managers and academics working in the field of management. The main emphasis is on European business affairs.

Fast Company
Gruner & Jahr U.S.A. Publishing
38 Commercial Wharf, Boston, Massachusetts, 02110–3883
T: +1 617 248 8000
F: +1 617 248 8090
www.inc.com
Frequency: monthly. Though only started in 1995, *Fast Company* has established itself as an important monthly business magazine, largely on the back of the dot-com boom. Its heady mix of company news, business biographies, and latest business practices make for compulsive reading.

Forbes Magazine
ISSN: 0015–6914
Forbes, Inc.
60 5th Avenue, New York, 10011
T: +1 212 620 2200
www.forbes.com
Frequency: weekly. A popular U.S. business magazine, with a heavy emphasis on personal finance and individual wealth creation. Its annual surveys of the best companies in the United States and the nation's people are very popular.

Fortune
ISSN: 0015–8259
Fortune, Inc.
Time and Life Building, Rockefeller Center, New York, 10020–1393
T: +1 800 621 8000
F: +1 212 522 7686
www.fortune.com
Issued 28 times a year, this is the most influential U.S. magazine for personal investors. Its influential surveys, including Fortune 500 and Global Most Admired, provide an accurate barometer of popular attitudes toward leading U.S. and international companies.

Harvard Business Review
ISSN: 0017–8012
Harvard Business School Press
60 Harvard Way, Boston, Massachusetts, 02163
T: +1 800 988 0886
F: +1 617 783 7555
www.hbr.org
The bimonthly *HBR* is a management journal with an outstanding reputation. It aims to advance the theory and practice of management by providing best practice models and techniques from around the world. Its articles are written by leading academics, consultants, managers, and management analysts. It covers all areas of business, including corporate strategy, management, finance, technology, and industry trends.

Inc.
ISSN: 0162–8968
Gruner & Jahr U.S.A. Publishing
38 Commercial Wharf, Boston, Massachusetts, 02110–3883
T: +1 617 248 8000
F: +1 617 248 8090
www.inc.com
Published 18 times a year, this magazine is a premier journal on entrepreneurship. Each issue includes articles on financial and personnel management, marketing, administration, sales, and operations from the unique perspective of small businesses. This magazine is a valuable publication for any executive or manager.

Long Range Planning
ISSN: 0024–6301
Elsevier Science
Customer Service Department, 6277 Sea Harbor Drive, Orlando, Florida, 32887–4800
T: +1 877 839 7126 or +1 407 345 4020
F: +1 407 363 1354
www.elsevier.com
Frequency: bimonthly. The aims of

1919

BUSINESS INFORMATION SOURCES

"If A is a success in life, then A equals x plus y plus z. Work is x; y is play; and z is keeping your mouth shut."
Albert Einstein

this journal are to assist senior managers, administrators, and academics who are involved in planning strategy, and to highlight new concepts and techniques in business and management. Its articles are practical in nature and contain findings from research and detailed case studies.

Management Decision
ISSN: 0025–1747
Emerald
44 Brattle Street, 4th Floor, Cambridge, Massachusetts, 02138
T: +1 888 622 0075
F: +1 617 354 6875
www.emeraldinsight.com
Frequency: ten issues per year. *Management Decision* publishes articles of interest to business managers, teachers, and students. It focuses on general management and strategic issues, with particular emphasis on practical applications.

Management Today
ISSN: 0025–1925
Management Publications
174 Hammersmith Road, London, W6 7JP, U.K.
T: +44 (0) 20 8606 7500
F: +44 (0) 20 8606 7301
www.clickmt.com
Frequency: monthly. *Management Today* covers a broad range of issues in the management field and is aimed at middle and senior level managers. It examines major developments in management, and carries interviews with leading business figures and profiles of successful companies.

McKinsey Quarterly
ISSN: 0047–5394
McKinsey & Company
55 East 52nd Street, 2nd Floor, New York, 10022

T: +1 212 446 7000
F: +1 212 446 8575
www.mckinseyquarterly.com
Frequency: quarterly. This is a journal of management and economics featuring the research of McKinsey consultants and selected outside authors. It is available only through a controlled circulation. Applications should be made to local offices or the U.S. office.

MIT Sloan Management Review
ISSN: 1532–9194
MIT Sloan School of Management
Room E60–100, 77 Massachusetts Avenue, Cambridge, Massachusetts, 01239–4307
T: +1 617 253 7170
F: +1 617 258 9739
www.sloanreview.mit.edu
Frequency: quarterly. Founded in 1959, it aims to provide senior managers with the best of current management theory and practice. It has a strong focus on corporate strategy and leadership.

Organizational Dynamics
ISSN: 0090–2616
Elsevier Science
Customer Service Department, 6277 Sea Harbor Drive, Orlando, Florida, 32887–4800
T: +1 877 839 7126 or +1 407 345 4020
F: +1 407 363 1354
www.elsevier.com
Frequency: quarterly. *Organizational Dynamics* was founded by the American Management Association. It is published as a forum for the dissemination of articles on organizational behavior and the problems of business and management.

SAM Advanced Management Journal
ISSN: 0036–0805
Society for the Advancement of Management
Texas A&M University, College of Business, FC111, 6300 Ocean Drive, Corpus Christi, Texas, 78412
T: +1 361 825 6045
F: +1 361 825 2725
www.cob.tamucc.edu/sam/amj

Frequency: quarterly. Aimed at the general manager, this journal publishes articles on business and management in a real-world setting written by business professionals.

Strategic Management Journal
ISSN: 0143–2095
Wiley
111 River St, Hoboken, New Jersey, 07030–5774
T: +1 201 748 6000
F: +1 212 850 6021
www.wiley.com
Frequency: monthly. *SMJ* focuses on all aspects of strategic management. Each issue publishes a range of articles, research notes, and commentaries.

Strategy + Business
ISSN: 1083–796X
Booz Allen & Hamilton, Inc.
101 Park Avenue, New York, 10178
T: +1 212 551 6222
F: +1 212 551 6008
www.strategy-business.com
Frequency: quarterly. *Strategy + Business* is published by the leading international consultancy Booz Allen & Hamilton. Its aim is to provide executives with commentary, research, and practical ideas that bridge the gap between theory and practice in contemporary global business.

Success
ISSN: 0745–2489
Success Publishing, Inc.
15 Fayetteville Street Mall, Suite 1110, Raleigh, North Carolina, 27601
T: +1 919 807 1100
www.SuccessMagazine.com
Formerly titled *High Technology Business*, this magazine is published ten times per year. Written for today's entrepreneur, its articles range from the aspects of running a successful business to marketing strategies and technology.

"There is no end to what you can accomplish if you don't care who gets the credit."

Florence Luscomb

The Top Twenty Business Publishers

ORGANIZATIONS
USA
Berrett-Koehler
235 Montgomery Street, Suite 650, San Francisco, California, 94104
T: +1 415 288 0260
F: +1 415 362 2512
E: *bkpub@bkpub.com*
www.bkpub.com

Penguin Putnam, Inc.
375 Hudson Street, New York
T: +1 800 788 6262
www.penguinputnam.com
A Pearson company. Imprints include: Viking, Penguin.

Perseus Books Group
387 Park Avenue South, New York, NY 10016
T: +1 212 340 8100
www.perseusbooks.com

Random House
1540 Broadway, New York, 10036
T: +1 212 782 9000
F: +1 212 302 7985
E: *customerservice@random.com*
www.randomhouse.com
Imprints include: Crown, Random House, Doubleday, Currency, Broadway.

International
AMACOM
1601 Broadway, New York, 10019
T: +1 212 586 8100
F: +1 212 903 8168
E: *customerservice@amanet.org*
www.amanet.org/books/index.htm

Blackwell Publishing, Inc.
350 Main Street, Malden, Massachusetts, 02148
T: +1 781 388 8200
F: +1 781 388 8210
E: *subscrip@blackwellpub.com*
www.blackwellpublishing.com

Butterworth-Heinemann
225 Wildwood Avenue, Woburn, Massachusetts, 01801
T: +1 800 366 2665
F: +1 800 446 6520
http://www.intl.elsevierhealth.com/bh/default.cfm

HarperCollins U.S.
10 East 53rd Street, New York, 10022
T: +1 212 207 7000
www.harpercollins.com
Imprint of HarperCollins Publishers.

Harvard Business School Press
60 Harvard Way, Boston, Massachusetts, 02163
T: +1 800 988 0886
F: +1 617 783 7555
E: *corpcustserv@hbsp.harvard.edu*
www.hbsp.harvard.edu

Irwin Publishing
325 Humber College Boulevard, Toronto, Ontario, M9W 7C3, Canada
T: +1 416 798 0424
F: +1 416 798 1384
E: *irwin@irwin-pub.com*
www.irwin-pub.com

Jossey-Bass
989 Market Street, San Francisco, California, 94103–1741
T: +1 415 433 1740
F: +1 415 433 0499
www.josseybass.com
A division of John Wiley.

Macmillan
The Macmillan Building, 4 Crinan Street, London, N1 9XW, U.K.
T: +44 (0) 20 7843 3600
F: +44 (0) 20 7843 4640
E: *mdl@macmillan.co.uk*
www.macmillan.co.uk
Includes Palgrave imprint.

McGraw-Hill Companies
Educational and Professional Publishing, 1221 Avenue of the Americas, New York, 10020
T: +1 212 512 2000
E: *webmaster@mcgraw-hill.com*
www.mcgraw-hill.com

Nicholas Brealey Publishing
1163 E Ogden Avenue, Suite 705–229, Naperville, Illinois, 60563
T: +1 630 499 0217
F: +1 630 898 3595
www.nbrealey-books.com

Oxford University Press, Inc.
198 Madison Avenue, New York, 10016
T: +1 212 726 6000
F: +1 212 726 6440
E: *custserv@oup-usa.org*
www.oup-usa.org

Quorum Books
88 Post Road West, P.O. Box 5007, Westport, Connecticut, 06881–5007
T: +1 800 225 5800
F: +1 203 750 9790
E: *customer-service@greenwood.com*
www.greenwood.com
Imprint of Greenwood Publishing Group

Routledge
29 West 35th Street, New York, 10001
T: +1 212 216 7800
F: +1 212 564 7854
E: *info@routledge-ny.com*
www.routledge-ny.com

Sage Publications
2455 Teller Road, Thousand Oaks, California, 91320
T: +1 805 499 0721
F: +1 805 499 0871
E: *market@sagepub.com*
www.sagepub.co.uk

Simon & Schuster
1230 Avenue of the Americas, New York, 10020
T: +1 212 698 7000
www.simonsays.com
Includes Scribner and The Free Press imprints.

Wiley
111 River St, Hoboken, New Jersey, 07030–5774
T: +1 201 748 6000
E: *bookinfo@wiley.com*
www.wiley.com

1921

"The First Duty of a newspaper is to be Accurate. If it is Accurate, it follows that it is Fair."
Herbert Bayard Swope

Training and Development

BOOKS

Accelerating Performance: Powerful New Techniques to Develop People

Sunny Stout Rostron
London: Kogan Page, 2002
256pp ISBN: 0749436425
This book is designed for trainers, coaches, facilitators and performance developers, consultants, and coaches involved in developing people. Rostron offers a fresh approach to the style and delivery of seminars, workshops, and lectures, offering practical suggestions for incorporating storytelling, drama, and music into performance development programs. Examples from the author's personal experience are included. Emphasis is placed on helping the facilitator or trainer to develop their skills and put together a personal toolkit of techniques for their own use.

The ASTD Training and Development Handbook: A Guide to Human Resource Development 4th ed.

Robert L. Craig, ed.
Maidenhead, United Kingdom: McGraw-Hill, 1996
1088pp ISBN: 007013359X
This edition of the American Society for Training and Development's classic guide presents the proven techniques of hundreds of industry leaders. These techniques will help you choose and develop your staff and create a learning organization. They can also help increase employee commitment to the organization, enhance employee computer literacy, and develop employee leadership skills.

Blended Learning: How to Integrate Online and Traditional Learning

Kaye Thorne
London: Kogan Page, 2003
160pp ISBN: 0749439017
This practical guide explains that "blended learning" is a solution that allows trainers to integrate online learning with a broad range of more traditional learning techniques. It suggests how to create an effective blended learning program, and the process is illustrated by a variety of case studies.

Designing and Delivering Training

David Simmonds
London, United Kingdom: Chartered Institute of Personnel and Development (CIPD), 2003
240pp ISBN: 0852929927
This textbook focuses on the blend between theory and practice in training. Topics covered include: the organizational context and business environment; the identification of training needs; the planning of training solutions; the design of training events; the delivery of training; incorporating new technology into the training process; the transfer of learning; the evaluation of training; the management and marketing of training activities; and the continuing professional development (CPD) of the training professional.

Developing Management Skills 6th ed.

David A. Whetten, Kim S. Cameron
Englewood Cliffs, New Jersey: Prentice Hall, 2005
704pp ISBN: 0131273205
Focusing on management skills relevant to most areas of both life and work, this book reviews studies of key management skills and describes a model and methodology to help develop important management skills. It is structured in four parts, covering personal skills, interpersonal skills, group skills, and specific communication skills. Individual chapters are organized on the basis of a five-step learning model comprising skill assessment, skill learning, skill analysis, skill practice, and skill application.

Developing Your People: Pain-free Solutions for Busy Managers

Suzy Siddons
London, United Kingdom: Chartered Institute of Personnel and Development (CIPD), 2001
128pp ISBN: 084645226X
This book examines the choices available for developing your staff, with an emphasis on practicality and cost effectiveness. Section One looks at deciding who needs developing and how. Section Two deals with planning a development program and motivating the staff it affects. Section Three considers the options, methods, and resources needed. Section Four looks briefly at ways in which managers can develop themselves.

Develop Your Training Skills

Leslie Rae
London, United Kingdom: Chartered Institute of Personnel and Development (CIPD), 2001
192pp ISBN: 0749435917

This book offers an introduction to training for those new to staff development and learning improvement. The text includes details on training methods, checklists, and action plans, and information relating to online as well as traditional training.

Effective Training: Systems, Strategies, and Practices 2nd ed.

P. Nick Blanchard, James W. Thacker
Englewood Cliffs, New Jersey: Prentice Hall, 2004
512pp ISBN: 0130327395
The authors discuss the theory and principles of training as they relate to organizational objectives and strategies. They emphasize the value of developing training programs that relate training to the overall strategy of the organization. Topics covered include overview of training in organizations; strategic planning, training, and organizational development; learning motivation and performance; needs analysis; training design; training methods; development and implementation of training; evaluation of training; key areas of organizational training; and management development.

Employee Training and Development 3rd ed.

Raymond A. Noe
Maidenhead, United Kingdom: McGraw-Hill, 2004
464pp ISBN: 0072992565
This guide to employee development aims to help companies become more competitive by increasing the role of training in the organization. It explores the strategic role of training, and focuses on ways of designing training programs that work, including those that facilitate the adoption of new technologies. This book manages to carefully assess older training methods that should be retained while presenting more cutting-edge approaches.

Evaluating Training: From Personal Insight to Organisational Performance 2nd ed.

Peter Bramley
London, United Kingdom: Chartered Institute of Personnel and Development (CIPD), 2003
160pp ISBN: 1843980304
This book reveals how to build evaluation into every stage of training. Topics covered include: the importance of evaluation;

changes in effectiveness and behavior; evaluation of learning—changes in knowledge, skills and attitudes; evaluation before designing a learning event; evaluation during the event; and the end-game—presenting an evaluation report, utilizing findings and ethical issues. Appendices look at the reliability of testing and approaches to evaluation.

Evaluation in Organizations
Darlene Russ-Eft, Hallie Preskill
Cambridge, Massachusetts: Perseus Books Group, 2001
416pp ISBN: 0738202681
This is the standard reference for anyone developing and launching evaluation programs in organizations.

The Fifth Discipline Fieldbook: Strategies and Tools for Building a Learning Organization
Peter M. Senge et al.
New York: Currency/Doubleday, 1994
592pp ISBN: 0385472560
Senge's concept of the learning organization has had an enormous impact on corporations because by promoting learning it makes change simpler to introduce. This workbook presents exercises to help organizations move in this direction, and provides detailed information on how to implement strategies such as building a shared vision, enhancing collaboration, and facing rather than avoiding tough questions.

Foundations of Human Resource Development
Richard A. Swanson, Elwood F. Holton, III
San Francisco, California: Berrett-Koehler, 2001
400pp ISBN: 1576750752
One of the best textbooks on HRD, this is a useful reference handbook for managers.

Handbook for Training Strategy 2nd ed.
Martyn Sloman
Brookfield, Vermont: Gower Publishing, 1999
288pp ISBN: 0566081288
Divided into three parts, the contents include: Part One, the role of training, competition through people, new human resources, and models for training; Part Two, the process of training, training and the organization, training and the individual, performance appraisal, design and delivery, and new approaches to measurement; Part Three, managing the training function, the role of the training function, and implications for the trainer.

How to Design and Deliver Training for the New and Emerging Generations
Susan El-Shamy
New York: Pfeiffer & Co., 2004
192pp ISBN: 078796977X
A training design and activity book that aims to help more mature trainers create lively training that will hold the attention of younger trainees. The different needs of younger learners are addressed in Part One, and Part Two offers games and activities that cater for younger generations; these are included on an accompanying CD-ROM.

How to Survive a Training Assignment
Stephen K. Ellis
Cambridge, Massachusetts: Perseus Books Group, 1988
160pp ISBN: 0201066475
This is an excellent short introduction to the skill of training staff effectively.

Human Resource Development: The New Trainer's Guide 3rd ed.
Edward E. Scannell et al.
Cambridge, Massachusetts: Perseus Books Group, 2000
224pp ISBN: 0738203289
A clear and concise step-by-step introduction to HRD, with useful practical examples and helpful techniques.

Mastering Employee Development
Richard Pettinger
New York: Palgrave, 2002
240pp (Palgrave Masters)
ISBN: 0333973585
This work discusses ways in which people learn; training needs analysis; training within companies and externally; monitoring and evaluation; mentoring, coaching and counseling; organization and management development; and government training and development policy. It is suitable for students of personnel and management topics at foundation, certificate, diploma, and undergraduate levels.

Now, Discover Your Strengths: How to Develop Your Talents and Those of the People You Manage
Marcus Buckingham, Donald O. Clifton
New York: Simon & Schuster, 2001
272pp ISBN: 0743201140
This book follows on from *First, Break All the Rules*. It is largely based around the "StrengthsFinder Profile," an Internet project that aims to uncover strengths and show how these can be translated into a career environment. Each book contains a

personal Internet access number so that readers can download the program. The authors have incorporated feedback from the program into the text, and combine this with practical advice on how to enhance existing skills.

Planning and Organizing Personal and Professional Development
Chris Sangster
Brookfield, Vermont: Gower Publishing, 2000
176pp ISBN: 0566082640
A practical step-by-step guide to personal and professional development that covers the strategy, techniques, and philosophy behind the processes. The book presents a route map for each of the three participants—the learner, the manager, or the mentor—in the training function, and a triangular model illustrates the interaction of each, placing particular emphasis on learning outcomes.

Principles of Human Resource Development 2nd ed.
Jerry W. Gilley et al.
Cambridge, Massachusetts: Perseus Books Group, 2002
400pp ISBN: 0738206040
This is a definitive guide to human resource development.

Rapid Instructional Design: Learning ID Fast and Right
George Piskurich
San Francisco, California: Jossey-Bass, 2006
364pp ISBN: 0787980730
The purpose of this book is to consider how to speed up both the learning and the practice of instructional design. Piskurich covers all the basics of the subject, from analysis to evaluation, but omits the theory. Instead he provides plenty of practical checklists, together with many hints on how to design better and more quickly in this age of technology-based training.

Running Training Like a Business: Delivering Unmistakable Value
David van Adelsberg, Edward A. Trolley
San Francisco, California: Berrett-Koehler, 1999
224pp ISBN: 1576750590
Drawing on their work with a wide range of organizations over six years, the authors explain what is involved in transforming the traditional training function into a training enterprise. They stress the importance of assessing the true cost of training and the return on training investment, and also outline ways in which training should be

1923

BUSINESS INFORMATION SOURCES

"All men who have turned out worth anything have had the chief hand in their own education."

Walter Scott

linked to the customer's business strategy in order to maximize the efficiency and effectiveness of delivery.

The Theory and Practice of Training 5th ed.

Roger Buckley, Jim Caple
London: Kogan Page, 2004
336pp ISBN: 0749441569
This book outlines the major instructional and training concepts and looks at their relationship to training in practice. Issues examined include: the role of training in organizations; proactive and reactive assessments of training needs; theoretical models of training; competence-based training; training objectives; training strategies and methods; validation, evaluation and assessment of training; the role of the trainer. Appendices cover: the methods for obtaining information about performance problems and job/task content; sampling; an example of a learning journal; an illustration of a tutor's review of a course; and an example of a checklist to assess trainer performance.

Training for a Smart Workforce

Rod Gerber, Colin Lankshear, eds.
New York: Routledge, 2000
224pp ISBN: 0415195527
This collection of essays takes a multi-disciplinary approach to workplace training for successful performance. The four parts cover megatrends (in work and social life), critical aspects for workplace education (including competence and literacy), pedagogic implications and actions (including identifying smart work practice and the transfer of learning), and directions (lifelong and life-broad learning).

Train Your Team Yourself: How to Design and Deliver Effective Inhouse Training Courses

Lisa Hadfield Law
Oxford, United Kingdom: How To Books, 2002
160pp ISBN: 1857037413
Many managers either provide no training for their team members, or send them on expensive courses that may not be very well suited to their needs. This book maintains that it may be better for managers to train their own team and describes how this can be done. It covers the principles of teaching and learning, the identification of training needs, presentations and visual aids, discussions and meetings, feedback, handling difficult team members, and team building.

MAGAZINES
Management Learning

ISSN: 1350–5076
Sage Publications
1 Oliver's Yard, 55 City Road, London, EC1Y 1SP, U.K.
T: +44 (0) 20 7324 8500
F: +44 (0) 20 7324 8600
www.sagepub.co.uk
This is an international journal containing articles with an academic slant, and covering all areas of managerial and organizational learning and development, including the nature and process of learning, learning outcomes, and learning and knowledge.

T+D

ISSN: 1535–7740
American Society for Training and Development (ASTD)
1640 King Street, Box 1443, Alexandria, Virginia, 22313–2043
T: +1 703 683 8100
F: +1 703 683 1523
www.astd.org
T + D aims to provide advice and tips for people who run training or development programs. Its articles are mainly of a practical nature.

INTERNET
American Society for Training and Development (ASTD)
www.astd.org
This site offers a job bank, a bookstore, and daily news clips covering developments in training. Some services are free; others require membership.

ORGANIZATIONS
USA
American Society for Training and Development (ASTD)

1640 King Street, Box 1443, Alexandria, Virginia, 22313–2043
T: +1 703 683 8100
F: +1 703 683 1523
E: *customercare@astd.org*
www.astd.org
An association of workplace learning and performance professionals, ASTD's members come from multinational corporations, medium-sized and small businesses, government, academia, consultancy firms, and product and service suppliers. It offers research and analysis, conferences, expositions, seminars, and publications. Though its primary focus is training and development, it also addresses issues of performance appraisal.

Europe
European Foundation for Management Development (EFMD)

88 Rue de Gachard, Brussels, B-1050, Belgium
T: +32 2 629 08 10
F: +32 2 629 08 11
E: *info@efmd.be*
www.efmd.be
Founded in 1971, EFMD is a network of organizations with interests in management education and development. Its member organizations include business schools, companies, public services, and employers' associations. Its aims include promoting partnerships between private companies and public sector organizations, disseminating information on management development, encouraging best practice in management education and development through international benchmarking, and the publication of research.

The Work Foundation

Peter Runge House, 3 Carlton House Terrace, London, SW1Y 5DG, U.K.
T: +44 (0) 870 165 6700
F: +44 (0) 870 165 6701
E: *customercentre@theworkfoundation.com*
www.theworkfoundation.com
Established in 2002, The Work Foundation is a new incarnation of The Industrial Society, an independent body with over 80 years' experience in management development and training. The Work Foundation operates under the belief that business success goes hand-in-hand with fair management practices. The services offered to members include an information service and employment law helpline; a publishing program of books, research reports, and videos; plus a training and consulting service, which includes the School of Coaching.

FOR MORE INFORMATION

☆ Choosing the Best Training Curriculum for You (pp. 426–427)
✔ Evaluating Training (pp. 478–479)
๖ Learning Organization (pp. 1804–1806)
๖ Management Development (pp. 1812–1814)
☆ Mentoring (pp. 414–415)
๖ Personnel Management and HR Management (pp. 1856–1859)
๖ Training Methods (pp. 1925–1926)
✔ Training Needs Analysis (pp. 476–477)

"There is too much education altogether." — William Paley

Training Methods

BOOKS

101 Ways to Make Training Active 2nd ed.
Mel Silberman
New York: Pfeiffer & Co., 2005
336pp ISBN: 0787976121
Trainer Mel Silberman offers over 100 suggestions on how to organize and perform active training sessions. Each of the 101 techniques is described and illustrated with a goal, a statement of purpose, a procedure, step-by-step instructions, and suggestions for other ways to use the strategy for both teaching and training.

The 2006 Pfeiffer Annual 41st ed.
Elaine Biech, ed.
San Francisco, California: Jossey-Bass, 2005
320pp ISBN: 0787978205
This two-volume set provides a collection of practical and useful materials written by and for professionals within the broad area described as human resources development. The main sections of the book cover experiential learning activities, inventories, questionnaires, surveys, and presentation and discussion resources.

The Accelerated Learning Fieldbook: Making the Instructional Process Fast, Flexible, and Fun
Lou Russell
San Francisco, California: Jossey-Bass, 2000
336pp ISBN: 0787946397
This course provides the tools needed to ensure that maximum learning and maximum retention are taking place in your training sessions. It considers ways to improve your communication skills and identify the best ways individual learners can learn, besides pointing out the necessity of rethinking personal beliefs that block learning. Among the other topics that it covers are how to use music to create focused learning environments, and how to ascertain the effectiveness of a learning session.

The Accelerated Learning Handbook: A Creative Guide to Designing and Delivering Faster, More Effective Training Programs
Dave Meier
Maidenhead, United Kingdom: McGraw-Hill, 2000
272pp ISBN: 0071355472
This book emphasizes learning by doing,

but doing things in an accelerated fashion. It suggests using color, music, and play to enhance creativity, and using computer-based learning to cut course development time. The author discusses practical techniques and ideas that will reduce the costs and time involved in training.

Active Training: A Handbook of Techniques, Designs, Case Examples, and Tips
Mel Silberman, Carol Auerbach
New York: Pfeiffer & Co., 1998
304pp ISBN: 0787939897
The book explores the learn-by-doing method of training, providing tips on how to design experience-based training programs ideal for adults who have been out of the classroom for a time. It focuses on an active approach as opposed to lectures, shows how trainers can learn to diagnose their mistakes, and offers numerous examples of ways in which trainers can improve their techniques.

Assessments A to Z: A Collection of 50 Questionnaires, Instruments, and Inventories
Bonnie Burn, Maggie Payment
San Francisco, California: Jossey-Bass, 2000
224pp ISBN: 0787945099
The first section of this book provides an introduction to the use of assessments. The second presents 50 assessments covering a range of management skills and techniques, including assertiveness, change, customer service, delegation, leadership, problem-solving, and time management. The final section looks at strategies for customizing or designing assessment tools.

The ASTD Handbook of Training Design and Delivery
George M. Piskurich
Maidenhead, United Kingdom: McGraw-Hill, 2000
640pp ISBN: 0071343105
A practical guide for trainers designing classroom, self-study, or technology-based training programs.

Complete Facilitator's Handbook
John Heron
London: Kogan Page, 1999
304pp ISBN: 0749427981
Intended to enable facilitators in all fields to achieve success, this book presents a

complete model, developed over the past 25 years. It gives six basic learning dimensions to three forms of decision making, and offers ideas for practical action. It also offers essential support to facilitators interested in developing their own style and the skills necessary to enable them to deal with any situation they may experience.

Creative Training Techniques Handbook: Tips, Tactics, and How-to's for Delivering Effective Training 3rd ed.
Robert Pike
Minneapolis, Minnesota: Lakewood Publications, 2003
304pp ISBN: 0874257239
This second edition adds valuable items such as a resource guide, outlines, and activity sheets to the myriad tips and techniques of the first edition. The aim of the book is to help you customize your training to meet the needs and capabilities of your audience. It presents step-by-step strategies for improving the training methods of instructors and their ability to make presentations that will motivate students to learn.

Designing Web-based Training: How to Teach Anyone Anything Anywhere Anytime
William Horton
Hoboken, New Jersey: Wiley, 2000
640pp ISBN: 047135614X
This volume explores the advantages of online training, examining the difficulties and rewards of developing distance learning courses and the intricacies of designing Web-based training. It is well illustrated, with more than 100 examples, and offers guidance about issues such as hardware and software options, graphic and content design, and tests for usability.

Energize Your Audience: 75 Quick Activities That Get Them Started and Keep Them Going
Lorraine L. Ukens
San Francisco, California: Jossey-Bass, 2000
208pp ISBN: 0787945307
The author presents 75 quick activities designed to engage the attention of an audience before training sessions, presentations, or meetings. For each of the exercises, which are divided up into

1925

BUSINESS INFORMATION SOURCES

"Education is what survives when what has been learned has been forgotten."

B. F. Skinner

ice-breakers, energizers, and group challenges, she gives full details of the objective and procedure, the group size, the time, materials, and preparation required, and opportunities for variation and discussion.

The Facilitator's Fieldbook

Thomas Justice et al.
New York: AMACOM, 1999
448pp ISBN: 0814470386
A practical manual for facilitators, for use in situations such as preparing brainstorms, meetings, or presentations.

Games Trainers Play

John W. Newstrom, Edward E. Scannell
Maidenhead, United Kingdom: McGraw-Hill, 1980
352pp ISBN: 0070464081
A practical, best-selling collection of innovative training exercises.

The Inspirational Trainer: Make Your Training Flexible, Spontaneous and Creative

Paul Z. Jackson
London: Kogan Page, 2001
208pp ISBN: 0749434686
Taking creativity as its starting point, this book describes an approach to training that draws particularly upon the theater but also upon sports, games, psychology, and a variety of other sources, to support the design and delivery of innovative, flexible training.

Managing Financial Resources 3rd ed.

Mick Broadbent, John Cullen
Woburn, Massachusetts: Butterworth-Heinemann, 2003
544pp ISBN: 0750657553
This book deals with the complicated issues of financial planning and control. Topics include performance measures and cost analysis, methods of improving profitability, and techniques of financial monitoring and control. Real examples and case studies are used throughout in order to illustrate points in a practical context.

Playing Along: 37 Group Learning Activities Borrowed from Improvisational Theater

Izzy Gesell
Duluth, Michigan: Whole Person Associates, 1997
160pp ISBN: 157025141X
Developed for group leaders who have no improvisational theater experience, this book presents step-by-step techniques that are designed to allow actors to solve problems on stage and build a learning environment through reducing resistance, creating cohesiveness, and promoting active participation in the learning process. These 5–10 minute exercises activate the learning skills of listening, affirming, imagining, and trusting.

Web Learning Fieldbook: Using the World Wide Web to Build Workplace Learning Environments

Valorie Beer
San Francisco, California: Jossey-Bass, 2000
304pp ISBN: 0787950238
This book and its accompanying Web site provide access to sample learning environments and links to related sites, as well as customizable electronic templates and tools that can be downloaded and used right away. Advice on how to incorporate Web-based learning into the workplace is also offered.

MAGAZINES

T+D

ISSN: 1535–7740
American Society for Training and Development (ASTD)
1640 King Street, Box 1443, Alexandria, Virginia, 22313
T: +1 703 683 8100
F: +1 703 683 1523
www.astd.org
T+D, the official journal of the American Society for Training and Development, features articles on a broad range of training issues. It also publishes contributions on other management topics and personal development, as well as surveys of work issues and media reviews.

Training and Management Development Methods

ISSN: 0951–3507
Emerald
44 Brattle Street, 4th Floor, Cambridge, Massachusetts, 02138
T: +1 888 622 0075
F: +1 617 354 6875
www.emeraldinsight.com
This journal is published five times a year in loose-leaf format. It looks at current practices and innovations in the field of training and development, and provides tried and tested examples of training methods, which can be collected to provide a useful practical manual and resource.

Training Journal

ISSN: 1465–6523
Fenman Ltd.
28 St. Thomas Place, Cambridgeshire Business Park, Ely, Cambridgeshire, CB7 4EX, U.K.
T: +44 (0) 1353 654 877
F: +44 (0) 1353 663 644
www.trainingjournal.co.uk
This is a journal for those involved in workplace training, development, and learning. The style is informal. The articles are usually fairly brief and practical in nature, and they often include checklists and action plans.

INTERNET
U.S. Department of Labor—Bureau of Labor Statistics
http://stats.bls.gov/oco/ocos021.htm
Designed for managers and specialists, the information on human relations, training, and labor relations provided by this site is thorough and informative.

FOR MORE INFORMATION

☆ Choosing the Best Training Curriculum for You (pp. 426–427)
🖱 Coaching, Counseling, and Mentoring (pp. 1698–1700)
🖱 Training and Development (pp. 1922–1924)

1926

BUSINESS INFORMATION SOURCES

     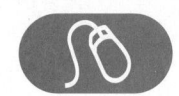

Venture Capital

BOOKS

Angel Financing: How to Find and Invest in Private Equity

Gerald A. Benjamin, Joel B. Margulis
Hoboken, New Jersey: Wiley, 1999
320pp (Wiley Investment)
ISBN: 0471350850
This book draws on extensive experience of the private investor market in the United States. It stresses the importance of careful planning and preparation to ensure the success of financial deals. It provides practical advice and information for entrepreneurs, investors, and intermediaries in four sections: the first focuses on how entrepreneurs can address the challenge of raising capital and finding workable strategies; the second examines the angel investor market; the third deals with the search for an investor; and the fourth provides insight into the investor's perspective on prospective deals. Detailed advice on preparing an investor-oriented business plan and an overview of securities law issues for nonlawyers are provided in appendices.

Angel Investing: Matching Startup Funds with Startup Companies

Mark Van Osnabrugge, Robert J. Robinson
San Francisco, California: Jossey-Bass, 2000
320pp ISBN: 0787952028
A comprehensive guide for anyone looking for funding from angel investors, this book presents key information in an accessible manner.

Directory of Venture Capital 2nd ed.

Kate E. Lister, Thomas D. Harnish
Hoboken, New Jersey: Wiley, 2000
400pp ISBN: 0471361046
The directory lists venture capital firms by state and provides detailed information on their preferences with regard to industry, stage of funding, geography, and size of company. The authors also provide information on the returns required by private equity investors, selecting the right lawyer, and important aspects of a venture partnership. Entrepreneurs will find the directory a good resource for locating the right venture capital firm to approach for funding.

Fundamentals of Venture Capital

Joseph W. Bartlett
Lanham, Maryland: Madison Books, 1999
176pp ISBN: 1568331266

A useful but technical introduction to venture capital, this title is aimed more at specialist advisors than potential entrepreneurs.

The VC Way: Investment Secrets from the Wizards of Venture Capital

Jeffrey Zygmont
Cambridge, Massachusetts: Perseus Books Group, 2002
240pp ISBN: 0738205923
This text offers a behind-the-scenes perspective of the venture capital market, revealing to investors how to strategize and invest in successful companies before their profits are certain. Zygmont also offers the reader a brief tutorial in creating a portfolio of holdings that may increase in value, as Apple and Yahoo did.

Venture Capital and Private Equity: A Casebook 3rd ed.

Josh Lerner et al.
Hoboken, New Jersey: Wiley, 2004
576pp ISBN: 0471230693
The book explains in detail the venture capital and private equity markets. Divided into four sections, the book covers the fundraising process required to start a venture capital fund, investment selection, and the relationship between the venture capitalist and entrepreneur, the various exit strategies available, and some key issues unique to the private equity market.

Venture Capital Funding: A Practical Guide to Raising Finance

Stephen Bloomfield
London: Kogan Page, 2005
272pp ISBN: 0749442913
Written in an informal and jargon-free style, this book offers step-by-step advice on how to attract venture capital funding for your business. To make the process seem less daunting, the process is broken down into a number of manageable sections.

Venture Capital Investing: The Complete Handbook for Investing in Private Businesses for Outstanding Profits 2nd ed.

David Gladstone, Laura Gladstone
Upper Saddle River, New Jersey: Prentice Hall, 2003
480pp ISBN: 013101885X
This classic serves as a primer on venture capital investing. It outlines the key

considerations for investing private capital, including an analysis of management, compensation, marketing and sales, financial statements and projections, and the production process. From due diligence and deal negotiation to the exit strategy, the author suggests a logical, step-by-step process that is filled with insights and actual examples from his experience as a venture capitalist. While most books are focused on how an entrepreneur can raise venture capital, this book provides an in-depth look at what it takes to be a successful investor in small private businesses.

MAGAZINES

European Venture Capital Journal

ISSN: 0954–1675
Thomson Financial Ltd.
Aldgate House, 33 Aldgate High Street, London, EC3N 1DL, U.K.
T: +44 (0) 20 7369 7897/7662
F: +44 (0) 20 7369 7330
www.evcj.com
This journal, published ten times a year, provides information on the European private equity market. The *U.K. Venture Capital Journal* merged with it in 1999.

Private Equity Analyst

Asset Alternatives
170 Linden Street, Wellesley, Massachusetts, 02482–7919
T: +1 781 304 1500
http://privateequity.dowjones.com
This monthly newsletter covers the private equity market, dealing mainly with venture capital, LBOs, mezzanine investing, and turnarounds.

Private Equity Week

ISSN: 1099–341X
Thomson Financial
195 Broadway, 10th Floor, New York, 10007
T: +1 646 822 2000
F: +1 646 822 3230
www.ventureeconomics.com
PEW is a weekly newsletter providing information on private equity deals in the venture capital market. It can be found on the Web at www.privateequityweek.com.

Venture Capital: An International Journal of Entrepreneurial Finance

ISSN: 1369–1066
Taylor & Francis Journals (U.S.)
325 Chestnut Street, Suite 800, Philadelphia, Pennsylvania, 19106

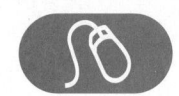

1927

BUSINESS INFORMATION SOURCES

"As an investor in small companies, I don't care how rich Microsoft is. I care about what my opportunities are."

Esther Dyson

T: +1 800 354 1420
F: +1 215 625 8914
www.tandf.co.uk
Venture Capital is a quarterly journal which publishes research-based papers from academics and practitioners on all aspects of private equity finance and on the venture capital process from decision to exit. Coverage is international, focusing on emerging venture capital markets in Eastern Europe and the Asian Pacific area as well as established markets in Western Europe and the United States.

Venture Capital Journal
ISSN: 0883–2773
Thomson Financial
195 Broadway, 10th Floor, New York, 10007
T: +1 646 822 2000
F: +1 646 822 3230
www.ventureeconomics.com
VCJ is a monthly journal covering the private equity and venture capital industry. It provides news and analysis of deals, company profiles, and interviews.

INTERNET
National Venture Capital Association
www.nvca.org
The National Venture Capital Association is a trade association providing advocacy, education, and networking opportunities for the venture capital industry. It boasts over 400 members representing the majority of venture firms invested in U.S.-based companies. The association's affiliate organization, American Entrepreneurs for Economic Growth (AEEG), is an advocacy group for over 14,000 C.E.O.s of emerging growth companies.

PriceWaterhouseCoopers MoneyTree Report
www.pwcmoneytree.com
This survey, sponsored by the accounting firm of PriceWaterhouseCoopers, provides a comprehensive list of venture capital investing in the United States by industry, stage of funding, geography, and type of financing on a quarterly basis. The report tracks venture capital firm investments and the enterprises receiving capital by region/state and industry.

U.S. Venture Partners (USVP)
www.usvp.com
Created in 1981, USVP aims to specifically help entrepreneurial ventures. In total, it has put over $1.8 billion into more than 370 companies, and their clients have gone on to become leaders in their respective fields.

vcapital
www.vcfodder.com
This is an action-packed site for entrepreneurs, with a distinct editorial voice. It features a "Dr VC" feature, whereby users can ask for specific advice, and encourages users to e-mail in their own stories of success and failure.

Venture Economics
www.ventureeconomics.com
News, statistics, product information, and a glossary of terms are to be found on this site, provided by a publisher of journals and research on the venture capital industry worldwide.

VentureOne
http://www.ventureone.com/
This site is a database of venture-backed investors and companies and includes upcoming events, publications, and information for the venture capital industry.

Venturewire
www.venturewire.com/default.asp
This Web site hosts a family of publications that are exclusively devoted to the private equity marketplace. *Venturewire Professional*, the site's flagship publication, features the latest news on fundings, acquisitions, venture capital firms, and key personnel changes in venture-backed businesses. Venturewire also publishes *Lifescience*, *Alert*, and *People* on a daily basis and provides the Research section as a source of in-depth coverage on specific industries.

vFinance, Inc. Venture Capital Resource Library
www.vfinance.com
This site is aimed at investors, entrepreneurs, and company C.E.O.s and provides access to databases of investors, angels, and business plans. Registration is required.

ORGANIZATIONS
USA
National Association of Investment Companies
733 15th Street NW, Suite 700, Washington, D.C., 20005
T: +1 202 289 4336
F: +1 202 289 4329
E: *NAICHQTRS@aol.com*
www.naicvc.com
NAIC is an industry association for venture capital and private equity firms. Its

members are privately owned equity investment firms, small business investment companies licensed by the United States Small Business Administration, and investment companies chartered by state and local governments.

National Association of Small Business Investment Companies
666 11th Street NW, Suite 750, Washington, D.C., 20001
T: +1 202 628 5055
F: +1 202 628 5080
E: *nasbic@nasbic.org*
www.nasbic.org
NASBIC is a nonprofit industry association which has represented and served the SBIC industry for over 40 years. It provides educational programs for investment professionals through the Venture Capital Institute and cooperates with other business associations. Its policies and priorities are established by a board of governors.

National Venture Capital Association
1655 North Fort Myer Drive, Suite 850, Arlington, Virginia, 22209
T: +1 703 524 2549
F: +1 703 524 3940
E: *lturner@nvca.org*
www.nvca.org
NVCA is a trade association with a membership of over 400 venture capital firms. It aims to foster understanding of the venture capital industry in the United States, to stimulate the flow of equity capital to growth companies, to promote professional standards, facilitate networking, and provide research data for members. NVCA publishes: *NVCA Today*, a quarterly review of legislative and regulatory developments; *The Venture Capital Review*, a biannual journal which provides an overview of trends in the industry; and the *Venture Capital Yearbook*.

Europe
British Business Angels Association
52–54 Southwark Street, London, SE1 1UN, U.K.
T: +44 (0) 20 7089 2305
F: +44 (0) 20 7089 2301
E: *liz@bbaa.org.uk*
www.bbaa.org.uk
BBAA, formerly NBAN (National Business Angels Network), is a nonprofit association sponsored by financial institutions and the Department of Trade and Industry in the United Kingdom. Through a network of

"Business? It's quite simple. It's other people's money." — Alexandre Dumas

associates across the country, it provides a service linking businesses seeking equity finance with investors seeking opportunities. A monthly bulletin of opportunities is sent to all registered investors, and an online service, BestMatch, is also provided.

British Venture Capital Association

Essex House, 12–13 Essex Street, London, WC2R 3AA, U.K.
T: +44 (0) 20 7025 2590
F: +44 (0) 20 7025 2951
E: *bvca@bvca.co.uk*
www.bvca.co.uk

The BVCA was founded in 1983 and is the representative body for the U.K. venture capital industry. It promotes private equity and venture capital for the benefit of entrepreneurs, investors, practitioners, and the economy as a whole. Its members are venture capital companies and professional firms involved in advising on venture capital transactions. Its wide variety of activities include training, workshops, lobbying, and research, and it produces publications.

European Private Equity and Venture Capital Association (EVCA)

Minervastraat 4, Zaventem, 1930, Belgium
T: +32 2 715 00 20
F: +32 2 725 07 04
E: *evca@evca.com*
www.evca.com

EVCA was founded in 1983 and now has over 850 members. Its aim is to promote and facilitate the development of the European venture capital industry through lobbying and initiatives such as conferences, training, and networking opportunities. The organization was involved in the creation of EASD (European Association of Security Dealers) and subsequently, EASDAQ (Automated Quotations), which in 2001 became NASDAQ Europe, the screen-based pan-European equities and securities market.

International

Australian Venture Capital Association

Level 5, 88 Philip Street, Sydney, New South Wales, 2000, Australia
T: +61 2 9251 3888
F: +61 2 9251 3808
E: *mbrs@avcal.com.au*
www.avcal.com.au

AVCAL was founded in 1992 to act as a forum for the venture capital industry in Australia and to encourage investment in growing businesses. Its members, numbering over 100, include venture capital firms, banks, incubators, angels, advisers, and government bodies. It organizes networking events and training courses, and sponsors a twice-yearly survey of venture capital investment.

Hong Kong Venture Capital Association

Room 34, 3rd Floor New Henry House, 10 Ice House Street, Hong Kong, Hong Kong
T: +852 2845 6100
F: +852 2526 2713
E: *enquiry@hkvca.com.hk*
www.hkvca.com.hk

The HKVCA was founded in 1987 to promote and protect the interests of, and provide a forum for, the venture capital industry in Hong Kong. It organizes meetings, conferences, and seminars, and conducts research studies.

FOR MORE INFORMATION

- Acquisitions, Takeovers, and Mergers (pp. 1670–1671)
- Avoiding the Mistakes of the Past: Lessons from the Startup World (pp. 164–165)
- Entrepreneurs (pp. 1745–1747)

1929

BUSINESS INFORMATION SOURCES

Working Abroad

BOOKS

Best Practices for Managers and Expatriates: A Guide on Selection, Hiring, and Compensation
Stan Lomax
Hoboken, New Jersey: Wiley, 2001
336pp ISBN: 0471392065
This book provides a detailed look at the career issues related to working abroad, including the type of person to select and how long the assignment should be. The book is designed as a guide for managers who have international assignments to fill or capacity to develop. It will also prove useful to those considering an expatriate assignment.

Dos and Taboos Around the World 3rd ed.
Roger E. Axtell, ed.
Hoboken, New Jersey: Wiley, 1993
208pp ISBN: 0471595284
Dos and Taboos provides facts, tips, and cautionary tales gathered from the experiences of more than 500 international business travelers. It includes information on protocol, customs, etiquette, hand gestures and body language, tipping, American jargon, and the international communications crisis. A section of advice for visitors to Eastern Europe and Russia, and a chapter on business gift-giving and gift-receiving, with country-by-country gift suggestions and precautions, are included.

Getting a Job Abroad: The International Jobseekers' Directory 7th ed.
Roger Jones
Oxford, United Kingdom: How To Books, 2003
336pp ISBN: 1857038517
The book lists country contact organizations worldwide to assist with the job-search process, and contains additional chapters on the recruitment rigmarole, short-term or long-term commitment, and preparation and acclimatization.

Global Résumé and CV Guide
Mary Anne Thompson
Hoboken, New Jersey: Wiley, 2000
288pp ISBN: 0471380768
This international approach will be of interest to managers seeking to work overseas and to multinational organizations. Experts from over 40 countries provide cultural dos and don'ts, information on business practices, and job hunting tips that will help create a résumé

tailored to the specific requirements of a target country. Standard coverage for each country includes a country overview, résumé specifics, résumé presentation, cover letters, job-information sources, Web sites, and interview advice.

Insider's Guide to Working in Europe: How to Develop a Successful International Career
Anne-Marie Boels
London: Bene Factum, 2000
208pp ISBN: 0952275481
This is a comprehensive guide for those seeking employment or wishing to do business abroad. It is not just a reference book but a combination of national details and statistics covering 48 European nations. It offers insights into national characteristics, culture, and fundamental dos and don'ts, gives advice on living conditions, notes important national variations, and points to further sources of information including over 320 Web sites. In addition, it offers advice on handling the culture shock of a long-term assignment in a new location (with or without families), and tips for those who travel regularly on business.

International HRM: Contemporary Issues in Europe
Chris Brewster, Hilary Harris, eds
London, United Kingdom: Chartered Institute of Personnel and Development (CIPD), 2003
224pp ISBN: 0852929838
This collection of edited papers from European experts in the field covers all aspects of international human resource management. The articles range from issues surrounding the strategic role of HRM in staffing, reward management, and performance management, to discussions of the dynamics of culture and gender in international management.

International Jobs: Where They Are, How to Get Them 6th ed.
Eric Kocher, Nina Segal
Cambridge, Massachusetts: Perseus Books Group, 2003
336pp ISBN: 0738207462
This guide navigates the reader around the international job market. The text contains listings of Web sites for each organization and a chapter on how to make effective use of the Internet in a global job search. Also

included are essays that tell you what some of these jobs are really like, and further advice to help you sort out which jobs present actual opportunities and which just sound good on paper.

Living and Working Abroad
David Hampshire
Wetherby, United Kingdom: Survival Books, 2001
400pp ISBN: 1901130851
David Hampshire offers a comprehensive and up-to-date work survey for employees, emigrants, students, business people, retirees, long-stay visitors, and anyone planning to spend some time abroad. The book contains huge amounts of practical advice concerning all aspects of working overseas. Important topics covered include how to obtain a residence or work permit, how to stretch your money further, how to get the best education for your family, and how to find the best job for you.

Mind Your Manners: Managing Business Cultures in the New Global Europe 3rd ed.
John Mole
Naperville, Illinois: Nicholas Brealey Publishing, 2003
288pp ISBN: 1857883144
This text is aimed at managers of any nationality intending to do business in the world's biggest market. It addresses such crucial issues as communication, leadership, decision making, meetings, and networking. Mole includes a toolkit to enable readers to test their own cultural responses.

Overseas Americans: The Essential Guide to Living and Working Abroad
William Beaver
Boulder, Colorado: Paladin Press, 2001
176pp ISBN: 1581602596
With the basic information that any American living abroad without significant corporate support may need to have, this book covers dealing with various U.S. government agencies, required documents, income tax questions, and many other topics. It also goes over less well-aired issues, like what to do if you are arrested, and there is a guide to over 100 Web sites geared toward the needs of expatriate workers.

"India will become the country of choice . . . It's already starting to happen."

Narayana Murthy

The Transplanted Executive: Why You Need to Understand How Workers in Other Countries See the World Differently

Christopher Earley, Miriam Erez
New York: Oxford University Press, Inc., 1997
208pp ISBN: 019508795X
The Transplanted Executive provides a comprehensive resource for managers of any nationality striving to understand the diversity of workplace values and traditions—and explains how these characteristics can be used to maximize employee efficiency, morale, and the bottom line. Each chapter focuses on a different management problem: effective communication; motivation of workers; turning groups into teams; leadership skills; and quality management production.

INTERNET
Control Risks Group
www.crg.com
This site belongs to a leading specialist international business risk consultancy operating in political risk analysis, confidential investigations, preemployment screening, security consulting, crisis management and response, and information security and investigations.

Embassy World
www.embassyworld.com
The embassies of each country in other countries and the embassies of other countries in that country are listed on this site. It also includes maps, an international telephone directory, and information on visas.

Employment Conditions Abroad
www.eca-international.com
This site introduces the information and support services offered by ECA International. These are designed to help both managers working abroad and those responsible for sending managers on international assignments. The services include country briefing reports, detailed data for salary calculations, and assistance in developing an expatriate policy.

MASTA
www.masta.org
MASTA is aimed at anyone who is interested in travel health issues, in particular the individual traveler who wants to know how to minimize the risks to his or her health. The aim is to present information in a way that is easily understood by the traveler. The site features

sections on immunization, things to know before you go, staying healthy away from home, information to have with you, and visa and passport information. There are links to related health sites for travelers.

Network for Living Abroad
www.liveabroad.com/articles
A selection of articles related to living abroad in various countries in Europe and Latin America is available on this noncommercial site, as well as valuable links to additional Web sites.

U.S. Expatriate Handbook
www.us-expatriate-handbook.com/contents.htm
This site offers the full text of John W. Adams's book *U.S. Expatriate Handbook: Guide to Living and Working Abroad* online. It is a convenient source for obtaining a basic understanding of the topic.

ORGANIZATIONS
USA
Association of Americans Resident Overseas
34 Avenue de New York, Paris, 75116, France
T: +33 1 47 20 24 15
F: +33 1 47 20 24 16
E: *aaromail@aaro-intl.org*
www.aaro.org
AARO is a public-service membership organization formed to protect the rights of Americans living and working abroad. It addresses issues including citizenship rights, tax treatment, Medicare and health insurance, and bureaucratic obstacles. Members receive a quarterly newsletter, group medical insurance, and the option of attending local events.

Employee Relocation Council
1717 Pennsylvania Avenue NW, Suite 800, Washington, D.C., 20006
T: +1 202 857 0857
F: +1 202 659 8631
E: *webmaster@erc.org*
www.erc.org
ERC is a membership organization, founded in 1964, for professionals who manage or support U.S. and international employee relocation.

Europe
Employment Conditions Abroad
One Rockefeller Plaza, Suite 325, New York, 10020

T: +1 212 582 2333
F: +1 212 582 0338
E: *eca@eca-international.com*
www.eca-international.com
ECA International is a leading membership organization for international human resources. It offers the information and consulting support required to manage international assignments. The organization has offices in 17 countries, including Australia, Hong Kong, South Africa, the United Kingdom, and many European countries. Details can be found on its Web site.

Farnham Castle International Briefing and Conference Centre
Farnham Castle, Farnham, Surrey, GU9 0AG, U.K.
T: +44 (0) 1252 720 418
F: +44 (0) 1252 719 277
E: *info@farnhamcastle.com*
www.intercultural-training.co.uk
The center offers a range of cross-cultural training programs, tailored country briefings, in-depth workshops on business cultures, and interactive workshops on working in a global environment. The issues covered range from the practical to the emotional, and program content can be tailored for individual expatriate employees, frequent business travelers, and home-based and multinational teams.

Medical Advisory Services for Travellers Abroad (MASTA)
Keppel Street, London, WC1E 7HT, U.K.
T: +44 (0) 20 7631 4408
E: *enquiries@masta.org*
www.masta.org
MASTA was set up in 1984 and aims to raise awareness of health issues associated with travel. While providing information for anyone who is interested in travel health issues, the organization focuses particularly on individual travelers who want to know how to minimize the risks to their health. The Web site features many helpful sections on health, visas, and immunization.

1931

BUSINESS INFORMATION SOURCES

FOR MORE INFORMATION

- International Management, Cross Cultural Management (pp. 1784–1786)
- ✔ Planning Overseas Assignments (pp. 460–461)
- Planning Your Career (pp. 1863–1864)
- ✔ Preparing for Business Abroad (pp. 570–571)
- Relocation (p. 1893)

INDEX

INDEX

Index

Text Credits

Best Practice

- pp. 57–58 Culture Clashes © Tim Hindle 2006
- pp. 53–56 China's Five Surprises © Edward Tse 2006
- pp. 71–72 Viewpoint: Seth Godin © Seth Godin 2006
- pp. 73–75 The Genius of Business © Peter Fisk 2006
- pp. 78–79 On Writing As an Essential Business Skill © John Simmons 2006
- pp. 80–81 On Value and Values: How a Blended Values Strategy Drives Sustainable Performance © Douglas K. Smith 2006
- pp. 82–84 How HR Adds Value © Dave Ulrich and Wayne Brockbank 2006
- pp. 101–103 How to Get Lucky © Donald N. Sull 2006
- pp. 112–115 The Only Sustainable Edge © John Seely Brown and John Hagel III 2006
- pp. 148–149 Viewpoint: Stan Davis © Stan Davis 2003, 2006
- pp. 153–154 Creating Value Through People © David Maister 2002, 2006
- pp. 155–157 Viewpoint: Robert Hormats © Global Business Network 2003, 2006
- pp. 174–175 Viewpoint: Paul Saffo © Global Business Network 2003, 2006
- pp. 194–195 Blogs and Business: What You Must Know © Andy Wibbels 2006
- pp. 196–197 Viewpoint: Howard Rheingold © Howard Rheingold 2006
- pp. 243–244 Viewpoint: Francis Fukuyama © Global Business Network 2003, 2006
- pp. 253–254 Viewpoint: Tom Brown © Thomas L. Brown 2006
- pp. 263–264 The One Thing You Need to Know © Marcus Buckingham 2006
- pp. 260–262 Viewpoint: Richard Boyatzis, Annie McKee, and David Smith © Richard Boyatzis, Annie McKee, and David Smith, 2006
- pp. 275–276 Learning the Art and Practice of Adaptive Leadership Through Case-in-Point © Sharon Daloz Parks 2006
- pp. 310–311 Viewpoint: Michael E. Gerber © Michael E. Gerber 2006
- pp. 316–317 Viewpoint: Paul Ormerod © Paul Ormerod 2006
- pp. 332–333 The Supply Chain © Peter Day 2006
- pp. 343–344 Viewpoint: Stewart Brand © Global Business Network 2003, 2006
- pp. 353–354 Trend Innovation Management © Matthias Horx 2006
- pp. 355–358 Adaptive Advantage © Global Business Network 2003, 2006
- pp. 359–361 Viewpoint: Clayton M. Christensen © Clayton M. Christensen 2006
- pp. 374–375 Corporate Responsibility: A Leadership Approach © Giles Gibbons 2006
- pp. 376–378 CSR: More than PR, Pursuing Competitive Advantage in the Long Run © John Surdyk 2006
- pp. 393–394 Viewpoint: Paul Hawken © Global Business Network 2003, 2006
- pp. 436–437 How NLP Can Contribute to Best Management Practice © Joseph O'Connor 2006

Management Checklists

Management Checklists © Chartered Management Institute 2002, 2006

Management Library

Ultimate Business Library © Stuart Crainer 2002
Writing the New Economy © John Middleton 2002

Business Thinkers

Business Thinkers © Chartered Management Institute 2002, 2006

Dictionary

Management terms © Chartered Management Institute 2002, 2006

Business Information Sources

Business Information Sources © Chartered Management Institute 2002, 2006

1971

Photo Credits